Contents

Whether you are a regular subscriber or a first-time user, we trust that you will find the 2005-2006 edition of the *World Travel Guide* concise, accurate and easy to use. Every country in the world is covered in the pages that follow – and in lavish detail. There are hundreds of maps, charts, city plans and colour photographs, as well as over a million words of relevant yet colourful information accessibly presented. No destination, no matter how far flung, obscure or recently emerged, will now be beyond your reach.

Whether you are a travel agent or tourist, a business traveller or conference planner, a librarian or student, you will have frequent questions about the world of travel which require instant and accurate answers. We have spent 24 years researching these for you and the results are spread over the following pages. Globally applicable, meticulously researched and user-friendly, we are sure that the *World Travel Guide* will function as a vital sales and reference tool for your business. But don't just take our word for it. A glance at the front cover, and the pages at the beginning of the appendices, will demonstrate the strength of the backing and endorsement for the publication from some of the world's leading travel-trade associations.

Every country in the book is listed alphabetically in the contents, from Afghanistan to Zimbabwe, together with the page number on which each country's entry begins. Alternative names of countries are also listed to avoid confusion eg French Polynesia - see Tahiti; Kampuchea - see Cambodia; Ivory Coast - see Côte d'Ivoire. Readers may also discover that smaller destinations may be found within a larger area, eg Bali – see Indonesia; Isle of Man – see United Kingdom; Crete - see Greece; or Dubai - see United Arab Emirates.

For more information on how each country's entry is laid out, see the introduction, 'How to Use this Guide'. For more information on the world, just start turning the pages!

Countries marked in red in the contents have been sponsored by the tourist board or tourism authority to help in the promotion of the destination for business and leisure travel. The presence of such sponsorship should not be taken to imply a different editorial approach.

EDITORIAL FEATURES

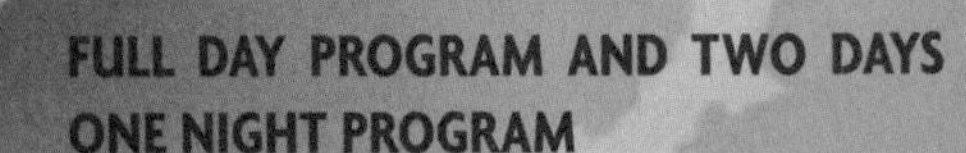

FULL DAY PROGRAM AND TWO DAYS ONE NIGHT PROGRAM

ACTIVITIES AT KING GEORGE ISLAND (Full day + Two days one night)

- Visit Villa Las Estrellas, (first site to be inhabited by civilians)
- Visit the Sea Lion colony in the Drake Sea
- Walk to the Chinese Station to observe Marine Birds, Penguins and Weddell Seals.
- Cross over to Ardley Island, where Papua Penguin colonies live.
- Return to Punta Arenas (Chile)

ONLY TWO DAYS ONE NIGHT PROGRAM:

- On the following day we visit different Antarctic Research Stations and will be able to speak to researchers about their work.
- If time permits, we can visit additional areas of attraction before returning to Punta Arenas (Chile).

HELICOPTER IN ATARCTICA

Once on King George Island you can catch our Bo –105 Helicopter that will fly you to nearby glaciers, where you can enjoy a wonderful sight of millenary ice fields in Antarctica.

SHIP IN ANTARTICA

Dap Mares has recently incorporated an Oceanographic Ship mainly oriented to support scientific expeditions to Antarctica and to provide logistic for different Antarctic Bases.

For General Conditions and pricing, please visit our web site at www.aeroviasdap.com

COLUMBUS
TRAVEL GUIDES

British Library Cataloguing in Publications Data
The World Travel Guide: Incorporating the ABTA/ANTOR Factfinder – 24th Edition
I. World Visitor's Guides
910'.2'02

ISBN: 1-902221-88-5
ISSN: 02678748

Columbus Travel Guides, Media House, Azalea Drive, Swanley, Kent BR8 8HU, United Kingdom
Tel: +44 (0) 1322 616 344. Fax: +44 (0) 1322 616 323. E-mail: booksales@nexusmedia.com
World Travel Guide website: www.gocoti.com; www.columbustravelguides.com

Printed by UP Group Ltd, Lithuania

Head of Editorial Marie Peyre
Project Editor Dominic Tombs
Assistant Editor Sophie Offord
Editorial Assistant Anna Tyler
USA Section Editor Jackie Finch
Contributors Gary Bowerman, Paul Deegan, Robin McKelvie, Dr Eve Speight

Design and Artwork Nigel Tansley, Anne Heppelthwaite, Toni Manuel, Peter Upsher
Cartography David Burles, AND Map Graphics Ltd
Production Mile Budimir, Michael Popejoy

Advertising Sales Manager Annette Cooper
Project Managers Gordon Green, Jason Vencatasen
Customer Liaison Officer Katie Butler

Sales & Marketing Manager Martin Newman
Office Manager Beverley Sansome

United States Booksales David Frank, President, SF Travel Publications, Roanoke, Virginia
US Travel Trade Book Sales Jill Hall
US Library Book Sales Donna Pinckney
US Customer Service Nancy Jarvis

Content Licensing Manager Adrian James

Publisher Peter Korniczky

Cover photo supplied by: **Tourism Authority of Thailand**

The Publishers would like to thank all the tourist offices, embassies, high commissions, consulates, airlines and other organisations and individuals who assisted in the preparation of this edition. Most of the photographs used in this publication were supplied by the respective tourist office, embassy or high commission. The Publishers would also like to thank other organisations and individuals whose photographs appear.

IMPORTANT NOTICE

The information in the World Travel Guide is compiled from many sources, including embassies, high commissions, tour operators, airlines, national tourist offices, health organisations and governmental bodies. Whilst every effort is made by the Publishers to ensure the accuracy of the information contained in this edition of the World Travel Guide, the Publishers accept no responsibility for any loss occasioned to any person acting or refraining from acting as a result of the material contained in this publication, or liability for any financial or other agreements which may be entered into with any advertisers, nor with any organisations or individuals listed in the text.

By its very nature much of the information contained in the publication is susceptible to change or alteration, for instance, in response to changing political, health and environmental situations. These changes or alterations are beyond the control of the Publishers. To assist users in obtaining up-to-date information, the Publishers have provided as many contact telephone and fax numbers as well as e-mail and website addresses as possible. In particular, the Timatic™ information is available in respect of many countries. In any case of doubt, or in response to any change in a domestic or international situation, users are urged to verify information upon which they are relying with the relevant authority.

Columbus Travel Guides are published by Nexus Media Communications a trading name of a division that is wholly owned subsidiary of Nexus Holdings Ltd. Registered office: Hanover House, 14 Hanover Square, London W1S 1HP

For security purposes, telephone conversations may from time to time be recorded.
This is to ensure that if necessary we can verify that we will deliver to all our clients all that has been promised verbally.

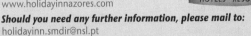

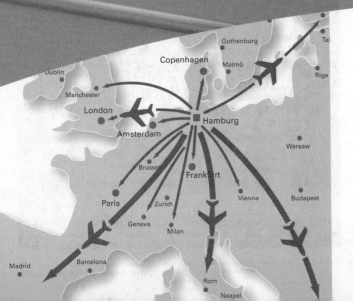

See pages 354-359 for more details of Ireland

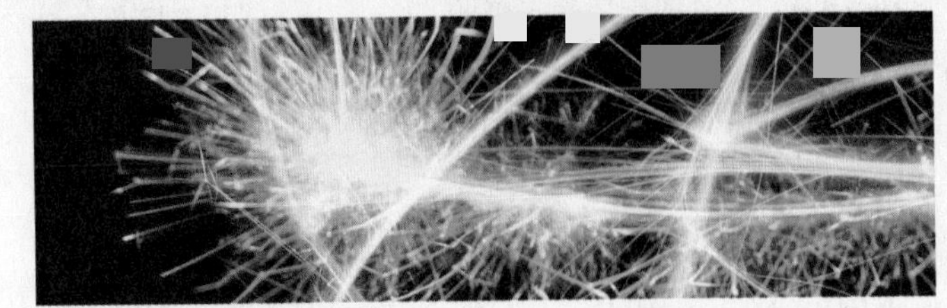

Cork 2005

European Capital of Culture

Hayfield Manor

Hayfield Manor Cork's first and only 5 star hotel is located opposite the historic University College Cork. Set in 2 acres of mature trees and gardens this country Manor hotel has many advantages of being only 1 mile from the city centre. All 88 Guestrooms and Suites are air conditioned. The Manor Room Restaurant serves Fine Dining cuisine while Perrotts is the casual dining option - glass walls overlooking the city and our bird aviary. The Manor Spa is exclusive to residents of the hotel. There are 4 meeting rooms, ample car parking and private back gardens. Cork is European Capital of Culture 2005.

- A member of Small Luxury Hotels of the World
- A member of Virtuoso Hotels and Resorts
- AA Irish Hotel of the Year 2004
- Black & White Hotel Bar of the Year 2004

www.hayfieldmanor.ie enquiries@hayfieldmanor.ie
Tel: + 353 21 4845900 Fax: + 353 21 4316839

*extra*ordinary

means lots extra... and nothing ordinary.

- 79 ensuite rooms and suites
- Full leisure centre
- 20 acres of 300 year old gardens
- Board Rooms & Syndicate rooms for 5-60
- Sherrard Suite maximum capacity 500
- State of the art facilities with touch button technology

...an exceptional venue committed to quality service.

Maryborough Hill, Douglas, Cork.
Tel: 00353 (0) 21 4365555
Fax: 00353 (0) 21 4365662
E-mail: info@maryborough.ie
Web site: www.maryborough.com

HOTEL ISAACS
CORK

Choice of 3 star accommodations - At one Cork City Centre address

- 47 en-suite standard and superior hotel bed rooms
- Two and three bedroom self-catering apartments
- Air Conditioned ground floor conference rooms.
- Greenes Restaurant and bar – dining alfresco
- Courtyard garden with a waterfall, floodlit by night!
- Limited car park spaces available (200 metres from hotel)
- 5 minutes from Bus & Train stations, shopping, tourist attractions, theatres and nightlife.

48 MacCurtain Street, Cork.
Tel: (00353)21-4500011 Fax: (00353)21-4506355
www.isaacs.ie

The Kingsley Hotel
Victoria Cross, Cork

Luxurious Living By The Lee 5 minutes from Cork City Centre

Two Nights Bed & Breakfast with a la carte dinner on one evening and an afternoon tea from *€175.00 pps*

Book on line www.kingsleyhotel.com

Cork..So much to do!

- Cork City Shopping
- Championship Golf Courses
- Cork Greyhound Stadium
- Blarney Castle
- Fota Wildife Park
- Great Nightlife
- Cork city Goal
- Cork Race Course Mallow
- Good Access to West Cork
- Cork Opera House
- The Titanic Trail Cobh

Winner of Jameson business hotel of the year 2004/2005
RAC blue ribbon award 2005/2006

www.kingsleyhotel.com
Victoria Cross, Cork, Ireland. Phone +353 21 4800555
Fax +353 21 4800526
Email: resv@kingsleyhotel.com

HOTEL
ANWB • Media
ANWB: see advertisement on outside back cover

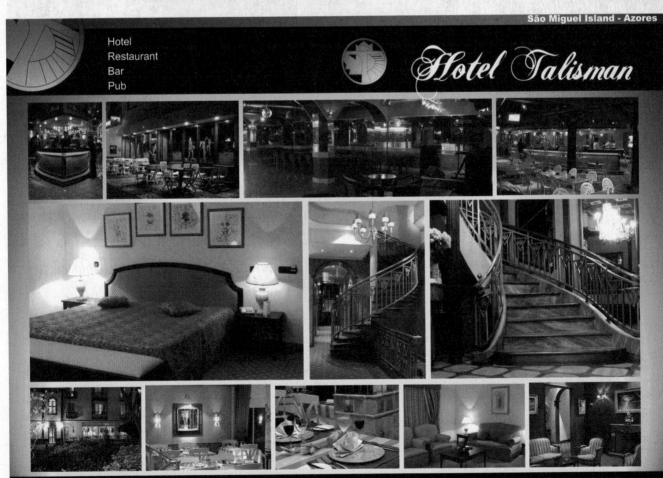

A New Star
Croatia is widely tipped to emerge as one of the major tourist attractions of the decade. Robin McKelvie finds out why.

© All images courtesy of Croatian National Tourist Board

When war engulfed the fledgling Republic of Croatia in 1991, it immediately brought an end to a booming tourist industry that had seen this corner of the former Yugoslavia develop as a major package holiday destination and emerge as a hub on the European backpacker circuit. A decade on since the end of the fighting and Croatia is now re-establishing itself as one of the continent's most fashionable destinations. And it's not just with package tourists, but also with a new breed of independent travellers keen to explore what the tourist office aptly hail as 'The Mediterranean as it Once Was'.

It is easy to see what attracts people to Croatia as the country enjoys an enviable climate and its sweeping coastline is blessed with some of the cleanest waters in the Mediterranean that's dotted with over 1,000 islands. Five decades of socialist rule slowed the economic development experienced across the Adriatic in Italy, leaving the coastline awash with Venetian-era towns, uninhabited islands and dolphins flitting on the water's edge. The shining star of the littoral region is Dubrovnik, once eulogised by Lord Byron as the 'Pearl of the Adriatic', but it is amply backed up by Split with its UNESCO World Heritage-listed Diocletian's Palace, and Trogir with its similarly vaunted old town, as well as a string of other attractive towns and cities on the coastline and islands.

Emerging Markets

Growth areas in Croatian tourism include the package tourist market, with the Dalmatia and the Kvarner Gulf regions experiencing ever-increasing visitor numbers. The main focus of this sector though is still on the northern region of Istria, an enclave that Tito earmarked for tourist development as early as the 1960s. The Istrian resort of Porec alone now caters for over 700,000 tourists a year as most of the big tour operators have moved back in since fighting stopped in 1995.

> *"With rapidly expanding infrastructure and one of the most marketable climates and landscapes in Europe, Croatia looks well placed to continue its inexorable rise."*

New parts of the country are developing as well. For example, ecotourism is flourishing in Istria's long forgotten hinterland - a lush, wooden oasis of rolling hills and vineyards that has won favourable comparisons with Tuscany. The government has set up bodies like the Istria County Tourism Association with the aim of promoting rural, small-scale ecotourism. The association already has over 180 members who between them have created around 1,500 beds as part of their 'agroturizam' drive.

Elsewhere, the capital of Zagreb - a graceful central European city with a population of one million - is emerging as a city break destination. Central Croatia also boasts the UNESCO World Heritage-listed Plitvice Lakes, a gurgling mass of waterways, fountains and streams that functions as a sort of natural Disneyland. Away to the east, the region of Slavonia was

See pages 189-192 for Croatia's family-run hotels!

the worst affected area of Croatia during the war, but is now starting to claw its way back. It may not have a coastline, but its rivers and waterways are becoming popular with fishermen and ornithologists, and the once cosmopolitan city of Osijek is regaining its confidence.

New types of tourism are also growing. Sailing, for example, has attracted the likes of Bill Gates, Bernie Ecclestone and Luciano Benetton who have all stationed yachts on the coast in recent years. There has been a conscious effort to enhance existing marinas and build new ones as Croatia rapidly becomes the 'New Greece' in terms of its popularity with mariners. The cruise ship market and adventure tourism are other sectors that have experienced a positive resurgence over recent years.

Positive Progress

The Croatian Tourist Office has been proactive since independence, most notably with its 'Mediterranean as it Once Was Campaign', and their efforts have been rewarded. Since 2000, visitor numbers to Croatia have been on the rise, with 7.8 million tourist visitors in 2001, 8.3 million in 2002 and over 8.8 million in 2003, a figure that exceeds the pre-war and pre-independence figure of less than 8.5 million in 1990.

As visitor numbers have increased, facilities have struggled to keep pace despite government efforts to rapidly improve infrastructure (as Yugoslavia, all main roads and railway lines tended to lead to Belgrade with little focus on the destinations along the way) and increase hotel capacity. Dubrovnik's hotel bed space was halved by the war and - despite massive demand for a resort town to accommodate the thousands of extra tourists that are arriving each year - only now is hotel capacity close to exceeding pre-war levels.

Another significant development is in accommodation and the shift away from the pre-war focus on concrete monoliths. Instead there has been an encouragement of smaller, more intimate options - many of which are family-run. Traditionally the pension (or 'sobe' as it is locally known) market has been strong, but the new family-run places often take a step up from pensions, with enhanced rooms and locally sourced meals available for guests. The most marked growth in this type of accommodation has been with inland Istria's agroturizam programme, but it looks set to continue around the country as families look for extra revenue streams and a new generation of travellers seek more 'authentic' experiences.

A key factor that has enabled recent growth has been the marked improvement in flight connections. State carrier Croatia Airlines once had a reputation for inflexibility and demand for peak season flights to this Adriatic gem simply outstripped supply. British Airways has recently entered the fray with London flights to Dubrovnik and, with partner airline GB Airways, to Split. Croatia Airlines have responded in 2005 by launching regional flights from all over the UK.

The budget carriers have so far been blocked from the lucrative Croatian market, but they have not been slow to react to the growing demand for travel to the region. Ryanair offers an alternative route to the Italian city of Trieste, which is particularly handy for onward travel to Istria. Independent travellers often fly into Trieste, work their way south and catch a ferry from Split, Dubrovnik or Zadar to a Ryanair destination in Italy. In 2004 EasyJet also launched a low cost route into Ljubljana in neighbouring Slovenia, opening up the market further still.

With EU membership now within tangible reach (many Croatian observers expect it to join as early as 2008), increasing flight options, rapidly expanding infrastructure and one of the most marketable climates and landscapes in Europe, Croatia looks well placed to continue its inexorable rise as it not only establishes itself on the tourist map of Europe, but also starts to challenge more established Mediterranean destinations.

Useful Contacts

Association of Family and Small Hotels of Croatia
Obala Hrvatskog Narodnog Preporoda 7/3, 21,000 Split, Croatia
Tel: 00385 21 317 880 Fax:00385 21 317 881 E-mail: info@omh.hr Website: www.omh.hr

See pages 189-192 for Croatia's family-run hotels!

By Gary Bowerman

World Cup 2006

'See you in Germany 2006!' is the marketing slogan. How very apt. Every four years, the World Cup enraptures the entire globe and soccer-mad Germany is already gearing up to host the 18th FIFA World Cup between 9 June-9 July 2006. The rest of the world will be watching in.

Held in Korea and Japan, a cumulative TV audience of 28.8 billion viewers in 213 countries watched the 2002 World Cup. But television isn't the only way to watch the tournament. Avid fans prefer the live action. Germany's National Tourist Office is preparing for a massive influx in visitors and spectators - and a huge boost to its tourism economy. And there is plenty for visitors to enjoy in this diverse country of 83 million people, including historic and beautiful cities such as the capital, Berlin, Munich and Cologne, the romantic Black Forest, scenic Rhine and Danube river cruises, 25 UNESCO heritage sites, charming medieval towns and castles and the soaring Bavarian Alps. The tourism and transport infrastructure is excellent, a friendly welcome is assured and Germany is experienced at holding such major events, having already hosted the World Cup back in 1974. And, of course, the sausages are world-famous, Black Forest Gateau is legendary and the beer is unrivalled.

The Tournament

In 2002, two Ronaldo goals won the final for Brazil, shattering German dreams of taking the World Cup back to defend in their homeland in 2006. Ronaldo was the undoubted star of the tournament in Japan/Korea, emerging as top-scorer with eight goals, but 2006 may see a new generation of footballing superstars. Watch out for such names as Robinho, Schweinsteiger, Tevez, Robben and, of course, England's Wayne Rooney. And, who could forget, Brazil's two Rons, Ronaldinho of Barcelona and Ronaldo of Real Madrid?

With the final group draw to be made in December 2005, several questions are already being raised. Can Brazil win a record sixth title? Will Germany become the seventh nation to triumph on home territory (a feat achieved as the then West Germany in 1974)? Can Asian teams sustain the rapid progress made in 2002? Could an African team win the title for the first time, in advance of the 2010 World Cup in South Africa?

Ticket Information

Germany's location at the heart of Europe (it has borders with nine countries) provides easy access for fans from around the world. Demand for tickets, therefore, is expected to be very high. On 1 February 2005, 812,000 match tickets went on sale via the Internet and organisers say "at least 300,000 more" will be made available - mostly by public ballot - before 15 January 2006, and yet more in the run-up to the tournament. The 12 World Cup stadiums boast a gross capacity of 3.37 million for the 64 matches. After deducting the customary VIP guests, media, security and restricted view seats, the total figure of available tickets for fans will be 2.93 million.

For more information, visit the official FIFA World Cup website: www.fifaworldcup.com. For accommodation bookings contact the 2006 FIFA World Cup Accommodation Services (tel: +0049 69 509586 400; e-mail: accommodation@ok2006.de).

The Host Cities

Matches will be held in 12 cities, with the opening ceremony and first match in Munich on June 9, 2006 and the final in Berlin on July 9. Other host cities are: Cologne, Dortmund, Frankfurt, Gelsenkirchen, Hamburg, Hanover, Kaiserslautern, Leipzig, Nuremberg and Stuttgart.

Berlin

Reunited in 1989, Germany's capital is one of Europe's favourite tourism cities. It has numerous museums and galleries, parks and Cold War remnants, such as the Checkpoint Charlie Museum and sections of the Berlin Wall.

Olympia Stadion: Built in the 1930s, it witnessed Jesse Owens' four gold medals at the 1936 Olympics and hosted several matches at the 1974 World Cup.

Nearest airports: Berlin Tegel, 8kms (Air Berlin, BA, DUO, Fly DBA); Berlin Schönefeld, 18kms (Aer Lingus, Easyjet, Ryanair).

Munich

Famous for its Oktoberfest and located near the beautiful German Alps, Munich is close to the fairytale castle of Neuschwanstein. One of Germany's most attractive cities, it is filled with museums, churches, galleries, palaces and beer gardens.

Allianz Arena: The brand new 66,000-seater stadium will be the home of both Bayern

Munich and TSV 1860 Munich from the start of the 2005/06 season.
Nearest airports: Munich, 25kms (Aer Lingus, BA, DUO, Easyjet, Lufthansa).

Cologne

Sat beside the River Rhine, Cologne is famous for its imposing twin-spired cathedral. The city has good shopping and plenty of museums (including the chocolate museum) and churches. The old town features the Kölsh brewery.
Rhein Energie Stadion: Reconstruction of the former Müngersdorfer Stadion, which was Germany's first completely covered stadium, is now complete and is the new home to FC Cologne.
Nearest airports: Cologne/Bonn, 15kms (BA, DUO, German Wings, Hapag Lloyd Express, Lufthansa); Düsseldorf, 40kms (Aer Lingus, Air Berlin, BA, Lufthansa).

Dortmund

Located in the industrial Ruhrgebiet region, Dortmund is a green city with a number of parks and botanical gardens. The football stadium is located at the Westfalen Park, which also hosts concerts, operas and sporting events.
Westfalen Stadion: Known as the Bundesliga's opera-house, it was originally built for the 1974 World Cup. Home to Borussia Dortmund, it is currently being enlarged to hold 60,000 people.
Nearest airports: Dortmund, 10kms (Air Berlin, Easyjet); Muenster, 50kms (Air Berlin); Dusseldorf, 55kms (Aer Lingus, Air Berlin, BA, Lufthansa).

Frankfurt

Germany's financial capital, Frankfurt is also the nation's transport hub. Straddling the River Main, it boasts a picturesque old town, excellent nightlife and the Sachsenhausen cider-making district.
Wald Stadion: The new stadium seats 48,000 people under a retractable roof. Home to Eintracht Frankfurt.
Nearest airports: Frankfurt Int'l, 12kms (Aer Lingus, BA, Lufthansa); Frankfurt Hahn, 90kms (Ryanair).

Gelsenkirchen

A large city located in the recently developed Ruhrgebeit industrial region, it offers a range of places to visit, including Movie World, an indoor ski centre, industrial heritage attractions and museums.
Arena Auf Schalke: Home to FC Schalke, it is one of Europe's finest and most modern stadiums and hosted the 2004 Champions League final.
Nearest airports: Dusseldorf, 40km (Aer Lingus, Air Berlin, BA, Lufthansa); Dortmund, 40km (Air Berlin, Eastjet).

Hamburg

Germany's second-largest city and Europe's second-largest port, Hamburg is an elegant, cosmopolitan city with magnificent promenades, excellent nightlife and the infamous Reeperbahn.
AOL Arena: The new stadium has a capacity of 50,000 and is home to Hamburger SV. It was awarded 5 stars by UEFA, an award held by two other German stadiums - Munich and Gelsenkirchen.
Nearest airports: Hamburg, 8kms (BA, Hapag Lloyd Express, Lufthansa); Hamburg (Lübeck), 55kms (Ryanair).

> "The sausages are world famous, Black Forest Gateau is legendary and the beer is unrivalled."

Hannover

Host city of World EXPO 2000, Hannover blends striking modern architecture with a historic Old Town and beautiful Baroque gardens.
AWD Arena: Reconstruction of the old Niedersachsen Stadium, home to Hannover 96.
Nearest airports: Hannover, 12kms (Air Berlin, BA, Lufthansa).

Kaiserslautern

Owes its name to Emperor Barbarossa, or 'the Kaiser', who - taken by the beauty of the countryside - built a palace in Lautern. Kaiserslautern is a modern city with a lively student scene.

Fritz-Walter-Stadion: Completed in 1920, the ground is named after Germany's 1954 World Cup captain and home to FC Kaiserslautern. The enlarged capacity is 48,500.
Nearest airports: Frankfurt Int'l, 90kms (Aer Lingus, BA, Lufthansa); Frankfurt Hahn, 90kms (Ryanair); Karlsruhe/Baden Baden, 100kms (Ryanair).

Leipzig

Cradle of East Germany's late-1980's revolution, Leipzig has received a makeover and is now a flourishing centre for trade fairs and conferences. The Renaissance and Baroque buildings, historical trading centre and shops have been exquisitely restored.
Zentral Stadion: The old Zentral Stadion was once Germany's largest stadium. The new incarnation seats 45,000.
Nearest airports: Leipzig/Halle, 14kms (Cirrus Airlines); Altenburg, 40kms (Ryanair).

Nuremberg

Modern metropolis meets old-world medieval city. The charming old town provides a backdrop for the world-famous Christkindl Christmas market. Also home to the German Railway Museum, Nazi Party rally grounds and the famous Germanic National Museum.
Franken Stadion: First opened its doors in 1991, the capacity has been increased to 45,500. Now home to FC Nuremberg.
Nearest airports: Nuremberg, 7kms (Air Berlin).

Stuttgart

Surrounded by green hills, forests and vineyards, Stuttgart is a lively city with several castles and palaces and the Porsche and Mercedes museums. Among its many festivals is the annual Canstatter Wasen beer booze-up.
Gottlieb-Daimler Stadion: The original Neckar stadium was built in 1933, and renovation will enlarge the capacity to 51,000. Now home to VFB Stuttgart.
Nearest airports: Stuttgart, 10kms (BA, Lufthansa, DUO, Hapag Lloyd Express).

Further Information
German Tourist Office: www.germany-tourism.co.uk
FIFA World Cup 2006: www.fifaworldcup.com.

© Tanzania Trade Centre

Everyone has their dream destinations, but there are a handful of jewels that invariably come in near the top of most people's wish lists. And with the U.S. dollar at a 10-year low, it's never been cheaper to experience many of them for yourself. Paul Deegan describes five all-time classic trips.

1. Kilimanjaro

The highest mountain in Africa is now viewed by many as the 'Attainable Everest'. One of the coveted 'Seven Summits' (a collection of peaks consisting of the highest mountain on each continent), Kilimanjaro is affordable, accessible and, more importantly, achievable even for mere mortals. You need a certain level of stamina to climb the mountain, as the summit-day is a lung-busting round trip of some 10-15 hours. But there's something more important than fitness on Kilimanjaro, and that's acclimatisation. The good news is that acclimatisation is in no way linked to strength. Almost everyone can acclimatise sufficiently in order to climb 'Kili' if they spend enough time at altitude prior to mounting a summit bid. The safest way to do this is by joining a trip that takes in nearby Mt Meru or Mt Kenya before attempting Kili. In return for your exertions, you'll be rewarded with a delightful hike through almost every type of terrain imaginable, from sub-tropical to sub-arctic, culminating in a sunrise panorama from the roof of Africa that will long linger in your memory.
Best Time Of Year To Visit: July to September and December to February.

2. Galapagos

Brought to the public's attention by Charles Darwin, the Galapagos is an archipelago that's literally lost in time. This is one of the very few places left on Earth where you can wander amongst wildlife that, for the most part, remain completely unafraid of humans. Visitors disembarking from cruise ships onto the islands are obliged to follow marked trails that have been established for over 40 years. Yet even after four decades of near-constant human traffic, blue-footed boobies continue to lay their eggs in the centre of the paths, such is their nonchalance toward Homo sapiens. Only the giant tortoise, who was driven to the edge of extinction as a result of being harvested for its meat and oil, remains shy of camera-toting visitors. Diving with hammerhead sharks, snorkelling with marine iguanas, swimming with sea lions and relaxing next to albatross and frigate birds are all possible in this Eden-like paradise. As for the giant tortoise, a visit to the world-class Charles Darwin Research Station (CDRS) helps to bring their story full circle. Although some sub-species of tortoise have become extinct, others are being reared and returned to their native islands.
Best Time Of Year To Visit: May to December.

3. Antarctica

Until the 1980s, Antarctica was as remote as the Moon: a place visited only by scientists prepared to overwinter in this desolate land in order to learn more about the history of the Earth. Then the break-up of the Soviet Union brought many ice-strengthened vessels and experienced Soviet crews onto the market. Suddenly, reasonably affordable 10-day cruises to the Antarctic Peninsula were being advertised in the national press. These days, adventurous travellers prepared to tough out a rough three-day crossing from Tierra del Fuego are rewarded by seashores teeming with tens of thousands of penguins, hundreds of seals and countless birdlife. Inflatable dinghies ferry passengers onto the continent for tours of

© IAATO Dick Filby

Travellers prepared to tough out a rough three-day crossing from Tierra del Fuego are rewarded by seashores teeming with tens of thousands of penguins, hundreds of seals and countless birdlife.

wildlife colonies and deserted whaling stations. Contrary to popular belief, the Antarctic Peninsula is not particularly cold, but it can be very wet. If passengers do return soaking wet, hot showers and heated cabins will have them snug and dry again in next to no time. Watching the ship making the incredible journey as it pushes through pack ice is a sight that more than makes up for the occasional bout of seasickness. If you can stay awake, then the 24 hours of daylight will allow you to keep an eye out for whales surfacing by the boat. If not, rest assured that the ship's tannoy will wake you from your slumber every time one of these gargantuan creatures is spotted by a member of the diligent crew.

Best Time Of Year To Visit: November to February.

4. Bhutan

With vast tracts of the Himalaya currently off-limits to trekkers and travellers, the Kingdom of Bhutan is an excellent choice for those who wish to gaze up at the world's highest and arguably most spectacular mountain range. The $200 daily fee imposed on foreigners can initially deter some potential visitors, but you should remember that this does include all your transport, lodging and meals. By imposing this fee, the authorities are able to limit the number of tourists and generate sufficient income to help improve medical, educational and other facilities in the country. In return, visitors are rewarded with the chance to interact with a predominantly Buddhist people who have not yet become jaded towards curious foreigners. Treks range from easy three-day hikes to the multi-week 'Snowman Trek', regarded as one of the toughest trails on the planet.

Best Time Of Year To Visit: October to December.

5. The Great Barrier Reef

The largest natural feature in the world, Australia's Great Barrier Reef is made up of nearly 3,000 coral reefs. It occupies an area greater than the United Kingdom, Switzerland and the Netherlands combined. Divers exploring the reef have often described the experience as akin to wandering around a submerged tropical garden. Extending for some 2,300km from the tip of Cape York to a point just north of Fraser Island, the reef is home to 1,500 species of fish, 400 variations of coral and around 4,000 types of mollusc. Several threatened species, including the dugong and green turtle, are found in the protected waters. The reef is a magnet for scientists, divers and sailors. Whale and dolphin watching, scuba-diving and snorkelling are all popular activities. People put off by the prospect of learning to dive in the cold and murky waters around the UK are often inspired by the crystal-clear aquatic conditions on the reef and decide to learn to dive during their visit to Australia.

Best Time Of Year To Visit: September to December.

© Tourism Australia

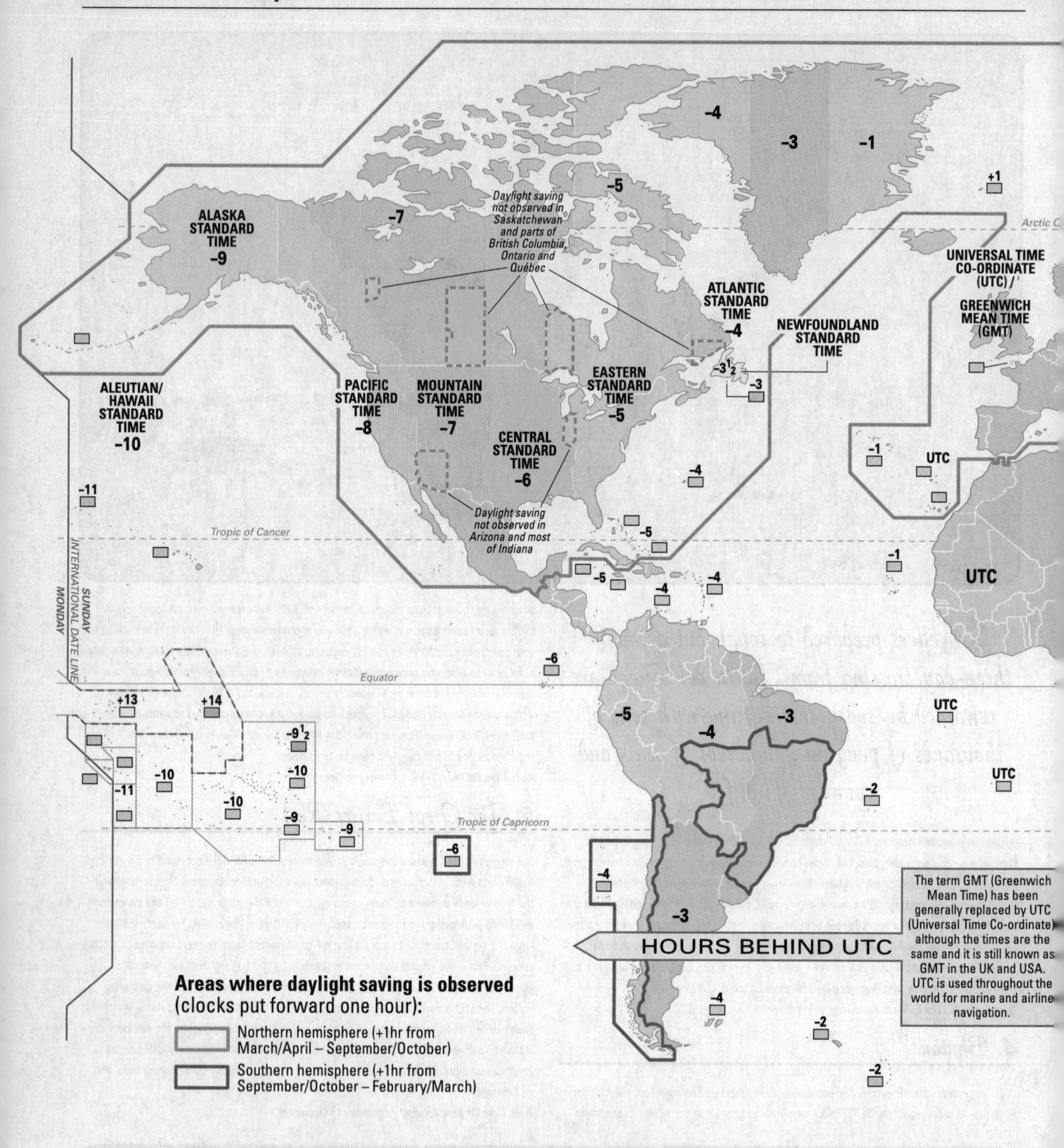

THE SUN AND THE EARTH

N
S
Sun directly overhead at noon over Tropic of Cancer
21 June (approx.): Summer solstice (NH) Winter solstice (SH)
1 July: Aphelion (earth furthest from sun) 152m km (94.5m miles)
Day
Night
23 Sept (approx.): Autumnal equinox (NH) Vernal equinox (SH)
SUN
21 Mar (approx.): Vernal equinox (NH) Autumnal equinox (SH)
1 Jan: Perihelion (earth closest to sun) 147m km (91.4m miles)
North Pole
22 Dec (approx.): Winter solstice (NH) Summer solstice (SH)
Sun directly overhead at noon over Tropic of Capricorn

NH: Northern hemisphere **SH:** Southern hemisphere

PHASES OF THE MOON

New moon
Last quarter
First quarter
EARTH
Average distance: 384,400 km (238,860 miles)
Moon as viewed from earth
Full moon

Sizes and distances are not to scale

SOLAR ECLIPSE

SUN
Maximum width of total eclipse on the earth's surface: 269 km (167 miles)
Umbra (total eclipse on earth)
Penumbra (partial eclipse on earth)
MOON
EARTH

An annular eclipse occurs when the apparent size of the moon is too small to fully cover the disc of the sun, resulting in a ring of sunlight remaining around the moon

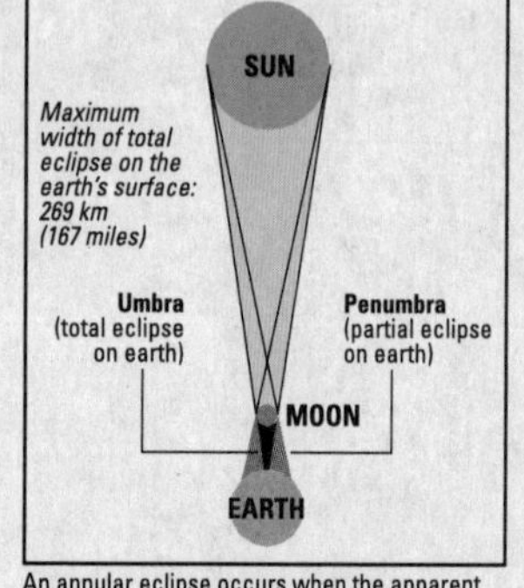

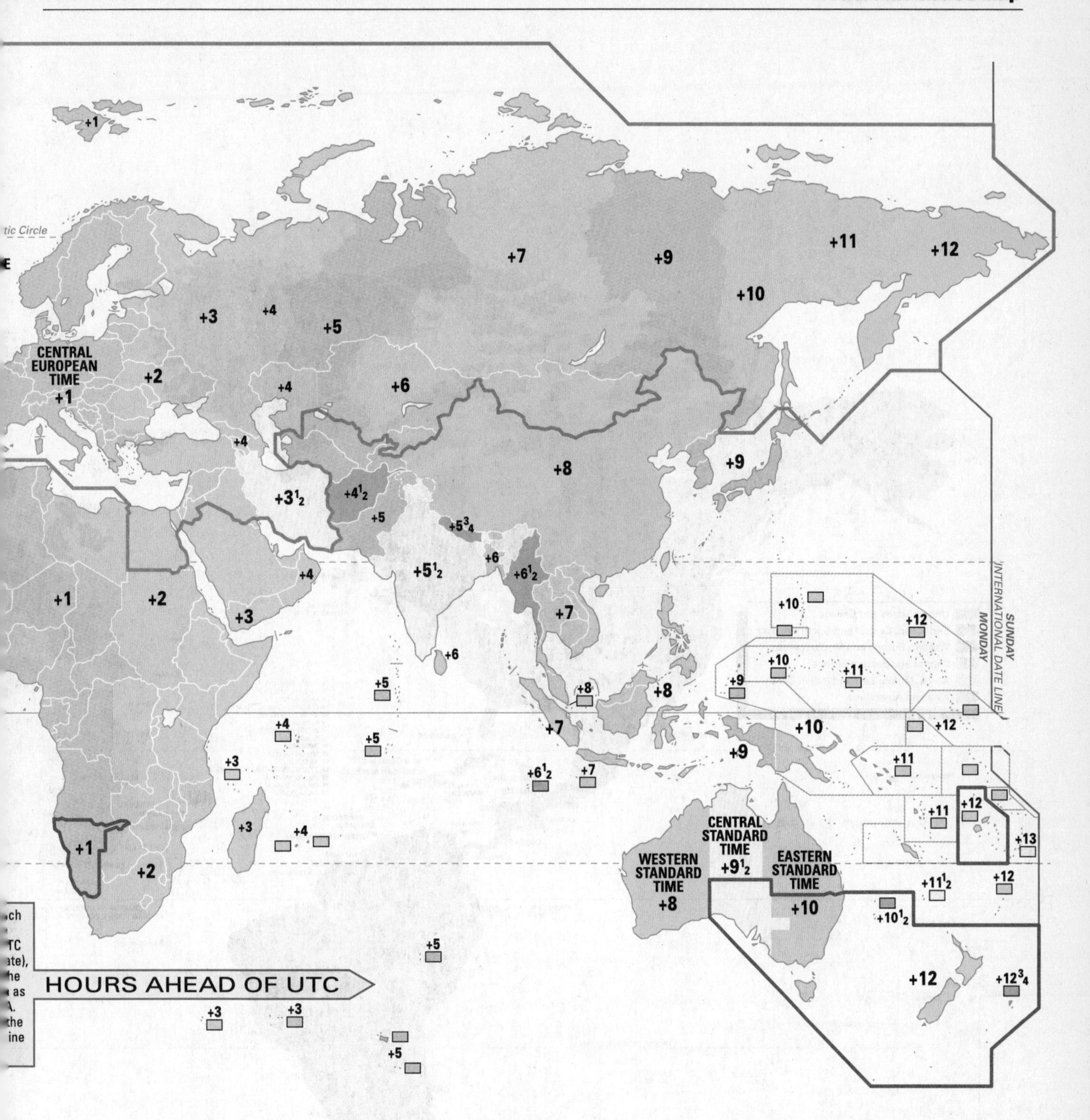

HOURS OF DAYLIGHT AND THE SEASONS

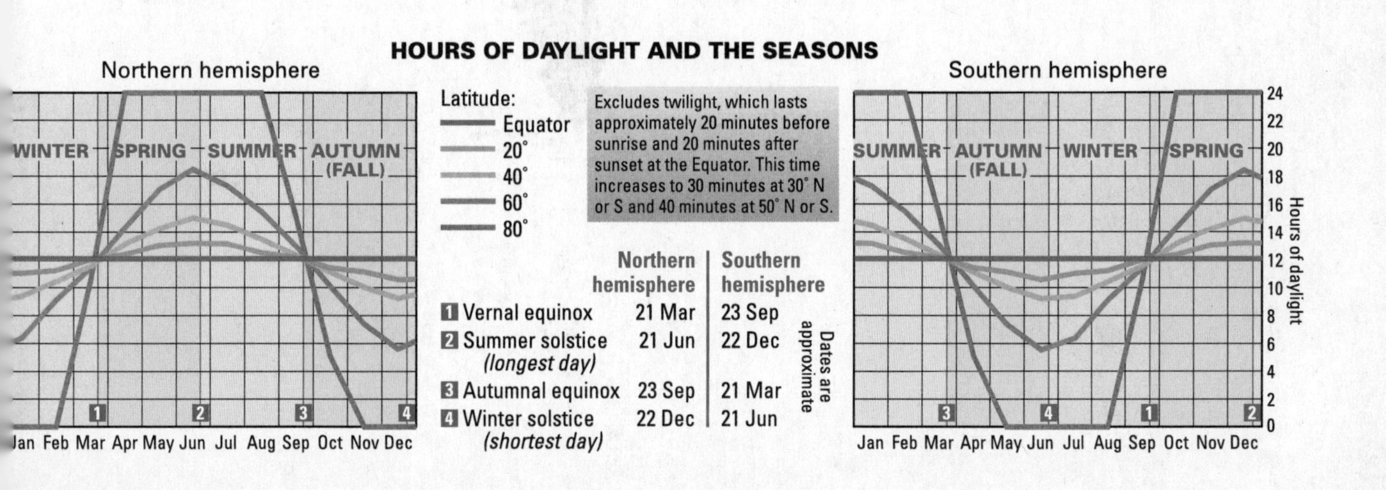

	Northern hemisphere	Southern hemisphere
1 Vernal equinox	21 Mar	23 Sep
2 Summer solstice *(longest day)*	21 Jun	22 Dec
3 Autumnal equinox	23 Sep	21 Mar
4 Winter solstice *(shortest day)*	22 Dec	21 Jun

United States and Canada
Caribbean, Central and South America
Western Europe and Mediterranean
Central and Eastern Europe
Africa, Middle East and Indian Ocean
Asia and Australasia
LINCOLN SEA
Ellesmere I.
Axel Heiberg I.
Parry Is.
Greenland (Den.)
GREENLAND SEA
BEAUFORT SEA
Banks I.
Victoria I.
Devon I.
BAFFIN BAY
Baffin I.
Jan Mayen (Nor.)
Alaska (US)
Great Bear Lake
Southampton I.
DAVIS STRAIT
ARCTIC CIRCLE
ICELAND
Great Slave Lake
HUDSON BAY
Faroe Is. (Den.)
BERING SEA
GULF OF ALASKA
CANADA
UNITED KINGDOM
IRELAND
L. Winnipeg
Aleutian Is.
Vancouver I.
L. Superior
Newfoundland I.
L. Huron
FRANCE
St-Pierre et Miquelon (Fr.)
L. Michigan
L. Ontario
ANDORRA
L. Erie
Long I.
UNITED STATES OF AMERICA
Azores (Port.)
PORTUGAL
SPAIN
Gibraltar (UK)
Bermuda (UK)
1 Puerto Rico (US)
2 Virgin Is. (US, UK)
3 Anguilla (UK)
4 St Maarten (Neths.); St-Martin (Fr.)
5 ST KITTS & NEVIS
6 Montserrat (UK)
7 ANTIGUA & BARBUDA
8 Guadeloupe (Fr.)
9 DOMINICA
10 Martinique (Fr.)
11 ST LUCIA
12 ST VINCENT & THE GRENADINES
13 Bonaire (Neths.)
14 Curaçao (Neths.)
15 Aruba (Neths.)
Madeira (Port.)
MOROCCO
Canary Is. (Sp.)
ALGERIA
Baja California
GULF OF MEXICO
BAHAMAS
WESTERN SAHARA
TROPIC OF CANCER
MEXICO
CUBA
Turks & Caicos Is. (UK)
DOMINICAN REPUBLIC
Hawaii (US)
Cayman Is. (UK)
HAITI
MAURITANIA
BELIZE
JAMAICA
MALI
CARIBBEAN SEA
CAPE VERDE
GUATEMALA
HONDURAS
SENEGAL
EL SALVADOR
NICARAGUA
BARBADOS
THE GAMBIA
BURKINA FASO
GRENADA
PACIFIC OCEAN
Panama Canal
TRINIDAD & TOBAGO
GUINEA-BISSAU
GUINEA
COSTA RICA
SIERRA LEONE
CÔTE D'IVOIRE
VENEZUELA
GUYANA
PANAMA
SURINAM
ATLANTIC OCEAN
LIBERIA
French Guiana (Fr.)
COLOMBIA
GHANA
TOGO
MONDAY
INTERNATIONAL DATE LINE
SUNDAY
EQUATOR
Galapagos Is. (Ec.)
ECUADOR
EQUATORIAL GUINEA
SÃO TOMÉ E PRÍNCIPE
KIRIBATI
Ascension (UK)
Tokelau (NZ)
PERU
BRAZIL
American Samoa (US)
SAMOA
Cook Is. (NZ)
BOLIVIA
St Helena (UK)
French Polynesia (Fr.)
Niue (NZ)
TROPIC OF CAPRICORN
PARAGUAY
Pitcairn Is. (UK)
Easter I. (Chile)
CHILE
URUGUAY
Islas Juan Fernández (Chile)
ARGENTINA
Tristan da Cunha (UK)
Gough I. (UK)
Falkland Is. (UK)
Bouvet (Nor.)
S. Georgia (UK)
Tierra del Fuego
SCOTIA SEA
Cape Horn
DRAKE PASSAGE
South Sandwich Is. (UK)

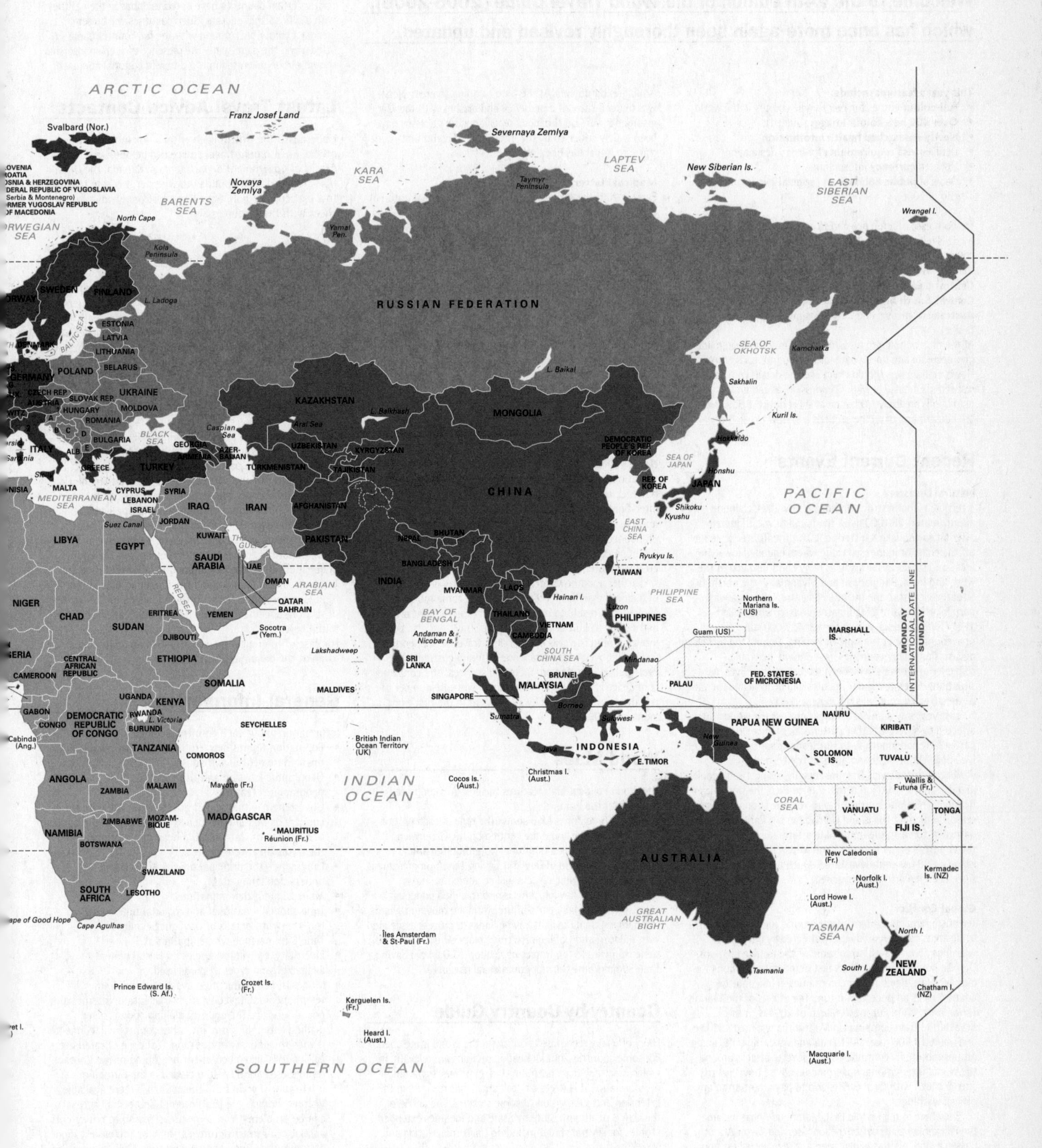
ARCTIC OCEAN
Svalbard (Nor.)
Franz Josef Land
Severnaya Zemlya
KARA SEA
LAPTEV SEA
New Siberian Is.
EAST SIBERIAN SEA
Wrangel I.
Novaya Zemlya
BARENTS SEA
Taymyr Peninsula
Yamal Pen.
North Cape
Kola Peninsula
SWEDEN
FINLAND
L. Ladoga
RUSSIAN FEDERATION
ESTONIA
LATVIA
BALTIC SEA
LITHUANIA
BELARUS
POLAND
GERMANY
CZECH REP
SLOVAK REP
UKRAINE
AUSTRIA
HUNGARY
MOLDOVA
ROMANIA
BULGARIA
BLACK SEA
GEORGIA
ARMENIA
AZER-BAIJAN
ITALY
ALB.
GREECE
TURKEY
MALTA
CYPRUS
SYRIA
LEBANON
ISRAEL
MEDITERRANEAN SEA
JORDAN
IRAQ
IRAN
Suez Canal
KUWAIT
LIBYA
EGYPT
SAUDI ARABIA
UAE
OMAN
QATAR
BAHRAIN
RED SEA
YEMEN
ARABIAN SEA
NIGER
CHAD
SUDAN
ERITREA
DJIBOUTI
Socotra (Yem.)
ETHIOPIA
CENTRAL AFRICAN REPUBLIC
CAMEROON
SOMALIA
UGANDA
KENYA
GABON
CONGO
DEMOCRATIC REPUBLIC OF CONGO
RWANDA
BURUNDI
L. Victoria
SEYCHELLES
Cabinda (Ang.)
TANZANIA
COMOROS
ANGOLA
ZAMBIA
MALAWI
Mayotte (Fr.)
MADAGASCAR
MOZAM-BIQUE
ZIMBABWE
NAMIBIA
BOTSWANA
MAURITIUS
Réunion (Fr.)
SWAZILAND
SOUTH AFRICA
LESOTHO
Cape Agulhas
Prince Edward Is. (S. Af.)
Crozet Is. (Fr.)
Kerguelen Is. (Fr.)
Heard I. (Aust.)
Îles Amsterdam & St-Paul (Fr.)
SOUTHERN OCEAN
INDIAN OCEAN
Caspian Sea
KAZAKHSTAN
Aral Sea
L. Balkhash
UZBEKISTAN
KYRGYZSTAN
TURKMENISTAN
TAJIKISTAN
AFGHANISTAN
PAKISTAN
MONGOLIA
L. Baikal
CHINA
NEPAL
BHUTAN
BANGLADESH
INDIA
MYANMAR
LAOS
THAILAND
VIETNAM
CAMBODIA
BAY OF BENGAL
Andaman & Nicobar Is.
Lakshadweep
SRI LANKA
MALDIVES
British Indian Ocean Territory (UK)
Cocos Is. (Aust.)
Christmas I. (Aust.)
SINGAPORE
MALAYSIA
BRUNEI
SOUTH CHINA SEA
Hainan I.
Sumatra
Borneo
Java
Sulawesi
INDONESIA
E. TIMOR
SEA OF OKHOTSK
Kamchatka
Sakhalin
Kuril Is.
Hokkaido
DEMOCRATIC PEOPLE'S REP OF KOREA
SEA OF JAPAN
Honshu
REP OF KOREA
JAPAN
Shikoku
Kyushu
EAST CHINA SEA
Ryukyu Is.
TAIWAN
PHILIPPINE SEA
Luzon
PHILIPPINES
Mindanao
PACIFIC OCEAN
Northern Mariana Is. (US)
Guam (US)
MARSHALL IS.
FED. STATES OF MICRONESIA
PALAU
INTERNATIONAL DATE LINE
MONDAY
SUNDAY
PAPUA NEW GUINEA
New Guinea
NAURU
KIRIBATI
SOLOMON IS.
TUVALU
Wallis & Futuna (Fr.)
CORAL SEA
VANUATU
TONGA
FIJI IS.
New Caledonia (Fr.)
AUSTRALIA
Kermadec Is. (NZ)
Norfolk I. (Aust.)
Lord Howe I. (Aust.)
GREAT AUSTRALIAN BIGHT
TASMAN SEA
North I.
South I.
NEW ZEALAND
Tasmania
Chatham I. (NZ)
Macquarie I. (Aust.)

How to Use this Guide

Welcome to the 24th edition of the *World Travel Guide* (2005-2006), which has once more again been thoroughly revised and updated.

This year's features include:

- **Full-colour** entries for every single country in the world;
- **Over 400 new colour images** sourced;
- **Newly-researched health information**;
- Detailed **visa requirements** for every destination
- Updated **currency** information
- Dates of **public holidays** and **special events** until the end of 2006

For both ease of reference and to enhance its appearance, the guide is regionally colour-coded. Each country is headed by a coloured box showing which region it belongs to. These are as follows: **Western Europe & Mediterranean**, dark blue; **Central & Eastern Europe**, light blue; **North America**, red; **Central, South America & Caribbean**, green; **Asia & Australasia**, mauve; and **Africa, Middle East & Indian Ocean**, orange.

At the time of going to press, every attempt has been made to give accurate and up-to-date information for each entry. However, travellers should check specific details with the respective Embassy or High Commission, as certain regulations are likely to change at short notice. Below is a brief description of all the sections and how to use them.

Recent Current Events

Natural Disasters

A terrible tsunami struck on Boxing Day 2004, claiming approximately 280,000 lives. The tsunami was triggered after an earthquake registering 9.0 on the Richter scale hit off the coast of Indonesia. Huge waves engulfed low-lying areas and struck as far away as Kenya and Tanzania in the west, and India, Bangladesh and Myanmar in the north. Situated closest to the quake's epicentre, Indonesia was particularly badly affected by the disaster which killed 111,171 in Indonesia, with a further 127,000 still unaccounted for at the time of writing. Despite the terrible devastation, many countries have shown incredible resilience and have slowly been rebuilding their lives. As situations develop, regular updates will be available for each of the affected countries on www.gocoti.com.

Last year saw many other areas around the world affected by severe weather patterns. September was a particularly bad month with Hurricanes Charley, Frances, Ivan and Jeanne battering areas of the US and the Caribbean. Jeanne was the most deadly, killing 1500 people and causing destruction across Puerto Rico, the Dominican Republic and Haiti. Hurricane Ivan was the strongest of the season, which hit the island Grenada in the Caribbean with particular force. In the immediate aftermath of the event, the country's prime minister Keith Mitchell assessed the island as '90 per cent devastated'. Much of the island has since been repaired and reopened.

Global Conflict

Terrorism remains a major threat around the world and some areas have been adversely affected by government warnings about travelling to some of the troubled regions. Despite holding the country's first democratic elections for over 50 years, fierce fighting continues in Iraq and the country faces an uncertain future. The effects of the War on Terror were felt in Europe in March of 2004 with the devastating train bombings in Madrid that claimed 191 lives and injured 1,800 more. Al-Qaeda and other militant Islamic groups reportedly continue to plan further attacks around the world. International governments advise travellers to stay in touch with local events and to pay attention to any official warnings.

Elsewhere in the Middle East, Mahmoud Abbas became the Palestinian leader after the long-serving Yasser Arafat passed away. This was widely seen as the region's best hope for peace in decades and both the Palestinians and the Israelis made tentative steps towards achieving that goal. At the time of going to press, the peace process was again hanging in the balance after a suicide bomb was detonated in Tel Aviv in February 2005. Abbas has vowed to clamp down on Islamic extremists and tensions remain high in the region.

And in Nepal, King Gyanendra sacked his entire government in February 2005 because he was unhappy with their efforts to stop the Maoist insurgency. He assumed control of the country himself and granted the Nepalese Army greater powers. At the time of going to press, Nepal was under a state of emergency and clashes with the Maoist insurgents were on the increase. Gyanendra's actions have been widely criticised by the international community and travel to Nepal has been affected.

Medical Matters

Early in 2005, health experts claimed that a repeat outbreak of the SARS virus on the scale of that which hit in 2003/04 was extremely unlikely. However, health officials have raised the alarm over their fears of a global bird flu pandemic. At the time of going to press, human cases of avian influenza had been contained to South-East Asia, but there is a very real threat that the virus could spread. Despite a large cull of poultry birds, cases of the virus continue to emerge in the region. The World Health Organization (WHO) has warned that if the virus mutates into a form that more easily transmits between humans, there could be a pandemic that many governments would be powerless to prevent. Travellers have been warned to avoid contact with live birds in areas known to be at risk of the disease.

Looking Forward

But on a positive note, globally, January 30 2005 heralded the first opportunity for Iraqis to vote in a multi-party election for 50 years. Millions turned out to help elect a transitional assembly. Issues surrounding the election do, however, remain contentious and it is also unlikely that inter-fighting and discord will diminish any time soon in Iraq. However, the majority of international leaders have pronounced the election as a milestone in Iraqi history and it is hoped that the country can now move towards a more positive future.

Further good news for the travel industry is that the rise of budget travel has forced airlines to become more competitive, resulting in a significant drop in flight prices – particularly to European destinations. There has also been a growing trend towards independent travel with operators responding well to the challenge, offering customers an ever-greater range of products and services. And consumer confidence is finally on the rise again with the number of worldwide arrivals rising by 12 per cent in the first eight months of 2004.

World Maps

The World Political Map features the colour coding used throughout the guide.

The World Time Zones Map shows the time in each part of the world. All time zones are centred on the Greenwich Meridian, zero degrees longitude. Note that in many countries, some form of Daylight Saving Time/Summertime is observed, during which clocks will be altered to make maximum use of daylight; this is also specified under each country's entry. Many parts of the world are moving towards standard regional Daylight Saving Times (a process associated with the formation of regional trade blocs, similar to the EU); some countries in the Tropics have adopted Daylight Saving Time/Summertime only for commercial reasons.

Country-by-Country Guide

Every officially recognised country in the world is included. For some countries, not all headed sections are relevant, in which case they have been omitted. In others, the amount of information it is necessary to convey has resulted in the extension and subdivision of some sections. The entry for the USA is dealt with State by State and includes extended profiles for several states, including California, Florida and New York.

Certain islands, states and territories do not have their own entry in the World Travel Guide but are instead grouped together; this applies particularly to island groups. In other cases, countries may, correctly or not, be known popularly by more than one name: for example, Sri Lanka/Ceylon and Myanmar/Burma. A further complication is caused by areas that are politically an integral part of a country with its own entry; thus the Balearic and Canary islands have their own subsections at the end of the Spain entry. If in doubt as to where information may be found, refer to the Contents pages. Certain countries have opted to enhance their entries with a sponsorship package; such countries will be set against a colour background with the full country name listed along the page spine. The presence of such sponsorship should not be taken to imply a different editorial approach.

Latest Travel Advice Contacts

Underneath the title of each entry a box indicates where official government travel advice can be obtained. Contact details of government departments in Canada, the UK and USA are given. If in doubt as to whether it is safe to travel to a particular region, travellers are strongly advised to check with these sources.

Maps

Each country section is headed by a full-colour map, with a smaller inset showing its location within a more general region. More detailed regional maps showing areas of particular interest to the tourist or business traveller have, where possible, also been introduced. In addition, there are two world maps at the beginning of the book.

Contact Addresses

Addresses are given in the following order: the name and address of the national tourist board or other relevant contact within the particular country; the diplomatic representative of the particular country in either the UK or mainland Europe; the name and address of the country's Tourist Board in the UK, where applicable; the British Embassy or High Commission in the particular country; the country's diplomatic representative and Tourist Board in the USA; the US Embassy in the country in question; the country's diplomatic representative and Tourist Board in Canada; and the Canadian Embassy or High Commission in the country. Addresses of Consulates or sections specifically handling visa applications can be found here.

For ease of reference, the country dialling code is now given at the beginning of this section.

General Information

Information about each country includes:

- Population figures derived from the most reliable and up-to-date official statistics
- Geographic location and the country's main geographical features
- Government – the type of government, the date the country gained independence (if applicable), the names of the head of state and the head of government and the dates they were elected
- Language – the principal official, spoken and understood languages
- Main religious denominations
- Time zone(s) – national and regional time zones, together with details of Daylight Saving Time/Summertime where appropriate
- Electricity, eg voltage, cycles (in Hertz) (where available), and types of plugs used
- Modes of communication available, including telephone, mobile (cellular), fax, telegram, Internet and postal services. The country dialling code is given: dialling this code from any other country will connect it with the country in question. (For ease of reference, this code is also given at the beginning of the Contact Addresses section.) Also included is the outgoing international code from the country, where available. Visitors should note that Internet and e-mail access can be problematic in some areas, owing to power cuts and lack of infrastructure. Fax may be the easiest mode of communication in some countries. The Press section lists the main English-language papers published in that country and, where none exist, the most important papers published in the national language(s)
- International radio services – website addresses for up-to-date information on international radio services available
- TIMATIC information – to access TIMATIC country information on Health and Visa regulations through the Computer Reservation System (CRS), type the appropriate command line listed in the TIMATIC box for each country

Passport/Visa

Information is presented by means of a quick-glance table on the passport and visa requirements for British and other EU nationals, as well as Australian, Canadian, Japanese and US nationals. Information, where available, is also given on the types and prices of visas and their validity, where to apply for visas, application requirements, the length of time an application takes to process and the procedures to be followed when renewing visas. There is also information on who to contact if seeking temporary residence. Information on passports and visas is provided mainly by Embassies and High Commissions based in London. Other relevant information is included where necessary.

In many cases, the same regulations for passports and visas (or other identity documents) apply equally to all countries that are members of a particular international organisation (such as the Commonwealth or the EU). Occasionally, in the notes following the charts, the organisation only, rather than the often-lengthy list of member states, will be referred to. For this reason, a table showing the membership (and contact details) of the Arab League, CIS countries, the Commonwealth, ECOWAS (Economic Community of West African States), the EU and other organisations may be found in the International Organisations section at the back of the book.

In the interest of clarity and brevity, various groups of people who are often exempt from passport and visa requirements have generally not been referred to in the charts or notes. These include holders of seamen's books, UN travel passes, service or diplomatic passports and stateless persons.

Unless otherwise stated in the chart, all travellers should be in possession of a return ticket and/or sufficient funds for the duration of their stay. In many cases they will be required to prove this on arrival in the country, or when they apply for their visa prior to departure.

Note: Although every effort has been made to ensure the accuracy of the information included in this section, entry requirements may be subject to change at short notice. If in doubt, check with the Embassy or High Commission concerned, being sure to state the nature of the visit (eg business, touristic, transit) and the intended length of stay, and to confirm exactly what documentation will be necessary for the application. Remember that transit visas may be required for stopovers.

Entry and other restrictions: Nationals of Israel and Taiwan (China) especially (though not exclusively) may be subject to restrictions when visiting other countries. Travellers whose passports indicate that they have entered these countries may also encounter difficulties. Some countries enforce stricter regulations for those crossing land borders than for those entering by air or sea. Travellers whose passports confer less than full British citizenship may also be subject to additional requirements. In such cases, it is advisable to check with the relevant Embassy or with the Foreign Office well in advance of travel.

British passports: Under the terms of the British Nationality Act 1981, which came into force on 1 January 1983, 'Citizenship of the United Kingdom and Colonies' has been divided into six categories. The three main categories are: British Citizen, for those closely connected with the UK (the holder has automatic right of abode in the UK); British Overseas Territories Citizen, for those with certain specific ties with one or more of the Overseas Territories; and British Overseas Citizen, for those citizens of the UK and Colonies who have not acquired either of the above citizenship. The other three categories are: British Nationals (Overseas), for former British Dependent citizens in Hong Kong who changed their status after the handover of Hong Kong to China in 1997; British Subjects; and British Protected Persons. Since 1 January 1983, no endorsement about immigration status has been necessary on passports issued to British Citizens, as they will automatically be exempt from UK immigration control and have the right to take up employment or to establish business in another member state of the EU.

Visitors should check with the relevant Embassy or High Commission if they have any queries regarding which level of citizenship is necessary to qualify for entry to any country destination without possession of a visa.

All applications and enquiries should be made to the following: Passport Office, Globe House, 89 Eccleston Square, London SW1V 1PN (tel: (0870) 521 0410), who also handle visa requirements relating to British Overseas Territories; or the Home Office Immigration & Nationality Policy Directorate, 3rd Floor, India Buildings, Water Street, Liverpool L2 0QN (tel: (0151) 237 5200); or its regional offices in Belfast, Glasgow, Newport and Peterborough.

The Schengen Agreement: Since March 1995, a 'borderless' region known as the Schengen area has been declared covering the following states: Austria, Belgium, Denmark, Finland, France, Germany, Greece, Iceland, Italy, Luxembourg, The Netherlands, Norway, Portugal, Spain and Sweden.

Schengen countries now issue standard Schengen visas, and nationals holding visas issued by one of the Schengen countries are, in principle, permitted to travel freely within the borders of all 15. However, since Schengen states are still free to decide their own visa requirements, entry regulations may vary and nationals not requiring a visa for one Schengen country may require one for other Schengen countries. This has various practical implications; for example, travellers may be refused entry to a Schengen country for which they do not require a visa if holding onward tickets to a country for which they do. If visiting more than one Schengen country, the traveller should apply for the Schengen visa to the Embassy/Consulate of the first or main country to be visited.

There are three types of Schengen visa: airport transit, transit and short-stay. For stays of over three months, a long-stay visa will be required; this will be valid only in the country of issue.

Money

The entries for each country provide information on currency denominations, currency restrictions, recent exchange rates for Sterling and the US Dollar, and banking hours.

The denominations of notes and coins given are correct at the time of writing, but new ones may be introduced or old ones withdrawn, particularly in countries with high rates of inflation. In some countries, certain foreign currencies may be accepted instead of, or in addition to, the local currency.

In most cases, UK Sterling and US Dollar bank notes and travellers cheques can be exchanged at banks and bureaux de change. In certain countries, some foreign currencies are more readily exchanged than others, and details are included where this is likely to affect a visitor carrying Sterling notes or travellers cheques. Banks may recommend US Dollars in preference to Pounds Sterling, depending on the exchange rates, and will also be able to offer up-to-date information as to the acceptability of Sterling in a particular country.

It is worth remembering that certain currencies can be reconverted into Sterling only at very disadvantageous rates; others cannot be reconverted at all. In some cases, banknotes of a very low value will not be negotiable in the UK, whilst denominations that are considered too high may attract a less favourable rate of exchange. However, US travellers can expect to get a better rate for US$100 notes than for US$5, but please note that many banks will refuse to exchange US$1 notes. Coins should not be brought back, as UK banks may not be able to exchange them. Some countries prohibit reconversion except at airports or borders, and then only up to a certain limit. It is often advisable to change only the amount needed to cover immediate expenses.

Currency restrictions permitting, it may be advisable to change enough money in the UK to cover practicalities such as taxi fares from the airport, in the event of the airport bank not being open (these banks do not always keep normal banking hours). Visitors should also note that each country has specific Public Holidays (see Public Holidays section).

Information has been given on the acceptability of credit and debit cards.

A selection of exchange rates, spanning the past year, has been included in each country entry. These figures are usually middle rates, ie the average of buying and selling prices. Some countries operate a two- or three-tiered exchange rate, in which case the rates quoted are the most advantageous, and are the ones that would apply to a foreign visitor. In other countries, there is an official rate of exchange, but visitors may often find the unofficial rates to be more to their advantage. It must be stressed that these figures are only a guide based on rates supplied by the Financial Times, or in some cases, from a country's Embassy.

Most countries permit the unlimited import of foreign currency, although it is often subject to declaration on arrival. In such cases, the export of foreign currency will usually be limited to the amount imported and declared. Some countries insist on the exchange of a certain quantity of foreign currency for each day of the visit; this may need to be done in advance. In some cases, receipts must be kept in order to reconvert surplus local currency on departure; in others, special forms or permits may be required.
Travellers should note that black market transactions are not necessarily favourable, in some cases illegal, and cannot be accounted for (which may cause problems when leaving a country). Changing money on the black market often results in severe punishment (including, in some places, a possible death sentence).

European Monetary Union (EMU) and the Euro: On 1 January 1999, the Euro became the official currency of 11 of the 15 member states of the European Union. Greece adopted the Euro in January 2001. 10 new countries joined the European Union on May 1 2004 and are set to join the European Monetary Union in the next couple of years: the 10 new countries are Cyprus, Czech Republic, Estonia, Hungary, Latvia, Lithuania, Malta, Poland, Slovak Republic and Slovenia. In all the countries belonging to the Eurozone, it is now possible to use one single currency. The new Euro coins and notes appeared on 1 January 2002. At the time of writing, three EU member-states – Denmark, Sweden and the United Kingdom – have not joined the single currency.

Duty Free

All duty free allowances, including differentials for EU and non-EU travellers, are given where applicable, as well as information on prohibited items and any other relevant details. Details given are not necessarily exhaustive and should only be used as a general guide. Further information may be obtained from the appropriate High Commission, Embassy or Tourist Board, HM Customs and Excise or the British Overseas Trade Board.

Following the introduction of the Single European Market in 1993, there are now no legal limits imposed on importing duty-paid tobacco and alcoholic products from one EU country to another. However, travellers may be questioned at customs if they exceed the amounts recommended and may be asked to prove that the goods are for personal consumption only.

Public Holidays

The holidays given are usually those when government offices, businesses and banks will close. Note that the dates for Islamic holidays are approximate, since they must accord with local sightings of the moon; similar variations of dating occur for Buddhist, Chinese and Hindu holidays.

In some cases, official dates for public holidays have not been fixed at the time of writing. Check with the respective Tourist Office, Embassy or High Commission for further details.

Health

Vaccination requirements and/or recommendations are presented in a quick-glance chart. Wherever an immunisation is considered 'advisable', it is strongly recommended that precautions are taken, even though they may not be strictly necessary. Occasionally this advice may conflict with guidance given by the relevant Tourist Board or Embassy, but it is felt that the advice of the Department of Health and the World Health Organization should be heeded, on the principle of safeguarding against even a minimal risk. Where immunisation is required, vaccination should be taken well in advance so that adequate intervals between doses can be maintained: rapid courses do not guarantee the same level of immunisation. Children and pregnant women may require special vaccination procedures. (See the immunisation chart in the Health appendix.)

Information has been compiled from several sources, including the Department of Health, the World Health Organization, the London School of Hygiene and Tropical Medicine and the British Medical Journal (official publication of the British Medical Association).
We would particularly like to thank Dr Eve Speight, MD, DFFP, for her help in updating the Health appendix.

Travel

This information is divided into sections for International and Internal travel.

International

The name and code of the major airline serving the country is given. In most cases, the approximate flight times from London and other major cities to the main airport are also given; it must be stressed that these figures are approximate and depend on a number of factors. Information is also supplied on the major international airports.

Where applicable, ferry and cruise ports will be mentioned and details given of international ferry services. In cases where a river runs through more than one country, services available from one country to the other will be specified.

Where applicable, the main international rail routes are detailed. The main border crossings and routes between countries are also listed.

Internal

Where appropriate, similar information is given on internal services and ports. This includes information on internal travel by air, sea, river/lake, rail and road, plus urban travel (travel facilities in and around the main cities).

Please note in regards to travelling by road that the validity of a visitor's national driving licence varies from country to country, therefore contact should be made with the motoring club or driver-licensing authority in the country of residence to determine whether or not an International Driving Permit is required. The International Driving Permit cannot be issued outside the country responsible for issuing the holder's national driving licence.

For some countries, a travel times chart has also been included, giving the approximate travel times between the capital and major destinations in the country.

Accommodation

Details are given on the range of available hotel accommodation, including government classifications, regulations etc, according to the latest information available at the time of writing. Details of the national hotel association are provided where possible, together with specific information on the national grading system. The national grading system should not be confused with local award schemes such as the AA or Michelin star systems. Information is also included on other types of accommodation, including self-catering, guest houses, camping/caravanning and youth hostels.

Resorts & Excursions

The country's main tourist regions and most popular resorts are described.

Note: In some cases, the divisions in the Resorts & Excursions section will not correspond exactly with administrative boundaries. These divisions have been made in an attempt to group towns or regions together for touristic purposes, and have no political significance.

Sport & Activities

The main activities available in the country concerned are outlined, with special emphasis on diving, trekking and golf – three activities that are increasingly popular with today's travellers. Contact details of diving and golf associations and the main official sporting organisations are given where applicable. In addition, the section aims to give an idea of the country's facilities as regards sport and activities, the ease with which they can be arranged and whether any special permits are required.
This section has been omitted for countries in which it is currently not possible to pursue sporting and outdoor activities, such as those parts of the world affected by natural disasters or civil war.

Social Profile

Areas covered in this section include Food & Drink, Nightlife, Special Events and Social Conventions (including Photography, Tipping and so on).

Business Profile

A brief description of the economy of each country, principal exports and imports and its major trading partners.

Also includes the best times to visit, the necessity or otherwise for visiting cards, prior appointments, translation/interpreter services and punctuality, the required style of dress for business meetings and business/office hours.

The National Chamber of Commerce in each country is able to offer detailed commercial advice and information to any prospective business traveller, and contact details, where possible, are listed, plus details of any other relevant organisation(s).

Where applicable, a brief description of the conference/convention facilities within the country is included, along with contact details of the national conference organisation.

Climate

A brief description of the country's climate, including clothing recommendations. The information is supplemented by at least one climate graph.

Appendices

Calendar of Events.
Dates for major travel-trade events around the world.

International Organisations
A list of organisations concerned with world trade and international cooperation, which can be used to supplement the Business Profile section of individual country entries.

Health
Essential information for anyone travelling abroad, particularly to tropical countries; supplements the information contained in the Health section of individual country entries.

The Disabled Traveller
Designed to provide the travel trade with information relevant to making travel arrangements for people with disabilities. A list of further sources of information/useful organisations is also given.

Religion
These four articles, World of Buddhism, World of Christianity, World of Islam and World of Judaism, are intended to give introductions to religious and cultural attitudes in countries where these religions are practised. They supplement the information contained in the Public Holidays, Social Profiles and Business sections.

Weather
A general introduction to the way in which weather conditions can affect individuals, and supplements the information contained in the Climate section of each country's entry. Information is included on humidity, wind and wind-chill factor, temperature range, precipitation and precautions.

Final Note
If there is anything that you would like to see expanded, clarified or included for the first time, or if you come across any information that is no longer accurate, we would be happy to hear from you. Such suggestions will be considered for future editions of the World Travel Guide. Address your suggestions to:

The Editor - World Travel Guide
Columbus Travel Guides
Media House, Azalea Drive, Swanley
Kent BR8 8HU, UK
Tel: 01322 661474. Fax: 01322 616327.
E-mail: travel.editorial@nexusmedia.com

Afghanistan

LATEST TRAVEL ADVICE CONTACTS

British Foreign and Commonwealth Office
Tel: (0870) 606 0290 Website: www.fco.gov.uk
US Department of State
Website: http://travel.state.gov/travel
Canadian Department of Foreign Affairs and Int'l Trade
Tel: (1 800) 267 8376 Website: www.dfait-maeci.gc.ca

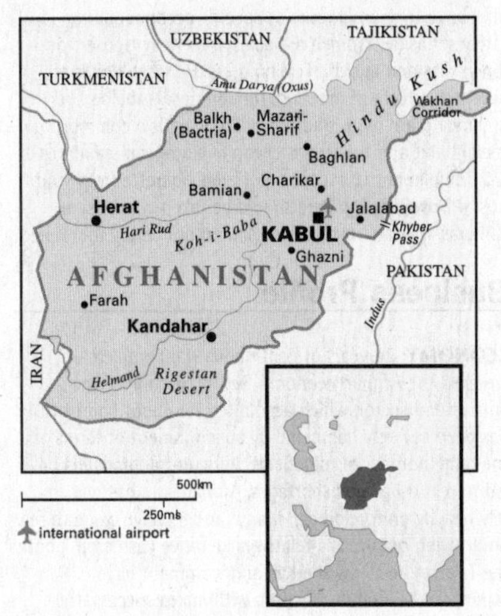

Location: Southwest Asia; northwest part of Indian subcontinent.

Country dialling code: 93.

Ministry of Foreign Affairs
Malak Azghar Road, Kabul, Afghanistan
Tel: (20) 293 005. Fax: (86) 6890 9988 *or* (80) 1459 2967.
E-mail: contact@afghanistan-mfa.net
Website: www.afghanistan-mfa.net

British Embassy
15th Street, Roundabout Wazir Akbar Khan, PO Box 334, Kabul, Afghanistan.
Tel: (70) 102 000. Fax: (70) 102 250 *or* 274.
E-mail: britishembassy.kabul@fco.gov.uk
Website: www.britishembassy.gov.uk/afghanistan
The British Embassy in Kabul is only able to provide limited consular assistance. The Embassy does not issue passports or visas.

Embassy of Afghanistan
31 Princes Gate, London SW7 1QQ, UK
Tel: (020) 7589 8891 *or* 8892 (consular section).
Fax: (020) 7581 3452 *or* 7581 3452 (consular section).
E-mail: afghanembassy@btinternet.com
Website: www.afghanembassy.co.uk
Open: Mon-Fri 0930-1500; 0930-1330 (visa applications).
The British High Commission in Islamabad deals with enquiries relating to Afghanistan (see *Pakistan* section).

Ariana Afghan Airlines
PO Box 76, Ansari Watt, AF-Kabul, Afghanistan
Tel: (20) 210 0351 or (873) 762 523 844/5 (drop country dialling code).
Fax: (873) 762 523 846 (drop country dialling code).
E-mail: flyariana@mail.com
Website: www.flyariana.com
Offers limited tourist information only.

Embassy of Afghanistan
2341 Wyoming Avenue, NW, Washington DC, 20008, USA
Tel: (202) 483 6410. Fax: (202) 483 6488.
E-mail: info@embassyofafghanistan.org
Website: www.embassyofafghanistan.org

TIMATIC CODES

Health
AMADEUS: **TI-DFT/JIB/HE**
GALILEO/WORLDSPAN: **TI-DFT/JIB/HE**
SABRE: **TIDFT/JIB/HE**

Visa
AMADEUS: **TI-DFT/JIB/VI**
GALILEO/WORLDSPAN: **TI-DFT/JIB/VI**
SABRE: **TIDFT/JIB/VI**

To access TIMATIC country information on Health and Visa regulations through the Computer Reservations System (CRS), type in the appropriate command line listed above.

Consulate General of Afghanistan
360 Lexington Avenue, 11th Floor, New York, NY 10017, USA
Tel: (212) 972 2276/7. Fax: (212) 972 9046.
E-mail: general@consulate.net (consul general) *or* info@consulate.net (general information)
Website: www.afghanconsulateny.org
The American Embassy in Islamabad deals with enquiries relating to Afghanistan (see *Pakistan* section).

General Information

Very little reliable information is available relating to some of the following sections; much of the infrastructure and services have been destroyed or ceased to function in the months of fighting. Those that were there before were severely limited and old-fashioned due to the years of civil war and occupation that had gone before.

AREA: 652,225 sq km (251,773 sq miles).

POPULATION: 22,930,000 (UN estimate 2002, including nomads).

POPULATION DENSITY: 35.2 per sq km.

CAPITAL: Kabul. **Population:** 2,766,800 (official estimate 2000).

GEOGRAPHY: Afghanistan is a landlocked country, sharing its borders with Turkmenistan, Uzbekistan and Tajikstan to the north, China to the northeast, Pakistan to the east and south and Iran to the west. On the eastern tip of the Iranian plateau, central Afghanistan is made up of a tangled mass of mountain chains. The Hindu Kush is the highest range, rising to more than 7500m (24,600ft). The Bamian Valley separates the Hindu Kush from Koh-i-Baba, the central mountain range and source of the Helmand River. To the north and southwest of these mountains, alluvial plains provide fertile agricultural soil. To the northeast is Kabul, the capital. The other major cities are Jalalabad, Kandahar, Mazar-i-Sharif and Herat.

GOVERNMENT: Republic. Civil war since 1992. **Head of State:** President Hamid Karzai since December 2001 (officially elected as president in October 2004).

LANGUAGE: The principal languages are Pashtu and Dari Persian. Some English and Russian may also be spoken.

RELIGION: Islamic majority (mostly Sunni), with Shi'ite, Hindu and Sikh minorities.

TIME: GMT + 4.5.

ELECTRICITY: 220 volts AC, 50Hz. Supplies may be seriously affected and powercuts frequent for the foreseeable future.

COMMUNICATIONS: At the time of writing, no telephone, fax, telex, telegram or postal services are generally available. **Telephone/Fax:** No IDD. In general, there is normally a severe shortage of lines for operator-connected international calls. **Mobile telephone:** *Afghan Wireless* (website: www.afghanwireless.com) operates a network covering cities like Kabul and Herat. **Telegram:** Under normal circumstances, these could be sent from the Central Post Office, Kabul (closes at 2100). **Post:** Prior to military action, airmail used to take one week to reach Europe. **Press:** The *Kabul New Times* is the main English-language newspaper.

Radio: BBC World Service (website: www.bbc.co.uk/worldservice) and Voice of America (website: www.voa.gov) can be received. From time to time the freq-uencies change and the most up-to-date can be found online.

Passport/Visa

Note: Please note that travellers are strongly advised by the British Foreign and Commonwealth Office and the US Department of State not to travel to Afghanistan.

	Passport Required?	Visa Required?	Return Ticket Required?
Full British	Yes	Yes	Yes
Australian	Yes	Yes	Yes
Canadian	Yes	Yes	Yes
USA	Yes	Yes	Yes
Other EU	Yes	Yes	Yes
Japanese	Yes	Yes	Yes

Note: *Regulations and requirements may be subject to change at short notice, and you are advised to contact the appropriate diplomatic or consular authority before finalising travel arrangements. Details of these may be found at the head of this country's entry. Any numbers in the chart refer to the footnotes below.*

Entry restrictions: Women of all nationalities should dress appropriately with a scarf to cover their heads and an overcoat for their bodies.

PASSPORTS: Valid passport required by all.

VISAS: Required by all except the following:
(a) travellers holding a re-entry permit issued by Afghanistan;
(b) transit passengers not leaving the airport and continuing their journey within two hours.

Types of visa and cost: *Single-entry:* £30. *Double-entry:* £40. *Multiple-entry:* £55 (up to three months); £115 (up to six months). Enquiries should be made at the Embassy for details about visiting Afghanistan.

Validity: Three or six months from date of issue. Duration of stay depends on purpose of visit.

Application to: Consulate (or Consular section at Embassy); see *Contact Addresses* section.

Application requirements: (a) Company or sponsorship letter with name and address of commissioning firm or person. (b) Application form. (c) Valid passport. (d) One passport-size photo. (e) Fee, (payable by cash (except when applying by post), postal order or cheque). (f) Registered SAE if replying by post. (g) Return or onward ticket and documents required for onward journey. (h) Sufficient funds for duration of stay.

Working days required: Two to five.

Money

Currency: Afghani (Af) = 100 puls. New bank notes were introduced in October 2002 in a bid to shore up the currency. The new notes are in denominations of Af1000, 500, 100, 50, 20, 10, 5, 2 and 1. The US Dollar is also widely accepted.

Credit & debit cards: Not accepted. There are no ATMs.

Travellers cheques: It is not currently recommended to take travellers cheques to Afghanistan; if necessary, however, to avoid additional exchange rate charges, travellers are advised to take travellers cheques in US Dollars, Euros or Pounds Sterling.

Currency restrictions: The import and export of local currency (in banknotes and coins) is permitted up to AF500. The import of foreign currency is unlimited if declared on arrival; export is permitted up to the amount imported and declared.

Exchange rate indicators: The following figures are included as a guide to the movements of the Afghani against Sterling and the US Dollar:

Date	Feb '04	May '04	Aug '04	Nov '04
£1.00=	78.27	76.80	79.22	81.42
$1.00=	43.00	43.00	43.00	43.00

Banking hours: Generally Sat-Wed 0800-1200 and 1300-1630, Thurs 0800-1330.

Duty Free

The following goods can be taken into Afghanistan without incurring customs duty:
A reasonable amount of tobacco products and alcoholic beverages for personal use; any amount of perfume.

Restricted items: The import of film cameras is possible only with a licence. The export of antiquities, carpets, furs and camera film is prohibited without a licence.

Public Holidays

2005: Jan 21 Eid al-Adha (Feast of the Sacrifice). **Feb 1** Mount Arafat Day. **Feb 19** Ashura (Martyrdom of Imam Hussein). **Mar 21** Navruz (Persian New Year). **Apr 18** Liberation Day. **Apr 21** Roze-Maulud (Birth of the Prophet). **Apr 28** Revolution Day; Loss of the Muslim Nation. **May 1** Labour Day. **Aug 19** National Day. **Nov 3-5** Eid al-Fitr (End of Ramadan).

2006: Jan 1 Eid-al-Adha (Feast of the Sacrifice). **Feb 9** Ashura (Martyrdom of Imam Hussain). **Feb 22** Mount Arafat Day. **Mar 20** Navruz (Persian New Year). **Mar 26** Roze-Maulud (Birth of the Prophet). **Apr 18** Liberation Day. **Apr 28** Revolution Day; Loss of the Muslim Nation. **May 1** Labour Day. **Aug 19** National Day. **Oct 24** Eid al-Fitr (End of Ramadan).

Note: Muslim festivals are timed according to local sightings of various phases of the moon and the dates given above are approximations. During the lunar month of Ramadan that precedes Eid al-Fitr, Muslims fast during the day and feast at night and normal business patterns may be interrupted. Some disruption may continue into Eid al-Fitr itself. Eid al-Fitr and Eid al-Adha may last up to several days, depending on the region. For more information, see the *World of Islam* appendix..

A B C D E F G H I J K L M N O P Q R S T U V W X Y Z

Health

	Special Precautions?	Certificate Required?
Yellow Fever	Yes	1
Cholera	2	No
Typhoid & Polio	3	N/A
Malaria	4	N/A

Note: *Regulations and requirements may be subject to change at short notice, and you are advised to contact your doctor well in advance of your intended date of departure. Any numbers in the chart refer to the footnotes below.*

1: A yellow fever vaccination certificate is required if arriving within six days of leaving or transitting countries with endemic or infected areas. Travellers arriving from non-endemic zones should note that vaccination is strongly recommended for travel outside urban areas, even if an outbreak of the disease has not been reported and they would normally not require a vaccination certificate to enter the country.
2: Following WHO guidelines issued in 1973, a cholera vaccination certificate is no longer a condition of entry to Afghanistan. However, cholera is considered a risk in this country and precautions are advised. Up-to-date advice should be sought before deciding whether these precautions should include vaccination, as medical opinion is divided over its effectiveness. See the *Health* appendix for further information.
3: Typhoid fever occurs and vaccination is advised. Polio eradication measures were being taken but will have been disrupted by the fighting. Polio should still, therefore, be assumed to be a threat.
4: Malarial risk, primarily in the benign *vivax* form, exists from May to November below 2000m (6562ft). The *falciparum* strain occurs in the south of the country. Chloroquine-resistant falciparum has been reported.
Food & drink: All water should be regarded as being potentially contaminated. Milk is unpasteurised and should be boiled. Powdered or tinned milk is available and is advised, but make sure that it is reconstituted with pure water. Avoid dairy products which are likely to have been made from unboiled milk. Only eat well-cooked meat and fish, preferably served hot. Pork, salad and mayonnaise may carry increased risk. Vegetables should be cooked and fruit peeled.
Other risks: *Cutaneous leishmaniasis* and *tick-borne relapsing fever* occur in Afghanistan. *Hepatitis A* and *E* are both present. *Hepatitis B* is endemic. *Typhus* occurs and *trachoma* is common. *Giardiasis* and other waterborne diseases are common. Outbreaks of *meningococcal disease* have been reported.
Rabies is present. For those at high risk, vaccination before arrival should be considered. If you are bitten, seek medical advice without delay. For more information consult the *Health* appendix.
Health care: Medical care was very limited before the fighting but now medicines are in even shorter supply and many hospitals have been damaged or destroyed. Doctors and hospitals demand immediate cash payment for most services. Medical insurance, covering emergency evacuation, is essential. International aid groups operate in some cities and villages.

Travel - International

Note: All but essential travel to Kabul is advised against. All travel to other parts of Afghanistan is very strongly advised against. The levels of threats, specific or otherwise, reported on an almost daily basis has, on occasion, led the Embassy to limit staff movement to essential travel only. The threat to Westerners from terrorist or criminal violence, including kidnappings, remains high. There have been a number of attacks against the UN, NGOs, ISAF, coalition forces and individuals. In addition, there is a widespread danger from mines and unexploded ordnance throughout Afghanistan.
AIR: Afghanistan's national airline is *Ariana Afghan Airlines (FG)* (website: www.flyariana.com). At the time of writing, there are regular flights from Kabul to Delhi (India), Dubai (UAE), Amritsar (India), Istanbul (Turkey), Tehran (Iran) and Sharjah (UAE). *Pakistan International Airlines (PK)* (website: www.piac.com.pk) also flies three times a week from Islamabad to Kabul. There is also a United Nations presence in the country, with aid mission flights in operation. For further information, consult a local embassy or the Foreign and Commonwealth Office (website: www.fco.gov.uk).
International airports: *Kabul Airport (KBL)* is 16km (10 miles) from the city. The airport was largely destroyed during the fighting at the end of 2001 but has now re-opened for limited international commercial flights as well as military and aid flights. Facilities include a bank, bar and restaurant. Taxis are available to the city centre (travel time - 30 minutes).
Departure tax: Af200. Children under two years of age are exempt.
ROAD: Overland travel is currently very dangerous in some parts of the country, with rural roads often unpaved, and the official advice is that it should be avoided. Prior to US bombing, buses used to operate along the Asia Highway, which links Afghanistan to Iran and Pakistan. There were also good road links from Mazar-i-Sharif and Herat to the countries in the north. It is, however, now known that 80 per cent of all roads and bridges have been destroyed. It will be a slow process to repair the damage.

Travel - Internal

AIR: At the time of writing there are no internal flights.
ROAD: Prior to the fighting, there were over 22,000km (13,000 miles) of roads, some of which were paved. This network has largely been destroyed. Traffic drives on the right. **Documentation:** International Driving Permit required.
URBAN: Buses, trolleybuses and taxis used to operate in Kabul but often proved unreliable. Since the fighting, some services have resumed, but are less reliable than ever due to the extensive infrastructure and vehicle destruction incurred.

Accommodation

In Kabul there are a very few hotels, like the Hotel Inter-Continental, that measure up to Western standards. Only basic accommodation is available elsewhere. In some rural areas there may still be hotels run by the provincial authority, but these are of a low standard.

Resorts & Excursions

Afghanistan's capital, **Kabul**, had preserved only a fraction of its historic past until the recent fighting, after which even less was still standing. It is estimated that at least one-third of all public buildings and approximately 40 per cent of the houses have been completely destroyed. The **Gardens of Babur** and a well-presented museum are among the few conventional attractions for tourists. The ancient walls of the citadel **Bala Hissar** remain too dangerous to circumnavigate. There are plans to re-open the **National Gallery** in the near future. Travel outside Kabul is not generally permitted to tourists but, if allowed, it is worth trying to visit the **Valley of Paghman**, 90 minutes by road west of the capital, where the rich had second houses; and, to the north, **Karez-i-Amir**, **Charikar** and the **Valley of Chakardara**.
Jalalabad, the capital of Nangarhar Province, used to be an attractive winter resort, with many cypress trees and flowering shrubs.
Consisting of two huge mountain ranges, the **Hindu Kush** is a wild and remote region. Although travelling by car is possible, the steepness of the routes makes vehicles prone to breakdowns. The Hindu Kush is best left for travellers prepared to rough it. For those who make the journey, the mountains, valleys and lakes provide stunning scenery. **Bamian** is the main centre. The second- to fifth-century Great Buddhas were destroyed here to international outcry in 2001. The **Red City** (Shahr-i-Zahak), 17km (11miles) from Bamian, is the location of the remains of another ancient citadel.
It should be noted that much of the land in Afghanistan is still mined and, therefore, trips outside urban areas are ill-advised and dangerous.

Social Profile

FOOD & DRINK: Indian-style cuisine. Most modern restaurants in Kabul offer international cuisine as well as Afghan specialities such as pilau and kebabs. Traditional foods and tea from chai khanas are found in all areas at low prices, which normally include service. Afghan dishes can be very good, but spicy, so visitors should consider this when ordering.
SHOPPING: Special purchases include Turkman hats, Kandahar embroidery, Istaff pottery, local glassware from Herat, nomad jewellery, handmade carpets and rugs, Nuristani woodcarving, silkware, brass, copper and silverwork. **Note:** Many craft items may only be exported under licence. **Shopping hours:** Generally Sat-Wed 0800-1200 and 1300-1630, Thurs 0800-1330.
SPECIAL EVENTS: The following is a selection of special events occurring in Afghanistan in 2005:
Jan 21 *Eid al-Adha* (Feast of the Sacrifice). **Mar 22** *Navrus* (New Days). **Apr 21** *Mawlid an-Nabi* (Birth of the Prophet). **Oct-Nov** *Ramadan*. **Nov 3-5** *Eid ul-Fitr* (End of Ramadan).
SOCIAL CONVENTIONS: Outside Kabul, Afghanistan is still very much a tribal society. Religion and traditional customs have a strong influence within the family, and there are strict male and female roles in society. It is considered insulting to show the soles of the feet. Guests may have to share a room as specific accommodation is rarely set aside. Women are advised to wear trousers or long skirts and avoid revealing dress. Handshaking is an acceptable form of greeting, though nose-rubbing and embracing are more traditional. Smoking is a common social habit and tobacco is cheap by European standards. It is a compliment to accept an offered cigarette from your host. **Photography:** Care should be taken when using cameras. Military installations should not be photographed.

Business Profile

ECONOMY: 24 years of continuous war completely wrecked the Afghan economy. Reconstruction of the agricultural sector, which accounted for about half of GDP, has been severely hampered by abandonment of farms and the huge number of minefields. Agricultural problems have led to recurring food shortages. Afghanistan has had to rely heavily on foreign aid. Many farmers have come to rely on growing opium as a relatively lucrative cash crop – both the Taleban and now the Karzai government have attempted to limit production, with mixed success. The industrial sector, which barely functions, was formerly concentrated in mining and some manufacturing. There are significant deposits of natural gas, coal, salt, barite and other ores. The small manufacturing sector produces textiles, chemical fertilisers, leather and plastics. Some trade links have been established with the former Soviet Central Asian republics but Pakistan and Saudi Arabia are now the strongest economic influences in the country. The Karzai government has applied for membership of the World Trade Organisation and is likely to receive observer status.
BUSINESS: Price bargaining is expected and oral agreements are honoured. Formal wear is expected and meetings should be pre-arranged. **Office hours:** Generally Sat-Wed 0800-1200 and 1300-1630, Thurs 0800-1330.
COMMERCIAL INFORMATION: The following organisations can offer advice: Afghan Chamber of Commerce and Industry, Mohammad Jan Khan Watt, Kabul (tel: (2) 290 090; fax: (01) 287 458); *or* the Federation of Afghan Chambers of Commerce and Industry, Daraulaman Wat, Kabul.

Climate

Although occupying the same latitudes as South-Central USA, the mountainous nature of much of Afghanistan produces a far colder climate. Being landlocked, there are considerable differences in temperature between summer and winter, and day and night in lowland regions and in the valleys. The southern lowlands have intensely hot summers and harsh winters.

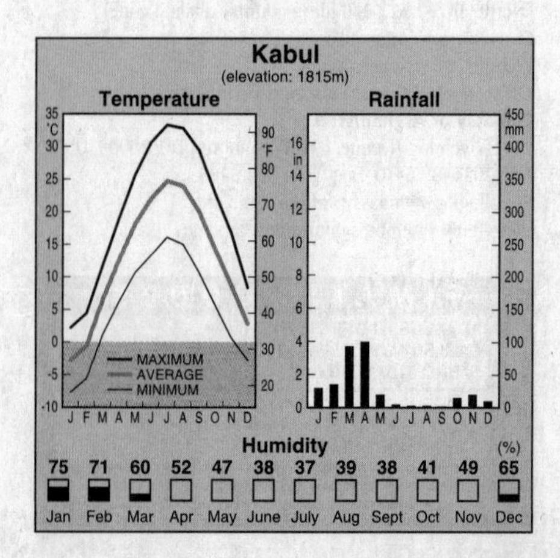

A B C D E F G H I J K L M N O P Q R S T U V W X Y Z

Albania

LATEST TRAVEL ADVICE CONTACTS

British Foreign and Commonwealth Office
Tel: (0870) 606 0290 Website: www.fco.gov.uk
US Department of State
Website: http://travel.state.gov/travel
Canadian Department of Foreign Affairs and Int'l Trade
Tel: (1 800) 267 8376 Website: www.dfait-maeci.gc.ca

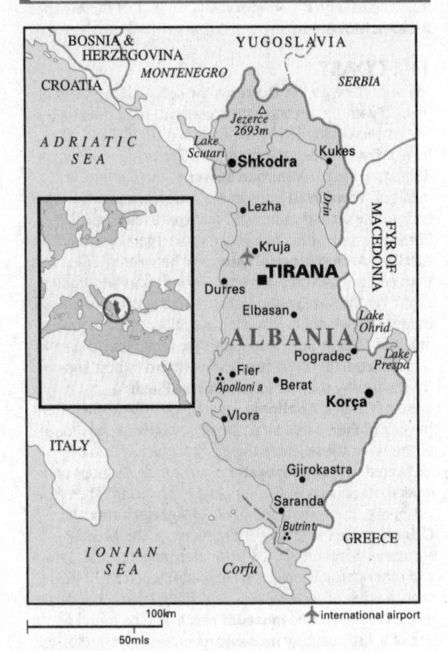

Location: Eastern Europe, Adriatic and Lonian Coast.

Country dialling code: 355.

Albturist
Vasopasga 8, Tirana, Albania
Tel: (42) 59746. Fax: (42) 33360.
E-mail: albturist@adn.net.al
Website: www.albaniantourism.com
Embassy of the Republic of Albania
2nd Floor, 24 Buckingham Gate, London SW1E 6LB, UK
Tel: (020) 7828 8897. Fax: (020) 7828 8869.
E-mail: amblonder@hotmail.com
Opening hours: Mon-Fri 0900-1530 (general enquiries); 0900-1200 (consular section).
Regent Holidays (UK) Ltd.
15 John Street, Bristol BS1 2HR, UK
Tel: (0117) 921 1711. Fax: (0117) 925 4866.
E-mail: regent@regent-holidays.co.uk
Website: www.regent-holidays.co.uk
British Embassy
Rruga Skenderbej 12, Tirana, Albania
Tel: (42) 34973-5. Fax: (42) 47697.
E-mail: visatiran@fco.gov.uk
Website: www.uk.al
Embassy of the Republic of Albania
2100 S Street, NW, Washington, DC 20008, USA
Tel: (202) 223 4942. Fax: (202) 628 7342.
E-mail: albaniaemb@aol.com
Embassy of the United States of America
Rruga Elbasanit Street 103, Tirana, Albania
Tel: (42) 47285. Fax: (42) 32222.
Website: www.usemb-tirana.rpo.at
Honorary Consulate of Canada
Rruga Dervish Hima, Tower Number 2, Apartment 22, Tirana, Albania
Tel: (42) 57274/5. Fax: (42) 57273.
E-mail: canadalb@canada.gov.al
The Canadian Embassy in Rome provides consular services for Albania.

TIMATIC CODES

Health	AMADEUS: **TI-DFT/JIB/HE** GALILEO/WORLDSPAN: **TI-DFT/JIB/HE** SABRE: **TIDFT/JIB/HE**
Visa	AMADEUS: **TI-DFT/JIB/VI** GALILEO/WORLDSPAN: **TI-DFT/JIB/VI** SABRE: **TIDFT/JIB/VI**

To access TIMATIC country information on Health and Visa regulations through the Computer Reservations System (CRS), type in the appropriate command line listed above.

General Information

AREA: 27,398 sq km (11,100 sq miles).
POPULATION: 3,141,000 (UN estimate 2002).
POPULATION DENSITY: 109.3 per sq km.
CAPITAL: Tirana. **Population:** 519,720 (2001).
GEOGRAPHY: Albania shares borders with Serbia and Montenegro to the north, with Macedonia (Former Yugoslav Republic of) to the northeast, and with Greece to the south; to the west are the Adriatic and Ionian Seas. Most of the country is wild and mountainous, with extensive forests. There are fine sandy beaches and, inland, many beautiful lakes.
GOVERNMENT: Democratic Republic since 1991. **Head of State:** President Alfred Moisiu since 2002. **Head of Government:** Prime Minister Fatos Nano since 2002. Gained independence from the Ottoman Empire in 1912.
LANGUAGE: The official language is Albanian. Some Albanians also speak Italian and English. Greek is widely spoken in the Gjirokastra and Saranda districts in south Albania.
RELIGION: Three religions coexist in Albania: Islam, Catholicism and Eastern Orthodox Christianity. The majority of the population is Muslim.
TIME: GMT + 1 (GMT + 2 from last Sunday in March to Saturday before last Sunday in October).
ELECTRICITY: 220 volts AC, 50Hz.
COMMUNICATIONS: Telephone: IDD is available to major towns. Country code: 355. Outgoing international code: 00. City codes: Tirana 42, Durresi 52, Elbasan 545, Shkodra 224, Gjirokastra 726, Korça 824, Kavaja 574. For other regions, international connections are made through the nearest city. **Mobile telephone:** GSM 900/1800 networks. Coverage is limited to main towns and coastal areas. Main network operators are *Albanian Mobile Communications* (website: www.amc.al) and *Vodafone Albania* (website: www.vodafone.al). **Internet:** Main ISPs include *Adanet* (website: www.albnet.net) and *Albania Online* (website: www.albaniaonline.net). Internet cafes exist in most towns. **Telegram/fax:** These services are offered in post offices and major hotels. **Post:** All mail to and from Albania is subject to delays. Letters can be sent recorded delivery to avoid loss. There are DHL offices in Tirana and Durres, offering services between Albania and other countries. The postal and telecommunications systems are undergoing extensive modernisation. Post office hours: Mon-Fri 0700-1400 and Sat 0800-1300.
Press: There are now about 400 newspapers and periodicals, many of which are independent. The main newspapers are published daily. *Rilindja Demokratike*, the organ of the ruling Democratic Party, has a circulation of 50,000. English-language newspapers published in Albania include the *Albanian Daily News*. Some Albanian newspapers contain a few pages in English; these include *Albania*, *Gazeta Shqiptare*, *Shekulli* and *Ekonomia*. Foreign newspapers are on sale in main towns.
Radio: BBC World Service (website: www.bbc.co.uk/worldservice) and Voice of America (website: www.voa.gov) can be received. From time to time the frequencies change and the most up-to-date can be found online.

Passport/Visa

	Passport Required?	Visa Required?	Return Ticket Required?
Full British	Yes	No	Yes
Australian	Yes	No	Yes
Canadian	Yes	No	Yes
USA	Yes	No	Yes
Other EU	Yes	No/1/2	Yes
Japanese	Yes	No	Yes

Note: *Regulations and requirements may be subject to change at short notice, and you are advised to contact the appropriate diplomatic or consular authority before finalising travel arrangements. Details of these may be found at the head of this country's entry. Any numbers in the chart refer to the footnotes below.*

PASSPORTS: A valid passport is required by all.
VISAS: Required by all except the following for stays of up to 30 days:
(a) nationals of countries referred to in the chart above, except **1.** nationals of Malta who must obtain a visa upon arrival;
(b) nationals of Bulgaria, Croatia, Israel, Korea (Rep), Malaysia, New Zealand, Norway, Romania, San Marino, Switzerland, and Turkey;
(c) transit passengers continuing their journey to a third country by the same or next connecting aircraft provided holding confirmed onward documentation and not leaving the airport.
Note: (a) Nationals of countries listed above pay an entry fee of €10 at Tirana airport or at the border crossing point, except nationals of Israel who must pay €30 and nationals of Poland and the Slovak Republic who may enter without charge. (b) **2.** Nationals of Macedonia (Former Yugoslav Republic of), Malta and Montenegro can obtain visas on arrival for free (Montenegro), 10 (Macedonia) or 30 (Malta).
Types of visa and cost: *Business* and *Tourist*: up to 54, depending on nationality of applicant and length and purpose of intended stay. Business visas are given for single- or multiple-entry.
Validity: Duration of visas is individually specified for each visit. The maximum length of stay is three months. Extentions are possible.
Application to: Consulate (or Consular Section at Embassy); see *Contact Addresses* section.
Application requirements: (a) Application form(s). (b) Valid passport. (c) Two passport-size photos. (d) Sufficient funds to cover duration of stay. *Business*: (a)-(d) and, (e) Letter from applicant's company. (f) Invitation from Albanian company.
Working days required: Two to three weeks.
Temporary residence: Application to be made to the Embassy of the Republic of Albania.

Credit: © Albanian Ministry of Territorial Planning and Tourism

Money

Currency: Lek (Lk) = 100 qindarka. Notes are in denominations of Lk5000, 1000, 500, 200 and 100. Coins are in denominations of Lk50, 20, 10, 5, 2 and 1.
Currency exchange: Currency can be exchanged at bureaux de change and banks. However, the best rate of exchange can be obtained from moneychangers who operate (legally) on the street, usually outside banks. US dollars are the preferred foreign currency.
Credit & debit cards: Rarely used. Cash is preferred in nearly all cases. However, American Express, Diners Club and MasterCard are accepted by some banks and hotels.
Travellers cheques: To avoid additional exchange rate charges, travellers are advised to take travellers cheques in US Dollars or Euros. They may not always be easily changed in all places.
Currency restrictions: The import and export of local currency is prohibited. The import of foreign currency is unlimited. The export of foreign currency is permitted up to US$5000 or up to the amount declared on arrival.
Exchange rate indicators: The following figures are included as a guide to the movements of the Lek against Sterling and the US Dollar:

Date	Feb '04	May '04	Aug '04	Nov '04
£1.00=	195.04	190.76	186.90	183.59
$1.00=	107.15	106.80	101.45	96.95

Banking hours: Mon-Fri 0800-1600.

Duty Free

The following items may be taken into Albania without incurring customs duty: *200 cigarettes or 50 cigars or 250g of tobacco; 1l of spirits or 2l of wine; 250ml of eau de toilette and 50ml of perfume.*
Prohibited items: Firearms, ammunition and narcotics. Special export permits are required for precious metals, antiques, national costumes of artistic or folkloric value, books and works of art which form part of the national heritage and culture.

Public Holidays

2005: Jan 1 New Year's Day. **Jan 21** Greater Bairam (Feast of the Sacrifice). **Mar 25** Good Friday. **Mar 28** Easter Monday.

May 1 May Day. **Nov 3-5** Lesser Bairam (End of Ramadan). **Nov 28** Independence and Liberation Day. **Dec 25** Christmas Day.
2006: Jan 1 New Year's Day. **Jan 10-13** Greater Bairam (Feast of the Sacrifice). **Apr 14** Good Friday. **Apr 17** Easter Monday. **May 1** May Day. **Oct 22-24** Lesser Bairam (End of Ramadan). **Nov 28** Independence and Liberation Day. **Dec 25** Christmas Day.
Note: Muslim festivals are timed according to local sightings of various phases of the moon and the dates given above are approximations. During the lunar month of Ramadan that precedes Lesser Bairam (Eid al-Fitr), Muslims fast during the day and feast at night and normal business patterns may be interrupted. Some disruption may continue into Lesser Bairam itself. Lesser Bairam and Greater Bairam (Eid al-Adha) may last anything from two to 10 days, depending on the region. For more information see the *World of Islam* appendix.

Health

	Special Precautions?	Certificate Required?
Yellow Fever	No	1
Cholera	No	No
Typhoid & Polio	2	N/A
Malaria	No	N/A

Note: Regulations and requirements may be subject to change at short notice, and you are advised to contact your doctor well in advance of your intended date of departure. Any numbers in the chart refer to the footnotes below.

1: A yellow fever vaccination certificate is required from travellers over one year of age arriving within 6 days after leaving or transiting countries with infected areas.
2: Immunisation against typhoid and poliomyelitis is recommended. Typhoid is more common in summer and autumn. Although the last major outbreak of poliomyelitis was in 1996, since when eradication activities have been conducted, a small risk still exists.
Food & drink: Mains water is normally chlorinated, and whilst relatively safe may cause mild abdominal upsets. Bottled water is advised, especially outside Tirana, and should be used for cleaning teeth, washing food, making ice and, of course, drinking. Drinking water outside main cities and towns is likely to be contaminated and sterilisation is considered essential. Milk is pasteurised and dairy products are safe for consumption. Local meat, poultry, seafood, fruit and vegetables are under the control of sanitary/hygiene authorities and are generally considered safe to eat. Avoid cooked food offered by street traders unless you are sure it is freshly prepared and piping hot.
Other risks: Immunisation against *hepatitis A* and *B* and *tetanus* is recommended. Campers and trekkers should avoid tick bites and consider immunisation against *tick-borne encephalitis*, which has been reported in the north. Long-term visitors should consider immunisation against *diphtheria* and check their BCG status.
Rabies is present. For those at high risk, vaccination before arrival should be considered. If you are bitten abroad seek medical advice without delay. For more information, see the *Health* appendix.
Health care: Medical facilities are very basic and there is a lack of supplies and doctors. If taking prescribed drugs, the visitor should bring a supply. There are no reciprocal agreements with the UK or USA. However, foreign travellers will be excluded from payment for emergency medical treatment and first aid. International travellers are strongly advised to take out full medical insurance before departure.

Travel - International

Note: Travel to the northeastern border areas between Albania and Kosovo is currently strongly advised against. For further advice contact your local government travel advice department.
AIR: The national carrier is *Albanian Airlines (LV)* (website: www.flyalbanian.com). Established in cooperation with *Tyrolean Airways*, the airline operates services to major European cities. Other airlines offering services to Tirana include *Ada Air*, *Alitalia*, *Austrian Airlines*, *Lufthansa*, *Malev Hungarian Airlines*, *Olympic Airways* and *Swiss*.
Approximate flight times: From Tirana to *London* is four to five hours (including stopover times, the shortest being via Zurich, 45 minutes, and via Rome, one to two hours). Passengers may travel via a number of cities including Athens, Belgrade, Budapest, Vienna and Zurich.
International airports: *Tirana Rinas (TIA)* is 29km (18 miles) from the capital. An *Albtourist* shuttle runs to the city centre every three hours (travel time – 30 minutes). Taxis are also available to and from the airport. There is a small duty-free shop, car hire, bank and light refreshments are available
Departure tax: US$10 is levied on all foreign nationals. Nationals of Albania pay Lk1000.
SEA: The main ports are Durres, Vlora and Saranda. Durres has ferry connections to Italy (to Bari is four-seven hours, to Brindisi and to Trieste is 23 hours, to Ancona is 16 hours) and to Slovenia (to Koper is 22 hours); Vlora has ferry connections to Bari (travel time – nine hours), Otranto and Brindisi; and Saranda has a connection with Corfu. Ferry services are run by *Adriatica Line* (website: www.adriatica.it) and *Agoudimos Lines* (website: www.agoudimos-lines.com), amongst others.
RAIL: There are no international passenger services at present.
ROAD: Road links to the Kosovo region are either closed or too dangerous to use, owing to political tensions in the region. There are possible crossings at Hani i Hotit (Podgorica in Montenegro), Bllata (Diber in the Former Yugoslav Republic of Macedonia), Qafa e Thaës (Struga and Ohrid in the Former Yugoslav Republic of Macedonia), Tushemisht (Ohrid in the Former Yugoslav Republic of Macedonia), Gorica (Resnja in the Former Yugoslav Republic of Macedonia), Kapshtica (Florina in Greece) and Kakavija (Ioanina in Greece). **Bus:** There are services to Istanbul, Sofia and Athens. **Documentation:** It is now permitted to travel in a private car. Parking places are generally available near hotels or at other designated areas. A fully comprehensive insurance policy is absolutely essential.

Travel - Internal

SEA: A fast ferry service links Durres and Vlora.
RAIL: The total rail network runs to approximately 720km (450 miles) and is single-track and unelectrified along the whole of its length. Trains are diesel, dilapidated and mostly overcrowded. Services operate from Tirana to Shkodra, Vlora, Fier, Ballsh and Pogradec. There are long-term plans to build railways connecting Pogradec with Kicevo (Macedonia, FYR) and Florina (Greece).
ROAD: There are around 18,000km (11,250 miles) of roads in Albania, but only 7450km (4656 miles) are considered main roads. Maintained by the State, they are supposed to be suitable for motor vehicles, although only 2850km (1781 miles) are paved and, of those, three-quarters are in very poor condition, with numerous potholes: 4-wheel drive vehicles are recommended. Motorways are planned for the future and the widening of existing roads has begun. All roads are used by pedestrians, cyclists, ox- and horse-drawn wagons, agricultural vehicles and herds of cattle and poultry, although the number of cars has increased considerably during the last decade. There are strict speed limits according to type of vehicle and type of road as well as within towns. Normal rules and international road signs apply. Traffic drives on the right. Visitors are advised to exercise extreme caution when driving, owing to the poor condition of the roads and the unpredictability of local drivers. Night-time driving should be avoided, as there have been reports of 'carjackings'. In addition, whilst petrol stations are available in urban areas, they are not common in the countryside.
Bus: This is the main form of transport within Albania. The main routes from Shkodra, Korça, Saranda, Gjirokastra, Peshkopia and Durres to Tirana are operated by private bus companies. **Documentation:** International Driving Permit and national driving licence are required.
URBAN: A cheap, flat-fare urban **bus** service operates in the main cities, although the buses are usually crowded. **Taxis** can be found in Tirana in front of the main hotels housing foreigners.
Travel Times: The following chart gives approximate travel times from **Tirana**(in hours and minutes) to other major cities/towns in Albania.

	Road
Durres	1.00
Elbasan	1.00
Shkodra	2.30
Berat	3.00
Vlora	3.00
Korça	4.00

Accommodation

Albturist runs the state-owned tourist hotels but many others are now privately run and increasing numbers are being built. For further information contact *Albturist* (see *Contact Addresses* section). Hotels are currently being classified in one of five categories according to the facilities offered.

Resorts & Excursions

TIRANA

Created in 1614 by Sulejman Bargjini, Tirana has only been the capital of Albania since 1920. The city has examples of early 19th-century architecture such as the **Ethem-Bey Mosque** (built 1789-1823) and the 35m-high (117ft) **clocktower** (1830). The old bazaar quarter was demolished in 1961 to make way for the **Palace of Culture**, which houses the **Opera and Ballet Theatre** and the **National Library**. The city centre and the government buildings on **Skanderbeg Square** date back to the Italian era, creating the impression of a provincial Italian town, while the **Pyramid**, which was built as a museum for Enver Hoxha (Albania's former communist leader), has been turned into an international Cultural Centre. Today, Tirana is not only the most populous city in Albania, but also the political, economic, cultural and spiritual centre of the country with national museums of archaeology, history and art. The **National Historical Museum** and the **National Art Gallery** are highly recommended, along with the **Exhibition of Folk Culture**. The best view over the city is from the **Martyrs' Cemetery** which contains the **Mother Albania Monument**.

THE COAST

The important port of **Durres** is the second largest city in Albania with the second largest concentration of industry. The city was colonised by the Greeks in 627 BC and was named *Epidamnos*, later becoming *Dyrrachium* under the Romans. From the **Venetian Tower** at the harbour, the medieval **Town Wall** leads to the **Amphitheatre** dating back to the second century BC and containing an early Christian crypt with a rare wall mosaic. There is also an excellent **Archaeological Museum**. Between the first and third centuries, Durres was an important port and trading centre on the *Via Egnatia* trading route between Rome and Byzantium (Istanbul). Following a number of earthquakes, much of ancient Durres sank into the sea or collapsed and was subsequently built over. Today the city is best known for the nearby beach resort of **Durres Plazh**.
In Roman times, **Apollonia**, located 12km (7.5 miles) from the city of **Fier**, was a large, prosperous city at the mouth of the **river Vjosa** where there is still much left to be excavated. The **amphitheatre**, a colonnade of shops and several other parts of the Roman city centre are open to the public. There are monuments of **Agonothetes** and **Odeon**, as well as an ancient portico and the **Mosaic House** with a fountain. Unfortunately, some of the statues and other portable objects were removed before 1946 and sent to other countries. Those remaining have been placed in the well-organised **museum** which is to be found on the site of a 13th-century **monastery**. In the courtyard of the monastery is a Byzantine-style church, the **Church of St Mary**, believed to have been built in the 14th century. Not far from Apollonia, on the route to Durres, is the **Monastery of Ardenica**.
Vlora is not only a major port, but of great historical importance, for it was here in 1912 that the Assembly was convened which first proclaimed Albania an independent state and set up the first national government, headed by Ismail Qemali. In recognition of this, it was proclaimed a 'Hero City' in 1962. The **Muradiye Mosque** (1538-42) was designed by the famous architect Mimar Sinan whose family originated in Albania. On a hill above the city is the tourist centre **Liria** which offers panoramic views of the beach and town.
Albania's southern coastline remains completely unspoilt. Situated opposite Corfu, **Saranda** is now much visited by day trippers who come to enjoy this previously inaccessible resort.
The ancient town of **Butrint** was once an important centre for the Illyrian tribes. It has been known as a settlement since 1000 BC and has belonged to both the Greek and Roman empires during its long history, leaving a rich legacy. Several sites dating from the first and fourth centuries AD can now be visited, among them a theatre, the **Temple of Aesculapius**, the **Nypheum**, the **Lion Gate**, the **Dionysus Altar**, Roman houses and baths. The **Baptistry**, with a floor of colourful mosaics, is not to be missed. The nearby tourist site of **Ksamil** offers magnificent views of **Butrint Lake**, the islands and citrus- and olive-tree plantations.

THE INTERIOR

Known as the 'city of a thousand windows', owing to the plethora of windows in the city's red-roofed houses, **Berat** has been declared a 'Museum City'. Built on the slopes of a mountain, the old Turkish part of the town is very picturesque, being largely encompassed by the medieval fortress. To house the growing population, a new town has been built further down the valley beside the largest textile combine in the country. The **Onufri Museum**, dedicated to the 16th-century painter and his contemporaries, houses restored icons in an orthodox church. There is also a magnificent castle near here.
Gjirokastra, in the far south, has also been designated a 'Museum City' as so many of the houses retain their traditional wood- and stonework. The narrow and winding cobbled streets ensure the virtual exclusion of motor traffic. The town is dominated by the 13th-century **Fortress** which was extended by Ali Pasha in 1811. It now contains the **National Museum of Weapons**; the collection ranges from medieval armour to a shot-down US reconnaissance aircraft (the museum was looted in 1997 but most of the collection is still there) and the view is not to be missed. The

surrounding area is renowned for its many mineral springs. **Korça** was the seat of government during Turkish rule. In the 18th century, the city was able to exploit its location at the crossroads of several caravan routes and became a major trading point. Standing at the foot of the dramatic Morava mountain near the Greek border, Korça is home to the **Mirahor Mosque**, dating back to 1466, the **Museum for Medieval Art**, the **Museum of Education** (where the first Albanian school was opened in 1887) and a listed, though decaying, bazaar quarter.

The charming resort of **Pogradec** near the Macedonian border stands beside **Lake Ohrid**, renowned for its clear water and rich in trout and carp. About 5km (3 miles) to the east is the tourist centre of **Drilon**, surrounded by extensive ornamental gardens.

Visible for miles around, **Kruja** is an attractive medieval town perched on top of a mountain north of Tirana. It was the centre of Albanian resistance to the Ottoman Turks under Skanderbeg, the national hero, and the **Skanderbeg Museum** is to be found inside the recently restored castle. The street leading up to the castle is built in the style of a medieval Turkish bazaar.

Situated on **Lake Scutari**, which divides Albania from Montenegro, **Shkodra** is dominated by the ruins of the **Fortress of Rozafa**, one of the ancient Ilyrian castles, built on a rock hill from which a spectacular panorama of the surrounding countryside, the lake and the **Lead Mosque** can be enjoyed. A museum is dedicated to one of the greatest Albanian writers, Migjeni. The **Mesi Bridge**, 8km (5 miles) from Shkodra, is also well worth a visit, as is the **Monument to Gjergj Kastrioti Skanderbeg** at his burial ground in **Lezha**.

Sport & Activities

Swimming may be enjoyed at Albania's many beaches; inland, the **hiking** opportunities are good. The mountains offer excellent **climbing** possibilities, although equipment may be hard to find. **Cycling** is also popular, although roads may be in bad condition.

Social Profile

FOOD & DRINK: Private restaurants are appearing rapidly in Albania. In the more popular places, it is necessary to reserve a table and to be punctual. Food is typically Balkan with Turkish influences evident on any menu – *byrek, kofte, shish kebab*. Albanian specialities include *fërgesë tirane*, a hot fried dish of meat, liver, eggs and tomatoes, and *tavë kosi* or *tavë elbasani*, a mutton and yoghurt dish. Fish specialities include the *koran*, a trout from Lake Ohrid and the *Shkodra carp*. In summer *tarator*, a cold yoghurt and cucumber soup, is particularly refreshing. Popular Albanian desserts include *oshaf*, a fig and sheep's milk pudding, cakes soaked in honey and candied fruits or *reçel*. Guests of honour are quite often presented with a baked sheep's head. A favourite in the south is *kukurec* (stuffed sheep's intestines). Continental breakfasts are usually served in hotels, but in the country the Albanian breakfast of *pilaf* (rice) or *paça* (a wholesome soup made from animals' innards) may not be to everyone's taste.

All bars and restaurants serve Albanian drinks such as *raki*, local red and white wines and different liqueurs. The Albanian cognac, with its distinctive aroma, is also popular. Many imported drinks can also be found, including Austrian canned beer, Macedonian wine and ouzo from Greece. Turkish coffee (*kafe Turke*) is popular with Albanians, but many bars also serve Italian espresso (*ekspres*).

NIGHTLIFE: The most popular form of nightlife is the *xhiro*, the evening stroll along the main boulevards and squares of each town and village. Cultural life takes the form of theatre, opera and concerts. Discos and games arcades are beginning to appear. Some hotels have taverns with music and dancing.

SHOPPING: Special purchases include carpets, filigree silver and copper, woodcarvings, ceramics and any kind of needlework. Old markets are often worth exploring. Bartering is very much the order of the day for foreigners as well as for locals. Some of the tourist hotels also have shops. **Shopping hours:** Generally Mon-Sat 0800-1200 and 1500-1900 (although regional variations are possible). Many shops are also open Sunday.

SPECIAL EVENTS: For information about special events in 2004, contact the Embassy (see *Contact Addresses* section). Annual events in Tirana include: *Marie Kraja* (Opera Festival), *Fall in Tirana Festival*, and the *Days of New Music Festival*.

SOCIAL CONVENTIONS: Nearly half of the population lives in urban areas, with the rest pursuing a relatively quiet rural existence. Some Albanian characteristics and mannerisms resemble those of the mainland Greeks, most notably in the more rural areas; for instance, a nod of the head means 'no' and shaking one's head means 'yes'. Handshaking is the accepted form of greeting. Albanians should be addressed with *Zoti* (Mr) and *Zonja* (Mrs). The former widespread greeting of *Shoku* (Comrade) has all but disappeared. Small gifts are customary when visiting someone's house, although flowers are not usually given. Any attempt to speak Albanian is greatly appreciated. Visitors should accept offers of raki, coffee or sweets. Dress is generally informal. Bikinis are acceptable on the beach; elsewhere women are expected to dress modestly although attitudes are becoming increasingly relaxed. Offices and restaurants are often unheated. Visitors should be aware that foreigners tend to be charged a lot more than locals, with this applying to entry fees as well as general merchandise. Smoking is permitted except where the sign *Ndalohet Duhani* or *Ndalohet pirja e duhanit* is displayed. It is also worth noting that the crime rate has risen, especially theft, and visitors should be careful not to display valuables. Passports which allow entry to EU countries without a visa, foreign currency and cameras are mostly at risk, although all possessions should be kept close at hand at all times. Avoid remote areas and streets, especially at night. **Tipping:** Previously frowned upon by the authorities, tips are gratefully received in restaurants or for any service provided.

Business Profile

ECONOMY: Albania is one of Europe's poorest countries and continues to face severe difficulties adjusting to the new Europe after decades of Stalinist isolation. More recently, conditions were worsened by regional political instability and the collapse of 'pyramid' investment schemes in 1997. Albania is blessed with appreciable natural resources – it is one of the world's largest producers of chromium and boasts reserves of copper, nickel, pyrites and coal. There are also oil deposits, both on and offshore. The agricultural sector, which accounts for 40 per cent of GDP and underwent some upheaval following de-collectivisation, has now settled down with all but a few farming enterprises in the private sector. New components of the economy, such as tourism, which were mostly set up with foreign investment, suffered badly in the wake of the 1997 upheaval – a great deal of Albania's hard-won economic progress was destroyed during that period. In the last five years, much of the damage has been restored but the black economy remains a huge influence over Albania, especially in view of the 40 per cent unemployment rate. Nonetheless, Albania has since received steady support from major foreign donors and it was admitted to the World Trade Organization in July 2000 – as much a valuable symbol of international recognition as a potential boost to the economy. The government hopes to join the EU in around 2010, although most observers consider this highly optimistic.

BUSINESS: Punctuality is expected. Business cards are common and European practices are observed. Nodding the head may mean 'No' and shaking it, 'Yes'. **Office hours:** Mon-Fri 0800-1600. All offices are closed on Saturday and Sunday.

COMMERCIAL INFORMATION: The following organisation can offer advice: Union of Chambers of Commerce & Industry of Albania, Rruga Kavajes 6, Tirana (tel/fax: (42) 22934; e-mail: uccial@abissnet.com.al; website: www.ccc.gov.al).

Climate

Temperate climate with warm and dry periods from June to September, cool and wet from October to May. April-June and mid-September to mid-October are the best months for visits.

Required clothing: Warm clothing and rainwear is advisable for winter. Lightweight for summer.

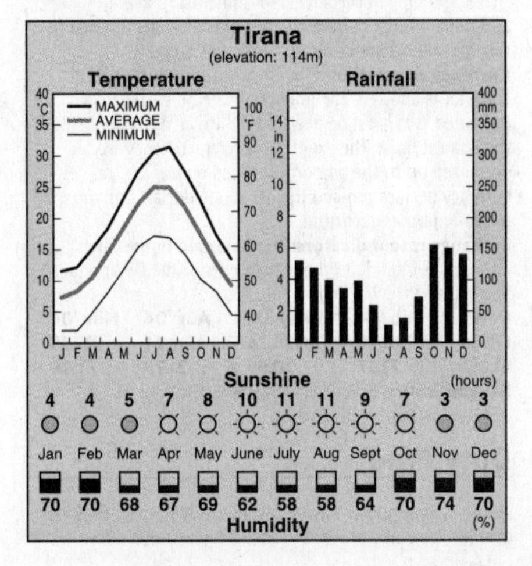

Algeria

LATEST TRAVEL ADVICE CONTACTS

British Foreign and Commonwealth Office
Tel: (0870) 606 0290 Website: www.fco.gov.uk

US Department of State
Website: http://travel.state.gov/travel

Canadian Department of Foreign Affairs and Int'l Trade
Tel: (1 800) 267 8376 Website: www.dfait-maeci.gc.ca

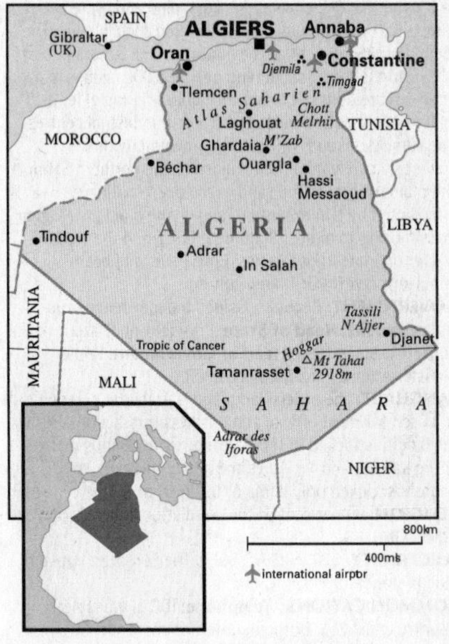

Location: North Africa, Mediterranean Coast.

Country dialling code: 213.

Ministère du Tourisme
Route Nationale 36, Ben Aknoun, Algiers, Algeria
Tel: (21) 792 301-7. Fax: (21) 792 632.
E-mail: mtazm@wissal.dz
Website: www.tourisme.dz

Office National du Tourisme (ONT)
2 rue Smail Kerrar, 1600, Algiers, Algeria
Tel: (21) 713 060. Fax: (21) 713 059.
E-mail: ont@wissal.dz
Website: www.ont.dz

Embassy of the People's Democratic Republic of Algeria
54 Holland Park, London W11 3RS, UK
Tel: (020) 7221 7800. Fax: (020) 7221 0448.
E-mail: mail@admi.freeserve.co.uk
Website: www.consalglond.u-net.com

Algerian Consulate
6 Hyde Park Gate, London SW7 5EW, UK
Tel: (020) 7589 6885. Fax: (020) 7589 7725.
E-mail: algerianconsulate@yahoo.co.uk
Website: www.algerianconsulate.org.uk

British Embassy
Hilton Hotel International, 7th Floor, Pins Maritimes, Palais des Expositions, El Mohammadia, Algiers, Algeria
Tel: (21) 230 068. Fax: (21) 230 067.
E-mail: visaenquiries.algiers@fco.gov.uk (visa enquiries)
Website: www.britishembassy.gov.uk/algeria

Embassy of the People's Democratic Republic of Algeria
2137 Wyoming Avenue, NW, Washington, DC 20008, USA
Tel: (202) 265 2800. Fax: (202) 667 2174.
E-mail: ambassadoroffice@yahoo.com
Website: www.algeria-us.org

Embassy of the United States of America
Street address: 4 Chemin Cheikh Bachir El-Ibrahimi, Algiers, Algeria
Postal address: BP 408, Alger-gare 16030, Algiers, Algeria
Tel: (21) 691 255/186/425. Fax: (21) 693 979.
E-mail: coltoneo@state.gov

Embassy of the People's Democratic Republic of Algeria
45 Daily Avenue, Ottawa, Ontario, K1N 6H3, Canada
Tel: (613) 789 8505 *or* 0282 *or* 5823 (consular section).
Fax: (613) 789 1406.
E-mail: ambalgcan@rogers.com
Website: www.embassyalgeria.ca

Canadian Embassy
Street address: 18 Mustapha Khalef Street, Ben Aknoun, 16035 Algiers, Algeria
Tel: (21) 914 951/60. Fax: (21) 914 973 (administration section) *or* 914 720 (commercial section).
E-mail: alger@dfait-maeci.gc.ca

A B C D E F G H I J K L M N O P Q R S T U V W X Y Z

General Information

AREA: 2,381,741 sq km (919,595 sq miles).
POPULATION: 31,070,000 (2002).
POPULATION DENSITY: 13.0 per sq km.
CAPITAL: Algiers (El Djezaïr). **Population:** 1,519,570 (1998).
GEOGRAPHY: Algeria is situated along the North African coast, bordered to the east by Tunisia and Libya, to the southeast by Niger, to the southwest by Mali, and to the west by Mauritania and Morocco. It is Africa's second-largest country, with 1200km (750 miles) of coastline. Along the coastal strip are the main towns, fertile land, beach resorts and 90 per cent of the population. Further south lies the area of the *Hauts Plateaux*, mountains of up to 2000m (6600ft) covered in cedar, pine and cypress forests with broad arable plains dividing the plateaux. The remaining 85 per cent of the country is the Sahara Desert in its various forms, sustaining only 500,000 people, many of whom are nomadic tribes with goat and camel herds. The oil and minerals boom has created new industrial centres like Hassi Messaoud, which have grown up within previously barely inhabited regions of the northern Sahara. The plains of gravel and sand in the deep south are interrupted by two mountain ranges: the dramatic *Hoggar* massif, rising to almost 3000m (9800ft), and the *Tassili N'Ajjer* or 'Plateau of Chasms'. Both have long been important centres of Tuareg culture.
GOVERNMENT: Republic. Gained independence from France in 1962. **Head of State:** President Abdelaziz Bouteflika since 1999. **Head of Government:** Prime Minister Ahmed Ouyahia since 2003.
LANGUAGE: The official language is Arabic, but French is still used for most official and business transactions. Berber (Amazigh) is spoken in the northern mountainous regions of the Kabylias and the Aures and also in the south. In general, English is spoken only in major business or tourist centres.
RELIGION: 99 per cent of the population adhere to Islam.
TIME: GMT + 1.
ELECTRICITY: 220 volts AC, 50Hz. The European two-pin plug is standard.
COMMUNICATIONS: Telephone: IDD is available. Country code: 213. Outgoing international code: 00. There are public telephones in all post offices, leading hotels and on many main streets. **Mobile telephone:** GSM 900 network is operated by AMN. Coverage is limited to main towns. There are some roaming agreements. Operators include *Orascom Telecom Algerie Spa (Djezzy)* (website: www.djezzygsm.com). **Fax:** Faxes may be sent from some more modern hotels. **Internet:** The main ISP is *Cerist* (website: www.cerist.dz). There are three Internet cafes: in Algiers, Constantine and Oran. **Telegram:** These can be sent from any post office from 0800-1900. The main post office in Algiers has a 24-hour service. **Post:** Mail posted in any of the main cities along the coast takes three to four days to reach Europe; posted elsewhere, it could take much longer. A letter delivery service operates Saturday to Thursday. Parcels sent by surface mail may take up to two months to reach Algeria. All parcels sent by air or surface mail are subject to long delays in customs. Post office hours: Generally Sat-Wed 0800-1700; Thurs 0800-1200; but the main post office in Algiers (5 boulevard Mohamed Khémisti) is open around the clock. **Press:** Daily newspapers are printed in Arabic or French. The main French-language dailies are *El-Moudjahid, El Watan, Liberté, Le Matin, Le Soir d'Algérie* and *La Tribune*. *Ach-Cha'ab* and *Al-Massa* are the leading Arabic-language dailies. Another daily, *Horizons*, has an English section.
Radio: BBC World Service (website: www.bbc.co.uk/worldservice) and Voice of America (website: www.voa.gov) can be received. From time to time the frequencies change and the most up-to-date can be found online.

TIMATIC CODES

Health	AMADEUS: **TI-DFT/JIB/HE** GALILEO/WORLDSPAN: **TI-DFT/JIB/HE** SABRE: **TIDFT/JIB/HE**
Visa	AMADEUS: **TI-DFT/JIB/VI** GALILEO/WORLDSPAN: **TI-DFT/JIB/VI** SABRE: **TIDFT/JIB/VI**

To access TIMATIC country information on Health and Visa regulations through the Computer Reservations System (CRS), type in the appropriate command line listed above.

Passport/Visa

	Passport Required?	Visa Required?	Return Ticket Required?
Full British	Yes	Yes	No
Australian	Yes	Yes	No
Canadian	Yes	Yes	No
USA	Yes	Yes	No
Other EU	Yes	Yes	No
Japanese	Yes	Yes	No

Note: Regulations and requirements may be subject to change at short notice, and you are advised to contact the appropriate diplomatic or consular authority before finalising travel arrangements. Details of these may be found at the head of this country's entry. Any numbers in the chart refer to the footnotes below.

Restricted entry: Entry and transit is refused to holders of Israeli passports.
Note: It is no longer compulsory to import a specific amount of currency for each day of the intended stay. However, all foreign currency imported must be declared and receipts retained for inspection.
PASSPORTS: Passport valid for at least six months required by all.
VISAS: Required by all except the following:
(a) nationals of Malaysia, Mauritania, Seychelles and Syrian Arab Republic for stays of up to three months;
(b) transit passengers continuing their journey by the same or first connecting aircraft within 24 hours provided holding sufficient funds, onward and return documentation and not leaving the airport. If transit exceeds 24 hours, a transit permit for up to 48 hours has to be obtained from airport authorities.
Note: Children under 15 years of age travelling on their parents' passports do not need a visa, although a letter of authorisation is required from the parents or guardian.
Types of visa and cost: *Tourist*, *Business* and *Transit*. The cost varies according to nationality. For British passport holders the costs are: *Single-entry*: £28; *Multiple-entry*: £35 (90 days). Contact the Consulate (or Consular section at Embassy) for details; see *Contact Addresses* section.
Validity: *Tourist*: approximately 30 days. *Transit*: maximum 48 hours. *Business*: up to 90 days. **Application to:** Consulate (see *Contact Addresses* section).
Application to: Consulate (see *Contact Addresses* section).
Application requirements: (a) Two completed application forms. (b) Two passport-size photos. (c) Passport valid for six months. (d) Fee. (e) Letter from current UK employer (and photocopy). (f) Pre-paid recorded delivery envelope for postal applications. *Tourist*: (a)-(f) and, (g) Letter of invitation from an Algerian national or a hotel booking. *Business*: (a)-(f) and, (g) Letter of invitation from the sponsoring company.
Working days required: At least three, 10 in peak periods and for postal applications. Express service available. For some nationals it might take longer depending on whether the application needs to be referred to Algeria.
Temporary residence: Apply to the authorities in Algeria.

Money

Currency: Dinar (AD) = 100 centimes. Notes are in denominations of AD1000, 500, 200, 100 and 50. Coins are in denominations of AD100, 50, 20, 10, 5, 2 and 1, and 50, 20, 10, 5 and 1 centimes.
Note: Because of the very strict adherence of the authorities to these regulations, visitors are strongly advised not to be associated with the black market, which tends to concentrate on the Euro and portable electronics.
Currency exchange: In the past, difficulties have arisen when trying to exchange currency in Algeria, with only one national bank (*La Banque Extérieure d'Algérie*) able to exchange foreign currency at branches in major business centres. Difficulties are now decreasing and it is possible, for example, to exchange currency at some of the larger hotels. However, the facilities for currency exchange remain quite limited.
Credit & debit cards: Very limited acceptance of American Express, Diners Club, MasterCard and Visa - and only in urban areas. Check with your credit or debit card company for details of merchant acceptability and other services that may be available.
Travellers cheques: Only top-class (4-star and above) hotels and government-run craft (souvenir) shops accept these, and only in certain establishments. To avoid additional exchange rate charges, travellers are advised to take travellers cheques in US Dollars or Euros.
Currency restrictions: The import and export of local currency is allowed. The import of foreign currency is unlimited, but must be declared on arrival and changed at the nearest bank. The export of foreign currency is permitted up to the amount declared on arrival. The currency declaration and the exchange declaration must be presented upon departure.
Exchange rate indicators: The following figures are included as a guide to the movements of the Dinar against Sterling and the US Dollar:

Date	Feb '04	May '04	Aug '04	Nov '04
£1.00=	130.28	126.26	132.24	137.25
$1.00=	71.57	70.69	71.78	72.48

Banking hours: Sun-Thurs 0900-1530.

Duty Free

The following goods may be taken into Algeria by persons over 17 years of age without incurring customs duty:
200 cigarettes or 50 cigars or 400g of tobacco; 1l of alcoholic beverages; 500ml of Eau de Cologne or 150ml of perfume in opened bottles.
Prohibited items: Gold, firearms, ammunition and narcotics may not be imported or exported. Jewellery, gold and firearms may not be exported.

Public Holidays

2005: Jan 1 New Year's Day. **Jan 21-23** Eid al-Adha (Feast of the Sacrifice). **Feb 10** Islamic New Year. **Feb 21** Ashoura. **Apr 21** Mouloud. **May 1** Labour Day. **Jun 19** Revolutionary Readjustment. **Jul 5** Independence Day. **Nov 1** Anniversary of the Revolution. **Nov 3-5** Eid al-Fitr (End of Ramadan).
2006: Jan 1 New Year's Day. **Jan 10-13** Eid al-Adha (Feast of the Sacrifice). **Jan 31** Islamic New Year. **Feb 9** Ashoura. **May 1** Labour Day. **Apr 11** Mouloud (Birth of the Prophet). **Jun 19** Revolutionary Readjustment. **Jul 5** Independence Day. **Nov 1** Anniversary of the Revolution. **Oct 22-24** Eid al-Fitr (End of Ramadan).
Note: Muslim festivals are timed according to local sightings of various phases of the moon and the dates given above are approximations. The Algerian observance of Ramadan (lasting one lunar month and culminating in the feast days of Eid al-Fitr) has recently relaxed, and restaurants and other business centres will be open during the day. However, in the towns and oases of the south where religious observance tends to be more orthodox, some difficulty might be had in finding eating places and getting transport during the daylight hours. For a more detailed description, see the *World of Islam* appendix.

Health

	Special Precautions?	Certificate Required?
Yellow Fever	Yes	1
Cholera	No	No
Typhoid & Polio	2	N/A
Malaria	3	N/A

Note: Regulations and requirements may be subject to change at short notice, and you are advised to contact your doctor well in advance of your intended date of departure. Any numbers in the chart refer to the footnotes below.

1: A yellow fever vaccination certificate is required by travellers over 1 year of age arriving within six days of transitting or leaving endemic or infected areas.
2: It is normally advised to get an immunisation course or booster against typhoid and sometimes poliomyelitis.
3: Malaria risk is limited. The benign *vivax* strain has been reported in Ihrir (Illizi Department).
Food & drink: Mains water is normally chlorinated, and whilst relatively safe may cause mild abdominal upsets. Bottled water is available and is advised for the first few weeks of stay. Drinking water outside main cities and towns is likely to be contaminated and sterilisation is considered essential. Milk is pasteurised and dairy products are safe for consumption. Powdered or tinned milk is available and is advised, but make sure that it is reconstituted with pure water. Local meat, poultry, seafood, fruit and vegetables are generally considered safe to eat.
Other risks: *Hepatitis A* occurs. *Hepatitis B, diphtheria* and *tuberculosis* are all present.
Rabies is present. For those at high risk, vaccination before arrival should be considered. If you are bitten, seek medical help without delay. For more information, consult the *Health* appendix.
Note: In 2003, there were three reported outbreaks of bubonic plague in western Algeria: El Kehailia, south of Oran, and in the areas of Mascara and Sidi Bel Abbes; the last reported case was on 10th July 2003.
Health care: Medical insurance is not always valid in Algeria and a medical insurance supplement with specific overseas coverage is recommended. Health care facilities are generally of a reasonable standard in the north but more limited in the south. Doctors and hospitals usually ask for immediate cash payment for their services. Emergency cases will be dealt with free of charge.

Travel - International

Note: Foreign travellers are advised against all holiday and non-essential travel to Algeria, owing to the continual threat of terrorism, which is greatest in rural areas in northern Algeria and in the desert and mountainous regions of the southeast (where a group of foreign tourists were abducted in 2003). It is advised that all travellers be extra cautious with personal security arrangements throughout their stay. *All* travel to the southeastern provinces of Tamanrasset, Djanet and Illizi is currently advised against.
Attacks from an armed insurgency of Islamist groups have

targeted security forces but have also launched indiscriminate attacks on civilians by bombs and raids on villages, and on buses and vehicles, sometimes at false vehicle checkpoints.
AIR: Algeria's national airline is *Air Algérie (AH)* (website: www.airalgerie.dz). Other airlines serving Algeria include *Alitalia, Egyptair, Royal Air Maroc, Saudia* and *Tunis Air*.
Approximate flight times: From Algiers to *London* is two hours 15 minutes.
International airports: *Algiers (ALG)* (Houari Boumediène) is 20km (12 miles) east of Algiers. Buses and trains operate to the city 0600-1900 (travel time – 30 minutes). Taxis are also available. Airport facilities include a bank and bureau de change, left luggage, shops, post office, tourist information, restaurants and car hire.
Oran (ORN) (Es Senia) is 10km (6 miles) from the city. Taxis are available to the city. Airport facilities include a bank, limited catering and car hire.
Annaba (AAE) (Les Salines) is 12km (7.5 miles) from the city. A bus service departs to the city every 30 minutes. Coach service is available on request and taxis are also available. Airport facilities include a restaurant, bank and car hire facilities.
Constantine (CZL) (Ain El Bey) is 9km (6 miles) from the city. There are bus and taxi links with the city and limited airport facilities.
Departure tax: None.
SEA: The main ports are Algiers, Annaba, Béjaia, Oran and Skikda. Regular shipping lines serve Algiers from Mediterranean ports. *Algérie Ferries* runs passenger services connecting Algeria to Marseille (France) and Alicante (Spain) (website: www.algerieferries.com).
RAIL: There is one daily train connecting Algiers with Tunis in Tunisia via Constantine and Annaba. A reservation is required for this route. First-class carriages are air conditioned; the train also carries a buffet car and couchettes. Another daily train runs between Algiers and Marrakech in Morocco. Stops en route are Oran, Fès, Mèknes, Rabat and Casablanca. Reservations are required and a supplement is charged. Air-conditioned coaches and light refreshments/buffet car are available. At present, services are interrupted owing to the closure of the border between Algeria and Morocco and through trains are not operating.
ROAD: Owing to border closures, land crossings between Morocco and Algeria are not possible at present. The main road entry points are Maghnia (Morocco), Souk-Ahras, Tebessa and El Kala (Tunisia), Fort Thiriet (Libya), In Guezzam (Niger) and Bordj Mokhtar (Mali). There is a good network of paved roads in the coastal regions and paved roads connect the major towns in the northern Sahara. Further south, the only substantial stretches of paved roads are on the two trans-Saharan 'highways', one of which runs to the west through Reggane and up through Morocco to the coast, while the other runs through Tamanrasset and Djanet on its way to Ghardaia and Algiers. The precise route taken by trans-Saharan travellers often depends on the season. Please note that many desert 'roads' are up to 10km- (6 mile-) wide ribbons of unimproved desert and are suitable only for well-maintained 4-wheel-drive vehicles. **Coach:** Services are run by *Altour* (www.altour.com) and *SNTF* with international routes to Tunisia and Morocco.
Documentation: International Driving Permit required.

Travel - Internal

AIR: *Air Algérie* operates frequent services from Algiers domestic airport (adjacent to Algiers International) to the major business centres of Annaba, Constantine and Oran. Less frequent services run from Algiers, Oran, Constantine and Annaba to the other less important commercial centres and gateway oases such as Ghardaia (six hours from Algiers) and Ouargla, as well as important oil towns such as In Amenas and Hassi Messaoud. Services are generally reliable, but air travel to the far south may be subject to delay during the dry summer months because of sand storms. Despite this, air is by far the most practical means of transport to the far south for the visitor with limited resources of time; Djanet and Tamanrasset are the oasis gateways to the *Tassili N'Ajjer* and the *Hoggar* respectively.
Note: The London office of *Air Algérie* (tel: (020) 7487 5903) can provide a timetable of services and prices, make reservations and issue tickets. There is an *Air Algérie* office in every Algerian town which is served by the airline. Reservations and itineraries can be arranged from these offices, but as some of the more isolated offices are not connected by computer, fax or telex, reservations should be confirmed well in advance. Offices are very busy in the major towns.
SEA: Government ferries service the main coastal ports: Algiers, Annaba, Arzew, Béjaia, Djidjelli, Ghazaouet, Mostaganem, Oran and Skikda.
RAIL: There are 4000km (2500 miles) of railway in Algeria, run by the *Société Nationale des Transports Ferroviaires (SNTF)*. Daily - but fairly slow - services operate in the northern part of the country between Algiers and Oran, Béjaia, Skikda, Annaba and Constantine. The southern routes connect once a day from Annaba to Tebessa via Souk Ahras, Constantine with Touggourt via Biskra (twice a day) and Mohammadia with Bechar. Trains on the southern routes only carry second-class coaches.
ROAD: Road surfaces are reasonably good. All vehicles travelling in the desert should be in good mechanical condition, as breakdown facilities are virtually non-existent. Travellers *must* carry full supplies of water and petrol. Traffic drives on the right. Travel by road (outside Algiers) in northern Algeria should be avoided, especially after dark.
Coach: Relatively inexpensive coaches, run by the SNTF, link major towns. Services are regular but this mode of travel is not recommended for long journeys, such as travel to the south from the coastal strip. Services leave from the coach stations close to the centres of Algiers and Oran. **Car hire:** Can be arranged at the airport on arrival or in most towns. Many hotels can also arrange car hire. **Documentation:** An International Driving Permit is required. A *carnet de passage* may be required if using your own car. Cars are allowed entry for three months without duty. Insurance must be purchased at the border.
URBAN: Municipal bus and tram services operate in Algiers, its suburbs and the coastal area. 10-journey *carnets* and daily, weekly or longer duration passes are available. There are also two public lifts and a funicular which lead up to the hill overlooking the old *souk* in Algiers. An underground system is planned. **Taxi:** It is advised not to use public transport other than taxis recommended by established hotels. All taxis are metered and are plentiful in most cities and major towns, though busy during the early evening in the main cities as many people use them to return home after work. The habit of sharing a taxi is widespread. The amount on the meter is the correct fare, but there are surcharges after dark. Travellers are advised not to use unlicensed taxis, as these are likely to be uninsured.

Accommodation

HOTELS: In general, good hotel accommodation in Algeria is limited. The business centres, and in particular Algiers, tend to have either extremely expensive luxury hotels or cheaper hotels primarily suited to the local population visiting on business or for social purposes. Algiers and Oran are full of the cheaper hotels, but they tend to be crowded and difficult to get into, even with a confirmed booking. For assurance on business, reserve rooms only at the best hotels.
Grading: All hotels are subject to government regulations and are classified by a star rating: deluxe (**5-star**), second class (**4/3-star**) and tourist class (**2/1-star**).
The Coast: The hotels in the resorts along the Mediterranean coast have increased in number, and many are of a reasonably high standard. Often, the good hotels in these resorts run their own nightclubs. Winter rates for coastal resorts apply from 1 October to 31 May, and summer rates for the remainder of the year.
The Oases: Good hotels in the gateway oases of the mid-south - such as Ghardaia and Ouargla - are few and far between, and during the season (any time other than high summer, which runs from late June to early September) it is vital to book well in advance.
The Far South: Hotels in the very far south are extremely limited. In Tamanrasset, better class hotels have been built since the oasis became a fashionable winter resort. Room availability is, however, limited.
CAMPING/CARAVANNING: Camping is free on common land or on the beaches but permission from the local authorities is necessary. Campsites with good facilities are found in Ain el-Turk, Annaba and Larhat.
YOUTH HOSTELS: There is a good network of (single sex) youth hostels throughout the country offering accommodation at budget rates. For more information, contact the Fédération Algérienne des Auberges de Jeunesse, 213 Rue Hassiba Ben Bouali, BP 15, El Annasser, Algiers (tel/fax: (21) 678 658/7).

Resorts & Excursions

THE NORTH

ALGIERS: The capital has been a port since Roman times and many impressive ruins can still be seen, such as those at **Djemila**, **Timgad** and especially Tipasa (see below), which are all in good condition because of the dry desert climate. Algiers was commercialised by the French in the mid-19th century and much of the fabric of the city dates from this time. However, it still has a *Maghreb* feel to it. The **Bardo Ethnographic and Local Art Museum** and the **National Museum of Fine Arts** are amongst the finest in North Africa.
Excursions: Within easy reach of Algiers along the coast lie some fine resorts. **Zeralda** is a beach resort with a holiday village and a replica nomad village. **Tipasa** has exceptional Roman, Punic and Christian ruins, and a Numidian mausoleum. The **Chiffa Gorges** and **Kabylia** in the mountains provide more rural scenery. Fig and olive groves in summer become ski resorts in the winter. To the east of Algiers, the **Turquoise Coast** offers rocky coves and long beaches within easy reach of the city, equipped with sports, cruise and watersports facilities. The **Sidi Fredj** peninsula has a marina, an open-air theatre and complete amenities including sporting facilities.
ORAN: The western coast around Algeria's second city has a similar range of beaches, historic remains and mosques. Along the coast from Oran, which is primarily a business centre and an oil depot, there are a number of resorts, many with well-equipped hotels. Notable beaches include **Ain El Turk**, **Les Andalouses**, **Canastel**, **Kristel**, **Mostaganem** and **Sablettes**. Les Andalouses is the most developed and offers all types of watersports facilities and nightclub entertainment as well as first-class accommodation.
THE HAUTS PLATEAUX: Tlemcen was an important imperial city from the 12th to 16th centuries. It stands in the wooded foothills of the Tellian Atlas and is a pleasant retreat from the stifling heat of high summer. Sights include the **Grand Mosque**, the **Mansourah Fortress** and the **Almohad ramparts**. **Constantine**, to the east, is a natural citadel lying across the **River Rhumnel**. Founded by the Carthaginians, who called it Cirta, it is the oldest continuously inhabited city in Algeria. Sights include the **Ahmed Bey Palace** (one of the most picturesque in the Maghreb) and the **Djamma el-Kebir Mosque**.

THE SAHARA

The Sahara is the most striking and also most forbidding feature of the country. Relatively uninhabited, the area is drawing increasing numbers of winter tourists.
Accommodation, though generally good value, is often scarce in oasis regions, and during the season it is advisable to book in advance. *Air Algérie* operates frequent flights from Algiers to Ghardaia, Djanet and Tamanrasset, as well as to several smaller towns, oases and oil settlements, but services can be delayed in high summer owing to adverse weather conditions. Roads are much improved, although summer sand storms and winter rains can make all but the major routes hazardous.
The best way to enter the south is to cross the **El Kautara Gorges** to the south of **Constantine**. The sudden glimpse of the Sahara through the El Kautara Gorges is breathtaking. These gorges are said to separate the winter areas from the land of everlasting summer and are called **Fouur Es Sahra** ('the Sahara's mouth') by the inhabitants.
Further down, most Algerian oases generally defy the European cliché of a small patch of palms forever threatened by encroaching dunes: they are often fairly large towns with highly organised, walled-in gardens with date palms, and mosques, shops and monuments.
Favourite starting places for exploring the Sahara are **Laghouat**, a town with a geometric plan, or the **M'Zab Valley**, which has seven typical holy towns and is inhabited by a Muslim fundamentalist sect called the Mozabites. Mozabite towns are distinguished by a characteristic minaret with four spires. The most famous among them is **Ghardaia**, coiled within a group of bare, ochre rocks. The streets, made of clay or paving stones, curl up through the blue and beige buildings towards the white obelisk of the minaret. Not far from Ghardaia, situated on a hill, is the holy town of **Beni-Isguen**, the four gates of which are constantly guarded. The special feature of this town is its permanent auction market. In the east of the M'Zab region is **Ouargla**, referred to as 'the golden key to the desert'. This town is well worth visiting for its malekite (an Islamic sect) minaret overlooking an expansive landscape. Further on is an oasis surrounded by palm trees and beyond that lie the beaches of the **Sebkha**.
Deeper into the south lies the town of **El Goléa**, referred to as 'the pearl of the desert' or 'the enchanted oasis' because of its luxuriant vegetation and abundant water. The town is dominated by an old *ksar* (fort) whose ruins are well preserved. Further south are the **Hoggar Mountains**, an impressive, jagged range reaching as far as Libya and surrounded by desert on all sides. It consists of a plateau made of volcanic rock. Eroded cliffs and granite needles form fascinating shapes in pink, blue or black basalt. At the top of the **Assekreu** nestles the famous refuge of Charles de Foucault at 2800m (9259ft). **Mount Tahat**, which belongs to the **Atakor Massif**, can be seen in the distance, reaching 3000m (9921ft) at its highest point. The picturesque capital, **Tamanrasset**, situated at the heart of the Hoggar Mountains, is full of life and character and is an important stopping place for commercial traffic travelling to and from West Africa. Being a large town with many hotels and restaurants, tourists often stay in 'Tam' (as it is sometimes called) and use it as a base for touring the Hoggar Mountains (the Assekreu and Charles de Foucault's hermitage) or hiking in the open desert to the south and west in the company of camel drivers who carry their luggage. It is also a popular winter holiday resort and a centre for oil exploration and exploitation. It is visited regularly by the camel caravans of *les hommes bleus*, blue-robed Touaregs, who are the ancient nomadic inhabitants of this wide region. They make their way around the

A B C D E F G H I J K L M N O P Q R S T U V W X Y Z

inscrutable desert through an ancient knowledge of landmarks passed on from father to son. These nomads have a fair complexion, a blue veil over the lower half of their faces and are often very tall.

The tiny oasis of **Djanet**, another watering hole for commercial traffic and trans-Saharan expeditions, can be found in the **Tassili N'Ajjer**, or 'Plateau of Chasms'. This is a vast volcanic plateau crossed by massive gorges gouged out by rivers which have long since dried out or gone underground. The Tassili conceals a whole group of entirely unique rupestrian paintings (rock paintings), which go back at least as far as the neolithic age. The paintings, depicting daily life, hunting scenes and herds of animals, have a striking beauty and reveal ways of life several thousand years old. They spread out over a 130,000 sq km surface (50,000 sq miles) and form an extraordinary open-air museum which has been miraculously conserved, owing to the pure quality of the air. Tours of the **Tassili Plateau** and the rupestrian paintings, as well as long-distance car treks in the **Ténéré** are available, lasting from one day to two weeks. These visits are organised by private agencies run by the Tuareg and most of them offer a high-quality service. Tourists are collected at the airport (either Djanet or Tamanrasset) and the agency provides them with transportation (usually in 4-wheel-drive vehicles), mattresses and food, although travellers must bring their own sleeping bags.

Sport & Activities

Horseracing and **football** are popular. The northern coastline offers **fishing**, **swimming**, **sailing** and **water-skiing**, mainly in Algiers and Annaba.

Social Profile

FOOD & DRINK: Algiers and popular coastal towns have a fair selection of good restaurants, serving mainly French and Italian-style food, though the spicy nature of the sauces sets the cuisine apart from its European counterparts. Even classic dishes will have an unmistakable Algerian quality. Fish dishes are exceptionally good. Menus generally feature a soup or salad to start, roast meat (lamb or beef) or fish as a main course and fresh fruit to finish. In the towns, stalls sell *brochettes* (kebabs) in French bread and covered in a spicy sauce (if desired). The range of foodstuffs in the south is more limited. Local cooking, which is often served for guests of a household, will often consist of roast meat (generally lamb), cous-cous with a vegetable sauce and fresh fruit to finish. Good-quality food is reasonably priced. The sale of alcohol is not encouraged. Alcohol is only available in the more expensive restaurants and hotels and is generally not cheap. There are no licensing hours and hotel bars tend to stay open for as long as there is custom. Algeria produces some good wines but very few of them seem to be served in the country itself. If available, try Medea, Mansourah and Mascara red wines and Medea, Mascara and Lismara rosés. The major hotels may have a reasonable cellar of European wines. All visitors are advised to respect Muslim attitudes to alcohol.
NIGHTLIFE: The main towns offer reasonable entertainment facilities, including hotel restaurants, nightclubs, discos, folk dancing and traditional music. In Algiers and Oran, some cinemas show English and French films.
SHOPPING: Possible souvenirs include leatherware, rugs, copper and brassware, local dresses and jewellery. Berber carpets are beautifully decorated, and from the Sahara comes finely-dyed basketwork and primitive-style pottery. Bargaining is customary in street markets and smaller shops. The rue Didouche Mourad is the best shopping street in Algiers. There are two state-run craft centres with fixed prices. One is located at Algiers airport. **Shopping hours:** Sat-Thurs 0900-1200 and 1400-1900. Some shops open on Fridays.
SPECIAL EVENTS: For a complete list of Special Events taking place in Algeria, contact the Ministère du Tourisme et de l'Artisanat (see *Contact Addresses* section). The following is a selection of special events occurring in Algeria in 2005:
Feb 28 *Sahara Marathon*, Tindouf. **Apr** *Tafsit* (Spring celebration), Tamrasset. **May** *Sbiba* (peace celebration), Djanet. **May** *Strawberry Festival*, Skikda. **Nov 3-5** *Eid al-Fitr* (End of Ramadan), nationwide.
SOCIAL CONVENTIONS: Courtesy should be adopted with new acquaintances. The provision and acceptance of hospitality are as important a part of Algerian culture as elsewhere in the Arab world. In the main cities, the urban population lives at a frantic pace much akin to European urban dwellers, but in the south and in rural areas people are much more open and friendly. Algerian women have strict social and dress codes. Western women should respect Muslim tradition and cover themselves as much as possible or they may incite hostility. Tourist visits should be avoided during Ramadan. For more information, see the *World of Islam* appendix. **Photography:** Military installations and personnel should not be photographed. Visitors are advised to make sure there is nothing that could be of a governmental or military nature around their prospective photographic subject. **Tipping:** 10 per cent is usual.

Business Profile

ECONOMY: Petroleum and natural gas are the most important industries in Algeria and account for all but a small fraction of the country's exports. Most of the country is covered by the Sahara Desert and despite investments in the agricultural sector (the main crops being wheat, potatoes, grapes, cereals and citrus fruits), Algeria is far from self-sufficient in foodstuffs and is vulnerable to drought. Most of the fertile land is located in the northern littoral region. The government has recently completed the process of breaking up state agricultural co-operatives and turning the land over to its occupants. Minerals, principally iron ore and phosphates, are the other major export. The country's principal trading partners are France, Germany, Italy and Spain – it currently supplies a quarter of European natural gas imports. This proportion is likely to increase with the construction of a new pipeline linking coastal terminals to newly developed Saharan gas fields. From Europe, Algeria imports most of its industrial equipment and consumer goods. The IMF and other Western donors have provided loans and aid packages, conditional on liberalising economic reforms and the sale of state-owned industrial assets – the government has, by and large, been prepared to meet these. As the security crisis has eased in the last few years, economic links between Algeria and the EU have grown. In April 2002, Algeria signed an Association Agreement with the EU, which aims to boost both-way trade.
BUSINESS: Suits should always be worn in winter months, shirt sleeves during the summer. Prior appointments are necessary for larger business firms. Businesspeople generally speak Arabic or French and, as a great deal of bargaining is necessary, it is rarely convenient to carry out transactions through an interpreter. Patience is always important. Visitors are usually entertained in hotels or restaurants, where Algerian businessmen are seldom accompanied by their wives. Only rarely are visitors entertained at home. If visiting during Ramadan (and this should be avoided if possible) care should be taken to observe local custom in public places (for a more detailed description, see the *World of Islam* appendix). The climate is best between October and May. **Office hours:** Generally Sat-Wed 0800-1200 and 1300-1600.
COMMERCIAL INFORMATION: The following organisation can offer advice: Chambre Algérienne de Commerce et d'Industrie, Palais Consulaire, BP 100, 6 boulevard Amilcar Cabral, Place des Martyrs, 6003 Algiers (tel: (21) 715 160 *or* 965 050 *or* 966 060; fax: (21) 710 714; e-mail: caci@wissal.dz; website: www.caci.com.dz).

Climate

Summer temperatures are high throughout the country, particularly in the south where it is both very dry and very hot. In the winter, the oases of the far south are pleasant and attract many visitors. The desert temperature drops dramatically at night. North of the Sahara, temperatures are very mild from September to May and vary little between day and night. South of the Sahara, temperatures are pleasant from October to April, but there are great variations between day and night. Coastal towns are prone to storms from the sea. Rainfall is relatively low throughout the country and in the far south it is virtually unknown.
Required clothing: Cotton and linen lightweights for winter months and for evenings in desert areas. Woollens and light rainwear are advised for the winter along the coast and the *Hauts Plateaux*.

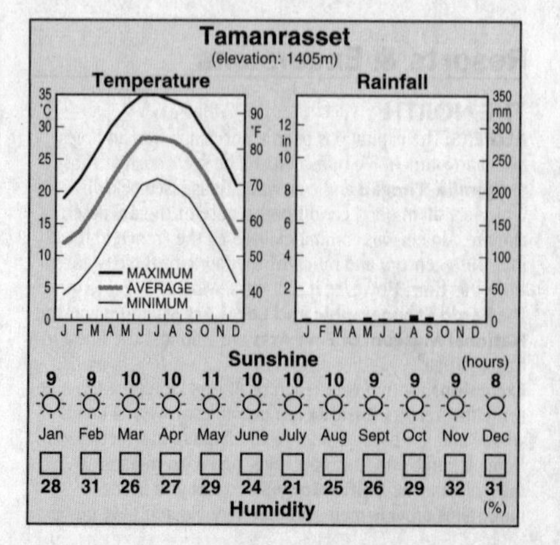

American Samoa

LATEST TRAVEL ADVICE CONTACTS

British Foreign and Commonwealth Office
Tel: (0870) 606 0290 Website: www.fco.gov.uk
US Department of State
Website: http://travel.state.gov/travel
Canadian Department of Foreign Affairs and Int'l Trade
Tel: (1 800) 267 8376 Website: www.dfait-maeci.gc.ca

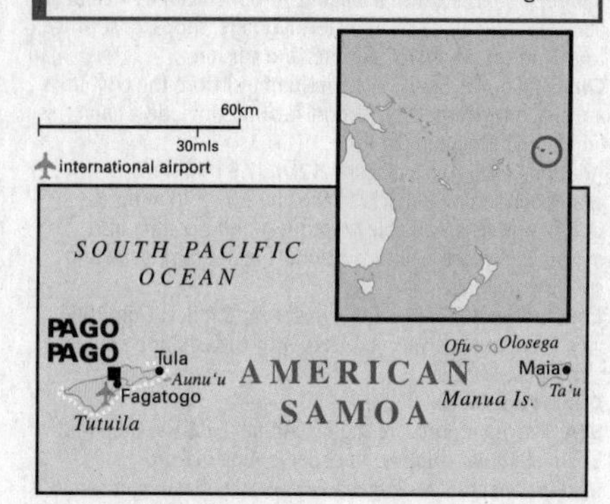

Location: South Pacific.

Country dialling code: 684.

American Samoa is an External Territory of the United States of America, and is represented abroad by US Embassies – see the *USA* section.
Office of Tourism
Department of Commerce, American Samoa Government, PO Box 1147, Pago Pago, American Samoa 96799
Tel: 699 9411. Fax: 699 9414.
E-mail: amerikasamoa@amerikasamoa.info
Website: www.amsamoa.com
South Pacific Tourism Organisation
Street address: Level 3, FNPF Place, 343-359 Victoria Parade, Suva, Fiji
Postal address: PO Box 13119, Suva, Fiji
Tel: (639) 330 4177. Fax: (639) 330 1995.
E-mail: info@spto.org. Website: www.spto.org
Also deals with enquiries from the UK.

General Information

AREA: 201 sq km (77.6 sq miles).
POPULATION: 57,291 (2000).
POPULATION DENSITY: 285.0 per sq km.
CAPITAL: Pago Pago. **Population:** 4,278 (2000).
GEOGRAPHY: American Samoa lies in the Pacific Ocean approximately 3700km (2300 miles) southwest of Hawaii. It comprises seven islands: Tutuila, the largest with an area of 53 sq miles; Ofu, Olosega and Ta'u, known as the Manu'a group; and Aunu'u, Rose and Swain's. The Manu'a group is volcanic in origin and dominated by high peaks. Rose and Swain's Islands are uninhabited coral atolls located to the east and north respectively of the other two island groups.
GOVERNMENT: US External Territory (Unincorporated). Gained a measure of self-government in 1977. **Head of State:** President George W Bush since 2001. **Head of Government:** Acting Governor Togiola Tulafono since 2003.
LANGUAGE: Samoan, but many islanders speak English.
RELIGION: Half of the population are Christian Congregational. There are also Roman Catholics, Latter Day Saints and Protestants, amongst others.
TIME: GMT - 11.
ELECTRICITY: 110V AC, 60Hz. US-style two-pin plugs.
COMMUNICATIONS: Telephone: IDD is available. Country code: 684. All outgoing calls must go through the international operator. **Mobile telephone:** GSM 1900 network operated by *Blue Sky* (www.blueskynet.as). US-style (non-GSM) network operated by *American Samoa Telecommunications Authority* (website: www.samoatelco.com). Roaming agreements do not exist at present. **Fax:** Hotels have facilities. **Internet:** Main ISP

TIMATIC CODES

Health	AMADEUS: **TI-DFT/JIB/HE** GALILEO/WORLDSPAN: **TI-DFT/JIB/HE** SABRE: **TIDFT/JIB/HE**
Visa	AMADEUS: **TI-DFT/JIB/VI** GALILEO/WORLDSPAN: **TI-DFT/JIB/VI** SABRE: **TIDFT/JIB/VI**

To access TIMATIC country information on Health and Visa regulations through the Computer Reservations System (CRS), type in the appropriate command line listed above.

is *American Samoa Telecommunications Authority* (see above for website). Internet cafes exist. **Telegram:** Facilities are available at main towns and hotels. **Post:** American Samoa is part of the US postal system and the same standard postal rates apply. The main Post Office in the Lumana'i Building in Fagatogo is open 24 hours. There are also branches in Leone and Faguita villages, open Mon-Fri 0800-1600 and Sat 0830-1200. **Press:** The island's own English-language newspaper is the *News Bulletin*, published from Monday to Friday. The *Samoa Journal and Advertiser* and *Samoa News* are also published in English.
Radio: BBC World Service (website: www.bbc.co.uk/worldservice) and Voice of America (website: www.voa.gov) can be received. From time to time the frequencies change and the most up-to-date can be found online.

Passport/Visa

	Passport Required?	Visa Required?	Return Ticket Required?
Full British	Yes	No	Yes
Australian	Yes	No	Yes
Canadian	Yes	No	Yes
USA	1	No	Yes
Other EU	Yes	No/2	Yes
Japanese	Yes	No	Yes

Note: Regulations and requirements may be subject to change at short notice, and you are advised to contact the appropriate diplomatic or consular authority before finalising travel arrangements. Details of these may be found at the head of this country's entry. Any numbers in the chart refer to the footnotes below.

PASSPORTS: Passport valid for at least 60 days beyond period of stay required by all except: **1.** nationals of the USA holding other proof of identity (bearing a photograph), a valid onward or return ticket for stays of up to 30 days and proof of sufficient funds for the duration of stay.
Note: Pago Pago is not a port of entry to the USA and passengers proceeding to the USA must comply with the appropriate regulations.
VISAS: Required by all except nationals of the following countries for stays of up to 30 days:
(a) nationals of countries mentioned in the chart above, except **2.** Cyprus, Czech Republic, Estonia, Greece, Hungary, Latvia, Lithuania, Malta, Poland and Slovak Republic who *do* need a visa.
(b) nationals of Andorra, Brunei, Iceland, Liechtenstein, Monaco, New Zealand, Norway, San Marino, Singapore and Switzerland.
Note: (a) All nationals must be in possession of a valid passport, documentation for onward travel, sufficient funds to cover their stay and a confirmed accommodation reservation.
Application to: US Consulate in plenty of time for prospective visits of more than 30 days (or Consular Section at US Embassy); see *Contact Addresses* section.
Temporary residence: Apply to Immigration Department in Pago Pago.

Money

Currency: US Dollar (US$) = 100 cents. See the *USA* section for information on denominations, travellers cheques and exchange rates.
Currency exchange: Exchange facilities are available at the airport and through trade banks. ATMs are located at the banking branches of the Amerika Samoa Bank and the Bank of Hawaii.
Credit & debit cards: American Express is widely accepted whereas MasterCard has more limited use. Check with your credit or debit card company for details of merchant acceptability and other services which may be available.
Currency restrictions: There are no restrictions on the import and export of local and foreign currencies.
Banking hours: Mon-Fri 0900-1500.

Duty Free

The following items may be imported into American Samoa without incurring customs duty:
200 cigarettes or 50 cigars or 454g of tobacco; one US Gallon or five bottles of alcohol; a reasonable amount of perfume.

Public Holidays

2005 Jan 1 New Year's Day. **Jan 19** Martin Luther King Day. **Feb 14** Presidents' Day/ Washington's Birthday. **Sep 5** Labour Day. **Oct 10** Columbus Day. **Nov 11** Veterans Day. **Nov 24** Thanksgiving Day. **Dec 25** Christmas Day.
2006 Jan 1 New Year's Day. **Jan 19** Martin Luther King Day. **Feb 13** Presidents' Day/ Washington's Birthday. **Sep 4** Labour Day. **Oct 9** Columbus Day. **Nov 11** Veterans Day. **Nov 23** Thanksgiving Day. **Dec 25** Christmas Day.

Health

	Special Precautions?	Certificate Required?
Yellow Fever	No	1
Cholera	No	No
Typhoid & Polio	2	N/A
Malaria	No	N/A

Note: Regulations and requirements may be subject to change at short notice, and you are advised to contact your doctor well in advance of your intended date of departure. Any numbers in the chart refer to the footnotes below.

1: A yellow fever vaccination certificate is required from travellers over one year of age arriving from - or within six days of transiting - infected areas.
2: Immunisation against typhoid is generally advised.
Food & drink: Mains water is normally chlorinated, and whilst relatively safe, may cause mild abdominal upsets. Bottled water is available and is advised for the first few weeks of the stay. Drinking water outside main cities and towns may be contaminated and sterilisation is advisable. Milk is pasteurised and dairy products are safe for consumption. Local meat, poultry, seafood, fruit and vegetables are generally considered safe to eat.
Other risks: *Hepatitis A* and *B* occur and vaccination is recommended. Outbreaks of *Japanese encephalitis* have been reported, as have epidemics of *dengue fever*.
Health care: There is no reciprocal Health Care Agreement with the UK. Health insurance is strongly recommended for all travellers.

Travel - International

AIR: The international airline is *Samoa Air (SE)* (website: www.samoaair.com). Other airlines operating between American Samoa and other destinations in the South Pacific include *Aloha Airlines*, *Hawaiian Airlines* and *Polynesian Airlines*.
Air passes: The *Polypass* (offered by Polynesian Airlines) allows the holder to fly between the Southern Pacific destinations of American Samoa, Fiji, Niue, Samoa, Tahiti and Tonga; Honolulu (Hawaii) and Los Angeles in the USA; Brisbane, Melbourne and Sydney in Australia; and Auckland, Christchurch and Wellington in New Zealand. The pass is valid for one year. Once a reservation has been made and travel begun, all travel must be completed within a maximum of 45 days. Tickets will be issued against the Polypass by any Polynesian Airlines office (a valid passport is also required). For further information, contact Polynesian Airlines (website: www.polynesianairlines.com).
Approximate flight times: From Pago Pago to *London* is 25 hours, depending on route taken and stopover times. A typical journey would probably involve stopovers in Los Angeles and Honolulu.
International airports: *Pago Pago (PPG)* is 12km (8 miles) from the city. Buses and taxis are available. Regular scheduled trips are available plus charters and sightseeing. Airport facilities include duty-free shops and a restaurant.
Departure tax: US$3.
SEA: The international port is Pago Pago (Tutuila), which is served by a number of passenger/cruise and cargo lines. Cruise lines include *Orient Line* and *P&O*.

Travel - Internal

AIR: *Samoa Air* (tel: 699 9106; fax: 699 1958; e-mail: alavigne@samoaair.com; website: www.samoaair.com) operates daily scheduled flights to Apia, Maota, Ofu, Olosega and Ta'u carrying up to 18 passengers.
SEA: There is a weekly ferry service from Pago Pago to the Manu'a Islands. A government-run excursion boat sails regularly around Tutuila, calling at the north coast villages of Afono, Vatia and Fagasa. Contact the local authorities for details.
ROAD: There are 150km (93 miles) of paved roads and 200km (125 miles) of unpaved or secondary roads throughout the islands. Traffic drives on the right. **Bus:** A local service operates between the airport and the centre of Pago Pago. The *Aiga* bus operates an inexpensive but unscheduled service between Fagatogo and outlying villages. **Taxi:** Plentiful; the government-fixed fares are displayed in all taxis. **Car hire:** Available; local companies impose a minimum age of 21 for drivers. **Documentation:** An International Driving Permit or valid national driving licence will be accepted.

Accommodation

HOTELS: There is a wide range of bed and breakfast, motel and hotel accommodation available in American Samoa, from international-standard hotels to simple guest houses. For further information, contact the Office of Tourism (see *Contact Addresses* section).
HOUSE-STAYS: Fale, Fala ma Ti ('Samoan home'). The Office of Tourism will help to make arrangements for visitors who wish to stay in a Samoan household. This will be of particular interest to those who wish to learn more of Samoan customs.

Resorts & Excursions

The harbour of **Pago Pago**, made famous by Somerset Maugham's short story *Rain*, is actually the crater of an extinct volcano. The visitor centre for the **national park** is situated in the **Pago Plaza** and the park itself is spread across three islands: **Ofu**, Ta'u and **Tutuila**. **Ta'u Island** is considered the birthplace of the Polynesian people and is therefore recognised as a sacred site. **Upolu** in neighbouring Samoa is sometimes visible. **Tula Village** is a traditional Samoan settlement. Situated at the far end of the eastern district of Tutuila, it overlooks a coastline of white sandy beaches and reefs that are exposed at low tide. **Amanave Village** is in an area renowned for the rugged beauty of its volcanic coastline. On the north coast of the island is the **Forbidden Bay**, claimed to be one of the most beautiful in the South Pacific. It can be reached from **Fagasa** on a trek or a boat trip. The traditional 'turtle and shark' legend is performed in **Vaitogi**. Mountain excursions are available at nearby **Aoloau**.

Sport & Activities

Watersports: American Samoa has many white sandy beaches offering safe **swimming**, with excellent facilities for **diving**, **snorkelling** and **kayaking**. The *Fagatele Bay National Marine Sanctuary* was established to protect the corals reefs and marine life in the area. Diving equipment can be hired easily and a number of companies provide dive courses and cruises to the best sites. Cruises to neighbouring Samoa are also available, and these can include an overnight stay in a local *Fale* (Samoan home). For further information, contact the Office of Tourism (see *Contact Addresses* section). Surfing can be done at *Alofay Bay*, *Carter Beach* and *Leone Bay*. The surrounding waters offer **game-fishing** for marlin, yellowfin tuna, wahoo and skip jack. Fully-equipped fishing boats can be hired through hotels or tour operators.
Hiking: The two coral atolls and five volcanic islands that make up American Samoa get twice as much rain as nearby Samoa, which makes American Samoa a lot greener. A number of marked trails lead into the lush interior of the islands, notably to the *National Park of American Samoa*. Guided trips to the volcanoes are also possible.
Other: Several hotels have **tennis** courts that are open to non-residents and there is a 9-hole **golf** course on Tutuila.

Social Profile

FOOD & DRINK: Restaurants offer a variety of cuisines, including American, Chinese, Japanese, Italian and Polynesian. There are also various drive-in restaurants. The Samoan feast, *fia fia*, consists of suckling pig, chicken, fish, *palusami* (coconut cream wrapped in taro leaves and cooked in the *umu*, or pit oven), breadfruit, coconut, bananas, lime and mango.
The national drink is *kava*, which is drunk in sacred ceremonies. If you become intimate with Samoans, you may be invited to a genuine *kava* ceremony. If you attend a genuine *kava* ceremony, do not sip until you tip a little *kava* from its coconut shell cup onto the ground immediately in front of you while saying *manuia* (mah-noo-ee-ah), meaning good luck. Do not drain your cup. Leave a little and tip it out before handing the cup back to the server. Remember that drinking *kava* is a solemn, sacred ceremony and should never be confused with a casual round of drinks in Western society. The taste may take a while to acquire. Most places have a 'happy hour' serving cheaper drinks (1630-1830).
NIGHTLIFE: There are many nightspots with music and dancing. Samoan *fia fias* – feasting and traditional dancing – are organised regularly by several establishments. Samoan village *fia fias* can be arranged through local tour operators. Visitors are usually welcome at any event in the villages and churches.
SHOPPING: Special purchases include handmade *tapa* cloth, the *puletasi* (women's dress) or *lavalava* (men's costume) made by local dressmakers, shell beads and purses, woodcarvings, woven *laufala* table and floor mats, carved kava bowls, Samoan records and duty-free goods.

Shopping hours: Mon-Fri 0800-1700 and Sat 0800-1300.
SPECIAL EVENTS: For further details of events in American Samoa, contact the Office of Tourism or South Pacific Tourism Organisation (see *Contact Addresses* section). The following is a selection of special events occurring in American Samoa in 2005:
Mar *St Patrick's Day Pago Pago Yacht Club Party*. **Mar 20** *Earth Day*. **Apr 13-16** *Easter Celebrations*, islandwide. **Apr 17** *Flag Day Celebrations*, islandwide. **May** *National Tourism Week*. **May 9** *Aso o Tina*. **Aug** *Annual Miss South Pacific Pageant*. **Oct/Nov** *Palolo Day*. **Oct 8** *White Sunday*. **Oct 31** *Halloween*. **Dec** *Holiday Performing Arts Festival*.
SOCIAL CONVENTIONS: Traditional Samoan society is still bound by very strict customs and, despite the younger generation's dissatisfaction with the old values, they are very much adhered to. The Government issues an official list of behaviour codes for both Samoas. Skimpy shorts or other revealing clothes should be avoided except when swimming or climbing coconut palms, although disapproval of shorts, if they are not *too* short, is on the wane. Samoan social behaviour conforms to strict and rather complicated rituals, to which the visitor will probably be introduced on arrival, and which should be respected. In the early evening hours, even if swimming offshore, be sure to avoid making any noise that could interrupt the Samoans' prayer period. Usually three gongs are sounded. The first is the signal to return to the house, the second is for prayer and the third sounds the all-clear. In some villages, swimming and fishing are forbidden on Sunday. A visitor who happens to be invited to stay in a Samoan household should be mindful of these customs. On leaving, making a gift, a *mea alofa* (literally a 'thing of love') of shirts, belts or dress-length fabrics is most appreciated. Samoans are extremely hospitable and visitors may receive more than one invitation to stay with neighbours. However, it is inappropriate to leave your first hosts before a pre-arranged date. **Tipping:** Not customary.

Business Profile

ECONOMY: The economy is based mainly on agriculture and fishing, with two tuna canneries providing employment for almost half the workforce; their output accounts for most of American Samoa's export revenue. Agricultural output is mainly for domestic consumption; a small surplus of fruit and vegetables is exported. Industrial estates have been built in an effort to encourage light industrial development. On these estates consumer goods, such as handicrafts, soap and perfume, are produced. The tourist industry is growing slowly; government employment accounts for the bulk of the country's service sector. The government's economic priorities have been to tackle the lack of infrastructure. Shortage of skilled workers and this lack of infrastructure have combined, along with its remote location, to inhibit American Samoa's economic development. American Samoa is a member of the South Pacific Commission.
BUSINESS: Lightweight or tropical suits for business visits. Ties need only be worn for formal occasions.
COMMERCIAL INFORMATION: The following organisation can offer advice: Department of Commerce, American Samoa Government, Pago Pago 1147, American Samoa 96799 (tel: 633 5155; fax: 633 4195; website: www.asg-gov.com/departments/doc.asg.htm).

Climate

Very warm, tropical climate. The heaviest rainfalls are usually between December and April. The climate is best during the winter months, May to September, when there are moderate southeast trade winds.
Required clothing: Lightweight cottons and linens throughout the year with warm wrap for cooler winter evenings, and rainwear for the wet season (December to April).

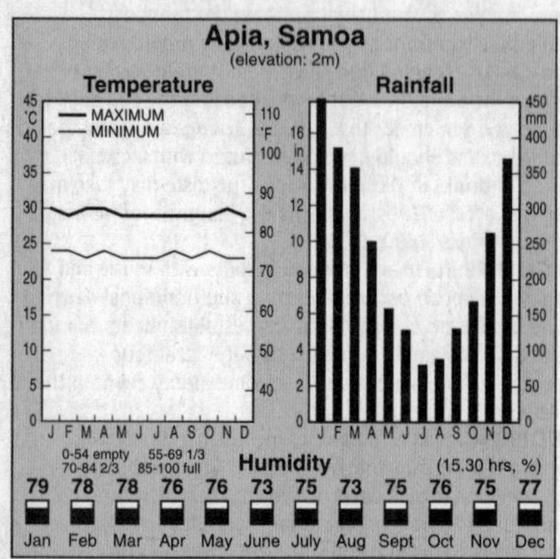

Andorra

LATEST TRAVEL ADVICE CONTACTS

British Foreign and Commonwealth Office
Tel: (0870) 606 0290 Website: www.fco.gov.uk
US Department of State
Website: http://travel.state.gov/travel
Canadian Department of Foreign Affairs and Int'l Trade
Tel: (1 800) 267 8376 Website: www.dfait-maeci.gc.ca

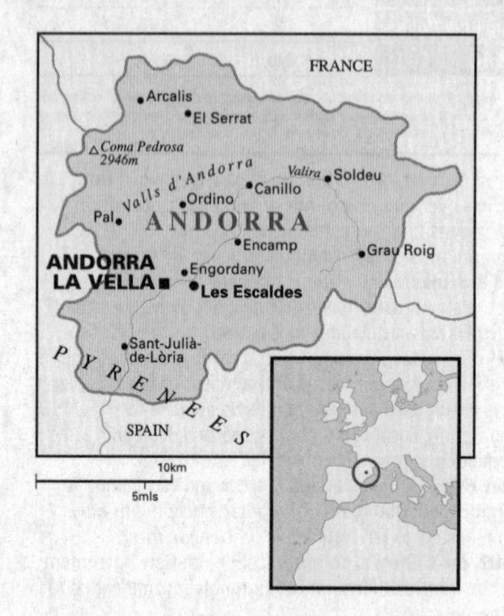

Location: Western Europe, border of France and Spain.

Country dialling code: 376.

Ministry of Presidency and Tourism
Carrer Prat de la Creu, 62 Andorra la Vella, Andorra
Tel: 875 702. Fax: 860 184.
E-mail: turisme@andorra.ad
Website: www.andorra.ad
Sindicat d'Iniciativa Oficina de Turisme (Tourist Office)
Carrer Dr Vilanova, Andorra la Vella, Andorra
Tel: 820 214. Fax: 825 823.
E-mail: sindicatdiniciativa@andorra.ad

Credit: © www.andorra.ad. Ministry of Presidency and Tourism

Embassy of the Principality of Andorra
63 Westover Road, London SW18 2RF, UK
Tel: (020) 8874 4806. Fax: (020) 8874 4902.
E-mail: andorra.embassyuk@btopenworld.com
Website: www.andorra.ad
Opening hours: Mon-Sat 0900-1700 (by appointment only).
This office is a general information bureau which also provides tourist information.
British Consulate
Casa Jacint Pons, 3/2 La Massana, Andorra
Tel/Fax: 839 840.
E-mail: britconand@mypic.ad *or* maestro@mypic.ad
Permanent Mission of the Principality of Andorra to the United Nations
2 United Nations Plaza, 25th Floor, New York, NY 10017, USA
Tel: (212) 750 8064. Fax: (212) 750 6630.
E-mail: andorra@un.int
Website: www.andorra.ad
The American and Canadian Embassies in Madrid deal with enquiries regarding Andorra (see *Spain* section).

TIMATIC CODES

Health
AMADEUS: **TI-DFT/JIB/HE**
GALILEO/WORLDSPAN: **TI-DFT/JIB/HE**
SABRE: **TIDFT/JIB/HE**

Visa
AMADEUS: **TI-DFT/JIB/VI**
GALILEO/WORLDSPAN: **TI-DFT/JIB/VI**
SABRE: **TIDFT/JIB/VI**

To access TIMATIC country information on Health and Visa regulations through the Computer Reservations System (CRS), type in the appropriate command line listed above.

General Information

AREA: 467.76 sq km (180.6 sq miles).
POPULATION: 67,159 (official estimate 2002).
POPULATION DENSITY: 143.6 per sq km.
CAPITAL: Andorra la Vella. **Population:** 20,724 (2002).
GEOGRAPHY: Andorra is situated in the eastern Pyrenees, bordered by France to the north and east and Spain to the south and west. It is roughly halfway between Barcelona and Toulouse. The landscape consists of gorges and narrow valleys surrounded by mountains. Much of the landscape is forested, but there are several areas of rich pastureland in the valleys. There are four rivers and several mountain lakes. Ski resorts and the spa town of Les Escaldes are Andorra's main attractions.
GOVERNMENT: Principality under the suzeraint of the President of France and the Spanish Bishop of Urgel. **Heads of State:** Co-Princes Joan Enric Vives i Sicilia (Bishop of la Seu d'Urgell) since 2003 and Jacques Chirac (President of France) since 1994. **Head of Government:** Marc Forné Molne since 1994.
LANGUAGE: The official language is Catalan. Spanish and French are also spoken.
RELIGION: Roman Catholic.
TIME: GMT + 1 (GMT + 2 from last Sunday in March to Saturday before last Sunday in October).
ELECTRICITY: Sockets: 240 volts AC, 50Hz. Lighting: 125 volts AC.
COMMUNICATIONS: Telephone: Telephone: Full IDD is available. Country code: 376. Outgoing international code: 0. **Mobile telephone:** GSM 900 network covers practically the whole country. Main operator is *STA* (website: www.sta.ad). **Internet:** ISPs include *Andorra Online* (website: www.andorraonline.ad). Internet cafes are readily available. **Post:** Internal mail services are free; international mail takes about one week within Europe. A *poste restante* service is available in Andorra la Vella. Post office hours: 0900-1300 and 1500-1700 in Andorra la Vella, otherwise variable. **Press:** Andorra has two daily newspapers, the *Diari d'Andorra*, and *El Periodic D'Andorra* and one weekly publication, the *Poble Andorra*.
Radio: BBC World Service (website: www.bbc.co.uk/worldservice) and Voice of America (website: www.voa.gov) can be received. From time to time the frequencies change and the most up-to-date can be found online.

Passport/Visa

	Passport Required?	Visa Required?	Return Ticket Required?
Full British	Yes	2	No
Australian	Yes	2	Yes
Canadian	Yes	2	Yes
USA	Yes	2	Yes
Other EU	1	2	No
Japanese	Yes	2	Yes

***Note:** Regulations and requirements may be subject to change at short notice, and you are advised to contact the appropriate diplomatic or consular authority before finalising travel arrangements. Details of these may be found at the head of this country's entry. Any numbers in the chart refer to the footnotes below.*

PASSPORTS: Valid passport required by all except:
1. nationals of France and Spain, providing they hold a valid national ID card.
VISAS: 2. There are no visa requirements for entry into Andorra; however, the relevant regulations for France or Spain should be followed, depending on which country is transited to reach Andorra. Visitors wishing to have their passport stamped with the Andorran coat of arms should apply to the Sindicat d'Initiativa in the capital.
Validity: Stays of up to three months are allowed without a visa.
Temporary residence: Apply in person at the Immigration Office, Carrer de les Boigues-Escaldes-Engordany.

Money

Currency: Although most currencies are accepted, the main currency in circulation is the Euro. See the *France* or *Spain* section for further details of exchange rates.
Single European currency (Euro): The Euro is now the official currency of 12 EU member states (including France and Spain). The first Euro coins and notes were introduced in January 2002 and completely replaced the French Franc on 17 February 2002, and the Spanish Peseta on 28 February 2002. Euro (€) = 100 cents. Notes are in denominations of €500, 200, 100, 50, 20, 10 and 5. Coins are in denominations of €2, 1 and 50, 20, 10, 5, 2 and 1 cents.
Currency exchange: Andorran banks and bureaux de change will exchange foreign currency.
Credit & debit cards: American Express, Diners Club, MasterCard and Visa are accepted, as well as Eurocheque

Credit: © www.andorra.ad. Ministry of Presidency and Tourism

cards. Check with your credit or debit card company for details of merchant acceptability and other services which may be available.
Travellers cheques: To avoid additional exchange rate charges, travellers are advised to take travellers cheques in Euros, Pounds Sterling and US Dollars.
Currency restrictions: There are no restrictions when entering or exiting the country, but French and Spanish authorities may carry out formalities on departure.
Banking hours: Mon-Fri 0900-1300 and 1500-1700, Sat 0900-1200.

Duty Free

Andorra is a duty-free zone, but travellers should check French/Spanish regulations as both these countries maintain customs control at the borders.
Prohibited/restricted items: Narcotics, firearms, ammunition, explosives (including fireworks), flick knives, pornography, horror comics, radio transmitters, certain foodstuffs, plants, flowers, animals and birds and items made from endangered species. No works of art can be exported without permission.

Public Holidays

2005: Jan 1 New Year's Day. **Jan 6** Epiphany. **Mar 14** Constitution Day. **Mar 25-28** Good Friday to Easter Monday. **May 1** Labour Day. **May 5** Ascension. **May 16** Whit Monday. **Jun 24** St John's Day. **Aug 15** Assumption of the Blessed Virgin. **Sep 8** National Day. **Nov 1** All Saints' Day. **Nov 4** St Charles' Day. **Dec 8** Immaculate Conception. **Dec 24** Christmas Eve. **Dec 25-26** Christmas. **Dec 31** New Year's Eve.
2006: Jan 1 New Year's Day. **Jan 6** Epiphany. **Mar 14** Constitution Day. **Apr 14-16** Good Friday to Easter Monday. **May 1** Labour Day. **May 25** Ascension. **Jun 5** Whit Monday. **Jun 24** St John's Day. **Aug 15** Assumption of the Blessed Virgin. **Sep 8** National Day. **Nov 1** All Saints' Day. **Nov 4** St Charles' Day. **Dec 8** Immaculate Conception. **Dec 24** Christmas Eve. **Dec 25-26** Christmas. **Dec 31** New Year's Eve.
Note: In July, August and September, parishes have their own public holidays, during which festivals are held.

Health

	Special Precautions?	Certificate Required?
Yellow Fever	No	No
Cholera	No	No
Typhoid & Polio	No	N/A
Malaria	No	N/A

Note: Regulations and requirements may be subject to change at short notice, and you are advised to contact your doctor well in advance of your intended date of departure. Any numbers in the chart refer to the footnotes below.

Other risks: Visitors should check their *tetanus* immunisation is up to date.
Rabies is present. For those at high risk, vaccination before arrival should be considered. If you are bitten, seek medical help without delay. For more information, consult the *Health* appendix.
Health care: For UK citizens, most health costs are covered by reciprocal health agreements but additional insurance is advised. Visitors should note that as entry to Andorra is usually through France or Spain, the health regulations of these countries should be complied with.

Travel - International

AIR: Andorra's two nearest international airports are *Barcelona (BCN)* in Spain, 225km (140 miles) from Andorra and *Toulouse (TLS)*, in France, 180km (112 miles) from Andorra. For more information on the airports and their facilities, consult the *Spain* and *France* sections. Shared taxis and buses are available.
RAIL: Routes from Perpignan, Villefranche, Toulouse and Barcelona go to *La Tour de Carol*, 20km (12 miles) from Andorra. The nearest station is *L'Hospitalet*, but buses run from both L'Hospitalet and La Tour de Carol (see *Road* below).
ROAD: Mountainous roads exist over the Envalira pass from Perpignan, Tarbes and Toulouse (France); and southwards to Barcelona and Lérida (Spain). Buses run regularly from Barcelona, Tarragona, Valencia and Madrid (Spain); and Toulouse (France). Taxis may also be taken and sharing is common practice to cut costs.
Bus: The journey from La Tour de Carol takes two hours 20 minutes and runs daily at 1045 and 1315. From L'Hospitalet the service takes two hours 40 minutes and runs early enough to permit a day-return trip from France. A seasonal service runs from Aix-les-Thermes and services may be available from Seo de Urgel in Spain. *Eurolines*, departing from Victoria Coach Station in London, serves destinations in Andorra. For further information about routes, prices and any special promotions, contact *Eurolines*, (tel: (08705) 143 219; e-mail: welcome@eurolines.co.uk; website: www.eurolines.com.

Travel - Internal

ROAD: A good road runs from the Spanish to the French frontiers through Saint Julià, Andorra la Vella, Escaldes-Engordany, Encamp, Canillo and Soldeu. There is one major east-west route and a minor road to El Serrat, which is closed in winter. **Bus:** There are buses and minibuses linking Andorra's villages on the 186km (115 miles) of road. Traffic drives on the right. **Documentation:** National driving licence accepted.

Accommodation

HOTELS: There are hundreds of hotels and guest houses, principally catering for the summer months and ski season, although some stay open all year round. Rooms during the summer months (July-August) should be booked well in advance. Hotels and restaurants are registered with the Tourist Office (*Sindicat d'Initiativa*) and are bound to keep to the registered prices and services. Information on hotels can be obtained from the Andorran Hotel Association (*Unió Hotelera d'Andorra*), Antic Carrer Major 18, Andorra la Vella (tel: 820 625; fax: 861 539; e-mail: uhotelera@uha.ad; website: www.uha.ad).
MOUNTAIN REFUGES: These offer cheap and basic accommodation; normally they will have one room available for visitors, and may or may not have a hearth and bunk beds. Enquire locally about locations and prices.
CAMPING: There are 25 campsites in Andorra, most of which are close to the main towns and are well signposted. Several have shops and other facilities. There are also facilities for caravans.

Resorts & Excursions

The country is mountainous, traversed by a main road which runs roughly north-east to south-west, along which most of the settlements are to be found. Many of these are villages or hamlets with Romanesque churches and houses built in the local style; others, off the main road, are even more unspoilt, and provide spectacular views across the rugged countryside. For the visitor, however, Andorra's two greatest attractions are that it is both a duty-free state and a centre for winter sports, a combination which has led to a great deal of overt commercialism, particularly in the main towns of Andorra la Vella and Escaldes-Engordany.
Andorra la Vella, the country's capital, lies at the junction of two mountain streams. Sights there include a fine 12th-century church and the **Casa de la Vall**, the ancient seat of government.
Adjoining the capital is the spa town of **Escaldes-Engordany** which also has examples of Romanesque architecture. These towns are also the centre of the colourful Andorran local festival in early September, in honour of the Virgin of Meritxell. Approximately 18km (11 miles) from Escaldes-Engordany, off the main road, is the hamlet of **El Serrat**, which commands a breathtaking view across the mountains. The town of **Encamp**, between the capital and the French frontier, is also worth a visit.
Ski resorts: There are several ski resorts in Andorra, most of which offer good facilities. The main centre is **Soldeu**, the first major settlement on the road after the French frontier at Port d'Envalira. Both nursery slopes and skiing for intermediates are available, with a good ski school offering tuition at reasonable prices.
There are also ski centres at **Pas de la Casa-Grau Roig**, on the French frontier, and at **Ordino-Arcalis** and **Arinsal-Pal**, all north of Andorra la Vella. Cross-country skiing is available in the resort of **La Rabassa**. Further information can be obtained from *Ski Andorra*, Edifici les columnes, 58-70 Avenida Tarragona, Andorra la Vella (tel: 864 389; fax: 865 910; e-mail: skiandorra@skiandorra.ad; website: www.skiandorra.ad). The Tourist Office (see *Contact Addresses* section) can provide details on prices and snow conditions.

Sport & Activities

There is excellent **skiing** (for further information, see *Resorts & Excursions* section). A bus service picks up skiers from hotels and inns, and takes them to the slopes, returning in the evening. There are many good nursery slopes. Other available activities include **horseriding**, **tennis**, **swimming**, **trout fishing**, **clay-pigeon shooting**, **hiking** and **rock climbing**. **Football**, **rugby**, **basketball**, **motorbike** and **car rallies** are the most popular spectator sports.

Social Profile

FOOD & DRINK: Cuisine is mainly Catalan, and generally expensive. Quality and prices in restaurants are similar to those in small French and Spanish resort towns. Local dishes include *coques* (flavoured flat cakes), *trinxat* (a

A B C D E F G H I J K L M N O P Q R S T U V W X Y Z

potato and cabbage dish), *truites de carreroles* (a type of mushroom omelette), local sausages and cheese, and a variety of pork and ham dishes.
Alcoholic drinks bought in shops and supermarkets are cheap (Andorra is a duty-free zone), but prices in bars can be high. They do, however, stay open late.
NIGHTLIFE: Andorra's many bars and hotels provide a variety of evening entertainment. Discos are open during both summer and winter.
SHOPPING: There is duty-free shopping for all goods. Petrol, alcohol, cameras and watches can be purchased at low prices. Electrical goods are very good value. **Shopping hours:** Mon-Sat 0900-2000, Sun 0900-1900.
SPECIAL EVENTS: For further details of events in Andorra, contact the Sindicat d'Iniciativa Oficina de Turisme (see *Contact Addresses* section). The following is a selection of special events occurring in Andorra in 2005:
Jan 1 *New Year's Day Concert*, Ordino. **Jan 17** *St Anthony's Day Festival*, Andorra La Vella. **Jan 26-29** *13th Trofeu Borrufa Ski Competition*. **Mar 27** *Mountain Triathlon*, Ordino. **Apr 25-May 4** *La Massana Comics*, exhibition of graphic stories with workshops, conferences, etc. **May 29** *Spring Concert by the Ordino Artistic Group*. **Jul-Aug** *Colours of Music 2005*, summer festival, Escaldes-Engordany. **Jul 16-18** *Roser Festival*, La Massana. **Aug 31** *Summer Trek*, Canillo. **Sep 18** *14th Andorran Gastronomic Display*, Ordino. **Oct 2-30** *22nd International Narciso Yepes Festival*.
SOCIAL CONVENTIONS: Normal social courtesies should be extended when visiting someone's home. Handshaking is the accepted form of greeting. Dress is informal and smoking is very common; customs are similar to those of Spain. **Tipping:** Service charges are usually included in the bill. Porters and waiters expect a further 10 per cent.

Business Profile

ECONOMY: Andorra's status as a low tax and duty-free zone has led to the development of a major trade in consumer goods. This trade, along with tourism and, more recently, financial services, are now the major components of the Andorran economy. There is a small but thriving agricultural sector farming potatoes, tobacco and livestock. There is also a small mining industry exploiting deposits of lead, iron and alum. The country's hydroelectric power plant supplies about a quarter of domestic needs; Andorra is dependent on imports of electricity and other fuels from France and Spain. Andorra's main trading partners are neighbouring France and Spain. In 1997, the country opened negotiations to join the World Trade Organisation. In June 2000, Andorra was identified by the Organization for Economic Cooperation and Development (OECD) – the world's 30 largest economies – as one of 35 'tax havens' whose financial laws are believed to encourage large-scale tax evasion and money-laundering. By March 2002, all but seven of the 35 had introduced measures to meet the OECD demands – Andorra was one of the seven and could now be subject to economic and financial sanctions.
BUSINESS: Suits are recommended at all times with white shirt and black shoes. Prior appointments are necessary and meetings tend to be formal. Punctuality is important. Lunch is usually after 1330 and can extend through the afternoon. Although English is quite widely spoken, a knowledge of Spanish/Catalan or French is very useful. **Office hours:** Mon-Fri 0800-1700. Some offices open Mon-Fri 0800-1500 (summer only).
CONFERENCES/CONVENTIONS: For information on conference and convention facilities, contact the Centre de Congressos i Exposicions, Plaça Poble, Andorra la Vella (tel: 861 131; fax: 861 489).

Climate

Temperate climate with warm summers and cold winters. Rain falls throughout the year.
Required clothing: Lightweights for the summer and warm mediumweights during winter. Waterproofing is advisable throughout the year.

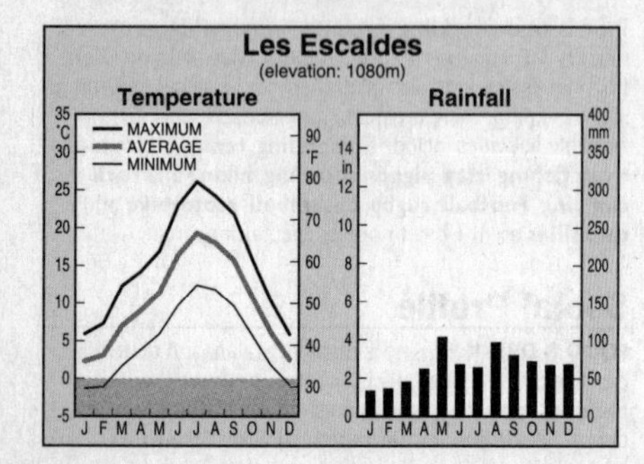

Angola

LATEST TRAVEL ADVICE CONTACTS

British Foreign and Commonwealth Office
Tel: (0870) 606 0290 Website: www.fco.gov.uk
US Department of State
Website: http://travel.state.gov/travel
Canadian Department of Foreign Affairs and Int'l Trade
Tel: (1 800) 267 8376 Website: www.dfait-maeci.gc.ca

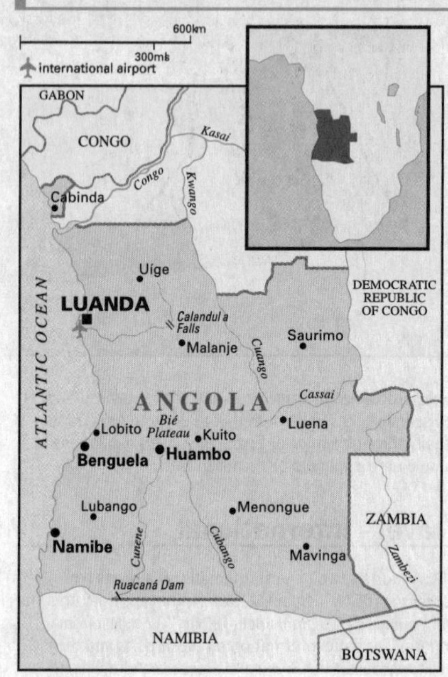

Location: Southwest Africa.

Country dialling code: 244.

Ministry of Hotels and Tourism
Largo 4 de Fevereiro, Palácio de Vidro, CP 1242, Luanda, Angola
Tel: (2) 310 899.
Website: www.angola.org
Embassy of the Republic of Angola
22 Dorset Street, London W1U 6QY, UK
Tel: (020) 7299 9850 *or* 7487 5125 (consulate). Fax: (020) 7486 9397 *or* 7299 9888 (consulate).
E-mail: embassy@angola.org.uk
Website: www.angola.org.uk
British Embassy
Street address: Rua Diogo 4, Luanda, Angola
Postal address: PO Box 1244, Luanda, Angola
Tel: (2) 334 582 *or* 392 991. Fax: (2) 333 331.
E-mail: postmaster.luanda@fco.gov.uk
Website: www.britishembassy.gov.uk/angola
Embassy of the Republic of Angola
2100-2108 16th Street, NW, Washington, DC 20009, USA
Tel: (202) 785 1156. Fax: (202) 785 1258.
E-mail: angola@angola.org
Website: www.angola.org
Embassy of the United States of America
Street address: 32 Rua Houari Boumedienne, CP 6468, Luanda, Angola
Tel: (2) 445 481 *or* 447 028 *or* 446 224 *or* 445 727.
Fax: (2) 446 924 *or* 390 515.
Website: http://luanda.usembassy.gov
Embassy of the Republic of Angola
189 Laurier Avenue East, Ottawa, Ontario K1N 6P1, Canada
Tel: (613) 234 1152.
Fax: (613) 234 1179.
E-mail: info@embangola-can.org
Website: www.embangola-can.org
Canadian Consulate
Street address: Rua Rei Katyavala 111-113, Luanda, Angola
Postal address: Consulado do Angola, CP 3360, Luanda, Angola
Tel: (2) 448 377 *or* 448 371 *or* 448 366.

TIMATIC CODES

Health	AMADEUS: **TI-DFT/JIB/HE** GALILEO/WORLDSPAN: **TI-DFT/JIB/HE** SABRE: **TIDFT/JIB/HE**
Visa	AMADEUS: **TI-DFT/JIB/VI** GALILEO/WORLDSPAN: **TI-DFT/JIB/VI** SABRE: **TIDFT/JIB/VI**

To access TIMATIC country information on Health and Visa regulations through the Computer Reservations System (CRS), type in the appropriate command line listed above.

Fax: (2) 449 494.
E-mail: consul.can@angonet.org *or* dwang@angonet.org
Website: www.angonet.org

General Information

AREA: 1,246,700 sq km (481,354 sq miles).
POPULATION: 13,184,000 (UN estimate 2002).
POPULATION DENSITY: 10.6 per sq km..
CAPITAL: Luanda. **Population:** 2,819,000 (UN estimate 2001).
GEOGRAPHY: Angola is bordered by the Democratic Republic of Congo to the north, Zambia to the east, Namibia to the south and the Atlantic Ocean to the west. Mountains rise from the coast, levelling to a plateau which makes up most of the country. The country is increasingly arid towards the south; the far south is on the edge of the Namib Desert. The northern plateau is thickly vegetated. Cabinda is a small enclave to the north of Angola proper, surrounded by the territories of the Democratic Republic of Congo and the Congo. The discovery of large oil deposits off the coast of the enclave has led to it becoming the centre of Angola's foreign business interests. The oil industry is based primarily at Malongo.
GOVERNMENT: Republic. Gained independence from Portugal in 1975. **Head of State:** President José Eduardo dos Santos since 1979. Prime Minister Fernando Dias dos Santos since 2002.
LANGUAGE: The official language is Portuguese. African languages (Umbundu, Kimbundu, Kikongo and Chokwe being the most common) are spoken by the majority of the population.
RELIGION: Mainly Roman Catholic (51 per cent). There are also other Christian minorities. Local Animist beliefs are held by a significant minority.
TIME: GMT + 1.
ELECTRICITY: 220 volts AC, 60Hz. Plugs are of the European-style round two-pin type.
COMMUNICATIONS: Telephone: Until recently, all international calls had to be made through the operator, booking in advance. Direct calls to Luanda (although not to the rest of the country) are increasingly available. Country code: 244. **Mobile telephone:** *Angola Telecom* and *Unitel* are the main service providers, with coverage restricted to areas around Luanda. **Fax:** Services are available at most major hotels. **Internet:** Local ISPs include *EBONET* (website: www.ebonet.net) and *NETANGOLA* (website: www.nexus.no). Internet roaming agreements exist. There are a few Internet cafes in Luanda. **Telegram:** Services are fairly reliable, but are occasionally subject to delay. **Post:** Airmail between Europe and Angola takes 5 to 10 days. Surface mail between Europe and Angola takes at least 2 months. There is a fairly reliable internal service. Most correspondence is by telex. **Press:** The daily newspaper is *O Jornal de Angola* (government controlled); *Diário da República* is the official government newsletter. There are some independent publications and journals. There are no English-language newspapers.
Radio: BBC World Service (website: www.bbc.co.uk/worldservice) and Voice of America (website: www.voa.gov) can be received. From time to time the frequencies change and the most up-to-date can be found online.

Passport/Visa

	Passport Required?	Visa Required?	Return Ticket Required?
Full British	Yes	Yes	Yes
Australian	Yes	Yes	Yes
Canadian	Yes	Yes	Yes
USA	Yes	Yes	Yes
Other EU	Yes	Yes	Yes
Japanese	Yes	Yes	Yes

Note: *Regulations and requirements may be subject to change at short notice, and you are advised to contact the appropriate diplomatic or consular authority before finalising travel arrangements. Details of these may be found at the head of this country's entry. Any numbers in the chart refer to the footnotes below.*

PASSPORTS: Passport valid for at least six months after intended period of stay required by all.
VISAS: Required by all.
Types of visa and cost: *Ordinary*, *Business* and *Transit*: £40 (single-entry); £80 (double-entry). *Express visa*: £110 (to process visas within two to three days).
Validity: Valid usually for 60 days from date of issue. Permitted length of stay is usually for a maximum of 30 days, but depends on application.
Application to: Consulate (or Consular Section at Embassy); see *Contact Addresses* section.
Application requirements: (a) Valid passport with two blank pages. (b) One application form. (c) Two passport-size photos with applicant's name on back. *Ordinary*: (a)-(c)

and, (d) Return ticket. (e) Letter from employer. (f) Recent bank statement. (g) Personal invitation letter from Angola (if sent by an Angolan citizen, must include an authenticated photocopy of their identity card; if sent by a non-Angolan citizen, must include a photocopy of their passport and work/residence visa or residence card).
Business: (a)-(c) and, (d) Photocopy of the company's Commercial License. (e) Photocopy of the company's most recent Industrial Tax receipt. (f) Photocopy of the company's registration. (g) Itinerary (Air Line or Travel Agent). *Transit*: (a)-(c) and, (d) Letter from the company *or* return ticket *or* itinerary.
Working days required: Up to 15 for all visa applications, although some visas may take more than one month. There is an express visa service (see above).
Temporary residence: Applications should be made to the Immigration Office in Angola.

Money

Currency: Kwanza (Kzr) = 100 centimos. Notes are in denominations of Kzr100, 50, 10 and 5. Coins are in denominations of Kzr1, 2, 5, 10, 20, 50, 100 and 50, 20 and 10 centimos.
Note: The Kwanza was devalued by a factor of 1000 in January 2000 (1 new Kwanza = 1000 old Kwanzas). New banknotes have now been introduced.
Currency exchange: Money should be exchanged at official bureaux de change only, which can be found throughout the country, but particularly in Luanda (changing money on the black market is illegal). US Dollars are also widely accepted.
Credit & debit cards: Credit cards are generally not accepted. American Express, Diners Club and Visa enjoy limited acceptance. Check with your credit or debit card company for details of merchant acceptability and other services which may be available.
Travellers cheques: Travellers cheques are not commonly used and Angolan banks charge very high commission fees.
Currency restrictions: All imported currency should be declared on arrival. The import of local currency is limited to Kzr15,000. The import of foreign currency is unlimited, subject to declaration on arrival. The export of local currency is prohibited. The export of foreign currency is limited to US$5000. Those travelling on return tickets purchased in Angola may export up to the equivalent of US$5000 per year.
Exchange rate indicators: The following figures are included as a guide to the movements of the Readjusted Kwanza against Sterling and the US Dollar:

Date	Feb '04	May '04	Aug '04	Nov '04
£1.00=	146.12	146.44	155.92	164.19
$1.00=	80.27	81.99	84.63	86.70

Banking hours: Mon-Fri 0845-1600.

Duty Free

The following items may be imported into Angola without payment of duty:
400 cigarettes or 500 grams of cigars or other tobacco products; 2 litres of wine and 1 litre of spirits; 250ml of eua de toilette or 50ml perfume, aftershave or similar; general items for personal use, gifts or souvenirs up to the value of US$500.
Prohibited items: Firearms and ammunition.

Public Holidays

2005 Jan 1 New Year's Day. **Jan 4** Martyrs of the Colonial Repression Day. **Feb 4** Start of Liberation War. **Mar 8** International Women's Day. **Apr 4** Peace and Reconciliation Day. **Apr 9** Good Friday. **Apr 12** Easter Monday. **May 1** Labour Day. **May 25** Africa Day. **Jun 1** International Children's Day. **Sep 17** Nation's Founder and National Hero's Day. **Nov 2** All Soul's Day. **Nov 11** Independence Day.
Dec 25 Christmas Day.
2006 Jan 1 New Year's Day. **Jan 4** Martyrs of the Colonial Repression Day. **Feb 4** Start of Liberation War. **Mar 8** International Women's Day. **Apr 4** Peace and Reconciliation Day. **Apr 14** Good Friday. **Apr 17** Easter Monday. **May 1** Labour Day. **May 25** Africa Day. **Jun 1** International Children's Day. **Sep 17** Nation's Founder and National Hero's Day. **Nov 2** All Soul's Day. **Nov 11** Independence Day.
Dec 25 Christmas Day.
Note: Holidays falling on a Saturday or Sunday are observed the following Monday.

Health

	Special Precautions?	Certificate Required?
Yellow Fever	Yes	1
Cholera	Yes	2
Typhoid & Polio	3	N/A
Malaria	4	N/A

Note: Regulations and requirements may be subject to change at short notice, and you are advised to contact your doctor well in advance of your intended date of departure. Any numbers in the chart refer to the footnotes below.

1: A yellow fever vaccination certificate is required from travellers over one year of age coming from infected areas. Pregnant women and infants under nine months should not be vaccinated and therefore should avoid exposure to infection. Travellers arriving from non-endemic zones should note that vaccination is strongly recommended for travel outside the urban areas, even if an outbreak of the disease has not been reported and they would normally not require a vaccination certificate to enter the country.
2: Following WHO guidelines issued in 1973, a cholera vaccination certificate is no longer a condition of entry to Angola. However, cholera is a serious risk in this country and precautions are essential. Up-to-date advice should be sought before deciding whether these precautions should include vaccination as medical opinion is divided over its effectiveness. For more information consult the *Health* appendix.
3: Typhoid fever is widespread; poliomyelitis is endemic.
4: Malaria risk, predominantly in the malignant *falciparum* form, exists all year throughout the country, even in urban areas, and is reported to be resistant to chloroquine and sulfadoxine-pyrimethamine. Mefloquine (MEF) is the recommended prophylaxis, at a weekly dose of 250mg.
Food & drink: All water should be regarded as being potentially contaminated. Water used for drinking, brushing teeth or making ice should have first been boiled or otherwise sterilised. Milk is unpasteurised and should be boiled. Powdered or tinned milk is available and is advised, but make sure that it is reconstituted with pure water. Avoid dairy products which are likely to have been made from unboiled milk. Only eat well-cooked meat and fish, preferably served hot. Pork, salad and mayonnaise may carry increased risk. Vegetables should be cooked and fruit peeled.
Other risks: *Hepatitis A* and *E* are widespread, *hepatitis B* is hyperendemic. Many insect-borne diseases, such as *onchocerciasis* (river blindness) and *trypanosomiasis* (sleeping sickness), exist all year throughout the country, including urban areas. *Bilharzia* (schistosomiasis) is present; avoid swimming and paddling in fresh water. Swimming pools which are well chlorinated and maintained are safe. *Meningitis* outbreaks occur. *Dengue fever* epidemics occur sporadically; natural foci of *plague* have been reported. Vaccination is advisable for long-staying visitors, who should also consider *hepatitis B* and *diphtheria* vaccines and check their BCG status. Take precautions against heat exhaustion and sunstroke.
Rabies is present. For those at high risk, vaccination before arrival should be considered. If you are bitten, seek medical advice without delay. For more information consult the *Health* appendix.
Health care: Full health insurance is essential and should include medical evacuation insurance. There are some hospital facilities in the main towns, but at the moment adequate medical facilities are virtually non-existent. However, there are some good private clinics in Luanda. Medical treatment is free although often inadequate, and visitors should travel with their own supply of remedies for simple ailments such as stomach upsets, as pharmaceutical supplies are usually extremely difficult to obtain.

Travel - International

Note: Despite the civil war having now ended, foreign travellers are still advised not to visit Angola unless on essential business, owing to the current political climate. For further advice visitors should contact their local government travel advice department.
AIR: Angola's national airline is *TAAG Angola Airlines (DT)*. Airlines serving Angola include *Aeroflot*, *Air France*, *British Airways* and *TAP Air Portugal*.
Approximate flight times: From *London* to Luanda is approximately 12 to 13 hours (including stopover in Brussels, Lisbon or Paris).
International airports: *Luanda (LAD)* is 4km (2.5 miles) from the city. There are no taxis; visitors must be met by their sponsors or use a transport service provided by their hotel. Airport facilities include a restaurant, bar, post office, currency exchange and 24-hour medical facilities with cholera and yellow fever vaccination available.
Departure tax: None.
SEA: The main ports are Malongo, Lobito, Luanda and Namibe.
RAIL/ROAD: Overland routes to neighbouring countries are generally not open, but conditions are subject to frequent change. Driving outside Luanda is not recommended and can be risky. Travellers should contact an embassy for advice on security along their planned routes. Plans to re-open the Benguela railway seem unlikely to come to fruition the country has become more stable.

Travel - Internal

Note: All travel in the country is very strictly controlled and limited, owing to the unstable political situation. Business travellers should contact an embassy or official representative before travelling. Most of the country is only accessible by air.
AIR: *TAAG Angola Airlines* operates flights within Angola. There are scheduled services between major towns. However, aircraft run by this airline may not be properly maintained, and travellers should aim to use flights run by reputable international organisations. Private jets are operated by some Portuguese, French and Italian business interests (trading most notably in oil and diamonds) in the north of the country, particularly to and from the Cabinda enclave, which is only accessible by air. Helicopter access to Cabinda is possible as well. Passengers on internal flights must carry official authorisation (*guia de marcha*).
Approximate flight times: From Luanda to *Benguela* and *Cabinda* is 50 minutes, to *Huambo* is one hour, to *Namibe* is one hour 45 minutes and to *Lubango* is one hour.
RAIL: Owing to the instability of the political situation, rail services are erratic, and tickets hard to purchase. Trains run on three separate routes inland from Luanda: to Malanje (daily) with short branches to Dondo and Golungo Alto; Lobito to Dilolo (the *Benguela Railway*, daily); and Namibe to Menongue (daily). There are no sleeping cars and no air conditioned services, though food and drink is available on some journeys. Children under 3 travel free and children aged three to 11 pay half fare.
ROAD: Traffic drives on the right. Driving outside of Luanda may be risky. There were once nearly 8000km (5000 miles) of tarred roads but much of the infrastructure was destroyed in the conflict after 1975. Many roads are unsuitable for travel at present, and local advice should be sought and followed carefully. It is hard to hire a car: taxis are the best way to travel. Car-jacking is a risk. Identity papers must be carried. **Documentation:** An International Driving Permit is required.
URBAN: Local buses run in Luanda. A flat fare is charged.

Accommodation

Many hotels in Angola have recently undergone refurbishment, and have air conditioning, a private bath or shower, a telephone, radio and TV. However, there is a general shortage of accommodation, and it is advisable to book well in advance (at least one month prior to departure); accommodation cannot be booked at the airport. Visitors should also note that accommodation in Luanda is expensive. Further information can also be obtained from the Ministry of Hotels & Tourism (see *Contact Addresses* section). There is also accommodation in Kissama National Park (see *Resorts & Excursions* section).

Resorts & Excursions

In the capital, **Luanda**, the main places to visit are the fortress (containing the **Museum of Armed Forces**), the **National Museum of Anthropology** and the **Museum of Slavery**, 25km (16 miles) along the coast from Luanda. Luanda itself is built around a bay and there are bathing beaches (the **Ilha** beaches) five minutes from the centre of the city. Approximately 45km (28 miles) south of Luanda is **Palmeirinhas**, a long, deserted beach. The scenery is magnificent, but bathing here is hazardous. Fishing is possible both here and at **Santiago** beach, 45km (28 miles) north of Luanda.
The **Kissama National Park** lies 70km (45 miles) south of Luanda, and is home to a great variety of wild animals. Accommodation is available in bungalows located in the middle of the park, but visitors must bring their own food. The park is closed during the rainy season.
The **Calandula Waterfalls**, located in the Malanje area, make an impressive spectacle, particularly at the end of the rainy season.

Sport & Activities

Watersports are available on the *Mussolo Peninsula*. **Fishing** is available in Santiago.

Social Profile

FOOD & DRINK: There are severe food and drink shortages at present. Tables should be booked well in advance in the few restaurants and hotels. Notice needs to be given for extra guests.
NIGHTLIFE: There are some nightclubs and cinemas in Luanda. Cinema seats should be booked in advance.
SHOPPING: Traditional handicrafts are sold in the city; shopping is not easy outside the main cities. **Shopping**

hours: These can vary, but are generally Mon-Fri 0900-1700.
SPECIAL EVENTS: The following is a selection of special events occurring in Angola in 2005:
Feb *Carnival Day*. **Mar** *Victory Day*. **Mar 2-4** *World Food Day*, Luanda. **Apr 14** *Youth Day*. **Aug 1** *Armed Forces Day*. **Dec 1** *Pioneer's Day*. **Dec 10** *Foundation of the MPLA Worker's Party Day*.
SOCIAL CONVENTIONS: Normal social courtesies should be observed. **Photography:** It is inadvisable to photograph public places, public buildings or public events. Copies of photography permits should be deposited with the British Embassy; permits should be carried at all times. **Tipping:** Where service charge is not added to the bill, 10 per cent is acceptable, although tipping is not officially encouraged. Tipping can be in kind (eg cigarettes).

Business Profile

ECONOMY: Angola is rich in natural resources, including oil, coffee and diamonds. In the years immediately after independence, economic development was stunted by the departure of 700,000 Portuguese colonists, who controlled the government and most of the economy. Thereafter, a quarter century of civil war reduced the country to ruins. The 2002 peace accord, which brought the war to an end, has allowed reconstruction to begin. In April 2003, the World Bank committed US$100 million to the Angolan reconstruction and rehabilitation programme. However, both the Bank and the IMF are reluctant to release funds until Angola's endemic corruption has been curtailed. Agriculture employs over 50 per cent of the population but production has declined so much that, from being a net exporter, Angola now imports over half its food requirements. Fishing, which almost ceased to exist, is now being rejuvenated with foreign aid. New oil and gas fields off the shore of Cabinda (an enclave in the north of the country) are being developed. However, Angola has only one refinery and so exports most of its oil in the crude form. The government is looking to a new cooperative agreement with Algeria and partial privatisation of the state oil firm, Sangol, to boost production and refining capacity. The only other industry of any size is diamond mining. Angola's largest trading partners are Portugal, Brazil, France and the USA, from whom it imports much of its food and almost all its manufactured equipment.
BUSINESS: Lightweight suits are recommended. Many Angolan businesspeople dress casually, wearing open-neck shirts. Any dark colours can be worn for social occasions. As Portuguese is the official language, a knowledge of this is an advantage in business transactions; French and Spanish are also useful. There are limited translation services. Avoid June to September as Angolans tend to take their holidays at this time. **Office hours:** Mon-Thurs 0730-1230 and 1430-1830, Fri 1430-1730; some offices open Sat 0830-1230.
COMMERCIAL INFORMATION: The following organisation can offer advice: Câmara de Comércio e Indústria de Angola (Chamber of Commerce and Industry), Largo do Kinaxixi 14, 1 Andar, CP 92, Luanda (tel: (2) 344 541; fax: (2) 344 629; e-mail: ccira@ebonet.net); *or* The US-Angola Chamber of Commerce, 1100 Connecticut Avenue, Suite 1000, NW, Washington, DC 20036, USA (tel: (202) 223 0540; fax: (202) 223 0551; e-mail: contactus@us-angola.org; website: www.us-angola.org).

Climate

The north of the country is hot and wet during the summer months (November to April); winters are slightly cooler and mainly dry. The south is hot throughout much of the year with a slight decrease in temperature in winter (May to Oct).
Required clothing: Lightweight cottons and linens throughout the year in the south. Tropical clothing for summers in the north. Nights can be cold, so warm clothing should be taken. Waterproofing is advisable for the rainy season throughout the country.

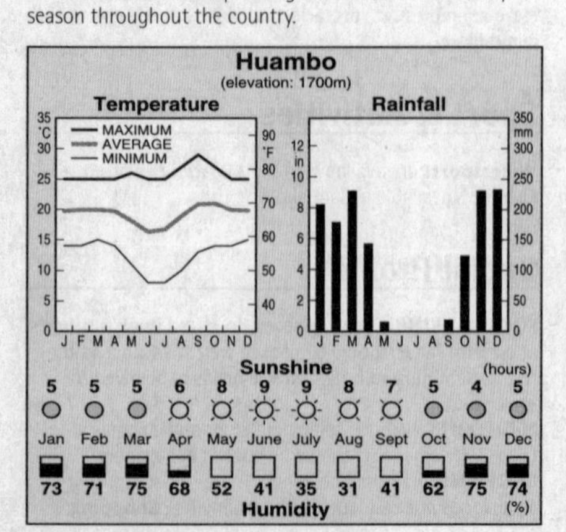

Anguilla

LATEST TRAVEL ADVICE CONTACTS

British Foreign and Commonwealth Office
Tel: (0870) 606 0290 Website: www.fco.gov.uk
US Department of State
Website: http://travel.state.gov/travel
Canadian Department of Foreign Affairs and Int'l Trade
Tel: (1 800) 267 8376 Website: www.dfait-maeci.gc.ca

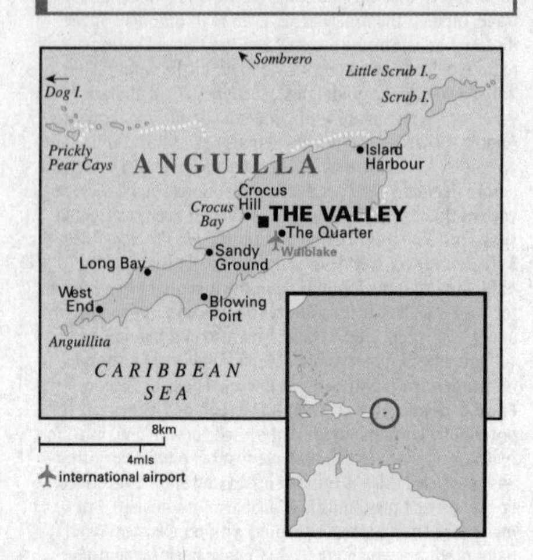

Location: Caribbean, Leeward Islands.
Country dialling code: 1 264.
Anguilla Tourist Board
PO Box 1388, Coronation Avenue, The Valley, Anguilla
Tel: 497 2759 *or* (800) 553 4939 (toll-free in USA).
Fax: 497 2710.
E-mail: atbtour@anguillanet.com
Website: www.anguilla-vacation.com
The UK Passport Service
London Passport Office, Globe House, 89 Eccleston Square, London SW1V 1PN, UK
Tel: (0870) 521 0410 (national advice line) *or* (020) 7901 2150/1. Fax: (020) 7901 2162 (visa section).
E-mail: info@passport.gov.uk
Website: www.passport.gov.uk
Opening hours: Mon-Fri 0745-1900, Sat 0915-1515 (passport office); Mon-Fri 0900-1600 (visa section).
Regional offices in: Belfast, Durham, Glasgow, Liverpool, Newport and Peterborough.
Personal callers for visas should go to the agency window in the collection room of the London office.
Anguilla Tourist Office
7A Crealock Street, London SW18 2BS, UK
Tel: (020) 8871 0012. Fax: (020) 7207 4323.
E-mail: anguilla4info@aol.com *or* info@river-communications.com
Website: www.anguilla-vacation.com
Immigration/Visa Office and Passport Office
James Ronald Webster Building, PO Box 60, The Valley, Anguilla
Tel: 497 2451 *or* 497 3994. Fax: 497 0310 (immigration).
E-mail: immigration@gov.ai
Tel: 497 7394. Fax: 497 2751 (passport office)
E-mail: passportoffice@gov.ai
Website: www.gov.ai
Anguilla Tourist Board
246 Central Avenue, White Plains, NY 10606, USA
Tel: (914) 287 2400. Fax: (914) 287 2404.
E-mail: mwturnstyle@aol.com
Website: www.anguilla-vacation.com
PR and marketing agency only; does not provide tourist information.

General Information

AREA: Anguilla: 91 sq km (35 sq miles). **Sombrero:** 5 sq km (2 sq miles). **Total:** 96 sq km (37 sq miles).
POPULATION: 11,430 (official estimate 2002).

TIMATIC CODES

Health	AMADEUS: **TI-DFT/JIB/HE** GALILEO/WORLDSPAN: **TI-DFT/JIB/HE** SABRE: **TIDFT/JIB/HE**
Visa	AMADEUS: **TI-DFT/JIB/VI** GALILEO/WORLDSPAN: **TI-DFT/JIB/VI** SABRE: **TIDFT/JIB/VI**

To access TIMATIC country information on Health and Visa regulations through the Computer Reservations System (CRS), type in the appropriate command line listed above.

POPULATION DENSITY: 124.2 per sq km (2002).
CAPITAL: The Valley. **Population:** 1,169 (2001).
GEOGRAPHY: Anguilla, the northernmost of the Leeward Islands, also comprises the island of Sombrero, lying 48km (30 miles) north of Anguilla, and several small islets or cays. The nearest islands are St Maarten, 8km (5 miles) south of Anguilla, and St Kitts and Nevis, 113km (70 miles) to the southeast. The islands are mainly flat – the highest point, Crocus Hill, is only 60m (213ft) above sea level – with, arguably, some of the best beaches in the world.
GOVERNMENT: United Kingdom Overseas Territory since 1980. **Head of State:** HM Queen Elizabeth II, represented locally by Governor Peter Johnstone since 2000. **Head of Government:** Chief Minister Osbourne Fleming since 2000.
LANGUAGE: English is the official and commercial language.
RELIGION: Roman Catholic, Anglican, Baptist, Methodist and Moravian, with Hindu, Jewish and Muslim minorities.
TIME: GMT - 4.
ELECTRICITY: 110/220 volts AC, 60Hz.
COMMUNICATIONS: Telephone: Full IDD is available. Country code: 1 264. Outgoing international code: 011. **Mobile telephone:** GSM800 and TDMA network. Network operators include *Cable & Wireless Caribbean Cellular* (website: www.caribcell.com). Unregistered roaming is available – visitors with TDMA handsets can make calls without registering, provided they can give a credit card number. **Fax:** *Cable & Wireless* operates fax services. **Internet:** ISPs include *Cable & Wireless* (website: www.cwwionline.com). **Telegram:** Cables may be sent from *Cable & Wireless (West Indies) Ltd* Public Booth, The Valley, which controls all British-owned cables in the area. **Post:** The General Post Office is in The Valley, open Mon-Fri 0800-1530 and closed at weekends. There is a 'travelling service' to other districts on Anguilla. Airmail to Europe takes from four days to two weeks **Press:** *The Light* is a weekly newspaper and *Anguilla Life Magazine* is published three times a year. *What We Do In Anguilla*, an official tourism guide, is published monthly.
Radio: BBC World Service (website: www.bbc.co.uk/worldservice) and Voice of America (website: www.voa.gov) can be received. From time to time the frequencies change and the most up-to-date can be found online.

Passport/Visa

	Passport Required?	Visa Required?	Return Ticket Required?
Full British	Yes	No	Yes
Australian	Yes	No	Yes
Canadian	Yes	No	Yes
USA	1	No	Yes
Other EU	Yes	No	Yes
Japanese	Yes	No	Yes

Note: *Regulations and requirements may be subject to change at short notice, and you are advised to contact the appropriate diplomatic or consular authority before finalising travel arrangements. Details of these may be found at the head of this country's entry. Any numbers in the chart refer to the footnotes below.*

PASSPORTS: Passport valid for six months after date of entry into Anguilla required by all except:
1. nationals of the USA with an original birth certificate and official photo ID.
VISAS: Required by all except the following:
(a) nationals of countries referred to in the chart above and nationals of their overseas territories;
(b) citizens of Commonwealth countries (except nationals of Bangladesh, Cameroon, Fiji, The Gambia, Ghana, Guyana, India, Jamaica, Kenya, Maldives, Mauritius, Mozambique, Nigeria, Pakistan, Papua New Guinea, Sierra Leone, Sri Lanka, Tanzania and Uganda who *do* require visas);
(c) nationals of Andorra, Argentina, Bahrain, Bolivia, Brazil, Chile, Costa Rica, East Timor, El Salvador, Guatemala, Honduras, Iceland, Israel, Korea (Rep), Marshall Islands, Mexico, Micronesia (Federated States of), Monaco, Nicaragua, Norway, Panama, Paraguay, San Marino, Switzerland, Uruguay, Vatican City, Venezuela and Zimbabwe.
Note: Nationals of the following countries require Direct Airside Transit Visas (DAVTs) to transit through Anguilla, even if not leaving the airport: Afghanistan, China (PR), Colombia, Congo (Dem Rep), Croatia, Ecuador, Eritrea, Ethiopia, Ghana, Iran, Iraq, Libya, Nigeria, Serbia and Montenegro, Somalia, Sri Lanka, Turkey and Uganda.
Types of visa and cost: *Tourist*, *Transit* and *Business*: £28.
Note: If applying by post, an extra £4 surcharge is requested for special delivery.
Validity: Three months from date of issue. Extensions can be granted in Anguilla.
Application to: Visa Section at UK Passport Office; see *Contact Addresses* section.

Application requirements: (a) Valid passport with two blank pages. (b) One application form (AV/BT). (c) Proof of onward or return ticket. (d) Fee payable in cash.
Working days required: Three to four weeks. An extra one to two days may be added if applying by post.

Money

Currency: Eastern Caribbean Dollar (EC$) = 100 cents. Notes are in denominations of EC$100, 50, 20, 10 and 5. Coins are in denominations of EC$1, and 25, 10, 5, 2 and 1 cents.
Note: The EC Dollar is tied to the US Dollar.
Currency exchange: Currency may be exchanged in the capital.
Credit & debit cards: American Express and Visa are widely used. Check with your credit or debit card company for details of merchant acceptability and other services which may be available.
Travellers cheques: To avoid additional exchange rate charges, travellers are advised to take travellers cheques in US Dollars.
Currency restrictions: The import of local and foreign currency is unlimited provided declared upon arrival. The export of local and foreign currency is limited to the amount imported and declared.
Exchange rate indicators: The following are included as a guide to the movements of the EC Dollar against Sterling and the US Dollar:

Date	Feb '04	May '04	Aug '04	Nov '04
£1.00=	4.91	4.82	4.97	5.11
$1.00=	2.70	2.70	2.70	2.70

Banking hours: Mon-Thurs 0800-1500, Fri 0800-1700.

Duty Free

The following goods can be taken into Anguilla without incurring customs duty:
200 cigarettes or 50 cigars or 225g of tobacco; 1.136l of wine or spirits.

Public Holidays

2005: Jan 1 New Year's Day. **Mar 25** Good Friday. **Mar 28** Easter Monday. **May 1** Labour Day. **May 16** Whit Monday. **May 27** Anguilla Day. **Jun 14** Queen's Birthday. **Aug 1** August Monday. **Aug 4** August Thursday. **Aug 5** Constitution Day. **Dec 19** Seperation Day. **Dec 25-26** Christmas.
2006: Jan 1 New Year's Day. **Apr 14** Good Friday. **Apr 17** Easter Monday. **May 1** Labour Day. **May 31** Anguilla Day. **Jun 5** Whit Monday. **Jun 11** Queen's Birthday. **Aug 7** August Monday. **Aug 10** August Thursday. **Aug 11** Constitution Day. **Dec 18** Separation Day. **Dec 25-26** Christmas.

Health

	Special Precautions?	Certificate Required?
Yellow Fever	No	1
Cholera	No	No
Typhoid & Polio	2	N/A
Malaria	No	N/A

Note: *Regulations and requirements may be subject to change at short notice, and you are advised to contact your doctor well in advance of your intended date of departure. Any numbers in the chart refer to the footnotes below.*

1: A yellow fever vaccination certificate is required from travellers over one year of age arriving from infected areas.
2: Polio vaccination is recommended.
Food & drink: Mains water is normally chlorinated, and whilst relatively safe may cause mild abdominal upsets. Bottled water is available and is advised. Local meat, poultry, seafood, fruit and vegetables are generally considered safe to eat.
Other risks: *Tetanus* vaccinations are recommended. *Hepatitis A* and *B*, *diphtheria* and *dengue fever* occur.
Health care: Primary health services can be obtained from the five district health clinics, where registered nurses provide care for minor emergencies. Family doctors hold clinics twice weekly. Secondary health care can be found at the 36-bed hospital located in The Valley. Minor emergency treatment is usually free for UK citizens with proof of UK residence. Health insurance is recommended as costs for other categories of treatment are high.

Travel - International

AIR: Anguilla is served by *LIAT (LI)* (Leeward Islands Air Transport) from Antigua, St Thomas (Antigua can be reached using *BWIA* from UK and US). *American Airlines* and *American Eagle* operate scheduled flights from Puerto Rico. *Air Anguilla, Caribbean Star, LIAT, TransAnguilla* and *WINAIR* operate several daily flights to and from St Maarten, St Thomas and St Kitts. *Caribbean Star* operates regular charter flights from Antigua and St Kitts. The main international gateways are Antigua, Puerto Rico and St Maarten.
Approximate flight times: From Anguilla to *London* is eight to 10 hours (including a stopover in Antigua), to *Los Angeles* is 10 hours and to *New York* is six hours.
International airports (turbo-prop only): *Wallblake Airport (AXA)* is in The Valley. Transport to the city centre is by taxi (travel time – five minutes). Facilities are limited but disabled facilities, light refreshments and tourist information are available.
Departure tax: US$20. Children: US$10 (five to 11 years of age); children under five years of age are exempt.
SEA: The main port is Road Bay where there is a jetty capable of handling ships of up to 1000 tonnes. Ferries operate between Blowing Point, Anguilla and Marigot on St Maarten at regular intervals between 0730-1815 (travel time – 20 minutes).
Departure tax: US$3.

Travel - Internal

ROAD: The road network is good but basic and the main road is asphalt, stretching throughout the 25km (16 miles) length of Anguilla. Unpaved roads lead to beaches. Traffic drives on the left and is restricted to 30-50kph (20-30mph). **Taxis** are available at the airport and seaports with fixed prices to the various hotels. Island tours can be arranged on an individual basis. In addition, there are numerous **car hire** agencies available. **Documentation:** Visitors must buy a temporary Anguillan licence. This can be issued by the car hire companies or the traffic department on presentation of a national driving licence, and currently costs US$20.

Accommodation

Accommodation on Anguilla ranges from luxury-class hotels to guest houses, apartments, villas, mid-range hotels and cottages. Many establishments are situated on the beach and offer boating, snorkelling, fishing and scuba-diving equipment. For more information, contact the Association at Old Factory Plaza, PO Box 1020, Coronation Avenue, The Valley (tel: 497 2944; fax: 497 3091; e-mail: ahta@anguillanet.com; website: www.ahta.ai). **Grading:** International standards apply.
Note: A government tax of 8 per cent is levied on all hotel bills as well as a 10 per cent service charge.

Resorts & Excursions

Anguilla is small and secluded; the main resorts are based around the hotels, many of which are situated off the islands' white coral beaches. Most excursions will be a leisurely exploration of other equally idyllic beaches. **Wallblake House** is an impressively restored plantation house whose foundations date back to 1787. Another historic landmark worth a visit is **The Fountain**, a huge underground cave with a constant supply of fresh water at **Shoal Bay**. The ruins of the **Dutch Fort**, built in the 1700s, are located at **Sandy Hill**, famous as the scene of fierce fighting during the second French invasion of Anguilla in 1796. The **Tomb of Governor Richardson** (1679-1742) at Sandy Hill is well preserved. Also of interest are the **Salt Ponds** at **Sandy Ground** and **West End**. Tours around the **Old Salt Mine and Pumphouse** at Sandy Ground are held at 1000 every Thursday.
There are over 30 beaches on Anguilla, some of which stretch for miles, dotted with hidden coves and grotto-like rock areas. Boats are available for charter. Some of the best beaches are **Rendezvous**, **Shoal Bay**, **Road Bay**, **Maundays Bay**, **Cove Bay**, **Meads Bay** and **Crocus Bay**. Visitors who enjoy solitude and privacy should charter a boat to **Sandy Island**, 15 minutes from Sandy Ground Harbour; or **Sombrero Island**, 48km (30 miles) northwest of Anguilla, which has a picturesque lighthouse.

Sport & Activities

Diving: There are about 16 dive sites around the island. These include *Frenchman's Reef*, a cliff edge inhabited by schools of reef fish; *Prickly Pear*, a beautiful canyon characterised by ledges and caverns, where nurse sharks can be seen; *The Coliseum*, a sandy area surrounded by lush hard coral formations; and *Little Bay*, a calm, sheltered site suitable for training and night dives. There are also several deliberately sunk wrecks, which attract schools of fish.
Watersports: Para-sailing, **windsurfing** and **water-skiing** facilities are available, and can be organised through Shoal Bay, individual hotels and Anguilla Watersports. **Shore fishing** and deep-sea fishing for marlin, tuna, swordfish and wahoo can be arranged by several operators. **Swimming with dolphins** can also be arranged. For further details contact Anguilla Tourist Board (see *Contact Addresses* section).
Other: Boat racing is the national sport. There are public **tennis** courts at some hotels. **Hiking** is popular, and **horse-riding** and **mountain biking** can both be arranged.

Social Profile

FOOD & DRINK: Restaurants offer a mixture of Continental, US and Anguillan dishes. Seafoods include lobster, conch and a variety of fish.
NIGHTLIFE: Anguilla's nightlife is centred around hotels and small local bars offering live music.
SHOPPING: There is a national *Arts and Crafts Centre*, and the island-built racing boats are world-famous. Souvenirs will also include shells and small models of island sloops. There are small boutiques offering resort clothing and accessories, swimwear and a gift shop offering international name brands in bone china, crystal and jewellery. **Shopping hours:** Mon-Sat 0900-1700. A few shops open on Sunday.
SPECIAL EVENTS: For a full list of special events, contact the Anguilla Tourist Board (see *Contact Addresses* section). The following is a selection of the special events occurring in 2005:
Feb 24-27 *Moonsplash* (annual music event that occurs on a full moon), Rendezvous Bay. **May 6-8** *Anguilla Regatta*. **May 27** *Anguilla Day*. **Jun 13** *Celebration of Her Majesty Queen Elizabeth's Birthday*. **Aug** *Carnival*.
SOCIAL CONVENTIONS: The Government is anxious to set limits to the commercialisation of the island and visitors will find that social life is centred on the tourist areas. The atmosphere is relaxed and English customs prevail. Beachwear should be confined to resorts. **Tipping:** 10 to 15 per cent in restaurants.

Business Profile

ECONOMY: Industries include fishing and fish processing, salt mining and boat manufacture (both traditional and contemporary crafts) and construction. Most of the island's agricultural produce is, however, for domestic consumption. The service sector, specifically tourism and financial services, are responsible for the great majority of economic output. The financial sector has been damaged by a series of scandals, which, along with growing competition from other Caribbean micro states, has put its future viability in question. Moreover, in June 2000, Anguilla was identified by the Organisation for Economic Cooperation and Development (OECD) – the world's 30 largest economies – as one of 35 'tax havens' whose financial laws are believed to encourage large-scale tax evasion and money laundering. Tourism accounts for approximately 40 per cent of GDP.
BUSINESS: Anguilla is a small island with few business opportunities as such; lightweight suits or shirt and tie should be adequate for meetings. **Office hours:** Mon-Fri 0800-1200 and 1300-1600.
COMMERCIAL INFORMATION: The following organisation can offer advice: Anguilla Chamber of Commerce, PO Box 321, The Valley (tel/fax: 497 2839; e-mail: acoci@anguillanet.com; website www.anguillachamber.com).

Climate

Hot throughout the year, tempered by trade winds in local areas. The average rainfall for the year is 14cm (35in) and the hurricane season is July to October.
Required clothing: Lightweight cottons throughout the year. Waterproofing is advisable during the rainy season.

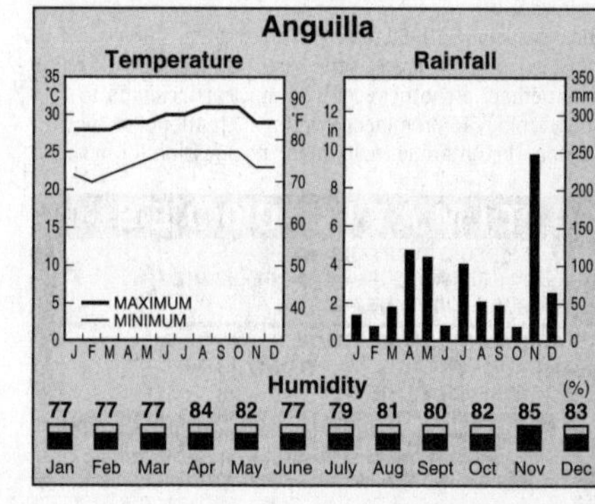

A B C D E F G H I J K L M N O P Q R S T U V W X Y Z

Antarctica

LATEST TRAVEL ADVICE CONTACTS

British Foreign and Commonwealth Office
Tel: (0870) 606 0290 Website: www.fco.gov.uk
US Department of State
Website: http://travel.state.gov/travel
Canadian Department of Foreign Affairs and Int'l Trade
Tel: (1 800) 267 8376 Website: www.dfait-maeci.gc.ca

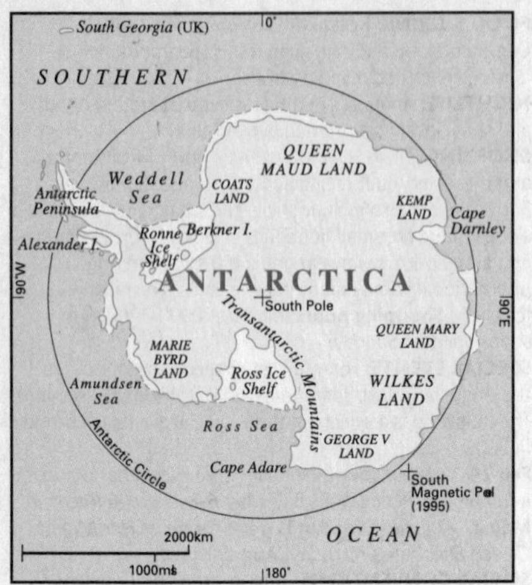

Location: South of 60 degrees latitude.

British Antarctic Survey
High Cross, Madingley Road, Cambridge CB3 0ET, UK
Tel: (01223) 221 400. Fax: (01223) 362 616.
E-mail: information@bas.ac.uk
Website: www.antarctica.ac.uk
International Association of Antarctica Tour Operators
PO Box 2178, Basalt, CO 81621, USA
Tel: (970) 704 1047. Fax: (970) 704 9660.
E-mail: iaato@iaato.org
Website: www.iaato.org

General Information

AREA: 13,661,000 sq km (5,274,126 sq miles).
GEOGRAPHY: Antarctica is the largest remaining wilderness on Earth and is still relatively untouched by human impact. It covers an area of 13.6 million sq km around the South Pole and is covered with an ice sheet 2.1km (1.3 miles) deep on average. The thickest ice is 4.7km (2.9 miles) deep. It has no permanent human population other than a small number of personnel at 37 research stations run by 18 different nations: Argentina, Australia, Brazil, Chile, China (PR), France, Germany, India, Japan, Korea (Rep), New Zealand, Poland, the Russian Federation, South Africa, Ukraine, the UK, USA and Uruguay.
The main human activity undertaken in Antarctica is scientific research, and it was at the British Halley research station that the hole in the ozone layer was discovered in 1985.
The constitutional position of Antarctica is governed by the terms of the Antarctic Treaty of 1959 (which came into effect in 1961), which was signed initially by Argentina, Australia, Chile, France, New Zealand, Norway, the UK, Belgium, Japan, South Africa, the USA and the former USSR. The first seven of these countries have historic claims to the ice-bound continent (none of which were or are generally recognised) and the Treaty preserves the status quo, neither recognising nor repudiating the old claims, but forbidding their expansion in any way. The terms of the Treaty also forbid, absolutely, the assertion of new claims. The Treaty applies to all land and ice shelves below 60 degrees South.
The discovery in 1985 by the British Antarctic Survey of a 'hole' in the ozone layer of the Earth's atmosphere did more than perhaps any other event, bar nuclear accidents, to bring ecology to prominence in the international political agenda. The Antarctic Treaty made no provision for mineral exploitation and in November 1988, an Antarctic Minerals Convention was carefully instigated. This was intended to regulate but not directly prevent the extraction of minerals, and angered environmental lobbyists. Several nations, led by Australia and France, declined to ratify the Convention. As a result, in 1991, the Antarctic Treaty nations agreed to add the Environmental Protocol to the Antarctic Treaty, which bans mining and provides for a fully comprehensive regime of environmental protection. The Protocol entered into force in 1998 after ratification by each of the 26 Antarctic Treaty nations.
In May 1994, the International Whaling Commission agreed to the creation of a whale sanctuary around Antarctica below 40 degrees South.
In May 1997, it was suggested by the World Meteorological Organization that the long-term outlook for the ozone layer over the Antarctic was improving. It will take some years for this to be conclusively proved, however.
Scientists from many nations collaborate on research projects in Antarctica. Every summer about 5000 of them travel to the continent to obtain vital information on the Earth's ecosystem. Antarctica's ice and sediment cores provide insights into how the world's climatic system functioned in the past. Studies of the Antarctic ice sheet help predict future sea levels, knowledge which is crucial to our future given that 50 per cent of the world's population lives in coastal areas. Information on the breakup of continents and the interaction between the Sun's wind and the outer limits of the Earth's atmosphere can be gained from studies here.
TOURISM IN ANTARCTICA: Tourism cruises are now available to Antarctica, to sub-Antarctic islands such as South Georgia and other polar regions, and are becoming increasingly popular. Itineraries vary according to the type of vessel. For trips beyond the Antarctic Peninsula an ice-strengthened ship is required. Most trips depart from Ushuaia (in Argentina) or Punta Arenas (in Chile). The passage from South America to the Antarctic Peninsula takes approximately two days. Activities on these tours typically include observing a variety of polar animals (including penguins, albatrosses, seals and whales), visiting scientific stations and historic sites, and witnessing the austere beauty of the Antarctic scenery. Some ice-strengthened ships also provide helicopters for accessing emperor penguin colonies. For further details, contact the International Association of Antarctica Tour Operators (see *Contact Addresses* section). Social Profile

Credit: © International Association of Antarctica Tour Operators

Social Profile

SPECIAL EVENTS: The following is a selection of special events occurring in Antarctica in 2005:
Feb 26 *The Last Marathon* (marathon on King George Island in sub-zero conditions). **Jun** *Midwinter's Day*. **Dec 25** *Christmas*. **Dec 31** *New Year's Eve*.

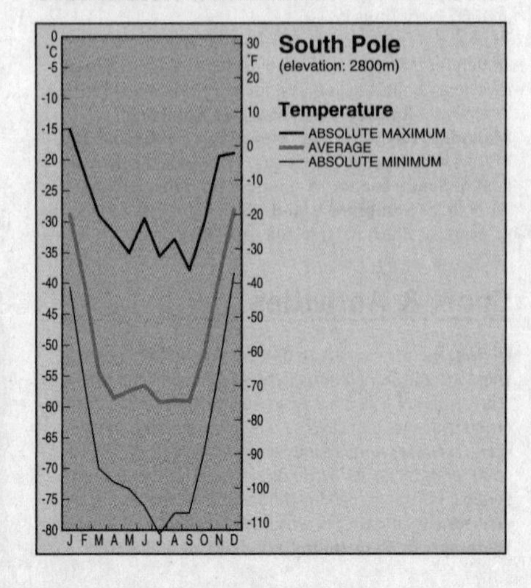

TIMATIC CODES

Health	AMADEUS: **TI-DFT/JIB/HE** GALILEO/WORLDSPAN: **TI-DFT/JIB/HE** SABRE: **TIDFT/JIB/HE**
Visa	AMADEUS: **TI-DFT/JIB/VI** GALILEO/WORLDSPAN: **TI-DFT/JIB/VI** SABRE: **TIDFT/JIB/VI**

To access TIMATIC country information on Health and Visa regulations through the Computer Reservations System (CRS), type in the appropriate command line listed above.

Antigua and Barbuda

LATEST TRAVEL ADVICE CONTACTS

British Foreign and Commonwealth Office
Tel: (0870) 606 0290 Website: www.fco.gov.uk
US Department of State
Website: http://travel.state.gov/travel
Canadian Department of Foreign Affairs and Int'l Trade
Tel: (1 800) 267 8376 Website: www.dfait-maeci.gc.ca

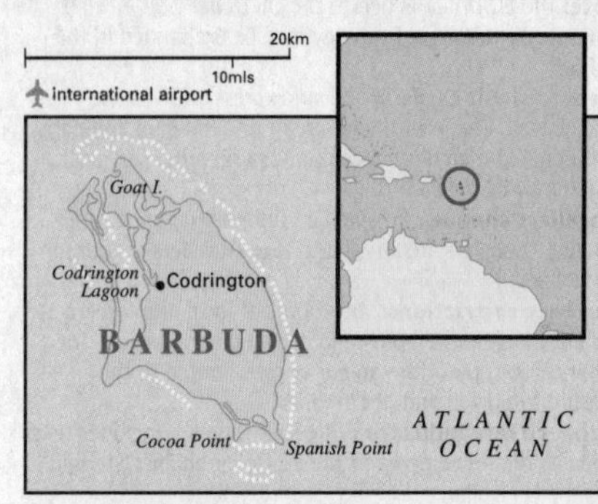

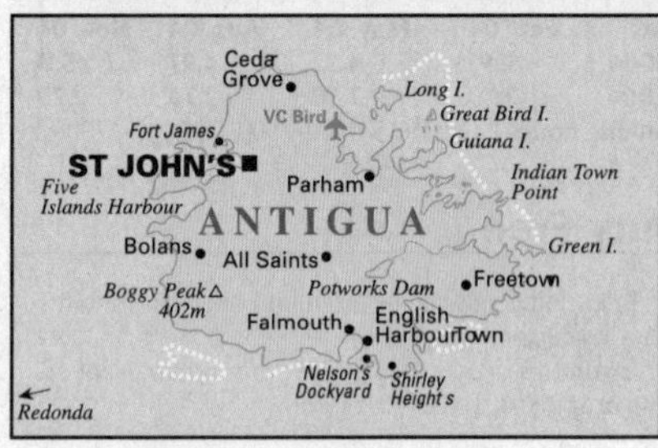

Location: Caribbean, Leeward Islands.

Country dialling code: 1 268.

Antigua and Barbuda Department of Tourism
Street address: Queen Elizabeth Highway, Government Complex, St John's, Antigua
Postal address: PO Box 363, St John's, Antigua
Tel: 462 0480.
Fax: 462 2483.
E-mail: deptourism@candw.ag
Website: www.antigua-barbuda.org
Ministry of Tourism
New Government Complex, Queen Elizabeth Highway, St John's, Antigua
Tel: 462 0787 *or* 462 0651.
Fax: 462 6398.
E-mail: deptourism@antigua.gov.ag
Website: www.antigua-barbuda.org
Antigua and Barbuda High Commission
15 Thayer Street, London W1U 3JT, UK
Tel: (020) 7486 7073.
Fax: (020) 7486 9970.
Website: www.antigua-barbuda.com
Antigua and Barbuda Tourist Office
Address and telephone number as above.
Fax: (020) 7486 1466.
E-mail: antbar@msn.com
Website: www.antigua-barbuda.com
Opening hours: Mon-Fri 0930-1230 and 1330-1500.
British High Commission
Street address: Price Waterhouse Cooper Centre, 11 Old Parham Road, St John's, Antigua
Postal address: PO Box 483, St John's, Antigua
Tel: 462 0008/9.
Fax: 562 2124.
E-mail: britishc@candw.ag
Embassy of Antigua and Barbuda
3216 New Mexico Avenue, NW, Washington, DC 20016, USA
Tel: (202) 362 5122 *or* 362 5166.

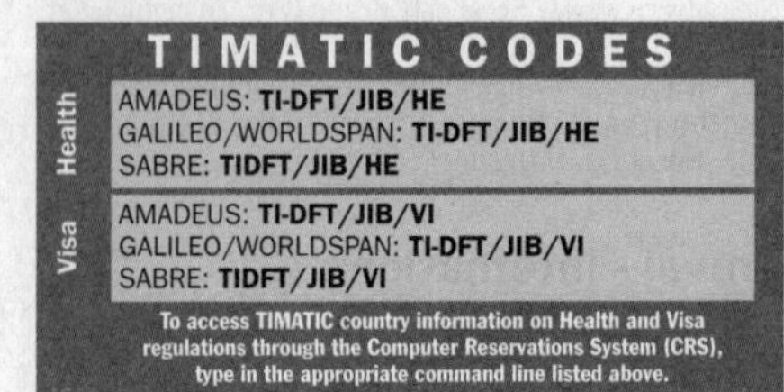
TIMATIC CODES

Health	AMADEUS: **TI-DFT/JIB/HE** GALILEO/WORLDSPAN: **TI-DFT/JIB/HE** SABRE: **TIDFT/JIB/HE**
Visa	AMADEUS: **TI-DFT/JIB/VI** GALILEO/WORLDSPAN: **TI-DFT/JIB/VI** SABRE: **TIDFT/JIB/VI**

To access TIMATIC country information on Health and Visa regulations through the Computer Reservations System (CRS), type in the appropriate command line listed above.

Fax: (202) 362 5225.
E-mail: embantbar@aol.com
Antigua and Barbuda Department of Tourism and Trade
610 Fifth Avenue, Suite 311, New York, NY 10020, USA
Tel: (212) 541 4117.
Fax: (212) 541 4789.
E-mail: info@antigua-barbuda.org
Website: www.antigua-barbuda.org
Offices also in: Miami and Washington, DC.
The United States Embassy in Bridgetown deals with enquiries relating to Antigua & Barbuda (see *Barbados* section).
High Commission for the Countries of the Organisation of Eastern Caribbean States
130 Albert Street, Suite 700, Ottawa, Ontario K1P 5G4, Canada
Tel: (613) 236 8952.
Fax: (613) 236 3042.
E-mail: echcc@travel-net.com
Website: www.oecs.org/ottawa
Antigua and Barbuda Department of Tourism and Trade
60 St Clair Avenue East, Suite 601, Toronto, Ontario M4T 1N5, Canada
Tel: (416) 961 3085.
Fax: (416) 961 7218.
E-mail: info@antigua-barbuda-ca.com
Website: www.antigua-barbuda.org
The Canadian High Commission in Bridgetown deals with enquiries relating to Antigua and Barbuda (see *Barbados* section).

General Information

AREA: Antigua: 280 sq km (108 sq miles); **Barbuda:** 161 sq km (62 sq miles); **Redonda:** 1.6 sq km (0.6 sq miles). **Total:** 441.6 sq km (170.5 sq miles).
POPULATION: 77,426 (2001).
POPULATION DENSITY: 175.3 per sq km.
CAPITAL: St John's. **Population:** 24,000 (UN estimate 2001).
GEOGRAPHY: Antigua & Barbuda comprises three islands; Antigua, Barbuda and Redonda. Low-lying and volcanic in origin, they are part of the Leeward Islands group in the northeast Caribbean. Antigua's coastline curves into a multitude of coves and harbours (they were once volcanic craters) and there are more than 365 beaches of fine white sand, fringed with palms. The island's highest point is Boggy Peak (402m, 1318ft); its capital is St John's. Barbuda lies 40km (25 miles) north of Antigua and is an unspoiled natural haven for wild deer and exotic birds. Its 8km-long (5-mile) beach is reputed to be amongst the most beautiful in the world. The island's village capital, Codrington, was named after the Gloucestershire family that once leased Barbuda from the British Crown for the price of 'one fat pig per year if asked for'. There are excellent beaches and the ruins of some of the earliest plantations in the West Indies. The coastal waters are rich with all types of crustaceans and tropical fish. Redonda, the smallest in the group, is little more than an uninhabited rocky islet. It lies 40km (25 miles) southwest of Antigua.
GOVERNMENT: Constitutional monarchy. Gained internal full independence in 1981. **Head of State:** HM Queen Elizabeth II, represented locally by Governor-General Sir James Carlisle since 1993. **Head of Government:** Prime Minister Baldwin Spencer since 2004.
LANGUAGE: English is the official language. English *patois* is widely spoken.
RELIGION: Anglican, Methodist, Moravian, Roman Catholic, Pentecostal, Baptist, Seventh Day Adventist and others.
TIME: GMT - 4.
ELECTRICITY: 220/110 volts AC, 60Hz. American-style two-pin plugs. Some hotels also have outlets for 240 volts AC; in this case European-style, two-pin plugs are used.
COMMUNICATIONS: Telephone: IDD is available to all numbers. Country code: 1 268. Outgoing international code: 011. **Mobile telephone:** GSM 900/1900 and TDMA networks. Network providers include *APUA PCS* (website: www.apuatel.com) and *Cable & Wireless Caribbean Cellular* (website: www.caribcell.com). Roaming agreements exist. Unregistered roaming is available – visitors with TDMA handsets can make calls without registering, provided they can give a credit card number. **Fax:** Services are widely available. Many hotels have fax facilities **Internet:** ISPs include *Cable & Wireless* (website: www.cwantigua.com). Facilities are available at the offices of Cable & Wireless in Long Street, St John's. **Telegram:** Facilities are offered by *Cable & Wireless* (West Indies). **Post:** *Poste Restante* service is available at the post office in St John's. Post office hours: Mon-Fri 0800-1200 and 1300-1600 **Press:** Some newspapers have political or governmental associations. All are in English. The main newspaper is the *Daily Observer*. *The Outlet* is published weekly and the *Antigua Sun* twice a week.
Radio: BBC World Service (website: www.bbc.co.uk/worldservice) and Voice of America (website: www.voa.gov) can be received. From time to time the frequencies change and the most up-to-date can be found online.

Passport/Visa

	Passport Required?	Visa Required?	Return Ticket Required?
Full British	Yes	No	Yes
Australian	Yes	No	Yes
Canadian	Yes	No	Yes
USA	Yes	No	Yes
Other EU	Yes	No/1	Yes
Japanese	Yes	No	Yes

Note: Regulations and requirements may be subject to change at short notice, and you are advised to contact the appropriate diplomatic or consular authority before finalising travel arrangements. Details of these may be found at the head of this country's entry. Any numbers in the chart refer to the footnotes below.

PASSPORTS: Passport valid for at least six months beyond period of stay required by all.
VISAS: Required by all except the following for stays of up to six months:
(a) nationals of countries referred to in the chart above,
1. except nationals of the Czech Republic, Latvia and the Slovak Republic;
(b) citizens of Commonwealth countries (except nationals of Bangladesh, Cameroon, The Gambia, Ghana, India, Mozambique, Nigeria, Pakistan, Sierra Leone and Sri Lanka, who *do* require a visa);
(c) nationals of Albania, Argentina, Brazil, Bulgaria, Chile, CIS, Korea (Rep), Liechtenstein, Mexico, Monaco, Norway, Peru, Romania, Surinam, Switzerland, Turkey and Venezuela;
(d) transit passengers continuing their journey within 24 hours by the same or next connecting aircraft provided holding valid onward or return documentation and not leaving the airport.
Note: Cruise ship passengers do not require a visa provided that they arrive in Antigua and Barbuda in the morning and depart the same evening.
Types of visa and cost: *Single-entry*: £24. *Multiple-entry*: £28.
Validity: *Single-entry:* Three months from date of issue. *Multiple-entry:* Six months from date of issue. Business visitors can stay as long as their business takes, provided it does not exceed six months.
Application to: Consulate (or Consular Section at Embassy or High Commission); see *Contact Addresses* section.
Application requirements: (a) One completed application form. (b) One passport-size photo. (c) Passport valid for at least six months. (d) Fee (payable by postal order, international money order or cash only), with an additional £4 for postal applications. (e) Confirmation of travel (return/onward ticket, letter from travel agent confirming date of travel etc). (f) For business visits, proof of sufficient funds, confirmation of accommodation and onward/return ticket.
Working days required: Three to five.
Temporary residence: Applications should be made to the Ministry of Foreign Affairs, St John's. However, it is advisable to enquire first at the Embassy or High Commission.

Money

Currency: Eastern Caribbean Dollar (EC$) = 100 cents. Notes are in denominations of EC$100, 50, 20, 10 and 5. Coins are in denominations of EC$1, and 50, 25, 10, 5, 2 and 1 cents. US currency is accepted almost everywhere.
Note: The EC Dollar is tied to the US Dollar.
Currency exchange: Although the EC Dollar is tied to the US Dollar, exchange rates will vary at different exchange establishments. There are international banks in St John's, and Sterling and US Dollars can be exchanged at hotels and in the larger shops.
Credit & debit cards: American Express, Diners Club, MasterCard and Visa are accepted. Check with your credit and debit card company for details of merchant acceptability and other services which may be available.
Travellers cheques: Can be exchanged at international banks, hotels and the larger stores. To avoid additional exchange rate charges, travellers are advised to take travellers cheques in US Dollars.
Currency restrictions: There are no limits on the import of local and foreign currency, provided declared on arrrival. The export of local and foreign currency is permitted up to the amount imported and declared.
Exchange rate indicators: The following figures are included as a guide to the movements of the EC Dollar against Sterling and the US Dollar:

Date	Feb '04	May '04	Aug '04	Nov '04
£1.00=	4.91	4.82	4.97	5.11
$1.00=	2.70	2.70	2.70	2.70

Banking hours: Mon-Thurs 0800-1300 and 1500-1700; Fri 0800-1200 and 1500-1700 (some banks open until midday on Saturday).

Duty Free

The following items may be taken into Antigua and Barbuda without incurring customs duty:
200 cigarettes or 50 cigars or 225g of tobacco; *1.137l of wine or spirits*.
Prohibited items: Firearms, ammunition, weapons and narcotics.

Public Holidays

2005 Jan 1 New Year's Day. **Mar 25** Good Friday. **Mar 28** Easter Monday. **May 2** Labour Day. **May 16** Whit Monday. **Jun 14** Queen's Birthday Celebrations. **Jul 4** Caricom Day. **Aug 4-5** Carnival. **Oct 7** Merchant Holiday. **Nov 1** Independence Day. **Dec 25-26** Christmas.
2006 Jan 1 New Year's Day. **Apr 14** Good Friday. **Apr 17** Easter Monday. **May 1** Labour Day. **Jun 6** Whit Monday. **Jun 12** Queen's Birthday Celebrations. **Jul 3** Caricom Day. **Aug 3-4** Carnival. **Oct 7** Merchant Holiday. **Nov 1** Independence Day. **Dec 25-26** Christmas.

Health

	Special Precautions?	Certificate Required?
Yellow Fever	No	1
Cholera	No	No
Typhoid & Polio	2	N/A
Malaria	No	N/A

Note: Regulations and requirements may be subject to change at short notice, and you are advised to contact your doctor well in advance of your intended date of departure. Any numbers in the chart refer to the footnotes below.

1: A yellow fever certificate is required from travellers aged one year or over arriving within six days from infected areas.
2: Vaccination against typhoid is advised.
Food & drink: Mains water is normally chlorinated, and whilst relatively safe may cause mild abdominal upsets. Bottled water is available and is advised for the first few weeks of the stay. Milk is pasteurised and dairy products are safe for consumption. Local meat, poultry, seafood, fruit and vegetables are generally considered safe to eat.
Other risks: *Hepatitis A* and *dengue fever* may occur. *Diphtheria*, *tuberculosis* and *hepatitis B* vaccinations are sometimes recommended.
Health care: Health insurance is strongly recommended as medical treatment is expensive. There are several GPs on the island as well as one hospital and one private clinic. Recompression chambers are on nearby Saba and St Thomas (travel by air ambulance).

Travel - International

AIR: Antigua & Barbuda is served by several scheduled international airlines, including *Air Canada*, *Air Jamaica*, *American Airlines*, *British Airways*, *BWIA*, *US Air* and *Virgin Atlantic*.
LIAT (Leeward Islands Air Transport), *Caribbean Star (8B)* and *BWIA* provide scheduled passenger flights from Antigua to over 20 destinations in the Caribbean. Subsidiary companies of *LIAT* (*Four Island Air Services Ltd* and *Inter Island Air Services Ltd*) run flights within the Leeward Islands.
Approximate flight times: From St John's to *Frankfurt/M* is nine hours 15 minutes, to *London* is eight hours, to *Los Angeles* is nine hours, to *Miami* is three hours and to *New York* is four hours.
International airports: *VC Bird International (ANU)*, formerly Coolidge International, is 8km (5 miles) northeast of St John's. The airport provides access to major international centres, such as Frankfurt/M, London, Miami, Montréal, New York and Toronto, with feeder services to all the Eastern Caribbean islands, the US Virgin Islands and Puerto Rico. Taxi services run to the town and hotels. Facilities include full outgoing duty-free shopping, restaurant, bar, car hire and currency exchange.
Departure tax: EC$50 or US$20. EC$35 for nationals of

CARICOM countries. EC$25 for nationals of Antigua and Barbuda. Children under 16 are exempt.
SEA: St John's has a deep-sea harbour served by cruise liners from the USA, Puerto Rico, the UK, Europe and South America. Fly-cruises from London are available with *Costa, Cunard, Holland America, Princess Cruises, Royal Caribbean* and *Royal Olympic*. Many smaller ships sail to other Caribbean islands.

Travel - Internal

AIR: A small airstrip at Codrington on Barbuda is equipped to handle light aircraft. *Carib Aviation* operates scheduled flights between Antigua and Barbuda.
SEA: Local boats are available for excursions.
ROAD: There are nearly 1000km (600 miles) of roads in the country, most of which are all-weather. Driving is on the left. The speed limit outside towns is 88kph (55mph).
Bus: The bus network is small, and buses are infrequent.
Taxi: Available everywhere with standardised rates. US Dollars are more readily accepted by taxi drivers. Taxi drivers are also qualified as tour guides for sightseeing trips. **Car hire:** This can be organised from your home country but is easy to do on arrival. There are several reputable car hire companies on Antigua (some of which also hire out mopeds and bicycles) including *Budget, Hertz, National, Thrifty* and local companies. Hire rates are for the day and there is no mileage charge.
Documentation: Local driver's permit is necessary. This can be obtained for a small fee (approximately US$12) from police stations on presentation of a valid national driving licence.
Travel times: The following chart gives approximate travel times (in hours and minutes) from **St John's** to other major towns, resorts or centres in Antigua.

	Road
VC Bird (airport)	**0.10**
Dickenson Bay	**0.10**
English Harbour	**0.35**
St James's	**0.35**
Royal Antiguan	**0.15**
Half Moon Bay	**0.30**
Long Bay	**0.35**
Jolly Beach	**0.20**
Shirley Heights	**0.35**

Accommodation

Accommodation must be booked well in advance during *Tennis Weeks, Antigua Sailing Week* and *Carnival* (see *Special Events* in the *Social Profile* section). No special accommodation facilities exist for students and young travellers and there are no official campsites in Antigua or Barbuda. Sleeping and living on the beaches is not permitted.
HOTELS: Hotel rates are considerably cheaper in the summer months (May to November). A government tax of 8.5 per cent is added to hotel bills, plus a service charge of 10 per cent. The majority of hotels are members of the Antigua Hotels and Tourist Association, PO Box 454, Island House, Newgate Street, St John's (tel: 462 0374 *or* 462 3703; fax: 463 3702; e-mail: ahta@candw.ag; website: www.antiguahotels.org). **Grading:** There is no official grading system but there is a wide choice of hotels available ranging from deluxe to standard. A full list of hotels and guest houses, with rates, is available from the tourist office and at VC Bird International Airport in Antigua.
Antigua: Most of the larger hotels have rooms with either full air conditioning or with fans and provide a choice of meal plans. The more luxurious establishments offer a large variety of watersports, tennis and evening entertainment. Guest houses, much cheaper than the hotels, provide basic but clean accommodation, sometimes with meals. Self-catering accommodation is available for the budget vacationer.
Barbuda: Accommodation on Barbuda is more limited but does include three major resort hotels and a number of guest houses.

Resorts & Excursions

ANTIGUA

Antiguans claim to have a different beach for every day of the year and their island's many beautiful soft, sandy beaches and coves certainly constitute its main attraction. The most popular resorts have hotels located either on beaches or close by, many of them taking their names from the beaches. However, for the more energetic, there is plenty to see and do away from the beaches. The island is rich in colourful bird and insect life; off-shore, beneath the waters of the Caribbean, are splendid tropical fish and coral and there are several sites of historic interest.
An excursion to **Great Bird Island** can be made from **Dickenson Bay**. Many hotels offer excursions in glass-bottomed boats for a leisurely view of the reef. A restored pirate ship sails around the island and takes passengers for day or evening trips; food, unlimited drink and entertainment are included.
Nelson's Dockyard in **English Harbour** is one of the safest landlocked harbours in the world. It was used by Admirals Nelson, Rodney and Hood as a safe base for the British Navy during the Napoleonic Wars. **Clarence House**, overlooking Nelson's Dockyard, was once the home of the Duke of Clarence, later King William IV. It is now the Governor General's summer residence and is periodically open to visitors. **Dow's Hill Interpretation Centre** provides visitors with a good overview of the island's history including information on the early Amerindians and the impact of slavery on Antigua's culture and economy.
Shirley Heights and **Fort James** are two examples of the efforts made by the British to fortify the colony during the 18th century. Shirley Heights was named after General Shirley, later Governor of the Leeward Islands in 1781. One of the main buildings, known as the **Block House**, was erected as a stronghold in the event of a siege by General Matthew in 1787. Close by is the cemetery, containing an obelisk commemorating the soldiers of the 54th Regiment.
St John's Cathedral appears on postcards and in almost all visitors' photographs. The church was originally built in 1683, but was replaced by a stone building in 1745. An earthquake destroyed it almost a century later and in 1845 the cornerstone of the present Anglican cathedral was laid. The figures of St John the Baptist and St John the Divine, erected at the south gate, were supposedly taken from one of Napoleon's ships and brought to the island by a British man-of-war.
The Market is in the west of St John's and makes a lively and colourful excursion, especially on busy Saturday mornings.
Indian Town, one of Antigua's national parks, is at the northeastern point of the island. Breakers roaring in with the full force of the Atlantic behind them have carved **Devil's Bridge** and have created blow-holes with foaming surf.
A lake now monopolises the countryside in the centre of Antigua. The result of the **Potworks Dam**, it is Antigua's largest artificial lake, with a capacity of one thousand million gallons.
Fig Tree Drive is a scenic route through the lush tropical hills and picturesque fishing villages along the southwest coast. Taxis will take visitors on a round trip. At **Greencastle Hill** there are megaliths said to have been erected for the worship of the Sun God and Moon Goddess. **Parham**, in the east of the island, is notable for its octagonal church, built in the mid-18th century, which still retains some stucco work.

BARBUDA & REDONDA

BARBUDA: Less developed than Antigua, Barbuda has a wilder, more spontaneous beauty. Deserted beaches and a heavily wooded interior abounding in birdlife, wild pigs and fallow deer are the main attractions of this unspoilt island. A visit to **Codrington**, the main village, makes an interesting excursion: the settlement is on the edge of a lagoon and the inhabitants rely largely on the sea for their existence.
REDONDA: This uninhabited rocky islet, lying about 56km (35 miles) northeast of Antigua, was once an important source of phosphates and guano (the remains of some of the mining buildings can still be seen), but for more than a century its chief claim to fame has been its association with a fairly harmless brand of English eccentricity. In 1865, Redonda was 'claimed' by Matthew Shiell as a kingdom for his son, Philippe. King Philippe I's 'successor', the poet John Gawsworth, appointed many leading literary figures of his day as dukes and duchesses of his kingdom; the lucky peers included JB Priestley, Dylan Thomas and Rebecca West. The current king lives in Sussex, but his subjects are not likely to produce any great works of fiction as they are all either goats, lizards or seabirds. The island is also well known amongst birdwatchers for its small population of burrowing owls, a bird now extinct on Antigua.

Sport & Activities

Watersports: Most resort hotels offer facilities for a range of watersports. Equipment for **snorkelling** and **scuba-diving** is cheap and easy to hire and most hotels also hire out **windsurfing** boards. The coastal waters offer a good selection of coral reefs and there are more than 365 beaches, all of them open to the public and suitable for **swimming**. Most of the larger hotels provide **water-skiing** and sunfish **sailboating** facilities. Antigua has excellent facilities for **sailing** and is famous for its international sailing regatta held once a year during April or May. Smaller regattas are held throughout the year, in particular a two-day event at the Jolly Harbour Yacht Club starting on Valentine's Day, a Cruise Race in July, and a two-day regatta in November. An annual Model Boat Race Competition is held in April. The less adventurous may wish to hire a dinghy and find their own secluded cove or sheltered beach and anchor for a day of peace and quiet. There is year-round **deep-sea fishing** for wahoo, kingfish, mackerel, dorado, tuna and barracuda. Yachts of all sizes can be chartered and an annual sportfishing tournament is held at the end of April to early May. Spear fishing is prohibited.
Crab-racing: A sport for the very lazy, crab-racing is staged in certain bars once or twice a week. A punter may win enough to pay for the next round of drinks, but stakes are moderate and the crabs are unlikely to make anyone a millionaire.
Golf: There are two first-class golf courses: the spectacular 18-hole golf course at *Cedar Valley* and *Jolly Harbour*. Daily, weekly and monthly memberships at Cedar Valley also include tennis privileges.
Other: The national game is **cricket**, which is played to the highest international standard. In Viv Richards, Antigua produced one of the finest cricketers the game has ever seen. January is the official start of the cricket season, as well as the beginning of the **netball** and **volleyball** seasons. There are also many lawn **tennis** courts and the *International Tennis Weeks* in January (men) and April (women) attract numerous professionals, some of whom stay for extended periods to train for the international tennis circuit.
Horseriding can be organised through hotels and there is a well-equipped riding club with competition facilities of an international standard. There is horseracing at Cassada Gardens. The annual **football** season runs from September through to February.
It is also possible to hire **bicyles**.

Social Profile

FOOD & DRINK: Casual wear is accepted in all bars and restaurants. There are no licensing restrictions, but excessive consumption of alcohol is frowned upon and further service will be refused. Antigua's gastronomic speciality is lobster, with red snapper and occasionally other fish running a close second when available. Larger hotels offer a wide selection of imported meats, vegetables, fruits and cheeses. Local specialities include barbecued free-range chicken, roast suckling pig, pilaffs, curries, mushrooms and saltfish.
Imported wines and spirits are available as well as imported sodas and local fruit drinks. Local drinks include ice-cold fruit juice, coconut milk, Antiguan-produced dark and light rums (*Cavalier*), rum punches, and beer from Antigua (*Wadadli*), Barbados (*Banks*) and Jamaica (*Red Stripe*). There is an 8.5 per cent government tax on most restaurant bills.
NIGHTLIFE: There is a wide choice of restaurants and bars around main tourist areas. Steel bands, combos and limbo dancers travel around hotels, performing nightly during the high season (November to April). There are five casinos on the island and two nightclubs/discos. Some hotels have their own discotheques.
SHOPPING: Uniquely Antiguan purchases include straw goods, pottery, *batik* and silk-screen printed fabrics, and jewellery incorporating semi-precious Antiguan stones. English bone china and crystal and French perfumes, watches and table linens are all available at very attractive prices. *Heritage Quay Complex* is a shopping and entertainment complex with 40 duty-free shops, a theatre, restaurants and a casino and supper club. It forms part of the newest development in central St John's.
Shopping hours: Mon-Sat 0800-1200 and 1300-1700, although some shops and chemists do not close for lunch; some shops close at noon on Thursday.
SPECIAL EVENTS: For a full list of special events, contact the Antigua Department of Tourism or the Antigua and Barbuda Tourist Office (see *Contact Addresses* section). The following is a selection of special events occurring in Antigua and Barbuda in 2005:
Jan 22-23 *Round the Island Race*, organised by the Antiguan Yacht Club. **Feb** *Horse & Dog Show*, Spring Hill Riding Club. **Apr 14-19** *Antigua Classic Yacht Regatta.* **Apr 24-30** *38th International Sailing Week* (sailing regatta including yacht-racing, the sunfish regatta and gala beach parties). **May 27** *Annual Tennis Week*, Curtain Bluff Hotel/*International Anglican Food Fair.* **Jun** *Wadadli Day Cultural Extravaganza/Olympic Day Run/Mr & Mrs Antigua Bodybuilding Championship.* **Jul** *Caribbean Comedy Festival.* **Jul 23-31** *48th Antigua Carnival Celebrations.* **Oct** *Heritage Day/National Warri Festival* (Antigua's national board game). **Nov** *Antigua Open Golf Tournament.* **Nov 1** *Independence Day.*

A B C D E F G H I J K L M N O P Q R S T U V W X Y Z

SOCIAL CONVENTIONS: Dress is informal unless formal dress is specifically requested. It is not acceptable to wear scanty clothing or beachwear in towns or villages. Relatives and good friends generally embrace. Friends tend to drop by unannounced, but an invitation is necessary for acquaintances or business associates. Although gifts will generally be well received, they are normally only given on celebratory occasions. Flowers are appropriate for dinner parties; bring a bottle only when specifically requested. Smoking is accepted in most public places. **Tipping:** 10 per cent is included on hotel bills for staff gratuities, plus an 8.5 per cent government tax. Taxi drivers expect 10 per cent of the fare, and dockside and airport porters expect US$0.50-1.00 per bag.

Business Profile

ECONOMY: Antigua was one of the first Caribbean islands to actively encourage tourism, beginning in the late 1960s; the late 1980s brought another phase of major development. Tourism and financial services are now the main components of the service sector, which accounts for over three-quarters of the Antiguan economy. Both have suffered problems in recent years - tourism because of repeated hurricanes, finance because of questionable associations with money-laundering operations. For instance, In June 2000, Antigua was identified by the Organisation for Economic Cooperation and Development (OECD) - the world's 30 largest economies - as one of 35 'tax havens' whose financial laws are considered inadequate. It has been told to tighten its regime or face sanctions.
Fears of an over-reliance on tourism and finance have led the government to try and diversify the economy into manufacturing, agriculture and fisheries. Local agriculture and fisheries have been promoted to reduce dependency on imported food - a range of fruit and vegetables is now produced and many fish farms have been established. There are numerous light industries producing such items as clothing, paper, furniture and household appliances. A final source of revenue for the government is the rent on two US military bases. Antigua & Barbuda has large trade and balance of payments deficits and relies heavily on foreign aid. The country's main trading partners are the USA, UK and Canada, as well as countries within the CARICOM Caribbean trading bloc, of which Antigua & Barbuda is a member.
BUSINESS: A lightweight suit, a long- or short-sleeved shirt and a tie are suitable for most business visits. Handshaking is the normal greeting for acquaintances and for formal introductions. Calling cards are expected from people who do not live on the islands. **Office hours:** Mon-Fri 0800-1200 and 1300-1630. **Government office hours:** Mon-Thurs 0800-1630, Fri 0800-1500.
COMMERCIAL INFORMATION: The following organisation can offer advice: Antigua and Barbuda Chamber of Commerce and Industry Ltd, PO Box 774, Corner of Popeshead Street and North Street, St John's, Antigua (tel: 462 0743; fax: 462 4575; e-mail: chamcom@candw.ag).
CONFERENCES/CONVENTIONS: Around 10 per cent of the members of the Antigua Hotels & Tourist Association (see *Accommodation* section for details) offer meeting facilities. Information is available direct from the Tourist Office. The following organisation can also offer advice: Alexander Parrish (Antigua) Ltd, PO Box 45, Travel Department, Redcliffe Street, St John's (tel: 462 0638; fax: 462 4457; e-mail: apal@candw.ag).

Climate

The islands enjoy a very pleasant tropical climate which remains warm and relatively dry throughout the year. **Required clothing:** Lightweight cottons or linen, with rainwear needed from September to December.

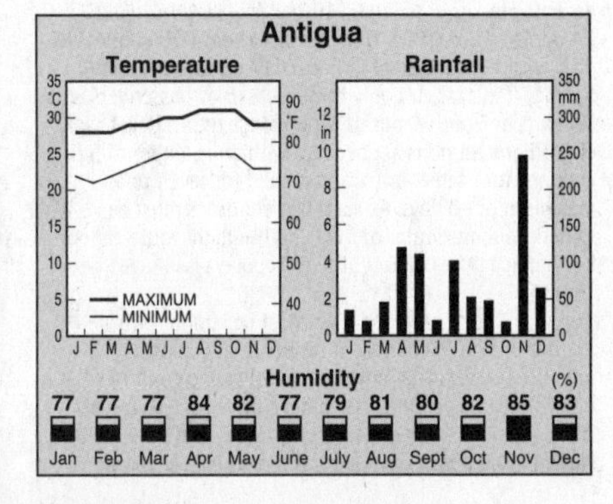

Argentina

LATEST TRAVEL ADVICE CONTACTS

British Foreign and Commonwealth Office
Tel: (0870) 606 0290 Website: www.fco.gov.uk
US Department of State
Website: http://travel.state.gov/travel
Canadian Department of Foreign Affairs and Int'l Trade
Tel: (1 800) 267 8376 Website: www.dfait-maeci.gc.ca

Location: Southeastern South America.

Country dialling code: 54.

Secretaría de Turismo y Deporte de la Nación (National Secretariat of Tourism and Sports)
Calle Suipacha 1111, 20, C1008AAW Buenos Aires, Argentina
Tel: (11) 4312 5621. Fax: (11) 4313 6834.
E-mail: info@turismo.gov.ar
Website: www.turismo.gov.ar
Embassy of the Argentine Republic and Tourist Board
65 Brooke Street, London W1K 4AH, UK
Tel: (020) 7318 1300. Fax: (020) 7318 1301.
E-mail: embar.ru@btclick.com
Website: www.argentine-embassy-uk.org
Argentine Consulate
27 Three Kings Yard, London W1K 4DF, UK
Tel: (020) 7318 1340. Fax: (020) 7318 1349.
E-mail: fclond@mrecic.gov.ar
British Embassy
Dr Luis Agote 2412, C1425EOF Buenos Aires, Argentina
Tel: (11) 4808 2200. Fax: (11) 4808 2274.
E-mail: askconsular.baires@fco.gov.uk *or* mailmaster.baires@fco.gov.uk
Website: www.britain.org.ar
Embassy of the Argentine Republic
1600 New Hampshire Avenue, NW, Washington, DC 20009, USA
Tel: (202) 238 6400 *or* 238 6460 (consular section).
Fax: (202) 332 3171.
E-mail: info@embajadaargentinaeeuu.org
Website: www.embassyofargentinausa.org
Consulate General in: New York.
Argentina Government Tourist Office
12 West 56th Street, New York, NY 10019, USA
Tel: (212) 603 0443. Fax: (212) 586 1786.
E-mail: ifegarra@turismo.gov.ar
Website: www.turismo.gov.ar
Embassy of the United States of America
Avenida Colombia 4300, Buenos Aires, C1425 GMN, Argentina
Tel: (11) 5777 4533. Fax: (11) 5777 4240 *or* 5777 4205.
E-mail: bue-publicopinion@state.gov
Website: http://buenosaires.usembassy.gov

TIMATIC CODES

Health
AMADEUS: **TI-DFT/JIB/HE**
GALILEO/WORLDSPAN: **TI-DFT/JIB/HE**
SABRE: **TIDFT/JIB/HE**

Visa
AMADEUS: **TI-DFT/JIB/VI**
GALILEO/WORLDSPAN: **TI-DFT/JIB/VI**
SABRE: **TIDFT/JIB/VI**

To access TIMATIC country information on Health and Visa regulations through the Computer Reservations System (CRS), type in the appropriate command line listed above.

Embassy of the Argentine Republic
90 Sparks Street, Suite 910, Ottawa, Ontario K1P 5B4, Canada
Tel: (613) 236 2351.
Fax: (613) 235 2659 *or* 563 7925 (commercial section).
E-mail: embargentina@argentina-canada.net
Website: www.argentina-canada.net
Consulates General in: Montréal and Toronto.
Canadian Embassy
Street address: Tagle 2828, C1425EEH Buenos Aires, Argentina
Postal address: Casilla de Correo 1598, 1000 Buenos Aires, Argentina
Tel: (11) 4808 1000. Fax: (11) 4808 1014.
E-mail: bairs-webmail@international.gc.ca
Website: www.buenosaires.gc.ca

General Information

AREA: 2,780,400 sq km (1,073,518 sq miles).
POPULATION: 37,486,938 (official estimate 2001).
POPULATION DENSITY: 13.0 per sq km (2001).
CAPITAL: Buenos Aires. **Population:** 2,776,138 (official estimate 2001).
GEOGRAPHY: Argentina is situated in South America, east of the Andes, and is bordered by Chile to the west, the Atlantic Ocean to the east and Uruguay, Bolivia, Paraguay and Brazil to the north and northeast. There are four main geographical areas: the Andes, the North and Mesopotamia, the Pampas and Patagonia. The climate and geography of Argentina vary considerably, ranging from the great heat of the Chaco (*El Chaco*), through the pleasant climate of the central Pampas to the sub-Antarctic cold of the Patagonian Sea. Mount Aconcagua soars almost 7000m (23,000ft) and waterfalls at Iguazú stretch around a massive semi-circle, thundering 70m (230ft) to the bed of the Paraná River. In the southwest is a small 'Switzerland' with a string of beautiful icy lakes framed by mountains.
GOVERNMENT: Federal and Democratic Republic. Gained independence from Spain in 1816. **Head of State and Government:** President Néstor Carlos Kirchner Ostoic since 2003.
LANGUAGE: Spanish is the official language. English is widely spoken with some French and German.
RELIGION: More than 90 per cent Roman Catholic, 2 per cent Protestant with small Muslim and Jewish communities.
TIME: GMT - 3 (GMT - 4 in summer).
ELECTRICITY: 220 volts AC, 50Hz. Lamp fittings are of the screw-type. Plug fittings in older buildings are of the two-pin round type, but some new buildings use the three-pin flat type.
COMMUNICATIONS: Telephone: IDD is available (but not generally in use). Country code: 54. Outgoing international code: 00. The system is often overburdened and international calls are expensive. Local calls can be made from public call-boxes, which are located in shops and restaurants and are identifiable by a blue sign outside. Public phones take 1 peso or 50 and 25 centavos coins or cards. Reduced tariffs apply from 2200-0800. **Mobile telephone:** GSM 1900 network. Network operators include *Telecom Personal* (website: www.telecompersonal.com.ar) and *Unifon* (website: www.unifon.com.ar). Roaming can be arranged. **Fax:** Most

Credit: © Argentinean National Secretariat of Tourism

large hotels have facilities. **Internet:** ISPs include *Ciudad Internet Prima* (website: www.ciudad.com.ar). Public access is available in Internet cafes in main towns. **Telegram:** A cable service to other Latin American countries exists, run by *All America Cables Limited*. **Post:** The main post office in Buenos Aires is located in Sarmiento 189 and is open Mon-Fri 0900-1930. Airmail to Europe takes between five and 10 days. Surface mail to Europe takes on average 20-25 days but can take as long as 50 days, so it is advisable to send everything airmail. Internal postal services are subject to delay. Post office hours: Mon-Fri 0800-2000, Sat 0800-1400. **Press:** The *Buenos Aires Herald* is the leading English-language newspaper in Latin America. Argentina's principal dailies include *Clarín*, *Crónica*, *El Cronista*, *La Nación*, *Página 12*, *Diario Popular*, *La Prensa*, *La Razón* and *Ámbito Financiero*.

Radio: BBC World Service (website: www.bbc.co.uk/worldservice) and Voice of America (website: www.voa.gov) can be received. From time to time the frequencies change and the most up-to-date can be found online.

Passport/Visa

	Passport Required?	Visa Required?	Return Required?
Full British	Yes	No	Yes
Australian	Yes	No	Yes
Canadian	Yes	No	Yes
USA	Yes	No	Yes
Other EU	Yes	No	Yes
Japanese	Yes	No	Yes

Note: Regulations and requirements may be subject to change at short notice, and you are advised to contact the appropriate diplomatic or consular authority before finalising travel arrangements. Details of these may be found at the head of this country's entry. Any numbers in the chart refer to the footnotes below.

PASSPORTS: Passport valid for six months required by all except nationals of Bolivia, Brazil, Chile, Paraguay and Uruguay who, for journeys that do not go beyond Argentina and these five countries, may use their national ID cards.
VISAS: Required by all except the following:
(a) nationals of the countries shown in the chart above for stays of up to 90 days;
(b) nationals of Andorra, Barbados, Bolivia, Brazil, Chile, Colombia, Costa Rica, Croatia, Dominican Republic, Ecuador, El Salvador, Guatemala, Haiti, Honduras, Iceland, Israel, Liechtenstein, Mexico, Monaco, New Zealand, Nicaragua, Norway, Panama, Paraguay, Peru, St Lucia, San Marino, Serbia & Montenegro, Singapore, South Africa, Switzerland, Trinidad & Tobago, Turkey, Uruguay, Vatican City and Venezuela for stays of up to 90 days;
(c) nationals of Grenada, Hong Kong (British Nationals Overseas), Jamaica and Malaysia for stays of up to 30 days;
(d) transit passengers holding confirmed onward or return tickets for travel provided continuing their journey within six hours and not leaving the airport.
Note: Visa exemptions mentioned above are for *tourist purposes only*. Business travellers are advised to contact the Argentinean Consulate before departure.
Types of visa and cost: *Tourist*: £16.65; *Business*: £27.75. Passengers requiring visas for transit only should still apply for tourist visas. The cost of visas changes monthly with exchange rates; further details can be obtained from the Consulate or Embassy (see *Contact Addresses* section).
Validity: Visas are generally valid for stays of up to 90 days. Extensions for a further 90 days are possible for some nationals; contact the Consulate (or Consular section at Embassy) for details.
Application to: Consulate, or Consular Section at Embassy (see *Contact Addresses* section).
Application requirements: *Tourist:* (a) Valid passport. (b) Application form. (c) One passport photo. (d) Fee; payable by cheque or postal order. (e) Return ticket. (f) Proof of sufficient funds (eg bank statement). *Business:* (a)-(e) and, (f) Letter of introduction from employer.
Note: Nationals of Australia, Hong Kong (British Nationals Overseas), Malaysia, The Netherlands, New Zealand, Poland, the UK and USA should travel with a UK company letter. It is advisable for nationals of all countries to contact the Consulate before travelling for business purposes, in particular, nationals of Belgium, Brazil, Czech Republic, Hungary, Iceland, Japan, St Lucia, Singapore, South Africa, and Trinidad & Tobago.
Working days required: 24 to 48 hours. An express service may be available for an added fee.
Note: Argentine minors travelling to or from Argentina, if unaccompanied by their parents, must carry their parents' or other legal guardian's authorisation to travel, which must be certified by an Argentine Consul if issued abroad. Fines will be levied if passengers do not comply with immigration requirements and passengers will be deported.
Temporary residence: Applicants for temporary residence, working holidays and long-stay business visits to Argentina should contact the Embassy or Consulate (see *Contact Addresses* section).

Money

Currency: Peso (P) = 100 centavos. Peso notes are in denominations of P100, 50, 20, 10, 5 and 2. Coins are in denominations of P5, 2 and 1 and 50, 25, 10, 5 and 1 centavos.
Currency exchange: While the US Dollar is generally (though not officially) accepted as legal tender, foreign currencies can be exchanged in banks and authorised *cambios* (bureaux de change), which are available in all the major cities.
Credit & debit cards: MasterCard and Visa are the most widely accepted; American Express and Diners Club are also taken. Check with your credit or debit card company for details of merchant acceptability and other services that may be available.
Travellers cheques: It is often difficult to exchange these in the smaller towns. To avoid additional exchange rate charges, travellers are advised to take travellers cheques in US Dollars.
Currency restrictions: The import and export of both local and foreign currency is unlimited. Gold must be declared. Note that currently there are certain restrictions for foreign currency transfers.
Exchange rate indicators: The following figures are included as a guide to the movements of the Peso against Sterling and the US Dollar:

Date	Feb '04	May '04	Aug '04	Nov '04
£1.00=	5.32	5.21	5.54	5.56
$1.00=	2.92	2.92	3.00	2.93

Note: The Government has changed the Peso fixed rate to the US Dollar, devaluating the local currency which is now under free flotation.
Banking hours: Mon-Fri 1000-1500.

Duty Free

The following goods may be imported into Argentina without incurring customs duty:
(a) Travellers over 18 years of age coming from Bolivia, Brazil, Chile, Paraguay or Uruguay, or residents returning to Argentina after less than one year's stay in these countries, may import the following goods to a value of US$100:
200 cigarettes and 25 cigars; 1l of alcohol; 2kg of foodstuffs.
(b) Travellers over 18 years of age coming from countries other than those listed above, or residents returning to Argentina after less than one year's stay in countries other than those above, may import the following goods to a value of US$300:
400 cigarettes and 50 cigars; 2l of alcohol; 5kg of foodstuffs.
Prohibited items: Animals and birds from Africa or Asia (except Japan) without prior authorisation, parrots and fresh foodstuffs, particularly meat, dairy products and fruit. Explosives, inflammable items, narcotics and pornographic material are also forbidden.
Note: All gold must be declared. It is wise to arrange customs clearance for expensive consumer items (cameras, computers, etc) to forestall any problems.

Public Holidays

2005: Jan 1 New Year's Day. **Mar 24** Maundy Thursday. **Mar 25** Good Friday. **Apr 4** Malvinas Day. **May 1** Labour Day. **May 25** National Day (Anniversary of the 1810 Revolution). **June 20** National Flag Day. **Jul 9** Independence Day. **Aug 17** Death of General José de San Martín. **Oct 12** Day of the Americas (Columbus Day). **Dec 8** Immaculate Conception. **Dec 25** Christmas Day. **Dec 31** New Year's Eve.
2006: Jan 1 New Year's Day. **Apr 3** Malvinas Day. **Apr 13** Maundy Thursday. **Apr 14** Good Friday. **May 1** Labour Day. **May 25** National Day (Anniversary of the 1810 Revolution). **Jun 19** National Flag Day. **Jul 9** Independence Day. **Aug 16** Death of General José de San Martín. **Oct 9** Day of the Americas (Columbus Day). **Dec 8** Immaculate Conception. **Dec 25** Christmas Day. **Dec 31** New Year's Eve.

Health

	Special Precautions?	Certificate Required?
Yellow Fever	1	No
Cholera	Yes	2
Typhoid & Polio	3	N/A
Malaria	4	N/A

Note: Regulations and requirements may be subject to change at short notice, and you are advised to contact your doctor well in advance of your intended date of departure. Any numbers in the chart refer to the footnotes below.

1: Yellow fever may occur in epidemics in forested areas (northeast only), but it is very rare.
2: Following WHO guidelines issued in 1973, a cholera vaccination certificate is not a condition of entry to Argentina. However, precautions are advised; some cases were reported in 1996. Up-to-date advice should be sought before deciding whether these precautions should include vaccination as medical opinion is divided over its effectiveness; see the *Health* appendix for more information.
3: Typhoid fever is not common but a risk exists.
4: Malaria risk, exclusively in the benign *vivax* form is low and exists in pockets in the provinces of Salta, Jujuy, Misiones and Corrientes. Protection in the form of 300mg of chloroquine prophylaxis administered weekly is advised.
Food & drink: Tap water is considered safe to drink. Drinking water outside main cities and towns may be contaminated and sterilisation is advisable. Pasteurised milk and dairy products are safe for consumption. Avoid unpasteurised milk as *brucellosis* occurs. Local meat, poultry, seafood, fruit and vegetables are generally considered safe to eat.
Other risks: *Hepatitis A* and *intestinal parasitosis* are widespread. Both *cutaneous* and *mucocutaneous leishmaniasis* occur. There is some risk of *dengue fever* and *anthrax*.
Rabies is present. For those at high risk, vaccination before arrival should be considered. If bitten, seek medical advice without delay. For more information consult the *Health* appendix.
Health care: Medical insurance is recommended as there are no reciprocal health agreements. Medical facilities are generally of a high standard, though of varying quality outside Buenos Aires. Immediate cash payment is often expected by doctors.

Travel - International

AIR: Argentina's national airline, *Aerolineas Argentinas (AR)* (website: www.aerolineas.com.ar), has resumed international flights, presently serving Auckland, London, Madrid, Miami, New York, Paris, Rome and Sydney in addition to regional services. Other airlines serving Argentina include *Aeroflot, Air Canada, Air France, Alitalia, American Airlines, British Airways, Iberia, KLM, Lan Chile, Lufthansa, Malaysian Airlines, Qantas, South African Airways, Swiss, VARIG* and *United Airlines*.
Approximate flight times: From Buenos Aires to *London* is 13 hours, to *Los Angeles* is 16 hours, to *New York* is 14 hours 15 minutes, to *Singapore* is 29 hours 30 minutes and to *Sydney* is 16 hours.
International airports: *Ezeiza Ministro Pistarini International Airport (EZE)* (tel: (11) 5480 6111), is 35km (22 miles) from Buenos Aires. There is a bus service to the city operating every 30 minutes between 0500-2300 (travel time – 45 minutes). Taxis are also available. Airport facilities include a 24-hour bank, restaurants, tourist information kiosk, bureau de change, duty-free shops and car hire (*Avis* and *Hertz*). There is also a coach connection to *Jorge Newbery* airport (locally called *Aeroparque*) for domestic flight connections.
Air passes: *The Mercosur Airpass:* Valid within Argentina, Brazil, Chile (except Easter Island), Paraguay and Uruguay. Participating airlines include *Aerolineas Argentinas (AR)* (however, flights on this airline cannot be combined with any others, as it has no agreements and its tickets are not accepted by other airlines), *Austral (AU), LAN-Chile (LA), LAPA (MJ), Pluna (PU), Transbrasil Airlines (TR)* and *VARIG (RG)* with the subsidiary airlines of *Nordeste (JH)* and *Rio Sul (SL)*. The pass can only be purchased by passengers who live outside South America, who have a return ticket. Only eight flight coupons are allowed with a maximum of four coupons for each country and is valid for seven to a maximum of 30 days. At least two countries must be visited (to a maximum of five) and the flight route cannot be changed. A maximum of two stopovers is allowed per country.
The Visit South America Pass: Must be bought outside South America in country of residence and allows unlimited travel to 36 cities in the following countries: Argentina, Bolivia, Brazil, Colombia, Chile (except Easter Island), Ecuador, Paraguay, Peru, Uruguay and Venezuela. Participating airlines include *Aer Lingus (EI), American*

Credit: © Argentinean National Secretariat of Tourism

Airlines (AA), British Airways (BA), Cathay Pacific (CX), Finnair (AY), IBERIA (IB), LAN-Chile (LA) and *Qantas (QF).* A minimum of three flights must be booked, with no maximum; the maximum stay is 60 days, with no minimum, and prices depend on the amount of flight zones covered. For both air passes children under 12 years of age are entitled to a 33 per cent discount and infants (under two years old) only pay 10 per cent of the adult fare. For further details contact one of the participating airlines.
Departure tax: Approximately US$18. For flights to Montevideo (Uruguay) and regional flights, the departure tax is US$8. Passengers in transit and children under two years of age are exempt. Visitors are advised to check with their airline or travel agent as the departure tax is subject to frequent changes. There is also an immigration tax of US$10 on all international flights.
SEA/RIVER: The main ports are Buenos Aires, Quequén and Bahía Blanca. Ferries and hydrofoils link Buenos Aires with Montevideo in Uruguay, and there are ferry connections down the Paraná River from Paraguay.
RAIL: The major direct international route is from Buenos Aires to Asunción in Paraguay. There are also direct rail links with Bolivia, Brazil, Chile and Paraguay. Services are often disrupted and delays can be expected.
ROAD: Argentina has a network of approximately 217,762km (136,101 miles) of roads, of which around 156,789km (97,993 miles) are paved. There are well-maintained road routes from Uruguay, Brazil, Paraguay, Bolivia and Chile. **Coach:** Direct daily services between Buenos Aires, Puerto Alegre, São Paulo and Rio de Janeiro.

Travel - Internal

AIR: Domestic flights from *Jorge Newbery (Aeroparque)* and *Córdoba (COR) (Pajas Blancas)* to destinations throughout Argentina are run by *Aerolíneas Argentinas (AR), Austral (AU)* (website: www.austral.com.ar) and *LAPA (MJ).* Air travel is the most efficient way to get around, but the services are very busy and can be subject to delay. You are advised to book in advance for all flights. *Aerolíneas* and *Austral* sell a 30-day 'Visit Argentina Pass', with four to eight coupons for flights within the country. It is also possible to buy a 60-day air pass with *LAPA.*
Domestic airports: *Buenos Aires Aeroparque Jorge Newbury (AEP)* is located on the bank of the Rio de la Plata, a few minutes away from the main financial and commercial district. There are frequent bus and taxi services to all areas of the city as well as a coach connection to *Ezeiza Ministro Pistarini* international airport. Airport facilities include a bank/bureau de change, left luggage, car rental and a tourist information kiosk.
Departure tax: Approximately US$6.05, but subject to frequent changes.
RAIL: Owing to severe underfunding of State railways and recent privatisation, many long haul services have been disrupted, although some suburban lines have been greatly improved. The domestic rail network extends over 43,000km (27,000 miles), which makes it one of the largest in the world. Children under three travel free and children aged three-11 pay half fare. There are three classes: air conditioned, first class and second class. There are restaurant and sleeping facilities for first-class passengers. Second-class rail travel is good value. There are six main rail routes from Buenos Aires: Buenos Aires–Rosario (where one branch goes to Tucumán and Jujuy via Córdoba and the second branch goes to Tucumán and Jujuy via La Banda), Buenos Aires–Rojas, Buenos Aires–Santa Rosa, Buenos Aires–Mar del Plata, Buenos Aires–Las Flores–Quequén Necochea and Buenos Aires–Bahía Blanca (where a branch goes to San Carlos de Bariloche). Rail travellers are warned that once out of Buenos Aires information is very hard to come by.
Special fares: The *Argempass* entitles visitors to unlimited first-class train travel, but is only sold in Argentina at railway booking offices. Passes are available for 30 days, 60 days and 90 days. A supplement is charged for sleeping car accommodation. The passes must be used within 30 days of purchase and are valid from the first day of use to the last day at 2400. Other discount tickets include: *Group Pass:* 10-25 per cent discount for a group of 10-25 people; *Family Pass:* 25 per cent discount for a parent and up to two children; *Youth Pass:* 25 per cent discount for people under 30 years of age; *Senior Pass:* 25 per cent discount for women aged 55 and over and men aged 60 and over; and *Student Pass:* 25 per cent discount for students.
ROAD: Major privatisation programmes have resulted in many trunk roads being upgraded, and roads are generally in good condition. Expect tolls on motorways. Rural roads, composed of packed dirt, become impassable after rain. Nonetheless, buses are considered to be a more reliable form of long-distance transport than trains. Traffic drives on the right. **Car hire:** There are a number of agencies in Buenos Aires (including *Avis, Dollar* and *Hertz*). Drivers must be at least 21 years of age (sometimes up to 25 years of age). **Documentation:** International Driving Permit is required and this must be stamped at the offices of the *Automóvil Club Argentino* (website: www.aca.org.ar). These documents must be carried at all times whilst driving: proof of ownership, proof of insurance and receipt for last

Credit: © Argentinean National Secretariat of Tourism

tax payment.
URBAN: Buenos Aires is generally well served by public transport. The city's underground, the Subte, was the first to be constructed in Latin America. Recently privatised, its old glitzy stations (adorned with ceramic tiles portraying scenes of Argentine life) are now being renovated. There are five lines, labelled A to E. Services operate from early morning to late at night on a fixed-fare basis; tokens can be purchased at booking offices.
Bus: Services are provided by *colectivo* buses operating 24 hours a day on an inexpensive flat fare; however, these are often crowded, particularly at rush hour, but are usually prompt. There are extensive bus services in other towns, including trolleybuses in Rosario. **Taxi:** Available in most cities and large towns and can either be hailed on the street or found at taxi ranks. They are usually recognisable by their yellow roofs.
Travel times: The following chart gives approximate travel times (in hours and minutes) from **Buenos Aires** to other major cities/towns in Argentina.

	Air	Road	Rail
Córdoba	1.10	9.00	12.00
Bariloche	2.10	22.00	36.00
Cataratas	1.30	17.00	24.00
Iguazú	1.40	20.00	-
Mendoza	1.50	17.00	30.00
Mar del Plata	0.40	4.00	4.00
Rio Gallegos	4.15	36.00	-
Rosario	0.50	4.00	4.00
Salta	2.00	15.00	20.00
Ushuaia	3.00	30.00	-

Accommodation

HOTELS: Hotels range in standard from the most luxurious in Buenos Aires to the lowest class in the rural areas. In Buenos Aires, the cheaper hotels can mostly be found around Avenida de Mayo. Generally service is excellent. All hotels add approximately 3 per cent tourism tax, 24 per cent service charge for food and drink and 15 per cent room tax. Check correct charges when booking. Most are air conditioned and have good restaurants. For further information, contact the Secretaría de Turismo de la Nación (see *Contact Addresses* section).
Grading: Maximum and minimum rates are fixed for **1-**, **2-** and **3-star** hotels, guest houses and inns; **4-** and **5-star** hotels are free to charge any rate they choose. All hotels, guest houses and inns, as well as campsites, are graded according to the number of beds available and the services supplied.
BED & BREAKFAST: Available in small family hotels in Buenos Aires and other cities. Maid service is generally included in the price, but laundry service often requires a small extra charge. Bed & breakfast hotels can also offer useful tourist advice.
SELF-CATERING: It is possible to rent cheap self-catering apartments and flats, with or without maid service, either by the day or week. Some can provide meals. Most apartments are in Buenos Aires.
CAMPING/CARAVANNING: Most resort cities welcome campers, and there are motels, campsites and caravan sites throughout Argentina. Campsites can be found in virtually every major region. Campervans can be hired.
YOUTH HOSTELS: There are youth hostels throughout Argentina, from Tilcaru in the north to El Calafate and Ushaia in the south. They are run by Hostelling International Argentina, Florida 835, C1005AAQ Buenos Aires(tel: (11) 4511 8712; fax: (11) 4312 0089; e-mail: raaj@hostels.org.ar; website: www.hostels.org.ar).

Resorts & Excursions

BUENOS AIRES

Argentina's capital city is located within the Capital Federal District and forms one of the world's largest metropolitan areas. Buenos Aires is an elegant shoppers' paradise and cosmopolitan centre that takes pride in its cultural establishments. There are now few reminders of the city's glorious past, although the immense **Catedral Metropolitana** (Metropolitan Cathedral), which contains the remains of San Martín, Argentina's liberator, is a notable exception. So is the famous **Teatro Colón**, the world's largest opera house (with a capacity of 2500 seats), which occupies an entire block on the massive Avenida 9 de Julio, the city's major thoroughfare with its **Obelisco** (obelisk) at the intersection with Avenida Corrientes (the traditional theatre, cinema and nightlife district). Also worth a visit are the **Isaac Fernández Blanco Museum of Spanish-American Art**, which houses an important silverware collection and is located in a beautiful neo-colonial mansion; the **Ambrosetti Museum** and the **Museum of Colonial History**. The old artists' quarter of **La Boca**, home of the tango, is located along a narrow waterway lined by meat-packing plants and warehouses. Visitors can see a tango show at one of several tango bars for approximately US$40-60. The **San Telmo** borough, one of the oldest parts of the city and particularly known for the **Manzana de las Luces** (Block of Enlightenment), has also preserved its artistic spirit. The city's oldest church, the **Jesuit Iglesia San Ignacio**, is located here. San Telmo has many cafes, antique shops, tango night spots and a Sunday flea market on **Plaza Dorrego**. Buenos Aires' open spaces are particularly notable in the northern part, where a succession of parks stretch for miles along the **River Plate**.
The **Palermo** neighbourhood contains the **Jardín Botánico Carlos Thays** (Botanical Gardens), the **Jardín Zoológico** (zoo), the **Campo de Polo** (polo grounds), the **Hipódromo** (racetrack) and the **Planetarium**.
The city's main shopping districts are located around the **microcentro** (north of Avenida de Mayo), which icludes popular tourist areas like the Florida and Lavalle pedestrian malls, the **Plaza San Martín**, and the commercial and entertainment areas of **Corrientes**, **Córdoba** and the fashionable **Santa Fe**. North of the microcentro is the chic and upper-class **Recoleta** borough, famous for its **Cementerio de la Recoleta** (where many members of Argentina's élite are buried) and the renowned **Museo Nacional de Bellas Artes** (Museum of Fine Arts), which has works by Renoir, Rodin, Monet, Van Gogh and numerous Argentine artists. Near the presidential palace, the neighbourhood known as **Puerto Madero** is now in serious competition with Recoleta to become the city's most chic quarter. Many of the port's 19th-century warehouses and docks have been transformed into Manhattan-style lofts, expensive restaurants, trendy nightclubs, new office blocks and a university campus.
Further southeast is the **Costanera Sur National Park**, a nature reserve close to the banking district.
Excursions: Argentina's most important devotional site (attracting millions of pilgrims every year), is the neo-gothic **Basílica Nuestra Señora de Luján** (whose day is 8 May), which is located 70km (43 miles) west of Buenos Aires. Around 113km (71 miles) west of the capital lies the village of **San Antonio de Areco**, the centre of Argentina's gaucho tradition and host to the **Día de la Tradición**, the country's biggest gaucho celebration held annually in November. The village is also known for its artisans, who specialise in *mate* (paraphernalia), *rastras* (silver-studded belts) and *facones* (knives). The country town of **Capilla del Señor** can be visited on a day trip with an old historic steam train (tickets should be purchased a week in advance).

THE ATLANTIC COAST

MAR DEL PLATA: Located approximately 400km (250 miles) from Buenos Aires, this is the main tourist resort on the Atlantic coast. Often referred to as 'Mardel', Mar del Plata's sandy beaches attract thousands of visitors during the December to March season. The many grandiose mansions testify to the city's upper-class origins. Interesting sites include the **Villa Normandy** (which has a distinctive French style), the **Iglesia Stella Maris** (a church with an impressive marble altar), the **Torre Tanque** (an 88m/289ft tower offering good views) and the **Villa Victoria** (once a literary salon). The **Banquina de Pescadores** is a picturesque wharf near the port with many restaurants and cafeterias. Mar del Plata is also the site of the largest gambling **casino** in Argentina.
ELSEWHERE: Other well-known resorts on the Atlantic coast include **Villa Gezell**, **Pinamar**, **Miramar** and **Necochea**, the latter being well known for the **Parque Miguel Lillo**, a large green space beside the beach, whose pine woods are popular for cycling and riding. New resorts are constantly springing up along this stretch of coastline. Most can offer deep-sea fishing and watersports.
Further south, some 650km (407 miles) from Buenos Aires, lies **Bahía Blanca**, the largest southern city, whose massive port makes it one of the country's major commercial centres.

THE PAMPAS

The area known as the Pampas consists mostly of flat agricultural land and contains the provinces of Buenos Aires and La Pampa as well as parts of Santa Fe and Córdoba. The area is well known for its horse-breeding tradition and cattle ranches.

LA PLATA: Located 56km (35 miles) southeast of Buenos Aires, La Plata is the capital of the Buenos Aires Province and an important administrative, commercial and cultural centre. It has one of the country's best universities.
South of La Plata lies the **Sierra de la Ventana**, whose scenic peaks attract many hikers and climbers. One of the most popular peaks for climbing excursions is the **Cerro de la Ventana** (1136m/3408ft), which is located within the **Ernesto Tornquist Provincial Park**.
SANTA FE: The capital of the Santa Fe Province is linked to **Paraná**, capital of the Entre Ríos Province, via a tunnel beneath the River Paraná (see below). Mainly important as an agricultural and industrial centre, Santa Fe's colonial past is still visible in its streets and squares, though there are also many modern buildings. The nearby city of **Rosario**, on the west bank of the River Paraná, was where the Argentinian flag was first raised and its biggest attraction is the impressive, boat-shaped **Monumento Nacional a la Bandera** (Monument to the Flag). **La Semana de la Bandera** (Flag Week) is celebrated annually in June. Nearby is the town of **Rufino**, an important centre for cattle raising. Walking and trekking are popular in the **Lihue Calel National Park**, an area consisting mostly of desert, located some 226km (142 miles) southwest of the city of **Santa Rosa**, and known for its pink granite rock formations (reaching up to 600m/1968ft).

MISIONES, EL CHACO & MESOPOTAMIA

The Misiones Province has a subtropical climate and is nearly surrounded by Paraguay and Brazil. It is most famous for its Jesuit missions and the spectacular Iguazú Falls. El Chaco is a sparsely populated area of nature reserves and parks. Mesopotamia usually refers to the area between the Paraná and Uruguay rivers and comprises the provinces of Entre Ríos and Corrientes.
POSADAS: The capital of the Misiones Province is joined to Paraguay by a modern bridge. The province is well known for its old Jesuit missions, and the most impressive Jesuit ruins can be visited at **San Ignacio Miní**, some 50km (32 miles) east of Posada. Jesuit carvings and art are on display at **Posada's Museo Regional**. The gigantic **Yacyreta Dam** lies 200km (125 miles) upstream from Posada.
IGUAZÚ FALLS: Puerto Iguazú is the gateway to the majestic Iguazú Falls (parts of which are located in neighbouring Brazil). The falls are located within the UNESCO World Heritage-listed **Iguazú National Park**, whose subtropical rainforest provides a habitat for over 2000 identified plant species and 400 bird species (for details of hiking trails, see the Sport & Activities section). The Iguauzú Falls are formed by the River Paraná which, before reaching the edge, divides into many channels. The most impressive of these is the **Garganta del Diablo** (Devil's Throat), which can be approached via a system of catwalks (some of which may occasionally be closed owing to flooding). At their highest point, the falls have a vertical drop more than one and a half times the full length of Niagara Falls. Visitors can catch a good view of the falls from a tower near the visitor centre, which also organises free trips to the **Isla San Martín**, another good lookout point from which to catch an extensive and crowd-free view.
EL CHACO: The capital of the Chaco Province is **Resistencia**, which prides itself on being a 'city of sculptures' (there are over 200 of them), and is a major crossroads for Paraguay and excursions through the Chaco to the northwest. The **Chaco National Park** is a large expanse of swamps, grasslands, palm savannahs and forest, which is rarely visited as camping is the only available accommodation. Interesting nature reserves within the area include **Estricta Colonia Benitez** (in eastern Chaco) and the **Pampa del Indio Provincial Park**. **Campo del Cielo** is an area famous for its meteorite fragments dating back some 6000 years.
FORMOSA: The capital of Formosa Province is a good starting point for excursions to the northern Chaco. Interesting buildings in the city include the **Casa de Gobierno**, which has been declared a national monument. Apart from Formosa's annual week-long *Fiesta del Río* (a nocturnal religious procession), one of the main regional attractions is the massive **Río Pilcomayo National Park**, an area of swamps, marshland and savannah on the Paraguayan border, whose **Laguna Blanca** is an ideal spot for birdwatching.
CORRIENTES: Corrientes, the capital of its namesake province, is one of Argentina's oldest cities. The **General Belgrano Bridge** over the **Paraná River** joins the city to **Resistencia**, the capital of the Chaco Province (see above). Among Corrientes' oldest churches, the **Santísima Cruz de los Milagros** and the **Convento de San Francisco** are worth a visit. In the north of the province lies the **Esteros del Iberá**, an area of marshland, lagoons and lakes providing a refuge for hundreds of bird species, reptiles and mammals such as swamp deer and **capibara** (the world's largest rodent). There are numerous remains of Jesuit settlements in the vicinity, notably at **Yapeyú**, the birthplace of José de San Martín. Cattle ranches (estancia) can be visited at **San Gará**, **Atalaya** and **San Juan Poriahú**. Well known for its fiestas and carnivals, the Corrientes is also the land of the *chamamé*, a characteristic type of rhythmic music derived from the polka, celebrated in the annual *National Chamamé Festival*.
PARANÁ: The capital of the Entre Ríos Province can be reached from Santa Fe via the **Hernandarias Tunnel** under the River Paraná. East of Paraná, near the border with Uruguay, **Concepción del Uruguay** has numerous spas and river beaches (on the River Uruguay), notably at **Banco Pelay** and **Itapo**. The nearby city of **Gualeguaychu** is famous for its carnival, which rivals those of Rio and Bahia in Brazil. Further north, some 360km (225 miles) from Buenos Aires, lies the **El Palmar National Park**, whose main attractions are the old yatay palms, some of which are nearly 800 years old.

CÓRDOBA, MENDOZA & THE ANDES

CÓRDOBA: Located on the bank of the **River Primero**, Córdoba has preserved much of its colonial past and character. Some of the most interesting colonial buildings include **El Cabildo** (the Town Hall) and the **Casa del Obispo Mercadillo**. One of the best streets in which to see colonial buildings is the **Calle Obispo Trejos**. Also worth seeing are the churches of the **Compañía de Jésus**, **San Francisco** and **San Roque**. Argentina's first university, the **Universidad Nacional de Córdoba** was founded here. The scenic mountain hinterland known as the **Sierras de Córdoba** is dotted with colonial hermitages and tourist towns: **Cosquín** hosts an annual folklore festival and **la Falda** is a popular resort for excursions to the **Sierra Chica**. Around Córdoba, numerous Jesuit churches can be visited: **Alta Gracia**, 35km (22 miles) southwest of the city, is one of the best known. Also of interest is the town of **Jesús María**, which hosts the *Fiesta Nacional de Doma y Folklore*, an annual celebration of gaucho horsemanship and customs.
MENDOZA: The Mendoza Province is Argentina's main wine-producing region and the annual grape harvest festival, the *Fiesta Nacional de la Vendimia*, is held in the provincial capital, Mendoza, at the end of February and the beginning of March. Founded in 1521, Mendoza is characterised by tree-lined streets and a large network (some 500km/32 miles) of irrigation channels. The **Andes** mountain ranges can be seen in the distance from many parts of the city, whose universities, museums, theatres and art galleries testify to a lively cultural life. Interesting museums include the **Museo Sanmartiniano** (for history) and the **Museo Popular Callejero** (architecture). Most wineries near Mendoza offer tours and tasting. Some of the province's main wine cellars are located in **San Rafael**. Near the border with Chile lies the famous **Mount Aconcagua** (6995m/22,944ft), the highest mountain in the Western hemisphere, located within the **Aconcagua National Park**. A good starting point for exploring the area is **Uspallata**, located in a serene valley surrounded by mountains. Some of the best ski resorts can be found at **las Leñas** (one of Argentina's most prestigious winter sports resorts, open from June to October), the **Valles del Plata** and **los Penitentes**. Also worth visiting is the striking **Puente del Inca**, a natural stone bridge over the River Mendoza; and **Cristo Redentor** (Christ the Redeemer), a famous monument in the high Andes, nearly 4000m (13,120ft) above sea level, offering magnificent views.
SAN JUAN: San Juan, capital of the San Juan Province was rebuilt after an earthquake in 1944. Today, the city is characterised by wide, tree-lined streets and fairly modern buildings. Around 60km (38 miles) southeast from here, the small town of **Vallecita** attracts large numbers of pilgrims who come to visit the famous **Difunta Correa** shrine (with the busiest times being around Easter and Christmas). The city of **Agustín del Valle Fértil** is a good base for excursions to the **Ischigualasto National Park**, a desert valley also referred to as 'the valley of the moon', owing to its distinctive rock formations and fossils dating back some 180 million years.

THE ANDEAN NORTHWEST

JUJUY: The capital of Jujuy Province, **San Salvador de Jujuy**, was once a stopover for colonial mule traders. It has an interesting Indian market, the **Mercado del Sur** and, at **Termas de Reyes**, thermal baths overlooking the scenic canyon of the **River Reyes**. North of the city lie the colourful dry landscapes of the **Quebrada de Humahuaca** and its isolated peasant villages. The indigenous village of **Purmamarca** is surrounded by the **Cerro de los Siete Colores** (Hill of Seven Colours), whose layers show different geological periods. Further up stands the **Paleta del Pintor** (Painter's Pallet), named after its view of the

multi-coloured surrounding mountains. The **Calilegua National Park** lies on the province's eastern border. It has abundant birdlife, some dense subtropical cloud forest and offers good views of the Gran Chaco from **Mount Hermoso** (3600m/11,808ft).
SALTA: The city of Salta, capital of Salta Province, is reputed to have the best preserved colonial architecture in Argentina. The most significant buildings are grouped around the central square, including the **Cathedral**, the **Cabildo** (Town Hall) – which houses the **Museo Histórico del Norte**, the **Museo Colonial** and the **Museo de Bellas Artes** – and the **Iglesia San Francisco**. The province is well known for its spectacular train journey, **el Tren a las Nubes** (Train to the Clouds), which ascends the Quebrada del Toro and climbs up to the *puna* (plateau). The climax of the trip is the crossing of the **la Polvorilla** viaduct (4182m/13,716ft above sea level). Around 100km (63 miles) south of Salta, the **Quebrada de Cafayete** is a landscape of barren sandstone known for its distinctive formations, such as the **Garganta de Diablo** (Devil's Throat). Surrounding Cafayete are many vineyards, which flourish in the warm, dry and sunny climate. **Los Cardones National Park** is known for its large cacti (cardó), reaching heights of up to 6m (20ft).
TUCUMÁN: Another Andean province offering green valleys with subtropical vegetation surrounded by snow-capped mountains. Within the **Tafí Valley** lies the **Parque de los Menhires**, named after its interesting collection of stones decorated by Tafí Indians. Also worth a visit are the ruins at **Quilmes**, an ancient fortified citadel built by Quilme Indians.
CATAMARCA: This province is flanked by the **Sierra del Colorado** in the west and the **Sierra Graciana** in the east, with **San Fernando del Valle del Catamarca** being the provincial capital. The region is popular for hiking, trekking and horseback riding tours to the surrounding mountains.
SANTIAGO DEL ESTERO: The provincial capital of Santiago del Estero Province, named after the province, is the country's oldest city, with numerous churches and old colonial buildings. The province is renowned for its spas and warm thermal pools, the most popular being at Río Hondo and las Aguas del Sol.

LA RIOJA: This province has a large variety of mountains, canyons, gorges and red-earthed plains. The **Talampaya Canyon** is one of its most famous natural attractions, owing mostly to its peculiar rock formations. The town of **Nonogasta** has many vineyards and wine cellars open to visitors. **La Puerta de Talampaya** is well known for its petroglyphs.

Credit: © Argentinean National Secretariat of Tourism

Credit: © Argentinean National Secretariat of Tourism

PATAGONIA

Comprising the provinces of Río Negro, Neuquén, Chubut and Santa Cruz, Patagonia – the southernmost portion of South America (located in both Argentina and Chile) – is a vast region with numerous parks and nature reserves. The Patagonian coast is home to large herds of seals, sea lions, blue whales and thousands of penguins.
RÍO NEGRO: One of the best-known resorts in the southern Lake District is **San Carlos de Bariloche**, which is surrounded by lakes, glaciers and forested mountains and which has both modern tourist amenities such as shopping areas and casinos, as well as hiking, mountaineering and picnic sites. Skiing is possible in **Gran Catedral**, a well-known resort with modern facilities. The nearby **Nahuel Huapi National Park** contains the massive **Nahuel Huapi Lake**, stretching over 100km (63 miles) to the border with Chile. Within the lake area lies the **Isla Victoria**, a natural sanctuary, which can be reached by private or organised boat trips. Travelling south, a road through spectacular scenery, passing the shores of three lakes, leads to **El Bolsón**, 130km (82 miles) from Bariloche, known for its hops and fruit orchards. The *Feria Artesanal*, a market held in El Bolsón on Saturday (and on Thursday during summer), provides a good opportunity to sample local dishes. Possible excursions within the area include the trail to the **Cabeza del Indio**, a rock formation resembling the 'noble savage', with good views of the **Río Azul** and **Lago Puelo** en route.
NEQUÉN: The town of **Junín de los Andes** is well known for trout fishing and offers good access to the **Lanín National Park** (see below). Nearby **San Martín de los Andes**, located on **Lake Lácar**, is close to one of Argentina's main winter sports destinations in **Cerro Chapelco**. San Martín is connected to Bariloche by a scenic road (also called 'the route of the seven lakes'), leading past seven lakes and through a landscape of snow-capped mountains, waterfalls and gigantic trees. The region's principal attraction is the **Lanín National Park**, a still fairly untouched area dominated by the extinct, snow-capped **Volcán Lanín** (3776m/12,386ft), and characterised by rare plant and animal species (including *raulí*, a type of beech, and *pehuén*, the monkey puzzle tree). On the northern shore of Nahuel Huapi National Park (see above) lies **Villa la Angostura**, a resort whose main interest is the nearby **Los Arrayanes National Park**.
Located on the Quetrihué peninsula (connected to Angostura by an isthmus), this park is best known for the **El Bosque de Arrayanes**, a forest of *arrayán* (cinnamon-barked) trees, many of which are over 100 years old. The **Siete Lagos** scenic road connects the park to San Martín de los Andes (see above).
CHUBUT: Puerto Madryn, founded by Welsh settlers, is a popular base for excursions to the nearby wildlife sanctuary at the **Peninsula Valdes** nature reserve in Chubut Province, where large numbers of sea lions, elephant seals and penguins frequent the beaches. Further north, the **Isla de los Pájaros** bird sanctuary is home to cormorants, flamingos and egrets. A number of trails and spots in the area provide opportunities for observing colonies of sea lions and elephant seals, notably at **Punta Delgada**, in the sheltered bay of **Caleta Valdés**, below the cliffs of **Punta Loma** and the nature reserves of **Punta Norte** and **Punta Pirámide** – the latter also being the main base for whale-sighting trips to the Gulf of San José; the best time to see whales is from August to December. The **Punta Tombo** reserve is known for its vast colonies of Magellanic penguins (around half a million of which use the reserve as a breeding ground from September to April). Further south, near the sunny town of Esquel, is **los Alerces National Park**, which protects vast stretches of the tall and long-lived (400 years) *alerce* conifer trees.
SANTA CRUZ: One of the province's main attractions is the UNESCO World Heritage-listed **los Glaciares National Park**, an area of great natural beauty, with rugged mountains and numerous glacial lakes, including **Lake Argentino**. Accessible from the busy tourist town of **El Calafate**, the park's centrepiece is the **Moreno Glacier**, one of the earth's few advancing glaciers. Huge icebergs calve and topple into Lake Argentino at the so-called **Canal de los Témpanos** (Iceberg Channel), and there are nearby catwalks and platforms from which to observe this event. It is also possible to visit the **Upsala Glacier** via a boat trip from Puerto Bandera along **Lake Onelli** and past floating icebergs.

TIERRA DEL FUEGO

Over half of this remote southern province belongs to Chile. Tierra del Fuego is the gateway to the Antarctic.
USHUAIA: The provincial capital is the world's most southernmost city, located in a dramatic setting, with jagged glacial peaks rising from sea level to nearly 1500m (4920ft). The **Museo del Fin del Mundo** (Museum of the End of the World) has exhibits dedicated to the Indians, nature, local history and the many shipwrecks that happened in the area. The nearby **Martial** is within walking distance and yields spectacular views of the city and the **Beagle Channel**. The city of **Río Grande** is mostly a petroleum service centre facing the South Atlantic and, though of no particular interest, the surrounding countryside offers good hiking opportunities (particularly around the **Garibaldi Pass**, where *lenga* tree forests show striking displays of red leaves during autumn). Some 18km (12 miles) west of Ushuaia, the **Tierra del Fuego National Park**, Argentina's only coastal national park, comprises rivers, lakes, forests and glaciers.
Ushuaia is also a major port for cruises departing to the Antarctic. Day-trips to Antartica, costing US$630 including return flights, lunch, and a tour, are possible from Malvinas Argentina International Airport.

Credit: © Argentinean National Secretariat of Tourism

Sport & Activities

Trekking: Argentina's vast landscapes, alpine parks, lakes and deserts offer spectacular opportunities for **walking** and trekking. The best trekking areas are the *Andean Lake District*, the *Sierras de Córdoba*, the *Sierra de la Ventana* (in Buenos Aires province) and *Patagonia*, a huge and sparsely populated region, dotted with glaciers and lakes, and home to several of Argentina's most popular national parks (see the *Resorts & Excursions* section). One of the

most popular tourist towns for starting excursions to the area is El Calafate.
Mountaineering: The Wild West frontier town of El Chaltén is a popular starting point for mountaineering trips to the *Fitzroy Range*. Good climbing is also possible at *Aconcagua* (near Mendoza) and the *Sierra de la Ventana* (for experienced climbers only).
Skiing: There is excellent skiing on the eastern slopes of the Andes, with an increasing number of ski resorts and runs. The season is generally from May to September. *Bariloche* is the oldest, most established and best-equipped ski resort. The runs at *San Antonio, San Bernado, La Canaleta, Puente del Inca* and *Las Cuevas* on the border of Argentina and Chile also offer exciting skiing. Other resorts include *Caviahue, Cerro Bayo, Cerro Chapelco, Vallecitos, las Leñas* and *Esquel*. Visitors are advised to book accommodation in advance.
Watersports: The rivers descending from the Andean ranges are attracting an increasing number of **whitewater rafting** enthusiasts. Some of the most popular include *Río Mendoza* and *Río Diamante* (Cuyo region); *Río Limay* and *Río Manso* (near Bariloche); and *Río Hua Hum* and *Río Meliquina* (near San Martín de los Andes). **Swimming** can be enjoyed in rivers, lakes and small resorts along the Atlantic coast; **water-skiing** along the *San Antonio River* in the Tigre Delta Region; **scuba-diving** in Patagonia; **yachting** and **boating** along the *River Plate*; and **fishing** on the Atlantic coast off the piers. Freshwater **fishing** (for trout and salmon) is particularly good along the *Paraná River* and in Argentina's many artificial lakes.
Other: By far the most popular spectator sport is **football**, which is followed obsessively throughout the country. *Palermo Park* in Buenos Aires has a **golf** course as well as public and professional **polo** grounds. The polo season is from October to December. **Rugby** is also practised by the immigrant population.

Social Profile

FOOD & DRINK: North American, Continental and Middle Eastern cuisine is generally available, whilst local food is largely a mixture of Basque, Spanish and Italian. Beef is of a particularly high quality and meat-eaters should not miss out on the chance to dine at a *parrillada*, or grill room, where a large variety of barbecue-style dishes can be sampled. Popular local dishes include *empanadas* (minced meat and other ingredients covered with puff pastry) and *locro* (pork and maize stew). In general, restaurants are good value. They are classified by a fork sign with three forks implying a good evening out. Hotel residents are usually asked to sign a charge slip.
Argentine wines are very good and inexpensive. Local distilleries produce their own brands of most well-known spirits. Whiskies and gins are excellent, as are classic and local wines. Caribbean and South American rum adds flavour to cocktails. There are no licensing laws.
NIGHTLIFE: Buenos Aires' nightlife is vibrant. There are many theatres and concert halls featuring foreign artists. Nightclubs featuring jazz and tango are plentiful. Tango lessons and dancing can be enjoyed at lively *milongas* (tango parties), throughout Buenos Aires. There are also many intimate *boîtes* (clubs) and many stage shows. There are casinos throughout Argentina.
SHOPPING: Buenos Aires has traditionally enjoyed a reputation as a shopper's paradise, possibly of even being the best shopping city in Latin America. Leather goods are a good buy, as are native crafts and souvenirs. **Shopping hours:** Mon-Fri 0900-1930, Sat 0830-1300.
SPECIAL EVENTS: For a full list of special events, contact the National Tourist Board. The following is a selection of special events occurring in Argentina in 2005:
Feb 28-Mar 5 *Buenos Aires Tango Festival*. **Mar** *Luis Palau Mendoza Festival*. **Mar 3-6** *Feriagro Argentina*. **Mar 21-26** *Holy Week*, Salta. **Apr 13-May 9** *Buenos Aires Book Fair*. **Jul 7** *International Video-Dance Festival*, Buenos Aires. **Jul 15-18** *FIA World Rally Championship*, Cordoba. **Aug 16-24** *Snow Festival*. **Oct 7-19** *International Guitar Festival*, Buenos Aires. **Nov 6** *Buenos Aires Pride*. **Nov 15-Dec 14** *Polo Argentine Open* (polo competition).
SOCIAL CONVENTIONS: The most common form of greeting between friends is kissing cheeks. When invited to somebody's house it is quite common to take a homemade dish or dessert. Dinner is usually served between 2100-2200. Avoid casual discussion of the Falklands/Malvinas war. Dress is not usually formal, though clothes should be conservative away from the beach. Formal wear is worn for official functions and dinners, particularly in exclusive restaurants. Smoking is prohibited on public transport, in cinemas and theatres. **Tipping:** Tips are theoretically outlawed but some hotels or restaurants will add 25 per cent service charge, plus a 21 per cent tax charge. In these cases, a minimal tip is still expected. Otherwise, 10 per cent on top of the bill will suffice. The same applies in bars. Taxi drivers tend to expect tips from visitors.

Business Profile

ECONOMY: Argentina is rich in natural resources and also has a large and profitable agricultural sector; the country is one of the world's major exporters of wheat and also produces maize, oilseeds, sorghum, soya beans and sugar. Beef is no longer the dominant trading commodity that it once was but animal products are still a valuable export earner. Agricultural goods aside, Argentina exports textiles and some metal and chemical products. These, along with oil refining and vehicle production, are also the main components of Argentina's manufacturing industry. Hydroelectricity and coal meet the bulk of the country's energy requirements. Brazil is the largest of Argentina's South American trading partners. There are also important trading relationships with the USA, which is the main source of manufactured products, and the countries of the former Soviet Union, which buy large quantities of grain. Elsewhere, trade with Japan and the EU – especially Germany and The Netherlands – has grown rapidly in recent years.
For all the potential of the Argentinian economy, it has been historically blighted by two major problems – high inflation and a massive foreign debt. The Menem government of the mid-1990s made a reasonable attempt to tackle these, using the orthodox market measures of dismantling the public sector, free competition, asset sales, and swingeing cuts in public spending. In addition, the value of Argentinian Peso was fixed to that of the US dollar. The immediate results were reductions in the national debt and the inflation rate – as well as considerable hardship for the poorer sections of the population. However, the policy of Peso-Dollar parity had unintended side effects which led to a sharp fall in exports and in government tax revenues as well as a large increase in government debt. With external debt topping US$130 billion in 2001, Argentina was on the point of defaulting on its overseas debts, potentially leading to a complete economic meltdown. At the end of the year, the government was forced to introduce draconian currency control measures – a substantial devaluation, along with a block on normal access to bank accounts – as it struggled to bring the situation under control. Since then, the Duhalde government, which took office at the end of 2001, has effectively stabilised the economy, which is now undergoing something of a resurgence. Estimated annual growth in mid-2004 was 9 per cent.
BUSINESS: Business cards are usually given and businesspeople expect to deal with someone of equal status. Punctuality is expected by visitors. Literature is in Spanish although many Argentinian businesspeople speak English as a second language. **Office hours:** Mon-Fri 0900-1200 and 1400-1900.
COMMERCIAL INFORMATION: The following organisation can offer advice: Cámara Argentina de Comercio (Chamber of Commerce), Avenida Leandro N. Alem 36, C1003AAN Buenos Aires (tel: (11) 5300 9000; fax: (11) 5300 9058; e-mail: centroservicios@cac.com.ar; website: www.cac.com.ar).
CONFERENCES/CONVENTIONS: For more information, contact the Secretaría de Turismo de la Nación (see *Contact Addresses* section).

Climate

The north is subtropical with rain throughout the year, while the Tierra del Fuego in the south has a sub-arctic climate. The main central area is temperate, but can be hot and humid during summer (December to February) and cool in winter.
Required clothing: European clothes for the main central area. Lightweight cottons and linens in the north. Warm clothes are necessary in the south and during winter months in the central area. Waterproofing is advisable for all areas.

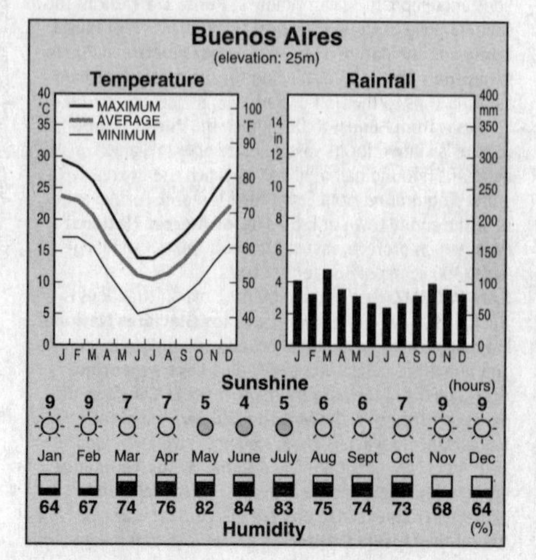

Armenia

LATEST TRAVEL ADVICE CONTACTS

British Foreign and Commonwealth Office
Tel: (0870) 606 0290 Website: www.fco.gov.uk
US Department of State
Website: http://travel.state.gov/travel
Canadian Department of Foreign Affairs and Int'l Trade
Tel: (1 800) 267 8376 Website: www.dfait-maeci.gc.ca

Location: Caucasus, east of Turkey.

Country dialling code: 374.

Ministry of Trade and Economic Development
5 M. Mkrtchian, 375010 Yerevan, Armenia
Tel: (1) 560 274 *or* 560 505 (tourism department).
Fax: (1) 526 577.
E-mail: minister@minted.am *or* tourgov@freenet.am
Website: www.minted.am/en
Armenia Visitor Information Centre
3 Nalbandyan Steet, Yerevan, Armenia
Tel/Fax: (1) 542 303/6.
E-mail: help@armeniainfo.am
Website: www.armeniainfo.am
Armintour
1 Pavstos Buzand Street, Yerevan, Armenia
Tel: (1) 582 282. Fax: (1) 560 815 *or* 542 407.
E-mail: armint@arminco.com
Website: www.armintour.com
Embassy of the Republic of Armenia
25A Cheniston Gardens, London W8 6TG, UK
Tel: (020) 7938 5435. Fax: (020) 7938 2595.
E-mail: armembuk@onetel.net.uk
Opening hours: Mon-Fri 900-1800 (general), 1000-1200 and 1500-1700 (consular section).
Armenian Tourist Office Representative
Sunvil House, 9 Upper Square, Old Isleworth, Middlesex, TW7 7BJ, UK
Tel: (020) 8568 8899. Fax: (020) 8560 9889.
E-mail: travel@sunvil.co.uk *or* discovery@sunvil.co.uk
Website: www.sunvil.co.uk
British Embassy
34 Baghramian Street, Yerevan 375019, Armenia
Tel: (1) 264 301. Fax: (1) 264 318.
E-mail: info.yerevan@fco.gov.uk
Website: www.britishembassy.am
Embassy of the Republic of Armenia
2225 R Street, NW, Washington, DC 20008, USA
Tel: (202) 319 1976 *or* 319 2983 (consular section).
Fax: (202) 319 2982 *or* 8330 (consular section).
E-mail: amembusadm@msn.com
Website: www.armeniaemb.org
Also deals with enquiries from Canada.

TIMATIC CODES

Health
AMADEUS: **TI-DFT/JIB/HE**
GALILEO/WORLDSPAN: **TI-DFT/JIB/HE**
SABRE: **TIDFT/JIB/HE**

Visa
AMADEUS: **TI-DFT/JIB/VI**
GALILEO/WORLDSPAN: **TI-DFT/JIB/VI**
SABRE: **TIDFT/JIB/VI**

To access TIMATIC country information on Health and Visa regulations through the Computer Reservations System (CRS), type in the appropriate command line listed above.

Embassy of the United States of America
18 Baghramyan Avenue, Yerevan 375019, Armenia
Tel: (1) 520 791 *or* 521 611 *or* 524 661. Fax: (1) 520 800.
E-mail: usinfo@arminco.com *or* consular@usa.am (consular section)
Website: www.usa.am
Also deals with enquiries from Canada.

General Information

AREA: 29,743 sq km (11,484 sq miles).
POPULATION: 3,330,099 (official estimate 2002).
POPULATION DENSITY: 111.9 per sq km.
CAPITAL: Yerevan. **Population:** 1,248,700 (official estimate 1999).
GEOGRAPHY: Armenia lies on the southern slopes of the Armenian Mountains in the Lesser Caucasus and is bordered by Georgia, Turkey, Azerbaijan and Iran. Its highest peak is Mount Aragats, 4090m (13,415ft), and even its deepest valleys lie 450-700m (1200-1870ft) above sea level. Its biggest lake is Lake Sevan in the east.
GOVERNMENT: Republic. Gained independence from the Soviet Union in 1991. **Head of State:** President Robert Kocharian since 1998. **Head of Government:** Prime Minister Andranik Markaryan since 2000.
LANGUAGE: Armenian. Russian is usually understood, but rarely used; Kurdish is sometimes used in broadcasting as 56,000 Kurds inhabit Armenia.
RELIGION: Armenia is the oldest Christian nation in the world, its conversion dating from the year AD 310. The Armenian Apostolic Church developed separately from both the Catholic and Orthodox branches of Christianity. It remains the dominant church, although there are Catholic and Protestant communities and a Russian Orthodox minority.
TIME: GMT + 3 (GMT + 4 from last Sunday in March to Saturday before last Sunday in October).
ELECTRICITY: 220 volts AC, 50Hz.
COMMUNICATIONS: Telephone: IDD is available to Yerevan. Country code: 374. Yerevan city code: 1. Outgoing calls to other CIS countries can be made by dialling with the appropriate codes, but only with difficulty. Outgoing international calls to other countries must be made through the operator. Some hotels and many businesses now have satellite links. **Mobile telephone:** GSM 900 network is in use. The main network operators include *Armentel* (website: www.armentel.com). Coverage is limited to Yerevan and the west of the country. **Fax:** Faxes can be sent from InfoCom offices and travel agencies. **Telegram:** Telegrams can be sent from post offices and larger hotels. **Internet:** ISPs include *Arminco* (website: www.arminco.com) and *Yerphi*, set up and run by the Yerevan Physics Institute Computer Center (website: www.yerphi.am). **Post:** International postal services are available to most countries but may be slow and unreliable. The main post office is located at 22 Sarya Str, Yerevan; post office opening hours are Mon-Fri 0900-1700. **Press:** The main newspapers are *Hayastan, Aravot, Azg* and *Yerkir*, all of which are published only in Armenian (Russian editions have been discontinued since the Russian minority in the republic has dropped from 8 per cent to less than 2 per cent in recent years). *Golos Armenii* (The Voice of Armenia) and *Respublika Armenia* survive as the main Russian-language papers. *Noyan Tapan*, an English-language weekly circulated primarily among the foreign missions and small foreign business community, is published by an independent information agency based in Yerevan.
Radio: BBC World Service (website: www.bbc.co.uk/worldservice) and Voice of America (website: www.voa.gov) can be received. From time to time the frequencies change and the most up-to-date can be found online.

Passport/Visa

	Passport Required?	Visa Required?	Return Ticket Required?
Full British	Yes	Yes	No
Australian	Yes	Yes	No
Canadian	Yes	Yes	No
USA	Yes	Yes	No
Other EU	Yes	Yes	No
Japanese	Yes	Yes	No

Note: *Regulations and requirements may be subject to change at short notice, and you are advised to contact the appropriate diplomatic or consular authority before finalising travel arrangements. Details of these may be found at the head of this country's entry. Any numbers in the chart refer to the footnotes below.*

PASSPORTS: Passport valid for at least four months required by all.
VISAS: Required by all except:
(a) nationals of CIS countries (except Turkmenistan, who *do* require a visa);
(b) nationals of Korea (Dem. Rep) and Serbia & Montenegro.
Types of visa and cost: *Ordinary/Tourist*: US$60, US$86 (three day express processing), US$95 (24-hour express processing). *Single-entry* (with official invitation): US$35. *Multiple-entry* (with official invitation): US$65. *Transit*: US$18 (single-entry); US$36 (double entry).
Note: There is no charge for diplomatic and official visas, or for those issued to persons under 18 years of age.
Validity: *Tourist/Ordinary*: 21 days. *Single-entry* and *Multiple-entry*: three months. *Transit*: three days. Visas must be used within 90 days of date of issue.
Application to: Embassy (or Consular Section at Embassy); see *Contact Addresses* section.
Application requirements: (a) Completed application form. (b) One recent passport-size photo. (c) Passport valid for at least four months. (d) Fee, payable by money order or certified cheque. (e) Postal applications should be sent by registered mail or by courier. *Single-entry/Multiple-entry*: (a)-(e) and, (f) Official invitation letter, duly authorised in Armenia (for stays over 21 days).
Working days required: Seven. Urgent visas can be processed in one or three days for a higher fee (see above).
Temporary residence: For stays of longer than three months, a residency permit must be obtained from the Foreign Ministry in Yerevan.

Money

Currency: Armenian Dram (AMD) = 100 luma. Dram notes are printed in denominations of AMD50,000, 20,000, 10,000, 5000, 1000, 500, 200, 100, 50, 25 and 10. Coins are in denominations of 500, 200, 100, 50, 20, 10 and 1 Dram, and 50 and 20 luma.
Note: The government is intending to phase out all banknotes less than 500 Dram.
Currency exchange: Foreign currencies can be exchanged at the airports, banks and most hotels and shops during normal opening hours. US Dollars are the most widely recognised foreign currency. Visitors using the national currency are advised to carry plenty of small change as some shops and, particularly markets, may be unable to accept large denominations. There are only five ATMs in Yerevan, operated by HSBC.
Credit & debit cards: These are accepted in a few large hotels. There are ATMs which accept Mastercard and Visa in Yerevan.
Travellers cheques: These are accepted in a few shops and hotels. Travellers are advised to take travellers cheques in US Dollars.
Currency restrictions: The import of local and foreign currency is unlimited, however cash amounts in excess of $10,000 or equivalent must be declared. The export of local and foreign currency is unlimited, however cash amounts in excess of US$10,000 or equivalent are prohibited and must be transferred via a bank.
Exchange rate indicators: The following figures are included as a guide to the movements of the Armenian Dram against Sterling and the US Dollar:

Date	Feb '04	May '04	Aug '04	Nov '04
£1.00=	1015.95	993.07	958.02	946.85
$1.00=	558.14	556.00	520.00	500.00

Banking hours: Mon-Fri 0900-1500. Exchange Offices are open until midnight and also operate at weekends and on public holidays.

Duty Free

The following goods may be imported into Armenia by persons of 18 years of age or older without incurring customs duty:
400 cigarettes; 2l or one bottle of alcoholic beverage; 5kg of perfume (or perfume to the value of US$500); other goods up to the amount of US$500, for personal use only.
Note: It is advisable to declare valuables on arrival.
Prohibited imports: Weapons and ammunition, narcotics, pornography, fruit and vegetables.
Prohibited exports: Weapons, ammunition, narcotics, pornography, fruit, vegetables, works of art and antiques (unless permission has been granted by the Ministry of Culture). An export tax of approximately US$10 is payable on each item. Contact the Embassy for further information (see *Contact Addresses* section).

Public Holidays

2005: Jan 1-2 New Year. **Jan 6** Armenian Orthodox Christmas. **Mar 8** International Women's Day. **Mar 25** Good Friday. **Apr 7** Motherhood and Beauty Day. **Apr 24** Genocide Memorial Day. **May 9** Victory and Peace Day. **May 28** First Republic Day. **Jul 5** Constitution Day. **Sep 21** Independence Day. **Dec 7** Earthquake Memorial Day. **Dec 31** New Year's Eve.
2006: Jan 1-2 New Year. **Jan 6** Armenian Orthodox Christmas. **Mar 8** International Women's Day. **Apr 7** Motherhood and Beauty Day. **Apr 14** Good Friday. **Apr 24** Genocide Memorial Day. **May 9** Victory and Peace Day. **May 28** First Republic Day. **Jul 5** Constitution Day. **Sep 21** Independence Day. **Dec 7** Earthquake Memorial Day. **Dec 31** New Year's Eve.

Health

	Special Precautions?	Certificate Required?
Yellow Fever	No	No
Cholera	No	No
Typhoid & Polio	1	N/A
Malaria	2	N/A

Note: *Regulations and requirements may be subject to change at short notice, and you are advised to contact your doctor well in advance of your intended date of departure. Any numbers in the chart refer to the footnotes below.*

1: Typhoid fever is common. Poliomyelitis eradication activities are underway but the disease should still be assumed to be a threat.
2: There is some risk of malaria from June to October in some villages in the Ararat Valley. No risk in main tourist areas.
Food & drink: All water should be regarded as being a potential health risk. Water used for drinking, brushing teeth or making ice should have first been boiled or otherwise sterilised. Only eat well-cooked meat and fish, preferably served hot. Pork, salad and mayonnaise may carry increased risk. Vegetables should be cooked and fruit peeled. Milk is pasteurised and dairy products should be safe for consumption, however, the incidence of communicable diseases among livestock is increasing because of a breakdown in vaccination programmes.
Other risks: *Diphtheria, hepatitis B* and *E, tick-borne encephalitis, brucellosis, echinococcosis* and *leishmaniasis* (cutaneous) may all occur. Visitors are advised to take precautions which may include vaccination.
There may be a risk of *rabies* although there has been no reported incidence in animals or humans since 1997. If you are bitten, seek medical advice without delay. For more information consult the *Health* appendix.
Health care: A reciprocal agreement for urgent medical treatment exists with the UK, although proof of UK residence is required. Power shortages and disrupted medical supplies have undermined normal health services to such a degree that travellers would be well advised to consider a health insurance policy guaranteeing emergency evacuation in case of serious accident or illness, as medical insurance is not often valid within the country. Doctors and hospitals often expect immediate cash payment for health services. Travellers are also advised to take a supply of those medicines that they are likely to require (but check first that they may be legally imported) as there is a severe shortage of even the most basic medical supplies, such as disposable needles, anaesthetics and antibiotics. Elderly travellers and those with existing health problems may be at risk owing to inadequate medical facilities.

Credit: © Discover Armenia

Travel - International

AIR: *Armenian International Airways (R3)* (website: www.armenianairways.com) operates weekly flights linking Yerevan with Athens, Beirut, Damascus and Frankfurt/M, and twice weekly flights to Amsterdam, Dubai and Paris. Lack of demand, unreliable fuel supplies and an uneconomic fare structure has resulted in greatly reduced services to other CIS republics. *British Mediterranean* (a franchise partner of *British Airways*) operates three flights per week from London to Yerevan. There are daily flights with *Siberian Airlines* from Yerevan to Istanbul and Moscow; these are often subject to delays and cancellations. For political reasons there are no direct international transport links between Armenia and Azerbaijan; Georgia is sometimes used as a stopover point.
International airports: *Zvartnots (EVN)* 10km (6 miles) from Yerevan. Buses and taxis are available to the city centre. Buses run every 15 minutes between 0700-2100 (travel time – 30 minutes).

Departure tax: US$20 per person (usually payable in local currency). Although this is normally paid at the airport, visitors staying in the large hotels may sometimes pay at their hotel, and present the receipt at the airport check-in desk. Transit passengers and children under 12 years of age are exempt.
RAIL: Armenia's rail links to Azerbaijan and Turkey have been closed indefinitely, but an international service still runs to Georgia (every other day) and to Iran. Passengers travelling to Georgia should be aware of the possibility of theft or robbery.
ROAD: A road link between Armenia and Iran, the Kajaran highway, has become the most important international road link. There are two highways linking Armenia to Georgia; these routes, especially the Yerevan-Tbilisi road, have a bad reputation for highway robbery, although efforts by the Georgian authorities to enforce law and order are reported to be paying off. The Azerbaijan and Turkey borders are both currently closed. It is possible to travel by road to the enclave of Nagorno Karabakh, however, it is essential to obtain a visa from the permanent representative of Nagorno Karabakh in Yerevan.

Credit: © Discover Armenia

Travel - Internal

Note: Internal travel, especially by air, may be disrupted by fuel shortages and other problems.
AIR: Yerevan has a small domestic airport as well as an international airport, which offers some flights to other destinations in Armenia.
RAIL: The main railway station is the Sasuntsi Davit Station on Tigran Mets Avenue. There are daily trains to most major towns.
ROAD: The road network comprises 7705km (4788 miles). Road surfaces can be very poor, even in the case of major highways, and care should be taken to avoid children and animals on the road. Supplies of petrol, diesel and oil are at present limited. It is common practice to flag down private cars as well as official taxis. Local drivers have a tendency to flout traffic regulations and ignore signals. Visitors should take care when driving or crossing the road. **Coach:** Coaches and minibuses run between the major centres of population.
URBAN: There is a small underground system in Yerevan. Buses and trolleybuses run in the city. Taxis are available in the city centre or can be ordered by telephone. Chauffeur-driven cars are available but are expensive. It is advisable to obtain them through official channels, such as hotels or travel agencies in Yerevan.

Accommodation

Hotels previously run by Intourist are now mostly being privatised. In Yerevan the new Armenia Hotel is an Armenian/Marriott joint venture, functioning exclusively in foreign currency and supplied with power from its own generators. The Hotel Hrazdan, mainly occupied by foreign missions, also has its own generator, but is state owned and functions primarily as a guest-house for official visitors. Private individuals may occasionally be allowed to stay there by special arrangement. The Hotel Dvin, opposite the Hrazdan, is less comfortable but has privileged supplies of electricity and running water. It has a satellite telephone service for guests. Armenia also has several B&Bs. Information on accomodation can be obtained from Armintour *or* the Armenian Visitor Information Centre (see *Contact Addresses* section). There are tourist information bureaux in the Armenia Hotel (Republic Square) and the newly refurbished Ani Plaza Hotel (19 Sayat Nova Avenue). Tours and other activities can be organised through these bureaux.

Resorts & Excursions

Armenia is an ancient country that was once counted as a great power, if only for a short period. The realm of King Tigranes II, in the 1st century BC, stretched from the Caspian Sea to Syrian Arab Republic and the Mediterranean, before it was conquered by the Romans.
YEREVAN: The present capital of Armenia, Yerevan is one of the oldest cities in the world, founded nearly 2800 years ago in the time of ancient Babylon. Sadly, little remains to remind the visitor of the city's ancient heritage. Most of the old town was demolished in the 1930s, ostensibly to upgrade standards of public health but, according to locals, more crucially with a view to facilitating the policing of the city. Yerevan was rebuilt using the attractive pinkish-brown volcanic tufa stone seen throughout the republic, in so-called 'Armenian national style' architecture - solid, sometimes imposing and essentially Soviet in character. **Mount Ararat** lies across the border in Turkey, although it is claimed as part of the territory of greater Armenia, and is where **Noah's Ark** is said to have settled after the Flood. Yerevan's **History and Art Museum** includes a section tracing the development of Armenian art from the seventh century to the present day. The history section features models and artefacts informing visitors about life in Armenia and the pre-Armenian state of Urartu. The Yerevan library of ancient manuscripts (*Materadaran*) houses over 12,000 texts, many beautifully illuminated and some dating as far back as the 9th century. The contents of the library testify to Armenia's long history of culture and education. The **Vernisaj** flea market, which takes place at weekends, is very popular with tourists. In the year AD 301, Armenia became the first country to adopt Christianity as the official state religion (with the exception of the now vanished kingdom of King Abgar of Edessa). Many of the most interesting sights in the republic are associated with the heritage of the Armenian apostolic church.
ECHMIADZIN: Some 20km (12 miles) west of Yerevan, Echmiadzin was the capital of Armenia from AD 180-340 and remains the site of the country's most important cathedral, and home of the church's Supreme Catholicos. The **Cathedral of St Gregory the Illuminator** is believed to stand on the site of a much older church, itself predated by a pagan shrine. The existing 17th-century cathedral is a fine example of Armenian ecclesiastical architecture, with its squat bell tower and elaborately carved dome. In addition to chalices, vestments and other religious artefacts, the cathedral's treasury contains a spearhead believed to have been used to pierce the side of the crucified Christ, and a chunk of wood from Mount Ararat, claimed to be part of a plank from Noah's Ark. There are a number of other churches at Echmiadzin, including the excavated remains of the seventh-century **Church of St Gregory** at **Zvartnots**. The building, reputed to have been of extraordinary beauty, was largely destroyed by an earthquake in the 10th century.
GEGARD: The **Gegard Monastery**, located 35km (22 miles) east of Yerevan in a steep, rocky valley, is one of Armenia's most dramatic sights. The monks, who still inhabit the monastery, occasionally sacrifice sheep on an open-air stone altar. 'Wishing trees' by the road approaching the site are decorated with coloured scraps of cloth, tied on by pilgrims and travellers hoping their prayers will be answered. A monastery has occupied this site since the fourth century AD, and the existing churches, all magnificently carved, date from the 13th century. Leading from the vaulted chambers of the main church and adjoining jamatoun, or meeting room, are two chapels hewn into the rock of the mountain itself. One of these contains a holy spring, the other a burial vault decorated with an ornate coat of arms. Higher up the slope, a passage leads into the mountainside to the 13th-century tomb of Prince Papak and his wife Rouzakan, a structure noted for its extraordinary acoustics.
GARNI: On the road between Gegard and Yerevan, Garni is the site of a temple to the Roman god Mithras. In the 1st century AD, Nero sent money and slaves to build the temple, as a tribute to the Armenian King Tiridates for his support in fighting off the Parthians. During the centuries following the conversion of the kings of Armenia to Christianity, the temple served as a royal summer palace. Repeated earthquakes have destroyed most of the original structure, but the temple's vertiginous position dominating the valley from a plateau 300m (984ft) above the **Azat River** is breathtakingly beautiful. A ruined 9th-century church stands near the restored temple, and a Roman bathhouse has recently been excavated, revealing a well-preserved mosaic floor.
LAKE SEVAN: Situated 70km (43 miles) east of Yerevan, Lake Sevan is the largest lake in the Caucasus, and much vaunted for its pure waters, stunning setting and delicious salmon trout. The principal lakeside resort is **Sevan** on the northern shore, once popular with Soviet tourists, now optimistically awaiting development to attract wealthy foreigners. Tragically, ill-considered irrigation and hydroelectric projects implemented during the 1970s have triggered an ecological crisis. The water level of the lake has dropped by as much as 16m (41ft). It is now feared that the ecology of Lake Sevan may be irreversibly damaged if radical action is not taken.
DILIZHAN: North of Sevan, further into the mountains, is Dilizhan, a resort much favoured during the Soviet period for the medicinal powers attributed to its mineral water. The authorities aspire in the long term to develop ski and spa resorts in this region, but at present, tourist infrastructure remains at a primitive level. A few kilometres east of Dilizhan, in a wooded gorge, is the **Agartsin Monastery**, believed to have been the major cultural centre in medieval Armenia, and one of the very few perfectly preserved examples of the architecture of its period (10th-13th centuries). The refectory building is particularly prized. 25km (16 miles) from Dilizhan, the 12th-century **Goshavank Monastery** features some of the finest examples of the delicate, lacey style of stone carving developed by medieval craftsmen in the region.
ELSEWHERE: In the northwest of the republic, **Gumri**, Armenia's second-largest city, and **Vanatsor** (known during the Soviet period as Leninakan and Kirovaken respectively) suffered badly in the 1988 earthquake and have yet to be rebuilt.

Sport & Activities

Hiking: Specialist tour operators in Yerevan can organise tailor-made walking tours in Armenia's spectacular countryside. Hotels will also often supply information. Outdoor pursuits are becoming more popular, and provision for tourists is improving.
Birdwatching: Rare species, including eagles, can be seen all over the country.

Social Profile

FOOD & DRINK: A restaurant and cafe culture is starting to flourish again in Armenia, with street stalls and privately run establishments replacing the colourless state restaurants typical of the Soviet era. New cafes and restaurants are now opening daily. Many of the cafes are in parks, and are very popular in summer with locals and tourists alike. Much Armenian cooking is based on lamb, either grilled and served as *shashlik* with flat bread, or prepared as soup (the most popular being *bozbash*, a dish which exists in infinite variations) or stew, often in combination with fruit or nuts. The newly butchered sheep carcasses hanging from trees near most *khorovats* (barbecued meat) stalls, although perhaps appearing somewhat gruesome to foreign visitors, testify to the freshness of the meat sizzling on the grill. A meal usually starts with a large spread of hors d'oeuvres, which may include peppers and vine leaves stuffed with rice and meat, pickled and fresh vegetables, salty white sheep's cheese eaten with fresh green herbs and flat bread, and various kinds of cured meat (*basturma*). Almost magical, health-giving properties are ascribed to dried apricots from the Caucasus. Another desert speciality is made from grape juice, dried into thin sheets of a deep, reddish brown colour, and then rolled up into long cylinders around walnuts or other nuts. The 'ishkan' salmon trout from Lake Sevan is proclaimed as a great delicacy, but it is now seldom available.
Armenian brandies are excellent. Production of Armenian wines and brandies suffered during Mikhail Gorbachev's anti-alcohol drive in the 1980s, but locals are still proud to inform visitors that Winston Churchill always insisted on Armenian in preference to French brandy, after first tasting it at the Yalta conference. During the season following the grape harvest, locals sell effervescent, mildly fermented grape juice from roadside stands. Coffee is served Turkish-style - strong and black in tiny cups - although in view of national sensibilities visitors would be ill-advised to refer to this cultural similarity.
NIGHTLIFE: There are restaurants and nightclubs featuring local music in Yerevan. Several new restaurants, clubs and discos have opened recently. There are several casinos. Opera, theatre and ballet performances are of a high standard, and tickets are cheap (about the equivalent of US$5).
SHOPPING: Although Armenia's economy is still relatively undeveloped, new shops are now opening. The *Vernisaj* flea market in Yerevan attracts sellers of all kinds of goods and is popular with tourists. **Shopping hours:** Mon-Fri 0900-1700. Shops stay open longer in the summer.
SPECIAL EVENTS: For details of events in Armenia, contact the Armenian Tourist Office (see *Contact Addresses* section). The following is a selection of special events occurring in Armenia in 2005:
Jan *New Year's Celebrations*, nationwide. **Jan 6** *Armenian Christmas*. **Jun** *Water Day*, nationwide. **Sep 21** *Independence Day*.
SOCIAL CONVENTIONS: Almost all entertaining takes place in private homes, and guests may find themselves subjected to overwhelming hospitality and generosity, as well as being expected to eat enormously and participate in endless toasts. Visitors invited to an Armenian's home should arrive bearing some kind of small gift, such as flowers and alcohol (preferably imported) or chocolates. Handshaking is the normal form of greeting. Business cards

are invariably exchanged at any kind of official meeting and not infrequently on first meeting people socially as well. Conversation tends to be highly politicised, and guests may be well advised to avoid expressing strong opinions. Women tend to be less retiring than in nearby Muslim countries.
Tipping: Expected by waiters and doormen in restaurants – sometimes in advance to ensure service. Taxi fares should always be negotiated before starting a journey, and visitors should be aware that rates proposed initially are likely to be unreasonably high, in the expectation that foreigners will have unlimited cash and little idea of how much they ought to be paying. It is therefore advisable to make enquiries about 'going rates' per kilometre of travel before entering into negotiations with taxi drivers. The same applies to market stall holders and so on.

Business Profile

ECONOMY: Armenia has recovered slowly from the massive economic crisis caused by the 1988 earthquake and the collapse of the Soviet Union but is still seriously affected by the results of the war with Azerbaijan, which include a partial economic blockade and border closures with Azerbaijan and Turkey. Other regional difficulties, such as upheavals in neighbouring Georgia, had a detrimental effect on the country's economy and Armenian foreign trade suffered badly as a result. Many people rely on subsistence agriculture. Mineral deposits including copper, zinc, gold, marble, bauxite and molybdenum have brought some foreign revenue and investment, although this sector is relatively undeveloped. The industrial sector comprises textile and chemical industries, aluminium production and some mechanical engineering. The government embarked on a reform programme in the mid-1990s, which included privatisation, a new fiscal structure and the introduction of a new currency, the Dram, to replace the Russian Rouble. The country remains dependent on foreign aid and remittances from émigrés but is steadily improving. The privatisation programme has since been extended to include major parts of the national infrastructure, such as the electricity grid. The volume of foreign investment is growing, despite concerns about widespread corruption and poor financial controls. The government has also signed important economic co-operation agreements with the Russian Federation and Iran. In the international arena, negotiations for Armenia to join the World Trade Organisation are reaching their final stages.
BUSINESS: Business is generally conducted formally, and visitors should dress smartly; appointments are necessary.
Office hours: Mon-Fri 0900-1800.
COMMERCIAL INFORMATION: The following organisations can offer advice: Ministry of Trade and Economic Development (see *Contact Addresses*); Ministry of Foreign Affairs, 1 Republic Square, Yerevan 375010 (tel: (1) 523 531; fax (1) 543 925; e-mail: info@armeniaforeignministry.com; website: www.armeniaforeignministry.com); *or* Chamber of Commerce and Industry, 11 Khanjyan Street, Yerevan 375010 (tel: (1) 560 184 *or* 587 871; fax: (1) 587 871; e-mail: armcci@arminco.com; website: www.armcci.am); *or* Armenian Development Agency, 17 Charents Street, Yerevan 375025 (tel: (1) 570 170; fax: (1) 542 272; e-mail: info@ada.am; website: www.businessarmenia.com).

Climate

Continental, mountain climate (over 90 per cent of the territory of the republic is over 900m/2286ft above sea level). During the summer, days can be hot and dry with temperatures falling sharply at night. Winters are extremely cold with heavy snow. May to June and September to October are good times to visit the country, as the weather is warm but mild.

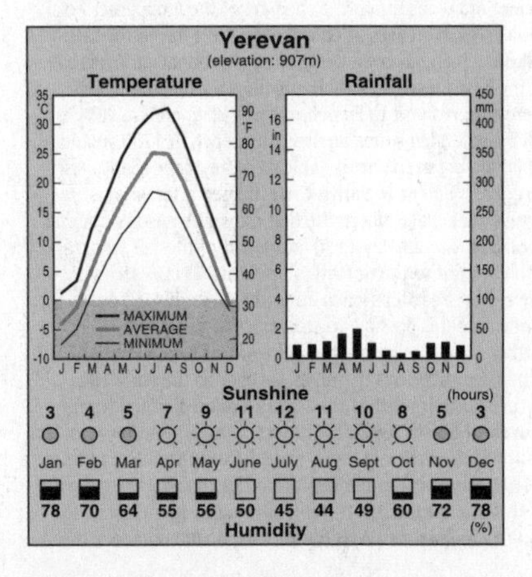

Aruba

LATEST TRAVEL ADVICE CONTACTS

British Foreign and Commonwealth Office
Tel: (0870) 606 0290 Website: www.fco.gov.uk

US Department of State
Website: http://travel.state.gov/travel

Canadian Department of Foreign Affairs and Int'l Trade
Tel: (1 800) 267 8376 Website: www.dfait-maeci.gc.ca

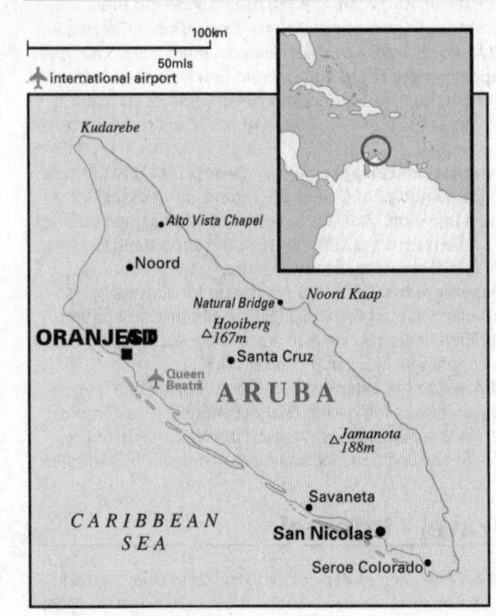

Location: South Caribbean.

Country dialling code: 297.

Aruba is a dependency of the Netherlands and represented abroad by Royal Netherlands Embassies – see *The Netherlands* section for embassy contact details.
Aruba Tourism Authority
Street address: 172 L G Smith Boulevard, Oranjestad, Aruba
Postal address: PO Box 1019, Oranjestad, Aruba
Tel: (58) 23777. Fax: (58) 34702.
E-mail: ata.aruba@aruba.com Website: www.aruba.com
Aruba Tourism Authority
Schimmelpenninckla an 1, 2517 JN The Hague, The Netherlands
Tel: (70) 302 8040. Fax: (70) 360 4877.
E-mail: ata.holland@aruba.com
Aruba Tourism Authority (UK Office)
c/o The Saltmarsh Partnership, The Copperfields, 25 Copperfield Street, London SE1 0EN, UK
Tel: (020) 7928 1600. Fax: (020) 7928 1700.
E-mail: geoff@saltmarshpr.co.uk Website: www.aruba.com
Aruba Tourism Authority
Ground Level, 1200 Harbor Boulevard, Weehawken, NJ 07087, USA
Tel: (201) 330 0800 *or* (800) 862 7822 (toll-free in USA and Canada). Fax: (201) 330 8757.
E-mail: ata.newjersey@aruba.com
Website: www.aruba.com
Aruba Tourism Authority
5875 Highway no 7, Suite 201, Woodbridge, Ontario L4L 1T9, Canada
Tel: (905) 264 3434 *or* (800) 268 3042 (toll-free in Ontario and Quebec). Fax: (905) 264 3437.
E-mail: ata.canada@aruba.com
Website: www.aruba.com

General Information

AREA: 193 sq km (74.5 sq miles).
POPULATION: 101,000 (UN official estimate 2000).
POPULATION DENSITY: 523.3 per sq km.
CAPITAL: Oranjestad. **Population:** 20,046 (1991).
GEOGRAPHY: Aruba is the smallest island in the Leeward group of the Dutch Caribbean islands, which also include Bonaire and Curaçao. They are popularly known as the ABCs. As the westernmost island of the group, Aruba is the final link in the long Antillean chain, lying 20km (12.5 miles) off the Venezuelan coast. The island is 30km (19.6 miles) long and 9km (6 miles) across at its widest and has a flat landscape dominated by Jamanota Mountain (188m/617ft). The west and southwest coast, known as Palm Beach, boasts 11km (7 miles) of palm-fringed powder-white sands, while in complete contrast the east coast has a desolate, windswept shoreline of jagged rocks carved into weird shapes by the pounding surf.
GOVERNMENT: Dependency of the Netherlands. In 1986 Aruba separated from the rest of the Netherlands Antilles. **Head of State:** Queen Beatrix of the Netherlands, represented locally by Governor-General Fredis Refunjol since 2004. **Head of Government:** Prime Minister Nelson Oduber since 2001.
LANGUAGE: The official language is Dutch. English and Spanish are also spoken. The islanders also speak Papiemento, which is a combination of Dutch, Spanish, Portuguese, English and Indian languages.
RELIGION: 80 per cent of the population are Roman Catholic.
TIME: GMT - 4.
ELECTRICITY: 110 volts AC, 60Hz.
COMMUNICATIONS: Telephone: IDD available. Country code: 297. Outgoing international code: 00. Payphones, from which international calls can be made are located all over the island. **Mobile telephone:** GSM 900/1800 network. Network operators include *Digicel* (website: www.digicelaruba.com) and *SETAR* (tel: 586 7138; website: www.setar.aw). Mobile phones can be hired from *SETAR*; a deposit and proof of identity are required. **Internet:** Internet cafes exist in Oranjestad. Main ISPs include *Setarnet* (website: www.setarnet.aw). **Fax/Telegram:** Most hotels offer fax and telegram services to residents. **Post:** Post office hours: 0730-1200 and 1300-1630. **Press:** The oldest established newspaper (in Dutch) is *Amigoe di Aruba* and the English-language papers are *Aruba Today*, and *The News*.
Radio: BBC World Service (website: www.bbc.co.uk/worldservice) and Voice of America (website: www.voa.gov) can be received. From time to time the frequencies change and the most up-to-date can be found online.

TIMATIC CODES

Health
AMADEUS: **TI-DFT/JIB/HE**
GALILEO/WORLDSPAN: **TI-DFT/JIB/HE**
SABRE: **TIDFT/JIB/HE**

Visa
AMADEUS: **TI-DFT/JIB/VI**
GALILEO/WORLDSPAN: **TI-DFT/JIB/VI**
SABRE: **TIDFT/JIB/VI**

To access TIMATIC country information on Health and Visa regulations through the Computer Reservations System (CRS), type in the appropriate command line listed above.

Passport/Visa

	Passport Required?	Visa Required?	Return Ticket Required?
Full British	Yes	No	Yes
Australian	Yes	No	Yes
Canadian	1	No	Yes
USA	2	No	Yes
Other EU	3	No	Yes
Japanese	Yes	No	Yes

***Note:** Regulations and requirements may be subject to change at short notice, and you are advised to contact the appropriate diplomatic or consular authority before finalising travel arrangements. Details of these may be found at the head of this country's entry. Any numbers in the chart refer to the footnotes below.*

PASSPORTS: Passport valid for at least three months after intended return to home country required by all except:
(a) **1.** nationals of Canada holding a birth certificate, baptismal certificate, valid driver's license, proof of Canadian citizenship or certificate of naturalisation;
(b) **2.** nationals of the USA holding an official birth certificate with a raised seal accompanied by photo ID, a certificate of naturalisation or an alien registration card (green card);
(c) **3.** nationals of Belgium, Luxembourg and The Netherlands, holding a National Identity Card.
VISAS: Required by all except the following:
(a) nationals of countries referred to in the chart above for up to three months;
(b) nationals of Andorra, Antigua & Barbuda, Argentina, The Bahamas, Barbados, Belize, Bolivia, Brazil, Brunei, Bulgaria, Chile, Costa Rica, Croatia, Dominica, Ecuador, El Salvador, Grenada, Guatemala, Guyana, Honduras, Hong Kong (SAR), Iceland, Israel, Korea (Rep), Liechtenstein, Macau (SAR), Malaysia, Mexico, Monaco, New Zealand, Nicaragua, Norway, Panama, Paraguay, San Marino, St Kitts & Nevis, St Lucia, St Vincent & the Grenadines, Singapore, Surinam, Switzerland, Trinidad & Tobago, Uruguay, Vatican City and Venezuela for stays of up to three months;
(c) many nationals can visit for a period of 14 days, as tourists only, provided they have a return or onward ticket, proof of sufficient funds for the length of stay and the necessary documents for returning to their home country. The list is extensive, however, so it is advisable to check with your nearest relevant Consulate or Embassy prior to making travel arrangements.
Note: (a) For stays of over 14 days and less than 30 days, the traveller will be issued with a Temporary Certificate of Admission by the Immigration authorities on arrival in Aruba. (b) All visitors require a return or onward ticket.
Types of Visa and Cost: *Single-entry:* approximately £16,

depending on the exchange rate.
Application to: Nearest Embassy of the Kingdom of the Netherlands *or* directly through the Department of Foreign Affairs, J E Irausquinplein 2A, Oranjestad, Aruba (tel: (58) 34705; fax: (58) 38108).
Application Requirements: (a) Passport valid for a minimum of three months after intended return to home country. (b) One fully completed application form. (c) Two recent, passport sized photos per person endorsed on passport, with daytime phone number and address written clearly on the back. (d) Fee; payable by postal order (to Royal Netherlands Embassy) or cash. Cheques are not accepted. (e) Proof of sufficient funds (three most recent bank statements) and return/onward tickets as well as any other necessary documents. (f) Letter of invitation. (g) Letter showing employment, salary, length of service and guarantee of employment upon return to country.
Note: (a) All visitors wishing to work in Aruba for a number of months must have a written permit from the Department of Immigration and Naturalisation. Further information and application forms for Written Permits can be obtained free of charge from the Department of Immigration and Naturalisation, Kaya Dek Cooper 11, Sint Nicolas (tel: (58) 43322; fax: (58) 43534). (b) Potential immigrants in Aruba are required to take an HIV test. (c) Visitors who are not nationals of the country of residence must submit a residency permit.
Working days required: Up to four weeks.

Money

Currency: Aruba Florin or Guilder (AFl) = 100 cents. Notes are in denominations of AFl500, 250, 100, 50, 25 and 10. Coins are in denominations of AFl 5, 1 and 50, 25, 10 and 5 cents.
Note: The Aruba Florin is tied to the US Dollar.
Currency exchange: The US Dollar is widely accepted. Other currencies can be exchanged in banks. Currency can also be obtained from ATMs in Oranjestad.
Credit & debit cards: Accepted by many shops and hotels. They can also be used in cash dispensers.
Travellers cheques: US Dollars or Euros are recommended.
Currency restrictions: The import and export of local and foreign currency is unlimited. The import of Dutch currency and currency from Surinam is prohibited. The Aruba Florin cannot be exchanged outside Aruba.
Exchange rate indicators: The following figures are included as a guide to the movements of the Aruba Florin/Guilder against Sterling and the US Dollar:

Date	Feb '04	May '04	Aug '04	Nov '04
£1.00=	3.25	3.20	3.29	3.38
$1.00=	1.79	1.79	1.79	1.79

Banking hours: Mon-Fri 0800-1600.

Duty Free

The following items may be taken into Aruba without incurring customs duty:
200 cigarettes or 50 cigars; 1l of spirits or 2.25l of wine or 3l of beer; gifts to a value of AFl100.
Note: A duty-free allowance is only available to persons over 16 years of age. The importation of leather goods and souvenirs from Haiti is not advisable. There are no restrictions on the import of perfume. Goods worth more than AFl500 must be declared.

Public Holidays

2005: Jan 1 New Year's Day. **Jan 25** GF Croe's Day. **Mar 18** National Anthem and Flag Day. **Mar 25-28** Easter. **Apr 30** Queen's Day. **May 1** Labour Day. **May 5** Ascension Day. **Dec 25-26** Christmas.
2006: Jan 1 New Year's Day. **Jan 25** GF Croe's Day. **Mar 18** National Anthem and Flag Day. **Apr 14-17** Easter. **Apr 30** Queen's Day. **May 1** Labour Day. **May 25** Ascension Day. **Dec 25-26** Christmas.

Health

	Special Precautions?	Certificate Required?
Yellow Fever	Yes	1
Cholera	No	No
Typhoid & Polio	No	N/A
Malaria	No	N/A

Note: *Regulations and requirements may be subject to change at short notice, and you are advised to contact your doctor well in advance of your intended date of departure. Any numbers in the chart refer to the footnotes below.*

1: A yellow fever vaccination certificate is required from travellers over 6 months of age arriving from infected areas.
Food & drink: Tap water is considered safe to drink. Milk is pasteurised and dairy products are safe for consumption. Local meat, poultry, seafood, fruit and vegetables are generally considered safe to eat.
Health care: There are excellent medical facilities and many hotels also have doctors on call. The main hospital is the Dr Horacio Oduber. In rare circumstances, air evacuation to Curaçao may be necessary. Full medical insurance is advised. There is no reciprocal health agreement with the UK.

Travel - International

AIR: Airlines serving Aruba include *Aerorepublica* (from Colombia), *American Airlines*, *Aserca Valencia* (from Venezuela), *Continental Airlines*, *Delta*, *Dutch Caribbean*, *KLM*, *Royal Arabian Airlines*, *United Airlines* and *US Airways*.
Approximate flight times: From Oranjestad to *London* is 11 hours 40 minutes (including a connection, normally in Amsterdam), to *Los Angeles* is 10 hours and to *New York* is four hours.
International airports: *Queen Beatrix (AUA)* is 3.5km (2.5 miles) southeast of Oranjestad. Airport facilities include a duty-free shop, bank, restaurants and left-luggage facilities. A taxi service is available between the airport and the town. Bus services run to the town centre.
Departure tax: US$36.75 per person for all passengers travelling to the USA; US$33.50 for all other destinations. Children under two years of age are exempt. Departure tax is normally included in the ticket price.
SEA: Aruba has extensive duty-free shopping and many cruise ships call in on their Caribbean itineraries. *Cunard*, *Holland America Lines*, *Majestic*, *Princess*, *Royal Caribbean* and *Sun Line* amongst others sail to Oranjestad.

Travel - Internal

SEA: Ferries depart daily to De Palm Island from the mainland. Crossings run every half an hour between 1000-1800.
ROAD: The road system throughout the island is very good. Driving is on the right and international signs are used.
Bus: *Arubus* operates an inexpensive and reliable public bus service between the towns and hotels on Eagle Beach and Palm Beach and the main bus station in Oranjestad; check with the tourist office or hotels for schedule. **Taxi:** The main taxi office is at Pos Abou. Taxis are not metered. Rates are fixed and should be checked before getting into the cab. There is no need to tip drivers except for help with unusually heavy luggage. **Car hire:** There are plenty of cars available for hire and touring by car or by 4-wheel drive jeep is one of the most pleasant ways to explore the island. Most major companies have offices in Aruba (including *Budget*, *Hertz*, *National* and *Thrifty*); there are also many well-established local car hire firms. It is possible to hire scooters, motorcycles and cycles. Minimum age for hiring a car is 21 to 25 depending on the firm. Hotels can assist with bookings. **Documentation:** A valid foreign licence or an International Driving Permit, held for at least two years, are both acceptable. Insurance is recommended.

Accommodation

HOTELS: The majority of hotels are in the Palm Beach and Eagle Beach resort area on the southwest coast, offering accommodation of a very high standard. Many of these luxury hotels have beach frontage and their own swimming pools, plus extensive sport, entertainment and shopping facilities. Rates are much lower in the summer, which is the island's low season. Some tour operators offer out-of-season accommodation packages. Rooms are subject to a 5 per cent government room tax and hotels also add a 16.6 per cent service charge. For more information, contact the Aruba Tourism Authority (see *Contact Addresses* section) *or* the Aruba Hotel and Tourism Association (AHATA), L G Smith Boulevard 174, PO Box 542, Oranjestad (tel: (58) 22607; fax: (58) 24202; e-mail: ahata@setarnet.net; website: www.ahata.net). The Aruba Tourism Authority provides a 24-hour customer service hotline (tel: (58) 39000) which is available to visitors wishing to make complaints or favourable comments about hotels and other establishments.
Grading: All hotels are graded into first class and deluxe.
GUEST HOUSES: There is limited scope for this kind of accommodation. Many guest houses are in the Noord area not far from the main hotel area. Contact the Tourism Authority for details (see *Contact Addresses* section).
SELF-CATERING: There are apartment complexes and a list is available through the Aruba Tourism Authority offices (see *Contact Addresses* section).

Resorts & Excursions

ORANJESTAD: Aruba's Dutch heritage is always present, and nowhere more so than in the capital of Oranjestad, characterised by pastel-coloured gabled buildings and a windmill brought piece by piece from Holland, now used as a restaurant. There are four museums here open to the public: the **Historical Museum**, the **Geological Museum**, the **Archaeological Museum** and the **Numismatic Museum**. The first is housed in the **Fort Zoutman**, the oldest building on Aruba (1796) with the **Willem III-Tower** having been added in 1868. The *Bonbini Festival* is held every Tuesday 1830-2030 throughout the year in the courtyard of the Historical Museum and offers the opportunity to get an insight into local customs, music and cuisine as well as a chance to get to know the islanders. Oranjestad has a daily market in the **Paardenbaai** (Schooner Harbour) where traders sell fresh fish straight from the boat, and fruit and vegetables from the mainland are available. The capital is also famous for its shopping district, centred on **Caya Gilberto François (Betico) Croes**.
One of the roads north from the capital runs inland, passing the **Bubali Bird Sanctuary**. Birdwatching and natural wildlife tours as well as archaeological and geological trips are available in various languages.
THE COAST: Aruba's principal attraction is its beaches; these include **Arashi Beach** (near California Point on the northwest tip, particularly good for snorkelling), **Bucuti Beach** (recently rated one of the top nine beaches in the Caribbean and one of the best 100 beaches in the world), **Spaans Lagoen** and **Commandeurs Baai**, **Bachelor's Beach** (good for windsurfing), and the particularly shallow areas of **Baby Beach** and the **Grapefield** (all on the south coast). Near Baby Beach, at Seroe Colorado, is **Rodger's Beach**, where the surf is a little stronger. Beaches on the north coast include **Boca Prins**, **Dos Playa** and **Andicouri**. One of the attractions on this shore is the **Natural Bridge**, an arch carved from coral cliffs by the crashing ocean surf. The bridge is the biggest and highest in the Caribbean and is Aruba's most famous natural wonder. So too is the surf on this coast, but visitors are warned that it can be very rough. Local advice concerning conditions for surfing on the island at any particular time should be followed carefully, but there will usually be one beach somewhere to suit all levels of skill and courage. Another favourite pastime is exploring the surrounding shallow water with specially equipped submarine vessels.
Not all of the coast is completely deserted; for instance, much of **Palm Beach**, the 11km (7 miles) of sand and palm trees on the west and southwest shores of the island, has now been developed into a unique hotel resort. Low-rise resort hotels are more common on **Eagle Beach**, located between the point to the west of **Druif Bay** and south of Palm Beach. Visitors after more isolated relaxation will need to seek out some of the more remote sunbathing and swimming spots (of which there are plenty).
On the northern tip of the island is the **California Lighthouse** set in an area of desolate sand dunes. Off this coast is the wreck of a German freighter from World War II which is now the home of countless exotic fish and a very popular spot for scuba-divers. The **Chapel of Alto Vista** at **Alto Vista** is another popular site on the north coast.
In the southeastern part of the island is Aruba's second-largest town, **San Nicolas**, which owed its prosperity to the oil refinery, once one of the largest in the world. To the east is the area known as **Seroe Colorado**, notable not only for several fine beaches but also for being the home of the local iguana community.
THE INTERIOR: The **Cunucu** is a land of cactus, windswept divi-divi trees, old villages and hamlets, unsignposted dirt roads stretching across the often mysterious landscape. The distinctive shape of the divi-divi trees (also known as *watapanas*) has become Aruba's unofficial trademark; blown by the northeasterly trade winds, the trees are forced to grow at alarming angles. The island can easily be driven round in a day, and cars can be hired without difficulty; see the *Travel – Internal* section for further information.
There are several systems of caves on Aruba. **Fontein** was once used by the Arawak Indians who were the original inhabitants of the island. On the walls of the caves are ancient drawings thought to be part of the Indian sacrificial rite. Nearby, the caves at **Guadirikiri** are a haven for bats. **Arikok**, which has been designated a national park, has by far the best preserved Indian drawings on the island. Also interesting is a visit to Frenchman's Pass, where Arawak Indians defended Aruba against the French in 1700. Inland – in fact almost in the geographical centre of the island – is the old settlement of **Santa Cruz**, named after what is allegedly the place where the first cross was raised on Aruba. **Hooiberg** (Mount Haystack) looms out of the flat landscape of the interior to the northwest of Santa Cruz. A series of several hundred steps leads up to the 165m (541ft) peak, from where it is possible to see across to Venezuela.
Northwest of Hooiberg is the old town of **Seroe Patrishi** with historical graves dating as far back as the early 18th century. Further north is the town of **Noord**, noted for its **Church of Santa Anna**, the oldest church on Aruba, with its beautiful 100-year-old hand-carved oak altar. The road from Noord turns north to the California Lighthouse (see above). North from Santa Cruz, turning back towards the coast, the road to **Casibari** and **Ayo** passes spectacular boulders, the

result of some unexplained geological catastrophe. The road continues to the coast at **Bushiribana**, centre of the island's former gold-mining industry. Gold was discovered here in 1824 and actively mined until the beginning of World War I. Kettles and ovens used in the smelting process have been preserved. Gold was also mined at **Balashi** in the south.
OUTLYING ISLANDS: Surrounded by spectacular corals and sealife, including Aruba's colourful parrotfish, **De Palm Island** is a five minute ferry ride from the mainland and is a popular site for diving and snorkelling. Ferries depart Oranjestad daily (see *Travel – Internal* section for further details). **Windjammer** beach, on the right side of the island, is a good place to snorkel. Facilities on the island include snorkel and dive hire and several bars and restaurants. **SeaTrek** is a new underwater park where marine life can be viewed. The **Renaissance Aruba Resort & Casino** is a luxury resort located on an island privately-owned by Mariott Hotels, offering guests a private paradise hideaway. For more information contact Renaissance Aruba Resort & Casino, L.G.Smith Blvd 82, Oranjestad (tel: (58) 36000; fax: (58) 25317; website: www.mariott.com).

Sport & Activities

Watersports: Swimming is possible all year round, though the Atlantic side of the islands is often wild and treacherous. Swimmers are advised to ask their hotel about safety before swimming anywhere other than the main beaches, the best of which are on the southern coast, and include *Palm Beach, Eagle Beach, Druif Beach, Baby Beach* and *Rodgers Bay*. Every year in June, Aruba hosts the *Hi-Winds Amateur World Challenge* **windsurfing** tournament. For details, contact the Aruba Tourism Authority (see *Contact Addresses* section). Equipment hire and windsurfing lessons are widely available. **Surfing** is popular on the northern coast, particularly at *Dos Playa* and *Andicouri* beaches, which have the best waves, but surfers are warned to pay attention to the strong currents in the area. Aruba has over 40 **dive** sites with good visibility (often up to 30m/100ft) and a rich marine life (manta rays, barracuda and the green moray). Wall diving, coral reef diving and wreck diving are all available, with water temperatures averaging at around 28°C (82°F). Scuba-diving qualifications can be taken on the island; further details are available from the Aruba Tourism Authority, who also publish a brochure, *Discover Scuba in Aruba*. Some of the best **snorkelling** spots are off the beaches of *Arashi, Boca Grandi* and *Baby Beach*, though snorkelling is possible in many other places. Snorkelling gear can be hired from water-sports centres at hotels, many of which organise combined **sailing** and snorkelling day trips. **Water-skiing** and **jet-skiing** are available, but restricted to certain areas. There is good **deep-sea fishing** in the area with a choice of half- or full-day trips. For information, enquire at hotels or at the waterfront in Oranjestad. Moonlight, sunset, dinner or dancing **cruises** are also available. There are a variety of **underwater tours** available in glass-bottomed boats or on the Atlantis Submarine (website: www.atlantisadventures.com).
Golf: *Tierra del Sol*'s par-71 championship 18-hole course was designed by the Robert Trent Jones II Group, renowned for protecting the natural ecology of their sites. The course is located on the northwestern tip of the island, near the California Lighthouse and affords magnificent views. A 9-hole course is located at the *Aruba Golf Club*.
Other: Horseriding is a popular pastime and **riding trips** are available in the *Cunucu* (countryside) or along the coast. **Cycling** tours are popular, and **bicycle hire** is available throughout the island. The island also has a **bowling alley**, the *Eagle Bowling Palace*, located in Oranjestad. This is a modern 12-lane facility which includes a cocktail lounge and snack bar.

Social Profile

FOOD & DRINK: Not much food is grown locally, but the variety in the local cuisine is extensive. Aruban specialities include *stobà* (lamb or goat stew), *cala* (bean fritters), *pastechi* (meat- or cheese-stuffed turnovers), *ayacas* (leaf-wrapped meat roll) and *sopi di pisca* (fish chowder). There is a very wide range of international cuisine and several of the more famous fast-food chains have premises on the island.
NIGHTLIFE: There is one drive-in and one indoor cinema screening current American, European and Latin American films. The highlight of Aruba's nightlife, however, is the casinos, of which there are 11, open from 1100 until the early morning. It is possible to take a dinner cruise. There are several bars and discos in Oranjestad, as well as nightclubs offering revues and live music. Themed nights and limbo dancing are a local speciality.
SHOPPING: As a 'free zone', duty on most items in Aruba is so low that shopping here can have obvious advantages. Stores carry goods from all parts of the world and there are some excellent buys, including perfume, linens, jewellery, watches, cameras, crystal, china and other luxury items plus a range of locally made handicrafts. **Shopping hours:** Mon-Sat 0800-1800; some shops close for lunch between 1200-1400.
SPECIAL EVENTS: For a full list of special events contact the Aruba Tourism Authority (see *Contact Addresses* section). The following is a selection of special events occurring in Aruba in 2005:
Jan 1 *51st Carnival Celebration*, countrywide. **Jan 7** *Torch Parade* (floats, costumes and lights). **Feb 6** *Grand 51st Carnival Parade* (culmination of the annual carnival), Oranjestad. **Feb 7** *Carnival Monday/Old Mask Parade and Burning of King Momito.* **Mar 20** *20th International Half-Marathon.* **Apr 24-30** *15th Eagle International Bowling Tournament.* **May 25-30** *Soul Beach Music Festival 2005.* **Jun 26** *20th International Triathlon.* **Jul 1-16** *16th Heineken Music Festival.* **Aug 13-16** *International Pro-Am Golf Tournament.* **Oct 22-23** *KLM Open Tournament.* **Dec** *Christmas Bazaars.* **Dec 5** *St Nicolas Day.*
SOCIAL CONVENTIONS: Much of the social activity takes place in hotels where the atmosphere will be informal, often American in feel. The islanders do not wear shorts in town though it is acceptable for visitors to do so. Bathing suits are strictly for beach or poolside. In the evenings people tend to dress up, especially when visiting the casinos. Jackets are not required for men, except for official government functions. **Tipping:** Hotels add a 15 per cent service charge to any food or beverage bill. Restaurants may add 15 per cent service to the bill; if not, 10 to 15 per cent is normal. Taxi fares do not include tips, but there may be charges for luggage and tips are well appreciated.

Business Profile

ECONOMY: Between 1824 and 1916, the economy was based on gold mining. Subsequently, an oil refinery opened in the mid-1920s and, once among the largest in the world, was the most important commercial operation on the island until its closure in 1985. However, it was re-opened in 1990, under an agreement with an American operator to establish transhipment (mainly between Venezuela and the USA), storage and refining facilities. Oil has now reassumed its central position in the Aruban economy. In the meantime, a sizeable tourism sector grew up. More recently, Aruba has been joined by offshore service industries, including finance and data processing. The country's free-port status, ship bunkering and repair facilities are the island's other main sources of revenue. However, in June 2000, Aruba was identified by the Organisation for Economic Cooperation and Development (OECD) – the world's 30 largest economies – as one of 35 'tax havens' whose financial laws are believed to encourage large-scale tax evasion and money laundering. The government has since addressed most of the OECD's concerns.
Light industry is limited to the production of some tobacco products, drinks and consumer goods. Agriculture is confined to small-scale activity, because of poor soil quality. Aruba is classed as an Associate Overseas Territory of the European Union. The most important trading partners are the Netherlands, USA, Colombia and Venezuela.
BUSINESS: Office hours: Mon-Fri 0800-1700.
COMMERCIAL INFORMATION: The following organisation can offer advice: Aruba Chamber of Commerce and Industry, JE Irausquin Boulevard, PO Box 140, Oranjestad (tel: (58) 21566; fax: (58) 33962; e-mail: registers@arubachamber.com; website: www.arubachamber.com).
CONFERENCES/CONVENTIONS: Information can be obtained from the following organisation: De Palm Tours NV, L G Smith Boulevard 142, Oranjestad (tel: (58) 24400; fax: (58) 23012; e-mail: info@depalmtours.aw; website: www.depalm.com).

Climate

With a mean temperature of 28°C (82°F), this dry and sunny island is made pleasantly cool throughout the year by constant trade winds. Showers of short duration occur during the months of October, November and December.

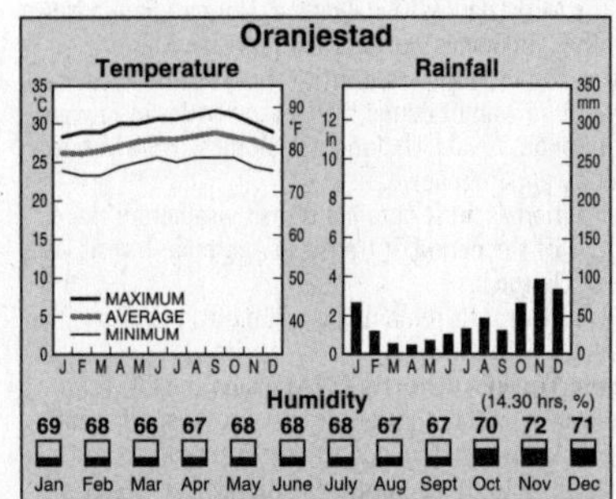

Australia

LATEST TRAVEL ADVICE CONTACTS

British Foreign and Commonwealth Office
Tel: (0870) 606 0290 Website: www.fco.gov.uk
US Department of State
Website: http://travel.state.gov/travel
Canadian Department of Foreign Affairs and Int'l Trade
Tel: (1 800) 267 8376 Website: www.dfait-maeci.gc.ca

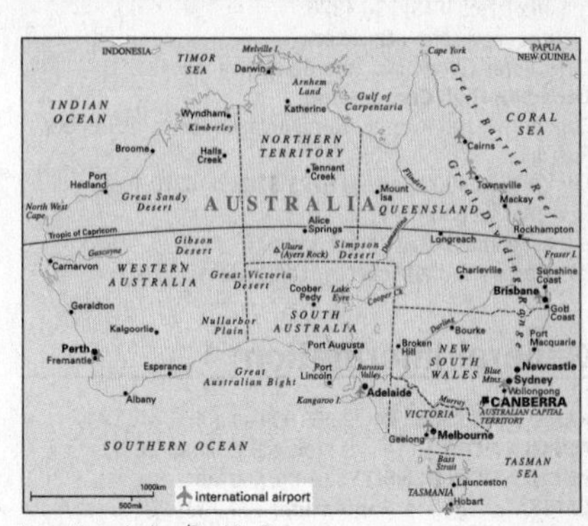

Location: Indian/Pacific Oceans.

Country dialling code: 61.

Note: Addresses of Tourist Representatives for individual States can be found at the head of each State entry.
Tourism Australia
Street address: Level 18, Tower 2 Darling Park, 201 Sussex Street, Sydney, NSW 2000, Australia
Tel: (2) 9360 1111 *or* 9361 1341 *or* 1215. Fax: (2) 9331 6469.
E-mail: corpaffairs@tourism.australia.com
Website: www.australia.com (consumer) *or* www.tourism.australia.com (corporate).
Australian High Commission
Australia House, The Strand, London WC2B 4LA, UK
Tel: (020) 7379 4334 *or* (09065) 508 900 (24-hr immigration and citizenship enquiries; calls cost £1 per minute).
Fax: (020) 7240 5333.
E-mail: firstenquiries.lhlh@dfat.gov.au
Website: www.australia.org.uk
Honorary Consulates in: Edinburgh and Manchester.
Tourism Australia
Gemini House, 10-18 Putney Hill, London SW15 6AA, UK
Tel: (020) 8780 2229 (trade enquiries only) *or* (0191) 501 4646 (brochure request line). Fax: (020) 8780 1496.
E-mail: info@tourism.australia.com
Website: www.australia.com
Opening hours: Mon-Fri 0900-1730.
British High Commission
Commonwealth Avenue, Yarralumla, Canberra, ACT 2600, Australia
Tel: (2) 6270 6666. Fax: (2) 6273 3236.
E-mail: bhc.canberra@uk.emb.gov.au
Website: www.britaus.net
Consular section: 39 Brindabella Circuit, Brindabella Business Park, Canberra Airport, ACT 2609, Australia
Tel: (1902) 941 555 (information line in Australia).
Fax: (2) 6257 5857.
Consulate in: Adelaide. *Consulates General in:* Brisbane, Melbourne, Perth and Sydney.
Embassy of the Commonwealth of Australia
1601 Massachusetts Avenue, NW, Washington, DC 20036, USA
Tel: (202) 797 3000 *or* (888) 990 8888 (visa information line; toll-free in the USA). Fax: (202) 797 3168.
E-mail: public.affairs@austemb.org
Website: www.austemb.org
Consulates General in: Atlanta, Chicago, Honolulu, Los Angeles, New York and San Francisco. *Honorary Consulates in:* Denver, Detroit, Houston and Miami.
All visa enquiries should be directed to the Embassy in Washington, DC or Consulate General in Los Angeles.
Tourism Australia
2049 Century Park East, Suite 1920, Los Angeles,

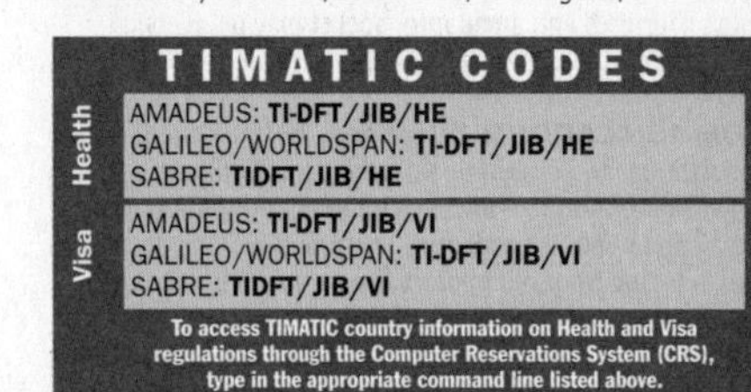

CA 90067, USA
Tel: (310) 229 4870. Fax: (310) 552 1215.
Website: www.australia.com

Embassy of the United States of America
Moonah Place, Yarralumla, ACT 2600, Australia
Tel: (2) 6214 5600. Fax: (2) 6214 5970.
E-mail: info@usembassy-australia.state.gov
Website: http://canberra.usembassy.gov
Consulates General in: Melbourne, Sydney and Perth.

Australian High Commission
50 O'Connor Street, 7th Floor, Suite 710, Ottawa, Ontario K1P 6L2, Canada
Tel: (613) 236 0841 *or* (888) 990 888 (visitor information; toll-free). Fax: (613) 236 4376.
Website: www.ahc-ottawa.org
Consulates General in: Toronto and Vancouver.

Canadian High Commission
Commonwealth Avenue, Yarralumla, Canberra, ACT 2600, Australia
Tel: (2) 6270 4000. Fax: (2) 6273 3285 *or* 6270 4060 (consular section).
E-mail: cnbra@dfait-maeci.gc.ca
Website: www.dfait-maeci.gc.ca/australia

General Information

AREA: 7,692,030 sq km (2,969,909 sq miles).
POPULATION: 19,546,792 (official estimate 2002).
POPULATION DENSITY: 2.54 per sq km.
CAPITAL: Canberra. **Population:** 309,900 (official estimate 1999).
GEOGRAPHY: Australia is bounded by the Arafura Sea and Timor Seas to the north, the Coral and Tasman Seas of the South Pacific to the east, the Southern Ocean to the south, and the Indian Ocean to the west. Its coastline covers 36,738km (22,814 miles). Most of the population has settled along the eastern and south-eastern coastal strip. Australia is the smallest continent (or the largest island) in the world. About 40 per cent of the continent is within the tropics and Australia is almost the same size as the mainland of the United States of America. The terrain is extremely varied, ranging from tortured red desert to lush green rainforest. Australia's beaches and surfing are world renowned, while the country is also rich in reminders of its mysterious past. These range from prehistoric Aboriginal art to Victorian colonial architecture. The landscape consists mainly of a low plateau mottled with lakes and rivers and skirted with coastal mountain ranges, highest in the east with the Great Dividing Range. There are rainforests in the far northeast (Cape York Peninsula). The southeast is a huge fertile plain. Further to the north lies the enormous Great Barrier Reef, a 2000km (1200 mile) strip of coral that covers a total area of 345,000 sq km. Although Australia is the driest land on Earth, it nevertheless has enormous snowfields the size of Switzerland. There are vast mineral deposits. More detailed geographical descriptions of each State can be found in the individual State entries.
GOVERNMENT: Constitutional Monarchy. Gained independence from the UK in 1901. **Head of State:** HM Queen Elizabeth II, represented locally by Governor-General Guy Stephen Montague Green since 2003. **Head of Government:** Prime Minister John Winston Howard since 1996. All individual States and Territories have their own autonomous legislative, executive and judicial systems (though certain powers remain under the jurisdiction of the Federal Government).
LANGUAGE: The official language is English. Many other languages are retained by minorities, including Italian, German, Greek, Vietnamese, Chinese dialects and Aboriginal languages.
RELIGION: 26 per cent Roman Catholic, 24 per cent Protestant and smaller minorities of all other major religions.
TIME: Australia spans three time zones:
1. GMT + 10 (GMT + 11 October to March, except Queensland).
2. GMT + 9.5 (GMT + 10.5 October to March, except Northern Territory).
3. GMT + 8.
Some States operate daylight saving time during the Australian summer. Clocks in these States are put forward by one hour in October and put back again in March.
ELECTRICITY: 220/240 volts AC, 50Hz. Three-pin plugs are in use, however sockets are different from those found in most countries and an adaptor socket may be needed. Outlets for 110 volts for small appliances are found in most hotels.
COMMUNICATIONS: Telephone: There are full facilities for national and international telecommunications. Full IDD is available. Country code: 61. Outgoing international code: 0011. Payphones are red, green, gold or blue. Only local calls can be made from red phones. Green, gold and blue phones also have International Direct Dialling (IDD) and Subscriber Trunk Dial (STD). The cost of a local phone call is 40c. Telstra Smart Phonecards are available at newsagents, supermarkets and chemists and can be bought in denominations of A$2, 5, 10 and 20 and used for local, STD or international calls. Creditphones, which take most major credit cards, can be found at airports, city-centre locations and many hotels. Multimedia payphones are available in parts of Sydney. A touch screen allows visitors to gain access to information services including tourist information which can be printed off for future reference. Phonecards for these telephones can be purchased from nearby shops. **Mobile telephone:** GSM 900 and 1800 networks in use. Network operators include *Vodafone* (website: www.vodafone.com.au), *Telstra* (website: www.telstra.com) and *Optus* (website: www.optus.net.au). Coverage extends to all major cities including good coverage in Tasmania; access in some of the more isolated, outback and rural areas is limited. US handsets are not compatible. **Fax:** Services are widely available from various retail outlets. Free collection by courier is available in Brisbane, Sydney, Melbourne, Perth and Adelaide. Fax number guides are available at post offices, and prices vary. Services are hard to find in the outback. **Internet:** Internet cafes are prevalent in all capital cities including over 24 outlets in Tasmania, and individual hotels may also provide facilities. ISPs include *Telstra BigPond* (website: www.bigpond.com), *Hunterlink* (website: www.pacific.net.au) and *Tassienet* for Tasmania (website: www.tassie.net.au). **Post:** There are post offices in all the main towns of every State. Opening hours are Mon-Fri 0900-1700. Some post office are also open Sat 0900-1200 . Stamps are often available at hotel and motel reception areas and selected newsagents. *Poste Restante* facilities are available at selected post offices throughout the country; mail is held for 30 days free of charge. **Press:** The main daily newspapers are *The Australian* and the *Australian Financial Review*. The weekly newspapers with the largest circulation are the *Sunday Telegraph* and the *Sunday Mail*. Newspapers generally have a high circulation throughout the continent.
Radio: BBC World Service (website: www.bbc.co.uk/worldservice) and Voice of America (website: www.voa.gov) can be received. From time to time the frequencies change and the most up-to-date can be found online.

Passport/Visa

	Passport Required?	Visa Required?	Return Ticket Required?
Full British	Yes	Yes	No
Australian	N/A	N/A	N/A
Canadian	Yes	Yes	No
USA	Yes	Yes	No
Other EU	Yes	Yes	No
Japanese	Yes	Yes	No

Note: Regulations and requirements may be subject to change at short notice, and you are advised to contact the appropriate diplomatic or consular authority before finalising travel arrangements. Details of these may be found at the head of this country's entry. Any numbers in the chart refer to the footnotes below.

Note: Australian visa regulations (including visa application charges) change from time to time. The information provided below is valid at the time of publication, but visitors should check that this information is still current by visiting the Department of Immigration online (website: www.immi.gov.au) *or* by calling the Australian Immigration and Citizenship 24-hour Information Service (tel: (09065) 508 900; calls cost £1 per minute).
PASSPORTS: Valid passport required by all.
VISAS: Required by all except the following:
(a) nationals of New Zealand;
(b) nationals of the following countries do not need to obtain a transit visa before travel if they are continuing their journey to a third country within eight hours of arriving in Australia: Andorra, Argentina, Austria, Belgium, Brunei, Canada, Denmark, Fiji, Finland, France, Germany, Greece, Hong Kong (SAR or BNO passport holders), Iceland, Indonesia, Ireland, Italy, Japan, Kiribati, Korea (Rep), Liechtenstein, Luxembourg, Malaysia, Malta, Marshall Islands, Mexico, Micronesia (Federated States of), Monaco, Nauru, The Netherlands, New Zealand, Norway, Papua New Guinea, The Philippines, Portugal, Samoa, San Marino, Singapore, Solomon Islands, South Africa, Spain, Sweden, Switzerland, Taiwan (if issued by the authorities in Taiwan), Thailand, Tonga, Tuvalu, UK (and its colonies), USA, Vanuatu, Vatican City and Zimbabwe.
All other nationals must obtain a transit visa before travel, irrespective of the period of transit in Australia. Transit visas are free of charge.
Note: Not all airports remain open all night; travellers should check with the airline.
Electronic Travel Authority (ETA) visas: The ETA is an electronically stored authority for travel to Australia that allows people from certain countries (see below) to visit Australia for up to three months for tourism, short-term business or elective study purposes. An ETA is *invisible* and therefore will not show up in your passport.
ETAs (Visitor and Business – Short Validity ETAs only) may, for some nationals, be obtained online from the main Department of Immigration and Multicultural and Indigenous Affairs (DIMIA; website: www.eta.immi.gov.au) *or* from over 10,000 travel agents and airline offices throughout the UK.
Please note, the Australian High Commission in London does not offer an automatic ETA service.
Only nationals of the following countries are eligible for an ETA: Andorra, Austria, Belgium, British Overseas Territories*, Brunei, Canada, Denmark, Finland, France, Germany, Greece, Hong Kong (SAR), Iceland, Ireland, Italy, Japan, Korea (Rep), Liechtenstein, Luxembourg, Malaysia, Malta, Monaco, The Netherlands, Norway, Portugal, San Marino, Singapore, Spain, Sweden, Switzerland, Taiwan*, UK, USA and Vatican City.
* Holders of these passports can only be processed for an ETA by external service providers if resident in, and applying in, their passport country.
Types of ETA and cost: *Tourist Visit/Business Visit (short-term)*: Free of charge; *Business Visit (long-term)*: £25.
Note: A service fee of A$20 is charged when applying for an ETA online through the DIMIA ETA website. Some travel agents and airlines issuing ETAs also charge a processing fee.
Validity of ETAs: *Tourist Visit* ETAs are valid for 12 months from date of issue (or until the passport expires, whichever comes first) and permit multiple entries into Australia for a stay of up to three months on each visit. *Short-term Business Visit* ETAs are valid for 12 months from date of issue (or until the passport expires, whichever comes first) for a single entry of up to three months. *Long-term Business Visit* ETAs are valid for 10 years (or the life of the passport) and permit multiple entries for a stay of up to three months for each visit.
Other types of visa and cost: Visitors not eligible for an ETA, or seeking a longer stay than an ETA offers, may apply for *Tourist Visit (Non ETA)* and *Temporary Business Short-stay* and *Temporary Business Long-stay (Non ETA)* visas. *Tourist Visit* and *Business Short-stay* visas cost £25; *Business Long-stay* visas cost £70.
Validity of non-ETA visas: For non-ETA visas, the validity varies according to the type of visa, the purpose of the trip and the validity of the passport. The validity will be stated on the visa label in your passport.
Application to: *ETA*: Authorised travel agents or airlines, by telephone or, in some cases, online through Australian Visas Ltd (see above). *Non-ETA*: Australian Embassies, High Commissions and Consulates; see *Contact Addresses* section. There is a new Tourist Short-Stay visa available online for passport holders of Cyprus, Czech Republic, Estonia, Hungary, Kuwait, Latvia, Lithuania, Poland, Slovak Republic, Slovenia and the United Arab Emirates.
Application requirements: *ETA*: (a) Valid passport. (b) Fee (if applicable). (c) Completed application form giving details of passport number and expiry date, airline, names of travellers etc (if applying by post). *Tourist Visitor (Non ETA)*: (a) Completed application form. Application forms for tourist and business visitor visas can be downloaded from the Department of Immigration (website: www.immi.gov.au). (b) An A4 stamped, self-addressed, registered envelope for return of passport. (c) Valid passport with two unused visa pages. (d) Fee (payable by credit card, cheque or postal order and made out to the Australian High Commission). (e) One or more recent passport photos as required. (f) Tourists over the age of 70 require a medical certificate. *Business Visitor (Non ETA)*: (a)-(e) and, (f) Applicant must provide proof of sponsorship and business interest. Business visa forms are also available from Australian Outlook, 3 Buckhurst Road, Bexhill on Sea, East Sussex TN40 1QF, UK.
Note: (a) Prior to lodging an application, visitors should confirm the current visa fees at www.immi.gov.au. (b) All travellers to Australia, except Australian citizens and permanent residents, must satisfy health and character requirements. (c) All travellers, including minors travelling on a parent's passport, require their own visa or ETA.
Working days required: *ETA*: When issued through DIMIA's ETA website (website: www.eta.immi.gov.au), or through travel agents or airline offices, ETAs are usually processed and valid immediately or within three working days. *Non-ETA*: 24 hours to three weeks. Processing may take even longer in busy periods.
Temporary residence: Applicants for temporary residence, working holidays and long-stay business visits to Australia should contact DIMIA online (website: www.immi.gov.au) *or* the High Commission online (website: www.australia.org.uk).

Money

Currency: Australian Dollar (A$) = 100 cents. Notes are in denominations of A$100, 50, 20, 10 and 5. Coins are in denominations of A$2 and 1, and 50, 20, 10 and 5 cents.

A B C D E F G H I J K L M N O P Q R S T U V W X Y Z

Currency exchange: Exchange facilities are available for all incoming and outgoing flights at all international airports in Australia. International-class hotels will exchange major currencies for guests. It is recommended that visitors change money at the airport or at city banks.
Credit & debit cards: American Express, Diners Club, MasterCard and Visa are accepted. Use may be restricted in small towns and outback areas. Check with your credit or debit card company for details of merchant acceptability and other services which may be available.
Travellers cheques: These are accepted in major currencies at banks or large hotels. However, some banks may charge a fee for cashing travellers cheques. To avoid additional exchange rate charges, travellers are advised to take travellers cheques in a major currency.
Currency restrictions: Export and import of coins/notes in Australian or foreign currency above A$10,000 must be declared to customs at the port of entry or departure. Export of local currency above A$2000 must have reserve bank approval.
Exchange rate indicators: The following figures are included as a guide to the movements of the Australian Dollar against Sterling and the US Dollar:

Date	Feb '04	May '04	Aug '04	Nov '04
£1.00=	2.39	2.53	2.57	2.40
$1.00=	1.31	1.42	1.39	1.26

Banking hours: Mon-Thurs 0930-1600, Fri 0930-1700. These hours may vary slightly throughout the country.

Duty Free

The following items may be taken into Australia by persons over 18 years of age without incurring customs duty:
250 cigarettes or 250g of tobacco or cigars; 1.125l of any alcoholic liquor; articles for personal hygiene and clothing, not including perfume or fur apparel; other goods to a value of A$400 (A$200 if under 18).
Prohibited items: There are very strict regulations against the import of non-prescribed drugs, weapons, firearms, wildlife, domestic animals and foodstuffs and other potential sources of disease and pestilence. There are severe penalties for drug trafficking. For further details on customs regulations, contact the information centre of the Australian Customs Service (tel: (2) 6275 6666 (from outside Australia) *or* (1 300) 363 263 (from anywhere in Australia); website: www.customs.gov.au). Customs information booklets can be obtained from the Australian High Commission or Embassy.

Public Holidays

2005: Jan 1 New Year's Day. **Jan 26** Australia Day. **Mar 25-28** Easter. **Apr 26** ANZAC Day. **Dec 25-26** Christmas.
2006: Jan 1 New Year's Day. **Jan 26** Australia Day. **Apr 14-17** Easter. **Apr 26** ANZAC Day. **Dec 25-26** Christmas.
Note: Nationwide holidays only. If these dates fall on a Saturday or Sunday, a day may be given in lieu. There are numerous individual State holidays – see individual state sections for details.

Health

	Special Precautions?	Certificate Required?
Yellow Fever	No	1
Cholera	No	No
Typhoid & Polio	No	N/A
Malaria	No	N/A

Note: *Regulations and requirements may be subject to change at short notice, and you are advised to contact your doctor well in advance of your intended date of departure. Any numbers in the chart refer to the footnotes below.*

1: A yellow fever certificate is required from travellers over one year of age arriving within six days of leaving or transiting countries with infected areas.
Food & drink: Standards of hygiene in food preparation are very high. Milk is pasteurised and meat and vegetables are considered safe to eat. Care should be taken, however, when sampling 'bush tucker' in outback areas as some insects and fauna are highly poisonous unless properly cooked.
Other risks: Occasional outbreaks of *dengue fever* and *Ross River fever* have occurred in rural areas in northern Australia in recent years. There have been reports of *Murray Valley encephalitis* in the Northern Territory. Corals, jellyfish and fresh water crocodiles may prove a hazard to the bather, and heat is a hazard in the northern and central parts of Australia. Insectivorous and fruit-eating bats have been found to harbour a virus related to the *rabies* virus and should be avoided. Venomous snakes and spiders exist throughout Australia and can be extremely dangerous. Medical assistance should be sought immediately if bitten.
Note: There are strict customs and health controls on entering and leaving the country, and Australian law can inflict severe penalties on health infringements. Australia reserves the right to isolate any person who arrives without the required certificates. Carriers are responsible for expenses of isolation of all travellers arriving by air who are not in possession of the required vaccination certificates. All arriving aircraft are sprayed before disembarkation to prevent the spread of disease-carrying insects.
Health care: Doctors and dentists are highly trained and hospitals are well equipped. There is a reciprocal health agreement with the UK, in emergencies only, which allows residents from the UK free hospital treatment. Passport or proof of UK residence, such as an NHS medical card or a UK driving licence, must be shown. Prescribed medicines, ambulances and treatment at some doctors' surgeries must be paid for. Personal insurance for illness and accidents is highly recommended for all visitors. Those wishing to benefit from the agreement should enrol at a *Medicare* office; this can be done *after* treatment.

Credit: © Northern Territory Tourist Commission

Travel - International

AIR: The national airline is *Qantas (QF)* (website: www.qantas.com.au). Approximately 30 international airlines fly to Australia.
Approximate flight times: From *London* to Adelaide is 24 hours 25 minutes, to Brisbane is 23 hours 25 minutes, to Cairns is 25 hours 45 minutes, to Darwin is 21 hours 25 minutes, to Melbourne is 23 hours, to Perth is 21 hours 50 minutes, to Sydney is 23 hours 30 minutes and to Townsville is 26 hours.
From *Los Angeles* to Sydney is 13 hours 30 minutes. From *New York* to Perth is 30 hours 10 minutes and to Sydney is 20 hours.
From *Singapore* to Sydney is eight hours and to Perth is five hours.
International airports: Adelaide, Brisbane, Cairns, Canberra, Darwin, Hobart, Melbourne, Perth and Sydney. All airports have a duty-free shop, bank/bureau de change, restaurant/bar, tourist information kiosk, car hire and taxi stand; these will almost always be available on arrival and departure of international flights.
Sydney Airport (SYD) (Kingsford Smith) (website: www.sydneyairport.com) is 8km (5 miles) south of the city (travel time – 30 minutes). *Airport Link* connects the airport to Sydney Central Station (travel time – 13 minutes). Coaches meet all incoming international and domestic flights, departing every 20-30 minutes. There are many courtesy guest shuttles; enquire at hotel when booking is made. The international terminal is separate from the domestic terminal. Passengers may be set down at city airline terminals and some city hotels, motels and guest houses on request. There are also buses and taxis.
Adelaide Airport (ADL) (website: www.aal.com.au) is 6km (4 miles) west of the city (travel time – 30 minutes). Coaches meet all international and domestic flights. Buses and taxis are available to the city and hotels. A new terminal is currently under construction.
Melbourne Airport (MEL) (Tullamarine) (website: www.melbourne-airport.com.au) is 22km (14 miles) northwest of the city (travel time – 30 minutes). Skybus Coach (24 hours) or taxis are available to the city centre. There are also regional bus links from the airport.
Perth Airport (PER) (website: www.perthairport.com) is 12km (7 miles) northeast of the city (travel time – 25 minutes). There are separate international and domestic terminals. Airport buses meet international and domestic flights. Taxis are available.
Brisbane Airport (BNE) (website: www.bne.com.au) is 13km (8 miles) northeast of the city (travel time – 35 minutes). Coach services are available to the city, Gold Coast, Sunshine Coast and major hotels. Coaches meet all international flights. A rail link between the airport and the city was introduced in 2001. Taxis are also available.
Darwin Airport (DRW) (website: www.darwinairport.com.au) is 13km (8 miles) northeast of the city (travel time – 20 minutes). Coaches and taxis meet all incoming international daytime flights.
Hobart Airport (HBA) (website: www.hobartairport.com) is 16km (10 miles) east of the city (travel time – 25 minutes). Coaches meet all incoming flights. Buses and taxis are available to the city. *Cairns Airport (CNS)* is 8km (5 miles) north of the city (travel time – 10 minutes). Coaches meet all incoming flights. There is also a shuttle taxi service, limousines, car hire and taxis.
Canberra Airport (CBR) (website: www.canberraairport.com.au) is 8km (5 miles) east of Canberra (travel time – 15 minutes). Taxis and shuttle buses are available to the city centre.
Boomerang Pass: For international travellers visiting Australia, certain airlines offer the *Boomerang Pass*, a zonal ticket permitting travel within Australia and to selected airports in Fiji, New Caledonia, New Zealand, Samoa, Solomon Islands, Tonga and Vanuatu. Participating airlines include *Air Pacific, Air Vanuatu, Australian Airlines, Polynesian Airlines* and *Qantas*. Passes must be purchased prior to arrival in Australia with a minimum of two passes per person. Nationals of countries in the South Pacific region are not eligible.
Departure tax: None.
SEA: Cruise liners dock at Sydney, Melbourne, Hobart, Perth (Port of Fremantle), Adelaide and Brisbane. International cruise lines calling at Australian ports include *Cunard, Norwegian Cruise Lines, Orient Lines, P&O, Princess Lines* and *Silver Sea*.

Travel - Internal

AIR: Australians rely on aviation to get from place to place as inhabitants of smaller countries rely on trains and buses. The network of scheduled services extends to more than 150,000km (95,000 miles) and covers the whole continent. Both first-class and second-class service is available, with meals and hostess service on many routes. Recent deregulation of Australia's domestic airlines means that flight services are more competitively priced. Aircraft can be chartered by pilots who pass a written examination on Australian air regulations and have their licences validated for private operations within Australia.
The major domestic airlines are: *Jetstar Airways* (website: www.jetstar.com.au), *Qantas* (website: www.qantas.com.au) and *Virgin Blue* (website: www.virginblue.com.au) which serve the major resorts and cities throughout Australia. In addition, *Rex Regional Express* (website: www.rex.com.au) operate throughout New South Wales, South Australia, Tasmania and Victoria; *Air North* (website: www.airnorth.com.au) operate throughout the Northern Territory; *Macair Airlines* (website: www.macair.com.au) operate throughout Queensland; *Skywest* (website: www.skywest.com.au) operate throughout Western Australia and several small airlines operate to the islands off Tasmania (see *Tasmania* section).
Nearly all the domestic airlines operate special deals or air-passes at greatly reduced prices.
Domestic airports: There are a great number of airports and landing strips throughout the country, including airports in all capital cities and regional centres such as *Alice Springs, Launceston* and *Uluru* (Ayers Rock). For further information contact the Tourism Australia (see *Contact Addresses* section).
SEA/RIVER: There are 36,738km (22,600 miles) of coastline and many lakes, inland waterways and inlets, all of which can be used for touring by boat. From paddle steamers along the Murray River to deep-sea fishing cruisers along the vast Barrier Reef, all are available for charter or passenger booking. Most tour operators also handle shipping cruises. The *Spirit of Tasmania* is an overnight car-ferry service linking Melbourne with Tasmania daily (website: www.spiritoftasmania.com.au).
RAIL: Over 40,000km (24,850 miles) of track cover the country. Due to the vastness of the country internal flights are a preferred option for travelling long distances, particularly as rail travel can be slow and relatively expensive. For further information on rail transport within the different States, see the individual State entries, or contact Rail Australia (website: www.railaustralia.com.au).
Two services span the continent from coast to coast. The twice-weekly *Indian Pacific* travels 4350km (2704 miles) on standard 1435mm (56.5-inch) gauge from Sydney on the east coast to Perth on the west coast, via Adelaide. The journey takes three days and three nights, crossing the Nullarbar Plain on the famous 478km (297 mile) stretch of straight track, the longest in the world. The *Ghan* travels 2979km (1891 miles) between Adelaide and Darwin, via Alice Springs. The service runs weekly in each direction and takes two nights. Both trains are fully air conditioned and soundproofed, with first- and second-class sleeping cars, a lounge car, bars and good restaurant facilities.
Other express service links (not always daily) from the state capitals are as follows:
The *Canberra Monaro Express* links Canberra with Sydney in four or five hours. The *XPT Express* runs from Melbourne

to Brisbane via Canberra and Sydney. The *Sunlander* and the *Queenslander* link Brisbane with Cairns (31 hours). The *Prospector* links Perth with Kalgoorlie and this is one of Australia's fastest trains (six to seven hours). The *Spirit of the Outback* runs Brisbane to Longreach via Rockhampton. There are also a number of scenic rail journeys available including the *Kuranda Scenic Railway* that links Cairns with Kuranda via a 34km (14-mile) climb through tropical rainforest; the *Great South Pacific Express* service along the East Coast from Sydney to Cairns via Brisbane has been temporarily suspended.
Several routes have motor-rail facilities. Long-distance trains are air conditioned and have excellent catering facilities and showers. Reservations for seats and sleeping berths are essential on all long-distance trains and are accepted up to six months in advance. **Luggage allowance:** All interstate rail passengers are allowed 50kg (111lb). Medium-sized suitcases and hand luggage can be placed in the passengers' compartments. Large suitcases must be carried in the guard's van and checked in 30 minutes prior to departure. **Sleeping berths:** Single and twin apartments are available for a surcharge on most inter-capital overnight services. All 'Twinettes' have two sleeping berths and wash basin. Twinettes are available either first-class or holiday-class; the first also offer individual showers. 'Roomette' (single compartment) cars have showers at the end of each car. These are first-class only. **Cheap fares:** Unlimited travel, valid for 14, 21 and 30 days, with seven day extensions available, is available with an *Austrailpass*, which must be purchased otside Australia, and can only be used by non-Australian passport holders. Only economy-class passes are available. Each State operator offers its own *Austrailpass* scheme. The *Austrail Flexi-Pass* is valid for eight, 15, 22 and 29 days within a six-month period, although it cannot be used on the *Ghan* or the *Indian Pacific*. The pass only offers economy-class accommodation. Both the *Austrailpass* and the *Austrail Flexi-Pass* must be purchased outside of Australia. The *East Coast Discovery Pass* offers six months' travel on the eastern coast. An *Austrailpass* does not include meal or sleeping berth charges. The passes must be used within 12 months of issue.
Representative in the UK: Rail Australia, c/o International Rail Limited, Chase House, Gilbert Street, Ropley, Hampshire SO24 0BY (tel: (0870) 751 5000; fax: (0870) 751 5005; e-mail: info@international-rail.com; website: www.international-rail.com). Most major tourist attractions can be reached by train; tickets for multiple destinations can be purchased from travel agents outside Australia.
ROAD: Traffic drives on the left. Road signs are international. The speed limit is 60kph (35mph) in cities and towns in most states but 50kph (31mph) in Victoria and Western Australia, 50kph/31mph in all suburban areas and 80-110kph (50-68mph) on country roads and highways unless signs indicate otherwise. Seat belts must be worn at all times and driving licences must be in the driver's possession when driving. Driving off major highways in the outback becomes more difficult between November and February because of summer rain, as many roads are little more than dirt tracks. Road travel is best between April and October. Distances between towns can be considerable, and apart from ensuring that all vehicles are in peak condition, it is advisable to carry spare water, petrol and equipment. Travellers are advised to check with local Automobile Associations before departure in order to obtain up-to-date information on road and weather conditions. Bicycle helmets must be worn by all cyclists.
Coach: Major cities are linked by an excellent national coach system, run by *Greyhound Pioneer* (website: www.greyhound.com.au). Tasmania also has its own coach service, *Tasmanian Redline Coaches* (website: www.redlinecoaches.com.au). There are numerous other companies operating State and Interstate services.
The main coach express routes are: Sydney to Adelaide, Melbourne (inland), Brisbane and Canberra; Canberra to Melbourne; Melbourne to Adelaide; Adelaide to Alice Springs, Perth and Brisbane; Darwin to Alice Springs, Cairns, Perth and Kakadu; Alice Springs to Ayers Rock; Cairns to Brisbane; Brisbane to Sydney (inland and coastal) and Melbourne.
Coach passes are available for travel on a variety of routes for between seven days and one year, such as the *All Australian*, the *Sunseeker*, the *Aussie Reef & Rock*, the *Coast to Coast* etc. The *Aussie Kilometre Pass* allows you to purchase your travel in kilometres and then travel in any direction on the national network to the distance purchased. It is advisable to purchase these passes before departure from country of origin.
Coaches are one of the cheapest ways to travel around Australia, as well as one of the most comfortable, with air conditioning, big adjustable seats and on-board bathrooms; some also have television and the latest videos.
Car Hire: Available at all major airports and major hotels to those over 21 years old. **Documentation:** An International Driving Permit is required by nationals of countries whose official language is not English. International, foreign or national driving permits are generally valid for three months. An International Driving Permit is only valid in conjunction with a valid national licence. Permits must be carried at all times while driving.
URBAN: Comprehensive public transport systems are provided in all the main towns. The State capitals have suburban rail networks, those in Sydney and Melbourne being particularly extensive, and trams run in Melbourne and Adelaide. Meter-operated taxis can be found in all major cities and towns. There is a minimum 'flagfall charge' and then a charge for the distance travelled. Taxi drivers do not expect to be tipped. A small additional payment may be required for luggage and telephone bookings. Some taxis accept payment by credit card. For further details, see individual State entries.
Travel times: The following chart gives approximate travel times (in hours and minutes) from **Sydney** to other major cities in Australia.

	Air	Rail	Coach
Canberra	0.45	4.00	5.00
Adelaide	1.40	25.00	22.00
Brisbane	1.20	15.00	15.00
Darwin	5.00	-	92.50
Melbourne	1.10	10.00	14.00
Perth	4.00	65.00	56.00
Hobart	2.05	-	-

Accommodation

HOTELS/MOTELS: Every State has a selection of hotels run by well-known and established international chains. More authentic accommodation can be found outside the cities. The smaller hotels are more relaxed, and offer more local flavour. The highways out of the State cities are lined with good quality motels offering self-contained family units, and often an in-house restaurant service.
Most hotels and motels provide rooms with telephones, private shower and/or bath, toilet, small fridge and tea- and coffee-making facilities. Check-out time is 1000 or 1100. Hotels/motels and motor inns have a licensed restaurant and a residents' bar; some may provide a public bar. Motels in rural areas will normally only be able to offer breakfast. Motor inns in rural areas will probably have a licensed restaurant, and possibly a residents' bar as well. Private hotels are not permitted to provide bars. The principal difference between a hotel and a motel in Australia is that a hotel must, by law, provide a public bar among its facilities. For this reason there are many motels which are hotels in all but name, offering an excellent standard of comfort and service but preferring to reserve their bar exclusively for the use of their guests, rather than for the public at large.
Grading: Hotels and motels in Australia are graded in a star rating system by the Australian Automobile Clubs. In most cases, different rooms will be offered at different rates depending on their size, aspect or facilities; this is particularly true of seafront hotels. In general, hotels in cities cost more than their rural counterparts. The fact that an establishment is unclassified does not imply that it is inferior, it may still be in the process of being classified. The following grading definitions are intended as a guide only and are subject to change:
5-star: International-style establishments offering a superior standard of appointments, furnishings and decor with an extensive range of first-class guest services including porterage and concierge. A variety of room styles and/or suites available. Choice of dining facilities, 24-hour room service and additional shopping or recreational facilities available; **4-star:** Exceptionally well-appointed establishments with high-quality furnishings and a high degree of comfort. Fully air conditioned. High standards of presentation and guest services provided. Restaurant and meals available on premises; **3-star:** Well-appointed establishments offering a comfortable standard of accommodation with above-average floor coverings, furnishings, lighting and ample heating/cooling facilities; **2-star:** Well-maintained establishments offering an average standard of accommodation with average furnishings, bedding, floor coverings, lighting and heating/cooling facilities; **1-star:** Establishments offering a basic standard of accommodation (simply furnished, adequate lighting) and resident manager. Motel units all have private facilities.
Note: Some hotels are graded with an additional open or hollow star. This indicates a slightly higher grade of facilities than the normal facilities for its classification. For more information on accommodation classification, contact the Australian Hotels Association, 24 Brisbane Avenue, Barton, ACT 2600 (tel: (2) 6273 4007; fax: (2) 6273 4011; e-mail: reception@aha.org.au; website: www.aha.org.au). Information is also available from the Australian Hotels Association, Level 5, 8 Quay Street, Sydney, NSW 2000 (tel: (2) 9281 6922; fax: (2) 9281 1857; e-mail: admin@aha-nsw.asn.au; website: www.aha-nsw.asn.au).
GUEST HOUSES/HOMESTAY/SELF-CATERING AND FARMSTAY HOLIDAYS: Service apartments and self-contained flats are available at main tourist resorts, especially along the east coast. Many of the less accessible areas have accommodation on farmsteads, from guest houses on the huge sheep stations to basic staff quarters on smaller arable farms, giving an insight into an alternative aspect of Australian life. There are many homes and farms which open their doors to foreign visitors and offer splendid hospitality. Bed & breakfast in private home accommodation is available throughout Australia, often at very low prices. Some companies offering budget bed & breakfast also offer tourist and general information services. For information on bed & breakfast accommodation, contact the Australian Bed & Breakfast Council (website: www.australianbedandbreakfast.com.au). Some hotels have self-catering apartments. For more information contact the Tourism Australia (see *Contact Addresses* section). Guest houses are not allowed to serve alcohol. **Grading:** Holiday units and apartments are classified according to a **5-star** system with criteria comparable to those for hotels and motels above.
COUNTRY PUB ACCOMMODATION: These offer drinks, meals and simple but comfortable accommodation for travellers. Pubs tend to be easy to find and advance reservations are not always necessary. However, standards may vary according to the type of pub and its location.
CAMPUS ACCOMMODATION: University colleges and halls of residence offer inexpensive accommodation for both students and non-students during the vacation periods (May, August and late November to late February).
CAMPING/CARAVANNING: Camping tours cover most of the country, especially the wilder areas. Participants generally join a group under an experienced guide team and everyone helps with cooking, washing, etc. All equipment and transport is supplied; some also provide portable showers. More rugged tours with Land Rovers are available, offering limited facilities, although company equipment is again provided with a driver/guide and cook. This can be one of the best ways to explore the Australian outback.
Campsite information is available from all major tourist centres. Camping is available in caravan parks, campsites, national parks and other areas. It is illegal to camp in undesignated areas.
With the constant threat of bushfire, a policy of 'no open fires' will sometimes be in force, especially during Fire Danger Season (Dec 1-Apr 30); check with local authorities for more information.
A number of companies can arrange **motor camper** rentals, with a range of fully-equipped vehicles. Full details can be obtained from the Tourism Australia (see *Contact Addresses* section). **Grading:** Caravan parks are classified according to a **5-star** system with criteria similar to those for hotels and motels above. Accommodation is also available at many of Australia's sheep stations.
YOUTH HOSTELS: Found throughout the country, but there are greater concentrations near cities and densely populated areas. Only YHA hostels meet Hostelling International standards. Further details may be obtained from the Australian Youth Hostel Association, National Office, PO Box 314, Camperdown, NSW 1450 (tel: (2) 9565 1699; fax: (2) 9565 1325; e-mail: yha@yha.org.au; website: www.yha.com.au). Other hostelling organisations in Australia include VIP Backpacker Resorts of Australia (with 130 hostels; website: www.backpackers.com) and Nomads (with 40 hostels; website: www.nomadsworld.com).

Resorts & Excursions

Australia's main tourist attractions are Sydney, the Great Barrier Reef, the Gold Coast of Queensland and Uluru (Ayers Rock), in the rugged outback of the Northern Territory. Other attractions in the continent range from the wild flowers of Western Australia to the vineyards of the Barossa Valley, and from Western Australia's ghost towns to the remarkable wildlife on the island of Tasmania. It is possible to visit the relatively undisturbed Aboriginal communities on Bathurst and Melville Islands, about 80km (50 miles) north of Darwin, providing valuable insights into the continent's ancient indigenous culture. The Australian coastline has thousands of miles of beautiful beaches. Information on resorts, excursions, places of interest, sports and activities within Australia is given under each individual State section.
NORFOLK ISLAND: Situated 1700km (1056 miles) off the east coast of Australia, Norfolk Island is not part of any State but is instead administered by the Australian government. The island is best reached by air from Sydney. Its history as one of the world's harshest penal colonies has left the island with some of Australia's finest Georgian colonial architecture.
Many of the island's small population are directly related to the mutineers of *HMS Bounty* who settled in the area. A variety of accommodation is available. There is excellent bushwalking and the island boasts 40 different plants and animals that are unique to the island.

Sport & Activities

The range of activity, adventure and special interest holidays is almost limitless. Detailed information is given under each individual State section. Below is a brief outline with practical information on some of the most popular sports and activities available in Australia. Further trade information can also be obtained via the Tourism Australia (website: www.australia.com).

Bushwalking: This is an Australian term coined in the 1920s to distinguish serious walkers from casual hikers. Australia's wilderness areas, national parks and vast tracts of sparsely populated countryside make bushwalking one of the country's most popular pastimes. Maps are widely available, either from the many guide books on offer or from State government offices. Fires are a threat during summer, and walkers must respect fire ban warnings. Outdoor clothing and equipment tends to be expensive. Each State and Territory has its own independent parks authority.

Self-drive tours: Three-quarters of Australia's land mass lies in the outback. 4-wheel-drive vehicles are a favourite means of transport and there are a number of scenic highways and roads leading to the often remote outback destinations. On such journeys, it is not unusual to drive for hours without seeing another person. It is advisable to take extra water and petrol in case of emergencies.

Diving: With 36,735km (22,826 miles) of coastline, Australia provides outstanding opportunities for watersports, particularly diving and **snorkelling**. The tropical waters along the 2500km (1500 miles) of the Great Barrier Reef and its multitude of tiny islands form one of the world's best known diving locations. Requirements for dive courses (which are widely available) vary from state to state, but generally, beginners must be at least 12 years of age and have a medical certificate of fitness in accordance with Australian standards. To obtain the basic scuba-diving qualification, visitors can participate in either a one-week full-time course or a two-week part-time course; tailor-made courses are also available. Certified divers must be able to produce their international certification card and log book for solo dives, unless they participate in fully supervised dives with a professional. For further information, contact Dive Directory, PO Box 5264, Cairns, Queensland 4870 (tel: (7) 4046 7304; fax: (7) 4031 1210; e-mail: info@dive-australia.com).

Fishing: The seas off the east coast are reputed to be one of the world's best game-fishing areas, and the waters off north Western Australia are also particularly abundant. The area north of Queensland is well-known for marlin fishing while the streams in the high country in New South Wales and Victoria are very good for trout. Newspapers and radio have comprehensive tide and fishing reports. Fishing licence requirements vary from state to state. For further information, contact the Australian Recreational and Sport Fishing Industry Confederation,
PO Box 854, Dickson ACT 2602
(tel: (2) 6257 1997; fax: (2) 6247 9314; e-mail: recfish@sportnet.com.au; website: www.recfishoz.com).

Surfing: There are surfing schools all over the country, offering instruction for beginners or advanced surfers. For details, contact Surfing Australia, PO Box 1613, Kingscliff, NSW 2487
(e-mail: crystalj@surfingaustralia.com; website: www.surfingaustralia.com).

Golf: Facilities are excellent and the settings often spectacular. For further details and a copy of the *Australian Golfers Handbook*, contact the Australian Golf Union, 153-155 Cecil Street, South Melbourne VIC 3205 (tel: (3) 9699 7944; fax: (3) 9690 8510; website: www.agu.org.au).

Skiing: Possible from May to mid-October in the mountainous areas of the southeast. The best skiing slopes are located on the eastern mountain ranges on the state borders of New South Wales and Victoria. For further information, contact Skiing Australia, Level 1, 1 Cobden Street, South Melbourne 3205
(tel: (3) 9696 2344; fax: (3) 9696 2399;
e-mail: info@skiingaustralia.org.au;
website: www.skiingaustralia.org.au).

Special interest holidays: A huge range of these are available – farming, flying and gliding, ballooning, cycling, rafting, pony trekking, gemstone fossicking, bungee jumping, camel treks, whale watching etc. For further details, see the individual State and Territory sections.

Credit: © Northern Territory Tourist Commission

Social Profile

FOOD & DRINK: There are numerous speciality dishes and foods including Sydney rock oysters, *barramundi* (freshwater fish), tiger prawns, macadamia nuts and *yabbies* (small freshwater lobsters). Beef is the most popular meat and lamb is also of a high quality. There is a wide variety of excellent fruits and vegetables. Service is European-style and varies from waitress and waiter service to self-service. Bistros, cafes, family-style restaurants and 'pub' lunches at the counter offer good food at reasonable prices. Some restaurants will allow guests to bring their own alcohol and are called 'BYO' restaurants. Australia also offers an enormous variety of cuisines, including Italian, French, Greek, Spanish, Chinese, Vietnamese, Malaysian, Thai, Japanese, Indian, African, Lebanese and Korean.
The major vineyards (wineries) are outside Perth, Sydney, Melbourne, Hobart, Canberra and Adelaide. The largest single wine-growing region is in the Barossa Valley, South Australia, two hours' drive from Adelaide, where high-quality red and white wines are produced. Most restaurants and hotels are licensed to serve alcohol; private hotels and guest houses cannot be licensed by law. Australian wines are good and inexpensive. Beer is served chilled. Licensing hours in public bars are 1000-2200 Mon-Sat, however most pubs are open until 2400; Sunday hours vary. Restaurants, clubs and hotel lounges have more flexible hours. Drinking age is 18 years or over.

SHOPPING: Special purchases include excellent local wines; wool, clothing, leather and sheepskin products; opal and other precious or semi-precious stones; and modern art sculpture and paintings. Exhibitions of bark paintings, boomerangs and other tribal objects are on view and for sale in Darwin, Alice Springs and the State capitals; many depict stories from the Dreamtime. Many cities and towns have small shops devoted to the sale of 'Australiana', where Australian souvenirs, ranging from T-shirts to boomerangs, can be bought. **Shopping hours:** Opening hours for most stores in the cities are Mon-Fri 0900-1730, Sat 0900-1700. Late-night shopping is available Friday to 2100 in Melbourne, Adelaide, Brisbane, Hobart and Darwin. Late-night shopping is available Thursday at the same times in Sydney, Canberra and Perth. Major stores in some states are open 1000-1600 Sunday. Corner stores, restaurants and snack bars are open in most cities until well into the night. For further information on shopping and trading, contact the ACT Office of Fair Trading (tel: (2) 6207 0400; fax: (2) 6207 0538; e-mail: fair.trading@act.gov.au; website: www.fairtrading.act.gov.au).

SPECIAL EVENTS: For a selection of festivals and special events occurring in each State and Territory throughout Australia consult the individual State and Territory sections.

SOCIAL CONVENTIONS: A largely informal atmosphere prevails; shaking hands is the customary greeting. Casual wear is worn everywhere except in the most exclusive restaurants, social gatherings and important business meetings. Most restaurants forbid smoking. **Tipping:** Not as common as it is in Europe and America nor is a service charge added to the bill in restaurants. 10 per cent for food and drink waiters is usual in top-quality restaurants, but is optional elsewhere. With taxis it is usual not to tip but round up the cost to the next dollar.

Business Profile

ECONOMY: Australia has a very diverse economy and a high standard of living. The service sector accounts for almost three-quarters of GDP, although other sectors of the economy contribute significantly to Australian export earnings. Approximately one-third of export earnings is derived from agricultural products, although the main agricultural industry, sheep farming, now appears to be in long-term decline. The other major export industry is mining; Australia has vast reserves of coal (of which it is now the world's leading exporter), oil, natural gas, nickel, zircon, iron ore, bauxite and diamonds, as well as uranium (Australian ore fuels many of the Western nations' nuclear power plants). Most Australian manufacturing is concentrated in processing of mineral products and in the iron, steel and engineering industries.
The country's service industries, which now account for the major part of the economy, have continued to grow, despite some damage in the wake of the 1997 Asian financial crisis, which severely affected many of Australia's major trading partners. The most important development in the economy in recent years has been a shift in trading patterns away from Britain and Europe towards the Pacific Rim – 60 per cent of Australian exports are now sold in that region. Australia's single largest trading partner is Japan, which takes approximately one-third of total exports, followed by the USA, South Korea, New Zealand, Singapore, Taiwan, China and then the EU nations (principally the UK and Germany). Japanese investment in Australia, particularly in property and tourist ventures, has reached the point where most of the eastern seaboard 'Gold Coast' is now Japanese owned. The Australian economy has continued to perform steadily during the last few years; annual growth in early 2004 was just over 3 per cent. Inflation and unemployment are stable at 3 and 7 per cent respectively.

BUSINESS: Suits are usually worn in Sydney and Melbourne. Brisbane business people may wear shirts, ties and shorts; visiting businesspeople should wear lightweight suits for the initial meeting. Prior appointments necessary. Punctuality is important. A great deal of business is conducted over drinks. Best months for business travel are March to November. **Office hours:** Mon-Fri 0900-1700.

COMMERCIAL INFORMATION: The following organisations can offer advice: Australia and New Zealand Chamber of Commerce UK, 30-35 Southampton Street, London WC2E 7HE, UK (tel: (020) 7379 0720; fax: (020) 7379 0721; e-mail: enquiries@anzcc.org.uk; website: www.anzcc.org.uk); *or* Australian Chamber of Commerce and Industry (ACCI), Commerce House, Level 3, 24 Brisbane Avenue, Barton, ACT 2600 (tel: (2) 6273 2311; fax: (2) 6273 3286; e-mail: acci@acci.asn.au; website: www.acci.asn.au); *or* International Chamber of Commerce, Level 3, 525 Collins St, Melbourne, VIC 3000 (tel: (3) 8608 2072; (3) 8608 2547).

CONFERENCES/CONVENTIONS: Tourism Australia is the first point of contact for information. There is also a nationwide organisation overseeing conference and convention activity throughout the country: Association of Australian Convention Bureaux (AACB), Level 2, 80 William Street, Sydney, NSW 2011 (tel: (2) 9360 3500; fax: (2) 9331 7767; website: www.aacb.org.au).

Climate

Australia is in the southern hemisphere and the seasons are opposite to those in Europe and North America. There are two climatic zones: the tropical zone (in the north above the Tropic of Capricorn) and the temperate zone. The tropical zone (consisting of 40 per cent of Australia) has two seasons, summer ('wet') and winter ('dry') while the temperate zone has all four seasons.

November-March: (spring-summer): Warm or hot everywhere, tropical in the north, and warm to hot with mild nights in the south.

April-September: (autumn-winter): Northern and central Australia have clear warm days, cool nights; the south has cool days with occasional rain but still plenty of sun. Snow is totally confined to mountainous regions of the southeast.

Note: For further details, including climate statistics, see under individual State entries.

Required clothing: Lightweights during summer months with warmer clothes needed during the cooler winter period throughout most of the southern States. Lightweight cottons and linens all year in the central/northern States with warm clothes only for cooler winter evenings and early mornings. Sunglasses, sunhats and sunblock lotion are recommended year round in the north of the country and during the summer months in the south.

Australian Capital Territory

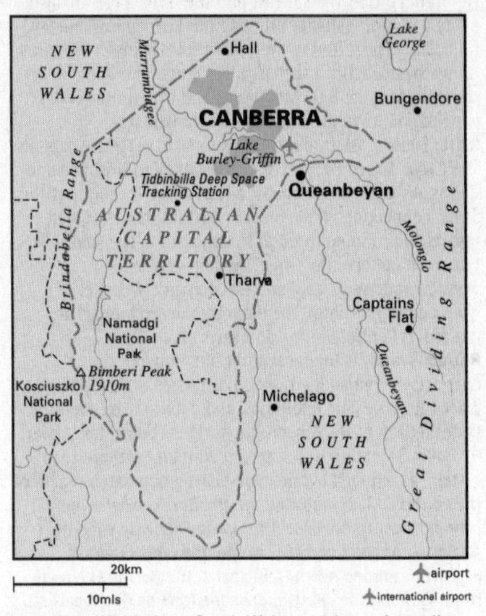

Location: Within New South Wales, southeast Australia.

Australian Capital Tourism
Street address: 5/2 Brindabella Circuit, Brindabella Business Park, Canberra International Airport, Canberra ACT 2609, Australia
Postal address: Locked Bag 2001, Civic Square, Canberra ACT 2608, Australia
Tel: (2) 6205 0666. Fax: (2) 6205 0629.
E-mail: visitcanberra@act.gov.au
Website: www.visitcanberra.com.au
Canberra and Region Visitors Centre
330 Northbourne Avenue, Dickson ACT, Australia
Tel: (2) 6205 0044. Fax: (2) 6205 0776.
E-mail: crvc@act.gov.au

General Information

AREA: 2400 sq km (1511 sq miles).
POPULATION: 310,800 (official estimate 2000).
POPULATION DENSITY: 131.7 per sq km.
CAPITAL: Canberra (also national capital). **Population:** 310,500 (official estimate 2000).
GEOGRAPHY: Canberra is located in the Australian Capital Territory on the western slopes of the Great Dividing Range, and was conceived in the early 1900s in order to create a capital city in a federal State separate from any of the uniting States. Spectacular green countryside is ringed by mountains nearly 600m (2000ft) above sea level. Lake Burley-Griffin, an artificial lake, is the main feature of this constantly expanding modern capital. Hills, trees and greenery remain prominent among the architecture of a city that is attractive, tidy, spacious and efficient as befits the national capital city.
TIME: GMT + 10 (GMT + 11 from last Sunday in August to last Saturday in March).

Public Holidays

The Australian Capital Territory observes all the public holidays observed nationwide (see the main Australia section) and, in addition, the following are observed:
2005: Mar 21 Canberra Day. **Jun 13** Queen's Birthday Celebrations. **Aug 1** Bank Holiday. **Oct 3** Labour Day.
2006: Mar 20 Canberra Day. **Jun 12** Queen's Birthday Celebrations. **Aug 7** Bank Holiday. **Oct 2** Labour Day.

Travel - International

AIR: Airlines serving Canberra include *Qantas, Regional Express* and *Virgin Blue. British Airways, Singapore Airlines* and *United Airlines* offer flights to Australia with connections through to Canberra.
International airports: *Canberra International Airport (CBR)* (website: www.canberraairport.com.au) is not an international point of entry to Australia but is linked to Sydney, Melbourne and Brisbane by convenient connections. Overseas visitors can book through one of the carriers listed above, changing aircraft after arrival in Australia. The city centre is 8km (5 miles) from the airport. Transport into the city is available by bus, taxi or rental car (travel time – 15 minutes).
RAIL: Through-trains run from Canberra to Sydney and Melbourne, with connections to other States. Economy *Austrailpass* tickets apply on both local and interstate systems, but must be purchased before travelling to Australia. For further information contact *Countrylink* (tel: (2) 6257 1576; fax: (2) 9224 4411; website: www.countrylink.nsw.gov.au). Other discount tickets include the *East Coast Discovery Pass*, which permits six months' one-way economy-class travel between main cities in the New South Wales area with unlimited stopovers. Prices depend on the route taken; see online (website: www.railpage.org.au) for more information.
ROAD: Coach: Main road links, which are used by coach services, connect Canberra to Sydney (travel time – four hours 15 minutes) and to Melbourne (travel time – seven hours 30 minutes), thereby allowing access to all other parts of the country. *All Australian* and other tickets apply. *Greyhound Pioneer* (website: www.greyhound.com.au) and *Murray's* (website: www.murrays.com.au) operate regular daily services from Canberra to Sydney, Adelaide and Melbourne.
URBAN: Bus: An internal bus network operates for the city of Canberra. Pre-purchase day tickets and 10-journey multi-tickets are available. There is a *City Sightseeing Bus* (double-decker) linking major attractions in the city that visitors can board or depart from at any point. **Taxi:** Radio-controlled, metered taxis are available at all hours.

Accommodation

For detailed information on accommodation in Canberra, contact the Canberra Accommodation Association (tel: (2) 6205 0044; fax: (2) 6273 2791; website: www.canberraaccommodation.com.au) *or* Canberra Getaways (tel: (2) 6205 0444) *or* Canberra Tourism & Events Corporation (see *Contact Addresses* section).
HOTEL/MOTEL: There is a wide range of accommodation in Canberra which boasts some of the most luxurious hotels in Australia, including well-known international chains. For those on a budget there are many well-located motels at reasonable prices.
BED & BREAKFAST: For more details, contact Canberra Tourism & Events Corporation (see *Contact Addresses* section).
SELF-CATERING: A wide range of apartments are available, many of which are serviced.
CAMPING/CARAVANNING: A number of companies can arrange motor camper rentals, with a range of fully equipped vehicles. Full details can be obtained from Canberrra Tourism & Events Corporation (see *Contact Addresses* section).
Note: For further coverage of the range of accommodation available, see *Accommodation* in the general *Australia* section.

Resorts & Excursions

CANBERRA

Canberra is an elegant city of wide streets, gardens and parkland. The **Old Parliament House** is impressive and complemented by its replacement, a grand modern edifice completed in 1988, Australia's bicentennial year. There are guided tours around Old Parliament House (home to the **National Portrait Gallery**) and the new **Parliament House**, where visitors can view both the Senate and House of Representatives. Parliament House also offers free guided tours daily where visitors can learn about the role and function of the Federal Parliament. The **Australian War Memorial** is deservedly one of the city's most popular attractions, and is the scene of the annual *ANZAC Parade*; it contains archives, galleries displaying relics, photographs and art. **Lake Burley Griffin**, a vast manmade waterway named after Canberra's architect, features prominently throughout the city area. Cruises and boating are popular. **Blundell's Cottage** (built 1858-60), which predates the lake, is a stone-slab construction calling to mind the location's earlier incarnation as a sheep station. The new, architecturally radical **National Museum of Australia** (located on the shores of the lake) displays a vast range of exhibits, chronicling Australian life from the first indigenous peoples through to modern times. It is a further cultural addition to the present **National Gallery of Australia**, **National Library of Australia** and **National Science and Technology Centre (Questacon)**. The **Australian Institute of Sport** offers guided tours by elite athletes and the interactive **Sportex Centre** with facilities for virtual rowing and virtual golfing. Some of Australia's deadliest and most colourful reptiles can be seen at Canberra's **Australian Reptile Centre**. The centre is open daily and, apart from the permanent displays, features special exhibitions. The **National Archives of Australia** hold archive material and Commonwealth records from Federation Day to the present. The Archives also feature special exhibitions and are open daily.
BEYOND CANBERRA: There are several hills in the immediate area of Canberra; from the 195m (650ft) **Telstra Tower**, topping the 825m high (2750ft) **Black Mountain**, there is an excellent view of the area for those who do not get dizzy in revolving restaurants (meal optional). Hot-air ballooning trips provide other ways of taking in the view. **Glenloch Sheep Station**, located in Belconnen on the outskirts of Canberra, is a popular tourist attraction. Activities include sheep shearing, boomerang throwing and sheep-dog demonstrations, rounded off with a traditional Australian barbecue lunch. The **Canberra Deep Space Communications Complex**, 40km (25 miles) southwest of Canberra, contains a collection of space models and memorabilia (including a sizeable piece of the moon) and interactive exhibits covering 40 years of space exploration. The **Snowy Mountains** are to the south of Canberra, in New South Wales, and provide excellent opportunities for winter skiing and summertime pursuits such as bushwalking, horseriding and watersports. Organised trips from Canberra are available; for details, contact the Canberra Tourism & Events Corporation (see *Contact Addresses* section).

NATIONAL PARKS & NATURE RESERVES

Approximately half of Australian Capital Territory consists of nature reserves and national parks. Just 40km (25 miles) southwest of the capital, the **Tidbinbilla Nature Reserve** in Tharwa, near the Canberra Deep Space Communications Complex, features a wealth of Australian fauna and wildlife in a natural bush setting. The park is open daily and a number of bushwalking trails are provided where visitors can observe kangaroos, wallabies, koalas, platypus, bush birds and water birds in their natural habitat; visitors are able to watch native birds being fed.
Further south is the **Namadgi National Park**, which is part of the Snowy Mountains and offers spectacular views and walking tracks. The park contains a number of prehistoric sites with Aboriginal rock paintings as well as a variety of rare sub-alpine species of flora and fauna.
The **Jerrabomberra Wetlands**, a well-known bird and wildlife sanctuary, are situated on the edge of **Lake Burley Griffin**. During drought in inland Australia, the wetlands, one of the most important bird habitats in the region, become a refuge for large numbers of water birds from surrounding areas. The **Murrumbidgee River** flows from the mountains in the south through the ACT; the **Murrumbidgee River Corridor** is a designated park area, popular for picnicking, walking and horseriding.
For further information contact the Environment ACT helpline (tel: (2) 6207 9777; website: www.environment.act.gov.au) *or* Environment Australia, GPO Box 787, Canberra, ACT 2601 (tel: (2) 6274 1111; fax: (2) 6274 1666; website: www.ea.gov.au).

Sport & Activities

Outdoor activities: The parks and nature reserves offer excellent facilities for **bushwalking**, **fishing** and **rock climbing**; the trails provided allow visitors to observe native animals and plants. A number of companies organise **whitewater rafting** trips (from one to four days) to the *Upper Murray*, *Murrumbidgee*, *Goodradigbee* and *Cottor* rivers. **Skiing** and cross-country skiing are possible during winter in the mountainous regions, particularly in the Snowy Mountains in the neighbouring State of New South Wales; trips from Canberra can be arranged.
Golf: Canberra has 9 golf courses open to visitors. The *Royal Canberra Golf Club*, located on the shores of Lake Burley Griffin, is ranked amongst the top 10 courses in Australia; visitors wishing to play must be guests of members or members of recognised golf clubs with a current handicap and a letter of introduction; booking is essential.
The *Federal Golf Club* features views to the Brindabella mountain ranges. The 41-year-old *Yowani Country Club* has a tree-lined course with extensive fairways and greens. The *Gold Creek Country Club*, Canberra's most popular course, designed by Bruce Devlin, hosts international championships and is Canberra's most popular public course. *Gungahlin Lakes* course is in a beautiful setting. The *Murrumbidgee Golf Club* offers a par 72 championship course in a country setting. The *Woodhaven Green Golf Course*, a 27-hole public course, has been established for 20 years.
Special interest holidays: There are over 20 cool-climate **wineries** located within 10-40 minutes' drive of the capital. In Canberra, special **balloon trips** are available to visitors wishing to see the city by air; spectacular displays of balloons can also be seen at the *Balloon Fiesta* held during the annual *Canberra Balloon Fiesta* (see *Social Profile* section).
Guided tours to working sheep properties, with demonstrations of **sheep-mustering**, **sheep-shearing** and even **boomerang-throwing**, are also available. For details, contact the Canberra Tourism & Events Corporation (see *Contact Addresses* section).

A B C D E F G H I J K L M N O P Q R S T U V W X Y Z

Social Profile

FOOD & DRINK: Restaurants and hotels serve trout from the streams and lakes of the Snowy Mountains. Beef and lamb come from the farmlands surrounding Canberra. The variety of cuisine available in Canberra is impressive, with over 300 restaurants offering food from all corners of the world, from Austria to Zanzibar.
NIGHTLIFE: Despite the daytime orderliness, nightlife is actively promoted by the large range of pubs, restaurants, nightclubs, acoustic venues and jazz, piano and wine bars. There are many film shows and a boutique casino.
SHOPPING: A wide range of goods, including Australian arts and crafts, is available from department stores and specialist shops. Galleries and museums are often open outside normal trading hours. **Shopping hours:** Opening hours for most stores in the city are 0900-1730 Mon-Wed and Fri, 0900-2100 Thurs, 0900-1700 Sat.
SPECIAL EVENTS: For further details of special events taking place in Canberra, contact Canberra Tourism & Events Corporation (see *Contact Addresses* section). The following is a selection of special events occurring in the Australian Capital Territory in 2005:
Jan 26 *Australia Day Tribute Performance.* **Feb 10-20** *National Multicultural Festival.* **Feb 19** *Canberra Symphony Orchestra Annual Prom.* **Feb 25-27** *Royal Canberra Show.* **Feb 27** *Tropfest*, short film festival. **Mar 12-21** *Canberra Balloon Fiesta.* **Mar 13** *Shannon's Wheels Expo.* **Apr 8-17** *Canberra & Region Heritage Festival.* **Apr 9-10** *Canberra Marathon.* **Apr 25** *Anzac Day*, Campbell. **Apr 28-Jun 8** *11th Canberra International Chamber Music Festival.* **May 2-15** *Innovation Festival*, showcasing the latest in technology and design. **Jul 15-Oct 9** *National Sculpture Prize & Exhibition.* **Aug 13-24** *Australian Science Festival*, Canberra. **Sep 17-Oct 16** *Floriade, Australia's Celebration of Spring*, Acton. **Nov 8-18** *Vintage Cellars National Wine Show of Australia*, Mitchell.

Business Profile

COMMERCIAL INFORMATION: The following organisation can offer advice: ACT & Region Chamber of Commerce & Industry, 12A Thesiger Court, Deakin, Canberra, ACT 2600 (tel: (2) 6283 5200; fax: (2) 6282 2436; e-mail: chamber@actchamber.com.au; website: www.actchamber.com.au).
CONFERENCES/CONVENTIONS: The National Convention Centre in Canberra has seating facilities for 2500. Other major convention centres include Australian Institute of Sport, Rydges Capital Hill and Parkroyal Canberra. For more information on conferences and conventions in Australian Capital Territory, contact the Canberra Convention Bureau Inc, Suite 405, Level 4, Optus Centre, 10 Moore Street, Canberra, ACT 2600 (tel: (2) 6247 7500; fax: (2) 6247 8155; e-mail: enquiry@canberraconvention.com.au; website: www.canberraconvention.com.au).

Climate

Warm during the summer months with cool, crisp and clear winters. Rainfall occurs throughout the year. Canberra averages more hours of sunshine per year than any other capital city in Australia.

Required clothing: Lightweights during summer months with warmer mediumweight clothes necessary in winter. Waterproofing advisable throughout the year, especially in winter. A top coat is necessary during winter months.

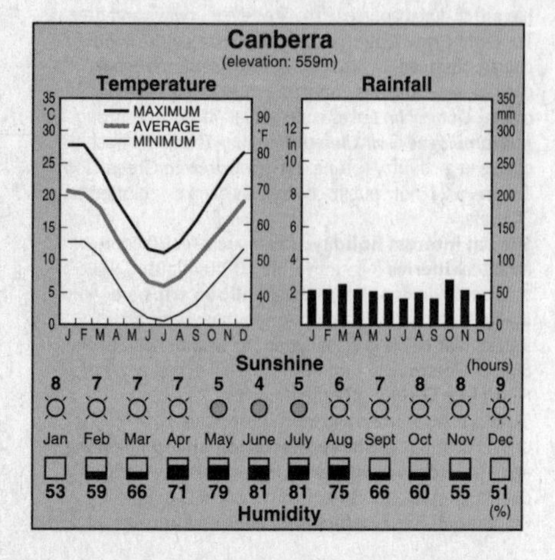

New South Wales

Location: Southeast Australia.

Tourism New South Wales
Street Address: Tourism House, Level Two, 55 Harrington Street, The Rocks, Sydney, NSW 2000, Australia
Postal Address: GPO Box 7050, Sydney, NSW 2001, Australia
Tel: (2) 9931 1111. Fax: (2) 9931 1424.
E-mail: visitor.callcentre@tourism.nsw.gov.au
Website: www.sydneyaustralia.com *or* www.tourism.nsw.gov.au (corporate site).
Tourism New South Wales
2nd Floor, Australia Centre, The Strand, London WC2B 4LG, UK
Tel: (0906) 863 3235 (brochure request line; calls cost 60p per minute) *or* (020) 7887 5003 (travel trade only).
Fax: (020) 7836 5266.
E-mail: london@tnsweurope.com
Website: www.sydneyaustralia.com
Provides trade and media marketing information only.
Sydney Convention & Visitors Bureau
c/o Axis Sales and Marketing, 421A Finchley Road, London NW3 6HJ, UK
Tel: (020) 7431 4045. Fax: (020) 7431 7920.
E-mail: sydney@axissm.com Website: www.scvb.com.au
The office provides information on conferences and incentives only.

General Information

AREA: 801,640 sq km (309,417 sq miles).
POPULATION: 6,463,500 (official estimate 2000).
POPULATION DENSITY: 8.1 per sq km.
CAPITAL: Sydney. **Population:** 4,085,600 (official estimate 2000).
GEOGRAPHY: The landscape ranges from the subtropical north to the Snowy Mountains in the south, which contain Australia's highest point, Mount Kosciuszko. There are over 1300km (800 miles) of coastline with golden beaches and picturesque waterways and rivers, including the 1900-km (1200-mile) Murray River.
TIME: GMT + 10 (GMT + 11 from last Sunday in October to first Saturday in March) except in the Broken Hill Area which keeps GMT + 9.5.

Public Holidays

New South Wales observes all the public holidays observed nationwide (see the main Australia section) and, in addition, the following are observed:
2005: Jun 13 Queen's Birthday Celebrations. **Oct 3** Labour Day.
2006: Jun 12 Queen's Birthday Celebrations. **Oct 2** Labour Day.
Note: The first Monday in August is also a public holiday in some parts of the state.

Travel - International

AIR: Sydney is an international gateway to Australia, and international flights from Europe, New Zealand, Asia, Africa and the Americas all serve the city. The main domestic airlines operating in New South Wales are: *Aeropelican Air Services, Air Link, Eastern Australian, Jetstar, Qantas, Rex – Regional Express, Sunshine Express* and *Virgin Blue*.
Approximate flight times: From Sydney to *Bangkok* is nine hours, to *London* is 25 hours, to *Los Angeles* is 13 hours 30 minutes, to *New York* is 21 hours 30 minutes, to *Paris* is 23 hours and to *Singapore* is eight hours.
International airports: *Sydney (SYD)* (website: www.sydneyairport.com.au) is Sydney's international airport; it is 8km (5 miles) from the city centre; travel time – 10 minutes by rail link or 20-30 minutes by car. For more information, see *Travel – International* in the main *Australia* section.
SEA: Sydney is a major international port, and cruise lines call from Europe, the Far East and the USA. There are also many day- and half-day cruises from Sydney Harbour (Circular Quay), offering everything from sightseeing tours to nearby attractions such as wildlife and aboriginal communities, the Blue Mountains and the Hunter Valley wine region, to night-time cabaret showboats.
RAIL: Sydney has through-trains to all other State capitals. The *Great South Pacific* connects Sydney to Brisbane and Cairns. An internal system of railways runs throughout the State, connecting all the most important towns, tourist resorts and running through to Canberra in the south. The two main rail operators are *Cityrail* (website: www.cityrail.nsw.gov.au) and *Countrylink* (website: www.countrylink.info). The main train interchanges are located at Central Station and Town Hall.
ROAD: Sydney is the focal point of a network that connects every major city. Road distances from many places, however, are enormous, and a journey by even the fastest coach to Darwin, on the northern coast, takes over 92 hours. The State is well served with an excellent road system, as required by the most heavily populated region of the country. Main highways are the *Barrier Highway*, running west to Adelaide, the *Hume Highway* running south to Canberra and Melbourne, the *New England Highway* running north to Brisbane, the *Pacific Highway* running along the coast to Brisbane (one of Australia's most popular touring routes), the *Princess Highway* running south along the coast to Melbourne, and the *Mitchell Highway* running northeast to Charleville and connecting with the routes to Mount Isa and Darwin in the north. The State is well served by national coach operators and regional bus lines.
URBAN: Sydney's extensive electrified suburban **rail** network includes a city-centre underground link, lightrail and a monorail link. The monorail runs in a loop, linking Darling Harbour and various tourist attractions. Lightrail services run from Sydney Central through Chinatown, Darling Harbour and other sights to Star City and Wentworth Park. There are also **bus** and **ferry** services (see the official bus and ferry website: www.sydneybuses.nsw.gov.au). Weekly and other period passes are available, as are multi-journey tickets. The *Sydney Explorer Bus* stops at over 20 attractions on its route and visitors can join or leave it at any point.
Discount travel tickets: There is a wide variety of saver passes for transportation to a range of tourist attractions. A special *Sydney Pass*, valid for three, five or seven days, offers unlimited travel on Sydney's public transport including sightseeing tours, *Sydney Ferries'* harbour cruises, *Manly Ferry, JetCat* and *RiverCat* services, the *Sydney, Bondi* and *Bay Explorer* buses and return travel to the airport. Prices start at A$100 for an adult three-day pass. Other passes include *Sydney/Bondi Explorer Ticket, Sydney Bonus Ticket, See Sydney and Beyond Pass* and *Sydney YES ticket*. For more information contact Tourism New South Wales (see *Contact Addresses* section).
Meter operated **taxis** service all major cities and towns. Taxi ranks can be found at transport terminals, major hotels and shopping centres or they can be hailed in the street.

Accommodation

HOTELS: Sydney offers an excellent choice of hotels for all budgets and tastes. They range from 5-star international chains to smaller hotels and budget backpacker-style hostels. Further outside the city, visitors can stay on one of the sheep stations to the west of the capital amongst some of the best sheep country in the world. The State is well travelled by Australians themselves, and so offers an excellent network of accommodation outside the larger cities, mostly of motel or similar class.
CAMPING/CARAVANNING: A number of companies can arrange motor camper rentals, with a range of fully-equipped vehicles. Contact Caravan and Camping Industry Association (NSW) PO Box H114, Harris Park, NSW 2150 (tel: (2) 9637 0599; fax: (2) 9637 0299; website: www.caravanaustralia.com.au) for further details.
Note: For further coverage of the range of accommodation available, see *Accommodation* in the general *Australia* section.

Resorts & Excursions

New South Wales is perhaps the most varied of all the States. The landscape ranges from snow-capped mountains with excellent skiing facilities to long, golden sandy beaches, and from the utter emptiness of the Outback to the cosmopolitan vitality of the State capital, Sydney.

SYDNEY

The State capital is perhaps best known abroad for the **Sydney Opera House** on Bennelong Point, a building

whose distinctive shape is echoed by the sails of the boats in the almost equally famous **Sydney Harbour**. Tours of the Opera House are available daily (0830-1700), except Christmas Day and Good Friday. The Opera House hosts many of Australia's opera, ballet and theatre companies and symphony orchestras. Sydney is also a major commercial and business centre with first-class conference and exhibition facilities. The city-centre skyline rivals that of Manhattan, with the added attraction that Sydney is far more likely to be seen under a clear blue sky. There is a spectacular view of the city and its surroundings from the 305m-high (1000ft) **Sydney Tower** above the **Centrepoint Shopping Complex** (daily 0900-2145). The city has a great number of concert halls, museums, art galleries and theatres. Among the many other interesting sights Sydney has to offer are the **Harbour Bridge** (the third-longest single span bridge in the world), **Taronga Zoo**, the **Royal Botanic Gardens**, the **Art Gallery of New South Wales** and the **Australian Museum**. **The Rocks** area (the site of Australia's first European settlement) has been largely restored to its original state and features cobbled streets, gas lamps, craft shops and small restaurants. This district of the city also contains one of Sydney's oldest buildings, **Cadman's Cottage** (1816), as well as the 'Lord Nelson' and the 'Hero of Waterloo', the city's oldest pubs. Tours around **Olympic Park** – venue of the 2000 Olympic Games – have become a popular visitor attraction, and include a visit to the **Olympic Village**.
Apart from exploring various quarters such as **Chinatown**, **Paddington** and **Kings Cross** on foot, there is **Darling Harbour**, one of Sydney's newest precincts, which is a five-minute monorail ride from the city centre. This bustling area contains numerous attractions including the **Harbourside Shopping Centre**, **Gavala Aboriginal and Cultural Education Centre**, **Panasonic IMAX Theatre**, the **Chinese Garden**, the **Powerhouse Museum** (design and science), the **National Maritime Museum**, **Cockle Bay Wharf** and the **Sydney Aquarium**. The city can also be enjoyed from the water, with harbour cruises departing from **Circular Quay**.
Other ways of seeing the city are from the bright red *Sydney Explorer Bus* which stops at 26 popular tourist spots on its 36km (22-mile) loop around the city, from the monorail train, or from a scenic flight aboard a seaplane or helicopter. The city has many beautiful green spaces including **Hyde Park**, **The Domain** and **Centennial Park** as well as the stunning **Botanic Gardens** with views of the Bridge, Opera House and Harbour. Sydney is also justly famous for its many excellent beaches in and around the city, such as **Manly**, on the north shore (15 minutes by JetCat), or **Bondi**, **Watson's Bay**, **Bronte**, **Clovelly** or **Coogee** to the south. Most beaches are within reach of public transport. For reasons of safety, people should swim in the areas marked with flags only. **Botany Bay**, the first foothold of British settlers, is still a botanist's delight with mangrove swamps and native wildlife as well as museums and picturesque walks.

BEYOND SYDNEY

New South Wales caters for all kinds of holiday, whatever the time of year. Visits to the **Hunter Valley** wine district and the **Blue Mountains** (a World Heritage Listed National Park), to the west of Sydney, are highly recommended. Home to famous wine makers such as *Wyndham Estate*, *Rosemount* and *McGuigans*, the Hunter Valley has over 80 wineries and many restaurants. Nearby **Port Stephens** is a great spot for watersports and dolphin and whale watching. **Lightning Ridge**, to the northwest, is a frontier town where the world's only source of black opal is to be found. The region of the Snowy Mountains in the southeast of the State, including **Mount Kosciuszko**, Australia's highest peak, is popular during the skiing season (June-October) as well as in summer for bushwalking. Resorts in the Snowy Mountain region include **Thredbo** and **Perisher Blue**, the latter incorporating **Guthega**, **Perisher Valley**, **Blue Cow** and **Smiggins**.
Uncommercialised and unpretentious, **Broken Hill** and the surrounding national parks of the New South Wales outback offer a taste of the original Australian wilderness. Featuring ancient landscapes, aboriginal culture and unusual flora and fauna, they are among the hightlights of the region. The **Menindee Lakes**, 113km (70 miles) from the town by a good road, cover an area of water eight times the size of Sydney Harbour with an abundance of birdlife and provide a major attraction for motor boat and sailing craft owners.

WORLD HERITAGE REGIONS

Areas listed according to the World Heritage Convention are internationally recognised as cultural and natural places of such outstanding value that they ought to be preserved for the benefit of humanity. Natural World Heritage areas often represent an important stage in the Earth's evolutionary history. For further information contact the Australian Heritage Council, GPO Box 787, Canberra, ACT 2601 (tel: (02) 6274 1111; fax: (02) 6274 2095; website: www.ahc.gov.au). New South Wales has several major World Heritage listed regions as outlined below (additional World Heritage areas are indicated in the *National Parks* section).
LORD HOWE ISLAND GROUP: This island group is situated 700km (400 miles) northeast of Sydney, covering 146,300 hectares (361,520 acres) and comprising **Lord Howe Island**, the **Admiralty Islands**, the **Mutton Bird Islands** and **Ball's Pyramid**. Lord Howe Island consists of rich lowland and mountains covered with lush vegetation, surrounded by white sandy beaches. **Mount Gower** and **Mount Lidgbird** (875m/2695ft and 777m/2394ft respectively) are both of volcanic origin and provide a stark contrast to the low-lying areas along the coast. Lord Howe Island has the southernmost coral reef in the world and boasts some of the rarest flora, bird and marine life. Owing to a strict conservation policy, the number of visitors on the island at any one time is limited to 393 and the number of cars is also restricted. The bicycle is the main mode of transport.
WILLANDRA LAKES REGION: This region covers 370,000 hectares (913,000 acres) of semi-arid country in the southwest centre of New South Wales and is renowned as one of the world's earliest known cremation sites; the archaeological discovery of skeletal remains and stone tools indicated that *homo sapiens* inhabited the area 40,000 years ago. The region also contains a system of Pleistocene lakes formed over the last two million years, most of which are fringed on the eastern shore by dunes. The area incorporates the **Mungo National Park**, which is open to visitors daily. The park offers good opportunities for walks along the famous **Walls of China**, orange-and-white dunes, as well as many native species of birds and animals.

NATIONAL PARKS

For further information about parks and nature reserves in New South Wales contact NSW National Parks Centre, 102 George Street, The Rocks, Sydney, NSW 2000 (tel: (2) 9253 4600 *or* (1300) 361 967 (in Australia only); fax: (2) 9251 9192; e-mail: info@npws.nsw.gov.au; website: www.nationalparks.nsw.gov.au).
GREATER METROPOLITAN AREA: Sydney Harbour National Park features forts, secluded beaches and spectacular views. Guided tours to historic buildings are available; the most popular trails for walkers are the 5Bluff' track to **Watson's Bay**, the 'Hermitage Foreshore' track to **Vaucluse** and the 'Manly' scenic walkway; the 'Fairfax' walk on **North Head** is suitable for wheelchair access. The **Royal National Park** is the oldest park in Australia and the second oldest in the world. **Wattamolla** and **Garie** are popular swimming spots while Garie, **Era** and **Burning Palms** are best for surfing. The park offers a variety of walking tracks along its 30km (19-mile) procession of headlands, cliffs, forests and beaches. Camping is possible at **Bonnie Vale**; for bush camping, a permit is required. **Ku-ring-gai Chase National Park** (40 minutes north of Sydney) is noted for its Aboriginal rock carvings (which can be seen on the 'Aboriginal Heritage Walk') and extensive walking tracks (one of which, the 'Discovery' track, has wheelchair access); beautiful water views and good sailing facilities are available at **West Head** and picnic areas can be found throughout the park. The park also includes a **koala sanctuary**. The **Blue Mountains National Park** (a World Heritage listed park), just 90 minutes drive west of Sydney, offers waterfalls and panoramic views featuring landmarks such as the 'Three Sisters'. There are numerous bushwalks on offer; the 'Fairfax Heritage Walk' at Blackheath is a wheelchair-friendly track to **Govetts Leap** lookout.
NORTHEAST: The **Myall Lakes National Park** near Port Stephens is the largest coastal lake system in the State and an important habitat for many species of waterbirds. Visitors are offered a range of activities, including a rainforest walk at **Mungo Brush**, campsites, caravans and cabins along the lake shores and beaches, as well as houseboat accommodation facilities. The mountainous **Barrington Tops National Park** in the Hunter wine-making region is crossed by six rivers and is known for its dramatic altitude variations, allowing visitors to experience snow-capped mountains and subtropical rainforests in a day's walk. The best views and walking trails are at **Gloucester Tops**, **Carey's Peak** and **Williams River**. The 'Riverside' walk is suitable for wheelchairs. **Mount Warning National Park**, 12km (7 miles) from Murwillumbah, offers a fantastic trek through rainforest communities, culminating in a challenging rock scramble, to reach the 1100m (3608ft) summit of the ancient volcano. Views from the top take in the expanse of the bowl-shaped Tweed Valley. **Dorrigo National Park** and **Border Ranges National Park**, both in tropical New South Wales, contain large stretches of rainforest, with walking tracks, educational tours, picnicking and camping all available; at Border Ranges, the rainforest grows on the rim of an extinct volcano.
CENTRAL: Rock climbing and mountain walks attract visitors to **Warrumbungle National Park**, near Coonabarabran, whose 'Grand High Tops' track through the remnants of ancient volcanoes ranks high among Australia's many spectacular walks. The park is noted for its bizarre rock outcrops.
OUTBACK: The **Mutawintji National Park**, situated 130km (82 miles) northeast of the old mining town of **Broken Hill**, offers the classic Outback experience. **Homestead Creek** is the main camping base (booking required) in this park on the back of an ancient mountain range, with spectacular gorges and a variety of native animals. Tours to the **Mutawintji Historic Site**, which contains an important collection of Aboriginal art engraved on a hillside, are also available. The nearby **Kinchega National Park** is similarly rich in Aboriginal sites and contains large areas of forest backwaters and lakes; camping and accommodation in former sheep shearers' quarters are possible (booking required).
SOUTHEAST: South of Sydney by 450km (281 miles), the **Kosciuszko National Park** and **Snowy Mountains National Park** feature some of Australia's highest mountains, including **Mount Kosciuszko** (the highest) as well as the great **Snowy**, **Murray** and **Murrumbidgee** rivers. Wintersports are popular from June to September while, in the summer, nature enthusiasts can enjoy rare alpine flora. The main attractions of **Morton National Park** are its waterfalls – one at **Fitzroy Falls**, the other at **Bundanoon**. Camping is possible (booking required).

SPORT & ACTIVITIES

Watersports: The coastline of New South Wales, stretching for over 2000km (1250 miles) to the north and south of Sydney, has excellent conditions for all kinds of watersports including **surfing**, **windsurfing**, **sea kayaking** and **scuba-diving**. In the Sydney area, the surf beaches of *Bronte* and *Coogee* to the south and *Collaroy* and *Palm Beach* to the north are particularly popular. *Byron Bay*, 800km (496 miles) north of Sydney, has outstanding surf conditions. Sydney Harbour has facilities for all kinds of maritime sports and there is an annual **yacht race** from Sydney to Hobart in Tasmania, starting on 26 December each year, covering over 2000km (1250 miles). The best beaches within easy reach of Sydney are at *Bondi* and *Manly*. Along the coast on the Pacific Highway, *Port Stephens*, some 200km (125 miles) north of Sydney, offers safe swimming beaches and a range of water-based activities. Further north still, the Great Lakes district and its most popular resort, *Port Macquarie*, is particularly well known for **fishing**, windsurfing and **houseboat holidays** (exploring the Great Lakes). A further 250km (150 miles) along the coastline is Coffs Harbour, a tropical resort town, famous for its fishing, **sailing** and **swimming** facilities, and adventure sports like **sky-diving** and **scuba-diving**. **Kayaking** and **whitewater rafting** enthusiasts may head to the *Gwydir* and *Nymbodia* rivers in the north west region or the streams of the *Kosciuszko National Park* in the Snowy Mountains (see below). Numerous companies offer scuba-diving or **snorkelling** trips on purpose-built boats to a choice of destinations along the New South Wales coast and as far as the famous Great Barrier Reef in the neighbouring State of Queensland. Good dive sites can be found at *Jervis Bay*, *Byron Bay*, *Lord Howe Islands* and *Coffs Harbour*. Specialist charters also provide **whale-** and **dolphin-watching** trips as well as great white **shark encounters** and **reef education** tours. The best time to see dolphins and whales is from May to December. *Port Stephens* is known for the bottlenose dolpins which live and play in the bay all year round. Most dolphin cruises depart from the region's largest township, *Nelson Bay*. Migrating whales can be spotted from Cape Byron between May and October.
Mountain sports: South of Sydney are the mountains of the Great Dividing Range, home to Australia's highest mountain, *Mount Kosciuszko* (2230m/7314ft). The *Snowy Mountains*, 526km (329 miles) south-west of Sydney, are a major destination for **skiing**, cross-country skiing and **snowboarding**. The season generally runs from June to October. In the summer, activities such as **mountain biking**, **riding**, **fishing** and **canoeing** are available. About 104km (65 miles) west of Sydney, the Blue Mountains consist of a landscape of forests, valleys, canyons, waterfalls and cliffs. Popular activities in this region include **abseiling**, **scenic flights**, **canyoning**, **climbing** as well as **bush-walking**, with many hidden trails for walkers to explore.
Urban climbing: It is possible to climb the Harbour Bridge in Sydney via a network of archways, catwalks and ladders. The resulting view of the harbour is spectacular. The whole climb takes around 3 hours and is open to those aged over 12. Climbs require special clothing and are in guided groups of 10 climbers. Further information is available from Bridgeclimb (website: www.bridgeclimb.com) or the tourist board (see *Contact Addresses* section).
Golf: The state has many international standard courses, including two of Australia's best-known golf courses – *Riverside Oaks* and *The Lakes* – are located in New South Wales. Tour operators can organise golfing trips to the province's best courses. For further information, contact Tourism New South Wales (see *Contact Addresses* section).

SOCIAL PROFILE

FOOD & DRINK: Cooking in New South Wales, and Sydney in particular, reflects the State's multicultural makeup with Thai, Vietnamese, Japanese, Greek, Italian and Indian cuisine all represented. Gourmet food and wine trails exist throughout the State.
Fine red and white wines come from the Hunter Valley. General licensing hours for public bars are Mon-Sat 1000-2200 with varying hours on Sunday.
NIGHTLIFE: Sydney is known for being a city that never sleeps, and has a diverse selection of bars, pubs, nightclubs and music venues. Kings Cross in Sydney is an exciting nightlife area. There are also some night-time cruises offering dinner and dancing. For further information on Sydney's nightlife see online (website: www.spraci.com *or* www.citysearch.com.au).
SHOPPING: Best buys are Australian opals, precious and semi-precious stones, Aboriginal arts and crafts, woollen and sheepskin goods and fashion by top Australian designers. **Shopping hours:** In Sydney, shops open Mon-Fri 0900-1730, Sat 0900-1600 and Sun 1000-1600. Many shops also stay open until 2100 on Thursday.
SPECIAL EVENTS: For a full list of special events, contact Tourism New South Wales (see *Contact Addresses* section, or visit www.events.nsw.gov.au *or* www.sydneyaustralia.com). The following is a selection of special events occurring in New South Wales in 2005:
Jan 8-30 *Sydney Festival.* **Feb 9** *Chinese New Year*, Dixon Street, Sydney. **Mar 5** *Sydney Gay and Lesbian Mardi Gras.* **Apr 1-10** *Food Week*, Orange. **Apr 2-15** *Royal Easter Show*, Sydney. **Apr 9** *Bundadoon Highland Gathering (Bundanoon Is Brigadoon)* (largest annual pipe band gathering in Australia). **Apr 24-May 2** *The National Trust Heritage Festival*, Sydney. **Aug 12-14** *Art, Food & All That Jazz*, Kingscliff. **Sep 18** *Camden Food, Wine and Music Festival.* **Sep 25** *Camden Jazz in the Vineyard.* **Dec 14** *Carrols by the Sea*, Bondi Beach.

Business Profile

COMMERCIAL INFORMATION: The following organisations can offer advice: State Chamber of Commerce (New South Wales), Level 12, 83 Clarence Street, Sydney, NSW 2000 (tel: (2) 9350 8100 *or* (1300) 137 157 (in Australia only); fax: (2) 9350 8199; website: www.thechamber.com.au); *or* the Department of State and Regional Developmment (website: www.sydneyaustralia.com).
CONFERENCES/CONVENTIONS: Sydney has launched a major initiative to become an important convention and meeting destination. The Sydney Convention and Exhibition Centre at *Darling Harbour* has facilities for up to 5000 people. Other major convention centres include Centrepoint Exhibition and Convention Centre, University of NSW, RAS Exhibition Centre, Sydney Opera House, Powerhouse Museum, Sydney Town Hall, University of Sydney, YWCA, Queen Victoria Building, Bankstown Town Hall, Bondi Surf Bathers' Life Saving Club, Curzon Hall, Film Australia, Hills Centre, Taronga Centre and the NSW Harness Racing Club. For more information on conferences and conventions in NSW contact the Australian Tourist Commission *or* the Sydney Convention & Visitors Bureau in London, UK (see *Contact Addresses* section) *or* the Sydney Convention & Visitors Bureau, Level 13, 80 William Street, Sydney, NSW 2011 (tel: (2) 9331 4045; fax: (2) 9360 1223; e-mail: info@scvb.com.au; website: www.scvb.com.au).

Climate

Warm semi-tropical summers, particularly in lower central area. Mountain areas in the west are cooler, particularly in winter. Rainfall is heaviest from March to June.

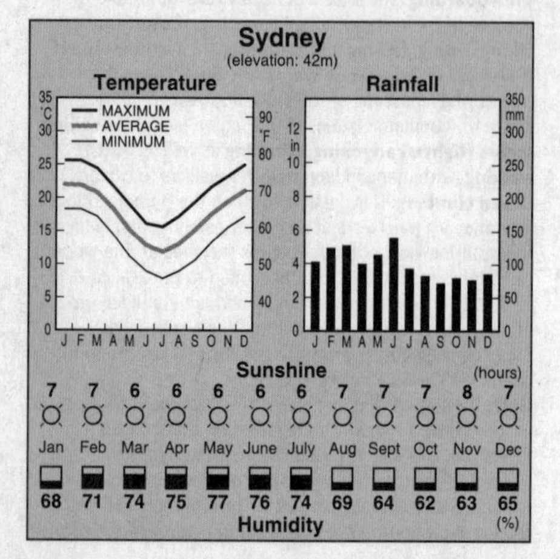

Northern Territory

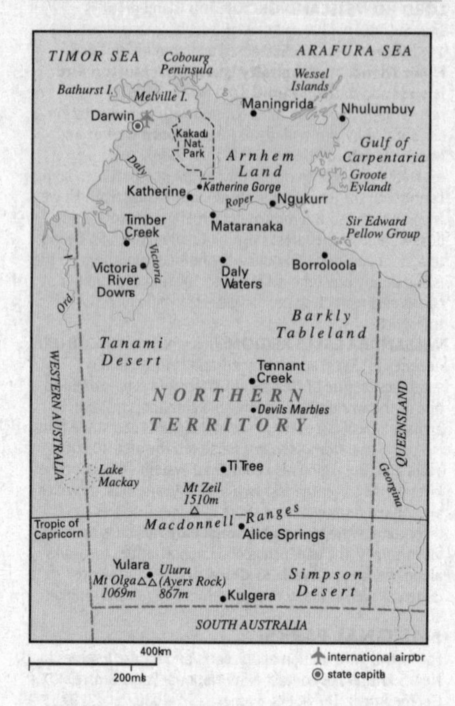

Location: Northern Australia.

Northern Territory Tourist Commission
Street address: Tourism House, 43 Mitchell Street, Darwin, NT 0800, Australia
Postal address: PO Box 1155, Darwin, NT 0801, Australia
Tel: (8) 8999 3900. Fax: (8) 8999 3888.
E-mail: nttc@nttc.com.au
Website: www.nttc.com.au *or* www.ntholidays.com

Northern Territory Tourist Commission
1st Floor, Beaumont House, Lambton Road, London SW20 0LW, UK
Tel: (020) 8944 2992. Fax: (020) 8944 2993.
E-mail: info@nttc.co.uk
Website: www.ntholidays.co.uk

Northern Territory Tourist Commission
3601 Aviation Boulevard, Suite 2100, Manhattan Beach, CA 90266, USA
Tel: (310) 643 2636. Fax: (310) 643 2637.
E-mail: nttc@myriadmarketing.com
Website: www.insidetheoutback.com

General Information

AREA: 1,349,130 sq km (520,902 sq miles).
POPULATION: 195,500 (official estimate 2000).
POPULATION DENSITY: 0.1 per sq km.
CAPITAL: Darwin. **Population:** 88,100 (estimate 1999).
GEOGRAPHY: A wilderness stretching roughly 1670km (1038 miles) north-south and 1000km (620 miles) east-west, the Northern Territory comprises nearly one-sixth of Australia. The geography of the Northern Territory is the closest to the popular image of the Great Australian Outback.
The northern area, centred on the capital, Darwin, is tropical with rich vegetation and a varied coastline. Beyond Darwin, 251km (155 miles) east, is World Heritage-listed Kakadu National Park, which is part of the 12,600 sq km (4500 sq mile) area of Arnhem Land. It is an area of vast flood plains and rocky escarpments steeped in natural and cultural heritage. Aboriginal people have lived here for at least 40,000 years. Katherine township is 314km (195 miles) from Darwin and a further 30km (20 miles) northeast is Nitmiluk (Katherine Gorge) National Park with 13 gorges towering up to 60m (200ft) high.
The southern part of the Northern Territory is centred on the town of Alice Springs, which is almost at the geographical centre of Australia and the starting point of many of the Red Centre's unique and natural wonders, including Uluru (Ayers Rock) and the Uluru-Kata Tjuta National Park. Other notable features of the Red Centre are King's Canyon, Ross River, Trephina, Ormiston and Glen Helen Gorge, the Olgas near Uluru (Ayers Rock) and the Devil's Marbles at Tennant Creek. There are also other parks and reserves with abundant bird and animal life.
TIME: GMT + 9.5.

Public Holidays

The Northern Territory observes all the public holidays observed nationwide (see the main Australia section) and, in addition, the following are observed:
2005 May 2 May Day. **Jun 13** Queen's Official Birthday. **Jul 1*** Alice Springs Show Day. **Jul 8*** Tennant Creek Show Day. **Jul 15*** Katherine Show Day. **Jul 22*** Darwin Show Day. **Aug 11** Picnic Day.
2006 May 1 May Day. **Jun 12** Queen's Official Birthday. **Jul 7*** Alice Springs Show Day. **Jul 14*** Tennant Creek Show Day. **Jul 21*** Katherine Show Day. **Jul 28*** Darwin Show Day. **Aug 7** Picnic Day.
Note: *Regional observance only.

Travel - International

AIR: The Northern Territory can be reached by international flights to Darwin from Bali, Bangkok, Brunei, East Timor, Europe, Japan, Kuala Lumpur, Singapore and the UK. At present there are several international carriers operating to the Northern Territory, including *British Airways*, *Garuda Indonesia*, *Qantas* and *Royal Brunei*. Only the latter two airlines fly directly to Darwin; the others require connections. There are several domestic airlines - *Airnorth*, *Jetstar*, *Qantas* and *Virgin Blue* - that cover the Territory from all capital cities within Australia with connections from most other towns. Smaller commuter airlines connect some of the remoter areas within the Territory.
Approximate flight times: From Darwin to *London* is 21 hours 25 minutes, to *Singapore* four hours 30 minutes, to *Bangkok* five hours, to *Bali* 90 minutes, to *Brunei* four hours and to *Timor* two hours. Connections are available from most Asian airports.
Airports: *Darwin Airport (DRW)* (website: www.darwinairport.com.au) is 13km (8 miles) from the city centre. The airport receives international flights. Airport buses and taxis operate services to the city. For further information, see the main Australia section.
Alice Springs Airport (ASP) (domestic flights only) is 15km (9 miles) from the city centre. Airport buses and taxis operate services to the city. Facilities include left luggage, bureau de change, bars and car hire.
Uluru/Ayers Rock Airport (AYQ) (domestic flights only) is 7km (4 miles) from the Uluru (Ayers Rock) resort. All scheduled flights are met by a free shuttle service to the resort. Taxi services are also available. Facilities include a gift shop and small refreshment kiosk.
Katherine Airport (KTR) (domestic flights only) is 11km (7 miles) from Katherine.
SEA: International cruise lines call at Darwin, the Northern Territory's only large port.
RAIL: The main rail service to the Territory is by the *Ghan* from Adelaide which travels to Darwin via Alice Springs; see *Travel* in the main *Australia* section for more information. There is no internal network.
ROAD: There are three main highways serving the Northern Territory: the *Stuart Highway*, south to Adelaide; the *Barkly Highway*, east to Mount Isa and Queensland; and the *Victoria Highway*, which runs west to join an unsealed road running across the top of the Western Desert which runs on to Perth. Off these roads there are many uncharted rough tracks often only suitable for 4-wheel-drive vehicles, and often ending in impassable desert. The dangers of travelling off main roads in the Northern Territory without a qualified guide cannot be stressed too strongly. **Coach:** The national coach services are run by *Greyhound/Pioneer Bus Australia* and *McCafferty's*, all of which serve the main townships within the Territory with direct services to all capital cities. Well-equipped coaches take over 92 hours to cover the distance from Darwin to Sydney; from Darwin, coaches depart daily to Kakadu National Park (travel time - four hours 50 minutes) and to Alice Springs (travel time - 19 hours).
URBAN: There are local **bus** services in Darwin (running Monday-Saturday) from the coach terminal located 1km (0.5m) from the city centre and in Alice Springs. Darwin Harbour ferries operate Monday-Friday.

Accommodation

The *Northern Territory Holiday Planner*, published by the Northern Territory Tourist Commission, gives details of tours, holidays and accommodation in the Territory for the travel trade. In addition there is a large selection of consumer brochures available from the Northern Territory Tourist Commission (see *Contact Addresses* section).
HOTELS: International-standard hotels are found in Darwin, Alice Springs and Uluru (Ayers Rock), and a good standard of hotel and motel accommodation can be found in all the major tourist areas and centres of population. 2001 saw the addition of 372 more hotel rooms and 85 apartment rooms in Darwin.
LODGES/MOTELS: Lodges and budget motels are

available in some of the remote areas.
CAMPING/CARAVANNING: The Northern Territory contains some of the most inhospitable country in the world. From Alice Springs, the nearest major town in any direction is Tenant Creek, 504km (313 miles) away, and consequently any car or caravan must be in prime mechanical condition. During the tropical summer from November to April, travel in the Outback is advisable only in suitable cross-country vehicles, as many conventional roads become impassable for ordinary cars. The Stuart Highway between Darwin and Alice Springs and through to Adelaide in South Australia is a fully sealed road accessible all year. A number of companies can arrange **motor camper** rentals, with a range of fully-equipped vehicles. Full details can be obtained from the Tourist Commission (see *Contact Addresses* section).
Note: For further coverage of the range of accommodation available, see *Accommodation* in the general *Australia* section.

Resorts & Excursions

The Northern Territory is a huge and diverse region. The north, the 'Top End' of Australia, is subtropical, with such high rainfall in the rainy season that much of it is accessible only by air. The south of the Territory is an arid desert, known as the 'Red Centre'.
Note: There are many places and objects in the Territory that are of special significance to the Aboriginal people and laws protecting these sacred sites carry heavy penalties for entering, damaging or defacing them. It is necessary to obtain a permit before entering Aboriginal lands, including by car. These permits are not issued lightly, nor are they generally issued for touristic purposes. Some areas that have historic significance to the Aborigines *are* open to the public – for example, **Uluru** (**Ayers Rock**) and **Corroboree Rock** near Alice Springs, and **Ubirr Rock** in Kakadu National Park (see *National Parks* section). Visitors are welcome at these places, but due respect should be shown for the site and its historical significance. For further information, maps and permit application advice, contact the Tourist Commission (see *Contact Addresses* section).

DARWIN AND THE TOP END

The territorial capital, **Darwin**, which was savaged by Cyclone Tracy on Christmas Eve 1974, has been rebuilt and has grown over the years to become a modern, multicultural, provincial city. Darwin and the rest of the Top End have two distinct seasons. In the tropical summer from November to April, monsoon conditions mean late afternoon thunderstorms, high humidity and heavy downpours. This is the green season when the waterfalls flow and the wildlife abounds. From May through to October is the 'dry' season, with unlimited sunshine and balmy evenings. The wetlands begin to dry out, confining the bird and animal life to ever smaller areas. The Top End is the area to see lush tropical vegetation, either in Darwin's **Botanical Gardens**, the **Crocodylus Park** just outside Darwin, or in the Territory's various national parks (see below). Also south of Darwin are the **Howard Springs** and **Berry Springs** nature parks, **Territory Wildlife Park** and the birds' haven **Fogg Dam Conservation Reserve**. There are many good opportunities for fishing near the city, for example at **Mindil Beach** or **Vestey's Beach**. The **Tiwi Islands**, comprising **Bathurst Island** and **Melville Island**, are Aboriginal islands rich in history and culture. The islands are a short flight from Darwin, but they are accessible only by organised one- or two-day tours.

THE RED CENTRE

Alice Springs is located in what is almost the geographical centre of the continent. A pleasant little town, set in red desert country, it is a popular tourist resort and a base for exploring the wonders of the Outback. There are many excellent hotels and motels, a casino, a variety of restaurants and varied sporting facilities ranging from golf and tennis to hot-air ballooning and tandem parachuting. The **Royal Flying Doctor Base** is open daily to the public (excluding public holidays) and the **School of the Air** is operational during the school term. There are also museums and preserved buildings which help the visitor to appreciate the history of this remote town. Not least among these are the **Dreamtime Gallery** and the **Aboriginal Arts & Culture Centre**. The **Telegraph Station Historical Reserve**, 3km (2 miles) north of the town, is an historical reserve featuring original buildings, restored equipment and an illustrated display including early photographs, papers and documents. **Anzac Hill War Memorial** lies just behind Alice Springs and provides a panoramic view of the town and surrounding ranges.
The region around Alice Springs is pitted with colourful gorges, canyons, valley pools and awe-inspiring chasms. These include **Standley Chasm**, 57km (35 miles) west of Alice, **Glen Helen Gorge**, 140km (9 miles) west, **Ormiston Gorge**, 130km (80 miles) west, **Kings Canyon**, 330km (205 miles) southwest and **N'Dhala Gorge**, 96km (59 miles) east, which is also notable for its ancient rock engravings. **Palm Valley** lies around one hour 30 minutes' drive to the southwest and **Rainbow Valley** to the southeast on the edge of the **Simpson Desert**.
Château Hornsby, the Northern Territory's only vineyard, is situated approximately 10km (6 miles) from the town centre and is a venue for tastings, barbecues, and Aboriginal corroborees.

ULURU (AYERS ROCK)

Alice Springs is the main base for tours to **Uluru** – approximately 460km (285 miles) or five hours' drive away – and the East and Western **MacDonnell Ranges**. Uluru is the world's largest monolith and plays an important part in Aboriginal mythology, in which it is believed to have been created by ancestors of the Aborigines. Visitors may still climb the rock, although to do so is considered a gross sacrilege by the indigenous people, or explore some of the fascinating caves at its base. Sunset and sunrise must be seen as the sun's rays change the rock's colour from blazing orange to red and even deep purple, depending on the atmospheric conditions. 22 km (13 miles) from Uluru (Ayers Rock) is the **Ayers Rock Resort** (**Yulara**) – a village built to cater for the growing number of visitors to the area. The resort contains top-class hotels, lodges, self-catering maisonettes, shops, bank, restaurants, post office, caravan park and campsites and caters for all the needs of the traveller. Tours depart throughout the day for the Rock, the nearby **Olgas** and **Uluru-Kata Tjuta National Park**, as well as other points of interest.
Uluru (Ayers Rock) has its own airport with daily flights to Alice Springs and direct connections to Sydney and other Australian cities. Car hire is available and all major coach companies service Ayers Rock on a daily basis.
Other points of interest in the Red Centre include Aboriginal tours to **Pitjantjatjara** country, and the **Ross River Homestead** for horseriding, log cabins and boomerang throwing. **Kings Canyon** (**Watarrka National Park**), four hours' drive southwest of Alice Springs, offers spectacular views, while visitors can discover the 'Lost City' (a maze of eroded earth domes) and the 'Garden of Eden' (a sheltered green waterhole) when walking around the canyon. Hotel accommodation is available at the Kings Canyon Resort. Campsite pitches are available at Kings Creek Station. **Tennant Creek** offers trail rides, half-day cattle drives and gold mine tours. An hour's drive from Tennant Creek is the impressive formation of 7m (23ft) boulders called **The Devil's Marbles**.

Credit: © Northern Territory Tourist Commission

NATIONAL PARKS

KAKADU NATIONAL PARK: This may be found about a Three-hour drive to the east of Darwin down the Arnhem Highway. The park includes the flood plains between the **Wildman** and the **Alligator Rivers**, which empty into **Van Diemen Gulf** to the north. It is bordered by the **Arnhem Land** escarpment, where the spectacular waterfalls of **Jim Jim** and **Twin Falls** cascade hundreds of feet into crystal-clear rock pools below. At **Ubirr** (**Obiri Rock**) and **Nourlangie Rock** are fascinating galleries of Aboriginal rock painting, many dating back over 20,000 years. These paintings show mythical and spiritual figures and an ancient lifestyle which still holds great significance for the Aboriginal people today.
Within the park there are several resort-style hotels and a number of camping and caravan sites from which to explore this beautiful area. Numerous creeks, rivers and *billabongs* provide excellent fishing, particularly for the much prized *barramundi*, which is found in abundance here. Thousands of birds inhabit the wetlands – over 275 species – and wildlife abounds throughout the year.
Aerial tours over the Arnhem Land escarpment depart daily and local fishing trips can be easily arranged. A popular way to explore the waterways is on a boat cruise on the **South Alligator River** or scenic **Yellow Water**, giving access to nature at its best. It is possible to spot crocodiles basking on the riverbanks, and the graceful *jabiru* (Australia's only stork) wading amongst the water lilies. Kakadu National Park is the habitat for all wildlife common to Northern Australia and as such provides a diverse and exciting experience in the tropical **Top End**. Tours and safaris from two to 21 days are available by air, coach or 4-wheel-drive from Darwin.
KATHERINE GORGE/NITMILUK NATIONAL PARK: The township of **Katherine** is in the area known as the 'Never Never' about 350km (220 miles) southeast of Darwin. This is pioneer territory, made famous by Mrs Aeneas Gunn in her book *We of the Never Never*. **Katherine Gorge**, some 30km (20 miles) northeast of the town, is one of Australia's great natural wonders and the famous boat cruises through the spectacular gorges, towering up to 60m (200ft) high, are a highlight of any visit to the region. There are, in fact, 13 gorges and each has its own glowing colours and fascinating outcrops, steep canyon walls above cool, blue waters. Marked walking tracks are well maintained for easy access to features of interest in the park. Canoeing, swimming and boat tours are all available (May to September) along with scenic helicopter rides over the gorges. There is a good range of accommodation both in the town and **Nitmiluk National Parks**, and campers and caravanners are also well catered for.
LITCHFIELD NATIONAL PARK: Only one hour 30 minutes' drive south of Darwin, **Litchfield National Park** is ideal for day trips or can be included in longer tours of the Top End. Six waterfalls provide the main attraction of the park. Other attractions include rainforest, bush walks, weathered sandstone formations, spring-fed streams, impressive cathedral termite mounds and wildlife, such as birds, possums, wallabies and lizards.

Sport & Activities

Bushwalking: The 'Top End' of the Northern Territory – a vast and beautiful region – contains several national parks and nature reserves, with one of the best walking destinations being the *Arnhem Land Plateau* (in Kakadu National Park); the *West MacDonnell Ranges* along *Larapinta Trail* are also good for bushwalking; see *National Parks* in *Resorts & Excursions* section for more information. Walkers are rewarded by regular sightings of buffalo and giant crocodiles. A camping permit is required outside established camping areas. Darwin is the usual starting point for excursions to the area. For further details, contact the Parks & Wildlife Commission of the NT, PO Box 496, Palmerston NT 0831 (tel: (8) 8999 5511; fax: (8) 8932 3849; website: www.nt.gov.au/ipe/pwcnt).
Watersports: The wetlands, with their numerous freshwater rivers and waterholes, offer excellent **fishing**, particularly the barramundi (renowned for its aggressive nature and fighting characteristics), which is so abundant that the Northern Territory is known as Australia's 'barramundi capital'. For details of state fishing regulations, contact the Department of Primary Industry and Fisheries, Fisheries Division, GPO Box 3000, Darwin, NT 0801 (tel: (8) 8999 2144; fax: (8) 8999 2065; e-mail: phill.hall@nt.gov.au; website: www.primaryindustry.nt.gov.au). Good **diving** can be found around Darwin Harbour and the offshore islands and reefs, including the *Cobourg Peninsula* (680km/423 miles from Darwin); the *Vernon Islands* (64km/40 miles from Darwin); and the seas around Nhulunbuy on the *Gove Pensinsula* (1114km/692 miles east of Darwin), where hundreds of islands and reefs are located. As an alternative to the sea, **swimming** holes can be found at *Jim Jim Falls* and nearby *Twin Falls* in Kakadu National Park. It is important to check that the area is safe for swimming, as salt-water crocodiles are found throughout the region. **Canoeing** is possible in *Katherine Gorge (Nitmiluk)* and on the *Victoria River*.

Social Profile

FOOD & DRINK: *Barramundi* (fish) is the local speciality. Dining out has been made even more special by the addition of new restaurants at Cullen Bay Marina, offering outdoor dining with beautiful ocean views. Cuisine from many countries, including Creole, Greek, Indian, Japanese, Malaysian, Mongolian and Thai, is available in Darwin's restaurants.

NIGHTLIFE: There is plenty of exciting nightlife in Darwin, which also boasts the *MGM Grand Darwin*, built in an extraordinary modern architectural style. This A$30-million casino complex also encompasses luxury accommodation, restaurants, discos and sporting and convention facilities and is surrounded by lush gardens perched along the shores of Mindil Beach. Alice Springs also has a casino.
SHOPPING: Darwin specialities include Aboriginal artefacts and Outback clothing. Aboriginal items, bush clothing and opals are available in Alice Springs. Darwin's markets are great attractions.
SPECIAL EVENTS: For a full list of events see the Northern Territory Tourist Commission (website: www.ntholidays.com). The following is a selection of special events occurring in the Northern Territory in 2005:
Apr 16-May 2 *Alice Springs Cup Carnival*. **Jun 16-19** *WordStorm, The Northern Territory's Writers' Festival*. **Jul 2-Aug 1** *Darwin Cup Carnival*. **Aug 11-28** *Darwin Festival*. **Sep 2-11** *Alice Springs Festival of the Desert*. **Sep 29-Oct 2** *Food & Wine Festival*, Darwin. **Oct 7** *Voyages Camel Cup*, Alice Springs. **Nov 20** *Christmas Craft Fair*, Darwin. **Dec 31** *New Year's Eve on the Wharf*, free entry and entertainment, alfresco dining and fireworks.

Business Profile

COMMERCIAL INFORMATION: The following organisation can offer advice: Northern Territory Department of Business, Industry and Resources Development, Second Floor, Development House, 76 The Esplanade, Darwin, NT 0800 (tel: (8) 8924 4280; fax: (8) 8999 5333; e-mail: info.dbird@nt.gov.au; website: www.dbird.nt.gov.au).
CONFERENCES/CONVENTIONS: Major convention centres in Darwin are The Beaufort Hotel, Darwin Performing Arts Centre, MGM Grand, Marrara International Indoor Sports Stadium and the Plaza Darwin. The Alice Springs Convention Centre boasts seven large function suites, that have a total capacity of 2000 persons, 140 hotel rooms and the latest conference facilities. For further details contact the Alice Springs Convention Centre, PO Box 2632, Alice Springs, NT 0871 (tel: (8) 8950 0200; fax: (8) 8950 0300; e-mail: info@aspcc.com.au; website: www.alicespringsconventioncentre.com.au). Other major convention centres in Alice Springs are Aruluen Arts Centre and Plaza Hotel Alice Springs. There is also a number of resort convention facilities outside the cities, such as at Ayers Rock Resort. For more information on conferences and conventions in the Northern Territory contact the Northern Territory Convention Bureau, PO Box 2531, Alice Springs, NT 0871 (tel: (8) 8951 8427; fax: (8) 8951 8550; e-mail: info@ntconventions.com.au; website: www.ntconventions.com.au).

Climate

Hot most of the year; the Top End has two seasons, dry and wet, whilst the Red Centre has the usual four: summer, autumn, winter and spring. Coastal areas have heavy monsoon rain from March-November.
Required clothing: Lightweight cottons and linens most of the year. Waterproofing is necessary in the northern areas during the rainy season. A warm sweater or jacket is advised for the centre during winter months, as evenings can be quite cool.

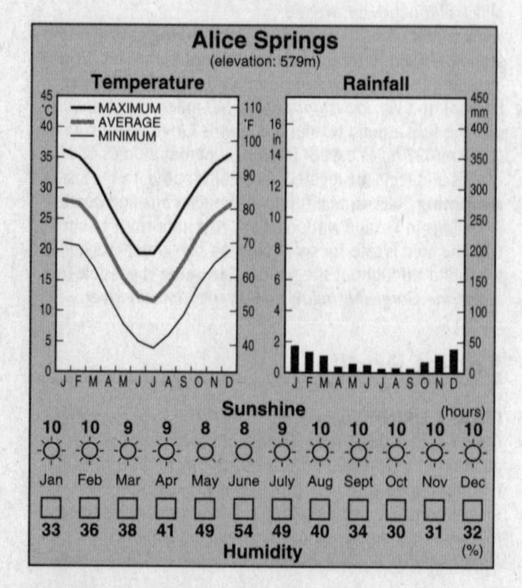

Queensland

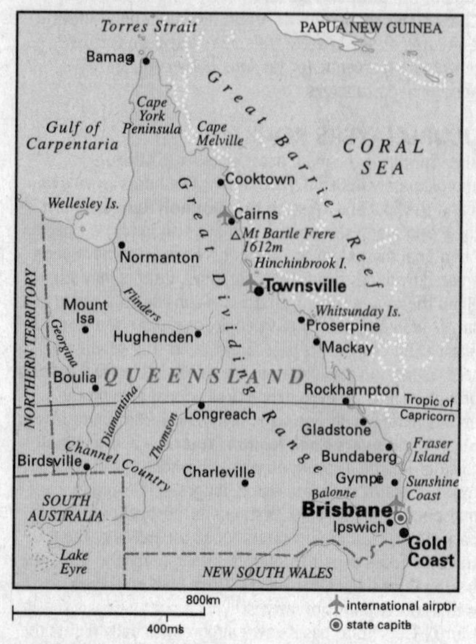

Location: Northeast Australia.

Tourism Queensland
Level 10, Tourism Queensland House, 30 Makerston Street, Brisbane, QLD 4000, Australia
Tel: (7) 3535 3535. Fax: (7) 3535 5246.
E-mail: tqinfo@tq.com.au
Website: www.queenslandholidays.com.au
Tourism Queensland
6th Floor, Australia Centre, Melbourne Place, Strand, London WC2B 4LG, UK
Tel: (020) 7240 0525. Fax: (020) 7836 5881.
E-mail: tq_london@tq.com.au (administration and marketing enquiries).
Website: www.queenslandholidays.co.uk

General Information

AREA: 1,730,650 sq km (668,207 sq miles).
POPULATION: 3,566,400 (official estimate 2000).
POPULATION DENSITY: 2.1 per sq km.
CAPITAL: Brisbane. **Population:** 1,626,900 (official estimate 2000).
GEOGRAPHY: Two and half times the size of Texas or seven times the size of the United Kingdom, Queensland, more than half of which lies above the Tropic of Capricorn, is known as the 'Sunshine State'. Within its borders are the Great Barrier Reef, numerous resort islands, kilometres of golden sandy beaches, national park forests, vast plains, lush rainforests, forested mountains and extensive wilderness areas.
TIME: GMT + 10.

Public Holidays

Queensland observes all the public holidays observed nationwide (see the main Australia section) and, in addition, the following are observed:
2005 May 2 Labour Day. **Jun 13** Queen's Birthday Celebrations. **Aug 12*** People's Day at the Brisbane Royal Show.
2006 May 1 Labour Day. **Jun 12** Queen's Birthday Celebrations. **Aug 11*** People's Day at the Brisbane Royal Show.
Note: *The Brisbane Royal Show is a holiday in Brisbane only.

Travel - International

AIR: There are several major air carriers serving Brisbane and Queensland including: *Air New Zealand*, *British Airways*, *Cathay Pacific*, *Garuda Indonesia*, *Malaysia Airlines*, *Qantas*, *Singapore Airlines*, *United Airlines* and *Virgin Atlantic*. For more flight details see *Travel* in the general *Australia* section. Domestic carriers include *Jetstar*, *Qantas* and *Virgin Blue*. Airlines such as *Macair Airlines* offer charter flights and feeder services to Queensland's main towns and Barrier Reef island resorts.
Aproximate flight times: Approximate flying time from Brisbane to *London* is 23 hours 30 minutes
International airports: *Brisbane International (BNE)* (website: www.bne.com.au) is 13km (8 miles) northeast of the city centre (travel time – approximately 35 minutes). Flights are available from Europe, Asia, the Far East, New Zealand, Canada and the USA. Airport buses, taxis and trains operate services to the city. Airport facilities include left luggage, first aid, banks, bureaux de change, bars, car hire (*Avis*, *Budget*, *Europcar*, *Hertz* and *Thrifty*), duty-free shops, restaurants and tourist information.
Townsville (TSV) is 5km (3 miles) from the city. Townsville is served by flights from Europe, Asia, New Zealand and the Far East.
Cairns (CNS) is 8km (5 miles) from the city. Cairns is an excellent gateway both to the Great Barrier Reef and the tropical north, and hosts flights from Europe, Asia, the Far East, New Zealand, Canada and the USA. Airport shuttle buses (travel time – 10-15 minutes) and taxis operate services to the city.
The extensive internal airline system means that Queensland is connected with nearly all major Australian gateways. Brisbane is connected directly to Sydney, Melbourne, Adelaide, Alice Springs and Darwin, as well as having links with Cairns, Mount Isa, Townsville and other smaller airstrips within the state. Cairns and Townsville also offer easy connections to the rest of Australia.
RAIL: Queensland has its own railway system, run by QR (website: www.qr.com.au), the main routes being the *Sunlander* and the *Queenslander* which connect coastal towns from Brisbane to Cairns. In addition, other services, such as the *Inlander*, *Westlander* and *Spirit of Outback* (from Brisbane to Longreach) open up the Outback to travellers. The *Spirit of the Tropics* provides more coastal services. The main tourist services are the famous *Kuranda Scenic Rail* and the *Gulflander*. The *Great South Pacific Express* running from Brisbane to Sydney or Cairns is a luxury service operated by Orient-Express Trains and Cruises. The new *Tilt Train* provides a faster service from Rockhampton to Brisbane. The main train stations are Central and Roma Street.
The *Sunshine Railpass* allows unlimited travel on Queensland's rail routes. Passes are valid for 14, 21 and 30 days in first- or economy-class, offering excellent travel facilities for those intending extensive travel throughout the state. The Queensland *Roadrail Pass*, for economy class only, offers 10 journeys over a 60-day period or 20 journeys over a 90-day period. For more information about rail travel and passes visit Queensland Rail Travel online (website: www.traveltrain.qr.com.au).
ROAD: There is a high standard of highways and road networks offering easy connections between towns and cities. The *Bruce Highway* runs down the whole east coast from Cairns to Brisbane and continues into New South Wales. An extensive **coach** network offers an easy and cheap way of getting around.
The inland areas can be explored with 4-wheel-drive vehicles, many of the interior roads being unsealed; 4-wheel-drive vehicles and guided self-drive tours are available. The other main highways running into the interior are the *Capricorn Highway* (Rockhampton–Winton), the *Flinders Highway* (Townsville–Mount Isa, connecting with the network in the Northern Territory) and the *Warrego Highway* (Brisbane–Charleville). The *Mitchell* and *Landsborough Highways*, which in places have unsealed road surfaces, run roughly north–south, connecting the main east–west highways and terminating at Sydney. The *Newell Highway* runs inland between Brisbane and Melbourne. For more information about driving in Queensland, visit Queensland Transport online (website: www.queensland-holidays.com.au/motoring_holidays).
URBAN: Brisbane's electrified **rail** system is easy to use for suburban services, particularly cross-river. There are also cross-river **ferries**, and a comprehensive **bus** network with zonal fares and 10-journey pre-purchase fares obtainable through newsagents. Day and other period tickets are also available. The *City Sights Bus* stops at 18 places of interest around the city, during a 90 minute tour, for A$20 (adult) and A$15 (children). In Cairns, bus services operate Mon-Sat and there is a touring bus that follows a circular route, *Cairns Red Explorer*, that departs from the Transit Centre. Day tickets are A$20 (adult) and A$10 (children). Taxis are also available.

Accommodation

HOTELS: International standard hotels are available in Brisbane, Cairns and the Gold Coast together with a high standard of hotel/motel accommodation throughout the state. Information regarding price and location of accommodation can be obtained through the Tourism Queensland website (see *Contact Addresses* section).
MOTELS: These are usually in or on the outskirts of towns and cities and normally offer self-contained rooms at reasonable rates.
SELF-CONTAINED APARTMENTS: These are available throughout the larger resort areas and offer a variety of facilities.
FARMSTAYS/HOMESTAYS: 'Holiday Host' services

A B C D E F G H I J K L M N O P Q R S T U V W X Y Z

operate throughout Australia, matching hosts with visitors, in stations, family homes and farm properties.
CAMPING/CARAVANNING: Parks are located in tourist areas around Queensland, and offer facilities of varying standards. Camping is permitted in parks, but permission must be sought from the National Parks Association of Queensland Inc, PO Box 1040, Milton, QLD 4064 (tel: (7) 3367 0878; fax: (7) 3367 0890; e-mail: npaq@npaq.org.au; website: www.npaq.org.au). A number of companies can arrange **motor camper** rentals, with a range of fully equipped vehicles. Full details can be obtained from Tourism Queensland (see *Contact Addresses* section).
YOUTH HOSTELS: Budget dormitory-style accommodation is available throughout Queensland.
Note: For further coverage of the range of accommodation available, see *Accommodation* in the general *Australia* section.

Resorts & Excursions

BRISBANE

Brisbane is the economic hub and State capital of Queensland, with a year-round warm subtropical climate. Australia's fastest growing city, it is the gateway to many coastal resorts and itself offers many attractions. Probably the most famous of these is the **Lone Pine Koala Sanctuary**,which can be reached via a river cruise. The **Botanic Gardens** is a splendid shady reserve at the south end of the city centre, accessible by a new footbridge. **City Hall** in **King George Square** houses an art gallery, museum and clocktower observation deck. Other buildings of note include the **State Parliament** House with its glittering copper roof, **St John's Cathedral**, **The Mansions** and the **Old Windmill**, the city's oldest surviving building and once a treadmill worked by convicts. The **Queensland Cultural Centre** at **South Bank** contains the **Queensland Art Gallery**, **Queensland Museum** and **Performing Arts Centre**. The **South Bank Parklands**, on the site of the 1988 World Expo, boasts an interesting **Maritime Museum** and an enormous artificial swimming beach. The **Brisbane Powerhouse** is a lively alternative arts venue, and the looming art deco **Castlemaine** Brewery offers enjoyable daily tours with samples of its famous product. Brisbane's many festivals are another major attraction; see *Social Profile* section for further information.

BEYOND BRISBANE

Probably the best beach area in the country, the **Gold Coast** region 80km (50 miles) south of Brisbane comprises 42km (25 miles) of white surf beaches, theme parks (**Sea World**, **Movie World** and **Dreamworld**), a casino, hotels and restaurants. It has year-round sunshine and lively tourist facilities. The partying never stops at **Surfers Paradise**, a Miami-style high-rise strip overlooking a crowded beach. Inland are lush green mountains, rainforests, walking trails and scenic villages. Nature lovers will also appreciate the **Lamington National Park** in the **McPherson Mountains**, and the **Currumbin Bird Sanctuary**. An hour's drive north from Brisbane, the **Sunshine Coast** offers miles of untouched wilderness, lakes, mountains and unspoilt beaches with surf ranging in condition from mild to wild. Arts and crafts trails, nature walks and awe-inspiring views can be found in the hinterland, where the **Glasshouse Mountains** can be found.
Cairns is the major gateway to the far north. As well as the **Barrier Reef**, there are rainforests in the **Atherton Tableland** to the west, and to the south is **Mission Beach** with 14km (9 miles) of white sandy beaches, looking out to **Dunk Island**. To the north, there is the charming old town of **Port Douglas** attracting many visitors, as well as **Daintree**, which has services to **Cape Tribulation National Park**, and **Cooktown**, close to **Endeavour National Park** where excellent examples of Aboriginal rock art can be found. Beyond this lies the wilderness of **Cape York Peninsula**. **Townsville** is North Queensland's largest city, boasting an international airport and a casino. Cruises are available to nearby islands, as are trips to the Barrier Reef for diving, walking or whitewater rafting. This pleasant city, its streets lined with palm trees and tropical flora, has a number of interesting attractions on offer, such as **ReefHQ**, the largest coral aquarium in the world, with a transparent walk-in tunnel, and **Magnetic Island**, a resort island with superb beaches, diving opportunities, bush-walking tracks and a koala sanctuary, only 8km (5 miles) offshore and a 25-minute ferry ride from the city centre.

GREAT BARRIER REEF

This playground and beauty spot is also one of the world's great natural wonders. It stretches for 2000km (1200 miles) along the Queensland coast, its width varying from 25km (15 miles) to 50km (30 miles). There is unique plant and animal life to be found, with visibility often as deep as 60m (200ft).
Dotted along the coast are 25 island resorts, lying on or between the Barrier Reef and the mainland. **Heron** and **Lady Elliot Islands** are coral cays renowned as the best diving spots on the reef. **Lizard**, **Bedarra** and **Orpheus Islands** are quiet, secluded and luxurious hideaways. **Hayman Island** is an international resort, with 5-star luxury facilities. **Long Island**, **Great Keppel Islands**, **South Molle**, **Hamilton** and **Lindeman Island** are all-year-round resorts with facilities for families. **Tropical Dunk Island** and **Brampton Island** are popular with honeymooners. **Fitzroy** and **Hinchinbrook Islands** offer unspoilt beauty. Camping facilities can be found at Fitzroy, **Hook** and **Keppel Haven** on **Great Keppel Island**. Outside the main reef areas, the islands of **Fraser**, **Moreton**, **Bribie**, **North and South Stradbroke** offer some of the best unpopulated surfing beaches and national parks in Australia.

Sport & Activities

Watersports: The geographic proximity to the *Great Barrier Reef* and the long stretches of golden beach in Queensland mean leisure pursuits are associated predominantly with the sea – from **surfing** off the beaches in the south or **scuba-diving** and **snorkelling** on the corals of the Reef to deep-sea **fishing** for black marlin and **sailing** round the islands. Many of the most exotic dive sites are within 20-35km (12-22 miles) north and south of Cairns. Some of the most popular are *Thretford Reef*; the *Ribbon Reefs* (comprising a string of 10 coral ramparts covering a huge area, including the *Cod Hole*, *Pixie Pinnacle* and *Dynamite Pass*); *Magnetic Island*; the *Pompey Complex*; the *Swain Reefs* (near Gladstone); *Great Keppel Island*; *Heron Island* (reputed to support a record diversity of tropical fish); and *Lady Elliot Island*. For further information, contact the Queensland Diving Association (tel: (7) 3823 1389; e-mail: qldiving@tpq.com.au).
Canoeing and **sea-kayaking** around the Great Barrier Reef are also popular. The best surfing can be found at *Surfers' Paradise*, the *Sunshine Coast*, *Bribie*, *Moreton* and the *Stradbroke Islands*.

Credit: © Tourism Queensland

Bushwalking: Given the high humidity encountered during the summer in the northern regions, the cooler southern parts tend to be more popular for walking. *Lamington National Park* has a well maintained, graded track system in the *McPherson Range* (on the border with New South Wales), which features tall rainforests, waterfalls and gorges. A 3-day circuit is possible around *Fraser Island*, which has rainforest, huge sand dunes and beautiful lakes. A series of fairly demanding trails lead to the summit of the state's highest mountain, *Mount Bartle Frere*. Popular day walks are available on the islands of Dunk, Green and Hinchinbrook. For further details contact the QLD Environmental Protection Agency, PO Box 155, Albert Street, Brisbane QLD 4002 (tel: (7) 3227 7111; fax: (7) 3225 1769; e-mail: nqic@epa.qld.gov.au; website: www.epa.qld.gov.au).
Golf: Many of Queensland's courses, especially those on the Gold Coast and Sunshine Coast, tend to be part of luxury resorts. There are however also several good public courses, including the *Palm Meadows Golf Club* (on the Gold Coast); the *Paradise Springs Golf Course* (in tropical northern Queensland); the *Palms Sanctuary Cove*; and the *Brisbane City Public Golf Course*.
Adventure sports: Queensland is Australia's centre for **paragliding** and **parasailing**, which can be practised all along the coast. **Abseiling** is possible in the *Lamington* and *Carnarvon* national parks. The *Sunshine Coast* and *Mount Tamborine* are the main destinations for **hang gliding**. The *Tully* and *Barron* rivers in the north are suitable for **whitewater rafting**. **Speed boating** trips can be arranged in Cairns.

Credit: © Tourism Queensland

Social Profile

FOOD & DRINK: The food of the area relies to a large extent on the sea and the subtropical climate for specialities in cuisine. Local delicacies include mud crabs, king and tiger prawns, mackerel and fresh *barramundi*, as well as avocados, mangoes, pawpaws, pineapples, strawberries, bananas and the highly recommended local speciality, the *macadamia nut*. In Fortitude Valley, just out of Brisbane city centre, there are a number of European, Asian and Chinese restaurants and trendy cafes.
Brisbane is supplied with local wines from vineyards at Stanthorpe to the southwest, producing both red and white wines, and from other Australian vineyards.
All beers on sale are brewed locally. Queensland is the home of *Bundaberg Rum*, a sweet rum brewed with local sugar cane.
NIGHTLIFE: Although much of the tourist activity is centred on the beaches and the Barrier Reef, Brisbane offers a wide selection of entertainment. Most of the large hotels have dinner and dancing facilities and there are several nightclubs in the city, especially in Southbank Parklands where discos and restaurants abound. The Gold Coast has many nightclubs, as well as Jupiter's Casino. Townsville has the spectacular Sheraton Breakwater Casino on Sir Leslie Thiess Drive, offering a full range of gaming facilities and high-quality entertainment.
SHOPPING: Good buys include opals, Aboriginal art and handicrafts, woollen clothing, sheepskin coats and wood products. **Shopping hours:** Mon-Fri 0800-2100, Sat 0800-

Credit: © Tourism Queensland

A B C D E F G H I J K L M N O P Q R S T U V W X Y Z

Credit: © Tourism Queensland

1700, although hours vary depending on the city. Shops in the Gold Coast, Brisbane City, Sunshine Coast and Cairns are open on Sundays.
SPECIAL EVENTS: The following is a selection of special events occurring in Queensland in 2005; for a full list, consult Tourism Queensland (see *Contact Addresses* section): **Jan 26** *Australia Day*. **Feb 4** *Brisbane International Motor Show*. **Mar 5** *Jazz Under the Stars at Cosmos*, Clareville. **Mar 20-28** *Gladstone Harbour Festival*. **Apr 30-May 2** *May Day Celebrations*, Outback. **Jul 15-17** *Boulia Camel Races*. **Jul 31** *Childers Multicultural Food, Wine & Arts Festival*. **Aug 6-13** *Hervey Bay Whale Festival*, Fraser Coast South Burnett. **Sep 10** *Kingaroy Peanut Festival*.

Business Profile

COMMERCIAL INFORMATION: The following organisation can offer advice: Queensland Chamber of Commerce and Industry, Industry House, 375 Wickham Terrace, Brisbane, QLD 4000 (tel: (7) 3842 2244; fax: (7) 3832 3195; e-mail: info@commerceqld.com.au; website: www.qcci.com.au).
CONFERENCES/CONVENTIONS: Brisbane's major convention centres are Brisbane Convention & Exhibition Centre, Brisbane Entertainment Centre, Brisbane City Hall, Queensland Cultural Centre, RNA Exhibition Grounds, Sheraton Brisbane Hotel, Hilton International Hotel and the Carlton Crest International Hotel. Cairns' major convention centres are Cairns Convention Centre, Cairns International, Cairns Civic Centre, Cairns Show Grounds, the Botanical Gardens, Sheraton Mirage Resort and Cairns Hilton. The Gold Coast also has some excellent convention facilities, especially the Hotel Conrad and Jupiter's Casino with seating for 2300. Smaller centres can be found elsewhere along the Gold Coast at Royal Pines Resort and Sheraton Mirage Gold Coast. For more information on conferences and conventions in Queensland contact Gold Coast Tourism Bureau, Level Two, 64 Ferny Avenue, Surfers' Paradise 4217 (tel: (7) 5592 2699; fax: (7) 5570 3144; e-mail: info@gctb.com.au; website: www.goldcoasttourism.com.au); *or* Brisbane Convention and Exhibition Centre, PO Box 3869, Brisbane, QLD 4101 (tel: (7) 3308 3000; fax: (7) 3308 3500; e-mail: sales@bcec.com.au; website: www.bcec.com.au); *or* Cairns Convention Bureau (Tourism Tropical North Queensland) PO Box 865, Cairns, QLD 4870 (tel: (7) 4031 7676, ext 218; fax: (7) 4051 0127; e-mail: crcb@tnq.org.au; website: www.cairnsconventionbureau.com).

Climate

Queensland straddles the Tropic of Capricorn which accounts for the pleasant climate throughout most of the region. Exceptions are the far north and the dry arid western Outback. Brisbane enjoys an average of 7.1 hours of sunshine daily in the winter. The period between November to March is generally humid throughout the state, but sea breezes temper the humidity and make for perfect holiday conditions.

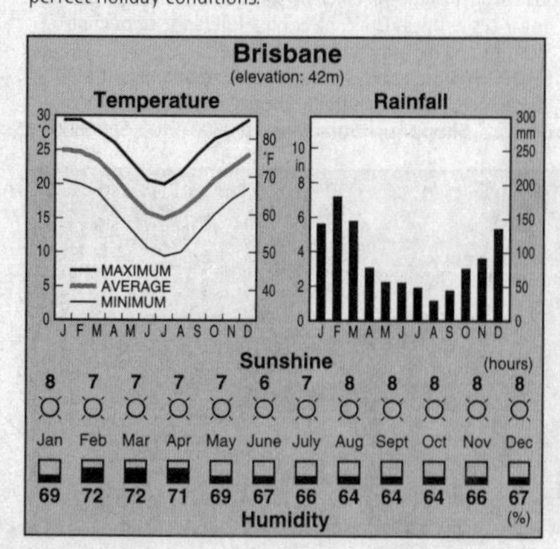

South Australia

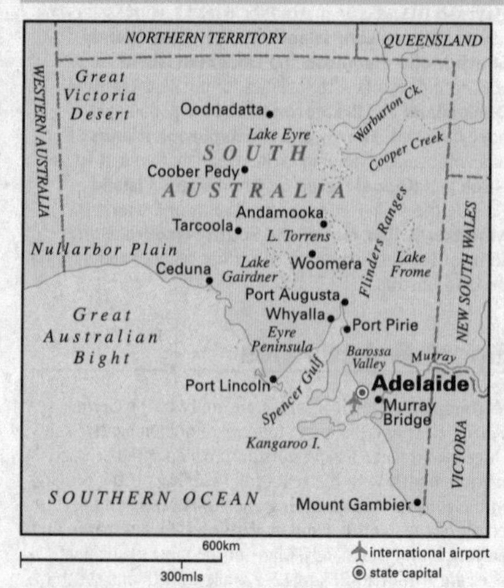

Location: Central Southern Australia.

South Australian Tourism Commission
Street address: Level 6, 50 Grenfell Street, Adelaide, SA 5000, Australia
Postal address: GPO Box 1972, Adelaide, SA 5001, Australia
Tel: (8) 8463 4500. Fax: (8) 8463 4535.
E-mail: satourism@saugov.sa.gov.au
Website: www.southaustralia.com
South Australian Visitor and Travel Centre
18 King William Street, Adelaide, SA 5000, Australia
Tel: (1 300) 655 276 (consumer enquiries) *or* (1 300) 363 544 (travel trade only). Fax: (8) 8303 2249.
E-mail: informationandbookings@southaustralia.com
Website: www.southaustralia.com
South Australian Tourism Commission
Gemini House, 10-18 Putney Hill, London SW15 6AA, UK
Tel: (020) 8780 8603. Fax: (020) 8780 1496.
E-mail: tbjordal@satc.australia.com
Website: www.southaustralia.com
South Australian Tourism Commission
17880 Skypark Circle, Suite 250, Irvine, CA 92614, USA
Tel: (949) 476 4081 *or* (888) 768 8428 (toll-free in USA).
Fax: (949) 476 4088.
E-mail: info@southoz.com
Website: www.southoz.com

General Information

AREA: 983,480 sq km (379,723 sq miles).
POPULATION: 1,527,421 (official estimate 2003).
POPULATION DENSITY: 1.6 per sq km.
CAPITAL: Adelaide. **Population:** 1,119,920 (official estimate 2003).
GEOGRAPHY: Except for the State capital of Adelaide, South Australia is sparsely inhabited – it is four times the area of the UK. It is the country's driest State, a region of rocky plains and desert landscape broken by the fertile wine-growing areas, which include the Barossa Valley. South Australia stretches upwards to the Northern Territory, and eastwards to Queensland, New South Wales and Victoria and westwards to Western Australia. The countryside ranges from the beach resorts of the Adelaide suburbs to the vast expanses of isolated, semi-desert outback; from the craggy mountains of Flinders Ranges to the meandering Murray River. Offshore is the popular Kangaroo Island.
TIME: GMT + 9.5 (GMT + 10.5 from last Sunday in October to third Saturday in March).

Public Holidays

South Australia observes all the public holidays observed nationwide (see the main Australia section) and, in addition, the following are observed:
2005: May 16* Adelaide Cup Day. **Jun 13** Queen's Birthday Celebrations. **Oct 3** Labour Day. **Dec 27** Proclamation Day.
2006: May 15* Adelaide Cup Day. **Jun 12** Queen's Birthday Celebrations. **Oct 2** Labour Day. **Dec 26** Proclamation Day.
Note: *The Adelaide Cup is a holiday in Adelaide only.

Travel - International

AIR: International carriers operating to Adelaide include *Air Paradise*, *Cathay Pacific*, *Garuda Indonesia*, *Malaysia Airlines*, *Qantas* and *Singapore Airlines*. Approximate flying time from *London* is 22 hours. Flights from Europe stop off in the Far East, usually Singapore, Kuala Lumpur or Bali. Adelaide is also linked to every other Australian State capital city. For more flight details see the main *Australia* section.
There is an excellent system of internal flights serving all regional towns, and the majority of flights are run by *Emu Air* (flights to Kangaroo Island), *Qantas*, *Rex Regional Express* and *Virgin Blue*. There are nine Government and 20 private airfields in the region.
International airports: *Adelaide Airport (ADL)* (website: www.aal.com.au), is 6km (4 miles) from the city centre, a drive of 15 minutes. Airport facilities include banks, bureaux de change, left luggage, restaurants, bars, shops and car hire (*Avis*, *Budget*, *Hertz* and *Thrifty*). A new international terminal is scheduled for completion in December 2005.
SEA: There are regular car-ferry services from Cape Jervis to Kangaroo Island (travel time – 45 minutes to one hour). Adelaide is an international port, with regular visits from several leading international cruise lines.
RAIL: Adelaide, where the popular *Ghan* train calls en route to Darwin (a scenic rail journey through a desert landscape), is a major terminal on the national rail network. *TransAdelaide* (website: www.transadelaide.com.au) offers comprehensive surburban rail services across the state. The main rail terminal is located at Keswick. The *Indian Pacific* from Sydney to Perth also stops in Adelaide, while the *The Overland* travels between Melbourne and Adelaide. Other tourist services are the *Cockle Train*, a scenic trip on vintage steam locomotives between Goolwa and Victor Harbour on the Fleurieu Peninsula, and the *Pichi Richi Steam Train* which leaves Quorn in the Flinders Ranges on a two hour 30 minutes round trip.
ROAD: The southern states are fully connected to the national system of **coach** lines that crosses Australia from all the state capitals. Typical coach journey times are as follows: from Adelaide to *Melbourne* is nine hours 30 minutes, to *Alice Springs* is 20 hours, to *Sydney* is 22 hours, to *Brisbane* is 33 hours 30 minutes, to *Perth* is 35 hours, and to *Darwin* is 46 hours. There are 95,225km (59,040 miles) of roads within the State. The main highways north are the *Stuart Highway* to Darwin via Coober Pedy and Alice Springs, and the *Birdsville Track* to Queensland. The other main State highways are the *Eyre Highway* west to Perth, the *Prince's Highway* along the coast to Melbourne and the *Stuart Highway* east to Canberra and Sydney. **Car hire:** Services are available at all the main hotels, the railway station and the airport. *Avis*, *Budget*, *Hertz* and *Thrifty Car Rental* are the main car hire companies. **Documentation:** Travellers need a current driving licence and either a cash deposit or credit card to make a booking. A minimum age requirement of 25 will probably be imposed.
URBAN: There is a fully integrated public transport system in Adelaide with **bus**, **tram** and local **rail** lines plus the *O-Bahn* bus system. The system is divided into zones. Pre-purchase booklets of cash-fare tickets and weekly and other passes are all available. The so-called *Metrotickets* are available for single, daily and multiple (up to 10) journeys. There are two free bus services, the *BeeLine* and the *City Loop*.

Accommodation

HOTELS: South Australia has many hotels and guest houses, ranging from budget hostels to 5-star international hotels. Bed & breakfast, farmstay and cottage accommodation is available throughout the State. Further information is available from the South Australian Visitor and Travel Centre (see *Contact Addresses*).
CAMPING/CARAVANNING: South Australia has approximately 200 caravan parks. Typical examples near Adelaide are as follows: Adelaide Caravan Park, West Beach, Marineland Village and Port Glanville Caravan Park. They all offer sites with full amenities and power. A number of companies can arrange **motor camper** rentals, with a range of fully equipped vehicles. Full details can be obtained from the South Australian Visitor and Travel Centre. In addition, there is a wide variety of holiday flats and apartments for rent in the State.
Note: For further coverage of the range of accommodation available in Australia, see *Accommodation* in the general *Australia* section.

Resorts & Excursions

ADELAIDE

Adelaide is home to more than two-thirds of the State's population. It has a 30km (18.6-mile) stretch of attractive coastline with excellent white sandy beaches. The best view of Adelaide and the surrounding countryside can be had from **Mount Lofty**, to the east of the city. Adelaide is a spacious city surrounded by parkland, golf courses and the botanical and zoological gardens. The city itself has a European atmosphere, primarily because of the large German and southern European minorities. The streets are filled with cafes (especially lively **Rundle Street**), European-style churches, art galleries and antique shops. Adelaide also has a vibrant nightlife along Rundle and Gouger Streets. One of the key attractions in the city is the **Festival Centre** complex in the parkland overlooking the **Torrens River**. It houses an excellent theatre company, and boasts a concert hall, two theatres, a restaurant and an amphitheatre. Another very popular attraction is the **Central Market** between Grote and Gouger streets. In March of even-numbered years, the world-renowned *Adelaide Bank Festival of Arts* is held, featuring everything from jazz to classical theatre and ballet, along with a diverse Edinburgh-style *Fringe Festival* (see *Social Profile* section). The **South Australian Museum** has the largest collection of Aboriginal artefacts in the world as well as a huge exhibition of Melanesian art and New Guinean wildlife. There is also a new permanent exhibition on the Antarctic Explorer, Sir Douglas Mawson. The **National Wine Centre**, featuring exhibitions, a tasting gallery and restaurant, opened in 2001 in the Botanic Gardens. **Tandanya – National Aboriginal Cultural Institute** offers a rounded view of Australia's indigenous culture. The swimming and skating on **Glenelg Beach** are popular Adelaide activities.

BEYOND ADELAIDE

55 km (34 miles) from Adelaide is Australia's wine cellar, the **Barossa Valley**, originally settled by German refugees in the 1830s and still indelibly marked by their influence. The main townships are **Tanunda**, **Angaston** and **Nuriootpa**, all notable for Lutheran churches and the vineyards where tours and tastings can be arranged. The other major wine regions in South Australia are the **Clare Valley**, **Riverland**, **McLaren Vale** and the **Coonawarra** wine district in the southeast.
Two routes through Australia's **Red Centre** begin near Adelaide, one being the Stuart Highway which goes to Darwin. The start of the **Great Ocean Road** begins at the haunting **Coorong Wetlands**, south of Adelaide, and goes on to Victoria.
Taking a **Murray River** steamer will afford the visitor a view of lush pastureland, limestone cliffs and the wine country. The Murray–Darling–Murrumbidgee river network is one of the largest in the world – 2600km (1615 miles) from source to sea – and brings irrigation to a wide area. The vegetation and wildlife evoke images of the Deep South in the USA.
Opposite Adelaide in the St Vincent Gulf lies Australia's third-largest island, **Kangaroo Island**. Off-road exploration of this natural wildlife sanctuary rewards the traveller with the chance to see penguins, koalas, wallabies and kangaroos as well as the large sea lion colony at **Seal Bay**; the rugged coastline is also noted for fine fishing. There is a variety of accomodation available, including a campsite.
Naracoorte Caves Conservation Park near the southeast border with Victoria is notable for its caves containing stalagmites, stalagtites, bats and fossils.
South Australia's best slice of the outback is to be found in the ancient Aboriginal heritage area of **Flinders Ranges**, a region of granite peaks and spectacular and colourful gorges, dotted with eucalyptus trees. In the centre of the Flinders area is the popular resort area of **Wilpena Pound**, a natural ampitheatre 16km (10 miles) long and 6km (3.7 miles) deep; accommodation is also available at **Arkaroola**, at the northern peak of the Flinders. The opal town of **Coober Pedy** is so hot that 45 per cent of the inhabitants live underground; even the church is underground, and in fact the name of the town means 'white man lives in a hole'. The area produces 90 per cent of the world's supply of opals and those who wish to dig for the semi-precious stones can obtain a miner's permit.

Sport & Activities

Wine tasting: Over 70 per cent of Australia's wine exports come from South Australia, where many of the region's wineries and cellars are open for tastings. The famous *Tasting Australia* wine and food festival is held bi-annually. For further information on the main wine-growing areas, see the *Resorts & Excursions* section.
Bushwalking: The remote *Flinders Ranges*, a vast area of plains, gorges and desert, located some 450km (280 miles) north of Adelaide, provides one of Australia's best gateways to the outback. The well-known *Heysen Trail*, the longest trail in Australia, which begins at Cape Jervis, winds its way north through scenic coastal areas to the Flinders Ranges. Bushwalkers can also head to the *Wilpena Pound*, a natural amphitheatre 16km (10 miles) long and 6km (3.7 miles) wide, with a possible two-day itinerary along well-marked tracks; or on a one-day climbing expedition to *St Mary's Peak*, a trek best tackled between May and October, when temperatures are milder and water more readily available

Credit: © South Australian Tourism Commission

(permits can be obtained from the ranger on site). More experienced walkers can embark on longer walks to the *Gammon Ranges National Park*, further north; the *Flinders Chase National Park* on Kangaroo Island; or the *Deep Creek Conservation Park* south of Adelaide. Further information can be obtained from the Department of Environment and Heritage, GPO Box 1047, Adelaide SA 5001 (tel: (8) 8204 9000; fax: (8) 8204 1919; e-mail: environmentshop@saugov.sa.gov.au; website: www.environment.sa.gov.au).
Watersports: The third-largest river in the world, the *River Murray*, winds its way through South Australia, providing opportunities for **cruises**, **houseboat hire**, **sailing** and **water-skiing**. The coast offers good **diving** facilities, with the best sites located near *Adelaide*, *Port Lincoln*, *Kangaroo Island*, *Yorke Peninsula*, *Eyre Peninsula* and several offshore islands and reefs. It is possible to wreck-dive and also dive with Great White Sharks. The best time for diving is between December and May. **Whale watching** is possible on the *Fleurieu Peninsula* around *Victor Harbor* and on the *Nullarbor* coast, where large colonies of Southern Right whales breed from June to October. **Fishing** is also good, and South Australia has a particularly abundant population of large snapper (with *Whyalla*, 397km/247 miles northwest of Adelaide, being the best region). Freshwater fishing can be undertaken on the Murray and Wakefield rivers. Game fishing is best around *Kangaroo Island* and *Port Lincoln*, the latter being known for its large concentration of giant great white pointer sharks. For **surfing** enthusiasts, South Australia offers uncrowded beaches and excellent waves, particularly at *Victor Harbor*, *Kangaroo Island* and the more remote *Yorke* and *Eyre* peninsulas (with Eyre's *Cactus Beach* attracting surfers from all over the world). The many deserted islands and beaches throughout the *Spencer Gulf* offer plenty of opportunities for **sailing cruises**.
Adventure sports: Ballooning is popular in the *Barossa Valley*, while the coast south of Adelaide is one of the country's major regions for **hang-gliding**. **Caving** is popular in the southeast and on Eyre Peninsula. It is possible to swim in an **underground lake** in the Nullabor caves.

Social Profile

FOOD & DRINK: The local delicacies are mainly German food in the Barossa region and, on the coast, crabs, whiting, crayfish and other seafood. Kangaroo steak is a speciality of the region and can be ordered in many Australian restaurants. Adelaide has a wide range of restaurants and cafes specialising in international cuisine, including US, Chinese, French, Greek, Italian, Indian, Indonesian, Japanese, Lebanese, Malaysian, Mexican, Mongolian and Vietnamese. Many of these offer alfresco dining. There are many excellent seafood restaurants.
There are many wine and food festivals throughout the region where local wines and beers can be tasted. One of these is the *Barossa Vintage Festival*, reminiscent in many ways of German beer festivals in Europe. There is also a brewery in Adelaide supplying stout and lagers, although whether in Adelaide itself, the hills or the outback, the pub experience should not be missed. South Australia contains one of the most important valley regions producing wines; from the reds of Coonawarra to the Rieslings of the Eden Valley. Although specialising in table wines, the state is noted for its sparkling reds and whites.
NIGHTLIFE: Adelaide has an extraordinary nightlife scene. The Adelaide Casino, once a grand Victorian railway station is now a haven for baccarat and roulette players amid its magnificent Corinthian columns (Mon-Fri 1000-0400 and continuously at weekends and on public holidays). There is also a concentration of nightclubs and discos on Hindley Street in the heart of the city, opposite Rundle Mall. Large crowds also flock to the cosmopolitan atmosphere of the pubs and cafes in Rundle Street.
SHOPPING: Excellent quality wines are available from the Barossa Valley, which attracts 60 per cent of Australia's wine-tasting tourists. Adelaide is a city which concentrates on culture, and is full of antique shops, art galleries and stores which sell Australia's finest opals, handmade chocolates and stockman's hats. Opening hours are the same as for the rest of Australia. There are also some street markets in Adelaide, the Central market being located adjacent to Victoria Square. This market, made up of 550 stalls, sells all kinds of produce including fruit, vegetables, fish, cheese, meat, spices and other exotic delights.
SPECIAL EVENTS: South Australia lives up to its name of the *Festival State* with a huge variety of festivals and special events taking place throughout the State all year round. For a full list of special events contact the South Australian Tourism Commission (see *Contact Addresses* section). The following is a selection of special events occurring in South Australia in 2005:
Jan 3-9 *Australian Hardcourt Championships*. **Jan 14-16** *Australian Open Road Championships* (cycling). **Jan 18-23** *Jacobs Creek Tour Down Under* (cycling). **Feb** *Jacob's Creek Open* (golf). **Feb 18-Mar 3** *Adelaide Film Festival*. **Mar** *Clipsal 500 Adelaide* (V8 touring cars). **Mar 4-6** *Womadelaide* (world music festival), Adelaide. **Mar 26-28** *Oakbank Easter Racing Carnival* (equestrian). **Apr 30-Jun 11** *The Great Australian Outback Cattle Drive*. **May** *Clare Valley Gourmet Weekend*. **Jun 10-25** *Adelaide Cabaret Festival*. **Jul 7-10** *Festival of Ideas*. **Sep 2-10** *Royal Adelaide Show*. **Sep 25-Oct 2** *World Solar Challenge*, racing by solar-powered vehicles from Darwin to Adelaide. **Oct 7-16** *Australian Master Games*. **Oct 21-30** *Tasting Australia*. **Nov 4-27** *FEAST 2005: Adelaide Lesbian & Gay Cultural Festival*.

Business Profile

COMMERCIAL INFORMATION: The following organisation can offer advice: Business SA, 136 Greenhill Road, Unley, SA 5061 (tel: (8) 8300 0000; fax: (8) 8300 0001; e-mail: enquiries@business-sa.com; website: www.business-sa.com.au).
CONFERENCES/CONVENTIONS: Adelaide's major convention centres are the recently upgraded Adelaide Convention Centre and Exhibition Hall, Adelaide Festival Centre, Hilton International Adelaide, Royal Showground and Exhibition Centre. For more information on conferences and conventions in South Australia contact the South Australian Tourism Commission *or* Adelaide Convention & Tourism Authority, GPO Box 351, Adelaide, SA 5001 (tel: (8) 8303 2333; fax: (8) 8303 2355; e-mail: acta@acta.com.au; website: www.acta.com.au).

Climate

Adelaide boasts a Mediterranean climate, perfect for enjoying the great Australian outdoors. Warm and temperate with long hot summers, short mild winters and low rainfall. The average temperature ranges from 15°C (58°F) in July, to 29°C (84°F) in January. One of the hottest places in the area in summer is Coober Pedy, 863km (536 miles) northwest of Adelaide, reaching temperatures of up to 45°C (113°F).
Required clothing: Lightweight cottons and linens in summer, warmer mediumweights in winter. Waterproofing is advisable throughout most of the year, particularly in winter.

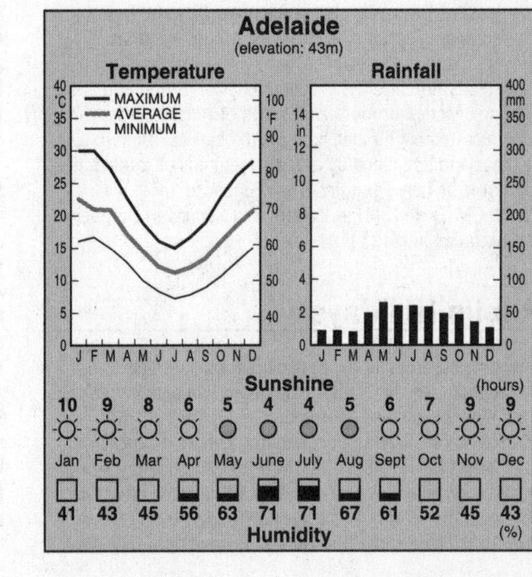

Tasmania

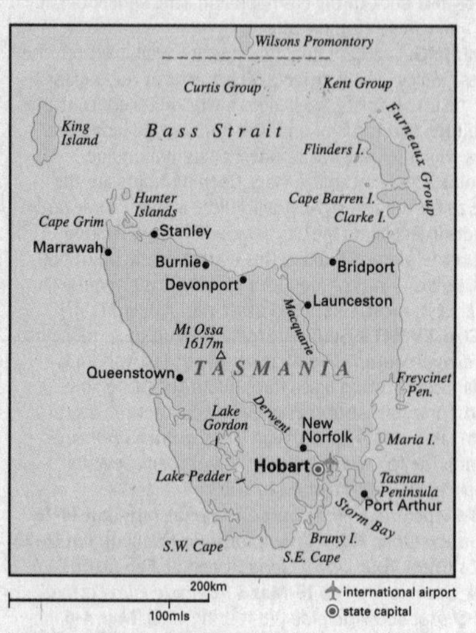

Location: South of mainland Australia.

Tourism Tasmania
Street Address: Level 2, 22 Elizabeth Street, Hobart, TAS 7001, Australia
Postal Address: GPO Box 399, Hobart, TAS 7000, Australia
Tel: (3) 6230 8235. Fax: (3) 6230 8353.
E-mail: reception@tourism.tas.gov.au
Website: www.discovertasmania.com.au *or* www.tourismtasmania.com.au

Tasmanian Travel Centre
60 Carrington Street, Sydney, NSW 2000, Australia
Tel: (1 300) 733 258 (reservations and enquiries; local call rate in Australia only). Fax: (2) 9202 2055.
E-mail: sydinfo@tourism.tas.gov.au
Website: www.tastravel.com.au *Office also in:* Melbourne.

Tourism Tasmania
12 Montpelier Place, London SW7 1HJ, UK
Tel: (020) 7584 6553. Fax: (020) 7584 6580
E-mail: sandra@sandraleach.co.uk
Website: www.discovertasmania.com

General Information

AREA: 68,400 sq km (26,409 sq miles).
POPULATION: 480,000 (official estimate 2003).
POPULATION DENSITY: 7.0 per sq km.
CAPITAL: Hobart. **Population:** 199,886 (official estimate 2003).
GEOGRAPHY: A separate island located 240km (149 miles) south of Melbourne across Bass Strait. Roughly heart-shaped, Tasmania is 296km (184 miles) long, ranging from 315km (196 miles) wide in the north to 70km (44 miles) in the south. The island has a diverse landscape comprising rugged mountains (snowcapped in winter), dense bushland (including the Horizontal Forest, so-called because the tree trunks are bent over parallel to the ground), tranquil countryside and farmland. Approximately 36 per cent of Tasmania is protected in national parks and other reserves, over half of this being the World Heritage-listed temperate wilderness in the west of the island. Located midway between Victoria and the northwest of Tasmania in Bass Strait lies King Island. This rich and fertile island, famous for its beef and dairy products, is regularly serviced by air carriers and is a popular tourist destination. To the northeast of Tasmania, also in Bass Strait, can be found Flinders Island, part of the Furneaux group of islands. Flinders Island is also popular with visitors and is particularly noted for its excellent coastal fishing and pristine beaches. Bruny Island, south of Hobart across the D'Entrecasteaux Channel, has superb beaches. The two parts of the island are joined by a narrow isthmus of sand-dunes, the home of Fairy Penguins from August to April.
TIME: GMT + 10 (GMT + 11 from first Sunday in October to last Saturday in March).

Public Holidays

Tasmania observes all the public holidays observed nationwide (see the main Australia section) and, in addition, the following are also observed:
2005: Feb 14* Royal Hobart Regatta. **Feb 23*** Launceston Cup. **Mar 14** Eight Hours Day. **Mar 29** Bank Holiday. **Jun 13** Queen's Birthday Celebrations. **Sep 30*** Burnie Show. **Oct 21*** Royal Launceston Show. **Oct 6*** Flinders Island Show. **Oct 20*** Hobart Show Day. **Nov 7*** Recreational Day. **Nov 25*** Devonport Show.
2006: Feb 13* Royal Hobart Regatta. **Feb 22*** Launceston Cup. **Mar 13** Eight Hours Day. **Apr 18** Bank Holiday. **Jun 12** Queen's Birthday Celebrations. **Oct 1*** Burnie Show. **Oct 12*** Launceston Show Day. **Oct 20*** Flinders Island Show Day. **Oct 26*** Hobart Show Day. **Nov 6*** Recreational Day. **Nov 24** Devonport Day. **Note:** *Regional observance only.

Travel - International

AIR: Most flights come from the Australian mainland. Direct flights to Hobart arrive from Brisbane, Melbourne and Sydney, with quick connections available from Adelaide, Cairns, Canberra, Darwin and Perth. Launceston, Devonport and Burnie also receive flights from the mainland. Airlines serving Tasmania include *Jetstar*, *Qantas*, *Rex Regional Express*, *Singapore Airlines* and *Virgin Blue*. The airport is 22km (14 miles) from Hobart city centre, a drive of about 35 minutes. *Island Airlines Tasmania* flies to Flinders Island. *TasAir* and *King Island Airlines* fly to King Island. Both islands are directly accessible from the Australian mainland, as well as from Tasmania.
International airports: *Hobart (HBA)* lies 16km (10 miles) east of Hobart (travel time - 15-20 minutes by taxi). Airport facilities include banks/ATMs, bars and car hire (*Avis*, *Budget*, *Hertz* and *Thrifty*).
SEA: There is an overnight ferry, the *Spirit of Tasmania*, which runs daily from Melbourne to Devonport on the northwest coast of the island (travel time - 10 hours), with additional day sailings during peak periods. Since January 2004, a new ferry service operates from Sydney to Devonport three times a week (travel time - 21 hours). Both services are operated by *Spirit of Tasmania* (website: www.spiritoftasmania.com).
RAIL: There are no passenger services. However, the West Coast Wilderness Railway runs a tourist service between Queestown and Strahan; it is a reconstruction of the original Abt railway that carried ore from the mines to the coast. In the northwest, the Don River Railway also runs regular excursions using both steam and diesel locomotives.
ROAD: All settlements on the island are linked by a road system running for 22,000km (13,670 miles) over which there are bus services connecting the main cities and towns. The main routes are: the *Lyell Highway* from Hobart to Queenstown; the *Huon Highway* from Hobart to Southport; the *Heritage Highway* from Hobart to Launceston; the *Tasman Highway* from Hobart along the east coast; and the *Bass Highway* linking the ports of the north and northwest coast. There are 11 pre-planned touring routes to help discover the unique Tasmanian scenery and natural attractions. **Coach:** Tasmania has its own coach services; *Tasmanian Redline Coaches*, which offers a *Tassie Bus Pass* to out-of-state visitors, and *Tasmania Wilderness Transport*, which serves the needs of bushwalkers. **Bicycle:** Helmets must be worn at all times.
URBAN: Local bus networks are operated in Hobart, Launceston and Burnie.

Accommodation

Tourism Tasmania publishes a booklet giving details of accommodation rates which is available from Tourism Australia (for address details, see the main *Australia* section). Information can also be obtained from the Australian Hotels Association, 176 New Town Road, New Town, Tasmania 7008 (tel: (3) 6278 1930; fax: (3) 6278 1971; e-mail: aha@australianhotels.asn.au; website: www.australianhotels.asn.au).
HOTELS, MOTELS AND GUEST-HOUSES: There are international hotels in Hobart and Launceston and a wide range of tourist hotels, motels and guest houses in all the major centres. Hotels tend to be slightly more expensive in Hobart and Launceston, and in the main tourist areas.
CAMPING/CARAVANNING: A number of companies can arrange campervan or motorhome rentals, with a range of fully equipped vehicles. Full details can be obtained from Tourism Tasmania. There are numerous camping and caravan sites in Tasmania. It should be noted that camping is not permitted in any roadside picnic or rest areas.
SELF-CATERING/FARM- AND HOMESTAYS: These are also widely available. More detailed information on the range of accommodation available in Australia may be found by consulting *Accommodation* in the main *Australia* section.
HOSTELS: There is an extensive network of backpacker hostels all over the island.
WILDERNESS LODGES: These are located in wilderness areas, and are designed to blend in with their surroundings. Some offer a high standard of comfort, while others are more humble in style. They also organise activities such as kayaking, wildlife viewing and guided walks.
Note: For further coverage of the range of accommodation available see *Accommodation* in the general *Australia* section.

Resorts & Excursions

HOBART: Tasmania's capital is Australia's second-oldest city after Sydney and is situated on the south side of the island. The city has strong links with the sea, typified by the wharves, jetties and warehouses - some dating back to the 19th century - which cluster around the waterfront. Examples of the island's history can be seen in the **Maritime Museum of Tasmania**, the convict-era buildings of **Battery Point** and the **Tasmanian Museum and Art Gallery**. The sweet-toothed will enjoy touring the **Cadbury Chocolate Factory**. **Mount Wellington**, towering 1270m (4170ft) to the west of the city, provides the backdrop to Hobart. From the lookout at the top (about 20km/12 miles by road) the clear air offers a spectacular view of Hobart, its suburbs, the **Derwent Estuary** and **Storm Bay**. Apart from the view, the area has picnic facilities and walking trails. The **Royal Tasmanian Botanical Gardens** offer a long walk through beautiful scenery.
BEYOND HOBART: The popular **Tahune AirWalk** is a 1.5 hour's drive from Hobart, offering a suspended 45m-high walkway above spectacular forest canopies. It is part of the **Huon Trail** which includes the Hastings thermal pool, caves and sheltered bays of the D'Entrecasteaux Channel. AirWalk admission fees are A$9 for adults and A$6 for children. **Launceston**, Tasmania's second city on the north of the island, retains much of its colonial Georgian/Edwardian flavour. It is the natural gateway for the rural beauty of the island, including the **Cataract Gorge** and the **Launceston Lake Wildlife Sanctuary**. **City Park** is frequented for its **Botanical Conservatory** and **Monkey Island** featuring Japanese mecaque monkeys. The new **Queen Victoria Museum and Art Gallery** at **Inveresk** near Launceston features original Tasmanian and Aboriginal art as well as various temporary exhibitions; entry fee is A$10. **Port Arthur**, 100km (82 miles) east of Hobart, is the site of a penal colony built in the early 19th century. Guided tours are available including a popular **ghost tour**. There is a new 1.5 hour trail along the cliffs and beaches. Not far away is **Eaglehawk Neck**, noted for its bizarre rock formations and the highest sea cliffs in the southern hemisphere.

National Parks

Tasmania is an island of wilderness; there are 20 national parks, including the world's last temperate-climate rainforest, and its wildlife includes the unique and fearsome little marsupial the Tasmanian Devil. Some of the more notable national parks include **Cradle Mountain/Lake St Clair**, famous for the **Overland Track** walk; **Mount Field**, known for **Russell Falls**, the **Tall Trees Walk** and autumnal colours of the only deciduous Australian tree - *nothofagus gunii*; **Freycinet** on Tasmania's east coast, which contains **Wineglass Bay** (one of the world's top ten beaches); **Narawntapu** (formerly **Aspestos Range** in northern Tasmania, renowned for its wildlife; **Franklin-Gordon Wild Rivers**, with walks, camping grounds and incredible views; **Ben Lomond**, Tasmania's main ski resort; the **Southwest**, a major part if the World Heritage Area, and **Walls of Jerusalem**.

Sport & Activities

Watersports: Boat or **sailing** cruises are popular ways to explore the port cities of Launceston and Hobart, as well as the outlying islands. **River cruises** can easily be arranged on Tasmania's the *Huon River*, with its orchards and salmon farms; the *Pieman* and *Arthur* rivers in the northwest of the island; or the mighty *Gordon River* which flows through the rainforest in the *World Heritage Area*. Options for more active visitors are **sea kayaking** (kayaks and equipment can be hired and guided voyages arranged) or **rafting** on the *Franklin*, *Derwent*, *Arthur*, *Picton*, *South Esk*, *Mersey* and *Meander* rivers. Trips last one-11 days. **Jet boating**, on flat water or on the rapids, is available on the *Derwent*, *Huon* or *King* rivers. Speeds average 70kph (43mph). **Diving** is a fantastic way to explore the shipwrecks and kelp forests near *King* and *Flinders Islands*. Professional dive operators around the islands and the east coast all offer equipment for hire.
Outdoor activities: Tasmania's air is reckoned to be the cleanest in the inhabited world. Its pristine scenery and balmy climate make it a delight for lovers of the outdoors. Furthermore, the island contains the largest expanse of temperate wilderness in the world, a unique landscape, rightly listed as a heritage site. On land, visitors can experience the spectacular countryside in a variety of ways. **Cycling** can be undertaken independently or on pre-arranged tours. A favourite route is from Devonport to Launceston via the dramatic *Elephant Pass*, and possibly all the way south to Hobart. Mountain bikers can opt for forest trails in the reserves, and those looking for strenuous activity can

ride 'The Wild Way' through the World Heritage Area. **All-terrain touring** to more remote and wilder areas can be arranged through specialist operators. Transport is in 4-wheel-drive vehicles or 4-wheel motorcycles, well suited to the island's extensive network of off-road trails. For aerial views, **wilderness flights** can be booked in Hobart; these travel over the mountains towards the southwestern wilderness.
Wildlife: Tasmania's 20 national parks are home to a rich variety of animals, many of them unique to the island. They include wombats, possums, platypus, wallabies, fairy penguins and the rare orange-bellied parrot. The Tasmanian Devil, a small, black, dog-like marsupial can be readily seen at night in the *Narawntapu-*, *Mount William-* and *Cradle National Parks*. Although it looks fierce, it is not usually harmful to humans. The hunt still continues for the so-called Tasmanian Tiger or *thylacine*, not sighted for 60 years and thought to be extinct. This creature, actually a marsupial wolf, is the state's official mascot.

Social Profile

FOOD & DRINK: Some of the best seafood in the world is available in Tasmania, including Angasi oysters, crayfish, scallops, Atlantic salmon and ocean trout. Freshwater wild brown trout is caught in the Tasmanian highlands. The island's cheese is excellent and renowned among conoisseurs. Goat, quail and venison are the area's speciality meats, and other specialities include apples, apricots, berry fruits and liqueur honey. Tasmanian wine, favoured by Sydney's top restaurants, has won several international awards, and two popular beers are produced, *Boags* and *Cascade*.
NIGHTLIFE: There are casinos in Hobart and Launceston. Hobart's waterfront area, Salamanca Place, is the home of many night-time haunts in its old stone warehouses. Small, traditional-style pubs, open all day and into the small hours of the morning, are a special feature here. Hobart boasts Australia's oldest theatre, the Royal Theatre, and the city's concert hall is the home of the Tasmanian Symphony Orchestra, considered to be Australia's best orchestra.
SPECIAL EVENTS: For a full list of special events contact Tourism Tasmania *or* the Australian Tourist Commission.

Business Profile

COMMERCIAL INFORMATION: The following organisation can offer advice: Tasmanian Chamber of Commerce and Industry (TCCI), Industry House, 30 Burnett Street, North Hobart, TAS 7000 (tel: (3) 6236 3600; fax: (3) 6231 1278; e-mail: admin@tcci.com.au; website: www.tcci.com.au).
CONFERENCES/CONVENTIONS: The major convention centres in Hobart are Wrest Point Federal Hotel, Casino and Convention Centre and Hobart Grand Chancellor Hotel. Launceston's major convention centres are Launceston Convention Centre/Albert Hall, Federal Launceston Country Club and Casino and Launceston International Hotel. For more information on conferences and conventions in Tasmania, contact Tourism Australia (see main *Australia* section) *or* the Tasmanian Convention Bureau, Level 3, 18 Elizabeth Street, Hobart, TAS 7000 (tel: (3) 6224 6852; fax: (3) 6223 8321; e-mail: mail@tasmania-conventions.org.au; website: www.tasmaniaconventions.com).

Climate

Similar climate to southern Australia, with warm, dry summers and cool, wet winters. However, climate in Tasmania is more variable and more changeable, with some areas (eg Hobart) receiving considerably less rainfall than others. Most of the rainfall is in the west of the island. There is often snow above 1000m (3280ft) in July and August.
Required clothing: Cottons and linens in summer, warmer mediumweights in winter. Waterproofing is advisable throughout the year, particularly in highland areas. Jumpers are recommended for the evenings, all year round.

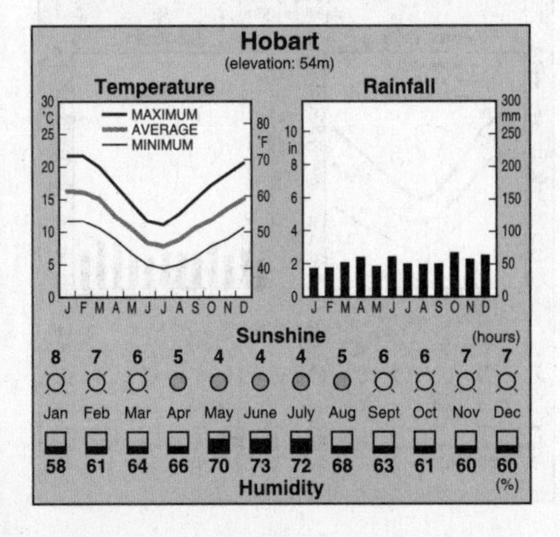

Victoria

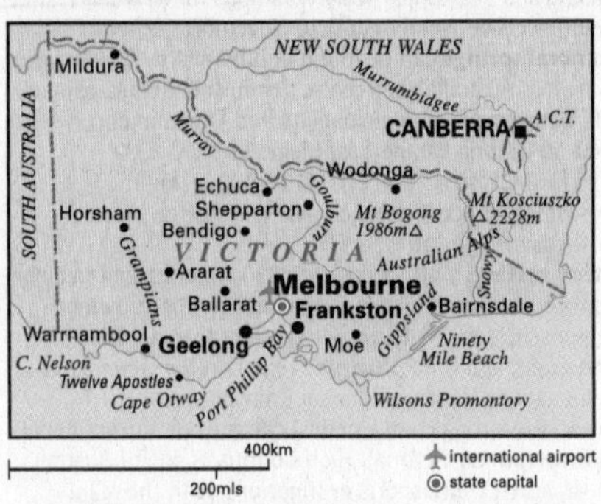

Location: Southeast Australia, south of New South Wales.

Tourism Victoria
GPO Box 2219T, 55 Collins Street, Melbourne, VIC 3000, Australia
Tel: (3) 9653 9777. Fax: (3) 9653 9722.
E-mail: planner@tourism.vic.gov.au
Website: www.visitvictoria.com *or* www.visitmelbourne.com *or* www.tourismvictoria.com.au (corporate).
Victoria Visitor Information Centre
Lower Level, Federation Square, Corner of Flinders and Swanston Streets, Melbourne, VIC 3000, Australia
Tel: (3) 9658 9658. Fax: (3) 9650 6168.
E-mail: tourism@melbourne.vic.gov.au
Website: www.thatsmelbourne.com.au
Tourism Victoria
Australia Centre, Melbourne Place, The Strand, London WC2B 4LG, UK
Tel: (020) 7438 4645 *or* (09068) 633 235 (brochure request line; calls cost 60p per minute). Fax: (020) 7379 9681.
E-mail: tourvic.london@tourism.vic.gov.au
Website: www.visitmelbourne.com/uk

General Information

AREA: 227,600 sq km (141,000 sq miles).
POPULATION: 4,765,900 (official estimate 2000).
POPULATION DENSITY: 21.0 per sq km.
CAPITAL: Melbourne. **Population:** 3,466,000 (official estimate 2000).
GEOGRAPHY: Victoria is Australia's most diverse state and its major agricultural and industrial producer. Located in the southeast, bordered by South Australia and New South Wales, its landscape consists of mountains, rainforests, deserts, snowfields, beaches, vineyards, wheatlands and market gardens. The Australian Alps are only three hours away from Melbourne and the Great Ocean Road to South Australia is a day's drive. Victoria has 32 national parks, amounting to a third of Australia's total.
TIME: GMT + 10 (GMT + 11 from third Sunday in October to third Saturday in March).

Public Holidays

Victoria observes all the public holidays observed nationwide (see the main Australia section) and, in addition, the following are also observed:
2005 Mar 14 Labour Day. **Jun 13** Queen's Official Birthday. **Nov 1*** Melbourne Cup Day.
2006 Mar 13 Labour Day. **Jun 12** Queen's Official Birthday. **Nov 2*** Melbourne Cup Day.
Note: *Melbourne metro area only.

Travel - International

AIR: The international airport at *Melbourne (MEL) (Tullamarine)* (website: www.melbourne-airport.com.au) receives flights from the UK (approximate flying time from London – 21 hours), Europe, Asia and the USA. Major international airlines serving Melbourne include *British Airways*, *KLM*, *Malaysia Airlines*, *Qantas* and *United Airlines*. The airport is 22km (14 miles) from the city (travel time – 35 minutes). For more flight details see the main *Australia* section. There are flights from Melbourne to all State capitals and many regional hubs. Domestic carriers include *Jetstar*, *Qantas*, *Regional Express* and *Virgin Blue*.
SEA: An overnight passenger/vehicle ferry from Tasmania to Melbourne departs daily (website: www.spiritoftasmania.com.au). There are also ferry services from Melbourne to Williamstown across Port Phillip Bay; between Southgate, Princes Walk and the Melbourne Aquarium and Crown entertainment complex; and across the headlands of Port Phillip Bay between the beach towns of Queenscliff and Sorrento. Melbourne is an increasingly popular port for international cruise ships.
RAIL: *V-Line* (website: www.vlinepassenger.com.au) operates state rail services, with links from Melbourne to Ballarat, Bendigo, Echuca, Geelong, Sale, Seymour, Swan Hill, Traralgon and Wodonga. Overnight trains link Melbourne and Sydney (13 hours), and an overnight train – *The Overland* – runs to Adelaide (12 hours). Trains run to other main centres including Canberra (eight hours 30 minutes), Brisbane (48 hours) and Perth (72 hours).
ROAD: Connected to all States by coach services. Main coach routes and travelling times are as follows: from Melbourne to *Canberra* is nine hours 30 minutes, to *Adelaide* is nine hours 30 minutes, to *Sydney* is 12 hours, to *Broken Hill* is 19 hours, to *Brisbane* is 25 hours. There is a well-developed road system covering 156,700km (97,400 miles) on which local buses operate.
URBAN: Melbourne has an extensive network of electric railways, linked in the city centre by an **underground** loop-line. There is also a **tram** network which has an integrated ticket structure with the **bus** and **rail** systems. Tickets should be purchased before boarding, or from onboard vending machines (trams only). Fares are zonal, with travel cards for daily or weekly travel and multi-journey tickets. The Melbourne *City Circle* tram, in distinct burgundy and gold colours, is free. The *Melbourne City Explorer Bus* and the *City Wanderer Bus* leave hourly to major attractions in the city and the visitor may join or leave at any stopping point in the journey.

Accommodation

HOTELS: A full range of accommodation is available in Victoria, ranging from international-standard hotels in Melbourne to farm-stay, home-stay and self-catering holidays throughout the region. Numerous historic bed & breakfast establishments, some of them supported by the National Trust of Australia, are also on offer. There are also new cutting-edge hotels now open in Victoria, including *Lindrum*, *Park Hyatt*, *The Hatton*, *The Prince* and *Westin*. For further information, contact the Australian Hotels Association Victoria, (tel: (3) 9822 0900; fax: (3) 9822 9099; website: www.ahha.com.au).
BED & BREAKFAST: These range from quiet lodges and cottages to farms and classic guest houses. **Farmstays** offer the opportunity to stay in a family homestead whilst participating in farm activities. Further information can be obtained from Tourism Victoria (see *Contact Addresses* section).
CAMPING/CARAVANNING: A number of companies can arrange motor camper rentals, with a range of fully equipped vehicles. Full details can be obtained from Parks Victoria, Level 10, 535 Bourke Street, Melbourne, VIC 3000 (tel: (3) 8627 4699; fax: (3) 9629 5563; e-mail: info@parks.vic.gov.au; website: www.parkweb.vic.gov.au). The Royal Automobile Club of Victoria (RACV) also produces a comprehensive guide to tourist park accommodation, available at RACV retail stores in Victoria and online (website: www.racv.com.au).
Note: For further coverage of the range of accommodation available, see *Accommodation* in the main *Australia* section.

Resorts & Excursions

MELBOURNE

Melbourne is a highly cosmopolitan city of over 3 million people with sizeable Italian and Greek minorities. Located in **Carlton Gardens** on the northern edge of the city centre, the ultramodern **Melbourne Museum** is Australia's largest museum. Its features include a living Forest Gallery, Aboriginal Centre, Children's Museum and IMAX Theatre. The chilling **Old Melbourne Gaol** has Ned Kelly's armour on display. The **National Gallery of Victoria: St Kilda Road** houses Australia's greatest collection of international fine art. The **NGV: Australian Art** is one of the attractions of **Federation Square**, a new city block devoted to culture. **Rialto Towers Observation Deck** offers panoramic views of the city and surrounds. Other places to visit include the **Royal Botanical Gardens**, **Parliament House**, the **Melbourne Cricket Ground** and the vibrant beach-side esplanade in **St Kilda** with its vibrant cafe culture. Also recommended are a trip to the races, a ride in one of Melbourne's trams, a river cruise down the **River Yarra**, or a visit to the huge **Melbourne Zoo**, with its intricately recreated animal habitats.

BEYOND MELBOURNE

35km (22 miles) from the State capital are the **Dandenong Ranges**, which provide excellent views of the city over the peaks from the **Summit Lookout**. At **Mount Dandenong** itself is the sanctuary named after William Ricketts, one of the early champions of Aboriginal rights. His haunting

A B C D E F G H I J K L M N O P Q R S T U V W X Y Z

carvings of Aboriginal faces still stare out over the forested landscape and are part of the **Galeena Beek Aboriginal Culture Centre**. Victoria was also the home of the outlaw Ned Kelly, often regarded as a national hero in Australia, and was the scene of the eventful days of bushranging during the gold rush of the 1850s and 1860s. **Sovereign Hill**, 120km (75 miles) northwest of Melbourne, is an old gold-rush town from this period, now restored to its original condition. Other towns of this era are **Ballarat** and **Bendigo**, respectively 115km (71 miles) and 150km (93 miles) from Melbourne. Nostalgia is also available in the shape of '**Puffing Billy**', a train of bright red carriages which runs along from Belgrave to Gembrook through the Dandenong Ranges. In the east of the State is **Gippsland Lakes**, a lush fertile region dotted with lakes and parkland. The west is drier, with huge sheep-grazing lands. Towards the centre are the **Grampian Mountains**, famous for wild flowers, birdlife and offering some of the world's finest rock climbing. Victoria is also home to **Brambuk**, a cultural centre exhibiting the arts, crafts and historical records of the Western Aboriginal people (open daily 1000-1700).

NATIONAL PARKS & NATURE RESERVES

Phillip Island Nature Reserve, 140km (87.5 miles) from Melbourne, is famous for its rich wildlife, particularly birds, koalas, fairy penguins (which can be seen marching up the beach in the evenings), and fur seals (large colonies of which can be observed at the **Seal Rocks Sea Life Centre**). Another famous wildlife sanctuary is in the **Wilson's Promontory National Park**, southeast of Melbourne on the southernmost tip of the Australian mainland. The **Port Campbell National Park**, southwest of Melbourne, contains some of the most beautiful - and dangerous - coastlines in Victoria. It is here that the awesome rock formations, **The Twelve Apostles**, can be seen from the stunning **Great Ocean Road**.

Sport & Activities

Bushwalking: The best-known destinations include *Bogong National Park* (with a possible six-day walk including the ascent of Mount Bogong, from October to April only); *Mount Feathertop* (a two-day circuit offering scenic mountain views, requiring walkers to be prepared for snowfalls at any time of the year); *Wilson's Promontory* (locally known as 'the Prom', a three-day circuit through beautiful stretches of coastline); and the *Grampians* (a spectacular region of sandstone mountain ranges, forests, valleys and heaths, particularly famous for its displays of wildflowers between August to November). Several **mineral springs** can be found around nearby *Daylesford*, known as Australia's spa centre. For further details, contact VIC Department of Sustainability and Environment, 240-50 Victoria Parade, East Melbourne VIC 3002 (tel: (3) 9412 4011; fax: (3) 9412 4803; e-mail: customer.service@dse.vic.gov.au; website: www.dse.vic.gov.au).

Wine tasting: Victoria has over 350 wineries, and tasting tours are widely available. Outstanding wine-growing regions include the *Yarra Valley*; the *Mornington Peninsula*; and the *Rutherglen* region in the Grampians. The Victorian Wineries Tourism Council (website: www.visitvictoria.com/wineries) can provide further details.

Wintersports: Victoria's High Country is one of Australia's most visited wintersports destinations, with the main snowfields only about four hours by car from Melbourne. The best destinations for **downhill skiing** and **snowboarding** include *Mount Buller, Falls Creek, Mount Hotham, Mount Buffalo* and *Mount Baw Baw*, all of which have excellent facilities. Other resorts, such as the *Bogong High Plains, Lake Mountain, Mount St Gwinear* or *Mount Torbreck*, are specifically designed for **cross country skiing**.

Watersports: Home to regular international regattas (such as *Sail Melbourne*), Melbourne's *Port Philip Bay* is one of the world's great **yachting** waterways. There are also some good beaches nearby and even better ones at *Westernport Bay, Ninety Mile Beach* (in the Gippsland Lakes area) and along the *Bellarine Peninsula* near Geelong. The best **diving** destinations include *Wilson's Promontory* (access to the sites is mostly by organised boat tours); *Cape Liptrap* (good for beginners); *Cape Patterson; Phillip Island; Cape Schanck; Apollo Bay; Cape Otway* (known for its crayfishing areas); *Port Fairy* (around which lie up to 30 stranded ships); and *Portland* (Victoria's westernmost town). **Whale watching** is possible at *Warrnambool*, 263km (163 miles) west of Melbourne, where migrating whales can be observed between May and July. **Surfing** enthusiasts may head to *Bells Beach* and *Jan Juc* on the Great Ocean Road near Torquay, where the *Rip Curl Pro & Quit Classic*, a triple-A world-rated international **surfing** contest, is held annually for a period of seven days over Easter. *Woolamai* in Phillip Island offers excellent surfing for the more experienced surfer.

Spectactor sports: Australian Rules Football, or 'Aussie Rules', a mixture between football and rugby, originated in Victoria. The climax of the season (starting in March) is the *Australian Football League Grand Final*, played in September at the famous *Melbourne Cricket Ground*, which also plays host to the highest standard of international and national **cricket** matches, and is ranked amongst cricket's most sacred pitches. The first Tuesday in November is declared a public holiday for the running, at Flemington, of the 3.2km- (two mile-long) *Melbourne Cup*, the highlight of Australia's racing year. This presitigious **horserace** offers the highest prizes in the southern hemisphere.

Other Activities: Northwest of Melbourne, *Sovereign Hill*, located within the country's most famous gold rush destination, offers visitors a chance to do their own **gold panning**. Further information on this area can be provided by Ballarat Tourism (website: www.ballarat.com).

Social Profile

FOOD & DRINK: There is an enormous variety of cuisine available in Melbourne and restaurants offering specific types can be found in sectionalised districts: Lygon Street for Italian, Little Bourke Street for Chinese, Lonsdale Street for Greek, Victoria Street for Vietnamese, Sydney Road for Turkish and Spanish, and Acland Street for Central European. Other cuisines that are well represented in the city's restaurants include French, American, Mexican, Lebanese, African, Malaysian, Afghan, Swiss and Mongolian.

NIGHTLIFE: Melbourne is home to a vibrant and varied entertainment culture that comes alive at night. There is everything from ballet, classical concerts and opera to plays in Melbourne's ornate theatres like the *Princess* and *Regent*, and street performers. There is an eclectic array of pubs, bars and nightclubs in and around Melbourne. Whatever your taste there is something to suit everyone, whether it's a laid-back beer in an authentic Aussie pub, a comedy night, live bands playing jazz and blues music or upmarket dance clubs. The *Crown Casino Complex*, located on the bank of the Yarra River in Melbourne is a complete amusement area that includes a casino, cinemas, restaurants, bowling-alley and nightclubs.

SHOPPING: Food products such as honeys, jams, chutneys and the local wines of *Yarra Valley* are popular buys. Tradtional sheepskins and the Australian's answer to the raincoat, the *drizabone*, can be found here. Melbourne is a major fashion centre, home to the world-famous surfing brand, *Quicksilver*, and shoppers looking for Australian and international designer wear should head for the city arcades or Howey Place. Unusual buys and bargains can be had at the Queen Victoria Market. **Shopping hours:** Sat-Wed 0900-1700, Thurs-Fri 0900-2100, Sun 1000-1700. All major supermarkets are open 24 hours.

SPECIAL EVENTS: 3For a full list, contact Tourism Victoria (see *Contact Addresses* section). The following is a selection of special events occurring in Victoria in 2005: **Jan 17-30** *Australian Open*, Melbourne. **Feb 19-20** *Honda Yarra Valley Grape Grazing Festival*, Yarra Valley, Dandenongs and the Ranges. **Feb 22-27** *Paynesville Jazz Festival/International Music Festival*, Melbourne. **Mar 3-6** *Australian Formula 1 Foster's Grand Prix*, Melbourne. **Mar 11-23** *Melbourne Food and Wine Festival*. **Mar 15-20** *Australian International Airshow*, Lara. **Mar 25-Apr 17** *Melbourne International Comedy Festival*. **May 3-5** *Warrnambool May Racing Carnival*. **May 5-15** *International Jazz Festival*, Melbourne. **May 6-14** *Shakespeare on the River Festival*, Phillip Island & Gippsland Discovery. **Oct 9** *Sorrento Spring Festival*, Melbourne's Bays & Peninsulas. **Nov 4-7** *Equitana Asia Pacific* (horse show), Melbourne.

Business Profile

COMMERCIAL INFORMATION: The following organisation can offer advice: Victorian Employers' Chamber of Commerce and Industry, Industry House, 486 Albert Street, East Melbourne, VIC 3002 (tel: (3) 8662 5333; fax: (3) 8662 5462; e-mail: webmaster@vecci.org.au; website: www.vecci.org.au).

CONFERENCES/CONVENTIONS: Melbourne, Australia's second-largest city and gateway to the southern region, has convention facilities to match international standards - the Melbourne Exhibition and Convention Centre is the largest exhibition space in the southern hemisphere with over 14,000 hotel rooms, 30 meeting rooms, 7300sq m of exhibition space and three state of the art theatres. The World Congress Centre, opened in 1990, also offers 28 meeting areas for up to 3500 delegates. A further exhibition complex linked by a walkway to the World Congress Centre, Melbourne, opened in 1996. Also, a casino-leisure complex, Crown Towers, opened in 1997. Major convention facilities include Dallas Brooks Conference Centre, Melbourne Hilton on the Park, Hyatt on Collins, the Radisson President Hotel and Convention Centre, Regent of Melbourne, Royal Exhibition Building and Convention Centre, Southern Cross Hotel, Melbourne Park Tennis Centre and Victorian Arts Centre. For more information on conferences and conventions in Victoria, contact the Australian Tourist Commission *or* the Melbourne Convention and Visitors Bureau, Level 12, IBM Centre, 60 City Road, Southbank, VIC 3006 (tel: (3) 9693 3333; fax: (3) 9693 3344; e-mail: mcvb@mcvb.com.au; website: www.mcmb.com.au) *or* Melbourne Convention and Visitors Bureau (UK Office), Suite 2, 42a Packhorse Road, Gerrards Cross, Bucks SL9 8EB, UK (tel: (01753) 481 540; fax: (01753) 481 600; e-mail: 106465.556@compuserve.com.au).

Climate

Hot summers and relatively cool winters. Rainfall is distributed throughout the year. Southern areas can have changeable weather even in summer, often with four seasons' weather in one day.

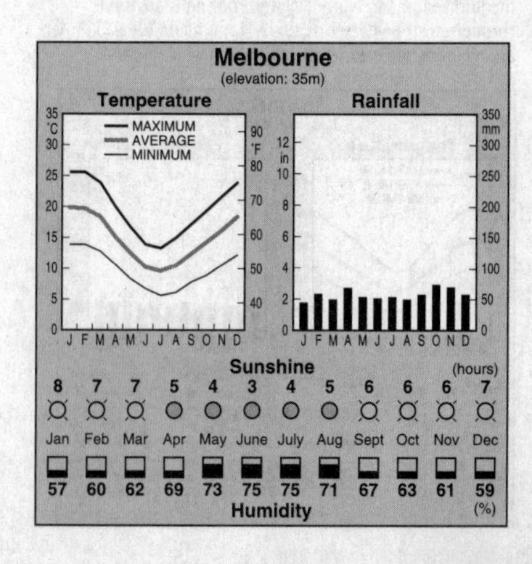

Western Australia

Credit: © Western Australian Tourism Commission

Location: Western part of Australia.

Western Australian Tourism Commission
Street address: 9th Floor, 2 Mill Street, Perth, WA 6000, Australia
Postal address: GPO Box X2261, Perth, WA 6847, Australia
Tel: (8) 9262 1700. Fax: (8) 9262 1702.
E-mail: welcome@westernaustralia.com
Website: www.westernaustralia.com
Tourism trade and tourism media enquiries only.
Western Australian Visitor Centre
Street address: Albert Facey House, Cnr of Wellington Street and Forrest Place, Perth, WA 6000, Australia
Postal address: GPO Box W2081, Perth, WA 6846, Australia
Tel: (8) 9483 1111 *or* (1 300) 361 351 (local call rate in Australia). Fax: (8) 9481 0190.
E-mail: travel@westernaustralia.com
Website: www.westernaustralia.com
Consumer enquiries only.
Western Australian Tourism Commission
Australia Centre, The Strand, London WC2B 4LG, UK
Tel: (020) 7240 2881 *or* (08705) 022 000 (helpline). Fax: (020) 7379 9826.
E-mail: westozuk@tourism.wa.gov.au
Website: www.westernaustralia.com

General Information

AREA: 2,529,880 sq km (976,787 sq miles).
POPULATION: 1,883,900 (official estimate 2000).
POPULATION DENSITY: 0.7 per sq km.
CAPITAL: Perth. **Population:** 1,381,100 (official estimate 2000).
GEOGRAPHY: Western Australia covers one-third of Australia; it is larger than Western Europe, but has a population only one-sixth that of London. It is bordered in the east by South Australia and the Northern Territory and in the west by the Indian Ocean, with the Timor Sea to the north. The west coast is nearer to Bali and Indonesia than to Sydney, making Perth a viable stopover destination en route to the rest of Australia. To the south, the nearest land mass is Antarctica, 2600km (1600 miles) away. It has mineral wealth in iron, bauxite, nickel, natural gas, oil, diamonds and gold. There are vast wheatlands, forests and deserts, and several national parks. A popular resort is Rottnest Island; there are also many excellent mainland beaches, particularly around Perth. Kimberley, in the far north, is one of the oldest geological areas on earth, a region where time and weather have formed deep gorges and impressive mountains, arid red plains and coastal sandstone rich in fossils. In the northwest there are two notable features: Wolf Creek Crater, an immense hole left in the desert by a giant meteorite 50,000 years ago, and the Bungle Bungles, an ancient sandstone massif covering 3000 sq km (1160 sq miles). Southeast of Perth, near Hyden, there is the 2700 million year-old Wave Rock.
TIME: GMT + 8.

Public Holidays

Western Australia recognises all the public holidays observed nationwide (see the main Australia section) and, in addition, the following are also observed:
2005: Mar 7 Labour Day. **Jun 6** Foundation Day.
Oct 3 Queen's Birthday Celebrations.
2006: Mar 6 Labour Day. **Jun 5** Foundation Day.
Oct 2 Queen's Birthday Celebrations.

Travel - International

AIR: There are international flights to Perth from Europe and Asia. International airlines serving Perth include *Air Mauritius, Air New Zealand, British Airways, Cathay Pacific Airways, Garuda Indonesia, Malaysia Airlines, Qantas, Royal Brunei, Singapore Airlines, South Africa Airlines* and *Thai Airways International*. Flying time from *London* is 18 hours. There are internal flights from all state capitals. Domestic carriers include *Airnorth, Qantas, Skywest* (within Western Australia only) and *Virgin Blue.*
International airports: *Perth International Airport (PER)* (website: www.perthairport.net.au) is 12km (7 miles) from the city (travel time - 25 minutes).
SEA: Port of Fremantle serves Perth. The port is 19km (11 miles) from Perth.
RAIL: Western Australia is served by *Transwa* rail service (website: www.transwa.wa.gov.au). An electric tram runs between Perth and Fremantle. The *Indian Pacific* service runs from Perth to Sydney twice a week; the journey takes three days and three nights.
ROAD: The highway network of Western Australia is almost entirely concentrated in the coastal areas. The main exception is the *Great Northern Highway* which runs from Perth to Port Headland on the northwest coast. Along the south coast is the *Eyre Highway*, which runs into South Australia. The *Brand/Northwest Coastal Highway* runs from Perth around the west coast to Kimberley. The journey between Perth and Sydney takes at least four days. Driving maps can be purchased via the Western Australian Tourism Commission (see *Contact Addresses* section). There is only one express **coach** route from Perth and it goes to Adelaide (travel time - 35 hours). *Integrity Coach Lines* and *South West Coachlines* run coach services throughout the southern part of Western Australia.
URBAN: *Transperth* (website: www.transperth.wa.gov.au) offers a fully integrated service across all **bus**, **train** and **ferry** services within Perth. Local trains run from Perth to Armadale, Midland, Fremantle and Joondalup. A zonal fare structure covers all transport modes; tickets issued on one mode are valid for transfer to any of the others (bus, rail and ferry). A free *CAT Clipper Bus* service circles the city centres of Perth and Fremantle Monday-Saturday.

Accommodation

The Western Australian Tourism Commission provides information to consumers and travel agents, which can be obtained from their offices.
HOTELS: There is a wide range of hotels and motels in Western Australia, including **5-star** (luxury), **4-star** (deluxe), **3-star** (standard) and **2-star** (economy).
HOLIDAY FLATS: An extensive range of holiday flats is available, both in Perth and the rest of the State.
CAMPING/CARAVANNING: There are many caravan parks and campsites in the State, most of which are located off the main highways. A number of companies also arrange **motor camper** rentals, with a range of vehicles. Full details can be obtained from the Western Australian Tourism Commission (see *Contact Addresses* section).
Note: For further coverage on the range of accommodation available see *Accommodation* in the general *Australia* section.

Resorts & Excursions

PERTH

Perth is sunny all year but pleasant owing to temperate breezes. Modern skyscrapers overshadow colonial buildings such as the **Town Hall** and **Perth Mint**. The **Swan River** winds through the city, and a cruise upriver to the vineyards is very popular with tourists. A futuristic tower resembling a giant swan, the **Swan Bells** houses the old bells from St Martin-in-the-Fields, London and is open daily for viewing. **Kings Park**, a beautiful park overlooking the town, the **Art Gallery of Western Australia** in James Street and the historic **His Majesty's Theatre** are also worth seeing. The most popular beach destinations are **Sorrento**, **Cottesloe**, **City**, **Scarborough** and the nude bathing beach at **Swanbourne**. 17km (11 miles) north of the city centre, **AQWA – The Aquarium of Western Australia** at **Hillary's Boat Harbour** showcases over 4000 sea creatures in their natural environments. South of Perth is **Cable's Water Ski Park** with thrilling water rides and **Adventure World**, a favourite family entertainment complex on **Bibra Lake** with thrill rides, native animals, parkland and waterways in beautiful surroundings.
Fremantle, 19km (12 miles) from the city, is a port full of historic houses and buildings such as the **Court House**, all of which have been superbly restored. Freo, as it is known, can be reached either by a one-hour boat trip or a 20-minute drive from Perth. The excellent **Western Australian Maritime Museum** and **Fishing Boat Harbour**, with its many outdoor seafood restaurants, are its other attractions.

BEYOND PERTH

Rottnest Island lies 20km (12.5 miles) offshore. This haven for watersports enthusiasts is connected to Fremantle by ferry services. The marsupial *quokka* is unique to the car-free island. Well to the east of Perth is the thriving gold-mining town of **Kalgoorlie** with its **Museum of the Goldfields**, and towns which were once the centre of Western Australia's gold rush, such as **Coolgardie**. Also interesting is **Wave Rock**, a 2700-million-year-old formation resembling a tidal wave, close to **Hyden**. The **Darling Ranges**, behind Perth, are popular with visitors and contain several national parks. The **Avon Valley**, a 90-minute drive from Perth, is an agricultural area. In this region can be found the town of **York** where the **York Motor Museum** and the **Residency Museum** are worth seeing. **Nanbung National Park**, 240km (150 miles) north of Perth, is well known for its amazing limestone pillars, **The Pinnacles**. At **Monkey Mia**, on the mid-western coast, there are wild bottlenose dolphins that come into the shallows to greet visitors. Also in the north of the State, **The Kimberley**, a wild semi-desert region rich in Aboriginal legends, has in recent years become a thriving diamond-mining centre. The city of **Broome**, on the north coast, is the pearl capital of the world. At the opposite end of the State is **Albany**, founded in 1827 and the first European settlement in Western Australia; it is noted for its blowholes and winter whale-watching. **Augusta**, to the west, is also visited by several species of whale.

Sport & Activities

Watersports: The long stretches of unspoilt coastline along the Timor Sea in the north and the Indian Ocean in the southwest offer a wide range of activities. Major destinations for **diving** include *Rottnest Island* (notably *Tortoise Bay*, *Jackson Rock* and *Transit Reef*); *Exmouth* (a good base for exploring the *Ningaloo Reef* and the *Muiron Islands*); the *Abroholos Islands* (three groups of islands rated amongst Australia's best dive sites); *Esperance* (the gateway to the *Recherche Archipelago*, which contains hundreds of islands); *Busselton* (good for jetty diving); and *Dunsborough* in the southwest (noted for its famous wreck dive to the *HMS Swan*). The best times for diving are from December to May (in the southern waters) and from March to August (in the northern waters). Encounters with friendly **dolphins** are particularly frequent at *Monkey Mia*, in the Gascoyne region, whose nearby *Shark Bay* – a World-Heritage listed area – is a habitat for turtles, manta rays, whales and sharks. Further north, at *Ningaloo Reef*, it is possible to **swim** with giant **whale shark**, the world's largest fish, which make frequent appearances between March and early June; access is by boat from *Coral Bay* or directly from the beaches. **Whale watching** is reputed to be particularly good in the *Cape to Cape* region, with an exceptionally long whale-watching season (lasting some six months). Perth ranks as one of Australia's top **surfing** destinations and there are many surfing beaches close to the city, such as *City Beach*, *Cottesloe* and *Scarborough*. Other challenging surfing destinations include *Yallingup* and *Margaret River*, whose ominously named beaches, such as *Suicide* and *Grunters*, should attract hardcore surfers only. **Canoeing** trips are also widely available on *Margaret River*.

Self-drive tours: Popular outback destinations that can be explored in **4-wheel-drive** vehicles include *The Pinnacles*, consisting of thousands of limestone pillars (260km/163 miles north of Perth); and the *Gibb River Road* through the rugged landscape of the *Kimberley* region.

Bushwalking: Walking in Western Australia can be particularly rewarding during spring (between September and November), when wild flowers blossom throughout the state. The *Bibbulmun Track* (963km/598 miles, from Kalamunda to Albany) has access to circuit walks through the southwestern karri forests as well as 48 acccommodation shelters along the route. For further details about the track check online (website: www.bibbulmuntrack.org.au). Other impressive routes can be found in the *Stirling Range*, an area containing over 500 species of wild flowers; throughout the *Pilbara* region, the major attractions of which are the spectacular red-walled chasms, subterranean pools and waterfalls of *Karijini National Park*; and in the northern *Kimberley* region, Western Australia's main outback destination, featuring a cliff-lined coast, rugged mountains and the spectacular *Purnululu* (*Bungle Bungle*) *National Park*, a 350-million-year old massif with distinctive bee-hive-like natural domes.

River cruises: Cruises on the *Swan River* from Perth travel either downstream, to the port of Fremantle, or – the more popular option – upstream, to the vineyards of *Swan Valley*. There are scenic and nature cruises in the *Kimberleys*, and on *Lake Argyle* (the largest fresh-water lake in Australia).

Wine tasting: The *Margaret River Wine Region* is Western Australia's best-known destination for wine lovers. Although producing less than 1 per cent of Australia's wine, the region is responsible for producing 15 per cent of the country's premium wine. The 50 or so wineries in the region are open for cellar door sales and tastings. Another up-and-coming wine region in Western Australia is in the southern *Mount Baker* region, some 50km (31 miles) from Albany. The *Swan Valley* wine region, on the outskirts of Perth, also attracts many visitors.

Adventure sports: Concentrated in *Kununurra* (Kimberley region) organised tours include **scenic flights**, **camping safaris** and **boat cruises**. At the *Walpole-Nornalup National Park* in the south, the imposing giant tingle trees in the 'Valley of the Giants' offer the possibility of a **tree-top-walk**, 38m above the forest on specially designed floorboards.

Social Profile

FOOD & DRINK: Excellent seafood comes from the coast around Perth, including king prawns, rock lobster (locals call this crayfish, dhufish, jewfish or barramundi), and special freshwater lobster called *marron*. There are excellent local wines in Western Australia and vineyards at Swan Valley, Mount Barker and Margaret River. A vibrant pavement coffee culture exists in Perth, and Fremantle's South Terrace is home to the aptly named *Cappuccino Strip* (and to the infamous *Redback* lager). There is also an abundance of international cuisine and interesting dining experiences; for example, eating fish and chips from a converted tram in Fremantle, sampling the excellent Asian food in Subiaco (Perth), enjoying a seafood barbecue in the bush or partaking of a culinary feast in a riverside restaurant along the Swan River. Tropical fruits are abundant - especially banana, mango and papaya.

NIGHTLIFE: There are many nightclubs in the Northbridge area of Perth, which is located within easy walking distance from the bus and train stations. Here you can find club venues to cater for all music tastes, including mainstream, hardcore, gay and alternative beats. The large Burswood Resort and Casino complex is also only minutes from Perth city centre. In addition there are many cinemas in Leederville, Fremantle and Perth, as well as several theatres (see the *Independent Theatre Association* for information; website: www.theatre.asn.au).

SHOPPING: Best buys are Argyle diamonds, opals and Aboriginal art. Shops are open all day Saturday and some shops in the suburbs are also open late night Thursday. Shops in Perth and Fremantle are open Friday and Sunday nights.

SPECIAL EVENTS: For a full list, contact the Western Australian Tourism Commission (see *Contact Addresses* section). The following is a selection of special events occurring in Western Australia in 2005:

Jan 1-8 *Hyundai Hopman Cup XVII* (international tennis competition). **Jan 9** *Summadayze*, dance festival, Perth. **Feb 1** *Leeuwin Concert Series*, Margaret River. **Feb 11-Mar 6** *52nd Perth International Arts Festival*. **Mar 26-27** *Western Australian Environmental Festival*, Peron. **May 13-15** *2005 Quilt Forest Rally*, Busselton. **Jun 4-6** *Western Australian Food & Wine Exhibition*, Perth. **Aug 6-7** *Multiplex Avon Descent* (boat race down Avon River from Northam to Bayswater). **Sep 28-Oct 1** *World Darts Federation World Cup*, Perth. **Oct 6-9** *Gravity Graves HQ*, action-sports competition, Perth.

Business Profile

COMMERCIAL INFORMATION: The following organisation can offer advice: Chamber of Commerce and Industry of Western Australia (CCIWA), PO Box 6209, East Perth, WA 6892 (tel: (8) 9365 7555; fax: (8) 9365 7550; e-mail: info@cciwa.com; website: www.cciwa.com).

CONFERENCES/CONVENTIONS: The major convention centres are the Hilton Hotel, Hyatt Regency Hotel, Observation City Resort Hotel, Perth International Hotel, Sheraton Hotel, the Superdrome and also Burswood Resort and Convention and Exhibition Centre, only 3km (2 miles) from the city centre with seating available for 2000 for conventions or 21,000 for exhibitions. For more information on conferences and conventions contact the Australian Tourist Commission or the Perth Convention Bureau, Level 7, 172 St Georges Terrace, Perth, WA 6000 (tel: (8) 9324 3355; fax: (8) 9324 3311; e-mail: info@pcb.com.au; website: www.pcb.com.au).

Climate

Hot summers (December-February), mild winters (June-August). North is tropical. South is subtropical to temperate. Rainfall varies from area to area.

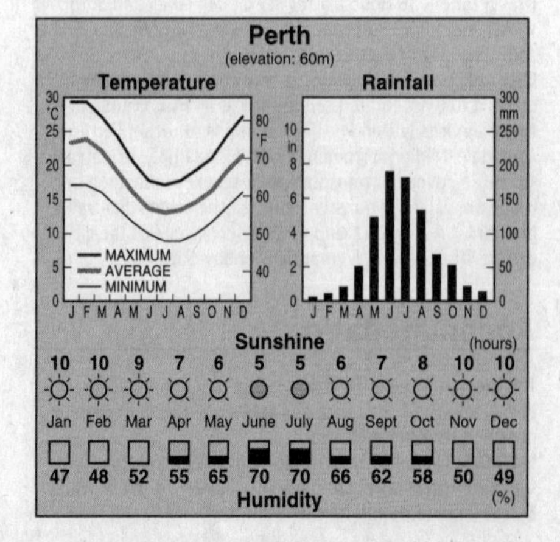

Austria

LATEST TRAVEL ADVICE CONTACTS

British Foreign and Commonwealth Office
Tel: (0870) 606 0290 Website: www.fco.gov.uk

US Department of State
Website: http://travel.state.gov/travel

Canadian Department of Foreign Affairs and Int'l Trade
Tel: (1 800) 267 8376 Website: www.dfait-maeci.gc.ca

Location: Central Europe.

Country dialling code: 43.

Oesterreich Werbung (Austrian National Tourist Office - ANTO)
Street address: Margaretenstrasse 1, A-1040 Vienna, Austria
Postal address: Postfach 83, A-1043 Vienna, Austria
Tel: (1) 588 660 (information). Fax: (1) 588 6620.
E-mail: holiday@austria.info
Website: www.austria.info

Austrian Embassy
18 Belgrave Mews West, London SW1X 8HU, UK
Tel: (020) 7235 3731. Fax: (020) 7344 0292.
E-mail: embassy@austria.org.uk
Website: www.bmaa.gv.at/london
Opening hours: Mon-Fri 0900-1200 (personal callers); 0900-1645 (telephone enquiries); 0900-1200 (visa section); 1400-1600 (telephone visa enquiries).

Austrian National Tourist Office (ANTO)
9-11 Richmond Buildings, Dean Street, London W1D 3BF, UK
Tel: (020) 7440 3830 *or* (0845) 101 1818 (holiday information and brochure request line). Fax: (020) 7440 3848.
E-mail: info@anto.co.uk
Website: www.austria.info/uk
No personal callers.

British Embassy
Jaurèsgasse 12, A-1030 Vienna, Austria
Tel: (1) 716 130. Fax: (1) 7161 36900 (commercial section).
E-mail: enquiries@britishembassy.at
Website: www.britishembassy.at
Consular section: Jaurèsgasse 10, A-1030 Vienna, Austria
Tel: (1) 7161 35151. Fax: (1) 7161 35900.
E-mail: visa-consular@britishembassy.at

Embassy of the Republic of Austria
3524 International Court, NW, Washington, DC 20008, USA
Tel: (202) 895 6700 *or* 895 6711 (consular section).
Fax: (202) 895 6750 *or* 895 6773 (consular section).
E-mail: austrianembassy@washington.nu
Website: www.austria.org

Austrian Tourist Office (ATO)
120 West 45th Street, 9th Floor, New York, NY 10036, USA
Tel: (212) 944 6880. Fax: (212) 730 4568.
E-mail: travel@austria.info
Website: www.austria.info/us

Austrian Tourist Office (ATO)
6520 Platt Avenue, PMB 561 West Hills, Los Angeles,

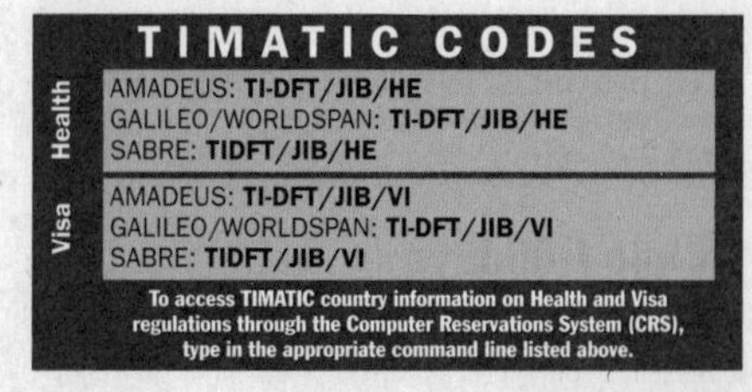
TIMATIC CODES

Health	AMADEUS: **TI-DFT/JIB/HE** GALILEO/WORLDSPAN: **TI-DFT/JIB/HE** SABRE: **TIDFT/JIB/HE**
Visa	AMADEUS: **TI-DFT/JIB/VI** GALILEO/WORLDSPAN: **TI-DFT/JIB/VI** SABRE: **TIDFT/JIB/VI**

To access TIMATIC country information on Health and Visa regulations through the Computer Reservations System (CRS), type in the appropriate command line listed above.

Credit: © Austrian National Tourist Office

CA 91307, USA
Tel: (818) 999 4030. Fax: (818) 999 3910.
E-mail: peter.katz@oewlax.com
Website: www.austria.info (general) *or* www.austria-tourism.biz (travel trade only).
Deals with travel trade and media enquiries only.
Embassy of the United States of America
Boltzmanngasse 16, A-1090 Vienna, Austria
Tel: (1) 313 390. Fax: (1) 313 392 919.
E-mail: embassy@usembassy.at
Website: www.usembassy.at
US Consulate
4th Floor, Parkring 12, A-1010 Vienna, Austria
Tel: (1) 313 392 351 *or* 900 510 300 (visa information line with live operators; €2,16 per minute). Fax: (1) 512 5835.
E-mail: consulatevienna@state.gov
Website: www.usembassy.at
Austrian Embassy
445 Wilbrod Street, Ottawa, Ontario K1N 6M7, Canada
Tel: (613) 789 1444. Fax: (613) 789 3431.
E-mail: ottawa-ob@bmaa.gv.at
Website: www.austro.org
Austrian National Tourist Office (ANTO)
Suite 400, 2 Bloor Street West, Toronto, Ontario M4W 3E2, Canada
Tel: (416) 967 4867 (travel trade only). Fax: (416) 967 4101.
E-mail: anto-tor@sympatico.ca
Website: www.austria.info/us
Canadian Embassy
Laurenzerberg 2, A-1010 Vienna, Austria
Tel: (1) 531 383 000. Fax: (1) 531 383 905 *or* 321.
Website: www.dfait-maeci.gc.ca

General Information

AREA: 83,858 sq km (32,378 sq miles).
POPULATION: 8,169,929 (official estimate 2002).
POPULATION DENSITY: 97.4 per sq km.
CAPITAL: Vienna (Wien). **Population:** 1,608,144 (official estimate 1999).
GEOGRAPHY: Austria is a landlocked country, bordered by Switzerland, Liechtenstein, Germany, the Czech Republic, the Slovak Republic, Hungary, Slovenia and Italy. It is a mountainous country, nearly half of which is covered with forests. Austria's nine Federal Provinces form a political entity, but reflect a diversity of landscapes falling into five sections: the Eastern Alps (62.8 per cent), the Alpine and Carpathian Foothills (11.3 per cent), the Pannonian Lowlands (11.3 per cent), the Vienna Basin (4.4 per cent) and the Granite and Gneiss Highlands or Bohemian Massif (10.1 per cent). Austria's highest mountain is Grossglockner (3798m/12,465ft). On its way from the Black Forest in southern Germany to the Black Sea, the River Danube flows approximately 360km (220 miles) through Austria. The vegetation changes according to the climate: the lower regions are densely wooded, with fir predominating above 1600ft and giving way to larch and stone-pine beyond 4000ft; the Alpine foothills consist predominantly of arable land and grassland (above 2000ft). The Pannonian region is characterised by scrub and heathland.
GOVERNMENT: Federal Republic. **Head of State:** President Heinz Fischer since 2004. **Head of Government:** Chancellor Wolfgang Schüssel since 2000.
LANGUAGE: German is the official language. Regional dialects are pronounced and within the different regions of the country one will encounter marked variations from *Hochdeutsch*, ie 'standard' German. There are Croatian and Slovene-speaking minorities in the Burgenland and southern Carinthia respectively.
RELIGION: 78 per cent Roman Catholic, 5 per cent Protestant, 4.5 per cent other denominations.
TIME: GMT + 1.
ELECTRICITY: 220 volts AC, 50Hz. Round two-pin European plugs are standard.
COMMUNICATIONS: Telephone: Full IDD facilities available. Country code: 43. Outgoing international code: 00. Call boxes are grey and found in all areas. International calls can be made from payphones with four coin slots. Trunk calls within Austria and to 40 countries are cheaper Mon-Fri 1800-0800 and approximately 35 per cent cheaper at the weekend (from 1300 Saturday to 0800 Monday). **Mobile telephone:** GSM 900/1800. Network operators include *One* (website: www.one.at), *Telering* (website: www.telering.at) and *T-mobile* (website: www.t-mobile.at). **Fax:** Widely available, especially in cities. **Internet:** There are many Internet cafes. ISPs include *Nextra* (website: www.nextra.at). **Telegram:** Facilities are available from any post office; telegrams can also be sent by dialling 10 from any phone. **Post:** Letters up to 20g and postcards within Europe are sent by airmail. Letters within Europe take two to four days, and to the USA four to six days. Stamps may be purchased in post offices or tobacco shops. Postcards and letters within Austria and Europe cost €0.55; to all other countries the cost is €1,25. Post boxes are yellow; red stripes mean that the box is also emptied weekends and bank holidays. A *Poste Restante* service is available at most post offices. Address mail to '*Postlagernd*' ('*Hauptpostlagernd*' if a main post office), followed by the person's name, town, and post code. Post office hours: generally Mon-Fri 0800-1200 and 1400-1800, and Sat 0800-1000, but main post offices and those at major railway stations are open for 24 hours, seven days a week, including public holidays. **Press:** Newspapers are in German. The *Wiener Zeitung*, established in 1703, is the oldest newspaper in the world. The national daily with the largest circulation is the *Neue Kronen-Zeitung*, followed by *Kurier*, *Der Standard* and *Die Presse*. English-language newspapers and magazines are also widely available, particularly in the big cities and tourist resorts.
Radio: BBC World Service (website: www.bbc.co.uk/worldservice) and Voice of America (website: www.voa.gov) can be received. Frequencies sometimes change and the most up-to-date can be found online.

Passport/Visa

	Passport Required?	Visa Required?	Return Ticket Required?
Full British	Yes	No	No
Australian	Yes	No/2	Yes
Canadian	Yes	No/2	Yes
USA	Yes	No/2	Yes
Other EU	1	No	No
Japanese	Yes	No/2	No

Note: *Regulations and requirements may be subject to change at short notice, and you are advised to contact the appropriate diplomatic or consular authority before finalising travel arrangements. Details of these may be found at the head of this country's entry. Any numbers in the chart refer to the footnotes below.*

Note: Austria is a signatory to the 1995 **Schengen Agreement**. For further details about passport and visa regulations in the Schengen area see the introductory section *How to Use This Guide*.
PASSPORTS: Passport valid for at least three months longer than the validity of visa required by all except:
1. nationals of EU countries, Liechtenstein, Monaco and Switzerland, who may enter with a valid national ID card.
VISAS: Required by all except the following:
(a) nationals of EU countries and nationals of Iceland, Liechtenstein, Norway and Switzerland for an unlimited period;
(b) **2.** nationals of American Samoa, Andorra, Argentina, Aruba, Australia, Bolivia, Bonaire, Brazil, British Overseas Territories, Brunei, Bulgaria, Canada, Chile, Cook Islands, Costa Rica, Croatia, Curaçao, East Timor, El Salvador, French Guiana, Greenland, Guadeloupe, Guam, Guatemala, Guernsey, Honduras, Israel (excluding nationals holding Palestinian passports), Japan, Jersey, Korea (Rep), Malaysia, Martinique, Mexico, Monaco, New Caledonia, New Zealand, Nicaragua, Niue, Northern Mariana Islands, Panama, Paraguay, Puerto Rico, Reunion, Romania, Saba, St Eustatius, St Maarten, San Marino, Singapore, Tahiti and her Islands, Uruguay, USA, US Virgin Islands, Vatican City and Venezuela for touristic stays of up to three months;
(c) transit passengers continuing their journey by the same or first connecting aircraft, provided holding valid onward or return documentation and not leaving the airport.
Note: Nationals of Afghanistan, Bangladesh, Congo (Dem Rep), Eritrea, Ethiopia, Ghana, Iran, Iraq, Liberia, Nigeria, Pakistan, Somalia and Sri Lanka passing through Austria *always* require a transit visa, even when not leaving the airport. Transit passengers are advised to check transit regulations with the relevant Embassy or Consulate before travelling.
Types of visa and cost: A uniform type of visa, the *Schengen* visa, is issued for all types of visit, costing £24.50.
Note: (a) Prices may change with the prevalent exchange rate, so visitors are advised to check the exact price before applying. (b) Spouses and children of EU nationals (providing spouse's passport and the original marriage certificate are produced), and nationals of some other countries, receive their visas free of charge; enquire at Embassy for details.
Validity: Validity according to documents presented. Visas can not be extended; a new application must be made each time.
Application to: Consulate (or Consular section at Embassy); see *Contact Addresses* section. Travellers visiting just one Schengen country should apply to the Consulate of that country; travellers visiting more than one Schengen country should apply to the Consulate of the country chosen as the main destination *or* the first country they will enter that requires them to have a visa (if they have no main destination).
Note: Visa applications can be sent by post or made in person. If using the latter method in the UK, an appointment will need to be arranged by telephone (tel: (020) 7344 3289) or online (e-mail: visa@austria.org.uk).
Application requirements: (a) Completed application form(s). (b) Passport valid for at least three months beyond the validity of the visa with at least one blank page for the visa sticker. (c) Fee (cash or postal order only). (d) Two passport-size photos. (e) Proof of transport (airline tickets, vehicle papers, train reservation etc). (f) Proof of intention to return to home country (applicants may submit return ticket or vehicle papers if returning by car). (g) Confirmed hotel or tour reservation or letter from business partner in Austria or letter of invitation from Austrian host. (h) An all-risk medical insurance policy covering duration of visa (minimum coverage: £15). (i) Proof of occupation/student status. (j) Proof of sufficient financial means to fund stay in Austria (minimum £30 per day per person). Applicants may submit travellers cheques, a confirmed hotel booking, bank statements or records from a similar financial institution. (k) For transit passengers, the visa from the destination country must be obtained first. (l) Postal applicants should enclose a self-addressed, prepaid envelope (registered or recorded delivery) for the return of the passport. (m) Original letter of invitation (*verpflichtungserklärung*), legalised by a notary public solicitor/competent authority, plus copy of Austrian passport/residence permit and proof of sufficient funds of host, *or*, letter from Austrian business partner, with company certifying financial responsibility for applicant during stay, *or*, confirmed hotel reservation/ confirmation of tour.
Note: All documents must be submitted in both their original form, plus one duplicate.
Working days required: Several weeks.
Temporary residence: Seek advice from the Austrian Embassy.

Money

Single European currency (Euro): The Euro is now the official currency of 12 EU member states (including Austria). The first Euro coins and notes were introduced in January 2002; the Austrian Schilling was in circulation until 28 February 2002, when it was completely replaced by the Euro. Euro (€) = 100 cents. Notes are in denominations of €500, 200, 100, 50, 20, 10 and 5. Coins are in denominations of €2, 1 and 50, 20, 10, 5, 2 and 1 cents.
Currency exchange: Foreign currencies and travellers cheques can be exchanged at all banks, savings banks and exchange counters at airports and railway stations at the official exchange rates.
Credit & debit cards: Most major credit cards and Eurocheque cards are accepted in large cities and tourist areas. However, credit and debit cards are less widely accepted in Austria than they are in the USA or the UK and some smaller hotels may require bills to be paid in cash.
Travellers cheques: These are widely accepted. To avoid additional exchange rate charges, travellers are advised to take travellers cheques in a major currency (Euros, US Dollars, Pounds Sterling).
Currency restrictions: No restrictions except for export of more than €7267.28, for which a permit is required.
Exchange rate indicators: The following figures are

included as a guide to the movements of the Euro against Sterling and the US Dollar:

Date	Feb '04	May '04	Aug '04	Aug '04
£1.00=	1.46	1.50	1.49	1.42
$1.00=	0.80	0.84	0.80	0.75

Banking hours: Banks in Vienna are open Mon-Wed and Fri 0800-1230 and 1330-1500; Thurs 0800-1230 and 1330-1730 (head offices do not close for lunch). Different opening hours may be kept in the various Federal Provinces. The exchange counters at airports and at railway stations are generally open from the first to the last flight or train, which usually means 0800-2200 including weekends.

Duty Free

The following goods can be taken into Austria without incurring customs duty by travellers over 17 years arriving from countries outside the EU:
200 cigarettes or 100 cigarillos or 50 cigars or 250g tobacco; 1l of spirits over 22 per cent or 2l of fortified wine or spirits up to 22 per cent or 2l of sparkling wine or liqueur and 2l of still wine; 500g of coffee or 200g of extracts, essences or concentrates of coffee; 50g of perfume or eau de toilette; goods up to a value of €175.
Abolition of duty free goods within the EU: On June 30 1999, the sale of duty free alcohol and tobacco at airports and at sea was abolished in all of the original 15 EU member states. Of the 10 new member states that joined the EU on May 1 2004, these rules already apply to Cyprus and Malta. There are transitional rules in place for visitors returning to one of the original 15 EU countries from one of the other new EU countries. But for the original 15, plus Cyprus and Malta, there are now no limits imposed on importing tobacco and alcohol products from one EU country to another (with the exceptions of Denmark, Finland and Sweden, where limits *are* imposed). Travellers should note that they may be required to prove at customs that the goods purchased are for personal use *only*.

Public Holidays

2005 Jan 1 New Year's Day. **Jan 6** Epiphany. **Mar 25** Good Friday. **Mar 28** Easter Monday. **May 1** Labour Day. **May 5** Ascension Day. **May 16** Whit Monday. **May 26** Corpus Christi. **Aug 15** Assumption. **Oct 26** National Day. **Nov 1** All Saints' Day. **Dec 8** Immaculate Conception. **Dec 25** Christmas Day. **Dec 26** St Stephen's Day.
2006 Jan 1 New Year's Day. **Jan 6** Epiphany. **Apr 14** Good Friday. **Apr 17** Easter Monday. **May 1** Labour Day. **May 25** Ascension Day. **Jun 5** Whit Monday. **Jun 15** Corpus Christi. **Aug 15** Assumption. **Oct 26** National Day. **Nov 1** All Saints' Day. **Dec 8** Immaculate Conception. **Dec 25** Christmas Day. **Dec 26** St Stephen's Day.

Health

	Special Precautions?	Certificate Required?
Yellow Fever	No	No
Cholera	No	No
Typhoid & Polio	No	N/A
Malaria	No	N/A

Note: *Regulations and requirements may be subject to change at short notice, and you are advised to contact your doctor well in advance of your intended date of departure. Any numbers in the chart refer to the footnotes below.*

Food & drink: Milk is pasteurised and dairy products are safe for consumption. Local meat, poultry, seafood, fruit and vegetables are generally safe to eat.
Other risks: Ticks often live in heavily afforested areas during the summer months in some of the more easterly parts of Austria and can create discomfort and, in very rare cases, serious infection to people who are bitten. Immunisation against *tick-borne encephalitis* is available and travellers likely to find themselves in these wooded areas should take a course of injections.
Rabies is present in Austria, although there have been no incidents reported in recent years. For those at high risk, vaccination before arrival should be considered. If you are bitten seek medical advice without delay. For more information consult the *Health* appendix.
Health care: The following emergency numbers are used: Police: 133; Ambulance: 144; Fire: 122. For UK nationals on a temporary visit to Austria, an E111 is not required – production of a British passport is sufficient to obtain medical treatment. For other EEA nationals (including Austrians), resident in the UK, an E111 is required. Visitors who are treated privately may receive a refund for part of the costs, up to the amount that would have been payable for public hospital treatment. Such refunds are available from Regional Health Insurance Offices (*Gebietskrankenkassen*) which also provide addresses of medical and dental practitioners. Referral to a public hospital will require an admission voucher issued by a doctor. In an emergency, UK nationals should show their passport to the hospital administration which will ascertain from the insurance office whether the costs of treatment will be met.

Travel - International

AIR: Austria has three national airlines, all of which are part of the Austrian Airlines Group (website: www.aua.com): *Austrian Airlines (OS)*, *Lauda Air (NG)* and *Tyrolean Airways (VO)*. *British Airways* offer frequent services to various destinations in Austria, as do low-cost airlines such as *Flybe* and *Ryanair*.
Approximate flight times: From Innsbruck to *London* is two hours and from Salzburg is one hour 50 minutes. From Vienna to *London* is two hours 10 minutes, to *Los Angeles* is 15 hours, to *New York* is nine hours, to *Singapore* is 14 hours and to *Sydney* is 25 hours.
International airports: *Vienna (VIE)* (Wien-Schwechat) (website: http://english.viennaairport.com) is 18km (11 miles) south-east of the city. Airport facilities include duty-free shops, banks, bureaux de change, post office, restaurants, cafes, left luggage, conference facilities, medical facilities, tourist information, car hire, car park and nursery. Airport buses run between the airport and the city centre (Hilton Hotel) every 20 minutes, 24 hours a day (travel time - 20 minutes); and between the airport and two stations (Vienna Südbahnhof and Vienna Westbahnhof) approximately every hour (0530-0010; travel time - 25 and 35 minutes respectively). Rail service is available at frequent intervals (from 0500-2258) to and from two other stations (Vienna Mitte and Vienna Nordbahnhof; travel time – 32 minutes). Local rail (*S-Bahn*) services also run to the Vienna railway stations of Südbahnhof (travel time – 20 minutes) and Nordbahnhof (travel time – 35 minutes). The *City Airport Train* travels express from the City Airport Terminal located at Vienna Mitte (travel time - 16 minutes). Taxis are available to the city and can be found north of the Arrivals Hall, costing approximately €25-30. A chaffeur-driven car service is also available from the Arrivals Hall.
Buses also run to Budapest four times a day (travel time – three hours 30 minutes); to Bratislava (Slovak Republic) about seven times a day (travel time – one hour).
Innsbruck (INN) (Kranebitten) (website: www.innsbruck-airport.com) is 5.5km (3.5 miles) west of the city. Airport facilities include duty free shopping, currency exchange, restaurant, medical facilities and car hire. Bus services are available every 20-30 minutes to the city centre (travel time – 20 minutes). Taxi services are also available.
Salzburg (SZG) (Maxglan) (website: www.salzburg-airport.com) is 4km (2.5 miles) west of the city. Airport facilities include duty-free shopping, currency exchange, post office, restaurants and snack bars, bar, left luggage, conference rooms and car hire. Bus no. 2 departs to the *Hauptbahnhof* (main railway station) in the city centre every 15 minutes on weekdays and every 30 minutes at the weekend (travel time - 20 minutes). It is also possible to go by train (travel time - 15-20 minutes). Taxis are available from the front of the main building for approximately €13.08 (travel time - 15 minutes). Some hotels have courtesy coaches.
Klagenfurt (KLU) (Wörther See) (website: www.klagenfurt-airport.at) is 4km (2.5 miles) from the city. Bus and taxi services are available. Airport facilities include a bar, duty-free shop and car hire.
Linz (LNZ) (website: www.linz-airport.at) is 10km (6 miles) from the city. Taxi and bus services are available. Airport facilities include a bar, duty-free shop, bank and car hire.
Graz (GRZ) (website: www.flughafen-graz.at) is 10km (6 miles) from the city. Taxis are available to the city (travel time – 20 minutes). Buses depart about 16 times a day and there are frequent train services. Airport facilities include a bar, restaurant, bank and car hire.
Note: Airports have fixed charges for portering.
Departure tax: None.
RAIL: *Österreichische Bundesbahnen (ÖBB)* (Austrian Federal Railways) operates a wide network of trains throughout and beyond Austria. International connections from Vienna include trains to Germany (Berlin), to the Russian Federation (Moscow, via Warsaw/Kiev and Minsk), to Romania (Bucharest, via Budapest), to Greece (Athens) or Turkey (Istanbul, via Belgrade) and to Italy (Venice, Milan or Rome). The most common routes are from Brussels or Paris (Eurostar connection from London) to Vienna (see *Channel Tunnel*, below, for further details). For further details contact Österreichische Bundesbahnen, Elisabethstraße 9, A-1010 Wien (tel: (1) 930 000; fax (1) 25000; e-mail: wien.ticketline@pv.oebb.at; website: www.oebb.at).
Rail passes: Several international rail passes permitting unlimited travel in a number of European countries are valid in Austria. The *Euro* and *Eurail* passes are available to non-European residents and must be bought outside Europe. The *Euro* pass is valid for travel over practically the whole of the European rail network, while the *Eurail* pass has more limited validity The *Interail* pass is available to European residents. Prices vary according to age, zones covered, time period, flexibility and class of travel. For more information, contact Rail Europe (tel: (08705) 848 848; website: www.raileurope.co.uk).
The Channel Tunnel: The quickest route by train from the UK is through the channel tunnel with connections from Brussels or Paris to Austria. *Eurostar* operates direct high-speed trains through the channel tunnel from London (*Waterloo International*) to Paris (*Gare du Nord*) and to Brussels (*Midi/Zuid*). From London to Paris, the journey time is 3 hours; from London to Brussels the journey time is 2 hours 40 minutes. From Brussels there is a morning train to Vienna leaving at 0828 (travel time - approximately 13 hours) and a night train leaving at 1910 (travel time - approximately 14 hours); from Paris (*Gare de l'Est*) there are two trains to Vienna, one at 0749 and another at 1717 (travel time - 14 hours 45 minutes). For further information and reservations contact *Eurostar* (tel: 0870 6000 792 (travel agents) *or* 08705 186 186 (public; within the UK) *or* 1233 617 575 (public; outside the UK); website: www.eurostar.com); *or* Rail Europe (tel: 08705 848 848). Travel agents can obtain refunds for unused tickets from Eurostar Trade Refunds, 2nd Floor, Kent House, 81 Station Road, Ashford, Kent TN23 1PD. Complaints and comments may be sent to Eurostar Customer Relations, Eurostar House, Waterloo Station, London SE1 8SE. General enquiries and information requests must be made by telephone.
ROAD: There are numerous and excellent road links with all neighbouring countries. For information on traffic regulations and required documentation, see the *Travel - Internal* section. **Coach:** Coaches run regularly to a large number of European destinations. *Eurolines*, departing from Victoria Coach Station in London, serves destinations in Austria. For further information, contact Eurolines, (tel: (08705) 143 219; e-mail: welcome@eurolines.co.uk; website: www.eurolines.co.uk). Some tour operators offer package holidays to Austria by coach from the UK. A full list is available from the Austrian National Tourist Office (see *Contact Addresses* section). **The Channel Tunnel:** *Eurotunnel* operates trains 24 hours per day through the Channel Tunnel between Folkestone in Kent (with direct access from the M20) and Calais in France. All vehicles from motorcycles to campers can be accommodated. Eurotunnel operates three to four passenger trains per hour at peak times. The journey takes approximately 35 minutes. For further information see *France, Travel - International* section *or* contact *Eurotunnel Reservations* (tel: (08705) 353 535; e-mail: callcentre@eurotunnel.com; website: www.eurotunnel.co.uk).
Car ferry: There are regular ferry services across the English Channel. The quickest and most practical route from London to Vienna is via the Dover-Ostend ferry (crossing time – three hours 30 minutes). The distance by road is approximately 1600km (1000 miles). It is one day's drive in summer, but can take longer in winter. Munich is four to five hours from Vienna; Milan and Zurich are a good day's drive.
RIVER: *DDSG-Blue Danube Schiffahrt* operates a passenger service on the Danube from Germany (Passau) to Vienna. For information and reservations, contact them at Friedrichstrasse 7, A-1010 Vienna (tel: (1) 588 800; fax: (1) 588 8440; e-mail: info@ddsg-blue-danube.at; website: www.ddsg-blue-danube.at). The German operator *Wurm und Köck* offers both passenger services and cruises to Linz. Overnight cruise packages from Passau to Linz include hotel accommodation for only slightly more than the regular one-way passenger fare. Evening and music cruises are available in the summer. For further information, contact *Wurm und Köck*, Untere Donaulände, 4020 Linz (tel: (732) 783 607; fax: (732) 783 60720; e-mail: info@donauschiffahrt.at; website: www.donauschiffahrt.at). *DDSG-Blue Danube Schiffahrt* also operates a hydrofoil service from the Praterlande hydrofoil dock in Vienna to Hungary (Budapest; travel time – 6 hours). *Ardagger* operates services between Linz and Germany (Krems) (tel: (7479) 64640; fax: (7479) 646 510; e-mail: dsa@pgv.at; website: www.tiscover.com/donauschiffahrt). *Brandner* concentrates its services between Melk and Krems. For further information, contact *Brandner* at Ufer 50, A-3313 Wallsee (tel: (7433) 259 021; fax: (7433) 259 025; e-mail: schiffahrt@brandner.at; website: www.ms-austria.at). A regular hydrofoil service also runs three times daily during the summer months from Vienna to the Slovak Republic (Bratislava) (travel time – 90 minutes). International rail tickets are valid on Danube river boats. More information on the above services, and connections to Serbia and Montenegro (Belgrade), Turkey (Istanbul) and Ukraine (Yalta), can be obtained from the Austrian National Tourist Office (see *Contact Addresses* section).

Travel - Internal

AIR: Vienna is connected to Graz, Klagenfurt, Linz and Salzburg by *Tyrolean Airways (VO)*. *Rheintalflug (WE)* also operates internal services. **Charter**: There are companies offering charter services for single- and twin-engined aircraft and executive jets.

RIVER/LAKE: A number of operators run cruises along the Danube, and from Switzerland (Bregenz) across Lake Constance. On some cruises, a passport is needed; they last from one to eight days depending on the itinerary. These services run between spring and autumn. **Ferries:** There are regular passenger boat services from mid-May to mid-September along the Danube and on Austria's lakes. The Danube steamer services are run by *DDSG Blue Danube Schiffahrt* (tel: (1) 588 800) and private companies.

RAIL: *Österreichische Bundesbahnen (ÖBB)* (Austrian Federal Railways) runs an efficient internal service, with a 5,700km network of tracks throughout Austria. There is a frequent intercity service from Vienna to Salzburg, Innsbruck, Graz and Klagenfurt, and regular motorrail services through the Tauern Tunnel. Information and booking can be obtained from railway stations *or* Austrian Federal Railways (see *Travel – International* for contact details). Local information can be obtained on (1) 1717. For bookings from the UK, contact *Deutsche Bahn* (German Rail) (tel: (0870) 243 5363; website: www.bahn.co.uk); *or* Rail Europe (tel: (08705) 848 848). The most scenic routes are Innsbruck–Brenner, Innsbruck–Buchs, Innsbruck–Bruck an der Mur–Vienna, Innsbruck–Feldkirch–Innsbruck, Innsbruck– Garmisch– Zugspitze, Innsbruck–Salzburg–Innsbruck, Linz–Selzthal–Amstetten–Linz, Salzburg–Zell am See–Innsbruck, Salzburg– Gmunden–Stainach–Salzburg, Salzburg–Vienna, Salzburg–Villach– Salzburg, Vienna–Puchberg am Schneeberg– Hochschneeberg–Vienna, Vienna–Bruck an der Mur–Innsbruck, Vienna–Klagenfurt–Udine–Trieste. Railways have fixed charges for portering. Tickets can be obtained from any station ticket office (*Reisebüro am Bahnhof*) or from most Austrian travel agents. For further information consult Austrian National Tourist Office (see *Contact Addresses* section). **Discount fares:** Throughout Austria, up to two children under six years who are accompanied or require no seat travel free and a third child qualifies for a 50 per cent discount. Children aged six to 15 pay half fare. The *Vorteilscard* is available to purchase, and offers a 45% discount on rail travel within a one-year period. This ID card can be purchased at all Austrian railway stations. Senior citizens (women 60 and over and men 65 and over) may buy train and bus tickets at half price after purchasing the *Vorteilscard* for approximately €25.50; those under 26 years of age pay approximately €17.90. Austria offers a number of discount rail passes including the *Euro Domino* and *Euro Domino Junior*, both valid for three to eight days within a 30-day period. The *Austrian Rail Pass* is available to foreigners. Reductions are also available for groups of more than six people. For more information, contact the *Austrian Railways Head Office* (see *Travel – International* section) or enquire locally.

ROAD: Austria has an excellent network of roads. Traffic drives on the right. Help is readily given by the Austrian Motoring Association (ÖAMTC); there is a fee for non-members. For emergency breakdowns, dial 120 *or* 123. Tolls must be paid on all Austrian motorways. Tourists can purchase either 10-day, two-monthly or one-year discs which are available at all major border crossings and at post offices. The weekly disc is valid for up to 10 days and costs approximately €7.63 for cars up to 3.5 tons. The two-month disc, valid for two consecutive calendar months costs €21.80 for cars below 3.5 tons. Heavy vehicles pay higher tariffs and motorcycles pay less. Seat belts must be worn and children under the age of 12 and under 150cm tall may not sit in the front seat unless a special child's seat has been fitted. Both driver and passenger on a motorcycle must wear helmets, and the vehicle must have lights on at all times. Speed limits are 50kph (31mph) in built-up areas (the speed limit in Graz is 30kph), 100kph (62mph) outside built-up areas and 130kph (81mph) on motorways. **Bus** and **coach** services are run by federal and local authorities, as well as private companies. There are over 1800 services in operation. Some 70 international coach services travel to or through Austria and 22 routes with timetables and prices can be found in the Austrian bus guide which can be consulted via the Austrian National Tourist Office. For further information, contact *Central Bus Information* (tel: (1) 794 440; e-mail: service@postbus.at; website: www.postbus.at). Coach excursions and sightseeing tours run from most major cities. **Car hire:** There are car hire firms with offices in most cities, as well as at airports and major railway stations. **Documentation:** National driving licences issued by EU countries, Norway, Iceland and Liechtenstein are accepted, and enable holders to drive in Austria for up to one year. UK licenses without a photo must be accompanied by some form of photo ID such as a passport. The minimum legal age for driving is 18. Car registration papers issue in the UK are also valid in Austria. A Green Card is compulsory.

URBAN: Vienna has an extensive system of **metro**, **bus**, **light rail** and **tramway** services. Most routes have a flat fare, and there are pre-purchase multi-journey tickets and passes. The *Vienna Card* entitles visitors to 72 hours of unlimited travel by underground, bus and tram. It also entitles the holder to reductions at several museums and other tourist attractions in the city as well as shops, cafes and wine taverns. The card can be purchased at hotels or at Vienna Transport's ticket offices. Those trams marked *schaffnerlos* on the outside of the carriage do not have conductors, but tickets can be bought from machines on board. Tickets are available from newspaper shops or tobacconists called Trafik. The classic way to travel round the capital is by **horse-drawn carriage** (*Fiaker*); fares should be agreed in advance. There are bus systems in all the other main towns, and also tramways in Linz, Innsbruck and Graz, and trolleybuses in Linz, Innsbruck and Salzburg.

Travel times: The following chart gives approximate travel times (in hours and minutes) from **Vienna** to other major cities/towns in Austria.

	Air	Road	Rail
Salzburg	0.45	3.00	3.18
Linz	0.45	2.00	1.54
Innsbruck	1.10	5.00	5.20
Bregenz	-	7.00	7.58
Klagenfurt	0.50	4.00	4.25
Graz	0.40	2.40	2.45

Accommodation

It is advisable to make enquiries and reservations well in advance (especially for July, August, Christmas and Easter). Room reservations are binding for the hotel-keeper and for the guest or travel agency. Compensation may be claimed if reserved rooms are not occupied. Hotels, *pensions* and other forms of tourist accommodation are classified by the Federal Chamber of Commerce and Industry. See the *Grading* section below for details. For further information contact the Austrian Hotel Association, Piaristengasse 16/7, A-1080 Vienna (tel: (1) 533 09520; fax: (1) 405 2584; e-mail: info@oehv.at; website: www.oehv.at).

HOTELS: 87 per cent of 5-star hotels and 50 per cent of 4-star hotels in Austria belong to the Austrian Hotel Association.

Grading: Classifications are according to the guidelines established by the International Hotel Association and relate to the facilities provided; 5-star for deluxe, 4-star for

A B C D E F G H I J K L M N O P Q R S T U V W X Y Z

first class, 3-star for standard, 2-star for economy and 1-star for budget. The facilities offered are as follows:
5-star hotels: Private bathrooms with shower or bath, hand basin and WC with all bedrooms. Telephone, alarm bell, colour TV in all bedrooms. Room service, day and night reception and foreign languages spoken. Restaurant, bars, lifts and garage space (in the cities) in all hotels; **4-star hotels:** Bedrooms with bath or shower, hand basin and WC. There is a telephone and alarm bell in all rooms, and TV in 50 per cent of them. Room service and day and night reception, dining rooms, foreign languages spoken, lifts in all hotels; **3-star hotels:** All new bedrooms and at least 70 per cent of older bedrooms with bath or shower, handbasin and WC. Foreign languages spoken at reception. Lifts and dining room; **2-star hotels:** 20 per cent of bedrooms should have a bath or shower and WC. 30 per cent should have at least a bath or shower. Toilet facilities may be shared. The dining room may serve as another public room. Some with reception and foreign language capability; **1-star hotels:** All rooms have hand basins. Toilet facilities and showers may be shared. The dining room may double as a general public room.
Note: Some hotels may still be under the old grades of A, B, C, etc. Full information and hotel list is available from the Austrian National Tourist Office.
SELF-CATERING: Holiday apartments, chalets, alpine huts and ski lodges are available for rent throughout Austria. For full details contact your local travel agent *or* the Austrian National Tourist Board (see *Contact Addresses* section).
FARM HOLIDAYS: There are approximately 29,000 farmhouses with a total of 300,000 beds providing accommodation. Lists of farmhouses taking paying guests for most provinces in Austria are available from the Austrian National Tourist Office. Listings include farms as well as pensions and inns with an attached farming operation.
CAMPING/CARAVANNING: There are approximately 500 campsites in Austria, all of which can be entered without any major formalities; approximately 160 sites are equipped for winter camping. Reductions for children are available, and for members of FICC, AIT and FIA. It is advisable to take along the camping carnet. Fees are charged on the usual international scale for parking caravans, motorbikes and cars. The parking of caravans without traction vehicle on or beside the public highways (including motorway parking areas) is prohibited. One can park caravans with traction vehicle beside public highways, if the parking regulations are observed. Some mountain roads are closed to caravans. For detailed information, contact the automobile clubs or Austrian National Tourist Office (see *Contact Addresses* section). The address of the Camping & Caravanning Club is Schubertring 1-3, A-1010 Vienna (tel: (1) 713 6151; e-mail: office@campingclub.at; website: www.campingclub.at).
Note: When camping in private grounds, permission from the landowner, police and municipal council is needed.
YOUTH HOSTELS: Youth hostels can be found throughout Austria and are at the disposal of anyone carrying a membership card of the International Youth Hostel Association. It is advisable to book in advance, especially during peak periods. For more details contact the Österreichische Jugendherbergsverband, Schottenring 28, A-1010 Vienna (tel: (1) 533 5353/4; fax: (1) 535 0861; e-mail: oejhv-zentrale@oejhv.or.at *or* backpacker-austria@oejhv.or.at; website: www.oejhv.or.at).
DISABLED TRAVELLERS: There are hotels with special facilities for disabled persons in towns all over Austria. Hotel guides for disabled travellers (including a special guide for Vienna) are available from Austrian National Tourist Office.

Resorts & Excursions

Austria is a country of startling contrasts, from the Austrian Alps in the west to the Danube Basin in the east. It is not only famous as one of the world's premier skiing regions, but also for its historical buildings, world-class museums and galleries, breathtaking scenery, magnificent mountains and established hiking trails. The nine Federal Provinces (**Vienna**, **Upper Austria** (*Oberösterreich*), **Burgenland**, **Lower Austria** (*Niederösterreich*), **Styria** (*Steiermark*), **Carinthia** (*Kärtnen*), **Salzburg**, **Tyrol** and **Vorarlberg**) divide the country along geographical and cultural lines. After Vienna, the western provinces of **Salzburg**, **Tirol** and **Vorarlberg** are the most popular tourist regions, although the southern province of **Carinthia** (bordering Italy and Slovenia) is now taking a larger share of the trade owing to its mild climate and attractive lakes.
Austria lends itself to walking, cycling and climbing as well as skiing, with an extensive network of hiking and mountain routes carefully signposted and cross-referenced to detailed maps. Alpine huts between 915m and 2744m, with resident wardens in the summer, are available for hire. Further information can be obtained from the Austrian Alpine Club (Österreichischer Alpenverein), Wilhelm-Greil-Strasse 15, 6010 Innsbruck (tel: (512) 595 470; fax: (512) 575 528; e-mail: office@alpenverein.at). Skiing facilities can be found in over 600 wintersport resorts between **Brand** in the west and **Semmering** in the east. Skiing enthusiasts of all ages and levels have a choice of more than 400 schools and top ski-instructors. It is possible to travel leisurely by boat from Passau on the German border to Vienna; this stretch of the Danube includes some of the finest scenery of its entire course.

VIENNA

The Austrian capital and one of the federal provinces is an important nexus for East-West trade and a frequent host to major congresses either in the **Vienna International Centre** (UNO City) or at the **Austria Centre Vienna**. Vienna is situated in the northeast of the country with the Danube River running through the northern suburbs of the city. The Ringstrasse forms the boundary of the elegant First District (the Innerstadt or Inner City), with its fine architecture, shops and hotels, much of it pedestrianised. Every major architectural style from the Baroque onwards can be found here, with especial importance given to the Art Nouveau (Secession) style which had its roots here. The Hapsburgs who ruled the country for six centuries resided in the Hofburg where the **Kaiser-Appartements** (**Imperial Apartments**) and the **Crown Jewels** are now open to the public. The **Spanish Riding School** in the Hofburg where the famous white Lipizzaner stallions perform finely executed dressage manoeuvres to Viennese classical music is very popular with tourists (closed during July and August). **Schloss Schönbrunn**, the sumptuous Imperial summer palace, can be compared with that at Versailles; its landscaped park is also home to the world's oldest zoo.
Many fine art collections like the **Kunsthistorisches Museum**, containing the works of Breughel, Dürer and Titian and the **Akademie der bildenden Künste** (with works by Hieronymus Bosch) are internationally renowned. There are more than 50 museums open to the public, including the **Natural History Museum**, the **Austrian Museum of Applied Arts**, the **Museum of the 20th Century**, the **Museum of Modern Art**, the **Museumsquartier**, the **Künstlerhaus**, the **Clock and Watch Museum** and the **Technology Museum**.
Immortalised in the film *The Third Man*, the **Ferris Wheel** (*Riesenrad*) in the **Prater amusement park** is also a popular attraction. Well worth a visit are **St Stephen's Cathedral**, the art collection at the **Belvedere Palace**, the **Chapel of the Hofburg**, the **Burgtheater** (known as '**Die Burg**'), the **Parliament**, the **Rathaus** (**Town Hall**), the **University** and the **Votive church** along the Ringstrasse. There are also memorial sites for Mozart, Haydn, Beethoven, Schubert, Strauss and Freud. On the southern and western edges of Vienna are the **Wienerwald** (**Vienna Woods**), ideal for both quiet time away from the city and rather wilder times at the many local **Heurigen** (wineries of the local vineyards).

BURGENLAND

Austria's youngest Federal Province in the easternmost part of the country is a popular tourist destination. The wooded hills in the south of the region form the foothills of the Austrian Alps. The northeast largely consists of expanses of the Central European Plain. The mild climate is especially well suited for the cultivation of wine.
EISENSTADT: The **Esterhazy Palace**, the **Cathedral** and the composer **Haydn's house** (now a museum), as well as the **Burgenländische Museum**, the **Berg** and the **Franciscan churches** are well worth a visit. A thoughtful atmosphere lies over the **Jewish Cemetery** and the area of the former **Jewish Ghetto**.
EXCURSIONS: The **Neusiedler-Seewinkle National Park** was Austria's first World Conservation Union approved national park, located in the area where the Austrian Alps meet the Euro-Asiatic (pannonishe) Plains. **Neusiedl am See's Local History Museum** is attractive, and **Mörbisch**, on **Neusiedl Lake**, hosts an important annual operetta festival. Raiding is the birthplace of Franz Liszt. *Passion plays* are staged every five years in St Margarethen. **Bad Tatzmannsdorf** is one of Austria's important spa centres. Storks return each year to nest in the chimneys at the wine-making centre of **Rust**.

STYRIA

Styria is a popular and especially attractive holiday destination stretching from Salzburg to the Hungarian border in the East. In the **Dachstein Gebirge** overshadowing the Enns Valley, skiing is possible all year round. The south of the province, known as the **Weinstrasse** (Wine Road), is dominated by large vineyards. Styria also has a wealth of green pine forests suitable for rambles and hikes during the summer.
GRAZ: A recent European Capital of Culture, Graz is also capital of the Styria region. From the 15th century, it was a major bulwark against the Turks and, in the 17th century adopted the Baroque before the rest of the Austrian empire. The city is compact and most important sights are within walking distance of the market square of the **Hauptplatz**. The **Landesmuseum Johanneum**, a large complex of museums, is one of the world's oldest, and includes the **Alte Galerie** with its superb Gothic paintings. The **Neue Galerie** in the **Herbenstrein Palace** displays 19th- and 20th-century paintings, including some works by Schiele and Klimt. The **Cathedral**, the **Mausoleum of Emperor** Ferdinand II (begun in 1614), the Leech Church, the pedestrian zone of the old quarter, the **Schlossberg** (**Castle Hill**) with its **Uhrtrum** (clock tower) and **Glockenturm** (bell tower) should also be seen. Some distance west of the city is **Schloss Eggenberg**, the 16th-century palace noted for its state rooms and museums. More than any other provincial centre Graz preserves the old *Kaffeehaus* culture where visitors can sit all day enjoying a leisurely coffee, watching the life of the city.
Excursions: Any itinerary should include a visit to the **Museum** and the **Convent at Leoben** and to the silver mine in **Oberzeiring**. **Piber** includes the stud farm for the famous Lipizzaner horses. **Stübing/Gratwein**, in the forests northeast of Graz, has an excellent open-air museum of furnished houses from all over the country. The **Weinstrasse** stretches from **Ehrenhausen** to **Elbiswald**. Also worth exploring are **Bruck an der Mur**, **Eisenerz**, **Murau**, **Oberzeiring**, **Schladming**, **Bad Aussee** and **Ramsau**.

CARINTHIA

Carinthia (Kärnten), with Austria's highest mountain, the **Grossglockner** (3798m/12,457ft) to the west and the **Karawanken Mountains** in the south, has a mild climate. The famous lakes reach temperatures of 28°C (82°F), and earned Carinthia the European Environment Award for their superb water quality.
From the **Wörther See** to the **Hohe Tauern National Park** (which extends into Tirol and Salzburg provinces), Carinthia offers a wide variety of excursions even in winter, when the lakes become skating rinks and the 10 ski resorts with 1000km (625-miles) of pistes open their doors to the public.
KLAGENFURT: The Provincial capital lies on the western edge of the **Wörthersee**, the largest lake in the region. The town is full of tradition, with more than 50 restored baroque arcades now housing shops and coffee houses. It is worth visiting the **Dom** (**Cathedral**), the museums and at least some of the 23 castles which encircle the town, now offering restaurants, cultural performances and even an animal sanctuary. The **Naturpark Kreuzbergl** overlooking the town offers trails, lakes and a way to see the Austrian hills without too much effort.
Excursions: Carinthia has a rich legacy of gothic and renaissance churches, fortresses, palaces, and museums; history is always close at hand. The **Wörthersee** has many good beaches and attractive campsites. The cathedrals, churches and monasteries of **Gurk**, **Maria Gail**, **Maria Saal** and **Viktring** are popular, as is the **City Museum** of **Friesach**. The hot spring at **Villach** is known for its curative properties. The **Hohe Tauern National Park** is one of the last large undisturbed mountain environments in Europe. Also worth visiting for a leisurely holiday are the towns of **Heiligenblut**, **Millstatt**, **Obervellach**, **Ossiach**, **St Veit an der Glan**, **Velden** and **Pörtschach**.

LOWER AUSTRIA

Lower Austria (Niederösterreich), to the north and west of Vienna, is the largest Federal Province, encompassing stark mountain scenery, the Alpine foothills, the Danube Valley and the hilly country north of the Danube with its meadows, lakes and ponds. The **Wachau Valley** of the **Danube River** with its vineyards and ruins is an attractive destination, less well known than other parts of the country; the most interesting stretch between Krems an der Donau and Melk can best be explored by bicycle or by riverboat.
ST PÖLTEN: The Provincial capital is home to a Cathedral, the bishop's residence, a Franciscan church, a church of the Carmelite Nuns, a museum and Baroque patrician houses.
EXCURSIONS: The spa of **Baden bei Wien** has a casino, a sulphur bath cure, a summer theatre and a harness-racing (trotting) course; the spa has long been popular with the Austrian aristocracy. **Krems an der Donau** has been a wine-growing town since the middle ages and the **Piaristenkirche** and the **Winestadt Museum** both feature important works of the 18th-century artist Johann Martin Schmidt. To the north of **Landstrasse** much of the original town layout remains, with numerous renaissance houses and small squares. **Melk an der Donau** is famous for its enormous Benedictine Abbey on the bluff above the town (although it was less well known as a pilot for the next phase of Nazi concentration camps). **Semmering** is both a spa and an attrative ski resort. **Bad Deutsch-Altenburg** boasts a museum and the Roman archaeological park **Carnuntum**. In **Dürnstein**, the castle ruins where Richard the Lionheart was imprisoned, the medieval town centre and the monastery church with its Baroque excess of statues of saints are part of every tour. The sights of **Retz** include subterranean wine-cellars, well-

restored medieval city walls, windmills and a Dominican church, and **Rohrau** is noted as Joseph Haydn's birthplace. The **Austrian Military Academy** (an old castle), the Cathedral, a Capuchin church and a former Jesuit church (now the city's museum) can be visited in **Wiener Neustadt**. The abbey, library, state rooms and chapter house at **Zwettl** are of some interest. **Burg Rosenau** hosts a **Museum of Freemasonry**. The **Thayatal National Park**, on the **Thaya River** on the border with the Czech Republic is a transborder protected area of what is left of the European forest. The **Donau-Auen National Park** to the east of Vienna is the last protected area of European rainforest.

SALZBURG PROVINCE

SALZBURG: An elegant and spacious baroque city, Salzburg is set against a backdrop of breathtaking mountain scenery. The snow-capped mountains of the **Hohe Tauern** rise in the south whereas the north offers the hills and lakes of the Salzkammergut. All sights are within walking distance of the old city centre, overlooked by the fortress **Hohensalzburg**, which can be reached either by walking up through the narrow, winding **Festungsgasse** or by taking the funicular. The **Altstadt** (the old city) was recently granted World Heritage Status by UNESCO and has now largely been pedestrianised. Considering its reputation as a 'typically Austrian city' it is ironic that it was either Bavarian or an independent city state, only coming under Hapsburg rule in 1816. Interesting sights include the Peterskirche (St Peter's Abbey, with cemetery and catacombs), the **Domkirche** (intended to rival St Peter's in Rome) and the **Alter Markt** (old market square). Salzburg's most famous son – although only after his death – is Wolfgang Amadeus Mozart, who is commemorated in the yearly *Salzburger Festspiele* which take place in the **Grosse** and **Kleine Festspielhäuser** (festival halls) as well as on the Cathedral square or in the University church. Mozart's birthplace (**Mozart Geburtshaus**) is in the Getreidegasse, also the city's main shopping street, while the family residence (**Mozart Wohnhaus**) is on the market square. Both are museums, with the residence offering a particularly detailed insight into his life and work. Like Vienna, Salzburg contains fine examples of Baroque architecture which stands second only to music in the country's cultural history. The Franciscan church, the **Nonnberg Convent**, the **Trinity Church**, **St Sebastian's Cemetery**, the **Church of Parsch**, the **Palace of the Prince-Archbishops**, the carillon, the **Town Hall**, the **Pferdeschwemme** (a fountain), the festival halls, the **Mirabell Palace** with its landscaped gardens, the **Mönchsberg** and the **Kapuzinerberg**, many museums, the theatre, **Hellbrunn Palace** with the fountains, **Leopoldskron** and **Klesshem Palaces**, **Maria Pein Pilgrimage Church**, the **Gaisberg** and the **Untersberg** provide many possible tours and walks.
EXCURSIONS: The original wealth of Salzburg and the province was based on the salt trade, and the mines and the **Celtic Museum** of **Hallein** are well worth a visit. **Badgastein** is a popular spa and winter resort, with a large casino, whilst **Kaprun** offers glacier skiing even in the summer. The **Zell-am-See** skiing area has an active nightlife. The **Open-Air Folklife Museum** at **Grossgmain** is also worth visiting, as are the **Eisriesenwelt** (ice caves, with wonderful ice sculptures) near **Werfen**. **Kremsmünster Monastery** is one of the country's oldest; founded in 877, the buildings are full of paintings, frescos and Renaissance statues. The monastery is also famous for its white wines.

UPPER AUSTRIA

The south of this Federal Province is dominated by the **Salzkammergut** lake district and the **Salzkammergut peaks** lie across the border of Upper Austria (Oberösterreich) and Salzburg province. This is an area less well known to tourists and, with its slower pace, is ideal for restful holidays. The north offers a relaxed holiday in the many quiet villages and farms – the **Mühlviertel**. Rolling plains, densely wooded highlands and lush meadows are interspersed with rocks of natural granite. The **Pyhrn-Eisenwurzen** region is more mountainous, while **Innviertel** (in the west) is an area of endless farmlands, rivers and forests. The many spas and convalescence centres of this region offer treatment for a wide range of illnesses.
LINZ: The Province's capital is an attractive town with a Baroque centre, straddling the **Danube**. Any tour should take in the 15th-century **Schloss** (castle) with its excellent museum, the numerous churches and museums, especially the **Neue Gallerie**. However, there are far more attractive offerings in the **Urfahr** suburb, with its interactive new technology **Ars Electronica Center**, and the narrow-gauge train, the **Pöstlingbergbahn**, which travels to the pilgrimage church of **Pöstlingberg** with its excellent views over the valley. The **Augustinian Monastery** of **St Florian** 7km (4 miles) from Linz was sponsored by the Hapsburgs and is an attractive day trip for Linz. The major Nazi concentration camp at **Mauthausen**, 20km (12 miles) east of Linz, is difficult to access by public transport but is well worth a day trip.
EXCURSIONS: Bad Ischl, a 19th-century spa town, is the hub of the region, near the three most scenic lakes (**Wolfgangsee**,**Traunsee** and **Hallstättersee**); the town offerings include a salt mine, several museums and the summer villa of Emperor Franz Josef. **Hallstatt** lent its name to a whole era in the Iron Age; surrounded by mountains it is known for its tranquility and scenery. The **Mondsee** is one of the warmest lakes in the Salzkammergut. **St Wolfgang** does not only offer an impressive altar, but a steam railway as well. **Gmunden**, the Nice of Upper Austria, is known for its many cultural festivals; located at the northern end of the **Traunsee**, the largest of the area's lakes, it has been famous for centuries for its porcelain. The old city centres of **Braunau** and **Schärding** are not to be missed. **Freistadt** has medieval forts, whilst **Grein** offers a navigation museum, **Clam Castle** and the old theatre. **Steyr**, with its old inner city, delights visitors with its **Working-World Museum** and the **Christkindl** pilgrimage church. The **National Park Kalkalpen** in the **Pyhrn-Eisenwurzen** region is primarily a mountainous environment; **Windischgarsten** is an attractive town from which to explore the park. Much of the interior of Upper Austria is little known to foreign tourists and many towns including **Bad Goisern**, **Gosau**, **Hinterstoder** and **Spital am Pyhrn** are attractive destinations for a quiet vacation. There are excellent skiing facilities throughout the province, mainly at smaller resorts.

TIROL

Situated in the heart of the Alpine region, this is the most mountainous province, with forests, hamlets and alpine pastures, beautiful valleys and mountain lakes. In summer it is a popular destination for hikers; in winter, all winter sports are on offer. Traditional Tirolean architecture is reflected in the villages, churches and castles.
INNSBRUCK: The Tirolean capital, and twice home of the Winter Olympics, is the centre of another internationally renowned ski complex comprising six major resorts. An 800-year-old university town, it has numerous fine buildings dating from Austria's cultural Renaissance in the 16th-18th centuries, and a 12th-century court castle. When Kaiser Maximilian based the imperial court here in the 1490s, the city became a European centre of culture and politics. For spectacular views over the town and southern Alps, take the funicular to Hungerburg and then the cable car to Hafelekar at 2334m (5928ft). Do not miss the **Goldenes Dachl** (**Golden Roof**), **Helbling House**, the **City Tower**, the **Hofburg** with its **Cenotaph of Kaiser Maximiloan**, and the **Court Church**, the parish **Church of St Jakob**, **Mount Isel**, the important **Tiroler Landesmuseum Ferdinandeum** and the **Tiroler Volkkunstmuseum**, the **Landestheater**, a conference centre and the Seegrube.
EXCURSIONS: Passion plays take place every five years in **Erl** (next staging: 2007) and **Thiersee** (next staging: 2005). A sight not to be missed is the **Mint Tower** at the **Hasegg Castle** in **Hall in Tirol**. In **Rattenberg**, a medieval atmosphere prevails from the glass factories which date back to this period. A visit to the **Cathedral Chapter** of **Stams** and its basilica is recommended. 15km (9 miles) from Innsbruck lies **Swarovski Crystal Worlds**, a museum/exhibition centre featuring unusual displays of crystal. **Kitzbühel** rose as a 16th-century silver and copper mining town and is now an exclusive resort with a lovely central area. **Seefeld** in Tirol is an attractive year-round sports destination. The **Schneewinkel Area** is excellent for all winter sports; **St Johann in Tirol** in particular is an old market town offering a wide variety of sports and fitness centres, with a good nightlife as well.

VORARLBERG

Situated at the far western tip of Austria, the scenery of the Vorarlberg is dramatically diverse. The glaciers of the **Silvretta mountain ranges** drop dramatically to the shores of **Lake Constance** with its lush vegetation. Vorarlbergers speak a dialect close to Swiss German; in 1918 they declared independence and requested union with Switzerland but this was refused by the Allied Powers.
BREGENZ: Bregenz in the summer lends itself to bicycle tours, swimming, sailing or sightseeing, whereas during the winter season visitors populate the numerous slopes and hiking trails of the Vorarlberg. The town is noted for its Upper City with the **St Martinstrum** (**St Martin's Tower**), the world's largest floating stage for summer opera productions, the **Congress Centre**, the **Mehrerau Abbey Church**, the **Vorarlberger Landesmuseum** with its superb 16th-century paintings and works by late-18th-century artist Angelika Kauffmann. A cable car runs to the viewing platform on **Mount Pfänder** where one can watch the flight of birds of prey as well as scenic views over **Lake Constance**.
EXCURSIONS: The historical old quarter of **Feldkirch** contains the **Cathedral St Nicholas**, the **Schattenburg** housing the **Local History Museum**, and the excellent **National Conservatoire**. In **Levis**, near Feldkirch, the **Castle Amberg** and the Hospital should not be missed. **Tosters'** sights include the castle ruin and the **St Corneli Church** with a 1000-year-old yew tree. Visitors should pay a visit to the famous Renaissance palace of **Hohenems**; the town is also known for its **Jewish Museum** and the only **Jewish Cemetery** in the Vorarlberg. A picturesque, completely restored farming village, **Schwarzenberg im Bregenzerwald** is the birthplace of the painter Angelika Kauffmann; the **Landesmuseum** and the church there are worth a visit. **Ischgl** is an attractive unsophisticated Tirolean village, with excellent après-ski in the winter.

Sport & Activities

Wintersports: Austria is one of Europe's major destinations for winter sports, particularly **skiing** and, more recently, **snowboarding**. The Austrian Alps take up approximately 60 per cent of the country's surface area and there are more than 800 winter sports resorts, with ski runs stretching some 22,000km (13,750 miles), and a further 16,000km (10,000 miles) of **cross-country skiing** trails. Every year, Austria hosts a number of prestigious international ski competitions. Besides skiing, many other types of winter sports can be enjoyed, such as **tobogganing**, **sleigh rides**, **curling** or **skating**. Full details of skiing packages and tours, resort information, snow reports and winter sports events can be obtained from the Austrian National Tourist Office (see *Contact Addresses* section), which also publishes several brochures, some of which, such as the *Winter Tour Finder*, can be ordered directly and free of charge from the Internet.
Walking tours: During summer, when the snow has melted, the Austrian Alps offer a vast network of **hiking** trails through varied landscapes, ranging from forests and green slopes to glaciers and rocks. Many rivers and lakes are suitable for **swimming** or **fishing** (the latter requiring a permit available from the local authorities). Detailed walking maps can be obtained either from the Austrian National Tourist Office or from the local tourist offices. Guides can be hired locally. Footpaths are recognisable by red-white-red markings displayed on trees and rocks. Interesting routes include the *Salt Road*, once used by Austria's salt merchants, from the salt mines in the Salzkammergut, through the Mühlviertel, via many historic towns and as far as the border with the Czech Republic; and the *Styrian Timber Road*, giving travellers an insight into the uses of wood. Near Vienna, a network of city paths (*Stadtwanderwege*) lead through the Vienna woods or the nearby Danube wetlands. The *Vorarlberg's* alpine pastures are well suited for gentle walks while the *Hohe Tauern National Park* is popular for more demanding **trekking**. Accommodation is widely available along the paths in the form of hotels, inns or mountain huts.
Mountaineering and climbing: Both are widely available throughout the Alps. For details of climbing associations and specialist operators, contact the Austrian National Tourist Office. Climbing tours are often combined with **hang-gliding** which has recently gained in popularity and can be practised in many locations in the mountains.
Cycling: Austria's infrastructure for cyclists is excellent. There are clearly marked cycling routes both in the cities and throughout the countryside. Tourist offices can provide detailed touring maps and the Austrian Federal Railways (*ÖBB*) offers substantial services to cyclists. Practically all local trains allow bicycles to be carried in the baggage car. For long-distance trains, cyclists should look out for a bicycle symbol next to the train number if they wish to take their bike. The ÖBB also offers a bicycle rental service (*Fahrrad am Bahnhof*) at 100 Austrian railway stations where visitors can rent bicycles directly from the station at a reduced fee. Along the cycling paths, many hotels and inns have lockable bicycle racks and other facilities for cyclists. Austria's mountains offer extensive and challenging trails for **mountain biking**. For further information on planning either an organised or independent cycling tour, contact the Austrian National Tourist Office; *or Radtouren in Österreich*, c/o Salzburger Land Tourismus Gmbh, Postfach 1, Wiener Bundesstrasse 23, A-5300 Hallwang bei Salzburg (tel: (662) 66 880; fax: (662) 668 866; e-mail: info@salzburgerland.com; website: www.salzburgerland.com).
Horseriding: There are many hotels and guest houses specialising in horseriding holidays (*reitferien*). Horses can be hired for short or longer periods and packages frequently include riding instruction.
Wine tours: The Austrian National Tourist Office has singled out three wine routes through Austria's main wine-growing regions – Lower Austria, Southern Styria and the Burgenland. In Lower Austria, a whole area in the northeast is known as the *Weinviertel* (wine quarter), where *Kellergassen* (wine cellars and wine-press buildings located outside the villages in the hillsides) and *Buschenschanken* (small wine taverns) can be visited. The Wachau region, a section of the Danube Valley approximately 50km (32 miles)

from Vienna, is reputed for its *Riesling* wines and the wine village of *Gumpoldskirchen*. Southern Styria enjoys a moist, warm climate and its token wine is the *Schilcher*, an onion-coloured to ruby-red wine. The Burgenland produces more than a quarter of Austria's wines and is known for sweet wines such as the *Ausbruch*. Most wine estates and cellars welcome visitors. Further information can be obtained from local tourist offices or the Austrian National Tourist Office; see also *Food & Drink* in the *Social Profile* section.

Social Profile

FOOD: Traditional Austrian dishes are *Wiener Schnitzel*, boiled beef (*Tafelspitz*), calf's liver with herbs in butter (*Geröstete Leber*), *Goulash*, *Kaiserschmarrn*, *Palatschinken* and *Salzburger Nockerln*, as well as various types of smoked and cured pork. Viennese cuisine is strongly influenced by southeast European cuisine, notably that of Hungary, Serbia, Romania and Dalmatia. Many of the simpler meals are often made with rice, potatoes and dumplings (*Knödel*) with sauces. The main meal of the day is lunch. *Mehlspeisen* is the national term for cakes and puddings, all of which are wonderfully appetising. There are more than 57 varieties of *Torte*, which is often consumed with coffee at around 1500. Open all day, the Austrian coffee shop (*Kaffeehaus*) is little short of a national institution and often provides the social focus of a town or neighbourhood.

Spirits such as whisky and gin, together with imported beers, tend to be on the expensive side, but local wines (often served in open carafes) are excellent and cheap. Most of the wines are white (*Riesling*, *Veltliner*) but there are also some good red wines from Baden and Burgenland, as well as imported wines from other European countries. Generally the strict registration laws mean that the quality of the wine will be fully reflected in its price. *Obstler* is a drink found in most German-speaking countries, and is made by distilling various fruits. It is usually very strong, and widely drunk as it is cheap and well flavoured. Most bars or coffee houses have waiter service and bills are settled with the arrival of drinks. All restaurants have waiter service.

Note: There are no national licensing laws in Austria, but each region has local police closing hours. Most coffee houses and bars serve wine as well as soft drinks and beers.

SHOPPING: High-quality goods such as handbags, glassware, chinaware and winter sports equipment represent the cream of specialist items found in Austria. A 20-32 per cent value-added-tax (called MwSt) is included in the list price of items sold. **Shopping hours:** Shops and stores are generally open from Mon-Fri 0800-1800 (with a one- or two-hour lunch break in the smaller towns). Some shops are open until 1930 on Thursday and on Saturday opening hours are until 1700.

NIGHTLIFE: Viennese nightlife offers something for every taste: opera, theatre and cabaret as well as numerous discos, bars and nightclubs. There are cinemas of all types, some of them of architectural interest, showing films in different languages. A good way to spend a summer evening is in one of the beer gardens found all over Austria. The wine-growing area around Vienna features wine gardens (*Heurigen*) where visitors can sample local wines in an open-air setting.

SPECIAL EVENTS: For a full list of events celebrated in Austria, contact the Austrian National Tourist Office (see *Contact Addresses* section). The following is a selection of special events occurring in Austria in 2005:

Jan *Johann Strauss Ball*. **Jan 1** *New Near Day's Concert in Vienna*. **Jan 5-6** *FIS Snowboarding World Cup Race*. **Jan 8-15** *International Ballooning Week*, Filzmoos. **Jan 14-16** *Snow Arena Polo*, Kitzbühel. **Jan 21-30** *Mozart Week*, Salzburg. **Jan 22-30** *Resonanzen Festival*, Vienna. **Jan 29** *Rainbow Ball*, Gay and Lesbian ball, Vienna. **Mar** *Formula 1: Austrian Grand Prix*. **Mar-May** *Vienna Spring Festival*. **May-Jun** *Daffodil Festival*. **Mar 12-21** *Swingin' Kitzbühel*, jazz festival. **Mar 15-19** *Davidoff Gourmet Festival*. **May 22** *Vienna City Marathon*. **Jun 27-Jul 29** *Jazz Festival*, Vienna. **Jul** *International Milka Chocolate Festival*, Bludenz. **Jul-Aug** *Lederhosen Festival*. **Jul 9-12** *International Youth & Music Festival*, Vienna. **Jul 12** *Styriarte Festival*, Graz. **Jul 25-Aug 31** *Salzburg Festival*. **Nov-Dec** *Christmas Market Schönbrunn*, Vienna. **Dec** *'Magic of Advent' Christmas Market*, Vienna.

SOCIAL CONVENTIONS: Austrians tend to be quite formal in both their social and business dealings. They do not use first names when being introduced, but after the initial meeting first names are often used. Handshaking is normal when saying hello and goodbye. It is considered impolite to enter a restaurant or shop without saying *Guten Tag* or, more usually, *Grüss Gott*; similarly, to leave without saying *Auf Wiedersehen* can cause offence. Social pleasantries and some exchange of small-talk is appreciated. If invited out to dinner, flowers should be brought for the hostess. The Church enjoys a high and respected position in Austrian society, which should be kept in mind by the visitor. It is customary to dress up for the opera or the theatre. **Tipping:** Widespread, but large amounts are not expected. On restaurant bills a service charge of 10 to 15 per cent is included, but it is usual to leave a further 5 per cent. Attendants at theatres, cloakrooms or petrol pumps, expect to be tipped €0.15-0.25. Railway and airports have fixed charges for portering. Taxi drivers expect €0.25-0.50 for a short trip and 10 per cent for a longer one.

Business Profile

ECONOMY: Austria is one of the most prosperous countries in the world. Manufacturing, including mining, accounts for nearly 30 per cent of GDP. Since World War II, much of the country's industrial capacity has been in state hands and only recently has been removed from under the protective wing of the state holding company, OIAG. Iron and steel, chemicals, metalworking and engineering all fall into this category. Agriculture has proved equally successful, with domestic products meeting 90 per cent of the country's food needs. Crops include sugar beet, potatoes, grain, grapes, tobacco, flax, hemp and wine. Austria has moderate deposits of iron, lignite, magnesium, lead, copper, salt, zinc and silver. Although there are some oil reserves and an extensive hydroelectric programme, Austria must import the bulk of its energy requirements. Austria was a member of the European Free Trade Association (EFTA) before it joined the EU in 1995; Germany is now Austria's largest trading partner by a considerable margin, followed by Italy, France, the UK and, outside the EU, Switzerland. Overall, the EU now accounts for approximately two thirds of total Austrian trade. The previously substantial trade with both the USA and the former USSR has fallen as a proportion of the total in recent years. After implementing austerity measures to cut government spending, Austria was able to meet the criteria for membership of the single European currency and joined it upon its inception at the beginning of 1999. Since then, in common with most of the EU, the economy has been sluggish. GDP growth was just over 2 per cent in 2002 and 2003.

BUSINESS: Austrians are quite formal in their business dealings. A working knowledge of German will be very advantageous. Best times to visit are the spring and autumn months. **Office hours:** Mon-Fri 0800-1230 and 1330-1730.

COMMERCIAL INFORMATION: The following organisation can offer advice: Wirtschaftskammer Österreich (Austrian Federal Economic Chamber), Wiedner Hauptstrasse 63, 1045, Vienna (tel: (1) 501 050 4226 *or* 590 900; fax: (1) 5010 5255; e-mail: callcenter@wko.at *or* awo.maerkte@wko.at; website: www.wko.at).

CONFERENCES/CONVENTIONS: Austria has 31 conference venues, including over 20 in Vienna and a floating conference centre, the *MS Mozart*, on the river Danube. The provincial capitals of Salzburg, Innsbruck, Graz, Linz, Bregenz, Klagenfurt and Eisenstadt also offer convention venues, as do several health and spa resorts. Furthermore there are approximately 70 hotels in Austria which specialise in the conference/convention field. For more detailed information, contact the Austrian National Tourist Office (see *Contact Addresses* section).

Climate

Austria enjoys a moderate continental climate: summers are warm and pleasant with cool nights, and winters are sunny, with snow levels high enough for widespread winter sports.

Required clothing: European clothes according to season. Alpine wear for mountain resorts.

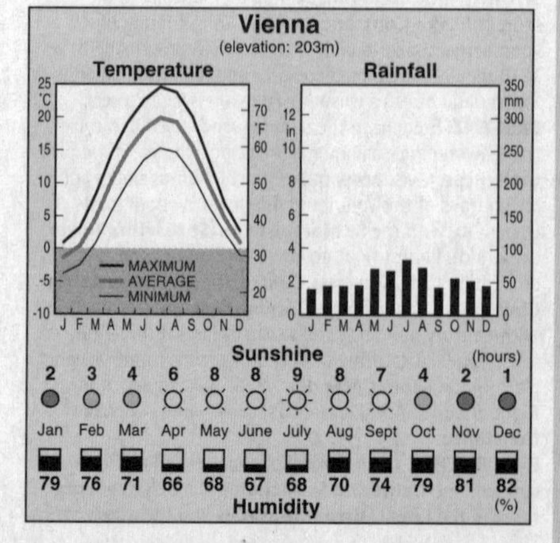

Azerbaijan

LATEST TRAVEL ADVICE CONTACTS

British Foreign and Commonwealth Office
Tel: (0870) 606 0290 Website: www.fco.gov.uk

US Department of State
Website: http://travel.state.gov/travel

Canadian Department of Foreign Affairs and Int'l Trade
Tel: (1 800) 267 8376 Website: www.dfait-maeci.gc.ca

Location: Caucasus, western Caspian Sea region.

Country dialling code: 994.

Ministry of Foreign Affairs
4 Shykhali Gurbanov Street, 370009 Baku, Azerbaijan
Tel: (12) 492 92 83. Fax: (12) 498 84 80.
E-mail: bkatl@mfa.gov.az
Website: www.mfa.gov.az

Embassy of the Azerbaijan Republic
4 Kensington Court, London W8 5DL, UK
Tel: (020) 7938 3412 or 5482 (consular section).
Fax: (020) 7937 1783.
E-mail: sefir@btinternet.com
Opening hours: 0930-1800.
Consular opening hours (located on the lower ground floor of above address): Mon-Fri 1000-1300.

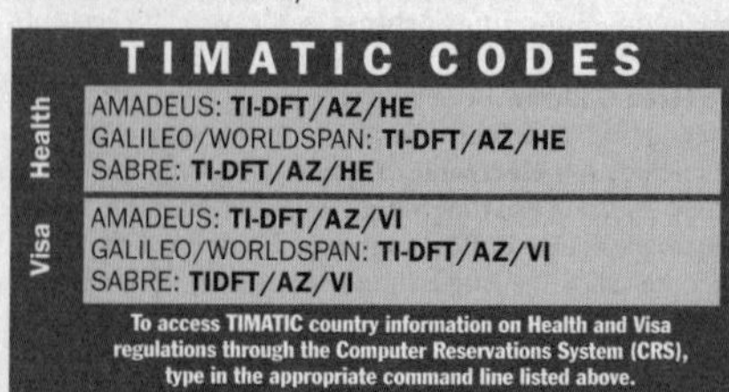

TIMATIC CODES

Health
AMADEUS: **TI-DFT/AZ/HE**
GALILEO/WORLDSPAN: **TI-DFT/AZ/HE**
SABRE: **TI-DFT/AZ/HE**

Visa
AMADEUS: **TI-DFT/AZ/VI**
GALILEO/WORLDSPAN: **TI-DFT/AZ/VI**
SABRE: **TIDFT/AZ/VI**

To access TIMATIC country information on Health and Visa regulations through the Computer Reservations System (CRS), type in the appropriate command line listed above.

British Embassy
45a Khagani Street, Baku, AZ1010 Azerbaijan
Tel: (12) 497 51 88/89/90. Fax: (12) 497 74 34 (general) or 492 27 39 (visa and consular section).
E-mail: office@britemb.baku.az
Website: www.britishembassy.az
Embassy of Azerbaijan
2741 34th Street, NW, Washington DC 20008, USA
Tel: (202) 337 3500 or 5912 (consular section). Fax: (202) 337 5911 or 5913 (consular section).
E-mail: azerbaijan@azembassy.com
Website: www.azembassy.com
Also deals with enquiries from Canada.
Embassy of the United States of America
83 Azadliq Avenue, AZ1007 Baku, Azerbaijan
Tel: (12) 498 03 35-7. Fax: (12) 465 66 71 or 498 37 55 (consular section).
E-mail: consularbaku@state.gov
Website: www.usembassybaku.org
The Canadian Embassy in Ankara deals with enquiries relating to Azerbaijan (see Turkey section).

General Information

AREA: 86,600 sq km (33,400 sq miles).
POPULATION: 8,347,000 (official estimate 2005)
POPULATION DENSITY: 90.1 per sq km.
CAPITAL: Baku. **Population:** 2,140,000 (2005)
GEOGRAPHY: Azerbaijan is bordered by the Russian Federation, Georgia and Iran, and is divided by the Republic of Armenia into a smaller western part in the Lesser Caucasus and a larger eastern part, stretching from the Greater Caucasus to the Mugan, Mili and Shirvan Steppes and bordered by the Caspian Sea in the east. Its highest peaks are Mount Bazar-Dyuzi (4114m/13497ft) and Sag-Dag (3886m/12749ft).
GOVERNMENT: Democratic Republic. Gained independence from the Soviet Union in 1991. **Head of State:** President Ilham Äliyev since 2003. **Head of Government:** Prime Minister Artur Rasizade since 2003.
LANGUAGE: Azerbaijani. Russian is widely spoken; English may be spoken in Baku and other main centres.
RELIGION: Mostly Shia Muslim although there are Russian Orthodox and Jewish communities.
TIME: GMT + 4.
ELECTRICITY: 220 volts AC, 50Hz.
COMMUNICATIONS: Telephone: IDD is available to anywhere in Azerbaijan. Country code: 994. International calls from Azerbaijan may be dialled directly from Baku; calls from other parts of the republic must be made through the operator. **Mobile telephone:** GSM 900 network covers the capital and main towns. Network operators include Azercell (website: www.azercell.com) and Bakcell. **Internet:** Access is widely available. Local ISPs include AdaNet (website: www.azdata.net), Azerin (website: www.azerin.com), AzEuroTel (website: www.azeurotel.com) and Bakinternet (website: www.bakinter.net). **Telegram:** Services are available at the main post office in Baku. **Fax:** Services are widely available especially at international hotels. **Post:** International postal services are sometimes disrupted. Delays occur, although letters should normally take 10 to 14 days to arrive. Parcels should be registered or sent by courier services to accelerate the process and ensure against loss. **Press:** The principal daily newspaper is *Azerbaijan*. Other newspapers include *Azerbaycan, Respublika, Bakinskii Rabochii* and *Azadliq*. **Radio:** BBC World Service (website: www.bbc.co.uk/worldservice) and Voice of America (website: www.voa.gov) can be received. From time to time the frequencies change and the most up-to-date can be found online.

Passport/Visa

	Passport Required?	Visa Required?	Return Ticket Required?
Full British	Yes	Yes	No
Australian	Yes	Yes	No
Canadian	Yes	Yes	No
USA	Yes	Yes	No
Other EU	Yes	Yes	No
Japanese	Yes	Yes	No

Note: Regulations and requirements may be subject to change at short notice, and you are advised to contact the appropriate diplomatic or consular authority before finalising travel arrangements. Details of these may be found at the head of this country's entry. Any numbers in the chart refer to the footnotes below.

PASSPORTS: Passport valid for at least three months after date of return required by all.
VISAS: Required by all except nationals of CIS countries (except nationals of Turkementistan who do require visas).
Types of visa and cost: Tourist, Private, Business and Transit: £27 (single-entry); £54 (double-entry); £167 (multiple-entry). Express visas: £35 (single-entry) or £230 (multiple-entry).
Note: Multiple-entry visas are only available for Business or Private visits.
Validity: Contact the Consulate (or Consular section at Embassy) for details of visa validity.
Application to: Consulate (or Consular Section at Embassy); see *Contact Addresses* section.

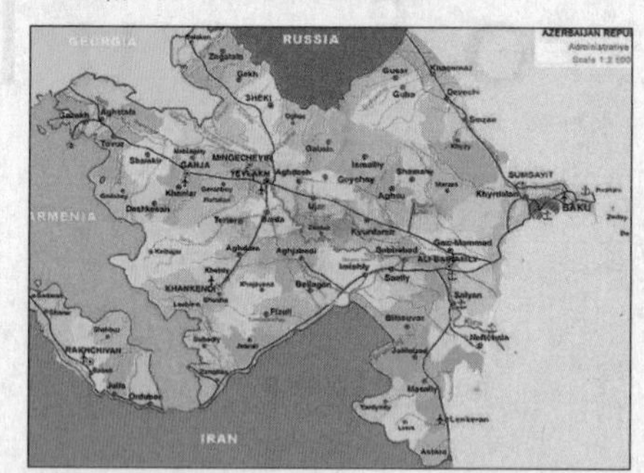

Application requirements: (a) Completed application form. (b) Two recent passport-size photos. (c) Valid passport. (d) Fee. Tourist: (a)-(d) and, (e) Letter of invitation from a travel agency in Azerbaijan or evidence of confirmed hotel reservation. Private: (a)-(d) and, (e) Letter of invitation from a person resident in Azerbaijan, processed through the Consular department of the Ministry of Foreign Affairs in Baku. Business: (a)-(d) and, (e) Letter of invitation from a company registered in Azerbaijan. Transit: (a)-(d) and, (e) Confirmed onward travel documentation. (f) Valid entry requirements for onward destination.
Note: Applications may be sent in by post, but must be collected from the Embassy either by the applicant or by a third party in possession of a letter of authorisation signed by the applicant.
Working days required: Three to four days for single-entry, five to seven days for multiple-entry and 48 hours for express visas.

Money

Currency: Manat (AM). Notes are in denominations of AM50,000, 10,000, 1000, 500, 100 and 50.
Currency exchange: US Dollar, Pound Sterling and the Euro are the preferred currencies and can be exchanged at the airport, bureaux de change, all hotels, some restaurants and major banks. However, many local hotels, exchange bureaux and restaurants will not accept dollar bills dated before 1992 or those which are torn or in any way disfigured. Travellers are advised to take banknotes in small denominations and change small amounts of money as required. Rates offered by banks and bureaux de change are unlikely to vary significantly.
Credit & debit cards: Generally Azerbaijan is a cash-only economy, however credit cards are accepted in the major hotels, some restaurants and all banks in Baku. Credit cards can be used to purchase tickets at the airport.
Travellers cheques: Generally not accepted.
Currency restrictions: The import and export of local currency is permitted for residents of Azerbaijan provided the amount is declared on the customs declaration. The import of foreign currency is unlimited although it must be declared on arrival. The export of foreign currency for non-residents is limited up to the amount declared on arrival. The export of foreign currency for residents is limited up to US$10,000 or equivalent; amounts in excess of US$1000 or equivalent are subject to 1 per cent tax.
Exchange rate indicators: The following figures are included as a guide to the movements of the Manat against Sterling and the US Dollar.

Date	Feb '04	May '04	Aug '04	Nov '04
£1.00=	8986.58	8806.37	9047.78	9298.07
$1.00=	4937.00	4930.50	4911.00	4910.00

Banking hours: Mon-Fri 0930-1730.

Duty Free

The following goods may be imported into Azerbaijan by persons aged over 16 years without incurring customs duty:
1000 cigarettes or 1000g of tobacco products; 1.5l of spirits and 2l of wine; a reasonable quantity of perfume for personal use; goods up to a value of US$10,000.
Note: On entering the country, tourists must complete a customs declaration form which must be retained until departure. This allows the import of articles intended for personal use, including currency and valuables which must be registered on the declaration form.
Prohibited imports: Weapons and ammunition, narcotics, live animals (subject to special permit), photographs and printed material directed against Azerbaijan, fruit and vegetables.
Prohibited exports: Weapons and ammunition, precious metals, works of art and antiques (unless permission has been granted by the Ministry of Culture) and furs.

Public Holidays

2005: Jan 1 New Year's Day. **Jan 20** Day of the Martyrs. **Mar 8** International Women's Day. **Mar 21** Novruz Bayramy. **May 9** Victory Day. **May 28** Republic Day. **Jun 15** Day of National Salvation. **Jun 26** Army and Navy Day. **Oct 18** Day of Independence. **Nov 12** Constitution Day. **Nov 17** Day of National Revival. **Dec 31** Day of Azeri Solidarity.
2006: Jan 1 New Year's Day. **Jan 20** Day of the Martyrs. **Mar 8** International Women's Day. **Mar 21** Novruz Bayramy **May 9** Victory Day. **May 28** Republic Day. **Jun 15** Day of National Salvation. **Jun 26** Army and Navy Day. **Oct 18** Day of Independence. **Nov 12** Constitution Day. **Nov 17** Day of National Revival. **Dec 31** Day of Azeri Solidarity.
Note: Muslim festivals are timed according to local sightings of various phases of the moon and the dates given above are approximations. During the lunar month of Ramadan that precedes Ramazan Bayram, Muslims fast during the day and feast at night and normal business patterns may be interrupted. Some disruption may continue into Ramazan Bayram itself. Ramazan Bayram and Kurban Bayram may last up to several days, depending on the region. For more information, see the *World of Islam* appendix.

Health

	Special Precautions?	Certificate Required?
Yellow Fever	No	No
Cholera	Yes	No
Typhoid & Polio	1	N/A
Malaria	2	N/A

Note: Regulations and requirements may be subject to change at short notice, and you are advised to contact your doctor well in advance of your intended date of departure. Any numbers in the chart refer to the footnotes below.

1: Immunisation against typhoid is usually recommended and immunisation against poliomyelitis is sometimes advised.
2: Limited malaria risk, exclusively in the benign vivax form,

exists during the summer in southern lowland areas, mainly in the area between the Kura and Arax rivers.
Other risks: *Cholera* and *hepatitis A* and B occur. Inoculation against *hepatitis A* and B, *diphtheria, tuberculosis* and *tetanus* is recommended before arrival. There may be some risk of *meningitis, tick-borne encephalitis* and *leishmaniasis* (cutaneous and visceral). *Rabies* is present. For those at high risk, vaccination before arrival should be considered. If you are bitten, seek medical advice without delay. For more information consult the *Health* appendix.
Food & drink: Water used for drinking should be regarded as being a potential health risk. Before drinking, brushing teeth or making ice it should be first boiled or otherwise sterilised. Some parts of Baku have their own water supply from natural mineral springs. Milk is pasteurised and dairy products are safe for consumption. Only eat well-cooked meat and fish, preferably served hot. Salad and mayonnaise may carry increased risk. Vegetables should be cooked and fruit peeled.
Health care: The health service provides free medical treatment for all citizens. However, state-run services in Azerbaijan are limited.
Reciprocal health agreements exist between the UK and Azerbaijan, enabling travellers to receive free or low-cost emergency care. If a traveller becomes ill during a organised tour in Azerbaijan, emergency treatment is free, with small sums to be paid for medicines and hospital treatment. If a longer stay than originally planned becomes necessary because of illness, the visitor has to pay for all further treatment - travel insurance is therefore recommended. It is advisable to take a supply of those medicines that are likely to be required (but check first that they may be legally imported). Private chemists in Baku stock a range of the more basic medicines. Travellers are advised to take out an insurance policy which includes emergency repatriation in case of serious illness or accident.

Travel - International

Note: Travel to the western region of Nagorno-Karabakh and to the militarily-occupied area around it is strongly advised against. For further advice visitors should contact their local government travel advice department.
AIR: The national airline is *Azerbaijan Airlines (AZAL) (J2)*, which operates regular flights to Ankara, London (via Istanbul), Kiev, Dubai, Tehran and Tel Aviv. Other airlines serving Azerbaijan include *Aeroflot, British Airways, Imair, Iran Air, Lufthansa, SAS, Turkish Airlines and United Airlines.* Flights into Baku from Moscow and St Petersburg are subject to frequent delays and cancellations.
International airports: *Baku Bina (BAK)* is 25km (16 miles) east of Baku (travel time - 40 minutes). Taxis and buses are available to the centre. Taxis usually cost AM40,000 (€6). Aiport facilities include car hire, bank/bureau de change, left luggage facilities and a VIP lounge.
Departure tax: None.
SEA: Shipping services from Baku across the Caspian Sea sail regularly to Turkmenbashi in Turkmenistan and to Bandar Anzali and Bandar Nowshar in Iran. Winter storms may disrupt these services.
RAIL: Azerbaijan is connected with Tbilisi in Georgia and Makhachkala in Dagestan (Russian Federation), as well as Moscow and other major cities in the CIS. There is a railway connecting the autonomous republic of Nakhichevan with Tabriz in Iran but there are not yet any connections to the main part of Azerbaijan. Rail travel is slow.
ROAD: There are routes from Azerbaijan to Iran, Georgia and the Russian Federation. It may be quicker to use public transport than to drive, owing to lengthy delays at the borders. **Bus:** There are regular services on the following routes: Baku–Tehran, Baku–Tbilisi and Baku–Derbent (Russian Federation).

Travel - Internal

Note: Internal travel to several regions close to the Armenian border is restricted; travellers must obtain special permission from the Ministry of the Interior to visit these areas. Travel to Nagorno-Karabakh and the occupied area around it is strongly advised against; official advice should be sought before departure.
ROAD: Azerbaijan's road network totals around 57,770km (34,346 miles). Nowadays, most of the roads are in good condition, 4-wheel-drive vehicles are recommended for journeys into the mountains, eg west of Kuba. Traffic drives on the right. Visitors should note that many local drivers do not adhere to traffic regulations. **Car hire:** Car hire facilities are available through Avis and Hertz in Baku.
Documentation: An International Driving Permit is required.
URBAN: Taxi fares should always be negotiated before starting a journey, and visitors should be aware that rates proposed initially are likely to be unreasonably high. There is an **underground** system totalling 28km (17.5 miles) but most visitors use taxis or private cars. **Buses** run from central Baku to the suburbs but sometimes they are overcrowded.

Accommodation

Most hotels are now private and standards of hygiene, service and catering have improved a great deal. Most hotels have satellite connection facilities, telephone and fax services. Many major hotel chains, including Hyatt Regency, Hyatt Park and Grand Hotel Europe are now represented in Azerbaijan.

Resorts & Excursions

BAKU & THE COAST

The medieval walled city - **Icheri Sheher** - within **Baku** has been restored, and retains a distinctly Middle-Eastern and relaxed atmosphere, with its tea-houses and busy street-life. Its attractive narrow streets and stone buildings spread up from the waterfront, where the 12th-century **Maiden's Tower** (Gyz-Galasy) looks out over the bay. Locals claim that the view from the top of the tower rivals the beauty of the Bay of Naples. Nearby are two *caravanserais* (inns), one dating from the 14th century, the other from the 16th century, originally built to accommodate travelling merchants from northern India and central Asia. The *caravanserais*, with their courtyards and vaulted roofs, have been restored and now function as restaurants. There are also a number of mosques located in the medieval city, one of which, the **Dzhuma Mosque**, houses the **Museum of Carpets and Applied Arts**, with a fine display of Azeri carpets, as well as jewellery, embroidery, woodcarving and filigree metalwork. The **Synyk Kalah Minaret** dates from 1093 and is the oldest building still standing in the city. Beyond the minaret is the 15th-century royal court complex, the **Palace of the Shirvan Shahs**. The palace, mausoleum and law courts are all open to the public. Equally distinctive are the opulent houses and public buildings built during the Baku oil boom at the turn of the 20th century. Millionaire oil merchants indulged themselves with neo-gothic, mock oriental and pseudo-renaissance fantasies in stone, developing a local architectural confidence which spilled over into the Soviet period; the Sabuchinsky railway station for example, dating from 1926, is designed to resemble an enormous madrassah (Islamic religious academy).
Excursions: A number of tourist sights are located near enough to Baku for one-day excursions to be feasible. Some 20km (12 miles) northeast of Baku is the **Surakhany Temple**, established by Parsee fire-worshippers living in Baku in the 18th century. The temple was predated by a much older **Zoroastrian shrine** on the same site. Surakhany remained a popular destination for Indian pilgrims until the revolution. Some of the pilgrims' cells now house a wax museum, intended to introduce the rudiments of fire worship to the uninitiated.
The **Apsheron Peninsula**, stretching out into the Caspian Sea beyond Baku, has several 14th-century fortresses, built by the Shirvan shahs fearing attack from the sea. Best preserved are those at **Ramana, Nardaran** and **Mardakan**. Ramana also features the remains of ancient oil fields where Zoroastrian fire-worshippers still occasionally stage ritual dances, leaping over the flames which rise from the oil-soaked ground over natural gas vents. The tip of the peninsula is a nature reserve.
The village of **Gobustan**, about 70km (43 miles) south of Baku, has an unique array of rock paintings, some of them 10,000 years old and spread over 100 sq km (39 sq miles) of caves and rocky outcrops. The subject matter includes hunting scenes, ritual dances, religious ceremonies, ships, animals and constellations, and many of the rocks are further adorned with signatures and remarks added by visiting Roman soldiers in the first century AD, suggesting that the area has a long history as a tourist attraction.

THE CAUCASUS

The city of **Shamakha**, 130km (80 miles) west of Baku in the foothills of the Caucasus, predated Baku as the principal trading centre and capital of the Shirvan shahs. Repeated earthquakes, most recently in 1902, and the ravages of invading armies, have destroyed most of the ancient city which was founded in the second century AD. A 10th-century mosque and a ruined fortress dating from the same period, the **Seven Domes Royal Mausoleum** and a modern carpet-weaving centre where traditional techniques are demonstrated, provide the main focus of tourist interest in the city.
Sheki is located 380km (236 miles) west of Baku close to the Georgian border. Archaeological evidence suggests that the city may be one of the oldest settlements in the Caucasus, dating back 2500 years. Tourists can still visit the 18th-century frescoed summer palace and the fortress built by a local warlord who declared Shekhi the capital of an independent khanate. Shekhi was famed for its silk, which is still produced locally, and the bazaars and *caravanserais* testify to its importance as a trading town. Some of the *caravanserais* have been restored and now function as hotels and restaurants.

Sport & Activities

Although travellers should avoid the Nagorno-Karabakh area and the border with Armenia, they can pursue various activities in other parts of the country. There are some good beaches in Baku, and visitors can also play chess at several outdoor **chess**-playing areas (where Gary Kasparov reputedly practised as a boy). The 70km-long (45 miles) Aspheron peninsula (northeast of Baku) has some of the country's best beaches and offers good **hiking** and coastal **walks**.

Social Profile

FOOD & DRINK: Azerbaijani food combines Turkish and central Asian elements. Dishes include the much celebrated *plov*, a delicious, spicy speciality made with pine nuts, vegetables and dried fruit, in addition to rice and mutton. Certain types of *plov* use chicken instead of mutton and include chestnuts. Grilled kebabs of various kinds are popular, including *lyulya kebab* made from spiced, minced lamb pressed onto skewers. These are often sold from roadside stalls. Meals often start with rich, heavy soups: *piti* is a mutton soup bulked out with chickpeas and slowly cooked in individual earthenware pots in the oven and served in the same pots. Also popular is *dogva* - a sharp, yoghurt and spinach-based soup containing rice and meatballs. Sturgeon, served both smoked and fresh, and caviar have traditionally been fished from the Caspian Sea. Rising pollution levels have given rise to alarm about falling fish stocks, but sturgeon is still widely available at a price. *Kutab* pastries stuffed with spinach or pumpkin and similar to Turkish *birekas* are another local speciality. Baku has a reasonable selection of Western style restaurants which have opened recently.
In the *chai khanas* (tea houses), men linger for hours drinking sweet black tea out of tiny glasses. Although the majority of Azeris are nominally Shia Muslims, alcohol is widely available. Wines and brandies are produced locally, Russian vodka is popular, and imported spirits represent a form of conspicuous consumption.
NIGHTLIFE: Several restaurants, late-night bars and nightclubs have opened in Baku in the last few years, catering largely for the foreign business community and wealthy local business people. Popular bars include *Chaplin*, *Finnegan's* and *Lancaster Gate*. Concerts, theatre, opera and ballet are a source of local pride and very popular.
SHOPPING: If visitors are intent on acquiring an Azeri carpet they are advised to visit the carpet-weaving centre at Nardaran. Locally produced silk, ceramics and other craftwork is also sold at the Sharg Bazary (a modern, covered market) in Baku. Prices here are likely to be negotiable. Any carpet or other artefact made before 1960 is subject to an export tax and must be certified for export by the Ministry of Culture. Items purchased at official art salons or tourist shops will already be duly certified. This is not true of goods sold at markets or by private individuals.
Shopping hours: Mon-Sat 0900-2000.
SPECIAL EVENTS: The following is a selection of special events occurring in Azerbaijan in 2005:
Jan 21 *Kurban Bayram* (Feast of the Sacrifice), nationwide. **Apr 7-9** *SportExpo 2005/AITF (International Travel & Tourism Fair)*. **Mar** *Novruz Bayramy* (Lunar New Year), nationwide. **Mar 16-19** *Autoshow Azerbaijan*, Baku. **May 19-21** *WCE* (exhibition and conference event on customs and security in international trade). **May 25-27** *InterFood 2005*, Baku. **Apr 20-22** *TransCaspian Transport and Logistics Expo*, Baku. **Sep** *Moda Azerbaijan* (fashion event), Baku.
SOCIAL CONVENTIONS: Visitors to Azerbaijan may find themselves the recipients of an unexpected bounty in the form of gifts of flowers, food and souvenirs. It is therefore advisable to travel equipped with suitable items - consumables or souvenirs - with which to reciprocate. Local women, particularly in rural areas, tend to be extremely retiring. They will serve a meal, but seldom eat with foreign guests. Visitors may present women with flowers, but overenthusiastic attempts to engage them in conversation may cause offence and embarrassment. Foreign women are treated with elaborate courtesy which can develop into excessive attention. It is therefore advisable for women to dress modestly, especially in the rural areas, and cultivate a certain coolness of manner. Handshaking is the normal form of greeting. Business cards are invariably exchanged at any kind of official meeting, and not infrequently on first meeting socially as well. **Tipping:** Expected by waiters and doormen in restaurants - sometimes in advance to ensure service. It is advisable to make enquiries about 'going rates' before entering into negotiations with taxi drivers, market stallholders, etc. It is also customary to tip car park supervisors.

Business Profile

ECONOMY: Political upheaval - especially the war in Nagorno-Karabakh - and disruption of trading links within the former USSR resulted in a dramatic fall in production levels in Azerbaijan. Since the late 1990s, the economy has undergone a mild recovery. Agriculture is an important part of the economy, in terms of both employment and production. Cotton, grain, fruit and vegetables are the major products; livestock rearing is the other main contributor to the sector. Traditionally, heavy industry, in the form of chemicals, steel and metal products, dominated the industrial sector but there are now also important light industrial operations devoted to food processing and textiles. However, the oil and gas industry offers the greatest promise for Azerbaijan's future economic development. Most of the reserves are located in the Caspian Sea basin and the Azeri government has signed a number of major deals with a variety of consortia for the exploration and development of various offshore fields; the state oil corporation retains a partial share in all of these. In the last few years, the contribution of the service sector - especially transport, telecommunications and trade-related activities - has grown sharply and now accounts for a large part of the economy. Azerbaijan left the Rouble zone in 1993, introducing its own currency, the Manat, the following year. A major privatisation programme was also put into effect that had transferred over three-quarters of productive activity into private ownership by 1998. As well as the IMF and the World Bank, which it joined in 1992, Azerbaijan has been accepted for membership of the Islamic Development Bank, the European Bank for Reconstruction and Development (as a 'country of operation') and a number of regional economic and trade organisations. The country's most important trading partners are now the Russian Federation, Iran, Turkey and Germany. Georgia and Hong Kong are key export markets (mainly for oil and gas products).
COMMERCIAL INFORMATION: The following organisation in the US can offer useful advice: US-Azerbaijan Chamber of Commerce, 1212 Potomac Street, NW, Washington DC 20007, USA (tel: (202) 333 8702; fax: (202) 333 8703; e-mail: chamber@usacc.org; website: www.usacc.org); or Chamber of Commerce and Industry, Istiglaliyat kucesi 31-33, 370001 Baku (tel: (12) 492 89 12; fax: (12) 497 19 97; e-mail: expo@chamber.baku.az).

Climate

Generally very warm, but low temperatures can occur, particularly in the mountains and valleys. Most of the rainfall is in the west.

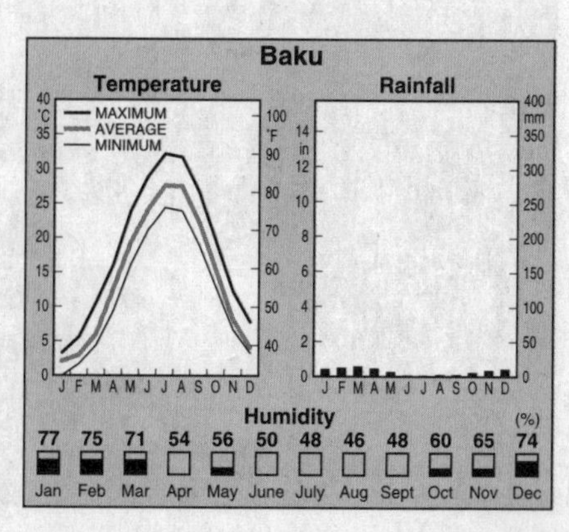

Bahamas

LATEST TRAVEL ADVICE CONTACTS

British Foreign and Commonwealth Office
Tel: (0870) 606 0290 Website: www.fco.gov.uk
US Department of State
Website: http://travel.state.gov/travel
Canadian Department of Foreign Affairs and Int'l Trade
Tel: (1 800) 267 8376 Website: www.dfait-maeci.gc.ca

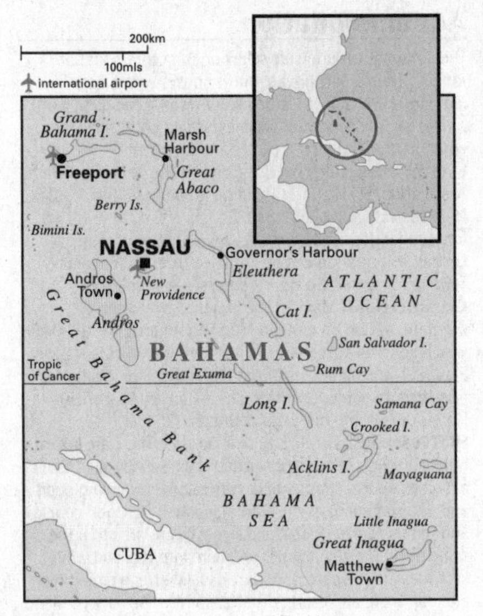

Location: Caribbean, southeast of Florida.

Country dialling code: 1 242.

Bahamas Ministry of Tourism
PO Box N-3701, Bay Street, Nassau, The Bahamas
Tel: 302 2000. Fax: 302 2098.
E-mail: tourism@bahamas.com
Website: www.bahamas.com
Bahamas High Commission
10 Chesterfield Street, London W1J 5JL, UK
Tel: (020) 7408 4488. Fax: (020) 7499 9937.
E-mail: information@bahamashclondon.com
Opening hours: Mon-Fri 0930-1730.
Bahamas Tourist Office
Bahamas House, 10 Chesterfield Street, London W1J 5JL, UK
Tel: (020) 7355 0800. Fax: (020) 7491 9459.
E-mail: info@bahamas.co.uk
Website: www.bahamas.co.uk
Embassy of the Commonwealth of The Bahamas
2220 Massachussetts Av., NW, Washington, DC 20008, USA
Tel: (202) 319 2660. Fax: (202) 319 2668.
E-mail: bahemb@aol.com
Bahamas Consulate General
Bahamas House, 231 East 46th St, New York, NY 10017, USA
Tel: (212) 421 6420. Fax: (212) 688 5926.
E-mail: bahamasconsulate@bahamasny.com
Website: www.un.int/bahamas
Bahamas Tourist Office
150 East 52nd Street, New York, NY 10022, USA
Tel: (212) 758 2777. Fax: (212) 753 6531.
E-mail: bmotny@bahamas.com
Website: www.bahamas.com
Embassy of the United States of America
Street address: 42 Queen Street, Nassau, The Bahamas
Postal address: PO Box N-8197, Nassau, The Bahamas
Tel: 322 1181/2. Fax: 328 7838 *or* 356 7174 (visa info.).
E-mail: visanassau@state.gov
Bahamas High Commission
50 O'Connor Street, Suite 1313, Ottawa, Ontario K1P 6L2, Canada
Tel: (613) 232 1724. Fax: (613) 232 0097.
E-mail: ottawa-mission@bahighco.com

TIMATIC CODES

Health
AMADEUS: **TI-DFT/NAS/HE**
GALILEO/WORLDSPAN: **TI-DFT/NAS/HE**
SABRE: **TIDFT/NAS/HE**

Visa
AMADEUS: **TI-DFT/NAS/VI**
GALILEO/WORLDSPAN: **TI-DFT/NAS/VI**
SABRE: **TIDFT/NAS/VI**

To access TIMATIC country information on Health and Visa regulations through the Computer Reservations System (CRS), type in the appropriate command line listed above.

Credit: © The Islands of The Bahamas Tourist Office

Bahamas Tourist Office
121 Bloor Street East, Suite 1101, Toronto, Ontario M4W 3M5, Canada
Tel: (416) 968 2999. Fax: (416) 968 6711.
E-mail: btoyyz@bahamas.com
Website: www.bahamas.com
Canadian Honorary Consulate
Street address: Shirley Street Shopping Plaza, Nassau, The Bahamas
Postal address: PO Box SS-6371, Nassau, The Bahamas
Tel: 393 2123/4. Fax: 393 1305.
E-mail: cdncon@bahamas.net.bs

General Information

AREA: 13,939 sq km (5382 sq miles).
POPULATION: 303,000 (official estimate 2000).
POPULATION DENSITY: 21.7 per sq km.
CAPITAL: Nassau. **Population:** 172,000 (1997).
GEOGRAPHY: The Bahamas consist of 700 low-lying islands, mostly islets (cays or keys) and rocks. The whole archipelago extends 970km (500 miles) southeastward from the coast of Florida, surrounded by clear, colourful waters. The soil is thin, but on the more developed islands, cultivation has produced exotic flowers. On other islands are large areas of pine forest, rocky and barren land, swamp and unspoilt beaches. The Bahamas are divided into two oceanic features, the Little Bahama Bank and the Great Bahama Bank.
GOVERNMENT: Constitutional monarchy. Gained independence in 1973. **Head of State:** HM Queen Elizabeth II, represented locally by Governor-General Dame Ivy Dumont since 2001. **Head of Government:** Prime Minister Perry Christie since 2002.
LANGUAGE: The official and national language is English.
RELIGION: The three main Christian denominations are Baptist, Anglican and Roman Catholic.
TIME: GMT - 5.
ELECTRICITY: 120 volts AC, 60Hz.
COMMUNICATIONS: Telephone: IDD is available. Country code: 1 242. New Providence and all islands have automatic telephone systems. The state telephone company, *BaTelCo*, offers both manual- and automatic-dial mobile radio telephones that allow callers to contact ships at sea. Phone cards can be purchased at discounted rates for international calls. **Mobile telephone:** Handsets must be registered with *BaTelCo* (tel: 394 4000; fax: 394 3573; e-mail: info@batelnet.bs). Visitors will need to purchase a SIM card if their provider has no agreement with *BaTelCo*. Handsets can be hired locally. **Fax:** This service is available to the public at the Centralised Telephone Office in East Street, Nassau or in Internet cafes. Machines can also be hired. **Internet:** There are a few Internet cafes on Grand Bahama Island and Nassau Island open seven days a week. Laptop connections are available, as are webcams and facilities for scanning and copying. The main ISP is *BaTelNet* (website: www.batelnet.bs). **Telegram:** Telegrams can be sent from most hotels, post offices and the CT Office. **Post:** Postal service to Europe takes up to 10 days. Post office hours: Mon-Fri 0900-1700 and Sat 0900-1230.
Press: The four daily newspapers are the *The Bahama Journal*, *Freeport News*, the *Nassau Guardian* and the *Tribune*. *The Punch* is published twice a week. Both *Bahamas Tourist News* and *What's On Magazine* are printed once a month. International newspapers available in The Bahamas include: *The Daily Telegraph*, *The Miami Herald*, *The New York Times*, *The Times*, *USA Today* and *Wall Street Journal*.
Radio: BBC World Service (website: www.bbc.co.uk/worldservice) and Voice of America (website: www.voa.gov) can be received. From time to time the frequencies change and the most up-to-date can be found online.

Credit: © The Islands of The Bahamas Tourist Office

Passport/Visa

	Passport Required?	Visa Required?	Return Ticket Required?
Full British	1	No/3	Yes
Australian	Yes	No/5	Yes
Canadian	1	No/5	Yes
USA	2	No/4	Yes
Other EU	Yes	No/3	Yes
Japanese	Yes	No/6	Yes

Note: *Regulations and requirements may be subject to change at short notice, and you are advised to contact the appropriate diplomatic or consular authority before finalising travel arrangements. Details of these may be found at the head of this country's entry. Any numbers in the chart refer to the footnotes below.*

PASSPORTS: Passport valid for at least six months from date of departure from The Bahamas required by all except:
(a) **1.** nationals of Canada and the UK and its colonies, provided holding a birth certificate, a citizenship card or a voter's card together with a photo ID for stays of up to three weeks. Passports, however, *are* required for re-entry into the UK;
(b) **2.** nationals of the USA, provided holding a passport not expired by more than five years, original or certified birth certificate, naturalisation certificate together with an official photo ID, for stays of up to eight months.
VISAS: Required by all except the following:
(a) **3.** nationals of EU countries for stays of up to three months (eight months for nationals of Belgium, Cyprus, Greece, Italy, Luxemburg, Malta, The Netherlands and the UK), except nationals of the Czech Republic, Estonia, Hungary, Latvia, Lithuania, Poland, the Slovak Republic and Slovenia who *do* need a visa;
(b) **4.** nationals of Iceland, Liechtenstein, Norway, San Marino, Switzerland, Turkey and the USA for stays of up to eight months;
(c) **5.** nationals of Commonwealth countries for stays of up to eight months (three months for nationals of Namibia and South Africa), except nationals of Brunei, Cameroon, Ghana, India, Mozambique, Nigeria and Pakistan who *do* need a visa;
(d) **6.** nationals of Chile, Israel, Japan, Korea (Rep) and Mexico for stays of up to three months;
(e) nationals of Argentina, Bolivia, Brazil, Costa Rica, Ecuador, El Salvador, Honduras, Nicaragua, Panama, Paraguay, Peru, Uruguay and Venezuela for stays of up to 14 days;
(f) nationals of French, Dutch, Portuguese and Ecuadorean overseas territories, and of Hong Kong (SAR), Monaco and Vatican City (who should contact the Consulate to find out the maximum length of visit without a visa);
(g) transit passengers continuing their journey by the same or next connecting aircraft within three days, provided holding confirmed onward documentation and passport.
Note: Nationals of Haiti and the Dominican Republic *do* need a visa when in transit.
Types of visa and cost: *Single-entry*: £15; *Multiple-entry*: £20 (three to six months); £30 (six to 12 months).

A B C D E F G H I J K L M N O P Q R S T U V W X Y Z

Validity: Usually three months. Applications for extension should be made to the Director of Immigration.
Application to: Consulate (or Consular Section at Embassy or High Commission); see *Contact Addresses* section.
Application requirements: (a) Completed application form. (b) Valid passport. (c) Proof of sufficient funds to cover stay. (d) Two passport-size photos. (e) Itinerary of trip. (f) Return or onward ticket and documents to enter any other country to which travel is planned. (g) Stamped self-addressed envelope if applying by post. (h) Proof of employment or enrolment in University. (i) Proof of hotel booking or letter of invitation if staying at a private home.
Note: Applications should be made in person.
Working days required: Dependent on nationality of applicant, a minimum of 24 to 48 hours, maximum of six weeks. Applications made by post and from some nationals may take longer to process. Enquire at the Consulate or Embassy for further details.
Temporary residence: Apply to the Director of Immigration, PO Box N-831, Nassau, The Bahamas (tel: (242) 322 7531; fax: (242) 326 0977).

Money

Currency: Bahamian Dollar (B$) = 100 cents. Notes are in denominations of B$100, 50, 20, 10, 5, 3 and 1, and 50 cents. Coins are in denominations of 25, 15, 10, 5 and 1 cents. The Bahamian Dollar has parity with the US Dollar and the latter is also accepted as legal tender.
Note: The Bahamian Dollar is tied to the US Dollar.
Currency exchange: Available in banks and at exchange bureaux and hotels. ATMs are located on the larger islands in airport terminals, at banks and casinos and at other convenient locations.
Credit & debit cards: American Express, Diners Club, MasterCard and Visa are accepted. Check with your credit or debit card company for details of merchant acceptability and other services which may be available.
Travellers cheques: To avoid additional exchange rate charges, travellers are advised to take travellers cheques in US Dollars.
Currency restrictions: Permission is required from the Central Bank of The Bahamas to import local currency, which may be exported up to a maximum of B$70. The import and export of foreign currency are unlimited.
Exchange rate indicators: The following figures are included as a guide to the movements of the Bahamian Dollar against Sterling and the US Dollar:

Date	Feb '04	May '04	Aug '04	Nov '04
£1.00=	1.82	1.79	1.84	1.90
$1.00=	1.00	1.00	1.00	1.00

Banking hours: Mon-Thurs 0930-1500, Fri 0930-1700.

Duty Free

The following goods may be taken into The Bahamas by persons aged over 18 years without incurring customs duty: *200 cigarettes or 50 cigars or 454g of tobacco; 1.136l of spirits and 1.136l of wine; goods up to the value of US$100.*
Note: Duty is payable on household items such as small electrical appliances (blenders, etc) which are taxed at 45 per cent of their cost. Laptop computers are considered to be personal effects and are therefore duty free.
Prohibited items: Firearms, ammunition, drugs and animals from countries with rabies.

Public Holidays

2005: Jan 1 New Year's Day. **Mar 25** Good Friday. **Mar 28** Easter Monday. **May 16** Whit Monday. **Jun 3** Labour Day. **Jul 10** Independence Day. **Aug 1** Emancipation Day. **Oct 12** National Heroes' Day. **Dec 25** Christmas Day. **Dec 26** Boxing Day.
2006: Jan 1 New Year's Day. **Apr 14** Good Friday. **Apr 17** Easter Monday. **Jun 2** Labour Day. **Jun 5** Whit Monday. **Jul 10** Independence Day. **Aug 7** Emancipation Day. **Oct 12** National Heroes' Day. **Dec 25** Christmas Day. **Dec 26** Boxing Day.

Health

	Special Precautions?	Certificate Required?
Yellow Fever	No	1
Cholera	No	No
Typhoid & Polio	2	N/A
Malaria	No	N/A

Note: *Regulations and requirements may be subject to change at short notice, and you are advised to contact your doctor well in advance of your intended date of departure. Any numbers in the chart refer to the footnotes below.*

1: A yellow fever vaccination certificate is required from travellers aged over one year travelling from an infected area.
2: Immunisation against typhoid is advised.
Food & drink: Tap water is safe to drink although it can often be salty in taste. Milk is pasteurised and dairy products are safe for consumption. Local meat, poultry, seafood, fruit and vegetables are generally considered safe to eat.
Other risks: *Diphtheria, tuberculosis* and *hepatitis B* vaccinations are sometimes recommended.
Health care: Medical facilities are on a par with the USA, but can be costly and therefore medical insurance is recommended.

Travel - International

AIR: The Bahamas' national airline is *Bahamasair (UP)*. Other airlines with regular flights to The Bahamas include *Air Canada, Air Jamaica, American Airlines, British Airways, Continental Airlines, Delta Airlines, TWA, United Airlines* and *USAir*. Charter airlines also fly regularly to the islands.
Approximate flight times: From Nassau to *Los Angeles* is eight hours, to *New York* is six hours, to *London* is nine hours and to *Singapore* is 26 hours.
International airports: *Nassau International (NAS)* is 16km (10 miles) west of the city. Taxi services are available. Airport facilities include banking, car hire, post office, bars, restaurants and duty free shops.
Freeport International (FPO) is 5km (3 miles) from the city. Taxis are available. Airport facilities include banking, car hire, car parking, bar/restaurant and a duty-free shop. The new international airport at Moss Town, Exuma, has been completed.
There are scheduled turbo-prop services between several airports in Florida and *Treasure Cay (TCB)* and *Marsh Harbour (MHH)*, Abaco Island; *Rock Sound (RSD)* and *Governor's Harbour (GHB)*, Eleuthera; and *Georgetown*

Credit: © The Islands of The Bahamas Tourist Office

(GGT), Exuma.
Departure tax: US$18 (for all passengers leaving from Freeport). Children under six years of age are exempt.
SEA: A large number of international passenger ships from New York and Miami call at Nassau. Nassau has direct passenger-cargo connections with the USA, the UK, the West Indies and South America. In addition, a large number of cruise ships call there. Facilities for cruisers in Nassau and some harbours of the Out Islands (Eleuthera, Andros and Exuma) are being improved. Contact Bahamas Tourist Office for an up-to-date list of cruise operators to The Bahamas, with all relevant contact numbers.

Travel - Internal

AIR: Charter services are available from *Bahamasair Charter (UP), Le Air Charter Ltd, Major's Air Service, Pinder's Charter Service* and *Sky Unlimited*.
Approximate flight times: From Nassau, New Providence Island to *Freeport* is 40 minutes, to *Marsh Harbour* or *Treasure Cay*, Abaco is 35 minutes, to *Governor's Harbour* is 30 minutes, and to *Georgetown* on Exuma is 40 minutes.
SEA: The Out Islands are served by a mail boat which leaves Nassau several times a week carrying mail and provisions to the islands. Passengers share facilities with the crew. Arrangements should be made through boat captains at Potters Cay. Air-conditioned ferries operate between Nassau, Eleuthera and Harbour Island. For further details contact *Bahamas Fast Ferries* (tel: 323 2166; fax: 322 8185; e-mail: info@bahamasferries.com; website: www.bahamasferries.com).
ROAD: Traffic drives on the left. **Bus:** The *jitney* (minibus) provides inexpensive touring and they operate in the hubs of Freeport and Nassau. However, there is no public transport on any of the smaller islands. Paradise Island is served by a bus service which stops at every hotel. A horse-drawn ride, which takes three passengers, is available along the streets of Nassau. **Taxis** are readily available and are the main form of transport on the smaller islands. Taxis in New Providence are metered and the rates are government controlled. **Car hire:** *Avis, Budget, Dollar* and *Hertz* are represented at the airports and in Nassau and Freeport. Motor scooter hire is also available. **Documentation:** International driver's licence. Drivers must be aged 21 or over. **Bicycles** can be rented by the day or by the week. **Documentation:** A national driving licence is valid for up to three months. Motorcycle riders and passengers are required to wear crash helmets.
Travel times: The following chart gives approximate travel times (in hours and minutes) from **Nassau** to other major centres.

	Air	Sea
Central Andros, Andros	**0.15**	**3.00**
Governor's Harbour, Eleuthera	**0.30**	**2.00***
Freeport, Grand Bahama	**0.30/0.45**	**12.00**
Marsh Harbour, Abaco	**0.45**	**11.00**
George Town, Exuma	**0.45**	**13.00**

Note: * By Bahamas Fast Ferries; all other travel times are by mail boat.

Accommodation

The Bahamas offer a wide selection of accommodation, ranging from small, private guest houses where only lodging is available, to large luxury resorts, complete with swimming pools, private beaches, sailing craft, skindiving equipment, full dining facilities and nightclub entertainment. Many hotels belong to The Bahamas Hotel Association, SG Hambros Building, Goodman's Bay, PO Box N-3318, Nassau (tel: 322 8381/2; fax: 502 4219; e-mail: info@bhahotels.com; website: www.bhahotels.com). Further information can be obtained from the Bahamas Tourist Office (see *Contact Addresses* section).
Classifications: Many of the larger resorts offer accommodation on either a Modified American Plan (MAP) which consists of room, breakfast and dinner, or European Plan (EP) which consists of room only. Accommodation is classified as Hotels, Colonies, Guest Houses, Apartment Hotels or Apartment/ Cottage Units.
HOTELS: Hotels vary in size and facilities. There are luxury hotels offering full porter, bell and room service, planned activities, sports, shops and beauty salons, swimming pools and entertainment; some have a private beach, golf course and tennis courts. Double and single rooms are often the same price. The small hotels are more informal and while activities are less extensive, they usually offer a dining room and bar. There are resorts situated on New Providence Island, which has sporting facilities and luxury accommodation. Some hotels include service charge on the bill.
COTTAGE COLONIES: Separate cottages or villas, with maid service, surrounding a main clubhouse with a bar and dining room – these are 'Cottage Colonies'. They are not equipped with kitchenette or facilities for the preparation of meals, although some have facilities for preparing beverages and light snacks. They offer the facilities of a hotel, such as a private beach/swimming pool, and are designed to offer maximum privacy.
GUEST HOUSES: Often less expensive than hotels and located near downtown Nassau. Many offer European Plan only, but restaurants are plentiful. Rooms may be with or without a bath. The Out Islands' hotels are small with a casual atmosphere.
APARTMENT HOTELS: These consist of apartment units with complete kitchen and maid service. Other hotel facilities (ie swimming pool, sporting activities, restaurant and bar, etc) are normally available on the premises.
APARTMENT/COTTAGE UNITS: These have complete kitchen facilities and some have maid service. Generally, there are no restaurant facilities and tenants are required to prepare their own meals. A few are situated in landscaped estates with their own beach, much like the cottage colonies but without the main clubhouse. Others offer inexpensive accommodation in less spacious but comfortable surroundings. Restaurant and bar facilities are not available.
CAMPING: Camping is not permitted on any of the islands of The Bahamas.

Resorts & Excursions

There are more than 700 islands in The Bahamas, many of which have escaped the notice of tourists. The islands offer clear warm water and sandy beaches. Several are relatively large – see individual entries for a description of some of these – but others are tiny and uninhabited. All the larger islands offer a high standard of accommodation and leisure facilities.

NASSAU

The capital of The Bahamas, Nassau, stands on **New Providence Island**. In the capital, tourists can shop in the bustling 'straw market', where local vendors create unique straw goods on the spot, or the more sophisticated shops in **Bay Street**. The 18th-century **Fort Charlotte** on West Bay Street has a moat, open battlements, dungeons and a magnificent view of the harbour. The nearby **Ardastra Gardens** have tropical flowers and pink flamingos. The **Queen's Staircase**, at the top of Elizabeth Avenue, is a 40m- (102ft-) climb up steps carved into the limestone leading to Fort Fincastle and the **Water Tower**. Built in 1793, **Fort Fincastle** is in the shape of a ship's bow. The Water Tower is the highest point on the island, 85m (216ft) above sea level. An elevator takes visitors to an observation deck for panoramic views. Many bars, restaurants and discos can be found along **Cable Beach**, a 2.5 mile-long stretch of golden sand, located just 3 miles outside the city. **Paradise Island** boasts some beautiful beaches, a 14-acre aquarium, the island's largest casino and a multitude of resorts. Sunbathing, diving, fishing and boating are the main daytime amusements on these islands.

THE MAIN ISLANDS

Grand Bahama Island: The main towns are **Freeport/Lucaya**, which has an airport, and **West End**. The island offers wide white sandy beaches, two casinos and good shopping facilities, entertainment and restaurants at the **International Bazaar** and **Port Lucaya**. The **Rand Memorial Nature Centre** offers an excellent nature walk and the **Garden of the Groves** has exotic flowers, waterfalls and colourful birds.

The Out Islands: These stretch across a huge area of clear ocean and are fringed with hundreds of kilometres of white sandy beaches. The islands have resort facilities for groups of up to 200 people and are ideal for a relaxing, secluded holiday. Though secluded, the islands are not isolated. They are served by the national flag carrier, *Bahamasair*, from Nassau and Freeport. The main Out Islands are described below.

Andros: The largest but probably the least known of the bigger islands. Laced with creeks and densely forested inland, the interior is still largely untouched and natural. Off the eastern shore is the 224km- (140 mile-) long coral barrier reef – the world's third longest. Beyond the reef, the ocean floor drops away steeply to a depth of more than 1.5km (1 mile); called the Tongue of the Ocean, deep-water fishing is a major attraction here.

The Abacos: A crescent-shaped chain of islands to the north of New Providence. Many of the towns here have the atmosphere of New England fishing villages. The islands are particularly noted for their tradition of shipbuilding, the original 200-year-old practice which can still be observed in **Man-O-War Cay**. **Treasure Cay** has an excellent golf course and here, as in the other major islands, there are excellent leisure facilities. Other attractions include **Alton Lowe's Museum** in **New Plymouth**, **Green Turtle Cay**, **Elbow Cay** and **Marsh Harbour**, the bare-boat charter centre of the northern Bahamas. Scuba-divers are drawn to **Pelican Cay National Park**, an underwater preserve where night dives can be arranged.

Eleuthera: A narrow island 177km (110 miles) long but seldom more than 3km (2 miles) wide. Attractions include the **Ocean Hole**, **Glass Window Bridge**, **Harbour Island** (with **Dunmore Town**, one of the oldest settlements in The Bahamas), **Spanish Wells**, off the northern tip of the island, **Preacher's Cave** and the underwater caves at **Hatchet Bay**. The scuba-diving from Eleuthera is particularly superb.

The Exumas: The waters surrounding this 160km- (100 mile-) long chain of islands have been described by yachtsmen as being the finest cruising region in the world. There are also spectacular reefs protected by the **Exuma Land and Sea Park**. Inland, several once-great plantation houses now stand ruined and deserted, although the names of their owners still live on in many local family surnames. In April, **Elizabeth Harbour** is the setting for the **Family Island Regatta**.

Cat Island: One of the eastern bulwarks of The Bahamas, Cat Island has 60m (200ft) cliffs (a rare height for The Bahamas), dense natural forest and pre-Columbian Arawak Indian caves. On **Mount Alvernia** is the Hermitage built by Father Jerome. The **Cat Island Regatta** takes place here during the August bank holiday.

Bimini: Lying between Andros and Florida, Bimini is widely regarded as one of the best fishing centres in the world. Hemingway used to live in **Alice Town** in Blue Marlin Cottage, and mementos of his life can be seen in the local museum.

Berry Island: Popular with fishing enthusiasts and also noted for its serene landscapes and white sand beaches. **Great Harbour Cay** has a championship golf course and a marina. Scuba-divers can admire the underwater rock formations and 5m (15ft) staghorn coral reefs off **Mamma Rhoda Rock**.

Blue Lagoon Island: An exotic lagoon where visitors can enjoy close encounters with friendly bottle-nosed dolphins. Regular 45-minute sessions include an educational talk and about 30 minutes of swimming in the water with the dolphins.

Long Island: This island lives up to its name, being almost 100km (60 miles) long but rarely more than 5km (3 miles) wide. The landscape consists of rugged headlands dropping sharply down to the sea, fertile pastureland, rolling hills and sandy beaches washed by surf. At **Conception Island**, divers can explore over 30 shipwrecks and tours are arranged from the **Stella Maris Resort Club** complex at the north end of the island. The **Long Island Regatta** at **Salt Pond** takes place here in May.

San Salvador: This was Columbus' first landing place in the New World. **Cockburn Town** is the main settlement, which is not far from the spot where Columbus is said to have landed, although other sites also claim this distinction. Game fishing and diving are the most popular pastimes.

Credit: © The Islands of The Bahamas Tourist Office

Sport & Activities

Watersports: These are exceptionally well catered for in The Bahamas: **sailing**, **parasailing**, **diving**, **swimming**, **snorkelling** and **water-skiing** are all widely available. The temperature of the sea rarely drops below 21°C (70°F) even in midwinter. Equipment is available from shops, hotels and marinas. **Surfing** can be done on Eleuthera and **windsurfing** in Nassau and on Grand Bahama. **Sport fishing** is popular throughout the islands. For further details on beaches and diving, see the *Resorts & Excursions* section.

Ball sports: Tennis, **squash**, **baseball**, **softball**, **basketball**, **volleyball**, **soccer**, **rugby**, **golf**, **American football** and **cricket** are all popular. Excellent facilities exist for **tennis** and **squash**.

Other: Eight 18-hole and one 9-hole **golf** courses are available and the islands are host to major tournaments. There are **gyms** and **fitness centres** which are open to visitors on Nassau/Paradise Island and on Grand Bahama Island. Good **spa facilities** and **yoga** tuition exist throughout the islands. A variety of **new age therapies** are available.

Social Profile

FOOD & DRINK: There is a wide choice of restaurants and bars. Specialities include conch, grouper cutlets, baked crab and red snapper fillets in anchovy sauce. Fresh fruit is available from the Out Islands, including sweet pineapple, mango, breadfruit and papaya. Table service is usual in restaurants.

Local drinks are based on rum. The local liqueur is *Nassau Royal*, served alone or in coffee.

NIGHTLIFE: Hotels have bars and nightclubs. Beach parties and discos are organised regularly. Live entertainment includes calypso, goombay music and limbo dancing. Nightclubs are found in Nassau and Freeport. There are four casinos: one on Cable Beach, another on Paradise Island; on Grand Bahama there is a casino in Freeport and one in Lucaya. All casinos feature restaurants and live entertainment.

SHOPPING: Special purchases include china, cutlery, leather, fabrics, spirits from Britain, Scandinavian glass and silver, Swiss watches, German and Japanese cameras and French perfume. Local products include all types of straw artefacts, seashell jewellery and woodcarvings. **Shopping hours:** Mon-Fri 0900-1700.

SPECIAL EVENTS: For a full list of special events, contact the Bahamas Ministry of Tourism (see Contact Addresses section). The following is a selection of special events occurring in The Bahamas in 2005:

Dec 26 2004-Jan 1 2005 *New Year's Junkanoo Festival*, Nassau. **Jan 14-17** *2nd Annual Jimmy Garvin Golf Event*. **Jan 30** *8th Annual Cacique Awards*. **Mar 25-28** *James Cistern Heritage Festival*. **Apr** *Annual National Youth Choir Concert*, Nassau. **Jul 31-Aug 5** *Bimini Native Fishing Tournament*. **Aug** *Annual Bernie Butler Basra Swim Race*, Grand Bahama Island. **Aug 1-4** *Emancipation Day Celebrations*, Nassau. **Nov** *Annual One Bahamas Music & Heritage Festival*, Nassau/Paradise Island. **Dec** *Annual Bahamas Wahoo Championships*; *Christmas Sailing Regatta*, Nassau/Paradise Island; *Festival Noelle*, Grand Bahama Island. **Dec 26** *Boxing Day Junkanoo Parade*, Nassau/Grand Bahama Island.

SOCIAL CONVENTIONS: The pace of life is generally leisurely. Informal wear is acceptable in the resorts with some degree of dressing up in the evenings, particularly for dining, dancing and casinos in Nassau or Freeport. Further from the main towns, dress is more casual, although there is still a tendency to dress up at night. Small outposts like Green Turtle Cay, for example, will not require more than a shirt and long trousers. It is not acceptable to wear beachwear in towns. **Tipping:** 15 per cent is usual for most services including taxis. Some hotels and restaurants, however, include service charge on the bill.

Business Profile

ECONOMY: One of the wealthiest countries in the Caribbean, The Bahamas depends heavily on its main industry of tourism. Other industries produce rum, oil, pharmaceuticals and salt. Transhipment through Freeport, which enjoys significant tax concessions as a free trade area, is another valuable source of revenue. The Bahamas also has a sizeable and growing offshore banking sector, although it has come under pressure as a result of competition from elsewhere and international efforts to tighten up on 'tax havens'. In June 2000, the Bahamas were identified by the Organisation for Economic Cooperation and Development (OECD) – the world's 30 wealthiest economies – as one of 35 countries whose financial laws were inadequate to prevent large-scale tax evasion and possible money laundering. The government has since taken measures to meet the OECD's requirements. Most foodstuffs and virtually all other products must be imported, mainly from the USA, although oil is purchased primarily from Indonesia and Saudi Arabia. Other than the USA, The Bahamas' major trading partners are the UK and Puerto Rico.

BUSINESS: Normal courtesies are observed, ie appointments are made and calling cards are exchanged. Office hours: Mon-Fri 0900-1700 and 0900-1730 (government offices).

COMMERCIAL INFORMATION: The following organisation can offer advice: Bahamas Chamber of Commerce, PO Box N-665, Shirley Street, Nassau (tel: 322 2145; fax: 322 4649; e-mail: bahamaschamber@bahamas.net.bs; website: www.bahamasb2b.com/bahamaschamber).

CONFERENCES/CONVENTIONS: Conference venues can seat up to 2000 people. Information may be obtained from the Bahamas Tourist Office *or* the Bahamas Ministry of Tourism in Nassau (see *Contact Addresses* section).

Climate

The Bahamas are slightly cooler than other Caribbean island groups owing to their proximity to the continental North American cold air systems.

Required clothing: Lightweight or tropical, cottons all year round. Light raincoats are useful during the wet season.

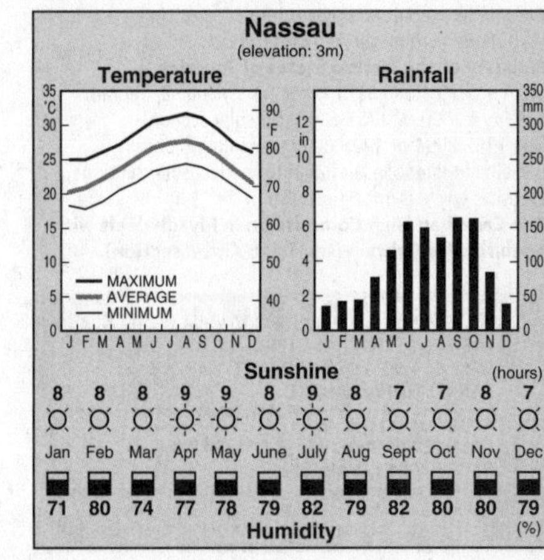

Bahrain

LATEST TRAVEL ADVICE CONTACTS

British Foreign and Commonwealth Office
Tel: (0870) 606 0290 Website: www.fco.gov.uk
US Department of State
Website: http://travel.state.gov/travel
Canadian Department of Foreign Affairs and Int'l Trade
Tel: (1 800) 267 8376 Website: www.dfait-maeci.gc.ca

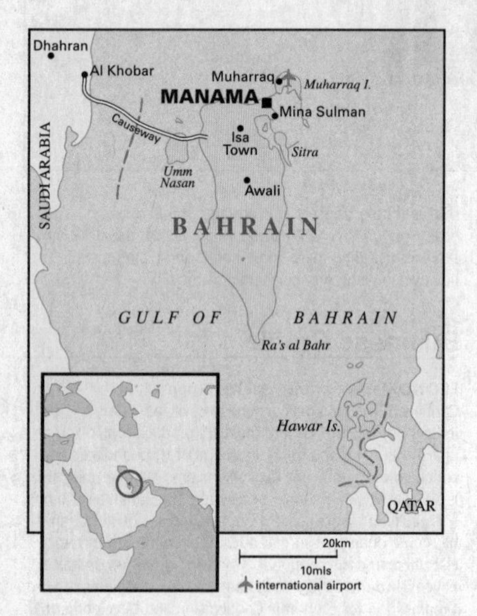

Location: Middle East, Gulf Coast.

Country dialling code: 973.

Kingdom of Bahrain Ministry of Tourism
PO Box 26613, Manama, Bahrain
Tel: (17) 201 203 *or* (17) 211 026.
Fax: (17) 211 717.
E-mail: btour@bahraintourism.com
Website: www.bahraintourism.com
Bahrain Tourism Company
PO Box 5831, Manama, Bahrain
Tel: (17) 530 530 *or* 1122.
Fax: (17) 530 867.
E-mail: btc@alseyaha.com
Website: www.alseyaha.com
Embassy of the Kingdom of Bahrain
30 Belgrave Square, London SW1X 8QB, UK
Tel: (020) 7201 9170. Fax: (020) 7201 9183.
E-mail: enquiries@bahrainembassy.co.uk
Website: www.bahrainembassy.co.uk
British Embassy
21 Government Avenue, PO Box 114, Manama 306, Bahrain
Tel: 1757 4100. Fax: 1757 4101 (commercial section) *or* 4161 (chancery) *or* 4121 (visa section).
E-mail: britemb@batelco.com.bh
Website: www.ukembassy.gov.bh
Embassy of the Kingdom of Bahrain
3502 International Drive, NW, Washington, DC 20008, USA
Tel: (202) 342 1111.
Fax: (202) 362 2192.
E-mail: info@bahrainembassy.org *or* consulate@bahrainembassy.org (consular section).
Website: www.bahrainembassy.org
Also deals with enquiries from Canada.
Embassy of the United States of America
Building 979, Road 3119, Block 331, Manama, Bahrain
Tel: 1724 2700 *or* 1727 6393 (consular section).
Fax: 1727 2594 *or* 1725 6242 (consular section).
E-mail: manamaconsular@state.gov (consular section).
Website: www.usembassy.gov.bh
The Canadian High Commission in Riyadh deals with enquiries for Bahrain (see ***Saudi Arabia*** **section).**

TIMATIC CODES

Health
AMADEUS: **TI-DFT/BAH/HE**
GALILEO/WORLDSPAN: **TI-DFT/BAH/HE**
SABRE: **TIDFT/BAH/HE**

Visa
AMADEUS: **TI-DFT/BAH/VI**
GALILEO/WORLDSPAN: **TI-DFT/BAH/VI**
SABRE: **TIDFT/BAH/VI**

To access TIMATIC country information on Health and Visa regulations through the Computer Reservations System (CRS), type in the appropriate command line listed above.

General Information

AREA: 710.9 sq km (274.5 sq miles).
POPULATION: 666,442 (official estimate 1999).
POPULATION DENSITY: 937.5 per sq km.
CAPITAL: Manama. **Population:** 140,401 (1992).
GEOGRAPHY: Bahrain is an archipelago of 33 islands in the Arabian Gulf, situated between Saudi Arabia's east coast and the Qatar peninsula. At the centre of the island is the highest point, Jebel Dukhan. The majority of Bahrain's oil wells are to be found in this area. The main island has the valuable asset of an adequate supply of fresh water, unique in the region, both on land and offshore. There are extensive date gardens to the north with irrigated vegetable and fruit gardens. The strategic 24km- (15-mile) long King Fahad Causeway links Bahrain with Saudi Arabia.
GOVERNMENT: Constitutional monarchy. Gained full independence from the UK in 1971 (had been a British Protectorate from 1861). **Head of State:** King Sheikh Hamad bin Isa al-Khalifa since 1999. **Head of Government:** Prime Minister Sheikh Khalifa bin Sulman al-Khalifa since 1971.
LANGUAGE: The official language is Arabic. English is widely spoken.
RELIGION: Islam is practised by around 85 per cent of Bahraini society (of which 60 per cent is Shi'ite and 40 per cent Sunni). There are also other faiths including Christianity, Hinduism, Judaism, Zoroastrianism and Buddhism.
TIME: GMT + 3.
ELECTRICITY: 230 volts AC, 50Hz (Awali, 110 volts AC, 60Hz). Lamp fittings are of both the bayonet and screw types. Plug fittings are normally of the 13-amp pin type.
COMMUNICATIONS: Telephone: Full IDD service is available to over 204 locations. Country code: 973. Outgoing international code: 00. Blue phone booths are coin-operated, red booths are phonecard operated and silver booths are operated by both cards and coins. Phonecards can be purchased in denominations of 500, 200, 100, 50 and 25 Dinars. Reduced rates are in operation Mon-Thurs 1900-0700 and all day on Friday. Facilities are provided for video conferencing, digital data networks, mobile links and satellite-linked skyphones for direct communication with airborne aircraft anywhere in the world. **Mobile Telephone:** GSM 900. Network operators include *Bahrain Telecommunications Company (BATELCO)*, which has handsets available for hire on a daily, weekly or monthly basis (website: www.batelco.com.bh). **Fax:** *BATELCO* operates a service from the Batelco Building on Government Avenue. **Internet:** ISPs include *BATELCO* (website: www.batelco.com.bh) and *GCC Online* (website: www.gcconline.com). E-mail facilities are available in Manama. **Telegram:** Bahrain possesses one of the most modern international communications networks in the Gulf. A 24-hour service is run by Cable & Wireless, Mercury House, Al-Khalifa Avenue, Manama, as well as at the airport. **Post:** Airmail service to Europe takes three to four days. The main post office is near Bab al-Bahrain in Manama; opening hours Sat-Thurs 0700-1930. Efficient one-day international courier services operate out of Bahrain. **Press:** There are two Arabic dailies – *Akhbar Al Khaleej* and *Al-Ayam*. The two English-language dailies are the *Bahrain Tribune* and *Gulf Daily News*. A number of Arabic and English-language business magazines are published locally. **Radio:** *Radio Bahrain* is broadcast in English 24 hours a day on 96.5 and 101 FM. *American Armed Forces Radio* can be heard on 104 FM and 107.9 Khz. There are four terres-trial channels, two in English and two Arabic channels.

Passport/Visa

	Passport Required?	Visa Required?	Return Ticket Required?
Full British	Yes	1	Yes
Australian	Yes	1	Yes
Canadian	Yes	1	Yes
USA	Yes	1	Yes
Other EU	Yes	1	Yes
Japanese	Yes	1	Yes

Note: *Regulations and requirements may be subject to change at short notice, and you are advised to contact the appropriate diplomatic or consular authority before finalising travel arrangements. Details of these may be found at the head of this country's entry. Any numbers in the chart refer to the footnotes below.*

Restricted entry: Holders of Israeli passports.
PASSPORTS: Valid passport for at least six months from date of departure required by all except the following:
(a) nationals of Kuwait, Oman, Qatar, Saudi Arabia and the United Arab Emirates holding a valid national ID card.
VISAS: Required by all except the following:
(a) nationals of Kuwait, Oman, Qatar, Saudi Arabia and the United Arab Emirates;
(b) transit passengers continuing their journey by the first connecting flight, provided holding confirmed tickets and appropriate travel documents and remaining within the transit area.

Note: 1. Nationals of EU countries (except nationals of Cyprus, the Czech Republic, Estonia, Hungary, Latvia, Lithuania, Malta, Poland, the Slovak Republic and Slovenia), Andorra, Australia, Brunei, Canada, Hong Kong, Iceland, Japan, Liechtenstein, Malaysia, Monaco, New Zealand, Norway, San Marino, Singapore, Switzerland, USA and the Vatican City may obtain visas on arrival for touristic or business stays of up to two weeks. The fee is approximately US$13. If working for a media company (eg, a newspaper or TV company) a special invitation from the Bahrain authorities is required.
Types of visa and cost: *Tourist*: £20 (two-week, single-entry), renewable for two further weeks once in Bahrain, at the General Directorate of Immigration and Passports, Manama. *Business*: £40 (four-week, multiple-entry), only available to British, Canadian and US nationals.
Validity: Three months from date of issue (*Tourist*); five years (*Business*).
Application to: Consulate (or Consular Section at Embassy); see *Contact Addresses* section.
Note: (a) No Objection Certificates are obtainable through various hotels, travel agencies and other companies licensed to carry out touristic activities in Bahrain. Organised groups are charged a fee of BD5 per person (approximately US$13). Long-term business visas should be arranged by the employing company in Bahrain. (b) Some visitors can now apply for an electronic visa in Bahrain, through the website www.evisa.gov.bh.
Application requirements: *Entry visa*: (a) Valid passport. (b) One passport-size photo. (c) One completed application form. (d) One registered, self-addressed envelope and cheque for £3 to cover return of passport if applying by post. (e) Fee, payable in cash or by company cheques only. (f) No Objection Certificate obtained by agent in Bahrain from the Ministry of Interior (only applies to certain nationals). *Tourist*: (a)-(e) and, (f) Letter stating the purpose and duration of the visit and the applicant's responsibility for all travel expenses. *Business*: (a)-(e) and, (f) Letter from the company stating the purpose and duration of of the visit and the applicant's responsibility for all travel expenses.
Working days required: Two.

Money

Currency: Dinar (BD) = 1000 fils. Notes appear in denominations of BD20, 10, 5, and 1, and 500 fils. Coins are in denominations of 100, 50, 25 and 10 fils.
Currency exchange: Currency can be exchanged at the airport, at most hotels and in banks and bureaux de change. Rates are more preferential at the bureaux de change than at the airport or at hotels. There are some ATMs in Manama that are connected to international networks.
Credit & debit cards: American Express, Diners Club, Master Card and Visa are accepted in hotels, major stores and restaurants. Smaller shops may prefer to deal in cash. Check with your credit or debit card company for details of merchant acceptability and other services which may be available.
Travellers cheques: To avoid additional exchange rate charges, travellers are advised to take travellers cheques in US Dollars.
Currency restrictions: There are no restrictions on the import or export of either local or foreign currency.
Exchange rate indicators: The following figures are included as a guide to the movements of the Dinar against Sterling and the US Dollar:

Date	Feb '04	May '04	Aug '04	Nov '04
£1.00=	0.69	0.67	0.69	0.71
$1.00=	0.38	0.38	0.37	0.37

Banking hours: Sat-Wed 0730-1200 and 1530-1730; Thurs 0730-1100. Government offices, businesses and most offices are closed on Friday, which is a weekly holiday.

Duty Free

The following goods may be imported into Bahrain by those aged 18 and over without incurring customs duty:
200 cigarettes and 50 cigars and 250g of tobacco in opened packets; 1l of alcoholic beverages and 6 bottles of beer (non-Muslim passengers only); 8oz of perfume; and gifts up to the value of BD250 (approximately US$600).
Prohibited items: Firearms, ammunition, drugs, methylated spirits, jewellery and all items originating in Israel may only be imported under licence.

Public Holidays

2005: Jan 1 New Year's Day. **Jan 21** Eid al-Adha (Feast of the Sacrifice). **Feb 10** Al-Hijrah (Islamic New Year). **Feb 19** Ashura. **Apr 21** Mouloud (Birth of the Prophet). **Nov 3-5** Eid al-Fitr (End of Ramadan). **Dec 16** National Day.
2006: Jan 1 New Year's Day. **Jan 10** Eid al-Adha (Feast of the Sacrifice). **Jan 31** Al-Hijrah (Islamic New Year). **Feb 9** Ashura. **Apr 11** Mouloud (Birth of the Prophet). **Oct 22-24** Eid al-Fitr (End of Ramadan). **Dec 16** National Day.

Note: Muslim festivals are timed according to local sightings of various phases of the moon and the dates given above are approximations. During the lunar month of Ramadan that precedes Eid al-Fitr, Muslims fast during the day and feast at night and normal business patterns may be interrupted. Many restaurants are closed during the day and there are restrictions on smoking and drinking. Some disruption may continue into Eid al-Fitr itself. Eid al-Fitr and Eid al-Adha may last anything from two to 10 days, depending on the region. For more information, see the *World of Islam* appendix.

Health

	Special Precautions?	Certificate Required?
Yellow Fever	No	No
Cholera	No	No
Typhoid & Polio	No	N/A
Malaria	No	N/A

Note: Regulations and requirements may be subject to change at short notice, and you are advised to contact your doctor well in advance of your intended date of departure. Any numbers in the chart refer to the footnotes below.

Food & drink: Water is treated and considered safe by the Ministry of Health in Bahrain, although visitors may prefer to drink bottled water. All modern hotels have their own filtration plants. Visitors are advised to eat well-cooked meat and fish, preferably served hot.
Other risks: *Typhoid fever* and *hepatitis A* occur; *hepatitis B* is endemic.
Health care: There is a comprehensive medical service, with general and specialised hospitals in the main towns. An emergency health service is provided free of charge or at a nominal fee. Pharmacies are well-equipped with supplies.

Travel - International

Note: Following the military action in Iraq, there is an increased risk of terrorism in Bahrain. The situation should be monitored closely. For further advice visitors should contact the relevant local government travel advice department.
AIR: The national carrier serving Bahrain is *Gulf Air (GF)*. Other airlines serving Bahrain include *Air India, American Airlines, British Airways, Cathay Pacific, KLM, Kuwait Airways, Qatar Airways, Royal Jordanian, Saudi Arabian Airlines, Thai Airways International, Turkish Airlines* and *Yemenia Yemen Airways*.
Approximate flight times: From Bahrain to *London* is approximately 7 hours 15 minutes, to *Los Angeles* is 18 hours 15 minutes and to *New York* is 13 hours 30 minutes.
International airports: *Bahrain International (BAH)* (Muharraq) (website: www.bahrainairport.com) is 6.5km (4 miles) northeast of Manama. Bus and taxi services run across the causeway to the main island (travel time - 15 minutes). Airport facilities include banks/bureaux de change, duty-free shops, first aid, restaurants, prayer room, car hire (*Avis, Budget, Europcar* and *Hertz*) and car parking.
Departure tax: BD3 (approximately US$8). Children under two years of age and transit passengers not leaving the airport are exempt.
SEA: There are three main ports of entry for *dhows* and other seafaring craft at Mina Salman, Mina Manama and Mina Muharraq. Passenger ferries operate between Iran and Bahrain. A port tax of BD3 may be payable.
ROAD: A car drive to Dhahran (Eastern Province of Saudi Arabia) takes approximately one hour 30 minutes from Bahrain using the King Fahad Causeway. A toll fee of approximately BD2 is payable by persons driving out of Bahrain. Normal Saudi Arabian visa regulations apply.

Travel - Internal

AIR: Several flights a week leave from Bahrain International Airport for other destinations within Bahrain. For further details contact a local travel or tour operator.
SEA: Transport between the smaller islands is by motorboat or *dhow*. For details, contact local travel agents.
ROAD: Manama is served by an excellent road system, largely created during the last few years. Traffic drives on the right. Road signs are written in English and Arabic. **Bus:** Routes now serve most of the towns and villages, with a standard fare of 50 fils. **Taxi:** Metered taxis are readily available. They can be hired in the street or from stands outside hotels and at major tourist attractions. They are identifiable by their orange side-wings and yellow number plates. Between 2200-0600 the minimum fare is BD1200. Taxis waiting outside hotels may charge more. Share-taxis which carry up to five passengers are also available. There are several designated pick-up points. Meters are not used and fares should always be agreed beforehand. Radio cabs are also available. **Car hire:** Most of the major international car hire companies operate in Bahrain with representatives at the airport and at big hotels. **Traffic regulations:** Speed restrictions are in place: 100kph (60mph) on highways and between 50-80kph (30-50mph) on all other roads.
Documentation: An International Driving Permit is necessary (must be obtained prior to arrival) and must be endorsed by the Traffic and Licensing Directorate.

Accommodation

Bahrain offers an impressive choice of world-class hotels. Hotel accommodation ranges from 5-star comfort, to family-run hotels and 1-star budget establishments. The deluxe hotels are well represented by international chains. Details of special packages are available from the Tourism Directorate (see *Contact Addresses* section).

Resorts & Excursions

Bahrain is an archipelago of 33 islands offering a blend of ancient and modern. Modern skyscrapers share the landscape with majestic mosques, embodiments of Islamic art, culture and architecture.
MANAMA: Manama, Bahrain's capital, is modern, dominated by a Manhattan-style skyline. The **souk** lies in the centre of the old town, near the archway of **Bab al-Bahrain** and, although much of the surrounding area is modern, the street layout and division of occupations still follow traditional lines: the gold souk, for example, is to be found to the southeast of the market area and is particularly impressive during the hours of darkness. The ancient city capital of **Bilad al-Qadim**, which dates from AD 900, is just outside the new city.
Excursions: To sample some of Bahrain's past, a visit to the **A'ali Burial Mounds** is recommended. This is the site for probably the largest prehistoric cemetery in the world with approximately 170,000 burial mounds dating from between 3000 BC and AD 600. Other sites of antiquity include **The House of Beit al-Jasra** (birthplace of the Amir, the ruler of Bahrain), **Beit al-Siyadi** (the 19th-century house of a pearl merchant), **Barbar Temple**, the ancient forts of **Arad**, **Bahrain**, and **Riffa**; the **National Museum** (tracing the archaeological development of Bahrain), **Bait al-Qur'an** (site of a rare collection of Islamic manuscripts), the **al-Fateh Grand Mosque** (Bahrain's largest mosque), the **Heritage Centre** (focusing on traditional Bahraini culture) and a number of **Oil Museums**. In the old quarter of the town, ancient houses still retain their 'wind towers'. Constructed 5-6m (16-20ft) above the house and open on all four sides, they act as primitive air-conditioning units. Other attractions include long stretches of sandy beach and coral reefs. The largest and most pleasant beach can be found at **Al Jazair**, complete with beach huts, pavillions, and picnic areas. Trips in traditional boats (*dhows*) can be taken across the islands to many locations, including **A'ali Village**, **al-Areen Wildlife Sanctuary** (containing endangered species such as Arabian Onyx), **al-Bander Resort**, **al-Dar Islands**, **Desert Camp**, **Jebel Dukhasn**, **King Fahad Causeway** and **Tree of Life**.

Sport & Activities

Watersports: Bahrain's year-round fine weather provides scope for a wide range of sea- or land-based activities. Facilities for **swimming**, **game fishing** (grouper and barracuda), **scuba-diving**, **snorkelling**, **water-skiing**, **windsurfing**, **parasailing** and **yachting** can be found on the islands.
Other: For those more at home on dry land there are **golf** courses, racecourses, riding and health clubs. Golf can be played at either the newly opened green golf course at Sakhir or the 18-hole sandy golf course at Awali. The **skating** rink and **bowling** alley at Busheri's in Budaiya has **snooker** tables and video rooms. There are expatriate **rugby** and **cricket** teams. **Football** is the national game and Bahrain has an olympic-sized stadium. **Horse racing**, **horse riding** and **camel racing** are also popular.

Social Profile

FOOD & DRINK: There is a good selection of restaurants serving all kinds of food, including American, Chinese, European, and Indian. Arabic food is mainly spicy and strongly flavoured. Lamb is the principal meat with chicken, turkey and duck. Salad and dips are common. Water, *arak* (grape spirit flavoured with aniseed) or beer are the most common drinks; the sale of alcohol is not encouraged although it is available to non-Muslims in nightclubs, good restaurants and luxury hotels, except during Ramadan. Strong Arabic coffee and tea is also widely available.
NIGHTLIFE: Restaurants, nightclubs and cinemas showing English and Arabic films can be found in the main towns.
SHOPPING: There is a wide range of modern shopping complexes with imported luxury goods. Pearls are the main local product. Famous red clay pottery is available from the village of A'ali. There are weavers at Bani Jamra village and basket-makers at Jasra village. **Shopping hours:** Sat-Thurs 0830-1230 and 1530-1930.
SPECIAL EVENTS: The following is a selection of special events occurring in Bahrain in 2005; for a complete list or further information, contact the Tourism Affairs and Ministry of Information (see *Contact Addresses* section): **Jan 22** *Mini Grand Prix & Desert Challenge*. **Jan 31** *Al Hijrah* (Islamic New Year). **Feb 5-9** *10th Islamic Trade Exhibition*. **Mar 1-31** *Festival of Ashura*, Manama. **Oct 22-24** *Eid al-Fitr* (End of Ramadan), nationwide. **Nov 22-24** *Jewellery Arabia Show*, Manama.
SOCIAL CONVENTIONS: Traditional beliefs and customs are strong influences and people are generally more formal than Westerners. Attitudes to women are more liberal than in most Gulf States. It is acceptable to sit cross-legged on cushions or sofas in people's homes but it is still insulting to display the soles of the feet or shoes or to accept food or anything else with the left hand. It is polite to drink two small cups of coffee or tea when offered. Guests will generally be expected to share a bedroom since guest bedrooms and privacy are almost unknown. Sports clothes may be worn in the street and short dresses are acceptable; however, revealing clothing should be avoided. Smoking is very common and cheap by European standards. **Tipping:** 10 per cent is expected by taxi drivers and waiters, particularly when service is not included, and is normal practice. Airport porters expect 100 fils for each piece of luggage.

Business Profile

ECONOMY: Oil dominates Bahrain's economy and, together with gas and petrochemicals, accounts for the bulk of exports and government revenue. That proportion is falling, however, as Bahrain seeks to diversify its economy and the reserves dwindle. Several successful industrial projects, including aluminium production, an iron-ore processing facility and an ammonia-methanol plant have been set up. In the service sector, the financial services industry has expanded dramatically in recent years, as companies trading in the region have set up their regional centres in Bahrain, where the relatively relaxed environment is an important factor in a region where rigorous social mores are often the norm. In June 2000, Bahrain was identified by the Organisation for Economic Cooperation and Development (OECD) - the world's 30 wealthiest economies - as one of 35 countries whose financial laws are believed to encourage large-scale tax evasion and possible money laundering. The government has since taken measures to meet the OECD's demands, thereby avoiding the threat of future sanctions. Most of Bahrain's trade is conducted with the major industrialised countries, particularly Japan, the USA and the larger EU states, plus Switzerland.
BUSINESS: Businessmen are expected to wear suits and ties. Business must be done on a personal introduction basis. Normal social courtesies should be observed but introductions and greetings are important and polite conversation is expected before business discussions begin. Bargaining is common practice: Arabs regard their word as their bond and expect others to do the same. The best time to visit is October to April. **Office hours:** Usually Sat-Wed 0800-1300 and 1500-1730. Some offices work Sat-Thurs 0800-1530. **Government office hours:** Sat-Wed 0700-1415.
COMMERCIAL INFORMATION: The following organisation can offer advice: Commercial Arbitration Centre, PO Box 16100, Adliya (tel: 1782 5540; fax: 1782 5580; e-mail: gccacct@batelco.com.bh; website: www.gccarbitration.net).

Climate

June to October, hot and humid (42°C), December to April, mild (10°-20°C). December through to March can be quite cool. Rainfall is slight and occurs mainly in winter. Spring and Autumn are the most pleasant months.
Required clothing: Lightweight cottons and linens from spring to autumn, mediumweight clothes from November to March. Warmer clothes are necessary in winter and on cool evenings.

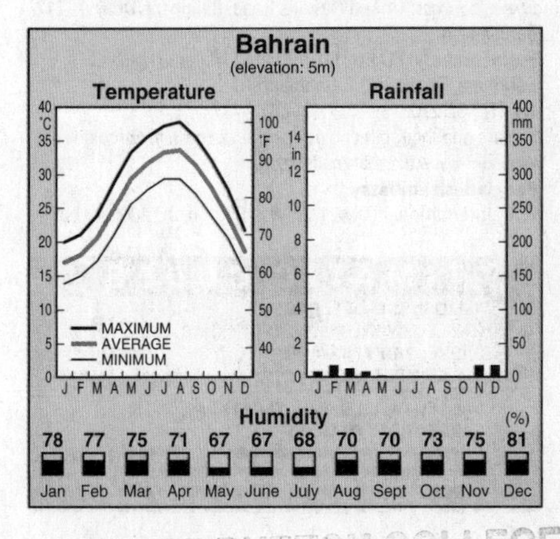

A B C D E F G H I J K L M N O P Q R S T U V W X Y Z

Bangladesh

LATEST TRAVEL ADVICE CONTACTS

British Foreign and Commonwealth Office
Tel: (0870) 606 0290 Website: www.fco.gov.uk
US Department of State
Website: http://travel.state.gov/travel
Canadian Department of Foreign Affairs and Int'l Trade
Tel: (1 800) 267 8376 Website: www.dfait-maeci.gc.ca

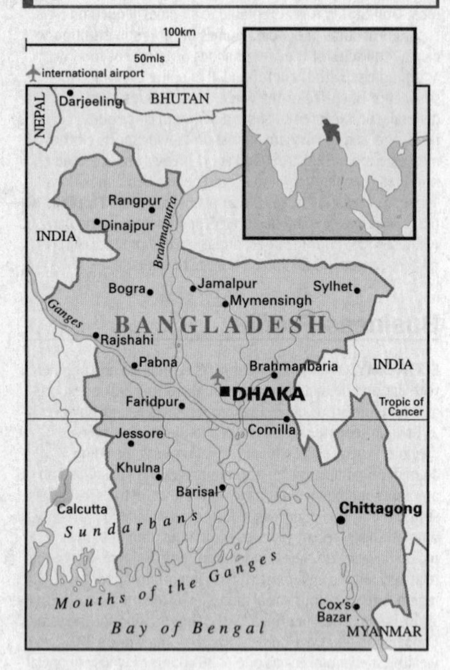

Location: South Asia.

Country dialling code: 880.

Bangladesh Parjatan Corporation (National Tourism Organisation)
233 Airport Road, Tejgaon, Dhaka-1215, Bangladesh
Tel: (2) 811 7855-9 *or* 9192. Fax: (2) 812 6501.
E-mail: bpcho@bangla.net
Website: www.bangladeshtourism.org
Bangladesh High Commission
28 Queen's Gate, London SW7 5JA, UK
Tel: (020) 7584 0081. Fax: (020) 7581 7477.
E-mail: bdesh.lon@dial.pipex.com
Website: www.bangladeshhighcommission.org.uk
Opening hours: Mon-Fri 1000-1730; Mon-Thurs 1030-1300, Fri 1030-1245 (visa section); 1500-1630 (visa collection).
Assistant High Commission
31-33 Guildhall Buildings, 12 Navigation Street, Birmingham B2 4BT, UK
Tel: (0121) 643 2386. Fax: (0121) 643 9004.
E-mail: bhcbham@aol.com
Opening hours: Mon-Fri 0930-1630.
Assistant High Commission
Cedar House, 3rd Floor, 2 Fairfield Street, Manchester M1 3GF, UK
Tel: (0161) 236 4853. Fax: (0161) 236 1522.
E-mail: bdoot.man@manc.go-legend.net
Opening hours: Mon-Fri 1000-1630; Mon-Fri 1000-1330 (consular section).
British High Commission
Street address: United Nations Road, Baridhara, Dhaka-1212, Bangladesh
Postal address: PO Box 6079, United Nations Road, Baridhara, Dhaka-1212, Bangladesh
Tel: (2) 882 2705-9. Fax: (2) 882 3437.
E-mail: ppabhc@citecho.net *or* dhaka.consular@fco.gov.uk
Website: www.ukinbangladesh.org
Bangladesh Embassy
3510 International Drive, NW, Washington, DC 20008, USA
Tel: (202) 244 0183. Fax: (202) 244 7830.
E-mail: bdootwash@bangladoot.org
Website: www.bangladoot.org
Embassy of the United States of America
Diplomatic Enclave, Madani Avenue, Baridhara, Dhaka 1212, Bangladesh
Tel: (2) 885 5500. Fax: (2) 882 3744 *or* 882 4449 (consular section).
Website: www.usembassy-dhaka.org
Bangladesh High Commission
275 Bank Street, Suite 302, Ottawa, Ontario K2P 2L6, Canada
Tel: (613) 236 0138/9. Fax: (613) 567 3213.
E-mail: bangla@rogers.com Website: www.bdhc.org
Canadian High Commission
House 16/A, Road 48, Gulshan-2, Dhaka-1212, Bangladesh
Tel: (2) 988 7091-7. Fax: (2) 882 3043 *or* 6585.
E-mail: dhaka@international.gc.ca
Website: www.dfait-maeci.gc.ca/bangladesh

TIMATIC CODES

Health
AMADEUS: **TI-DFT/DAC/HE**
GALILEO/WORLDSPAN: **TI-DFT/DAC/HE**
SABRE: **TIDFT/DAC/HE**

Visa
AMADEUS: **TI-DFT/DAC/VI**
GALILEO/WORLDSPAN: **TI-DFT/DAC/VI**
SABRE: **TIDFT/DAC/VI**

To access TIMATIC country information on Health and Visa regulations through the Computer Reservations System (CRS), type in the appropriate command line listed above.

General Information

AREA: 147,570 sq km (56,977 sq miles).
POPULATION: 130,200,000 (official estimate 2000).
POPULATION DENSITY: 882.3 per sq km.
CAPITAL: Dhaka. **Population:** 3,612,850 (1991).
GEOGRAPHY: TThe People's Republic of Bangladesh, formerly East Pakistan, is bordered to the west and northwest by West Bengal (India), to the north by Assam and Meghalaya (India), to the east by Assam and Tripura (India) and by Myanmar (Burma) to the southeast. The landscape is mainly flat with many bamboo, mango and palm-covered plains. A large part of Bangladesh is made up of alluvial plain, caused by the effects of the two great river systems of the Ganges (Padma) and the Brahmaputra (Jamuna) and their innumerable tributaries. In the northeast and east of the country the landscape rises to form forested hills. To the southeast, along the Burmese and Indian borders, the land is hilly and wooded. About one-seventh of the country's area is under water and flooding occurs regularly.
GOVERNMENT: Republic. Gained independence from Pakistan in 1971. **Head of State:** President Iajuddin Ahmed since 2002. **Head of Government:** Prime Minister Khaleda Zia since 2001.
LANGUAGE: The official language is Bengali (Bangla). English is widely spoken especially in government and commercial circles. Tribal dialects are also spoken.
RELIGION: 88 per cent Muslim, 10 per cent Hindus and 2 per cent Buddhist and Christian minorities. Religion is the main influence on attitudes and behaviour. Since 1988, Islam has been the official state religion.
TIME: GMT + 6.
ELECTRICITY: 220/240 volts AC, 50Hz. Plugs are of the British 5- and 15-amp, two- or three-pin (round) type.
COMMUNICATIONS: Telephone: Limited IDD available. Country code: 880. Outgoing international code: 00. Public telephone booths are located at the principal marketplaces and in post offices in the main towns. **Mobile telephone:** GSM 900. Main network operators include *Aktel* (website: www.aktel.com), *Grameen Phone* (website: www.grameenphone.com) and *Sheba Telecom* (website: www.shebatel.com). Coverage is limited to main towns. **Fax:** There are facilities at major hotels in Dhaka and services are now widely available in all large towns. **Internet:** Public Internet services exist in the main towns and there are also a few Internet cafes. Hotels in Dhaka and Chittagong offer Internet access (mainly to guests). Main ISPs include *BanglaNet* (website: www.bangla.net) and *Proshikanet* (website: www.proshikanet.com). **Telegram:** Telegrams may be sent from main post offices and there are three charge rates. **Post:** Airmail takes three to four days to Europe; surface mail can take several months. Post boxes are blue for airmail and red for surface mail. **Press:** There are eight daily English-language papers, the most popular being the *Bangladesh Observer*, followed by the *Daily Star*, the *Financial Express*, the *Independent* and the *New Nation*. The main English-language weeklies are the *Bangladesh Gazette*, the *Dhaka Courier* and *Holiday*. The main Bengali dailies are *Ittefaq*, *Janakantha*, *Prothan Alo* and *Sangbad*. . **Radio:** BBC World Service (website: www.bbc.co.uk/worldservice) and Voice of America (website: www.voa.gov) can be received. From time to time the frequencies change and the most up-to-date can be found online.

Passport/Visa

	Passport Required?	Visa Required?	Return Ticket Required?
Full British	Yes	Yes	Yes
Australian	Yes	Yes	Yes
Canadian	Yes	Yes	Yes
USA	Yes	Yes	Yes
Other EU	Yes	Yes	Yes
Japanese	Yes	Yes	Yes

Note: Regulations and requirements may be subject to change at short notice, and you are advised to contact the appropriate diplomatic or consular authority before finalising travel arrangements. Details of these may be found at the head of this country's entry. Any numbers in the chart refer to the footnotes below.

Restricted entry: The government of Bangladesh refuses admission and transit to nationals of Israel.
PASSPORTS: Passport valid for three months after departure required by all.
VISAS: Required by all except the following:
(a) nationals of Bangladesh or former Bangladeshi nationals holding British passports, provided they have the statement 'no visa required for travel to Bangladesh' stamped in their passport by the Bangladesh High Commission;
(b) nationals of China (PR), Hong Kong (SAR) and Macau (SAR) for stays of up to 30 days;
(c) nationals of The Bahamas, Congo (Dem Rep), Eastern Caribbean States, Fiji, The Gambia, Guyana, Honduras, Jamaica, Lesotho, Malawi, Seychelles, Solomon Islands and Vatican City;
(d) transit passengers continuing their journey by the same or first connecting aircraft provided holding valid onward or return documentation and not leaving the airport.
Note: Tourist and business travellers who do not have a mission for Bangladesh in their country of origin can obtain visas on arrival at Chittagong, Dhaka and Zia international airports, provided holding return air tickets and any other documentation necessary. Citizens of countries where there is a Bangladesh Mission must obtain a visa before going to Bangladesh.
Types of visa and cost: *Tourist* and *Business*. Prices vary according to nationality; contact the Embassy for more details (see *Contact Addresses* section). For UK passport holders: £40 (single-entry); £52 (double-entry); £75 (triple-entry); £104 (multiple-entry). Visas are issued free for nationals of India and Japan.
Validity: *Single-entry*: three months; *Double-entry* and *Triple-entry*: six months. *Multiple-entry*: twelve months. Stays are for a maximum of 90 days each.
Application to: Consular Section at Embassy or High Commission; see *Contact Addresses* section.
Application requirements: (a) Valid passport. (b) Completed application form. (c) Three passport-size photos. (d) Fee, payable in cash (application in person) or postal order (postal application). (e) Letter from employer confirming applicant's identity and position in the company. (f) For postal applications, self-addressed pre-paid registered envelope or pre-paid return courier. *Tourist*: (a)-(f) and, (g) Printed itinerary. (h) Hotel reservation letter, or invitation letter, which should be on official letterhead or, if it is from a private individual, have their bank statement attached. *Business*: (a)-(f) and, (g) Invitation from a business organisation in Bangladesh. (h) Letter from the sponsoring organisation in the UK detailing their financial responsibility for the applicant.
Working days required: Three. At least seven days for postal applications. Application times are longer (two to three weeks) for non-British or Irish nationals and journalists.

Money

Currency: Bangladeshi Taka (Tk) = 100 paisa. Notes are in denominations of Tk500, 100, 50, 20, 10, 5, 2 and 1. Coins are in denominations of Tk5 and 1 and 50, 25, 10 and 5 paisa.
Currency exchange: All foreign currency exchanged must be entered on a currency declaration form. Hotel bills must be paid in a major convertible currency or with travellers cheques. Many shops in the cities will offer better rates of exchange than the banks.
Credit & debit cards: Limited acceptance of American Express, Diners Club and MasterCard outside the capital. Check with your credit or debit card company for details of merchant acceptability prior to travel.
Travellers cheques: Can be exchanged on arrival at Dhaka Airport. To avoid additional exchange rate charges, travellers are advised to take travellers cheques in US Dollars or Pounds Sterling.
Currency restrictions: The import and export of local currency is limited to Tk100. Reconversion of local currency is permitted up to Tk500 or 25 per cent of the amount exchanged on arrival. The import of foreign currency is allowed but amounts greater than US$150 must be declared on arrival. The export of foreign currency is limited to US$150 or the amount declared on arrival.
Exchange rate indicators: The following figures are included as a guide to the movements of the Taka against Sterling and the US Dollar:

Date	Feb '04	May '04	Aug '04	Nov '04
£1.00=	107.07	105.78	109.22	112.91
$1.00=	58.82	59.23	59.28	59.62

Banking hours: Sun-Wed 0900-1500, Thurs 0900-1300. Selected banks may open on Saturdays.

Credit: © Bangladesh Parjatan Corporation

Duty Free

The following goods may be imported into Bangladesh without incurring customs duty:

200 cigarettes or 50 cigars or 225g of tobacco; two bottles of alcoholic beverages or one bottle if not travelling for touristic purposes (non-Muslims only); 250ml of perfume; gifts up to the value of Tk500.

Note: Duty free items may be bought at the duty free shop at Dhaka Airport on arrival.

Prohibited items: Firearms and some animals.

Public Holidays

2005: Jan 1 New Year's Day. **Jan 21** Eid ul-Adha (Feast of the Sacrifice). **Feb 10** Islamic New Year. **Feb 21** International Mother Language Day. **Mar 26** Independence Day. **Apr 14** Bangla New Year. **Apr 21** Eid-e-Milad-un Nabi (Birth of the Prophet). **Apr 29** Buddha Purnima. **May 1** Labour Day. **Sep 1** Shab-e Barat (Ascension of the Prophet). **Oct 11** Durga Puja (Dashami). **Oct 30** Shab e-Qadr (Evening of Destiny). **Nov 3-5** Eid al-Fitr (End of Ramadan). **Nov 7** National Revolution Day. **Dec 26** Victory Day.

2006: Jan 1 New Year's Day. **Jan 10** Eid ul-Adha (Feast of the Sacrifice). **Jan 31** Islamic New Year. **Feb 21** International Mother Language Day. **Mar 26** Independence Day. **Apr 11** Eid-e-Milad-un Nabi (Birth of the Prophet). **Apr 14** Bangla New Year. **May 1** Labour Day. **May 13** Buddha Purnima. **Aug 22** Shab-e Barat (Ascension of the Prophet). **Oct 2** Durga Puja (Dashami). **Oct 19** Shab e-Qadr (Evening of Destiny). **Oct 22-24** Eid al-Fitr (End of Ramadan). **Nov 7** National Revolution Day. **Dec 26** Victory Day.

Note: (a) Muslim festivals are timed according to local sightings of various phases of the moon and the dates given above are approximations. During the lunar month of Ramadan that precedes Eid al-Fitr, Muslims fast during the day and feast at night and normal business patterns may be interrupted. Many restaurants are closed during the day and there are restrictions on smoking and drinking. Some disruption may continue into Eid al-Fitr itself. Eid al-Fitr and Eid ul-Azha may last anything from two to 10 days, depending on the region. (b) Buddhist festivals are declared according to local astronomical observations and it is not possible to forecast the date of their occurrence exactly.

Health

	Special Precautions?	Certificate Required?
Yellow Fever	No	1
Cholera	2	No
Typhoid & Polio	3	N/A
Malaria	4	N/A

Note: *Regulations and requirements may be subject to change at short notice, and you are advised to contact your doctor well in advance of your intended date of departure. Any numbers in the chart refer to the footnotes below.*

1: A yellow fever certificate is required of all persons (including infants) arriving by air or sea within six days of departure from an infected area, or a country with infection in any part, or a country where the WHO judges yellow fever to be endemic or present; or has been in such an area in transit; or has come by an aircraft which has come from such an area and has not been properly disinfected. Those arriving without a required certificate will be detained in quarantine for six days. For further information, see the *Health* appendix.

2: Following WHO guidelines issued in 1973, a cholera vaccination certificate is no longer a condition of entry to Bangladesh. However, cholera is a serious risk in this country and precautions are essential. Up-to-date advice should be sought before deciding whether these precautions should include vaccination as medical opinion is divided over its effectiveness; see the *Health* appendix.

3: Vaccination against typhoid is advised.

4: Malaria risk exists throughout the year in the whole country with the exception of Dhaka City. The malignant *falciparum* form is reported to be highly resistant to chloroquine and resistant to sulfadoxine-pyrimethamine. Seek advice on recommended prophylaxis at least one month before travelling.

Food & drink: All water should be regarded as being potentially contaminated. Water used for drinking, brushing teeth or making ice should have first been boiled or otherwise sterilised. Milk is unpasteurised and should be boiled. Powdered or tinned milk is available and is advised, but make sure that it is reconstituted with pure water. Avoid all dairy products. Only eat well-cooked meat and fish, preferably served hot. Salad and mayonnaise may carry increased risk. Vegetables should be cooked and fruit peeled.

Other risks: *Dengue fever, visceral leishmaniasis, TB* and *hepatitis A, B* and *E* are present. *Japanese encephalitis* occurs. *Rabies* is present. For those at high risk, vaccination before arrival should be considered. If bitten abroad seek medical advice without delay. For more information consult the *Health* appendix.

Health care: There is no reciprocal health agreement with the UK and health insurance is essential. Visitors can also be treated at military hospitals.

Travel - International

Note: All but essential travel to the Chittagong Hill Tracts (excluding Chittagong City) is advised against because of the risk of being caught up in clashes between rival tribal groups, settlers and the military. There is a threat from terrorism and there have been attacks carried out in public places. There have been a number of serious incidents in the Sylhet area. Nationals should avoid demonstrations and large gatherings such as *hartals* (political strikes). There is a danger of street crime, including armed robbery.

AIR: Bangladesh's national airline is *Biman Bangladesh Airlines (BG)*. International carriers serving Bangladesh include: *Aeroflot, British Airways, Emirates, Gulf Air, Indian Airlines, Kuwait Airways, Malaysia Airlines, Pakistan International Airlines, Royal Nepal Airlines, Saudi Airways, Singapore Airlines* and *Thai Airways*.

Approximate flight times: From Dhaka to *London* (direct) is nine hours, to *Los Angeles* is 21 hours and to *New York* is 23 hours.

International airports: *Dhaka International (DAC)* (Zia International). The airport is 20km (11 miles) north of the city (travel time – 45 minutes). Biman Bangladesh coaches run every hour from 0800-2200. To return, pick up the coach from the Tejgaon old airport building, the Golden Gate or Zakaria hotels. Parjatan Coaches are also available. Bus and taxi services are available to the city. Airport facilities include restaurants, post office, banks, duty-free shops and car hire.

Other international airports include *Sylhet (ZYL)* (Osmani International Airport) and *Chittagong (CGP)* (MA Hannan International Airport).

Departure tax: Tk300. Children under two years of age and passengers in immediate transit are exempt.

SEA: Ferries from Myanmar and India run to the southern coastal ports. For details contact the Embassy or High Commission of the People's Republic of Bangladesh. The main seaport is Chittagong.

RAIL: Rail connections (there are no through-trains) link Bangladesh with India (West Bengal and Assam). Cycle-rickshaw, bus or porter services provide the cross-border connections.

ROAD: Overland crossings include the Benapol-Haridispur border (for Calcutta), the Chilihari-Haldibari border (for Darjeeling) and the Tamabil-Dawki border (for Shillong). The crossing at Benapol is the easiest and most used. It is advisable to check when the frontier posts will be open. Conditions are likely to be difficult during the monsoon season. All other frontier posts between the two countries are currently closed. Overland travel is not currently possible between Bangladesh and Myanmar. **Coach:** A direct daily service has recently been introduced between Dhaka and Calcutta via Benapol. For further details, contact Bangladesh Road Transport Corporation (tel: (2) 955 5553; fax: (2) 955 5786-8).

Travel - Internal

AIR: Internal services are operated by *Aero Bengal Airlines, Air Parabat, Biman Bangladesh Airlines (BG)* and *GMG Airlines*. Regular flights are run between Dhaka and several other main towns. These are cheap, and most routes are served at least two or three times a week. Airline buses connect with terminals.

Domestic airports: These include *Barisal, Cox's Bazar, Ishwdi, Jessore, Rajshahi* and *Saidpur*.

Departure tax: Tk25.

SEA/RIVER: The country has about 8433km (5240 miles) of navigable waterways and water transport, if a little slow, is the least expensive method of getting around Bangladesh. Ferries operate between southern coastal ports and the Ganges River delta, where there are five major river ports: Barisal, Chandpur, Dhaka, Khulna and Narayanganj. Passages should be booked well in advance; for details contact local port authorities. River services are operated by the Bangladesh Inland Waterway Transport Corporation (BIWTC), who run 'Rocket' ferries and launches on a number of routes. A ferry operates from Dhaka to Khulna four times a week (travel time – 28 hours).

RAIL: A rail system of approximately 2800km (1740 miles) connects major towns, with broad gauge in the west of the country and narrow gauge in the east. A slow but efficient network, operated by *Bangladesh Railway*, is limited by the geography of the country, but river ferries (see above) provide through links. Services are being upgraded. The main line is Dhaka–Chittagong, with several daily trains, some of which have air conditioned cars. An inter-city express service is available between main towns. For details contact the Embassy or High Commission for the People's Republic of Bangladesh (see *Contact Addresses* section).

ROAD: There are approximately 6240km (3877 miles) of roads, of which 3840km (2386 miles) are paved. It is possible to reach virtually everywhere by road, but given the geography of the country, with frequent ferry crossings being a necessity, together with the poor quality of many of the roads, road travel can be very slow. Traffic drives on the left. **Bus:** The Bangladesh Road Transport Corporation (BRTC) provides a countrywide network of bus services. All major towns are served; fares are generally low. **Taxi:** Generally available at airports and major hotels. Fares should always be agreed upon before travelling. **Car hire:** Cars may be hired at Dhaka airport, the Bangladesh Tourism Corporation Office or from the major hotels. However, in the major cities, it is relatively easy and inexpensive to hire chauffeur-driven cars. **Documentation:** International Driving Permit required.

URBAN: There are **bus** services, which are usually very crowded and unreliable, in Dhaka, provided by the Bangladesh Road Transport Corporation. The Central Bus Station is on Station Road (Fulbaria); there are also several other terminals that are, in general, for long-distance services. Buses and bus stations do not generally have signs in English. There are also an estimated 10,000 independent 'auto-rickshaw' 3-wheeler taxis (avoid night-time use). Conventional taxis are also available.

Travel times: The following chart gives approximate travel times (in hours and minutes) from **Dhaka** to other major cities/towns in Bangladesh.

	Air	Road	Rail
Chittagong	0.35	6.00	6.00
Sylhet	0.30	7.00	7.00
Rajshahi	0.45	12.00	13.00
Khulna	-	10.00	-
Rangpur	-	11.30	11.30
Dinajpur	-	12.00	13.00
Jessore	0.30	9.00	-

Accommodation

HOTELS: There are a few 5-star hotels in Dhaka, Chittagong and Cox's Bazar. All rates are for European Plan. The Bangladesh Parjatan Corporation (see *Contact Addresses* section) manages several modern hotels throughout the country. Bills are usually paid in hard currency or with travellers cheques.

GUEST HOUSES: Government-owned and private guest houses are available to hire throughout the country. Enquire at the Bangladesh Parjatan Corporation (see *Contact Addresses* section).

Resorts & Excursions

The country is divided into five administrative areas: Dhaka (North Central); Rajshahi (Northwest); Khulna (Southwest); Barisal (South); and Chittagong (Southeast). Formerly, 'Dhaka' was spelt 'Dacca'.

DHAKA (NORTH)

Dhaka, the historic city and capital of Bangladesh, lies on the Buriganga River. The river connects the city with all major inland ports in the country, contributing to its trade and commerce, as it has done for centuries.

The old part of the city, to the south of the centre and on the banks of the river, is dominated both by the commercial bustle of the waterfront and several old buildings. These include the uncompleted 17th-century **Lalbagh Fort**, the spectacular **Ahsan Manzil palace museum**, the **Chotta Katra** and a large number of mosques. To the north of this region is the European quarter (also known as British City), which contains the **Banga Bhavan**, the presidential palace, several parks, the **Dhakeswari Temple** and the **National Museum**. To the north and the east are to be found the commercial and diplomatic regions of Dhaka. The **Zoo** and **Botanical Gardens** are a bus or taxi ride into the suburbs. The waterfront has two main water transport terminals at Sadarghat and Badam Tali, located on the Buckland Road

Bund. The famous 'Rocket' ferries dock here and boats can also be hired. There are many buildings of interest along the river and in the old part of the city. The **Khan Mohammed Mirdha Mosque** and the **Mausoleum of Pari Bibi** are worth a visit, as are the **Baldha Gardens** with their collection of rare plants. There are dozens of mosques and bazaars to visit – the **Kashaitully Mosque** is especially beautiful.
The modern part of the city comprises the diplomatic and commercial regions and is to be found further north in areas such as Motijheel and Gulshan.
City tours of Dhaka and its environs are available: contact the Bangladesh Parjatan Corporation for further information.
Excursions: Sonargaon, about 30km (20 miles) east of Dhaka, was the capital of the region between the 13th and early 17th centuries and retains a number of historical relics of interest, although many of these are now in ruins. The **Rajendrapur National Park**, about 50km (30 miles) north of the capital, is noted for its varied birdlife.
Northwest of Dhaka is **Dhamrai** which contains several Hindu temples. Further north still is **Mymensingh**, at the centre of a region famous for its supply of high-quality jute. The **Madhupur National Park and Game Sanctuary** is situated about 160km (99 miles) from Dhaka. North of Dhaka is **Sylhet**, known as 'the land of two leaves and a bud' because of its long renown as a tea-growing area. **Srimongol** is the main centre of the Sylhet tea gardens. Nearby **Madhabkunda** is noted for panoramic scenery and enchanting waterfalls. Around 43km (27 miles) from Sylhet are the ruins of **Jaintiapur**, once the capital of an ancient kingdom. **Tamabil** is a border outpost on Sylhet-Shilong Road. There are excellent views of the surrounding area, including some spectacular waterfalls across the Indian border. **Zaflong** is a scenic spot nearby, set amidst tea gardens and beautiful hills.

RAJSHAHI (NORTHWEST)

Rajshahi Division, in the northwest of the country, is often ignored by tourists, but it contains a large number of archaeological sites. The most important of these are at **Paharpur**, where the vast Buddhist monastery of **Somapuri Vihara** and the **Satyapir Vita** temple are located; there is also a museum. Other places of interest in the region include the ancient Hindu settlement of **Sherpur**, near Bogra; **Mahastanagar**, also near Bogra, which dates back to the third century BC; **Vasu Vihara**, 14km (9 miles) to the northwest, the site of an ancient but now ruined monastery; **Rajshahi**, on the Ganges, which has a museum displaying many of the archaeological relics of the area; and **Gaur**, very close to the border with the Indian state of West Bengal, which contains a number of old mosques. **Bogra** is a useful base for visiting the archaeological sites of **Paharpur**, **Mahastanagar** and **Sherpur**, although not intrinsically interesting itself. The Bangladesh Parjatan Corporation (NTO) offers package tours to these sites.

KHULNA (SOUTHWEST)

Khulna Division is principally marshland and jungle. The city of the same name is the administrative capital of the division and is mainly a commercial centre, particularly for river traffic. The principal place of interest in this area of the country is the **Sundarbans National Park**, a supreme example of lush coastal vegetation and the variety of wildlife which it can support. The most famous inhabitants of this region are the Royal Bengal tigers, but spotted deer, monkeys and a great variety of birds are also to be found here. Tours (usually for 10 people or more) are organised by the Bangladesh Parjatan Corporation during the winter; otherwise, boats can be hired from **Khulna** or **Mongla**, which is the main port for the Khulna region. Accommodation is available at Heron Point. Other places of interest include the mosque of **Sat Gombud**, and the town of **Bagerhat** (home of Khan Jahan Ali, a well-known Sufi mystic).

BARISAL (SOUTH)

Barisal is the administrative centre of the division of the same name. Situated in an area dissected by rivers, it is the most important river port in the south of the country. Just 10km (6 miles) outside Barisal, at **Madubashah**, is a lake and bird sanctuary. **Kuakata** is the most outstanding tourist attraction. It is a scenic beauty spot on the southernmost tip of Bangladesh in the district of Patuakhali and has a wide sandy beach which is an ideal vantage point to watch the sun rise and set.
Other attractions include two pre-Moghul mosques: one, which boasts nine domes, is situated at the village of **Qasba Guarnadi** and the other, built in 1464, is near **Patuakhali**.

CHITTAGONG (SOUTHEAST)

Chittagong, the second-largest city in the country, is the principal city of the southeastern administrative division of Bangladesh. It is a thriving port set amid lovely natural surroundings studded with green-clad knolls, coconut palms, mosques and minarets, against the background of the blue waters of the Bay of Bengal.
The Old City retains many echoes of past European settlements, mainly by the Portuguese, as well as many mosques. These include the 17th-century **Shahi Jama-e-Masjid** – which closely resembles a fort – set astride a hilltop, and the earlier **Qadam Mubarek Mosque**. The **Chilla of Bada Shah** stands to the west of Bakshirhat in the old city. The higher ground to the northwest was, in due course, settled by the British, and this is now where most of the city's commercial activity is conducted. The **Dargah of Sah Amanat** is a holy shrine located in the heart of the town.
Excursions: Approximately 8km (5 miles) from Chittagong is the picturesque **Foy's Lake** in the railway township of **Pahartali**. The **Tomb of Sultan Bayazid Bostami**, a holy shrine situated on a hillock in **Nasirabad**, is situated 6km (4 miles) to the northwest of the town. At its base is a large tank with several hundred tortoises, supposedly the descendants of evil spirits.
Northeast of Chittagong is **Rangamati**, a place of scenic beauty and unspoiled tribal life. It is perched on the bank of the manmade **Kaptai Lake**. In the extreme south of Bangladesh is **Cox's Bazar**, a thriving regional tourist centre and beach resort, with a mixed population of Bengali and Burmese origin. The town has many thriving cottage industries for weaving and cigar making. This is also where the world's longest and broadest beach, **Inani Beach**, can be found; it is 120km (75 miles) long and 55m (180ft) to 90m (300ft) broad (depending on the tide). It has not, however, been fully developed for tourism. The main tourist beach is **Patenga**, which is also broad and long. Bangladesh Parjatan Corporation offers excellent accommodation and catering facilities (see *Contact Addresses* section).

Sport & Activities

Wildlife: Bangladesh has several national parks with abundant wildlife (including the rare Royal Bengal tiger) and many species of exotic birds. Tours (usually for groups of 10 or more people) are organised by the Bangladesh Parjatan Corporation (see *Contact Addresses* section). For further details, see the *Resorts & Excursions* section.
Watersports: Located in the Rangamati Hill District, *Kapati Lake* offers good opportunities for **sailing**, **swimming** and **fishing**. A range of watersports is also available on the coast, particularly at *Cox's Bazar* (see *Resorts & Excursions* for details). Boating enthusiasts may head to *Sunderbands National Park*, large parts of which are only accessible by rowing boat.
Spectator sports: Cricket, **hockey** and **football** are among the most popular national sports. The Dhaka Metropolitan Soccer League season begins in April. Games are held in the city stadium and playgrounds. Floodlit **badminton** courts can be found almost everywhere and visitors are welcome to join the locals at one of their favourite games.

Social Profile

FOOD & DRINK: There are plenty of good restaurants in Dhaka and main towns around the country. Western food can be found in most hotels and in some large restaurants. Local specialities include a variety of curries such as korma, bhuna, masala gosht, kashmiri and tikka. Dishes are usually served with rice, naan or *paratha* (griddle-fried flat breads). Kebabs are widely available. Seafood and fresh-water fish are in natural abundance and smoked *hilsa*, fresh *bhetki*, *chingri* and prawns are definitely worth trying. Desserts tend to be sweet and milky including *misti dhohi* (sweetened yoghurt), *zorda* (sweet rice with nuts) and *ros malai* (round sweets floating in thick milk).
Alcoholic drink is expensive and strict Muslim customs severely limit availability and drinking times, although leading hotels have bars which will serve alcohol. Local drinks included *chai* (milky sweet tea), *lassi* (yoghurt drink) and coconut water.
NIGHTLIFE: Leading hotels have bars, but Western-style nightclubs do not exist. Displays of local dance and music are occasionally to be seen, particularly during religious festivals. Traditional theatre can be seen in major cities and the Dhaka City Corporation has recently opened a modern theatre hall called *Dhaka Mohanagor Natya Mancha*.
SHOPPING: Bangladesh is famous for its pink pearl. Handloom fabrics, silks, printed saris, coconut masks, bamboo products, mother-of-pearl jewellery, leather crafts, wood and cane handicrafts and folk dolls are popular purchases. Duty-free shops are available in Dhaka and international airports. **Shopping hours:** Generally Sat-Thurs 0900-2000, Fri 0900-1230 and 1400-2000 (shops in tourist districts often stay open later).
SPECIAL EVENTS: The following is a selection of special events occurring in Bangladesh in 2005; for a complete list or further information, contact the Bangladesh Parjatan Corporation (see *Contact Addresses* section): **Feb 21** *National Mourning Day*, Dhaka. **Mar** *Holi* (Spring Festival). **Apr** *Pahela Baishakh* (Bengal New Year); *Langalbandh Mela* (Hindu festival), Sonargaon. **Oct 22-24** *Eid al Fitr* (End of Ramadan), nationwide. **Dec 25** *Bara Din* (Big Day), Dhaka.
SOCIAL CONVENTIONS: In someone's home it is acceptable to sit crossed-legged on cushions or the sofa. If a visitor wishes to bring a gift, money must not be given as it may cause offence. Religious customs should be respected by guests. For instance, women should not be specifically photographed unless it is certain that there will be no objection. Women should wear trousers or long skirts; revealing clothes should be avoided, particularly when visiting religious places. Dress is generally informal for men. **Photography:** In rural areas people are becoming more used to tourists, however, permission should be requested before photographs are taken of individuals. Do not photograph military installations. **Tipping:** Most services expect a tip in hotels; give 10 per cent for restaurant staff and 5 per cent for taxi drivers.

Business Profile

ECONOMY: With few mineral resources, overcrowded Bangladesh depends mainly on a subsistence agriculture, which suffers frequent and severe damage from cyclones and flooding. Tea and jute are the main cash crops – Bangladesh supplies about 90 per cent of the world's raw jute – production of both of which has dipped in recent years, again largely owing to the weather. There are large reserves of natural gas and some deposits of low-grade coal, which meet the bulk of domestic energy requirements. Offshore gas production in the Bay of Bengal will improve the country's overall energy situation and provide a valuable source of export revenue. Most of the manufacturing workforce is based in jute-related industries; the remainder works in textiles, chemicals and sugar. However, Bangladesh will continue to rely heavily on foreign aid – at present this derives from a variety of sources coordinated by the World-Bank-led 'Paris Club' of donors. The country's economic stability and consistent growth during the last decade has improved its international status. The major outstanding problem is corruption – measuring corruption is at best an inexact science but Bangladesh is widely recognised to be among the worst offenders. The informal 'hundi' banking system is especially vulnerable to illicit transfers and laundering. In May 2003, the government established a national commission to tackle the problem.
The USA is substantially the largest export market followed by Italy, Japan, Singapore and the UK. Japan, Canada and Singapore are the country's main suppliers of imports, which are mostly manufactured goods. Bangladesh is a member of the seven-strong South Asian Association for Regional Co-operation – the main economic grouping in the region.
BUSINESS: Tropical-weight suits or shirt and tie are recommended. Suits are necessary when calling on Bengali officials. Cards are given and usual courtesies are observed. Visitors should not be misled by the high illiteracy rate and low educational level of most of the population. Given the opportunity, Bangladeshis prove to be good businesspeople and tough negotiators. The best time to visit is October to March. **Office hours:** Sun-Thurs 0900-1700 and 0800-1430 (government offices).
COMMERCIAL INFORMATION: The following organisation can offer advice: Federation of Bangladesh Chambers of Commerce and Industry, 60 Motijheel Commercial Area, Dhaka-1000 (tel: (2) 956 0102/3 *or* 0598; fax (2) 861 3213; e-mail: fbcci@bol-online.com; website: www.fbcci-bd.org).

Climate

Very hot, tropical climate with a monsoon season from April to October when temperatures are highest; rainfall averages over 2540mm. The cool season is between November and March.
Required clothing: Lightweight cottons and linens throughout the year. Warmer clothes are needed in the evenings during the cool season. Waterproofs are necessary during the monsoon season.

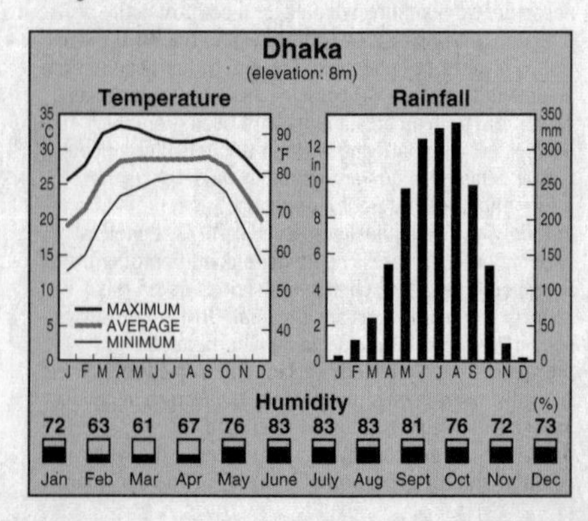

Barbados

LATEST TRAVEL ADVICE CONTACTS

British Foreign and Commonwealth Office
Tel: (0870) 606 0290 Website: www.fco.gov.uk

US Department of State
Website: http://travel.state.gov/travel

Canadian Department of Foreign Affairs and Int'l Trade
Tel: (1 800) 267 8376 Website: www.dfait-maeci.gc.ca

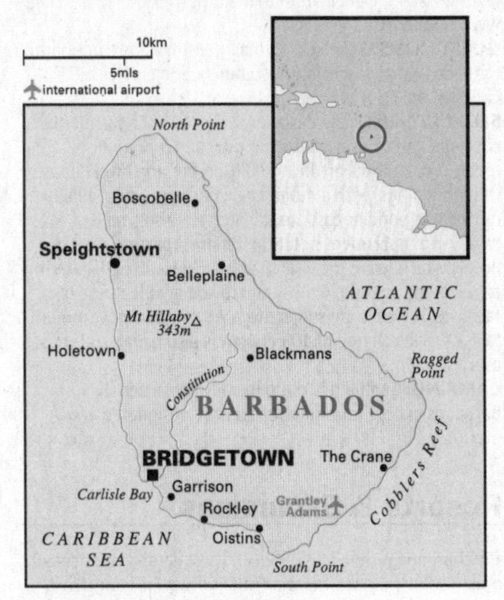

Location: Caribbean, Windward Islands.

Country dialling code: 1 246.

Ministry of Tourism
Sherbourne Conference Centre, Two Mile Hill, St Michael, Barbados
Tel: 430 7500. Fax: 436 4828.
E-mail: barmot@sunbeach.net Website: www.barmot.gov.bb

Barbados Tourism Authority
PO Box 242, Harbour Road, Bridgetown, Barbados
Tel: 427 2623. Fax: 426 4080.
E-mail: btainfo@barbados.org Website: www.barbados.org

Barbados High Commission
1 Great Russell Street, London WC1B 3ND, UK
Tel: (020) 7631 4975. Fax: (020) 7323 6872.
E-mail: london@foreign.gov.bb
Website: www.foreign.gov.bb
Opening hours: Mon-Fri 0930-1730 (general enquiries); 1000-1600 (visa section).

Barbados Tourism Authority
263 Tottenham Court Road, London W1T 7LA, UK
Tel: (020) 7636 9448. Fax: (020) 7637 1496.
E-mail: btauk@barbados.org
Website: www.barbados.org/uk

British High Commission
Street address: Lower Collymore Rock, St Michael, Bridgetown, Barbados
Postal address: PO Box 676, St Michael, Bridgetown, Barbados
Tel: 430 7800. Fax: 430 7860 (consular section and management).
E-mail: britishhcb@sunbeach.net
Website: www.britishhighcommission.gov.uk/barbados

Embassy of Barbados
2144 Wyoming Avenue, NW, Washington, DC 20008, USA
Tel: (202) 939 9200. Fax: (202) 332 7467.
E-mail: washington@foreign.gov.bb
Website: www.barbados.org

Barbados Tourism Authority
800 Second Avenue, 2nd Floor, New York, NY 10017, USA
Tel: (212) 986 6516 *or* (800) 221 9831 (toll-free in USA). Fax: (212) 573 9850.
E-mail: btany@barbados.org
Website: www.barbados.org

Embassy of the United States of America
Street address: Canadian Imperial Bank of Commerce Building, Broad Street, Bridgetown, Barbados
Postal address: PO Box 302, Bridgetown, Barbados
Tel: 436 4950 *or* 431 0225 (consular section). Fax: 429 5246 *or* 431 0179 (consular section).
E-mail: consularbridge2@state.gov *or* douglasar@state.gov
Website: http://bridgetown.usembassy.gov

Barbados High Commission
130 Albert Street, Suite 1204, Ottawa, Ontario K1P 5G4, Canada
Tel: (613) 236 9517/8. Fax: (613) 230 4362 *or* 236 3528.
E-mail: ottawa@foreign.gov.bb
Website: www.foreign.gov.bb

Barbados Tourism Authority
105 Adelaide Street West, Suite 1010, Toronto, Ontario M5H 1P9, Canada
Tel: (416) 214 9880. Fax: (416) 214 9882.
E-mail: canada@barbados.org
Website: www.barbados.org/canada

Canadian High Commission
Street address: Bishop's Court Hill, St Michael, Bridgetown, Barbados
Postal address: PO Box 404, St Michael, Bridgetown, Barbados
Tel: 429 3550. Fax: 437 7436 (administration section) *or* 429 3780 (public affairs section).
E-mail: bdgtn@international.gc.ca
Website: www.international.gc.ca/barbados

TIMATIC CODES

Health	AMADEUS: TI-DFT/BGI/HE GALILEO/WORLDSPAN: **TI-DFT/BGI/HE** SABRE: **TIDFT/BGI/HE**
Visa	AMADEUS: **TI-DFT/BGI/VI** GALILEO/WORLDSPAN: **TI-DFT/BGI/VI** SABRE: **TIDFT/BGI/VI**

To access TIMATIC country information on Health and Visa regulations through the Computer Reservations System (CRS), type in the appropriate command line listed above.

Credit: © Barbados Tourism Authority

General Information

AREA: 430 sq km (166 sq miles).
POPULATION: 267,000 (2000).
POPULATION DENSITY: 620.9 per sq km.
CAPITAL: Bridgetown. **Population:** 5,928 (1990).
GEOGRAPHY: Barbados is the most easterly of the Caribbean chain of islands. It lies well to the east of the West Indies. To the west, beaches are made of fine white sand and there are natural coral reefs. Along the east coast there is a lively surf as the sea pounds the more rocky shoreline. Barbados is predominantly flat with only a few gently rolling hills to the north. The coral structure of the island acts as a natural filter and the waters of Barbados are amongst the purest in the world.
GOVERNMENT: Constitutional monarchy. Gained independence from the UK in 1966. **Head of State:** HM Queen Elizabeth II, represented locally by Governor-General Sir Clifford Husbands since 1996. **Head of Government:** Prime Minister Owen S Arthur since 1994.
LANGUAGE: The official language is English. Local Bajan dialect is also spoken.
RELIGION: Mainly Christian, with an Anglican majority, Roman Catholic minority, plus small Jewish, Hindu and Muslim communities.
TIME: GMT - 4.
ELECTRICITY: 110 volts AC, 50Hz. American-style two-pin plugs are in use.
COMMUNICATIONS: Telephone: Inward IDD service is available and outward IDD is available from most telephones. Country code: 1 246. Outgoing international code: 011. Hotels have telephones available to both residents and non-residents. There are cardphones at the airport, the seaport, the university campus, in Bridgetown and at the offices of Barbados External Telecommunications (BET) in Wildey and Bridgetown. Payphones exist throughout the island, although it may be better to use cardphones for overseas calls. Overseas calls may also be made from the offices of BET at Wildey, St Michael. Local calls are free when calling from a residence. Collect overseas calls can be made from cardphones and payphones. **Mobile telephone:** TDMA and GSM 1900 networks. Network provider is *Cable & Wireless Caribbean Cellular* (website: www.candw.com.bb/barbados). Unregistered roaming is available – visitors with TDMA handsets can make calls without registering, provided they can give a credit card number. **Fax:** Available at hotels. BET provides services for members of the public. **Internet:** There are about 20 Internet cafes throughout Barbados. The major ISPs are *Cable & Wireless BET* (website: www.cwwionline.com), *CariAccess*, *CaribSurf* (website: www.caribsurf.com) and *Sunbeach*. **Telegram:** Services are provided by Barbados External Telecommunications (BET). The Cable & Wireless office is at Lower Broad Street (Mon-Fri 0700-1900, Sat 0700-1300). There is a 24-hour service at Wildey, St Michael. **Post:** Deliveries are made twice a day in Bridgetown and once a day in rural areas. Post boxes, which are red, are plentiful. Post office hours: Mon-Fri 0800-1700 at Bridgetown main office; other branches are open Mon 0730-1200 and 1300-1500, Tues-Fri 0800-1200 and 1300-1515. **Press:** The main dailies are *The Barbados Advocate*, *East Caribbean News* and *The Nation*. Foreign newspapers are also available. **Radio:** BBC World Service (website: www.bbc.co.uk/worldservice) and Voice of America (website: www.voa.gov) can be received. From time to time the frequencies change and the most up-to-date can be found online.

Passport/Visa

	Passport Required?	Visa Required?	Return Ticket Required?
Full British	Yes	No/2	Yes
Australian	Yes	No/3	Yes
Canadian	1	No/3	Yes
USA	1	No/4	Yes
Other EU	Yes	2	Yes
Japanese	Yes	No/5	Yes

Note: Regulations and requirements may be subject to change at short notice, and you are advised to contact the appropriate diplomatic or consular authority before finalising travel arrangements. Details of these may be found at the head of this country's entry. Any numbers in the chart refer to the footnotes below.

PASSPORTS: Passport valid for duration of intended stay required by all.
Note: 1. As of 1 March 2004, nationals of Canada and the USA require a valid passport to enter Barbados.
VISAS: Tourist visas are required by all except the following:
(a) **2.** nationals of EU countries for stays of up to six months (nationals of the Czech Republic, Estonia, Hungary, Lithuania, Poland and Slovenia for stays of up to 28 days), except nationals of Latvia, Malta and the Slovak Republic who *do* need a visa;
(b) **3.** nationals of commonwealth countries for stays of up to six months (nationals of Botswana for stays of up to 60 days), except nationals of Cameroon, India, Malta, Mozambique, Namibia, Nauru, Pakistan and Papua New Guinea who *do* need a visa;
(c) **4.** nationals of Armenia, Brazil, Iceland, Israel, Liechtenstein, Mali, Mauritania, Monaco, Norway, San Marino, Switzerland, Tunisia, Uruguay, USA, Vatican City and Zimbabwe for stays of up to six months;
(d) nationals of Turkey for stays of up to three months;
(e) **5.** nationals of Argentina, Chile, Colombia, Hong Kong, Japan, Korea (Rep) and Panama for stays of up to 90 days;
(f) nationals of Costa Rica for stays of up to 30 days;
(g) nationals of CIS countries for stays of up to 28 days (nationals of Armenia for stays of up to six months), except nationals of Kyrgyzstan and Tajikistan who *do* need a visa);
(h) nationals of Albania, Bulgaria, Croatia, Cuba, Mexico, Nicaragua, Peru, Romania and Venezuela for stays of up to 28 days.
Types of visa and cost: *Tourist*: £18 (single-entry); £22 (multiple-entry).
Validity: Three months from date of issue.
Application to: Consulate (or Consular Section at Embassy or High Commission); see *Contact Addresses* section.
Application requirements: (a) One application form. (b) One passport-size photo. (c) Valid passport. (d) Evidence of return or onward flight. (e) Company letter where required. (f) Fee; payable by cash or postal order. (g) Special delivery, addressed envelope for postal applications.
Working days required: Two (in person and by post).
Temporary residence: Enquire at the Immigration Office in Barbados.

Money

Currency: Barbados Dollar (Bd$) = 100 cents. Notes are in denominations of Bd$100, 50, 20, 10, 5 and 2. Coins are in denominations of Bd$1, and 25, 10, 5 and 1 cents.
Note: The Barbados Dollar is tied to the US Dollar.
Currency exchange: The best exchange rates are available at commercial banks. The island is served by the Barbados National Bank and a range of at least six international banks, each with a main office in Bridgetown and further branches in Hastings, Holetown, Speightstown and Worthing. ATMs are available.
Credit & debit cards: American Express, Barclaycard, Carte Blanche, Diners Club, Eurocard, MasterCard and Visa are accepted in the resorts, but cash is preferred for customs duty payment. Discover Card may be used in certain places. Check with your credit or debit card company for details of merchant acceptability and other services that may be available.
Travellers cheques: Accepted by all banks and most hotels. To avoid additional exchange rate charges, travellers

are advised to take travellers cheques in US Dollars or Pounds Sterling.
Currency restrictions: The import of local currency is unlimited, subject to declaration. The export of local currency is prohibited. The import and export of foreign currency is limited to the amount declared on arrival.
Exchange rate indicators: The following figures are included as a guide to the movements of the Barbados Dollar against Sterling and the US Dollar:

Date	Feb '04	May '04	Aug '04	Nov '04
£1.00=	3.64	3.57	3.68	3.78
$1.00=	2.00	2.00	2.00	2.00

Banking hours: Generally Mon-Thurs 0800-1500, Fri 0800-1700.

Duty Free

The following items may be taken into Barbados by persons aged over 18 years without incurring customs duty:
200 cigarettes or 250g tobacco or other tobacco products; 750ml of spirits and 750ml of wine; 150ml of perfume and 300ml of all other scents; gifts up to a value of Bd$100.
Note: For certain items it is now possible, on presentation of airline tickets and travel documents, to obtain duty-free goods any time from the day of arrival in the country. However, tobacco, alcohol and electronic goods must still be bought under the old system immediately prior to embarkation. A permit must be obtained from the Ministry of Agriculture and Consumer Affairs in order to import meat and meat products.
Prohibited items: Foreign rum and matches, fresh fruit and vegetables (only if grown in or conveyed through certain areas; contact the Ministry of Agriculture and Consumer Affairs for further information) and articles made of camouflage material.

Public Holidays

2005: Jan 1 New Year's Day. **Jan 21** Errol Barrow Day. **Mar 25** Good Friday. **Mar 28** Easter Monday. **Apr 28** National Heroes' Day. **May 1** Labour Day. **May 16** Whit Monday. **Aug 1** Emancipation Day; Kadooment Day. **Nov 30** Independence Day. **Dec 25-26** Christmas.
2006: Jan 1 New Year's Day. **Jan 21** Errol Barrow Day. **Apr 14** Good Friday **Apr 17** Easter Monday. **Apr 28** National Heroes' Day. **May 1** Labour Day. **Jun 5** Whit Monday. **Aug 7** Emancipation Day/ Kadooment Day. **Nov 30** Independence Day. **Dec 25-26** Christmas.

Health

	Special Precautions?	Certificate Required?
Yellow Fever	No	1
Cholera	No	No
Typhoid & Polio	2	N/A
Malaria	No	N/A

Note: *Regulations and requirements may be subject to change at short notice, and you are advised to contact your doctor well in advance of your intended date of departure. Any numbers in the chart refer to the footnotes below.*

1: A yellow fever vaccination certificate is required from travellers over one year of age coming from countries with infected areas.
2: A small risk of typhoid exists.
Food & drink: The water in Barbados is considered by some to be the purest in the world; it is filtered naturally by limestone and coral and pumped from underground rivers. Milk is pasteurised and dairy products are safe for consumption. Local meat, poultry, seafood, fruit and vegetables are generally considered safe to eat.
Other risks: Immunisation against *tetanus* and *hepatitis A* are usually recommended; *hepatitis B* may also be recommended for long-term travellers. A low risk of *dengue fever* exists. *Hay fever* and *asthma* can be exacerbated during the sugar cane harvesting season. *Leptospirosis* may occur during the rainy season (October/November). It is also important to note that there is a high prevalence of HIV (Human Immunodeficiency Virus), particularly amongst the 20 to 45 age group, of which it is the second-biggest killer. All necessary precautions should be undertaken.
Health care: Excellent medical facilities are available in Barbados, with both private and general wards. Barbados has a reciprocal health agreement with the UK, which entitles UK nationals to free hospital and polyclinic treatment, ambulance travel and prescribed medicines for children and elderly patients. However, prescribed medicines for those other than children or the elderly and all dental treatment must be paid for. To receive treatment, UK nationals must show their UK passport or NHS medical card, as well as their temporary entry permit. Medical insurance is recommended for all other nationals.

Travel - International

AIR: Barbados is served by a number of international airlines including *Air Canada*, *Air Jamaica*, *American Airlines*, *British Airways*, *BWIA*, *Canadian Airlines* and *Virgin Atlantic*. *BWIA*, *Caribbean Star* and *LIAT* run flights to most of the neighbouring islands.
Approximate flight times: From Barbados to *Miami* is 3 hours 30 minutes, to *New York* is 5 hours, to *London* is 7 hours 30 minutes and to *Los Angeles* is 9 hours.
International airports: *Barbados (BGI)* (Grantley Adams International) is 16km (10 miles) southeast of Bridgetown, in Christ Church. Airport porters are ubiquitous and charge Bd$1 for transporting luggage between the luggage claim area and the street. Facilities include a bank, post office, bureaux de change, bar, shops and restaurant. The outgoing duty-free shop carries a range of items including jewellery, perfumes, china, crystal, cameras, shoes and clothing. There is a regular bus service to the city (travel time - 45 minutes) which departs every 30 minutes (0600-2400), and a 24-hour taxi service (travel time - 30 minutes).
Departure tax: Bd$25 for all departures. Passengers in transit who will be remaining in Barbados for less than 24 hours and children aged under 12 are exempt.
SEA: Barbados, which has a deep-water harbour at Bridgetown, is a port of call for a number of British, European and US cruise lines. Cruises call at the Bridgetown Cruise Ship Terminal, which is a multi-purpose marketplace containing duty-free shops, a local goods market, restaurant and bar, customs, immigration, health services and police facilities. Other services include a bureau de change, car hire, ATM and a communications centre with telephones, facsimile machines and mobile phone hire. For details, contact the Tourist Office. There is a small departure tax.

Travel - Internal

AIR: There are no internal services.
ROAD: Barbados has a good network of roads which covers the entire island, but there are many potholes (except on the main highway) on the roads and care should be taken. In rural areas, roads are often narrow, unlit or lack sufficient grip. Driving time to the east coast from Bridgetown has been greatly reduced following the completion of the trans-insular highway. Traffic drives on the left. Speed limits are posted in kilometres per hour (40, 60 and 80 kph maximum) and are lower than in the UK. The road journey from Bridgetown to Speightstown takes about 30 minutes and to Holetown or Oistins about 20 minutes. **Bus:** Buses are frequent and provide comprehensive coverage of the island at a flat rate of approximately Bds$1.50 for all journeys. Although cheap, buses are crowded during the rush hours. All buses terminate at Speightstown. **Mini vans:** Licensed mini vans, identifiable by their 'ZR' licence plate, operate around the island and can be flagged down by tourists and locals. There are no fixed schedules, but service is frequent. **Taxi:** Taxis do not have meters but fares are regulated by the Government. Listings are available from the Tourist Office. It is advised to check the fare before travel. The fare can usually be paid in US dollars (fixed exchange rate: Bd$2 - US$1) as well as in Barbados dollars. **Car hire:** Anything from a mini-moke to a limousine may be hired at the airport, at offices in Bridgetown and at main hotels. Petrol is comparatively cheap. Cars may be hired by the hour, day or week. Cars can be booked by calling a car hire agency, which will then send a car over to the applicant's hotel. *Courtesy Car Rentals* is the only car hire agency situated at the airport, and is located in the Arrivals Hall. **Documentation:** A Barbados driving permit is required. This can be obtained from car hire companies, the Ministry of Transport (Mon-Fri 0830-1430), the airport (every day 0800-2200) or police stations in Hastings, Worthing and Holetown. There is a registration fee of Bd$10. A valid national licence or an International Driving Permit should also be held.
URBAN: Bridgetown has a local bus network and taxis are available.

Accommodation

HOTELS: Accommodation includes uncompromising luxury and many first-class hotels. Hotel prices range to suit all budgets. Generally the luxury hotels are in the west, while the medium-priced ones can be found along the southwest coast. The east coast, owing to its exposure to the trade winds and wild Atlantic Ocean, has only a small number of hotels and guest houses. However, it is this area that is chosen by the Bajans for their own holidays. Hotel prices are higher in the winter than in the summer. The high season is from 16 December to 15 April, the low season runs for the remainder of the year. Rates are subject to a 7.5 per cent government tax; a service charge of 10 per cent is also applicable at most hotels. Most hotels have air conditioning, many have swimming pools and housekeeping apartments. Most rates are for room only.
Grading: There is a hotel inspection and grading system, as well as standard services, the main ones being European Plan (EP), which is room only, and Modified American Plan (MAP), where breakfast and dinner are included with the price of the room. In addition, the Tourist Authority information gives full details on facilities. Further information is available from the Barbados Tourism Authority (see *Contact Addresses* section); *or* from the Barbados Hotel and Tourism Association, Fourth Avenue, Belleville, St Michael, W1 (*street address*) *or* PO Box 711C, Bridgetown, St Michael, W1 (*postal address*) (tel: 426 5041; fax: 429 2845; e-mail: info@bhta.org; website: www.bhta.org).
GUEST HOUSES: There are small guest houses throughout Barbados, particularly in Christchurch. Some offer self-catering facilities.
SELF-CATERING: There is a large number of apartments, cottages and villas available for hire, and a number of modern complexes are being built on the northwest coast. Older buildings, with a more local character, are available on the less popular east coast. There are also smaller, family-run apartment hotels and many apartment-style hotels which leave the visitor with a choice of self-catering or restaurant eating. Almost all provide a wide range of facilities. All rates are subject to a 7.5 per cent government tax; a service charge of 10 per cent is also payable at most establishments.
CAMPING: Camping is not generally permitted in Barbados except for organised trips by designated youth groups.

Resorts & Excursions

The dramatic differences between the east and west coast must not be missed. The east (Atlantic side) is less developed and ruggedly beautiful. The west coast is the Caribbean side, where there is more hotel development, but the coastline remains elegant and attractive. The sea is calm and clear and this is the coast where watersports come into their own. Barbados is actively promoting ecotourism. The Barbados National Trust has implemented programmes to support this venture, owning and/or administering 10 sites that are open to the public. Various hiking, cycling and walking events are available and information can be obtained from the Barbados National Trust, Wildey House, Wildey, St Michael, Barbados (tel: 436 9033 *or* 426 2421; fax: 429 9055; e-mail: natrust@sunbeach.net).
Bridgetown: The island was discovered by the Portuguese in 1536, but throughout its colonial history, which ended with the Declaration of Independence in 1966, Barbados was under British sovereignty. This is strongly reflected in the old capital of Bridgetown which has a decidedly English character; so much so that there is even a miniature of London's Trafalgar Square, complete with a statue of Lord Nelson. The city is small and there are many excellent walking tours. Places worth a visit include the **Fairchild Market**, **St Michael's Cathedral** (built in 1789), **Belleville**, **Government House**, the **Barbados Museum**, the **Old Synagogue** and the **Garrison Savannah**. **Temple Yard** has a Rastafarian street market.
St John: There is a breathtaking view of the east coast from **St John's Parish Church**. The church's cemetery contains the grave of Ferdinando Paleologus, a possible descendant of the Byzantine Emperors.
Codrington College: Situated near Consett Bay, and one of the oldest schools of theology in the Western hemisphere, built in 1745.
Morgan Lewis Mill: Also in the east, this is a splendid example of a Dutch windmill from the days of the sugar cane planters. It has been completely restored and is open to the public.
Newcastle Coral Stone Gates: Situated in St Joseph, these gates were erected by 20th Century Fox for the film *Island in the Sun*, and the area affords a commanding view of the magnificent east coast beaches.
The East Coast Road: One of the most exciting drives on the island, with the Atlantic crashing over treacherous reefs on to the rugged and beautiful coast.
Andromeda Gardens: The array of exotic plants grown along terraced gardens makes this the prettiest area of St Joseph.
Welchman Hall Gully: Owned by the National Trust, this botanic garden in St Thomas is home to many rare fruit and spice trees.
Holetown (St James): The monument in the town gives the date of the founding of Barbados' first settlement by the English as being 1605, although this event in fact took place in 1627. There are still a few structures dating from that time. **St James**, the first church, still retains a 17th-century font, and a bell inscribed 'God bless King William, 1696'.
Harrison's Cave (St Thomas): This eerie, luminous cavern makes a spectacular excursion. Completely lit, one can see

every part from a special train which takes the visitor on a mile-long ride underground. It is open every day 0900-1600.
Flower Forest: A 50-acre botanical garden in which can be found almost every plant that grows on Barbados. The grounds offer pleasant walks and spectacular views of **Chalky Mountain**, the Atlantic Ocean and **Mount Hillaby**.
Bathsheba: Small pastel-coloured houses cling to the chalky cliffs that rise above the Atlantic.
Potteries: This village is famous for its ceramic artworks.
Gun Hill Signal Station: Notable both for its splendid view of **St George's Valley** and for the lion carved out of a rock by a British soldier in the days when **Gun Hill** was an army look-out point.
St George's Church: 18th-century, and worth a visit for its wonderful altarpiece.
Platinum Coast: This beautiful stretch of coast is also known as **Millionaires Row**. There are fine beaches of white sand and clear, turquoise waters.
Speightstown: Typical West Indian village, with attractive wooden houses, shops and old churches.
Animal Flower Cave: A cavern carved out by the sea with coral rock tinted almost every imaginable colour.
Farley Hill: Once a fine plantation house, now in ruins, still covered in hibiscus and poinsettias.
St Nicholas Abbey: Another plantation house, graced with Persian arches and well-kept gardens.
The Atlantic Coast: Take the inland road through sugar-cane country with little churches and tiny towns with pretty houses. See the dramatic view from **Crane Beach**.
Sam Lord's Castle: Once an old plantation house, but now a hotel, beautifully decorated with furniture made from Barbados mahogany.
Barbados Wildlife Reserve: Wildlife, some indigenous and some introduced to the island, roams free in a mahogany forest. Animals that visitors may expect to see during their visit include green monkeys, tortoises, deer, wallabies, pelicans and otters. There is also a screened aviary where peacocks, turkeys, toucans, macaws, lovebirds, parrots and an iguana may be viewed.

Sport & Activities

Watersports: Barbados is fringed by coral reefs which host a variety of marine life and offer excellent **scuba-diving** and **snorkelling**. Sea horses, frog fish, giant sand eels and the hawksbill turtle are among the creatures to be found around the island. Dive operators will provide equipment, advice and guided tours. Carlisle Bay near Bridgetown has 200 wrecks and is a good venue for beginners. Folkstone Marine Park features the popular wreck of the *Stavronikita*. The best conditions for **windsurfing**, **jet-skiing**, **parasailing** and **water-skiing** are on the south and west coasts. Crane Beach on the southeastern side is a pink-tinged stretch of sand that is ideal for **bodysurfing** but too rough for swimming. There is also good, regular **surfing** at the Soup Bowl, South Point and Rockley Beach. All watersports are easy to arrange.
Fishing: Boat chartering is available for game fishing, spin fishing and inshore fishing. Game fishing tournaments are held regularly, with the highlight of the deep-sea season being the *Mutual/Mount Gay International Tournament* in April.
Golf: There are three 18-hole courses (*Royal Westmoreland*, designed by Robert Trent Jones Junior, *Sandy Lane* and the *Barbados Golf Club*) and three 9-hole courses (*Rockley*, *Almond Beach Village* and *Belair*). Reservations are usually required and instruction is available at all levels.
Spectator sports: Cricket is the national obsession and can be enjoyed virtually all year round, both at national and club level. Test matches and the Inter-Caribbean Shield competition are played at the *Kensington Oval* in Bridgetown. Many of the great names of West Indian cricket are from Barbados, most notably Sir Garfield Sobers. There are 20 **horse racing** meetings at the *Garrison Savannah* during the year's two main seasons (January to March and May to October), the highlight of which is the *Sandy Lane Gold Cup Race*, held on the first Saturday in March. **Polo** is played to a high level throughout the year.
Other: Stables and horses are available and **horseriding** along the beach at sunset can be arranged. *The Barbados National Trust* organises regular guided **hikes**, as advertised in their 'Calendar of Hikes'. The hikes, which last for approximately three hours, begin at 0600, 1530 and 1730. Participants on evening (moonlight) walks need to bring a torch. For further details, contact the tourist board (see *Contact Addresses* section).

Social Profile

FOOD & DRINK: There are a great many restaurants offering both international and traditional Bajan cuisine at a variety of prices. Local specialities include flying fish,

Credit: © Barbados Tourism Authority

lobster and crane chubb. The sea urchin (oursin or sea egg) is a particular speciality. Other local foods include sweet potatoes, plantains, breadfruit, yams and such fruits as avocados, pears, soursops, pawpaws, bananas, figs and coconuts. An exchange 'Dine Around' system is operated between some hotels of the same class and guests can eat at other hotels for no extra cost.
Local drink specialities include all types of rum-based cocktails, rum punch, planters punch, pina coladas and sangria. The local beer is *Banks*. The two most famous rums are *Cockspur's Five Star* and, for the connoisseur, *Mount Gay* (the oldest rum blend on the island). There are numerous bars which emulate the British pub and serve genuine British bitter and stout.
NIGHTLIFE: Nightclubs, discos and bars provide entertainment including limbo dancing, fire-eaters, steel bands and dance bands. There is a small cover charge. As in all Caribbean countries, swinging nightspots tend to come and go with seasons. Coastal boat trips with live entertainment are very popular; most sail twice daily and run buffets, bars and live music.
SHOPPING: Shopping is a delight and there is a wide range of goods with visitors being able to take some purchases home duty-free on production of their passport and air ticket. Liquor and cigarettes are sent to the airport or port for collection on departure. Other items can be taken away at point of purchase. Prices tend to be on the high side, though for such things as jewellery, clothing and ceramics, the high quality often makes the expense worthwhile. Special purchases include rum, straw goods, coral and shell jewellery, prints (*batik*) and woodcraft.
Shopping hours: Mon-Fri 0900-1700, Sat 0830-1600 (supermarkets are open longer on Saturdays).
SPECIAL EVENTS: All details are available in *The Visitor*, published weekly, and *The Sunseeker*, published fortnightly, available in most hotels. The following is a selection of special events occurring in Barbados in 2005; for a complete list and exact dates, contact the Barbados Tourism Authority (see *Contact Addresses* section):
Jan 10-16 *Barbados Jazz Festival*. **Feb** *Barbados International Polo Challenge 2005*. **Feb 13-20** *Holetown Festival*. **Mar** *Barbados Sandy Lane Gold Cup*. **Mar 24-27** *Congaline Festival*. **Mar 26-28** *Oistins Fish Festival*. **May 27-Jun 3** *International Folk Festival*. **May 28-29** *Barbados Rally Carnival*. **Nov 20** *National Fun-Walk*. **Dec 2-4** *Run Barbados Festival*.
SOCIAL CONVENTIONS: Social attitudes, like administration and architecture, tend to echo the British provincial market town. However, the optimistic attitude, laid-back manner and wonderful sense of humour of the Bajans is well appreciated by many tourists. Casual wear is acceptable in most places. Dressing for dinner in hotels and restaurants is suggested. Smoking is generally unrestricted.
Tipping: In restaurants or nightclubs, tips are usually 10 to 15 per cent. Porters' tips are at the customer's discretion.

Business Profile

ECONOMY: The Bajan economy traditionally relied on sugar production but persistently low world market prices forced the government to promote economic diversification. Most effort has concentrated on tourism, which is now the largest employer on the island and continues to show steady growth. Cotton, flowers and plants are being developed as export products. New light industrial projects, such as electronic components, have fared less well, mainly as a result of falling demand in the USA – the principal export market. The island's other important industry is oil. Two-thirds of offshore output is exported, with the remainder assigned for domestic consumption. Exploration activities have been intensified since the mid-1990s. In the service sector, Barbados has developed an 'offshore' financial industry that now accounts for 15 per cent of GDP. Barbados receives some overseas aid from British and US sources and is a member of the Caribbean economic community, CARICOM, which has boosted regional trade. The island has a good transport and communications infrastructure, which should assist future economic development. The main trading partners are the USA, UK and the other CARICOM nations.
BUSINESS: Lightweight tropical suits and shirt and tie are recommended. European courtesies should be observed.
Office hours: Mon-Fri 0800-1600.
COMMERCIAL INFORMATION: The following organisation can offer advice: Barbados Chamber of Commerce and Industry, 1st Floor, Nemwil House, Collymore Rock, St Michael, W1 (tel: 426 2056 *or* 0747; fax: 429 2907; e-mail: bdscham@caribsurf.com; website: www.bdscham.com) *or* Barbados Investment & Development Corporation, PO Box 1250, Pelican House, Princess Alice Highway, Bridgetown (tel: 427 5350; fax: 426 7802; e-mail: bidc@bidc.org; website: www.bidc.com).
CONFERENCES/CONVENTIONS: For the business traveller, conference organiser or incentive group, there is a number of hotels with conference and meeting facilities. There is also a selection of conference centres, the newest being the Sherbourne Conference Centre. Located 3km (2 miles) from Bridgetown, it is adjacent to the main highway linking the south and west coast. The centre is fully air conditioned and equipped to handle seminars, meetings, international conferences, trade shows and exhibitions. Restaurants and cafe facilities are available to seat 120 and 300 persons respectively. For more information, contact the Barbados Conference Services Ltd, Sherbourne Conference Centre, Two Mile Hill, St Michael (tel: 467 8200; fax: 431 9795; e-mail: sales@sherbournecentre.com; website: www.sherbournecentre.com).

Climate

The balmy, tropical climate is cooled by constant sea breezes but is still sunnier and drier than the other islands. The dry season is from December to June; during the so-called wet season (July to November) some brief rain showers are likely. Average sunshine hours per day are eight to 10 from November to March and eight to nine from April to October.
Required clothing: Lightweight cottons are advised; beachwear is not worn in towns.

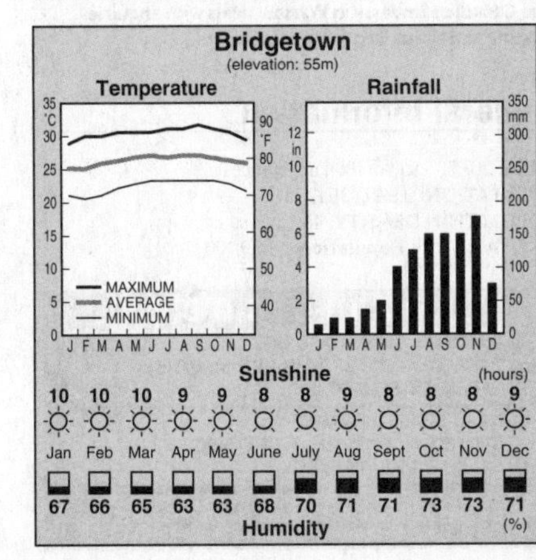

A B C D E F G H I J K L M N O P Q R S T U V W X Y Z

Belarus

LATEST TRAVEL ADVICE CONTACTS

British Foreign and Commonwealth Office
Tel: (0870) 606 0290 Website: www.fco.gov.uk

US Department of State
Website: http://travel.state.gov/travel

Canadian Department of Foreign Affairs and Int'l Trade
Tel: (1 800) 267 8376 Website: www.dfait-maeci.gc.ca

Location: Eastern Europe.

Country dialling code: 375.

Belintourist
19 Masherov Avenue, 220004 Minsk, Belarus
Tel: (17) 226 9840 *or* 9056 *or* 9971 (tourism).
Fax: (17) 223 1143.
E-mail: incoming@belintourist.by (tourism) *or* marketing@belintourist.by (marketing).
Website: www.belintourist.by

Embassy of Belarus
6 Kensington Court, London W8 5DL, UK
Tel: (020) 7937 3288 *or* 7938 3677 (visa section).
Fax: (020) 7361 0005.
E-mail: uk@belembassy.org
Website: www.belembassy.org/uk
Opening hours: Mon-Fri 0900-1800; 0930-1230 (visa section).

British Embassy
Karl Marx 37, 220030 Minsk, Belarus
Tel: (17) 210 5920/1 *or* 229 2310 (visa and consular section). Fax: (17) 229 2306 *or* 2311 (visa section).
E-mail: britinfo@nsys.by
Website: www.britishembassy.gov.uk/belarus

Embassy of Belarus
1619 New Hampshire Avenue, NW, Washington, DC 20009, USA
Tel: (202) 986 1604 *or* 1606 (consular section).
Fax: (202) 986 1805.
E-mail: usa@belarusembassy.org
Website: www.belarusembassy.org

United States Embassy
46 Starovilenskaya Street, 220002 Minsk, Belarus
Tel: (17) 210 1283. Fax: (17) 234 7853.
E-mail: minskinfo@state.gov
Website: http://minsk.usembassy.gov

Embassy of the Republic of Belarus
130 Albert Street, Suite 600, Ottawa, Ontario K1P 5G4, Canada
Tel: (613) 233 9994. Fax: (613) 233 8500.
E-mail: belamb@igs.net

The Canadian Embassy in Warsaw deals with enquiries relating to Belarus (see *Poland* section).

General Information

AREA: 207,595 sq km (80,153 sq miles).
POPULATION: 9,990,435 (2001).
POPULATION DENSITY: 48.1 per sq km.
CAPITAL: Minsk. **Population:** 1,699,100 (2001).

TIMATIC CODES

Health	AMADEUS: **TI-DFT/MSQ/HE** GALILEO/WORLDSPAN: **TI-DFT/MSQ/HE** SABRE: **TIDFT/MSQ/HE**
Visa	AMADEUS: **TI-DFT/MSQ/VI** GALILEO/WORLDSPAN: **TI-DFT/MSQ/VI** SABRE: **TIDFT/MSQ/VI**

To access TIMATIC country information on Health and Visa regulations through the Computer Reservations System (CRS), type in the appropriate command line listed above.

GEOGRAPHY: Belarus is bordered by Latvia, Lithuania, Poland, Ukraine and the Russian Federation. It is covered largely by forests and lakes which are rich in wildlife and is crossed by major rivers such as the Dnieper.
GOVERNMENT: Republic since 1991. **Head of State:** President Aleksandr Lukashenka since 1994. **Head of Government:** Prime Minister Henadz Navitski since 2001.
LANGUAGE: The official languages are Belarusian and Russian.
RELIGION: Christian, mainly Eastern Orthodox and Roman Catholic with small Protestant, Jewish and Muslim communities.
TIME: GMT + 2 (GMT + 3 from last Sunday in March to Saturday before last Sunday in October).
ELECTRICITY: 220V, 50Hz. Adaptors are recommended.
COMMUNICATIONS: Telephone: IDD is available to all major cities, including Minsk (17) and Brest (162). Country code: 375. To make international calls it is necessary to dial 8, wait for a tone, then dial 10. Calls from Belarus to some countries must be booked through the international operator. Public telephones take cards. Grey booths are for internal calls and blue ones for international calls. **Mobile telephone:** GSM 900 network covers Minsk and other towns. Main operators are *Velcom* (website: www.velcom.by) and *MTS* (website: www.mts.by). Coverage is limited to main towns. Handsets can be hired at the airport (*Belcel* office) and in Minsk. **Fax:** Services are available in all larger hotels in Minsk and other big cities. Faxes can also be sent from any of the state telegraph offices or from business centres. There are some public fax facilities. **Internet:** There are a few Internet cafes in Minsk. Access is also available at some post offices. Local ISPs include *Belpak* (website: www.belpak.by) and *Solo* (website: www.solo.by). **Telegram:** These can be sent from hotels and telephone offices. **Post:** Airmail to Western Europe takes a minimum of 10 days. Larger hotels offer *Poste Restante* services. The Central Post Office (Minsk, Skoriny 10; open 0730-2300) and the Yubileynaya and Planeta hotels in Minsk offer express mail services. DHL Worldwide Express and Federal Express also have branches in Minsk. **Press:** The English-language paper *Belarus Today* is published weekly. The principal dailies are *Belorusskaya Niva, Narodnaya Hazeta* and *Respublika*, all printed in Belarusian and Russian. *Sovetskaya Beloroussiya* is printed in Russian. *Zvyazda* is printed in Belarusian.
Radio: BC World Service (website: www.bbc.co.uk/worldservice) and Voice of America (website: www.voa.gov) can be received. From time to time the frequencies change and the most up-to-date can be found online.

Passport/Visa

	Passport Required?	Visa Required?	Return Ticket Required?
Full British	Yes	Yes	No
Australian	Yes	Yes	No
Canadian	Yes	Yes	No
USA	Yes	Yes	No
Other EU	Yes	Yes/1	No
Japanese	Yes	Yes	No

Note: *Regulations and requirements may be subject to change at short notice, and you are advised to contact the appropriate diplomatic or consular authority before finalising travel arrangements. Details of these may be found at the head of this country's entry. Any numbers in the chart refer to the footnotes below.*

PASSPORTS: Passport valid for six months after departure required by all.
VISAS: Required by all except the following:
(a) nationals of the CIS (except nationals of Turkmenistan, who *do* require visas);
(b) nationals of Cuba, Macedonia, Mongolia, **1.** Poland and Serbia & Montenegro, provided arriving from their country of origin, holding return tickets and travelling for touristic purposes for up to 30 days;
(c) transit passengers continuing their journey to a third country provided holding valid onward or return documentation and not leaving the airport.
Note: All foreign nationals must hold medical insurance and register their passports at the local police station within three days of their arrival. If staying at a hotel, reception will do this automatically.
Types of visa and cost: *Visitor* and *Business*: £40 (single-entry); £72 (double-entry); £104 (triple-entry); £200 (multiple-entry). *Tourist*: £19 (individual); £10 per person (group). *Transit*: £15 (single-entry); £27 (double-entry); £39 (triple entry); £50 (multiple-entry); £10 per person (group). Express visas are available for a higher fee.
Note: (a) *Tourist* visas are only available to those booking through a travel agency in Belarus or from a travel agency in another country which has an agreement with Belarus state travel and can supply state travel vouchers. (b) Children travelling on their parents' passports do not need a visa but must be accounted for on parents' visa application form.
Validity: *Visitor* and *Business*: 90 days (single-, double-, and triple-entry); one year (multiple-entry). *Tourist*: 30 days. *Transit*: 48 hours.
Application to: Nearest Consulate (or Consular section at Embassy); see *Contact Addresses* section. Visas can be obtained at Minsk-2 International Airport in exceptional cases, such as illness or death of a Belarusian relative, only provided the traveller is met at the airport by their official sponsor with the original letter of invitation or tourist vouchers. In this case, the fee may be higher.
Application requirements: (a) Valid passport with at least one blank page. (b) One application form. (c) One recent passport-size photo. (d) Fee (postal order or cheque only). (e) Stamped, self-addressed envelope for return of passport if applying by post, sent by recorded delivery. *Tourist*: (a)-(e) and, (f) Copy of tourist voucher. (g) Copy of the confirmation from a Belarusian travel agency, including registration number. *Business*: (a)-(e) and, (f) Letter of invitation from a registered Belarusian company, written on headed paper, including registration number, date of issue, official's signature, corporate seal and expected duration of stay. *Visitor*: (a)-(e) and, (f) Invitation from Belarusian resident endorsed by a local Belarusian Visa and Registration office. *Transit*: (a)-(e) and, (f) Visa for destination country, or, if no visa required, copy of the ticket or itinerary.
Note: Nationals of EU countries, Andorra, Argentina, Bahrain, Brazil, Bulgaria, Canada, Chile, Croatia, Iceland, Japan, Korea (Rep), Kuwait, Liechtenstein, Norway, Oman, Qatar, Saudi Arabia, South Africa, Switzerland, United Arab Emirates and Uruguay no longer need to submit formal letters of invitation to obtain *Visitor* and *Business* visas.
Working days required: Five, or 48 hours for express processing.

Money

Currency: The Belarusian Rouble (BYR). The Belarusian Rouble was devalued by a factor of 1000 on 1 Jan 2000 (1 new Rouble = 1000 old Roubles). Old banknotes are still in circulation and are worth one-thousandth of their face value. Notes are in denominations of BYR50,000, 20,000, 10,000, 5000,1000, 500, 100, 50, 10 and 5.
Currency exchange: Foreign currency should only be exchanged at banks, money-changing kiosks and official bureaux de change, and all transactions must be recorded on the currency declaration form which is issued on arrival. It is wise to retain all exchange receipts. Most aspects of a tour, including accommodation, transport and meals, are paid before departure (through *Belintourist* or a recognised tour operator), so large amounts of spending money are not necessary. The US dollar or Euros are the preferred foreign currencies. Some foreign currencies may be hard to exchange.
Credit & debit cards: Major European and international credit cards, including American Express, MasterCard and Visa are accepted in some larger hotels and at foreign currency shops and restaurants. Check with your credit or debit card company for details of merchant acceptability and other services which may be available.
Travellers cheques: May be accepted at larger banks, but cash is easier to exchange. To avoid exchange rate charges, travellers cheques should be taken in US dollars or Euros.
Currency restrictions: The import and export of local currency is prohibited. All remaining local currency must be reconverted at the point of departure. The import of foreign currency is unlimited, subject to declaration. The export of foreign currency is limited to the amount declared on arrival. Foreign banknotes and coins must be exported within two months of import.
Exchange rate indicators: The following figures are included as a guide to the movements of the Belarusian Rouble against Sterling and the US Dollar:

Date	Feb '04	May '04	Aug '04	Nov '04
£1.00=	3929.92	3858.87	3985.92	4130.16
$1.00=	2159.00	2160.50	2163.50	2181.00

Banking hours: Mon-Fri 0930-1730.

Duty Free

The following goods may be imported into Belarus without incurring customs duty by persons of 18 years and above: *1000 cigarettes or 1000g of tobacco products; 1.5l of spirits and 2l of wine; a reasonable quantity of perfume for personal use; other goods up to a value of US$10,000.*
Note: On entering the country, tourists must complete a customs declaration form which must be retained until departure. This records the import of articles intended for personal use, including currency and valuables. Customs inspection can be long and detailed.
Prohibited imports: Weapons and ammunition, narcotics, photographs and printed matter directed against Belarus, and fruit and vegetables. Contact the Embassy for further details of import restrictions (see *Contact Addresses* section).
Prohibited exports: Weapons and ammunition, precious metals, works of art and antiques (unless special permission has been granted by the Ministry of Culture) and furs.

Public Holidays

2005: Jan 1 New Year's Day. **Jan 7** Orthodox Christmas. **Mar 8** International Women's Day. **Mar 15** Constitution Day. **Mar 25-28** Catholic Easter. **Apr 29-May 2** Orthodox Easter. **May 1** Labour Day. **May 9** Victory Day. **Jul 3** Independence Day. **Nov 2** Dzyady. **Nov 7** Day of the October Revolution. **Dec 25** Christmas Day.
2006: Jan 1 New Year's Day. **Jan 7** Orthodox Christmas. **Mar 8** International Women's Day. **Mar 15** Constitution Day. **Apr 14-17** Catholic Easter. **Apr 21-24** Orthodox Easter. **May 1** Labour Day. **May 9** Victory Day. **Jul 3** Independence Day. **Nov 2** Dzyady. **Nov 7** Day of the October Revolution. **Dec 25** Christmas Day.

Health

	Special Precautions?	Certificate Required?
Yellow Fever	No	No
Cholera	No	No
Typhoid & Polio	1	N/A
Malaria	No	N/A

Note: Regulations and requirements may be subject to change at short notice, and you are advised to contact your doctor well in advance of your intended date of departure. Any numbers in the chart refer to the footnotes below.

1: Immunisation against poliomyelitis and typhoid is sometimes advised.
Other risks: Extensive epidemics of *diphtheria* were reported in the 1990s and immunisation may be recommended. There may be some risk of *tick-borne encephalitis*. Long-staying travellers should take precautions against *hepatitis A*. Certain foods should be avoided, especially dairy produce, mushrooms and fruits of the forest, as they may contain high levels of radiation as a long-term legacy of the Chernobyl disaster. Tap water should be filtered and boiled before drinking.
Rabies is present. For those at high risk, vaccination before arrival should be considered. If you are bitten, seek medical advice without delay. For more information consult the *Health* appendix.
Health care: There is a reciprocal health agreement with the UK. Hospital treatment, some dental treatment and some other medical treatment is normally free. Visitors can expect to pay for prescribed medicines. A UK passport must be shown to receive medical treatment. It is advisable to take out adequate health insurance. If the visitor does not have insurance, then medical insurance must be purchased from the State for US$1 per day. It is also advisable to carry an adequate supply of prescribed medicines which may be unobtainable in Belarus.

Travel - International

Note: Visitors should be aware of the potential for pickpockets and muggers and take necessary precautions. However, the majority of visits to Belarus are trouble-free.
AIR: The national airline is *Belavia* (B2), 5 Hobart Place, London SW1W 0HU, UK (tel: (020) 7393 1202; fax: (020) 7393 1203; e-mail: england@belavia.by; website: www.belavia.by). Other airlines serving Belarus include *Austrian Airlines*, *El Al Israel Airlines*, *LOT Polish Airlines* and *Lufthansa*.
Approximate flight times: From Minsk to *London* is 3 hours, to *Frankfurt/M* or *Vienna* is 2 hours 25 minutes, to *Moscow* is 1 hour 30 minutes and to *Zurich* is 3 hours.
International airports: *Minsk 2 (MSQ)* is 43km (27 miles) east of the city centre. Buses and taxis are available to the city centre (travel time - 60 minutes). Airport facilities include banks and bureaux de change, bars, car hire (*Avis*), duty-free shops, nursery, post office and restaurants.
Departure tax: None.
RAIL: All trains arrive and depart from Minsk Central Railway Station located in the centre of Minsk. There are several lines from Berlin via Warsaw and Brest with connections to Minsk. Another line runs from Vienna via Warsaw and Brest. Further direct trains are available from other cities including Kaliningrad, Moscow, Odessa, Riga and Vilnius.
ROAD: Tourists may drive their own cars or may hire cars from some larger hotels. Those entering by car should have their visas registered at the hotel, motel or campsite where they stay for the first night and are advised to insure their vehicle with a Belarusian insurance company, some of which have offices at crossing points and in major cities. There are also a number of other national and international insurance companies. The petrol supply is restricted and only 4-star and diesel are available. Petrol stations accept cash. The supply of petrol and service stations is best on the major routes (Europa highways/motorways) through the country. **Coach:** Coaches run from many points across Europe. There are three international bus stations in Minsk: Central Bus Station, Eastern (Vostochnaya) Bus Station and Moscow (Moskovskaya) Bus Station.

Travel - Internal

RAIL: There are 5488km (3410 miles) of track in use. Services run regularly from Minsk to all other towns. For more information contact Belarus Railways.
ROAD: Belarus has a road network of 51,547km (32,219 miles), most of which is hard-surfaced, although there are potholes and lighting is bad. Traffic drives on the right.
Regulations: International traffic signs and regulations are in use. Driving under the influence of alcohol is strictly forbidden. Speed limits are 60kph (37mph) in towns and cities and 90kph (55mph) on country lanes. There are frequent radar traps. **Documentation:** International Driving Permit required.
URBAN: Public transport is cheap and efficient. The city of Minsk has an underground system with two lines that cover central Minsk (16 stations). It is in the process of being expanded. Trains run between 0600-0100, buses, trams and trolleybuses between 0535-0055. Tickets for buses, trams and trolleybuses can be purchased at news-stands or kiosks and are to be punched on board. Entry to the underground is by tokens which are obtainable from stations. Taxis are available and carry a maximum of four passengers; fares can vary greatly.

Accommodation

HOTELS: There are 1-star hotels in Pinsk and other district centres of Belarus. Brest, Gomel, Grodno, Minsk, Mogilev and Vitebsk have 2-, 3- and 4-star hotels. The following organisations provide information on accommodation in Belarus: Belintourist (see *Contact Addresses* section); *or* Minsktourist Association, Tankavaya Street 30, Minsk (tel: (17) 223 7360; fax: (17) 223 9868; e-mail: info@minsktourist.com).
CAMPING: There are limited facilities for camping in Belarus. However, camping is permitted outside towns anywhere in the countryside, provided consideration is shown for other countryside users.

Resorts & Excursions

MINSK

The capital of Belarus, situated 340km (213 miles) northeast of Warsaw and 120km (75 miles) southeast of Vilnius, was first mentioned in 1067, but little of the old city now survives except a few 17th-century buildings. The city grew to be an important axis of communication and suffered badly during World War II. Modern Minsk is symmetrically designed with wide embankments flanking the **Svisloch River**. The cultural scene is very diverse with the Belarusian Ballet and good museums such as the **National Museum of Belarusian History and Culture**, the **National Arts Museum**, the **Museum of History of the Great Patriotic War** and the **Museum of Old Belarusian Culture**. Museums generally open Tues-Sun 1000-1900. The suburb of **Troitskoye Predmestye** should not be missed; it gives an insight into the way Minsk once looked – 19th-century houses with colourful facades line the streets. There are also excellent examples of Baroque architecture such as the **Cathedral of the Holy Spirit** (1642), the **Cathedral of St Peter and Paul** (1613) and the **Maryinsky Cathedral**, which has been rebuilt to its original shape.
EXCURSIONS: About 22km (14 miles) from the capital is the picturesque village of **Raubichi** with an interesting ethnographic museum housed in a disused church. Not far from Raubichi (10km/6 miles) is the idyllic **Minsk Lake** dotted with numerous islets and surrounded by dense pines. The **Museum of Folk Architecture** is situated in Ozerto (15km/ 10 miles southwest of Minsk), and features original pieces of century-old buildings from different regions in Belarus. The **Dudutki Museum of Material Culture** is to be found 40km/25 miles from the capital city and is the only private museum in Belarus showing traditional crafts and ways of life. The onion-shaped domes of Russian Orthodox churches dominate the landscape throughout the country, but especially around **Logoysk** (40km/25 miles from Minsk), **Krasnoe** (60km/38 miles from Minsk) and **Molodechno** (80km/50 miles from Minsk). The memorial at **Khatyn** commemorates its destruction by the German army during World War II.

BEYOND MINSK

Wide plains, picturesque villages, ancient castles and monasteries, deep forests, scenic landscapes, and thousands of lakes await visitors. Belintourist offers several one- and two-week itineraries with different themes catering for nature-lovers, culture fans and sport enthusiasts.
The village of **Zhirovitsa**, 190km (119 miles) from Minsk, is renowned for the beautiful 15th-century **Monastery of the Assumption**. Part of the monastery complex is a convent and a theological seminary (17th-18th century).
120km (75 miles) from Minsk is the small town of **Mir** where one can see the **Jewish Cemetery** and the 15th-century **Mir Castle** (a UNESCO-listed World Heritage Site). Nearby, historic **Nesvizh** still retains its old buildings. The former residence of the Radzivill family is one of the most attractive palaces in the country. It is surrounded by a large park with numerous lakes and elaborate gardens. Only a short walk away is the imposing Catholic Church designed by the 16th-century Italian architect Bernardoni.
Vitebsk, situated 270km (169 miles) from Minsk is the birthplace of the painter Marc Chagall. There is a cultural centre named after him, and his family house has been turned into a museum. The centre of Christianity during the time of Rus (the first Russian state) lay in the Slavic town of **Polotsk**. An excellent example of architecture of the period is the **Church of St Sophia**. Also worth a visit are the two castles nearby.
Brest is a popular place to visit. One of the highlights is a tour of the **Brest Fortress** which was used to repel the German forces during World War II. Inside the Fortress is a museum which chronicles its history back to the 13th century. This history is further illustrated by a fascinating selection of exhibits in the **Museum of History and Archaeology**. In the surrounding countryside, time appears to have stood still for centuries; 500-year-old trees can be found in the nature reserve **Balvezhskaya Pushcha**. Wild European bison roam the area. Brest also has a famous puppet theatre that is worth seeing.
In **Grodno**, the fifth-largest city of Belarus, major sites are the Old Town centre, the **Kalozh-Church** and the **Old Castle** (both from the 11th century). The north and northwest, near the borders of Lithuania and Latvia, are dominated by the **Braslav Lake District**. It is a good area for watersports, with a total of 30 lakes situated in an atmospheric forest. Accommodation in the area is usually in small dachas along the lakeshore. **Belavezha Wood** is one of the last sites where rare animals such as bisons, bears and wolves can still be seen living in their natural habitat. Long scenic hiking trails are scattered throughout the **Nature Reserve of Berezinsky**, stretching from the source of the Berezina to **Palik Lake**. Primeval forests, marshland, deep rivers and a rich fauna and flora dominate this unique region, hence its UNESCO listing as a protected biosphere.

Sport & Activities

Minsk was one of the venues of the 1980 Olympic games and has excellent sports facilities. **Tennis**, **gymnastics**, **athletics**, **swimming**, **football** and **ice hockey** are just some of the sports which are on offer. Excellent **cross-country skiing** is available in the nature reserve near the Minsk campsite. **Skating** is also popular. **Hiking** is possible throughout Belarus. The *Braslav Lake District* situated in the north and northeast of the country is ideal for **boating** holidays. Several of the 30 lakes are connected by canals.

Social Profile

FOOD & DRINK: Belarusian *borshch*, a soup made with beetroot, is served hot with sour cream. Other excellent specialities are *filet à la Minsk* and Minsk cutlet. Regional cooking is often based on potatoes with mushrooms and berries as favourite side dishes. Local dishes well worth trying are *dracheny*, a tasty potato dish with mushrooms, and *draniki* which is served with pickled berries. There is also a good selection of international and Russian specialities available.
Beloveszhskaya Bitters are made from over 100 different herbs and have an interesting flavour. A favourite drink is *chai* (black tea). Coffee is generally available with meals and in cafes, although standards vary. Some bars are open until the early hours of the morning.
NIGHTLIFE: A thriving cultural scene with opera, ballet, theatre, circus and puppet theatre can be found in Minsk. Brest also has a renowned puppet theatre. Tickets can be bought in advance at underground stations or at the Central Theatre Ticket Office (Skoriny 13; opening hours: Mon-Sat 0930-2000, Sun 1100-1700). Same-day tickets are only available at the venue in question. Minsk has a reasonable selection of restaurants. There are also discos, music venues and bars.
SHOPPING: Wooden caskets, trinket boxes, straw items, decorative plates and other handicraft items are good buys. Typical Russian souvenirs like the wooden *matreshka* dolls and original *samovars* are also available. Scarina Avenue is the main street with antique shops and two department stores. Only Belarusian Roubles are accepted. However, nearly every shop has a currency exchange counter. Some shops are closed on Sunday, but tourist shops are usually open every day. Antiquities, valuables, works of art and manuscripts other than those offered for sale in souvenir shops require an export licence. **Shopping hours:** Mon-Sat 0900-1900. In big cities shops are open daily and many open 24 hours a day.
SPECIAL EVENTS: The following is a selection of special events occurring in Belarus in 2005; for a complete list and exact dates, contact the Embassy (see *Contact Addresses* section): **Jan** *National Convention of Belarusian Composers*. **Jun** *Festival of Poetry*, Lake Svityaz. **Jul 14-20** *14th International Festival - 'Slavic Bazaar in Vitebsk'*. **Oct** *International*

Theatre Festival. **Nov** *Belarusian Musical Autumn*, Minsk.
SOCIAL CONVENTIONS: Handshaking is the usual form of greeting. Hospitality is part of the tradition and people are welcoming and friendly. Company or business gifts are well received. Smoking is acceptable unless stated otherwise. **Tipping:** 10 per cent is usual. In some hotels in Minsk and other cities a 10 to 15 per cent service charge is added to the bill. Porters expect a tip of US$1-2.

Business Profile

ECONOMY: Despite a paucity of natural resources, Belarus enjoyed a relatively high level of prosperity during the Soviet era compared to other ex-Soviet republics. However, the last 12 years have brought continuous decline. The main agriculture crops are sugar beet, grain and potatoes; livestock breeding is also substantial. The manufacturing industry is focused on the production of agricultural machinery vehicles and chemicals, most of which have been exported in the past. Apart from a few oil and gas deposits, Belarus has no energy reserves and relies on imports, most of which come from the Russian Federation. Like other Soviet republics, Belarus suffered a sharp decline in output and a variety of other problems following the dissolution of the Soviet Union; this was then followed by a period of stabilisation, which took hold during the mid-1990s as the government and people adjusted to new economic circumstances. A new currency, the Belarusian Rouble, was introduced at the beginning of 1995. The economy recorded GDP growth of 6.8 per cent in 2004, however, it still suffers from high inflation of about 28 per cent. Reluctance to implement measures recommended by the IMF, World Bank and the EBRD (which Belarus joined in 1992) has limited access to these sources of finance. The government has since been engaged in a tentative programme of privatisation. In 2002, 200 state-owned enterprises in the Minsk area were privatised; the government has (under Russian pressure) committed itself to selling major national enterprises.
Membership of the World Trade Organization is another government objective. Belarus' trade is largely conducted with the countries of the former Soviet Union. In 2002, these accounted for two-thirds of Belarusian trade (nearly 80 per cent of that was with Russia). Most of the remaining trade was with the EU, USA and Japan. Belarus has been trying to develop its trade links with the Arab world, especially Iraq and the Syrian Arab Republic, with limited results.
BUSINESS: For business meetings, visitors should dress smartly. English is widely used in management circles and knowledge of German might also be useful. Appointments should be made well in advance and should be confirmed nearer the time. Cards should have a Russian translation on the back. Business transactions are likely to take quite a long time. **Office hours:** Mon-Fri 0830-1730.
COMMERCIAL INFORMATION: The following organisation can offer advice: Belarusian Chamber of Commerce and Industry, ul. Ya. Kolasa 65, 220113 Minsk (tel: (17) 226 0473; fax: (17) 226 2604; e-mail: secret@mdbcci.belpak.minsk.by; website: www.cci.by).
CONFERENCES/CONVENTIONS: The 3-star Hotel Yubileynaya offers conference facilities for up to 250 persons, including simultaneous translation services. This facility is operated by Belintourist (see *Contact Addresses* section). The following organisation can also give information regarding conferences and conventions in Belarus: Ministry of Foreign Affairs, ul Lenina 19, 220030 Minsk (tel: (17) 227 2922; fax: (17) 227 4521; e-mail: mail@mfabelar.gov.by; website: www.mfa.gov.by).

Climate

Temperate continental climate.
Required clothing: Medium- to heavyweights in winter. Waterproofs are advisable throughout the year.

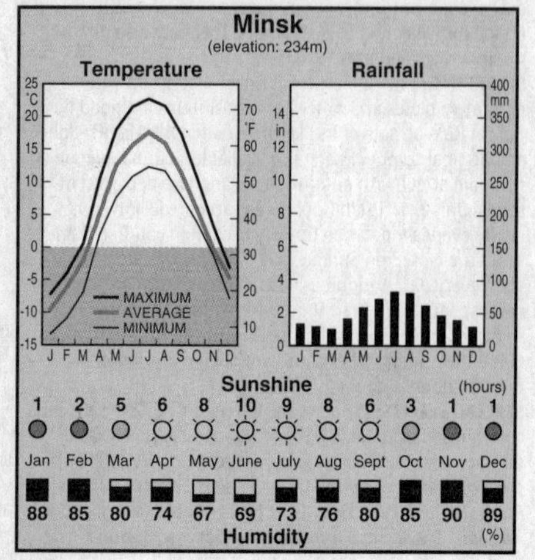

Belgium

LATEST TRAVEL ADVICE CONTACTS

British Foreign and Commonwealth Office
Tel: (0870) 606 0290 Website: www.fco.gov.uk
US Department of State
Website: http://travel.state.gov/travel
Canadian Department of Foreign Affairs and Int'l Trade
Tel: (1 800) 267 8376 Website: www.dfait-maeci.gc.ca

Location: Western Europe.

Country dialling code: 32.

Office de Promotion du Tourisme (Belgian Tourist & Information Office - Brussels & Wallonia)
rue Marché-aux-Herbes 63, B-1000 Brussels, Belgium
Tel: (2) 504 0390. Fax: (2) 513 0475.
E-mail: info@opt.be
Website: www.belgium-tourism.net
Toerisme Vlaanderen (Tourism Flanders-Brussels)
Grasmarkt 63, B-1000, Brussels, Belgium
Tel: (2) 504 0390. Fax: (2) 513 0474.
E-mail: info@toerismevlaanderen.be
Website: www.visitflanders.com *or* www.toervl.be
Brussels International – Tourism and Congress
Hôtel de Ville, City Hall, Grand-Place, B-1000 Brussels, Belgium
Tel: (2) 513 8940. Fax: (2) 513 8320.
E-mail: tourism@brusselsinternational.be
Website: www.brusselsinternational.be
Embassy of the Kingdom of Belgium
103-105 Eaton Square, London SW1W 9AB, UK
Tel: (020) 7470 3700 (general enquiries) *or* (09065) 508 963 (recorded visa information; calls cost £1 per minute) *or* 547 777 (visa appointments; calls cost £1.50 per minute).
Fax: (020) 7470 3795.
E-mail: belembvisa@ntlworld.com (visa section).
Website: www.diplobel.org/uk
Opening hours: Mon-Fri 0900-1300 and 1400-1700.
Office de Promotion du Tourisme (Belgian Tourist Office – Brussels & Wallonia)
217 Marsh Wall, London E14 9FJ, UK
Tel: (0906) 302 0245 (calls cost 60p per minute) *or* (0800) 954 5245 (brochure request line; toll-free in UK) *or* (020) 7531 0391 (trade enquiries only). Fax: (020) 7531 0393.
E-mail: trade@belgiumtheplaceto.be *or* info@belgiumtheplaceto.be
Website: www.belgiumtheplaceto.be
Toerisme Vlaanderen (Tourism Flanders - Brussels)
Flanders House, 1a Cavendish Square, London W1G 0LD, UK
Tel: (020) 7307 7730 (travel trade and press only) *or* (0800) 954 5245 (brochure request line; toll-free in UK) *or* (09063) 020 245 (live operator; calls cost 60p per minute). Fax: (020) 7307 7731.
E-mail: office@visitflanders.co.uk
Website: www.visitflanders.co.uk

TIMATIC CODES

Health
AMADEUS: **TI-DFT/BRU/HE**
GALILEO/WORLDSPAN: **TI-DFT/BRU/HE**
SABRE: **TIDFT/BRU/HE**

Visa
AMADEUS: **TI-DFT/BRU/VI**
GALILEO/WORLDSPAN: **TI-DFT/BRU/VI**
SABRE: **TIDFT/BRU/VI**

To access TIMATIC country information on Health and Visa regulations through the Computer Reservations System (CRS), type in the appropriate command line listed above.

British Embassy
rue d'Arlon 85 Aarlenstraat, B-1040 Brussels, Belgium
Tel: (2) 287 6211. Fax: (2) 287 6360 (press and public affairs section) *or* 6270 (consular section).
E-mail: brussels.visa.section@fco.gov.uk *or* consularsection.brussels@fco.gov.uk *or* ppa@britain.be
Website: www.britishembassy.gov.uk/belgium
Consulates in: Liège and Ghent.
Embassy of the Kingdom of Belgium
3330 Garfield Street, NW, Washington, DC 20008, USA
Tel: (202) 333 6900. Fax: (202) 333 3079 *or* 333 5457 (consular section).
E-mail: washington@diplobel.org
Website: www.diplobel.us
Consulates General in: Atlanta, Los Angeles and New York.
Belgian Tourist Office
220 East 42nd Street, Suite 3402, New York, NY 10017, USA
Tel: (212) 758 8130. Fax: (212) 355 7675.
E-mail: info@visitbelgium.com
Website: www.visitbelgium.com
Embassy of the United States of America
Regentlaan 27 boulevard du Régent, B-1000 Brussels, Belgium
Tel: (2) 508 2111 *or* 788 1200 (visa information and appointments service) *or* 508 2537 (consular section).
Fax: (2) 511 2725.
Website: http://brussels.usembassy.be
Embassy of Belgium
360 Albert Street, Room 820, Ottawa, Ontario K1R 7X7, Canada
Tel: (613) 236 7267. Fax: (613) 236 7882.
E-mail: ottawa@diplobel.org
Website: www.diplomatie.be/ottawa
Consulate in: Toronto
Consulate General in: Montréal.
Honorary Consulates in: Edmonton, Halifax (Dartmouth), Vancouver and Winnipeg.
Wallonia–Brussels Tourism Promotion Office (Belgium)
43 rue de Buade, bureau 525, Québec City, Québec G1R 4A2, Canada
Tel: (418) 692 4939 *or* (877) 792 4939 (toll-free in USA and Canada). Fax: (418) 692 4974.
E-mail: opt.walbru.quebec@videotron.net
Website: www.belgique-tourisme.qc.ca
Canadian Embassy
2 avenue de Tervueren, 1040 Brussels, Belgium
Tel: (2) 741 0611. Fax: (2) 741 0643.
E-mail: jps@dfait-maeci.gc.ca
Website: www.dfait-maeci.gc.ca/canadaeuropa/brussels

General Information

AREA: 30,528 sq km (11,787 sq miles).
POPULATION: 10,263,414 (official estimate 2001).
POPULATION DENSITY: 336.2 per sq km.
CAPITAL: Brussels (Bruxelles, Brussel). **Population:** 964,405 (2001).
GEOGRAPHY: Belgium is situated in Europe and bordered by France, Germany, Luxembourg and The Netherlands. The landscape is varied, the rivers and gorges of the Ardennes contrasting sharply with the rolling plains which make up much of the countryside. Notable features are the great forest of Ardennes near the frontier with Germany and Luxembourg and the wide, sandy beaches of the northern coast, which run for over 60km (37 miles). The countryside is rich in historic cities, castles and churches.
GOVERNMENT: Constitutional monarchy. The Kingdom of Belgium was established in 1830. In 1993, Belgium became a federal state comprising three autonomous regions. **Head of State:** King Albert II since 1993. **Head of Government:** Prime Minister Guy Verhofstadt since 1999.
LANGUAGE: The official languages are Dutch, French and German. Dutch is slightly more widely spoken than French, and German is spoken the least.
RELIGION: Mainly Roman Catholic, with small Protestant and Jewish communities.
TIME: GMT + 1 (GMT + 2 from last Sunday in March to Saturday before last Sunday in October).
ELECTRICITY: 220 volts AC, 50Hz. Plugs are of the round two-pin type.
COMMUNICATIONS: Telephone: Fully automatic IDD. For operator services, dial 1324. Country code: 32. Outgoing international code: 00. There are call boxes in all major towns and country districts. Some coinless cardphones and credit card phones are also available. Telecards are available from newsagents, railway stations and post offices. **Mobile telephone:** GSM 900 and 1800 networks provide coverage all over Belgium. Main operators include *BASE* (website: www.base.be), *Mobistar* (website: www.mobistar.be) and *Proximus* (website: www.proximus.be). **Internet:** Internet cafes are widely available. ISPs include *Belgacom* (website: www.belgacom.net). **Post:** Airmail takes two to three days to other West European destinations. *Poste Restante* facilities are available in main cities. Post office hours: Mon-Fri 0900-1600. **Press:** Principal daily newspapers are *La Lanterne*, *La Meuse*, *Le Soir* (French) and *De Gentenaar*, *De Standaard*, *Het Laatste Nieuws*, *Het Nieuwsblad*

(Dutch). There is an English-language magazine, *The Bulletin*, printed in Belgium.
Radio: BBC World Service (website: www.bbc.co.uk/worldservice) and Voice of America (website: www.voa.gov) can be received. From time to time the frequencies change and the most up-to-date can be found online.

Passport/Visa

	Passport Required?	Visa Required?	Return Ticket Required?
Full British	Yes	No	No
Australian	Yes	No	Yes
Canadian	Yes	No	Yes
USA	Yes	No	Yes
Other EU	1/2/3	No	No
Japanese	Yes	No	Yes

Note: *Regulations and requirements may be subject to change at short notice, and you are advised to contact the appropriate diplomatic or consular authority before finalising travel arrangements. Details of these may be found at the head of this country's entry. Any numbers in the chart refer to the footnotes below.*

Note: Belgium is a signatory to the 1995 **Schengen Agreement**. For further details about passport/visa regulations within the Schengen area, see the introductory section, *How to Use this Guide*.
PASSPORTS: Passport valid for at least three months beyond the period of intended stay required by all except:
(a) **1.** nationals of EU countries with a valid national ID card (except for nationals of Cyprus, Czech Republic, Estonia, Hungary, Latvia, Lithuania, Poland, Slovak Republic, Slovenia, Sweden and the UK, who *always* require a valid passport);
(b) nationals of Andorra, Liechtenstein, Monaco, San Marino and Switzerland, in possession of a national ID card.
(c) **2.** nationals of Andorra, Austria, France, Liechtenstein, Luxembourg, Monaco, Portugal, San Marino, Spain and Sweden with passports expired up to five years previously;
(d) **3.** nationals of Germany with a passport expired up to one year previously.
VISAS: Required by all except the following for stays of no more than three months within a six-month period:
(a) nationals referred to in the chart and under passport exemptions above;
(b) nationals of Argentina, Bolivia, Brazil, holders of BNO (British National Overseas) passports and 'look-alike' passport holders of British Overseas Territories (except Gribraltar), plus British Indian Ocean Territory, Henderson Islands, Pitcairn, Ducie & Oeno and the St Helen Islands and dependencies, Brunei, Bulgaria, Chile, Costa Rica, Croatia, El Salvador, Guatemala, Honduras, Hong Kong (SAR), Iceland, Israel, Korea (Rep), Macau (SAR), Malaysia, Mexico, New Zealand, Nicaragua, Norway, Panama, Paraguay, Romania, Singapore, Uruguay, Vatican City and Venezuela;
(c) nationals remaining within the airport on transit, except for the following nationals, who *always* require an Airport Transit visa: Afghanistan, Angola, Bangladesh, Congo (Dem Rep), Eritrea, Ethiopia, Ghana, Guinea, India, Iran, Iraq, Lebanon, Nigeria, Pakistan, Sierra Leone, Somalia, Sri Lanka, Sudan, Syrian Arab Republic and Turkey, if not possessing a valid residence permit for the EU member states or Andorra, Canada, Iceland, Japan, Liechtenstein, Monaco, Norway, San Marino, Switzerland or the USA.
Types of visa and cost: A uniform type of visa, the *Schengen* visa, is issued for tourist, business and private visits. All visas cost either £26 (short stay; up to 90 days) or £38 (long stay).
Note: Spouses and children (under 18 years) of EU nationals receive their visas free of charge (enquire at Embassy for details). The original marriage certificate, the spouse's passport and the birth certificate(s) for the child(ren) must be produced. Additional documents may also be required.
Validity: *Short-stay* (single- and multiple-entry): usually valid for six months from date of issue for stays of a maximum 30 or 90 days per entry. *Transit* (single- and multiple-entry): valid for a maximum of five days per entry, including the day of arrival. Visas cannot be extended and a new application must be made each time. *Schengen* collective visas are also available for group visits, subject to rules and regulations.
Application to: Consulate (or Consular Section at Embassy); see *Contact Addresses* section. The consulate operates an appointment system and all applicants must make an appointment before attending the visa section (tel: (09065) 540 777; for those who reside in the London area). Travellers visiting just one *Schengen* country should apply to the Consulate of that country; travellers visiting more than one *Schengen* country should apply to the Consulate of the country chosen as the main destination *or* the country they will enter first and to which they require a visa (if they have no main destination).
Application requirements: (a) Passport or official travel documents valid for at least three months after proposed stay with blank pages to affix visa stamp. (b) Completed application form. (c) One passport-size photo. (d) Proof of sufficient funds to cover stay and to cover return to country of origin/transit to onwards country, plus funds to cover any possible medical expenses. This includes access to at least €38 per day if residing with an individual in Belgium, or €50 per day if residing in a hotel. If applying with a guarantor, the guarantor must have a minimum net income (enquire at Embassy for further details). (e) Valid travel insurance, with a minimum cover of €30,000. (f) Proof of purpose of stay such as a letter of invitation from a host in Belgium, a return ticket or hotel booking. (g) Letter from employer or from solicitor or bank manager if self-employed. If a student, letter from school or college confirming attendance. (h) Stamped, self-addressed registered envelope for postal applications. If visiting friends or family in Belgium, sponsorship from person in Belgium must be submitted along with business letter (with proof that national is a paid employee), providing evidence of sponsor's income, and certified at the Town Hall at which sponsor is registered. (i) Fee payable by postal order only, or cash if in person. (j) Return ticket(s) to country of residence for some nationalities. (k) Documents substantiating the purpose and circumstances of the proposed visit. *Business*: (a)-(k) and, (l) Invitation letter from overseas business associate.
Note: Nationals may identify a Belgian national or alien residing or established legally, and for a long period, in Belgium, as guarantor for subsistence and medical/travel costs incurred, if national cannot guarantee their own ability to do so. The person acting as guarantor does not necessarily have to be the person who invites the national. If the national chooses to be covered by an undertaking of responsibility, the national must, within six months of the undertaking being legalised, report to the Belgian diplomat or Consular authorities. This rule also applies to nationals exempt from a visa requirement but wishing to gain access to the *Schengen* states on the basis of an undertaking of responsibility. Consult the nearest Consular section for the list of documents to be submitted that are necessary to legalise any undertaking of responsibility.
Working days required: 48 hours to eight weeks, depending on nationality and resident status, and whether applying by post or in person. Certain nationals must apply in person (contact Consulate or Consular section at Embassy for further details). Visa processing can, on some occasions, take up to three months.
Temporary residence: Persons wishing to take up temporary residence should make a special application to the Belgian Embassy.

Credit: © Tourisme Vlaanderen

Money

Single European currency (Euro): The Euro is now the official currency of 12 EU member states (including Belgium). The first Euro coins and notes were introduced in January 2002; the Belgian Franc was still in circulation until 28 February 2002, when it was completely replaced by the Euro. Euro (€) = 100 cents. Notes are in denominations of €500, 200, 100, 50, 20, 10 and 5. Coins are in denominations of €2, 1 and 50, 20, 10, 5, 2 and 1 cents.
Credit & debit cards: American Express, Diners Club, MasterCard and Visa are accepted as well as Eurocheque cards. Check with your credit or debit card company for details of merchant acceptability and other services which may be available. ATMs are plentiful.
Travellers cheques: Widely accepted. To avoid additional exchange rate charges, travellers are advised to take travellers cheques in Euros, Pounds Sterling or US Dollars.
Currency restrictions: There are no restrictions on the import and export of either local or foreign currency.
Exchange rate indicators: The following figures are included as a guide to the movements of the Euro against Sterling and the US Dollar:

Date	Feb '04	May '04	Aug '04	Nov '04
£1=	1.46	1.50	1.49	1.42
$1=	0.80	0.84	0.80	0.75

Banking hours: Mon-Fri 0900-1600.

Duty Free

The following goods may be taken into Belgium without incurring customs duty by travellers aged over 17 years arriving from non-EU countries:
200 cigarettes or 100 cigarillos or 50 cigars or 250g of tobacco; 2l of wine, 1l of spirits or 2l of sparkling wine or 2l of non-sparkling wine or 2l of fortified wine; 50g of perfume and 250ml of eau de toilette; other goods up to €64.45 or €24.79 for nationals under 15 years (subject to change – contact the Embassy for up-to-date information); 500g of coffee or 200g of coffee extract; 100g of tea or 40g of tea extract.
Prohibited items: Unpreserved meat products. Other unpreserved foodstuffs must be declared.
Abolition of duty-free goods within the EU: On June 30 1999, the sale of duty free alcohol and tobacco at airports and at sea was abolished in all of the original 15 EU member states. Of the 10 new member states that joined the EU on May 1 2004, these rules already apply to Cyprus and Malta. There are transitional rules in place for visitors returning to one of the original 15 EU countries from one of the other new EU countries. But for the original 15, plus Cyprus and Malta, there are now no limits imposed on importing tobacco and alcohol products from one EU country to another (with the exceptions of Denmark, Finland and Sweden, where limits *are* imposed). Travellers should note that they may be required to prove at customs that the goods purchased are for personal use *only*.

Public Holidays

2005: Jan 1 New Year's Day. **Mar 28** Easter Monday. **May 1** Labour Day. **May 5** Ascension Day. **May 15** Whit Sunday. **May 16** Whit Monday. **Jul 11*** Flemish Community Holiday. **Jul 21** Independence Day. **Aug 15** Assumption of the Blessed Virgin Mary. **Sep 27*** French Community Holiday. **Nov 1** All Saints' Day. **Nov 11** Armistice Day. **Dec 25** Christmas Day.
2006: Jan 1 New Year's Day. **Apr 17** Easter Monday. **May 1** Labour Day. **May 25** Ascension Day. **Jun 4** Whit Sunday. **Jun 5** Whit Monday. **Jul 11*** Flemish Community Holiday. **Jul 21** Independence Day. **Aug 15** Assumption of the Blessed Virgin Mary. **Sep 27*** French Community Holiday. **Nov 1** All Saints' Day. **Nov 11** Armistice Day. **Dec 25** Christmas Day.
Note: *Observed by the respective communities.

Health

	Special Precautions?	Certificate Required?
Yellow Fever	No	No
Cholera	No	No
Typhoid & Polio	No	N/A
Malaria	No	N/A

Note: *Regulations and requirements may be subject to change at short notice, and you are advised to contact your doctor well in advance of your intended date of departure. Any numbers in the chart refer to the footnotes below.*

Other risks: *Rabies* is present in a small number of animals. If you are bitten, seek medical advice without delay. For those at high risk, vaccination before arrival should be considered. For more information consult the appendix, *Health* section.
Health care: Medical care is expensive but of a high standard. There is a reciprocal health agreement with the UK. It allows UK citizens a refund of up to 75 per cent of medical costs. To take advantage of the agreement, UK citizens should obtain form E111 from the post office *before* departure.

Travel - International

AIR: Following the bankruptcy of Belgium's international carrier, *Sabena*, in 2001, Belgium's regional airline, *DAT* (*Delta Air Transport*), has launched its new European airline *SN Brussels Airlines (SN)*. 53 European destinations are served as well as others worldwide. For further information, check online (website: www.flysn.com).
Approximate flight times: From Brussels to *London* is 50 minutes and from Antwerp is 50 minutes. From Brussels to *Los Angeles* is 16 hours and to *New York* is 7 hours.
International airports: *Brussels Zaventem (BRU)* (website: www.brusselsairport.be) is 12km (8 miles) northeast of the city (travel time - 35 minutes). The *Airport City Express* train connects all three main railway stations (Brussels North, Central and South) with the airport, running every 15 minutes, 0600-0000 (travel time - 15-20 minutes). The airport station is located on level one below the terminal. Other trains also depart frequently for the city and for destinations all over Belgium. Coaches depart from the airport bus station on ground level for major cities in Belgium, France and The Netherlands. Buses run regularly to and from the city and the bus station is located below the Arrivals Hall. Taxis to the city cost approximately €30, and are only available from outside the Arrivals Hall; all licensed taxis are recognisable by their yellow and blue license emblems. Hotel courtesy coaches go to Holiday Inn, Novotel and Sofitel. There are helicopter services to and from Antwerp, Ghent and Kortrijk. Airport facilities include car parking, car hire (*Alamo*, *Avis*, *Budget*, *Europcar*, *Hertz* and *Sixt*), post office, banks, bureaux de change, bars, restaurants, incoming and outgoing duty-free shops, medical facilities, computer and fax facilities and conference and business facilities.
Antwerp (ANR) (Deurne) (website: www.antwerpairport.be) is 2km (1.2 miles) east of the city. There is a regular bus service (no. 16) to Central Station. Taxis are available. Airport facilities include an outgoing duty-free shop, car hire (*Budget* and *Hertz*), bank and bar/restaurant.
Ostend (OST) (website: www.ost.aero), 5km (3 miles) from the city, has car parking facilities, car hire, bureau de change, restaurant, bar and duty-free shop.
Charleroi (CRL) (*Brussels South Charleroi*) (website: www.charleroi-airport.com) is 5km (3 miles) from Charleroi and 46km (29 miles) from Brussels. Airlines serving the airports include Ryanair, which operates cheap flights to several European destinations from Charleroi. Buses depart every 30 minutes to Charleroi (travel time - 10 minutes). There are regular coaches to Brussels (travel time - 45 minutes). Airport facilities include automatic money changer, car hire (*Avis*, *Europcar*, *Hertz* and *TC Location*), cafe, business lounge and duty-free shop.
Liège (LGG). There are taxis and a regular bus service to the centre, 5km (3 miles) away.
Departure tax: None.
SEA: Antwerp is one of Europe's busiest commercial ports, but passenger services generally operate out of Ostend or Zeebrugge. *P&O Ferries* (tel: (08705) 202 020; website: www.ponsf.com) operates between Hull and Zeebrugge (travel time - 14 hours).
RAIL: The Belgium national railway, *Société Nationale des Chemins de Fer Belges (SNCB)* (website: www.sncb.be), operates frequent day and night trains to destinations in Andorra, Austria, Czech Republic, Denmark, France, Germany, Hungary, Italy, Luxembourg, The Netherlands, Poland, Switzerland and the UK. High-speed trains - *Trains à Grande Vitesse* or *TGV* - operate between Belgium and France, connecting Brussels with destinations in Brittany, on the French Atlantic coast, the Côte d'Azur and the French Alps. Cities that can be reached from Brussels by TGV include Bordeaux, Cannes, Chambéry, Lyon, Marseille, Nice, Perpignan, Rennes and Valence. TGV trains depart from Brussels and need to be booked in advance. Further high-speed trains are operated by *Thalys* (website: www.thalys.com), a service jointly run by the the Belgium, French, German and Dutch national railways. The main international Thalys trains link Brussels to Amsterdam (The Netherlands), Cologne (Germany) and Paris (France).
Rail passes: International rail passes include the Eurail and Euro passes, available to non-European residents and permitting unlimited travel in most European countries for a period of one or two months; and the *Interrail* pass, permitting unlimited travel in Europe to European residents. The *Benelux five-day Tourrail ticket* offers five days of unlimited travel within a period of 30 days by rail in Belgium, Luxembourg and The Netherlands. The *Rail Plus Senior card* is available to people aged over 60 and entitles the buyer to reductions of up to 25 per cent on international tickets in 19 European countries. For further information, contact *Rail Europe* (tel: (08705) 848 848; e-mail: reservations@raileurope.co.uk; website: www.raileurope.co.uk) *or Belgian National Railways* (tel: (020) 7593 2332; fax: (020) 7593 2333; e-mail: belrail@aol.com; website: www.raileurope.be *or* www.b-rail.be).
Channel tunnel: *Eurostar*, a service provided by the railways of Belgium, France and the UK, operates direct high-speed trains from London (*Waterloo International*) via the Channel Tunnel to Brussels (*Midi/Zuid*). The travel time from London to Brussels is 2 hours 40 minutes. For further information and reservations contact *Eurostar* (tel: (0870) 160 0052 (travel agents) *or* (08705) 186 186 (public; within the UK) *or* (+44 1233) 617 575 (public; outside the UK); e-mail: sales.enquiries@eurostar.co.uk; website: www.eurostar.com); *or Rail Europe* (tel: (08705) 848 848). Travel agents can obtain refunds for unused tickets from Eurostar Internet Contact Center, 2nd Floor, Kent House, 81 Station Road, Ashford, Kent TN23 1PP. Complaints and comments may be sent to Eurostar Customer Relations Travel Centre, 1-1-G Eurostar House, Waterloo Station, London SE1 8SE, UK. General enquiries and information requests must be made by telephone.
ROAD: There are good road links from most of the European countries. *Eurolines*, departing from Victoria Coach Station in London, serves destinations in Belgium. For further information, contact, *Eurolines* (52 Grosvenor Gardens, London SW1; tel: (08705) 143 219; website: www.eurolines.com *or* www.nationalexpress.com). **Channel Tunnel:** From the UK, all road vehicles are carried through the tunnel in shuttle trains running between the two terminals, one near Folkestone in Kent, with direct road access from the M20, and one just outside Calais with links to the A16/A26 motorway (Exit 13). Each shuttle is made up of 12 single- and 12 double-deck carriages, and vehicles are directed to single-deck or double-deck carriages depending on their height. There are facilities for cars and motorcycles, coaches, minibuses, caravans, campervans and other vehicles over 1.85m (6.07ft). Bicycles are provided for. Passengers generally travel with their vehicles. Heavy goods vehicles are carried on special shuttles with a separate passenger coach for the drivers. Terminals and shuttles are well equipped for disabled passengers. Passenger Terminal buildings contain a variety of shops, restaurants, bureaux de change and other amenities. The journey takes about 35 minutes from platform to platform and around 1 hour from motorway to motorway. Eurotunnel runs up to four passenger shuttles per hour at peak times, 24 hours per day. Services run every day of the year. For further information about departure times of shuttles at the French terminal, contact Eurotunnel Customer Information in Coquelle (tel: (3) 2100 6100). Motorists pass through customs and immigration before they board, with no further checks on arrival. Fares are charged according to length of stay and time of year and whether or not you have a reservation. The price applies to the car, regardless of the number of passengers or size of the car. Promotional deals are frequently available, especially outside the peak holiday seasons. Tickets may be purcased in advance from travel agents, or from Eurotunnel Customer Services in France or the UK with a credit card. For further information, brochures and reservations, contact Eurotunnel Customer Services UK, PO Box 2000, Folkestone, Kent CJ18 8XY (tel: (0800) 096 9992; e-mail: callcentre@eurotunnel.com; website: www.eurotunnel.co.uk).

Travel - Internal

AIR: As Belgium is such a small country, there are no internal flights. Bus services operate between Brussels airport to Antwerp, Ghent and Liège; see *Travel – International* section.
RAIL: SNCB operates a dense railway network with regular trains on most lines. On the main lines there are more frequent trains. For more information contact SNCB (website: www.b-rail.be). **Fares:** First- and second-class, single and return tickets are available. However, a return ticket is double the single fare and is only valid on the day of issue. Children from six to 11 years pay half price.
Discount travel: Weekend return fares are available from Friday (after 1900) to Sunday for the outward journey and on Saturday and Sunday for the return journey (on long holiday weekends, these periods are extended). A 50 per cent reduction card, valid for one month, is for sale. It entitles the holder to buy an unlimited number of half-price single tickets.
Go Pass offers 10 second-class trips for persons aged under 26 and *Multi Pass* (valid for one day) offers one return trip between any two stations for a minimum of two people and a maximum of five. The *Rail Pass* offers two people 10 single trips within 1 year. The *Golden Rail Pass* offers six first-class single journeys, between any two stations, to people aged 60 and over. Enquire at Rail Europe (tel: (08705) 848 848) for further information. For information on timetables, routes and special passes contact Belgian National Railways (tel: (020) 7593 2332; fax: (020) 7593 2333; e-mail: belrail@aol.com; website: www.b-rail.be).
Runabout tickets: The *Five-day B-Tourrail* ticket permits five days of unlimited travel within a period of 30 days on Belgian Rail. Principal stations in Belgium (and throughout Europe) are able to issue single and return tickets valid from the border to principal foreign stations (in conjunction with a *Tourrail* ticket). For details of *Benelux Tourrail* tickets, see the *Travel – International* section. The *Euro Domino* pass permits unlimited travel in any one European country for a period of three to eight days in any calendar month.
ROAD: There are many different brands of petrol available, and prices vary. Traffic drives on the right. Main towns are connected by toll-free motorways. It is compulsory for seat belts to be worn in the front and back of vehicles. Children under 12 are not permitted to travel in the front seat of a car. A warning triangle must be displayed at the scene of a breakdown or accident. It is compulsory to carry a fire extinguisher or first aid kit in all vehicles. The speed limit on motorways and dual carriageways is 120kph (75mph) with a minimum speed of 70kph (45 mph), on single carriageways outside built-up areas is 90kph (55mph), and in built-up areas is 50kph (31mph). Trams always have priority on roads. **Bus:** Extensive regional bus services are operated by the bus companies which publish regional timetables. There are long-distance stopping services between towns. **Taxi:** Plentiful in all towns. The tip is included in the final meter price. If there are no taxi stands, taxi companies may be telephoned for an extra charge of about €2.5. **Car hire:** Both self-drive and chauffeur-driven cars are available. The minimum age is 23 and the person must possess a valid full licence with at least one year of validity (and which will be required upon collection of the car). **Documentation:** A national driving licence is acceptable. EU nationals taking their own cars to Belgium must obtain a Green Card. The Green Card tops insurance cover up to the level of cover provided by the car owner's domestic policy.
URBAN: There is a good public transport system in all the major towns and cities, with underground, tram and bus services in Antwerp and Brussels, bus and tramways in Charleroi, Ghent and Ostend and bus systems elsewhere. There is a standard flat-fare system, with discounts for 5- and 10-journey multi-ride tickets. 1-day tickets and multi-mode tourist travelcards are also available.
Travel times: The following chart gives approximate travel times from **Brussels** (in hours and minutes) to other major cities and towns in Belgium and neighbouring countries.

	Air	Road	Rail
Paris	0.50	-	1.20
Amsterdam	0.40	-	3.00
Rome	2.00	-	20.00
Cologne	-	-	3.00
London	0.55	-	3.18
Arlon	-	3.00	2.20
Antwerp	-	0.40	0.41
Bruges	-	1.00	0.53
Ghent	-	0.50	0.28
Liège	-	1.10	1.22
Ostend	-	1.20	1.10
Namur	-	1.00	0.56

Accommodation

HOTELS: Belgium has a large range of hotels from luxury to small family pensions and inns. The best international-class hotels are found in the cities. For more information on hotels in Belgium, contact Belgian Tourist Office - Brussels & Ardennes or Tourism Flanders-Brussels (see *Contact Addresses* section) *or* one of the three regional hotel associations run by Horeca: Brussels-Flanders offices, BP 4, Anspachlaan 111, 1000 Brussels (tel: (2) 513 6484; fax: (2) 513 8954; e-mail: fed.brussel@horeca.be *or* fed.vlaanderen@horeca.be; website: www.horeca.be); Ardennes office, 83 Chaussée de Charleroi, 5000 Namen (tel: (81) 721 888; fax: (81) 737 689; e-mail: info@horecawallonie.be).
Grading: The Belgian Tourist Board issues a shield to all approved hotels by which they can be recognised. This must be affixed to the front of the hotel in a conspicuous position. Hotels which display this sign conform to the official standards set by Belgian law which protects the tourist and guarantees certain standards of quality. Some hotels are also graded according to the Benelux system in which standard is indicated by a row of 3-pointed stars, from the highest (**5-star**) to the minimum (**1-star**). However, membership of this scheme is voluntary, and there may be first-class hotels which are not classified in this way. If an establishment providing accommodation

facilities is classified under category H or above (1, 2, 3, 4 or 5 stars), it may call itself hotel, hostelry, inn, guest house, motel or other similar names. Benelux star ratings comply with the following criteria:
5-star: Luxury hotel, meeting the highest standards of comfort, amenities and service, 24-hour room service, à la carte restaurant, gift shop, parking and baggage service, travel and theatre booking service. **4-star:** First-class hotel, with lift, facilities for breakfast in the room, day and night reception, telephone in every room, radio, bar. **3-star:** Very good hotel, with lift (if more than two floors), day reception, guest wing (food and drink optional). **2-star:** Average-class hotel, with private bath and WC in at least 25 per cent of rooms, baggage handling facilities, food and drink available. **1-star:** Plain hotel, washstand with hot and cold water in every room, breakfast facilities available. **CAT H:** Very plain hotel, meets all the fire safety requirements and provides moderate standards of comfort, at least one bathroom for every 10 rooms and accessible to guests at night.
FARM HOLIDAYS: In some regions of the country, farm holidays are now available. In the Polders and the Ardennes visitors can (for a small cost) participate in the daily work of the farm. Further information can be obtained either from the Flemish Federation for Farmhouse and Rural Tourism, Minderbroederstraat 8, B-3000 Leuven (tel: (16) 242 158; fax: (16) 242 187; e-mail: hoevetoerisme@boerenbond.be; website: www.hoevetoerisme.be) *or* Belsud, 61 rue du Marché-aux-Herbes, 1000 Brussels (tel: (2) 504 0390; e-mail: info@opt.be; website: www.belgium-tourism.net). Belsud also provides information on bed & breakfast and self-catering accommodation.
SELF-CATERING: There are ample opportunities to rent furnished villas, flats, rooms, or bungalows for a holiday period. There is a particularly wide choice in the Ardennes and on the coast. These holiday houses and flats are comfortable and well-equipped. Rentals are determined by the number of bedrooms, the amenities, the location and the season. On the coast, many apartments, studios, villas and bungalows are classified into five categories according to the standard of comfort they offer. Estate agents will supply full details. For the Ardennes region, enquiries should be made to the local tourist office or to Belsud (for contact details, see above under *Farm Holidays*). Addresses of local tourist offices and lists of coastal estate agents can be obtained from Tourism Brussels-Ardennes/Tourism Flanders-Brussels.
YOUTH HOSTELS: There are two youth hostel associations: the Vlaamse Jeugdherbergcentrale (VJHC) (website: www.vjh.be) which operates in Flanders, and the Centrale Wallonne (CWAJ) (website: www.laj.be) operating in the French-speaking area. The hostels of the former are large, highly organised and much frequented by schools and youth groups; the hostels of the CWAJ are smaller and more informal, similar in some ways to those in France. A complete list of youth hostels and other holiday homes for young people can be obtained from Belgian Tourist Office - Brussels & Ardennes *or* Tourism Flanders-Brussels (see *Contact Addresses* section).
CAMPING/CARAVANNING: The majority of campsites are in the Ardennes and on the coast; many of these are excellent. A list of addresses, rates and other information can be obtained from the Belgian Tourist Office - Brussels & Ardennes or Tourism Flanders-Brussels (see *Contact Addresses* section). The local *Verblijftaks* or *Taxe de Séjour* is a tax usually included in the rates charged. On the coast during the summer season, a supplement of about 25 per cent is charged on the majority of tariffs. Camping out in places other than the recognised sites is permitted, provided the agreement of the landowner or tenant has been obtained.

Resorts & Excursions

The anachronistic images of 'boring Belgium' have been well and truly banished over the last decade as the country promotes its key destinations, along with a string of new attractions. Belgium always had a lot more going for it than the faceless political and bureaucratic buildings that litter its capital, Brussels, with a string of engaging cities in Bruges, Ghent, Liège - and Brussels itself - that offer impressive architecture, lively nightlife, first-rate cuisine and numerous other attractions for visitors. Then there is reinvented Antwerp, now a hotbed of fashion and modern design, and the more bucolic charms of the chocolate box beauty of the mountainous Ardennes region to the east, as well as the sweeping sand of the coastline resorts of the western seaboard.

BRUSSELS

Brussels is home to the European Union and NATO, amongst many other institutions, but beyond their facelessness, the city's architecture is a smorgasbord, with the gothic **Grand Place** the undoubted highlight. Other key sights in Brussels include **St Michael and St Gudule's Cathedral** and the **Mont des Arts** park, which links the upper and lower parts of the city. Then there is the elegant **Place Royale**, built between 1774 and 1780 in the style of Louis XVI, the **Museum of Ancient Art** and the **Museum of Modern Art**. The **Manneken-Pis**, and his less heralded sister the **Janneken Pis**, are statues that hint at the exuberance and irreverence of the 'Bruxellois', a spirit that reaches its zenith in the city's numerous bars which, along with the 1000 types of Belgian beer, are not to be missed. Among other areas worth exploring are the **Îlot Sacré**, the picturesque area of narrow streets to the northeast of the Grand-Place; the fashionable **boulevard de Waterloo**; the administrative quarter, a completely symmetrical park area commanding a splendid view of the surrounding streets; the **Grand Sablon**, the area containing both the flamboyant Gothic structure of the **Church of Our Lady of Sablon** and the Sunday antique market and, lastly, the **Petit Sablon**, a square surrounded by Gothic columns, which support 48 small bronze statues commemorating medieval Brussels guilds. A more modern attraction is the bizarre **Atomium**, a futuristic, atom-shaped aluminium tower built for the 1958 World Fair. One important out-of-town attraction is the **Battle of Waterloo site**, 18km (11 miles) to the south of Brussels, commemorating the battle that shaped the future of both Belgium and modern Europe, of which Brussels is now such a crucial hub. The *Brussels Card* now gives the visitor free access to 30-plus museums and also the use of public transport throughout the Brussels-Capital region, within a 72-hour period. This 'culture pass' is available at all participating museums - at the six sales offices of the Brussels Public Transport Company (STIB), at certain hotels and at the Brussels International Tourism Office (see Contact Addresses section), costing just €30.

FLANDERS

ANTWERP: Although still Europe's second-largest port, the city of Antwerp has moved on from its purely industrial past. Today, the inhabitants, or *Sinjoors* as they are known, are at the cutting edge of fashion and design with countless boutiques and shopping outlets across the city. This energy also surfaces in the trendy bars and hip nightclubs that have now joined the more traditional charms of the beer and gin bars that still pull in the more reserved drinkers. Beyond modern Antwerp the more traditional attractions complement the new, with the impressive **Grote Markt**, containing the **Town Hall** and the **Brabo Fountain**, which commemorates the legend of the city's origin and also the 18th-century **Groenplaats**, with its Rubens statue. The work of local artistic luminary Peter Paul Rubens surfaces all over Antwerp, most notably at the **Royal Museum of Fine Arts**, home to what is arguably the world's finest collection of his work. The **Rubens' House**, the magnificent 17th-century house where the painter lived and worked, contains works by the painter and his associates as do many other museums and churches. Antwerp's maritime heritage can be explored on tours of the port and also at the **Steen**, a 12th-century fortress now housing the **National Maritime Museum**, that overlooks the buzzing new city of today.
BRUGES: Bruges is a pure picture postcard with a perfectly preserved 'medieval heart' that can be explored from the comfort of a canal boat ride, which takes tourists around the myriad of waterways that lead to the city often being referred to as the 'Venice of the North'. Bruges offers a variety of attractions such as the **Lake of Love**, which in the Middle Ages was the city's internal port, the 14th-century **Town Hall** featuring a façade decorated with bas-reliefs and statues of a Biblical nature; the **Cathedral of the Holy Saviour**, a fine example of 13th-century Gothic architecture and home to many treasures; and the **Grote Markt** which was formerly the commercial hub of the city. Bruges boasts several good museums, including the **Groeninge Museum** which houses a comprehensive and fascinating collection of six centuries of Flemish paintings, from Jan van Eyck to Marcel Broodthaers. The **Memling Museum**, housed in the medieval **Saint John's Hospital**, is dedicated to the painter Hans Memling. The city is close to some excellent beaches and the fertile Polder region, dotted with abbeys and parks. The year 2002 was a big one for Bruges as its lively cultural and artistic scene was recognised with the award of *European City of Culture*.
GHENT: Bruges' perennial poor cousin has plenty to offer visitors today, with the lack of tourist crowds an attraction in itself. This old cloth centre was once the largest medieval city in Europe after Paris. The medieval heart of Ghent boasts many historic buildings, including three abbeys. Key attractions include **St Bavo's Cathedral**, place of Charles V's baptism and home to **The Adoration of the Mystical Lamb**, the Van Eyck brothers' masterpiece; the **Town Hall**, where the Treaty of Ghent was signed in 1576; the **Castle of the Counts**, a medieval castle surrounded by the **Lieve canal**; the 15th-century **Cloth Hall**; the medieval town centre with its old guild houses; the **Museum of Fine Arts**, and the **Museum of Industrial Archaeology**.
THE COAST AND WEST FLANDERS: The Belgian

Credit: © Tourisme Vlaanderen

coastline is a largely sandy affair that stretches for 67km (42 miles) from **Knokke** near the Dutch border to **De Panne** on the French border, with over a dozen resorts. Bathing in the sea is free on all beaches and there are facilities for sailing, sand yachting, riding, fishing, rowing, golf and tennis. Some of the best resorts are **Bredene**, **De Haan**, **De Panne**, **Lombardsijde**, **Nieuwpoort**, **Wenduine**, **Westende** and the town of **Ostend**, where Queen Victoria once took to the waters. **Knokke**, **Middelkerke** and **Ostend** are the liveliest resorts. Visiting the World War I battlefields is an increasingly popular activity, with a number of sites open with varying degrees of facilities. The killing fields of **Ypres** are the most accessible with a war museum, monuments, military cemeteries and the battlefields themselves all located around the town.

WALLONIA

LIÈGE: Liège opens up the other half of Belgian culture as it is a major city of Wallonia, the French-speaking portion of Belgium. A popular tourist destination, situated on the banks of the **Meuse**, with many reminders of a colourful and affluent past, Liège was independent for much of its history, ruled over by prince-bishops for 800 years. The view from the **Citadel** covers the old town, the most impressive part of the city. Liège boasts many fine museums with the highlights being **The Museum of Wallonian Life**, showcasing the unique culture of Wallonia; the **Museum of Wallonian Art**; the **Museum of Modern Art**, displaying the works of Corot, Monet, Picasso, Gauguin and Chagall, to name but a few; and the **Curtius Museum**, housing a large collection of coins, Liège furniture and porcelain. Liège's most notable buildings are the **Church of St James**, an old abbey church of mixed architecture, including an example of the Meuse Romanesque style, with fine Renaissance stained glass and the 18th-century **Town Hall**.
TOURNAI: The second-oldest city in Belgium dates back to the days of the Romans. World War II damaged much of the old town, but the **Cathedral of Our Lady** (12th century), boasts an impressive Belfry, which is the oldest in Belgium. The **Museum of Fine Arts** is one of the finest in Belgium, with works by Rubens and Bruegel, while the **Natural History Museum** is also worth visiting. **Minibel**, 28km (17 miles) outside the city at the **Château of Beloeil**, offers a display of scaled-down reproductions of many of Belgium's most interesting treasures and curiosities.
THE ARDENNES: This mountainous area is famous for its cuisine, forests, lakes, streams and grottoes. The **River Meuse** makes its way through many important tourist centres. The town of **Dinant**, in the Meuse valley, boasts a medieval castle, while its most famous landmark is the Gothic church of **Notre-Dame**. **Annevoie** has a castle and some beautiful water gardens, while **Yvoir Godinne** and **Profondeville** are well known for watersports. The old university town of **Namur**, with cobbled streets in its centre, has a cathedral, castle and many museums. Houyet offers kayaking and other assorted outdoor activities. The **River Semois** passes through **Arlon** and **Florenville**; nearby are the ruins of **Orval Abbey**, **Bouillon** and its castle, **Botassart**, **Rochehaut** and **Bohan**. The **Amblève Valley** is one of the wildest in the Ardennes and the grottoes in the **Fond de Quarreux** are one of the great

attractions of the region. Among these is the **Merveilleuse grotto** at **Dinant** and the cavern at **Remouchamps**. There are prehistoric caverns at **Spy**, **Rochefort**, **Hotton** and **Han-sur-Lesse**.

Sport & Activities

Cycling: A new network of cycling paths has been developed in the Ardennes region. Known as *RAVeL* (*Réseau Autonome des Voies Lentes* or 'independent network of slow paths'), the system is made up of disused railway lines and old canal towpaths, now reserved and adapted for the exclusive use of pedestrians, cyclists and wheelchair users. It will eventually consist of 2000km (1240 miles) of paths, which will be linked to similar paths in neighbouring countries. For further information, contact RAVeL (website: http://ravel.wallonie.be). Flanders, the more northerly and flatter part of the country, is just as well-equipped for cyclists. There are many kilometres of signposted cycling routes. Bicycles can be hired at larger railway stations and can be reserved in advance. They can very often be carried on trains at no extra expense. Many hotels will make arrangements for luggage to be taken to the next destination during cycling tours. Contact the tourist boards for further information (see *Contact Addresses* section).

Outdoor activities: Although a highly developed country, Belgium has some beautiful countryside. The hilly country in the Ardennes region features forests, lakes and caves. Flanders offers opportunities for coastal and forest walks. For further information about marked trails, contact the tourist boards (see *Contact Addresses* section). Numerous other activities can be practised, including **canoeing**, **kayaking**, **horseriding**, **caving**, **climbing** and **fishing**. A range of **watersports** is also available on the coast.

Brewery tours: Belgium is renowned for its hundreds of varieties of high-quality beer. There are beers of all colours and types, brewed using different methods and ingredients – wheat beers, fruit beers, red beers, amber ales and 'spontaneously fermented beers', to mention but a few. Each beer has its own distinctive glass and label. Six kinds of trappist beer, brewed by monks to ancient recipes, are made in Belgium. Some breweries are open to the public. Trappist breweries open to the public include the *Bières de Chimay* brewery at Bailleux and the *Rochefortoise* brewery at Eprave. Visits to the Rochefortoise brewery must be booked by fax and confirmed two days in advance. These beers can all be sampled in Belgium's many cafes, pubs and restaurants.

Gastronomy: Belgium's large number of excellent restaurants testifies to the high esteem in which the Belgians place good food. The country has the highest number of Michelin stars per head of the population, and is the only country in the world where US fast food chains have been consistently losing money. The visitor has an array of fine restaurants, sophisticated cafes, and pubs to choose from. Specialist tour operators offer gastronomy trips where visitors can learn how to cook Flemish dishes using local produce and beers.

Chocolate: Belgian chocolate has an excellent reputation. Some chocolate factories are open to the public, though it is often necessary to book in advance. The *Chocolate and Cocoa Museum* on the Grand-Place in Brussels is open from Tuesday to Sunday. The *Chocolaterie Jacques* in Eupen near Liège is open to the public from Monday to Saturday. Groups of more than 10 people need to book in advance.

World Wars I and II: Flanders contains Passendale and Ypres. These battlefields can be visited, and there are many museums commemorating the war dead and informing the visitor about the terrible events. The *In Flanders Fields Museum* (tel: (5) 723 9220) is an authority on the region and the impact the war made upon it. In Ypres at 2000 each day, the Last Post is sounded under the Menin Gate. A number of commemorative events are organised by the regional tourist boards.

Social Profile

FOOD & DRINK: Belgian cuisine is similar to French, based on game and seafood. Each region in Belgium has its own special dish. Butter, cream, beer and wine are generously used in cooking. Belgian chocolate, waffles and chips - preferably served with mayonnaise - are famous. Ardennes sausages and ham are renowned. Most restaurants have waiter service, although self-service cafes are becoming quite numerous. Restaurant bills always include drinks, unless they have been taken at the bar separately. In the latter case this is settled over the counter. Tips are also included in the final bill, although an additional tip may be left at the discretion of the individual.

Local beers are very good. Two of the most popular are *Lambic*, made from wheat and barley, and *Trappist*. Fruit beers, such as *Kriek* cherry beer, are a speciality. Under a new law, the majority of cafes now have licences to serve spirits. Beers and wines are freely obtainable everywhere and there are no licensing hours.

NIGHTLIFE: As well as being one of the best cities in the world for eating out (both for its high quality and range), Brussels has a very active and varied nightlife. It has 10 theatres producing plays in both Dutch and French. These include the *Théâtre National* and the *Théâtre Royal des Galeries*. The more avant-garde theatres include the *Théâtre Cinq-Quarante* and the *Théâtre de Poche*. Brussels' 35 cinemas, numerous discos and many night-time cafes are centred on two main areas: the uptown Porte Louise area and the downtown area between Place Roger and Place de la Bourse. Nightclubs include the famous *Chez Paul*, *Le Crazy*, *Le Grand Escalier* and *Maxim*; jazz clubs include *Bloomdido Jazz Cafe* and *The Brussels Jazz Club*. Programmes and weekly listings of events can be found in the *BBB Agenda* on sale at tourist offices. This also covers information on the many festivals that take place in Brussels itself. Tourism Brussels-Ardennes/Tourism Flanders-Brussels should be consulted about folk music or drama festivals elsewhere in Belgium – the most famous of which is the *Festival of Flanders* for classical music concerts. The other large cities of Belgium, such as Antwerp, Ghent, Kortrijk, Leuven, Liège, Mons and Namur, all have similar (though less extensive) nightlife facilities.

SHOPPING: Special purchases include ceramics and hand-beaten copperware from Dinant; Belgian chocolates; crystals from Val Saint Lambert; diamonds; jewellery from Antwerp; lace from Bruges, Brussels and Mechelen

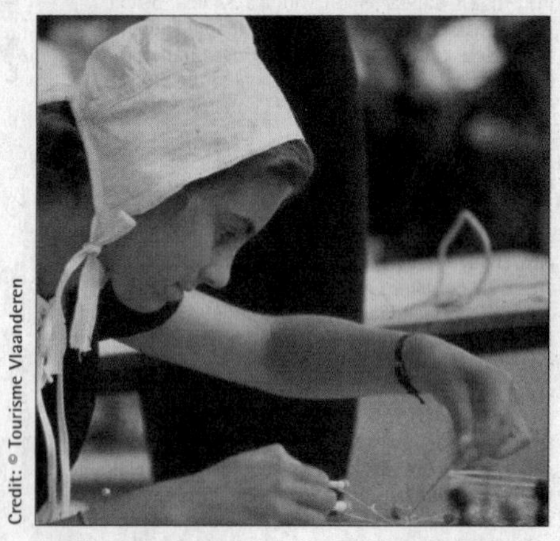
Credit: © Tourisme Vlaanderen

(Malines), woodcarvings from Spa and *bandes dessinées* (comic-strip books) by a number of talented Belgian cartoon artists from Brussels. Main shopping centres are located in Antwerp, Bruges, Brussels, Ghent, Liège, Mechelen, Mons, Namur and Ostend. **Shopping hours:** Mon-Sat 1000-1800/1900. Department stores often remain open longer, up to 2100 on Friday. Outside main areas, some shops may close at lunchtime.

SPECIAL EVENTS: The following is a selection of special events occurring in Belgium in 2005; for further information, contact Tourism Brussels-Ardennes and Tourism Flanders-Brussels (see *Contact Addresses* section): **Jan 21-30** *50th Belgium Antiques Fair*. **Feb 6-8** *Carnaval de Binche*, Hainaut. **Feb 13** *Grand Feu de Bouge*, spectacular bonfire on the first Sunday of Lent, Namur. **Mar 6** *Carnaval du Laetare*, Stavelot. **Mar 8-Sep 8** *"Made in Belgium"*, exposition celebrating 175 years of independence, Brussels. **Mar 28** *129th Cavalcade in Herve*, Liege. **Apr 29-30** *Liege Jazz Festival*. **May 7** *Belgium Gay Pride*, Brussels. **May 14-16** *Brussels Jazz Marathon/350th Military March at Saint Roch*, Thuin. **May 16** *Matrimonial High Tea*, Ecaussines. **Jun 11-12** *Days of the 4 Processius*, Tournai. **Jun 18-19** *7th Napoleonic Bivouac at Waterloo*, yearly reconstruction of a Napoleonic bivouac and the battle of Placenoit. **Jun 22-25** *European March of Memory & Friendship*, 30km march. **Jul 1** *Ommegang Pageant*, Brussels. **Dec** *European Christmas Markets*, countrywide.

SOCIAL CONVENTIONS: Belgians will often prefer to answer visitors in English rather than French, even if the visitor's French is good. It is customary to bring flowers or a small present for the hostess, especially if invited for a meal. Dress is similar to other Western nations, depending on the formality of the occasion. If black tie/evening dress is to be worn, this is always mentioned on the invitation. Smoking is generally unrestricted. **Tipping:** A service charge of 16 per cent is usually included in hotel or restaurant bills. Cloakroom attendants and porters may expect a tip per item of luggage. A tip is generally included in taxi fares.

Business Profile

ECONOMY: The economies of Belgium and Luxembourg have been unified since 1921, when the two governments signed a Convention of Economic Union; this is distinct from the Benelux Union (which includes The Netherlands) and the EU (Belgium being a founder member of both). The country's traditional industries of steel, motor vehicles and textiles suffered from the recession of the 1980s. While important, these no longer play the central economic role of the past. Coal mining ceased when the last mine was closed in 1992. Nuclear power accounts for almost two-thirds of Belgium's energy consumption; the remainder is generated from imported fuel products. Manufactured goods and machinery are the largest export sectors, with the major markets inside the EU – including France, Germany, The Netherlands and the UK. These are also Belgium's main source of imported goods. Belgium relies particularly heavily on export earnings – 70 per cent of GDP is exported, one of the highest proportions in the world. Successive Belgian governments have been keen proponents of the process of European integration, including the introduction of a single European currency, which Belgium adopted upon its inception in 1999. The Verhofstadt government has managed to reduce Belgium's high unemployment level to around 7 per cent, while keeping inflation below 2 per cent. Growth is sluggish at present, at just over 1 per cent.

BUSINESS: Suits should always be worn and business is conducted on a formal basis, with punctuality valued and business cards exchanged. Transactions are usually made in French or English. **Office hours:** Mon-Fri 0830-1730.

COMMERCIAL INFORMATION: The following organisations can offer advice: Chambre de Commerce et d'Industrie de Bruxelles, 500 avenue Louise, 1050 Brussels (tel: (2) 648 5002; fax: (2) 640 9328; e-mail: info.ccib@ccib.irisnet.be; website: www.ccib.irisnet.be); *or* Kamer van Koophandel Antwerpen-Waasland (Chamber of Commerce and Industry Anterpen-Waasland), Markgravestraat 12, 2000 Antwerp (tel: (3) 232 2219; fax: (3) 233 6442; e-mail: info@kvkaw.voka.be); website: www.kkna.be); *or* Belgian-Luxembourg Chamber of Commerce, Riverside House, 27-29 Vauxhall Grove, London SW8 1SY, UK (tel: (020) 7820 7839; fax: (020) 7793 1628; e-mail: info@blcc.co.uk; website: www.blcc.co.uk); *or* Belgian Foreign Trade, 30 Boulevard du Roi Albert II, Boîte 36, 1000 Brussels (tel: (2) 206 3511; fax (2) 203 1812; e-mail: info@abh-ace.org; website: www.abh-ace.org). The Flanders Foreign Investment Office (FFIO) is an agency of the Flemish government and promotes Flanders as an investment location for foreign businesses. For further information, contact FFIO, Regentlaan 40, B-1000 Brussels (tel: (2) 227 5311; fax: (2) 227 5310; e-mail: flanders@ffio.be; website: www.ffio.com).

CONFERENCES/CONVENTIONS: There is an extensive range of meeting venues throughout the country. In 1994, Belgium was the seventh most popular conference destination, whilst Brussels was the third most popular city. For more information or assistance in organising a conference or convention in Belgium, contact the Flanders-Brussels Convention Bureau, Grasmarkt 61, 1000 Brussels (tel: (2) 504 0355; fax: (2) 504 0480; e-mail: congres@meetingpoint.be; website: www.meetingpoint.be); *or* Brussels International (Brussels Convention Bureau), Rue de la Violette, 18 1000 Brussels (tel: (2) 549 5050 *or* 5052; fax: (2) 549 5059; e-mail: mice@brusselsinternational.be; website: www.brusselsinternational.be).

Climate

Seasonal and similar to neighbouring countries, with warm weather from May to September and snow likely during winter months.

Required clothing: Waterproofs are advisable at all times of the year.

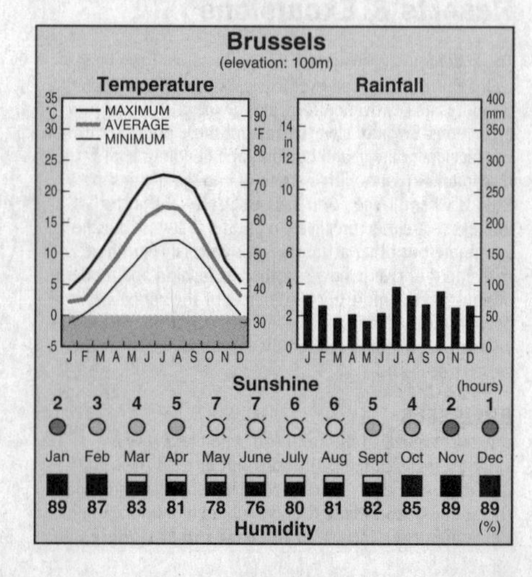

Belize

LATEST TRAVEL ADVICE CONTACTS

British Foreign and Commonwealth Office
Tel: (0870) 606 0290 Website: www.fco.gov.uk

US Department of State
Website: http://travel.state.gov/travel

Canadian Department of Foreign Affairs and Int'l Trade
Tel: (1 800) 267 8376 Website: www.dfait-maeci.gc.ca

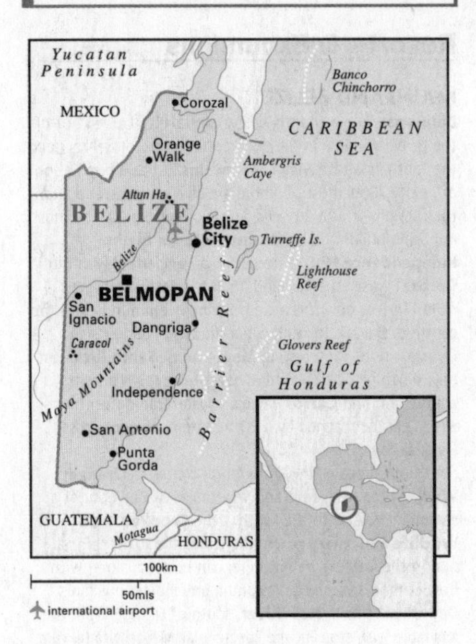

Location: Central America, Caribbean coast.

Country dialling code: 501.

Belize Tourism Board
New Central Bank Building, Level 2, Gabourel Lane,
PO Box 325, Belize City, Belize, CA
Tel: (22) 31913 *or* 1800 624 0686 (toll-free within CA).
Fax: (22) 31943.
E-mail: info@travelbelize.org
Website: www.travelbelize.org

Belize Tourism Industry Association (BTIA)
Street address: 10 North Park Street, Belize City, Belize, CA
Postal address: PO Box 62, Belize City, Belize, CA
Tel: (22) 75717 *or* 71144. Fax: (22) 78710.
E-mail: info@btia.org
Website: www.btia.org

Belize High Commission
3rd Floor, 45 Crawford Place, London W1H 4LP, UK
Tel: (020) 7723 3603. Fax: (020) 7723 9637.
E-mail: bzhc-lon@btconnect.com
Website: www.bzhc-lon.co.uk
Opening hours: Mon-Fri 1000-1800; 1000-1300 (consular section).

Caribbean Tourism Organisation
22 The Quadrant, Richmond, Surrey TW9 1BP, UK
Tel: (020) 8948 0057. Fax: (020) 8948 0067.
E-mail: ctolondon@caribtourism.com
Website: www.caribbean.co.uk

British High Commission
PO Box 91, Embassy Square, Belmopan, Belize, CA
Tel: (8) 222 146/7. Fax: (8) 222 761.
E-mail: brithicom@btl.net
Website: www.britishhighbze.com

Embassy of Belize
2535 Massachusetts Avenue, NW, Washington, DC 20008, USA
Tel: (202) 332 9636. Fax: (202) 332 6888.
E-mail: ebwreception@aol.com (consular section).
Website: www.embassyofbelize.org

Caribbean Tourism Organisation
80 Broad Street, 32nd Floor, New York, NY 10004, USA
Tel: (212) 635 9530. Fax: (212) 635 9511.
E-mail: ctony@caribtourism.com
Website: www.doitcaribbean.com

Embassy of the United States of America
Street address: 29 Gabourel Lane, Belize City, Belize, CA
Postal address: PO Box 286, Belize City, Belize, CA
Tel: (22) 77161. Fax: (22) 35423 (consular section).
E-mail: embbelize@state.gov
Website: http://belize.usembassy.gov

High Commission for Belize
350 Albert Street, Suite 2120, Ottawa K1R 1A4, Canada
Tel: (613) 232 2826 *or* 9505. Fax: (613) 232 4279.
E-mail: hcbelize@bellnet.ca

Canadian Consulate
Street address: 80 Princess Margaret Drive, Belize City, Belize, CA
Postal address: PO Box 610, Belize City, Belize, CA
Tel: (22) 31060 *or* 33722. Fax: (22) 30060.
E-mail: cdncon.bze@btl.net

TIMATIC CODES

Health
AMADEUS: **TI-DFT/BZE/HE**
GALILEO/WORLDSPAN: **TI-DFT/BZE/HE**
SABRE: **TIDFT/BZE/HE**

Visa
AMADEUS: **TI-DFT/BZE/VI**
GALILEO/WORLDSPAN: **TI-DFT/BZE/VI**
SABRE: **TIDFT/BZE/VI**

To access TIMATIC country information on Health and Visa regulations through the Computer Reservations System (CRS), type in the appropriate command line listed above.

General Information

AREA: 22,965 sq km (8867 sq miles).
POPULATION: 240,204 (2000).
POPULATION DENSITY: 10.5 per sq km.
CAPITAL: Belmopan City. **Population:** 8,130 (2000). Belize City (the former capital) has a population of 49,050.
GEOGRAPHY: Belize is situated at the base of the Yucatan Peninsula in Central America and borders Mexico and Guatemala, with the Caribbean Sea to the east. The country's area includes numerous small islands (Cayes) off the coast. The coastal strip is low and swampy, particularly in the north, with mangroves, many salt and freshwater lagoons and some sandy beaches crossed by a number of rivers. To the south and west rises the heavily forested Maya mountain range, with the Cockscomb range to the east and the Mountain Pine Ridge in the west. More than 65 per cent of the area of the country is forested. The land to the west along the borders with Guatemala is open and relatively scenic compared to much of the interior. The shallow offshore Cayes straddle a coral reef second only in size to the Great Barrier Reef of Australia.
GOVERNMENT: Constitutional monarchy. Gained independence from the UK in 1981. **Head of State:** HM Queen Elizabeth II represented locally by Governor-General Sir Colville Young since 1993. **Head of Government:** Prime Minister Said Musa since 1998.
LANGUAGE: English is the official language, but Spanish is spoken to some extent by over half the population. Garifuna (Carib), Maya and Ketchi are also spoken as well as a German dialect (by the Mennonites).
RELIGION: The people of Belize are mainly Roman Catholic (approximately 60 per cent of the population). Other denominations include Anglican, Mennonite, Methodist, Pentecostal and Seventh Day Adventist.
TIME: GMT - 6.
ELECTRICITY: 110 volts AC, 60Hz. American-style two-pin plugs.
COMMUNICATIONS: Telephone: IDD is available. Country code: 501. Outgoing international code: 00. **Mobile telephone:** Coverage is available in all six districts. *Belize Telecommunications Ltd* has a GSM 1900 network. Handsets can be hired from *Belize Telecommunications Ltd (BTL)*. **Fax:** *BTL* public booth in Belize City and some government and company offices have facilities available. **Internet:** ISPs include *BTL* (website: www.btl.net) and *Belize Web* (website: www.belizeweb.com). There is an e-mail service centre in the BTL office in central Belize City and Internet cafes in urban centres and popular tourist centres. **Telegram:** Full services are available from BTL public booth and post offices and major hotels in Belize City, Belmopan and San Ignacio. **Post:** Mail to Europe takes up to five days. **Press:** The major weeklies include *Amandala, The Belize Times, Government Gazette, The Reporter* and *The San Pedro Sun. Belize Today* is a monthly official paper published in English.
Radio: BBC World Service (website: www.bbc.co.uk/worldservice) and Voice of America (website: www.voa.gov) can be received. From time to time the frequencies change and the most up-to-date can be found online.

Passport/Visa

	Passport Required?	Visa Required?	Return Ticket Required?
Full British	Yes	No	Yes
Australian	Yes	No	Yes
Canadian	Yes	No	Yes
USA	Yes	No	Yes
Other EU	Yes	No/1	Yes
Japanese	Yes	Yes/1	Yes

Note: *Regulations and requirements may be subject to change at short notice, and you are advised to contact the appropriate diplomatic or consular authority before finalising travel arrangements. Details of these may be found at the head of this country's entry. Any numbers in the chart refer to the footnotes below.*

PASSPORTS: Passport valid for six months beyond the intended length of stay required by all.
VISAS: Required by all except the following for stays of up to 30 days:
(a) nationals indicated in the chart above and nationals of their overseas territories (except **1.** nationals of Czech Republic, Estonia, Hungary, Japan, Latvia, Lithuania, Poland, Slovak Republic and Slovenia who *do* need a visa);
(b) nationals of Commonwealth countries and nationals of their overseas territories (except nationals of Bangladesh, Cameroon, The Gambia, Ghana, India, Mozambique, Nauru, Nigeria, Pakistan, Sierra Leone and Sri Lanka who *do* need a visa);
(c) nationals of Caribbean Community Member States (CARICOM), except nationals of Haiti who *do* need a visa;
(d) nationals of Chile, Costa Rica, Guatemala, Iceland, Mexico, Norway, Tunisia and Uruguay.
Note: (a) All travellers are required to show evidence of sufficient funds (minimum £50 per day) and proof of return or onward ticket at the point of entry. (b) Each individual traveller regardless of age must make a separate visa application.
Types of visa and cost: *Tourist* and *Business*. *Single-entry*: £20 (three months); £30 (six months). *Multiple-entry*: £30 (three months); £40 (six months); £50 (one year).
Validity: *Single-entry*: Three or six months. *Multiple-entry*: Three months, six months or one year.
Application to: Consulate (or Consular Section at Embassy or High Commission); see *Contact Addresses* section.
Application requirements: (a) Application form. (b) One recent passport-size photo. (c) Valid passport. (d) Copies of tickets or a confirmed travel itinerary. (e) Copies of confirmed hotel reservations or full contact details of family or friends in Belize. (f) Copies of most recent bank statements. (g) Fee, payable by bank draft or postal order; personal cheques are not accepted (you may pay in cash if the application is made in person). (h) £5 to cover postal applications, where applicable. *Business*: (a)-(h) and, (i) Letter from financial officer. (j) Letter of introduction from company or organisation and supporting documents.
Note: The visa recipient is advised to carry all evidence submitted in support of the application for possible inspection by the immigration official upon entry into Belize.
Working days required: Visas issued in person will be ready for the following day. Allow two to four weeks if clearance is needed from the Belize Immigration and Nationality Services.
Temporary residence: Apply to Immigration and Nationality Department, Belmopan.

Money

Currency: Belize Dollar (Bz$) = 100 cents. Notes are in denominations of Bz$100, 50, 20, 10, 5 and 2. Coins are in denominations of Bz$1, and 100, 50, 25, 10, 5 and 1 cents.
Note: The Belize Dollar is tied to the US Dollar at US$1 = Bz$2.
Currency exchange: Currency can be exchanged at most banks, hotels and travel agencies and some businesses. ATMs in Belize generally do not accept foreign cards.
Credit & debit cards: American Express, MasterCard (limited) and Visa are accepted. Check with your credit or debit card company for details of merchant acceptability and other services which may be available. Most establishments will add a 5 per cent service charge to the bills of customers using credit cards.
Travellers cheques: These can be exchanged, commission will usually be charged.
Currency restrictions: The import and export of local currency is limited to Bz$100. The import of foreign currency is unlimited, provided declared on arrival. The export of foreign currency is limited to the equivalent of Bz$400 for residents, and up to the amount imported and declared for non-residents. Visitors are advised to carry a minimum of Bz$75 for each day they intend to stay.
Exchange rate indicators: The following figures are included as a guide to the movements of the Belize Dollar against the Pound Sterling and the US Dollar:

Date	Feb '04	May '04	Aug '04	Nov '04
£1.00=	3.60	3.54	3.64	3.74
$1.00=	1.98	1.98	1.98	1.98

Banking hours: Mon-Thurs 0800-1300, Fri 0800-1630.

Duty Free

The following goods may be taken into Belize without incurring customs duty:
200 cigarettes or 50 cigars or 250g of tobacco; 568ml of alcoholic beverages; one bottle of perfume for personal use.
Prohibited items: The following items may not be exported from Belize: pre-Columbian articles, marine products, unprocessed coral or turtle shells.

Public Holidays

2005: Jan 1 New Year's Day. **Mar 9** Baron Bliss Day. **Mar 25-28** Easter. **May 1** Labour Day. **May 24** Commonwealth Day. **Sep 10** St George's Caye Day. **Sep 21** Independence Day. **Oct 12** Columbus Day. **Nov 19** Garifuna Settlement Day. **Dec 25-26** Christmas.
2006: Jan 1 New Year's Day. **Mar 9** Baron Bliss Day. **Apr 14-17** Easter. **May 1** Labour Day. **May 24** Commonwealth Day. **Sep 10** St George's Caye Day. **Sep 21** Independence Day. **Oct 9** Columbus Day. **Nov 19** Garifuna Settlement Day. **Dec 25-26** Christmas.

Health

	Special Precautions?	Certificate Required?
Yellow Fever	No	1
Cholera	2	No
Typhoid & Polio	3	N/A
Malaria	4	N/A

Note: *Regulations and requirements may be subject to change at short notice, and you are advised to contact your doctor well in advance of your intended date of departure. Any numbers in the chart refer to the footnotes below.*

1: A yellow fever vaccination certificate is required from all travellers coming from infected areas. Pregnant women and children under nine months should not normally be vaccinated.
2: Following WHO guidelines issued in 1973, a cholera vaccination certificate is no longer a condition of entry into Belize. However, imported cases of cholera were reported in 1996 and precautions are essential. Up-to-date advice should be sought before deciding whether these precautions should include vaccination as medical opinion is divided over its effectiveness.
3: Typhoid fever is a risk and immunisation is advised.
4: Malaria risk exists throughout the year, excluding Belize district and urban areas, predominantly in the benign *vivax* form. The risk is highest in the western and southern regions. A weekly dose of 300mg of chloroquine is the recommended prophylaxis.
Food & drink: While tap water is generally regarded as safe for consumption, purified water is readily available and is advised for the first few weeks of stay. Milk is unpasteurised and should be boiled. Powdered or tinned milk is available and is advised, but make sure that it is reconstituted with pure water. Avoid all dairy products. Only eat well-cooked meat and fish, preferably served hot. Pork, salad and mayonnaise may carry increased risk. Vegetables should be cooked and fruit peeled.
Other risks: *Amoebic* and *bacillary dysenteries* and other *diarrhoeal* diseases are very common. *Hepatitis A, B* and *C* occur. *Dengue fever* may also be present. *Cutaneous* and *mucocutaneous leishmaniasis* occur. Snakes may be a hazard.
Rabies is present. For those at high risk, vaccination before arrival should be considered. If you are bitten, seek medical advice without delay. For more information, consult the *Health* appendix.
Note: Visitors applying for residency will require an AIDS test (foreign tests may not be acceptable).
Health care: There are seven government hospitals – one in Belmopan, one in Belize City and one in each of the other five main district towns. Medical services in rural areas are provided by rural health care centres, and mobile clinics operate in remote areas. International travellers are strongly advised to take out medical insurance before departing for Belize.

Travel - International

AIR: International services, mainly of a regional nature, are provided by *American Airlines, Continental, Grupo TACA, Maya Island Air* and *Tropic Air*. There are flights from the USA, Guatemala and other Central American countries.
Approximate flight times: To Belize from *London* (via Miami) is 11 hours; from *Los Angeles* is eight hours; from *Miami* is two hours; from *Guatemala City* is two hours; from *Cancun* is one hour 30 minutes; and from *New York* is five hours.
International airports: The *Philip S W Goldson International Airport (BZE)* is 16km (10 miles) northwest of Belize City. Taxis are available to the city (travel time – 15 minutes); prices should be agreed with the driver beforehand. Facilities include duty-free shops, bank, shops, restaurant and bar. There is an airport bus to the city centre (travel time – 30 minutes).
Note: Belmopan, the capital, is 84km (52 miles) from Belize City by road.
Departure tax: US$20 is levied on all passengers, apart from transit passengers travelling on within 48 hours and children under 12 years of age.
SEA: Main ports include Belize City, Corozal, Dangriga, Punta Gorda and San Pedro. Belize has greatly improved its port facilities, but these cater for cargo vessels and no cruise lines call. There are regular ferry services between Punta Gorda and Puerto Barrios and Livingston in Guatemala, or from Dangriga and Placencia to Puerto Cortés in Honduras.
ROAD: There are road links with Chetumal on the Mexican border and Melchor de Mencos in Guatemala. Regular scheduled bus services serve these routes, leaving between every half hour or hour for Belize City. Border crossing fees may apply.

Travel - Internal

AIR: Local services link the main towns. *Maya Island Air* and *Tropic Air* fly three times daily from the municipal airstrip at Belize City to Ambergris Caye. There are also scheduled flights daily to each of the main towns, and charter rates are offered to all local airstrips, of which there are 25. *Island Air (WP)* offers scheduled flights between the mainland and San Pedro. Several companies have charters from Belize City to the outlying districts.
SEA: The sugar industry runs motorboat links along the coast. There is a scheduled boat service from Belize City to Ambergris Caye, Caye Chapel and Caye Caulker. Small boats irregularly ply between the small Cayes off the coast. This transport used to be the only means of travel to the interior, along the Belize, Hondo and New rivers, but services have dwindled since the advent of better roads.
ROAD: Approximately 1600km (1000 miles) of all-weather roads link the eight towns in the country, though torrential rain seasonally severs these links, particularly at ferry points. Belize has a less developed network of roads than the rest of Central America but it is steadily being improved, especially in the north, as is the Belize stretch of the road to Mexico, while the Belize-Belmopan road is in generally good condition. Traffic drives on the right. **Bus:** There are good and inexpensive daily bus services to all the large towns, and to both the Mexican and Guatemalan borders. Many of the buses are modern and air conditioned. See the tourist board website for details of schedules (see *Contact Address* section). **Car hire:** *Avis, Budget, Hertz* and *National* operate in Belize City and there are many other companies in Ladyville, Dangriga and San Ignacio. 4-wheel-drive vehicles are recommended for excursions south of Belize City. **Documentation:** A national driving licence is acceptable.
Travel times: The following chart gives approximate travel times (in hours and minutes) from **Belize City** to other major cities/towns in the country.

	Air	Road	Sea
Northern Border	2.20	-	-
Corozal Town	-	2.00	-
Orange Walk Town	1.15	-	-
Belmopan	0.20	1.00	-
Benque Viejo	-	1.45	-
San Ignacio	-	1.30	-
Dangriga	0.30	3.30	-
Punta Gorda	0.45	8.00	-
San Pedro, Ambergris	0.15	-	1.30
Caye Caulker	-	0.45	-
Placencia	0.30	4.00	7.00

Accommodation

HOTELS: Belize has few first-class hotels, but smaller establishments give good value. There are mountain lodges in the interior and resort hotels on the Caribbean coast. Most accommodation establishments are listed by the Belize Tourism Industry Association (see *Contact Addresses* section). The BTIA represents more than 50 per cent of all establishments.
Grading: Hotels have been divided into three categories according to price and standard. Rates are subject to change without notice. It is advisable to confirm reservations and rates in advance. Classes of hotels are as follows: **Expensive:** All hotels provide a private bath/shower and have a restaurant and bar. There is air conditioning in all rooms. Some rooms also have a phone and TV. **Moderate:** All hotels provide a private bath/shower and full or partial air conditioning. **Budget:** Nearly all provide a private bath/shower, though sometimes baths/showers are shared. On the Barrier Reef Cayes there are numerous resort hotels of roughly the same standard as those given above.
APARTMENTS: Long-stay visitors can rent apartments on a monthly basis.
CAMPING/CARAVANNING: There are budget campsite facilities in Belize, Cayo and Corozal districts and a slightly more expensive campsite in the Toledo district. There is a caravan site in Corozal Town, and also outside San Ignacio. Camping on the beach is forbidden. Camping on private beach yards in Caye Caulker and in Tobacco Caye is available.

Resorts & Excursions

MAINLAND BELIZE

Belmopan is the country's new capital city, carved out of the tropical jungle in the geographic centre of Belize, near the foothills of the **Maya Mountains**. It has a population of nearly 7000, most of whom are civil servants, and is in the first phase of a 20-year development period. The most imposing building is the **National Assembly** on **Independence Hill**, patterned in an ancient Mayan motif.
Corozal was settled around 1850 by Mestizo refugees from Mexico; now it is a well-planned community and the centre of Belize's thriving sugar industry. Just outside Corozal are two interesting Mayan ruins: **Santa Rita**, just 1 mile north of Corozal with a view of the town and its waterfront; and **Cerros**, once a coastal trading centre which can be reached by a 20-minute boat ride across Corozal Bay.
South of Corozal is the agricultural centre of **Orange Walk**, where fresh fruit and vegetables can be bought at the markets. Also to the south is the **Crooked Tree Wildlife Sanctuary** where the jabiru stork (the largest bird in the western hemisphere) can be seen, along with howler monkeys, crocodiles and many indigenous birds. Day cruises of the **New River**, south of Orange Walk, are available with stops at the spectacular Mayan citadel ruin of **Lamanai** and the **Temple of the Masks**, where visitors can see the tremendous head of the sun god, Kinich Ahau, carved into the limestone. One of the most famous Mayan ruins in Belize is **Altun Ha**, located 50km (31 miles) north of Belize City on the Northern Highway. The site was a major ceremonial centre and trading centre in the Classic period (AD 250-900) and an extraordinary head of the sun god, ornately carved in jade, was found here and is now a national symbol of Belize. **Mountain Pine Ridge Forest Reserve** is located south of the Western Highway about 115km (70 miles) from Belize City. It is an area of fine views and secluded streams, and contains the **Hidden Valley Falls**, which plunge 500m (1600ft) into the valley. Inland from Belize City on the Belize River, is the **Community Baboon Sanctuary** with one of the few robust black howler monkey populations in Central America.
San Ignacio, surrounded by hills, is the administrative centre for the Cayo district. Not far from San Ignacio are several Mayan sites including **El Pilar** and the magnificent **Xunantunich** with its 1500-year-old **El Castillo**, the second-tallest building in Belize. The **canaa** of the **Caracol** Mayan site in **Cayo** is the tallest Mayan building in Belize. This site has been claimed to rival such other famous sites as Tikal in neighbouring Guatemala. Also in Cayo are the waters of **Rio on Pools** in the Mountain Pine Ridge Forest Reserve. Near the town of **San Antonio**, located in the Toledo District inland from **Punta Gorda**, is the Mayan site of **Lubaantum**, where the famous perfectly carved crystal skull was found in a temple vault.

COASTAL BELIZE

Belize City is over 300 years old and serves as the main commercial area and seaport. It is the country's biggest city, and is a mixture of colonial architecture, functional wooden buildings and historic cathedrals. Sights include the oldest Anglican cathedral in Latin America, **St John's**, and **Government House**, the Belize City residence of the British Governor, built in 1814. Around 32km (20 miles) south of the city is **Belize Zoo** on the Western Highway, with more than 100 species of indigenous animals, including monkeys, jaguars and tapirs.
Cerros is located on the fringe of a beautiful expanse of blue-green water which is ideal for watersports. Across the bay is an archaeological site. **Dangriga** (Stann Creek) provides a good base for excursions to the offshore islands and nearby forests. Natural waterfalls can be seen at the **Cockscomb Basin Wildlife Sanctuary** situated at the foothills of the **Maya Mountains**. Close by lies the diving and snorkelling haven, **Southwater Caye**.
Placencia is a village situated at the tip of the 20km- (12

mile-) long Placencia peninsula. Its protected lagoon and sandy beaches make it an ideal place for fishing, swimming and sunbathing.
The fishing village of **Punta Gorda** is the southernmost outpost of Belize. 40km (25 miles) north of here off the Southern Highway is the Mayan ruin of **Nim Li Punit**, with the tallest carved **stele** in Belize.

THE BELIZE CAYES

The cayes (pronounced 'keys') are islands and/or mangroves located between the mainland and the barrier reef, on the barrier reef, and on or within the barrier reef perimeters of the offshore atolls. Although the mangrove cayes are normally uninhabitable for humans, they do provide an ideal habitat for birds and marine life. The island cayes, which are distinguishable by their palm trees, have provided the foundation for the development of many fine resorts to serve watersports enthusiasts and marine naturalists.
Ambergris Caye, with its many beaches and the fishing village of **San Pedro**, is the most popular tourist destination. Along with the other Cayes, it is a paradise for divers with access to one of the most unspoilt coral reefs in the world; **Hoi Chan Marine Reserve** is a popular dive site where southern stingray and nurse sharks can be observed in shark ray alley. Situated 58km (36 miles) north of Belize City, it is accessible by daily scheduled air flights and boat transfers. **Caye Caulker** has an extensive underwater cave system which has made it popular with divers, whilst those who wish to explore the reef without getting wet can see photographs of reef fish at the museum. On **Half Moon Caye** at **Lighthouse Reef** is the **Red-Footed Booby Bird Sanctuary**, founded in 1982 to protect the booby and other birds and animals. There are many other Cayes with facilities for those interested in fishing, diving and seeing wildlife.

NATIONAL PARKS

Belize has a rich natural geography, from jungle forests, karst terrain and swampy mangroves to tropical beaches. Consequently, the country is eager to promote ecotourism and there exists a number of protected areas, including marine reserves and national parks. 12 miles southeast of Belmopan, the **Blue Hole National Park** pays tribute to the curious **Blue Hole**, a collapsed water sinkhole, 7.6m (25 feet) deep, of intense colour. The park is a natural forest reserve that is home to an abundance of birds, animals and **St Herman's Cave**, an ancient Mayan cave. **Five Blues Lake National Park** is situated at the foot of the spectacular Mayan Mountains and covers over 1619 hectares (4000 acres) of tropical forest. The eponymous lake is a collapsed cave system, known as a cenote or blue hole, and appears in an array of aqua hues. There is an amazing wealth of wildlife and fauna to be seen here. At the junction to the Cayo District from the Hummingbird and Western highways, lies **Guanacaste National Park**, taking its name from the giant Guanacaste trees at the edge of the reserve. With over a hundred species of bird and highlighted trails with information on the trees and plants within the forest, the park is popular as an introduction to the diverse environment of Belize.
Laughing Bird Caye National Park is a shelf atoll, ideal for diving, but is also a habitat for the unusual laughing gulls. The Caye is situated 21km (13 miles) southeast of Placencia Village in the Stann Creek District.
The **Rio Bravo Conservation and Management Area** contains 81,745 hectares (202,000 acres) of preserved forests and marshlands, which provides a home for a rich array of birds and endangered species, including Jaguars, Pumas, Black Howler Monkeys, Margays, Ocellated Turkeys and Brocket Deer. Over 40 Mayan ruins have also been discovered here. The conservation park is located near the Orange Walk district of Belize.

MAYAN ARCHAEOLOGICAL SITES

Travellers wishing to follow 'La Ruta Maya' ('the pathways into Mayan culture') will find some unspoilt and rarely visited Mayan ruins in and around Belize. **Lamanai** (Submerged Crocodile) is one of the largest Mayan centres, and, as an archaeological reserve, also contains a museum, the remains of two 16th-century Spanish churches and a 19th-century sugar mill. The site is situated on the banks of the New River Lagoon in the North of Belize and accommodation is available in local guest houses and jungle lodges.
Altun Ha (Water of the Rock) has two main plazas, over 13 temples and a large jade head of the Sun God Ahau (one of the largest carved Mayan jade objects). Several tour operators run trips to the site, which is located near the Belize district and is inaccessible by public transport.
Situated in the Chiquibul Rain Forest of the Cayo District, **Caracol** (Snail) is home to the tallest manmade structure in Belize; **Canaa** (Sky Place) **Pyramid** rises 43m (140ft) high. Although hard to get to during the rainy season, trips and the necessary entry permits can be organised with travel agents in Belize.
Cerros (Maya Hills) lies on a peninsula overlooking Corozal Bay and consists of three large acropolises dominated by pyramid structures. The impressive ruins of **Xunantunich** (Stone Woman) include six plazas, 25 temples and palaces, and the 43m-(130 foot) high 'El Castillo' (The Castle). To access the site requires taking a bus 8 miles west of San Ignacio town and a ferry over the Mopan River, before walking a further 1.6km (1 mile) to the grounds. It is advisable to book the trip through a travel operator or company. For further details, contact the Belize Tourist Board (see *Contact Addresses* section).

Sport & Activities

Watersports: Belize ranks among the best **scuba-diving** and **snorkelling** destinations in the western Caribbean. At a length of 296km (185 miles), Belize's *Barrier Reef* is the longest in the Western hemisphere and offers divers a nearly continuous wall of coral (stretching almost 224km (140 miles) from Mexico to the Sapodilla Cayes). The best developed sections of the reef are south of *Columbus Reef*. Some of the best dive sites include *Lighthouse Reef*, where divers can explore walls with spectacular drops of thousands of feet; and the *Blue Hole* (see *Resorts & Excursions*, *National Parks* section). Boats to both sites can be hired. Visitors can either arrange diving trips with an offshore resort, sign on with one of the live-aboard boats or hire a charter boat from one of many dive resorts along the coast. Visitors should also be aware of the restrictions on the removal of coral, orchids and turtles, and on spearfishing in certain areas. Wrecks and treasures are also government-protected. For further information and a list of dive operators, contact the Belize Tourist Board (see *Contact Addresses* section). **Swimming** is good off the Cayes and on the southeast coast, where many places have developed as diving and watersport resorts (see *Resorts & Excursions* section). All kinds of **fishing**, including game fishing (for snapper, barracuda, marlin and bonito), can be enjoyed all year round. Belize's 20 river systems and smaller streams are ideal for **kayaking** and **canoeing**, and trips (which usually also involve birdwatching or wildlife viewing) can be arranged via local travel agents, operators or hotels.
Other: Birdwatching is popular since hundreds of bird species can be observed, particularly in the national parks notably, the *Cockscomb Basin Wildlife Sanctuary*, *Crooked Tree Wildlife Sanctuary*, *Silk Grass Greek Road* and the *Mountain Pine Ridge*. **Caving** and **archaeology** are also popular pastimes.

Social Profile

FOOD & DRINK: There is a selection of restaurants which serve international, Chinese, Creole and Latin American food. Service and quality vary but the food is generally cheap. Bars are plentiful and local drinks include coconut rum mixed with pineapple juice. The local *Belikin* beer is worth sampling.
NIGHTLIFE: There is live dancing late in the evenings at Bellevue Hotel and quiet music at Fort George Bar overlooking the harbour. In addition, there are popular nightclubs throughout Belize that feature local bands at weekends.
SHOPPING: Handicrafts, woodcarvings and straw items are on sale. Jewellery in pink and black coral, and tortoiseshell (not to be imported to the USA) used to be good buys, but now there are severe restrictions on the export of these and some other goods in the interests of wildlife conservation. 'In-Bond' stores carry watches, perfumes and other duty-free purchases, but Belize is not comparable in size to other free ports in the Caribbean. **Shopping hours:** Mon-Sat 0800-1200, 1300-1630 and 1900-2100.
SPECIAL EVENTS: For further details, contact the Belize Tourism Board (see *Contact Addresses* section). The following is a selection of special events celebrated annually in Belize:
Feb 9 *San Pedro Carnival*. **Mar 25-28** *Easter Fair*, San Ignacio. **Mar 26** *Holy Saturday Cycling Classic*. **May 7-9** *Cashew Festival*. **Jun 25-27** *Lobster Festival*. **Aug 5-8** *International Costa Maya Festival*. **Aug 12** *Deer Dance Festival*. **Nov** *Garifuna Settlement Day*, nationwide. **Dec** *Boxing Day Celebrations*, nationwide.
SOCIAL CONVENTIONS: British influence can still be seen in many social situations. Flowers or confectionary are acceptable gifts to give to hosts if invited to their home for a meal. Dress is casual, although beachwear should not be worn in towns. It may be inadvisable to discuss politics, particularly if of a partisan nature. **Tipping:** Few places add service charges, and 10 per cent is normal. Taxi drivers are not tipped.

Business Profile

ECONOMY: Agriculture is the most important economic sector – the main products are citrus fruit, bananas and sugar cane. Timber is also important, especially mahogany and other tropical hardwoods. Fishing and livestock are being developed. The fastest-growing area of the Belize economy has been the service sector, particularly 'offshore' activities, including the lightly regulated banking sector and a 'flag of convenience' shipping register. However, these have started to cause political difficulties for the Belizean government. In June 2000, Belize was identified by the Organisation for Economic Cooperation and Development (OECD) – the world's 30 wealthiest economies – as one of 35 'tax havens' whose financial laws are believed to encourage large-scale tax evasion and money laundering. The government has since taken measures to meet the OECD's demands. Tourism, fuelled by foreign investment, has also expanded in recent years, although not at the rate the government had originally hoped – net tourist expenditure in Belize is approximately US$100 million annually. Industry is dominated by the processing of agricultural products (for example, the production of rum from sugar) and light industries such as textiles. The country has no natural energy resources, although the search for oil reserves continues both on- and offshore, and hydroelectric projects are underway. The USA is the largest single trading partner, providing half of all imports and taking about 60 per cent of Belizean exports. The UK and other EU countries are other important trading partners. Belize is a member of CARICOM, the Caribbean economic community, and provides some transit facilities for trade to and from other countries in the region. Belize is a significant recipient of overseas aid from Britain, the EU and North America.
BUSINESS: Lightweight, tropical suits are often worn. Appointments should be made and calling cards are acceptable. October to March are the best months for visits. **Office hours:** Mon-Thurs 0800-1200 and 1300-1700, Fri 0800-1200 and 1300-1630.
COMMERCIAL INFORMATION: The following organisation (with which 80 per cent of all businesses are associated) can offer advice: Belize Chamber of Commerce and Industry, PO Box 291, 63 Regent Street, Belize City (tel: (22) 73148 *or* 70668; fax: (22) 74984; e-mail: bcci@btl.net; website: www.belize.org); *or* Belize Trade & Investment Development Service (BELTRAIDE), 14 Orchid Garden Street, Belmopan City, Cayo, Belize (tel: (8) 222 832; fax: (8) 222 837; e-mail: beltraide@belize.gov.bz; website: www.belizeinvest.org.bz).
CONFERENCES/CONVENTIONS: Facilities are available at a number of venues, and information can be obtained from the Ministry of Tourism, Investment and Culture, 14 Constitution Drive, Belmopan (tel: (8) 223 393/4; fax: (8) 223 815; e-mail: tourismdpt@btl.net).

Climate

Subtropical with a brisk prevailing wind from the Caribbean Sea. High annual temperatures and humidity. Dry and hot climate from January to April, with rainy season from June.

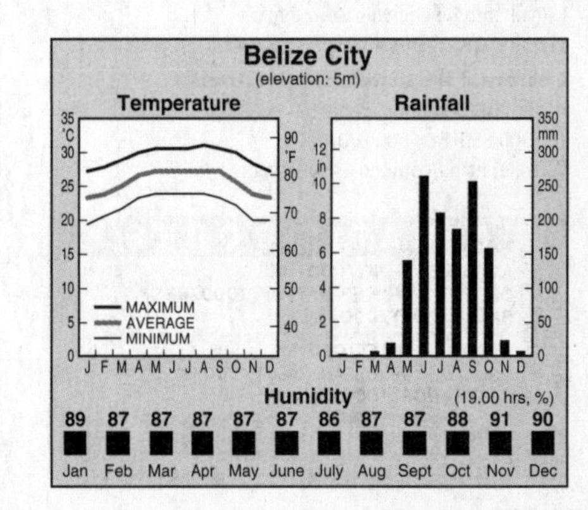

Benin

LATEST TRAVEL ADVICE CONTACTS

British Foreign and Commonwealth Office
Tel: (0870) 606 0290 Website: www.fco.gov.uk

US Department of State
Website: http://travel.state.gov/travel

Canadian Department of Foreign Affairs and Int'l Trade
Tel: (1 800) 267 8376 Website: www.dfait-maeci.gc.ca

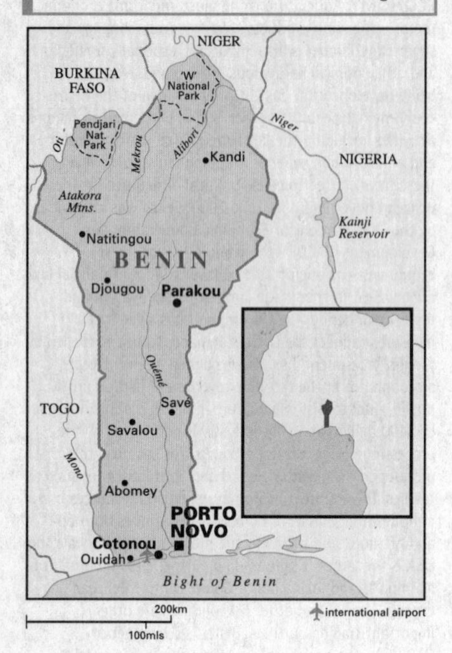

Location: West Africa.

Country dialling code: 229.

Ministry of Culture, Craft Industry and Tourism
01 BP 2037, Cotonou, Benin
Tel: 307 010. Fax: 307 031.
E-mail: sq@tourisme.gouv.bj
Website: www.tourisme.gouv.bj

Honorary Consulate of Benin
Dolphin House, 16 The Broadway, Stanmore,
Middlesex HA7 4DW, UK
Tel: (020) 8954 8800. Fax: (020) 8954 8844.
E-mail: l.landau@btinternet.com
Opening hours: Mon-Fri 1000-1230 and 1400-1630.

Embassy of the Republic of Benin
87 avenue Victor Hugo, 75116 Paris, France
Tel: (1) 4500 9882 *or* 4222 3191 (consular section).
Fax: (1) 4501 8202 *or* 4222 3919 (consular section).
E-mail: ambassade@ambassade-benin.org *or*
consulat-paris@ambassade-benin.org
Website: www.ambassade-benin.org

The British High Commission in Lagos deals with enquiries relating to Benin (see *Nigeria* section).

Embassy of the Republic of Benin
2124 Kalorama Road, NW, Washington, DC 20008, USA
Tel: (202) 232 6656 *or* 2611 (consular section).
Fax: (202) 265 1996.
E-mail: info@beninembassyus.org
Website: www.beninembassyus.org

Embassy of the United States of America
01 BP 2012, Cotonou, Benin
Tel: 300 650. Fax: 300 670.
Website: http://cotonou.usembassy.gov

TIMATIC CODES

Health
AMADEUS: **TI-DFT/COO/HE**
GALILEO/WORLDSPAN: **TI-DFT/COO/HE**
SABRE: **TIDFT/COO/HE**

Visa
AMADEUS: **TI-DFT/COO/VI**
GALILEO/WORLDSPAN: **TI-DFT/COO/VI**
SABRE: **TIDFT/COO/VI**

To access TIMATIC country information on Health and Visa regulations through the Computer Reservations System (CRS), type in the appropriate command line listed above.

Embassy of the Republic of Benin
58 Glebe Avenue, Ottawa, Ontario K1S 2CR, Canada
Tel: (613) 233 4429. Fax: (613) 233 8952.
E-mail: ambaben@benin.ca
Website: www.benin.ca
Consulates in: Montréal and Vancouver.

The Canadian Embassy in Abidjan deals with enquiries relating to Benin (see *Côte d'Ivoire* section).

General Information

AREA: 112,622 sq km (43,484 sq miles).
POPULATION: 6,059,000 (official estimate 1999).
POPULATION DENSITY: 53.8 per sq km.
CAPITAL: Porto Novo (administrative). **Population:** 200,000 (1994). (Cotonou is the economic capital with an estimated population of 750,000 in 1994.)
GEOGRAPHY: Benin is situated in West Africa and is bordered to the east by Nigeria, to the north by Niger and Burkina Faso, and to the west by Togo. Benin stretches 700km (435 miles) from the Bight of Benin to the Niger River. The coastal strip is sandy with coconut palms. Beyond the lagoons of Porto Novo, Nokoue, Ouidah and Grand Popo is a plateau rising gradually to the heights of the Atakora Mountains. From the highlands run two tributaries of the Niger, while southwards the Ouémé flows down to Nokoue lagoon. Mono River flows into the sea at Grand Popo and forms a frontier with Togo.
GOVERNMENT: Republic. Gained independence from France in 1960. **Head of State and Government:** President Mathieu Kérékou since 1996.
LANGUAGE: The official language is French. However, many ethnic groups have their own languages: Bariba and Fulani are spoken in the north, Fon and Yoruba in the south. Some English is also spoken.
RELIGION: 35 per cent Animist/traditional, 35 per cent Christian (mainly Roman Catholic) and the majority of the rest are Muslim.
TIME: GMT + 1.
ELECTRICITY: 220 volts AC, 50Hz.
COMMUNICATIONS: Telephone: IDD is available. Country code: 229. Outgoing international code: 00. There is an additional charge for calls made from a coin box. **Mobile telephone:** GSM 900 network. Operators include *Libercom*, *Spacetel-Benin* (website: www.spacetelbenin.com) and *Telecel Benin* (website: www.telecel.com). Handsets can be hired locally. Further information can be obtained from the *Office de Postes et dés Télécommunications du Bênin* (website: www.opt.bj). **Internet:** *OPT* has just launched its own ISP (website: www.opt.bj). Public access is available in Cotonou. **Post:** Airmail takes three to five days to reach Europe. Surface mail letters or parcels take from six to eight weeks. There are good *poste restante* facilities at most main post offices. Post office hours: Mon-Sat 0800-1400. **Press:** Exclusively in French. The fortnightly *Journal Officiel de la République du Bénin* is issued by the government information bureau. *La Nation* is the daily official newspaper. Other dailies include *Le Matinal* and *Le Point au Quotidien*.
Radio: BBC World Service (website: www.bbc.co.uk/worldservice) and Voice of America (website: www.voa.gov) can be received. From time to time the frequencies change and the most up-to-date can be found online.

Passport/Visa

	Passport Required?	Visa Required?	Return Ticket Required?
Full British	Yes	Yes	No
Australian	Yes	Yes	No
Canadian	Yes	Yes	No
USA	Yes	Yes	No
Other EU	Yes	Yes	No
Japanese	Yes	Yes	No

Note: *Regulations and requirements may be subject to change at short notice, and you are advised to contact the appropriate diplomatic or consular authority before finalising travel arrangements. Details of these may be found at the head of this country's entry. Any numbers in the chart refer to the footnotes below.*

Restricted entry: All visitors over one year of age are required to produce a yellow fever certificate on entry to Benin.
PASSPORTS: Valid passport required by all except nationals of the following countries in possession of a national identity card: Burkina Faso, Cameroon, Central African Republic, Chad, Congo, Côte d'Ivoire, Gabon, Ghana, Madagascar, Mali, Mauritania, Niger, Rwanda, Senegal and Togo.
VISAS: Required by all except the following:
(a) nationals of ECOWAS member countries;
(b) those in transit continuing their onward journey within 24 hours, provided holding confirmed tickets and not leaving the airport.
Note: All children of nationals who require a visa, issued with their own passport, *do* require a visa.
Types of visa and cost: *Tourist* and *Business*. Visas cost £35 for 15 days; £45 for 30 days; £55 for 90 days.
Validity: Visas are valid for a 15-, 30- or 90-day period within three months of date of issue.
Application to: Consulate (or Consular Section at Embassy); see *Contact Addresses* section.
Application requirements: (a) Valid passport. (b) Application form completed in duplicate. (c) Two passport-size photos. (d) Pre-paid registered envelope large enough to fit passport, if applying by post. (e) Fee. (f) For a Business visa, a letter from the applicant's company.
Working days required: Callers at the Consulate are usually able to obtain visas on the same day.
Temporary residence: Enquire at Consulate (or Consular Section at Embassy).

Money

Currency: CFA (*Communauté Financiaire Africaine*) Franc (CFAfr) = 100 centimes. Notes are in denominations of CFAfr10,000, 5000, 2000, 1000 and 500. Coins are in denominations of CFAfr250, 100, 50, 25, 10, 5 and 1. Benin is part of the French Monetary Area. Only currency issued by the *Banque des Etats de l'Afrique de l'Ouest* (Bank of West African States) is valid; currency issued by the *Banque des Etats de l'Afrique Centrale* (Bank of Central African States) is not. The CFA Franc is tied to the Euro.
Currency exchange: Currency can be exchanged at banks and in major hotels.
Credit & debit cards: American Express, Diners Club, MasterCard and Visa are accepted on a limited basis. Check with your credit or debit card company for details of merchant acceptability and other services which may be available. Some banks may advance cash or visa cards.
Travellers cheques: To avoid additional exchange rate charges, travellers are advised to take travellers cheques in Euros or Pounds Sterling.
Currency restrictions: The import of local currency is unlimited, subject to declaration. The export of local currency is unlimited for EU residents; other nationalities must declare currency that is to be exported (proof of origin might be demanded). The import of foreign currency is unlimited, subject to declaration. The export of foreign currency is limited to the equivalent of CFAfr100,000.
Exchange rate indicators: The following figures are included as a guide to the movements of the CFA Franc against Sterling and the US Dollar:

Date	Feb '04	May '04	Aug '04	Nov '04
£1.00=	961.13	983.76	978.35	936.79
$1.00=	528.01	550.79	531.03	494.69

Banking hours: Mon-Fri 0800-1100 and 1500-1700. Some banks may open on Saturday.

Duty Free

The following items may be imported into Benin by travellers aged over 15 without incurring customs duty:
200 cigarettes or 25 cigars or 250g of tobacco; 1 bottle of wine and 1 bottle of spirits; 500ml of eau de toilette and 250ml of perfume.

Public Holidays

2005: Jan 1 New Year's Day. **Jan 10** Traditional Day. **Jan 21** Tabaski (Feast of the Sacrifice). **Mar 28** Easter Monday. **Apr 21** Prophet's Birthday. **May 1** Labour Day. **May 5** Ascension Day. **May 16** Whit Monday. **Aug 1** Independence Day. **Aug 15** Assumption. **Oct 26** Armed Forces Day. **Nov 1** All Saints' Day. **Nov 3-5** Eid al-Fitr (End of Ramadan). **Nov 30** National Day. **Dec 25** Christmas Day.
2006: Jan 1 New Year's Day. **Jan 10** Traditional Day/Tabaski (Feast of the Sacrifice). **Apr 11** Prophet's Birthday. **Apr 17**

Easter Monday. **May 1** Labour Day. **May 25** Ascension Day. **Jun 5** Whit Monday. **Aug 1** Independence Day. **Aug 15** Assumption. **Oct 22-24** Eid al-Fitr (End of Ramadan). **Oct 26** Armed Forces Day. **Nov 1** All Saints' Day. **Nov 30** National Day. **Dec 25** Christmas Day.
Note: Muslim festivals are timed according to local sightings of various phases of the moon and the dates given above are approximations. For further details, see the *World of Islam* appendix.

Health

	Special Precautions?	Certificate Required?
Yellow Fever	Yes	1
Cholera	Yes	2
Typhoid & Polio	3	N/A
Malaria	4	N/A

Note: Regulations and requirements may be subject to change at short notice, and you are advised to contact your doctor well in advance of your intended date of departure. Any numbers in the chart refer to the footnotes below.

1: A yellow fever vaccination certificate is required by all travellers over one year of age. Risk occurs in all rural areas, but especially in Atakora and Borgou.
2: Following WHO guidelines issued in 1973, a cholera vaccination certificate is no longer a condition of entry to Benin. However, cholera is a serious risk in this country and precautions are essential. Up-to-date advice should be sought before deciding whether these precautions should include vaccination as medical opinion is divided over its effectiveness; see the *Health* appendix.
3: Vaccination against typhoid is advised.
4: Malaria is a risk all year throughout the country. It occurs predominantly in the malignant *falciparum* form. Resistance to chloroquine is common. A weekly dose of 250mg of mefloquine is recommended.
Food & drink: All water should be regarded as being potentially contaminated. Water used for drinking, brushing teeth or making ice should have first been boiled or otherwise sterilised. Milk is unpasteurised and should be boiled. Powdered or tinned milk is available and is advised, but make sure that it is reconstituted with pure water. Avoid all dairy products. Only eat well-cooked meat and fish, preferably served hot. Pork, salad and mayonnaise may carry increased risk. Vegetables should be cooked and fruit peeled.
Other risks: *Hepatitis A* and *E* are widespread. *Hepatitis B* is hyperendemic. *Hepatitis C* occurs. *Meningococcal meningitis* is a risk, depending on the area and the time of year. Immunisation against *hepatitis B*, *diphtheria* and *meningococcal A* and *C* is sometimes recommended.
Bilharzia (schistosomiasis) is present. Avoid swimming and paddling in fresh water; swimming pools which are well chlorinated and maintained are safe.
Onchoceriasis (river blindness) exists and precautions are recommended. *TB* occurs. *Haemorrhagic fevers* can be a risk in rural areas; rat-contaminated food should be avoided. The hot, dusty, windy environmental conditions in November and December may exacerbate respiratory problems.
Rabies is present. For those at high risk, vaccination before arrival should be considered. If you are bitten, seek medical advice without delay. For more information consult the *Health* appendix.
Health care: Medical facilities are limited, especially outside the major towns, and not all medicines are available. Doctors and hospitals often expect immediate cash payment for health services. Medical insurance is strongly recommended.

Travel - International

AIR: *Air Burkina, Air France, Air Gabon, Air Ivoire, Cameroon Airlines* and *Delta Airlines* all run services to and from Benin. Benin also has a shareholding in *Air Afrique (RK).*
International airports: *Cotonou Cadjehoun (COO)* is 5km (3 miles) west of the city. Taxis and limousines are available to the city (travel time – 15-20 minutes). Airport facilities include duty-free shop, restaurant, bar, post office, business centre, 24-hour medical facilities, bank and car hire (*Benin Limousine* and Hertz *Benin*).
Departure tax: None.
SEA: Several shipping lines run regular cargo services from Marseille to Cotonou. Local shipping from Lagos arrives in Porto Novo.
RAIL: The railway line from Parakou (via Gaya) to Niamey in Niger, currently under construction, will provide the first rail link into Niger.
ROAD: There are at least three good main roads: one connecting Cotonou with Niamey in Niger; another connecting Lagos with Porto Novo, Cotonou, Lomé and Accra; and a third connecting Parakou with Kara in Togo. Buses and taxis are available.

Travel - Internal

AIR: Government aeroplanes run services between Cotonou, Parakou, Natitingou, Djougou and Kandi. It is also possible to charter two-seater aeroplanes.
RAIL: Benin has about 600km (400 miles) of rail track. Trains run from Cotonou to Pobé, Ouidah and Parakou. Food is available on some services. Upholstered seats are available only in first-class cars and these exist only on the route to Parakou. Children aged under four travel free and children aged four to nine pay half fare. Approximate travel times from Cotonou to *Parakou* is 12 to 14 hours, to *Segboroué* is two hours 30 minutes and to *Pobé* is four hours.
ROAD: The roads are in reasonably good condition and many of those which run from Cotonou to Dassa, and Parakou to Malanville, are paved. Tracks are passable during the dry season but often impassable during the rainy season. Traffic drives on the right. Minibus and bush taxi services run along major road routes. Minibuses are cheaper but slower. **Car hire:** A number of local firms are available in Cotonou. **Documentation:** An International Driving Permit is required.
URBAN: Taxis are widely available in the main towns. Taxi fares should be agreed in advance.

Accommodation

Main towns and urban areas have a variety of hotels. Top-end hotels are, however, mainly found in and around the capital. There are also some campsites in and around Cotonou. There are a few establishments (*campements*) for **game viewing** at Porga near Pendjari National Park.

Resorts & Excursions

Abomey, situated about 100km (60 miles) northeast of the capital, was once the capital of a Fon kingdom and contains an excellent museum covering the history of the Abomey kingdoms (with a throne made of human skulls) and the **Fetish Temple**. Nearby is the **Centre Artisanal** where local craft products are sold at reasonable prices. Cotonou has a market, the **Dan Tokpa**, which is normally open every four days. The museum here is well worth a visit. The lake village of **Ganvie**, 18km (11miles) northwest of Cotonou, has houses built on stilts and a water-market. About 32km (20 miles) to the west is the town of **Ouidah**, notable for its old Portuguese fort and the **Temple of the Sacred Python**.
Porto Novo, the capital, is the administrative centre of the country, containing many examples of colonial and pre-colonial art and architecture. The **Ethnological Museum** is probably the most notable place of interest for a visitor. The northwest of the country is the home of the Somba people, whose goods can be bought at the weekly market at **Boukombe**.
Benin has two national parks. **Pendjari** is normally only open between December and June and has a wide range of wildlife including cheetahs, hippos and crocodiles. Accommodation is available. The **'W' National Park** straddles the frontier region between Niger, Benin and Burkina Faso and is less well developed.

Sport & Activities

There are limited facilities for **watersports** on the coast, but visitors should note that tides and currents can render the sea very dangerous and at certain places only the strongest swimmers should venture in. There are good beaches at *Grand Popo* and *Ouidah*. In Cotonou, several hotels have **swimming** pools, and **tennis** is available at the Club du Benin and **sailing** at the Yacht Club. A dug-out **canoe** or **motorboat** can be hired on Nakoue Lagoon.
Wildlife: The country's two national parks, *Pendjari* and *'W'*, are the best places to view **wildlife**. For further details see the *Resorts and Excursions* section.

Social Profile

FOOD & DRINK: There is a selection of restaurants and hotels in Cotonou, serving French food with table service, although some also serve local African specialities, particularly seafood.
NIGHTLIFE: Cotonou offers several nightclubs, but elsewhere there is little nightlife except during festivals.
SHOPPING: In Cotonou, along the marina, there are many stalls selling handicrafts and souvenirs. The Dan Tokpa market borders the Cotonou Lagoon and is stocked with many goods from Nigeria and elsewhere, as well as traditional medicines and artefacts. Crafts and local goods can be purchased in many towns and villages elsewhere, particularly in markets. Good buys include ritual masks, tapestries, elongated statues and pottery. **Shopping hours:** Mon-Sat 0900-1300 and 1600-1900.
SOCIAL CONVENTIONS: Normal courtesies are appreciated; it is customary to shake hands on arrival and departure. However, religious beliefs play a large part in society and these should be respected. Voodoo is perhaps the most striking and best-known religion, and has acquired considerable social and political power. Only priests can communicate with voodoos and spirits of the dead. If travelling, it is advisable to clear itineraries with district or provincial authorities. Casual wear is acceptable in most places. **Tipping:** It is normal to tip 10 per cent of the bill in hotels and restaurants.

Business Profile

ECONOMY: Since the transition to democratic government in 1991, Benin has undergone a remarkable economic recovery. A large injection of external investment from both private and public sources has alleviated the economic difficulties of the early 1990s, caused by global recession and persistently low commodity prices (although the latter continues to affect the economy). Benin's economy is principally agricultural – it is self-sufficient in basic foodstuffs, the main export commodities being cotton, peanuts, coffee and palm oil. The manufacturing sector is confined to some light industry, mainly involved in processing primary products and the production of consumer goods. A planned joint hydroelectric project with neighbouring Togo is intended to reduce Benin's dependence on imported energy (mostly from Ghana), which currently accounts for a significant proportion of the country's imports. The service sector has grown quickly, stimulated by economic liberalisation and fiscal reform. Membership of the CFA Franc Zone offers reasonable currency stability, as well as access to French economic support. Benin sells its products mainly to France and, in smaller quantities, to India, Korea, Japan and The Netherlands. The country's leading suppliers are France and Germany. Benin is also a member of the West African economic community ECOWAS.
BUSINESS: It is essential to be able to conduct conversations in French. Normal courtesies should be observed and punctuality is especially important. Lightweight tropical suits should be worn. **Office hours:** Mon-Fri 0800-1230 and 1500-1830.
COMMERCIAL INFORMATION: The following organisation can offer advice: Chambre de Commerce et d'Industrie du Bénin, Avenue du Général de Gaulle, 01 BP 31, Cotonou (tel: 312 081 *or* 314 386; fax: 313 299; e-mail: ccib@bow.intnet.bj).

Climate

The south has an equatorial climate with four seasons. It is hot and dry from January to April and during August, with rainy seasons through May to July and September to December. The north has more extreme temperatures, hot and dry between November and June, cooler and very wet between July and October.
Required clothing: Lightweight cottons and linens. A light raincoat or an umbrella is necessary in rainy seasons and warmer clothes are advised for cool evenings.

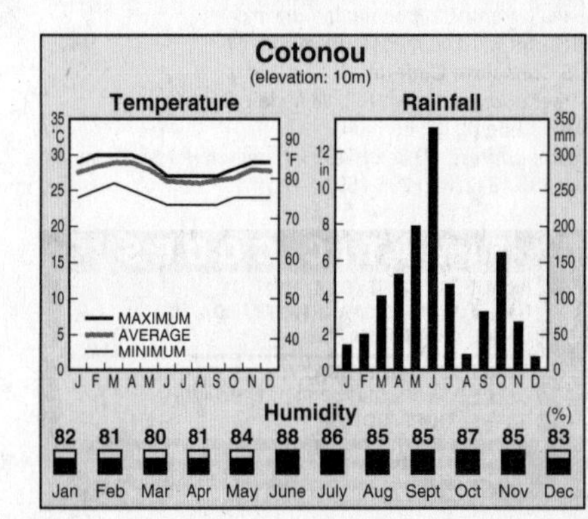

Bermuda

LATEST TRAVEL ADVICE CONTACTS

British Foreign and Commonwealth Office
Tel: (0870) 606 0290 Website: www.fco.gov.uk
US Department of State
Website: http://travel.state.gov/travel
Canadian Department of Foreign Affairs and Int'l Trade
Tel: (1 800) 267 8376 Website: www.dfait-maeci.gc.ca

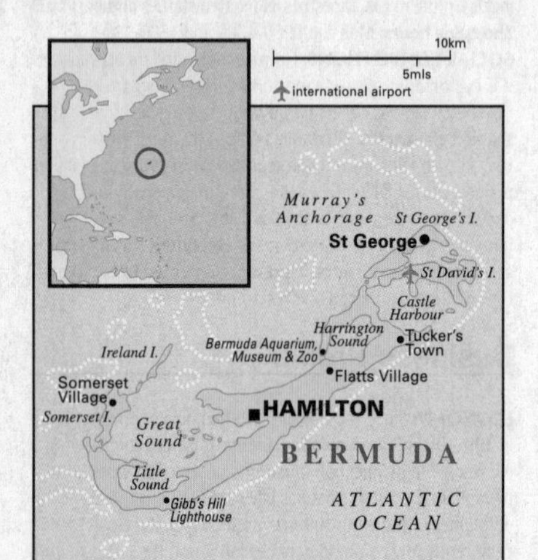

Location: Western Atlantic Ocean.

Country dialling code: 1 441.

Bermuda is a British Crown Colony, and is represented abroad by British Embassies – see *United Kingdom* section.
Department of Tourism
Street address: Global House, 43 Church Street, Hamilton HM 12, Bermuda
Postal address: PO Box HM465, Hamilton HM BX, Bermuda
Tel: 292 0023. Fax: 292 7537.
E-mail: travel@bermudatourism.com
Website: www.bermudatourism.com
Department of Immigration
Government Administration Building, Parliament Street, Hamilton, Bermuda
Tel: 295 5151. Fax: 295 4115.
Website: www.gov.bm
The UK Passport Service
London Passport Office, Globe House, 89 Ecclestone Square, London SW1V 1PN, UK
Tel: (0870) 521 0410 (24-hour national advice line) *or* (020) 7901 2150 (visa enquiries for British Overseas Territories).
Fax: (020) 7271 8403.
E-mail: info@passport.gov.uk *or* london@ukpa.gov.uk
Website: www.passport.gov.uk *or* www.ukpa.gov.uk
Opening hours: Mon-Fri 0730-1900; Sat 0900-1600.
Regional offices in: Belfast, Durham, Glasgow, Liverpool, Newport and Peterborough.
Personal callers for visas should go to the agency window in the collection room of the London office.
Bermuda Department of Tourism
c/o Hills Balfour LTD, Notcutt House, 36 Southwark Bridge Road, London SE1 9EU, UK
Tel: (020) 7202 6378. Fax: (020) 7928 0722.
E-mail: bermudatourism@hillsbalfour.com
Website: www.bermudatourism.co.uk
Bermuda Department of Tourism
675 Third Avenue, 20th Floor, New York, NY 10017, USA
Tel: (212) 818 9800. Fax: (212) 983 5289.
E-mail: frontdesk@bermudatourism.com
Website: www.bermudatourism.com
US Consulate General
Street address: Crown Hill, 16 Middle Road, Devonshire DV 03, Bermuda
Postal address: PO Box HM325, Hamilton HM BX, Bermuda
Tel: 295 1342. Fax: 295 1592.

TIMATIC CODES

Health
AMADEUS: **TI-DFT/BDA/HE**
GALILEO/WORLDSPAN: **TI-DFT/BDA/HE**
SABRE: **TIDFT/BDA/HE**

Visa
AMADEUS: **TI-DFT/BDA/VI**
GALILEO/WORLDSPAN: **TI-DFT/BDA/VI**
SABRE: **TIDFT/BDA/VI**

To access TIMATIC country information on Health and Visa regulations through the Computer Reservations System (CRS), type in the appropriate command line listed above.

Bermuda Department of Tourism
Suite 1004, 1200 Bay Street, Toronto, Ontario M5R 2A5, Canada
Tel: (416) 923 9600. Fax: (416) 923 4840.
Website: www.bermudatourism.com
The Canadian Consulate in New York deals with enquiries relating to Bermuda (see *USA* section).

General Information

AREA: 53 sq km (20.59 sq miles).
POPULATION: 61,688 (official estimate 2000).
POPULATION DENSITY: 1,163.9 per sq km.
CAPITAL: Hamilton. **Population:** 1100 (1991).
GEOGRAPHY: Bermuda consists of a chain of some 180 coral islands and islets lying 1046km (650 miles) off the coast of North Carolina, in the Atlantic Ocean. 10 of the islands are linked by bridges and causeways to form the principal mainland. There are no rivers or streams and the islands are entirely dependent on rainfall for fresh water. Coastlines are characterised by a succession of small bays with beaches of fine pale pink coral sand. The surrounding waters are a vivid blue-green. Inland there is an abundance of subtropical plants and flowers.
GOVERNMENT: British Crown Colony since 1684. Gained internal autonomy in 1968. **Head of State:** HM Queen Elizabeth II, represented locally by Governor Sir John Vereker since 2002. **Head of Government:** Prime Minister Alex Scott since 2003.
LANGUAGE: English is the official language. There is a small community of Portuguese speakers.
RELIGION: Anglican, Episcopal, Roman Catholic and other Christian denominations.
TIME: GMT - 4 (GMT - 3 from first Sunday in April to last Sunday in October).
ELECTRICITY: 120 volts AC, 60Hz. American (flat) two-pin plugs are standard.
COMMUNICATIONS: Telephone: IDD is available. Country code: 1 441. Outgoing international code: 011. The internal telephone system is operated by the Bermuda Telephone Company. Bermuda numbers dialled from within Bermuda should be prefixed with the last two digits of the country code (29 or 23) but there are no conventional area codes. **Mobile telephone:** GSM 1900. Operators are *A&T Wireless* (www.attwireless.bm) and *Mobility LTD* (www.mobilityltd.bm). Coverage is excellent. TDMA and AMPS (800 MHz) networks operated by *Cellular One* (website: www.cellularone.bm) and *Mobility Ltd*. **Fax:** This service is available from many hotels and offices. **Internet:** ISPs include *Logic Communications* (website: www.logic.bm) and *NorthRock Communications* (website: www.northrock.bm). There are Internet cafes in Hamilton and St George. **Telegram:** *Cable & Wireless Ltd* operates Bermuda's international telecommunications system. Cablegrams may be sent from the *C&W* office in Hamilton. **Post:** Most letters will automatically travel airmail even if surface rates are paid, although paid-for airmail will be given priority. Airmail letters to Europe take five to seven days. *Poste restante* facilities are available. Post office hours: Mon-Fri 0830-1700. In addition, the General Post Office in Hamilton is open on Saturday mornings until 1200. **Press:** The main newspapers are *The Mid-Ocean News* (weekly), *The Royal Gazette* (daily) and *The Bermuda Sun* (twice weekly).
Radio: BBC World Service (website: www.bbc.co.uk/worldservice) and Voice of America (website: www.voa.gov) can be received. From time to time the frequencies change and the most up-to-date can be found online.

Passport/Visa

	Passport Required?	Visa Required?	Return Ticket Required?
Full British	Yes	No	Yes
Australian	Yes	No	Yes
Canadian	1	No	Yes
USA	1	No	Yes
Other EU	Yes	No/1	Yes
Japanese	Yes	No	Yes

Note: *Regulations and requirements may be subject to change at short notice, and you are advised to contact the appropriate diplomatic or consular authority before finalising travel arrangements. Details of these may be found at the head of this country's entry. Any numbers in the chart refer to the footnotes below.*

Note: Before entering Bermuda, it is essential to be in possession of either a return or onward ticket to a country to which one has a legal right of entry. Anyone arriving in Bermuda and intending to return to their own country via another one which requires a visa *must* obtain such a visa before arrival in Bermuda. Visitors are advised to check details with the British Overseas Territories Visa Section (see *Contact Addresses* section).
Restricted entry: Admission will be refused to travellers intending to immigrate from Bermuda to the USA. Those who intend to visit the USA must possess an onward ticket to a country beyond the USA and the necessary documents to enter that country.
PASSPORTS: Passport valid for six months after date of entry into Bermuda required by all except:
1. nationals of Canada and the USA with an original birth certificate and official photo ID.
VISAS: Required by all except the following:
(a) nationals of countries referred to in the chart above, and of their overseas territories, except nationals of the Slovak Republic and Slovenia, who *do* need a visa;
(b) citizens of Commonwealth countries (except nationals of Ghana, Jamaica, Nigeria, Pakistan and Sri Lanka who *do* need a visa);
(c) nationals of Andorra, Angola, Argentina, Benin, Bhutan, Bolivia, Brazil, Burkina Faso, Burundi, Cape Verde, Central African Republic, Chad, Chile, Colombia, Comoro Islands, Congo (Dem Rep), Congo (Rep), Costa Rica, Cote d'Ivoire, Dominican Republic, East Timor, Ecuador, El Salvador, Equatorial Guinea, Eritrea, Ethiopia, Gabon, Guatemala, Guinea, Guinea-Bissau, Honduras, Iceland, Indonesia, Israel, Korea (Rep), Laos, Libya, Liechtenstein, Madagascar, Mali, Mexico, Micronesia (Federated States of), Monaco, Mynamar, Nepal, Nicaragua, Niger, Norway, Panama, Paraguay, Peru, The Phillippines, Puerto Rico, Rwanda, San Marino, São Tomé e Principe, Senegal, Sudan, Surinam, Switzerland, Taiwan (China), Thailand, Togo, Turkey, Uruguay, Vatican City, Venezuela and Zimbabwe.
Note: (a) Visa controlled nationals who have the right to reside in the United States (Permanent Resident), Canada (Landed Immigrant status) or the United Kingdom (no limit on stay in the United Kingdom), and are in possession of proof of such status and a valid passport, do *not* require Bermuda entry visas. (b) Transit passengers from countries mentioned above must continue to a third country within five hours by the same aircraft, hold confirmed onward tickets and documentation and not leave the airport.
Types of visa and cost: *Tourist*: £28.
Validity: The permitted length of stay is initially three months. For extensions, permission should be sought from the immigration authorities in Bermuda (see address below).
Application to: Visa Section at UK Passport Office; see *Contact Addresses* section.
Application requirements: (a) Valid passport with two blank pages. (b) One application form. (c) Proof of onward or return ticket. (d) Fee payable in cash.
Working days required: Four weeks. Processing by post may take longer.
Temporary residence: Persons intending to take up residence and/or employment will require prior authorisation from the Department of Immigration, Government Administration Building, 30 Parliament Street, Hamilton HM 12 (tel: 295 5151 *and/or* ext 1378; fax: 295 4115).

Money

Currency: Bermuda Dollar (Bda$) = 100 cents. Notes are in denominations of Bda$100, 50, 20, 10, 5 and 2. Coins are in denominations of Bda$1, and 25, 10, 5 and 1 cents.
Note: The Bermuda Dollar is tied to the US Dollar.
Currency exchange: US Dollars are generally accepted at parity. It is illegal to exchange money other than at authorised banks or bureaux de change.
Credit & debit cards: American Express, Diners Club and MasterCard are accepted at most large hotels, shops and restaurants. Check with your credit or debit card company for details of merchant acceptability and other services which may be available.
Travellers cheques: US Dollar cheques are widely accepted. To avoid additional exchange rate charges, travellers are advised to take travellers cheques in US Dollars.
Currency restrictions: There is no limit to the import of local or foreign currency, provided declared on arrival. The export of local currency is limited to Bda$250. The export of foreign currency is subject to the amount imported and declared.
Exchange rate indicators: The following figures are included as a guide to the movements of the Bermuda Dollar against Sterling and the US Dollar:

Date	Feb '04	May '04	Aug '04	Nov '04
£1.00=	1.82	1.79	1.84	1.89
$1.00=	1.00	1.00	1.00	1.00

Banking hours: Mon 0930-1600, Tue-Thurs 0830-1600, Fri 0830-1630.

Duty Free

The following goods may be taken into Bermuda by travellers aged over 18 years without incurring customs duty:
200 cigarettes and 50 cigars and 454g of tobacco; 1137ml (1qt) of spirits and 1137ml (1qt) of wine.
Prohibited items: Spear guns for fishing. All visitors should declare any prescribed drugs on arrival as regulations are strictly observed. Clearance of merchandise and sales materials for use at trade conventions must be arranged in advance with the hotel concerned.

Public Holidays

2005: Jan 1 New Year's Day. **Jan 3** New Year's Day Holiday (forwarded to Monday). **Mar 25** Good Friday. **May 24** Bermuda Day. **Jun 13** Queen's Birthday Celebrations. **Jul 28** Emancipation Day. **Sep 5** Labour Day. **Nov 11** Remembrance Day. **Dec 25** Christmas Day. **Dec 26** Boxing Day. **Dec 27** Christmas Day Holiday (forwarded to Tuesday).
2006: Jan 1 New Year's Day. **Apr 14** Good Friday. **May 24** Bermuda Day. **Jun 12** Queen's Birthday Celebrations. **Jul 29** Emancipation Day. **Sep 4** Labour Day. **Nov 11** Remembrance Day. **Dec 25-26** Boxing Day.

Health

	Special Precautions?	Certificate Required?
Yellow Fever	No	No
Cholera	No	No
Typhoid & Polio	No	N/A
Malaria	No	N/A

Note: *Regulations and requirements may be subject to change at short notice, and you are advised to contact your doctor well in advance of your intended date of departure. Any numbers in the chart refer to the footnotes below.*

Health care: Health insurance is essential as medical costs are very high. There is a fully-equipped 237-bed hospital near Hamilton.

Travel - International

AIR: Bermuda has no national airline, but *British Airways* operates regular weekly flights to and from London Gatwick and Bermuda. Other airlines serving Bermuda include *Air Canada, American Airlines, Continental Airlines, Delta, Iberia, United* and *US Airways*.
Approximate flight times: To Bermuda from *London* is 7 hours 45 minutes and from *New York* is 1 hour 45 minutes.
International airports: *Bermuda International (BDA)* (website: www.bermudaairport.com), is 16km (10 miles) from Hamilton (travel time – 30 minutes). Bermuda Hosts (buses) meet all arrivals. Taxis are also available. There are duty-free shops, cafes, bar and bureaux de change at the airport. Duty-free goods may also be purchased in town shops for collection at the airport on departure.
Departure tax: A tax of Bda$25 is included in air tickets. Children under two years and passengers in immediate transit are exempt.
SEA: Many cruise lines call at Bermuda including *Carnival, Celebrity Cruises, Cunard Line, Norwegian Cruise Lines, Princess Cruises, Radisson Seven Seas* and *Royal Caribbean International*. Cruises operate in the summer months of April to October and suspend services during the winter.

Travel - Internal

SEA: Ferries run on a regular daily schedule across Hamilton Harbour and to points on the West End and East (in summer months).
ROAD: The main island has an extensive road network, but foreign visitors may not drive cars in Bermuda. Motorcycles and scooters may be hired (see below). Caution should be taken as many roads are narrow and winding. Outside main urban areas, there is also little street lighting. The speed limit is 35kph (22mph) and traffic drives on the left. **Bus:** Buses are modern, frequent and punctual. Bermuda's state-run buses (painted pink) are a pleasant and inexpensive way to visit points of interest. The trip from Hamilton to the town of St George's, the northeastern tip of Bermuda, takes about 30 minutes, with the ride from Hamilton to Somerset, Bermuda's westernmost point, taking about 45 minutes. It is essential to have the correct fare in coins. A route and schedule map is available free, and books of tickets are available at sub-post offices. **Taxi:** All taxis are metered with government-set rates, with a surcharge after midnight; there is a maximum of four passengers per taxi. Taxis displaying small blue flags are driven by qualified guides approved by the Department of Tourism. A 25 per cent surcharge operates between midnight and 0600.
Carriages: Horse-drawn carriages are available in Hamilton. **Motorcycle/bicycle hire:** Lightweight motor-assisted bicycles ('livery cycles') may be hired throughout the island; a driving licence is not required for this. Crash helmets must be worn. Third party insurance is compulsory. Bicycles can also be hired. The Department of Tourism produces a comprehensive sheet giving details of prices and supplies. Minimum age limit is 16 years.
Travel times: The following chart gives approximate travel times from **Hamilton** (in hours and minutes) to other major towns and the airport on Bermuda.

Credit: © Bermuda Tourism

	Road	Sea
Airport	0.30	-
St George's	0.30	-
Somerset	0.45	0.30
Naval Dockyard	0.45	-

Accommodation

The Bermuda Department of Tourism issues a booklet *Where to stay in Bermuda* listing all accommodation. Another leaflet gives rates and added taxes. Reduced rates are available during the *Rendezvous*, or 'low' season, which runs from November to March, and there are many special package tours for speciality holidays. Visitors will be charged 7.25 per cent government room occupancy tax. A service charge between 10 and 15 per cent may also be added to the room rate in hotels.
HOTELS: Hotels are all of a high standard. The top resort hotels offer a range of facilities including shops, restaurants, organised entertainment, beauty salon and taxi rank. They usually have their own beach or beach club and pool. Several have their own golf course. Hotels usually offer a choice of meal plans. Information is available from the Bermuda Hotel Association, 61 King Street, Hamilton MH 19 (tel: 295 2127; fax: 292 6671; website: www.bermudahotels.com). **Grading:** There is no formal grading system in Bermuda, only MAP, AP, BP, CP and EP. MAP is Modified American Plan; breakfast and dinner included with the price of the room, plus, in some places, British-style afternoon tea. AP is American Plan; room, breakfast, lunch and dinner. BP is Bermuda Plan; room and full breakfast only. CP is Continental Plan; room and light breakfast. EP is European Plan; room only. Large hotels with many facilities make up about 7 per cent of accommodation in Bermuda. Smaller hotels (around 16 per cent) have fewer than 150 rooms. Normally less expensive than the self-contained resorts, they have limited on-site facilities for shopping and entertainment and are less formal.
GUEST HOUSES: Generally, guest houses taking fewer than 12 guests are usually small private homes. Some incorporate several housekeeping units (see below), while others provide shared kitchen facilities. Most of the larger establishments are old Bermudian residences with spacious gardens which have been converted and modernised. A few have their own waterfront and/or pool. Guest houses make up 50 per cent of accommodation in Bermuda. **Grading:** Larger guest houses may offer the Bermuda Plan or a slightly stripped-down version of the CP (Continental Plan) – room and light breakfast. EP (European Plan) consists of room only. All guest houses offer an informal atmosphere.
COTTAGE COLONIES: These are typically Bermudian and feature a main clubhouse with dining room, lounge and bar. The cottage units are spread throughout landscaped grounds and offer privacy and luxury. Though most have kitchenettes for beverages or light snacks, they are not self-catering units. All have their own beach and/or pool.
CLUB RESORTS: These are noted for privacy and luxury and are for members or by invitation only. There are two club resorts on the main island.
SELF-CATERING: Housekeeping cottages are large properties situated in landscaped estates with their own beach and pool, much like cottage colonies, but without a main club-house. They are considered to be luxury units. All have kitchen facilities but BP or a reduced CP is available at some establishments.
APARTMENTS: Apartments are smaller and less expensive with fewer amenities than housekeeping cottages. Most holiday apartments are nonetheless comfortable. Some have a pool; all have a kitchen and a minimal daily maid service.
CAMPING/CARAVANNING: There are no camping facilities for visitors in Bermuda.

Credit: © Bermuda Tourism

Resorts & Excursions

HAMILTON: The colony's capital city, situated at the end of Bermuda's **Great Sound** on the inner curve of the 'fish hook' is an interesting place to explore. Here, between Parliament Street and Court Street, is the **Cabinet Building** where the Senate – the Upper House of Bermuda's Parliament – meets. The Lower Chamber of Parliament is housed in the **Sessions House** in Hamilton and is open to the public. Front Street is Hamilton's main street which runs along the water's edge from **Albuoy's Point**, site of the Ferrydock and the Royal Bermuda Yacht Club, to King Street in the east. Located on Queen Street in Hamilton is **Perot's Post Office**. The Perot stamp, Bermuda's first postage stamp, was printed by Bermuda's Postmaster from 1818 to 1862. In the summer months there are usually up to three cruise ships moored at the city's piers. Ferry trips are available round Hamilton Harbour, and also longer cruises to Great Sound and the rural village of Somerset. The restored 19th-century **Fort Hamilton** welcomes visitors to

its formidable ramparts, cannon, underground web of limestone tunnels and spectacular view of Hamilton. In **Hamilton parish** is the Bermuda **Aquarium** and **Natural History Museum and Zoo**, based at **Flatts Village**.
ELSEWHERE: In **Somerset**, on the western end of the island, **Fort Scaur** is a good place to picnic, fish, swim and enjoy the panoramic view of the picturesque Great Sound. At the far eastern end of the chain of islands is the 17th-century town of **St George**, Bermuda's first capital, founded in 1612. It has been the focus of considerable recent restoration; today, the town's narrow winding lanes and historic landmarks appear much as they did more than three centuries ago. At the corner of Duke of Clarence Street and Featherbed Alley is a working model of a 17th-century printing press. Also to be seen are the **Confederate Museum**, a hotel for Confederate officers during America's Civil War; the **Stocks & Pillory**; and the replica of the *Deliverance*, one of Bermuda's first ships. St George also has many excellent pubs, restaurants and shops. **Gates Fort**, which dates back to 1620, is built on a promontory overlooking the sea and offers a spectacular view of the ocean and harbour. Nearby is **Fort St Catherine**, built in 1622, the largest and one of the most fascinating of the island's fortifications. At the very tip of Bermuda, on the western side, is **Ireland Island**, with a **Maritime Museum** which displays relics of sunken wrecks and the neo-classical buildings of the **Royal Naval Dockyard**. Two of the best known caves are **Crystal Caves** and **Leamington Caves**, made up of sprawling underground systems and crystalline tidal pools. They are open daily in season. The best view of the island is from **Gibb's Hill Lighthouse**, in Southampton parish. Two notable churches on the island include **Old Devonshire Church** and **St Peter's Church**, on Duke of York Street in old St George. Everywhere on the island there are circles of stone, called **Moongates**, a design brought to Bermuda in the 19th century by a sea captain who had seen them on a voyage to China. Oriental legend has it that honeymooners should walk through them and make a wish.

Credit: © Bermuda Tourism

Sport & Activities

Watersports: Bermuda's most famous beaches lie along the island's southern edge. Some of the most beautiful are at *Chaplin, Horseshoe Bay, Stonehole* and *Warwick Long Bay*. **Snorkelling** and **scuba-diving** are popular. Visibility underwater is often as much as 61m (200ft). Experienced scuba-divers can go below for a historic 'tour' of old wrecks, cannons and other remnants of past disasters on the reefs. All necessary equipment is easy to hire - visitors should note, however, that spear guns are not allowed. For **sailing** enthusiasts, the *Blue Water Cruising Race* - from Marion, Massachusetts, to Bermuda - takes place in June bi-annually, in odd-numbered years. The *Newport to Bermuda Ocean Yacht Race* is also held bi-annually, in even-numbered years; this world-famous *June Blue Water Classic* (fondly referred to as the 'Thrash to the Onion Patch') attracts scores of the finest racing craft afloat. The week-long festivities, which follow the arrival of the boats, are held at the Royal Bermuda Yacht Club. In August, the *Non-Mariners Race* is held. Sailboats and skippers are available for hire from 'Sail Yourself' charter agencies. Bermuda is one of the world's finest **fishing** centres, especially for light-tackle fishing. Equipment may be rented for shore fishing and there are charter boats for reef and deep-sea fishing. For deep-sea aficionados, wahoo, amberjack, marlin and tuna abound. On the reefs, there are amberjack, great barracuda, grey snapper and yellowtail. Shore fishermen can test their skills on bonefish and pompano. The best fishing is from May to November, when trophies are awarded.
Golf: There are seven 18-hole courses, including the *Mid-Ocean Club*, which is world-renowned for its challenge and beauty, and *Port Royal*, situated in oceanside terrain. There is one 9-hole layout, Ocean View. For information on Amateur, Professional and Pro-Am tournaments, write to the Bermuda Golf Association, PO Box 433, Hamilton (tel: 238 1367; fax: 238 0938; e-mail: info@bermudagolf.org; website: www.bermudagolf.org).
Tennis: There are almost 100 courts on the island, with a variety of surfaces. Most of the larger Bermuda hotels have their own courts, many of them floodlit for night play. Tournaments are held all year round and several are open to visitors.
Cricket: The annual *Cup Match*, an island-wide, two-day public holiday (played since 1902 in July/August), is held once a year, when the St George's and Somerset Cricket clubs vie for the Championship Cup.
Soccer: A hugely popular sport amongst Bermudians, who even have some of their nationals playing in UK football leagues. The season in Bermuda runs from the end of September through April and the matches themselves are usually played each weekend and on some weeknights on a variety of soccer fields. For further information, contact the Bermuda Football Association, PO Box HM 745, Hamilton, HM CX (tel: 295 2199; fax: 295 0773; e-mail: bfa@northrock.bm).

Credit: © Bermuda Tourism

Social Profile

FOOD & DRINK: Hotel cooking is usually international with some Bermudian specialities such as Bermuda lobster (in season September to mid-April), mussel pie, conch stew, cassava pie, *Wahoo* steak, *Hoppin' John* (black-eyed peas and rice), fish chowder laced with sherry, peppers, rum and shark. Other seafoods include rockfish, red snapper, guinea chick (shiny lobster) and yellowtail. Peculiar to Bermuda is the Bermuda onion; other fine home-grown products include pawpaw and strawberries in January and February, and a variety of local citrus fruit. Traditional Sunday breakfast is codfish and potatoes while desserts include sweet potato pudding, bay grape jelly and a syllabub of guava jelly, cream and sherry. There is a vast variety of restaurants, cafes, bars and taverns to suit all pockets. Service will vary although generally table service can be expected.
Local drinks and cocktails have Caribbean rum as a base, and have colourful names such as *Dark and Stormy* and the famous *Rum Swizzle*. British, European and US beer is available. It is normal in bars to pay for each drink and to tip the barman. In restaurants, drinks are added to the bill.
NIGHTLIFE: Most hotels offer a variety of entertainment. Dancing, barbecues, nightclubs and discos are all available. There are also island cruises such as the *Hawkins Island Don't Stop the Carnival Party*, which enables exclusive access to Hawkins Island (it is accessible only by boat) for entertainment - even the locals attend. Local music is a mixture of Calypso and Latin American, and steel band music is very popular. All the latest listings can be found in *Preview Bermuda* and *This Week in Bermuda*.
SHOPPING: The best buys are imported merchandise such as French perfumes, English bone china, Swiss watches, Danish silver, American costume jewellery, German cameras, Scottish tweeds, and various spirits and liqueurs. Bermuda-made articles include handicrafts, pottery, cedar ware, fashions, rum, honey, Bermuda Rum cakes, Sherry Peppers condiments, records and paintings by local artists. Antique shops may have the odd good bargain and shops in the countryside offer many souvenirs. Bathing suits, sports clothes, straw hats and, of course, Bermuda shorts, are other good buys. There is no sales tax or VAT. **Shopping hours:** Mon-Sat 0900-1700, with some closing early on Thursday. Shops at the Royal Naval Dockyard are open on Sun 1000-1700.
SPECIAL EVENTS: Bermuda's many annual events include concerts, marathons, cricket matches, regattas, golf and tennis tournaments, and horse shows. The following is a selection of special events occurring in Bermuda in 2005; for a full list of special events, contact Bermuda Tourism (see *Contact Addresses* section):
Jan 13-31 *Festival of the Performing Arts*. **Jan 13-Feb 26** *Bermuda Festival*. **Jan 14-16** *Bermuda International Race Weekend*. **Feb 5-6** *Champion of Champions Harness Racing*. **Mar 7-12** *Ladies/Men's Amateur Match Play Championships*. **Mar 18-24** *International Film Festival*. **Mar 25** *Annual Good Friday Kite Festival*. **Mar 26** *Cat Fanciers' Association Cat Shows*. **Mar 27** *Open Karate Championships*. **Apr 4-9** *Virtual Spectator Bermuda Masters 2005 Squash Championship*. **May 24** *Bermuda Day Parade*. **Jun 13** *Queen's Birthday Parade*. **Jun 17-21** *Marion Bermuda Ocean Race*. **Jul 28-29** *Cup Match Cricket Festival*. **Sep 5** *Labour Day*, parade, stalls and games, Union Square, Hamilton. **Oct 13-16** *Bermuda Open for Men*, golf. **Nov 6-13** *World Rugby Classic*.
SOCIAL CONVENTIONS: Many of Bermuda's social conventions are British influenced, and there is a very English 'feel' to the islands. It is quite customary to politely greet people on the street, even if they are strangers. Casual wear is acceptable in most places during the day, but beachwear (including short tops and 'short' shorts) should be confined to the beach. Almost all hotels and restaurants require a jacket and tie in the evenings; check dress requirements in advance. Non-smoking areas will be marked. Drinking alcohol in public outside of a licensed premise is prohibited. **Tipping:** When not included in the bill, 15 per cent generally for most services. Hotels and guest houses add a set amount per person in lieu of tips to the bill.

Business Profile

ECONOMY: Bermuda's economy is dominated by two industries - tourism and international financial services - which together account for approximately 90 per cent of GDP. Offshore banking and related services have been the mainstay of the financial sector, although in recent years, insurance has grown to the point where Bermuda is now the world's third-largest insurance market. Tax receipts from several thousand offshore companies registered in Bermuda, plus customs duties, go some way to offsetting the island's large annual visible trade deficit of around US$500 million. The small light-manufacturing base in Bermuda is engaged in boat building, ship repair and perfume and pharmaceutical production. There is some agriculture, concentrated in the growing of fruit and vegetables, although most of Bermuda's food is imported along with all its oil, machinery and most manufactured goods. Bermuda has recently established an important diamond market. The USA is the largest trading partner followed by Japan, Germany and the UK.
BUSINESS: Lightweight suits or shirt and tie are acceptable, as are Bermuda shorts, when worn in the appropriate manner. Visiting cards and, occasionally, letters of introduction are used. Codes of practice are similar to those in the UK. **Office hours:** Mon-Fri 0900-1700.
COMMERCIAL INFORMATION: The following organisations can offer advice: Bermuda Chamber of Commerce, PO Box HM 655, Hamilton HMCX (tel: 295 4201; fax: 292 5779; e-mail: info@bermudacommerce.com; website: www.bermudacommerce.com) *or* Bermuda International Business Association (BIBA) Century House, 16 Par-La-Ville Road, Hamilton HM 08 (tel: 292 0632; fax: 292 1797; e-mail: info@biba.org; website: www.biba.org).
CONFERENCES/CONVENTIONS: The Bermuda Department of Tourism (see *Contact Addresses* section) can give information, including advice on customs arrangements for the speedy handling of materials. The Chamber of Commerce can also offer assistance; *Special Groups* and *Incentive Services* (published by the Department of Tourism) is a list of members' services available to organisers.

Climate

Semi-tropical, with no wet season. The Gulf Stream which flows between Bermuda and the North American continent keeps the climate temperate. A change of seasons comes during mid-November to mid-December and from late March through to April. Either spring or summer weather may occur and visitors should be prepared for both. Showers may be heavy at times but occur mainly at night. Summer temperatures prevail from May to mid-November with the warmest weather in July, August and September - this period is occasionally followed by high winds. Visitors should note that such high winds between June and November can (albeit rarely) turn into hurricanes and tropical storms.
Required clothing: Lightweight cottons and linens. Light waterproofs or umbrellas are advisable and warmer clothes for cooler months.

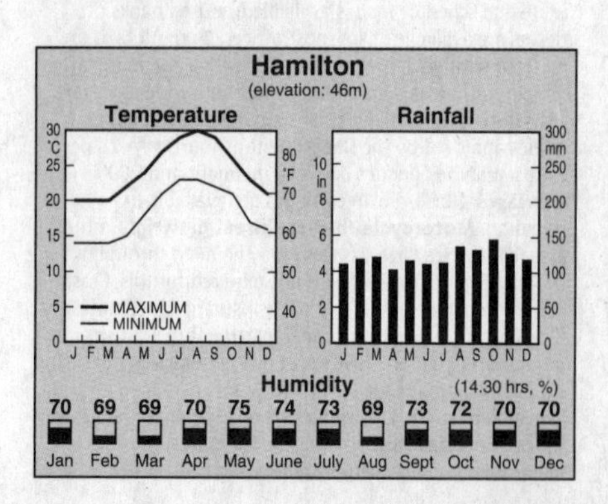

Bhutan

LATEST TRAVEL ADVICE CONTACTS

British Foreign and Commonwealth Office
Tel: (0870) 606 0290 Website: www.fco.gov.uk

US Department of State
Website: http://travel.state.gov/travel

Canadian Department of Foreign Affairs and Int'l Trade
Tel: (1 800) 267 8376 Website: www.dfait-maeci.gc.ca

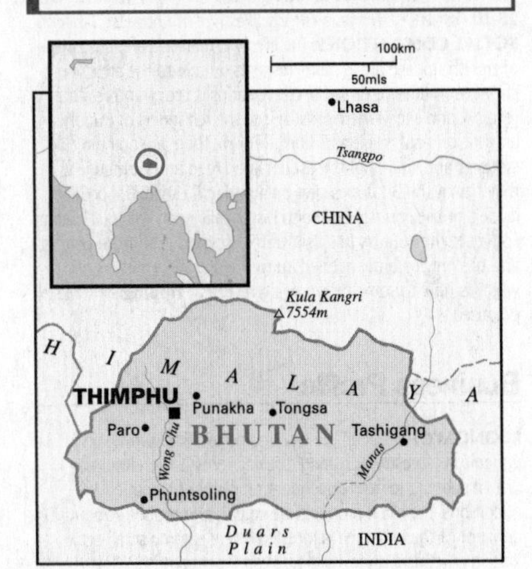

Location: South Asia (between Assam in northeast India and China).

Country dialing code: 975.

Department of Tourism
PO Box 126, Thimphu, Bhutan
Tel: (2) 323 251/2. Fax: (2) 323 695.
E-mail: tab@druknet.bt Website: www.tourism.gov.bt

Bhutan Tourism Corporation Limited (BTCL)
PO Box 159, Thimphu, Bhutan
Tel: (2) 323 517 *or* 392. Fax: (2) 323 392 *or* 322 479.
E-mail: btcl@druknet.bt
Website: www.kingdomofbhutan.com

Royal Bhutanese Embassy
Chandragupta Marg, Chanakyapuri, New Delhi 110 021, India
Tel: (11) 2688 9230 *or* 9807-9. Fax: (11) 2687 6710.
E-mail: bhutan@del2.vsnl.net.in *or* bhutanembassy_del@yahoo.com

Embassy of India
India House Estate, Thimphu, Bhutan
Tel: (2) 322 161 Fax: (2) 323 195 or 325 341.
E-mail: eoiss@druknet.bt
Website: www.eoithimphu.org

United Nations Development Programme
United Nations Building, GPO Box 162, Thimphu, Bhutan
Tel: (2) 322 424 *or* 315. Fax: (2) 322 657 *or* 328 526 (resident representative).
E-mail: fo.btn@undp.org *or* webmaster.bt@undp.org
Website: www.undp.org.bt

Bhutan Tourism Corporation Limited (BTCL)
c/o Far Fung Places, 1914 Fell Street, San Francisco, California 94117, USA
Tel: (415) 386 8306. Fax: (415) 386 8104.
E-mail: info@farfungplaces.com
Website: www.farfungplaces.com *or* www.kingdomofbhutan.com

The Permanent Mission of the Kingdom of Bhutan to the United Nations
2 United Nations Plaza, 27th Floor, New York, NY 10017, USA
Tel: (212) 826 1919. Fax: (212) 826 2998.
E-mail: pmbnewyork@aol.com *or* bhutan@un.int

General Information

AREA: 46,500 sq km (17,954 sq miles).
POPULATION: 654,269 (official estimate 2001).
POPULATION DENSITY: 14.1 per sq km.

TIMATIC CODES

Health	AMADEUS: TI-DFT/PBH/HE GALILEO/WORLDSPAN: **TI-DFT/PBH/HE** SABRE: **TIDFT/PBH/HE**
Visa	AMADEUS: **TI-DFT/PBH/VI** GALILEO/WORLDSPAN: **TI-DFT/PBH/VI** SABRE: **TIDFT/PBH/VI**

To access TIMATIC country information on Health and Visa regulations through the Computer Reservations System (CRS), type in the appropriate command line listed above.

CAPITAL: Thimphu. **Population:** 27,000 (official estimate 1990).
GEOGRAPHY: Bhutan is located in the eastern Himalayas, bordered to the north by China and to the south, east and west by India. The altitude varies from 300m (1000ft) in the narrow lowland region to 7000m (22,000ft) in the Himalayan plateau in the north, and there are three distinct climatic regions. The foothills are tropical and home to deer, lion, leopards and the rare golden monkey as well as much tropical vegetation including many species of wild orchids. The Inner Himalaya region is temperate; wildlife includes bear, boar and sambar and the area is rich in deciduous forests. The High Himalaya region is very thinly populated, but the steep mountain slopes are the home of many species of animals including snow leopards and musk deer.
GOVERNMENT: Constitutional Monarchy. **Head of State and Government:** Druk Gyalpo ('Dragon King') Jigme Singye Wangchuk since 1972.
LANGUAGE: Dzongkha is the official language. A large number of dialects are spoken, owing to the physical isolation of many villages. Sharchop Kha, from eastern Bhutan, is the most widely spoken. Nepali is common in the south of the country. English has been the language of educational instruction since 1964 and is widely spoken.
RELIGION: Mahayana Buddhism is the state religion; the majority of Bhutanese people follow the Drukpa school of the Kagyupa sect. Those living in the south are mainly Hindu.
TIME: GMT + 6.
ELECTRICITY: 220 volts AC, 50Hz.
COMMUNICATIONS: Telephone: Services are restricted to the main centres. Country code: 975. All other calls must go through the international operator. Outgoing international code: 00. **Mobile telephone:** GSM 900 network operated by B-Mobile launched in Summer 2003. **Internet:** The main ISP is *DrukNet* (website: www.druknet.bt). There are four Internet cafes in Thimphu. **Post:** Airmail letters to Bhutan can take up to two weeks. Mail from Bhutan is liable to disruption, although this is due not to the inefficiency of the service but rather to the highly prized nature of Bhutanese stamps which often results in their being steamed off the envelopes enroute. **Press:** There are very few papers, but *Kuensel*, a government news bulletin, is published weekly in English and *The Bhutan Review* is published monthly in English by the Human Rights Organisation of Bhutan.
Radio: BBC World Service (website: www.bbc.co.uk/worldservice) and Voice of America (website: www.voa.gov) can be received. From time to time the frequencies change and the most up-to-date can be found online.

Passport/Visa

	Passport Required?	Visa Required?	Return Ticket Required?
Full British	Yes	Yes	Yes
Australian	Yes	Yes	Yes
Canadian	Yes	Yes	Yes
USA	Yes	Yes	Yes
Other EU	Yes	Yes	Yes
Japanese	Yes	Yes	Yes

Note: *Regulations and requirements may be subject to change at short notice, and you are advised to contact the appropriate diplomatic or consular authority before finalising travel arrangements. Details of these may be found at the head of this country's entry. Any numbers in the chart refer to the footnotes below.*

Restricted entry: Tourists to Bhutan are obliged to use *Druk Air* (the only airline serving Bhutan) either on entering or leaving the country. The government may refuse entry to those wishing to visit for mountaineering, publicity and other research activities.
PASSPORTS: Valid passport required by all.
VISAS: Required by all except nationals of India.
Note: (a) There are two ways of entering Bhutan: by air to Paro Airport or by road to the Bhutanese border town of Phuntosholing. All travellers entering the country by road must ensure that they have the necessary documentation for transiting through that part of India to Phuntsholing. (b) Visitors are required to book with a registered tour operator in Bhutan which can be done directly through an affiliated travel agent abroad. (c) A yellow fever certificate is required by all if arriving within six days from an infected area.
Types of visa and cost: *Tourist*: US$20 (payable in hard currency).
Validity: Visas are initially granted for stays of up to 15 days. The Bhutan Tourism Corporation Limited (BTCL) can apply for an extension of tourist visas for an additional fee per person.
Application to: Visa applications for all tourists processed by the travel/tour agent through the Tourism Authority of Bhutan (TAB). Only once the visa has been cleared can visitors travel to Bhutan. Visas are issued (stamped in passport) on arrival at Paro Airport or at Phuntsholing check post.
Application requirements: (a) Application forms, which may be obtained from the BTCL, who should be contacted directly (see *Contact Addresses* section). (b) Faxed details of passport to the BTCL prior to arrival. (c) All necessary documents for transiting India (see *Note* above). (d) Confirmed onward or return ticket. (e) Sufficient funds for length of stay (Mar-May, Sep-Nov: US$200 per day; Jun-Aug, Dec-Feb: US$165 per day). (f) Fee. (g) Two passport-size photos.
Working days required: Visa clearance takes at least 10 days to process and should be applied for at least 60 days prior to arrival in Bhutan.

Money

Currency: 1 Ngultrum (NU) = 100 chetrum (Ch). The Ngultrum is pegged to the Indian Rupee (which is also acccepted as legal tender). Notes are in denominations of NU500, 100, 50, 20, 10, 5, 2 and 1. Coins are in denominations of NU1, and 100, 50, 25, 10 and 5 chetrum. US Dollars are also widely accepted throughout the kingdom.
Currency exchange: Leading foreign currencies are accepted but travellers cheques are preferred and receive a better exchange rate. Major hotels in Thimphu and Phuntsholing, and the Olathang Hotel in Paro, will also exchange foreign currency.
Credit & debit cards: American Express and Diners Club have very limited acceptability. Check with your credit or debit card company for details of merchant acceptability and other services which may be available.
Travellers cheques: These can be exchanged in any branch of the Bank of Bhutan or at all BTCL hotels. Travellers are advised to take travellers cheques in US Dollars.
Currency restrictions: None, but foreign currency must be declared on arrival.
Exchange rate indicators: The following figures are included as a guide to the movements of the Ngultrum/Indian Rupee against Sterling and the US Dollar:

Date	Feb '04	May '04	Aug '04	Nov '04
£1.00=	82.44	79.70	85.22	85.15
$1.00=	45.29	44.62	46.26	44.96

Banking hours: Mon-Fri 0900-1300. Some smaller branches may be open Saturday or Sunday for currency exchange.

Duty Free

Duty-Free: The following goods may be taken into Bhutan by travellers aged 17 years or over without incurring customs duty: *400 cigarettes and 150g of tobacco; 2l of spirits.*
Prohibited items: Firearms, narcotics, plants, gold and silver bullion and obsolete currency. The export of antiques, religious objects, manuscripts, images and anthropological materials is strictly prohibited and closely monitored by the Bhutanese authorities.
Note: Cameras, videos, mobile telephones and all other electronic equipment for personal use must be registered with the authorities on arrival and will be checked by customs on departure.

Public Holidays

2005: Aug 8 Independence Day. **Nov 11** Birthday of HM Jigme Singye Wangchuck. **Dec 17** National Day of Bhutan.
Aug 8 2006 Independence Day. **Nov 11** Birthday of HM Jigme Singye Wangchuck. **Dec 17** National Day of Bhutan.
Note: The traditional Buddhist holidays are observed, including Winter Solstice, Day of Offerings, Losar (New Year), Shabdung Kuchoey, Birthday of Drukgyal Sumpa, Lord Buddha's Paranirvana, Coronation Day, Birthday of Guru Rinpoche, First Sermon of Lord Buddha, Death of Drukgyal Sumpa, Thimphu Drubchen, Thimphu Tsechu, The Blessed Rainy Day, Dasain and the Descending Day of Lord Buddha, Birthday of his Majesty the King, The Meeting of Nine Evils and the National Day. Buddhist festivals are declared according to local astronomical observations and it is not possible to forecast the date of their occurrence.

Health

	Special Precautions?	Certificate Required?
Yellow Fever	Yes	1
Cholera	Yes	2
Typhoid & Polio	3	N/A
Malaria	4	N/A

Note: *Regulations and requirements may be subject to change at short notice, and you are advised to contact your doctor well in advance of your intended date of departure. Any numbers in the chart refer to the footnotes below.*

1: A yellow fever vaccination certificate is required by all travellers if coming from an infected area.
2: Following WHO guidelines issued in 1973, a cholera vaccination certificate is no longer a condition of entry to Bhutan. However, cholera is a serious risk in this country and precautions are essential. Up-to-date advice should be sought before deciding whether these precautions should

A B C D E F G H I J K L M N O P Q R S T U V W X Y Z

include vaccination as medical opinion is divided over its effectiveness; see the *Health* appendix.
3: Typhoid fever is common. Poliomyelitis eradication has begun and is reducing the risk, although it must still be assumed to be a risk.
4: Malaria risk exists throughout the year in the southern belt of the following five districts: Chirang, Samchi, Samdrupjongkhar, Sarpang and Shemgang. Resistance to chloroquine and sulfadoxine/
pyrimethamine has been reported in the malignant *falciparum* form of the disease.
Food & drink: All water should be regarded as being potentially contaminated. Water used for drinking, brushing teeth or making ice should have first been boiled or otherwise sterilised. Milk is unpasteurised and should be boiled. Powdered or tinned milk is available and is advised, but make sure that it is reconstituted with pure water. Avoid all dairy products. Only eat well-cooked meat and fish, preferably served hot. Pork, salad and mayonnaise may carry increased risk. Vegetables should be cooked and fruit peeled.
Other risks: *Hepatitis A* and *E* occur; *hepatitis B* is endemic. *Giardiasis* is common. *Meningitis* is a sporadic risk and vaccination is advised. *TB exists. Visceral leishmaniasis* is prevalent and a small risk of *Japanese encephalitis* exists in southern lowland areas. *Altitude sickness* may be a problem. *Rabies* is present. For those at high risk, vaccination should be considered. If you are bitten, seek medical advice without delay. For more information consult the *Health* appendix.
Health care: There is no reciprocal health agreement with the UK. Full medical insurance is strongly advised. Medical facilities are good but scarce.

Travel - International

AIR: *Druk Air (KB)* (Royal Bhutan Airlines, website: www.drukair.com.bt), the national airline of Bhutan, is the only airline serving Bhutan and has just two 72-seater planes. It is compulsory for all visitors to Bhutan to travel at least one way by *Druk Air*. Owing to the changeable Himalayan weather, travellers may experience delays.
Druk Air operates flights from New Delhi and Calcutta (India), Dhaka (Bangladesh), Bangkok (Thailand), Khathmandu (Nepal) and Yangon (Myanmar). The airline flies two-five times a week to each of the above destinations. Additional flights are offered during the high seasons (from March to April and from September to October).
International airports: *Paro (PBH)*, Bhutan's only airport, is located in a deep valley, some 2190m (7300ft) above sea level, surrounded by hills and high mountains. Operating conditions are fairly difficult and the approach into Paro airport is entirely by visual flight rules. Buses and taxis are available to the city centre (travel time – 90 minutes).
Departure tax: NU300.
RAIL: The nearest railhead is Siliguri (India).
ROAD: The road from Bagdogra (West Bengal) enters Bhutan at the border town of Phuentsholing, which is 179km (111 miles) from Thimphu.

Travel - Internal

AIR: *Druk Air* operates an hour-long scenic mountain flight – the so-called 'Kingdom of the Sky' – which offers visitors spectacular views of the mountains, lakes and waterfalls that are part of Bhutan's beautiful scenery. The plane's seating capacity is 72, with 32 window seats. However, there are no domestic airline routes within Bhutan.
ROAD: Traffic drives on the left. The country has a fairly good internal road network with 3100km (1926 miles) of surfaced road. The main routes run north from Phuntsholing to the western and central regions of Paro and Thimphu, and east-west, across the Pele La Pass linking the valleys of the eastern region. The northern regions of the High Himalayas have no roads. **Bus:** Those services which were formerly government owned are now privately run, though yaks, ponies and mules are the chief forms of transportation. The main routes are from Phuntsholing to Thimphu, Thimphu to Bumthang, Bumthang to Tashigang, Tashigang to Samdrup Jongkar and from Tongsa to Gaylegphug.
Documentation: International Driving Permit is required.
Travel times: The following chart gives approximate travel times (in hours and minutes) from **Thimphu** to other major towns in the country.

	Road
Paro	1.30
P'sholing	6.00
W'phodrang	2.15
Punakha	2.30
Bumthang	8.45
Tongsa	6.45

Accommodation

There are comfortable hotels, cottages and guest houses (many constructed to accommodate foreign guests during the coronation of the present King in 1974). Hotels have hot and cold running water, electricity and room telephones. All hotels run by the Bhutan Tourism Corporation Limited are decorated in traditional Bhutanese style and are now equipped with international direct dial telephones and fax machines. For further information, contact the BTCL (see *Contact Addresses* section).

Resorts & Excursions

The Kingdom of Bhutan has adopted a very cautious approach to tourism in an effort to avoid the negative impacts of tourism on the country's culture and environment. All tourists must travel on a pre-planned, pre-paid, guided package tour. Independent travel is not permitted. The package rate is fixed and controlled by the Government and is followed by all travel agents.
Thimphu, the capital of Bhutan, lies at a height of over 2400m (8000ft) in the fertile valley traversed by the **Wangchhu River**. In many ways it resembles a large, widely dispersed village rather than a capital. The **Tashichhodzong** is the main administrative and religious centre of the country; it was rebuilt in 1961 after being damaged by fire and earthquake. Its hundred-odd spacious rooms house all the government departments and ministries, the **National Assembly Hall**, the **Throne Room of the King** and the country's largest monastery, the summer headquarters of the Je Khempo and 2000 of his monks. The yearly *Thimphu Festival* is held in the courtyard directly in front of the National Assembly Hall. The **Handicraft Emporium** displays a wide assortment of beautifully handwoven and crafted products which make unique souvenirs. **Simtokha**, 8km (5 miles) from Thimphu, has Bhutan's most ancient *Dzong* (fortified monastery).
The small town of **Phuntsholing** is a commercial and industrial centre as well as the gateway to Bhutan. A short walk from the hotel is the **Kharbandi Monastery**. Bhutan is well known for its stamps, and the best place to buy them is in Phuntsholing where the **Philatelic Office of Bhutan** has its headquarters. The first and only department store of Bhutan is also in Phuntsholing. **Punakha** is the former capital of the country; situated at a lower altitude, it enjoys a comparatively benign climate. The valley contains many sacred temples, including **Machin Lhakhag** where the remains of Ngawang Namgyal, the unifier of Bhutan, are entombed. **Tongsa** is the ancestral home of the Royal family. The Dzong at Tongsa commands a superb view of the river valley and contains a magnificent collection of rhino horn sculptures. The district of **Wangdiphodrang** is known for its slate carving and bamboo weaving.
A visit to the **Paro Valley**, where the **Taktsang** (Tiger's Nest) **Monastery** clings dizzily to the face of a 900m (2952ft) precipice, is highly recommended. Other attractions in the area include the **Drukgyul Dzong**, further up the Paro Valley (now in ruins after the earthquake in 1954), which once protected Bhutan against numerous Tibetan invasions; and the **Paro Watchtower**, which now houses the **National Museum of Bhutan**. The temperate **Punakha Valley** houses many sacred temples, including the **Machin Lhakhag** in the **Punakaha Dzong**. The 3100m-(10,170ft) high **Dochu La Pass** commands a breathtaking view of the eastern Himalayan chain.
Bumthang is the starting point for four- and seven-day cultural tours through the rural villages, including **Mongar**. **Tashigang**, a silk-spinning district, has an interesting *dzong*.
Useful information can be obtained from Bhutan Yodsel Tours and Treks (website: www.bhutaan.com) *or* Yarkay Tours & Treks (website: www.aaboutbhutan.com).

Sport & Activities

Much of the pleasure of visiting Bhutan is enjoying the breathtaking scenery by **trekking** around the valleys and the mountain gorges. The rivers offer superb trout **fishing**. The country boasts over 320 varieties of **birds**, including the rare black-necked crane. The *Manas Game Sanctuary* has a wide variety of **wildlife** (a special permit is necessary). **Archery** is popular.

Social Profile

FOOD & DRINK: Restaurants are relatively scarce and most tourists eat in their hotels. Meals are often buffet-style and mostly vegetarian. Cheese is a very popular ingredient in dishes and the most popular cheeses are *dartsi* (cow's milk cheese), sometimes served in a dish with red chillies (*ema dartsi*), and yak cheese. Rice is ubiquitous, sometimes flavoured with saffron. The most popular drink is *souza* (Bhutanese tea).
SHOPPING: Markets are held regularly, generally on Saturday and Sunday, and are a rich source of local clothing and jewellery, as well as foodstuffs. The handicraft emporium on the main street in the capital is open daily except Sunday. The Motithang Hotel in Thimphu has a souvenir shop. Silversmiths and goldsmiths in the Thimphu Valley are able to make handcrafted articles to order. **Shopping hours:** Mon-Sun 0900-2000 (closed Tue).
SPECIAL EVENTS: Buddhist festivals, full of masks, dancing and ritual, generally centre on *Dzongs* (fortified monasteries) in cobbled courtyards, the most famous of which is at Paro. More than 40 religious or folk dances are performed by the monks recounting tales of Buddhist history and myth. Formal dress is required for all festivals. For a complete list of special events, contact the Tourism Corporation of Bhutan (see *Contact Addresses* section). The following is a selection of special events occurring in Bhutan in 2005:
Feb 13-17 *Festival of Punakha Dromchoe*. **Mar 18-20** *Festival of Gom Kora Tshechu*, Trashiyangtse/*Festival of Chhukha Tshechu*, Chhukha. **Apr 9-13** *Festival of Paro Tshechu*. **Jul 4-6** *Festival of Nimalung Tshechu*, Bumthang. **Sep 30-Oct 2** *Festival of Wangdue Tshechu*. **Nov 27-28** *Festival of Mongar Tshechu*. **Dec 28-30** *Festival of Trongsa Tshechu*/*Festival of Lhuentse Tshechu*.
SOCIAL CONVENTIONS: The lifestyle, manners and customs of the Bhutanese are in many respects unique to the area. The strongest influence on social conventions is the country's state religion, and everywhere one can see the reminders of Buddhism and the original religion of Tibet, Bonism. There are no rigid clan systems, and equal rights exist between men and women. The majority of the Bhutanese live an agrarian lifestyle. The political leaders of the country have also historically been religious leaders. For years, the country has deliberately isolated itself from visitors, and has only recently opened up to the outside world, a policy which is now to some extent being reversed. **Tipping:** Not widely practised.

Business Profile

ECONOMY: Almost all the working population is involved in agriculture, forestry or fishing. The economy is therefore mainly one of subsistence and dependent on clement climatic conditions. The main products are cereals and timber – about 60 per cent of the land area is forested. There is some small-scale industry – contributing no more than 5 per cent of GDP – producing textiles, soap, matches, candles and carpets. Recent economic policy has concentrated on export industries, of which electric power generation and transmission is the major earner. Tourism and stamps are major sources of foreign exchange. India accounts for nearly 90 per cent of imports and nearly 70 per cent of exports. However, during the 1990s, Bhutan also developed valuable trading links with Bangladesh. Bhutan is a member of the South Asian Association for Regional Cooperation, which seeks to improve economic and commercial links in the region.
BUSINESS: Lightweight or tropical suit or a shirt and tie for the south. In the capital, a full business suit and tie are recommended. The best time to visit for business is October and November.
COMMERCIAL INFORMATION: The following organisation can offer advice: Bhutan Chamber of Commerce and Industry, PO Box 147, Doybum Lam, Thimphu (tel: (2) 322 742 *or* 324 254; fax: (2) 323 936; e-mail: bsdbcci@druknet.bt; website: www.bcci.com.bt).
CONFERENCES/CONVENTIONS: The BTCL can offer advice (see *Contact Addresses* section).

Climate

There are four distinct seasons similar in their divisions to those of Western Europe. The Monsoon occurs between June and August when the temperature is normally between 8° and 21°C (46°-70°F). Temperatures drop
dramatically with increases in altitude. Days are usually very pleasant (average about 10°C/50°F) with clear skies and sunshine. Nights are cold and require heavy woollen clothing, particularly in winter. Generally, October, November and April to mid-June are the best times to visit – rainfall is at a minimum and temperatures are conducive to active days of sightseeing. The foothills are also very pleasant during the winter.
Required clothing: Lightweight cottons in the foothills, also linens and waterproof gear, light sweaters and jackets for the evenings. Upland areas: woollens for evenings, particularly during the winter months.

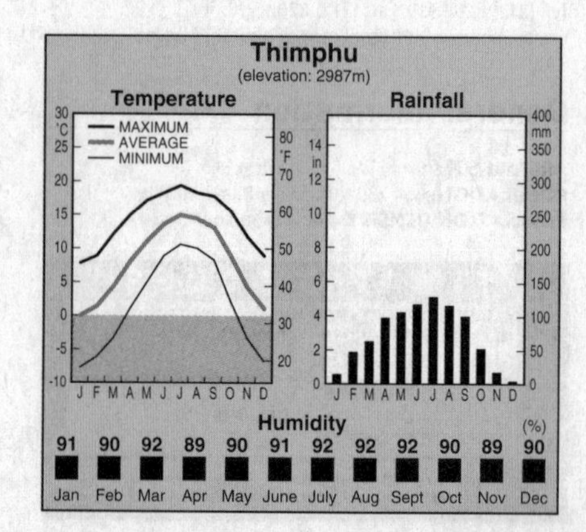

Bolivia

LATEST TRAVEL ADVICE CONTACTS

British Foreign and Commonwealth Office
Tel: (0870) 606 0290 Website: www.fco.gov.uk
US Department of State
Website: http://travel.state.gov/travel
Canadian Department of Foreign Affairs and Int'l Trade
Tel: (1 800) 267 8376 Website: www.dfait-maeci.gc.ca

Location: South America.

Country dialling code: 591.

Viceministerio de Turismo
Avenida Mariscal Santa Cruz, Edificio Cámara de Comercio, Piso 11, La Paz, Bolivia
Tel: (2) 233 4849. Fax: (2) 235 0526.
E-mail: xalvarez@desarrollo.gov.bo *or* xalvarez@turismo.bolivia.bo
Website: www.turismobolivia.bo

Embassy and Consulate of the Republic of Bolivia
106 Eaton Square, London SW1W 9AD, UK
Tel: (020) 7235 4248 *or* 2257. Fax: (020) 7235 1286.
E-mail: info@embassyofbolivia.co.uk
Website: www.embassyofbolivia.co.uk
Opening hours: Mon-Fri 0930-1730 (general enquiries); 0930-1300 (consular and visa enquiries).

British Embassy
Avenida Arce 2732, Casilla 694, La Paz, Bolivia
Tel: (2) 243 3424. Fax: (2) 243 1073.
E-mail: ppa@megalink.com
Website: www.britishembassy.gov.uk/bolivia

Embassy of the Republic of Bolivia
3014 Massachusetts Avenue, NW, Washington, DC 20008, USA
Tel: (202) 483 4410. Fax: (202) 328 3712.
E-mail: webmaster@bolivia-usa.org
Website: www.bolivia-usa.org

Embassy of the United States of America
Avenida Arce 2780, Casilla 425, La Paz, Bolivia
Tel: (2) 216 8000. Fax: (2) 216 8111.
E-mail: consularlapaz@state.gov (consular section).
Website: http://lapaz.usembassy.gov

Bolivian Embassy
Suite 416, 130 Albert Street, Ottawa, Ontario K1P 5G4, Canada
Tel: (613) 236 5730. Fax: (613) 236 8237.
E-mail: embolivia-ottawa@rree.gov.bo

Bolivian Consulate
10316-124 Street, 2nd Floor, Edmonton, Alberta T5N 1R2, Canada
Tel: (780) 447 1177. Fax: (780) 452 1114.
E-mail: dr.c.pechtel@deavila.ca

TIMATIC CODES

Health
AMADEUS: **TI-DFT/LPB/HE**
GALILEO/WORLDSPAN: **TI-DFT/LPB/HE**
SABRE: **TIDFT/LPB/HE**

Visa
AMADEUS: **TI-DFT/LPB/VI**
GALILEO/WORLDSPAN: **TI-DFT/LPB/VI**
SABRE: **TIDFT/LPB/VI**

To access TIMATIC country information on Health and Visa regulations through the Computer Reservations System (CRS), type in the appropriate command line listed above.

The Consulate of Canada
Street address: Calle Victor Sarijinez, No 2678 Edificio Barcelona, 2nd Floor, Plaza España (Sopocachi), La Paz, Bolivia
Postal address: PO Box 10345, La Paz, Bolivia
Tel: (2) 241 5021 *or* 4517. Fax: (2) 241 4453.
E-mail: lapaz@international.gc.ca

General Information

AREA: 1,098,581 sq km (424,164 sq miles).
POPULATION: 8,328,700 (official estimate 2000).
POPULATION DENSITY: 7.6 per sq km.
CAPITAL: Legal: Sucre. **Population:** 223,436 (official estimate 2000). **Administrative:** La Paz. **Population:** 1,004,440 (official estimate 2000).
GEOGRAPHY: Bolivia is a landlocked country bordered by Peru to the northwest, Brazil to the north and east, Paraguay to the southeast, Argentina to the south and Chile to the west. There are three main areas: the first is a high plateau known as the 'Altiplano', a largely barren region lying approximately 4000m (13,000ft) above sea level. It comprises 10 per cent of the country's area and contains 70 per cent of the population, nearly one-third of whom are urban dwellers. The second area is a fertile valley situated 1800m (5900ft) to 2700m (8850ft) above sea level. The third area comprises the lowland tropics which stretch down to the frontiers with Brazil, Argentina and Paraguay, taking up some 70 per cent of the land area. Rainfall in this region is high, and the climate is hot.
GOVERNMENT: Republic. Gained independence from Spain in 1825. **Head of State and Government:** President Carlos Diego Mesa Gisbert (2003).
LANGUAGE: The official languages are Spanish, Quechua and Aymará. English is also spoken by a small number of officials and businesspeople in commercial centres.
RELIGION: Roman Catholic with a Protestant minority.
TIME: GMT - 4.
ELECTRICITY: 110/220 volts AC in La Paz, 220 volts AC, 50Hz in the rest of the country. Most houses and hotels have two-pin sockets for both electrical currents. Variations from this occur in some places.
COMMUNICATIONS: Telephone: IDD is available. Country code: 591. Outgoing international code: 00. **Mobile telephone:** GSM 1900 network. Network operators include *Entel SA* (website: www.entelmovil.com.bo) and *Nuevatel PCS de Bolivia SA* (website: www.nuevatel.com). **Fax:** Services available. **Internet:** ISPs include *Megalink* (website: www.megalink.com). There are Internet cafes in main towns. **Telegram:** Facilities are available from the West Coast of America Telegraph Company; head office at Edificio Electra, Calle Mercado 1150, La Paz. **Post:** Airmail to Europe takes three to four days. A *poste restante* service is available. **Press:** The Bolivian Times is published weekly in English. The main papers published in La Paz are *El Diario, Hoy, Presencia, La Razón* and *Última Hora*.
Radio: BBC World Service (website: www.bbc.co.uk/worldservice) and Voice of America (website: www.voa.gov) can be received. From time to time the frequencies change and the most up-to-date can be found online.

Passport/Visa

	Passport Required?	Visa Required?	Return Ticket Required?
Full British	Yes	1	Yes
Australian	Yes	1	Yes
Canadian	Yes	1	Yes
USA	Yes	1	Yes
Other EU	Yes	1	Yes
Japanese	Yes	1	Yes

Note: *Regulations and requirements may be subject to change at short notice, and you are advised to contact the appropriate diplomatic or consular authority before finalising travel arrangements. Details of these may be found at the head of this country's entry. Any numbers in the chart refer to the footnotes below.*

PASSPORTS: Passport valid for at least one year beyond the intended length of stay required by all except holders of an identity card issued to nationals of Argentina, Paraguay, Peru and Uruguay.
VISAS: Required by all except the following, provided travelling for touristic purposes:
(a) **1.** nationals of countries mentioned in the chart above (except nationals of Malta who *do* require a visa);
(b) nationals of Andorra, Argentina, Brazil, Chile, Colombia, Costa Rica, Ecuador, Holy See, Iceland, Liechtenstein, Mexico, Monaco, New Zealand, Netherlands Antilles, Norway, Panama, Paraguay, Peru, The Philippines, Serbia & Montenegro, Switzerland, Turkey, Uruguay and Venezuela;
(c) transit passengers (except nationals of China (PR)) continuing their journey by the same or first connecting aircraft within 24 hours, provided holding valid onward or

Credit: © Sky Bolivia

return documentation and not leaving the airport.
Note: (a) All nationals travelling on business *do* need a Specific Purpose visa. (b) Nationals not requiring a tourist visa are usually allowed to stay for a period of 30 to 90 days; check with the Embassy (or Consular section at Embassy). (c) In addition to a visa, nationals of the following countries also require special authorisation: Afghanistan, Cambodia, Congo (Dem Rep), Korea (DPR), Iran, Iraq, Laos, Libya, Nigeria, Pakistan, Sudan and the Syrian Arab Republic.
Types of visa and cost: *Tourist/Transit*: cost depends on nationality; enquire at the Embassy (or Consular section at Embassy). *Specific Purpose:* £61.50. *Student*: £31.
Validity: Tourist visas are valid for 30 days but can be extended for up to 90 days (depending on nationality) from the date of entry. Specific Purpose visas are valid for 30 days and can be renewed for 60 or 90 additional days at the immigration office in Bolivia. Student visas are valid for 60 days. Transit visas are valid for 15 days.
Application to: Consulate (or Consular section at Embassy); see *Contact Addresses* section.
Application requirements: (a) One passport-size photo. (b) Completed application form. (c) Passport with remaining validity of at least one year. (d) Fee, payable by cash or cheque. (e) Return airline ticket or travel itinerary as proof of onward travel. (f) A yellow fever vaccination certificate may be required (see *Health* section). (g) For Specific Purpose visas, a letter of introduction from the relevant company or institution as proof of business intentions and the dates of travel. *Student*: (a)-(g) and, (h) Medical certificate proving that applicant possesses no contagious diseases.
Working days required: One to two for nationals requiring tourist visas without special authorisation. Approximately six weeks for all other nationals requiring tourist visas and special authorisation from the Bolivian Ministry of Foreign Affairs.
Temporary residence: Enquire at Bolivian Consulate.

Money

Currency: 1 Boliviano (Bs) = 100 centavos. Notes are in denominations of Bs200, 100, 50, 20, 10 and 5. Coins are in denominations of Bs2 and 1, and 50, 20, and 10 centavos.
Note: The Boliviano is tied to the US Dollar.
Currency exchange: Money can be changed in hotels and *casas de cambio*.
Credit & debit cards: American Express, Diners Club, MasterCard and Visa have very limited acceptance. Check with your credit or debit card company for details of merchant acceptability and other services which may be available.
Travellers cheques: US Dollar travellers cheques are probably the best form of currency to take to Bolivia at present. Sterling cheques can sometimes be exchanged, but only with difficulty.
Currency restrictions: There are no restrictions on the import or the export of either local or foreign currency, subject to declaration.
Exchange rate indicators: The following figures are included as a guide to the movements of the Boliviano against Sterling and the US Dollar:

Date	Nov '03	Feb '04	May '04	Aug '04
£1.00=	13.18	14.30	14.13	14.60
$1.00=	7.77	7.86	7.91	7.92

Banking hours: Mon-Fri 0830-1200 and 1430-1800. Some banks open Sat 0830-1200.

Duty Free

The following goods may be taken into Bolivia without incurring customs duty by persons aged 18 and over:
400 cigarettes and 50 cigars or 500g of tobacco; 3l of alcoholic beverages; new articles up to US$1000;

A B C D E F G H I J K L M N O P Q R S T U V W X Y Z

photographic camera, non-professional camcorder and accessories, tape recorder, electronic memo book, mobile phone and portable computer for personal use; sporting gear.

Public Holidays

2005: Jan 1 New Year's Day. **Feb 2** Carnival. **Mar 25** Good Friday. **May 1** Labour Day. **May 26** Corpus Christi. **Aug 6** Independence Day. **Sep 2** Labour Day. **Nov 1** All Saints' Day. **Dec 25** Christmas Day.
2006: Jan 1 New Year's Day. **Feb 27** Carnival. **Apr 14** Good Friday. **May 1** Labour Day. **Jun 15** Corpus Christi. **Aug 6** Independence Day. **Sep 2** Labour Day. **Nov 1** All Saints' Day. **Dec 25** Christmas Day.
Note: There are other additional holidays celebrated in individual provinces and towns. For further details, contact the Embassy *or* the Viceministerio de Turismo (see *Contact Addresses* section).

Health

	Special Precautions?	Certificate Required?
Yellow Fever	Yes	1
Cholera	2	No
Typhoid & Polio	3	N/A
Malaria	4	N/A

Note: *Regulations and requirements may be subject to change at short notice, and you are advised to contact your doctor well in advance of your intended date of departure. Any numbers in the chart refer to the footnotes below.*

1: A yellow fever vaccination certificate is required from travellers arriving from infected countries. Vaccination is recommended for incoming travellers from non-infected zones visiting risk areas such as the Departments of Beni, Cochabamba, Santa Cruz and the subtropical part of the La Paz Department.
2: Following WHO guidelines issued in 1973, a cholera vaccination certificate is no longer a condition of entry to Bolivia. However, cases of cholera were reported in 1996 and precautions are essential. Up-to-date advice should be sought before deciding whether these precautions should include vaccination as medical opinion is divided over its effectiveness; see the *Health* appendix for more information.
3: A moderate to high risk of typhoid exists, especially outside main cities and tourist areas.
4: Malaria risk exists throughout the year below 2500m, in the Departments of Beni, Pando, Santa Cruz and Tarija, and provinces of Lacareja, Rurenabaque, and North and South Yungas in the La Paz Department. Resistance to chloroquine and sulfadoxine-pyrimethamine has been reported. The disease occurs predominantly in the benign *vivax* form but *falciparum* malaria occurs in Beni and Pando, especially within the localities of Guayaramerín, Puerto Rico and Riberalta. There is lower-risk Malaria in Cochabamba and Chuquisaca.
Food & drink: Water used for drinking, brushing teeth or making ice should be boiled or otherwise sterilised. Milk is unpasteurised and should be boiled. Powdered or tinned milk is available and is advised, but make sure that it is reconstituted with pure water. Avoid all dairy products which are likely to have been made from unboiled milk. Only eat well-cooked meat and fish, preferably served hot. Pork, salad and mayonnaise may carry increased risk. Vegetables should be cooked and fruit peeled.
Other risks: *Diarrhoeal* diseases and *hepatitis A* are common. *American trypanosomiasis* (*Chagas disease*) and cutaneous and mucocutaneous leishmaniasis occur. *Hepatitis B* and *C*, *Japanese encephalitis* and *TB* are a risk. Epidemics of *viral encephalitis* and *dengue fever* may occur. *Plague* has been reported in natural foci.
Rabies is present. For those at high risk, vaccination before arrival should be considered. If you are bitten, seek medical advice without delay. For more information consult the *Health* appendix.
Health care: There is no reciprocal health agreement with the UK. Medical insurance is strongly recommended. All travellers, but especially those with heart conditions, should allow time to acclimatise to the high altitude of La Paz. In case of a medical emergency, La Paz has a good US clinic.

Credit: © Sky Bolivia

Travel - International

Note: There are no restrictions on travel throughout Bolivia, but unpredictable bouts of social unrest can affect main tourist areas and internal travel. Transport strikes can affect movement in and out of the country. It is best to avoid demonstrations and respect roadblocks.
AIR: The national airline is *Lloyd Aéreo Boliviano (LB)*. Other airlines serving Bolivia include *American Airlines*, which flies from major European cities to *La Paz* via Miami. *British Airways* flies to Miami and Rio, from where connecting *LAB* or *Varig* flights to Bolivia are available.
Approximate flight times: From La Paz to *London* is 14 hours 30 minutes and from Santa Cruz is 14 hours 40 minutes.
International airports: *La Paz (LPB)* (El Alto) is 14km (8.5 miles) southwest of La Paz. Coach services to the city depart whenever there are scheduled flight arrivals (travel time - 20 minutes). Services from the city to the airport depart from Plaza Isabel La Católica. Minibus and taxis are also available.
Santa Cruz (VVI) (Viru-Viru) is 16km (10 miles) from the centre of Santa Cruz. Restaurant and duty-free facilities are available.
The Visit South America Pass: *The Visit South America Pass*: Must be bought outside South America in country of residence and allows unlimited travel to 36 cities in the following countries: Argentina, Bolivia, Brazil, Colombia, Chile (except Easter Island), Ecuador, Paraguay, Peru, Uruguay and Venezuela. Participating airlines include *Aer Lingus (EI)*, *American Airlines (AA)*, *British Airways (BA)*, *Cathay Pacific (CX)*, *Finnair (AY)*, *IBERIA (IB)*, *LAN-Chile (LA)* and *Qantas (QF)*. A minimum of three flights must be booked, with no maximum; the maximum stay is 60 days, with no minimum, and prices depend on the amount of flight zones covered. Children under 12 years of age are entitled to a 33 per cent discount and infants (under two years old) only pay 10 per cent of the adult fare. For further details, contact one of the participating airlines.
Departure tax: US$25. Payable in US Dollars for all non-residents. For visitors staying longer than 90 days: US$50.
SEA: Although it is a member of the International Maritime Organisation, Bolivia is wholly landlocked. However, it is possible to reach ports in Argentina, Brazil, Chile, Paraguay and Peru by ship, and from there there are rail connections to La Paz or Santa Cruz. The nearest seaport is Arica in the extreme north of Chile.
LAKE: Steamers cross Lake Titicaca to the Peruvian port of Puno from Guaqui, the most important port on the lake. Situated 90km (56 miles) from La Paz, it is accessible both by road and rail, though services are generally slow.
RAIL: There is a twice-weekly connection from La Paz to Buenos Aires (Argentina), and a twice-monthly connection to Arica (Chile). There is also a weekly train to Calama (Chile) with bus connections to Antofagasta.
ROAD: The Pan-American Highway which links the Argentine Republic with Peru crosses Bolivian territory from the south to the northwest. Driving in the rainy season may be hazardous. During recent years, much attention has been given to new roads, and the principal highways are now well maintained.

Travel - Internal

AIR: Airlines operating internal flights are *AeroXpress*, *LAB* and *TAM* (the military airline). Because of the country's topography and tropical regions, air travel is the best method of transport, although delays, cancellations and general unreliability is highly possible. *La Paz* (El Alto) - which is the highest airport in the world - and *Santa Cruz* (Viru-Viru) are the chief internal airports.
Departure Tax: Usually Bs15, but variable depending on airport and destination. It is advisable to check locally.
RIVER/LAKE: Double-decker passenger boats operate between the various small islands on Lake Titicaca and traverse the many rivers of the Amazon basin (the main thoroughfares being Ichilo, Mamoré, Beni, Madre de Dios and Guaporé rivers); most of them leave from Copacabana.
RAIL: Bolivia has 3697km (2297 miles) of track which goes to make up separate and unconnected networks in the eastern and western parts of the country. Since privatisation, the railway services have been reduced and services are, by and large, slow and disorganised. The Eastern network is particularly inefficient. Some trains have restaurant cars, but there are no sleeping-car services. The railways have recently renewed their rolling stock with Fiat railway carriages from Argentina. There are joint plans with the Brazilians to link Santa Cruz and Cochabamba.
ROAD: The internal road system covers 50,419km (31,330 miles). Work is in progress to improve the condition of major highways, since the overall road network is rather poor, due to the lack of paved roads. Traffic drives on the right. **Bus:** Long bus trips off the main routes can be erratic. Most long-distance bus trips are overnight. **Taxi:** All have fixed rates and sharing taxis is a common practice. Tipping is not necessary. **Car hire:** *Hertz* and local companies exist in La Paz. **Documentation:** An International Driving Permit is required. This can be issued by Federación Inter-Americana de Touring y Automóvil on production of a national licence, but it is wiser to obtain the International Permit before departure.
URBAN: Bus services in La Paz are operated by a confederation of owner-operators. There are also some fixed route taxi 'Trufi' and 'Trufibus' systems which show coloured flags for particular routes. Fares are regulated. In some cases, catching a 'truck' can prove a better means of transport, being half the price of a bus and usually more reliable - although less comfortable.
Travel times: The following chart gives approximate travel times from **La Paz** (in hours and minutes) to other major cities/towns in Bolivia.

	Air	Road	Rail
Cochabamba	0.25	6.00	7.00
Santa Cruz	0.50	24.00	-
Tarija	1.00	18.00	-
Sucre	0.35	11.00	13.00
Potosí	0.40	12.00	12.00
Beni	0.35	-	-

Accommodation

It is important to arrive in La Paz as early as possible in the day as accommodation, particularly at the cheaper end of the market, can be hard to find.
HOTELS: Bolivia has several deluxe and first-class hotels. Service charges and taxes amounting to 25-27 per cent are added to bills. Rates are for room only, except where otherwise indicated. There is a wide range of middle-range hotel accommodation available, generally of good value. For details contact la Cámara Departamental de Hotelería (the Bolivian Chamber of Hotel Management), Calle Panamá, esquina Plaza Uyuni, edificio Shopping Miraflores, 3°, oficina 303, La Paz (tel: (2) 222 2618; tel/fax: (2) 222 6290).
GUEST HOUSES: Several pensions in La Paz, Cochabamba and Santa Cruz provide visitors with reasonable comfort at a reasonable price.
CAMPING/CARAVANNING: There are few camping areas anywhere in South America. However, adventurous travellers may often find adequate lodging for the small fee usually charged at most US or European campsites. Despite no formal organisation or marked zones, camping is possible in Bolivia. Mallasa, Valencia and Palca in the river gorge below the suburb of La Florida are recommended, also Chinguihue, 10km (6 miles) from the city. For details, contact the Viceministerio de Turismo (see *Contact Addresses* section).

Resorts & Excursions

La Paz, the seat of national government, is situated 3632m (11,910ft) above sea level and is the world's highest capital city. **Mount Illimani** stands in the background. The city contains many museums and is well provided with modern and comfortable hotels. Nearby attractions include **Lake Titicaca**, the **Yungas Valleys**, the **Chacaltaya** ski resort and the exceptional rock formations in the **Moon Valley**.
Cochabamba, known as the garden city, is 2558m (8390ft) above sea level and boasts a long tradition of local culture

and folklore.

The state of **Santa Cruz** is rich in natural resources; the city itself, despite considerable modernisation, still retains much of its colonial past and is characterised by its ethnic diversity (owing to the large number of immigrants it has attracted in recent years). Santa Cruz, which shares many historical links with neighbouring Argentina and Brazil, is Bolivia's fastest-growing city, as well as the centre of the country's economic growth. This region around the city is rich in tradition and folklore and the nearby rainforest offers abundant opportunities to lovers of outdoor activities (such as fishing or swimming). The area's rich cuisine is also to be sampled.

Potosí is known as the imperial city and is situated at the foot of **Rich Mountain**, famed for its mineral wealth. In early colonial times, Potosí was the most important and populous city on the continent, and is now one of its greatest historical memorials. The **House of Coins** is just one example of this.

Oruro is a traditional mining centre, and preserver of many relics of a colonial past. Every year the town hosts one of the most extraordinary and faithful expressions of folklore in South America during the famous *carnival* (February/March).

Sucre, in the state of **Chuquisaca**, played an important part in the struggle for independence, and is rich in museums, libraries and historical archives. Among the most important are the **Cathedral Museum**, the **National Library**, the **Colonial Museum**, the **Anthropological Museum**, the **Natural History Museum** and the **Recoleta Convent**.

Tarija stands 1957m (6480ft) above sea level. The area enjoys an excellent climate, and is festive and hospitable. With its beautiful flowers and fine wines, Tarija is the ideal place for finding peace and quiet.

The states of **Beni** and **Pando**, situated in the heart of the Bolivian jungle, occupy a region which offers the visitor landscapes of warmth and colour. The **'Golden' Pantiti**, with many navigable rivers, a popular place for excursions by both land and water. Good fishing is also possible in the region. The major towns in the area are **Cobija** and **Trinidad**.

Sport & Activities

An increasing number of local and international tour operators offer customised adventure tours to Bolivia, with a strong focus on trekking, mountaineering, ecotourism, and wildlife and jungle tours. For further information, contact the Viceministerio de Turismo (see *Contact Addresses* section).

Trekking: Bolivia's large range of geographical regions and climates makes for an exceptional variety of ecosystems, flora and fauna. There are currently 10 national parks and eight protected areas, as well as another dozen or so areas that are being re-evaluated for park or protected area status. La Paz is the most popular starting point for trekking excursions, many of which follow ancient Inca routes through the *Cordillera Real* and end up in the *Yungas* - an area of deep valleys that separates the high Andes from the Amazon basin. Well-known trekking routes include the *La Cumbre* to *Coroico* trail (three days); the *Taquesi* route through the Cordillera Real (two days), also known as the *Inca Trail*; and the *El Camino de Oro* route (six days) starting at Sorata and ending at the *Río Tipuani* gold fields. Good maps of Bolivia can be obtained from the *Instituto Geográfico Militar* in La Paz and other major cities.

Jungle tours: Most treks to the Amazon jungle start from *Rurrenabaque* (235km/145 miles northeast of La Paz). Typical jungle trips include a motorised canoe trip up the rivers *Beni* and *Tuichi*, with rainforest walks and camping en route. Most tours are led by local guides who have an intimate knowledge of the indigenous plants and wildlife (which includes hundreds of species of tropical birds). Further popular itineraries for treks in the Amazon region include expeditions to the *pampas* (good for wildlife viewing); the remote *Parque Nacional Noel Kempff*; and river trips along the *Río Mamoré*.

Mountaineering: The best opportunities are in the *Cordillera Real*, which has several peaks above 5000m (14,500ft). Climbing excursions (complete with mules, porters and guides) can also be booked in Sorata, which is set in a beautiful valley with an abundance of trees and flowers. **Mountain bike tours** are also available (website: www.hoodoobiketours.com).

Skiing: At an altitude of 5486m (18,000ft), *Mount Chacaltaya* (55km/35 miles from La Paz) is reputedly the world's highest ski resort. Visitors should note, however, that lift and accommodation facilities are fairly basic and that low oxygen levels and icy snow often make for difficult conditions. The best time to attempt skiing here is from April to June.

Fishing: Bolivia is reputed to offer some of the best lake fishing in the world, especially for trout.

Social Profile

FOOD & DRINK: Bolivian food is distinctive and is generally good. National dishes include *empanada salteña* (a mixture of diced meat, chicken, chives, raisins, diced potatoes, hot sauce and pepper baked in dough), *lomo montado* (fried tender loin steak with two fried eggs on top, rice and fried banana), *picante de pollo* (southern fried chicken, fried potatoes, rice, tossed salad with hot peppers), *chuño* (naturally freeze-dried potato used in soup called *chairo*) and *lechón al horno* (roast suckling pig served with sweet potato and fried plantains). Dishes are dominated by meat. *Ilajhua* (a hot sauce consisting of tomatoes and pepper pods) will often be used to add spice and flavour to dishes. International- and local-style restaurants are available in La Paz and other main towns. Bolivian beer, especially *paceña*, is one of the best on the continent. *Chicha*, made from fermented cereals and corn, is very strong. Mineral water and bottled drinks are available. Local bars are increasing in number and are unrestricted with no licensing hours.

NIGHTLIFE: La Paz has many nightclubs, which generally open around midnight. There are also numerous *whiskerias*, local bars. On Fridays and Saturdays there are folk music and dancing shows, which start late in the evening. Cochabamba and Santa Cruz have several discos.

SHOPPING: Special purchases include woodcarvings, jewellery, llama and alpaca blankets, Indian handicrafts and gold and silver costume jewellery. **Shopping hours:** Mon-Fri 0930-1230 and 1500-1930; Sat 1000-1500.

SPECIAL EVENTS: For a complete list of events and festivals, contact the Embassy (see *Contact Addresses* section). In many places, a festival is associated with a local holiday. The following is a selection of special events occurring in Bolivia in 2005:

Feb *Carnival*, Oruro, Sucre, Santa Cruz and Tarija. **Feb 1-2** *Festividad de le Virgen de la Candelaria*, Aisquille and Coloni, Cochabamba. **Mar 28-Apr 2** *Seminario Nacional del Medio*, Ambiente, Santa Cruz. **Apr 19-21** *Congreso Latinoamericano de Alcades*, Santa Cruz. **Jun 20-21** *Solsticio de Invierno*, Samaipata, Santa Cruz. **Sep** *Festival Internacional de Cultura/Entrade de la Virgen de Guadalupe*, Sucre, Chuquisaca. **Sep 12-13** *Fiesta Virgen Dolorosa*, Tarija. **Dec** *Navidad*, Tarija.

SOCIAL CONVENTIONS: Normal social courtesies in most Bolivian families and respect for traditions should be observed. Remember to refer to rural Bolivians as *campesinos* rather than Indians, which is considered an insult. Western dress and diet are gradually being adopted by the *campesinos* (although great poverty remains further to the north); a suit and tie for men and dress for women should be worn for smart social occasions. Casual wear is otherwise suitable. Smoking is accepted except where indicated. **Tipping:** It is customary to add 10 per cent as a tip to the 13 per cent service charge added to hotel and restaurant bills. Porters also expect tips for each piece of luggage.

Business Profile

ECONOMY: Bolivia has the second-lowest per capita income in Latin America. Agriculture employs nearly half the working population, although it suffers from relatively low productivity. The main cash crops are soya, sugar and coffee, while beef and hides from the extensive livestock-rearing industry are valuable export earners. The other key primary product is timber. Bolivia has developed a unique system of sustainable development, which allows for commercial exploitation of high-quality tropical hardwoods without over-depleting the forests. There is also a substantial unregistered and illegal trade in coca, the plant source for cocaine, which provides a livelihood for many peasants - its economic value is thought to be approximately US$1 billion annually. This is a major political issue in the country.

Bolivia has large mineral deposits, especially of tin - of which it is one of the world's leading producers - and also natural gas, petroleum, lead, antimony, tungsten, gold and silver. Oil and gas deposits serve to meet much of the country's energy needs and are increasingly valuable export commodities. Reliance on primary products has made Bolivia vulnerable to fluctuations in world commodity prices. Having accepted international demands during the 1990s to liberalise its economy and open it up to foreign competition, the Bolivians have been frustrated by a perceived lack of 'reciprocity' - in other words, access to foreign markets for Bolivian products. Bolivia is a member of the Latin American Integration Association, the River Plate Basin Alliance and, most importantly, of the Andean Pact. The country's largest trading partners are neighbouring Brazil, Argentina and Chile, along with the USA, followed by Japan and the EU countries.

Credit: © Sky Bolivia

BUSINESS: Suit or a shirt and tie should be worn. Appointments should be made in advance. **Office hours:** Mon-Fri 0830-1200 and 1430-1830; Sat 0900-1200 (some offices).

COMMERCIAL INFORMATION: The following organisations can offer advice: Cámara Nacional de Industrias, Edificio Cámara Nacional de Comercio, Piso 14, Avenida Mariscal, Santa Cruz 1392, La Paz (tel: (2) 237 4477; fax: (2) 236 2766; e-mail: cni@caoba.entelnet.bo; website: www.bolivia-industry.com) *or* Cámara Nacional de Comercio de La Paz, Avenida Mariscal, Santa Cruz 1392, Edificio Cámara Nacional de Comercio, Piso 1, La Paz (tel: (2) 237 8606; fax: (2) 239 1004; e-mail: cnc@boliviacomercio.org.bo; website: www.boliviacomercio.org.bo).

Climate

Bolivia has a temperate climate but with wide differences between day and night. The wettest period is November to March, which, in extreme circumstances, may induce landslides in mountainous areas, and cause certain roads to become impassable. The northeast slopes of the Andes are semi-tropical. Visitors often find La Paz uncomfortable because of the thin air due to high altitude. The mountain areas can become very cold at night.

Required clothing: Lightweight linens with a raincoat. A light overcoat is necessary at night, particularly in the Altiplano and the Puna.

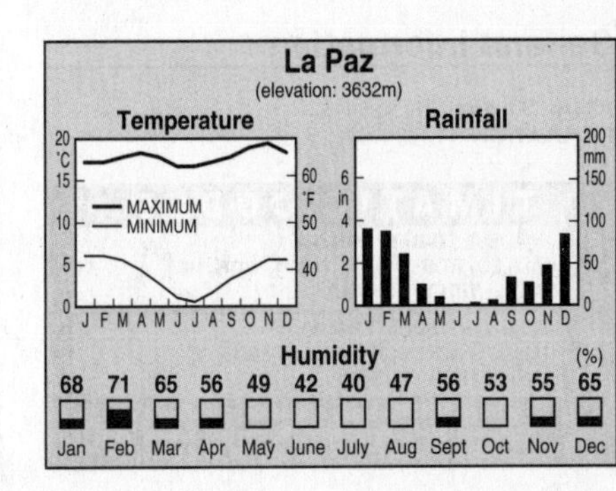

Bonaire

LATEST TRAVEL ADVICE CONTACTS

British Foreign and Commonwealth Office
Tel: (0870) 606 0290 Website: www.fco.gov.uk

US Department of State
Website: http://travel.state.gov/travel

Canadian Department of Foreign Affairs and Int'l Trade
Tel: (1 800) 267 8376 Website: www.dfait-maeci.gc.ca

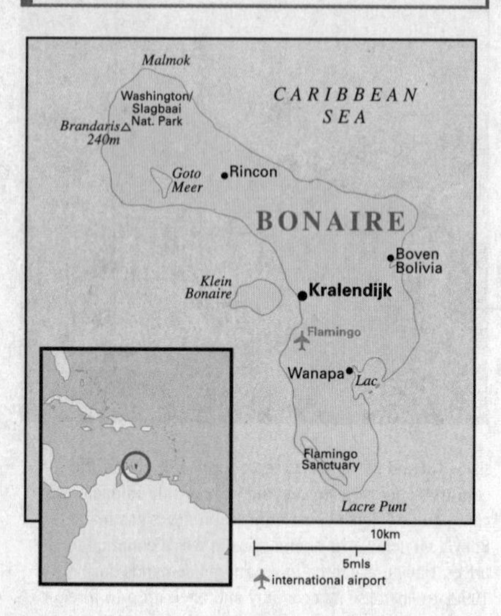

Location: Caribbean, 80km (50 miles) north of Venezuela.

Country dialling code: 599.

Bonaire is part of the Netherlands Antilles represented abroad by Royal Netherlands Embassies – see *The Netherlands* section.

Tourism Corporation Bonaire
Kaya Grandi 2, Kralendijk, Bonaire, NA
Tel: (717) 8322 *or* 8649. Fax: (717) 8408.
E-mail: gm@tourismbonaire.com
Website: www.infobonaire.com

Office of the Minister Plenipotentiary of the Netherlands Antilles
PO Box 90706, Badhuisweg 173-175, 2597 JP The Hague, The Netherlands
Tel: (70) 306 6111. Fax: (70) 306 6110.
E-mail: serphos@kgmna.nl

Tourism Corporation Bonaire, European Office
PO Box 472, NL 2000, Al-Haarlem, The Netherlands
Tel: (23) 543 0705. Fax: (23) 543 0730.
E-mail: europe@tourismbonaire.com
Website: www.infobonaire.com

Caribbean Tourism Organisation
22 The Quadrant, Richmond, Surrey, TW9 1BP, UK
Tel: (020) 8948 0057. Fax: (020) 8948 0067.
E-mail: ctolondon@carib-tourism.com
Website: www.doitcaribbean.com *or* www.onecaribbean.org

The British Consulate in Jansofat deals with enquiries relating to Bonaire (see *Curaçao* section).

Tourism Corporation Bonaire
10 Rockefeller Plaza, Suite 900, New York, NY 10020, USA
Tel: (212) 956 5912 *or* (800) 266 2473 (toll-free in USA and Canada). Fax: (212) 956 5913.
E-mail: usa@tourismbonaire.com
Website: www.infobonaire.com

The US Consulate in Curaçao deals with enquiries relating to Bonaire (see *Curaçao* section).
The Canadian Consulate in Curaçao deals with enquiries relating to Bonaire (see *Curaçao* section).

General Information

AREA: 290 sq km (112 sq miles).
POPULATION: 14,169 (1996).

TIMATIC CODES

Health	AMADEUS: **TI-DFT/BON/HE** GALILEO/WORLDSPAN: **TI-DFT/BON/HE** SABRE: **TIDFT/BON/HE**
Visa	AMADEUS: **TI-DFT/BON/VI** GALILEO/WORLDSPAN: **TI-DFT/BON/VI** SABRE: **TIDFT/BON/VI**

To access TIMATIC country information on Health and Visa regulations through the Computer Reservations System (CRS), type in the appropriate command line listed above.

POPULATION DENSITY: 49 per sq km.
CAPITAL: Kralendijk. **Population:** 1800 (2002).
GEOGRAPHY: Bonaire is the second-largest island in the Netherlands Antilles and is located 80km (50 miles) north of Venezuela and 48km (30 miles) east of Curaçao. The landscape is flat and rocky and, owing to low annual rainfall, Bonaire has a fairly barren desert climate. The island has small beautiful beaches and safe waters.
GOVERNMENT: Part of the Netherlands Antilles; dependency of The Netherlands. **Head of State:** Queen Beatrix of the Netherlands, represented locally by Governor Frits Goedgedrag since 2002. **Head of Government:** Prime Minister Etienne Ys since 2002. The Netherlands Antilles consist of Bonaire, Curaçao, Saba, St Eustatius and St Maarten. The capital of the island group is Willemstad, Curaçao.
LANGUAGE: Dutch is the official language. Papiamento (a mixture of Portuguese, African, Spanish, Dutch and English) is the commonly used *lingua franca*. English and Spanish are also widely spoken.
RELIGION: Predominantly Roman Catholic with a Protestant minority. There are many evangelical churches of different denominations, and a new mosque has also been erected on the island.
TIME: GMT - 4.
ELECTRICITY: 127 volts AC, 50Hz.
COMMUNICATIONS: Telephone: IDD is available. Country code: 599. Outgoing international code: 00. It is cheaper to make international calls from phone booths in the Telbo building than from resorts. **Mobile telephone:** *Communications Systems Curaçao NV* operates GSM 1900 coverage, and *Curaçao Telecom NV* (website: www.curacaotelecom.com) and *Seltel NV* operate GSM 900 and GSM 900/1800, respectively, across the whole of the Netherlands Antilles. Mobile telephones can be hired on the island from *Cell Rent* or *Cellularone*. The local network provider is *Obersi Electronics*. **Internet:** ISPs include *Bonairelive* (website: www.bonairelive.net) which operates an Internet Access Center. There are three Internet cafes in Kralendijk and a coin-operated Internet kiosk at the Harborside Mall and also in Kralendijk. **Telegram:** Facilities are available in the post office in Kralendijk and main hotels. **Post:** Airmail to and from Europe takes 4 to 6 days. Surface mail takes up to 6 weeks. **Press:** The main Dutch-language newspapers are *Algemeen Dagblad*, *Amigoe*, *Bala*, *Extra*, *La Prensa*, *Nabo*, *Telegraaf* and *Vigilante* are published in Papiamento.
Radio: BBC World Service (website: www.bbc.co.uk/worldservice) and Voice of America (website: www.voa.gov) can be received. From time to time the frequencies change and the most up-to-date can be found online.

Passport/Visa

	Passport Required?	Visa Required?	Return Ticket Required?
Full British	Yes	1	Yes
Australian	Yes	2	Yes
Canadian	Yes	2	Yes
USA	Yes	2	Yes
Other EU	Yes	1/2	Yes
Japanese	Yes	2	Yes

Note: Regulations and requirements may be subject to change at short notice, and you are advised to contact the appropriate diplomatic or consular authority before finalising travel arrangements. Details of these may be found at the head of this country's entry. Any numbers in the chart refer to the footnotes below.

PASSPORTS: Passport valid for at least three months after intended return to home country required by all.
VISAS: Required by all except the following:
(a) **1.** nationals of Belgium, Bolivia, Burkina Faso, Chile, Costa Rica, Czech Republic, Ecuador, Germany, Hungary, Israel, Jamaica, Korea (Rep), Luxembourg, Malawi, Mauritius, The Netherlands, Niger, The Philippines, Poland, San Marino, Slovak Republic, Spain, Swaziland, Togo and the UK for touristic stays of up to three months;
(b) **2.** all other nationals for touristic stays of up to 14 days, except nationals of Albania, Bosnia & Herzegovina, Bulgaria, Cambodia, China (PR) (except Hong Kong SAR), CIS, Colombia, Cote d'Ivoire, Croatia, Cuba, Dominican Republic, Estonia, Ghana, Guinea-Bissau, Haiti, Kenya, Korea (Dem Rep), Latvia, Libya, Lithuania, Macedonia (Former Yugoslav Republic of), Mali, Nigeria, Romania, Serbia & Montenegro and Vietnam who *always* need a visa;
(c) most nationals continuing to a third country within 24 hours by the same means of transportation and not leaving the airport and holding tickets with reserved seats and documents for their onward journey.
Note: All stays can be extended locally by the same period that they are valid for.
Types of visa and cost: All visas, regardless of duration of stay or number of entries permitted on visa, cost £15.
Validity: Visas are generally issued for as long as duration of stay, up until a maximum 90 days from date of issue.
Application requirements: (a) Valid passport with at least one blank page. If passport is new, the old passport must also be submitted. (b) One fully completed application form. (c) One recent passport-size photo per person endorsed on passport. (d) Fee, payable by postal order (to Royal Netherlands Embassy) or cash. Cheques are not accepted. (e) Evidence of sufficient funds amounting to a minimum of £30 for each day of stay (cash not accepted), eg original bank statements, credit card with credit limit statement, traveller's cheques. (f) A recent and original letter from employer, stating commencement date, with last payslip. If self-employed, submit letter from solicitor, accountant or company house. If unemployed, submit social benefit booklet. If in education, submit a recent and original letter from school/college/university, confirming attendance. (g) Valid medical or travel insurance. *Tourist*: (a)-(g) and, (h) Invitation from family or proof of hotel booking. (i) Return or onward ticket. *Business*: (a)-(g) and, (h) Invitation from Dutch company confirming duration and purpose of stay.
Application to: Nearest Embassy of the Kingdom of The Netherlands. All further information about visa requirements may be obtained from The Royal Netherlands Embassies which formally represent the Netherlands Antilles; see *Contact Addresses* in *The Netherlands* section.
Working days required: Applications should be lodged at least one month prior to departure.
Temporary residence: Enquire at the office of the Lieutenant Governor of the Island Territory of Bonaire, Plaza Reina Wilhelmina 1, Kralendijk, Bonaire. In certain cases, Dutch Europeans may be permitted to reside in the Netherlands Antilles without having to apply for a residence permit. However, it is best to consult the nearest Dutch Embassy/Consulate in advance to ascertain whether this is applicable taking into consideration the individual circumstances of the traveller.

Money

Currency: Netherlands Antilles Guilder or Florin (NAG) = 100 cents. Notes are in denominations of NAG250, 100, 50, 25, 10 and 5. Coins are in denominations of NAG5, 2.5, 1, 0.5, 0.25, 0.1, 0.05 and 0.01 cents. The US Dollar is accepted everywhere although change is given in Guilders. Notes in denominations greater than US$20 will only be accepted in banks.
Note: The Netherlands Antilles Guilder is tied to the US Dollar.
Currency exchange: Most major currencies, including US Dollars, Pounds Sterling and Euros, are easily exchanged. ATMs are located around the island.
Credit & debit cards: American Express, Diners Club, MasterCard and Visa are accepted in larger establishments. Check with your credit or debit card company for details of merchant acceptability and other services which may be available.
Travellers cheques: To avoid additional exchange rate charges, travellers are advised to take travellers cheques in US Dollars.
Currency restrictions: There are no restrictions on the import or export of local or foreign currency. The import of Dutch or Surinam silver coins is forbidden.
Exchange rate indicators: The following figures are included as a guide to the movement of the Netherlands Antilles Guilder against Sterling and the US Dollar:

Date	Feb '04	May '04	Aug '04	Nov '04
£1.00=	3.18	3.20	3.26	3.38
$1.00=	1.78	1.79	1.77	1.79

Banking hours: Mon-Fri 0900-1200 and 1400-1600.

Duty Free

The following items may be imported into Bonaire by persons aged 15 years or over without incurring customs duty:
200 cigarettes or 100 cigarillos (or of 3g each) or 50 cigars or 250g of tobacco; 2l of alcoholic beverages or 2l of wine; an unlimited quantity of perfume; gifts up to a value of NAG100.
Note: If the total value of goods per passenger exceeds NAG500, a declaration should be made on a customs form and cleared at the freight department. It should also be noted that the import of leather articles from Haiti is not advisable.

Public Holidays

2005: Jan 1 New Year's Day. **Jan 19** Carnival Rest Day. **Mar 25-28** Easter. **Apr 30** Queen's Birthday Celebrations and Rincon's Day. **May 1** Labour Day. **May 5** Ascension Day. **Sep 6** Bonaire Day. **Dec 25-26** Christmas.
2006: Jan 1 New Year's Day. **Jan 19** Carnival Rest Day. **Apr 14-17** Easter. **Apr 30** Queen's Birthday Celebrations and

Rincon's Day. **May 1** Labour Day. **May 25** Ascension Day. **Sep 6** Bonaire Day. **Dec 25-26** Christmas.

Health

	Special Precautions?	Certificate Required?
Yellow Fever	No	1
Cholera	No	No
Typhoid & Polio	2	N/A
Malaria	No	N/A

Note: *Regulations and requirements may be subject to change at short notice, and you are advised to contact your doctor well in advance of your intended date of departure. Any numbers in the chart refer to the footnotes below.*

1: A yellow fever certificate is required from all travellers over six months of age coming from infected areas.
2: Polio and typhoid are not endemic in Bonaire, however, precautions are advised as a few areas of risk exist within the general region of the Caribbean.
Food & drink: All mains water on the islands is distilled from seawater, and is thus safe to drink. Bottled mineral water is widely available. Milk is pasteurised and dairy products are safe for consumption. Local meat, poultry, seafood, fruit and vegetables are generally considered safe to eat.
Other risks: *Hepatitis A* is present. Outbreaks of *dengue fever* occur in the area.
Health care: The San Francisco Hospital is equipped to deal with emergencies and has a decompression chamber and an ambulance aircraft.

Travel - International

AIR: The national airline of the Netherlands Antilles is *DCA* (website: www.flydca.net). *DCA* offers direct services from Miami to Bonaire's Flamingo Airport once a week. *DCA* flies daily to Curaçao, from where there are international connections. *KLM* offers direct flights twice a day from Amsterdam to Bonaire, as well as daily flights from Amsterdam to Curaçao and Aruba, with connections to Bonaire. *American Eagle* has flights six times a week between Puerto Rico and Bonaire, and three times a week from Aruba. *Air Jamaica* operates from Montego Bay on Mondays, Wednesdays and Saturdays. *American Airlines* operates direct flights to Curaçao from many US cities, with connections to Bonaire. There is also *BonairExcel*, which operates seven daily flights to Curaçao and three daily flights to Aruba, although connections with *KLM* sometimes occur.
Approximate flight times: From Bonaire to *London* is 11 hours, to *Amsterdam* is 9 hours 30 minutes, to *Los Angeles* is 10 hours and to *New York* is 4 hours. Times vary considerably depending on connections.
International airports: *Flamingo Airport (BON)* is 4km (2.5 miles) from Kralendijk. Taxis are available.
Departure tax: US$5.75 to destinations within the Netherlands Antilles and US$20 for international flights.
SEA: There are no international boat connections to Bonaire, except for a passenger ferry between Bonaire and Curaçao. However, Bonaire is regularly visited by cruise ships operated by *Holland America, Majestic, P&O, Silver Sea* and *Windjammer* during high season (December to April).

Travel - Internal

ROAD: A good **taxi** service exists on the island. Rates are government controlled. There are numerous car hire firms located at hotels, the airport and Kralendijk. Reservations should be made in advance to get the best rates. Pick-ups and mini-vans are available for shore divers. **Car hire** tax is US$4 per day, plus 5 per cent on the rental fee. Bikes and motorbikes can also be hired without any difficulty. Traffic drives on the right. Roads are reasonably good, although jeeps may be needed for extensive touring of the island.
Documentation: A national driving licence is acceptable if held for at least two years, although drivers must be at least 21 years of age (minimum age varies according to hire company and type of car). Drivers under a certain age may also be restricted as to what type of car they may hire, and most cars are manual/standard transmission.

Accommodation

HOTELS: There are excellent hotels and resorts on the island with good facilities for the holidaymaker, particularly in the provision of watersports equipment, etc. Advance booking is essential. For further information, contact the Bonaire Hotel and Tourism Association (BONHATA), PO Box 358, Kaya Gob Debrot 67, Kralendijk (tel: (717) 5134; fax: (717) 8534; e-mail: info@bonhata.org; website: www.bonhata.com).
GUEST HOUSES: The visitor can opt for accommodation in beach villas or private apartments. Various property companies can be contacted – details are available from BONHATA (see address above).
Note: Rates for accommodation will be approximately 20 to 40 per cent cheaper in the off-peak season (15 April to15 December). A room tax of around US$5.50-6.50 per person per night is added to the bill. An additional service charge of 10 to 15 per cent may also be levied.

Resorts & Excursions

Bonaire is a place for privacy and rest. The island is ideal for those who want to enjoy a beautiful coastline and the full range of watersports facilities, but do not demand too much by way of sophisticated restaurants and nightspots. Bonaire's **Marine Park** is centred on a spectacular coral reef, which is maintained and protected throughout the year by marine experts. There are frequent slide shows on underwater sports and conservation in the hotels and at watersports centres in Kralendijk.
The salt flats change colour according to fluctuations in the resident algae population, from a breathtaking fuchsia to a subtle pink. Slave huts nearby were inhabited by the salt workers until the abolition of slavery in 1863. The beautiful lagoon of **Goto Meer** is a haven for flocks of flamingos. Bonaire has its own 5463 hectares (13,500 acres) game reserve, the **Washington/Slagbaai National Park**, including **Mount Brandaris**, the island's highest point at 241m (790ft). There are two routes through the park, each enabling the visitor to see the interesting flora and fauna the island has to offer, in particular, the birdlife. In **Kralendijk** itself, there are several sites worth visiting, including the lively and interesting fruit and vegetable market. There are some handsome buildings along the waterfront, such as **Fort Oranje**. **Klein Bonaire**, situated half a mile off Bonaire's west coast, is a popular destination for sail charters or for lunch or evening picnics. For more information on activities and sightseeing in Bonaire, contact the Tourism Corporation Bonaire (see *Contact Addresses* section).

Sport & Activities

Watersports: Kayaking, **scuba-diving**, **snorkelling**, **windsurfing** and **water-skiing** are all available with facilities and tuition as necessary. The waters around the island are clear, safe and teeming with fish of every size and hue. **Fishing** and **sailing** charters are popular; half- or full-day cruises can be arranged round the bay or to Klein Bonaire, the island's tiny uninhabited sister isle. Every second week of October there is a sailing regatta during which there is a carnival atmosphere on the island. The focus of the regatta is the marina, just a few minutes out of Kralendijk: berthing facilities for various types of vessel, a shipyard, and a drydock make Bonaire a pleasure boater's retreat.
Other: The main hotels and sporting centres on the island have **tennis** facilities and **mountain bikes** are available for hire. **Birdwatching** trips and **horseriding** are also popular. There are two-day spas on the island offering sea salt baths.

Social Profile

FOOD & DRINK: The restaurants serve predominantly Creole cooking, particularly seafood dishes, including conch shell meat, grilled spicy fish and lobster. Island specialities include iguana soup and *kabrito stoba* (goat stew). A variety of Chinese, French, Indonesian, Italian and international cooking can also be found. There are several hotels, restaurants and bars in Kralendijk to choose from. Restaurants and bars are usually closed by midnight.
NIGHTLIFE: This is centred on both the main hotels and restaurants. Having eaten, evening entertainment includes dancing or listening to reggae groups or calypso steel bands at the many oceanside bars and cafes. The island has two discos and two casinos.
SHOPPING: The reductions on duty-free imports make the purchase of some perfume, jewellery or alcohol well worthwhile. Bonaire prides itself on its unique, specialist stores. Watches, Dutch cheese, fine China and Cuban cigars are usually sold. **Shopping hours:** Mon-Sat 0800-1200 and 1400-1800. Larger supermarkets are open Mon-Sat 0800-1900, with some open Sun 1100-1400.
SPECIAL EVENTS: The following is a selection of special events occurring in Bonaire in 2005; for a complete list and exact dates consult Tourism Corporation Bonaire (see *Contact Addresses* section):
Jan *Carnival* season opens; *Marathon Jump-up*, Rincon; *Tumba Festival Contest*, Kralendijk. **Jan 1-6** *Maskarada* (New Year). **Feb-Mar** *Carnival*. **Feb 22** *Carnival Adult Parade*, Kralendijk. **Apr 1** *Simadam* (harvest) *Festival*, Rincon. **Apr 15-22** *Dive into Earth Week*. **Apr 30** *Queen's Birthday Windsurfing Race*; *Cycle Bonaire* (70km Road

Credit: © Dutch Caribbean Travel Center

Race). **May** *Bonaire Mountain Bike Challenge Race*. **Jun 5-19** *Bonaire Dive Festival*. **Jun 8** *Angola Construction Sailing Competition*, Kas di Regatta. **Jul 4** *Annual Bonaire Arts Day*. **Aug** *Family Month*; *Copa Cultimera*, Sorobon. **Sep** *Bonaire Bikers MC Flag Day Weekend 2005*. **Sep 6** *Bonaire Day*. **Sep 18** *Underwater Cleanup*. **Oct 3-10** *38th Annual International Sailing Regatta*. **Dec** *King of the Caribbean Pro-Am Windsurfing Competition*.
SOCIAL CONVENTIONS: Dutch customs are still prevalent throughout the islands, although they are increasingly subject to US influence. Dress is casual and lightweight cottons are advised. Bathing suits should be confined to beach and poolside areas only. Nudity is prohibited on beaches except at Sorobon Beach Resort, a privately owned nudist resort. **Tipping:** There is normally a 10 per cent service charge in restaurants and a 6 per cent tax. Tipping is not widely practised but porters are usually given 50 cents-US$1 per bag; taxi drivers are generally given 10 per cent of the fare.

Business Profile

ECONOMY: During the 1950s, Bonaire began a gradual climb out of chronic economic depression, aided by investment in tourism and the revival of a long-dormant salt industry. The economy gained a further boost in the mid-1970s, when the Bonaire Petroleum Corporation (Bopec) set up an oil transfer depot with a deep-water port, with facilities for transferring oil from ocean-going to coastal tankers. However, plans to build a refinery in Bonaire have been indefinitely shelved. Other economic activities on Bonaire include rice processing and shipping. There is also some agriculture – Bonaire grows a variety of fruit and vegetables; in particular, it is a major producer and exporter of aloes. Bonaire has benefited from the offshore financial industry, which has built up among the island group, although most of the companies engaged in the sector are located on Curaçao and St Maarten. As part of the Kingdom of The Netherlands, Bonaire is an overseas territory in association with the EU; it also holds observer status at the regional CARICOM trading bloc.
BUSINESS: General business practices prevail. **Office hours:** Mon-Fri 0730-1200 and 1330-1630.
COMMERCIAL INFORMATION: The following organisation can offer advice: Bonaire Chamber of Commerce and Industry, PO Box 52, Princess Marie-Straat, Kralendijk (tel: (717) 5595; fax: (717) 8995).
CONFERENCES/CONVENTIONS: For information regarding conference facilities, contact Tourism Corporation Bonaire (see *Contact Addresses* section).

Climate

Hot throughout the year, but tempered by cooling trade winds. The average temperature is 28°C (82°F) and the average rainfall is 50cm (20 inches) per year.
Required clothing: Lightweights with warmer top layers for evenings; showerproof clothing is advisable throughout the year.

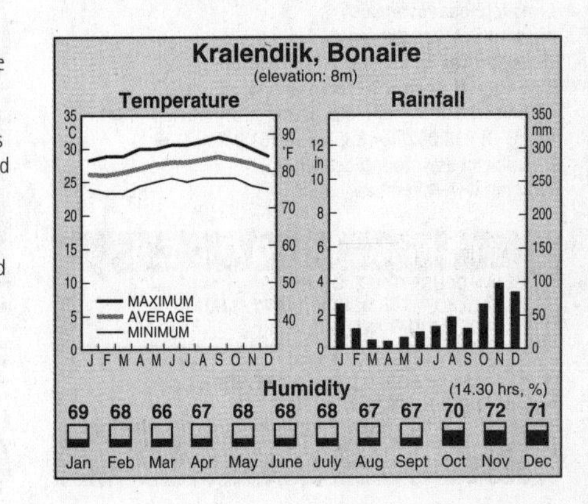

Bosnia & Herzegovina

LATEST TRAVEL ADVICE CONTACTS

British Foreign and Commonwealth Office
Tel: (0870) 606 0290 Website: www.fco.gov.uk
US Department of State
Website: http://travel.state.gov/travel
Canadian Department of Foreign Affairs and Int'l Trade
Tel: (1 800) 267 8376 Website: www.dfait-maeci.gc.ca

Location: Southeastern Europe.

Country dialling code: 387.

Ministry of Foreign Affairs
Cumuorija 5, 71000 Sarajevo, Bosnia & Herzegovina
Tel: (33) 200 582. Fax: (33) 472 188.
E-mail: info@mvp.gov.ba *or* consular.info@mvp.gov.ba (consular section).
Website: www.mvp.gov.ba
Embassy of Bosnia & Herzegovina
5-7 Lexham Gardens, London W8 5JJ, UK
Tel: (020) 7373 0867. Fax: (020) 7373 0871.
Opening hours: Mon-Fri 0900-1700; Mon-Fri 1000-1300 (consular section, personal callers).
British Embassy
Tina Ujevica 8, 71000 Sarajevo, Bosnia & Herzegovina
Tel: (33) 282 200. Fax: (33) 666 131.
E-mail: britemb@bih.net.ba
Consular section: Petrakijina 11, 71000 Sarajevo, Bosnia & Herzegovina
Tel: (33) 208 229. Fax: (33) 204 780.
E-mail: visaenquiries@sarajevo.mail.fco.gov.uk *or* consularenquiries@sarajevo.mail.fco.gov.uk
Website: www.britishembassy.ba
Embassy of Bosnia & Herzegovina
2109 East Street, NW, Washington, DC 20037, USA
Tel: (202) 337 1500 *or* 6473/6479 (consular section).
Fax: (202) 337 1502 *or* 2909 (consular section).
E-mail: info@bhembassy.org *or* consularaffairs@bhembassy.org (consular section).
Website: www.bhembassy.org
Embassy of the United States of America
Alipašsina 43, Sarajevo, Bosnia & Herzegovina
Tel: (33) 445 700. Fax: (33) 659 722.
E-mail: bhopa@state.gov
Website: www.usembassy.ba
Other offices in: Banja Luka and Mostar.
Embassy of Bosnia & Herzegovina
130 Albert Street, Suite 805, Ottawa, Ontario K1P 5G4
Tel: (613) 236 0028 *or* 8557. Fax: (613) 236 1139.
E-mail: embassyofbih@bellnet.ca
Website: www.bhembassy.ca

TIMATIC CODES

Health
AMADEUS: **TI-DFT/SJJ/HE**
GALILEO/WORLDSPAN: **TI-DFT/SJJ/HE**
SABRE: **TIDFT/SJJ/HE**

Visa
AMADEUS: **TI-DFT/SJJ/VI**
GALILEO/WORLDSPAN: **TI-DFT/SJJ/VI**
SABRE: **TIDFT/SJJ/VI**

To access TIMATIC country information on Health and Visa regulations through the Computer Reservations System (CRS), type in the appropriate command line listed above.

Canadian Embassy
Grbavicka 4, 2nd Floor, 71000 Sarajevo, Bosnia & Herzegovina
Tel: (33) 222 033. Fax: (33) 222 044.
E-mail: sjevo@international.gc.ca

General Information

AREA: 51,129 sq km (19,741 sq miles).
POPULATION: 4,126,000 (UN estimate 2002).
POPULATION DENSITY: 80.7 per sq km.
CAPITAL: Sarajevo. **Population:** 416,497 (1991).
GEOGRAPHY: Roughly triangular in shape, and the geopolitical centre of the former Yugoslav Federation, Bosnia & Herzegovina shares borders with Serbia & Montenegro in the east and southeast, and Croatia to the north and west, with a short Adriatic coastline of 20km (12 miles) in the southeast, but no ports.
GOVERNMENT: Parliamentary Democracy. Under the terms of the 1995 Dayton Peace agreement, Bosnia & Herzegovina consists of two entities: *Federacija Bosne i Hercegovine* (the Federation of Bosnia & Herzegovina) and *Republika Srpska* (the Serbian Republic). Each has its own president, although there is also a three-member rotating presidency, elected every four years. The presidency then appoints a Chairman of the Council of Ministers. **Heads of State:** The presidency of Bosnia & Herzegovina consists of two Members and one Chairperson: one Bosniak, one Serb and one Croat. Current Members and Chairman are: Dragan Covic (since 2002), Sulejman Tihic (since 2002) and Borislav Paravac (since 2003). The chair rotates every eight months.
Head of Government: Chairman of the Council of Ministers Adnan Terzic (since 2003).
LANGUAGE: The official languages are Bosnian, Serbian and Croatian. The Croats and Bosniaks use the Latin alphabet, whereas the Serbs use the Cyrillic.
RELIGION: 40 per cent Muslim, 31 per cent Orthodox, 15 per cent Roman Catholic, 4 per cent Protestant and 10 per cent other denominations and religions.
TIME: GMT + 1 (GMT + 2 from last Sunday in March to last Sunday in October).
ELECTRICITY: 220 volts AC, 50Hz. Two-pin plugs are in use.
COMMUNICATIONS: Telephone: Country code: 387. Outgoing international code: 99. The national network of telecommunications is operated by *bh telecom* (website: www.telecom.ba). **Mobile telephone:** GSM 900 network. Coverage is reasonable. Network operators include *GSMBIH*, *Mobilna Srpske* and *Eronet* (website: www.eronet.ba). **Internet:** Local ISPs include *bih.net* (website: www.bih.net.ba) and *Inecco* (website: www.inecco.net). There are few Internet cafes; however hotels might provide facilities. **Post:** International and internal postal services are now fully restored. *BH Post* (tel: (33) 252 613; website: www.bhp.ba) is the government-run postal service and the only internationally recognised service in the country. *HPT Mostar* is the local Croatian postal service, while *Srpske Poste* is maintained by the Serbian government in Banja Luka. Post office hours: Generally Monday to Friday 1000-1700. Normal post takes approximately one week to reach its destination, while heavier packages could take up to 10 days. Coins, bank notes, precious metals and stones, narcotics, alcohol, firearms and ammunition are not permitted to be sent by mail. **Press:** The main newspaper for the Federation of Bosnia and Herzegovina, *Dnevni Avaz*, is published in Sarajevo. Serbian newspapers include *Glas Srpski* and *Nezavisne Novine*, both published in Banja Luka. *Dnevni List* and the weekly *Hratska Rijec* are Croatian-language papers, published in Banja Luka and Sarajevo respectively.
Radio: BBC World Service (website: www.bbc.co.uk/worldservice) and Voice of America (website: www.voa.gov) can be received. From time to time the frequencies change and the most up-to-date can be found online.

Passport/Visa

	Passport Required?	Visa Required?	Return Ticket Required?
Full British	Yes	No	Yes
Australian	Yes	No	Yes
Canadian	Yes	No	Yes
USA	Yes	No	Yes
Other EU	Yes	No	Yes
Japanese	Yes	No	Yes

Note: *Regulations and requirements may be subject to change at short notice, and you are advised to contact the appropriate diplomatic or consular authority before finalising travel arrangements. Details of these may be found at the head of this country's entry. Any numbers in the chart refer to the footnotes below.*

PASSPORTS: Valid passport required by all.
VISAS: Required by all except the following for a stay of up to 90 days:
(a) nationals of countries referred to in the chart above, except nationals of Cyprus, Czech Republic, Estonia, Hungary, Latvia, Lithuania, Malta, Poland and Slovak Republic who *do* require a visa;
(b) nationals of Andorra, Brunei, Croatia, Iceland, Korea (Rep), Kuwait, Liechtenstein, Macedonia (Former Yugoslav Republic of), Malaysia, Monaco, New Zealand, Norway, Qatar, Russian Federation, San Marino, Serbia & Montenegro, Turkey and Vatican City.
Types of visa and cost: *Tourist*, *Business* and *Private*: £20 (single-entry); £36 (multiple-entry for up to 90 days); £45 (multiple-entry for more than 90 days).
Application to: Consulate (or Consular Section at Embassy); see *Contact Addresses* section.
Application requirements: (a) Passport or official travel document valid for at least three months beyond the expiry date of the visa. (b) One completed application form. (c) Two passport-size photos. (d) Return/onward ticket. *Tourist*: (a)-(d) and, (e) Copy of the invoice from tour operator. *Private*: (a)-(d) and, (e) Invitation letter from host, endorsed by the authorities. *Business*: (a)-(d) and, (e) Invitation letter from the host company in Bosnia & Herzegovina, endorsed by the Chamber of Commerce.
Note: Applicants from certain countries might have to submit evidence of cash assets (such as a recent bank statement), as well as evidence of a negative HIV test.
Working days required: Approximately three weeks, as all applications are now sent to Bosnia & Herzegovina for approval.
Temporary residence: Enquire at the Ministry of Interior in Bosnia & Herzegovina.

Money

Currency: Bosnia & Herzegovina Konvertibilna Marka (KM) = 100 pfeninga. Notes are in denominations of KM200, 100, 50, 20, 10, 5 and 1 and 50 pfenings. Coins are available in denominations of KM2 and 1, and 50, 20 and 10 pfenings.
Currency exchange: The Euro and US Dollar are the preferred foreign currencies. The Pound Sterling is of relatively little value in the republic and rarely used. Included in the Dayton Peace Agreement, signed in 1995, were provisions for a Central Bank of Bosnia & Herzegovina. This bank acts as a currency board and is the sole authority for the issue of the Konvertibilna Marka.
Credit & debit cards: These are not readily accepted. Check with your credit or debit card company for details of merchant acceptability. There are a few ATMs (in Sarajevo and Mostar).
Travellers cheques: Bosnia & Herzegovina is generally a cash-only economy and travellers cheques are not easily exchanged.
Currency restrictions: The import and export of local currency are limited to KM200,000. There are no restrictions on the import and export of foreign currencies.
Exchange rate indicators: The following figures are included as a guide to the movements of the Konvertibilna Marka against Sterling and the US Dollar:

Date	Feb '04	May '04	Aug '04	Nov '04
£1.00=	2.86	2.93	2.91	2.79
$1.00=	1.57	1.64	1.58	1.47

Banking hours: Mon-Fri 0800-1900.

Duty Free

The following goods may be imported into Bosnia & Herzegovina without incurring customs duty:
200 cigarettes or 20 cigars or 200g of tobacco; 1l of wine or spirits; one bottle of perfume; gifts to the value of €76.70.

Public Holidays

2005: Jan 1 New Year's Day. **Jan 6-7** Orthodox Christmas. **Jan 14-15** Orthodox New Year. **Jan 27** St Sava's Day. **Feb 2** Kurban Bajram. **Mar 1** Independence Day. **Apr 9-12** Easter. **Aug 15** Velika gospa (Western Christian Assumption). **Nov 1** All Saints' Day. **Nov 25** National Statehood Day. **Dec 25** Christmas.
2006: Jan 1 New Year's Day. **Jan 6-7** Orthodox Christmas. **Jan 14-15** Orthodox New Year. **Jan 27** St Sava's Day. **Feb 2** Kurban Bajram. **Mar 1** Independence Day. **Apr 14-17** Easter. **May 1** Labour Day. **Aug 15** Velika gospa (Western Christian Assumption). **Nov 1** All Saints' Day. **Dec 25** Christmas.
Note: In addition to the above dates, the government of Bosnia & Herzegovina has decided to allow its citizens two working days per year to fulfil their religious needs. These days are not considered official holidays and the measure has been introduced to respect the religious and ethnic diversity of the country.

Health

	Special Precautions?	Certificate Required?
Yellow Fever	No	No
Cholera	No	No
Typhoid & Polio	1	No
Malaria	No	N/A

Note: Regulations and requirements may be subject to change at short notice, and you are advised to contact your doctor well in advance of your intended date of departure. Any numbers in the chart refer to the footnotes below.

1: Immunisation or tablets against typhoid and polio are recommended; immunisation against typhoid may be less important for short stays in first-class conditions.
Food & drink: Water is generally considered safe to drink, although bottled water is recommended. Local meat, poultry, seafood, fruit and vegetables are generally considered safe to eat, although it is advisable to peel vegetables and fruit and only eat cooked meat and fish, preferably served hot. Unpasteurised milk must be boiled. Avoid dairy products that are likely to have been made from unboiled milk.
Other risks: *Hepatitis A* occurs and vaccination is usually advised. Immunisation against *hepatitis B, diphtheria, tuberculosis* and *tick-borne encephalitis* is recommended. *Rabies* is present. For those at high risk, vaccination before arrival should be considered. If you are bitten, seek medical advice without delay. For more information, consult the *Health* appendix.
Health care: Facilities are limited, especially outside Sarajevo and other major towns. There is no reciprocal healthcare agreement for British nationals; the E111 form is not valid. All medical and dental care must be paid for in cash, at the point of treatment. Tourists are strongly advised to take out full travel and medical insurance before travelling to Bosnia & Herzegovina.

Travel - International

Note: There continues to be a threat from terrorism to Western targets. Visitors must be particularly vigilant in public places and tourist sites. Unexploded landmines remain a real danger and travellers should be careful not to stray from roads and paved areas. If travelling within the Republika Srpska, visitors must remain vigilant and avoid drawing attention to their presence. All public demonstrations or gatherings must be eschewed.
AIR: The national airlines are *Air Bosna (JA)*, which operates flights from Amsterdam, Belgrade, Copenhagen, Gothenburg, Istanbul, London and Stockholm to Sarajevo, and *Air Srpska (R6)*, which operates regularly from Banja Luka to Belgrade and Zurich, with plans to expand the service to destinations in Germany and France. Other airlines serving Sarajevo include *Adria Airways, Air France, Austrian Airlines, Croatia Airlines, KLM, Lufthansa, Malev Hungarian Airlines* and *Turkish Airlines*. Flights from London are also operated by *Adria Airlines* (via Ljubljana) and *Croatia Airlines* (via Zagreb).
International airports: *Sarajevo (SJJ)* is the main international airport. *Banja Luka (BNX)* and *Mostar (OMO)* also receive a small number of international flights (from Vienna and Zagreb).
Departure tax: US$12. Transit passengers not leaving the airport transit area are exempt.
RAIL: The railway system was badly damaged during the civil war but restoration is underway. Rail services now link Sarajevo, Mostar, Doboj and Banja Luka to Zagreb, Belgrade, Ljubljana and Ploce. However, services are slow; the Sarajevo–Zagreb journey takes around nine hours.
ROAD: Bosnia & Herzegovina's road network is still in the process of being reconstructed, following massive damage during the 1992-1995 civil war. It is possible to enter the country by car from Croatia. Drivers from the UK should note that Green Card motor insurance is not extended to Bosnia & Herzegovina; compulsory third-pary insurance is available at border crossing points. There are frequent bus services from Sarajevo to many Eastern and Central European cities, including London (website: www.eurolines.com).
Note: The border crossing from Croatia at Bosanski Brod is now open.

Travel - Internal

RAIL: Rail links between the Federation of Bosnia & Herzegovina and the Republika Srpska have been restored. In addition, a few local services are operating.
ROAD: Travel by road is the usual means of transport in Bosnia & Herzegovina. Road conditions are still poor, but many roads are now being restored. The safety and condition of urban roads is generally fair, although rural road maintenance is seriously lacking. The risk of landmines has decreased in the last few years, as most mines remaining from the war are now clearly marked. However, visitors are still advised to exercise caution when travelling outside main cities and towns. Caution should also be taken when driving at night or during winter. Drivers should keep to the main roads. The emergency number for roadside assistance is 987. The capital, Sarajevo, is the nodal point for all Bosnia & Herzegovina's main communications routes, which go west to Banja Luka, and then to Zagreb, capital of Croatia; north to Doboj, and then to Osijek in Croatia; east to Zvornik, and then to Belgrade in Serbia & Montenegro; south to Mostar, and then the Adriatic Sea; and southeast to Foca, and then to Podgorica (formerly Titograd). **Documentation:** An International Driving Permit is required.

Accommodation

There are a number of national and international hotels, particularly in Sarajevo and the major cities. Other types of accommodation, including bed & breakfast and guest houses, are also available. Facilities in the smaller towns have improved in recent years and it is now possible to find hotels and other types of accommodation in most areas.

Resorts & Excursions

Note: The civil war not only caused numerous deaths and casualties but led to the devastation of the country's historic towns. However, the rebuilding process is underway and travellers are again visiting the country.
Historically, Bosnia & Herzegovina was a melting pot of different cultures, with Christians, Muslims and Jews co-existing peaceably in this area for many centuries. The country's architecture was diverse and fascinating – beautiful churches and mosques existed in equal measure.
The 500 years of Turkish rule left their trace, mainly in the capital, **Sarajevo**. The Turkish quarter and the town centre have been largely rebuilt and the city, although scarred by war, is coming back to life. The colourful bazaars are also part of the Ottoman heritage. **Travnik** in Bosnia was known as the town of the wazirs at the time of the Ottoman Empire. Much of the town was spared in the war and it is still possible to visit the **medieval castle**. The **many-coloured mosque** near the base of ul Hendek is alleged to contain hairs from Muhammad's beard.
The reconstruction of **Mostar**, once a prime tourist destination, has begun; however, most of the town's monuments were destroyed in the war, including all the 16th- and 17th-century mosques and the famous Turkish bridge. A few medieval buildings and cobbled streets remain. **Banja Luka**, the capital of the Republika Srpska, still contains a **16th-century fort** and an **amphitheatre**. There are several spas in the Republika Srpska area, most of which are operating again. **Bijeljina**, **Dubica**, **Laktasi**, **Srebrenica**, **Telic** and **Visegrad** all have natural mineral springs and medical facilities.

Sport & Activities

Opportunities for outdoor activities, especially **hiking**, **rafting** and **fishing**, exist in Bosnia & Herzegovina. But even though the country's large areas of forest, streams and mountains have much to offer to nature and outdoor enthusiasts, the effects of the civil war are still burdening Bosnia & Herzegovina with difficult transport links, poor roads and the considerable danger of landmines (which are apparently taking a heavy toll on wildlife). It will therefore take some years before the country's potential for activity holidays can be further developed. In past years, mountain health spa resorts such as *Bjelasnica*, *Igman* and *Jahorina* were renowned for good **skiing**, while the Adriatic Coast was known for its beaches, many of them suitable for **swimming** and other types of watersports. **Fishing** is unrestricted on the coast. For rivers and lakes, a special permit (which can be issued by hotels and regional authorities) is needed, with regulations differing in individual regions.

Social Profile

FOOD & DRINK: The traditional cuisine of the region includes obvious Turkish influences. Specialities are *bosanski lonac* (Bosnian meat and vegetable stew), *lokum* (Turkish delight) and *rakija* (old Serbian brandy) as well as *halva* (crushed sesame seeds in honey).
NIGHTLIFE: Bosnia & Herzegovina's nightlife, particularly in Sarajevo, is widely reputed to be excellent. In the capital, the cosmopolitan atmosphere is tangible. The city apparently has more cafes per capita than any other European city and a relaxed cafe culture is prominent. There are many opportunities for nightlife activities, from cinemas and clubs to opera and theatre performance. There are also frequent festivals, showcasing such popular pastimes as jazz and film.
SHOPPING: Traditional purchases include woodcarvings, brass coffee-pots, ceramics, handmade carpets, woollen goods, wines, folk-art, tapestries, embroidery and leather boxes. **Shopping hours:** 0800-2000.
SPECIAL EVENTS: The following is a selection of special events occurring in Bosnia & Herzegovina in 2005:
Feb 7-Mar 21 *Winter Festival*. **Mar** *Festival of Bosnian Orchestras*. **Jun-Jul** *Days of Culture*, New Town Sarajevo. **Jul 12-16** *Language Week*. **Aug 19-27** *Sarajevo Film Festival*. **Sep** *TheaterFest*. **Nov 2-6** *Jazz Fest Sarajevo*.
SOCIAL CONVENTIONS: Bosnia & Herzegovina is charaterised by its ethnic and religious diversity and visitors should respect the customs and traditions of the various ethnic and religious groups. The main ethnic groups are the Bosniaks (48 per cent, also sometimes referred to as Bosnian Muslims), the Serbs (37.1 per cent) and the Croats (14.3 per cent). As a sign of acknowledgement of the three main religious communities (Islamic, Orthodox and Roman Catholic), the Government of Bosnia & Herzegovina allows its citizens to take off two working days per year for religious purposes. Visitors should be aware that drinking alcohol in public may be considered offensive by Muslims. Visitors should avoid expressing opinions about the war or other sensitive issues. **Tipping:** Tipping is customary for taxis, as well as in hotels and restaurants; the bill is often rounded up.

Business Profile

ECONOMY: The collapse of the internal Yugoslav market at the beginning of the 1990s placed the Bosnian economy in serious difficulty, especially as it relied heavily on the sale of its agricultural produce and mineral ores to the rest of the Yugoslav federation. The main agricultural products are tobacco and fruit; livestock rearing is also important. There are extensive mineral resources, particularly of copper, lead, zinc and gold, plus iron ore and lignite coal. The civil war that broke out in 1992 then brought the economy to a virtual standstill. Reconstruction was backed by US$5 billion dollars of international aid. Although the division of the economy between two jurisdictions has made economic policy-making difficult, the Bosnian economy as a whole recorded exceptional growth during the 1990s (at some stages, exceeding 30 per cent annually). A central bank has been set up and a common currency, Konvertibilna Marka (fixed in value to the Deutschmark and hence to the Euro), successfully introduced.
Initially, most of the post-war international aid was directed to the Muslim-Croat region. The *Republika Srpska* managed to get much of its industrial sector working again but relied heavily on the support of Yugoslavia. The war between NATO and Yugoslavia in the late 1990s thus set the Bosnian Serb economy back once again. Since then, the central government has received a series of loans, totalling approximately US$250 million, from the IMF. Bosnia has begun a slow transformation to a market economy. The government is hoping that opening up the economy will attract both inward investment and, equally important, the return of the country's skilled and professional workforce – most of whom have been living in exile since the war.
COMMERCIAL INFORMATION: Information can be obtained from the following organisations: Foreign Trade Chamber of Bosnia & Herzegovina, Branislava Djurdjeva 10, Sarajevo (tel: (33) 663 636; fax: (33) 214 292; e-mail: cis@komorabih.com; website: www.komorabih.com); *or* Central Bank of Bosnia & Herzegovina, Marsala Tita 25, 71000 Sarajevo (tel: (33) 278 100; fax: (33) 278 299; e-mail: contact@cbbh.ba; website: www.cbbh.gov.ba).

Climate

Dominated by mountainous and hilly terrain, and drained by major rivers to the north (Sava) and east (Drina), Bosnia & Herzegovina has a climate that is as variable as the rest of the former Yugoslav federation, with moderate continental climatic conditions generally the norm (very cold winters and hot summers).
Required clothing: In winter, heavyweight clothing and overcoat. In summer, lightweight clothing and raincoat required, with mediumweight clothing at times in the colder and wetter north, and at higher altitudes elsewhere.

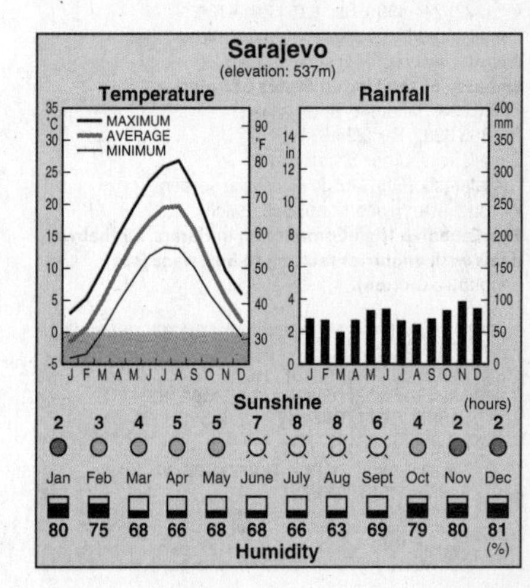

A B C D E F G H I J K L M N O P Q R S T U V W X Y Z

Botswana

LATEST TRAVEL ADVICE CONTACTS

British Foreign and Commonwealth Office
Tel: (0870) 606 0290 Website: www.fco.gov.uk
US Department of State
Website: http://travel.state.gov/travel
Canadian Department of Foreign Affairs and Int'l Trade
Tel: (1 800) 267 8376 Website: www.dfait-maeci.gc.ca

Location: Central southern Africa.

Country dialling code: 267.

Department of Tourism
Private Bag 0047, Gaborone, Botswana
Tel: 395 3024. Fax: 390 8675.
E-mail: botswanatourism@gov.bw
Website: www.botswanatourism.org
Botswana High Commission
6 Stratford Place, London W1C 1AY, UK
Tel: (020) 7499 0031 *or* 7647 1000 *or* (09065) 508 954 (recorded visa information; calls cost £1 per minute).
Fax: (020) 7495 8595 *or* 7409 7382.
Opening hours: Mon-Fri 0900-1300 and 1400-1700.
Department of Tourism UK Representation Office
c/o Southern Skies Marketing, Old Boundary House, London Road, Sunningdale, Berkshire SL5 0DJ, UK.
Tel: (01344) 298 980. Fax: (0870) 706 0116.
E-mail: botswanatourism@southern-skies.co.uk
Website: www.botswanatourism.org.uk
British High Commission
Street address: Plot 1079-1084 Main Mall off Queens Road, Gaborone, Botswana
Postal address: Private Bag 0023, Gaborone, Botswana
Tel: 395 2841. Fax: 395 6105.
E-mail: bhc@botsnet.bw
Website: www.britishhighcommission.gov.uk/botswana
Embassy of the Republic of Botswana
1531-33 New Hampshire Avenue, NW, Washington, DC 20036, USA
Tel: (202) 244 4990. Fax: (202) 244 4164.
E-mail: mgradikgokong@botswanaembassy.org
Website: www.botswanaembassy.org
Embassy of the United States of America
PO Box 90, Gaborone, Botswana
Tel: 395 3982. Fax: 395 6947.
E-mail: ircgaborone@state.gov *or* consulargaboro@state.gov (consular section).
Website: http://gaborone.usembassy.gov
The Canadian High Commission in Harare, Zimbabwe, deals with enquiries relating to Botswana (see *Zimbabwe* section).

TIMATIC CODES

Health	AMADEUS: **TI-DFT/GBE/HE** GALILEO/WORLDSPAN: **TI-DFT/GBE/HE** SABRE: **TIDFT/GBE/HE**
Visa	AMADEUS: **TI-DFT/GBE/VI** GALILEO/WORLDSPAN: **TI-DFT/GBE/VI** SABRE: **TIDFT/GBE/VI**

To access TIMATIC country information on Health and Visa regulations through the Computer Reservations System (CRS), type in the appropriate command line listed above.

General Information

AREA: 581,730 sq km (224,607 sq miles).
POPULATION: 1,680,863 (2001).
POPULATION DENSITY: 2.9 per sq km.
CAPITAL: Gaborone. **Population:** 186,007 (2001).
GEOGRAPHY: Botswana is bordered to the south and east by South Africa, to the northeast by Zimbabwe, to the north and west by Namibia and touches Zambia just west of the Victoria Falls. The tableland of the Kalahari Desert covers most of Botswana. National parks cover 17 per cent of the country, with 38 per cent of the country dedicated to wildlife areas. To the northwest is the Okavango Delta, the largest inland delta in the world. The Moremi Game Reserve occupies two-thirds of the delta's area. The Chobe National Park in the north includes the Savute and Linyanti regions. To the far southwest is the Kgalagadi Transfrontier National Park, which ranges across the borders of Botswana, South Africa and Namibia, but is managed as a single entity. The majority of the population lives in the southeast around Gaborone, Serowe and Kanye along the South African border. The vast arid sandveld of the Kalahari occupies much of north, central and western Botswana. The seasonal rains bring a considerable difference to the vegetation, especially in the Makgadikgadi Pans and the Okavango Delta in the north. The latter, after the winter floods, provides one of the wildest and most beautiful nature reserves in Africa.
GOVERNMENT: Republic since 1966. **Head of State and Government:** President Festus Gontebanye Mogae since 1998.
LANGUAGE: English is the official language. Setswana is the national language.
RELIGION: The majority of the population holds animistic beliefs, 30 per cent are Christian. There are small Muslim communities and the Bahá'í Faith is also represented.
TIME: GMT + 2.
ELECTRICITY: 220-240 volts AC, 50Hz. 15- and 13-amp plug sockets are in use.
COMMUNICATIONS: Telephone: IDD is available to over 80 countries. Country code: 267. Outgoing international code: 00. There are very few public phone boxes. **Mobile telephone:** GSM 900 network. Local providers include *Mascom Wireless* (website: www.mascom.bw) and *Orange Pty LTD* (www.orange.co.bw). Coverage is limited to the main inhabited areas. **Fax:** Widely available in urban areas, although there are very few facilities in wildlife areas. **Internet:** Local ISPs include *IBIS* and *Mega* (website: www.mega.bw). **Telegram:** There are facilities in Gaborone and other large centres (usually in major hotels and main post offices). **Post:** There are post offices in all towns and the larger villages, open weekdays 0815-1245 and 1400-1600 and Sat 0800-1100. Services are slow but cheap. Airmail service to Europe takes from one to three weeks. There are post offices in all the main towns, although there are no deliveries and post must be collected from boxes. **Press:** The daily newspaper is the *Dikgang tsa Gompieno* (*Botswana Daily News*), published in Setswana and English. Other English-language newspapers include *The Botswana Gazette*, *The Botswana Guardian*, *Mmegi* (*The Reporter*) and *The Midweek Sun*, all published weekly. **Radio:** BBC World Service (website: www.bbc.co.uk/worldservice) and Voice of America (website: www.voa.gov) can be received. From time to time the frequencies change and the most up-to-date can be found online.

Passport/Visa

	Passport Required?	Visa Required?	Return Ticket Required?
Full British	Yes	No	Yes
Australian	Yes	No	Yes
Canadian	Yes	No	Yes
USA	Yes	No	Yes
Other EU	Yes	1	Yes
Japanese	Yes	No	Yes

Note: *Regulations and requirements may be subject to change at short notice, and you are advised to contact the appropriate diplomatic or consular authority before finalising travel arrangements. Details of these may be found at the head of this country's entry. Any numbers in the chart refer to the footnotes below.*

PASSPORTS: Passports valid for at least six months required by all.
VISAS: Required by all except the following for stays of up to 90 days:
(a) nationals referred to in the chart above (except **1.** nationals of Czech Republic, Estonia, Hungary, Latvia, Lithuania, Poland, Slovak Republic and Slovenia, who *do* need a visa);
(b) nationals of Commonwealth countries (except nationals of Bangladesh, Cameroon, Ghana, India, Mozambique, Nigeria, Pakistan and Sri Lanka, who *do* need a visa);
(c) nationals of Iceland, Liechtenstein, Norway, San Marino, Serbia & Montenegro, Switzerland and Uruguay and Zimbabwe;
(d) transit passengers provided continuing their journey by the same or first connecting aircraft and not leaving the airport.
Types of visa and cost: *General Entry*: £60 (single- or multiple-entry).
Validity: Maximum of 90 days from the date of issue.
Application to: Consulate (or Consular Section at Embassy or High Commission); see *Contact Addresses* section.
Application requirements: (a) Two completed application forms. (b) Two recent colour passport-size photos. (c) Passport valid for at least six months, with at least one blank page. (d) Fee (cash or postal order only). (e) Tourists must be able to produce evidence of their itinerary in Botswana. (f) Letter of invitation or letter of offer of employment if travelling on business.
Working days required: One to three.
Temporary residence: Anyone wishing to stay for more than 90 days should contact the Immigration and Passport Control Officer, PO Box 942, Gaborone.

Money

Currency: Pula (P) = 100 thebe. Notes are in denominations of P100, 50, 20 and 10. Coins are in denominations of P5, 2 and 1, and 50, 25, 10 and 5 thebe. Various gold and silver coins were issued to mark the country's 10th anniversary of independence, and are still legal tender.
Currency exchange: Money should be exchanged in banks at market rates. There are five commercial banks in the country (Bank of Baroda, Barclays Bank of Botswana, First National Bank, Stanbic Bank Botswana and Standard Charted Bank) with branches in major towns and villages. Owing to limited facilities in small villages, it is advisable to change money at the airport or in major towns, where credit card cash advances may also be available. There are also Exchange Bureaus at major border posts.
Credit & debit cards: American Express, Diners Club, MasterCard and Visa are widely accepted. However, the majority of tourist facilities accept credit cards. Check with your credit or debit card company for details of merchant acceptability and other services which may be available.
Travellers cheques: To avoid additional exchange rate charges, travellers are advised to take travellers cheques in US Dollars or Pounds Sterling. Most hotels accept travellers cheques, but the surcharge may be high.
Currency restrictions: There are no restrictions on the import of local or foreign currencies, provided declared on arrival. Export of local currency is limited to P50 and foreign currencies up to amount declared on arrival.
Exchange rate indicators: The following figures are included as a guide to the movements of the Pula against Sterling and the US Dollar:

Date	Feb '04	May '04	Aug '04	Nov '04
£1.00=	8.43	8.89	8.78	8.35
$1.00=	4.63	4.98	4.76	4.41

Banking hours: Mon-Fri 0900-1530; Sat 0815-1045. Most banks work these core hours with occasional regional differences.

Duty Free

The following goods may be imported into Botswana without incurring customs duty:
400 cigarettes and 50 cigars and 250g of tobacco; 2l of wine and 1l of spirits; 50ml of perfume and 250ml of eau de toilette; goods up to the value of P500.

Public Holidays

2005: Jan 1 New Year. **Mar 25-28** Easter. **May 1** Labour Day. **May 5** Ascension Day. **Jul 1** Sir Seretse Khama Day. **Jul 15-16** President's Day. **Sep 30** Botswana Day. **Dec 25-26** Christmas.
2006: Jan 1 New Year. **Apr 14-17** Easter. **May 1** Labour Day. **May 25** Ascension Day. **Jul 1** Sir Seretse Khama Day. **Jul 15-16** President's Day. **Sep 30** Botswana Day. **Dec 25-26** Christmas.

Health

	Special Precautions?	Certificate Required?
Yellow Fever	No	3
Cholera	No	No
Typhoid & Polio	1	N/A
Malaria	2	N/A

Note: *Regulations and requirements may be subject to change at short notice, and you are advised to contact your doctor well in advance of your intended date of departure. Any numbers in the chart refer to the footnotes below.*

1: Risk of typhoid fever exists throughout the region especially if travelling outside cities. Botswana is practically free of poliomyelitis.
2: Malaria risk exists from November to May/June in the northern part of the country (Boteti, Chobe, Ngamiland, Okavango and Tutume districts/subdistricts), predominantly in the malignant *falciparum* form. Some of the *falciparum*-related cases have been reported as chloroquine-resistant; in which case, the recommended prophylaxis in risk areas is mefloquine.
3: A yellow fever vaccination certificate is required from all travellers over one year of age travelling from infected areas.
Food & drink: Tap water is considered safe to drink, although drinking water outside main cities and towns may be contaminated and sterilisation is advisable. Mineral water is available in most tourist centres. Milk is pasteurised and dairy products are safe for consumption. Local meat, poultry, seafood, fruit and vegetables are generally considered safe to eat.
Other risks: *Hepatitis A, C* and *TB* occur. *Hepatitis B* is hyperendemic. *Bilharzia* (*schistosomiasis*) is endemic. Avoid swimming and paddling in fresh water; swimming pools which are well chlorinated and maintained are safe. *Trypanosomiasis* (sleeping sickness) is transmitted by tsetse flies in the Moremi Wildlife Reserve, Ngamiland and western parts of the Chobe National Park. Protective clothing and insect repellent are recommended. *Tick-bite fever* can be a problem when walking in the bush. It is advisable to wear loose-fitting clothes and to search the body for ticks. The disease may be treated with tetracycline, though pregnant women and children under eight years of age should not take this medicine. Natural foci of *plague* have been reported. In recent years, there has been a high prevalence of *HIV/AIDS* cases detected; indeed, Botswana has a prevalence rate of 39 per cent (statistics: end of 2002), the highest in the world. Visitors should therefore take necessary precautions.
Rabies is present in animals. For those at high risk, vaccination before arrival should be considered. If you are bitten, seek medical advice without delay. For more information, consult the *Health* appendix.
Health care: The dust and heat may cause problems for asthmatics and people with allergies to dust. Those with sensitive skin should take precautions. Botswana's altitude, 1000m (3300ft) above sea level, reduces the filtering effect of the atmosphere. Hats and sunscreen are advised.
The public health system is made up of 23 district health teams, three referral hospitals (Francistown, Gaborone and Lobatse), 12 district hospitals, 17 primary hospitals, 222 clinics, 330 health posts and 740 mobile stops. All main towns have chemists, and pharmaceutical supplies are readily available. Health insurance is essential. There is a government medical scheme and medicines supplied by government hospitals are free.

Travel - International

Note: Although most visits to Botswana are trouble-free, there is, unfortunately, an increasing incidence of violent crime (on the street but also in the percentage of burglaries).
AIR: The national airline is *Air Botswana (BP)* which only operates within Africa. The airline's agent in the UK is *British Airways* (tel: (0845) 773 3377). There are no direct flights from London to Gaborone but regular connections can be made from Johannesburg, Windhoek, Harare and Victoria Falls. Other airlines serving Botswana include *South African Airways*.
Approximate flight times: From Gaborone to *London* is 15 hours (including stopovers).
Departure tax: None.
International airports: *Sir Seretse Khama International (GBE)* is 15km (9 miles) northwest of Gaborone. There are no regular bus services to and from the airport but several hotels run minibuses (combis). Taxis are available to the city centre (travel time - 15 minutes). Airport facilities include left luggage, bank (*Barclays Bank* available for all flights), bar, snack bar, restaurant, post office, shops and car hire (*Avis* and *Imperial*). There is a major airport at Kasane (north Botswana) and at Selebi-Phikwe which take international flights.
Maun International Airport (MUB) receives direct flights from Johannesburg, Windhoek and Gaborone. This gateway to the Okavango Delta is served by *Air Botswana*, *Air Namibia* and several charters. For information on charters, see the *Travel – Internal* section.
RIVER: A car ferry operates across the Zambezi River to Zambia.
RAIL: There are good connections between South Africa and Botswana (Johannesburg–Mafikeng–Ramatlhabama–Gaborone) and Botswana and Zimbabwe (Gaborone–Francistown–Bulawayo–Harare). From Gaborone to Bulawayo takes 20 hours; passengers are advised to take their own food and drink as the buffet has a limited range.

There are three classes, and sleeping compartments are available. First-class cars have comfortable reclining seats. Complicated formalities may be necessary for crossing the border from Zimbabwe and to or from South Africa, where the South African Customs Union agreement is in operation. Botswana has assisted in the construction of the Limpopo line from Zimbabwe to Mozambique, an act which will speed up the availability of alternative routes into Botswana. Other plans include extending the network into Namibia.
ROAD: There are reasonable roads running roughly along the same routes as the railway, linking Botswana with South Africa and Zimbabwe. There is also road access from Namibia. **Bus:** Services are available from Namibia and Zimbabwe. Frequent services also operate between Gabarone and Johannesburg.

Travel - Internal

AIR: Major areas of the country are linked by air. There are airports in Francistown, Ghanzi, Jwaneny, Kasane, Maun, Pont Drift and Selebi-Phikwe. Many visitors use charter companies based in Maun to fly to the various lodges in Botswana. These include *Delta Air*, *Mack Air*, *Moremi Air Services*, *Northern Air*, *Sefofane* and *Wildlife Helicopters*. *Kalahari Air Services*, PO Box 41278, Gaborone (tel: 395 1804 *or* 3593) offers charters within Botswana and to Lesotho, Namibia, South Africa, Swaziland, Zambia and Zimbabwe.
RAIL: The main railway line runs between Ramatlhabama and Francistown. Work on upgrading and extending the rail network continues. In Botswana, children under seven travel free and children aged seven to 11 pay half fare.
ROAD: Botswana has good tarmac roads on the following routes: running from south to north from Lobatse to Francistown up to Ramokgwebana and from Lobatse to Jwaneng; running from Francistown to Kazungula via Nata. There are over 2500km (1500 miles) of bitumised roads in the country. Others are either gravel or sand tracks. Drivers should be careful as many drivers ignore safety rules. There are plans to construct a road network with more major highways. Reserve fuel and at least 20l of water, plus emergency supplies, should always be carried on journeys into more remote areas, and visitors are advised to make careful enquiries before setting out. Wildlife and stray livestock may occasionally pose a hazard, especially in more remote areas. **Bus:** There are bus services between Gaborone and Francistown, and from Francistown to Nata and Maun. Buses from Francistown to Maun run every day. The journey takes about six hours. Timetables can be obtained from bus operators. **Taxi**: There is taxi service in all major towns, and it is generally safe. Prices should, however, be agreed before embarking on journey. **Car hire:** Services are available in Gaborone, Francistown or Maun. 4-wheel-drive vehicles are necessary in many areas. Traffic drives on the left and seat belts must be worn. It is advisable to keep the petrol tank at least half full as distances between towns can be long. There is a speed limit of 120kph (75mph) outside built-up areas, and about 60kph (37mph) in built-up areas. Speed limits are strongly enforced with high fines. **Documentation:** An International Driving Permit is not legally required, but is recommended for stays of up to six months, or a UK licence is needed and must be carried at all times; thereafter, a Botswana driving licence must be obtained, which will be issued without a test if a valid British licence is produced.
URBAN: Public transport within towns consists of share-taxis or minibus services operating at controlled flat fares. Exclusive use of taxis is sometimes available at a higher charge although fares should always be agreed before setting off.
Travel times: The following chart gives approximate travel times from **Gaborone** (in hours and minutes) to other major cities and towns in Botswana.

	Air	Road	Rail
Francistown	0.50	5.00	6.35
Selebi-Phikwe	1.00	4.30	-
Jwaneng	-	1.30	-
Orapa	-	5.00	-
Lobatse	0.20	0.45	1.50
Maun	1.30	12.00	-
Kasane	2.50	13.30	-
Tshabong	2.00	15.00	-
Ghanzi	1.25	11.00	-

Accommodation

HOTELS: Although there is no grading system, all hotels generally maintain a reasonable standard, particularly those in main centres in the east of the country. The largest number of hotels and motels are in or near Gaborone, Francistown Kasane and Maun, some with air conditioning, swimming pools and facilities for films, bands and entertainment. Many other hotels have fairly basic amenities.
SAFARI LODGES & CAMPS: The majority of the safari lodges are found in the Chobe National Park, Moremi Game Reserve and Okavango Delta and there are a few lodges and camps in the Makgadikgadi Pans and Tuli Block. Standards are generally high, with luxury and comfort being the order of the day. Some lodges are permanent structures but the majority are tented. The tents are luxurious and spacious with ensuite facilities. Most lodges only accommodate between 10 and 28 people so the emphasis is on personalised service. Along the banks of the Chobe river near Kasane, there are also luxury hotels and lodges. It is recommended to spend at least two nights at each lodge and do a circuit of the various tourist regions in the country. Charter flights on 6-seater planes are the standard means of transfer. Visitors can also do a mobile safari, camping in a variety of different regions. Standards on these vary from simple to luxurious.
CAMPING: There are campsites at Chobe National Park, Makgadikgadi Pans National Park, Moremi Game Reserve and Nxai Pan National Park. These campsites need to be pre-booked with the Department of Wildlife and National Parks. Permission should be sought before camping on private land. Grass fires should not be started, and all litter should be buried or removed. The presence of lions and other dangerous animals in all the National Parks and Game Reserves as well as in some of the more remote areas makes it advisable to exercise extreme care, such as keeping tents zipped up and not walking around at night. It is not permitted to leave your vehicle in a national park or game reserve unless in a designated camping or picnic area. A booklet entitled *Where To Stay In Botswana*, giving details of prices and facilities, may be obtained from the

Credit: © Botswana Tourism

Department of Tourism (see *Contact Addresses* section).
The following is an umbrella organisation comprising hotels and lodges, travel agents, tour operators and airlines: The Hotel and Tourism Association of Botswana (HATAB), Private Bag 00423, Gaborone (tel: 395 7144 *or* 395 6498; fax: 390 3201; e-mail: hatab@info.bw).
NOTE: For further information on accommodation in Botswana, see the *Resorts & Excursions* section.

Resorts & Excursions

Botswana is a vast, flat dry land - as big as France but with a population of only 1.6 million, many of whom live in or near the two main cities of Gaborone and Francistown. Over 80 per cent of the country is semi-desert, but, in spite of this, abundant wildlife thrives, and with so few people, Botswana boasts the largest percentage of land given over to wildlife in the world – a remarkable 17 per cent is national park, and with the many huge private concessions in the Okavango Delta and Tuli Block, it reaches a staggering 38 per cent. All national parks and game reserves have camping areas. For all information and reservations within the National Parks, contact the Department of Wildlife and National Parks, PO Box 20346, next to Police Station, Maun (tel: 686 1265; fax: 686 1264 *or* 686 0053); and Gaborone (tel: 318 0774; fax: 318 0775; e-mail: dwnp@gov.bw *or* dwnp.parrogabs@gov.bw; website: www.botswanatourism.org).

THE SOUTHEAST

GABORONE: The capital, Gaborone, is situated in the southeast of the country. There is an excellent **National Museum** open from Tues-Fri 0900-1800 and weekends 0900-1700, with natural history and ethnological exhibitions. As well as permanent displays, there are also temporary exhibitions and various symposia and conferences. Gaborone has several good bookshops and libraries, including the **University of Botswana Library**, which has a 'Botswana Room' devoted solely to publications on the country. There are good craft shops and markets in the town, where pottery, basketwork, leatherwork and handwoven objects can be bought.
Excursions: The 600 hectare **Gaborone Game Reserve**, along the Ngotwane River, about 5km east of central Gaborone, is nothing like as good for game as the major parks, but does have a number of species of antelope. 10km southwest of the city is the privately operated, 3000 hectare **Mokolodi Nature Reserve**, where visitors can go on guided game walks amongst the elephant, cheetah, leopard and antelope. Both reserves have small numbers of white rhino. The **St Claire Lion Park**, 14km from the city on the Lobatse road, is a good place to see the animals up close, but in a situation far from a natural environment. It also has a vulture restaurant, children's playground, riding and other entertainments.
The **Gaborone Dam** is a centre for watersports, and day trips can be made to see local crafts at **Oodi**, **Thamaga** and **Pilane**. A trip to the weaving centre at **Lentswe-La-Odi**, just north of Gaborone, is especially recommended. Local craftwork can be bought here at a fraction of its cost in the big cities. The centre is a non-profitmaking organisation, with proceeds going back to the craftspeople. **Mochudi**, also north of Gaborone, is the regional capital of the Bakgatla tribe. The **Phuthadikobo Museum** chronicles the history of the Bakgatla people in fascinating detail.
SEROWE: Halfway between Gaborone and Francistown, Serowe is one of the largest villages in Botswana, the seat of the Bangwato tribe, and the birthplace of Botswana's charismatic first president, Sir Seretse Khama. He is buried in the local graveyard. The **Khama III Memorial Museum**, located in the Red House at the base of the Serowe Hill has memorabilia of the Khama Family. On Khama III's grave (Sir Seretse's grandfather) is a bronze duiker sculpted by the famous South African artist Anton van Wouw.
Thathaganyana Hill is home to the ruins of an 11th-century settlement.
Nearby, the small **Khama Rhino Sanctuary** houses almost all of Botswana's rhino collection, gathered here to protect them from poachers. There are also 28 other animal species and over 150 bird species.
THE TULI BLOCK: This patchwork of private game ranches and concessions covers about 120,000 hectares in the southeastern corner of the country adjacent to South Africa. It is quite different to anywhere else in Botswana, with ruggedly beautiful countryside famed for both its birdwatching potential and its large herds of elephant. The pot pourri of rocks, varying in age from 2700 million to 3700 million years old, makes for incredible scenery. Horseriding safaris are available, as are mountain bike tours. Mashatu main camp and Mashatu tented camp are in the area.

THE NORTHEAST

FRANCISTOWN: Francistown is a stopping-off point for visitors on the way to the Okavango, Moremi and Chobe game reserves. The area has been inhabited for about 80,000 years, but the town was created in 1867 with the discovery of gold. There are still mines working in the area. The **Supa-Ngwao Museum** has displays on local history, an information centre and a craft shop with books and maps. There are several reasonable hotels and restaurants, and some of Botswana's best nightlife, which is still somewhat limited.
MAKGADIKGADI AND NXAI PANS: Situated only 37km (23 miles) north of the main Francistown to Maun road, the entrance to Nxai Pan National Park marks the start of a vast area (roughly the size of Portugal) once covered in giant, shallow salt lakes. Only rare shallow islands of palms and baobabs break the flatness of the countryside. The 2578 sq km park, incorporating the Nxai and Kgama-Kgama Pans, is grassland, teeming with plain animals such as zebra and wildebeest.
The sands of the **Makgadikgadi Pans**, part of which is protected by a 4900 sq km national park, gleam white with salt in the dry season and transform into a shimmering lake in the rainy season, when thousands of brilliant pink flamingos arrive to paddle in the brine. Herds of zebra and wildebeest also come to drink here. When the Makgadikgadi loses its water, the animals move on to the **Boteti River**, where they remain until the following rainy season, which heralds their movement northwards again to the Nxai Pan. A new cultural village, **Planet Baobab**, has been established close to the Nxai Pan, and luxury camps in this area include Jack's Camp and San Camp. Non-game-viewing activities include quad biking in the dry season.

THE NORTHWEST

KASANE: Both border crossing and safari town, Kasane lies on the Chobe River between the Chobe National Park and the Zimbabwean border. It is a pleasant little town, with a good range of lodges, hotels and campsites including the Chobe Chilwero, Chobe Game Lodge, Chobe Valley Lodge and Cresta Mowana (all in the luxury end of the market); and Chobe Safari Lodge, Kasane Marina Lodge and Kubu Lodge (standard accommodation). It also has an airport, used mainly by charter flights, taking people deep into the Delta or southern Chobe; most international arrivals use Victoria Falls, only 40 minutes' drive away, in Zimbabwe. Like Maun, Kasane has a wide range of tour operators and facilities such as banks.
CHOBE NATIONAL PARK: This area of 10,566 sq km (4081 sq miles) is the home of a splendid variety of wildlife, including elephants who move in their thousands along the well-worn paths of the **Chobe River** every afternoon to drink. Chobe boasts the highest elephant population in the world, with an estimated 45,000 to 90,000 elephants. There are also large herds of buffalo to be seen at the river's edge, as well as hippo, lechwe, kudu, impala, roan and puku. The tourists, like the elephants, all tend to congregate in a narrow, 20km (12 mile) strip in the north of the park, doing game drives from the lodges in Kasane. It is undoubtedly spectacular, but it is also very crowded with other vehicles and boats.
In an effort to spread people and elephants out and save the river's ecosystem, the park authorities are now pumping water to a series of waterholes in the **Nogatsaa** area, about 65km (40 miles) south. As yet, there are only simple campsites in this dry area, but better facilities are being planned.
Further south and west, the **Linyanti Marshes** are a mini-version of the Okavango, a river twisted by a volcanic fault to splay out into a lush green, animal rich oasis. Nearby, the **Savuti** area marks the northern shore of what was once the giant superlake which covered most of Botswana, its flat dry lakebed now a sea of grass, scattered by rocky kopjes beloved of leopards and baboons.
With the exception of certain sections, which are closed in the rainy season during November to April, the park is open throughout the year. The best time to visit it is between May and September when it is possible to see several thousand animals in a day. In the Linyanti region, the camps include Kings Pool Camp, Selinda Camp, Zibalianja and Lebala Lodge.
Although this is the most developed of Botswana's parks and reserves, many of the roads in the area are passable only by 4-wheel-drive vehicles.
THE TSODILO HILLS: Situated northwest of the Okavango Delta close to the border with the Caprivi Strip (Namibia), these four granite ridged hills (Male, Female and Child Hills, plus a fourth, unnamed and said to be the first, discarded wife) are considered to be a sacred site by the Basarwa (San or Bushmen), who regard them as the final resting place of the dead, and the home of the gods. Known to have been inhabited for at least 100,000 years, they have been decorated with around 4000 rock paintings, mostly portraying animal life; the eldest of the paintings is believed to date back more than 4000 years. The hills are reached by air or road but there are no camping facilities or water supplies so visitors should allow for water, food and fuel needs. The Caprivi strip is currently suffering from security problems, so visitors should seek advice before travelling in this area.

THE DELTA

MAUN: On the southern edge of the Okavango Delta, nearly 950km northwest of Gaborone, Maun is the main jumping-off point for most tourists visiting Botswana. It is a sprawling, scruffy little town, founded in 1915 as the administrative centre for the Batawana people. It has an international airport and a number of reasonable hotels, including Riley's Hotel, Sedia Hotel and Maun Lodge while lodges include Crocodile Camp, Audi Camp and Island Safari Lodge. Okavango River Lodge is a campsite. Most hotels have a swimming pool as well as bar and restaurant. This is also the best place to book safaris, with many tour operators' offices, a National Park office and the only banks for several hundred miles.
There is an 8 sq km game reserve with several pleasant walking trails along the Thamalakane River near Riley's Hotel.
OKAVANGO DELTA: Undoubtedly the most striking region in the north of the country, situated in the **Kgalagadi** (or **Kalahari**) **Desert** and easily accessible from Maun. It is the greatest inland delta system in the world. The region is extremely beautiful, covering an area of about 15,000 sq km (5600 sq miles) and composed of vast grass flats, low tree-covered ridges and a widespread network of narrow waterways opening into lagoons. The thick reeds and grasses which thrive in these waters make much of the delta section impenetrable except by dug-out canoe (*mokoro*), which is the local people's traditional form of transport. The waters are clear, and crocodiles, hippos and hundreds of fabulous birds can be seen, as well as elephants, zebras and giraffes.
The few people who live here are mainly fishermen, in the west. The only part of the park that is officially protected is the Moremi National Park in the east (see below). Most of the land in the delta is carved up into giant private concessions, scattered by luxury lodges and camps, including Mombo, Xigera, Kwetsani, Xudum, Rann's, Gubanare, Chiefs Camp, Khwai River Lodge, Eagle Island

Camp, Xaxanaxa, Shinde, Camp Okavango, Camp Moremi, Xugana, Tsaro, Nxabega and Sandibe. Bizarrely, with the channels and lagoons shifting every season, these lodges, as the only permanent landmarks, have become an integral part of mapping and navigating in the Delta.

The Delta has three main areas – the **Panhandle**, a 15km- (9 mile-) wide fault in the northwest, where the fishing is superb but the game-viewing less spectacular; the central **permanent swamp**, with its maze of pans and watermeadows; and the arid **seasonal swamps** to the south and east. Although the Delta is home to about 36 species of large mammals, 480 species of birds, 80 species of fish and a wealth of flora, it is not the best place in Africa to find big game – there is plenty there, but it is often hard to see.

The Delta has its own micro-climate with three main seasons. It is warm to hot and dry in August to November, which is when the game-viewing is at its best, but the water is too low for many mokoro trips. December to March is hot and wet, the game vanishes into the undergrowth, but the bird and plant life is at its best. Many lodges close. April to August is cooler and dry, but with flood waters from the Angolan Highlands still fuelling the river channels.

MOREMI GAME RESERVE: This beautiful park covers 1812 sq km (700 sq miles) in the northeast corner of the Okavango Delta. It comprises permanently swamped areas, seasonally swamped areas and dry land. It not only offers water activities such as boat trips but also top game-viewing and incredible scenery, with giant bullrushes fringing hidden lagoons shining blue between the solid trunks of the baobabs, tottering termite mounds and the cracked red mud plains. Small boats travel around the delta, visiting lagoons like **Xaxanaxa**, **Gcobega** and **Gcodikwe**, with their abundance of birdlife. Elephant, hippo, buffalo, lion and most other game can be viewed in abundance. Fishing, walking and night drives are possible outside the park boundaries. South of here, the **Gcwihaba Caverns**, about 240km (150 miles) from **Tsau**, contain beautiful stalactites. The name means 'Hyena's Hole' in the Quing language of the Bushmen.

THE CENTRE AND SOUTH

CENTRAL KALAHARI GAME RESERVE: This remote and virtually unexplored reserve was set up as a refuge both for animals and the country's few remaining San (Bushmen) people. The terrain is very varied, with open plains, salt pans, sand dunes and mopane scrub in the north (which also has the best game-viewing), bushveld in the centre and woodland in the south. There are five designated but undeveloped campgrounds. Self-drivers with 4-wheel-drive vehicles can go year-round with a permit. The **Deception Valley** area is used by several upmarket mobile safari operators.

KHUTSE GAME RESERVE: This 2500 sq km (965 square mile) expanse of dry savannah land in the centre of the Kalahari incorporates a series of shallow pans, which, when filled with water, attract hundreds of bird species as well as an abundance of springbok and ostrich, giraffe, gemsbok, lion, leopard and the rare brown hyena, amongst others. It joins the southern boundary of the Central Kalahari National Park, about 240km (150 miles) northwest of Gaborone. Camping facilities are basic, and water, food and fuel should be brought. Many of the campsites are on the edge of the pan, which enables one to game-watch from the comfort of a camp chair. There are still a few small bands of *Basarwa* (San) living in this region, one of the last Stone Age races on earth, some of whom guide visitors around the reserve and teach them about edible and moisture-bearing plants and how many of the animals survive despite the lack of water.

KGALAGADI TRANSFRONTIER NATIONAL PARK: This remote park straddles the border with South Africa in the southwest of the country, the first of a number of '**peace parks**' planned to cross national boundaries and re-open ancient animal migration routes. The park has deep fossil river beds and high sand dunes, and the area is also known for its salt pans which reflect amazing colour changes during the day. Many herds of gemsbok and springbok (as well as other species of antelope), cheetah and famous black-maned Kalahari lion can be seen here and brown hyenas and jackals occur in abundance. The best time to visit is from March to May. It can be reached by a paved road from Gaborone to **Tsabong**, after which a 4-wheel-drive vehicle is necessary. The main entrance, easiest access point and accommodation are all on the South African side of the border in what was the Kalahari Gemsbok National Park. At present there is no accommodation on the Botswanan side and you will need to take a tent and all supplies, including water and fuel.

Sport & Activities

Wildlife: Botswana's magnificent wildlife can be observed in the national parks; for details of these, see the *Resorts & Excursions* section. Visits can be arranged independently or with tour operators. 4-wheel-drive vehicles tend to be expensive to hire, and budget travellers are not encouraged.

Credit: © Botswana Tourism

Botswana is particularly good for **horseback safaris** and it is also possible to go on elephant-back safaris. Entry permits are required for all reserves. Visits can be booked up to 12 months in advance through Embassies and High Commissions *or* through the Parks and National Reserves Office in Gaborone (see *Resorts & Excursions* section).

The best time of year to visit the parks is between April and October; the game is more difficult to see in the rainy months when the grass is high and there is plenty of water around, so the game does not have to rely on the waterholes and moves off into the more remote areas of the parks. In the dry winter season, however, the animals congregate around water sources. For further details, contact the Department of Tourism (see *Contact Addresses* section).

Watersports: Fishing trips, **water-skiing**, **motorboat** and **canoe** hire are available to varying degrees. Near to Gaborone is a dam with a yacht club offering **sailing**, water-skiing and fishing; use of facilities is available to visitors at the invitation of a club member.

Social Profile

FOOD & DRINK: Restaurants and bars can be found in main towns, often within hotels. Millet and sorghum porridge constitutes much of the cuisine. Visitors to Botswana may encounter *Morama* (an underground tuber), the *Kalahari* truffle and the *Mopane* worm (boiled, cooked or deep-fried). Most lodges and safari camps also have restaurants and licensed bars, although food is generally basic outside major hotels and restaurants. The standard of food in lodges and camps is generally very good.

There is local beer and in general no restrictions on alcohol. Traditional drinks include Palm wine (which is extremely strong) and *Kgadi* (made from distilled sugar or fungus).

NIGHTLIFE: Most people get up early in the morning, and nightlife is not very extensive. However, there are some bars and restaurants in Gaborone. The city also has a cinema. Maun has a handful of restaurants and a small cinema.

SHOPPING: Woodcarvings, handcrafted jewellery, woven goods and attractive basketry are recommended. **Shopping hours:** Mon-Fri 0800-1800; Sat 0830-1300.

SPECIAL EVENTS: The following is a selection of special events celebrated annually in Botswana:

Mar 1-Aug 31 *Lost in the Kalahari*, Mabuasehube Game Reserve. **Apr** *Botswana Defence Force Day*. **Apr 16-24** *Maitisong Festival*, Gaborone. **Jul 16** *President's Day* (celebrated with traditional dancing, musical events, including performances by the Defence Force Band, and karate shows). **Jul 25-27** *National Music Eisteddfod*, Selebi-Phikwe. **Sep 30** *Botswana Day* (marked by colourful parades). **Nov-Dec** *Flowers in the Kalahari Desert*, Khutse Game Reserve.

SOCIAL CONVENTIONS: As most people in Botswana follow their traditional pattern of life, visitors should be sensitive to customs which will inevitably be unfamiliar to them. Outside urban areas, people may well not be used to visitors. Casual clothing is acceptable and, in urban centres, normal courtesies should be observed.

Photography: Airports, official residences and defence establishments should not be photographed. Permission should be obtained to photograph local people.

Tipping: A discretionary 10 per cent in urban centres. In many places, a service charge is automatically added. It is customary to tip the game guide and lodge staff while on safari.

Business Profile

ECONOMY: As a key foreign exchange earner, livestock farming is the most important part of Botswana's agricultural sector. In addition, there is substantial subsistence agriculture, cultivating maize, sorghum and millet. The country's other main export industry is mining, extracting diamonds (of which Botswana is the world's largest producer by value), nickel, gold, cobalt, copper, salt and coal (the principal source of energy) and soda ash. The small manufacturing sector is largely devoted to the production of food products and textiles. Botswana is economically closely connected to South Africa and is a member of the Southern African Customs Union (SACU). It also hosts the Southern African Development Conference, which is the principal mechanism for economic co-operation.

The bulk of the country's imports come from within SACU, other African countries and Korea. Europe is the key export market. Prudent management and the successful development of new mineral resources have afforded Botswana healthy economic growth of around 5 per cent since the late 1990s. But the vulnerability of the agricultural sector to bad weather and commodity price fluctuations has led the government to seek to develop a service sector, with tourism and financial services as the best prospects. However, the HIV/AIDS epidemic, which is extremely serious in Botswana and mainly afflicts the productive, young and middle-aged population, is starting to have a negative effect on the country's economy.

BUSINESS: Lightweight or tropical suits should be worn. **Office hours:** Mon-Fri 0800-1700 April-October; 0730-1630 October-April. **Government office hours:** 0730-1630 all year round.

COMMERCIAL INFORMATION: The following organisation can also offer advice: Botswana Export Development & Investment Authority (BEDIA), Plot 28, Matsitama Road, The Main Mall, Gaborone (tel: 3918 1931; fax: 3918 1941; website: www.bedia.co.bw).

Climate

Mainly temperate climate. Summer, between October and April, is very hot and combined with the rainy season. Dry and cooler weather exists between May and September with an average temperature of 25°C (77°). Early mornings and evenings may be cold and frosty in winter. Annual rainfall decreases westwards and southwards.

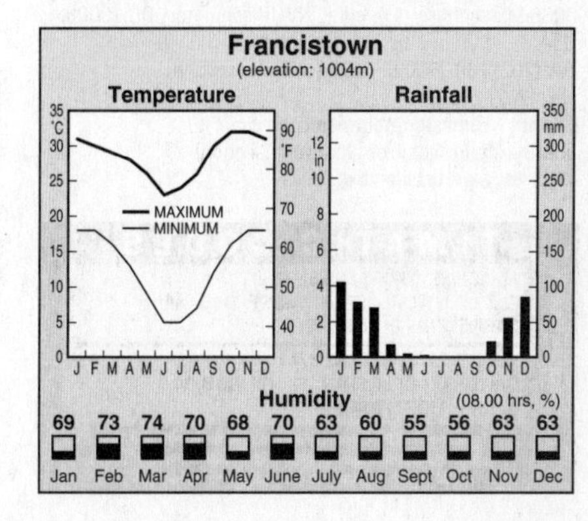

Brazil

LATEST TRAVEL ADVICE CONTACTS

British Foreign and Commonwealth Office
Tel: (0870) 606 0290 Website: www.fco.gov.uk
US Department of State
Website: http://travel.state.gov/travel
Canadian Department of Foreign Affairs and Int'l Trade
Tel: (1 800) 267 8376 Website: www.dfait-maeci.gc.ca

Location: South America.

Country dialling code: 55.

EMBRATUR – Instituto Brasileiro do Turismo (Brazilian Tourist Institute)
SCN, Quadra 02, Bloco 'G', 70712-907 Brasilia, DF, Brazil
Tel: (61) 429 7704. Fax: (61) 429 7710.
E-mail: presedencia@embratur.org.br
Website: www.embratur.gov.br
Brazil Embassy
32 Green Street, London W1K 7AT, UK
Tel: (020) 7399 9000. Fax: (020) 7399 9100 *or* 9102 (commercial section).
E-mail: info@brazil.org.uk
Website: www.brazil.org.uk
Opening hours: Mon-Fri 0900-1300 and 1400-1800 (embassy).
Brazilian Consulate General
6 St Alban's Street, London SW1Y 4SQ, UK
Tel: (020) 7930 9055. Fax: (020) 7839 8958.
E-mail: visa@cgbrasil.org.uk
Website: www.brazil.org.uk
Opening hours: Mon-Fri 1000-1600 (personal callers).
British Embassy
Setor das Embaixadas Sul, Quadra 801, Lote 8, Conjunto K, 70408-900, Brasília, DF, Brazil
Tel: (61) 329 2300. Fax: (61) 329 2369.
E-mail: contato@reinounido.org.br
Website: www.reinounido.org.br
British Consulate General
Praia do Flamengo, 284 (2nd floor), 22210-030, Rio de Janeiro, RJ, Brazil
Tel: (21) 2555 9600. Fax: (21) 2555 9672.
E-mail: consular.rio@fco.gov.uk or britishconsulaterio@terra.com.br
Website: www.reinounido.org.br *or* www.uk.org.br
Consulates in: Belo Horizonte, Curitiba, Pôrto Alegre, Recife and São Paulo.
Brazilian Embassy
3006 Massachusetts Avenue, NW, Washington, DC 20008, USA
Tel: (202) 238 2700 *or* 2828 (consular section).
Fax: (202) 238 2827.
E-mail: webmaster@brasilemb.org *or* consular@brasilemb.org (consular section).
Website: www.brasilemb.org

TIMATIC CODES

Health	AMADEUS: **TI-DFT/BSB/HE** GALILEO/WORLDSPAN: **TI-DFT/BSB/HE** SABRE: **TIDFT/BSB/HE**
Visa	AMADEUS: **TI-DFT/BSB/VI** GALILEO/WORLDSPAN: **TI-DFT/BSB/VI** SABRE: **TIDFT/BSB/VI**

To access TIMATIC country information on Health and Visa regulations through the Computer Reservations System (CRS), type in the appropriate command line listed above.

Consulate General of Brazil
1185 Avenue of the Americas, 21st Floor, New York, NY 10036, USA
Tel: (917) 777 7777. Fax: (212) 827 0225.
E-mail: consulado@brazilny.org
Website: www.brazilny.org
Embassy of the United States of America
Avenida das Nações, Quadra 801, Lote 3, 70403-900 Brasília, DF, Brazil
Tel: (61) 312 7000. Fax: (61) 312 7676.
Website: www.embaixada-americana.org.br
Consulates General in: Rio de Janeiro and São Paulo.
Consulate in: Recife.
Brazilian Embassy
450 Wilbrod Street, Ottawa, Ontario K1N 6M8, Canada
Tel: (613) 237 1090. Fax: (613) 237 6144.
E-mail: mailbox@brasembottawa.org *or* consular@brasembottawa.org
Website: www.brasembottawa.org
Brazilian Consulate General
Centre Maruivie, Suite 1700, 2000 Mansfield Street, Montréal, Québec H3A 3A5, Canada
Tel: (514) 499 0968-70. Fax: (514) 499 3963.
E-mail: geral@consbrasmontreal.org
Website: www.consbrasmontreal.org
Consulate also in: Toronto.
Canadian Embassy
SES, Avenida das Nações, Quadra 803, Lote 16, 70410-900 Brasília, DF, Brazil
Tel: (61) 424 5400. Fax: (61) 424 5490.
E-mail: brsla@dfait-maeci.gc.ca
Website: www.canada.org.br *or* www.dfait-maeci.gc.ca/brazil
Consulates General in: Rio de Janeiro and São Paulo.

General Information

AREA: 8,547,404 sq km (3,300,170.9 sq miles).
POPULATION: 176,876,443 (official estimate 2003).
POPULATION DENSITY: 20.7 per sq km.
CAPITAL: Brasília. **Population:** 2,051,146 (2000).
GEOGRAPHY: Brazil covers almost half of the South American continent and it is bordered to the north, west and south by all South American countries except Chile and Ecuador; to the east is the Atlantic. The country is topographically quite flat and at no point do the highlands exceed 3000m (10,000ft). Over 60 per cent of the country is a plateau; the remainder consists of plains. The River Plate Basin (the confluence of the Paraná and Uruguay rivers, both of which have their sources in Brazil) in the far south is more varied, higher and less heavily forested. North of the Amazon are the Guiana Highlands, partly forested, partly stony desert. The Brazilian Highlands of the interior, between the Amazon and the rivers of the south, form a vast tableland, the Mato Grosso, from which rise mountains in the southwest that form a steep protective barrier from the coast called the Great Escarpment, breached by deeply cut river beds. The population is concentrated in the southeastern states of Minas Gerais, Rio de Janeiro and São Paulo. The city of São Paulo has a population of over 10 million, while over 5.5 million people live in the city of Rio de Janeiro.
GOVERNMENT: Federal Republic. **Head of State and Government:** President Luiz Inácio Lula da Silva since 2003.
LANGUAGE: The official language is Portuguese, with different regional accents characterising each State. Spanish, English, Italian, French and German are also spoken, particularly in tourist areas. Four linguistic roots survive in the indigenous areas: Gê, Tupi-guarani, Aruak and Karib.
RELIGION: There is no official religion, but approximately 70 per cent of the population adhere to Roman Catholicism. A number of diverse evangelical cults are also represented, as are animist beliefs (particularly spiritism, umbanda and candomblé).
TIME: Brazil spans several time zones:
Eastern Standard Time: GMT - 3 (GMT - 2 from third Sunday in October to third Saturday in March).
Western Standard Time: GMT - 4 (GMT - 3 from third Sunday in October to third Saturday in March).
North East States and East Parà: GMT - 3.
Amapa and West Parà: GMT - 4.
Acra State: GMT - 5.
Fernando de Noronha Archipelago: GMT - 2.
ELECTRICITY: Brasília and Recife 220 volts AC; Rio de Janeiro and São Paulo 127 volts AC or 220 volts in larger hotels. Plugs are of the two-pin type. Most hotels provide 110-volt and 220-volt outlets, transformers and adaptors.
COMMUNICATIONS: Telephone: Full IDD services are available for the whole country and abroad. Country code: 55. Outgoing international code: 00. *Embratel* is one of the main telecommunication services in Brasil (website: www.embratel.com.br). Offices of Embratel are in Rio de Janeiro and São Paulo. Rio's airport provides 24-hour telecommunication services. Public telephones take telephone cards (*cartões telefônicos*), most of which cost R$20. Some older telephones may require metal discs (*fichas*), which can be obtained from cash desks or newspaper kiosks. International calls from Brazil are expensive: to the UK, the rate is approximately US$3 per minute, to the USA and Canada it is approximately US$2.50 per minute. 25 per cent cheaper calls can be made daily from 2000-0500. **Mobile telephone:** US-style analogue and digital networks exist. There are many different network providers, including *Claro* (website: www.claro.com.br) and *Vivo* (website: www.vivo.com.br). GSM 1800 networks have recently been established. Main operators include *Oi* (website: www.oi.com.br) and *TIM Brasil* (website: www.timbrasil.com.br). **Fax:** Facilities are available in the main post offices of major cities and some 5-star hotels. **Internet:** ISPs include *Terra* (website: www.terra.com.br). Hotels generally provide Internet access to guests. Internet cafes can be found in main towns and cities, and there are often Internet booths at airports. In smaller towns, public access is sometimes available at post offices. **Telegram:** International telegram facilities exist in many cities but are heavily taxed. **Post:** Services are reasonably reliable. Sending mail registered or franked will eliminate the risk of having the stamps steamed off. Airmail service to Europe takes four to six days. Surface mail takes at least four weeks. Post office hours: Mon-Sat 0900-1300.
Press: In Rio de Janeiro, there is an English-language publication, the *Rio Visitor*, which gives tourist information. *The Brazil Post* is a global news service providing information on the latest stories and current affairs in Brazil (website: www.noticiasdomundo.com). International magazines and newspapers are also available throughout the country.
Radio: BBC World Service (website: www.bbc.co.uk/worldservice) and Voice of America (website: www.voa.gov) can be received. From time to time the frequencies change and the most up-to-date can be found online.

Passport/Visa

	Passport Required?	Visa Required?	Return Ticket Required?
Full British	Yes	1/2	Yes
Australian	Yes	Yes	Yes
Canadian	Yes	Yes	Yes
USA	Yes	Yes	Yes
Other EU	Yes	1/2	Yes
Japanese	Yes	Yes	Yes

Note: *Regulations and requirements may be subject to change at short notice, and you are advised to contact the appropriate diplomatic or consular authority before finalising travel arrangements. Details of these may be found at the head of this country's entry. Any numbers in the chart refer to the footnotes below.*

Restricted entry: (a) Nationals from certain countries require consultation with, and approval from, the Brazilian Ministry of External Relations prior to being issued with visas. In these cases, an extra fee of £20 applies and the processing time is a minimum of 15 days. (b) Passports issued by Bhutan, Central African Republic, Chinese Taipei and Comoros Islands are not recognised by the Brazilian Government. Holders of such passports should hold a Laissez-Passer issued by the Brazilian authorities. For further details, check with the nearest Consulate or Consular section of Embassy.
PASSPORTS: Passports valid for at least six months from date of entry required by all except nationals of Argentina, Chile, Paraguay and Uruguay arriving in Brazil directly from their own countries and holding a national identity card.
Note: Persons under 18 years of age when not accompanied by both parents must have a birth certificate (an original or authenticated photocopy). This must be in English, French, Portuguese or Spanish, otherwise an official translation must be presented as well. When travelling alone or with one parent, a declaration from the absent parent(s) must be presented authorising the journey and giving the name and address of the person in Brazil who will be responsible for the minor. In the case of divorced or deceased parents, papers attesting to full custody must be presented.
VISAS: Required by all except the following:
(a) nationals mentioned under passport exemptions above;
(b) **1.** nationals of EU countries (except nationals of Cyprus, Czech Republic, Estonia, Latvia, Lithuania, Malta and Slovak Republic who *do* require a visa) for touristic stays of up to 90 days;
(c) nationals of Andorra, Argentina, The Bahamas, Barbados, Bolivia, Chile, Colombia, Costa Rica, Ecuador, Iceland, Israel, Korea (Rep), Liechtenstein, Malaysia, Mexico, Monaco, Morocco, Namibia, New Zealand, Norway, Panama, Paraguay, Peru, The Philippines, San Marino, South Africa, Surinam, Switzerland, Thailand, Trinidad & Tobago, Tunisia,

Turkey, Uruguay, Vatican City and Venezuela for touristic stays of up to 90 days;
(d) transit passengers continuing their journey to a third country by the same or first connecting flight, provided holding onward documentation and not leaving the airport.
Note: (a) Visa exemptions mentioned above are for touristic purposes only. All those travelling on business *do* need a visa (except **2.** nationals of the UK, members of the EU listed under visa exemptions above, Argentina, Chile, Colombia, Costa Rica, Ecuador, Iceland, Israel, Korea (Rep), Mexico, Monaco, Morocco, Norway, Paraguay, Peru, The Philippines, San Marino, South Africa, Surinam, Switzerland, Thailand, Tunisia, Turkey, Uruguay and the Vatican City). The length of stay permitted is normally up to 90 days but can be extended to a maximum of 180 days in any 12-month period at the discretion of the Brazilian Immigration Authorities. First entry into Brazil must be within 90 days of receiving the visa. (b) All travellers must be in possession of onward or return tickets and sufficient funds to cover their stay.
Types of visa and cost: *Tourist*: cost varies according to nationality. Generally, it is around £16. Other prices, based on reciprocity, are £28 (for nationals of Australia); £32 (for nationals of Canada and Nigeria); free, but £80 processing fee (for nationals of the USA); £40 (for nationals of Japan and the Russian Federation). *Business*: £48 (£80 for nationals of the USA). *Transit*: contact the Consulate for details of cost. Postal applications, and those via courier or travel agent, cost an additional £8. Some countries must pay an extra £20.
Validity: 90 days from date of issue. Tourist visas can be used for multiple entry within the period of validity. For an extension of the up to three month tourist visas, apply in Brazil, although this is always at the discretion of the Brazilian Immigration Authorities.
Application to: Consulate (or Consular section at the Embassy); see *Contact Addresses* section.
Application requirements: *Tourist/Transit*: (a) Valid passport for at least six months. (b) Application form. (c) Proof of sufficient funds to cover duration of stay or return or onward tickets (photocopy, or letter from carrier giving flight details). (d) One passport-size photo. (e) Certificate of vaccination against yellow fever is compulsory for travellers who have entered the following countries within three months prior to arrival: Angola, Benin, Bolivia, Burkina Faso, Cameroon, Colombia, Congo (Dem Rep), Congo (Rep), Ecuador, French Guiana, Gabon, The Gambia, Ghana, Guinea, Guinea-Bissau, Liberia, Nigeria, Peru, Sierra Leone, Sudan and Venezuela. (f) Fee (paid at any post office with a Giro slip obtainable from the Consulate). (g) If participating in conferences, seminars, an artistic or sports event, a letter from the organisers is required. *Business*: (a)-(g) and, (h) Letter from applicant's company stating the purpose and duration of the visit and confirming financial responsibility for the applicant.
Note: For postal applications, travellers should also submit a special delivery or guaranteed delivery, self-addressed, pre-paid envelope and a written request stating nationality, status and length of residence in the UK (where applicable) and validity of the British visa (where applicable).
Working days required: Depends on nationality. A minimum of three working days in person, 10 by post, 15 for those who require consultation.
Temporary residence: Apply to Consulate (or Consular section at Embassy).

Credit: © Brazilian Tourist Board

Money

Currency: Real/Reais (R$) = 100 centavos. Notes are in denominations of R$100, 50, 10, 5 and 1. Coins are in denominations of R$1, and 50, 25, 10, 5 and 1 centavos.
Currency exchange: All banks and *cambios* exchange recognised travellers cheques and foreign currency. There is an extensive network of ATMs around the country. The US Dollar is the most widely accepted foreign currency.
Credit & debit cards: Most major international cards are accepted. Check with your credit or debit card company for details of merchant acceptability and other services which may be available.
Travellers cheques: Exchangeable at hotels, banks and tourist agencies. Tourists cannot exchange US travellers cheques for US banknotes but they may, however, benefit from a 15 per cent discount when paying hotel or restaurant bills in foreign currency or travellers cheques. To avoid additional exchange rate charges, travellers are advised to take travellers cheques in US Dollars.
Currency restrictions: The import and export of local currency is unlimited although it may be subject to prior approval by Brazil Central Bank. The import of foreign currency is unlimited, provided amounts over US$1000 are declared on arrival; the export of foreign currency is limited to US$4000 per person (amounts in excess of this need special approval from the Brazilian Central Bank).
Exchange rate indicators: The following figures are included as a guide to the movements of the Brazilian Real against Sterling and the US Dollar:

Date	Feb '04	May '04	Aug '04	Nov '04
£1.00=	5.31	5.46	5.56	5.17
$1.00=	2.92	3.06	3.02	2.73

Banking hours: Mon-Fri 1000-1600.

Duty Free

Duty Free: The following goods may be imported into Brazil without incurring any customs duty:
400 cigarettes or 25 cigars; 2l of alcohol; up to US$500 worth of goods bought duty free in Brazilian airports.
Prohibited items: Meat and dairy products; fruit and vegetables; and plants or parts of plants.

Public Holidays

2005: Jan 1 New Year's Day. **Jan 20*** Founding of Rio de Janeiro. **Jan 25*** Founding of São Paulo. **Feb 25 - Mar 1** Carnival. **Apr 14** Good Friday. **Apr 21** Tiradentes. **May 1** Labour Day. **Jun 5** Corpus Christi. **Sep 7** Independence Day. **Oct 12** Our Lady Aparecida, Patron Saint of Brazil. **Nov 2** All Souls' Day. **Nov 15** Proclamation of the Republic Day. **Dec 24** Christmas Eve (half day). **Dec 25** Christmas Day. **Dec 31** New Year's Eve (half day).
2006: Jan 1 New Year's Day. **Jan 20*** Founding of Rio de Janeiro. **Jan 25*** Founding of São Paulo. **Feb 19-23** Carnival.

A B C D E F G H I J K L M N O P Q R S T U V W X Y Z

Mar 25 Good Friday. **Apr 21** Tiradentes. **May 1** Labour Day. **May 26** Corpus Christi. **Sep 7** Independence Day. **Oct 12** Our Lady Aparecida, Patron St of Brazil. **Nov 2** All Soul's Day. **Nov 15** Republic Day. **Dec 24** Christmas Eve (half day). **Dec 25** Christmas Day. **Dec 31** New Year's Eve (half day).
Note: *Regional observances only.

Health

	Special Precautions?	Certificate Required?
Yellow Fever	Yes	1
Cholera	Yes	2
Typhoid & Polio	3	No
Malaria	4	N/A

Note: *Regulations and requirements may be subject to change at short notice, and you are advised to contact your doctor well in advance of your intended date of departure. Any numbers in the chart refer to the footnotes below.*

1: A yellow fever vaccination certificate is required from all travellers over nine months old arriving within from infected regions. The following areas are regarded as infected: Angola, Bolivia, Cameroon, Colombia, Congo (Dem Rep), Ecuador, Gabon, The Gambia, Ghana, Guinea, Liberia, Nigeria, Peru, Sierra Leone and Sudan. Vaccination is strongly recommended for those intending to visit rural areas in the states of Acre, Amapá, Amazonas, Goiás, Maranhão, Mato Grosso, Mato Grosso do Sul, Pará, Rondônia, Roraima, Tocantins, and certain areas of Minas Gerais, Parana and São Paulo. If in any doubt, please contact the Brazilian Consulate General (see *Contact Addresses* section).
2: Following WHO guidelines issued in 1973, a cholera vaccination certificate is no longer a condition of entry to Brazil. However, cases of cholera were reported in 1996 and precautions are essential. Up-to-date advice should be sought before deciding whether these precautions should include vaccination as medical opinion is divided over its effectiveness; see the *Health* appendix for more information.
3: Immunisation against typhoid is recommended.
4: Malaria risk exists throughout the year (77 per cent *vivax* form and 23 per cent *falciparum* form) below 900m (2953ft) in Acre, Amapá, Amazonas, Maranhão (western part), Mato Grosso (northern part), Pará (except Belém City), Rondônia, Roraima and Tocantins states, as well as some larger cities. The malignant *falciparum* form of the disease is reportedly highly resistant to both chloroquine and sulfadoxine-pyrimethamine. A weekly dose of 250mg of mefloquine is the recommended prophylaxis.
Food & drink: All water should be regarded as being potentially contaminated. Water used for drinking, brushing teeth or making ice should have first been boiled or otherwise sterilised. Pasteurised milk and cheese is available in towns and is generally considered safe to consume. Milk outside of urban areas is unpasteurised and should be boiled; powdered or tinned milk is available and is advised in rural areas, but make sure that it is reconstituted with pure water. Avoid dairy products which are likely to have been made from unboiled milk. Only eat well-cooked meat and fish, preferably freshly prepared and served hot. Pork, salad and mayonnaise may carry increased risk. Vegetables should be cooked and fruit peeled.
Other risks: *Bilharzia* (schistosomiasis) is present. Snakes and leeches may be a hazard. Avoid swimming and paddling in fresh water; swimming pools that are well-chlorinated and maintained are safe. Other infectious diseases prevalent in Brazil include *trypanosomiasis* (*Chagas disease*) and *mucocutaneous leishmaniasis* (on the increase). *Visceral leishmaniasis* is endemic (especially in the northeast). *Onchocerciasis* (especially northern Brazil) and *Bancroftian filariasis* are also present. *Hepatitis A, B* and *D*, *Brazilian purpuric fever* and *brucellosis* all occur. There are epidemics of *meningococcal meningitis* in and around the Rio area. Air pollution, especially in São Paulo City, may aggravate chest complaints.
Rabies is present. For those at high risk, vaccination before arrival should be considered. If you are bitten, seek medical advice without delay. For more information, consult the *Health* appendix.
Health care: There is no reciprocal health agreement with the UK or USA. Full insurance is strongly recommended as medical costs are high. English-speaking medical staff are found mainly in São Paulo and Rio de Janeiro. The main hospital in São Paulo is the Hospital das Clinicas.

Travel - International

AIR: Brazil's national airlines are *TAM (KK)*, *Varig (RG)* and *VASP (VP)*. Other airlines serving Brazil include: *Aerolineas Argentinas, Air France, Alitalia, American Airlines, British Airways, Continental Airlines, Iberia, Japan Airlines, KLM, LAN-Chile, Lufthansa, Pluna, South African Airways, SAS, SWISS, TAP Air Portugal* and *United Airlines*.
Approximate flight times: From *London* to São Paulo and to Rio de Janeiro is approximately 11 hours. From *Los Angeles* to Rio de Janeiro is 14 hours. From *New York* to Rio de Janeiro is 10 hours. From *Sydney* to Rio de Janeiro is 20 hours..
International airports: *Brasilia International (BSB)* is 11km (7 miles) south of the city. Buses run regularly to the city centre (travel time - 30 minutes). Taxis are also available (travel time - 15 minutes). Airport facilities include left luggage, first aid, snack bar, post office, banks/bureaux de change, bar, restaurant, shops and car hire (*Disbrave, Hertz, Interlocadora, Localiza, Locarauto* and *Unidas*).
Rio de Janeiro (Galeão) *(GIG)* is 20km (13 miles) north of the city. Public buses operate 0530-2330 to the city (travel time - 40 minutes). There is an airport shuttle bus which stops at all major resorts and hotels, running every hour. Taxis are also available. Airport facilities include left luggage and lockers, bank, bureau de change, duty-free shops, a pharmacy and a small 24-hour hospital, restaurant, snack bar, car parking, tourist information, post office and car hire companies (*Avis, Hertz, Interlocadora, Localiza, Mega-Rent-Car* and *Unidas*).
São Paulo (Guarulhos) *(GRU)* is 25km (16 miles) northeast of the city. An airport bus runs every 30 minutes (travel time - 30 minutes). Taxis are also available. The airport provides the following 24-hour facilities: left luggage and lockers, duty-free shops, banks, bureau de change, pharmacies, restaurants, snack bar, post office and car hire (*Budget, Localiza* and *Unidas*).
Information on Brazilian airports can be found on the following website (www.infraero.gov.br).
Air passes: *The Mercosur Airpass*: Valid within Argentina, Brazil, Chile (except Easter Island), Paraguay and Uruguay. Participating airlines include *Aerolineas Argentinas (AR)* (however, flights on this airline cannot be combined with any others, as it has no agreements and its tickets are not accepted by other airlines), *Austral (AU), LAN-Chile (LA), LAPA (MJ), Pluna (PU), Transbrasil Airlines (TR)* and *VARIG (RG)*, with the subsidiary airlines of *Nordeste (JH)* and *Rio Sul (SL)*. The pass can only be purchased by passengers who live outside South America, who have a return ticket. Only eight flight coupons are allowed with a maximum of four coupons for each country and is valid for seven to a maximum of 30 days. At least two countries must be visited (to a maximum of five) and the flight route cannot be changed. A maximum of two stopovers is allowed per country.
The Visit South America Pass: Must be bought outside South America in country of residence and allows unlimited travel to 36 cities in the following countries: Argentina, Bolivia, Brazil, Colombia, Chile (except Easter Island), Ecuador, Paraguay, Peru, Uruguay and Venezuela. Participating airlines include *Aer Lingus (EI), American Airlines (AA), British Airways (BA), Cathay Pacific (CX), Finnair (AY), IBERIA (IB), LAN-Chile (LA)* and *Qantas (QF)*. A minimum of three flights must be booked, with no maximum; the maximum stay is 60 days, with no minimum, and prices depend on the amount of flight zones covered. For both air passes, children under 12 years of age are entitled to a 33 per cent discount and infants (under two years old) only pay 10 per cent of the adult fare. For further details, contact one of the participating airlines.
Departure tax: None.
SEA: The main port is Rio de Janeiro, which is used by many international cruise ships. Other popular ports include Manaus, Fortaleza, Recife, Salvador and Vitória. Passenger services are limited although *Grimaldi Freighter* do offer sailings from Europe. For more information about freighter services between the UK and Brazil, contact The Cruise People, 88 York Street, London W1H 1QT, UK (tel: (020) 7723 2450; fax: (020) 7723 2486; e-mail: cruise@dial.pipex.com; website: www.cruisepeople.co.uk). Most major international cruiselines sail to Brazilian ports, including: *Celebrity, Crystal, Cunard, Holland America, Mediterranean Shipping, Orient Lines, P&O, Princess, Seabourn* and *Swan Hellenic*.
RAIL: Limited rail services link Brazil with Argentina, Bolivia and Chile, although travelling by train is not a popular option. The main international routes include Rio de Janeiro–Buenos Aires, Rio de Janeiro–Santiago, Rio de Janeiro–São Paulo–Montevideo, São Paulo–Bauru–Corumba–Santa Cruz–La Paz, São Paulo–Antofagasta.
ROAD: It is possible to drive or take a bus to Brazil from the USA, but it is wise to check any changes in political status or requirements in Central America before travelling. It is also possible to travel from Rio de Janeiro to other Latin American countries. The journeys tend to be long; for example, from Rio de Janeiro to Buenos Aires (Argentina) is 44 hours. For further information, contact *Embratur* (see *Contact Addresses* section).

Credit: © Brazilian Tourist Board

Travel - Internal

AIR: There is a shuttle service between São Paulo and Rio de Janeiro, a regular service from São Paulo to Brasília, and a shuttle service from Brasília to Belo Horizonte. There are air services between all Brazilian cities, Brazil having one of the largest internal air networks in the world. At weekends it is advisable to book seats as the services are much used. The monthly magazine *Panrotas* (website: www.panrotas.com.br) gives all timetables and fares for internal air travel. Air taxis are available between all major centres.
Domestic airports: *São Paulo* (Viracopos) *(VCP)*, 96km (60 miles) southwest of the city. Airport facilities include banking, a duty-free shop and a restaurant.
São Paulo (Congonhas) *(CGH)*, 14km (8 miles) from the city.
Manaus (Internacional Eduardo Gomes) *(MAO)*, 14km (9 miles) from the city. There are coach services into the city and to other destinations.
Salvador (Dois de Julho) *(SSA)*, 36km (22 miles) from the city. 24-hour taxi facilities are available. Airport facilities include banking, a duty-free shop and a restaurant.
The Brazilian Airpass: The airpass is available through *Varig Brazilian Airlines* and can be purchased only outside of Brazil and only in conjunction with a British Airways or Varig international carrier ticket. Only one airpass may be purchased per person. The pass costs up to US$560 for one to five coupons. Extra coupons cost US$100 each, up to a

maximum of nine coupons; validity is for 21 days from first date of travel. The same route cannot be travelled twice and coupons have variable values. Further information is available from Varig Brazilian Airlines in the UK (tel: (0845) 603 7601; website: www.varig.co.uk). It is also possible to buy an airpass with TAM, Transbrasil and VASP and use any international carrier.

Departure tax: None.

SEA/RIVER: Ferries serve all coastal ports. River transport is the most efficient method of travel in the Amazon Delta. The government-owned *Empresa de Navegação de Amazônia* (ENASA) has now virtually suspended its passenger-boat services, but private companies have stepped in and provide constantly improving services on rivers throughout the country. Boat trips from the mainland to the popular and beautiful islands of Ilha Grande, Ilhabela and Ilha de Santa Catarina are also possible.

RAIL: Limited rail connections exist to most major cities and towns, but there has been a substantial decline in the provision of long-distance services from the 18 major regional networks. Most (95 per cent) of Brazil's 22,000km (13,640 miles) of rail lines are located within 480km (300 miles) of its Atlantic coastline. Because of the great distances and the climate, some of these journeys can be uncomfortable. Daytime and overnight trains with restaurant and sleeping-cars link São Paulo and Rio de Janeiro. Brazil's most scenic rail routes are from Curitiba to Paranagua (originating in São Paulo) and from São Paulo to Santos. Other major rail routes include Belo Horizonte-Itabira-Vitoria (with buffet car), Campo Grande-Ponte Pora (with restaurant car), Porto Santana-Serra do Navio (second-class only), Santos Ana Costa-Juquia (second-class only), São Luis A Guarda-Parauapebas (with buffet car), Curitiba-Foz do Iguacu, São Paulo-Panorama (second-class only), São Paulo-Presidente Prudente (first-class, air-conditioned, buffet and sleeping cars available), Araguari-Campinas (restaurant or buffet car) and Santa Maria-Pôrto Alegre (with restaurant car). Children under three travel free. Children from three to nine pay half fare.

ROAD: Brazil has 1,940,400km (1,202,800 miles) of roads. Traffic drives on the right. **Bus:** Inter-urban transport is very much road-based (accounting for 97 per cent of travel), compared with air (2.2 per cent) and rail (less than 1 per cent). High-quality coaches have been increasingly introduced on the main routes, which are well served. Services connect all inhabited parts of the country. Standards and timetables vary, and the visitor must be prepared for overnight stops and long waits between connecting stages. **Car hire:** Available in all major centres but rates are expensive and the whole procedure very bureaucratic. Parking in cities is very difficult and it is best to avoid driving through the often congested urban areas if at all possible. **Documentation:** International Driving Permit required.

URBAN: There are extensive bus services in all the main centres, often with air-conditioned express executive coaches running at premium fares. Rio and São Paulo both have two-line metros and local rail lines, and there are trolleybuses in São Paulo and a number of other cities. Trolleybuses are increasingly being introduced as an energy-saving measure. Fares are generally regulated with interchange possible between some bus and metro/rail lines for instance, on the feeder bus linking the Rio metro with Copacabana. **Taxi:** In most cities these are identified by red number plates and are fitted with meters. Fares are inexpensive, costing a little more with the 'special' taxis with air conditioning and better comfort. Willingness to accept a taxi driver's advice on where to go or where to stay should be tempered by the knowledge that places to which he takes a visitor are more than likely to give him a commission – and the highest commissions will usually come from the most expensive places. Taxis are metered and passengers should insist that the meter is turned on.

Travel times: The following chart gives approximate travel times (in hours and minutes) from **Rio de Janeiro** to other major cities/towns in Brazil.

	Air
Belo Horizonte	0.50
Brasília	1.30
Campo Grande	3.30
Curitiba	1.30
Fortaleza	4.25
Foz de Iguaçu	3.00
Manaus	5.00
Natal	3.00
Porto Alegre	2.00
Recife	2.45
Salvador	2.00
São Paulo	0.55

Accommodation

HOTELS: Accommodation varies according to region. First-class accommodation is, by and large, restricted to the cities of the south and is generally expensive. For further information, contact the Associacão Brasileira da Industria de Hoteis, sala 213, Avenida das Americas, 3.120 Bl.1, Rio de Janeiro (tel/fax: (21) 3410 5131; website: www.riodejaneirohotel.com.br). There are also a number of *pousadas*, small, privately run hotels that are less expensive than the major hotels.

Credit: © Brazilian Tourist Board

Rio de Janeiro/São Paulo: Many modern hotels, ranging from the very expensive deluxe hotels to moderately priced hotels. It is vital to book well in advance for the Carnival (which takes place annually in February/March).

Brasília: Small number of good hotels. Most tourists visit Brasília by air from Rio or São Paulo for a day trip, or make a single-night stopover.

Bahia (Salvador): Small number of good hotels, some moderately priced hotels, several demi-pensions. The Bahia carnival takes place after Christmas (from December to March).

Amazon Basin: This region is being developed in part as a tourist attraction and has numerous lodges. Visitors are reminded that hotel tariffs are subject to alteration at any time, and are liable to fluctuate according to changes in the exchange rate.

Note: The best guide to hotels in Brazil is the 'Guia do Brasil Quatro Rodas', which includes maps available from EMBRATUR and from any news-stand in Brazil. **Grading:** The Brazilian Tourist Board (EMBRATUR) has a star-rating system for hotels used by most establishments in towns. The classification is not, however, the standard used in Europe and North America. **5-star** is the grade for deluxe hotels. **3-star** hotels are good value for money and offer well-kept accommodation, whilst a **1-star** hotel can only offer basic amenities.

CAMPING/CARAVANNING: Cars may be hired, and camping arranged on safari tours or group 'exploration' trips in the Amazon region. The road network in Brazil is good and is being expanded, but since many parts are wild, or semi-explored, it is wise to drive on main roads, to camp with organised groups under supervision and with official permits, or otherwise to stay in recognised hotels. The country is peaceful, but because it is so large there is a real danger of getting lost, or being injured or killed by natural accident or lack of local survival skills.

The Camping Clube do Brasil has 52 sites in 14 states. Those with an 'international camper's card' pay only half the rate of a non-member (about €4 per person). For those on a low budget, service stations can be used as campsites. These are equipped with shower facilities and can supply food. For further information, contact Camping Clube do Brasil, Divisao de Campings, Rua Senador Dantas 75, 29 andar, 20000 Rio de Janeiro (tel: (21) 210 3171; fax: (21) 2262 3143; e-mail: ccb@campingclube.com.br; website: www.campingclube.com.br).

YOUTH HOSTELS: There are over 90 youth hostels *(albergues de juventude)*. For further information, contact Federação Brasileira dos Albergues da Juventude, Rua General Dionisio 63, Botafogo, 22271-050 Rio de Janeiro (tel: (21) 2286 0303; fax: (21) 2286 5652; e-mail: info@hostel.org.br; website: www.hostel.org.br).

OTHER TYPES OF ACCOMMODATION: Eco-Hotels: Owing to a recent government initiative to invest in ecotourism, there are now a relatively small number of 'eco-hotels' available, located mostly in or near the Amazonian rainforest. Some provide visitors with luxury accommodation built on treetops and also arrange informative tours to the surrounding area; prices tend to be very high. **Budget:** *Dormitórios*, which have several beds to a room, cost as little as US$5 per night, though standards are correspondingly basic (with shared bathroom facilities); a *pousada* (small guest house) costs approximately US$10 per night. Rooms with bathrooms are called *apartamentos*, those without a bathroom are called *quartos*.

Resorts & Excursions

THE INTERNATIONAL GATEWAYS TO BRAZIL

RIO DE JANEIRO: Known as the *cidade maravilhosa* (the marvellous city), Rio has one of the most beautiful settings in the world. The city's spectacular harbour is dominated by the famous rocky outcrop, **Pão de Açúcar (Sugar Loaf)**, and, further up, the **Corcovado (Hunchback)** peak, rising 709m (2326ft) above the **Baía de Guanabara** and providing the focal point for the classic Rio skyline. The **Cristo Redentor (Christ the Redeemer) statue** stands on top of Corcovado. Pão de Açúcar can be reached by two cable cars ascending 396m (1300ft) above Rio and the Baia de Guanabara (one leaves approximately every 30 minutes). Flocks of tourists arriving by tour buses can sometimes spoil the view, so visitors should avoid the busiest times (between 1000-1100 and 1400-1500). The Corcovado peak is located within the **Parque Nacional da Tijuca**, and is accessible by cog train (leaving from the Rua Cosme Velho). From the top there are magnificent views of Rio. Taxis also take visitors up to the peak and driving there will take up to an hour. Rio's other landmarks are its numerous beaches, most notably the infamous **Copacabana** and **Ipanema**. Beach life is a ritual in Brazil and different beach sections reflect different ways of life and fashions. **The Girl from Ipanema** beach is particularly popular with young people and is located at Posto Nine in Ipanema. Owing to strong waves and undertows, swimming off Ipanema can be dangerous. Rio's other main beaches include **Arpoador**, **Barra da Tijuca**, **Botafogo**, **Flamengo**, **Leblon**, **Leme**, **Pepino** and **Vidigal**.

Rio has many interesting museums, including the **Museu Histórico Nacional**, located in the **São Tiago Fortress**. The **Museu de Arte Moderna do Rio de Janeiro** contains Brazil's most important collection of modern art. The **Museu de Arte Contemporânea de Niterói**, designed by famous architect Oscar Niemeyer and overlooking Boa Viagem beach, showcases contemporary Brazilian art. The **Museu do Folclore Edison Carneiro** displays folk art and art naif. The **Museu do Índio** contains some 14,000 objects made by Brazilian Indians and is one of the nation's most important Indian heritage museums. The **Museu da República** is set in the well-restored **Palácio do Catete** and reveals a fascinating insight into Brazilian history.

SÃO PAULO: The view from the top of São Paulo's tallest building, the **Edificio Italiano** reveals South America's largest city (over 9 million inhabitants) and Brazil's financial, commercial and industrial heartland. Famed throughout the continent for its abundant nightlife and shopping, São Paulo's rapidly growing population resides in a sprawling urban maze characterised by perpetual traffic jams and a chronic lack of space. While São Paulo's concrete jungle is a far cry from the colour and charm of other Brazilian cities, there are some cultural attractions on offer, notably the **MASP – Museu de Arte de São Paulo** with an internationally renowned collection of impressionist paintings (with works by Van Gogh and Degas amongst many others).

THE BRAZILIAN NORTHEAST

The Northeast of Brazil is famed for its beautiful beaches and distinct history and folklore. Known as the 'Golden Coast', this region contains the states of Alagoas, Bahia, Ceará, Maranhão, Paraíba, Pernambuco, Piauí, Rio Grande do Norte and Sergipe.

SALVADOR DA BAHIA: The state capital is split into upper and lower sections. **Cidade Alta**, the heart of the old city, is perched at the top of a 50m-high cliff, linked to **Cidade Baixa** by steep streets, a funicular railway and the marvellous Art-Deco Elevador Lacerdo. The majority of Salvador's museums, palaces and churches are concentrated within Cidade Alta and thus the city is ideal for exploring on foot. This UNESCO World Heritage Site boasts a staggering number of churches, including the impressive **Church of São Francisco** and the fascinating **Church of Bonfim**, where middle-class matrons rub shoulders with the peasantry as they gather to worship. However, religion in Bahia is not limited to the established church. The state's African legacy extends to *candomble*, a fusion of African and Catholic religions. *Candomble* followers dress in white and honour hundreds of native deities in *terreiros* (or cult houses) all over the city, it is possible to witness ceremonies as some *terreiros* accept visitors as long as they dress

accordingly and are respectful.
Salvador has some of the best museums in Brazil and next to the opulent **Catedral Basilica** is the **Museu Afro-Brasileiro**, a fascinating insight into afro-Brazilian culture, with sections on *candomble*, *capoeira* and *Carnaval*. Other interesting museums include the **Casa de Jorge Amado**, Bahia's best-known novelist, the **Museu da Cidade** and the **Museu de Arte Sacra**, the latter housed in a 17th-century convent.
Avid shoppers should head for the **Mercado Modelo** for a wide variety of goods including many examples of local handicrafts. The local cuisine (*comida bahiana*) is among the best in Brazil, focusing on rich African flavours.
Salvador is also renowned for being the hub of Brazilian music and Salvador's central district of **Pelourinho** is home to numerous bars and clubs showcasing live music and *afoxé* (Salvador's carnival bands).
ELSEWHERE: Also in Bahia state, the **Diamantina National Park** is also well worth a visit; it contains several underground lakes (such as **Lago Azul**) and spectacular waterfalls (such as **Veu da Noiva**). The towns of **Ilhéus** and **Aracaju** with their ornate churches and colonial architecture are also worth a visit.
Piauí State contains the UNESCO World Heritage site of the **Serra da Capivara National Park**, which contains ancient cave paintings estimated to be over 25,000 years old.
Alagoas state capital, **Maceiô**, is deservedly proud of its fantastic beaches, reputedly the finest in all of Brazil.
Pernambuco state capital, **Recife**, has been the beneficiary of sizeable investment to promote tourism. However despite being one of the most visited cities in the Brazilian Northeast, it still suffers from a poor infrastructure and the influx of rich, foreign tourists has made begging and street crime a real problem in the city. A world away is the nearby historical town of **Olinda**, infamous for its *Carnaval* celebrations and one of Brazil's eight UNESCO World Heritage Sites.
Rio Grande do Norte's state capital, **Natal**, is divided between the commercial section of the city and its beach suburbs – clean, safe and good for surfing. Natal has several large markets and is famous for its cotton and leather handicrafts.
Ceara's capital, **Fortaleza**, sprawls lazily along a spectacular coastline. Blessed with excellent restaurants and an abundance of attractions for the visitor, the city is also a great place to organise a trip to **Jericocoara**. Just four hours by car, this heavenly village is nestled between a dazzling white sand-dune desert and a balmy turquoise sea.

THE INTERIOR

Few tourists venture far from Brazil's spectacular beaches but a trip into the interior reveals a different Brazil, one with a great deal to offer the visitor.
MINAS GERAIS: As its name suggests, this was so called after the abundant gold and diamond mines that transformed the state into a treasure trove of gold and also of baroque art. During the 18th century, the stream of riches from this region was so relentless that the Portuguese lacked sufficient ships to transport it to Europe. Almost all the gold that gilded altars in cathedrals and churches from as far north as **Olinda** came from Minas. In towns such as **Ouro Preto**, **Tiradentes**, **Sabará** and **Mariana**, this tidal wave of wealth resulted in the construction of hundreds of churches and civic buildings in lavish baroque style. All of the cidades históricas are immaculately preserved examples of Brazil's colonial heritage and are accessible by road from the state capital **Belo Horizonte**. This region's highlight for art-lovers is Aleijadinho's interpretation of 'The Passion' at the **Basilica de Bom Jesus de Matosinhos**. Set in gardens that gently slope towards **Matosinhos** town, the work is positioned in six small domed chapels filled with life-size statues that dramatise the scenes. All of the figures, including the 12 magnificent soapstone statues of prophets from the Old Testament, are more poignant for being sculpted by an artist almost completely disabled by the advanced stages of leprosy and who, therefore, knew it to be his final work.
ELSEWHERE: Brasília, the country's capital, was built on land originally covered by *cerrado* (sub-tropical forest) and is renowned for its futuristic architecture, most notable in the **Praça dos Três Poderes**, **Palácio do Planalto** and the **National Congress**. Attracting far fewer visitors than the huge cities of Rio and São Paulo or the tropical paradise of the Northeast, Brasília has little to offer the visitor interested in Brazilian history and culture. However, it is Brazil's future and it is up to the individual to decide whether it is as attractive as Brazil's colourful past.
Mato Grosso is the gateway to the **Pantanal**, a vast area of wetlands approximately half the size of France and Brazil's largest ecological reserve. Flooded by the **Rio Paraguai** during the wet season (October to March), this region is the best place in Brazil to see wildlife. However, the region is sparsely populated, with few towns or villages and only one major road (the 'Transpantaneira'). Therefore, in order to get the most out of the area, wildlife enthusiasts should choose an organised tour with experienced guides.

Credit: © Brazilian Tourist Board

THE SOUTH

PORTO ALEGRE: In the rich southern state of **Rio Grande do Sul**, this city caters for thousands of tourists each year, the majority of whom come from nearby Argentina. The capital has excellent museums, art galleries and restaurants to entertain the visitor, as well as delightful surrounding countryside. To the west, travellers can visit the ruins of the 300-year-old Jesuit missions, abandoned when the Jesuits were expelled from Spain. One of the most fascinating is **Saõ Miguel das Missões**, yet another UNESCO World Heritage Site, located 58km (36 miles) from the town of **Santo Angelo** (a good starting point for visiting the missions). The most popular beaches in this area are the *Tramandai* and *Torres*, respectively 126km (78 miles) and 209km (130 miles) from Pôrto Alegre. In addition, the region's **Gramado** and **Canela Mountains** provide ample opportunities for walking and trekking.
ELSEWHERE: The state of Santa Catarina, with its island capital of **Florianópolis**, has superb beaches at **Laguna**, **Itapena** and **Camburiu**. The island is famous for its excellent surfing and watersports facilities are particularly good in the area. Further inland **Blumenau** and **Joinville** are both living testaments to the last century's massive influx of German immigration with both towns constructed in predominantly German architecture. Germanic culture is still vibrant in small towns like **Pomerode** (near Blumenau) where German remains the lingua franca with Portuguese only used in government offices. Blumenau's annual three-week *Oktoberfest* is not to be missed.
Paraná is a prime coffee-producing state with a bright modern capital, **Curitiba**, whose public transport system could be the envy of European capitals like London or Paris. Efficient trams run throughout the city and travellers are encased in glass tunnels that protect them from the elements as they wait for the next tram. However, Curitiba is relatively compact and (weather permitting) easy to explore on foot with most areas of interest found in the historic centre. Curitiba is famous for its parks, two of which are worth seeking out; visitors will be fascinated by the riot of vivid plumage in the aviaries of the **Passeio Público**, where several species of local birds are kept. A fascinating insight into frontier life and the endeavours of countless European immigrants, who moved here during the last 150 years, is the **Museu de Imigração Polenesa** in the centre of **Bosque João Paulo**. The museum's best exhibits are the log cabins, built by Polish immigrants in the 1880s and relocated here over 100 years later.
The train journey between **Curitiba** and **Paranaguá** is a spectacular journey through dense jungle, its route strewn with memorials for the many workers who perished from tropical diseases as they constructed the tracks. Accessible by road or air from Curitiba are the world-famous **Iguazu Falls**, a spectacular set of 70m waterfalls, including the impressive **Garganta del Diablo** (Devil's Throat). Standing near the waterfalls is a humbling experience. The deafening roar of 5000 cubic metres of water cascading down each second accompanies a perpetual (and in summer temperatures, welcoming) mist that envelopes visitors. The area encompasses two national parks, each boasting hundreds of species of plant and animal life, and spans the borders of two countries, Argentina and Brazil, divided by the **River Paraná**. For a good view of the entire set of falls, visit the Brazilian side of the Park in **Foz de Iguazu** and photograph the spectacle. To get close enough to stare into the watery abyss, visit the Argentine side. Unfortunately, there is no access to Brazil from the Argentine Park or vice versa, so visitors wishing to see both parks must travel overland to the border crossing, about 10km south. Due to Foz de Iguazu's proximity to both the Argentine and Paraguayan borders, it is possible to visit both countries in a day trip from Foz.
THE NORTHERN INTERIOR AND AMAZON: Almost entirely covered with dense rainforest, Brazil's northern interior is split into the vast regions of **Amazonas**, **Pará**, **Acre** and **Rondônia**. These massive federal states easily outstrip the land resources of many European countries and, combined, cover over 3,400,000 sq km (1,300,000 sq miles) of endless jungle filled with countless species of life.
RONDÔNIA AND ACRE: Created in 1991 Rondônia has suffered extensive deforestation. There are still natural wonders hidden away such as the stunning **Teotonio** and **Santo Antônio Falls**, accessible from capital **Porto Velho**. Other attractions include river trips to the **Forte Principe de Beira** or to Bolivia, where air taxis operate to La Paz from Guayaramerin.
Territorially annexed from Bolivia in the early 20th century, Acre is a state of contrasts with a funky capital in **Rio Branco**, a thriving market and university town on the river. Because of its student population, Rio Branco has good nightlife and its geographical position as a trading post has made the town an important handicrafts centre.
AMAZONAS: The state capital, Manaus, was transformed by the 19th-century rubber boom and nowhere is this more evident than in the **Teatro Amazonas**, built in 1896 in the elaborate style of the Italian Renaissance. In front of the theatre, a marble square is designed to reflect the four continents represented by four great ships. Along **Avenida Sete de Setembro** are numerous museums worth a visit; the **Museo de Indio**, **Museo de Amazonas** and the marvellous colonial mansion that houses the **Centro Cultural de Palacio Rio Negro**, an extensive archive of naturalist Alexandre Ferreira. The city is easy to navigate and offers the visitor both fine restaurants and tax-free bargains in the free trade zone. As a major port for river-traffic with arrivals and departures to Colombia, Peru and Venezuela, Manaus is an excellent starting point for river trips and guided tours into the rainforest. 25 million years ago, the volcanic activity that created the Andes blocked the Amazon's path to the Pacific, sending it on the 6400km journey to the Atlantic and thus creating the vast Amazon basin. Upriver from Manaus, the rivers **Amazon** and **Negro** meet but their waters (yellow and black respectively) run parallel for many miles in different-coloured channels.
PARA AND AMAPA: The Eastern Amazon region is split between the states of **Para** and **Amapa**. Para's state capital **Belem** was founded in 1616. Situated at the Atlantic end of the Amazon estuary at the mouth of the **Rio Tocantins**, Belem is a thriving port city with an exquisite historical centre, dotted with splendid churches and elegant parks. **The Goeldi Museum** boasts the largest collection of tropical plants in the world. The docks are the location of the early-morning **Ver O Peso** (See the Weight) market, which was originally a slave market but still exists these days although the stalls now mostly sell fruit and produce.

Sport & Activities

Jungle treks: The Amazon rainforest is the world's largest biological reserve. It contains one-third of all living species on the earth and is crossed by 10 of the world's 20 largest rivers, including the *River Amazon* (the largest river in the world). The usual base for trips to the Amazon is the city of Manaus, where numerous tour operators can arrange anything from standard day trips to month-long expeditions to more remote areas. It is best to hire a local guide (trips without guides are only allowed on certain trails). During the rainy season (February to April), the flooded rainforest can be explored by boat or canoe. Several jungle lodges and hotels offer **ecotourism** packages, though many of these tend to be expensive. River cruises to the so-called 'wedding of the waters', where the clear waters of the Rio Negro meet the muddy Amazon, are popular. For information on wildlife, see the *Resorts & Excursions* section.

Hiking and climbing: The best time for **hiking** and **climbing** is from April to October. Rio de Janeiro is the centre of Brazilian rock climbing: over 300 climbs can be reached within 40 minutes from the city centre. There are many great hiking trails in the national parks and along the coastline. The *Iguaçu Falls* on the Parana River near the junction of Brazil, Argentina and Paraguay is one of the world's greatest waterfalls, with 275 cataracts. Boat trips to the falls from Rio are available and take 2 days. Good aerial views can be enjoyed from a **helicopter tour** of the falls that can be booked on location.

Watersports: Brazil is one of the world's top **surfing** destinations. The best places to surf in Brazil include *Joaquina Beach* (near Florianópolis in Santa Catarina state, which hosts the annual Brazilian surfing championships); *Saquarema* (in Rio state); *Búzios* (a chic resort area on the Cabio Frio Peninsula); *Itacoatiara*; and a string of beaches near Rio de Janeiro. There are hundreds of beaches along the coastline suitable for many types of watersports, some of the best being at *Buzios*; *Angra* (on the Costa Verde, which is fairly uncrowded, with access to hundreds of offshore islands); *Fortaleza*; *Niteroi* (near Rio, with three good beaches); and *Itamaraca Island* (north of Recife). **Diving** can be practised in *Fernando de Noronha* (a small archipelago off Brazil's north eastern coast in Pernambuco state, where a strict environmental protection programme allows a maximum of 420 visitors at a time); *Angra dos Reis* (a seaside village in Rio de Janeiro state, part of Ilha Grande Bay, with possible diving trips to 300 surrounding islands); *Bonito* (located in the fairly untouched and undeveloped Panatal region); *Recife* (the 'birthplace' of Brazil, offering excellent diving in the vicinity); and *Parcel Manoel Luís*. Diving clubs are located all along the coastline. For further information, contact the Brazilian Tourist Board - EMBRATUR (see *Contact Addresses* section).

Golf: Rio de Janeiro's spectacular location makes for a number of dazzling golf courses. The *Gávea Golf & Country Club*, located beneath the massive Gávea rock and next to São Conrado beach, has an 18-hole course; non-members are not allowed at *Itanhangá Golf Club* has a 9- and an 18-hole course, located near Barra da Tijuca beach.

Carnaval and music: Such a Brazilian cultural anomaly that it deserves a section by itself. *Carnaval* is held four days before Ash Wednesday each year and lasts from four days in the South, to two weeks in northern cities such as Salvador and Recife. Brazilians themselves remark that the Recife and Olinda celebrations are the most distinctive but it is cities like Rio or Salvador that receive the most foreign visitors. However in every town and village in Brazil, Carnaval is a time to celebrate and the visitor will see processions and *blocos* in every region during Carnaval time.

Accommodation is traditionally prepaid in four- or five-day blocks and overland travel during Carnaval is notoriously difficult, although always entertaining!

Music: Brazil is the perfect place to sample the samba, bossa nova or lambada and the major cities, particularly Rio de Janeiro, are full of cafes with live music and dancing. *Gefieiras* are samba parlours where visitors can either watch or join in. In Rio, many gefieiras are located on the south side. The *Copacabana* beach, where parties are staged nearly 24 hours a day, is also a good location for sampling some Latin American entertainment. An exciting way to experience the genuine samba is by attending a rehearsal at the *escolas de samba* (samba schools), which open their doors to visitors a couple of months before the beginning of Rio de Janeiro's *carneval*. *Bandas*, the non-professional equivalent of the samba schools, are also a good place to practice. Tickets for the carnival go on sale two weeks before the beginning. The best costumes and most spectacular samba parades can be seen at the *Sambódromo* (Sambadrome), a stadium on Rua Marquês de Sapucaí, where 14 samba schools parade on Carnival Sunday and Monday; the parades go on for 24 hours and tickets should be bought well in advance. It is possible for visitors to take part in a parade. One week of preparation should be allowed and hotels can often make all the necessary arrangements. During carnival, foreign visitors should be alert to pickpockets and not carry more money than needed.

Football: A good way to experience the Brazilian *Maracana Stadium*, the largest in the world.

Social Profile

FOOD & DRINK: Many regional variations are very different from North American and European food. One example is Bahian cookery, derived from days when slaves had to cook scraps and anything that could be caught locally, together with coconut milk and palm oil. Specialities include *vatapá* (shrimps, fish oil, coconut milk, bread and rice), *sarapatel* (liver, heart, tomatoes, peppers, onion and gravy) and *caruru* (shrimps, okra, onions and peppers). From Rio Grande do Sul comes *churrasco* (barbecued beef, tomato and onion sauce), *galleto al primo canto* (pieces of cockerel cooked on the spit with white wine and oil). From Amazonas comes *pato no tucupi* (duck in rich wild green herb sauce) and *tacacá* (thick yellow soup with shrimps and garlic). In the northeast, dried salted meat and beans are the staple diet. In Rio de Janeiro, a favourite dish is *feijoada* (thick stew of black beans, chunks of beef, pork, sausage, chops, pigs' ears and tails on white rice, boiled green vegetables and orange slices). Types of establishment vary. Table service is usual in most restaurants and cafes and a service charge of 10 per cent is added to most bills. If resident in a hotel, drinks and meals can often be charged to an account.

All kinds of alcoholic drink are manufactured and available and there are no licensing hours or restrictions on drinking. Beer is particularly good and draught beer is called *chopp*. The local liqueur is *cachaça*, a type of rum popular with locals, but not so much with visitors. This phenomenally strong spirit is often mixed with sugar, crushed ice and limes to make *caipirinha*, a refreshing if intoxicating cocktail, and the Brazilian national drink. Southern Brazilian wine is of a high quality. Some bars have waiters and table service. Brazilian coffee is served in espresso-sized cups and is extremely popular.

NIGHTLIFE: The best entertainment occurs in Rio de Janeiro and São Paulo. In Rio, the major clubs do not present their main acts until after midnight, and the daily paper gives current information; small clubs (*boites*) provide nightly entertainment throughout the city. São Paulo nightlife is more sophisticated, with greater choice; the shows tend to start earlier.

SHOPPING: In Rio and São Paulo, major shops and markets stay open quite late in the evening. Rio and Bahia specialise in antiques and jewellery. Special purchases include gems (particularly emeralds), jewellery (particularly silver), souvenirs and permissible antiques, leather or snakeskin goods. Fashions and antiques, crystal and pottery are a speciality of São Paulo. Belém, the city of the Amazon valley, specialises in jungle items, but be careful that you are not purchasing objects that have been plundered from the jungle, contributing to the general destruction. Check for restrictions on import to your home country of goods made from skins of protected species. **Shopping hours:** Mon-Sat 0900-1900. Supermarkets are open Mon-Sat 0800-2200. Major shopping centres also open on Sundays 1500-2200. All the above times are subject to local variations and many shops open until late in the evenings, especially in December.

SPECIAL EVENTS: There are a number of lavish festivals throughout the year in Brazil, the two most notable being Bahia's *Carnival* just after Christmas (from December to March) and the *Carnival* in Rio de Janeiro (February/March), widely regarded as the most spectacular and extravagant in the world. The following is a selection of special events occurring in Brazil in 2005; further details of other special events may be obtained from the Brazilian Tourist Board (EMBRATUR) (see *Contact Addresses* section):

Feb 3-8 *Bahia Carnival*. **Feb 4-8** *Carnival*, Rio de Janeiro. **Feb 5-6** *Carnival*, São Paulo. **Mar 21-25** *Holy Week Processions*, Ouro Preto. **May 21-30** *Festa Do Divino Espírito Santo*. **Jun 27** *Rio de Janeiro Pride*. **Sep 8** *Festa de Nossa Senhora dos Remédios*. **Sep 18-26** *International Fishing Festival*, Cáceres. **Oct 24** *Formula One: Brazilian Grand Prix*.

SOCIAL CONVENTIONS: Handshaking is customary on meeting and taking one's leave, and normal European courtesies are observed. Frequent offers of coffee and tea are customary. Flowers are acceptable as a gift on arrival or following a visit for a meal. A souvenir from the visitor's home country will be well received as a gift of appreciation. Casual wear is normal, particularly during hot weather. In nightclubs, smart-casual (eg blazer, no tie) is acceptable. For more formal occasions the mode of dress will be indicated on invitations. Smoking is acceptable unless notified otherwise. The Catholic Church is highly respected in the community, something which should be kept in mind by the visitor. **Tipping:** 10 to 15 per cent is usual for most services not included on the bill. Tipping taxi drivers is not normal practice.

Business Profile

ECONOMY: Brazil has the world's 10th largest economy. Agriculture remains the largest sector in terms of employment and Brazil is the world's second-largest exporter of agricultural products, principally coffee, sugar, soya beans, orange juice, beef, poultry and cocoa. Sisal, tobacco, maize and cotton are also produced. Orange juice and coffee are key export earners. There is also a substantial industrial sector, concentrated in machinery, electrical goods, construction materials, rubber and chemicals, and vehicle production. The country also possesses large mineral reserves including iron ore - of which Brazil is the world's largest exporter - bauxite, gold, titanium, manganese, copper and tin. Plans to develop Brazil's potentially vast oil and gas resources will serve to reduce the country's large current energy import bill but face opposition both at home and abroad on environmental grounds.

After difficulties throughout the 1980s, as the economy adjusted to new liberal economic policies, Brazil recorded a fairly strong economic performance during most of the 1990s. Industrial efficiency and financial management were improved while the government bolstered its coffers through a programme of privatisation. However, little of this money was directed towards investment and Brazil has suffered the consequences of years of under-investment in infrastructure and public services. In 1994, the government introduced a new currency, the Real, to replace the Cruzeiro. Despite several bouts of serious speculative attack - the 1997 Asian financial crisis, the 1999 Mexico financial crisis and in the run-up to the 2002 election - the Real has survived with the support of several bail-outs from the IMF and World Bank, which have, as ever, demanded austerity measures in return. The Lula government, which took office with a series of radical social programmes at the beginning of 2003, was soon forced to make budget cuts. Its main target has been the country's costly pension system, which is now being overhauled.

The economy has recorded slow growth - below 2 per cent - during the last two years. Inflation remains stubbornly high but not unmanageable, at 15 per cent. Brazil's principal trading partners are the USA, Japan and Germany, as well as its fellow members of the newly formed southern Latin American trading bloc, MERCOSUR. Brazil also has important trading links with a number of Arab countries, notably Saudi Arabia.

BUSINESS: Business suits are worn when meeting senior officials and local heads of business, for semi-formal social functions and in exclusive restaurants and clubs. Exchange of business cards is usual. **Office hours:** Mon-Fri 0900-1800.

COMMERCIAL INFORMATION: The following organisations can offer advice: International Chamber of Commerce, Rua Timbiras 1200, 3 andar, 30140-060 Belo Horizonte (tel/fax: (31) 3273 7021; e-mail: camint@camint.com.br; website: www.camint.com.br); *or* Brazilian-American Chamber of Commerce (BACC), 509 Madison Avenue, Suite 304, New York, NY 10022, USA (tel: (212) 751 4691; fax: (212) 751 7692 *or* 751 8929; e-mail: info@brazilcham.com; website: www.brazilcham.com); *or* American Chamber of Commerce for Brazil, Rua da Paz, 1431 CEP 04713-001 São Paulo (tel: (11) 5180 3804; fax: (11) 5180 3777; e-mail: amhost@amcham.com.br; website: www.amcham.com.br); *or* trade and commercial sections of Brazilian Embassies (some of which also incorporate a Brazilian Chamber of Commerce; for contact numbers, see *Contact Addresses* section).

Climate

Varies from arid scrubland in the interior to the impassable tropical rainforests of the northerly Amazon jungle and the tropical eastern coastal beaches. The south is more temperate. Rainy seasons occur from January to April in the north, April to July in the northeast and November to March in the Rio/São Paulo area.

Required clothing: Lightweight cottons and linens with waterproofing for the rainy season. Warm clothing is needed in the south during winter (June to July). Specialist clothing is needed for the Amazon region. Warm clothing is advised if visiting the southern regions in winter time. The sunlight is extremely bright and sunglasses are recommended.

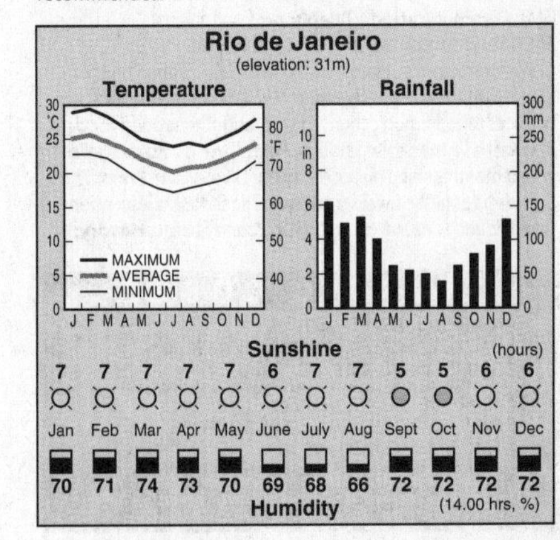

British Overseas Territories

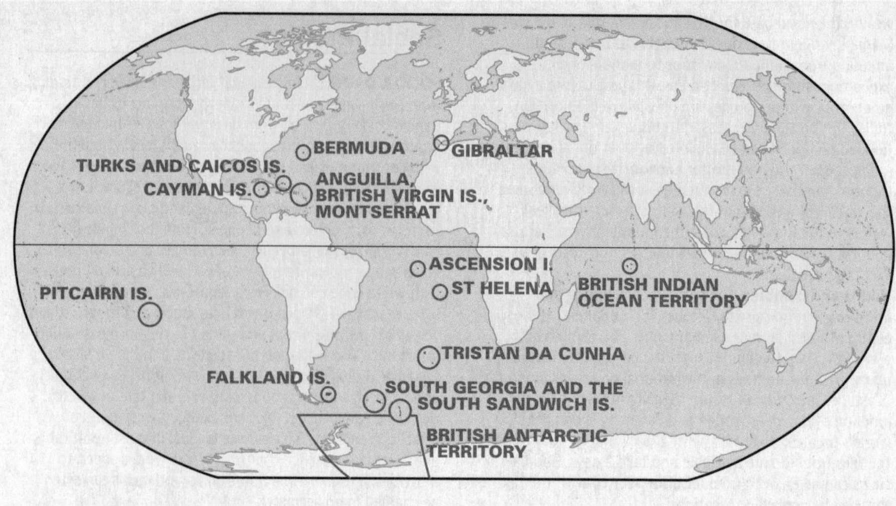

LATEST TRAVEL ADVICE CONTACTS

British Foreign and Commonwealth Office
Tel: (0870) 606 0290 Website: www.fco.gov.uk

US Department of State
Website: http://travel.state.gov/travel

Canadian Department of Foreign Affairs and Int'l Trade
Tel: (1 800) 267 8376 Website: www.dfait-maeci.gc.ca

Scattered throughout the world are several British Overseas Territories. Most of these have their own sections in the *World Travel Guide*, but basic information is given here on the others. For more information, contact:

The UK Passport Service
London Passport Office, Globe House, 89 Eccleston Square, London SW1V 1PN, UK
Tel: (0870) 521 0410 (national advice line) *or* (020) 7901 2150 (visa enquiries for British Overseas Territories).
Fax: (020) 7271 8403 *or* 7901 2162.
E-mail: info@passport.gov.uk *or* london@ukpa.gov.uk
Website: www.passport.gov.uk *or* www.ukpa.gov.uk
Opening hours: Mon-Fri 0730-1900, Sat 0900-1600 (appointments only).
Regional offices in: Belfast, Durham, Glasgow, Liverpool, Newport and Peterborough.

Royal Commonwealth Society
18 Northumberland Avenue, London WC2N 5BJ, UK
Tel: (020) 7930 6733. Fax: (020) 7766 9222.
E-mail: reception@rcsint.org
Website: www.rcsint.org

British Foreign and Commonwealth Office
Overseas Territories Department, Room WH3/417, King Charles Street, London SW1A 2AH, UK
Tel: (020) 7008 2749. Fax: (020) 008 2108.
E-mail: otdenquiries@fco.gov.uk
Website: www.fco.gov.uk

Resorts & Excursions

British Overseas Territories: From 1998, what were once known as British Dependent Territories became United Kingdom Overseas Territories, enjoying the same rights as nationals of Gibraltar and the Falklands Islands, with full British citizenship and residence within the UK. All territories are required to adhere to EU standards, particularly regarding financial regulations and human rights.

British Crown Dependencies: These include the Isle of Man and the Channel Islands, which are dependencies of the British Crown, whilst exercising considerable self-government in domestic affairs. The following countries all have their own sections in the *World Travel Guide*: **Anguilla**, **Bermuda**, **British Virgin Islands**, **Cayman Islands**, **Falkland Islands**, **Gibraltar**, **Montserrat**, **Turks & Caicos Islands**.

Ascension Island

Administrator's Office
Georgetown, Ascension Island, South Atlantic Ocean, ASCN 1ZZ
Tel: 6311 (office). Fax: 6152.
E-mail: aigenquiries@ascension.gov.ac
Website: www.ascension-island.gov.ac

Location: South Atlantic. **Area:** 88 sq km (34 sq miles). **Population:** 1100 (2003). **Population density:** 12.5 per sq km. **Geography:** Ascension Island lies 1207km (750 miles) northwest of St Helena and is of purely volcanic origin. The island is famous for green turtles and is also a breeding ground for Wideawakes (Sooty Tern). **Religion:** Anglican and Roman Catholic. **Time:** GMT. **Communications: Telephone:** Country code: 247. The *BBC World Service* and their contractors *Merlin Communications* operate their Atlantic Relay Station on the island. *Cable & Wireless* (website: www.cw.com/ascension) operates telecommunications services and the *European Space Agency* has a monitoring station. **Post:** There is a Royal Mail ship with a monthly shipping service to the UK available. **Press:** *The Islander* is published weekly. **Money:** The St Helena/Ascension Island Pound is equivalent to the UK Pound Sterling. **History:** A dependency of St Helena, the island was first occupied in 1815 and remained under British Admiralty control until 1922. Its airfield was built by US forces during World War II. The main importance of the island is as a communications centre and a military base, but attempts are being made to attract tourists to what was once a closed island. The island's administrative costs are borne collectively by the user organisations. The Royal Air Force has a facility supporting its garrison in the Falklands and there is a small US Air Force base on the island. Public services are provided by *Ascension Island Services*.

TIMATIC CODES

Health	AMADEUS: **TI-DFT/GDT/HE** GALILEO/WORLDSPAN: **TI-DFT/GDT/HE** SABRE: **TIDFT/GDT/HE**
Visa	AMADEUS: **TI-DFT/GDT/VI** GALILEO/WORLDSPAN: **TI-DFT/GDT/VI** SABRE: **TIDFT/GDT/VI**

To access TIMATIC country information on Health and Visa regulations through the Computer Reservations System (CRS), type in the appropriate command line listed above.

British Antarctic Territory

British Foreign and Commonwealth Office
(see *Contact Addresses* section).

Location: Within the Antarctic Treaty area (between 20° west and 80° west of longitude). **Area:** Approximately 1,709,400 sq km (660,003 sq miles) of land. **Population:** There are no permanent inhabitants, and the territory is used only for scientific purposes. The population is about 50 in the winter, rising to about 400 in summer. The region is administered by the Overseas Territories Department at the British Foreign and Commonwealth Office; see also the *Antarctica* section. **Geography:** The territory also includes the South Shetlands and the South Orkneys.

British Indian Ocean Territory

British Foreign and Commonwealth Office
(see *Contact Addresses* section).

Location: The Territory consists of the Chagos Archipelago, 1930km (1199 miles) northeast of Mauritius, which includes the coral atoll of Diego Garcia. **Area:** 60 sq km (23 sq miles) of land and over 54,400 sq km (21,100 sq miles) of sea. **Population:** There are no permanent inhabitants; however, the original inhabitants, who were forcibly evicted in the 1960s, were given permission to return, although the exact details of the rights of the islanders remains in dispute. In September 2003, there were approximately 3000 people stationed in the Territory, consisting of US and British military personnel and their supporting workforce. **Time:** GMT + 6. **Money:** UK Pound Sterling; the US Dollar is also accepted. **History:** Under the terms of the 1966 agreement, the islands are used jointly by the US and UK governments for military purposes. A Fisheries Commission was formed between the UK and Mauritius in 1994.

Pitcairn Islands

Office of the Governor of Pitcairn, Henderson, Ducie and Oeno Islands
c/o British High Commission, 44 Hill Street, Thorndon, PO Box 1812, Wellington, New Zealand
Tel: (4) 924 2888. Fax: (4) 473 4982.
E-mail: PPA.Mailbox@fco.gov.uk

Pitcairn Islands Administration
Private Box 105696, Auckland, New Zealand
Tel: (9) 366 0186. Fax: (9) 366 0187.
E-mail: admin@pitcairn.gov.pn
Website: www.government.pn

Location: Central South Pacific. **Area:** 35.5 sq km (13.7 sq miles). **Population:** 45 in Pitcairn (2003). **Population density:** 10.3 per sq km (2003). **Geography:** Equidistant from Panama and New Zealand. The group includes the uninhabited islands of Oeno, Henderson and Ducie. **Language:** English and Pitcairn; the latter is a mixture of English and Tahitian, and became an official language in 1997. **Religion:** Seventh Day Adventist. **Time:** GMT - 8.5. **Communications: Telephone:** No direct dialling. Telephone calls must be booked via the international operator. **Press:** The *Pitcairn Miscellany* is a monthly four-page mimeographed news sheet. **Money:** New Zealand money is used on the island. This is on a par with the Pitcairn dollar. There are no banking facilities, but personal and travellers' cheques may be cashed at the Island Secretary's office. **Health:** A yellow fever vaccination certificate is required of all travellers over one year of age coming from infected areas. **Travel:** Although plans were approved for further development on the islands, designed to attract and accommodate more travellers, there is still no airfield, and the number of ships stopping at Pitcairn is decreasing: this increasing isolation is a concern. **History:** Pitcairn officially became a British settlement in 1887. Since 1989, Henderson has been included in the UNESCO World Heritage List as a bird sanctuary. An exclusive economic zone (EEZ) was declared in 1992 including 370km (200 nautical miles) of the islands' waters.

South Georgia and The South Sandwich Islands

The Commissioner for South Georgia and the South Sandwich Islands
Government House, Stanley, Falkland Islands, South Atlantic, via United Kingdom
Tel: (+500) 27433. Fax: (+500) 27434.
E-mail: gov.house@horizon.co.fk
Website: www.sgisland.org

Location: South Atlantic. **Area: South Georgia:** 3592 sq km (1387 sq miles); **South Sandwich Islands:** 311 sq km (120 sq miles). **Population:** There are no permanent inhabitants. **Geography:** South Georgia lies about 1309km (864 miles) southeast of the Falkland Islands, and the South Sandwich Islands lie about 640km (400 miles) southeast of South Georgia, of which 50 per cent is comprised of permanent ice. The South Sandwich Islands consist of a chain of 11 volcanic islands some 350km long. Parts of the islands are protected areas or Sites of Special Scientific Interest, with varied wildlife. **Time:** GMT - 2. **Communications:** All telephone, fax and e-mail communications are through international satellite systems. Public telephone and fax facilities are not available. **Post:** Mail can be posted using South Georgia stamps, but the postal service may take up to two months. **Money:** The South Georgia and South Sandwich Islands Pound is the official currency but the UK Pound Sterling and US Dollars are also in use on the island. Mastercard and Visa are accepted at the museum shop. **Health:** The islands have no hospital facilities or rescue services. Sunburn may be a problem and visitors should take sufficient precautions. Former whaling stations are still emitting wind-blown debris that contains asbestos dust. It is therefore prohibited to enter or approach these stations within 200 metres. **Travel:** There are no road or air links; sole passage to the islands is by sea. However, the South Sandwich Islands' Antarctic climate means that in winter, the islands may be surrounded by pack ice, which may make landing very difficult. All visitors must apply to the Commissioner, in advance of travel, for permission to land, and landing on South Georgia will require a fee of £55. On arrival, all visitors must report to the Marine Officer at King Edward Point, Cumberland, Bay East. **History:** In 1775, Captain Cook claimed South Georgia for the British Crown and the island was annexed by Britain in 1908. In 1927, Argentina laid claim to South Georgia. Dependencies of the Falkland Islands up until 1985, the islands are now a distinct British Overseas Territory governed by the Commissioner, who is also the Governor of the Falkland Islands. There is a local administrator who is Harbour Master, Fishery Officer and Customs and Immigration Officer (amongst other titles). In 1993, the British government announced an extension of its territorial jurisdiction of the waters surrounding the islands. The British Antarctic Survey carries out scientific research on behalf of the Government of the Territory; the small British garrison, stationed there following a brief Argentine occupation in 1982, has now departed. The economy is driven by fisheries and ecotourism. South Georgia has the greatest concentration of Antarctic and sub-Antarctic wildlife on earth, and this, set against the island's extraordinary, glaciated mountain scenery, makes it a unique destination for ecotourism. Most tourists visiting the islands do so as part of a cruise. For details of cruises to Antarctica, contact the International Association of Antarctic Tour Operators based in the USA (tel: (970) 704 1047; fax: (970) 704 9660; e-mail: iaato@iaato.org; website: www.iaato.org).

St Helena

Office of the Governor
The Castle, Jamestown, St Helena, South Atlantic Ocean
Tel: 2555 *or* 2525. Fax: 2598.
E-mail: OCS@helanta.sh
Tourist Office
Main Street, Jamestown, St Helena STHL 1ZZ, South Atlantic Ocean Tel: 2158. Fax: 2159.
E-mail: help@sthelenatourism.com
Website: www.sthelenatourism.com
Location: South Atlantic Ocean. **Area**: 122 sq km (47 sq miles). **Population:** 4647 (2000); official estimate. **Population density:** 59.9 per sq km. **Capital:** Jamestown (population 884). **Geography:** Located approximately 1930km (1200 miles) west of the Angolan coast. The island has a rare flora and fauna with some 40 species that are unique to St Helena. **Religion:** Mostly Anglican. **Time:** GMT. **Communications: Telephone:** Country Code: 290. Credit card calls are permitted to Canada, the UK and the USA. Euro, Mastercard and Visa are accepted as payment of telephone calls. *Cable & Wireless* operates. **Press:** The *St Helena Herald* is published weekly. **Money:** The St Helena Pound is equivalent to the UK Pound Sterling. Visa is accepted by some businesses and shops. Travellers cheques can be cashed at the Finance Department Cash Office, The Castle, Jamestown. **Health:** A yellow fever vaccination certificate is required for all travellers over one year of age coming from infected areas in Africa. There is no National Health Service but there is a reciprocal health agreement with the UK, which entitles all those with proof of UK residence (ie NHS medical card) to hospital treatment in out-patient clinics during normal clinic times at local rates. **Travel:** There are no railways or airfields, but the *RMS St Helena* visits the island 25 times a year. All effort is currently concentrating on constructing an airport on St Helena (on Prosperous Bay Plain) by 2008. In October 1999, the UK and the USA announced that Wideawake Airfield on Ascension Island should be opened on a limited basis to civilian aircraft. Negotiations to bring this into effect are ongoing. Roads on St Helena are nearly all single lanes. Driving is on the left-hand side of the road. **History:** St Helena was discovered on 21 May 1502 by the Portuguese navigator Joan da Nova. In 1658, Richard, Lord Protector, authorised for the British East India Company to colonise and fortify the island. Later, Napoleon Bonaparte was exiled here in 1815 until his death in 1821. In 1834, the island became a crown colony. St Helena depends on aid from the UK, although fishing, livestock, handicrafts and timber are important to the economy.

Tristan da Cunha

Administrator's Office
Settlement of Edinburgh of the Seven Seas, Tristan da Cunha, South Atlantic Ocean
Tel: +870 (682) 087 155. Fax: +870 (682) 087 158.
E-mail: hmg@cunha.demon.co.uk
Location: South Atlantic. **Area:** 98 sq km (38 sq miles). **Population:** 290 (2000). **Population density:** 2.96 per sq km. **Geography:** Tristan da Cunha lies 2778km (1726 miles) west of Cape Town, South Africa. It is the most remote uninhabited island in the world. The group also includes Inaccessible Island, the three Nightingale Islands and Gough Island. **Religion:** Anglican with a small Roman Catholic minority. **Time:** GMT. **Communications:** Calls have to be placed through the international operator, unless made via satellite links. There is a public satellite telephone. **Money:** Pound Sterling is used for currency. **Travel:** There is no airport. All passengers must arrive by boat, if weather BRITISH OVERSEAS TERRITORIES - O/M
conditions permit. **History:** The island was discovered in 1506 by the Portuguese navigator Tristao da Cunha, and garrisoned in 1816 to prevent its possible use as a rescue base for Napoleon Bonaparte. A dependency of St Helena, Tristan da Cunha's economy is based on fishing and fish processing, handicrafts and stamps. The island no longer requires British aid for its day-to-day expenses. The Government and the lobster fishing industry are the only employers.

United Kingdom Crown Dependencies

The **Isle of Man** and the **Channel Islands** are not integral parts of the United Kingdom but are dependencies of the Crown and enjoy a high degree of internal self-government. Information on these islands has been placed at the end of the *United Kingdom* section. **Guernsey** and **Jersey** have their own separate sections.

British Virgin Islands

LATEST TRAVEL ADVICE CONTACTS

British Foreign and Commonwealth Office
Tel: (0870) 606 0290 Website: www.fco.gov.uk
US Department of State
Website: http://travel.state.gov/travel
Canadian Department of Foreign Affairs and Int'l Trade
Tel: (1 800) 267 8376 Website: www.dfait-maeci.gc.ca

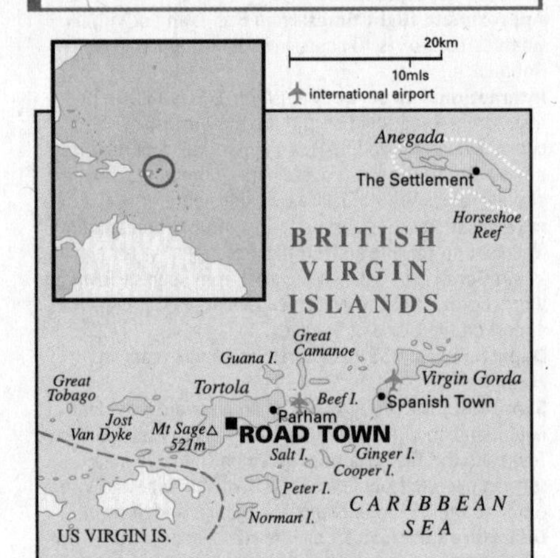

Location: Caribbean, Leeward Islands.

Country dialling code: 1 284 49.

The British Virgin Islands are a British Overseas Territory represented abroad by British Embassies – see *United Kingdom Section*.
Office of the Governor of the British Virgin Islands
Governor's Office, PO Box 702, Waterfront Drive, Road Town, Tortola, British Virgin Islands
Tel: 42345 *or* 42370. Fax: 44490.
E-mail: bvigovernor@gov.vg
Website: www.bvi.gov.vg
British Virgin Islands Tourist Board
PO Box 134, 2nd Floor, Akara Building, De Castro Street, Road Town, Tortola, British Virgin Islands
Tel: 43134. Fax: 43866.
E-mail: bvitourb@surfbvi.com
Website: www.bvitouristboard.com
The UK Passport Service
London Passport Office, Globe House, 89 Eccleston Square, London SW1V 1PN, UK
Tel: (0870) 521 0410 (national advice line) *or* (020) 7901 2150 (visa enquiries for British Overseas Territories).
Fax: (020) 7271 8403 *or* 7901 2162.
E-mail: info@passport.gov.uk *or* london@ukpa.gov.uk
Website: www.passport.gov.uk *or* www.ukpa.gov.uk
Opening hours: Mon-Fri 0730-1900, Sat 0900-1600 (appointments only).
Regional offices in: Belfast, Durham, Glasgow, Liverpool, Newport and Peterborough.
Personal callers for visas should go to the agency window in the collection room of the London office.
British Virgin Islands Tourist Board
15 Upper Grosvenor Street, London W1K 7Pj, UK
Tel: (020) 7355 9585. Fax: (020) 7355 9587.
E-mail: infouk@bvi.org.uk
Website: www.bvitouristboard.com
Offices also in: Düsseldorf and Milan.
No personal callers.
British Virgin Islands Tourist Board
1270 Broadway, New York, NY 10001, USA
Tel: (212) 696 0400 *or* (800) 835 8530 (toll-free in USA and Canada). Fax: (212) 563 2263.
E-mail: ny@bvitouristboard.com
Website: www.bvitourism.com
Offices in: Atlanta and Los Angeles.
Also deals with enquiries from Canada.
The US Embassy in Bridgetown deals with enquiries related to the British Virgin Islands (see *Barbados* section).

TIMATIC CODES

Health	AMADEUS: **TI-DFT/VU/HE** GALILEO/WORLDSPAN: **TI-DFT/VU/HE** SABRE: **TIDFT/VU/HE**
Visa	AMADEUS: **TI-DFT/VU/VI** GALILEO/WORLDSPAN: **TI-DFT/VU/VI** SABRE: **TIDFT/VU/VI**

To access TIMATIC country information on Health and Visa regulations through the Computer Reservations System (CRS), type in the appropriate command line listed above.

General Information

AREA: 153 sq km (59 sq miles).
POPULATION: 21,000 (2002).
POPULATION DENSITY: 137.3 per sq km.
CAPITAL: Road Town, Tortola. **Population:** 13,568 (1991).
GEOGRAPHY: The 60-plus islands, rocks and cays of the British Virgin Islands, only 16 of which are inhabited, make up the larger part of an archipelago forming the northern extremity of the Leeward Islands in the eastern Caribbean. They are situated approximately 100km (62 miles) east of Puerto Rico, adjoining the US Virgin Islands. The islands are volcanic in origin, with the exception of Anegada, which is formed of coral and limestone and is the lowest lying. The topography is otherwise mountainous, the highest point being Tortola's Sage Mountain, which rises to 550m (1800ft). There are remnants of a primeval rainforest on Tortola.
GOVERNMENT: British Overseas Territory since 1672. **Head of State:** HM Queen Elizabeth II, represented locally by Governor Tom Macan since 2002. **Head of Government:** Chief Minister Orlando Smith since 2003.
LANGUAGE: English.
RELIGION: Mainly Christian, including Methodist (45 per cent), Anglican (21 per cent) and Roman Catholic (6 per cent).
TIME: GMT - 4.
ELECTRICITY: 110/60 volts AC, 60Hz. American two-pin plugs are used.
COMMUNICATIONS: Telephone: IDD is available. Country code: 1 284 49. There are no area codes. Outgoing international code: 00. **Mobile telephone:** GSM 900/1900 operated by *Caribbean Cellular Telephone* (website: www.bvicellular.com). Handsets can be hired. **Fax:** *Cable & Wireless* provides a service. **Internet:** ISPs include *Cable & Wireless* (website: www.candw.vg) and *Caribsurf* (website: www.caribsurf.com). Services are available in some hotels. There are a few Internet cafes. **Post:** Airmail to Europe takes up to a week. **Press:** The *BVI Beacon*, *The BVI StandPoint* and the *Island Sun* are published weekly. The tourist board publishes *The Welcome* every two months.
Radio: BBC World Service (website: www.bbc.co.uk/worldservice) and Voice of America (website: www.voa.gov) can be received. From time to time the frequencies change and the most up-to-date can be found online.

Passport/Visa

	Passport Required?	Visa Required?	Return Ticket Required?
Full British	Yes	No	Yes
Australian	Yes	No	Yes
Canadian	1	No	Yes
USA	1	No	Yes
Other EU	Yes	No	Yes
Japanese	Yes	No	Yes

Note: Regulations and requirements may be subject to change at short notice, and you are advised to contact the appropriate diplomatic or consular authority before finalising travel arrangements. Details of these may be found at the head of this country's entry. Any numbers in the chart refer to the footnotes below.

PASSPORTS: Passport valid for duration of stay required by all except:
1. nationals of Canada and the USA with an original birth certificate and official photo ID.
VISAS: Required by all except the following for stays of up to 30 days:
(a) nationals of countries referred to in the chart above and their overseas territories;
(b) citizens of Commonwealth countries (except nationals of Cameroon, Guyana, Mozambique, Nigeria and Pakistan, who do require visas);
(c) nationals of Andorra, Argentina, Bolivia, Brazil, Chile, Costa Rica, Croatia, East Timor, Ecuador, El Salvador, Guatemala, Honduras, Hong Kong (SAR), Iceland, Korea (Rep), Liechtenstein, Marshall Islands, Mexico, Micronesia (Federated States of), Monaco, Nicaragua, Norway, Panama, Paraguay, Romania, San Marino, Serbia & Montenegro, Switzerland, Tunisia, Turkey, Uruguay, Vatican City and Venezuela.
Types of visa and cost: *Tourist*, *Business*, *Transit*: £28.
Validity: All visitors are initially allowed for a stay of up to 30 days, but extensions to a maximum of six months can be granted by the British Virgin Islands Immigration Department, Road Town, Tortola, British Virgin Islands (tel: 43471).
Application to: UK Passport Agency (see *Contact Addresses* section) or the nearest British Consulate or Embassy.
Application requirements: (a) Valid passport. (b) One application form. (c) Proof of onward or return ticket. (d)

Fee payable in cash.
Working days required: Generally four weeks.
Temporary residence: Work permit and residence permit required. For further details, contact the Immigration authorities in the British Virgin Islands.

Money

Currency: US Dollar (US$) = 100 cents.
Notes are in denominations of US$1000, 500, 100, 50, 20, 10, 5, 2 and 1. Coins are in denominations of 50, 25, 10, 5 and 1 cents.
Credit & debit cards: Major credit cards are accepted in some establishments. Check with your credit or debit card company for details of merchant acceptability and other services which may be available.
Travellers cheques: Accepted in some places, particularly US Dollar cheques. All cheques are liable to a 10c stamp duty.
Currency restrictions: The import of local and foreign currency is unlimited, subject to declaration. The export of local and foreign currency is restricted to the amount declared on import.
Exchange rate indicators: The following figures are included as a guide to the movements of the US Dollar against Sterling:

Date	Feb '04	May '04	Aug '04	Nov '04
£1.00=	1.82	1.79	1.84	1.89

Banking hours: Mon-Fri 0900-1400. Barclays Bank opens until 1500 and Chase Manhattan until 1600.

Duty Free

The following goods can be imported by passengers of 18 years and above without incurring customs duty:
200 cigarettes or 50 cigars or 230g of tobacco; 0.94l of wine or spirits.
Note: (a) Import licences are required for a small number of goods, mostly foodstuffs. (b) Heavy fines and long jail sentences are imposed for the possession, sale or use of narcotics.

Public Holidays

2005: Jan 1 New Year's Day. **Mar 14** Commonwealth Day. **Mar 25-28** Easter. **May 16** Whit Monday. **Jun 11** Sovereign's Birthday. **Jul 1** Territory Day. **Oct 21** St Ursula's Day. **Dec 25-26** Christmas.
2006: Jan 1 New Year's Day. **Mar 13** Commonwealth Day. **Apr 14-17** Easter. **Jun 5** Whit Monday. **Jun 12** Sovereign's Birthday. **Jul 1** Territory Day. **Oct 21** St Ursula's Day. **Dec 25-26** Christmas.

Health

	Special Precautions?	Certificate Required?
Yellow Fever	No	No
Cholera	No	No
Typhoid & Polio	1	N/A
Malaria	No	N/A

Note: Regulations and requirements may be subject to change at short notice, and you are advised to contact your doctor well in advance of your intended date of departure. Any numbers in the chart refer to the footnotes below.

1: A small risk of typhoid exists in some rural areas.
Food & drink: Mains water is normally chlorinated and, whilst relatively safe, may cause mild abdominal upsets whilst your body adjusts. Bottled water is available and is advised for the first few weeks of stay. Milk is pasteurised and dairy products are safe for consumption. Local meat, poultry, seafood, fruit and vegetables are generally considered safe to eat.
Other risks: Outbreaks of *dengue fever* and *dengue haemorrhagic fever* can occur, and *bacillary* and *amoebic dysentery* are common in the Caribbean. *Hepatitis A* has been reported in the northern Caribbean.
Rabies is present, particularly in the mongoose. If you are bitten, seek immediate medical advice. Anyone at high risk should consider vaccination before departure.
Health care: There is only one hospital on the British Virgin Islands, as well as Government Community Clinics. Since medical facilities are limited, certain medical cases may be transferred to hospitals in the US Virgin Islands, Puerto Rico or mainland USA. There is a reciprocal health agreement with the UK. Hospital and other medical treatment for persons aged 70 or over and school-age children is normally free on presentation of proof of UK residence. Other visitors are charged for all services at rates applicable to residents and are advised to take out medical insurance before departure.

Travel - International

AIR: There are no direct flights from the USA, Canada, Europe or South America to the British Virgin Islands' main airport, the Terrence B Lettsome, located on Beef Island. British Virgin Islands are served from the UK via Antigua. *British West Indies Airways, Virgin Atlantic* and *British Airways* fly to Antigua. The islands are also accessible via St Maarten and Miami. Connecting flights from Antigua are available with *Air St Thomas, Air Sunshine, American Airlines/American Eagle, Cape Air, LIAT* and *Windward Island Airways International.*
Approximate flight times: From Beef Island or Virgin Gorda to *London* is 10 hours, including stopover time in Antigua.
International airports: *Beef Island (EIS)* is 14.5km (9 miles) from Road Town on Tortola; the islands are connected via a road bridge. An airport bus departs three times a day to the city (travel time - 20 minutes). Taxis are also available. Airport facilities include light refreshments/bar, restaurant, tourist information and hotel reservations, car hire and left luggage.
Virgin Gorda (VIJ) is 3.5km (2 miles) from Spanish Town on Virgin Gorda. Taxis are available. There is also an unpaved airport on the island of Anegada.
Departure tax: US$10. Children under five years are exempt.
SEA: The British Virgin Islands' main ports are West End, Beef Island and Road Town on Tortola, as well as Spanish Town and the Yacht Harbour on Virgin Gorda. Regular services operate from Road Town, Jost Van Dyke and Virgin Gorda to the US Virgin Islands (St Thomas and St John).
Departure tax: US$5 for all international departures, US$7 for cruise ship passengers.

Travel - Internal

AIR: *Clair Aero Services* operates between Tortola and Anegada (travel time - 15 minutes). *Fly BVI* operates between Tortola and Virgin Gorda, with occasional flights to Anegada.
SEA: Yacht charter is one of the major industries, and bareboats can be hired for all cruises. A permit is required for all charter boat passengers. Local boats can be hired for special tours. The high season is from December to April. For current prices and a full list of boats for charter and hire, contact the British Virgin Islands Tourist Board (see *Contact Addresses* section). **Ferries:** The main routes are from Tortola to Marina Cay, Jost Van Dyke, Peter Island and Virgin Gorda (Bitter End and Spanish Town).
ROAD: There is a good network, although due to steep and narrow mountain roads, plus poor driving standards, conditions may be precarious. Driving is on the left and there is a maximum speed limit of 64kph (40mph) throughout all the islands. **Taxi:** The *BVI Taxi Association* operates a wide selection of vehicles on a range of standard journeys at fixed rates. All drivers are capable tour guides. Taxis can also be hired on an hourly or daily basis. **Car hire:** There are many car hire companies in the British Virgin Islands, including the most well-known companies.
Documentation: A temporary British Virgin Islands licence is required; this will be issued on production of a current foreign licence for a fee of US$10. Otherwise, a temporary driving permit may suffice. Insurance and British Virgin Islands licences are available from car hire companies.
Travel times: The following chart gives approximate travel times (in hours and minutes) from **Beef Island, Tortola** to other major destinations in the British Virgin Islands and the surrounding area:

	Air	Sea
Virgin Gorda	0.05	0.30
Peter Island	-	0.30
Guana Island	-	0.20
Jost van Dyke	-	0.40
St Thomas (USVI)	0.15	0.45
San Juan (PR)	0.45	-

Note: PR = Puerto Rico; USVI = US Virgin Islands.

Accommodation

HOTELS: A wide range of hotel accommodation is available; a full list can be obtained from the British Virgin Islands Tourist Board (see *Contact Addresses* section). There

Credit: © British Virgin Islands Tourist Board

is a 7 per cent hotel accommodation tax added to all hotel bills. For further information, contact the British Virgin Islands Chamber of Commerce and Hotel Association, PO Box 376, Wickham's Cay, Road Town, Tortola (tel: 43514; fax: 46179; e-mail: bbchand.ccha@surfbvi.com; website: www.bvihotels.org).
Grading: Although there is no grading structure, many hotels in the Caribbean offer accommodation according to one of a number of plans. FAP is Full American Plan; room with all meals (including afternoon tea, supper, etc). AP is American Plan; room with three meals. MAP is Modified American Plan; breakfast and dinner included in the price of the room and, in some places, British-style afternoon tea. CP is Continental Plan; room and breakfast only. EP is European Plan; room only.
SELF-CATERING: Villas, houses and cottages can be hired on a weekly or longer basis. Information on properties is available from the Tourist Board.
CAMPING: Only permitted on authorised sites. Details of sites and facilities are available from the Tourist Board. Backpacking is actively discouraged.

Resorts & Excursions

There are over 60 islands, rocks and cays in the British Virgin Islands archipelago but only 16 are inhabited. All of them, apart from Anegada, are volcanic in origin. In general, the atmosphere is quiet and uncommercialised, with miles of beautiful unspoilt beaches and concealed bays offering privacy and peace. The islands are situated in one of the finest sailing areas in the world. The scenery ranges from jagged mountain peaks covered with frangipani to banana and mango groves and palm trees. **Tortola**, a major yachting centre, with a population of approximately 16,000, is the largest island of the group. It is linked by a bridge to **Beef Island**, site of the international airport. **Road Town**, on the south coast of Tortola, is the capital of the British Virgin Islands. It has a colourful market and delightful West Indian-style houses. Other attractions on the island are the **Sage Mountain National Park** and the **J R O'Neal Botanic Gardens**. Many of the best beaches are on the northern part of the island, with names such as **Smugglers' Cove**, **Long Bay** and **Brewer's Bay**. **Cane Garden Bay** is host to a number of bars and nightspots. There is an excellent view of the island and its coast from **Sage Mountain**, 550m (1800ft) above sea level.
Other islands worth visiting are the coral island of **Anegada**, famous for the many shipwrecks in the surrounding waters and a favourite diving area; **Salt Island**, where salt is harvested each year and a bag sent to HM Queen Elizabeth II; **Norman Island**, with caves and a wealth of local sea-shanties and tales of treasure; and **Virgin Gorda**. On this island are found the famous **Baths**, a unique rock formation of dimly lit grottoes and caves. Most of its attractions can be reached only by foot or boat. The smaller islands have strange names that are often the result of an historical connection with smuggling and piracy - for example, **Fallen Jerusalem**, **Necker Island** (owned by Richard Branson), **Great Camanoe**, **Great Dogs** and **Ginger Island**.

Sport & Activities

Diving: The clear waters and unspoilt reefs provide ideal diving conditions, and qualified instructors are widely available. There are over 60 dive sites, many of which are within the *Underwater National Park System*. Night diving can be especially spectacular. Vertical walls, underwater pinnacles, coral reefs, caverns and wrecks, notably the *RMS Rhone*, which sank in 1867 off Salt Island, can all be visited. The marine life includes most Caribbean and Atlantic species of tropical fish and marine invertebrates. Humpback whales, dolphins, turtles and manta rays also make occasional appearances. Certification is necessary for equipment rental and air fills. When diving or **swimming**, it is important not to over-exert, especially if unused to swimming in sea conditions, if unfit, or if having consumed alcohol. There is, however, a Virgin Islands Search & Rescue (VISAR) to respond to emergencies. Coral reefs are very fragile and divers should take great care not to touch the reefs or remove anything, dead or alive, from the ecosystem. For further details on how to protect the marine environment, contact the British Virgin Islands Association of Reef Keepers (tel: 53237; e-mail: info@arkbvi.org; website: www.arkbvi.org).
Sailing: This is extremely popular. There are numerous modern marinas, and the Yacht Club in Road Town, Tortola, organises races and regattas and offers instruction in sailing and navigation. Yacht charter and one-day sailing trips are widely available. Day trips are also being offered on the *Gli Gli*, an authentic replica of a traditional Carib Indian dugout canoe. The highlight of the sail racing season in the British Virgin Islands is the *BVI Spring Regatta*, the largest regatta in the prestigious Caribbean Ocean Racing

Credit: © British Virgin Islands Tourist Board

Triangle (CORT) series. The race and its shore-side activities and entertainment attract large crowds of spectators and party-goers. For entry forms and further information, contact the Royal BVI Yacht Club (tel: 43286; fax: 46117; e-mail: rbviyc@caribsurf.com; website: www.rbviyc.net).
Fishing: Charters can be arranged for offshore fishing trips. Removing fish or other marine life is illegal for non-residents without a recreational fishing permit, obtainable from the Ministry of Natural Resources and Labour (tel: 43701, ext 2147; fax: 4283; e-mail: nrl@gov.vg).
Outdoor pursuits: In spite of the steep terrain, **hiking** is growing in popularity. There is a trail up *Sage Mountain* on Tortola, as well as along *Ridge Road*, with its dramatic views. A route runs up *Gorda Peak* on Virgin Gorda, and a hiking trail has recently been established on Jost Van Dyke. **Horseriding** can be arranged. On Tortola, tours to the *Sage Mountain National Park* and *Cane Garden Bay* begin near Meyers on the Ridge Road. Trips are also available through Virgin Gorda's unusual landscape. **Cycling** and **mountain biking** are possible, with bicycles for hire in most of the islands' resorts.

Social Profile

FOOD & DRINK: There is no shortage of excellent restaurants and inns serving local and international dishes. Most food is imported but local island specialities are often available. These include lobster and fish chowder, snapper, mussel pie, conch stew, shark and other fish delicacies. In addition to the hotels, eateries can be found on Tortola, Virgin Gorda and Jost van Dyke.
All kinds of rum punch and cocktails are served, plus a wide selection of imported beers, wines and spirits. Local spirits include *Pusser's Rum* (originally produced for the Royal Navy's pursers).
NIGHTLIFE: Many hotels have special nights with live music or dancing. There are several bars offering live music and/or DJs on both Virgin Gorda and Tortola. A full moon party takes place on the beach at Apple Bay, Tortola every month. There is one cinema (on Tortola). The British Virgin Islands Tourist Board publishes details of all forthcoming events in its publication, *The Welcome*, which appears every two months.
SHOPPING: Special purchases include carved wooden items, straw-work, jewellery made from conch (pronounced 'konk') shell, seeds and the attractive *batik* material, designed and made locally.
SPECIAL EVENTS: For a full list of special events contact the Tourist Board (see *Contact Addresses* section). The following is a selection of special events occurring in the British Virgin Islands in 2005:
Mar 26-28 *Virgin Gorda Easter Festival.* **Mar 28-Apr 3** *BVI Spring Regatta & Sailing Festival.* **May 27-30** *Music Festival/Whit Weekend Festival.* **Jul 3-10** *Highland Springs HIHO 2005 - Surffestival.* **Jul 4** *Fisherman's Day.* **Jul 22-Aug 1** *Emancipation Celebrations.* **Sep 3-4** *Jost Van Dyke Festival.*
SOCIAL CONVENTIONS: The British Virgin Islands remain linked to the British Commonwealth, and the islanders reflect many British traditions and customs. The development of tourism proceeds with great caution; hence the unspoilt charm of these islands and cays remains the chief attraction. The pace of life is very easygoing and visitors can expect old-fashioned British courtesies. Shaking hands is the customary form of greeting. Dress is informal for most occasions apart from the formal requirements of some hotels. Beachwear should be confined to the beach or poolside. **Tipping:** All hotels add a 10 to 12 per cent service charge.

Business Profile

ECONOMY: Tourism and financial services are the islands' main economic activities. Agricultural production is limited by poor soils, and relies mainly on livestock rearing, but some fruit and vegetables are produced for export, along with fish, livestock, gravel and sand. Rum is an important export commodity, and its distilling is the principal industrial activity. There is also a small mining industry, producing salt and materials for the construction industry. Tourism employs one-third of the working population directly or indirectly. The hotel and restaurant sector is particularly strong, with many customers arriving on day-trips as well as extended stays. The majority of visitors come from the USA - 350,000 annually - but the Government is looking to attract custom from elsewhere, as well as trying to dampen the islands' reputation as a resort for the wealthy.
The offshore financial sector, which has been operating since the mid-1980s, has been a spectacular success, by virtue of the British connection, benign legislation and political uncertainty in rival centres (notably Hong Kong and Panama). However, in the last three years, the Government has been forced to respond to international pressure to tighten its regulatory regime in order to prevent money-laundering. The British Virgin Islands' main trading partners are the US Virgin Islands, the USA and Puerto Rico.
BUSINESS: A shirt and tie are required for the summer months, with lightweight suits being acceptable at all other times. Best time to visit is December to April. **Office hours:** Mon-Fri 0900-1700. **Government office hours:** Mon-Fri 0830-1630.
COMMERCIAL INFORMATION: The following organisations can offer advice: Development Bank of the Virgin Islands, PO Box 275, 1 Wickham's Cay, Road Town, Tortola (tel: 43737; fax: 43119; e-mail: devbankbvi@surfbvi.com); *or* the Chamber of Commerce and Hotel Association (see *Accommodation* section).
CONFERENCES/CONVENTIONS: The British Virgin Islands Tourist Board can offer advice (see *Contact Addresses* section).

Climate

The climate is subtropical and tempered by trade winds. There is little variation between summer and winter. Rainfall is low, varying slightly from island to island. Night-time temperatures drop to a comfortable level. Visitors should note that the British Virgin Islands are susceptible to hurricanes and earthquakes, although these are by no means a frequent occurrence. The primary hurricane season is from June to November.
Required clothing: Tropical lightweights. Dress is generally informal but beachwear is confined to beaches.

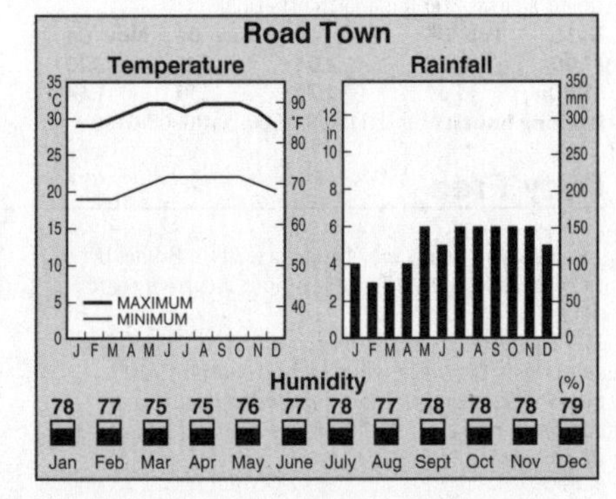

Brunei

LATEST TRAVEL ADVICE CONTACTS

British Foreign and Commonwealth Office
Tel: (0870) 606 0290 Website: www.fco.gov.uk
US Department of State
Website: http://travel.state.gov/travel
Canadian Department of Foreign Affairs and Int'l Trade
Tel: (1 800) 267 8376 Website: www.dfait-maeci.gc.ca

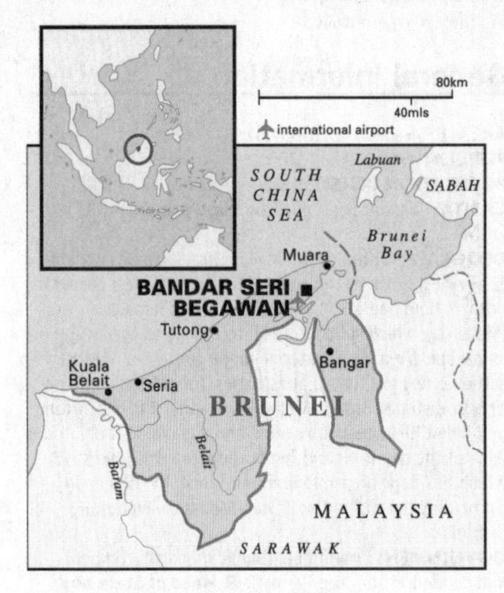

Location: South-East Asia, island of Borneo.

Country dialling code: 673.

Brunei Tourism
Jalan Menteri Besar, Bandar Seri Begawan BB3910, Brunei Darussalam
Tel: (2) 382 825 *or* 830 *or* 831. Fax: (2) 382 824.
E-mail: info@tourismbrunei.com
Website: www.tourismbrunei.com
High Commission of Brunei Darussalam
19-20 Belgrave Square, London SW1X 8PG, UK
Tel: (020) 7581 0521 (ext 111/137 for consular section).
Fax: (020) 7235 9717 *or* 7590 7822 (consular section).
E-mail: bhcl@brunei-high-commission.co.uk
Opening hours: Mon-Fri 0930-1300 and 1400-1630.
Also provides tourist information.
British High Commission
Street address: Unit 2.01, 2nd Floor, Block D, Kompleks Yayasan Sultan, Haji Hassanal Bolkiah, Jalan Pretty, Bandar Seri Begawan BS8711, Brunei Darussalam
Postal address: PO Box 2197, Bandar Seri Begawan BS8674, Brunei Darussalam
Tel: (2) 222 231 *or* 223 121 *or* 226 001 (consular/management section). Fax: (2) 234 315.
E-mail: brithc@brunet.bn
Website: www.britishhighcommission.gov.uk/brunei
Embassy of Brunei Darussalam
3520 International Court, NW, Washington, DC 20008, USA
Tel: (202) 237 1838. Fax: (202) 885 0560.
E-mail: info@bruneiembassy.org
Website: www.bruneiembassy.org
Permanent Mission of Brunei Darussalam to the United Nations
771 First Avenue, UN Plaza, New York City, NY 10017, USA
Tel: (212) 697 3465 or 3828. Fax: (212) 697 9889 *or* 3828.
E-mail: info@bruneimission-ny.org *or* brunei@un.int
Website: www.brunei.gov.bn
Embassy of the United States of America
Street address: 3rd Floor, Teck Guan Plaza, Jalan Sultan, Bandar Seri Begawan BS8811, Brunei Darussalam
Postal address: PO Box 2991, Badar Seri Begawan BS8675, Brunei Darussalam
Tel: (2) 220 384. Fax: (2) 225 293.
E-mail: amembassybrunei@state.gov *or* consularbrunei@state.gov
Website: http://bandar.usembassy.gov/

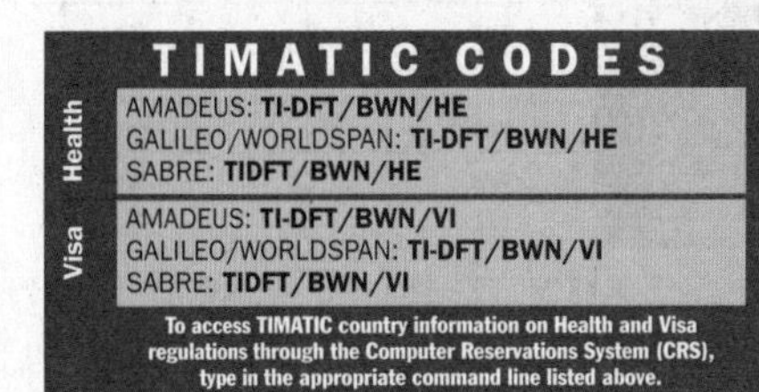
TIMATIC CODES

Health
AMADEUS: **TI-DFT/BWN/HE**
GALILEO/WORLDSPAN: **TI-DFT/BWN/HE**
SABRE: **TIDFT/BWN/HE**

Visa
AMADEUS: **TI-DFT/BWN/VI**
GALILEO/WORLDSPAN: **TI-DFT/BWN/VI**
SABRE: **TIDFT/BWN/VI**

To access TIMATIC country information on Health and Visa regulations through the Computer Reservations System (CRS), type in the appropriate command line listed above.

High Commission of Brunei Darussalam
395 Laurier Avenue East, Ottawa, Ontario K1N 6R4, Canada
Tel: (613) 234 5656. Fax: (613) 234 4397.
E-mail: bhco@bellnet.ca
Website: www.pmo.gov.bn
Canadian High Commission
Street address: 5th Floor, Jalan McArthur Building, 1 Jalan McArthur, Bandar Seri Begawan, BS8675 Brunei Darussalam
Postal address: PO Box 2808, Bandar Seri Begawan BS8711, Brunei Darussalam
Tel: (2) 220 043. Fax: (2) 220 040.
E-mail: hicomcda@brunet.bn *or* bsbgn@international.gc.ca
Website: www.brunei.gc.ca

General Information

AREA: 5765 sq km (2226 sq miles).
POPULATION: 332,844 (2001).
POPULATION DENSITY: 57.7 per sq km.
CAPITAL: Bandar Seri Begawan. **Population:** 27,285 (2001).
GEOGRAPHY: Brunei is a small coastal state just 443km (277 miles) north of the equator in the northwest corner of Borneo, bordered on all landward sides by Sarawak (Malaysia), which splits Brunei into two parts. The landscape is mainly equatorial jungle cut by rivers. Most settlements are situated at estuaries. The state is made up of four districts: Brunei-Muara (the capital district), Tutong and Belait (Brunei's centre of oil and gas exploitation, in the west of the country); and Temburong, the eastern district, which has large areas of virgin rainforest. The islands in Brunei Bay fall within the Brunei-Muara or Temburong districts.
GOVERNMENT: Traditional Islamic monarchy. Gained independence from the UK in 1959. **Head of State and Government:** Sultan Haji Hassan al Bolkiah Muizaddin Waddaulah since 1967.
LANGUAGE: Malay is the official language. English is widely used and Chinese dialects are also spoken.
RELIGION: Most of the Malay population are Sunni Muslims. There are also significant Buddhist, Confucianist, Daoist and Christian minorities. Large numbers of the indigenous groups practise traditional animist forms of religion.
TIME: GMT + 8.
ELECTRICITY: 220/240 volts AC, 50Hz. Plugs are either round or square three-pin.
COMMUNICATIONS: Telephone: Full IDD is available. Country code: 673. Outgoing international code: 00. Public telephones are available in most post office branches and main shopping areas and there is a private internal service. There are both coin and card operated public telephones in Brunei. Telephone cards can be obtained at post offices or at the Telecom office. **Mobile telephone:** GSM 900 network. *DST Communications Sdn Bhd* (website: www.dst-group.com) operates. There is good coverage around main cities and business areas, particularly in the northwest. **Internet:** ISPs include *BruNet* (website: www.brunet.bn). A wireless network supporting ISDN lines is being launched, initially in the Rimba-Gadong area. **Telegram:** Facilities are available from the government telecommunications office in Bandar Seri Begawan. **Post:** Airmail letters to Europe take two to five days. Registered, recorded and express postal services ('Speedpost') are all available. Post office opening hours: Mon-Thurs 0745-1630. **Press:** The only independent English-language newspaper is the daily *Borneo Bulletin*. The Government publishes a *Daily News Digest* and a fortnightly *Brunei Darussalam Newsletter*, both in English.
Radio: BBC World Service (website: www.bbc.co.uk/worldservice) and Voice of America (website: www.voa.gov) can be received. From time to time the frequencies change and the most up-to-date can be found online.

Passport/Visa

	Passport Required?	Visa Required?	Return Ticket Required?
Full British	Yes	1	Yes
Australian	Yes	2	Yes
Canadian	Yes	3	Yes
USA	Yes	4	Yes
Other EU	Yes	1	Yes
Japanese	Yes	3	Yes

Note: *Regulations and requirements may be subject to change at short notice, and you are advised to contact the appropriate diplomatic or consular authority before finalising travel arrangements. Details of these may be found at the head of this country's entry. Any numbers in the chart refer to the footnotes below.*

Restricted entry: Nationals of Israel may not be granted entry to Brunei.
PASSPORTS: Passport valid for at least six months from date of departure required by all. Travellers must be entitled to return to home country.
VISAS: Required by all except the following:
(a) **1.** nationals of the United Kingdom holding full British passports, and nationals of Germany for up to 30 days. Nationals of Belgium, Denmark, France, Italy, Luxembourg, The Netherlands, Spain and Sweden for up to 14 days (nationals of other EU countries *do* require a visa);
(b) **2.** nationals of Australia are advised to obtain visas before arrival although it may be possible to obtain one at Brunei International Airport for a stay of maximum 14 days (a visa is required for longer stays);
(c) **3.** nationals of Canada, Indonesia, Japan, Korea (Rep), Liechtenstein, Maldives, Norway, Oman, The Philippines, Switzerland and Thailand for up to 14 days;
(d) **4.** nationals of the USA for up to 90 days;
(e) nationals of Malaysia, New Zealand and Singapore for touristic stays of up to 30 days.
Note: A return ticket is necessary for visa-free trips. All visitors must possess sufficient funds to support themselves whilst in the country and a yellow fever vaccination certificate is required from travellers aged one year and over who have visited infected or endemic areas within the previous six days.
Types of visa and cost: *Short Visit:* £5.70 (single-entry); £11.40 (multiple-entry). Cost changes frequently and depends on prevailing exchange rate.
Validity: Single-entry: three months. The validity of multiple-entry visas is at the discretion of the Consulate.
Application to: Consulate (or Consular section at Embassy or High Commission); see *Contact Addresses* section.
Application requirements: (a) Passport valid for six months from date of departure with at least four blank pages. (b) One passport-size photo. (c) Application form. (d) Fee, payable by cash, bank draft or postal order. (e) A letter from employer stating purpose of visit if on business. (f) Copy of onward or return ticket. (g) Stamped, self-addressed envelope for postal applications. (h) Confirmed onward or return tickets (copies of flight itinerary or travel agent's booking confirmation).
Working days required: Three. Applications which need to be referred to Brunei can take up to two months for processing.

Money

Currency: Brunei Dollar (Br$) = 100 cents. Notes are in the denominations Br$10,000, 1000, 500, 100, 50, 25, 10, 5 and 1. Coins are in the denominations 50, 20, 10, 5 and 1 cents. The Brunei Dollar is officially on a par with the Singapore Dollar.
Currency exchange: Foreign currencies and travellers cheques can be exchanged at any bank.
Credit & debit cards: American Express, Diners Club, MasterCard and Visa are generally accepted by hotels, department stores and major establishments. Check with your credit or debit card company for details of merchant acceptability and other services that may be available.
Travellers cheques: To avoid additional exchange rate charges, travellers are advised to take travellers cheques in US Dollars or Pounds Sterling. Hotels and many department stores will also cash travellers cheques.
Currency restrictions: The import of local currency is unlimited. The export of local currency is limited to Br$1000 in notes. The Singapore Dollar may be imported and exported up to the equivalent of Br$1000. Indian banknotes may not be imported. Free import of other foreign currencies, subject to declaration. Export of foreign currencies for foreigners is unlimited up to amount imported and declared.
Exchange rate indicators: The following figures are included as a guide to the movements of the Brunei Dollar against Sterling and the US Dollar:

Date	Feb '04	May '04	Aug '04	Nov '04
£1.00=	3.08	3.04	3.15	3.10
$1.00=	1.69	1.70	1.71	1.64

Banking hours: Mon-Fri 0900-1500; Sat 0900-1100.

Duty Free

The following goods may be imported into Brunei by travellers aged over 17 years without incurring customs duty:
200 cigarettes or 225g tobacco products; 1l bottle of spirits or 1l bottle of wine (by non-Muslims for personal consumption only, provided declared at customs upon arrival); 1.1l of perfume and 0.8l of eau de toilette.

Public Holidays

2005: Jan 1 New Year's Day. **Jan 21** Hari Raya Haji (Feast of the Sacrifice). **Feb 9** Chinese New Year. **Feb 10** Hijriah (Islamic New Year). **Feb 23** National Day. **Apr 21** Maulud (Birth of the Prophet). **May 31** Anniversary of Royal Brunei Malay Regiment. **Jul 15** Sultan's Birthday. **Sep 1** Israk Mikraj (Ascension of the Prophet). **Oct 3** Start of Ramadan. **Nov 3-5** Hari Raya Aidilfitri (End of Ramadan). **Dec 25** Christmas.
2006: Jan 1 New Year's Day. **Jan 10** Chinese New Year. **Jan 29** Hari Raya Haji (Feast of the Sacrifice). **Jan 31** Hijriah (Islamic New Year). **Feb 23** National Day. **Apr 11** Maulud (Birth of the Prophet). **May 31** Anniversary of Royal Brunei Malay Regiment. **Jul 15** Sultan's Birthday. **Aug 22** Israk Mikraj (Ascension of the Prophet). **Sep 24** Start of Ramadan. **Oct 22-24** Hari Raya Aidilfitri (End of Ramadan). **Dec 25** Christmas.
Note: Muslim festivals are timed according to local sightings of various phases of the moon and the dates given above are approximations. During the lunar month of Ramadan that precedes Hari Raya Puasa, Muslims fast during the day and feast at night and normal business patterns may be interrupted. Restaurants are closed during the day and Muslims are prohibited from smoking and drinking. Some disruption may continue into Hari Raya Puasa itself. Hari Raya Puasa and Hari Raya Haji may last anything from two to 10 days.

Health

	Special Precautions?	Certificate Required?
Yellow Fever	No	1
Cholera	Yes	2
Typhoid & Polio	3	N/A
Malaria	4	N/A

Note: *Regulations and requirements may be subject to change at short notice, and you are advised to contact your doctor well in advance of your intended date of departure. Any numbers in the chart refer to the footnotes below.*

1: A yellow fever vaccination certificate is required from travellers aged one year and over who have visited infected or endemic areas within the previous six days.
2: Following WHO guidelines issued in 1973, a cholera vaccination certificate is no longer a condition of entry to Brunei. However, precautions are still advisable. Up-to-date information should be sought before deciding whether these precautions should include vaccination as medical opinion is divided over its effectiveness; see the *Health* appendix.
3: Typhoid fever occurs.
4: There is a slight risk of malaria in border areas. No prophylaxis is recommended.
Food & drink: All water should be regarded as being potentially contaminated. Water used for drinking, brushing teeth or making ice should have first been boiled or sterilised. Milk is unpasteurised and should be boiled. Powdered or tinned milk is available and advised, but should be reconstituted with pure water. Avoid all dairy products. Only eat well-cooked meat and fish, preferably served hot. Pork, salad and mayonnaise may carry increased risk. Vegetables should be cooked and fruit peeled.
Other risks: *Amoebic* and *bacillary dysentery* and *hepatitis A* and *E* may occur. *Hepatitis B* is highly endemic in the region. *Dengue fever* and *Japanese encephalitis* occur occasionally. Epidemics of *Avian influenza* (bird flu) were reported in early 2004 in flocks of poultry in parts of Asia, and human cases were confirmed. Visitors to Asia should be mindful of prolonged exposure or the consumption of poultry that has not been cooked to a high internal temperature. In recent months, Asia has seen a resurgence in such cases .
Health care: Medical insurance is advised. Medical facilities are of a high standard. The health administration of Brunei reserves the right to vaccinate arrivals not in possession of required certificates and to take any other action deemed necessary to ensure arrivals present no health risk.

Travel - International

Note: All involvement with drugs of any kind must be avoided: possession of even very small quantities can lead to imprisonment or the death penalty.
AIR: Brunei's national airline is *Royal Brunei Airlines (BI)*; it flies to Bali, Bangkok, Beijing, Brisbane (four times a week), Calcutta, Darwin (twice weekly), Dubai, Frankfurt/M, Hong Kong, Jakarta, Jeddah, Kota Kinabalu, Kuala Lumpur (daily), Kuching, London (daily), Manila, Perth (three times a week), Singapore, Surabaya and Taipei. Air carriers to Brunei include: *Garuda Indonesia, Lufthansa, Malaysia Airlines, Singapore Airlines, Philippines Airlines* and *Thai*

Airways International.
Approximate flight times: From Brunei to *London* is 17 hours, to *Los Angeles* is 18 hours 30 minutes including stopover in Hong Kong, to *New York* is 23 hours 20 minutes including stopover in Hong Kong, to *Singapore* is two hours and to *Sydney* is 12 hours 40 minutes including stopover in Perth.
International airports: *Bandar Seri Begawan (BWN)* is 11km (7 miles) south of the city. Airport facilities include a bank, bureaux de change, car hire (*Avis*, *Hertz* and *National Car Systems*), duty-free shops, post office, restaurants and shops. Taxi services are available to the city with surcharges after 2200. Lower rates are charged by taxis leaving from the airport car park.
Departure tax: Br$5 for flights to Indonesia, Malaysia, The Philippines or Singapore; Br$12 (just over £4) for all other destinations. This is payable in local currency in cash, at the airport check-in desk.
SEA: Ports at Muara and Kuala Belait are the entry points for sea cargo. There are passenger services between Singapore and Muara port. Ships and water taxis run a service between Bandar Seri Begawan and the Malay city of Labuan (Sabah).
ROAD: There are access roads into Brunei from Sarawak at various locations, although some are unpaved.

Travel - Internal

Note: It is easy to get lost in the Rainforest and visitors are advised to use well-known and recognised guides, and to also stay on the designated footpaths.
AIR: There are no internal air services.
SEA/RIVER: There are water taxi services to Kampong Ayer, with stations at Jalan Kianggeh and Jalan McArthur. Water taxis are the most common form of transport in Kampong Ayer, Brunei's renowned water village. Fares are negotiable. Regular water taxi and boat services also ply between Bandar Seri Begawan and Bangar (in Temburong), Limbang (in Sarawak), Labuan and some towns in the Malaysian state of Sabah.
ROAD: There are approximately 1800km (1080 miles) of roads in the country; the best-developed road network is in the Brunei-Muara district, including a coastal highway which runs from Muara to Jerudong and then on to Tutong. Traffic drives on the left. **Bus:** Services operate to Seria (91km; 57 miles) from Bandar Seri Begawan), Kuala Belait (16km; 10 miles) from Seria), Tutong (48km; 30 miles) from Bandar Seri Begawan) and Muara (27km; 17 miles) from Bandar Seri Begawan). There is a bus station in the town centre and the city bus system is well maintained and inexpensive. There are six bus routes in Bandar Seri Begawan, operating from 0630 until 1800. **Car hire:** Self-drive or chauffeur-driven cars are available at the airport and major hotels. It is important to specify whether an air-conditioned car is required. **Documentation:** An International Driving Permit is required to hire a car. A temporary licence to drive in Brunei is available on presentation of a valid driving licence from the visitor's country of origin.
URBAN: **Taxis** are available in Bandar Seri Begawan, in the multi-storey car park at Jalan Central. There are also airport taxis and taxis in most hotels and shopping centres. Fares are usually metered; if not, they should be agreed before the journey. There is a 50 per cent surcharge after 2300. Tipping is not necessary.

Accommodation

Accommodation outside the main towns is not readily available. Hotel accommodation in Bandar Seri Begawan ranges from those of international standard to budget accommodation. Visitors should, however, note that budget accommodation is in scarce quantity and mid-range accommodation may be a better option. Service apartments combining home comforts with hotel luxury are also growing in popularity. Contact the High Commission of Brunei Darussalam (Consular and Tourist Information Section) for further information (see *Contact Addresses* section).

Resorts & Excursions

There are beaches with facilities at Kuala Belait, Lumut Beach near Tutong and at Muara. Brunei is a heavily forested state, and most activity is either on the coast or at the estuaries.
BANDAR SERI BEGAWAN: The principal tourist sights in the capital are: the minaret crowning the golden-domed **Sultan Omar Ali Saifuddien Mosque**, which stands in the middle of its own artificial lagoon, affording a fine view over the town and stilt village; the **Churchill Memorial**, incorporating the **Churchill Museum and Aquarium**; the ancient **Tomb of Sultan Bolkiah**, the fifth sultan, known as the 'singing admiral' for his love of both music and conquest; the **Brunei Museum**; and the **Malay Technology Museum** showing traditional crafts.
Kampong Ayer is the water village on the outskirts of the capital, reputed to be the largest collection of stilt habitations in the world; visitors can walk freely around the wooden walkways between the houses, which combine traditional architecture with modern facilities such as Internet connections.
EXCURSIONS: Outside the capital within the Brunei-Muara district, **Jerudong Theme Park**, best reached by road, offers free modern amusements and rides next to a beach. Other beaches can be found at **Muara** and **Serasa**, where watersports are popular. Local travel agents offer half-day boat tours to **Pulau Selirong**, a mangrove island 45 minutes from Muara by boat, where wildlife includes proboscis monkeys, macaques, kingfishers and eagles. Other islands in Brunei Bay offer beaches and watersports.
ELSEWHERE: Tasek Merimbun, Brunei's largest lake, is in a hill resort in the Tutong District just over an hour's drive from Bandar Seri Begawan; it offers peaceful picnicking, birdwatching facilities and jungle trails. Many unspoiled jungle areas in other districts are accessible only by boat. There are splendid traditional longhouses in the Temburong district, which contains large tracts of virgin rainforest. Travel agents offer day or overnight tours to the **Ulu Temburong National Park** with forest canopy trails on wooden walkways; trips can include rafting and swimming. In the Belait district near **Kampong Labi**, there are more traditional longhouses including **Rampayoh**. River safaris up the **Belait River** offer opportunities to visit remote forest communities, longhouses, hot springs and waterfalls. Recreational parks in the Belait district include **Luagan Lalak**, where there is a picnic area and a wooden walkway across the lake. The **Billionth Barrel Monument** near **Kuala Belait** is a testament to the continuing importance of oil to Brunei's economy.

Sport & Activities

Watersports: Swimming, **sailing**, **jet skiing**, **skindiving** and **fishing** are popular, especially around Brunei Bay and its islands. **Scuba-diving** training and certification, and sailing schools, **water-skiing** and **wake boarding** courses are available. Most hotels will have details of activities on offer.
Other: The *Mentiri Golf Club* has an international standard, 18-hole, par 72 **golf** course. There are facilities for watching or participating in **tennis**, **polo**, **football** and **hockey**. The *Hassanal Bolkiah National Stadium* is Olympic-sized and includes a track and field complex for **running**, amongst other features.

Social Profile

FOOD & DRINK: European food is served in hotel restaurants, along with Malaysian, Chinese and Indian dishes. Local food is similar to Malay cuisine with fresh fish and rice, often quite spicy. Alcohol is prohibited, although alcohol may be imported in certain quantities if reported to Customs.
SHOPPING: Special purchases include handworked silverware, brassware and bronzeware such as jugs, trays, gongs, boxes, napkin rings, spoons and bracelets; and fine handwoven sarongs, baskets and mats of pandan leaves. Shopping centres at Bandar Seri Begawan, Seria and Kuala Belait offer local products and imported items. The 'Tamu' Night Market in Bandar Seri Begawan is open from early morning to late at night and sells many fruits, spices, poultry and vegetables, as well as antiques. Food is available there at the lowest prices in town. **Shopping hours:** Mon-Sat 0800-2100.
SPECIAL EVENTS: Most festivals are religious celebrations or mark the anniversaries of important historical events. For a complete list of special events, contact Brunei Tourism (see *Contact Addresses* section). The following is a selection of special events celebrated annually in Brunei:
Jan 28-30 *Chinese New Year*. **Feb 23** *National Day Celebrations*. **Oct 22-24** *Hari Raya Haji* (End of Ramadan).
SOCIAL CONVENTIONS: Shoes should be removed when entering Muslim homes and institutions and visitors should not pass in front of a person at prayer or touch the Koran, the Muslim holy book. Traditionally, a Bruneian shakes hands lightly, bringing his hands to his chest. However, any physical contact between members of opposite sexes is avoided. Non-Muslims should not be found in the company of a Muslim member of the opposite sex in private: sexual contact, or even compromising behaviour, between non-Muslims and Muslims is punishable by deportation. There are many honorific titles in Brunei: *Awang* (abbreviated to Awg), for instance, is equivalent to 'Ms' or 'Mrs'. *Adat* (customary law) governs many occasions and ceremonies. Food may be served without cutlery: eat using the right hand only. Avoid giving or receiving with the left hand or pointing the soles of one's feet towards companions. Gifts (particularly food) should only be passed with the right hand, although it is acceptable to use the left hand under the right wrist for support. It is also considered impolite to point with the index finger (the right thumb should be used instead) or to beckon someone with your fingers (the whole hand should be waved instead, with the palm facing downwards). The right fist should never be smacked into the left palm, and children (or adults) should not be patted on the head. It is widely regarded as discourteous to refuse refreshment when it is offered by a host, or to eat or drink in public places, especially during Ramadan when Muslims are fasting. Visitors should note that there are severe penalties for all drug offences, and that the legal system in Brunei is partly based on Shariah law and can, occasionally, apply to non-Muslims, including visitors. Dress is informal except for special occasions. Women should ensure that their head, knees and arms are covered. **Tipping:** Most hotels and restaurants add 10 per cent to the bill.

Business Profile

ECONOMY: Brunei's economy depends on its oil and natural gas deposits, which are mostly offshore, and its investments. Although these are not extensive by world standards, Brunei's small population enjoys a very high standard of living. The government has made recent efforts to diversify the economy, mainly by providing tax concessions on foreign investment; timber, paper, fertilisers, petrochemicals and glass are the most promising candidates for development in the growing industrial sector. However, these have been fairly limited to date. Some 15 per cent of the land is under cultivation, with rice, cassava and fruit as the main crops. Japan, which takes half of the oil produced by Brunei, is the country's largest single trading partner, followed by Korea, Singapore, Thailand and Australia. Brunei belongs to the Association of South East Asian Nations (ASEAN) and subscribes to its major projects, including the plan to establish a free-trade zone among member states in around 2010/2015. In 1995, Brunei joined the IMF and World Bank, making available technical and consultative advice from those institutions (it hardly needs their financial support). The Asian financial crisis in 1997 had little effect on Brunei, because of the country's lack of indebtedness. However, it has since become apparent that a substantial proportion of the country's financial resources, which are under the exclusive control of the royal family, have been dissipated through individual profligacy.
BUSINESS: Suits are recommended. Business visits are best made outside the monsoon season (between November and December). The services of a translator will not normally be required as English is widely spoken. **Office hours:** Mon-Thurs 0745-1215 and 1330-1630, Sat 0900-1200. **Government office hours:** Mon-Thurs and Sat 0745-1215 and 1330-1630.
COMMERCIAL INFORMATION: The following organisations can offer advice: Brunei Darussalam International Chamber of Commerce and Industry, PO Box 2285, Bandar Seri Begawan (tel: (2) 236 601); *or* National Chamber of Commerce and Industry of Brunei Darussalam, PO Box 115, Bandar Seri Begawan, BS8670 (tel: (2) 227 297-8; fax: (2) 221 565).

Climate

Very hot, humid tropical climate most of the year. Heavy rainfall in the monsoon season, November to December. Average temperature is 28°C (82°F).
Required clothing: Lightweight cottons and linens. Waterproofing is advisable all year.

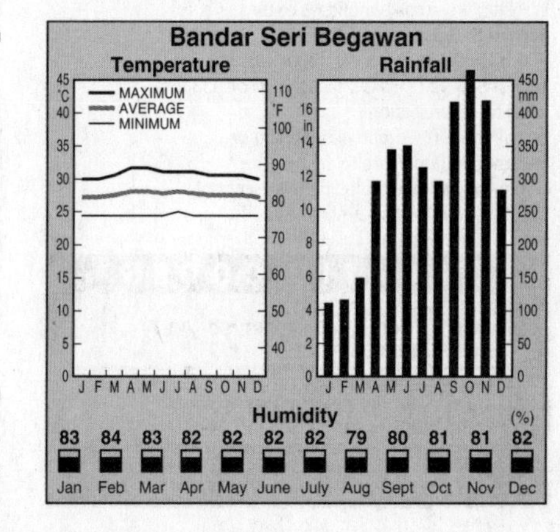

Bulgaria

LATEST TRAVEL ADVICE CONTACTS

British Foreign and Commonwealth Office
Tel: (0870) 606 0290 Website: www.fco.gov.uk
US Department of State
Website: http://travel.state.gov/travel
Canadian Department of Foreign Affairs and Int'l Trade
Tel: (1 800) 267 8376 Website: www.dfait-maeci.gc.ca

Location: Eastern Europe.

Country dialling code: 359.

National Tourist Information Centre
1 Sveta Nedelia Square, Sofia 1000, Bulgaria
Tel: (2) 987 9778.
Fax: (2) 989 6939.
E-mail: webmaster@bulgariatravel.org
Website: www.bulgariatravel.org
Embassy of the Republic of Bulgaria
186-188 Queen's Gate, London SW7 5HL, UK
Tel: (020) 7584 9400 *or* 9433 *or* 7581 4903 (tourism department).
Fax: (020) 7584 4948 *or* 7589 4875 (commercial department).
E-mail: info@bulgarianembassy.org.uk
Website: www.bulgarianembassy.org.uk
Opening hours: Mon-Fri 0900-1800 (general enquiries).
Visa section: Tel: (09065) 540 819 (recorded information; calls cost £1 per minute) *or* (020) 7584 9433 (individual enquiries; from Mon-Fri 1230-1330 only).
Fax: (09065) 540 819 (application service; calls cost £1 per minute).
E-mail: consul@bulgarianembassy.org.uk
Opening hours: 0930-1150 (visa applications; closed Wednesday and weekends).
Also provides tourist information.
Balkan Holidays
Sofia House, 19 Conduit Street, London W1S 2BH, UK
Tel: (0845) 130 1114 *or* (020) 7543 5555. Fax: (020) 7543 5577.
E-mail: res@balkanholidays.co.uk
Website: www.balkanholidays.co.uk
British Embassy
9 Moskovska Street, Sofia 1000, Bulgaria
Tel: (2) 933 9222. Fax: (2) 933 9250 *or* 933 9263 (visa/consular section).
E-mail: britembinf@mail.orbitel.bg *or* britembcon@mail.orbitel.bg *or* britembvisa@mail.orbitel.bg (visa section).
Website: www.british-embassy.bg

TIMATIC CODES

Health	AMADEUS: **TI-DFT/SOF/HE** GALILEO/WORLDSPAN: **TI-DFT/SOF/HE** SABRE: **TIDFT/SOF/HE**
Visa	AMADEUS: **TI-DFT/SOF/VI** GALILEO/WORLDSPAN: **TI-DFT/SOF/VI** SABRE: **TIDFT/SOF/VI**

To access TIMATIC country information on Health and Visa regulations through the Computer Reservations System (CRS), type in the appropriate command line listed above.

Embassy of the Republic of Bulgaria
1621 22nd Street, NW, Washington, DC 20008, USA
Tel: (202) 387 0174 *or* 7969 (consular office).
Fax: (202) 234 7973.
E-mail: office@bulgaria-embassy.org *or* consulate@bulgaria-embassy.org (visas).
Website: www.bulgaria-embassy.org
Embassy of the United States of America
16 Kozyak Street, Sofia 1407, Bulgaria
Tel: (2) 937 5100. Fax: (2) 937 5320.
E-mail: irc@usembassy.bg
Website: www.usembassy.bg
Embassy of the Republic of Bulgaria
325 Stewart Street, Ottawa, Ontario K1N 6K5, Canada
Tel: (613) 789 3215. Fax: (613) 789 3524.
E-mail: mailmn@storm.ca
Website: www.bulway.ca
The Consulate of Canada
9 Moskovska Street, Sofia 1000, Bulgaria
Tel: (2) 969 9710. Fax: (2) 981 6081.
E-mail: general@canada-bg.org *or* consular@canada-bg.org

General Information

AREA: 110,994 sq km (42,855 sq miles).
POPULATION: 7,845,499 (official estimate 2002).
POPULATION DENSITY: 70.7 per sq km (2002).
CAPITAL: Sofia. **Population:** 1,096,389 (2001).
GEOGRAPHY: Bulgaria is situated in Eastern Europe and bordered to the north by the River Danube and Romania, to the east by the Black Sea, to the south by Turkey and Greece and to the west by Serbia and the Former Yugoslav Republic of Macedonia. The Balkan Mountains cross the country reaching to the edge of the Black Sea and its golden beaches. The land is heavily cultivated, covered with forests and crossed by rivers. Although Bulgaria lies in the very southeast corner of Europe, the climate is never extreme in summer, even on the red-earthed plains of Southern Thrace. The Black Sea resorts have some of the largest beaches in Europe and offer sunbathing from May until October, while in winter heavy falls of snow are virtually guaranteed in the mountain skiing resorts.
GOVERNMENT: Democratic Republic since 1990. **Head of State:** President Georgi Sedefchov Parvanov since 2002. **Head of Government:** Prime Minister Simeon Borisov Sakskoburggotski since 2001.
LANGUAGE: Bulgarian is the official language and the Cyrillic alphabet is used. Turkish and Macedonian are amongst the minority languages. English, German, French and Russian are spoken in major tourist resorts and hotels.
RELIGION: The majority of the population are Christian, the main denomination being Bulgarian Orthodox Church with a membership of 80 per cent of the population. Eastern Orthodox Chrisitianity is considered to be the traditional religion in Bulgaria. There is also a significant Muslim minority (9 per cent) and a small Jewish community.
TIME: GMT + 2 (GMT + 3 from last Sunday in March to Saturday before last Sunday in October).
ELECTRICITY: 230 volts AC, 50Hz. Plugs are two-pin.
COMMUNICATIONS: Telephone: Telephone: IDD is available to main cities. Country code: 359. Outgoing international code: 00. Calls from some parts of the country must be placed through the international operator. There are many public telephones in the main towns. The national network of telecommunications is operated, for the present, by Bulgarian Telecommunications Company (BTC) (website: www.btc.bg). **Mobile telephone:** GSM 900/1800, with good to patchy coverage in most urban centres. Network operators include *MobilTEL* (website: www.mobiltel.bg) and *GloBul* (website: www.globul.bg). **Fax:** Facilities are available at *BTA* (Bulgarina Telegraph Agency) offices and most post offices. **Internet:** The main ISPs are *Geo Enterprise* (website: www.geobiz.com) and *bol.bg* (website: www.bol.bg). There are Internet cafes and centres in Sofia and Plovdiv. **Telegram:** International services are available. **Post:** Airmail to Western Europe takes from four days to two weeks. The General Post Office in Sofia, at 4 Gurko Street, is open 24 hours. Post office hours: Usually Mon-Fri 0830-1730. **Press:** The weekly newspaper, *Sofia Echo*, is available in English, as is the business publication *Pari* (Money). Both of these are published weekly and are available in print or Internet versions. The most popular dailies include *Duma* (Word), *Trud* (Labour) and *24 Chasa* (24 Hours).
Radio: BBC World Service (website: www.bbc.co.uk/worldservice) and Voice of America (website: www.voa.gov) can be received. From time to time the freq-uencies change and the most up-to-date can be found online.

Passport/Visa

	Passport Required?	Visa Required?	Return Ticket Required?
Full British	Yes	No/1	No
Australian	Yes	No/2	No
Canadian	Yes	No/2	No
USA	Yes	No/2	No
Other EU	Yes	No/1	No
Japanese	Yes	No/2	No

Note: *Regulations and requirements may be subject to change at short notice, and you are advised to contact the appropriate diplomatic or consular authority before finalising travel arrangements. Details of these may be found at the head of this country's entry. Any numbers in the chart refer to the footnotes below.*

PASSPORTS: Passport with at least one blank page valid for at least three months beyond departure required by all.
VISAS: Required by all except the following:
(a) **1.** nationals of EU countries for stays of up to 90 days within each six-month period (except nationals of Estonia, Ireland and the UK;
(b) Nationals of Chile, Iceland, Malaysia and Norway for stays of up to 90 days within a six-month period; the UK who may stay for up to 30 days within a six-month period).
Note: UK nationals living overseas *do* need a visa.
(c) **2.** nationals of Andorra, Australia, Canada, Israel, Japan, Liechtenstein, Monaco, New Zealand, Switzerland, USA and Vatican City for stays of up to 30 days within each six-month period;
(d) nationals of Croatia, Korea (Rep), Macedonia (Former Yugoslav Republic of), Romania, San Marino and Tunisia.
Types of visa and cost: *Single-entry*: £34. *Multiple-entry*: £41 (three months); £61 (six months); £81 (12 months). *Urgent single-entry*: £44. *Transit*: £28 (single-entry); £41 (double-entry); from £54 (multiple entry).
Note: Nationals of Afghanistan, Angola, Bangladesh, Congo (Dem Rep), Eritrea, Ethiopia, Ghana, Iran, Iraq, Liberia, Nigeria, Pakistan, Somalia, Sri Lanka and Sudan must apply for an airport transit visa and may not leave the airport transit lounge. They need to present a valid flight reservation to get the visa.
Validity: Single-entry visas for tourist visits are normally valid for three months from date of issue for a maximum stay of 30 days. Multiple-entry visas are for business visits and are normally valid for three months from date of issue. *Transit*: Up to 24 hours. Enquire at the Embassy for further details.
Application to: Consulate (or Consular section at Embassy); see *Contact Addresses* section. Applications should be made in person or by courier, not by post.
Application requirements: (a) Valid passport. (b) Application form. (c) One passport-size photo. (d) Return ticket or documentation for next destination. (e) Fee, payable in cash or by postal order only. (f) UK Resident visa (if applicable). (g) Prepaid tourist vouchers from the travel agency. (h) Proof of sufficient funds (at least €50 a day). *Transit*: (a)-(h) and, (i) Visa issued by country of final destination. (j) Proof of paid fare for onward destination. (k) For motor vehicle transit, proof of an extra €200 for each entry. (l) Proof of a secured return trip. *Business*: (a)-(h) and, (i) Letters from the applicant's company and from the Bulgarian business partner, endorsed by the Bulgarian Chamber of Commerce. *Private*: (a)-(h), and (i) A letter of invitation by a Bulgarian citizen endorsed by the local authorities.
Working days required: Urgent single-entry visas take up to five days to be processed and should be applied for in person if resident in the UK.
Temporary residence: Enquire at the Bulgarian Embassy.

Money

Currency: Lev (Lv) = 100 stotinki. Notes are in denominations of Lv50, 20, 10, 5, 2 and 1. Coins are in denominations of 50, 20, 10, 5, 2 and 1 stotinki.
Note: (a) The Lev is tied to the Euro at a fixed rate; €1 = Lv1.955. (b) Notes dated 1997 and earlier are now out of circulation.
Currency exchange: A *bordereaux* receipt indicating the amount of currency exchanged will be given, and must be kept until departure. Visitors are advised to exchange money at banks and at large hotels. Travellers should not change currency on the black market , and they should exercise caution when exchanging money in bureaux de change since some have been known to dupe customers with misleading rates of exchange. There is now a large network of ATMs that accept international credit and debit cards, although it is best to check with the relevant bank/card provider prior to travel.
Credit & debit cards: Major international credit cards are accepted in larger hotels and car hire offices, and in some restaurants and shops, mainly in Sofia. Check with your credit or debit card company for details of merchant acceptability and other services that may be available. However, Bulgaria is still a country that operates mainly on currency, rather than credit cards.

Travellers cheques: Accepted in major hotels and restaurants. To avoid additional exchange rate charges, travellers are advised to take travellers cheques in US Dollars or Pounds Sterling.
Currency restrictions: The import and export of local currency is prohibited. The import of foreign currency is unlimited, provided declared on arrival. The export of foreign currency is limited to the amount declared on arrival. Local currency can be exchanged at the airport on production of a *bordereaux*.
Note: Travellers should check the currency regulations just prior to departure, as they may change.
Exchange rate indicators: The following figures are included as a guide to the movements of the Lev against Sterling and the US Dollar:

Date	Feb '04	May '04	Aug '04	Nov '04
£1.00=	2.86	2.92	2.91	2.79
$1.00=	1.57	1.63	1.58	1.47

Banking hours: Mon-Fri 0900-1600.

Duty Free

The following goods may be taken into Bulgaria by all persons irrespective of age without incurring customs duty: *200 cigarettes or 50 cigars or 250g of tobacco*; *1l of spirits and 2l of wine*; *50g of perfume and 100g eau de toilette*; *reasonable amount of gifts*.
Prohibited items: Any foodstuffs for personal consumption originating from cloven-footed animals, due to the outbreak of Foot & Mouth disease in the UK in 2001.

Public Holidays

2005: Jan 1 New Year's Day. **Mar 3** National Day (Day of Liberation). **Mar 25** Good Friday. **Mar 28** Easter Monday. **May 1** Labour Day. **May 6** St George's Day (Day of Bulgarian Army). **May 24** St Cyril and Methodius Day (Day of Culture and Literacy). **Sep 6** The Unification of Bulgaria. **Sep 22** Independence Day. **Nov 1** Day of the Spiritual Leaders of Bulgaria. **Dec 24-26** Christmas.
2006: Jan 1 New Year's Day. **Mar 3** National Day (Day of Liberation). **Apr 14** Good Friday. **Apr 16** Easter Monday. **May 1** Labour Day. **May 6** St George's Day (Day of Bulgarian Army). **May 24** St Cyril and Methodius Day (Day of Culture and Literacy). **Sep 6** The Unification of Bulgaria. **Sep 22** Independence Day. **Nov 1** Day of the Spiritual Leaders of Bulgaria. **Dec 24-26** Christmas.

Health

	Special Precautions?	Certificate Required?
Yellow Fever	No	No
Cholera	No	No
Typhoid & Polio	1	N/A
Malaria	No	N/A

Note: Regulations and requirements may be subject to change at short notice, and you are advised to contact your doctor well in advance of your intended date of departure. Any numbers in the chart refer to the footnotes below.

1: It is sometimes advised to get immunisation against typhoid and poliomyelitis.
Food & drink: Mains water is normally chlorinated and, whilst relatively safe, can cause mild abdominal upsets. Some travellers may prefer to drink bottled water for the first few weeks of their stay. Milk is pasteurised and dairy products are safe for consumption. Local meat, poultry, seafood, fruit and vegetables are considered safe to eat.
Other risks: *Hepatitis B* is endemic. *Hepatitis C* may occur. *Tick-borne encephalitis* exists. Immunisation against *hepatitis A*, *diphtheria* and *tuberculosis* is sometimes recommended. *Bacillary dysentery* and *typhoid fever* are common, especially in summer.
Rabies is present. For those at high risk, vaccination before arrival should be considered. If you are bitten, seek medical advice without delay. For further information, consult the *Health* appendix.
Health care: There is a reciprocal health agreement with the UK. On production of a UK passport and an NHS medical card, hospital and other medical and dental care will normally be provided free of charge; prescribed medicines must be paid for and can be supplied by public pharmacies. Basic medical supplies are widely available but specialised treatments may not be.

Travel - International

AIR: Bulgaria's national airline is *Bulgaria Air*. Other airlines serving Bulgaria include *Aeroflot*, *Air France*, *Alitalia*, *Austrian Airlines*, *British Airways*, *El Al Israel Airlines*, *KLM*, *LOT Polish Airlines*, *Lufthansa*, *MALEV Hungarian Airlines*, *Olympic Airlines* and *Swiss*.
Approximate flight times: From Sofia to *London* is 3 hours and to *New York* is 14 hours.
International airports: *Sofia (SOF)* (website: www.sofia-airport.bg) is 10km (6 miles) east of the city (travel time – 20 minutes). Buses run approximately every 10 minutes to the city centre during the day and every 20 minutes between 2100-0030. Coaches are available by arrangement through tour operators. Taxis are also available, although taxi drivers may not use their meters and travellers are advised to agree on the fare beforehand. The airport itself only advises its passengers to use the taxi company *OK Supertrains*. Airport facilities include banks and currency exchange (24 hours), post office, duty-free shop, nursery, restaurant, bar and car hire is located in the public area of the Arrivals Hall (*Avis*, *Hertz*, *Sixt* and *Tany Rent*).
Varna (VAR) is 9km (5.5 miles) from the city. A bus service to Varna city centre departs every 20 minutes. A coach service is available by arrangement with various tour operators. A taxi service is also available. Airport facilities include outgoing duty-free shop, banking and currency exchange (24 hours), a restaurant, bar and car hire by prior arrangement with travel agents.
Bourgas (BOJ) is 13km (8 miles) from the city. A bus service departs every 20 minutes to the city centre. A coach service is available by prior arrangement with tour operators. A taxi service is also available. Airport facilities include outgoing duty-free shop, banking and currency exchange (24 hours), a restaurant, bar and car hire (by prior arrangement).
Departure tax: None except for US nationals who will be charged US$20.
SEA: The main international ports are Bourgas and Varna on the Black Sea.
RIVER: The official crossing points into Romania are by ferry from Vidin to Calafat and by road bridge from Ruse to Giurgiu.
RAIL: There are frequent services between Sofia and Budapest, Belgrade, Bucharest, Thessaloniki and Istanbul. Sofia is also directly connected with Paris, Vienna, Munich and Berlin. Dining car facilities are available on all routes. For details contact RILA (website: www.bdz-rila.com).
ROAD: Main entry points include Koulata and Novo Selo (from Greece); Ruse, Kardom, Durankulak and Silistra (from Romania); Svilengrad and Kapitan Andrikeevo (from Turkey); Kalotina, Zlatarevo and Vrashkachuka (from Serbia & Montenegro) and Guyeshevo (from the Former Yugoslav Republic of Macedonia). Foreign citizens entering Bulgaria in a motor vehicle must have documentation to prove their ownership of the vehicle. They must also state their proposed border crossing and pay suitable road tax. **Bus:** There are daily bus connections from other cities, including Istanbul, Athens and Thessaloniki to Sofia. *Eurolines*, departing from Victoria Coach Station in London, serves destinations in Bulgaria. For further information, contact *Eurolines* (4 Cardiff Road, Luton, Bedfordshire L41 1PP; tel: (0990) 143 219; fax: (01582) 400 694; e-mail: welcome@eurolinesuk.com; website: www.eurolines.com *or* www.nationalexpress.com).

Travel - Internal

AIR: *Bulgaria Air* operates domestic services connecting Sofia with the coast and main towns. The journeys from Sofia to Bourgas and Varna can be made in about one hour. Air travel is comparatively cheap, and is only slightly more expensive than rail travel.
RIVER: Regular boat and hydrofoil services along the Bulgarian bank of the Danube link many centres, including Vidin, Lom, Kozloduj, Orjahovo, Nikopol, Svishtov, Tutrakan and Silistra.
RAIL: There are over 4200km (2625 miles) of railways in the country. Bulgarian State Railways connects Sofia with main towns. Reservations are essential and first-class travel is advised. For details, contact the State Railway Office (website: www.bdz.bg).
ROAD: There are over 13,000km (8000 miles) of roads linking the major centres; their quality is variable and some main roads have major potholes, plus driving standards are generally poor. Traffic drives on the right. International road signs are used, although roadworks are often not signposted. Night driving can be dangerous owing to poor lighting. Foreign drivers are sometimes liable to extra road tolls. Additionally, if the vehicle is stolen in Bulgaria, import duty and related taxes must be paid: insurance may be taken to cover this. Speed limits are strictly adhered to: 50kph (30mph) in built-up areas, 90kph (55mph) outside built-up areas and 120kph (75mph) on motorways. In addition, the driver may be banned from driving in Bulgaria for up to three years. The nationwide alcohol limit is 0.05 per cent; on-the-spot fines of between Lv50-150 are imposed for offences. Spare parts are easily available. There are large numerous petrol stations. It should also be observed that car-theft is on the increase in Bulgaria, and all cars should ideally be fitted with alarms and other visible security measures. Car-jacking is also becoming more frequent, usually occurring at night, and with some criminals even impersonating traffic policeman in the

Credit: © Bulgarian Tourism Authority

process. It is best to drive in daylight. **Bus:** There is a good network of buses that are cheap and convenient; but visitors should be aware that timetabling can be erratic. **Taxi:** Available in all towns and also for intercity journeys. Vehicles may not be in top condition. Vehicles are metered, unless they are privately owned. Taxi meters may be rigged so that foreign passengers can be overcharged; foreign visitors should therefore take great caution in determining the correct fare before travel. A 5 to 10 per cent tip is appreciated. **Car hire:** Available through hotel reception desks. Available car hire companies include *Avis* and *Hertz*. There are no fly-drive arrangements through the airlines. Payment is usually in hard currency. **Documentation:** An International Driving Permit is required. A Green Card is compulsory.
URBAN: Bus, tramway and trolleybus services operate in Sofia; in addition, a metro is under construction. Flat fares are charged and tickets must be pre-purchased. Buses and taxis operate in all the main towns. There are also trolleybuses in Plovdiv and Varna.
Travel times: The following chart gives approximate travel times from **Sofia** (in hours and minutes) to other major cities/towns in Bulgaria.

	Air	Road	Rail
Varna	1.00	8.00	7.00
Bourgas	1.00	7.00	6.00
Plovdiv	0.40	2.00	2.00
Ruse	-	9.00	8.00
Turnovo	-	3.30	-
Vitosha	-	0.30	-
Borovets	-	1.30	-
Pamporovo	-	3.30	-
Golden Sands	*0.45	*7.00	-
Albena	*0.45	*7.00	-
Sunny Beach	**0.35	**6.30	-

Note: *From Varna Airport. **From Bourgas Airport.

Accommodation

HOTELS: Advance booking is advisable. **Grading:** Hotels are classified according to the European star-grading system, but standards are comparatively low. Special care has been taken in some hotels to conform to international standards. For further information, contact the Bulgarian Hotel and Restaurant Association, Triaditsa 5b, 1000 Sofia (tel: (2) 987 6586; fax; 988 0578; e-mail: bhra_office@abv.bg; website: www.bhra-bg.org).
GUEST HOUSES: Accommodation is available in small villas with private rooms, particularly near the coast.
CAMPING/CARAVANNING: Campsites are classified from I to III, and the top two categories have hot and cold water, showers, electricity, grocery stores, restaurants, telephones and sports grounds. The camping areas are located in main tourist areas.
YOUTH HOSTELS: These are situated in over 30 main towns. For information, contact USIT Colours, 35 Vassil Levski Boulevard, Sofia 1000 (tel: (2) 981 1900; e-mail: sofia@usitcolours.bg; website: www.usitcolours.bg). USIT Colours is affiliated to the International Youth Hostel Federation.

Resorts & Excursions

SOFIA & THE WEST

SOFIA: Dating back to the fourth century BC, the ancient capital of Sofia has a wealth of different architectural styles including Greek, Roman, Byzantine, Bulgarian and Turkish. The city boasts many theatres and museums (including those of archaeology and ethnography), opera houses and art galleries (including the **National Gallery of Painting and Sculpture** housed in the former Royal Palace), as well as universities, open-air markets, parks (over 300 of them, including the **Borisova Park**) and sports stadiums. Visitors should see the extraordinary **Alexander Nevsky Memorial Church** (which dominates the city with its goldleaf dome), built to celebrate Bulgaria's liberation from the Turks in the Russo-Turkish war at the end of the last century. The crypt hosts an exhibition of beautiful icons and the choir is excellent and well worth hearing. Other churches in Sofia include **St Sophia**, which is Byzantine and dates from the sixth century; **St George**, which dates back to the fifth century and contains 14th-century frescoes; **St Petka Samardshijska**, which is 14th century, and **St Nedelya**. There is an archaeological museum housed in the nine cupolas of the **Bouyouk Mosque** (the largest in Sofia). The **Banya Bashi Mosque** is also worth a visit. An example of modern architecture is the **Alexander Batenberg Square**, which contains the **Government Buildings** and some Roman remains nearby (discovered when an underpass was being constructed), together with a reconstruction of the city as it was in Roman times. Other attractions include the Turkish baths and the markets at

Credit: © Bulgarian Tourism Authority

Hali (covered market), **Georgi Kirkov** and **Kristal Square** (flea market and antique shops).

RILA: Rila Monastery is 121km (75 miles) from Sofia, perched high up on the side of a mountain in the middle of thick pine forests. Rila has a fascinating collection of murals, woodcarvings, old weapons and coins; and manuals and Bibles written on parchment. The monastery itself is notable for its delicate and unusual architectural features. Originally founded in the 10th century by the hermit and holy man, Ivan Rilsky, the monastery acted as a repository and sanctuary for Bulgarian culture during the 500-year Turkish occupation from 1396. Fire has destroyed most of the early architecture and the present buildings date from the 19th century, with the exception of the 14th-century **Hrelio's Tower**. There is good accommodation in the monastery and a nearby hotel. Rila is an excellent starting place for climbs and hikes in the surrounding countryside.

ELSEWHERE: The mountain of **Vitosha** on the outskirts of Sofia is a National Park with chairlifts and cable cars to help with the ascent as it is approximately 1800m (6000ft) high. Here, the medieval church of **Boyana**, a UNESCO World Heritage Site, can be seen, with its beautiful and ancient frescoes painted around the year 1200 and thought to be some of the oldest in Bulgaria.

South of Sofia is **Blagoevgrad**, home of the Pirin State Ensemble (the world-renowned folkloric group), and **Sandansky**, an ancient spa town and birthplace of the Roman gladiator, Spartacus. Further south still, travellers can visit two of Bulgaria's museum towns: **Melnik** is known for its wine cellars, 18th to 19th century architecture and its proximity to **Rozhen Monastery** with its beautifully carved altar, stained-glass windows, murals and icons; and the museum town of **Bansko** at the foot of the Pirin Mountains contains the **Holy Trinity Church** with its carved ceilings and murals, and its monastery-like houses with high stone walls.

CENTRAL BULGARIA

PLOVDIV: Founded in 342 BC and the country's second-largest city, the museum town of **Plovdiv** is divided by the Maritsa River and contains both an old quarter and a new commercial section. The old part contains many buildings dating from the 18th and 19th centuries (and earlier) in typical National Revival style. It is possible to wander along the narrow cobbled streets and see Roman ruins (including an amphitheatre), picturesque medieval houses and 17th-century buildings with their upper sections hanging out into the street and almost touching those opposite. The **Archaeological Museum** has collections of gold Thracian artefacts, including cooking utensils, and the **Ethnographic Museum** is also worth seeing, as are the churches of **St Marina** and **St Nedelya**.

ELSEWHERE: 8 km (5 miles) from Plovdiv is **Batchkovo Monastery**, founded in the 11th century, with some rare frescoes, icons, manuscripts and coins. **Batchkovo** lies within the area known in ancient times as Thrace (partly occupied by the **Rhodope Mountains**) and many items of archaeological interest have been discovered, including wonderful gold Thracian objects.

The town of **Kazanluk** has a **Museum of Rose Production** and is the centre of Bulgaria's major export: attar of roses. The valley of Kazanluk itself has countless archaeological and historic treasures – Greek, Roman, Thracian and Ottoman.

Veliko Turnovo, ancient capital of the Second Bulgarian Empire (1187-1393), is another museum town, situated on three hills circled by the **River Yantra**. It contains extraordinary collections of historic works of art, including church relics. Turnova has many fine examples of houses built in the National Revival style (18th to 19th century), many of which were designed by master builder Kolyo Phicheto and typically seem to grow out of the steep slopes flanking the river. The **Preobrazhenski Monastery** is quite close, as is the open-air folk museum at **Etar**. The picturesque village of **Arbanassi**, a museum town located 4km (2.5 miles) from Turnovo, was a wealthy merchants' town between the 16th and 18th centuries and is noted for its unique stone-built houses, its two monasteries, **St Nikola** and **Holy Virgin** and, in particular, the beautiful murals of the **St Elija Chapel**. 8 km (5 miles) northwest of Plovdiv, the museum town of **Koprivshtitsa** is one of Bulgaria's best-preserved towns, with primary coloured examples of National Revival architecture apparent everywhere. The town is perhaps best known for its *Great Koprivshtitsa Folklore Festival*, held every four years. Further museum towns to the east of Plovdiv include **Tryavna**, again with many examples of houses in the National Revival style; **Kotel**, which is located in a small valley in the Balkan mountain range, and is famous as a centre for carpet making; and **Zheravna**, in the Eastern Balkan range, containing beautiful 17th-century wooden houses.

THE BLACK SEA COAST

The Bulgarian **Black Sea Riviera** resorts are ideal for the traditional seaside family holiday. Swimming is generally safe, as even at 150m (500ft) away from the shore, the water is only shoulder-high. Areas where currents are a problem are clearly marked. The Black Sea has half the salt content of the Mediterranean. Some of the sand is pulled by currents from as far away as the Mediterranean, flowing through the Bosphorus and Dardenelles. Special children's pools have been installed on many of the beaches; swings, slides, playdomes and donkey rides are also available and most resorts offer a wide range of watersports.

Resorts: There are dozens of attractive resorts on the Black Sea Riviera. **St Constantine Resort** is Bulgaria's oldest Black Sea spa, centred on the Grand Hotel Varna, the largest and most luxurious hotel on the Riviera. **Albena**, named after a famous local beauty, is situated on the edge of a lovely forest, and is Bulgaria's newest resort (a showcase and vivid monument to contemporary Bulgarian design), with good food and lively nightlife. **Golden Sands**, Bulgaria's second-largest resort, has good facilities and probably the best nightlife on the Black Sea Riviera. **Sunny Day** offers a wide range of beauty and health treatments in two of its four hotels. In a forested setting overlooking the sea, it is only 15km (9 miles) from **Varna**, the Black Sea capital founded in the sixth century BC, which contains many Roman and Byzantine remains. **Sunny Beach** is a large purpose-built family resort with beautiful and safe beaches. Close to Sunny Beach is the seventh-century fishing village of **Old Nessebur** with its wooden fishermen's houses and its famed four dozen Byzantine churches. The Black Sea port town of **Burgas** has a **Maritime Park** and an extensive beach.

WINTER RESORTS

Borovets is a World Cup venue. It is only 70km (45 miles) from Sofia, at 1350m (4300ft) in the Rila Mountains and is the oldest and largest mountain resort in Bulgaria. There, the 2400m (8000ft) *Yastrebets* (Hawk's Nest) is a steep, twisting red trail for the advanced skier, in operation from November until April. Seven comfortable, friendly and well-run hotels provide most of the accommodation and there is a village of timber-framed houses (each sleeping six) nearby. In Bulgarian resorts, hotels usually provide most of the nightlife. There is a disco in the Mousalla. There is also a wine bar and some folk taverns (*mehana*); sleigh rides through the snow are also available.

At **Pamporovo**, in the Rhodope Mountains near Plovdiv, there is one of the finest ski schools in Europe. Pamporovo is also the most southerly ski resort in Europe. The major ski runs start from the top of the **Snejanka Peak**.

Vitosha, 1800m (6000ft) high and home of the National Ski School based on the FIS methods, overlooks Sofia. Two of the six ski runs have been approved for international competitions. All the resorts have been purpose-built to blend in with the magnificent natural scenery of mountains and forest. Equipment on hire is modern and well maintained.

The most recent resort is **Bansko**, a small town in southwest Bulgaria at the foothills of the Pirin Mountain. There are slalom and giant slalom runs available, as well as a 5km- (3.1 mile-) cross-country track.

NATIONAL PARKS

Bulgaria has a number of national parks which abound in rare flora and fauna, bird species (including vultures, eagles and falcons), as well as endangered animal species such as bears, wolves and red deer. Facilities for nature and outdoor enthusiasts have improved in recent years, with different types of accommodation, including small hotels, lodges, private chalets and camping becoming increasingly available. Guided tours or private visits are possible; for some areas, a permit is required. For details, contact the Ministry of Economy (Tourist Department) *or* Balkan Holidays (see *Contact Addresses* section).

The **Pirin National Park** is situated on the highest part of the Pirin mountain range. The landscape varies from the ancient Baikusheva pine forests to crystalline lakes and limestone rocks. Many rare plant species, such as the near extinct *Edelweiss*, are preserved within the park, which also contains nearly 180 glacier lakes. In the southwest, the **Rila National Park** covers nearly half of the Rila mountain range and is renowned for its seven lakes and its 10th-century monastery. **Vitosha National Park**, just outside Sofia, is home to many species of butterflies and offers shelter to wolves, bears and wild cats. The **Vratchansky Balkan National Park**, in the northwest, has spectacular rock formations, waterfalls and ancient caves. It incorporates the **Vratchansky Karst Nature Reserve**, whose caves provide a habitat for many species of bats. The **Central Balkan National Park**, located to the northeast of Sofia and reached via the **Troyan Pass**, is noted for the **Raiskoto Praskalo** waterfall – the highest in Bulgaria - and its 50 protected plant species, many of them native to these mountains. The small **Sinite Kamani National Park** has spectacular rock formations. The **Shoumen Plateau National Park** near the town of Shoumen has a varied landscape of thick forests and steep rock formations and is home to the Shumenska Krepost archaeological reserve. Situated near the River Danube close to the town of Rousse, the **Roussenski Lom National Park** is known for its rich wildlife and fauna. The **Strandzha National Park** in the southeast is Bulgaria's largest. It borders the Black Sea and is famous for its oak and beech forests. The nearby **Ropotamo Reserve** on the banks of the River Ropotamo has a diverse landscape ranging from cliffs and forests to sandy beaches, dunes and swamps; the Arkutino swamp is a shelter for many rare bird species.

WORLD HERITAGE SITES

Bulgaria has nine UNESCO-listed World Heritage Sites. The **Thracian Kazanluk Tomb**, located in the Valley of Roses near the town of **Kazanluk**, has perfectly preserved murals dating from the fourth century BC. The **Sveshtari Tomb** is situated in an archaeological reserve near the town of **Razgrad**; it was built 2300 years ago for a Thracian king. The **Madara Horseman**, an image carved into a rock of a horseman piercing a lion with his spear dates from the early Middle Ages (eighth century); it is located on the **Madara Plateau** in the Danube plain. The 13th-century **Boyana Church** is located at the foot of the Vitosha mountain in the Sofia suburb of **Boyana** and is famous for its murals, which include replicas of icons from Constantinople.

The **Ivanovo Rock Monasteries** near the city of **Ruse** stretch for more than 5km (3.1 miles) and consist of cells, churches and chapels dug into the rocks by hermit monks who settled there between the 11th and 14th centuries. **Old Nessebur** is one of Europe's oldest towns (for details, see The *Black Sea Coast* section). The 11th-century **Rila Monastery** is set on Rila Mountain, 121km (75 miles) from Sofia (for details, see *Sofia & The West* section). The **Sreburna Lake** nature reserve is located near the Danube river, 16km (10 miles) west of the town of Silistra. It stretches over an area of 600 hectares (1482 acres) and is listed for its unique fauna and wildlife, including the rare Dalmatian pelican, the cormorant and the ibis. Thanks to swift preventative measures, the park seems to have escaped unscathed from the recent Danube cyanide spill. The **Pirin National Park** (for details, see *National Parks* section) is a protected area of 27,400 hectares (67,678 acres).

Sport & Activities

Special interest tours: Most towns and cities have a national history and ethnographic museum. Visits to the old **museum towns** and ancient **monasteries** provide an excellent opportunity to experience Bulgaria's rich historical and cultural traditions; some museum towns, such as Koprivshtitsa and Plovdiv, offer **painting** and **photography** courses.

Wintersports: Bulgaria is a fast-growing **skiing** destination and the country's three major ski resorts have been improved in recent years. Snowfall is consistently heavy from December until April. The ski areas may not be as extensive as the Alps, but for novice and intermediate skiing, Bulgaria offers excellent conditions. Off-piste skiing is good and **cross-country skiing** is becoming increasingly popular, with many trails leading through pine forests. (For details of the main ski resorts and facilities, see Winter Resorts in the *Resorts & Excursions* section.)

Watersports: The Black Sea coast has over 370km (232 miles) of coastline with sandy beaches. Owing to its low salt

content, it is ideal for **swimming**. A wide range of watersports, including **water-skiing**, **sailing** and **surfing** are available. **Whitewater rafting**, **canoeing** and **kayaking** are possible on the Rivers *Arda*, *Ossam*, *Stackevska* and *Struma* during springtime. The quieter waters of the *Danube* are particularly suitable for canoeing and kayaking.
Hiking: There are over 35,000km (21,749 miles) of waymarked paths in Bulgaria. one- or two-week trips through the wild mountains can be arranged. Guides are provided and accommodation is usually in mountain chalets, guest houses or camps. (See also National Parks in the *Resorts & Excursions* section.)
Outdoor pursuits: Organised **mountaineering** and **climbing** trips can be arranged by specialised companies in the areas of Vratsa, Veliko Tarnovo, Trojan, Maliovitza and Roussenski Lom. The steep rocks of the *Pirin*, *Rhodope*, *Rila* and *Stara Planina* are popular with expert climbers.
Bulgaria has twice hosted the **orienteering** World Championships and a national orienteering cup takes place annually on the *Shoumensko Plateau*. Numerous companies also offer organised **caving** trips to the country's numerous caves and spectacular subterranean rock formations (many of which have ancient cave paintings). **Horseriding** has traditionally been popular in Bulgaria and there is a choice of one- or two-week tours available; possible itineraries include the Danube Valley, the Balkan, Rila and Stara Planina mountains and the Valley of Roses. It is also possible to travel the country by horse and cart. For **mountain biking** enthusiasts, the Rhodope mountains provide excellent trails, while **cycling** along the Black Sea coast is a popular family activity.
There are also generally good facilities for **tennis** and **mini-golf** in the major resorts.
Cruises: Luxury cruises along the Danube sailing through seven countries in two air-conditioned river liners, each accommodating 236 passengers, is available. This interesting tour includes transit to Passau or Vienna, to begin either a two- or three-week cruise to Ruse in eastern Bulgaria, with excursions at all points of call. Afterwards, there is a choice of touring Bulgaria by coach, or staying on the Black Sea Riviera, or at a mountain resort inland. The return trip home is by air.
Health spas: Bulgaria has many mineral water spas and increasing interest is being shown in spa holidays. There are over 500 springs. For further details, contact Balkan Holidays (see *Contact Addresses* section).

Social Profile

FOOD & DRINK: The main meal is eaten in the middle of the day. Dinner is a social occasion, with dancing in many restaurants. Food is spicy, hearty and good. National dishes include cold yoghurt soup with cucumbers, peppers or aubergines stuffed with meat, *kebapcheta* (small, strongly spiced, minced meat rolls). A lot of meals include meat, potatoes and cheese. Fruit is particularly good and cheap throughout the year. *Banitsa* is a pastry stuffed with fruit or cheese. There is a wide variety of national dishes, as well as Western European standard dishes, which can be chosen on the spot at any restaurant. All good hotels have restaurants and there are many attractive folk-style restaurants and cafes throughout the country.
Coffee, heavily sweetened, is particularly popular. Drinks are also made from infusions of mountain herbs and dried leaves, particularly lime. White wines include *Evksinograde*, *Karlouski Misket* and *Tamianka*. Heavy red wines include *Mavroud* and *Trakia*. Liquors include the rather potent *mastika* and *rakia*.
NIGHTLIFE: Some restaurants have folk dancing and music. Opera is performed at the State Opera House in Sofia; other classical concerts include the National Folk Ensemble. There are nightclubs with floor shows and dancing in Sofia, as well as in most major towns and all the resorts.
SHOPPING: The main shopping area of Sofia is the Vitosha Boulevard. Bulgarian products, handicrafts, wines, spirits and confectionery can all be purchased. **Shopping hours:** Shops and stores are generally open Mon-Fri 1000-2000, Sat 1000-1400.
SPECIAL EVENTS: For a complete list of special events, contact the National Tourist Information Centre *or* the Embassy (see *Contact Addresses* section). The following is a selection of special events celebrated annually in Bulgaria:
Dec 31-Jan 1 *Ladouvane*, various towns. **Jan** *International Folklore Festival*, Pernik. **Mar** *Martenitsas* (Festival of Spring), nationwide; *Musical Days*, Ruse. **May** *Festival for Authentic Thrace Region Folklore*, Haskovo. **May-Jun** *Sofia Musical Weeks*. **Jun** *Festival of the Rose*, Kazanluk. **Jun-Aug** *The Varna Summer Festival*; *Golden Orpheus International Pop Music Festival*, Sunny Beach. **Jul** *European Cultural Month*, Plovdiv. **Aug** *International Folklore Festival*, Plovdiv; *Quadrennial National Folklore Festival*, Koprivstitsa; *National Folklore Festivities*, Rhodope Mountains; *International Folklore Festival*, Bourgas. **Sep** *Art, Crafts and Chamber Music*, Plovdiv; *Apolonia Arts Festivities*, Sozopol. **Oct** *St Dmitri's Day*, various towns. **Nov** *Katya Popova International Laureate Festival*, Pleven. **Dec** *Saint Barbara*, various towns.
SOCIAL CONVENTIONS: Normal courtesies should be observed and handshaking is the normal form of greeting. Dress should be conservative but casual. If invited to the home, a small souvenir from one's homeland is an acceptable gift. Do not give money. Remember that a nod of the head means 'No' and a shake means 'Yes'. **Tipping:** Until recently not applicable, but 10 to 12 per cent is now customary.

Business Profile

ECONOMY: Bulgaria has a strong agricultural sector, in which the main products are wheat, maize, barley, sugar beet, grapes and tobacco, although its relative importance has declined in recent years. Attar (oil) of roses is exported from the Valley of Roses near Kazanluk to perfumers across the world. The country is also one of the world's leading wine exporters. Mineral deposits include coal, iron ore, copper, manganese and zinc. Coal, supplemented by gas supplied by pipeline from the Russian Federation, meets most of the country's energy requirements. Manufacturing industry is concentrated in engineering, metals, chemicals and petrochemicals and, more recently, electronics and biotechnology. Bulgaria is a major producer of bulk carriers and forklift trucks. In the service sector, tourism and road transport are both important foreign exchange earners. In general, Bulgaria has suffered the usual problems experienced by centrally planned economies adjusting to market conditions. Successive governments have followed the path taken by other former Communist governments, under which most of industry and agriculture was privatised, trade liberalised and reforms of the fiscal and banking systems instituted. However, some key privatisations (tobacco, telecoms, banking) have already, or are, experiencing difficulties, possibly threatening the stability of the government. The value of the Bulgarian Lev was fixed to the Deutschmark by the currency control board created in 1997; it is now linked to the Euro. The economy grew at a healthy 4.3 per cent in 2004; inflation has been brought down to single figures reducing unemployment to 12.67 per cent. In 1990, Bulgaria joined the IMF, which has had a major influence on the country's economic policy, along with the World Bank and the European Bank for Reconstruction and Development. Bulgaria has applied to become a full member of the EU and should join in 2007. The Russian Federation, Germany, Italy and Greece are Bulgaria's major trading partners.
BUSINESS: Suits and prior appointments are necessary. Interpreters can be organised through tourist agencies. If arranged in advance through foreign trading organisations, services are free. It is common for the visiting business person to offer hospitality to the contact in Bulgaria.
Office hours: Mon-Fri 0900-1730.
COMMERCIAL INFORMATION: The following organisation can offer advice: Bulgarian Chamber of Commerce and Industry, 42 Parchevich Street, 1058 Sofia (tel: (2) 987 2631; fax: (2) 987 3209; e-mail: bcci@bcci.bg; website: www.bcci.bg).
CONFERENCES & CONVENTIONS: The National Tourist Information Centre (see *Contact Addresses* section) can offer advice.

Climate

Varies according to altitude. Summers are warmest with some rainfall, with the south feeling the influence of the Mediterranean. Winters are cold with snow. It rains frequently during spring and autumn.
Required clothing: Mediumweights most of the year; warmer outdoor wear necessary in winter.

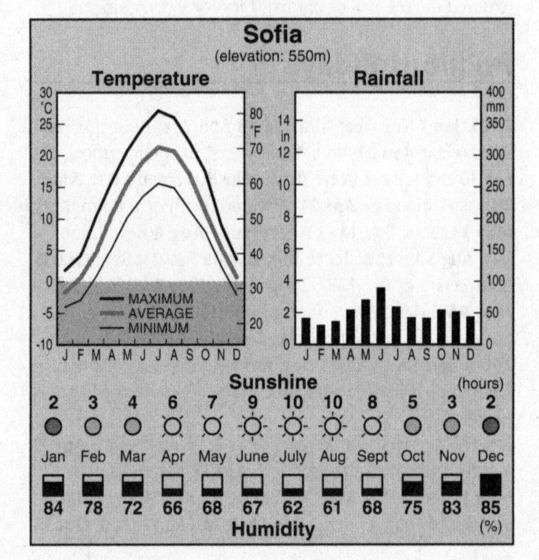

Burkina Faso

LATEST TRAVEL ADVICE CONTACTS

British Foreign and Commonwealth Office
Tel: (0870) 606 0290 Website: www.fco.gov.uk
US Department of State
Website: http://travel.state.gov/travel
Canadian Department of Foreign Affairs and Int'l Trade
Tel: (1 800) 267 8376 Website: www.dfait-maeci.gc.ca

Location: West Africa.

Country dialling code: 226.

Direction du Tourisme et de l'Hôtellerie
BP 624, Ouagadougou 01, Burkina Faso
Tel: 5030 6396. Fax: 5033 0964.
Ambassade du Burkina Faso
16 Place Guy d'Arezzo, 1180 Brussels, Belgium
Tel: (2) 345 9912. Fax: (2) 345 0612.
E-mail: ambassade.burkina@skynet.be
Website: www.ambassadeduburkina.be
Since the Honorary Consulate of Burkina Faso in London closed in 2002, all enquiries should be directed here.
British Honorary Consulate
Hotel Yibi, 10 BP 13593, Ouagadougou 10, Burkina Faso
Tel: 5030 7323. Fax: 5030 5900.
E-mail: ypi@cenatrin.bf
Provides only limited assistance.
The British Embassy in Abidjan normally deals with enquiries relating to Burkina Faso (see *Côte d'Ivoire* section).
Embassy of Burkina Faso
2340 Massachusetts Avenue, NW, Washington, DC 20008, USA
Tel: (202) 332 5577. Fax: (202) 667 1882.
E-mail: ambawdc@verizon.com
Website: www.burkinaembassy-usa.org
Embassy of the United States of America
Street address: 602 avenue Raoul Follereau, Ouagadougou 01, Burkina Faso
Postal address: 01 BP 35, Ouagadougou 01, Burkina Faso
Tel: 5030 6723.
Fax: 5031 2368 *or* 5030 7775 (consular section).
E-mail: amembouaga@state.gov *or* consularouaga@state.gov (consular section).
Website: http://ouagadougou.usembassy.gov
Embassy of Burkina Faso
48 Range Road, Ottawa, Ontario K1N 8J4, Canada
Tel: (613) 238 4796. Fax: (613) 238 3812.
E-mail: burkina.faso@sympatico.ca
Website: www.ambaburkina-canada.org
Honorary Consulate: Toronto.
Canadian Embassy
Street address: 586 Rue Agostino Neto, Canadian Development Centre, Ouagadougou 01, Burkina Faso
Postal address: 01 BP 548, Ouagadougou 01, Burkina Faso
Tel: 5031 1894. Fax: 5031 1900.
E-mail: ouaga@dfait-maeci.gc.ca
Website: www.dfait-maeci.gc.ca/burkina_faso

TIMATIC CODES

Health	AMADEUS: **TI-DFT/OUA/HE** GALILEO/WORLDSPAN: **TI-DFT/OUA/HE** SABRE: **TIDFT/OUA/HE**
Visa	AMADEUS: **TI-DFT/OUA/VI** GALILEO/WORLDSPAN: **TI-DFT/OUA/VI** SABRE: **TIDFT/OUA/VI**

To access TIMATIC country information on Health and Visa regulations through the Computer Reservations System (CRS), type in the appropriate command line listed above.

General Information

AREA: 274,200 sq km (105,870 sq miles).
POPULATION: 12,624,000 (UN estimate 2002).
POPULATION DENSITY: 46 per sq km (2002).
CAPITAL: Ouagadougou.**Population:** 709,736 (1996).
GEOGRAPHY: Burkina Faso is situated in West Africa and bordered to the north and west by Mali, to the east by Niger, to the southeast by Benin and to the south by Togo, Ghana and Côte d'Ivoire. The southern part of the country, less arid than the north, is wooded savannah, gradually drying out into sand and desert in the north. The Sahara desert is relentlessly moving south, however, stripping the savannah lands of trees and slowly turning the thin layer of cultivatable soil into sun-blackened rock-hard *lakenite*. Three great rivers, the Mouhoun, Nazinon and Nakambé (Black, Red and White Volta), water the great plains. The population does not live in the valleys along the river banks due to the diseases prevalent there.
GOVERNMENT: Republic. Gained independence from France in 1960. Changed its name from Upper Volta to Burkina Faso (Land of Dignity) in 1984. **Head of State:** President Blaise Compaoré since 1987. **Head of Government:** Prime Minister Paramanga Ernest Yonli since 2000.
LANGUAGE: The official language is French. Several other languages such as Mossi, Mooré, Dioula, Peul, Fulfuldé and Gourmantché are also spoken.
RELIGION: More than 50 per cent follow animist beliefs; 30 per cent are Muslim and fewer than 12 per cent Christian (mostly Roman Catholic).
TIME: GMT.
ELECTRICITY: 220 volts AC, 50Hz. Two-pin plugs are standard.
COMMUNICATIONS: Telephone: IDD is available. Country code: 226. Outgoing international code: 00. **Mobile telephone:** GSM 900 networks operated by *Celtel Burkina Faso* (website: www.msi-cellular.com), *Onatel* (website: www.onatel.bf) and *Telecel Faso SA* (website: www.telecelfaso.bf). Coverage available in the five main towns. Handsets can be hired (against a large deposit); contact *Onatel* for further information. **Internet:** Available in some hotels and Internet cafes. There are three Internet cafes in Ouagadougou and one in Bobo Dioulassou. ISPs include *Cenatrin* (website: www.cenatrin.bf) and *FasoNet*. Power cuts can hamper Internet usage. **Telegram:** There are limited facilities outside Ouagadougou. Main hotels have facilities. **Post:** There are few post offices, but stamps can often be bought at hotels. *Poste Restante* facilities are available but a charge is made for letters collected. There is no local delivery, and all other mail must be addressed to a box number. Airmail to Europe takes up to two weeks. Post office opening hours: Mon-Fri 0730-1230 and 1500-1730. The main post office in the capital is open Mon-Sat 0830-1200 and 1500-1830. **Press:** French-language only. The main daily newspapers are *L'Express du Faso*, *L'Observateur Paalga*, *Le Pays* and *Sidwaya Quotidien*.
Radio: BBC World Service (website: www.bbc.co.uk/worldservice) and Voice of America (website: www.voa.gov) can be received. From time to time the frequencies change and the most up-to-date can be found online.

Passport/Visa

	Passport Required?	Visa Required?	Return Ticket Required?
Full British	Yes	Yes	Yes
Australian	Yes	Yes	Yes
Canadian	Yes	Yes	Yes
USA	Yes	Yes	Yes
Other EU	Yes	Yes	Yes
Japanese	Yes	Yes	Yes

Note: *Regulations and requirements may be subject to change at short notice, and you are advised to contact the appropriate diplomatic or consular authority before finalising travel arrangements. Details of these may be found at the head of this country's entry. Any numbers in the chart refer to the footnotes below.*

PASSPORTS: Valid passport required by all except nationals of ECOWAS countries, when holding national identity cards.
VISAS: Required by all except:
(a) those mentioned under passport exemptions above, for up to 90 days;
(b) those persons continuing their journey within 24 hours to another country, provided holding onward tickets and the appropriate travel documents and not leaving the airport.
Types of visa and cost: *Tourist*, *Business* and *Transit*: €26 (three months); €48 (12 months). Visa costs vary with the exchange rate. Visitors should contact the nearest Embassy for up-to-date prices.
Validity: Visas are valid for three or 12 months from the date of entry and permit multiple entry.
Application to: Nearest Consulate (or Consular Section at Embassy); see *Contact Addresses* section.
Application requirements: (a) Valid passport. (b) Three application forms. (c) Three passport-size photos. (d) Fee, payable in cash or by postal order only. (e) For postal applications, arrangements must be made for the passport to be returned by a courier service. (f) Company letter if on business.
Working days required: Visas can be granted within one day if papers are in order.
Temporary residence: Application to be made to the Central Government of Burkina Faso. Enquire at Consulate or Embassy for further information.

Money

Currency: CFA (*Communauté Financiaire Africaine*) Franc (CFAfr) = 100 centimes. Notes are in denominations of CFAfr10,000, 5000, 2500, 1000 and 500. Coins are in denominations of CFAfr250, 100, 50, 25, 10, 5 and 1. Burkina Faso is part of the French Monetary Area. Only currency issued by the *Banque des Etats de l'Afrique de l'Ouest* (Bank of West African States) is valid; currency issued by the *Banque des Etats de l'Afrique Centrale* (Bank of Central African States) is not. The CFA Franc is tied to the Euro.
Currency exchange: Can be exchanged in banks and major hotels.
Credit & debit cards: Diners Club and MasterCard have limited acceptance. Check with your credit or debit card company for details of merchant acceptability and other services which may be available.
Travellers cheques: To avoid additional exchange rate charges, travellers are advised to take travellers cheques in Euros or US Dollars. Banks often require proof of purchase, so all receipts should be kept as a precautionary measure. It is advised to take at least some Euros in cash.
Currency restrictions: No restrictions on import of local or foreign currency, provided declared on arrival. The export of local and foreign currency is allowed up to the amount imported and declared for non-residents.
Exchange rate indicators: The following figures are included as a guide to the movements of the CFA Franc against Sterling and the US Dollar:

Date	Feb '04	May '04	Aug '04	Nov '04
£1.00=	961.13	983.76	978.35	936.79
$1.00=	528.01	550.79	531.03	494.69

Banking hours: Mon-Fri 0730-1230 and 1530-1730.

Duty Free

The following items may be imported into Burkina Faso by persons over 15 years of age without incurring customs duty:
200 cigarettes or 25 cigars or 100 cigarillos or 250g of tobacco; 0.75l of spirits and 0.75l of wine; 500ml of eau de toilette and 250ml of perfume.
Note: Permission from the Ministry of Administration is required for the use of photo-, film- or video cameras.

Public Holidays

2005: Jan 1 New Year's Day. **Jan 3** Anniversary of the 1966 Coup d'État. **Jan 21** Aid El Kébir (Feast of the Sacrifice). **Feb 10** El am Hejir (New Year). **Mar 8** Women's Day. **Mar 28** Easter Monday. **Apr 21** Mouloud (Birth of the Prophet). **May 1** Labour Day. **May 5** Ascension. **Aug 4** Revolution Day. **Aug 5** Independence Day. **Aug 15** Assumption. **Oct 15** Anniversary of the 1987 Coup d'État. **Nov 1** All Saints' Day. **Nov 3-5** Aid El Segheir (End of Ramadan). **Dec 11** Proclamation of the Republic. **Dec 25** Christmas.
2006: Jan 1 New Year's Day. **Jan 3** Anniversary of the 1966 Coup d'État. **Jan 10** Aid El Kébir (Feast of the Sacrifice).
Jan 31 El am Hejir (New Year). **Mar 8** Women's Day. **Apr 11** Mouloud (Birth of the Prophet). **Apr 17** Easter Monday. **May 1** Labour Day. **May 25** Ascension. **Aug 4** Revolution Day. **Aug 5** Independence Day. **Aug 15** Assumption. **Oct 15** Anniversary of the 1987 Coup d'État. **Oct 22-24** Aid El Segheir (End of Ramadan). **Nov 1** All Saints' Day. **Dec 11** Proclamation of the Republic. **Dec 25** Christmas.
Note: Muslim festivals are timed according to local sightings of various phases of the moon and the dates given above are approximations. During the lunar month of Ramadan that precedes Aid El Segheir, Muslims fast during the day and feast at night, and normal business patterns may be interrupted. Many restaurants are closed during the day and there may be restrictions on smoking and drinking. Some disruption may continue into Aid El Segheir itself. Aid El Segheir and Aid El Kébir may last anything from two to 10 days, depending on the region. For more information, refer to the *World of Islam* appendix.

Health

	Special Precautions?	Certificate Required?
Yellow Fever	Yes	1
Cholera	Yes	2
Typhoid & Polio	3	N/A
Malaria	4	N/A

Note: *Regulations and requirements may be subject to change at short notice, and you are advised to contact your doctor well in advance of your intended date of departure. Any numbers in the chart refer to the footnotes below.*

1: A yellow fever vaccination certificate is required from all travellers over one year of age. High-risk areas are rural areas, particularly the Poni province. Vaccinations against the A, C and W135 strains are highly recommended.
2: Following WHO guidelines issued in 1973, a cholera vaccination certificate is no longer a condition of entry to Burkina Faso. However, cholera is a serious risk in this country and precautions are essential. Up-to-date advice should be sought before deciding whether these precautions should include vaccination as medical opinion is divided over its effectiveness; see the *Health* appendix.
3: Typhoid immunisation or boosters are recommended. Poliomyelitis is endemic.
4: Malaria risk exists all year throughout the country, predominantly in the malignant *falciparum* form. Resistance to chloroquine has been reported. A weekly dose of 250mg of mefloquine is the recommended prophylaxis.
Food & drink: Water is scarce and all found water should be regarded as being potentially contaminated. Drinking water outside main cities and towns is likely to be contaminated and sterilisation is considered essential. Milk is unpasteurised and should be boiled. Powdered or tinned milk is available and is advised, but make sure that it is reconstituted with pure water. Avoid all dairy products made from unboiled milk. Only eat well-cooked meat and fish, preferably served hot. Pork, salad and mayonnaise may carry increased risk. Vegetables should be cooked and fruit peeled.
Other risks: *Bilharzia* (schistosomiasis) is present. Avoid swimming and paddling in fresh water; swimming pools that are well chlorinated and maintained are safe. *Onchoerciasis* (river blindness) and *trypanosomiasis* (sleeping sickness) occur. Vaccination against *meningococcal meningitis*, *tetanus* and *hepatitis A* is recommended. *Hepatitis B* is hyperendemic. *Hepatitis E*, *TB* and *dengue fever* occur. *HIV/Aids* is prevalent. The hot, dusty environment can exacerbate breathing problems. *Rabies* is present. For those at high risk, vaccination before arrival should be considered. If you are bitten, seek medical advice without delay. For more information, consult the *Health* appendix.
Health care: Health insurance is strongly recommended.

Travel - International

AIR: Burkina Faso's national airline is *Air Burkina (2J)*. Other airlines serving Burkina Faso include *Air Algérie*, *Air France* and *Air Ivoire*. There are regular flights from Paris and Brussels to Ouagadougou.
Approximate flight times: There are no direct flights from the UK or the USA. To Ouagadougou from *London* (via Paris) is 8 hours 15 minutes; from *New York* (via Paris) is 12 hours 20 minutes.
International airports: *Ouagadougou (OUA)* is 8km (5 miles) from the city. Taxi and bus services are available to the city. Airport facilities include banks, post office, shops, restaurants and car hire. *Borgo*, 16km (10 miles) from Bobo Dioulasso, handles mainly domestic flights (see

Travel – Internal).
Departure tax: None.
RAIL: The only route is the international line from Abidjan, Côte d'Ivoire, running through to Ouagadougou. There are around three trains a week between the two capitals. The line has recently been taken over by a French company. Work is underway to extend the line from Ouagadougou to Tambao on the Mali border, but this project may have to be cancelled to meet foreign debt requirements.
ROAD: Routes are from Benin, Côte d'Ivoire, Ghana, Mali, Niger and Togo, although these are often barely adequate. Regular bus services run during the dry season, from Bobo to Bamako in Mali, and from Ouagadougou to Niamey in Niger and to Abidjan in Côte d'Ivoire. The road from Ghana is being improved. Bush taxis also serve most routes.

Travel - Internal

AIR: *Borgo*, 16km (10 miles) from Bobo Dioulasso, is the principal domestic airport. Flights run to Bamako, Bouake and Tambao on *Air Volta*. Air taxis are available. Passenger and postal flights are also operated by *Air Inter-Burkina*.
RAIL: Services have been indefinitely suspended.
ROAD: In general, roads are impassable during the rainy season (July to September). Police checkpoints are a common cause of delays. Traffic drives on the right. It is inadvisable to drive at night, as there are few street lights and some vehicles do not have headlights. Visitors should be aware that there have been recent incidents involving armed groups stopping vehicles to rob them in the north of the country (including the Gorom-Gorom to Djibo road in February 2004). **Bus:** Buses and vans are called *cars* in Burkina Faso. Regular bus services are operated in the dry season to all major towns and it is necessary to book at least 48 hours in advance. These buses are also cheap and plentiful. **Taxi:** Shared taxis are available in major centres; fares are negotiable. **Car hire:** Available from hotels in Ouagadougou. Car hire is still a recent phenomenon in Burkina Faso, and vehicles may be in poor condition. Visitors are therefore advised to lease cars for a day or two before committing themselves to a longer contract. Chauffeur-driven cars are also available. **Documentation:** A temporary licence to drive is available from local authorities on presentation of a valid national driving licence, but an International Driving Permit is recommended.

Accommodation

There are hotels in Ouagadougou and Bobo Dioulasso with some air-conditioned rooms and additional facilities. Elsewhere there are small lodges. There is also a group of tourist-class bungalows at Arly National Park. Camping may be allowed in certain areas. Information can be obtained from the Direction du Tourisme et de l'Hôtellerie (see *Contact Addresses* section). **Grading:** Hotels are rated by the Government in stars.

Resorts & Excursions

The capital, **Ouagadougou**, has an interesting **Ethnography Museum** containing a substantial collection of Mossi artefacts, the town being the centre of one of the many ancient Mossi kingdoms. Other museums include the **National Museum** in the Lycée Bogodogo and the **Snake Museum** in the Collège de la Salle. There is also a tourist office in the town. The Moro-Naba ceremony, with traditional costumes and drums, takes place outside the **Moro-Naba Palace** every Friday morning around 0600. Excursions from Ouagadougou include a wildlife-viewing trip to a small artificial lake 18km (11 miles) to the north. **Pabre**, an ancient Mossi village, is a short distance from another large reservoir north of the city. At **Sabou**, crocodiles can be seen at close quarters. However, as far as viewing wildlife is concerned, the three national parks – at **Kabore Tembi**, at **'W'** near the Benin and Niger border, and at **Arli** – are the most important. South of Ougadougou, near Po, the **Ranch de Nazinga** is a game reserve with a large population of elephants, antelopes, monkeys, baboons and warthogs.
Bobo Dioulasso is the largest town inhabited by the Bobo people in Burkina Faso, with attractive streets and a bustling market, the **Grand Marché**. Other city attractions are the **Musée Provincial du Houët** with regional relics, arts and crafts, and the **Grande Mosquée** in the Kibidwé district. Excursions outside the city include the scenic sacred fish pond of **La Mare aux Poissons Sacrés de Dafra**, 8km (5 miles) southeast of the city; the excellent bathing pond of **La Guinguette**, located in **La Fôret de Kou**, 18km (11 miles) from the city; and the **Mare aux Hippopotames**, 66km (41 miles) northeast of the city, where visitors may be taken out in a **pirogue** to view the hippos for a small fee.
Southwest of Bobo Dioulasso is the town of **Banfora**, from where the impressive **Karfiguéla Waterfalls** can be seen, located 12km (3 miles) northwest of the town. Approximately 50km (31 miles) west of Banfora is the town of **Sindou**, the area where the extraordinary **Sindou Rock Formations** can be seen.

Sport & Activities

Wildlife: The national parks and reserves are the best places to view **wildlife**; for further details, see the *Resorts & Excursions* section. Tour operators in Ouagadougou can organise trips of varying duration. Entrance fees are payable to all reserves.
Outdoor pursuits: The best areas for **hiking** are in the southwest of the country near Banfora. Excellent views of the whole region can be had from the top of the *Banfora Escarpment*. The *Sénoufo* region west of Banfora is also very pleasant, as is the *Lobi* region around Gaoua, southeast of Bobo Dioulasso. **Mountain bike** trips can be arranged in the areas around *Bobo Dioulasso* and *Banfora*, in the *Lobi* region and in the *Nazinga Ranch* south of Ouagadougou.
Other: There are a couple of hotels with **swimming** pools in Ouagadougou open to non-residents for a small fee. Owing to endemic bilharzia, it is not safe to swim in most rivers, lakes or standing water. **Golf** can be played at the course on the *Route de Pô*. **Tennis** courts are in Ouagadougou and visitors can play at the Burkina Faso Club on invitation by a member. Permits are not usually required for **fishing**, although the use of poison, explosives and nets with mesh smaller than 3cm (1.2 inches) is prohibited. **Horses** are available for hire at the Club Hippique in Ouagadougou. **Football** is very popular. Several new stadiums are being planned, including a major new stadium in Ouagadougou.

Social Profile

FOOD & DRINK: Outside hotels, there are few restaurants in Ouagadougou and in Bobo Dioulasso. Staple foods include sorghum, millet, rice, maize, nuts, potatoes and yams. There are many popular dishes incorporating a sauce, eg rice with sauce, beef and aubergine with sauce, etc. Local vegetables and strawberries are available in season. Specialities include *brochettes* (meat cooked on a skewer) and chicken dishes. Beer is very reasonably priced.
NIGHTLIFE: Nightlife is particularly good in Ouagadougou and Bobo Dioulasso. There are several nightclubs in Ouagadougou, some with live music, and several cinemas, both open-air and air conditioned. Bobo Dioulasso has a lively street-cafe scene, good open-air bars and restaurants and a number of open-air and air-conditioned discos.
SHOPPING: Good markets exist in Bobo Dioulasso, Dori, Gorom-Gorom, Oahigouya and Ouagadougou. Bargaining in the traditional marketplace is recommended. Purchases include wooden statuettes, bronze models, masks, worked skins from the tannery in Ouagadougou, jewellery, fabrics, hand-woven blankets and leather goods and crafts ranging from chess sets to ashtrays. **Shopping hours:** Mon-Sat 0800-1400 and 1600-1700. Some shops may be open Sunday and there are daily markets in the main towns.
SPECIAL EVENTS: At around 0600 on Fridays, Nabayius Gou ('the Emperor goes to war') is a traditional 'drama' performed at the Moro-Naba Palace in Ouagadougou depicting the magnificently bedecked emperor being restrained by his wife and subjects as he sets off to make war with his brother. Traditional music and dancing can also be seen on festivals and holidays, especially in the southwest region which is rich in folklore.
The following is a selection of special events occurring in Burkina Faso in 2005:
Feb 26-Mar 5 *FESPACO Pan-African Film and Television Festival*, Ouagadougou. **Mar 20-27** *Internet Festival*. **Oct-Nov** *International Arts and Crafts Fair*, Ouagadougou. **Nov 4-6** *End of Ramadan*, nationwide.
SOCIAL CONVENTIONS: Women are always expected to dress modestly since this is a Moslem country. Within the urban areas, many French customs prevail. Dress should be casual and appropriate for hot weather. Lounge suits for men and formal wear for women are required for evening entertainment. Burkina Faso is a fascinating country because of its diversity: over 60 ethnic groups dwell in this country, proud to be Burkinabé, and yet, keen to preserve their own social and cultural idiosyncrasies. Outside the cities, little has changed for centuries and visitors should respect local customs and traditions. **Tipping:** Service is generally included in the bill (about 10 to 15 per cent) although it is customary to tip taxi drivers, porters and hotel staff. Tipping is more expected in the better-class restaurants.

Business Profile

ECONOMY: Burkina Faso's economy is predominantly agricultural, employing 80 per cent of the population and contributing to approximately half the total output. During years unaffected by drought – a frequent and recurring problem – it maintains subsistence agriculture (sorghum, millet, maize and rice), plus cash crops of cotton, groundnuts, sesame and shea-nuts, which are valuable export earners. Mineral deposits, including gold and manganese, have been located, although comparatively little has been exploited – in August 1999, the country's largest gold mine was closed as being unviable. Burkina Faso has a small manufacturing sector producing textiles, sugar and flour. New hydroelectric schemes should reduce the country's dependence on imported fuels. Economic policy has been dominated by the liberalisation measures implemented by the Compaoré government since the late 1990s, with particular stress on the reduction of the state sector, trade liberalisation and attraction of foreign investment. The economy has been growing at approximately 6 per cent annually since 2000, although it is still very poor, with an average annual per capita income of US$220 and depends heavily on overseas aid, particularly from France and the EU. Burkina Faso belongs to the CFA Franc Zone, which fixes the value of the local currency to that of the Euro (formerly the French Franc). Imports outweigh exports in value by a factor of five. Over one-third of exports are bought by France, which provides a similar quantity of Burkina Faso's imports. Outside the EU, neighbouring Côte d'Ivoire is Burkina's main trading partner.
BUSINESS: Suits should be worn for government and official business, otherwise a shirt and tie should suffice. Most officials prefer to wear national dress. French is the main language spoken in business circles and if the visitor does not have a command of French, interpreter services should be sought from the British Embassy. **Office hours:** Mon-Fri 0700-1230 and 1500-1730.
COMMERCIAL INFORMATION: The following organisation can offer advice: Chambre de Commerce, d'Industrie et d'Artisanat du Burkina Faso, 01 BP 502, Ouagadougou 01 (tel: 5030 6114/5; fax: 5030 6116; website: www.ccia.bf).

Climate

Tropical. The dry season lasts from November to February and the rainy season from June to October. The best months are November to February when the *Harmattan* wind blows from the east producing dry and cool weather. Rainfall is highest in the southwest and lowest in the northeast.
Required clothing: Lightweights and rainwear for the rainy season. Plenty of scarves and handkerchiefs are recommended during the months when the *Harmattan* blows.

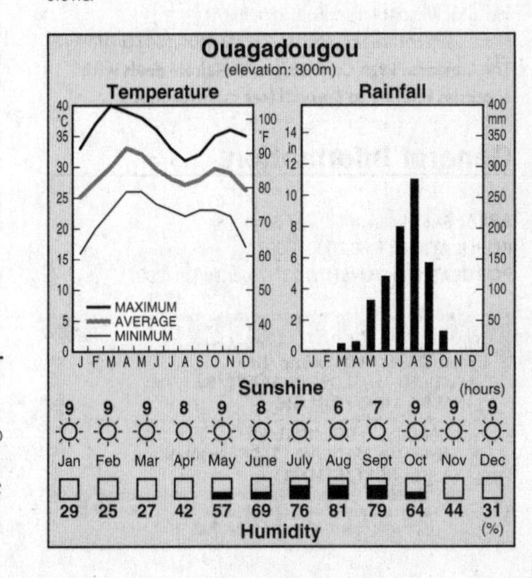

A B C D E F G H I J K L M N O P Q R S T U V W X Y Z

Burundi

LATEST TRAVEL ADVICE CONTACTS

British Foreign and Commonwealth Office
Tel: (0870) 606 0290 Website: www.fco.gov.uk

US Department of State
Website: http://travel.state.gov/travel

Canadian Department of Foreign Affairs and Int'l Trade
Tel: (1 800) 267 8376 Website: www.dfait-maeci.gc.ca

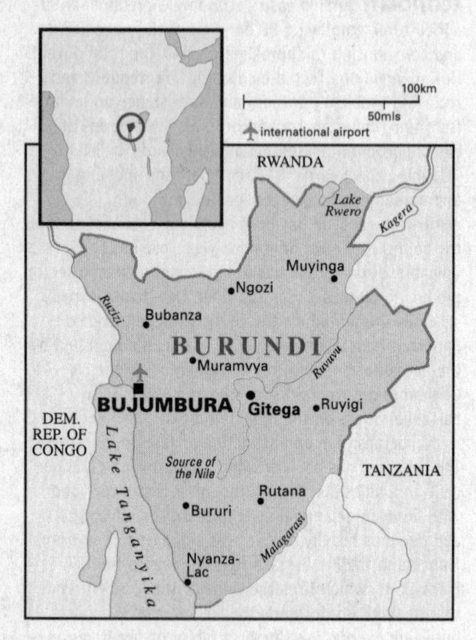

Location: Central Africa.

Country dialling code: 257.

Office National du Tourisme
2 avenue des Euphorbes, BP 902, Bujumbura, Burundi
Tel: 222 023. Tel/Fax: 229 390.
E-mail: ontbur@cbinf.com

Embassy of the Republic of Burundi
46 square Marie-Louise, 1000 Brussels, Belgium
Tel: (2) 230 4535. Fax: (2) 230 7883.
E-mail: ambassade.burundi@skynet.be

The British Embassy in Kigali deals with enquiries relating to Burundi (see *Rwanda* section).

Embassy of the Republic of Burundi
Suite 212, 2233 Wisconsin Avenue, NW,
Washington, DC 20007, USA
Tel: (202) 342 2574. Fax: (202) 342 2578.
E-mail: burundiembassy@erols.com
Website: www.burundiembassy-usa.org

Embassy of the United States of America
BP 1720, avenue des Etats-Unis, Bujumbura, Burundi
Tel: 223 454. Fax: 222 926.
Website: http://bujumbura.usembassy.gov

Embassy of the Republic of Burundi
325 Dalhousie Street, Suite 815, Ottawa, Ontario K1N 7G2, Canada
Tel: (613) 789 0414. Fax: (613) 789 9537.
E-mail: amabottawa@yahoo.ca *or* ambabucanada@infonet.ca

The Canadian High Commission in Nairobi deals with enquiries relating to Burundi (see *Kenya* section).

General Information

AREA: 27,834 sq km (10,747 sq miles).
POPULATION: 6,602,000 (2002).
POPULATION DENSITY: 237.2 per sq km (2002).

TIMATIC CODES

Health
AMADEUS: **TI-DFT/BJM/HE**
GALILEO/WORLDSPAN: **TI-DFT/BJM/HE**
SABRE: **TIDFT/BJM/HE**

Visa
AMADEUS: **TI-DFT/BJM/VI**
GALILEO/WORLDSPAN: **TI-DFT/BJM/VI**
SABRE: **TIDFT/BJM/VI**

To access TIMATIC country information on Health and Visa regulations through the Computer Reservations System (CRS), type in the appropriate command line listed above.

CAPITAL: Bujumbura. **Population:** 235,440 (1990).
GEOGRAPHY: Burundi is a land-locked country in the heart of Africa, a little south of the equator, on the eastern shore of Lake Tanganyika. It is bordered by Rwanda to the north, by the Democratic Republic of Congo to the west and by Tanzania to the south and east. The interior is a broken plateau sloping east to Tanzania and the valley of the River Malagarasi. The southern tributary of the Nile system rises in the south of the country. The landscape is characterised by hills and valleys covered with eucalyptus trees, banana groves, cultivated fields and pasture. In the east, the fertile area gives way to savannah grassland, and tea and coffee are now grown on mountainsides.
GOVERNMENT: Republic. Gained independence from Belgium in 1966. **Head of State and Government:** President Domitien Ndayizeye since 2003. A transitional government currently presides over Burundi: Burundi is in a state of civil war.
LANGUAGE: The official languages are French and Kirundi, a Bantu language. Swahili and English are also spoken.
RELIGION: More than 65 per cent of the population are Christian, the majority of which are Roman Catholic; there are Anglican and Pentecostalist minorities. 40 per cent adhere to animist beliefs. There is also a small (1 per cent) Muslim community.
TIME: GMT + 2.
ELECTRICITY: 220 volts AC, 50Hz.
COMMUNICATIONS: Telephone: IDD is available. Country code: 257. Outgoing international code: 00. Outgoing international calls must be made through the international operator (16). **Mobile telephone:** GSM 900 networks are operated by *Telcel Burundi* (website: www.telecel.com), *SAFARIS* and *Spacetel*. Coverage is mainly over the west of the country. **Internet:** ISPs include the Government-run *CBI Net*. New Internet providers are currently being set up in Bujumbura. There are a few Internet cafes in Bujumbura. **Telegram:** Facilities are available from *Direction des Télécommunications* in Bujumbura. **Post:** The main post office in Bujumbura is open Mon-Fri 0730-1200 and 1400-1730, Sat 0830-1200. **Press:** No English-language newspapers are published. Most publications are in French (such as *Le Renouveau du Burundi*) or local languages (such as *Ubumwe* in Kirundi). The two main newspapers are government-controlled. **Radio:** BBC World Service (website: www.bbc.co.uk/worldservice) and Voice of America (website: www.voa.gov) can be received. From time to time the frequencies change and the most up-to-date can be found online.

Passport/Visa

	Passport Required?	Visa Required?	Return Ticket Required?
Full British	Yes	Yes	Yes
Australian	Yes	Yes	Yes
Canadian	Yes	Yes	Yes
USA	Yes	Yes	Yes
Other EU	Yes	Yes	Yes
Japanese	Yes	Yes	Yes

Note: *Regulations and requirements may be subject to change at short notice, and you are advised to contact the appropriate diplomatic or consular authority before finalising travel arrangements. Details of these may be found at the head of this country's entry. Any numbers in the chart refer to the footnotes below.*

PASSPORTS: Valid passport for at least six months required by all.
VISAS: Required by all except nationals of Congo (Dem Rep), Rwanda and Uganda. Passengers arriving at Bujumbura airport from countries where Burundi does not have diplomatic representation can obtain visas on arrival, providing they have previously informed their travel agency of their passport number, identity and flight details. Those who are continuing onto a third country within 72 hours may also obtain a visa upon arrival. It is better to obtain a visa in advance from the nearest Burundi embassy.
Types of visa and cost: *Tourist* or *Business*: US$80 or US$40 (non-US citizens); single- or multiple-entry. The validity of the visa is at the discretion of the Immigration Department. A transit visa is not required for passengers continuing their journey to a third country if staying up to 24 hours, provided holding valid onward documentation and not leaving the airport. If staying up to 72 hours, a fee of US$10 is required. A Re-entry Permit is required for all alien residents.
Application to: Consulate (or Consular section at Embassy); see *Contact Addresses* section.
Application requirements: (a) Valid passport. (b) Three application forms (requests for application forms should be accompanied by a stamped, self-addressed envelope). (c) Three passport-size photos. (d) Return ticket or copy of flight itinerary, plus proof of accommodation. (e) Fee, payable in cash, postal order or company cheque. (f) Stamped, self-addressed envelope for recorded delivery. (g) For *business* visas, a letter from the applicant's employer and the sponsoring company in Burundi. (h) Yellow fever vaccination certificate, if applicable.
Working days required: Two. Applications should be made as far as possible in advance of the intended date of departure. A rush fee of US$25 is available.

Money

Currency: Burundi Franc (Bufr) = 100 centimes. Notes are in denominations of Bufr5000, 1000, 500, 100, 50, 20 and 10. Coins are in denominations of Bufr10, 5 and 1.
Currency exchange: All exchange transactions must be conducted through one of the main banks in Bujumbura or Gitega.
Credit & debit cards: Major credit cards have very limited acceptance.
Travellers cheques: To avoid additional exchange rate charges, travellers are advised to take travellers cheques in US Dollars or Euros. Commission rates are usually high.
Currency restrictions: The import and export of local currency is limited to Bufr2000. The import and export of foreign currency is unlimited, subject to declaration.
Exchange rate indicators: The following figures are included as a guide to the movements of the Burundi Franc against Sterling and the US Dollar:

Date	Feb '04	May '04	Aug '04	Nov '04
£1.00=	1929.47	1893.27	1952.90	2007.33
$1.00=	1060.00	1060.00	1060.00	1060.00

Banking hours: Mon-Fri 0800-1130 and 1500-1600; Sat 0830-1230.

Duty Free

The following goods may be taken into Burundi without incurring customs duty:
1000 cigarettes or 1kg of tobacco; 1l of alcoholic beverages.
Note: A deposit may be required for items such as cameras, recorders and typewriters.

Public Holidays

2005: Jan 1 New Year's Day. **Feb 5** Unity Day. **Mar 12** Labour Day. **May 5** Ascension. **Jul 1** Independence Day. **Aug 15** Assumption. **Oct 13** Anniversary of Rwagasore's Assassination. **Oct 21** Anniversary of President Ndadaye's Assassination. **Nov 1** All Saints' Day. **Dec 25** Christmas Day.
2006: Jan 1 New Year's Day. **Feb 5** Unity Day. **Mar 12** Labour Day. **May 25** Ascension. **Jul 1** Independence Day. **Aug 15** Assumption. **Oct 13** Anniversary of Rwagasore's Assassination. **Oct 21** Anniversary of President Ndadaye's Assassination. **Nov 1** All Saints' Day. **Dec 25** Christmas Day.

Health

	Special Precautions?	Certificate Required?
Yellow Fever	Yes	1
Cholera	Yes	2
Typhoid & Polio	3	N/A
Malaria	4	N/A

Note: *Regulations and requirements may be subject to change at short notice, and you are advised to contact your doctor well in advance of your intended date of departure. Any numbers in the chart refer to the footnotes below.*

1: A yellow fever vaccination certificate is required from travellers over one year of age arriving from infected areas. The country is officially considered endemic for yellow fever. Travellers arriving from non-endemic zones should note that vaccination is strongly recommended for travel outside the urban areas, even if an outbreak of the disease has not been reported and they would normally

not require a vaccination certificate to enter the country.
2: Despite WHO guidelines issued in 1973, a cholera vaccination certificate may still be a condition of entry to Burundi. Cholera is a serious risk in this country and precautions are essential; there was a serious outbreak in the Rumonage District in 1999, and there have been several clusters of Cholera cases in 2004. Up-to-date advice should be sought before deciding whether these precautions should include vaccination as medical opinion is divided over its effectiveness; see the *Health* appendix.
3: Vaccines against poliomyelitis and typhoid are advised.
4: Malaria risk exists throughout the year, predominantly in the malignant *falciparum* form, in the whole country. Resistance to chloroquine has been reported. The recommended prophylaxis is mefloquine.
Food & drink: All water should be regarded as being potentially contaminated. Water used for drinking, brushing teeth or making ice should have first been boiled or otherwise sterilised. Milk is unpasteurised and should be boiled. Powdered or tinned milk is available and is advised, but make sure that it is reconstituted with pure water. Avoid dairy products that are likely to have been made from unboiled milk. Only eat well-cooked meat and fish, preferably served hot. Pork, salad and mayonnaise may carry increased risk. Vegetables should be cooked and fruit peeled.
Note: Visitors may be asked to show proof of vaccination against meningococcal meningitis.
Other risks: *Hepatitis A* and *E*, *dysentery* and *typhoid fever* are widespread. *Hepatitis B* is hyperendemic. *Meningitis* is present all year (see note above). *Bilharzia* (schistosomiasis) is present; avoid swimming and paddling in fresh water. Swimming pools that are well chlorinated and maintained are safe. *Onchocerciasis* (river blindness) is present, as is *human trypanosomiasis* (sleeping sickness) in certain areas. *HIV/Aids* is prevalent. *Rabies* is present. For those at high risk, vaccination before arrival should be considered. If you are bitten, seek medical advice without delay. For more information, consult the *Health* appendix.
Health care: Medical insurance, including repatriation, is essential. Medical supplies are limited.

Travel - International

Travel Warning: All but essential travel to Bujumbura is advised against due to the high threat from indiscriminate attacks by rebel groups and all travel to other parts of Burundi, unless with an organised UN Mission, particularly in Bujumbura Rural Province.
AIR: Burundi's national airline is *Air Burundi (8Y)*. Other airlines serving Bujumbura include *Ethiopian Airlines*, *Kenya Airways* and *KLM*. There are no direct flights from Europe or the USA at present.
International airports: *Bujumbura International (BJM)* is 11km (7 miles) north of the city. Taxis are available to and from the city. Airport facilities include banks/bureaux de change, bars, duty-free shops, post office, light refreshments and car hire.
Departure tax: US$20.
LAKE: Cargo/passenger ferries ply Lake Tanganyika between Kigoma (Tanzania) and Mpulungu (Zambia) calling at various ports including Bujumbura, when political conditions permit. There are normally some ferries to Kalemi (Congo, Dem Rep). There are three classes. Ferries can often be delayed depending on the cargo being loaded or unloaded.
ROAD: It is normally possible to drive into Burundi from Congo (Dem Rep), either from the north or south. Roads from Rwanda are reasonable, but from Tanzania, poor. However the viability of crossing these borders depends on prevailing political conditions, and border areas can be very dangerous.

Travel - Internal

Note: There is a risk of street crime in Bujumbura, including muggings at gunpoint, car break-in, etc. It is advised not to walk in the streets after dark, especially since there is a curfew throughout the country (from 2300-0600), nor to carry large amounts of money. Attacks on public transport in the provinces are reported on most days, and the risk of being a victim of indiscriminate violence is high, with foreigners being occasional targets. Public transport outside Bujumbura is reported to be dangerous.
AIR: There are no scheduled internal flights at present.
ROAD: Most roads are sealed. There are main roads east from Bujumbura to Muramvya (once the royal city of Burundi) and south to Gitega. Both journeys can be completed without too much strain during the dry season, but any road travel can be difficult in the rainy season. Traffic drives on the right. Travellers should exercise extreme caution when travelling on roads to Kayanza, Ngozi and Kirundo. Roads can be subject to ambushes and are often closed during military operations; major roads are closed after 1600. All roads outside of Bujumbura City are unsafe to travel. **Bus:** There are services around Bujumbura and main towns only. Japanese-style minibuses operate between towns and are normally cheaper and less crowded than share-taxis; departures (when the vehicle is full) are normally from bus stands. **Taxi:** *Tanus-tanus* (truck taxis) are usually available but they are often crowded. **Car hire:** It may be possible to arrange some form of car hire via a local garage. **Documentation:** Driving licences issued by the UK are acceptable.

Accommodation

HOTELS: Almost all the hotels in the country are situated in the capital, Bujumbura, although there are a few in Gitega, Kirundo, Muyinga and Ngozi. Elsewhere in the country there is virtually no accommodation for visitors. For information contact the Office National du Tourisme (see *Contact Addresses* section); *or* NITRA, BP 1402, 7 place de l'Indépendence, Bujumbura (tel: 222 321; fax: 220 704; e-mail: nitra@usan-bu.net).
CAMPING: Currently very dangerous. Generally frowned upon, particularly near towns. Permission should always be obtained from the local authorities.

Resorts & Excursions

The capital port-city of **Bujumbura**, situated on the shore of **Lake Tanganyika**, is a bustling town with a population of some 300,000 inhabitants. The area was colonised by Germany at the end of the 19th century, and there is still architecture dating from that period of Burundi's history, including the **Postmaster's House**. Other attractions include three museums and the **Islamic Cultural Centre**. Various cafes and restaurants line the lake, where (in normal circumstances) there are some opportunities for watersports, including sailing, water-skiing and fishing. There is an excellent market. Around 10km (6.2 miles) south of the city, a stone marks the historic meeting-place of Stanley and Livingstone.
Other points of interest in the country include the former royal cities of **Muramvya** and **Gitega** (with its **Chutes de la Kagera** waterfall and its recently renovated **National Museum**), and the monument near **Rutovu**, in Bururi Province, which marks Burundi's claim to the source of the Nile.

Sport & Activities

General: Soccer is the national game. Burundians also excel in **track and field** events, often competing at an international level. People of all ages play the ancient game of **urubugu**, *or* **mancala**. It is played with pebbles or seashells on hollows scooped out on the ground, or with seeds on expensive, elaborately carved wooden boards.

Social Profile

FOOD & DRINK: The choice is limited. Meals in Bujumbura's hotels are reasonable, but expensive and of fairly average quality. The French and Greek restaurants in the town are good. There are few restaurants outside the capital and Gitega.
NIGHTLIFE: There are several nightclubs, restaurants and bars in Bujumbura.
SHOPPING: Local crafts, particularly basketwork, make excellent buys. **Shopping hours:** Mon-Fri 0830-1200 and 1500; Sat 0830-1230.
SOCIAL CONVENTIONS: Normal social courtesies apply. However, outside the cities people may not be used to visitors, and care and tact must be used in respect of local customs. Inhabitants of major towns generally have a more modern way of life. Dress should be reasonably conservative. **Tipping:** As a rule, no service charge is levied automatically; 10 per cent is the recommended tip.

Business Profile

ECONOMY: Subsistence agriculture employs 90 per cent of the workforce and accounts for approximately half of the total economic output. Cassava and sweet potatoes are the main subsistence crops, while coffee (the country's leading export), tea and cotton are the main cash crops. Hides and skins also produce valuable income. The country's small mining industry produces gold, tin, tungsten and tantalum. Deposits of vanadium, uranium and nickel – perhaps 5 per cent of known global reserves – have also been located and are due to be exploited in the near future. Oil deposits are believed to be present, although the quantities are unknown. Manufacturing is confined to small textile concerns. Burundi has economic cooperation agreements with Rwanda and the Democratic Republic of Congo through the Economic Community of the Great Lakes Countries and is a member of the Common Market for Eastern and Southern Africa (COMESA) and of the International Coffee Organisation. As one of the poorest countries in the world, with an annual per capita income of just US$100, Burundi remains heavily dependent on foreign aid, principally from France, Germany, Belgium (these three are also its major sources of imports), the EU and the World Bank. It appeared, in 2001, that Burundi's future prospects had been improved by the largely successful implementation of the Mandela peace accord. However, sustainable peace between the Tutsi minority, who dominates government, and the Hutu majority, has looked increasingly doubtful, and has hampered Burundi economic development - GDP plummeted to -1.3 per cent in 2004. Burundi's major export markets are the countries of the CFA Franc zone, which take approximately one-third of the total, followed by Belgium-Luxembourg, the USA, UK, France and The Netherlands.
BUSINESS: Lightweight suits are necessary. April to October and December to January are the best times to visit. **Office hours:** Mon-Fri 0730-1200 and 1400-1730.
COMMERCIAL INFORMATION: The following organisation can offer advice: Chambre de Commerce et de l'Industrie du Burundi, BP 313, Bujumbura (tel: 222 280; fax: 227 895).
CONFERENCES/CONVENTIONS: The following is the main organisation: Intercontact, BP 982, 19 rue de l'Industrie, Bujumbura (tel: 226 618 *or* 226 666; fax: 226 603).

Climate

A hot equatorial climate is found near Lake Tanganyika and in the Ruzizi River plain. It is often windy on the lake. The rest of the country is mild and pleasant. Burundi has two rainy seasons – the major one from February to April, with a minor rainy season between September and December, and two dry seasons: the long dry season from May to August and the shorter dry season between December and February.
Required clothing: Lightweight cottons and linens with waterproofs for the rainy season. Warm clothes are recommended for the evening.

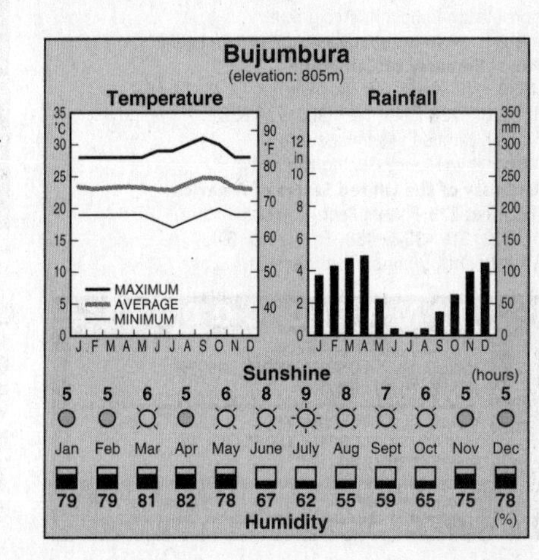

Cambodia

LATEST TRAVEL ADVICE CONTACTS

British Foreign and Commonwealth Office
Tel: (0870) 606 0290 Website: www.fco.gov.uk

US Department of State
Website: http://travel.state.gov/travel

Canadian Department of Foreign Affairs and Int'l Trade
Tel: (1 800) 267 8376 Website: www.dfait-maeci.gc.ca

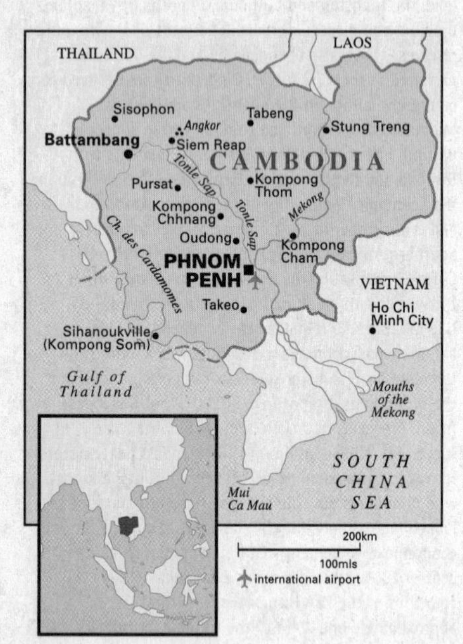

Location: South-East Asia.

Country dialling code: 855.

Ministry of Tourism
3 Monivong Boulevard, Phnom Penh 12258, Cambodia
Tel: (23) 211 593 *or* 222 409. Fax: (23) 212 837 *or* 213 741.
E-mail: info@mot.gov.kh Website: www.mot.gov.kh

Diethelm Travel (Cambodia) Ltd
No 65, Street 240, PO Box 99, Phnom Penh, Cambodia
Tel: (23) 219 151. Fax: (23) 219 150.
E-mail: dtc@dtc.com.kh Website: www.diethelm-travel.com

Orbitours Pty Ltd
Street address: 3rd Floor, 73 Walker Street, North Sydney, NSW 2060, Australia
Postal address: PO Box 834, North Sydney, NSW 2059, Australia
Tel: (2) 8913 0755. Fax: (2) 9956 7707.
E-mail: info@adventureworld.com.au
Website: www.orbitours.com.au

Royal Embassy of Cambodia
Wellington Building, 28-32 Wellington Road,
St John's Wood, London NW8 9SP, UK
Tel: (020) 7483 9063 *or* 9064 (consular section).
Fax: (020) 7483 9061.
E-mail: cambodianembassy@btconnect.com
Website: www.cambodianembassy.org.uk

British Embassy
27-29 Street 75, Phnom Penh, Cambodia
Tel: (23) 427 124 *or* 428 153. Fax: (23) 427 125.
E-mail: britemb@online.com.kh *or*
consular.phnompenh@fco.gov.uk
Website: www.britishembassy.gov.uk/cambodia

Royal Embassy of Cambodia
4530 16th Street, NW, Washington, DC 20011, USA
Tel: (202) 726 7742. Fax: (202) 726 8381.
E-mail: cambodia@embassy.org
Website: www.embassy.org/cambodia

Embassy of the United States of America
16 Street 228, Phnom Penh, Cambodia
Tel: (23) 216 436 *or* 438. Fax: (23) 216 437.
Website: http://phnompenh.usembassy.gov

TIMATIC CODES

Health	AMADEUS: **TI-DFT/JIB/HE** GALILEO/WORLDSPAN: **TI-DFT/JIB/HE** SABRE: **TIDFT/JIB/HE**
Visa	AMADEUS: **TI-DFT/JIB/VI** GALILEO/WORLDSPAN: **TI-DFT/JIB/VI** SABRE: **TIDFT/JIB/VI**

To access TIMATIC country information on Health and Visa regulations through the Computer Reservations System (CRS), type in the appropriate command line listed above.

Canadian Embassy
Villa 9, R.V. Senei Vinnavut Out (formerly Street 254), Sangkat Chaktomuk, Khan Daun Penh, Phnom Penh, Cambodia
Tel: (23) 213 470 ext 426. Fax: (23) 211 389.
E-mail: pnmpn@dfait-maeci.gc.ca
Website: www.dfait-maeci.gc.ca/cambodia
The embassy is shared with the Australian Embassy. Under the Consular Sharing Agreement, the Australian Embassy has consular responsibility for Canadian citizens in Cambodia.

General Information

AREA: 181,035 sq km (69,898 sq miles).
POPULATION: 13,311,000 (official estimate 2001).
POPULATION DENSITY: 73.5 per sq km.
CAPITAL: Phnom Penh. **Population**: 999,804 (1998).
GEOGRAPHY: Cambodia shares borders in the north with Laos and Thailand, in the east with Vietnam and in the southwest with the Gulf of Thailand. The landscape comprises tropical rainforest and fertile cultivated land traversed by many rivers. In the northeast area rise highlands. The capital is located at the junction of the Mekong and Tonle Sap rivers. The latter flows from a large inland lake, also called Tonle Sap, situated in the centre of the country. There are numerous offshore islands along the southwest coast.
GOVERNMENT: Constitutional monarchy since 1993. **Head of State**: King Norodom Sihamoni since 2004. **Head of Government**: Prime Minister Hun Sen since 1998.
LANGUAGE: Khmer is the official language and spoken by 95 per cent of the population. Chinese and Vietnamese are also spoken. French was widely spoken until the arrival of the Pol Pot regime and is still taught in schools, but English is now a more popular language to learn among the younger generation.
RELIGION: 90 per cent Buddhist (Theravada), the remainder Muslim and Christian. Buddhism was reinstated as the national religion in 1989 after a ban on religious activity in 1975.
TIME: GMT + 7.
ELECTRICITY: 230 volts AC, 50Hz. Power cuts are frequent. Outside Phnom Penh, electrical power is available only in the evenings from around 1830-2130.
COMMUNICATIONS: Telephone: IDD is available to Cambodia. At present, outgoing international calls can not be made. Country code: 855. Phnom Penh code: 23. Prepaid telephone cards are available in post offices, hotels and supermarkets for public phones around Phnom Penh and Siem Reap. **Mobile telephone:** GSM 900 and 1800 networks cover Phnom Penh and other main cities. Main network operators include Cambodia Shinawatra, CamGSM (MobiTel; website: www.mobitel.com.kh) and Samart (Hello GSM). **Fax:** Service is available in hotels and Internet shops. **Internet:** ISPs include OnlineCOM (website: www.online.com.kh). Internet cafes are available in Phnom Penh and Siem Reap. **Post:** Airmail to Europe takes four to five days, and seven to 10 days to the USA. The Post & Telephone Office (PTT) in Phnom Penh is located across from the Hotel Monorom at the corner of Achar Mean Boulevard and 126 Street and is open 0700-1200 and 1300-2300. The main post office in Phnom Penh is located on the western side of 13 Street between 98 Street and 102 Street, open 0630-2100. General post office hours: Mon-Fri 0730-1200 and 1430-1700. **Press:** The *Phnom Penh Post* (fortnightly), *Cambodia Times* (weekly) and *Cambodia Daily* are printed in English.
Radio: BBC World Service (website: www.bbc.co.uk/worldservice) and Voice of America (website: www.voa.gov) can be received. From time to time the frequencies change and the most up-to-date can be found online.

Passport/Visa

	Passport Required?	Visa Required?	Return Ticket Required?
Full British	Yes	Yes	No
Australian	Yes	Yes	No
Canadian	Yes	Yes	No
USA	Yes	Yes	No
Other EU	Yes	Yes	No
Japanese	Yes	Yes	No

Note: *Regulations and requirements may be subject to change at short notice, and you are advised to contact the appropriate diplomatic or consular authority before finalising travel arrangements. Details of these may be found at the head of this country's entry. Any numbers in the chart refer to the footnotes below.*

PASSPORTS: Passport valid for at least six months at time of entry required by all.
VISAS: Required by all.
Note: Visitors arriving by air can obtain a visa for stays of up to 30 days on arrival at *Phnom Penh International Airport*, Phnom Penh or *Siem Reap International Airport*, Angkor. Visas are also available from Immigration at the border posts of Bavet, Poi Pet and Koh Kong. Visitors are advised to check current situation before travelling.
Types of visa and cost: *Tourist* (single-entry): $22 ($20 in Cambodia). *Business* (single-entry): $27 ($25 in Cambodia).
Note: Children up to the age of 12, when travelling on their parent's passport, may obtain a visa without charge.
Validity: All visas are valid for a one month period, and visas issued by the Embassy must be used within three months of date of issue. Extensions of up to one extra month for *Tourist* visas or three to six years for *Business* visas may be granted by the Ministry of the Interior at the Immigration Office in Phnom Penh.
Application to: Consulate (or Consular section of Embassy); see *Contact Addresses* section. Tourists on package tours will normally have their visas arranged by the tour operator.
Note: Applications by post will only be accepted through a recognised visa courier. For further details, contact the nearest Consulate (or Consular section of Embassy); see *Contact Addresses* section.
Application requirements: (a) One completed application form. (b) Two passport-size photos. (c) Valid passport. Children need a passport and visa also. (d) Fee in cash only. (e) Self-addressed prepaid envelope if applying by post.
Note: (a) Children travelling on their parent's passport must submit an extra photo. (b) Nationals of Afghanistan, Algeria, Bangladesh, Iran, Iraq, Pakistan, Saudi Arabia, Sri Lanka and Sudan also need a return ticket. For *Tourist* visas, a letter of guarantee from the travel agent, and for *Business* visas, a business letter.
Working days required: Two.

Money

Credit: © Cambodian Ministry of Tourism

Currency: Riel (CRI) = 100 sen. Notes are in denominations of CRI100,000, 50,000, 20,000, 10,000, 5000, 2000, 1000, 500 and 100.
Currency exchange: US Dollars and Thai Baht are widely accepted and exchanged, but other currencies are generally not recognised.
Credit & debit cards: Limited acceptance, but can be used in upmarket hotels and restaurants catering to visitors. There are no ATMs in Cambodia. It is always best to carry cash (US dollars if necessary).
Travellers cheques: Limited acceptance. Travellers cheques are generally not recommended. Travellers cheques in US dollars can be changed at the official rate at the Foreign Trade Bank in Phnom Penh, and other larger banks and hotels.
Currency restrictions: Import and export of local currency is prohibited. Foreign currency may be exported up to the limit declared at customs on arrival. Amounts over US$10,000 have to be declared.
Exchange rate indicators: The following figures are included as a guide to the movements of the Riel against Sterling and the US Dollar:

Date	Feb '04	May '04	Aug '04	Nov '04
£1.00	7262.80	7126.54	7065.41	7290.74
$1.00	3990.00	3990.00	3835.00	3850.00

Banking hours: Mon-Fri 0800-1530. Some banks are open on Saturdays.

Duty Free

The following goods may be taken into Cambodia without incurring customs duty:
A reasonable amount of tobacco products or spirits.

Public Holidays

2005: Jan 1 New Year's Day. **Jan 7** Victory Day. **Feb 5** Meak Bochea Day. **Mar 8** Women's Day. **Apr 14-16** Cambodian New Year. **Apr 25** Visaka Buja Day (Birth of Buddha). **May 1** Labour Day. **May 19** Royal Ploughing Day Ceremony. **Jun 1** International Children's Day. **Jun 18** Queen's Birthday. **Sep 24** Constitution and Coronation Day. **Oct 14-14** Pchum Ben Day. **Oct 23** Paris Peace Agreement. **Oct 30-Nov 1** King's Birthday. **Nov 7-9** Water Festival. **Nov 9** Independence Day.
2006: Jan 1 New Year's Day. **Jan 7** Victory Day. **Feb 5** Meak Bochea Day. **Mar 8** Women's Day. **Mar 30** Cambodian New Year. **May 1** Labour Day. **May 7** Visaka Buja Day (Birth of Buddha); Royal Ploughing Day Ceremony. **Jun 1** International

Children's Day. **Jun 18** Queen's Birthday. **Sep 24** Constitution and Coronation Day. **Oct 14-14** Pchum Ben Day. **Oct 23** Paris Peace Agreement. **Oct 30-Nov 1** King's Birthday. **Nov 9** Independence Day. **Nov 25-27** Water Festival.
Note: The religious festivals are determined by the Buddhist lunar calender and are therefore variable.

Health

	Special Precautions?	Certificate Required?
Yellow Fever	No	1
Cholera	Yes	2
Typhoid & Polio	3	N/A
Malaria	4	N/A

Note: *Regulations and requirements may be subject to change at short notice, and you are advised to contact your doctor well in advance of your intended date of departure. Any numbers in the chart refer to the footnotes below.*

1: A yellow fever vaccination certificate is required by travellers arriving from infected areas.
2: Following WHO guidelines issued in 1973, a cholera vaccination certificate is no longer a condition of entry to Cambodia. However, cholera is a serious risk in this country and precautions are essential. Up-to-date advice should be sought before deciding whether these precautions should include vaccination as medical opinion is divided over its effectiveness; see the *Health* appendix for further information.
3: Immunisation against typhoid is recommended. Polio vaccination should be up-to-date.
4: Malaria risk exists all year outside the capital and close around Tonle Sap. Malaria does occur in the tourist areas of Angkor Wat. The malignant *falciparum* strain predominates and is reported to be highly resistant to chloroquine and sulfadoxine-pyrimethamine. Resistance to mefloquine has been reported from the western provinces. The recommended prophylaxis is mefloquine (including within the Angkor Wat area) but doxycycline in the western provinces.
Food & drink: All water should be regarded as being potentially contaminated. Water for drinking, brushing teeth or making ice should first be boiled or otherwise sterilised. Milk is unpasteurised and should be boiled. Powdered or tinned milk is available and is advised, but make sure that it is reconstituted with pure water. Avoid dairy products which are likely to have been made from unboiled milk. Only eat well-cooked meat and fish, preferably served hot. Pork, salad and mayonnaise may carry increased risk. Vegetables should be cooked and fruit peeled.
Other risks: *Bilharzia* (schistosomiasis) is present. Avoid swimming and paddling in fresh water; swimming pools which are well chlorinated and maintained are safe. *Giardiasis*, *dysentery*, *typhoid fever* and *dengue fever* are common throughout Cambodia. *Hepatitis A* occurs, *hepatitis B* is hyperendemic. *Japanese encephalitis* occurs in rural areas from May to October and is relatively common in the highlands. Epidemics of *avian influenza* (bird flu) were reported in Asia in 2004 and again in 2005, and some human cases were confirmed. Human cases were also reported in humans in 2005. Visitors should avoid bird farms or markets where contact with poultry might occur.
Rabies is present. For those at high risk, vaccination before arrival should be considered. If you are bitten, seek medical advice without delay. For more information, consult the *Health* appendix.
Health care: Health insurance, including emergency evacuation, is absolutely essential. Doctors and hospitals expect cash payments for any medical treatment.

Travel - International

Note: The greatest risks facing the traveller to Cambodia derive from road traffic accidents, armed robbery after dark, landmines and unexploded ordnance in rural areas. Public order is fragile; however, most visits to Cambodia are trouble-free.
AIR: *Bangkok Airways* and *Thai International* fly to Phnom Penh from Bangkok. *Malaysia Airlines* flies from Kuala Lumpur, *Vietnam Airlines* from Hanoi, *Aeroflot* from Moscow, *Silkair* from Singapore and *Lao International Aviation* from Vientiane.
Approximate flight times: From *London* to Phnom Penh takes 12 hours 30 minutes (with a stopover in Bangkok).
International airports: *Pochentong* (PNH) is 8km (5 miles) from Phnom Penh. A bus service (travel time - 15 minutes) and taxis (travel time - 10 minutes) to the city are available. Taxi fares are approximately US$8 and motorbikes are US$1. For pre-arranged tours a pick-up service is available. Airport facilities include left luggage, banks/bureaux de change, bars, shops, post office and light refreshments.
Departure tax: US$25 levied on international departures at Phnom Penh and Siam Reap International Airports; US$20 elsewhere; US$15 for holders of Cambodian passports. Children less than 4 years of age are exempt.
SEA: The port of Phnom Penh, and the ocean port at Sihanoukville, can be reached via the Mekong delta through Vietnam. This route is served by regular passenger ferry crossings.
RAIL/ROAD: The Thai border is now open for overland access. The main highway links the capital with the Vietnam border. Border checkpoints include Poipet, Cham Yeam (Thailand), Bavet, Kaam Samhar (Vietnam) and Stung Treng (Laos).

Travel - Internal

Note: Visitors should be aware that there is a danger of road traffic accidents, armed robbery after dark, landmines and unexploded ordnance whilst travelling in Cambodia. All necessary precautions should be undertaken. In terms of armed robbery (particularly in Phnom Penh and Sihanoukville) after dark, the greatest danger faces those travelling on motorcycles, especially regarding bag-snatching. There have also been violent incidents around popular tourist spots such as Street 154/174 of Phnom Penh. In terms of landmines, visitors should not stray off main routes, particularly in rural areas.
AIR: Internal flights operate between Phnom Penh and Siem Reap for Angkor (travel time - 45 minutes), Battambang, Koh Kong, Sihanoukville and Stung Treng. The upgraded *Siem Reap Airport*, the main gateway for visitors going to see the ancient temples at Angkor, is a 7 to 10-minute taxi ride from the city. Taxi fares are approximately US$5. Other airports include *Bottambang, Mondulkiri, Phnom Penh, Rattanakhiri* and *Stung Treng.*
Departure tax: US$20 for foreign nationals.
SEA: Government-run ferries depart from the Psar Cha Ministry of Transport Ferry Landing between 102 and 104 Streets and go to Kompong Cham, Kratie, Stung Treng, Kompong Chhnang and Phnom Krom. Boats are also available from Phnom Penh to Siem Reap, a route popular with travellers. Due to the present rise in crime, inter-city boat travel should be restricted to the fast boats to Kompong Cham and Kratie. Some boats have been reported as poorly maintained and over-crowded; some are reported to not contain life-jackets. Care should be taken to ensure the best and most safety-conscious boat travel available is selected.
RAIL: Some rail services operate; they are cheap but take much longer than the buses. There are plans to restore the international service to Bangkok, but a great deal of repair work is needed. If possible, other modes of transport with better maintained infrastructure should be taken.
ROAD: Traffic drives on the right. Most roads are in very poor condition, although the highway to Vietnam is open. It is possible to drive from Phnom Penh to Ho Chi Minh City in a day but there are formalities involved regarding the use of the same vehicle all the way. Right-hand drive vehicles (quite common in Cambodia) are not allowed entry to Vietnam. Both Cambodian and Vietnamese visas must be obtained in advance and the Vietnamese visa must mention 'Moc Bai' (the border point on the Vietnamese side) as a point of entry/exit, otherwise travellers run the risk of being turned back. Care should be taken while driving as Cambodian drivers are prone to recklessness and accidents are relatively frequent. The safety of road travel outside urban areas varies greatly from region to region. If travel is undertaken in vehicle convoy during daylight hours only, potential risks can be reduced. Other vehicles cannot always be relied on to use headlights. Cattle often stray onto the roads. In Siem Reap, the local police have banned rental outlets from hiring motorcycles to tourists. Reliable information about security should be obtained before considering extensive road journeys. **Bus**: Buses to Phnom Penh suburbs are available from 182 Street and the bus station is open 0530-1730. **Taxi**: Taxis can be hired in main cities. However, *cyclo's* (tricycles) or *motodops* (motorcycles) are a slow but inexpensive way to see the city and some of the drivers, especially those found outside main hotels, speak a little French or English. **Car hire**: Official visitors can arrange to hire a government car and driver. Enquiries about car hire should be addressed to the Ministry of Tourism (see *Contact Addresses* section).
Documentation: An International Driving Permit is not recognised in Cambodia, but car hire is generally not recommended. Visitors are advised to hire a car with a driver instead which is only slightly more expensive than car hire.

Accommodation

There is now a variety of good hotels available. The capital Phnom Penh and Siem Reap have numerous luxury hotels offering high standards and a range of recreational facilities. Hotels and guest houses are also available throughout the country, but standards generally tend to be basic. Camping is not permitted in Cambodia. For further information on accommodation, contact the Ministry of Tourism (see *Contact Addresses* section).

Resorts & Excursions

Since the ousting of the Pol Pot regime, many aspects of Khmer cultural life have revived. The famed *National Ballet* has been re-established by the surviving dancers and performs classical dances for visiting groups. **Buddhist temples**, such as **Preah Vihear**, close to the border with Thailand in the Dongrek mountains, have re-opened and are the sites of various celebrations, especially during the Cambodian New Year.
The interrogation centre of the Pol Pot regime in **Phnom Penh** is now the chilling **Toul Sleng Museum of Genocide**, also called S-21 (security office 21). Other attractions in the capital are the **Royal Palace**, with its famous **Silver Pagoda** (whose floor consists of 5000 silver tiles), and the recently restored **National Museum** (which includes bronze and stone sculptures from the Angkor period). River cruises, some also now offering dolphin watching, operate on the Mekong and Tonle Sap rivers near the capital. The famous and magnificent temples at **Angkor**, in the country's northwest, are hard and dangerous to reach by road, but may be reached by regular flights from Phnom Penh, Ho Chi Minh City, Singapore, Kuala Lumpur and Bangkok. This ancient and astounding temple complex is what remains of the capital of the once mighty Khmer civilisation. **Angkor Wat** itself, built AD 879-1191 to honour the Hindu god Vishnu, is often hailed as one of the most extraordinary architectural creations ever built, with its intricate bas reliefs, strange acoustics and magnificent soaring towers. **Oudong**, 30km (19 miles) from Phnom Penh, is located on a hill overlooking vast plains and is famous for the burial chedis of the Khmer kings. **Tonle Bati**, 42km (26 miles) from Phnom Penh, is located near a lake close to the ancient temple of **Ta Phrom**. The **Preah Vihear temple**, in the **Preah Vihear** province and on the border with Thailand, is now open to members of the public. The temple is a fine example of Khmer architecture from the 12th century. For more information, contact the Ministry of Tourism (see *Contact Addresses* section).
Sihanoukville is a popular beach resort town and may be reached by bus or air from Phnom Penh.

Sport & Activities

River tours: Trips on the Mekong and Tonle Sap rivers are becoming increasingly popular, one highlight being the opportunity to see Cambodia's famous freshwater dolphins near Kratié.
Trekking: There are still many thousands of unexploded landmines in more remote areas of Cambodia. Trekking is therefore still fairly limited, though some marked routes are available around Ratanakiri. In rural areas, travellers are strongly advised to seek local advice and not stray from the main paths. There is also the opportunity for **elephant rides** in Ratanakiri and Mondulkiri, although once again, a tour guide is needed.
Watersports: A range of watersports, including **swimming**, is available at Sihanoukville. **Snorkelling** is also good in this location.

Social Profile

FOOD & DRINK: Food stalls are also common in Phnom Penh and can usually be found in and around the Central Market, O Ressei Market and Tuol Tom Pong Market. Khmer cuisine is very similar to Thai, but with fewer spices involved. Popular dishes include fish, soup and salad, almost always incorporating Cambodia's favourite flavours of coriander, lemongrass and mint. There is also a plethora of sweet dishes. Common ingredients used in Cambodian cuisine include nuts, banana, coconut, the *durian* fruit (known for its distinctive odour), jackfruit, *longan* fruit, lychee, pineapple and *Rambutan* (which has translucent white flesh) fruit, to name just a few.
NIGHTLIFE: The major hotels offer entertainment, and weekly Apsara dance performances are often held from November to March in some hotel gardens. The *Holiday International Hotel* is a popular nightclub which also offers a karaoke bar and casino. For further information, contact Diethelm Travel (see *Contact Addresses* section).
SHOPPING: Antiques, woodcarvings, *papier mâché* masks, brass figurines, *kramas* (checked scarves), material for *sarongs* and *hols*, and items and jewellery made of gold, silver and precious stones are Cambodia's best buys. Visitors are advised that there are strict controls on the export of antiques - and stone carvings in particular. The Central Market, Tuol Tom Pong Market and the Old Market are among the best places for buying jewellery and the Fine Arts School sells many of the above goods in its shop. Clothing and materials are available at the Central Market.
Shopping hours: Mon-Fri 0800-2100.
SPECIAL EVENTS: The following is a selection of special events celebrated annually in Cambodia:
Jan/Feb *Têt*, Vietnamese and Chinese New Year. **Feb**

Meak Bochea Festival. **Feb 9-12** *Chaul Chhnam*, three-day celebration of the Cambodian New Year. **May 3** *Visaka Bochea*, Anniversary of the Buddha's Birth. **May 26** *Chrat Prea Nongkoal*, ceremonial beginning of the sowing season. **Jul-Sep** *Buddhist 'Lent'*. **Oct 2-4** *Pchum Ben*, offerings made to dead ancestors. **Oct** *Bonn Kathem* (religious festival). **Nov 10-11** *Angkor Wat Lighting Concert Hideki Togi* (*God's Banquet*). **Nov 15-17** *Festival of the Reversing Current* (The Water Festival), pirogue canoe races are held in Phnom Penh; *Bon Om Tuk*, Phnom Penh and Siem Reap.
SOCIAL CONVENTIONS: Sensitivity to politically-related subjects in conversation is advisable. Avoid pointing your foot at a person or touching someone on the head. Women should wear long clothing that covers the body.
Photography: Permitted, with certain restrictions, such as the photographing of military installations, airports and railway stations. It is polite to ask permission before photographing Cambodian people, especially monks.
Tipping: Tips are appreciated in hotels and restaurants where no service charge has been added, and by tour guides.

Business Profile

ECONOMY: The Cambodian economy was all but destroyed by the war in South-East Asia, following the rule of the Khmer Rouge between 1975 and 1979. Since the ousting of the Khmer Rouge from power by the Vietnamese in 1979, Cambodia has undergone a slow process of recovery. Restoration of agriculture – the foundation of the Cambodian economy and the main source of employment – has been slow but steady. Rice is the staple; other products include maize, sugar cane, cassava and bananas. The timber industry has also grown quickly on the back of heavy foreign investment and meets both domestic fuel demands and export markets - but at the expense of worrying deforestation. Timber is, along with rubber, the source of most of Cambodia's export earnings. Other mineral resources, which include phosphates, iron ore, bauxite, silicon and manganese, are limited. There is a small but fast-growing industrial sector concentrated in the production of consumer goods, processed foods and light manufacturing. This has largely relied on foreign investment, most of which has come from elsewhere in East Asia (especially Thailand), as more developed economies seek to take advantage of Cambodia's lower labour costs. Japan and Australia have supplanted the former Soviet Union as Cambodia's largest trading partners. GDP growth has reached 6 per cent annually since 2000, with construction activity particularly extensive, especially in the capital. The effects of the 1997 currency crisis on the economy were transitory, given the relatively undeveloped state of the Cambodian economy. Cambodia aspires to the status of an Asian 'tiger' economy and has joined, along with its neighbour Vietnam, the Association of South-East Asian Nations (ASEAN), now the principal regional economic co-operation body.
BUSINESS: Shirt and tie should be worn. Some knowledge of French would be useful. **Business hours**: Mon-Fri 0700-1700.
COMMERCIAL INFORMATION: For advice and information, contact The Royal Embassy of Cambodia in Paris (see *Contact Addresses* section).

Climate

Tropical monsoon climate. Monsoon season is from May to November. The most pleasant season is the dry season, from November/December to April. In the north, winters can be colder, while throughout most of the country temperatures remain fairly constant. There is often seasonal flooding in Phnom Penh and the rest of Cambodia in late-July and early-August; travel may be disrupted.
Required clothing: Lightweight clothing and cottons are worn all year. Rainwear is essential during the rainy season.

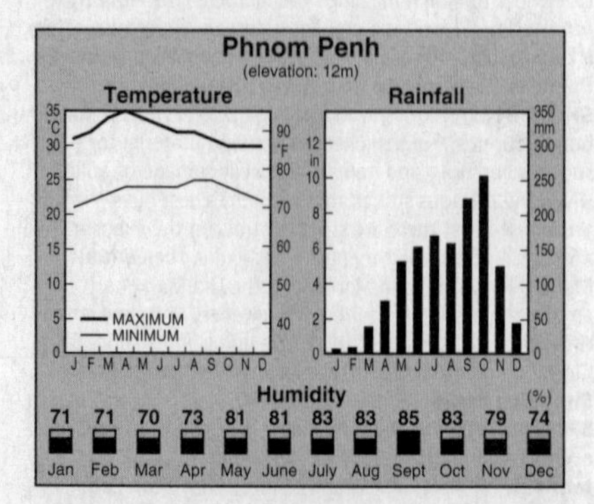

Cameroon

LATEST TRAVEL ADVICE CONTACTS

British Foreign and Commonwealth Office
Tel: (0870) 606 0290 Website: www.fco.gov.uk
US Department of State
Website: http://travel.state.gov/travel
Canadian Department of Foreign Affairs and Int'l Trade
Tel: (1 800) 267 8376 Website: www.dfait-maeci.gc.ca

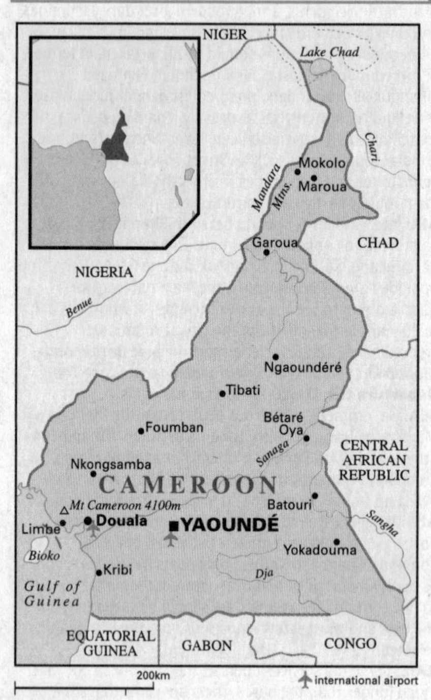

Location: Central Africa.

Country dialling code: 237.

Ministère du Tourisme
BP 266, Yaoundé, Cameroon
Tel: 224 4411. Fax: 221 1295.
E-mail: mintour@camnet.cm Website: www.mintour.gov.cm
Cameroon High Commission
84 Holland Park, London W11 3SB, UK
Tel: (020) 7727 0771. Fax: (020) 7792 9353.
Opening hours: Mon-Fri 0930-1600; 0930-1230 (visa applications).
British High Commission
Street address: Avenue Winston Churchill, Yaoundé, Cameroon
Postal address: BP 547, Yaoundé, Cameroon
Tel: 222 0545 *or* 222 0796. Fax: 222 0148.
E-mail: bhc.yaounde@fco.gov.uk
Website: www.britcam.org
Consulate in: Douala.
Embassy of the Republic of Cameroon
2349 Massachusetts Avenue, NW, Washington, DC 20008, USA
Tel: (202) 265 8790. Fax: (202) 387 3826.
E-mail: cdm@ambacam-usa.org
Website: www.ambacam-usa.org
Embassy of the United States of America
Rue Nachtigal, BP 817, Yaoundé, Cameroon
Tel: 223 4014 *or* 0512 *or* 222 2589 *or* 222 1794.
Fax: 223 0753.
E-mail: consularyaound@state.gov
Website: http://yaounde.usembassy.gov
High Commission for the Republic of Cameroon
170 Clemow Avenue, Ottawa, Ontario K1S 2B4, Canada
Tel: (613) 236 1522. Fax: (613) 235 3885.
E-mail: cameroon@rogers.com
Website: www.haut-commissariat-cameroun-ottawa.ca
Canadian High Commission
Street address: Immeuble Stamatiades, Place de l'Hôtel de Ville, Yaoundé, Cameroon
Postal address: BP 572, Yaoundé, Cameroon
Tel: 223 2311. Fax: 222 1090.
E-mail: yunde@international.gc.ca
Website: www.dfait-maeci.gc.ca/cameroon

TIMATIC CODES

Health	AMADEUS: **TI-DFT/JIB/HE** GALILEO/WORLDSPAN: **TI-DFT/JIB/HE** SABRE: **TIDFT/JIB/HE**
Visa	AMADEUS: **TI-DFT/JIB/VI** GALILEO/WORLDSPAN: **TI-DFT/JIB/VI** SABRE: **TIDFT/JIB/VI**

To access TIMATIC country information on Health and Visa regulations through the Computer Reservations System (CRS), type in the appropriate command line listed above.

General Information

AREA: 475,442 sq km (183,569 sq miles).
POPULATION: 16,018,000 (2003).
POPULATION DENSITY: 33.7 per sq km (2003).
CAPITAL: Yaoundé (constitutional). **Population**: 649,000 (1987). Douala (economic). **Population**: 810,000 (1987).
GEOGRAPHY: Situated on the west coast of Africa, Cameroon is bordered to the west by the Gulf of Guinea, to the northwest by Nigeria, to the northeast by Chad (with Lake Chad at its northern tip), to the east by the Central African Republic and to the south by Congo, Gabon and Equatorial Guinea. The far north of the country is a semi-desert broadening into the vast Maroua Plain, with game reserves and mineral deposits. This is bordered to the west by the lush Mandara Mountains. The Benue River rises here and flows westwards into the Niger. The country to the northwest is very beautiful; volcanic peaks covered by bamboo forest rise to over 2000m (6500ft), with waterfalls and villages scattered over the lower slopes. Further to the south and west are savannah uplands, while dense forest covers the east and south. The coastal strip is tropical and cultivated. Cameroon derives its name from the 15th-century Portuguese sailor Fernando Po's description of the River Wouri: *Rio dos Cameroes* ('river of shrimps').
GOVERNMENT: Republic. Gained independence in 1961. **Head of State**: President Paul Biya since 1982; won a new seven-year term in 2004. **Head of Government**: Prime Minister Peter Mafany Musonge Mafani since 1996.
LANGUAGE: The official languages are French and English. They are given equal importance in the Constitution but French is the more commonly spoken. Spanish is spoken in some urban centres. There are 24 major African language groups.
RELIGION: 53 per cent Christian (mainly Roman Catholic), 25 per cent traditional animist beliefs, 22 per cent Muslim.
TIME: GMT + 1.
ELECTRICITY: 110/220 volts AC, 50Hz. Plugs are round two-pin; bayonet light-fittings are used.
COMMUNICATIONS: Telephone: Telephone: IDD is available to and from Cameroon. Country code: 237. Outgoing international code: 00. International calls can be made from *CAMTEL* offices. Telephones can usually be found in post offices and restaurants, and there are telephone booths in the towns. Phonecards are available. The main towns in Cameroon are linked by automatic dialling, although this service is often unreliable. **Mobile telephone:** GSM 900 network provides coverage mainly in Yaoundé, Douala and the southwest of the country. Network operators include *Mobile Telephone Networks Cameroon (MTNC)* and *Orange Cameroun SA*. **Fax:** Available at *CAMNET* offices. **Internet:** ISPs include *Camnet* (website: www.camnet.cm). Internet cafes, which are on the increase, exist in the main towns. Charges are significantly higher outside Yaoundé and Douala. **Telegram:** Facilities are available at Yaoundé and Douala post offices and at larger hotels but service is slow. **Post:** Stamps can only be obtained from post offices. Mail takes about a week to reach addresses in Europe. Post office hours: Mon-Fri 0730-1530. **Press:** The main newspaper is the (government-controlled) *Cameroon Tribune*, published daily in French and English. Other English-language newspapers include the *Cameroon Post* (weekly), *Cameroon Times* (weekly) and *The Herald* (three times a week). **Radio:** BBC World Service (website: www.bbc.co.uk/worldservice) and Voice of America (website: www.voa.gov) can be received. From time to time the frequencies change and the most up-to-date can be found online.

Passport/Visa

	Passport Required?	Visa Required?	Return Ticket Required?
Full British	Yes	Yes	Yes
Australian	Yes	Yes	Yes
Canadian	Yes	Yes	Yes
USA	Yes	Yes	Yes
Other EU	Yes	Yes	Yes
Japanese	Yes	Yes	Yes

Note: *Regulations and requirements may be subject to change at short notice, and you are advised to contact the appropriate diplomatic or consular authority before finalising travel arrangements. Details of these may be found at the head of this country's entry. Any numbers in the chart refer to the footnotes below.*

Restricted entry: A yellow fever vaccination certificate must be presented on arrival by all travellers.
PASSPORTS: Passport valid for a minimum of six months required by all.
VISAS: Required by all except the following:
(a) nationals of Central African Republic, Chad, Congo (Rep),

Mali and Nigeria for stays not exceeding 90 days;
(b) those in transit continuing their journey on the first or same aircraft within 24 hours provided holding onward tickets and not leaving the airport.
Types of visa and cost: *Tourist* and *Short-stay*: £33.25 (three months). *Business*: £33.25 (three months); £66.50 (six months). *Transit*: £33.25 (five days). All visas are for multiple-entries.
Validity: *Tourist* and *Short-stay* visas are valid for up to three months; *Business* visas for up to six months. *Transit* visas are valid for up to five days.
Application to: Consulate (or Consular section at Embassy); see *Contact Addresses* section. Visas are also available on arrival for countries where Cameroon has no diplomatic representation.
Application requirements: (a) Passport valid for six months. (b) Two completed application forms. (c) Two passport-size photos. (d) International Certificate of Vaccination for Yellow Fever; (e) Return ticket or letter of confirmation from travel agent. (f) Copy of recent bank statement or letter from the bank verifying that applicant has sufficient funds. (g) For a business visa, a letter from applicant's company and a letter from business partners in Cameroon that must be legalised by the local police. (h) Appropriate fee.
Working days required: Two if the application is delivered in person; several for postal applications.
Temporary residence: Applicants must have Residence and Work Permits. Apply to immigration authorities in Cameroon.

Money

Currency: CFA (*Franc de la Communauté Financière Africaine*) Franc (CFAfr) = 100 centimes. Notes are in denominations of CFAfr10,000, 5000, 2000, 1000 and 500. Coins are in denominations of CFAfr250, 100, 50, 25, 10, 5 and 1. Cameroon is part of the French Monetary Area. Only currency issued by the *Banque des États de l'Afrique Centrale* (Bank of Central African States) is valid; currency issued by the *Banque des États de l'Afrique de l'Ouest* (Bank of West African States) is not. The CFA Franc is tied to the Euro.
Currency exchange: Euros are the easiest currency to exchange. US Dollars are the next most acceptable. Travellers should bring cash in preference to travellers cheques.
Credit & debit cards: Major credit cards are accepted on a very limited basis (some airline offices and hotels will take them). Cards cannot be used in banks to obtain cash advances.
Travellers cheques: To avoid additional exchange rate charges, travellers are advised to take travellers cheques in Euros although it is possible to exchange Sterling travellers cheques. Commission rates tend to be high.
Currency restrictions: Import of local currency is limited to CFAfr20,000. Import of foreign currency is unlimited. Export of local currency is limited to CFAfr20,000 if travelling for touristic purposes, or CFAfr450,000 if travelling for business purposes. There is no limit on the export of foreign currency.
Exchange rate indicators: The following figures are included as a guide to the movements of the CFA Franc against Sterling and the US Dollar:

Date	Feb '04	May '04	Aug '04	Nov '04
£1.00=	961.130	983.76	978.35	936.79
$1.00=	528.010	550.79	531.03	494.69

Banking hours: Mon-Fri 0730-1530.

Duty Free

The following goods may be taken into Cameroon without incurring any customs duty:
400 cigarettes or 50 cigars or five packets of tobacco; one bottle of alcoholic beverage; five bottles of perfume.
Note: Sporting guns require a licence.

Public Holidays

2005: Jan 1 New Year's Day. **Jan 21** Eid al-Adha (Festival of Sacrifice). **Feb 11** Youth Day. **Mar 25-28** Easter. **Apr 21** Eid Milad Nnabi (Prophet's Anniversary). **May 1** Labour Day. **May 5** Ascension. **May 20** National Day. **May 21** Sheep Festival. **Aug 15** Assumption. **Oct 1** Unification Day. **Nov 3-5** Djoulde Soumae (End of Ramadan). **Dec 25** Christmas.
2006: Jan 1 New Year's Day. **Jan 13** Eid Al Adha (Festival of Sacrifice). **Feb 11** Youth Day. **Apr 11** Eid Milad Nnabi (Prophet's Anniversary). **Apr 14-17** Easter. **May 1** Labour Day. **May 20** National Day. **May 21** Sheep Festival. **May 25** Ascension. **Aug 15** Assumption. **Oct 1** Unification Day. **Oct 22-24** Djoulde Soumae (End of Ramadan). **Dec 25** Christmas.
Note: Muslim festivals are timed according to local sightings of various phases of the moon and the dates given above are approximations. During the lunar month of Ramadan that precedes Djoulde Soumae (Eid al-Fitr), Muslims fast during the day and feast at night and normal business patterns may be interrupted. Many restaurants are closed during the day and there may be restrictions on smoking and drinking. Some disruption may continue into Djoulde Soumae itself. Djoulde Soumae may last anything from two to 10 days, depending on the region.

Health

	Special Precautions?	Certificate Required?
Cholera	Yes	2
Typhoid & Polio	3	N/A
Malaria	4	N/A

Note: *Regulations and requirements may be subject to change at short notice, and you are advised to contact your doctor well in advance of your intended date of departure. Any numbers in the chart refer to the footnotes below.*

1: A yellow fever vaccination certificate is required of all travellers over one year of age.
2: Following WHO guidelines issued in 1973, a cholera vaccination certificate is no longer a condition of entry to Cameroon. However, cholera is a serious risk in this country and precautions are essential. In June 2004, 2924 cases of cholera were confirmed in littoral to West Regions areas, since January of the same year. Although this has since abated, visitors should continue to monitor the situation. Up-to-date advice should be sought before deciding whether these precautions should include vaccination as medical opinion is divided over its effectiveness. For more information, see the *Health* appendix.
3: Immunisation against diphtheria, hepatitis A and typhoid is recommended. Poliomyelitis is endemic and inoculation is advised. Vaccines are also sometimes advised for hepatitis B, meningococcal meningitis, rabies and tuberculosis.
4: Malaria risk exists all year throughout the country, predominantly in the malignant *falciparum* form. Resistance to chloroquine and sulfadoxine-pyrimethamine has been reported. The recommended prophylaxis is mefloquine.
Food & drink: Water precautions are recommended outside of main hotels but all water should be regarded as being potentially contaminated. Water used for drinking, brushing teeth or making ice should have first been boiled or otherwise sterilised. Bottled water is readily available. Milk is unpasteurised and should be boiled. Powdered or tinned milk is available and is advised, but make sure that it is reconstituted with pure water. Avoid dairy products which are likely to have been made from unboiled milk. Only eat well-cooked meat and fish, preferably served hot. Pork, salad and mayonnaise may carry increased risk. Vegetables should be cooked and fruit peeled.
Other risks: *Hepatitis B* is hyperendemic in the region. *Hepatitis A* and *E*, *dysentery*, *dengue fever* and *typhoid fever* are widespread. *Lassa fever* may be spread via rat populations in rural areas. *Onchocerciasis* (river blindness) exists and *cutaneous* and *visceral leishmaniasis* may be found in drier areas. *Human trypanosomiasis* (sleeping sickness) is reported in certain locations. *Bilharzia* (schistosomiasis) is present. Avoid swimming and paddling in fresh water; swimming pools which are well chlorinated and maintained are safe. *Meningococcal meningitis* risk exists during the dry season (December to June) in northern areas. *Paragonimiasis* (oriental lung fluke) has been reported. *HIV/Aids* is prevalent.
Rabies is present. For those at high risk, vaccination before arrival should be considered. If you are bitten, seek medical advice without delay. For more information, consult the *Health* appendix.
Health care: There are roughly 250 hospitals in Cameroon, although health facilities are not recommended to foreign travellers. Sanitation levels are low, even in the best hospitals and clinics. Facilities outside Yaoundé and Douala are extremely limited. International travellers are strongly advised to take out full medical insurance before departure.

Travel - International

Travel Warning: All travel to the border area with Nigeria is advised against (in the region of Bakassi Peninsula), since this area is still subject to a territorial dispute between the two countries and tensions are rife, with localised violent incidents often occurring with little warning. All non-essential travel to the border area with the Central African Republic is advised against. The border area with Congo (Rep) is closed. In addition, there is a danger of mugging and banditry in Cameroon, including car-hijacking and robbery, often armed and violent, particularly in Douala, Yaoundé, Kribi and Maroua. Jewellery and valuables should not be worn or carried in more isolated, poor regions of Cameroon (notably Yaoundé, la Briquetterie and Mokolo).
AIR: Cameroon's national airline is *Cameroon Airlines* (UY). Other airlines serving Cameroon include *Air France*, *Air Gabon*, *British Airways*, *Kenya Airways* and *Nigeria Airways*. There are connections to many destinations across Africa, including regular flights to Benin, Côte d'Ivoire, Nigeria, South Africa and Togo. There are also direct flights, once a week, to Brussels and Zurich, as well as five flights per week to Paris.
Approximate flight times: From Douala to *Paris* is six hours 40 minutes; from Yaounde to *Paris* is eight hours 35 minutes; from Douala to *London* is nine hours 15 minutes.
International airports: *Aeroports de Cameroon SA* (*ADC*) oversees the seven airports, including *Douala International*, *Garoua International* and *Yaoude Nsimalen International*. *Douala* (*DLA*) is situated 10km (6 miles) southeast of the city. Taxis to the city are available at a cost of approximately CFAfr3000. Facilities include a duty free shop, bar, post office, bank, shops and buffet/restaurant.
Yaounde Nsimalen International (NSI) airport is situated 25km (15.5 miles) from the city. Taxis to the city are available at a cost of approximately CFAfr3000 (travel time – 20 minutes).
Departure tax: Around US$15.
SEA: Cargo boats from Douala to Malabo (Equatorial Guinea) sometimes accept passengers. Speedboats and cargo boats ply the coastal route between Idendao (northern Cameroon) and Oron (Nigeria). However, these services are not regulated.
RIVER: There are ferry services across the Ntem River, on the border with Gabon. Pirogues also operate across this river to Equatorial Guinea.
RAIL: There is a rail route running from Douala to Nkongsamba, with a branch line leading off from Mbanga to Kumba. The Trans-Cameroon railway runs from Douala to Ngaoudere, with a branch line from Ngoumen to Mbalmayo. There are plans to extend the rail network from Mbalmayo to Bangui in the Central African Republic.
ROAD: There are road connections to Chad, the Central African Republic, Equatorial Guinea, Gabon and Nigeria. Travel on these routes is rough, and should not be attempted in the rainy season. 4-wheel-drive vehicles are recommended. Drivers should avoid travelling at night. Problems might be experienced at the borders with Gabon and the Central African Republic. Armed robberies have been reported in the three provinces of Adamaoua, the north and the far north (bordering Chad). Gendarmerie detachments are posted along the road between Maroua and Chad. The Trans-Africa Highway from Kenya to Nigeria is still under construction; the border area with Nigeria, neighbouring the Bakassi peninsula, should be avoided. The border with the Republic of Congo has been closed. **Bus**: Minibuses and bush taxis run from Yaoundé and Douala to all neighbouring countries (except where borders are closed). It may be necessary to change at the border.

Travel - Internal

Note: Petty theft is common on trains, coaches and bush-taxis, and visitors to Cameroon who rely on its transport are urged to remain vigilant.
AIR: This is the most efficient means of national transport. There are daily flights between Douala and Yaoundé; less regular flights to other interior towns, served by *Unitair*.
Departure tax: CFAfr500.
RAIL: *Cameroon Railways* (CAMRAIL) is the national service provider. Services are good, if relatively slow, and it is much quicker to go by train than by bus. There are daily services from Yaoundé to Ngaoundéré on the 'Gazelle du Nord', that runs from Douala to Ngaoundéré via Yaoundé and Belabo. Daily trains also run from Yaoundé to Douala, with onward connections to Nkongsamba. Couchettes are available, as are first- and second-class seats. Trains usually have a restaurant car. Tickets must be booked on the day of travel.
ROAD: There are paved roads from Douala to Yaoundé, Limbé, Buéa, Bafoussam and Bamenda and between main centres. Other roads are generally poorly maintained and become almost impassable during the rainy season. Many vehicles are poorly lit and badly driven. Traffic drives on the right. Night driving is not recommended. Car hijackings and violent muggings are increasingly common, particularly in the three provinces of Adamaoua, the North and the far North, so sensible precautions should be taken. Driving on the Yaoundé/Douala trunk road should be avoided, since accidents are common there. Roadside assistance is non-existent. Travellers should consult official government advice services for further information about security while driving. **Bus**: Modern coach services are available between Yaoundé and Douala, Bafoussam and Bamenda, Foumban and Dschanga. Bus services also exist between other main centres and more rural areas but tend to be unreliable and are often suspended during the rainy season. Bus services also have a reputation for being dangerous, as road safety is not a priority for Cameroon drivers and accidents are common. **Car hire**: This is limited and expensive and is available in Douala, Yaoundé and Limbé, with or without a driver. **Documentation**: An International Driving Permit is not a legal requirement but recommended, especially for those hiring a car. By law, a driving licence must be carried when driving; a Cameroonian licence can be obtained within 24 hours for a small fee.

URBAN: Taxis and share-taxis are available at reasonable fixed rates (none are metered). A 10 per cent tip is optional. City taxis do not generally comply with basic security norms and seatbelts are often absent. Violent assaults on taxi passengers are not uncommon, so the choice of taxi must be considered carefully. However, they are cheap and fast.

Accommodation

HOTELS: Good accommodation of international standard is available in Bamenda, Douala, Garoua, Maroua and Yaoundé. The good hotels (government-rated 2-star and above) have air conditioning, sports facilities and swimming pools; most rooms have showers. Some large hotels will accept major credit cards. Rates are for the room only. Cheaper accommo-dation is also available. *Campement* accommodation, is available just outside Waza National Park, north of Maroua in the far north of the country. Hotel facilities are in heavy demand; it is advisable to book in advance and obtain written confirmation of your booking. For more information on hotels in Cameroon, contact the Ministry of Tourism (see *Contact Addresses* section).
CAMPING: Permitted in Boubandjidah National Park, on the banks of Mayo Lidi River, and near the entrance of Waza National Park. Elsewhere, camping is considered unsafe due to the possibility of robberies.

Resorts & Excursions

THE CENTRE & EAST

Yaoundé, the capital city, stands on seven hills. There are modern hotels and many markets, shops and cinemas. Museums include the **Musée des Bénédictins**, a collection of traditional arts and crafts housed in a Benedictine Monastery on Mont Fébé, and the newer **National Museum of Yaoundé**. To the northwest, jungle-clad mountains rise to an altitude of 1000m (3280ft). **Mont Fébé**, which overlooks the city, has been developed as a resort, with a luxury hotel, nightclub, casino, gardens and golf course. Its high altitude ensures a pleasant climate. Further on are the **Nachtigal Falls** on the **River Sanga**; continue to **Bertoua**, **Yokadouma** and **Moloundou** with its abundant wildlife, most notably a small population of lowland gorillas.

THE WEST

Douala, Cameroon's economic capital, is 24km (15 miles) from the sea, on the left bank of the Wouri and dominated by Mount Cameroon. The cathedral, the shopping avenues, the **Artisanat National** (a craft/souvenir market), **Deido market**, the harbour, the museum, **Wouri Bridge** and the electric coffee-grading plant are worth visiting.
Buéa is a charming town situated on the slopes of **Mount Cameroon** (4095m/14,435ft), West Africa's highest mountain and the highest active volcano in Africa. For those interested in climbing the mountain, which is relatively easy, a permit from the local tourist office is necessary (these are not issued during the rainy season from March to November).
Bamenda, in the highlands north of Dschang, has a museum and a craft market. **Foumban**, northeast of Dschang, has many traditional buildings dating from its period of German colonisation, including **Bafut Fon's Palace**, which includes a craft centre. There is also the **Musée du Palais**, whose collection includes bejewelled thrones, armaments, musical instruments and dancing masks, the **Musée des Arts et des Traditions Bamoun**, and a market. The town serves as an excellent base for experiencing the Bamileke region's colourful Bamoun festivals and feast days.
Kribi, a small port and beach resort south of Douala, has perhaps the finest beach in Cameroon, **Londji Beach**. It is also a convenient starting point for tours to local villages and the **Campo Game Reserve** region. Buffaloes, lions and elephants roam the virgin forests inland.

THE NORTH

North Cameroon presents unexpected natural landscapes, with an average altitude of 1500m (4900ft) and plains, reaching an altitude of 300m (1000ft), covered by savannah. **Maroua** is located in the foothills of the **Mandara Mountains**, along the **Mayo River**. Places worth visiting include the market, the **Diamare Museum** (mainly an ethnographic museum where local craftwares are on sale: jewellery, tooled leather articles etc), the various African quarters and the banks of the Mayo Kaliao.
Mokolo is a picturesque town in a rugged rocky landscape. Approximately 55km (34 miles) away is the village of **Rhumsiki**, which features a maze of paths linking the small farms known as the Kapsiki; the Kirdi live here, whose customs and folklore have changed little for centuries. Going further north, there is a very typical village called **Koza** located at an altitude of 1100m (3600ft). **Mabas** gives a panoramic view on the large Bornou plain of Nigeria and where there are still see primitive blast furnaces.

NATIONAL PARKS AND RESERVES

The **Kalamaloué Reserve** is small but offers opportunities for viewing several species of antelopes, monkeys and warthogs; some elephants cross the reserve. **Waza National Park** covers 170,000 hectares (420,079 acres) and is open from mid-November to mid-June. There is a forest area and a vast expanse of grassy and wet plains, called *Yaeres*. Elephants, giraffes, antelopes, hartebeest, cobs, lions, cheetahs and warthogs are numerous. There is also a rich variety of birds. Accommodation and other facilities are available. A vehicle and a guide are required for entrance to the park. The **Bénoué National Park**, situated just off the Ngaoundere-Garoua main road, covers 180,000 hectares (444,790 acres) and has buffalo, hippopotamuses, crocodiles, hyena, giraffes, panthers, lions and a variety of primates, and can be visited all year round.
Korup National Park is home to Africa's oldest and most biologically diverse rainforest. Accessible by bush taxi, it is located in the westernmost corner of the country, along the Nigerian border near the town of **Mundemba**, which is about 150km (93miles) northwest of Douala. A wide variety of primates, birds, trees and other plants, including dozens of recently discovered species are there. Travellers should dress to cope with the 100 per cent humidity and the fording of waist-high pools.
The **Bouba Ndjidah National Park** is situated on the banks of **Mayo Lidi River** in the far north of the country; bordering Chad. Its wildlife includes elan and buffalo, black rhinoceroses, elephants and lions. There are several other parks and reserves which are not open to the public. Dinosaur fossils have been discovered here.

Sport & Activities

Wildlife: There are seven national parks and several reserves, which offer excellent opportunities to see some of the richest **flora and fauna** in Africa. Antelopes, hartebeest, warthogs and lions are amongst the species inhabiting the parks, and there are also numerous types of birds.
Photo safaris: A range of tours including photo safaris are organised by the Ministry of Tourism (see *Contact Addresses* section): a seven to 10-day tour of northern Cameroon sets out from *Ngaoundéré* and includes sports activities at *Ngaoundaba Ranch*, safari photography at *Bénoué* and *Waza National Parks*, visits to *Garoua*, the volcanic landscapes of *Rhumsiki*, the traditional village of *Oudjila*, the *Maga Dam* and a crafts workshop at *Maroua*, before returning to *Garoua*. An organised tour of western Cameroon and the *Bamileke region* sets out from *Douala* and includes visits to *Nkongsamba* coffee plantations, *Batié* and *Dschang* mountain towns, and *Foumban* with its museums of arts, crafts and culture, before returning to *Douala*.
Hiking and trekking: *Mount Cameroon*, the highest mountain in West Africa and Africa's highest active volcano, is a popular **mountaineering** destination. No special equipment is required but permits and guides are compulsory. The climb to the summit takes approximately three-four days; huts are available en route for accommodation. The best time to attempt the climb is in the dry season, between November and May. In Mindif, a park south of the northern town of Maroua, there is a huge rock known as *Le Dent de Mindif*, which is highly regarded for rock **climbing**. For those favouring really strenuous exercise, an **international marathon** is held annually at the mountain. Favourite hiking areas include the northern region near Mora (not far from the Nigerian border) and the highland area around Bamenda in the southwest. The Mandara Mountains west of Maroua are a good area for trekking. A permit is not required, but it is advisable to take a guide. A variety of **trails**, featuring coastal terrain, a focus on biodiversity, adventure or riverside terrain, are offered by *Jungle Village* in *Limbe Botanic Gardens*.
Other: Fishing is good in many rivers and coastal areas. **Swimming** in the sea and swimming pools of luxury hotels, which generally also have **tennis** courts, is available. A **golf** course is available to hotel residents in Yaoundé. **Football** is a very popular spectator sport.

Social Profile

FOOD & DRINK: Local food is excellent; French or Lebanese cuisine is also available. Luxury items can be extremely expensive. The country abounds in avocado pears, manioc leaves, citrus fruits, pineapples and mangoes. Prawns are in plentiful supply in the south. Many dishes are served with rice, *couscous* or mashed potato. There are many restaurants in big towns and cities, with good service. Most international hotels have bars.
NIGHTLIFE: In Douala and Yaoundé particularly, nightclubs and casinos can be found independently or within most good hotels. There are also some cinemas. Hotel bars stay open as long as there is custom.
SHOPPING: Local handicrafts include highly decorated pots, drinking horns, jugs, bottles and cups, great earthenware bowls and delicate pottery, dishes and trays, mats and rugs woven from grass, raffia, jewellery and camel hair or cotton and beadwork garments. **Shopping hours**: Mon-Sat 0730-1800.
SPECIAL EVENTS: Local entertainment troupes may be seen in most regional towns. For further information on special events, contact the Ministry of Tourism (see *Contact Addresses* section). The following is a selection of special events celebrated annually in Cameroon:
Jan *Mt Cameroon Race*. **May** *Cameroon National Festival*. **Oct** *Eid al-Fitr* (End of Ramadan). **Nov** *Nso Cultural Week*, including horse races through Kumbo.
SOCIAL CONVENTIONS: Handshaking is the customary form of greeting. In the north, where the population is largely Muslim, Islamic traditions should be respected. Visitors should never step inside a Muslim prayer circle of rocks. In other rural areas, where traditional beliefs predominate, it is essential to use tact. **Photography**: Cameras should be used with discretion, particularly in rural areas. Always ask permission before taking a photograph. Do not photograph airports, military establishments, official buildings, or military personnel in uniform. **Tipping**: The average tip for porters and hotel staff should be about 10 per cent, otherwise service charges are usually inclusive.

Business Profile

ECONOMY: Cameroon has enjoyed broad economic success since independence, by virtue of consistent agricultural performance and the rapid growth of its oil industry, although it has suffered some reverses through persistently low world commodity prices. The main agricultural products are cocoa (of which Cameroon is one of the world's largest producers), coffee, bananas, cotton, palm oil, wood and rubber. There are sizeable but largely unexploited deposits of iron ore, bauxite, copper, chromium, uranium and other metals. Hydro-electric projects meet almost all the country's energy needs, so that oil and gas are largely treated as export products. There are some offshore oil deposits, although the largest are located near the disputed Bakassi peninsula. The manufacturing industry is concentrated on processing of primary products – most of these are indigenous, although imported raw materials (such as Guinean bauxite, which feeds the aluminium industry) also play an important role. Wood and timber products, oil and coal, and food and drinks are the main sectors. During the 1990s, the government opened up much of the economy to competition. The economy has been growing steadily at an annual rate of approximately 5 per cent since 2000. France and The Netherlands are the major export markets, followed by Germany, the USA and fellow members of the Central African Customs and Economic Union, of which Cameroon is a member. The IMF agreed a structural adjustment programme with Cameroon in 1995; this was extended beyond the normal three-year term and continues to set the ground rules for the country's economic policy. The capital, Douala, now hosts one of sub-Saharan Africa's few stock exchanges, which was opened in 2002.
BUSINESS: Office hours: Mon-Fri 0730-1700.
Government office hours: Mon-Fri 0730-1530.
COMMERCIAL INFORMATION: The following organisation can offer advice on commercial information and on organising conferences and conventions: Chambre de Commerce, BP 36, Yaoundé (tel: 222 4776; fax: 222 155).

Climate

The south is hot and dry between November and February. The main rainy season is from July to October. Temperatures in the north vary. On the Adamaoua Plateau, temperatures drop sharply at night; the rainy season is from May to October. Grassland areas inland are much cooler than the coast with regular rainfall.
Required clothing: Lightweight cotton clothes, canvas or light leather shoes or sandals. Rainwear is necessary for coastal areas.

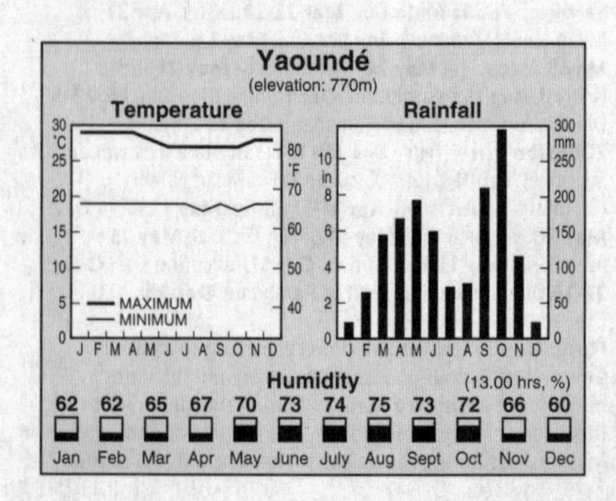

Canada

LATEST TRAVEL ADVICE CONTACTS

British Foreign and Commonwealth Office
Tel: (0870) 606 0290 Website: www.fco.gov.uk

US Department of State
Website: http://travel.state.gov/travel

Canadian Department of Foreign Affairs and Int'l Trade
Tel: (1 800) 267 8376 Website: www.dfait-maeci.gc.ca

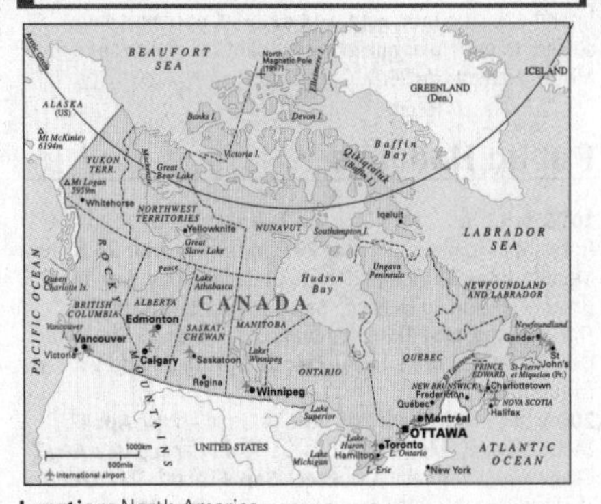

Location: North America.

Country dialling code: 1.

Canadian Tourism Commission
55 Metcalfe Street, Suite 600, Ottawa, Ontario K1P 6L5, Canada
Tel: (613) 946 1000. Fax: (613) 952 2320 (general).
Website: www.canadatourism.com
E-mail: trdc@ctc-ctc.ca

Canadian High Commission
Immigration division: 38 Grosvenor Street, London W1K 4AA, UK
Tel: (020) 7258 6600 *or* (020) 7258 6699 (recorded visa information). Fax: (020) 7258 6533.
Website: www.canada.org.uk *or* www.cic.gc.ca
Opening hours: Mon-Fri 0800-1100 excluding public holidays (personal callers only).
Cultural section: Canada House, 5 Pall Mall East, Trafalgar Square, London SW1Y 5BJ, UK
Tel: (020) 7258 6366. Fax: (020) 7258 6434.
E-mail: ldn-ld@international.gc.ca
Website: www.international.gc.ca/canadaeuropa/united_kingdom

Visit Canada Centre
PO Box 170, Ashford, Kent, TN24 0ZX, UK
Tel: (0906) 871 5000 (Mon-Fri 0900-1730, recorded information line; calls cost 60p per minute).
Fax: (0870) 165 5665.
E-mail: visitcanada@dial.pipex.com
Website: www.travelcanada.ca
Deals with consumer enquiries.

Canadian Tourism Commission
Address as for Visit Canada Centre (see above).
Tel: (0870) 161 5151 (travel trade only).
Fax: (0870) 165 5665.
E-mail: visitcanada@dial.pipex.com *or* gomediacanada@ctc-cct.ca (travel trade only).
Website: www.travelcanada.ca
Canadian Tourism Commission deals with marketing and trade enquiries only. Consumer enquiries should be directed to the Visit Canada Centre.

British High Commission
80 Elgin Street, Ottawa, Ontario K1P 5K7, Canada
Tel: (613) 237 1530 *or* 2008 (visa section).
Fax: (613) 237 7980 *or* 232 2533 (visa section).
E-mail: visaenquiries@britainincanada.org *or* generalenquiries@britainincanada.org
Website: www.britainincanada.org
Consulates General in: Montréal, Toronto and Vancouver.

Canadian Embassy
501 Pennsylvania Avenue, NW, Washington, DC 20001, USA
Tel: (202) 682 1740. Fax: (202) 682 7726.
E-mail: webmaster@canadianembassy.org
Website: www.canadianembassy.org

TIMATIC CODES

Health	AMADEUS: **TI-DFT/JIB/HE** GALILEO/WORLDSPAN: **TI-DFT/JIB/HE** SABRE: **TIDFT/JIB/HE**
Visa	AMADEUS: **TI-DFT/JIB/VI** GALILEO/WORLDSPAN: **TI-DFT/JIB/VI** SABRE: **TIDFT/JIB/VI**

To access TIMATIC country information on Health and Visa regulations through the Computer Reservations System (CRS), type in the appropriate command line listed above.

Canadian Consulate General
1251 Avenue of the Americas, New York, NY 10020, USA
Tel: (212) 596 1628. Fax: (212) 596 1793.
E-mail: cngny-td@international.gc.ca
Website: www.dfait-maeci.gc.ca/can-am/new_york
Consulate in: Miami. *Consulates General in*: Atlanta, Boston, Buffalo, Chicago, Dallas, Detroit, Los Angeles, Minneapolis and Seattle.

Embassy of the United States of America
490 Sussex Drive, Ottawa, Ontario K1N 1G8, Canada
Tel: (613) 238 5335.
Fax: (613) 688 3080 *or* 3082 (consular section).
E-mail: ottawareference@state.gov
Website: www.usembassycanada.gov
Consulates General in: Calgary, Halifax, Montréal, Québec, Toronto, Vancouver and Winnipeg.

For major regional Tourist Information Offices, see individual *Provinces/Territories* sections.

General Information

AREA: 9,984,670 sq km (3,855,101 sq miles).
POPULATION: 31,629,700 (official estimate 2003).
POPULATION DENSITY: 3.5 per sq km.
CAPITAL: Ottawa. **Population**: 1,063,664 (2001, including Hull).
GEOGRAPHY: Canada is bordered to the west by the Pacific Ocean and Alaska, to the east by the Atlantic Ocean, to the northeast by Greenland, and to the south by the 'Lower 48' of the USA. The polar ice cap lies to the north. The landscape is diverse, ranging from the Arctic tundra of the north to the great prairies of the central area. Westward are the Rocky Mountains, and in the southeast are the Great Lakes, the St Lawrence River and Niagara Falls. The country is divided into 10 provinces and three territories. A more detailed description of each province can be found under the separate provincial entries.
GOVERNMENT: Constitutional Monarchy. **Head of State**: HM Queen Elizabeth II, represented by Governor-General Adrienne Bing Chee Clarkson since 1999. **Head of Government**: Prime Minister Paul Martin since 2003.
LANGUAGE: Bilingual: English and French. The use of the two languages reflects the mixed colonial history – Canada has been under both British and French rule.
RELIGION: 75 per cent of the population belong to the Christian faith: Anglican, Roman Catholic and United Church of Canada. There are numerous other active denominations and religions.
TIME: Canada spans six time zones. Information on which time zone applies where may be found in the regional entries following this general introduction. The time zones are:
Pacific Standard Time: GMT - 8.
Mountain Standard Time: GMT - 7.
Central Standard Time: GMT - 6.
Eastern Standard Time: GMT - 5.
Atlantic Standard Time: GMT - 4.
Newfoundland Standard Time: GMT - 3.5.
From the first Sunday in April to the last Sunday in October, one hour is added for Daylight Saving Time (except in Saskatchewan).
ELECTRICITY: 110-120 volts AC, 60Hz. American-style (flat) two-pin plugs are standard.
COMMUNICATIONS: Telephone: Most public telephones operate using 25-cent coins. There is a reduced rate Mon-Fri 1800-0900, Sat 1200 to Mon 0900. For long-distance calls, telephone cards are available. Credit card telephones are to be found in larger centres. Full IDD is available. Country code: 1. Outgoing international code: 011. **Mobile telephone:** Digital PCS (1900MHz) services area available in and around major centres, while older analogue and digital cellular networks are available in less populated areas. A 'dual mode' handset is required outside the digital service areas. Network operators include *Bell Mobility* (website: www.bellmobility.ca), *Telus Mobility* (website: www.telusmobility.com) and *Rogers AT&T* (website: www.rogers.com). GSM network operators include *Microcell*, operating under the *Fido* brand name (website: www.canadagsm.com) and *Rogers AT&T*. Handsets can be hired from *Roadpost* (tel: (905) 272 5665 *or* (888) 290 1616 (toll-free within North America); website: www.roadpost.com), although it may be cheaper to buy a pay-as-you-go phone. **Fax:** Services are available in commercial bureaux and most hotels all day at locally agreed rates. **Internet:** ISPs include *Inter.net* (website: www.ca.inter.net) and *Sympatico* (website: www.sympatico.ca). There are Internet cafes all over the country. Internet terminals are usually available at airports and in photocopy shops. **Telegram:** These are handled by *Telegrams Canada*. Messages may be telephoned toll-free to 1-866-TEL-GRAM (1-866-835-4726; toll-free within Canada and the USA) for delivery anywhere in Canada or the USA. Billing arrangements may be made at the time the message is phoned in. Pricing and other information is available from *Telegrams Canada* (website: www.telegrams.ca) **Post:** All mail from Canada to outside North America is by air. Stamps are available in hotels, some pharmacies and local stores, or in vending machines outside post offices and shopping centres. *Poste Restante* facilities are available. *Intelpost* is offered at main postal offices for satellite transmission of documents and photographs. Post office hours: generally Mon-Fri 0930-1700, Sat 0900-1200, but times vary according to province and location; city offices will have longer hours. **Press:** The main national daily newspaper is *The Globe and Mail*. *The National Post* also has national distribution. Daily newspapers published in the larger population centres have a wide local and regional circulation. French-language dailies are published in seven cities, including Montréal, Ottawa and Québec. In Alberta, the main English-language newspapers are the *Calgary Herald*, *The Calgary Sun*, *The Edmonton Journal* and *The Edmonton Sun*; in British Columbia, the *Vancouver Sun*; in

Credit: © Travel Alberta

Manitoba, the *Winnipeg Free Press* and *The Winnipeg Sun*; in New Brunswick, the *Daily Gleaner* and *The Times Transcript*; in Newfoundland & Labrador, the *Telegram* and *The Western Star*; in Nova Scotia, *The Chronicle-Herald* and *The Daily News*; in Ontario, *The Ottawa Citizen*, *Ottawa Sun*, *The Toronto Star* and the *The Toronto Sun*; in Prince Edward Island, the *Guardian* and the *Journal Pioneer*; in Québec, *The Gazette* (daily); in Saskatchewan, the *Daily Herald*, *Leader Post*, *Star-Phoenix* and the *Times-Herald* ; and in Yukon, *The Whitehorse Star*.
Radio: BBC World Service (website: www.bbc.co.uk/worldservice) and Voice of America (website: www.voa.gov) can be received. From time to time the frequencies change and the most up-to-date can be found online.

Passport/Visa

	Passport Required?	Visa Required?	Return Ticket Required?
Full British	Yes	No/4	Yes
Australian	Yes	No	Yes
Canadian	1	N/A	N/A
USA	2	No	No
Other EU	3	5	Yes
Japanese	Yes	No	Yes

Note: *Regulations and requirements may be subject to change at short notice, and you are advised to contact the appropriate diplomatic or consular authority before finalising travel arrangements. Details of these may be found at the head of this country's entry. Any numbers in the chart refer to the footnotes below.*

Restricted entry and transit: The Government of Canada refuses admission to holders of passports, identity or travel documents issued by Bophuthatswana, Ciskei, Transkei, Venda or the All Palestine government.
Note: Visitors to Canada must satisfy an examining officer at the Port of Entry that they are genuine visitors, in good health, with no criminal convictions, and have sufficient funds to maintain themselves during their stay in Canada and to return to their country of origin, as well as evidence of confirmed onward reservations out of Canada. Persons under 18 years of age who are unaccompanied by an adult should bring with them a letter from a parent or guardian giving them permission to travel to Canada.
PASSPORTS: Passport valid for at least one day beyond the intended departure date from Canada required by all except the following:

A B C D E F G H I J K L M N O P Q R S T U V W X Y Z

(a) **1.** Canadian citizens holding a Canadian Certificate of Identity, Canadian birth certificate or a certificate of Canadian citizenship;
(b) permanent residents of Canada with proof of status, ie Permanent Resident Card, Record of Landing, Returning Resident Permit or a Refugee Travel Document issued by the Government of Canada to refugees who have been resettled in Canada;
(c) **2.** citizens of the USA holding proof of citizenship (eg US birth certificate or US naturalisation papers);
(d) persons entering from St Pierre & Miquelon or the USA who are legal permanent residents of the USA and hold a US alien registration card (Green Card);
(e) **3.** citizens of France who are residents of and entering from St Pierre & Miquelon;
(f) nationals who are residents of and entering from Greenland.
Note: Identity/travel documents issued to non-national residents of the country of issue, refugees or stateless persons are recognised for travel to Canada.
VISAS: Required by all except the following for stays of up to six months:
(a) nationals of countries indicated in the chart above, including **4.** citizens of British dependent territories (except holders of passports endorsed 'British Subjects' and 'British Protected Persons', who *do* require a visa);
(b) **5.** nationals of EU countries (except Czech Republic, Estonia, Hungary, Latvia, Lithuania, Poland and Slovak Republic, who *do* require a visa);

Credit: © Travel Alberta

(c) nationals of Andorra, Antigua & Barbuda, Bahamas, Barbados, Botswana, Brunei, French Overseas Possessions and Territories, Greenland, Guernsey, Hong Kong (SAR), Iceland, Jersey, Korea (Rep), Liechtenstein, Mexico, Monaco, Namibia, New Zealand, Niue, Norway, Papua New Guinea, St Kitts & Nevis, St Lucia, St Vincent & the Grenadines, Samoa, San Marino, Singapore, Solomon Islands, Swaziland, Switzerland and Vatican City;
(d) those visiting Canada who, during that visit, also visit the USA or St Pierre & Miquelon (a French Overseas Territory) and return directly to Canada as visitors within the period authorised on their initial entry (or any extension thereto).
Types of visa and cost: *Visitor*: C$75 (single-entry); C$150 (multiple-entry). *Family*: C$400 (for families of six or more persons). *Transit*: gratis. Transit visas are necessary for all nationals who require a visitor visa. Although transit visas are not required by British citizens, they may be required by foreign nationals with British passports; check with the Embassy or High Commission for details. *Employment*: C$150 (individual); C$450 (group of three or more). *Student*: C$125. For further information, contact the High Commission. Prices are subject to frequent change.
Validity: Up to six months depending on circumstances of individual applicant. The determination regarding length of stay in Canada can only be decided by the examining officer at the port of entry. If no actual departure date is indicated within the visitor's passport, then the visitor will be required to depart within three months from the date of entry. Visitors must effect their departure from Canada on or before the date authorised by the examining officer on arrival. If an extension of stay is desired, an application must be made in writing to the nearest Canada Immigration Centre well before the expiry of the visitor visa. Multiple-entry visas cannot be valid longer than passport. Transit visas are only allocated if a national's flight/onward journey is continuing within 24 hours. Single-entry visas can be used multiple times by nationals of St Pierre & Miquelon and the USA.
Note: A single-entry visa is still valid if used to visit the USA.
Application to: Consulate (or Consular section at Embassy or High Commission); see *Contact Addresses* section.
Application requirements: (a) Valid passport. (b) Proof of immigration status in country of residence. (c) Application form. (d) Two recent passport-size photos. (e) Proof of sufficient funds for length of stay (this may entail providing a letter from one's employer, mortgage statements or bank statements or letter of invitation from a Canadian resident). (f) Evidence of employment (in some cases). (g) Details of travel plans. (h) Visa processing fee payable in bankers draft only. (i) For those applying by post, an 8" x 6", registered, self-addressed envelope with £1 (C$2) stamp. *Transit*: (a)-(i) and, (j) Onward/return tickets.
Note: (a) Children under 16 years must have information with them on the people responsible for their welfare, if travelling alone; this includes a letter of permission to travel from guardian(s), and also a letter from the custodian in Canada. (b) Depending on circumstance and nationality, certain applicants may need to undergo a medical examination in order to receive their visas; this must be carried out by a physician on Canada's list of Designated Medical Practitioners.
Temporary residence: A work permit is required for temporary residence in Canada. Persons who wish to proceed to Canada for the purposes of study or temporary employment should contact the nearest Canadian High Commission, Embassy or Consulate, as authorisation is normally required prior to arrival. Those taking up temporary employment will require an Employment Authorization, for which a fee is charged. Persons going for study purposes must obtain a Student Authorization; a charge is made for this service.
Working days required: Applications should be made at least one month prior to the intended date of departure; eight weeks if applying by post. Certain nationals are subject to longer processing times.

Money

Currency: Canadian Dollar (C$) = 100 cents. Notes are in denominations of C$1000, 100, 50, 20, 10 and 5. Coins are in denominations of C$2 and 1, and 50, 25, 10, 5 and 1 cents.
Credit & debit cards: Most international credit and debit cards are accepted.
Travellers cheques: To avoid additional exchange rate charges, travellers are advised to take travellers cheques in Canadian Dollars; these are widely negotiable.
Currency restrictions: There are no restrictions on the import or export of either local or foreign currency. The export of silver coins over C$5 is prohibited.
Exchange rate indicators: The following figures are included as a guide to the movements of the Canadian Dollar against Sterling and the US Dollar:

Date	Feb '04	May '04	Aug '04	Nov '04
£1.00 =	2.42	2.47	2.41	2.42
$1.00 =	1.33	1.38	1.31	1.31

Banking hours: Mon-Wed and Fri 1000-1500, Thurs 0800-2100 (most banks). Business accounts can only be set up on presentation of a letter of credit from a home bank. Some banks in major centres have extended hours; visitors should check locally.

Duty Free

The following goods may be taken into Canada by non-residents without incurring customs duty:
200 cigarettes and 50 cigars or cigarillos and 200g of loose tobacco and 200 tobacco sticks per person over 18 years of age; one bottle (1.1l) of spirits or wine or 24 bottles or cans (355ml) of beer or ale per person over 18 years of age if entering Alberta, Manitoba and Québec, and over 19 years if entering British Columbia, New Brunswick, Newfoundland & Labrador, Northwest Territories, Nova Scotia, Ontario, Prince Edward Island, Saskatchewan and Yukon; gifts to the value of C$60 per gift (excluding advertising matter, tobacco or alcoholic beverages).
Prohibited items: The import of firearms, explosives, endangered species of animals and plants, animal products, meat, dairy, food and plant material is subject to certain restrictions and formalities. The import of soft shell turtles from any country and articles from Haiti made of animal skins (eg drums) is prohibited. The plant Qhat (Kat), although legal in the UK and various other locations, is illegal in Canada. Enquire at the Canadian High Commission or Embassy for further details.
Note: There is a Goods and Services Tax (GST) of 7 per cent on all goods and services. Visitors may reclaim this tax on accommodation and any goods purchased and taken out of the country. The goods must be available for inspection on leaving the country. The total amount on each receipt for eligible exported goods must be at least C$50 and the total purchase amount (before taxes) must be at least C$200. However, GST is not reclaimable on food, drink, tobacco or any form of transport. To claim a rebate, a GST form must be completed, with all original receipts and aircraft boarding pass attached, and posted to the address on the form. Forms are available in hotels and tourist offices. In Québec, the provincial sales tax can be reclaimed at the same time as GST on the GST form (see Shopping in the *Social Profile* section for further information on provincial sales tax). GST forms should be sent to Visitor Rebate Program, Canada Customs & Revenue Agency, Summerside Tax Centre, Suite 104, 275 Pope Road, Summerside PE C1N 6C6, Canada (tel: (902) 432 5608 outside Canada *or* (800) 668 4748 in Canada; website: www.ccra-adrc.gc.ca/visitors).
For cameras, radios, gramophones, typewriters etc, a deposit may be requested at the port of entry; this will be refunded to the owner upon submission of proof of export.
Canada Customs require nationals to declare whether they intend to visit a farm within 14 days. UK nationals were subject to particular questioning, following their Foot and Mouth epidemic in 2001.

Public Holidays

2005: Jan 1 New Year's Day. **Jan 2** New Year's Day (forwarded to Monday). **Mar 25** Good Friday. **Mar 28** Easter Monday. **May 23** Victoria Day. **Jul 1** Canada Day. **Aug 1** Civic Holiday (excluding Québec). **Sep 5** Labour Day. **Oct 10** Thanksgiving. **Nov 11** Remembrance Day. **Dec 25** Christmas Day (forwarded to Monday). **Dec 26** Boxing Day (forwarded to Tuesday).
2006: Jan 1 New Year's Day. **Apr 14** Good Friday. **Apr 17** Easter Monday. **May 22** Victoria Day. **Jul 1** Canada Day. **Aug 7** Civic Holiday (excluding Québec). **Sep 4** Labour Day. **Oct 9** Thanksgiving. **Nov 11** Remembrance Day. **Dec 25** Christmas Day. **Dec 26** Boxing Day.

Health

	Special Precautions?	Certificate Required?
Yellow Fever	No	No
Cholera	No	No
Typhoid & Polio	No	N/A
Malaria	No	N/A

Note: *Regulations and requirements may be subject to change at short notice, and you are advised to contact your doctor well in advance of your intended date of departure. Any numbers in the chart refer to the footnotes below.*

Other risks: In the summer months, extremely high temperatures can be reached, so visitors at this time may wish to guard against the problems of heat and sunstroke. *Rabies* is present in animals. For those at high risk, vaccination before arrival should be considered. If you are bitten, seek medical advice without delay. For more information, consult the *Health* appendix.
Health care: There is no reciprocal health agreement with the UK, but doctors will continue medication for prescriptions issued in Europe. Private health insurance of up to C$50,000 is absolutely essential as hospital charges are very high (from US$1000-2000 a day, often with 30 per cent surcharge for non-residents imposed in some provinces). Health facilities are excellent (similar to the USA). Personal first-aid kits should be carried by travellers to more remote northern areas. Dial 911 for emergencies.
Note: Visitors intending to stay in Canada for more than 6 months - either as tourists, students or employees - may be required to take a medical examination. Visitors working in an occupation in which protection of public health is essential may be required to undergo a medical examination even if employment is only temporary. Check with the Canadian Consulate or High Commission for further information.

Travel - International

AIR: Canada's principal national airline is *Air Canada (AC)* (website: www.aircanada.ca).
Approximate flight times: From *London* to Calgary is eight hours 45 minutes, to Halifax is seven hours five minutes, to Montréal is six hours 30 minutes, to Toronto is seven hours 15 minutes and to Vancouver is nine hours 20 minutes.
From *Los Angeles* to Montréal is seven hours 20 minutes, to Toronto is five hours 15 minutes and to Vancouver is two hours 50 minutes.
From *New York* to Montréal is one hour 15 minutes, to Toronto is one hour 20 minutes and to Vancouver is five hours 30 minutes.
From *Singapore* to Montréal is 23 hours 45 minutes, to Toronto is 21 hours 35 minutes and to Vancouver is 26 hours.
From *Sydney* to Montréal is 23 hours, to Toronto is 20 hours 30 minutes and to Vancouver is 18 hours 20 minutes.
International airports: Canada has 13 international airports. All have full banking and catering facilities, duty-free shops and car hire. Airport-to-city bus and taxi services

and, in some cases, rail links, are available.
Calgary (YYC) (website: www.calgaryairport.com) is 20km (12.5 miles) from the city (travel time - 45 minutes).
Edmonton (YEG) (website: www.edmontonairports.com) is 28km (17 miles) from the city (travel time - 30 minutes).
Gander (YQX) (website: www.ganderairport.com) is 3km (2 miles) from the city (travel time - 10 minutes).
Halifax (YHZ) (website: www.hiaa.ca) is 35km (21 miles) from the city (travel time - 30 minutes). *Hamilton* (YHM) (website: www.yhm.com) is 10km (6 miles) from the city (travel time - 20 minutes).
Montréal (YUL) (Dorval) (website: www.admtl.com) is 25km (16 miles) from the city (travel time - 25 minutes).
Ottawa (YOW) (Macdonald-Cartier) (website: www.ottawa-airport.ca) is 15km (8 miles) from the city (travel time - 20 to 45 minutes).
St John's (YYT) (website: www.stjohnsairport.com) is 8km (5 miles) from the city (travel time - 10 to 15 minutes).
Saskatoon (YXE) (website: www.yxe.ca) is 7km (4.5 miles) from the city (travel time - 15 minutes). *Toronto (YYZ)* (Lester B Pearson) (website: www.gtaa.com) is 27km (17 miles) from the city (travel time - 30 minutes).
Vancouver (YVR) (website: www.yvr.ca) is 13km (8 miles) from the city (travel time - 20 to 45 minutes).
Winnipeg (YWG) (website: www.waa.ca) is 10km (6 miles) from the city (travel time - 20 minutes).
Departure tax: Vancouver has an Airport Improvement Fee (AIF) which is C$15 for international departures and approximately C$10 for departures to other North American destinations, including Hawaii and Mexico. Montréal (Dorval) has a departure tax of C$10 for international departures. Transit passengers and children under two years of age not occupying a seat are exempt. Edmonton, Halifax, Ottawa, St John's, Toronto and Winnipeg levy an AIF of C$10, which is included in the ticket price. Calgary's AIF is C$12.
Note: In 2002, a new Air Travellers Security Charge (ATSC) was introduced, which helps to pay for the additional security following 11 September 2001. This charge is levied on all passengers departing from any Canadian airport for domestic, national and international flights. The charge is currently C$24 per person for national and international departures and C$12 per person per flight for all domestic services to a maximum of C$24 per person per ticket.
SEA: The principal Canadian ports on the Atlantic Ocean (east coast) are Halifax (Nova Scotia), St John (New Brunswick) and St John's (Newfoundland). Montréal and Québec have ports on the St Lawrence Seaway, which links the Atlantic Ocean with the Great Lakes and the industrial heartland of Canada and the USA. Toronto's port is on the northwestern shore of Lake Ontario. The port of Vancouver is on the west coast. All are served by international shipping lines, but Montréal (website: www.port-montreal.com) is the only port for passenger liners from Europe.
RAIL: The Canadian rail system connects to the USA at several points. Major routes are: New York–Montréal, New York–Buffalo–Niagara Falls–Toronto, Chicago–Sarnia–London–Toronto, Cleveland–Buffalo–Niagara Falls–Toronto and Detroit–Windsor–Toronto. *VIA Rail Canada*, the country's main rail operator, issues a discount pass for rail travel within Canada and the USA: the *North American Rail Pass* (available to anyone) is valid for 30 days and allows 12 days' unlimited travel within that 30-day period on VIA trains in Canada and practically any *Amtrak* train in the USA, with direct access to over 900 Canadian and US cities and towns. For details of ticket prices and reservations, contact VIA Rail in Canada (tel: (1 888) 842 7245 (toll-free in Canada); website: www.viarail.ca) *or* their UK representative *1st Rail* (tel: (0845) 644 3552/3; website: www.1strail.com).
ROAD: The only road access to Canada is through the southern border with the USA or from the west through Alaska. Apart from private motoring, the most popular way of travelling by road is by bus. The biggest coach company in the world is the *Greyhound Bus Company* (see the Coach section in *Travel – Internal*) and this is one of the most common routes to Canada from the USA. There are many crossing points from the USA to Canada, but some of the most common are: New York to Montréal/Ottawa; Detroit to Toronto/Hamilton; Minneapolis to Winnipeg; Seattle to Vancouver/Edmonton/Calgary.

Travel - Internal

AIR: Air Canada has a low-cost airline called *Tango* that offers reduced flights from most Canadian provinces and Fort Lauderdale, Orlando and Tampa in Florida, USA to a number of internal destinations. For further information about *Tango* services contact Air Canada, PO Box 64239, Thorncliffe Outlet, 5512 Fourth Street, NW, Calgary, Alberta, T2K 6J0 (tel: (800) 315 1390 (toll-free in Canada); fax: (866) 584 0380; website: www.flytango.com).
There are also around 75 airlines operating local services, the principal ones being: *Air Nova* (for eastern Canada) (website: www.airnova.ca), and *Air Alliance*, *Air Ontario* and *West-Jet* (website: www.westjet.com) (for central Canada). Reductions are available for those aged 13 to 21, with substantial reductions for those under 12.
Departure tax: From C$5 to C$28, depending on the airport of departure and the destination.
Note: In 2002 a new Air Travellers Security Charge (ATSC) was introduced, which helps to pay for the additional security following 11 September 2001. This charge is levied on all passengers departing from any Canadian airport for domestic, national and international flights. The charge is currently C$24 per person for national and international departures and C$12 per person per flight for all domestic services to a maximum of C$24 per person per ticket.
SEA/RIVER/LAKE/CANAL: Canada has many thousands of miles of navigable rivers and canals, a vast number of lakes and an extensive coastline. The whole country is well served by all manner of boats and ships, particularly the east and west coasts, where the ferries are fast, frequent and good value. The St Lawrence Seaway provides passage from the Atlantic Ocean to the Great Lakes. For further details, see individual regional entries *or* contact the Visit Canada Centre (see *Contact Addresses* section).
RAIL: *VIA Rail Canada* operates extensive services across Canada. The regional railways are *Algoma Central*, *British Columbia Railway*, *Great Canadian Railtour Company*, *Ontario Northland*, *Québec North Shore & Labrador*, *Toronto Hamilton & Buffalo Railway* and *White Pass & Yukon Route*. Children under two years of age not occupying a separate seat may travel free (one per adult) and children two to 11 years of age pay half fare. Persons over 60 years of age and students carrying an International Student Card (ISIC), will receive a 10 to 50 per cent discount (depending on the type of ticket); student discount fares also apply to young people aged 12 to 17.
VIA Rail operates a Western transcontinental service (the *Canadian*) between Toronto (Ontario) and Vancouver (British Columbia), running three times weekly east and west, transiting Winnipeg, Saskatoon, Edmonton and Jasper. Passengers are drawn to this route by the spectacular scenery of the three mountain ranges which are passed en route - the Rockies, the Selkirks and the Coastal. The route also features views of ancient glaciers, large lakes and waterfalls. All trains operating between Vancouver and Toronto include showers in sleeping cars. The transcontinental service can be accessed by regular services from the Atlantic provinces and from Québec City and Montréal. Rapid intercity services are available between Québec, Montréal, Halifax, Toronto, Windsor and Ottawa. On these journeys, the fare price includes a meal, snacks and drinks. *VIA Rail* also operates an overnight Eastern transcontinental service between Montréal (Québec) and Halifax (Nova Scotia). Long-distance trains are extremely comfortable, with full restaurant services, air conditioning, spacious reclining seats, etc.
The Rocky Mountaineer service (website: www.rockymountaineer.com) offers the opportunity to travel between Calgary, Banff, Jasper and Vancouver during daylight hours, enabling passengers to view the extraordinary passing scenery. Customers can purchase either a one-way or round-trip fare. A one-way trip takes two days and covers approximately 443km (275 miles) each day. Included in the price is a one-night stopover in Kamloops, bus transfer from train to Kamloops hotel, two continental breakfasts, two light lunches and complimentary beverages (coffee, tea, fruit juices and soft drinks). Alcoholic beverages, films and souvenirs are available on board at an additional cost.
For visitors seeking a route into the Canadian wilderness, the *Polar Bear Express* (Toronto–North Bay–Cochrane–Moosonee) runs daily (except Friday) from late June to early September. Passengers are advised to make hotel reservations in Moosonee in advance. Particularly scenic routes include Sault Ste. Marie–Eton–Hearst (with superb views of the Montréal River and hundreds of lakes), Winnipeg–Hudson Bay–Churchill, Edmonton–Jasper–Prince George–Prince Rupert (with exceptional scenery between Burns Lake and Prince Rupert), North Vancouver–Squamish (a one-day 87km round-trip (54 miles) tour of the Howe Sound on a steam locomotive to the logging town of Squamish where there are many First Nation arts and crafts and the 374m- (1000ft-) Shannon Falls), Victoria–Courtenay (along sheer cliffs to Malahat Summit with good views of Vancouver Island) and Vancouver–Whistler–Lillooet–Prince George (along the fjord-like coast of Howe Sound, then the craggy cliffs and rushing white-water streams in the heavily forested Cheakamus Canyon to Alta Lake, then the snow-covered mountains looming over the verdant forests and farmlands of the Pemberton Valley, before the final descent into Fraser River Canyon).
VIA Rail also offers tailor-made adventure rail trips (*VIA Adventures*) to far-flung destinations, some of which are inaccessible by road, offering drop-off and pick-up services and special facilities for carrying bulky items such as canoes and bicycles.
Discount Rail Passes: The *Canrailpass* must be purchased outside Canada and a valid passport presented at time of purchase; it allows unlimited journeys on the Canadian railway system (except for the Bras d'Or tourist train) for 12 days (up to three extra days can be added to the pass at any time) within a 30-day period, and is only valid on *VIA Rail* trains. There is also a *Student Canrailpass* available to holders of International Student Cards (ISIC) and a *Senior Canrailpass* available to persons aged 60 and over. There is a reduced fare for children. The *Alaska Pass* (website: www.alaskapass.com) offers eight-, 12-, 15- and 22-day travel within Alaska and British Columbia, including travel on *Alaska Ferry*, *Alaska Railroad*, *Greyhound Canada*, *Holland America Motorcoaches* and *White Pass & Yukon Railroad*.
For more information on rail itineraries, timetables, fares and special discounts, contact *VIA Rail* in Canada (tel: (416) 366 8411; website: www.viarail.ca); *or* the Visit Canada Centre (see *Contact Addresses* section).
ROAD: The road network covers vast distances as the country is over 7600km (4800 miles) from west to east and 4800km (3000 miles) from north to south. The longest road is the Trans-Canada Highway (website: www.transcanadahighway.com), running west to east for 8000km (5000 miles). On country roads, visitors should be mindful of wild animals that may be roaming, eg deer or moose. Petrol and oil are sold by the litre, and costs per litre should be obtained at time of travel. The *Canadian Automobile Association* (tel: (613) 247 0117; fax: (613) 247 0118; website: www.caa.ca) is affiliated to most European organisations, giving full use of facilities to members. Road signs are international. Right turns on red lights are not permitted in some parts of Québec. Traffic drives on the right. Road speeds (per hour) and distances are in kilometres, and speeds are: 100kph (60mph) on motorways, 80kph (55mph) on rural highways and 50kph (30mph) in cities. Many road signs throughout the country are bilingual (English and French). Seatbelts are compulsory for all passengers. Radar detection devices are strictly prohibited in many states and may not be carried in automobiles. Studded tyres are illegal in Ontario, but are permitted without seasonal limitations in the Northwest Territories, Saskatchewan and Yukon, and are allowed only in winter in other provinces.
Note: The official date on which winter begins, for this and other purposes, will vary from province to province.

Credit: © Travel Alberta

Coach: One of the cheapest and most convenient ways of travelling the country apart from private motoring is by coach. Each region is well served by a large network of coach lines, the most extensive being the *Greyhound Bus Company*, which covers more than 193,000km (120,000 miles) of North America. *Greyhound's Canada Pass* ticket must be purchased outside of North America and entitles the holder to unlimited travel over periods of seven, 10, 15, 21, 30, 45 and 60 days in Alberta, British Columbia, Manitoba, Northwest Territories, Ontario, Saskatchewan and Yukon and as far east as Montréal. The *Greyhound Canada Pass PLUS* offers unlimited travel for seven, 10, 15, 21, 30, 45 and 60 days throughout all of Canada, including the area east of Montréal to the Maritimes. The *Greyhound Canada Pass* includes all scheduled routes on *Greyhound* plus *Greyhound Lines Inc*: Montréal to New York and Vancouver to Seattle; *Voyageur Colonial*: Toronto to Montréal/Ottawa and North Bay to Montréal; *Brewster Transportation*: Banff to Jasper; Adirondack Trailways: New York to Buffalo to Toronto; *Canada Coach Services*: Toronto to Niagara Falls and Buffalo and Toronto to Detroit; *Grey Goose Bus Lines*: routes between Manitoba and Ontario; *Laidlaw Coach Lines*: services on Vancouver Island; *Saskatchewan Transportation Co*: Alaska to Saskatoon; and *VIA Rail*: Toronto to Ottawa to Montréal. The *Canada Pass PLUS* includes all these previous routes, plus *Orleans Express*: serving Montréal, Québec City and Rivière du Loup; Acadian Lines: Amherst to Truro and

A B C D E F G H I J K L M N O P Q R S T U V W X Y Z

Halifax; and SMT Lines: routes through New Brunswick. For further information, contact *Greyhound Canada* (tel: (403) 265 9111 *or* (800) 661 8747 (toll-free in USA and Canada); e-mail: canada.info@greyhound.ca; website: www.greyhound.ca). The *Go Canada* pass, which includes hostel accommodation, costs £396 for 15 days/nights and £588 for 30 days/nights.
Gray Line is another bus company that offers excursions to major Canadian resorts (website: www.grayline.ca). Canada also has regional bus services, the most important of which are:
Atlantic Canada: Acadian Lines, CN Roadcruiser, SMT Eastern and Terra Nova Transport.
Central Canada: Canada Coach Lines, Grey Goose Bus Lines Limited, Orleans Express, Saskatchewan Transportation, Voyageur and Voyageur Colonial.
West Canada: Brewster Transport and Vancouver Island Coach Lines.
Other coach companies operating in Canada include:
Gray Coach: Toronto to Niagara Falls and Buffalo; *Arctic Frontier Carriers*: Hay River to Yellowknife.
Besides long-distance travel, all these companies operate a range of services, such as regional tours and escorted sightseeing for groups. *RoutPass* offers 14-, 15-, 16- and 20-day passes for unlimited bus travel in eastern Canada. Children are not charged if under five years old; half the adult fare is charged for children aged five to 11 years old. Persons aged over 65 are eligible for reductions on fares in some provinces. Contact individual operators for details.
Bus: Metropolitan buses operate on a flat-fare system (standard fares, irrespective of distance travelled). Fares must be paid exactly, which means that drivers do not carry change or issue tickets. Transfers should be requested when boarding a bus.
Car Hire: Available in all cities and from airports to full licence holders over 21 years of age. Major companies from which cars can be booked in the UK for use in Canada are *Alamo, Avis, Budget, Dollar, Hertz, National* and *Thrifty*.
Documentation: It is advised to apply for an International Driving Permit. Visitors may drive on their national driving licences for up to three months in all provinces, with the following exceptions: Yukon – one month; Prince Edward Island – four months; British Columbia, New Brunswick and Québec – six months.
Travel times: The following chart gives approximate travel times from **Ottawa** (in hours and minutes) to other major cities/towns in Canada.

	Air	Road	Rail
Toronto	1.00	5.00	4.00
Montréal	0.30	2.00	2.00
Edmonton	4.30	50.00	50.00
Québec	1.00	6.00	6.00
Halifax	2.00	24.00	24.00
Winnipeg	2.30	32.00	32.00
Calgary	4.00	50.00	-
Vancouver	5.00	62.00	75.00
Regina	5.00	40.00	-

Accommodation

There is a wide range of accommodation from hotels to hostels. Standards are high, with full facilities. International hotel chains are represented in major cities, but advance booking is essential. Guest houses, farm vacations, bed & breakfast establishments and self-catering lodges are available throughout the country. Hunting and fishing trips to the wilderness areas of the north are often best arranged through 'Outfitters'. These are guides (often licensed by the local tourist office) who can arrange supplies, tackle, transport and accommodation. For further information, contact the Visit Canada Centre (see *Contact Addresses* section) *or* the Hotel Association of Canada, Suite 1206, 130 Albert Street, Ottawa, Ontario K1P 5G4 (tel: (613) 237 7149; fax: (613) 237 8928; e-mail: info@hotelassociation.ca; website: www.hotelassociation.ca). **Grading**: There is no national system of accommodation grading. Some provinces operate their own voluntary grading programmes; see the individual Provinces/Territories sections for details.
CAMPING/CARAVANNING: Camping facilities in the National Parks are generally only open from mid-May until the end of September. For further information, contact Canadream Campers (website: www.canadream.com). Mobile trailers and caravans are extremely popular ways of traversing the enormous expanse of the Canadian landscape. There are two different types of vehicle available: a 'motorhome' is a vehicle with connected driving cab and living space, equipped for up to five adults; whilst a 'camper' is a vehicle with a separate driving cab, more like a truck with a caravan on the back, equipped for up to three adults. There are different models according to the size of the accommodation and facilities required, but most have a fridge, cooker, sink, heater, fitted WC and showers. All vehicles are fitted with power steering. Petrol consumption is about 24km (15 miles) per imperial gallon (but petrol costs half as much as it does in Europe). Hiring is available to those who hold full licences and are aged over 25. The cost of hire can vary according to the season. High season runs from June to the end of September, and low season runs for the rest of the year. Full details can be obtained from the Visit Canada Centre (see *Contact Addresses* section).
YOUTH HOSTELS: There are youth hostels in major cities and national parks across the country. For further information, contact Hostelling International Canada (tel: (613) 237 7884; fax: (613) 237 7868; e-mail: info@hostellingintl.ca; website: www.hihostels.ca).

Resorts & Excursions

Canada offers a huge range of attractions, from large cosmopolitan cities such as Montréal and Toronto in the south, to isolated Inuit (Eskimo) settlements dotted around the frozen shores of Hudson Bay. The contrasting Pacific and Atlantic seaboards and the thousands of lakes and rivers of the interior provide superb watersports and fishing. The Rocky Mountains and other ranges offer breathtaking scenery on a grand scale. Some of the best resorts are in the series of great National Parks which preserve the wildlife and forests of Canada in their virgin state. Those in the north provide basic amenities for tours of the beautiful northern wilderness. A taste of the pioneering west can be had in the rich farming and grain regions of central Canada. Further north are the New Frontier of Yukon, the Northwest Territories and Nunavut. For a more detailed description of the historic sites and natural attractions of each region, see *Resorts & Excursions* in the individual Provinces/Territories sections.

Sport & Activities

Outdoor pursuits: Canada's vast wilderness areas and rich natural beauty offer scope for all kinds of outdoor activities. From **fishing** in the countless lakes and rivers to **trekking** in the back country, **long-distance canoeing**, **horse riding**, **rafting** and **skiing**, there are wonderful opportunities for those with a pioneering spirit. All activities are easy to arrange, given Canada's well-developed infrastructure: outfitters, guides, equipment hire and charters can be organised practically anywhere. Activities are often best pursued in national parks, of which there are about 41 in the whole of Canada, with other conservation areas and provincial parks adding to the range of facilities. At least one of the parks is larger than Switzerland (Wood Buffalo Park in Alberta and the Northwest Territories) and seven of them have been listed by UNESCO as World Heritage Sites. The national parks are administered by Parks Canada, 25 Eddy Street, Gatineau, Québec K1A 0M5 (tel: (819) 997 0055 *or* (888) 773 8888 (toll-free in USA and Canada); e-mail: information@pc.gc.ca; website: www.pc.gc.ca). Each national park has an information centre where advice on outdoor activities can be obtained, as can weather reports and bear sightings. Permits are required for fishing and camping and can be bought at these centres. Regulations common to all national parks include prohibitions on firearms, snowmobiles and off-road vehicles. Natural features may not be removed or damaged and hunting is also forbidden in most parks. Permits are required for all motor vehicles (approximately C$5-10 per person per day). Regional and national passes are available. Camping regulations vary, but in general, an overnight permit is required, whether or not the traveller camps at a campsite. Visitors intending to fish should note that regulations apply regarding closed seasons, quotas and equipment. Fishing permits are also usually required from the provincial authorities. For further information, contact regional tourist boards *or* the Visit Canada Centre (see *Contact Addresses* section).
Hiking: All the national parks and most of the provincial parks have well-marked and well-maintained trails. Maps may be obtained from information centres, but those intending to go into the back country should obtain the appropriate map from the *Canadian Topographical Series*. Walkers should not venture into the wilder areas without ensuring that they are fit and properly equipped. Canada's long-distance footpaths include the *Voyageur Trail* along the northern shores of Lakes Superior and Huron and the 690km- (428 mile-) *Bruce Trail* from Queenstown on the Niagara River to Tobermory on the Bruce Peninsula.
Canoeing: Regional tourist boards can supply lists of outfitters who will help make arrangements. Aeroplane and boat drop-offs, and boat and equipment hire, are among the services offered, and maps can be supplied. The most challenging canoeing is in the northern areas, in the Northwest Territories and British Columbia, while the rivers and lakes in Ontario are often easier to negotiate. Further advice and information can be obtained from the Canadian Recreational Canoeing Association, PO Box 398, 446 Main Street West, Merrickville, Ontario K0G 1N0 (tel: (613) 269 2910 *or* (888) 252 6292 (toll-free in Canada); fax: (613) 269 2908; e-mail: info@paddlingcanada.com; website: www.paddlingcanada.com). Excellent facilities for **sailing** and other watersports are available throughout the country.
Wintersports: Both **downhill** and **cross-country skiing** can be enjoyed in innumerable resorts throughout Canada. Most cities are close to ski resorts. Prices of ski passes and accommodation tend to be lower than in Europe. Ottawa's Rideau Canal features the world's largest **skating** rink, and this is an activity that is popular throughout.
Other: Ice hockey is played at the highest level and top-class competition can be enjoyed as a spectator sport in all cities throughout Canada. **Canadian football**, which is similar to American football, is played everywhere, but European football (**soccer**) is becoming increasingly popular. Professional **baseball** is enjoyed in several cities in the summer months. Facilities for **golf** and **tennis** are excellent throughout the country. Most large hotels have some sports facilities. A number of tour operators offer all-in-one golfing packages.

Social Profile

FOOD & DRINK: Canadian cuisine is as varied as the country. The hundreds of miles of coastline offer varied seafood, and the central plains provide first-class beef and agricultural produce. Some more unusual produce might include elk, bison and caribou. The colonial influence is still strong, with European menus available in all major cities. The French influence in Québec is easily discernible in the many restaurants which specialise in French cuisine. Waiter service in restaurants is common. Dress requirements and billing procedures vary. Spirits may only be purchased from specially-licensed liquor stores or restaurants displaying the sign 'Licensed Premises' if alcohol is served on the premises. Many allow customers to bring their own beer or wine. A wide variety of alcohol is sold in most hotels, restaurants and bars. A selection of European/US wines and spirits are imported, although the Canadians also enjoy their own, such as rye whisky. Bars may have table or counter service and payment is generally made after each drink. Opening hours vary from province to province. The legal age for drinking in bars is 18 or 19 depending on local regulations. See also *Social Profile* in the individual Provinces/ Territories sections.
NIGHTLIFE: Every major provincial capital in the more populated areas has nightclubs, and hotel dinner/dancing. Montréal, Ottawa, Toronto, Vancouver and Winnipeg are centres for ballet, opera and classical music, with visits from leading orchestras and internationally renowned performers. Entertainment in the more remote towns is scarce.
SHOPPING: Fine examples of Canadian craftware are available, such as art woodcarvings, pottery, cottons and native artefacts. Some countries have restrictions against the import of endangered animal species products, such as polar bear, seal, walrus etc, so visitors should check entry regulations in their home country before departure. A 7 per cent goods and service tax (GST) is levied on most goods and services in Canada. In addition, most provinces (except Alberta, Northwest Territories and Yukon) levy a provincial service tax (PST) of 5 to 7 per cent in shops, restaurants and short-term accommodation. In the provinces of Newfoundland, Nova Scotia and New Brunswick, a 15 per cent harmonised sales tax (HST) has replaced the GST and PST. Visitors to Canada are entitled to claim a rebate of GST and HST (except on food, drink, tobacco and transport). The province of Quebec also allows visitors to apply for a rebate of its provincial sales tax (TVQ). For further information, see the special note under the *Duty-Free* section *or* contact Canada Border Services Agency (CBSA) (website: www.cbsa-asfc.gc.ca). **Shopping hours**: Mon-Sat 0900-1800, with late-night shopping in some stores Thur-Fri, up to 2100. Some shops and stores are also open on Sunday, and some are open 24 hours a day.
SPECIAL EVENTS: A list of some of the major festivals and special events may be found in the individual Provinces/Territories sections.
SOCIAL CONVENTIONS: Handshaking predominates as the normal mode of greeting. Close friends often exchange kisses on the cheeks, particularly in French areas. Codes of practice for visiting homes are the same as in other Western countries: flowers, chocolates or a bottle of wine are common gifts for hosts and dress is generally informal and practical according to climate. It is common for black tie and other required dress to be indicated on invitations. Exclusive clubs and restaurants often require more formal dress. Smoking has been banned in most public areas. Most restaurants, theatres and cinemas, if they permit smoking, have large 'no smoking' areas. **Tipping**: Normal practice is usually 15 per cent of the bill, more if service is exceptional. Waiters, barbers, hairdressers and taxi drivers should be tipped this amount. Porters at airports and railway stations, cloakroom attendants, bellhops, doormen and hotel porters generally expect C$1 per item of luggage. Tipping your server is standard practice in bars and nightclubs.

Business Profile

ECONOMY: Canada is the seventh-largest trading nation and a member of the G8 group of major industrial economies. The country has immense natural resources and a high standard of living. Agriculture and fisheries are particularly important; Canada exports more than half of its agricultural produce – principally grain and oil seeds – and is the world's leading exporter of fish. Timber is another important sector, given that more than 40 per cent of the land area is forest. As a mineral producer, Canada exports crude oil and natural gas, copper, nickel, zinc, iron ore, asbestos, cement, coal and potash. Energy requirements are met by a mixture of hydroelectric (two-thirds), nuclear and oil-fired generating stations.
Manufacturing covers a wide range of industries from heavy engineering and chemicals to vehicle production and agro-business to office automation and commercial printing.
After running a substantial trade deficit throughout much of the 1990s, Canada now enjoys a net trade surplus, currently estimated at US$40 billion for the year 2000-2001. Slightly more than 75 per cent of the country's trade is with the USA, making this the world's largest single bilateral trade route. In common with most OECD countries, GDP growth slowed during 2002 to just over 1 per cent although the outlook for the next few years is rather better. The 1989 free trade agreement signed with the USA formed the basis for the North American Free Trade Agreement (NAFTA); Mexico has joined as the third signatory and other Latin American countries may sign up in due course. After the USA, Canada's trade partners are, in order of descending volume: Japan, the UK, Germany, Taiwan and France.
BUSINESS: Usual courtesies observed including exchange of business cards, making appointments, etc. **Office hours:** Mon-Fri 0900-1700.
COMMERCIAL INFORMATION: The following organisations can offer advice: Canada-United Kingdom Chamber of Commerce, 38 Grosvenor Street, London W1K 4DP, UK (tel: (020) 7258 6576 *or* 7258 6572 (trade information service; enquiries cost £10 plus VAT for non-members); fax: (020) 7258 6594; e-mail: info@canada-uk.org; website: www.canada-uk.org); *or* Canadian Chamber of Commerce, Head Office, Delta Office Tower, 350 Sparks Street, Suite 501, Ottawa, Ontario K1R 7S8 (tel: (613) 238 4000; fax: (613) 238 7643; e-mail: info@chamber.ca; website: www.chamber.ca). Each province and territory has its own regional chamber of commerce; consult the individual Provinces/Territories sections for more information.
CONFERENCES/CONVENTIONS: All the major business centres, ie Calgary, Edmonton, Montréal, Ottawa, Toronto and Vancouver, offer extensive convention and conference facilities. For general information on conferences and conventions in Canada, contact the Meetings and Incentive Officer at the Canadian High Commission in London (see *Contact Addresses* section). Consult the individual Province/Territories sections for more information.

Climate

Note: Summer thunderstorms are common throughout Canada. Occasionally, these may become 'severe'. Tornados also occur throughout Canada, with May to September being prime months. The peak season is June and early July in southern Ontario, Alberta, southeastern Québec, and a band stretching from southern Saskatchewan and Manitoba, through to Thunder Bay. The interior of British Columbia and western New Brunswick are also tornado zones. Earth tremors occur in the western mountains. Forest fires can occur at any time, regardless of the season, particularly in the grasslands and forests of western Canada. Climate graphs for the various provinces and territories may be found in the relevant entries below.
Required clothing: *March*: Moderate temperatures. Winter clothing with some mediumweight clothing.
April: Milder days but the evenings are cool. Mediumweight clothing including a topcoat is recommended.
May: Warm days but cool at night. Mediumweight and summer clothing recommended.
June: Warm, summer clothing with some mediumweight clothing for cool evenings. The weather in June is ideal for travel and all outdoor activities.
July/August: These are the warmest months of the year. Lightweight summer clothing is recommended.
September: Warm days and cool evenings. Light- to mediumweight clothing recommended.
October: Cool, with the first frost in the air.
November: Cool to frosty. Medium- to heavyweight clothing is recommended. First signs of snow. Motorists should have cars prepared for winter and snow tyres are recommended. *December/January/February*: Winter temperatures. Winter clothing is necessary (eg overcoat, hat, boots and gloves). Heavy snowfall in most provinces.

Alberta

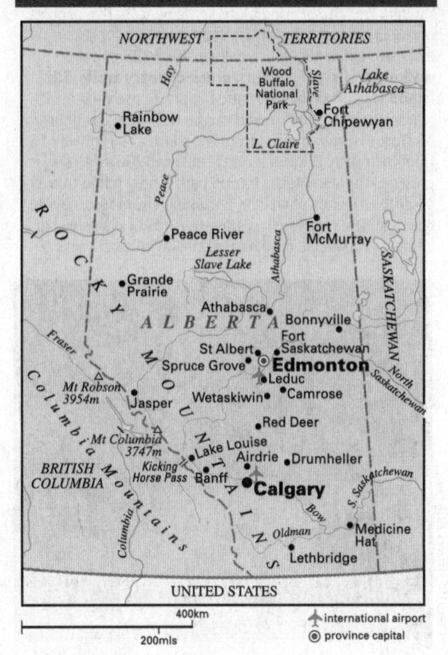

Location: Western Canada.

Travel Alberta
Suite 300, Sunlife Place, 10123, 99 Street, Edmonton, Alberta T5J 3H1, Canada
Tel: (780) 427 4321 *or* (800) 252 3782 (toll-free in USA and Canada). Fax: (780) 427 0867.
E-mail: info@travelalberta.com
Website: www.travelalberta.com
Travel Alberta UK
11 Cornflower Way, Southwater, West Sussex RH13 7WB, UK
Tel: (01403) 754 424. Fax: (01403) 754 423.
E-mail: amanda@tdservices.com
Website: www.explorealberta.com *or* www.travelalberta.com
Edmonton Tourism
World Trade Centre Edmonton, 9990 Jasper Avenue, Suite 500, Edmonton, Alberta, T5J 1P7, Canada
Tel: (780) 426 4715. Fax: (780) 425 5283.
E-mail: info@edmonton.com
Website: www.edmonton.com

General Information

AREA: 638,233 sq km (246,422 sq miles).
POPULATION: 2,974,807 (2001).
POPULATION DENSITY: 4.3 per sq km.
CAPITAL: Edmonton. **Population**: 951,395 (2001).
GEOGRAPHY: Alberta is the most westerly of the 'prairie and plains' provinces, bordered to the west by British Columbia and the Rockies, to the southeast by the badlands and prairie, while in the north, along the border with the Northwest Territories, there is a wilderness of forests, lakes and rivers. The western, Rocky Mountain border rises to 3747m (12,293ft), has permanent icefields covering 340 sq km (122 sq miles) and releases meltwaters which supply the Mackenzie River flowing into the Arctic Ocean, and the Saskatchewan River flowing into Hudson Bay.
LANGUAGE: Although Canada is officially bilingual (English and French), English is more commonly spoken in Alberta.
TIME: GMT - 7 (GMT - 6 in summer).
Summer officially lasts from the first Sunday in April to the Saturday before the last Sunday in October.

Public Holidays

Public holidays as for the rest of Canada (see general *Canada* section), with the following dates also observed:
2005: Feb 21 Alberta Family Day. **Aug 1** Heritage Day.
2006: Feb 20 Alberta Family Day. **Aug 7** Heritage Day.

Travel - International

AIR: The province is served by *Air Canada (AC)* and others including *Air North, Alaska Air Lines, American Airlines, Austrian Airlines, Continental Airlines, KLM, Lufthansa, Martinair, Northwest Airlines, SAS, United Airlines* and *WestJet*. For fares and schedules, contact airlines.
Approximate flight times: From Edmonton/Calgary to *London* is eight hours 30 minutes, to *Los Angeles* is three hours, to *New York* is five hours and to *Sydney* is 15 hours.
International airports: *Edmonton (YEG)* (tel: (780) 890 8900; website: www.edmontonairports.com) is 28km (17 miles) from the city. A bus service to the city operates every 20 minutes (travel time – 40 minutes).
Calgary (YYC) (tel: (403) 735 1200; website: www.calgaryairport.com) is 20km (12.5 miles) from the city. A bus service to the city operates every 30 minutes (travel time – 20 minutes).
Both Edmonton and Calgary also receive domestic services; and both have duty-free shops, banks, restaurants and car parking.
RAIL: *VIA Rail* (tel: (1-888) 842 7245; website: www.viarail.ca) serves Edmonton and Jasper three times a week. The *Canadian*, the Western transcontinental train, crosses the province thrice weekly originating from Toronto, Ontario in the east through Edmonton and Jasper, to Vancouver in the west and vice versa. This train connects with the *Skeena* service at Jasper with a thrice-weekly service to Prince Rupert, British Columbia. The seasonal *Rocky Mountain Railtours* (website: www.rkymtnrail.com) is the only other rail service operating into the province. This is a two-day, all-daylight tour from either Calgary, Banff or Jasper to and from Vancouver, running between mid-April and mid-October (tel: (604) 606 7245; toll-free in Canada and USA only).
ROAD: Coach: *Greyhound Canada* (tel: (800) 661 8747) runs coach services into Alberta, thereby connecting Edmonton with all other major capitals. The main *Greyhound* terminals are at Banff, Calgary, Edmonton, Fort McMurray, Grand Prairie, Lethbridge and Red Deer. Coaches are also operated in Alberta by *Brewster Transportation and Tours* (Banff) (website: www.brewster.ca) and *Gray Line Sightseeing Tours* (Calgary), which organise coach tours in the area. A coach is operated between the two city centres of Calgary and Edmonton by *Red Arrow* (on behalf of VIA Rail) six times a day (tel: (1-800) 232 1958; website: www.redarrow.pwt.ca). **Car hire**: Available in all large towns and at Edmonton and Calgary airports. National driving licences are accepted in Alberta.
Note: When visiting in late autumn, winter or spring, travellers are advised to ensure their vehicle has snow tyres or to carry chains. It is also advisable to have an adequate supply of antifreeze when crossing through mountain passes.
URBAN: Buses and the light rail system in Calgary are operated on a flat-fare system. Exact fares are required if tickets are purchased on boarding; pre-purchased single- and multi-journey tickets are available. Edmonton, where there is a similar fares system, has buses, trolleybuses and a light rail route. Local buses operate in all other major towns.
Travel times: The following chart gives approximate travel times from **Edmonton** (in hours and minutes) to other major cities/towns in Alberta.

	Air	Road	Rail
Calgary	**0.45**	**3.00**	**-**
Banff	**-**	**5.00**	**-**
Jasper	**-**	**4.30**	**5.20**

Credit: © Travel Alberta

Accommodation

Accommodation ranges from top-quality hotels to motorway motels, lodge estates and hostels. Banff National Park is famous for its two baronial-quality hotels, offering approximately 2000 rooms. Many lodges offer various levels of self-catering, often in conjunction with fishing and hiking trips. Several agencies offer bed & breakfast and ranch vacations throughout Alberta. For information on bed & breakfast accommodation, contact the Alberta Bed & Breakfast Association (website: www.bbalberta.com); *or* Bed & Breakfast Association of Greater Edmonton (BBAGE) (tel: (780) 432 7116; website: www.bbedmonton.com). Travel Alberta can provide a comprehensive guide to the province's accommodation (see *Contact Addresses* section). **Grading**: *Canada Select* star ratings (blue stars), and *Access Canada* (showing as A1, A2, A3 and A4 in the amenity symbols; for those who are senior or disabled), are both optional programmes that accommodations can participate from. However, much of Alberta's accommodation is at present

already supervised by the provincial government under a voluntary scheme to ensure high standards of cleanliness, comfort, construction and maintenance of furnishings and facilities. Look for the 'Approved Accommodation' sign which means that the establishment conforms to these standards. For more information on accommodation in Alberta, contact Travel Alberta *or* the Alberta Hotel & Lodging Association, Suite 401, Centre 104, 5241 Calgary Trail, Edmonton, Alberta T6H 5G8 (tel: (780) 436 6112; fax: (780) 436 5404; e-mail: info@ahla.ca; website: www.ahla.ca).
CAMPING/CARAVANNING: The northern area of Alberta contains hundreds of lakes and forests, with abundant game such as deer, moose, bears and the rare trumpeter swan. There are numerous campsites in the National Parks. The permanent facilities tend to be more basic in the north. A number of companies can arrange **motor camper** rentals, with a range of fully-equipped vehicles. Full details can be obtained from Travel Alberta (see *Contact Addresses* section); see also Camping/Caravanning in the general *Canada* section.

Resorts & Excursions

Alberta is represented by six tourism regions, divided principally by their geographic characteristics. The province's most famous region, the Alberta Rockies, takes up a relatively small part of the province and is identified by its numerous alpine attractions. Both of Alberta's major cities are represented by their own tourism regions.

CENTRAL ALBERTA

EDMONTON: The capital of Alberta, located at the centre of the province, was originally established as a remote trading post by the Hudson Bay Company in 1795. From then on, Edmonton experienced relatively little growth until the Klondike Gold Rush of 1897. Overnight, Fort Edmonton became the supply area for the thousands of gold seekers heading up the treacherous Klondike Trail to the Yukon. The discovery of oil in the Edmonton area in 1947 assured the city of its future, making it one of the fastest-growing metropolitan areas in Canada. The spacious well-planned city is also famed for its huge parks, which sit on the banks of the **North Saskatchewan River**. Edmonton's love affair with its past is reflected in Canada's largest historical park, **Fort Edmonton Park**. This is a complex of reproductions of the city's frontier days and reaches its apogee in the annual 'Klondike Days' extravaganza, held each July, when Edmontonians relive the days of the Gold Rush. **West Edmonton Mall** is the largest shopping mall in the world, with theatres, restaurants, nightclubs, amusement areas (including a miniature golf course, ice rink, swimming pool, waterpark and amusement park), aviaries, aquariums and museums. Edmonton also boasts **Fantasyland**, the world's largest indoor amusement park, and Canada's largest planetarium, the **Space & Science Centre** which also has an IMAX experience and Challenger centre. There are several theatres and art galleries. On a clear day, an estimated 6500 sq km (2500 sq miles) of Alberta can be seen from **Vista 33** at the **Alberta Telephone Tower**. The **Ukrainian Cultural Heritage Village** is just outside the city. Other attractions include the **Valley Zoo** to the west of Edmonton and the **John Janzen Nature Centre** nestled in the **River Valley Park**.

Credit: © Travel Alberta

BEYOND EDMONTON: In the town of St Albert, 30km (19 miles) northwest from downtown Edmonton, is the historic **log cabin of Father Lacombe** and Alberta's oldest surviving structure. It was at one time the centre of a thriving French-speaking Métis settlement (native peoples of mixed heritage). Today, St Albert is known for its extensive parklands, which include 40km (25 miles) of **walking trails** and groomed **cross-country trails**. **Elk Island National Park** is located approximately 45km (29 miles) east of Edmonton and can be reached via Highway 16 (Yellowhead Highway) from the south and Highway 15 from the north. Originally established in 1906 as an elk preserve, this completely fenced park is now home to over 44 different kinds of wildlife (including elk, moose, coyote, bear and beaver) as well as massive herds of plains bison. Camping is possible for a maximum stay of two weeks.

Credit: © Travel Alberta

SOUTHERN ALBERTA

CALGARY: The province's second city is situated at the western end of the Great Plains in the foothills of the Rocky Mountains. It is probably the fastest growing city in Canada, and hosted the 1988 Winter Olympics. The heart of the city is a pedestrian mall with excellent shopping and restaurants; the **Glenbow Museum**, art galleries and theatres are nearby. The **Calgary Zoo and Prehistoric Park** is one of the best in North America. **Heritage Park** offers a chance to explore an authentic Alberta frontier town as it was 80 years ago. There are panoramic views of the Rocky Mountains from the **Calgary Tower**.
BEYOND CALGARY: The historic site of **Cochrane Ranche**, established in 1881, sits 30km (19 miles) west of Calgary. By 1888, operations had expanded to such an extent that the ranch billed itself as 'the largest ranch in the Dominion'. The site is now an historic landmark. On Alberta's southwestern border with the USA is **Waterton Lakes National Park**, joined to **Glacier National Park** in Montana to form the **Waterton-Glacier International Peace Park**. Scenic views of the stunning lake and scenery can be experienced on a cruise boat tour around the lake. Visitors should note that the park is a natural habitat for many species of wildlife, including bears; and that caution, particularly with bears, should be exercised. The Canadian Heritage National Parks Department publishes leaflets on safety precautions in backcountry areas. For details, contact one of the travel authorities under Canada's *Contact Addresses* section. In south-central southern Alberta, the remains of dinosaurs first discovered in 1874 in the banks of the **Red Deer River**, can be seen on the 48km- (30 mile-) **Dinosaur Trail** near **Drumheller**. A few minutes from the downtown area is the **Royal Tyrrell Museum of Palaeontology**, with hands-on exhibitions, ongoing site work and one of the world's largest collections of dinosaur remains. Southwest of Drumheller, the **Dinosaur Provincial Park** continues this theme with reconstructed skeletons of duck-billed dinosaurs. To the south of Calgary, 50km (36 miles) south of Lethbridge, **Head-Smashed-In Buffalo Jump** is among the largest and best-preserved jump sites in the world; it was used by the native people for more than 10,000 years to drive thousands of buffalo to their deaths, thus providing them with food, shelter and clothing. The top of the cliff provides an unparalleled view of the surrounding prairie.

WESTERN ALBERTA

THE ROCKIES: The city of Calgary is the major stopping-off point en route to **Banff National Park**, 130km (80 miles) to the west in the heart of the Canadian Rockies. Banff, the first of the country's national parks and now a UNESCO World Heritage Site, is a spectacular wilderness area with mountain, river and lake scenery – notably **Lake Louise**. Along with **Jasper National Park** to the north, it offers a huge range of activities, including boating, canoeing, raft tours, fishing and hiking. The major ski resort in the Rockies, it hosts the annual **Banff Festival of the Arts**. The small town of **Jasper** is mainly used as a stocking-up point for the numerous hikers on their way into the mountains. Set in magnificent mountain scenery, it is an ideal starting point for trips to **Pyramid Lake**, the **Miette Hotsprings** and **Maligne Canyon** as well as **Maligne Lake**. For the bold of heart, there is even alpine scuba-diving. **Horseshoe Lake**, **Patricia Lake** and **Lake Annette** are three of the more popular locations. Divers should be experienced and employ the 'buddy' system as the water is cold and visibility is often limited. The local Rangers Station opposite the railway station can supply maps and other information. one-day permits for these parks cost C$5 per adult, with children aged six years and under admitted free of charge. The **Icefields Parkway** (Highway 93), runs the length of the two parks, affording magnificent views of the lakes, forests and the glaciers of the **Columbia Icefield**, which incorporates the McKinley Glacier and the Columbia Glacier. Visitors can take a bus trip to the top of the latter or go on foot to the bottom edge of it. It should be noted, though, that the temperature drops noticeably when approaching the glacier and that the hiking trail can be difficult in parts. The Parkway provides the best access to the wilderness trails in the area.
NORTHERN ALBERTA: In the far north of the province, the remote **Wood Buffalo National Park** straddles the border with Canada's Northwest Territories. The park is located 1310km (819 miles) north of Edmonton and 228km (143 miles) north of **Fort McMurray**. Wood Buffalo is Canada's largest national park (it is bigger than Switzerland) and was granted World Heritage status by UNESCO in 1983. The park's vast expanses of boreal plains make it a perfect habitat for many rare species of wildlife, including the world's largest free-roaming bison herd. Within the park, the **Peace-Athabasca Delta** is one of the world's largest inland freshwater deltas and a major nesting area for migratory waterfowl, such as the whooping crane. The park offers a variety of activities to visitors, including wildlife viewing, walks on secluded forest trails and canoe trips on the mighty **Athabasca**, **Peace** and **Slave** rivers.

Sport & Activities

Outdoor pursuits: The Rocky Mountains in the southwest of the province, the wilderness in the north, the large open spaces of the prairies and Alberta's many lakes and rivers offer scope for a wide variety of outdoor activities. The four contiguous national parks situated in the southern part of the Rockies (*Banff*, *Jasper*, *Kootenay* and *Yoho*) are an obvious starting point for visitors in search of the great outdoors. **Skiing**, both **cross-country** and **downhill**, is a major pastime in the Rockies in the winter. **Snowboarding** is also very popular. Other snow-based activities include **dog sledding** (trekking along mountain trails with teams of huskies under the supervision of experienced guides), **ski-joring** (being pulled along on skis by teams of huskies), **wildlife tracking**, **igloo building** and **snowshoeing**. Longer treks allow the visitor to penetrate deeper into the pristine wilderness. Accommodation is usually in log cabins or winter camps. Visitors should note that certain regulations apply to national parks and that some activities are not allowed (snowmobiles are prohibited for example); for further details, see *Sport & Activities* in the main Canada section. Provincial parks, such as Kananaskis or Mount Robson may offer the visitor more freedom in this respect.
Watersports: There are excellent facilities for **whitewater rafting**, **fishing** and **canoeing** in particular. **Boats** can also be hired privately for recreational purposes.
Rodeos: The *Calgary Stampede*, one of Canada's biggest rodeos, is held in July each year and attracts many competitors and spectators. Lasting for 10 days, it includes stage shows and agricultural exhibits, and offers one of the largest prizes in North America. Many other rodeos are held in Alberta.
Spectator sports: Ice hockey, **baseball** and **football** are very popular. The Calgary Flames, Alberta's premier hockey team, attract a large following. For general information about sport and activities in Canada, see the main *Canada* section.

Social Profile

FOOD & DRINK: Alberta's prairie is ideal for cattle rearing and its Western beef is world famous. Beef is barbecued, braised, grilled, minced and skewered with different complements such as onions, mushrooms, green peppers, rice, sauces and beans. Unusual beef dishes are stew (combination of diced steak, garden vegetables and biscuits cooked in rich gravy) and *beef mincemeat* (combines chopped suet, fruits and spices) used in pies and tarts and as a traditional Christmas dish served with ice-cream, cream or rum sauce. Wild berries and nuts are used in desserts. During the season, try the blueberry muffins from local bakeries. Honey is made from alfalfa and clover nectar and is a widely used sweetener and breakfast food. Apart from traditional foods, Alberta's towns and cities offer an excellent range of international cuisine.
Alcohol is sold in 'liquor stores', although beer may be obtained in the majority of hotels. The minimum legal drinking age is 18 years old.
NIGHTLIFE: Both Edmonton and Calgary have a rich

variety of night-time entertainment. Nightclubs, cabarets, taverns, lounges and that infamous Alberta watering hole, the beer parlour, combine to provide constant local and international entertainment. Calgary and Edmonton boast full-scale orchestras.
SHOPPING: Alberta is the only province (apart from the Northwest Territories and Yukon) that does not apply an extra sales tax on all purchases over and above the general sales tax of 7 per cent. Artwork available in the province includes pottery, ceramics, sculptures and paintings. There are numerous malls in Edmonton, including Heritage Mall and the huge West Edmonton Mall (see *Resorts & Excursions* section). Speciality shops can be found in the Old Strathcona district, from boutiques to a farmers market. The Kensington district - Calgary's village in the city - has over 140 excellent shops and restaurants. **Shopping hours**: Mon-Fri 1000-1700; Sat 1000-2100 (malls are generally open until 2100).
SPECIAL EVENTS: For full details, contact Travel Alberta (see *Contact Addresses* section). The following is a selection of special events occurring in Alberta in 2005: **Jan-Feb** *Banff/Lake Louise Winter Festival*. **Jan 14-16** *Ice Magic – Annual Ice Sculpture Competition and Exhibition*, Banff. **Feb 26** *Athabasca Winterfest 2005*. **Mar 11** *Cody Snyder's Bullbustin*. **Jun** *Jazz City International Music Festival*, Edmonton; *Calgary International Jazz Festival*. **Jul 1** *Canada Day Celebrations*. **Jul 15-16** *Peace Fest*. **Aug** *Canadian Death Ride 2005*, Grand Cache and Edmonton. **Aug 19** *Jasper Heritage Rodeo*. **Sep 9** *Waynefest Folk Festival*. **Oct 22** *Jasper Root Romp*. **Dec 10** *Farmer's Market Christmas Bazaar*, Drumheller.

Business Profile

COMMERCIAL INFORMATION: The following organisation can offer advice: Alberta Chambers of Commerce, 1808 Merrill Lynch Tower, 10025-102A Avenue, Edmonton City Centre, Alberta T5J 2Z2 (tel: (780) 425 4180; fax: (780) 429 1061; website: www.abchamber.ca).
CONFERENCES/CONVENTIONS: Banff, Calgary, Edmonton and Jasper offer conference and convention venues. Information can be obtained from the Visit Canada Centre (see general *Canada* section) *or* Travel Alberta (see *Contact Addresses* section). The following organisations can also offer assistance and advice: Calgary Conventions & Visitors Bureau, Suite 200, 238 11th Avenue SE, Calgary, Alberta T2G 0X8 (tel: (403) 263 8510; fax: (403) 262 3809; e-mail: fay@tourismcalgary.com; website: www.visitor.calgary.ab.ca); *or* Banff/Lake Louise Tourism Bureau, PO Box 1298, Banff, Alberta T1L 1B3 (tel: (403) 762 8421; fax: (403) 762 8163; website: www.banfflakelouise.com); *or* Edmonton Tourism (see *Contact Addresses* section); *or* Jasper Tourism and Commerce, PO Box 98, 409 Patricia Street, Jasper, Alberta T0E 1E0 (tel: (780) 852 3858; fax: (780) 852 4932; e-mail: jaspercc@incentre.net; website: www.jaspercanadianrockies.com).

Climate

Summer, between May and September, is warm, while winters are cold, with particularly heavy snowfalls in the Rockies. Spring and summer evening temperatures can be cool.
Required clothing: Light- to mediumweights during warmer months. Heavyweights are worn in winter, with alpine wear in mountains. Waterproof wear is advisable throughout the year.

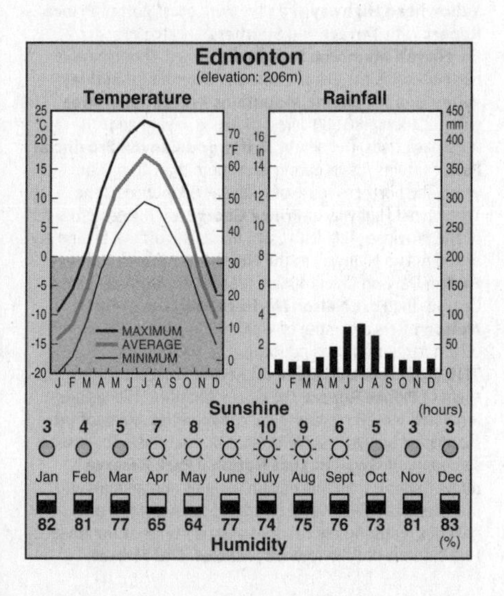

British Columbia

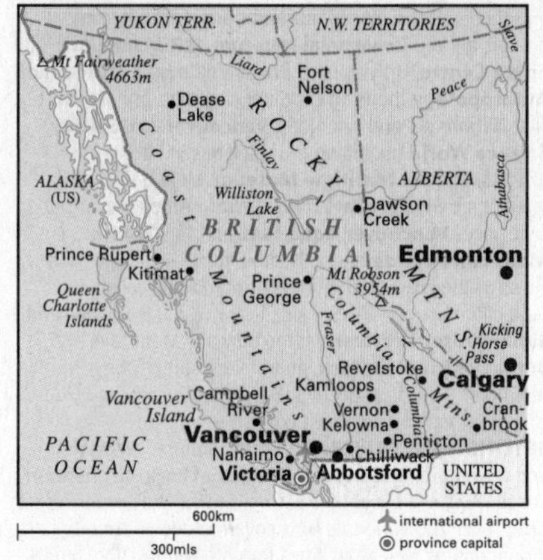

Location: Western Canada.

Tourism British Columbia
12th Floor, 510 Burrard Street, Vancouver, British Columbia V6C 3A8, Canada
Tel: (604) 660 3757 *or* (800) 435 5622 (reservation and information line). Fax: (604) 660 3383.
Website: www.HelloBC.com
Tourism British Columbia
3rd Floor, British Columbia House, 3 Regent Street, London SW1Y 4NS, UK
Tel: (0906) 871 5000 (Visit Canada Centre; calls cost 60p per minute) *or* (020) 7930 6857 (trade and media enquiries).
Fax: (020) 7930 2012.
E-mail: info@tourismbc.co.uk (travel trade only).
Website: www.HelloBC.com

General Information

AREA: 892,677 sq km (344,662 sq miles).
POPULATION: 3,907,738 (2001).
POPULATION DENSITY: 4.17 per sq km.
CAPITAL: Victoria. **Population**: 311,902 (2001).
GEOGRAPHY: British Columbia is Canada's most westerly province, bordered to the south by the USA (Washington, Idaho and Montana states), to the east by Alberta, to the north by the Northwest Territories and the Yukon, and to the west by the Pacific Ocean and the 'Alaskan Panhandle'. It is mainly covered by virgin forests, and encompasses the towering Rocky Mountains (rising to 3954m/12,972ft), vast expanses of semi-arid sagebrush, lush pastures on Vancouver Island's east coast, farmland in the Fraser River delta, and fruitland in the Okanagan Valley. The highest mountain is Fairweather at 4663m (15,298ft). Between the eastern and coastal mountains is a lower central range. The coastal range sinks into the Pacific, with larger peaks emerging at Vancouver and Queen Charlotte islands. The Columbia River flows from the Rockies into Washington State and out into the Pacific Ocean.
LANGUAGE: Although Canada is officially bilingual (English and French), English is more commonly spoken in British Columbia.
TIME: GMT - 8. Small areas of the province near the Alberta border are GMT - 7.

Public Holidays

Public holidays as for the rest of Canada (see general *Canada* section), except Easter Monday and Boxing Day, with the following dates also observed:
2005: Aug 1 British Columbia Day.
2006: Aug 7 British Columbia Day.

Travel - International

AIR: Airlines that operate in British Columbia include the following: *Air Canada, American Airlines, Belair, Cathay Pacific Airways, Continental Airlines, Helijet Airways, KLM Royal Dutch Airlines, Lufthansa, Northwest Airlines, Pacific Coastal Airlines, Seair, Singapore Airlines, Westcoast Air, WestJet* and *United Airlines*.
International airports: *Vancouver (YVR)* (website: www.yvr.ca) is 15km (9 miles) southwest of the city. It is served by airlines from the USA, Europe and the Far East. The journey to the city centre takes about 25 minutes. Airport facilities include banks and ATMs, a post office, business centre, restaurant, car parking, garage, car rental, nursery and duty free shop.
The other major airports are *Abbotsford, Campbell River, Castlegar, Comox, Cranbrook, Fort St John, Kamloops, Kelowna, Nanaimo, Penticton, Prince George, Prince Rupert, Quesnel* and *Victoria*.
SEA: Vancouver is an international passenger port, with regular sailings to the Far East and ports on the USA's northwestern coast.
Ferry services to and from all coastal ports in British Columbia are available from the following shipping lines: *Alaska Ferries, BC Ferries, Washington State Ferries* and seven independent companies. Ferry services link three points on Vancouver Island with Vancouver city's north (Horseshoe Bay) and south (Tsawwassen) terminals on the mainland, including *BC Ferries'* spectacular car and passenger service from Tsawwassen to Swartz Bay on the southern tip of Vancouver Island just north of Victoria. Foot passengers can take coaches which travel from Vancouver city centre to Victoria city centre. *BC Ferries* operates a total of 25 routes between 46 ports of call in coastal British Columbia, including a scenic, luxury, 15-hour, one-way, daylight voyage from Port Hardy on the northern tip of Vancouver Island along the Inside Passage to Prince Rupert, a crossing from Prince Rupert to the Queen Charlotte Islands (see *Sport & Activities* and *Resorts & Excursions* sections), and the new Discovery Coast Passage, a summer route between Port Hardy and Bella Coola on the mid-coast mainland that runs either direct in a day or with stops at various inlets. There is also a high-speed catamaran from Victoria to Seattle (USA), the *Victoria Clipper*, leaving twice a day. The crossing takes two hours 30 minutes. For further information on ferries, contact *BC Ferries* (tel: (250) 386 3431 or (888) 223 3779 (toll-free in British Columbia); fax: (250) 381 5452; website: www.bcferries.com) *or* consult *The Ferry Traveller*, a website with general ferry information (tel: (604) 733 9113; fax: (604) 733 6888; e-mail: info@ferrytravel.com; website: www.ferrytravel.com).
RAIL: *VIA Rail* (website: www.viarail.ca) train routes to and within British Columbia are: Edmonton to Prince Rupert via Jasper (Alberta); Victoria to Courtenay; Vancouver to Edmonton via Kamloops and Jasper, and on to Toronto

Credit: © Tourism British Columbia

three times a week (*Western Transcontinental*).
ROAD: The Trans-Canada Highway reaches British Columbia via Calgary (Alberta) and continues through the south of the province to Vancouver, over to Nanaimo, and onto Victoria. The other main highways are numbers 3, 5, 6, 16, 95 and 97. Apart from Highway 97 and the remote scenic Highway 37, which run northwards to the Yukon, the province's road network is concentrated in the south. Road signs are international. There are good roads south to Seattle in the USA. **Bus**: *Translink* supplies buses to the Greater Vancouver area as part of an integrated public transport service. For timetable details, contact *Translink* (tel: (604) 953 3333; website: www.translink.bc.ca). *BC Transit* provides a network of buses to many communities in British Columbia, including the major cities of Victoria and Whistler. Timetable details are available (tel: (250) 385 2551; fax: (250) 995 5639; e-mail: Lorill_Garner@bctransit.com; website: www.bctransit.com). *Gray Line* and *Laidlaw* coaches provide services on Vancouver Island including sightseeing routes (tel: (800) 318 0818 (toll-free in Canada) *or* (250) 388 5248).
URBAN: Most of Vancouver's public transport network is operated by *Translink* (tel: (604) 453 4500; website: www.translink.bc.ca), including buses, commuter rail services between Vancouver and Mission, *SkyTrain* between Vancouver and Surrey, and *SeaBuses* between Vancouver and North Vancouver. Ferries between the mainland and Vancouver Island are provided by *BC Ferries*. Buses in Victoria are run by *BC Transit*.
TRAVEL TIMES: The following chart gives approximate travel times from **Vancouver** (in hours and minutes) to other major cities/towns in British Columbia.

	Air	Road	Rail
Victoria	0.25	3.30	-
Kamloops	0.55	4.00	9.00
Whistler	0.30	2.00	-
Prince George	1.00	10.00	-

Accommodation

Accommodation ranges from top-class hotels in Victoria and Vancouver and motels beside the main southern highways to simple cabins high up in the Rockies. Cottages and cabins are widely available on Vancouver Island. 'Ranch Holidays' are popular in the Cariboo Chilcotin Coast tourism region of central British Columbia. Bed & Breakfast accommodation can be found by contacting the Old English B & B Registry, 1226 Silverwood Crescent, North Vancouver, British Columbia V7P 1J3 (tel: (604) 986 5069; fax: (604) 986 8810; e-mail: relax@oldenglishbandb.bc.ca; website: www.oldenglishbandb.bc.ca) or Western Canada Bed & Breakfast Innkeepers Association, PO Box 74534, 2803 West 4th Avenue, Vancouver, British Columbia V6K 4P4 (e-mail: info@wcbbia.com; website: www.wcbbia.com). Tourism British Columbia has an annual guide listing all the agencies providing accommodation in the province. **Grading**: Standards are overseen by Tourism British Columbia and approved hotels display a white 'Approved Accommodation' sign to indicate that Tourism BC's standards of courtesy, comfort and cleanliness have been met. For more information, contact Tourism British Columbia *or* British Columbia & Yukon Hotels' Association, 2nd Floor, 948 Howe Street, Vancouver, British Columbia V6Z 1N9 (tel: (604) 681 7164; fax: (604) 681 7649; e-mail: hotel@bcyha.com; website: www.bcyha.com).

CAMPING/CARAVANNING: There are nearly 10,000 campsites situated in over 150 parks and recreation areas.

Credit: © Tourism British Columbia

Most campsites do not have power supply link-ups for caravans. Several of the parks are designated as 'Nature Conservancy Areas', where all motor vehicles are banned and transport must be on foot. The type of parkland available varies from sandy beaches with vehicle access, to lakes and glaciers reached only by aircraft or boat. All campsites have a time limit of 14 days and reservations are recommended. A number of companies can arrange **motor camper** rentals, with a range of fully-equipped vehicles. Full details can be obtained from Tourism British Columbia *or* British Columbia Lodging and Campgrounds Association, Suite 209, 3003 St John's Street, Port Moody, British Columbia V3H 2C4 (tel: (604) 945 7676; fax: (604) 945 7606; e-mail: info@bclca.com; website: www.bclca.com) *or* Discover Camping (website: www.discovercamping.ca). See also Camping/Caravanning in the general *Canada* section.

Resorts & Excursions

VANCOUVER, COAST & MOUNTAINS

VANCOUVER: Canada's third-largest city and a major port, is situated in the southwest corner of British Columbia (also called 'BC'), overlooking the Burrard Inlet on the Pacific Ocean and backed by the **Coastal Mountain Range**. Downtown Vancouver has one of the largest Chinese quarters in North America (celebrated by the new **Chinese Cultural Centre**), and large German and Ukrainian populations. **Gastown**, the reconstructed old centre of Vancouver, is a pleasant array of cobblestone streets, cafes and shops. Of the several museums and galleries, most notable are the **Centennial Museum**, **H R MacMillan Space Centre**, University of British Columbia's **Museum of Anthropology** (housing excellent examples of northwest First Nations art and artefacts), **Vancouver Art Gallery**, **Science World** (including four galleries of hands-on exhibits) and the **Maritime Museum**. More points of interest are **Stanley Park**, one of North America's largest civic parks, **Vancouver Aquarium**, and the **Grouse Mountain Skyride** on the North Shore. The latter offers views of the city and the fjords of the Pacific coast. Adjoining Vancouver's east side is the city of **Burnaby**, and **Simon Fraser University**, atop Burnaby Mountain. **Burnaby Mountain Park**, on the west side of the mountain, affords a spectacular view of the city and Gulf Islands on Vancouver's west coast.

BEYOND VANCOUVER: During the summer, **Whistler** and the adjoining **Garibaldi Provincial Park**, just north of Vancouver, are a delight for naturalists. The year-round resort offers over 200 varied ski runs covering two enormous mountains, as well as facilities for golf, windsurfing, tennis, mountain biking, and river rafting. Skiing and snowboarding are available nine months of the year. Northwest of Vancouver, accessed by ferry, are the coastal towns of **Sechelt**, **Powell River** and **Lund**, popular for their sunny beaches and surrounding fjords and recreational areas. 150km (93 miles) east of Vancouver is the town of **Hope** and BC's **Fraser Canyon**. The Trans-Canada Highway (Highway 1) links the Greater Vancouver Area with the dramatic river country of British Columbia's western interior and the historic **Cariboo Gold Rush route**. In the Fraser Canyon, the **Hell's Gate Airtram** takes visitors down to the edge of the spectacular **Fraser River**, where visitors can learn about the lifecycle of the spawning salmon. River rafting tours can be arranged at numerous points along the river as well as on the more remote shores of the **Nahatlatch River**, 30 minutes' drive northwest of **Boston Bar**. The towns of **Lytton** and **Lillooet** are regaled as having some of BC's warmest summertime weather, averaging around 40°C (104°F). Both towns are rich in First Nations' history and culture.

VANCOUVER ISLAND, VICTORIA & THE GULF ISLANDS

VANCOUVER ISLAND: British Columbia's provincial capital, **Victoria**, lies at the southern tip of the heavily forested and mountainous **Vancouver Island**. This most English of Canadian towns is distinguished by Victorian and neo-classical architecture and well-appointed residential areas. In the harbour area are the impressive **Legislative Buildings** and the **Royal British Columbia Museum**. Also worth visiting are **Maltwood Art Gallery**, **Thunderbird Park** and **Craigdarroch Castle** (an impressive 19th-century landmark mansion home). City life is enhanced by more than 60 recreational parks, which are spread throughout the islands. Some 21km (13 miles) to the north, the **Butchart Gardens** have delightful English, Italian and Japanese gardens set in a former limestone quarry. **Nanaimo**, north of Victoria, is home to one of the province's largest collection of heritage buildings. Near Vancouver Island's northern tip is the rural town of **Port Hardy** and the connecting ferry service to British Columbia's northernmost destinations. Just south of Port Hardy is the town of **Port McNeill**, a popular ecotourism destination that is known for its caving and hiking activities. **Pacific Rim National Park**, 306km (192 miles) north of Victoria on the west coast, is a popular ecological attraction, with sandy beaches offering good swimming and wilderness trails through deep, hilly forests. Two of the hiking trails in Pacific Rim are wheelchair-accessible. The remote towns of **Tofino** and **Ucluelet** offer first-rate whale-watching opportunities. In March, the **Pacific Rim Whale Festival** celebrates the yearly migration of Pacific grey whales from Baja California, Mexico to Vancouver Island.

THE GULF ISLANDS: Known for their breathtaking beauty and quaint seaside villages, the Gulf Islands include **Saltspring Island**, home to a flourishing art colony; the **Pender Islands** which are linked together by a bridge and have several good sandy beaches; and **Mayne Island**, whose history dates back to the Cariboo Gold Rush, when prospectors gathered at Miners Bay and rowed across the formidable waters of the Georgia Strait. **Galiano Island's Bellhouse Park** is home to more than 130 different species of birds and is a naturalist's paradise with numerous rare and protected plants. At the northeastern edge of Vancouver Island is a lesser known collection of Gulf Islands. **Cormorant Island's Alert Bay** is comprised of a large First Nations and Finnish population. Influenced by the migration of Finnish settlers at the beginning of the 20th century, the town is a delight for photographers.

THE THOMPSON OKANAGAN REGION

Known as BC's 'playground', the azure blue waters of **Lake Okanagan** and the stunning vistas of the surrounding vineyards are only two of the major draws to this area. The northern tip of Mexico's **Sonora Desert** actually ends here – in the rich, lush countryside of British Columbia's interior. The Okanagan's fall wine tours attract visitors from across Europe and North America. Winter activities include the choice of more than four regional ski resorts. With over 60 courses in the region, the Thompson Okanagan is also a golfer's paradise, with panoramic views guaranteed to enrich the sporting experience. For those wishing to immerse themselves in other sports, the region also offers a host of outdoor activities, including mountain biking and canoeing, at the World Heritage site, **Mount Robson Provincial Park**. At the northern tip of the **Okanagan Valley**, **Shuswap Lake** offers resort-like summer weather and excellent boating opportunities. Those seeking close proximity to nature can observe black bears meander and munch on berries in their natural environment; prime viewing areas include **Wells Gray Provincial Park**, as well as rural roads nears Kamloops and Merritt.

CARIBOO CHILCOTIN COAST REGION

North of the ranching town of **Williams Lake** (540km, 338 miles north of Vancouver) lie the vast tracts of untamed lakeland, forest and wilderness of the **Cariboo**. The arid, desert-like terrain is best known for its guest ranch accommodations and winter lodge facilities. Heli-skiing is a favourite activity in the **Cariboo** and **Chilcotin Ranges**. Backcountry excursions into BC's mountains are best planned through trained and experienced outfitters. Near **William's Lake**, **100 Mile House** is an historic marker of the Cariboo Gold Rush days, when pioneers measured journeys by the distance of a day's horse ride and the relative distance from the Gold Rush town of **Lillooet**, otherwise known as 'Mile 0'.

KOOTENAY ROCKIES REGION

Nestled at the western base of Canada's Rockies are the rich, fertile valleys and plains of the province's easternmost border. The checkerboard landscape of **Rossland** and **Castlegar** are reminiscent of its European origins, as is this area's mixture of cultures and heritage. The scenery is best enjoyed by car, as many of the local sites can be accessed by circle driving tours. Accessible from any number of points, the **Silvery Slocan Circle Driving Tour** takes visitors past numerous historic landmarks, such as the historic logging town of **Kaslo**, which populates the hills and shoreline of **Kootenay Lake** and the city of **Nelson**, which is home to 350 heritage buildings. The ghost town of **Sandon** is located at the heart of the circle tour, accessible by a small road that winds through farmlands and rainforest. The **Nikkei Internment Centre** in **New Denver**, also on this route, acknowledges the history of the Japanese-Canadian internments during World War II. At the northern edge of the Kootenay Rockies region, Highway 1 links the city of **Revelstoke** with the eastern mountain resort of Banff, in the province of Alberta. The **Revelstoke Railroad Museum** includes interpretive displays of Canada's dramatic efforts to establish a rail system across the Rocky Mountains. The town of **Golden**, 148km (93 miles) from Revelstoke, is the last major stopping point before ascending **Roger's Pass** and the spectacular countryside of **Glacier National Park**.

THE NORTHERN BRITISH COLUMBIA REGION

BC's most northern region is a haven for recreational vehicle owners. Highway 16, better known as the **Yellowhead Highway**, links the west coast port of **Prince Rupert** with **Terrace** and **Smithers**. Located near Terrace is the **Nisga'a Memorial Lava Bed**, a sacred Aboriginal site. Further east is the delicate sub-alpine terrain of **Bulkley valley**, and the **Babine Mountains Recreational Area**, with 32,400ha (80,060 acres) of hiking, biking and horseback trails. The nearby **Driftwood Canyon Provincial Park** contains fossils dating back more than 10 million years. The northern route of Highway 97 intersects the Yellowhead Highway at **Prince George**, on the eastern side of the province. A 'Mile 0' Cairn marks the official beginning of the Alaska Highway at the **Northern Alberta Railway Park** in Dawson Creek, 406km (254 miles) north of Prince George. The **Fort Nelson Heritage Museum** in **Fort Nelson** offers a glimpse of what life was like 200 years ago on a northern fur-trading route.

THE QUEEN CHARLOTTE ISLANDS: Adjacent to the town of **Prince Rupert**, the Queen Charlotte Islands are inhabited by several Aboriginal communities. Many of the islands are only accessible by boat or floatplane. The coastal sanctuary of **Gwaii Haanas National Park Reserve** is home to more than one million seabirds and animals and includes a UNESCO World Heritage Site. Art stores and galleries featuring the carvings and paintings of the Haida First Nations dot the towns of **Masset**, **Old Masset**,

Queen Charlotte City and **Sandspit**. Northern BC's spectacular west coast is best appreciated by ferry, which links Prince Rupert with Vancouver Island's Port Hardy. BC's information centres can provide Visitor Information Centres can provide information on journey times and destinations.

Sport & Activities

Hiking and trekking: Practically every type of walking activity is available in Canada's most mountainous province, with its long, jagged coastline, extensive interior forests and numerous lakes and rivers. Seven national parks and more than 450 provincial parks offer superb opportunities to observe wildlife and experience pristine wilderness. Long-distance **hiking** trails include the beautiful West Coast Trail in the Pacific Rim National Park (Vancouver Island), so much in demand that a quota system is in place; and the *Juan de Fuca Marine Trail*, also on Vancouver Island. Giant trees may be seen in the old coastal rainforests on the Island and the Pacific coast. Ample camping and other facilities exist in the national parks.

Skiing and snowboarding: There are excellent facilities for skiing and other snow-based activities in the Rocky Mountains. Canada's best-known ski resort is *Whistler*, which has over 200 marked runs; this and some other resorts (including *Cypress Mountain*, *Hemlock* and *Valley Ski Resort*) lie conveniently close to Vancouver. Other well-known centres include *Mount Washington* on Vancouver Island, *Red Mountain* in Rossland (home to Canada's Olympic ski medallists), the *Kimberley Alpine Resort* and *Big White Ski Resort* in the Okanagan Valley. Other activities on offer include snowboarding, **glacier skiing** (in summer), **heli-skiing** and **snowcat skiing** (where skiers are taken to remote areas by snowcat). **Cross-country skiing** is widely practised, and **ski touring** in the back country through snow-covered forests is popular; accommodation is often in simple huts. The hundreds of watersheds among the Rocky Mountains have provided British Columbia with countless rivers and lakes in every park area.

Watersports: Sailing, **canoeing** and **whitewater rafting** are all available. *Campbell River* on Vancouver Island is world-famous for **salmon fishing**.

Ocean-based activities: The famous *Inside Passage* from the southern end of Vancouver Island to Prince Rupert in the north provides excellent opportunities for protected **ocean cruising**, which can be done by charter yacht, ocean kayak, ferry or cruise ship. For independent sailors, there are many anchorages and marinas providing facilities for safe moorage and other services. Beautiful views of the fjord-indented coastline and the snow-capped *Coast Mountains* beyond are one of the attractions of sailing here. **Whale-watching** cruises providing the chance to view killer whales are also available; at certain times of the year, grey whales can be seen on their way to the Gulf of Alaska.

First Nations: There is a number of cultural centres which introduce visitors to the heritage of the First Nations people. Of particular interest in this respect are the *Queen Charlotte Islands*, home to the Haida people who were nearly eradicated by smallpox when they first came into contact with Europeans. Nowadays around 2000 of the Haida live here, many of whom produce highly regarded art and craft items.

Winery tours: The Thompson Okanagan region has a variety of vineyard and winery tours to offer along the Okanagan Wine Route.

Credit: © Tourism British Columbia

Credit: © Tourism British Columbia

Social Profile

FOOD & DRINK: The cuisine of the province is enhanced by English traditions. The Pacific Ocean yields a great variety of seafood, including King Crab, oysters, shrimp and other shellfish, as well as cod, haddock and salmon (coho, spring, chum, sockeye and pink) which are smoked, pan-fried, breaded, baked, canned or barbecued, and complemented by local vegetables. Fruits grown in the province include apples, peaches, pears, plums, apricots, strawberries, blackberries, the famous Bing cherries, cranberries and loganberries. *Victoria creams*, a famous chocolate delicacy derived from a recipe dating back to 1885, are exported worldwide from British Columbia. The original confectioners shop is situated in Victoria on Vancouver Island.

Sparkling wines are produced in the Okanagan Valley and all the usual alcoholic beverages are widely available. Spirits, beer and wine can be served in licensed restaurants, dining rooms, pubs and bars. Taverns (pubs) are open until 0100, bars and cabarets until 0200. The minimum drinking age is 19.

NIGHTLIFE: Major cities and towns have top-class restaurants, nightclubs and bars, sometimes in pub style. Vancouver has an active theatre life. Better nightspots are often found in hotels.

SHOPPING: Vancouver is a shopper's paradise. *Robson Street* offers fashion boutiques, souvenir and speciality shops. *Yaletown* is the shopping ground of Vancouver's young and aspirational, with designer fashions, art galleries and trendy home decor shops. Other popular areas include *Chinatown*, *Gastown* and *Granville Island*. Indoor shopping downtown includes the *Pacific Centre*, *Royal Centre* and the *Sinclair Centre*, while *Metrotown* is a large suburban mall (with over 500 shops and food outlets). Popular handicrafts include Pacific Northwest and Inuit arts and crafts: soapstone sculptures, carved masks, totem poles, pottery, jewellery and prints. **Shopping hours**: Mon-Sat 1000-1800 (Thurs-Fri until 2100), Sun 1200-1700.

SPECIAL EVENTS: For a full list of special events in British Columbia, contact Tourism British Columbia (see Contact Addresses section). The following is a selection of special events occurring in British Columbia in 2005:

Jan *108th Annual Winter Carnival*, Rockies; *Ice Wine Festival*, Okangan. **Jan 1** *Polar Bear Swim*, Vancouver. **Mar 5** *14th Annual Children's Festival*, Northern BC. **Apr 8-17** *World Ski and Snowboard Festival*, Whistler. **May 23** *67th Annual Victoria Highland Games*, Victoria. **Jun 2-Sep 25** *Bard on the Beach*, Vancouver. **Jul 22-Aug 2** *18th Annual Vancouver International Comedy Festival*, Vancouver. **Aug** *Summerfest*, *Cariboo Chilcotin*; *Eldorado Gold Panning Championships*, Cariboo Chilcotin; *Okanagan Summer Wine Festival*, Silver Star Mountain; *Abbotsford International Airshow*. **Aug-Sep** *2005 Championship Golf Tournament*, Vancouver. **Sep** *Whistler Comedy Festival*. **Sep-Oct** *World Championship Sand Sculpture Competition*, Harrison Hot Springs. **Sep** *Vancouver Fringe Festival*. **Oct** *Adams River Sockeye Salmon Run*, Okanagan. **Dec 4-5** *17th Annual North American Native Arts & Crafts Festival*, Vancouver.

Business Profile

COMMERCIAL INFORMATION: The following organisation can offer advice: Ministry of Small Business & Economic Development, Marketing, Investment & Trade, Ste 730 999 Canada Place, Vancouver, BC V6C 3E1 (tel: (604) 844 1900; fax: (604) 660 4092; e-mail: enquirybc@gems3.gov.bc.ca).

CONFERENCES/CONVENTIONS: There are conference/convention centres in Penticton, Vancouver, Victoria and Whistler as well as over 200 hotels throughout the province which can offer meeting facilities. For more information on conferences and conventions in British Columbia, contact Tourism British Columbia in London (see *Contact Addresses* section).

Climate

The southern coast is one of the mildest regions in Canada, with very warm summers and relatively mild winters. Heavy snowfalls in the Rockies.

Required clothing: Lightweights for most of the summer, with warmer clothes sometimes necessary in the evenings. Mediumweights are worn during winter, with Alpine wear in the mountains. Waterproof clothing is advisable throughout the year.

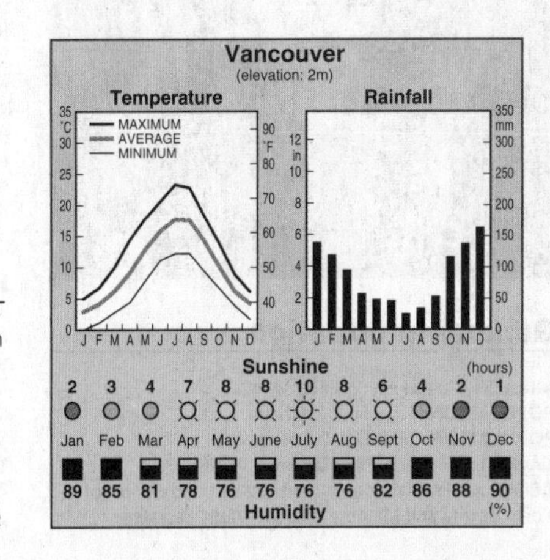

A B C D E F G H I J K L M N O P Q R S T U V W X Y Z

Manitoba

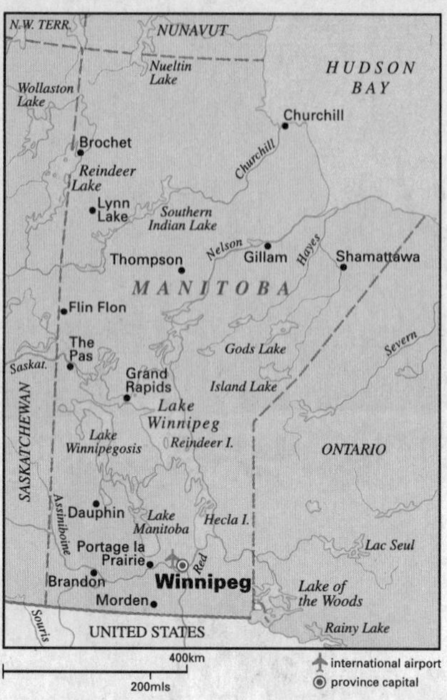

Location: Central Canada.

Travel Manitoba
7th Floor, 155 Carlton Street, Winnipeg, Manitoba R3C 3H8, Canada
Tel: (204) 945 3777 *or* (800) 665 0040 (toll-free USA and Canada). Fax: (204) 945 2302.
Website: www.travelmanitoba.com

Credit: © Travel Manitoba

General Information

AREA: 547,704 sq km (211,468 sq miles).
POPULATION: 1,119,583 (2001).
POPULATION DENSITY: 2.1 per sq km.
CAPITAL: Winnipeg. **Population**: 698,210 (2003).
GEOGRAPHY: Manitoba is bordered by the US states of North Dakota and Minnesota to the south, Saskatchewan to the west, Ontario to the east, and the Northwest Territories and Nunavut to the north. The province is also known as Heartland Canada. The landscape is diverse, ranging from rolling farmland to sandy beaches on the shores of Lake Winnipeg, and from the desert landscape of the south to northern parkland covered by lakes, forests and sub-Arctic tundra.
LANGUAGE: Although Canada is officially bilingual (English and French), English is commonly spoken in Manitoba.
TIME: GMT - 6 (GMT - 5 in summer).
Summer officially lasts from the first Sunday in April to the Saturday before the last Sunday in October.

Public Holidays

Public holidays are as for the rest of Canada (see general *Canada* section).

Travel - International

AIR: The following airlines run inter-provincial and international (US) flights: *Air Canada (AC), Jetsgo, Northwest Airlines* and *WestJet*. For timetables and fares, contact the airline offices.
International airports: *Winnipeg International Airport (YWG)* (website: www.waa.ca) is 10km (6 miles) northwest of the city centre. There is a regular bus service every 20 minutes (travel time - 20 minutes). Airport facilities include duty-free shop, post office, shops, hotel, restaurant, banks, car rental and car parking.
SEA: The only major coastal port is Churchill on Hudson Bay, which is frozen from November to early June. In summer, there are services to Nunavut and Ontario.
RAIL: Winnipeg is the most central hub of *VIA Rail*'s Canadian network. The *Western Transcontinental* connects Vancouver in the west to Toronto in the east, passing through Winnipeg three times a week in each direction. A thrice weekly train runs northwards within Manitoba from Winnipeg to The Pas (the interchange station for services to Lynn Lake), Thompson and Churchill. For timetables and fares, contact a local *VIA Rail* office.
ROAD: Excellent road services connect Manitoba with Ontario (through Kenora), Saskatchewan (Regina) and the USA (Grand Forks and Bismarck, North Dakota). The road system within Manitoba is also excellent and covers over 19,794km (12,300 miles). **Bus**: Services are run by local authorities, and interstate services are run by *Beaver*, *Grey Goose Bus Lines* and *Greyhound*. For timetables and fares, contact local offices. **Taxi**: Available in all larger towns. Taxi drivers expect a 15 per cent tip. **Documentation**: National driving licences are accepted.
URBAN: There are comprehensive bus services in Winnipeg. A flat fare is charged. There are good bus services in other towns.

Accommodation

Manitoba has a wide selection of accommodation, ranging from first-class hotels in Winnipeg to guest houses and farm holiday camps. Farm vacations are controlled by their own association, ensuring high standards. Bed & breakfast accommodation is available at a reasonable price. For all accommodation details, contact Travel Manitoba (see *Contact Addresses* section) *or* the Manitoba Hotel Association, Canada Select Suite 1505, 155 Carlton Street, Winnipeg, Manitoba R3C 3H8 (tel: (204) 942 0671; fax: (204) 942 6719; e-mail: jerry@manitobalodging.com; website: www.canadaselect.mb.ca).
CAMPING/CARAVANNING: The parklands and the enormous spread of lakes and forests in northern Manitoba are major attractions. Further details on privately operated campgrounds can be obtained from Manitoba Association of Campgrounds and Parks, Box 68, St Malo, MB R0A 1T0 (tel/fax: (204) 347 5543; e-mail: info@macap.mb.ca; website: www.macap.mb.ca). For information about Manitoba's provincial parks, contact (tel: (1-800) 214 6497; website: www.gov.mb.ca). Camping facilities are widespread. A number of companies can arrange **motor camper** rentals, with a range of fully-equipped vehicles. Full details can be obtained from Travel Manitoba (see *Contact Addresses* section).

Resorts & Excursions

Manitoba, landlocked on three sides, comprises eight tourism regions. Most of Manitoba's population can be found in the southern regions of the province, although Churchill, at its most northern border, remains one of Manitoba's more popular tourist attractions.
THE WINNIPEG REGION: Almost equidistant from the Pacific and Atlantic Oceans, the provincial capital stands in the heart of the vast prairie which covers much of the southern part of the province. This 'Gateway to the North' at the confluence of the **Red** and **Assiniboine rivers** is one of Canada's most culturally and racially diverse cities, with a well-known ballet troupe and symphony orchestra. Places of note include the **Legislative Building** with Manitoba's symbol, the **Golden Boy**, balancing triumphantly on its dome; the **Manitoba Museum** which recreates past and present life on the prairies; and **The Forks National Historic Site**, a 13.6 acre park with river walks, historic port, market, theatrical tours, restaurants and concerts. **St Boniface** is the French Quarter of Winnipeg. In the suburbs, the **Royal Canadian Mint**, with its high-tech building, and **Lower Fort Garry**, an old fur-trading post, are both worth visiting. Paddlesteamers offer excursions through Winnipeg's urban and residential areas on the Red and Assiniboine rivers. The famous Winnie the Pooh was named after Winnipeg. A statue commemorates the bear in **Assiniboine Park** along with the only known oil painting of the cub. Additionally, the park offers a **zoo**, **sculpture garden**, **English gardens** and **conservatory**.
THE CENTRAL PLAINS REGION: West of Winnipeg, the highway cuts through the wheat belt. **Fort la Reine Museum** and the **Pioneer Village** at **Portage la Prairie** reconstruct the town's days as an 18th-century trading post.
THE INTERLAKE REGION: On the eastern edge of the Interlake Region is **Lake Winnipeg**, with good sandy beaches and boats for hire. The western shore of the lake was once New Iceland, a self-governing area settled by thousands of Icelanders fleeing volcanic eruptions in their homeland. **Gimli** has the largest Icelandic population outside Iceland, and stages an annual Icelandic festival in August. **Hecla/Grindstone Provincial Park**, a group of wooded islands on the lake, offers a resort and conference centre as well as good hiking, golfing and camping facilities.
THE EASTERN REGION: East of the capital along the Trans-Canada Highway is the German-speaking Mennonite town of **Steinbach**. The **Mennonite Heritage Village** provides a close-up view of early Mennonite life.
Whiteshell Provincial Park has over 2500 sq km (1000 sq miles) of wilderness, and the **Alfred Hole Goose Sanctuary** nearby is home to four different species of wild geese. The more developed resort towns of **Falcon Lake** and **West Hawk Lake** have good facilities for swimming and sailing.
THE PARKLAND REGION: En route to the great northern wilderness, **Riding Mountain National Park** is a vast recreational area providing wildlife viewing, biking, backpacking, and horseback riding on 300km (190 miles) of hiking trails. Golfing, swimming and shopping are available. Bison still roam the range near **Lake Audy** in the park. Ukrainian immigrants colonised the farming area around **Dauphin** in the 1890s and their influence is still felt in the cuisine and costume of the area, notably during the annual **National Ukrainian Festival**.
THE WESTERN REGION: Densely wooded parklands are home to moose and wood bison, the **Spirit Sands**, a 5 sq km tract of blowing sand dunes towering over 30m, the **International Peace Garden** dedicated to the long-standing peace between Canada and the USA, located at the North Dakota border and Canada's longest free suspension foot bridge in **Souris**.
THE NORTHERN REGION: Just north of the 53rd parallel, is the town of **The Pas**, a jumping-off point for trips to the lakes and rivers of the northern interior. Further east, near the border with Saskatchewan is the mining and lumbering town of **Flin Flon**, noted for its abundant fishing opportunities, and **Grass River Provincial Park**, a huge granite wilderness with excellent canoeing adventures.
Churchill, a sub-Arctic seaport in the far northeast, is best reached by air across the vast flatlands running into **Hudson Bay**. It is known for its bird-watching opportunities and the beluga whales that congregate at the mouth of the **Churchill River** in the summertime. It is an ideal spot to view the **aurora borealis** (northern lights) in winter and to take an organised tour by **tundra buggy** in the autumn, and see why the area is known as the polar bear capital of the world. **Wapusk National Park** is a remote area with a severe sub-Arctic climate and home to one of the world's largest known polar bear den sites, in addition to hundreds of thousands of waterfowl and shorebirds.
THE PEMBINA VALLEY REGION: Panoramic valleys and rolling hills recapture the centuries-old past of the North West Mounted Police. The rough and tumble of the **Manitoba Stampede** is as exciting as **Morden's Corn and Apple Festival** is appetising.

Sport & Activities

Outdoor pursuits: The easternmost of the 'prairie provinces', Manitoba is dominated in the south by its two huge lakes, Lake Winnipeg and Lake Manitoba. Altogether, the province has over 100,000 lakes and 175 provincial parks. There are ample opportunities for all types of **watersports** on the lakes and rivers. Rivers offering particularly good **canoeing** include Bloodvein River in

Credit: © Travel Manitoba

Atikaki Provincial Wilderness Park, which flows through wild rice marshes into Lake Winnipeg; and Seal River in the north, one of the most challenging canoe routes in Canada. **Fishing** for trout, northern pike, walleye, channel catfish and Arctic grayling is especially popular. Several of the northern lakes are only accessible by air, and remote fly-in lodges are the answer for an angler's wilderness dream. There are some excellent **beaches** around the lakes, the best known being *Grand Beach* on Lake Winnipeg, one of North America's top 10 beaches. Backed by high, grass-topped sand dunes, the beach is a favourite **swimming** spot amongst local people, owing to its shallow water and easy access from Winnipeg. **Sailboarding**, **windsurfing** and **sailing** are also available here. In the northern part of the province, there are unique opportunities to observe **wildlife**. Churchill, on the shore of Hudson Bay, is known as the 'Polar Bear Capital of the World'. The best months to see them are October and early November. Special trips in 'tundra buggies' enable visitors to view the bears and other creatures (including Arctic foxes, birds and caribou) at close range. In summer, thousands of **beluga whales** congregate in the mouth of the Churchill River and in Hudson Bay, and some 200 species of birds use the environment as a nesting habitat during spring. The **northern lights** (aurora borealis) can best be seen here between January and April. Other sports on offer include **golf** (there are over 125 golf courses in Manitoba, 27 of these in Winnipeg) and **hiking**. **Cross-country skiing** is available throughout the winter months at the provincial and national parks.

For general information about sport and activities in Canada, see the main *Canada* section.

Social Profile

FOOD & DRINK: Winnipeg offers opportunities to experience the cuisine of the many and diverse cultures that typify the city in restaurants or at numerous festivals showcasing the food and culture of the region, such as the *Folklorama 'A Taste of Winnipeg'* Icelandic festival (see Special Events section). Rural Manitoba also offers a wide choice of restaurants from the very expensive to the moderately priced, with good home cooking. It is customary to tip waiters 15 per cent of the bill. The minimum age for drinking is 18, but those under 18 can drink with a meal if it is purchased by a parent or guardian. Off-licence alcohol is available only from government outlets. Opening hours are generally 1100-2100.

NIGHTLIFE: Winnipeg's nightlife is vibrant. Many cinemas, theatres, clubs, restaurants and bars also provide entertainment. Winnipeg is home to a mixture of performing arts: the Royal Winnipeg Ballet, the Winnipeg Symphony Orchestra, Manitoba Opera and several theatre, dance and music companies. The city also offers dining and moonlit dancing cruises aboard riverboats on its scenic Red and Assiniboine rivers. The main stages at Club Regent and McPhillips Street Station casinos also feature entertainment.

SHOPPING: There are several nationally known department stores in Winnipeg, with branches throughout Manitoba. City and provincial centres have a variety of unusual shops and boutiques. North of The Pas is a Native American handicraft shop where visitors can watch Native American women making moccasins, mukluks, jackets and jewellery. At the Rock Shop in Souris, costume jewellery made from rock from a local quarry can be bought, and the visitor may obtain a permit to collect his own rock. **Shopping hours**: Mon-Fri 0930-2130, Sat 0930-1800, Sun 1200-1800.

SPECIAL EVENTS: For a complete list of special events, contact Travel Manitoba (see *Contact Addresses* section). The following is a selection of special events occurring in Manitoba in 2005:

Feb 11-20 *Festival du Voyageur*, Winnipeg. **Feb 16-20** *Northern Manitoba Trapper's Festival*. **Apr 4-10** *Winnipeg Comedy Festival*. **Jun** *Winnipeg International Children's Festival*. **Jun 23-Jul 2** *Red River Exhibition*, Winnipeg. **Aug** *Opaskwayak Indian Days*, The Pas; *Islendingadagurinn*, Gimli (Icelandic Festival of Manitoba). **Aug 6-19** *Folklorama*, Winnipeg (Canada's Cultural Celebration). **Sep** *Pembina's Threshermen's Reunion*, Winkler. **Sep 22-Oct 1** *Winnipeg International Writers' Festival*. **Nov-Dec** *Santa's Village*, Manitoba.

iBusiness Profile

COMMERCIAL INFORMATION: The following organisation can offer advice: Manitoba Chamber of Commerce, 227 Portage Avenue, Winnipeg, Manitoba R3B 2A6 (tel: (204) 948 0100; fax: (204) 948 0110; e-mail: mbchamber@mbchamber.mb.ca; website: www.mbchamber.mb.ca).

CONFERENCES/CONVENTIONS: For information on conferences and conventions in Winnipeg, contact Destination Winnipeg, Tourism Division, 279 Portage Avenue, Winnipeg, Manitoba R3B 2B4 (tel: (204) 943 1970 *or* (800) 665 0204 (toll-free in USA and Canada); fax: (204) 942 4043; e-mail: wpginfo@destinationwinnipeg.ca; website: www.destinationwinnipeg.ca).

Climate

Summers are warm and sunny. Winters are cold, particularly in the north. Rainfall is highest in May.

Required clothing: Light- to mediumweights during warmer months, heavyweights in winter. Waterproofing is advisable throughout the year.

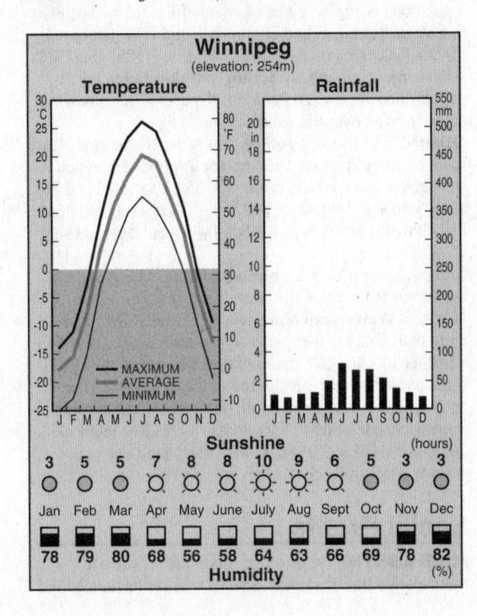

New Brunswick

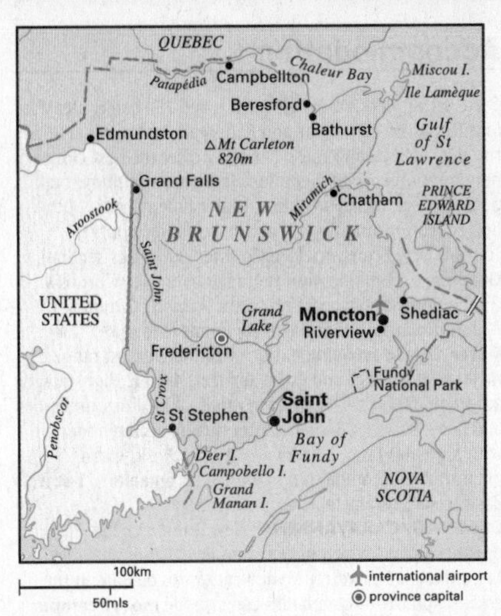

Location: East coast of Canada.

Tourism New Brunswick
Street address: 670 Centennial Building, 5th Floor, Fredericton, New Brunswick E3B 1G1, Canada
Postal address: PO Box 6000, Fredericton, New Brunswick E3B 5H1, Canada Fax: (506) 453 7127.
Information centre:
Street address: 26 Roseberry Street, Campbellton, New Brunswick E3N 2G4, Canada
Postal address: PO Box 12345, Campbellton, New Brunswick E3N 3T6, Canada
Tel: (800) 561 0123 (toll-free in USA and Canada).
Fax: (506) 789 2044.
Website: www.tourismnewbrunswick.ca

General Information

AREA: 71,569 sq km (27,632 sq miles).
POPULATION: 729,498 (2001).
POPULATION DENSITY: 10.1 per sq km.
CAPITAL: Fredericton. **Population**: 46,466 (1996).
GEOGRAPHY: New Brunswick, which is below the Gaspé Peninsula, shares its western border with Maine and has 2250km (1400 miles) of coast on the Gulf of St Lawrence and the Bay of Fundy. Its landscape comprises forested hills with rivers cutting through them. The main feature is St John River Valley in the south. Northern and eastern coastal regions give way to the extensive drainage basin of the Miramichi River in the central area.
LANGUAGE: New Brunswick is officially bilingual (English and French) with approximately 33 per cent of the population being French speaking.
TIME: GMT - 4 (GMT - 3 in summer).
Daylight saving officially lasts from the first Sunday in April to the Saturday before the last Sunday in October.

Public Holidays

Public holidays are the same as for the rest of Canada (see general *Canada* section), with the following dates also observed:
2005: Aug 1 New Brunswick Day.
2006: Aug 7 New Brunswick Day.

Travel - International

AIR: *Greater Moncton Airport (YQM)* hosts international flights operated by *Canada 3000 (2T)* to St Petersburg (Florida) and to Paris (France). International connections can often be made via Halifax (Nova Scotia). Fredericton, Saint John and Moncton are connected to Montréal by inter-provincial flights operated by *Air Canada* and its local affiliate *Air Nova*. There are airports offering local services at *Bathurst, Charlo, Fredericton, Miramichi, Moncton, Saint John* and *Saint-Léonard*.

SEA: Ferries run from Nova Scotia to Saint John, from Maine to the Fundy Islands and from Québec to Dalhousie near Campbellton. Prince Edward Island is now accessible via the Confederation Bridge. There is a full coastal ferry service between all ports in the province. For timetables, contact the local tourist information office.

RAIL: *VIA Rail* runs six times a week from Montréal to Halifax, three times via Mont Joli and via Saint John.

ROAD: The Trans-Canada Highway follows the St John River Valley from Edmundston in the north to Moncton in the east, with the majority of the highways branching off it. There are over 16,000km (10,000 miles) of roads in the province.

Accommodation

There are around 200 hotels/motels and 250 bed & breakfast inns. The main centres of population are on the coast and in the river valleys, and these generally offer the best choice of hotel or motel accommodation. There are also numerous guest houses, bed & breakfast establishments and youth hostels. For information on accommodation, contact Tourism New Brunswick (see *Contact Addresses* section).
Grading: Accommodation is graded by the New Brunswick Grading Authority according to the *Atlantic Canada Accommodations Grading Program* as follows:
5-star: Deluxe accommodation with the greatest range of facilities, amenities and guest services; **4-star**: High-quality accommodation with extended range of facilities, amenities and guest services; **3-star**: Better quality accommodation with a greater range of services; **2-star**: Basic, clean, comfortable accommodation with extra amenities; **1-star**: Basic, clean, comfortable accommodation.
CAMPING/CARAVANNING: New Brunswick has 11 provincial parks which have extensive camping facilities. More than 100 privately owned campsites operate in the area. A number of companies can arrange **motor camper** rentals, with a range of fully-equipped vehicles. Full details can be obtained from New Brunswick Investment and Exports, Tourism Section (see *Contact Addresses* section).

Resorts & Excursions

New Brunswick is a maritime province with three coastlines – on **Chaleur Bay**, the **Northumberland Strait** and the **Bay of Fundy**. Routes along these coasts can provide an interesting introduction to the area.

SOUTH

BAY OF FUNDY COASTAL DRIVE REGION: Saint John, New Brunswick's largest city, has been a shipbuilding centre since the last century. Replicas of sailing ships can be seen in the **New Brunswick Museum**. Other historic sites include the **Loyalist House** and the **Old County Courthouse**. The city was also a bastion for the British Loyalists, who flocked there in May 1783 to escape from the victorious American rebels after the War of Independence. The **Reversing Falls** are a natural phenomenon caused by the powerful tidal waters of the **Bay of Fundy** finding an upstream outlet into the rocky river gorge. The coastline is battered by the tempestuous 14m- (46ft-) tides of the Bay of Fundy, resulting in dramatic scenery such as the **Hopewell Cape**'s sandstone '**flowerpots**' – enormous rock formations that have been likened to flowerpots because of their shape and peculiar sprouts of green foliage. Visitors should stay alert to the powerful incoming tide however, which can rise as much as 14m (46ft). **St Andrews** has some well-preserved 18th-century houses as well as **The Blockhouse**, built in 1812 to defend the town from US incursions.
Blacks Harbour has a ferry to the little-known and unspoilt **Fundy Islands**, of which **Grand Manan**, the largest, boasts beautiful rare flora and fauna. Whales and dolphins can often be spotted from the shoreline. It is also a centre for collecting **dulse** (edible seaweed) which is a speciality of the province. **Deer Island** and **Campobello Island** are reached by ferry from **Letete**. To the east of Saint John is **Fundy National Park**, the area's most popular resort. Much of it is set on a plateau 300m (985ft) above sea level with 110km (69 miles) of hiking trails and 700 campsites. The huge range of organised activities there includes an **Arts and Crafts School**. Rowboats and canoes can be rented to navigate the tidal flats where tides can rise by 14m (46ft) a day. At low tide, guided walks of the ocean floor are led by naturalists. The park is situated on the major Atlantic bird migratory route, providing good birdwatching opportunities.
The Fundy tides cause an impressive tidal bore at **Moncton**, the province's second-largest city. At **Magnetic Hill**, a popular natural attraction, an optical illusion makes it seem as if cars are being 'pulled' uphill. Family entertainments are provided at the **Magic Mountain Water Theme Park** and **Crystal Palace Amusement Park**.

WEST

THE RIVER VALLEY REGION: The **St John River Valley** provides a scenic route to the capital, with the uncluttered resort of **Grand Lake** on the way. **Fredericton**, 110km (70 miles) upriver from Saint John and the Bay of Fundy, is the province's capital. It is the legislative and academic centre of New Brunswick and possesses some fine neo-classical and Victorian architecture, such as the **Legislative Building**, **Christ Church Cathedral** and **Government House**. The **Beaverbrook Art Gallery** is one of the finest in Canada with an extensive collection of Canadian, British and Renaissance paintings. Salvador Dali's painting *St James the Great* forms the centrepiece of the collection. Cruises on the St John River are possible. On Saturdays, the **Farmer's Market** is the focus for Frederictonians and visitors alike. North of the city, the highly developed resort of **Mactaquac Provincial Park** offers a huge range of outdoor activities. Nearby, **King's Landing Historical Settlement**, a reconstructed loyalist village, is also worth visiting for its insights into the 17th-century pioneering lifestyle.

CENTRAL

MIRAMICHI RIVER ROUTE: Salmon fishing on the **Miramichi River** is recommended. There are also numerous walking tours and trails along the river. The Aboriginal town of **Metepenagiag (Red Bank First Nation)**, just outside of the town of **Miramichi**, is New Brunswick's oldest town, with archaeological finds that date back more than 3000 years.

EAST

THE ACADIAN COASTAL DRIVE REGION: The eastern shoreline, once a French stronghold, has a temperate climate and some excellent beaches, particularly near **Kouchibouguac National Park**, where a network of boardwalks protects the fragile sand dune ecology: the park is the home of more than 223 species of birds, and ocean canoe trips are offered to view nearby seal colonies. **La Dune de Bouctouche**, one of the world's last surviving white sand dunes, has an award-winning eco-visitor centre. In the south, **Shediac** hosts an annual lobster festival; at **Parlee Beach** nearby is the largest and best beach in the province. North of this, the area around Tracadie is still a French-speaking enclave and deep-sea fishing charters are available here. A 500-acre **Acadian Village** at **Caraquet** recreates the lifestyle of the 18th-century Breton settlers.

Sport & Activities

Outdoor pursuits: Visitors interested in an active holiday in New Brunswick may obtain more details from the numerous Adventure Outlets and Adventure Stations (recognisable by an Adventure Lighthouse symbol) located throughout the province. The Tourism section also offers a special 'Day Adventure Programme', with over 100 activities available that can be done in one day (tel: (800) 561 0123; toll-free in USA and Canada).
A new network of **walking**, **hiking** and **biking** trails includes the *International Appalachian Trail*, a network of paths linking to the Appalachian Trail in the US at Mount Katahdin; *Le Petit Temis*, a cycling and hiking trail stretching from Edmundston to Riviere-du-Loup in Québec; the *Fundy Trail Parkway*, 27km (17 miles) of hiking and cycling trails along the Bay of Fundy; and the *Acadian Coastal Trail*, a network of walking and biking routes beginning at Dalhousie. **Whale watching** is extremely popular due to the Bay of Fundy's boast of more whale species, more often, than anywhere else in the world; the waters of the *Bay of Fundy* are home to over 15 species, including the rare right whale. Whale-watching tours depart from different regions around the province.
Watersports: New Brunswick's beaches are renowned for their warm water and there are 42 so-called 'ocean hot spots' which are particularly good for **swimming**, notably *Parlee Beach* and *Kelly's Beach* (in Kouchibouguac National Park). There are plenty of opportunities for **fishing** in New Brunswick's 3814km (19,884 miles) of rivers and streams. The *Mirimachi River*, in particular, is famous for salmon fishing. Deep-sea fishing boats are open for charter. The booklet 'Fish New Brunswick', which gives details on fish species, seasons and regulations, is available free of charge from the Department of Natural Resources and Energy, Fish and Wildlife Branch, PO Box 6000, Fredericton NB, E3B 5H1 (tel: (506) 453 3826; e-mail: dnrweb@gnb.ca). **Sailing** and **skindiving** are popular, and the annual *Renforth Regatta* attracts **rowing** crews from all over the world.
Other: One of the best **golf** centres is the picturesque resort town of St Andrews-by-the-Sea. For information on golf courses, contact the New Brunswick Golf Association, PO Box 1555, Station A, Fredericton, NB E3B 5G2 (tel: (506) 451 1349; fax: (506) 451 1348; e-mail: nbgolf@nbnet.nb.ca; website: www.golfnb.com).
Grand Manan Island is a **birdwatching** paradise and was the favourite haunt of the famous ornithologist, James Audubon. **Wintersports** are also well catered for, with more than 9000km (5600 miles) of **snowmobile** trails and a further 1000km (621 miles) of **cross-country skiing** trails. Snowmobiling is restricted to the designated trails and requires a valid trail permit, obtainable from the New Brunswick Federation of Snowmobile Clubs (tel: (506) 325 2625; fax: (506) 325 2627; e-mail: nbfsc@nb.aibn.com; website: www.nbfsc.com).

Social Profile

FOOD & DRINK: The province is famous for seafood, particularly Atlantic salmon with its delicate flavour, served with butter, new potatoes and *fiddleheads* (young fronds of ostrich fern served with butter and seasoned or used cold in salads). Apples, blueberries and cranberries are common dessert ingredients. Home-made baked beans and steamed brown bread are served as traditional Saturday-night supper. *Rapée pie*, made with chicken, is an Acadian speciality for Sundays or festivals. Shediac is reputed to be the lobster capital of the world. Fredericton, Saint John and Moncton offer international cuisine as well as local specialities like New Brunswick *dulse*, an edible seaweed. The minimum drinking age is 19 years old.
NIGHTLIFE: Music is very much a part of the lives of New Brunswick citizens. Many bars and clubs throughout the province, especially in Fredericton, Saint John and Moncton, feature live music, much of it with a French, Scottish and Irish flavour. The area has recently acquired a reputation for jazz and blues.
SHOPPING: Special purchases include local and provincial handicrafts which are especially worthwhile in New Brunswick. The best markets in Saint John are between Charlotte and Germain streets, forming the *Old City Market*. This is open all week, with farmers taking over on Friday and Saturday. Moncton has three large shopping areas: Champlain Place, Moncton Mall and Highfield Square.
Shopping hours: Mon-Sat 0900-1730; 1000-2200 in malls.
SPECIAL EVENTS: There are many seasonal festivities; for full details, contact Tourism New Brunswick (see *Contact Addresses* section). The following is a selection of special events occurring in New Brunswick in 2005:
Mar 3-5 *Saint-Quentin Winter Carnival*. **Apr** *Salon du Livre*, Edmunston. **May** *Salon de la Forêt*, Edmundston. **Jun** *Dory Boat Festival*, Petit-Rocher; *Edmunston Jazz and Blues Festival*. **Jul 22-24** *24th New Brunswick Highland Games & Scottish Festival*. **Sep 9-11** *Atlantic Balloon Fiesta*, Sussex. **Sep 14-18** *Harvest Jazz and Blues Festival*, Fredericton. **Nov** *Festival of Christmas Magic*, Fredericton.

Business Profile

COMMERCIAL INFORMATION: The following organisations can offer advice: Atlantic Provinces Chamber of Commerce, Suite 21, 236 St George Street, Moncton, New Brunswick E1C 1W1 (tel: (506) 857 3980; fax: (506) 859 6131; e-mail: info@apcc.ca; website: www.apcc.ca); *or* Greater Moncton Chamber of Commerce, Suite 100, 910 Main Street, Moncton, New Brunswick E1C 1G6 (tel: (506) 857 2883; fax: (506) 857 9209; e-mail: info@gmcc.nb.ca; website: www.gmcc.nb.ca). There are also Chambers of Commerce representing New Brunswick and Fredericton.
CONFERENCES/CONVENTIONS: For information on conferences and conventions in New Brunswick, contact Business New Brunswick, PO Box 6000, Fredericton, New Brunswick E3B 5H1 (tel: (506) 444 5228; fax: (506) 444 4586; e-mail: www@gnb.ca; website: www.gnb.ca); *or* Fredericton Tourism, PO Box 130, City Hall, 397 Queen Street, Fredericton, New Brunswick E3B 4Y7 (tel: (506) 460 2020; fax: (506) 460 2042; e-mail: webmaster@fredericton.ca; website: www.city.fredericton.nb.ca); *or* Tourism Saint John, PO Box 1971, 11th Floor, City Hall, Saint John, New Brunswick E2L 4L1 (tel: (506) 658 2990; fax: (506) 632 6118; e-mail: visitsj@saintjohn.ca; website: www.tourismsaintjohn.com); *or* Moncton Convention & Visitors Bureau (tel: (506) 853 3590; fax: (506) 856 4352).

Climate

Summer is warm with cooler evenings. Autumn is relatively mild. Winters are cold with heavy snows.

Required clothing: Light- to mediumweights during summer months, heavyweights in winter. Waterproofing is advisable all year.

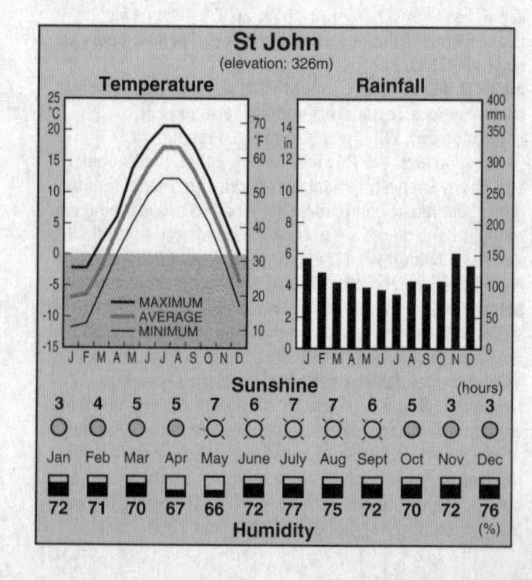

Newfoundland and Labrador

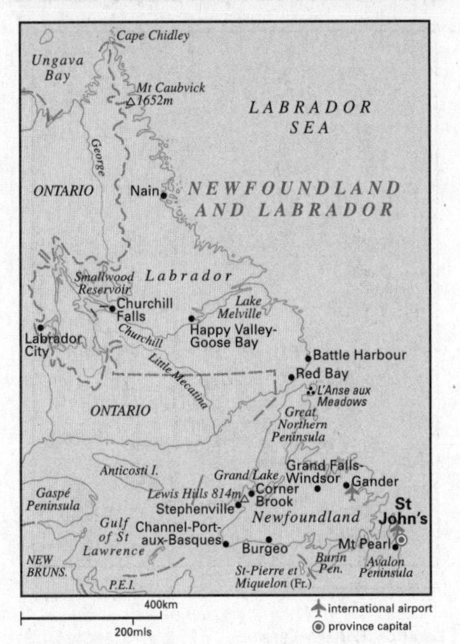

Location: Eastern Canada.

Department of Tourism, Culture and Recreation
PO Box 8700, St John's, Newfoundland A1B 4J6, Canada
Tel: (709) 729 2808. Fax: (709) 729 0057.
Website: www.gov.nl.ca/tourism
E-mail: apeddle@gov.nl.ca

General Information

AREA: 405,720 sq km (156,648 sq miles).
POPULATION: 512,930 (2001; excludes Labrador).
POPULATION DENSITY: 1.36 per sq km.
CAPITAL: St John's. **Population**: 177,500 (2001).
GEOGRAPHY: Newfoundland and Labrador is the most easterly Canadian province. It consists of the Island of Newfoundland and the mainland plateau region of Labrador which borders the province of Québec. The province stretches approximately 1700km (1063 miles) north to south, and has approximately 17,000km (10,625 miles) of coastline, much of it rugged and heavily indented with bays and fjords. The interior of Newfoundland is a combination of forest, heath, lakes and rivers spread over a terrain that ranges from mountainous in the west to rolling hills in the centre and east. Labrador is also mountainous in the west, although its rivers are larger and wilder.
LANGUAGE: Although Canada is officially bilingual (English and French), 95 per cent of this province speaks English as a first language.
TIME: Newfoundland: GMT - 3.5 (GMT - 2.5 in summer).
Labrador: GMT - 4 (GMT - 3 in summer).
Summer officially lasts from the first Sunday in April to the Saturday before the last Sunday in October.

Public Holidays

Public holidays as for the rest of Canada (see general *Canada* section), with the following dates also observed:
2005: Jun 24 Discovery Day. **Jul 1** Remembrance Day (Beaumont Hamel, 1916). **Aug 1** St John's Regatta Day (only in St John's).
2006: Jun 24 Discovery Day. **Jul 1** Remembrance Day (Beaumont Hamel, 1916). **Aug 7** St John's Regatta Day (only in St John's).

Travel - International

AIR: *Air Canada (AC)* operates regular services to Newfoundland and Labrador. *Air Labrador*, *CanJet*, *Interprovincial Airlines*, *Jazz* and *WestJet* operate services within the province and to the Maritime Provinces.
International airports: *Gander (YQX)* is 3km (2 miles) from the city centre. Airport facilities include car parking, restaurant, duty-free shop and banks.
St John's (YYT) is 8km (5 miles) from the city centre (travel time - 15 minutes).
Other major airports are at *Churchill Falls*, *Deer Lake*, *Happy Valley-Goose Bay*, *St Anthony*, *Stephenville* and *Wabush*.

SEA: A year-round daily passenger and vehicle ferry service runs between North Sydney, Nova Scotia and Port aux Basques on Newfoundland's southwest coast (crossing time - six hours). Summer services run three times a week between North Sydney and Argentia on Newfoundland's Avalon Peninsula, mid-June to mid-September (crossing time - 12 hours). Reservations can be made with *Marine Atlantic* (tel: (800) 341 7981 (toll-free in USA and Canada) *or* (709) 695 4200; fax: (902) 564 7480; e-mail: info@marine-atlantic.ca; website: www.marine-atlantic.ca). There is also a summer ferry to the French islands of St Pierre & Miquelon from Fortune on Newfoundland's Burin Peninsula (crossing time - 90 minutes) (tel: (800) 563 2006 (toll-free in USA and Canada) *or* (709) 832 0429).
Intra-provincial ferries connect island communities with larger towns. A seasonal twice-daily summer ferry (tel: (709) 729 2830) connects Blanc Sablon in southern Labrador and St Barbe on Newfoundland's Great Northern Peninsula with an 80-minute crossing. Remote communities on the Labrador coast and Newfoundland's south coast are also served by coastal boats. All intra-provincial ferry services can be checked online (website: www.gov.nf.ca/ferryservices).
RAIL: A passenger service provided by *The Québec North Shore & Labrador Railway* operates between Sept Isles in Québec and Labrador City in western Labrador (tel: (709) 944 8205).
ROAD: A modern paved highway (Route 1, the Trans-Canada Highway) crosses Newfoundland from Port aux Basques in the southwest to the capital of St John's in the east. Distance is 905km (565 miles). Paved secondary roads connect most communities to the main highway. Visitors can reach western Labrador along a partially paved highway from Baie Comeau, Québec. Route 500, a seasonal gravel highway dubbed the 'Freedom Road' by residents, connects Labrador City and Wabush in the west with the interior town of Churchill Falls and Happy Valley-Goose Bay in east-central Labrador. There are limited services along this road. **Coach**: *DRL Coachlines* (website: www.drlgroup.com) operate a daily scheduled bus service between St John's and Port aux Basques (Route 1). Stops along the route include Gander, Grand Falls-Windsor and Corner Brook. Route 510 connects communities along Labrador's southeast coast between L'Anse au Clair on the Quebec/Labrador border and Cartwright. The road is paved for the first 85km to Red Bay and is Class A gravel from there to Charlottetown (160km). From L'Anse au Claire to Cartwright is 400km.

Accommodation

There are over 500 establishments in the province with a total of more than 7000 rooms. Many towns offer hotel or bed & breakfast accommodation, although this is often seasonal. Most of the settlements in the province are on the coast rather than the wild interior (where some cabins and lodges are, however, available). As St John's is now an 'oil boom town', accommodation there can be hard to come by, and advance reservations are recommended. For information on hotels and bed & breakfast accommodation, contact the Department of Tourism, Culture and Recreation (see *Contact Addresses* section). **Grading**: Accommodation is graded according to the *Canada Select Accommodations Grading Program* as follows: **5-star**: Deluxe accommodation with the greatest range of facilities, amenities and guest services; **4-star**: High-quality accommodation with extended range of facilities, amenities and guest services; **3-star**: Better quality accommodation with a greater range of services; **2-star**: Basic, clean, comfortable accommodation with extra amenities; **1-star**: Basic, clean, comfortable accommodation.
CAMPING/CARAVANNING: The wildness of the province offers superb camping facilities, both for motorhomes and tents. Both national parks (Gros Morne in western Newfoundland and Terra Nova in eastern Newfoundland) as well as 13 provincial and 56 private campgrounds provide camping services. Facilities on campsites are basic rather than luxurious, the emphasis being on seclusion and privacy. Full details can be obtained from the Department of Tourism, Culture and Recreation (see *Contact Addresses* section).

Resorts & Excursions

The province of Newfoundland and Labrador consists of the Island of Newfoundland and the mainland plateau region of Labrador which borders the province of Québec. Most areas are accessible by road, with the exception of Newfoundland's northwestern interior and Labrador's northern extremities. Visitors should consult the provincial tourism office for information on tours to these remote regions.

ISLAND OF NEWFOUNDLAND

SOUTHEAST: Home to the majority of Newfoundland's population, the **Avalon Peninsula** is full of historic settlements dating back to the 17th century. **Trinity** records the history of European explorers' first encounter with the ancient Beothuk people. The town of **Placentia**, like many of the older towns of this region, was established by Basque fishermen almost 500 years ago. It later became the French capital of Newfoundland in the 17th and 18th centuries. On Newfoundland's southeast coast lies the seabird ecological reserve of **Witless Bay**, which is home to thousands of Atlantic Puffins and over one million northern seabirds. The provincial capital and a busy port, **St John's** is the region's economic and communications centre, with a good natural harbour that is bounded by hills. **Water Street** is one of the oldest shopping streets in North America and still bustles with activity. **Signal Hill**, the reception point for Guglielmo Marconi's first transatlantic radio transmission from England in 1901, is Canada's second-largest national historic site and offers a good view of the town and harbour to the west. The **Quidi Vidi Battery** is worth visiting. **The Rooms** (opened in 2005) include the old Newfoundland museum (formerly located at 285 Duckworth Street, A1C 1G9, St John's), the provincial archives and the provincial art gallery.

Credit: © Newfoundland and Labrador Tourism

CENTRAL: Terra Nova National Park is an area of scenic rugged coastline adjoining **Bonavista Bay**, which also boasts an 18-hole golf course. The **Burin Peninsula** in the south has some beautiful coastal villages. At **Fortune**, a ferry runs to the island of **St Pierre**, which is officially part of France. A current passport is required to embark at Fortune. Fishing trips to the remote and barely accessible interior can be arranged at **Gander** and **Grand Falls-Windsor**. An interpretive centre and excavation site at **Boyd's Cove** on the **Kittiwake Coast** recounts the history of Newfoundland's mysterious Beothuk people, who once populated much of Newfoundland's shores. Driving tours through the Kittiwake coastal area begin at Gander and wind through the fishing communities of Bonavista Bay and Notre Dame Bay. The **Banting Interpretive Centre** at **Musgrave Harbour** honours the life and history of the Canadian scientist Sir Frederick Banting, co-discoverer of insulin. Icebergs can be seen from the sandy shores of **Cape Freels**. Further south are the communities of Greenspond, a small fishing village that dates back to the 17th century, and **Indian Bay**, which is known for its sport fishing opportunities. Blueberry fields abound in Indian Bay, which is a popular stopping point during the warm sunny months of August and September.
NORTHWEST: The **Long Range Mountains** dominate the western seaboard, along which runs a 715km- (444 mile-) coastal road affording good views of the fjords, mountains and beaches. **Corner Brook**, the island's second city, set in a deep inlet halfway up the coast, is an outfitting centre for expeditions to the lakes and rivers of the interior, many of which are accessible only by air. **Wiltondale Pioneer Village** demonstrates everyday life in the 19th century. Newfoundland's west coast, the **French Shore**, has vibrant folk traditions.
The **Great Northern Peninsula** is a wilderness area of outstanding scenic beauty. It is best seen from **Gros Morne National Park**, a blend of rugged mountains, deep fjords and bays on the **Gulf of St Lawrence**. There are regularly scheduled boat tours. A national historic site at nearby **Port au Choix** pays homage to the Maritime Archaic People, whose local history dates back more than 5000 years. At the northernmost tip of the peninsula at **L'Anse aux Meadows** (which, like Gros Morne, is a UNESCO World Heritage Site) lie the restored remains of the earliest European settlement in the New World, a group of six **sod houses** built by Norsemen around the year AD 1000.

Credit: © Newfoundland and Labrador Tourism

A B C D E F G H I J K L M N O P Q R S T U V W X Y Z

LABRADOR

The largely undisturbed wilderness of **Labrador**, which lies northwest of the Island of Newfoundland, has only 27,000 inhabitants, and can be reached by air or by ferry from the port of **St Barbe** on Newfoundland's northern coast. The 16th-century Basque whaling station of **Red Bay** on Labrador's southern coast is the oldest industrial complex in the New World. Close by, the **Labrador Straits Museum** has displays on the Maritime Archaic Indians who built a burial mound nearby at **L'Anse-Amour** around 5500 BC. Much of Labrador is undeveloped and, except in the few isolated towns and Inuit, Innu and Métis coastal villages, uninhabited. There are two principal road systems in Labrador, one which connects the inland mining town of **Labrador City** with the eastern inlet of **Happy Valley-Goose Bay**, and a coastal highway that extends along the eastern coastline and links most of the region's Atlantic fishing villages. Both provide opportunities for short day tours. Longer trips to the Labrador interior can be arranged through the many tour operators and outfitters that service the Labrador region. Winters can be bitterly cold in Labrador and travellers should come prepared. **Labrador City**, near the Labrador-Quebec border, is a favourite destination for snowmobiling, cross-country and downhill skiing.

Credit: © Newfoundland and Labrador Tourism

Sport & Activities

Outdoor pursuits: Newfoundland's coastline offers a wide range of **boating** excursions and other water-based activities, as well as a rich concentration of marine life. More than 360 species of bird have been spotted here, but the province is most famous for its 60 major seabird colonies that are the summer nesting sites of millions of puffins, gannets, kittiwakes, murres and petrels. Many birds and whales can be seen in the *Witless Bay Ecological Reserve*, which visitors can travel through by boat or **kayak**. Caribou, black bears and - very rarely - polar bears can be found in the *Avalon Wilderness Reserve*, while *Cape St Mary's Ecological Reserve* is best known for its golden-headed gannets. Illustrated talks, guided walks and nature hikes with experienced naturalists can be booked at the visitor centre.

Whale watching is very popular around the waters of **Bay Bulls and Witless Bay**, which are home to a large population of humpback whales as well as smaller pods of fin and minke whales. Eastern Newfoundland, a region of sheltered coves and sandy beaches, is a popular destination for **sailing** and **swimming**. In the interior, **salmon fishing** is particularly good in the *Exploits* and *Gander rivers*. The salmon fishing season runs from 24 May to 15 September. A qualified guide is required for visitors intending to fish in licensed rivers in Newfoundland and in all waters in Labrador. The Gros Morne National Park offers **hiking**, **trekking** and **climbing** and over 100km (65 miles) of hiking trails. The *T'Railway Park* comprises over 900km (565 miles) of hiking trails between Port aux Basques and St John's, through widely varied landscapes. **Skiing** is popular at the Island of Newfoundland's *Marble Mountain*, 8km (5 miles) east of Corner Brook, the province's second city. Labrador ski resorts include *Smokey Mountain* (near Labrador City), and *White Hills* (at Clarenville) in eastern Newfoundland. The best **cross-country skiing** trails can be found in Labrador.

Folk music: Newfoundland, and particularly St John's, is famous for its folk music, and there are plenty of bars in the provincial capital where visitors can see live performances by local bands. The *Newfoundland and Labrador Folk Festival* takes place annually during the first weekend in August.

Social Profile

FOOD & DRINK: The province boasts a hearty cuisine making full use of fat pork, molasses, salt fish, salt meat, boiled vegetables and soups. Fish is a staple food, predominantly cod made into stews and fish cakes, or fried, salted, dried and fresh. Salmon, trout, halibut and hake are also available. *Brewis* is a hard water biscuit that needs soaking in water to soften, then gentle cooking; often salt or fresh cod is served with *scrunchions*, which are bits of fat pork, fried and crunchy. Another speciality is *damper dog* (a type of fried bread dough), *cod sound pie* (made from tough meat near the cod's backbone), *crubeens* (Irish pickled pigs' feet) and *fat back and molasses dip* (rich mixture of pork fat and molasses for dipping bread). Pies, jams, jellies and puddings are made from wild berries. The minimum drinking age is 19.

NIGHTLIFE: A St John's pub crawl is a real cultural experience, with a particularly strong English and Irish influence. Water Street and Duckworth Street offer fine restaurants and nightclubs. Newfoundland also has its own music, mostly English and Irish, which can be found everywhere in local festivals, nightclubs, bars, taverns and concerts. George Street in St John's has become a club and restaurant zone and holds a variety of seasonal festivals. However, on the whole, night entertainment in many regions is scarce.

SHOPPING: Water Street and Duckworth Street in downtown St John's are a must for any shopper - Water Street is one of the oldest shopping streets in North America, and European merchants, sailors and privateers have bartered here since the 16th century. Handicrafts, Grenfell parkas and Labradorite jewellery are the best known products of the Newfoundland and Labrador area.

Shopping hours: Mon-Wed 1000-1700, Thurs-Fri 1000-2200, Sat 1000-1800, Sun 1200-1700. (Malls generally open Mon-Sat 1000-2200.)

SPECIAL EVENTS: For full information on special events, contact Department of Tourism, Culture and Recreation (see *Contact Addresses* section). The following is a selection of special events occurring in Newfoundland and Labrador in 2005:

Feb 25-26 *Alexis Sled Dog Race*, Port Hope Simpson. **Feb** *Pasadena Winter Carnival*. **May 21** *Polar Bear Dip*, Port Hope Simpson. **Jun 19** *National Aboriginal Day*, Happy Valley - Goose Bay. **Jul 1** *Canada Day*, nationwide. **Aug 12-14** *Ramea Rock Island Music Festival*. **Oct 28-Nov 5** *Grand Falls Windsor Red Maple Festival*.

SOCIAL CONVENTIONS: Newfoundland society shows the dominant influence of northern European - especially English and Irish, but also French - settlers in its dialects, folk music and dance. Aboriginal peoples with distinct cultures and traditions include the Mi'kmaq on Newfoundland and the Inuit, Innu and Métis in Labrador. Geographical isolation nurtured a fiercely independent spirit in the province, which joined the Canadian Union as late as 1949.

Business Profile

COMMERCIAL INFORMATION: The following organisations can offer advice: Atlantic Provinces Chamber of Commerce, Suite 21, 236 St George Street, Moncton, New Brunswick E1C 1W1 (tel: (506) 857 3980; fax: (506) 859 6131; e-mail: info@apcc.ca; website: www.apcc.ca); *or* St John's Board of Trade, PO Box 5127, St John's, Newfoundland A1C 5V5 (tel: (709) 726 2961; fax: (709) 726 2003; e-mail: mail@bot.nf.ca; website: www.bot.nf.ca); *or* Department of Innovation, Trade and Rural Development, Head Office, Confederation Building, PO Box 8700, St John's, Newfoundland A1B 4J6 (tel: (709) 729 7000; fax: (709) 729 7244; e-mail: ITRDinfo@gov.nl.ca).

CONFERENCES/CONVENTIONS: For information on conferences and conventions in St John's only, contact the Meetings and Conventions Co-ordinator, Department of Tourism, Culture and Recreation, PO Box 8700, St John's, Newfoundland A1B 4J6 (tel: (709) 729 0862; fax: (709) 729 0870).

Climate

Very cold winters and mild summers.

Required clothing: Light- to mediumweights in warmer months, heavyweights in winter. Waterproofing is advisable throughout the year.

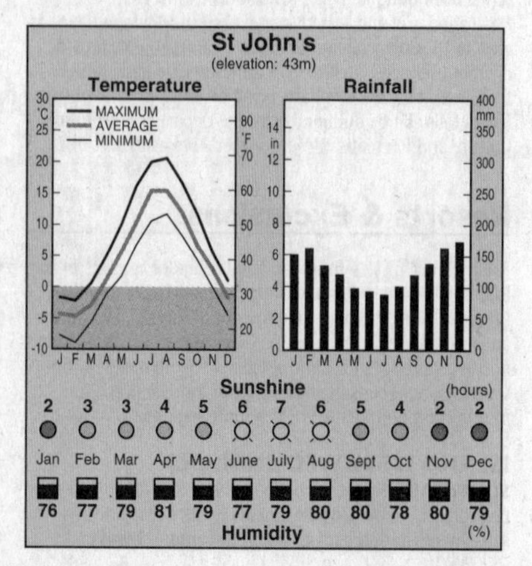

North West Territories

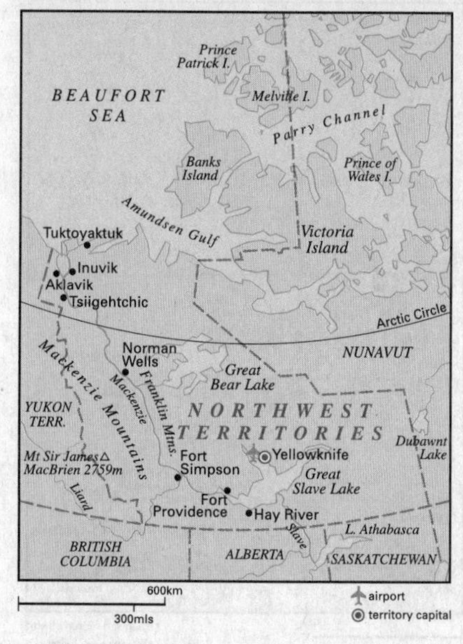

Location: Northern Canada.

On 1 April 1999 the former Northwest Territories was divided, creating two new territories: Nunavut (which means 'our land' in Inuktitut) in the east, and the Northwest Territories in the west.

Northwest Territories Tourism
PO Box 610, Yellowknife, Northwest Territories X1A 2N5, Canada
Tel: (867) 873 7200 *or* (800) 661 0788 (toll-free in Canada and USA). Fax: (867) 873 4059.
E-mail: arctic@explorenwt.com
Website: www.explorenwt.com

General Information

AREA: 1,004,471 sq km (387,826 sq miles).
POPULATION: 37,360 (2001).
POPULATION DENSITY: 0.03 per sq km.
CAPITAL: Yellowknife. **Population**: 18,028 (official estimate 2000).

GEOGRAPHY: The Northwest Territories stretch from the Mackenzie Mountains on the Yukon border to the open barrenlands to the east, from the shores and islands of the Arctic Ocean to the woodlands in the south. Canada's longest river, the Mackenzie, flows 1800km (1125 miles) from Great Slave Lake to its delta on the Beaufort Sea.

LANGUAGE: Although Canada is officially bilingual (English and French), English is more commonly spoken in the Northwest Territories.

TIME: West of 102°W: GMT - 8 (GMT - 7 in summer). Summer officially lasts from the last Sunday in April to the Saturday before the last Sunday in October.

Public Holidays

Public holidays are as for the rest of Canada (see general *Canada* section), although Victoria Day is not listed and the following holidays are also observed:
2005: Aug 1 Civic Holiday. **2006: Aug 7** Civic Holiday.

Travel - International

AIR: The best way to reach the more remote areas within the Territory is by air. Float planes are commonly used to reach the northern lakes. The largest operators into the region are *Air Canada* and *First Air* (website: www.firstair.ca). Numerous regional airlines offer scheduled and charter services to communities within the Northwest Territories.

Airports: *Yellowknife Airport (YZF)* is less than 1km (0.6 miles) from the town centre (travel time - 10 minutes). International visitors will need to fly to Calgary or Edmonton (in Alberta) or Winnipeg (in Manitoba) and board a domestic flight to Yellowknife.

SEA/LAKE/RIVER: Ferry crossings for road travellers are provided free during the summer months by the territorial government for the Mackenzie River at Fort Providence, for the Mackenzie and Arctic Red Rivers at Tsiigehtchic, for the Liard River at Fort Simpson and for the Peel River at Fort McPherson. During winter, ice bridges are provided at these crossings, but no crossing is available for some weeks in

Credit: © Northwest Territories Tourism

spring and autumn each year during the break-up and freeze-up of the ice. Cruises are available on Great Slave Lake and from Yellowknife to Inuvik on the Mackenzie River during the summer. Speedboat tours, guided canoe trips and river rafting trips are offered on Great Slave Lake, the Mackenzie Delta, the Nahanni River and other more remote rivers. Sail boats are available on Great Slave Lake for charter or package tours.

ROAD: The major routes are along the Dempster Highway from the Yukon to the Mackenzie Delta, the Mackenzie Highway from Alberta to the Great Slave Lake region, and the Liard Highway from British Columbia to the junction of the Liard and Mackenzie Rivers, near Fort Simpson. During the winter months, ice roads providing supply routes to remote communities almost double the size of the highway network. **Documentation**: International driver's licences are accepted in the Northwest Territories. Drivers should ensure that their insurance is valid and take advice on precautions for driving in cold weather conditions. Ice roads require special vehicles. **Coach**: There are two bus companies running scheduled services in the region: *Frontier Coachlines* (tel: (867) 874 2566; fax: (867) 874 2388) serves Yellowknife, Fort Smith and Fort Simpson from Hay River. *Greyhound Canada* (tel: (800) 661 8747; toll-free in USA and Canada) runs services from Edmonton, Alberta to Hay River and Yellowknife. Companies offering charter and organised bus tours for groups include the *Arctic Tour Company*, Box 325, Tuktoyaktuk, Northwest Territories X0E 1C0 (tel: (867) 977 2230; fax: (867) 977 2276; e-mail: atc@auroranet.nt.ca), whose tours include a 5-day Dempster Highway tour, Beluga whale watching and viewing of the Aurora Borealis (Northern Lights).

Accommodation

HOTELS: Although most of the towns have hotels and bed & breakfast establishments open all year, accommodation can be scarce and often quite basic. There can be long distances between settlements of any size, especially in the Arctic zone. 'Lodges' designed for outdoor activity holidays can be found in many settlements. For details, contact Northwest Territories Tourism for an *Explorers' Guide* (see *Contact Addresses* section).

CAMPING/CARAVANNING: Campsites are generally open from late May to September and are run by both government and private organisations. Some outfitters have established 'outposts' (semi-permanent camps) with tents, beds and meals, usually offered as part of organised trips. A number of companies can arrange **motor camper** rentals, with a range of fully-equipped vehicles. Full details can be obtained from Northwest Territories Tourism (see *Contact Addresses* section).

Resorts & Excursions

Most of the province's population and commercial activity is based in Yellowknife and around the Great Slave Lake. The smaller communities to the north of Yellowknife are largely populated by aboriginal people living a more traditional way of life. The Inuit and Dene comprise almost 50 per cent of the Territories' population and tend to live in or around small communities that have existed for hundreds or thousands of years. Four of the Northwest Territories' five tourism regions are featured below.

NORTHERN FRONTIER REGION

Yellowknife, the Territories' capital, is a small city perched on the pre-Cambrian shield, which adjoins the **Great Slave Lake**. The city's main industries are government/service industries and mining. Two major gold finds were made here in the 1930s, followed more recently by the discovery of diamonds north of Yellowknife. The **Prince of Wales Northern Heritage Centre** showcases northern Canadian culture and wildlife, with temporary art exhibitions. Boats and canoes can be hired for trips on the **Mackenzie River** and the **Great Slave** and **Great Bear Lakes**. These tours often follow old trapping and fur-trading routes. An experienced guide is essential. Near the capital are the Dene (aboriginal) settlements of **Dettah**, **Rae-Edzo** and **Wekweti**, or **Rock Lake** (formally known as **Snare Lake**), where a largely traditional way of life is still maintained.

DEH CHO REGION: Two highways serve the Big River Country to the west of Yellowknife and visitors may view this area from the road or fly deep into the interior. In the far southwestern corner of this territory lies **Nahanni National Park**, a UNESCO World Heritage Site in the **Mackenzie Mountains**. Access to the park itself is by air from **Fort Simpson**, **Fort Liard (BC)** or **Watson Lake (Yukon)** as there are no roads in the wilderness area. Several operators offer boat and raft tours on the river taking in the magnificent 100m high (312ft) **Virginia Falls** (twice the height of Niagara).

SOUTH SLAVE LAKE REGION

Wood Buffalo National Park, south of the Great Slave Lake, is a noted centre for naturalists and birdwatchers. The Waterfalls Route, a 325km (203 mile) driving route beginning at the NWT/Alberta border on Highway 1, links the traveller with more than seven unusual territorial parks and waterfalls. **Twin Falls Territorial Park**, just north of **Enterprise**, has two waterfalls, **Louise Falls** and **Alexandra Falls**, which are linked together by a 3km- (1.9 mile-) hiking trail along the spectacular **Hay River Canyon**.

INUVIK REGION: The Arctic coastline and islands of the territory have a spectacular landscape and fascinating history. The cliffs and valleys of **Tuktut Nogait**, the Territories' newest National Park, harbour birds of prey and offer lush habitat for caribou and musk oxen. **Inuvik**, in the far northwest, sits on the majestic **Mackenzie River Delta** and is accessible by road from **Dawson City** in the **Yukon** (at limited times of the year). Cruises on the Delta and the Inuvialuit and Dene settlements such as **Aklavik** are the main attractions. **Aulavik**, on **Banks Island**, includes archaeological sites dating back more than 3000 years. Much of this rough and forbidding terrain is best visited as part of a package tour or with other experts.

Sport & Activities

Stretching up to the Beaufort Sea in the Arctic from a latitude of 60°N, the Northwest Territories are part of Canada's remote north, inhabited largely by native peoples but visited by intrepid adventurers. The territories consist largely of wilderness, punctuated in places by human settlements. An experienced guide is usually advisable for expeditions. For more general information about sport and activities in Canada, see the main *Canada* section.

Watersports: Canoeing and **whitewater rafting** are particularly popular. Tours and trips can be arranged to suit all levels of ability, although the area is most attractive to advanced canoeists. A favourite destination is the *Nahanni River* in the southern *Mackenzie Mountains*, featuring falls, rapids and torrents flowing through a highland wilderness. A trip along its entire length would take 10 to 20 days. The *Mackenzie River* itself offers good canoeing, as do other rivers in the area. Those in the west are more popular, while in the east the rivers are less often tackled. River reports are available on a daily basis; contact Northwest Territories Tourism for details (see *Contact Addresses* section). Novice canoeists are advised to go with a guide. **River cruises** can be taken on the Mackenzie River, with the opportunity to stop off at Dene (Aboriginal) settlements and traditional camps, or on the *Thomsen River*, Banks Island, through spectacular unspoiled scenery. **Fishing** on the thousands of clear, unpolluted lakes is a very popular sport. Chief catches are trout, great northern pike and grayling. Numerous operators offer drop-off and pick-up flights to remote areas.

Other: Photographers and **wildlife enthusiasts** have exceptional opportunities to observe and record unusual sights. *Wood Buffalo National Park*, south of *Great Slave Lake*, hosts Canada's largest herd of free-roaming bison. Over 700,000 barren-ground caribou migrate across the Northwest Territories and special tours can be arranged to their calving grounds along the shore of the *Beaufort Sea*. Musk oxen inhabit the tundra, moose live in the boreal forests, grizzly bears roam freely and Dall's sheep graze in the mountains. Beluga whales, polar bears, birds and sea mammals can be observed near the coast. During the brief spring, hosts of tiny wild flowers cover the tundra area; a macro lens is needed to photograph them. Five national parks provide trails for **hiking** and other facilities. Sandy hills known as 'eskers' offer easy hiking with good viewpoints. More challenging hiking can be found on the *Canol Heritage Trail*, through mountains and valleys to the Yukon. The **northern lights** (*aurora borealis*) can be seen in winter on clear nights from September to January. In midsummer the light lasts all night, and the landscape takes on a surreal quality.

Social Profile

FOOD & DRINK: Arctic char, grayling, musk ox and caribou are specialities. Most alcohol is imported and supplies vary from town to town. Hotels and restaurants in main towns normally have a good selection, including Canadian whiskies.

SHOPPING: There are over 40 co-operatives in the Territories specialising in handicrafts, furs, fisheries, print shops and retailing. First Nations handicrafts and footwear are made locally for sale. The often higher cost of goods (an increase of up to 20 per cent on the rest of Canada) is due to the supply and distribution charges caused by the large distances involved.

SPECIAL EVENTS: For full information about special events, please contact Northwest Territories Tourism (see *Contact Addresses* section). The following is a selection of special events occurring in the Northwest Territories in 2005:

Jan 3 *Sunrise Festival*, Inuvik. **Feb 26-29** *Kamba Winter Carnival*. **Mar 26-28** *Caribou Carnival* (dogsled race, skating, snowshoeing), Yellowknife. **Apr** *47th Muskrat Jamboree* (muskrat skinning and snow shoe races), Invuik. **Apr 17-20** *Wha Ti Spring Festival*. **May** *White Fox Jamboree*. **Jun** *Funk Fest*, Yellowknife; *Summer Solstice/Midnight Madness*, Inuvik. **Jul** *Folk on the Rocks*, Yellowknife; *Wood Block Music Festival*, Fort Good Hope. **Aug** *Overlander Sports Yellowknife Marathon*; *Wha Ti Annual Golf Tournament*. **Sep** *Fort Smith Fall Fair*.

Credit: © Northwest Territories Tourism

Business Profile

COMMERCIAL INFORMATION: The following organisation can offer advice: Yellowknife Chamber of Commerce, 4807 49th Street, Yellowknife, Northwest Territories X1A 3T5 (tel: (867) 920 4944; fax: (867) 920 4640; e-mail: admin@ykchamber.com; website: www.ykchamber.com).

Climate

The region experiences a diverse climate. The north has Arctic and sub-Arctic winters whereas the south is more temperate with mild summers and cold winters.

Required clothing: Winter weather requires down-filled and other polar-temperature gear. Special clothing is required for adventure expeditions. Good-quality windproof and waterproof clothes, warm jerseys, gloves and moulded-sole shoes are needed at all times of the year. In the summer, thinner clothes are required.

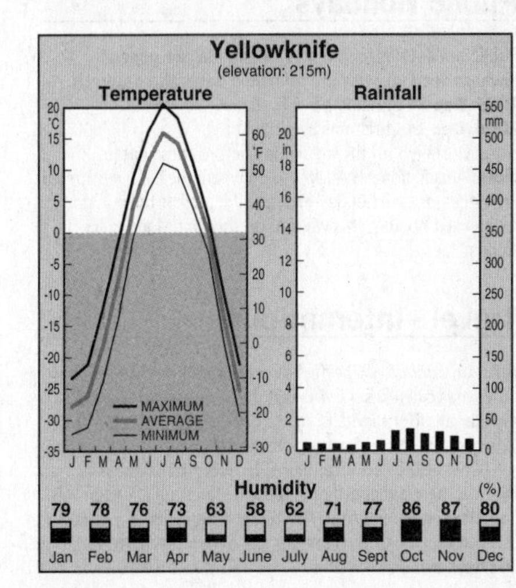

Nova Scotia

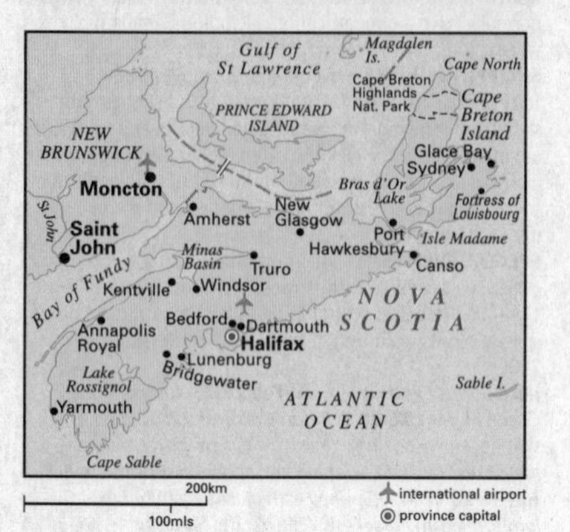

Location: East coast of Canada.

Tourism Nova Scotia
6th Floor, World Trade and Convention Centre, PO Box 456, 1800 Argyle Street, Halifax, Nova Scotia B3J 2R5, Canada
Tel: (902) 424 5000 *or* (800) 565 0000 (toll-free in USA and Canada). Fax: (902) 424 2668.
Website: www.novascotia.com
E-mail: explore@gov.ns.ca

General Information

AREA: 52,841 sq km (20,402 sq miles).
POPULATION: 908,007 (2001).
POPULATION DENSITY: 17.2 per sq km.
CAPITAL: Halifax. **Population**: 359,183 (official estimate 2001).
GEOGRAPHY: Nova Scotia comprises the peninsula of Nova Scotia, connected to the mainland by a narrow isthmus, and Cape Breton Island in the northern part of the province, linked by the world's deepest causeway which is 1.6km (1 mile) long. The Atlantic batters the eastern shore. The Bay of Fundy separates the southern part of the peninsula from the mainland, with the Gulf of St Lawrence to the north. The northeast is rural and rocky, while the south and southwest are lush and fertile. The Fundy region's red soil was originally part of the present North African continent. Much of the province is covered by rivers. The land rises to 540m (1770ft) on the northeast islands.
LANGUAGE: Although Canada is officially bilingual (English and French), English is the main language spoken in Nova Scotia.
TIME: GMT - 4 (GMT - 3 in summer).
Summer officially lasts from the first Sunday in April to the Saturday before the last Sunday in October.

Credit: © Nova Scotia Tourism, Culture and Heritage

Public Holidays

Public holidays as for the rest of Canada (see general *Canada* section), with the following dates also observed:
2005: Dec 24 Christmas Eve (half-day).
2006: Dec 24 Christmas Eve (half-day).
Note: Observed on the last Friday before these dates.
Note: An additional holiday is given where there is a recognised Provincial or Civil holiday in a specific area. If there is no recognised holiday, this will fall on the first Monday in August.

Travel - International

AIR: *Air Canada (AC)* offers direct flights from London and other major centres. *Air Transat* and *Continental Express Airlines* all offer flights from major European centres. *Air Canada* flies to Halifax from Ottawa, Montréal and Toronto. *Air Nova* also offers local flights between Halifax and Sydney. There are also flights into Halifax from all major Canadian cities, and from Amsterdam, Berlin, Boston, Detroit, Düsseldorf, Frankfurt, Hamburg, London, Munich, Newark and Reykjavik.
International airports: *Halifax (YHZ)* (website: www.hiaa.ca), 42km (26 miles) from the city. Airport facilities include duty-free shops, car hire, currency exchange, ATMs and restaurants.
SEA: There are regular sailings to Nova Scotia from Portland and Bar Harbor, Maine (USA), New Brunswick, Prince Edward Island and Newfoundland. North America's fastest ship *The Cat* (website: www.catferry.com) operates between Yarmouth and Bar Harbor in the USA (travel time - two hours 45 minutes). Several ferries and shipping lines offer local services in and around the province. Enquire locally for further details. A growing number of cruise lines also visit Halifax as part of the New Atlantic Frontier itinerary. Ferry and cruise operators include *Bay Ferries* and *Northumberland Ferries* (website: www.nfl-bay.com), *Marine Atlantic* (website: www.marine-atlantic.ca) and *Scotia Prince Cruises* (website: www.scotiaprince.com).
RAIL: *VIA Rail* trains run from Montréal to Halifax (the *Ocean* line) six times a week with bus connections to the rest of Nova Scotia.
ROAD: The Trans-Canada Highway enters the province from New Brunswick and ends at North Sydney on the northeast coast. Smaller provincial highways branch off it and circumnavigate the coastline. Ferry services or causeways connect most islands with the mainland. **Bus**: *Acadian Lines* provides services throughout the province. There are connections with *SMT Eastern* from New Brunswick, *Voyageur* from Quebec and Ontario, and *Greyhound* from the USA. **Car hire**: There are agencies at Halifax and Sydney airports and throughout the province.
URBAN: Comprehensive bus services are provided in the Halifax-Dartmouth area by *Metro Transit*, which operates a zonal fare system. There are connections with the harbour ferry on both sides.

Accommodation

Nova Scotia offers a wide range of accommodation and campsites. Advance reservations are recommended, especially during the summer. All establishments are inspected and recommended by Tourism Nova Scotia. Farmhouse holidays are possible and many Nova Scotians provide bed & breakfast for visitors in the tourist season (late April to November). For information and reservations, call Nova Scotia's 'Check-in and Reservation Service' (tel: (800) 565 0000 (toll-free in USA and Canada) *or* (902) 425 5781; fax: (902) 424 2668; website: www.novascotia.com *or* www.checkinnovascotia.com).
Grading: Some accommodation is graded on a voluntary basis according to the *Canada Select Accommodations Grading Program* as follows: **5-star**: Deluxe accommodation with the greatest range of facilities, amenities and guest services; **4-star**: High-quality accommodation with extended range of facilities; **3-star**: Better-quality accommodation with a greater range of services; amenities and guest services;
2-star: Basic, clean, comfortable accommodation with extra amenities; **1-star**: Basic, clean, comfortable accommodation.
CAMPING/CARAVANNING: Much of Nova Scotia is luxuriant parkland, and one of the best ways to see the province is by motorhome or camper; a number of companies can arrange rentals, with a range of fully-equipped vehicles. Full details can be obtained from Tourism Nova Scotia (see *Contact Addresses* section), which also publishes a comprehensive guide to the province.

Resorts & Excursions

HALIFAX

The provincial capital is the commercial, administrative and maritime centre for the whole of Atlantic Canada. Situated at the mouth of the **Bedford Basin**, it is the second-largest natural harbour in the world (after Sydney in Australia) and has a long and distinguished history as a naval and military base. Harbour tours and deep-sea fishing charters are available. Despite the city's boom over the past 15 years, the historic **Waterfront Area**, comprising important 18th- and 19th-century buildings, has been kept intact. Excellent shopping, nightlife and restaurants are to be found in both the old and new sections of the city. Worth seeing are **Province House**, the birthplace of Canadian democracy in 1819; **St Paul's**, the oldest Protestant church in Canada; the **Museum of Natural History**; the **Maritime Museum of the Atlantic** (featuring Titanic exhibits) and the 17-acre Victorian **Halifax Public Gardens**. The 1km- (0.6 mile-) long **Boardwalk** is also worth a visit. Halifax itself is dominated by the **Citadel**, a star-shaped granite fortress built in 1749 and one of Canada's most visited National Historic Sites. It is known for its kilted regiment and changing of the guard display. A good view of the city and harbour can be had from its ramparts.

ELSEWHERE

Touring Nova Scotia is easy. The 560km- (350 mile-) long peninsula features a series of interconnecting scenic routes, each one with a different view of a celebrated shore. The **Cabot Trail**, voted North America's most spectacular ocean drive by the American Bus Association, is a ribbon of road around the northern highlands of the province which passes through **Cape Breton Highlands National Park**. The **Lighthouse Route** travels the southern shore where seafaring traditions are especially strong. The **Evangeline Trail** is a rural road that goes through the beautiful **Annapolis Valley**, known for its orchards, forts and Victorian mansions. The **Sunrise Trail** follows the Northumberland Strait which features 35 sandy beaches and the warmest waters north of the Carolinas.
Dartmouth, across the mouth of the harbour from Halifax, is a vibrant and green community featuring many parks and walking trails and with easy access to the unspoiled coastal beauty of the Eastern Shore. West of Halifax, a coastal road skirts around the fishing villages set in the deep bays and inlets of the southern shore. En route to the port of **Yarmouth** are: **Peggy's Cove**, known for its rugged and beautiful coastal scenery and as Canada's most photographed lighthouse; **Mahone Bay**; and **Lunenburg**, a German settlement established in 1753 and now a listed UNESCO World Heritage Site. North of **Liverpool** on this route is **Kejimkujik National Park**, which offers wilderness trails, canoeing and winter sports.
After Yarmouth, the coastal road runs northeast by French-speaking Acadian villages such as **Metaghan** and **Church Point**, which are dotted along the Bay of Fundy. Nearby, **Port Royal** and **Fort Anne** are the sites of some of the earliest French settlements in Canada. **Grand Pré National Park** commemorates the expulsion of 2000 Acadians from Nova Scotia in 1755 and is the site of **Longfellow's Memorial**. From **Amherst**, the gateway town to the province, a coastal road on the north shore leads to Cape Breton Island (see below) across a 1.6km- (1 mile-) long causeway. The north shore displays strong Scottish influences. Street signs in **Pugwash** are in English and Gaelic and highland games are held annually in **Antigonish**. **Cape Breton Island** attracts many nature lovers. Some of the island's most spectacular scenery can be found at the **Cape Breton Highlands National Park**. There is superb inland sailing in the **Bras d'Or Lakes**. **Sydney**, a centre of shipping and industry, is the island's main city. Southeast of this is the **Fortress of Louisbourg**, North America's largest historical restoration. **Baddeck** on Cape Breton Island is home to the **Alexander Graham Bell Museum**. Bell (1847-1922) made Baddeck his home in the latter part of his life and his final resting place.

Credit: © Nova Scotia Tourism, Culture and Heritage

Sport & Activities

Outdoor pursuits: Nova Scotia's system of 120 provincial parks encompasses nearly 35,000 hectares (86,500 acres) of forested landscapes, heritage sites and beaches (scattered along an 8050km- (5000 mile-) long coastline). A network of interconnecting scenic routes provides easy access to these areas (see *Resorts & Excursions* section). Amongst the wide range of possible outdoor activities, **watersports** predominate. **Sailing**, **kayaking** and **canoeing** (along the coast or on the myriad inland kayaking routes, particularly those in *Kejimkujik National Park*), **swimming** (notably at *Melmerby Beach* in the Northumberland Strait) and **deep-sea fishing** are all popular. Anglers intending to fish in Nova Scotia's 9000 freshwater lakes require a valid fishing licence, which is obtainable from any Department of Natural Resources office in the province. **Tidal bore rafting** is available on the *Minas Basin*, located in the *Bay of Fundy* (see also the *New Brunswick* section), which has one of the highest tides in the world. The *Fundy Shore Eco Tour* is a self-guided nature and heritage tour featuring 37 observation points. **Dolphin-** and **whale-watching** tours leave from a string of ports along the coast - those from *Digby Neck* (two daily trips from June to early October) and *Westport* are among the best. **Fossil hunting** enthusiasts may sign up for a cliff tour at *Joggins*, while visitors interested in **geology** can look for amethyst, agate, quartz and jasper around *Parrsboro*. The *Provincial Wildlife Park* at Shubenacadie is home to the province's most characteristic **wildlife**, which includes moose, bear, cougar, coyote, the Sable Island horse and the bald eagle (of which

Credit: © Nova Scotia Tourism, Culture and Heritage

Nova Scotia has a particularly high population). Tourism Nova Scotia (see *Contact Addresses* section) provide a range of brochures (for example, the 'Complete Guide for Doers and Dreamers') to help visitors with planning an active holiday. For general information about sport and activities in Canada, see *Sports & Activities* in the main *Canada* section.

Social Profile

FOOD & DRINK: Seafood features strongly on most menus; popular local dishes include scallops, fried, baked or grilled, and usually served with tartar sauce. Fish and clam chowders and *solomon gundy* (a herring dish) are also popular and, of course, lobster and salmon. *Lunenburg sausage* exemplifies the German influence, as do *hugger in buff, fish and scrunchions, Dutch mess* and *house bunkin* - all names for tasty combinations of fish and potatoes covered in cream sauce with onions and salt pork. Desserts make use of plentiful fruit and berries and include a stewed fruit and dumplings dish called *grunt*, and baked apple dumplings wrapped in pastry and served with cream, sugar or lemon sauce. Beer and alcoholic beverages are sold by the glass in licensed restaurants (food must also be ordered) and in licensed lounges (opening hours generally 1100-1400). Beer by the bottle and draught beer is sold by the glass in taverns, pubs and beverage rooms, which offer great snacks and light meals; opening hours are normally from 1000 until early morning the next day. The Pub District in Halifax is said to be one of the best in North America, with over 55 establishments; the minimum drinking age is 19 years old.

NIGHTLIFE: Nightclubs are mostly centred in Halifax. Scottish bagpipe music and Gaelic songs can be heard all over the territory in concerts, bars, hotels and restaurants. Professional and amateur theatre is very popular; details of forthcoming attractions are available from Tourism Nova Scotia.

SPECIAL EVENTS: For full information on special events, contact Tourism Nova Scotia (see *Contact Addresses* section). The following is a selection of special events occurring in Nova Scotia in 2005:

Feb 11-13 *Pictou Winter Carnival.* **Mar 11-20** *Winter Fest*, Ingonish - Cabot Trail. **Apr 6** *Tartan Day Celebrations*, Pictou. **May 29-Jun 12** *Scotia Festival of Music*, Halifax. **Jun 24-26** *Luenburg Summer Opera Festival.* **Jul 7-11** *Halifax Highland Games and Scottish Festival.* **Aug 13** *Firefighter's Fair and Roast Beef Supper*, Hubbards - Lighthouse Route. **Sep 30-Oct 2** *Great Scarecrow Festival and Antiques Fair*, Mahone Bay. **Oct 7-15** *Celtic Colours International Festival.* **Dec 31** *Farewell to 2005*, nationwide.

Business Profile

COMMERCIAL INFORMATION: The following organisation can offer advice: Atlantic Provinces Chamber of Commerce, Suite 21, 236 St George Street, Moncton, New Brunswick E1C 1W1 (tel: (506) 857 3980; fax: (506) 859 6131; e-mail: info@apcc.ca; website: www.apcc.ca).

Credit: © Nova Scotia Tourism, Culture and Heritage

CONFERENCES/CONVENTIONS: Nova Scotia has a wide range of conference and convention venues. The Halifax Metro Centre arena in downtown Halifax has facilities for 10,000 people. Connected to this is the World Trade & Convention Centre, a striking landmark building made of brick and glass with a sumptuous interior. It has three convention floors, all with excellent catering and audio-visual facilities, and enough room for 2600 people at a stand-up reception, or 1700 for a banquet. A number of hotels in Halifax and Dartmouth offer good meeting facilities. The Dartmouth Sportsplex arena is another excellent large group facility. The city of Sydney offers Centre 200, an arena and convention complex built in celebration of Sydney's bicentennial in 1985, with various flexible meeting rooms for trade shows, receptions and banquets for up to 800. There are also some meeting facilities in more rural settings: The Pines Resort, overlooking the Annapolis Basin and the Bay of Fundy; Dundee Resort, overlooking the Bras D'Or Lakes; Keltic Lodge, overlooking Cape Smoky and the Atlantic Ocean; Liscombe Lodge, tucked into the evergreens where the Liscomb River meets the sea; and Lansdowne Lodge, east of Truro along the Glooscap Trail and near the beautiful Upper Stewiacke Valley. For more information, contact the Greater Halifax Conventions and Meetings Bureau, Suite 423, 1800 Argyle Street, Halifax B3J 3N8, Nova Scotia (tel: (902) 422 9334 *or* (877) 422 9334 (toll-free in USA and Canada); fax: (902) 492 3175; e-mail: info@destinationhalifax.com; website: www.meethalifax.com).

Climate

Moderately cold winters, warm summers and long, mild autumns. Nova Scotia has a mild overall climate due to ocean currents.

Required clothing: Light- to mediumweights in summer months. Heavyweights in winter. Waterproofing is advisable all year.

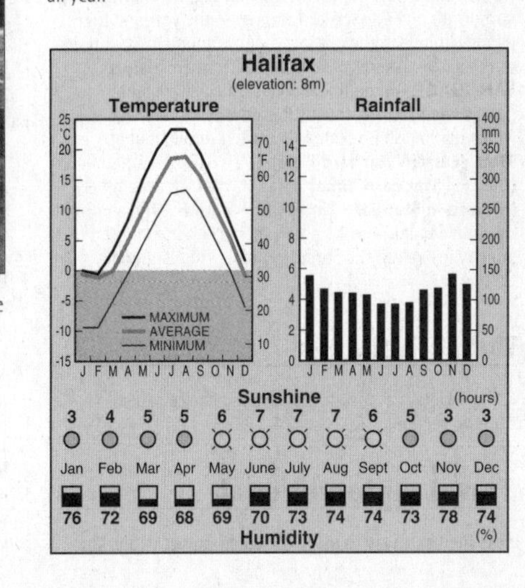

Nunavut

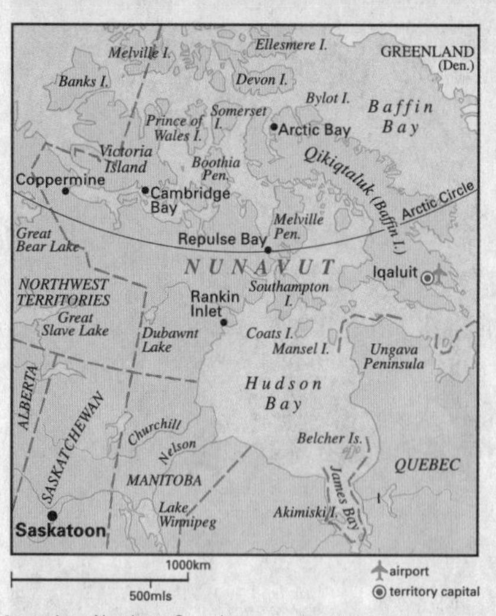

Location: Northern Canada.

On 9 July 1993, the Government of Canada and representatives of the Inuit of Nunavut signed the Nunavut Act in Kugluktuk (Coppermine), Northwest Territories. From 1 April 1999 the Inuit of the Nunavut area of Canada's Arctic took on the responsibility of managing their own affairs, and those of the non-Inuit also living there.

Nunavut Tourism
PO Box 1450, Iqaluit, Nunavut Territory X0A 0H0, Canada
Tel: (867) 979 6551 *or* (866) 686 2888 (toll-free in USA and Canada). Fax: (867) 979 1261.
E-mail: info@nunavuttourism.com
Website: www.nunavuttourism.com

Credit: © Nunavut Tourism

General Information

AREA: 2,241,919 sq km (865,605 sq miles).
POPULATION: 26,745 (2001).
POPULATION DENSITY: 0.01 per sq km.
CAPITAL: Iqaluit. **Population**: 5,500 (2001).
GEOGRAPHY: The Nunavut Territory covers one-fifth of Canada, stretching from Ellesmere Island off Greenland's north coast to a border that runs north from the Saskatchewan / Manitoba border and then angles west to the arctic coast near Amundsen Gulf. The mainland portion of the territory is an untouched wilderness, where the stark northern tundra changes into cliffs and plateaux along the Northwest Passage. To the north and east, the Arctic Islands are surrounded by pack ice for most of the year and the region extends to the glaciers, jagged mountains and fjords of the eastern shores of Baffin and Ellesmere Islands.
LANGUAGE: Although Canada is officially bilingual (English and French), Inuktitut is an official language in Nunavut. English is commonly spoken throughout.
TIME: (Eastern Standard Time) GMT - 6 (GMT - 5 in summer).
(Central Standard Time) GMT - 7 (GMT - 6 in summer).
(Mountain Standard Time) GMT - 8 (GMT - 7 in summer).
Daylight Saving Time (summer) officially lasts from the first Sunday in April to the Saturday before the last Sunday in October.

Public Holidays

Public holidays as for the rest of Canada (see general *Canada* section).

Travel - International

AIR: The usual way to reach the communities within the Territory is by air, although an increasing number of expedition cruise ships are putting in to Nunavut each summer. Float planes are rarely used owing to tidal areas, but do provide access to some northern lakes. The three airlines providing scheduled flights into the region are *Calm Air* (website: www.calmair.com), *Canadian North (CP)* (website: www.cdn-north.com) and *First Air* (website: www.firstair.ca). Other carriers provide scheduled or charter flights within Nunavut which are generally timed to meet inbound flights. These include *Adlair Aviation, Air Nunavut, Kenn Borek Air, Kivalliq Air, Skyward Air* and *Unalik Aviation.*
Airports: *Iqaluit Airport (YFB)* is less than 1km (0.6 miles) from the town centre (travel time – five minutes). International visitors will need to fly to Ottawa (Ontario), Montréal (Québec), Edmonton (Alberta) or Winnipeg (Manitoba) to board domestic flights to the Nunavut entry airports – Iqaluit, Cambridge Bay or Rankin Inlet.
SEA/LAKE/RIVER: There is no water access to Nunavut for visitors except on cruises during the open water season – July to September. A number of tour operators offer Northwest Passage, Hudson Bay and High Arctic cruises each year.
ROAD: There are no roads to Nunavut and only one road in Nunavut, between the communities of Nanisivik and Arctic Bay – 21km (13 miles) in length.

Accommodation

HOTELS: All communities have accommodation facilities, hotels, hostels and/or bed & breakfast establishments open all year. The accommodation and facilities may be shared, and are often quite basic. There are, however, full service hotels in the larger centres that also have meeting and conference facilities. Iqaluit, the capital, now hosts approximately 260 rooms, including hotels and bed & breakfast establishments. 'Lodges' designed for outdoor activity holidays or naturalist trips can be found in some areas. Nunavut Tourism publishes an annual vacation planner detailing accommodation and other tourism services in Nunavut (see *Contact Addresses* section).
CAMPING: Backpacking and tent camping is a popular summer activity. Ellesmere Island National Park, Auyuittuq National Park and Katannilik Territorial Park are particularly popular with hikers.

Resorts & Excursions

The majority of the population, and most commercial activity, is based around the communities, where most of the people are Inuit still living a subsistence life of fishing and hunting. The Inuit comprise 85 per cent of the Territory's population. The Arctic coastline and islands of Nunavut have a spectacular landscape of tundra, glaciated mountains and deep fjords. **Baffin Island** has some of the best of the area's rugged beauty; it is most accessible in **Auyuittuq National Park**, a haven for experienced hikers, skiers and climbers with its frozen peaks and glaciers. From **Iqaluit**, trips across the frozen tundra by dog sled with an Inuit guide and overnight accommodation in an igloo can be arranged. **Pond Inlet** or **Arctic Bay** are particularly popular as destinations to visit the floe edge and to view arctic marine mammals. A trip to **Cambridge Bay** on **Victoria Island** will afford the visitor the opportunity to view musk ox or tundra swans in their natural environment, or join an arctic cruise on the **Northwest Passage**. Contact Nunavut Tourism (see *Contact Addresses* section) for a complete listing of operators.

Sport & Activities

Nunavut's sparsely populated and untouched Arctic wilderness is best visited as part of a package tour or in the company of an experienced guide. Individual travellers should note that they are likely to be exposed to a number of hazards, including severe cold, reduced hours of daylight and potentially aggressive wildlife, including bears. Before setting out on individual trips, travellers should contact Nunavut Tourism for advice (see *Contact Addresses* section). The 'Nunavut Handbook', which is also available on the Internet (website: www.arctic-travel.com), contains a wealth of practical information. Nunavut Tourism also publishes 'The Nunavut Travel Planner' brochure, which contains a directory of tour operators and outfitters, plus a brief description of their offerings. To learn about Nunavut's fauna, flora, culture and history, **nature and cultural tours** offer a good overview of the territory. **Wildlife viewing** plays an important part in most tours and wildlife is particularly abundant in the summer at the so-called 'floe edge', where the land ice meets the open sea and the blooming plankton attract large schools of shrimp and fish as well as seals, whales and polar bears. The method of transport depends on the season: in summer, **boating** (in an Inuit freighter canoe, a kayak, a high-powered, motorised dinghy or a larger boat) is the most common, while, in spring, **dog sledding** (in the company of experienced local Inuit guides) or **snowmobiling** are widespread. The seasonal variations in light and temperature, and the dramatic scenery, provide rewarding conditions for **photography** enthusiasts. One of the best times for taking photographs is during the sunlit nights (between 2000 and 0300 in spring and summer), when shadows are long and colour and texture are particularly well defined. **Inuit art tours** offer visitors an opportunity to learn about native carving, tool-fashioning, jewellery-making and hat-making (out of Quivviuq wool collected from the land). Some of the best **hiking** destinations include the mountains of *Auyuittuq National Park*, the willow forest of *Katannilik Park, North Ellesmere National Park* (which has particularly rich wildlife), the new *Sirmilik National Park* (surrounding the scenic community of Pond Inlet) or the trail from *Kugluktuk* (Coppermine) to the *Bloody Falls.* **Fishing** enthusiasts should note that catch-and-release is practised in all areas and that possession limits are based on regular and seasonal evaluation of stock. Chief catches are Arctic char and lake trout. For general information about sport and activities in Canada, see the main *Canada* section.

Social Profile

FOOD & DRINK: Arctic char, mussels, clams, shrimp, musk ox and caribou are specialities. Local *bannock* (a mixture of flour and water blended into a dough and cooked slowly in a frying pan) dates from the old prospecting rations which kept for weeks in an easily transportable form. Other unusual specialities include *muktuk* (skin of the whale). Alcohol is controlled in Nunavut and in some communities is prohibited. Hotels and restaurants in Iqaluit are licensed.
SHOPPING: There are general retail stores in almost all communities in Nunavut; some specialise in handicrafts, furs, fisheries and Inuit Art. The high cost of goods (an increase of up to 50 per cent on the rest of Canada) is due to the supply and distribution costs caused by the large distances that goods must be transported by air or sea.
Shopping hours: Mon-Fri 1000-2000, Sat 1000-1800 (although these may vary regionally).
SPECIAL EVENTS: For full details, contact Nunavut Tourism (see *Contact Addresses* section). The following is a selection of special events occurring in Nunavut in 2005:
Mar *Nunavut Snow Challenge*, Iqaluit. **Jul 2-6** *Nunavut Midnight Sun Marathon and Road Races.* **Aug** *Kitikmeot Northern Games.*

Business Profile

COMMERCIAL INFORMATION: For further information, contact Baffin Regional Chamber of Commerce, Building 607, Iqaluit, Nunavut Territory X0A 0H0 (tel: (867) 979 4656; fax: (867) 979 2929).
CONFERENCES/CONVENTIONS: Contact Nunavut Tourism for further information (see *Contact Addresses* section).

Climate

Owing to the vast size of the territory, there are great variations in the weather. Winters can be severe – the northernmost community of Grise Fiord has a mean January temperature of -35°C (-31°F) and a mean July temperature of 10°C (50°F). Summers are milder, but the temperature can drop suddenly.
Note: Conditions in all parts of the territory can become hazardous. Local advice concerning weather conditions should be followed very carefully. Nevertheless, the summer months are suitable for a wide range of activities.
Required clothing: Winter weather requires down-filled and other polar-temperature gear. Special clothing is required for adventure expeditions. Good-quality windproof and waterproof clothes, warm jerseys, gloves and moulded sole shoes are needed at all times of the year. In the summer, thinner clothes are required. Sunglasses and protective lotion are strongly advised. Mosquitoes are a significant irritant in some areas during July and August. A mosquito net and repellent are essential.

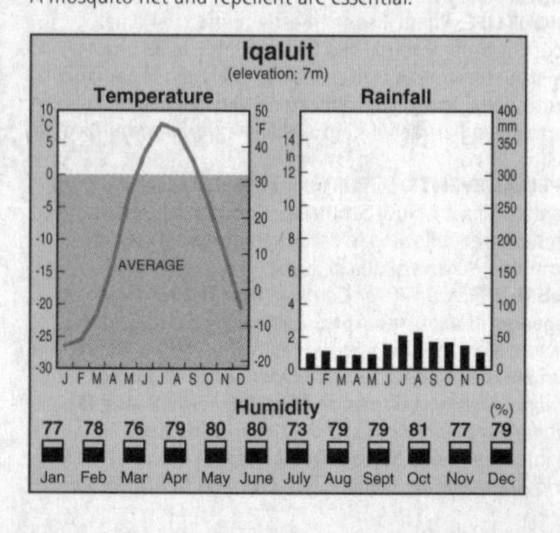

Ontario

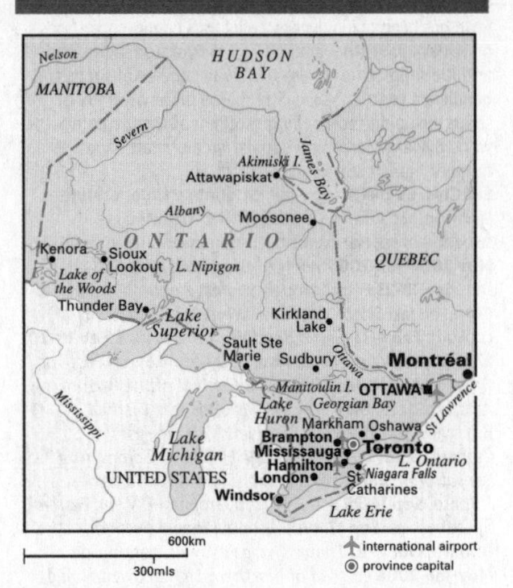

Location: Eastern central Canada.

Ontario Tourism Marketing Partnership/Ministry of Tourism & Recreation
10th Floor, Hearst Block, 900 Bay Street, Toronto, Ontario M7A 2E1, Canada
Tel: (416) 326 9326 *or* (800) 668 2746 (toll-free in USA and Canada). Fax: (416) 326 9338.
E-mail: general_info@mtr.gov.on.ca
Website: www.ontariotravel.net

Tourism Toronto
PO Box 126, 207 Queens Quay West, Suite 590, Toronto, Ontario M5J 1A7, Canada
Tel: (416) 203 2600. Fax: (416) 203 6753.
E-mail: toronto@torcvb.com
Website: www.torontotourism.com
Also incorporates Conferences and Conventions Bureau.

Ontario Tourism Marketing Partnership
4 Vencourt Place, Hammersmith, London W6 9NU, UK
Tel: (020) 8237 7998 *or* (01622) 832 180 (brochure request line).
Fax: (020) 8237 7999.
E-mail: tanya@mcclusky.co.uk
Website: www.ontariotravel.net

General Information

AREA: 916,734 sq km (353,951 sq miles).
POPULATION: 11,410,046 (2001).
POPULATION DENSITY: 11.7 per sq km.
CAPITAL: Toronto (provincial). **Population**: 4,682,897 (2001). Ottawa (federal). **Population**: 1,063,664 (2001; statistic combined with Hull).
GEOGRAPHY: Ontario is an eastern-central province bordered by Manitoba and Québec, with a northern coastline on James Bay and Hudson Bay; it also shares the shores of the Great Lakes with the USA. The two main populated areas, around Toronto and Ottawa, are in the southern spur, and the north remains a landscape of forests and lakes. The province contains the Niagara Falls, one of the most spectacular sights in the world.
LANGUAGE: Although Canada is officially bilingual (English and French), English is more commonly spoken in Ontario.
TIME: East of 90°W: GMT - 5 (GMT - 4 in summer). **West of 90°W:** GMT - 5.
Summer officially lasts from the first Sunday in April to the Saturday before the last Sunday in October.

Public Holidays

Public holidays as for the rest of Canada (see general *Canada* section), with the following dates also observed: **2005: Aug 1** Simcoe Day. **2006: Aug 7** Simcoe Day.

Travel - International

AIR: International air services are available through *Air Canada (AC)* and *British Airways* from Toronto and by *Air Canada* from Ottawa. Many other international airlines offer direct services into Toronto. Charter airlines often offer an economical alternative to the scheduled airlines. *Air Transat* and *Royal* operate charter flights to Toronto. Local air services are operated by a number of operators, including *Air Ontario* and *Bearskin Airlines*, as well as by *Air Canada*. These connect all of the large towns. For rates and routes, contact local offices.

International airports: *Ottawa (YOW)* (Macdonald-Cartier) (website: www.ottawa-airport.ca) is 13km (8 miles) south of the city. A regular bus service departs every 30 minutes (travel time - 45 minutes). Taxis are also available (travel time - 20 minutes). *Toronto (YYZ)* (Lester B Pearson) (website: www.gtaa.com) is 27km (17 miles) northwest of the city. A regular bus service departs every 20 to 30 minutes (travel time - 20 to 30 minutes). Taxis are also available.
SEA: The only port on James Bay with rail links to the south is Moosonee, which is also the base for a limited local air service. The principal ports receiving sailings from the USA are Windsor (to Detroit/Lake St Clair); Sarnia (to Port Huron/St Clair River); Leamington (to Sandusky/Lake Eire); Kingston, Brockville, Cornwall and Ogdensburg (to the USA across the St Lawrence Seaway); and Wolfe Island to New York. The principal ferry operators in the province are *Ontario Ministry of Transportation* (website: www.mto.gov.on.ca), *Owen Sound Transportation Company* (Tobermory-Manitoulin Island), *Pelee Island Transportation Services* (Toronto-Niagara), *Toronto Islands Ferries*, *Waterways Transportation Services* (Toronto-Niagara) and local river authorities. For timetables and rates, contact local offices.
RAIL: *VIA Rail* (website: www.viarail.com) connects Toronto to western Canada. Several corridor services connect Toronto, Windsor and Ottawa with Montréal and Québec City in Québec. Links to the USA are with *Amtrak* (website: www.amtrak.com) and *VIA Rail*. Services run from Toronto to New York via Niagara Falls, and to Chicago via Windsor and Sarnia. *VIA Rail* also serves all the major cities of the province, concentrating in the southern region, which holds most of the population. *Ontario Northland Rail* (website: www.ontc.on.ca) runs services from Toronto to Timmins, with a connection at Porquis for Cochrane and Kapuskasing. From Cochrane, services run northeast to Moosonee and west to Hearst. For details, contact local offices.
ROAD: There are several bridges connecting Canadian and US territories, notably at Cornwall, Fort Erie, Fort Frances, Niagara Falls, Rainy River, Sarnia, Sault Ste Marie and Windsor. A tunnel also connects Windsor to Detroit. The domestic highway network is excellent around the Great Lakes, but does not extend to the north of the province. Good trunk roads run throughout. **Bus**: Services linking most towns are operated by *Go-Transit*, *Greyhound Canada*, *Ontario Northland*, *PMCL*, *Trentway-Wagar Bus Lines* and *Voyageur Colonial*. **Car hire**: Facilities are available from all hotels, at Ottawa and Toronto airports, and at main railway stations (including *Avis*, *Budget*, *Discount*, *Hertz*, *National* and *Thrifty*). Drivers must be over 21 years old and the wearing of seatbelts is strictly enforced.
URBAN: Bus, trolleybus, metro and tramway services are provided by the *Toronto Transit Commission*. Flat fares are charged and there are free transfers. Pre-purchase tokens and multi-tickets may be obtained. Services are integrated with those of the regional *Go-Transit* bus and rail system. Bus services in Ottawa, Carleton and surrounding areas are provided by *OC Transpo*. A flat fare operates with a premium on express routes. There are free transfers, and pre-purchase multi-journey tickets and passes are sold. An unlimited 1-day pass (cost: C$7.75) is available for use on all forms of transport within the Toronto Metropolitan area.
TRAVEL TIMES: The following chart gives approximate travel times from **Toronto** (in hours and minutes) to other major cities/towns and tourist destinations in the surrounding area.

	Air	Road	Rail
Niagara Falls		**1.50**	**2.00**
Ottawa	**1.00**	**4.50**	**4.00**
Windsor	**1.10**	**4.00**	**4.30**
London	**0.40**	**2.30**	**2.15**
Sudbury	**1.05**	**5.00**	**8.00**
Sault Ste Marie	**1.25**	**9.00**	-
Thunder Bay	**1.45**	**15.00**	-

Accommodation

Most of the accommodation is in the southern spur of the province where the majority of the population is located.
HOTELS: Hotel costs vary according to class. Both Ottawa and Toronto have international-standard hotels. For further information, contact Ontario Accommodation Association, 347 Pido Road, Unit 2, RR6 Peterborough, Ontario K9J 6X7 (tel: (705) 745 4982 *or* (800) 461 1972 (toll-free in the USA, the UK and Canada); fax: (705) 745 4983;
e-mail: info@ontarioaccommodation.com;
website: www.ontarioaccommodation.com). **Grading**: Accommodation is graded on an entirely voluntary basis by Tourism Ontario, a private non-profitmaking federation of food service, accommodation, recreation and travel associations and businesses. There are over 1000 participating members (there are also several other associations of a less general nature). Tourism Ontario grades hotels in Ontario according to a 5-star system as follows: **5-star**: Provides deluxe accommodation. Marked superiority in extent and quality of facilities, amenities and guest services; **4-star**: Provides superior quality furnishings

Credit: © Ontario Tourism

and a complete range of facilities, amenities and guest services; **3-star**: Provides better quality furnishings and a more extensive range of facilities, amenities and guest services; **2-star**: Provides more furnishings and some facilities, amenities and guest services; **1-star**: Provides basic furnishings and very limited or no facilities, amenities and guest services. Just over 75 per cent of participating hotels are in the 3- or 4-star category.
BED & BREAKFAST: For help with bed & breakfast accommodation, contact the Federation of Ontario Bed & Breakfast Accommodation (FOBBA), PO Box 437, 253 College Street, Toronto, Ontario M5T 1R5 (tel: (416) 515 1293; e-mail: info@fobba.com; website: www.fobba.com).
SELF-CATERING: Furnished cottages are available throughout the region.
CAMPING/CARAVANNING: The best way to explore the wilderness of the north with its lakes and forestry is to hire a **motorhome** or **camper**. A number of companies can arrange rentals of fully-equipped vehicles. Full details can be obtained from Ontario Tourism (see *Contact Addresses* section) or Ontario Private Campground Association, RR5 Owen Sound, Ontario N4K 5N7 (tel: (519) 371 3393; fax: (519) 371 0080; e-mail: opca@campgrounds.org; website: www.campgrounds.org).
RESORTS: For information on Ontario's many and varied resorts, contact Resorts Ontario, 29 Albert Street North, Orillia, Ontario L3V 5J9 (tel: (705) 325 9115 *or* (800) 363 7227 (toll-free in USA and Canada); fax: (705) 325 7999; e-mail: escapes@resorts-ontario.com; website: www.resorts-ontario.com).

Resorts & Excursions

OTTAWA

The federal capital is situated on the south bank of the **Ottawa River** facing the French-speaking city of Hull in Québec. The imposing Gothic-style **Parliament Buildings** overlook the confluence of the rivers **Ottawa**, **Rideau** and **Gatineau** and are surmounted by the 92m (302ft) **Peace Tower**, affording a panoramic view of the city and its surroundings. Guided tours are available. The colourful **Changing of the Guard** ceremony takes place here daily in July and August. **Confederation Square**, site of the **National War Memorial**, is the focal point of central Ottawa. The **National Arts Center**, a hexagonal complex on the banks of the Rideau Canal, houses an opera

A B C D E F G H I J K L M N O P Q R S T U V W X Y Z

company, theatres, studios and restaurants. The **Rideau Canal** and the **Rideau-Trent-Severn Waterway** are part of a complex of recreational lakes and canals linking Ottawa to Lake Ontario and Georgian Bay. Outstanding among the city's many museums and galleries are the **National Gallery of Canada**, the **National Museum of Science and Technology**, the **Canadian Museum of Nature**, the **Canadian War Museum** and the **Museum of Civilisation** (over the bridge in nearby Hull).

Excursions: Gatineau Park, an 88,000 acre (35,612 hectare) wilderness area, is only a 15-minute drive north of Parliament Hill. Southeast of the city, **Upper Canada Village** is a reconstructed 19th-century town consisting of historic buildings salvaged from threatened sites on the St Lawrence Seaway.

Credit: © Ontario Tourism

TORONTO

The provincial capital is Canada's largest city. Its accelerated growth in recent years, with a huge influx of immigrants, has resulted in one of the most vibrant and cosmopolitan cities on the continent. The city is laid out on a rectangular grid broken only by the **Don River** and **Humber River**, the banks of which provide a host of recreational amenities. The **CN Tower**, the world's tallest free-standing structure, has glass-fronted elevators rising 553m (1815ft) to indoor and outdoor observation decks that afford a 120km- (75 mile-) panoramic view on a clear day. The twin gold towers of the **Royal Plaza** make it the most eye-catching of the many avant-garde commercial buildings in the city. Toronto's latest attraction, **SkyDome**, at the foot of the CN Tower, is a multi-purpose entertainment complex and sports stadium and was the world's first to have a retractable roof – baseball's **World Series** has been played here more than once. It is home to the **Toronto Blue Jays** baseball team and the **Argonauts** football team. It also hosts a multitude of events including rock concerts, opera, exhibitions, cricket, wrestling and motorshows. Tours of the SkyDome are available. The nearby **Air Canada Centre** is the home of the **Maple Leafs** hockey team and the **Raptors** basketball team. Together with modern developments, the city has seen the renovation of old neighbourhoods, particularly the tree-lined streets of Victorian houses characteristic of the city. **Yorkville**, the hip part of town in the 1960s, now caters to the tastes of the city's upwardly mobile, but is a good spot to go window shopping or enjoy a cup of coffee. **Queen Street**, further south towards the lake, attracts a younger, more style-conscious crowd. In the eastern suburbs, the spectacular **Ontario Science Centre** and the **Metro Toronto Zoo** are both worth seeing. The **Art Gallery of Ontario** and the **Royal Ontario Museum** are also noteworthy. **Casa Loma** was originally the home of Lord and Lady Pellatt. It was designed by architect Edward Lennox to Sir Henry Pellatt's specific requirements and Scottish stone masons were hired to build it. The castle offers fantastic views of downtown Toronto from the landscaped gardens. Ferries to the **Toronto Islands** depart from **Harbourfront**, one of a group of recreational, shopping and arts complexes, including the artificial island of **Ontario Place**. **Canada's Wonderland** is a huge theme park to the northwest of the city.

THE REST OF THE PROVINCE

Niagara Falls provides a spectacular day's outing from Toronto, and the storybook village of **Niagara-on-the-Lake** offers a tranquil environment in which to enjoy the many wines of this region. Heading west, the north shore of Lake Erie is dotted with resorts and good beaches; **St Thomas** and **Port Stanley** are particularly popular. North of this, between Lake Erie, Lake Ontario and Lake Huron, are **London** and **Stratford**, home of Canada's annual Shakespeare festival. **Kitchener-Waterloo** offers the chance to see Ontario's pioneer past in the Mennonite settlers of this region. Further north, **Midland** commands a spectacular view of the **Georgian Bay Lake District**, a popular resort area. Various minor ski resorts are located around Georgian Bay, mostly on the Niagara Escarpment. About 2.5 hours north of Toronto is the protected wilderness of **Algonquin Park**, Ontario's oldest provincial park; 7600 sq km (2934 sq miles) of forest and lakeland provide the perfect environment for outdoor recreation, particularly canoeing and hiking.

At the eastern end of **Lake Superior**, **Sault Ste Marie** straddles the US border and is an important commercial centre. It is also a good starting point for trips to the northern and western wildernesses. A railway (Algoma) and the Trans-Canada Highway head westwards around the north shore of Lake Superior. The principal attraction here is the **Lake Superior Provincial Park**, a region with many beautiful ravines, lakes and waterfalls but chiefly famed for the **Agawa Rock Pictographs**. Nearby is the hunting and fishing resort of **White River**.

The Highway continues to **Thunder Bay**, the western terminus of the St Lawrence Seaway. Fantastic canyons and rock formations can be seen between Thunder Bay and **Lake Nipigon**; the lake itself and the town of the same name are popular resorts in the heart of historic Native American country.

The far north and west of the province is a largely uninhabited wilderness of lakes, swamps and forests. The main trans-Canadian railway crosses Ontario at about 50°N; north of that, there are very few roads and only one railway line, which follows the **Moose River** to **Moose Factory**, one of several small settlements on the shores of **James** and **Hudson Bays**.

Sport & Activities

Outdoor pursuits: Canada's 'heartland' province of Ontario has its southern border running along the Great Lakes and its northern edge on Hudson Bay. There are six national parks and 260 provincial parks. It is particularly well known for **canoeing**, and has more canoe routes than any other region in the world – more than 1496km (930 miles) of routes in northern Ontario alone. Good locations for canoeing include *Kilarney* and *Algonquin Provincial Parks* in the south of Ontario near Lake Huron, the latter being within three hours' drive of Toronto. There are excellent facilities for all other types of *watersports*. *Horseriding*, *hiking* and *cycling* can also be easily arranged. Hiking is particularly good on the Bruce Peninsula on Lake Huron, where the views are spectacular. *Diving* is popular on the peninsula, owing to the many wrecks in the lake. Favourite cycling destinations include the Bruce Peninsula and the wine route on the Niagara Peninsula, which takes in several wineries. For details of cycling routes, contact the relevant tourist board (see *Contact Addresses* section). In winter, sports enthusiasts can choose from **cross-country skiing** (for which there are very good facilities), **dog sledding**, **snowmobiling** (along special trails) and other snow-based activities. There are ample opportunities to observe **wildlife** in the parks and less populated areas. Among the wildlife unique to Ontario are the monarch butterflies which stop off at *Point Pelee* on Lake Erie in September during their annual migration. These colourful insects cover the trees, providing an amazing spectacle. Polar bears can be seen in *Polar Bear Provincial Park* in northern Ontario, only accessible by light aircraft in summer. The bears come ashore when the ice melts in June and stay for around four months.

Spectator sports: These include **ice hockey**, **baseball** and **horseracing**. For general information about sport and activities in Canada, see the main *Canada* section.

Social Profile

FOOD & DRINK: International cuisine can be enjoyed in all major towns but for a more traditional fare, try Haliburton pheasant or one of the dazzling varieties of fish from the countless lakes and rivers. Toronto is rated as one of the best cities for dining out on the continent. Bars and restaurants offer an international selection of alcohol. Ontario has extensive vineyards providing much of Canada's wine. Each autumn, the *Niagara Grape* and *Wine Festival* is held in Niagara-on-the-Lake. The minimum drinking age is 19 years old. Alcohol is sold in Provincial Liquor Control Board outlets. Domestic beer is available at Brewer's Retail. Domestic wines are also sold through company stores. Liquor and beer stores are run and operated by the Government. Licensing hours are daily 1100-0200. Beer and liquor stores are open on Sundays. It is illegal to consume alcohol unless you are in a residence or a licensed establishment.

NIGHTLIFE: Both main cities have establishments offering all forms of entertainment, from quiet clubs featuring a lone pianist, through Latin American combos to dance and rock bands and big-name international entertainers. Toronto is recognised as the third most important theatre centre after London and New York, and cabaret/dinner theatres are also especially popular in Toronto. Toronto is also known as a good jazz and blues town. Both Toronto and Ottawa host jazz festivals in the summer. Theatres with classical entertainment are also found in Ottawa.

SHOPPING: Toronto offers everything from antiques to luxury lingerie, if the visitor has the money and time to spend. There are large suburban shopping centres and the *Eaton Centre*, a glass-domed galleria in the heart of the city, is linked to 4.8km (3 miles) of interconnecting underground shopping malls with 1000 retail outlets. Toronto's villages are full of colourful streets of renovated Victoriana, with garment shops, art galleries, antique stores and open-air cafes in summer. The run-down Queen Street Strip has been taken over by collector's comic-book shops, punk day-glo leather emporia, sci-fi bookstores, junk and antique shops. Ottawa also has a wide choice of shops and handicraft centres. Sparks Street Mall offers a variety of shops including those selling excellent authentic native work. Byward Market is a popular area of craft shops, farmers' market stalls and cafes.

SPECIAL EVENTS: For a full list, contact Ontario Tourism (see *Contact Addresses* section). The following is a selection of special events occurring in Ontario in 2005:

Nov 2004-Jan 2005 *Winter Festival of Lights*, Niagara Falls. **Jan 18-23** *Peterborough Snofest Annual Winter Carnival*. **Jan** *Sioux Mountain Winter Festival*, Sioux Lookout. **Feb 4-13** *Grand Bend Winter Carnival*. **Feb 18-20** *57th Annual Winterama*. **Mar 1-30** *Maple Syrup Festival*, Oakville. **Apr 18-May 2** *Kiwians Festival of the Performing Arts*, Stratford. **May 5-14** *1000 Islands Jazz Festival*, Brockville. **Jun 11-26** *Niagara New Vintage Festival*, St Catharines. **Jul 15-16** *Cambridge Highland Games*. **Aug 7** *Sensational Sounds of Summer Sunday Music Series*, Toronto. **Sep 16-25** *54th Niagara Grape and Wine Festival*, St Catharines. **Sep 17** *49th Annual Pioneer Festival*, Toronto. **Oct 8-10** *Thanksgiving Festivals*, nationwide. **Nov-Jan 2006** *Festival of Northern Lights*, Owen Sound. **Dec** *Christmas Celebrations*, nationwide.

Business Profile

COMMERCIAL INFORMATION: The following organisation can offer advice: Ontario Chamber of Commerce, 180 Dundas Street West, Suite 505, Toronto, Ontario M5G 1Z8 (tel: (416) 482 5222; fax: (416) 482 5879; e-mail: info@occ.on.ca; website: www.occ.on.ca).

CONFERENCES/CONVENTIONS: Ontario offers a wide range of conference venues. Ottawa usually hosts between 35 and 40 major international conferences per year. The following organisations can provide assistance and information:

For conferences in Toronto: Toronto Convention & Visitor Association, PO Box 126, Suite 590, 207 Queen's Quay West, Toronto, Ontario M5J 1A7 (tel: (416) 203 2600; fax: (416) 203 6753; e-mail: toronto@torcvb.com; website: www.torontotourism.com).

For conferences in Niagara Falls: Niagara Falls Tourism, Marketing Department, 5515 Stanley Avenue, Niagara Falls, Ontario L2G 3X4 (tel: (905) 356 6061 or (800) 563 2557; toll-free in USA and Canada); fax: (905) 356 5567; e-mail: info@niagarafallstourism.com; website: www.discoverniagara.com).

For conferences in Hamilton: The New City of Hamilton, Economic Development Department, 8th Floor, 1 James Street South, Hamilton, Ontario L8P 4R5 (tel: (905) 546 4222; fax: (905) 546 4107; e-mail: economicdevelopment@hamilton.ca; website: www.city.hamilton.on.ca).

For conferences in Ottawa: Ottawa Tourism and Convention Authority, Suite 1800, 130 Albert Street, Ottawa, Ontario K1P 5G4 (tel: (613) 237 5158 (tourism information) or 237 5150 (administration); fax: (613) 237 7339; e-mail: info@tourottawa.org; website: www.tourottawa.org).

Climate

Summers can be very warm, while spring and autumn are cooler. Winters are cold with snowfall.

Required clothing: Light- to mediumweights during warmer months, heavyweights in winter. Waterproofing is advisable throughout the year.

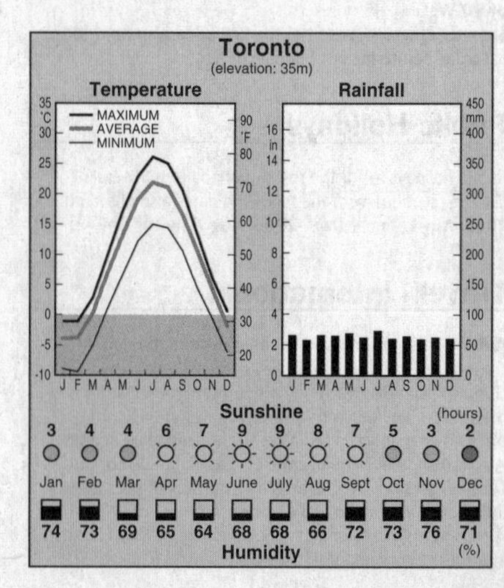

Prince Edward Island

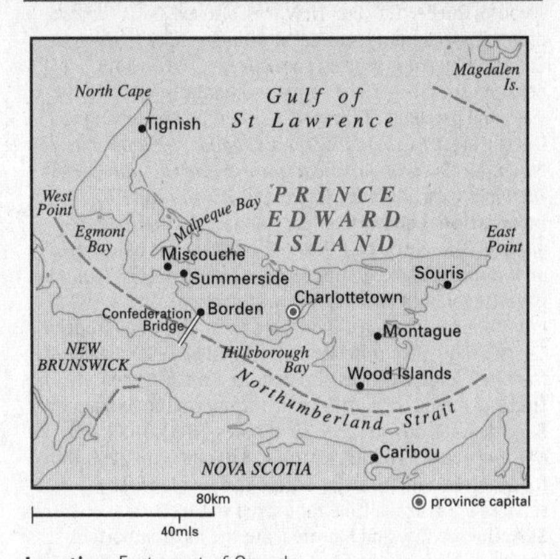

Location: East coast of Canada.

Tourism Prince Edward Island
PO Box 2000, Charlottetown, Prince Edward Island C1A 7N8, Canada
Tel: (902) 368 5540. Fax: (902) 368 4438.
E-mail: tourpei@gov.pe.ca
Website: www.gov.pe.ca

General Information

AREA: 5660 sq km (2185 sq miles).
POPULATION: 135,294 (2001).
POPULATION DENSITY: 23.77 per sq km.
CAPITAL: Charlottetown. **Population**: 32,531 (1999).
GEOGRAPHY: Prince Edward Island is a crescent-shaped island in the Gulf of St Lawrence comprising red farm fields, northern evergreen forests and white sand beaches. It is 224km (139 miles) long and between 6km (4 miles) and 65km (40 miles) wide.
LANGUAGE: English and some French are spoken.
TIME: GMT - 4 (GMT - 3 in summer).
Summer officially lasts from the first Sunday in April to the Saturday before the last Sunday in October.

Public Holidays

Public holidays as for the rest of Canada (see general *Canada* section).

Travel - International

AIR: *Charlottetown (YYG)* (website: www.flypei.com) airport is 3km (2 miles) from the city. *Air Canada, Jazz, Jetsgo* and *Prince Edward Air* operate here. There are no local internal flights.
SEA: *Northumberland Ferries* (website: www.nfl-bay.com) sail from Wood Islands on the southeast coast to Caribou in Nova Scotia from May to mid-December (travel time – 75 minutes). Advance reservations are not accepted. *CTMA Ferry* (website: www.ctma.ca) sails to Souris on the east coast from the Magdalen Islands in Québec from early April to the end of January (travel time – five hours). Advance reservations are recommended during the summer schedule from mid-June to early September (tel: (888) 986 3278).
RAIL: There are no passenger services on the island.
ROAD: The Confederation Bridge connects Borden-Carleton, Prince Edward Island with Cape Jourimain, New Brunswick. The bridge, which is 13km (8 miles) long, takes approximately 10 to 12 minutes to cross and is open 24 hours a day. A toll of C$39 per car is payable on return over the bridge only. Ferry services no longer operate on this route. There are three scenic drives following the coast of the Island: Lady Slipper Drive (west), Blue Heron Drive (central) and King's Byway (east). Seatbelts for adults and children are mandatory on Prince Edward Island.

Accommodation

HOTELS: Prince Edward Island offers a wide range of quality accommodation, from conventional hotels to lodges and family farms. Most of the towns have excellent hotels and one is never far from the sea.
BED & BREAKFAST: Standards for Bed & Breakfast and Country Inn accommodation are overseen by the Bed & Breakfast and Country Inns Association. For further information, contact Visitor Information Services, PO Box 940, Charlottetown, Prince Edward Island C1A 7M5 (tel: (902) 368 4444; fax: (902) 368 6613; e-mail: viccharlottetown@gov.pe.ca; website: www.gov.pe.ca).
Grading: Owners of accommodation in Prince Edward Island are invited to participate in the Canada Select Rating Program. Participation in the grading system is voluntary. For further information, contact the Canada Select Rating Program, Quality Tourism Services, 375 University Avenue, Unit 1B, Charlottetown, Prince Edward Island C1A 4N4 (tel: (902) 566 3501; fax: (902) 566 3575; e-mail: qts@qts.pe.ca; website: www.canadaselect.com). The star ratings are based on the extent of facilities, quality of facilities, extent of services and amenities. **5-star**: Exceptional quality accommodation; among the best in the country with outstanding facilities, amenities and guest services; **4-star**: High-quality accommodation; extended range of facilities, amenities and guest services; **3-star**: Better quality accommodation; greater range of facilities and services; **2-star**: Basic, clean and comfortable with some amenities; **1-star**: Basic, clean, comfortable accommodation.
CAMPING/CARAVANNING: There are over 65 travel parks for camping near sandy beaches or in the interior. Camping fees vary, depending on the facilities offered. Most private sites accept reservations. For rates, reservations and other information on provincial parks, contact the Department of Tourism, Parks Division, PO Box 2000, Charlottetown, Prince Edward Island C1A 7N8 (tel: (902) 368 5540 *or* (888) 734 7529; fax: (902) 368 4438; e-mail: tourpei@gov.pe.ca; website: www.gov.pe.ca); for rates and information on the National Parks, contact Parks Canada, 2 Palmers Lane, Charlottetown, Prince Edward Island C1A 5V6 (tel: (902) 566 7626; e-mail: sharon.larter@pc.gc.ca). For general information, contact Canadian Heritage (tel: (819) 997 0055; website: www.pch.gc.ca). A number of companies can arrange **motor camper** rentals, with a range of fully-equipped vehicles. Full details can be obtained from the Tourism Prince Edward Island (see *Contact Addresses* section).

Credit: © Tourism Price Edward Island

Resorts & Excursions

Charlottetown, the provincial capital, is a well-designed colonial seaport with tree-lined streets and rows of woodframe houses. Main places of interest are **Province House**, a fine Georgian building of Nova Scotia sandstone, the site of the 1864 discussions that led to the Canadian Confederation, and the **Confederation Centre of the Arts**, which houses art galleries, theatres, a restaurant and a museum. Founders' Hall, located on Charlottetown waterfront, is a newly opened attraction which tells the story of Canada from the 1864 Charlottetown Conference to the present day.
A tourist route known as the **Blue Heron Drive** heads westwards from Charlottetown to **Port-la-Joye-Fort Amherst**, the original French settlement on the Island, and on to **Prince Edward Island National Park**, 45km (25 miles) of fine white sand beaches and red sandstone capes on the north coast. **Green Gables**, the farmhouse immortalised in the book *Anne of Green Gables* by Lucy Maud Montgomery, is now a museum in **Cavendish**, located within the park. Further along the route, through **Stanley Bridge** where there is a large marine aquarium, is **New London**, where the author was born and wrote; there is now a museum in the house where she lived.
Dunstaffnage, halfway between Charlottetown and Prince Edward Island National Park has a **car museum** worth visiting. A second tourist route, the **Lady Slipper Drive**, circles Prince County, home to most of the province's French-speaking residents. The route passes through **Miscouche**, which has an **Acadian Museum**, and **Mont Carmel**, which has an **Acadian Pioneer Village**. **West Point**, on the western tip of Prince Edward Island, has **Cedar Dunes Provincial Park**, with a century-old wooden lighthouse and a connecting complex housing a museum, restaurant, handicraft shop and guest-rooms. A third route, the **King's Byway**, traverses the hilly farming region of the eastern interior. It passes through **Souris**, where ferries depart regularly for the Québecois **Magdalen Islands**; and **North Lake**, where boats can be chartered for what is claimed to be some of the best tuna fishing in the world. Seal-watching tours have become very popular in the King's Byway region. **Point Prim**, located on a long promontory to the southeast, has the oldest lighthouse on the Island, built in 1846 and still in use. In the interior of the Island, accessible by this route, is **Milltown Cross**, offering the **Buffaloland Provincial Park**, home of bison and white-tailed deer, and the **Harvey Moore Migratory Bird Sanctuary**, home to many varieties of duck and geese.

Sport & Activities

Watersports: Prince Edward Island has a 805km- (500 mile-) long shoreline with numerous bays and sandy beaches, the best and prettiest of which can be found in the *Prince Edward Island National Park*. The park's northern shore (situated in Queen's County), where the beaches are protected by cliffs and sand dunes, is particularly well suited for **swimming**, and attracts thousands of visitors during the summer. **Deep-sea fishing** is a popular sport and chartered boats are widely available from July to September. Although the most common type of charters are for cod, mackerel and flounder, the waters around Prince Edward Island are particularly renowned for tuna. The tuna season begins in mid-August, and many tuna charters are available. Fishing equipment and bait are provided by the captain, but anglers are reminded that if they catch large fish such as tuna, the catch belongs to the captain. Those bringing in tuna may be offered a free charter for one day. **Sea kayaking** in 1- and 2-seater kayaks around the island's coast offers good views and an opportunity to observe some of the local **wildlife** which includes seals, porpoises, eagles, osprey and cormorants. Several operators on the islands offer guided kayaking tours.
Other: Cycling has become increasingly popular in recent years and Tourism Prince Edward Island (see *Contact Addresses* section) can offer advice about recommended cycling routes, which include trails along heritage roads and the 275 km- (170 mile-) *Confederation Trail*. The warm waters of the Gulf of St Lawrence and the Northumberland Strait have a moderating influence on the island's climate and help to create one of the longest **autumn foliage viewing** periods in northeastern North America. The best time to go on these scenic forest walks is from mid-September until late October. There are excellent facilities for **skiing** and **cross-country skiing** at *Brookvale Provincial Ski Park*, which hosted the 1991 Canada Winter Games. Prince Edward Island has over 1000km (625 miles) of **snowmobiling** trails. The main line, the *Confederation Trail*, runs from Tignish in the west to Souris in the east, with several interconnecting lines branching off to virtually every corner of the province. Service stations can be found along the way. Prince Edward Island has excellent **golfing** facilities. There are 26 courses, designed to challenge golfers of varying skill, which include the *Links at Crowbush Cove* and *Brudenell River Resort*.
For general information about sport and activities in Canada, see the main *Canada* section.

Social Profile

FOOD & DRINK: Shellfish – lobster in particular – is a mainstay of the dinner table. Lobsters are steamed or boiled and included in casseroles and salads. Lobster suppers are a tradition on Prince Edward Island and they are often held in church basements or community halls where fresh lobster is served, along with home-made chowder, rolls, cakes and pies. 'Seconds' are available of everything except lobster. Oysters are also popular; they may be served with tangy sauce, deep-fried, in pies, scalloped, in soufflés, soups and stews. Prince Edward Island is famous for its new potatoes – small, round potatoes – and a favourite with locals are new potatoes boiled with their skins, then mashed and served with lots of butter, salt and pepper. The Island offers plenty of plain, wholesome, home-cooked food in restaurants. Service is informal and friendly. There are also many seafood outlets where fresh fish and shellfish can be bought in season and taken away for cooking on barbecues or camp fires. Waiters expect a 10 to 15 per cent tip. Most dining rooms are licensed to sell alcohol. Licensed premises are open until 0200. Off-licences (liquor stores) are open 6 days a week from 1000-2200 during the summer months. Hours of operation vary in winter. Only persons over 19 years of age may buy alcohol.
NIGHTLIFE: Lounges on the Island usually have some live entertainment for all or part of the week. Theatres, located mainly in Charlottetown, Victoria, Georgetown, Mont Carmel and Summerside, offer cultural, musical or light entertainment.
SHOPPING: The Island's crafts include highly original pottery, weaving, leatherwork, woodwork, quilting, hand-painted silk and jewellery. Various guilds preserve the

A B C D E F G H I J K L M N O P Q R S T U V W X Y Z

standards of production. There are also several antique dealers, second-hand stores, auctions, yard sales and flea markets. Main shopping centres can be found in Charlottetown, Summerside, Montague and Cavendish.
Shopping hours: Mon-Thurs and Sat 0900-1700, Fri 0900-2100 (although these may vary depending on the area and the time of year).
SPECIAL EVENTS: For a more complete list, contact Tourism Prince Edward Island (see *Contact Addresses* section). The following is a selection of special events occurring on Prince Edward Island in 2005:
Feb 11-13 *Jack Frost Children's Winterfest*, Charlottetown. **Mar** *Celebration On Ice*, Charlottetown. **May-Oct** *The Charlottetown Festival*. **Jun-Jul** *Festival of Lights*, Charlottetown. **Jul** *PEI Bluegrass and Oldtime Music Festival*, Rollo Bay. **Jul-Aug** *Celtic Festival*, Summerside; *Woodleigh Medieval Faire*, Burlington; *Indian River Festival* (fine music series). **Aug** *Atlantic Fiddlers Festival*, Abram Village. **Sep** *Annual 70-mile (112km) Coastal Yard Sale*, southeastern PEI. **Sep 16-18** *International Shellfish Festival*. **Nov** *Annual Christmas Auction*, Summerside; *Christmas Ceilidh*, Sturgeon.
Dec *Souris Christmas Parade*.

Business Profile

COMMERCIAL INFORMATION: The following organisation can offer advice: Atlantic Provinces Chamber of Commerce, Suite 21, 236 St George Street, Moncton, New Brunswick E1C 1W1 (tel: (506) 857 3980; fax: (506) 859 6131; e-mail: info@apcc.ca; website: www.apcc.ca).
CONFERENCES/CONVENTIONS: For information on conferences and conventions on Prince Edward Island, contact the Visit Canada Centre (see main Canada *Contact Addresses* section) *or* Meetings Prince Edward Island, 129 Queen Street, Charlottetown, Prince Edward Island C1A 4B3 (tel: (902) 368 3688; fax: (902) 368 3108; e-mail: info@meetingspei.com; website: www.meetingspei.com).

Credit: © Tourism Price Edward Island

Climate

Temperate climate with cold winters (mean January/February daytime high of -3°C/26°F) and warm summers (mean July/August daytime high of 23°C/73°F).
Required clothing: Light- to mediumweights in warmer months, heavyweights in winter. Waterproof wear is advisable all year.

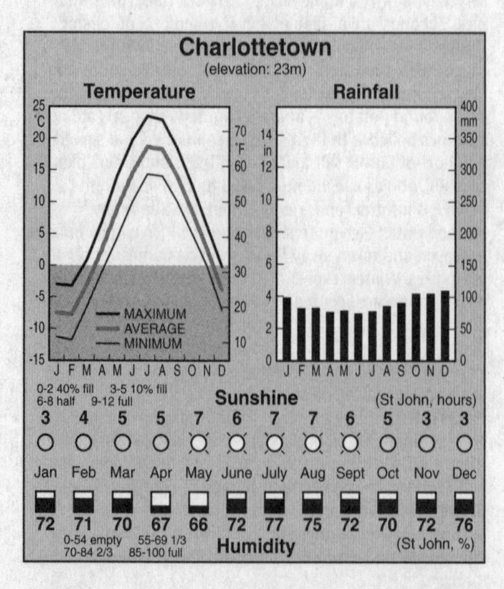

Quebec

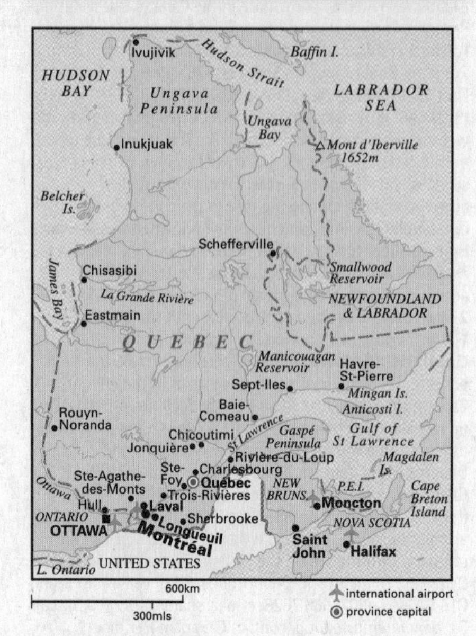

Location: Eastern Canada.

Tourisme Québec
Street address: 1255 Peel Street, Office 100, Montréal, Québec H3B 4V4, Canada
Postal address: PO Box 979, Montréal, Québec H3C 2W3, Canada
Tel: (514) 873 2015 *or* (877) 266 5687 (toll-free in USA and Canada). Fax: (514) 864 3838.
E-mail: info@bonjourquebec.com
Website: www.bonjourquebec.com
Tourisme Québec
Centre Infotouriste de Québec, 12 rue Sainte-Anne, Québec City, Québec G1R 3X2, Canada
Tel: (514) 873 2015 *or* (877) 266 5687 (toll-free in USA and Canada). Fax: (514) 864 3838.
Destination Québec
Suites 11-16, 35-37 Grosvenor Gardens House, Grosvenor Gardens, London SW1W 0BS, UK
Tel: (020) 7233 8011. Fax: (020) 7233 7203.
E-mail: traveltrade@destinationquebec.co.uk *or* dquk@destinationquebec.co.uk
Website: www.quebec4u.co.uk
Deals with trade enquiries only. Members of the public should contact the Destination Québec brochure service by telephone or e-mail
Destination Québec Brochure Service
PO Box 1939, Maidenhead, Berks SL6 1AJ, UK
Tel: (08705) 561 705 (24-hour brochure hotline).
E-mail: brochures@quebectourism.co.uk

General Information

AREA: 1,357,812 sq km (524,252 sq miles).
POPULATION: 7,237,479 (2001).
POPULATION DENSITY: 5.26 per sq km.
CAPITAL: Québec City. **Population**: 682,757 (2001).
GEOGRAPHY: The Province of Québec is in the east of Canada, with coasts on the North Atlantic and Hudson and James Bays; the St Lawrence Seaway, the major shipping channel of the Canadian east coast, cuts through the populous south; the cities of Québec and Montréal (Canada's second-largest city) stand beside it. In the north, the Laurentians resort area has snow-covered mountains in winter and scenic lakes. The far north is a spread of forest and lakes.
LANGUAGE: French is the official language and 82 per cent of the population speak it as a first language; 35 per cent of the population speak English either as a first language or in addition to French.
TIME: GMT - 5 (GMT - 4 in summer).
Summer officially lasts from the first Sunday in April to the Saturday before the last Sunday in October.

Public Holidays

Public holidays are as for the rest of Canada (see general *Canada* section) with the following dates also observed:
2005: Jan 2 New Year. **Jun 24** Quebec National Day or St Jean Baptiste Day.
2006: Jan 2 New Year. **Jun 24** Quebec National Day or St Jean Baptiste Day.

Travel - International

AIR: *Air Canada (AC)* and other international carriers fly into Montréal. Commuter services between Montréal and Toronto, Québec City and New York also exist. *Air Canada* offers services from Montréal and Québec City to other Canadian business centres. Local air services operate between the cities in the south and float planes serve the lakes and parkland of the north. Other airlines serving Québec are *Air Canada Jazz, Air Creebec, Air Inuit, Air Nova, Air Ontario, American Airlines, Delta Airlines, First Air, Northwest Airlines, Tango* and *US Airways*.
International airports: Montréal has two international airports, *Trudeau (YUL)*, 25km (16 miles) west of Montréal, and *Mirabel (YMX)*, 53km (33 miles) northwest of Montréal (website for both airports: www.admtl.com). All international scheduled flights are from Montréal-Trudeau. Charter flights are from Montréal-Mirabel. Several daily trans-border US services also operate from Montréal-Trudeau. A regular shuttle service connects the two airports. Buses leave *Trudeau* every 30 minutes (0700-0100) and *Mirabel* every 90 minutes (0100-2330 and until 2200 Thurs) for Montréal and its major hotels. Taxi and limousine services are also available for a fixed flat fee.
SEA: Québec City and Montréal are the most important Canadian ports on the St Lawrence Seaway, which links the Atlantic Ocean with the Great Lakes and the industrial heartland of Canada and the USA. Several international passenger carriers sail to both ports; European carriers dock only at Montréal. Most of the province's lakes and rivers (notably the Ouatouais, the Richelieu and the Saguenay) are served by local ferries, some of which are able to take heavy lorries. For schedules and fares, enquire locally.
RAIL: *VIA Rail* connects Montréal and Québec City to Toronto with fast, regular services. It also offers services to Halifax from Montréal and Québec City. Links to the USA are with *Amtrak* and *VIA Rail*. *VIA Rail* connects all major provincial towns, and *Amtrak* operates two daily trains to the USA. *VIA Rail* services also connect the major cities in the south of the province, with thrice-daily mainline services from Montréal to Québec.
ROAD: The best way of travelling into and around Québec by road is by long-distance coach, especially *Orléans Express* (website: www.orleansexpress.com). The services in the southern region are especially frequent. Motorhomes and campers are best for seeing the northern parklands, and the area is connected to the south by several good highways, although the most extensive network is around the populous areas in the south.
URBAN: Montréal's bus and metro services are fully integrated and operate on a flat-fare system. Tickets for single journeys are not usually issued unless a transfer is required. For transfers from metro to bus, transfer-tickets should be obtained from machines before leaving the underground. If transferring from bus to metro, ask the bus driver for a ticket. Passes and multi-ticket books are sold and metro fares are the lowest in North America. Québec City's bus services operate on a flat-fare system. No change is carried on board. Pre-purchase passes are available. There are good bus services in other towns.

Accommodation

HOTELS: The majority of the population live in the south of the province, where all the large cities offer an extensive choice of hotel accommodation. Some of the best hotels in the country are in Montréal and Québec City. Outside the cities, accommodation takes on a more rural flavour; lakeside lodges and cabins are very popular. Accommodation is often possible in private homes. All accommodation establishments are required to have a classification certificate from the Minister of Regional Development & Tourism. All accommodation is awarded 1 to 6 stars according to their facilities and level of comfort, while bed & breakfast establishments (*gîtes*) are awarded 1 to 6 suns for their atmosphere, architecture and welcome. The precise definition of the star allocation system varies according to the type of accommodation. For further information, contact Tourisme Québec (see *Contact Addresses* section).
BED & BREAKFAST: There are numerous organisations in Québec that provide information regarding bed & breakfast accommodation, including Réseau des Gîtes Classifiés, 10 Rue de la Chapelle, La Malbaie G5A 3A3 (tel: (418) 665 2323; fax: (418) 665 6996; e-mail: aggite@gites-classifies.qc.ca; website: www.gites-classifies.qc.ca); *or* Fédération des Agricotours du Québec, 4545 avenue Pierre de Coubertin, PO Box 1000, Succ. M, Montréal H1V 3R2 (tel: (514) 252 3138; fax: (514) 252 3173; e-mail: info@agricotours.qc.ca; website: www.agricotours.qc.ca).
CAMPING/CARAVANNING: Northern Québec is a vast area of forest and lakes and one of the best areas for wilderness camping in Canada. A number of companies can arrange motor camper rentals with a range of fully-equipped vehicles. Full details can be obtained either from

Tourisme Québec *or* from the Fédération Québécoise de Camping et de Caravaning, 4545 avenue Pierre de Coubertin, PO Box 1000, Succ. M. Montréal H1V 3R2 (tel: (514) 252 3003; fax: (514) 254 0694; e-mail: camping-caravaning@fqcc.qc.ca; website: www.campingquebec.com).

Resorts & Excursions

Outside the major centres of population in the southwest, Canada's largest province consists of hilly agricultural land along the banks of the **St Lawrence** and vast tracts of barren mountains in the north. The one-hour drive along St Lawrence from Québec to the outskirts of **Charlevoix** follows a breathtaking route of towering rock faces, looming canyons and craggy fjords. More than 100,000 lakes provide excellent fishing (chiefly for trout and salmon), whilst in the northern tundra of Québec's Far North (Nouveau-Québec), caribou and other game are hunted. Information on itineraries, equipment, transport and accommodation in this region can be obtained from La Fédération des Pourvoyeurs du Québec Inc, Suite 270,
5237 Boulevard Hamel, Québec G2E 2H2 (tel: (418) 877 5191; fax: (418) 877 6638; e-mail: fpq@fpq.com; website: www.fpq.com).

MONTRÉAL

Canada's second-largest city, on a 48km- (30 mile-) long island, is a sophisticated cosmopolitan metropolis with a 65 per cent francophone population. Careful central planning for Expo '67 and the 1976 Olympic Games have produced a spacious and beautiful modern city. A series of underground shopping and recreation complexes, linked by walkways and the metro, is centred on **Place Ville-Marie**. The **Place des Arts** is the home of the Montréal Symphony Orchestra and several theatres offering year-round drama, music, ballet and opera. Both the **Montréal Museum of Fine Arts** and the **Museum of Contemporary Arts** have good collections. **Vieux-Montréal**, the historic waterfront section, has been carefully restored. Main places of note here are: **Place Jacques-Cartier**, the former French governor's residence; **Château Ramezay**; the city's oldest church, **Notre-Dame-de-Bonsecour**; and **Pointe-à-Callière**, the **Montréal Museum of Archaeology and History**. Another museum of note is the **Stewart Museum**, which is dedicated to the exploration and discovery of the New World. It is located on the Ile Sainte-Hélène, in Montréal's only fort. **Mont-Royal Park** is the city's highest point, offering an excellent vista from the centre of Montréal. Behind-the-scenes tours of the **Olympic Park**, site of the 1976 games, are available. The park is also home to the world's tallest leaning building, the **Botanical Gardens** and the **Biodôme**. The area around **St-Denis** is renowned for its many jazz cafes and small restaurants.

QUÉBEC CITY

With its old city walls, the characteristic green copper roofs and fortified **Citadel**, the provincial capital is one of the most European cities in North America; in 1985 it was declared a World Heritage Site by UNESCO. It is the cradle of French culture in Canada with a 95 per cent French-speaking population. The city is split into two levels, connected by stone stairways and a municipal lift.
Surrounded by the old city walls is the 'Upper Town' with some fine 18th- and 19th-century architecture, notably the **Place D'Armes** and the **Château Frontenac**. The latter is a first-class hotel. In front of the Château Frontenac is a wide promenade with 310 wooden steps leading up to the Citadel which affords incredible views across the St Lawrence River. Small street cafes, cobblestoned streets and shaded squares emphasise the European air of the 'Upper Town'. In the 'Lower Town', the network of 17th-century streets centred on **Place Royale** has recently been restored.

THE REST OF THE PROVINCE

Sainte-Agathe-des-Monts, 100km (60 miles) north of Montréal, is the hub of a resort area providing some of the best skiing in North America. Further north, the **Mont-Tremblant Park** provides boating, hunting and camping as well as wintersports. Northwest of this is **La Verendrye Wildlife Reserve**, a protected lakeland wilderness; and further on, the mining territory centred on **Rouyn-Noranda**. **L'Île d'Orléans**, east of Québec City, is a region of picturesque Québécois villages. In front of the Ile d'Orléans are the **Montmorency Falls** and further east, the **Shrine of Sainte-Anne-de-Beaupré** and **Mont Sainte-Anne**. The latter is the main ski resort in the famous Laurentians (or Laurentides) skiing region, which is also a provincial park.
Heading northeast from Québec along the southern bank of the St Lawrence, the main route leads first through the farming region of **Bas-Saint-Laurent** and from there to the **Gaspé Peninsula**. The major attractions here are the **Rocher Percé** in the **Gaspé Provincial Park** and **Forillon National Park**.
Across the mouth of the river is the **Duplessis Peninsula**, site of some of the earliest landfalls in the New World.

Credit: © Tourisme Quebec

Remains left by these Viking sailors can be seen in the museum at **Sept-Îles**, the largest city in the area. The bizarre geological formations of the nearby **Mingan Archipelago** are best explored by boat.
The **Magdalen Islands**, 215km (134 miles) east of the Gaspé peninsula in the Gulf of St Lawrence, offer miles of white sandy beaches and a host of unspoilt fishing villages.

Sport & Activities

Outdoor pursuits: At roughly 1.5 million sq km (524,252 sq miles), Québec is Canada's biggest province. Its landscapes are diverse, with 6000km (3750 miles) of coastline, numerous rivers, mountain ranges and countless lakes and forests. The province's 22 natural parks and 14 wildlife reserves provide opportunities for all types of outdoor activities. A variety of **watersports** can be practised, from **whitewater rafting** to gentle **boating**, and canoes, kayaks, sailboards and other equipment can be hired in the parks. Detailed maps of **canoe-camping** itineraries are available at information centres. Excellent watersports facilities exist on the St Lawrence River, especially for **sailing**, **swimming** and **water-skiing**. Several different species of whale can be observed in the mouth of the river at different times of the year, and **whale-watching** dinghy trips are available for visitors wishing to observe these creatures at close hand. The *St Lawrence River Valley* is also good for moderate **cycling**, while the terrain in the *Laurentides* region is more challenging. There are many marked cycling routes, and the cycling network, La Route Verte (the 'Green Circuit') so far boasts more than 3000km (1865 miles) of marked paths and designated roadways. **Mountain bike** enthusiasts will find plenty of trails in the parks and nature reserves, especially *Parc de la Jacques-Cartier* and *Mont-Sainte-Anne* near Québec City.
Wintersports facilities are outstanding. There are around 200 downhill and cross-country ski centres in the province. The season is long and there is plenty of snow. International **downhill skiing** competitions are held to the north of Montréal at Mont-Tremblant and at Mont-Sainte-Anne near Québec City. **Cross-country skiing** is very popular, and trails are extensive. *La Traversée de Charlevoix* is the most challenging trail east of the Rocky Mountains. There are ample opportunities for **snowmobiling** on some of these trails. Other winter activities include **snowshoe trekking**, **dog sledding**, **ice fishing** and **ice climbing**. Various activities are available in the far north of the province, including **wildlife viewing** and **air safaris**.
Gastronomy: Québec people take their food very seriously, and there are many opportunities to partake in the delights of the local cuisine. Several food and drink festivals take place each year. One of the highlights of the culinary year is the maple harvest which takes place from March until the end of May. Québec produces some 80 per cent of Canada's maple syrup total. *Érablières* (maple farms) and *cabanes à sucre* (sugar shacks) are situated all over the province and most are open to the public in the season. Visitors can watch the harvest and sample maple toffee (made by pouring molten syrup onto fresh snow). Barn dance parties are held and meals featuring local specialities are served. These celebrations are popular with locals and visitors alike. For further details, contact Tourisme Québec (see *Contact Addresses* section).
Other: Excellent **golf** facilities exist throughout the province. For further information, contact the Québec Golf Association (tel: (514) 633 1088; fax: (514) 633 1074; e-mail: golfquebec@golfquebec.org; website: www.golfquebec.org). Facilities for other sports, including tennis and fishing are very good. For general information about sport and activities in Canada, see the main *Canada* section.

Social Profile

FOOD & DRINK: Québec proudly reflects a tradition of French culture, never more so than in the restaurants and cuisine of the province. French food here is as excellent as anywhere in Europe. Immigrants from many countries provide a vast selection. English, Greek, Italian, Japanese and Spanish cuisine are all available in Montréal and Québec. International menus are found at all the larger hotels, but the best food is found by wandering around the backstreets of the cities and sampling the small but excellent restaurants scattered throughout both cities.
Specialist dishes include *ragoût de boulettes* (pork meatballs with seasoning) and *cretons du Québec* (chilled minced pork). The Île d'Orléans is an island northeast of Québec City that provides abundant fruit and vegetables for the city. Québec follows French tradition in having excellent standards of wine and spirits to complement the high standards of cuisine. Some spirits and rarer wines are imported from Europe. Wines and spirits based on maple sap are a speciality of the region, among them maple cider and maple whiskey. Local mead is said to be good. Taverns and brasseries serve alcoholic beverages from 1200-0300 every day. Cocktail lounges and cabarets stay open until 0200 and 0300, respectively, in Québec and Montréal. The minimum drinking age is 18 years old.
NIGHTLIFE: Québec City and Montréal offer some of the best nightclubs and cabarets to be found anywhere in Canada. In Montréal, the action seldom begins before 2200 and usually continues until 0300 the next morning. Nightlife is concentrated in the western part of the downtown area along Crescent and Bishop Streets and around Ste-Catherine Street, where there are many bars, restaurants and clubs of all kinds. For a particularly French flavour, try the many clubs, bars, restaurants, cafes and bistros further east around Saint-Denis and Saint-Laurent.
SHOPPING: Québec City and Montréal have excellent shopping facilities, both in large department stores and small street markets. Specialities include furs, Native American crafts, haute couture, antiques, specialist fashion boutiques and discount retail outlets. **Shopping hours**: Mon-Wed 0900-1800, Thurs-Fri 0900-2100, Sat 0900-1700. Most shops are open on Sunday.
SPECIAL EVENTS: For further details and exact dates of special events, contact one of Québec's tourist offices (see *Contact Addresses* section). The following is a selection of special events occurring in Québec during 2005:
Jan 22-Feb 6 *La Fête des Neiges* (including ice sculptures, skating and sliding), Montréal. **Jan 28-Feb 13** *Québec City Winter Carnival*. **Feb 17-27** *Montréal High Lights Festival* (lively arts performances). **Mar 1-13** *Festivalissimo* (Latin and Portuguese cultural event), Montréal. **May** *La Fête du Chocolat de Bromont* (chocolate festival). **Sep-Oct** *La Biennale de Montréal* (celebration of contemporary artists). **Nov** *Montréal International Autoshow*. **Dec** *Christmas Celebrations*, nationwide.

Business Profile

COMMERCIAL INFORMATION: The following organisation can offer advice: Board of Trade of Metropolitan Montréal, 380 St Antoine Street West, Suite 6000, Montréal, Québec H2Y 3X7 (tel: (514) 871 4000; fax: (514) 871 1255; e-mail: info@ccmm.qc.ca; website: www.ccmm.qc.ca).
CONFERENCES/CONVENTIONS: Montréal is a major meeting and convention centre and an extensive information booklet is available from Tourisme Montréal, CP 979, Montréal, Québec H3L 2W2 (tel: (514) 873 2015; fax: (514) 864 3838; website: www.tourisme-montreal.org). For information about conferences and conventions in Québec City, contact Tourisme Québec *or* Greater Québec Area Tourism & Convention Bureau, 2nd Floor, 399 St-Joseph Street East, Québec City, Québec G1K 8E2 (tel: (418) 641 6654; fax: (418) 641 6578; website: www.quebecregion.com).

Climate

Summer months (Jun to Aug) are hot with cooler evenings. Autumn and spring are cooler and winters are very cold and snowy.

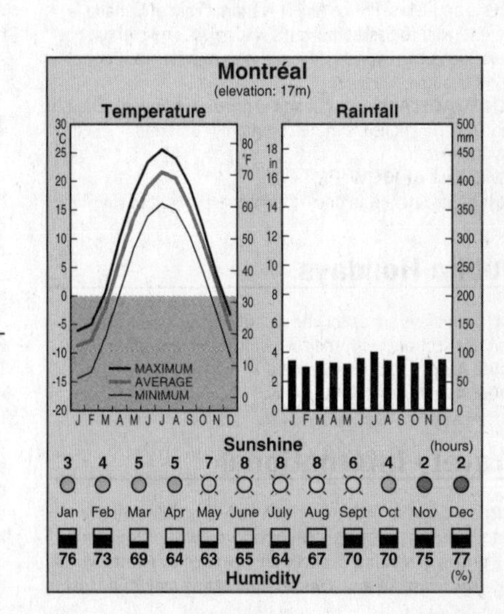

Saskatchewan

Location: Central Canada.

Tourism Saskatchewan
1922 Park Street, Regina, Saskatchewan S4N 7M4, Canada
Tel: (306) 787 2300 *or* (877) 237 2273 (toll-free in USA and Canada). Fax: (306) 787 5744.
E-mail: travel.info@sasktourism.com
Website: www.sasktourism.com

Tourism Saskatoon
6-305 Idylwyld Drive North, Saskatoon, Saskatchewan S7L 0Z1, Canada
Tel: (306) 242 1206 *or* (800) 567 2444 (toll-free in USA and Canada). Fax: (306) 242 1955.
E-mail: info@tourismsaskatoon.com
Website: www.tourismsaskatoon.com
Also deals with convention enquiries.

Tourism Regina
Box 3355, Highway 1 East Regina, Saskatchewan S4P 3H1, Canada
Tel: (306) 789 5099 *or* (800) 661 5099 (toll-free in USA and Canada). Fax: (306) 789 3171.
E-mail: info@tourismregina.com
Website: www.tourismregina.com
Also deals with convention enquiries.

General Information

AREA: 570,113 sq km (220,121 sq miles).
POPULATION: 978,933 (2001).
POPULATION DENSITY: 1.5 per sq km.
CAPITAL: Regina. **Population:** 178,225 (2001).
GEOGRAPHY: Saskatchewan is bordered by Manitoba to the east, the Northwest Territories to the north, Alberta to the west and the US States of North Dakota and Montana to the south. Its landscape is mainly prairie, parkland, forests and lakes. Prince Albert National Park of Canada is the gateway to Saskatchewan's wilderness. The highest elevation is the Cypress Hills in the southwest, 1392m (4566ft) above sea level.
LANGUAGE: Although Canada is officially bilingual (English and French), English is more commonly spoken in Saskatchewan.
TIME: East of 106°W: GMT - 6.
Most of Saskatchewan does not observe Daylight Saving Time.

Public Holidays

Public holidays are as for the rest of Canada (see general *Canada* section), with the following dates also observed:
2005: Aug 1 Saskatchewan Day.
2006: Aug 7 Saskatchewan Day.

Travel - International

AIR: *Air Canada (AC)* provides a daily scheduled service connecting Saskatoon and Regina to the rest of the world. The principal regional services are operated by *Points North Air*, *Transwest Air* and *WestJet* connecting major Canadian centres as well as serving the northern communities.
International airports: *Saskatoon (YXE)* (website: www.yxe.ca) is 7km (4.5 miles) from the city centre (travel time - 15 minutes). Airport facilities include car hire, car parking, restaurant and gift shop.
Regina International Airport (YQR) (website: www.yqr.ca) is 5km (3 miles) from the city centre. Airport facilities include car rental, restaurants and gift shops.
RIVER: Ferry services operate from various locations connecting communities within the province. Houseboats may also be chartered in certain areas.
RAIL: *VIA Rail*, Canada's national passenger train service, operates the Winnipeg–Saskatoon–Edmonton link.
ROAD: Saskatchewan has six travel corridors, namely the Northern Woods and Water Route (9 and 55) east-west, Yellowhead Highway (16) east-west, the Trans-Canada Highway (1) east-west, Red Coat Trail (13) east-west, CanAm International Highway north-south and the Saskota International Highway (9) north-south. Saskatchewan has more road surface than any other province in Canada - a total of 250,000km (150,000 miles). **Bus**: A scheduled motorcoach service is provided by *Greyhound Bus Lines*, *Moose Mountain Bus Lines* and *Saskatchewan Transportation Company* (website: www.stcbus.com). Charter motorcoach services are also available from a number of cities and operators. **Car hire**: Hire cars are available in most cities. Saskatchewan law requires that anyone driving or riding in a motor vehicle must wear available seatbelts at all times.

Accommodation

The majority of accommodation suitable for travellers is found in the south and central portion of the province, especially in Regina, Saskatoon, Moose Jaw, Prince Albert, Swift Current, Weyburn, Melfort, Yorkton, Estevan and the Battlefords. The parklands in the northern part of the province have mainly camping-style accommodation, as well as northern lodges and cabins, some with all the modern facilities. 'Houseboat charters' on the lakes are a special feature of Saskatchewan. For further information on hotels in Saskatchewan, contact the Hotels Association of Saskatchewan, 302 20AD Broad Street, Regina, Saskatchewan S4P 1Y3 (tel: (306) 522 1664; fax: (306) 525 1944; e-mail: lorane.has@sasktel.net; website: www.hotelsofsask.com). Accommodation reservations can be made through Tourism Saskatchewan (see *Contact Addresses* section). The *Saskatchewan Accommodation, Resort and Campground Guide* is available through Tourism Saskatchewan and is a comprehensive directory of hotels/motels, parks, campgrounds, lakeside accommodation, bed & breakfast and vacation farms that are available throughout the province. **Grading**: Saskatchewan Tourism's annual guide uses the following definitions when describing accommodation: **Mod**: Modern room. Includes private bathroom facilities with wash basin, bathtub and/or shower and flush toilet; **Smod**: Semi-modern room. Includes wash basin only and a pressurised hot and cold water supply; **Nmod**: Non-modern room. Has no plumbing facilities; **Lhk**: Light housekeeping unit. Includes kitchen facilities as well as living and sleeping quarters.
CAMPING/CARAVANNING: The parklands offer some of the best camping landscapes in Canada. There are 34 provincial parks in the categories of wilderness, recreational, natural environment and historical parks, two national parks, as well as 101 regional parks, all offering different rates of service with some offering accommodation for those without recreational vehicles or tents. For details, contact the local park authorities.
A number of companies can arrange **motor camper** rentals, with a range of fully-equipped vehicles. Full details can be obtained from Tourism Saskatchewan (see *Contact Addresses* section).

Resorts & Excursions

Half of this vast province comprises designated provincial forest. There are 80 million acres (32 million hectares) of it north of the 54th parallel, offering unequalled opportunities for outdoor enthusiasts. The south and centre enjoy a more mellow landscape, ranging from prairie and grasslands to badlands and breathtaking river valleys.

REGINA

The provincial capital was once called 'Pile of Bones' but was renamed in honour of Queen Victoria. Its centrepiece is the **Wascana Centre**, a huge urban park (one of the largest in North America) containing the **McKenzie Art Gallery** and **Saskatchewan Centre of the Arts**. The park also provides an impressive setting for the **Legislative Building**, the **Royal Saskatchewan Museum** and the **Kramer/IMAX Theatre**. Regina is the home of Canada's only training academy for Royal Canadian Mounted Police ('The Mounties') and the **RCMP Centennial Museum**.

SASKATOON: Built on both banks of the South Saskatchewan River, Saskatoon is one of Canada's fastest-growing urban centres. The **Western Development Museum**, **Wanuskewin Heritage Park**, **Forestry Farm Park**, **Mendel Art Gallery** and the **Ukrainian Museum of Canada** are its main attractions.

ELSEWHERE

The Trans-Canada Highway provides the best means of touring the far south, connecting the cities of **Swift Current**, **Moose Jaw** and **Regina**. Moose Jaw, once a quiet trading post, achieved notoriety during Prohibition in the 1920s, when it played host to gangsters, including Al 'Scarface' Capone, and played a pivotal role in the distilling, bootlegging and rum running business. The **Tunnels of Moose Jaw** tours provide an excellent account of the town's turbulent and exciting history. Another popular Moose Jaw attraction is the **Temple Gardens Mineral Spa and Resort**. Visitors can take the waters (drawn from porous rock formations more than 1350m (4500ft) below ground) in the hot indoor and outdoor mineral pools. The Highway follows the cavernous **Qu'Appelle Valley**, a sunken garden studded with lakes that runs two thirds of the way across the province. East of Regina, **Fort Qu'Appelle** and the lakeside recreation parks of **Katepwa Point** and **Echo Valley**, as well as **Buffalo Pound** to the west are worth visiting. On the west side of the province is **Swift Current**, which hosts an annual **Frontier Days Festival**; and, further west across low-scrub prairie, the afforested oasis of **Cypress Hills Park** (the highest point of land between Labrador and the Rocky Mountains).
The Yellowhead Highway, running eastwards from Saskatoon to **Yorkton**, near the border with Manitoba, is a good way to tour Saskatchewan's grain belt. This region was once settled by Ukrainians, as testified by the many silver-domed Orthodox churches, such as that at **Veregin**. Other attractions en route include the **Duck Mountain** and **Good Spirit Lake Provincial Parks**. There is a pioneer village at the **Western Development Museum** in **North Battleford**, northwest of Saskatoon, and **Fort Battleford National Historic Park**, is located 5km (3 miles) southeast of North Battleford. **Manitou Beach** has the **Manitou Springs Mineral Spa**, where visitors may relax and float effortlessly in the very salty, warm, mineral-rich waters which are pumped from **Little Manitou Lake** into pools in the spa and are believed to provide relief from a variety of ailments. But Saskatchewan's main attractions are the endless forests and thousands of lakes of the north, accessible by the Northern Woods and Water Route. There are few permanent settlements and many regions are accessible only by air. **Prince Albert** is the main gateway. The closest park is **Prince Albert National Park of Canada**, a hilly, forested area with hundreds of lakes, ponds and rivers, consisting of nearly 30 per cent water. Animal species that can be seen in the park include bison (in the southwest corner), white pelicans (**Lavallée Lake**), lynx, timber wolf, elk, moose and black bear. Its most developed area is at **Waskesiu Lake**, which has lodge and cottage accommodation and good facilities for camping, recreation and watersports, including water-skiing, sailing, canoeing and kayaking. Further off to the northwest is **Meadow Lake**, which has good accommodation and facilities for hunting and winter sports. The small airport at **Lac la Ronge**, about 238km (149 miles) north of Prince Albert, is the main base for flights to the very remote northern lakes, such as **Wollaston** and **Athabasca**. Excellent fishing and canoeing opportunities are available on **Lac la Ronge** and on the **Churchill River** which passes nearby, as well as many rivers and lakes throughout Saskatchewan.

Sport & Activities

Outdoor pursuits: Saskatchewan's two national parks, *Prince Albert National Park of Canada* in the north and *Grasslands National Park* in the southwest, cover nearly 5,000,000 acres (2,000,000 hectares) between them. Opportunities for **wildlife viewing** are plentiful, with wolves, moose and caribou inhabiting the northern forests, while elk and deer can be found further south. When the snow melts, parklands are used for **horseriding**, **camping**, **canoeing**, **cycling** and **hiking**. The south of the province is particularly good for **birdwatching**. The Network Reserve sites of *Chaplin Lake* and *Quill Lakes* are home to over 300 species including rare ferruginous hawks, peregrine falcons and Hudsonian godwits. Saskatchewan boasts nearly 100,000 lakes and the province is named after the Native American word for river systems (Kis-is-ska-tche-wan). **Sailing**, **water-skiing**, **swimming** and **fishing** are especially popular in summer months. The fishing season is from May to March, and ice fishing is popular in the winter. There are over 68 species of fish found in Saskatchewan and 100,000 lakes, rivers and streams.
Wintersports are practised in the region, including **skiing**, **skating**, **curling** and **ice hockey**. There are at least 13 **downhill** and over 25 **cross-country skiing** areas. With over 250 courses, **golf** can be played throughout the province.

Social Profile

FOOD & DRINK: Whitefish and pickerel are marketed by Native American co-operatives. Wild rice harvested by Native Americans is an excellent accompaniment to the abundant wild fowl which includes partridge, prairie chicken, wild duck and goose. 'Saskatoon' berries, similar to blueberries, are used for jams, jellies and 'saskatoon pie', eaten with fresh country cream. Other wild berries include pinchberries and cranberries which make a tart and tangy jelly, ideal with wild fowl meals. A good selection of restaurants can be found in all the province's cities and major towns catering to all tastes and budgets. The minimum drinking age is 19 years old. Alcohol is sold only in licensed stores, licensed restaurants, cocktail lounges, dining and beverage rooms. Retail outlets operate throughout the province.
NIGHTLIFE: There are several nightclubs in the major cities; bars and restaurants in most main towns have live entertainment as well as music and dancing. The best times for nightlife are during the annual summer fairs held regularly in all the major towns. The days of the settlers and cowboys are recreated with people dressing in costumes and eating traditional foods. The emphasis changes in each town and according to the time of year. An example can be found in the capital, Regina, with a festival lasting several days – *Buffalo Days* (see *Special Events* below).
SHOPPING: There are many small craft stores that offer pottery, silkscreens, rock jewellery, potash clocks, embroidered leather and denim.
SPECIAL EVENTS: For more information on special events in Saskatchewan, contact Tourism Saskatchewan (see *Contact Addresses* section). The following is a selection of special events occurring in Saskatchewan in 2005:
Jan *Annual Snowmobile Rally*, Cut Knife. **Apr 8-10** *International Film Festival for Young People*. **Jun 17-19** *Cameco Victoria Park Summer Festival*. **Jun 24-Jul 3** *Jazz Festival*, Saskatoon. **Aug 4-14** *Saskatoon International Fringe Festival*. **Aug 18-20** *Folkfest 2005 - One World; The Heart of the Community*. **Oct 20-23** *Canadian Cowboy's Association Rodeo Finals*. **Dec 2-4** *Sundog Arts and Entertainment Fair*. **Dec 4-10** *Festival of Trees*, Prairieland Park.

Business Profile

COMMERCIAL INFORMATION: The following organisation can offer advice: Saskatchewan Chamber of Commerce, 1920 Broad Street, Regina, Saskatchewan S4P 3V2 (tel: (306) 352 2671; fax: (306) 781 7084; e-mail: info@saskchamber.com; website: www.actionsask.com) *or* Saskatchewan Economic and Co-operative Development, 1925 Rose Street, Regina, Saskatchewan S4P 3P1 (tel: (306) 787 1605 (general enquiries); fax: (306) 787 1620; website: www.ir.gov.sk.ca).
CONFERENCES/CONVENTIONS: For information or assistance, contact the Visit Canada Centre *or* Tourism Saskatoon *or* Tourism Regina (see *Contact Addresses* sections for *Canada* and *Saskatchewan*).

Climate

Temperate in the south with cold winters in the north. The highest rainfall occurs between April and June. Summers are hot and dry with long hours of sunshine, but winter temperatures are generally cold and snowy until early March, but sunny.
Required clothing: Light- to mediumweights during warmer months. Heavyweights are worn in winter. Waterproof wear is advisable throughout the year.

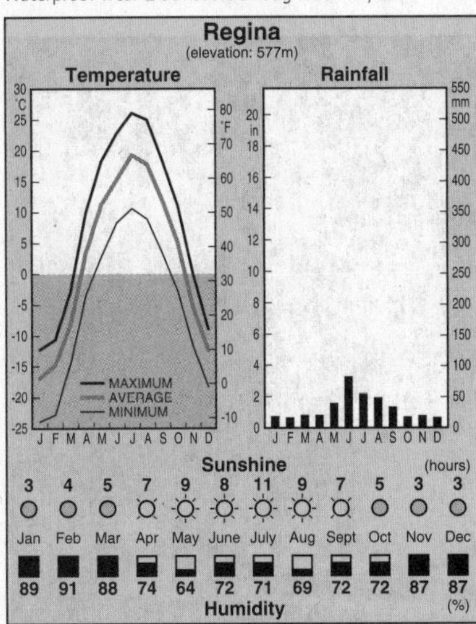

Yukon Territory

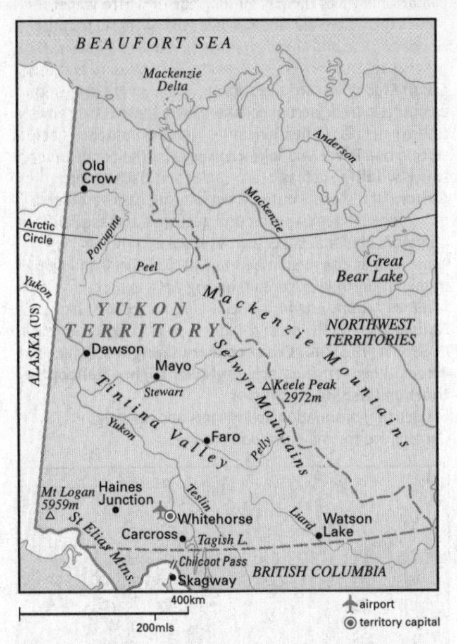

Location: Northwest Canada.

Tourism Yukon
Street address: 1st Floor, 100 Hanson Street, Whitehorse, Yukon Y1A 2C6, Canada
Postal address: PO Box 2703, Whitehorse, Yukon Y1A 2C6, Canada
Tel: (867) 667 5340 *or* (800) 661 0494 (toll-free) *or* (800 789 8566 (brochure request).
Fax: (867) 667 3546.
E-mail: vacation@gov.yk.ca
Website: www.touryukon.com
Yukon First Nations Tourism Association
Street address: One 1109 First Avenue, Whitehorse, Yukon Y1A 5G4, Canada
Postal address: PO Box 4518, Whitehorse, Yukon Y1A 2R8
Tel: (867) 667 7698.
Fax: (867) 667 7527.
E-mail: yfnta@yknet.yk.ca.org
Website: www.yfnta.org

General Information

AREA: 531,844 sq km (205,345 sq miles).
POPULATION: 28,674 (2001).
POPULATION DENSITY: 0.06 per sq km.
CAPITAL: Whitehorse. **Population**: 24,031 (1997).
GEOGRAPHY: The Yukon Territory, Canada's 'last frontier', is a largely mountainous and forested wilderness located in the northwest of the country. It borders the US State of Alaska to the west, Canada's Northwest Territories to the east and British Columbia to the south. The Yukon Territory is bisected by the valley of the Yukon River, which passes to the west of the Mackenzie Mountains. Mount Logan, in the St Elias Range on the border with Alaska, is the second-highest peak in North America at 5959m (19,550ft).
LANGUAGE: Although Canada is officially bilingual (English and French), English is more commonly spoken in the territory.
TIME: GMT - 8 (GMT - 7 in summer).
Summer officially lasts from the first Sunday in April to the Saturday before the last Sunday in October.

Public Holidays

Public holidays are as for the rest of Canada (see general *Canada* section), with the following dates also observed:
2005: Feb 25 Heritage Day. **Aug 15** Discovery Day.
2006: Feb 24 Heritage Day. **Aug 14** Discovery Day.

Travel - International

AIR: The main international services are run by *Air Canada (AC)*. They also operate a daily domestic service between Whitehorse and Vancouver. There are also flights between Frankfurt and Whitehorse with the airline Thomas Cook/*Condor*. *Zip* also provides a connecting service from Regina and Whitehorse to other parts of Canada, eg Montréal, Ottawa and Vancouver (website:

Credit: © Tourism Yukon

www.aircanada.com). *Air North*, the main local carrier, provides services from Whitehorse to Inuvik, Dawson City, Old Crow, Juneau and Fairbanks, with connecting flights to Anchorage in Alaska (tel: (867) 668 2228; fax: (867) 668 6224; e-mail: reservations@flyairnorth.com; website: www.flyairnorth.com). Other scheduled carriers include *First Air*, which operates from Whitehorse to Fort Simpson and Yellowknife in the Northwest Territories (tel: (613) 839 3340; fax: (613) 839 5690; e-mail: reservat@firstair.ca; website: www.firstair.ca). *Era Aviation* provides a non-stop service in summertime between Whitehorse and Anchorage, Alaska (tel: (800) 866 8394; (toll-free in USA and Canada) *or* (907) 266 8394; website: www.era-aviation.com). The Yukon also has many companies offering charter air services; contact Tourism Yukon for a complete listing.
SEA: Cruise ships and passenger and vehicle ferries operate from Bellingham in Washington (USA) and Vancouver and Prince Rupert in British Columbia, arriving at Skagway in Alaska and connecting with Whitehorse by motorcoach, or train/motorcoach combination. Whitehorse is approximately 180km (113 miles) from Skagway. Ferry information can be obtained by phone (tel: (800) 642 0066; toll-free in USA and Canada).
ROAD: The major road in the region is the Alaska Highway, running from Alaska to British Columbia through Whitehorse. The Dempster Highway connects Dawson City with Inuvik in the north. The Klondike Highway connects Skagway, Alaska to Dawson City, Yukon. **Bus/Coach**: Scheduled bus services are available between most Yukon communities. *Greyhound Canada* operates services six times a week from Edmonton, Alberta and Vancouver, British Columbia to Whitehorse during the summer.

Accommodation

HOTELS: There are 86 hotel/motels with approximately 2500 rooms in the Yukon Territory. Because of the heavy tourist flow through the region in summer, reservations should be considered. The majority of hotels and motels are located in the larger centres, but facilities are available along the highways and in the smaller communities. Some hotels are closed for the winter. Whilst not mandatory, some Yukon Territory accommodation have opted to be graded through the Canada Select Program. For further information, contact Tourism Yukon.
BED & BREAKFAST: There are many bed & breakfast properties in the Yukon Territory. For further information, contact Tourism Yukon (see *Contact Addresses* section); *or* the Bed & Breakfast Association of Yukon, PO Box 31518, Whitehorse, Yukon Y1A 6K8 (tel: (867) 667 2171 or (877) 735 3281 (toll-free in USA and Canada); fax: (867) 667 2171; website: www.yukonbandb.com).
CAMPING/CARAVANNING: Camping is advised only in summer and allowed only on government or private campsites. A number of companies can arrange **motor camper** rentals, with a range of fully-equipped vehicles. Full details can be obtained from Tourism Yukon.

Credit: © Tourism Yukon

Resorts & Excursions

WHITEHORSE: Yukon's capital (since 1953) lies on the west bank of the Yukon River, the water route taken by thousands of eager prospectors during the Klondike Gold Rush of 1898. The majority of the territory's population is concentrated here. The **McBride Museum** houses many of the artefacts of the gold rush era, including **Sam McGee's Cabin**. On the river itself, the **SS Klondike**, a restored sternwheeler vessel, is open for viewing. The **MV Schwatka** offers a two-hour cruise of the **Miles Canyon**.
ELSEWHERE: Carcross, an hour's drive south of Whitehorse, lies between the Nares and Bennett Lakes at the foot of Nares Mountain; the **Caribou**, Yukon's oldest hotel, can be found here. Carcross connects to Skagway in Alaska via the **Klondike Highway**. **Kluane National Park and Reserve**, in the southwest corner of the territory, has the highest mountains in Canada (the highest at 5959m (19,545ft) is Mount Logan) and the largest non-polar icefields in the world. Special flightseeing tours of this park can be arranged from Whitehorse and a variety of other Yukon Territory communities.
Near Skagway (Alaska) is **Dyea**, the starting point of the famous **Chilkoot Trail**, where hikers can retrace the footsteps of the gold rush stampeders. **Dawson City**, at the heart of the Klondike, can be reached by road or by the Yukon River. In its brief heyday at the turn of the century, Dawson was hailed as the 'Paris of the North', having then some 30,000 inhabitants; in 1996, the population was approximately 2100. Many areas of the city have now been designated national historic sites, with buildings such as the **Commissioner's Residence** and the **Palace Grand Theatre** bearing witness to its former glories. Each summer the latter produces an authentic 1898 vaudeville show – the 'Gaslight Follies'. Tours on the **Yukon River** on the miniature stern-wheeler **Yukon Lou** visit the **Sternwheelers Graveyard** and **Pleasure Island**. Visitors can pan gold at **Guggieville** or **Claim 33** on Bonanza Creek, the site of the original claim which sparked off the 1898 Gold Rush. In the north of the territory are two further national parks, **Ivvavik** and **Vuntut**. Ivvavik has a non-glaciated landscape with abundant wildlife, significant archaeological sites and the Firth River. The recently established **Vuntut National Park** currently has no facilities or visitor information centre. Camping and hiking are possible, but there are no developed trails; visitors should be self-sufficient and arrange transportation and accommodation well in advance. The village of **Old Crow** has very limited bed & breakfast and cabin facilities. Owing to the lack of a tourist infrastructure, most visitors might prefer to undertake expeditions to the wild backcountry of the Yukon Territory in the company of a licensed outfitter or guide.

Sport & Activities

The Yukon Territory, in Canada's far northwest, consists mainly of mountain ranges cut by the mighty Yukon River and its tributaries. This unspoilt wilderness is relatively well served by roads left over from the days of Canada's gold rush and from an attempt to exploit oil reserves, which facilitates access by adventure seekers.
Watersports: Canoeing is particularly popular. In summer, the tributaries of the *Yukon River* (including the *Teslin*, the *Big Salmon* and the *Pelly*) offer fast-flowing, flat water. Most trips are easy to arrange because starting and ending points have roadside access. There is also the advantage of being able to re-supply from communities located along the riverbank. Trips ranging from a few hours to several weeks can be organised. There is no shortage of **white water** for more experienced canoeists. While wild rivers such as the *Bonnet Plume* and the *Firth* must be reached by bush plane, other spectacular rivers, such as the *Tatchenshini* and the *South Macmillan* are accessible by road. Simple riverside campsites provide accommodation. River travellers are advised to leave details of their itineraries with the authorities before setting out. **River** and **lake cruises** offer the opportunity to see **wildlife** such as bears, eagles and Dall's sheep.
Other: All the usual outdoor pursuits are easily arranged, either independently or through outfitters and specialist operators. National parks such as *Kluane* in the far southwest (containing more than 4000 glaciers) and *Ivvavik* in the far northwest, contain **hiking** trails and other facilities. *Mount Logan*, in the St Elias Range in Kluane National Park, is the second-highest peak in North America at 5959m (19,550ft). **Cross-country skiing** is possible in in winter. Other activities include **glacier flights**, **helicopter tours** and **fishing**.
For general information about sport and activities in Canada, see the main *Canada* section.

Credit: © Tourism Yukon

Social Profile

FOOD & DRINK: Some of Yukon's food is very distinctive but difficult to produce commercially. Moose meat is cooked in several ways from steaming to smoking or pot roasting, and accompanied by *sourdough* and vegetables. Dall sheep, mountain goat, caribou and porcupine are also eaten. Wild fish features on most menus. There are restaurants throughout the area, but the best selection is in Whitehorse, Dawson City and Watson Lake. Most alcohol is imported from other areas of Canada and the USA. A local speciality is *hooch* (a blend of imported and Canadian rum); it is only available in the Yukon Territory. Whitehorse is home to the *Chilkoot Brewing Company* which produces unique beers and ales.
NIGHTLIFE: Nightlife is best during the historical festivals and carnivals reflecting the pioneer spirit that explored the region. However, Dawson City has legalised gambling, live vaudeville theatre and a floor show at *Gertie's* featuring Cancan girls and honky-tonk piano.
SHOPPING: Special items include First Nation moccasins, jewellery, art and carvings. Check with Revenue Canada or the Visitor Reception Centres to determine qualification for the Goods Service Tax rebate. **Shopping hours**: Mon-Wed and Sat 1000-1800, Thurs-Fri 1000-2100.
SPECIAL EVENTS: For full details, contact Tourism Yukon (see *Contact Addresses* section). The following is a selection of special events occurring in Yukon in 2005:
Feb 13 *Yukon Quest International Sled Dog Race*, Whitehorse. **Mar 11-20** *International Federation of Sleddog Sports World Championships*, Dawson. **Mar 17-20** *Thaw-Di-Gras Spring Carnival*, Dawson. **May 21-22** *Dawson City International Gold Show*. **Jun 21** *Aboriginal Day Celebrations*. **Jun 24** *Jean Baptiste Day*. **Jul 22-24** *Dawson City Music Festival*. **Aug 10-15** *Discovery Days Celebrations*, Dawson City. **Sep 9-10** *Klondike Trail International Road Relay*, Whitehorse. **Oct 15** *Octoberfest*, Watson Lake. **Dec** *Dawson City Traditional Christmas Party*.

Business Profile

COMMERCIAL INFORMATION: The following organisation can offer advice: Yukon Chamber of Commerce, 201-208 Main Street, Whitehorse, Yukon Territory Y1A 2A9 (tel: (867) 667 2000; fax: (867) 667 2001; e-mail: ycc@yukonchamber.com; website: www.yukonchamber.com).
CONFERENCES/CONVENTIONS: For information on conferences and conventions in the Yukon Territory, contact the Visit Canada Centre or Yukon Convention Bureau, 208-100 Main Street, Whitehorse, Yukon Y1A 2A7 (tel: (867) 668 3555; fax: (867) 668 3550; e-mail: info@ycb.ca; website: www.meetingsyukon.com).

Climate

Summers are warm with almost continuous daylight during June. Winters are bitterly cold.
Required clothing: *Summer* – days can be hot, but sweaters and light jackets are advised for the evenings. *Spring and Autumn* – coats and gloves are required for outdoor activities. *Winter* – thermal underwear, wool sweaters, parkas, wool gloves or mittens and mukluks or felt-lined boots are advised for the winter.

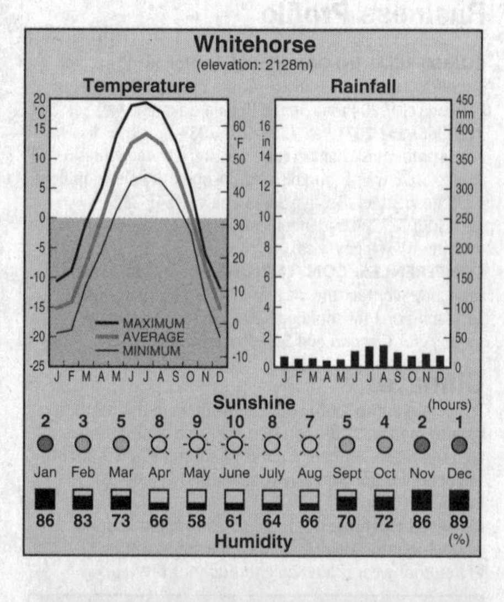

Credit: © Tourism Yukon

Cape Verde

LATEST TRAVEL ADVICE CONTACTS

British Foreign and Commonwealth Office
Tel: (0870) 606 0290 Website: www.fco.gov.uk

US Department of State
Website: http://travel.state.gov/travel

Canadian Department of Foreign Affairs and Int'l Trade
Tel: (1 800) 267 8376 Website: www.dfait-maeci.gc.ca

Location: Atlantic Ocean, off coast of West Africa.

Country dialling code: 238.

ACI (Agência Cabo-verdiana de Promoção do Investimento, do Turismo e das)
Rua Cruz do Papa, Achada Santo António, PO Box 89C, Praia, Santiago, Cape Verde
Tel: 260 4111 *or* 262 1488 *or* 2689.
Fax: 262 2657.
E-mail: cvinvestment@cvtelecom.cv
Website: www.virtualcapeverde.net

Embassy of the Republic of Cape Verde
Avenue Jeanne 29, 1050 Brussels, Belgium
Tel: (2) 643 6270.
Fax: (2) 646 3385.
E-mail: emb.caboverde@skynet.be

The British Embassy in Dakar deals with enquiries relating to Cape Verde (see *Senegal* **section).**

British Consulate
c/o Shell Cabo Verde, Sarl, Avenida Amilcar Cabral CP4, São Vincente, Cape Verde
Tel: 232 6625-7.
Fax: 232 6629.
E-mail: antonio.a.canuto@scv.sims.com

Embassy of the Republic of Cape Verde
3415 Massachusetts Avenue, NW, Washington, DC 20007, USA
Tel: (202) 965 6820.
Fax: (202) 965 1207.
E-mail: ambacvus@verison.net
Website: www.virtualcapeverde.net
Also deals with enquiries from Canada.

Embassy of the United States of America
Street address: Rua Abilio Macedo 6, Praia, Santiago, Cape Verde
Postal address: PO Box 201, Santiago, Cape Verde
Tel: 261 5616.
Fax: 261 1355.
E-mail: praiaconsularpraia@state.gov (consular enquiries)
Website: http://capeverde.usembassy.gov

The Canadian Embassy in Dakar deals with enquiries relating to Cape Verde (see *Senegal* **section).**

TIMATIC CODES

Health	AMADEUS: **TI-DFT/JIB/HE** GALILEO/WORLDSPAN: **TI-DFT/JIB/HE** SABRE: **TIDFT/JIB/HE**
Visa	AMADEUS: **TI-DFT/JIB/VI** GALILEO/WORLDSPAN: **TI-DFT/JIB/VI** SABRE: **TIDFT/JIB/VI**

To access TIMATIC country information on Health and Visa regulations through the Computer Reservations System (CRS), type in the appropriate command line listed above.

General Information

AREA: 4036 sq km (1558 sq miles).
POPULATION: 434,625 (2000).
POPULATION DENSITY: 112.5 per sq km.
CAPITAL: Cidade de Praia. **Population**: 94,757 (2000).
GEOGRAPHY: Cape Verde is situated in the Atlantic Ocean, 600km (450 miles) west-northwest of Senegal and comprises 10 volcanic islands and five islets in two groups: *Barlavento* (Windwards) and *Sotavento* (Leewards). In the former group are the islands of São Vicente, Santo Antão, São Nicolau, Santa Luzia, Sal and Boa Vista, along with the smaller islands of Branco and Raso; the Sotavento group comprises the islands of Santiago, Maio, Fogo and Brava, along with the smaller islands of Rei and Rombo. Most have mountain peaks; the highest being Pico do Cano, an active volcano, which is on Fogo. The islands are generally rocky and eroded, and have never been able to support more than subsistence agriculture (maize, bananas, sugar cane and coffee are the main crops); low rainfall over the last 10 years has crippled food production and forced the islands to depend on international aid.
GOVERNMENT: Republic. Gained independence from Portugal in 1975. **Head of State**: President Pedro Pires since 2001. **Head of Government**: Prime Minister José Maria Neves since 2001.
LANGUAGE: The official language is Portuguese. Creole is spoken by most of the inhabitants. Some English, French and Spanish are spoken.
RELIGION: 92.8 per cent of the population are Roman Catholic with a Protestant minority of one per cent.
TIME: GMT - 1.
ELECTRICITY: 220 volts AC, 50Hz.
COMMUNICATIONS: Telephone: IDD is possible to main cities. Country code: 238. Improvements to rural areas are in progress and the islands have around 22,900 telephones. **Mobile telephone:** GSM 900 network operated by *Cabo Verde Telecom*. **Fax:** Services are available at post offices and major hotels. **Internet:** Major hotels offer laptop connections. Public access is available at the offices of *Cabo Verde Telecom*. Privately-run business centres in the main towns offer e-mail, Internet and fax facilities. **Post:** Postal facilities can be slow with deliveries to Europe normally taking over a week. **Press:** Newspapers are in Portuguese. There are no daily newspapers. The weekly newspapers with the highest circulation figures are *Horizonte* and the independent *A Semana*.
Radio: BBC World Service (website: www.bbc.co.uk/worldservice) and Voice of America (website: www.voa.gov) can be received. From time to time the frequencies change and the most up-to-date can be found online.

Passport/Visa

	Passport Required?	Visa Required?	Return Ticket Required?
Full British	Yes	Yes	Yes
Australian	Yes	Yes	Yes
Canadian	Yes	Yes	Yes
USA	Yes	Yes	Yes
Other EU	Yes	Yes	Yes
Japanese	Yes	Yes	Yes

Note: *Regulations and requirements may be subject to change at short notice, and you are advised to contact the appropriate diplomatic or consular authority before finalising travel arrangements. Details of these may be found at the head of this country's entry. Any numbers in the chart refer to the footnotes below.*

PASSPORTS: Passport valid for at least six months required by all.
VISAS: Required by all except the following:
(a) nationals of ECOWAS countries;
(b) former nationals of Cape Verde, their spouses and children, provided holding proof of origin;
(c) those continuing their journey to a third destination provided holding onward documentation and not leaving the airport.
Types of visa and cost: *Transit*, *Tourist*, *Business*: €38 (single entry); €72 (multiple-entry, for *Business* visas only). Prices may fluctuate - enquire at nearest Embassy or Consulate for details.
Validity: Valid for six months from date of issue for visits of up to 90 days.
Note: US nationals can obtain visas valid for five years.
Application to: Consulate (or Consular Section at Embassy); see *Contact Addresses* section. Visitors from countries where there is no Cape Verdean Embassy or Consulate can obtain visas at Cape Verdean Border Services offices at the airports on Praia and Sal.
Application requirements: (a) Two passport-size photos. (b) One application form. (c) Valid passport. (d) Fee. (e) Return/onward ticket.
Working days required: Where there are no complications, visas may be issued immediately; however, it is advisable to anticipate up to two days' delay.

Money

Currency: Cape Verde Escudo (CVEsc) = 100 centavos. Notes are in denominations of CVEsc5000, 2000, 1000 and 500. Coins are in denominations of CVEsc200, 100, 50, 20, 10, 5 and 1.
Currency exchange: Available at the airport and in local banks. Currency cannot be reconverted, except in Portugal. There are ATMs at the airport on Sal.
Credit & debit cards: Rarely used. A few major hotels accept Visa. Currency can be obtained in banks from credit cards but charges are very high.
Travellers cheques: Accepted in main towns and tourist areas. To avoid additional exchange rate charges, travellers are advised to take travellers cheques in Pounds Sterling or US Dollars.
Currency restrictions: The import and export of local currency is prohibited. The import of foreign currency is unlimited, subject to declaration on arrival and on departure. The export of foreign currency is limited to the equivalent of CVEsc1,000,000 or the amount declared on arrival, whichever is the larger.
Exchange rate indicators: The following figures are included as a guide to the movements of the Cape Verde Escudo against Sterling and the US Dollar:

Date	Feb '04	May '04	Aug '04	Nov '04
£1.00=	198.32	194.60	166.92	158.31
$1.00=	108.95	108.95	90.60	83.60

Banking hours: Mon-Fri 0800-1500.

Duty Free

The following goods may be taken into Cape Verde without incurring customs duty:
A reasonable amount of perfume, lotion and eau de cologne in opened bottles.
Note: There is, in principle, no free import of tobacco products and alcoholic beverages.

Public Holidays

2005: Jan 1 New Year's Day. **Jan 20** Heroes' Day. **Feb 7** Carnival. **May 1** Labour Day. **Jul 5** Independence Day. **Aug 15** Assumption (Day of Our Lady of Grace). **Sep 12** National Day. **Nov 1** All Saints' Day. **Dec 25** Christmas Day.
2006: Jan 1 New Year's Day. **Jan 20** Heroes' Day. **Feb 27** Carnival. **May 1** Labour Day. **Jul 5** Independence Day. **Aug 15** Assumption (Day of Our Lady of Grace). **Sep 12** National Day. **Nov 1** All Saints' Day. **Dec 25** Christmas Day.

Health

Special	Precautions?	Certificate Required?
Yellow Fever	No	No
Cholera	No	1
Typhoid & Polio	2	2
Malaria	3	N/A

Note: *Regulations and requirements may be subject to change at short notice, and you are advised to contact your doctor well in advance of your intended date of departure. Any numbers in the chart refer to the footnotes below.*

1: Following WHO guidelines issued in 1973, a cholera vaccination certificate is not a condition of entry to Cape Verde. However, cholera is a risk in this country and precautions could be considered. Up-to-date advice should be sought before deciding whether these precautions should include vaccination as medical opinion is divided over its effectiveness. For more information, see the *Health* appendix.
2: Typhoid fever is widespread and vaccination may be necessary. Polio vaccination may also be advised.
3: There is a limited risk of malaria from September to November on São Tiago Island.
Food & drink: All water should be regarded as being potentially contaminated. Water used for drinking, brushing teeth or making ice should have first been boiled or otherwise sterilised. Milk is unpasteurised and should be boiled. Powdered or tinned milk is available and is advised, but make sure that it is reconstituted with pure water. Avoid all dairy products. Only eat well-cooked meat and fish, preferably served hot. Pork, salad and mayonnaise may carry increased risk. Vegetables should be cooked and fruit peeled.
Other risks: *Hepatitis A* and *E* are highly endemic in sub-saharan Africa, but have very low occurrence in Cape Verde, but precautions are still advisable. *Hepatitis B* is hyperendemic in the region. Vaccination against *tetanus* is advised. *Giardia* occurs.
Health care: Health insurance, including emergency repatriation cover, is advised, although in-patient treatment is free in general wards on presentation of a passport. Treatment is private and expensive on the smaller islands.

Travel - International

AIR: The national airline is *TACV – Transportes Aéreos de Cabo Verde (VR)*, which offers flights to several European cities, including Amsterdam, Lisbon, Madrid, Paris, Porto and Verona, as well as to Las Palmas (Canary Islands). Discounts are available for frequent flyers and their families. Other airlines serving Cape Verde include *South African Airlines* and *TAP Air Portugal*. Information on international and internal flights, and flight tickets may be obtained from Cape Verde Travel, TACV's agent in the UK (tel: (01964) 536 191; fax: (01964) 536 192; e-mail: enquiries@capeverdetravel.com; website: www.capeverdetravel.com).

Approximate flight times: From *London* to Lisbon (Portugal) is two hours and from *Lisbon* to Sal is four hours; from *Boston* to Sal is eight hours; from *Paris* to Sal is six hours. Note that the stopover in Lisbon will sometimes be overnight if flying by *TAP Air Portugal*. The most convenient routes from *London* are via Paris and Amsterdam, where there are direct connections with no stopover time.

International airports: *Amilcar Cabral (SID)* on Sal, 2km (1 mile) south of Espargos, is the only airport with a runway long enough to take jets; there are six others throughout the islands. Airport facilities include several banks, duty free shops, refreshments, tourist information, car hire and left luggage facilities. Taxis are available to the city centre and to resort areas.

Francisco Mendes Airport now also has a paved runway in Praia, Santiago.

Departure tax: None.

SEA: Mindelo and Praia are the principal ports. São Vicente is served by passenger and cargo ships, but sea services are not frequent and may be costly.

Travel - Internal

AIR: *TACV – Cabo Verde Airlines* is the main domestic carrier. There are internal flights available to all inhabited islands except Brava and San Antao. The *Cape Verde Airpass*, available from TACV to passengers booking their long-distance tickets through the airline or their agents, offers discounted flights within Cape Verde. A minimum of two internal flights must be booked and the pass is valid for 22 days. These must be purchased with transatlantic tickets. Private charters are available from the *Cape Verde Express* air-taxi service.

SEA: There is a regular ferry service connecting Santiago, Fogo and Brava. There is also a daily ferry service operating between the port of Mindelo, São Vincente and Santo Antao. Cargo ships may also accept passengers. Sea conditions around Cape Verde are sometimes treacherous, due to many submerged rocks. Travel by sea to the southern islands of Brava and Fogo can be particularly disrupted.

ROAD: There are over 2250km (1400 miles) of roads on the islands, of which one-third are cobbled. There is a road improvement programme. Road conditions and driving standards are generally of a reasonable quality. Traffic drives on the right. Taxi fares should be agreed in advance. Drivers can be hired to see the main sights on the islands. Buses are satisfactory. **Car hire:** Available on the main islands. **Documentation:** An International Driving Permit is recommended and legally required.

TRAVEL TIMES: The following chart gives the approximate travel times (in hours and minutes) from **Cidade de Praia** to other major cities/towns in Cape Verde:

	Air	Sea
Saõ Vicente	0.45	-
Sal	0.45	-
Maio	0.15	-
Boa Vista	0.30	-
Fogo	0.40	-
Brava	-	12.00
São Nicolau	0.50	-

Accommodation

The range of accommodation is increasing rapidly. There are international hotels on the main islands. Otherwise there are small hotels on the smaller islands. There are also pensions. For further information, contact PROMEX (see *Contact Addresses* section) or local travel agencies.

Resorts & Excursions

The Cape Verde islands count as Africa's most westerly point. First discovered by the Portuguese in the 15th century, they have since featured on the routes of seafarers and traders sailing between Europe, Africa and Latin America, and their culture today reflects this mix. The climate is mainly dry (especially in the Leeward Islands) and years of deforestation, overcultivation and rather unpredictable weather have left the country's economy relatively fragile. Evidently, the islands are no longer as verdant as they were when the Portuguese named them, but they offer much to interest the traveller: long, white sand beaches, a vibrant creole culture and good conditions for watersports. Their isolation has left them unspoilt and comparatively undiscovered. The Government is now trying to develop the tourist industry, and the infrastructure is being expanded to accommodate the increasing number of visitors attracted to this unusual but attractive destination. Cape Verde has nine inhabited islands. **Santiago**, the largest and most populated of these, has a mountainous, lush interior fringed by small sandy beaches. The island's capital, **Praia**, is a lively, pleasant town with a good nightlife. Other attractions include **Cidade Velha**, the first Portuguese settlement on Cape Verde. There are ruins and old buildings and, on the hill above, the **Fort Real de San Felipe**, an old Portuguese fort. The attractive fishing village of **Tarrafal** features one of the island's best beaches and contains the **old colonial prison** where the Portuguese dictator, Salazar, held dissidents from all over his empire in the first two-thirds of the 20th century. This is currently being restored. The island of **Sal**, characterised by its fine white sand beaches, attracts most of the package tourists. There are three dive schools, and windsurfing conditions are excellent. The famous **salt pits**, after which the island is named, produced salt for much of the former Portuguese empire. **São Vicente** is home to the deep-water port of **Mindelo**, a lively town with old colonial buildings and a thriving local music scene. Cape Verde's most famous daughter, Cesaria Evora (an internationally-known singer who performs in the traditional style), hails from the island, as do many other leading local musicians. São Vicente's carnival is the liveliest in Cape Verde, while the traditional **Baia das Gatas** festival, which usually falls in August, has become internationally renowned for the standard of its music. The other islands in the archipelago are quieter and more appealing to nature lovers. **Boa Vista** features shallow seas and the 16km- (10 mile-) pristine **Santa Monica beach**. **Sao Nicolau** has a dramatic landscape of steep rocky peaks in its interior with black sand beaches around its edge. **Maio** is isolated and quiet with simple fishing villages, white sand beaches and sand dunes. Sea turtles lay their eggs on the beaches. **Brava**, a lush island with more rainfall than most, offers beautiful views of the coast from its plateau and an abundance of unique plant life. There are no facilities for watersports. The mountainous island of **Fogo** features an active volcano and black sandy beaches. Coffee, grapes and local wine are amongst the island's produce. **Santo Antão**'s spectacular scenery and rugged coastline attract mainly walkers and climbers, especially given that there are no beaches. It is one of Cape Verde's greener islands and its interior contains forested hills. Many of the deep flat-bottomed valleys are the craters of extinct volcanoes, long overgrown by trees and tropical vegetation. Visitors should make sure they sample Cape Verdean rum or *grog*, produced on Santo Antão.

Sport & Activities

Hiking: The islands' spectacular scenery is ideal for hiking. The volcanic island of Fogo offers good hikes with excellent views, while the scenery on Santo Antão is particularly lush. *Ribeira Grande Mountain* on Santo Antão takes a day to climb but is well worth the effort. It is advisable to take a guide. There are also excellent walks on Brava and São Nicolau. **Birdwatching** trips can be arranged.

Watersports: Sailing charters can be arranged, depending on time, weather and number of passengers. **Surfing** and **windsurfing** are both available on Sal, although the surfing is not generally suitable for beginners. **Diving** is gaining in popularity. There are several dive centres, mainly on the islands of Sal and Boavista, with qualified personnel and equipment. These islands also offer good wreck sites. Water temperatures are good all year round, though the seas can be rough. Some boats and equipment are available for **fishing**. Visitors could consider taking their own equipment.

Live music: There is no shortage of live Cape Verdean music played in bars and clubs. Local musicians may hope to follow in the footsteps of their internationally known compatriots such as Cesaria Evora. Music is an integral part of daily life in the islands.

Social Profile

FOOD & DRINK: There is an increasing number of restaurants and cafes. The main local culinary speciality is *cachupa*, a mess of maize and beans. Another delicious Cape Verdean treat is *pastel com diablo dentro* ('pastry with the devil inside') - a mix of tuna, onions, tomatoes, and pastry made from boiled potatoes and corn flour. Fruits include mangoes, bananas, papayas, *goiabas* (guavas), *zimbrão*, *tambarinas*, *marmelos*, *azedinhas*, *tamaras* and *cocos*.

Local beer, wine and spirits are commonly available; grogue is a popular choice. Soft drinks are expensive.

NIGHTLIFE: Some hotels provide evening entertainment. Small villages will have a lively taverna. Most nightlife is on the main islands: there are 21 nightclubs in Cape Verde – eight on Santiago, seven on Sal, five on São Vicente and one on Fogo. Praia has a cultural centre at which local Cape Verdean artists and instrumentalists perform.

SHOPPING: There are daily markets. The Santa Catarina market is held Wednesday and Saturday. Coconut shells are carved by local craftsmen; there is also pottery, lacework and basketry. **Shopping hours**: Mon-Fri 0800-1300 and 1500-1900, Sat 0900-1300.

SPECIAL EVENTS: Many Saints' days are celebrated all over the islands, and towns and villages have their own local festivals; further details may be obtained from ACI (see *Contact Addresses* section). The following is a selection of special events celebrated annually in Cape Verde: **Feb** *Carnival* (with Street Parades), Praia and Mindelo. **May** *Festa de Santa Cruz*. **May-Jun** *Tabanka*, São Tiago and Fogo. **Jun** *Festival of the Solstice*. **Jul** *Independence Day Celebrations*; *Festa do Municipio de Boa Vista*. **Aug** *Festival Baia das Gatas*; *Festival of Music of Praia de Santa Cruz*.

SOCIAL CONVENTIONS: The usual European social courtesies should be observed. **Tipping**: It is normal to give 10 per cent for good service.

Business Profile

ECONOMY: About one-quarter of the working population is engaged in agriculture. Maize and beans are the main crops; a variety of fruit and vegetables are also grown. The agricultural sector is especially vulnerable to the periodic droughts that afflict the islands, often lasting for several years. Meanwhile, throughout the 1990s, the fishing industry has received substantial international aid, reflected in the result that the islands' catches now contribute almost half of the total export earnings. Cape Verde joined the International Whaling Commission in 2002 and, with the incentive of an aid package from Japan, has supported the resumption of commercial whaling. The small industrial sector is dominated by fish processing and canning factories, to which electrical and other machinery, chemicals and textiles have recently been added. Mining is confined to salt and pozzolana (used in cement production). Future economic development is being focused on tourism, transhipment facilities and 'offshore' financial services. A further vital source of national income are the remittances provided by émigré communities – some 700,000 Cape Verdeans live abroad, mainly in the USA. Portugal, The Netherlands, Brazil, the USA and Japan meet the bulk of Cape Verde's import requirements. Cape Verde is a member of the West African Economic Community (ECOWAS).

BUSINESS: All correspondence should be in English or French. Most of Cape Verde's business links are with Portugal. **Office hours**: Mon-Fri 0800-1230 and 1430-1800.

COMMERCIAL INFORMATION: The following organisations can offer advice: Câmara de Comercio Industria, Agricultura e Serviços de Barlavento, Rua de Luz 31, CP 728, Mindelo, São Vicente (tel: 328 495; fax: 328 496; e-mail: camara.com@mail.cvtelecom.cv; website: www.cciasb.com); *or* Câmara de Comercio Industria e Servicos de Sotavento, Largo Pinheiro Chagas, Edificio Shopping Moeda, Praia, Santiago (tel: 617 234 *or* 615 352; fax: 617 235; e-mail: cciss@cvtelecom.cv); *or* Centro de Promoção Turística, do Investimento e das Exportações (PROMEX; see *Contact Addresses* section).

CONFERENCES/CONVENTIONS: The following organisation can offer advice: Ministry for Education, Science, Youth and Sport, Palácio do Governo, Santiago, Praia (tel: 610 507; fax: 612 764). The larger hotels on the main islands can provide conference facilities.

Climate

Generally temperate, but rainfall is very low.

Required clothing: Lightweight throughout the year, tropical for midsummer.

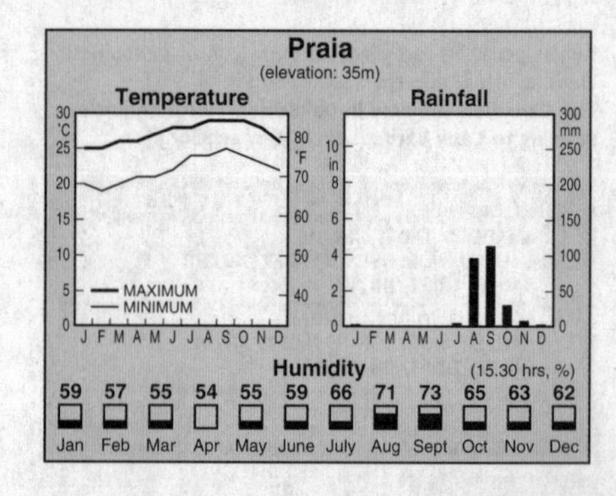

Cayman Islands

LATEST TRAVEL ADVICE CONTACTS

British Foreign and Commonwealth Office
Tel: (0870) 606 0290 Website: www.fco.gov.uk
US Department of State
Website: http://travel.state.gov/travel
Canadian Department of Foreign Affairs and Int'l Trade
Tel: (1 800) 267 8376 Website: www.dfait-maeci.gc.ca

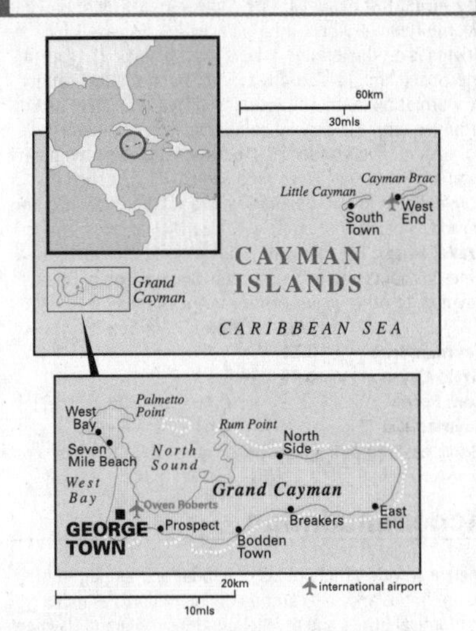

Credit: © Cayman Islands Department of Tourism

Location: Caribbean, south of Cuba, 720km (480 miles) southwest of Miami.

Country dialling code: 1 345.

Cayman Islands Department of Tourism
Street address: 2nd Floor, Corporate Office, Hospital Road, George Town BWI, Grand Cayman
Postal address: PO Box 67 GT, George Town, Grand Cayman
Tel: 949 0623. Fax: 949 4053. E-mail: pr@caymanislands.ky
Website: www.caymanislands.ky *or* www.divecayman.ky
Cayman Islands Government Office and Department of Tourism
6 Arlington Street, London SW1A 1RE, UK
Tel: (020) 7491 7772 (government office) *or* 7491 7771 (department of tourism). Fax: (020) 7491 7944 (government office) *or* 7409 7773 (department of tourism).
E-mail: info-uk@caymanislands.ky (general enquiries) *or* info@cigo.co.uk (government office).
Website: www.caymanislands.co.uk
The UK Passport Service
London Passport Office, Globe House, 89 Eccleston Square, London SW1V 1PN, UK
Tel: (0870) 521 0410 (national advice line) *or* (020) 7901 2150 (visa enquiries for British Overseas Territories).
Fax: (020) 7271 8403 *or* 7901 2162.
E-mail: info@passport.gov.uk *or* london@ukpa.gov.uk
Website: www.passport.gov.uk *or* www.ukpa.gov.uk
Opening hours: Mon-Fri 0730-1900, Sat 0900-1600 (appointments only).
Regional offices in: Belfast, Durham, Glasgow, Liverpool, Newport and Peterborough.
Personal callers for visas should go to the agency window in the collection room of the London office.
Cayman Islands Department of Tourism
3 Park Avenue, 39th Floor, New York, NY 10016, USA
Tel: (212) 889 9009. Fax: (212) 889 9125.
E-mail: pbush@caymanislands.ky
Website: www.caymanislands.ky
Offices also in: Chicago and Houston.
Cayman Islands Department of Tourism
Suite 306, 234 Eglinton Avenue East, Toronto, Ontario M4P 1K5, Canada
Tel: (416) 485 1550 *or* (800) 263 5805 (toll-free in Canada).
Fax: (416) 485 7578.
E-mail: info-canada@caymanislands.ky
Website: www.caymanislands.ky/canada

TIMATIC CODES

Health
AMADEUS: **TI-DFT/JIB/HE**
GALILEO/WORLDSPAN: **TI-DFT/JIB/HE**
SABRE: **TIDFT/JIB/HE**

Visa
AMADEUS: **TI-DFT/JIB/VI**
GALILEO/WORLDSPAN: **TI-DFT/JIB/VI**
SABRE: **TIDFT/JIB/VI**

To access TIMATIC country information on Health and Visa regulations through the Computer Reservations System (CRS), type in the appropriate command line listed above.

General Information

AREA: 262 sq km (102 sq miles).
POPULATION: 40,900 (official estimate 2000).
POPULATION DENSITY: 156.1 per sq km.
CAPITAL: George Town. **Population**: 20,626 (1999).
GEOGRAPHY: The Cayman Islands are situated in the Caribbean, 290km (180 miles) northwest of Jamaica, 240km (480 miles) south of Cuba and 770km (480 miles) south of Miami. The island country comprises Grand Cayman, the largest and most populous of the islands, and the sister islands of Little Cayman and Cayman Brac, which lie approximately 143km (89 miles) northeast of Grand Cayman and are separated from each other by a channel about 11km (7 miles) wide. The islands are peaks of a subterranean mountain range extending from Cuba towards the Gulf of Honduras. The beaches are said to be the best in the Caribbean, the most notable being Seven Mile Beach on Grand Cayman. Tall pines line many of the beaches; those located on the east and west coasts are equally well protected offshore by the Barrier Reef.
GOVERNMENT: British Crown Colony since 1670. **Head of State**: HM Queen Elizabeth II, represented locally by Governor Bruce Dinwiddy since 2002.
LANGUAGE: English is the official language, with a distinctive 'brogue' reflecting heritage of Welsh, Scottish and English ancestors still distinguishing the speech of the Caymanian people. The number of Jamaican residents in the workforce means the Jamaican patois and accompanying heavier accent is also common. Spanish, particularly regional dialects of Central America and Cuba, is also widely spoken.
RELIGION: Mainly Presbyterian with Anglican, Roman Catholic, Seventh Day Adventists, Pilgrims, Pilgrim Holiness Church of God, Jehovah's Witnesses and Bahai minorities on Grand Cayman; Baptists on Cayman Brac.
TIME: GMT - 5.
ELECTRICITY: 120 volts AC, 60Hz. American-style (flat) two-pin plugs are standard.
COMMUNICATIONS: Telephone: A modern telephone system links the Cayman Islands to the world by submarine cable and satellite. Full IDD is available. A Cardphone service is available at select locations on all three islands. Pre-paid phonecards in values of CI$10, CI$15 and CI$30 can be purchased at the *Cable & Wireless* main office in Anderson Square in George Town and at the *Cayman Brac* post office and petrol stations. Country code: 1 345. Outgoing international code: 00. **Mobile telephone:** TDMA network. Network providers are *Cable & Wireless Caribbean Cellular*, *Digicel Cayman LTD* (website: www.digicelcayman.com) and *Wireless Ventures LTD* (website: www.attwireless.com), offering GSM 850/1900, GSM 900/1800 and GSM 850/1900, respectively. Unregistered roaming is available – visitors with TDMA handsets can make calls without registering, provided they can give a credit card number. **Fax:** Available at most hotels and banks. Some businesses also have public facilities. **Internet:** ISPs include *Cable & Wireless* (website: www.cwinternet.ky). There are many Internet cafes throughout the Cayman Islands and many hotels also offer Internet facilities. **Telegram:** Services are provided by *Cable & Wireless (West Indies) Limited* under government franchise. Public telegraph operates daily 0730-1800, accepting cables from any country. **Post:** Mail is not delivered to private addresses in the Cayman Islands, but collected from numbered PO boxes. *Poste Restante* mail should be addressed 'General Delivery' at the post office. Post office hours: Mon-Fri 0830-1530, Sat 0830-1200.
Press: *The Caymanian Compass* is published week-days.
Radio: BBC World Service (website: www.bbc.co.uk/worldservice) and Voice of America (website: www.voa.gov) can be received. From time to time the frequencies change and the most up-to-date can be found online.

Passport/Visa

	Passport Required?	Visa Required?	Return Ticket Required?
Full British	1	No	Yes
Australian	Yes	No	Yes
Canadian	1	No	Yes
USA	1	No	Yes
Other EU	Yes	No	Yes
Japanese	Yes	No	Yes

Note: *Regulations and requirements may be subject to change at short notice, and you are advised to contact the appropriate diplomatic or consular authority before finalising travel arrangements. Details of these may be found at the head of this country's entry. Any numbers in the chart refer to the footnotes below.*

PASSPORTS: 1. Passport valid for period of stay required by all except nationals of Canada, the UK and the USA, provided holding proof of nationality (such as a birth certificate or a notarised affidavit of citizenship) and provided return or onward ticket shows that the visitor will leave the Cayman Islands within one month.
VISAS: Any person resident in the USA or Canada who arrives in the Cayman Islands directly from the USA or Canada and who, on landing, can produce a valid US Alien Registration Card may be permitted to enter and remain without a visa for up to 30 days. A visa is required by all except the following for a period of up to 30 days:
(a) nationals of countries mentioned in the chart above;
(b) nationals of Commonwealth countries (except nationals of Bangladesh, Cameroon, The Gambia, Ghana, India, Nigeria, Pakistan, Sierra Leone, Sri Lanka, and Uganda who *do* require a visa);
(c) nationals of Andorra, Argentina, Bahrain, Brazil, Chile, Costa Rica, Dominican Republic, Ecuador, El Salvador, Guatemala, Iceland, Israel, Kuwait, Liechtenstein, Mexico, Monaco, Norway, Oman, Panama, Peru, San Marino, Saudi Arabia, Switzerland and Venezuela;
(d) transit passengers continuing their journey by the same or first connecting aircraft provided holding onward or return documentation and not leaving the airport.
Note: (a) Cruise ship passengers do not require visas to enter the Cayman Islands. (b) Visitors are prohibited from engaging in any form of employment unless holding a Work Permit. A short-term Work Permit can usually be obtained within one to two weeks.
Types of visa and cost: *Tourist*, *Transit* and *Business*. All visas cost £28.
Validity: Three months, though this may vary. Visitors may remain in the Cayman Islands for up to one month,

although an extension of up to six months may then be applied for, provided return tickets and proof of financial means/funding is submitted on arrival or at the immigration department.
Application to: Nearest Embassy.
Application requirements: (a) Two application forms. (b) Valid passport. (c) Sufficient funds to cover duration of stay.
Working days required: Dependent upon nature of application. Allow three weeks.

Credit: © Cayman Islands Department of Tourism

Money

Currency: Cayman Islands Dollar (CI$) = 100 cents. Notes are in denominations of CI$100, 50, 25, 10, 5 and 1. Coins are in denominations of 25, 10, 5 and 1 cents.
Note: The Cayman Islands Dollar is tied to the US Dollar at a fixed rate of CI$1 = US$1.25 although bank charges for currency exchange may result in minor fluctuations.
Currency exchange: US Dollars circulate freely and are the best currency to exchange. ATMs accepting Visa and MasterCard with Cirrus affiliation are located at Cayman National Bank and other banks, and at Owen Roberts International Airport.
Credit & debit cards: All major credit cards are widely accepted. Check with your credit or debit card company for details of merchant acceptability and other services which may be available.
Travellers cheques: Readily accepted. To avoid additional exchange rate charges, travellers are advised to take travellers cheques in US Dollars.
Currency restrictions: No restriction on import or export of foreign or local currency apart from import of Jamaican dollars, which is restricted to J$20.
Exchange rate indicators: The following figures are included as a guide to the movement of the Cayman Islands Dollar against Sterling and the US Dollar:

Date	Feb '04	May '04	Aug '04	Nov '04
£1.00=	1.50	1.47	1.51	1.56
$1.00=	0.82	0.83	0.82	0.82

Banking hours: Mon-Thurs 0900-1600, Fri 0900-1630. Some banks are open on Saturday mornings.

Duty Free

The following goods may be taken into the Cayman Islands by travellers over the age of 18 without incurring customs duty:
200 cigarettes or 50 cigars or 225g of tobacco; 1l of alcoholic beverages (including wines).
Prohibited items: Base or counterfeit coins, instruments and appliances for gambling, narcotics and utensils.
Note: A permit from the commissioner of police/district commissioner is required for the import of firearms, ammunition and explosives (besides gun powder and blasting powder).
Visitors should be aware that products made from farmed green sea turtles available in limited selections at the *Cayman Turtle Farm Ltd* are offered for local consumption. The importation of genuine sea turtle products is strictly prohibited by any countries that have signed the *Convention on International Trade in Endangered Species (1978)*, including the USA, Canada and the UK.
The export of lobster, conch or conch meat is prohibited (unless in transit). There are also a number of marine and animal specimens that may not be taken from the Islands; it is best to check prior to travel.

Public Holidays

2005: Jan 1 New Year's Day. **Jan 27** National Heroes Day. **Feb 9** Ash Wednesday. **Mar 25** Good Friday. **Mar 28** Easter Monday. **May 16** Discovery Day. **Jun 13** Queen's Birthday. **Jul 4** Constitution Day. **Nov 11** Remembrance Day. **Dec 25** Christmas Day. **Dec 26** Boxing Day.
2006: Jan 1 New Year's Day. **Jan 27** National Heroes Day. **Mar 1** Ash Wednesday. **Apr 14** Good Friday. **Apr 17** Easter Monday. **May 15** Discovery Day. **Jun 12** Queen's Birthday. **Jul 3** Constitution Day. **Nov 11** Remembrance Day. **Dec 25** Christmas Day. **Dec 26** Boxing Day.

Health

	Special Precautions?	Certificate Required?
Yellow Fever	No	No
Cholera	No	No
Typhoid & Polio	1	N/A
Malaria	No	N/A

Note: Regulations and requirements may be subject to change at short notice, and you are advised to contact your doctor well in advance of your intended date of departure. Any numbers in the chart refer to the footnotes below.

1: Immunisation against typhoid is advised.
Other risks: Outbreaks of *dengue fever* and *dengue haemorrhagic fever* can occur. *Hepatitis A* has been reported in the northern Caribbean. Immunisations against *TB*, *diphtheria* and *hepatitis B* and *C* are sometimes advised.
Health care: Modern medical facilities are available, particularly on Grand Cayman and Cayman Brac, including government-operated hospitals on both islands. There is also an island-wide, 24-hour 911 (*or* 555) emergency service. Serious cases may be transferred to Miami. Health costs are similar to the UK. Private insurance is recommended. Insect repellent is useful to counter mosquitoes and sandflies.
Note: Divers should note that the George Town Hospital also has a two-man, double-lock decompression chamber staffed by trained operators supervised by a physician experienced in treating diving-related accidents.

Travel - International

AIR: The Cayman Islands national airline is *Cayman Airways (KX)* (website: www.caymanairways.com). *Cayman Airways* flies to Grand Cayman and Cayman Brac from Miami, Tampa, Houston and Kingston (Jamaica). *British Airways* operates four scheduled flights per week from London Heathrow to Grand Cayman. *Air Jamaica* flies to the Cayman Islands from Kingston and Montego Bay. Airlines operating from mainland USA to Grand Cayman include *Air Canada*, *American Airlines*, *Continental Airlines*, *Delta Airlines*, *Northwest Airlines* and *USAir*.
Approximate flight times: From *London* to Grand Cayman is 10 hours and from *Miami* to Grand Cayman is one hour five minutes. From *Miami* to Cayman Brac is one hour 35 minutes.
International airports: *Grand Cayman (GCM) (Owen Roberts International Airport)* is 2km (1 mile) east of the city. Taxis are available to the centre (travel time - 10 minutes), operating from 0600 to 2300, for a fare of about US$10. There is also an airport bus available that must be pre-booked. Airport facilities include an outgoing duty free shop for all international departures, banks/bureaux de change, post office, car hire (*Avis*, *Budget*, *Coconut* and *Hertz*) and a bar/restaurant (open for all arrivals and departures).
Cayman Brac (CYB) (Gerard Smith Airport) is 8km (5 miles) from the town. Taxis meet all flights (travel time - 10 minutes).
Departure tax: CI$20 or US$25. Travellers under 12 years of age and transit passengers continuing their journey within 24 hours are exempt.
SEA: Grand Cayman is one of the most popular Caribbean ports and a busy port of call for leading international cruise lines operating from North America, Mexico and Europe. The Cayman Islands are legally supposed to limit the number of cruise passengers to 6000 (three to four ships) per day. Tuesday, Wednesday and Thursday are the busiest days in port. There is no cruise ship dock and passengers are ferried ashore by tenders to the North or South dock terminals in George Town. Cruise lines serving the Cayman Islands include *Carnival*, *Crystal Cruises*, *Cunard*, *Fred Olsen*, *Norwegian*, *P&O Cruises*, *Royal Caribbean* and *Seven Seas*.

Travel - Internal

AIR: The main island of Grand Cayman is connected to Cayman Brac and to Little Cayman by internal flights run by *Cayman Airways* and *Island Air* and to Little Cayman by *Island Air* , plus a service between Cayman Brac and Little Cayman.
ROAD: A good road network connects the coastal towns of all three main islands. **Bus**: Public minibuses operate from George Town to West Bay (every 15 minutes), to Bodden Town (every 30 minutes) and to East End and North Side (every hour). Fares are CI$1.50 to CI$2 each way. The bus terminal is located opposite the public library on Edward Street in central George Town. Services are normally from 0600-2300 (until midnight at weekends for most routes). There are 38 minibuses operated by 24 licensed operators. Routes are colour coded (with colours marked on the front and rear of the buses). Public buses have blue licence plates and standard fares are displayed inside. **Mopeds and scooters**: Available for hire on Grand Cayman and Cayman Brac. Riders are required by law to wear a helmet at all times. The average fee is US$27.50 per day, which includes helmet and permit. **Bicycles**: Available for hire on all three islands. On Cayman Brac and Little Cayman, most hotels have bicycles available for complimentary guest use. **Taxi**: There are large fleets of taxis operating from all resorts, the cruise dock at George town and the international airports. **Car hire**: Most major car hire companies are represented in George Town. 4-wheel-drive vehicles are also available. Driving is on the left and drivers must be over 21 years of age. Speed limits are strictly enforced and seat belts must be worn at all times. Full insurance is required and must be arranged with the car hire company; some companies will not insure drivers under 25. **Documentation**: A temporary local driving licence is required, which will be issued at a nominal charge on presentation of a valid licence from the traveller's country of origin.
Travel times: The following chart gives approximate travel times (in hours and minutes) from **George Town**, Grand Cayman, to other major centres in the islands.

	Air	Road	Sea
Cayman Brac	0.30	-	-
Little Cayman	0.45	-	-
Rum Point	-	0.45	1.15
Cayman Kai	-	0.45	-

Note: Cayman Brac to Little Cayman is 10 minutes by air.

Accommodation

There is a wide variety of accommodation, ranging from luxury hotels and self-catering condominiums to more economical hotels and dive lodges. Most of Grand Cayman's condominiums are superbly situated on beaches and coastal areas and guests can walk out of the apartments onto beautiful beaches with crystal clear water. Many condominiums have been built in the last few years and are equipped with the latest fittings and furnishings, as well as central facilities such as swimming pools and tennis courts.
HOTELS: The leading hotels are located on the coast. Some of the best known overlook Grand Cayman's renowned *Seven Mile Beach*, a dazzling stretch of fine powdery sand said to be one of the world's most beautiful beaches. There is also a fine selection of diving resort hotels. Hotels providing accommodation with 100 rooms are considered large in the Cayman Islands and are generally only found on Grand Cayman. Prices are seasonal, being higher in the winter than in the summer (when some hotels offer free accommodation for children under 12). The high season begins on 15 December and usually runs through to 15 April. During that time, visitors should expect to pay up to 50 per cent more for a room. A 10 per cent government accommodation tax is payable to the hotel on departure. Most also add a service charge (about 10 per cent). For more information, contact the Cayman Islands Department of Tourism (see *Contact Addresses* section). **Grading**: A government board of control monitors standards in various hotels and establishments. Hotels vary in standard from *luxury* (very comfortable, with some outstanding features) to *tourist class* (budget hotel).
SELF-CATERING: There is a wide variety of apartments and villas available, from the most luxurious to the relatively austere. The Department of Tourism can give full details of these, and also of beach cottages for families, and dive lodges.

Resorts & Excursions

There are three islands in this British Overseas Territory, which has long been associated with buccaneers and pirates.

GRAND CAYMAN

Most of the population lives on this island, surrounded by water rich in colourful marine life and spectacular coral reefs. There is a 6km- (4 mile-) stone wall at Bodden Town, known as Grand Cayman's 'Wall of China', built to protect residents from pirate attacks. **Seven Mile Beach** is the main tourist centre. Although highly developed, it retains its charm and the new developments are not as overwhelming as in some places. The peculiar rock formation at **Hell** evolved from skeletons of shells and corals solidified by salt and lime deposits. A close examination reveals petrified forms of sea life supposedly up to 20 million years old. Close by Seven Mile Beach is the unique **Cayman Turtle Farm**. Owing to conservation pressures, turtle meat is now usually only consumed locally (for more information, see Shopping in the *Social Profile* section). The capital of Grand Cayman is **George Town**. Along the harbour front are traditional Caymanian gingerbread-style buildings and, close by, modern banks and finance houses. **The Cayman Islands National**

Museum, based in the centre of George Town, offers a complete history of the islands. The **Pedro St James** historic site on Grand Cayman features an historically accurate restoration of the early 19th-century Pedro St James great house and grounds in Savannah. The site has a visitor centre and a multimedia theatre, and also organises historic tours. A 45-minute drive from George Town is the popular **Queen Elizabeth II Botanic Park** with a 2-acre heritage garden, visitors information centre, two-acre lake, and 2.5-acre floral garden with a vivid array of cacti, shrubs and native flowers. The park has become an important habitat for the endangered Cayman blue iguana. Other wildlife that can be spotted are tri-coloured herons, black-necked stilts, cattle egrets and rare West Indian whistling ducks.

CAYMAN BRAC

This island, (pronounced 'brack', which means 'bluff' in Gaelic) is inhabited by fewer than 1500 people. It gets its name from the huge cliff which rises 42m (140ft) from the sea on the eastern side of the island. The Brac, which is 143km (89 miles) northeast of Grand Cayman, is about 19km (12 miles) long, and not much more than a mile wide. The rocky cliffs provide excellent opportunities for exploring an area riddled with caves, some of which have barely been explored. The dozens of wrecks scattered around the Brac attract many divers. The island also has a rare bird sanctuary and provided the basis for Robert Louis Stevenson's classic novel *Treasure Island*.

LITTLE CAYMAN

Home to approximately 170 people, and many more wild birds and iguanas, Little Cayman is 11km (7 miles) southeast of Cayman Brac. This tiny island is just 16km (10 miles) long, and at no point more than 3km (2 miles) wide. Expert anglers consider it the world's best place for bone fishing.

Sport & Activities

Diving and snorkelling: There are over 40 professional dive operators in the Cayman Islands, and few other island groups offer as many easily accessible dive sites. On *Seven Mile Beach*, diving begins 183m (200 yards) from the shore. Diving shops and boats can be found at most hotels. Some diving resorts offer an underwater photography service, including camera rentals, training and repairs, along with overnight processing of slides. The Islands' main hospital in George Town, Grand Cayman's capital, has a decompression chamber. Dive sites in the Cayman Islands range from shallow dives near offshore reefs to the celebrated *North Wall* off Grand Cayman – a sheer drop to the bed of the ocean. The famous *Stingray City* offers divers and snorkellers the opportunity to come into close contact with the friendly southern stingray. Various locations also offer wreck diving, particularly Cayman Brac, where a Russian warship (renamed *MV Captain Keith Tibbets*) was intentionally sunk. The abundance of fish, marine and coral life around the islands is protected by strict conservation measures. Those not wishing to dive can enjoy the reefs from the *Atlantis Submarine*, which offers hour-long underwater trips for up to 46 passengers. The Cayman Islands Department of Tourism can provide further information (see *Contact Addresses* section) or see online (website: www.divecayman.ky).

Fishing: The deep waters around Grand Cayman are a migratory path for numerous species of large fish, including marlin, tuna, dolphin, swordfish and wahoo. Fishing is possible all year round. The best fishing is between Grand Cayman's west coast and the banks, 7.5km (12 miles) offshore; the *Trench*, 6 to 13km (4 to 8 miles) off the west coast, is particularly good. The inshore lakes of Little Cayman, the smallest of the three islands which make up the Cayman Islands, are known for tarpon and bonefish. The *Million Dollar Month* fishing festival, which established the Cayman Islands as a leading game-fishing destination, has now been replaced by an annual international fishing tournament (see Special Events in the *Social Profile* section).

Golf: The *Brittania Golf Club* has a course designed by Jack Nicklaus that can be played either as a 9-hole championship course or as an 18-hole course with the unique Cayman Ball (half the weight of the standard ball and travelling half as far), although regular golf balls can also be used. The 18-hole championship golf course, the *Links at Safehaven*, is an 18-hole, par 71 course, measuring 6039m (6605 yards). Created by Roy Case, it is reminiscent of a Scottish links course. The clubhouse features a restaurant, a patio bar and a golf shop.

Motorsports: The *Family Recreation and Motorsports Park* at Breakers offers a 12 hectare- (30 acre-) racetrack which claims to be the best in the Caribbean, with family recreation areas and a nature reserve; no alcohol is permitted in the park. The *Lakeview Raceway* in George Town features stock car racing on the first Sunday of every month.

Social Profile

FOOD & DRINK: Restaurants are excellent, with several outstanding gourmet establishments. Specialities are turtle steaks, turtle soup, conch chowder and conch salad, red snapper, sea bass and lobster. There is also a strong Jamaican influence, with popular dishes including Jerk curry, rice and peas, and plantain. There are various standards of restaurants with good service, most of which accept credit cards.

Bars and restaurants are well stocked with all beverages normally consumed in America and Europe. Draught beer is available in a few bars.

NIGHTLIFE: Grand Cayman has a lively nightlife with comedy clubs, bars and nightclubs. Music is varied and clubs offer everything from live DJs to salsa, reggae, calypso and disco. Concerts are held at the Lions Centre in Red Bay and theatre productions are shown at either the Harquail Theatre on West Bay Road or the Prospect Playhouse in Red Bay. Dinner cruises onboard a replica pirate ship and 19th-century tall ship can be booked through local watersports operators. For further information about entertainment on the Islands, visitors should consult the free local *What's Hot* magazine or the *What's Happenin* column in the Friday issue of the *Caymanian Compass* newspaper.

SHOPPING: As a shopping centre, George Town, with its fascinating boutiques and duty-free shops, is now one of the leading centres in the Caribbean region. Delicious local foods can be bought or sampled at the Farmers Market Cooperative on Thomas Russell way or Frankie's Fresh Fruits and Juices on Red Bay Road. Half a dozen modern and sophisticated shopping centres have recently been established offering a choice of North American and European fashion brands, furnishings and household goods. Local products include the Tortuga Rum company speciality rum and rum cake, shell jewellery, Caymanite (the island's semi-precious stone), tropical fruit and woodcarvings. Special purchases include china, crystal, silver, French perfume and local crafts of black coral, sculptures, tortoise and turtle shell jewellery (turtles are bred at Cayman Turtle Farm, which also undertakes conservation measures). Travellers should note that turtle products cannot be imported, even by persons in transit, into any country which has signed the Convention on International Trade in Endangered Species – this includes the USA, Canada and the UK. Many luxury goods and essential foodstuffs are duty free but duty of up to 20 per cent is charged on other items. **Shopping hours**: Mon-Sat 0900-1700.

SPECIAL EVENTS: The following is a selection of special events occurring in the Cayman Islands in 2005; for information and a complete list, contact the Cayman Islands Department of Tourism (see *Contact Addresses* section):

Jan *International Underwater Film Festival*, Grand Cayman. **Feb** *Little Cayman Annual Mardi Gras Festival*. **Mar 5-6** *Marathon, Half-Marathon and Relay events*. **Mar** *Rundown. A satirical look at island life*. **Apr 10** *Cayman Brac Turtle Triathalon*. **Apr 23** *Earth Day Reef Watch and Beach Clean Ups*. **Apr** *Cayfest*; *Annual Eco-Art Party*. **May 5-8** *22nd Annual Batabano Carnival*. **Jun 10-11** *5th Annual Deloitte Cayman International Sevens*. **Jun** *Jazz Festival*. **Jul** *6th Annual Hyatt/Kendall Jackson Golf Classic*. **Aug** *3rd Annual Cayman Islands Sand Sculpting Competition*. **Nov** *29th Annual Pirates Week Festival*. **Nov** *GIMISTORY* (storytelling festival). **Dec 4** *Cayman Islands Marathon*. **Dec 31** *New Year's Under the Stars*, Pageant Beach.

SOCIAL CONVENTIONS: The mode of life on the Cayman Islands is a blend of local traditions and of US and British patterns of behaviour. Handshaking is the usual greeting. Because of the large number of people with a similar surname (such as Ebanks and Bodden), a person may be introduced by his Christian name (such as Mr Tom or Mr Jim). Flowers are acceptable as a gift on arrival or following a visit for a meal. Dinner jackets are seldom worn. Short or long dresses are appropriate for women in the evenings. It is normal to prescribe the required mode of dress on invitation cards. Casual wear is acceptable in most places, but beachwear is best confined to the beach to avoid offence. Topless bathing is prohibited. **Tipping**: For most services, 5 to 10 per cent is normal. Hotels and apartments state the specific amount. Restaurant bills usually include 10 to 15 per cent in lieu of tipping.

Business Profile

ECONOMY: The Cayman Islands have no direct taxation and have become important as an offshore financial centre and a tax haven. The finance industry has grown rapidly since the late 1980s when many companies relocated to the islands from Panama, which was racked by political instability. Good communications and infrastructure helped to sustain its growth, to the point where the islands are now the world's fifth largest banking centre. A key agreement on information exchange signed with the US government in 1990 – extended in 2001 – has spared the Cayman Islands many of the problems (money laundering and large-scale tax avoidance) that have bedevilled other aspirant offshore financial centres. Nor has it been subject to the critical scrutiny of the OECD which has been leading the global assault on cross-border financial malpractice. Tourism is the islands' other main source of revenue. There is little agriculture, and most of the foodstuffs for the islands are imported. Industry is confined to construction and food-processing. The standard of living on the islands is generally high, and the per capita income is the highest in the region. The healthy state of the economy has attracted migrant workers from Jamaica, Europe and North America who now make up 30 per cent of the working population. The USA is substantially the islands' largest trading partner, followed by the UK, Japan and The Netherlands Antilles. The Cayman Islands have observer status at the Caribbean Common Market, CARICOM, and associate membership of the European Union.

BUSINESS: Business suits are recommended when calling on senior officials and local heads of business and also for semi-formal or formal functions. Exchange of calling cards is usual and letters of introduction are sometimes used. It is generally easy to gain access to offices of senior government officials, politicians and business executives. Civil servants are precluded from accepting gifts except for diaries or calendars at Christmas. Monetary gifts or expensive presents are not encouraged in the private sector. **Office hours**: Mon-Fri 0900-1700.

COMMERCIAL INFORMATION: For advice, contact the Cayman Islands Chamber of Commerce, PO Box 1000 GT, Grand Cayman (tel: 949 8090; fax: 949 0220; e-mail: info@caymanchamber.ky; website: www.caymanchamber.ky).

CONFERENCES/CONVENTIONS: Many hotels have conference facilities. Contact the Cayman Islands Department of Tourism for details (see *Contact Addresses* section).

Credit: © Cayman Islands Department of Tourism

Climate

Very warm, tropical climate throughout the year. High temperatures are moderated by trade winds. The rainy season is from May to October but showers are generally of short duration. The hurricane season is from June to November and, since the islands are low-lying, there is a high risk of flooding if a storm hits them.

Required clothing: Lightweight cottons and linens and a light raincoat or umbrella for the rainy season. Warmer clothes may be needed on cooler evenings.

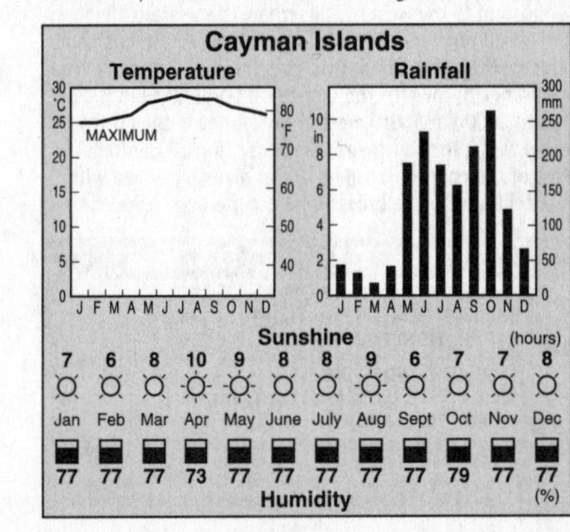

Central African Republic

LATEST TRAVEL ADVICE CONTACTS

British Foreign and Commonwealth Office
Tel: (0870) 606 0290 Website: www.fco.gov.uk

US Department of State
Website: http://travel.state.gov/travel

Canadian Department of Foreign Affairs and Int'l Trade
Tel: (1 800) 267 8376 Website: www.dfait-maeci.gc.ca

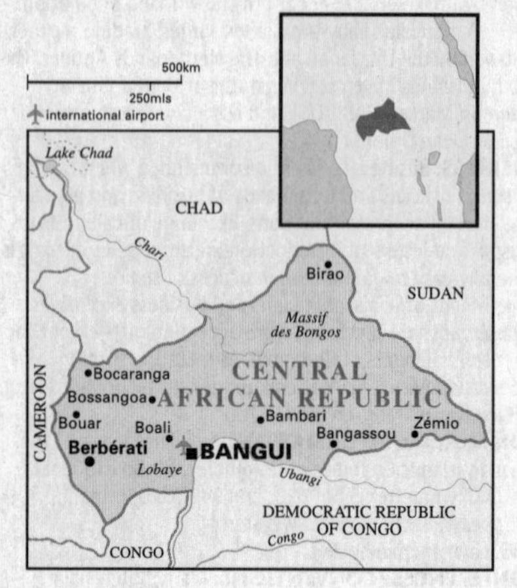

Location: Central Africa.

Country dialling code: 236.

Ministère Chargé du Dévéloppement du Tourisme et de l'Artisanat
Ave. B. Boganda, BP 655, Bangui, Central African Republic
Tel: 610 216. Fax: 618 053.
Embassy of the Central African Republic
30 rue des Perchamps, 75016 Paris, France
Tel: (1) 4224 4256. Fax: (1) 4251 0021.
The British High Commission in Yaoundé deals with enquiries relating to the Central African Republic (see *Cameroon* **section).**
Embassy of the Central African Republic
1618 22nd Street, NW, Washington DC 2008, USA
Tel: (202) 483 7800. Fax: (202) 332 9893.
Embassy of the United States of America
BP 924, Avenue David Dacko, Bangui, Central African Republic
Tel: 610 200. Fax: 614 494.
E-mail: emb-usa@intnet.cf
The Embassy is not currently open. Until service resumes, the US Embassy in Yaoundé and N'djamena (see Cameroon and Chad sections) are dealing with enquiries relating to the Central African Republic.
Consulate of the Central African Republic
6111 du Boisé (4-F) Street, Montréal H35 2U8, Canada
Tel: (514) 731 8459.
The Canadian High Commission in Yaoundé (see *Cameroon* **section) deals with enquiries relating to the Central African Republic.**

General Information

AREA: 622,984 sq km (240,535 sq miles).
POPULATION: 3,819,000 (UN estimate 2002).
POPULATION DENSITY: 6.1 per sq km.
CAPITAL: Bangui. **Population**: 524,000 (1994).
GEOGRAPHY: The Central African Republic is bordered to the north by Chad, to the east by Sudan, to the south by the Democratic Republic of Congo and the Republic of Congo, and to the west by Cameroon. It is a large, landlocked territory of mostly uninhabited forest, bush and game reserves. The Chari River cuts through the centre from east to north; towards the Cameroon border the landscape rises to 2000m (6560ft) west of Bocaranga in the northwest corner, while the southwest has dense tropical rainforest. Most of the country is rolling or flat plateau covered with dry deciduous forest, except where it has been reduced to grass savannah or destroyed by bush fire. The northeast becomes desert scrubland and mountainous in parts.
GOVERNMENT: Republic. **Head of State**: President François Bozizé since 2003. **Head of Government**: Prime Minister Celestin Leroy Gaombalet since 2003.
LANGUAGE: The national language is Sango, but French is the official administrative language and is essential for business. Another 68 languages and dialects have been identified in addition to these.
RELIGION: One-half of the population is Christian. There is a small Islamic minority of 15 per cent. Animist beliefs are fostered by an estimated 24 per cent of the population.
TIME: GMT + 1.
ELECTRICITY: 220 volts AC, 50Hz.
COMMUNICATIONS: Telephone: IDD is available, although some calls are still directed through the operator. Country code: 236. **Mobile telephone:** GSM 900 network is operated by Nationlink Telecom RCA (www.nationlinks.net) and *Telecel Centrafrique* (website: www.telecel.com). Coverage is limited to the capital, Bangui. **Internet:** ISPs include *Bangui 2000, Fateb* and *Socatel* (website: www.socatel.intnet.cf). **Telegram:** Telegrams may be sent Sat 1430-1830, Sun 0800-1830. **Post:** There is a post office in each prefecture. Local postal services are unreliable. Both postal and telecommunications services are in the course of development. Airmail services to Europe take approximately one week, although it is often much longer; surface mail can take up to three months. *Poste Restante* facilities are available in Bangui. Post office hours: Mon-Fri 0730-1130 and 1430-1630; Sat 1430-1830; Sun 0800-1100, open for stamps and telegrams only. **Press:** There are seven daily newspapers, including *Le Citoyen* (an independent publication), *E Le Songo* and *Le Novateur* (an independent publication). The weekly publications have limited distribution and are in French.
Radio: BBC World Service (website: www.bbc.co.uk/worldservice) and Voice of America (website: www.voa.gov) can be received. From time to time the frequencies change and the most up-to-date can be found online.

Passport/Visa

	Passport Required?	Visa Required?	Return Ticket Required?
Full British	Yes	Yes	Yes
Australian	Yes	Yes	Yes
Canadian	Yes	Yes	Yes
USA	Yes	Yes	Yes
Other EU	Yes	Yes	Yes
Japanese	Yes	Yes	Yes

Note: Regulations and requirements may be subject to change at short notice, and you are advised to contact the appropriate diplomatic or consular authority before finalising travel arrangements. Details of these may be found at the head of this country's entry. Any numbers in the chart refer to the footnotes below.

PASSPORTS: Passport valid for six months after entry into the Central African Republic required by all.
VISAS: Required by all except the following:
(a) nationals of Cameroon, Chad, Congo (Rep), Equatorial Guinea and Gabon, provided travelling from their own countries;
(b) transit passengers continuing their journey by the same or first connecting aircraft provided holding valid onward or return documentation and not leaving the airport.
Note: Nationals of Lebanon are visa-exempt if in possession of written proof their status as businessperson, banker or technician.
Types of visa and cost: *Tourist/Business* and *Transit*: €50 (for stays of up to 30 days); €152 (for stays of up to three months). Fees paid in other currencies depend on exchange rates.
Validity: *Tourist* and *Business* visas are valid for stays of maximum three months. For transit through the Central African Republic, enquire at the Consulate (or Consular sections at Embassy).
Application to: Consulate (or Consular section at Embassy); see *Contact Addresses* section.
Application requirements: (a) Two application forms. (b) Fee. (c) Two passport-size photos. (d) Return/onward ticket. (e) Letter from company stating that applicant will resume work on returning. (f) Yellow fever vaccination certificate. (g) Stamped, self-addressed envelope.
Working days required: Normally two unless application is referred to the authorities in the Central African Republic.

Money

Currency: CFA (*Communauté Financiaire Africaine*) Franc (CFAfr) = 100 centimes. Notes are in denominations of CFAfr10,000, 5000, 2000, 1000 and 500. Coins are in denominations of CFAfr500, 100, 50, 25, 10, 5 and 1. The Central African Republic is part of the French Monetary Area. Only currency issued by the *Banque des Etats de l'Afrique Centrale* (Bank of Central African States) is valid; currency issued by the *Banque des Etats de l'Afrique de l'Ouest* (Bank of West African States) is not. The CFA Franc is tied to the Euro.
Currency exchange: Currency can be exchanged at banks in Bangui and Berbérati.
Credit & debit cards: Not generally accepted.
Travellers cheques: To avoid additional exchange rate charges, travellers are advised to take travellers cheques in Euros. Even so, commission rates can be very high.
Currency restrictions: Import and export of local currency from Benin, Burkina Faso, Côte d'Ivoire, Mauritania, Niger, Senegal and Togo is unlimited; for all other countries the import and export of local currency is limited to CFAfr75,000. The import of foreign currency is unlimited. The export of foreign currency is limited to the amount imported and declared.
Exchange rate indicators: The following figures are included as a guide to the movements of the CFA Franc against Sterling and the US Dollar:

Date	Feb '04	May '04	Aug '04	Nov '04
£1.00=	961.13	983.76	978.35	936.79
$1.00=	528.01	550.79	531.03	494.69

Banking hours: Mon-Fri 0700-1230.

Duty Free

The following goods may be imported by visitors over 18 years of age into the Central African Republic without incurring customs duty:
1000 cigarettes or cigarillos or 250 cigars or 2kg of tobacco (for women, cigarettes only); five bottles of alcoholic beverages; five bottles of perfume.
Note: Firearms must be declared before entering. When leaving the Central African Republic, any animal skins and diamonds must be declared.

Public Holidays

2005: Jan 1 New Year's Day. **Mar 28** Easter Monday. **Mar 29** Anniversary of the Death of Barthélemy Boganda. **Aug 13** Independence Day. **Aug 15** Assumption. **Nov 1** All Saint's Day. **Dec 1** National Day. **Dec 25** Christmas.
2006: Jan 1 New Year's Day. **Mar 29** Anniversary of the Death of Barthélemy Boganda. **Apr 17** Easter Monday. **Aug 13** Independence Day. **Aug 15** Assumption. **Nov 1** All Saints' Day. **Dec 1** National Day. **Dec 25** Christmas Day.

Health

	Special Precautions?	Certificate Required?
Yellow Fever	Yes	1
Cholera	Yes	2
Typhoid & Polio	3	N/A
Malaria	4	N/A

Note: Regulations and requirements may be subject to change at short notice, and you are advised to contact your doctor well in advance of your intended date of departure. Any numbers in the chart refer to the footnotes below.

1: A yellow fever vaccination certificate is required from travellers over one year of age.
2: Following WHO guidelines issued in 1973, a cholera vaccination certificate is not a condition of entry to the Central African Republic. However, cholera is a serious risk in this country and precautions are essential. Up-to-date advice should be sought before deciding whether these precautions should include vaccination as medical opinion is divided over its effectiveness. See the *Health* appendix for more information.
3: Immunisation against typhoid is usually recommended.
4: Risk of malaria (and of other insect-borne diseases) exists all year throughout the country. The malignant *falciparum* form is prevalent. Resistance to chloroquine and sulfadoxine-pyrimethamine has been reported. The recommended prophylaxis is mefloquine.
Food & drink: All water should be regarded as being potentially contaminated. Water used for drinking, brushing teeth or making ice should have first been boiled or otherwise sterilised. Milk is unpasteurised and should be boiled. Powdered or tinned milk is available and is advised, but make sure that it is reconstituted with pure water. Avoid dairy products which are likely to have been made from unboiled milk. Only eat well-cooked meat and fish, preferably served hot. Pork, salad and mayonnaise may carry increased risk. Vegetables should be cooked and fruit peeled.
Other risks: *Hepatitis A* and *E* are present and *hepatitis B* is hyperendemic. *Diarrhoeal* illnesses are common. *Cutaneous* and *visceral leishmaniasis* occur during the dry season. *Bilharzia* (schistosomiasis) is present. Avoid swimming and paddling in fresh water; swimming pools which are well-chlorinated and maintained are safe. *Onchocerciasis* (river blindness) and *African*

TIMATIC CODES

Health
AMADEUS: **TI-DFT/JIB/HE**
GALILEO/WORLDSPAN: **TI-DFT/JIB/HE**
SABRE: **TIDFT/JIB/HE**

Visa
AMADEUS: **TI-DFT/JIB/VI**
GALILEO/WORLDSPAN: **TI-DFT/JIB/VI**
SABRE: **TIDFT/JIB/VI**

To access TIMATIC country information on Health and Visa regulations through the Computer Reservations System (CRS), type in the appropriate command line listed above.

trypanosomiasis (sleeping sickness) are also prevalent. *Meningococcal meningitis* is particularly prevalent during the dry season in December, especially in the north of the country. In March 2004, two districts (Nana Bongila with 39 cases/five deaths and Zere with four cases/two deaths) had attack rates above the epidemic threshold. Vaccination is strongly recommended. There is also a high incidence of HIV/AIDS; sensible precautions should be taken.
Rabies is present. For those at high risk, vaccination before arrival should be considered. If you are bitten, seek medical advice without delay. For more information, consult the *Health* appendix.
Health care: Full health insurance is essential, and should include air evacuation to Europe in case of serious accident or illness. Medical facilities are severely limited outside the major centres and visitors should travel with their own supply of remedies for simple ailments such as stomach upsets: pharmaceutical supplies are usually very difficult to obtain.

Travel - International

Note: There is still great political tension in the Central African Republic and it is advisable to avoid all non-essential travel to this country (especially outside Bangui). For further advice, contact your local government travel advice department.
AIR: The main airlines serving the Central African Republic are *Air France (AF)* (website: www.airfrance.com) (once a week), Benin Golf Air (twice-weekly), Cameroon Airlines (three times a week) and Sudan Airways. Both operate one flight a week from Paris to Bangui. *Sudan Airways* offer a route from London or Paris via Khartoum to Bangui. There are regular flights from Bangui to various African cities, including Libreville and N'Djaména.
Approximate flight times: From *London* to Bangui is 10 hours 50 minutes (including approximately one hour stopover in Paris). There are also connections between Bangui and Douala (Cameroon), Lagos (Nigeria), and other West African destinations.
International airport: *Bangui M'Poko (BGF)* is 7km (4 miles) southeast of Bangui of the city (travel time - 30 minutes). Taxis are available to the city (travel time - 15 minutes), during flight hours for a fare of about CFAfr2500. A bus service to the city meets all flights. Airport facilities include a restaurant, post office, bar and car hire/parking.
Departure tax: CFAfr10,000 is levied on all passengers.
RIVER: The route by ferry along the Ubangi to Bangui from the Congo (Rep) or the Congo (Dem Rep) is run by ACCF (Tel: 610 967) and SOCATRAF (Tel: 614 315). However, it is not operating at present, owing to rebel activity in the northern part of the Democratic Republic of Congo. A car/passenger ferry normally operates across the Ubangi between the Central African Republic and the Democratic Republic of Congo, Bangui-Zongo and Bangassou-Ndu. Fares are very low, although the service breaks down frequently and may be disrupted by political instability. It is sometimes possible to hire a boat, although this is expensive. Visitors may not cross the river to the Congo (Dem Rep) on Saturday or Sunday, as the customs posts in that country do not operate at the weekend.
ROAD: Road access is from the Congo (Dem Rep), Chad and Cameroon. There are reasonable all-weather roads from Yaoundé (Cameroon) and N'Djaména (Chad). The border with Cameroon may be closed; it is necessary to check locally near the time of travel. Theoretically, all borders are open; however, non-residents can experience difficulty obtaining permission to cross them.

Travel - Internal

Note: Identification (eg residence permit or certified copy of passport) must be carried on persons at all times. Failure to do so can result in detention by police. Incidents of theft and robbery occur regularly, and armed gangs are known to operate in the outlying areas of Bangui.
AIR: Scheduled flights sometimes operate to Berbérati. However, most domestic flying is limited to chartered planes. Contact *Minair* (Tel: 611 963 *or* 612 236) *or BADICA* (Tel: 613 726/7) for details.
RIVER: Ferries sail from Bangui to several towns further up the Ubangi.
ROAD: Good roads connect the few main towns (although few are paved), but the majority are often impassable during the rainy season and travellers should expect delays. Most roads will require a 4-wheel-drive to render them passable. Outside the urban areas, motor vehicles are rare and spare parts virtually impossible to find. Traffic drives on the right. Travellers must carry as large a petrol supply as possible, since deliveries to stations outside the towns are infrequent. **Bus**: Local services run between towns; they are a cheap but sometimes gruelling way to travel. It is also possible to pay for a lift on the numerous goods trucks which drive between the main towns. **Car hire**: Self-drive or chauffeur-driven cars are available. **Documentation**: International Driving Permit required.
URBAN: Limited bus services run in Bangui on a two-zone tariff. Taxis are only available in the urban areas; they do not have meters and fares must be negotiated.

Accommodation

HOTELS: There are good hotels in Bangui, some of which are very exclusive and expensive. The better hotels have air conditioning and swimming pools. Pre-booking is essential - ideally several weeks in advance. Outside Bangui, accommodation of any standard may be difficult to find, although guest houses exist in smaller towns, principally Bangassou, Boali, Bambari and Bossangoa.
CAMPING AND CARAVANNING: Most of the country is unpopulated or traversed by nomadic herdsmen, and there are few organised facilities for camping and caravanning. Sufficient provisions should be carried with vehicles at all times.

Resorts & Excursions

BANGUI

At the beginning of the century, the present-day capital, Bangui, was a modest village beside the **River Ubangi**; it now extends over 15 sq km (5 sq miles). Built on a rock, it is shaded by tropical greenery and features many modern buildings. Places of interest include the colourful **Central Market** (renowned for its malachite necklaces), the **Boganda Museum**, the **Arts and Crafts School**, the cathedral and the **Saint Paul Mission**, whose small brick church overlooks the river, and the **Hausa quarter**. The **Grande Corniche** leads to the banks of the Ubangi and provides a picturesque view of the fishermen's round huts and canoes.

ELSEWHERE

The **Lobaye Region**, 100km (60 miles) from the capital, is inhabited by indigenous forest tribes living in encampments of small, low huts made of lianas and roofed with leaves. There are coffee plantations on the fringe of the forest. A number of similar villages can also be found in the **M'Baiki Region**, 100km (60 miles) southwest of Bangui. The **Boali Waterfalls** are 90km (55 miles) northwest of Bangui, near the charming and picturesque village of **Boali**. They are 250m (820ft) wide and 50m (165ft) high, with a stunning view from the restaurant at the top. The nearby hydroelectric power plant can also be visited. At Bouar, in the east of the country, there is an area of burial mounds with many upright megaliths (*tanjunu*) thought to be thousands of years old. In **Bangassou**, near the **Ubangi River** on the border with the Democratic Republic of Congo, are the extraordinary **Kembe Falls** on the **River Kotto**.
Note: Travel outside Bangui can be dangerous, and travellers should take suitable precautions.

Sport & Activities

Wildlife: There are opportunities to view wildlife in the country's national parks, most of which are accessible by 4-wheel-drive vehicles from Birao, in the far north of the country between the Chad and Sudanese borders, during the dry season only. It is also possible to charter light aircraft to travel to these areas. The three most important parks are *Manovo-Gounda St Floris*, known for its high concentration of hippos; *Bamingui-Bangoran* in the north; and *Dzanga-Sangha* in the southwest. The game population of these National Parks is impressive, although the activities of poachers have led to a considerable decrease in recent years - elephants and rhinos being the worst affected species. It is possible to view gorillas in Bayanga. There is no accommodation available: all supplies, including bedding, must be taken.
Outdoor pursuits: Travellers can also participate in **archery**, **fishing**, **mountain-** and **rock-climbing**, **golf** and **swimming**. **Basketball** is Africa's most popular sport and a good way to forge connections with the people of the Central African Republic.

Social Profile

FOOD & DRINK: Western food is only available in the capital, Bangui. Most of the top-class hotels have good restaurants. The standard of these restaurants is high, but they do tend to be expensive. Otherwise travellers must call at local villages and barter for provisions. Local food is basic. Many dishes contain okra (*gombo*), although other popular ingredients include rice, bananas and cassava.
Bars are numerous in Bangui with both table and counter service. Drinking and smoking are not encouraged in Muslim society; in Muslim areas, drinking is best done in private. Elsewhere, there are numerous beer halls offering beverages of a high standard. Two of the most popular brews are palm wine and banana wine.
NIGHTLIFE: The few hotels in Bangui have expensive clubs catering for tourists and businessmen; local nightlife is centred on the district known as 'Kilomètre Cinq'.
SHOPPING: Bangui has reasonable shopping facilities, notably for ebony, gold jewellery, butterfly collections and objets d'arts made from butterfly wings. However, one of the best methods of finding bargain souvenirs is by bartering with villagers outside the urban areas for their handmade goods. **Shopping hours**: Mon-Sat 0800-1200 and 1600-1900. Some shops close on Monday. The market in Bangui is open 0730-dusk.
SPECIAL EVENTS: The Central African Republic celebrates all Christian festivals and, in the north, all Muslim ones. New Year's Day is also a day of celebration throughout the country.
SOCIAL CONVENTIONS: Dress is informal. Care should be taken to dress modestly in Muslim areas, and Muslim customs should be respected and observed; visitors should not, for instance, show the soles of their feet when sitting. Shorts are also generally frowned upon, and women are expected to dress modestly. It is customary to shake hands. Women are strictly segregated, especially in towns. In Muslim areas, visitors should not smoke or drink in public during Ramadan. **Photography**: Film is expensive and should be sent abroad for developing. Show caution and discretion when photographing local people; ask for permission. Do not photograph military installations or government buildings. **Tipping**: 10 per cent is appropriate for most services.

Business Profile

ECONOMY: Agriculture, upon which most of the population depends, is concentrated on subsistence crops plus coffee, cotton and wood as cash crops for export. Livestock and tobacco are also exported. The main cash earner is timber, which has been heavily exploited with little government restriction. The country's mining industry is largely devoted to diamonds; a small quantity of gold is also produced. Other deposits, including uranium, copper, manganese and iron ore, are yet to be exploited. The small manufacturing sector is devoted to the processing of primary products to produce food and drinks, wood products and textiles. The overall economic development of the Central African Republic has been limited by an adverse climate, poor infrastructure and low world commodity prices. With a per capita annual income of just US$260, the Central African Republic is one of Africa's poorest countries; the economy grew at a modest 1.5 per cent in 2001. The Central African Republic is a member of the Central African Economic and Customs Union (CEEAC), the main regional trading organisation. France provides extensive economic and financial aid and is the country's main trading partner. Belgium and Luxembourg are both important export markets.
BUSINESS: A knowledge of French is essential. Interpreter and translation services may be available at large hotels. Business cards should be in French and English. Formal wear is expected (suits and ties for men). The best months for business visits are between November and May. **Office hours**: Mon-Fri 0730-1530.
COMMERCIAL INFORMATION: The following organisation can offer advice: Chambre de Commerce et d'Industrie (CCI), Boulevard Charles de Gaulle, BP 823, Bangui (tel: 611 668; fax: 613 570; e-mail: ccici@africaonline.co.ci).

Climate

Hot all year with a defined dry season. Especially hot in the north, with greater humidity in the south. The rainy season is mainly from May to October. Heavy rainfall is typical in the southwestern forest areas.
Required clothing: Linens and tropical waterproof clothing.

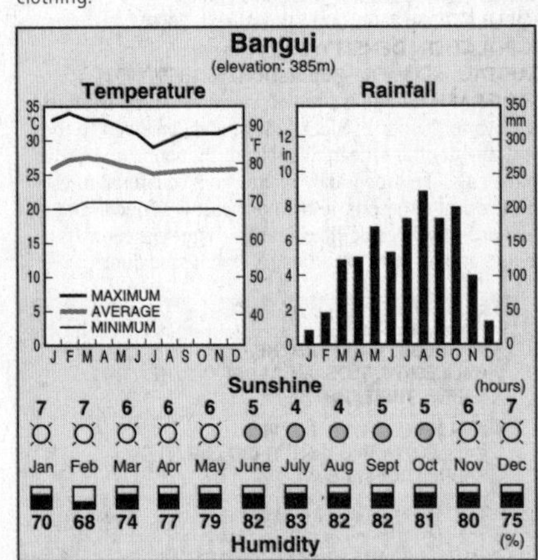

Chad

LATEST TRAVEL ADVICE CONTACTS

British Foreign and Commonwealth Office
Tel: (0870) 606 0290 Website: www.fco.gov.uk

US Department of State
Website: http://travel.state.gov/travel

Canadian Department of Foreign Affairs and Int'l Trade
Tel: (1 800) 267 8376 Website: www.dfait-maeci.gc.ca

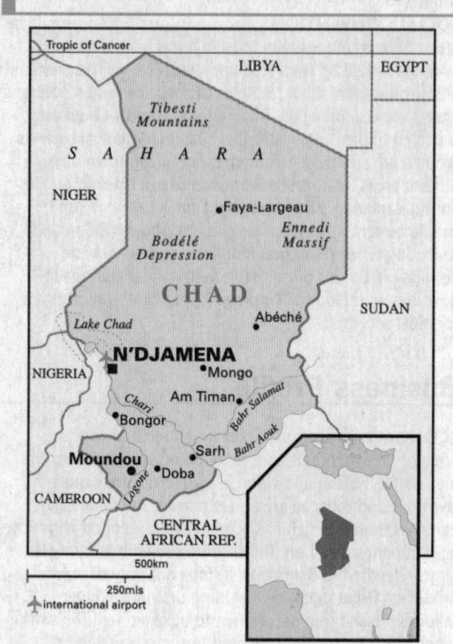

Location: Central Africa.

Country dialling code: 235.

Direction du Tourisme
BP 86, N'Djaména, Chad Tel: 522 303. Fax: 524 419.
Embassy of the Republic of Chad
Boulevard Lambermont 52, B 1030 Brussels, Belgium
Tel: (2) 215 1975. Fax: (2) 216 3526.
E-mail: ambassade.tchad@chello.be
Embassy of the Republic of Chad
65 rue des Belles Feuilles, 75116 Paris, France
Tel: (1) 4553 3675. Fax: (1) 4553 1609.
The British High Commission in Yaoundé deals with enquiries relating to Chad (see *Cameroon* section).
Tel: 523 970 *or* 520 172. *Emergency assistance only.*
Embassy of the Republic of Chad
2002 R Street, NW, Washington, DC 20009, USA
Tel: (202) 462 4009. Fax: (202) 265 1937.
E-mail: info@chadembassy.org
Website: www.chadembassy.org
Also deals with enquiries from Canada.
Embassy of the United States of America
BP 413, avenue Félix Eboué, N'Djaména, Chad
Tel: 517 009 *or* 524 727 *or* 516 211. Fax: 515 654.
E-mail: consularndjame@state.gov
Website: http://ndjamena.usembassy.gov
The Canadian Embassy in Yaoundé deals with enquiries relating to Chad (see *Cameroon* section).

General Information

AREA: 1,284,000 sq km (495,800 sq miles).
POPULATION: 8,348,000 (UN estimate 2002).
POPULATION DENSITY: 6.5 per sq km.
CAPITAL: N'Djaména. **Population**: 530,965 (1993).
GEOGRAPHY: Chad is situated in central Africa, bordered by Libya to the north, Niger, Nigeria and Cameroon to the west, the Central African Republic to the south, and Sudan to the east. The topography ranges from equatorial forests to the driest of deserts. In the northeast lies Ennedi, and to the north the volcanic Tibesti range - largely sheer cliffs, ravines and canyons set among Saharan sand dunes.

TIMATIC CODES

Health
AMADEUS: **TI-DFT/JIB/HE**
GALILEO/WORLDSPAN: **TI-DFT/JIB/HE**
SABRE: **TIDFT/JIB/HE**

Visa
AMADEUS: **TI-DFT/JIB/VI**
GALILEO/WORLDSPAN: **TI-DFT/JIB/VI**
SABRE: **TIDFT/JIB/VI**

To access TIMATIC country information on Health and Visa regulations through the Computer Reservations System (CRS), type in the appropriate command line listed above.

GOVERNMENT: Republic. Gained independence from France in 1960. **Head of State**: President Idriss Déby since 1990. **Head of Government**: Prime Minister Moussa Faki since 2003.
LANGUAGE: The official languages are French and Arabic. Other widely spoken African languages include Sara (in the south). The territory's boundaries enclose a small but highly diverse population.
RELIGION: 50 per cent Muslim, 30 per cent Christian, 20 per cent Animist.
TIME: GMT + 1.
ELECTRICITY: 220 volts AC, 50Hz.
COMMUNICATIONS: Telephone: Country code: 235. It may be necessary to go through the operator. **Mobile telephone:** GSM 900 network covers the N'Djaména area, and other small clusters, mainly in the south. Network operators include *Celtel Tchad* (website: www.msi-cellular.com) and *Tchad Mobile SA (Libertis)*. **Fax:** Services are available in large hotels in main cities. **Internet:** Limited facilities are available in N'Djaména. **Telegram:** Available in major post offices in N'Djaména, Sarh, Moundou and Abéché. **Post:** Airmail takes about one week. Post office hours: Mon-Fri 0700-1130 and 1530-1830, Sat 0730-1100. **Press:** Newspapers are printed in French and generally have a low circulation. Dailies include *Info-Tchad* and *Le Progrès*. **Radio:** BBC World Service (website: www.bbc.co.uk/worldservice) and Voice of America (website: www.voa.gov) can be received. From time to time the frequencies change and the most up-to-date can be found online.

Passport/Visa

	Passport Required?	Visa Required?	Return Ticket Required?
Full British	Yes	Yes	Yes
Australian	Yes	Yes	Yes
Canadian	Yes	Yes	Yes
USA	Yes	Yes	Yes
Other EU	Yes	Yes	Yes
Japanese	Yes	Yes	Yes

Note: Regulations and requirements may be subject to change at short notice, and you are advised to contact the appropriate diplomatic or consular authority before finalising travel arrangements. Details of these may be found at the head of this country's entry. Any numbers in the chart refer to the footnotes below.

PASSPORTS: Passport valid at least six months required by all.
VISAS: Required by all except those continuing their journey within 48 hours by the same or first connecting aircraft provided holding tickets with reserved seats and valid travel documents.
Types of visa and cost: *Ordinary visa* (includes visas issued for business or touristic purposes): €70 (single-entry); €100 (multiple-entry).
Validity: One month.
Note: Single parents or adults travelling alone with children should be aware that documentary evidence of parental responsibility may be requested.
Application to: Consulate (or Consular section at Embassy); see *Contact Addresses* section for details. In countries with no Chadian representation, French consulates may deal with applications.
Application requirements: (a) Valid passport. (b) Two passport-size photos. (c) Two application forms. (d) Letters of recommendation from employer (for business visits). (e) Valid return ticket. (f) Fee. (g) Yellow fever vaccination certificate, provided upon arrival. Failure to do so may result in a further vaccination being administered, for which a charge will be made.
Working days required: Three.

Money

Currency: CFA (*Communauté Financiaire Africaine*) Franc (CFAfr) = 100 centimes. Notes are in denominations of CFAfr10,000, 5000, 2000, 1000 and 500. Coins are in denominations of CFAfr250, 100, 50, 25, 10, 5 and 1. Chad is part of the French Monetary Area. Only currency issued by the *Banque des Etats de l'Afrique Centrale* (Bank of Central African States) is valid; currency issued by the *Banque des Etats de l'Afrique de l'Ouest* (Bank of West African States) is not. The CFA Franc is tied to the Euro.
Currency exchange: It is advisable to bring US Dollars or Euros rather than Sterling into the country. CFA Francs can be difficult to exchange outside the French Monetary Area.
Credit & debit cards: Diners Club, MasterCard and Visa are accepted at two hotels in N'Djaména. It may not be possible to obtain cash advances at banks on credit cards.
Travellers cheques: May be exchanged at one or two banks in N'Djaména. To avoid additional exchange rate charges, travellers are advised to take travellers cheques in Euros.
Currency restrictions: If importing or exporting local currency from other countries in the French monetary area, there are no restrictions; the import or export of local currency from any other country is limited to CFAfr10,000. Import of foreign currency is unrestricted, provided declared upon arrival. Export of foreign currency is limited to the amount imported and declared.
Exchange rate indicators: The following figures are included as a guide to the movements of the CFA Franc against Sterling and the US Dollar:

Date	Feb '04	May '04	Aug '04	Nov '04
£1.00 =	961.13	983.76	978.35	936.79
$1.00 =	528.01	550.79	531.03	494.69

Banking hours: Mon-Sat 0700-1300, Fri 0700-1030.

Duty Free

The following goods may be imported into Chad without incurring customs duty for passengers over 18 years of age:
400 cigarettes (or cigarillos) or 125 cigars or 500g of tobacco (women are permitted to import cigarettes only); three bottles of wine and one bottle of spirits.
Note: There is free export of 1000 cigarettes or 250 cigars or 1kg of tobacco.

Public Holidays

2005: Jan 1 New Year's Day. **Jan 21** Eid al-Adha (Feast of the Sacrifice). **Mar 25** Easter Monday. **Apr 13** National Day. **May 1** Labour Day. **May 25** Liberation of Africa (anniversary of the OAU's foundation). **Aug 11** Independence Day. **Nov 1** All Saint's Day. **Nov 3-5** Eid al-Fitr (End of Ramadan). **Nov 28** Proclamation of the Republic. **Dec 1** Day of Liberty and Democracy. **Dec 25** Christmas Day.
2006: Jan 1 New Year's Day. **Jan 13** Eid al-Adha (Feast of the Sacrifice). **Apr 17** Easter Monday. **Apr 13** National Day. **May 1** Labour Day. **May 25** Liberation of Africa (anniversary of the OAU's foundation). **Aug 11** Independence Day. **Nov 1** All Saints' Day. **Oct 22-24** Eid al-Fitr (End of Ramadan). **Nov 28** Proclamation of the Republic. **Dec 1** Day of Liberty and Democracy. **Dec 25** Christmas Day.
Note: Muslim festivals are timed according to local sightings of various phases of the moon and the dates given above are approximations. During the lunar month of Ramadan that precedes Eid al-Fitr, Muslims fast during the day and feast at night and normal business patterns may be interrupted. Many restaurants are closed during the day and there may be restrictions on smoking and drinking. Some disruption may continue into Eid al-Fitr itself. Eid al-Fitr and Eid al-Adha may last anything from two to 10 days, depending on the region. For more information, see the *World of Islam* appendix.

Health

	Special Precautions?	Certificate Required?
Yellow Fever	Yes	1
Cholera	Yes	2
Typhoid & Polio	3	N/A
Malaria	4	N/A

Note: Regulations and requirements may be subject to change at short notice, and you are advised to contact your doctor well in advance of your intended date of departure. Any numbers in the chart refer to the footnotes below.

1: A yellow fever certificate is required from travellers over one year of age.
2: Following WHO guidelines issued in 1973, a cholera vaccination certificate is no longer a condition of entry to Chad. However, cholera is a serious risk in this country and precautions are essential. A current Cholera outbreak is affecting N'Djaména, Chari Baguirmi, Karem and Lac. Up-to-date advice should be sought before deciding whether these precautions should include vaccination as medical opinion is divided over its effectiveness. See the *Health* appendix for more information.
3: Immunisations or boosters for typhoid and polio are recommended.
4: Risk of malaria (and of other insect-borne diseases) exists all year throughout the country. The malignant *falciparum* form is prevalent. Resistance to chloroquine is reported. The recommended prophylaxis is mefloquine.
Food & Drink: All water should be regarded as being potentially contaminated. Water used for drinking, brushing teeth or making ice should have first been boiled or otherwise sterilised. Milk is unpasteurised and should be boiled. Powdered or tinned milk is available and is advised, but make sure that it is reconstituted with pure water. Avoid all dairy products. Only eat well-cooked meat and fish, preferably served hot. Pork, salad and mayonnaise may carry increased risk. Vegetables should be cooked and fruit peeled.
Other risks: *Bilharzia* (schistosomiasis) is present, but only in the south and southeast of the country. Avoid swimming and paddling in fresh water; swimming pools which are well chlorinated and maintained are safe. *River blindness*

(onchocerciasis) and *sleeping sickness* (trypanosomiasis) are also prevalent. *Meningococcal meningitis* occurs, particularly in the savannah areas during the dry season (November to May). Immunisation is compulsory. A recent outbreak in the Iriba district resulted in 15 cases and four deaths - above the epidemic threshold. Immunisation against *diphtheria* and *hepatitis B* should be considered for longer visits.
Hepatitis A and *E* are widespread in the region (especially in the north and east of Chad). Between June and August 2004 there were 672 cases/21 deaths of *acute jaundice syndrome* (AJS) in Coz Amer, where lies a camp of Sudanese refugees - and the *Hepatitis E* virus has been confirmed. *HIV/AIDS* is prevalent.
Rabies is present. For those at high risk, vaccination before arrival should be considered. If you are bitten, seek medical advice without delay. For more information, consult the *Health* appendix.
Health care: Medical facilities are poor, particularly in the north, and health insurance (to include emergency repatriation) is essential.

Travel - International

Note: It is advised against all travel to the area bordering the Darfur region of Sudan where, due to the conflict in Darfur, the security situation in the region is extremely unstable. All travel to the Borkou-Ennedi-Tibesti provinces in the north of the country, and to the area bordering the Central African Republic where there have been recent armed clashes/reports of increased rebel activity, is advised against. The Sudan and Libyan borders are subject to closure. Terrorists are active in neighbouring countries, including Algeria, and in March 2004, Chadian forces fought with members of an African extremist group in the northern Tibesti region of Chad.
AIR: There are at least two flights a week from Paris to Chad and several times a week from Congo, Ethiopia and Central African Republic. Airlines serving Chad include *Afriqiyah Airways*, *Air France*, *Cameroon Airlines*, *Ethiopian Airlines*, and *Sudan Airways*.
Approximate flight times: From N'Djaména *to Paris* is five hours 30 minutes. There are no direct flights or good connections for those travelling from London. Overnight transit costs may be covered by some airlines.
International airports: *N'Djaména (NDJ)* is 4km (2.5 miles) northwest of the city. Taxis are available, operating 24 hours, for a fare of about CFAfr5000. Airport facilities include a post office, car hire, refreshments and bar, as well as restaurants.
Departure tax: CFAfr5000 (tourist tax) and CFAfr3000 (security tax). Students and transit passengers continuing their journey within 24 hours are exempt.
RAIL: There is no railway network in Chad. There have been long-standing plans for a rail link with Cameroon but construction is not yet underway.
ROAD: There are routes from Cameroon, Central African Republic, Niger and Nigeria. The border between Cameroon and Chad is the River Logone, which flows into Lake Chad. Boats ply across the river (there is no bridge). Access from Nigeria is via a sliver of northern Cameroon. There is a road from N'Djaména via Sarh to the Central African Republic. The road from N'Djaména to Maidguri in Niger is paved. Roads can be inaccessible during the rainy season. It is not possible, or advisable, to cross the border from Sudan. Care should be taken when travelling in the area around the border with Cameroon as there have been reports of armed bandits. **Bus**: Minibuses and bush taxis operate between N'Djaména and Kousséri in Cameroon. Rudimentary public transport is available to the Central African Republic, Niger and Nigeria, although it may be necessary to change vehicles at the border.

Travel - Internal

AIR: At present, the only internal flights are chartered by private companies. Enquire at the Direction de la Promotion Touristique for further details; see *Contact Addresses* section.
ROAD: Travel by road outside N'Djaména is possible by 4-wheel-drive vehicle and permits are usually needed. Buses run fairly regularly to Sarh during the dry season. Security conditions and a lack of housing, food, petrol and vehicle repair facilities have resulted in the Government restricting travel, especially in the central and northern areas of the country. Petrol is expensive. Many roads urgently need repair, and are impassable during the rainy season, especially in the south. It is advised to travel in convoy, keep doors locked, carry spare fuel and supplies, and not travel after dark, due to the potential for highway bandits. Traffic drives on the right. For travel to all areas outside N'Djaména, authorisation from the Ministry of the Interior is required, which is usually granted without difficulty after a few days. **Documentation**: International Driving Permit required for car hire (which is expensive) as well as an official *autorisation de circuler*.
URBAN: The city of N'Djaména has an adequate road system and there are limited self-drive and chauffeured car hire facilities. Minibuses and taxis operate in N'Djaména, with a flat fare charged. A 10 per cent tip is expected by taxi drivers.

Accommodation

There are several good hotels in N'Djaména, but accommodation elsewhere is very limited. There are some small hotels at Sarh, a modern hotel complex in Zakouma National Park, and various small hunting hotels in the southwest. It is advisable to book in advance and prospective travellers should contact the Embassy in Paris for the latest information (see *Contact Addresses* section).

Resorts & Excursions

N'DJAMÉNA

Chad's capital is slowly regaining its pre-war reputation as one of Central Africa's liveliest cities. Bullet holes in buildings serve as a reminder of troubled times, but the atmosphere here is increasingly upbeat. The historic quarter, with its colourful daily market, is fascinating and a good place to pick up colourful Chadian rugs and jewellery. The **National Museum** has collections of the Sarh culture dating back to the 9th century. There is a distinctive difference between the Arab section of town (very quiet at night) and the area where the southerners live (lively and full of bars).

ZAKOUMA NATIONAL PARK

This is located on an immense plain, across which the *Bahr Salamat* and its tributaries flow from north to south. Here, visitors may view what is left of the wildlife (the area has suffered greatly at the hands of poachers).

LAKE CHAD

This was once the centre of Africa's lucrative salt trade but is now shrinking (literally) and sparsely populated. The lake is best seen during the August to December period, when the water level is highest and the occasional hippo or crocodile can be seen drifting by.

SARH

Situated 550km south of N'Djaména, Sarh is Chad's second-largest city and has gained a reputation as a strong sugar-cane and cotton-growing region. Things to see include the small **National Museum** and the **Centre Artisanal**, where woodcarvings and traditional paintings and embroideries can be purchased.

MOUNDOU

Chad's up-and-coming city, due to an oil rush from the Doba basin, is known for its **Gala Brewery**, that produces some of the best beer in the country. Although Moundou lies 400km south of the capital, the trip may take up to a day to complete by road.

ABÉCHÉ

Lying 890km east of N'Djaména, Abéché is surrounded by desert. Former capital of the powerful Ouadaï sultanate, the town has retained much of its oriental charm with interesting mosques, cobbled narrow streets and old markets.

TIBESTI MOUNTAINS

Home of the fierce Toubou tribe, this astonishing region of chasms and crags has seldom been seen by non-Muslims and remains closed to travellers. The range is said to be home to the best racing camels in the world. The inhabitants are distantly related to the Tuareg of the Western Sahara, and were made famous by Herodotus as the 'Troglodytes' - stocky but immensely agile cave-dwellers.

Social Profile

FOOD & DRINK: N'Djaména offers a fair selection of restaurants serving mainly French and African food. Chad's excellent beer, *Gala*, is brewed in Moundou and is widely available in the non-Muslim parts of the capital. Standard European-style service is normal. Outside the capital, restaurants tend to be cheap and cheerful and there is an acute shortage of some foodstuffs. Visitors should exercise caution with street market food.
NIGHTLIFE: Lively dancing and music is to be found in the capital, where there is an increasing number of nightclubs. *Pari-matches* take place on most Saturdays and Sundays in N'Djaména (non-Muslim areas): groups of women hire bars and sell drinks all day. Outside N'Djaména, nightlife is limited, although bars and open-air dancing can generally be found.
SHOPPING: Chad has an excellent crafts industry. Items include camel-hair carpets, all kinds of leatherware, embroidered cotton cloths, decorated calabashes, knives, weapons, pottery and brass animals. **Shopping hours**: Tues-Sat 0900-1230 and 1600-1930. Food shops open Sunday morning. The market in the capital is open from 0730 until dusk.
SPECIAL EVENTS: Celebrations in Chad are largely confined to Muslim feasts and festivals, and private, tribe-specific ceremonies.
SOCIAL CONVENTIONS: Chadians are a relaxed and friendly people, but respect for traditional beliefs and customs is expected. Dress is informal but conservative in respect of Muslim laws. There is strict segregation of women in the Muslim areas. It is customary to shake hands. The left hand should never be used for offering or accepting food, nor should the sole of the foot be exposed in the presence of a Muslim. Identification should be carried at all times; failure to do so may result in detention by police. **Photography**: It is necessary to obtain a permit from the Ministry of Information in order to take photographs. Photographing military sites, airports and official buildings is prohibited. Other photography requires a government permit. **Tipping**: 10 per cent is normal for most services (US Dollars are the preferred currency).

Business Profile

ECONOMY: Chad is one of the world's poorest countries, with a per capita annual income of just US$200. Civil war, poor infrastructure, few natural resources and droughts have hampered any development of the economy during the last few decades. Subsistence level farming occupies 70 per cent of the population, producing mainly sorghum, millet and groundnuts. Cotton is the main cash crop. Nonetheless, there are chronic food shortages which can, in many areas, only be met by international food aid. Agro-industrial operations, most of which are based in the south of the country, dominate the small industrial sector. Mineral deposits including tungsten, tin, bauxite, gold and iron ore have been located: only natron (hydrated sodium carbonate) is mined in commercial quantities. However, the country now has a unique opportunity to transform its economic fortunes following the discovery of large oil deposits in the Doba Basin in the southwest. A 1000km pipeline linking the fields to the Cameroonian port of Kribi (Chad is landlocked) was due on stream in 2003. Chad is expected to earn around US$3 billion over 25 years, which will increase national income by around 50 per cent. France is by far the largest trading partner, followed by Nigeria, The Netherlands, Italy, the USA, the UK, Cameroon and Germany. Chad is a member of the Central African Economic and Customs Union (CEEAC).
BUSINESS: A knowledge of French is essential as there are no professional translators available. Best months for business visits are between November and May. **Office hours**: Mon-Thurs 0700-1530, Fri 0700-1200.
COMMERCIAL INFORMATION: The following organisation can offer advice: Chambre de Commerce, d'Industrie, d'Agriculture, des Mines et d'Artisanat, 13 avenue du Colonel Moll, BP 458, N'Djaména (tel: 525 264; fax: 525 263).

Climate

Hot, tropical climate, though temperatures vary in different areas. The southern rainy season lasts from May to October and the central rains from June to September. The north has little rain all year. The dry season is often windy and cooler during the evenings.
Required clothing: Linens and tropical waterproof clothing.

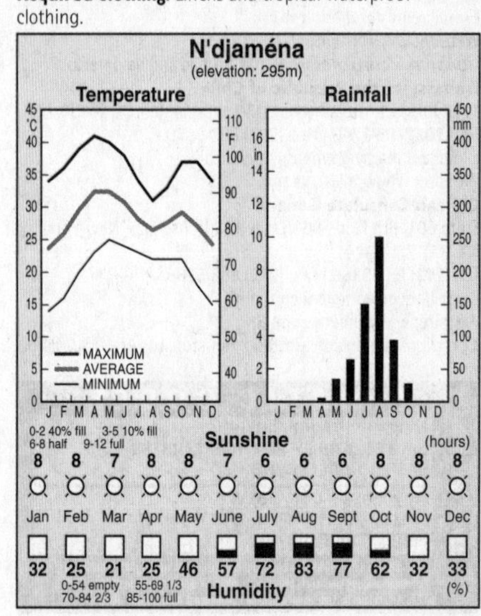

A B C D E F G H I J K L M N O P Q R S T U V W X Y Z

Chile

LATEST TRAVEL ADVICE CONTACTS

British Foreign and Commonwealth Office
Tel: (0870) 606 0290 Website: www.fco.gov.uk

US Department of State
Website: http://travel.state.gov/travel

Canadian Department of Foreign Affairs and Int'l Trade
Tel: (1 800) 267 8376 Website: www.dfait-maeci.gc.ca

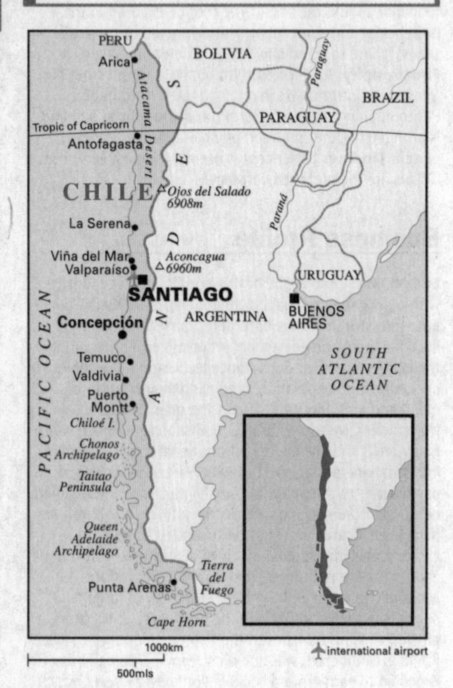

Location: West coast of South America.

Country dialling code: 56.

Servicio Nacional de Turismo (SERNATUR) (Tourist Office)
Avenida Providencia 1550, PO Box 7500548, Santiago, Chile
Tel: (2) 731 8310 *or* 8300 *or* 8336/7. Fax: (2) 236 4054.
E-mail: info@sernatur.cl
Website: www.sernatur.cl

Embassy and Consulate of the Republic of Chile
12 Devonshire Street, London W1G 7DS, UK
Tel: (020) 7580 6392 (embassy) *or* 7580 1023 (visa section and tourist office).
Fax: (020) 7436 5204.
E-mail: embachile@embachile.co.uk (embassy) *or* cglonduk@congechileuk.demon.co.uk (consulate).
Website: www.echileuk.demon.co.uk
Opening hours: Mon-Fri 0900-1730; Mon-Thurs 0930-1700, Fri 0930-1400 (consulate, by appointment only).

British Embassy
Casilla 72D, Avenida el Bosque Norte 0125, Las Condes, Santiago, Chile
Tel: (2) 370 4100.
Fax: (2) 370 4170 (consular) *or* 370 4180 (commercial).
E-mail: embsan@britemb.cl
Website: www.britemb.cl
Honorary consulates in: Punta Arenas and Valparaiso.

Embassy of the Republic of Chile
1732 Massachussets Avenue, NW, Washington, DC 20036, USA
Tel: (202) 785 1746. Fax: (202) 887 5579.
E-mail: embassy@embassyofchile.org
Website: www.chile-usa.org

Chilean Consulate General
Suite 601, 6th Floor, 866 United Nations Plaza, New York, NY 10017, USA
Tel: (212) 980 3366. Fax: (212) 888 5288.
E-mail: recepcion@chileny.com
Website: www.chileny.com
Consulates in: Boston, Chicago, Houston, Los Angeles, Miami, Philadelphia, Puerto Rico, San Francisco and Washington.

Embassy of the United States of America
Street address: Avenida Andrés Bello 2800, Las Condes, Santiago, Chile
Postal address: Casilla 27-D, Santiago, Chile
Tel: (2) 232 2600 *or* 330 3005 (consular information hotline).
Fax: (2) 330 3710.
Website: www.usembassy.cl

Embassy of the Republic of Chile
50 O'Connor Street, Suite 1413, Ottawa, Ontario K1P 6L2, Canada
Tel: (613) 235 4402 *or* 9940. Fax: (613) 235 1176.
E-mail: echileca@chile.ca
Website: www.chile.ca

Chilean Consulate General
1010 Sherbrooke Street West, Suite 710, Montréal, Québec H3A 2R7, Canada
Tel: (514) 499 0405. Fax: (514) 499 8914.
E-mail: cgmontca@qc.aira.com
Website: www.chilemtl.ca
Consulates General in: Toronto and Vancouver.

Canadian Embassy
Nueva Tajamar 481, North Tower, Piso 12, Santiago, Chile
Tel: (2) 362 9660. Fax: (2) 362 9663.
E-mail: stago@international.gc.ca
Website: www.dfait-maeci.gc.ca/chile
The visa section is in the southern tower on the 14th Floor.

TIMATIC CODES

Health	AMADEUS: **TI-DFT/JIB/HE** GALILEO/WORLDSPAN: **TI-DFT/JIB/HE** SABRE: **TIDFT/JIB/HE**
Visa	AMADEUS: **TI-DFT/JIB/VI** GALILEO/WORLDSPAN: **TI-DFT/JIB/VI** SABRE: **TIDFT/JIB/VI**

To access TIMATIC country information on Health and Visa regulations through the Computer Reservations System (CRS), type in the appropriate command line listed above.

General Information

AREA: 756,096 sq km (291,930 sq miles).
POPULATION: 15,589,147 (2002 official estimate).
POPULATION DENSITY: 20 per sq km.
CAPITAL: Santiago (de Chile). **Population**: 4,668,473 (2002).
GEOGRAPHY: Chile is situated in South America, bordered to the north by Peru, to the east by Bolivia and Argentina, to the west by the Pacific and to the south by the Antarctic. The country exercises sovereignty over a number of islands off the coast, including the Juan Fernández Islands and Easter Island. Chile is one of the most remarkably shaped countries in the world; a ribbon of land, 4200km (2610 miles) long and nowhere more than 180km (115 miles) wide. The Andes and a coastal highland range take up one-third or half of the width in parts, and run parallel with each other from north to south. The coastal range forms high, sloped cliffs into the sea from the northern to the central area. Between the ranges runs a fertile valley, except in the north where transverse ranges join the two major ones, and in the far south where the sea has broken through the coastal range to form an assortment of archipelagos and channels. The country contains wide variations of soil and vast differences of climate. This is reflected in the distribution of the population, and in the wide range of occupations from area to area. The northern part of the country consists mainly of the Atacama Desert, the driest in the world. It is also the main mining area. The central zone is predominantly agricultural. The south is forested and contains some agriculture; further south, the forests on the Atlantic side give way to rolling grassland on which sheep and cattle are raised.
GOVERNMENT: Republic. Gained independence from Spain in 1810. **Head of State and Government**: President Ricardo Lagos Escobar since 2000.
LANGUAGE: The official language is Spanish, but English is widely spoken.
RELIGION: Predominantly Christian, of which 72 per cent are Roman Catholic.
TIME: Mainland and Juan Fernández Islands: GMT - 5 (GMT - 4 from second Sunday in October to second Saturday in March).
Easter Island: GMT - 7 (GMT - 6 from second Sunday in October to second Saturday in March).
ELECTRICITY: 220 volts AC, 50Hz. Three-pin plugs and screw-type bulbs are used.
COMMUNICATIONS: Telephone: Full IDD available. Country code: 56. Outgoing international code: 00. *Compañia de Teléfonos de Chile* provides most services, though there are a few independent companies. Cheap rate is applicable Mon-Fri 1800-0500 and all day Saturday, Sunday and public holidays. **Mobile telephone:** GSM 1900 network. Operators include *Entel PCS* (website: www.entelpcs.cl), *Telefonia Movil* and *Telefónica Movil de Chile*. **Fax:** *ITT Communicaciones*, *Telex Chile* and *Transradio Chilena* provide services in main towns.
Internet: ISPs include *Entel Chile* (website: www.entelchile.net). There are some Internet cafes in the main towns. **Telegram:** *Telex Chile*, *Transradio Chilena* and *ITT Communicaciones Mundiales* provide services in main towns. **Post:** Daily airmail services to Europe take approximately three to four days. Post office hours in Santiago: Mon-Fri 0900-1800; Sat 0900-1300. **Press:** Spanish dailies include *El Mercurio*, *La Nación* and *Las Ultimas Noticias*.
Radio: BBC World Service (website: www.bbc.co.uk/worldservice) and Voice of America (website: www.voa.gov) can be received.

Passport/Visa

	Passport Required?	Visa Required?	Return Ticket Required?
Full British	Yes	No/1	Yes
Australian	Yes	1/2	Yes
Canadian	Yes	1/2	Yes
USA	Yes	1/2	Yes
Other EU	Yes	1	Yes
Japanese	Yes	No/1	Yes

Note: *Regulations and requirements may be subject to change at short notice, and you are advised to contact the appropriate diplomatic or consular authority before finalising travel arrangements. Details of these may be found at the head of this country's entry. Any numbers in the chart refer to the footnotes below.*

PASSPORTS: Valid passport required by all except:
(a) nationals of Argentina, Brazil, Colombia, Paraguay and Uruguay, provided not entering under commercial contract or as students or as immigrants, can enter with a special identity card (*Cédula de Identitad*) for short-term visits (except foreign residents of these countries who *do* need a passport); (b) Chinese residents of Taiwan (China) and nationals of Taiwan, Mexico and Peru who have an official travel document issued by the Organisation of American States. Documents have to remain valid for six months after departure.
Note: Passports issued to children must contain a photo and state the nationality.
VISAS: As regulations are subject to change at short notice it is advisable to check with the Chilean Consulate for the latest information. At present, a visa is not required by the following:
(a) **1**. nationals of countries mentioned in the chart above for a touristic stay of up to 90 days (except nationals of Greece, who can stay up to 60 days, and nationals of Latvia, who *do* need a visa);
(b) nationals of Andorra, Antigua & Barbuda, The Bahamas, Barbados, Bolivia, Bulgaria, Croatia, Dominican Republic, Ecuador, El Salvador, Grenada, Guatemala, Honduras, Iceland, Israel, Jamaica, Korea (Rep), Liechtenstein, Mauritius, Mexico, Monaco, New Zealand, Nicaragua, Norway, Panama, St Kitts & Nevis, St Lucia, San Marino, Serbia & Montenegro, South Africa, Surinam, Switzerland, Tonga, Turkey and Venezuela for stays of up to 90 days;
(c) nationals of Indonesia and Peru for stays of up to 60 days;
(d) nationals of Belize, Costa Rica, Malaysia and Singapore for touristic stays of up to 30 days;
(e) transit passengers continuing their journey on the same or first connecting aircraft provided holding required travel documents for onward destination and not leaving the airport transit lounge.
Note: 2. Nationals of Australia, Canada, Mexico and the USA entering Chile for touristic purposes will be charged a processing fee payable on arrival and in cash only.
Types of visa and cost: *Tourist*, *Visitor*, *Residence*. Cost varies according to nationality of applicant.
Validity: Tourist and Visitor (up to 90 days depending on nationality); Residence (enquire at Embassy).
Application to: Consulate (or Consular section at Embassy); see *Contact Addresses* section.
Application requirements: (a) Valid passport. (b) Evidence of sufficient funds to cover stay. (c) Return or onward ticket. (d) Fee.
Working days required: Up to 15.
Temporary residence: Not readily granted. Enquire at the Consulate or Consular Section of the Embassy (see *Contact Addresses* section).

Money

Currency: Chilean Peso (peso) = 100 centavos. Notes are in denominations of peso20,000, 10,000, 5000, 2000 and 1000. Coins are in denominations of peso500, 100, 50, 10, 5 and 1.
Currency exchange: Foreign exchange transactions can be conducted through commercial banks, *casas de cambio*, or authorised shops, restaurants, hotels and clubs. Visitors should not be tempted by the premiums of 10 to 15 per cent over the official rate offered by black marketeers. *Casas de cambio* are open daily 0900-1900.
Credit & debit cards: American Express, Diners Club, MasterCard and Visa are accepted. Check with your credit or debit card company for details of merchant acceptability and other services which may be available.
Travellers cheques: Must be changed before 1200 except in *casas de cambio* (which in any case tend to offer better rates than banks). There may be some difficulty exchanging travellers cheques outside major towns. To avoid additional exchange rate charges, travellers are advised to take travellers cheques in US Dollars.
Currency restrictions: There are no restrictions on the import and export of either local or foreign currency.
Exchange rate indicators: The following figures are included as a guide to the movements of the Chilean Peso

against Sterling and the US Dollar:

Date	Feb '04	May '04	Aug '04	Nov '04
£1.00=	1060.75	1143.55	1178.64	1112.08
$1.00=	582.75	640.25	639.75	587.25

Banking hours: Mon-Fri 0900-1400.

Duty Free

The following goods may be imported into Chile without incurring customs duty:
400 cigarettes and 500g of tobacco and 50 large cigars or 50 small cigars; 2.5l of alcohol (only for visitors over 18 years of age); a reasonable quantity of perfume.
Prohibited items: Parrots.

Public Holidays

2005: Jan 1 New Year's Day. **Mar 25** Good Friday. **Mar 26** Holy Saturday. **May 1** Labour Day. **May 21** Navy Day. **May 23*** Corpus Christi. **Jun 29** St Peter and St Paul. **Aug 15** Assumption. **Sep 5** Reconciliation Day. **Sep 18** Independence Day. **Sep 19** Army Day. **Oct 12** Dia de la Raza (Columbus Day). **Nov 1** All Saints' Day. **Dec 8** Immaculate Conception. **Dec 25** Christmas Day.
2006: Jan 1 New Year's Day. **Apr 14** Good Friday. **Apr 15** Holy Saturday. **May 1** Labour Day. **May 21** Navy Day. **Jun 12*** Corpus Christi. **Jun 29** St Peter and St Paul. **Aug 15** Assumption. **Sep 4** Reconciliation Day. **Sep 18** Independence Day. **Sep 19** Army Day. **Oct 12** Dia de la Raza (Columbus Day). **Nov 1** All Saints' Day. **Dec 8** Immaculate Conception. **Dec 25** Christmas Day.
Note: *Corpus Christi dates for 2005 and 2006 are actually May 26 and Jun 15 respectively. However, the holiday is observed on the Monday closest to these dates.

Health

	Special Precautions?	Certificate Required?
Yellow Fever	1	No
Cholera	No	No
Typhoid & Polio	2	N/A
Malaria	No	N/A

Note: *Regulations and requirements may be subject to change at short notice, and you are advised to contact your doctor well in advance of your intended date of departure. Any numbers in the chart refer to the footnotes below.*

1: Immunisation against Yellow Fever is required if going to Easter Island within six days of visiting infected countries.
2: Immunisation against typhoid and Polio are sometimes advised.
Food & drink: All water should be regarded as being potentially contaminated. Water used for drinking, brushing teeth or making ice should have first been boiled or otherwise sterilised. Milk is pasteurised and is safe to drink without boiling, except in very remote areas of the countryside. Only eat well-cooked meat and fish, preferably served hot. Pork, salad and mayonnaise may carry increased risk. Vegetables should be cooked and fruit peeled.
Other risks: Immunisation against *tetanus* and *hepatitis A* is advised. Epidemic outbreaks of *meningococcal meningitis* occur. *Chagas' disease* has been reported in rural areas but other insect-borne diseases are largely absent.
Rabies is present in animals. For those at high risk, vaccination before arrival should be considered. If you are bitten, seek medical advice without delay.
Health care: Health insurance is essential.

Travel - International

AIR: Chile has one privately owned national airline: *LAN-Chile (LA)* (website: www.lan.com), which deals with international flights. Its subsidiary, *Lanexpress (LU)*, deals with domestic flights.
Approximate flight times: From Santiago to *London* is 16 hours 30 minutes.
International airports: *Santiago (SCL)* (Arturo Merino Benitez) (website: www.aeropuertosantiago.cl). The airport is 17km (11 miles) northwest of Santiago (travel time – 30 minutes). Bus services to the city centre operate 24 hours a day. Return is from the underground stations Los Héroes, Estación Central and Las Rejas or Moneda/corner of San Martín. Taxis to the city are also available. Official taxis are blue with official documentation. Airport facilities include bar, bureaux de change, restaurants, car hire, post office and tourist office.
Air passes: *The Mercosur Airpass*: Valid within Argentina, Brazil, Chile (except Easter Island), Paraguay and Uruguay. Participating airlines include *Austral (AU), LAN-Chile (LA), LAPA (MJ), Pluna (PU), Transbrasil Airlines (TR)* and *VARIG (RG)*, with the subsidiary airlines of *Nordeste (JH)* and *Rio Sul (SL)*. The pass can only be purchased by passengers who live outside South America and who have a return ticket. Only eight flight coupons are allowed with a maximum of four coupons for each country and is valid for seven to a maximum of 30 days. At least two countries must be visited (to a maximum of five) and the flight route cannot be changed. A maximum of two stopovers is allowed per country.
The Visit South America Pass: Must be bought outside South America in country of residence and allows unlimited travel to 36 cities in the following countries: Argentina, Bolivia, Brazil, Chile (except Easter Island), Colombia, Ecuador, Paraguay, Peru, Uruguay and Venezuela. To be eligible, passengers must fly with *Lan* airlines (*LanChile, LanEcuador* or *LanPeru*). A minimum of three flights must be booked, with no maximum; the maximum stay is 60 days, with no minimum, and prices depend on the amount of flight zones covered. There is no discount for children, although infants travelling without need of a seat may do so free of charge. For further details, contact one of the participating airlines.
Departure tax: US$26 for distances over 500km.
SEA: The principal port is Empremar in Valparaiso. Important shipping lines are *Compañía Chilena de Navegación Interoceánica (CCNI)* (website: www.ccni.cl); *Compañía Argentina de Navegación Dodero (CADND)* (from Buenos Aires); *Compañía Sud Americana de Vapores (CSAV)* (from New York and European ports) (website: www.csav.cl); *Delta Line Cruises* (from the USA via the Panama Canal); *Holland America Line*; *Norwegian Cruise Line*; and *Silversea Cruises*.
RAIL: Some rail connections with neighbouring countries use buses for part of the journey. There are trains running between Arica and Tacna in Peru and La Paz in Bolivia.
ROAD: The Pan American Highway enters Chile through Arica. TEPSA buses come to Chile from as far north as Ecuador. There are also services from Argentina and Brazil to Santiago.

Travel - Internal

AIR: There are frequent services to main towns. The southern part of the country relies heavily on air links. Reservations are essential. Internal passenger air services are operated by the domestic subsidary of *LAN-Chile, Lanexpress (LU)*, as well as by a number of air taxi companies. Services connecting the main towns are frequent during weekdays, and are fairly regular. There are one-month 'Visit Chile' tickets available from *Lanexpress* and *LAN-Chile* covering the north and the south of the country. Air passes sold in conjunction with *LAN* transatlantic flights cost US$250 for the first three coupons and US$60 per additional coupon (up to a maximum of six). A coupon is worth one sector of a flight. When travelling long haul with another airline, the costs are US$350 and US$80 per additional coupon. Passes must be obtained abroad and it is advisable to make reservations well in advance. An air taxi runs a daily service during the summer months to the Juan Fernández Islands from Valparaíso and Santiago.
Departure tax: Peso4,521 or 3,444. For distances under 270km, the departure tax is peso1,781.
SEA: Coastal passenger shipping lines are unreliable and infrequent. Boat services run from Valparaíso to Easter Island and Robinson Crusoe Island (part of the Juan Fernández Islands) once a month.
RAIL: The state railway (run by the *State Railway Company*, website: www.efe.cl) runs between Santiago and Temuco. Principal trains also carry vehicles. Children under 1.20m in height travel free. Train fares are from £10-53.
ROAD: Chile has about 80,000km (49,460 miles) of good roads. The Pan American Highway crosses the country from north to south (a total of 3455km or 2147 miles) from the Peruvian border to Puerto Montt. It is advisable in remoter areas to carry spare petrol and an additional spare tyre. Traffic drives on the right. **Bus**: Intercity buses are cheap and reliable. There is a luxury north-south service running most of the length of the country. **Taxi**: Most have meters, but for long journeys fares should be agreed beforehand. A surcharge of 50 per cent applies on Sundays after 2100. Taxis in Santiago are black and yellow. Tipping is not expected. **Car hire**: Self-drive cars are available at the airport and in major city centres. They are hired on a daily basis, plus a mileage charge and 20 per cent tax. A large guarantee deposit is often required. The Automóvil Club de Chile, Andrés Bello 1863, Santiago can supply road maps (tel: (2) 431 1000; fax: (2) 431 1160; e-mail: acchinfo@automovilclub.cl; website: www.cmet.net/acchi). **Documentation**: An International or Inter-American Driving Permit is necessary.
URBAN: Santiago has three metro lines, as well as bus, minibus and shared 'Taxibus' services. A fourth and fifth metro line is under construction. Fares on the metro depend on the time of day in which travel occurs. 10-journey tickets (*carnets*) are available. Taxis are plentiful and can be flagged down in the streets. The different tariffs are displayed in the taxis. Taxi drivers do not expect tips. The buses and minibuses have flat fares. There is a higher rate for shared taxis. There are bus and taxi services in most towns.
Travel times: The following chart gives approximate travel times from **Santiago** (in hours and minutes) to other major cities/towns in Chile.

	Air	Road	Rail
Arica	2.40	28.00	-
Concepción	1.30	9.00	7.00
Portillo	2.30	-	-
Puerto Montt	1.45	11.00	17.00
Punta Arenas	3.25	120.00	-
Viña del Mar	-	2.00	-
Easter Island	5.00	-	-

Accommodation

HOTELS: Chile offers excellent accommodation. Several new luxury hotels have recently opened in Santiago and throughout the country. Chile's famous hospitality is very apparent in provinces where it is common to see the owner or manager sit down to dinner with guests. Advance bookings are essential in resort areas during the high season.
The cost of accommodation in Santiago is higher than in the provinces. Rates in Valparaíso, Viña del Mar and other holiday resorts may be increased during the summer holiday from January to March. Members of foreign motoring organisations can obtain discounts at hotels by joining the Automóvil Club de Chile (see address in *Travel – Internal* section). The address of the Chilean National Hotel Association is HOTELGA, Nueva Tajamar 481, Oficina 806, North Tower, Las Condes, Santiago (tel: (2) 203 6625; fax: (2) 203 6626).
Grading: Hotels in Chile are graded from **5 to 2 stars**. A description of the facilities included in the Chilean hotel system is as follows: **5-star**: Luxurious rooms with air conditioning, private bathroom and 24-hour room service; garden; restaurant; bar; swimming pool; laundry services; shops; conference rooms; recreational and medical facilities. **4-star**: Rooms with air conditioning and private bathroom; restaurant; bar; laundry services; tourist information; conference rooms; medical and recreational facilities. **3-star**: Rooms with private bathrooms; laundry services; first aid and continental breakfast. **2-star**: 30 per cent of rooms with private bathroom.
Government tax: VAT of 19 per cent is levied on all hotel bills, except those paid in foreign currencies by foreign visitors for which an export bill is required.
CAMPING/CARAVANNING: Camping facilities exist throughout Chile. A list of campsites may be obtained from Chilean embassies. Official sites are expensive.
YOUTH HOSTELS: There are 13 hostels in Chile. Membership of the *Asociación Chilena de Albergues Turísticos Juveniles*, Av. Hernando de Aguirre 201, of. 602, Providencia (tel: (2) 233 3220; fax: (2) 233 2555; e-mail: hostelling@hostelling.cl; website: www.hostelling.cl), is required; many hostels are extremely crowded and it is advised to book in advance where possible.

Resorts & Excursions

NORTHERN REGION

Arica, near the northern border with Peru, is an excellent tourist centre. It has good beaches and the famous **San Marcos Cathedral**. Conditions in the area are ideal for deep-sea fishing. The unique landscape of **Altiplano**, near Arica, where vast volcanoes, salt marshes and lakes exist together upon a 12,000 ft plateau, is home to the indigenous Aymara Indians. Llamas and alpacas can be seen here. The nearby UNESCO World Biosphere Reserve, **Lauca National Park**, is worth visiting. Travelling south through the Atacama Desert, excursions can be made to the hot springs of **Mamina** and to the oasis of the **Pica Valley**. The port of **Antofagasta** is the stopping point for air services and for most shipping lines. From here, a visit can be made to **Chuquicamata**, the world's largest opencast copper mine, and also to the archaeological oasis town of **San Pedro de Atacama** and to the geysers at **El Tatio**.
Further south is **Coquimbo**, situated in one of the best harbours on the coast. Nearby is the beautiful bathing resort of **Los Vilos**. 9 miles north of Coquimbo is **La Serena**, the provincial capital. This charming and well laid-out town is graced with fine buildings and streets, and good reproductions of the attractive Spanish colonial style of architecture. The town is at the mouth of the **Elqui River** and excursions can be made from here to the rich fruit-growing region of the **Elqui Valley**, which is also full of reminiscences of the Chilean Nobel Prize Winner, Gabriela Mistral. Tours can also be arranged to the **Tololo Observatory**, the largest in the southern hemisphere.

CENTRAL REGION AND THE ISLANDS

This is the most temperate and pastoral region of the country, where the snow-capped peaks of the **Andes** provide a backdrop for rolling green fields, vineyards and orange groves. **Valparaíso**, the principal port, has many attractions. Only 8km (5 miles) to the north is **Viña del Mar**, Chile's principal and most fashionable seaside resort with casinos, clubs and modern hotels. The **Valparaíso Sporting Club** offers a race course, polo grounds and playing fields. From Valparaíso there are excellent road and rail services to **Santiago**, where visitors will find all the

A B C D E F G H I J K L M N O P Q R S T U V W X Y Z

conveniences of a modern capital city, including good hotels to suit all tastes. The Virgin Mary guards the city from the peak of the 860m (2822ft) **Cerro San Cristóbal** (Saint Christopher's Hill), in the northeast of the city, where a zoo, gardens, restaurants and fine views of the city can be found; the **Club Hípico** and the **Prince of Wales Country Club** provide sporting facilities. From Santiago it is also possible to visit ski resorts such as **Portillo**, **Farellones**, and the newest and most fashionable, **Valle Nevado**.
Immediately south of Santiago are the many vineyards where excellent Chilean wine is produced.
PACIFIC ISLANDS: 650km (403 miles) west of Valparaiso are the **Juan Fernández Islands**, which can be reached either by plane or boat from the Chilean mainland. Alexander Selkirk was shipwrecked here in the early 18th century, and Defoe based his novel *Robinson Crusoe* on Selkirk's adventures.
Easter Island is another Pacific Chilean possession, situated 3800km (2361 miles) west of the mainland. It is most famous for the Moai, gigantic stone figures up to 9m (30ft) tall which are found all over the island. Other sites include the crater of the volcano **Rano Kao**, the rock carvings at **Oronco**, and the museum in the main town of **Hanga Roa**. The best method of travel to the island is by air. Tour guides and guest house keepers tend to meet every plane, so although it is possible to book good hotel accommodation from Santiago or Valparaiso, it is not essential. Many of the hotels specialise in catering for groups and will arrange tours if asked. Tours can also be arranged with a tour guide.

SOUTHERN REGION

A visit to the impressive waterfalls at **Laguna de Laja** is recommended. **Temuco** marks the beginning of the **Lake District**, where **Lake Villarica** and the **Trancura** and **Cincira** rivers combine to create beautiful scenery, and an angler's paradise. **Lake Todos los Santos** is also well worth a visit. At the southernmost end of the railway line and the Pan American Highway, there is the picturesque town of **Puerto Montt** and, nearby, the colourful small fishing port of **Angelmo**. Inveterate travellers will wish to go on to visit **Chiloé Island**, and should not miss the UNESCO Biosphere Reserve of **Torres del Paine National Park** (located in Chilean Patagonia), which is simply one of the most beautiful, unspoiled and remote places on the planet. The whole area of **Magallanes** and **Tierra del Fuego** is worth exploring during the summer season.

Sport & Activities

Trekking: One of Chile's most popular regions for trekking is the Lake District, which lies some 900km (560 miles) south of Santiago, and where several of the country's national parks can be visited. The *Lago Verde Trail* in the *Parque Nacional Huerquehue* leads through beech forests, past waterfalls and offers good views of the *Volcán Villarica*. The fairly remote *Parque Nacional Queulat* (characterised by glaciers, fjords and volcanic peaks) is a popular destination for adventure travel package tours. Guided hikes, ecology tours and boat trips are available at *Parque Nacional Conguillio*. The *Parque Nacional Torres del Paine*, which lies 400km (250 miles) northwest of Punta Arenas, offers abundant wildlife and spectacular scenery consisting of huge glaciers, fjords, waterfalls and blue lakes dotted with icebergs. In many cases, visitors intending to trek through Chile individually must register with local rangers or at the nearest CONAF (*Corporación Nacional Forestal*) office. At the *Parque Nacional Torres del Paine*, solo treks are not allowed.
Wildlife: Naturalists wishing to follow in the footsteps of Charles Darwin (who wrote extensively about Chile's fauna and flora) may head to the *Juan Fernández Islands* (located in the Pacific, some 965km/600 miles west of Santiago). The islands contain numerous indigenous plants and animals, most notably the Juan Fernández fur seal and the Juan Fernández hummingbird. The *Parque Nacional Lauca* (155km/95 miles from Arica) is filled with flamingos, rheas (an ostrich-like bird) and llamas. Guanacos (or *llama guanicoe*) roam freely in the Parque Nacional Torres del Paine (see above), which is also a good place to observe giant condors. Magellanic penguins can be seen at *Chiloé Island* (485km/300 miles from Santiago), a region of evergreen forests and fjords much admired by Darwin. The abundant coastal wildlife of Patagonia and Tierra del Fuego includes large colonies of sea elephants, sea lions and penguins.
Climbing: The Lake District's *Volcán Villarrica* and *Volcán Osorno* are the most popular destinations. Various companies offer guided ascents, but ice gear is required. Guides are compulsory.
Fishing: This is particularly good in the Lake District and in Patagonia, South America's southernmost region. The lakes near *Puerto Montt*, a port city whose economy is mainly based on fishing, offer excellent trout fishing.
Whitewater rafting: The *Maipo*, *Claro*, *Trancura* and *Bio-Bio* rivers are the main destinations and specialist operators can organise week-long trips. The scenery around the Bio-Bio includes hot springs and waterfalls, but the construction of several dams along the river will change conditions.
Watersports: Chile's coastline is indented by many bays and fjords where various types of watersports, including **swimming**, **diving**, **water-skiing** and **boating** can be enjoyed.
Equestrian sports: As an alternative to walking, guided **horseback** trips are widely available in Chile's national parks. The *International Horsemanship Championship* is held in Viña del Mar in January. The two main horseraces of the year are the *Derby* (Viña del Mar, January) and *el Ensayo* (Santiago, October).
Skiing: *Portillo* (150km/95 miles northeast of Santiago) is a world-famous ski resort offering both downhill and cross-country skiing and **ice skating** (on the spectacular *Laguna del Inca*). Other ski slopes in the area can be found at *Farellones-El Colorado*, *La Parva* and *Valle Nevado*. The best time to ski is August (with the season running from June to September).
Glacier cruises: Departing from Puerto Montt, glacier cruises follow a spectacular route through Chile's Inside Passage, the Beagle Channel and around Cape Horn, passing through glacial valleys (notably at *Laguna San Rafael*), fjords and past huge icebergs. Passengers can disembark at various points en route, notably at Puerto Natales and on the Argentinian portion of Tierra del Fuego.
Antarctic trips: Chile's southernmost city, *Punta Arenas* (located 2170km/1350 miles south of Santiago), is one of the most widely used departure points for trips to Antarctica.

Social Profile

FOOD & DRINK: Santiago has many international restaurants; waiter service is usual. The evening will often include floor shows and dancing. Examples of typical national dishes are *empanada* (combination of meat, chicken or fish, with onions, eggs, raisins and olives inside a flour pastry), *humitas* (seasoned corn paste, wrapped in corn husks and boiled), *cazuela de ave* (soup with rice, vegetables, chicken and herbs), *bife a lo pobre* (steak with french fries, onions and eggs) and *parrillada* (selection of meat grilled over hot coals, often including delicacies such as intestines, udders and blood sausages). Seafood is good. Best known are the huge lobsters from Juan Fernández Islands. Abalone, sea urchins, clams, prawns and giant *choros* (mussels) are also common.
Chile is famous for its wine. *Pisco* is a powerful liqueur distilled from grapes after wine pressing. Grapes are also used to make the sweet brown *chicha* as well as *aguardiente*, similar to brandy. Beer is drunk throughout the country.
NIGHTLIFE: While many restaurants and hotels offer entertainment, there are also a number of independent discos and nightclubs. **Casinos**: The Municipal Casino in Viña del Mar offers large gambling salons, full cabaret and boîte with Chile's best dance bands. A casino operates in Gran Hotel in Puerto Varas between September and March. Arica also has a casino operating throughout the year with baccarat, roulette, black jack, a restaurant and late night cabaret performances.
SHOPPING: Special purchases include textiles such as colourful handwoven ponchos, vicuna rugs and copper work. Chilean stones such as lapis lazuli, jade, amethyst, agate and onyx are all good buys. **Shopping hours**: Mon-Fri 1000-2000, Sat 1000-1400. Large shopping malls are open daily 1000-2100.
SPECIAL EVENTS: The following is a selection of special events occurring in Chile in 2005:
Jan *Feast Day of St Sebastian*, Yumbel. **Jan-Feb** *Semanas Musicales de Frutilar*, Trilla. **Feb** *Festival Costumbrista*, Castro. **Mar** *Los Andes International Fair*. **Apr** *Fiesta de Cuasimodo* (traditional religious festival). **Jul** *Fiesta de la Tirana*. **Sep** *Independence Day Celebrations*, Rancagua. **Oct** *Saint's Day of St Francis of Assisi*. **Dec 26** *La Fiesta Grande*, Andacollo.
Note: Dates for special events in Chile change frequently.
SOCIAL CONVENTIONS: Handshaking is the customary form of greeting. Most Chileans use a double surname and only the first part should be used in addressing them. Normal courtesies should be observed when visiting local people. It is very common to entertain at home and it is acceptable for invitees to give small presents as a token of thanks. Informal, conservative clothes are acceptable in most places but women should not wear shorts outside resort areas. **Tipping**: Restaurants and bars add 10 per cent to the bill. However, waiters will expect a 10 per cent cash tip in addition.

Business Profile

ECONOMY: With well-developed industrial and service sectors, Chile has one of Latin America's strongest economies. However, it still depends on export of primary commodities for a large proportion of its export earnings. Chile has a large surplus of fruit and vegetables available for export to North America and Europe but is not entirely self-sufficient in agricultural produce. The industrial base has grown substantially over the last 30 years. Imported oil and natural gas provide most of Chile's energy requirements, but coal and hydro-electricity also make an important contribution. The service sector has developed rapidly in recent years, especially financial services, following the government's introduction in the mid-1990s of a unique comprehensive pension scheme. Chile's economic performance has been strong since 2000 with annual growth around 7 per cent and low inflation; unemployment hovers just below 10 per cent. The USA is the largest trading partner, followed by Japan, Brazil, Germany and the UK. Chile is a member of the Latin American Integration Association (ALADI), the southern free trade zone (Mercosur), and the Rio Group. This latter organisation, established in 1987, comprises a dozen Latin American countries with common interests in promoting free trade, suppressing corruption and drug trafficking, and other matters. The country was also admitted in 1994 to the Asia-Pacific Economic Cooperation Forum and may be the first South American country to join the North American Free Trade Area (NAFTA, presently comprising the USA, Canada and Mexico). A bilateral free trade agreement between the US and Chile was concluded during 2003.
BUSINESS: Businesspeople should wear formal clothes in dark colours for official functions, dinners, smart restaurants and hotels. Dress is usually stipulated on invitations. There is a tendency to formality with many Old World courtesies. Best months for business visits are April to December. **Business hours**: Mon-Fri 0900-1830.
COMMERCIAL INFORMATION: The following organisations can offer advice: Cámara de Comercio de Santiago de Chile AG, Monjitaf 392, Santiago (tel: (2) 360 7000; fax: (2) 633 2879; e-mail: rrii@ccs.cl; website: www.ccs.cl) *or* the Cámara Nacional de Comercio de Chile, Merced 230, Santiago (tel: (2) 365 4000; fax: (2) 365 4001; e-mail: cnc@cnc.cl; website: www.cnc.cl).
CONFERENCES/CONVENTIONS: Information on conferences and conventions can be obtained from the Santiago Convention Bureau, Officina 64, Avenida El Bosque Norte 0140, Las Condes, Santiago (tel/fax: (2) 333 8085 *or* 333 7977; e-mail: info@scb.cl; website: www.scb.cl); *or* the Camara Nacional de Comercio de Chile, Merced 230, Santiago (tel: (2) 365 4000; fax: (2) 365 4001; e-mail: cnc@cn.cl; website: www.cn.cl).

Climate

Ranges from hot and arid in the north to very cold in the far south. The central areas have a mild Mediterranean climate with a wet season (May to August). Beyond Puerto Montt in the south is one of the wettest and stormiest areas in the world.
Required clothing: Lightweight cottons and linens in northern and central areas. Rainwear is advised during rainy seasons. Mediumweights and waterproofing are needed in the south.

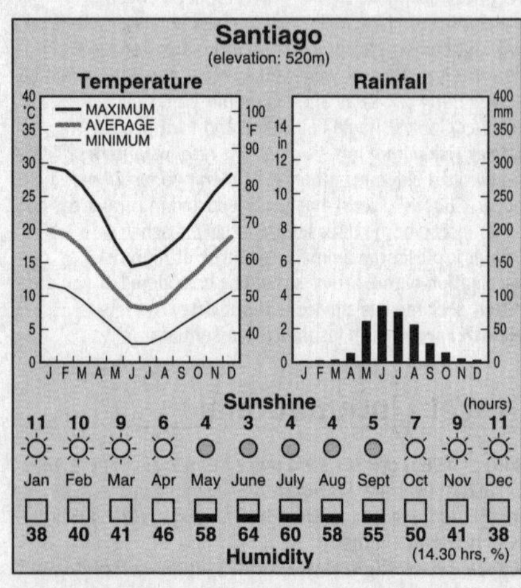

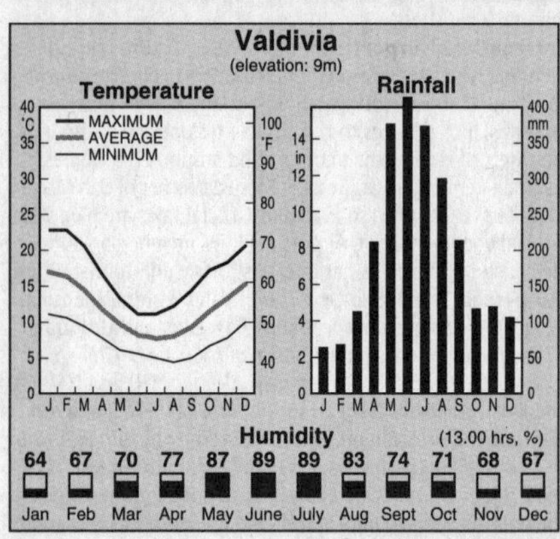

China

LATEST TRAVEL ADVICE CONTACTS

British Foreign and Commonwealth Office
Tel: (0870) 606 0290 Website: www.fco.gov.uk

US Department of State
Website: http://travel.state.gov/travel

Canadian Department of Foreign Affairs and Int'l Trade
Tel: (1 800) 267 8376 Website: www.dfait-maeci.gc.ca

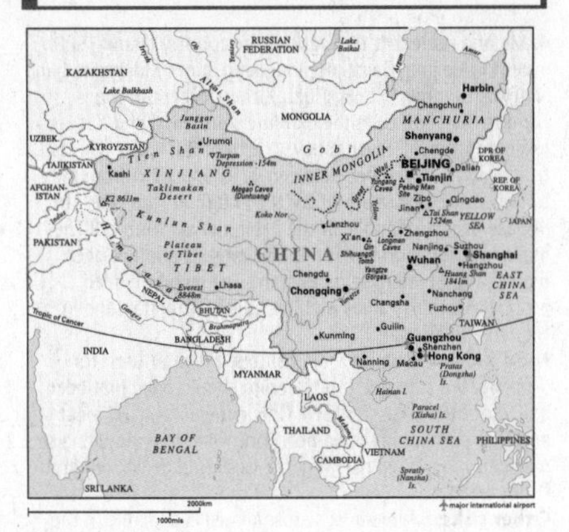

Location: East Asia.

Country dialling code: 86.

China National Tourism Administration (CNTA)
9A Jianguomennei Avenue, Beijing 100740, People's Republic of China
Tel: (10) 6520 1114. Fax: (10) 6512 2096.
E-mail: webmaster@cnta.gov.cn
Website: www.cnta.com

China International Travel Service (CITS)
CITS Building, No.1 Dongdanbei Avenue, Beijing 100800, People's Republic of China
Tel: (10) 6255 2991 *or* 8522 7930. Fax: (10) 6522 2862.
E-mail: shuyu@cits.com.cn
Website: www.cits.net

Tibet Tourism Administration
18 Yuanlin Road, Lhasa, Tibet 850001, People's Republic of China
Tel: (891) 633 5472. Fax: (891) 633 4632.

Tibet Tourism Office
Room M021 Poly Plaza, 14 Dongzhimen Nandajie, Beijing 100027, People's Republic of China
Tel: (10) 6500 1188 (ext 3423) *or* 6593 6538.
Fax: (10) 6593 6538 *or* 6503 5802.
E-mail: tibettour2001@sina.com
Website: www.tibettour.net.cn

Tibet Tourism Bureau Shanghai Office
Suite B, 2/F, QiHua Tower, 1375 Middle Huaihai Road, Shanghai 200031, People's Republic of China
Tel: (21) 6431 1184 *or* 6321 1729. Fax: (21) 6323 1016.
E-mail: ttbshanghai@163.net
Website: www.tibet-tour.com

Embassy of the People's Republic of China
49-51 Portland Place, London W1B 1JL, UK
Tel: (020) 7299 8426. Fax: (020) 7436 9178.
E-mail: press@chinese-embassy.org.uk
Website: www.chinese-embassy.org.uk
Opening hours: Mon-Fri 0900-1230 and 1330-1700.
Consular and Visa section: 31 Portland Place, London W1B 1QD, UK
Tel: (020) 7631 1430 (telephone enquiries: 1400-1600 only) *or* (09001) 880 808 (recorded visa and general information; calls cost 60p per minute). Fax: (020) 7636 9756.
Opening hours: Mon-Fri 0900-1200.

Consulate General of the People's Republic of China
Denison House, 49 Denison Road, Rusholme, Manchester M14 5RX, UK
Tel: (0161) 225 5355 *or* 248 9304. Fax: (0161) 257 2672.
E-mail: chinaconsul_man_uk@mfa.gov.cn
Website: http://manchester.chineseconsulate.org/eng

TIMATIC CODES

Health	AMADEUS: **TI-DFT/JIB/HE** GALILEO/WORLDSPAN: **TI-DFT/JIB/HE** SABRE: **TIDFT/JIB/HE**
Visa	AMADEUS: **TI-DFT/JIB/VI** GALILEO/WORLDSPAN: **TI-DFT/JIB/VI** SABRE: **TIDFT/JIB/VI**

To access TIMATIC country information on Health and Visa regulations through the Computer Reservations System (CRS), type in the appropriate command line listed above.

Consulate General of the People's Republic of China
55 Corstorphine Road, Edinburgh EH12 5QG, UK
Tel: (0131) 337 9896 *or* 3220. Fax: (0131) 337 7866.
E-mail: chinaconsul_eb_uk@mfa.gov.cn
Website: www.chinese-embassy.org.uk

China National Tourist Office (CNTO)
71 Warwick Road, London SW5 9HB, UK
Tel: (020) 7373 0888 *or* (09001) 600 188 (brochure request and general information; calls cost 60p per minute).
Fax: (020) 7370 9989.
E-mail: london@cnta.gov.cn
Website: www.cnta.gov.cn

British Embassy
11 Guang Hua Lu, Jian Guo Men Wai, Beijing 100600, People's Republic of China
Tel: (10) 5192 4000. Fax: (10) 6532 1937/8/9.
E-mail: commercialmail@beijing.fco.gov.uk (commercial section).
Website: www.uk.cn
Consular section: 21st Floor, Kerry Centre 1, Guang Hua Lu, Jian Guo Men Wai, Beijing 100020, People's Republic of China
Tel: (10) 8529 6600. Fax: (10) 8529 6080.
E-mail: pekingvisamail@fco.gov.uk
Consulates General in: Chongqing, Guangzhou and Shanghai.

Embassy of the People's Republic of China
2300 Connecticut Avenue, NW, Washington, DC 20008, USA
Tel: (202) 328 2500. Fax: (202) 328 2582.
E-mail: chinaembassy_us@fmprc.gov.cn
Website: www.china-embassy.org
Visa section: Room 110, 2201 Wisconsin Avenue, NW, Washington, DC 20007, USA
Tel: (202) 338 6688. Fax: (202) 588 9760 (visa section).
E-mail: chnvisa@bellatlantic.net
Consulates General in: Chicago, Houston, Los Angeles, New York and San Francisco.

China National Tourist Office CNTO
Suite 6413, 350 Fifth Avenue, New York, NY 10118, USA
Tel: (212) 760 8218 (information and trade enquiries).
Fax: (212) 760 8809.
E-mail: info@cnto.org
Website: www.discoverchinaforever.com
Office also in: Los Angeles.

Embassy of the United States of America
3 Xiu Shui Bei Jie, Beijing 100600, People's Republic of China
Tel: (10) 6532 3831. Fax: (10) 6532 5141 *or* 3178 (consular/visa section).
E-mail: BeijingWebmaster@state.gov *or* BeijingWebcomments@state.gov
Website: www.usembassy-china.org.cn
Consulates in: Chengdu, Guangzhou, Hong Kong, Shanghai and Shenyang.

Embassy of the People's Republic of China
515 St Patrick Street, Ottawa, Ontario K1N 5H3, Canada
Tel: (613) 789 3434. Fax: (613) 789 1414 (visa section and 24-hour recorded information line).
Website: www.chinaembassycanada.org
Consulates General in: Calgary, Toronto and Vancouver

China National Tourist Office (CNTO)
480 University Avenue, Suite 806, Toronto, Ontario M5G 1V2, Canada
Tel: (416) 599 6636 *or* (866) 599 6636 (toll-free in Canada).
Fax: (416) 599 6382.
E-mail: cnto@tourismchina-ca.com
Website: www.tourismchina-ca.com

Canadian Embassy
19 Dongzhimenwai Dajie, Chao Yang District, Beijing 100600, People's Republic of China
Tel: (10) 6532 3536 *or* 6532 3031/2 (immigration).
Fax: (10) 6532 3034 *or* 1684 (immigration) *or* 5544 (consular section).
E-mail: beijing-co@international.gc.ca *or* bejing-cs@international.gc.ca (consular section) *or* beijing-immigration@international.gc.ca (visa section).
Website: www.beijing.gc.ca
Consulates in: Guangzhou, Hong Kong, Mongolia (emergencies only) and Shanghai.

General Information

AREA: 9,572,900 sq km (3,696,100 sq miles).
POPULATION: 1,284,530,000 (official estimate 2002). Roughly a quarter of the world's population lives in China.
POPULATION DENSITY: 134.2 per sq km.
CAPITAL: Beijing (Peking). **Population**: 10,839,000 (2000). The largest city in the country, Shanghai, has a population of over 12 million and, as of 2000, 22 other cities had a population of over two million and 42 cities had a population of one to two million.
GEOGRAPHY: China is bordered to the north by Russia and Mongolia; to the east by Korea (Dem Rep), the Yellow Sea and the South China Sea; to the south by Vietnam, Laos, Myanmar, India, Bhutan and Nepal; and to the west by India, Pakistan, Afghanistan, Tajikistan, Kyrgyzstan and

Credit: © National Tourism Administration of the People's Republic of China

Kazakhstan. China has a varied terrain ranging from high plateaux in the west to flatlands in the east; mountains take up almost one-third of the land. The most notable high mountain ranges are the Himalayas, the Altai Mountains, the Tian Shan Mountains and the Kunlun Mountains. On the border with Nepal is the 8848m-(29,198ft-) high Mount Qomolangma (Mount Everest). In the west is the Qinghai/Tibet Plateau, with an average elevation of 4000m (13,200ft), known as 'the Roof of the World'. At the base of the Tian Shan Mountains is the Turpan Depression or Basin, China's lowest area, 154m (508ft) below sea level at the lowest point. China has many great river systems, notably the Yellow (Huang He) and Yangtze Kiang (Chang Jiang). Only 10 per cent of all China is suitable for agriculture.
GOVERNMENT: People's Republic. China comprises 22 Provinces, five Autonomous Regions, two Special Administrative Regions and four Municipalities directly under Central Government. **Head of State:** President Hu Jintao since 2003. **Head of Government**: Premier Wen Jiabao since 2003. Jiang Zemin, however, retains much actual power in China.
LANGUAGE: The official language is Mandarin Chinese. Among the enormous number of local dialects, large groups speak Cantonese, Fukienese, Xiamenhua and Hakka in the south. Mongolia, Tibet and Xinjiang, which are autonomous regions, have their own languages. Translation and interpreter services are good. English is spoken by many guides.
RELIGION: The principal religions and philosophies are Buddhism, Daoism and Confucianism. There are 100 million Buddhists and approximately 60 million Muslims, five million Protestants (including large numbers of Evangelicals) and four million Roman Catholics, largely independent of Vatican control.
TIME: GMT + 8. Despite the vast size of the country, Beijing time is standard throughout China.
ELECTRICITY: 220 volts AC, 50Hz. Two-pin sockets and some three-pin sockets are in use.
COMMUNICATIONS: Telephone: IDD is available. Country code: 86. Outgoing international code: 00. Antiquated internal service with public telephones in hotels and shops displaying a telephone unit sign. It is often easier to make international phone calls from China than it is to make calls internally. **Mobile telephone:** GSM 900 and 1800 networks provide coverage in Beijing, Guangzhou (Canton) and Shanghai; GSM 900 networks also exist in most other major urban areas in the southeastern and eastern regions including Chengdu and Chongqing. Networks are operated by *China Mobile* and *China Unicom* (website: www.chinaunicom.com.cn). **Fax:** A growing number of hotels offer fax facilities but are often incoming only. Rates are generally high. Faxes can also be sent from Internet cafes. **Internet:** ISPs include *Eastnet China Ltd* (website: www.eastnet.com.cn). There are Internet cafes in main towns. **Post:** Service to Europe takes from between two days and one week. Tourist hotels usually have their own post offices. All postal communications to China should be addressed 'People's Republic of China'. **Press:** The main English-language daily is the *China Daily*. There is also the weekly news magazine *Beijing Review*, with editions in English, French, German, Japanese and Spanish. National newspapers include *The Guangming Daily* and *The Worker's Daily*, with many provinces having their own local dailies as well.

Radio: BBC World Service (website: www.bbc.co.uk/worldservice) and Voice of America (website: www.voa.gov) can be received. From time to time the frequencies change and the most up-to-date can be found online.

Passport/Visa

	Passport Required?	Visa Required?	Return Ticket Required?
Full British	Yes	Yes	Yes
Australian	Yes	Yes	Yes
Canadian	Yes	Yes	Yes
USA	Yes	Yes	Yes
Other EU	Yes	Yes	Yes
Japanese	Yes	1	Yes

Note: *Regulations and requirements may be subject to change at short notice, and you are advised to contact the appropriate diplomatic or consular authority before finalising travel arrangements. Details of these may be found at the head of this country's entry. Any numbers in the chart refer to the footnotes below.*

Note: (a) China does not recognise dual nationality (eg US-Chinese, Canadian-Chinese). (b) Travellers are required to complete a health declaration certificate on arrival in China. HIV-positive travellers are not permitted to enter the country.
PASSPORTS: Required by all. Passport must be valid for at least six months for a single or double entry within three months of the date of visa issue; at least nine months for multiple entries within six months.
VISAS: Required by all except:
(a) **1.** nationals of Brunei, Japan and Singapore for stays of up to 15 days;
(b) transit passengers (except nationals of the UK and USA, who *always* require a visa) continuing their journey by the same or first connecting plane to another country within 24 hours who hold valid onward documentation and do not leave the airport.
Types of visa and cost: *Tourist/Business/Transit* (UK nationals): £30 (single-entry); £45 (double-entry); £60 (multiple-entry for business visas only; six months); £90 (multiple entry for business visas only; 12 months *and* two to five years). *Group* (at least five people): £24 per person. Visa charges for other nationals vary; check with Embassy for further information.
Validity: *Tourist*, *Business* and *Group* visas are normally valid for three months from the date of issue (single and double-entry). Multiple-entry visas are normally valid for six months, 12 months or two to five years. The validity of *Business* visas varies. *Transit* visas are generally valid for up to seven days.
Application to: Consulate (or Consular section at Embassy); see *Contact Addresses* section. Visas should be applied for in person at least one month before departure. Group visas will usually be obtained by the tour operator or travel agent.
Application requirements: (a) Completed application form. (b) One recent passport-size photo. (c) Valid passport with at least one blank page. (d) Fee (payable in cash or by postal order only). *Tourist*: (a)-(d) and, (e) Return airline ticket or travel information about itinerary and confirmation of hotel reservation in China. *Business*: (a)-(d) and, (e) Official invitation (letter/fax) from a Chinese government department or a government-approved company indicating duration of stay and purpose of visit (original copies must be submitted for multiple-entry visas). *Student*: (a)-(d) and, (e) JW-201 or JW-202 form issued by the Ministry of Education of China, and letter of admission from Chinese university/college. *Group* (five people or more): (a)-(d) and, (e) Confirmation letter or fax from an authorised Chinese travel company. A list of all group members should be presented in triplicate. Photocopies of all group passports with the visa form number for each member. The serial number given to group members should be listed in order on the group visa form. There should be a front page covering information about the group. *Transit*: (a)-(d) and, (e) Visa for the next country of destination and letter from employer (if applicable).
Working days required: Three (72 hours). Two weeks for Group visas. Applications should be made at least one month in advance. A same-day service may be available at an extra cost of £20 per person, or a 48-hour service at £15 per person. Visas, however, cannot be issued on the same day unless the same-day airline ticket or itinerary is presented.
Note: (a) The majority of visits to China tend to be organised through the official state travel agency *CITS* (China International Travel Service). This liaison with *CITS* is generally handled by the tour operator organising the inclusive holiday chosen by the visitor, though it is possible for individuals to organise their own itinerary. Once the tour itinerary details have been confirmed to the visitor or visiting group, finances to cover accommodation and the cost of the tour must be deposited with *CITS* through a home bank. Once again, for package trips, all the necessary formalities for a visit to China can be handled by the tour operator concerned. (b) Those wishing to visit Tibet are strongly advised to join a travel group. Individual travellers need a special permit and should obtain permission to visit Tibet or Xinjiang by fax from the following organisation before applying for a visa: Tourist Bureau of Tibet (see *Contact Addresses* section).
Temporary residence: Enquiries should be addressed to the Chinese Embassy.

Money

Currency: 1 Renminbi Yuan (RMBY) = 10 chiao/jiao or 100 fen. Notes are in denominations of RMBY100, 50, 10, 5, 2 and 1, and 5, 2 and 1 chiao/jiao. Coins are in denominations of RMBY1, 1.5 chiao/jiao and 5, 2 and 1 fen.
Currency exchange: RMBY is not traded outside China. Foreign banknotes and travellers cheques can be exchanged at branches of The Bank of China. In hotels and *Friendship Stores* for tourists, imported luxury items such as spirits may be bought with Western currency. Scottish and Northern Irish banknotes cannot be exchanged.
Credit & debit cards: American Express, Diners Club, East-American Visa, Federal Card, JCB Card, MasterCard, Million Card and Visa are valid in major provincial cities in designated establishments. However, the availability of ATMs is often limited, and the acceptance of credit cards is often unlikely.
Travellers cheques: To avoid additional exchange rate charges, travellers are advised to take travellers cheques in US Dollars.
Currency restrictions: Import and export of local currency is limited to RMBY6000. Import of foreign currency is up to US$1000 (US$5000 for non-residents). Higher amounts should be declared upon arrival. Export of foreign currency is limited to the amount imported and declared.
Exchange rate indicators: The following figures are included as a guide to the movements of the Renminbi against Sterling and the US Dollar:

Date	Feb '04	May '04	Aug '04	Nov '04
£1.00=	15.07	14.78	15.24	15.67
$1.00=	8.28	8.28	8.27	8.28

Banking hours: Mon-Fri 0900-1700, Sat 0800-1130.

Duty Free

The following items may be imported into China by passengers staying less than six months without incurring customs duty:
400 cigarettes (600 cigarettes for stays of over six months); two bottles (up to 75cl) of alcoholic beverages (four bottles for stays of over six months); a reasonable amount of perfume for personal use.
Prohibited items: Arms and ammunition (prior approval may be obtained courtesy of the travel agency used), pornography (photographs in mainstream Western magazines may be regarded as pornographic), radio transmitters/receivers, exposed but undeveloped film, fruit and certain vegetables (tomatoes, aubergines and red peppers), political and religious pamphlets (a moderate quantity of religious material for personal use is acceptable). Any printed matter directed against the public order and the morality of China.
Note: Customs officials may seize audio and videotapes, books, records and CDs to check for pornographic, political or religious material. Baggage declaration forms must be completed upon arrival noting all valuables (such as cameras, watches and jewellery); this may be checked on departure. Receipts for items such as jewellery, jade, handicrafts, paintings, calligraphy or other similar items should be kept in order to obtain an export certificate from the authorities on leaving. Without this documentation, such items cannot be taken out of the country.

Public Holidays

2005: Jan 1-2 New Year. **Feb 9-11** Spring Festival, Chinese New Year. **May 1** Labour Day. **Oct 1** National Day.
2006: Jan 1-2 New Year. **Jan 29-31** Spring Festival, Chinese New Year. **May 1** Labour Day. **Oct 1** National Day.
Note: In addition to the above, other holidays may be observed locally and certain groups have official public holidays on the following dates:
Mar 8 International Women's Day. **May 4** National Youth Day. **May 23** Tibet Liberation Day. **Jun 1** International Children's Day. **Aug 1** Army Day.

Health

	Special Precautions?	Certificate Required?
Yellow Fever	Yes	1
Cholera	Yes	2
Typhoid & Polio	3	N/A
Malaria	4	N/A

Note: *Regulations and requirements may be subject to change at short notice, and you are advised to contact your doctor well in advance of your intended date of departure. Any numbers in the chart refer to the footnotes below.*

1: A yellow fever vaccination certificate is required from all travellers arriving within six days of leaving an infected area.
2: Following WHO guidelines issued in 1973, a cholera vaccination certificate is not a condition of entry to China. However, cholera is a slight risk in this country and precautions could be considered. Up-to-date advice should be sought before deciding whether these precautions should include vaccination as medical opinion is divided over its effectiveness. For more information, see the *Health* appendix. A strain of *Bengal cholera* has been reported in western areas.
3: Poliovirus transmission has been shown by reliable data to have been completely interrupted since 1994 through eradication programmes.
4: Malaria risk exists throughout the country below 1500m except in Beijing, Gansu, Heilongjiang, Inner Mongolia, Jilin, Ningxia, Qinghai, Shanxi, Tibet (Xizang, except in the Zangbo River Valley in the extreme southeast) and Xinjiang (except in the Yili River Valley). North of 33°N, the risk lasts from July to November, between 33°N and 25°N from May to December, and south of 25°N throughout the year. The disease occurs primarily in the benign *vivax* form but the malignant *falciparum* form is also present and has been reported to be multidrug-resistant. The recommended prophylaxis in risk areas is chloroquine, or mefloquine in Hainan and Yunnan.
Food & drink: Outside main centres, all water used for drinking, brushing teeth or freezing should have first been boiled or otherwise sterilised. Only eat well-cooked meat and fish, preferably served hot. Pork, salad and mayonnaise may carry increased risk. Vegetables should be cooked and fruit peeled.
Other risks: *Bilharzia* (schistosomiasis) is endemic in the central Yangtze river basin. Avoid swimming and paddling in fresh water; swimming pools that are well chlorinated and maintained are safe. There is some risk of *plague*. *Hepatitis E* is prevalent in northeastern and northwestern China and *hepatitis* A is common across the country. *Hepatitis B* is highly endemic. *Tuberculosis* is common in indigenous populations. *Oriental liver fluke* (clonorchiasis), *oriental lung fluke* (paragonimiasis) and *giant intestinal fluke* (fasciolopsiasis) are reported, and *brucellosis* also occurs. *Bancroftian* and *brugian filariasis* are still reported in southern China, *visceral leishmaniasis* is increasingly common throughout, and *cutaneous leishmaniasis* has been reported from Xinjiang. *Haemorrhagic fever with renal syndrome* is endemic. Precautions should be taken against *Japanese encephalitis*, particularly in rural areas. *Mite-borne* or *scrub typhus* may be found in scrub areas of southern China. *Altitude sickness* can be a problem in parts of Gansu, Qinghai, Sichuan, Tibet, Xinjiang and Yannan. There are still habitual occurrences of *avian influenza* (bird flu) and the *SARS* virus.
Rabies is present, although the Government policy that bans dogs and cats from main cities makes this less of a risk in these areas. For those at high risk, vaccination before arrival should be considered. If you are bitten, seek medical advice without delay. For more information, consult the *Health* appendix.
Health care: Medical costs are low. Many medicines common to Western countries are unavailable in China. Medical facilities in international hospitals are excellent. There are many traditional forms of medicine used in China, the most notable being acupuncture. Medical insurance is strongly advised.

Travel - International

AIR: The national airline is *Air China* (CA) (website: www.airchina.com.cn). Airlines serving China include: *British Airways*, *Finnair*, *KLM*, *Lufthansa*, *Northwest Airlines*, *Singapore Airlines* and many others.
Note: Travellers should ensure that they re-confirm their return flight reservations, as overbooking by airlines has led to people being stranded in China.
Approximate flight times: From Beijing to *London* is approximately 10 hours, to *New York* is 22 hours, to *Los Angeles* is 12 hours, and to *Sydney* is 12 hours.
International airports: *Beijing/Peking (BJS/PEK)* airport (Capital International Central) is 28km (18 miles) northeast of the city (travel time – 40 minutes by bus and taxi).
Guangzhou/Canton airport (Baiyun) is 7km (4 miles) from the city (travel time – 20 minutes).
Shanghai Hongqiao (SHA) airport is 13km (8 miles) southwest of the city (travel time – 25 to 40 minutes).
Shanghai Pudong (PVG) airport, in the eastern financial district, is 30km (19 miles) from the city centre (travel time – 50 minutes by bus or taxi). Pudong is a major international airport with a magnetic levitation train and an underground link (due for expansion in 2005, when Pudong will be connected with Hongqiao).
Facilities at the above airports include taxis, public and shuttle buses, duty free shops, banks/bureaux de change, post offices, business facilities, bars and restaurants. There are also airports at other major cities.

Departure tax: RMBY90. Children under 12 and transit passengers (proceeding within 24 hours) are exempt.
SEA: Principal seaports are Fuzhou (Foochow), Guangzhou (Canton), Hong Kong/Kowloon, Qingdgo (Tsingtao) and Shanghai. *Pearl Cruises* operates over 20 cruises a year to China. Other cruise lines include *Holland America, NCL Asia Cruisetours, Princess, Seabourn* and *Silversea*. There are regular ferry services linking most Chinese ports with Kobe in Japan and the west coast of Korea (Dem Rep). Ferry services operate between Weihai, Qingdao, Tianjin and Shanghai in China to Incheon in Korea (Dem Rep).
RAIL: International services run from Beijing to Moscow (Russian Federation), on both the Trans-Mongolian Railway (via Ulaanbaatar in Mongolia) and the Trans-Manchurian Railway (via Zabaikalsk in northern China). There are also services from Beijing to Pyongyang (Korea, Dem Rep). Owing to demand, it may be necessary to book up to two months in advance. A regular train service runs from Hong Kong to Guangzhou (Canton), and is of a higher standard than internal trains in China. There are several trains daily. Services between Shanghai-Kowloon/Hong Kong (travel time - 29 hours) and Beijing-Kowloon/Hong Kong (travel time - 30 hours) both run on alternate days. There are twice-weekly trains from Almaty in Kazakhstan to Urumqi. There are three types of fare: hard sleeper, soft sleeper and deluxe soft sleeper.
Note: Travellers on the Trans-Mongolian or Trans-Manchurian Railways are strongly advised to search their compartments and lock the doors before departure, owing to an increase in smuggling via this route.
ROAD: The principal road routes into China follow the historical trade routes through Myanmar, India, the former Soviet republics and Mongolia. It is also possible to travel from Pakistan to Xinjiang on the Karakoran highway.

Travel - Internal

AIR: Most long-distance internal travel is by air. The *Civil Aviation Administration of China (CAAC)* operates along routes linking Beijing to over 80 other cities by 14 regional airlines, covering all major cities and some sites. CAAC controls several other private carriers including *China Eastern, China Northern, China Southern, Great Wall* and *Yunnan Airlines*. Tickets will normally be purchased by guides and the price will be included in any tour costs. Independent travellers can also book through the local Chinese International Travel Service (CITS), which charges a small commission, or alternatively buy tickets in booking offices. It is advisable to purchase internal air tickets well in advance if travelling during May, September or October. The tourist price for a ticket is 70 per cent on a train ticket and 100 per cent on an air ticket. There are many connections to Hong Kong from Beijing/Guangzhou (Peking/Canton) as well as other cities. Safety records are variable.
Note: Where possible, travellers are advised to fly in UK or North American aircraft which are used by larger airlines.
Departure tax: RMBY50.
SEA/RIVER: All major rivers are served by river ferries, especially the Yangzi. Coastal ferries operate between Dalian, Tianjin (Tientsin), Qingdao (Tsingtao) and Shanghai. There are regular ferry services between mainland China and Hong Kong, conditions on which vary.
RAIL: Railways provide the principal means of transport for goods and people throughout China. The routes are generally cheap, safe and well maintained. The major routes are from Beijing to Guangzhou, Shanghai, Harbin, Chengdu and Urumqi. There are three types of train, of which Express is the best. There are four types of fare: hard seat, soft seat (only on short-distance trains such as the Hong Kong to Guangzhou (Canton) line), hard sleeper and soft sleeper. Children under 1m (3ft) tall travel free and those under 1.3m (4ft) pay a quarter of the fare.
ROAD: It is possible to reach 80 per cent of settlements by road. Roads are not always of the highest quality. Distances should not be underestimated and vehicles should be in prime mechanical condition as China is still very much an agricultural nation without the mechanical expertise or services found in the West. From Beijing to Shanghai is 1461km (908 miles), and from Beijing to Nanjing (Nanking) is 1139km (718 miles). Traffic drives on the right. **Bus**: Reasonable services are operated between the main cities. Buses are normally crowded, but reach parts of the country that trains do not. There are some more expensive luxury buses. **Car hire**: Available, but most rental companies' policy of retaining the driver's passport makes self-drive car hire impossible in practice for visitors. Cars with a driver can be hired on a daily or weekly basis. Driving standards are erratic.
URBAN: There is a metro system in Shanghai and limited metro services in Beijing and Tianjin, and tramways and trolleybuses in a number of other cities. New lines are under construction in Beijing. Guides who accompany every visitor or group will ensure that internal travel within the cities is as trouble-free as possible. Most cities have public transit systems, usually bus. **Taxi**: Taxis are available in large cities but can be hard to find. It is best to check if the taxi is metered. If not, then it is important to agree a fare beforehand, especially at railway stations where it is best to bargain before getting into the taxi. Visitors should write down their destination before starting any journey. Taxis can be hired by the day. Most people travel by bicycle or public transport. In most cities, bicycles or other types of rickshaws are available for short rides.
Travel times: The following chart gives approximate travel times (in hours and minutes) from **Beijing** to other major cities/towns in China.

	Air	Rail
Tianjin	0.50	1.40
Wuhan	1.45	16.00
Xian	1.55	22.00
Nanjing	1.40	15.30
Shanghai	1.50	20.00
Chengdu	2.25	60.00
Kunming	3.20	80.00
Guangzhou	3.00	37.00
Urumqi	4.00	95.00

Credit: © National Tourism Administration of the People's Republic of China

Accommodation

HOTELS: China has 4418 tourist hotels with 386,000 rooms, among which 2349 hotels have been star-graded according to international standards. Most of the hotels have comfortable and convenient facilities including air conditioning and private bathrooms, Chinese and Western restaurants, coffee shops, bars, banqueting halls, conference rooms, multi-function halls, ballrooms, swimming pools, bowling alleys, beauty parlours, massage rooms, saunas, clinics and ticket booking offices. Some even include shopping and business malls, banks and post offices. For further information, contact the China Tourism Hotel Association, 9A Jianguomennei Avenue, Beijing 100740 (tel: (10) 6520 1114 or 6512 2905; fax: (10) 6512 2851) *or* China Hotel and Buyers' Guide (website: www.hotelschina.com).
DORMITORIES: These are found in most tourist centres and provide cheaper accommodation for budget travellers. Standards range from poor to adequate.
YOUTH HOSTELS: China is currently constructing a network of hostels, covering in particular Beijing, Guandong, Guangxi, Shangai and Yunnam. For more information, contact the IYHF (tel: (20) 8668 1851 *or* 8734 5080; e-mail: yhachina@yahoo.com.cn; website: www.yhachina.com).

Resorts & Excursions

China is a vast country, with long travel times between the many cultural, historical and natural wonders of the land, 23 of which have already been declared UNESCO World Heritage Sites. Altogether there are 26 provinces, each with their own dialect and regional characteristics. The western provinces of Xinjiang, Tibet, Qinghai, Sichuan and Yunnan occupy an enormous area of land, and Sichuan alone is about the size of France. *China International Travel Services (CITS)*, the state travel agency, tends to organise a good deal of the tours in China, although more and more specialist operators are running packages so visitors are now presented with a considerable choice of excursions. Independent travel is becoming both easier and more popular, a trend likely to increase with China's accession to the World Trade Organization in 2001. For full details of independent travel in China, contact the China National Tourist Office (CNTO) or China International Travel Service (CITS) (see *Contact Addresses* section). Individual visitors wishing to travel to Tibet should note that they must obtain permits in advance from one of the Tibet Tourist Authority's Tourism Offices (see *Contact Addresses* and *Passport/Visa* sections).

BEIJING

The entire area of Beijing within the city limits is - in many ways - one great historic museum. The original city plan was divided in four. The innermost rectangle is the **Forbidden City**, now a museum and public park, but formerly the residence of the Ming and Qing emperors. The second rectangle forms the boundaries of the **Imperial City**, enclosing residences and parks for the former senior government officials. The outer rectangle forms the outer city with its markets and old residential districts. The **Imperial Palace**, lying inside the Forbidden City and surrounded by a high wall and broad moat, is probably China's greatest surviving historical site. Dating from the 15th century, the Palace was home to a total of 24 emperors and, today, its fabulous halls, palaces and gardens house a huge collection of priceless relics from various dynasties. The surviving **city walls** are impressive monuments, as are the traditional **hutongs**, enclosed neighbourhoods of alleys and courtyards. Other points of interest are the **Coal Hill** (Mei Shan), a beautiful elevated park with breathtaking views; **Beihai Park**, the loveliest in Beijing; **Tiananmen Square**, the largest public square in the world, surrounded by museums, parks, the zoo and Beijing University; the **Temple of Heaven**, an excellent example of 15th-century Chinese architecture; the **Summer Palace**, the former court resort for the emperors of the Qing Dynasty reconstructed in traditional style in the early 1900s after Western attacks, looking out over the **Kunming Lake**; the **Great Wall** (see below), the section at **Badaling** being some 72km (45 miles) from Beijing; and the **Ming Tombs**, where 13 out of the 16 Ming emperors chose to be buried. Two magnificent tombs here have been excavated, one of which is open to the public.

BEYOND BEIJING: The **Great Wall**, built up in stages over 2000 years and said to be the only manmade structure visible from the moon, is a spectacular sight which should not be missed. Stretching for a distance of 5400km (3375 miles), it starts at the Shanhaiguan Pass in the east and ends at the Jiayuguan Pass in the west. The section at Badaling, built in stone and brick and dating back to the Ming Dynasty, is roughly 8m (26ft) high and 6m (20ft) wide. **The Yungang Caves** near **Datong**, west of Beijing, have awe-inspiring monumental Buddhist effigies carved into them. Equally impressive is the nearby **Hanging Temple**, clinging to a cliff, and the **Yingxian Pagoda**, China's oldest surviving wooden pagoda.
Beidaihe, a small seacoast resort with beaches, temples and parks, is a popular vacation area 277km (172 miles) from Beijing, favoured by the ruling elite. Attractions include the **Yansai Lake** and **Shan Hai Guan**, a massive gateway at the very start of the Great Wall, as well as elegant colonial-era villas.
Chengde is the former summer retreat of the Qing emperors and a UNESCO World Heritage Site. There are many temples and parks, including the remains of the **Qing Summer Palace** with its impressive **Imperial Garden**. The **Eight Outer Temples**, lying at the foot of the hills to the northeast of the Palace, include the architectural styles of the Mongolians, Tibetans and other subject peoples.

THE NORTHERN PROVINCES

XI'AN: The capital of Shaanxi Province and often regarded as the true historic capital of China, Xi'an was once amongst the most magnificent cities in the world. For 11 dynasties, from the 11th century BC, the city was also the capital of China. It was the starting point of the ancient trade route with the West known as the **Silk Road** (see *Silk Road* section) and is now, after Beijing, the most popular tourist attraction in China. The city is most famous for the **Tomb of Emperor Qin Shi Huangdi**, who first united China under the Qin Dynasty in 200 BC, and its terracotta figures - over 6000 life-sized **Terracotta Warriors** and horses buried along with the emperor. Many other tombs from the Han and Tang Dynasties are still unexcavated. Despite damage inflicted during the Cultural Revolution, there are still numerous tombs, pavilions, museums and pagodas to be seen, such as the **Big Wild Goose Pagoda** with its spiral staircase, and the **Small Wild Goose Pagoda**.

BEYOND XI'AN: Luoyang, lying east of Xi'an and its historical twin capital, has a fine museum of treasures. The fifth-century **Longmen Buddhist Caves** are among some of China's finest, lined with carved effigies and monuments. **Kaifeng**, east of Luoyang and a Northern Song Dynasty capital, has a **Jewish quarter** formerly home to indigenous Chinese Jews, the **Xiangguo Monastery**, the **Iron Pagoda**

A B C D E F G H I J K L M N O P Q R S T U V W X Y Z

from AD 1049, **Fan Bo Pagoda** (c. AD 977), and other relics of ancient courts and poets.

JINAN: The capital of Shandong Province, Jinan is known as the 'City of Springs'; these provide the main tourist attraction. The city also has Buddhist relics, parks and lakes. Of particular interest is the **Square Four Gate Pagoda**, the oldest stone pagoda in China. Outside the city, **Mount Taishan**'s 72 peaks make up a mountain park with ancient pine and cypress trees, spectacular waterfalls, 1800 stone sculptures and a kilometre-long mountain stairway known as the '**Ladder to Heaven**'.

BEYOND JINAN: Qingdao is a former Treaty Port annexed by Germany. Like elsewhere in Asia, the Germans brought breweries, creating China's ubiquitous Tsingtao Lager in 1902, but also built the fine German Concession buildings; there are also attractive traditional areas. **Laoshan**, east of Qingdao, is a fine mountain region with a famous monastery, the **Taiqing Palace**. In **Qufu**, close to Qingdao, the **Mansion of Confucius** was home to the sage's descendants, and the enormous **Temple of Confucius**, with its many pavilions, was a centre for his worshippers. Today, the buildings store and display important historical records, art and cultural artefacts. Confucius's tomb is in a cemetery just north of Qufu.

FAR NORTHEASTERN REGIONS: Shenyang was once an imperial capital. Remains from this period include the **Imperial Palace** and two interesting tombs. The **North Imperial Tomb**, about 20km (13 miles) from the city, is the burial place of the founding father of the Qing (Ch'ing) Dynasty. **Dalian** is China's third port. Formerly occupied by the Soviets, it is an airy and interesting bi-cultural city with some Russian architecture. **Hohhot** (meaning 'green city' in Mongolian) is the capital of the Inner Mongolia Autonomous Region, and one of the most colourful cities in China, with unique local architecture including the **Five-Pagoda Temple**. Tours of the grasslands can also be arranged. Harbin, the capital of Heilongjiang Province, is a Russian-style industrial city. Harbin is host to the annual *Harbin Summer Music Festival* and a winter *Ice Festival* of ice sculptures (see *Special Events* section).

FAR NORTHWESTERN REGIONS: Lanzhou is an oasis on the Silk Road (see *Silk Road* section), and capital of Gansu Province, but the ugly city is chiefly noteworthy as a centre to visit the 34 early Buddhist caves at **Bingling**. The **White Pagoda Mountain Park** is also an attractive retreat. **Dunhuang**, a 2000-year-old town on the edge of the desert, once an important Silk Road caravan stop, is famous for the **Mogao Caves**, some of the oldest Buddhist shrines in China and a UNESCO World Heritage Site. These ancient murals and hand-carved shrines are a national treasure and represent a thousand years of devotion to Buddha between the fifth and 14th centuries. Some 500 exist today, and large areas of frescoes can still be seen. Also worth a visit when in Dunhuang are the **Crescent Lake**, the **Yang Guan Pass** and the **Mingsha Hill**.

Credit: © National Tourism Administration of the People's Republic of China

Turpan and **Urumqi** are situated in the far northwest on the edge of the vast deserts of Xinjiang Province. These Muslim cities, lying on the Silk Road, are well known for the distinctive Islamic culture of the inhabitants. Turpan has a distinct and well-preserved architectural character, and is surrounded by spectacular scenery and interesting sites, including two ruined cities. Turpan is also the hottest place in China, lying in the Turpan Depression, the second-lowest point on earth next only to the Dead Sea. Nearby are the **Flaming Mountains**, which glow brightly at sunset. Urumqi is the capital of the Xinjiang Uygur Autonomous Region. The city is inhabited by people of 13 different nationalities, including Mongolian, Kazakh, Russian, Tartar and Uzbek. The majority of the inhabitants are Muslim Uygurs who speak a Turkish language completely unrelated to Chinese. Northwest of Urumqi, a few hours' bus ride away, is the beautiful **Lake of Heaven**, a clear turquoise-coloured lake set in the midst of the **Tian Shan** range of mountains. Museums in both cities trace their fascinating histories.

THE EASTERN PROVINCES

SHANGHAI: This is one of the world's largest cities and one of China's most famous - more like New York or Paris than Beijing. Lying on the estuary of the **Chang Jiang (Yangtze) River**, it is the centre of China's trade and industry. European-style architecture, traditional Chinese buildings and sleek modern developments all co-exist in this cosmopolitan metropolis. The **Yuyuan Gardens** date back over 400 years: although relatively small, they are impressive thanks to their intricate design, with pavilions, rockeries, ponds and a complete traditional theatre woven together in an ornate maze. The gardens are reached via the **Town God Temple Bazaar**, a touristy but impressive warren of lanes and stalls. The **French Concession** area has quiet, characterful colonial parks and neighbourhoods, while the **Bund** along the **Huangpu River** has the celebrated strip of Art Deco towers. From here, the dynamic new Pudong Development Area and the **Oriental Pearl Tower** can be viewed across the water.

HANGZHOU: Situated about 190km (120 miles) south of Shanghai, Hangzhou is one of China's seven ancient capital cities. Known as 'Paradise on Earth', Hangzhou was also described by Marco Polo as 'the most beautiful and magnificent city in the world'. Today's city is a beauty spot still visited by Chinese and foreign tourists in great numbers. By far the most attractive excursion, however, is to the **West Lake** area, dotted with weeping willows and peach trees, stone bridges, rockeries and painted pavilions. Here can be found the **Pagoda of Six Harmonies**, various tombs and sacred hills, monasteries and temples, not least the **Linyin Temple**.

NANJING: Another former capital of China, Nanjing (meaning 'southern capital') is now capital of Jiangsu Province. The city lies on the Chang Jiang (Yangtze) River at the foot of **Zijinshan** (Purple Mountain). It abounds with temples, tombs, parks and lakes, museums, and monuments - foremost amongst them being the **Tomb of the Ming Emperor**, where lies the body of Zhu Yuanzhang, founding father of the Ming Dynasty and the only Ming emperor to be buried outside Beijing. The mausoleum of China's first president, Dr Sun Yat-sen, is also here. Other places of interest are the ruins of the **Ming Palace**, the **Ming city wall**, the **Yangtze River Bridge** with its observation deck, the **Purple and Gold Mountains Observatory** and the **Tombs of the Southern Tang Dynasty**, known as the 'Underground Palace'.

SUZHOU: This is one of China's oldest cities, dating back some 2500 years. An old proverb says that 'in Heaven there is Paradise; on earth, Suzhou'. Its riverside streets are reminiscent of Venice and there are many famous water gardens. There are over 400 historical sites and relics under the protection of the Government, such as the **Blue-Waves Pavilion Garden** on the outskirts, the **Lion-Grove Garden** which has rockeries resembling lions, the **Humble Administrator's Garden** and the **Garden of the Master of the Nets**. The **Grand Canal** and **Tiger Hill** are also worth a visit. There are numerous silk mills producing exquisite fabrics, and the local embroidery.

WUXI: This industrial and resort city on the north bank of **Lake Tai**, some 125km (75 miles) west of Shanghai, has some celebrated lakeside parks and gardens. **Yangzhou** to the west, supposedly once governed by Marco Polo, has a fine poetic tradition of gardens such as the **Xu Garden** and others along the **Narrow West Lake**, and old merchant houses. To the southwest, on **Huangshan Mountain** in the southern Anhui Province, trees cling to breathtaking rocky precipices amongst seas of cloud and clear natural springs and lakes. A UNESCO World Heritage Site for its natural beauty and wildlife, the mountain has a cablecar linking the summit and base.

WUHAN: Wuhan spans the Chang Jiang (Yangtze) River. As the capital of Hubei Province, it is an industrial centre. There are also Buddhist temples, lakes and parks, as well as the **Yellow Crane Tower** and the **Provincial Museum**, home to the famous **Chime Bells**, manufactured over 2400 years ago. Nearby in **Danjiangou City**, **Wudang** or **Taihe Mountain** houses an ancient building complex with temples, nunneries, palaces and pavilions.

THE CENTRAL PROVINCES

CHENGDU: This booming capital of mountainous, distinctive Sichuan Province lies at the foot of the Tibetan plateau. Attractions include Tang Dynasty shrines, the house of the celebrated poet **Du Fu**, ancient parks and bamboo forests (the last stronghold of the **giant panda**), Buddhist temples and an ancient Buddhist monastery. Chengdu is a base for visiting **Emei Shan**, a famous mountain to which Buddhist pilgrims flock every year, and the holy mountains of **Gongga** and **Siguniang**. There is also the spectacular **Grand Buddha** of **Leshan**, a 70.7m- (225ft-) high coloured sculpture carved out of a cliff, so enormous that 100 people can fit on its instep, with the **Grand Buddha Temple** and **Lingbao Pagoda** beside it. In the **Jiuzhaigou Ravine** in northern Sichuan Province, there is a vast nature reserve where giant pandas can be seen in their natural habitat. The six official 'scenic spots' among the snowy peaks include **Shuzheng**, with waterfalls and 40 lakes of different colours where swimming and boating are allowed. Further north, the concentration of mineral salts in the water at **Huanglong** (Yellow Dragon) nature reserve has created beautifully coloured natural talpatate ponds and rock formations.

CHONGQING: Located east of **Dazu**, Chongqing is perched magnificently above the Chang Jiang (Yangtze) River. A prosperous rather than beautiful city, it is a natural starting point for excursions to the **Yangtze Gorges**, whose most popular stretches are further east with poetic names like **Witches Gorge** and **Shadowplay Gorge**. These natural wonders are due to be completely submerged by 2009 after the completion of the Three Gorges Dam.
In Dazu County, the **Dazu Rock Carvings** represent the pinnacle of Chinese rock art.

THE SOUTHERN PROVINCES

FUZHOU: Situated in Fujian Province on the southeast coast opposite Taiwan, this beautiful city lies on the banks of the **Min River**. Dating back some 1400 years (to the Tang Dynasty), the city has numerous parks and temples, including the **White Pagoda** and **Black Pagoda**, and maritime reminders of its past as a colonial Treaty Port. Fuzhou also has hot springs dotted throughout the city. Further south, **Mount Wuyi** is an outstanding area of natural beauty and the cradle of neo-Confucianism.

GUANGZHOU (CANTON): Sometimes known as the 'City of Flowers', Guangzhou is a subtropical metropolis on the south coast. As a Special Economic Zone only 182km (113 miles) from Hong Kong, Guangzhou is developing at breakneck speed, but it has more established attractions, since it dates back to 221 BC and first welcomed European traders in 1516. Parks, museums, temples, hot springs and colonial architecture - especially on **Shamian Island** - are the main attractions. The **Chenhai Tower**, a 15th-century observation tower overlooking the **Pearl River**, the **Huaisheng Mosque** built by Arab merchants in AD 650, and the **Tomb of the King of Southern Yue**, a 2000-year-old relic of one of the region's short-lived splinter kingdoms, are also worth visiting. Other attractions for those drawn by the gold rush mentality of Shenzhen include theme parks such as the **World of Splendid China** (with miniatures of Chinese heritage sites), and the **China Folk Culture Villages**.

CHANGSHA: The capital of Hunan Province is close to the birthplace of Mao Zedong at **Shaoshan**. Most attractions revolve around Mao's early life and there are museums and schools dedicated to him. One notable exception is the **Han Tomb** whose contents - including the 2000-year-old remains of a woman - are now in the **Hunan Provincial Museum**.

LUSHAN MOUNTAIN: Lying approximately 150km southeast of Wuhan, this is a well-known scenic area and summer resort with tranquil scenery and a comfortable climate. The mountain has been a haven for poets and hermits for centuries, and more recently for Chiang Kaishek, Mao Zedong, Harry Truman and other dignitaries. At its centre is **Guling Town**, at an altitude of 1167m.

GUILIN: Located to the northwest of Guangzhou (Canton), Guilin is famous for its spectacular landscape of bizarre limestone formations, echoed so evocatively in the paintings and wall-hangings well known in the area. Steep monolithic mountains rise dramatically from a flat landscape of meandering rivers and paddy fields. Visitors can climb the hills, take river trips and visit the parks, lakes and caves. Further north is the **Wulingyuan** basin, centred on the town of **Zhangjiajie**, which contains dense primeval forest and several thousand steep mountain peaks, as well as **Yellow Dragon Cave**, Asia's largest, with gnarled stalactites.

KUNMING: The capital of Yunnan Province, which borders Vietnam, Myanmar and Laos, has its own distinctive identity as a newer, showcase city with some temples and very pretty lakeside parks. It is known as the 'City of Eternal

Spring' or the 'Geneva of the Orient' because of the pleasant alpine climate. Outside of Kunming are the major attractions of **Xi Shan**, the holy mountain, and the petrified limestone forest called **Shilin**, 120km (75 miles) southeast of Kunming. The ancient city of **Lijiang**, further west in Yunnan Province, is dominated by the Naxi ethnic people, and was the subject of the celebrated documentary *Beyond The Clouds*.

HAINAN ISLAND: This tropical island off the south coast of Guangdong Province has some fine beaches, palm groves, fresh seafood and coconuts. In 1989, Hainan Island became a separate province in its own right, and is now one of several Special Economic Zones, although it is not yet the 'Hawaii of China' it aspires to be.

TIBET (XIZANG)

Known as 'the Roof of the World', Tibet has only been open to tourists since 1980. Although it is possible to go to Tibet as an independent traveller (provided a permit is obtained), it is much more straightforward to go as part of a tour group on an organised itinerary. The scenery is spectacular and Tibetan culture is uniquely fascinating: its tradition of esoteric Buddhism is followed across Asia and is of great historical importance. The Cultural Revolution, driven by Han Chinese, inflicted serious damage on Tibet's cultural identity, but despite this, it has preserved its own way of life and religious traditions, helped in some cases by apologetic Chinese attempts at restoration. Visitors should note, though, that the Chinese government has been actively settling Tibet with Han Chinese for some time, and many people they see or meet will not be Tibetans. Some travellers may experience health problems as a result of the altitude, so it is wise to consult a doctor prior to departure.

LHASA: Known as 'city of the gods', Lhasa stands at an altitude of 3700m (12,000ft). Its wonderful light and clear skies are peculiar to its high mountainous terrain, but for six months of the year it is bitterly cold. The main highlights for tourists lie in the **Potala** or **Red Palace**, home to successive Dalai Lamas, which dominates Lhasa and the valley. This 7th-century edifice, built on a far more ancient site, is now a unique museum whose exhibits include labyrinths of dungeons beneath the Palace, gigantic bejewelled Buddhas and vast treasure hoards, 10,000 chapels with human skull and thigh-bone wall decorations and wonderful Buddhist frescoes, with influences from India and Nepal. The Potala Palace is a UNESCO World Heritage Site. Other buildings of interest include the **Drepung Monastery**, the **Norbulingka** (Summer Palace) and the **Jokhang Temple**, with its golden Buddhas. Ask permission before taking photographs in Buddhist temples.
Note: Individual visitors wishing to travel to Tibet should note that they must obtain permits in advance from one of the Tibet Tourist Authority's Tourism Offices (see *Contact Addresses* and *Passport/Visa* sections). However, local border officials have been known to demand additional fees, sometimes violently. The Chinese authorities react strongly to overseas visitors becoming involved with any political activity for Tibetan independence, including taking photographs or videotaping demonstrations, or taking Tibetan nationals' correspondence or parcels out of the country.

THE SILK ROAD

This ancient trading route was opened up by Han Dynasty power from 138 BC when Emperor Han Wudi sent a mission into Central Asia and launched westwards extensions of the Great Wall into the Gobi Desert. Used by silk merchants from the 2nd century AD until its decline in the 16th century, the Silk Road is open in parts to tourists eager to explore its heritage. This long string of caravan trails, oases, roads and mountain passes, stretched from northern China, through bleak and foreboding desert and mountainous terrain to the ports on either the Caspian Sea or Mediterranean Sea, and was the conduit for goods and ideas passing between ancient China and the West. The Mongols later used the Silk Road to bind their vast empire, as Marco Polo found when he travelled it in the 13th century.

The two main routes are split into the north route and the south route: the north starting in China at Xi'an, running through the Gansu Corridoor, Dunhuang, Jade Gate Pass to the neck of the Gobi desert, following the Tianshan mountains round the fringes of the Taklimakan desert to Kashgar (Xinjiang province), across the Pamirs to Samarkand or Tashkent (Uzbekistan) onto the Caspian Sea. The south route runs with the north until the Jade Gate Pass and then stretches round the southern edges of the Taklimakan desert to Kashgar and then over the **Karakorum mountain range** (see Karakorum Highway in the *Pakistan* section) into India.

The Silk Road was a major highway for the spread of Buddhism into East Asia, and later for the growth of Islam, and consequently a number of monasteries, grottos, stupas, minarets and other ruins dating back to the early centuries can still be seen along the way. Other attractions of the route are the diverse scenery, various minority peoples and romantic cities.

Within China, the main sights are found in Xinjiang Province, including the Buddhist grottos at Dunhuang and ancient relics at Turpan, such as the ruins of the city of Jiaohe and the lively Sunday market at Kashgar. Travel along the Silk Road can be quite difficult due to the terrain, harsh climate and lack of developed infrastructure. Visitors to the region are advised to travel with an organised tour company or travel agent.

Sport & Activities

Cycling: An estimated 300 million Chinese people use the bicycle as a means of transport and, not surprisingly, bicycle hire shops can be found everywhere, even in smaller towns. Visitors should note that car traffic has been increasing in China, particularly in Beijing, where traffic and pollution levels are high. Major roads outside cities also tend to be busy.
Hiking and trekking: China's main natural attractions are its scenic mountains, waterfalls, caverns and great rivers and lakes. No permit is required for hiking, although a trekking permit is compulsory (and fairly expensive) for visiting more remote areas. For details of the necessary practicalities for individual hiking or trekking and for a list of specialised tour operators, contact the China National Tourist Office (see *Contact Addresses* section). The Qinghai-Tibet Plateau (also known as 'the roof of the world') is one of the world's most famous **mountaineering** destinations. Some of the world's highest mountains define the southern border of Tibet, including *Mount Everest* (or *Qoomolangma*), 8848m (29,021ft), *Namcha Barwa*, 7756m (25,445ft), around which the Brahmaputra River carves a fantastic gorge to enter India, and *Gurla Mandhata*, 7728m (25,355ft). Among the 14 peaks on earth above 8000m, five are located in Tibet. The Tibetan approach to Mount Everest provides far better views than the Nepal side. Some 27,000 sq km around Everest's Tibetan face have been designated as the *Qoomolangma Nature Reserve*. For foreign travellers, the Everest Base Camp has become the most popular trekking destination in Tibet. The two access points are *Shegar* and *Tingri*, along the Friendship Highway to Nepal, but visitors should note that these treks are very demanding and that the altitude requires some acclimatisation. 4-wheel-drive vehicles can also take visitors all the way to base camp along the Shegar track. For practicalities on how to enter Tibet, see Tibet in the *Resorts & Excursions* section or the *Passport/Visa* section.
Winter sports: It is possible to ice skate on Beijing's lakes during winter. **Downhill** and **cross-country skiing** can be practised in the North-east provinces.
Martial arts: The ancient 'shadow art' of **Tai Chi**, a series of linked movements performed in a slow relaxed manner using the entire body whilst focusing the mind, is traditionally practised in towns throughout China, particularly in the early morning hours, and visitors wishing to learn or participate are welcome.

Social Profile

FOOD & DRINK: Chinese cuisine has a very long history and is renowned all over the world. Cantonese (the style the majority of Westerners are most familiar with) is only one regional style of Chinese cooking. There are eight major schools of Chinese cuisine, named after the places where they were conceived: Anhui, Fujian, Guangdong, Hunan, Jiangsu, Shandong, Sichuan and Zhejian. For a brief appreciation of the cuisine, it is possible to break it down into four major regional categories:
Northern Cuisine: Beijing, which has developed from the Shandong school, is famous for *Peking Duck*, which is roasted in a special way, and eaten in a thin pancake with cucumber and a sweet plum sauce. Another speciality of the North of China is *Mongolian Hotpot*, which is a Chinese version of fondue. It is eaten in a communal style and consists of a central simmering soup in a special large round pot into which is dipped a variety of uncooked meats and vegetables, which are cooked on the spot. A cheap and delicious local dish is *shuijiao*, which is pasta-like dough wrapped round pork meat, chives and onions, similar in idea to Italian ravioli. These can be bought by the jin (pound) in street markets and small eating houses, and are a good filler if you are out all day and do not feel like a large restaurant dinner. It should, however, be noted that in the interests of hygiene, it is best to take your own chopsticks.
Southern Cuisine: Guangdong (Cantonese) food is famous for being the most exotic in China. The food markets in Guangzhou are a testimony to this, and the Western visitor is often shocked by the enormous variety of rare and exotic animals that are used in the cuisine, including snake, dog, turtle and wildcat.
Eastern Cuisine: Shanghai and Zhejiang cooking is rich and sweet, often pickled. Noted for seafood, hot and sour soup, noodles and vegetables.
Western Cuisine: Sichuan and Hunan food is spicy, often sour and peppery, with specialities such as diced chicken stirred with soy sauce and peanuts, and spicy *doufu* (beancurd).
One of the best-known national drinks is *maotai*, a fiery spirit distilled from rice wine. Local beers are of good quality, notably *Qingdao*, which is similar to German lager. There are now some decent wines, which are produced mainly for tourists and export.
NIGHTLIFE: Visitors can follow itineraries drawn up in advance, when sampling the nightlife of the larger cities, including a selection of prearranged restaurant meals and visits to Chinese opera, Chinese state circus, ballet and theatre. Local Chinese will tend to only drink socially with a formal meal so bars and nightclubs will generally only be found in the more cosmopolitan cities and major towns. Karaoke (written *OK* on Chinese signs) is a popular form of evening entertainment.
SHOPPING: All consumer prices are set by the Government, and there is no price bargaining in shops and department stores, although it is possible to bargain fiercely in small outdoor markets (of which there are many) for items such as jade, antique ceramics and also silk garments. All antiques over 100 years old are marked with a red wax seal by the authorities, and require an export customs certificate. Access to normal shops is available, offering inexpensive souvenirs, work clothes, posters and books; this will prove much easier if accompanied by an interpreter, although it is possible to point or get the help of a nearby English-speaker. Items are sometimes in short supply, but prices will not vary much from place to place. In large cities such as Beijing and Shanghai, there are big department stores with four or five floors, selling a wide range of products. The best shopping is in local factories, shops and hotels specialising in the sale of handicrafts. Arts and crafts department stores offer local handicrafts. Special purchases include jade jewellery, embroidery, calligraphy, paintings and carvings in wood, stone and bamboo. It is advisable to keep receipts, as visitors may be asked to produce them at Customs prior to departure.
Shopping hours: Mon-Sun 0900-1900.
SPECIAL EVENTS: *Spring Festival* is the most important festival in the year for the Chinese, when families get together and share a sumptuous meal on the eve of the Chinese new year. Homes are festooned with banners and pictures to bring good fortune. Other activities associated with the festival include the lion dance, the dragon-lantern dance and stilt walking. For a full list of events, contact the China National Tourism Administration (see *Contact Addresses* section). The following is a selection of special events occurring in China in 2005:
Jan 5-Feb 28 *Harbin Ice and Snow Festival*. **Feb 9-11** *Spring Festival* (Chinese New Year), nationwide. **Feb 9** *Tibetan New Year*. **Feb 25-26** *Great Prayer Festival*, Tibet. **Apr 4-6** *Qintong Boat Festival*, Yangzhou. **Apr 11** *Hainan International Coconut Festival*. **Apr 13-15** *Water Splashing Festival*, Yunnan Province. **Apr 25** *Fujian Mazu Festival*, Meizhou Island. **May 23** *Saga Dawa Festival*, Tibet. **Jun 24-26** *Torch Festival of the Yi Minority*, Yunnan. **Jul 25-Aug 25** *Wutai Mountain Tourist Month*, Shanxi Province. **Aug** *Qingdao International Beer Festival; Horse Race Festival*, Qingtan, Tibet; *Shoton Festival*, Tibet. **Sep 10-15** *Shaolin International Martial Arts Festival*, Henan Province. **Sep 26-Oct 10** *Qufu International Confucius Culture Festival*.
SOCIAL CONVENTIONS: Cultural differences may create misunderstandings between local people and visitors. The Chinese do not usually volunteer information and the visitor is advised to ask questions. Hotels, train dining cars and restaurants often ask for criticisms and suggestions, which are considered seriously. Do not be offended by being followed by crowds, this is merely an open interest in visitors who are rare in the remoter provinces. The Chinese are generally reserved in manner, courtesy rather than familiarity being preferred. The full title of the country is 'The People's Republic of China', and this should be used in all formal communications. 'China' can be used informally, but there should never be any implication that another China exists. Although handshaking may be sufficient, a visitor will frequently be greeted by applause as a sign of welcome. The customary response is to applaud back. Anger, if felt, is expected to be concealed and arguments in public may attract hostile attention. In China, the family name is always mentioned first. It is customary to arrive a little early if invited out socially. Toasting at a meal is very common, as is the custom of taking a treat when visiting someone's home, such as fruit, confectionery or a souvenir from a home country. If it is the home of friends or relatives, money may be left for the children. If visiting a school or a factory, a gift from the visitor's home country, particularly something which would be unavailable in China (a text book if visiting a school, for example), would be much appreciated. Stamps are also very popular as gifts,

as stamp-collecting is a popular hobby in China. A good gift for an official guide is a Western reference book on China. Conservative casual wear is generally acceptable everywhere and revealing clothes should be avoided since they may cause offence. Visitors should avoid expressing political or religious opinions. **Photography**: Not allowed in airports. Places of historic and scenic interest may be photographed, but permission should be sought before photographing military installations, government buildings or other possibly sensitive subjects. **Tipping**: Not officially encouraged but accepted.

Business Profile

ECONOMY: The vast Chinese economy has developed in fits and starts since the founding of the People's Republic in 1949. Its basic structure is mostly that of a developing country, with the majority of the population employed on the land. However, there is a significant industrial base and expanding pockets of advanced manufacturing and technological enterprises, concentrated on the eastern coast and the Special Administrative/Economic Zones (including Hong Kong and Macau).

The economy has undergone rapid and consistent growth of approximately 8 to 9 per cent annually since the introduction of economic reforms in the late 1980s. However, the new wealth has not been evenly distributed and there are now major disparities between what are sometimes known as the 'blue China' – the coastal cities and Special Zones – and the inland 'brown China' of low-grade agriculture, antiquated industrial operations and widespread social and economic deprivation. Although modernisation of the agricultural sector is underway, there has been a major shift of population from the countryside to the cities. And the government is still prepared to undertake massive engineering projects such as the Three Gorges Dam project, which may displace anything up to one million people.

China is the world's largest producer of rice and a major producer of cereals and grain. Large mineral deposits, particularly coal and iron ore, provide the raw material for an extensive steel industry. China is self-sufficient in oil and is developing a petrochemicals industry. Other important minerals include tungsten, molybdenum, tin, lead, bauxite (aluminium), phosphates and manganese. In the last 10 years, central government policy has switched the emphasis in development from heavy to light industry and promoted the evolution of a service sector. Chemicals and high technology industries have grown particularly quickly. The fundamental changes that have taken place in the Chinese economy were introduced under what was described as the 'socialist market economy', under which market mechanisms were introduced to attract foreign investment and improved trade terms. Foreign companies were encouraged both to sell products in China and to establish joint ventures – under certain conditions – with Chinese commercial organisations. Such problems as emerged were put into perspective by the 1997 Asian economic crisis. China, because of its vast domestic market and highly regulated banking system, did not suffer nearly as badly as many of the region's smaller economies. Government targets for production and growth continued to be met and still are. In 2003, the economy accelerated to reach 10 per cent growth, the trade balance showed a healthy surplus, and price inflation was negligible. China's major imports are energy-related products, telecommunications, electronics and transport. Minerals and manufactured goods are the principal exports. The economy has already begun to show the benefits of China's recently acquired membership of the World Trade Organisation in 2001. (This was a major foreign policy objective for the Jiang government.) The country's principal trading partners are Germany, Japan and the USA.

BUSINESS: Weights and measures are mainly metric, but several old Chinese weights and measures are still used. Liquids and eggs are often sold by weight. The Chinese foot is 1.0936 of an English Foot (0.33m). Suits should be worn for business visits. Appointments should be made in advance and punctuality is expected. Visiting cards should be printed with a Chinese translation on the reverse. Business visitors are usually entertained in restaurants where it is customary to arrive a little early and the host will toast the visitor. It is customary to invite the host or hostess to a return dinner. Business travellers in particular should bear in mind that the government of the United Kingdom recognises the government of the People's Republic of China as being the only government of China, as do the United Nations. Best months for business visits are April to June and September to October. **Office hours**: Mon-Fri 0800-1700, midday break of one to two hours.

COMMERCIAL INFORMATION: The following organisation can offer advice: China Council for the Promotion of International Trade (CCPIT). *London office*: 40-41 Pall Mall, London SW1Y 5JQ, UK (tel: (020) 7321 2044; fax: (020) 7321 2055; website: www.ccpit.org). *Beijing office*: 1 Fu Xing Men Wai Jie, Beijing 100860 (tel: (10) 6801 3344; fax: (10) 6801 1370; e-mail: ccpit@ccpit.org; website: www.ccpit.org).

CONFERENCES/CONVENTIONS: The following organisations can offer advice: China International Travel Service (CITS) *or* Department of Marketing and Promotion, China National Tourism Administration (see *Contact Addresses* section).

Climate

China has a great diversity of climates. The northeast experiences hot and dry summers and bitterly cold winters. The north and central region has almost continual rainfall, hot summers and cold winters. The southeast region has substantial rainfall, with semi-tropical summers and cool winters. Central, southern and western China are also susceptible to flooding, China is also periodically subject to seismic activity.

Required clothing: *North* – heavyweight clothing with boots for the harsh northern winters. Lightweight clothing for summer. *South* – mediumweight clothing for winter and lightweight for summer.

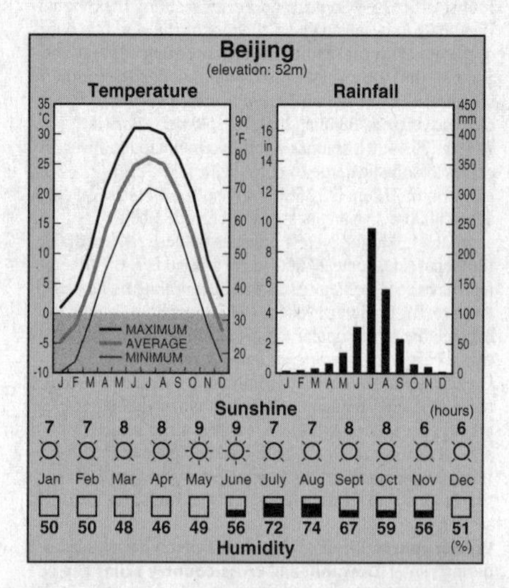

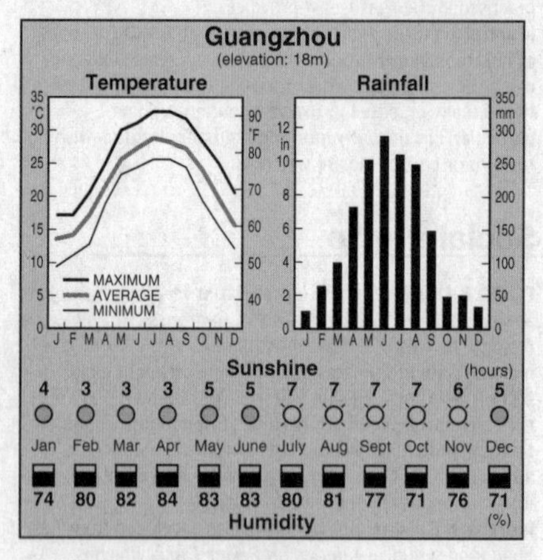

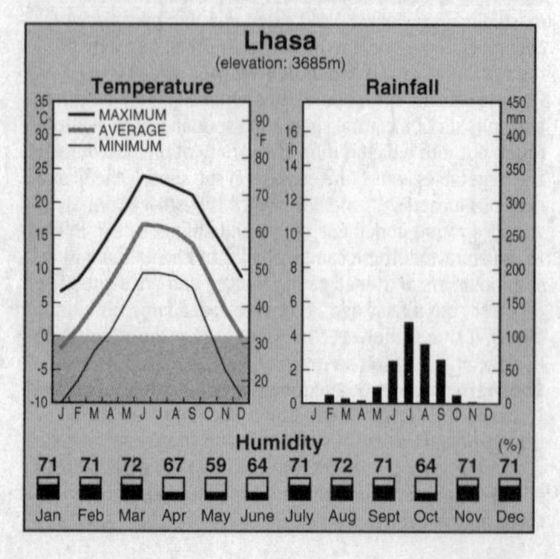

China - Hong Kong

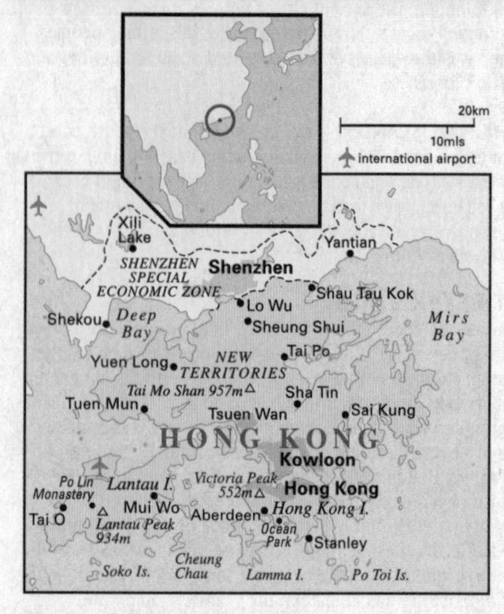

Location: East Asia.

Country dialling code: 852.

On 1 July 1997, Hong Kong became a Special Administrative Region of China in an arrangement that will last for 50 years. Operating under a 'one country, two systems policy', Hong Kong maintains its own political, social and economic systems. English remains an official language and Hong Kong's border with China still exists.

Hong Kong Tourism Board
9th to 11th Floor, Citicorp Centre, 18 Whitfield Road, North Point, Hong Kong
Tel: 2807 6543 *or* 2508 1234 (multilingual tourist information).
Fax: 2806 0303.
E-mail: info@hktb.com
Website: www.discoverhongkong.com

Hong Kong Economic and Trade Office
6 Grafton Street, London W1S 4EQ, UK
Tel: (020) 7499 9821. Fax: (020) 7495 5033.
E-mail: general@hketolondon.gov.hk
Website: www.hketolondon.gov.hk

Hong Kong Tourism Board
6 Grafton Street, London W1S 4EQ, UK
Tel: (020) 7533 7100. Fax: (020) 7533 7119.
E-mail: lonwwo@hktb.com
Website: www.discoverhongkong.com

British Consulate General
1 Supreme Court Road, Central, Hong Kong
Tel: 2901 3000. Fax: 2901 3066 (general enquiries) *or* 2901 3008 (press & public affairs enquiries) *or* 2901 3347 (visa enquiries).
E-mail: information@britishconsulate.org.hk
Website: www.britishconsulate.org.hk

Embassy of the People's Republic of China
2300 Connecticut Avenue, NW, Washington, DC 20008, USA
Visa section: Room 110, 2201 Wisconsin Avenue, NW, Washington, DC 20007, USA
Tel: (202) 328 2500 *or* 338 6688 (visa section).
Fax: (202) 328 2582 *or* 588 9760 (visa section).
E-mail: chinaembassy_us@fmprc.gov.cn
Website: www.china-embassy.org
Consulates General in: Chicago, Houston, Los Angeles, New York and San Francisco.

Hong Kong Tourism Board
115 East 54th Street, 2nd Floor, New York, NY 10022, USA
Tel: (212) 421 3382. Fax: (212) 421 8428.
E-mail: nycwwo@hktb.com
Website: www.discoverhongkong.com

Consulate General of the United States of America
26 Garden Road, Hong Kong
Tel: 2523 9011. Fax: 2845 1598.
Website: http://hongkong.usconsulate.gov

Embassy of the People's Republic of China
515 St Patrick Street, Ottawa, Ontario K1N 5H3, Canada
Tel: (613) 789 3434. Fax: (613) 789 1911.
E-mail: chinaemb_ca@mfa.gov.cn
Website: www.chinaembassycanada.org
Consulates General in: Calgary, Toronto and Vancouver.

Hong Kong Tourism Board
Ground Floor, 9 Temperance Street, Toronto, Ontario M5H 1Y6, Canada
Tel: (416) 366 2389. Fax: (416) 366 1098.
E-mail: yyzwwo@hktourismboard.com
Website: http://discoverhongkong.com/canada

Consulate General of Canada
Street address: 11-14th Floors, Tower 1, Exchange Square, 8 Connaught Place, Central, Hong Kong

HONG KONG: Central & Wan Chai

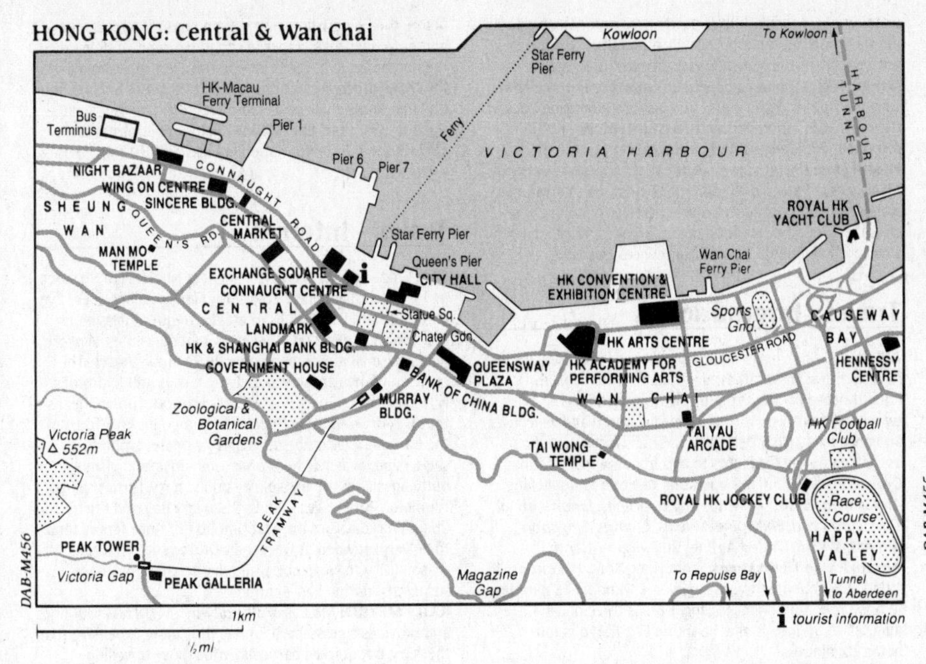

HONG KONG: Kowloon

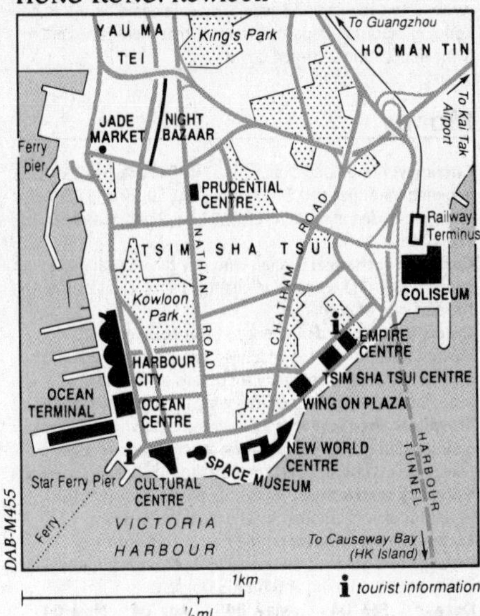

Postal address: PO Box 11142, Hong Kong
Tel: 2810 4321. Fax: 2810 6736.
E-mail: hkong@dfait-maeci.gc.ca *or* webmaster.hkong@dfait-maeci.gc.ca
Website: www.hongkong.gc.ca

General Information

AREA: 1098 sq km (424 sq miles).
POPULATION: 6,787,000 (official estimate 2002).
POPULATION DENSITY: 6181.2 per sq km.
GEOGRAPHY: Hong Kong is located in East Asia, just south of the Tropic of Cancer. Hong Kong Island is 32km (20 miles) east of the mouth of Pearl River and 135km (84 miles) southeast of Canton. It is separated from the mainland by a good natural harbour. Hong Kong Island was ceded to Britain in 1842 by the Treaty of Nanking; and the Kowloon Peninsula (south of Boundary Street and Stonecutters Island) in 1860 by the Convention of Peking. The area of Boundary Street to Shenzhen River and a group of 260 islands, now known as the New Territories, were leased to Britain in 1898 for a period of 99 years. The New Territories (plus the 260 islands) comprise 891 sq km (380 sq miles). Shortage of land suitable for development has led to reclamation from the sea, principally from the seafronts of Hong Kong Island and Kowloon.
GOVERNMENT: Special Administrative Region of the People's Republic of China since 1997. **Head of Government:** Chief Executive Tung Chee-Hwa.
LANGUAGE: Chinese and English are the official languages, with Cantonese most widely spoken. English is spoken by many, particularly in business circles.
RELIGION: Buddhist, Confucian and Taoist, with Christian and Muslim minorities, but there are also places of worship for most other religious groups.
TIME: GMT + 8.
ELECTRICITY: 220 volts AC, 50Hz.
COMMUNICATIONS: Telephone: Directory enquiries services are computerised. For directory enquiries, dial 1081 (English) *or* 1083 (Chinese). Full IDD is available. Country code: 852. Outgoing international code: 001. Local public telephone calls can be made either with phonecards or coins. Local calls are free from private phones. **Mobile telephone:** GSM 900 and 1800 networks provide excellent coverage, even to most of the smaller outlying islands. Mobile telephones also function all over the underground network, thanks to transmitters installed in the tunnels. Main network operators include *New World Mobility* (website: www.nwmobility.com), *Peoples Telephone Co Ltd* (website: www.peoplesphone.com.hk), *SmarTone Mobile Comms Ltd* (website: www.smartone.com.hk) and *Sunday* (website: www.sunday.com). **Fax:** *HK Telecom International Ltd* and the post office provide services. Bureaufax and international services are also available. **Internet:** ISPs include *ABC Net* (website: www.hkabc.net), *HKNet* (website: www.hknet.com) and *Hong Kong Internet Service* (website: www.hkispa.org.hk). Internet cafes are plentiful nationwide. **Post:** Regular postal services are available. Airmail to Europe takes three to five days. *Poste Restante* facilities are available. Post office hours: Mon-Fri 0800-1800; Sat 0800-1400. **Press:** English-language dailies include *Asian Wall Street Journal*, *International Herald Tribune* and *South China Morning Post*.
Radio: BBC World Service (website: www.bbc.co.uk/worldservice) and Voice of America (website: www.voa.gov) can be received. From time to time the frequencies change and the most up-to-date can be found online.

Passport/Visa

	Passport Required?	Visa Required?	Return Ticket Required?
Full British	Yes	No/1	Yes
Australian	Yes	No/2	Yes
Canadian	Yes	No/2	Yes
USA	Yes	No/4	Yes
Other EU	Yes	No/3	Yes
Japanese	Yes	No/4	Yes

Note: *Regulations and requirements may be subject to change at short notice, and you are advised to contact the appropriate diplomatic or consular authority before finalising travel arrangements. Details of these may be found at the head of this country's entry. Any numbers in the chart refer to the footnotes below.*

Entry restrictions: All visitors must show evidence of sufficient funds to support themselves during their stay.
PASSPORTS: Passport valid for at least six months after the period of intended visit required by all.
VISAS: Required by all except the following:
(a) **1.** British Citizens for stays of up to 180 days (British Overseas Citizens, British Subjects, British Protected Persons and nationals of British Dependent Territories may stay for up to 90 days);
(b) **2.** nationals of Commonwealth countries for stays of up to 90 days (except nationals of Samoa, South Africa, Sri Lanka and Uganda for stays of up to 30 days, and nationals of Bangladesh, Cameroon, India, Lesotho and Mozambique for stays up to 14 days): nationals of Grenada, Nigeria, Pakistan, Sierra Leone and the Solomon Islands *do* require a visa;
(c) **3.** nationals of EU countries for stays of up to 90 days (except **1.** British citizens for stays of up to 180 days);
(d) **4.** nationals of Andorra, Anguilla, Bermuda, Brazil, Cayman Islands, Chile, Colombia, Ecuador, Egypt, Faroe Islands, Greenland, Iceland, Israel, Japan, Korea (Rep), Liechtenstein, Monaco, Montserrat, Norway, Romania, St Helena and Dependencies, St Kitts & Nevis, San Marino, Switzerland, Turkey, Turks & Caicos Islands, USA, Venezuela and Zimbabwe for stays of up to 90 days;
(e) nationals of Argentina, Bolivia, Cape Verde, Costa Rica (except holders of a provisional passport and holders of 'Documento de Identidad Y Viaje' issued by the Costa Rican Government, who *do* require a visa), Dominican Republic, El Salvador, Guatemala, Honduras, Indonesia, Mexico, Morocco, Paraguay, Peru (except for holders of Peruvian special resident's passports, who *do* require a visa), Thailand, Tunisia, United Arab Emirates, Uruguay (except holders of passports issued under decree 289/90, who *do* require a visa) and Yemen for stays of up to 30 days;
(f) nationals of Algeria, Angola, Bahrain, Benin, Bhutan, Bosnia & Herzegovina, Burkina Faso, Burundi, Central African Republic, Chad, Comoro Islands, Congo (Dem Rep), Congo (Rep), Côte d'Ivoire, Croatia, Djibouti, Equatorial Guinea, Ethiopia, Gabon, Guinea, Guinea-Bissau, Haiti, Jordan, Kuwait, Macedonia (Former Yugoslav Republic of), Madagascar, Mali, Marshall Islands, Mauritania, (Federated States of) Micronesia, Mongolia, Niger, Oman, Palau, The Philippines, Qatar, Rwanda, São Tomé e Principe, Saudi Arabia, Surinam, Togo, US Territory of Pacific Islands and Vatican City for stays of up to 14 days;
(g) People in transit not leaving the airport transit area except for nationals of Eritrea, Iraq, Liberia, Pakistan (except holders of Diplomatic and Official passports) and Sierra Leone who *do* require a transit visa;
(h) all other nationals for stays of up to seven days (except for nationals of Eritrea, Iraq, Liberia, Pakistan (except holders of Diplomatic and Official passports) and Sierra

Credit: © Hong Kong Tourism Board

Leone who *do* require a visa at all times).
Note: For clarification or further information, contact the Hong Kong Immigration Department, 2nd Floor, Immigration Tower, 7 Gloucester Road, Wan Chai, Hong Kong (tel: 2824 6111; fax: 2877 7711; e-mail: enquiry@immd.gov.hk; website: www.immd.gov.hk). Their booklet *Do you need a Visa for Hong Kong?* is also available from the Hong Kong Economic and Trade Office in London (see *Contact Addresses* section).
Types of visa and cost: *Tourist*; *Business* (single- and multiple-entry); visas generally cost HK$135, but this varies according to nationality and nature of visit. Enquire at the Chinese Consulate (or Consular section at the Embassy) or the Hong Kong Immigration Department for details. *Transit*: HK$70.
Validity: Three months. Extensions are possible for about HK$135. Enquire at the Immigration Department in Hong Kong or at the nearest Chinese Embassy (or Consular Section).
Application to: Chinese Consulate (or Consular Section at the Embassy), Hong Kong Economic Office or the Hong Kong Immigration Department.
Application requirements: (a) Passport valid for at least six months with photocopies of the relevant pages of information. (b) Completed application form. (c) Valid travel documents (onward or return tickets, unless on transit to China (PR) or Macau (SAR), and accommodation bookings). (d) Sufficient funds to cover duration of stay. (e) Two passport-size photos. (f) Evidence of employment (employment certificate, company letter etc). (g) Fee. (h) For business visas, a letter of invitation from a ministry, firm or an official Hong Kong organisation is required.
Working days required: Five (if the application is

processed by a Chinese Consulate or Embassy); four to six weeks if the application needs to be considered by the Hong Kong Immigration Department. Note that there is no refund if the application is turned down.

Money

Currency: Hong Kong Dollar (HK$) = 100 cents. Notes are in denominations of HK$1000, 500, 100, 50, 20 and 10. Coins are in denominations of HK$10, 5, 2 and 1, and 50, 20 and 10 cents.
Currency exchange: Foreign currency can be changed in banks, hotels and bureaux de change. Banks usually offer the best rate of exchange.
Credit & debit cards: American Express, Diners Club, MasterCard and Visa are widely accepted. Check with your credit or debit card company for details of merchant acceptability and other services which may be available.
Travellers cheques: Accepted almost everywhere. To avoid additional exchange rate charges, travellers are advised to take travellers cheques in Pounds Sterling, US Dollars or Euros.
Currency restrictions: There are no restrictions on the import or export of either local or foreign currency.
Exchange rate indicators: The following figures are included as a guide to the movements of the Hong Kong Dollar against Sterling and the US Dollar:

Date	Feb '04	May '04	Aug '04	Nov '04
£1.00=	14.15	13.93	14.36	14.72
$1.00=	7.78	7.80	7.79	7.77

Banking hours: Mon-Fri 0900-1630, Sat 0900-1230.

Duty Free

The following goods may be imported into Hong Kong by persons aged over 18 years without incurring customs duty:
Non-residents: *200 cigarettes or 50 cigars or 250g of tobacco*; *1l of wine or spirits*; *reasonable quantity of other items for personal use*.
Residents: *60 cigarettes or 15 cigars or 75g of tobacco*; *750ml of still wine*; *reasonable quantity of other items for personal use*.
Note: (a) Antibiotic drugs are prohibited unless confirmed by a medical note. (b) The import of animals is strictly controlled.
Prohibited items: Firearms, narcotics, psychotropic drugs, counterfeit items, ammunition, copyright-infringed goods, plants, endangered species (dead or alive) and products deriving from them, game, poultry and fireworks and other explosives.

Public Holidays

2005: Jan 1 New Year's Day. **Feb 9-11** Chinese New Year. **Mar 25** Good Friday. **Mar 28** Easter Monday. **Apr 5** Ching Ming Festival. **May 1** Labour Day. **May 15** Lord Buddha's Birthday. **Jun 11** Tuen Ng (Dragon Boat) Festival. **Jul 1** Hong Kong Special Administrative Region Establishment Day. **Sep 19** Chinese Mid-Autumn Festival. **Oct 1** National Day. **Oct 11** Chung Yeung Festival. **Dec 25** Christmas Day. **Dec 26** Boxing Day.
2006: Jan 1 New Year's Day. **Jan 29-31** Chinese New Year. **Apr 5** Ching Ming Festival. **Apr 14** Good Friday. **Apr 17** Easter Monday. **May 1** Labour Day. **May 5** Lord Buddha's Birthday. **May 31** Tuen Ng (Dragon Boat) Festival. **Jul 1** Hong Kong Special Administrative Region Establishment Day. **Oct 1** National Day. **Oct 10** Chinese Mid-Autumn Festival. **Oct 30** Chung Yeung Festival. **Dec 25** Christmas Day. **Dec 26** Boxing Day.
Note: Religious festivals are timed according to the lunar calendar and variations may occur. The above represent all holidays on which banks, schools, public offices and government departments close. There are also statutory holidays on which all employees receive a day's holiday. For further details of these dates, contact the Hong Kong Tourism Board.

Health

	Special Precautions?	Certificate Required?
Yellow Fever	No	No
Cholera	No	No
Typhoid & Polio	1	N/A
Malaria	2	N/A

Note: *Regulations and requirements may be subject to change at short notice, and you are advised to contact your doctor well in advance of your intended date of departure. Any numbers in the chart refer to the footnotes below.*

1: Vaccination against typhoid and polio is advised.
2: There may be a slight risk of malaria in the rural areas although prophylaxis is not considered necessary.
Food & drink: All water direct from government mains in Hong Kong exceeds the United Nations WHO standards and is fit for drinking. However, all hotels also provide bottled water in guest rooms. Milk is pasteurised and dairy products are safe for consumption. Local meat, poultry, seafood, fruit and vegetables are generally considered safe to eat.
Other risks: *Japanese encephalitis* may occur in the New Territories between April and October. Immunisation against *hepatitis A, B, diphtheria* and *TB* is sometimes recommended. *Dengue fever* is increasing.
Health care: Charges are made for all services and treatment. All visitors are advised to take out private health insurance. Hotels have a list of government-accredited doctors. First-class Western medicine is practised. Excellent dental care is available. For emergency medical services, dial 999.

Travel - International

AIR: Hong Kong's major international airline is *Cathay Pacific (CX)* (website: www.cathaypacific.com), which flies to Hong Kong thrice-daily from London Heathrow and Los Angeles, twice-daily from New York (JF Kennedy Airport) and Vancouver, and once a day from Delhi and Toronto. *Cathay Pacific's* associated airline for flights to and from mainland China is *Dragonair*. Other airlines operating to Hong Kong include *Air Canada, British Airways, China Airlines, Japan Airlines, KLM, Lufthansa, Philippine Airlines, Qantas, Singapore Airlines, SWISS, United Airlines* and *Virgin Atlantic*.
Approximate flight times: From Hong Kong to *London* is 12 hours 50 minutes, to *Los Angeles* is 14 hours 15 minutes, to *New York* is 17 hours, to *Singapore* is three hours 40 minutes, to *Sydney* is nine hours, and to *Tokyo* is four hours 20 minutes.
International airports: *Hong Kong International Airport (HKG)* (Chek Lap Kok) (website: www.hongkongairport.com) is located on Lantau Island, 34 km (21 miles) from central Hong Kong. It is one of 10 Airport Core Programme (ACP) projects, one of the largest infrastructural projects ever undertaken in the world. It includes the 2.2km (1.4 miles) Tsing Ma Bridge, the world's largest road and rail suspension bridge, linking Lantau Island to the mainland New Territories. About three-quarters of the 12,480 sq km (7800 sq miles) airport site was constructed from land reclaimed from the sea, with the rest formed from the excavation of the existing islands of Chek Lap Kok and Lam Chau. The airport terminal building, designed by the British architect Sir Norman Foster, is Hong Kong's largest single building and its wing-like roof and glass walls have been hailed as a landmark in modern architecture.
Rail, bus and taxi links from *Hong Kong International Airport* to central Hong Kong leave from the Transportation Centre adjacent to the passenger terminal and cross the Tsing Ma bridge to the mainland New Territories. The easiest connection is via the *Airport Express Line (AEL)*, an all-seater business class high-speed train. The *AEL* leaves the airport every 10 minutes, operating from 0545-0048. It is a 23-minute journey to Hong Kong station, also stopping at Kowloon, with free shuttle buses running from the rail stations to various hotels (a single ticket to Hong Kong station from the airport costs HK$90). Many bus routes operate between the airport and Hong Kong and Kowloon, including nine Airbus services. Fares range between HK$20-45. High-speed ferries run between Chek Lap Kok Ferry Pier and Tuen Mun, with a shuttle bus from the pier to the airport. Ferries operate from 0600-2200 and cost HK$15. There are also 18 pick-up bays for coaches providing group and organised tour hotel transfers, and a car park for more than 3000 vehicles. Taxis to Hong Kong are readily available. *China Travel Service* and a number of other coach companies offer a variety of travel services for journeys to mainland China or Macau.
Facilities at *Hong Kong International Airport* include tourist information desks and computer kiosks, several currency exchange counters, banks and ATMs, food and drink outlets, a post office and medical centre, good physical accessibility for passengers with disabilities and a large Hong Kong Sky Mall shopping centre with duty free shopping available. *Hong Kong International* is also one of only a few airports to have an Automated People Mover (APM), a driverless train at basement level that transports passengers between terminals.
Departure tax: None.
SEA: A large number of cruise ships visit Hong Kong port. The following is a list of those that are UK-based; *Crystal, Cunard, P&O, Radisson Seven Seas, Seabourn* and *Silversea*. Ferries and hovercraft link Hong Kong with mainland China. Departures are from the Hong Kong ferry terminal in Kowloon to Shenzhen or Guangzhou. Enquire locally for details. There are more than 100 daily scheduled sailings each way to Macau. The journey can be made by jetfoil, turbocat, jumbocat, hoverferry or catamaran. Travel time by jetfoil – 55 minutes; by catamaran – one hour 10 minutes. See also the *Macau* section.
RAIL: The *Kowloon–Canton Railway Corporation (KCR)* operates a service from Kowloon to Guangzhou (formerly Canton), several times a day. There are also services from Hong Kong to Foshan and Changping. Restaurant cars are only available if travelling first class. Local KCRC trains run regularly (every five to 10 minutes) to Lo Wu, the last stop before the Chinese border. It is then possible to cross the border to Shenzhen, a special economic zone, in China over the border. To go as far as Lo Wu, travellers must hold a visa for China, otherwise it is only possible to get to Sheung Shui. Children under three years old travel free. Children aged three to nine years pay half fare. For more information, contact the KCRC information line (tel: 2688 1333; website: www.kcrc.com).

Travel - Internal

SEA: Cross-harbour passenger services (shortest route seven to 10 minutes) are operated by *Star Ferries* (sailing every five minutes) from 0630-2330. There are frequent passenger and vehicle services on other cross-harbour routes. *Wallah wallahs* (small motorboats) provide 24-hour service. The outlying islands are served daily by ferries and hydrofoils. However, the opening of the Cross Harbour Tunnel means that *wallah wallahs* are decreasing in popularity. Tours of the harbour and to Aberdeen and Yaumatei typhoon shelters are available by *Watertours* junks, and visits to outlying islands are possible by public ferry. Ferries sail to Tuen Mun, Sha Lo Wan, Tai O, Discovery Bay and Cheung Chau. Weekdays are the best time to go, since ferries tend to be very crowded at weekends. During the typhoon season (May to November), all ferry services may be suspended during bad weather.
RAIL/METRO: *Mass Transit Railway (MTR)* has four lines and provides a cross-harbour line. It is more expensive than the ferry, but quicker, particularly for those travelling further into Kowloon than Tsimshatsui or to Lantau Island. Trains run between 0600-0100. A single ticket costs HK$4-11. For visitors staying for a week or more it is worth getting an *Octopus Card*, an electronic ticket from which the cost of the journey is automatically deducted when it is placed on a sensor. The card costs HK$50, and value can be added to the card at machines in any MTR station. Any other credit remaining is also refunded when the card is handed in. At present, the card may be used on MTR services, as well as on the Kowloon-Canton Railway, major bus routes and some ferries. The *Airport Express Tourist Octopus Card* is valid for three days, entitling passengers to one Airport Express journey and three days of unlimited travel by MTR. Plans are underway to extend its use to other routes and means of transport as Hong Kong's transport system becomes more and more integrated. For further details, contact the MTR information line (tel: 2881 8888; website: www.mtr.com.hk). The Kowloon– Canton Railway Corporation (KCR) has 13 stations within Hong Kong. Trains run between 0530-0025 from Hung Hom (Kowloon) to Shenzhen in China; see *Travel – International* section for more information. KCR also run the Light Rail (LR) which connects the north west new territories Tuen Mun and Yuen Long. LR trains run from 0545-0030. For further information, contact Light Rail (tel: 2468 7788).
ROAD: Traffic drives on the left. **Bus**: The *Octopus Card* (see above) can be used on buses. Routes run throughout the territory, with cross-harbour routes via the tunnels. These, however, are often very crowded. Exact change is required. Air-conditioned coaches operate along certain Hong Kong and Kowloon routes. **Minibus**: These can pick up passengers and stop on request except at regular bus stops and other restricted areas. **Trams**: The *Octopus Card* (see above) can be used on trams. They are only available on Hong Kong Island, running from Kennedy Town to Shau Kei Wan (via Happy Valley racecourse). Double decker trams are also available. All trams run from 0600-0100 and fares are HK$2. *Peak Tram* on the Island is a cable tramway to the upper terminus on Victoria Peak. **Taxi**: These are plentiful in Hong Kong and Kowloon. There is an extra charge (HK$10) for the Cross Harbour Tunnel. Red taxis serve Hong Kong Island and Kowloon, green ones the New Territories, and blue ones Lantau Island. Maxicabs, however, operate on fixed routes without fixed stops. Many drivers speak a little English, but it is wise to get your destination written in Chinese characters. **Rickshaws**: These are gradually disappearing and are now purely a tourist attraction. It is advisable to agree the fare in advance. **Car hire**: A wide selection of self-drive and chauffeur-driven cars are available, although car hire is not that popular in Hong Kong. **Documentation**: An International Driving Permit is recommended, although it is not legally required. A valid national licence is accepted for up to 12 months. Minimum age is 18 years. Third Party insurance is compulsory.
Travel times: The following chart gives approximate travel times (in hours and minutes) from **Hong Kong Island** to main tourist districts and outlying islands.

	Road	Metro	Sea
Kai Tak	0.35	-	-
Kowloon	0.20	0.04	0.10
Causeway Bay	0.10	-	-
Lantau Is.	-	-	1.00
Aberdeen	0.20	-	-
Cheung Chau	-	-	1.00

Accommodation

HOTELS: Hong Kong offers a wide range of luxury hotels with all the major international chains represented. Smaller hotels specialising in 'family style' hospitality can be a cheaper alternative. There are also a number of fairly new hotels in the New Territories, providing a range of recreational facilities. Guest house accommodation, with good standards and facilities, is also available. In spite of the large number of hotel rooms available in Hong Kong, visitors are strongly advised to make an advance booking, especially during the peak season (May until November). There is a Hotel Reservation Centre at Hong Kong International Airport on Chek Lap Kok island (open daily from 0600-0100) which can offer assistance. A 10 per cent service charge and 5 per cent government tax are added to the bill. 80 member hotels belong to the Hong Kong Hotels Association, 508-511 Silvercord Tower II, 30 Canton Road, Tsimshatsui, Kowloon (tel: 2375 3838; fax: 2375 7676; e-mail: info@hkha.org; website: www.hkha.org). **Grading**: Though there is no grading structure as such, hotel members of the HKTA fall into one of four categories: High Tariff A Hotels, High Tariff B Hotels, Medium Tariff Hotels and Hostels/Guest houses.
SELF-CATERING: Resort houses on the outlying islands can be hired.
CAMPING/CARAVANNING: Permitted in the countryside, though permission is required within the Country Park protection area.
YOUTH HOSTELS: There are four main YMCA/YWCAs in Hong Kong. The YMCA in Kowloon is at 41 Salisbury Road, Tsimshatsui, Kowloon (tel: 2268 7000; fax: 2739 9315; e-mail: info@ymcahk.org.hk; website: www.ymcahk.org.hk). For further details, contact the Hong Kong Tourism Board (see *Contact Addresses* section). There are numerous youth hostels in Hong Kong, all of which are outside the city. Contact Hong Kong Youth Hostels Association Ltd, Room 225-227, Block 19, Shek Kip Mei Estate, Shamshuipo, Kowloon (tel: 2788 1638; fax: 2788 3105; e-mail: info@yha.org.hk; website: www.yha.org.hk).

Resorts & Excursions

Hong Kong is a popular tourist destination as well as being one of the world's major business centres. This tax-free, bustling port and commercial centre comprises **Hong Kong Island**, **Kowloon Peninsula**, the **New Territories** and the many **Outlying Islands**. Transportation is modern and well-organised and most tours and sightseeing trips are completed the same day. A tour of the New Territories takes about six hours, one of Hong Kong Island about four. Other popular excursions include sport and recreation tours and night tours, such as a dinner cruise and a tram tour with cocktails served. Contact the Hong Kong Tourism Board for further details (see *Contact Addresses* section).
HONG KONG ISLAND: The island is an eclectic mix of modern skyscrapers, colonial buildings and traditional temples. **Central** is the financial and commercial hub of the island and the main point for catching the famous **star ferry** to the Kowloon Peninsula. A unique way to experience the buzz of city life is by riding the 800m-long **central-mid-levels** escalator (the world's longest covered outdoor escalator) which transports tens of thousands of people each day and has created its own escalator culture of cafes and restaurants. Central is also a major shopping and entertainment area with the trendy night spots of **Lang Kwai Fong** and **SoHo**. Nearby, along Hollywood Road is **Man Mo Temple**, the country's oldest Chinese temple that honours the gods of literature (Man) and war (Mo). One of the best ways to view the incredible density and scale of the city is from **Victoria Peak**. Reached by the **Peak Tram**, that rises 386m up the mountainside within eight minutes, the summit offers an exceptional panorama, whether by day or night. At the foot of the tram lies **Government House**, the residence of 25 British Governors from 1855 until Hong Kong's handover to China in 1997. Other vestiges of this colonial past are seen in **St John's Cathedral**, thought to be the oldest Christian church in the Far East, and the **Flagstaff House Museum of Tea Ware**. Located in **Hong Kong Park**, the museum is an imposing colonial-style building housing ancient Chinese artefacts used in tea-making.
Wan Chai district is renowned for its small shops and markets, as well as fashionable restaurants and bars. The impressive 78-storey **Central Plaza** stands here (Hong Kong's tallest building) and visitors can view the city from the Sky Lobby on its 46th floor. After 1800 each day, neon lights upon the building's rooftop change colour every hour to denote the time of evening. Nearby is the vast **Hong Kong Convention and Exhibition Centre**, where the handover ceremony took place. The **Golden Bauhinia monument** outside the centre symbolises this momentous occasion. **Causeway Bay** is the main embarkation point for the cross-harbour tunnel. Attractions in the area include the **Happy Valley Racetrack**, many local teahouses, department stores and the **Noon Day Gun**, that has fired at midday since the 1840s.
The south of the island is characterised by a more relaxed pace of life, and beautiful bays and harbours. **Aberdeen Harbour** can be toured by traditional fishing junks and sampans. It is perhaps best known, however, for its neon-lit **Jumbo Floating Restaurant** (one of the largest in the world). Situated near the harbour is **Ocean Park**, a popular amusement park with roller coaster rides, large reef aquariums, performing dolphins and killer whales, as well as giant pandas. **Repulse Bay** is renowned for its pristine beach, overlooked by the **Tin Hau Temple**, and **Stanley** is well worth a trip for its outdoor markets.
KOWLOON: Considered as Hong Kong's 'tourist mecca', **Tsim Sha Tsui** is packed with tourist hotels, shops and markets. **Nathan Road** is a smart and fashionable shopping street, considered the equivalent of Fifth Avenue or the Champs Elysées. Near to the star ferry pier stands the old **Clock Tower** – the remaining piece from the Kowloon-Canton railway station that was re-located to Hung Hom in 1975. Worth visiting are the **Hong Kong Museum of Art**, which has exhibitions of jade, ceramic and calligraphy, and the **Hong Kong Space Museum**, with a Space Theatre. **Kowloon Park** features a Sculpture Walk with local and international exhibits, as well as Chinese and ornamental gardens. For a more spiritual retreat, tourists should visit either the **Chi Lin Nunnery**, a spectacular Tang Dynasty-style complex, or **Wong Tai Sin Temple**, built in honour of a shepherd who earned immortality. Many fortune-tellers congregate here. Further into Kowloon City, **Mong Kok** and **Yau Ma Tei** offer unique bustling markets. In Yau Ma Tei, **Temple Street** is a normal commercial road until 1400 when makeshift stalls and carts appear for the **Night Market**, selling everything from electrical goods to incense sticks. Mong Kok (thought to be the world's most densely populated urban area) heaves with selling and buying. Exotic fish and amphibians are sold at the **Goldfish Market**, and near the **Yuen Po Street Bird Garden**, intricate bamboo birdcages and songbirds can be purchased.
NEW TERRITORIES: The territories cover 796 sq km (306 sq miles) between Kowloon and Mainland China, and are a contrast of hilly woodlands, wildlife reserves, sandy bays, new towns and lively markets. **Sha Tin** is home to **Sha Tin Racecourse**, that normally stages horse races at the weekend, and the **Hong Kong Heritage Museum**, which includes many interactive exhibits. The **Ten Thousand Buddhas Monastery**, situated in the hills above Sha Tin, in fact houses around 13,000 small Buddha statues, and is well worth visiting.
Many historical and interesting sights are scattered among the New Territories. A beautifully designed complex, located in **Tuen Mun**, features pavilions, bonsai trees, lotus ponds and a Taoist temple that contains lanterns from Beijing's Imperial Palace. Built in 1486, **Tsui Shing Lau Pagoda** in **Yuen Lang** district is the only historic pagoda in Hong Kong. The **Waterfront Park** in **Tai Po** has a futuristic **Lookout Tower** that provides breathtaking views across **Tolo Harbour**. Further north, on the border with China, is the fantastic **Fung Ying Seen Koon Temple**, built in the traditional Taoist style with a double-tiered roof of orange tiles.

OUTLYING ISLANDS: Hong Kong has over 260 outlying islands but only a few are inhabited. **Lantau Island** is famed for its **Giant Buddha** that sits upon **Ngong Ping Plateau** at the **Po Lin Monastery**. At 26m high and weighing in at 202 tonnes of bronze, it is the world's largest seated outdoor Buddha. Monks prepare vegetarian lunches at the monastery for visitors. Tanka boat people who live in traditional stilt-houses at the fishing village of **Tai O** can be visited. The island also boasts the white sandy beach, **Cheung Sha**, and the amazing **Shek Pik Reservoir Dam**. Day trips to Lantau and tours can be arranged from Hong Kong Island.
Lamma Island is renowned for its seafood and there are many restaurants and cafes along the sea front. The walk to the village of **Yung Shue Wan** provides a wonderful hilltop vista of Hong Kong's distant skyline. **Cheung Chau** and **Peng Chau** are still traditional fishing islands with simple temples and unspoilt beaches. Cheung Chau holds an annual **Bun Festival** in celebration of Pak Tai (a god that influences good sailing and fishing). Bamboo towers covered in steamed buns are constructed as an offering to the god.
Numerous other islands can be visited as a tranquil alternative to the frenetic energy of the rest of Hong Kong. For more information, contact the Hong Kong Tourism Board (see *Contact Addresses* section).

Sport & Activities

Horseracing: This is the most popular sport among local people. Race meetings, at which vast sums of money change hands, are held from September to June, Saturday or Sunday afternoon, and Wednesday evening. The two main **racecourses** are at *Happy Valley* (Hong Kong Island) and *Shatin* (New Territories). The tourism board organises horseracing tours which allow visitors to enjoy the races from the members-only enclosures.
Hiking and trekking: *MacLehose Trail*, the longest trail, at 100km (62 miles), crosses the New Territories, taking in Hong Kong's highest peak, *Tai Mo Shan* (985m/3231ft). It can be joined at 10 different points, all of them accessible by public transport, and is recommended for experienced hikers. The 70km- (43 mile-) *Lantau Trail* runs around Lantau Island, via Lantau Peak (934m/3064ft) and Po Lin Monastery, home to the world's tallest seated Buddha. The *Hong Kong Trail* runs through five country parks on Hong Kong Island, and the *Wilson Trail* runs for 78km from the south of Hong Kong Island to the north of the New Territories, necessitating a ferry ride across the harbour. A popular walk is the *Dragon's Back* on Hong Kong Island, which follows a ridge, giving spectacular views. This can be concluded with dinner in one of the restaurants in Shek-O village. On these trails and on other walks, visitors can escape from the urban bustle that characterises the rest of the territory and enjoy tranquillity and beautiful views.
Wildlife: In 1841, Lord Palmerston - who was then foreign secretary - wrote that Hong Kong was 'nothing but a barren island without a house upon it'. Today, the situation is different, although many people will be surprised to learn that less than 30 per cent of the territory's land area is developed. Owing to the foresight of a former Governor, many of Hong Kong's natural areas have been protected, and there are 22 country parks which cover approximately 110,000 acres (40,000 hectares) of land. There is a wide variety of vegetation, including native and imported species of trees. Although there are no longer large mammals such as tigers and elephants to be seen, it is possible to spot macaque monkeys, wild boar, civet cats, barking deer and the Chinese pangolin, a scaly mammal which resembles an armadillo. Hong Kong's prime **birdwatching** site is at the *Mai Po* marshes near Yuen Long in the east of the New Territories. The area is now administered by the World Wide Fund for Nature (WWF) and visitors are required to obtain a permit to enter. Black-headed gulls, Saunders gull, osprey, Dalmatian pelicans and Chinese pond herons all visit the site to feed on the fish in the mud flats and mangroves there, and many other species can also be seen. Hong Kong's waters are home to the Chinese pink dolphin, which can be observed near Lantau Island.
Golf: All golf clubs and their facilities in Hong Kong are for members only, although visitors can play for a limited time at an extra cost. Major tournaments are held at the renowned *Hong Kong Golf Club* in Fanling, which also allows visitors to join as day members. The *Jockey Club Kau Sai Chau* public golf course, beautifully located on an island, was designed by Gary Player. The Hong Kong Tourism Board organises sports and recreation tours on Tuesdays and Fridays which include trips to various golf courses (see *Contact Addresses* section).
Watersports: There are over 30 highly-acclaimed **beaches** throughout the territory. Excellent **skindiving**, **water-skiing**, **sailing**, **kayaking**, **windsurfing**, and **fishing** (from a boat or at a reservoir) are available. Watersports equipment can be hired from beaches and hotels in Stanley and Sai Kung, and from other centres.
Other: Cyclists will enjoy the *Tolo Harbour Cycling Track*, running from Sha Tin to Tai Po, an easy ride through scenic countryside. Bikes are available for rental near KCR stations. Most of the outlying islands do not allow cars and are therefore very peaceful. They are best visited in the week because they attract many visitors at weekends. Spectator sports such as **soccer**, **rugby** and **cricket** are also popular. **Jogging** facilities are provided by some hotels. The Clinic at Adventis Hospital holds jogging sessions every Sunday. There are also good facilities for **squash**, **tennis**, **riding**, **bowling** and **ice skating**, as well as health-centre facilities.

Social Profile

FOOD & DRINK: Hong Kong is one of the great centres for international cooking. Apart from Chinese food, which is superb, there are also many Indian, Vietnamese, Filipino, Singapore/Malaysian and Thai restaurants. It is the home of authentic Chinese food from all the regions of China, which may be sampled on a sampan in Causeway Bay, on a floating restaurant at Aberdeen, in a Kowloon restaurant, in a street market or at a deluxe hotel. Hotels serve European and Chinese food but there are also restaurants serving every type of local cuisine.
Chinese regional variations on food include Cantonese, Northern (Peking), Chiu Chow (Swatow), Shanghai, Sichuan and Hakka. Cantonese is based on parboiling, steaming and quick stir-frying to retain natural juices and flavours. The food is not salty or greasy and seafoods are prepared especially well, usually served with steamed rice. Specialities include *Dim Sum* (savoury snacks, usually steamed and served in bamboo baskets on trolleys). These include *Cha siu bao* (barbecue pork bun), *Har gau* (steamed shrimp

dumplings) and *Shiu mai* (steamed and minced pork with shrimp). The emphasis in Northern food is on bread and noodles, deep-frying and spicy sauces. Specialities include *Peking duck* and hotpot dishes. Shanghainese food is diced or shredded, stewed in soya or fried in sesame oil with pots of peppers and garlic. *Chiu Chow* is served with rich sauces and Hakka food is generally simple in style with baked chicken in salt among the best dishes. Sichuan food is hot and spicy with plenty of chillies. A speciality is barbecued meat.

The Chinese do not usually order a drink before dinner. Popular Chinese wines and spirits are *Zhian Jing* (a rice wine served hot like sake), *Liang hua pei* (potent plum brandy), *Kaolian* (a whisky) and *Mao toi*. Popular beers are the locally brewed *San Miguel* and *Tsingtao* (from China), with imported beverages widely available.

NIGHTLIFE: There are many nightclubs, discos, hostess clubs, theatres and cinemas. Cultural concerts, plays and exhibitions can be seen at Hong Kong's City Hall which also has a dining room, ballroom and cocktail lounge. The Hong Kong Cultural Centre, including a 2100-seat Concert Hall, 1750-seat Grand Theatre, a studio theatre with 300 to 500 seats and restaurants, bars and other facilities, has become the major venue for cultural concerts, plays and operas. Hong Kong Art Centre in Wan Chai supplements the City Hall's entertainment with culture in the form of Chinese opera, puppet shows, recitals and concerts. American, Chinese, European and Japanese films with subtitles are shown at a number of good air-conditioned cinemas. Two daily papers, the *Hong Kong Standard* and the *South China Morning Post*, contain details of entertainment. An unusual event to watch is night horseracing held Wednesday nights from September to May. For further details, contact the Hong Kong Tourism Board (see *Contact Addresses* section).

SHOPPING: Whether one is shopping in modern air-conditioned arcades or more traditional street markets, the range of goods available in Hong Kong is vast. Many famous-name shops have opened in Hong Kong, bringing the latest styles in great variety. Places that display the QTS sign (Quality Tourism Services) are the best guarantee of satisfaction. Bargaining is practised in the smaller shops and side stalls only. There are excellent markets in Stanley on Hong Kong Island, which is in a beautiful setting in a small village on the coast, and in Temple Street, Kowloon, which is a night market. Tailoring is first class. Except for a few items, such as liquor and perfume, Hong Kong is a duty-free port. **Shopping hours**: Hong Kong Island (Central & Western): 1000-1900 (1000-2000 along Queen's Road). Hong Kong Island (Causeway Bay & Wan Chai): 1000-2130. Kowloon (Tsimshatsui & Yau Ma Tei and Mong Kok): 1000-2100. Many shops are open Sunday. Shopping hours may vary greatly.

SPECIAL EVENTS: For a complete list of special events, contact the Hong Kong Tourism Board (see *Contact Addresses* section). The following is a selection of special events occurring in Hong Kong in 2005:

Jan 22-23 *Dragon Dance and Lion Dance Championships*. **Feb 9** *Chinese New Year Night Parade*. **Feb 10** *Lunar New Year Fireworks Display*. **Feb 17-Mar 20** *Hong Kong Arts Festival*. **Mar 11-20** *Hong Kong Flower Show*. **Mar 18-20** *International Rugby World Cup* Sevens. **Apr 5** *Ching Ming Festival*. **May 1** *Tin Hau Festival*. **May 15** *Birthday of Lord Buddha*. **Jun 11** *Tuen Ng (Dragon Boat) Festival*. **Aug 11** *Seven Sisters Festival*. **Aug 19** *Hungry Ghosts Festival*. **Sept 18** *Chinese Mid-Autumn Festival; Moon Festival*.

Note: A festival in Hong Kong is a major event on a scale hardly understood in the West. During Chinese New Year festivities, there is total disruption of everyday life.

SOCIAL CONVENTIONS: Handshaking is the common form of greeting. In Hong Kong, the family name comes first, so Wong Man Ying would be addressed as Mr Wong. Most entertaining takes place in restaurants rather than in private homes. Normal courtesies should be observed when visiting someone's home. During a meal, a toast is often drunk saying *Yum Sing* at each course. There may be up to 12 courses served in a meal, and although it is not considered an insult to eat sparingly, a good appetite is always appreciated and it is considered cordial to taste every dish. It is customary to invite the host to a return dinner. Informal wear is acceptable. Some restaurants and social functions often warrant formal attire. Smoking is widely acceptable and only prohibited where specified.

Tipping: Most hotels and restaurants add a 10 per cent service charge and an additional 5 per cent gratuity is also expected. Small tips are expected by taxi drivers, doormen and washroom attendants.

Business Profile

ECONOMY: The mainstays of Hong Kong's economy are light manufacturing, shipping and financial services. The last of these is now the most important as Hong Kong has developed into a major international financial centre. Manufacturing is concentrated in textiles, consumer electronics and other consumer goods (Hong Kong is the world's largest producer of children's toys). The shipping industry is assisted by Hong Kong's natural deep-water harbour, probably the best in the region. Much regional trade is still conducted through Hong Kong.

Within months of the handover of the territory to China in July 1997, a financial crisis which affected the whole region started to take hold. With a more mature and stable banking system than most of the rest of the region, Hong Kong showed few immediate ill effects. However, the severe impact on many of the territory's major trading partners and the depression of the regional economy was sure to cause some damage, and did so in the form of a 7 per cent drop in output during 1999. There was some recovery during 2000, but unexpectedly this did not last and by mid-2002, the economy was contracting at an annual rate of 1.5 per cent. Unemployment, meanwhile, had grown to 8 per cent.

The USA, Japan, Taiwan, Singapore and Germany are Hong Kong's main trading partners.

BUSINESS: Businesspeople are generally expected to dress smartly. Local businesspeople are usually extremely hospitable and speak English. Appointments should be made in advance and punctuality is appreciated. Business cards are widely used with a Chinese translation on the reverse. Most top hotels provide business centres for visiting businesspeople, with typing, duplication, translation and other services. **Office hours**: Mon-Fri 0900-1300 and 1400-1700, Sat 0900-1300. Some Chinese offices open earlier than 0900 and close later than 1700.

COMMERCIAL INFORMATION: The following organisations can offer advice: Hong Kong Trade Development Council, 16 Upper Grosvenor Street, London W1K 7PL, UK (tel: (020) 7616 9500; fax: (020) 7616 9510; e-mail: london.office@tdc.org.hk; website: www.tdctrade.com); *or* Hong Kong Trade Development Council, 38th Floor, Office Tower, Convention Plaza, 1 Harbour Road, Wan Chai (tel: 2584 4333; fax: 2824 0249; *or* Hong Kong General Chamber of Commerce, 22nd Floor, United Centre, 95 Queensway (tel: 2529 9229; fax: 2527 9843; e-mail: chamber@chamber.org.hk; website: www.chamber.org.hk).

CONFERENCES/CONVENTIONS: The Hong Kong Convention and Incentive Travel Bureau is a division of the Hong Kong Tourist Association, which specialises in promoting Hong Kong as a leading venue with a special East/West position; it publishes lavish and detailed brochures showcasing the region for conference and incentive planners, together with a glossy catalogue of promotional material and a directory of associations and societies in Hong Kong. There are venues with seating for up to 12,500 persons. For further information, contact the Hong Kong Convention and Exhibition Centre, 1 Expo Drive, Wanchai, Hong Kong (tel: 2582 8888; fax: 2802 7284; e-mail: info@hkcec.com; website: www.hkcec.com.hk).

Climate

Hong Kong experiences four distinct seasons, with the climate influenced in winter by the north-northeast monsoon and in summer by the south-southwest monsoon. Summers are very hot, with the rainy season running from June to August. Spring and autumn are warm with occasional rain and cooler evenings. Winter can be cold, but most days are mild. There is a risk of typhoons and tropical storms from April to October, although direct hits are rare.

Required clothing: Lightweight cottons and linens are worn during warmer months, with warmer clothes for spring and autumn evenings. It should be noted that even during the hottest weather, a jacket or pullover will be required for the sometimes fierce air conditioning indoors. Warm mediumweights are best during winter. Waterproofing is advisable during summer rains.

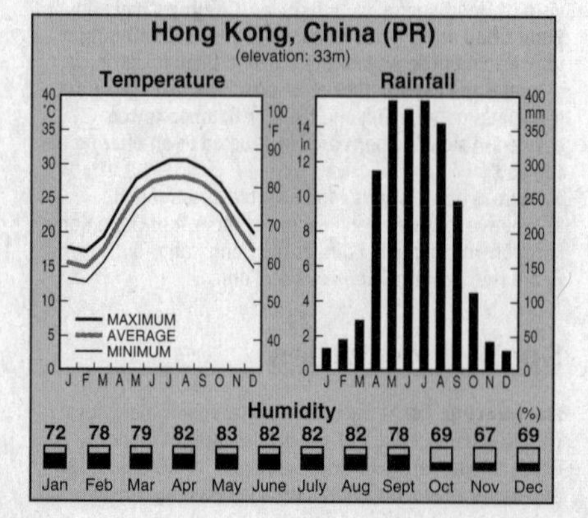

China: Macau

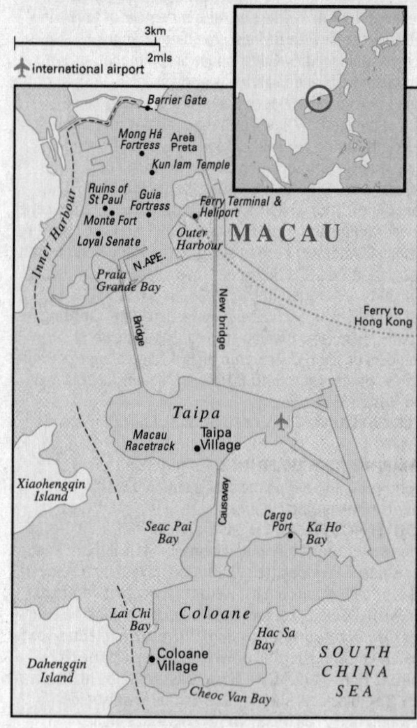

Location: South China coast.

Note: On 20 December 1999, Macau became a Special Administrative Region of China. Operating under a 'one country, two systems' policy, Macau will maintain its own political, social and economic systems in an arrangement that will last for 50 years. Portuguese and Chinese will both remain the official languages.

Country dialling code: 853.

Direcção dos Serviços de Turismo (Macau Government Tourist Office)
Alameda Dr. Carlos D'Assumpcao 335-341, Edificio 'Hot Line', 12 andar, Macau
Tel: 315 566 *or* 333 000 (tourist hotline). Fax: 510 104.
E-mail: mgto@macautourism.gov.mo
Website: www.macautourism.gov.mo

Government Head Quarters of Macau SAR
Avenida da Praia Grande, Macau
Tel: 989 5313 *or* 989 5316. Fax: 726 886.
E-mail: info@macau.gov.mo
Website: www.macau.gov.mo

Macau Government Tourist Office (MGTO)
c/o Representation Plus, 11 Blades Court, 121 Deodar Road, London SW15 2NU, UK
Tel: (020) 8877 4504/1. Fax: (020) 8874 4219.
E-mail: sharon@representationplus.co.uk
Website: www.macautourism.gov.mo

Public Security Forces Bureau
Calcada dos Quarteis, Quartel de San Francisco, Macau
Tel: 559 999. Fax: 559 998.
E-mail: info@fsm.gov.mo Website: www.fsm.gov.mo

The British Consulate General in Hong Kong deals with enquiries relating to Macau (see *Hong Kong* within the *China (PR)* section).

Embassy of the People's Republic of China
2300 Connecticut Avenue, NW, Washington, DC 20008, USA
Tel: (202) 328 2500. Fax: (202) 328 2582.
E-mail: chinaembassy_us@fmprc.gov.cn
Visa section: Room 110, 2201 Wisconsin Avenue, NW Washington, DC 20007, USA
Tel: (202) 338 6688. Fax: (202) 588 9760.
E-mail: chnvisa@bellatlantic.net
Website: www.china-embassy.org
Consulates General in: Chicago, Houston, Los Angeles, New York and San Francisco.

Macau Government Tourist Office
3601 Aviation Boulevard, Suite 2100, Manhattan Beach, Los Angeles, CA 90266, USA
Tel: (310) 643 2630 *or* (866) 656 2228 (toll-free in USA and Canada). Fax: (310) 643 2627.
E-mail: macau@myriadmarketing.com
Website: www.macautourism.gov.mo
Also deals with enquiries from Canada.

The Consulate General of the United States of America in Hong Kong deals with enquiries relating to

Macau (see *Hong Kong* within the *China (PR)* section).
Embassy of the People's Republic of China
515 St Patrick Street, Ottawa, Ontario K1N 5H3, Canada
Tel: (613) 789 3434. Fax: (613) 789 1414.
Website: www.chinaembassycanada.org
Consulates General in: Calgary, Toronto and Vancouver.
The Consulate General of Canada in Hong Kong deals with enquiries relating to Macau (see *Hong Kong* within the *China (PR)* section).

General Information

AREA: 26.80 sq km (10.35 sq miles).
POPULATION: 441,637 (official estimate 2002). 96 per cent of the population is Chinese and 4 per cent is Portuguese, European and from other regions.
POPULATION DENSITY: 16,479 per sq km.
CAPITAL: Macau.
GEOGRAPHY: Macau is situated on a tiny peninsula at the mouth of the Pearl River. Two bridges of 2.5km (1.5 miles) and 4.5km (2.8 miles) respectively link it to its nearest island, Taipa, which in turn is joined to the island of Côloane by a 2.2 km- (1.3 mile-) long causeway. At the extreme northern end of the peninsula, on a narrow isthmus, is the imposing gateway (*Portas do Cerco*, or Border Gate), which leads to the Zhuhai and Zhongshan areas of the People's Republic of China. Some 60km (37.5 miles) to the east-northeast, across the mouth of the river, is Hong Kong.
GOVERNMENT: Special Administrative Region of the People's Republic of China since 1999. **Head of State**: President Jiang Zemin since 1999. **Head of Government**: Chief Executive Edmund H W Ho.
LANGUAGE: The official languages are Chinese (Cantonese) and Portuguese. English is widely spoken by those engaged in trade, tourism and commerce.
RELIGION: The main religions are Buddhism, Roman Catholicism and Protestantism. The majority are Buddhists, while 7 per cent are Catholics.
TIME: GMT + 8.
ELECTRICITY: Usually 220 volts AC, 50Hz.
COMMUNICATIONS: Telephone: IDD service is available. Country code: 853. Outgoing international code: 00. International facilities are available at the General Post Office at Leal Senado Square, Macau City, the Central Post Offices in Taipa and Colôane, as well as all phone booths. **Mobile telephone:** Dual band GSM network covers the whole territory. Main operators are *CTM* (website: www.macau.ctm.net), *Hutchison Telephone Company* (website: www.hutchisonmacau.com) and *SmarTone* (website: www.smartone.com.mo). **Fax:** Major hotels have facilities. **Internet:** ISPs include *MacauWeb* (www.macauweb.com). **Telegram:** Services available at larger hotels and telecommunication offices, as well as all phone booths. **Post:** Airmail to Europe takes five to seven days. Automatic vending machines are available at various locations for stamps. **Press:** Newspapers are in Portuguese or Chinese, including Portuguese dailies *Hoje Macau* and *Jornal Tribuna de Macau*, and Chinese dailies *Macau Daily News* and *Va Kio Pou*. There are English-language papers from Hong Kong.
Radio: BBC World Service (website: www.bbc.co.uk/worldservice) and Voice of America (website: www.voa.gov) can be received. From time to time the frequencies change and can be found online.

Passport/Visa

	Passport Required?	Visa Required?	Return Ticket Required?
Full British	Yes	No/1	No
Australian	Yes	No/2	No
Canadian	Yes	No/2	No
USA	Yes	No/2	No
Other EU	Yes	No/1	No
Japanese	Yes	No/2	No

Note: Regulations and requirements may be subject to change at short notice, and you are advised to contact the appropriate diplomatic or consular authority before finalising travel arrangements. Details of these may be found at the head of this country's entry. Any numbers in the chart refer to the footnotes below.

PASSPORTS: Passport valid for at least one month required by all, except nationals of China who have a China Identity Card or travel permit and nationals of Hong Kong (SAR) who have a Hong Kong Identity Card (HKIC).
VISAS: Required by all except the following:
(a) **1.** nationals of all EU countries (UK nationals for stays of up to six months), Andorra, Egypt, Iceland, Israel, Korea (Rep), Lebanon, Norway, Romania and Tanzania for stays of up to 90 days;
(b) **2.** nationals of Australia, Brazil, Canada, Chile, India, Indonesia, Japan, Kiribati, Liechtenstein, Malaysia, Mexico, Monaco, Namibia, New Zealand, The Philippines, Samoa, Seychelles, Singapore, South Africa, Switzerland, Thailand, Turkey, Uruguay and the USA for stays of up to 30 days;
(c) nationals of China (PR) with valid Macau entry/departure documents, including residents of Hong Kong (SAR), Taiwan (China) and overseas Chinese for stays of up to 30 days;
(d) holders of a Hong Kong Identity Card (HKIC) or Hong Kong Permanent Identity Card or those with a Hong Kong Re-entry Permit for stays of up to one year.
Types of visa and cost: *Individual*: MOP100 (MOP50 for children under 12). *Family*: MOP200. *Group*: MOP50 per person for bona fide groups of 10 people or more and children of 12 years of age or less.
Validity: 30 days. Can be extended on application.
Application to: Individual visitors requiring a visa may obtain it upon arrival in Macau for a fee of MOP100. Visas can also be obtained from Consulates or Embassies of China (PR); see *China* section. For other enquiries, contact the Public Security Forces Bureau (see *Contact Addresses* section).

Money

Currency: Pataca (MOP) = 100 avos. Notes are in denominations of MOP1000, 500, 100, 50, 20 and 10. Coins are in denominations of MOP10, 5, 2 and 1, and 50, 20 and 10 avos. Hong Kong dollars are widely accepted.
Note: The Pataca is loosely pegged to the Hong Kong Dollar.
Currency exchange: Foreign currency may be exchanged at hotels, banks and licensed bureaux de change. Numerous ATMs are available for cash withdrawal by credit card.
Credit & debit cards: MasterCard and Visa are accepted. Check with your credit or debit card company for details of merchant acceptability and other services which may be available.
Travellers cheques: These may be exchanged at banks, bureaux de change and at many hotels. To avoid additional exchange rate charges, travellers are advised to take travellers cheques in US Dollars, Pounds Sterling or Euros.
Currency restrictions: There are no restrictions on the import or export of either local or foreign currency.
Exchange rate indicators: The following figures are included as a guide to the movements of the Pataca against Sterling and the US Dollar:

Date	Feb '04	May '04	Aug '04	Nov '04
£1.00=	14.58	14.35	14.79	14.80
$1.00=	8.01	8.03	8.03	8.03

Banking hours: Mon-Fri 0900-1700, Sat 0900-1200.

Duty Free

The following goods may be imported into Macau without incurring customs duty:
200 cigarettes or 50 cigars or 250g of tobacco products; 1l of wine and 1l of spirits; other goods up to a value of MOP10,000; one camera and five rolls of film and one film camera and two reels of film; clothing articles, jewellery and sports articles; one video cassette recorder; binoculars; one portable musical instrument; one portable record player and 10 records; one portable radio; one tape recorder; one portable typewriter; and one portable computer.
Restricted imports: Fish, shellfish, meat and all plants require an import permit.
Prohibited items: Firearms, ammunition, gunpowder and explosives, narcotics, drugs, chemicals and pharmaceutical products, dangerous goods, radioactive substances/irradiating apparatus, endangered species of animals and plants and pesticides.
Note: There is a 5 per cent duty on the import of electrical appliances and equipment. There are no export duties, but as travel is almost invariably via Hong Kong, the relevant Hong Kong import/export regulations must be observed (see *Hong Kong* within the *China (PR)* section).

Public Holidays

2005: Jan 1 New Year's Day. **Feb 9-11** Chinese New Year. **Mar 25** Good Friday. **Mar 28** Easter Monday. **Apr 5** Ching Ming Festival. **May 1** Labour Day. **May 15** Feast of Buddha (feast of the bathing of Lord Buddha). **Jun 11** Dragon Boat Festival (Tuen Ng). **Sep 19** Mid-Autumn Festival. **Oct 1-2** National Day of the People's Republic of China. **Oct 11** Chung Yeung Festival. **Nov 2** All Souls' Day. **Dec 8** Feast of the Immaculate Conception. **Dec 20** Macau Special Administrative Region Establishment Day. **Dec 22** Winter Solstice. **Dec 24-25** Christmas.
2006: Jan 1 New Year's Day. **Jan 29-31** Chinese New Year. **Apr 5** Ching Ming Festival. **Apr 14** Good Friday. **Apr 17** Easter Monday. **May 1** Labour Day. **May 5** Feast of Buddha (feast of the bathing of Lord Buddha). **May 31** Dragon Boat Festival (Tuen Ng). **Oct 7** Mid-Autumn Festival. **Oct 1-2** National Day of the People's Republic of China. **Oct 30** Chung Yeung Festival. **Nov 2** All Souls' Day. **Dec 8** Feast of the Immaculate Conception. **Dec 20** Macau Special Administrative Region Establishment Day. **Dec 21** Winter Solstice. **Dec 24-25** Christmas.

Credit: © Macau Government Tourist Office

Health

	Special Precautions?	Certificate Required?
Yellow Fever	No	No
Cholera	No	No
Typhoid & Polio	1	N/A
Malaria	No	N/A

Note: Regulations and requirements may be subject to change at short notice, and you are advised to contact your doctor well in advance of your intended date of departure. Any numbers in the chart refer to the footnotes below.

1: Vaccination against Typhoid and Polio are recommended, but not essential.
Food & drink: Tap water is generally regarded as safe, but bottled water may be advisable for the first few days. Milk is pasteurised, but avoid dairy products which are likely to have been made from unboiled milk. Vegetables should be cooked and fruit peeled.
Health care: Health insurance is recommended. There are good medical facilities, and religious orders or hotels will also give assistance.
Other risks: *Japanese encephalitis* may occur in the New Territories between April and October. *Diarrhoeal diseases*, *hepatitis A* and *B* and *Oriental lung fluke* (paragonimiasis) may occur in this area. Immunisation against *hepatitis A*, *B*, *diphtheria* and *tuberculosis* is sometimes recommended. *Rabies* is present.

Travel - International

AIR: The territory has its own airline, *Air Macau (NX)* (website: www.airmacau.com.mo), which operates regional flights. Other airlines serving Macau include *Air China*, *China Eastern Airlines*, *EVA Airways*, *Shangdong Airlines*, *Silk Air*, *TransAsia Airways* and *Xiamen Airlines*. A variety of charter airlines operate from Japan.
Approximate flight times: Flights from Europe and North America are usually via Hong Kong. From Hong Kong to *London* is 14 hours; for other flight times, see *Hong Kong (SAR)* in the *China (PR)* section.
International airports: *Macau International Airport (MFM)* (website: www.macau-airport.gov.mo) is 7km (5 miles) southeast of the city. Buses run to the city and Macau-Hong Kong ferry terminal via major hotels (travel time – 45 minutes). Bus fares cost MOP4-6. Taxis to the city centre are also available for approximately MOP40 (travel time - 15 minutes). Airport facilities include banks and bureaux de change, car hire, duty-free shops and restaurants.
An *ExpressLink* service is also available, allowing fast, trouble-free transfer between Macau and Hong Kong airports. Ferries depart approximately every 15 minutes (travel time – 55 minutes). On arrival at Macau Ferry Terminal, passengers travel by a special shuttle bus to the enclave's airport. Travellers should allow approximately one hour between ferry arrival time in Macau and departure time from Macau International Airport.
Departure tax: MOP80 per person (MOP50 per child aged two to 12) for destinations in China (PR), and MOP130 (MOP80 per child aged two to 12) for other destinations. Children under two are free, and transfer/transit passengers departing Macau within 24 hours are exempt. Payment *must* be made in local currency, and credit cards are not accepted.
Helicopter: *East Asia Airlines* and *Helicopters Hong Kong Limited* (website: www.helihongkong.com) operate daily flights (every 30 minutes; 0930-2259) between Hong Kong and Macau (travel time - 16 minutes). Cost: HK$1600 (weekdays) or HK$1700 (weekends and public holidays) one way. Helicopters depart from the Macau Maritime and Heliport Terminal, situated in the Outer Harbour.
SEA: A wide variety of vessels sail the 60km (37 mile) distance between Macau and Hong Kong: jetfoils, jumbocats, turbocats, hover-ferries and catamarans. There are more than 100 scheduled sailings each way throughout the day, while jetfoils operate round the clock. Passengers are advised to be at the terminals at least 30 minutes before the scheduled departure time in order to complete

immigration formalities; there is always a standby queue for a prior boat for passengers who arrive unexpectedly early. Jetfoils depart every 15 minutes from 0700 and every 30 minutes between 1730/1800-0400 (travel time - 55 minutes). Turbocat services take one hour. Catamaran services take one hour 10 minutes. For further details, contact First Ferry Macau (tel: 2131 8181; e-mail: ferry_ideas@nwff.com.hk; website: www.nwff.com.hk).
Tickets to Hong Kong can be bought in Macau up to seven days in advance. For travel from Hong Kong to Macau, jetfoil and jumbocat tickets can be bought up to 28 days in advance. A computerised booking system is available from Hong Kong MTR Travel Service Centres in the MTR stations of Admiralty, Central, Tsim Shat Sui, Causeway Bay, Mongkok, Tseun Wan and Kowloon Bay.
Telephone bookings for jetfoil services can be made by holders of American Express, Diners Club, MasterCard and Visa (tel: (+852) 2859 6596); further information can be obtained from the Far East Hydrofoil Company Ltd (tel: (+852) 2859 3351 *or* 790 7039 (in Macau)).
The baggage allowance is 10kg per person on high-speed ferries and, in general, is limited to hand-carried items. Tour operators can arrange luggage-handling where required. Porters are available for heavy luggage.
There are also turbojet and ferry services to Fu Yong ferry terminal in Shenzhen, China (travel time - one hour).
ROAD: The crossing point into China is via the Barrier Gate (Portas de Cerco) (open 0730-0000 daily). Buses run frequently to and from this point from 0800-1830 (travel time - two hours 30 minutes).

Travel - Internal

SEA: There are several daily harbour tours in Chinese Junks between the Inner and Outer harbours (travel time - 30 minutes). Tours depart from Pier 1 and cost MOP10 (children under 12 travel free).
ROAD: Traffic drives on the left. There are two bridges: one to Taipa Island, and a bridge carrying a four-lane highway from the international airport to the Macau-China border at Zhuhai. **Bus**: Services operate frequently around Macau and to the islands. The fare on all routes around the island is MOP2.5. The airport bus from Macau costs MOP6. **Car hire**: Available through several agencies. Drivers must be over 21. Passports may be required, as well as a credit card for a deposit. Chauffeur-driven limousines are also available. **Documentation**: An International Driving Permit is required. **Taxi**: Most taxis are black with a cream-coloured top, but some are all-yellow radio taxis. The fare is MOP10 for the first 1500m travelled, then MOP1 per 200m. There is a surcharge of MOP2 between Taipa and Colôane and MOP5 between Macau and Colôane. From the airport, a surcharge of MOP5 is added and each item of luggage is MOP3. **Rickshaws** and **pedicabs** (bicycles with a two-seater section at the back) are also available for hire. The ferry terminal and the Hotel Lisboa are the two main pick-up locations. Prices should be agreed in advance. It is worth remembering that many of the attractions in Macau are located on hilltops, beyond the reach of even the strongest-legged pedicab driver. **Bicycles** can be hired on Taipa Island and cost approximately MOP20 per hour. They may not be taken to the mainland.

Accommodation

There are various types of accommodation, ranging from first-class to economy-class hotels, plus inns, villa-apartments housed in new buildings, and older colonial hotels. At weekends, the hotels, villas and inns are usually full, so it is wise to make a reservation. There are currently about 9000 hotel rooms in Macau. Most hotels are air conditioned and rooms have private baths. A 10 per cent service charge is added to hotel bills, plus a 5 per cent government tax. For further information, contact the Macau Hotels Association, c/o Emperor Hotel, Rua de Xangai, Macau (tel: 781 888; fax: 782 287).

Resorts & Excursions

MACAU: The most famous sight in Macau is probably the ruins of the **Church of St Paul's**, originally built in 1602 and rebuilt in 1835 after a disastrous typhoon. The Jesuit citadel of **São Paulo do Monte** is almost directly in the centre of Macau. It forms the strong central point of the old city wall, and was instrumental in preventing the Dutch from conquering the city in 1622. The 17th-century **Guia Fortress** stands on the highest point in Macau; its lighthouse is the oldest on the China coast. Standing at 130ft high over the Praia Grande Bay, the **Gate of Understanding** (designed by Charters Almeida) is a symbolic structure which represents the goodwill between China and Portugal.
The complex of temples known as **Kun Iam Tong** dates from the time of the Ming Dynasty, about 400 years ago, and contains, amongst other works of art, a small statue of Marco Polo. The oldest Chinese temple in the territory is that of the **Goddess A-Ma**, which dates back at least six centuries. It has some excellent multicoloured bas-relief stone carvings. The **Macau Museum** seeks to embody the life of Macau and its people from the first settlement to the present day. The museum contains a vast collection of historic and social memorabilia.
The finest expression of Portuguese architecture is probably the **Leal Senado**, the Senate Chamber. The **Public Library**, off the main staircase, and the main chamber itself, are well worth a visit. The **Sun Yat Sen Memorial Home**, the former residence of the Revolutionary leader who overthrew the Ching Dynasty in 1910, is now a museum. **São Domingo's Church**, built in the 17th century, is one of the most beautiful religious buildings in Macau. It has recently reopened after a large-scale renovation programme which has transformed the church. A new **Museum of Sacred Art** has opened on three floors of the renovated belfry, and is home to 300 works of sacred art that illustrate the history of the Roman Catholic church in Asia. Other churches of interest include those of **Santo Agostinho**, **São Jose** and **São Lourenco**. Opposite Santo Agostinho church is the neo-classical **Dom Pedro V Theatre** and **Macau Club**, which still host plays and formal functions. The restored colonial buildings around the sqaure of Santo Agostinho are also worth seeing. Other monuments of note in Macau include those in honour of Jorge Alvares and Vasco da Gama. The **Chinese Garden of Lou Lim Ieoc** offers a relaxing alternative.
The **Macau Tower** is an entertainment and convention centre situated on the waterfront on the **Nam Van Lakes**. The 338m tower is the 10th tallest in the world and provides panoramic views of the region.

ELSEWHERE: Taipa and Colôane represent Macau's traditional countryside, with beach resorts, ancestral Chinese villages, and pine-forested hills with nature trails and picnic areas. A lot of 'old' Macau is preserved on the islands, including fishing boat-building yards, colonial mansions, Chinese temples and floating fisherfolk communities.
Taipa: Taipa village is a busy, colourful place with interesting shops and colonial Portuguese offices in narrow streets and alleys, where many traditional crafts are still followed. The **Taipa House Museum** is a group of five colonial-style houses which have been newly restored and converted. One house is an art gallery; another, furnished in 1920s style, shows how a Macanese family used to live; the other houses contain costumes, crafts and traditional artefacts. Nearby, a small amphitheatre offers typical Macanese entertainment. **Pou Tai Un Temple** is the largest temple on the islands and has a very good vegetarian restaurant.
Colôane: Colôane has several beaches, as well as **Seac Pai Van Park**, which has nature trails threading among the hills, and a walk-in aviary with rare and beautiful species. **A-Ma Statue** has recently been unveiled on the highest point on the island, from which there are spectacular views. Colôane Village has interesting Chinese temples, the **Chapel of St Francis Xavier** (a classic, Portuguese-style chapel built in 1928) and good restaurants.

Sport & Activities

Racing: This takes place at the *Canidrome* on Avenida General Castelo Branco on Monday, Thursday, weekends and some public holidays. The Canidrome is the only greyhound racing stadium in Asia and its excellent facilities include two grandstands, several private boxes and a VIP lounge. Over 300 dogs take part in races on each racing day. The *Macau Jockey Club* organises flat **horse races** at its track on the island of Taipa. Free shuttle buses take visitors from the Hotel Lisboa to the pier and the racecourse on racing days. The grandstand is air conditioned.
The Far East's gala **motorcycle** and Formula III **car racing** event, the *Macau Grand Prix*, is held during the third week in November. Near the Grand Prix circuit is the *Macau Grand Prix Museum*.
Gambling: For the majority of travellers, gambling is Macau's great attraction. Although it is well known that a large proportion of Macau's GDP comes from gambling, people regularly travel to the country in the hope of hitting the jackpot. There are nine official casinos, all operated under Government franchise and all open 24 hours a day. Both familiar western games and popular eastern games are on offer, and an assortment of slot machines are available - these are called 'hungry tigers' by the locals.
Compared to western casinos, the atmosphere is unglamorous, with the emphasis on serious betting. There is a minimum bet, currently 50 patacas on all games. Further information is available from the Macau Government Tourist Board (see *Contact Addresses* section), who also sell a detailed leaflet called *A-O-A Macau Gambling Guide*.
Other: An 18-hole **golf** course is available at the Macau Golf and Country Club, Colôane. **Go-karting** is available on Taipa Island. **Swimming** pools are found in major hotels and public pools are available in Macau, Colôane Island and Taipa. The best beach in the territory is at **Hac Sa** on Colôane. Despite the black colour of its sand, it has good facilities, including showers, toilets and good restaurants nearby. A **bowling centre** and ice rink is available at Future Bright Amusement Centre. **Squash** courts are available at the Oriental Macau and Royal hotels, as well as the Westin Resort. Courts and equipment for **badminton** and **tennis** are available for hire.

Social Profile

FOOD & DRINK: Most restaurants have table service. Hotels, inns and restaurants offer a wide variety of food. Some specialise in Portuguese dishes, while others offer cuisine from China, Japan, Korea and Indonesia. Local Macau food is spicy, a unique combination of Chinese and Portuguese cooking methods with influences of Indian and African spices. Dishes include *bacalhau* (cod served baked, grilled, stewed or boiled), *caldo verde* and *sopa a alentejana* (rich soups with vegetables, meat and olive oil), 'African chicken' (grilled with hot spices), *galinha a portuguesa* (chicken baked with potatoes, onions, eggs and saffron - the appearance of curry without the spice), *minche* (minced meat with fried potato and onion), Macau sole (fried fish usually served with salad) and *feijoados* (from Brazil, stews of kidney beans, pork, potatoes, cabbage and spicy sausage). The speciality of *dim sum* (Chinese savoury snacks steamed and served in bamboo baskets on trolleys) includes *cha siu bao* (steamed pork dumplings), *har gau* (steamed shrimp dumplings) and *shui mai* (steamed and minced pork with shrimp). Alcohol is easily obtainable. There are no licensing laws. All restaurants offer a variety of Portuguese red and white wines and sparkling *vinho verde*, as well as port and brandy, all at low prices.
NIGHTLIFE: Most of the nightlife is centred on the hotels, many of which have nightclubs with cabaret, Portuguese folk dancing, lively dance bands, discos, international menus and bars. In summer there are several open-air *esplanadas* serving soft drinks. Many locals, however, tend to relax in the evening in some of the many lively restaurants (see *Food & Drink* section).
Gambling is a big attraction for visitors to Macau and the casinos are open 24 hours, providing famous entertainers, baccarat, blackjack, roulette and Chinese games like *fantan* and *dai-siu* (big and small). See the *Sport & Activities* section for further information.
SHOPPING: Macau's most popular buys are jewellery (particularly gold and jade), Chinese antiques, porcelain, pottery, electronic gadgetry, cameras, watches and beading work. They are available at duty free prices because Macau is a free port and no sales tax is charged. Bargaining is expected on many items although most shops will have the same minimum price. Other popular buys are Chinese herbs and medicines, dried seafood (such as sharks' fins), abalone, Chinese and Macau pastries, and locally-made knitwear sold at stalls. When purchasing antiques, gold and jewellery, it is advisable to patronise shops recommended by the Goldsmiths' and Jewellers' Association and the Macau Government Tourist Office. A warranty and a receipt should be asked for when buying jewellery, gold, cameras, watches and electrical goods. The main shopping area is located along the Avenida do Infante D Henrique and Avenida Almeida Ribeiro, São Domingos Market, Rua de Palha, Rua do Campo and Rua Pedro Nolasco da Silva. Antiques and unique gifts may be found in Macau's flea market in the lanes around Rua das Estalagens (near St Paul's Ruins). There is an Artisan's Fair every Saturday evening in *Santo Agostinho Square*. Excursions can be made across the Chinese border to Zhuhai, where the first floor of the Gongbei market is well known for antiques, ceramics and fabrics. Software is also a good buy in Zhuhai. **Shopping hours**: Generally Mon-Sun 1000-2000. Some shops may close on the first day of every month.
SPECIAL EVENTS: The Macau Government Tourist Office can supply details of the many festivals celebrated in Macau. Festivals which are also official public holidays are listed in the Public Holidays section. The following is a selection of special events occurring in Macau in 2005: **Mar 11** *Feast of the God Toutei.* **Mar-Apr** *Macau Arts Festival.* **May 13** *Procession of Our Lady Fatima.* **May 18** *International Museum Day.* **May 15** *Feast of the Bathing of Lord Buddha.* **Jun** *Macau Lotus Flower Festival.* **Jun 11** *Macau International Dragon Boat Races.* **Jun 19** *Feast of Kuan Tai.* **Aug 11** *Feast of Maidens.* **Aug 18** *Feast of Hungry Ghosts.* **Sep-Oct** *International Fireworks Festival.* **Sep 18** *Mid-Autumn Festival.* **Oct** *International Music Festival.* **Oct 11** *Festival of Ancestors.* **Nov 17-20** *Macau Grand Prix.* **Dec 4** *Macau International Marathon and Half Marathon.* **Dec 22** *Winter Solstice.*

SOCIAL CONVENTIONS: Entertaining generally takes place in restaurants and public places. It is rare to be invited to a private home, unless the person is wealthy. Spirits are standard gifts in return for hospitality. Apart from the most formal occasions in restaurants and nightclubs, casual wear is acceptable. **Tipping**: A 10 per cent service charge will be added to most hotel and restaurant bills, but a small tip should also be left.

Business Profile

ECONOMY: Macau has long been an important distribution outlet for Chinese products and, in this respect, is similar to Hong Kong. Agriculture is negligible and there are very few natural resources (Macau relies almost entirely on imported oil to meet its energy needs.) The territory has an active manufacturing and export sector, the main products of which are textiles, toys, optical products, rubber, ceramics, china, furniture and footwear. Macau is also well known in the region for its extensive gambling facilities: the associated tourism has become a major source of income. Together, gambling and tourism account for about two-thirds of Macau's GDP. Trade between Macau and the neighbouring Chinese Special Economic Zone of Zhuhai has grown rapidly and contributed substantially to Macau's present trade surplus. However, key infrastructure projects (notably the new airport and the Nam Van land reclamation project) have, in different ways, fallen far short of expectations. China, Hong Kong and the USA are the territory's major trading partners. The Sino-Portuguese agreement, under which Macau reverted to Chinese rule in December 1999, guarantees the continuation of Macau's economic status for a minimum of 50 years. Macau's currency, the Pataca, has been retained indefinitely.
BUSINESS: Businesspeople are expected to dress smartly. Calling cards are essential, appointments should be made in advance and punctuality is appreciated. The World Trade Centre (16th Floor, 918 Edificio World Trade Centre, 918 Avenida da Amizade (tel: 727 666; fax: 727 633; e-mail: wtcmc@macau.ctm.net) offers assistance and various facilities for businesses, including a VIP Club restaurant. **Office hours**: Mon-Thurs 0900-1300 and 1430-1745, Fri 0900-1300 and 1430-1800.
COMMERCIAL INFORMATION: The following organisation can offer advice: Associação Comercial de Macau, 16th Floor, Edificio ACM 5, Rua de Xangai 175 (tel: 576 833; fax: 594 513).
CONFERENCES/CONVENTIONS: Macau's major meetings venues include the Conference Centre at the University of Macau (with seating for up to 764), the Forum (a multipurpose complex with seating for up to 4035), the Tourist Activities and Conference Centre (with seating for up to 600) and Macau Landmark (featuring a unique 'skyroof'). The majority of hotels also have facilities, and support services can be provided by the World Trade Centre (see above). A new cultural centre (website: www.ccm.gov.mo) was inaugurated in March 1999 on the Outer Harbour waterfront. It includes two auditoria, one seating 1200 people and the other 500 people. The territory's newest convention venue is the conference centre in the Macau Tower, the world's 10th tallest building (website: www.macautower.com.mo). The tower also features a revolving restaurant, an entertainment area and shopping facilities. For further information, contact the Macau Government Tourist Office (see *Contact Addresses* section).

Climate

Subtropical climate with very hot summers and a rainy period during the summer months. Most rain occurs in the afternoon. Winds can reach gale force and typhoons are not unknown. The best season is autumn (October to December), when days are sunny and warm and the humidity low.

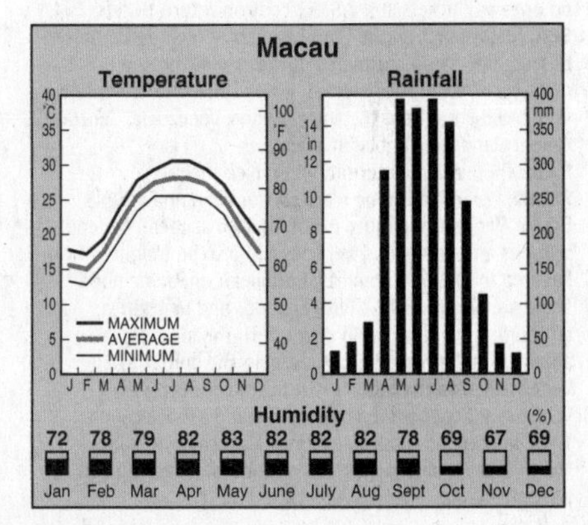

Colombia

LATEST TRAVEL ADVICE CONTACTS

British Foreign and Commonwealth Office
Tel: (0870) 606 0290 Website: www.fco.gov.uk
US Department of State
Website: http://travel.state.gov/travel
Canadian Department of Foreign Affairs and Int'l Trade
Tel: (1 800) 267 8376 Website: www.dfait-maeci.gc.ca

Location: Northwest South America.

Country dialling code: 57.

Ministerio de Comercio, Industria y Turismo
Calle 28, 13A-15, Bogotá, DC, Colombia
Tel: (1) 606 7676 *or* 382 1309. Fax: (1) 696 7521.
Website: www.mincomercio.gov.co
Fondo de Promoción Turística de Colombia
Calle 16A 78-55 Of. 604
Tel: (1) 611 4330. Fax: (1) 236 3640.
E-mail: turismocolombia@andinet.com
Website: www.turismocolombia.com
Embassy of the Republic of Colombia
Flat 3A, Three Hans Crescent, London SW1X 0LN, UK
Tel: (020) 7589 9177. Fax: (020) 7581 1829.
E-mail: mail@colombianembassy.co.uk
Website: www.colombianembassy.co.uk
Opening hours: Mon-Fri 0900-1800.
Colombian Consulate
3rd Floor, 35 Portland Place, London W1B 1AE, UK
Tel: (020) 7637 9893. Fax: (020) 7637 5604.
E-mail: info@colombianconsulate.co.uk
Website: www.colombianconsulate.co.uk
Opening hours: Mon-Fri 0900-1330 (personal callers); 1500-1700 (telephone enquiries).
British Embassy
Carrera 9, 76-49, Piso 8-10, Bogotá, DC, Colombia
Tel: (1) 326 8300. Fax: (1) 326 8302.
E-mail: bogota.info@fco.gov.uk
Website: www.britain.gov.co
Honorary Consulates in: Cali and Medellín.
Embassy of the Republic of Colombia
2118 Leroy Place, NW, Washington, DC 20008, USA
Tel: (202) 387 8338. Fax: (202) 232 8643.
E-mail: emwas@colombiaemb.org
Website: www.colombiaemb.org
Consulate in: New York.

TIMATIC CODES

Health
AMADEUS: **TI-DFT/JIB/HE**
GALILEO/WORLDSPAN: **TI-DFT/JIB/HE**
SABRE: **TIDFT/JIB/HE**

Visa
AMADEUS: **TI-DFT/JIB/VI**
GALILEO/WORLDSPAN: **TI-DFT/JIB/VI**
SABRE: **TIDFT/JIB/VI**

To access TIMATIC country information on Health and Visa regulations through the Computer Reservations System (CRS), type in the appropriate command line listed above.

Embassy of the United States of America
Street address: Calle 22D-bis, 47-51, Santa Fe de Bogotá, DC, Colombia
Postal address: Carrera 45, 22D-45, Santa Fe de Bogotá, DC, Colombia
Tel: (1) 315 0811 *or* 315 1566 (consular section).
Fax: (1) 315 2197.
E-mail: nib@estate.gov
Website: http://bogota.usembassy.gov
Embassy of the Republic of Colombia
360 Albert Street, Suite 1002, Ottawa, Ontario K1R 7X7, Canada
Tel: (613) 230 3760. Fax: (613) 230 4416.
E-mail: embajada@embajadacolombia.ca
Website: www.embajadacolombia.ca
Canadian Embassy
Street address: Carrera 7, 115-33, 14th Floor, Santa Fe de Bogotá, Colombia
Postal address: General Apartado, Aereo 110067, Bogotá, Colombia
Tel: (1) 657 9800. Fax: (1) 657 9912 (general).
E-mail: bgota@dfait-maeci.gc.ca
Website: www.bogota.gc.ca

General Information

AREA: 1,141,748 sq km (440,831 sq miles).
POPULATION: 44,583,577 (official estimate 2003).
POPULATION DENSITY: 39.0 per sq km.
CAPITAL: Santa Fe de Bogotá. **Population**: 6,260,862 (1999).
GEOGRAPHY: Colombia is situated in South America, bordered to the north by the Caribbean, to the northwest by Panama, to the west by the Pacific Ocean, to the southwest by Ecuador and Peru, to the northeast by Venezuela and to the southeast by Brazil. The Andes Mountains extend into the country in three ranges running south to north, dipping finally into the lowlands of the Caribbean coast. Along the southern part of the Pacific coast run wide, marshy lowlands rising to a relatively low but rugged mountain chain. East of this range, the southwestern coastal lowlands extend in a low trough running from the port of Buenaventura on the Pacific coast to the Caribbean. East of this rise the slopes of the Western Cordillera which, with the Central Cordillera range, runs north to the Caribbean lowlands from Ecuador, separated by a valley, filled in the south by volcanic ash to a height of 2500m (8202ft). Further north lies the fertile Cauca Valley, which extends to Cartago where it becomes a deep gorge running between the Cordilleras to the Caribbean lowlands. The Eastern Cordillera, the longest range, rises north of the Ecuadorean border and runs north then northeast towards Venezuela. Flat grassy prairies in the east along with the jungles and towering rainforests of the Amazon make up over half the country's area. There are also two small islands, San Andrés and Providencia, located 700km (430 miles) north of the Colombian coast, that have belonged to Colombia since 1822.
GOVERNMENT: Republic. Gained independence from Spain in 1819. **Head of State and Government**: President Álvaro Uribe Vélez since 2002.
LANGUAGE: Spanish is the official language. Local Indian dialects and some English, French, German and Italian are also spoken.
RELIGION: Christianity, with 92 per cent Roman Catholic; small Protestant and Jewish minorities.
TIME: GMT - 5.
ELECTRICITY: Mostly 110 volts AC, 60Hz. American-style two-pin plugs.
COMMUNICATIONS: Telephone: IDD service to most areas; calls to smaller centres must be made through the international operator. Country code: 57. Outgoing international code: 90. Many public telephones now work only with phone cards produced by *Empresa de Teléfonos de Bogotá (ETB)*, which can be bought in many shops and kiosks. **Mobile telephone:** AMPS/TDMA networks exist. Operators include *Bellsouth* (website: www.bellsouth.com.co) and *Comcel* (website: www.comcel.com.co). **Fax:** Hotels have facilities. **Internet:** ISPs include *Cablenet* (website: www.tvcable.com). Internet cafes exist in the main cities. **Telegram:** Facilities are available through national ENDT telecommunications offices. **Post:** Post offices are marked *Correos*. Post office opening hours: Mon-Sat 0800-1200. There are two types of service: urban post (green letter boxes) and inter-urban and international (yellow boxes). Letters and packets sent by airmail normally take five to seven days to reach their destination. **Press:** Spanish dailies include *El Espacio*, *El Nuevo Siglo*, *La República* and *El Tiempo*.
Radio: BBC World Service (website: www.bbc.co.uk/worldservice) and Voice of America (website: www.voa.gov) can be received. From time to time the frequencies change and the most up-to-date can be found online.

Passport/Visa

	Passport Required?	Visa Required?	Return Ticket Required?
Full British	Yes	No	Yes
Australian	Yes	No	Yes
Canadian	Yes	No	Yes
USA	Yes	No	Yes
Other EU	Yes	No/1	Yes
Japanese	Yes	No	Yes

Note: *Regulations and requirements may be subject to change at short notice, and you are advised to contact the appropriate diplomatic or consular authority before finalising travel arrangements. Details of these may be found at the head of this country's entry. Any numbers in the chart refer to the footnotes below.*

PASSPORTS: Passport valid for at least six months required by all.
VISAS: Required by all except the following for up to 180 days:
a) **1.** nationals listed in the table above (except for nationals of the Czech Republic, Estonia, Hungary, Republic of Ireland, Latvia, Poland and Slovenia);
b) nationals of Andorra, Antigua & Barbuda, Argentina, The Bahamas, Barbados, Belize, Bolivia, Brazil, Chile, Costa Rica, Dominica, Dominican Republic, Ecuador, El Salvador, Grenada, Guatemala, Guyana, Honduras, Iceland, Indonesia, Israel, Jamaica, Korea (Rep), Liechtenstein, Malaysia, Mexico, Monaco, New Zealand, Norway, Panama, Paraguay, Peru, The Philippines, Romania, San Marino, St Kitts & Nevis, St Lucia, St Vincent & the Grenadines, Singapore, Switzerland, Trinidad & Tobago, Turkey, Uruguay and Venezuela.
Types of visa and cost: *Tourist*: £30 (depends on nationality). *Temporary visitor*: £75. *Business*: £120. *Student*: £30. For other types and costs contact the Consulate or Consular section at Embassy.
Validity: *Tourist* and *Temporary Visitor*: valid six months. *Business*: valid four years for multiple entries with maximum stays of six months each. *Student*: valid five years with multiple entry.
Application to: Consulate (or Consular section at Embassy); see *Contact Addresses* section.
Application requirements: (a) Valid passport with at least one blank page to affix the visa (two pages for business visas). (b) Three recent passport-size photos. (c) Two copies of application form. (d) Onward or return tickets. (e) Proof of sufficient funds to cover stay (such as latest bank statements). (f) Fee, payable by bank deposit only. (g) For postal applications, a pre-paid self-addressed special delivery envelope or prepaid courier service. *Tourist*: (a)-(g) and, (h) Letter of Invitation from a Colombian national or resident, or proof of hotel accommodation. *Temporary Visitor*: (a)-(g) and, (h) Letter of invitation from a sponsoring organisation or a Colombian national or resident. *Business*: (a)-(g) and, (h) Letter form company stating applicant's position, purpose and duration of visit, and taking responsibility for travel expenses, if self-employed, letter must also include bank references and names of commercial contacts in Colombia. (i) Company's UK registration certificate.
Note: Photocopies of all the above documentation are required All documents will need to be translated into Spanish, and some of them will need to be legalised by the Consulate. Nationals will be required to undergo an interview prior to being issued with a visa. Contact the nearest Colombian Consulate or Consular section at Embassy for further details
Working days required: Depends on the visa issued. Five for Tourist and Business visas; one week for Temporary Visitors Visas. It is generally advised to allow plenty of time for applications.
Temporary residence: Enquire at Consulate or Counsular section of Embassy for further details; see *Contact Addresses* section.

Money

Currency: Colombian Peso (peso) = 100 centavos. Notes are in denominations of peso50,000, 20,000, 10,000 and 5000. Coins are in denominations of peso1000, 500, 200, 100 and 50.
Currency exchange: The exchange rate tends to be lower on the Caribbean coast than in Bogotá, Medellín and Cali. The US Dollar is the easiest currency to exchange at hotels, banks, shops and travel agencies, but all establishments charge an exchange fee.
Credit & debit cards: All major cards are accepted, but check with your credit or debit card company for details of merchant acceptability and other services which may be available.
Travellers cheques: These are not always easy to change in the smaller towns, except at branches of the Banco de la República. To avoid additional exchange rate charges, travellers are advised to take travellers cheques in US Dollars.
Currency restrictions: The import and export of local currency is unlimited. The import of foreign currency is unlimited subject to declaration on arrival. The export of foreign currency is limited to US$25,000.
Exchange rate indicators: The following figures are included as a guide to the movements of the Colombian Peso against Sterling and the US Dollar:

Date	Feb '04	May '04	Aug '04	Nov '04
£1.00=	4985.66	4829.17	4804.89	4696.66
$1.00=	2739.00	2703.75	2608.03	2480.15

Banking hours: Mon-Fri 0900-1500.

Duty Free

The following goods may be taken into Colombia by people up to 18 years of age without incurring customs duty:
200 cigarettes and 50 cigars and up to 50g of tobacco; two bottles of alcoholic beverage; a reasonable quantity of perfume.
Prohibited items: Ammunition and firearms, unless prior authorisation has been obtained, and item(s) are declared on arrival. Vegetables, plants or plant material; meat and food products of animal origin.

Public Holidays

2005: Jan 1 New Year's Day. **Jan 6*** Epiphany. **Mar 19*** St Joseph's Day. **Mar 24** Maundy Thursday. **Mar 25** Good Friday. **May 1** Labour Day. **May 5*** Ascension. **May 26*** Corpus Christi. **Jun 17** Sagrado Corazon (Sacred Heart). **Jun 29*** Saint Peter and Saint Paul. **Jul 20** Independence Day. **Aug 7** Battle of Boyacá. **Aug 15*** Assumption. **Oct 12*** Dia de la Raza (Columbus Day). **Nov 1*** All Saints' Day. **Nov 11*** Independence of Cartagena City. **Nov 24** Thanksgiving. **Dec 8** Immaculate Conception. **Dec 25** Christmas Day.
2006: Jan 1 New Year's Day. **Jan 6*** Epiphany. **Mar 19*** St Joseph's Day. **Apr 13** Maundy Thursday. **Apr 14** Good Friday. **May 1** Labour Day. **May 5*** Ascension. **Jun 15*** Corpus Christi. **Jun 16** Sagrado Corazon (Sacred Heart). **Jun 29*** Saint Peter and Saint Paul. **Jul 20** Independence Day. **Aug 7** Battle of Boyacá. **Aug 15*** Assumption. **Oct 12*** Dia de la Raza (Columbus Day). **Nov 1*** All Saints' Day. **Nov 11*** Independence of Cartagena City. **Nov 23** Thanksgiving. **Dec 8** Immaculate Conception. **Dec 25** Christmas Day.
Note: * When they do not fall on a Monday, these holidays are observed the following Monday.

Health

	Special Precautions?	Certificate Required?
Yellow Fever	1	No
Cholera	2	No
Typhoid & Polio	3	N/A
Malaria	4	N/A

Note: *Regulations and requirements may be subject to change at short notice, and you are advised to contact your doctor well in advance of your intended date of departure. Any numbers in the chart refer to the footnotes below.*

1: Vaccination is recommended for travellers who visit the following areas considered to be endemic for yellow fever: middle valley of the Magdalena River, eastern and western foothills of the Cordillera Oriental from the frontier with Ecuador to that with Venezuela, Urabá, the foothills of the Sierra Nevada, eastern plains (Orinoquia) and Amazonia.
2: Following WHO guidelines issued in 1973, a cholera vaccination certificate is not a condition of entry to Colombia. However, there may be a risk of cholera in this country; autochthonous cases were reported in 1996, and precautions should be considered. Up-to-date advice should be sought before deciding whether these precautions should include vaccination as medical opinion is divided over its effectiveness. See the *Health* appendix.
3: Typhoid immunisation or boosters are recommended.
4: Malaria risk exists throughout the year in rural and jungle areas below 800m. There is high risk in the following municipalities: Urabá-Bajo Cauca, Amazonia, Orinoquia and Pacífico. The highest risk is in the following departments: Amazonia, Chocó, Córdoba, Guainía, Guaviare, Putumayo and Vichada. The malignant *falciparum* form of the disease is reported to be highly resistant to chloroquine in Amazonia, Pacífico and Urabá-Bajo Cauca. The recommended prophylaxis is chloroquine plus proguanil in Amazonia and Pacífico, and in Urabá-Bajo Cauca, mefloquine.
Food & drink: All water should be regarded as being potentially contaminated outside major cities. Water used for drinking, brushing teeth or making ice should have first been boiled or otherwise sterilised. Milk may be unpasteurised in places and should be boiled. Powdered or tinned milk is available and is advised, but make sure that it is reconstituted with pure water. Avoid dairy products which are likely to have been made from unboiled milk. Only eat well cooked meat and fish, preferably served hot. Pork, salad and mayonnaise may carry increased risk. Vegetables should be cooked and fruit peeled.
Other risks: *American trypanosomiasis* (Chagas disease), as well as *cutaneous* and *mucocutaneous leishmaniasis* occur in Colombia. *Hepatitis A*, *B* and *C* occur. *Dengue fever* and *TB* are also found. For further details, see the *Health* appendix.
Rabies is present. For those at risk, vaccination before arrival should be considered. If you are bitten, seek medical advice without delay.
Health care: Health facilities in the main cities are good. In rural areas, services can be very limited. Travellers are strongly advised to take out full medical insurance. There are nine firms in Colombia offering prepaid medical care and medical insurance which may be purchased from travel agents, a list of which is available from the Embassy.

Travel - International

Note: All travel to Choco, Putumayo, Meta, Narino, Caqueta and Norte de Santander departments, and to the rural areas of Arauca, Sucre, Bolivar, Antioquia and Cauca departments, is strongly advised against. There is a high risk to personal safety in these areas. The threat from terrorism, especially Colombian domestic groups, is high. Visitors are urged to be extremely vigilant, particularly in public places used by foreigners, such as hotels, bars, restaurants, nightclubs and shopping malls - or avoid them all together. There is a serious risk of kidnapping and crime. All travellers intending to visit Magdalena, Cesar, La Guajira, Atlantico, Santander, Norte de Santander and Amazona areas, should possess yellow fever inoculations and carry vaccination certificates. Colombian Immigration officials may insist upon seeing such proof.
AIR: Colombia's national airline is *Avianca (AV)* (website: www.avianca.com.co). *Avianca* and *British Airways* each operate flights, Monday to Saturday, to Bogotá. During the summer season, *British Airways* only operate flights Wednesday, Friday and Sunday. Other airlines flying to Colombia include *Air France*, *American Airlines*, *Continental Airlines* and *Iberia* but, as with *Avianca*, some may not fly directly there but with other airlines as part of a Code Share agreement.
Approximate flight times: From *London* to Bogotá is 11 hours 45 minutes, from *Los Angeles* is 10 hours 30 minutes, from *New York* is six hours 30 minutes, and from *Sydney* is 29 hours.
International airports: *Bogotá* (El Dorado) *(BOG)* is situated 12km (8 miles) east of the city. Buses to the city depart every 20 minutes from 0600-2200 (travel time - 30 minutes). Taxis are also available (travel time - 30 to 40 minutes). Airport facilities include bank, duty-free shop, bar, restaurant, tourist information and car hire (*Auto Renta*, *Avis* and *Hertz*).
Barranquilla (Ernesto Cortissoz) *(BAQ)* is 10km (6 miles) from the city. Car hire is available.
Cali (Palmaseca) *(CLO)* is 19km (10 miles) from the city.
Cartagena (Crespo) *(CTG)* is 2km (1 mile) from the city.
Departure tax: Either collected upon ticket issuance or levied upon embarkation. Transit passengers continuing their journey on the same day are exempt. US$19 or possibly more - payable by cash only.
The Visit South America Pass: This must be bought outside South America in country of residence and allows unlimited travel to 36 cities in the following countries: Argentina, Bolivia, Brazil, Colombia, Chile (except Easter Island), Ecuador, Paraguay, Peru, Uruguay and Venezuela. Participating airlines include *Aer Lingus (EI)*, *American Airlines (AA)*, *British Airways (BA)*, *Cathay Pacific (CX)*, *Finnair (AY)*, *IBERIA (IB)*, *LAN-Chile (LA)* and *Qantas (QF)*. A minimum of three flights must be booked, with no maximum; the maximum stay is 60 days, with no minimum, and prices depend on the amount of flight zones covered. Children under 12 years of age are entitled to a 33 per cent discount and infants (under two years old) only pay 10 per cent of the adult fare. For further details, contact one of the participating airlines.
Note: All air tickets purchased in Colombia for destinations outside the country are liable to a total tax of 15 per cent on one-way tickets and 7.5 per cent on return tickets.
SEA: Major ports on the Caribbean coast include Cartagena, Baranquilla, Santa Marta and Turbo. Buenaventura is the main port on the Pacific coast. Many ships and cruise lines visit these ports from the USA, Mexico, Venezuela, Central America and the Caribbean Islands.
RAIL: There are no international rail connections.
ROAD: Colombia can be reached from Panama via the Darien Gap, but the route is not advised as it can be long, arduous and dangerous. Vehicles can also be freighted from Panama to one of Colombia's Caribbean or Pacific ports. There are also road links with Ecuador and Venezuela, although travellers should check with the local embassy about safety of roads before crossing the border to Venezuela. **Coach/bus**: *TEPSA* buses connect with Venezuela. Coaches are comfortable and services good. There are second-class buses from Maracaibo to Santa Marta and Cartagena, but this method of travelling can be uncomfortable.

Travel - Internal

Note: Visitors should take sensible precautions when travelling outside major cities in Colombia, as violence and kidnapping occur. Check with your local embassy before entering the country to assess the current situation.
AIR: There is an excellent internal air network connecting major cities, including those in the Caribbean coastal area. There are also local helicopter flights. There are flights between the mainland and the islands of San Andrés and Providencia operating from most major Colombian cities. Services are offered by *Avianca*, *SAM* , and several smaller companies. San Andrés is a regular stop for *Avianca*, *Lacsa* and *Sahsa* airlines.
Departure tax: peso6800-8500, usually included in the ticket price.
SEA: There is a ferry service between the mainland and the islands of San Andrés and Providencia, leaving from the Muelle de los Pegasos. The journey is long (72 hours) but cheap. Information about other sailings to San Andrés can be obtained from the Maritima San Andrés office.
RIVER: The Magdalena River is the main artery of Colombia. Some cargo boats take passengers, though this is a slow way to travel. It is possible to hire boats for particular trips. Paddle steamers no longer run services up and down the river and hiring can be expensive. From Leticia, on the Peruvian border, a number of operators run sightseeing tours and jungle expeditions up the Amazon.
RAIL: Although trains still carry freight, inter-city passenger services are virtually non-existent. Services have been frequently suspended during recent years owing to operators' financial difficulties. The main route is between Bogotá and Santa Marta on the Caribbean coast, east of Barranquilla. Because of the distances, it is easier to take a plane if speed is important.
ROAD: A good highway links Santa Marta in the east with Cartagena, and passes Barranquilla en route. The Trans-Caribbean Highway has placed Barranquilla only five hours away from Venezuela. Northeast of Santa Marta, in the Guajira Peninsula, roads are usually passable except during rainy periods. There is highway transportation between the coastal cities and the capital and other cities of the interior, but much of the highway is rutted. **Bus**: Approximately 40 companies with modern buses and minibuses provide transportation between coastal towns and cities. There are also *collectivos* (taxi-buses) for shorter distances which can often be a cheaper alternative. **Car hire**: *Avis*, *Budget*, *Hertz* and *National* have car hire offices, but driving in cities is not recommended. Traffic drives on the right. **Documentation**: An International Driving Permit is required.
URBAN: Bogotá has extensive trolleybus, bus and minibus services, and a funicular railway; flat fares are charged. There are also shared taxis (*buseta*) which are not expensive and stop on demand. Drivers are authorised to add a supplement for out-of-town trips and to airports. At hotels, the green and cream coloured taxis are available for tourists. They are more expensive than the others, but some of the drivers may have a working knowledge of English. Passengers should insist that meters are used. For those without a meter the fare should be agreed before starting a journey.
Travel times: The following chart gives approximate travel times from **Bogotá** (in hours and minutes) to other major towns/cities in Colombia.

	Air
Cartagena	**1.15**
Barranquilla	**1.15**
Medellín	**1.15**
Manizales	**1.00**
Cali	**1.00**
Bucaramanga	**0.45**
Cúcuta	**1.00**
Pereira	**1.00**
Leticia	**2.00**

Accommodation

HOTELS: It is advisable to choose hotels recommended by the official Colombian Hotel Organisation, COTELCO, Carrera 7, no. 60-92, Bogotá (tel: (1) 310 3640; fax: (1) 310 3509; e-mail: cotelco@cotelco.org; website: www.cotelco.org). Two tariffs are levied: 'European tariff' from May to November, and 'American tariff' from December to April, which is much higher. It is advisable to make reservations well in advance. There are several hotels and *residencias* on the island of San Andrés, and one on Providencia. Prices rise on average 10 per cent a year; visitors are advised to check current prices when making reservations. A five per cent tax is added to all hotel bills throughout the country. **Grading**: There is a star grading system similar to that operating in Europe.
CAMPING/CARAVANNING: Camping is possible in Colombia, although there are very few official camping areas. Two of the better campsites in the country are *Camping del Sol* and *Camping de Covenas*.

Resorts & Excursions

BOGOTÁ: The capital and largest city is situated almost in the centre of the country at an altitude of 2600m (8600ft). Bogotá reflects a blend of Colombian tradition and Spanish colonial influences. Many historical landmarks have been preserved, such as the **Capitol Municipal Palace** and the cathedral on the main square, the **Plaza Bolivar**. Bogotá also contains the **Gold Museum**, with its unique collection of over 100,000 pre-Colombian artworks. Around 50km (32 miles) south of Bogotá lies Zipaquirá, an area well-known for its many salt mines, one of which contains the famous **Salt Cathedral** (capable of accommodating 8400 people). **Guatavita**, a two-hour bus drive from Bogotá, is best known for its **Laguna de Guatavita**, the ritual centre and sacred lake of the Muisca Indians.
MEDELLÍN: Colombia's second city, with over 1.5 million inhabitants, lies 1300m (4264ft) above sea level in a narrow valley of the central mountain range. It is primarily industrial, and is the centre of the coffee and textile trades. The region has acquired a reputation for violence owing to the war between the Government and the drug barons.
CALI: The centre of the principal sugar-producing region of the country, where modern technology blends with colonial tradition. Deposits of coal and precious metals are found in this area.
BARRANQUILLA: A busy port and Colombia's fourth city, Barranquilla is located towards the mouth of the Magdalena River. It is one of the nation's main commercial centres. There is a colourful market in a side channel of the Magdalena.
CARIBBEAN COAST: The main tourist resorts on Colombia's 1600km- (1000 mile-) long Caribbean coast lie near **Santa Marta**, one of the first major cities founded by the Spanish in South America. Its modern hotels, white beaches and proximity to fashionable beach resorts now make it a popular base for visitors wishing to explore the coast. The **Tayrona National Park**, some 35km (22 miles) south of Santa Marta, is one of the country's most popular parks. Its major attraction is its deep bays, shaded with coconut trees, beautiful beaches and several coral reefs. **Cartagena**, an ancient walled fortress city on the north coast, is also worth a visit, particularly for its fascinating **Old Town**. Tourist facilities have been considerably developed in recent years, particularly at **El Laguita**, an L-shaped pensinsula, now packed with hotels and expensive restaurants. Some 35km (22 miles) west lie the **Islas del Rosario**, an archipelago of about 25 small coral islands now declared a national park. Cruises and tours are widely available and can be booked in Cartagena. Easily reached from Cartagena, by plane or boat, are the islands of **San Andrés** and **Providencia**, nearly 500km (300 miles) north of the Colombian coast. San Andrés was once the headquarters of the English pirate Captain Henry Morgan, the scourge of the Caribbean. The islands are duty-free, and consequently often crowded, but there are still several less spoilt parts. Popular excursions include visits by boat to **Johnny Cay** and the **Aquarium**.
THE AMAZON BASIN: Almost one-third of Colombia's territory is covered by the Amazon Basin, an area of thick tropical forest in the southeast, with no roads and inhabited mostly by Indians. The most popular base for tourists wishing to explore the area is **Leticia**, a small town with well-developed tourist facilities, located on the banks of the **Amazon River** and close to the border with Brazil and Peru. Jungle trips, notably to the nearby **Amacayu National Park**, are widely available and often include visits to Indian tribes.
ELSEWHERE: Colombia has much to offer those interested in archaeology. **San Augustín Archaeological Park** contains a great number of relics and massive stone statues. The traditional city of **Popayan** is the birthplace of many of Colombia's most illustrious statesmen. As well as containing many fine colonial houses and churches, it is also noted for its Holy Week procession. Tierradentro, in the southwest of the country, has beautiful manmade burial caves painted with pre-Colombian geometric patterns. In the same region, **Silva** is a beautiful Indian town. The country also contains much unspoilt countryside; the **Guajira Peninsula** is home to more than 100,000 nomadic Indians.

Sport & Activities

Watersports: Water-skiing, **boating**, **sailing** and **skindiving** can all be practised on the coast (check with authorities before diving, as sharks and barracudas have caused fatalities). **Fishing** is excellent all year round; a licence is required. **Other: Football** is Colombia's main sport, with major league games played throughout the year. **Tennis** is popular; most hotels have facilities. **Mountain climbing** begins 48km (30 miles) east of Santa Marta, with peaks of up to nearly 6000m (19,000ft). A major **cycle race**, the Tour of Colombia, takes place every March and April. **Boxing** and **bullfighting** (the latter at Bogotá, Cali, Medellín, Manizales and Cartagena) are popular sports. **Golf** clubs allow visitors to use their facilities. Good **skiing** can be found on the slopes of *Nevado del Ruiz* (5400m/ 17,700ft), 48km (30 miles) from Manizales.

Social Profile

FOOD & DRINK: Restaurants offering international cuisine and table service is the norm. Local dishes are varied and tasty, with a touch of Spanish influence. Recommended dishes are *ajiaco* (chicken stew with potatoes, served with cream, corn on the cob and capers); *arepas* (corn pancakes made without salt, eaten in place of bread); *bandeja paisa* (meat dish accompanied by cassava, rice, fried plantain and red beans), served in the area of Medellín. Seafood (*mariscos*) is plentiful on the Caribbean coast -lobsters in particular are renowned for their flavour. It is safest to drink bottled water. Colombians rarely drink alcohol with meals. *Gaseosa* is the name given to non-alcoholic, carbonated drinks. For a small black coffee, you should ask for a tinto, but this term is also used to describe red wine or *vino tinto*. Colombian wines are generally of poor quality. Chilean and Argentinian wines are available in restaurants at reasonable prices. Colombia produces many different types of rum (ron). *Canelazo*, a rum-based cocktail taken hot or cold, is recommended. There are no licensing hours.
NIGHTLIFE: Bogotá's *Colon Theatre* presents ballet, opera, drama and music, with international and local groups. There are many nightclubs and discos in the major towns of Colombia.
SHOPPING: Special purchases include local handicrafts, cotton, wood and leather goods, woollen blankets, ruana, and travelling bags. Hotel shops carry excellent gold reproductions of ancient Colombian jewellery. Colombia produces first-grade stones, and the emeralds are among the most perfect in the world. **Shopping hours**: Mon-Sat 0900-1200 and 1400-1830.
SPECIAL EVENTS: For a complete list, contact the Colombian Embassy (see *Contact Addresses* section). The following is a selection of special events occurring in Colombia in 2005: **Jan** *Festival of Blacks and Whites*, Pasto. **Feb** *Barranquilla Carnival*. **Feb-Mar** *Cartagena Film Festival*. **Mar** *International Caribbean Music Festival*, Cartagena; *Latin American Bogotá Theatre Festival*. **Mar 21-28** *Easter Week in Popayan*. **Jun** *Cumbia Festival*, El Banco; *Porro Festival*, San Pelayo. **Aug** *Medellín Flower Fair*; *Colombiamoda* (fashion event), Medellín; *Sea Festival*, Santa Marta; *Guabina and Tiple Festival*, Veléz. **Oct** *Rock in the Park*, Bogotá. **Nov** *National Folk and Tourist Festival*, San Martín; *Colombian National Beauty Contest*, Cartagena. **Dec 25-Jan 6 2006** *Cali Fair*.
SOCIAL CONVENTIONS: Normal courtesies should be observed. It is customary to offer guests black Colombian coffee, well sugared, called *tinto*. Spanish style and culture can still be seen in parts of the country, although in Bogotá, North American attitudes and clothes are becoming prevalent. Casual clothes can be worn in most places; formal attire will be necessary for exclusive dining rooms and social functions. Smoking is allowed except where indicated. The visitor is advised that many of the main cities in Colombia are notorious for street crime, particularly at night. Drug-related crimes are a serious problem throughout the country and the visitor should be wary of the unsolicited attention of strangers. **Tipping**: Taxi drivers expect 10 per cent tips. Porters at airports and hotels are usually given c. pesos500 per item. Many restaurants, bars and cafes add 10 per cent service charge to the bill or suggest a 10 per cent tip. Maids and clerks in hotels are also tipped. Bogotá's shoeshine boys live on their tips and expect about 1000 pesos.

Business Profile

ECONOMY: Agriculture is extensive and varied; it accounts for 75 per cent of export earnings. Coffee has traditionally been the principal crop (Colombia is the world's second-largest producer) but as production has declined and prices fallen, other products have partially replaced it, including sugar, bananas, cut flowers and cotton. Illegal farming of cocoa is also widespread in the more remote parts of the country. The country is self-sufficient in consumer goods and exports of manufactured goods have been steadily increasing. Colombia has sizeable oil reserves, which are now on stream. Coal deposits are the largest in Latin America, although development of these has been slow. Recent economic performance has been moderate, with annual growth of just over 1 per cent during 2002. In the same year, inflation was 7 per cent, although official unemployment is still close to 20 per cent (the true figure is probably rather higher). The ongoing internal conflict, which shows little sign of resolution at present, is a huge millstone around the country's neck. Colombia is a member of the Andean Pact and of the *Asociación Latinoamericana de Integración* (ALADI), which is seeking to regularise tariffs throughout South America. In addition, Colombia is establishing a three-country free trade zone with Venezuela and Mexico; by 2002, these two, plus the USA, were Colombia's largest trading partners.
BUSINESS: Businesspeople are expected to dress smartly. English is widely understood in many business circles but a command of Spanish is always appreciated. Business visitors

will sometimes be invited out to dinner, which may be preceded by a long cocktail party, with a meal starting around 2300. The best months for business visits are March to November. The business community generally takes holidays from September to February, the driest months. It is advisable to avoid Barranquilla in June and July. **Office hours**: Mon-Fri 0800-1200 and 1400-1700.
COMMERCIAL INFORMATION: The following organisations can offer advice: Confederación Colombiana de Cámaras de Comercio (CONFECAMARAS) (National Chamber of Commerce), Apdo Aéreo 29750, Carrera 13, 27-47, Oficina 502, Santa Fe de Bogotá (tel: (1) 346 7055; fax: (1) 346 7026; e-mail: andresbernal@confecamaras.org.co; website: www.confecamaras.org.co); *or* Proexport Colombia, Edificio Bancafe, Calle 28, 13A-15, Piso 37, Santa Fe de Bogotá (tel: (1) 341 2066; fax: (1) 561 1776; e-mail: proexport@proexport.com.co; website: www.proexport.com.co) *or* Colombian Government Trade Bureau, 1901 L Street, Suite 700, NW, Washington DC, 20036, USA (tel: (202) 887 9000; fax: (202) 223 0526; e-mail: coltrade@coltrade.org; website: www.coltrade.org).
CONFERENCES/CONVENTIONS: For advice and assistance with conferences and conventions in Colombia, contact the CORFERIAS (National Centre of Trade Fairs), Carrera 40, 22C-67, Santa Fe de Bogotá (tel: (1) 381 0000; fax: (1) 428 5551; e-mail: info@corferias.com; website: www.corferias.com).

Climate

The climate is very warm and tropical on the coast and in the north, with a rainy season from May to November. This varies according to altitude. It is cooler in the upland areas and cold in the mountains. Bogotá is always spring-like, with cool days and crisp nights.
Required clothing: Lightweight cottons and linens with waterproofing during rainy season in coastal and northern areas. Medium- to heavyweights are needed in upland and mountainous areas.

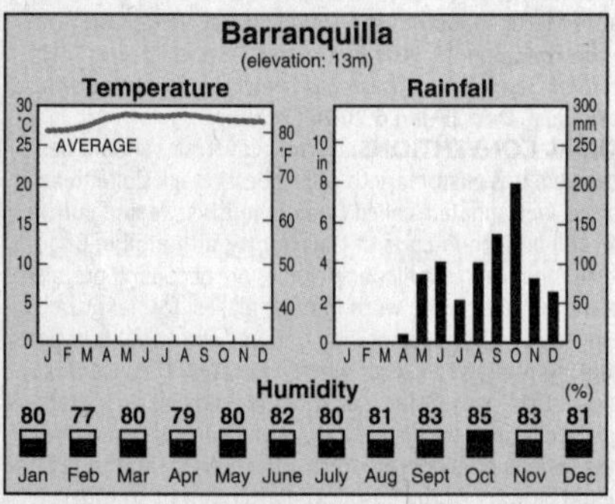

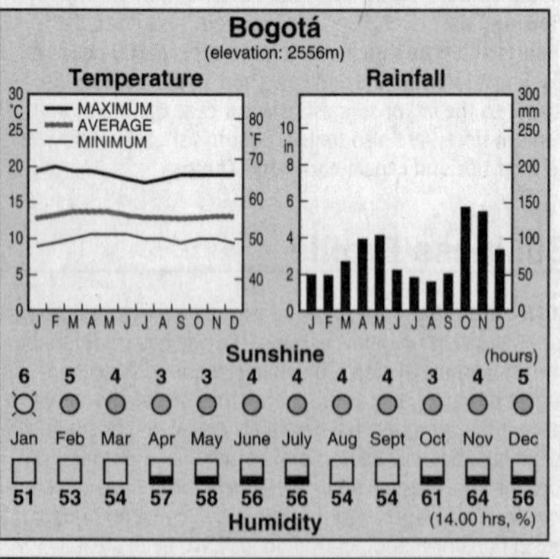

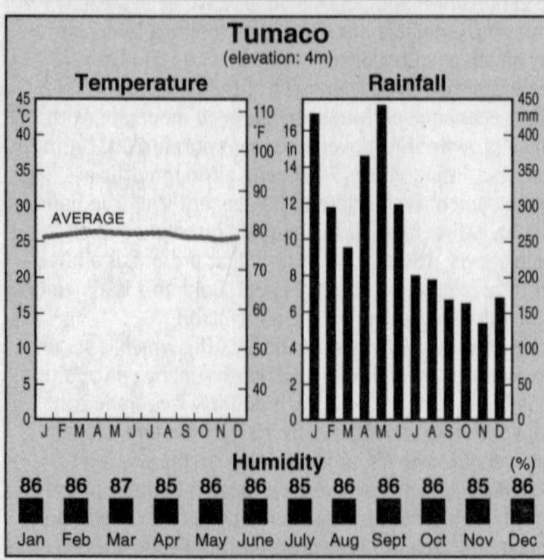

Comoro Islands

LATEST TRAVEL ADVICE CONTACTS

British Foreign and Commonwealth Office
Tel: (0870) 606 0290 Website: www.fco.gov.uk

US Department of State
Website: http://travel.state.gov/travel

Canadian Department of Foreign Affairs and Int'l Trade
Tel: (1 800) 267 8376 Website: www.dfait-maeci.gc.ca

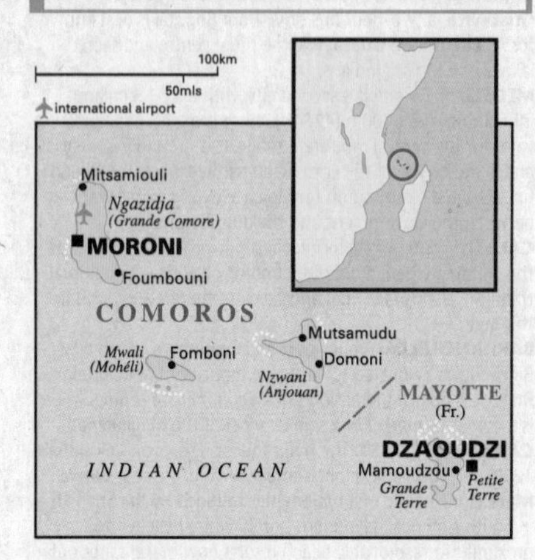

Location: Indian Ocean, between the East African coast and Madagascar.

Country dialling code: 269.

Direction Générale du Tourisme et de l'Hôtellerie (Ministry of Tourism)
BP 97, Moroni, Comoros
Tel: 744 242/65. Fax: 744 241.
Societe Comorienne de Tourisme et Hôtellerie (COMOTEL)
Itsandra Hotel, BP 1027, Moroni, Comoros
Tel: 732 365.
Embassy of the Federal Islamic Republic of the Comoros
20 rue Marbeau, 75016 Paris, France
Tel: (1) 4067 9054.
Opening hours: Mon-Fri 1000-1600.
The British Embassy in Antananarivo deals with enquiries relating to the Comoro Islands (see Madagascar section).
The US Embassy in Port Louis deals with most enquiries relating to the Comoro Islands (see Mauritius section).
Permanent Mission of the Comoros to the United Nations
866 United Nations Plaza, Suite 418, New York, NY 10017, USA
Tel: (212) 750 1637. Fax: (212) 750 1657.
E-mail: comoros@un.int or aboudmatimoud@aol.com
Website: www.un.int/comoros
Also deals with enquiries from Canada.
The Canadian High Commission in Dar es Salaam deals with enquiries relating to the Comoro Islands (see Tanzania section).

General Information

AREA: 1862 sq km (719 sq miles).
POPULATION: 747,000 (UN estimate 2002).
POPULATION DENSITY: 401.2 per sq km.
CAPITAL: Moroni. **Population**: 60,200 (2003).
GEOGRAPHY: The Comoro archipelago is situated in the Indian Ocean north of Madagascar and consists of four main islands of volcanic origin, surrounded by coral reefs: Ngazidja (formerly Grande Comore), Nzwani (formerly Anjouan), Mwali (formerly Mohéli) and Mayotte. The latter is administered by France but is claimed by the Federal Islamic Republic of the Comoros. Land can only support subsistence agriculture but the surrounding seas are rich in marine life.
GOVERNMENT: Federal Islamic Republic. **Head of State**: President Assoumani Azali, since the military coup of April 1999. **Head of Government**: Prime Minister Hamada Madi 'Boléro' since 2001. Parliament has been dissolved.
LANGUAGE: The official languages are French, Arabic and Comorian, a blend of Arabic and Swahili.
RELIGION: Muslim (mostly Sunni) with Roman Catholic minority.
TIME: GMT + 3.
ELECTRICITY: 220 volts AC, 50Hz.
COMMUNICATIONS: Telephone: Outgoing international calls must be made through the international operator. Country code: 269. **Mobile telephone:** GSM 900 network *Societe Nationale des Postes et Telecommunications* (HURI) (website: www.snpt.km) provides limited coverage. **Internet:** Main ISP is *ComNet* (website: www.snpt.km). A few hotels have Internet access. **Post:** Mail to Western Europe takes at least one week. **Press:** There are no English-language newspapers. The main (weekly) papers are *Al Watwan* (state-owned) and *La Gazette des Comores* (independent). *L'Archipel* (independent) is published monthly. **Radio:** BBC World Service (website: www.bbc.co.uk/worldservice) and Voice of America (website: www.voa.gov) can be received. From time to time the frequencies change and the most up-to-date can be found online.

TIMATIC CODES

Health	AMADEUS: **TI-DFT/JIB/HE** GALILEO/WORLDSPAN: **TI-DFT/JIB/HE** SABRE: **TIDFT/JIB/HE**
Visa	AMADEUS: **TI-DFT/JIB/VI** GALILEO/WORLDSPAN: **TI-DFT/JIB/VI** SABRE: **TIDFT/JIB/VI**

To access TIMATIC country information on Health and Visa regulations through the Computer Reservations System (CRS), type in the appropriate command line listed above.

Passport/Visa

	Passport Required?	Visa Required?	Return Ticket Required?
Full British	Yes	Yes	Yes
Australian	Yes	Yes	Yes
Canadian	Yes	Yes	Yes
USA	Yes	Yes	Yes
Other EU	Yes	Yes	Yes
Japanese	Yes	Yes	Yes

Note: *Regulations and requirements may be subject to change at short notice, and you are advised to contact the appropriate diplomatic or consular authority before finalising travel arrangements. Details of these may be found at the head of this country's entry. Any numbers in the chart refer to the footnotes below.*

PASSPORTS: Passport valid for at least six months required by all.
VISAS: Required by all except those continuing their journey by the same or first connecting aircraft without leaving the airport and holding documents certifying onward/return travel.
Types of visa and cost: *Ordinary*: US$10.
Validity: Two weeks.
Application to: Visas are issued at the Frontier Post in Comores or by some of their diplomatic representations, such as Antananarivo, Cairo and Paris.
Application requirements: (a) Application form (provided at airport). (b) Valid passport. (c) Two passport-sized photos. (d) Fee (payable in Comoros Francs, Euros or US Dollars only). (e) Return/onward tickets.

Money

Currency: Comoros Franc (Cfr) = 100 centimes. Notes are in denominations of Cfr10,000, 5000, 2500, 1000 and 500. Coins are in denominations of Cfr20, 10, 5, 2 and 1, and 20 centimes. The Comoros Franc is part of the French Monetary Area and Euros are also commonly used. The Comoros Franc is tied to the Euro.
Currency exchange: Foreign currency may be exchanged in banks in the towns. Banking facilities are very limited on Mwali.
Credit & debit cards: There is limited acceptance of most international credit cards (mainly in upmarket hotels), but check with your credit or debit card company for details of merchant acceptability and other services which may be available.
Travellers cheques: The Banque Internationale des Comores (BIC) is the only bank that will change travellers cheques. To avoid additional exchange rate charges, travellers are advised to take travellers cheques in Euros.
Currency restrictions: There are no restrictions on the import and export of either local or foreign currency.
Exchange rate indicators: The following figures are included as a guide to the movements of the Comoros Franc against Sterling and the US Dollar:

Date	Feb '04	May '04	Aug '04	Nov '04
£1.00=	720.84	737.82	733.76	702.59
$1.00=	396.01	413.09	398.27	371.02

Banking hours: Mon-Thurs 0800-1400; Fri 0800-1100.

Duty Free

The following goods may be imported into the Comoro Islands by persons 18 years of age and over without incurring customs duty:
400 cigarettes or 100 cigars or 500g of tobacco; one

bottle of alcoholic beverage; one bottle of perfume.
Prohibited items: Plants or soil, except on presentation of an import permit issued from the Comoro Islands' Agriculture Department, together with a phytosanitary certificate of the place of origin.

Public Holidays

2005: Jan 21 Eid al-Adha (Feast of the Sacrifice). **Feb 10** Muharram (Islamic New Year). **Feb 19** Ashoura. **Mar 18** Anniversary of the Death of President Said Mohamed Cheikh. **May 25** Anniversary of the Organisation of African Unity. **May 29** Anniversary of the Death of President Ali Soilih. **Jul 6** Independence Day. **Nov 3-5** Eid al-Fitr (End of Ramadan). **Nov 26** Anniversary of the Death of President Ahmed Abdallah. **Dec 25** Christmas Day.
2006: Jan 13 Eid al-Adha (Feast of the Sacrifice). **Jan 31** Muharram (Islamic New Year). **Feb 9** Ashoura. **Mar 18** Anniversary of the Death of President Said Mohamed Cheikh. **May 25** Anniversary of the Organisation of African Unity. **May 29** Anniversary of the Death of President Ali Soilih. **Jul 6** Independence Day. **Oct 22-24** Eid al-Fitr (End of Ramadan). **Oct 24** Anniversary of the Death of President Ahmed Abdallah. **Dec 25** Christmas Day.
Note: Muslim festivals are timed according to local sightings of various phases of the moon and the dates given above are approximations. During the lunar month of Ramadan that precedes Eid al-Fitr, Muslims fast during the day and feast at night and normal business patterns may be interrupted. Many restaurants are closed during the day and there may be restrictions on smoking and drinking. Some disruption may continue into Eid al-Fitr itself. Eid al-Fitr and Eid al-Adha may last anything from two to 10 days, depending on the region. For more information see the section *World of Islam*.

Health

	Special Precautions?	Certificate Required?
Yellow Fever	No	1
Cholera	Yes	2
Typhoid & Polio	3	N/A
Malaria	4	N/A

Note: Regulations and requirements may be subject to change at short notice, and you are advised to contact your doctor well in advance of your intended date of departure. Any numbers in the chart refer to the footnotes below.

1: Some travellers from areas infected with yellow fever have been asked to provide vaccination certificates, but this is not an official policy.
2: Following WHO guidelines issued in 1973, a cholera vaccination certificate is not an official condition of entry to the Comoro Islands. However, outbreaks of cholera still occur periodically. Up-to-date advice should be sought before deciding whether precautions should include vaccination, as medical opinion is divided over its effectiveness; see the *Health* appendix.
3: Typhoid fevers are present.
4: Malaria risk exists all year throughout the whole country, predominantly in the malignant *falciparum* form. Resistance to chloroquine has been reported. The recommended prophylaxis is mefloquine.
Food & drink: All water should be regarded as being potentially contaminated. Water used for drinking, brushing teeth or making ice should have first been boiled or otherwise sterilised. Milk is unpasteurised and should be boiled. Powdered or tinned milk is available and is advised, but make sure that it is reconstituted with pure water. Avoid dairy products which are likely to have been made from unboiled milk. Only eat well-cooked meat and fish, preferably served hot. Pork, salad and mayonnaise may carry increased risk. Vegetables should be cooked and fruit peeled.
Other risks: *Hepatitis A* and *E* are widespread. *Hepatitis B* is hyperendemic. Both *cutaneous* and *visceral leishmaniasis* may be found. Outbreaks of *yellow fever* occur periodically.
Health care: There is no reciprocal health agreement with the UK. In order to secure even basic medical care, visitors are strongly advised to take out comprehensive health insurance.

Travel - International

AIR: Airlines operating to the Comoro Islands include *Air Austral, Air Madagascar, Air Tanzania Corporation, Sudan Airlines* and *Yemenia Yemen Airways. Air France* operates regularly from Paris via Réunion.
Approximate flight times: To Moroni from *London* takes a minimum of 20 hours; this includes stopovers (usually in Paris and Réunion).
International airports: *Moroni International Prince Said Ibrahim (HAH)*, 25km (16 miles) north of the city. Taxis are available to the town (travel time – 30 minutes). Airport facilities (available for international flights) include bars and light refreshments, left luggage facilities and a post office. There are no money-changing facilities at the airport.
Departure tax: None.
SEA: There are irregular sailings from East Africa (Mombasa, Kenya), Madagascar, Mauritius, Réunion or Zanzibar to Moroni or Mutsamudu. These are mostly cargo ships which might carry passengers.

Travel - Internal

AIR: Each island has an airfield. Small private operators, such as *Aéromarine* and *Air Archipel*, operate services between Moroni, Mwali (Mohéli) and Nzwani (Anjouan).
SEA: The islands are linked by regular ferry services. Travellers can hire motorboats, sailing craft and canoes in port villages and towns. A boat can be especially useful for Mwali (Mohéli) where the road system is rudimentary.
ROAD: Bush taxis (*taxis-brousses*), hired vehicles or private cars are the only forms of transport on the islands. Traffic drives on the right. All the islands have tarred roads. 4-wheel-drive vehicles are advisable for the outlying islands and in the interior, especially in the rainy season. Roads are narrow and domestic animals often roam free, so visitors should drive slowly. Share-taxis provide transport in and around towns.
Car hire: Available on Ngazidja (Grande Comore).
Documentation: An International Driving Permit is required.

Accommodation

Although accommodation on the Comoro Islands is being upgraded, there are only a few hotels and pensions, located mostly in Moroni and Mutsamudu, which handle the needs of travelling businesspeople, government officials and other visitors. Room sharing is quite common. There are simple shelters (*gîtes*) on the slopes of Karthala (an active volcano).

Resorts & Excursions

NGAZIDJA (GRANDE COMORE): The capital **Moroni** is a charming, peaceful town containing a few broad squares and modern government buildings, as well as old, narrow, winding streets and a market place. There are numerous fine mosques including the **Vendredi Mosque**, from the top of which there is an attractive view.
The more energetic may climb to the top of **Mount Karthala** and then descend into the crater of this active volcano. The crater is claimed to be the largest still active anywhere in the world. It is usual to make one overnight stop at the shelter provided.
Itsandra, a fishing village 6km (4 miles) from Moroni, has a fine beach and there are opportunities to see dances performed by the local men. The town was once the ancient capital of the island, complete with royal tombs and a fortress. There are hot sulphur springs at **Lac Salé** and a 14th-century village at **Iconi**. **Mitsamiouli**, a town in the north of the island, is known both for its good diving facilities and for having the best Comoran dancers. There are many bats and spiders on the island, the former often appearing in broad daylight.
MWALI (MOHÉLI): Dhows (Arab sail boats) are built on the beach at **Fomboni** on the smallest of the main islands. There is a fine waterfall at **Miringoni**. Giant turtles may be seen at **Niumashuwa Bay**.
NZWANI (ANJOUAN): This island is notable for its waterfalls and abundant vegetation. The main town of **Mutsamudu** is built in Swahili-Shirazi style, complete with 17th-century houses with carved doors, twisting alleyways, mosques and a citadel. The ancient capital of **Domoni** is also worth a visit. The best beaches are in the **Bimbini** area. There are perfume distilleries at **Bambao**.
MAHORE (MAYOTTE): This French-administered island is surrounded by a coral reef and has good beaches and excellent scuba-diving facilities. Tourists may explore the lagoon (claimed to be the largest in the world) by dugout canoe. The town of **Dzaoudzi** contains some old fortifications worthy of a visit. **Pamanzi** is a forested islet 5km (3 miles) offshore, fragrant with a wealth of vegetation. At **Sulu**, a waterfall plunges straight into the sea. There are the remains of an old mosque at **Tsingoni**. Elsewhere, there are 19th-century sugar refineries. For further information, see the *French Overseas Possessions* section.
Note: Travel to Mayotte from the Comoros Islands may be problematic owing to the fact that this is disputed territory.

Sport & Activities

Watersports: There is excellent **diving** in the archipelago. The *Trou du Prophète in Misamiouli* on Ngazidja, *Niumashuwa Bay* on Mwali and *Pamanzi* islet off Mahore are particularly fine. There are many excellent beaches on all the islands and Galawa Beach on Grande Comore has a diving school. Other good beaches include *Bouni, Chomoni* (near a sheltered bay), *Galawa, Itsandra* and the palm-fringed *Planet Plage*. **Pirogue** (canoe) **races** are occasionally staged in the lagoon that surrounds Mahore. **Sailing** boats and **canoes** are available for hire in many ports.
Hiking: *Dziani Boundouni*, a sulphurous crater lake at the centre of the sparsely populated island of Mwali (Mohéli) can be reached on day-walks from its capital, Fomboni. Fit hikers may also head up to the *Mt Karthala* crater on Grande Comore (guides can be hired locally). Owing to political instability, visitors are advised to check the latest travel advice from an official organisation (such as an embassy) before contemplating a trip to Mohéli.
Wildlife: The Comoro Islands' distinctive (and now protected) green turtle can be seen in the marine reserve off Mohéli's southern coast. Trips by motorised pirogues can be arranged with local fishermen from Niumashuwa.

Social Profile

FOOD & DRINK: Restaurants serve good food with spiced sauces, rice-based dishes, cassava, plantain, couscous, barbecued goat meat, plentiful seafood and tropical fruits. There may be restrictions on drink within Muslim circles.
SHOPPING: Comoran products can be purchased at Moroni on Ngazidja (Grande Comore). These include gold, pearl and shell jewellery, woven cloth, embroidered skull-caps (*koffia*) and slippers, carved chests, panels and *portes-croix* (lecterns), pottery and basketry. Most items can be bought in the villages where they are made. **Shopping hours**: Mon-Sat 0800-1200 and 1500-1800.
SPECIAL EVENTS: Most festivals and events in Comoro are connected to Muslim celebrations, most notably *Eid al-Adha* (Feast of the Sacrifice) and *Eid al-Fitr* (End of Ramadan). *Bastille Day* (**Jul 14**) and *Christmas Day* (**Dec 25**) are also celebrated.
SOCIAL CONVENTIONS: Religious customs should be respected, particularly during Ramadan. Dress should be modest although the French residents and tourists tend to be fairly relaxed about what they wear. **Tipping**: Normally 10 per cent.

Business Profile

ECONOMY: The bulk of the working population is employed in agriculture, which produces vanilla and cloves (the main exports), basil, ylang-ylang (an essence extracted from trees) and copra. There is a small fishing industry and a minimal industrial base devoted mainly to processing vanilla. The tourism industry has grown rapidly during the last 10 years to the extent that the service sector as a whole now accounts for half of total domestic output: chronic political instability on the islands has, however, probably prevented the industry from reaching its full potential. Moreover, the agricultural economy is vulnerable to low world commodity prices. Substantial French aid remains essential. France is also the country's major trading partner, providing almost half of the Comoros' imports and taking two-thirds of its exports. China, Kenya, Tanzania and Madagascar are the other major importers into the islands. Per capita income is estimated at US$380. The economy grew slowly at 1.5 per cent in 2001.
BUSINESS: Lightweight suit or shirt and tie required. Business is conducted in French or Arabic; English is seldom spoken. **Office hours**: Mon-Thurs 0730-1430, Fri 0730-1100, Sat 0730-1200.
COMMERCIAL INFORMATION: The following organisation can offer advice: Chambre de Commerce, d'Industrie et d'Agriculture, BP 763, Moroni (tel: 730 958; fax: 731 983; e-mail: pride@snpt.km).

Climate

The climate is tropical and very warm. Coastal areas are hot and very humid (December to March), interspaced with rains and seasonal cyclones. The upland areas are cooler, particularly at night, and have higher rainfall.
Required clothing: Lightweight cottons and linens with waterproofing during the rainy season. Warmer garments and rainwear are needed for the mountains.

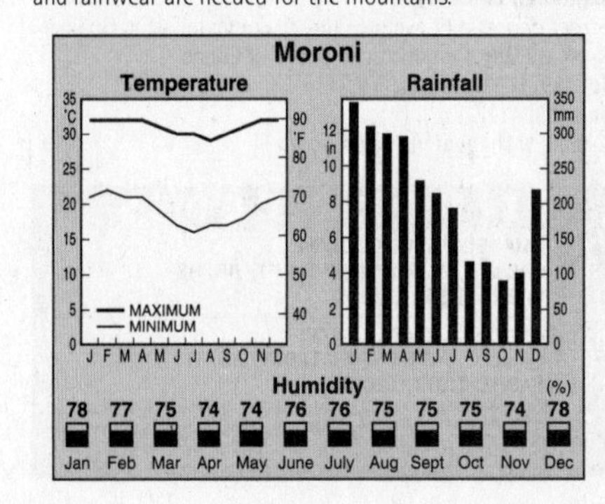

A B C D E F G H I J K L M N O P Q R S T U V W X Y Z

Congo (Democratic Republic)

LATEST TRAVEL ADVICE CONTACTS

British Foreign and Commonwealth Office
Tel: (0870) 606 0290 Website: www.fco.gov.uk
US Department of State
Website: http://travel.state.gov/travel
Canadian Department of Foreign Affairs and Int'l Trade
Tel: (1 800) 267 8376 Website: www.dfait-maeci.gc.ca

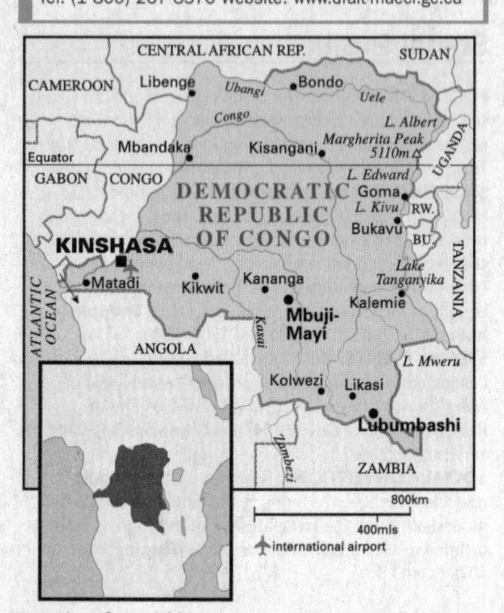

Location: Central Africa.

Country dialling code: 243.

Ministry of Foreign Affairs and International Co-operation
Street address: 1 place de l'Indépendance, Kinshasa-Gombe, Democratic Republic of Congo
Tel: (12) 32450.
Office National du Tourisme
2 A/B Avenue des Oranges, BP 9502, Kinshasa-Gombe, Democratic Republic of Congo
Tel: (12) 30070.
Embassy of the Democratic Republic of Congo
281 Gray's Inn Road, London WC1 X8QF, UK
Tel: (020) 7278 9825.
Fax: (020) 7833 9967.
Opening hours: Mon-Fri 0930-1400.
British Embassy
Street address: 83 avenue Roi Baudouin, Kinshasa-Gombe, Democratic Republic of Congo
Tel: (98) 169 100/111/200.
Fax (88) 46102.
E-mail: ambrit@ic.cd
Embassy of the Democratic Republic of Congo
1726 M Street, Suite 601, NW, Washington, DC 20036, USA
Tel: (202) 234 7690/1.
Fax: (202) 234 2609.
Embassy of the United States of America
310 Avenue des Aviateurs, Kinshasa-Gombe, Democratic Republic of Congo
Tel: (81) 225 5872.
Fax: (81) 301 0560.
E-mail: AEKinshasaConsular@state.gov
Website: http://usembassy.state.gov/kinshasa
Embassy of the Democratic Republic of Congo
18 Range Street, Ottawa, Ontario K1N 8J3, Canada
Tel: (613) 230 6391 *or* 6582.
Fax: (613) 230 1945.
Canadian Embassy
Street address: 17 avenue Pumbu, Commune de la Gombe, Kinshasa One, Democratic Republic of Congo
Tel: (89) 50310-2.
Fax: (88) 41277.
E-mail: knsha@dfait-maeci.gc.ca

TIMATIC CODES

Health	AMADEUS: **TI-DFT/JIB/HE** GALILEO/WORLDSPAN: **TI-DFT/JIB/HE** SABRE: **TIDFT/JIB/HE**
Visa	AMADEUS: **TI-DFT/JIB/VI** GALILEO/WORLDSPAN: **TI-DFT/JIB/VI** SABRE: **TIDFT/JIB/VI**

To access TIMATIC country information on Health and Visa regulations through the Computer Reservations System (CRS), type in the appropriate command line listed above.

General Information

AREA: 2,344,885 sq km (905,365 sq miles).
POPULATION: 51,201,000 (UN estimate 2002).
POPULATION DENSITY: 21.8 per sq km.
CAPITAL: Kinshasa. **Population**: 5,253,000 (UN estimate 2001).
GEOGRAPHY: The Democratic Republic of Congo is the third-largest country in Africa and is bordered to the north by the Central African Republic and Sudan, to the east by Uganda, Rwanda, Burundi and Tanzania, to the south by Zambia and Angola, and to the west by the Republic of Congo and the Angolan enclave, Cabinda. The country has a coastline of only 27km (17 miles), at the outlet of the Congo River, which flows into the Atlantic. The country straddles the Equator and has widely differing geographical features, including mountain ranges in the north and west, a vast central plain through which the Congo River flows, and the volcanoes and lakes of the Kivu region. The river has given rise to extensive tropical rainforests on the western border with the Republic of Congo.
GOVERNMENT: Republic. Gained independence from Belgium in 1960. **Head of State**: President Joseph Kabila since 2001. Kabila took over following the assassination of his father, Laurent-Désiré Kabila.
LANGUAGE: The official language is French. There are many local languages, the most widely spoken being Lingala, Swahili, Tshiluba and Kikongo.
RELIGION: Predominantly Roman Catholic, with a minority of Protestant and traditional beliefs.
TIME: Kinshasa and Mbandaka: GMT + 1.
Haut-Zaïre, Kasai, Kivu and Shaba: GMT + 2.
ELECTRICITY: 220 volts AC, 50Hz.
COMMUNICATIONS: Telephone: IDD is available. Country code: 243. Outgoing international code: 00. Internal telephone service is often unreliable and exists only in major towns. Satellite or cellular telephones are often used by international organisations. **Mobile telephone:** GSM 900 and 1800 network cover Kinshasa. Network operators include *Celtel Congo*, *SAIT Telecom SPRL* (OASIS) and *Vodacom Congo* (website: www.africanwireless.com). Roaming agreements exist. Using a handset in public can attract unwanted attention and make the user a target for robbery. **Fax:** A few hotels have facilities; business centres in the capital may be cheaper however. **Internet:** Can be accessed, though power shortages may cause difficulties. There are Internet cafes in Kinshasa. **Telegram:** These can be sent from chief telegraph offices, but are unreliable and sometimes subject to delays – particularly internal. **Post:** Post office opening hours: Mon-Sat 0800-1700. The country is included in the Universal Postal Union and the African Postal Union. Airmail to Europe takes four to 18 days but can take much longer. **Press:** The main newspapers are *L'Analyste*, *Boyoma* and *Mjumbe*.
Radio: BBC World Service (website: www.bbc.co.uk/worldservice) and Voice of America (website: www.voa.gov) can be received.

Passport/Visa

	Passport Required?	Visa Required?	Return Ticket Required?
Full British	Yes	Yes	Yes
Australian	Yes	Yes	Yes
Canadian	Yes	Yes	Yes
USA	Yes	Yes	Yes
Other EU	Yes	Yes	Yes
Japanese	Yes	Yes	Yes

Note: Regulations and requirements may be subject to change at short notice, and you are advised to contact the appropriate diplomatic or consular authority before finalising travel arrangements. Details of these may be found at the head of this country's entry. Any numbers in the chart refer to the footnotes below.

PASSPORTS: Passport valid for at least three months required by all.
VISAS: Required by all except transit passengers continuing their journey by the same or first connecting aircraft within 48 hours, provided holding valid onward or return documentation and not leaving the airport.
Types of visa and cost: *Tourist* and *Business*. *Single-entry*: £40 (one month); £73 (two months); £105 (three months); £145 (six months). *Multiple-entry*: £65 (one month); £97 (two months); £121 (three months); £194 (six months). *Transit*: £24 (seven days).
Validity: Three months from date of issue.
Application to: Consulate (or Consular section at Embassy); see *Contact Addresses* section.
Application requirements: (a) Passport valid for at least six months. (b) One application form. (c) One passport-size photo. (d) Yellow fever vaccination certificate. (e) Stamped, self-addressed envelope (or cost of return postage) for postal applications. (f) Fee (payable on submission of documents for application of visa; cash or postal orders only). (g) Return or onward travel documentation or itinerary from travel agent. *Tourist*: (a)-(g) and, (h) Letter from employer/university giving proof of status. (i) Letter from bank/building society giving proof of sufficient funds.
Working days required: Two days minimum, in person or by post.

Money

Currency: Franc Congolais (FC) = 100 centimes. Owing to the precarious nature of the economy, the denominations of the currency are subject to rapid change.
Note: The Franc Congolais has been revalued.
Currency exchange: Because of the parlous state of the economy, the only true repository of value is the US Dollar. Free circulation of foreign currencies is now allowed within the country. Note that purchase of airline tickets within the country can be made only with money exchanged officially.
Credit & debit cards: The use of MasterCard and Visa is limited to Kinshasa's major hotels. Credit cards cannot be used to obtain cash advances at banks.
Travellers cheques: Not recommended. Commission fees are very high, and travellers cheques are not accepted outside Kinshasa.
Currency restrictions: The import and export of local currency is prohibited. The import of foreign currency is limited to US$10,000. The export of foreign currency is unlimited.
Exchange rate indicators: The following figures are included as a guide to the movements of the Franc Congolais against Sterling and the US Dollar:

Date	Feb '04	May '04	Aug '04	Nov '04
£1.00=	701.71	701.05	723.12	823.76
$1.00=	385.50	392.50	392.50	435.00

Banking hours: Mon-Fri 0800-1130.

Duty Free

The following items may be imported into the Democratic Republic of Congo without incurring customs duty:
100 cigarettes or 50 cigars or 227g of tobacco; one bottle of alcoholic beverage; a reasonable amount of perfume for personal use; cameras if temporarily imported by tourists.
Note: Radios, tape recorders, record players and gifts are subject to duty. An import licence is required for arms and ammunition.

Public Holidays

2005: Jan 1 New Year's Day. **Jan 4** Commemoration of the Martyrs of Independence. **Jan 17** National Hero's Day. **May 1** Labour Day. **May 17** National Liberation Day. **Jun 30** Independence Day. **Nov 17** Army Day. **Nov 24** New Regime Anniversary. **Dec 25** Christmas Day.
2006: Jan 1 New Year's Day. **Jan 4** Commemoration of the Martyrs of Independence. **Jan 17** National Hero's Day. **May 1** Labour Day. **May 17** National Liberation Day. **Jun 30** Independence Day. **Nov 17** Army Day. **Nov 24** New Regime Anniversary. **Dec 25** Christmas Day.

Health

	Special Precautions?	Certificate Required?
Yellow Fever	Yes	1
Cholera	2	No
Typhoid & Polio	3	N/A
Malaria	4	N/A

Note: Regulations and requirements may be subject to change at short notice, and you are advised to contact your doctor well in advance of your intended date of departure. Any numbers in the chart refer to the footnotes below.

1: A yellow fever vaccination certificate is required by travellers over one year of age.
2: Following WHO guidelines issued in 1973, a cholera vaccination certificate is not an official condition of entry to the Democratic Republic of Congo. However, cholera is a serious risk in this country and precautions are essential. Up-to-date advice should be sought before deciding whether these precautions should include vaccination as medical opinion is divided over its effectiveness.
3: Immunisation or boosters for typhoid are recommended and vaccination against poliomyelitis is sometimes advised.
4: Malaria risk, predominantly in the malignant *falciparum* form, exists throughout the year in the whole country. The malignant form is reported to be highly resistant to chloroquine and sulfadoxine-pyrimethamine. Mefloquine is the recommended prophylaxis.
Food & Drink: All water should be regarded as being a potential health risk. Water used for drinking, brushing teeth or making ice should have first been boiled or otherwise sterilised. Milk is unpasteurised and should be boiled. Powdered or tinned milk is available and is advised, but make sure that it is reconstituted with pure water.

Avoid dairy products that are likely to have been made from unboiled milk. Only eat well-cooked meat and fish, preferably served hot. Pork, salad and mayonnaise may carry increased risk. Vegetables should be cooked and fruit peeled.
Other risks: *Bilharzia* (schistosomiasis) is present. Avoid swimming and paddling in fresh water; swimming pools which are well chlorinated and maintained are safe.
Hepatitis A, B and *E* are present and *meningococcal meningitis* may occur. *Plague* is present in natural foci. There is a very high risk of *diarrhoeal diseases*, the *dysenteries* and various *parasitic worm infections*; observe strict food and drink caution. *Leishmaniasis* and human *trypanosomiasis* (sleeping sickness) are present. *Ebola* outbreaks have occurred. Avoid tick bites which spread *African tick typhus*. Wear shoes to avoid soil-borne parasites. *Rabies* is present. For those at high risk, vaccination before arrival should be considered. If you are bitten, seek medical advice without delay.
Health care: Government expenditure on health is low and the quality of hospitals is poor. It is advisable to take specific personal medicines as well as supplies such as syringes and drip needles, as medical facilities are available only in larger centres. Doctors and hospitals expect cash payment in full for health services. Health insurance is *essential* and it is advisable to include cover for emergency air evacuation.

Travel - International

Travel Warning: All travel to the eastern and northeastern Democratic Republic of Congo (including entering from Uganda or Rwanda) is not advised. A reported coup attempt occurred during the early hours of 11 June 2004 in Kinshasa, although this was unsuccessful. and there have continued to be violent demonstrations against the international community in Kinshasa.
AIR: Airlines serving the Democratic Republic of Congo include *Air France, Air Gabon, Cameroon Airlines, Ethiopian Airlines, Kenya Airways, KLM* and *South African Airways.*
Approximate flight times: From Kinshasa to *London* is 10 hours 30 minutes including stopover in Brussels.
International airports: *Kinshasa (N'Djili) (FIH)* is 25km (15 miles) east of the city. Buses run to and from the city. Taxis are available. Airport facilities include 24-hour bank/bureau de change, post office, restaurant and car hire (*Avis, Budget, Europcar, Hertz* and *InterRent*), but all services may well be erratic and unreliable.
Departure tax: None.
SEA/RIVER: The international port is Matadi on the Congo River. There are no passenger services to or from Matadi at present. Ferries usually operate across the Congo River from Brazzaville to Kinshasa, although services are sporadic at present. In peacetime, there are ferries along the Oubangui River to the Central African Republic.
RAIL: In peacetime, there are rail services to Dar es Salaam in Tanzania and Lobito in Angola; and connections to Zambia, Zimbabwe, Mozambique and South Africa.
ROAD: Most of the Democratic Republic of Congo's borders are closed or very dangerous. Even in peacetime, the roads are mostly in bad condition and impassable in the rainy season. There are connecting roads to surrounding countries.

Travel - Internal

Note: There are indefinite restrictions on tourist travel within or across the country. A permit from the Ministry of the Interior is required for all travel outside the capital. Government curfews are in force in Kinshasa. There are safety concerns about all public transport.
AIR: There are connections from *N'Djili Airport* (Kinshasa) to over 40 internal airports and 150 landing strips. Small planes may be available for charter.
RIVER: Over 1600km (1000 miles) of the Congo River are navigable and, in normal circumstances, there are services from Kinshasa to the upriver ports of Kisangani and Ilébo. Services at present, however, are unreliable owing to political instability and fuel shortages.
RAIL: The main internal railway runs from Lubumbashi to Ilébo, with a branch to Kalemie and Kindu, and from Kinshasa to the port of Matadi. Rail services are generally subject to disruption. There is no air conditioning.
ROAD: Traffic drives on the right. Owing to poor maintenance, the roads are among the worst in Africa and only achieve a fair standard around the main towns. It is wise to check that bridges are safe before crossing. Vehicle thefts, including hijackings at gunpoint, occur. **Bus**: Services run between the main towns but are crowded and unreliable. **Taxi**: Available in Kinshasa but unreliable. **Car hire**: Available on a limited basis at the airport.
Documentation: International Driving Permit required.
URBAN: Conventional bus services in Kinshasa can be severely overcrowded. Minibuses and converted truck-buses also offer public transport, and are known as *fula fulas*. Pick-up trucks are known as 'taxibuses'. A better standard of transport is provided by shared taxis, which are widely available. There is little or no public transport in most other large centres.

Accommodation

The difficult terrain has resulted in relatively few settlements except along river banks. Accommodation is essentially restricted to the main cities, and is virtually non-existent in the interior. For further details, contact the Embassy. The few hotels that cater for visitors are expensive and generally booked up well in advance. The majority of hotels are in Kinshasa, with others in Boma, Bukavu, Kerning, Kisangani, Kolwezi, Lubumbashi, Matadi, Mbandaka, Mbanzangunu and Muanda.

Resorts & Excursions

KINSHASA & THE WEST

KINSHASA: The capital does not have many sights of historic interest, but the visitor interested in the past should not miss the prehistoric and ethnological museums at **Kinshasa University**, an ensemble of light, rectangular, well laid-out buildings standing on a hillside. A brightly coloured chapel crowns the top of the hill. Nearby is a corner of the equatorial forest surrounding a beautiful lake called **Ma Vallée** with a tavern on its banks.
Other attractions include the fishing port of **Kinkole**, the **Gardens of the Presidential Farm of Nsele** made of pagodas, and the extensive pools where angling and swimming may be enjoyed. In both the markets and the suburbs of Kinshasa, there are craftspeople who produce wood and metal items. The **National Museum** includes some unique pieces of national art.
SOUTHWEST CONGO & BANDUNDU: The **Inkisi Falls** (60m/197ft high) at Zongo and the caves in the region of **Mbanza-Ngungu** may be visited in one day, but it is preferable to stay for two or three days, for Mbanza-Ngungu is a pleasant resort with a good climate. While in the Mbanza-Ngungu area the visitor should stop at Kisantu to visit the **Frère Gillet Botanic Gardens** with their world-famous rare orchids.
Further west are the wild slopes and gorges of the **River Kwilu**, 120km (75 miles) from Mataoi; on the right bank of the river is a spot of rugged beauty called **Inga**. The woods, caves and waterfalls of **Boma** and equatorial **Mayumbe** and the **Tombs of Tshela** can be visited on the way to the ocean beach of **Moanda**.
Less easily accessible is the upper valley of the **Kwango** in the southwest. A long journey through a region of unspoiled natural beauty leads to the **Tembo** (formerly Guillaume) **Falls**.

CENTRAL & EASTERN CONGO

KASAI & SHABA: In the south, the **Upemba National Park** straddles the **River Lualaba**, northeast of **Bukama**, and includes several lakes inhabited by hippos, crocodiles and numerous aquatic birds. Here too are fishermen, cattle farmers and peasants, as well as a number of mining communities. **Kananga** and **Mbuji-Mayi** are typical tropical towns; **Kalemie** and the banks of **Lake Tanganyika** are reminiscent of the French Riviera.
The whole of the south is dotted with freshwater lakes such as **Munkamba**, **Fwa** and **Kasai**; there are also numerous impressive waterfalls, such as **Kiobo**, on the **River Lufira**, and **Lofol**, 384m (1259ft) high, north of Lubumbashi.
UPPER CONGO & THE KIVU: The high plateaux of Congo extend across the eastern part of the country, around lakes Tanganyika, Kivu, Edward, Albert and Bukavu. **Bunia** is a small, pretty town featuring villas, restaurants and hotels. In the north is the **Garamba National Park**, covering 400,000 hectares and featuring lions, leopards, elephants, rhinos and giraffes. **Lake Albert**, which contains more fish than any other lake in Africa, lies at an altitude of over 618m (2027ft). It can be reached from Bunia, which is also the point of departure for numerous excursions into the forests and mountains, native villages, the **Caves of Mount Hoyo** and the **Escaliers de Venus Falls**.
Lake Edward is the home of birds of all sizes and colours. The highest peak in the **Ruwenzori range** is the **Pic Marguerite**, at an altitude of 5119m (15,795ft). The snowline is at 533m (1776ft). This region is also inhabited by gorillas and by the extremely rare okapi. The mountain scenery between **Goma** and **Beni** was regarded as some of the most spectacular in Africa, although the volcanic eruption of **Nyiragongo**, 3470m (11,385ft) in January 2002, damaged the surrounding area to some extent.
VIRUNGA NATIONAL PARK: Covering an area of 12,000 sq km (4633 sq miles), this comprises an immense plain bounded by two jagged mountain ranges that serve as a natural enclosure for the animals which roam at liberty in this huge natural reserve. Game includes numerous lions, elephants, buffaloes, warthogs, antelopes and hippos.

Social Profile

FOOD & DRINK: There are a number of good restaurants in Kinshasa and Lubumbashi, but prices are high. Hotels and restaurants which cater for tourists are generally expensive and serve international and national dishes. A typical speciality is *moambe* chicken, cooked in fresh palm oil with rice and spinach. The capital Kinshasa offers Belgian, French and local cuisine but, again, restaurants are expensive and cater essentially for businesspeople.
NIGHTLIFE: Kinshasa is the best place for nightlife, especially in the sprawling township of the *Cité*, where most of the population live. In spite of recent political turmoil, the local music scene is thriving. There are hundreds of dance clubs in Kinshasa. Congolese music is popular throughout Africa as well as in Europe and the USA.
SHOPPING: Local craftware includes bracelets, ebony carvings and paintings. The large towns all have markets and shopping centres, selling everything from fresh ginger to baskets and African carvings. **Shopping hours**: Mon-Sat 0800-1800.
SOCIAL CONVENTIONS: Casual clothes are widely suitable although scanty beachwear should be confined to the beach or poolside. **Photography**: A permit is required. Even then, local authorities are likely to be sensitive. Avoid official areas, airports and riverbanks. **Tipping**: 10 per cent service charge is added to hotel and restaurant bills.

Business Profile

ECONOMY: With rich agricultural land and extensive mineral and energy deposits, the Democratic Republic of Congo is potentially one of the richest countries on the African continent. However, decades of chronic neglect at the hands of the corrupt Mobutu left it as one of the poorest, with a per capita annual income of just US$150. Such plans as the Kabila governments may have had for development have been undermined by the civil war. Moreover, no significant development aid – essential to rebuild the country's infrastructure – can be expected until the conflict has ended.
At least two-thirds of the population are engaged in subsistence farming. Industry runs well below capacity due to a lack of spare parts and foreign exchange with which to buy them. The country could be one of the world's largest producers of copper and cobalt, but production is far short of its potential; what is produced is sold by the warring party in control of the mine to finance continued fighting. (In some cases, mining concessions have been handed over to a government ally in exchange for military support: Zimbabwe, which controls several copper mines in the south is the most notable example.) The mining sector can also produce manganese, zinc, uranium and tin. There are also some oil deposits located off the short Atlantic coastline. Manufacturing for domestic consumption dominates the industrial sector, producing textiles, cement, food and beverages, wood products and plastics.
BUSINESS: Businesspeople should wear lightweight suits. Interpreter and translation services are available as business is mainly conducted in French. The best time to visit is in the cool season (which varies from one part of the country to another). **Office hours**: Mon-Fri 0730-1500, Sat 0730-1200.
COMMERCIAL INFORMATION: The following organisation might be able to offer advice: Chambre de Commerce, d'Industrie et d'Agriculture de la République Démocratique du Congo, BP 7247, 10 avenue des Aviateurs, Kinshasa (tel: (12) 22286).

Climate

Varies according to distance from the Equator, which lies across the north of the country. The dry season in the north is from December to March, and in the south May to October. The annual temperatures are warm and humidity is high.
Required clothing: Lightweight clothes are recommended all year, with rainwear during the rainy season.

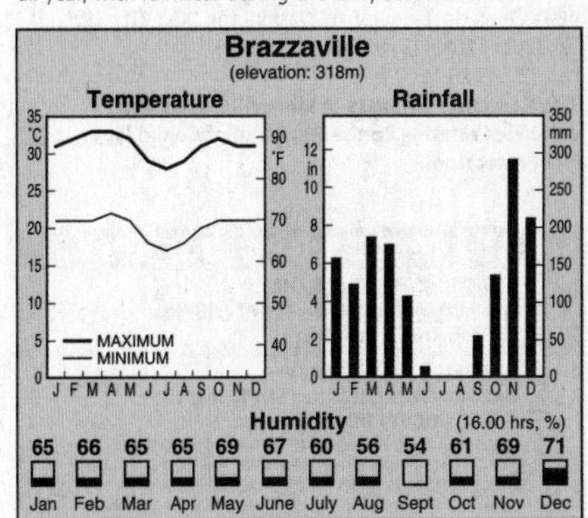

Congo (Republic of)

LATEST TRAVEL ADVICE CONTACTS

British Foreign and Commonwealth Office
Tel: (0870) 606 0290 Website: www.fco.gov.uk
US Department of State
Website: http://travel.state.gov/travel
Canadian Department of Foreign Affairs and Int'l Trade
Tel: (1 800) 267 8376 Website: www.dfait-maeci.gc.ca

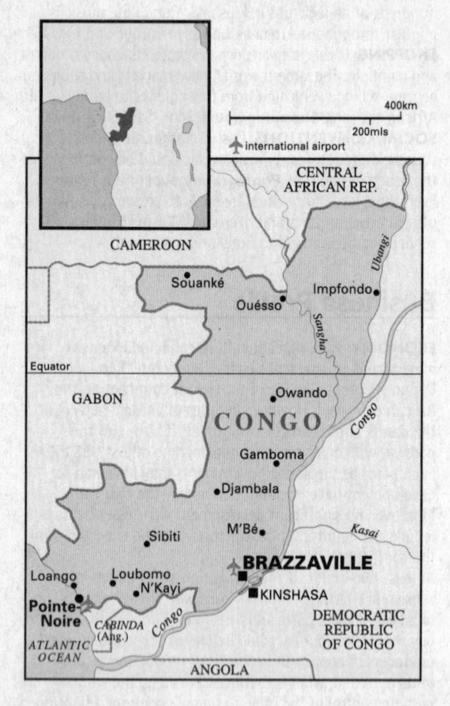

Location: West coast of Central Africa.

Country dialling code: 242.

Ministry of Culture, Arts and Tourism
BP 20480, Brazzaville, Congo
Tel: 814 022.
Fax: 814 025.
Direction Generale du Tourisme et des Loisirs
BP 456, Brazzaville, Congo
Tel: 830 953.
Honorary Consulate of the Republic of Congo (Brazzaville)
Arena, 24 Southwark Bridge Road, London SE1 9HF
Tel: (020) 7922 0695.
Fax: (020) 7401 2566 *or* 2545.
Opening hours: Mon-Fri 1030-1530.
Embassy of the Republic of Congo and Tourist Office
37 bis rue Paul Valéry, 75116 Paris, France
Tel: (1) 4500 6057. Fax: (1) 4067 1733.
British Honorary Consulate
Et-Lisa Avenue Foch (á côté de DHL), Brazzaville, Congo
Tel: 620 893.
Fax: 838 543.
E-mail: vorick@congonet.cg
Offers limited services.
The British Embassy in Kinshasa deals with enquiries relating to the Republic of Congo (see the *Congo (Dem Rep)* **section).**
Embassy of the Republic of Congo
4891 Colorado Avenue NW, Washington DC 20011, USA
Tel: (202) 726 0825 *or* 5500.
Fax: (202) 726 1860.
The Canadian Embassy in Libreville deals with enquiries relating to the Republic of Congo (see *Gabon* **section).**

TIMATIC CODES

Health	AMADEUS: **TI-DFT/JIB/HE** GALILEO/WORLDSPAN: **TI-DFT/JIB/HE** SABRE: **TIDFT/JIB/HE**
Visa	AMADEUS: **TI-DFT/JIB/VI** GALILEO/WORLDSPAN: **TI-DFT/JIB/VI** SABRE: **TIDFT/JIB/VI**

To access TIMATIC country information on Health and Visa regulations through the Computer Reservations System (CRS), type in the appropriate command line listed above.

General Information

AREA: 342,000 sq km (132,047 sq miles).
POPULATION: 3,633,000 (UN estimate 2002).
POPULATION DENSITY: 10.6 per sq km.
CAPITAL: Brazzaville. **Population**: 856,410 (1996).
GEOGRAPHY: Congo is situated in Africa, bordered to the north by Cameroon and the Central African Republic, to the south and east by the Democratic Republic of Congo, to the southwest by the Atlantic, and to the west by Gabon. The Cabinda Enclave, belonging to Angola, lies to the southwest, on the Atlantic coast. Vast areas are swamps, grassland or thick forests with rivers being virtually the only means of internal travel. The vast River Congo and its major tributaries form most of the country's border with the Democratic Republic of Congo, drawing much of its water from the swamplands in the north of the country. The narrow sandy coastal plain is broken by lagoons, behind which rise the Mayombe Mountains. Most of the population lives in the south of the country.
GOVERNMENT: Republic. Gained independence from France in 1960. **Head of State and Government:** President Denis Sassou-Nguesso since 1997.
LANGUAGE: The official language is French. Other major languages are Lingala, Munukutuba and Kikongo. English is spoken very little.
RELIGION: The majority follow animist belief systems (50 per cent), with most of the remainder being Christians (mainly Roman Catholic). There are small Protestant and Muslim minorities.
TIME: GMT + 1.
ELECTRICITY: 220 volts AC, 50Hz.
COMMUNICATIONS: Telephone: IDD service is available in major cities only. Country code: 242. Outgoing international code: 00. Links with Western Europe are generally poor. **Mobile telephone:** GSM 900 networks are operated by *CelTel Congo* (website: www.msi-cellular.com) or *Libertis Telecom.* Coverage is mainly limited to Brazzaville and Pointe Noire. **Fax:** Large hotels may be able to provide services. **Internet:** ISPs include *Africances* and *Congonet* . Facilities are available at hotels. **Telegram:** Services are available in cities at the main post offices and some hotels. **Post:** There is an unreliable internal service. Post office hours: Mon-Fri 0730/0800-1200 and 1430-1730; and (for stamps and telegrams) Mon-Sat 0800-2000; Sun and public holidays 0800-1200. **Press:** Daily papers, which are all published in French, include *ACI Actualité, Aujourd'hui* and *Mweti Journal de Brazzaville.*
Radio: BBC World Service (website: www.bbc.co.uk/worldservice) and Voice of America (website: www.voa.gov) can be received. From time to time the frequencies change and the most up-to-date can be found online.

Passport/Visa

	Passport Required?	Visa Required?	Return Ticket Required?
Full British	Yes	Yes	Yes
Australian	Yes	Yes	Yes
Canadian	Yes	Yes	Yes
USA	Yes	Yes	Yes
Other EU	Yes	Yes	Yes
Japanese	Yes	Yes	Yes

Note: Regulations and requirements may be subject to change at short notice, and you are advised to contact the appropriate diplomatic or consular authority before finalising travel arrangements. Details of these may be found at the head of this country's entry. Any numbers in the chart refer to the footnotes below.

PASSPORTS: Passport valid for at least three months required by all.
VISAS: Required by all except nationals of Gabon.
Note: Nationals of Congo possessing dual nationality *do* require visas if travelling on their other passport.
Types of visa and cost: *Tourist* and *Business*: £40 for 15 days; £60 for one month; £100 for three months (Business only). All visas are multiple entry.
Validity: Dependent on length of visa.
Application to: Consulate (or Consular section at Embassy); see *Contact Addresses* section.
Application requirements: (a) Valid passport. (b) One completed application form. (c) One passport-size photo in colour. (d) Return or onward ticket. (e) Fee, payable in cash or by postal order. (f) Yellow fever vaccination certificate for travellers aged over one year. (g) Stamped, self-addressed envelope (or cost of return postage) for postal applications. *Tourist*: (a)-(g) and, (h) Authorised lodging certificate, provided a resident or national of the Republic of Congo, or a hotel reservation. (i) Proof of sufficient funds (credit card, pay slips, proof of employment). *Business*: (a)-(g) and, (h) Letter from employer verifying the applicant's identity, purpose of travel and length of stay, giving the name and address of a contact in the Republic of Congo and taking responsibility for the applicant.
Note: (a) Applications made by post must be accompanied by a cheque for £5 to cover postal charges (UK and Republic of Ireland only). (b) Vaccination certificates for cholera and tetanus may also be required. (c) All journalists, photographers and researchers must obtain written permission to carry out filming or research *before* entering the country.
Working days required: Visas issued immediately for applications made in person or 24 hours after date of receipt for postal applications.

Money

Currency: CFA Franc (CFAfr) = 100 centimes. Notes are in denominations of CFAfr10,000, 5000, 2000, 1000 and 500. Coins are in denominations of CFAfr250, 100, 50, 25, 10, 5 and 1. Congo is part of the French Monetary Area. Only currency issued by the *Banque des États de l'Afrique Centrale* (Bank of Central African States) is valid; currency issued by the *Banque des États de l'Afrique de l'Ouest* (Bank of West African States) is not. The CFA Franc is tied to the Euro.
Credit & debit cards: Diners Club and MasterCard all have limited use. Check with your credit or debit card company for details of merchant acceptability and other services which may be available.
Travellers cheques: To avoid additional exchange rate charges, travellers are advised to take travellers cheques in Euros or Pounds Sterling.
Currency restrictions: The import and export of local currency is prohibited, except between countries of the Central African group. The import of foreign currency is unrestricted, although amounts over £234/US$335 must be declared upon arrival. Export of foreign currency is restricted to the amount imported.
Exchange rate indicators: The following figures are included as a guide to the movements of the CFA Franc against Sterling and the US Dollar:

Date	Feb '04	May '04	Aug '04	Nov '04
£1.00=	961.13	983.76	978.35	936.79
$1.00=	528.01	550.79	531.03	494.69

Banking hours: 0620-1300 Monday to Friday (counters close at 1130).

Duty Free

The following items may be imported into Congo by visitors over 18 years of age without incurring customs duty:
200 cigarettes or one box of cigars or tobacco (women are permitted to import cigarettes only); one bottle of spirits and one bottle of wine; a reasonable quantity of perfume in opened bottles.
Note: If importing expensive items such as watches and cameras, it is advisable to present the receipt.

Public Holidays

2005: Jan 1 New Year's Day. **Mar 8** Congolese Women's Day. **May 1** Labour Day. **Jun 10** Commemoration of the National Sovereign Conference. **Aug 15** National Day. **Dec 25** Christmas.
2006: Jan 1 New Year's Day. **Mar 8** Congolese Women's Day. **May 1** Labour Day. **Jun 10** Commemoration of the National Sovereign Conference. **Aug 15** National Day. **Dec 25** Christmas.

Health

	Special Precautions?	Certificate Required?
Yellow Fever	Yes	1
Cholera	Yes	2
Typhoid & Polio	3	N/A
Malaria	4	N/A

Note: Regulations and requirements may be subject to change at short notice, and you are advised to contact your doctor well in advance of your intended date of departure. Any numbers in the chart refer to the footnotes below.

1: A yellow fever vaccination certificate is required for all travellers over one year of age.
2: Following WHO guidelines issued in 1973, a cholera vaccination certificate is no longer a condition of entry to Congo. However, cholera is a serious risk in this country and precautions are essential. Up-to-date advice should be sought before deciding whether these precautions should include vaccination as medical opinion is divided over its effectiveness; see the *Health* appendix.
3: Immunisations or boosters for typhoid and poliomyelitis are advised.
4: Malaria risk exists all year throughout the country, predominantly in the malignant *falciparum* form. Resistance to chloroquine and sulfadoxine-pyrimethamine

has been reported. A weekly dose of 250mg of mefloquine is the recommended prophylaxis.
Food & Drink: All water should be regarded as being potentially contaminated. Water used for drinking, brushing teeth or making ice should have first been boiled or otherwise sterilised. Milk is unpasteurised and should be boiled. Powdered or tinned milk is available and is advised, but make sure that it is reconstituted with pure water. Avoid dairy products which are likely to have been made from unboiled milk. Only eat well cooked meat and fish, preferably served hot. Pork, salad and mayonnaise may carry increased risk. Vegetables should be cooked and fruit peeled.
Other risks: *Bilharzia (*schistosomiasis) is present. Avoid swimming and paddling in fresh water; swimming pools which are well chlorinated and maintained are safe. *River blindness* (onchocerciasis) and *sleeping sickness* (trypanosomiasis) are also prevalent. *Hepatitis A* is widespread and *hepatitis B* is hyperendemic.
Meningococcal A and *C* have been reported and immunisation is recommended. There are sometimes outbreaks of *ebola haemorrhagic fever.*
Rabies is present. For those at high risk, vaccination before arrival should be considered. If you are bitten, seek medical advice without delay. For more information, consult the *Health* appendix.
Health care: Medical and dental facilities are generally very limited outside Brazzaville. Health insurance is essential.

Travel - International

Travel Warning: All but essential travel outside the main cities of Brazzaville and Pointe-Noire is advised.
AIR: *Aero Benin, Air France, Air Service Gabon* and *Cameroon Airlines* operate international services to Congo.
Approximate flight times: From *London* to Brazzaville is approximately 11 hours (including up to three hours for stopover in Paris).
International airports: *Brazzaville (BZV)* (Maya Maya) is 4km (2 miles) northwest of the city. Buses and taxis are available to the city. Airport facilities include a restaurant and car hire (*Europcar, Hertz* and *InterRent*).
Pointe-Noire (PNR) is 5.5km (3.5 miles) from the city. Taxis are available to the city.
Departure tax: None.
SEA/RIVER: Cargo ships dock at Pointe-Noire. An hourly car ferry operates between Kinshasa (Democratic Republic of Congo) and Brazzaville across the Congo River (travel time – 20 minutes). Ferries operate to and from the Central African Republic on the Ubangi.
ROAD: There is a road connection from Lambaréné in Gabon to Loubomo and Brazzaville. The road from Cameroon is usable only during the dry season. There is a good road between Pointe Noire and Cabinda (Angola). Entry can also be made via the Democratic Republic of Congo. **Documentation**: A *carnet de passage en douane* is needed to cross land borders between Congo and the neighbouring countries. Further information can be obtained from national motoring organisations.

Travel - Internal

AIR: The national airline, *Lina Congo (GC)*, operates regular services from Brazzaville to Pointe-Noire, with stops in Loubomo and Ouesso. Private charters are available.
Departure tax: CFAfr 3400 on internal flights.
RIVER: Inland steamers ply from Brazzaville up the Congo and Ubangi. Rivers are vital to internal transport.
RAIL: *Congo-Océan* railway company operates services between Brazzaville and Pointe-Noire (travel time – up to three days). Known as the 'Peace Train', this service endured a long suspension due to civil war, and still incurs occasional disruptions. Services between Mbinda and Pointe Noire are also due to resume soon. Advance booking is recommended. Children under five years travel free. Half-fare is charged for children aged five to nine.
ROAD: Roads are mostly earth tracks, sandy in dry season and impassable in the wet, suitable for 4-wheel drive vehicles only. There are 1207km (750 miles) of paved roads. Traffic drives on the right. Poorly marked army checkpoints, often manned by undisciplined soldiers, exist throughout the country. Travel at night on unfamiliar roads can be dangerous and should be avoided. **Car hire**: There are several car hire firms represented in Brazzaville, lists of which can be obtained from main hotels. **Documentation**: An International Driving Permit is required.
URBAN: Brazzaville has a minibus and taxi service. Taxis are also available in Pointe-Noire and Loubomo. Taxi fares have a flat rate and fares should be agreed beforehand.

Accommodation

There are five good hotels in Brazzaville, three in Loubomo and four in Pointe-Noire. Prices and advance bookings can be obtained via *Air France*. Outside the towns mentioned above, accommodation for visitors is limited. For further details, contact the Direction Générale du Tourisme et de l'Hôtellerie (see *Contact Addresses* section).

Resorts & Excursions

The capital city of **Brazzaville** is situated on the west side of **Malebo Pool** on the **River Congo**. Sights to see include the beautiful **Basilique Sainte Anne**, the colourful suburb of **Poto Poto**, the **Temple Mosque**, the markets at **Oluendze** and **Moungali**, the **National Museum**, the **Municipal Gardens** and the house constructed for de Gaulle when Brazzaville was the capital of Free France. There is a golf course at the **Cité du Djoué**. The first church in Congo was built in 1882 by a French priest and is located in **Linzolo**, 30km (19 miles) from the capital. The city is also home to the regional seat of the **World Health Organization** and a good market. 150km (90 miles) north of the capital is the historic village of **M'Bé**, the capital of King Makoko. Also in this region is **Lac Bleu** with good fishing available and the **Valley of Butterflies**.
To the south of Brazzaville are the **Congo Rapids** (9km/6 miles away by tarred road), the **Loufoulakari Falls** and the **Trou de Dieu**, above which there is a panoramic view of the surrounding countryside. The main town on the coast is **Pointe-Noire** (with its lively evening market), and there are several good beaches close by in the region known as the **Côte Sauvage**. Around 20km (12 miles) from the city are the villages of **Loango** and **Diosso**. Loango was the main embarkation port for slaves and it is estimated that more than 2 million people were transported from here. The **Gorges of Diosso**, spectacular cliffs formed by the erosion of the sea and the wind, are worth visiting.
The landscape in the north of the country is distinguished by huge tracts of virgin forest with an abundance of wildlife. The forest is also home to several indigenous tribes who have maintained their traditional way of life.

Social Profile

FOOD & DRINK: Restaurants provide mostly French cuisine, and the coast has excellent fish, giant oysters and shrimps. The main hotels in Brazzaville have good restaurants serving French cuisine, and there are also restaurants specialising in Italian, Lebanese and Vietnamese dishes. Some restaurants, such as those at Nanga Lake and Grand Hotel in Loubomo, specialise in African dishes such as *piri piri chicken* (with pepper), *Mouamba chicken* in palm oil, palm cabbage salad and cassava leaves, *saka saka* (ground cassava leaves cooked with palm oil and peanut paste) and *Maboke* (freshwater fish cooked in large *marantacee* leaves). Pointe-Noire and Loubomo also have restaurants and bars, usually in hotels, with table service. Some bars also have counter service.
NIGHTLIFE: Local groups are popular in the main towns. Brazzaville and Pointe-Noire have several nightclubs.
SHOPPING: In Brazzaville, there are shops and colourful markets. An arts and crafts centre at Poto Poto sells, amongst other things, local paintings and carved wooden masks and figures. The two main markets are Moungali and Ouenze. Avenue Foch is crowded with street vendors. Basketwork can be bought at the villages of Makana and M'Pila (3km/2 miles from Brazzaville), with pottery and an open-air market. **Shopping hours**: Mon-Sat 0800-1200 and 1500-1800. Some shops close on Monday afternoon and a few will open on Sunday morning.
SPECIAL EVENTS: For full details of events in 2005, contact the Direction Générale du Hotellerie (see *Contact Addresses* section).
SOCIAL CONVENTIONS: Normal courtesies should be observed when visiting people's homes. Gifts are acceptable as a token of thanks, especially if invited for a meal. Dress should be casual, and informal wear is acceptable in most places. Mini-skirts and shorts should not be worn in most public places, however. Artistic carving, both traditional and modern dance, as well as folk songs, play an important part in Congolese culture, which is strongly based on tradition. There are large numbers of foreigners resident in Congo, working as technical assistants, businesspeople and traders. **Photography**: It is forbidden to photograph public buildings. **Tipping**: Normally 10 per cent in hotels and restaurants. Porters and taxi drivers do not expect tips.

Business Profile

ECONOMY: About 60 per cent of the country is covered by tropical forest, roughly half of which can be exploited economically. Forestry is thus an important part of the economy and, along with agriculture, employs about two-thirds of the working population. Both subsistence (cassava, plantains) and cash crops (sugar, palm oil, coffee, cocoa) are grown; even so, Congo continues to depend on a large quantity of imported food. A further 20 per cent of the workforce is employed in various industries, of which the most important is oil. The first field came on stream in 1960 and the industry now accounts for 90 per cent of Congo's export earnings; it also allows the country a trade balance under normal circumstances, even though the oil sector's contribution to GNP has dropped from 40 per cent in 1985 to its current level of about 20 per cent. Strengthening of the non-oil economy remains the main long-term objective. Unfortunately, the government's economic planning and reforms have been undermined by political instability, erratic implementation of the programme, and fractious relations with the IMF and World Bank (which have underwritten it). The USA is the largest oil purchaser, followed by France and Spain. France provides two-thirds of Congo's imports, consisting largely of machinery, transport equipment, chemicals, iron and steel as well as foodstuffs. Italy, Spain and Japan are also important trading partners in the industrialised world. Annual per capita income, at US$640, is relatively high by regional standards. Congo is a member of the CFA Franc Zone and of the Central African Economic and Customs Union (CEEAC).
BUSINESS: Jackets and ties are not usually worn by men on business visits but are expected when visiting government officials. A knowledge of French is essential as there are no professional translators available. Normal courtesies should be observed and the best months for business visits are January to March and June to September. **Office hours**: Usually Mon-Fri 0700-1400, Sat 0700-1200.

Climate

Equatorial climate with short rains from October to December and long rains between mid-January and mid-May. The main dry season is from June to September.
Required clothing: Practical lightweight cottons and linens with a light raincoat or umbrella in the rainy season.

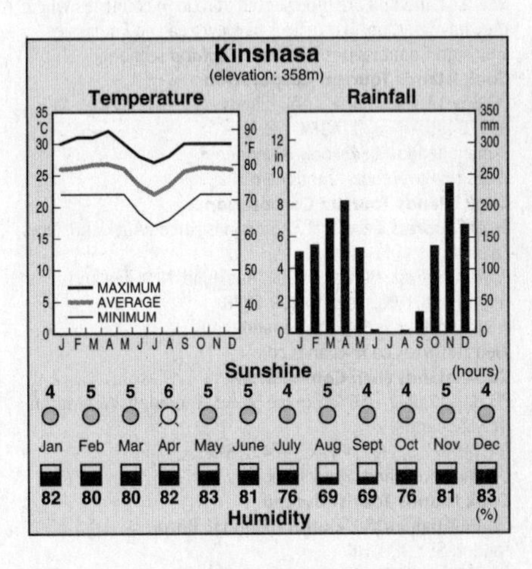

Cook Islands

LATEST TRAVEL ADVICE CONTACTS

British Foreign and Commonwealth Office

US Department of State

Canadian Department of Foreign Affairs and Int'l Trade

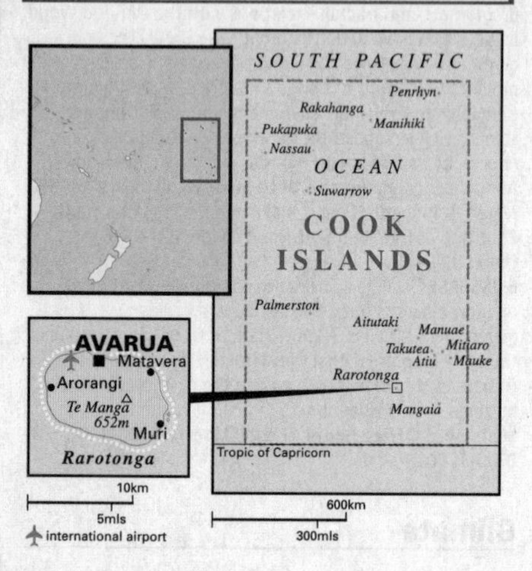

Location: South Pacific, Polynesia.

Country dialling code: 682.

The Cook Islands are self governing 'in free association' with New Zealand and are represented abroad in countries where they have no Consular offices by New Zealand Embassies and High Commissions (see *New Zealand* section).

Cook Islands Tourism Corporation
PO Box 14, Rarotonga, Cook Islands
Tel: 29435. Fax: 21435.
E-mail: headoffice@cook-islands.com
Website: www.cook-islands.com

Cook Islands Tourism Corporation
Street address: Level 1, 127 Symonds Street, Auckland, New Zealand
Postal address: PO Box 37391, Auckland, New Zealand
Tel: (9) 366 1106. Fax: (9) 309 1876.
E-mail: nzmanager@cook-islands.com
Website: www.cook-islands.com

Cook Islands High Commission
PO Box 12, 242 - 56 Mulgrave Street, Thorndon, Wellington, New Zealand
Tel: (4) 472 5126/7. Fax: (4) 472 5121.
E-mail: cookislands@cookhicom.org.nz

Cook Islands Tourist Bureau
c/o Hills Balfour, 36 Southwark Bridge Road, London SE1 9EU, UK
Tel: (020) 7202 6365 (consumer line) *or* 6376 (trade enquiries).
Fax: (020) 7928 0722.
E-mail: cooks@hillsbalfour.com
Website: www.cook-islands.com

Cook Islands Tourism Corporation
1133-160A Street, White Rock, Vancouver, British Colombia V4A 7G9, Canada
Tel: (604) 541 9811 *or* (888) 994 2665 (toll-free in USA and Canada). Fax: (604) 541 9812.
E-mail: canadamanager@cook-islands.com
Website: www.cook-islands.com

General Information

AREA: 237 sq km (91.5 sq miles).
POPULATION: 18,400 (official estimate 2002).
POPULATION DENSITY: 77.6 per sq km.
CAPITAL: Avarua (on Rarotonga). **Population**: 10,337 (1996, the whole island of Rarotonga).
GEOGRAPHY: The Cook Islands are situated 3500km (2200 miles) northeast of New Zealand and 1000km (600 miles) southwest of Tahiti in the South Pacific, forming part of Polynesia. The islands fall into two groups: the scattered Northern Group are all coral atolls while the Southern Group is of volcanic origin. Rarotonga is the largest and highest island with a rugged volcanic interior, its highest peak being Te Manga, at 652m (2140ft). Coral reef surrounds the island and the population lives between reef and hills where rich soil supports both tropical and subtropical vegetation. Most of the island is covered by thick evergreen bush. Most of the larger islands include lagoons surrounded by small areas of fertile land, above which rise volcanic hills. The best beaches found on Aitutaki are also part of the eight-island Southern Group. The Northern Group comprises seven islands, the largest being Penrhyn, Manihiki and Pukapuka. The Cook Islands have been used as the setting for several films, the best known being *Merry Christmas Mr Lawrence*.
GOVERNMENT: Self-governing state in 'free association' with New Zealand. (New Zealand retains responsibility for external affairs.) Gained self-governing status in 1965.
Head of State: HM Queen Elizabeth II, represented locally by Apenera Short since 1991. New Zealand is represented locally by High Commissioner Rob Moore-Jones since 1998.
Head of Government: Prime Minister Robert Woonton since 2002.
LANGUAGE: The official languages are English and Cook Islands Maori.
RELIGION: Mainly Cook Islands Christian Church (58 per cent); also Roman Catholic, Latter Day Saints, Seventh Day Adventists and Assembly of God.
TIME: GMT - 10.
ELECTRICITY: 220 volts DC, 50Hz.
COMMUNICATIONS: Telephone: IDD is available. Country code: 682. Outgoing international code: 00 (operator assistance may be required). **Mobile telephone:** GSM 900 network provided by Telecom Cook Islands (website: www.telecom.co.ck). Travellers arriving from New Zealand, Australia and Samoa can arrange roaming with their own network providers. **Fax:** Many Cook Island organisations have facilities. **Internet:** There are Internet facilities in Avarua at the Telecom Cook Islands office (open 24 hours a day) and at the post office. ISPs include *Telecom Cook Islands* (website: www.oyster.net.ck). **Telegram:** Services are provided by Telecom Cook Islands in Rarotonga; the most convenient way to use them is via one's hotel. **Post:** Post office hours: Mon-Fri 0800-1600. **Press:** The daily *Cook Islands News* is published in Maori and English. *The Cook Islands Herald* and *Cook Islands Star* are also available. **Radio:** BBC World Service (website: www.bbc.co.uk/worldservice) and Voice of America (website: www.voa.gov) can be received. From time to time the frequencies change and the most up-to-date can be found online.

TIMATIC CODES

Health	AMADEUS: **TI-DFT/JIB/HE** GALILEO/WORLDSPAN: **TI-DFT/JIB/HE** SABRE: **TIDFT/JIB/HE**
Visa	AMADEUS: **TI-DFT/JIB/VI** GALILEO/WORLDSPAN: **TI-DFT/JIB/VI** SABRE: **TIDFT/JIB/VI**

To access TIMATIC country information on Health and Visa regulations through the Computer Reservations System (CRS), type in the appropriate command line listed above.

Passport/Visa

	Passport Required?	Visa Required?	Return Ticket Required?
Full British	Yes	1/2	Yes
Australian	Yes	1/2	Yes
Canadian	Yes	1/2	Yes
USA	Yes	1/2	Yes
Other EU	Yes	1/2	Yes
Japanese	Yes	1/2	Yes

Note: *Regulations and requirements may be subject to change at short notice, and you are advised to contact the appropriate diplomatic or consular authority before finalising travel arrangements. Details of these may be found at the head of this country's entry. Any numbers in the chart refer to the footnotes below.*

PASSPORTS: Valid passport required by *all*, including nationals of New Zealand. Passports should be valid for six months after the initial 31-day stay in the Cook Islands.
VISAS: 1. Not required by visitors for tourist stays of up to 31 days and they are issued on arrival. Confirmed onward/return tickets and documentation are required, as are accommodation arrangements and proof of adequate finances for duration of stay.
2. All nationals arriving in the Cook Islands for business purposes or sourcing investment possibilities *do* require a 21-day work visa and this can be issued on arrival. Business must be completed within that period.
Validity: Visitors can extend length of stay on a monthly basis up to an additional five months, providing they have sufficient funds, use licensed accommodation and are not taking up employment. A fee is payable with each application within 14 days before the expiry of the permit. three-month extensions cost NZ$70 and five-month extensions may be obtained for a fee of NZ$120. For visitors wanting to stay longer than six months, a visa must be applied for from their country of residence. There is no fee for applicants aged under 15 years.
Application to: Cook Islands Representative (see *Contact Addresses* section) *or* the Principal Immigration Officer (see *Temporary residence* below).
Application requirements: A return ticket and proof of sufficient funds are required for those wishing to extend their stay in the Cook Islands.
Temporary residence: Applicants should refer to the Principal Immigration Officer, PO Box 105, Rarotonga (tel: 29347; fax: 21247; e-mail: tutai@immigration.gov.ck; website: www.mfai.gov.ck).

Money

Currency: New Zealand Dollar (NZ$) = 100 cents, supplemented by notes and coins minted for local use which are not negotiable outside the Cook Islands. Notes are in denominations of NZ$100, 50, 20, 10 and 5. Coins are in denominations of NZ$2 and 1, and 50, 20, 10 and 5 cents.
Currency exchange: Exchange facilities are available at the airport, banks and in some larger stores and hotels. EFTPOS and ATM machines are available at both *ANZ* and *Westpac* banks on Rarotonga and Aitutaki, and also major stores and restaurants.
Credit & debit cards: American Express, Diners Club, MasterCard and Visa are all accepted. Check with your credit or debit card company for details of merchant acceptability and other services which may be available.
Travellers cheques: Accepted in hotels and some shops.
Currency restrictions: There are no restrictions on the import of either local or foreign currency. Local currency can be exported up to NZ$250. Foreign currency can be exported up to the amount imported and declared subject to bank authorisation.
Exchange rate indicators: The following figures are included as a guide to the movements of the New Zealand Dollar against Sterling and the US Dollar:

Date	Feb '04	May '04	Aug '04	Nov '04
£1.00=	2.72	2.89	2.76	2.64
$1.00=	1.49	1.62	1.50	1.39

Banking hours: Mon-Thur 0900-1500; Fri 0900-1600. Some banks are open Sat 0900-1100.

Duty Free

The following goods may be taken into the Cook Islands by travellers over the age of 18 without incurring customs duty:
200 cigarettes or 20 cigars or 250g of tobacco; 2l of spirits or wine or 4.5l of beer; goods up to the value of NZ$250.
Prohibited items: Fruit, meat and livestock (unless arriving from New Zealand); firearms, gunpowder, ammunition, cartridges and cartridge cases, unless prior permission is obtained from the Minister of Police; fireworks.

Public Holidays

2005: Jan 1-4 New Year. **Mar 25** Good Friday. **Mar 28** Easter Monday. **Apr 25** ANZAC Day. **Jun 6** Queen's Birthday. **Jul 25** Gospel Day (Rarotonga). **Aug 4** Constitution Day. **Oct 26** Gospel Day. **Dec 25** Christmas Day. **Dec 26** Boxing Day.
2006: Jan 1-2 New Year. **Apr 14** Good Friday. **Apr 17** Easter Monday. **Apr 25** ANZAC Day. **Jun 5** Queen's Birthday. **Jul 25** Gospel Day (Rarotonga). **Aug 4** Constitution Day. **Oct 26** Gospel Day. **Dec 25** Christmas Day. **Dec 26** Boxing Day.

Health

	Special Precautions?	Certificate Required?
Yellow Fever	No	No
Cholera	No	No
Typhoid & Polio	1	N/A
Malaria	No	N/A

Note: *Regulations and requirements may be subject to change at short notice, and you are advised to contact your doctor well in advance of your intended date of departure. Any numbers in the chart refer to the footnotes below.*

1: Typhoid immunisations should be up-to-date.
Food & drink: Tap water is relatively safe but may cause mild abdominal upsets. Bottled water is available and is advised for the first few weeks of the stay. Milk is pasteurised and dairy products are safe for consumption. Local meat, poultry, seafood, fruit and vegetables are generally considered safe to eat.
Other risks: *Hepatitis A* occurs in the region and *hepatitis B* is endemic. Inoculation against *Tetanus* is recommended. Bathers should be aware of the possible hazard caused by sharp *coral reefs*.
Health care: There is no direct reciprocal health agreement with the UK, but such an agreement exists with New Zealand, which may, in some circumstances, also apply to the Cook Islands; enquire at the Cook Islands Representative

(see *Contact Addresses* section). There is one government hospital (on Rarotonga).

Travel - International

AIR: The Cook Islands are served by *Air New Zealand (NZ)* (website: www.airnz.co.nz), which offers regular flights from New Zealand, Tahiti and Fiji. There are also frequent connections from Australia, North America and Europe. For details, contact the Cook Islands Tourist Bureau (see *Contact Addresses* section).

Air passes: *The Visit the South Pacific Pass* is valid for many airlines operating in the South Pacific, including most of the larger ones, such as *Air Caledonie, Air Marshall Islands, Air Nauru, Air Niugini, Air Pacific, Air Vanuatu, Polynesian Airlines, Qantas, Royal Tongan Airlines* and *Solomon Airlines*. Offering reductions of up to 40 per cent on normal airfares, this sector-based pass allows for flexible island-hopping between the destinations of the Cook Islands, Fiji, Nauru, New Caledonia, Samoa, Tahiti, Tonga, Vanuatu and the more remote Melanesian and Micronesian islands, together with major cities in Australia (Brisbane, Melbourne and Sydney) and New Zealand (Auckland, Christchurch and Wellington). It is only available for people resident outside of the South Pacific. The journey must be started outside the South Pacific and only one stopover in Australia is allowed. A minimum of two sectors must be bought before departure (extra sectors can be purchased enroute). There is a maximum of one pass per person, and passes must be used within six months of the first day of travel. Children pay 75 per cent of the adult fare and infants under two years of age pay 10 per cent of the adult fare. For details and conditions, contact the South Pacific Tourist Organisation (website: www.spto.org).

Approximate flight times: From Rarotonga to *London* is 24 hours (*Air New Zealand* flies via Los Angeles and Auckland).

International airports: *Rarotonga (RAR)* is 3km (2 miles) west of Avarua (travel time - 10 minutes). Hotel coaches meet each flight. Taxis and buses are also available. The airport facilities are open according to flight arrivals and departures and include 24 hour luggage storage facilities, duty-free shops, bank/bureau de change, bars, shops and car rental (*Avis* and *Budget*).

Departure tax: NZ$25 for passengers over 12 years of age; NZ$10 for passengers aged two to 12 years.

SEA: Cargo lines operating to the Cook Islands are run by *Express Cook Islands Line Shipping Ltd* and *Hawaii-Pacific Maritime Ltd.*

Travel - Internal

AIR: *Air Rarotonga (GZ)* (website: www.airraro.com) runs regular inter-island services to Aitutaki, Atiu, Mangaia, Mauke, Manihiki, Mitiaro and Penrhyn. Services do not operate on Sundays.

Inter-island flight times: From Rarotonga to *Aitutaki* is 50 minutes, to *Atiu* is 45 minutes, and to *Mauke* and *Mitiaro* is 50 minutes. The *Discover Cook Islands Pass* offers discount travel around the islands. For more information, contact the Cook Islands Tourism Corporation (see *Contact Addresses* section).

ROAD: Traffic drives on the left. There are two main roads that circle the island; the Ara Tapu sealed road that runs through villages and past beaches and the older inland road which winds through local farmlands. **Bus**: The 'Round the Island Bus' operates regular services around Rarotonga from Monday to Saturday. Buses are available from a number of hotels on the islands. **Taxi**: Available on Rarotonga. **Car hire**: Several companies offer cars for hire from a number of shops and hotels. Motor scooter and bicycle hire is also popular. **Documentation**: Drivers of all vehicles are required to have a current Cook Islands driver's licence, which costs NZ$10 and is obtainable from the Police Station in Avarua on presentation of an international or Commonwealth licence.

Accommodation

HOTELS: Accommodation of a high standard is increasing yearly. There are several resorts, hotels and a number of villas, motels, bungalows and self-catering apartments. Most are situated close to, if not on, a beach. Advance booking is essential, and it is probably wiser to book via an inclusive tour operator specialising in Pacific destinations. For more information on hotels, contact the Cook Islands Tourism Corporation (see *Contact Addresses* section).

CAMPING: This is not permitted.

Resorts & Excursions

The developed resorts are situated on **Rarotonga** and **Aitutaki**, and provide various amenities (see *Sport & Activities* section). The best swimming beaches are at **Muri Lagoon** and **Titikaveka**. A variety of tours are available, including lagoon cruises, inland trekking, historical tours, guided walking trips, sightseeing by air, and horse-drawn and motorised drives around the islands. A scenic drive into the **Takuvaine/Avatiu Valleys** offers a panorama of lush tropical scenery. **Papua (Wigmore's) Waterfall**, the only waterfall on the island, is located at **Vaimaanga**. The museum at **Takamoa** has excellent examples of Cook Islands handicrafts. The three-hour 'cultural village tour' offers the opportunity to enjoy demonstrations in weaving, coconut husking, fire making, carving and other Cook Islands traditions.

During the year, various festivals take place. These are generally celebrated with singing and dancing, often with a strange mixture of traditional ritual grafted on to the somewhat later Christian music and ceremony. The choirs of the Cook Islands are renowned. Places of historical interest include: the **Takamoa Mission House**, built in 1842, and believed to be the second-oldest building in the South Pacific; the old **Palace of Makea** at **Taputapuatea**; **Pa's Palace** in **Takitumu**, which is built of coral and lime; and **Arai-Te-Tonga** (*Marae*), consisting of stone structures which, in the islands' pre-European history, formed a *koutu*, or royal court, where the investiture of chiefs took place. This spot is still regarded as sacred.

Sport & Activities

Watersports: Scuba-diving and **snorkelling** are excellent in the clear waters of the islands' many lagoons. Visibility is seldom less than 30m (100ft) and the scenery is quite varied, with canyons, caves, 73 types of live coral and a rich marine life. A maximum of 10 persons can dive at any one site at any one time. There are four dive companies operating in Rarotonga and Aitutaki, usually offering two diving trips a day. Divers must have a recognised diving certificate. Some of the best dive sites include the *Matavera Drop-off*; the *Ngatangiia Swimthroughs* (particularly well known for its unusual and rare fish species); *Koromiri Coral Garden*; *Mataora Wreck* (purposely sunk in December 1990); *Papua Canyon* (known for its eagle ray population); and *Sand River*. **Whale watching** can also be practised in the Cook Islands: the humpback whale season is from July to October. In addition to observing the whales from a boat, it is possible to swim with them wearing a snorkel; for details, contact local operators. **Game fishing** excursions (usually five-hour trips) are available. Visitors can also watch flying fish being netted at night in outrigger canoes equipped with bright lights. Visitors are welcome at Rarotonga Sailing Club, where **sailing** races are held on Saturday afternoons from October to May. **Kayaking** tours in the lagoon are also available, as are **lagoon cruises** to the coral reefs in glass-bottomed boats or in a semi-submersible vessel.

Walking: The island of Rarotonga offers a wide range of walks for all ages and fitness levels. There are 13 marked trails, and guides should be hired for all routes leading into the inland area of Rarotonga. Details are available from hotels and other tourist establishments. The most popular trails include the **Cross Island Trek** (a four-and-a-half-hour trek through the centre of the island on paths known to be historical war paths of ancestral warriors); **Pa's Mountain Walk** (a four- to five-hour walk through the lush interior); **Te Kou Trek** (a five-hour trek with steep ascents and good views); and the **Ikurangi Trek** (a four-hour trek for experienced hikers only, also providing the opportunity for rock climbing around the top of the mountain). The **Takitumu Conservation Area Walk** also offers **birdwatching**. Guided **lagoon reef walks** are possible at low tide along Rarotonga's coral fringe.

Other: The Rarotonga Golf Club has a nine-hole **golf** course. In addition, lawn **bowls** has an enthusiastic following and is a long-established sport in Rarotonga. Two-and-a-half-hour **pony treks** to Wigmores Waterfall leave twice daily with a maximum of six people per trip (advance booking is recommended).

Social Profile

FOOD & DRINK: There are restaurants in hotels, and a variety of independent eating places as well, as a result of the increasing tourist trade. Local produce includes a wide variety of citrus and tropical fruits, island chestnuts and garden vegetables. Seafood features on many restaurant menus and so does coconut as the coconut palms produce an abundant supply of fruit all year round. Local meat and poultry are available. At larger resorts you can try the traditional Polynesian feast known as the '*Umukai*', which involves baking food in an underground oven and is usually accompanied with traditional entertainment by local people.

NIGHTLIFE: Island feast and dance groups feature at various hotels and details are available from local tourist information offices or hotel receptionists.

SHOPPING: Best buys are woodcarvings, pearls, shell craft, woven products, pottery, hats and baskets made out of coconut fibre. Coins and stamps are considered to be valuable collectors' items. Another popular buy is a brightly coloured, all-purpose wrap-around cloth garment worn by both men and women called a *Pareu*, and ideal for casual wear in the hot climate. *Island Craft* (website: www.islandcraft.com) has factories in Avarua where hand-carved items can be purchased. The art of carving may be observed in Punanganui Market Place. There is also a wide range of duty-free items. **Shopping hours**: Mon-Fri 0800-1600, Sat 0800-1200. Some stores near tourist areas remain open for longer.

SPECIAL EVENTS: The following is a selection of special events occurring in the Cook Islands in 2005; for a complete list, contact the Cook Islands Tourism Corporation (see *Contact Addresses*):

Feb *Cultural Festival Week*. **Mar-Jun** *Rugby Football Union*. **Apr** *Cooks Islands Dance Festival Week*; *Rarotonga Tin-Man Triathlon*. **May** *World Day Athletics*; *Athletics Vaka Challenge*. **Jun** *Cross Country Run*; *Olympic Day Fun Run*. **Jul** *National Cross Country Championship*; *Song Quest*. **Jul-Aug** *Constitution Celebrations* (with float parade, sporting events and inter-island competitions); *Te Maeva Celebrations* (national celebrations including Tangi Kaara (drumming) competitions). **Sep** *Westpac Bank Half Marathon*. **Oct** *Westpac Bank Round Rarotonga Road Race*; *Cook Islands Squash Tournament*; *Gospel Day* (open-air performances of biblical stories, commemorating the arrival of Christianity on the islands). **Oct-Nov** *Cook Islands Tivaevae Exhibition* (local quilting). **Nov** *Tiare Festival Week* (flower and floral competitions). **Dec 31** *New Year's Eve Celebrations*.

SOCIAL CONVENTIONS: Dress code is informal, though modest attire should be worn when visiting towns or villages. Women are expected to wear dresses for church services and social functions. **Tipping**: Tradition says that all gifts require something in return and tipping is therefore not practised.

Credit: © Tipani Tours

Business Profile

ECONOMY: Tourism is the principal industry. The islands are economically underdeveloped, largely due to their isolation, and depend on extensive aid from New Zealand. Fresh fruit is the islands' main export product. The Government is seeking to build up the islands' infrastructure as a precursor to further development.

BUSINESS: Tropical or lightweight suits are necessary.

Office hours: Mon-Fri 0800-1600.

COMMERCIAL INFORMATION: The following organisation can offer advice: Chamber of Commerce, PO Box 242, Rarotonga (tel: 20925; fax: 20969).

Climate

Weather can be quite changeable from day to day and varies throughout the islands. It is generally hot throughout the year, although the trade winds provide some moderating influence. Rainfall is heaviest in Rarotonga, while the northern atolls tend to be drier. The coolest months are June to August, while November to March marks the warmer season, which also has the highest rainfall.

Required clothing: Lightweight cottons and linens throughout the year. Warmer clothes are advised for the evenings. Rainwear is advised in the rainy season.

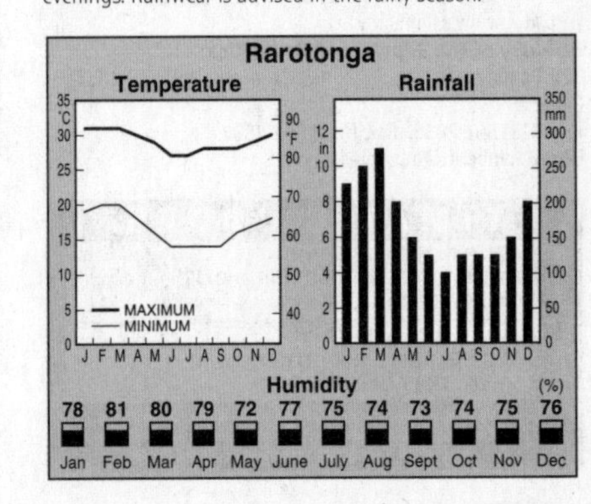

Costa Rica

LATEST TRAVEL ADVICE CONTACTS

British Foreign and Commonwealth Office
Tel: (0870) 606 0290 Website: www.fco.gov.uk
US Department of State
Website: http://travel.state.gov/travel
Canadian Department of Foreign Affairs and Int'l Trade
Tel: (1 800) 267 8376 Website: www.dfait-maeci.gc.ca

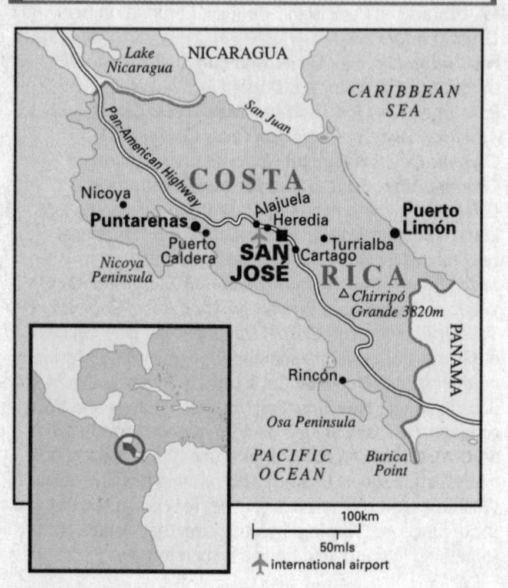

Location: Central America.

Country dialling code: 506.

Instituto Costarricense de Turismo (ICT)
Street address: Costado Este del Puente Juan Pablo II, Sobre Autopista General Cañas, San José, Costa Rica
Postal address: Apartado 777, 1000 San José, Costa Rica
Tel: 299 5800. Fax: 291 5648.
Website: www.visitcostarica.com
Cámara Nacional de Turismo (CANATUR)
Apartado 828, 1000 San José, Costa Rica
Tel: 234 6222. Fax: 253 8102.
E-mail: info@canatur.org
Website: www.costarica.tourism.co.cr
Embassy and Consulate of the Republic of Costa Rica
Flat 1, 14 Lancaster Gate, London W2 3LH, UK
Tel: (020) 7706 8844. Fax: (020) 7706 8655.
E-mail: costarica@btconnect.com *or* crconsulate@btconnect.com
Website: www.visitcostarica.com
Opening hours: Mon-Fri 1000-1500 (embassy); 1000-1300 (consulate).
British Embassy
Apartado 815-1007, 11th Floor, Edificio Centro Colón, San José, Costa Rica
Tel: 258 2025. Fax: 233 9938.
E-mail: britemb@racsa.co.cr
Website: www.britishembassycr.com
Embassy of the Republic of Costa Rica
2114 S Street, NW, Washington, DC 20008, USA
Tel: (202) 234 2945 *or* 328 6628 (consular enquiries).
Fax: (202) 265 4795.
E-mail: embassy@costarica-embassy.org
Website: www.costarica-embassy.org
Embassy of the United States of America
Street address: Calle 120, Avenida 0, Pavas, San José, Costa Rica
Postal address: PO Box 920-1200, San José, Costa Rica
Tel: 519 2000. Fax: 519 2305 (embassy) *or* 232 7944 (public affairs).
E-mail: info@usembassy.or.cr *or* consular@usembassy.or.cr
Website: www.usembassy.or.cr
Embassy of the Republic of Costa Rica
325 Dalhousie Street, Suite 407, Ottawa, Ontario K1N 7G2, Canada
Tel: (613) 562 2855. Fax: (613) 562 2582.
E-mail: embcrica@travel-net.com
Website: www.costaricaembassy.com
Consulates in: Montréal and Toronto.
Canadian Embassy
Street address: Oficentro Ejecutivo La Sabana, Tower Five, 3rd Floor, San José, Costa Rica
Postal address: Apartado Postal 351-1007, Centro Colón, San José, Costa Rica
Tel: 242 4400. Fax: 242 4410.
E-mail: sjcra@international.gc.ca
Website: www.dfait-maeci.gc.ca/sanjose

TIMATIC CODES

Health
AMADEUS: **TI-DFT/JIB/HE**
GALILEO/WORLDSPAN: **TI-DFT/JIB/HE**
SABRE: **TIDFT/JIB/HE**

Visa
AMADEUS: **TI-DFT/JIB/VI**
GALILEO/WORLDSPAN: **TI-DFT/JIB/VI**
SABRE: **TIDFT/JIB/VI**

To access TIMATIC country information on Health and Visa regulations through the Computer Reservations System (CRS), type in the appropriate command line listed above.

General Information

AREA: 51,100 sq km (19,730 sq miles).
POPULATION: 3,925,331 (2000).
POPULATION DENSITY: 79.2 per sq km.
CAPITAL: San José. **Population**: 328,293 (official estimate 2002).
GEOGRAPHY: Costa Rica, lying between Nicaragua and Panama, is a complete coast-to-coast segment of the Central American isthmus. Its width ranges from 119km to 282km (74 to 176 miles). A low thin line of hills, that rises between Lake Nicaragua and the Pacific Ocean in Nicaragua, broadens and rises as it enters northern Costa Rica, eventually forming the high, rugged, mountains of volcanic origin in the centre and south. The highest peak is Chirripó Grande, which reaches 3820m (12,530ft). More than half the population live on the Meseta Central, a plateau with an equitable climate. It is rimmed to the southwest by the Cordillera range, and provides the setting for the country's capital, San José. There are lowlands on both coastlines, mainly swampy on the Caribbean coast, with grassland savannah on the Pacific side merging into mangrove towards the south. Rivers cut through the mountains, flowing down to both the Caribbean and the Pacific.
GOVERNMENT: Republic. Gained independence from Spain in 1821. **Head of State and Government**: President Abel Pacheco de la Espriella since 2002.
LANGUAGE: Spanish is the official language. English is widely spoken. Some French, German and Italian are also spoken.
RELIGION: Almost entirely Christian, with Roman Catholic majority.
TIME: GMT - 6.
ELECTRICITY: 120 volts AC, 60Hz. Two-pin plugs are standard.
COMMUNICATIONS: Telephone: IDD is available. Country code: 506. Outgoing international code: 00. Telephone booths are available all over the country. **Mobile telephone:** GSM 1800/3G network is operated by *Instituto Costarricense de Electricidad (ICE)*. Handsets can be hired, although this can be difficult and time-consuming. **Fax:** Facilities are available in San José at the *Radiográfica Costarricense SA* (opening hours: 0700-2200). **Internet:** There are Internet cafes and some hotels also provide facilities. **Telegram:** Since the abolition of the inland telegram service in the UK, the Costa Rican Government Telegram Company will not accept telegrams destined for the UK. **Post:** Airmail letters to Western Europe usually take between six and 10 days. **Press:** Daily newspapers printed in Spanish include *Diario Extra, El Heraldo, La Nación, La Prensa Libre* and *La República*. One weekly paper is printed in English - *The Tico Times*.
Radio: BBC World Service (website: www.bbc.co.uk/worldservice) and Voice of America (website: www.voa.gov) can be received. From time to time the frequencies change and the most up-to-date can be found online.

Passport/Visa

	Passport Required?	Visa Required?	Return Ticket Required?
Full British	Yes	1	Yes
Australian	Yes	3	Yes
Canadian	Yes	2	Yes
USA	Yes	2	Yes
Other EU	Yes	2/3	Yes
Japanese	Yes	2	Yes

Note: Regulations and requirements may be subject to change at short notice, and you are advised to contact the appropriate diplomatic or consular authority before finalising travel arrangements. Details of these may be found at the head of this country's entry. Any numbers in the chart refer to the footnotes below.

PASSPORTS: Passport valid for at least six months at date of entry required by all.
VISAS: Required by all except the following:
(a) **1**. nationals of the UK and its dependencies for stays of up to 90 days;
(b) **2**. nationals of Argentina, Austria, Belgium, Brazil, Canada, Czech Republic, Denmark, Finland, France, Germany, Greece, Hungary, Israel, Italy, Japan, Korea (Rep), Liechtenstein, Luxembourg, Monaco, The Netherlands, Norway, Panama, Paraguay, Poland, Portugal, Puerto Rico, Romania, Spain, Sweden, Switzerland, Trinidad & Tobago, Uruguay and USA for a stay of up to 90 days;
(c) **3**. nationals of Antigua & Barbuda, Australia, Bahamas, Barbados, Belize, Bolivia, Bulgaria, Chile, Dominica, El Salvador, Estonia, Grenada, Guatemala, Guyana, Honduras, Iceland, Ireland, Jamaica, Kenya, Mexico, New Zealand, Philippines, Russian Federation, St Kitts & Nevis, St Lucia, St Vincent & The Grenadines, San Marino, Singapore, Slovak Republic, South Africa*, Surinam, Taiwan (China), Turkey, Vatican City and Venezuela for stays of up to 30 days;
(d) transit passengers continuing their journey to a third country by the same or first connecting flight within 12 hours, provided holding confirmed onward tickets and not leaving the airport (except nationals of China (PR) who *do* need a transit visa authorised by the Immigration Department in San José).
Note: (a) *Persons holding passports issued by the former homelands of Transkei and Venda *do* need a visa authorised by the Immigration Department in San José. (b) Nationals of countries listed above must obtain an exit visa from the Immigration Department in San José at least three weeks before leaving Costa Rica. Those who stay for less than 30 days are exempt if in possession of a disembarkation card. (c) All other nationals require a visa. In some cases, an authorisation from the Immigration Department in San José is also necessary and visitors should consult the Consulate for an up-to-date list. Temporary visitors must hold return or onward tickets, except those holding a visa showing an exit ticket is not required.
Types of visa and cost: *Tourist*. Visas cost approximately £15. All passengers requiring a visa must hold documents required for the next destination.
Validity: Visas are valid for 30 or 90 days depending on nationality. Contact the Immigration Department in Costa Rica for renewal or information on the extension procedure.
Application to: Consulate (or Consular section of Embassy; see *Contact Addresses* section). Applications should be made in person.
Application requirements: (a) Completed application form. (b) Two passport-size photos. (c) Passport valid for six months at time of entry. (d) Proof of sufficient funds to cover duration of stay. (e) Return or onward ticket.
Working days required: One to two, depending on nationality of applicant. Some visas need the authorisation of the Immigration Department in Costa Rica (ask the Consulate or Consular section of Embassy for details) and may take up to three weeks.
Temporary residence: Apply to the Consulate or Consular section of Embassy.

Money

Currency: Costa Rican Colón (c) = 100 céntimos. Notes are in denominations of c10,000, c5000, c2000, 1000 and 500. Coins are in denominations of c100, 50, 25, 20, 10 and 5. US Dollars are also widely accepted.
Currency exchange: Visitors should consult their banks for the current rate of exchange (there is no direct local quotation for sterling; the cross rate with the US Dollar is used). ATMs are available throughout the country.
Credit & debit cards: Diners Club, MasterCard and Visa are all accepted; American Express slightly less so, but check with your credit or debit card company for details of merchant acceptability and other services which may be available.
Travellers cheques: To avoid additional exchange rate charges, travellers are advised to take travellers cheques in US Dollars.
Currency restrictions: There are no restrictions on the import and export of either local or foreign currency (but only US Dollars are exchangeable).
Exchange rate indicators: The following figures are included as a guide to the movements of the Costa Rican Colón against Sterling and the US Dollar:

Date	Feb '04	May '04	Aug '04	Nov '04
£1.00=	767.80	771.40	815.38	861.56
$1.00=	421.81	431.89	442.58	454.96

Banking hours: Mon-Fri 08000900-1500/1700.

Duty Free

The following goods may be imported into Costa Rica without incurring customs duty:
400 cigarettes or 50 cigars or 500g tobacco; 3l of alcoholic beverages (people aged over 18 only); a reasonable quantity of perfume for personal use.

Public Holidays

2005: Jan 1 New Year's Day. **Mar 19** Feast of San José (San José only). **Mar 24-27** Easter. **Apr 11** Anniversary of the

Battle of Rivas. **May 1** Labour Day. **May 26** Corpus Christi. **Jun 29** Saint Peter and Saint Paul. **Jul 25** Guanacaste Annexation. **Aug 2** Virgin of Los Angeles, Feast of Patroness of Costa Rica. **Aug 15** Mothers' Day and Assumption. **Sep 15** Independence Day. **Oct 12** Dia de la Raza (Columbus Day). **Dec 8** Immaculate Conception. **Dec 24** Christmas Eve. **Dec 25** Christmas Day. **Dec 31** New Year's Eve.
2006: Jan 1 New Year's Day. **Mar 19** Feast of San José (San José only). **Apr 11** Anniversary of the Battle of Rivas. **Apr 14-17** Easter. **May 1** Labour Day. **Jun 15** Corpus Christi. **Jun 29** Saint Peter and Saint Paul. **Jul 25** Guanacaste Annexation. **Aug 2** Virgin of Los Angeles, Feast of Patroness of Costa Rica. **Aug 15** Mothers' Day and Assumption. **Sep 15** Independence Day. **Oct 12** Dia de la Raza (Columbus Day). **Dec 8** Immaculate Conception. **Dec 24** Christmas Eve. **Dec 25** Christmas Day. **Dec 31** New Year's Eve.
Note: Most businesses close for the whole of Holy Week and between Christmas and New Year.

Health

	Special Precautions?	Certificate Required?
Yellow Fever	No	No
Cholera	1	No
Typhoid & Polio	2	N/A
Malaria	3	N/A

Note: *Regulations and requirements may be subject to change at short notice, and you are advised to contact your doctor well in advance of your intended date of departure. Any numbers in the chart refer to the footnotes below.*

1: Following WHO guidelines issued in 1973, a cholera vaccination certificate is no longer a condition of entry into Costa Rica. However, cases of cholera were reported in 1996 and precautions should be considered. Up-to-date advice should be sought before deciding whether these precautions should include vaccination as medical opinion is divided over its effectiveness; consult the *Health* appendix for further information.
2: Typhoid is very common throughout the area.
3: Malaria risk exists throughout the year, mostly in the benign *vivax* form, in the rural areas below 700m, especially in the cantons of Matina, Los Chiles (Alajuela province) and Talamanca (Limón province). Lower transmission risk exists in 20 cantons in the provinces of Guanacaste, Alajuela and Heredia. There is negligible or no risk of malaria in the other cantons of the country.
Food & drink: Mains water is normally heavily chlorinated and, whilst relatively safe, may cause mild abdominal upsets. Drinking water outside main cities and towns may be contaminated and sterilisation is advisable. Bottled water is available and is advised for the first few weeks of the stay. Milk is pasteurised and dairy products are safe for consumption. Local meat, poultry, seafood, fruit and vegetables are generally considered safe to eat.
Other risks: *Hepatitis A, B* and *C* occur. *Paragonimiasis* (oriental lung fluke) and *lymphatic* and *bancroftian filiariasis* have been reported in Costa Rica. *Dengue fever* occurs. *Cutaneous* and *mucocutaneous leishmaniasis* have also been reported.
Rabies is widespread throughout Central America. For those at high risk, vaccination before arrival should be considered. If you are bitten, seek medical advice without delay. For more information, consult the *Health* appendix.
Health care: Health insurance is recommended. Reliable medical services are available in Costa Rica. Standards of health and hygiene are among the best in Latin America.

Travel - International

AIR: The Costa Rican national airline is *Taca International Airlines (TA)* (website: www.taca.com) (an amalgamation of the airlines Aviateca, Lacsa, Nica and Taca). *Taca International* flies direct to Costa Rica from Miami, New Orleans, Los Angeles, New York, Mexico and other destinations in Central and South America. The *Visit Central America Pass* is available from *Grupo Taca* and is an economical way to travel to Costa Rica from the USA and from Costa Rica to other Central American countries. Other airlines include *American Airlines, British Airways, Continental, Delta* and *KLM*.
Approximate flight times: From San José to *London* is 12 hours (including stopover time), to *Los Angeles* is 11 hours and to *New York* is seven hours.
International airports: *Juan Santamaría (SJO)* is 17km (11 miles) northwest of the city. Coaches depart every 20 minutes (0500-2400); return pickups stop at various hotels. Buses depart to the city every 15 minutes (travel time - 20 minutes). Some hotels have shuttle services to the airport; these are 24 hours and free of charge. Taxis are also available to the city (travel time - 15 minutes). The airport in Liberia has been upgraded and may be used for some international flights.
Departure tax: US$26 (or the equivalent in Costa Rican Colon) payable if staying more than 24 hours.
SEA: Cruise lines calling at Costa Rican ports include *Carnival, Celebrity, Costa, Crystal, Cunard, Delphin, Hapag, Holland America, Mediterranean Shipping, NCL, Princess, Radisson, Regal, Royal Caribbean, Royal Olympic, Seabourn, Silversea, Sun* and *Wind Star*. The port of Puntarenas has been redeveloped recently.
ROAD: The Inter-American Highway runs through Costa Rica from La Cruz on the Nicaraguan border through San José to Progreso on the Panamanian border.

Travel - Internal

AIR: *SANSA* (website: www.flysansa.com), a national airline, operates services between San José and provincial towns and villages. A bus is provided from the airline offices in San José to the airport. A number of smaller airlines also provide internal flights, such as *Nature Air*.
ROAD: The standard of the roads is generally very good. There are 35,583km (22,110 miles) of all-weather highways including 663km (412 miles) of the Inter-American Highway and highways linking San José with the other principal towns. Traffic drives on the right. **Bus**: Regular services to most towns, but buses are often crowded so pre-booking is advisable. Costa Rica offers a wide variety of sightseeing tours. Most tour companies feature bilingual guides and round-trip transportation from hotels. For full details, contact the Instituto Costarricense de Turismo (see *Contact Addresses* section). **Taxi**: Numerous and inexpensive in San José. The taxis are coloured red (except those serving the Juan Santamaría International Airport, which are orange). Taxis are usually metered. **Car hire**: Major car hire companies as well as local firms have offices in San José. Distances are measured in kilometres. A speed limit of 88kph (55mph) is enforced on most highways.
Documentation: Drivers must have a national licence or International Driving Permit.
URBAN: San José has privately run bus services, charging fares on a two-zone system.
Travel times: The following chart gives approximate travel times (in hours and minutes) from **San José** to other major cities/towns.

	Air	Road
Alajuela	-	0.30
Cartago	-	0.30
Heredia	-	0.20
Puntarenas	-	2.00
Liberia	0.25	3.00
Quepos	0.30	3.30
Puerto Limón	0.25	3.00

Accommodation

HOTELS: There is a good range of reasonably priced hotel accommodation. Most proprietors speak English. San José has many hotels, from the extravagant to the smaller, family-run hotels in the less fashionable districts. There are several good hotels out of town near the airport. Larger hotels have swimming pools and other sports facilities. The majority have their own restaurants which are generally good and reasonably priced. Hotel tariffs are liable to alteration at any time. A 3 per cent sales tax plus 3 per cent tourism tax is added to hotel prices. Outside the capital, charges and the standard of comfort are lower. **Grading**: Hotels are graded from **A** to **D** according to price range. The A-grade category accounts for 20 per cent of all hotels and costs from the equivalent of US$100. About 20 per cent of hotels are in the B-range and cost US$50-70. C-grade hotels cost US$30-50 and D-range hotels, about 30 per cent, cost US$10-30. For further information check with the Costa Rica Chamber of Hotels online (website: www.costaricanhotels.com).
CAMPING/CARAVANNING: Facilities exist at San Antonio de Belén, 8km (5 miles) from San José. There is also a camping and caravan site close to Alajuela. Most, but not all, national parks allow camping at designated sites (see *Resorts & Excursions* section).

Resorts & Excursions

Costa Rica is the Central American state forming the land-bridge between North and South America and it has a surprising diversity of terrain (see *General* section). In the cities and towns, the country's Spanish heritage provides the main features of interest. Elsewhere, Costa Rica's national parks are its greatest glory.

SAN JOSÉ: The capital was founded in 1737 and is a pleasant mixture of traditional and modern Spanish architecture. Places of interest include the **Teatro Nacional**, the **Palacio Nacional** (where the legislative assembly meets), and the **Parque Central**, east of which is

Credit: © Costa Rica Tourist Board

the Cathedral. The **National Museum** and the **Museum of Gold** are also worth a visit. There are numerous other parks in the city, including the **Parque Nacional**, the **Parque Bolivar** and the **Parque Morazán**.
Excursions: San José is a good centre for excursions into the beautiful **Meseta Central** region. The nearby town of **Cartago** was founded in 1563, but there are no old buildings as earthquakes destroyed the town in 1841 and 1910. However, some of the reconstruction was in the colonial style. Excursions can be made from here to the crater of **Irazú** and to the beautiful valley of **Orosi**, with its colonial church.

CARIBBEAN COAST: There are numerous beaches, ports and towns worth visiting. The biggest is **Puerto Limón**; others include **Guapiles**, **Tortuguero**, **Barra del Colorado**, **Cahuita** and **Puerto Viejo**.

PACIFIC COAST: Costa Rica's principal Pacific port for freight is **Puntarenas**. The beaches around it are rather poor, although **San Lucas Island**, just off the port, has magnificent beaches. Another island worth a visit is **Isla del Coco** where a great hoard of treasure is supposed to have been buried by pirates. **Puerto Caldera**, a few miles south of Puntarenas, has recently become the country's premier port of call for cruise liners. **Quepos**, **Nicoya**, **Liberia** and **Samara** are the region's other major towns. There are beautiful beaches in the **Guanacaste** area, near Quepos in the Central Pacific and near **Golfito** in the South.

Credit: © Costa Rica Tourist Board

NATIONAL PARKS
Well-kept and well-guarded national parks and nature reserves cover nearly 26 per cent of the country's territory. Information and permits can be obtained from: Fundación de Parques Nacionales, 300 Metros Norte, 175 Metros Este, Iglesia Santa Teresita, San José (tel: 257 2239; fax: 222 4732; e-mail: fpn_cr@racsa.co.cr; website: www.fpncostarica.org). In addition to the following, **Manuel Antonio National Park** and the **Barra del Colorado National Wildlife Refuge** are worth a visit, and many of the tiny islands in the **Gulf of Nicoya**, near Puntarenas, are 'biological protection areas'.
Braulio Carrillo National Park: Located in the central region of the country just 23km (14 miles) north of San José. It has five kinds of forest, some with characteristic rainforest vegetation. Orchids and ferns, jaguars, ocelots and the Baird tapir may be seen here. There are trails through the park and many lookouts.
Poás Volcano National Park: As the name suggests, this

park contains the smouldering **Poás Volcano**. It contains the only dwarf cloudforest in Costa Rica. The crater of the volcano is 1.5km (1-mile) wide and contains a hot-water lake which changes colour from turquoise to green to grey. Access is possible by road.
Tortuguero National Park: This park protects the Atlantic green turtle egg-laying grounds; it is in an area of great ecological diversity. Its network of canals and lagoons serves as waterways for transportation and exploration. There are camping facilities and lodges.
Santa Rosa National Park: The last large stand of tropical dry forest in Central America can be found here. There are 10 habitats including extensive savannahs and deciduous and non-deciduous forests. In addition to its abundant wildlife, recreational facilities are provided on some of the beaches.
Corcovado National Park: The virgin rainforest in this park contains many endangered species. It has the largest tree in Costa Rica, a ceibo which is 70m (230ft) high. Additionally there is **Cano Island Biological Reserve**, a bird sanctuary.
Cahuita National Park: This park protects the only coral reef on Costa Rica's Carribbean coastline. Its other attractions include howler and white-faced monkeys, racoons and 500 species of fish.
Chirripó National Park: The centrepiece here is Costa Rica's highest mountain. Most notably the park is home to the quetzal, said to be Latin America's most beautiful bird.

Credit: © Costa Rica Tourist Board

Sport & Activities

Ecotourism: Partly in order to continue to encourage ecotourism, the Costa Rican authorities have set aside a large proportion of the country (around 26 per cent of the total land area) as national parks and protected areas. There is good road access to most of these areas, and public transport is available. Nature trails and tracks are well developed. The country has a stunning variety of landscapes, micro-climates, flora and fauna, and nature lovers will not be disappointed. The highland area in the centre consists of four mountain ranges. Some of the country's great attractions are its eight **active volcanoes**. The sight of *Arenal*, in the Sierra Volcánica Guanacaste in the northwest, erupting at night is truly spectacular. In the foothills of *Rincón de la Vieja*, the mud pools bubble permanently. It is possible to bathe in the hot springs in this area. The central highlands are the most accessible for the visitor, and feature *Poás*, whose crater contains a boiling sulphurous lake, and *Irazú*, its desolate landscape resembling the surface of the moon. The country's tallest peaks are in the non-volcanic Cordillera de Talamanca near Panama, and include the impressive *Chirripó* (12,533ft/3828m). The upper slopes of the mountains are often covered by **cloudforest**, characterised by the algae, mosses and lichens on the permanently wet surfaces. Numerous orchids and ferns grow here, but the forests' most notable inhabitant is the Resplendent Quetzal (a bird). Lower down is the **rainforest**. Best visited in the company of an experienced guide (in part, because it is so easy to get lost), these forests are filled with elusive **wildlife**. Among the creatures they harbour are monkeys, armadillos, sloths, crocodiles, and birds such as toucans, parrots and macaws. Sea turtles can be observed in the *Tortuguero* region at certain times of the year. Depending on what the visitor wants to see, it is best to visit in the dry season (from December to April). For further information, see the *Climate* section.
Watersports: The most popular adventure sport is **white-water rafting**. Outfitters and guides can arrange trips. The *Reventazón River* (class III) is suitable for beginners, while more experienced rafters can tackle the Pacuare (class IV) and the *Pascua* (class V) rivers. The best times to go are from May to November. *Lake Arenal* was recently voted one of the world's top **windsurfing** spots. Situated at 5580ft (1700m) above sea level, the lake offers its best windsurfing between April and December. *Puerto Soley* on the northern Pacific coast offers good **ocean windsurfing**. **Kayaking** and **ocean kayaking** are gaining in popularity. **Surfing** is possible at many beaches, being especially popular at *Pavones* on the Pacific coast and at *Playa Naranjo* in the northwest. This part of the country also offers excellent **diving** and **snorkelling**, with more than 20 local dive sites.

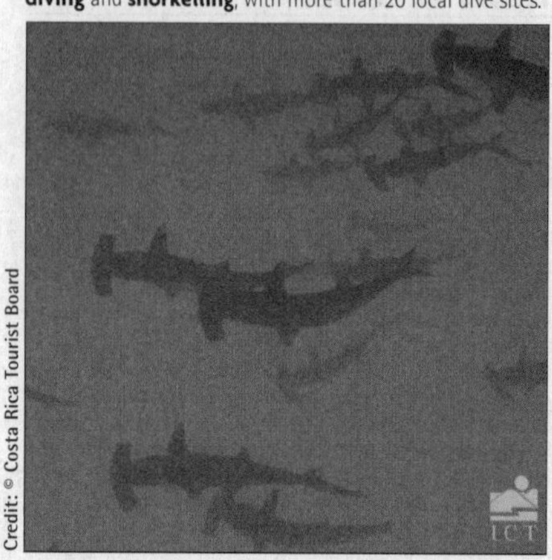

Credit: © Costa Rica Tourist Board

Tuition and equipment hire are widely available. *Cocos Island*, praised by Jacques Cousteau, and *Caño Island* off the southwest coast, are also good diving areas.
Fishing: The Pacific coast, from the Gulf of Papagayo to Golfito offers excellent **sport fishing**. Sailfish, marlin, tuna and wahoo are among the catches. The *Tortuguero Canals* and the area around *Barra del Colorado* offer good **freshwater game fishing**, while trout can be caught in the country's mountain streams.
Other activities: Mountain biking can be done on the trails in the forests and national parks. Hotels have equipment for hire and some specialist operators organise trips. **Horseriding** is also easily arranged. Because a different type of saddle and stirrups are used, even experienced riders may need to take some time to get used to their mounts. Beginners should arrange to have tuition beforehand, as working ranch horses are often used on rides. **Canopy touring** is becoming popular as well; it entails being attached to a harness and 'flying' through the jungle canopy via a series of cables. **Bungee jumping** and **ballooning** are also available.

Social Profile

FOOD & DRINK: Restaurants in towns and cities serve a variety of foods including Chinese, French, Italian, Mexican and North American. Food is satisfactory, from the most expensive to the cheapest eating places (which are generally found west of the city centre). Food *sodas* (small restaurants) serve local food. Common dishes include *casado* (rice, beans, stewed beef, fried plantain, salad and cabbage), *olla de carne* (soup of beef, plantain, corn, yuca, nampi and chayote), *sopa negra* (black beans with a poached egg) and *picadillo* (meat and vegetable stew). Snacks are popular and include *gallos* (filled tortillas), *tortas* (containing meat and vegetables), *arreglados* (bread filled with same) and *pan de yuca* (speciality from stalls in San José).
There are many types of cold drink made from fresh fruit, milk or cereal flour, for example, *cebada* (barley flour), *pinolillo* (roasted corn) and *horchata* (corn meal with cinnamon). Imported alcoholic and soft drinks are widely available. Coffee is good value and has an excellent flavour.
NIGHTLIFE: San José especially has many nightclubs, venues with folk music and dance, theatres and cinemas.
SHOPPING: Special purchases include wood and leather rocking chairs (which dismantle for export), as well as a range of local crafts available in major cities and towns. Local markets are also well worth visiting. Prices are slightly higher than in other Latin American countries. Best buys are wooden items, ceramics, jewellery and leather handicrafts.
Shopping hours: Mon-Sat 0900-1800/1900. There may be variations between areas.
SPECIAL EVENTS: For a complete list of special events for 2005, contact the Instituto Costarricense de Turismo (see *Contact Addresses* section). The following is a selection of special events celebrated annually in Costa Rica:
Dec-Jan *Fiestas del Fin del Año* (week-long festivities). **Jan** *International Tennis Tournament*, San José; *Festival of Alajuetila*. **Feb-Mar** *Orchid Show*, Cartago. **Mar** *Día del Boyero* (Day of the Oxcart Driver), San Antonio de Escazú; *National Craft Fair*, San José; *South Carribean Music Festival*, Puerto Viejo. **Mar 19** *San José Day*. **Apr 11** *Juan Santa María's Day*. **Jun 29** *Feast of St Peter and St Paul*. **Aug** *Arrival of Pilgrims*, Cartago. **Aug 2** *Virgin of Los Angeles Day*. **Oct** *Carnival Week*, Puerto Limón.
SOCIAL CONVENTIONS: Handshaking is common and forms of address are important. Christian names are preceded by *Don* for a man and *Doña* for a woman. Normal courtesies should be observed when visiting someone's home and gifts are appreciated as a token of thanks, especially if invited for a meal. For most occasions casual wear is acceptable, but beachwear should be confined to the beach. **Tipping**: It is not necessary to tip taxi drivers. All hotels add 10 per cent service tax plus 3 per cent tourist tax to the bill by law. Restaurants add a 10 per cent service charge. Tipping is expected by hotel staff, porters and waiters.

Business Profile

ECONOMY: About half of Costa Rica's export earnings are derived from agriculture (coffee, bananas, meat, sugar and cocoa). Staple crops are also grown for domestic consumption. Manufacturing industry consists of food-processing, textiles, chemicals and plastics and is steadily expanding with government encouragement. New industries include aluminium production, following the discovery of a large bauxite deposit; and a rapid move into the computer industry, as a result of which, microprocessors have become a valuable export. Oil and hydroelectricity meet the bulk of the country's energy needs. Tourism dominates the service sector and is the most important source of foreign exchange earnings. The economy is nearly static at present with annual growth under one per cent. Costa Rica receives some international aid through international bodies such as the IMF, the Inter-American Development Bank (IDB) and from the USA, which is Costa Rica's main trading partner. Costa Rica is also a member of the Central American Common Market.
BUSINESS: Customs tend to be conservative. Advance appointments, courtesy and punctuality are appreciated. It is preferable to have some knowledge of Spanish, although many locals speak English. Best months for business visits are November and December; avoid the last week of September, which is the end of the financial year.
Government office hours: Mon-Fri 0800-1600.
COMMERCIAL INFORMATION: The following organisations can offer advice: Cámara de Comercio de Costa Rica (Chamber of Commerce), Apartado 1114-1000, 1000 San José (tel: 221 0005; fax: 223 157; e-mail: servicio@camara-comercio.com; website: www.camara-comercio.com); *or* Cámara de Industrias de Costa Rica (Chamber of Industries), 350 metros sur de la Fuente de la Hispanidad, San Pedro de Montes de Oca, Apartado 10003, San José (tel: 281 0006; fax: 234 6163; e-mail: cicr@cicr.com; website: www.cicr.com); *or* Costa Rican-American Chamber of Commerce, Apartado 4946-1000, San José (tel: 220 2200; fax: 220 2300; e-mail: chamber@amcham.co.cr; website: www.amcham.co.cr); *or* Promotora de Comercio Exterior de Costa Rica (PROCOMER), Apartado 1278-1007, San José (tel: 256 7111; fax: 233 4655; e-mail: info@procomer.com; website: www.procomer.com).

Climate

In the Central Valley, where the main centres of population are located, the average temperature is 22°C (72°F). In the coastal areas, the temperature is much hotter. The rainy season starts in May and finishes in November. The 'warm' dry season is December to May, though temperature differences between summer and winter are slight.
Required clothing: Lightweight cottons and linens most of the year, warmer clothes for cooler evenings. Waterproofing is necessary during the rainy season.

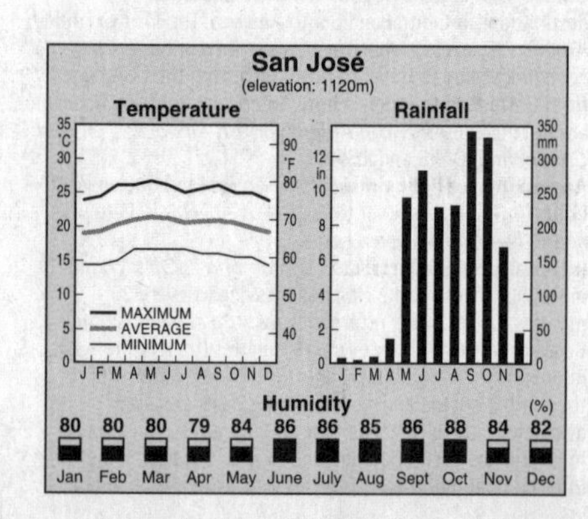

Côte d'Ivoire

LATEST TRAVEL ADVICE CONTACTS

British Foreign and Commonwealth Office
Tel: (0870) 606 0290 Website: www.fco.gov.uk

US Department of State
Website: http://travel.state.gov/travel

Canadian Department of Foreign Affairs and Int'l Trade
Tel: (1 800) 267 8376 Website: www.dfait-maeci.gc.ca

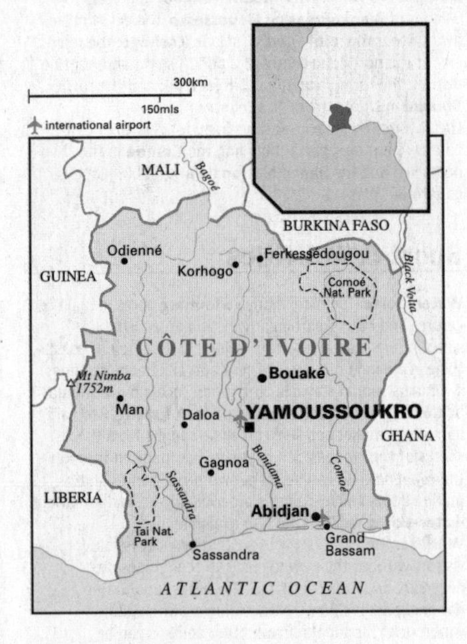

Location: West African coast.
Country dialling code: 225.
Office Ivoirien du Tourisme et de l'Hôtellerie
2nd Floor, ex-EECI Building, place de la République, Abidjan 01 BP 8538, Côte d'Ivoire
Tel: 2025 1600. Fax: 2032 0388.
E-mail: oith@tourismeci.org
Website: www.tourismeci.org
Embassy of the Republic of Côte d'Ivoire
2 Upper Belgrave St, London SW1X 8BJ, UK
Tel: (020) 7201 9601. Fax: (020) 7462 0087.
Opening hours: Mon-Fri 0930-1300 and 1400-1730.
British Embassy
Street address: Immeuble 'Bank of Africa', 3rd to 4th Floors, angle Avenue Terrasson de Fougeres et Rue Gourgas, Abidjan-Plateau, Abidjan, Côte d'Ivoire
Postal address: 01 BP 2581, Abidjan 01, Côte d'Ivoire
Tel: 2030 0800 *or* 0824 (visa section). Fax: 2030 0834 or 0828 (visa section).
E-mail: britemb@aviso.ci
Embassy of the Republic of Côte d'Ivoire
2424 Massachusetts Avenue NW, Washington DC 20008, USA
Tel: (202) 797 0300. Fax: (202) 244 3088.
Also deals with tourism enquiries.
Embassy of the United States of America
Street address: 5 rue Jesse Owens, Abidjan 01, Côte d'Ivoire
Postal address: 01 BP 1712, Abidjan 01, Côte d'Ivoire
Tel: 2021 0979. Fax: 2022 3259.
E-mail: abidjancons@state.gov (consular section).
Website: http://abidjan.usembassy.gov
Embassy of the Republic of Côte d'Ivoire
9 Marlborough Avenue, Ottawa, Ontario K1N 8E6, Canada
Tel: (613) 236 9919. Fax: (613) 563 8287.
E-mail: embaci@ican.net
Consulates in: Montréal, Toronto and Vancouver.
Canadian Embassy
Street address: Immeuble Trade Centre Building, 6th and 7th floors, 23 avenue Noguès, Plateau, Abidjan 01, Côte d'Ivoire
Postal address: 01 BP 4104, Abidjan 01, Côte d'Ivoire
Tel: 2030 0700. Fax: 2030 0725.
E-mail: abdjn@dfait-maeci.gc.ca
Website: www.dfait-maeci.gc.ca/abidjan

TIMATIC CODES

Health	AMADEUS: **TI-DFT/JIB/HE** GALILEO/WORLDSPAN: **TI-DFT/JIB/HE** SABRE: **TIDFT/JIB/HE**
Visa	AMADEUS: **TI-DFT/JIB/VI** GALILEO/WORLDSPAN: **TI-DFT/JIB/VI** SABRE: **TIDFT/JIB/VI**

To access TIMATIC country information on Health and Visa regulations through the Computer Reservations System (CRS), type in the appropriate command line listed above.

General Information

AREA: 322,462 sq km (124,503 sq miles).
POPULATION: 16,365,000 (UN estimate 2002).
POPULATION DENSITY: 50.8 per sq km.
CAPITAL: Yamoussoukro (administrative and political capital since 1983). **Population**: 299,243 (1998). Abidjan (former capital). **Population**: 2,877,948 (1998).
GEOGRAPHY: Côte d'Ivoire shares borders with Liberia, Guinea, Mali, Burkina Faso and Ghana. There are 600km (370 miles) of coast on the Gulf of Guinea (Atlantic Ocean). The southern and western parts of the country are forested, with undulating countryside rising to meet the savannah plains of the north and the mountainous western border. Three rivers, the Sassandra, the Bandama and the Comoé, run directly north-south and, on their approach to the coast, flow into a series of lagoons. Birdlife is plentiful throughout the country, but particularly so near the coast.
GOVERNMENT: Republic. Gained independence from France in 1960. In 1999, the army took power and installed a National Council for Public Salvation. **Head of State**: President Laurent Gbagbo since 2000. **Head of Government**: Prime Minister Seydou Diarra since 2003.
LANGUAGE: The official language is French. The main African languages are Yacouba, Senoufo, Baoulé, Betie, Attie, Agni and Dioula (the market language).
RELIGION: 34 per cent Christian, 27 per cent Muslim, 15 per cent traditional beliefs. It is important to note, however, that these percentages are based on census results in 1998, of which some Muslim foreign workers may have been excluded - therefore, the Muslim percentage may be higher than is indicated here.
TIME: GMT.
ELECTRICITY: 220 volts AC, 50Hz. Round two-pin plugs are standard.
COMMUNICATIONS: International telecommunications are available in major towns/centres.**Telephone:** IDD is available. Country code: 225. Outgoing international code: 00. **Mobile telephone:** GSM 900 network. Network operators include *Loteny Telecom* (website: www.telecel.net) and *Orange Côte D'Ivoire* (website: www.orange.ci). **Internet:** ISPs include *Aviso*, *Africa On Line* and *Globeaccess*. Public access is available at Internet cafes in Abidjan. **Fax:** Facilities are available at some major hotels, but are not yet widespread. **Post:** Airmail to Europe takes up to two weeks. Post office opening hours: Mon-Fri 0730-1200 and 1430-1800. **Press:** All newspapers are in French. The main dailies include *Fraternité Matin*, *L'Inter*, *Le Jour*, *Le National*, *Notre Voie*, *Le Patriote* and *Soir Info*.
Radio: BBC World Service (website: www.bbc.co.uk/worldservice) and Voice of America (website: www.voa.gov) can be received. From time to time the frequencies change and the most up-to-date can be found online.

Passport/Visa

	Passport Required?	Visa Required?	Return Ticket Required?
Full British	Yes	Yes	Yes
Australian	Yes	Yes	Yes
Canadian	Yes	Yes	Yes
USA	Yes	Yes/1	Yes
Other EU	Yes	Yes	Yes
Japanese	Yes	Yes	Yes

Note: Regulations and requirements may be subject to change at short notice, and you are advised to contact the appropriate diplomatic or consular authority before finalising travel arrangements. Details of these may be found at the head of this country's entry. Any numbers in the chart refer to the footnotes below.

PASSPORTS: Passports valid for six months after intended length of stay required by all except nationals of Benin, Burkina Faso, Mali, Mauritania, Niger, Senegal and Togo holding national ID cards.
VISAS: Required by all except the following:
(a) nationals of other ECOWAS countries for stays of up to three months;
(b) **1.** nationals of Central African Republic, Chad, Congo (Rep), Morocco, Seychelles, Tunisia and the USA for stays of up to three months;
(c) transit passengers leaving on the same or first connecting flight within, 12 hours, provided holding onward or return documentation and not leaving the airport.
Types of visa and cost: Prices vary according to nationality. Prices given are for UK nationals. *Tourist*, *Business* and *Transit*: £35 (single-entry); £45 (multiple-entry).
Validity: Three months.
Application to: Consulate (or Consular section at Embassy); see *Contact Addresses* section.
Application requirements: *Tourism*: (a) Valid passport. (b) One application form. (c) One passport-size photo. (d) Evidence of hotel booking or faxed letter of invitation from a Côte d'Ivoire resident. (e) Return ticket or travel itinerary. (f) Stamped, self-addressed, registered envelope for return of passport (if applying by post). (g) Fee.
Business: (a)-(g) and, (h) Fax from home company confirming financial responsibility for the applicant and an invitation letter faxed from Côte d'Ivoire.
Note: A yellow fever vaccination certificate is required for all travellers over one year of age.
Working days required: 48 hours, although it may take longer, depending on nationality.

Money

Currency: CFA (*Communauté Financiaire Africaine*) Franc (CFAfr) = 100 centimes. Notes are in denominations of CFAfr10,000, 5000, 2000, 1000 and 500. Coins are in denominations of CFAfr250, 100, 50, 25, 10, 5 and 1. Côte d'Ivoire is part of the French Monetary Area. Only currency issued by the *Banque des États de l'Afrique de l'Ouest* (Bank of West African States) is valid; currency issued by the *Banque des États de l'Afrique Centrale* (Bank of Central African States) is not. The CFA Franc is tied to the Euro.
Currency exchange: Currency can be exchanged at the airport as well as at main banks and hotels.
Credit & debit cards: American Express and MasterCard are widely accepted; Diners Club and Visa have more limited use. Check with your credit or debit card company for details of merchant acceptability and other facilities which may be available.
Travellers cheques: These are accepted in hotels, restaurants and some shops.
Currency restrictions: The import of local currency is unlimited. The export of local currency is limited to amounts up to the value of CFAfr10,000. The import of all foreign currency other than Euros must be declared. The export of foreign currency is limited to amounts up to the equivalent of CFAfr25,000 or the amount imported and declared on arrival. There is no restriction on the re-export of unused travellers cheques and letters of credit.
Exchange rate indicators: The following figures are included as a guide to the movements of the CFA Franc against Sterling and the US Dollar:

Date	Feb '04	May '04	Aug '04	Nov '04
£1.00=	961.13	983.76	978.35	936.79
$1.00=	528.01	550.79	531.03	494.69

Banking hours: Mon-Fri 0800-1500.

Duty Free

The following goods may be imported into Côte d'Ivoire by passengers over 15 years of age without incurring customs duty:
200 cigarettes or 25 cigars or 250g of tobacco or 100 cigarillos; 1 bottle of wine; 1 bottle of spirits; 0.5l of toilet water and 0.25l of perfume.
Restricted items: Duty must be paid on video cameras, which may be imported for personal use only. A deposit must be paid on entry and is refundable on departure. Limits are placed on certain other personal effects; contact the Consulate prior to departure.

Public Holidays

2005: Jan 1 New Year's Day. **Jan 21** Eid al-Adha (Feast of the Sacrifice). **Mar 28** Easter Monday. **Apr 21** Mouloud (Birth of the Prophet). **May 1** Labour Day. **May 5** Ascension. **May 16** Whit Monday. **Aug 7** Independence Day. **Aug 15** Assumption. **Sep 1** Lailat al Miraj (Ascent of the Prophet). **Nov 1** All Saints' Day. **Nov 3-5** Eid al-Fitr (End of Ramadan). **Nov 9** Day of Mourning. **Nov 15** Peace Day. **Dec 7** Félix Houphouët-Boigny Remembrance Day. **Dec 25** Christmas.
2006: Jan 1 New Year's Day. **Jan 13** Eid al-Adha (Feast of the Sacrifice). **Apr 11** Mouloud (Birth of the Prophet). **Apr 17** Easter Monday. **May 1** Labour Day. **May 25** Ascension. **June 5** Whit Monday. **Aug** Lailat al Miraj (Ascent of the Prophet). **Aug 7** Independence Day. **Aug 15** Assumption. **Oct 22-24** Eid al-Fitr (End of Ramadan). **Nov 1** All Saints' Day. **Nov 9** Day of Mourning. **Nov 15** Peace Day. **Dec 7** Félix Houphouët-Boigny Remembrance Day. **Dec 25** Christmas.
Note: (a) Holidays that fall on a Sunday are often observed on the following day. (b) Muslim festivals are timed according to local sightings of various phases of the moon and the dates given above are approximations. During the lunar month of Ramadan that precedes Eid al-Fitr, Muslims fast during the day and feast at night and normal business patterns may be interrupted. Some disruption may continue into Eid al-Fitr itself. Eid al-Fitr and Eid al-Adha may last anything from two to 10 days, depending on the region. For more information, see the *World of Islam* appendix.

Health

	Special Precautions?	Certificate Required?
Yellow Fever	Yes	1
Cholera	Yes	2
Typhoid & Polio	3	N/A
Malaria	4	N/A

Note: *Regulations and requirements may be subject to change at short notice, and you are advised to contact your doctor well in advance of your intended date of departure. Any numbers in the chart refer to the footnotes below.*

1: A yellow fever vaccination certificate is required from travellers over one year of age coming from all countries.
2: Following WHO guidelines issued in 1973, a cholera vaccination certificate is no longer a condition of entry to Côte d'Ivoire. However, cholera is a serious risk in this country and precautions are essential. Up-to-date advice should be sought before deciding whether these precautions should include vaccination, as medical opinion is divided over its effectiveness; see the *Health* appendix for more information.
3: Immunisation against typhoid is usually advised.
4: Malaria risk (and risk of other insect-borne diseases) exists throughout the year in the whole country, including urban areas. The malignant *falciparum* form is prevalent. Resistance to chloroquine and sulfadoxine-pyrimethamine has been reported. A weekly dose of mefloquine is the recommended prophylaxis.
Food & drink: All water should be regarded as being potentially contaminated. Water used for drinking, brushing teeth or making ice should have first been boiled or otherwise sterilised. Milk is unpasteurised and should be boiled. Powdered or tinned milk is available and is advised, but make sure that it is reconstituted with pure water. Avoid dairy products which are likely to have been made from unboiled milk. Only eat well cooked meat and fish, preferably served hot. Pork, salad and mayonnaise may carry increased risk. Vegetables should be cooked and fruit peeled.
Other risks: *Bilharzia* (schistosomiasis) is present. Avoid swimming and paddling in fresh water; swimming pools which are well chlorinated and maintained are safe.
Hepatitis B is hyperendemic and *hepatitis A* and *E* are widespread. *Meningitis* risk is present depending on area visited and time of year. *Sleeping sickness* (trypanosomiasis) is reported. There have been recent cases of *ebola*. There is a high incidence of *HIV/AIDS*.
Rabies is present. For those at high risk, vaccination before arrival should be considered. If you are bitten, seek medical advice without delay. For more information, consult the *Health* appendix.
Health care: Health care facilities in the main towns are up to international standards but expensive; medical insurance is essential.

Travel - International

Travel warning: Travellers are currently advised against all travel to Côte d'Ivoire. Clashes have particularly been noted in the West. Renewed fighting could lead to a backlash in Abidjan. The situation is volatile and liable to change at short notice. For further advice, contact your local government travel advice department.
AIR: Airlines serving Côte d'Ivoire include *Air Burkina*, *Air France*, *Egyptair*, *Kenya Airways*, *South African Airways* and *Trans African Airlines*. Côte d'Ivoire has a shareholding in *Air Afrique*, although the future of this airline, due to financial difficulties, is still under negotiation. It is recommended that visitors re-confirm returns flights 72 hours in advance.
Approximate flight times: From Abidjan to *London* is six hours, to *New York* is 12 hours.
International airports: *Abidjan (ABJ)* (Félix Houphouët-Boigny) is 16km (10 miles) (website: www.aeria.ci) southeast of Abidjan (travel time - 25 minutes). Buses and taxis are available to the city (travel time - 25 minutes). Airport facilities include duty-free shop, restaurant, shops, banks/bureaux de change, post office and car hire (*Avis*).
Yamoussoukro (ASK) (San Pedro) has been upgraded to international standard.
Departure tax: CFAfr3000 for African destinations and CFAfr5000 for all other departures (from Abidjan airport - prices differ according to airport flown from).
SEA: There are no regular passenger sailings but cargo liners provide limited accommodation for passengers travelling from Europe.
RAIL: There are two through-trains with sleeping and restaurant cars from Abidjan to Ouagadougou (Burkina Faso) daily (travel time - 25 to 27 hours). Those intending to travel should be aware that the Burkina Faso rail network is under constant threat of closure because of financial difficulties: check with the appropriate authorities before finalising arrangements.
ROAD: There are road links of varying quality from Kumasi (Ghana) and from Burkina Faso, Guinea and Liberia and Mali. Borders close at night. **Bus**: Frequent services operate to Accra (Ghana) and Ouagadougou (Burkina Faso). There is a service approximately once a week to Bamako (Mali); the journey can be very long (36 to 96 hours). Bush **taxis** also operate on these routes.

Travel - Internal

AIR: *Air Ivoire (VU)* (website: www.airivoire.com) operates regular internal flights from Abidjan to all major towns.
Departure tax: CFAfr800.
RAIL: The Abidjan–Ouagadougou railway is one of the most efficient in Africa and runs trains daily from Abidjan to Bouaké and Ferkessédougou. Children under four years of age travel free. Children aged between four and nine pay half fare.
ROAD: Côte d'Ivoire has a good road system by West African standards, with 68,000km (42,250 miles) of roads, 5600km (3480 miles) of which are surfaced. However, drivers should be extra aware of potholes and poorly lit vehicles. Petrol stations are frequent except in the north. Traffic drives on the right. **Bus**: Small private buses and bush taxis operate throughout the country; they are comfortable and efficient, although often extremely overcrowded. There are also larger coaches for the longer journeys. **Taxi**: These are available in main cities, although often of unsound mechanical condition. **Car hire**: Cars may be hired in Abidjan, main towns and at the airport.
Documentation: Insurance is compulsory for the driver. The driver requires a UK or most other (applicable) national driving licences, accompanied by attestation from the Embassy of the issuing country that it is genuine.
URBAN: Extensive bus and boat services are operated in Abidjan by *SOTRA* on a two-tiered fare structure. Taxis are usually red and metered; rates are doubled from 0000-0600.
Travel times: The following chart gives approximate travel times (in hours and minutes) from **Abidjan** to other major towns in the Côte d'Ivoire.

	Air	Rail
Abengourou	0.35	-
Agboville	-	2.00
Bondoukou	1.20	-
Bouaké	1.20	6.00
Bouna	1.20	-
Boundiali	2.35	-
Daloa	1.00	-
Dimbokro	-	4.00
Gagnoa	0.50	-
Guiglo	2.15	-
Korhogo	1.30	-
Man	0.50	-
Odienne	2.20	-
San Pedro	1.00	-
Sassandra	0.45	-
Seguela	1.20	-
Tabou	1.20	-
Touba	1.00	-
Yamoussoukro	0.30	-

Accommodation

Hotels and restaurants are expensive in the larger towns. There are several hotels of international standard in Abidjan. In general, there is a choice between luxury, medium-range and cheaper accommodation in the larger towns. In all cases it is advisable to book in advance. For further information, contact the Office Ivoirien du Tourisme et de l'Hôtellerie (see *Contact Addresses* section). **Grading**: Hotels are graded from **1** to **5 stars**.

Resorts & Excursions

YAMOUSSOUKRO: The new administrative and political capital is Yamoussoukro, about 230km (143 miles) north of Abidjan. The town has a lively market, an international-standard golf course and several buildings of architectural interest, including the **Palace and Plantations of the President** and the **Mosque**. Also of architectural interest but, above all, of statistical interest, is the **Cathédrale Notre-Dame-de-la-Paix**. Fractionally smaller than St Peter's in Rome, it incorporates a greater area of stained glass than the total area of stained glass in France. Roman Catholicism is a minority religion in Côte d'Ivoire (some say that the Cathedral could accommodate every Roman Catholic in the country several times over). Yamoussoukro was the birthplace of Félix Houphouët-Boigny, who was Côte d'Ivoire's President for 33 years. The cathedral was paid for almost entirely out of his own pocket.

ELSEWHERE: The former capital and largest city, **Abidjan** is dominated by the **Plateau**, the central commercial district. The older, more traditional heart of the city is **Treichville**, home of many bars, restaurants and nightclubs as well as the colourful central market. There is a very good museum, the **Ifon Museum**. Suburbs have grown up along the banks of the lagoon; these include **Cocody**, **Marcory** and **Adjamé**. About 100km (60 miles) east of the former capital is the beach resort of **Assouinde**; other places being developed as tourist attractions include **Tiagba**, a stilt town; **Grand Bassam**, whose sandy beaches make the place a favourite weekend retreat for the inhabitants of Abidjan; and **Bondoukou**, one of the oldest settlements in the country.
In the west of the country is the attractive town of **Man**, situated in a region of thickly forested mountains and plateaux. The nearby waterfalls are a popular attraction, as are climbs to the peak of **Mount Tonkoui** and visits to the villages of **Biankouma** and **Gouessesso**, 55km (34 miles) away. Other towns of interest include **Korhogo**, the main city of the north and centre of a good fishing and hunting district; the former capital of **Bingerville**; and the town of **Bouaké** in the centre of the country.
Locally organised package tours include visits to one of the country's national parks, including the **Comoé** in the northeast and the **Banco National Park**, 3000 hectares of equatorial forest.

Sport & Activities

Watersports: There are many **swimming** pools in main centres and hotels, particularly in Abidjan and the surrounding coastal resorts. All along this stretch of coast there is a dangerous deep current and all but the strongest swimmers should stay near the shore. Local advice should be taken. There is good coastal and river **fishing**. Red carp, barracuda, mullet and sole can all be caught from the shores of the lagoons. Sea trips can be organised through travel agencies to catch sharks, swordfish, bonito and marlin. Boats and instructors are available in Abidjan, where **water-skiing** facilities are also available.
Wildlife: The national parks are largely inaccessible for visitors without their own vehicles. Local guides are necessary and easily available. The largest and oldest national park is *Comoé National Park*, where lions, waterbucks, hippopotami and other animals can be observed. A landing strip nearby facilitates access.
Hiking: Although much of Côte d'Ivoire has been deforested, there is good hiking in the west near Man (nicknamed the 'city of 18 mountains'). A guide is necessary for longer walks.
Other: Most major centres have a **golf** course. In Abidjan, there is a course at the *Hôtel Ivoire* on the Riviera. Many hotels have **tennis** courts.

Social Profile

FOOD & DRINK: Abidjan and other centres have restaurants serving Caribbean, French, Italian, Lebanese and Vietnamese food. There is a growing number of African restaurants catering for foreigners. Traditional dishes are *kedjenou* (chicken cooked with different vegetables and sealed in banana leaves), *n'voufou* (mashed bananas or yam mixed with palm oil and served with aubergine sauce) and *attieké* (cassava dish). The best area for spicy African food is the Treichville district of Abidjan. The blue pages of the Abidjan telephone book have a special restaurant section. There are no restrictions on drinking. *Bangui* is a local palm wine.
NIGHTLIFE: There are nightclubs in most major centres. Abidjan is the most lively area with its hotels and lagoon-side tourist resorts. There are also theatres, casinos and bars. Traditional entertainment is offered in some hotels.
SHOPPING: In the markets, hard bargaining is often necessary to get prices down to reasonable levels. Special purchases include wax prints, Ghanaian *kente* cloth, indigo fabric and woven cloth, wooden statuettes and masks, bead necklaces, pottery and basketware. **Shopping hours**: Mon-Fri 0800-1200 and 1430-1830, Sat 0800-1200 and 1500-1900.
SPECIAL EVENTS: For a full list of festivals and other special events to be held in Côte d'Ivoire, contact the Embassy, Consulate or the Office Ivoirien du Tourisme et de l'Hôtellerie (see *Contact Addresses* section). The following is a selection of special events occurring in Côte d'Ivoire in 2005:
Feb *Festival of Masks*, Man Region. **Mar** *Bouaké Carnival*. **Apr** *Fête du Dipri*, Gomon. **Oct 22-24** *Eid el-Fitr* (End of Ramadan), nationwide. **Dec 7** *National Day Celebrations*.
SOCIAL CONVENTIONS: One of the most striking features of Côte d'Ivoire, distinguishing it from many other African countries, is the extreme ethnic and linguistic variety. The size of each of the 60 groups – which include the Akar, Kron, Nzima, Hone, Voltaic and Malinke peoples – varies widely and the area they occupy may cover a whole region. With very few exceptions every Ivoirian has a mother tongue which is that of the village, along with traditions, family and social relations within their ethnic group. French has become the official language of schools, cities and government and therefore has an influence on lifestyle even at a modest level. Handshaking is normal. Tropical lightweight clothes are essential, a light raincoat in the rainy season and a hat for

the sun. Casual wear is widely acceptable but beachwear should be confined to the beach or poolside. Dress tends to err on conservative - men wearing long trousers and women wearing knee-length or longer skirts, dresses and trousers. Ties need only be worn for formal occasions. Small tokens of appreciation, a souvenir from home or a business gift with the company logo are always welcome. Normal courtesies should be observed and it is considered polite to arrive punctually for social occasions. There are no restrictions on smoking. Snakes are regarded as sacred by some ethnic groups. **Tipping**: Most hotels and restaurants include a service charge in the bill; if not, 15 per cent is acceptable.

Business Profile

ECONOMY: Côte d'Ivoire is the world's largest producer of cocoa and among the largest producers of coffee. Other important cash crops include cotton, rubber, fruit and vegetables; a variety of vegetables are also produced for domestic consumption. The timber industry has declined from previous levels due to excessive exploitation, although the Government has now limited production in order to protect the remaining forests. A light industrial sector has grown up processing primary agricultural products and produces textiles, chemicals and sugar - again, these are aimed towards export markets. Newly discovered offshore oil and gas deposits will boost the country's industrial sector as well as meeting the country's future energy needs. Côte d'Ivoire already has an established oil refining operation which, along with cigarette manufacture, forms the main components of the country's industrial economy. It will also reduce Côte d'Ivoire's reliance on imported fuel to supplement the hydroelectric installations that are its main source of power. A service sector is gradually developing, centred on tourism, financial services (exploiting the dominant role of the Abidjan stock exchange in the region) and telecommunications. Côte d'Ivoire is one of the more prosperous economies in West Africa, although its recent progress has been undermined by severe political instability and the difficulty in meeting the standards of international donars. GDP was -1.9 per cent in 2004. The country is a member of all the main regional economic organisations, including the Economic Community of West African States (ECOWAS) and the various bodies associated with the CFA Franc zone. Côte d'Ivoire's main trading partner is France. Other important trading relations are maintained with The Netherlands, Nigeria, Germany and Italy.
BUSINESS: French is predominantly used in business circles, although executives in larger businesses may speak English. Translators are generally available. Punctuality is expected, although the host may be late. Visiting cards are essential and given to each person met. It is usual for business visitors to be entertained by local hosts in a hotel or restaurant. Businessmen need only wear cotton safari suits. **Office hours**: Mon-Fri 0730-1200 and 1430-1800, Sat 0800-1200.
COMMERCIAL INFORMATION: The following organisation can offer advice: Chambre de Commerce et d'Industrie de Côte d'Ivoire, 01 BP 1399, 6 avenue Joseph Anoma, Abidjan 01 (tel: 2033 1600; fax: 2032 3942; e-mail: mail@ccici.org).
CONFERENCES/CONVENTIONS: In Abidjan, the *Palais des Congrès* which is part of the *Inter-Continental Hotel* can host conferences for more than 3000 persons. The political capital Yamoussoukro has a capacity for over 5000. For details, contact the Office Ivoirien du Tourisme et de l'Hôtellerie (see *Contact Addresses* section).

Climate

Dry from December to April, long rains from May to July, a short dry season from August to September, short rains in October and November. In the north, the climate is more extreme - rains (May to October) and dry (November to April). **Required clothing:** Tropical lightweights; warmer clothing for evenings.

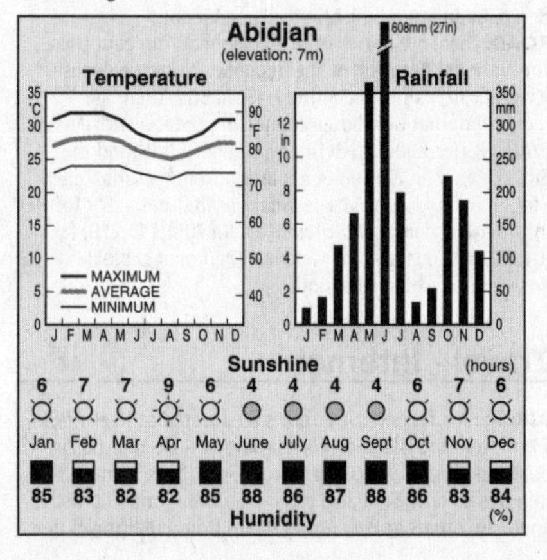

Croatia

British Foreign and Commonwealth Office
Tel: (0870) 606 0290 Website: www.fco.gov.uk
US Department of State
Website: http://travel.state.gov/travel
Canadian Department of Foreign Affairs and Int'l Trade
Tel: (1 800) 267 8376 Website: www.dfait-maeci.gc.ca

Location: Southeastern Europe.

Country dialling code: 385.

Ministry of Tourism
Prislje 14, 10000 Zagreb, Croatia
Tel: (1) 616 9180. Fax: (1) 616 9181.
E-mail: tanja.runtic@mmtpr.hr
Website: www.mmtpr.hr
Croatian National Tourist Board
Iblerov Trg 10/4, 10000 Zagreb, Croatia
Tel: (1) 469 9333. Fax: (1) 455 7827.
E-mail: info@htz.hr
Website: www.croatia.hr
Embassy of the Republic of Croatia
21 Conway Street, London W1T 6BN, UK
Tel: (020) 7387 2022 *or* 1144 (consular section).
Fax: (020) 7387 0310 *or* 0936 (consular section).
E-mail: info-press@croatianembassy.co.uk *or* consular-dept@croatianembassy.co.uk
Website: http://uk.mvp.hr
Croatian National Tourist Office
2 The Lanchesters, 162-164 Fulham Palace Road, London W6 9ER, UK
Tel: (020) 8563 7979. Fax: (020) 8563 2616.
E-mail: info@cnto.freeserve.co.uk
Website: www.croatia.hr
British Embassy
Ivana Lucica 4, 10000 Zagreb, Croatia
Tel: (1) 600 9100. Fax: (1) 600 9111.
E-mail: british.embassyzagreb@fco.gov.uk
Consular and Visa section: Alexandera von Humboldta 4, 10000 Zagreb, Croatia
Tel: (1) 600 9122. Fax: (1) 600 9298.
E-mail: zagreb.visaenquiries@fco.gov.uk
Website: www.britishembassy.gov.uk/croatia
Consulates in: Dubrovnik and Split.
Embassy of the Republic of Croatia
2343 Massachusetts Avenue, NW, Washington, DC 20008, USA
Tel: (202) 588 5899. Fax: (202) 588 8936.
E-mail: amboffice@croatiaemb.org *or* consular@croatiaemb.org *or* public@croatiaemb.org
Website: www.croatiaemb.org

TIMATIC CODES

Health
AMADEUS: **TI-DFT/JIB/HE**
GALILEO/WORLDSPAN: **TI-DFT/JIB/HE**
SABRE: **TIDFT/JIB/HE**

Visa
AMADEUS: **TI-DFT/JIB/VI**
GALILEO/WORLDSPAN: **TI-DFT/JIB/VI**
SABRE: **TIDFT/JIB/VI**

To access TIMATIC country information on Health and Visa regulations through the Computer Reservations System (CRS), type in the appropriate command line listed above.

Consulates General in: Chicago, Los Angeles, New York and St Paul.
Honorary Consulates in: Minnesota, New Orleans and Seattle.
Croatian National Tourist Office
350 Fifth Avenue, Suite 4003, New York, NY 10118, USA
Tel: (212) 279 8672 *or* (800) 829 4416 (toll-free in USA).
Fax: (212) 279 8683.
E-mail: cntony@earthlink.net
Website: www.croatia.hr
Embassy of the United States of America
Ul Thomasa Jeffersona 2, 10010 Zagreb, Croatia
Tel: (1) 661 2200. Fax: (1) 661 2373.
E-mail: irc@usembassy.hr
Website: www.usembassy.hr
Embassy of the Republic of Croatia
229 Chapel Street, Ottawa, Ontario K1N 7Y6, Canada
Tel: (613) 562 7820. Fax: (613) 562 7821.
E-mail: croatia.emb@bellnet.ca
Website: www.croatianemb.ca
Consulate General in: Mississauga.
Canadian Embassy
Prilaz Gjure Dezelica 4, 10000 Zagreb, Croatia
Tel: (1) 488 1200 *or* 1211 (consular section).
Fax: (1) 488 1230.
E-mail: zagrb@international.gc.ca
Website: www.canadaeuropa.gc.ca/croatia

General Information

AREA: 56,542 sq km (21,831 sq miles).
POPULATION: 4,437,460 (official estimate 2004).
POPULATION DENSITY: 78.4 per sq km.
CAPITAL: Zagreb. **Population**: 779,145 (official estimate 2004).
GEOGRAPHY: Croatia stretches along the Adriatic coast (narrowing north-south; the major ports being Rijeka, Pula, Zadar, Sibenik, Split and Dubrovnik) with a larger inland area (running west-east from Zagreb to the border with Serbia & Montenegro). The northern two-thirds of this border are formed by the River Danube. The country borders Slovenia and Hungary to the north, Serbia & Montenegro to the east and Bosnia & Herzegovina.
GOVERNMENT: Republic. Independence from the Federal Republic of Yugoslavia proclaimed in 1991. **Head of State**: President Stjepan Mesic since 2000. **Head of Government**: Prime Minister Ivo Sanader since 2003.
LANGUAGE: Croatian, written in the Latin alphabet (although the cyrillic script is still in use in parts).
RELIGION: Roman Catholic Croats (76.5 per cent of the total population) and Eastern Orthodox Serbs (11 per cent), as well as small communities of Protestants, Jews and Muslims.
TIME: GMT + 1 (GMT + 2 from last Saturday in March to Saturday before last Sunday in October).
ELECTRICITY: 220 volts AC, 50Hz.
COMMUNICATIONS: Telephone: IDD is available. Country code: 385. Outgoing international code: 00. Telephone booths are operated by phonecards available at post offices, news stands and in some tourist shops. **Mobile telephone:** GSM 900 network covers the whole country. Network operators include *HT Mobile Communications LLC (CRONET)* (website: www.ht.hr) and *VIPnet d.o.o.* (website: www.vipnet.hr). Both have roaming partners worldwide. **Fax:** Services are widely available. **Post:** Post offices are open Mon-Fri 0700-1900 and Sat 0700-1300. Some may be open until 2200 in larger cities. Stamps are available in post offices and from news stands. **Internet:** The main ISP is *Hrvatske Telekomunikacije* (website: www.tel.hr). Internet cafes can be found in Zagreb and other main towns. **Press:** There are no English-language newspapers at present. The main local newspapers are *Novi List* (Rijeka), *Slobodna Dalmacija* (Split) and *Vecernji List* (Zagreb).
Radio: BBC World Service (website: www.bbc.co.uk/worldservice) and Voice of America (website: www.voa.gov) can be received. From time to time the frequencies change and the most up-to-date can be found online.

Passport/Visa

	Passport Required?	Visa Required?	Return Ticket Required?
Full British	Yes	No	Yes
Australian	Yes	No	Yes
Canadian	Yes	No	Yes
USA	Yes	No	Yes
Other EU	No/1	No	Yes
Japanese	Yes	No	Yes

***Note:** Regulations and requirements may be subject to change at short notice, and you are advised to contact the appropriate diplomatic or consular authority before finalising travel arrangements. Details of these may be found at the head of this country's entry. Any numbers in the chart refer to the footnotes below.*

See contents section at front of book

Restricted entry and transit: Croatia does not recognise passports issued by Chinese Taipei, Palestine and the Turkish Republic of Cyprus.

PASSPORTS: Passport valid for at least length of stay required by all, except:

1. nationals of EU countries, and nationals of Bosnia & Herzegovina, Iceland, Liechtenstein, Monaco, Norway, San Marino and Switzerland, with valid national photo ID cards.

VISAS: Required by all except the following for stays of up to 90 days:

(a) nationals listed in the chart above (including the Sovereign Military Order of Malta, although such passport holders may not enter Croatia with national ID cards);

(b) nationals of Andorra, Argentina, Bolivia, Bosnia & Herzegovina, Brazil, Brunei, Bulgaria, Chile, Costa Rica, Ecuador, El Salvador, Guatemala, Honduras, Hong Kong (SAR), Iceland, Israel, Liechtenstein, Macau (SAR), Macedonia (Former Yugoslav Republic of), Malaysia, Mexico, Monaco, New Zealand, Nicaragua, Norway, Panama, Paraguay, Romania, San Marino, Serbia & Montenegro*, Singapore, Switzerland, Turkey, Uruguay, Vatican City and Venezuela;

(c) nationals of Korea (Rep) for tourist/business stays of up to 30 days;

Credit: © Croatian National Tourist Board

(d) transit passengers continuing their journey by the same or first connecting aircraft within 48 hours, provided holding confirmed onward and return documentation and not leaving the airport.*

Note: (a) * Nationals of Serbia & Montenegro are only visa-exempt on a temporary basis until 31 December 2005. (b) * Some nationals always require a visa, even when transiting; contact the Consulate for further information.

Types of visa and cost: *Travel/Transit*: £15 (single-entry); £19 (double-entry); £30 (multiple-entry). *Business permit*: £15. *Group*: £4 per person.

Validity: *Travel*: Valid for a one-year period, with continuous stay or the overall duration of repeated entries not exceeding 90 days, during a six-month period starting from day of entry. *Business*: Valid for one year; can be issued to members of a foreign company provided it is registered in Croatia. For further information on company registration, contact the Croatian Chamber of Economy (see *Business Profile* section). *Transit*: Valid for a six-month period for up to five days maximum; can sometimes be multiple-entry. *Airport Transit*: One or more transit through the Airport International Transit area over a period not exceeding 24 hours. *Group*: Five to 50 persons based on submission of group travel documents, for one entry or transit not exceeding a 30-day period.

Application to: Consulate (or Consular section at Embassy); see *Contact Addresses* section.

Application requirements: (a) Valid passport. (b) Completed application form. (c) Passport-size photo (30 x 35mm and in colour). (d) Proof of sufficient funds to cover duration of stay (minimum of € 102 per day). (e) Proof of accommodation within Croatia or documentation regarding the purpose and means of travel (such as business/invitation letter, return or onward ticket, holiday arrangements).

Working days required: One day to four weeks, depending on nationality and type of visa required. *Multiple-entry* visas: Four to six weeks.

Money

Currency: Kuna (K) = 100 Lipa. Notes are in denominations of K1000, 500, 200, 100, 50, 20, 10 and 5. Coins are in denominations of K25, 5, 2 and 1, and 50, 20, 10, 5, 4, 2 and 1 lipa.

Currency exchange: Foreign currency can be exchanged in banks, by authorised dealers and post offices. ATMs are widespread.

Credit & debit cards: All major credit cards are widely accepted. Check with your credit or debit card company for details of merchant acceptability and other facilities which may be available.

Travellers cheques: To avoid additional exchange rate charges, travellers are advised to take travellers cheques in US Dollars, Pounds Sterling or Euros.

Currency restrictions: The import and export of local currency is limited to K15,000 (in banknotes up to K500). The import and export of foreign currency is unlimited.

Exchange rate indicator: The following figures are included as a guide to the movements of the Kuna against Sterling and the US Dollar:

Date	Feb '04	May '04	Aug '04	Nov '04
£1.00=	11.24	11.15	10.94	10.85
$1.00=	6.17	6.24	5.93	5.73

Banking hours: Mon-Fri 0700-1900, Sat 0700-1300. Some banks may open on Sundays in larger cities.

Duty Free

The following goods may be taken into Croatia without incurring customs duty:

200 cigarettes or 50 cigars or 250g of tobacco; 1l of wine and 1l of spirits; 250ml of eau de cologne and 1 bottle of perfume.

Note: (a) Valuable professional and technical equipment must be declared on arrival. (b) Articles of archaeological, historical, ethnographic, artistic and other scientific or cultural value require an export licence issued by the Croatian authorities. (c) Passengers carrying firearms (for hunting and sporting purposes) or radios for communication (CB, walkie-talkie) must hold a valid passport.

Public Holidays

2005: Jan 1 New Year's Day. **Mar 25-28** Easter. **May 1** Labour Day. **Jun 10** Corpus Christi. **Jun 22** Anti-Fascist Resistance Day. **Jun 25** Croation National Day. **Aug 5** Victory Day and National Thanksgiving Day. **Aug 15** Assumption. **Oct 8** Independence Day. **Nov 1** All Saints' Day. **Nov 3-5*** End of Ramadan. **Dec 25-26** Christmas.

2006: Jan 1 New Year's Day. **Apr 14-17** Easter. **May 1** Labour Day. **Jun 15** Corpus Christi. **Jun 22** Anti-Fascist Resistance Day. **Aug 5** Victory Day and National Thanksgiving Day. **Aug 15** Assumption. **Oct 8** Independence Day. **Oct 22-24*** End of Ramadan. **Nov 1** All Saints' Day. **Dec 25-26** Christmas.

Note: *The end of Ramadan, while not an official public holiday, is celebrated as such by the Muslim community, and some shops and businesses may be closed on this day.

Health

	Special Precautions?	Certificate Required?
Yellow Fever	No	No
Cholera	No	No
Typhoid & Polio	1	N/A
Malaria	No	N/A

Note: *Regulations and requirements may be subject to change at short notice, and you are advised to contact your doctor well in advance of your intended date of departure. Any numbers in the chart refer to the footnotes below.*

1: Immunisation against both diseases may be advised unless staying solely in first-class accommodation.

Food & drink: Mains water is normally chlorinated, and whilst relatively safe, may cause mild abdominal upsets. Bottled water is available and is advised for the first few weeks of the stay. Milk is pasteurised and dairy products are safe for consumption. Local meat, poultry, seafood, fruit and vegetables are generally considered safe to eat.

Other risks: *Hepatitis A* occurs. Precautions should be taken against tick bites. Immunisation against *tick-borne encephalitis* is advised.

Rabies is present. For those at high risk, vaccination before arrival should be considered. If you are bitten, seek medical advice without delay. For more information, consult the *Health* appendix.

Health care: For UK nationals, hospital and other medical treatment as well as some dental treatment is normally free on presentation of a UK passport. UK residents who are not nationals, and are visiting the country for a short stay, should take an E111 form to cover any medical care. Prescribed medicines must be paid for. All other international travellers are advised to take out full medical insurance.

Travel - International

AIR: Croatia's national airline is *Croatia Airlines (OU)* (website: www.croatiaairlines.hr) which flies directly from London Heathrow to Zagreb daily. *British Airways* also operates direct flights three times a week from London Gatwick to Dubrovnik. Other airlines serving Croatia include *Aeroflot, Air France, Fly Bosnia, KLM, LOT, Lufthansa, Malaysia Airways* and *Swiss*. *Croatia Airlines* operates direct flights from the UK (London and Manchester) to Dubrovnik, Pula and Split in the summer.

Approximate flight times: From Zagreb to *London* is two hours 30 minutes, to *New York* is 10 hours 35 minutes.

International airports: *Zagreb (ZAG)* (Pleso International) (website: www.zagreb-airport.hr) is 17km (10 miles) southeast of the city. An airport bus runs 0700-2000 to the city centre (travel time - 25 minutes); taxis are also available (travel time - 20 minutes). Airport facilities include left luggage, banks/bureaux de change, restaurants, snack bars, bars, business lounge, duty-free shops, post office, tourist information, first aid and car hire (including *Avis, Europcar, Hertz* and *National*).

Dubrovnik (DBV) is 18km (11 miles) southeast of the city. An airport bus runs to the city (travel time - 20 minutes). Airport facilities include banks/bureaux de change, a post office, bars, duty-free shop, shops and car hire.

Split (SPU) is 25km (16 miles) northwest of the city. An airport bus runs to the city (travel time - 40 minutes). Airport facilities include banks/bureau de change, post office, car hire, duty-free shops and bar/restaurant.

Pula (PUY) is 8km (5 miles) northwest of the city. An airport bus runs to the city (travel time - 15 minutes). Airport facilities include bureau de change, car hire, duty-free shop and snack bar/restaurant.

Departure tax: None.

SEA: Passenger and car ferry services run to Italy. The main routes are: Split–Ancona, Zadar–Ancona, Split–Pescara and Dubrovnik–Bari. Fast hydrofoil services operate on some routes. The main ferry lines are *Adriatica* (website: www.adriatica.it), *Jadrolinija* (website: www.jadrolinija.hr) and *SEM Marina* (website: www.sem-marina.hr).

RAIL: Direct trains run from Austria, Germany, Hungary, Italy, Serbia & Montenegro, Slovenia and Switzerland. Express services run from Zagreb to major cities including Berlin, Budapest, Munich, Venice and Vienna.

ROAD: There are routes from all neighbouring countries. The National Autoclub of the Republic of Croatia (website: www.hak.hr) can provide information. **Bus:** There are regular international buses connecting Croatia with Austria, Bosnia & Herzegovina, Germany, Hungary, Italy and the Slovak Republic. *Eurolines*, departing from Victoria Coach Station in London, serves destinations in Croatia. For further information, contact *Eurolines* (tel: (08705) 143 219; fax: (01582) 400 694; e-mail: welcome@eurolines.co.uk; website: www.eurolines.com).

Travel - Internal

AIR: The main domestic airports are located at *Rijeka (RJK)*, 27km from the Island of Krk (travel time - 35 minutes by bus) and at *Split (SPU)*, 25km from Split (travel time - 30 minutes by bus). Split also receives international flights. There are others at *Pula (PUY)*, 10km from Pula (travel time

CROATIA
HOTEL
For information please contact :
HOTEL CROATIA, Marketing & Sales Dpt.
Frankopanska 10, 20210 CAVTAT, Croatia
Tel: +385/20/475 555, 478 055, Fax: +385/20/478 213,
E-mail: info@hoteli-croatia.hr,
Website: www.hoteli-croatia.hr
Hotel Croatia lies in a beautiful position on a peninsula overlooking the Adriatic sea on one side an the picturesque old town of Cavtat on the other, 5 km from Dubrovnik International Airport. The world famous medieval city of Dubrovnik (18 km) can be seen from some hotel terraces.
480 rooms and 7 suites, several a la carte restaurants and bars, night bar, casino, shopping center, quiet salon, indoor & outdoor swimming pools, sport facilities, fitness room, sauna, massage, beauty salon, hairdresser, walking & jogging paths.
Convention and banqueting facilities, 6 conference halls to accommodate 30 - 800 persons, large exhibition area - all supported by latest audio & visual equipment. Salons and terraces feature facilities for receptions and cocktails.
Offering spacious, air-conditioned rooms and excellent facilities, Hotel Croatia is ideal for business & leisure travellers.

– 15 minutes by bus) and *Dubrovnik (DBV)*, 22km from Dubrovnik (travel time – 30 minutes by bus).

SEA: There are regular connections between the main ports and the offshore islands. Rijeka, Zadar, Split and Dubrovnik are linked by passenger and car ferries.

RAIL: The network connects all major cities except Dubrovnik. However, it is often quicker to travel by bus.

ROAD: In 1996, there were 27,247km of roads in Croatia, including 495km of motorways. A 10-year road-building programme was announced in that year. Unexploded ordinance may remain in Eastern Slavonia and the former Krajina; motorists should avoid these areas. A toll is payable on motorways. Unleaded petrol is available. **Regulations**: Traffic drives on the right. Speed limits are 130kph (81mph) on motorways, 100kph (62mph) on dual carriageways, 50kph (31mph) in built-up areas and 80kph (50mph) outside built-up areas. Heavy fines are imposed for speeding. **Documentation**: National or International Driving Permit. All motorists should also carry a valid passport as proof of identity at all times. A Green Card should be carried by visitors (except EU nationals) taking their own car into Croatia. Without it, insurance cover is limited to the minimum legal cover; the Green Card augments this to the level of cover provided by the car owner's domestic policy. National registration in country of origin is required for all foreign vehicles. **Bus**: There are regular services to destinations all over Croatia. Timetable information is available from Zagreb Central Bus Station (website: www.akz.hr; see links from tourist board website: www.croatia.hr).

Accommodation

HOTELS: Once again a major European tourism destination, Croatia has the best of its hotels on its Adriatic coast. Elsewhere, deluxe hotels are only to be found in Zagreb, plus the Plitvice Lakes tourist area on the border with Bosnia & Herzegovina near Bihac, although the situation is rapidly changing. For further information, contact the Croatian Association of Hoteliers, Vladimira Nazora 3, Opatija (tel/fax: (51) 711 415 *or* 567; e-mail: huh@ri.tel.hr; website: www.huh.hr). **Grading**: Hotels in Croatia are now officially graded by the Ministry of Tourism into five categories according to the standard of accommodation: **5-star**: Luxury. **4-star**: Deluxe. **3-star**: First class. **2-star**: Moderate. **1-star**: Basic and budget. Many hotels are still in the process of upgrading their facilities to match EU standards. For a list of classified hotels, contact the Croatian National Tourist Board (see *Contact Addresses* section).

CAMPING AND CARAVANNING: There are over 148 campsites in Croatia, including some naturist camps.

Private accommodation: Private accommodation is increasingly availabe in Croatia. It is even possible to stay in some lighthouses.

Resorts & Excursions

With 1778km (1111 miles) of mainland coast, emerald-blue waters, secluded pebble beaches and countless unspoilt islands, Croatia is an ideal destination for lovers of sea and sunshine who want to avoid the crowds. For ease of reference, the country has been divided into the following regions: Istria, Kvarner, Northern Dalmatia, Central Dalmatia, Southern Dalmatia and Inland Croatia. In addition, the cities of Zagreb, Dubrovnik and Split are each given a brief description.

MAIN CITIES

ZAGREB: Croatia's economic, cultural and administrative heart sits on the north bank of the river **Sava**. Its historic nuclei, **Gradec** and **Kaptol**, in **Gornji Grad** (Upper Town), were founded in the Middle Ages. Here, a labyrinth of peaceful cobbled streets links the city's oldest and finest monuments: the **Cathedral**, **St Mark's Church** (noted for its red, white and blue tiled roof) and the **Sabor** (seat of the Croatian Parliament). At the foot of the Upper Town lie **Trg Bana Jelacic**, the main square, and **Dolac**, the colourful open-air market. The main square links the Upper Town to **Donji Grad** (Lower Town), the commercial centre of modern-day Zagreb, with theatres, shops, cinemas, museums and cafes. A number of important 19th-century public buildings are located here, including **Glavni Kolodvor** (Main Train Station), the imposing neo-Baroque **Croatian National Theatre** and the **Academy of Arts and Sciences**. Regarding museums, the **Museum of Arts and Crafts** traces Croatian craftsmanship from the Renaissance up to the present day, while the **Mimara Museum** presents a rich collection of painting, sculpture and ceramics from abroad. Also worth visiting are the **Museum of Zagreb**, the **Archaeological Museum** and the **Gallery of Naïve Art**. The city boasts one of Europe's very first planned parks: **Maksimir**, a magnificent feat of landscaping, with lakes, pavilions and sculptures, dating back to 1794.

DUBROVNIK: Unanimously considered the jewel of Croatia, Dubrovnik is best known for its well-preserved historic centre contained within 13th-century city walls, its terracotta rooftops, and a stunning location overlooking the Adriatic. Today a UNESCO World Heritage Site, the city was a wealthy independent republic up until 1808. The finest monuments date back to those golden years: the 16th-century **Rector's Palace**, the **Franciscan Monastery** (home to Europe's oldest pharmacy), and a number of delightful baroque churches, including the **Cathedral**, **St Blaise's Church** and the **Jesuit Church**. Also worth visiting is the **Maritime Museum**, which highlights Dubrovnik's former importance as a world naval power. Each summer, from mid-July to late August, the city hosts the **Dubrovnik Summer Festival**, featuring various cultural events plus open-air evening performances of theatre, jazz and classical music.

SPLIT: The city of Split was founded in the third century AD by the Roman Emperor Diocletian. Today, the traffic-free historic centre lies within the imposing walls of **Diocletian's Palace**, now a UNESCO World Heritage Site. A vibrant cafe scene focuses on the Roman **Peristil**, presided over by the majestic **Cathedral** with its 13th-century Romanesque bell tower. The **Museum of Croatian Archaeological Monuments** displays early Croatian religious art, while the **Meštrovic Gallery** celebrates the country's best-known 20th-century sculptor. On the hill above town, **Marjan**, an extensive nature reserve planted with pine woods and fragrant Mediterranean shrubs, affords stunning views over the Adriatic. During the **Split Summer Festival**, held annually from mid-July to mid-August, the city becomes an open-air stage with nighttime opera and concerts.

THE COAST

ISTRIA: Istria is the largest peninsula on the Croatian coast and, thanks to its easy transport links with nearby Italy and Austria, has also become the country's major tourist destination. The region's administrative centre and chief port, **Pula**, was founded by the Romans in the fifth century BC. Several interesting buildings remain from this period, notably the **Arena**, a well-preserved amphitheatre, which hosts summer concerts and the annual film festival. The city

A B C D E F G H I J K L M N O P Q R S T U V W X Y Z

is a good starting point for excursions to **Brijuni National Park**, an archipelago of 14 unspoilt islands. It is possible to stay overnight on the largest island, **Veli Brijun**, where a range of tourist facilities is available. On the west coast of Istria lies Croatia's most visited resort, **Porec**. Fortunately the large hotel complexes of **Plava Laguna** and **Zelena Laguna** are situated out of town a little way along the coast, leaving the historic centre intact. Built on a small peninsular, Porec dates back to Roman times, and its star attraction is the UNESCO World Heritage-listed **Euphrasius Basilica**, decorated with stunning sixth-century Byzantine mosaics. Istria's second most popular resort, **Rovinj**, was originally built on a small island, though the narrow strait that separated it from the mainland was filled in during the 18th century. Just out of town lies Zlatni Rt, a blissful park affording access to several secluded coves for bathing. Also by the sea, midway between Porec and Rovinj, lies **Vrsar**, home to **Koversada**, Europe's largest nudist resort. Inland Istria, with romantic hill towns such as **Motovun** and **Groznjan**, makes an ideal day trip from the coast.
KVARNER: The economic and administrative centre of this popular and busy island region is **Rijeka**, Croatia's largest port. Other than **Trsat Castle**, built on a hilltop commanding splendid views out to sea, Rijeka has little of architectural interest, its main claim to fame being the exuberant celebrations it puts on each year in February for **Carnival**. The main touristic centres of the Kvarner region are **Opatija**, **Crikvenica** and **Novi Vinodolski** (sometimes referred to as the 'three rivieras'), all of which have extensive pebble beaches complemented by good accommodation and recreational facilities. Opatija, Croatia's oldest tourist resort, was popular with the Austro-Hungarian nobility and some of its former *fin-de-siecle* elegance remains. Of the many islands scattered throughout the Kvarner Bay, **Krk**, connected to the mainland by a road bridge, is the most developed as well as the largest, with clean beaches and extensive tourist facilities. Further out lie **Rab**, home to the delightful medieval **Rab Town** with a number of elegant Romanesque bell towers; **Cres**, which contains the **Vransko Lake** and is popular with nature lovers; and **Lošinj**, which has pine woods and numerous bays with beaches. Inland from Rijeka, the **Risnjak National Park** is located in the mountains of **Gorski Kotar** and rises to 1528m (510ft) above sea level, making it a popular destination for hiking and climbing.
NORTHERN DALMATIA: The chief city and port in the region is **Zadar**, the historic centre of which is made up of narrow cobbled streets, some Roman remains and several interesting churches, notably the 12th-century Romanesque **Cathedral**. However, the region's main attraction is the **Kornati National Park**, an archipelago consisting of over 90 islands scattered over an area of 300 sq km. Virtually uninhabited, the islands display a harsh, rocky landscape practically devoid of vegetation. Most visitors arrive on organised day trips by boat, though several renovated stone cottages provide 'Robinson Crusoe'-type holiday accommodation. Inland from Zadar, on the southern slopes of the **Velebit Massif**, lies **Paklenica National Park**, a popular destination for hiking and climbing. The region's second city is **Sibenik**, worth seeing for its 15th-century UNESCO-listed **Cathedral**, and a good base for visiting **Krka National Park**. Here, the river **Krka** has sculpted a picturesque canyon, famed for its spectacular **Skradinski buk** (Skradin Waterfalls) and the islet of **Visovac**, home to a **Franciscan Monastery**, which can be visited by boat.
CENTRAL DALMATIA: Croatia's second-largest city, **Split** (see *Main Cities* section) is also the economic and cultural capital of Central Dalmatia. Nearby, the tiny medieval city of **Trogir**, founded by the Greeks in the third century BC, is a UNESCO World Heritage Site noted for its beautiful Venetian Gothic stone buildings. Regarding sea and sunshine, the resorts of the **Makarska Riviera**, centred around the pretty town of **Makarska**, boast long stretches of pebble beaches and are able to accommodate large numbers of holidaymakers. However, the highlight of Central Dalmatia has to be its islands, which are less exploited than those in the north of the country. Taking Split as a base, the closest island, **Brac**, is best known for its magnificent beach, **Zlatni Rat** (Golden Cape), close to the well-equipped but unspoilt resort of **Bol**. **Hvar**, possibly Dalmatia's most beautiful island, is renowned for its rugged coastline, excellent wines and lavender fields. The largest settlement, **Hvar Town**, is built around a picturesque harbour presided over by a hilltop fortress. Chic cafes and restaurants focus on the main square, lined with elegant 15th-century 'palaces' and the much-photographed Renaissance **Cathedral**. Hvar Town claims to have more hours of sunshine than any other resort on the Adriatic, and hotels offer free accommodation in the unlikely event of a snowfall. Slightly less sophisticated, but equally well equipped with hotels and bathing areas, is the friendly town of **Jelsa**. **Vis**, Croatia's most remote inhabited island, is wild and unspoilt. Due to its former status as a Yugoslav military base, it was closed to foreigners until 1989 and therefore has very limited tourist facilities.
SOUTHERN DALMATIA: The chief centre of the southernmost region of Croatia is **Dubrovnik** (see *Main Cities* section). Nearby, a group of tiny traffic-free islands known as the **Elaphites,** offer secluded beaches and basic tourist amenities. Further up the coast, the island of **Korcula** is reigned over by the beautifully preserved **Korcula Town**, a marvel of medieval urban planning which has charmed foreign visitors since the first tourists arrived in the 1920s. During summer, regular performances of the colourful *Moreška* sword dance are staged here. Nearby, the village of **Lumbarda** is home to one of Croatia's few sand beaches. On the island of **Mljet**, the green and unspoilt **Mljet National Park** boasts dense indigenous forests and two interconnected saltwater lakes – **Veliko Jezero** and **Malo Jezero**. In the centre of the larger lake sits the exquisite **St Mary's Island**, crowned by a **Benedictine Monastery**. A series of paths, perfect for mountain biking or hiking, runs round the lakes and through the woods. **Lastovo**, like Vis (see *Central Dalmatia* section), is a remote island and former home to a Yugoslav military base, hence the lack of tourist facilities. Back on the mainland, south of Dubrovnik, **Cavtat** is a pretty holiday resort with numerous hotels and pebble beaches. South from here lies the border with **Montenegro**.

INLAND CROATIA

While the vast majority of tourists head straight for the coast, inland Croatia also holds several places of interest, notably the capital, **Zagreb** (see *Main Cities* section). North of Zagreb lies **Zagorje**, a rural area of undulating hills and vineyards with several castles open to the public, the most visited being **Veliki Tabor** and **Trakocšan**. East of Zagreb lies the flat fertile region of Slavonia, the major city of which, **Osijek**, makes an ideal base for visiting **Kopacki Rit Nature Park**, a vast expanse of wetland popular with birdwatchers. South of Zagreb, on the edge of the Dalmatian hinterland, lies one of Croatia's biggest tourist attractions, the UNESCO-listed **Plitvice Lakes National Park**. Situated in a densely forested valley, the park features 16 beautiful blue-green lakes joined together by a succession of spectacular waterfalls. There are numerous hotels, motels and campsites in the area, although tourism development has thankfully been combined with strict environmental preservation policies.

Sport & Activities

Watersports: Fishing permits are available from hotels or local authorities. Local information is necessary. Freshwater angling and fishing with equipment needs a permit. 'Fish-linking' with a local small-craft owner is popular. **Sailing** is possible along the coast. Berths and boats can be hired at all ports. Permits are needed for boats brought into the country. **Sea kayaking** is also popular around the islands off the coast. The coast is also an increasingly popular **diving** destination, with ever more dive centres.
Other: Skiing and **spa resorts** exist at Delnice and Platak. **Football** and **basketball** are two of the most popular spectator sports. **Rock climbing** is possible (the Paklencia National Park is particularly good for this), and there are good **hiking** areas.

Social Profile

FOOD & DRINK: The Adriatic coast is renowned for the variety of seafood dishes, including scampi, *prstaci* (shellfish) and *brodet* (mixed fish stewed with rice), all cooked in olive oil and served with vegetables. In the interior, visitors should sample *manistra od bobica* (beans and fresh maize soup). Much Croatian food contains cheese and oil, often mixed with other ingredients in pies or 'donuts'.
The regional wines are good. Italian espresso is also popular and cheap.
SHOPPING: Traditional handicrafts like embroidery, woodcarvings and ceramics make good souvenirs. Tourists can reclaim VAT on expenditure of more than K500. Visitors should ensure that all receipts are retained after any purchase is made, as financial police do have the power to fine visitors without relevant documents. This is to prevent VAT evasion by shopkeepers. **Shopping hours**: Mon-Fri 0800-2000, Sat 0800-1400/1500. Some shops in cities may now open on Sundays.
SPECIAL EVENTS: The following is a selection of special events occurring in Croatia in 2005; for further details contact the Croatian National Tourist Board (see *Contact Addresses* section):
Jan *International Carnival of Rijeka*. **Feb-Mar** *Kvarner Riviera Carnival*. **Apr** *Kontrapunkt Future Jazz Festival*, Zagreb. **Jun-Jul** *International Children's Festival*, Sibenik. **Jul** *Urban Festival*, Zagreb; *Zagreb International Folk Festival*. **Jul-Aug** *Zagreb Summer Festival*; *Dubrovnik Summer Festival*; *Split Summer Festival*; *Istrian Cultural Summer*. **Aug-Sep** *International Puppet Festival*, Zagreb. **Sep** *Vinkovci Autumn Festival*. **Sep-Oct** *Varazdin Baroque Evenings*.
SOCIAL CONVENTIONS: People normally shake hands upon meeting and leaving. Smoking is generally acceptable but there are restrictions in public buildings and on public transport. **Photography**: Certain restrictions exist. **Tipping**: 10 per cent is expected in hotels, restaurants and taxis.

Business Profile

ECONOMY: After Slovenia, Croatia was the most developed republic of the former Yugoslavia. With substantial support and investment from abroad, the Croatian economy recovered well after the break up of Yugoslavia and several years of civil war. Industry is the most important sector in the economy, producing textiles, chemicals, processed foods, finished metal goods and construction materials. Agriculture, which produces maize, wheat and sugar beet, is important for domestic purposes but has never contributed significantly to the export economy. Mineral deposits of exploitable size include oil, coal and natural gas. Croatia also has an important tourism industry, based on the Dalmatian coast: after being all but wiped out by the civil war, it has recovered and prospered; it now accounts for about 15 per cent of GDP and has been largely responsible for Croatia's recent economic progress. Annual GDP growth is around 4 per cent. After independence, the government introduced a programme of privatisation and other market reforms inline with those adopted throughout eastern Europe. Croatia joined the IMF in January 1993, the European Bank for Reconstruction and Development and the World Trade Organisation. In May 1994, the Government introduced a new currency, the Kuna: low inflation has allowed the government to keep its value reasonably stable. The country's most important trading partners are Germany, Italy, Austria, Slovenia and Bosnia & Herzegovina.
BUSINESS: In many ways one of the more conservative areas of the former Yugoslav Federation, Croatia tends towards formal business protocol, but this image of Western-style efficiency is often belied by the fact that things go very slowly on account of the cumbersome bureaucracy. Communication, however, is no problem as English and German are widely used as second languages. Business cards including professional or academic titles should be exchanged just after formal introductions. There is also a large number of local agents, advisers, consultants and, to a lesser extent, lawyers, willing to act for foreign companies, but none should be engaged before being thoroughly checked in advance. Croatia has created a more liberal framework for foreign investments so that foreign investors are guaranteed special rights and incentives for investing in Croatia. **Office hours**: Mon-Fri 0830-1630.
COMMERCIAL INFORMATION: The following organisation can offer advice: Croatian Chamber of Economy, Trg Rooseveltov 2, 10000 Zagreb (tel: (1) 456 1555; fax: (1) 482 8380; e-mail: hgk@hgk.hr; website: www.hgk.hr).
CONFERENCES/CONVENTIONS: The Croatian National Tourist Board can offer advice through their Convention Bureau (see *Contact Addresses* section), which also has a Zagreb Convention Bureau located at Koptol 4, 10000 Zagreb (tel: (1) 489 8555; e-mail: info@zagreb-convention.hr; website: www.zagreb-convention.hr).

Climate

Croatia has a varied climate, with continental climate conditions in the north and Mediterranean ones on the Adriatic coast.
Required clothing: Lightweights with rainwear for summer. Mediumweights for winter with heavier clothing for inland areas.

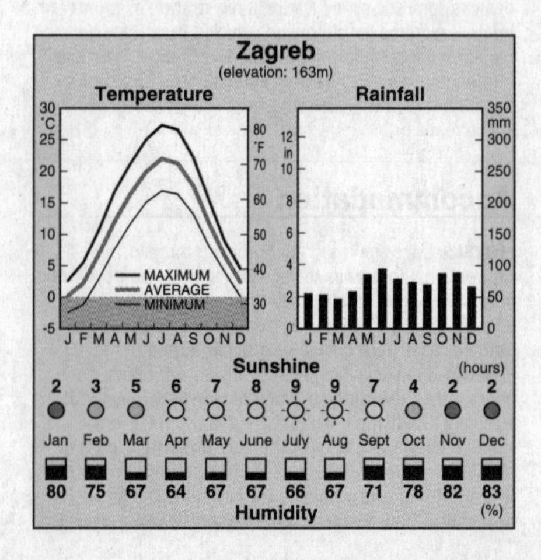

Cuba

LATEST TRAVEL ADVICE CONTACTS

British Foreign and Commonwealth Office
Tel: (0870) 606 0290 Website: www.fco.gov.uk

US Department of State
Website: http://travel.state.gov/travel

Canadian Department of Foreign Affairs and Int'l Trade
Tel: (1 800) 267 8376 Website: www.dfait-maeci.gc.ca

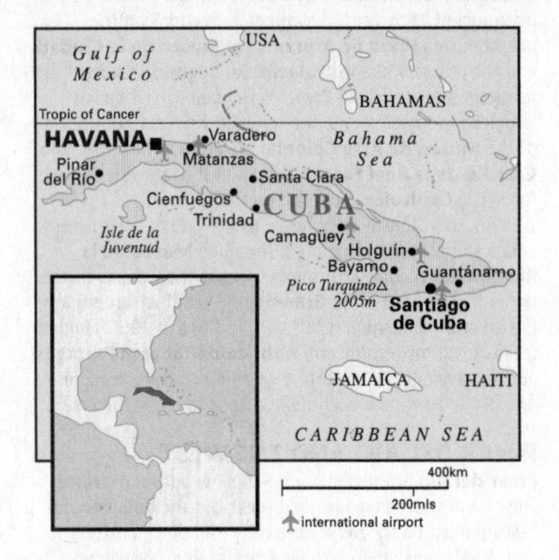

Location: Northwest Caribbean.

Country Dialling Code: 53.

Ministerio de Turismo
Malecón y G, Vedado, Havana, Cuba
Tel: (7) 833 3755. Fax: (7) 831 1825.
Website: www.cubatravel.cu

Embassy of the Republic of Cuba
167 High Holborn, London WC1V 6PA, UK
Tel: (020) 7240 2488. Fax: (020) 7836 2602.
E-mail: embacuba@cubaldn.com
Website: www.cubaldn.com
Opening hours: Mon-Fri 0900-1700.

Cuban Consulate
167 High Holborn, WC1V 6pA London, UK
Tel: (0870) 240 3675 (recorded information line; calls cost 60p per minute). Fax: (020) 7836 2602.
Opening hours: Mon-Fri 0930-1230.

Cuba Tourist Board
154 Shaftesbury Avenue, London WC2H 8JT, UK
Tel: (020) 7240 6655 *or* (09001) 600 295 (24-hour brochure request line; calls cost 60p per minute). Fax: (020) 7836 9265.
E-mail: tourism@cubasi.info Website: www.cubatravel.cu

British Embassy
Calle 34 No 702/4, Entre 7 ma Avenida y 17, Miramar, 11300 Havana, Cuba
Tel: (7) 204 1771. Fax: (7) 204 8104.
E-mail: embrit@ceniai.inf.cu
Website: www.britishembassy.gov.uk/cuba

Cuban Interests Section
2630 16th Street, NW, Washington DC 20009, USA
Tel: (202) 797 8518-20. Fax: (202) 797 8521.
E-mail: secconscuba@worldnet.att.net

US Interests Section
c/o The Embassy of Switzerland, Entre Calle L y M, Calle Calzada, Vedado, 10400 Havana, Cuba
Tel: (7) 833 3551-9 *or* 1196/8 (visa section).
Fax: (7) 833 1084.

Embassy of the Republic of Cuba
388 Main Street, Ottawa, Ontario, K1S 1E3, Canada
Tel: (613) 563 0141. Fax: (613) 563 0068.
E-mail: cuba@embacuba.ca Website: www.embacuba.ca

Canadian Embassy
Calle 30, No 518, Esquina a 7ma, Avenida Miramar, Havana, Cuba
Tel: (7) 204 2516. Fax: (7) 204 1069 (visa section).
E-mail: havan@dfait-maeci.gc.ca
Website: www.havana.gc.ca

TIMATIC CODES

Health	AMADEUS: **TI-DFT/JIB/HE** GALILEO/WORLDSPAN: **TI-DFT/JIB/HE** SABRE: **TIDFT/JIB/HE**
Visa	AMADEUS: **TI-DFT/JIB/VI** GALILEO/WORLDSPAN: **TI-DFT/JIB/VI** SABRE: **TIDFT/JIB/VI**

To access TIMATIC country information on Health and Visa regulations through the Computer Reservations System (CRS), type in the appropriate command line listed above.

General Information

AREA: 110,860 sq km (42,803 sq miles).
POPULATION: 11,251,000 (official estimate 2002).
POPULATION DENSITY: 101.5 per sq km.
CAPITAL: Havana. **Population**: 2,189,716 (1999).
GEOGRAPHY: Cuba is the largest Caribbean island, about the size of England, and the most westerly of the Greater Antilles group, lying 145km (90 miles) south of Florida. A quarter of the country is fairly mountainous. West of Havana is the narrow Sierra de los Organos, rising to 750m (2461ft) and containing the Guaniguanicos hills in the west. South of the Sierra is a narrow strip of 2320 sq km (860 sq miles) where the finest Cuban tobacco is grown. The Trinidad Mountains, starting in the centre, rise to 1100m (3609ft) in the east. Encircling the port of Santiago are the rugged mountains of the Sierra Maestra. A quarter of the island is covered with mountain forests of pine and mahogany.
GOVERNMENT: Socialist Republic. Gained independence from Spain in 1898. **Head of State and Government**: President Fidel Castro Ruz since 1959.
LANGUAGE: The official language is Spanish.
RELIGION: Roman Catholic majority. There are also minority Afro-Cuban religions.
TIME: GMT - 5.
ELECTRICITY: 110/220 volts AC, 60Hz. American-style flat two-pin plugs are generally used, except in certain large hotels where the European round two-pin plug is standard.
COMMUNICATIONS: Telephone: IDD to Havana only. Country code: 53. Outgoing international code: 119. Phonecards for both internal and external calls are readily available from shops and kiosks. Some calls must be made through the international operator, and may be subject to delays. **Mobile telephone:** Phones from the UK cannot be used. Cellular handsets can be hired from *Cubacel*. Roaming agreements exist with Canada and some European and Latin American countries, although not with the USA or UK. For further details, check online (website: www.cubacel.com). GSM 900 network by *C_Com* has limited coverage. **Fax:** Services are widely available. **Internet:** Available at hotels and some Internet cafes. ISPs are limited. The main providers include *Cubaweb* (website: www.cubaweb.cu). **Telegram:** These may be sent from all post offices in Havana and from RCA offices in major hotels in large towns. **Post:** Letters to Western Europe can take several weeks. It is advisable to use the airmail service. **Press:** Papers are in Spanish, although the Communist Party daily newspaper, *Granma*, publishes a weekly edition, called *Granma International*, in English, German, Portuguese and French. There is also a fortnightly international newspaper, *Prisma*, published in Spanish and English. All media is government-controlled.
Radio: BBC World Service (website: www.bbc.co.uk/worldservice) and Voice of America (website: www.voa.gov) can be received. From time to time the frequencies change and the most up-to-date can be found online.

Passport/Visa

	Passport Required?	Visa Required?	Return Ticket Required?
Full British	Yes	1	Yes
Australian	Yes	1	Yes
Canadian	Yes	1	Yes
USA	Yes	1	Yes
Other EU	Yes	1	Yes
Japanese	Yes	1	Yes

Note: Regulations and requirements may be subject to change at short notice, and you are advised to contact the appropriate diplomatic or consular authority before finalising travel arrangements. Details of these may be found at the head of this country's entry. Any numbers in the chart refer to the footnotes below.

PASSPORTS: Passports valid for at least six months after the departure date from Cuba required by all nationals without diplomatic representation in Cuba.
Note: Persons of Cuban origin who are nationals of other countries must travel with a Cuban passport if they left Cuba after 1970.
VISAS: Required by all except:
a) those nationals whose countries have signed visa-exemption agreements with Cuba (contact the Consulate for further information);
b) **1**. holders of a **Tourist Visa Card**. Certain tour operators, travel agencies and airlines can issue a Tourist Visa Card valid for one single trip of up to 30 days, although the stay can be extended in Cuba. Stipulations are that the traveller pre-books and pre-pays hotel accommodation in Cuba through an officially recognised tour operator. The card must be bought in the country where the trip has been arranged. All passengers must hold tickets and other documentation required for their onward or return journey unless holding special annotation issued by a Cuban Consulate;
c) transit passengers continuing their journey to a third country within 72 hours, provided they hold confirmed onward tickets and US$50 per day.
Note: (a) All business travellers (except journalists, those attending a conference or those wishing to study) need a visa, regardless of nationality. (b) Neither visa exemptions nor tourist visa card facilities are applicable to foreign passport holders born in Cuba, unless holding a document proving withdrawal of Cuban citizenship.
Exit permits: Required by those whose stay in Cuba exceeds 90 days.
Types of visa and cost: *Tourist visa card*: £15. All visas are £49.99.
Note: (a) With the exception of Tourist Visa Cards, all visas have an additional charge of £15 for expenses in connection with visa authorisation.
Validity: Tourist visa cards must be used within 180 days of issue, with one entry permitted. Tourist visa cards and tourist and business visas are valid for 30 days from date of entry; extensions of a further 30 days are possible.
Application to: Consulate (or Consular section at Embassy); see *Contact Addresses* section. Application forms for tourist visa cards can be obtained from certain tour operators and travel agents.
Application requirements: *Tourist Visa Card*: (a) One completed application form. (b) Photocopy of valid passport. (c) Photocopy of return ticket or travel agent voucher for pre-paid package tour, plus proof of accommodation. (d) Fee (payable in cash or by postal order). *Business*: (a) Valid passport. (b) Two completed application forms. (c) Two passport-size photos. (d) Details of business contact in Cuba. (e) Letter of invitation from Cuban company, organisation or institution. (f) Fee (payable in cash, by postal order or bank counter-cheque). *Journalist*: (a) Valid passport with photocopy. (b) Two completed application forms. (c) Two passport-size photos. (d) A sponsor letter from employer and a written version of your journalistic project, plus a list of photographic/filming equipment that applicant is intending to bring into Cuba. (e) Fee (payable by postal order or bank counter-cheque).
Note: (a) All applications by post require a self-addressed envelope; recorded mail or special delivery is especially recommended.
Working days required: *Tourist visa card*: One day (seven days for postal applications). *Tourist visa*: Seven to 10 days. *Business visa*: 10 days (two weeks for postal applications). *Journalist visa*: Six weeks minimum.
Temporary residence: Enquire at Embassy.

Money

Currency: Cuban Peso (peso) = 100 centavos. Notes are in denominations of peso100, 50, 20, 10 and 5. Coins are in denominations of peso1, and 20, 5, 2 and 1 centavos. The US dollar was also introduced as legal tender in 1993 forming a vital part of the economy. But as of November 8 2004, Cuba has banned the use of US dollars in commercial transactions - a response to the US's tighter embargoes. Dollars must now be exchanged for Cuban pesos where a 10 per cent commission will be charged. In some tourist and large urban areas, the Euro is also accepted. Hard currency must be used in most transactions.
Currency exchange: Money should be exchanged at official foreign exchange bureaux, banks or international air- and seaports, which issue receipts for transactions. ATMs are currently only available in Varadero and Havana, but cash can be obtained in banks with visa credit or debit cards.
Credit & debit cards: MasterCard and Visa are increasingly accepted, provided they are not issued by a US bank, but check with your credit or debit card company for details of merchant acceptability and other services which may be available. American Express and other cards issued by US banks are not accepted.
Travellers cheques: US Dollar, Sterling and other major currencies are accepted, but US Dollar cheques issued by US banks are not acceptable (including overbranded cheques from other banks worldwide). The white exchange paper received upon encashment must be retained.
Currency restrictions: The import and export of local currency is prohibited. The import of foreign currency is unlimited, subject to declaration of amounts exceeding US$5000 on arrival; export is allowed up to the amount imported and declared. Generally, a maximum of pesos10 may be reconverted to foreign currency for re-export at the end of the stay but it may only be reconverted on presentation of a correctly filled out official exchange record.
Exchange rate indicators: The following figures are included as a guide to the movements of the Cuban Peso against Sterling and the US Dollar:

Date	Feb '04	May '04	Aug '04	Nov '04
£1.00=	1.87	1.79	1.84	1.89
$1.00=	0.99	1.00	1.00	1.00

Banking hours: Mon-Fri 0830-1200 and 1330-1500, Sat 0830-1030. Hours may vary and banks may be open all day in larger cities.

A B C D E F G H I J K L M N O P Q R S T U V W X Y Z

Duty Free

The following goods may be taken into Cuba by persons aged 18 years and over without incurring customs duty:
200 cigarettes or 50 cigars or 250g of tobacco; 3 bottles of alcoholic beverages; gifts up to a value of US$50 (articles up to US$200 will be subject to customs duty payments); 10kg of medicines.
Prohibited items: Natural fruits, seeds, beans or vegetables; meat and dairy products; weapons and ammunition; video cassettes and household appliances; all pornographic material and drugs.
Note: Electrical items with heavy power consumption may be confiscated and returned upon departure.

Public Holidays

2005: Jan 1 Liberation Day. **Jan 2** Victory of Armed Forces. **May 1** Labour Day. **May 20** Independence Day. **Jul 25-27** Days of Rebeliousness. **Oct 10** Anniversary of the beginning of the War of Independence in 1868. **Dec 25** Christmas Day.
2006: Jan 1 Liberation Day. **Jan 2** Victory of Armed Forces. **May 1** Labour Day. **May 20** Independence Day. **Jul 25-27** Day of Rebeliousness. **Oct 10** Anniversary of the beginning of the War of Independence in 1868. **Dec 25** Christmas.

Health

	Special Precautions?	Certificate Required?
Yellow Fever	No	No
Cholera	No	No
Typhoid & Polio	1	N/A
Malaria	No	N/A

Note: *Regulations and requirements may be subject to change at short notice, and you are advised to contact your doctor well in advance of your intended date of departure. Any numbers in the chart refer to the footnotes below.*

1: Typhoid may be a risk in remote rural areas.
Food & drink: Mains water is chlorinated and, whilst relatively safe, may cause mild abdominal upsets. Bottled water is available and is advised for the first few weeks of stay. Milk is pasteurised and dairy products are safe for consumption. Local meat, poultry, seafoods and fruit are generally considered safe to eat.
Other risks: *Hepatitis A* has been reported in the northern Caribbean Islands, and immunoglobin is not always readily available. *Human fascioliasis* is endemic. *Dengue fever* may occur in the area as well as outbreaks of *dengue haemorrhagic fever* and *meningitis*, particularly in urban areas such as Havana. Rabies is present. For those at high risk, vaccination should be considered. If you are bitten, seek medical advice without delay. For more information, consult the *Health* appendix.
Health care: Cuba's medical services are very good and some emergency treatment may be available to visitors at no cost. However, health insurance is necessary, as foreigners must pay most of their own health care costs. Some hospitals may ask for proof of ability to pay for treatment prior to receiving sufficient medical attention.

Travel - International

AIR: Cuba's national airline is *Cubana (CU)* (website: www.cubana.cu). Other airlines serving Cuba include *Aeroflot, Air France, Air Jamaica, British Airways, Continental Airlines, Mexicana* and *SA*.
Approximate flight times: From Havana to *London* is eight hours, to *Los Angeles* is nine hours and to *New York* is six hours.
International airports: *Havana (HVA)* (José Martí International) is 15km (9 miles) southwest of the city. Bus and taxi services to the city are available (travel time: bus - one hour; taxi - 20 to 30 minutes). Airport facilities include duty-free shops, bank and bureau de change, tourist information/hotel reservation, restaurants and bars, and car hire.
There are also nine other international airports.
Departure tax: 25 Convertible Pesos. Transit passengers departing within the same day and not leaving the transit area, plus children under two years, are exempt.
SEA: Due to the US blockade, there are no scheduled passenger ships and only some cruise ships call at Cuba. It is possible, however, to call in on a private yacht, although the authorities must be contacted prior to arrival.

Travel - Internal

AIR: *Cubana* operates scheduled services between most main towns but advance booking is essential as flights are limited. It is advised that, where possible, internal flights are undertaken with internationally recognised tour operators.
RAIL: The principal rail route is from Havana to Santiago de Cuba, with two daily trains. There are also through trains from Havana to other towns. Previously, the rail network connected the vast majority of the country but has been badly affected by natural disasters and now only certain parts of the country are accessible by rail.
ROAD: Sightseeing can be pre-arranged, although internal travel arrangements may be made through any of the several ground handlers. Roads are signposted and adequate, although often poorly lit. Traffic drives on the right. **Bus**: Most tours will include travel by air-conditioned buses. Cuba's national bus service *Astro* (Asociaciones de Transportes por Omnibus) connects all the main towns and suburbs at least once or twice a day; fares are low and services are reliable, but the buses can be very crowded, especially during the rush hour. Four seats are saved for tourists or foreign visitors on each bus. Increasingly popular, however, are the state-operated, air-conditioned *Viazul* 'tourist buses' (website: www.viazul.cu), which connect most major cities and tourist destinations daily. These must be paid for in US dollars (larger offices should accept payment by credit/debit card). **Taxi**: Taxis and chauffeur-driven cars can work out to be as cheap as the bus or train. An influx of comfortable, modern cars makes this a viable form of transport. It is usual to order them through the hotel. All official taxis have meters but, in private taxis, fares should be pre-arranged. Especially in and around the airports, and old Havana, many bogus tour agents/taxi companies operate, so visitors should ensure any taxis used are officially recognised. **Car hire**: There are several good and inexpensive car hire companies with representatives at most hotels, and due to Cuba's well-maintained road system, this is often regarded as one of the best forms of getting around the island. Bicycles can be hired. **Documentation**: Valid national driving licence required. Drivers must be aged 21 or over.
URBAN: Buses, minibuses and plentiful shared taxis operate in Havana at low flat fares. Buses are frequent but often very crowded, and foreigners may have difficulty paying the fare in pesos.
Travel Times: The following chart gives approximate travel times (in hours and minutes) from **Havana** to other major towns in Cuba.

	Air	Road
Varadero	0.15	2.00
Trinidad	0.20	5.00
Santiago de Cuba	1.15	17.00
Playas del Este	-	0.30
Pinar del Rio	0.15	2.00

Accommodation

The range of accommodation available is expanding, although the budget traveller is still not largely catered for. The best hotels are in Havana, Trinidad, Cayo Coco or at Varadero Beach. Since many visitors to Cuba go as part of a package holiday, the hotel will have been selected in advance. The hotels are clean, functional and adequate. Contact the Cuba Tourist Board for further information (see *Contact Addresses* section).
CASAS PARTICULARES: Also known as private houses, these are - as the name suggests - similar to bed & breakfast. In certain towns only (most notably not in Varadero), it is possible for Cubans to rent out rooms to visitors. The rooms normally have a private bathroom and the deal often includes breakfast. It may also be possible to have other meals there as well, which are much more varied and plentiful than those offered in many of the state-operated restaurants. It can be a good, and cheaper, way to get more of a feel for the Cuban way of life and to get a glimpse of the 'real Cuba'. Legal *casas particulares* are recognised by a blue triangle on a white background on the front door.

Resorts & Excursions

Cuba has undergone a transformation since it first opened its doors to global tourism after almost three decades of isolation. Most noteworthy has been the rapid growth in private accommodation, the extensive network of *casas particulares* allowing the independent traveller the opportunity, not only to experience life more as it is lived by the average Cubano, but also to explore corners of the country that had previously been inaccessible or off-limits. Good news for the tourist is the growing choice of resorts and the number of new or refurbished hotels that are opening in towns across the country. While ecotourism is still in its infancy and much of the island's extraordinary natural beauty remains to be discovered, the government is already making strides in the right direction.

HAVANA

One of the largest and most vibrant cities in the Caribbean (with a population of over two million), **Havana** (**La Habana**) boasts an old town which features on UNESCO's World Heritage List. Much of the money made from tourism is currently being pumped back into restorative works in the city and its buildings. The surrounding 19th-century district of densely packed, crumbling houses and narrow streets has its own appeal, as does the high-rise city centre (**Vedado**). The most famous of the hotels here is the **Nacional**, still patronised by Hollywood film stars. Dating from the same period is **Miramar**, the leafy embassy district reminiscent of Miami. The sea wall, known as the **Malecón**, extends for 8km and is a popular meeting point for locals, especially after dusk. Havana's best beaches, the **Playas del Este**, are about 20km from the centre.
Havana is closely associated with the US writer, Ernest Hemmingway. One of his favourite haunts was the bar, **La Bodeguita del Medio**, only a stone's throw from the city's magnificent 18th-century cathedral. Overlooking the neighbouring **Plaza de Armas** is the **Museo de la Ciudad** and the recently opened **Palacio del Segundo Cabo**, former residence of the Captains General, which boasts wonderful rooftop views. The splendidly refurbished rooms of the **Museo de Arte Colonial** are also worth a visit. The **Castillo de la Real Fuerza** is the oldest of Havana's three forts. The **Capitolio**, modelled on the Capitol in Washington DC, was once home to the Cuban government and is sumptuously decorated. The huge **Museo de la Revolución** occupies the former presidential palace. Outside under a glass case is the **Granma**, the yacht which brought Castro and the leading rebels back to Cuba in 1956. Guided tours of the tobacco factory (**Fábrica de Tabacos Partagás**) are also available. It is worth enjoying a relaxing drink on one of the Habana Vieja hotel rooftops to enjoy the views.

PINAR DEL RÍO AND THE WEST

Pinar del Río is arguably Cuba's most beautiful province. The countryside is amazingly diverse, but the outstanding feature must be the *mogotes* (oddly rounded limestone mountains, covered in lush vegetation). The caves here, notably the **Cueva del Indio**, are well worth a visit, with stalactites and stalagmites and underground rivers. The town of **Pinar del Río** should be explored in its own right, and is home to several cigar factories that are open to the public. The tobacco plantations at **Vuelta Abajo**, a short distance southwest of Pinar del Río can also be visited during the growing season from December to April. The road from **Viñales** to the coast makes a scenic drive.
Isla de la Juventud (Isle of Youth) is the largest of the 350 islands making up the **Canarreos archipelago**, administered from the capital, **Nueva Gerona**. Once known as 'Parrot Island', the Isle of Youth was a hideout for pirates, including the notorious Englishman, Captain Henry Morgan. It is also supposed to have inspired Robert Louis Stevenson's *Treasure Island*. In the same archipelago is **Cayo Largo**, another of Cuba's well-known tourist resorts, considered to have some of the best beaches in the Caribbean.
Varadero, a sheltered peninsula on Cuba's north coast, is the island's best-known beach resort. Apart from the 20km (12.5 miles) of fine white sand, there are excellent opportunities for scuba-diving. The amenities are first rate. **Guama**, in the south of **Matanzas Province**, is a reconstruction of an Amero-Indian village. There are boat trips along the **Treasure Lake** (**Laguna del Tesoro**), while most visitors will also enjoy the crocodile nursery. This part of Mantanzas is also famous for bird life and the attractive beaches of **Playa Girón** and **Playa Larga**, location for the disastrous Bay of Pigs invasion in 1961.

TRINIDAD AND THE CENTRE

Cienfuegos is a prosperous modern city built around a fine harbour at the foot of the **Escambray Mountains**. Its 19th-century core was built with the help of French settlers from Louisiana, which explains why many of the town's finest buildings are reminiscent of New Orleans. The main sights around **Parque José Martí** include the cathedral and the late 19th-century **Teatro Tomás Terry**, worth exploring for its florid interior. Closer to the harbour are the castle, **Castillo de Jagua** and the **Palacio de Valle**. Built in an appealing mixture of architectural styles, with Moorish influences to the fore, it is now a restaurant with a roof-top terrace that affords splendid views of the bay and surrounding countryside. **Trinidad** retains the atmosphere of an old colonial town, despite the influx of tourists. Founded in the year 1514, it was one of Cuba's seven original towns, and the presence of many beautiful buildings dating from the 17th to 19th centuries accounts for its place on UNESCO's World Heritage List. The main attractions include the elegant **Parque Martí** and several museums in the colonial mansions, the best of which, the **Museo Romántico**, having been beautifully refurbished in period style. The **Taller Alfarero**, a ceramics workshop where traditional techniques are still used, is also worth visiting. Many tourists stay not in Trinidad itself but at the nearby beach resort of **Playa Ancón**. Mention should also be made of the **Torre de Manaca Iznaga** (50m/165ft), a lookout tower offering great views of the **Valley of the Sugar Mills** (**Valle de los Ingenios**) and the **Escambray Mountains**.
Santa Clara is a bustling city in the heart of an important

agricultural region. Santa Clara is closely associated with the revolutionary hero Ernesto 'Ché' Guevara who captured the town for the Cuban revolution days before the resignation of the dictator, General Batista. Understandably, the government promotes this lively town; it is also investing in the area's other potential attractions, which include **Remedios** and the beaches around **Cayo Las Brujas**. **Sancti Spíritus** has a laid-back feel and a good range of state and private accommodation. The bridge over the **Yayabo River** is made of stone – the oldest one on the island. Strolling through the sleepy streets while admiring the colonial architecture is the main attraction. The best example of the style is the **Colonial Art Museum**.

SANTIAGO DE CUBA AND THE EAST

Camagüey is one of the more heavily promoted towns of the island. Its attractions include a number of churches and museums and a thriving (and very photogenic) peso market. Camagüey lies in the centre of a fertile plain, exploited for sugar. The unspoilt Camagüey archipelago is also known as **Jardines del Rey**. Within the natural park are some 20km of landscaped white-sand beaches, the best known of which are **Cayo Coco** and **Cayo Guillermo**, the latter a favourite haunt of Ernest Hemmingway who came to fish here.

Bayamo was the birthplace of the 19th-century revolutionary, Manuel de Cépedes, who launched Cuba's struggle for independence here in 1868-9. Modern Bayamo is a delightful little town with one of the few pedestrianised centres on the island. From here it is possible to explore the nature trails of the **Parque Nacional del Granma** around the fishing hamlet of **Cabo Cruz**.

Holguín is familiar to most tourists for its airstrip, but the old colonial town is worth a couple of hours at least for its attractive squares and streets. Also falling within the province are the beach resorts of **Guarda la Vaca** and **Esmeralda**, both of which are well served with amenities.

Santiago de Cuba, 780km (485 miles) from Havana, was the island's first capital. It owed this distinction to a superb deepwater harbour, the majestic **Sierra Maestra Mountains** forming a dramatic backdrop. Despite losing its primacy early in the day, Santiago was never eclipsed by Havana thanks to the French plantation owners and their slaves who arrived in the 18th century, turning the region over to coffee and sugar production. Santiago consequently acquired a cosmopolitan flavour that accounts for its cultural importance, especially in music – the **Son** originated here. In July, the town hosts one of the most spectacular carnivals in the country, which has even spawned its own museum. Highlights of Santiago's old quarter (around the square, **Parque Céspedes**) are the cathedral, the **Casa de Diego Velázquez**, one of Cuba's oldest colonial mansions, and the **Museo Emilio Bacardí**. Adjacent to the square is the **Casa Granda Hotel**, located adjacent to the square in the area, a favourite haunt of the British author Graham Greene.

The **Moncada Barracks**, where Fidel Castro and his revolutionary insurgents launched an abortive uprising in 1953, is the most visited sight outside the town centre. After soaking up Santiago's heady atmosphere, visitors should venture into the surrounding countryside. Excursions on offer include the **Castillo del Morro**, once an important fortress and now a museum of piracy with superb vistas of the surrounding countryside. The shrine to the Virgin of **Cobre** is housed in a magnificent basilica. This important centre of pilgrimage was the focus of Pope John Paul II's visit to Cuba in 1998. **Baracoa** lies between two bays on Cuba's eastern tip and is one of the island's most beautiful towns. Tradition has it that Christopher Columbus planted a wooden cross here after coming ashore in 1492. It was later transferred to the **Church of Our Lady of the Assumption** where it is still on view. Until the 1960s, when a road connecting it to the mainland was constructed, Cuba's oldest European settlement was accessible only by boat. The town's role as a former Spanish outpost is evidenced by its three forts, the **Fuerte Matachín** (now housing the municipal museum), the **Castillo de Seboruco** (now a hotel), and the **Fuerte de la Punta** (which now also houses a restaurant).

Sport & Activities

All sporting events are free for Cubans. The country participates in many sports in the Olympic Games. **Baseball** is the national sport; **soccer** and a variety of **ball games** are also played. There are many stadiums, and both playing and watching sport is one of the national pastimes.

Watersports: Diving can be practised at major resorts and at some lesser-known locations. The 21 km-/13 mile-long *Varadero Beach*, one of Cuba's best-developed resorts, offers good diving and **snorkelling**. For those not wanting to venture underwater, **boat tours** to the reef are available. *Cayo Largo*, an island to the south of Cuba, also has a beautiful beach, with facilities for snorkelling, diving, **windsurfing** and **fishing**. Lesser-known resorts offering good facilities include *Cayo Coco*, an island off the northern coast, and *Guardalvaca*, to the north of Holguín. The *Isla de la Juventud*, a large island to the south of Cuba, offers excellent reef diving. Wildlife, including turtles and iguanas, can be observed on the coral keys to the east. There is also very good diving from resorts in the *Pinar del Río* province in the northwest of the island, an area characterised by clear water and long white-sand beaches. Beautiful corals can be seen off the coast. Some of the best fishing is to be had off the more remote beaches, which can be difficult to get to without one's own transport. Local dive operators offer organised dives, equipment hire and tuition.

Trekking and horseriding: Although possible in some of the more remote areas of the island, permits may be required. Check with the authorities before departure. There are few marked trails, so it is best to hire a local guide. There are three main mountain ranges in the west, centre and east of the island. Beautiful and unspoilt scenery can be found all over Cuba. *Pico Turquino*, Cuba's highest mountain, is in the *Sierra Maestra* range, offering good hikes and treks. The *Sierra de Cubitas* range near Camagüey is characterised by river gorges and cliffs, while the *Escambray Mountains* near Trinidad contain dense rainforest. *Guama*, on the Zapata peninsula is an extensive marshy area, which hosts many interesting varieties of birds, including parrots. The *Cordillera de Guaniguanico* in the north of the island features spectacular scenery with rivers and limestone mountains and caves. Horseriding is available at special tourist ranches at Baconao and Trinidad.

Social Profile

FOOD & DRINK: Restaurants (both table- and self-service) are generally inexpensive. Cuisine is continental or Cuban with a strong emphasis on seafood. Cuban food uses more garlic and less chilli than elsewhere in the Caribbean. Favourite dishes are omelettes, often stuffed with meat and/or cheese; maize fritters; a thick soup made of chicken or black beans; roast suckling pig; chicken and rice; plantains baked or fried; and local Cuban ice cream. Tour food served in hotels is not always exciting but it is adequate and will include chicken, fish, cheese, papaya, pineapple, vegetables and green salads. Desserts are sweet and include pastries, flans, caramel custard, guava paste and cheese.

Bars generally have waiter and counter service. Cuban coffee is very strong, but weaker, British-style coffee is available. Cuban beer is tasty but weak. Spirits are reasonably priced; rum is good and plentiful and used in excellent cocktails such as *daiquiris* and *mojitos*.

NIGHTLIFE: Nightlife is concentrated in Havana, Varadero Beach and in the major tourist resorts. Cuba is renowned for its salsa dancing and visitors can attend dance classes or swing their hips with the locals at the *Tropicana* and *Varadero Mambo* nightclubs. Even medium-sized bars usually have a house band playing Cuban classics. There is a choice of floor show entertainments, nightclubs and theatres. The *Tropicana* nightclub stages spectacular open-air shows. Theatre, opera and ballet are staged all year round in Havana and seats are very cheap. Cinemas show films in Spanish, but some have subtitles.

SHOPPING: Special purchases include cigars, rum, coffee and local handicrafts. The main hotels have a few luxury shops. There are duty-free shops at the airport and in the centre of Havana. **Shopping hours**: Mon-Sat 0900-1800, Sun 0900-1200.

SPECIAL EVENTS: The following is a selection of special events occurring in Cuba in 2005. All events take place in Havana unless otherwise stated.

Jan *Winter CUBALLET*. **Jan-Jul** *FolkCuba* (traditional music and dance). **Jan-Aug** *Cubadanza*. **Feb** *Havana Cigar Festival* (trade fair); *International Book Fair*. **Mar** *International Festival of Electro-Acoustic Music*. **Apr** *Percuba 2005* (16th International Percussion Festival). **May** *CUBADISCO*; *Tourism Convention*. **Jul** *Fiesta del Fuego* (Caribbean Festival), Santiago de Cuba. **Jul-Aug** *Havana Carnival*. **Aug** *Summer Cuba Ballet*. **Sep** *International Transport Exhibition*.

Oct *International Ballet Festival*; *Festival of Ibero-American Culture*. **Nov** *International Havana Exhibition*; *International Choir Festival*. **Dec** International Festival of New Latin American Cinema; *International Jazz Festival*.

SOCIAL CONVENTIONS: Handshaking is the normal form of greeting. Cubans generally address each other as *compañero*, but visitors should use *señor* or *señora*. Some Cubans have two surnames after their Christian name and the first surname is the correct one to use. Normal courtesies should be observed when visiting someone's home and a small gift may be given if invited for a meal. Formal wear is not often needed and hats are rarely worn. Men should not wear shorts except on or near the beach. Women wear light cotton dresses or trousers during the day and cocktail dresses for formal evenings. **Tipping**: Moderate tipping is expected. However, as more foreigners pass through Cuba, many people who would not normally merit them have begun to demand tips. Some discretion may be required.

Business Profile

ECONOMY: The agricultural component of Cuba's economy is dominated by sugar, of which it is one of the world's largest exporters. However, due to persistently low world prices throughout the 1980s and 1990s, the Government has attempted to diversify into other crops. Tobacco (Cuban cigars are renowned throughout the world) and citrus fruits are the most successful of these. Cuban industry is largely devoted to the processing of agricultural products but also produces cement, fertilisers, textiles, prefabricated buildings, agricultural machinery and domestic consumer goods. Tourism, the only significant service industry, has proved to be a growth industry and a vital source of foreign exchange; the Government has invested heavily in developing infrastructure for that purpose. Development of the Cuban economy has long been hampered by the blockade imposed by successive American governments (even though bilateral US-Cuban trade is estimated at US$300 million annually, mostly in telecommunications traffic and various financial instruments, such as credit cards). While the Soviet Union was able to provide aid and markets, especially for Cuba's sugar output, this was not an insurmountable hurdle. However, during the last decade, since the demise of the USSR, Cuba has faced increasing economic difficulties. In June 2001, the lack of markets and low-world price forced the government to close down half the country's sugar mills. Nevertheless, domestic reforms of the previously rigid state-controlled structure – opening up to foreign investment and creating export-processing zones – have allowed erratic growth (2.6 per cent in 2004) to take place. A substantial informal dollar economy also grew up during the 1990s. As with the political structure in Cuba, most observers are awaiting what form of government emerges after Castro to determine which direction the economy will take. Argentina, Canada, China and Spain are Cuba's main trading partners.

BUSINESS: Courtesy is expected and hospitality should not be lavish, being offered to groups rather than individuals. Best months for business visits are November to April. **Office hours**: Mon-Fri 0830-1230 and 1330-1630, some offices also open on alternate Saturdays from 0800-1700.

COMMERCIAL INFORMATION: The following organisation can offer advice: *Cámara de Comercio de la República de Cuba*, Calle 21, No 661, esq. Calle A, Vedado, Havana (tel: (7) 551 321/2/4 or 551 654 or 551 452 or 551 746; fax: (7) 333 042; website: www.camaracuba.cubaweb.cu).

CONFERENCES/CONVENTIONS: Modern facilities are available at Havana International Conference Center, Pabexpo, ExpoCuba and the Varadero Plaza America. Further information can be obtained from Cubanacan UK Ltd,
Unit 49, Skylines, Limeharbour, London E14 9TS, UK
(tel: (020) 7537 7909 *or* 536 8173; fax: (020) 7537 7747; e-mail: administration@cubanacan.co.uk *or* director@cubanacan.co.uk; website: www.cubanacan.cu)
or Buró de Convenciones de Cuba, COCAL, Edificio Focsa, Calle M entre la 17 y 19, Vedado, La Habana (tel: (7) 552 923 *or* 662 629; fax: (7) 334 261; e-mail: marketing@buroconv.mit.tur.cu; website: www.cubameeting.org)

Climate

Hot, sub-tropical climate all year. Most rain falls between May and October and hurricanes can occur in autumn (August to November). Humidity varies between 75 per cent and 95 per cent. Cooler months are January to April when the least rain falls.

Required clothing: Lightweight cottons and linens most of the year; the high humidity makes it unwise to wear synthetics close to the skin. Light waterproofs are advisable all year round.

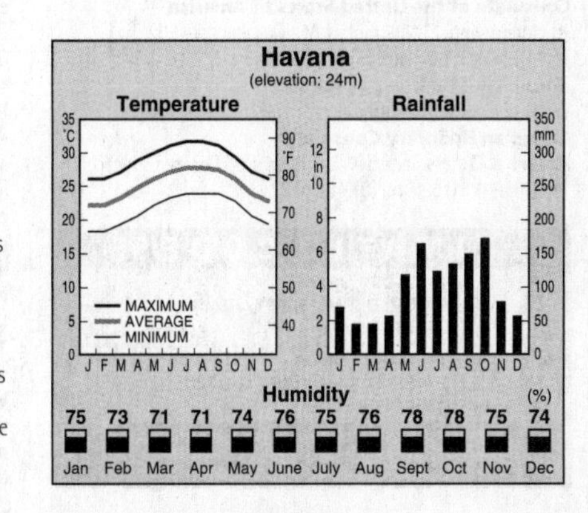

Curaçao

LATEST TRAVEL ADVICE CONTACTS

British Foreign and Commonwealth Office
Tel: (0870) 606 0290 Website: www.fco.gov.uk
US Department of State
Website: http://travel.state.gov/travel
Canadian Department of Foreign Affairs and Int'l Trade
Tel: (1 800) 267 8376 Website: www.dfait-maeci.gc.ca

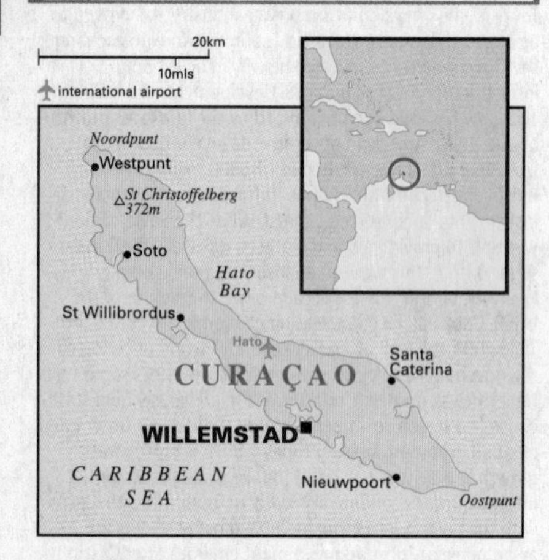

Location: Caribbean, 56km (35 miles) north of Venezuela.

Country dialling code: 599.

Curaçao is part of the Netherlands Antilles, represented abroad by Royal Netherlands Embassies (see *The Netherlands* section).

Curaçao Tourism Development Bureau
Pietermaai 19, PO Box 3266, Willemstad, Curaçao, NA
Tel: (9) 434 8200. Fax: (9) 461 2305.
E-mail: ctdbcur@ctdb.net
Website: www.curacao-tourism.com *or* www.ctb.an

Office of the Minister Plenipotentiary of the Netherlands Antilles
PO Box 90706, Badhuisweg 173-175, 2597 JP The Hague, The Netherlands
Tel: (70) 306 6111. Fax: (70) 306 6110.
E-mail: serphos@kymna.nl

Curaçao Tourism Development Bureau (UK Representative)
c/o Axis Sales & Marketing Ltd, 421A Finchley Road, London NW3 6HJ, UK
Tel: (020) 7431 4045. Fax: (020) 7431 7920.
E-mail: destinations@axissm.com
Website: www.curacao-tourism.com

Caribbean Tourism Organisation
22 The Quadrant, Richmond, Surrey, TW9 1BP, UK
Tel: (020) 8948 0057. Fax: (020) 8948 0067.
E-mail: ctolondon@caribtourism.com
Website: www.caribbean.co.uk

British Consulate
Jan Sofat 38, PO Box 3803, Curaçao, NA
Tel: (9) 747 3322. Fax: (9) 747 3330.
E-mail: britconcur@attglobal.net

Curaçao Tourist Bureau
7951 SW, Sixth Street, Suite 216, Plantation, Florida 33324, USA
Tel: (954) 370 5887 *or* (800) 328 7222 (toll-free in USA and Canada). Fax: (954) 723 7949.
E-mail: jbgrossman@aol.com
Website: www.curacao-tourism.com *or* www.curacao.com
Also deals with enquiries from Canada.

Consulate of the United States of America
JB Gorsiraweg 1, Willemstad AN, Curaçao, NA
Tel: (9) 461 3066. Fax: (9) 461 6489.
E-mail: info@amcongencuracao.an
Website: www.amcongencuracao.an

Canadian Honorary Consulate
Maduro & Curiel's Bank, NV, 2-4 Plaza JoJo Correa, Curaçao, NA
Tel: (9) 466 1115. Fax: (9) 466 1122.

TIMATIC CODES

Health	AMADEUS: **TI-DFT/JIB/HE** GALILEO/WORLDSPAN: **TI-DFT/JIB/HE** SABRE: **TIDFT/JIB/HE**
Visa	AMADEUS: **TI-DFT/JIB/VI** GALILEO/WORLDSPAN: **TI-DFT/JIB/VI** SABRE: **TIDFT/JIB/VI**

To access TIMATIC country information on Health and Visa regulations through the Computer Reservations System (CRS), type in the appropriate command line listed above.

General Information

AREA: 444 sq km (171 sq miles).
POPULATION: 152,700 (1996).
POPULATION DENSITY: 344 per sq km.
CAPITAL: Willemstad. **Population**: 125,000 (UN estimate 2001, including the suburbs).
GEOGRAPHY: Curaçao, the largest island in the Netherlands Antilles, is geographically part of the Dutch Leeward Islands, also known as the Dutch Antilles. It is flat, rocky and fairly barren owing to its low rainfall. There are many excellent beaches.
GOVERNMENT: Part of the Netherlands Antilles; dependency of The Netherlands. The Netherlands Antilles consist of Bonaire, Curaçao, Saba, St Eustatius and St Maarten. The capital of the island group is Willemstad, Curaçao. **Head of State:** HM Queen Beatrix of the Netherlands, represented locally by Governor Frits Goedgedrag since 2002. **Head of Government:** Prime Minister Etienne Ys since 2002.
LANGUAGE: Dutch is the official language. Papiamento (a mixture of Dutch, Spanish, Portuguese, English, Arawak Indian and several African languages) is the *lingua franca*; English and Spanish are also widely spoken.
RELIGION: The majority of the population is Roman Catholic, with Protestant minorities, both evangelical and other low-church denominations. There is also a Baha'i temple and a synagogue.
TIME: GMT - 4.
ELECTRICITY: 110/130 volts AC, 50Hz.
COMMUNICATIONS: Telephone: Good IDD service to Europe. Country code: 599. Outgoing international code: 00. **Mobile telephone:** TDMA network exists. GSM GSM 900/1900 networks operated by *AT&T Wireless, Curaçao Telecom NV* (website: www.curacaotelecom.com), *East Caribbean Cellular, Setel NV* and *Telcell NV*. Handsets can be hired at the airport post office. There is a 5 per cent tax. **Internet:** There is an Internet cafe in Willemstad. Local ISPs include *Curanet* (website: www.cura.net) and *IBM*. **Telegram:** Facilities available in most large hotels and in the post office in Willemstad. **Post:** Airmail to Western Europe takes four to six days. **Press:** The English-language newspaper is the *Business Journal* (monthly).
Radio: BBC World Service (website: www.bbc.co.uk/worldservice) and Voice of America (website: www.voa.gov) can be received. From time to time the frequencies change and the most up-to-date can be found online.

Passport/Visa

	Passport Required?	Visa Required?	Return Ticket Required?
Full British	Yes	1	Yes
Australian	Yes	2	Yes
Canadian	Yes	2	Yes
USA	Yes	2	Yes
Other EU	Yes	1/2	Yes
Japanese	Yes	2	Yes

Note: *Regulations and requirements may be subject to change at short notice, and you are advised to contact the appropriate diplomatic or consular authority before finalising travel arrangements. Details of these may be found at the head of this country's entry. Any numbers in the chart refer to the footnotes below.*

PASSPORTS: Passport or official travel documents valid for at least three months after intended return to home country required by all.
VISAS: Required by all except the following:
(a) **1.** nationals of Belgium, Bolivia, Burkina Faso, Chile, Costa Rica, Czech Republic, Ecuador, Germany, Hungary, Israel, Jamaica, Korea (Rep), Luxembourg, Malawi, Mauritius, The Netherlands, Niger, The Philippines, Poland, San Marino, Slovak Republic, Spain, Swaziland, Togo and the UK for touristic stays of up to three months;
(b) **2.** all other nationals for touristic stays of up to 14 days, except nationals of Albania, Bosnia & Herzegovina, Bulgaria, Cambodia, China (PR) (except Hong Kong SAR), CIS, Colombia, Cote d'Ivoire, Croatia, Cuba, Dominican Republic, Estonia, Ghana, Guinea-Bissau, Haiti, Kenya, Korea (Dem Rep), Latvia, Libya, Lithuania, Macedonia (Former Yugoslav Republic of), Mali, Nigeria, Romania, Serbia & Montenegro and Vietnam who *always* need a visa;
(c) most nationals continuing to a third country within 24 hours by the same means of transportation and not leaving the airport and holding tickets with reserved seats and documents for their onward journey.
Note: All stays can be extended locally by the same period that they are valid for.
Types of visa and cost: All visas, regardless of duration of stay or number of entries permitted on visa, cost £15.
Validity: Visas are generally issued for as long as duration of stay, up until a maximum 90 days from date of issue.
Application to: Nearest Embassy of the Kingdom of The Netherlands. All further information about visa requirements may be obtained from The Royal Netherlands Embassies, which formally represent the Netherlands Antilles; see *Contact Addresses* in *The Netherlands* section.
Application requirements: (a) Valid passport with at least one blank page. If passport is new, the old passport must also be submitted. (b) One fully completed application form. (c) One recent passport-size photo per person endorsed on passport. (d) Fee, payable by postal order (to Royal Netherlands Embassy) or cash. Cheques are not accepted. (e) Evidence of sufficient funds amounting to a minimum of £30 for each day of stay (cash not accepted), eg original bank statements, credit card with credit limit statement, traveller's cheques. (f) A recent and original letter from employer, stating commencement date, with last payslip. If self-employed, submit letter from solicitor, accountant or company house. If unemployed, submit social benefit booklet. If in education, submit a recent and original letter from school/college/university, confirming attendance. (g) Valid medical or travel insurance. *Tourist*: (a)-(g) and, (h) Invitation from family or proof of hotel booking. (i) Return or onward ticket. *Business*: (a)-(g) and, (h) Invitation from Dutch company confirming duration and purpose of stay.
Working days required: Applications should be lodged at least one month prior to departure.
Temporary residence: Enquire at the office of the Lieutenant Governor of the Island Territory of Curaçao, Concordiastraat 24, Willemstad, Curaçao. In certain cases, Dutch Europeans may be permitted to reside in the Netherlands Antilles without having to apply for a residence permit. However, it is best to consult the nearest Dutch Embassy/Consulate in advance to ascertain whether this is applicable based on the individual circumstances of the traveller.

Money

Currency: Netherlands Antilles Guilder or Florin (NAG) = 100 cents. Notes are in denominations of NAG250, 100, 50, 25, 10 and 5. Coins are in denominations of 100, 50, 25, 10, 5, 2.5 and 1 cents. US Dollars are accepted everywhere. However, it is best to take notes in small denominations; US$50 and US$100 notes are not always easy to change.
Note: The Netherlands Antilles Guilder or Florin is tied to the US Dollar.
Currency exchange: Available in banks and bureaux de change. There are some ATMs.
Credit & debit cards: Major credit cards are widely accepted. Check with your credit or debit card company for details of merchant acceptability and other services which may be available. Debit cards are accepted in large shops and supermarkets.
Travellers cheques: Widely accepted. To avoid additional exchange rate charges, travellers are advised to take travellers cheques in US Dollars.
Currency restrictions: The import and export of local and foreign currency is unlimited. The import of Dutch or Surinam silver coins is forbidden.
Exchange rate indicators: The following figures are included as a guide to the movement of the Netherlands Antilles Guilder against Sterling and the US Dollar:

Date	Feb '04	May '04	Aug '04	Nov '04
£1.00=	3.26	3.20	3.29	3.39
$1.00=	1.79	1.79	1.79	1.79

Banking hours: Mon-Fri 0800-1530.

Duty Free

The following items may be taken into Curaçao by those over 15 years of age without payment of duty:
200 cigarettes or 100 cigarillos (of 3g each) or 50 cigars or 250g of tobacco; 2l of alcoholic beverages or 2l of wine; an unlimited amount of perfume; gifts up to the value of NAG100.
Note: If the total value of the goods per passenger exceeds NAG500, a declaration should be made on customs forms and cleared at the freight department. The importation of leather articles from Haiti is not advisable.
Prohibited: Dogs and cats from Central and South America, except from Surinam; monkeys from the South American continent.

Public Holidays

2005: Jan 1 New Year's Day. **Feb 7** Carnival Monday. **Mar 25** Good Friday. **Mar 28** Easter Monday. **Apr 30** Queen's Birthday. **May 1** Labour Day. **May 5** Ascension. **Jul 2** Curaçao Flag Day. **Oct 21** Antillean Day. **Dec 24** Christmas Eve (half day). **Dec 25-26** Christmas. **Dec 31** New Year's Eve (half day).
2006: Jan 1 New Year's Day. **Feb 6** Carnival Monday. **Apr 14** Good Friday. **Apr 17** Easter Monday. **Apr 30** Queen's Birthday. **May 1** Labour Day. **May 25** Ascension. **Jul 2** Curaçao Flag Day. **Oct 21** Antillean Day. **Dec 24** Christmas Eve (half day). **Dec 25-26** Christmas. **Dec 31** New Year's Eve (half day).

Health

	Special Precautions?	Certificate Required?
Yellow Fever	No	1
Cholera	No	No
Typhoid & Polio	2	N/A
Malaria	No	N/A

Note: *Regulations and requirements may be subject to change at short notice, and you are advised to contact your doctor well in advance of your intended date of departure. Any numbers in the chart refer to the footnotes below.*

1: A yellow fever certificate is required from travellers over six months of age coming from infected areas.
2: Immunisation against typhoid is sometimes advised.
Food & drink: All mains water on the island is distilled from sea water and is thus safe to drink. Bottled mineral water is widely available. Milk is pasteurised and dairy products are safe for consumption. Local meat, poultry, seafood, fruit and vegetables are generally considered safe to eat.
Other risks: *Hepatitis A* and *B* occur and immunisation is sometimes recommended. *Dengue fever* may occur. There are potential risks from sea *urchins*, *jellyfish* and *coral* whilst swimming.
Health care: There are three hospitals on Curaçao as well as some medical centres. The largest, St Elizabeth, is well equipped. Health insurance is recommended.

Travel - International

AIR: The national airline of the Netherlands Antilles is *Air DCA*, formerly known as *Air ALM (LM)*. It operates to Amsterdam, Miami, Caracas and the larger Caribbean islands. *KLM* operates daily flights to Curaçao from Amsterdam. Other airlines serving Curaçao include *Air Jamaica*, *American Airlines* and *Avianca Airlines*.
Approximate flight times: From Curaçao to *London* is 11 hours (depending on connection time), to *Los Angeles* is 12 hours and to *New York* is 6 hours.
International airports: *Curaçao* (CUR) (Hato) is 12km (7 miles) from Willemstad. Buses to the city centre operate daily 0600-2300 (travel time - 45 minutes). Taxis are also available (travel time - 30 minutes). Airport facilities include duty-free shop, bar, restaurant, light refreshments, banks/bureaux de change, ATMs, post office, hotel reservation facilities and car hire. Taxis are available to Willemstad (travel time - 20 minutes).
Departure tax: NAG36 (US$20) per person.
SEA: International cruise lines calling at Curaçao include *Air Tours/Sun Cruises*, *Carnival*, *Deutsche Seetouristik*, *Holland America*, *Norwegian Cruise Lines*, *Princess*, *Royal Caribbean* and *Royal Cruise Line*.

Travel - Internal

AIR: *Windward Islands Air International (WM)* operates to Saba, St Eustatius and St Maarten. *ALM* operates regularly between Curaçao, Bonaire and Aruba.
Departure tax: NAG10 (US$6.00) to other islands in the Netherlands Antilles; children under two years of age and passengers transiting within 24 hours are exempt.
ROAD: Traffic drives on the right. A good public **bus** service runs throughout the island and many of the main hotels provide their own **minibus** services to Willemstad. **Taxi**: These are plentiful as are **car hire** firms (both international and local), which are located at the airport and in the main hotels, as well as in the capital. Taxis are easily recognisable by their signs and also the letters TX on registration plates. There is a 25 per cent surcharge after 2300. Prices should be agreed in advance. **Documentation**: An International Driving Permit is required.

Accommodation

HOTELS: There are a few luxury hotels on Curaçao, all offering air conditioning, restaurants, swimming pools and/or beach access, and a choice between European Plan (room only) and Modified American Plan (half-board). Most also offer some sort of in-house entertainment, a baby-sitting service and cable TV. Some have their own casinos. Out-of-town hotels provide their guests with free transport to and from Willemstad. A 7 per cent government tax and 12 per cent service charge are normally levied on all hotel bills. For more information, contact the Curaçao Hospitality and Tourism Association (CHATA), PO Box 6115, Kurason di Komérsio (tel: (9) 465 1005; fax: (9) 465 1052; e-mail: information@chata.org; website: www.chata.org).
GUESTHOUSES: For details of more modest accommodation - guest houses, commercial hotels and self-catering - contact the Curaçao Tourism Development Bureau (see *Contact Addresses* section).
CAMPING AND CARAVANNING: There are a few campsites. However, these sometimes only take larger groups that have been organised in advance.

Resorts & Excursions

WILLEMSTAD: The capital is noted for its brightly coloured, Dutch-style houses and a range of other interesting and complementary architectural styles, including *cunucu* houses (based on African-style mud and wattle huts), thatched cottages and country houses. It has been declared a UNESCO World Heritage Site, and is one of the finest shopping centres in the Caribbean. Monuments of interest in the city include the **Statue of Manuel Piar**, a famous freedom fighter, and two statues associated with World War II: one given by the Dutch royal family to the people of Curaçao (in recognition of their support), and one in commemoration of those who lost their lives. The mustard-coloured **Fort Amsterdam**, now the seat of government of the Netherlands Antilles, stands at the centre of historic Willemstad, which from 1648 to 1861 was a fortified town of some strategic importance. The fort's church, still standing, doubled as a storehouse for provisions saved in case of siege. Other specially designed storerooms for food, sails and other essentials may still be seen. A cannonball is still embedded in the church's southwest wall. Nearby is the present **Governor's Residence**, dating back to the Dutch colonial days. Also worth seeing are the **Queen Emma Pontoon** bridge and the **Queen Juliana Bridge**. The latter spans the harbour at a height of 490m (1600ft). The harbour itself has a floating market where colourful barges full of agricultural produce can be seen. Nearby is the new market building, the design of which is very striking. The market comes to life after 0600 on a Saturday morning. The architecture of the **Scharloo** area, reached by crossing the **Wilhelmina Drawbridge**, is fascinating, dating from as early as 1700. The **Mikvé Israel Synagogue** is the oldest in the Americas and, like the Jewish **Beth Heim Cemetery**, is worth a visit. Its courtyard museum has a fine collection of historical artefacts.
ELSEWHERE: Besides the excellent beaches and hotel resorts, the island itself has a number of other points of interest. Just outside Willemstad is the modern site of the Netherlands Antilles University and, further along the western road, is the **Landhuis Papaya** (a country house), the **Ceru Grandis** (a three-storey plantation house) and the driftwood beach of **Boca San Pedro**. Also of note is **Boca Tabla**, the thundering underwater cave of the north coast and the picturesque fishing village of **Westpoint**. **St Christoffel National Park**, occupying the most northwestern part of the island, is a nature reserve dominated by the **St Christoffel Mountain**. There are several caves decorated with Arawak Indian paintings, some unusual rock formations and many fine views across the countryside - the ruins of the **Zorguliet Plantation** and the privately owned **Savonet Plantation** and the **Savonet Museum** may be seen at the base of the mountain; the latter dates back to the 18th century and is still in use today. The indigenous flora includes orchids and some very interesting evergreens. As well as the interesting birdlife, iguanas and the shy Curaçao deer may also be observed at the park. Well worth a visit are the interesting **Caves of Hato**. Magnificent stalactite formations, wall paintings and underground streams with cascading waterfalls can be seen within the 4900m (16,076ft) labyrinth.

Sport & Activities

Watersports: As with the other islands of the Caribbean, watersports are widely promoted and facilities on Curaçao itself are well developed. There are excellent beaches for **swimming** along the sheltered southwestern coast (some charge an entrance fee). **Windsurfing**, **sailing** and **water-skiing** are popular on the island and the hotels and watersports centres are well equipped. **Snorkelling**, **scuba-diving** and **deep-sea fishing** are also popular and there are plenty of opportunities to participate in these sports. The waters make it particularly worthwhile as they are teeming with underwater life. Tuition is available.
Other: Other sports available include **tennis**, **squash** and **golf** (at the Shell 9-hole golf course and the new 18-hole course near the Blue Bay golf resort). **Horseriding** can also be arranged.

Social Profile

FOOD & DRINK: Traditional Dutch food (particularly using fresh seafood and cheeses) is popular, as well as the exciting flavours of Creole food (*criollo*) which also makes good use of the great variety of fresh fish. French, Italian and other international cuisines are also on offer. Restaurant styles vary from informal bistro to the very expensive. A wide variety of alcohol is available. 'Curaçao' liqueur, which is made from the sun-dried peel of a bitter orange and a mixture of spices is a popular local drink.
NIGHTLIFE: There are several discos run by hotels on the island and some hotels have a casino. Performances of drama and music can be found at the *Centro Pro Arte*.
SHOPPING: Curaçao (and other Netherlands Antilles islands) is a thriving centre for duty-free shopping. An enormous range of imported goods are on sale at considerably reduced prices. Locally made curios are available for the tourist. A particularly popular souvenir is the 'Curaçao' liqueur (see *Food & Drink* section). **Shopping hours**: Mon-Sat 0830-1200 and 1400-1800. Hours may vary.
SPECIAL EVENTS: For a complete list of special events, contact the Curaçao Tourism Development Bureau (see *Contact Addresses* section). The following is a selection of special events occurring in Curaçao in 2005:
Feb *Carnival* (including *Tumba Festival*, *Teener Parade*, *Banda Bou Parade* and *Grand Carnival Parade*). **Apr** *Great Seú March*. **May** *Annual Curaçao Jazz Festival*. **Aug** *Curaçao Salsa Festival*. **Oct** *Carribean Jazz Fest*, Willemstad. **Dec** *Festival of Lights*; *St Nicolas Day*; *Regatta*, from St Barbara to St Anna Bay.
SOCIAL CONVENTIONS: The social influences are predominantly Dutch, combined with Indian and African traditions. Dress for men should include tropical lightweight suits for business appointments and formal wear for evening engagements. Similarly, women should take some evening wear, but dress for daytime is casual. Swimwear should be confined to the beach and poolside only.
Tipping: Hotels add a 5 to 10 per cent government tax and a 12 per cent service charge. Bar staff, waiters, porters and doormen expect a 10 per cent tip.

Credit: © Dutch Caribbean Travel Center

Business Profile

ECONOMY: Curaçao is the most prosperous of the Netherlands Antilles island group. The capital, Willemstad, is at the centre of a network of 'offshore' banking facilities and other financial services. Curaçao also houses one of the largest dry docks in the western Caribbean. Oil refining and transhipment are the other key economic activities. Import substitution has also been successfully pursued and a wide range of consumer goods are now produced locally. Venezuela, which supplies most of the crude oil for the refineries, and the USA are the island's principal trading partners.
BUSINESS: Suits should be worn and punctuality is essential. **Office hours**: Mon-Fri 0730-1200 and 1330-1630.
COMMERCIAL INFORMATION: The following organisation can offer advice: Curaçao Chamber of Commerce and Industry, PO Box 10, Kaya Junior Salas 1, Willemstad (tel: (9) 461 1451 *or* 461 3918; fax: (9) 461 5652; e-mail: management@curacao-chamber.an; website: www.curacao-chamber.an).
CONFERENCES/CONVENTIONS: There are facilities at the World Trade Centre, Conference Centre Kura Hulanda and Tres Tan Conference Centre. For further information, contact the Curaçao Tourism Development Bureau (see *Contact Addresses* section).

Climate

Hot throughout the year, but tempered by cooling trade winds. The main rainy season is from October to December. The annual mean temperature is 27.5°C (81.5°F), rainfall is 515mm and humidity is 75.9 per cent. The island lies outside the Caribbean 'hurricane belt'.

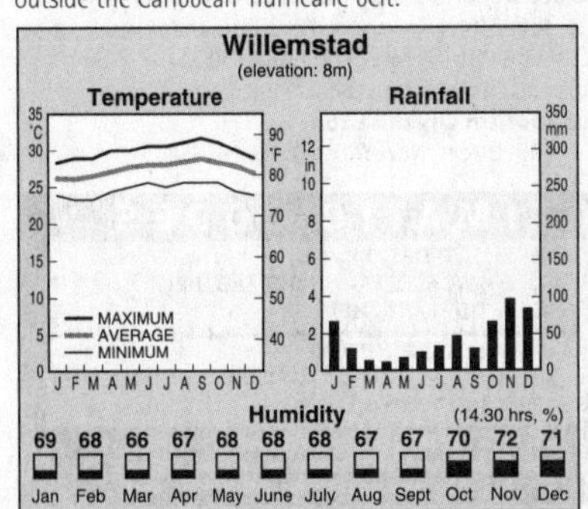

A B C D E F G H I J K L M N O P Q R S T U V W X Y Z

Cyprus

LATEST TRAVEL ADVICE CONTACTS

British Foreign and Commonwealth Office
Tel: (0870) 606 0290 Website: www.fco.gov.uk
US Department of State
Website: http://travel.state.gov/travel
Canadian Department of Foreign Affairs and Int'l Trade
Tel: (1 800) 267 8376 Website: www.dfait-maeci.gc.ca

Location: Europe, eastern Mediterranean.

Country dialling code: 357.

Cyprus Tourism Organisation
Leoforos Lemesou 19, PO Box 24535, 1390 Nicosia, Cyprus
Tel: (2) 269 1100. Fax: (2) 233 4696
E-mail: visitcyprus@cto.org.cy
Website: www.visitcyprus.org.cy
High Commission of the Republic of Cyprus
93 Park Street, London W1K 7ET, UK
Tel: (020) 7499 8272 *or* 7491 2955 *or* 7629 6288 (Cyprus Trade Centre) *or* 5350 (consular section).
Fax: (020) 7491 0691.
E-mail: cyphclondon@dial.pipex.com *or* presscounsellor@chclondon.com
Website: www.cyprus.gov.cy
Opening hours: Mon-Fri 0930-1700; 0930-1300 (consular section).
Honorary High Commission
Delta Travel, Unit Five, University Precinct, Oxford Road, Manchester M13 9RN, UK
Tel: (0161) 276 3013. Fax: (0161) 273 3855 *or* 274 3555.
E-mail: sales@deltatravel.co.uk
Cyprus Tourism Organisation
17 Hanover Street, London W1S 1YP, UK
Tel: (020) 7569 8800. Fax: (020) 7499 4935.
E-mail: informationcto@btconnect.com
Website: www.visitcyprus.org.cy
British High Commission
Alexander Pallis Street, PO Box 21978, 1587 Nicosia, Cyprus
Tel: (2) 286 1100 *or* 1369 (visa enquiries). Fax: (2) 286 1125.
E-mail: infobhc@cylink.com.cy
Website: www.britain.org.cy
Embassy of the Republic of Cyprus
2211 R Street NW, Washington DC 20008, USA
Tel: (202) 462 5772 *or* 232 8993 (press office).
Fax: (202) 483 6710.
E-mail: info@cyprusembassy.net
Website: www.cyprusembassy.net
Consulate General of the Republic of Cyprus
13 East, 40th Street, New York, NY 10016, USA
Tel: (212) 686 6016/7. Fax: (212) 686 3660.
E-mail: consulgenofcyprus@earthlink.net
Cyprus Tourism Organisation
13 East, 40th Street, New York, NY 10016, USA
Tel: (212) 683 5280. Fax: (212) 683 5282.
E-mail: gocyprus@aol.com
Website: www.visitcyprus.org.cy
Also deals with enquiries from Canada.
Embassy of the United States of America
Street address: Metochiou and Ploutarchou Street, Engomi, 2407 Nicosia, Cyprus
Postal address: PO Box 24536, 1385 Nicosia, Cyprus
Tel: (2) 239 3939.
Fax: (2) 278 0944.
E-mail: info@americanembassy.org.cy *or* consularnicosia@state.gov
Website: www.americanembassy.org.cy
Consulate General of the Republic of Cyprus
365 Bloor Street East, Suite 1010, PO Box 43, Toronto, Ontario M4W 3L4, Canada
Tel: (416) 944 0998. Fax: (416) 944 9149.
E-mail: consulcy@rogers.com
The Canadian High Commission in Damascus deals with enquiries related to Cyprus (see *Syrian Arab Republic* **section).**

TIMATIC CODES

Health	AMADEUS: **TI-DFT/JIB/HE**
	GALILEO/WORLDSPAN: **TI-DFT/JIB/HE**
	SABRE: **TIDFT/JIB/HE**
Visa	AMADEUS: **TI-DFT/JIB/VI**
	GALILEO/WORLDSPAN: **TI-DFT/JIB/VI**
	SABRE: **TIDFT/JIB/VI**

To access TIMATIC country information on Health and Visa regulations through the Computer Reservations System (CRS), type in the appropriate command line listed above.

General Information

AREA: 9251 sq km (3572 sq miles, including Turkish-occupied territory).
POPULATION: 793,100 (2001, including Turkish-occupied region).
POPULATION DENSITY: 119.3 per sq km
CAPITAL: Nicosia (Lefkosia). **Population**: 205,633 (2001, excluding Turkish-occupied portion).
GEOGRAPHY: Cyprus is an island in the eastern Mediterranean. The landscape varies between rugged coastlines, sandy beaches, rocky hills and forest-covered mountains. The Troodos Mountains in the centre of the island rise to almost 1952m (6400ft) and provide good skiing during the winter. Between these and the range of hills which run eastward along the north coast and the 'panhandle' is the fertile Messaoria Plain. The Morphou Basin runs around the coast of Morphou Bay in the west.
GOVERNMENT: Republic since 1960. **Head of State and Government**: President Tassos Papadopoulos since 2003.
LANGUAGE: The majority (approximately 80 per cent) speak Greek and approximately 20 per cent speak Turkish. The Greek Cypriot dialect is different from mainland Greek. Turkish is spoken by Turkish Cypriots. English, German and French are also spoken in tourist centres.
RELIGION: Greek Orthodox, with Muslim minority.
TIME: GMT + 2 (GMT + 3 from last Sunday in March to Saturday before last Sunday in October).
ELECTRICITY: 240 volts AC, 50Hz. Square 13-amp three-pin plugs (UK-type) are used.
COMMUNICATIONS: Telephone: Full IDD is available. Country code: 357. Outgoing international code: 00. Telecard (C£3, 5 or 10 denominations) or coin-operated public telephones are installed at various central locations in towns and villages. Call Direct (cheaper than ordinary collect calls) is available to most EU countries, as well as Australia, USA and Canada. **Mobile telephone:** GSM 900/1800/3G network. Main operators include *CYTA* (website: www.cytamobile-vodafone.com) and *Scancom* (www.scancomcyprus.com). **Fax:** This is available at district post offices in Nicosia, Larnaca, Limassol and Pafos. **Internet:** ISPs include *Avacomnet* (website: www.avacom.net), *Cytanet* (website: www.cytanet.com.cy), *Logosnet* (website: www.logosnet.com.cy) and *Spidernet* (website: www.spidernet.net). Public access is available in Internet cafes located in the cities, for instance Nicosia, Larnaca, Limassol, Pafos and Ayia Napa. **Telegram:** There are telegraph links to the international network through major hotels and the Central Telegraph Office, Egypt Avenue, Nicosia. A 24-hour service is provided with three charge rates. **Post:** There are daily airmail services to all developed countries. Service to Europe takes three to four days. *Poste Restante* facilities are available in main cities and resorts. District Post office opening hours: Mon-Fri 0730-1330 and 1500-1800 except Wednesday, Saturday 0830-1030 during the winter period (1 Sep to 30 Jun); Mon-Fri 0730-1330 and 1600-1900 except Wednesday, Sat 0830-1030 during the summer period (1 Jul to 31 Aug). Other post office opening hours: Mon-Fri 0730-1330, Thurs 1500-1800 at other times. **Press:** Newspapers published in English are the *The Blue Beret*, *Cyprus Financial Mirror*, *Cyprus Mail* (daily), *Cyprus Today* (Turkish Cypriot) and *Cyprus Weekly*. Most others are in Greek and most English papers are available.
Radio: BBC World Service (website: www.bbc.co.uk/worldservice) and Voice of America (website: www.voa.gov) can be received. From time to time the frequencies change and the most up-to-date can be found online.
In addition, the CTO sponsors programmes for tourists Mon-Sat on 603kHz (498m) and FM94.8. The times are as follows: German 0800; English 0830; French 0900; Swedish 0930; Arabic 1000.

Passport/Visa

	Passport Required?	Visa Required?	Return Ticket Required?
Full British	Yes	No	Yes
Australian	Yes	No	Yes
Canadian	Yes	No	Yes
USA	Yes	No	Yes
Other EU	1	No	Yes
Japanese	Yes	No	Yes

Note: *Regulations and requirements may be subject to change at short notice, and you are advised to contact the appropriate diplomatic or consular authority before finalising travel arrangements. Details of these may be found at the head of this country's entry. Any numbers in the chart refer to the footnotes below.*

Resricted Entry: (a) Holders of Former Yugoslav Republic passports bearing the stamp 'Macedonia'. (b) Holders of passports issued by the 'Turkish Republic of Northern Cyprus'.
PASSPORTS: Passport valid for at least three months beyond the period of intended stay required by all except:
(a) **1.** nationals of EU countries, Iceland, Liechtenstein, Norway and Switzerland who hold a valid national identity card with the bearer's photograph;
(b) holders of Laissez-passer issued by the United Nations (nationals of Egypt and Israel can enter Cyprus with a Laissez-passer provided they hold an entry permit previously obtained by the Immigration Department in Nicosia);
(c) holders of travel documents issued by the Government of the Republic of Cyprus to Cypriot nationals;
(d) holders of documents issued to stateless persons and recognised refugees.
VISAS: Required by all except the following for stays of up to 90 days:
(a) nationals of countries referred to in the chart above;
(b) nationals of Andorra, Argentina, Bolivia, Brazil, Brunei, Bulgaria, Chile, Costa Rica, Croatia, El Salvador, Guatemala, Honduras, Hong Kong (SAR), Iceland, Israel, Korea (Rep), Liechtenstein, Macau (SAR), Malaysia, Mexico, Monaco, New Zealand, Nicaragua, Norway, Panama, Paraguay, Romania, San Marino, Singapore, Switzerland, Uruguay, Vatican City and Venezuela;
(c) transit passengers continuing their onward journey by the same or first connecting aircraft within 24 hours, provided holding valid onward or return documentation and not leaving the airport, except nationals of Afghanistan, Bangladesh, Congo (Dem Rep), Eritrea, Ethiopia, Ghana, Iran Iraq, Nigeria, Pakistan, Somalia, Sri Lanka and Turkey, who require an *Airport Transit* visa.
Types of visa and cost: *Tourist/Business*: C£6 (free of charge to nationals of Egypt, Russian Federation, Syrian Arab Republic and Ukraine, provided holding onward or return tickets and sufficient funds to cover the duration of their stay). Multiple-entry visas are only issued to those who require it for business purposes and cost C£20. *Transit*: C£6. *Airport Transit*: C£6.
Validity: *Tourist/Business*: three months. *Transit*: five days.
Application to: In person to the Consulate (or Consular section at Embassy or High Commission); see *Contact Addresses* section.
Application requirements: (a) Passport valid at least six months after returning from Cyprus. (b) One completed application form. (c) One passport-size photo. (d) Proof of sufficient funds to cover duration of stay. (e) Onward or return ticket and evidence of hotel reservation or letter of invitation from resident of Cyprus. (f) Fee (payable by cash or postal order only, subject to rate of exchange). *Business*: (a)-(f) and, (g) Introductory letter from the applicant's company, giving details of salary. (h) Official letter of invitation from a company in Cyprus.
Working days required: In most cases, personal applications will be processed on the same day or within 24 hours after an interview, but it may take up to a minimum of 10 days if application needs to be referred to Cyprus (depending on nationality, eg Iraq and Turkey).
Temporary residence: Nationals of any country coming to Cyprus for employment or studies must secure an employment or student's permit through the Migration Officer, Nicosia prior to arrival. Applications should be submitted by the prospective employers or the directors of the schools.

Money

Currency: Cyprus Pound (C£) = 100 cents. Notes are in denominations of C£20, 10, 5 and 1. Coins are in denominations of 50, 20, 10, 5, 2 and 1 cents.
Currency exchange: Visitors wishing to obtain non-Cypriot currency at Cypriot banks for business purposes are advised that this is only possible by prior arrangement. ATMs operate 24 hours in main towns and tourist areas.
Credit & debit cards: All major credit cards are accepted

at most places. Check with your credit or debit card company for details of merchant acceptability and other services which may be available.
Travellers cheques: May be cashed in all banks. To avoid additional exchange rate charges, travellers are advised to take travellers cheques in Pounds Sterling or Cyprus Pounds.
Currency restrictions: The import of local currency is unrestricted, subject to declaration; foreign currency for amounts over US$1000 (or the equivalent in other currency) must be declared. The export of local and foreign currency is limited to the amount declared on arrival. Local currency withdrawn from Cypriot banks may be exported provided a holding certificate is obtained by the bank.
Exchange rate indicators: The following figures are included as a guide to the movements of the Cyprus Pound against Sterling and the US Dollar:

Date	Feb '04	May '04	Aug '04	Nov '04
£1.00=	0.86	0.88	0.86	0.83
$1.00=	0.47	0.49	0.46	0.44

Banking hours: Generally Mon-Fri 0830-1230 in June, July and August; Mon-Fri 0815-1230 and Mon 1515-1645 rest of year. Certain central banks may also open Tues-Fri in the afternoon. Banks in Larnaca and at Pafos International Airport are open all day.

Duty Free

The following goods may be imported into Cyprus without incurring customs duty:
200 cigarettes or 50 cigars or 250g of tobacco; 1l of spirits or 750ml of wine; 150ml of perfume and 150ml of eau de toilette; goods (excluding jewellery) up to C£50.
Prohibited imports: Agricultural products and propagating stock, ie natural fruits and flowers; an assortment of meat and dairy products imported from certain Asian and African countries.
Abolition of duty free goods within the UK: On June 30 1999, the sale of duty-free alcohol and tobacco at airports and at sea was abolished in all of the original 15 EU member states. Of the 10 new member states that joined the EU on May 1 2004, these rules already apply to Cyprus and Malta. There are transitional rules in place for visitors returning to one of the original 15 EU countries from one of the other new EU countries. But for the original 15, plus Cyprus and Malta, there are now no limits imposed on importing tobacco and alcohol products from one EU country to another (with the exceptions of Denmark, Finland and Sweden, where limits *are* imposed). Travellers should note that they may be required to prove at customs that the goods purchased are for personal use *only*.

Public Holidays

2005: Jan 1 New Year's Day. **Jan 6** Epiphany. **Mar 14** Green Monday. **Mar 25** Greek National Day. **Apr 1** Greek Cypriot National Day. **Apr 29** Greek Orthodox Good Friday. **May 1** Labour Day. **May 2** Greek Orthodox Easter Monday. **Jun 20** Pentecost (Kataklysmos). **Aug 15** Assumption. **Oct 1** Cyprus Independence Day. **Oct 28** Greek National Day (Ochi Day). **Dec 24-26** Christmas.
2006: Jan 1 New Year's Day. **Jan 6** Epiphany. **Feb 6** Green Monday. **Mar 25** Greek National Day. **Apr 1** Greek Cypriot National Day. **Apr 21** Greek Orthodox Good Friday. **Apr 24** Greek Orthodox Easter Monday. **May 1** Labour Day. **May 12** Pentecost (Kataklysmos). **Aug 15** Assumption. **Oct 1** Cyprus Independence Day. **Oct 28** Greek National Day (Ochi Day). **Dec 24-26** Christmas.

Health

	Special Precautions?	Certificate Required?
Yellow Fever	No	No
Cholera	No	No
Typhoid & Polio	No	No
Malaria	No	No

Note: *Regulations and requirements may be subject to change at short notice, and you are advised to contact your doctor well in advance of your intended date of departure. Any numbers in the chart refer to the footnotes below.*

Food & drink: Milk is pasteurised and tap water is generally safe to drink. Powdered and tinned milk are available. Only eat well-cooked meat and fish, preferably served hot. Pork, salad and mayonnaise may carry increased risk. Vegetables should be cooked and fruit peeled.
Other risks: Immunisation against *hepatitis A* is sometimes recommended.
Health care: Health facilities are generally of a good standard. The emergency departments of all hospitals are manned with English-speaking personnel, although it is advisable to seek the assistance of an interpreter for more complex medical matters. Emergency medical treatment, administered in the Accident and Emergency department, is free to international tourists. International travellers are, however, advised to take out full medical insurance before departure. No health agreement exists with the UK.

Credit: © Cyprus Tourism Organisation

Travel - International

Note: Since October 1974, the Cyprus government has declared the ports of Famagusta (Ammochostos), Karavostassi and Kyrenia, and the airport of Ercan, all in the northern part of the island, as illegal 'ports of entry' to Cyprus.
AIR: Over 40 airlines, including *Cyprus Airways (CY)* (website: www.cyprusair.com.cy), the national airline of Cyprus, operate scheduled flights within, to and from Cyprus.
Approximate flight times: From Pafos and Larnaca to *London* is four hours 30 minutes, to *Paris* is three hours 30 minutes, to *Zurich* is three hours, to *Frankfurt* is three hours 30 minutes, to *Athens* is one hour 40 minutes and to *Stockholm* is five hours.
International airports: *Larnaca (LCA)* is 5km (3 miles) south of the city. Taxis are available outside the airport terminal. Airport facilities include outgoing duty-free shop, tourist information, bank/bureau de change, bars and restaurants, Cyprus Hotel Information and Reservation Office, first aid, car hire and post office.
Pafos (PFO) is 15km (9 miles) east of the city (travel time - 25 minutes). Airport facilities include special facilities for disabled people and car hire facilities.
Departure tax: None.
SEA: Passenger ships from the ports of Limassol and Larnaca connect Cyprus with various Greek and Middle Eastern ports, including Piraeus, Rhodes, Heraklion, Haifa, Port Said, Jounieh and many Greek islands. Services are reduced during the winter months. For detailed information on ferry boats and shipping lines, contact the Cyprus Tourism Organisation (see *Contact Addresses* section). Several cruise lines call at Cyprus, including *Classical Cruises, Costa, Cunard Line, Euro Cruises, Norwegian Cruise Lines, Princess* and *Swan Hellenic Cruises. Louis Cruise Lines* sail to Egypt and the Holy Land (tel: (25) 570 000 *or* (0800) 018 3883 toll-free UK; e-mail: sales@louiscruises.com; website: www.louiscruises.com). *Paradise Cruises* also operate many cruises to Egypt, Greece and Lebanon (tel: (25) 357 604; fax: (25) 370 298; e-mail: cruises@paradise.com.cy; website: www.paradise.com.cy).

Travel - Internal

ROAD: Bus: Services connect all towns and villages on the island every day except Sunday. Service is efficient and cheap. Although the local buses are sometimes slow, they are a good way of seeing the more remote villages. **Taxi:** These run 24 hours a day between all the main towns on the island. Fares are regulated by the Government and all taxis have meters. *Transurban Service Taxis* offers an excellent, cheap service using seven-seat taxis running fixed routes between main points. Taxis run to a timetable and delivery is door to door. Fares under this system are often one-tenth of the usual rate. **Car hire:** Cars are one of the best ways to explore the island. They may be hired at airports and commercial centres, but should be reserved well in advance during the summer season. Reduced tariffs are offered if cars are hired for more than a week. Road signs are in both Greek and English. Traffic drives on the left. Although most roads are of a good standard, the driving standards of others may be of a lower standard than that in the UK or elsewhere. It should also be noted that there are strict repercussions for those not wearing seatbelts or a crash helmet, or using a mobile telephone/under the influence of alcohol whilst driving.
Motorcycles: Riders and pillion passengers should always wear crash helmets if the motorcycle is over 50cc.
Documentation: An International Driving Permit or national driving licence is accepted for one year.
URBAN: Nicosia has its own privately run bus company operating efficient services at flat fares, which offers a comprehensive service covering the urban area of Limassol and linking the port with the tourist area. For more details, contact the *Limassol Urban Bus Company (E.A.L.) Limited*, PO Box 51117 (tel: (25) 354 050; fax: (25) 354 060; e-mail: ealstores@cytanet.com.cy). Taxis are widely available: a 15 per cent surcharge is in operation from 2300-0600. Tipping is expected.
Travel times: The following chart gives approximate travel times (in hours and minutes) from **Nicosia** to other main towns and tourist centres in Cyprus.

	Road
Limassol	1.00
Pafos	2.15
Larnaca	0.50
Ayia Napa	1.10
Platres	1.30
Protaras	2.00
Polis	2.30

Accommodation

HOTELS: There are over 500 hotels and hotel apartments scattered throughout the island. There are also simple hotels that are ungraded. A VAT charge of 15 per cent is added to bills. Room service costs up to 54 cents per order, or more for 5-star hotels. Air-conditioning facilities can be hired for about C£2.15 per unit. Most hotels and hotel apartments offer discounts during the low season, which for seaside resorts is from 6 November to 15 March (excluding the period 20 December to 6 January) and for hill resorts from 1 October to 30 June. There are discounts for children occupying the same room as their parents: *under one year*, by private arrangement; *one to six years*, 50 per cent discount; *six to 10 years*, 25 per cent discount. Some hotels may only charge 80 per cent of the daily room rate for single occupancy of a double room. Visitors should check discounts with their hotel prior to arrival. **Grading**: Hotels range from deluxe **5-star** to **1-star**. Hotel apartments are classified A, B or C. The range of accommodation in Cyprus is classified by the Cyprus Tourism Organisation as consisting of hotels with a star-classification system; this indicates facilities offered, physical criteria, room size and the cost, according to the class chosen.
For further information, contact the Cyprus Tourism Organisation, which controls and regulates hotels (see

Contact Addresses section); or the Cyprus Hotel Association, PO Box 2772, 1303 Nicosia (tel: 22 152 820; fax: 22 375 460; e-mail: chaniccy@cylink.com.cy). The Hotel Association also has an office at Larnaca International Airport (tel: 24 643 186; fax: 24 643 058).

GUEST HOUSES: Located mainly in Nicosia, Limassol, Pafos and Larnaca. The Cyprus Agrotourism Company (tel: 22 340 071; fax: 22 339 723; website: www.agrotourism.com.cy) offers traditional countryside accommodation.

CAMPING/CARAVANNING: There are seven organised camping sites, at Polis (open March to October), Kalymnos Beach, Forest Beach (open June to October), Feggari (open all year round), Geroskipou Zenon Gardens (open April to October) and Ayia Napa (open April to October). Facilities available in camping sites include showers, toilets, washing facilities, mini-market, and usually a snackbar or restaurant. Rates for camping sites range between C£1-C£1.50 per day for a tent or caravan space, plus C£1-C£1.50 per person daily for service and taxes.

YOUTH HOSTELS: There are youth hostels in Nicosia, Larnaca and Pafos in Cyprus open to members of the International Youth Hostels Association. Non-members are also accepted, but on arrival at the hostel they will be provided with a guest card. For further details, contact the Cyprus Youth Hostel Association, 34 Theodotu Street, PO Box 24040, 1700 Nicosia (tel: 2267 0027 *or* 2267 5574; fax: 2267 2896; e-mail: montis@logos.cy.net).

Credit: © Cyprus Tourism Organisation

Resorts & Excursions

NICOSIA (LEFKOSIA)

The capital of Cyprus since the 12th century, Nicosia stands at the heart of the **Mesaoria Plain**. It is currently divided by the 'Green Line', a UN buffer zone that separates the Turkish-occupied north of the island and the Government-controlled south. The Old City, which is being renovated in part, is defined by 16th-century walls built by the Venetians. Among attractions and points of interest are the **Cyprus Museum**, a storehouse of the island's archaeological treasures, the **Folk Art Museum**, the new **Archbishop's Palace**, **St John's Cathedral**, Byzantine churches, the **Byzantine Museum/Makarios Cultural Centre** and the **Ömeriye Mosque**. The city hosts the annual **International State Fair** (end of May) and the **Nicosia Arts Festival** (beginning of June).

Excursions: The Nicosia area has some interesting excursion possibilities, including the **Royal Tombs** and **Agios Irakleidios Monastery** at **Tamassos**; the five-dome church and the mosque in **Peristerona**; the **Panagia Chrysospiliotissa Church**, in a cliff-side cave near **Deftera**. Further into the rugged **Pitsylia Region**, in the hills southwest of Nicosia, is **Machairas Monastery**, close to the restored and protected traditional villages of **Fikardou**, **Gourri** and **Lazanias**.

LARNAKA & THE SOUTHEAST

An industrious resort town, Larnaka has Cyprus' main international airport on its doorstep, a harbour with deep-water berths and a marina. The seafront promenade is fringed with palm trees and cafes and tavernas. Places of interest include the **Agios Lazaros Church** and its associated **Byzantine Museum**, **Larnaka Fort**, the **District Archaeological Museum**, the **Pierides Museum** (a private archaeological museum), the **Natural History Museum**, the **Tornaritis-Pierides Palaeontology Museum** and the scant ruins of ancient **Kition**. During the feast of **Kataklysmos** (the Greek Orthodox Whitsun), celebrated throughout Cyprus but with especial enthusiasm in Larnaka, crowds throng the shore for watersports, singing, dancing, eating and drinking.

Excursions: Near the airport is the **Hala Sultan Tekkesi**, a historic mosque standing in beautiful gardens on the edge of **Larnaka Salt Lake** (dry in summer), a winter home of migratory flamingoes. Nearby, in Kiti, **Panagia Angeloktisti Church** contains a superb sixth-century Byzantine mosaic of the Virgin and Child.

In the hills to the west is the village of **Lefkara**, famous for its handmade lace, and the **Convent of Agios Minas**. Off the Limassol–Nicosia road are the hilltop **Stavrovouni Monastery**, and the Crusader-era **Chapelle Royal** near Pyrga. Further west, on a hillside at **Choirokoitia**, are the remains of a neolithic village from 5800 BC, one of the earliest settlements in Cyprus.

East of Larnaka, **Larnaka Bay** has a sand beach lined with hotels. Beyond the bay, and the **Dekeleia** British Sovereign Base Area, much of **Famagusta (Ammochostos) District**, including the town of the same name, lies across the Cypriot divide in the Turkish-occupied zone (the Turks call Famagusta 'Gazimagusa'). The part still under Government control includes the fertile **Kokkinochoria** (Red Villages) belt, where potatoes and other vegetables are grown for export. On the coast south of Famagusta lie busy resorts, speckled with golden sand beaches, that are ideal for children, like those at **Fig Tree Bay** and **Flamingo Bay**.

Agia Napa has a 16th-century monastery – and an increasingly boisterous reputation as a major clubbing resort. It also attracts families to its beaches, Waterworld leisure centre and Go-Karts track. Boat tours leave from the harbour. Family-oriented **Protaras** and **Pernera** resorts have good beaches, with cafes and beach bars. Other attractions in the area include watersports and rock climbing. Around **Cape Gkreko**, the coastline becomes indented with rocky coves and small sandy beaches, ideal for snorkelling and scuba-diving (both for experienced practitioners), explorations by boat and picnics. The **Potamos Creek** fishing harbour presents a scene of colourful fishing boats. Inland, the small town of **Paralimni** provides entertainment in its restaurants, dance clubs and cafes.

LIMASSOL (LEMESOS) & THE SOUTHWEST

The second-largest city in Cyprus, Limassol is the island's main industrial centre and port. It is also the focus of Cyprus' wine industry. In September, the town holds a wine festival, at which wine and food are served free. During the pre-Lenten Carnival, Limassol bursts into celebration, with bands, gaily decorated floats and dancing. The city is an important tourist destination, and has beaches like **Dassoudi Beach** and those at nearby **Germasogeia**, backed by cafes and tavernas. **Limassol Castle** stands guard over the old harbour and houses the **Cyprus Medieval Museum**. There is also a **Folk Art Museum**, the **Limassol District Archaeological Museum** and, in the **Municipal Gardens**, a small zoo.

Excursions: There are several places of historical and archaeological interest around Limassol. **Amathus**, just outside the city to the east, was once the capital of a city-kingdom, but is now in ruins and partly covered by the sea. The **Acropolis**, **Necropolis** and the remains of an early Christian basilica can be seen, and excavation continues in the lower part of the ancient city. Further east lies **Agios Georgios Alamanos Convent** and the black sands of **Governor's Beach**.

West of Limassol, at **Fassouri**, are extensive citrus orchards and the **Water Mania** leisure park. Nearby **Kolossi Castle** was the headquarters of the Crusader Knights of St John of Jerusalem. The ancient city of **Kourion**, on a steep hillside near **Episkopi**, has a superbly sited Graeco-Roman theatre where concerts and Shakespearean plays are performed in summer. Kourion contains other interesting sites, including the House of **Eustolios**, which has beautiful mosaics; the **Acropolis**, the ruins of the Roman-era forum; the **Christian Basilica**; and public buildings. Beyond Kourion to the west are the city's stadium and the **Sanctuary of Apollo Ylatis**. All of these sites lie within the **Akrotiri-Episkopi** British Sovereign Base Area.

South of Limassol, on the **Akrotiri Peninsula** (and also inside the British military base), **Lady's Mile Beach** is a long stretch of excellent sand. Nearby **Akrotiri Salt Lake** (dry in summer) is a winter home to thousands of flamingos; on its southern shore stands the **Agios Nikolaos ton Gaton Convent**.

PAFOS & THE WEST

The booming main town and year-round resort in the west consists of **Upper Pafos**, built on a rocky escarpment that commands a superb view of the coastline, and **Lower Pafos**, with a taverna-fringed harbour and a long seafront lined with hotels. Pafos is rich in ancient sites, in particular a cluster of excavated Roman villas near the harbour, among them the **House of Dionysos** and the **Villa of Theseus**, that contain superb mosaic floors, and the **Tombs of the Kings**. Other attractions include the **Pafos District Museum**, the **Byzantine Museum**, **Pafos Fort** commanding the harbour, the remains of the Byzantine castle of **Saranda Kolones**, and **Panagia Chrysopolitissa Church**, the largest early Christian basilica on the island. **Pafos Aquarium** is of more recent origin.

Excursions: Pafos is a good base for exploring the rugged west of the island. To the east and northeast, the land rises through vineyards and the **Pafos Forest** to **Cedar Valley**, part of the **Tripylos Nature Reserve**, centred on the **Stavros tis Psokas Forest Station**. Wild mountain sheep (moufflon) are being protected here. The **Panagia Chrysorrogiatissa Monastery** is situated in scenic surroundings and is an interesting stop on the way.

A main road skirts the foothills on the edge of this area, passing close to **Agios Neofytos Monastery**, and finally descending to the north coast at **Polis**, a small town that until recently was virtually undeveloped and is now a bustling resort, though it retains traces of its former 'alternative' character. Nearby, at the fishing port and resort of **Latchi (Lakki)**, tavernas around the harbour serve freshly caught fish. Westwards, at the edge of the **Akamas Peninsula**, are the **Baths of Aphrodite**, a grotto containing a freshwater pool – legend says the Greek goddess of love bathed here. Going east from Polis, around **Chrysochou Bay**, the barely developed coast as far as the UN buffer zone at **Kato Pyrgos** gives an idea of what Cyprus looked like before mass tourism began on the island.

On the coast north of Pafos, **Coral Bay** is a fast-growing resort around a small but good beach. Further on in this direction, the fishing harbour at **Agios Georgios** is overlooked by cliffs into which ancient tombs are cut; at the top is an excavated early Christian basilica. At **Lara Bay**, beyond the rugged **Avgas Gorge**, a reserve has been established to protect the dwindling number of loggerhead turtles that nest here.

In the opposite direction, southeast of Pafos, **Geroskipou** village – now little more than a suburb of sprawling Pafos – is the home of 'Greek Delight' (like 'Turkish Delight') and has a small **Folk Museum**. Farther along, at **Kouklia**, are the ruins of ancient **Palaia Pafos** and the **Temple of Aphrodite**. At the coast are **Petra tou Romiou (Rock of Aphrodite)** and a busy small resort at **Pissouri Bay**.

TROODOS MOUNTAINS

The scenery in the forested – or, more accurately, reafforested – mountains is spectacular. **Platres**, 1230m (4035ft) above sea level on the southern slopes, is the ideal base for excursions. It lies on the approaches to **Mount Olympus**, at 1952m (6404ft), the highest peak in Cyprus, with a summit that is invariably snow-covered in winter and has skiing slopes and facilities.

Prodromos, the highest village on the island, 1530m (5019ft) above sea level, is reputed to grow the best apples. **Pedoulas** in the fertile **Marathasa Valley** is famous for cherries (and in spring for cherry blossom) and other fruits. **Kalopanagiotis** also has orchards. **Moutoullas** is a source of mineral water bottled and sold locally as well as exported to the Middle East. **Omodos**, a restored conservation village, has the **Stavros Monastery** and a small **Folk Art Museum**. **Foini** is a centre of local craft pottery. On the northeastern slopes, **Kakopetria**, 730m (2395ft) above sea level and a touring centre like Platres, has a traditional quarter that is being protected and restored. **Agros** produces rose water, mineral water and wine. The **Commandaria Region**, midway down the southern slopes, where the grapes for the Commandaria sweet red dessert wine are grown, has attractive villages like **Zoopigi**, where almond and walnut trees grow.

Other places of interest include **Kykkos Monastery**, which houses a golden icon of the Virgin Mary; **Throni tis Panagias**, uphill from the monastery, where the tomb of the late Archbishop Makarios III, the first President of Cyprus, occupies a setting that commands a magnificent view; the small but prettily situated **Kaledonia Falls**; and the monasteries of **Mesa Potamos** and **Trooditissa**.

UNESCO has listed nine Byzantine churches in the mountains as World Heritage Sites for their magnificently frescoed interiors. These are **Panagia tis Asinou** near **Nikitari**, one of the finest examples of Byzantine art in the Levant; **Stavros tou Agiasmati** near **Platanistasa**; **Agios Ioannis Lampadistis** in **Kalopanagiotis**; **Panagia tou Araka** near **Lagoudera**; **Agios Nikolaos tis Stegis** southwest of **Kakopetria**; **Panagia tis Podythou** outside **Galata**; **Archangelos Michail** at **Pedoulas**; **Panagia tou Moutoulla** in Moutoullas; and **Timiou Stavrou** in **Pelendri**.

Sport & Activities

Cycling: A cheap and effective way of seeing the island. Facilities for renting bicycles are available in all towns and resorts, although the quality of the bicycles can vary considerably. The terrain offers many opportunities for mountain biking. The *Cyprus Cycling Federation* organises various non-racing activities and events; PO Box 24572, CY 1301, Nicosia (tel: (22) 663 344; fax: (22) 661 150; e-mail: ccf@cytanet.com.cy; website: www.geocities.com/cyclingcy). The *Cyprus Tourism Organisation* (see *Contact Addresses* section) can also provide free maps.

Hiking and trekking: The many unspoilt areas in Cyprus make the land ideal for hiking. Recommended Nature Trails include *Atalante*, *Kaledonia* and *Persephone* in the Troodos area and *Aphrodite* and *Adonis* in the Akamas area, with other trails in the forests of Machairas and Limassol.

Watersports: Opportunities abound for **windsurfing**, **paragliding** and **swimming**. Recommended beaches

include *Geroskipou*, *Dasoudi* and *Larnaca* (all of which are public beaches). Some or all offer full facilities to swimmers and include bars, restaurants and changing rooms. **Sailing**, **diving**, **water-skiing** and **scuba-diving** are also available at specific locations. The *Cyprus Federation of Underwater Activities*, PO Box 21503, 1510 Nicosia (tel: (22) 754 647; fax: (22) 755 246) and *Cydive* (tel: (26) 934 271; fax: (26) 935 307; e-mail: cydive@spidernet.com.cy; website: www.cydive.com) can provide information on diving facilities, for instance at *Protaras*, *Larnaca*, *Limassol* and *Polis* (near Pafos). **Fishing** can be practised on Cyprus, although a licence needs to obtained from the *Department of Fisheries*, Aiolou 13, CY, Nicosia (tel: (22) 807 861; fax: (22) 775 955 *or* 777 830). Licences cost C£3 for each reservoir or C£10 for all reservoirs.
Skiing and snowboarding: Cyprus is also becoming established as a destination for winter sports with some hoteliers and tour operators, offering off-peak incentives. Both Platres and Kakopetria are conveniently placed for the skiing season on *Mount Olympus*, which usually lasts from January to mid-March, but Troodos is actually the nearest resort to the skiing area; it has hotels and cafes. Although Cyprus is not well known for its skiing, the Troodos Mountains offer excellent winter sports facilities and there are four ski-lifts on Mount Olympus. The *Ski-Club*, which is based in Troodos, has its own shelter and accepts tourists as temporary members. Ski equipment can be hired there, PO Box 22185, CY 1518, Lefkosia (tel: (22) 675 340).
Other: Golf can be played on three courses on the island: the *Tsada Golf Club*, an 18-hole course, situated near Tsada village, 15 minutes' drive north of Pafos town; *The Secret Valley Golf Club*, also 18-hole, situated 18km (11 miles) east of Pafos and 49km (30 miles) from Limassol; and the *Aphrodite Hills* 18-hole course in Limassol. A number of hotels also offer limited golfing facilities; in this instance, *Cyplon Travel Ltd* in the UK can provide further information at Cyplon House, 561-563 Green Lanes, London N8 ORL, UK (tel: (020) 8348 8866; fax: (020) 8348 7939; e-mail: sales@cyplon.co.uk; website: www.cyplon.co.uk). **Tennis** courts are available in most towns and in the grounds of many hotels; the *Cyprus Tennis Federation* can provide further information at PO Box 23931, CY 1687, Nicosia (tel: (22) 666 822, mornings; fax: (22) 668 016; e-mail: cytennis@spidernet.com.cy; website: www.cyprustennis.com).

Credit: © Cyprus Tourism Organisation

Credit: © Cyprus Tourism Organisation

Social Profile

FOOD & DRINK: Major resorts have bars and restaurants of every category. At larger hotels, the indigenous cuisine tends to have an 'international flavour' although authentic local dishes may also be available. All over the island there are restaurants offering genuine Cypriot food. Charcoal-grilled meat is very popular, as is fresh seafood. Dishes include *kebabs* (pieces of lamb or other meat skewered and roasted over a charcoal fire), *dolmades* (vine leaves stuffed with minced meat and rice) and *tava* (a tasty stew of meat, herbs and onions). One of the best ways of enjoying Cypriot food is by ordering *mezze* (snacks), a large selection of a number of different local dishes. However, the cuisine varies according to whether the visitor eats in the North or the Republic of Cyprus. Fresh fruit is plentiful and cheap, and very sweet desserts such as *baklava* are widely available. Waiter service is normal and counter service is common in bars.
There are no licensing hours. Cyprus produces excellent wines, spirits and beer which can only be bought in the south. Coffee is Greek-style (short, strong and unfiltered), though cappuccino is available in most restaurants and bars. Traditional English tea can be bought everywhere. The highlight of the wine year is the annual wine festival in Limassol, usually held in September, when free wine flows and local food is on offer.
SHOPPING: Cypriot purchases include handmade lace, woven curtains and tablecloths, silks, basket work, pottery, silverware and leather goods. Jewellery is an art which has been practised on the island since the Mycenean period; craftspeople working in contemporary and traditional styles produce some very fine pieces. Silver spoons and forks are a traditional symbol of Cypriot hospitality. *Lefkara* lace is famous throughout the world as one of the products most closely associated with Cypriot workmanship; the name originates from the village Lefkara, situated on a hill on the Nicosia-Limassol road. Other products include the simple baskets which have been made on the island for years, leather goods and pottery. The local wines and brandy also make good purchases. Imported goods sell at competitive prices, including cameras, perfume, porcelain, crystal and, of course, the finest English fabrics. Shirts made to measure or ready to wear can be found at very low prices. **Shopping hours**: Shops are closed Wednesday and Saturday after 1400 as well as all day Sunday. Otherwise opening hours are 0800-1300 and 1600-1930 (summer, or until 1900 spring and autumn); 0800-1300 and 1430-1800 (winter). On Fridays, shops are generally open until 2000/2030.
SPECIAL EVENTS: The following is a selection of special events occurring in Cyprus in 2005:
Jan 24-25 *Agios Neofytos Days*, (traditional festival) Paphos. **Feb 16** *Carnival Monday*, Larnaca. **Feb 25-27** *28th Troodos International Skie Competition*. **Mar 3-13** *Apokreo & Limassol Carnivals*. **Mar 14** *Green Monday*. **Mar 25** *Greek National Day celebrations*. **Apr 1** *Greek-Cypriot National Day*. **Apr 15-17** *4th Cyprus Amateur Open Championships*. **Apr 25-30** *Greek Orthodox Easter*. **May 14-15** *Anthesteria Flower Festival*. **Jun 5** *11th Children's Festival*, Agia Napa. **Jun 17-22** *Pentecost-Kataklysmos Fair* (Flood Festival). **Jul 1-31** *Larnaka International Festival*. **Aug** *Ancient Greek Drama Festival*, Pafos. **Aug 14-15** *Assumption Day celebrations*. **Aug 30-Sep 11** *Wine Festival*, Lemesos. **Sep 23** *Autumn Equinox*, Limassol. **Sep 27** *World Tourism Day*. **Oct 28** *Greek National Day celebrations*. **Dec** *Christmas Festivities*. **Dec 21-24** *Re-enactment of Christ's Birth*, Paphos.
In addition to the events listed above, a number of saints' days based on the Greek Orthodox Church are celebrated throughout the year. For a complete list of events and saints' days, contact the Cyprus Tourism Organisation (see *Contact Addresses* section).
SOCIAL CONVENTIONS: Respect should be shown for religious beliefs. Those visitors who leave the confines of their hotel and beach to explore Cyprus will find a warm reception waiting for them in the many villages. It is customary to shake hands and other normal courtesies should be observed. It is viewed as impolite to refuse an offer of Greek coffee or a cold drink. It is acceptable to bring a small gift of wine or confectionery, particularly when invited for a meal. For most occasions, casual attire is acceptable. Beachwear should be confined to the beach or poolside. More formal wear is required for business and in more exclusive dining rooms, social functions, etc.
Photography: Photography is forbidden near military camps or installations. A licence from the appropriate authorities is required to photograph museum artefacts - this can sometimes be purchased from the museum's ticket desk. No flash photography is allowed in churches with murals or icons. **Tipping**: A service charge is added to all bills, but tipping is still acceptable and remains at the discretion of the individual.

Business Profile

ECONOMY: The southern, Greek-Cypriot region has a strong agricultural sector, producing fruit and vegetables, potatoes, barley, citrus fruit and grapes for export. However, the south's principal exports are clothing, footwear and textiles, which dominate the region's light manufacturing industry. Tourism is the main component of the southern service economy but, in recent years, financial services - including 'offshore' enterprises - have also assumed an important role. The UK's sovereign military bases on the southern coast and near the partition boundary are a major source of revenue for the south. Economic development of the northern occupied part of Cyprus has been severely limited by lack of diplomatic recognition and it continues to rely heavily on economic support from Turkey. The profile of the northern occupied part of Cyprus's agricultural sector is similar to that of the south; manufacturing is relatively insignificant; tourism relies heavily on visitors from the Turkish mainland. Both parts of the island rely on imported raw fuels for their energy supplies. The decision of the north to allow visits across the partition may presage the development of a cross-border economy, but this may take some time. This concession on the part of the north was driven mainly by the acceptance of the south into the European Union in 2004, as part of the wave of new entrants which brought the EU up to 25 members. Turkey, which ultimately controls the fate of the northern part of Cyprus, is an aspirant member of the EU, and a solution to the present division of the island is an essential precursor to their own accession. The EU accounts for the bulk of southern Cyprus trade: Lebanon, Egypt, the Gulf States and Libya are the other trading partners.
COMMERCIAL INFORMATION: The following organisation can offer advice: Cyprus Chamber of Commerce and Industry, 38 Grivas Digenis Avenue, Chamber Building, PO Box 21455, 1509 Nicosia (tel: (22) 889 800; fax: (22) 669 048; e-mail: chamber@ccci.org.cy; website: www.ccci.org.cy).
CONFERENCES/CONVENTIONS: Many hotels have facilities; seating for up to 1200 people is available. Nicosia is a popular destination for budget-priced conferences and has a number of modern facilities. Advice can be obtained from the Cyprus Tourism Organisation in London (see *Contact Addresses* section).

Climate

Warm Mediterranean climate. Hot, dry summers with mild winters during which rainfall is most likely.
Required clothing: Lightweight cottons and linens during summer months; warmer mediumweights and rainwear during the winter.

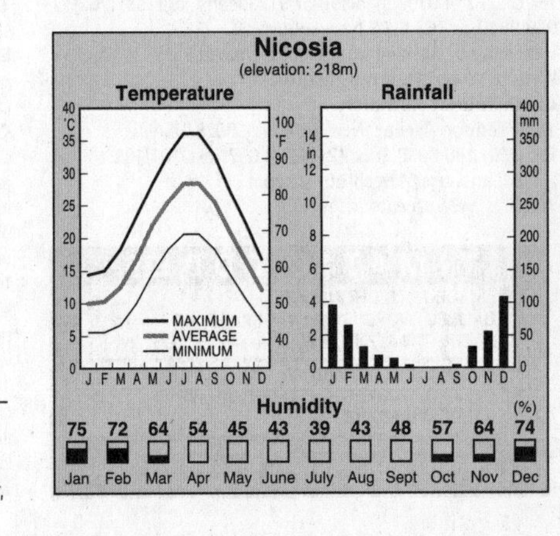

A B C D E F G H I J K L M N O P Q R S T U V W X Y Z

Czech Republic

LATEST TRAVEL ADVICE CONTACTS

British Foreign and Commonwealth Office
Tel: (0870) 606 0290 Website: www.fco.gov.uk

US Department of State
Website: http://travel.state.gov/travel

Canadian Department of Foreign Affairs and Int'l Trade
Tel: (1 800) 267 8376 Website: www.dfait-maeci.gc.ca

Location: Central Europe.

Country dialling code: 420.

Czech Tourist Authority
Vinohradská Suite 46, PO Box 32, 120 41 Prague 2, Czech Republic
Tel: (2) 2158 0111. Fax: (2) 2424 7516.
E-mail: ic@czechtourism.cz
Website: www.czechtourism.com *or* www.czechtourism.cz

Prague Information Service
Betlemské Namêsti 2, 11698 Prague 1, Czech Republic
Tel: (2) 12 444. Fax: (2) 2222 1721.
E-mail: tourinfo@pis.cz
Website: www.prague-info.cz

Embassy of the Czech Republic
28 Kensington Palace Gardens, London W8 4QY, UK
Tel: (020) 7243 1115 *or* (09069) 101 060 (24-hour recorded visa information; calls cost £1 per minute). Fax: (020) 7727 9654 *or* 7243 7926 (consular section).
E-mail: london@embassy.mzv.cz or visa.london@embassy.mzv.cz
Website: www.czechembassy.org.uk
Opening hours: Mon-Thurs 0830-1715; Fri 0830-1600; Mon-Fri 0900-1100 (visa application); 1315-1500 (visa collection).

Czech Tourist Authority
Morley House, 320 Regent Street, W1B 3BG, London, UK
Tel: (020) 7631 0427 *or* (09063) 640 641 (24-hour enquiry line; calls cost 60p per minute). Fax: (020) 7631 0419.
E-mail: info-uk@czechtourism.com
Website: www.czechtourism.com

British Embassy
Thunovská 14, 118 00 Prague 1, Czech Republic
Tel: (2) 5740 2111. Fax: (2) 5740 2296.
E-mail: info@britain.cz Website: www.britain.cz

Embassy of the Czech Republic
3900 Spring of Freedom Street, NW, Washington, DC 20008, USA
Tel: (202) 274 9100 (general) *or* 9123 (consular). Fax: (202) 966 8540 *or* 363 6308 (visa enquiries).
E-mail: amb_washington@embassy.mzv.cz
Website: www.mzv.cz/washington

Czech Tourist Authority
1109 Madison Avenue, New York, NY 10028, USA
Tel: (212) 288 0830. Fax: (212) 288 0971 ext. 101/105.
E-mail: info-usa@czechtourism.com
Website: www.czechtourism.com

TIMATIC CODES

Health	AMADEUS: **TI-DFT/JIB/HE** GALILEO/WORLDSPAN: **TI-DFT/JIB/HE** SABRE: **TIDFT/JIB/HE**
Visa	AMADEUS: **TI-DFT/JIB/VI** GALILEO/WORLDSPAN: **TI-DFT/JIB/VI** SABRE: **TIDFT/JIB/VI**

To access TIMATIC country information on Health and Visa regulations through the Computer Reservations System (CRS), type in the appropriate command line listed above.

Embassy of the United States of America
Trziste 15, 118 01 Prague 1, Czech Republic
Tel: (2) 5753 0663. Fax: (2) 5753 4028 (consular section).
E-mail: consprg@state.gov (consular section) *or* webmaster@usembassy.cz Website: www.usembassy.cz

Embassy of the Czech Republic
251 Cooper Street, Ottawa, Ontario K2P 0G2, Canada
Tel: (613) 562 3875. Fax: (613) 562 3878.
E-mail: ottawa@embassy.mzv.cz
Website: www.czechembassy.org

Czech Tourist Authority
401 Bay Street, Suite 1510, Toronto, Ontario M5H 2Y4, Canada
Tel: (416) 363 9928. Fax: (416) 363 0239.
E-mail: info-ca@czechtourism.com
Website: www.czechtourism.com

Canadian Embassy
Muchova 6, 160 00 Prague 6, Czech Republic
Tel: (2) 7210 1800. Fax: (2) 7210 1890.
E-mail: canada@canada.cz
Website: www.canada.cz

Credit: © Czech Tourist Authority

General Information

AREA: 78,866 sq km (30,450 sq miles).
POPULATION: 10,203,269 (2002).
POPULATION DENSITY: 129.4 per sq km.
CAPITAL: Prague. **Population**: 1,161,938 (2002).
GEOGRAPHY: The Czech Republic is situated in central Europe, sharing frontiers with Germany, Poland, the Slovak Republic and Austria. Only about one-quarter of the size of the British Isles, the republic is hilly and picturesque, with historic castles, romantic valleys and lakes, as well as excellent facilities to 'take the waters' at one of the famous spas or to ski and hike in the mountains. Among the most beautiful areas are the river valleys of the Vltava (Moldau) and Labe (Elbe), the hilly landscape and rocky mountains. Bohemia, to the west, is one of two main regions. Besides Prague, the Czech capital, tourists are drawn to the spa towns of Karlovy Vary and Mariánské Lázne, and to the very beautiful region of south Bohemia. The Elbe flows through eastern Bohemia from the Krkonoɕse/Giant mountains, one of the most popular skiing regions. The eastern part, the rich agricultural area of Moravia offers a variety of wooded highlands, vineyards, folk art and castles. There are many historic towns such as Olomouc, Kromeríz and Telc. Brno is Moravia's administrative and cultural centre.
GOVERNMENT: Republic since 1993. **Head of State**: President Václav Klaus since 2003. **Head of Government**: Prime Minister Stanislav Gross since 2004.
LANGUAGE: The official language is Czech. English and German are also spoken.
RELIGION: Mostly Roman Catholic and some Protestant, including churches such as the Reformed, Lutheran, Methodist, Unity of Czech Brothers and Baptist. There is a small community of Jews, mainly in Prague. According to the March 2001 national Census, 60 per cent of the population profess no religious beliefs.
TIME: GMT + 1 (GMT + 2 during the European/continental summertime).
ELECTRICITY: Generally 220 volts AC, 50Hz. Most major hotels have standard international two-pin razor plugs. Lamp fittings are normally of the screw type.
COMMUNICATIONS: Telephone: Full IDD is available. Country code: 420. Outgoing international code: 00. There are public telephone booths, including special kiosks for international calls. Surcharges can be quite high on long-distance calls from hotels. Most of the public telephone boxes take phonecards, which can be purchased at all Telecom points of sale and at newsagent and tobacconist shops. **Mobile telephone:** GSM 900/1800. Network operators include *Cesky Mobil* (website: www.oskarmobil.cz), *Eurotel* (website: www.eurotel.cz) and *T Mobile* (website: www.t-mobile.cz). Coverage extends all over the country. **Fax:** Services are available in most hotels and offices and some shops. **Internet:** There are Internet cafes in Prague. Local ISPs include *Tiscali* (website: www.tiscali.cz). Roaming agreements exist. **Telegram:** Facilities are available at all main towns and hotels. **Post:** There is a 24-hour service at the main post office in Prague at 14 Jindrisská Street, Prague 1. *Poste Restante* services are available throughout the country. Post office hours: Mon-Fri 0800-1800. **Press:** The *Prague Post* and *Prague Wochenblatt* (both weekly) are published in English. The main Czech dailies include *Mladá Fronta Dnes, Moravskoslezský den, Právo* and *Veèerník Praha*.
Radio: BBC World Service (website: www.bbc.co.uk/worldservice) and Voice of America (website: www.voa.gov) can be received. From time to time the frequencies change and the most up-to-date can be found online.

Passport/Visa

	Passport Required?	Visa Required?	Return Ticket Required?
Full British	Yes	No	No
Australian	Yes	No/2	No
Canadian	Yes	No/2	No
USA	Yes	No/2	No
Other EU	1	No	No
Japanese	Yes	No/2	No

***Note:** Regulations and requirements may be subject to change at short notice, and you are advised to contact the appropriate diplomatic or consular authority before finalising travel arrangements. Details of these may be found at the head of this country's entry. Any numbers in the chart refer to the footnotes below.*

PASSPORTS: Passport valid for 90 days from issue date of visa for visas up to 90 days; at least 455 days for visas over 90 days. For nationals who do not require a visa, passport must be valid for 90 days beyond the expected length of stay except for:
1. EU and EEA nationals with valid national ID cards (who may also travel with a passport valid only for the duration of stay in the Czech Republic).
Note: Minors are allowed to travel on their parents' passports up until aged 15 years.
VISAS: Required by all except the following:
(a) nationals listed in the chart above (including French Overseas Territories for stays of up to 90 days);
(b) **2.** nationals of Andorra, Argentina, Bolivia, Brazil, Brunei, Chile, Costa Rica, Croatia, El Salvador, Guatemala, Honduras, Hong Kong (SAR), Israel, Korea (Rep), Macau (SAR), Malaysia, Mexico, Monaco, New Zealand, Nicaragua, Panama, Paraguay, San Marino, Switzerland, Uruguay, Vatican City and Venezuela for up to 90 days;
(c) nationals of Bulgaria, Romania and Singapore for up to 30 days;
(d) transit passengers continuing their journey within 24 hours and not leaving the airport, providing holding onward tickets and relevant travel documentation. *Airport transit/transit visas are, however, *always* required for nationals of Afghanistan, Bangladesh, Congo (Dem Rep), Eritrea, Ethiopia, Ghana, Iran, Iraq, Lebanon, Nigeria, Pakistan, Somalia, Sri Lanka and the Syrian Arab Republic (this does not apply if the above national holds a valid residence visa or permit of any EU country, Iceland, Liechtenstein or Norway, or holds a permanent or long-term residence permit in Andorra, Canada, Japan, Monaco, San Marino, Switzerland or the USA);
(e) holders of a UN laissez-passer for as long as is necessary.
Note: (a) EU and EEA nationals, and those who do not require visas, whose stay will exceed 30 days, must register with the Alien and Border Police within 30 days of arrival. All other nationals must register with the Alien and Border Police within three days of arrival, regardless of intended length of stay. Generally, accommodation providers will arrange this for their guests. (b) British Overseas Citizens require visas as do holders of British Travel Documents (blue) under the 1951 Geneva Convention, and holders of British Travel Documents (brown) for tourism and business trips, and must apply in person.
Types of visa and cost: *Single-entry*, *Multiple-entry*, *Single-transit*, *Double-transit*, *Multiple-transit* and *Airport-transit*. Prices vary according to the nationality of the applicant and according to currency rates. For UK nationals, single-entry visas cost £17, multiple-entry visas cost £63, for stays not exceeding 90 days. *Single-transit*: £17; *double-transit*: £25. There are no visa fees for nationals of Albania, Ecuador, Japan, Seychelles and South Africa, or for children under 15 years of age.
Validity: *Single-* and *multiple-entry*: Six months from date of issue for a visit of a specified period not exceeding 90 days. *Transit* (also available: double-transit and multiple-transit): Six months from date of issue for a visit of a specified period not exceeding five days.
Application to: Consulate (or Consular section at the Embassy); see *Contact Addresses* section for details. Please note that some nationals must apply in person for a visa and submit slightly different application requirements (see below). Check with the Embassy for further details.

Application requirements: (a) One original application form. (b) One recent passport-size photo. (c) Passport valid for at least 90 days beyond the requested length of visa, with at least one blank page and a photocopy of the data page. (d) Fee (payable in cash, by banker's draft or by postal order only). (e) Proof of sufficient funds (eg recent bank statement or letter from host or sponsor). (f) Postal applications should be accompanied by a self-addressed envelope pre-paid for special delivery. (g) Valid travel insurance policy covering emergency hospital treatment and repatriation. *Business*: (a)-(g) and, (h) Letter from employer or invitation letter from company in the Czech Republic. *Student*: (a)-(g) and, (h) Letter from school or college confirming that you are a student and confirmation of available accommodation.

Note: All documents must be submitted in both original form, plus one photocopy.

Working days required: Seven (in person); 14 (by post); maximum 30.

TEMPORARY RESIDENCE: EU citizens may apply if intending to stay longer than three months, filed with the Alien & Border Police in the Czech Republic. The process will take about 60 to 180 days.

Money

Currency: Koruna (Kc) or Crown = 100 haler. Notes are in denominations of Kc5000, 2000, 1000, 500, 200, 100, 50 and 20. Coins are in denominations of Kc50, 20, 10, 5, 2 and 1, and 50, 20 and 10 hellers.

Currency exchange: Foreign currency (including travellers cheques) can be exchanged at all bank branches and at authorised exchange offices, main hotels and road border crossings.

Credit & debit cards: Major cards such as American Express, Diners Club, Discover, Visa, MasterCard and others may be used to exchange currency and are also accepted in some hotels, restaurants and shops. Check with your credit or debit card company for details of merchant acceptability and other services which may be available.

Travellers cheques: These are widely accepted. To avoid additional exchange rate charges, travellers are advised to take travellers cheques in US Dollars, Euros or Pounds Sterling.

Currency restrictions: The import and export of local currency is limited to Kc200,000 or 10 golden coins. The import and export of foreign currency is unlimited.

Exchange rate indicators: The following figures are included as a guide to the movements of the Koruna against Sterling and the US Dollar:

Date	Feb '04	May '04	Aug '04	Nov '04
£1.00=	48.81	48.30	46.91	44.22
$1.00=	26.82	27.04	25.46	23.35

Banking hours: Generally Mon-Fri 0800-1800. Some banks close early on Fridays.

Duty Free

The following goods may be imported into the Czech Republic without incurring customs duty:

200 cigarettes or 100 cigarillos or 50 cigars or 250g tobacco (if over 16 years of age); 1l of spirits and 2l of wine (if over 18 years of age); 50g of perfume or 250ml of eau de toilette; gifts up to a value of 175 (if over 15 years of age) or 90 (if under 15 years of age); foods, fruits, flowers and medication for personal use.

Note: The export of cultural heritage pieces is only possible with prior approval by the Czech Ministry of Culture.

Abolition of duty free goods within the EU: On 30 June 1999, the sale of duty-free alcohol and tobacco at airports and at sea was abolished in all of the original 15 EU member states. Of the 10 new member states that joined the EU on May 1st 2004, these rules already apply to Cyprus and Malta. There are transitional rules in place for visitors returning to one of the original 15 EU countries from one of the other new EU countries. But for the original 15, plus Cyprus and Malta, there are now no limits imposed on importing tobacco and alcohol products from one EU country to another (with the exceptions of Denmark, Finland and Sweden, where limits *are* imposed). Travellers should note that they may be required to prove at customs that the goods purchased are for personal use only.

Public Holidays

2005: Jan 1 New Year's Day. **Mar 28** Easter Monday. **May 1** May Day. **May 8** Liberation Day. **Jul 5** Day of the Apostles St Cyril and St Methodius. **Jul 6** Anniversary of the Martyrdom of Jan Hus. **Sep 28** Czech Statehood Day. **Oct 28** Independence Day. **Nov 17** Freedom and Democracy Day. **Dec 24-26** Christmas.

2006: Jan 1 New Year's Day. **Apr 17** Easter Monday. **May 1** May Day. **May 8** Liberation Day. **Jul 5** Day of the Apostles St Cyril and St Methodius. **Jul 6** Anniversary of the Martyrdom of Jan Hus. **Sep 28** Czech Statehood Day. **Oct 28** Independence Day. **Nov 17** Freedom and Democracy Day. **Dec 24-26** Christmas.

Health

	Special Precautions?	Certificate Required?
Yellow Fever	No	No
Cholera	No	No
Typhoid & Polio	No	No
Malaria	No	No

Note: *Regulations and requirements may be subject to change at short notice, and you are advised to contact your doctor well in advance of your intended date of departure. Any numbers in the chart refer to the footnotes below.*

Food & drink: Mains water is normally chlorinated and, whilst relatively safe, may cause mild abdominal upsets. Bottled water is available and advised. Milk is pasteurised and dairy products are safe for consumption. Local meat, poultry, seafood, fruit and vegetables are generally considered safe to eat.

Other risks: *Tick-borne encephalitis* exists in rural forested areas during summer months. Immunisation against *hepatitis A* and *B* is sometimes advised. *Rabies* is present. For those at high risk, vaccination before arrival should be considered. If you are bitten, seek medical advice without delay. For further information, consult the *Health* appendix.

Health care: There is a reciprocal health agreement with the UK. On production of a UK passport, hospital and other medical care will be provided free of charge in case of illness or accident. Prescribed medicine and dental treatment will be charged for. Other international agreements exist for free health care and visitors are advised to check with their national health authorities. Medical insurance is advised in all other cases.

Travel - International

AIR: The national airline is *Czech Airlines (OK)* (website:

www.csa.cz). There are also several small airlines. Information can be obtained from Czech Airlines, City Service Centre, V Celnici 5, 11000 Prague 1 (tel: (2) 3900 7007 (reservations office); e-mail: Call.Centre@csa.cz). The airline also has an office in London (tel: (0870) 444 3747 (reservations); e-mail: lon@czechairlines.com).
Approximate flight times: From Prague to *London* is four hours 10 minutes; to *New York* is 10 hours 40 minutes.
International airports: *Prague (PRG)* (Ruzyne) is 20km (12 miles) northwest of the city. Transport to/from city: Airport bus (*Cedaz*) every 30 minutes from 0600-2100 (travel time - 30 minutes); 119 and 254 buses run approximately every 10 minutes, from 0425-2340 (travel time - 20 minutes) to the nearest metro station, Dejvická (there are also night-buses in operation); mini-bus taxis to the city centre (24-hour service, surcharge at night). Big hotels operate frequent shuttle-bus services during the summer months to the major hotels in the city. Airport facilities include duty-free shops; post office; banks/bureaux de change; restaurant and bar; car parking and car hire (*Alamo, Alimex CR, Avis, Budget, CS-Czechocar, Dvorak, Europcar, Hertz* and *Sixt*).
RAIL: The Czech Republic forms part of the European InterCity network. The most convenient routes to the Czech Republic from Western Europe are via Berlin, Cologne, Frankfurt, Nuremburg, Munich, Vienna, Würzburg or Zurich to Prague. The *Vindobona Express* is a once-daily through train that travels from Vienna to Prague (main station) and on to Berlin. Rail travel information is available from Czech Railways (tel: (2) 2461 4030; e-mail: info@cdrail.cz; website: www.cdrail.cz).
ROAD: The Czech Republic can be entered via Germany, Poland, the Slovak Republic or Austria. **Bus:** There is an international bus network covering most European cities. There are connections to Amsterdam, Frankfurt/M, London, Munich, Vienna and other main cities from the Florenc and Zelivskeho Bus Terminals (Metro stations). Kingscourt Express runs services Monday to Saturday between London Victoria to Prague and Brno (tel: (2) 6671 3032; fax: (2) 6671 2177; website: www.eurobus.cz). Eurolines (4 Cardiff Road, Luton, Bedfordshire L41 1PP; tel: (08705) 143 219; fax: (01582) 400 694; website: www.eurolines.com *or* www.nationalexpress.com) also operate services between Prague and other european cities.

Travel - Internal

AIR: *Czech Airlines (OK)* operates an extensive domestic service. There are regular domestic flights from Prague to Ostrava, Brno and Karlovy Vary.
RIVER: Navigable waterways can be found in the country and the main river ports are located at Prague, Ústí nad Labem and Decin.
RAIL: The rail network is operated by *Czech Railways* (*Ceské Drahy*, see above). There are several daily express trains between Prague and main cities and resorts. Reservations should be made in advance on major routes. Fares are low, but supplements are payable for travel by express trains.
ROAD: Traffic drives on the right. Speed limits are 31mph (50kph) in built-up areas, 55mph (90kph) outside built-up areas and 80mph (130kph) on motorways. Motorways run from Prague to Plzen, Podebrady to Bratislava (Slovak Republic) via Brno. Users of the Czech motorways have to buy a *vignette* (season ticket), which costs approximately Kc800 for each year. A 10-day *vignette* is now available at approximately Kc100. **Bus**: The extensive bus network mostly covers areas not accessible by rail and is efficient and comfortable. Buses are mostly run by the State Bus Company; see online for timetables (website: www.vlak-bus.cz). **Car hire**: Self-drive cars may be hired through *Avis, Hertz* and other companies. Seat belts are compulsory and drinking is absolutely prohibited. Many petrol stations open 24 hours. There is a road emergency service available by calling 154. **Documentation**: A valid national driving licence. If this has no photocard, an International Driving Permit is also required.
URBAN: Public transport is excellent. See online (website: www.dp-praha.cz) for timetables and other information on transport in Prague. There is a **metro** service in Prague that runs from 0500-0000. Three flat fares are charged. There are also **tram** and **bus** services (for which tickets must be purchased in advance from tobacconist shops, newsagents, metro stations, information centres or travel agents). Night trams and buses run from 0000-0430 in Prague. Buses, trolleybuses and trams also exist in Brno, Ostrava, Plzen and several other towns. Most services run from 0430-0000. All the cities operate flat-fare systems and tourist passes can be purchased in advance that are valid for a number of journeys. Tickets should be punched in the appropriate machine on entering the tram or bus. A separate ticket is required when changing routes. There is a fine for fare evasion. Blue badges on tram and bus stops indicate an all-night service. Taxis are available in all the main towns and are metered, higher fares are charged at night. For further information about public transport in Prague, contact the Czech Tourist Authority (Prague Information Line); see *Contact Addresses* section.
Travel times: The following chart gives approximate travel times (in hours and minutes) from **Prague** to other major towns/cities in the Czech Republic.

	Air	Road	Rail
Brno	0.45	2.15	4.45
Karlovy Vary	0.30	2.00	4.45
Ostrava	1.00	6.45	6.00

Accommodation

The Czech Republic is able to offer a full range of accommodation to suit every pocket. There is a wide range of hotels, graded from **1 to 5 stars**, boarding hostels and private apartments. Many campsites are also open during the summer. For further information on the range of accommodation available, contact the Czech Tourist Authority (see *Contact Addresses* section) *or* visit www.travelguide.cz *or* www.discoverczech.com.
YOUTH HOSTELS: There 35 youth hostels in the Czech Republic, with several in Prague. Contact the International Youth Hostel Federation in the Czech Republic, check online for more information (website: www.iyhf.cz/iyhf).

Resorts & Excursions

Although for most visitors, Prague is the Czech Republic, there is far more to see and do throughout the country. Tourism is still in its infancy but the strides forward since the Velvet Revolution in 1989 have been remarkable. There are over 3000 castles, palaces and other historic monuments throughout the country. Equally characteristic are the country's many important churches from the Gothic to the Baroque periods. Spas have been an important cultural phenomenon since the 19th century and, indeed, there are 176 spas in the country today. The Czech Republic has three National Parks, 24 Protected Landscape Areas, 113 National Nature Reserves, 453 Nature Reserves, 99 National Nature Monuments and 850 Nature Monuments, most of which have only been founded since 1990. The country is divided into two provinces: Bohemia in the west and Moravia in the east.

PRAGUE

Picturesquely sited on the banks of the **Vltava (Moldau) River**, Prague has always played an important part in the history of Europe. It is noted for magnificent Gothic, Baroque, Romanesque, Belle Epoque/Art Nouveau and Cubist architecture, as well as its cultural scene of elegance. Since the fall of Communism, Prague has rapidly regained its cafe culture and is again very much the 'Paris of the East'. The city's historical centre, never bombed in World War II, is a UNESCO World Cultural Heritage Site. This includes the **Hradcany** complex of **Prazsky hrad (Prague Castle)**, including Palace rooms like the **Vladislavsky sál (Vladislav Hall)** which was once used by Bohemian knights for jousting, the **Katedrála sv Víta (St Vitus Cathedral)** and the Basilica of sv Jirí (St George Basilica). Views over the Vltava, spanned by many bridges, including the famous medieval **Karluv most (Charles Bridge)**, contribute to Prague's reputation as a 'fairytale city'. The **Lesser Town (Mala Strana)** beneath the castle is a quarter of winding, narrow streets with palaces from the 17th and 18th centuries and small artisan houses. The **Old Town (Stare Mesto)** across the Charles Bridge includes important tourist sites like the **Old Town Hall (Staromestska radnice)** with its astronomical clock and the Gothic **Tyn Church** behind the square. The area around **Vaclavske namesti (Wenceslas Square)** is the principal shopping area of the city. To the south is **Vysehrad** with its **Slavin Cemetery** honouring the intellectuals and artists, and its Cubist villas.
EXCURSIONS: Near to Prague is a grim reminder of the horrors of World War II - the site of the 'show' concentration camp at **Terezin**, which is now a museum. Also in the area are the castles of **Karlstejn**, **Krivoklat** and **Konopiste**. Near **Karlstejn** is the **Cesky kras (Bohemian Karst)**, a region of limestone caves, of which **Konepruské jeskyne** is open to the public. The historic silver mining town of **Kutna Hora** with the dominating Gothic cathedral of **sv Barbora (St Barbara)** is another UNESCO Cultural Heritage Site. North of Prague at the confluence of the **Vltava** and the **Labe rivers** is **Melník** with its **Zamek (Castle)** built by the Lobkowitz family; this area is now returning to its former role as an important wine-making region.

BOHEMIA

Heavy industrialisation in Northern Bohemia has taken its toll and many of the forests suffer greatly from the effects of acid rain. A start to correcting this situation has been made but it will be many years before significant results are shown. However, the north remains a popular destination with Czech and German tourists. Much of the area's interest lies in the sandstone 'rock-cities' (spectacular mini-canyons and steep bluffs of volcanic rocks in a densely forested area) of the **Cesky Svycarsko (Bohemian Switzerland)** especially around Tisa, the **Cesky raj (Bohemian paradise)** between **Turnov** and **Jicin** and the area around **Broumov**. The **Krkonoše (Giant) Mountains National Park** of northeast Bohemia offers superb scenery, excellent hiking and many downhill and cross-country ski and snowboarding facilities; **Spindleruv Mlyn**, on the banks of **River Labe**, is the most visited mountain town in the park. Southwest of Prague, **Plzen**, the second-largest city in Bohemia, boasts eclectic architecture from the Gothic to Art Nouveau, interesting museums and galleries like the **Brewery Museum** and the **Západoceské Galérie** (one of the best art galleries outside Prague), and the world-famous *Pilsner* beer to which the town has given its name; beer had been brewed since the town's foundation in 1295 but it was only in 1842 that the Pilsner style was established. Guided tours of the **Plzensky Prazdroj brewery** are available.
The **Trebonsko** region of south Bohemia is made up of peat bogs and marshes, with linked fish-farming ponds dating from the 15th century; carp is the traditional Christmas Day dish in the Czech lands and fish farming still dominates the region. Trebon is a perfect medieval spa town right in the middle of the area of fish ponds. The enormous **Zamek (Castle)** was built by Peter Vok, the last Rozmberk heir, who was fond of alchemy, sex and drugs; its large 'English park' now provides walks for the spa patients.
Southern Bohemia, with its lakes and woods, has for a long time been a favourite holiday place for families, since it has many recreational facilities and points of historic interest. The country is also famed for its caves: the rock formation of the mountain ranges form underground rivers and chambers decorated above and below with stalactites and stalagmites. **Ceske Budejovice (Budweis)**, whose wealth was founded on silver mines, and the salt route from Linz to Prague boasts one of Europe's largest town squares. However, it is the local beer, *Budvar (Budweiser)* which is the town's main claim to fame. The medieval town of **Cesky Krumlov** (a UNESCO Cultural Heritage Site) has its enormous castle perched on a ridge above the young **River Vltava**, and the region to the border is full of castles, monasteries and churches. The **Sumava/Bohemian Forest** towards the German border is the country's largest National Park, and with the **Bavarian Forest** across the border forms the largest forest complex in Europe. The park includes glacial lakes, many areas of virgin forest and important historic monuments. Good wintersports centres include **Zelezna Ruda**, **Spicak**, **Zadov**, **Churanov** and **Kramolin**. The northern shore of **Lake Lipno** has many small popular summer resorts and is a good location for exploring the **Sumava**.
In western Bohemia, the health resorts or spas remain one of the country's primary attractions, with their many springs, graceful colonnades and parks, spectacular houses and hotels. By the 19th century, the combination of their cures and their position at the meeting point of the two German-speaking empires made them the focal point of central Europe. Beethoven, Wagner, Edward VII and Goethe all admired the resort of **Marianske Lazne (Marienbad)**, whilst the town of **Karlovy Vary (Karlsbad)**, the king of the spas, has attracted the crowned heads of Europe to bathe in its sulphurous waters. **Frantiskovy Lazne**, however, is the most typical spa town, laid out in perfect symmetry with delightful parks and 24 springs used to cure heart disease and infertility. There is also a nature reserve near the town.

MORAVIA

Brno, the capital of Moravia, dates from the 13th century and has the fine **Moravian Museum**; an important **Augustinian Monastery** where the great geneticist, Mendel, was Abbot; the **Capuchin Church** with its mummies; and the Gothic **Spilberk Castle**. A large number of international trade fairs take place in the **Brno Exhibition Centre**. To the northeast is the **Moravsky krás**, the area of great limestone caves around **Blansko**. To the northwest, the Gothic castle of **Pernstejn** is probably closest to most people's idea of what a medieval castle should look like; the hour-long train journey to it up the **Svratka Valley** is an attractive trip. Southwest of Brno, three towns in particular stand out as tourist locations: **Moravsky Krumlov** with its **Mucha Gallery**, including great pictures, such as 'Slovanska epopej' (The Slav Epic), **Slavkov** (Austerlitz), near the Napoleonic battlefield, and **Bucovice**, whose castle features the remarkable **zajeci sal (The Hall of Hares)** with murals of hares revenging themselves on men and dogs.
In the **Vysocina (Bohemian-Moravian Uplands)** to the east, the towns of **Telc** (a UNESCO Cultural Heritage Site) and **Slavonice** are two of the most perfect examples of Renaissance towns in Europe. Telc, including the **Zamec (Castle)**, was completely rebuilt after the fire of 1530; medieval arcades surround the town square with its gabled and pedimented houses. Slavonice is another old town founded on silver mining. In **Zdar nad Sazavou**, about

40km (25 miles) northeast of **Jihlava**, the Cistercian monastery and pilgrimage church dedicated to sv Jan Nepomucky (St John of Nepomuk) was designed by Prague-born Giovanni Santini, one of the greatest artists of the Czech Counter-Reformation, who married Gothic and Baroque forms, often with a humour lacking in other architects. Nearby in **Ostrov nad Oslavou**, he designed a *hostinec* (pub) shaped like the letter 'W' to honour a fellow architect, and the village church at **Obyctov**, shaped like a turtle, one of the Virgin Mary's more obscure symbols.

The area between the small wine-making towns of **Lednice** and **Valtice** was once a possession of the Grand Dukes of Liechtenstein. Several impressive castles, landscaped parks and structural follies are dotted over an area of 250 sq km (96 sq miles), broken up by numerous ponds and forests. To the west, the area between **Znojmo** and **Vranov** on the **River Dyji** (**Thaya** in German) is an area of untouched river valley, now a joint National Park on both sides of the Austrian border. Northeast of Brno, **Kromeriz** (also accessible as a day trip from Prague) is a beautifully preserved Baroque town; its great Bishop's Palace includes an important art collection (including paintings from the auction after the execution of the English Charles I), and superb water gardens which run down to the banks of the **Morava** river.

Despite many ecological disaster zones and the great – and unpleasant – industrial centre of **Ostrava**, northern Moravia has much to offer the independent traveller.

Olomouc, now happily recovered from its era as a Soviet garrison, is once again an attractive university town noted as much for its parks as for its Baroque churches, sculptures and fountains. The surrounding **Haná** region is strongly agricultural, with many villages having attractive harvest festivals in late September. In the extreme north, the **Jeseniky Mountains** are an eastern extension of the Bohemian **Krkonose**. **Lazne Jesenik** is one of the many famous Czech Silesian spas founded in the 19th century; this area is excellent for hiking, with rocky outcrops, cave systems and monuments. To the east of Ostrava, the hilly **Beskydy** region (which extends through Poland into the Ukraine) is the area of the *Vlachs* (Wallachs), whose culture still survives in folklore and architecture. This area is excellent for hiking and winter sports. The excellent open-air *skansen* (Folk Museum) at **Roznov pod Radhostem**, begun in 1925, is the largest in the country; another good *skansen* is at **Velke Karlovice**. *Valchs* architecture can be found to the south in the villages in the **Vsetinska Becva valley**, including **Bzove**, **Jezerne** and **Ratkov**.

Sport & Activities

Outdoor pursuits: The Czech Republic has a wealth of beautiful areas to explore. More than 10 per cent of the country's surface area is occupied by the three national parks and the 1200 protected natural areas. **Skiing** is a very popular activity, and there are many well-established resorts. The most frequented areas for downhill skiing are in the *Krkonoše* (Giant Mountains) in northern Bohemia, where *Pec pod Snezkou*, *Spindlorov Mlyn* and *Harachov* are the main resorts. Facilities are also to be found in the *Jeseniky* and *Besniky* ranges, and in the *Orlické Hory* (Eagle Mountains). **Cross-country skiing** is also a widespread sport, and facilities and tracks are to be found not only in the *Krkonoše*, but also in the *Šumava* (Bohemian Forest) in southern Bohemia. In summer, these areas become havens for hikers, and contain well-marked trails. The *Krkonoše* are the Czech Republic's highest mountain range, with the country's highest peak, *Snezka* (1602m/5255ft). Several other peaks exceed 1500m (4920ft). Less strenuous walks can be pursued in other natural areas, such as the *Beskidy* range. **Rock climbers** should go to the sandstone rock formations in the north (*Cesky raj*, *Adršpach Rocks* and *Ceskosaské švycarsko*). **Cavers** should go to the *Moravsky Kras* (Moravian karst) near Brno, where there are interesting caves. **Cycling** is emerging as a popular pastime, and the network of cycle tracks is growing. Southern Bohemia is a good region for this. **Horse Riding** is very popular, with many stables offering riding holidays or treks. Contact the Czech Horse Riding Federation for more information (tel: (2) 2051 1105; fax (2) 3335 4399; e-mail: info@cjf.cz).

Watersports: There are many lakes, both natural and artificial, and a variety of watersports can be pursued there. South Bohemia and Lednice-Valtice (south Moravia) contain extensive **fishing** lakes. For more information on fishing, contact the Czech Angling Federation (tel: (2) 7481 1751; fax: (2) 7481 1754; e-mail: radacrs@ipnet.cz). **Canoeing** is done on rivers such as the *Luznice*, upper *Vltava* and *Sazava*. **Windsurfing** and **sailing** equipment can be hired at various locations.

Golf: This sport is increasingly popular, with some beautiful courses. Contact the Czech Golf Federation for more information (tel: (2) 5731 7865; fax: (2) 5731 8618; e-mail: cgf@cgf.cz; website: www.cgf.cz).

Spas: The many thermal springs and mineral baths in Bohemia and Moravia have been frequented by patients seeking cures for various ailments for centuries. Nowadays, advanced medical techniques are combined with traditional methods of treatment. The best known spas are at Karlovy Vary, Marianské Lazne and Frantijskovy Lazné (see the *Resorts & Excursions* section for details). There are world-famous radioactive springs in Jáchymov, which specialises in the treatment of disorders of the nervous system, while Janské Lazne in the *Krkonoše* is also a very popular resort. In northern Moravia, the most significant spas are at Jesenik and Luhacovice, where Vincenc Priessnitz, a local doctor, developed methods of treatment which are still followed today. All the spa resorts are located in beautiful surroundings. For further information on spa stays, contact the Czech Tourist Authority (see *Contact Addresses* section).

Social Profile

FOOD & DRINK: Food is often based on Austro-Hungarian dishes; *(Wiener) Schnitzel* and pork are very popular. Specialities include *bramborak*, a delicacy of a potato pancake filled with garlic and herbs and Prague ham. Meat dishes are mostly served with *knedliky*, a type of large dough dumpling, and *zeli* (sauerkraut). Western-style fresh vegetables are often missing in lower-class restaurants. There is a wide selection of restaurants, beer taverns and wine cellars.

Popular beverages include beers (lager, dark ales, pilsner), red, white and sparkling wines from Bohemia and Moravia, fruit juices and liqueurs. Particular specialities include *becherovka* (herb brandy) and two Moravian favourites, *slivovice* (plum brandy) and *merunkovice* (apricot brandy). There are no rigid licensing hours.

NIGHTLIFE: Theatre and opera are of a good standard all over Eastern Europe. Much of the nightlife takes place in nightclubs, bars and casinos which are to be found in major cities.

SHOPPING: Souvenirs include Bohemian glass and crystal, pottery, porcelain, wooden folk carvings, hand-embroidered clothing, and food items. There are a number of excellent shops specialising in glass and crystal, while various associations of regional artists and craftspeople run their own retail outlets (pay in local currency). Other special purchases include pottery (particularly from Kolovec and Straznice); china ornaments and geyserstone carvings from Karlovy Vary; delicate lace and needle embroidery from many Moravian towns; and blood-red garnets and semi-precious stones from Bohemia. **Shopping hours**: Mon-Fri 0800-1800, Sat 0800-1200. Supermarkets and food shops in large towns and cities are open from 0600. The number of shops also open on Sunday is constantly increasing.

SPECIAL EVENTS: The Czech nation is one of the most musical in Central Europe. Throughout the year there are many occasions to enjoy music in concert halls, theatres, stately homes and churches. Regular music festivals and concert cycles also take place. Most towns have their own folk festivals, with dancing, local costumes and food. These tend to be in the summer months leading up to the harvest festivals in September. For further details, check with the Czech Tourist Authority and travel agencies (who can also arrange music festival tours). The following is a selection of special events occurring in the Czech Republic in 2005:

Jan *FIS Cross Country Skiing World Cup*. **Jan-Feb** *6th Music Theatre* Festival, Prague. **Feb 11-28** *Shrovetide* (celebrating the coming of Spring). **Apr 14-24** *Junior World Ice Hockey Championships*, Èeské Budijovice. **May 12-Jun 6** *60th International Prague Spring Music Festival*. **May 22** *11th Prague International Marathon*. **May 23-28** *Khamoro 2005* (Roma festival). **Jun** *Royal Silver in Kutná Hora*. **Jun 3-5** *Pardubice Folklore Festival*. **Jul 15-Aug 27** *International Music Festival*, Èeské Krumlov. **Aug 12-14** *Napoleon Celebrations*. **Aug 18-28** *Jazz at the End of the Summer*, Èeské Krumlov. **Sep** *International Carlsbad Folklore Festival*. **Oct 1-2** *22nd Jazzfest*, Karlovy Vary. **Dec** *Christmas Celebrations*. **Dec 31** *New Year's Eve Celebrations*, nationwide.

SOCIAL CONVENTIONS: Dress should be casual, but conservative, except at formal dinners and at quality hotels or restaurants. **Tipping**: A 5 to 10 per cent tip is usual.

Business Profile

ECONOMY: Under Soviet control, the former Czechoslovak economy was subject to a particularly high level of state control, lacking even the small-scale private enterprise that existed to some extent in all other Eastern European economies. In the aftermath of the 'Prague Spring', especially, economic development was concentrated for political reasons on heavy industry at the expense of traditional strengths in light and craft-based industries. In the immediate post-Soviet era at the beginning of the 1990s, these inefficient and, in some cases, redundant industrial monoliths appeared to be a considerable impediment to the growth of the economy. The other problem was a dearth of natural resources – the country relied heavily on the former Soviet Union for most of its raw materials, particularly oil.

After a period of political and economic crisis, which ended with the separation of the Czech and Slovak Republics and a dispute with the Soviets over oil supplies, the Czech government pushed ahead with a rapid programme of market reforms, including a programme of mass privatisation and a major overhaul of the country's financial system. The Government identified priority industries for development. These included: aircraft and vehicles, electronics, nuclear energy, gasification of coal, transport and communications, as well as traditionally strong light industries such as textiles, leather, ceramics and glass, and a variety of agricultural and service industries.

Although more than three-quarters of economic output is now in private hands, the State retains a major influence through minority shareholdings and state-owned banks (which in turn own parts of major corporations) in the economy. The results have been fairly good, with the exception of a mild recession during 1997-98. The Czech Republic has recorded steady growth within, on the whole, a sound fiscal and monetary environment. Annual growth is now slowly climbing at 2.9 per cent. The country joined the European Union along with nine other countries, in May 2004. Trade links with Austria and Germany in particular, and with the EU generally, have grown substantially. The Czech Republic has already acquired membership of the IMF, World Bank and the European Bank for Reconstruction and Development.

BUSINESS: Businessmen wear suits. A knowledge of German is useful as English is not widely spoken among the older generation. Long business lunches are usual. Avoid visits during July and August as many businesses close for holidays. **Office hours**: Mon-Fri 0800-1600.

COMMERCIAL INFORMATION: The following organisation can offer advice: Hospodárská Komora Ceské Republiky (Economic Chamber of the Czech Republic), Freyova 27, 190 00 Prague 9 (tel: (2) 9664 6111; fax: (2) 9664 6222; e-mail: info@komora.cz; website: www.hkcr.cz *or* www.komora.cz).

CONFERENCES/CONVENTIONS: The Prague International Congress Centre can seat up to 15,000 people. There are also facilities in many hotels throughout the country. Trade fairs are held in Brno. Information can be obtained from the Brno Trade Fairs and Exhibitions, V'ystaviste 1, 647 00 Brno (tel: (5) 4115 1111; fax: (5) 4115 3070; e-mail: info@bvv.cz; website: www.bvv.cz); *or* Prague Convention Bureau, Rytírská 26, 110 00 Prague 1 (tel: (2) 2423 5159; fax: (2) 2423 4399; e-mail: info@pragueconvention.cz).

Climate

The weather is quite unsettled, with generally cold winters and mild summers. Spring and summer have the highest rainfall.

Required clothing: Mediumweights, heavy topcoat and overshoes for winter; lightweights for summer.

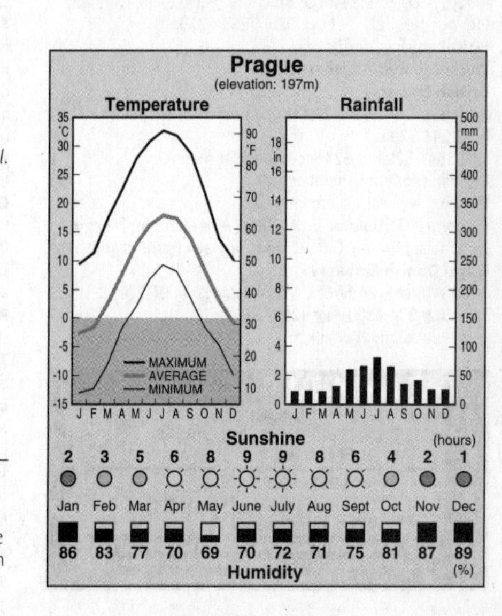

Denmark

LATEST TRAVEL ADVICE CONTACTS

British Foreign and Commonwealth Office
Tel: (0870) 606 0290 Website: www.fco.gov.uk

US Department of State
Website: http://travel.state.gov/travel

Canadian Department of Foreign Affairs and Int'l Trade
Tel: (1 800) 267 8376 Website: www.dfait-maeci.gc.ca

Location: Western Europe.

Country dialling code: 45.

Danmarks Turistråd (Danish Tourist Board)
Islands Brygge 43, 3. sal, DK-2300 Copenhagen S, Denmark
Tel: 3288 9900. Fax: 3288 9901.
E-mail: dt@dt.dk
Website: www.visitdenmark.com
Government organisation dealing with policy and development: not for general tourist information.

Wonderful Copenhagen Convention and Visitors Bureau
Gammel Kongevej 1, DK-1610 Copenhagen V, Denmark
Tel: 3325 7400 *or* 7022 2442 (tourist information and booking). Fax: 3325 7410.
E-mail: woco@woco.dk *or* touristinfo@woco.dk
Website: www.visitcopenhagen.com

Royal Danish Embassy
55 Sloane Street, London SW1X 9SR, UK
Tel: (020) 7333 0200.
Fax: (020) 7333 0270 *or* 0266 (visa section).
E-mail: lonamb@um.dk
Website: www.denmark.org.uk
Opening hours: Mon-Thurs 0900-1630 and Fri 0900-1600; consular enquiries Mon-Fri 1500-1600 (telephone).

Danish Tourist Board
55 Sloane Street, London SW1X 9SY, UK
Tel: (020) 7259 5959 (Mon, Wed and Fri 1000-1300) *or* (09001) 600 109 (24-hour brochure request line; calls cost 60p per minute). Fax: (020) 7259 5955.
E-mail: dtb.london@dt.dk
Website: www.visitdenmark.com

British Embassy
Kastelsvej 36-40, DK-2100 Copenhagen Ø, Denmark
Tel: 3544 5200.
Fax: 3544 5293 or 5246 (commercial section).
E-mail: info@britishembassy.dk
Website: www.britishembassy.dk
Honorary Consulates in: Åbenraa, Ålborg, Århus, Esbjerg, Fredericia, Herning, Odense and Tórshavn (Faroe Islands).

Royal Danish Embassy
3200 Whitehaven Street, NW, Washington, DC 20008, USA
Tel: (202) 234 4300. Fax: (202) 328 1470.
E-mail: wasamb@um.dk

TIMATIC CODES

Health
AMADEUS: **TI-DFT/JIB/HE**
GALILEO/WORLDSPAN: **TI-DFT/JIB/HE**
SABRE: **TIDFT/JIB/HE**

Visa
AMADEUS: **TI-DFT/JIB/VI**
GALILEO/WORLDSPAN: **TI-DFT/JIB/VI**
SABRE: **TIDFT/JIB/VI**

To access TIMATIC country information on Health and Visa regulations through the Computer Reservations System (CRS), type in the appropriate command line listed above.

Website: www.denmarkemb.org

Royal Danish Consulate General
One Dag Hammerskjold Plaza, 885 Second Avenue, 18th Floor, New York, NY 10017-2201 USA
Tel: (212) 223 4545. Fax: (212) 754 1904.
E-mail: information@denmark.org
Website: www.denmark.org

Danish Tourist Board
PO Box 4649, Grand Central Station, New York, NY 10063, USA
Tel: (212) 885 9700. Fax: (212) 885 9710.
E-mail: info@goscandinavia.com
Website: www.goscandinavia.com *or* www.visitdenmark.com
Also deals with enquiries from Canada. Not open to public.

Embassy of the United States of America
Dag Hammarskjølds Allé 24, DK-2100 Copenhagen Ø, Denmark
Tel: 3341 7100. Fax: 3543 0223.
E-mail: info@usembassy.dk
Website: www.usembassy.dk

Royal Danish Embassy
47 Clarence Street, Suite 450, Ottawa, Ontario KIN 9K1, Canada
Tel: (613) 562 1811. Fax: (613) 562 1812.
E-mail: ottamb@um.dk
Website: www.danish-embassy-canada.com
Consulate Generals in: Montreal and Toronto.
Honorary Consulates in: Calgary, Edmonton and Vancouver.

Canadian Embassy
Kristen Bernikowsgade 1, 1105 Copenhagen K, Denmark
Tel: 3348 3200. Fax: 3348 3220.
E-mail: copen@international.gc.ca
Website: www.canada.dk
Consulate in: Nuuk.

Credit: © Danish Tourist Board & Cees Van Roeden

General Information

AREA: 43,098 sq km (16,640 sq miles).
POPULATION: 5,383,507 (official estimate 2003).
POPULATION DENSITY: 124.9 per sq km.
CAPITAL: Copenhagen. **Population:** 1,085,813 (2003).
GEOGRAPHY: Denmark is the smallest Scandinavian country, consisting of the Jutland peninsula, north of Germany, and over 400 islands of various sizes, some inhabited and linked to the mainland by ferry or bridge. The landscape consists mainly of low-lying, fertile countryside broken by beech woods, small lakes and fjords. Greenland and the Faroe Islands are also under the sovereignty of the Kingdom of Denmark, although both have home rule. The Faroe Islands are a group of 18 islands in the North Atlantic inhabited by a population of 47,120 (2001), whose history dates back to the Viking period. Fishing and sheep farming are the two most important occupations. Tórshavn (population 18,812 (2001)), the capital of the Faroes, is served by direct flights from Copenhagen. During the summer months, there are direct flights from Aberdeen and Glasgow.
GOVERNMENT: Constitutional monarchy. **Head of State:** Queen Margrethe II since 1972. **Head of Government:** Prime Minister Anders Fogh Rasmussen since 2001.
LANGUAGE: The official language is Danish. Many Danes also speak English, German and French.
RELIGION: Predominantly Evangelical Lutheran with a small Roman Catholic minority.
TIME: GMT + 1 (GMT + 2 from last Sunday in March to Saturday before last Sunday in October).
ELECTRICITY: 230 volts AC, 50Hz. Continental two-pin plugs are standard. On many campsites, 110-volt power plugs are also available.
COMMUNICATIONS: Telephone: Full IDD is available. Country code: 45. Outgoing international code: 00. There are no area codes. **Mobile Telephone:** GSM 900 and 1800 networks. Network operators include *Orange* (website: www.orange.dk) *Sonofon* (website: www.sonofon.dk), and *TeleDanmark* (website: www.tdc.dk). **Fax:** Available from many main post offices and from major hotels. **Internet:** ISPs include *Business Net Danmark and Telepassport*. Internet cafes are available in most urban areas. **Telegram:** The Copenhagen Central Telegraph Office is open 24 hours a day. Telegrams can also be sent by phone; dial 122. **Post:** All telephone and postal rates are printed at the post offices. All post offices offer *Poste Restante* facilities. Post office opening hours: Mon-Fri 0900-1730, some are open Sat 0900-1200. **Press:** Newspapers are largely regional; the main papers in the capital include *Berlingske Tidende, Dagbladet Information, Ekstra Bladet* and *Politiken*. English-language newspapers and magazines are also available.
Radio: BBC World Service (website: www.bbc.co.uk/worldservice) and Voice of America (website: www.voa.gov) can be received. From time to time the frequencies change and the most up-to-date can be found online.

Passport/Visa

	Passport Required?	Visa Required?	Return Ticket Required?
Full British	1/2	No/3	No
Australian	Yes	No	Yes
Canadian	Yes	No	Yes
USA	2	No	Yes
Other EU	1/2	No	No
Japanese	Yes	No	Yes

Note: *Regulations and requirements may be subject to change at short notice, and you are advised to contact the appropriate diplomatic or consular authority before finalising travel arrangements. Details of these may be found at the head of this country's entry. Any numbers in the chart refer to the footnotes below.*

Note: Denmark is a signatory to the 1995 **Schengen Agreement**. For further details about passport/visa regulations within the Schengen area, see the introductory section, *How to Use this Guide*.
PASSPORTS: Passport valid for three months after the last day of stay required by all except the following:
(a) **1.** nationals of Finland, Iceland, Norway and Sweden in possession of identification papers (eg driver's licence or identity card), provided travelling entirely within Scandinavia;
(b) **2.** nationals of other EU countries holding a valid national ID card and holders of a Gibraltar Identity Card issued to British Citizens or British Dependent Citizens for tourist visits of up to three months.
Note: For nationals of EU countries and the USA, passports need to be valid for duration of stay.
VISAS: Required by all except the following for stays of up to three months:
(a) nationals of countries referred to in the chart above;
(b) nationals of Andorra, Argentina, Bermuda (provided holding a British Dependent Territories passport), Bolivia, Brazil, Brunei, Bulgaria, Chile, Costa Rica, Croatia, El Salvador, Guatemala, Honduras, Hong Kong (SAR), Iceland, Israel, Korea (Rep), Liechtenstein, Macau (SAR), Malaysia, Mexico, Monaco, New Zealand, Nicaragua, Norway, Panama, Paraguay, Romania, San Marino, Singapore, Switzerland, Uruguay, Vatican City and Venezuela;
(c) holders of a UN Laissez-passer.
Note: 3. (a) Holders of the following also *do not* require a visa: 'British Citizen' passports, including those from the Channel Islands and Isle of Man, with the endorsement 'Holder has the right of re-admission' *or* 'Holder is entitled to re-admission to the United Kingdom' *or* 'Holder has the right of abode in the United Kingdom', provided holders of such passports have not stayed outside the UK for more than two years (including the expected stay in Denmark); 'British Dependent Territories Citizens' passports (BDTC) issued to persons with the right of abode in Gibraltar with the endorsement 'Holder is defined as a UK national for Community purposes'; British National Overseas passports (BNO) with permanent residence in Hong Kong are visa exempt for up to three months. (b) Holders of the following *do* require a visa: 'British Protected Persons' passports endorsed 'Holder is subject to control under the Immigration Act 1971'.
Airport transit: Passengers continuing their journey by the same or first connecting aircraft within the international zone of the *Schengen* airport, without gaining access to the national territory of the *Schengen* member state, may not require a transit visa, provided they are holding valid onward or return documentation.
Nationals of the following countries *always* need a visa to transit through a Danish airport: Afghanistan, Bangladesh, Congo (Dem Rep), Eritrea, Ethiopia, Ghana, India (not required for Indian nationals in possession of a valid visa to an EU or EEA country, USA or Canada), Iran, Iraq, Nigeria, Pakistan, Somalia and Sri Lanka (the above list is subject to changes; please check with the Embassy or Consular section at Embassy). However, if any of these nationals are residents in an EU member state, an EEA country, the USA or Canada, and hold permission to return a minimum of three months

Credit: © Danish Tourist Board + Klaus Bentzen

after transiting Denmark, a visa is not required.
Types of visa and cost: *Tourist*, *Business*, *Transit*, *Airport Transit*: £23. An additional fee of £11 is payable for applications lodged at Honorary Consulates.
Note: (a) Spouses and children of EU and EEA nationals (providing spouse's passport and the original marriage certificate/proof of joint household are produced), and nationals of some other countries, if related in direct line of ascent or descent to such nationals or their spouses, receive their visas free of charge.
Validity: Validity depends on type of visa, nationality and purpose of visit. For further information, contact the Consulate (or Consular section at Embassy); see *Contact Addresses* section.
Application to: Consulate (or Consular section at Embassy); see *Contact Addresses* section. Applications should be made in person. Travellers visiting just one Schengen country should apply to the Consulate of that country; travellers visiting more than one Schengen country should apply to the Consulate of the country chosen as the main destination *or* the country they will enter first (if they have no main destination).
Application requirements: (a) Passport valid for a minimum of three months after expiry of visa, or official travel document valid for at least six months, both with a blank page for the visa sticker. (b) One signed and completed application form, containing parental consent for minors (if applicable). (c) One passport-size colour photograph on light background. (d) Fee, payable in cash or cheque with a cheque guarantee card. (e) Proof of purpose of visit and accomodation, eg a letter from relatives or a hotel reservation (e-mails not accepted). (f) Evidence of occupation, eg letter from employer or university or, if unemployed, benefit booklet. (g) Evidence of sufficient funds for duration of stay, eg original, recent bank statement, travellers cheques, credit card statement with credit limit. (h) A prepaid and self-addressed envelope (special delivery) if the visa is to be returned by post. (i) Valid health insurance. (j) Residents of the UK who are returning to the UK after a visit to Denmark are required to hold a residence work permit valid for at least three months beyond the validity of the visa (at least six months for holders of travel documents). *Business*: (a)-(j) and, (k) The original invitation from the business contact in Denmark.
Note: Some further documents and guarantees might be required for the processing of visas. All applications must initially be made in person at the Embassy/Consulate and by first arranging an appointment through the appointment booking system (for UK, tel: (09065) 540 755). For further information, contact the *Schengen* information line (for UK, tel: (0900) 160 0115).
Working days required: Applications can take several weeks to be processed (applicants may apply up to 12 weeks before the start of their trip).
Temporary residence: Persons wishing to stay in Denmark for more than three months should make their application *in their home country* well in advance of their intended date of departure.

Money

Currency: Danish Krone (DKR) = 100 øre. Notes are in denominations of DKR1000, 500, 200, 100 and 50. Coins are in denominations of DKR20, 10, 5, 2 and 1, and 50 and 25 øre.
Currency exchange: There are plenty of ATMs. Personal cheques cannot be used by visitors to Denmark. Some banks may refuse to exchange large foreign bank notes.
Credit & debit cards: American Express, Diners Club, MasterCard and Visa are widely accepted, as well as Eurocheque cards. Check with your credit or debit card company for details of merchant acceptability and other services which may be available.
Travellers cheques: Can be cashed by banks and hotels, and can be used at most restaurants and shops. To avoid additional exchange rate charges, travellers are advised to take travellers cheques in Euros, Pounds Sterling or US Dollars.
Currency restrictions: No limitations on the import of either local or foreign currencies, although declarations should be made for large amounts. Export of local currency over DKr50,000 is allowed if it can be proved that the amount was declared on import, or acquired by the conversion of foreign currency. There is no limit on the export of foreign currency, apart from gold coins.
Exchange rate indicators: The following figures are included as a guide to the movements of the Danish Krone against Sterling and the US Dollar:

Date	Feb '04	May '04	Aug '04	Nov '04
£1.00=	10.91	11.16	11.09	10.61
$1.00=	5.99	6.25	6.02	5.60

Banking hours: Mon, Wed and Fri 1000-1600; Thurs 1000-1800. Some banks in Copenhagen are open Mon-Fri 0930-1700. Some bureaux de change are open until midnight.

Duty Free

The following goods may be imported into Denmark without incurring customs duty by:
(a) Non-Danish residents arriving from an EU country with duty-paid goods purchased in an EU country:
1.5l of spirits or 20l of wine (over 22 per cent); 90l of table wine; 300 cigarettes or 150 cigarillos or 75 cigars or 400g of tobacco; other commodities, including beer: no limit.
(b) Residents of non-EU countries entering from outside the EU (excluding Greenland) with goods purchased in non-EU countries:
1l of spirits or 2l of sparkling wine (maximum 22 per cent); 2l of table wine; 200 cigarettes or 100 cigarillos or 50 cigars or 250g of tobacco; 500g of coffee or 200g of coffee extracts; 100g of tea or 40g of tea extracts; 50g of perfume; 250ml of eau de toilette; other articles, including beer: up to DKr700.
Note: Alcohol and tobacco allowances are for those aged 17 or over only, coffee and coffee extracts allowances are for those aged 15 or over. It is forbidden to import fresh foods into Denmark unless vacuum packed.
Abolition of duty free goods within the EU: On 30 June 1999, the sale of duty-free alcohol and tobacco at airports and at sea was abolished in all of the original 15 EU member states. Of the 10 new member states that joined the EU on May 1 2004, these rules already apply to Cyprus and Malta. There are transitional rules in place for visitors returning to one of the original 15 EU countries from one of the other new EU countries. But for the original 15, plus Cyprus and Malta, there are now no limits imposed on importing tobacco and alcohol products from one EU country to another (with the exceptions of Denmark, Finland and Sweden, where limits *are* imposed). Travellers should note that they may be required to prove at customs that the goods purchased are for personal use *only*.

Public Holidays

2005: Jan 1 New Year's Day. **Mar 24** Maundy Thursday. **Mar 25** Good Friday. **Mar 28** Easter Monday. **Apr 22** Common Prayer Day. **May 5** Ascension. **May 16** Whit Monday. **Jun 5** Constitution Day. **Dec 24-26** Christmas. **Dec 31** New Year's Eve.
2006: Jan 1 New Year's Day. **Apr 13** Maundy Thursday. **Apr 14** Good Friday. **Apr 17** Easter Monday. **May 12** Common Prayer Day. **May 25** Ascension. **Jun 5** Whit Monday; Constitution Day. **Dec 24-26** Christmas. **Dec 31** New Year's Eve.

Health

	Special Precautions?	Certificate Required?
Yellow Fever	No	No
Cholera	No	No
Typhoid & Polio	No	No
Malaria	No	No

Note: *Regulations and requirements may be subject to change at short notice, and you are advised to contact your doctor well in advance of your intended date of departure. Any numbers in the chart refer to the footnotes below.*

Note: *Diabetic diets* are catered for at many restaurants. See *Food & Drink* in the *Social Profile* section.
Health care: Medical facilities in Denmark are excellent. The telephone number for emergencies is 112. Local tourist offices will tell visitors where to contact a doctor or dentist. Copenhagen has an emergency dental service outside office hours; fees are paid in cash.
Only medicine prescribed by Danish or other Scandinavian doctors can be dispensed at a chemist (*Apotek*). Many medicines that can be bought over the counter in the UK can only be obtained with prescriptions in Denmark.
There is a reciprocal health agreement with the UK. In addition to the free emergency treatment at hospitals and casualty departments allowed to all foreign visitors, this allows UK citizens on presentation of a UK passport (form E111 is not necessary if on a temporary visit to Denmark) free hospital treatment if referred by a doctor, and free medical treatment given by a doctor registered with the Danish Public Health Service. It may occasionally be necessary to pay at the time of treatment; if this is so, receipts should be kept to facilitate refunds. The Agreement does not apply in the Faroe Islands. To obtain refunds, UK citizens should apply (with receipts) to the *Kommunens Social og Sundhedsforvaltning* before leaving Denmark. No refund is possible on amounts under DKr 500 (although there is a 50 per cent refund for under 18s).

Travel - International

AIR: The national airlines are *SAS (SK)* (website: www.sas.se) and *Mærsk Air (DM)* (website: www.maersk-air.com). The major carriers are *SAS* and *British Airways*.
Approximate flight times: From Copenhagen to *London* is 1 hour 50 minutes (from Århus to *London* is 1 hour 40 minutes), to *Los Angeles* is 11 hours 15 minutes, to *New York* is 7 hours 40 minutes, to *Singapore* is 15 hours 5 minutes and to *Sydney* is 22 hours 50 minutes.
International airports: *Copenhagen (CPH)* (Kastrup) (website: www.cph.dk) is 8km (5 miles) southeast of the city (travel time – 15 to 30 minutes). A new rail link between the airport and main railway station in Copenhagen has facilitated travel to the city (travel time – 12 minutes). There are also high-speed Intercity trains to Funen (travel time – 1 hour) and Jutland (travel time – 2 hours) with additional connections to Malmø (Sweden) on a 30-minute journey via the Øresund link. There are also regular bus services from the airport departing every 10 to 20 minutes (travel time – 20 minutes). Airport facilities include an outgoing duty-free shop, a wide range of car hire firms (*Avis*, *Budget*, *Europcar*, *Hertz* and *Sixt*), bank/bureau de change, and several restaurants and bars. Direct scheduled flights to Copenhagen operate from Aberdeen, Birmingham, Dublin, London Gatwick, London Heathrow, London Stansted, Manchester and Newcastle.
Århus (AAR) (Tirstrup) (website: www.aar.dk) is 44km (27 miles) from the city. Buses connect with flight arrivals; taxis are also available. Airport facilities include a duty-free shop, a wide range of car hire firms, bank/bureau de change, a post office and a restaurant. Direct scheduled flights to Århus operate from London Heathrow.
Billund Airport (BLL) (Billund) (website: www.billund-airport.dk) is approximately 2km (1.3 miles) from Legoland. Direct scheduled flights to Billund operate from London Gatwick and Manchester.
Departure Tax: None.
SEA: Denmark's major ports are Copenhagen, Esbjerg, Frederikshavn, Hanstholm and Hirtshals. There are regular ferries to and from the Faroe Islands, Germany, Iceland, Norway, Poland, Sweden and the UK. *DFDS Seaways* (website: www.dfdsseaways.co.uk) sail from Harwich to Esbjerg three times a week all year round. They also operate services between Harwich and Cuxhaven, Copenhagen and Oslo and Copenhagen and Gdansk. The major ferry operators from Germany, Norway and Sweden are *Color Line*, *Flyvebådene*, *Scandlines* and *Stena Line*. North Jutland is connected to the Faroes, Iceland, Norway and Scotland during the summer by ferries sailing once a week. There are no departure taxes when leaving Denmark by sea. Cruise lines calling at Copenhagen include *CTC*, *Lauro*, *Lindblad Travel*, *Norwegian Cruise Line* and *Royal Viking*.
RAIL: Copenhagen is connected by rail to all other major European cities, and typical express journey times from Copenhagen are: to *London* 26 hours; to *Hamburg* 4 hours 30 minutes; to *Berlin* 11 hours 25 minutes. All international trains connect with ferries where applicable.
ROAD: All the major road networks of Europe connect with ferry services to Copenhagen; it is advisable to book ferries in advance. The completion of the 18km (11 mile-long) toll Great Belt bridge and tunnel, linking Copenhagen (which is situated on the island of Sjælland) with the island of Funen, now provides the first seamless surface connection from the European continent to Copenhagen. It includes the world's second-longest suspension bridge at 6.5km (4 miles) long. A second bridge and tunnel, the Øresund connection, links Copenhagen with Malmø in Sweden. This consists of an 8km (5 mile) bridge and an 8km (5 mile) tunnel linked by an artificial island. Tolls are applicable for both bridges.
Eurolines, departing from Victoria Coach Station in London, serves destinations in Denmark. For further information, contact Eurolines, 4 Cardiff Road, Luton, Bedfordshire LU1 1PP, UK (tel: (08705) 143 219; fax: (01582) 400 694; website: www.eurolines.com *or* www.nationalexpress.com).
See *Travel – Internal* for information on **documentation** and traffic regulations.

Travel - Internal

AIR: The network of scheduled services radiates from *Copenhagen* (Kastrup). Other airports well served by

A B C D E F G H I J K L M N O P Q R S T U V W X Y Z

A B C D E F G H I J K L M N O P Q R S T U V W X Y Z

domestic airlines include Ålborg, Århus, Billund, Esbjerg, Karup, Rønne, Skrydstrup, Sønderborg and Thisted. Domestic airports are generally situated between two or more cities which are within easy reach of each other. Domestic flights are usually of no more than 30 minutes' duration. Limousines are often available. Discounts are available on certain tickets bought inside Denmark. Family, children and young person's discounts are also available.
SEA: There are frequent ferry sailings from Kalundborg to Århus, Ebeltoft to Sjællands Odde and Rønne to Copenhagen. The larger ferries usually have restaurants or cafes and may have TV, video and cinema lounges, shops, play areas for children and sleeping rooms. Local car ferries link most islands to the road network.
RAIL: The main cities on all islands are connected to the rail network: Ålborg, Copenhagen, Esbjerg, Herning, Horsens, Odense and Randers. *Danish State Railways (DSB)* (tel: 7013 1418; e-mail: dsb@dsb.dk; website: www.dsb.dk) operates a number of express trains called *Lyntogs* which provide long-distance, non-stop travel; it is often possible to purchase newspapers, magazines and snacks onboard these trains. Payphones are also available. There is also a new type of intercity train called the *IC3*, which is even faster and more direct. Seat reservations are compulsory. Children under 10 years old travel free. There are also price reductions for persons over 65 and groups of eight people or more. The *Englænderen* boat-train runs between Esbjerg and Copenhagen and connects with ferries from the UK. DSB passenger fares are based on a zonal system. The cost depends on the distance travelled; the cost per kilometre is reduced the longer the journey. The *Scanrail Pass* allows unlimited travel within Denmark, Finland, Norway and Sweden. First-class prices for adults are approximately £297 for 21 days and £167 for five days out of 15. As elsewhere in Europe, *Inter-Rail* passes are valid in Denmark. Bus and ferry and, of course, rail tickets may be purchased at all railway stations.
ROAD: The road system in the Danish archipelago makes frequent use of ferries. Country buses operate where there are no railways, but there are few private long-distance coaches. Motorways are not subject to toll duty. Emergency telephones are available on motorways and there is a national breakdown network similar to the AA in Britain called *Falck*, which can be called out 24 hours a day. There are petrol stations on motorways, generally with other services such as restaurants. Many petrol stations are automatic. A maximum of 10 litres of petrol is allowed to be kept as a reserve in suitably safe containers. The Danish Motoring Organisation is *Forenede Danske Motorejere (FDM)*, Firskovvej 32, PO Box 500, 2800 Kgs. Lyngby (tel: 7013 3040; fax: 4527 0993; e-mail: fdm@fdm.dk; website: www.fdm.dk). Speed limits are 110kph (66mph) on motorways, 80kph (48mph) on other roads and 50kph (30mph) in built-up areas (signified by white plates with town silhouettes). Speed laws are strictly enforced, and heavy fines are levied on the spot; the car is impounded if payment is not made. **Cycling:** There are cycle lanes along many roads and, in the countryside, many miles of scenic cycle track. Bikes can easily be taken on ferries, trains, buses and domestic air services. **Car hire:** Available to drivers over the age of 20, and can be reserved through travel agents or airlines. However, many car rental firms will only hire vehicles out to drivers over 25 years of age. **Regulations:** Traffic drives on the right. The wearing of seat belts is compulsory. Motorcyclists must wear helmets and drive with dipped headlights at all times. Headlamps on all vehicles should be adjusted for right-hand driving. All driving signs are international. **Documentation:** A national driving licence is acceptable. EU nationals taking their own cars to Denmark are strongly advised to obtain a Green Card. Without it, insurance cover is limited to the minimum legal cover in Denmark; the Green Card tops this up to the level of cover provided by the car owner's domestic policy.
URBAN: Car repair is often available at petrol stations; costs include 25 per cent VAT on labour and materials, which is not refunded when you leave the country. **Parking:** Parking in cities is largely governed by parking discs, available from petrol stations, post offices, tourist offices, banks and some police stations. These allow up to three hours parking in car parks. Kerbside parking is allowed for one hour Mon-Fri 0900-1700, Sat 0900-1300 unless stated otherwise. The hand of the disc should point to the quarter hour following time of arrival. The disc is to be placed on the side of the screen nearest the kerb. Where discs do not apply, parking meters regulate parking. Parking on a metered space is limited to three hours Mon-Fri 0900-1800, Sat 0900-1300. Meter charges differ according to the area of the city.
Travel Times: The following chart gives approximate travel times from **Copenhagen** (in hours and minutes) to other major cities/towns in Denmark.

	Air	Road	Rail
Ålborg	0.45	6.00	4.30
Århus	0.30	4.30	3.08
Billund	0.50	5.00	-
Esbjerg	1.00	5.00	3.12
Odense	0.35	3.00	1.45
Sønderborg	0.30	5.30	3.45

Accommodation

Contact the Danish Tourist Board (see *Contact Addresses* section) for information on booking hotels and for details of the savings from the use of a *Scandinavian Bonus Pass* (which must be applied for in advance) or *Inn Cheques*.
HOTELS: Travellers without reservations can book at one of the provincial tourist offices. Denmark's fine beaches attract many visitors, and there are hotels and pensions in all major seaside resorts. For more information or a list of hotels, contact HORESTA (Association of the Danish Hotel, Restaurant and Tourism Industry), Vodroffsvej 46, DK-1900 Frederiksberg C (tel: 3524 8080; fax: 3524 8086; e-mail: horesta@horesta.dk; website: www.danishhotels.dk *or* www.horesta.dk) *or* the Danish Tourist Board (see *Contact Addresses* section). **Grading:** Hotels are graded with **1 to 5 stars**. Approximately 470 hotels and holiday centres (some 85 per cent of Denmark's total hotel capacity) that are members of HORESTA are taking part in the grading scheme. The Danish Tourist Board publishes an annual list of about 1000 establishments, describing facilities and tariffs; quoted prices are inclusive of *MOMS* (VAT). **Green Key certificates:** A number of hotels and hostels in Denmark are also participating in a grading scheme based on environmental concerns. To receive an eco-friendly certificate (a so-called 'Green Key'), participating establishments have to fulfil 55 strict ecological criteria. For further details and a list of Green Key hotels and hostels, contact The Green Key (see HORESTA address above; website: www.dengroennenoegle.dk).
INNS: Excellent inns are to be found all over the country. Some are small and only cater for local custom, but others are tailored for the tourist and have established high culinary reputations for both international dishes and local specialities. For further details, contact the Danish Tourist Board.
BED AND BREAKFAST: There are private rooms to let, usually for one night, all over Denmark. Signs along the highway with *Zimmer frei* or *Vårelse* on them indicate availability of accommodation; those who call in and enquire will find that arrangements are easily made. In Copenhagen, rooms can be booked in person through the Tourist Information Department for a small fee. Local tourist offices may be contacted, either by writing or in person.
SELF-CATERING: Chalets are available in various parts of the country.
CAMPING/CARAVANNING: Campers must purchase a camping carnet, available at campsites. Over 500 campsites are officially recognised and graded for facilities and shelter. Prices vary greatly; it is half price for children under four years. **Grading: 1 to 5 stars** controlled by the Danish Camping Board; approved sites carry the sign of a pyramid-shaped tent. **5-star sites:** Fulfil the highest requirements. **3-star sites:** Showers, razor points, shops, laundry facilities, kitchen facilities. **1-star sites:** Fulfil minimum requirements for sanitary installations, drinking water etc. For more information and a list of campsites, contact the Danish Tourist Board (see *Contact Addresses* section).
YOUTH AND FAMILY HOSTELS: There are 100 Youth and Family Hostels scattered around the country, all of which take members of affiliated organisations. A membership card from the National Youth Hostel Association is required. Hostels are classified from **1 to 5 stars**. For a list of youth and family hostels contact Danhostel, Vesterbrogade 39, DK-1620 Copenhagen V, Denmark (tel: 3331 3612; fax: 3331 3626; e-mail: ldv@danhostel.dk; website: www.danhostel.dk); *or* the Danish Tourist Board (see *Contact Addresses* section).
FARMHOUSE HOLIDAYS: Rooms are often available for rent in farmhouses. Visitors stay as paying guests of the family and, although it is not expected, are welcome to help with the daily chores of the farm. Alternatively, in some cases, separate apartments are available close to the main farmhouse. Many farms have their own fishing streams. All holiday homes and farmhouses are inspected and approved by the local tourist office.
HOME EXCHANGE: Introductions between families interested in home exchange for short periods can be arranged. The major expense for participants is travel, plus a fee of DKr500. The best period (because of school holidays) is from late June to early August. The following organisation can provide further information: HomeLink Denmark, Dansk Bolig Bytte, PO Box 53, Bernstorffsvej 71A, DK-2900 Hellerup (tel: 3961 0405; fax: 3961 0525; e-mail: bed@bbdk.dk; website: www.bbdk.dk).

Resorts & Excursions

Denmark has an abundance of picturesque villages and towns, historic castles and monuments, and a coastline which varies delightfully from broad sandy beaches to small coves and gentle fjords. Throughout the country, rolling hills and gentle valleys provide a constant succession of attractive views; there are cool and shady forests of beech trees, extensive areas of heathland, a beautiful lake district, sand dunes and white cliffs

Credit: © Danish Tourist Board & Jorgen Schytte

resembling those of Dover; nor should one forget the Danish islands, each of which has its own unique attractions. Though there are few holiday resorts of the kind found in, say, France or Spain (the nearest equivalent being the '*Holiday Centre*' (HC), a purpose-built coastal resort), the Danes, who are taking strong measures to keep their coastline clean and tidy, are keen for visitors to sample the many unspoilt beaches.
There are now various *Sommerlands* in locations all over Denmark; these are activity parks where a flat entrance fee covers the visitor for use of all the many and varied facilities inside.

COPENHAGEN

The largest urban centre in Scandinavia, Copenhagen is a city of copper roofs and spires, founded in 1167. It has many old buildings, fountains, statues and squares, as well as the singular attraction of the **Little Mermaid** at the harbour entrance. The *Copenhagen Card* gives unlimited travel on buses and trains and free entry to a large number of museums and places of interest.
A number of organised tours are available, taking in most of the famous sights. These include the Vikingland tour to the **Viking Ship Museum**; a Royal tour to the **Christianborg Palace** (the seat of Parliament), **Rosenborg Castle** and **Amalienborg Palace**; a coach tour to old-world **Bondebyen** and its open-air museum; and even a brewery tour, which takes in the famous **Carlsberg** brewery, including an exhibition on the history of brewing and on this particular brewery. **Tivoli**, Copenhagen's world-famous amusement park, is open from late April to mid-September. **Bakken** (in the deer park north of Copenhagen) and the **Charlottenlund Aquarium** are both worth a visit.

JUTLAND

This area comprises the greater part of Denmark, extending 400km (250 miles) from the German border to its northernmost tip. Jutland's west coast has superb sandy beaches but bathing there is, however, often unsafe, due to the changing winds and tides. Care should be exercised, and any advice or notices issued by local authorities should be heeded. Also in Jutland is the major port of **Esbjerg**, which receives daily ferries from the UK. Main towns and resorts include Aalborg, Århus, Esbjerg, Frederikshavn, Holstebro, Kolding, Randers, Silkeborg, Vejle and Viborg.
Excursions: Aalborg contains the largest Viking burial ground, as well as a cathedral, monastery and castle. The largest Renaissance buildings in Denmark are in Aalborg. **Århus** has a collection of more than 60 17th- and 18th-century buildings – houses, shops, workshops and so on – from all over the country, re-erected on a spacious landscaped site; as well as **Marselisborg Castle** and a museum of prehistory. Esbjerg and **Fanø** are also historically interesting and have a number of fine beaches.
Rosenholm, **Clausholm** and **Vœrgard** castles are all worth a visit, while **Legoland** (Billund), which is open from April to October, provides good entertainment for children.

FYN (FUNEN)

Known as the 'Garden of Denmark', Fyn (Funen) has some of Denmark's most picturesque and historic castles and manor houses, set in age-old parks and gardens. Odense is famous as the birthplace of the great fairytale writer Hans Christian Andersen (1805-1875). Fyn (Funen) is connected to Jutland by bridges. Main towns and resorts include Odense, Nyborg, Svendborg, Middelfart and Bogense.
Excursions: Castles and churches are the main attraction in Fyn (Funen). **Egeskov Castle** is a superb moated

Renaissance castle, which is fairytale in every detail. Other castles in the area include **Nyborg** (seat of the former National Assembly) and **Valdemar**, which houses a naval museum. There are also a number of beautiful beaches, particularly on the southern islands of **Langeland**, **Tåsinge** and **Ærø**. **Odense** has a festival every July and August celebrating the life and works of Hans Christian Andersen. Visitors can see the **Hans Christian Andersen Museum** and his childhood home. Other museums include a major railway museum and **Fyn Village**, a major cultural centre. Also in Odense is the **Brandts Klaedefabrik**, a major cultural centre.

LOLLAND, FALSTER, MØN & BORNHOLM

Lolland is generally flat, Falster less so, while Møn is a haven of small hills and valleys, with the **Møn Klint** chalk cliffs a breathtaking sight. **Bornholm** is set apart from the rest, 150km (90 miles) east of the Danish mainland, and is made up of fertile farmland, white beaches and rocky coastlines. Other towns worth visiting include Nakskov, Nykobing, Nysted, Rønne, Sakskøbing and Stege.

Excursions: Knuthenborg Park on Lolland is Denmark's largest, with 500 species of trees, flowers and plants; it also contains a safari park. **Corselitse** and the **Pederstrup Museum** are also worth a visit. **Bornholm** contains **Hammershus**, Denmark's largest castle ruin (built in 1260), as well as many fine churches. The small town of **Svaneke** was awarded the European Gold Medal in Architectural Heritage Year (1975).

ZEALAND (SJÆLLAND)

Denmark's capital, Copenhagen, is on Zealand (Sjælland) and thus there is much commercial activity on the island. But there are also fine beaches, lakes, forests and royal palaces. Other towns worth visiting include Slagelse, Nastved and Frederikssund.

Excursions & sightseeing: The old fortress of **Kronborg** can be found at **Helsinør** (**Elsinore**), famed not only as the most imposing edifice in Scandinavia, but also as the setting for Shakespeare's *Hamlet*. **Frederiksborg Castle**, equally as impressive, is to be seen at **Hillerød**, which houses the **National History Museum**. The 12th-century cathedral at **Roskilde** and the **Viking Museum** are both worth a visit, while at **Skjoldenasholm**, there is a fine **Tram Museum**. Excellent beaches can be found in Sjælland, particularly in the north of the island.

Sport & Activities

Cycling: Many local tourist offices offer all-inclusive cycling trips, with everything (including bicycle rental, detailed route descriptions, maps, ferry tickets and accommodation) arranged in advance. Prices are lower for those bringing their own bicycles. The routes are laid out by local experts. For independent cyclists, a wide range of detailed cycling maps is available. Bicycles can be hired from local tourist offices or bicycle shops. Bicycles are allowed on all Danish ferries and several small passenger boats (in most cases, against payment), most trains (InterCity trains require prior reservation and reservations are not possible on Interregional trains), buses (which have room for up to four bicycles, although prams have priority) and aeroplanes (special packing requirements apply). For details, contact the Danish Cyclists' Association (*Dansk Cyklist Forbund*), Rømersgade 5-7, DK-1362 Copenhagen K (tel: 3332 3121; fax: 3332 7683; e-mail: dcf@dcf.dk; website: www.dcf.dk).

Horseriding: It is possible to hire horses at riding schools and centres almost everywhere in Denmark. Many riding schools offer riding holidays with half or full board.

Golf: Denmark has around 130 golf courses. Foreign visitors are welcome, on presentation of a valid membership card from their home club. For further information, contact the Danish Golf Union (*Dansk Golf Union*), Idrættens Hus, Brøndby Stadion 20, DK-2605 Brøndby (tel: 4326 2700; fax: 4326 2701; e-mail: info@dgu-golf.dk; website: www.dgu-golf.dk).

Health resorts: These are widespread throughout Denmark. Some offer medical and physiotherapeutic treatment, others simply recreation in beautiful and quiet surroundings.

Fishing: Denmark has excellent facilities for both **freshwater** and **saltwater** fishing. Sea fishing tours can be arranged with local fishermen at many Danish harbours (for instance in Copenhagen, Elsinore or Frederikshavn); large groups may charter a boat for themselves. Fishing off the shores of Denmark's 7500km- (5000 mile-) long coastline is widely available. Anglers must not take up position within 50m (164ft) of a dwelling place. Fishing rights in lakes and streams are usually privately owned but are often let to local societies which issue day- or week-cards. A fishing licence is required in all cases (except for under 18s and over 65s, who are free) and can be obtained from Danish post offices, local tourist offices and angling shops. Special licences for tourists (valid from one day to one week) are available. Anglers are obliged to inform themselves about fishing restrictions and closed seasons. For further information and addresses of angling societies, contact the Danish Sports Fishing Association (*Danmarks Sportsfiskerforbund*), Worsåesgade 1, DK-7100 Vejle (tel: 7582 0699; fax: 7582 0209; e-mail: post@sportsfiskerforbundet.dk; website: www.sportsfiskeren.dk).

Nude bathing: This is quite common at Danish seaside resorts. At beaches where nude bathing is not officially permitted, bathers are requested to show consideration and follow the directions of the local guards. The only beaches where it is actually prohibited are *Henne Strand* and *Holmsland Klit* (both on Jutland's western coast). At *Bellevue Beach* in the metropolitan area, walking in the nude is prohibited while bathing or sunbathing in the nude is not. See online for more information (website: www.strandguide.dk).

Watersports: The long inlets and protected shores on the Danish coast offer easy conditions for **windsurfing** (and are thus particularly suitable for beginners). Facilities for **sailing** are excellent: over 500 yachting harbours can be found along the coast and anchorage is allowed at a further 500 islands. Boat hire facilities are widespread. Detailed handbooks and marine charts are available from the Danish Yachting Association (*Dansk Sejlunion*) (tel/fax: 4326 2182; e-mail: ds@sailing.dk; website: www.sejlsport.dk) *or* the National Survey and Cadastre (*Kort & Matrikelstyrelsen*) (tel: 3587 5050; e-mail: kms@kms.dk; website: www.kms.dk); charts are available for direct download from the KMS Internet site.

Note: All waterscooter traffic is under general prohibition within the Danish sea territory.

Social Profile

FOOD & DRINK: *Smørrebrød* is a highly popular traditional Danish dish that is often eaten for lunch. It consists of a slice of dark bread with butter, topped with slices of meat, fish or cheese and generously garnished. It bears no resemblance to traditional sandwiches and needs to be eaten sitting down with a knife and fork. Buffet-style lunch (the *koldt bord*) is also popular with a variety of fish, meats, hot dishes, cheese and sweets, usually on a self-service basis. Danes do not mix the various dishes on their plates but have them in strict order. A normal Danish breakfast - or *morgen-complet* - consists of coffee or tea and an assortment of breads, rolls, jam and cheese, often also sliced meats, boiled eggs and warm Danish pastries. Given its geographical position, it is not surprising that shellfish also forms an important part of Danish cuisine. Apart from traditional dishes, French or international cuisine is the order of the day. In Copenhagen, superb gourmet restaurants can be found, whilst Ålborg is noted for its impressive number of restaurants. Most towns have 'fast food' outlets for hamburgers and pizzas, and the sausage stalls on most street corners, selling hot sausages, hamburgers, soft drinks and beer, are popular.

Danish coffee is delicious. Denmark also has many varieties of beer, famous breweries being Carlsberg and Tuborg. Most popular is *pilsner* (a lager) but there are also darker beers. The other national drink is *akvavit*, popularly known as *snaps*, which is neither an aperitif, cocktail nor liqueur and is meant to be drunk with food, preferably with a beer chaser. It is served ice cold and only accompanies cold food. There are no licensing hours.

Note: The Danish Hotel and Restaurant Association displays signs indicating restaurants where the needs of **diabetics** are given special attention. It consists of the words '*Diabetes mad – sund mad for alle*' ('Food for Diabetics – healthy food for everyone') encircling a chef's head.

NIGHTLIFE: There is a wide selection of nightlife, particularly in Copenhagen, where the first morning restaurants open to coincide with closing time at 0500. Jazz and dance clubs in the capital city are top quality and world-famous performers appear regularly. There are numerous beer gardens.

SHOPPING: Copenhagen has excellent shopping facilities. Special purchases include Bing & Grøndal and Royal Copenhagen porcelain, Holmegård glass, Bornholm ceramics, handmade woollens from the Faroe Islands and Lego toys. Visitors from outside the EU can often claim back on some of the *MOMS* (VAT) on goods purchased that are sent straight to their home country from the shop in Denmark. **Shopping hours:** Mon-Fri 0900/1000-1730/1800; Sat 0900-1700. Supermarkets are often open Mon-Fri 0900-2000. Opening hours vary from town to town since shops can regulate their own hours. At some holiday resorts, shops are open Sunday and public holidays.

SPECIAL EVENTS: Festivals take place throughout the summer in nearly every town in Denmark, featuring street festivities and performing artists. For a complete list of festivals and cultural events in the different regions (published in several languages) contact the Danish Tourist Board (see *Contact Addresses* section). The following is a selection of special events occurring in Denmark in 2005:

Jan 15 *Opening of the Royal Danish Opera at Dokøen*, Copenhagen. **Feb 6-7** *Shrove Tide Tilting at the barrel*, close to Copenhagen. **Mar 11-13** *Holmboe in Horsens* (classical music festival), Mid Jutland. **Apr 21-24** *Odense Folk Festival*. **May 28** *Half-marathon across the Great Belt*, Korsør. **Jun 21-Jul 3** *Viking* Plays, Lindholm Høje, Ålborg, north Jutland. **Jun 30-Jul 3** *Roskilde Festival* (music festival). **Aug 3-7** *Post Danmark Rundt* (bicycle race). **Sep** *Champion of the Baltic* (regatta and boat race), Bornholm. **Oct 14** *Night of Culture* (various locations). **Nov 10-13** *Silkeborg's International Puppet Theatre Festival*. **Dec** *Christmas Markets and Celebrations* (countrywide). **Dec 3-4 & 10-11** *Hans Christian Andersen Christmas Market*, Odense.

SOCIAL CONVENTIONS: Normal courtesies should be observed. Guests should refrain from drinking until the host toasts his or her health. Casual dress is suitable for most places but formal wear is required at more exclusive dining rooms and social functions. Smoking is restricted on public transport and in some public buildings. **Tipping:** Hotels and restaurants quote fully inclusive prices and tipping is not necessary. Taxi fares include tips. Railway porters and washroom attendants receive tips.

Business Profile

ECONOMY: The standard of living is generally high, with annual GDP per capita of US$30,000. Compared to most industrialised countries, Denmark retains a large and important agricultural sector, two-thirds of whose produce is exported. Danish manufacturing depends on imports of raw materials and components. Iron, steel and the production of other metals are the most important industries, followed by electronics, chemicals and biotechnology, paper and printing, textiles, furniture and cement. Food processing and drinks also make a significant contribution. Since the discovery of offshore oil and gas reserves in the 1980s, production has gradually increased to the point where the country can meet all its domestic energy needs. Most of Denmark's trade is conducted within the EU, of which it is a member, although it has proved reluctant (in rather the same manner as the UK) to adopt measures which are perceived as threatening to its sovereignty. It has thus so far refused to join the single European currency zone. Recent economic performance has been steady: inflation (2 per cent) and unemployment (6 per cent) are near the EU average; in 2004, current annual growth remained at 0 per cent. Germany is substantially the largest trading partner followed by Sweden and the UK; outside the EU, Norway and the USA are important trading partners. Denmark is a member of the Nordic Union. Its links with Scandinavia will be further enhanced by the new road and rail system linking it to Sweden across the Øresund Strait: this is one of Europe's largest engineering infrastructure projects.

BUSINESS: English is widely used for all aspects of business. Local businesspeople expect visitors to be punctual and the approach to business is often direct and straightforward. Avoid business visits from mid-June to mid-August, which are prime holiday periods. **Office hours:** Mon-Fri 0800/0900-1600/1700 (some offices close earlier Fri).

COMMERCIAL INFORMATION: The following organisations can offer advice: Handelskskammeret (Danish Chamber of Commerce), Børsen, DK-1217 Copenhagen K (tel: 7013 1200; fax: 3332 5216; e-mail: hts@hts.dk; website: www.hts.dk).

CONFERENCES/CONVENTIONS: For information and brochures regarding conference facilities, contact Wonderful Copenhagen Convention & Visitors Bureau *or* the Danish Tourist Board (see *Contact Addresses* section).

Climate

Summer extends from June to August. Winter is from December to March, wet with long periods of frost. February is the coldest month. Spring and autumn are generally mild. The *Faroe Islands* are under the influence of the warm current of the Gulf Stream, and they enjoy a very mild climate for the latitude. Winters are warm, but the islands are cloudy, windy and wet throughout the year. Summers are cool, but with little sunshine.

Required clothing: Lightweight for summer and heavyweight for winter snows.

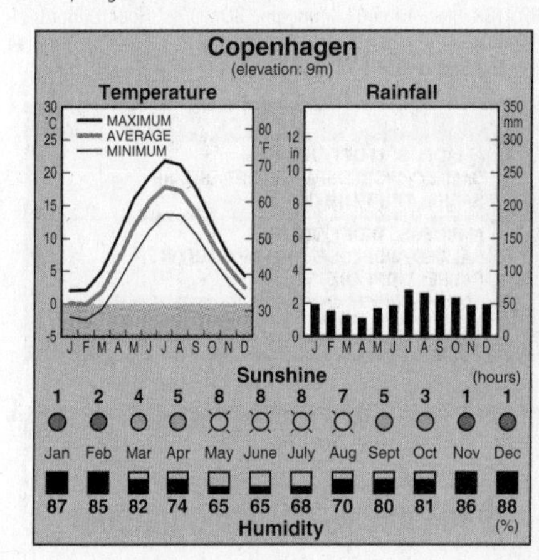

A B C D E F G H I J K L M N O P Q R S T U V W X Y Z

Djibouti

LATEST TRAVEL ADVICE CONTACTS

British Foreign and Commonwealth Office
Tel: (0870) 606 0290 Website: www.fco.gov.uk

US Department of State
Website: http://travel.state.gov/travel

Canadian Department of Foreign Affairs and Int'l Trade
Tel: (1 800) 267 8376 Website: www.dfait-maeci.gc.ca

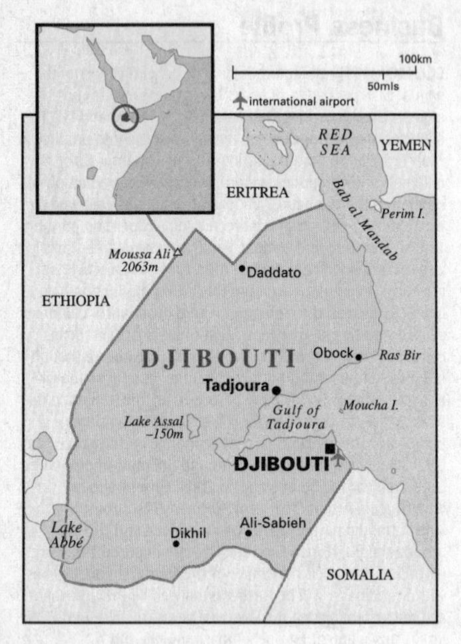

Location: Northeast Africa, Gulf of Aden.

Country dialling code: 253.

Office National du Tourisme de Djibouti (ONTD) (Djibouti National Tourist Office)
place du 27 juin, BP 1938, Djibouti, Djibouti
Tel: 352 800 *or* 353 790. Fax: 356 322.
E-mail: onta@intnet.dj
Website: www.office-tourisme.dj

Embassy of the Republic of Djibouti
26 rue Emile Menier, 75116 Paris, France
Tel: (1) 4727 4922. Fax: (1) 4553 5053.
Opening hours: Mon-Fri 0900-1600

British Consulate
BP 169, rue de Djibouti, Djibouti, Djibouti
Tel: 385 007 *or* 325 543.
E-mail: martinet@intnet.dj

Embassy of the Republic of Djibouti
1156 15th Street, Suite 515, NW, Washington DC 20005, USA
Tel: (202) 331 0270. Fax: (202) 331 0302.
E-mail: usdjibouti@aol.com
Also deals with enquiries from Canada.

Embassy of the United States of America
Street address: Plateau du Serpent, boulevard Maréchal Joffre, Djibouti, Djibouti
Postal address: Ambassade Americaine, BP 185, Djibouti, Djibouti
Tel: 353 995. Fax: 353 940.

Canadian Consulate
BP 1188, Place Lagarde, Immeuble BDMO, 1st Floor, Djibouti, Djibouti
Tel: 353 859 *or* 351 581. Fax: 350 014.

TIMATIC CODES

Health	AMADEUS: **TI-DFT/JIB/HE** GALILEO/WORLDSPAN: **TI-DFT/JIB/HE** SABRE: **TIDFT/JIB/HE**
Visa	AMADEUS: **TI-DFT/JIB/VI** GALILEO/WORLDSPAN: **TI-DFT/JIB/VI** SABRE: **TIDFT/JIB/VI**

To access TIMATIC country information on Health and Visa regulations through the Computer Reservations System (CRS), type in the appropriate command line listed above.

General Information

AREA: 23,200 sq km (8958 sq miles).
POPULATION: 693,000 (UN estimate 2002).
POPULATION DENSITY: 29.9 per sq km.
CAPITAL: Djibouti. **Population:** 547,100 (official estimate 2003).
GEOGRAPHY: Djibouti is part of the African continent, bordered to the northeast and east by the Red Sea, the southeast by Somalia, the southwest by Ethiopia and to the north by Eritrea. The country is a barren strip of land around the Gulf of Tadjoura, varying in width from 20km (12 miles) to 90km (56 miles), with a coastline of 300km (188 miles), much of it white sandy beaches. Inland is semi-desert and desert, with thorn bushes, steppes and volcanic mountain ranges.
LANGUAGE: The official languages are Arabic and French. Afar and Somali are spoken locally. English is spoken by hoteliers, taxi drivers and traders.
GOVERNMENT: Republic. Gained independence from France in 1977. **Head of State:** President Ismail Omar Guelleh since 1999. **Head of Government:** Prime Minister Dileita Mohamed Dileita since 2001.
RELIGION: Predominantly Muslim with Roman Catholic, Protestant and Greek Orthodox minorities.
TIME: GMT + 3.
ELECTRICITY: 220 volts AC, 50Hz.
COMMUNICATIONS: Telephone: IDD available. Country code: 253. Outgoing international code: 00. **Mobile telephone:** AMPS network offers coverage of the capital and 40km (25 miles) around it. Handsets can be hired at the main post office. A GSM 900 service is available through *Djibouti Telecom SA* (website: www.intnet.dj). **Fax:** There are no public facilities. **Internet:** Services are accessible in the main post office and some hotels. There is at least one Internet cafe in Djibouti. ISPs include the *Société des Télécommunications Internationales de Djibouti* (website: www.intnet.dj). **Telegram:** Telegrams can be sent from the main post office from 0700-2000. Telegram services are also available at the Telegraph office. **Post:** Letters and parcels to western Europe can take about one week by airmail or up to three weeks by surface mail **Press:** Djibouti has no daily papers. A weekly newspaper, *La Nation de Djibouti*, is published in French. There is at least one Arabic newspaper. Other weekly newspapers published in French include *Le Progrès*, *Le Renouveau*, *La Republique* and *Le Temps*. **Radio:** BBC World Service (website: www.bbc.co.uk/worldservice) and Voice of America (website: www.voa.gov) can be received. From time to time the frequencies change and the most up-to-date can be found online.

Passport/Visa

	Passport Required?	Visa Required?	Return Ticket Required?
Full British	Yes	Yes	No
Australian	Yes	Yes	No
Canadian	Yes	Yes	No
USA	Yes	Yes	No
Other EU	Yes	Yes	No
Japanese	Yes	Yes	No

Note: *Regulations and requirements may be subject to change at short notice, and you are advised to contact the appropriate diplomatic or consular authority before finalising travel arrangements. Details of these may be found at the head of this country's entry. Any numbers in the chart refer to the footnotes below.*

PASSPORTS: Passport valid for six months beyond date of departure required by all.
VISAS: Required by all except transit passengers not disembarking and continuing their journey by the same aircraft or ship.
Types of visa and cost: *Entry* (*visa de séjour*); *Tourist* (*visa de tourisme*); *Business* (*visa d'affaires*); *Transit* (*visa de transit*). All visas cost €50.
Validity: From one day to three months. An extension may be granted in Djibouti on request to the Headquarters of the Police Nationale.
Application to: The Embassy in Paris (see *Contact Addresses* section). 10-day transit visas can be issued at the point of entry to visitors holding confirmed return air tickets. A fee will be charged. This facility is only available to nationals from countries where Djibouti has no diplomatic representation. Contact the Embassy in Paris for further information.
Application requirements: (a) Valid passport. (b) Two application forms completed in French. (c) Two passport-size photos. (d) Fee of €50 plus €5 to cover postage within France or €6 to cover postage from abroad; the amount should be sent in the form of a postal or money order, not a cheque. (e) Return or onward ticket. *Business*: (a)-(e) and, (f) Letter from the employer or a letter of invitation from the company in Djibouti.
Working days required: 48 hours for personal applications. Four to five days for postal applications.

Money

Currency: Djibouti Franc (Djf) = 100 centimes. Notes are in denominations of Djf10,000, 5000, 2000, 1000 and 500. Coins are in denominations of Djf500, 100, 50, 20 and 10.
Currency exchange: Currency can be exchanged at major banks and hotels, or at authorised bureaux de change in the capital. The bureaux de change are open all day, while the banks have limited opening hours.
Credit & debit cards: These are only accepted by airlines and some of the larger hotels.
Travellers cheques: To avoid additional exchange rate charges, travellers are advised to take travellers cheques in US Dollars or Euros. Euro and Sterling cheques are not accepted unless marked as 'External Account' or 'Pour Compte Etranger'. The majority of banks are in the place du 27 juin area.
Currency restrictions: There are no restrictions on the import or export of either foreign or local currency.
Exchange rate indicators: The following figures are included as a guide to the movements of the Djibouti Franc against Sterling and the US Dollar:

Date	Feb '04	May '04	Aug '04	Nov '04
£1.00=	318.54	312.57	322.50	333.10
$1.00=	175.00	175.00	175.05	175.90

Banking hours: Sat-Thurs 0715-1145.

Duty Free

As for France (see *France* section). Firearms must be declared on entry and exit.

Public Holidays

2005: Jan 1 New Year's Day. **Jan 21** Eid al-Adha (Feast of the Sacrifice). **Feb 10** El-am-Hejir (Islamic New Year). **Apr 21** Mouloud (Birth of the Prophet). **May 1** Labour Day. **Jun 27** Independence Day. **Nov 3-5** Eid al-Fitr (End of Ramadan). **Dec 25** Christmas Day.
2006: Jan 1 New Year's Day. **Jan 13** Eid al-Adha (Feast of the Sacrifice). **Jan 31** El-am-Hejir (Islamic New Year). **May 1** Labour Day. **May 11** Mouloud (Birth of the Prophet). **Jun 27** Independence Day. **Oct 22-24** Eid al-Fitr (End of Ramadan). **Dec 25** Christmas Day.
Note: Muslim festivals are timed according to local sightings of various phases of the moon and the dates given above are approximations. During the lunar month of Ramadan that precedes Eid al-Fitr, Muslims fast during the day and feast at night and normal business patterns may be interrupted. Many restaurants are closed during the day and there may be restrictions on smoking and drinking. Some disruption may continue into Eid al-Fitr itself. Eid al-Fitr and Eid al-Adha may last anything from two to 10 days, depending on the region. For more information, see the appendix *World of Islam* section.

Health

	Special Precautions?	Certificate Required?
Yellow Fever	Yes	1
Cholera	Yes	2
Typhoid & Polio	3	N/A
Malaria	4	N/A

Note: *Regulations and requirements may be subject to change at short notice, and you are advised to contact your doctor well in advance of your intended date of departure. Any numbers in the chart refer to the footnotes below.*

1: A yellow fever vaccination certificate is required from travellers over one year of age coming from infected areas.
2: Following WHO guidelines issued in 1973, a cholera vaccination certificate is no longer a condition of entry to Djibouti. However, cholera is a serious risk in this country and precautions are essential. Up-to-date advice should be sought before deciding if these precautions should include vaccination as medical opinion is divided over its effectiveness. For more information, consult the Health appendix.
3: Immunisation against typhoid is usually advised.
4: Malaria risk, predominantly in the malignant falciparum form, exists throughout the year in the whole country. Resistance to chloroquine has been reported.
Food & drink: Mains water is normally heavily chlorinated and, whilst relatively safe, may cause mild abdominal upsets. Bottled water is available and is advised for the first few weeks of the stay. Drinking water outside main cities and towns is likely to be contaminated and sterilisation is considered essential. Milk is unpasteurised and should be boiled. Powdered or tinned milk is available and is advised, but make sure that it is reconstituted with pure water. Avoid dairy products which are likely to have been made from unboiled milk. Only eat well-cooked meat and fish,

preferably served hot. Pork, salad and mayonnaise may carry increased risk. Vegetables should be cooked and fruit peeled.
Other risks: *Diarrhoeal disease, giardiasis, dysentery* and *typhoid fever* are widespread throughout the country. *Hepatitis A, B* and *E* occur and precautions should be taken. Visitors should also consider immunisation against *diphtheria. Meningococcal meningitis* risk exists, depending on area and time of year.
Rabies is present. For those at high risk, vaccination before arrival should be considered. If you are bitten, seek medical advice without delay. For more information, consult the *Health* appendix.
Health care: Health insurance is advisable. Doctors and hospitals may expect immediate cash payment for any form of medical treatment.

Travel - International

AIR: *Air France (AF)* (website: www.airfrance.com) operates three flights a week from Paris to Djibouti, stopping enroute in Jeddah. Djibouti-based *Daallo Airlines (D3)* operates flights to Paris and services to Ethiopia, Kenya, Saudi Arabia and Somalia. Other airlines offering services to Djibouti include *Air Kenya, Air Tanzania, Djibouti Airlines, Ethiopian Airlines* and *Yemenia Yemen Airways*.
Approximate flight times: From Djibouti to *London* is 10 hours (including stopovers).
International airports: *Djibouti (JIB)* is 5km (3 miles) south of the city. Taxis are available. Airport facilities include duty-free shops, restaurants, left luggage, tourist information, car hire (*Maril*), bureau de change and a craft shop.
Departure tax: None.
RAIL: The *Djibouti–Ethiopian Railway* operates regular trains between Addis Ababa and Dire Dawa with one train daily connecting with Djibouti; in theory, tourists and businesspeople can use this service (for which they should book first-class tickets only), but it is not recommended as trains are old, fairly unreliable and the volatile security situation in Ethiopia is causing considerable risks to all travellers.
ROAD: There are roads from Djibouti to Assab (Eritrea) and going west into Ethiopia via Dikhil. Travellers using them should be aware that road conditions are generally poor (the roads are more often dirt tracks than asphalted) and personal security might be at risk when travelling – particularly to Ethiopia (see *Travel – Internal* section for information on documentation required). Visitors are also advised to check transit regulations as political conditions in Ethiopia and Eritrea are changeable. Travel to neighbouring Somalia (which has bus links with Djibouti) is *not* recommended due to the highly unstable political situation in Somalia.

Travel - Internal

AIR: Private charters may be available.
SEA: Ferry services sail daily to Tadjoura and Obock (on the northeast coast of the Gulf of Tadjoura) from Djibouti (3 hours).
RAIL: The only service is provided by daily train to the border with Ethiopia (see *Travel – International* section).
ROAD: 4-wheel-drive vehicles are recommended for the interior. There is a new highway from Djibouti to Tadjoura. Traffic drives on the right. **Bus:** Buses operate from Djibouti to most towns and villages throughout the country. Buses leave when they are full. **Car hire:** Available in Djibouti and at the airport. 4-wheel-drive vehicles are also available. It is advisable to carry water and petrol on any expedition off main routes.
Documentation: An International Driving Permit is recommended, although not legally required. A temporary licence to drive is available from local authorities on presentation of a valid British or Northern Ireland driving licence. Insurance is not required.
URBAN: A minibus service operates in Djibouti, stopping on demand. A flat-fare system is used. **Taxi:** These are available in Djibouti and from the airport to the town; also in Ali-Sabieh, Dikhil, Dorale and Arta. Fares increase by 50 per cent after dark.

Accommodation

Hotels in Djibouti tend to be expensive and the few cheap hotels are somewhat rundown. There is a small number of first-class hotels.
Outside Djibouti, accommodation is limited, although attention is being given to upgrading and adding to the accommodation available in the hinterland. The rest shelter at Ali-Sabieh, a provincial town in the hills, has been enlarged, and a large shaded terrace and simple cooking facilities have also been added. Countrywide, however, much remains to be done. The Government would like to establish a network of rest houses similar to the one at Ali-Sabieh throughout the country. In addition, it hopes to build several beach shelters.

Resorts & Excursions

DJIBOUTI: Djibouti is a late 19th-century city with a distinctly Arabic feel. Attractions include the lively **Central Market** (Le Marché Central) near the Mosque, and many good local restaurants. Also worth seeing is the **Tropical Aquarium** with underwater exhibits from the Red Sea (open daily 1600-1830), and the Presidential Palace. Nearby are beaches at **Dorale**, 11km (7 miles), and **Kor Ambado**, 14km (9 miles). Djibouti lies within a geological feature known as the **Afar Triangle**, one of the hottest and most desolate places on Earth. Part of the **Great Rift Valley** system, it is a wedge of flat desert pushing into the Ethiopian Massif. Much of it is below sea level. **Lake Assal**, 100km (60 miles) to the southwest of Djibouti city, is one of the lowest surface areas anywhere on the planet (150m (570 ft) below sea level); and is reachable only by 4-wheel-drive vehicle.
BEYOND DJIBOUTI: Located 95km (59 miles) south-west of Djibouti lies **Ali-Sabeh**, a major stop for the mainline train between Djibouti and Addis Ababa. The journey from the capital crosses two stunning desert plains; **Petit Bara** and **Grand Bara**. The large market draws visitors to the city. Straddling the Ethiopian frontier is **Lake Abbé**, the home of thousands of flamingos and pelicans. On the opposite side of the **Gulf of Tadjoura**, an excellent place for scuba-diving, fishing and underwater photography, are the towns of **Obock** and **Tadjoura**, a town with seven mosques. In the hinterland is the **Goda Mountains National Park**.

Sport & Activities

Watersports: The beaches at *Doralé* and *Khor-Ambade*, which are both about 15km (10 miles) from Djibouti, offer safe **swimming**. Also just outside the city is the *Ambouli* palm grove, a pleasant place to stroll during the cooler parts of the day. Another good beach can be found at *Ghoubet al Kharab*, which is about an hour's drive from Lake Assal, and where black-lava cliffs border the beach. The *Gulf of Tadjoura* (especially Obock) contains many species of fish and coral and is ideal for **diving**, **snorkelling** and **underwater photography**; in many places, the coral reefs are easily accessible from the beaches. The best time for these activities is from September to May when the waters of the Red Sea are clear. **Waterskiing** and **windsurfing** can also be arranged.
Wildlife: Geology and **wildlife** enthusiasts may head to the wilderness around *Lake Abbé* (accessible by 4-wheel-drive vehicles only), a gathering place for flamingos and pelicans and the location of strange natural steaming chimneys. It is possible to **windsurf on wheels** in the desert areas.
Note: Hunting is forbidden throughout the country.

Social Profile

FOOD & DRINK: There are restaurants to suit all tastes, serving Arab, Chinese, French and Vietnamese local specialities. Alcoholic beverages will be limited in Muslim areas (particularly during Ramadan).
SHOPPING: Lively and colourful local markets are well worth visiting and local crafts and artefacts can be bought. **Shopping hours:** Daily 0730-1200 and 1600-1900.
SPECIAL EVENTS: Friday is a holiday for offices and government institutions. Djibouti observes all Islamic holidays.
SOCIAL CONVENTIONS: Casual wear is widely acceptable, but visitors are reminded that Djibouti is a Muslim country and certain codes of behaviour should be observed. **Tipping:** A 10 per cent service charge is usually added to bills. Tipping is rare and never requested. Not usual for taxi drivers. A tariff is normally set but visitors will be charged at a higher rate.

Business Profile

ECONOMY: Djibouti's economic output fell by one-third during the 1990s, largely due to the chaos which afflicted the Horn of Africa. Little of the mainly desert land will support crops and agriculture, and is therefore concentrated in livestock-rearing; this is mostly conducted by nomadic tribes. There is a small industrial sector devoted to light manufacturing of locally consumed products. Djibouti's economic potential lies in the development of its service sector; in particular, transport facilities and banking. The deep-water port on the Bab-El-Mandeb Straits, which has developed as a major refuelling and transhipment facility, is vitally important to the country, as it is on the major oil route between the Gulf of Aden and the Red Sea. In addition, the Government hopes to develop Djibouti as a general trading centre between Africa and the Middle East and as an important telecommunications hub for the region. However, at present, the country remains dependent on foreign aid, the bulk of which comes from France and Saudi Arabia. Unemployment, which affects perhaps half the workforce, is a particular problem. The country's main trading partners are France, Saudi Arabia, Ethiopia, Somalia, Yemen and Thailand.
BUSINESS: Suits should be worn. French and Arabic are the main languages used in business. A knowledge of either of these languages is essential. Business entertainment will often take place in hotels or restaurants. **Office hours:** Sat-Thurs 0620-1300.
COMMERCIAL INFORMATION: The following organisation can offer advice: Chambre de Commerce et d'Industrie de Djibouti, BP 84, Djibouti (tel: 351 070 or 350 826; fax: 350 096; e-mail: cicid@intnet.dj.
CONFERENCES/CONVENTIONS: Information can be obtained from the Chambre de Commerce et d'Industrie de Djibouti (see address above).

Climate

Extremely hot and particulary arid between June and August when the dusty *Khamsin* blows from the desert. Between October and April it is slightly cooler, with occasional light rain.

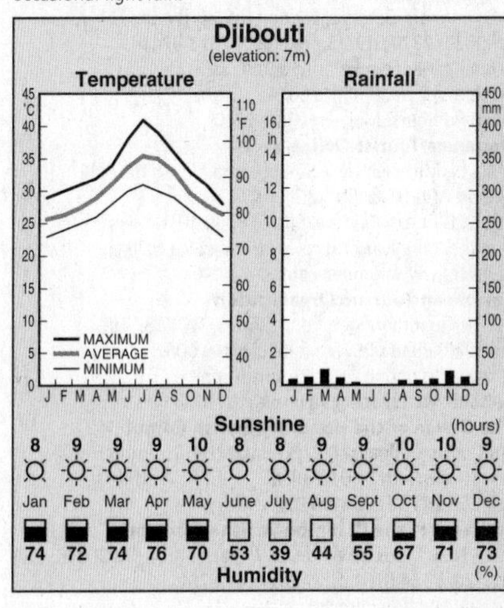

A B C D E F G H I J K L M N O P Q R S T U V W X Y Z

Dominica (Commonwealth of)

LATEST TRAVEL ADVICE CONTACTS

British Foreign and Commonwealth Office
Tel: (0870) 606 0290 Website: www.fco.gov.uk
US Department of State
Website: http://travel.state.gov/travel
Canadian Department of Foreign Affairs and Int'l Trade
Tel: (1 800) 267 8376 Website: www.dfait-maeci.gc.ca

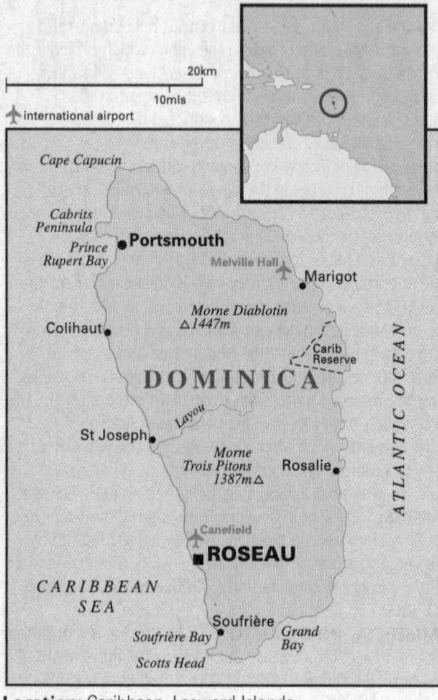

Location: Caribbean, Leeward Islands.

Country dialling code: 1 767.

National Development Corporation (NDC) – Division of Tourism
PO Box 293, Valley Road, Roseau, Commonwealth of Dominica
Tel: 448 2045. Fax: 448 5840.
E-mail: tourism@dominica.dm
Website: www.dominica.dm
Office for the High Commission for the Commonwealth of Dominica
1 Collingham Gardens, London SW5 0HW, UK
Tel: (020) 7370 5194/5. Fax: (020) 7373 8743.
E-mail: highcommission@dominica.co.uk
Website: www.dominica.co.uk
Opening hours: Mon-Fri 0930-1730.
Dominica Tourist Office
MKI Ltd, Mitre House, 66 Abbey Road, Bush Hill Park, Enfield, Middlesex EN1 2QE, UK
Tel: (020) 8350 1004. Fax: (020) 8350 1011.
E-mail: dominica@ttg.co.uk *or* mki@ttg.co.uk
Website: www.dominica.dm
Caribbean Tourism Organisation
22 The Quadrant, Richmond, Surrey, TW9 1BP, UK
Tel: (020) 8948 0057. Fax: (020) 8948 0067.
E-mail: ctolondon@caribtourism.com
Website: www.caribbean.co.uk
The Office of the Honorary British Consul
c/o Courts Dominica Ltd, PO Box 2269, Roseau, Commonwealth of Dominica
Tel: 255 2407. Fax: 448 7817.
Embassy of the Commonwealth of Dominica
3216 New Mexico Avenue, NW, Washington, DC 20016, USA
Tel: (202) 364 6781. Fax: (202) 364 6791.
E-mail: embdomdc@aol.com
Dominica Tourist Office
110-64 Queens Boulevard, Forest Hills, NY 11375, USA
Tel: (718) 261 9615 *or* (888) 645 5637 (toll-free, US residents only). Fax: (718) 261 0702.

TIMATIC CODES

Health	AMADEUS: **TI-DFT/JIB/HE** GALILEO/WORLDSPAN: **TI-DFT/JIB/HE** SABRE: **TIDFT/JIB/HE**
Visa	AMADEUS: **TI-DFT/JIB/VI** GALILEO/WORLDSPAN: **TI-DFT/JIB/VI** SABRE: **TIDFT/JIB/VI**

To access TIMATIC country information on Health and Visa regulations through the Computer Reservations System (CRS), type in the appropriate command line listed above.

E-mail: dominicany@msn.com
Website: www.dominica.dm
High Commission for the Eastern Caribbean States
130 Albert Street, Suite 700, Ottawa, Ontario K1P 5G4, Canada
Tel: (613) 236 8952. Fax: (613) 236 3042.
E-mail: echcc@travel-net.com
Website: www.oecs.org/ottawa
Also deals with tourism enquiries.
The Canadian High Commission in Bridgetown deals with enquiries relating to Dominica (see *Barbados* **section).**

General Information

AREA: 751 sq km (290 sq miles).
POPULATION: 71,727 (2001).
POPULATION DENSITY: 95.5 per sq km.
CAPITAL: Roseau. **Population:** 26,000 (UN estimate 2001).
GEOGRAPHY: Dominica is a large and mountainous island, geographically part of the Leeward Islands, though historically it has been grouped with the Windward Islands for administrative purposes, with volcanic peaks, mountain streams and rivers, dense forests, quiet lakes, waterfalls, geysers and boiling volcanic pools. There are beaches of both black (volcanic) and golden sands, while orchids and untamed subtropical vegetation grow in the valleys. Guadeloupe lies to the north and Martinique to the south.
GOVERNMENT: Republic. Gained independence from the UK in 1978. **Head of State:** Nicholas Liverpool since 2003. **Head of Government:** Roosevelt Skerrit since 2004.
LANGUAGE: The official language is English, but Creole French, the national language, is spoken by most of the population.
RELIGION: Almost entirely Christian, with a Roman Catholic majority.
TIME: GMT - 4.
ELECTRICITY: 220/240 volts AC, 50Hz. Three-pin European-style plugs are usual.
COMMUNICATIONS: Telephone: IDD available. Country code: 1 767. Outgoing international code: 1 for USA, Canada and *most* Caribbean islands; 011 for other countries. **Mobile telephone:** TDMA network. Network providers include *Cable & Wireless Dominica* (website: www.cwdom.dm) and *Wireless Ventures (Dominica) Ltd.* Unregistered roaming is available – visitors with TDMA handsets can make calls without registering, provided they can give a credit card number. Handsets can be hired. **Fax:** Services are available through the *Cable & Wireless Company*. Opening hours: Mon-Sat 0700-2000. **Internet:** Access is available at the offices of *Cable & Wireless* in Roseau, at an Internet cafe and in some hotels. The main ISPs are *Cable & Wireless* (CWDom) (website: www.cwdom.dm) and *Marpin*. **Post:** There are no *Poste Restante* facilities. Post office hours: Mon 0830-1300 and 1430-1700, Tues-Fri 0830-1300 and 1430-1600. **Press:** Newspapers are in English. These include *The Chronicle*, *The Independent Newspaper*, the *Official Gazette*, *The Sun* and *The Tropical Star*, all of which appear weekly.
Radio: BBC World Service (website: www.bbc.co.uk/worldservice) and Voice of America (website: www.voa.gov) can be received. From time to time the frequencies change.

Credit: © Dominica Tourism Board

Passport/Visa

	Passport Required?	Visa Required?	Return Ticket Required?
Full British	Yes	No/3	Yes
Australian	Yes	No/4	Yes
Canadian	1	No/4	Yes
USA	1	No/5	Yes
Other EU	Yes/2	No/3/5	Yes
Japanese	Yes	No/5	Yes

Note: Regulations and requirements may be subject to change at short notice, and you are advised to contact the appropriate diplomatic or consular authority before finalising travel arrangements. Details of these may be found at the head of this country's entry. Any numbers in the chart refer to the footnotes below.

PASSPORTS: Passport valid for at least six months required by all except the following:
(a) **1.** nationals of Canada and the USA holding proof of citizenship bearing a photograph and return or onward tickets;
(b) **2.** nationals of France holding National Identity Cards (*Carte d'Identité*) for stays of up to two weeks.
VISAS: Required by all except the following:
(a) **3.** nationals of EU countries for stays of up to six months (except Austria, Czech Republic, Estonia, Finland, Hungary, Latvia, Lithuania, Poland, Slovak Republic and Slovenia for stays of up to 21 days);
(b) **4.** nationals of Commonwealth countries for stays of up to six months;
(c) **5.** nationals of Argentina, China (PR), Costa Rica, Israel, Japan, Korea (Rep), Malta, Mexico, Norway, Surinam, Taiwan (China), USA and Venezuela for stays of up to six months;
(d) nationals of *all other countries* for tourist stays of up to 21 days, provided they have a return ticket and satisfy the immigration officer that they do not wish to stay for longer. For an extension, visitors should apply to the Immigration Department at the Police Headquarters in Roseau, Dominica.
Types of visa and cost: *Single-entry:* £15.
Application to: Consular section at Embassy.
Application requirements: (a) Valid passport. (b) Two passport-size photos. (c) Return ticket or receipt from travel agent. (d) Fee (plus extra £5 if require return of passport by registered mail). (e) Letter explaining the length of stay required.
Temporary residence: A work permit must be obtained.

Money

Currency: East Caribbean Dollar (EC$) = 100 cents. Notes are in denominations of EC$100, 50, 20, 10 and 5. Coins are in denominations of EC$1, and 50, 25, 10, 5, 2 and 1 cents. US Dollars and Pounds Sterling are also legal tender.
Note: The Eastern Caribbean Dollar is tied at a fixed rate to the US Dollar.
Currency exchange: Foreign currencies can be exchanged at banks and bureaux de change.
Credit & debit cards: American Express, MasterCard (limited) and Visa are accepted. Check with your credit or debit card company for details of merchant acceptability and other services which may be available.
Travellers cheques: Accepted by most hotels. To avoid additional exchange rate charges, travellers are advised to take travellers cheques in US Dollars.
Currency restrictions: The import of local and foreign currency is unlimited, subject to declaration on arrival. The export of local and foreign currency is limited to the amount declared on arrival. If holding a credit card, export is limited to EC$2500 and any currency in excess of this will require proof of conversion.
Exchange rate indicators: The following figures are included as a guide to the movements of the East Caribbean Dollar against Sterling and the US Dollar:

Date	Feb '04	May '04	Aug '04	Nov '04
£1.00=	4.91	4.82	4.97	5.11
$1.00=	2.70	2.70	2.70	2.70

Banking hours: Mon-Thurs 0800-1500, Fri 0800-1600.

Duty Free

The following goods may be imported into Dominica without incurring customs duty by passengers aged 18 and above:
200 cigarettes or equivalent of tobacco products; 2l of alcoholic beverages; tools for professional use.
Prohibited items: Various plants including bananas, coconuts, coffee and avocados. A licence is needed to import firearms.

Public Holidays

2005: Jan 1-2 New Year. **Feb 7** Carnival. **Mar 25** Good Friday. **Mar 28** Easter Monday. **May 2** Bank Holiday. **May 16** Whit Monday. **Aug 1** August Monday. **Nov 3** Independence Day. **Nov 4** Community Service Day. **Dec 25** Christmas Day. **Dec 26** Boxing Day.
2006: Jan 1-2 New Year. **Feb 27-28** Carnival. **Apr 14** Good Friday. **Apr 17** Easter Monday. **May 1** Bank Holiday. **Jun 5** Whit Monday. **Aug 7** August Monday. **Nov 3** Independence Day. **Nov 4** Community Service Day. **Dec 25** Christmas Day. **Dec 26** Boxing Day.

Health

	Special Precautions?	Certificate Required?
Yellow Fever	No	1
Cholera	No	No
Typhoid & Polio	2	N/A
Malaria	No	N/A

Note: *Regulations and requirements may be subject to change at short notice, and you are advised to contact your doctor well in advance of your intended date of departure. Any numbers in the chart refer to the footnotes below.*

1: A yellow fever vaccination certificate is required from travellers over one year of age coming from infected areas.
2: Typhoid may be a risk in rural areas.
Food & drink: Mains water is normally chlorinated and, whilst relatively safe, may cause mild abdominal upsets. Bottled water is available and is advised for the first few weeks of the stay. Drinking water outside main towns may be contaminated and sterilisation is advisable. Milk is pasteurised and dairy products are safe for consumption. Local meat, poultry, seafood, fruit and vegetables are generally considered safe to eat.
Other risks: *Hepatitis A* is common, as are *bacillary* and *amoebic dysentries*. Outbreaks of *dengue fever* occur in the area, as well as *dengue haemorrhagic fever*.
Health care: As visitors are required to pay up front for treatment, international travellers are strongly advised to take out full medical insurance.

Credit: © Dominica Tourism Board

Travel - International

AIR: The main airline to serve Dominica is *LIAT (LI)*. Other airlines serving Dominica include *American Eagle* and *Caribbean Star*. There are currently no direct, non-stop flights from Europe or the USA, mostly because the two airports are too small for jets. Popular routes from Europe are via Antigua, Barbados, Guadeloupe, Martinique or Puerto Rico, then a local flight to Dominica.
Approximate flight times: From Roseau to *London* via Antigua is approximately 10 hours (depending on length of stopover), to *Los Angeles* is 10 hours and to *New York* is seven hours.
International airports: (turbo-prop only): *Melville Hall (DOM)*, the older of the two airports, is approximately 64km (40 miles) northeast of Roseau.
Canefield (DCF) is approximately 5km (3 miles) north of Roseau. Airport facilities include snack bars, tourist information office, shops, left luggage and car hire (*Avis* and *Budget*).
Departure tax: US$14 or equivalent. Transit passengers continuing their journey on the same day and children under 12 years of age are exempt.
SEA: *Geest* and several other island-hopping freight lines stop in Dominica. Generally, passenger accommodation is comfortable but numbers are limited, so book well in advance. *L'Express des Îles*, a scheduled ferry service, connects Dominica with Guadeloupe, St Lucia and Martinique on a 300-seat catamaran. *Caribbean Ferries* also operate regular services between Dominica, Guadeloupe and Martinique. There is an EC$20 departure tax. Cruise liners stop at Woodbridge Bay, 5km (3 miles) outside Roseau. A new cruise ship jetty has been developed and opened at Prince Rupert Bay, Portsmouth.

Travel - Internal

ROAD: There are more than 700km (450 miles) of well-maintained roads on the island and there is little traffic outside Roseau. Traffic drives on the left. There is a 32kmph (20mph) speed limit in towns and villages. **Bus:** Services connect all towns and villages. **Taxis** are efficient. **Car hire:** Available (see *Travel – International* section) but some roads can be difficult. Visiting drivers must be between 25 and 65 years old and have had at least two years' driving experience in order to apply for a local driver's permit; permits cost US$12 or EC$30 for one month, and US$23 or EC$60 for three months. Jeep and minibus tours operated by local firms offer the best means of sightseeing; all vehicles chartered for this purpose must be hired for at least three hours. **Documentation:** International Driving Permit recommended. A valid foreign licence can be used to get a Temporary Visitor's Permit.
Travel Times: The following chart gives approximate travel times (in hours and minutes) from **Roseau** to other places in Dominica.

	Road
Canefield Airport	**0.15**
Melville Hall Airport	**1.15**
Portsmouth	**1.00**

Accommodation

HOTELS: The number of hotels has expanded in recent years; most are small- to medium-sized, and well equipped; the largest has 170 rooms. There are three hotels at the fringe of an area designated as a National Park. Information can be obtained from the Dominica Hotel and Tourism Association (e-mail: dhta@marpin.dm; website: www.dhta.org).
Grading: Many of the hotels offer accommodation according to one of a number of 'Plans' widely used in the Caribbean; these include Modified American Plan (MAP), which consists of room, breakfast and dinner, and European Plan (EP), which consists of room only.
APARTMENTS/COTTAGES: These offer self-catering, full service and maid service facilities and are scattered around the island.
GUEST HOUSES: There is a variety of guest houses and inns around the island which offer a comfortable and very friendly atmosphere. There is a 5 per cent government tax and 10 per cent service charge on rooms.
CAMPING/CARAVANNING: Facilities are available. Overnight safari tours are run by local operators.

Resorts & Excursions

Roseau, on the southwest coast, is the main centre for visitors. From hotels around here, it is possible to arrange jeep safari tours for seeing the hinterland of the country. Canoe trips up the rivers can also be arranged. The beaches are mainly of black volcanic sand, but there are a few white-sand beaches on the northeast of the island.
Morne Trois Pitons National Park, covering 7000 hectares (17,000 acres) in the south-central part of Dominica, was established in July 1975. Places of interest in the park include the **Boiling Lake**, the second-largest actively boiling lake in the world, and the **Emerald Pool**, **Middleham Falls**, **Sari Sari Falls**, **Trafalgar Falls**, **Freshwater Lake**, **Boeri Lake** and the **Valley of Desolation**.
Cabrits Historical Park was designated a park in 1987. Attractions include the **Cabrits Peninsula**, which contains the historical ruins of **Fort Shirley** and **Fort George**, 18th- and early 19th-century forts, and a museum at Fort Shirley. Other places of interest include the **Carib Indian Territory**, home to the only remaining Carib Indians in the Caribbean, the **Sulphur Springs**, the **Central Forest Reserve**, **Botanical Gardens**, **Titou Gorge**, **L'Escalier Tête Chien**, several areas of rainforest and a variety of fauna and flora.

Sport & Activities

Hiking: Dominica is characterised by a lush, green landscape and a mountainous interior covered in dense tropical forests. Some of the best hiking trails can be found in the *Morne Trois Pitons National Park* (containing crater lakes, spectacular waterfalls and the world's second-largest boiling lake, which can be reached after a strenuous four-hour walk). The Dominican authorities adhere to strict nature conservation policies and a number of brochures, including special hiking guides, are available and recommended; contact the National Development Corporation (see *Contact Addresses* section) for details.
Ecotourism: Several resorts, usually located in the rainforest or the mountains, specialise in ecological holidays, offering guided educational trips to Dominica's many natural attractions.
Watersports: There are good opportunities for **scuba-diving** and **snorkelling**, the latter being very popular in the *Soufrière* area, south of the capital Roseau, where volcanic cliffs drop into the sea. Visibility is usually up to 80m

Credit: © Dominica Tourism Board

A B C D E F G H I J K L M N O P Q R S T U V W X Y Z

(263ft). In some places you can reach good snorkelling sights by **kayaking** along the coast. Equipment may be hired through hotels and local tour operators. **Whale and dolphin watching** is on offer, from boats or in the sea. Special diving excursions take visitors to the best spots. Divers need to have a certified diving qualification or be engaged in a training course conducted by one of the island's dive authorities. Spear fishing is prohibited and divers should also refrain from taking any living organism from the seabed or removing any artefacts from sunken wrecks. **Swimming** is possible in the sea or in the island's secluded rock pools, notably at *Trafalgar Falls*, *Emerald Pool* and *Titou Gorge*, where two hot springs filter into a rock pool fed by a river. There are facilities for **parasailing**, **windsurfing** and **water-skiing** at coastal hotels. 15-minute parasailing flights are available for parties of four or more. Windsurfing boards may be hired. Speedboats can be hired for water-skiing. **Motor boats** and **sailing boats** can also be chartered along the coast and **fishing charters** can be arranged for larger groups. For further information on watersports, contact the National Development Corporation (see *Contact Addresses* section).

Credit: © Dominica Tourism Board

Social Profile

FOOD & DRINK: In general, it is wise to order the speciality of the house or of the day to ensure freshness. Island cooking includes Creole, Continental and American dishes. Creole dishes include *tee-tee-ree* (tiny freshly spawned fish), *lambi* (conch), *agouti* (a rodent), *manicou* (pig- and wild pigeon-smoked meats) and *crabbacks* (backs of red and black crabs stuffed with seasoned crab meat). *Bello Hot Pepper Sauce* is made locally and served everywhere with almost everything. Food prices on Dominica are usually reasonable. Restaurants close at about midnight weekdays but are open later at weekends. Root vegetables, such as yams and turnips, are often referred to as 'provisions' on a menu.
Island fruit juices are excellent as are rum punches, particularly coconut rum punch (made from fresh coconut milk, sugar, rum, bitters, vanilla and grenadine). *Sea Moss* is a non-alcoholic beverage made from sea moss or seaweed, with a slightly minty taste. Spirits, local rum especially, are inexpensive. Wines (mainly French and Californian) are expensive. There is a wide choice of beers available. There are no licensing hours.
NIGHTLIFE: Some hotel lounges stay open until 2300 and there is music at weekends at several hotels. A favourite haunt in Roseau, *La Robe Creole*, has dance music nightly with live bands at weekends. Popular local discos include *The Warehouse*, *Scorpio* and *Doubles International*. There are often folklore evenings with authentic costumes and music. Hotel staff will generally be able to advise visitors as to the best places.
SHOPPING: There is no duty-free shopping, but there are some excellent buys to be found among local handicrafts, including hats, bags and rugs made from vetiver grass joined with wild banana strands. The *Carib Reserve Crafts Centre* produces bags made from two layers of reeds that are buried in the ground to achieve a three-colour effect and covered with a layer of broad banana-type leaf to make them waterproof. **Shopping hours:** Mon-Fri 0800-1300 and 1400-1600, Sat 0800-1300.
SPECIAL EVENTS: For a complete list of special events, contact the Dominica Tourist Office (see *Contact Addresses* section). The following is a selection of special events occurring in Dominica in 2005:
Jan 1 *New Year's Day Celebrations*. **Feb** *Carnival* ('*Mas Dominik*'). This entails two weeks of celebrations, culminating in an explosion of parades. **May** *Art, Craft and Flower Festival*; *International Sports Fishing Tournament*. **Jun** *Fete Isidore*; *Fete Mawen*. **Jun-Jul** *Dominica Dive Fest*, Roseau. **Jul** *Emancipation Festival*. **Oct** *National Independence Day Celebrations*; *World Creole Music Festival*. **Oct** *Creole Day*. **Dec** *Christmas Festival*.
SOCIAL CONVENTIONS: Casual dress is normal, but swimwear is not worn on the streets in town. Evening clothes are informal but conservative. The Catholic Church is one of the most dominant social influences.
Photography: Visitors should ask before taking photographs of local people. **Tipping:** A 10 per cent service charge is added by most hotels and some restaurants. Other less touristic places do not add service to the bill and therefore tipping is discretionary; 10 to 15 per cent of the bill is acceptable. Taxi rates are set by law and therefore taxi drivers do not expect tips.

Business Profile

ECONOMY: Much of the land is under cultivation, with bananas, coconuts, citrus fruits and cocoa as the main produce. The banana industry, which is the country's main export earner, has been under serious pressure following a World Trade Organization ruling outlawing the preferential access to its main European markets that Dominica had previously enjoyed. This, and the -1 per cent GDP rate during 2001, have given added urgency to the Government's efforts to diversify the country's economic base and improve the country's inadequate infrastructure. At present there is a little light industry producing vegetable oil, canned juices, cigarettes, soap and other consumer goods largely for domestic consumption. In the service sector, tourism initially developed rather more slowly in Dominica than elsewhere in the Caribbean but it has become a vital component of the economy. The government has sought to promote Dominica as an Ecotourism destination. In recent years, the Government has been trying to promote an offshore financial services industry; in a highly competitive market, it has enjoyed limited success. Dominica is a member of the Caribbean economic bloc CARICOM and of the Organisation of East Caribbean States. Substantial overseas aid is provided by the USA, the UK and the EU. The island's largest trading partners are the UK, the USA, Canada and Japan; Barbados and Guadeloupe are the largest within the Caribbean region.
BUSINESS: Businesspeople should usually dress smartly and dealings will be formal, initially at least. **Government office hours:** Mon 0800-1300 and 1400-1700, Tue-Fri 0800-1300 and 1400-1600.
COMMERCIAL INFORMATION: The following organisations can offer advice: Dominica Association of Industry and Commerce (DAIC), PO Box 85, 6 Cross Lane, Roseau (e-mail: daic@marpin.dm); *or* the National Development Corporation (see *Contact Addresses* section).

Climate

Hot, subtropical climate throughout the year. The main rainy season is between June and October, when it is hottest.
Required clothing: Lightweight cottons and linens. Waterproofing is advisable throughout most of the year.

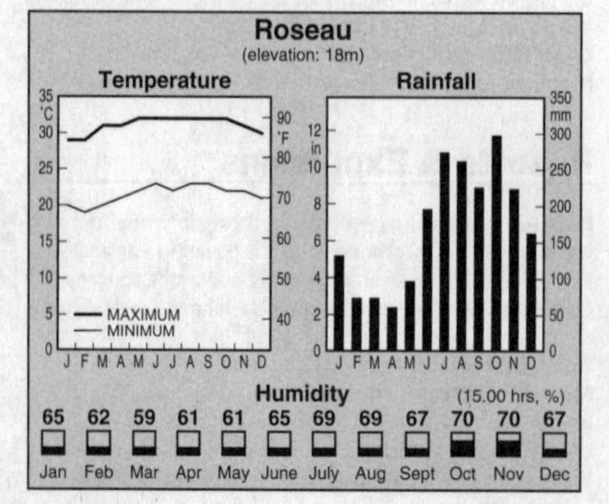

Dominican Republic

LATEST TRAVEL ADVICE CONTACTS

British Foreign and Commonwealth Office
Tel: (0870) 606 0290 Website: www.fco.gov.uk
US Department of State
Website: http://travel.state.gov/travel
Canadian Department of Foreign Affairs and Int'l Trade
Tel: (1 800) 267 8376 Website: www.dfait-maeci.gc.ca

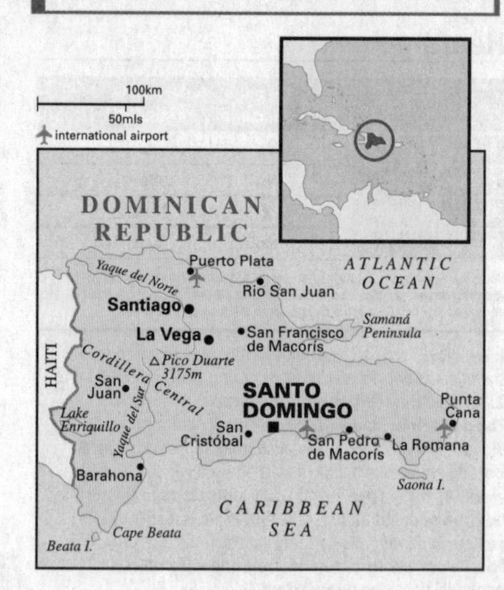

Location: Caribbean, island of Hispaniola, east of Cuba.

Country dialling code: 1 809.

Secretaría de Estado de Turismo (Ministry of Tourism)
Street address: Avenida México esq, 30 de Marzo, Oficinas Gubernanentales Bloque B, Santo Domingo, Dominican Republic
Postal address: Apdo 497, Santo Domingo, Dominican Republic
Tel: 221 4660. Fax: 682 3806.
Website: www.dominicana.com.do
Embassy of the Dominican Republic
139 Inverness Terrace, Bayswater, London W2 6JF, UK
Tel: (020) 7727 6285 *or* 7727 6214 (consular section) *or* (09065) 508 945 (recorded tourist cards information; calls cost 60p per minute). Fax: (020) 7727 3693.
E-mail: info@dominicanembassy.org.uk
Website: www.dominicanembassy.org.uk
Opening hours: Mon-Fri 1000-1400.
Honorary Consulate of the Dominican Republic
539 Martin's Building, 4 Water Street, Liverpool L2 3SX, UK
Tel: (0151) 236 0722. Fax: (0151) 255 0990.
Opening hours: Tues-Fri 0930-1230.
Dominican Republic Tourist Board
18-21 Hand Court, High Holborn, London WC1V 6JF, UK
Tel: (020) 7242 7778. Fax: (020) 7405 4202.
E-mail: inglaterra@sectur.gov.do
Website: www.dominicanrepublic.com
British Embassy
Avenida 27 de Febrero 233, Edificio Corominas Pepin, 7th Floor, Santo Domingo, Dominican Republic
Tel: 472 7111 *or* 472 7905. Fax: 472 7574.
E-mail: brit.emb.sadom@codetel.net.do
Embassy and Consulate of the Dominican Republic
1715 22nd Street, NW, Washington, DC 20008, USA
Tel: (202) 332 6280. Fax: (202) 265 8057.
E-mail: embdomrepusa@msn.com *or* embassy@us.serex.gov.do *or* consular@us.serex.gov.do.
Website: www.domrep.org
Dominican Republic Tourist Board
136 East 57th Street, Suite 803, New York, NY 10022, USA
Tel: (212) 588 1012. Fax: (212) 588 1015.
E-mail: newyork@sectur.gov.do
Website: www.dominicanrepublic.com
Embassy of the United States of America
Calle César Nicolás Pensón y Calle Leopoldo Navarro, Santo

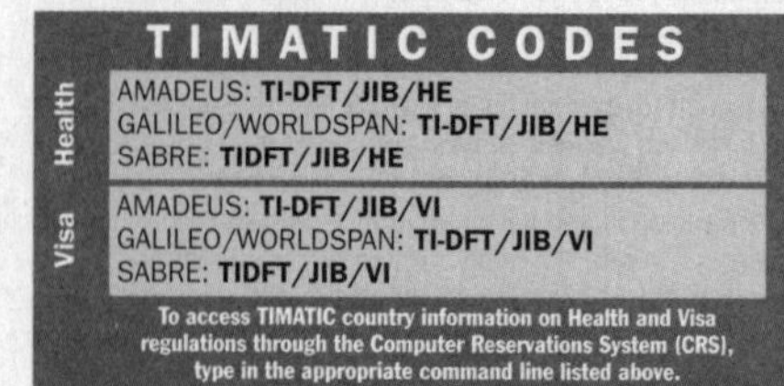
TIMATIC CODES
Health
AMADEUS: **TI-DFT/JIB/HE**
GALILEO/WORLDSPAN: **TI-DFT/JIB/HE**
SABRE: **TIDFT/JIB/HE**
Visa
AMADEUS: **TI-DFT/JIB/VI**
GALILEO/WORLDSPAN: **TI-DFT/JIB/VI**
SABRE: **TIDFT/JIB/VI**
To access TIMATIC country information on Health and Visa regulations through the Computer Reservations System (CRS), type in the appropriate command line listed above.

Domingo, Dominican Republic
Tel: 221 2171. Fax: 686 7437.
E-mail: infovisas@codetel.net.do (consular section).
Website: www.usemb.gov.do
Embassy of the Dominican Republic
130 Albert Street, Suite 418, Ottawa K1P 5G4, Canada
Tel: (613) 569 9893. Fax: (613) 569 8673.
E-mail: info@drembassy.org
Website: www.drembassy.org
Consulates in: Montreal and Toronto
Dominican Republic Tourist Board
2080 rue Crescent, Montréal, Québec H3G 2B8, Canada
Tel: (514) 499 1918 *or* (800) 563 1611 (toll-free).
Fax: (514) 499 1393.
E-mail: montreal@sectur.gov.do
Website: www.dominicanrepublic.com
Canadian Embassy
Street address: Capitán Eugenio de Marchena 39, La Esperilla, Santo Domingo, Dominican Republic
Postal address: A.P. 2054, Santo Domingo, Dominican Republic
Tel: 685 1136. Fax: 682 2691.
E-mail: sdmgo@dfait-maeci.gc.ca
Website: www.dfait-maeci.gc.ca/dominicanrepublic
Consulate in: Puerto Plata

Credit: © The Dominican Republic Tourist Board

General Information

AREA: 48,072 sq km (18,696 sq miles).
POPULATION: 8,230,722 (2002).
POPULATION DENSITY: 175.9 per sq km.
CAPITAL: Santo Domingo. **Population:** 1,822,028 (2002).
GEOGRAPHY: The Dominican Republic is in the Caribbean, sharing the island of Hispaniola with Haiti and constituting the eastern two-thirds of land. The landscape is forested and mountainous, with valleys, plains and plateaux. The soil is fertile with excellent beaches on the north, southeast and east coasts, rising up to the mountains.
GOVERNMENT: Republic. Gained independence in 1884.
Head of State and Government: President Hipolito Mejía Domínguez since 2000.
LANGUAGE: Spanish is the official language. Some English and French are spoken.
RELIGION: Almost all Christian, with 89 per cent Roman Catholic; there are small Protestant and Jewish minorities.
TIME: GMT - 4.
ELECTRICITY: 110 volts AC, 60Hz. American-style two-pin plugs are in use.
COMMUNICATIONS: Telephone: Full IDD available. Country code: 1 809. Outgoing international code: 011. CODETEL, Dominican Republic's telecommunications company, has produced the *Comunicard*, which enables tourists visiting the country to phone anywhere abroad from any touchtone phone. For further information, contact CODETEL, Av Tiradentes 1169, Santo Domingo (tel: 220 5168; fax: 549 4721; e-mail: ayuda@codetel.com.do; website: www.codetel.net.do). **Mobile telephone:** GSM 1900 network exists; the main network provider is Orange (website: www.orange.com.do). **Fax:** There are facilities at most locations and many hotels and telecommunications centres offer this service. **Internet:** ISPs include *Caribbean Internet* (website: www.caribe.net, *Tricom* (website: www.tricom.net) and *Verizon* (website: www.verizon.net.do). **Telegram:** These may be sent from RCA Global Communications Inc, Santo Domingo, or from ITT-America Cables and Radio Inc, Santo Domingo. Large hotels have facilities. **Post:** Airmail takes about 10 days to reach western Europe. It is advisable to post all mail at the Central Post Office in Santo Domingo to ensure rapid handling. **Press:** All daily papers are in Spanish and include *Hoy*, *Listín Diario* and *El Nacional*. The English-language *Santo Domingo News* is published weekly on Wednesday and may be obtained in hotels. *Dominicana News*, a monthly Tourism Promotion Council publication, has the main Dominicana tourism industry items.
Radio: BBC World Service (website: www.bbc.co.uk/worldservice) and Voice of America (website: www.voa.gov) can be received. From time to time the frequencies change and the most up-to-date can be found online.

Passport/Visa

	Passport Required?	Visa Required?	Return Ticket Required?
Full British	Yes	3	Yes
Australian	Yes	3	Yes
Canadian	1	3	Yes
USA	1	3	Yes
Other EU	2	3	Yes
Japanese	Yes	4	Yes

Note: *Regulations and requirements may be subject to change at short notice, and you are advised to contact the appropriate diplomatic or consular authority before finalising travel arrangements. Details of these may be found at the head of this country's entry. Any numbers in the chart refer to the footnotes below.*

PASSPORTS: Passports valid for six months after date of departure required by all except:
(a) **1.** nationals of Canada and the USA holding appropriate ID such as a Birth Certificate or a Driver's Licence accompanied by a photo ID document, provided travelling for business or touristic purposes;
(b) **2.** nationals of Belgium, France, Germany, Luxembourg and The Netherlands holding a National Identity Card at the discretion of immigration.
Note: These nationals will also require *Tourist Cards*, which may be purchased on arrival.
Tourist Cards: Issued to travellers visiting the Dominican Republic for touristic purposes for stays of up to two weeks. Tourist Cards can be applied for in advance at a cost of £8, or can be issued on arrival at a cost of US$10, though this can be a lengthy process. Extensions of up to three months are possible by visiting the Immigration Department in Santo Domingo; failure to do so will result in a surcharge at the airport upon departure. Nationals of the following countries are eligible for a Tourist Card:
(a) **3.** nationals of the countries mentioned in the chart above (except nationals of Cyprus, Estonia, Japan, Latvia, Malta and Slovak Republic, who *do* need a visa);
(b) nationals of Andorra, Antigua & Barbuda, Aruba, The Bahamas, Barbados, Bolivia, Brazil, Costa Rica, Croatia, Curaçao, Dominica, El Salvador, Guadeloupe, Guatemala, Guyana, Honduras, Jamaica, Macedonia (Former Yugoslav Republic of), Martinique, Mexico, Monaco, Norway, Paraguay, Puerto Rico, Reunion, Russian Federation, St Kitts & Nevis, St Lucia, St Maarten, St Vincent & the Grenadines, San Marino, Serbia & Montenegro, Surinam, Switzerland, Trinidad & Tobago, Turks & Caicos Islands, Ukraine, US Virgin Islands and Venezuela.
Application to: Consulate (or Consular section at Embassy); see *Contact Addresses* section.
Application requirements: (a) Photocopy of the photo page of the passport, containing personal details of the applicant. (b) Fee, payable by postal order or bank draft. Applicant's name and address must be written on the back. (c) Stamped, self-addressed A5 envelope for postal applications.
Note: Some foreign nationals with permanent legal residency in countries such as the UK need to get a verbal note from the Embassy of the Dominican Republic, and possibly travel visa-free. In the UK, the passport containing the stamp of right to remain in the UK must be presented along with £50 in person.
Working days required: Seven.
VISAS: Required by all except:
(a) holders of a Tourist Card;
(b) **4.** Residents, regardless of nationality, of Argentina, Chile, Ecuador, Iceland, Israel, Japan, Korea (Rep), Liechtenstein, Peru and Uruguay, may enter the Dominican Republic without a visa or Tourist Card.
Note: In addition to a valid visa, nationals of China (PR) require an authorisation from the Director of the Migration/Immigration Department.
Types of visa and cost: *Tourist* (single entry): £130. *Business* (single entry): £200. There is no charge for visas for nationals of Italy, Mexico, Norway, Panama, Spain and the USA. *Student*: £60.
Validity: Tourist visas and single-entry business visas are valid for 60 days. Multiple-entry business visas are valid for up to one year.
Application to: Consulate (or Consular section at Embassy); see *Contact Addresses* section. Multiple entry visas can only be applied for once in the Dominican Republic.
Application requirements: (a) Valid passport. (b) Completed application form. (c) Four passport-size photos. (d) Fee (payable by cash or postal order). (e) Three months of bank account statements, plus any other proof of sufficient funds. (f) Stamped, registered self-addressed envelope for postal applications. *Tourist*: (a)-(f) and, (g) Flight itinerary and reservation. *Business*: (a)-(f) and, (g) Reference letter or letter of invitation from a company in the Dominican Republic. Those applying for business visas must also submit a letter of invitation from a company in the Dominican Republic. Students must also submit a duly signed request letter to the ambassador, proof of support by parents, health certificate and a certificate of 'Good Behaviour' from the applicants' country of residence, which is valid for 30 days from the date of issue.
Note: All minors under 13 years, travelling alone or with anyone but both parents, must present written authorisation from the parent(s) or legal guardian(s) not accompanying them. This authorisation should contain passport numbers of traveller(s), and details of onward and return dates. This must then be legalised by the nearest Dominican Embassy or Consulate. This will incur a charge of £55.
Working days required: Approximately four weeks for visas which have to be referred to the authorities in the Dominican Republic, unless requested by fax (the cost of which must be paid by the applicant).
Temporary residence: Consult the Consulate or Consular section at the Embassy; see *Contact Addresses* section.

Money

Currency: Dominican Republic Peso (peso) = 100 centavos. Notes are in denominations of peso2000, 1000, 500, 50, 20, 10 and 5. Coins are in denominations of peso1, and 50, 25, 10, 5 and 1 centavos.
Currency exchange: The peso is not available outside the Dominican Republic. Currencies of Canada, France, Germany, Italy, Japan, Mexico, The Netherlands, Spain, Switzerland, UK, USA and Venezuela may be converted into local currency. At departure, up to 30 per cent of the exchanged currency can be reconverted into US Dollars at any bank, provided original receipts are shown. All exchange must be done through official dealers such as banks and hotels approved by the Central Bank.
Credit & debit cards: American Express, Diners Club, MasterCard and Visa are all accepted. Check with your credit or debit card company for details of merchant acceptability and other services which may be available.
Travellers cheques: Travellers cheques are accepted by some banks. To avoid additional exchange rate charges, travellers are advised to take travellers cheques in US Dollars.
Currency restrictions: The import and export of local currency is prohibited; the import of foreign banknotes is allowed provided they are declared on arrival. Foreign currencies up to the amount imported and declared may also be exported. The import and export of travellers cheques is unlimited.
Exchange rate indicators: The following figures are included as a guide to the movements of the Dominican Peso against Sterling and the US Dollar:

Date	Feb '04	May '04	Aug '04	Nov '04
£1.00=	90.28	80.91	72.77	53.02
$1.00=	49.60	45.30	39.50	28.00

Banking hours: Mon-Fri 0800-1800.

Duty Free

The following goods may be imported into the Dominican Republic without incurring customs duty by travellers over 16 years of age:
200 cigarettes or one box of cigars; one unopened bottle (maximum 2l) of alcoholic beverage; two bottles of perfume (opened) for personal use.
Prohibited items: All animal products, agricultural and horticultural products and drugs.

Credit: © The Dominican Republic Tourist Board

Public Holidays

2005: Jan 1 New Year's Day. **Jan 6** Epiphany. **Jan 21** Our Lady of Altagracia. **Jan 26** Duarte's Birthday. **Feb 27** Independence Day. **Mar 25** Good Friday. **May 1** Labour Day. **May 26** Corpus Christi. **Aug 16** Restoration Day. **Sep 24** Our Lady of las Mercedes. **Nov 6** Constitution Day. **Dec 25** Christmas Day.
2006: Jan 1 New Year's Day. **Jan 6** Epiphany. **Jan 21** Our Lady of Altagracia. **Jan 26** Duarte's Birthday. **Feb 27** Independence Day. **Apr 14** Good Friday. **May 1** Labour Day. **Jun 15** Corpus Christi. **Aug 16** Restoration Day. **Sep 24** Our Lady of las Mercedes. **Nov 6** Constitution Day. **Dec 25** Christmas Day.

Health

	Special Precautions?	Certificate Required?
Yellow Fever	No	No
Cholera	No	No
Typhoid & Polio	1	N/A
Malaria	2	N/A

Note: *Regulations and requirements may be subject to change at short notice, and you are advised to contact your doctor well in advance of your intended date of departure. Any numbers in the chart refer to the footnotes below.*

1: Typhoid may be a risk in rural areas. Vaccination against typhoid and polio is recommended.
2: Malaria risk, exclusively in the malignant *falciparum* form, exists throughout the year in rural areas of the western provinces of Castañuelas, Hondo Valle and Pepillo Salcedo. Chloroquine is the recommended prophylaxis.
Food & drink: All water should be regarded as being potentially contaminated and sterilisation should be considered essential. Water used for drinking, brushing teeth or making ice should have first been boiled or otherwise sterilised. Milk is pasteurised. Powdered or tinned milk is available. Only eat well-cooked meat and fish, preferably served hot. Pork, salad and mayonnaise may carry increased risk. Vegetables should be cooked and fruit peeled.
Other risks: *Bilharzia* (schistosomiasis) is endemic. Avoid swimming and paddling in fresh water; swimming pools which are well chlorinated and maintained are safe. *Diffuse cutaneous leishmaniasis* has been reported. *Hepatitis A* and *B* may occur. Outbreaks of *dengue fever* occur in the area. *Rabies* may be present. For those at high risk, vaccination before arrival should be considered. If you are bitten, seek medical advice without delay. For more information, consult the *Health* appendix.
Health care: Health insurance (to include emergency repatriation) is strongly recommended. Medical care is limited and variable in quality. An emergency service is available in Santo Domingo.

Credit: © The Dominican Republic Tourist Board

Travel - International

AIR: The Dominican Republic's national airline is *Air Santo Domingo (EX)* (website: www.airsantodomingo.com). *American Airlines* offers daily flights from London via Miami. Direct flights from the USA are operated by *American Airlines* (from New York) and *Continental Airlines* (from New Jersey). *Iberia* operates every day to Santo Domingo via Madrid. Other airlines operating flights from Europe are *Air France*, *Condor* and *Martinair*.
Approximate flight times: From *London* to Santo Domingo is 11 hours (including stopover).
International airports: *Santo Domingo (SDQ)* (Internacional de las Americas), 30km (18 miles) east of the city (travel time – 30 minutes). Taxi services are available to Santo Domingo. Airport facilities include outgoing duty-free shop, post office, bank/bureau de change, restaurants, bars and car hire.
Puerto Plata International Airport (POP) (Internacional General Gregorio Luperón). Airport facilities include outgoing duty-free shop, banking and exchange facilities, restaurant, bar and car hire (*Avis*).
Punta Cana International Airport (PUJ) is 10 to 30 minutes' travel time from the Punta Cana and Bávaro resorts. Airport facilities include gift shops, duty-free shop and taxi.
Departure tax: US$10. Passengers in direct transit and children under two years of age are exempt. A 'stay tax' is also levied on all passengers staying longer than three months: peso60.48 (three to nine months); peso100.80 (nine to 12 months) or peso160.16 - peso600.32 (one year or more).
Note: When buying an international air ticket in the Dominican Republic a tax of approximately 12 per cent is levied on the carrier by the Government. This expense is passed on directly to the customer on the price of the ticket. If the ticket is bought outside the Dominican Republic, there is no tax.
SEA: Cruise lines calling at the Dominican Republic include *Holland America*, *Seabourn* and *Windjammer*.
ROAD: There are three routes from Haiti: on the road from Port-au-Prince to Santo Domingo at Jimani/Malpasse; on the road from Cap-Haitian to Santiago at Dajabón/Ouanaminthe; and a third route near the centre of the island at Elías Piñá/Belladere. The borders are open from 0800-1600.

Travel - Internal

AIR: There are regular flights between Santo Domingo, Santiago, Samaná, Punta Cana and Puerto Plata by *Air Santo Domingo*. Planes may also be chartered. For more information, contact the airline directly.
ROAD: Traffic drives on the right. There is a reasonable network of roads, including the *Sanchez Highway* running westwards from Santo Domingo to Elias Pina on the Haitian frontier; the *Mella Highway* extending eastwards from Santo Domingo to Higuey in the southeast, and the *Duarte Highway* running north and west from Santo Domingo to Santiago and to Monte Cristi on the northwest coast. Not all roads in the Dominican Republic are all-weather and 4-wheel-drive vehicles are recommended for wet weather. Checkpoints near military installations are ubiquitous, though no serious difficulties have been reported (those near the Haitian border are most likely to be sensitive). The speed limit is up to 60kph in cities and 80-100kph on motorways. **Bus:** Cheap and efficient air-conditioned bus and coach services run from the capital to other major towns. **Car hire:** There are several car hire companies in Santo Domingo (including *Avis*, *Budget*, *Dollar*, *Europcar*, *Hertz* and *National*). Minimum age for car hire is 25. A credit card is required for car-hire transactions. Insurance is compulsory. **Documentation:** A national or International Driving Permit is accepted, but is only valid for 90 days.
URBAN: Santo Domingo has flat-fare bus and minibus services, and an estimated 7000 share-taxis called *Carro de Conchos*. These operate a 24-hour service, stop on demand and charge higher fares. In old Santo Domingo, the streets are narrow with blind corners, so care should be taken, particularly as Dominican drivers have a tendency to use their horns rather than their brakes. Horse-drawn carriages are available for rent in most cities for tours around parks and plazas.
Travel times: The following chart gives approximate travel times (in hours and minutes) from Santo Domingo to other major cities and towns in the Dominican Republic.

	Air	Road
Santiago	**0.30**	**3.00**
Puerto Plata	**0.45**	**3.15**
Samaná	**0.35**	**3.30**
La Romana	**0.25**	**2.00**
Punta Cana	**0.30**	**3.30**
Barahona	**-**	**3.30**

Accommodation

HOTELS: Following a period of intensive development, the Dominican Republic now boasts over 55,000 hotel rooms, making it the largest room supply in the entire Caribbean. The southeast coast is noted for its modern hotels and beautiful beaches. In the capital, the choice ranges from clean and cheap to plush, with rates remaining the same all year because of steady business traffic. At resort hotels winter prices are higher, and in summer, prices drop by up to 10 per cent. Hotels outside Santo Domingo and La Romana are considerably less expensive, whatever the season. A service charge of 10 per cent and a 12 per cent sales tax will be added to all bills. **Grading:** There is a **5-star** grading system, but visitors should note that even the highest grade is somewhat lower in standard than is general in the Caribbean. For further information, contact the *Asociación Nacional de Hoteles y Restaurantes* (ASONAHORES), Calle President Gonzalez esq, Avenida Tiradentes, Edificio la Cumbre, Santo Domingo, Dominican Republic (tel: 540 4676; fax: 540 4727 *or* 6753; e-mail: cpt@codetel.net.do *or* asonahores@codetel.net.do; website: www.drhotels.com).
GUEST-HOUSES: Guest houses are very economical, and best found after arrival in the country
SELF-CATERING: Self-catering establishments are available in Puerto Plata at very reasonable rates.
CAMPING: There are no official sites. Camping is only possible in rural areas with permission from the landowner. National Parks are also available for camping with the permission of the National Parks Office.

Resorts & Excursions

SANTO DOMINGO: The colonial part has been carefully restored to retain its original charm, and is home to the first university, cathedral and hospital built in the New World. The modern city of Santo Domingo, by contrast, is a thriving port city, equipped with discos, gambling casinos, shops and the **Cultural Plaza**, which houses the **Gallery of Modern Art** and the **National Theatre**. Just a few miles east of the city is a remarkable cave complex, **Los Tres Ojos de Agua** (**The Three Eyes of Water**), so-called because it contains three turquoise lagoons on three different levels, each fed by an underground river and surrounded by countless stalactites, stalagmites and lush tropical vegetation.
SOUTHERN COAST: To the west of Santo Domingo is **San Cristóbal**, where the first constitution was signed on 6 November 1844. It is probably the most visited city, particularly by those wishing to get a closer look at the historical sites linked to the life of Trujillo, the dictator who governed the country with an iron fist from 1930-61. In the church and **Caves of Santa Maria**, the patron saint's day is celebrated with drums and dance rituals. One hour 45 minutes east of Santo Domingo is the city of **La Romana**, home to the understated elegance and graceful charm of the 7000-acre **Casa de Campo** resort, designed by Oscar de la Renta. Nestled within the resort is **Altos de Chavón**, a reconstructed 15th-century Mediterranean-style village of culture and art which is perched high on a cliff overlooking the tropical **Chavón River** and the **Caribbean Sea**. Altos de Chavón hosts major events in a 5000-seat Greek amphitheatre, built in the traditional design of Epidaurus. Near **Punta Cana**, is **Manatí Park**, a new theme park which includes a zoo, gardens, a recreated Taino village and a variety of exotic animals. The popular destination of **Barahona** is a humid area with beautiful beaches of white sand. **Cabritos Island**, a national park in the centre of **Lake Enriquillo**, is the greatest preserve of the wild American Crocodile, large populations of flamingos and two species of iguana. **Azúa de Compostela** was founded in 1504 by Diego Velázquez, who later conquered Cuba. In particular, the ruins of the colonial city in **Pueblo Viejo** are well worth a visit.
NORTHERN COAST: The Northern, or **Amber Coast**, is so named because some of the most beautiful amber in the world is mined here. The **Amber Museum** houses a good display of amber pieces found in this area. **Puerto Plata** (the **Silver Port**) has some of the finest beaches in the Caribbean Islands. It was founded in 1504 and boasts colonial architecture. The **Fort San Felipe** was built in the 1600s by the Spanish to protect the settlement from pirates. The Atlantic coast of the country is renowned for its miles of unspoilt beaches that surround Puerto Plata, the most popular being **Sosúa**. Just 3km (2 miles) from the town is the **Playa Dorada** resort complex. Just outside, in **Puerto Plata**, is the **Costambar Beach Resort**, with 5km (3 miles) of beach. **Mount Isabel de Torres** features a cable car which climbs over 760m (2500ft) above sea level. The breathtaking view of the Atlantic and the port of Puerto Plata is well worth the seven-minute ride up to the top of the mountain. 10 sq km (4 sq miles) of botanical gardens can be explored here. **Río San Juan** is still an undeveloped area awaiting the adventurer to discover **Playa Grande** (with a few resorts under construction), the beautiful **Playa Caletón** and the **Gri-Gri lagoon**.
The **Samaná Peninsula** is located on the northern portion of the island, approximately two hours from Puerto Plata's international airport. **Samaná**, with its transparent blue waters, miles of unspoilt beaches, and dozens of caves, is a romantic paradise. Other resorts include **The Gran Bahía Beach Resort**, **Cayo Levantado** and **El Portillo Beach Club**.

Credit: © The Dominican Republic Tourist Board

Sport & Activities

Baseball: This is not only the national sport, but also a national obsession, and even the smallest communities have floodlit stadiums. The centre of the country's baseball is the industrial seaport of *San Pedro de Macoris*. Many Dominican players go on to play in the US major leagues. Juan Marichal, whose pitching exploits for the San Francisco Giants landed him a place in the Baseball Hall of Fame, is now the country's Director of Sports. The professional winter season runs from October to January. Visitors should ask local people or look in the local paper for schedules and the nearest game.
Watersports: The opportunities for watersports in the Dominican Republic are excellent. Although some shores are rough and rocky, there are magnificent stretches of beach suitable for **swimming**. For **scuba-diving** and **snorkelling** enthusiasts, there is reef diving, good visibility, warm waters, wrecks, caverns and a rich marine life. Good dive sites include *Sosúa* (near Puerto Plata); *Cabrera* (freshwater cave diving with an underground lake); *Las Terrenas*; the *Sasmaná peninsula*; *Punta Rucia* (good for coral diving); *La Caleta National Underwater Park* (accessible by boat from Boca Chica); *Catalina* and *Saona islands* (accessible by boat from La Romana); and *Barahona* (an area currently being developed for ecotourism). Experienced divers can also join the North Caribbean Research Group and participate in a government-funded project to recover and remove artefacts from sunken ships, some dating back to the 16th century (e-mail: info@oldship.com). Snorkelling and diving equipment can be borrowed or hired from dive operators and resort hotels. Small **sailing** craft are available through hotels in Santo Domingo and most other resorts in the country. **Boat trips** to the marine caves of the *Gri Gri Lagoon* near Sosúa are a popular tourist attraction. Hotels also organise charter boats for **offshore fishing** for marlin, sailfish, dorado, benittos and other game fish. **River fishing** in flat-bottomed boats with guides can be arranged at *La Romana, Boca de Yuma* and on the north coast. **Windsurfing** is particularly good at Sosuá, which also hosts the *Professional Windsurfing Association World Cup*.
Adventure sports: The Dominican Republic was quick to jump onto the adventure sports bandwagon and, hence, has well-developed facilities for the usual range of adrenalin-generating sports. **Whitewater rafting** is available on the *Río Yaque del Norte* in Jarabacoa. The best places for **tubing**, in which participants individually float down the rapids in oversized rubber tubes, are on the *Río Jamao del Norte*, the *Río Yaque del Norte* and the *Río Isabela* in Santo Domingo. **Cascading** involves climbing up to the top of a waterfall and rapelling down the cascade tied to a rope; the best places to do this are *Cascada del Limón, Cascada Ojo de Agua, El Salto de Baiguate* and *El Salto de Jimenoa*. **Canyoning**, which is cascading minus the rope (meaning that practitioners climb up a river gorge and then jump into the river below), is popular at *La Madajagua* in Imbert and the *Jarabacoa* area.
Trekking and hiking: The best places for trekking are Jarabacoa, the *Constanza Valley*, and the *Nuevo Valley*. Hiking and climbing enthusiasts may join the locals' annual pilgrimage to the Caribbean's highest mountain, the *Pico Duarte* (3210m/10,700ft), which they can conquer either on foot or by riding a mule. Similar tours can also be made at *El Mogote, Mount Isabel de Torres, Pico Yaque* and, in the southwest, the *Sierra de Bahoruco*.
Horseriding: Dominicans love horseriding and their country offers some of the best riding in the Caribbean. Regular **polo** games are held at *Sierra Prieta* in Santo Domingo and at *Casa de Campo* near La Romana, where guests can join in the twice-weekly competitions.
Golf: There are nine championship golf courses (and several others under construction), many of which are bordered by the ocean on one side and the mountains on the other. Following on from the *42nd Caribbean Golf Championships*, which were held in the Dominican Republic in 1998, the country continues to actively promote itself as a major international golf destination. Some of the best courses can be found at *Casa de Campo, Dientes de Perro* (Teeth of the Dog), *Gran Diablo Links* (the planned location for the country's first Golf Academy), *Playa Dorada* (designed by Robert Trent Jones), *La Romana Country Club* and *Santo Domingo Country Club*. For more information, contact the Federation of Dominican Golf (FEDOGOLF), Aut. Duarte KM 201, Santo Domingo (tel: 231 4719 *or* 231 4720; e-mail: fedogolf@enel.net; website: www.fedogolf.org.do).

Social Profile

FOOD & DRINK: Native Dominican cooking combines Spanish influences with local produce. Beef is expensive (Dominicans raise fine cattle, but most is exported) and local favourites are pork and goat meat. There is plenty of fresh fish and seafood, island-grown tomatoes, lettuce, papaya, mangoes and passion fruit and all citrus fruits are delicious. Local dishes include *la bandera* (meaning 'the flag', comprising white rice, red beans, stewed meat, salad and fried plaintain), *chicharrones* (crisp pork rind), *chicharrones de pollo* (small pieces of fried chicken), *casava* (fried yucca), *moro de habichuelas* (rice and beans), *sopa criolla dominicana* (native soup of meat and vegetables), *pastelón* (baked vegetable cake) and *sancocho* (stew with anything up to 18 ingredients).
Presidente (Dominican beer) is very good, as are rum drinks such as the local *Brugal* or *Bermudez. Rum añejo* (old, dark rum) with ice makes a good after-dinner drink. Native coffee is excellent and very strong. Locally produced beer and rums are cheaper than imported alcohol which tends to be expensive.
NIGHTLIFE: Choice varies from a Las Vegas-style revue, discos and casinos to a quiet cafe by the sea in Santo Domingo. Hotels offer more traditional shows, including folk music and dancing. Popular dances are the *merengue*, played very loudly almost everywhere; *bachata*, which is becoming very popular in tourist hotspots; *perico ripiao*; and the *salsa*. *The Malecón*, along a seaside boulevard in Santo Domingo, is known as the world's longest disco. Concerts and other cultural events are often held at the *Casa de Francia* and *Plaza de la Cultura* in Santo Domingo, among other venues.
SHOPPING: Best buys are products made on the island including amber jewellery and decorative pieces. These are a national speciality, some pieces encasing insects, leaves or dew drops within ancient petrified pine resin. Larimar or Dominican turquoise is another popular stone. Milky blue and polished pink pieces of conch shell are also made into jewellery. Rocking chairs, woodcarvings, macramé, pottery, Taino artefacts, Creole dolls, baskets, limestone carvings and cassettes of salsa and merengue also make good buys. Bargaining is recommended. **Shopping hours:** Mon-Sat 0800-1200 and 1400-1800.
SPECIAL EVENTS: Carnivals, fiestas and festivals are held frequently all year round, both in larger cities as well as among the rural communities. As in many Latin American countries, Carnival is a traditional event. Merengue is the national music and the Merengue Festival draws large numbers of nationals as well as international musicians and spectators. For a complete list of events, contact the Tourism Promotion Council (see *Contact Addresses* section). The following is a selection of special events occurring in the Dominican Republic in 2005:
Feb *Sosua and Cabarete Gastronomic Festival*; *Carnival*, Santo Domingo and various locations. **Mar** *Santo Domingo Music Festival*. **Jun** *Puerto Plata Cultural Festival*. **Jul** *Santo Domingo Merengue Festival*; *Central American University Games*, Santo Domingo. **Oct** *Puerto Plata Jazz Festival*. **Oct/Nov** *Puerto Plata Merengue Festival*.
SOCIAL CONVENTIONS: The Dominican lifestyle is more American than Latin, with short siestas and without long, late lunches. The non-Latin ambience is indicated by the fact that, though the culture is rich in Roman Catholic and Spanish influences, 72-hour divorces may be obtained. Daytime dress is generally casual but beachwear and shorts are only acceptable in resorts and at pools. Evenings tend to be smarter, with jackets (although not necessarily ties) recommended for men at better restaurants, hotels and for social functions. **Tipping:** Hotel and restaurant bills automatically include a 10 per cent service charge (on top of a 12 per cent charge for tax purposes) but an additional tip may be given as an appreciation of good service. Taxi drivers on the fixed routes do not expect tips.

Business Profile

ECONOMY: Sugar, coffee and cocoa are the main agricultural cash crops. The mining industry produces ferro-nickel, gold and silver. These primary products are the basis of the Dominican Republic's economy and its main export commodities. Exploration of other potential deposits has been underway since the early 1990s but, although some gold and silver has been located, the expected oil deposits have failed to materialise. Industry is mainly concentrated in production of food and drinks, chemicals and refining of imported oil. In the service sector, tourism has had a major impact on the Dominican Republic's economy during the last 20 years and now contributes one-sixth of total output. The economy grew slowly but steadily during most of this period, but has recently experienced some problems. Growth turned negative in 2003 and unemplyment rose to 16.5 per cent, while the Dominican peso has lost a third of its value against the dollar. (A major cause is the collapse of the international sugar market.) The country relies on substantial foreign aid, principally from the USA and the Inter-American Development Bank. The Dominican Republic is a member of CARICOM, the major regional reading bloc. The USA is substantially the Dominican Republic's main trading partner, followed by Venezuela, Mexico, The Netherlands and Japan.
BUSINESS: It is usual for businesspeople to dress smartly and to deal formally with each other at first, although the general atmosphere is informal. Spanish is the main business language and a knowledge of it will be of assistance. Enquire at hotel for interpreter services. **Office hours:** Mon-Sat 0800-1200 and 1400-1800. **Government office hours:** Mon-Fri 0800-1500.
COMMERCIAL INFORMATION: The following organisation can offer advice: Cámara de Comercio y Producción de Santo Domingo, Apartado Postal 815, Arz. Nouel 206, Santo Domingo (tel: 682 2688; fax: 685 2228; e-mail: camara.sto.dgo@codetel.net.do; website: www.ccpsd.org.do).

Climate

Hot with tropical temperatures all year with coastal areas being warmer than central regions. There are two rainy seasons; the first is from May to August and is the heaviest, whilst the second from November to December is the lightest. Hurricanes may sometimes occur during these periods.

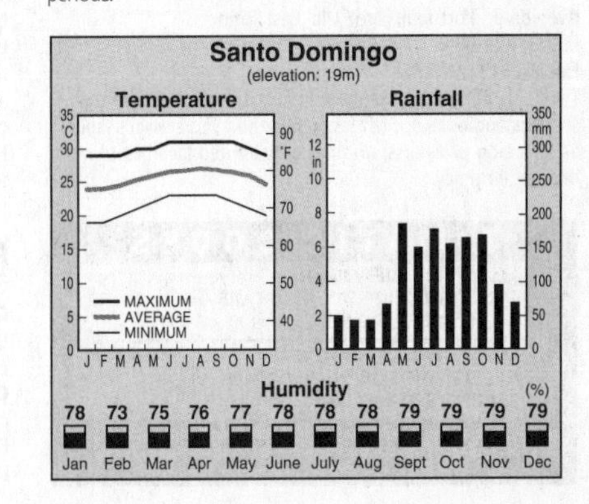

East Timor

LATEST TRAVEL ADVICE CONTACTS

British Foreign and Commonwealth Office
Tel: (0870) 606 0290 Website: www.fco.gov.uk

US Department of State
Website: http://travel.state.gov/travel

Canadian Department of Foreign Affairs and Int'l Trade
Tel: (1 800) 267 8376 Website: www.dfait-maeci.gc.ca

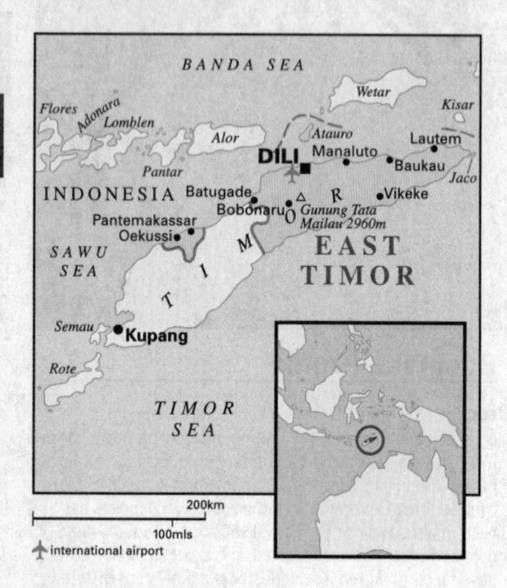

Location: South-East Asia.

OFFICIAL NAME OF COUNTRY: The Democratic Republic of Timor-Leste.

Country dialling code: 670.
Due to the fact that East Timor only became fully independent on 20 May 2002 and the fact that the UN is still playing a significant role in the running of the country, some information and details, including diplomatic representation, may be unclear or impossible to obtain at the time of writing. For further information, please check the following links:

Ministry of Foreign Affairs and Cooperation
GPA Building 1, Ground Floor, Rua Avenida Presidente Nicolau Lobato, PO Box 6, Dili, East Timor
Tel: (3) 339 600 *or* 610 *or* 625. Fax: (3) 339 025.
E-mail: administration@mnec.gov.tl.net
Website: www.mfac.gov.tp

UN Development Programme (UNDP)
Street address: UN Agency House, Caicoli Street, Dili, East Timor
Postal address: UNDP Timor-Leste, PO Box 2436, Darwin, NT 0801, Australia.
Tel: (3) 312 481 (general enquiries) *or* 418 ext. 2044 (media section).
Fax: (3) 312 408.
E-mail: registry.tp@undp.org
Website: www.undp.east-timor.org

Embassy of East Timor
Avenue de Cortenbergh, Cortenberghlaan 12, 1040 Brussels, Belgium
Tel: (2) 280 0096.
Fax: (2) 280 0377.

Embassy of East Timor
3415 Massachusetts Avenue, NW, Washington, DC 20007, USA
Tel: (202) 965 1515.
Fax: (202) 965 1517.

US Embassy
Avenida do Portugal, Farol, Dili, East Timor
Tel: (3) 324 684.
Fax: (3) 313 206/008.
The British Embassy, like most in East Timor, offers limited services and does not offer consular and visa services (such as replacing passports) and has only limited facilities to help in an emergency.

TIMATIC CODES

Health	AMADEUS: **TI-DFT/JIB/HE** GALILEO/WORLDSPAN: **TI-DFT/JIB/HE** SABRE: **TIDFT/JIB/HE**
Visa	AMADEUS: **TI-DFT/JIB/VI** GALILEO/WORLDSPAN: **TI-DFT/JIB/VI** SABRE: **TIDFT/JIB/VI**

To access TIMATIC country information on Health and Visa regulations through the Computer Reservations System (CRS), type in the appropriate command line listed above.

General Information

AREA: 14,609 sq km (5641 sq miles).
POPULATION: 779,000 (UN estimate 2003).
POPULATION DENSITY: 50.5 per sq km.
CAPITAL: Dili. **Population:** 50,800 (estimate 2003).
GEOGRAPHY: East Timor makes up the eastern half of the island of Timor (the western half belongs to Indonesia) which is situated off the northern coast of Western Australia. Also included within East Timor is the Oekussi Ambeno enclave on the northwest coast of the island, as well as the islands of Ataúro (Pulo Cambing) and Jaco (Pulo Jako). East Timor is mountainous in the interior.
GOVERNMENT: Republic. Declared full independence 20 May 2002 after the UN Transitional Authority in East Timor (UNTAET) had run the country for nearly three years during its transition to independence. Prior to UNTAET, the country had been under Indonesian control since 1975. **President:** Xanana Gusmao since May 2002. **Prime Minister:** Mari Alkatiri since May 2002.
LANGUAGE: Tetum is the main dialect and is the official language along with Portuguese; English is often used for administrative purposes (due to the high numbers of English- speaking relief and UN workers still working in East Timor). More than 30 other languages are also used in East Timor.
RELIGION: Christian majority with 86 per cent Catholic. Islam and animist beliefs are also practised.
TIME: GMT + 8.
ELECTRICITY: 220 V, 50 Hz. Electricity supplies may be erratic with many power cuts.
COMMUNICATIONS: Telephone: International calls can be made from and to Dili. The code for Dili is 390. **Mobile telephone:** Coverage provided by *Timor Telecom International* in and around Dili and other main urban areas. International roaming agreements are stilll being set up but cannot be relied upon as yet. In some parts of the country, however, telephone communication may still only be possible with satellite telephones. **Fax:** Facilities exist in Dili in major organisations and hotels. **Internet:** Facilities are not generally available to the public at the present time. **Post:** A limited postal service does exist. **Press:** The *Timor Post* is published daily in English; *Tais Timor* is published every fortnight in English.
Radio: BBC World Service (website: www.bbc.co.uk/worldservice) and Voice of America (website: www.voa.gov) can be received. From time to time the frequencies change and the most up-to-date can be found online.

Passport/Visa

Note: Potential travellers are advised against all non-essential travel to East Timor and to monitor the situation regularly. The following visa information was obtained from the UK Foreign and Commonwealth website.

	Passport Required?	Visa Required?	Return Ticket Required?
Full British	Yes	1	Yes
Australian	Yes	1	Yes
Canadian	Yes	1	Yes
USA	Yes	1	Yes
Other EU	Yes	1	Yes
Japanese	Yes	1	Yes

Note: *Regulations and requirements may be subject to change at short notice, and you are advised to contact the appropriate diplomatic or consular authority before finalising travel arrangements. Details of these may be found at the head of this country's entry. Any numbers in the chart refer to the footnotes below.*

VISAS: 1. Visas are currently not necessary as long as travellers have a valid passport. Upon arrival, an entry permit valid for 30 days will be issued. If the traveller can prove that he/she has valid grounds for staying in East Timor, they can then obtain an extension.
Types of visa and cost: From 19 April 2003, East Timor began to charge a fee for visas issued on arrival. They cost US$30 for stays of 30 days and less; extensions cost US$30 for each subsequent period of 30 days. Fines of US$50 apply to each 30-day period if advance payment and extension of visas have not been sought and approved. There is a US$10 fee for airport tax, paid at the airport on the day of departure.

Money

Currency: The US Dollar is the official currency. For local transactions, the Indonesian Rupiah may be accepted in border areas, but this should not be relied on.
Currency exchange: Travellers should take plenty of hard currency in cash. Both the Australian ANZ bank and the Portuguese Banco Nacional Ultramarino have branches in Dili. Cirrus/Maestro credit cards can be used to withdraw US Dollars from an ATM.
Credit & debit cards: These can only currently be used in the very few expensive hotels in East Timor. Check with your credit or debit card company for further details of merchant acceptability and other services which may be available.
Travellers cheques: Travellers cheques are not widely exchangeable. Only some top-of-the-range hotels may be able to exchange them.
Currency restrictions: Import is allowed, although amounts of US$5000 and above must be declared.
Exchange rate indicators: The following figures are included as a guide to the movements of the US Dollar against Sterling:

Date	Feb '04	May '04	Aug '04	Nov '04
£1.00=	1.82	1.79	1.84	1.89

Banking hours: Information not currently available.

Duty Free

Information not available at the time of writing.

Public Holidays

2005: Jan 1 New Year's Day. **Mar 25** Good Friday. **May 20** Independence Day. **Aug 15** Assumption. **Aug 30** Consultation Day. **Sep 20** Liberation Day. **Nov 1** All Saints' Day. **Nov 12** Santa Cruz Day (memorial day for the 1991 massacre in the cemetery of the Santa Cruz church). **Dec 8** Immaculate Conception. **Dec 25** Christmas.
2006: Jan 1 New Year's Day. **Apr 14** Good Friday. **May 20** Independence Day. **Aug 15** Assumption. **Aug 30** Consultation Day. **Sep 20** Liberation Day. **Nov 1** All Saints' Day. **Nov 12** Santa Cruz Day (memorial day for the 1991 massacre in the cemetery of the Santa Cruz church). **Dec 8** Immaculate Conception. **Dec 25** Christmas.

Health

	Special Precautions?	Certificate Required?
Yellow Fever	No	1
Cholera	Yes	2
Typhoid & Polio	3	N/A
Malaria	4	N/A

Note: *Regulations and requirements may be subject to change at short notice, and you are advised to contact your doctor well in advance of your intended date of departure. Any numbers in the chart refer to the footnotes below.*

1: A yellow fever vaccination certificate is advisable for travellers coming from infected areas. The countries and areas included in the yellow fever endemic zones are considered by East Timor as infected areas. For a map of yellow fever endemic zones, see the *Health* appendix.
2: Following WHO guidelines issued in 1973, a cholera vaccination certificate is no longer a condition of entry to East Timor. However, cholera is a serious risk in this country and precautions are essential. Up-to-date advice should be sought before deciding whether these precautions should include vaccination as medical opinion is divided over its effectiveness, see the *Health* appendix.
3: Poliomyelitis is endemic. Typhoid occurs frequently.
4: Malaria risk exists throughout the year. Some resistance to chloroquine has been reported.
Other risks: *Dengue fever* (there has been a particularly large outbreak of this in 2005) and *Japanese encephalitis* occur. *Tuberculosis* and *hepatitis A* are prevalent and *rabies* may also be present.

Food & drink: All water should be regarded as a potential health risk. Water used for drinking, brushing teeth or making ice should have first been boiled or otherwise sterilised. Milk is unpasteurised and should be boiled. Powdered or tinned milk is available and is advised, but make sure that it is reconstituted with pure water. Avoid dairy products that are likely to have been made from unboiled milk. Only eat well-cooked meat and fish, preferably served hot. Salad and mayonnaise may carry increased risk. Vegetables should be cooked and fruit peeled.
Health care: Medical services in East Timor are extemely limited. There are currently no optical or dental services. It is essential to take out comprehensive medical and travel insurance which includes emergency repatriation cover.

Travel - International

Note: East Timor shares a threat from terrorism with the rest of South-East Asia. Attacks could be indiscriminate and against civilian targets. Demonstrations and large crowds should be avoided. There remains the potential for trouble in border areas and these may wish to be bypassed.
AIR: *Airnorth (4N)* (website: www.airnorth.com.au) flies daily from Darwin, Australia to Dili. *Qantas* (website: www.qantas.com.au) also flies to Dili.
Approximate flight times: From *Darwin* to Dili is 2 hours 15 minutes.
International airports: *Comoro Airport (DIL)*, Dili. Some international flights use *Baucau Airport (BCH)* in the province of Baucau.
Departure tax: US$10.
ROAD: The border crossings at Batugede and Oesilo, into Indonesian West Timor, are open. Roads and driving conditions are very poor (including in Dili) and drivers must take extreme caution. To drive, travellers need a valid driver's licence or permit either from their country or issued in East Timor, and detailing which class of vehicle they are entitled to drive. Third-party motor vehicle insurance is not available.

Travel - Internal

SEA: There is one weekly barge between Oekusi and Dili, carrying both freight and passengers.
ROAD: Bus links are bad. Most of the buses that existed prior to 1999 were destroyed in the fighting; the few that survived are in very bad technical shape and chronically overcrowded. The roads are generally in very bad condition and driving can be very hazardous. Car hire is available in Dili. Mountain bikes may be a viable form of transport outside of the capital.

Accommodation

HOTELS AND MOTELS: Hotel rooms and other accommodation are still very limited and very expensive, especially for independent travellers. A government tax of 12 per cent is added to all bills.

Resorts & Excursions

East Timor is made up of 13 provinces. Colonial architecture, Portuguese fortresses and other remains from the 100-year-long Portuguese occupation can be found all over the country. However, many towns and villages were destroyed during the Indonesian occupation and the fighting in 1999, which are slowly being rebuilt. Many houses are still built on stilts in the traditional way, using local materials such as grass, bamboo, tree trunks and palm leaves.
DILI: The capital of Portuguese East Timor, Dili is today the administrative capital of the new country. Colonial architecture abounds in Dili, along with a **Portuguese castle** dating from 1627. Another attraction is the **State Museum of East Timor**, founded in 1995, with one-tenth of its collection still surviving. The collection includes religious woodcarvings, wood figures, traditional crafts, musical instruments and paintings. Most of the city was destroyed in 1999, with any surviving buildings bearing considerable war wounds. UNTAET led restoration works by rebuilding the most important government and official buildings. There are many **catholic churches** in Dili and a famous, large statue of Christ on a hilltop near **Cape Fatucama**. Outside the city, there are numerous beautiful beaches, the most popular being **Areia Branca** ('white sand').
BAUCAU: The second-largest city in East Timor, Baucau is still charming despite the devastation it has incurred, with Portuguese colonial architecture and caves used by the Japanese during the occupation in World War II. Due to its location, Baucau is always comfortably cool and the beaches 5km (3 miles) from the city are breathtaking. The four-hour journey between Dili and Baucau is well worth taking, offering some of the finest coastal views.
Elsewhere: Oecussi province belongs to East Timor politically, yet is a part of Indonesian West Timor culturally and geographically; it was 95 per cent destroyed during the fighting and the remaining inhabitants mostly live in small hamlets and villages. Its capital, **Pantemakassar**, was the first Portuguese settlement and, as such, has special meaning for the East Timorese. A sleepy little town, it lies between the coast and the mountains. Coral reefs off the nearby coast offer the opportunity for diving and snorkelling. Mountain biking and hiking are possible in the interior or in the mountains.

Social Profile

FOOD & DRINK: The staple diet for most East Timorese is similar to that of Indonesians – rice and spices – although, at present, there may be difficulty in obtaining a variety of foods outside main urban areas due to the unstable political situation, the financial situation of many of the people and internal logistical difficulties. In Dili, there are a number of restaurants and cafes serving 'western' cuisine, catering to the foreigners living and working there.
SHOPPING: Batik and embroidered fabrics in traditional patterns and colours are a good souvenir buy; others include woodcarvings and silverwork.
SPECIAL EVENTS: Celebrations of Christian festivals, plus commemorations of landmark dates in East Timor's recent independence are the most common special events (see *Public Holidays* section).
SOCIAL CONVENTIONS: Most social courtesies are fairly formal. Many conventions will be similar to those of Indonesia (despite their political and religious differences) and many old East Timorese conventions will doubtless come to the fore in the coming years.

Business Profile

ECONOMY: Subsistence agriculture, forestry and fishing sustain most of the population. The sole export products are coffee beans and sandalwood. The economy as a whole was chronically underdeveloped as a result of centuries of neglect by the Portuguese. The Indonesians built some basic infrastructure (roads, power, telecommunications), but most of that was destroyed or removed by the Indonesians themselves and their client militias in the aftermath of the August 1999 vote for independence. Since then, East Timor's principal source of income has been international aid. However, the country's originally poor economic prospects have been transformed by the discovery of large oil and gas fields in the Timor Sea, which lies between Timor itself and the north coast of Australia. Under the terms of a deal negotiated between East Timor and the Australian government, the East Timorese will receive a fixed income of around US$180 million from 2006. (Additional oil and gas deposits have also been discovered in the same area.) There are some doubts about the integrity of the deal. In any event, until then, East Timor will remain one of the region's poorest nations, with a per capita annual income of US$500 (2001 estimate).
COMMERCIAL INFORMATION: Limited information and advice is available from the Department for Economic Affairs and Planning (website: www.gov.east-timor.org).

Climate

Tropical monsoon climate. It is very hot and dry from July to November with the western monsoon bringing the rains from December to March. It is cooler and more humid in the mountain region.
Required clothing: Lightweights with rainwear throughout the year. Warmer clothes are needed for cool evenings and mountain areas.

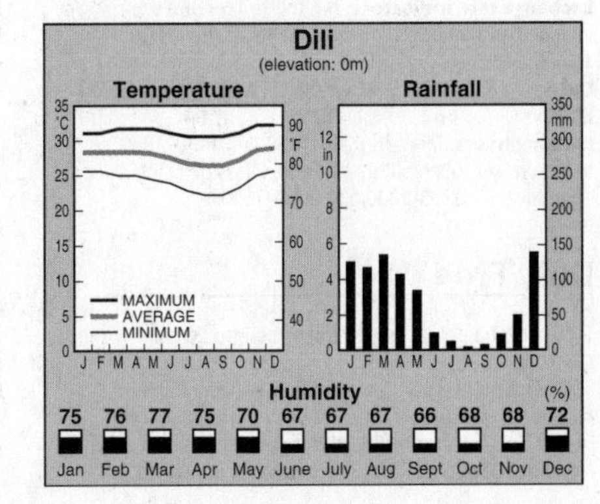

Ecuador

LATEST TRAVEL ADVICE CONTACTS

British Foreign and Commonwealth Office
Tel: (0870) 606 0290 Website: www.fco.gov.uk
US Department of State
Website: http://travel.state.gov/travel
Canadian Department of Foreign Affairs and Int'l Trade
Tel: (1 800) 267 8376 Website: www.dfait-maeci.gc.ca

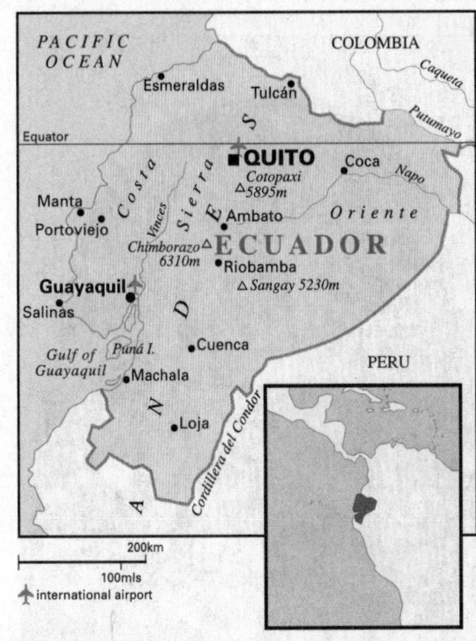

Location: South America.

Country dialling code: 593.

Ministerio de Turismo (Ministry of Tourism)
Avenida Eloy Alfaro N32-300 y Carlos Tobar, Quito, Ecuador
Tel: (2) 222 8304. Fax: (2) 222 9330.
E-mail: info@vivecuador.com *or* ministra@turismo.gov.ec
Website: www.vivecuador.com
Cámara Provincial de Turismo (CAPTUR)
Av. Amazonas y Patria (esq.), Edificio Cofiec, Piso 3, Quito, Ecuador
Tel: (2) 223 1198 *or* 222 9330. Fax: (2) 250 7682.
E-mail: captur@captur.com
Website: www.captur.com
Embassy of the Republic of Ecuador
Flat 3B, Hans Crescent, London SW1X 0LS, UK
Tel: (020) 7584 1367. Fax: (020) 7823 9701.
E-mail: embajada.ecuador@btclick.com
Opening hours: Mon-Fri 0930-1300.
British Embassy
Street address: Piso 14, Edificio Citiplaza, Avenida Naciones Unidas y República de El Salvador, Quito, Ecuador
Postal address: PO Box 17-17-830, Quito, Ecuador
Consular Section: Piso 12, Edificio Citiplaza, Avenida Naciones Unidas y República de El Salvador, Quito, Ecuador
Tel: (2) 297 0800/1. Fax: (2) 297 0809.
E-mail: britembq@uio.satnet.net *or* consuio@uio.satnet.net
Website: www.britembquito.org.ec
Honourary Consulates in: Galápagos and Guayaquil.
Embassy of the Republic of Ecuador
2535 15th Street, NW, Washington, DC 20009, USA
Tel: (202) 234 7200 *or* 234 7166. Fax: (202) 667 3482 *or* 265 9325.
E-mail: embassy@ecuador.org *or* consuladodc@ecuador.org
Website: www.ecuador.org
Embassy of the United States of America
Patria y Avenida 12 Octubre, Quito, Ecuador
Tel: (2) 256 2890. Fax: (2) 250 2052 *or* 256 1524 (consular section).
Website: www.usembassy.org.ec
Honourary Consulate in: Guayaquil.

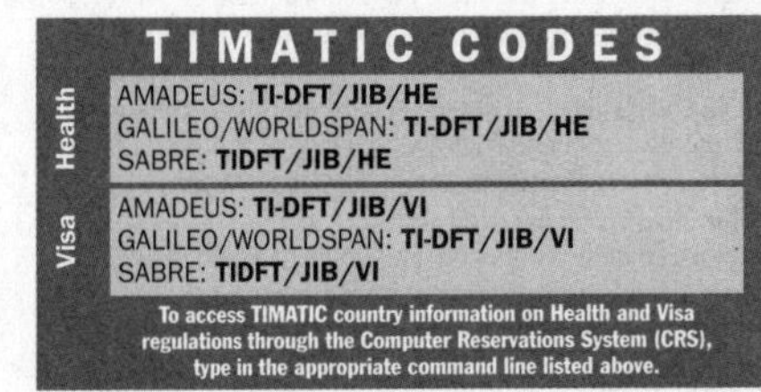
TIMATIC CODES

Health
AMADEUS: **TI-DFT/JIB/HE**
GALILEO/WORLDSPAN: **TI-DFT/JIB/HE**
SABRE: **TIDFT/JIB/HE**

Visa
AMADEUS: **TI-DFT/JIB/VI**
GALILEO/WORLDSPAN: **TI-DFT/JIB/VI**
SABRE: **TIDFT/JIB/VI**

To access TIMATIC country information on Health and Visa regulations through the Computer Reservations System (CRS), type in the appropriate command line listed above.

Embassy of the Republic of Ecuador
Suite 316, 50 O'Connor Street, Ottawa, Ontario K1P 6L2, Canada
Tel: (613) 563 8206. Fax: (613) 235 5776.
E-mail: mecuacan@rogers.ca
Consulates in: British Columbia, Montréal and Toronto.

Canadian Embassy
Street address: Avenida 6 de Diciembre, 2816 y Paul Rivet, Edificio Josueth Gonzales, 4th Floor, Quito, Ecuador
Postal address: PO Box 17-11-8512, Quito, Ecuador
Tel: (2) 250 6162 *or* 223 2040. Fax: (2) 250 3108.
E-mail: quito@dfait-maeci.gc.ca
Website: www.dfait-maeci.gc.ca/ecuador *or* www.quito.gc.ca
Honourary Consulate in: Guayaquil.

Credit: © Klein Tours

General Information

AREA: 272,045 sq km (105,037 sq miles).
POPULATION: 12,810,000 (official estimate 2002).
POPULATION DENSITY: 44.7 per sq km.
CAPITAL: Quito. **Population:** 1,399,378 (2001).
GEOGRAPHY: Ecuador is bordered to the north by Colombia, to the east and south by Peru, and to the west by the Pacific Ocean. There are three distinct zones: the *Sierra* or uplands of the Andes, running from the Colombian border in the north to Peru in the south (of this there are two main ranges - the Eastern and Western Cordilleras, which are divided by a long valley); the *Costa*, a coastal plain between the Andes and the Pacific with plantations of bananas, cacao, coffee and sugar; and the *Oriente*, the upper Amazon basin to the east, consisting of tropical jungles threaded by rivers. The latter, although comprising 36 per cent of Ecuador's land area, contains only 3 per cent of the population. Colonisation is, however, increasing in the wake of the oil boom.
GOVERNMENT: Democratic republic since 1978. **Head of State and Govenment:** President Lucio Edwin Gutiérrez Borbúa since 2003.
LANGUAGE: Spanish is the official language but Quechua and other indigenous languages are common. Some English is spoken.
RELIGION: More than 90 per cent are nominally Roman Catholic.
TIME: GMT - 5 (Galapagos Islands GMT - 6).
ELECTRICITY: 110/120 volts AC, 60Hz.
COMMUNICATIONS: Telephone: Country code: 593. Outgoing international code: 00. **Mobile telephone:** AMPS network is operated by *Otecel*, and AMPS-TDMA network is operated by *Conecel*. A GSM 850 network was set up in 2003. **Internet:** ISPs include *Interactive* (website: www.interactive.net.ec). **Telegram:** These may be sent from the chief telegraph office in main towns. **Post:** Airmail to western Europe and the USA takes up to one week, but incoming deliveries are less certain. **Press:** Dailies are in Spanish and include *El Comercio* (website: www.elcomercio.com) and *Hoy* (website: www.hoy.net), published in Quito; and *El Telégrafo* (website: www.telegrafo.com.ec) and *El Universo* (website: www.eluniverso.com), published in Guayaquil. There are two English-language newspapers, *Inside Ecuador* and *Q*, though both are published irregularly. International newspapers and magazines are available at international airports, main post offices and in some bookshops.
Radio: BBC World Service (website: www.bbc.co.uk/worldservice) and Voice of America (website: www.voa.gov) can be received. From time to time the frequencies change and the most up-to-date can be found online.

Passport/Visa

	Passport Required?	Visa Required?	Return Ticket Required?
Full British	Yes	1	Yes
Australian	Yes	1	Yes
Canadian	Yes	1	Yes
USA	Yes	1	Yes
Other EU	Yes	1	Yes
Japanese	Yes	1	Yes

Note: Regulations and requirements may be subject to change at short notice, and you are advised to contact the appropriate diplomatic or consular authority before finalising travel arrangements. Details of these may be found at the head of this country's entry. Any numbers in the chart refer to the footnotes below.

PASSPORTS: Passport valid for at least six months required by all, except nationals of Colombia with an identity card.
Note: Passports must be carried at all times.
VISAS: Required *only* by:
(a) nationals of Afghanistan, Algeria, Bangladesh, China (PR), Costa Rica, Cuba, Guatemala, Honduras, India, Iran, Iraq, Jordan, Korea (Dem Rep), Korea (Rep), Lebanon, Libya, Nigeria, Pakistan, Palestinian Authority Area, Sri Lanka, Sudan, Syrian Arab Republic, Tunisia, Vietnam and Yemen;
(b) **1.** all nationals wishing to remain in Ecuador for more than three months.
Note: (a) Nationals listed above also require a visa even when in transit, unless continuing their journey to a third country by the same or first connecting flight or within 48 hours, provided holding confirmed onward tickets and not leaving the airport. As this list may change at short notice, visitors to Ecuador are advised to check with the nearest Consulate *before* travelling. (b) Those with visas must register with the Ministry of Government and the Director General of Migration in Ecuador within 30 days of their entry.
Types of visa and cost: *Tourist*: £40. *Business*: £153.
Validity: *Tourist* visas are valid for up to six months; *Business* visas are valid as long as necessary.
Application to: Consulate (or Consular section at Embassy); see *Contact Addresses* section.
Application requirements: (a) Completed application form. (b) Two passport-size photos. (c) Valid passport. (d) Fee. (e) Return ticket. (f) Proof of economic solvency; for instance, the applicant's last three bank statements. *Tourist*: (a)-(f) and, (g) Letter of invitation from an Ecuadorian resident or proof of hotel reservation. *Business*: (a)-(f) and, (g) Letter from applicant's firm and sponsoring company.
Working days required: Applications must be made in person (an appointment is necessary) and a visa is usually issued on the same day.
Temporary residence: Persons wishing to stay longer than six months should apply to the Consulate for details.

Money

Currency: US Dollar (US$) = 100 cents. Notes are in denominations of US$100, 50, 20, 10, 5, 2 and 1. Coins are in denominations of US$1 and 50, 25, 10, 5 and 1 cents. The US Dollar replaced the Sucre as the official currency of Ecuador in September 2000.
Currency exchange: Foreign currencies can be exchanged at banks and at exchange houses (*casas de cambio*), the latter being generally the best option. It may be difficult to exchange money in the Oriente. The rate of commission varies between 1 per cent and 4 per cent, so it is worth shopping around. ATMs are available in large urban areas.
Credit & debit cards: American Express, Diners Club, MasterCard and Visa are accepted. Check with your credit or debit card company for details of merchant acceptability and other services which may be available.
Travellers cheques: Travellers cheques are generally accepted in the larger cities and can be exchanged into currency at most banks.
Currency restrictions: There are no restrictions on the import and export of either local or foreign currency.
Exchange rate indicators: The following figures are included as a guide to the movements of the US Dollar against Sterling:

Date	Feb '04	May '04	Aug '04	Nov '04
£1.00=	1.82	1.79	1.84	1.89

Banking hours: Mon-Fri 0900-1330 and 1430-1830; some banks are also open Sat 0930-1400. Casos de cambio are open Mon-Fri 0900-1800, Sat 0900-1200.

Duty Free

The following goods may be imported into Ecuador without incurring customs duty:
300 cigarettes or 50 cigars or 200g of tobacco; 1l of alcohol; a reasonable amount of perfume; gifts and personal effects up to US$200 (for stays of up to seven days) or US$500 (for stays of two years onwards).
Note: Prior permission is required for the import of firearms, ammunition, fresh or dry meat and meat products, plants and vegetables.

Public Holidays

2005: Jan 1 New Year's Day. **Mar 24** Maundy Thursday. **Mar 25** Good Friday. **May 1** Labour Day. **May 24** Battle of Pichincha. **May 26** Corpus Christi. **Jul 24** Simon Bolivar Day. **Aug 10** Independence Day. **Nov 2** All Souls' Day. **Dec 25** Christmas Day. **Dec 31** New Year's Eve.
2006: Jan 1 New Year's Day. **Apr 13** Maundy Thursday. **Apr 14** Good Friday. **May 1** Labour Day. **May 24** Battle of Pichincha. **Jun 15** Corpus Christi. **Jul 24** Simon Bolivar Day. **Aug 10** Independence Day. **Nov 2** All Souls' Day. **Dec 25** Christmas Day. **Dec 31** New Year's Eve.
Note: Ecuador's Carnival (in March/April), the Foundation of Guayaquil (usually in October), the Foundation of Cuenca (usually in November) and the Foundation of Quito (usually in December) are not official public holidays, but are widely observed. Other holidays, in addition to the above, may be marked locally.

Health

	Special Precautions?	Certificate Required?
Yellow Fever	Yes	1
Cholera	2	No
Typhoid & Polio	3	N/A
Malaria	4	N/A

Note: Regulations and requirements may be subject to change at short notice, and you are advised to contact your doctor well in advance of your intended date of departure. Any numbers in the chart refer to the footnotes below.

1: A yellow fever vaccination certificate is required from all travellers over one year of age arriving from infected areas. Travellers arriving from non-endemic zones should note that vaccination is strongly recommended for travel outside the urban areas, even if an outbreak of the disease has not been reported and they would normally not require a vaccination certificate to enter the country.
2: Following WHO guidelines issued in 1973, a cholera vaccination certificate is no longer a condition of entry to Ecuador. However, cholera is a serious risk in this country and precautions are essential. Up-to-date advice should be sought before deciding whether these precautions should include vaccination as medical opinion is divided over its effectiveness; see the *Health* appendix for further information.
3: Typhoid poses some risk in rural areas.
4: Malaria risk, predominantly in the benign *vivax* form, is high throughout the year below 1500m in 148 cantons in 19 provinces. A high proportion of *falciparum* cases in Esmeraldas Province are reportedly resistant to chloroquine. There is no risk in Guayaquil or Quito.
Food & drink: All water should be regarded as being potentially contaminated. Water used for drinking, brushing teeth or making ice should have first been boiled or otherwise sterilised. Bottled water is available. Milk is unpasteurised and should be boiled. Powdered or tinned milk is available and is advised, but make sure that it is reconstituted with pure water. Avoid dairy products which are likely to have been made from unboiled milk. Only eat well-cooked meat and fish, preferably served hot. Pork, salad and mayonnaise may carry increased risk. Vegetables should be cooked and fruit peeled.
Other risks: *Endemic onchocerciasis* occurs in rural areas. *Hepatitis A* and *B* are hyperendemic and inoculation with gamma globulin is highly recommended. *Hepatitis D* is endemic in the Amazon Basin. *Dengue fever* might occur. *Altitude sickness* is a risk flying directly into Quito (2800m). *Rabies* is present. For those at high risk, vaccination before arrival should be considered. If you are bitten, seek medical advice without delay. For more information, consult the Health appendix.
Health care: Medical facilities outside the major towns are extremely limited. Health insurance (to include emergency repatriation) is strongly recommended.

Travel - International

Note: Travel to the northern border, including the provinces of Sucumbios and Orcllana, is advised against. Armed groups are active in these areas and there is a high risk of kidnapping and crime. Staying overnight in Baros, due to the threat of the Tungurahue volcano erupting, is also advised against. There is an ongoing risk of disruptions to travel due to social and political unrest.
AIR: Ecuador's national airline, *TAME (EQ)* (website: www.tame.com.ec), connects Ecuador with the USA and some South American countries. *American Airlines (AA)*

operates daily flights from London Heathrow to Guayaquil, via Miami or New York.
Approximate flight times: From Quito to *London* is 17 hours, to *Los Angeles* is 9 hours and to *New York* is 9 hours 30 minutes.
International airports: *Quito (UIO)* (Mariscal Sucre) is 8km (5 miles) from the city centre. A bus service operates frequently, 1100-0300 (travel time 20 to 30 minutes). Return is from Avenida 10 de Agosto. Taxis are also available. The airport facilities include a medical department, bars, car hire, duty-free shops, post office and restaurants.
Guayaquil (GYE) (Simón Bolivar) is 5km (3 miles) from the city. There are bus and taxi services into the city.
Departure tax: US$25.
The Visit South America Pass: This must be bought outside South America in country of residence and allows unlimited travel to 36 cities in the following countries: Argentina, Bolivia, Brazil, Colombia, Chile (except Easter Island), Ecuador, Paraguay, Peru, Uruguay and Venezuela. Participating airlines include *Aer Lingus (EI)*, *American Airlines (AA)*, *British Airways (BA)*, *Cathay Pacific (CX)*, *Finnair (AY)*, *IBERIA (IB)*, *LAN-Chile (LA)* and *Qantas (QF)*. A minimum of three flights must be booked, with no maximum; the maximum stay is 60 days, with no minimum, and prices depend on the amount of flight zones covered. Children under 12 years of age are entitled to a 33 per cent discount and infants (under two years old) only pay 10 per cent of the adult fare. For further details, contact one of the participating airlines or visit www.oneworld.com.
SEA: There are regular passenger/cargo services from Europe, including *Hamburg-South American*, *Johnson Lines*, *Knutsen* and *Royal Netherlands* which take 20 to 22 days from Rotterdam and Le Havre. Others sail from Antwerp, Genoa and Liverpool, and the US West Coast (*Delta Line Cruises*). Guayaquil is the main port for both passengers and freight. However, it is becoming increasingly difficult to secure this kind of passage.
ROAD: The Pan-American Highway bisects the country from the Colombian border at Rumichaca south to Quito and on to Riobamba, Cuenca, Loja and ending at Macará near the border with Peru. **Bus:** *Panamericana Internacional* operates direct services to Caracas, Venezuela (tel: (2) 250 1585). *Rutas de América* operates direct services to Colombia, Peru and Venezuela with connections to Argentina, Bolivia, Brazil, Chile, Paraguay and Uruguay (tel/fax: (2) 254 8142; fax: (2) 250 3612). Visitors should remember to carry their passports at all times as there may be frequent controls, both within Ecuador and at border crossings.

Travel - Internal

AIR: The national airline, *TAME*, flies frequently between Guayaquil, Quito and other destinations throughout the country. A number of small airlines serve the coast and eastern part of the country. Flying is the usual mode of transport for intercity travel. Other airports include *Coca*, *Cuenca*, *Esmeraldas*, *Lago Agrio* and *Manta*.
Departure tax: 12 per cent of the ticket price, paid with the ticket.
Galápagos Islands: There are daily flights to the Galápagos Islands on national airlines from both Quito and Guayaquil; note that non-Ecuadorians have to pay more for their tickets on this route (US$100 for adults and US$50 for children is charged for visiting any national park). The main airports in the Galápagos are *Baltra* and *Caráquez*.
SEA/RIVER: Ecuador's rocky coastline makes coast-hopping an inefficient and even dangerous means of transport for visitors. Several navigable rivers flow eastwards into the Amazon basin. Dugout canoes, which carry up to about 25 people, are widely used as a means of transport in roadless areas, particularly in the Oriente jungles and in the northwest coastal regions. There are few passenger services between the mainland and the Galápagos Islands; once there, however, tourist boats, local mail steamers and hired yachts may be used to travel between islands.
RAIL: The journey from Guayaquil to Quito offers spectacular views, as the train climbs to 3238m (10,623ft) in 80km (50 miles), reaching its highest point at Urbina (3609m/11,841ft). Railway enthusiasts will also enjoy the particularly scenic sections on the Alausi-Duran and Ibarra-San Lorenzo sections. Landslides caused by heavy rain frequently disrupt train services. Always check for further details on arrival in the country.
ROAD: Traffic drives on the right. An extensive network of roads spreads out from the main north-south axis of the Pan-American Highway. The Government and *PetroEcuador* are developing highways into the Oriente. In general, road improvements are being put into effect rapidly but, due to the effect of earthquakes and flooding (in the south) during the last 10 years, conditions remain variable; potholes and cracks in the road are sometimes sizeable. The roads between Quito and Guayaquil and between Quito, Latacunga, Ambato and Riobamba are completely paved. A road connects Quito, Otavalo, Ibarra and Tulcán, the frontier with Colombia. **Bus:** Long-distance buses leave from central bus stations (*terminal terrestre*) but timetables can be unreliable. Tickets should be bought in advance to secure a seat. Buses generally tend to be crowded and fairly uncomfortable. **Taxis:** These are widely available, particularly in larger cities and towns. Fares tend to be low but should be negotiated in advance. Taxis are metered in Quito, but rarely elsewhere. Taxis may be hired for a whole day. **Car hire**: *Avis*, *Budget* and *Hertz* car hire companies all operate in Ecuador. **Documentation:** An International Driving Permit is not required.
URBAN: Guayaquil and Quito have bus and minibus services operating at flat fares.
Travel Times: The following chart gives approximate travel times (in hours and minutes) from **Quito** to other major cities and towns in Ecuador.

	Air	Road	Rail
Guayaquil	0.50	7.00	7.00
Cuenca	1.30	9.30	-
Ambato	-	2.30	-
Riobamba	-	3.30	3.00
Esmeraldas	1.00	7.00	-
Puerto Ayora	2.30	-	-

Accommodation

HOTELS: Hotel rooms should be booked at least one week in advance. Outside the main towns, a more or less standard price is charged per person for one night in a *provision residencia*, or a hotel. There is, however, a minimum charge per person. A 10 per cent service charge and 5 per cent tax are added to upper- and middle-range hotel bills. Cheaper hotels usually charge 5 per cent at the most. Hotel accommodation is very limited on the Galápagos Islands. Further information is available through the national hotel association, Federación Hotelera del Ecuador (AHOTEC), Avenida América 5378 y Diguja, Edificio San Francisco, Piso 2, Quito (tel: (2) 244 3425; fax: (2) 245 3942; e-mail: ahotec@interactive.net.ec). **Grading:** Hotels in Ecuador have been graded into three main categories according to standard and price bracket. All categories provide at least basic facilities.
CAMPING/CARAVANNING: Camping facilities in Ecuador are run by US or European agencies, but these are very limited. Camping is prohibited on the Galápagos Islands except in one of the three designated campsites. A permit is required and can be obtained from the park offices.

Credit: © Klein Tours

Resorts & Excursions

QUITO

Ecuador's capital (and second-largest) city has a setting of great natural beauty, overshadowed by the volcano **Pichincha** with its twin peaks of **Ruco** and **Guagua**. Quito is located at 2850m (9348 ft) above sea level and some visitors may suffer from altitude sickness during the first hours after arrival. Quito used to be a major Inca city that was destroyed shortly before the arrival of the Spanish conquistadors. Although no Inca traces remain, the city has preserved much of its Spanish colonial character, the cathedral in the **Plaza de la Independencia** (the oldest church in South America) and the many old churches and monasteries being among the most notable instances. Also in the plaza is the **Municipal Palace**, the **Archbishop's Palace** and the **Palacio Presidencial**. Many of the city's famous churches and monasteries contain priceless examples of Spanish art and sculpture, particularly the **Monasterio de San Francisco** (located in the beautiful plaza of the same name) and the **Jesuit church of La Compañía**. Most of Quito's colonial churches are located in the Old Town, parts of which have been listed by UNESCO as a World Heritage Site. Perhaps the best preserved colonial street is the historic alley of **la Ronda**. Other places in Quito worth visiting include the **Parque la Alameda** (a

Credit: © Klein Tours

triangular-shaped park), the **astronomical observatory**, the **School of Fine Arts** and the modern **Palacio Legislativo**. As the cultural and political capital, Quito has a number of museums of colonial and modern art. The **Museo del Banco Central**, located in the **Casa de la Cultura**, has a vast archaeological repertory as well as displays of colonial furniture and religious art. Also of interest is the **Museo Guayasamín**, home to many fine works of Ecuador's renowned modern artist Oswaldo Guayasamín.

THE ANDEAN HIGHLANDS

The Pan-American Highway traverses the country from north to south, a spectacular route which passes through all the principal cities of the Andean Highlands. **Tulcán**, centre of a rich farming area, is the northernmost of these. Further south is **Chota**, still inhabited by the descendants of former African slaves who retain some of their tribal customs (the city's population being made up largely of Africans). Chota's Indian market (particularly good for traditional art and weavings) is renowned throughout Ecuador. The peak of **Mount Imbabura** signals the approach to the valley of **Otavalo** (95km/60 miles from Quito), the town of the same name being famed for its craftwork and Indian market (which is at its biggest on Saturdays). Approaching Quito, one passes a granite monument which marks the Equator. South of Quito, the region of **Latacunga** and **Ambato** has much fine scenery, marked by an avenue of volcanoes. Two active ones are located within the **Parque Nacional Sangay**, a national park of outstanding beauty which has been listed by UNESCO as a World Heritage Site. The park is characterised by a variety of landscapes, ranging from rain forests to glaciers, as well as numerous indigenous animal species, such as the mountain tapir and the Andean condor. Located within Sangay park, the **Tunguraha** volcano (5016m/16,453ft) is popular with tourists, especially at night, since it became active again in 1999. West of Latacunga, the **Parque Nacional Cotopaxi** is Ecuador's most visited national park. It includes the active Cotopaxi volcano which, at 5895m (19,345ft), is the world's highest active volcano. All have refuges at the snow-line where intrepid walkers can make overnight stays. Visitors are, however, advised to be cautious when setting out on walking or trekking trips as robberies have been reported in certain areas; experienced mountain guides are available. Further south, the city of **Cuenca** was founded in 1577 and still contains many examples of Spanish colonial architecture. Contrasting with this, a vast cathedral has recently been built. The nearby ancient Inca settlement at **Ingapirca**, 50km (32 miles) north of Cuenca, is worth visiting. In the highlands of southern Ecuador, **Loja** is the last city of importance on the Pan-American Highway, being originally a trading station on the Spanish 'gold road'. Not far from Loja, the **Parque Nacional Podocarpus** is, along with Ecuador's other national parks, a popular destination for walking and climbing.

THE COAST

GUAYAQUIL: Ecuador's biggest city, Guayaquil is also the chief port and commercial centre. A good starting point for sightseeing is the **Rotonda**, the city's most historic landmark, which faces the beautiful garden promenade of **Paseo de las Colonias**. Across the malecón are the **Government Palace** and city hall, while, at the northern end, one can find the ancient fortress of **la Planchada**. Other places of interest include the **Church of Santo Domingo**, the old residential section of **Las Penas** and the **Municipal Museum**.
THE LITTORAL: This is a narrow coastal belt, 560km (350 miles) in length. The chief ports provide visitors with some of the best resorts for deep-sea fishing on the west coast. Particularly attractive are the towns of **Playas Posoria** and

Salinas, while **Esmeraldas**, one of the country's most important ports, is also known for its beautiful beaches. The relaxing island of **Muisne** is also becoming a popular destination. The region of **Santo Domingo de los Colorados**, situated some 90km (55 miles) west of Quito, is the domain of the Colorados Indians who still practise many of their ancient customs.

THE ORIENTE

El Oriente is the term used by Ecuadorians to refer to the Amazon basin in eastern Ecuador. This is a primeval world of virgin forests and exotic flora and fauna, still mainly inhabited by Indians. In January 1999, the Ecuadorian President issued a decree blocking future oil exploration, mining and colonisation by oil companies of the **Cuyabeno-Imuya** and **Yasuni** national parks. These parks are home to thousands of indigenous people, including the Huaorani, the Tagaeri, the Taromenare, the Secoyas and the Sionas. In recent years, the region has experienced ongoing conflicts between oil companies seeking to develop the area and indigenous communities afraid that development will lead to the destruction of their ancestral homeland and loss of their traditional way of life. The principal towns of the area are **El Puyo**, **Lago Agrio**, **Macas**, **Sucúa**, **Tena** and **Zamora**. Tourist excursions are available along the rivers, which provide the principal method of transport. One of the main rivers in this region is the **Napo** which, like most of the rivers in the Oriente, is a tributary of the Amazon (which lies further east in Peru). **Baños** is worth visiting, taking its name from the numerous springs and pools of hot and cold mineral waters. It is also the gateway to the Amazon region, passing through the spectacular gorge of the **River Pastaza**.

GALÁPAGOS ISLANDS

Situated about 1000km (625 miles) west of the Ecuadorian mainland, the islands are bleak, barren and rocky. Made famous by Charles Darwin's scientific voyage in the 'Beagle' during the 19th century, the islands' unique wildlife – which includes giant tortoises, lizards and iguanas – remains the most interesting feature for the modern-day visitor. Some 50 per cent of the islands' species are found nowhere else in the world. The islands have been turned into a national park in an attempt to preserve their natural state and, in 1978, UNESCO declared the Galápagos to be 'the universal natural heritage of humanity'. In 1998, the Government enacted a law for the 'Special Regime for the Conservation and Sustainable Development of the Galápagos Province', which states that the protection of the area is a state responsibility. Accommodation and travel can generally be arranged either inclusively from the visitor's home country or through local tour operators once in Ecuador. It is advisable to shop around and take advice before booking as the quality of service and reliability can vary greatly. For further information, contact the Galápagos Tour Operators Association (ASOGAL), Avenida de los Shyris 247 y Gaspar de Villarroel (tel: (2) 441 550; fax: (2) 436 625; e-mail: asogal@ecnet.ec; website: www.asogal.com). Accommodation is extremely limited and food is not cheap. There are a few small restaurants. Boat trips around the islands can be arranged locally.

Sport & Activities

Rainforest treks: Travellers wishing to explore the rainforest of the lower Amazon basin, and its abundant plant and animal life, should head to the Oriente region (see *Resorts & Excursions* section). It is probably best to do this as part of an organised tour, which can be booked with a number of local operators providing tailor-made itineraries and experienced guides. The presence of hundreds of waterways, many of which are tributaries of the great *River Amazon*, means that such tours invariably involve travelling by boat. Usually, these are large motorised canoes travelling up the main rivers (such as the *Aguarico* or the *Napo*), although trips on non-motorised boats along the smaller waterways are also available, which is a far better way to observe the wildlife. Several indigenous communities living in the region have preserved their traditional lifestyles and are actively engaged in resisting the ongoing attempts by oil companies to develop and exploit the Ecuadorian rainforest.
Hiking: There are some good hiking trails in *Cotopaxi National Park*, one of them following the shores of *Lago Limpiopungo*, located at an altitude of 3800m (12,465ft).
Climbing: Several tour operators based in Baños, Ecuador's tourist mecca for adventure sports and trips to the rainforest, also offer climbing expeditions to the volcanoes. Experienced climbers may head to the *Cotopaxi* volcano which, at 5985m (19,345ft), is one of the world's highest and is best reached from Quito.
Wildlife: Apart from the rainforest, Ecuador's rich wildlife is best represented in the Galápagos Islands, whose most famous inhabitants are the giant Galápagos tortoises (weighing up to 272kg/600lb). Adventure tours around the islands are available, either in large cruise ships or in smaller ships and yachts (advance booking is essential). The amount of time visitors are allowed to stay on the islands is regulated by the Government. For further details on the Galápagos Islands, see the *Resorts & Excursions* section.
Watersports: There are 2800km (1750 miles) of coastline along the mainland, with beach resorts offering various types of watersports. Good **snorkelling** is available via chartered boat trips around the *Isla de la Plata* (located in the *Parque Nacional Machalilla*, Ecuador's only coastal national park). **Fishing** is particularly good off the western coast. **Whitewater rafting** is also popular in and around Baños.
Scenic train journeys: Several of Ecuador's railway routes, particularly those in the Andes, pass through spectacular mountain scenery, often at dramatic altitudes. The Ecuadorian custom of riding on the roof of the train makes the views even more breathtaking. One of the most famous routes, whose climax is the precipitous 'Devil's Nose' passage, is from Riobamba down to the Pacific coast. Train schedules are fairly erratic and visitors should check locally prior to travelling.

Social Profile

FOOD & DRINK: Best of the jungle fruits include *chirimoya*, with a delicious custard-like inside; *mamey*, which has a red, sweet, squash-like meat; and *pepinos*, a sweet white and purple striped cucumber-like fruit. Specialities include *llapingachos* (pancakes stuffed with mashed potato and cheese); shrimp or lobster ceviche. This is traditionally accompanied by popcorn and chifles (thinly sliced and fried green bananas); *locro* (stew of potatoes and cheese); *humitas* (flavoured sweetcorn tamale); and the national delicacy of roasted guinea pig. Bakeries offer delicious sweet pastries and *empanadas* (hot crispy meat- or cheese-filled pastries). Another popular snack is *patacones* (squashed fried green bananas). You will often find that most Ecuadorian homes have a special pounding stone for making this tasty snack. Restaurants have waiter service and there are cafe-style bars.
Ecuador has some of the best beer in South America. The most popular brand is *Pilsner*. International drinks and whiskies are available, but expensive. An Ecuadorian speciality is a unique fruit juice called *naranjilla* – a taste somewhere between citrus and peach. Good Chilean wine is available, but expensive. The best local drink is *canelazo*, made from sugar cane, alcohol, lemon, sugar and cinnamon. Another local drink is *pisco*, made from fresh lemon. Alcohol cannot be sold after 0200.
NIGHTLIFE: There is little nightlife except in Quito and Guayaquil where there are excellent restaurants and other attractions. In smaller towns, social life takes place in the home and in private clubs. The cinema is the most popular form of entertainment.
SHOPPING: Bargaining is acceptable in small shops and in markets, but prices are usually fixed in 'tourist stores'. A few stores around the major hotels have fixed prices. In the Province of Azuay, the cities of Cuenca and Gualaceo offer a wide variety of handicrafts at *ferias* or special market days. The top attractions are the *ferias* of Otavalo, Ambato, Latacunga, Saquisili and Riobamba, most held once a week. They offer the visitor excellent bargains for Indian crafts and silver. Principal silver stores are in Quito. Special purchases include native woodcarvings, varnished and painted ornaments made of bread dough, Indian tiles, woollen and orlon rugs, blankets, baskets, leather goods, *shigras* (shoulder bags) and hand-loomed textiles, indigenous art and native weapons. **Shopping hours:** Mon-Fri 1000-2000, Sat 0800-2100 (times are for shopping malls; local stores may have shorter opening hours). Some shops open Sunday.
SPECIAL EVENTS: For a full list of special events, contact one of the Ecuadorian tourism authorities (see *Contact Addresses* section). The following is a selection of special events celebrated annually in Ecuador:
Jan 6 *Epiphany*. **Feb** *Festival of Fruits and Flowers*, Ambato; *Carnival* (three-day national celebration). **Mar** *Peach Festival*, Azuay. **Apr** *Holy Week*. **May 24** *Battle of Pichincha Day*. **Jun** *Corpus Christi* (harvest festivals in mountain villages); *Festival of the Friendly Rooster*, Chimborazo. **Jun 24** *Festival of John the Baptist*, especially in Otavalo. **Jul 24** *Simón Bolivars' Birthday*. **Aug 10** *Independence Day*. **Sep** *Festival of Yamor* (native masks, costumes and dances), Otavalo; *Banana's Fair*, Machala. **Oct 9** *International Fair*, Guayaquil (celebration of town's independence). **Nov 2** *All Souls' Day* (visits to cemeteries). **Nov 3** *Independence of Cuenca*. **Nov 30-Dec 8** *Quito Bullfighting Fair*. **Dec 6** *Founding of Quito* (bullfights, folklore exhibits and sporting events). **Dec 24** *Christmas Eve* (costume pageants). **Dec 31** *New Year's Eve*.
Note: Booking hotels during fiestas and festivals can be difficult. Visitors should book well in advance.
SOCIAL CONVENTIONS: Casual wear is widely acceptable, but businesspeople are expected to dress smartly. It is important to be punctual when arriving for meetings. Smart clothes are often required when visiting hotel dining rooms and better restaurants. Beachwear should only be worn on the beach and revealing clothes should not be worn in towns. Smoking is widely accepted.
Photography: A tip may be requested if you wish to take someone's photograph and it is better to seek permission first. **Tipping:** 10 per cent service charge is usually added to the bill in hotels and restaurants. Taxi drivers do not expect tips.

Business Profile

ECONOMY: Ecuador's economy rests on the twin pillars of oil and agriculture. Some commentators believe that the potential fluctuation in oil prices leaves the country susceptible to market crashes. It is the world's largest exporter of bananas and also grows coffee, cocoa, palm oil and sugar in significant quantities. The timber industry yields valuable hardwoods and the country is also a leading producer of balsa wood. Fishing is another important sector: seafood exports have expanded rapidly to the point where Ecuador is now the world's second-largest producer of shrimps. The mining sector produces gold, silver, copper and other metals, but it is the discovery of substantial new oil reserves in the mid-1990s that could transform Ecuador's economy. In August 1997, work began to expand the trans-Ecuadorian pipeline. The other main components of the industrial sector are food processing, chemicals and textiles. Ecuador pursued an isolationist foreign and trade policy for many years until a programme of economic reform was begun during the 1990s. In November 1992, Ecuador withdrew from OPEC and, in August 1995, joined the World Trade Organization. Since then, the country's increasing oil revenues have largely been devoted to paying off the country's substantial foreign debt. In addition, after a period of poor relations with the IMF, Ecuador has sold many former state assets as part of a deal with the IMF in 2002 to secure future funding. Ecuador is a member of the main regional integration bodies: the Andean Union and ALADI (*Asociación Latinoamericana de Integración*). The USA is the largest single trading partner, accounting for over 40 per cent of Ecuadorian exports and supplying around one-third of imports. Other significant trading partners are Japan, Colombia, Germany, Italy and Korea (Rep).
COMMERCIAL INFORMATION: The Federación Nacional de Cámaras de Comercio del Ecuador can offer advice. This chamber usually swaps location (between Quito and Guayaquil) every two years; it has been in Quito since March 2004: Amazonas y República, Edificio las Cámaras, Apartado 17-01-202, Quito (tel: (2) 244 3787; fax: (2) 243 5862; website: www.ccq.org.ec). In 2006, in will be in Guayaquil: Francisco de Orellana y Miguel Alciras, Ciudadela Kennedy Norte, Edificio Las Cámaras, Guayaquil (tel: (4) 268 2771; fax: (4) 268 2725).
CONFERENCES/CONVENTIONS: For more information, contact Centro de Exposiciones Quito de la Federación Ecuatoriana de la Pequeña Industria de Pichincha, Avenidas Amazonas y Atahualpa no 34-332, Centro de Exposiciones, Quito (tel: (2) 244 3388; fax: (2) 244 3742; e-mail: capeipi@interactive.net.ec; website: www.capeipi.com).

Climate

Warm and subtropical. Weather varies within the country due to the Andes mountain range and coastal changes. Andean regions are cooler and it is especially cold at nights in the mountains. Rainfall is high in coastal and jungle areas. In the Galápagos, the weather is dry and mild.
Required clothing: Lightweight cottons and linens, and rainwear in subtropical areas. Warmer clothes are needed in upland areas.

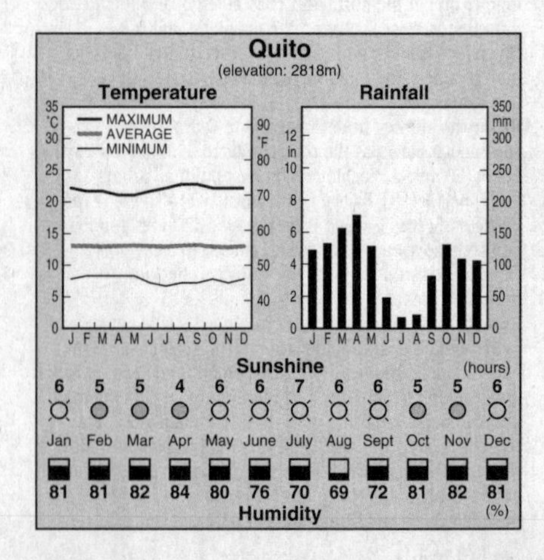

Egypt

LATEST TRAVEL ADVICE CONTACTS

British Foreign and Commonwealth Office
Tel: (0870) 606 0290 Website: www.fco.gov.uk

US Department of State
Website: http://travel.state.gov/travel

Canadian Department of Foreign Affairs and Int'l Trade
Tel: (1 800) 267 8376 Website: www.dfait-maeci.gc.ca

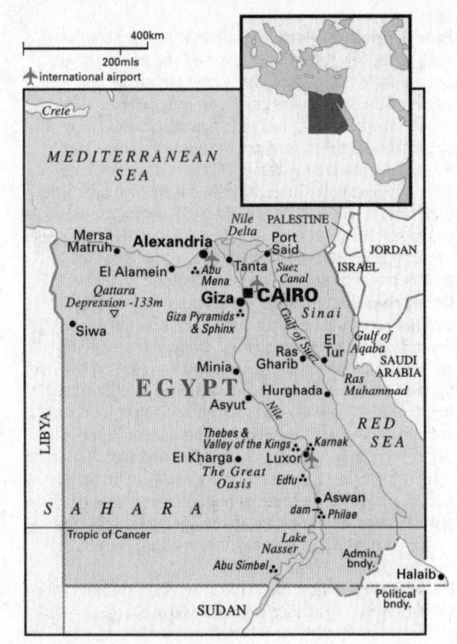

Location: Middle East, North Africa.

Country dialling code: 20.

Ministry of Tourism
Cairo International Convention Centre, Nasr City, Nasr Road, Gate 1, Cairo, Egypt
Tel: (2) 404 7004/3. Fax (2) 263 7199.
E-mail: contact@touregypt.net
Website: www.touregypt.net

Egyptian Tourist board
Misr Travel Tower, Abassia Square, Abassia, Cairo, Egypt
Tel: (2) 285 4509 *or* 284 1970. Fax: (2) 285 4363.
E-mail: contact@touregypt.net
Website: www.touregypt.net

Embassy of the Arab Republic of Egypt
26 South Street, London W1K 1DW, UK
Tel: (020) 7499 3304. Fax: (020) 7491 1542.
E-mail: etembuk@hotmail.com
Opening hours: Mon-Fri 0930-1630 (1000-1500 during Ramadan).

Egyptian Consulate
2 Lowndes Street, London SW1X 9ET, UK
Tel: (020) 7235 9777 *or* (09065) 508 933 (24-hour recorded visa information; calls cost £1 per minute). Fax: (020) 7235 5684.
E-mail: info@egyptianconsulate.co.uk
Website: www.egyptianconsulate.co.uk
Opening hours: Mon-Fri 0930-1230 (lodging applications); 1430-1600 (visa collection).

Egyptian State Tourist Office
Egyptian House, 3rd Floor, 170 Piccadilly, London W1V 9EJ, UK
Tel: (020) 7493 5283 *or* (09001) 600 299 (24-hour brochure service; calls cost 60p per minute). Fax: (020) 7408 0295.
E-mail: info@visitegypt.org.uk
Website: www.egypttreasures.gov.eg

British Embassy
7 Ahmad Ragheb, Garden City, Cairo, Egypt
Tel: (2) 794 0850-8. Fax: (2) 795 1235.
E-mail: webmaster@britishembassy.org.eg
Website: www.britishembassy.org.eg
Consulate General in: Alexandria.
Honorary Consulates in: Luxor and Suez.

TIMATIC CODES

Health	AMADEUS: **TI-DFT/JIB/HE** GALILEO/WORLDSPAN: **TI-DFT/JIB/HE** SABRE: **TIDFT/JIB/HE**
Visa	AMADEUS: **TI-DFT/JIB/VI** GALILEO/WORLDSPAN: **TI-DFT/JIB/VI** SABRE: **TIDFT/JIB/VI**

To access TIMATIC country information on Health and Visa regulations through the Computer Reservations System (CRS), type in the appropriate command line listed above.

Credit: © Corel Corporation

Embassy of the Arab Republic of Egypt
3521 International Court, NW, Washington, DC 20008 USA
Tel: (202) 895 5400. Fax: (202) 244 4319 *or* 5131.
E-mail: embassy@egyptembdc.org
Website: www.egyptembassy.us

Egyptian Tourist Authority
630 Fifth Avenue, Suite 2305, New York, NY 10111, USA
Tel: (212) 332 2570. Fax: (212) 956 6439.
E-mail: info@egypttourism.org
Website: www.egypttourism.org

Embassy of the United States of America
5 Latin America Street, Garden City, Cairo, Egypt
Tel: (2) 797 3300. Fax: (2) 797 3200.
E-mail: consularcairo@state.gov (visa enquiries).
Website: www.usembassy.egnet.net

Embassy of the Arab Republic of Egypt
454 Laurier Avenue East, Ottawa, Ontario K1N 6R3, Canada
Tel: (613) 234 4931. Fax: (613) 234 4398.
E-mail: egyptemb@sympatico.ca
Website: www.egyptembassy.ca
Consulate in: Montréal.

Egyptian Tourist Authority
1253 McGill College Avenue, Suite 250, Montréal, Québec H3B 2Y5, Canada
Tel: (514) 861 4420. Fax: (514) 861 8071.
E-mail: eta.mgr@biz.videotron.ca
Website: www.egyptourguide.com

Canadian Embassy
Street address: 26 Kamel El Shenawy Street, Garden City, Cairo, Egypt
Postal address: PO Box 1667, Cairo, Egypt
Immigration and visa section: 6 Mohamed Fahmy El Sayed, Garden City, Cairo, Egypt
Tel: (2) 794 3110. Fax: (2) 796 3548 (administrative section) *or* 794 4224 (visa section).
Website: www.dfait-maeci.gc.ca/cairo

General Information

AREA: 1,002,000 sq km (386,874 sq miles).
POPULATION: 67,886,000 (official estimate 2001).
POPULATION DENSITY: 67.8 per sq km.
CAPITAL: Cairo (El Qahira). **Population:** 7,388,000 (official estimate 2002).
GEOGRAPHY: Egypt is bordered to the north by the Mediterranean, to the south by Sudan, to the west by Libya, and to the east by the Red Sea and Israel. The River Nile divides the country unevenly in two, while the Suez Canal provides a third division with the Sinai Peninsula. Beyond the highly cultivated Nile Valley and Delta, a lush green tadpole of land that holds more than 90 per cent of the population, the landscape is mainly flat desert, devoid of vegetation apart from the few oases that have persisted in the once fertile depressions of the Western Desert. Narrow strips are inhabited on the Mediterranean coast and on the African Red Sea coast. The coast south of Suez has fine beaches and the coral reefs just offshore attract many divers. The High Dam at Aswan now controls the annual floods that once put much of the Nile Valley under water; it also provides electricity.
GOVERNMENT: Republic. **Head of State:** President Muhammad Hosni Mubarak since 1981. **Head of Government:** Ahmed Nazif since 2004.
LANGUAGE: Arabic is the official language. English and French are widely spoken.
RELIGION: According to the 1986 census, over 94 per cent of the population follows Islam; the majority of the rest is Christian. All types of Christianity are represented, especially the Coptic Christian Church. There is also a small Jewish minority.
TIME: GMT + 2 (GMT + 3 from May to September).
ELECTRICITY: Most areas 220 volts AC, 50Hz. Certain rural parts still use 110 to 380 volts AC.
COMMUNICATIONS: Telephone: Full IDD is available. Country code: 20. Outgoing international code: 00. **Mobile telephone:** GSM 900. Coverage is limited to Cairo, Alexandria and along the north coast line of the Red Sea from Suez to Sharm el-Sheikh and the major towns along the Nile. Network operators include *ECMS-MobiNil* (website: www.mobinil.com) and *Vodafone Egypt Telecommunications* (website: www.vodafone.com.eg). **Fax:** Several of the major hotels in Cairo have introduced fax facilities; check with the hotel concerned before travelling. **Telegram:** International telegram services are available from the Central Post Offices in Cairo, Alexandria, Luxor and Aswan and main hotels. **Internet:** There are Internet cafes in the main cities, including Cairo, Alexandria, Dahab and Luxor. Tourists can also access the Internet in hotels. The main ISPs include *Internet Egypt* (website: www.internetegypt.com), *EUN*, *Rite* and *Ritesec*. **Post:** The postal system is efficient for international mail. Airmail takes about five days to western Europe, and eight to 10 days to the USA. There are *Poste Restante* facilities at the Central Post Office; a small fee is charged when mail is collected. All post offices are open daily 0830-1500 except Friday, and the Central Post Office in Cairo is open 24 hours. **Press:** The most influential Egyptian daily is *Al-Ahram*; others include *Al-Akhbar* and several weekly and periodical publications. Two daily newspapers – *Le Journal d'Alexandrie* and *Le Progrès Egyptien* – are published in French. The English-language daily newspaper is the *Egyptian Gazette*. The *Middle East Observer* is the main weekly English-language business paper.
Radio: BBC World Service (website: www.bbc.co.uk/worldservice) and Voice of America (website: www.voa.gov) can be received. From time to time the frequencies change and the most up-to-date can be found online.

Passport/Visa

	Passport Required?	Visa Required?	Return Ticket Required?
Full British	Yes	Yes	No
Australian	Yes	Yes	No
Canadian	Yes	Yes	No
USA	Yes	Yes	No
Other EU	Yes/1	Yes	No
Japanese	Yes	Yes	No

Note: *Regulations and requirements may be subject to change at short notice, and you are advised to contact the appropriate diplomatic or consular authority before finalising travel arrangements. Details of these may be found at the head of this country's entry. Any numbers in the chart refer to the footnotes below.*

PASSPORTS: Passport valid for at least three months from date of departure required by all except:
1. nationals of Belgium, France, Germany ("Kinderausweis" given to children is also accepted and need only be valid upon arrival), Italy and Portugal travelling with national ID cards.

A B C D E F G H I J K L M N O P Q R S T U V W X Y Z

VISAS: Required by all except the following:
(a) nationals of Kuwait, who are allocated a six months' residence permit upon arrival;
(b) Palestinians holding an Egyptian residence card, provided the stay outside Egypt does not exceed six months;
(c) nationals of Bahrain, Djibouti, Guinea, Jordan (only with a passport with at least five years' validity), Libya, Oman, Saudi Arabia, the United Arab Emirates and Yemen for stays of up to three months;
(d) nationals of Malaysia for stays of up to 15 days;
(e) those continuing their journey to a third country within 24 hours, provided holding confirmed tickets.
Note: (a) The amount of stay permitted in Egypt in which visa exemptions apply to such nationals varies. It is advised to contact the nearest Embassy/Consulate prior to travel to confirm the details. (b) Those in possession of a residence permit to Egypt are not required to obtain an entry visa if they leave Egypt and return within the validity of their residence permit or within six months, whichever period is less. (c) Nationals of Afghanistan, Iran, Lebanon, The Philippines and holders of Palestinian documents must not leave the airport transit lounge if travelling enroute to onward destination (and must do so by the same or first connecting aircraft). All other nationals must remain within the airport.
Types of visa and cost: *Tourist* and *Business* (single- and multiple-entry). Cost varies according to nationality. For UK nationals: *Tourist*: £15 (single-entry); £18 (multiple-entry); *Business*: £53 (single-entry); £91 (multiple-entry). For US nationals: All visas £12. For Canadian nationals: *Tourist*: £15 (single-entry); £18 (multiple-entry). *Business*: £40 (single-entry); £70 (multiple-entry). Processing fees for other nationals vary considerably; check with the appropriate Consulate (or Consular section of Embassy) for details.
Validity: Varies, but are usually valid for six months from the date of issue for stays of up to three months. Visas cannot be post-dated. Visas can be extended (for over one month) one week before the end of the permitted stay in Egypt at Immigration.
Application to: Consulate (or Consular section at Embassy); see *Contact Addresses* section.
Application requirements: (a) Passport valid for at least six months with at least one blank page. (b) Application form, completed and signed. (c) One recent passport-size photo. (d) Postal applicants must enclose a registered- or recorded-delivery, self-addressed envelope and pay by postal order only. (e) Fee, payable by cash or postal order. (f) Business letter for Business visa.
Working days required: Same day for personal applications; seven days or more from day of receipt for postal applications. Processing may take longer (estimated six to eight weeks) for the following nationals, who require pre-approval from the relevant authorities in Cairo: Algeria, Bangladesh, China (PR), Eritrea, Ethiopia, Iran, Iraq, Lebanon, Morocco, Somalia, Sudan and Tunisia.
Note: Visitors from all countries except the EU and the USA must register with the police within one week of arrival in Egypt, although this service is usually undertaken by the hotel.

Money

Currency: Egyptian Pound (E£) = 100 piastres. Notes are in denominations of E£100, 50, 20, 10, 5 and 1. Coins are in denominations of 50, 25, 20, 10 and 5 piastres.
Currency exchange: Available at banks and official bureaux de change. There are five national banks and 78 branches of foreign banks.
Credit & debit cards: American Express, Diners Club, MasterCard and Visa are accepted. Check with your credit or debit card company for details of merchant acceptability and other services which may be available.
Travellers cheques: To avoid additional exchange rate charges, travellers are advised to take travellers cheques in US Dollars, Euros or Pounds Sterling.
Currency restrictions: The import and export of foreign currency is unlimited. The import of local currency is unlimited. The export of local currency is prohibited.
Exchange rate indicators: The following figures are included as a guide to the movements of the Egyptian Pound against Sterling and the US Dollar:

Date	Feb '04	May '04	Aug '04	Nov '04
£1.00=	11.22	11.03	11.48	11.81
$1.00=	6.16	6.18	6.23	6.24

Banking hours: Sun-Thurs 0830-1400.

Credit: © Corel Corporation

Duty Free

The following goods may be imported into Egypt without incurring customs duty:
200 cigarettes or 25 cigars or 200g of tobacco; 1l of alcoholic beverages; 1l of perfume or eau de cologne; gifts up to EGP500.
Note: Persons travelling with valuable electronic equipment such as cameras, video cameras or computers may be required to list these in their passports to ensure that they will be exported on departure.
Prohibited items: Narcotics, firearms, cotton, gold and silver purchased locally unless for personal use only and in small quantities; for a full list, contact the Egyptian Commercial Office, 23 South Street, London W1L 2XD (tel: (020) 7499 3002; fax: (020) 7493 8110).

Public Holidays

2005: Jan 7* Coptic Christmas Day. **Jan 21** Grand Feast. **Feb 10** Islamic New Year. **Apr 25** Sinai Liberation Day (Sinai only). **May 1** Labour Day. **May 2** Sham el-Nassim (Coptic Easter). **Jun 18** Liberation Day. **Jul 23** Revolution Day. **Aug 15** Wafa'a el Nil (Flooding of the Nile). **Sep 11*** Coptic New Year. **Oct 6** Armed Forces Day. **Oct 24** Suez Victory Day. **Nov 3** Bairam Feast (End of Ramadan). **Dec 23** Victory Day.
2006: Jan 7* Coptic Christmas Day. **Jan 10** Grand Feast. **Jan 31** Islamic New Year. **Apr 24** Sham el-Nassim (Coptic Easter). **Apr 25** Sinai Liberation Day (Sinai only). **May 1** Labour Day. **Jun 18** Liberation Day. **Jul 23** Revolution Day. **Aug 15** Wafa'a el Nil (Flooding of the Nile). **Sep 11*** Coptic New Year. **Oct 6** Armed Forces Day. **Oct 22** Bairam Feast (End of Ramadan). **Oct 24** Suez Victory Day. **Dec 23** Victory Day.
Note: (a)*These holidays are not official, although Coptic Christians may observe them. (b) Muslim festivals are timed according to local sightings of various phases of the moon and the dates given above are approximations. During the lunar month of Ramadan that precedes the Bairam Feast, Muslims fast during the day and feast at night and normal business patterns may be interrupted. Some restaurants are closed during the day but most tourist attractions and hotels are not affected. Some disruption may continue into the three-day Grand Feast itself. For more information, see the *World of Islam* appendix.

Health

	Special Precautions?	Certificate Required?
Yellow Fever	No	1
Cholera	Yes	2
Typhoid & Polio	3	N/A
Malaria	4	N/A

Note: *Regulations and requirements may be subject to change at short notice, and you are advised to contact your doctor well in advance of your intended date of departure. Any numbers in the chart refer to the footnotes below.*

1: A yellow fever vaccination certificate is required from travellers over one year of age coming from infected areas (see below). Those arriving in transit from such areas without a certificate will be detained at the airport until their onward flight departs. The following countries and areas are regarded by the Egyptian health authorities as being infected with yellow fever: all countries in mainland Africa south of the Sahara with the exception of Lesotho, Mauritania, Mozambique, Namibia, South Africa, Swaziland and Zimbabwe (and including Chad, Mali and Niger); Sudan south of 15°N (location certificate issued by a Sudanese official is required in order to be exempt from vaccination certificate); São Tomé e Principe. *Also* Belize, Bolivia, Brazil, Colombia, Costa Rica, Ecuador, French Guiana, Guyana, Panama, Peru, Surinam, Trinidad & Tobago and Venezuela.
2: Following WHO guidelines issued in 1973, a cholera vaccination certificate is no longer a condition of entry to Egypt and the country is currently not listed as infected. However, sporadic cases of cholera have been reported and precautions could be considered. Up-to-date advice should be sought before deciding whether these precautions should include vaccination as medical opinion is divided over its effectiveness; see the *Health* appendix for further information.
3: Vaccination against typhoid and polio is advised.
4: Limited malaria risk, in the malignant *falciparum* and benign *vivax* forms, exists from June to October in the El Faiyoum area. There is no risk in Cairo or Alexandria at any time.
Food & drink: Mains water is normally chlorinated and, whilst relatively safe, may cause mild abdominal upsets. Bottled water is available and is advised for the first few weeks of the stay. Milk is unpasteurised and should be boiled. Powdered or tinned milk is available and is advised, but make sure that it is reconstituted with pure water. Avoid dairy products which are likely to have been made from unboiled milk. Only eat well-cooked meat and fish, preferably served hot. Pork, salad and mayonnaise may carry increased risk. Vegetables should be cooked and fruit peeled. Drinking water outside main cities and towns carries a greater risk and should always be sterilised.
Other risks: Precautions against *hepatitis A* and *E* and *diphtheria* should be considered. Immunisation against *hepatitis B* is sometimes advised. *Dengue fever* occurs in epidemics. *Bilharzia* (schistosomiasis) is present in the Nile Delta and the Nile Valley. Avoid swimming and paddling in fresh water; swimming pools which are well chlorinated and maintained are safe. *Filariasis* may occur in the Nile Delta. There may be a danger of snakes and scorpions in certain areas. Sandstorms are also a risk in some parts. *Rabies* is present. For those at high risk, vaccination before arrival should be considered. If you are bitten, seek medical advice without delay. For more information, consult the *Health* appendix.
Health care: Public hospitals and chemists are open to tourists. Health insurance is strongly advised.

Travel - International

AIR: The national airline is *Egypt Air (MS)* (website: www.egyptair.com.eg). All the main carriers service Egypt, including *Air France, British Airways, JAT, KLM, Lufthansa, Olympic Airways* and *SWISS*. Charter services fly direct from London Gatwick to Egypt. British Mediterranean (a franchise partner of British Airways) operates daily services from London to Alexandria.
Approximate flight times: From Cairo to *London* is 4 hours 45 minutes (from Luxor to *London* is 5 hours 35 minutes), from Cairo to *Los Angeles* is 16 hours 40 minutes, to *New York* is 14 hours 25 minutes, to *Singapore* is 12 hours 35 minutes, and to *Sydney* is 20 hours.
International airports: *Cairo International (CAI)*, 24km (15 miles) northeast of the city at Heliopolis (travel time – 1 hour). There are bus services every 30 minutes, and taxis are available. Special limousines are offered by local and international operators. Hotel cars may also be available. Airport facilities include incoming and outgoing duty-free shops selling a wide range of goods, several car hire firms, post office, bank/bureau de change, restaurants and bar, hotel reservation service, souvenir shops, bookshop and travel insurance services.
Borg El Arab (HBE), has replaced El Nouzha airport as the main international airport for Alexandria. It lies 60 km (37 miles) southwest of Alexandria. Airport facilities include a duty-free shop, bank and exchange services, VIP lounge, post office and restaurant.
Luxor Airport (LXR) is 5.5km (3.5 miles) from Luxor. There is a regular bus service to the city centre (travel time – 15 minutes). Special limousine and local taxi services are available. Airport facilities include car hire, bank and exchange services, and a bar and restaurant. Improvement works have taken place and are expected to continue to meet the increasing tourist flow.
Departure tax: None.
SEA: The main coastal ports are Alexandria, Nuweiba, Port Said and Suez. The Saudi Sea Transport Company runs a regular car ferry service between Suez and Jeddah. A ferry service usually travels twice a week up the Nile between Wadi Halfa (Sudan) and Egypt High Dam, but is occasionally suspended. For further information, contact the Nile Valley Association (tel: (2) 578 9256). There is also a ferry service that operates twice-daily between South Sinai and Aqaba (Jordan). There are special rates for children under 12 and under three years of age. For more information, contact the Cairo Navigation Agency (tel: (2) 574 5755 *or* 575 5568). The *Black Sea Shipping Company* sails from Odessa. Other main passenger lines are *Arab Express Shipping, Egyptian Navigation Company* (website: www.enc.com.eg), *Gulf Agency Company* (website: www.gulfagencycompany.com)

and *Orient Shipping Ltd.* Many cruise ships stop over in Egypt as part of their African itinerary. Main cruise line operators include *Cunard Line*, *Orient Lines*, *Princess Cruises*, *Royal Caribbean* and *Silversea Cruises*.
RAIL: There are no international rail links to any of Egypt's northwestern neighbours. The railheads at Aswan and Wadi Halfa, Sudan are connected by a ferry across Lake Nasser.
ROAD: The road border between Libya and Egypt is open. There are two border crossings between Israel and Egypt: one runs from Cairo via El Arish to Rafiah on the north Sinai coast; and the other from Cairo via Suez and Taba to Eilat. Daily coaches leave early in the morning from Tel Aviv and Jerusalem in Israel for travel via El Arish/Rafiah to Cairo and vice versa. There are no direct buses from Eilat to Cairo; it is necessary to change in Taba. The crossing from Taba to Eilat is now open 24 hours a day. Passengers in taxis and rented cars are not permitted to cross the borders between Israel and Egypt. Privately owned vehicles may be taken across other borders, provided the appropriate documentation is obtained. All private vehicles entering Egypt must have a three month *triptyche* or *Carnet de passage en douane* from an automobile club in the country of registration. The driver must hold an international drivers' licence. Visas should normally be obtained in advance; however, travellers entering Egypt via Taba may be able to obtain visas at the border. Contact the Tourist Office for further details of entry restrictions (see *Contact Addresses* section).

Credit: © Corel Corporation

Travel - Internal

AIR: *Egypt Air* operates daily flights between Cairo, Alexandria, Luxor, Aswan, Abu Simbel, and Hurghada. For information on schedules, contact local offices *or* see online (website: www.egyptair.com.eg). *Air Sinai* operates services from Cairo to Eilat, El Arish, Hurghada, Luxor, Ras El Nakab, St Catherine, Sharm el-Sheikh and Taba.
SEA/RIVER: There are slow and fast ferry services linking Hurghada with Sharm el-Sheikh in Sinai. Slow ferries operate daily on Mon, Wed, Fri (travel time – 5 to 6 hours). Fast ferries operate daily on Mon, Tues and Sat (travel time – 1 hour 30 minutes). The traditional Nile sailing boats, *feluccas*, can be hired by the hour for relaxed sailing on the Nile. Regular Nile cruises operate between Luxor and Aswan, and sometimes between Cairo and Aswan, usually for the following periods: four nights, five days (standard tour); six nights, seven days (extended tour), and 14 nights, 15 days (full Nile cruise). There are over 160 individually owned boats of all categories operating on the Nile.
RAIL: A comprehensive rail network run by Egyptian State Railways (tel: (02) 574 9474 *or* 575 3555) offering a high standard of service is operated along an east-west axis from Sallom on the Libyan border to Alexandria and Cairo, and along the Nile to Luxor and Aswan. There are also links to Port Said and Suez. There are frequent trains from Cairo to Alexandria, and also several luxury air-conditioned day and night trains with sleeping and restaurant cars from Cairo to Luxor and Aswan for the Nile Valley tourist trade. For the overnight train, bookings should be made one week in advance through a travel agent or through Abela Egypt, Ramses Station, Ramses Square, Cairo (tel: (2) 574 9274 *or* 574 9474; fax: (2) 574 9074; e-mail: info@sleepingtrains.com; website: www.sleepingtrains.com). On Egyptian state railways, children under four years travel free. Children aged four to nine years pay half fare. Holders of Youth Hostel cards can get reductions. For details of other possible reductions, contact the Tourist Office.
ROAD: Traffic drives on the right. Besides the Nile Valley and Delta, which hold an extensive road network, there are paved roads along the Mediterranean and African Red Sea coasts. The road looping through the Western Desert oases from Asyut to Giza is now fully paved. The speed limit is usually 90kph (56mph) on motorways and 100kph (62mph) on the desert motorway from Cairo to Alexandria (there are substantial fines for speeding). Private motoring in the desert regions is not recommended without suitable vehicles and a guide. For more details, contact the Egyptian Automobile Club in Cairo. **Bus:** The national bus system serves the Nile Valley and the coastal road. Main routes are from Cairo to St Catherine, Sharm el-Sheikh, Dahab, Ras Sudr, El-Tour, Taba and Rafah; from Suez to El-Tour and Sharm el-Sheikh; and from Sharm el-Sheikh to Taba, Neweiba, El-Tour, Dahab and St Catherine. Coach services operate between Cairo and Agami, Marakia-Mrabila, Marina-Aidda Sidy Abd El Rahman, Matrouh, Ma'amoura Beach and Hurghada. **Taxi:** These are available in all the larger cities and are metered (see also *Urban* below). Long-distance group taxis for all destinations are cheap. Fares should be agreed in advance. **Car hire:** This is available through *Avis*, *Budget*, *Europcar*, *Hertz*, *Thrifty* and local companies. The driver must be at least 25 years of age. **Documentation:** Visitor's own insurance and an International Driving Permit are required to drive any motor vehicle. *Carnet de Passage* or a suitable deposit is necessary for the temporary import of visitor's own vehicle. All vehicles (including motorcycles) are required by law to carry a fire extinguisher and a red hazard triangle.
URBAN: The government-owned *Cairo Transport Authority* runs buses and tram services in Cairo and also operates cross-Nile ferries. There is a central area flat fare. In addition, there are other buses and fixed-route shared taxi and minibus services run by private operators. Vehicles normally wait at city terminals to obtain a full load, but there are frequent departures. Fares are three to four times higher than on the buses. Cairo's suburban railways have been upgraded to provide a rapid transit network, including Africa's first underground railway. Alexandria also has buses and tramways, with first- and second-class accommodation and distance-regulated fares.
TRAVEL TIMES: The following chart gives approximate travel times (in hours and minutes) from **Cairo** to other major cities/towns in Egypt.

	Air	Road	Rail
Alexandria	0.30	3.00	2.30
Luxor	1.00	12.00	17.00
Aswan	2.00	16.00	19.00a*
Port Said	0.45	3.00	3.00
St Catherine	0.30	4.00	-
Hurghada	1.00	8.00	-
Sharm el-Sh'k	1.30	7.00	-
Marsa Matr'h	1.30	5.00	9.00
Arish	1.00	5.00	9.00
Ismailia	-	2.00	2.30
Suez	-	4.00	4.00
New Valley	2.00	12.00	-

*Overnight journey.

Accommodation

Tourism is one of Egypt's main industries and accommodation is available around all the major attractions and the larger cities. Egypt has all types of accommodation on offer, from deluxe hotels to youth hostels, at prices to suit all budgets.
HOTELS: The main cities have moderately priced quality hotels, which *must* be booked well in advance, especially during the winter months. Smaller hotels are very good value. Hotel bills are subject to a tax and service charge of 12 per cent. For further information and a copy of the 'Egyptian Hotel Guide', contact the Egyptian Hotel Association, 8 El Sad El Ali Street, Dokki, Giza, Cairo (tel: (2) 761 1400; fax: (2) 761 1333; e-mail: eha@link.net; website: www.egypttourism.org).
CAMPING/CARAVANNING: Travel through the desert wilderness is available through local tour operators. It should be borne in mind that desert travel is extremely hazardous without an experienced guide, ample supplies of water and a vehicle in good mechanical condition. There are only a few official campsites in the country. Tourists are advised to contact the local tourist offices on arrival for further details. The tourist office in Cairo is at 5 Adly Street, Cairo (tel: (2) 391 3454). There is also an office at Cairo International Airport (tel: (2) 291 4255 ext. 2223).
YOUTH HOSTELS: There are 15 youth hostels altogether, which are located mainly in large towns, on the coast and in popular tourist regions. Further information can be obtained from the Egyptian Youth Hostels Associaton, 1 El-Ibrahimy Street, Garden City, Cairo (tel: (2) 794 0527 *or* 796 1448; fax: (2) 795 0329; e-mail: booking@hihostels.com).

Resorts & Excursions

Travellers have marvelled at Egypt's archaeological wonders for centuries, ever since the Ancient Greeks visited the pyramids. Today, the ancient wonders attract millions of tourists each year to the pyramids, temples, mosques and great monuments of the Nile Valley, as well as the stunning diving resorts of the Red Sea.

CAIRO

Known as the greatest city in the Islamic world, Cairo's ancient monuments and medieval customs thrive in a cosmopolitan, modern city. A blend of Arab, African and European influences, Africa's largest city has a population of at least 18 million. Situated on the Nile, the city is polluted and overcrowded, and getting around poses many challenges, although it has greatly improved with the ever-expanding underground Metro system.
In **Islamic** (or **Medieval**) **Cairo**, narrow congested streets are filled with donkey carts, spice traders and imposing mosques. A central landmark is **Midan Hussain**, a large open square with tea houses around the perimeter, and dominated by the sacred **Mosque of Sayyidna Al-Hussain**. Adjacent is the famous **Khan-el Khalili**, one of the world's largest bazaars, pulsing with commerce and crammed with spices, coppersmiths, perfume and trinkets. Bargaining has been a way of life in these alleyways since the late 14th century and it is easy to get taken in by silver-tongued salesmen. Here, **Fishawi's tea house** has been in business for over 200 years, and is still a great people-watching venue.
Nearby is **Al-Azhar Mosque**, containing the oldest university in the world (AD 970). The pre-Ottoman **Madrassa and Mausoleum of Al-Ghouri**, has Sufi dancing, and opposite is **Wakala of Al-Ghouri**, an attractively preserved cultural centre. Exhibits in the **Museum of Islamic Art** bring Islamic Cairo to life, with arts, ceramics, mosaics and calligraphy.
The **Citadel** was home to Egypt's rulers for 700 years; an imposing medieval fortress offering sweeping views of the city. Within it is the **Midan Salah al-Din** with the unmissable **Sultan Hassan** and **Rifai Mosques**. The **Mohammad Ali Mosque** has classic Ottoman minarets and interior. Within the Citadel, other attractions include the **Military National Museum**, **Al-Gawhara Palace and Museum** and the **National Police Museum**.
City of the Dead (**Northern Cemetery**) is a Mamluk necropolis with hundreds of thousands of tombs dating from the 12th century. Many thousands more live here in something resembling a shanty town amongst the ornate mausoleums.
Sharia Talat Harb street and **Midan Tahrir** (**Liberation Square**) are typical of the more modern, commercial centre of Cairo – filled with concrete and cars, and containing countless hotels, restaurants, office blocks and museums. Here is one of the country's greatest attractions; the **Museum of Egyptian Antiquities** housing over 130,000 exhibits, including Pharaonic and Byzantine art and sculpture, the **Mummy Room** and the celebrated **Tutankhamun** exhibition.
Behind the museum, bridges cross the Nile, and riverside

Credit: © Corel Corporation

walks along the corniche bring some relief from traffic. Here, river taxis travel to local docks, and *feluccas* (sail boats) are available for private trips.
The south is home to the Coptic Orthodox Christians, forming 10 per cent of the population. Originally a Roman fortress town called Babylon, it was greatly significant to early Christians. Here, the **Coptic Museum** has exhibits from AD 300 to AD 1000, in the world's greatest collection of Coptic art. The **Hanging Church**, **Monastery of St George** and the churches of **St Sergius** and **St Barbara** are all in the same area. The **Ben Ezra Synagogue** is one of the oldest in Egypt, and represents the remains of the Jewish community.
The small island of **Gezira** is a modern upmarket area with the **Opera House** (a US$30 million arts complex) containing the **Museum of Modern Art**, and the **Cairo Tower** with great city views. The adjacent neighbourhood of **Zamalek** contains elegant town houses and embassies.
On the southwest outskirts of the city is **Giza** with **Cairo Zoo** and the **University**. But Cairo is most famous for the **Great Pyramids**, Egypt's most visited monuments. Of the three main pyramids (**Cheops**, **Chephren** and **Mycerinus**), the largest is 137m (449ft) high and contains some 3 million blocks of stone. Exploring the interiors is possible via labyrinthine tunnels and staircases. Adjacent is the bewitching **Sphinx**, as named by the ancient Greeks, with the head of a woman and body of a lion. Erosion was partly rectified by restoration, which finished in 1998. Early morning and late afternoon are a little less crowded, and every evening there are *son et lumière* - extravagant light shows telling the story of ancient Egypt. Camels, horses and donkeys can be hired to explore the site.
ELSEWHERE: There are more ancient tombs and pyramids outside the city - more difficult to get to but much less crowded. There are remains of the Old Kingdom's capital **Memphis**; the necropolis at **Saqqara**, with the **Step Pyramid** older than those at Giza, with well-preserved wall reliefs and royal tombs. **Dahshur** has only been open to foreigners since 1996, and is famous for its **Bent Pyramid** and a huge field of royal tombs.
In contrast to ancient sights, the **Camel Market** (**Souq al-Gamaal**), is held every morning at **Birqash**, around 35km (21 miles) from the city, located on the edge of the Western Desert. Hundreds of camels are sold daily, most having been brought from Sudan.
Oases: Egypt's six oases can provide relief from cities. All have accommodation and can be accessed by public transport. The desert forms 94 per cent of the country's area, yet only 1 per cent of the population lives in it. The largest and most developed oasis is **Kharga**, with a Berber community, temples and museums. **Dhakla Oasis** has hot springs, and camel rides over the sand dunes. The nearby village of **Bashandi** sells handicrafts made by local girls. The smallest is **Farafra**, an ancient fort town; **Bahariyya** is made up of several small villages, famed for its olives and dates. **Al-Faiyum Oasis** is 100km (60 miles) southwest of Cairo, and the area contains small pyramids, the old city of **Karanis**, and temples. **Siwa** is the furthest west and remote, but the most picturesque and idyllic. The community is traditional and Berber-speaking.

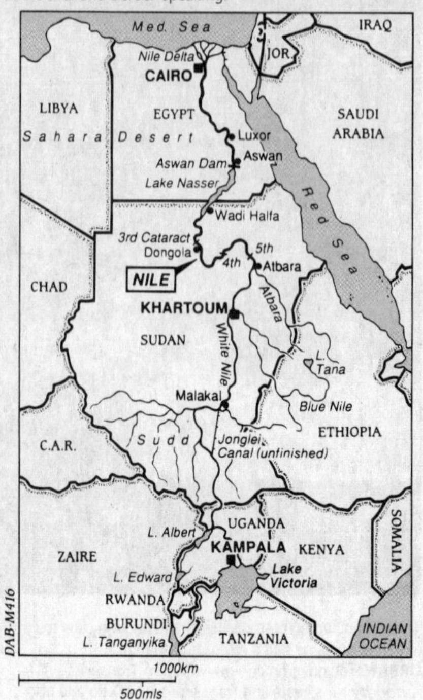

THE NILE

Many tour operators offer Nile cruises, usually between Luxor and Aswan, and generally lasting around five days. It is also possible to get a cruise to **Minia** (a charming town with Roman, Greek and Pharaonic ruins, including the Beni Hassan archaeological area) and/or through to Cairo. *Felucca* trips offer the same route – with more basic facilities. For further information, see the *Sport & Activities* section.
LUXOR: Once the ancient city of **Thebes** and powerhouse of upper Egypt, Luxor has grown into a large town, awash with hotels, restaurants and souvenir shops, with most of its economy coming from tourism.
A highlight is the **Karnak Temple**, covering an immense 100 acres (40.5 hectares). Of the three temple enclosures, the grandest is the **Precinct of Amun**, the main place of worship. The **Great Hypostyle Hall** is 6000 sq m (64,584 sq ft) and filled with immense stone pillars. The whole site has colossal statues, reliefs, obelisks and halls and, of course, the **Avenue of the Sphinxes**. There are nightly *son et lumière* shows.
Along the riverbank, **Luxor Temple** is guarded by a huge statue of **Ramses II**, and although a fraction of the area of **Karnak**, it also contains countless columns, statues and sphinxes. A pleasant walk north along the corniche brings you to the **Luxor Museum** where a small, interesting collection of relics from the Theban Temples and Necropolis can be viewed. The recently opened **Mummification Museum** has exhibits of human, reptile and bird mummies, as well as explanations of how they are made.
On the **West Bank** of the Nile is the vast **Theban Necropolis**, containing some of the world's finest tombs: the **Valley of the Kings**; **Valley of the Queens**; and **Tombs of the Nobles**. Highlights include the **Tomb of Tutankhamun**; **Ramses II**, and the **Tomb of Nefertari**, reputed to be the country's finest, which is newly restored and allows only 150 visitors a day for 10 minutes. Nearby is **Deir el-Bahri** (Northern Monastery), a picturesque temple set amidst the amphitheatre of the **Theban Hills**.
Along the Nile, felucca owners tout for custom, and it is possible to hire one for a brief sunset cruise to **Banana Island**, or even to organise a trip upriver to Aswan. Hot-air balloon trips are also available, offering the best views of Luxor.
Around Luxor Temple, shopping is dominated by tourist bazaars with enthusiastic salesmen. The more traditional *souk*, with household goods, spices and clothes, is on **Sharia el-Birka**. Cafes and stalls sell hot food, and there are rooftop terraces overlooking the river. A livestock market is held every Tuesday morning at **El-Hebel**, a village 4km (2.4 miles) from Luxor.
ASWAN: A beautiful winter resort, relaxing Aswan is the southernmost city in the country; the gateway to Africa, and steeped in Nubian culture. Although the sights are not the country's finest, the town's riverside location is picturesque and peaceful. It has a busy tourism scene although it is less aggressive than Luxor.
The corniche provides attractive riverside walks, and a stop-off for many cruise ships. In the evenings, floating restaurants provide a lively gathering place, and the world-famous folkloric dance troupe performs nightly during winter months at the **Cultural Centre**. Southernmost is the **Old Cataract Hotel** (famous as the location of the film 'Death on the Nile'). **Sharia el-Souq** is the atmospheric market stretching for streets, with spices, food and clothes, as well as predictable tourist souvenirs.
Elephantine Island is easily accessible by river taxi. Formerly Egypt's frontier town, recent excavations of this ancient site have revealed temples and a fortress. **Aswan Museum** contains exhibits found in Nubia and Aswan. The **Nilometre** on the south of the island, dating back to Pharaonic times, was used to measure the height of the Nile.
Further south is the tiny **Island of Plants**, presented to Lord Horatio Kitchener in the 1890s in recognition of his military services. Importing exotic flowers and plants from India and Malaysia, he created a beautiful botanical garden, open daily to the public, attracting a wide variety of birds.
On the **West Bank** of the Nile lies the **Monastery of St Simeon**, which resembles a fortress. Nearby is the domed granite and sandstone Mausoleum of **Aga Khan**.
Beyond Aswan: Outside the city are the **Aswan Dam**, built by the British at the beginning of the century, and the **Temple of Philae**, on the **Island of Philae**. The Temple is one of Egypt's most famous attractions, and after being under threat from flooding from the High Dam, UNESCO moved it stone by stone to a higher point on the island.
Further afield is **Abu Simbel**, the magnificent **Sun Temple of Ramses II**, also rescued from flooding by UNESCO. Ramses had four gigantic statues of himself built in order to intimidate travellers entering Egypt from Africa, especially the Nubians.
Kom Ombo, 30km (18 miles) north of Aswan, is a largely Nubian settlement, known for its **Temple of Haroeris and Sobek**. Nearby is the **Darow Camel Market**, held every Tuesday morning and mainly frequented by tribesmen from the northern Sudanese deserts.
Edfu is famed for the largest and best preserved Pharaoronic Temple in Egypt, the **Temple of Horus**. It is a favoured starting/stopping point for felucca trips to and from Luxor.

ALEXANDRIA

The Northern Coast is dominated by Alexandria, conquered and designed by Alexander the Great. More Mediterranean than Arabic, it was always considered affluent and liberal, and still attracts wealthy Cairenes as a summer retreat. Egypt's second city is less chaotic than Cairo, and famed for its numerous Hellenistic and Roman relics from the age when it was the cultural capital of Europe.
The newly constructed **Bibliotheka Alexandria**, costing over US$300m, is the greatest library in the ancient world and a major research centre for scholars. Relics from the third century BC are exhibited in the **Graeco-Roman Museum**, and there is a recently excavated **Roman Amphitheatre**. **Fort Qait Bey** is a 15th-century fort built on the foundations of the **Pharos Lighthouse**, one of the Seven Wonders of the World. The modern **Mosque of Abu al-Abbas Mursi** dominates the main square on **Sharia Tatwig**, and other places of interest include the **Museum of Fine Arts**, and **Montazah Palace** with attractive gardens, often the summer venue of theatre performances.
Swimming and diving are popular, although beaches tend to be overcrowded in summer. **Ma'amoura** is a more liberal and Westernised beach, and further out of the city **Agami** and **Hannoville** are cleaner and less crowded. Diving is possible on **Montazah** beach.
Beyond Alexandria: The ancient city of **Rosetta**, 65km (39 miles) away from Alexandria, is famed for being where the Rosetta Stone was discovered (now housed in the British Museum) and has attractive Ottoman, 'Delta Style' architecture.
El Alamein is a small coastal village 100km (60 miles) west of Alexandria and an easy day-trip. Famous as the scene of a decisive Allied victory, which determined the fate of Egypt and Britain's Empire, there is a **War Museum**, **Cemetery** and **Memorial** to the soldiers who died in battle.
Further west is the coastal resort of **Mersa Matrouh**, which has a good beach, although it can be overcrowded in summer.

SINAI & THE RED SEA COAST

A great example of modern engineering, the **Suez Canal** links the Red Sea with the Mediterranean. Completed in 1869, it has repeatedly been the cause of dispute, most recently when blocked during the 1967 war with Israel. **Port Said** is the main city. Anyone travelling to Sinai by road would cross the Suez on a small shuttle boat, or under the tunnel.
The Red Sea Coast sits strategically between Africa and Asia, rich in mineral wealth and revered as the place of miracles and prophets in Judaism, Islam and Christianity. God is said to have appeared to Moses here, and thought to have delivered the Israelites from the Egyptian army into the Red Sea. These days, the region is revered for its spectacular

Credit: © Corel Corporation

diving resorts, beaches, stunning coastline and vast deserts. This area has some of the best diving and snorkelling in the world, and has a more liberal atmosphere than the rest of Egypt.
The coastline attracts tourists ranging from top-class package deals, to backpackers in campsites: **Sharm el-Sheikh** is a large resort, and is best for diving. **Na'ama Bay** is much better developed and upmarket, with private beaches. A few kilometres north is **Shark Bay**, a quieter resort camp. The beaches at **Dahab** are spectacularly framed by jagged mountains. Holiday villages within a Bedouin settlement are close by. **Nuweiba** is a port city, with a plethora of resorts, and is famous for Olin the dolphin, with which people can pay to swim. Local Bedouins offer jeep safaris into the interior. Between here and **Taba**, there are many small, quiet resorts that threaten to be overshadowed by a huge new tourist development, **Taba Heights**. On the west of the Red Sea Coast, the biggest diving resort is **Hurghada**, once a fishing village and now a major commercial tourist centre. **Ras Muhammed** is the southernmost point on the peninsula, fringed with lagoons and reefs, and is now a **National Park**.
Little is accessible in **Sinai**'s interior, a barren area with rocks and sands, and the best way to explore this is by treks or safari by camel or jeep. One of the highlights is **St Catherine's Monastery**, now home to Greek Orthodox monks. St Catherine was the legendary martyr of Alexandria, who was tortured and beheaded for her Christianity. It has been a place of pilgrimage since the 4th century. Within the monastery is the 'burning bush' from which God is said to have appeared to speak to Moses.
Mount Sinai, revered as the site of God's revelation of the Ten Commandments, is a craggy and sheer-faced mount of grey and red, dramatic and steep. Care should be taken when ascending. Other places to visit in this region include **Oyun Musa** ('Springs of Moses'), **Qalat al-Gindi**, an 800-year-old fortress, and **Hammam Fara'un**'s hot springs and isolated beach.

Sport & Activities

Diving: The Red Sea coast and the Gulf of Aqaba are deservedly popular among divers, owing to their rich marine life and shipwrecks. A large variety of coral, tiny florescent fish, giant turtles, Napoleon wrasse and nurse sharks are just some of the species inhabiting the area. The main dive centres are on the Sinai Peninsular at *Sharm el-Sheikh* and *Ras Muhammad*, a national park since 1983. Equipment may be hired and training is available for all levels of ability. Near Sharm el-Sheikh, there is a famous World War II wreck, the *SS Thistlegorm* and the nearby *Straits of Tirian* host spectacular offshore reefs, as well as two more wrecks. Live-aboard packages are available from some operators. Conditions vary according to the time of year: in February and March, the extra plankton in the water attracts manta rays and in November and December, the visibility is particularly good. A twice-weekly tour for E£5 can be taken to four islands in the Red Sea, namely *Abou Kizan*, *The Emerald*, *The Rocky Island* and *The Two Brothers*. For further information, see the *Resorts & Excursions* section or contact the Egyptian State Tourist Office (see *Contact Addresses* section).
Note: The Red Sea coral reefs are all protected by law and persons removing 'souvenirs' will incur heavy fines.
Nile cruises: There are numerous cruise steamers on the Nile, the majority of which provide a very high standard of service. Vessels usually carry between 50 and 100 passengers, with the facilities varying according to the size of the individual vessel. Contacting a specialist operator is recommended for choosing a Nile cruise. Normally visitors can only book the complete package through a tour operator. Traditional *feluccas* may also be chartered. For further information, see *Nile Cruises* in the *Resorts & Excursions* section *or* contact the Egyptian State Tourist Office (see *Contact Addresses* section).
Other: Tennis, **croquet** and **horseriding** clubs are found in both Alexandria and Cairo. For details, ask at the hotel. There is a public **golf** club at the foot of the Giza pyramids and there is a *Gary Player* course at Soma Bay on the Red Sea. Most courses either adjoin or are part of hotels, for instance, the *Mena House*, which is 15 minutes from Cairo. Other courses include the *Alexandria Sporting Club* (30 minutes from Alexandria); *Jolie Ville* (five minutes from Sharm el-Sheikh); *Royal Valley Golf Course* (25 minutes from Luxor); *The Steigenberger Golf Club* (30 minutes from Hurghada). The Egyptian State Tourist Office can provide further information (see *Contact Addresses* section).

Social Profile

FOOD & DRINK: Egyptian cuisine is excellent, combining many of the best traditions of Middle Eastern cooking, and there are both large hotel restaurants and smaller specialist ones throughout the main towns. Some of the larger hotels in Cairo and its environs have excellent kitchens serving the best cosmopolitan dishes. In the centre of Cairo, American-style snack bars are also spreading. Local specialities include *foul* (bean dishes), stuffed vine leaves, roast pigeon, grilled aubergines, kebabs and *humus* (chickpeas). Restaurants have waiter service, with table service for bars.
Although Egypt is a Muslim country, alcohol is available in cafe-style bars and good restaurants. The legal drinking age is 21.
NIGHTLIFE: Sophisticated nightclubs, discos, casinos and good restaurants can be found in Cairo, Alexandria and most large towns. The nightlife in Luxor and Aswan often includes barbecues along the Nile.
SHOPPING: The most interesting shopping area for tourists in Cairo is the old bazaar, *Khan-el-Khalili*, specialising in reproductions of antiquities. Jewellery, spices, copper utensils and Coptic cloth are some of the special items. There are also modern shopping centres available, particularly near Tehrir Square. **Shopping hours:** *Winter:* Tues, Wed, Fri and Sat 0900-1900, Mon and Thurs 0900-2000. During Ramadan, hours vary, with shops often closing on Sunday. *Summer:* Tues, Wed, Fri-Sun 0900-1230 and 1600-2000.
SPECIAL EVENTS: For a complete list containing organiser details, contact the Egyptian State Tourist Office (see *Contact Addresses* section). The following is a selection of special events occurring in Egypt in 2005:
Jan 7 *Coptic Christmas*. **Feb 22** *Abu Simbel Festival*. **May 2** *Mohammed's Birthday*. **May 2** *Shem al Nessim*. **Sep 20-30** *Experimental Theatre Festival*. **Oct 1-14** *Moulid of Sayyida Zeinab*. **Oct 10-12** *Aida at Giza*. **Nov 30-Dec 10** *Cairo International Film Festival*.
SOCIAL CONVENTIONS: Islam is the dominant influence and many traditional customs and beliefs are tied up with religion. The people are generally courteous and hospitable and expect similar respect from visitors. Handshaking will suffice as a greeting. Because Egypt is a Muslim country, dress should be conservative and women should not wear revealing clothes, particularly when in religious buildings and in towns (although the Western style of dress is accepted in modern nightclubs, restaurants, hotels and bars in Cairo, Alexandria and other tourist destinations). Official or social functions and smart restaurants usually require more formal wear. Smoking is very common.
Photography: Tourists will have to pay a fee to take photographs inside pyramids, tombs and museums.
Tipping: 10 to 12 per cent is added to hotel and restaurant bills but an extra tip of 5 per cent is normal. Taxi drivers generally expect 10 per cent.

Business Profile

ECONOMY: On taking power in 1952, President Nasser quickly instituted a Soviet-style command economy that was closed to Western investment. After Nasser's death, his successor, Anwar Sadat, gradually dismantled the existing system in favour of a policy of *infitah* (openness) towards investment. Egypt's economy underwent rapid growth during the 1970s with the swift expansion of the oil industry, tourism and the Suez Canal. During the 1990s, stern fiscal policies, agreed with the IMF and World Bank, and further market-oriented measures brought the Egyptian economy to its current condition. As of mid-2004 annual growth had fallen to 3 per cent, inflation was about 4 per cent, while official unemployment was 10 per cent (although there is considerable under-employment). Egypt's major industries are textiles, fertilisers, rubber products and cement. There are also steel production works and several vehicle-assembly plants. The main crops are cotton, rice, wheat, sugar, maize and a range of fruit and vegetables. Egypt's major trading partners are the USA and the major EU economies (especially Italy and Germany). Expansion of the tourist sector was briefly hampered by the activities of Islamic fundamentalists. Agriculture, which relies on irrigation from the Nile, employs one-third of the working population. Foreign aid, especially from the USA, is an important source of government funds.
COMMERCIAL INFORMATION: The following organisations can offer advice: Egyptian-British Chamber of Commerce, PO Box 4EG, 4th Floor, 299 Oxford Street, London W1A 4EG, UK (tel: (020) 7499 3100; fax: (020) 7499 1070; e-mail: info@theebcc.com; website: www.theebcc.com); *or* Federation of Egyptian Chambers of Commerce, 4 Midan el-Falaky Square, Cairo (tel: (2) 795 1136; fax: (2) 795 7940); *or* Cairo Chamber of Commerce (address as for the Federation; tel: (2) 354 2943; fax: (2) 355 7940).
CONFERENCES/CONVENTIONS: Cairo has many hotels and three large meeting halls (seating up to 2000 people), which are equipped for use as conference centres. The new Cairo International Conference Centre, 12km (7 miles) east of Cairo International Airport, has seating for 2500 people, with an exhibition hall, banquet hall and comprehensive facilities. There is also a new convention centre at Alexandria University, which has a main hall with seating for 2400. For more information on conference facilities in Egypt, contact the Egyptian State Tourist Office (see *Contact Addresses* section); *or* Cairo International Conference and Exhibition Centre, Nasr Road, Nasr City, Cairo (tel: (2) 263 4631 *or* 263 4632; fax: (2) 263 4640; website: www.cicc.egnet.net); *or* Egyptian General Company for Tourism and Hotels, 6th floor, 4 Latin America Street, Garden City, Cairo (tel: (2) 795 7867; fax: (2) 796 4830).

Climate

Hot, dry summers with mild, dry winters and cold nights. Rainfall is negligible except on the coast. In April, the hot, dusty *Khamsin* wind blows from the Sahara.
Required clothing: Lightweight cottons and linens during summer, with warmer clothes for winter and cooler evenings.

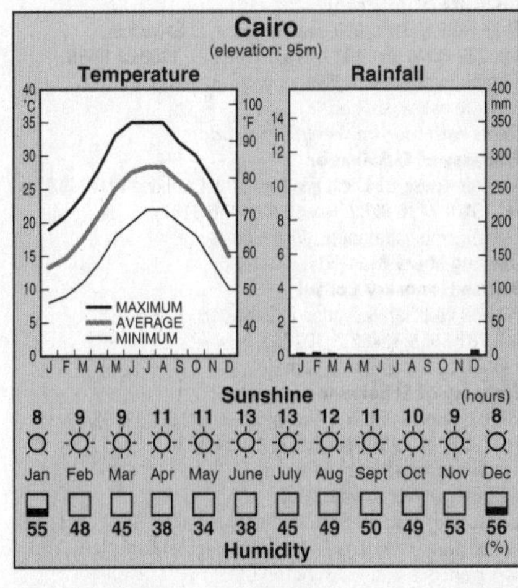

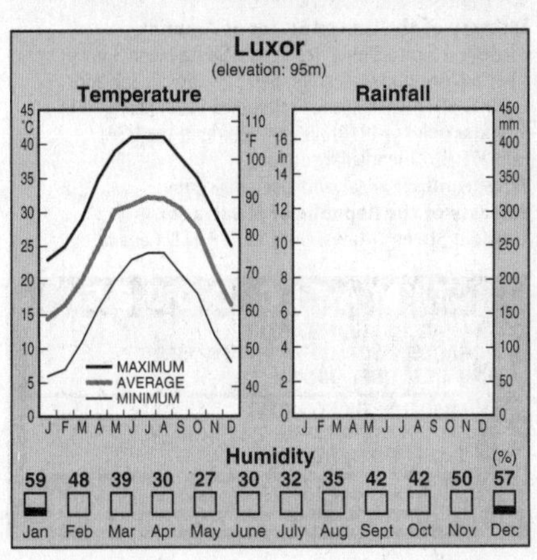

El Salvador

LATEST TRAVEL ADVICE CONTACTS

British Foreign and Commonwealth Office
Tel: (0870) 606 0290 Website: www.fco.gov.uk

US Department of State
Website: http://travel.state.gov/travel

Canadian Department of Foreign Affairs and Int'l Trade
Tel: (1 800) 267 8376 Website: www.dfait-maeci.gc.ca

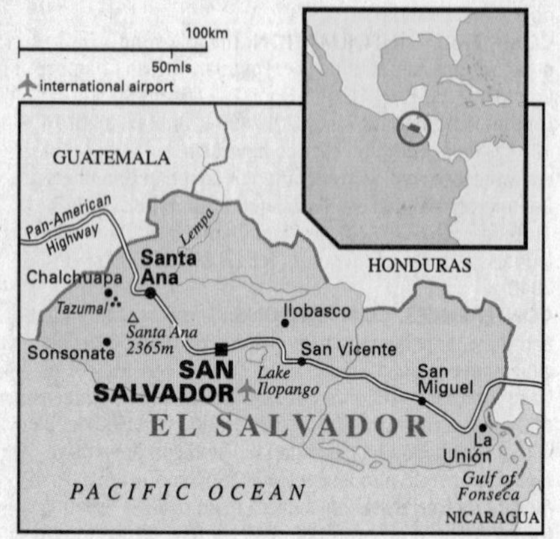

Location: Central America.

Country dialling code: 503.

The British Embassy in San Salvador is now closed indefinitely. However, the British Embassy in Guatemala City, Guatemala may be able to provide limited assistance.

Corporacion Salvadoreña de Turismo (CORSATUR) (Salvadorian Tourism Corporation)
Avenida el Espino 68, Urbanización Madre Selva, Santa Elena, Antigua Cuzatan, El Salvador
Tel: 243 7835. Fax: 243 7844.
E-mail: corsatur@salnet.net
Website: www.elsalvadorturismo.gob.sv
Promotes El Salvador abroad.

Instituto Salvadoreño de Turismo (ISTU) (Salvadorian Institute of Tourism)
Calle Rubén Darío 619, San Salvador, El Salvador
Tel: 222 8000 (ext 131 or 151). Fax: 222 1208 *or* 8455.
E-mail: informacion@istu.gob.sv
Website: www.istu.gob.sv
Deals with tourism within El Salvador.

Embassy of El Salvador
Mayfair House, 39 Great Portland Street, London W1W 7JZ, UK
Tel: (020) 7436 8282. Fax: (020) 7436 8181.
E-mail: embajadalondres@rree.gob.sv
Opening hours: Mon-Fri 0900-1600.

British Honorary Consul
PO Box 242, San Salvador, El Salvador
Tel: 281 5555. Fax: 271 1026.
E-mail: claims@gibson.com.sv

Embassy of El Salvador
2308 California St, NW, Washington, DC 20008, USA
Tel: (202) 265 9671/2. Fax: (202) 234 3834.
E-mail: correo@elsalvador.org
Website: www.elsalvador.org
Consulates also in: Boston, Chicago, Dallas, Houston, Long Island (New York), Los Angeles, Las Vegas, Miami, New York, San Francisco and Washington DC.

Embassy of the United States of America
Boulevard Santa Elena, Residencia Santa Elena Sur, La Libertad, Antiguo Cuscatlán, San Salvador, El Salvador
Tel: 900 6011 (with special telefonica calling card, in El Salvador only) *or* (818) 755 8425 (line in the USA).
Fax: 278 5522 (consular section).
Website: http://sansalvador.usembassy.gov

Embassy of the Republic of El Salvador
209 Kent Street, Ottawa, Ontario K2P 1Z8, Canada
Tel: (613) 238 2939. Fax: (613) 238 6940.
E-mail: embajada@elsalvador-ca.org

Canadian Embassy
Centro Financiero Gigante, 63 Avenida Sur y Alameda Roosevelt, Torre A, Lobby 2, San Salvador, El Salvador
Tel: 279 4655. Fax: 279 0765.
E-mail: ssal@international.gc.ca
Website: www.dfait-maeci.gc.ca/elsalvador

TIMATIC CODES

Health
AMADEUS: **TI-DFT/JIB/HE**
GALILEO/WORLDSPAN: **TI-DFT/JIB/HE**
SABRE: **TIDFT/JIB/HE**

Visa
AMADEUS: **TI-DFT/JIB/VI**
GALILEO/WORLDSPAN: **TI-DFT/JIB/VI**
SABRE: **TIDFT/JIB/VI**

To access TIMATIC country information on Health and Visa regulations through the Computer Reservations System (CRS), type in the appropriate command line listed above.

General Information

AREA: 21,041 sq km (8124 sq miles).
POPULATION: 6,517,300 (official estimate 2002).
POPULATION DENSITY: 314.6 per sq km.
CAPITAL: San Salvador. **Population:** 485,847 (official estimate 2001).
GEOGRAPHY: El Salvador is located in Central America and is bordered north and west by Guatemala, north and east by Honduras and south and west by the Pacific Ocean. Most of the country is volcanic uplands, along which run two almost parallel rows of volcanoes. The highest are Santa Ana at 2365m (7759ft), San Vicente at 2182m (7159ft) and San Salvador at 1943m (6375ft). Volcanic activity has resulted in a thick layer of ash and lava on the highlands, ideal for coffee planting. Lowlands lie to the north and south of the high backbone.
GOVERNMENT: Republic. **Head of State and Government:** Elias Antonio Saca since 2004.
LANGUAGE: The official language is Spanish. English is widely spoken.
RELIGION: 78 per cent Roman Catholic; there are also some other Christian denominations.
TIME: GMT - 6.
ELECTRICITY: 110 volts AC, 60Hz.
COMMUNICATIONS: Telephone: IDD available. Country code: 503. IDD is available to Europe, the USA and certain international ports. Outgoing international code: 0. **Mobile telephone:** GSM 850, 900 and 1950 networks. Network operators include *CTE Telecom Perosnal SA de CV* and *Digicel SA de CV* (website: www.digicel.com.sv). **Fax:** Large hotels and Telecom offices have facilities. **Internet:** Internet access is readily available throughout El Salvador. ISPs include *NetSat Express* (website: www.netsatx.net) and *Pointe Communications* (website: www.telscape.com). **Post:** Airmail to Europe takes up to seven days. Post office hours: Mon-Fri 0900-1600. **Press:** Six daily newspapers are published in San Salvador, including *El Diario de Hoy* and *La Prensa Gráfica*. There are several provincial papers. **Radio:** BBC World Service (website: www.bbc.co.uk/worldservice) and Voice of America (website: www.voa.gov) can be received. From time to time the frequencies change and the most up-to-date can be found online.

Passport/Visa

	Passport Required?	Visa Required?	Return Ticket Required?
Full British	Yes	No	Yes
Australian	Yes	No	Yes
Canadian	Yes	No	Yes
USA	Yes	No	Yes
Other EU	Yes	No	Yes
Japanese	Yes	No	Yes

Note: *Regulations and requirements may be subject to change at short notice, and you are advised to contact the appropriate diplomatic or consular authority before finalising travel arrangements. Details of these may be found at the head of this country's entry. Any numbers in the chart refer to the footnotes below.*

PASSPORTS: Passport valid for at least six months after day of departure required by all.
VISAS: Required by all except the following for stays of up to 90 days:
(a) nationals of countries mentioned in the table above;
(b) nationals of all British, French and Dutch overseas territories, and nationals of Hong Kong (when the passport is marked 'Nationality: British Citizen' *only*);
(c) nationals of Andorra, Antigua & Barbuda, Argentina, The Bahamas, Bahrain, Barbados, Belize, Brazil, Brunei, Bulgaria, Chile, Costa Rica, Croatia, Guam, Guatemala, Honduras, Iceland, Israel, Korea (Rep), Kuwait, Liechtenstein, Macedonia, Madagascar, Malaysia, Marshall Islands, Mexico, Monaco, New Zealand, Nicaragua, Norway, Panama, Paraguay, Qatar, Romania, St Kitts & Nevis, St Lucia, St Vincent & the Grenadines, San Marino, Sao Tomé e Principe, Singapore, Solomon Islands, South Africa, Switzerland, Taiwan (China), Trinidad & Tobago, Turkey, Tuvalu, Uruguay, Vanuatu and Vatican City;
(c) transit passengers continuing their journey within 12 hours by the same or first connecting aircraft provided holding valid onward or return documentation and not leaving the airport.
Note: Nationals of Afghanistan, Albania, Algeria, Armenia, Angola, Bangladesh, Bolivia, Bosnia & Herzegovina, Botswana, China (PR), Colombia, Congo, Congo (Rep), Cuba, East Timor, Ecuador, Eritrea, Ethiopia, Ghana, Haiti, India, Indonesia, Iran, Iraq, Jordan, Korea (Dem Rep), Laos, Lebanon, Liberia, Libya, Mali, Mongolia, Mozambique, Nepal, Nigeria, Oman, Pakistan, Palestinian Authority, Peru, Sierra Leone, Somalia, Sri Lanka, Sudan, Syrian Arab Republic, Vietnam and Yemen need authorisation from the immigration authorities in El Salvador and their visa processing time can therefore take up to three weeks. Applicants should apply in plenty of time.
Types of visa and cost: *Tourist* and *Business*: US$30 (single entry); US$45 (multiple-entry, valid six months); US$60 (multiple-entry, valid 12 months).
Validity: *Tourist* and *Business*: single entry, valid up to 30 days; multiple-entry, valid either six or 12 months. Visas can be renewed at the Immigration Office in El Salvador.
Application to: Consulate (or Consular section at Embassy); see *Contact Addresses* section.
Application requirements: (a) Completed application form. (b) One passport-size photo. (c) Valid passport. (d) For tourist visas, a photocopy of the return ticket is necessary or, if the tickets have not yet been purchased, an original letter from the travel agency stating that the tickets are being purchased, or a travel itinerary. (e) Fee, payable in cash (US$ *only*) or by cheque (in US dollars, made payable to 'Direccion General de Tesoreria'). Visa fees are non-refundable. *Business*: (a)-(e) and, if from a country listed above as requiring authorisation from El Salvador, (f) Letter of invitation from the company being visited in El Salvador and a letter from the company the applicant is representing, both translated into Spanish.
Working days required: Tourist and business visas are normally issued within 24 hours. If authorisation from the Immigration Department in El Salvador is needed, processing time is approximately 21 days.
Temporary residence: Apply to Ministry of Interior in San Salvador.

Money

Currency: Colón (¢) (colloquially 'Peso') = 100 centavos. Notes are in denominations of ¢200, 100, 50, 25, 10 and 5. Coins are in denominations of ¢1, and 50, 25, 10, 5 and 1 centavos. Due to the introduction of the US Dollar into the country, dollars have been accepted as dual currency since January 2001 and are now widely used and will eventually completely replace the Colón.
Note: Visitors should reconvert all unspent Colónes before entering Guatemala or Honduras, as they are neither exchanged nor accepted in these countries.
Currency exchange: Visitors are advised to change currency only at banks and official bureaux de change.
Credit & debit cards: American Express, MasterCard and Visa are widely accepted, whilst Diners Club has more limited use. Check with your credit or debit card company for details of merchant acceptability and other services which may be available.
Travellers cheques: These may be cashed at any bank or hotel on production of a passport.
Currency restrictions: No restrictions on import and export of local currency. Import of foreign currency is unlimited, but declaration is advised. Export of foreign currency is unlimited but limited to the amount declared on import for larger amounts.
Exchange rate indicators: The following figures have been included as a guide to the movements of the Colón against Sterling and the US Dollar:

Date	Feb '04	May '04	Aug '04	Nov '04
£1.00=	15.93	15.63	16.12	16.57
$1.00=	8.75	8.75	8.75	8.75

Banking hours: Generally Mon-Fri 0900-1700; Sat 0900-1300.
Note: Most banks are closed for balancing on Jun 29-30 and Dec 30-31. These dates may vary for individual banks.

Duty Free

The following goods may be imported into El Salvador without incurring customs duty:
200 cigarettes or 50 cigars; 2l of alcoholic beverages; up to 6 units of perfume; gifts to the value of US$500.
Note: There are restrictions on import and export of fruit, vegetables, plants and animals.

Public Holidays

2005: Jan 1 New Year's Day. **Mar 23-27** Holy Week. **May 1** Labour Day. **Aug 4** Transfiguration Bank Holiday. **Aug 5-6** Festival El Salvador del Mundo (San Salvador only). **Sep 15** Independence Day. **Oct 12** Columbus Day. **Nov 2** All Souls' Day. **Nov 5** Cry of Independence Day. **Dec 24** Christmas Eve. **Dec 25** Christmas Day. **Dec 31** New Year's Eve.

2006: Jan 1 New Year's Day. **Apr 12-16** Holy Week. **May 1** Labour Day. **Aug 4** Transfiguration Bank Holiday. **Aug 5-6** Festival El Salvador del Mundo (San Salvador only). **Sep 15** Independence Day. **Oct 9** Columbus Day. **Nov 2** All Souls' Day. **Nov 5** Cry of Independence Day. **Dec 24** Christmas Eve. **Dec 25** Christmas Day. **Dec 31** New Year's Eve.

Health

	Special Precautions?	Certificate Required?
Yellow Fever	No	1
Cholera	2	No
Typhoid & Polio	3	N/A
Malaria	4	N/A

Note: *Regulations and requirements may be subject to change at short notice, and you are advised to contact your doctor well in advance of your intended date of departure. Any numbers in the chart refer to the footnotes below.*

1: A yellow fever vaccination certificate is required from travellers over six months of age coming from infected areas.
2: Following WHO guidelines issued in 1973, a cholera vaccination certificate is no longer a condition of entry into El Salvador. However, cases of cholera were reported in 1996 and precautions are essential. Up-to-date advice should be sought before deciding whether these precautions should include vaccination, as medical opinion is divided over its effectiveness.
3: Typhoid is common and vaccination against typhoid and polio is advised.
4: Very low malaria risk, predominantly in the benign *vivax* form, exists all year in Santa Ana Province and in rural areas of migratory influence.
Food & drink: All water should be regarded as being potentially contaminated. Water used for drinking, brushing teeth or making ice should have first been boiled or otherwise sterilised. Milk is unpasteurised and should be boiled. Powdered or tinned milk is available and is recommended, but make sure that it is reconstituted with pure water. Avoid dairy products that are likely to have been made from unboiled milk. Only eat well-cooked meat and fish, preferably served hot. Pork, salad and mayonnaise may carry increased risk. Vegetables should be cooked and fruit peeled.
Other risks: *Dengue fever* (including *dengue haemorrhagic fever*) is reported to be on the increase. Travellers should ask their doctor for advice before travelling. *Visceral leishmaniasis* occurs in this country, as well as *cutaneous* and *mucocutaneous leishmanisis*. *Hepatitis A* occurs and precautions should be taken; see the *Health* appendix for further information.
Rabies is widespread, particularly in dogs and bats. If you are bitten, seek medical advice without delay. For persons at high risk of exposure on a continuing basis, it may be advisable to have a course of rabies vaccine. Persons taking animals to El Salvador should be certain that the animals are immunised against rabies.
Health care: There are about 50 state-run hospitals with a total of more than 7000 beds. Medical facilities are limited and doctors and hospitals expect immediate cash payment. Health insurance is essential as there is no reciprocal health agreement with the UK.

Travel - International

Note: There are very high crime rates in El Salvador. Visitors who arrange to be met at the airport and accompanied during their trip encounter few problems. Great care must be taken if travelling alone or at night.
AIR: El Salvador's national airline is *Taca International Airlines (TA)* (website: www.taca.com). *American Airlines* operates daily flights from London Heathrow to El Salvador via Miami and via Washington. *United Airlines* operates flights from London Heathrow to El Salvador via Washington. Other airlines include *Air France*, *Continental*, *COPA*, *Delta*, *Iberia* and *Northwest Airlines*.
Approximate flight times: From San Salvador to *London*, excluding stopover time in USA (usually overnight), is 10 hours 20 minutes.
International airports: *San Salvador (SAL)* (El Salvador International) is 62km (38 miles) from the city. Coaches to the city operate every 30 minutes (travel time – 40 minutes). Taxis to the city are also available. Airport facilities include a restaurant, duty-free shops, car hire, disabled facilities, pharmacy, bank/bureau de change, tourist information and left luggage.
Departure tax: US$22 (including a US$2.65 Immigration Tax), payable in US Dollars or Colóns. Children under two years are exempt, but *do* need to pay the Immigration Tax.
SEA: The principal ports are *Acajutla*, *La Unión* and *La Libertad* on the Pacific coast.
RAIL: There are currently no rail links to Guatemala. Contact the Embassy for passage details.

Credit: © Corsatur

ROAD: There are frequent buses from San Salvador to Guatemala City and Tegucigalpa. If arriving at the border during off-duty hours (from Mon-Fri 1200-1400, 1800-0800 and Saturday from 1200 to Monday 0800), a duty must be paid.

Travel - Internal

AIR: Services are available from San Salvador to San Miguel, La Unión and Usulután.
RAIL: There are over 600km (372 miles) of railways, linking San Salvador with Acajutla, Cutuco, San Jerónimo and Angiuatu.
ROAD: Traffic drives on the right. There are more than 12,000km (7440 miles) of roads around the country; a third of this network is either paved or improved to allow all-weather use. Car hijacking and burglaries are frequent in El Salvador (especially in the cities) and drivers are advised to travel by day only and with the doors locked at all times. New cars, particularly with foreign licence plates, are frequent targets. There are petrol stations in every town and at motorway junctions. **Bus:** A good service exists between major towns, although there can be delays if the weather is bad. Buses can be hailed. **Car hire:** Available in San Salvador and from the airport. **Documentation:** A national or International Driving Permit is required. A vehicle may remain in the country for 30 days, and for a further 60 days on application to the Customs and Transport authorities.
URBAN: Bus: City buses offer a good service, but are often crowded. **Taxi:** Plentiful but not metered, so it is advisable to agree the fare beforehand. Taxis are yellow and can usually be found cruising the streets looking for pick ups. Alternatively, head to the town square (or similar), where taxis usually congregate between fares. Many large hotels have their own taxi services.
Travel Times: The following chart gives approximate travel times (in hours and minutes) from **San Salvador** to other major cities/towns in El Salvador.

	Road
Costa del Sol	1.30
Santa Ana	1.15
San Miguel	3.00

Accommodation

The main hotels are in the capital, and accommodation should be booked in advance. Due to a high crime rate, foreign visitors should seek advice from the Embassy before leaving. Lake Coatepeque is a popular resort in Western El Salvador, which has good hotels, restaurants and lodging houses. Contact the El Salvador Hotel Association for more information (website: www.elsalhoteles.com).
Grading: Hotels in El Salvador can be classified into three groups: deluxe, first-class and budget hotels.

Resorts & Excursions

Note: El Salvador's infrastructure was badly affected by the earthquake in Jan 2001. This has resulted in years of ongoing work and you should consult Government travel warnings for up-to-date information on specific conditions in the country.

SAN SALVADOR: Situated 680m (2240ft) above sea level, the capital, San Salvador, is the second-largest city in Central America, with a population of over 600,000. Founded by the Spaniard Pedro De Alvarado in 1525, the city is a blend of modern buildings and colonial architecture, broad plazas and monuments, amusement parks and shopping centres. The most important public buildings are downtown. Standing within a short distance of each other are the **Catedral Metropolitana** (metropolitan cathedral), the **Palacio Nacional** (national palace), the **National Treasury** and the **Teatro Nacional** (national theatre). Among the many beautiful colonial churches to be seen are **St Ignatius Loyola** (once the shrine of the 'Virgin of Guadalupe') with a traditional Spanish colonial facade, the **Juayua** and the **Suchitoto**. The amusement park on San Jacinto Mountain can be reached by cable car and gives a panoramic view of the city.
Balboa Park, 11km (7 miles) from the capital, and the 1200m (3900ft) rock formation, the **Puerta del Diablo** (devil's doorway), just south of Balboa Park, also give a bird's-eye view of San Salvador.
EXCURSIONS: From San Salvador, excursions can be made by road to **Panchimalco**, 15km (9 miles) south of the capital, around which live the Pancho Indians (pure-blooded descendants of the original Pipil tribes), who retain many of their old traditions and dress. The village of **San Sebastián**, approximately one hour by car from San Salvador, is known for its beautiful woven materials. The village is situated near **Lake Ilopango**, the largest of El Salvador's lakes, surrounded by volcanoes and mountains, and is a popular destination for outdoor and watersports' enthusiasts. The mountain village of **Ilobasco**, northeast of the capital, is renowned for its beauty and its craftwork.
ARCHAEOLOGICAL SITES: El Salvador has a number of ancient archaeological sites from the Maya civilisation, some dating back to the third century BC. The Mayan village of **Joya de Cerén** was buried under volcanic ash 1400 years ago and is now a UNESCO World Heritage Site. Also close to the capital is the **San Andrés** region, where fertile soil once housed Mayan settlements and where the architectural jewel, the acropolis, is a highlight. El Salvador's earliest people lived between 300 BC and AD 1200 at **Chalchuapa** in the Tazumal region, 78km (46 miles) from San Salvador. During this period, five important ceremonial centres were built: **Pampe**, **El Trapiche**, **Las Victorias**, **Casablanca** and the beautiful ruins at **Tazumal**, which boasts structures over 30m (90ft) high and a ball court where the Maya practised an unusual sporting rite. Other interesting sites include the pre-Columbian **Tehuacán** site near **San Vicente**; the monumental **Santa Leticía** sculptures near the town of **San Miguel**; and the pre-Columbian village of **Quelepa**, also in San Miguel.
VOLCANOES & PARKS: There are more than 25 volcanoes in El Salvador, only three of which – the **Izalco**, **San Miguel** and **Santa Ana** (the largest) – are still considered active. The extinct **San Salvador** volcano is within close proximity of the capital. Another extinct volcano, the easily accessible **Cerro Verde** in the west, is located within the **Cerro Verde National Park**, also home to the popular and beautiful **Lake Coatepeque**, which sits on top of a volcanic crater. The nearby **Santa Ana** volcano, which is still active and last erupted in 1966, is located near the town of Santa Ana, whose cathedral is the most famous in El Salvador. Also within the area is **El Imposible National Park**, the country's most important ecological reserve, where varied

vegetation and fauna offer a refuge for numerous bird and wildlife species, including the rare Black Hawk Eagle.
THE COAST: El Salvador has a 320km- (200 mile-) Pacific Coast with resort hotels, unspoiled beaches, fishing villages and pine views. Beaches include **la Barra de Santiago**, **los Cóbanos**, **el Cuco**, **el Sunzal** and **el Tamarindo**. The best resorts tend to be found along the **Costa del Sol**, easily accessible via a modern highway. For details on sports and activities that can be pursued on the coast and elsewhere in El Salvador, see the *Sport & Activities* section.

Sport & Activities

Watersports: The eastern coast is renowned for having the most attractive beaches, the best of which include *El Icacal* and *El Tamarindo*. **Surfing** is popular, with the biggest waves rolling in at *Punta Roca* and *Los Cóbanos*. **Boat excursions** on the Gulf of Fonseca, a large stretch of water shared by El Salvador, Honduras and Nicaragua, are also possible, including stopovers at the many volcanic islands dotting the Gulf. For an inland resort, the western region of *Lake Coatepeque* at the foot of the Santa Ana volcano is recommended and offers a range of watersports. It also has several good hotels, restaurants and lodging houses. **Canoeing** and **whitewater rafting** are possible on some of the rivers, notably the *Tórtola*. Visitors can also practise **fishing**, **sailing** and **boat racing**, which is available in private clubs only.
Other: Organised **cultural tours** to El Salvador's archaeological sites, as well as **hiking** and **trekking** expeditions to the volcanoes, lakes and parks can be booked through private operators. **Ecological tours** to study the fauna and wildlife in the parks and nature reserves are also available. For details, contact CORSATUR (see *Contact Addresses* section).

Credit: © Corsatur

Social Profile

FOOD & DRINK: There are numerous Chinese, Mexican, Italian, French and local restaurants, plus several fast-food chains. The food market (one of the biggest and cleanest in Central and Latin America) has many stalls selling cheap food.
NIGHTLIFE: San Salvador has a few nightclubs and cocktail lounges with dinner and dancing, some of which require membership. There are many cinemas, some showing English-language films with subtitles; there are also some 'jukebox' dance-halls and theatres.
SHOPPING: Various goods can be bought at the Mercado Cuartel crafts market, including towels in Maya designs. Other shopping centres can be found at Basilea, Galerias Escalón, Metrocentro, Metrosor and Villas Españolas.
Shopping hours: Mon-Sat 1000-1900.
SPECIAL EVENTS: For full details of special events and festivals in El Salvador, contact the National Tourism Institute or Embassy (see *Contact Addresses* section). The following is a selection of special events celebrated annually in El Salvador:
Jan *Sugar Cane Festival*, Cojutepeque; *Street Festival of Ahuachapán*. **Apr** *Semana Santa*. **May** *Flower Fiesta*, Panchimalco. **May 3** *Day of the Cross*. **May 10** *Mothers Day*. **Jun 17** *Fathers Day*. **Jun 22** *Teachers Day*. **Jul** *July Festival*, Santa Ana. **Aug** *August Festival* (El Salvador del Mundo), San Salvador. **Aug 6** *La Bajada* (The Descent). **Sep** *El Salvador Independence Day*. **Oct** *Balm Festival*, Santa Tecla. **Nov** *Straw Festival*, Zacatecoluco; *Carnival*, San Miguel. **Dec 12** *Feast of the Indians*.
SOCIAL CONVENTIONS: Visitors should not point their finger or their foot at anyone. First names should not be used to address someone unless invited to do so. Conservative casual wear is acceptable. **Photography:** Sensitive (eg military) areas should not be photographed. **Tipping:** 10 per cent in hotels and restaurants; 15 per cent is appropriate for smaller bills. Taxi drivers do not expect tips, except when the taxi has been hired for the day.

Business Profile

ECONOMY: The long-running civil war caused a significant decline in El Salvador's mainly agricultural economy. Although there has been a steady recovery since the political settlement took hold, El Salvador remains one of the poorest economies in the region. The economy is also still vulnerable to the vagaries of the regional climate – hurricanes, floods and drought. The principal commercial crop is coffee, which is the country's major export earner. Other important crops are cotton, sugar, maize, beans and rice; in addition, shrimps and honey have become important export commodities. There is a sizeable manufacturing sector – the largest in Central America – producing footwear, textiles, leather goods and pharmaceuticals. Hydroelectricity and imported oil are the main sources of energy. Tourism is the main service industry. Remittances from Salvadorans working abroad are a vital source of income for many families. The Flores government adopted a number of radical measures in an effort to kick-start the economy, including fixing the Colón (the Salvadoran currency) to the US dollar. It has also made substantial investments in national infrastrusture and the education system, but these will take some time to show results. In 2004, GDP growth was 1.4 per cent. El Salvador still relies heavily on aid from the US and the EU, as well as loans from the International Monetary Fund. El Salvador is a member of the Central American Common Market. The USA is the country's largest trading partner, followed by Guatemala, Germany and Japan.
BUSINESS: Businesspeople are expected to wear suits. Although some local businesspeople speak English, a good knowledge of Spanish is important. Visiting cards are essential. The best months for business visits are September to March, avoiding the Christmas period. **Office hours:** Mon-Fri 0900-1730, Sat 0800-1200.
COMMERCIAL INFORMATION: The following organisations can offer advice: Cámara de Comercio e Industria de El Salvador, Ard. Hermanos Bon, 79124, Castellon, (tel: 356 500; fax: 356 510; e-mail: camarainforma@camaracs.es *or* cocints@camaracs.es; website: www.camaracs.es); *or* Banco Central de Reserva de El Salvador, CENTREX, Alameda Juan Pablo Segundo, Entre 15 y 17 Avenida Norte, San Salvador (tel: 281 8000; fax: 281 8113; e-mail: comunicaciones@bcr.gob.sv; website: www.bcr.gob.sv).

Climate

Hot, subtropical climate affected by altitude. Coastal areas are particularly hot, with a rainy season between May and October. Upland areas have a cooler, more temperate climate.
Required clothing: Lightweight cottons and rainwear during the wet season in coastal areas. Waterproof clothing is advisable all year round. Warm clothing should be taken for higher altitudes.

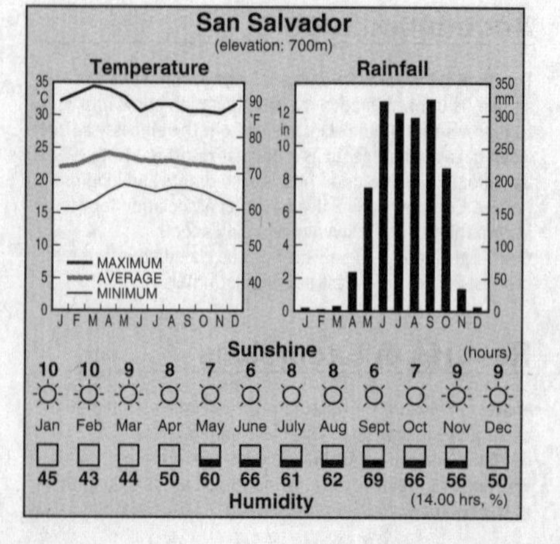

Equatorial Guinea

LATEST TRAVEL ADVICE CONTACTS

British Foreign and Commonwealth Office
Tel: (0870) 606 0290 Website: www.fco.gov.uk
US Department of State
Website: http://travel.state.gov/travel
Canadian Department of Foreign Affairs and Int'l Trade
Tel: (1 800) 267 8376 Website: www.dfait-maeci.gc.ca

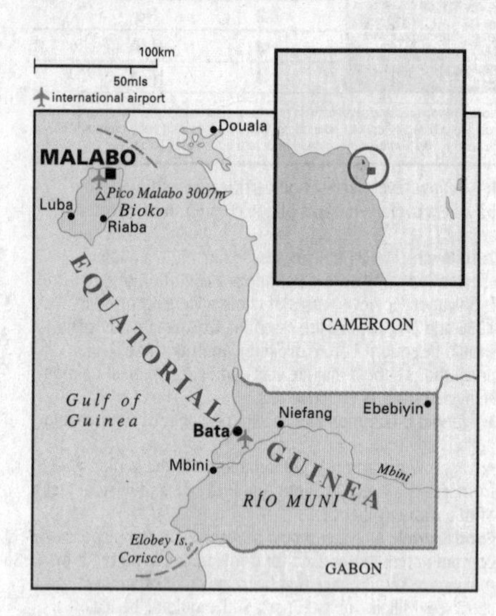

Location: West Coast of Central Africa, Gulf of Guinea.

Country dialling code: 240.

Embassy of the Republic of Equatorial Guinea
29 Boulevard de Courcelles, 75008 Paris, France
Tel: (1) 5688 5454 *or* 1075. Fax: (1) 5688 1048 *or* 5458.
The British Consulate in Yaoundé deals with enquiries relating to Equatorial Guinea (see *Cameroon* **section).**
Embassy of Equatorial Guinea
2020 16th Street, NW, Washington, DC 20009, USA
Tel: (202) 518 5700. Fax: (202) 518 5252.
E-mail: eg_africa@yahoo.com
The Embassy of the United States of America in Yaoundé deals with enquiries relating to Equatorial Guinea (see *Cameroon* **section).**
The Canadian Embassy in Libreville deals with enquiries from Canadian and Australian citizens relating to Equatorial Guinea (see *Gabon* **section).**

General Information

AREA: 28,051 sq km (10,831 sq miles).
POPULATION: 481,000 (UN estimate 2002).
POPULATION DENSITY: 17.1 per sq km.
CAPITAL: Malabo. **Population:** 33,000 (2001).
GEOGRAPHY: Equatorial Guinea is bordered to the south and east by Gabon, to the north by Cameroon and to the west by the Gulf of Guinea. The country also comprises the island of Bioko, formerly Fernando Poo, 34km (21 miles) off the coast of Cameroon, and the small offshore islands of Corisco, Great Elobey, Small Elobey and Annobón (formerly Pagalu). The mainland province, Rió Muni, is mainly forest, with plantations on the coastal plain and some mountains. Bioko rises steeply to two main peaks in the north and south. The southern area is rugged and inaccessible. Cultivation and settlements exist on the other slopes; above the farming land, the forest is thick. The beaches around the islands are extremely beautiful.
GOVERNMENT: Republic. Declared independence from Spain in 1968. **Head of State:** President Teodoro Obiang Nguema Mbasogo since 1979. **Head of Government:** Miguel Abia Biteo Borico since 2004.
LANGUAGE: Spanish and French are the official languages.

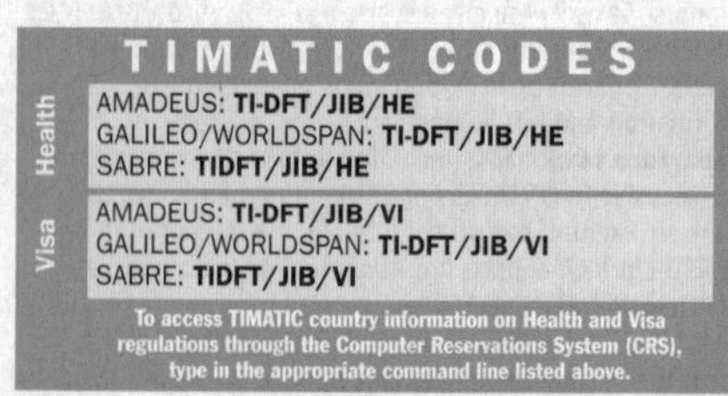
TIMATIC CODES

Health
AMADEUS: **TI-DFT/JIB/HE**
GALILEO/WORLDSPAN: **TI-DFT/JIB/HE**
SABRE: **TIDFT/JIB/HE**

Visa
AMADEUS: **TI-DFT/JIB/VI**
GALILEO/WORLDSPAN: **TI-DFT/JIB/VI**
SABRE: **TIDFT/JIB/VI**

To access TIMATIC country information on Health and Visa regulations through the Computer Reservations System (CRS), type in the appropriate command line listed above.

The main African dialects spoken are Fang and Bubi (which is common on Bioko).
RELIGION: No official religion, but around 90 per cent are Roman Catholic, with an animist minority.
TIME: GMT + 1.
ELECTRICITY: 220/240 volts AC.
COMMUNICATIONS: Telephone: IDD is available. Country code: 240. Operator assistance may be required when making international calls from the country. **Mobile telephone:** GSM 900 network, operated by *GETESA*. Coverage limited to Malabo and a few other inhabited areas. **Internet:** Main ISP is run by *GETESA* (website: www.getesa.com). **Post:** Service to Western Europe takes up to two weeks. **Press:** Spanish language weekly publications include *Hoja Parroquial* and *El Sol*, produced in Equatorial Guinea. There's also the state-owned *Ebano* and the privately-owned *La Nacion* and *La Opinion*.
Radio: BBC World Service (website: www.bbc.co.uk/worldservice) and Voice of America (website: www.voa.gov) can be received. From time to time the frequencies change and the most up-to-date can be found online.

Passport/Visa

	Passport Required?	Visa Required?	Return Ticket Required?
Full British	Yes	Yes	Yes
Australian	Yes	Yes	Yes
Canadian	Yes	Yes	Yes
USA	Yes	No	Yes
Other EU	Yes	Yes	Yes
Japanese	Yes	Yes	Yes

Note: *Regulations and requirements may be subject to change at short notice, and you are advised to contact the appropriate diplomatic or consular authority before finalising travel arrangements. Details of these may be found at the head of this country's entry. Any numbers in the chart refer to the footnotes below.*

PASSPORTS: Passport valid for a minimum of six months required by all.
VISAS: Required by all except nationals of the USA.
Types of visas and cost: *Tourist*, *Business* and *Transit*: €80.
Validity: Enquire at Embassy (or Consular section at Embassy); see *Contact Addresses* section.
Application to: Consulate (or Consular section at Embassy); see *Contact Addresses* section.
Application requirements: (a) Passport valid for at least six months after return date (and photocopy). (b) One completed application form. (c) Two passport-size colour photos. (d) Original copy of return ticket or proof of confirmed airline reservation. (e) Yellow fever vaccination certificate. (f) Fee, payable in cash, money order or company cheque. (g) Self-addressed, stamped envelope for postal applications. *Tourist*: (a)-(g) and, (h) Proof of hotel booking. *Business*: (a)-(g) and, (h) Letter of invitation from the company in Equatorial Guinea declaring responsibility for the applicant. *Private*: (a)-(g) and, (h) Letter of invitation, stamped by the Director General of Security in Marabo. *Transit*: (a)-(g) and, (h) Valid visa for the destination country.
Working days required: 48 hours (shorter if application is urgent; longer in exceptional circumstances or if applying by post).

Money

Currency: CFA (*Communauté Financiaire Africaine*) Franc (CFAfr or XAF) = 100 centimes. Notes are in denominations of CFAfr10,000, 5000, 1000 and 500. Coins are in denominations of CFAfr500, 100, 50, 25, 10 and 5.
Currency exchange: Equatorial Guinea is part of the French Monetary Area. Only currency issued by the *Banque des Etats de l'Afrique Centrale* (Bank of Central African States) is valid; currency issued by the *Banque des Etats de l'Afrique de l'Ouest* (Bank of West African States) is not. The CFA Franc is tied to the Euro. Foreign currencies are best exchanged at banks, of which, however, there are few. Receipts for currency exchange should be retained.
Credit & debit cards: Diners Club is accepted on a limited basis. Check with your credit or debit card company for details of merchant acceptability and other services which may be available.
Travellers cheques: Travellers cheques are generally not recommended.
Currency restrictions: The import of local and foreign currency is unrestricted provided declared on arrival. The export of local currency is limited to CFAfr50,000. The export of foreign currency is limited to the amount declared on arrival. It is worth remembering that CFA Franc notes cannot easily be exchanged outside the CFA Franc area.
Exchange rate indicators: The following figures are included as a guide to the movements of the CFA Franc against Sterling and the US Dollar:

Date	Feb '04	May '04	Aug '04	Nov '04
£1.00=	961.13	983.76	978.35	936.79
$1.00=	528.01	550.79	531.03	494.69

Banking hours: Mon-Sat 0800-1200.

Duty Free

The following goods may be imported into Equatorial Guinea without incurring customs duty:
200 cigarettes or 50 cigars or 250g of tobacco; 1l of wine; 1l of alcoholic beverages; a reasonable amount of perfume.

Public Holidays

2005: Jan 1 New Year's Day. **Mar 8** Women's Day. **Mar 25** Good Friday. **May 1** Labour Day. **May 25** Africa Day. **May 26** Corpus Christi. **Jun 5** President's Day. **Aug 3** Armed Forces Day. **Aug 15** Constitution Day. **Oct 12** Independence Day. **Dec 10** Human Rights Day. **Dec 25** Christmas.
2006: Jan 1 New Year's Day. **Mar 8** Women's Day. **Apr 14** Good Friday. **May 1** Labour Day. **May 25** Africa Day. **Jun 5** President's Day. **Jun 15** Corpus Christi. **Aug 3** Armed Forces Day. **Aug 15** Constitution Day. **Oct 12** Independence Day. **Dec 10** Human Rights Day. **Dec 25** Christmas.

Health

	Special Precautions?	Certificate Required?
Yellow Fever	Yes	1
Cholera	2	No
Typhoid & Polio	3	N/A
Malaria	4	N/A

Note: *Regulations and requirements may be subject to change at short notice, and you are advised to contact your doctor well in advance of your intended date of departure. Any numbers in the chart refer to the footnotes below.*

1: Equatorial Guinea is listed as one of the countries in the endemic zone and a yellow fever vaccination should be considered. You should also note that most countries require a yellow fever vaccination certificate from travellers coming from infected areas.
2: Following WHO guidelines issued in 1973, a cholera vaccination certificate is no longer a condition of entry to Equatorial Guinea. However, cholera is a serious risk in this country and precautions are essential. Up-to-date advice should be sought before deciding whether these precautions should include vaccination as medical opinion is divided over its effectiveness; see the *Health* appendix for further information.
3: Immunisation against typhoid and poliomyelitis is advised.
4: Malaria risk, predominantly in the malignant *falciparum* form, exists all year throughout the country. Resistance to chloroquine has been reported.
Food & drink: All water should be regarded as being potentially contaminated. Water used for drinking, brushing teeth or making ice should have first been boiled or otherwise sterilised. Milk is unpasteurised and should be boiled. Powdered or tinned milk is available and is advised, but make sure that it is reconstituted with pure water. Avoid dairy products which are likely to have been made from unboiled milk. Only eat well-cooked meat and fish, preferably served hot. Pork, salad and mayonnaise may carry increased risk. Vegetables should be cooked and fruit peeled.
Other risks: *Diarrhoeal* diseases, including *giardiasis*, as well as *typhoid fevers*, are common. *Hepatitis A*, *B* and *E* occur. *Bilharzia* (schistosomiasis) is present. Avoid swimming and paddling in fresh water; swimming pools which are well-chlorinated and maintained are safe. *Onchocerciasis* (river blindness) is present. *Trypanosomiasis* (sleeping sickness) has recently been reported. *Meningococcal meningitis* may occur, especially during the dry season.
Rabies is present. For those at high risk, vaccination before arrival should be considered. If you are bitten, seek medical advice without delay. For more information, consult the *Health* appendix.
Health care: Medical insurance including emergency repatriation is strongly advised.

Travel - International

AIR: *Iberia (IB)* (website: www.iberia.com) operates direct flights from Madrid to Malabo three times a week. *Cameroon Airlines (UY)* operates regular flights to Malabo from London, Paris and Rome. Other airlines serving Equatorial Guinea include *Air Afrique*, *Air Gabon*, *Nigeria Airways* and *Spanair*.
Approximate flight times: From Malabo to *Madrid* is five hours 40 minutes.
International airports: There are international airports at *Malabo (SSG/FGSL)* (Santa Isabel) 7km (4 miles) from the city centre, and *Bata (BSG)*, 6km (3.7 miles) from the city centre. Both airports have basic facilities.
Departure tax: None.
SEA: The main ports are Malabo and Bata. Passenger services operate to Douala (Cameroon).
ROAD: Roads link Equatorial Guinea with Cameroon and Gabon (bush taxis are available), although road surfaces are not always good. Most travellers enter from Douala in Cameroon.

Travel - Internal

AIR: The country's national airline operates flights between Malabo and Bata every day except Sunday, and it is advisable to book in advance. Light aircraft can be chartered in Malabo with international pilot's qualifications.
Note: It is reported that maintenance procedures used on internal flights are not always properly observed.
SEA: There is a ferry between Malabo, Bata and Douala. The trip takes about 12 hours. There are four classes of fare.
ROAD: Not all roads are paved, although the majority are. On Bioko, the north is generally better served with tarred roads. **Minibuses** run from Bata to Mbini and Acalayong on the coastal road. **Bush taxis** connect Malabo with the island's two other main towns, Luba and Riaba, and also run from Bata to Mongomo and Ebebiyin; they can be hired hourly or daily. There are some **car hire** facilities.

Accommodation

Malabo, Bata, Luba and Ebebiyan each offer several hotels of variable standards. In Malabo, there are also a few hostels offering basic but cheap accommodation with shared bathroom facilities (two of which are located in Avenida de las Naciónes). For more information, contact the Embassy in Paris (see *Contact Addresses* section).

Resorts & Excursions

Belying its troubled political past, Equatorial Guinea is a country of luscious vegetation and much beautiful scenery, including tropical forests and snow-capped volcanoes. The capital, **Malabo**, located on **Bioko Island** and overlooked by the striking **Pico Malabo** volcano, is a small but attractive town, with pleasant Spanish colonial architecture, open plazas and a lively market. Frederick Forsyth wrote his novel *The Dogs of War* in Malabo. The **Spanish Cultural Centre** is worth a visit.
The smaller town of **Luba** (one hour's drive from Malabo) has some lovely deserted, white sand beaches and breathtaking vistas. **Bata** is the principal town in the mainland and, though not particularly interesting in itself, is close to some beautiful deserted beaches, notably those at **Mbini**, 50km (32 miles) south of Bata.

Sport & Activities

Swimming: Equatorial Guinea has several beautiful beaches with excellent conditions for swimming. Some of the best beaches can be found near Bata, the principal town on the mainland, and at Mbini, where beaches are usually deserted.
Hiking: The island of Bioko has a number of secluded hiking trails, particularly in the southern half. **Mountain climbing** is possible at the spectacular *Pico Malabo* volcano on Bioko. As this is a military area, a government permit is required and travellers should always check with the authorities before undertaking an expedition to the volcano.

Social Profile

FOOD & DRINK: There are few restaurants in Equatorial Guinea and those that exist are mainly restricted to Malabo and Bata and do not necessarily open every day. Most restaurants serve Spanish or continental cuisine.
Beer is usually expensive, though a local sugar cane brew, *malamba*, can be sampled very cheaply.
SHOPPING: Shopping hours: Mon-Sat 0800-1300, 1600-1900.
SPECIAL EVENTS: Events celebrated in Equatorial Guinea coincide with Christian or traditional religious ceremonies. The following is a special event celebrated annually in Equatorial Guinea:
Oct 12 *Independence Day* (usually sees public celebrations in major towns).
SOCIAL CONVENTIONS: Foreign visitors (especially

Europeans) are a comparative rarity in Equatorial Guinea and are liable to be met with much curiosity and, possibly, suspicion. Foreign cigarettes are appreciated as gifts. A knowledge of Spanish is useful. **Photography:** A permit is required. Care should be taken when choosing subjects. Photographing the presidential palace, airports, harbours and other sensitive areas should be avoided. **Tipping:** Unless service charges are added to bills, 10 to 15 per cent.

Business Profile

ECONOMY: Equatorial Guinea produces timber, cocoa, coffee, bananas and spices for export, and is self-sufficient in other basic food products. Manufacturing industry is confined to timber processing. During the 1990s, the long overdue development of the country's oil and gas reserves – which now account for about a quarter of GDP – produced spectacular economic growth (up to 20 per cent annually) and such growth has persisted at a steady rate. Equatorial Guinea also has confirmed deposits of gold, uranium, iron ore, tantalum and manganese. Intervention by the IMF in the mid-1990s has led to restructuring of the public and financial sectors. A long legacy of maladministration, corruption (the country's largest companies are still largely owned by members of the ruling family) and the lack of even the most basic services have made progress difficult. Nonetheless, Equatorial Guinea has made considerable economic progress in the last decade and will continue to do so for some time yet, on the basis its oil infrastructure. The USA, Cameroon, Liberia and Spain are the country's main trading partners. Equatorial Guinea is a member of the Central African Customs and Economic Union (CEEAC) and the CFA Franc Zone, and receives large injections of foreign aid from a variety of sources.
COMMERCIAL INFORMATION: The following organisation can offer advice: Cámara de Comercio, Agrícola y Forestal de Malabo, Avenida de la Independencia 43, Apartado Postal 51, Bioko (tel: (9) 2343; fax: (9) 4462).

Climate

Tropical climate all year round. Rainfall is heavy for most of the year, decreasing slightly in most areas between December and February.
Required clothing: Lightweight cottons and linens.

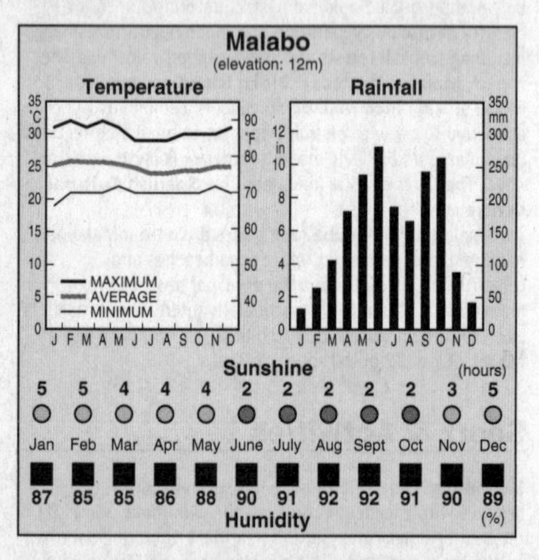

Eritrea

LATEST TRAVEL ADVICE CONTACTS

British Foreign and Commonwealth Office
Tel: (0870) 606 0290 Website: www.fco.gov.uk
US Department of State
Website: http://travel.state.gov/travel
Canadian Department of Foreign Affairs and Int'l Trade
Tel: (1 800) 267 8376 Website: www.dfait-maeci.gc.ca

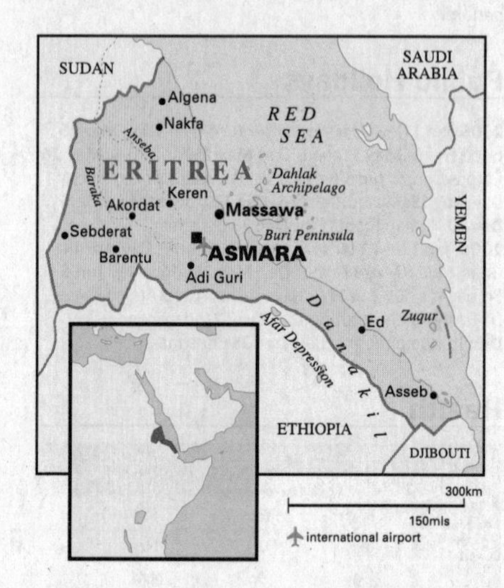

Location: Northeast Africa, on the Red Sea coast.

Country dialling code: 291.

Ministry of Tourism
PO Box 1010, Asmara, Eritrea
Tel: (1) 126 997. Fax: (1) 126 949.
E-mail: eritrea_tourism@cts.com.er *or* eritrea_tourism@cnet.com.er
Website: www.shaebia.org/mot.html
Eritrean Tour Service (ETS)
Street address: 61 Hartnet Avenue, Asmara, Eritrea
Postal address: PO Box 889, Asmara, Eritrea
Tel: (1) 124 999. Fax: (1) 126 366 *or* 127 695.
Embassy of the State of Eritrea
96 White Lion Street, London N1 9PF, UK
Tel: (020) 7713 0096. Fax: (020) 7713 0161.
E-mail: eriemba@freeuk.com *or* eriemba@eriembauk.com
Opening hours: Mon-Fri 0930-1300 (visa application); 1400-1600 (visa collection).
British Embassy
Street address: 66-68 Mariam Ghimbi Street, House 24, Asmara, Eritrea
Postal address: PO Box 5584, Asmara, Eritrea
Tel: (1) 120 145. Fax: (1) 120 104.
E-mail: asmara.enquiries@fco.gov.uk
Embassy of the State of Eritrea
1708 New Hampshire Avenue, NW, Washington, DC 20009, USA
Tel: (202) 319 1991. Fax: (202) 319 1304.
E-mail: sessahaie@embassyeritrea.org
Embassy of the United States of America
179 Allah Street, PO Box 211, Asmara, Eritrea
Tel: (1) 120 004. Fax: (1) 127 584.
Embassy of the State of Eritrea
75 Albert Street, Suite 610, Ottawa, Ontario K1P 5E7, Canada
Tel: (613) 234 3989. Fax: (613) 234 6213.
E-mail: embassy.eritrea@rogers.com
Canadian Consulate
Street address: 87-89 Warsay Street, Asmara, Eritrea
Postal address: PO Box 3962, Asmara, Eritrea
Tel: (1) 181 940 *or* 186 490. Fax: (1) 186 488.
E-mail: mkcc@cts.com.er
The Canadian Embassy in Addis Ababa also deals with enquiries relating to Eritrea (see *Ethiopia* section).

TIMATIC CODES

Health
AMADEUS: **TI-DFT/JIB/HE**
GALILEO/WORLDSPAN: **TI-DFT/JIB/HE**
SABRE: **TIDFT/JIB/HE**

Visa
AMADEUS: **TI-DFT/JIB/VI**
GALILEO/WORLDSPAN: **TI-DFT/JIB/VI**
SABRE: **TIDFT/JIB/VI**

To access TIMATIC country information on Health and Visa regulations through the Computer Reservations System (CRS), type in the appropriate command line listed above.

General Information

AREA: 121,144 sq km (46,774 sq miles).
POPULATION: 3,991,000 (official estimate 2002).
POPULATION DENSITY: 32.9 per sq km.
CAPITAL: Asmara. **Population:** 400,000 (official estimate 2003).
GEOGRAPHY: Eritrea stretches along the Red Sea for almost 1000km (625 miles). To the south and west it borders Ethiopia, to the southeast Djibouti and to the northwest Sudan. The low-lying coastal area is very humid. The mountainous interior is largely cultivated.
GOVERNMENT: Independent State since 1993. **Head of State and Government:** President Isaias Afewerki since 1993.
LANGUAGE: Arabic and Tigrinya are the main business languages. Various dialects such as Afar, Bilien, Hedareb, Kunama, Nara, Rashaida, Saho and Tigre are also spoken. English is rapidly becoming the language of business and education; Italian and Arabic are also spoken.
RELIGION: Roughly half Ethiopian Orthodox Christians and half Muslim, but some have traditional beliefs.
TIME: GMT + 3.
ELECTRICITY: 110/220 volts AC; there are occasional power surges.
COMMUNICATIONS: Telephone: IDD is available to Asmara, Massawa and Assab. Country code: 291. Outgoing international code: 00. Operator assistance may be required. All larger cities are connected via the internal system. **Mobile telephone:** GSM 900 was launched in 2004 by Eritel. **Fax:** These can be sent and received at the Telecommunications Office in Harnet Street (Asmara); some hotels also provide services. **Internet:** The main ISPs are *EWAN Technical Solutions* and the Eritrean PTO working with USAID's Leland project. There is Internet access in the main towns. **Telegram:** International services are available in the office in Asmara. **Post:** International post services have not been resumed with all countries. Delays are likely **Press:** The *Eritrea Profile* is published weekly in English. *Hadas Eritrea* is published three times a week in English, Arabic and Tigrinya. A pro-government youth paper called *Tirigta* is published once a week.
Radio: BBC World Service (website: www.bbc.co.uk/worldservice) and Voice of America (website: www.voa.gov) can be received. From time to time the frequencies change and the most up-to-date can be found online.

Passport/Visa

	Passport Required?	Visa Required?	Return Ticket Required?
Full British	Yes	Yes	Yes
Australian	Yes	Yes	Yes
Canadian	Yes	Yes	Yes
USA	Yes	Yes	Yes
Other EU	Yes	Yes	Yes
Japanese	Yes	Yes	Yes

Note: *Regulations and requirements may be subject to change at short notice, and you are advised to contact the appropriate diplomatic or consular authority before finalising travel arrangements. Details of these may be found at the head of this country's entry. Any numbers in the chart refer to the footnotes below.*

PASSPORTS: Passport valid for a minimum of three months beyond intended departure date required by all.
VISAS: Required by all except the following:
(a) nationals of Kenya and Uganda;
(b) transit passengers continuing their journey to a third country within six hours, provided holding valid onward or return documentation and not leaving the airport transit lounge.
Types of visas and cost: *Tourist:* £25 (single-entry only). *Business:* £40 (single-entry); £55 (multiple-entry for up to three months); £80 (multiple-entry for up to six months). *Transit:* £10. An additional fee of £5 is payable for express service visas.
Validity: *Single-entry business visas:* up to one month. Extensions are possible. Apply to the Foreign Ministry in Asmara. Apply on arrival in Eritrea. *Transit visas:* 24 hours.
Application to: Consulate (or Consular section at Embassy); see *Contact Addresses* section.
Application requirements: (a) Application form. (b) Valid passport. (c) One passport-size photo. (d) Fee. (e) Yellow fever certificate, if arriving within six days of visiting an infected area (except for passengers in transit and not leaving the airport). (f) Stamped, self-addressed registered envelope for postal applications. *Tourist:* (a)-(f) and, (g) A valid onward ticket and travel documents. (h) Proof of travellers cheques of minimum US$40 per day, or bank statement. *Business:* (a)-(f) and, (g) Company letter stating the purpose of the visit.
Working days required: One. Five hours for express service.

Money

Currency: Nakfa (Nkfa/ERN) = 100 cents. Notes are in denominations of Nkfa100, 50, 25, 10, 5 and 1. Coins are in denominations of Nkfa100, 50, 25,10, 5 and 1.
Note: The IMF and the World Bank have recognised the circulation of Nakfa in both coin and paper note denominations.
Note: * Values are given against the Euro rather than Sterling as accurate exchange rate against Sterling is not available.
Currency exchange: US Dollar bills are the most convenient form of exchange. Foreign currencies can be exchanged at the Commercial Bank of Eritrea in Asmara (which provides the best exchange rate), private currency exchange offices and major hotels.
Credit & debit cards: Diners Club and MasterCard are accepted on a limited basis. Check with your credit or debit card company for details of merchant acceptability.
Travellers cheques: These are generally accepted.
Currency restrictions: Import and export of local or foreign currency is unrestricted.
Exchange rate indicators: The following is included as a guide to the movements of the Nakfa against the Euro* and the US Dollar:

Date	Feb '04	May '04	Aug '04	Nov '04
€1.00=	-	15.97	16.68	25.56
$1.00=	13.50	13.50	13.50	13.50

Banking hours: Mon-Fri 0800-1200 and 1400-1800, Sat 0800-1230.

Duty Free

The following goods may be imported into Eritrea without incurring customs duty:
200 cigarettes or 50 cigars or 250g of tobacco; 1l of alcoholic beverages.

Public Holidays

2005: Jan 1 New Year's Day. **Mar 8** Women's Day. **May 24** Independence Day. **Jun 20** Martyrs' Day. **Sep 1** Anniversary of the Start of the Armed Struggles.
2006: Jan 1 New Year's Day. **Mar 8** Women's Day. **May 24** Independence Day. **Jun 20** Martyrs' Day. **Sep 1** Anniversary of the Start of the Armed Struggles.

Health

	Special Precautions?	Certificate Required?
Yellow Fever	Yes	1
Cholera	2	No
Typhoid & Polio	3	N/A
Malaria	4	N/A

Note: Regulations and requirements may be subject to change at short notice, and you are advised to contact your doctor well in advance of your intended date of departure. Any numbers in the chart refer to the footnotes below.

1: A yellow fever vaccination certificate is required from travellers arriving within six days from infected areas. Travellers arriving from non-endemic zones should note that vaccination is strongly recommended for travel outside the urban areas, even if an outbreak of the disease has not been reported and they would normally not require a vaccination certificate to enter the country.
2: Following WHO guidelines issued in 1973, a cholera vaccination certificate is no longer a condition of entry to Eritrea. However, cholera is a serious risk in this country and precautions are essential. Up-to-date advice should be sought before deciding whether these precautions should include vaccination, as medical opinion is divided over its effectiveness; see the *Health* appendix for further information.
3: Typhoid is widespread, especially in rural areas and poliomyelitis is endemic. Vaccination against both is advised.
4: Malaria risk, predominantly in the malignant *falciparum* form, exists throughout the year in all areas below 2000m (682ft). Highly chloroquine-resistant *falciparum* has been reported. There is no malaria risk in Asmara.
Food & drink: All water should be regarded as being potentially contaminated. Water used for drinking, brushing teeth or making ice should have first been boiled or otherwise sterilised. Milk is unpasteurised and should be boiled. Powdered or tinned milk is available and is advised, but make sure that it is reconstituted with pure water. Avoid dairy products which are likely to have been made from unboiled milk. Only eat well-cooked meat and fish, preferably served hot. Pork, salad and mayonnaise may carry increased risk. Vegetables should be cooked and fruit peeled.
Other risks: *Bilharzia* (schistosomiasis) is present. Avoid swimming and paddling in fresh water; swimming pools which are well-chlorinated and maintained are safe. *Hepatitis A* and *E* are widespread and *hepatitis B* is hyperendemic. Vaccinations against *hepatitis B* and *tetanus* are recommended. *Meningococcal meningitis* is a risk, particularly in savannah areas and during the dry season. Endemic foci of *onchocerciasis* (river blindness) exist. *Rabies* is present. For those at high risk, vaccination before arrival should be considered. If you are bitten, seek medical advice without delay. For more information, consult the *Health* appendix.
Health care: Time is needed to acclimatise to the high altitude and low oxygen level. Those who suffer from heart ailments or high blood pressure should consult a doctor before travelling. Medical services are limited throughout the country: modern facilities are not always available and supplies can be irregular. Visitors should bring a supply of any necessary drugs and prescriptions. Chemists can be found in larger towns. The country has an extensive network of health workers. Regional and district clinics and the central hospital in Asmara deal with emergencies. Health insurance is strongly advised.

Travel - International

Note: All travel to the border areas with Ethiopia and Sudan is advised against. This advice includes Tesseney, near the Sudan border, where there was a bomb attack on March 1 2004 in a hotel. Visitors should avoid the area north of Afabet in the Sahel region, and along one road in the west of the country. There is a continuing threat to Western targets from terrorism in Eritrea as there is in other countries in East Africa and the Horn. You should be aware that travel restrictions may limit the ability to offer immediate consular assistance (for UK nationals) outside Asmara, Keren, Dekemhare, Mendeferra and Massawa.
AIR: Eritrea's national airline is *Eritrean Airlines*. Other airlines operating to Eritrea include *Egyptair* (from Cairo), *Lufthansa* (from Frankfurt), *Saudi Arabian Airlines* (from Jeddah), *Sudan Airways* (from Khartoum) and *Yemenia* (from Sanaa). Flights from Europe and the USA can be booked through Ericommerce International Ltd, Robin House, 2A Iverson Road, London NW6 2HE, UK (tel: (020) 7372 7242; fax: (020) 7624 6716; e-mail: info@ericommerce.com; website: www.ericommerce.com).
Approximate flight times: From Asmara to *London* is seven hours.
International airports: *Asmara (ASM)* is 6km (4 miles) from the city. Buses and taxis are available to the city centre. Airport facilities include left luggage, bank/bureau de change, post office, bars, duty-free shop and restaurants.
Departure tax: US$15.
SEA: There are two main ports, Assab and Massawa, both on the Red Sea, but there are very limited scheduled passenger services. There is a weekly ferry service from Massawa to Jeddah.
ROAD: Currently, there are no safe land routes into Eritrea. Previously, it was accessible by bus from Sudan, and another bus route went from Asmara to Djibouti.

Travel - Internal

AIR: Internal flights operate between Asmara and Assab but are limited. *Assab (ASA)* is 15 km (9 miles) from Assab. Buses and taxis travel to the town (travel time – 15 to 30 minutes).
Departure tax: Domestic: ERN15. International: ERN60 (nationals). US$15 for all others.
RAIL: The only existing railway line between *Ak'ordat*, *Asmara* and the port of *Massawa*, was left non-operational after the war with Ethiopia. However, work is currently underway to restore it and most of the section running from Asmara to the coast is now functioning.
ROAD: The infrastructure suffered badly during the protracted fighting. Repairs and a modernisation programme are currently underway. Reasonable roads still connect all business centres and holiday resorts. 4-wheel-drive vehicles are recommended on all other roads and tracks. An extension of the existing road system is planned. Traffic drives on the right. **Bus:** Services connect all larger towns and cities. **Taxi:** These can be found in the capital and at the airport. Fares are higher at night (usually double) and should be negotiated in advance as taxis are not metered. **Car hire:** Cars can be booked through the Eritrean Tour Service (see *Contact Addresses* section). **Documentation:** An International Driving Permit is required.

Accommodation

The capital, Asmara, has several good hotels which can sometimes offer seminar rooms and small exhibition spaces. Similar standard hotels can be found in Assab and Massawa. It is advisable to book in advance. Meals are available in all hotels. There are also hotels and guest houses in smaller towns; prices are, in general, slightly lower than those in the main centres. When making reservations, check for service charges and sales taxes. Hotel bills must be paid in hard currency. For further information, contact the Eritrean Tour Service (see *Contact Addresses* section).

Resorts & Excursions

ASMARA: Eritrea's capital, Asmara, was only a small cluster of villages at the beginning of the 19th century. In 1897, the Italian colonial government moved the administration there from Massawa. Today, Italian architecture prevails in the city. The magnificent **Cathedral** (1922), built in the Lombardian style, is not far from a bustling market. Fruit and vegetables, bric-a-brac, spices, used furniture, ceramics, handicrafts and clothes are sold on the stalls. There are a number of churches and mosques which can be visited. Marble from the Italian **Carrara quarry** was used to build the largest mosque, **Khalufa el Rashidin**. Gold and silver jewellery is on offer at the nearby market. Palms and colourful bougainvillaea line the main avenues. The **National Avenue** is the major thoroughfare of the city; an ideal place to meet people and enjoy the numerous cafes and bars. The Avenue is also the address for the **Government Administrative Centre**, the **Asmara Theatre** (built 1918), the **Catholic Cathedral** and the **Town Hall**. The former residence of the colonial rulers, the *Ghibi* or palace, is used today as the **National Museum**. The **University** and the **Mai Jahjah Fountain** are also interesting.
ELSEWHERE: The road from Asmara to **Massawa**, 105km (65 miles), is both spectacular and beautiful. It descends from 2438m (8000ft) to sea level, with hairpin bends on the escarpment, and magnificent views over the coastal desert strip. It passes the famous Orthodox **Monastery of Debre Bizen**. Massawa was an important centre in ancient times and remains, and to this day, the largest natural deep-water port on the Red Sea. If Asmara is an 'Italian' city, Massawa is 'Turko-Egyptian', reflecting the periods of Ottoman and Egyptian rule from the 16th century to the late 19th century. Dams connect the islands of Batsi and Twalet with the main part of the city.
The port and old town of **Batsi** were damaged during the civil war but are still impressive. The **Iman Hanbeli Mosque** escaped damage. **Batsi Island** is a good area for restaurants, cafes and bars; visitors can take a small boat to **Sheikh Said Island** (also known as **Isola Verde**), a favourite picnic spot. **Twalet** has fine examples of Italian architecture. There is also a badly damaged *Ghibi* or palace. It was originally built in the 15th century, but has been much altered and restored since then. It was badly damaged in the civil war and is again in need of restoration. The **Port Club** has a restaurant, a museum, a small library and sporting facilities. North of Massawa is the white sandy beach of **Gergussum**. It is a good place to sunbathe or swim.
From here, it is not far to **Emberemi**, famous for the mausoleums of **Sheikh el Amin** and **Muhammad Ibn Ali**. It is an important pilgrimage site. **Nakfa** in Satel province is famous as the main site and symbol of resistance during the war with Ethiopia. The nearby towns of **Denden**, **Orota** and **Afabet** still bear the scars of fighting although much rebuilding has been completed. **Keren**, in the Province of Senhit, is like a miniature Asmara. The **Forto** was built during the Turkish period. Also of interest are the religious sites of the **Tomb of Said Abu Bakr el Mirgani** and the Mariam de Arit. **Debre Sina**, near **Elabered** on the Asmara-Keren road, is also a noteworthy monastery. The modern city of **Asseb** in the southeasterly Province of Denkalia has many pleasant beaches.
The Turkish and Egyptian colonial periods left numerous interesting buildings and sites in **Akordat** (Barka Province). Here is situated the tomb of **Said Mustafa wad Hasan**. **Qohaito**, **Metera** and **Rora Habab** are also important archaeological sites.

Social Profile

FOOD & DRINK: Italian cuisine dominates in the restaurants of the larger cities. Massawa is renowned for its excellent seafood, especially prawns and lobster. Staple food includes *kitcha*, a thin bread made from wheat, and *injera*, a spongy pancake. Local specialities are often very spicy.
Tea and espresso are drunk black with a lot of sugar. In some regions, coffee is served with ginger or black pepper and sugar. Fruit juices (banana, mango and papaya) are available.
SHOPPING: Good buys are gold and silver jewellery (sold by weight), woodcarvings, leather items, spears, drums, carpets and wicker goods. A certain amount of bargaining is expected in marketplaces but prices at shops in towns are usually fixed. **Shopping hours:** Mon-Sat 0830-1300, 1430-2030 (regional variations occur).
SPECIAL EVENTS: The following is a selection of special events celebrated annually in Eritrea:
Jan 7 *Leddet* (Christmas). **Jan 19** *Timket* (Epiphany). **Feb** *Fenkil* (a remembrance of the last days of the war fought to

A B C D E F G H I J K L M N O P Q R S T U V W X Y Z

liberate the city of Massawa). **Aug** *Eritrean Festival* (exhibitions, musical shows and dances, a cultural event that lasts about 10 days). **Sep 11** *Kiddus Johannes* (Orthodox New Year). **Sep 27** *Meskel* (Finding of the True Cross).

SOCIAL CONVENTIONS: Handshaking is the normal form of greeting. Casual tourist wear is suitable for most places, but visitors should dress modestly. For business, a suit is most appropriate. Tea or coffee is offered frequently to visitors. Smoking is not popular with traditional or elderly Eritreans. Shoes should be taken off in churches and, particularly, in mosques. **Tipping:** Hotels and restaurants add a service charge, usually around 10 per cent. Tipping is fairly common, in small amounts. Taxi drivers are not usually tipped.

Business Profile

ECONOMY: The long-running Ethiopian civil war left Eritrea, which was, until 1991, the northernmost province of Ethiopia, with its economy in a parlous condition. Since the split from Ethiopia in 1993, Eritrea has been engaged in a series of military campaigns which have stunted its economic development. The most recent border war with Ethiopia cost Eritrea several hundred million dollars in damage to the country's fragile infrastructure and parts of its agricultural economy. Agriculture sustains the bulk of the population with indigenous grains, maize, wheat and sorghum as the main crops. However, reconstruction has been hampered by the legacy of war (damage to land, mines, lack of equipment) and poor rainfall, and the country still needs substantial food aid. The small industrial economy produces glass, cement and textiles. The Government has been developing fishing and mineral industries, particularly as there are thought to be significant oil and gas deposits within Eritrea's territorial waters (which may in part explain its petulance over border disputes). Exploration rights have been granted by the Government to several major multinational oil companies to conduct surveys of the area. With an average annual per capita income of just US$160, Eritrea is one of the world's poorest countries. But, albeit from a low base, the economy has been expanding rapidly since the end of the Ethiopian war. However, erratic rainfall and below-average cereal production has slumped growth somewhat: growth rate was 2 per cent in 2004. Eritrea has been granted admission to the ACP group of Third World countries, which receive preferential access to certain European Union markets, and it is now a member of the International Monetary Fund. In 1997, Eritrea introduced its own currency, the Nakfa, in place of the Ethiopian Birr; this has been construed as a deliberate provocation since Nakfa is the location of a battle where Ethiopia suffered great losses at the hands of Eritrean rebels.

BUSINESS: Local businesspeople tend to speak English or Italian. A knowledge of French can also be useful. Business cards are not always exchanged. May to October is best for business visits. **Office hours:** Mon-Thurs 0700-1200, 1400-1800, Fri 0700-1130, 1400-1800. In other towns, hours may vary slightly.

COMMERCIAL INFORMATION: The following organisation can offer advice: Eritrean National Chamber of Commerce, PO Box 856, Abiot Av 46, Asmara (tel: (1) 121 589 or 121 388 or 122 456; fax: (1) 120 138; e-mail: encc@eol.com.er).

Climate

Summer months (April to August) can be hot with temperatures reaching up to 40°C (100 °F) on the western plateau. Although temperatures rarely drop below 18°C (64 °F) along the coast, winters in the central and western plateau regions (December to February) can be freezing with dramatic temperature differences between day and night. The short rainy season is usually between March to April and a longer one from late June to the beginning of September.

Required clothing: Lightweight and mediumweight clothing is recommended but warm clothes may be needed because the temperature drops at night. An umbrella and a raincoat are recommended during the rainy season.

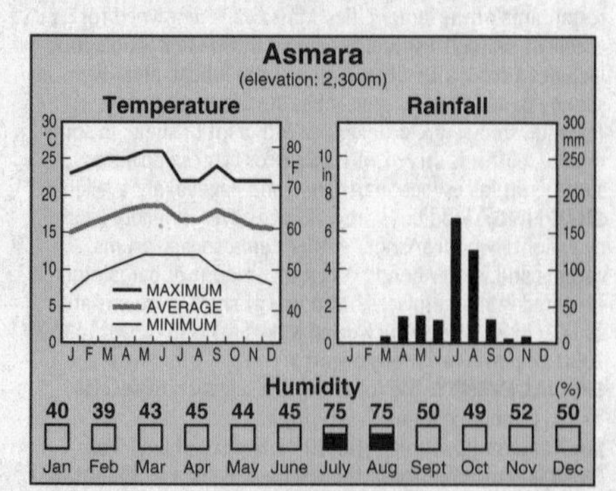

Estonia

LATEST TRAVEL ADVICE CONTACTS

British Foreign and Commonwealth Office
Tel: (0870) 606 0290 Website: www.fco.gov.uk

US Department of State
Website: http://travel.state.gov/travel

Canadian Department of Foreign Affairs and Int'l Trade
Tel: (1 800) 267 8376 Website: www.dfait-maeci.gc.ca

Location: Northern Europe.

Country dialling code: 372.

Estonian Tourist Board
1315 Liivalaia Street, 10118 Tallinn, Estonia
Tel: (6) 279 770. Fax: (6) 279 777.
E-mail: info@visitestonia.com
Website: www.visitestonia.com
Tourist information can be obtained within Estonia (tel: 8 1188).

Embassy of the Republic of Estonia
16 Hyde Park Gate, London SW7 5DG, UK
Tel: (020) 7589 3428. Fax: (020) 7589 3430.
E-mail: embassy.london@estonia.gov.uk
Website: www.estonia.gov.uk
Opening hours: Mon-Fri 0900-1700 (embassy); Mon and Fri 1000-1300, Tue and Thurs 1300-1600 (consular section).

British Embassy
Wismari 6, 10136 Tallinn, Estonia
Tel: (6) 674 700. Fax: (6) 674 724/5 (consular section).
E-mail: information@britishembassy.ee
Website: www.britishembassy.ee

Embassy of the Republic of Estonia
2131 Massachusetts Avenue, NW, Washington, DC 20008, USA.
Tel: (202) 588 0101. Fax: (202) 588 0108.
E-mail: info@estemb.org
Website: www.estemb.org

Consulate of the Republic of Estonia
600 Third Avenue, 26th Floor, New York, NY 10016, USA
Tel: (212) 883 0636. Fax: (212) 883 0648.
E-mail: nyconsulate@nyc.estemb.org
Website: www.nyc.estemb.org

Embassy of the United States of America
Kentmanni 20, 15099 Tallinn, Estonia
Tel: (6) 688 100. Fax: (6) 688 134 *or* 267 (consular section).
E-mail: tallinn@usemb.ee *or* VisaTallinn@state.gov
Website: www.usemb.ee

Embassy of the Republic of Estonia
260 Dalhousie Street, Suite 210, Ottawa, Ontario K1N 7E4, Canada
Tel: (613) 789 4222. Fax: (613) 789 9555.
E-mail: embassy.ottawa@mfa.ee
Website: www.estemb.ca

The Office of the Canadian Embassy
Toom Kooli 13, 2nd Floor, 10130 Tallinn, Estonia
Tel: (6) 273 311 *or* 310 (visa section). Fax: (6) 273 312.
E-mail: Tallinn@canada.ee

TIMATIC CODES

Health	AMADEUS: **TI-DFT/JIB/HE** GALILEO/WORLDSPAN: **TI-DFT/JIB/HE** SABRE: **TIDFT/JIB/HE**
Visa	AMADEUS: **TI-DFT/JIB/VI** GALILEO/WORLDSPAN: **TI-DFT/JIB/VI** SABRE: **TIDFT/JIB/VI**

To access TIMATIC country information on Health and Visa regulations through the Computer Reservations System (CRS), type in the appropriate command line listed above.

General Information

AREA: 45,227 sq km (17,462 sq miles).
POPULATION: 1,356,045 (official estimate 2003).
POPULATION DENSITY: 30 per sq km.
CAPITAL: Tallinn. **Population:** 397,150 (official estimate 2003).
GEOGRAPHY: Estonia is the most northerly of the three Baltic Republics and is bordered to the north and west by the Baltic Sea, to the east by the Russian Federation and to the south by Latvia. The country is one of great scenic beauty with many forests, more than 1400 lakes and 1500 islands. Smaller than Lithuania and Latvia, it has nevertheless the longest coastline of all the Baltic States.
GOVERNMENT: Republic since 1918. Regained independence in 1991. **Head of State:** President Arnold Rüütel since 2001. **Head of Government:** Prime Minister Juhan Parts since 2003.
LANGUAGE: Estonian is the official language. Most people also speak Russian, which is the mother tongue of around 30 per cent of the population. However, since independence the indiscriminate use of Russian could on occasion cause offence. In addition to Russian, the most common foreign languages are English, Finnish and German.
RELIGION: Predominantly Protestant (Lutheran).
TIME: GMT + 2.
ELECTRICITY: 220 volts AC, 50Hz. European-style two-pin plugs are in use.
COMMUNICATIONS: Telephone: IDD service is available. Country code: 372. To make international calls, dial 8, wait for the long tone and then dial 00. An English directory enquiries service is available (tel: 8 1182). Public telephones, which are plentiful, are operated by phonecards, available from kiosks. **Mobile telephone:** GSM 900 and 1800 networks cover the whole country. Main operators include *AS EMT* (website: www.emt.ee), *Radiolinja Eesti* (website: www.radiolinja.ee) and *TELE2* (website: www.tele2.ee). **Fax:** Services are available at telephone offices and some post offices, as well as in hotels. **Internet:** Public access is available at Internet cafes and libraries in main towns and cities. There is free Internet access at Tallinn Airport. Local ISPs include *Delfi Online* (website: www.delfi.ee) and *Sünerkom* (website: www.zzz.ee). **Post:** Post to Western Europe takes up to six days. Post office hours: Mon-Fri 0900-1800, Sat 0930-1500. *Poste Restante* is available at the central post office in Tallinn located at Narva 1. **Press:** Newspapers are published in Estonian, the most popular being *Eesti Ekspress*, *Postimees* and *SL Õhtuleht*. The English-language newspaper *The Baltic Times* is published in Latvia and available weekly. There are a growing number of city guides published in English.
Radio: BBC World Service (website: www.bbc.co.uk/worldservice) and Voice of America (website: www.voa.gov) can be received. From time to time the frequencies change and the most up-to-date can be found online.

Passport/Visa

	Passport Required?	Visa Required?	Return Ticket Required?
Full British	1	No	No
Australian	Yes	No/2	No
Canadian	Yes	No/2	No
USA	Yes	No/2	No
Other EU	1	No	No
Japanese	Yes	No/2	No

Note: *Regulations and requirements may be subject to change at short notice, and you are advised to contact the appropriate diplomatic or consular authority before finalising travel arrangements. Details of these may be found at the head of this country's entry. Any numbers in the chart refer to the footnotes below.*

PASSPORT: Passport valid for three months beyond intended period of stay except:
1. EU nationals and nationals of Iceland, Liechtenstein, Norway and Switzerland with valid personal ID cards.
VISA: Required by all except the following:
(a) nationals of the EU and Iceland, Liechtenstein, Norway and Switzerland with valid passport or personal ID card;
(b) **2.** nationals of Andorra, Argentina, Australia, Bolivia, Brazil, Brunei, Bulgaria, Canada, Chile, Costa Rica, Croatia, El Salvador, Guatemala, Honduras, Hong Kong (SAR), Israel, Korea (Rep), Japan, Macau (SAR), Malaysia, Mexico, Monaco, New Zealand, Nicaragua, Panama, Paraguay, Romania, San Marino, Singapore, Uruguay, USA, Vatican City and Venezuela for stays of up to three months;
(c) nationals of South Africa when holding a visa for Latvia or Lithuania.
Note: Participants in organised excursions are allowed to enter Estonia for up to 12 hours based on a name list affirmed by the captain of the vessel, and previously presented to the Estonian Border Guard Board.
Types of visa and cost: *Short-term*: Single-entry: £14 (up

to 30 days); £24 (up to 90 days); Multiple-entry: £17 (up to 30 days); £24 (up to 90 days); £34 (up to one year). *Transit*: £17. *Airport transit*: £14.
Validity: *Transit*: Up to 48 hours. *Single-entry*: Up to six months. *Multiple-entry*: Up to five years. In the case of South Africans, visas for Estonia are also valid for Latvia and Lithuania and vice versa.
Applications to: Consulate (or Consular section at Embassy); see *Contact Addresses* section. Applications must be made in person.
Application requirements: (a) One completed application form. (b) Passport valid for at least three months after expiry of visa, and with at least two blank pages. (c) One colour passport-size photo. (d) Fee. (e) Health insurance (with coverage of at least 160,000 EEK) valid for entire duration of stay. (f) Documents confirming purpose of visit (visa invitation, letter of invitation, travel vouchers, documents confirming employment or similar). (g) Proof of sufficient funds (equal to one-fifth of the minimum monthly wage [currently €33] for every day of planned stay in Estonia). (h) Documents confirming accommodation.
Note: All documents must be original.
Working days required: Up to 30. Postal applications are possible if there is no Estonian Embassy in country of residence.

Money

Currency: 1 Kroon (ekr) = 100 sents. Notes are in denominations of ekr500, 100, 50, 25, 10, 5, 2 and 1. Coins are in denominations of ekr1 and 5, and 50, 20, 10 and 5 sents.
Currency exchange: All major currencies can be exchanged at banks and bureaux de change. The value of the Kroon has been tied to the Euro. There are ATMs in most towns.
Credit & debit cards: Credit cards are widely accepted. Check with your credit or debit card company for details of merchant acceptability and other services which may be available.
Travellers cheques: Travellers cheques can be changed in banks in most larger towns. To avoid additional exchange rate charges, travellers are advised to take travellers cheques in US Dollars, Pounds Sterling or Euros.
Currency restrictions: The import and export of local and foreign currency is limited to ekr80,000 or equivalent.
Exchange rate indicators: The following figures are included as a guide to the movements of the Estonian Kroon against Sterling and the US Dollar:

Date	Feb '04	May '04	Aug '04	Nov '04
£1.00=	22.97	23.47	23.34	22.34
$1.00=	12.59	13.14	12.67	11.79

Banking hours: Mon-Fri 0900-1600, Sat 0900-1500; hours may vary.

Duty Free

The following goods may be imported into Estonia without incurring customs duty, by persons aged 18 or over:
200 cigarettes or 50 cigars or 250g tobacco; 1l of alcohol over 22 per cent or 2l of alcohol up to 22 per cent and 2l of wine; 10kg of foodstuffs.
Note: Restrictions apply to certain items, including plants and vegetable products, firearms, diamonds and antiques. Contact the authorities for further information (tel: (6) 967 436; e-mail: info@customs.ee; website: www.customs.ee).
Abolition of duty free goods within the EU: On June 30 1999, the sale of duty free alcohol and tobacco at airports and at sea was abolished in all of the original 15 EU member states. Of the 10 new member states that joined the EU on May 1 2004, these rules already apply to Cyprus and Malta. There are transitional rules in place for visitors returning to one of the original 15 EU countries from one of the other new EU countries. But for the original 15, plus Cyprus and Malta, there are now no limits imposed on importing tobacco and alcohol products from one EU country to another (with the exceptions of Denmark, Finland and Sweden, where limits *are* imposed). Travellers should note that they may be required to prove at customs that the goods purchased are for personal use *only*.

Public Holidays

2005: Jan 1 New Year's Day. **Feb 24** Independence Day. **Mar 25** Good Friday. **May 1** May Day. **Jun 23** Victory Day. **Jun 24** Midsummer's Day. **Aug 20** Restoration of Independence Day. **Dec 25-26** Christmas.
2006: Jan 1 New Year's Day. **Feb 24** Independence Day. **Apr 14** Good Friday. **May 1** May Day. **Jun 23** Victory Day (Anniversary of the Battle of Võnnu). **Jun 24** Midsummer's Day. **Aug 20** Restoration of Independence Day. **Dec 25-26** Christmas.

Health

	Special Precautions?	Certificate Required?
Yellow Fever	No	No
Cholera	No	No
Typhoid & Polio	No	N/A
Malaria	No	N/A

Note: *Regulations and requirements may be subject to change at short notice, and you are advised to contact your doctor well in advance of your intended date of departure. Any numbers in the chart refer to the footnotes below.*

Other risks: *Hepatitis A* occurs. Cases of *diphtheria* have been reported. Vaccination against *tick-borne encephalitis* is advisable if visiting forested areas. Precautions should be taken against *tuberculosis*, as cases of this disease have increased. *HIV* testing is required for foreigners requesting work permits or residency.
Rabies is present. For those at high risk, vaccination before arrival should be considered. If you are bitten, seek medical advice without delay. For more information, consult the *Health* appendix.
Health care: Medical insurance is recommended.

Travel - International

AIR: Estonia's national airline is *Estonian Air (OV)* (website: www.estonian-air.ee), which operates six direct flights a week (everyday except Saturday) between Gatwick and Tallinn. For more information, contact the *Estonian Air* office in the UK (tel: (020) 7333 0196; fax: (020) 7333 0068; e-mail:lon@maersk-air.com). *Aeroflot, Air Baltic, Finnair, Lithuanian Airlines* and *SAS* also operate flights to Tallinn. Flights to Tallinn via Moscow, Helsinki, Riga or Stockholm are available from all major European cities. Connections to the USA are via Helsinki and New York or Los Angeles.
Approximate flight times: From Tallinn to *London* is approximately three hours, to *Frankfurt/M* is approximately 2 hours 30 minutes, to *Los Angeles* is approximately 22 hours (via Helsinki), and to *New York* is approximately 13 hours 30 minutes (via Helsinki).
International airports: *Tallinn (TLL)* (website: www.tallinn-airport.ee) is located 5km (3 miles) northwest of the city. Buses run between the city and the airport (travel time - 15 minutes). A shuttle bus to the main hotels and the city centre meets all flights. Taxis are also available. The airport facilities include banks/bureaux de change, duty-free shops, shops, post office, restaurants, two business lounges, tourist information and car hire (*Avis, Baltic, Budget, Europcar, Finest, Hertz, National* and *Sixt*).
Departure tax: None.
SEA: Ferries operated by *Eckerö Line* (website: www.eckeroline.fi), *Silja Line* (website: www.silja.com) and *Tallink* (website: www.tallink.ee) run several times a day between Helsinki (Finland) and Tallinn (travel time - 3 hours 45 minutes). Express catamarans (operated by *Nordic Jet, Silja Line* and *Tallink AutoExpress*) and hydrofoils (operated by *Lindaline*) also ply this route (travel time - 1 hour 45 minutes). Express services run only in the high season. Tallink operates daily from Stockholm (Sweden) to Tallinn (travel time - 11 hours). *Silja Line* operates ferries from Tallinn to Rostock (Germany) in high season (travel time - 21 hours).
RAIL: *Estonian Railways (Eesti Raudtee)* (website: www.evr.ee) is underdeveloped, although there is a route on the EVR Express between St Petersburg (Russian Federation) and Tallinn. There is no longer a train route between Estonia and Latvia. Travel is slower than by bus. Children up to seven years may travel free if accompanied by an adult and not taking a separate seat.
ROAD: There are direct routes along the Baltic coast into Latvia, Lithuania and Kaliningrad, and also east into the Russian Federation. Routes into the Baltic states are via Poland and Belarus or Poland and Lithuania; border points: Terespol (Poland) - Brest (Belarus) and Ogrodniki (Poland) - Lazdijai (Lithuania). **Bus:** Long-distance services run regularly to Riga, Vilnius, Kaliningrad and St Petersburg. *Eurolines*, 4 Cardiff Road, Luton, Bedfordshire LU1 1PP, UK (tel: (08705) 143 219; fax: (01582) 400 694; website: www.eurolines.com *or* www.nationalexpress.com) operate to other European cities, including Berlin, Hamburg, Kiel, Kyiv, Minsk, Moscow, Oslo, Riga, St Petersburg and Warsaw.

Travel - Internal

AIR: There are domestic flights from Tallinn to the islands of Saaremaa and Hiiumaa (this service does not operate during the winter).
SEA/RIVER: Frequent ferry services connect the mainland with the larger islands, and boats operate on Lake Peipsi and the Emajõgi River.
RAIL: The rail system is underdeveloped but most major

Credit: © Estonian Tourist Board

cities are connected to the network. Rail services to Tartu take about three hours (express trains 2 hours 30 minutes) from Tallinn.
ROAD: Estonia has a high density of roads although there are few major highways. Signs are not illuminated and fairly small, so driving at night is best avoided. Car headlights must be used 24 hours a day. Lead-free and 4-star petrol are now widely available and a good network of petrol stations (many of them open 24 hours) has been developed. Payment is in local currency or by credit card. Traffic drives on the right. The minimum driving age is 18. **Bus:** There is a wide network covering most of the country, including express services. Prices are very low and buses are still the most important means of transport. **Taxi:** Private taxis must display the name of the company and their number on the roof. Fares should be agreed upon beforehand. *Marshrut-taxis* are minibuses which operate on fixed routes stopping on request. They can take up to 10 people. **Car hire:** Can be arranged at the airport or in Tallinn. **Regulations:** Speed limits are 120kph (74mph) on some roads in summer, 90kph (55mph) outside built-up areas and 50kph (31mph) in built-up areas. The consumption of alcohol while driving is strictly forbidden. **Documentation:** EU nationals should be in possession of an EU or national driving licence and insurance.
URBAN: Taxis in Tallinn are inexpensive. All parts of the city can also be reached by bus, trolley-bus and tram. Tickets can be bought in stalls in the main shopping areas.

Accommodation

HOTELS: Since independence, there has been a scramble from Western and Estonian firms to turn the old state-run hotels into modern Western-standard enterprises. Many more joint ventures with firms from all over Western Europe and the United States will ensure that the standard of accommodation in Estonia rapidly reaches Western European levels. Outside Tallinn, which for the time being is the main location of the current expansion, Estonia enjoys an adequate range of acceptable accommodation, left over from the pre-independence days or built by Estonian entrepreneurs, including large hotels and smaller pension-type establishments. For more details, contact the Estonian Hotel and Restaurant Association, Kirku 6, 10130, Tallinn (tel: (6) 411 428; fax: (6) 411 425; e-mail: info@ehrl.ee; website: www.ehrl.ee).
CAMPING: There are over 80 campsites in Estonia. The most popular include: Camping & Motel Peoleo, 12km (7.5 miles) south of Tallinn; Camping Valgerand in Pärnu; and Camping Malvaste on Hiiumaa Island. Standards are improving, though not yet as high as in Western European countries.
RURAL ACCOMMODATION: The Estonian Rural Tourism Association provides accommodation in the countryside across Estonia, from farm-stays to local bed & breakfasts. For further information, contact the Estonian Rural Tourism Association, Vilmsi 53b, 10147 Tallinn (tel: (6) 009 999; e-mail: eesti@maaturism.ee; website: www.maaturism.ee).
YOUTH HOSTELS: The majority of youth hostels have saunas and seminar facilities. For further information, contact the Estonian Youth Hostels Association, Natva mnt., 10120 Tallinn, Estonia (tel: (6) 461 455; fax: (6) 461 595; e-mail: eyha@online.ee; website: www.baltichostels.net/eyha.html).

Credit: © Estonian Tourist Board

Resorts & Excursions

TALLINN: An ancient Hanseatic city and the capital of Estonia, Tallinn has a wealth of historical and architectural monuments, particularly in the old town centre which is dominated by the soaring steeple of the medieval **Town Hall** (14th to 15th centuries), the oldest in northern Europe. More than two-thirds of the original **City Wall** still stands and a superb view of the narrow streets, the gabled roofs and the towers and spires of old Tallinn is afforded from **Toompea Castle**, situated on a cliff top. A favourite recreation spot is **Kadriorg Park**, which contains the palace built for Peter the Great. The **Open Air Museum** offers visitors a glimpse into the way of rural life in the 18th and 19th centuries.

PÄRNU: About two hours' drive from Tallinn is Pärnu, a small town situated on the banks of the **Pärnu River** where it emerges into the Gulf of Riga. Established in the 13th century, the town is known as a seaport and a health resort. Among its attractions are its theatre and its 3km- (2 mile-) long sandy beach, which is very popular with Estonians.

TARTU: Estonia's second-largest city lies about 176km (110 miles) from Tallinn on the **Emajõgi River**. The city has a very old university and other sights include the **Vyshgorod Cathedral** (13th to 15th centuries), the **Town Hall** (18th century) and the university's **Botanical Garden**.

NARVA: One of the oldest towns in Estonia. Situated on the western banks of the **River Narva**, it was first mentioned in the chronicle of Novgorod. The **Herman Castle** is the oldest architectural monument and the city museum, which is situated in the castle, is well worth seeing.

BEYOND THE CITIES: Haapsalu is a small town on the western coast and has been a well-known resort since the 19th century. It is the ideal place to get away from it all with its romantic wooden houses and tree-lined avenues. **Saaremaa** is the largest island in Estonia. On here and on Hiiumaa (Estonia's second-largest island) one can see old windmills, stone churches, fishing villages and a restored Episcopal castle dating back to the 13th century. **Mustvee**, situated on the shores of the beautiful and vast **Lake Peipsi**, and **Kuremäe**, the site of the only functioning convent in Estonia, are also well worth a visit.

NATIONAL PARKS: Lahema National Park (70km/44 miles from Tallinn) is one of Estonia's three national parks, with almost totally unspoiled and untouched forest and swamps, picturesque old fishing villages and historic manor houses. The other two national parks are the **Soomaa National Park** and the **Vilandsi National Park**. There are also several nature reserves and protected areas. For further details, see *Sport & Activities* section.

Sport & Activities

Nature and Wildlife: Estonia is an unspoilt, sparsely populated country, nearly half of which is covered with forests. Around a dozen national parks and protected areas provide opportunities for nature lovers to explore the countryside. Information centres at each reserve can provide advice and maps. Popular among both Estonians and tourists is *Lahemaa National Park*, the country's largest national park. Situated on the northern coast, it contains limestone cliffs, waterfalls, lakes and forests. **Bog walks** can be undertaken in this area. Walkways on wooden boards give visitors the opportunity to observe the special flora and fauna of the deep peat bogs. In *Soomaa National Park*, near Pärnu, the ancient bogs (said to be inhabited by witches) can be explored in traditional canoes. Estonian **wildlife** includes large mammals such as lynx, bears, wolves and elk. Birdlife is abundant, and **birdwatchers** are well catered for in reserves such as the *Käina Bay Bird Reserve* and *Matsalu Nature Reserve*. Eagles, storks and a variety of wetland birds are among the species to be seen. Butterflies are also numerous in parts of Estonia.

Trainspotting: Owing to the wide-gauge track, unusual trains can be spotted, an activity popular amongst local people. The *National Railway Museum* in Haapsalu is a source of information for trainspotters. Behind the museum, a 'train graveyard' contains vehicles of special interest to train buffs. There is even the opportunity to spend the night in a former luxury sleeping car, used to transport Communist Party members in the Soviet era, and now turned into a youth hostel.

Watersports: Swimming is popular all over Estonia. The beaches are often long and wide with white sand; pools and lakes abound in the interior of the country. In the north of the country, it is possible to find small coves used for **nude bathing**, though there are no designated areas for this. **Fishing** is very popular and **boating** widely practised.

Other: Good **hiking** and **cycling** spots include Saaremaa Island, which has remained particularly unspoiled, owing to the fact that, in the Soviet era, even Estonians required a visa to visit it. **Horseriding** is widely practiced. Otepää in the southeast, with its lakes and forests, is a good location for all outdoor activities in the summer and for **skiing** in the winter. **Canoeing** can be arranged with specialist companies. Trips usually last one to three days and the price includes equipment hire. There is an international-standard **golf** course at Niitivälja, 34km (21 miles) from Tallinn. It is closed in winter. **Basketball** is also very popular, as are **cross-country skiing** and **football**.

Social Profile

FOOD & DRINK: Hors d'oeuvres are very good and often the best part of the meal. Local specialities include *sült* (jellied veal), *täidetud vasikarind* (roast stuffed shoulder of veal) and *rosolje* (vinaigrette with herring and beets). Braised goose stuffed with apples and plums is also a Baltic speciality. The legal drinking age is 21.

NIGHTLIFE: Tallinn is used to entertaining daytrippers from Finland and has a wide range of restaurants, cafes and bars. There is also an opera and ballet theatre.

SHOPPING: Amber and local folk-art are good buys. **Shopping hours:** Mon-Fri 0900-2100. Many shops are also open at the weekend.

SPECIAL EVENTS: For detailed information on major events and festivals occurring in Estonia, contact the Estonian Embassy or the tourist office (see *Contact Addresses* section). The following is a selection of special events occurring in 2005:

Jan 8-9 *World Cup in Cross-Country Skiing.* **Feb 13** *Tartu Marathon*, Tehvandi Ski Stadium. **Apr 9-10** *11th International Pärnu Film and Video Festival.* **Apr 25-May 1** *The University Spring Festivities.* **May 5-7** *Nordic Poetry Festival.* **Jun 3-Aug 26** *3rd Pärnu Organ Festival.* **Jun 30-Jul 3** *25th International Hanseatic Days.* **Jul 2-Aug 4** *David Oistrakh Festival.* **Jul 14-17** *15th International Folklore Festival Pärnumaa Pirand.* **Jul 16-Aug 3** *Glasperlenspiel Music Festival.* **Aug 12-13** *Saku Suverull.*

SOCIAL CONVENTIONS: Handshaking is customary. Normal courtesies should be observed. The Estonians are proud of their culture and their national heritage, and visitors should take care to respect this sense of national identity. **Tipping:** Taxi fares and restaurant bills include a tip.

Business Profile

ECONOMY: Economic autonomy was a key demand from Estonia during the negotiations that led to its independence. The Baltic states were the most prosperous areas of the former Soviet Union and they were keen to develop economic links with their Western neighbours outside the straitjacket of central planning. Other than oil-shale, which is present in significant quantities and provides the basis of the country's power generation, Estonia has few raw materials of its own and relies mostly on imported commodities to produce finished goods. Light machinery, electrical and electronic equipment and consumer goods are the main products. Fishing, forestry and dairy farming dominate the agricultural sector. Estonia's infrastructure, particularly the road network, is well-developed by regional standards. Post-Soviet economic policy has followed a customary pattern of deregulation and privatisation. In June 1992, Estonia became the first former Soviet Republic to introduce its own currency, the Kroon, which is the legal tender and is now fixed in value to the Euro. Estonia's service sector was the most developed in the former USSR, and has since expanded further with increased tourism and Western investment. There is also a thriving financial services industry. Overall, trade with the West has increased dramatically, particularly with Scandinavia; Finland, Sweden and Germany are important trading partners. Despite this, Estonia still has fundamental economic links with the Russian Federation, and the 1998 Russian economic crisis led to a recession in Estonia the following year. Growth in 2004, however, was around 5 per sent.

In 1999, Estonia joined the World Trade Organisation, adding to its previous membership of the IMF, World Bank and the European Bank for Reconstruction and Development. In May 2004, Estonia, along with its Baltic neighbours and seven other countries, achieved a long-cherished ambition when it joined the European Union.

BUSINESS: Prior appointments are necessary. Business is conducted formally. Business cards are exchanged after introduction. **Office hours:** Mon-Fri 0800-1800.

COMMERCIAL INFORMATION: The following organisation can offer advice: Estonian Chamber of Commerce and Industry, Toom Kooli 17, 10130 Tallinn (tel: (6) 460 244; fax: (6) 460 245; e-mail: koda@koda.ee; website: www.koda.ee).

Climate

Temperate climate, but with considerable temperature variations. Summer is warm with relatively mild weather in spring and autumn. Winter, which lasts from November to mid-March, can be very cold. Rainfall is distributed throughout the year with the heaviest rainfall in August. Heavy snowfalls are common in the winter months.

Required clothing: Light- to mediumweights are worn during the summer months. Medium- to heavyweights are needed during winter. Rainwear is advisable all year.

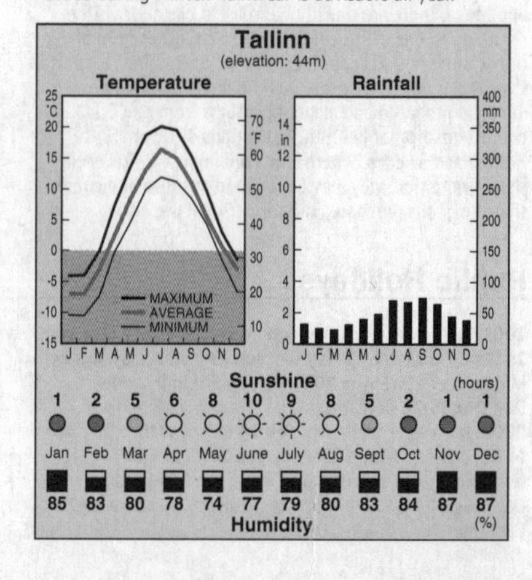

Ethiopia

LATEST TRAVEL ADVICE CONTACTS

British Foreign and Commonwealth Office
Tel: (0870) 606 0290 Website: www.fco.gov.uk

US Department of State
Website: http://travel.state.gov/travel

Canadian Department of Foreign Affairs and Int'l Trade
Tel: (1 800) 267 8376 Website: www.dfait-maeci.gc.ca

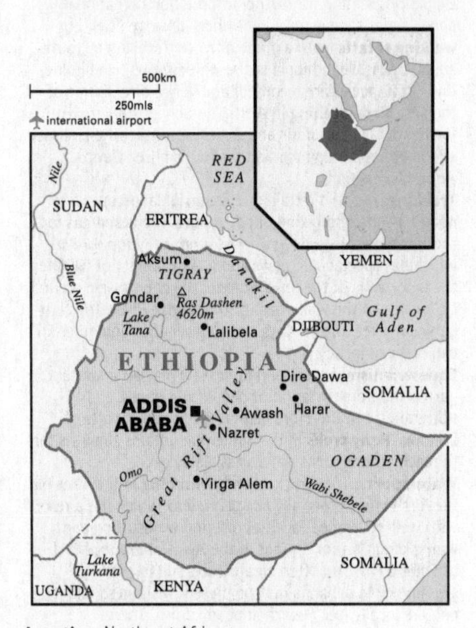

Location: Northeast Africa.

Country dialling code: 251.

Ethiopian Tourism Commission
PO Box 2183, Addis Ababa, Ethiopia
Tel: (1) 517 470. Fax: (1) 513 899.
E-mail: tour-com@telecom.net.et *or* info@tourismethiopia.org
Website: www.tourismethiopia.org

Embassy of the Federal Democratic Republic of Ethiopia
17 Princes Gate, London SW7 1PZ, UK
Tel: (020) 7589 7212. Fax: (020) 7584 7054 *or* 7838 3889.
E-mail: info@ethioembassy.org.uk
Website: www.ethioembassy.org.uk
Opening hours: Mon-Fri 0900-1600 (general); Mon-Fri 0900-1600 (visa applications and collections).

Ethiopian Airlines
1 Duke's Gate, Acton Lane, London W4 5DX, UK
Tel: (020) 8987 9086 (administration) *or* 7000 (reservations).
E-mail: lonsm@ethiopianairlines.com *or* reservation@ethiopianairlines.com
Website: www.flyethiopian.com

British Embassy
Street address: Fikre Mariam Abatechan Street, Addis Ababa, Ethiopia
Postal address: PO Box 858, Addis Ababa, Ethiopia
Tel: (1) 612 354. Fax: (1) 610 588 (general) *or* 614 154 (visa section).
E-mail: BritishEmbassy.AddisAbaba@fco.gov.uk
Website: www.britishembassy.gov.uk/ethiopia

Embassy of the Federal Democratic Republic of Ethiopia
3506 International Drive, NW, Washington, DC 20008, USA
Tel: (202) 364 1200. Fax: (202) 587 0195.
E-mail: info@ethiopianembassy.org
Website: www.ethiopianembassy.org

Embassy of the United States of America
Street address: Entoto Street, Addis Ababa, Ethiopia
Postal address: PO Box 1014, Addis Ababa, Ethiopia
Tel: (1) 174 000 *or* 242 424 (visa section). Fax: (1) 174 001.
E-mail: usemaddis@state.gov
Website: http://addisababa.usembassy.gov

TIMATIC CODES

Health
AMADEUS: **TI-DFT/JIB/HE**
GALILEO/WORLDSPAN: **TI-DFT/JIB/HE**
SABRE: **TIDFT/JIB/HE**

Visa
AMADEUS: **TI-DFT/JIB/VI**
GALILEO/WORLDSPAN: **TI-DFT/JIB/VI**
SABRE: **TIDFT/JIB/VI**

To access TIMATIC country information on Health and Visa regulations through the Computer Reservations System (CRS), type in the appropriate command line listed above.

Embassy of the Federal Democratic Republic of Ethiopia
151 Slater Street, Suite 210, Ottawa, Ontario K1P 5H3, Canada
Tel: (613) 235 6637. Fax: (613) 235 4638.
E-mail: infoethi@magi.com

Canadian Embassy
Street address: Nifas Silk Lasto Kefle Ketema, Keble 04, House 122, Addis Ababa, Ethiopia
Postal address: PO Box 1130, Addis Ababa, Ethiopia
Tel: (1) 713 022. Fax: (1) 713 033.
E-mail: addis@international.gc.ca

General Information

AREA: 1,133,380 sq km (437,600 sq miles).
POPULATION: 65,370,000 (official estimate 2001).
POPULATION DENSITY: 57.7 per sq km.
CAPITAL: Addis Ababa. **Population:** 2,084,588 (1994).
GEOGRAPHY: Ethiopia is situated in northeast Africa, bordered by Eritrea, Sudan, Kenya, Somalia and Djibouti. It is the 10th-largest country in Africa and about twice the size of France. The central area is a vast highland region of volcanic rock forming a watered, temperate zone surrounded by hot, arid, inhospitable desert. The Great Rift Valley, which starts in Palestine, runs down the Red Sea and diagonally southwest through Ethiopia, Kenya and Malawi. The escarpments on either side of the country are steepest in the north where the terrain is very rugged. To the south, the landscape is generally flatter and more suited to agriculture.
GOVERNMENT: Federal Republic. **Head of State:** President Girma Wolde Giorgis since 2001. **Head of Government:** Prime Minister Meles Zenawi since 1995. Ethiopia is the only African country never to have been colonised by Europeans.
LANGUAGE: Amharic is the official language, although about 80 other native tongues are spoken. English is widely used and some Arabic, Italian and French is spoken.
RELIGION: Ethiopian Orthodox (*Tewahido*) and Coptic Church mainly in the north; Islam, mainly in the east and south. There are also significant Evangelical, Protestant and Roman Catholic communities.
TIME: GMT + 3.
ELECTRICITY: 220 volts AC, 50Hz.
COMMUNICATIONS: Telephone: IDD is available. Country code: 251. Outgoing international code: 00. **Mobile telephone:** The PTO, *ETA*, provides a GSM 900 network. Coverage is limited. **Fax:** Facilities are available in major hotels and at the Telecommunications Head Office in Addis Ababa. **Telegram:** International services from local offices and hotels in Addis Ababa. **Internet:** There are Internet cafes in Addis Ababa. Some top-end hotels may also offer services. The main ISP is the PTO *ETC*, although connections may be difficult. **Post:** Service to and from Europe takes up to two weeks. Post office hours: Mon-Fri 0800-1600. **Press:** Amharic newspapers published in the capital include *Addis Zemen*. The English-language daily in Ethiopia is *The Ethiopian Herald*. A number of other weeklies - many of them in English - are also available.
Radio: BBC World Service (website: www.bbc.co.uk/worldservice) and Voice of America (website: www.voa.gov) can be received. From time to time the frequencies change and the most up-to-date can be found online.

Passport/Visa

	Passport Required?	Visa Required?	Return Ticket Required?
Full British	Yes	Yes	Yes
Australian	Yes	Yes	Yes
Canadian	Yes	Yes	Yes
USA	Yes	Yes	Yes
Other EU	Yes	Yes	Yes
Japanese	Yes	Yes	Yes

Note: *Regulations and requirements may be subject to change at short notice, and you are advised to contact the appropriate diplomatic or consular authority before finalising travel arrangements. Details of these may be found at the head of this country's entry. Any numbers in the chart refer to the footnotes below.*

PASSPORTS: Passport valid for six months required by all.
VISAS: Required by all except the following:
(a) nationals of Djibouti and Kenya for stays of up to three months;
(b) transit passengers continuing to a third country within 12 hours, provided not leaving the airport and holding valid travel documents for onward destination.
Types of visa and cost: *Tourist*: £12 (single-entry); £18 (multiple-entry, three months); £24 (multiple-entry, six months). *Business*: £12 (single-entry); £18 (multiple-entry, three months); £30 (multiple-entry, six months); £60 (multiple-entry, one year). *Transit*: £12 (single-entry); £18 (double-entry).
Validity: *Tourist* and *Business*: Single-entry visas are valid for one month, multiple-entry visas are valid for three, six or twelve months. Applications for extensions should be made to the Immigration Department in Ethiopia. *Transit*: Seven days.
Application to: Consulate (or Consular section at Embassy); see *Contact Addresses* section.
Application requirements: (a) Completed application form. (b) Passport valid for at least six months (containing residence permit, if applicable). (c) One passport-size photo. (d) Fee (payable by cash, banker's draft or postal order). (e) Proof of sufficient funds to cover stay (US$50 or equivalent per day of stay). (f) Return or onward ticket. (g) For postal applications, a self-addressed, special delivery envelope. *Business*: (a)-(g) and, (h) Letter from sponsor, accepting financial responsibility for applicant. *Student*: (a)-(g) and, (h) Letter from educational institution, or invitation from Ethiopian reference.
Note: A yellow fever vaccination, whilst advisable, is not compulsory. Consult the embassy for up-to-date advice on whether applications will be accepted without the certificate.
Working days required: Three to four. Applications should be made well in advance.
Exit permit: Required by all nationals of Ethiopia and visitors staying more than 30 days.

Money

Currency: Ethiopian Birr (Birr) = 100 cents. Notes are in denominations of Birr100, 50, 10, 5 and 1. Coins are in denominations of 50, 25, 10, 5 and 1 cents.
Currency exchange: US Dollar bills are the most convenient currency to exchange.
Credit & debit cards: Diners Club and MasterCard are accepted on a very limited basis (only the Hilton Hotel is certain to accept them). Check with your credit or debit card company for details of merchant acceptability and other services which may be available.
Travellers cheques: To avoid additional exchange rate charges, travellers are advised to take travellers cheques in US Dollars or Pounds Sterling.
Currency restrictions: The import of local currency is limited to Birr100. The export of local currency up to Birr100 is permitted, provided the traveller holds a re-entry permit. The import and export of foreign currency is unlimited, subject to declaration on arrival.
Exchange rate indicators: The following figures are included as a guide to the movements of the Birr against Sterling and the US Dollar:

Date	Feb '04	May '04	Aug '04	Nov '04
£1.00=	15.65	15.23	15.80	16.28
$1.00=	8.60	8.53	8.58	8.60

Banking hours: Mon-Fri 0800-1600, Sat 0800-1200.

Duty Free

The following goods may be imported into Ethiopia without incurring customs duty:
100 cigarettes or 50 cigars or 227g of tobacco; 1l of alcoholic beverages; 2 bottles or 500ml of perfume; gifts up to the value of Birr100.
Note: Export certificates are required for skins, hides and antiques.

Public Holidays

2005: Jan 7* Ethiopian Christmas. **Jan 19*** Timket (Epiphany). **Jan 21** Eid-al Adha (Arafat). **Mar 2** Battle of Adowa. **Apr 21** Mouloud (Birth of the Prophet). **Apr 25*** Ethiopian Good Friday. **May 2*** Ethiopian Easter. **May 28** Downfall of the Dergue. **Sep 11*** Ethiopian New Year (Enkutatash). **Sep 27*** Finding of the True Cross (Meskel). **Nov 3-5** Eid al-Fitr (End of Ramadan).
2006: Jan 7* Ethiopian Christmas. **Jan 10** Eid-al Adha (Arafat). **Jan 19*** Timket (Epiphany). **Mar 2** Battle of Adowa. **Apr 11** Mouloud (Birth of the Prophet). **Apr 14*** Ethiopian Good Friday. **Apr 17*** Ethiopian Easter. **May 28** Downfall of the Dergue. **Sep 11*** Ethiopian New Year (Enkutatash). **Sep 26*** Finding of the True Cross (Meskel). **Oct 22-24** Eid al-Fitr (End of Ramadan).
Note: (a) *Indicates Coptic holidays. (b) Ethiopia still uses the Julian calendar, which is divided into 12 months of 30 days each, and a 13th month of five or six days at the end of the year; hence the date for Christmas. The Ethiopian calendar is seven years and eight months behind our own. (c) Muslim festivals are timed according to local sightings of various phases of the moon and the dates given above are approximations. During the lunar month of Ramadan that precedes Eid al-Fitr, Muslims fast during the day and feast at night and normal business patterns may be interrupted. Some disruption may continue into Eid al-Fitr itself. Eid al-Fitr and Eid al-Adha may last anything from two to 10 days, depending on the region. For more information, see the *World of Islam* appendix.

Health

	Special Precautions?	Certificate Required?
Yellow Fever	Yes	1
Cholera	2	No
Typhoid & Polio	3	N/A
Malaria	4	N/A

Note: *Regulations and requirements may be subject to change at short notice, and you are advised to contact your doctor well in advance of your intended date of departure. Any numbers in the chart refer to the footnotes below.*

1: A yellow fever vaccination certificate is required from travellers over one year of age coming from infected areas. Ethiopia is listed in the endemic zone for yellow fever and travellers arriving from non-endemic zones should note that vaccination is strongly recommended for travel outside the urban areas, even if an outbreak of the disease has not been reported and they would normally not require a vaccination certificate to enter the country.
2: Following WHO guidelines issued in 1973, a cholera vaccination certificate is no longer a condition of entry to Ethiopia. However, cholera is a serious risk in this country and precautions are essential. Up-to-date advice should be sought before deciding whether these precautions should include vaccination as medical opinion is divided over its effectiveness; see the *Health* appendix for more information.
3: Typhoid is widespread. Poliomyelitis is endemic. Vaccination against both is advised.
4: Malaria risk, predominantly in the malignant *falciparum* form, exists throughout the year in all areas below 2000m (6562ft). Highly chloroquine-resistant *falciparum* is reported. No malaria risk exists in Addis Ababa.
Food & drink: All water should be regarded as being potentially contaminated. Water used for drinking, brushing teeth or making ice should have first been boiled or otherwise sterilised. Milk is unpasteurised and should be boiled. Powdered or tinned milk is available and is advised, but make sure that it is reconstituted with pure water. Avoid dairy products which are likely to have been made from unboiled milk. Only eat well-cooked meat and fish, preferably served hot. Pork, salad and mayonnaise may carry increased risk. Vegetables should be cooked and fruit peeled.
Other risks: *Diarrhoeal* diseases, including giardiasis, and *typhoid fevers* are common. *Bilharzia* (schistosomiasis) is present. Avoid swimming and paddling in fresh water; swimming pools which are well-chlorinated and maintained are safe. *Onchocerciasis* (river blindness) occurs. *Trypanosomiasis* (sleeping sickness) has been reported. *Hepatitis A* and *E* are widespread; *hepatitis B* is hyperendemic. *Meningococcal meningitis* risk is present, particularly in dry areas and during the dry season. *Visceral leishmaniasis* may be found in the drier areas. *Trachoma* is widespread. Immunisation against *diphtheria* is also recommended.
Rabies is present. For those at high risk, vaccination before arrival should be considered. If you are bitten, seek medical advice without delay. For more information, consult the *Health* appendix.
Health care: The high altitude and low oxygen level of much of Ethiopia needs time to be acclimatised to. Those who suffer from heart ailments or high blood pressure should consult a doctor before travelling. Health insurance is strongly advised; see the *Health* appendix.

Travel - International

Travel warning: Travel within 20km of the border areas of Tigray and Afar is advised against. All travel to the Gambella Region, where continuing unrest and sporadic violence has led to many deaths since December 2003, is advised against. Crossing the Ethiopia/Somalia border by road is also advised against, as is all but essential travel in the area east of the Harar to Gode line.
AIR: Ethiopia's national airline is *Ethiopian Airlines (ET)* (website: www.flyethiopian.com), which operates three flights a week from London, with a stopover either in Frankfurt/M or in Cairo. *Lufthansa* operates four flights a week from London to Addis Ababa via Frankfurt. Addis Ababa is also served by *British Airways*, *KLM*, *SAS* and *United Airlines*.
Approximate flight times: From Addis Ababa to *London* is 10 hours.
International airports: *Addis Ababa (ADD)* (Bole International) is 8km (5 miles) southeast of the city (travel time – 25 minutes). A coach service departs regularly to the city. Taxis are also available. Airport facilities include duty-free, car hire, banks, bureaux de change, left luggage, post office, first aid facilities, restaurant and bar.
Departure tax: US$20, payable in US Dollars only. Exact amount only. Transit passengers not leaving the airport are exempt.
RAIL: A 784km- (487 mile-) rail service between Djibouti and Addis Ababa is run jointly by the two governments.
ROAD: The main route is via Kenya. There is an all-weather road from Moyale on the border via Yabelo, Dila and Yirga to Addis Ababa. The following border points are also open: Dewale/Galafi (from Djibouti) and Humera/Metema (from Sudan).

Travel - Internal

AIR: *Ethiopian Airlines* runs internal flights to over 40 towns, although services may be infrequent. Airports throughout Ethiopia are currently being upgraded in a step to encourage tourism. *Ethiopian Airlines* also operates an *Historic Route Service* for tourists taking in the country's world-famous historic sites.
Departure tax: Birr10.
RAIL: The only operative line runs between Addis Ababa and Djibouti, via Dire Dawa and Harar. Travellers should be prepared for occasional delays.
ROAD: A good network of all-weather roads exists to most business and tourist centres. Otherwise, 4-wheel-drive vehicles are recommended. Frequent fuel shortages can make travel outside Addis Ababa very difficult. Vehicle travel after dark outside Addis Ababa is risky. Traffic drives on the right. **Bus:** Services are run by the Government as well as private companies and they operate throughout the country. The bus terminus can provide schedules and tickets, although it is unusual for tourists to attempt to use this service. Bus trips can be slow as there is often a lengthy wait to assemble a convoy (necessary in more dangerous areas). **Taxi:** Available in Addis Ababa and other major towns. Painted blue and white, they sometimes offer service on a shared basis. Fares should be negotiated before travelling. There are also minibus taxis which offer cheap and frequent shared travel in Addis Ababa. **Car hire:** This is available from *Avis* and *Hertz* in Addis Ababa. **Documentation:** A British driving licence is valid for up to one month, otherwise the visitor needs to obtain a temporary Ethiopian driving licence on arrival.

Accommodation

Good hotels can be found in Addis Ababa and other main centres, although they tend to be better in the north than in the south. Some offer facilities for small exhibitions and conferences. There are hotels in the other larger towns; prices are, in general, slightly lower than those in the main centres. There is a 5 to 10 per cent service charge. For more information, contact the Ethiopian Commission for Tourism (see *Contact Addresses* section).

Resorts & Excursions

ADDIS ABABA: Ethiopia's capital is located at an altitude of 2440m (8000ft) in the central highlands. Places of interest include the university, **St George's Cathedral**, the **Ethnology Church Museum**, the **Menelik Mausoleum**, the **Trinity Church**, the **Old Ghibi Palace** and the market, one of the largest in Africa.
AKSUM: The ancient royal capital of the earliest Ethiopian kingdom lies in the north of the country. It is renowned for multi-storeyed ancient carved granite obelisks, for important archaeological remains and for the church, which claims to house the Lost Ark of the Covenant.
NATIONAL PARKS: There are nine national parks in Ethiopia: the **Simien Mountain National Park** (in the northern mountain massif); the **Awash National Park** (east of the capital); the **Omo** and **Mago National Parks** (southwest of the capital); the **Shalla-Abijatta Lakes National Park** (south of the capital); the **Gambella National Park** (Ilubabor region); the **Nechi Sar National Park** (Gambo region); **Yangudi-Rassa National Park** (Harerge region); and the **Bale Mountains National Park**, on high southern moorland country, which has its own unique flora and fauna.
ELSEWHERE: The **Blue Nile Falls** (also called **Tissisat**) are one of the most spectacular waterfalls in Northern Africa. They are situated about 35km (22 miles) from Bahar Dar. **Gondar** was the capital of Ethiopia from 1632 to 1855 and is the site of many ruined castles. Close by is **Lake Tana**, on which 37 islands stand and is the largest lake in Ethiopia. **Lalibela** is famous for its 12th-century, rock-hewn churches. **Harar** is a famous Muslim walled city and the centre for the coffee trade. **Dire Dawa**, near Harar, is an important trading centre on the Addis Ababa–Djibouti railway line. The Rift **Valley Lakes** in Ziway, Langano, Awasso, Abiyata, Shalla, Abaya and Chamo offer unique scenery and beautiful beaches. **Langano** is one of the most popular lakeside resorts.

Sport & Activities

Safaris: Wildlife safaris to the national parks are organised by a number of tour operators (see the *Resorts & Excursions* section for further information on national parks). Safaris are usually in 4-wheel-drive vehicles, but **walking safaris** (with a guide only) or travelling by **mule** are also possible. Ethiopia is also noted for its rich birdlife (over 850 species are recorded) and hence offers some of the best **birdwatching** in Africa, notably at *Abiyata*. For further details on safaris and trekking, contact the Embassy or the Ethiopian Commission for Tourism (see *Contact Addresses* section).
Trekking: The wild terrain and beautiful landscapes offer good trekking and hiking opportunities. The best areas for these activities include *Simien Mountains National Park*, which has spectacular views and a large variety of wildlife; the moorlands of the *Bale Plateau*; the countryside around *Lalibela*; and the wilderness of the *Awash River*. Trips last between three and 10 days, and English-speaking guides can be hired locally.
Equestrianism: Horses and mules still play an important part in the transportation of people and goods, and horseriding can therefore be practised in most parts of Ethiopia. **Pony treks** in the Simien Mountains allow visitors to reach remote areas not accessible by car.
Watersports: There is excellent **swimming** in the lakes of the *Rift Valley*, especially *Lake Langano*, which has a resort with well-developed facilities offering windsurfing and waterskiing. Natural springs in the *Awash National Park* or at *Sodere Filwoha* often create pools suitable for swimming. As bilharzia may be present, visitors should enquire locally (see *Health* appendix for further information). The rivers and streams of the *Bale Mountains*, in the southeast, and the many lakes in the *Rift Valley* provide excellent **fishing**, particularly for trout. Local fishermen offer trips in their own boats. Dugout **canoes** or traditional **papyrus boats** can also be hired. **Sailing** and organised **boat trips** are available on the spectacular *Lake Tana*, which contains 37 islands, many of which also have monasteries that can be visited. **Whitewater rafting** is possible on parts of the *Omo River* and the *Blue Nile*.
Cycling: Expeditions can be made to various sites, for instance the *Bale National Park*. Bicycle Africa can provide further information (website: www.ibike.org/bikeafrica).

Social Profile

FOOD & DRINK: Menus in the best hotels offer international food and Addis Ababa also has a number of good Chinese, Italian and Indian restaurants. Ethiopian food is based on dishes called *we't* (meat, chicken or vegetables, cooked in a hot pepper sauce), served with or on *injera* (a flat spongy bread). Dishes include *shivro* and *misir* (chickpeas and lentils, Ethiopian-style) and *tibs* (crispy fried steak). There is a wide choice of fish including sole, Red Sea snapper, lake fish, trout and prawns. Traditional restaurants in larger cities serve food in a grand manner around a brightly coloured basket-weave table called a masob. Before beginning the meal, guests will be given soap, water and a clean towel, as the right hand is used to break off pieces of *injera* with which the *we't* is gathered up. Cutlery is not used.
Ethiopian coffee from the province of Kaffa, with a little rue added for extra aroma, is called 'health of Adam'. Local red and dry white wines are worth trying. *Talla* (Ethiopian beer) has a unique taste and European-style lager is widely available. *Kaitaka* (a pure grain alcohol), cognac (a local brandy) and *tej* (an alcoholic drink based on fermented honey) are unique.
SHOPPING: Special purchases include local jewellery (sold by the actual weight of gold or silver), woodcarvings, illuminated manuscripts and prayer scrolls, wood and metal crosses, leather shields, spears, drums and carpets. In marketplaces, a certain amount of bargaining is expected, but prices at shops in towns are fixed. **Shopping hours:** Mon-Fri 0800-1300, 1400-2000; Sat 0900-1300, 1500-1900 (with local variations).
SPECIAL EVENTS: The principal annual events are Islamic and Coptic religious festivals. For dates, see *Public Holidays* section. The following is a selection of special events occurring in Ethiopia in 2005:
Jul 23 *Birthday of Haile Selassie.* **Nov 2** *Anniversary of the Crowning of Haile Selaissie.*
SOCIAL CONVENTIONS: Casual wear is suitable for most places, but Ethiopians tend to be fairly formal and

conservative in their dress. Private informal entertaining is very common. Most religious houses are not open to women. **Photography:** In the smaller towns, the locals may expect a small payment in return for being photographed. Video photography in famous tourist attractions occasionally carries a small charge. Photography may be prohibited in airports and near military camps. **Tipping:** In most hotels and restaurants, a 10 per cent service charge is added to the bill. Tipping is a fairly frequent custom, but amounts are small.

Business Profile

ECONOMY: Ethiopia is one of the world's least developed countries, with an average annual per capita income of US$100, minimal infrastructure and a serious shortage of skilled labour. Economic development has also been hampered by the effects of the long-running civil war and, more recently, a series of military clashes with both neighbours (notably Eritrea) and internal opposition. The Eritrean war is estimated to cost Ethiopia around US$3 billion – half the country's entire annual economic output. To this litany of ill-fortune can be added severe drought and flooding, which have hampered post-war reconstruction work. The economy is largely dependent on subsistence agriculture, which employs almost 90 per cent of the workforce. Coffee is the main export earner. After the end of the civil war, the government set about dismantling the command economy established by the Mengistu regime, not least in an attempt to tackle the country's huge debt burden. Not surprisingly, Ethiopia relies on substantial quantities of food aid. The manufacturing and service sectors are both small. However, there is one bright prospect in the form of a large natural gas field, development of which is now beginning and which promises substantial future revenues. Ethiopia's main trading partners are the USA, which buys most of its coffee crop, and Germany.
BUSINESS: Businesspeople should wear suits and ties for business visits. English is widely used for trade purposes but Italian and French are also useful. Nonetheless, knowledge of a few words of Amharic will be appreciated. Some of the more useful are *Tena Yistillign* – 'Hello'; *Ow* – 'Yes'; *Aydellem* – 'No'; and *Sintinew* – 'How much is this?'. Normal courtesies should be observed and business cards can be used. Best months for business visits are October to May. **Office hours:** Mon-Fri 0800-1200, 1300-1700.
COMMERCIAL INFORMATION: The following organisations can offer advice: Commercial Bank of Ethiopia, PO Box 255, Unity Square, Addis Ababa (tel: (1) 515 004; fax: (1) 514 522; website: www.combanketh.com); *or* Addis Ababa Chamber of Commerce, PO Box 2458, Mexico Square, Addis Ababa (tel: (1) 513 882 *or* 515 055; fax: (1) 511 479; e-mail: aachamber1@telecom.net.et; website: www.addischamber.com); *or* Ethiopian Trade Promotions Section, 17 Princes Gate, London SW7 1PZ, UK (tel: (020) 7589 7217; fax: (020) 7584 7054; e-mail: info@ethioembassy.org.uk; website: www.ethioembassy.org.uk).
CONFERENCES/CONVENTIONS: Information is available from the United Nations Conference Centre, PO Box 3001, Addis Ababa (tel: (1) 514 874 *or* 514 945; fax: (1) 513 155; e-mail: uncc-aa@un.org; website: www.un.org).

Climate

Hot and humid in the lowlands, warm in the hill country and cool in the uplands. Most rainfall is from June to September.
Required clothing: The lightest possible clothing in lowland areas; medium- or lightweight in the hill country. Warm clothing may be needed at night to cope with the dramatic temperature change.

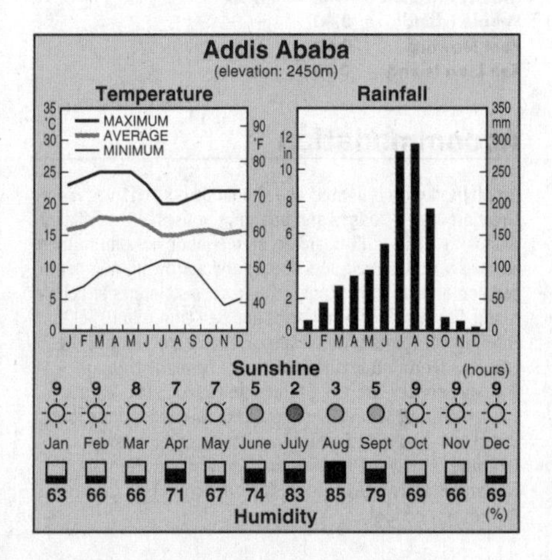

Falkland Islands

LATEST TRAVEL ADVICE CONTACTS

British Foreign and Commonwealth Office
Tel: (0870) 606 0290 Website: www.fco.gov.uk
US Department of State
Website: http://travel.state.gov/travel
Canadian Department of Foreign Affairs and Int'l Trade
Tel: (1 800) 267 8376 Website: www.dfait-maeci.gc.ca

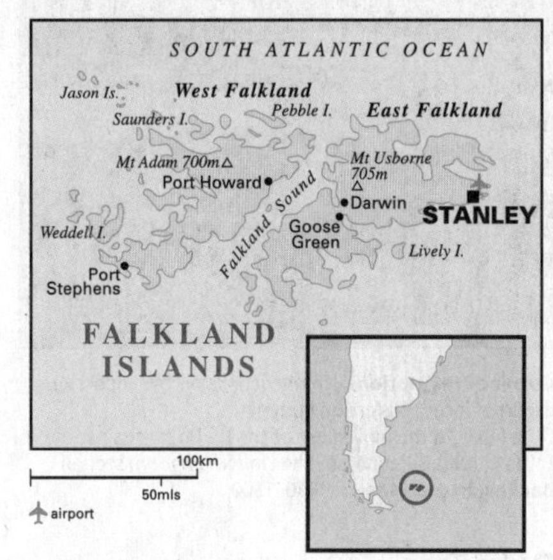

Location: South Atlantic.

Country dialling code: 500.

The Falkland Islands is a British Overseas Territory represented abroad by British Embassies – see *United Kingdom* section.
Falkland Island Development Corporation (FIDC)
PO Box 580, Shackleton House, West Hillside, Stanley, Falkland Islands
Tel: 27211. Fax: 27210.
E-mail: develop@fidc.co.fk
Website: www.fidc.co.fk *or* www.falklandislands.com
Falkland Islands Tourist Board
Shackleton House, Stanley, Falkland Islands, FIQQ 1ZZ
Tel: 22215. Fax: 22619.
E-mail: jettycentre@horizon.co.fk
Website: www.tourism.org.fk
Falkland Islands Government Office (incorporating the Falkland Islands Development Corporation and the Falkland Islands Tourist Board)
Falkland House, 14 Broadway, London SW1H 0BH, UK
Tel: (020) 7222 2542. Fax: (020) 7222 2375.
E-mail: representative@falklands.gov.uk
Website: www.falklandislands.com
Opening hours: Mon-Fri 0900-1730.
The Falkland Islands Government Office issues visas and visitor forms, helps to promote trade and investment in the Islands, offers RAF flight bookings to the Islands, assists immigrants and promotes the Falkland Islands' interests in all respects.
Government House
Stanley, Falkland Islands, FIQQ 1ZZ
Tel: 27433. Fax: 27434.
E-mail: gov.house@horizon.co.fk
British Foreign and Commonwealth Office
Overseas Territories Department, King Charles Street, London SW1A 2AH, UK
Tel: (020) 7008 1500. Fax: (020) 7008 2879.
E-mail: otdenquiries@fco.gov.uk *or* consular.fco@gtnet.gov.uk
Website: www.fco.gov.uk

General Information

AREA: 12,173 sq km (4700 sq miles).
POPULATION: 2,913 (2001).
POPULATION DENSITY: 0.24 per sq km.
CAPITAL: Stanley. **Population:** 1,981 (2001).

TIMATIC CODES

Health
AMADEUS: **TI-DFT/JIB/HE**
GALILEO/WORLDSPAN: **TI-DFT/JIB/HE**
SABRE: **TIDFT/JIB/HE**

Visa
AMADEUS: **TI-DFT/JIB/VI**
GALILEO/WORLDSPAN: **TI-DFT/JIB/VI**
SABRE: **TIDFT/JIB/VI**

To access TIMATIC country information on Health and Visa regulations through the Computer Reservations System (CRS), type in the appropriate command line listed above.

GEOGRAPHY: The Falkland Islands are located 560km (350 miles) off the east coast of South America and consist of two main islands and hundreds of small outlying islands, amounting to approximately 3 million acres (1.2 million hectares). Generally, the main islands are mountainous, with low-lying and undulating terrain in the south of East Falkland. The highest mountain is Mount Usborne at 712m (2312ft).
GOVERNMENT: British Overseas Territory since 1833. Not recognised by Argentina, which considers the Falkland Islands to be part of Argentina. Existing Constitution adopted in 1985. **Head of State:** Queen Elizabeth II, represented locally by Governor Howard Pearce since 2002. The Governor presides over the Executive Council, the country's ruling body. The Executive Council consists of two official members and three elected members. Elections are held every four years.
LANGUAGE: English.
RELIGION: Christian.
TIME: GMT - 3 (GMT - 4 from third Sunday in April to first Saturday in September).
ELECTRICITY: 240 volts AC, 50Hz.
COMMUNICATIONS: Telephone: IDD available. Country code: 500. Outgoing international code: 00. External communication links and Internet services are provided by *Cable & Wireless* plc (website: www.cw.com). Telephone links to the Islands, which are by satellite, provide clear and rapid links to the outside world. The *Cable & Wireless* office is open daily 0800-2000 for acceptance of traffic and sale of phone cards for use in the international telephone service booths situated in the office. **Mobile telephone:** There is currently no network coverage on the Falkland Islands. **Fax:** A system spans the Islands providing international direct-dialling facilities, together with high-speed data services. **Radio:** Remote areas still keep in contact by radio. **Internet:** There is an Internet cafe in Stanley. The main ISPs are *Cable & Wireless* and *U-Net*. **Post:** Airmail to Europe takes four to seven days. **Press:** There are no daily papers on the Falkland Islands, but *Penguin News* (weekly) and *Teaberry Express* (weekly) are published in Stanley and all British national newspapers are also available. *The Falkland Islands Gazette* is a government publication. The *Falkland Islands News Network* relays news daily via fax. **Media:** Satellite television channels are widely available.
Radio: BBC World Service (website: www.bbc.co.uk/worldservice) and Voice of America (website: www.voa.gov) can be received. From time to time the frequencies change and the most up-to-date can be found online.

Credit: © Falkland Islands Tourism

Passport/Visa

	Passport Required?	Visa Required?	Return Ticket Required?
Full British	Yes	No	Yes
Australian	Yes	No	Yes
Canadian	Yes	No	Yes
USA	Yes	No	Yes
Other EU	Yes	No	Yes
Japanese	Yes	No	Yes

Note: Regulations and requirements may be subject to change at short notice, and you are advised to contact the appropriate diplomatic or consular authority before finalising travel arrangements. Details of these may be found at the head of this country's entry. Any numbers in the chart refer to the footnotes below.

PASSPORTS: Passport valid for a minimum of three months beyond departure required by all.
VISAS: Required by all except the following for stays of up to four months:
(a) nationals of countries mentioned in the chart above;
(b) nationals of Andorra, Argentina, Bolivia, Brazil, Chile, Hong Kong (SAR), Iceland, Israel, Korea (Rep), Liechtenstein, New Zealand, Norway, Paraguay, San Marino, South Africa, Switzerland, Uruguay and Vatican City.
Note: All nationals (including non-visa nationals) must obtain a visitors permit, normally valid for four weeks. An extension may be granted by applying to the Immigration Office on arrival and providing proof of sufficient funds and accommodation during stay. A visitors permit is issued after

A B C D E F G H I J K L M N O P Q R S T U V W X Y Z

Credit: © Falkland Islands Tourism

completing a visitors form and requires proof of return tickets, sufficient funds and accommodation. Visitors permits can be obtained from the Falkland Islands Government Office in London (see *Contact Addresses* section), the nearest British Consulate (or Consular section at the Embassy) *or*, on arrival, at the Falkland Islands Immigration Office, 3 H. Jones Road, Stanley, Falkland Islands (tel: 27340; fax: 27342; e-mail: gov.house@horizon.co.fk; website: www.falklands.gov.fk).
Types of visa and cost: One type of visa is issued for all types of travel. The cost is £20.
Note: All persons leaving the Falkland Islands by air are charged an Embarkation Tax of £20.
Validity: Usually six months from the date of issue for stays of up to four months.
Application to: Falkland Islands Government Office (see *Contact Addresses* section), the nearest British Consulate (or Consular section at the Embassy) *or* the Falkland Islands Immigration Office.
Application requirements: (a) Application form. (b) Passport valid for a minimum of six months. (c) Two passport-size photographs. (d) Proof of sufficient funds for the duration of stay, accommodation booking and onward/return tickets. (e) Fee.
Working days required: Within 24 hours if applying in person. Two to four weeks for applicants applying by post. It is advisable, however, to apply in plenty of time.

Credit: © Falkland Islands Tourism

Money

Currency: Falkland Islands Pound (Fl£) and the British Pound Sterling (£) = 100 pence. Notes are in denominations of £50, 20, 10 and 5. Coins are in denominations of £1 and 2, and 50, 20, 10, 5, 2 and 1 pence.
Currency exchange: Exchange facilities are available in Stanley and the Standard Chartered Bank. British Pound Sterling cheques up to £50 from Barclays, Lloyds, Midland and National Westminster banks can be cashed on production of a valid cheque card. Falklands currency cannot be exchanged anywhere outside the Islands.
Credit & debit cards: American Express, MasterCard and Visa are accepted in the Upland Goose Hotel, the Malvina House Hotel, various shops and The Falkland Island Travel Service Ltd.
Travellers cheques: May be changed at the Standard Chartered Bank and at some commercial outlets. To avoid additional exchange rate charges, travellers are advised to take travellers cheques in Pounds Sterling.
Currency restrictions: No restrictions on the import and export of local and foreign currency.
For a guide to the movement of the US Dollar against the Falkland Islands Pound, see the *United Kingdom* section.
Banking hours: Mon-Fri 0830-1500.

Duty Free

The following items may be imported into the Falkland Islands without incurring customs duty:
200 cigarettes or 50 cigars or 250g tobacco; 1l of alcoholic beverage over 38.8 per cent proof or 2l up to 38.8 per cent proof and 2l of sparkling or still table wine; 10l of beer or cider.
Restricted items: Import licences are required from the Department of Agriculture for plants, meat, poultry and dairy produce. An import licence is required from the Falkland Islands' Policy Authority for firearms and ammunition.
Prohibited items: Drugs, pornography and counterfeit goods.

Public Holidays

2005: Jan 3 New Year's Day. **Mar 25** Good Friday. **Apr 21** Queen's Birthday. **Jun 14** Liberation Day. **Oct 3** Spring Holiday. **Dec 8** Battle Day. **Dec 25-28** Christmas.
2006: Jan 1 New Year's Day. **Apr 14** Good Friday. **Apr 21** Queen's Birthday. **Jun 14** Liberation Day. **Oct 2** Spring Holiday. **Dec 8** Battle Day. **Dec 25-28** Christmas.

Health

	Special Precautions?	Certificate Required?
Yellow Fever	1	No
Cholera	No	No
Typhoid & Polio	No	N/A
Malaria	No	N/A

Note: *Regulations and requirements may be subject to change at short notice, and you are advised to contact your doctor well in advance of your intended date of departure. Any numbers in the chart refer to the footnotes below.*

1: Although not an official requirement, the Ministry of Defence recommends inoculation against yellow fever in case flights are diverted to a risk area.
Other risks: *Hepatitis A* occurs; *viral hepatitis* occurs but is rare.
Health care: Hospital, dental and other medical treatments are free, as are prescribed medicines and ambulance travel to visitors whose country has a reciprocal NHS agreement.

Credit: © Falkland Islands Tourism

Otherwise, medical insurance is recommended. Proof of residence in the UK (eg medical card or UK driving licence) or an E111 form for other nationals are required to benefit from free treatments.

Travel - International

AIR: Travel to and from the Islands is courtesy of the UK Ministry of Defence. There are seven flights in any four-week period by Tristar from RAF *Brize Norton*, Oxfordshire, in the UK. Tour operators and travel agents will make the necessary arrangements if the holiday is booked through them; independent travellers need to contact a travel coordinator at the Falkland Islands Government Office (see *Contact Addresses* section). Return flights from the UK are via Ascension Island. The other option is to fly *British Airways* from London Gatwick to Santiago and connect with a *LanChile* flight (once a week only, on Saturdays) to Punta Arenas and Puerto Montt in southern Chile and then on to Stanley. Bookings for this flight can be made through *British Airways*, *LanChile* or agents. The Falkland Islands Tourist Board can provide up-to-date information on changes to the normal schedule.
Approximate flight times: From *Brize Norton* to Mount Pleasant is 18 hours (including a refuelling stop at Ascension Island); from Mount Pleasant to *Punta Arenas* (Chile) is five hours.
International airports: *Mount Pleasant Airport (MPN)* is approximately 56km (35 miles) from Stanley. There are limited duty-free facilities at the airport. Buses connect the airport and Stanley.
Departure tax: £20. Children under two years of age are exempt.
SEA: Cruise companies operating to the Falklands include Carriage Travel and Zegrahm Expeditions. The main shipping company operating to and from the UK is Darwin Shipping, The Falkland Islands Company, West Store Complex, Ross Road, Stanley, F1QQ 1ZZ (tel: 27633; fax: 27626; e-mail: darwin@horizon.co.fk; website: www.the-falkland-islands-co.com).

Travel - Internal

AIR: Most of the settlements and offshore islands in the Falklands can be reached by light aircraft. This service is run by the *Falkland Islands Government Air Service (FIGAS)* (tel: 27219; fax: 27309; e-mail: figas.fig@horizon.co.fk *or* fwallace@figas.gov.uk). *FIGAS* operates Islander aircraft from the airport. There are no fixed schedules but daily flights operate to all parts of the Islands, subject to demand.
SEA: Boats may be chartered for day trips from Stanley and elsewhere in the Islands. Some settlements may be able to offer the use of landing vessels or other craft to reach the outlying Islands. There are plenty of tour operators and guides to choose from in Stanley. Contact the Falkland Islands Tourist Board for further information (see *Contact Addresses* section).
ROAD: Outside the capital, overland travel is difficult and vehicles can frequently get bogged down. However, there is one road linking Stanley, the Mount Pleasant airport complex and Goose Green, and an all-weather track linking Stanley, Port Louis and Port San Carlos. A similar track on West Falkland links Port Howard, Chartres, Fox Bay, Hill Cove and Roy Cove. 4-wheel-drive vehicles are the best form of transport in this terrain. But road networks are continually improving. **Bus:** There are routes to and from the airport, and also in and around Stanley. **Taxi:** Taxi services are available. **Car hire:** 4-wheel-drive vehicles and other vehicles can be hired.
Travel times: The following chart gives approximate travel times from Stanley to other islands in the surrounding area.

	Air	Road
Mount Pleasant	0.15	0.50
Pebble Island	0.40	-
Port Howard	0.40	-
Sea Lion Island	0.30	-

Accommodation

Accommodation is limited and should be booked in advance. There are hotels, lodges and boarding houses in the Falkland Islands, as well as full-board accommodation on a farm. There are two hotels, three guest houses and a growing number of bed and breakfasts in Stanley. There are also lodges at Pebble Island, Port Howard, San Carlos and Sea Lion Island. Self-catering accommodation is also available throughout the Islands. All ground arrangements can be made through Stanley Services Limited, Stanley (tel: 22622; fax: 22623; e-mail: office@stanley-services.co.fk). Falkland Islands Tourist Board can help with finding available accommodation
Grading: A new grading system is now in use. Contact the Falkland Islands Tourist Board for full details (see *Contact Addresses* section).

Resorts & Excursions

Stanley: The capital has pubs, snack bars and restaurants, as well as a golf and race course. Houses on the seafront overlook Stanley Harbour where many different sea birds can be seen. **Government House**, **Stanley Museum** and the **Cathedral** are also worth visiting.
Coastal areas: These offer a chance (in good weather) to explore ships and wrecks abandoned over the years in the often fierce weather conditions that characterise the local waters. South Atlantic Marine Services Ltd in Stanley can also arrange wreck and kelp reef diving expeditions (see *Sports & Activities* section). 19th-century sailing ships and iron vessels can be seen at Stanley and Darwin. Stanley used to be a safe anchorage for whalers and merchant vessels travelling around the Horn, though not all of them made it. The marine birdlife is varied, including five species of penguins. The views in winter are spectacular due to the 'grey beards', winter waves that can reach a height of 4.5m (15ft).
Inland areas: These offer opportunities to observe the varied wildlife. Activities such as horseriding and walking can also be enjoyed, often in complete solitude. Fishing is a popular and rewarding experience, with the Falkland waters being particularly good for sea trout and the Falkland mullet in the shallow estuaries.
Battle sites: Many visitors come to the Islands to see places made famous by the events of the Falkland Islands conflict. As well as the battlefields at Goose Green, San Carlos, Fitzroy, Pebble Island, Mount Tumbledown, Wireless Ridge, Sapper Hill and Stanley itself, there are also military cemeteries, memorials and museums.
Islands: Pebble Island is well known for its penguin colonies, sheep farms, South American horse tack and Southern sea lions. **Port Howard** is famous for its Falkland Island knitwear and sheep farming. **San Carlos** will be of interest to military historians and horse riders. One of the most ecologically balanced islands is **Sea Lion Island** which has a resident population of two and amazing wildlife, including elephant seals, sea lions and King penguins, as well as Killer whales offshore.

Sport & Activities

Walking tours: Stanley's history is closely associated with the days when great sailing ships and early steam vessels called into port on their journeys around Cape Horn. A self-guided *Maritime History Trail* has been set up in the capital. A half-day trail leads from Stanley to Cape Pembroke, offering an interesting introduction to the Falkland Islands' birdlife. For further information and a copy of the *Trail Guide*, contact the Falkland Islands Tourist Board (see *Contact Addresses* section).
Battlefield tours: Trips to several of the **Battlefield** sites associated with the 1982 conflict (including *Wireless Ridge*, *Mount Tumbledown* and *Sapper Hill*) can be arranged.
Wildlife: Migratory species, such as penguins, arrive to breed in September and depart late March/early April. The young are born and reared in the islands throughout the southern summer.
Boat trips: Tours around Stanley Harbour in an inflatable craft, as well as various types of fishing tours are available. A number of lodges have motor boats for taking guests to view wildlife and places of interest. Tours around Kidney Island and Sparrow Cove can also be arranged. *South Atlantic Marine Services Ltd* can provide further information (tel: 21145; fax: 22674; e-mail: sams@horizon.co.fk.
Fishing: The sea trout season runs from September to the end of April, but September to October and mid-March to mid-April are acknowledged as best for encountering good runs of sea trout. Falklands Mullet is available throughout the period. A licence costing £10 per annum is required. It is obtainable from the Stanley Post Office and a log book is issued with it which needs to be returned to the Fisheries Department before departure. Visitors are advised that a catch and return policy applies, that barbless hooks are used and that 12 is the maximum number of fish allowed to be taken. The best locations in West Falkland are Warrah and Chartres, while in East Falkland, San Carlos and Murrel are notable.
Golf: There are facilities at Darwin Lodge on Darwin, and at the following courses: Fox Bay, Goose Green, Hill Cove, Port Howard and Stanley.

Social Profile

FOOD & DRINK: Almost everything is home-cooked and many traditional recipes have been handed down through several generations. Food, generally British in character, includes large 'camp breakfasts' and *smoko* (tea and coffee with homemade cakes) with lunch and dinner. Local specialities include lamb, mutton, beef, sea trout, mullet and home-grown vegetables.
NIGHTLIFE: There is a variety of clubs and societies which welcome visitors. There are several pubs in Stanley, as well as restaurants and cafes.
SHOPPING: Costs tend to be slightly higher as much has to be imported, though smaller luxury goods may be cheaper. There is a good range of shops in Stanley selling the same type of goods found in a small town in Britain and a variety of souvenirs. Sweaters made from pure Falkland Wool and local art work, coins, stamps and books are also sold. Fresh vegetables are available all year round but many Islanders are virtually self-sufficient. Print film is available but it is advisable to bring a supply. **Shopping hours:** Shopping hours vary, but shops are generally open Mon-Sun 0830-1800.
SOCIAL CONVENTIONS: The lifestyle in the Falkland Islands resembles that of a small English or Scottish village/town and communities on the Falkland Islands are highly self-contained. The influx of the British Forces has obviously had an effect on the Islands. More people now visit the Islands for a variety of reasons (see the *Sport & Activities* section). The islanders themselves have benefited from the additional amenities offered by the Forces. The Government runs a radio station for the islanders (FIBS), in conjunction with the British Forces Broadcasting Service; this broadcasts all day on FM and MW. The Forces also run a television network around the islands, another example of the close links that have built up between the Islands and the British Forces Government. The population is very keen to remain under British sovereignty. **Tipping:** If no service charge has been added to the bill, 10 per cent is appropriate. Taxi drivers expect a tip.

Business Profile

ECONOMY: The economy is dominated by fishing and sheep-farming. The poor quality of the land precludes large scale crop-growing. Productivity in sheep-farming has increased sharply since the mid-1980s with improved working practices. However, it is the fishing sector that now accounts for the islands' much improved economic performance. The industry has grown substantially since 1982, assisted by the introduction of a licensing system in Falklands territorial waters. The presence of large quantities of squid, a very popular dish in several parts of the world, has fuelled an economic boom and the emergence of a 'squidocracy' – a group of individuals living on the islands who have become extremely wealthy as a result. There are some concerns about stock depletion, and controls have now been introduced. Other plans for the Falklands' economic development have proved less successful. Restrictions on Antarctic development have undermined the islands' hope of deriving benefit from being an enroute staging post. The search for suspected oil and gas reserves began in earnest in 1995 after the signing of an agreement between the British and Argentinians; test drilling started in 1998 but no viable deposits have yet been located. However, as long as the squid last, the Falklands economic outlook remains bright. Despite the improvement in relations with Argentina, trade between the islands and the mainland is small and most trade is still conducted with Britain.
BUSINESS: Punctuality for meetings is expected. **Office hours:** 0800-1200, 1300-1630 (Government); 0800-1200, 1300-1700 (Private).
COMMERCIAL INFORMATION: For advice, contact the Falkland Islands Development Corporation (FIDC) (see *Contact Addresses* section) *or* the Falkland Islands Chamber of Commerce (e-mail: commerce@horizon.co.fk.
CONFERENCES/CONVENTIONS: For details, contact the Falkland Islands Tourist Board (see *Contact Addresses* section).

Climate

The climate is temperate and largely conditioned by the surrounding sea being cooled by the Antarctic Current.
Required clothing: A windproof jacket is essential, as is a stout pair of walking boots when crossing the rugged terrain. Because the air is so clear and unpolluted, suntan lotion is advisable.

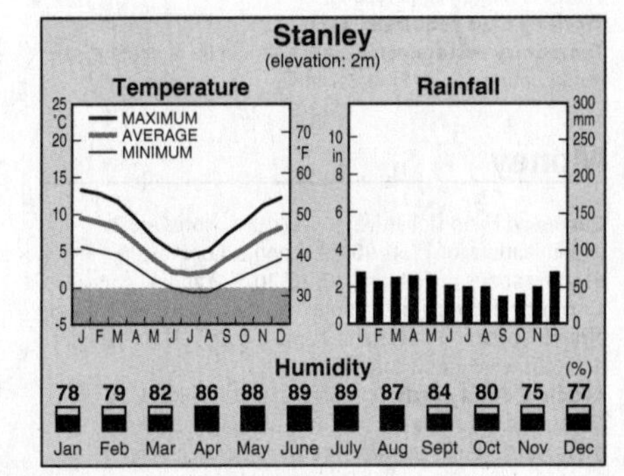

Fiji

LATEST TRAVEL ADVICE CONTACTS

British Foreign and Commonwealth Office
Tel: (0870) 606 0290 Website: www.fco.gov.uk
US Department of State
Website: http://travel.state.gov/travel
Canadian Department of Foreign Affairs and Int'l Trade
Tel: (1 800) 267 8376 Website: www.dfait-maeci.gc.ca

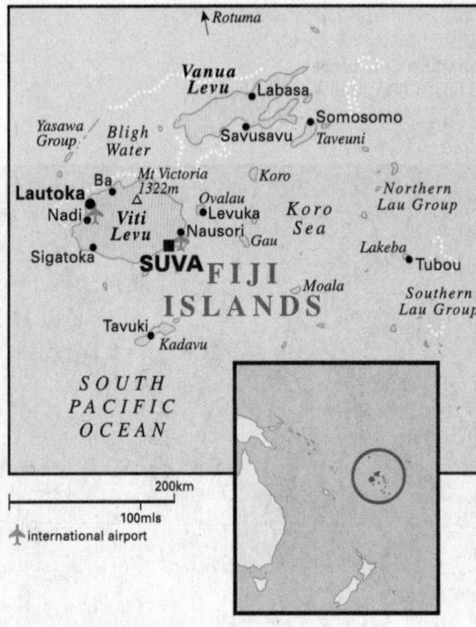

Location: South Pacific, Melanesia.

Country dialling code: 679.

Ministry of Tourism, Culture, Heritage and Civil Aviation
3rd Floor, Civic Towers Buildings, PO Box 1260, Suva, Fiji
Tel: 331 2788. Fax: 330 2060.
E-mail: infodesk@fijifvb.gov.fj
Website: www.bulafiji.com
Fiji Visitor Bureau - Nadi Office
Street address: Suite 107, Colonial Plaza, Namaka, Nadi, Fiji
Postal address: PO Box 9217, Nadi Airport, Nadi, Fiji
Tel: 672 2433. Fax: 672 0141.
E-mail: infodesk@bulafiji.com Website: www.bulafiji.com
Fiji Visitors Bureau - Suva Office
PO Box 92, Thomson Street, Suva, Fiji
Tel: 330 2433. Fax: 330 0970 *or* 330 2751.
E-mail: infodesk@bulafiji.com
Website: www.bulafiji.com
South Pacific Tourism Organisation
PO Box 13119, Suva, Fiji
Tel: 330 4177. Fax: 330 1995.
Website: www.spto.org
Also deals with enquiries from the UK.
Fiji High Commission
34 Hyde Park Gate, London SW7 5DN, UK
Tel: (020) 7584 3661. Fax: (020) 7584 2838.
E-mail: mail@fijihighcommission.org.uk
Website: www.fijihighcommission.org.uk
Opening hours: Mon-Thurs 0930-1300, 1400-1700, Fri 0930-1300, 1400-1600; Mon-Fri 0930-1230 (consular section).
Fiji Visitors Bureau
c/o Hills Balfour, Notcutt House, 36 Southwark Bridge Road, London SE1 9EU, UK
Tel: (020) 7202 6365. Fax: (020) 7928 0722.
E-mail: fiji@hillsbalfour.com
Website: www.bulafiji.com
British High Commission
PO Box 1355, Victoria House, 47 Gladstone Road, Suva, Fiji
Tel: 322 9100. Fax: 322 9132.
E-mail: consularsuva@fio.gov.uk
Website: www.britishhighcommision.gv.uk/fiji
Embassy of the Republic of Fiji
Suite 240, 2233 Wisconsin Avenue, NW, Washington, DC

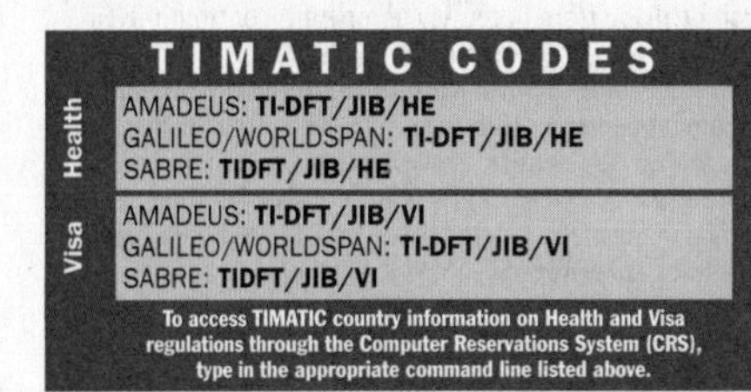
TIMATIC CODES

Health
AMADEUS: **TI-DFT/JIB/HE**
GALILEO/WORLDSPAN: **TI-DFT/JIB/HE**
SABRE: **TIDFT/JIB/HE**

Visa
AMADEUS: **TI-DFT/JIB/VI**
GALILEO/WORLDSPAN: **TI-DFT/JIB/VI**
SABRE: **TIDFT/JIB/VI**

To access TIMATIC country information on Health and Visa regulations through the Computer Reservations System (CRS), type in the appropriate command line listed above.

20007, USA
Tel: (202) 337 8320. Fax: (202) 337 1996.
E-mail: fijiemb@earthlink.net
Website: www.fijiembassy.org

Fiji Visitors Bureau
Suite 220, 5777 West Century Boulevard, Los Angeles, CA 90045, USA
Tel: (310) 568 1616 *or* (800) 932 3454 (toll-free in USA and Canada). Fax: (310) 670 2318.
E-mail: infodesk@bulafiji-americas.com
Website: www.bulafiji.com *or* www.bulafijiislands.com
Also deals with enquiries from Canada.

Embassy of the United States of America
PO Box 218, 31 Loftus Street, Suva, Fiji
Tel: 331 4466. Fax: 330 0081.
E-mail: usembsuva@connect.com.fj
Website: www.amembassy-fiji.gov

Canadian Consulate
PO Box 10690, Nadi Airport, Nadi, Fiji
Tel: 672 2400. Fax: 672 1936.

Credit: © Fiji Visitors Bureau

General Information

AREA: 18,376 sq km (7095 sq miles).
POPULATION: 819,000 (official estimate 2002).
POPULATION DENSITY: 44.6 per sq km.
CAPITAL: Suva. **Population:** 77,366 (1996).
GEOGRAPHY: Fiji is located in the South Pacific, 3000km (1875 miles) east of Australia and approximately 1930km (1200 miles) south of the Equator. It comprises 322 islands, 105 of which are uninhabited (some are little more than rugged limestone islets or tiny coral atolls). The three largest are Viti Levu (Great Fiji), Vanua Levu (Great Land of the People), both of which are extinct volcanoes rising abruptly from the sea, and Taveuni. There are thousands of streams and small rivers in Fiji, the largest being the Rewa River on Viti Levu, which is navigable for 128km (80 miles). Mount Victoria, also on Viti Levu, is the country's highest peak, at 1322m (4430ft).
GOVERNMENT: Republic since 1987. **Head of State:** President Ratu Josefa Iloilo since 2000. The President is appointed for a five-year term by the Great Council of Chiefs (Bosu Levu Vakaturaga), a traditional body with roughly 70 members, consisting of every hereditary Fijian chief (or *ratu*). **Head of Government:** Prime Minister Laisenia Qarase since 2000.
LANGUAGE: The principal languages are Fijian and Hindustani, but English is widely spoken and is also taught in schools. Chinese and Urdu are heard in the markets.
RELIGION: Methodist and Hindu with Roman Catholic and Muslim minorities. A strictly fundamentalist Methodist version of Christianity is enshrined in, and informs, the Fijian Constitution.
TIME: GMT + 12.
ELECTRICITY: 240 volts AC, 50Hz. Larger hotels also have 110-volt razor sockets.
COMMUNICATIONS: Telephone: IDD is available. Country code: 679. Outgoing code: 05. International calls can be made from hotels via an operator, or from the Fiji International Telecommunications (*FINTEL*) office at 158 Victoria Parade in Suva. **Mobile telephone:** GSM 900. Roaming agreements in operation. Network provider is *Vodafone Fiji* (website: www.vodafone.com.fj). Phone rentals are available from the airport. **Fax:** The *FINTEL* office in Suva also offers fax services. Major hotels have facilities. **Internet:** ISPs include *Fiji Online*, a subsidiary of Telecom Fiji (website: www.fijionline.com), and *fiji.net*. There are Internet cafes in Suva, Nadi and Lautoka. **Telegram:** Facilities are available at major hotels in Suva and at the *FINTEL* office on Victoria Parade. **Post:** Airmail to Europe takes up to 10 days. Post office hours: Mon-Fri 0800-1630, Sat 0800-1300. **Press:** The main English-language daily is the *Fiji Times*, which claims to be 'the first newspaper published in the world today' – a reference to Suva's position just to the west of the International Date Line; the other main English language paper is the *Fiji Daily Post*. *Fiji Calling* is the bi-annual tourist newspaper, which may be of interest to visitors.
Radio: BBC World Service (website: www.bbc.co.uk/worldservice) and Voice of America (website: www.voa.gov) can be received. From time to time the frequencies change and the most up-to-date can be found online.

Passport/Visa

	Passport Required?	Visa Required?	Return Ticket Required?
Full British	Yes	No	Yes
Australian	Yes	No/2	Yes
Canadian	Yes	No/2	Yes
USA	Yes	No	Yes
Other EU	Yes	No/1	Yes
Japanese	Yes	No	Yes

Note: *Regulations and requirements may be subject to change at short notice, and you are advised to contact the appropriate diplomatic or consular authority before finalising travel arrangements. Details of these may be found at the head of this country's entry. Any numbers in the chart refer to the footnotes below.*

Restricted entry: Entry will be denied to persons who have been deported or removed from another country.
PASSPORTS: Passport valid for at least six months beyond intended period of stay required by all except nationals of Fiji when holding a Certificate of Identity including a photograph of the bearer. Holders of the certificate must obtain approval from the Fiji Immigration Department before arrival.
VISAS: Required by all except the following who are issued a visitor's permit valid for one month (extendable to four months) on arrival:
(a) nationals of countries shown in the chart above, except **1.** nationals of Lithuania who *do* need a visa;
2. (b) nationals of Commonwealth countries (except nationals of Cameroon, Mozambique, Namibia and Sri Lanka who *do* need a visa);
(c) nationals of Argentina, Brazil, Bulgaria, Chile, Colombia, Iceland, Indonesia, Israel, Korea (Rep), Liechtenstein, Marshall Islands, Mexico, Micronesia (Federated States of), Moldova, Monaco, Norway, Paraguay, Peru, The Philippines, Romania, Russian Federation, Switzerland, Taiwan (China), Thailand, Tunisia, Turkey, Ukraine, Uruguay, Venezuela, Vatican City and Zimbabwe;
(d) transit passengers continuing their journey to a third country within three hours, provided holding valid onward or return documentation and not leaving the airport.
Note: All visitors must hold onward or return tickets and sufficient funds to cover stay.
Types of visa and cost: *Single-entry*: £45. *Multiple-entry*: £80.
Validity: Visas are valid for stays of up to three months, but can be extended on application to: Immigration Dept, Level 3, Suvavou House, Victoria Parade, Suva (*street address*); *or* PO Box 2224, Government Buildings, Suva, Fiji (*postal address*) (tel: 331 2622; fax: 330 1653).
Application to: Consular section of High Commission or Embassy; see *Contact Addresses* section.
Application requirements: (a) Valid passport. (b) Completed application form. (c) Three passport-size photos. (d) Onward/return air ticket. (e) Copy of travel ticket/itinerary. (f) Fee payable by bankers' draft, bank cheque or by cash (if application is made in person). (g) Police clearance report (proof of no criminal record) from local police station (must be in English). (h) Sufficient funds for duration of stay.
Note: Applicants must make their own arrangements for collection/return of passport.
Working days required: Seven to 21.
Temporary residence: Enquiries should be directed to the High Commission or Embassy of Fiji.

Money

Currency: Fijian Dollar (F$) = 100 cents. Notes are in denominations of F$50, 20, 10, 5 and 2. Coins are in denominations of F$1, and 50, 20, 10, 5, 2 and 1 cents.
Currency exchange: Exchange facilities are available at the airport, at trading banks and at most hotels. ATMs may not accept foreign credit cards.
Credit & debit cards: American Express, Diners Club, MasterCard and Visa are accepted at a number of establishments. Check with your credit or debit card company for details of merchant acceptability and other services which may be available.
Travellers cheques: To avoid additional exchange rate charges, travellers are advised to take travellers cheques in Australian Dollars or Pounds Sterling.
Currency restrictions: There are no restrictions on the import of foreign or local currency, provided declared on arrival. Unspent local currency can be re-exchanged on departure up to the amount of foreign currency imported. The export of local currency is limited to F$500. The export of foreign currency as cash is limited to the equivalent of F$500.
Exchange rate indicators: The following figures are included as a guide to the movements of the Fijian Dollar against Sterling and the US Dollar:

Date	Feb '04	May '04	Aug '04	Nov '04
£1.00=	3.10	3.19	3.19	3.10
$1.00=	1.70	1.79	1.75	1.64

Banking hours: Mon-Thurs 0930-1500, Fri 0930-1600. Restricted Foreign Exchange Dealers (authorised to issue foreign currency and travellers cheques for travel-related purposes only): Mon-Fri 0830-1700, Sat 0830-1200.

Duty Free

The following items may be imported by persons 17 years of age and over into Fiji without incurring customs duty:
500 cigarettes or 500g of tobacco goods; 2l of spirits or 4l of wine or 4l of beer; 114ml of perfume for personal use; goods to the value of F$400.
Prohibited items: All categories of firearms, ammunition and all narcotics. The import of vegetables, seeds, meat and dairy products requires a special permit from the Ministry of Agriculture, Fisheries and Forests. The import of meat and dairy products from Tasmania is not permitted.

Public Holidays

2005: Jan 1 New Year's Day. **Mar 25** Good Friday. **Mar 26** Easter Saturday. **Mar 28** Easter Monday. **Apr 25** Birth of the Prophet Muhammad. **May 6** National Youth Day. **May 30** Ratu Sir Lala Sukuna Day. **Jul 13** Queen's Birthday. **Oct 10** Fiji Day. **Nov 1** Diwali. **Dec 25-26** Christmas.
2006: Jan 1 New Year's Day. **Apr 11** Birth of the Prophet Muhammad. **Apr 14** Good Friday. **Apr 15** Easter Saturday. **Apr 17** Easter Monday. **May 5** National Youth Day. **May 29** Ratu Sir Lala Sukuna Day. **Jun 5** Queen's Birthday. **Oct 13** Fiji Day. **Oct 21** Diwali. **Dec 25-26** Christmas.
Note: (a) Muslim and Hindu festivals are timed according to local sightings of various phases of the moon and therefore dates can only be approximations. (b) Some holidays are annually set by the Government, or moved to either Friday or Monday, if the normal day of observance falls on a weekend.

Health

	Special Precautions?	Certificate Required?
Yellow Fever	No	1
Cholera	No	2
Typhoid & Polio	3	N/A
Malaria	No	N/A

Note: *Regulations and requirements may be subject to change at short notice, and you are advised to contact your doctor well in advance of your intended date of departure. Any numbers in the chart refer to the footnotes below.*

1: A yellow fever vaccination certificate is required from travellers over one year of age arriving within 10 days of leaving infected areas.
2: Following WHO guidelines issued in 1973, a cholera vaccination certificate is not a condition of entry to Fiji. However, cholera is a serious risk in this country and precautions are essential. Up-to-date advice should be sought before deciding whether these precautions should include vaccination, as medical opinion is divided over its effectiveness; see the *Health* appendix for more information.
3: Vaccination against typhoid and polio is advised.
Food & drink: Mains water is normally heavily chlorinated, and, whilst relatively safe, may cause mild abdominal upsets. Bottled water is available and is advised for the first few weeks of the stay. Milk is pasteurised and dairy products are safe for consumption. Local meat, poultry, seafood, fruit and vegetables are generally considered safe to eat.
Other risks: *Diarrhoeal diseases* are common. *Hepatitis A* occurs. *Hepatitis B* is endemic. *Dengue fever* may occur.
Health care: The main hospitals are located in Ba, Labasa, Lautoka, Levuka, Savusavu, Sigatoka, Suva and Taveuni, with clinics and medical representations elsewhere throughout the islands. Medical insurance is recommended.

A B C D E F G H I J K L M N O P Q R S T U V W X Y Z

Travel - International

AIR: The national airline is *Air Pacific (FJ)* (website: www.airpacific.com), which operates to the Pacific Island nations as well as to Australia, New Zealand and the USA. Other airlines serving Fiji include *Air New Zealand, American Airlines, Korean Air, Polynesian Airlines, Qantas* and *United Airlines*.
Approximate flight times: From Nadi to *London* is 27 hours 45 minutes (plus connection/stopover time), to *Los Angeles* is nine hours 30 minutes and to *Sydney* is three hours 45 minutes.
International airports: *Nadi (NAN)* is 8km (5 miles) north of Nadi town on Viti Levu island. A bus to the city operates 0700-1830 (travel time - 20 mintues). Taxis are also available. Airport facilities include banks/bureaux de change, duty-free shop, 24-hour bar, restaurant, left luggage office (24-hour), tourist information, post office and car hire (*Avis, Budget, Central, Hertz* and *Roxy*).
Suva (SUV) is actually at Nausori, 21km (13 miles) from Suva.
Nadi is where most international flights arrive, while Suva is the internal hub. Buses and taxis are available at both airports.
Air passes: *The Polypass* (offered by *Polynesian Airlines*) allows the holder to fly between the Southern Pacific destinations of American Samoa, Fiji, Niue, Samoa, Tahiti and Tonga; Honolulu (Hawaii) and Los Angeles in the USA; Brisbane, Melbourne and Sydney in Australia; and Auckland, Christchurch and Wellington in New Zealand. The pass is valid for one year. Once a reservation has been made and travel begun, all travel must be completed within a maximum of 45 days. Tickets will be issued against the Polypass by any *Polynesian Airlines* office (a valid passport is also required). For further information, contact *Polynesian Airlines* (website: www.polynesianairlines.com).
The *Visit the South Pacific Pass* is valid for many airlines operating in the South Pacific, including most of the larger ones, such as *Air Caledonie, Air Marshall Islands, Air Nauru, Air Niugingi, Air Pacific, Air Vanuatu, Polynesian Airlines, Qantas, Royal Tongan Airlines* and *Solomon Airlines*. Offering reductions of up to 40 per cent on normal airfares, this sector-based pass allows for flexible island-hopping between the destinations of the Cook Islands, Fiji, Nauru, New Caledonia, Samoa, Tahiti, Tonga, Vanuatu and the more remote Melanesian and Micronesian islands, together with major cities in Australia (Brisbane, Melbourne and Sydney) and New Zealand (Auckland, Christchurch and Wellington). It is only available for people resident outside of the South Pacific. The journey must be started outside the South Pacific and only one stopover in Australia is allowed. A minimum of two sectors must be bought before departure (extra sectors can be purchased enroute). There is a maximum of one pass per person, and passes must be used within six months of the first day of travel. Children under 12 years of age pay 75 per cent of the adult fare. For details and conditions, contact the South Pacific Tourist Organisation (see *Contact Addresses* section).
Departure tax: F$30. Children under 12 years of age and transit passengers leaving within 12 hours are exempt.
SEA: The international ports are Suva and Lautoka (Viti Levu). Passenger lines serving Fiji include *Crystal, Cunard, Peter Deilmann, Princess Cruises, Seabourn* and *Society*. Several cargo lines stop at Fiji including *Bank Line* and *Pacific Forum Line*. There are regular sailings to Kiribati, Nauru, Samoa and Tuvalu.

Travel - Internal

AIR: Fiji's domestic airlines, *Air Fiji, Air Pacific* and *Sun Air* operate shuttle services around the islands, particularly between Nadi and Suva (Nausori) with additional regular flights to Vanua Levu, Kadavu and Taveuni. The flight time from Nadi to Suva is approximately 30 minutes. *Air Fiji* also operates from Suva to Ovalau, Koro, Cicia in the Lau group and Gau, and from Nadi to Labasa. A *Discover Fiji* ticket is available which gives virtually unlimited flights (Rotuma and Funafuti in Tuvalu not included) for 30 days. Contact *Air Fiji*, PO Box 1259, Suva (tel: 331 3666 or 331 5055; fax: 330 0771; e-mail: suvasales@airfiji.com.fj; website: www.airfiji.net). *Sun Air* operates daily flights to Malololailai (for Musket Cove and Plantation Village), Kadavu, Labasa, Taveuni and Savusavu (tel: 723 016; fax: 723 611; e-mail: sunair@connect.com.fj; website: www.fiji.to). *Pacific Crown Aviation* operates a helicopter service out of Suva which is available for charter.
SEA: Government and local shipping companies operate freight and passenger services linking the outer islands. Cruises to offshore islands leave Nadi/Lautoka and Suva. A ferry goes back and forth regularly from Suva to Labasa, and to Ovalau and Koro Island. Yachts and cabin cruisers are available for charter. Inter-island trips can take anything from a few hours to a few weeks, and are usually very inexpensive. In general, timetables are not posted. Persons

Credit: © Fiji Visitors Bureau

wishing to travel about the islands in this way should enquire at the offices of one of the local shipping agents, being sure to confirm all arrangements with the captain once the vessel is in port. A number of ferries now operate between the major islands, greatly reducing travel times. These boats can take between 300 and 500 passengers and have a full range of facilities, including bar, TV lounge and snack bar. A new F$2.5 million catamaran has recently been launched by Beachcomber island resort and will provide two cruises from Fiji, servicing Lautoka, Nadi, Nanu-i-ra, Savusavu and Wananvu.
ROAD: Traffic drives on the left. There are about 5000km (3100 miles) of roads, 1500km (930 miles) of which are paved and useable all year round. The approximate driving time from Nadi to Suva is three hours (on a tar-sealed road). The main roads on Viti Levu follow the coast, linking the main centres. **Bus:** Local open-windowed buses operate across Viti Levu and the other main islands between all towns and on suburban routes. Express air-conditioned buses operate between Suva and Nadi and between Suva and Lautoka. **Taxi:** These are metered in towns. A fare table for long distances is required. **Car hire:** Car hire is available. **Documentation:** International Driving Permit required if driving a locally registered vehicle.

Accommodation

HOTELS: There are a good number of luxury hotels, the majority of which are located in Douba, Lautoka, Nadi, Raki Raki, Sigatoka, Suva and Tavua and off Viti Levu at Ovalau and Savusavu. There are also many small, inexpensive hotels throughout the islands. Increasing numbers of establishments are offering dormitory accommodation at cheap rates. Small resort islands include Beachcomber, Castaway, Mana, Plantation Islands and Treasure. A 5 per cent hotel tax is levied on all hotel services charged to guests' accounts, including meals in hotel restaurants. For information, contact the Fiji Visitors Bureau (see *Contact Addresses* section), which can supply listings of hotels, their cost and facilities; *or* the Fiji Hotel Association, PO Box 13560, 42 Gorrie Street, Suva (tel: 330 2980 *or* 330 2975; fax: 330 0331; e-mail: info@fha.com.fj; website: www.fha.com.fj). **Grading:** A star system is used to indicate the price range, as follows: 3-star (deluxe), 2-star (medium) and 1-star (budget).
GUEST HOUSES: These are known as *Budgetels*. They are clean, comfortable and most have a licensed bar, pool and restaurant; some are air conditioned with kitchens. There is also a youth hostel in Suva.

Resorts & Excursions

There is much of scenic and historic worth in Fiji, including its copra, ginger, sugar cane and cocoa plantations. The capital, **Suva**, has many old shops and markets selling various artefacts and handicrafts. Places of historic interest include the **National Museum**, situated in the lush surrounds of **Thurston Gardens** next to **Government House**, and the old **Parliament Buildings**. Other sites of note include the **Cultural Centre** at **Orchid Island**, the mysterious earthworks just outside Suva, and the protected **Bouma Forest Park** and **Taveuni Island Reserve**. Just 11km (7 miles) from Suva, visitors can enjoy the beauty of the protected **Colo-I-Suva Forest Park**. Other natural attractions include the acres of orchids and flowering plants in the **Garden of the Sleeping Giant** at the foot of the **Sabeto Mountains** and the **Sigatoka Sand Dunes** off the main Queens Highway on Viti Levu.
Cruises on large schooners or yachts to the different islands can be arranged, and coach tours around the main islands are also available. For the hardy, hiking in the mountains with dramatic views of the islands is another option.
Tavarua is one of Fiji's main tourist destinations, with over 50 resorts and hotels and excellent facilities for snorkelling and scuba-diving. The Outrigger Reef Resort is located in Korotogo near the scenic town of Sigatoka. It combines the qualities of mainland and island, with over 200 hotels and resorts.

Sport & Activities

Watersports: Particularly well known for their soft coral reefs, Fiji's islands offer excellent **scuba-diving** and **snorkelling**. On Viti Levu, the best dive sites are found on the Coral Coast and Pacific Harbour (both on the western side), where the well-known *Beqa Lagoon*, the crater of an extinct volcano that measures 16km (10 miles) across, is often frequented by groups. About 12km (7 miles) off the Viti Levu coast, *Vatulele* is known for its red prawns, regarded as sacred by local people. Northwest of Viti Levu, divers may head to the Yasawa and Mamanuca island groups; to the south lies Kadavua, where the *Astrolabe, Namalata, Solo* and *Tavuki* reefs are located. Vanua Levua and Taveuni are particularly good for land-based diving, and ecologically-minded operators have buoyed dozens of sites to prevent damage from anchors. The best sites around these islands include the *Somosomo Straits* (home to the *Great White Wall*, one of Fiji's most famous dive sites) and the *Rainbow Reef* (where over 20 dive sites can be found). Live-aboard dive tours are available to the more remote islands, such as Ngau, which has no resorts and where the local chief has to grant permission to dive in the waters. Many hotels and resorts also offer opportunities to go **sailing**, **windsurfing**, **waterskiing**, **canoeing**, **kayaking**, **parasailing** and **game fishing**. **Surfing** is a popular activity and surfers have a seemingly endless choice of locations to choose from. The famous 'Cloud Breaker' (6-metre wave) was found offshore at Tavarua, attracting surfers from around the world. Fiji's waves typically break on coral reefs. Most of the well-known spots are on or near Viti Levu and can often only be reached by boat. Tavarua Island is another favourite surfing spot. There are several surf camps, notably on Beqa and Yanuca islands. Visitors should note that there are dangerous rip tides along the reefs, and should take appropriate precautions.
Adventure sports: The mangrove-lined tidal corridors can be explored on **jet-boating** trips, which depart every 15 minutes from Port Denauru, 7km (4 miles) from Nadi Town. **Bamboo rafting** (referred to locally as a *bilibili* ride) is available along the streams and rivers.
Hiking: Fiji's network of marked nature trails can be explored either individually or on organised guided walks. Activities such as **birdwatching** (as for example in the *Colo-i-Suva Forest Park*), **ecotourism** (studying the local fauna and flora) and **swimming** at the waterfalls are often combined with hiking tours. Visitors are reminded to respect local customs when passing through villages (see *Social Conventions* in the *Social Profile* section). The *Lavena Coastal Walk* starts at Lavena and follows the southeastern coastline of Taveuni, ending at the *Wainabau Waterfalls*; the *Vidawa Forest Walk* is a guided trip through the *Bouma Forest Park*. Marked trails (including wooden walkways and bridges) also exist in the *Kula Eco Park*, an area of coastal rainforest rich in wildlife (including fruit bats, parrots and marine turtles).

Social Profile

FOOD & DRINK: International cuisine is available, but the local cooking is Fijian and Indian. Local dishes include *kakoda* (a marinated local fish steamed in coconut cream and lime), *rourou* (a taro leaf dish), *kassaua* (tapioca, often boiled, baked or grated and cooked in coconut cream with sugar and mashed bananas) and *duruka* (an unusual

Credit: © Fiji Visitors Bureau

asparagus-like vegetable in season during April and May). Breadfruit is also common. Indian curries are served in all major hotels. A number of hotels and restaurants also serve the Fijian *lovo* feast of meat, fish, vegetables and fruit cooked in covered pits. Table service is normal, although some establishments offer buffet-style food at lunchtime. Hotels often serve meals to non-residents. A wide range of drinks are available. Local beers are *Carlton*, brewed in Suva, and Fiji Bitter, brewed in Lautoka. Local wines include *Meridan Moselle* and *Suvanna Moselle*. South Pacific Distilleries produce *Booth's Gin*, *Bounty Fiji Golden Rum*, *Cossack Vodka* and *Old Club Whisky*. Throughout Fiji, the drinking of *yaqona* (pronounced yanggona) or *kava* is common. In the past, the drink was prepared by virgins, who chewed the root into a soft pulpy mass before adding water. It is made from the root of the pepper plant and the *yaqona* drinking ceremony is still important in the Fijian tradition, although it has also become a social drink. Bars and cocktail lounges have table and/or counter service. Only licensed restaurants, clubs and hotel bars can serve alcohol.

NIGHTLIFE: Major hotels and resorts have live bands and dancing during the evening. There are also nightclubs with entertainment, especially in Suva. Cinemas show English-language and Indian films. Most social activity, however, is in private clubs and visitors can obtain temporary membership through hotels. Hotels offer Fijian entertainment (*meke*) on a rotation basis.

SHOPPING: Favourite buys are filigree jewellery, woodcarvings (such as *kava* bowls) and polished coconut shells, seashells, woven work (such as mats, coasters, hats, fans and trays), tapa cloth and pearls. Bargaining is not a rule in shops. Some shopkeepers will give a discount with large purchases. Duty-free items are available and include cameras, televisions, watches, binoculars, clocks, lighters, hi-fi equipment, pewter, crystal and porcelain. **Shopping hours:** Mon-Fri 0800-1700, Sat 0800-1300 (some shops have half-day closing on Wednesday and are open later on Friday).

SPECIAL EVENTS: For further details, contact the Fiji Visitors Bureau (see *Contact Addresses* section). The following is a selection of special events occurring in Fiji in 2005:

Jan *New Year Celebrations*. **Feb** *Hindu Holi* (Festival of Colours); *Super League Two-Day World Sevens Championship*, Suva. **Mar/Apr** *Ram Naumi* (Birth of Lord Rama), Suva Bay. **Apr** *Fiji International Jazz Festival*, Coral Coast. **Jun** *Taveuni Arts Festival* (three-day festival of arts, handicrafts, game-fishing, and boat races). **Jul** *Bula Festival*, Prince Charles Park, Nadi. **Aug** *Hibiscus Festival*, Albert Park, Suva; *Indian Firewalking Ceremony*, Suva. **Sep** *Sugar Festival*, Lautoka; *Heaven to Heaven Fiji International Triathlon*. **Oct** *Indian Firewalking*, Mahi Devi Temple, Suva; *Coral Coast Bilibili Race*, Sigatoka. **Oct 21** *Diwali Festival*. **Dec** *Suva Carnival*.

SOCIAL CONVENTIONS: Fijians are a very welcoming, hospitable people and visitors should not be afraid to accept hospitality. The ethnic variety of Fiji society can be seen mainly in the towns. There are powerfully built Fijians dressed in wrap-around *sulus*, numerous Indians, men in Western clothes, women wearing colourful *saris* and a scattering of European, Chinese and other Pacific Islanders. One celebrated tradition is the practice of fire-walking which has its origin in legend, although the Indian variant is performed for religious reasons. Tourists can pay to see these ceremonies but the ritual remains a religious penance and not merely a tourist attraction. Informal casual wear is generally acceptable, as are swimsuits, as long as they are worn on beaches and not in towns. Smoking is only restricted where specified. **Tips about visiting villages:** The Fiji Visitors Bureau has the following advice for travellers visiting Fijian villages: visitors should be aware that they cannot just stroll into a village, which would be an intrusion of privacy. It is customary to purchase a bundle of unpounded *yaqona* (kava) – the traditional *sevusevu* (gift) – before visiting; half a kilo, which is an appropriate amount for a gift, costs approximately $10. When approaching the village, visitors should not enter immediately but wait nearby until someone comes to greet them and ask the purpose of their visit. They will then be taken to the Chief or *Turaga Ni Koro* (Headman), to whom the kava should be offered. Visitors who are accepted by the Chief will be assigned a guide and host. Once inside the village, please also note the following: visitors should dress modestly and not wear shorts or hats and women should not have their shoulders bare; shoes should always be taken off when entering someone's house or any other village building; visitors should speak softly and not raise their voices too much as this may be interpreted as expressing anger; visitors should show respect but be cautious about praise as Fijians will feel obliged to make a gift of an object if visitors show too much liking for it; Fijians wil always, out of custom, ask visitors to stay or eat with them, but if one has already been invited, new invitations should be politely declined and possibly arranged for a later date; visitors who spend a night in the village should reward their host with a useful gift of similar value for each member of the party; it is not recommended to give money. **Tipping:** Small tips only for special services.

Business Profile

ECONOMY: The Fijian economy has a sizeable subsistence agricultural economy as well as producing cash crops, of which sugar is the most important. In 2002, the government began a wholesale reorganisation of the state-owned sugar monopoly, which was close to collapse through years of inefficiency and the state of the world sugar market. Fisheries and timber, especially mahogany (of which Fiji is the world's second-largest producer) are also vital export earners. The industrial sector exploits low-grade copper deposits. There are also a number of light industrial enterprises producing goods such as cement, paint, cigarettes, biscuits, flour, nails, barbed wire, furniture, matches and footwear, mainly for domestic consumption. Tourism is the main service industry, and was severely affected by recent political upheavals, although visitors are gradually returning. Foreign trade and investment have both declined, while many ethnic Indian members of the business community have left the country. GDP growth in 2002 was 4.8 per cent. Fiji's largest trading partners are Australia, New Zealand, Japan, the UK and the USA; more recently, closer economic relations have been forged with other Asian countries, including China, Korea (Rep) and Taiwan.

BUSINESS: Lightweight or tropical suits are acceptable.

Office hours: Mon-Fri 0830-1700 (some businesses/government offices close 30 minutes earlier every day, and one hour earlier on Fridays).

COMMERCIAL INFORMATION: The following organisation can offer advice: Suva Chamber of Commerce, PO Box 337, Suva (tel: 338 0975; fax: 338 0854.

Climate

Tropical. Southeast trade winds from May to October bring dry weather. The rainy season is from December to April.

Required clothing: Lightweight for summer, rainwear for the wet season.

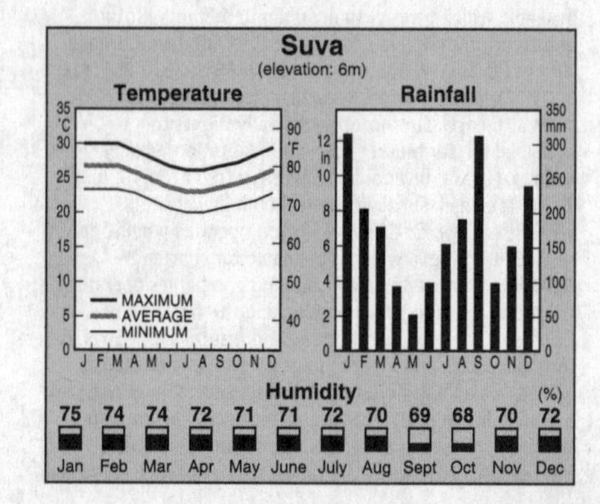

Finland

LATEST TRAVEL ADVICE CONTACTS

British Foreign and Commonwealth Office
Tel: (0870) 606 0290 Website: www.fco.gov.uk

US Department of State
Website: http://travel.state.gov/travel

Canadian Department of Foreign Affairs and Int'l Trade
Tel: (1 800) 267 8376 Website: www.dfait-maeci.gc.ca

Credit: © Helsinki City Tourist & Convention Bureau

Location: Scandinavia, Europe.

Country dialling code: 358.

Matkailun Edistämiskeskus (Finnish Tourist Board)
Head Office: Töölönkatu 11, PO Box 625, 00101 Helsinki, Finland
Tel: (9) 417 6911. Fax: (9) 4176 9333/99.
E-mail: mek@mek.fi
Website: www.finland-tourism.com *or* www.visitfinland.com
Tourist Information: Eteläesplanadi 4, 00131 Helsinki, Finland
Tel (9) 4176 9300. Fax: (9) 4176 9301.
E-mail: mek.espa@mek.fi

Embassy of Finland
38 Chesham Place, London SW1X 8HW, UK
Tel: (020) 7838 6200. Fax: (020) 7235 3680 *or* 7838 9703 (consular section).
E-mail: sanomat.lon@formin.fi
Website: www.finemb.org.uk
Opening hours: Mon-Fri 0830-1230, 1330-1630; 0900-1200 (consular affairs in person), 1400-1600 (consular telephone enquiries).

Finnish Tourist Board
PO Box 33213, London W6 8JX, UK
Tel: (020) 7365 2512 (information and brochures) *or* 8600 5680 (press and trade section). Fax: (020) 8600 5681.
E-mail: finlandinfo.lon@mek.fi *or* mek.lon@mek.fi
Website: www.visitfinland.com/uk

British Embassy
Itäinen Puistotie 17, 00140 Helsinki, Finland
Tel: (9) 2286 5100. Fax: (9) 2286 5262.
E-mail: visa.mail.helsinki@fco.gov.uk
Website: www.britishembassy.fi

Embassy of Finland
3301 Massachusetts Avenue, NW, Washington, DC 20008, USA
Tel: (202) 298 5800. Fax: (202) 298 6030.
E-mail: info@finland.org
Website: www.finland.org
Consulates General in: Los Angeles and New York.

TIMATIC CODES

Health	AMADEUS: **TI-DFT/JIB/HE** GALILEO/WORLDSPAN: **TI-DFT/JIB/HE** SABRE: **TIDFT/JIB/HE**
Visa	AMADEUS: **TI-DFT/JIB/VI** GALILEO/WORLDSPAN: **TI-DFT/JIB/VI** SABRE: **TIDFT/JIB/VI**

To access TIMATIC country information on Health and Visa regulations through the Computer Reservations System (CRS), type in the appropriate command line listed above.

Finnish Tourist Board
PO Box 4649, Grand Central Station, New York, NY 10163, USA
Tel: (212) 885 9700. Fax: (212) 885 9710.
E-mail: mek.usa@mek.fi *or* info@goscandinavia.com
Website: www.gofinland.org *or* www.goscandinavia.com.
Also deals with enquiries from Canada.

Embassy of the United States of America
Itäinen Puistotie 14, 00140 Helsinki, Finland
Tel: (9) 616 250 *or* 6162 5730 (consular). Fax: (9) 6162 5800.
E-mail: arc@usembassy.fi *or* consular@usembassy.fi *or* webmaster@usembassy.fi
Website: www.usembassy.fi

Embassy of Finland
Suite 850, 55 Metcalfe Street, Ottawa, Ontario K1P 6L5, Canada
Tel: (613) 288 2233. Fax: (613) 288 2244.
E-mail: embassy@finland.ca
Website: www.finland.ca
Consulate General in: Toronto.
Honorary Consulate Generals in: Vancouver.
Honorary Consulates in: Calgary, Edmonton, Halifax, Montréal, Québec, Regina, St John, Sault Ste Marie, Sudbury, Thunder Bay, Timmins and Winnipeg.

Canadian Embassy
Street address: Pohjoisesplanadi 25B, 00101 Helsinki, Finland
Postal address: PO Box 779, 00101 Helsinki, Finland
Tel: (9) 228 530. Fax: (9) 601 060.
Website: www.dfait-maeci.gc.ca/canadaeuropa/finland

General Information

AREA: 338,145 sq km (130,559 sq miles).
POPULATION: 5,206,295 (official estimate 2002).
POPULATION DENSITY: 15.4 per sq km.
CAPITAL: Helsinki. **Population:** 559,716 (official estimate 2002).
GEOGRAPHY: Finland is situated in the far north of Europe. Bordered to the west by Sweden and the Gulf of Bothnia, to the north by Norway, to the east by the Russian Federation and to the south by the Gulf of Finland, it is the fifth-largest country in Europe. There are about 30,000 islands off the Finnish coast, mainly in the south and southwest, and inland lakes containing a further 98,000 islands. The Saimaa lake area is the largest inland water system in Europe. Of the total land area, 10 per cent is under water, and 65 per cent is forest, the country being situated almost entirely in the northern coniferous zone. In the south and southwest, the forest is mainly pine, fir and birch. In Lapland, in the far north, trees become more sparse and are mainly dwarf birch. 8 per cent of the land is cultivated.
GOVERNMENT: Republic. **Head of State:** President Tarja Halonen since 2000. **Head of Government:** Prime Minister Matti Vanhanen since 2003.
LANGUAGE: There are two official languages: Finnish, spoken by 93.6 per cent of the population, and Swedish, spoken by 6 per cent of the population. About 1700 people speak Same (Lapp). English is taught as the first foreign language.
RELIGION: 85 per cent Evangelical Lutheran, 10 per cent others including Finnish Orthodox, Baptists, Methodists, Free Church, Roman Catholic, Jews and Muslims.
TIME: GMT + 2 (GMT + 3 from last Saturday in March to Saturday before last Sunday in October).
ELECTRICITY: 230 volts AC, 50Hz. Continental two-pin plugs are standard.
COMMUNICATIONS: Telephone: Full IDD is available. Country code: 358. Outgoing international code: 990, 994 or 999. For international number enquiries and tariff information within Finland, callers should dial 020 208. **Mobile telephone:** GSM 900/1800 networks available. Main operators include *OY Radiolinja AB* (website: www.radiolinja.fi) and *Sonera* (website: www.sonera.fi). **Fax:** Many hotels and businesses have fax facilities. Also available in post offices in Helsinki. **Internet:** ISPs include *Kolumbus* (website: www.elisa.net) and *Sonera* (website: www.sonera.fi). Public access is available in Internet cafes. There are also many Internet booths in Helsinki. **Telegram:** These can be left with the nearest post office or hotel desk. **Post:** Letters and postcards sent by airmail usually take about three days to reach destinations within Europe. Stamps are available from post offices, book and paper shops, stations and hotels. Visitors can have mail sent to them via *Poste Restante*, Central Post Office, Mannerheimintie 11, 00100 Helsinki, which is open Mon-Fri 0800-2100, Sat 0900-1800, Sun 1100-2100. Generally, post offices are open Mon-Fri 0900-1700, closed Saturday. During winter, many town offices are open 0900-1800.
Press: There are over 200 daily newspapers, with the most popular including *Aamulehti*, *Helsingin Sanomat*, *Ilta-Sanomat* and *Iltalehti*. *Apu* and *Seura* are weekly illustrated news magazines and are two of several periodicals. *Kauppalehti* is one of the leading business newspapers. There are no English-language newspapers published in Finland, but most UK and US daily newspapers are available, as well as international papers in many different languages.
Radio: BBC World Service (website: www.bbc.co.uk/worldservice) and Voice of America (website: www.voa.gov) can be received. From time to time the frequencies change and the most up-to-date can be found online.

Passport/Visa

	Passport Required?	Visa Required?	Return Ticket Required?
Full British	No/10	No	No
Australian	Yes	No	No
Canadian	Yes	No	No
USA	Yes/6	No	No
Other EU	1-5 & 7-9	No	No
Japanese	Yes/6	No	No

Note: Regulations and requirements may be subject to change at short notice, and you are advised to contact the appropriate diplomatic or consular authority before finalising travel arrangements. Details of these may be found at the head of this country's entry. Any numbers in the chart refer to the footnotes below.

Note: Finland is a signatory to the 1995 **Schengen Agreement**. For further details about passport/visa regulations within the Schengen area, see the introductory section, *How to Use this Guide*.
PASSPORTS: Passport valid for at least three to six months required by all except the following provided they hold a valid national ID card:
(a) **1.** nationals of EU countries (except Cyprus, the Czech Republic, Estonia, Greece, Hungary, Latvia, Lithuania, Malta, Poland, the Slovak Republic, Slovenia and Sweden), including the French Overseas Departments of Guadeloupe,

Martinique and Réunion but excluding Greenland and the Faroe Islands;
(b) nationals of Liechtenstein, San Marino and Switzerland.
Note: The following nationals may also be able to enter Finland with documents other than a passport, although this should be checked prior to arrival, since passport exemptions are not guaranteed in these cases:
(a) **2.** Nationals of Croatia and Slovenia with Yugoslavian passports issued prior to the states becoming independent.
(b) **3.** Nationals of Denmark with an emergency passport;
(c) **4.** Nationals of Estonia with a temporary travel document;
(d) **5.** Nationals of Germany and Lithuania with a child document in lieu of passport (Germany also with repatriation certificate);
(e) **6.** Nationals of Japan and the USA with re-entry permits to their respective countries (USA also with refugee travel documents);
(f) **7.** Nationals of Latvia with ID documents for stateless persons, or with alien's passport;
(g) **8.** Nationals of The Netherlands with a *Titre de Voyage*;
(h) **9.** Nationals of Poland with an emergency travel document;
(i) **10.** Nationals of the UK with a certificate of identity or identity card. Passports must be blue and issued after Jan 1 1983, bearing "British Citizen" on page one, and/or "Holder has a right of abode in the UK" on page five. EU passports must bear "European Community" or "European Union" on the front cover and "British Citizen" on the page of personal data.

Credit: © Helsinki City Tourist & Convention Bureau

VISAS: Required by all except the following for a period of up to three months:
(a) nationals listed in the chart and under passport exemptions (with national ID cards) above;
(b) nationals of Andorra, Argentina, Bolivia, Brazil, Brunei, Bulgaria, Chile, Costa Rica, Croatia, El Salvador, Guatemala, Honduras, Hong Kong (SAR), Iceland, Israel, Korea (Rep), Macau (SAR), Malaysia, Mexico, Monaco, New Zealand, Nicaragua, Norway, Panama, Paraguay, Romania, Singapore, Uruguay, Vatican City and Venezuela. Visas are required for stays exceeding three months and by all who wish to work during their stay except nationals of Denmark, Iceland, Norway and Sweden;
(c) holders of a UN or EU laissez-passer.
Types of visa and cost: A uniform type of visa, the *Schengen* visa, is issued for tourist, business and private visits. All visas are £24 (€35), regardless of duration of stay or whether single-, double- or multiple-entry. Visa fees may vary with the rate of exchange. The transfer of a visa costs £14.
Note: Spouses and children of EU nationals (providing spouse's passport and the original marriage certificate/children's full birth certificate is produced), and nationals of some other countries, receive their visas free of charge (enquire at Embassy for details).
Validity: Transit visas are valid for up to five days. Single-entry and double-entry visas are valid for up to 90 days. Multiple-entry visas are valid for up to one year. Applications for renewal or extension should be made to the Embassy or Authorities in Finland.
Application to: Consulate (or Consular section at Embassy); see *Contact Addresses*. Visas must be applied for in person at Embassy of *Schengen* country visited. If visiting more than one *Schengen* country, apply to the Embassy of the main destination *or* to the Embassy of the country entered first (if there is no main destination).
Application requirements: (a) One completed, signed application form. (b) One passport-size photo. (c) Passport valid for at least three months from the date of return. An alien's spouse and children under 16 years may travel with passport holder if their names and dates of birth are in the passport, plus photo of spouse and photos of any children under seven years. (d) Re-entry permit into the UK valid for at least three months (for applicants applying at the Finnish Embassy in London). (e) Valid travel insurance other than E111. (f) Hotel reservation or original invitation from either a family or company in Finland. (g) Reservation of travel tickets (possibly original return tickets also) and proof of funds. (h) Fee (non-refundable; payable in advance in cash or by postal order only). *Business*: (a)-(h) and, (i) Letter of invitation from the Finnish company confirming length and purpose of stay and a letter from current employer. For minors under 18 years, letter from college/university and written permission from both parents, plus copy of parents' passports.
Note: All documents should be submitted both in their original form and with photocopy attached.
Working days required: Up to two weeks, although sometimes longer.
Temporary residence and work: Apply to Finnish Embassy. Work permits and Residence permits should be arranged well in advance. EU nationals are allowed to live and work in Finland without visas or permits for up to three months; for periods exceeding three months, they can obtain a residence permit (a work permit is not required) from the local police station. Contact the Directorate of Immigration for more information (website: www.uvi.fi).
Note: Those wishing to visit the CIS from Finland are advised to obtain their visa in their country of origin; applications made in Helsinki take at least eight working days.

Money

Single European currency (Euro): The Euro is now the official currency of 12 EU member states (including Finland). The first Euro coins and notes were introduced in January 2002; the Finnish Markka was still in circulation until 28 February 2002, when it was completely replaced by the Euro. Euro (€) = 100 cents. Notes are in denominations of €500, 200, 100, 50, 20, 10 and 5. Coins are in denominations of €2 and 1, and 50, 20, 10, 5, 2 and 1 cents.
Currency exchange: Foreign currency and travellers cheques can be exchanged in banks and at bureaux de change at ports, stations and airports.
Credit & debit cards: American Express, Diners Club, MasterCard and Visa enjoy wide acceptance, as well as Eurocheque cards. Check with your credit or debit card company for details of merchant acceptability and other services which may be available. Up-to-date information is available in Helsinki from American Express (tel: (9) 6132 0400) *or* Diners Club (tel: (9) 693 991).
Travellers cheques: Travellers cheques are also accepted in banks and some shops. To avoid additional exchange rate charges, travellers are advised to take travellers cheques in Euros, Pounds Sterling or US Dollars.
Currency restrictions: Unrestricted import of local and foreign currency. Export of local and foreign currency is limited to the amount imported for non-residents, and to €1,682 or equivalent for residents.
Exchange rate indicators: The following figures are included as a guide to the movements of the Euro against Sterling and the US Dollar:

Date	Feb '04	May '04	Aug '04	Nov '04
£1.00=	1.46	1.50	1.49	1.43
$1.00=	0.80	0.84	0.81	0.75

Banking hours: Mon-Fri 0915-1615 (regional variations may occur).

Duty Free

The following items may be imported into Finland from non-EU countries without incurring customs duty:
200 cigarettes or 50 cigars or 250g of tobacco or 100 cigarillos; 2l of alcoholic beverages of less than 22 per cent by volume or 1l of alcoholic beverages of more than 22 per cent by volume or 2l of wine or 16l of beer; 50g of perfume and 250ml of eau de toilette; non-commercial goods to a value of €185.
The following items may be imported into Finland from EU countries without incurring customs duty:
300 cigarettes or 150 cigarillos or 75 cigars or 400g of tobacco; 1l of alcoholic beverages of more than 22 per cent by volume and 3l of alcoholic beverages of less than 22 per cent by volume and 5l of wines and 64l of beer.
Note: The import of alcoholic beverages over 22 per cent is only allowed by persons aged 20 years or over; alcoholic beverages up to 22 per cent may be imported by persons aged 18 years or over.
Restricted items: The import and export of certain foods, plants, medicines, firearms and works of art are subject to certain restrictions and formalities. The import of drinks containing more than 60 per cent alcohol by volume is prohibited. Contact the Finnish Tourist Board for further details (see *Contact Addresses* section).
Abolition of duty free goods within the EU: On 30 June 1999, the sale of duty-free alcohol and tobacco at airports and at sea was abolished in all of the original 15 EU member states. Of the 10 new member states that joined the EU on May 1st 2004, these rules already apply to Cyprus and Malta. There are transitional rules in place for visitors returning to one of the original 15 EU countries from one of the other new EU countries. But for the original 15, plus Cyprus and Malta, there are now no limits imposed on importing tobacco and alcohol products from one EU country to another (with the exceptions of Denmark, Finland and Sweden, where limits *are* imposed). Travellers should note that they may be required to prove at customs that the goods purchased are for personal use *only*.

Public Holidays

2005: Jan 1 New Year's Day. **Jan 6** Epiphany. **Mar 25-28** Easter. **May 1** May Day. **May 5** Ascension. **Jun 25** Midsummer's Day. **Nov 1** All Saints' Day. **Dec 6** Independence Day. **Dec 24-26** Christmas.
2006: Jan 1 New Year's Day. **Jan 6** Epiphany. **Apr 14-17** Easter. **May 1** May Day. **May 25** Ascension. **Jun 24** Midsummer's Day. **Nov 1** All Saints' Day. **Dec 6** Independence Day. **Dec 24-26** Christmas.

Health

	Special Precautions?	Certificate Required?
Yellow Fever	No	No
Cholera	No	No
Typhoid & Polio	No	N/A
Malaria	No	N/A

Note: Regulations and requirements may be subject to change at short notice, and you are advised to contact your doctor well in advance of your intended date of departure. Any numbers in the chart refer to the footnotes below.

Other risks: *Hepatitis A* occurs. Cases of *diphtheria* have been reported. Campers and trekkers should take precautions against tick bites and consider immunisation against *tick-borne encephalitis*.
Health care: There is a reciprocal health agreement with the UK. For UK nationals on a temporary visit, an E111 form is not required. Production of a British passport is sufficient to obtain medical treatment. Other EU nationals generally need to present an E111 form or the new European Health Insurance Card that is set to replace the paper E111, E119 and E128 cards. There are charges for visits to the doctor, hospital and dental treatment, and prescribed medicines. Some of these charges may, however, be partially refunded by the Finnish Sickness Insurance Department (*Kansaneläkelaitoksen Paikallistoimisto – KELA*; tel: (20) 434 5058; website: www.kela.fi). On production of the required documents, visitors seeking treatment will generally be charged approximately €11-22 for a visit to a doctor at a municipal health centre (outside regular hours, patients may be liable to an additional €15 charge), €22 for a visit to a hospital outpatient clinic and €26 per day for hospitalisation (charges may vary depending on the municipality). Those receiving private treatment should keep the receipt and submit it to the local KELA office as they may be entitled to a partial refund. For emergency dental treatment, visitors should contact the dentist on duty at the municipal health centre. A standard fee will be charged. Prescribed drugs may be obtained from any pharmacy and are charged at the full amount, though costs may be partially claimed back from the local KELA. For most prescribed medicines, a 50 per cent refund is available on amounts exceeding around €8. For emergencies, dial 112. For general information about health care and doctors who make house calls, dial 10023 (24-hour helpline; obtainable in Finland only). The pharmacy at Mannerheimintie 96, Helsinki (tel: 0203 20200 *or* 4178 0317) is open 24 hours.

Travel - International

AIR: The national airline of Finland is *Finnair (AY)* (website: www.finnair.com). Finland is served by many international airlines including *Air Canada, Air France, American Airlines, British Airways, Cathay Pacific Airways, IBERIA, IcelandAir, KLM, Lufthansa, Malaysia Airlines, Qantas, SWISS* and *United Airlines*.
Approximate flight times: From Helsinki to *London* is two hours 55 minutes, to *New York* is eight hours, to *San Francisco* is 10 hours 10 minutes, to *Singapore* is 14 hours, to *Toronto* is eight hours 45 minutes and to Zurich is two hours 55 minutes.
International airports: *Helsinki (HEL)* (Helsinki-Vantaa) (website: www.ilmailulaitos.com) is Finland's principal international airport, 18km (11 miles) north of the city (travel time – 25 minutes). *Finnair City Bus* and other services operate to the city regularly (travel time – 35 minutes). Taxi services are available. Some Helsinki hotels run courtesy coaches. Airport facilities include banks/bureaux de change, duty-free shops, car hire (*Avis, Budget, Europcar* and *Hertz*), hotel reservation service, VIP lounge, a 24-hour electronic information system with four channels, conference rooms, restaurants, cafes and bars. The other international airports are *Turku (TKU)*, 7km (5 miles) north of the city; *Tampere (TMP)*, 15km (9 miles) from the city; and *Rovaniemi (RVN)*, 10km (6 miles) from the city.
Departure tax: None.
SEA: Car ferries sail daily from Stockholm and other Swedish ports with *Anedin, Birka, Eckerö, Finnlines* (website: www.finnlines.fi), *Silja* (website: www.silja.fi) and *Viking Lines*. Other major Finnish ports are Naantali , Turku

and Vaasa. There are also ferry services to Finland from Rostock and Travemünde (Germany) and Tallinn (Estonia). Cruise lines with ships docking in Finnish ports include *Birka Line, Costa, Crystal, Cunard, Eckerö Line, Fred Olsen, Kristina Cruises, Norwegian Cruise Line, P&O, Princess, Radisson, Seabourn* and *Silversea*.
RAIL: Rail-sea links exist from Hamburg, Copenhagen and Stockholm to Helsinki or Turku. There is a rail connection between Haparanda/Tornio in the north from Sweden, and daily trains to Moscow and St Petersburg.
ROAD: Most direct road routes include sea ferry links from Sweden or Germany, though there is a northern land link via northern Norway or Sweden to Finnish Lapland, which involves travel within the Arctic Circle. **Coach:** There are coach services from many European cities, including direct services from London to Helsinki or Turku and Gothenburg with a sea link from Sweden.

Travel - Internal

AIR: There are 22 domestic airports in Finland. Finnair runs an excellent network of domestic services. For further information, contact their UK Head Office, 14 Clifford Street, London W1S 4BX, UK (tel: (0870) 241 4411; fax: (020) 7629 7289 *or* (0870) 787 4988; website: www.finnair.com). Other domestic airlines include *Blue 1* (website: www.blue1.com) and *Golden Air* (website: www.goldenair.se).
Cheap fares: There are some money-saving offers available. These include: *Group discounts* which vary between 15 per cent and 35 per cent, depending on the size of the group; *Senior Citizens' fares* giving special rates (with some restrictions) for persons over 65; *Junior fares* giving special rates for children aged 12 to 16; and *Youth fares* giving special rates (with some restrictions) for persons aged 17 to 25. There are special 'Midnight Sun' packages to Rovaniemi (Lapland) in June and July. For further information, contact Norvista, 31-5 Kirby Street, London EC1N 8TE, UK (tel: (0870) 744 7315; fax: (0870) 744 7310; e-mail: reservations@norvista.co.uk; website: www.norvista.co.uk); *or* the Finnish Tourist Board (see *Contact Addresses* section).
RIVER/LAKE: Traffic on the inland waterways is serviced by regular water buses and ferries. There is a wide choice of routes and distances. Popular routes are the 'Silver Line' between Hämeenlinna and Tampere and the 'Poet's Way' between Tampere and Virrat. *Saimaa Ferries* operate lake routes from Lieksa, Koli and Joensuu. There are also regular services on Lake Päijänne and Lake Inari. *Lake Päijänne Cruises* run services from Lahti, Heinola and Jyväskylä and *Roll Cruises* operate from Kuopio and Savonlinna. On Lake Pielinen, there are regular services, also by car ferry. Overnight accommodation in small cabins and meals and refreshments are available on lake cruises. For more detailed information on schedules and routes, contact the Finnish Tourist Board (see *Contact Addresses* section).
RAIL: There are 6000km (3700 miles) of rail network with modern rolling stock. *VR Ltd* (website: www.vr.fi) operates an extensive rail service around Finland. The 'Pendolino' fast train runs at a maximum speed of 220km (132 miles) per hour and is designed to operate on all main routes by the end of 2006. Current lines include Helsinki–Turku, Helsinki–Tampere–Jyväskylä, Jyväskylä–Kuopio and Helsinki–Seinäjoki–Oulu. Other trains include express trains (for which seats must be booked in advance), night and car-carrier trains, regional trains and InterCity trains (InterCity2 trains have double-decker cars). Rail travel is cheap and efficient. Children under six years of age travel free of charge, children aged six to 16 pay half price.
Cheap fares: Special tickets offering discounts are available including: *Group tickets* (minimum of three people), giving 20 per cent discount, valid for one month; Finnrail pass, giving unlimited travel for three, five or 10 days within a period of one month, first- or second-class; *Finnish Senior Citizens Rail Card* for persons over 65 years of age, entitling the holder to a 50 per cent discount (passport has to be shown); *Student Rail Discounts*, entitling the student to 50 per cent discounts with a valid student card; *Scanrail Pass*, valid for 21 days for travel in the Scandinavian countries with reductions of 25 to 50 per cent for young people according to age; *Inter-Rail Ticket*, valid in Finland as well as the rest of Europe; *Eurail Passes* and *Euro Domino* passes are also accepted.
For further details and reservations, contact the Finnish Tourist Board (see *Contact Addresses* section) *or* Finnish Railways, PO Box 488, 00101 Helsinki (tel: 3072 0902; fax: 3072 0111; e-mail: yhteyskeskus@vr.fi; website: www.vr.fi).
ROAD: There are 77,000km (47,000 miles) of road. The main roads are passable at all times and are surfaced with asphalt or oil and sand. There are weight restrictions on traffic from April to May in southern Finland, and from May to early June in northern Finland. Traffic drives on the right. Horn-blowing is frowned upon. In some areas, warnings of elk, deer and reindeer crossing will be posted. Drivers involved in an elk or reindeer collision should report the event to the Police immediately. **Bus:** This is an excellent means of transport.

Credit: © Finnish Tourist Board

Coach services are run by *ExpressBus* (a consortium of 30 bus companies; website: www.expressbus.com) and there are more than 300 services daily from Helsinki and connections can be made to the most remote and isolated parts of the country. In Lapland, buses are the major means of surface travel. Bus stations have restaurants and shops. Baggage left at one station is dispatched to its destination, even when bus transfers and different bus companies are involved. One child under four is carried free (children aged four to 11 years pay half fare). Seats for coaches can be reserved in advance by paying the full fare and reservation fee. Timetables are widely available. **Cheap fares:** Group tickets are sold for groups travelling at least 80km (50 miles) and including at least three persons (at least one of whom is aged over 12 years). There is a 50 per cent discount for students when travelling a minimum of 80km. The state post office also runs a bus service with routes that serve the rural areas. Up-to-date details of bus services may be obtained from Matkahuolto (website: www.matkahuolto.fi). **Taxi:** Available in every city and from airports or major hotels. Taxi drivers are not tipped. Taxis have a yellow *taksi* sign which is lit when the taxi is vacant. They can be booked at taxi ranks or signalled from the street. Fares are more expensive at nights (Sun-Fri 2000-0600, Sat 1600-0600). **Car hire:** Cars can be rented in Helsinki and other places. The minimum age varies from 19 to 25 years of age depending on the company and all must have a minimum of one year's driving experience. The rates usually include oil, maintenance, liability and insurance, but no petrol. A few caravans are for hire. **Regulations:** Seat belts must be worn by the driver and all passengers (front and back seat). Car headlights must be kept on at all times. Cars towing caravans may not exceed 80kph (50mph). Cars and caravans must have the same tyres. Studded tyres are allowed from 1 October to 30 April or when weather conditions are appropriate. From 1 December until 28 February, snow tyres are a legal requirement for vehicles under 3.5 tonnes. It is possible to hire tyres. Further information can be obtained from *Autoliitto* (Automobile and Touring Club of Finland), Hämeentie 105A, 00550 Helsinki (tel: (9) 7258 4400; fax: (9) 7258 4460; e-mail: autoliitto@autoliitto.fi; website: www.autoliitto.fi). If involved in an accident, immediately contact the Finnish Motor Insurer's Bureau (*Liikennevakuutuskeskus*), Bulevardi 28, 00120 Helsinki (tel: (9) 6804 0611; fax: (9) 6804 0474; e-mail: uk.ic@vakes.fi).
Documentation: National driving licence or International Driving Permit and insurance required.
URBAN: Efficient and integrated bus, metro and tramway services, suburban rail lines and ferry services to Suomenlinna Islands are operated in Helsinki. A common fares system applies to all the modes (including the ferries) with a zonal flat fare and free transfer between services. Multi-trip tickets are sold in advance, as are various passes. The peninsular location of the city has led to an emphasis on public transport. Tram no. 3 passes most of the main tourist attractions – a free brochure in English is available for those who wish to take the trip. **Helsinki Card:** This is available for one, two or three days. Once purchased, it gives free travel on public transport and free entry to about 50 museums and other sights in the city. The card comes with a guidebook giving details of the museums, sights and other discounts on offer. Enquire at the Tourist Board for prices and further details.
Travel times: The following chart gives approximate travel times (in hours and minutes) from **Helsinki** to other major cities/towns in Finland.

	Air	Road	Rail
Tampere	0.35	2.50	1.48
Turku	0.30	2.40	1.50
Rovaniemi	1.15	13.30	9.07

Accommodation

Further details on accommodation and grades of accommodation are given in the publications available from the Finnish Tourist Board.
HOTELS: There is usually a sauna and often a swimming pool in Finnish hotels and motels. The price level varies from district to district, being higher in Helsinki and some areas of Lapland. Many hotels and motels usually include breakfast in their rates. The service fee is usually included in the bill. This is 15 per cent of the room rate; for meals and drinks it is 14 per cent on weekdays and 15 per cent on Friday evenings, Saturdays, Sundays, holidays and the eve of holidays.
Advance reservations are advisable in the summer months. Details of hotels are listed in the brochures available from Finnish Tourist Board offices. Accommodation at reduced rates is often possible, especially for groups and during weekends. Reductions are also possible for guests participating in special schemes run by hotel chains throughout Scandinavia. Information can also be obtained from the Finnish Hotel and Restaurant Association, Merimiehenkatu 29, 00150 Helsinki (tel: (9) 622 0200; fax: (9) 6220 2090; e-mail: shr@shr.fi; website: www.shr.fi).
Summer hotels: During summer (1 June to 31 August), when the universities are closed, student accommodation becomes available to tourists. Rooms are modern and clean and become the 'summer hotels' of Finland. They are located around the country in major cities. The price level of 'summer hotels' is less than that of regular hotels.
BED & BREAKFAST: There are approximately 100 bed & breakfast host families in Finland. Accommodation ranges from rooms in main buildings to cottages and outbuildings. Children aged under four years are free of charge; those aged up to 11 years pay half the price. A list of B&Bs can be supplied by the Finnish Tourist Board (see *Contact Addresses* section) and the brochure *Finland Country Holidays – Bed & Breakfast*, published by Lomarengas, who can also take bookings (tel: (9) 5766 3300; fax: (9) 5766 3355; e-mail: sales@lomarengas.fi; website: www.lomarengas.fi). The brochure also includes information on farm holidays.
FARMHOUSE HOLIDAYS: More than 500 farmhouses take guests on a bed & breakfast and full- or half-board basis. They are in rural settings and almost always close to water. The guest rooms may be without modern conveniences but are clean, and there is usually a bathroom in the house. Some farms also have individual cottages for full-board guests, or apartments with kitchen, fridge and electric stove for those wishing to cater for themselves. The guests can join the farm family for meals, take a sauna twice a week, row, fish, walk in the forests or join in the work of the farm. Full-board rates include two hot meals, coffee twice a day and a sauna twice a week (children receive a 50 to 75 per cent reduction). The majority of farms are in central and eastern Finland, some on the coast and in the Åland Islands.
Grading: Farmhouses are graded on a scale from **1 to 5 stars**.
SELF-CATERING: There are over 200 Holiday Villages in Finland, many in the luxury class with all modern conveniences. These villages consist of self-contained first-class bungalows by a lake and offer varied leisure activities, such as fishing, rowing, hiking and swimming. The best villages are open all year round and can be used as a base for winter holidays and skiing. Some of the villages also have hotels and restaurants. Those in the top-price bracket have several rooms, TV and all modern conveniences. There are also approximately 5000 individually owned holiday cottages for hire, ranging from the humblest fishing hut on the coast or in the archipelago to the luxury villas of the inland lakes. They are all furnished and have cooking utensils, crockery and bed linen as well as fuel for heating, cooking and lighting and, in many cases, a sauna and a boat. Most cottages inland are near a farm where the tourist can buy food. Reductions are available out of season. Enquire at tourist offices for details.
Grading: Classification is from **1 to 5 stars**.
YOUTH HOSTELS: There are about 100 youth hostels in Finland. Many of them are only open in the summer from 10 June to 15 August, and about 50 of them are also open in winter. Some of the hostels are in empty educational establishments, with accommodation and fairly large rooms, but a lot of them also offer 'family rooms'. The hostels do not usually provide food, but coffee and refreshments are available at most and some have self-service kitchens. There are no age restrictions and motorists may use the hostels. Sheets can be hired. For more information, contact The Finnish Youth Hostel Association, Yrjönkatu 38B-15, 00100 Helsinki (tel: (9) 565 7150; fax: (9) 5657 1510; e-mail: info@srm.inet.fi; website: www.srmnet.org). **Grading:** Youth hostels are classified into four categories according to their facilities.
CAMPING/CARAVANNING: There are about 350 campsites in Finland. The majority have cooking facilities, kiosks and canteens where food, cigarettes and sweets can be bought. Campsites are generally along waterways, within easy reach of the main roads and towns. Camping outside official campsites is allowed providing not causing damage to crops or other items, and at least 150m from human habitations. The camping season starts in late May or early June and ends in late August or early September. In southern Finland, it is possible to sleep under canvas for about three months and in the north for about two months. Most campsites have indoor accommodation, camping cottages, and holiday cottages suitable for family accommodation. Prices depend on the classification of the campsite and are charged for a family, ie two adults, children, car, tent and trailer. The charge includes basic facilities, such as cooking, washing, etc. If a camper has an international camping card (FICC), a national camping card is not required. Further details can be obtained from: the

Finnish Tourist Board (see *Contact Addresses* section); *or* from Camping in Finland (website: www.camping.fi).
Grading: Sites are classified into five grades.

Resorts & Excursions

Over the country as a whole, there are marked differences in climate and landscape, with corresponding regional variations in traditions, culture and food. Seasonal variations are particularly marked in the north; in Lapland, for instance, the winter sports season lasts until May, and the midnight sun shines night and day for the whole of June and part of July. Autumn is also worth seeing for, in September, the first frosts produce the vivid colours of 'Ruska'. In southern Finland, spring comes earlier and summer is longer. At midsummer, daylight lasts for 19 hours and there are generally many hours of warm sun.

HELSINKI

There are approximately half a million inhabitants in the Helsinki Metropolitan Area, making it the most densely populated region in Finland. The area comprises four towns, **Helsinki** (the capital), **Espoo**, **Vantaa** and **Kauniainen**. However, only half of the 800 sq km (300 sq miles) that it occupies is actually developed. The rest consists of parks, forests, shoreline and lakes. In many places, there are historical sights – old manors and churches – as well as buildings by the best-known of Finnish architects, including **Dipoli Hall** at the **Helsinki University of Technology** in **Otaniemi**, an internationally acknowledged 20th-century masterpiece.

FINNISH ARCHIPELAGO AND ÅLAND ISLANDS

Finland is surrounded in the south, southwest and west by the **Baltic**, the **Gulf of Finland** and the **Gulf of Bothnia**. The coastline is highly indented and its total length is 4600km (2760 miles). Around the coast is a vast archipelago of thousands of islands.
The coast and archipelago are largely composed of granite rocks, either grey or red, but these are generally low-lying. In many places there are long unspoiled sandy beaches. There are no tides to speak of, so the appearance of the seashore does not differ much from the lakeshores. In addition, the seawater is not very salty as very little water of high salt content passes through the Danish straits, and the many rivers, as well as the rainfall, contribute more water to the Baltic than is lost by evaporation. A special feature of the Baltic is that the land is constantly rising from the sea, as much as 9mm a year in the narrow part of the Gulf of Bothnia - a long-term result of the end of the Ice Age. The archipelago can be explored by local cruises from many coastal towns.
Southwest Finland and the **Åland Islands** are the warmest part of the country and more deciduous trees grow here than anywhere else in the country. Fruit and vegetables are cultivated extensively and 20 per cent of the country's fields are here.
For historical reasons, a large proportion of the Swedish-speaking population of Finland lives in this region and is concentrated in the Åland Islands, the **Turku Archipelago** and on the south coast. The region is often spoken of as the cradle of Finnish civilisation and the area has a larger concentration of granite churches and manors than elsewhere.
Main towns & resorts: Hämeenlinna, Hamina, Hanko, Hyvinkää, Kotka, Kouvola, Kuusankoski, Lohja, Mariehamn and Åland Islands, Naantali, Parainen, Pori, Porvoo, Rauma, Riihimäki, Tammisaari, Turku and Uusikaupunki.

FINNISH LAKELAND

The majority of Finland's 180,000 lakes are situated between the coastal area and the eastern frontier covering an area some 100km- (60 mile-) wide. The lakes are a veritable maze with their profusion of bays, headlands and islands. Sometimes they open out into broader stretches. They are linked to each other by rivers, straits and canals forming waterways which in former times were a principal means of communication. Nowadays, they are attractive routes for the tourist. As the lakes are usually shallow and the surrounding land is not high, the water soon becomes warm in summer. Many summer festivals of all kinds take place in the lakeland area, often in beautiful country settings.
EASTERN LAKELAND: The eastern region is an area of interconnected lakes which is dominated by **Lake Saimaa**, a vast expanse of water. Dotted over their surface are no fewer than 33,000 islands and the shoreline is 50,000km (80,000 miles) long. A network of waterways joins the lively Savo towns, such as Savonlinna with its medieval **Olavinlinna Castle**, the best preserved in Scandinavia. The *Savonlinna Opera Festival* is held annually in July. In addition to operas performed to international standards, there are a number of concerts. **Kuopio** is known for its food speciality, *kalakukko* (a rye bread pie with fish and pork filling).
WESTERN LAKELAND: Jyväskylä, **Tampere**, **Lahti** and **Hämeenlinna** region. This area comprises two major waterways, the oldest of which, the Finnish *Silverline*, runs between Hämeenlinna, birthplace of Sibelius, and Tampere, through fertile agricultural lands which are fairly densely populated. Lahti, a winter sports centre, lies at one end of **Lake Päijänne** where the land is higher and steep rocky cliffs rise to as much as 200m (650ft). At the other end is Jyväskylä, famous for its modern architecture.

FOREST FINLAND

The remoteness of Forest Finland has meant that the beauty of the wild, vast forests, rivers and lakes has remained unspoilt. It is a popular area for canoe and hiking trips, and rapid-shooting. **Northern Karelia**, the southernmost part of Forest Finland, lies in the 'bulge' to the east of **Lake Pielinen**. The **Koli Heights** (347m/1138ft), the highest point in Northern Karelia, overlook the lake. A large percentage of the Finnish Orthodox population lives here, and the region has preserved its own special character, customs and food. One speciality is known far beyond the region, the *Karjalan piirakka*, a Karelian (rice and potato) pasty. **Kainuu**, the district around **Lake Oulujärvi**, is wild and beautiful with vast forests, marshes, deep lakes and rapids. **Vuokatti**, near Sotkamo village, specialises in cross-country skiing.
Main towns & resorts: Iisalmi, Imatra, Joensuu, Jyväskylä, Kajaani, Kuopio, Lahti, Lappeenranta, Lieksa, Mikkeli, Nurmes, Outokumpu, Savonlinna, Tampere, Valkeakoski and Varkaus.

OSTROBOTHNIA

The west coast area of Ostrobothnia, with its long sandy beaches (of which the dunes of **Kalajoki** are the best known), is an agricultural region with a sunny climate and less rain than elsewhere. There are islands between **Vaasa** and **Kokkola** with old fishermen's villages. **Hailuoto Island**, with its interesting fauna, can be reached by ferry from **Oulu**, the area's chief commercial and university centre. Picturesque old wooden houses are still a feature of the coastal towns. Traditions are maintained in many local festivals where *Pelimannit* play music handed down through the generations. A number of Swedish-speaking Finns live on the coast. **Seinäjoki** has administrative buildings designed by Alvar Aalto. **Ähtäri Wildlife Park** is 80km (130 miles) southeast of Seinäjoki. The region just south of the Arctic Circle along the eastern frontier is centred round **Kuusamo**. In **Oulanka National Park**, rivers with rapids run through gorge-like valleys. Seine fishing (using vertical nets) takes place on **Lake Kitkajärvi**. In summer, there are numerous hiking routes. **Ruka Fell** is a popular winter sports centre.
Main towns & resorts: Kokkola, Oulu, Pietersaari, Raahe, Seinäjoki and Vaasa.

LAPLAND

Finnish Lapland is a place for those who wish to enjoy the peace and quiet of a remote area either in the comfort of first-class accommodation out in the wilds or in more primitive conditions. Lapland can offer gastronomic delights such as salmon and reindeer prepared in many ways, and the rare golden cloudberry. It is a very large area of 100,000 sq km (38,000 sq miles). Between the many rivers are vast uninhabited areas and swamps. In the valleys, pine and spruce grow, but the most northerly regions are treeless tundra or low-fell birch scrub. Many fells have gently rounded treeless tops. There are only four towns in the province: **Rovaniemi** (the provincial capital), **Kemijärvi**, **Tornio** and **Kemi**. The whole of the rest of Lapland is very sparsely populated with a density of only slightly over two persons per sq km. Of the 200,000 inhabitants, about 3900 are Lapps and 600 Skolt Lapps, the latter belonging to the Orthodox church. About 200,000 reindeer roam freely on the fells. They are the property of 5800 different owners. There are reindeer round-ups from September to January. Special reindeer-driving competitions take place in March with participants from all over Lapland.
As regards scenery and communications, Lapland can be roughly divided into two areas: Eastern and Western Lapland.
EASTERN LAPLAND: Suomutunturi, on the Arctic Circle, is a well-known winter sports centre, as are **Pyhätunturi**, **Luostotunturi** and **Saariselkä Fells**. At **Porttikoski** and **Simo**, there are traditional lumberjack competitions in summer. Further north, **Tankavaara** is a gold-panning centre. Inari village lies on the third-largest lake in Finland, **Lake Inari**, with 3000 islands, on one of which stands an old Lapp sacrificial palace. The **Sami Museum** is devoted to the history of the Lapps. In the wilds lies **Pielpajärvi Church**. The **River Lemmenjoki** flows into Lake Inari and is another well-known gold-panning region. The **Lemmenjoki National Park** has marked routes for hikers.
WESTERN LAPLAND: The scenery differs from Eastern Lapland and the ground is higher. The fells rise in bare and impressive ranges. Among the best known are **Yllästunturi**, **Olostunturi** and **Pallastunturi**. All of them are winter sports centres but are attractive in other seasons and are especially popular among hikers. **Haltia Fell**, the highest in Finland, at 1300m (4265ft), and **Saana Fell**, 1029m (3376ft), lie on the border between Finland, Norway and Sweden. In the north is the Lapp village of **Hetta**, scene of colourful festivities on Lady Day in March.
Main towns & resorts: Kemi, Kemijärvi, Rovaniemi and Tornio.

SKI RESORTS

The major ski resorts include: **Pallastunturi**, **Saariselkä**, **Pallas**, **Levi**, **Ylläs** and **Luosto/Pyhä** (in the North); **Rovaniemi**, **Ruka**, **Iso-Syöte**, **Vuokatti**, **Koli** and **Tahko** (in central Finland); and **Himos** and **Lahti** (in the south). All of the major resorts are easily accessible from the nearest airports or railway stations; the number of slopes varies from five to 36, while cross-country skiing trails vary in total length from around 100 to 250km (63 to 157 miles). For further details, contact the Finnish Tourist Board (see *Contact Addresses* section), which also publishes a special brochure on winter activities; see also *Sport & Activities* section.

Sport & Activities

Winter sports: One of Finland's most popular sports is **cross-country skiing**, with marked and often illuminated tracks all over the country. There are also some 120 **downhill skiing** resorts, offering instruction, equipment hire and extensive *après-ski* facilities. For details, see the *Resorts & Excursions* section. Many resorts have halfpipes and 'snowboard streets' for **snowboarding** enthusiasts. **Off-piste skiing** (for experienced skiers only) is available through private companies. The skiing season is from January to February (southern Finland) and December to March/April (central and northern Finland). The lakes and the ground freeze between November and May and the coastal waters freeze in December. Northernmost Finland is above the Arctic Circle and enjoys a spell of polar night (*kaamos*) when the sun does not rise; many skiing slopes are artificially lit during this time. **Dog- or reindeer-sledge safaris, snowmobile tours** and **icebreaker cruises** often involve overnight stays in log cabins or Lap tents (*kota*), located in the Arctic wilderness. Although remote, kotas are warm and comfortable.
Outdoor pursuits: Around 65 per cent of Finland's surface area is forested. The north has coniferous forests, streams and open country; central Finland is characterised by its many lakes; the east has forests and deep gullies; and the south, though more densely populated, still offers forests and attractive coastal trails for hiking. The midnight sun period in Lapland is particularly popular. In early autumn, Finland's trees and vegetation take on the beautiful hues and colours of the *ruska* season, especially beautiful in Lapland. Finland has 31 national parks, the largest of which, such as *Lemmenjoki* and *Pallas-Ounastunturi*, are in the north. There are also seven national hiking areas, specifically designed for outdoor recreation. These offer a network of trails and extensive recreational facilities (including accommodation ranging from campsites to log cabins). **Cliff abseiling**, **bear trails**, **bird- and reindeer-watching** (notably in *Salla Reindeer Park*) and **pony treks** are also possible. Finland hosts several international **orienteering** competitions every year, and races are open to all.
Sailing: Visitors arriving in Finland under their own sail traditionally proceed past the west coast of the Åland Islands (see *Resorts & Excursions* section) to either Hanko, Helsinki or Kotka. Hidden rocks make the Finnish archipelago quite treacherous and only experienced sailors with up-to-date charts should navigate them. Foreign pleasure craft entering Finnish waters are subject to Finnish immigration laws. The Finnish Maritime Administration publishes a number of useful guides and brochures. For further information and charts, contact the Finnish Maritime Administration, Porkkalankatu 5, PO Box 171, 00181 Helsinki (tel: (9) 204 481; fax: (9) 2044 84355; website: www.fma.fi). For information on **sailing courses**, contact the Finnish Yachting Association, Radiokatu 20, 00093, Slu (tel: (9) 348 121; fax: (9) 3481 2369).
Lake cruises: Many lakes in the eastern *Saimaa Lake District* are large enough for bigger vessels. Cruises ranging from a few hours to a few days are available from June to August. The *Saimaa Canal*, the waterway leading from the Gulf of Finland through Russian territory to the Saimaa lake region, is also open to foreign visitors (but subject to special safety and travel regulations). For details, contact the Board of Management of the Saimaa Canal, Itäinen, Kanavatie 2, 53420 Lappeenranta, Finland (tel: (5) 458 5170; fax: (5) 020 4483 110; e-mail: saimaankanavan.hoitokunta@fma.fi).
Canoeing: Good areas for canoeing include *Saimaa*, *Lake Oulujärvi* and *Lake Inari*. Owing to strong currents, guides are recommended for trips to remote areas. City tourist offices can supply ready-planned canoeing routes. All canoeists should use charts of the coastal regions and inland waterways. Further information can be obtained from the Finnish Canoe Federation, Olympiastadion, Eteläkaarre, 00250 Helsinki (tel: (9) 494 965; fax: (9) 499 070; website: www.kanoottiliitto.fi).
Fishing: The low salt content of the sea around Finland means that those fishing in the coastal regions can catch both sea and freshwater fish. Overall, the Gulf of Finland is excellent for salmon, trout, pike and perch. The lakes and inland waterways are particularly good for trout, perch, bream and roach. For river fishing, the *Tornio* and *Teno*

salmon rivers in the Gulf of Bothnia are best. Visitors over 18 years are required to purchase a general fishing licence for all areas (except the Åland Islands); they are valid for one year and can be obtained from postal bank offices and from post offices. In addition, permission from owners of fishing waters must be obtained. Fishing permits, information and maps are available from Metsähallitus (tel: (0205) 647 702; e-mail: natureinfo@metsa.fi).
Cycling: Finland has few mountains and little traffic. Some cycling routes follow old country roads and, in the cities, there are special cycling lanes. Bicycles can be taken to the start of a route by public transport. Along the cycling routes, campsites, hostels and other forms of accommodation are available. **Mountain biking** is popular in the lake districts, where bicycles can be hired from campsites, hotels, hostels and tourist information offices. A useful cyclists' road map (with details of bike centres and connections to ferries and boats) is available.
Golf: Finland has around 100 courses. The season runs from May to October, although in some areas (such as Rovaniemi) it is possible to play **snow golf** in winter. The best 18-hole courses are in the Helsinki region. Visitors should bring a membership card from their own golf club.
Horseriding: There are around 150 riding schools in Finland, most of them located outside the towns and cities. **Harness racing** is very popular, with competitions held throughout the year; the main track at Vermo, just outside Helsinki, hosts 65 races a year (the main ones being the *Finlandia Race* in April and the *Great Finnish Derby* in September).
Special interest: The **sauna** is perhaps one of the best-known Finnish traditions, and the country has an estimated 1.6 million of them – nearly one for every three inhabitants. Most hotels, holiday villages, campsites and even log cabins come equipped with a sauna, usually built close to the water. During winter, when the water freezes, it is not uncommon to cut a hole (*avanto*) into the ice through which seasoned sauna fans may take a dip. **Sauna tours**, notably to the sauna village of **Muurame**, are possible. Health-conscious travellers can also go on a spa tour, taking in some of Finland's spas at, for instance, *Naantali* or *Haikko*.
Architecture tours put particular emphasis on buildings and designs by the internationally acclaimed *Alvar Aalto*, one of Finland's most famous architects. **Design tours**, focusing particularly on glassware, jewellery and household items as well as fireplaces and log houses, often include a visit to Helsinki's *Iittala Glass Museum* or *Glassworks*.

Credit: © Finnish Tourist Board

Social Profile

FOOD & DRINK: Potatoes, meat, fish, milk, butter and rye bread are the traditional mainstays of the Finnish diet, but food in Finland has been greatly influenced both by Western (French and Swedish) and Eastern (Russian) cooking. Tourists can expect excellent fresh fish dishes on menus. Examples are pike, trout, perch, whitefish, salmon and Baltic herring. All are in abundance most of the year. Crayfish (a Finnish speciality) is available from July to August. One should also try reindeer meat, smoked or in other forms. Regional dishes include *kalakukko*, a kind of fish and pork pie, baked in a rye flour crust, and *karjalan piirakat*, a pasty of rye flour stuffed with rice pudding or potato and eaten with egg butter. Various kinds of thick soups are also popular.
In restaurants (*ravintola*), the menu is continental with several Finnish specialities. Restaurant prices are moderate if the set menu is chosen. Most restaurants have a special menu for children, or other half-price meals. Inexpensive lunches are served at places called *kahvila* and *baari* (the latter is not necessarily a licensed bar). Information about **gourmet trails** may be obtained from Finnish Tourist Board offices; two are planned – for east and west Finland. The trails have been designed so that both can be covered in two to four days. Visitors on the trails will visit a variety of eating places from large chain hotels to inns and farmhouses, with the emphasis on the smaller, more personal places. Additionally in Lapland, *Lappi à la carte* consists of three gourmet routes. An English route map with details is available from the Tourist Board.
Restaurants are divided into two classes: those serving all kinds of alcohol and those serving only beers and wines. Waiter service is common although there are many self-service snack bars. Bars and cafes may have table and/or counter service and all internationally known beverages are available. The Finnish berry liqueurs, *mesimarja* (arctic bramble), *lakka* (cloudberry) and *polar* (cranberry), as well as the Finnish vodka (usually served ice cold with meals), are well worth trying. Finnish beer (grades III and IV A) is of a high quality and mild beers are served in most coffee bars. There are strict laws against drinking and driving. In restaurants, beer is served from 0900 and other liquor from 1100. All alcohol is served until half an hour before the restaurant closes. Nightclubs are open to serve drinks until 0200 or 0400. Service begins at 1100 and continues until the restaurant closes. The age limit for drinking is 18 years, but consumers must be 20 before they can buy the stronger alcoholic beverages.
Restaurant classification: Prices for alcohol vary according to the restaurant's classification.
E: Elite price category.
G: General price category.
S: Self-service price category.
A: Fully licensed.
B: Licensed for beer and wine.
SHOPPING: Finnish handicrafts, jewellery, handwoven *ryijy* rugs, furniture, glassware, porcelain, ceramics, furs and textiles are amongst the many Finnish specialities. Excellent supermarkets and self-service shops can be found all over the country. Helsinki railway station has the first underground shopping centre in the country, where the shops are open 0800-2200 (Sun and public holidays 1200-2200). At the Katajanokka boat harbour, there is a shop selling glass, china, wooden articles and textiles. **Duty free:** Anyone permanently resident outside the EU can claim back purchase tax at the time of departure. Repayment can be made (on presentation of a special chèque provided by the retailer) at the following gateways: Helsinki, Turku, Tampere, Mariehamn, Vaasa and Rovaniemi airports; onboard ferries and ships operated by *Polferries*, *Silja Line*, *Vaasaferries* and *Viking Line*; and at the main checkpoints on the land borders with Sweden, Norway and the Russian Federation.
Shopping hours: Mon-Fri 0900-1800, Sat 0900-1500. Shops are generally open on Sunday from June to August. Many shops are also open 0900-2100 during the week and Sat 0900-1800.
SPECIAL EVENTS: For a full list of special events, contact the Finnish Tourist Board (see *Contact Addresses* section). The following is a selection of special events occurring in Finland in 2005:
Feb 21-27 *Oulu Children's Theatre Festival*. **Mar 4-12** *Musica nova Helsinki*. **Apr 20-24** *April Jazz Espoo*. **Jun 28-Jul 7** *Kimito Island Music Festival*. **Jul 27-31** *Eteläpohjalaiset Spelit at Suupohja* (folk music festival), Teuva. **Aug 19-Sep 9** *Helsinki Festival*. **Oct 18-23** *Espoo International Piano Festival*. **Nov 3-6** *Tampere Jazz Happening*.
SOCIAL CONVENTIONS: Handshaking is customary. Normal courtesies should be observed. It is customary for the guest to refrain from drinking until the host or hostess toasts their health with a 'kippis' or a 'skol'. Casual dress is acceptable. Black tie will usually be specified when required. Finns appear sometimes to be rather reserved and visitors should not feel alarmed if there is a lack of small talk during the first half hour or so. Shoes must usually be removed when entering someone's home. **Tipping:** A 15 per cent service charge is included in the bill in hotels. Restaurants and bars have a 14 per cent service charge weekdays and a 15 per cent weekends and holidays. The obligatory cloakroom or doorman fee is usually clearly indicated. Taxi drivers, washroom attendants and hairdressers are also tipped.

Business Profile

ECONOMY: Finland is a highly industrialised country, producing a wide range of industrial and consumer goods. Timber and related industries are a key component of the economy, accounting for 40 per cent of all Finnish exports, but the country is consequently vulnerable to fluctuations in world market prices and demand levels for timber, paper and finished products such as furniture. Per capita annual income is currently just under US$25,000. Agriculture is relatively important by the standards of most European industrialised economies and, despite its climatic and geographical conditions (which only allow a very short growing season), Finland enjoys virtual self-sufficiency in basic foodstuffs such as grain, dairy products and root crops. The largest industrial sector is engineering, where traditional 'metal bashing' industries are relatively important by the standards of most industrialised countries. Mining is relatively small, although exportable quantities of gold are produced and diamond deposits were discovered in 1994. Industry is heavily dependent on imported components. Apart from paper and woodworking, the principal exports are machinery and transport equipment, metal ores and textiles. Engineering products and consumer goods are the country's main imported products. The service sector is notable for the spectacular growth of mobile communications to which Finns are now among the world's highest per capita subscribers. A number of Finnish companies are also prominent in parts of the global telecommunications equipment market. After a sharp decline in GDP growth in 2001 from 6 per cent to under 1 per cent, caused by a collapse in exports, Finland has undergone a gradual recovery. Annual growth as of 2004 was 1.9 per cent. Unemployment rates remain stubbornly high at 9 per cent: efforts to reduce it now form a centrepiece of government economic policy. Through its geographical position and political neutrality, Finland has developed unique trading links with East and West. Its principal parners are now Germany, Sweden and the UK. Finland joined the EU along with Sweden and Austria in January 1995. Since then, after meeting the required fiscal and budgetary targets, Finland has joined the European Monetary Union and adopted the Euro at its inception in 2001. Finland is also a member of the Nordic Council and the Organisation for Economic Co-operation and Development.
BUSINESS: Businesspeople are expected to dress smartly. Most Finnish businesspeople speak English and/or German. Finnish is a complex language related to Hungarian and Estonian; details of available courses may be obtained from the Council for the Instruction of Finnish for Foreigners, Pohjoisranta 4 A 4, 00171 Helsinki (tel: (9) 134 171; fax: (9) 135 9335). Local tourist boards and travel agents will be able to assist in finding translation services. Punctuality is essential for business and social occasions. Calling cards are common. Best months for business visits are February to May and October to December. **Office hours:** Mon-Fri 0800-1615.
COMMERCIAL INFORMATION: The following organisation can offer advice: FINPRO, Finland Trade Centre, Embassy of Finland, 177-179 Hammersmith Road, London W6 8BS, UK (tel: (020) 8600 7260; fax: (020) 8600 7261; e-mail: uk@finpro.fi; website: www.finpro.fi/uk); *or* Keskuskauppakamari (Central Chamber of Commerce of Finland), PO Box 1000, 00101 Helsinki (tel: (9) 696 969; fax: (9) 650 303; e-mail: keskuskauppakamari@wtc.fi; website: www.kauppakamari.fi).
CONFERENCES/CONVENTIONS: Finland is among the world's top-20 conference destinations. In addition to conference centres and hotels, there are luxury cruise ships and spas offering full convention facilities. The Finland Convention Bureau helps and advises conference organisers. They can be reached at Fabianinkatu 4 B 11, 00130 Helsinki (tel: (9) 668 9540; fax: (9) 6689 5410; e-mail: info@fcb.fi; website: www.finlandconventionbureau.fi). Information may also be obtained from the Finnish Tourist Board, who produce a brochure entitled *Meeting Planner's Guide to Finland*.

Climate

Temperate climate, but with considerable temperature variations (see below). Summer is warm with relatively mild weather in spring and autumn. Winter, which lasts from November to mid-March, is very cold. In the north (see the chart for Sodankyla), the snow cover lasts from mid-October until mid-May, but, in the brief Arctic summer, there may be up to 16 hours of sunshine a day. Rainfall is distributed throughout the year with snow in winter, but the low humidity often has the effect of making it seem warmer than the temperature would indicate (even in Lapland, the temperature can rise to over 30°C). During warm weather, gnats and mosquitos can be a hazard, particularly in the north of the country. Bring a good supply of insect repellant. The *Twilight* season lasts for two months in the north during winter.
Required clothing: Light- to mediumweights in warmer months. Medium- to heavyweights in winter, with particularly warm clothing needed for the Arctic north. Waterproofing is essential throughout the year.

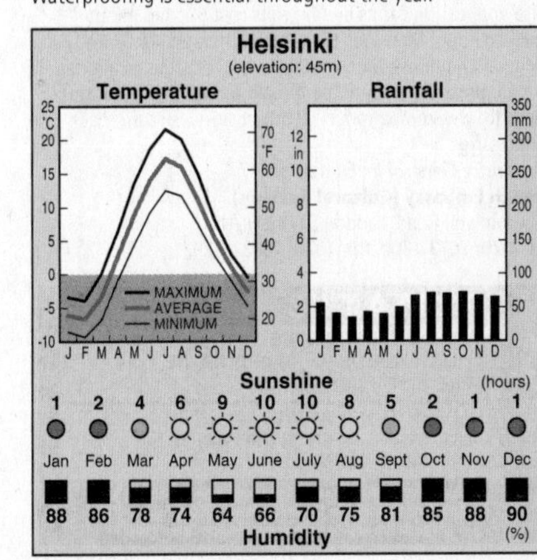

France

LATEST TRAVEL ADVICE CONTACTS

British Foreign and Commonwealth Office
Tel: (0870) 606 0290 Website: www.fco.gov.uk

US Department of State
Website: http://travel.state.gov/travel

Canadian Department of Foreign Affairs and Int'l Trade
Tel: (1 800) 267 8376 Website: www.dfait-maeci.gc.ca

Location: Western Europe.

Country dialling code: 33.

For information on French Overseas Departments, Overseas Territories and Overseas *Collectivités Territoriales*, consult the *French Overseas Possessions* section. See also the individual sections on *French Guiana, Guadeloupe, Martinique, New Caledonia, Réunion* and *Tahiti and Her Islands.*

Direction du Tourisme (Department of Tourism)
23 Place Catalogne, 75014 Paris, France
Tel: (1) 4437 3600. Fax: (1) 4437 3636.
E-mail: cnt@tourisme.gouv.fr
Website: www.tourisme.gouv.fr

Maison de la France (French Government Tourist Office)
20 avenue de l'Opéra, 75001 Paris, France
Tel: (1) 4296 7000. Fax: (1) 4292 7011.
Website: www.franceguide.com

Embassy of the French Republic
58 Knightsbridge, London SW1X 7JT, UK
Tel: (020) 7073 1000. Fax: (020) 7073 1059.
E-mail: press@ambafrance.org.uk
Website: www.ambafrance-uk.org

French Consulate General
21 Cromwell Road, London SW7 2EN, UK
Visa section: 6A Cromwell Place, London SW7 2EW, UK
Tel: (020) 7073 1200 (consular section) *or* 1250 (visa section) *or* 7073 1295 (visa applications in progress; 1500-1700 only) *or* (09065) 508 940 (visa information service; calls cost £1 per minute) *or* 266 654 (24-hour visa application form request service; calls cost £1.50 per minute) *or* 540 700 (24-hour automated visa appointment booking service). Fax: (020) 7073 1201 *or* (09001) 669 932 (visa application forms by fax; calls cost 60p per minute).
Opening hours: Mon-Wed 0845-1500, Thurs and Fri 0845-1200 (general enquiries); Mon-Fri 0845-1130 (visa applications).
E-mail: presse.londres-amba@diplomatie.fr (information).
Website: www.ambafrance-uk.org *or* www.consulfrance-londres.org
Consulate General in: Edinburgh.

French Embassy (Cultural Section)
23 Cromwell Road, London SW7 2EL, UK
Tel: (020) 7073 1300. Fax: (020) 7073 1326.

TIMATIC CODES

Health	AMADEUS: **TI-DFT/JIB/HE** GALILEO/WORLDSPAN: **TI-DFT/JIB/HE** SABRE: **TIDFT/JIB/HE**
Visa	AMADEUS: **TI-DFT/JIB/VI** GALILEO/WORLDSPAN: **TI-DFT/JIB/VI** SABRE: **TIDFT/JIB/VI**

To access TIMATIC country information on Health and Visa regulations through the Computer Reservations System (CRS), type in the appropriate command line listed above.

E-mail: culturel@ambafrance.org.uk
Website: www.instutute-francais.org.uk
Opening hours: Mon-Thur 0900-1300, 1400-1730; Fri 0900-1400.

Maison de la France (French Government Tourist Office)
178 Piccadilly, London W1J 9AL, UK
Tel: (09068) 244 123 (information line; calls cost 60p per minute) *or* (020) 7399 3520 (travel trade only). Fax: (020) 7493 6594.
E-mail: info.uk@franceguide.com
Website: www.franceguide.com

British Embassy
35 rue du Faubourg St Honoré, 75383 Paris, France
Consular section: 18 rue d'Anjou, 75008 Paris, France
Tel: (1) 4451 3100 *or* 3301/3 (visa section).
Fax: (1) 4451 3234 *or* 3128 (visa section) *or* 3127 (consular section).
E-mail: visamailparis.visamailpavis@fco.gov.uk
Website: www.amb-grandebretagne.fr
Consulates General in: Bordeaux, Lille, Lyon and Marseille.
All post should be addressed to the main British Embassy.

Embassy of the French Republic
4101 Reservoir Road, NW, Washington, DC 20007, USA
Tel: (202) 944 6000. Fax: (202) 944 6166.
E-mail: info-washington@diplomatie.gouv.fr *or* impotsl@ambafrance-us.org
Website: www.ambafrance-us.org *or* www.consulfrance-washington.org (consular section).
Consulates General in: Atlanta, Boston, Chicago, Houston, Los Angeles, Miami, New Orleans, New York and San Francisco.

French Government Tourist Office
444 Madison Avenue, 16th Floor, New York, NY 10022, USA
Tel: (212) 838 7800 *or* (514) 288 6989 (travel trade only) *or* 288 1904 (public information service). Fax: (212) 838 7855.
E-mail: info.us@franceguide.com
Website: www.franceguide.com

Embassy of the United States of America
2 avenue Gabriel, 75382 Paris Cedex 08, France
Consular section: 2 rue St Florentin, 75382 Paris Cedex 01, France
Tel: (1) 4312 2222. Fax: (1) 4266 9783.
Website: www.amb-usa.fr
Consulates General in: Marseille and Strasbourg.

Embassy of the French Republic
42 Sussex Drive, Ottawa, Ontario K1M 2C9, Canada
Tel: (613) 789 1795. Fax: (613) 562 3735.
Website: www.ambafrance-ca.org
Consulates General in: Moncton, Montréal, Québec, Toronto and Vancouver.

French Government Tourist Office
1981 Avenue McGill College, Suite 490, Montréal, Québec H3A 2W9, Canada
Tel: (514) 876 9881. Fax: (514) 845 4868.
E-mail: canada@franceguide.com
Website: www.franceguide.com

Canadian Embassy
35 avenue Montaigne, 75008 Paris, France
Tel: (1) 4443 2900 *or* 2916 (immigration and visas). Fax: (1) 4443 2999 *or* 2993 (immigration and visas).
Website: www.amb-canada.fr
Honorary Consulates in: Lyon, Nice, St-Pierre (St-Pierre et Miquelon) and Toulouse.

General Information

AREA: 543,965 sq km (210,025 sq miles).
POPULATION: 59,481,919 (official estimate 2002).
POPULATION DENSITY: 109.3 per sq km.
CAPITAL: Paris. **Population:** 2,125,246 (1999).
GEOGRAPHY: France, the largest country in Europe, is bordered to the north by the English Channel (*La Manche*), the northeast by Belgium and Luxembourg, the east by Germany, Switzerland and Italy, the south by the Mediterranean (with Monaco as a coastal enclave between Nice and the Italian frontier), the southwest by Spain and Andorra, and the west by the Atlantic Ocean. The island of Corsica, southeast of Nice, is made up of two *départements*. The country offers a spectacular variety of scenery, from the mountain ranges of the Alps and Pyrénées to the attractive river valleys of the Loire, Rhône and Dordogne and the flatter countryside in Normandy and on the Atlantic coast. The country has some 2900km (1800 miles) of coastline.
GOVERNMENT: Republic since 1792. **Head of State:** President Jacques Chirac since 1995. **Head of Government:** Prime Minister Jean-Pierre Raffarin since 2002.
LANGUAGE: French is the official language, but there are many regional dialects. Basque is spoken as a first language by some people in the southwest, and Breton by some in Brittany. Many people, particularly those connected with tourism in the major areas, will speak at least some English.
RELIGION: Approximately 77 per cent Roman Catholic with a Protestant minority.
TIME: GMT + 1 (GMT + 2 from last Sunday in March to last Sunday in October).
ELECTRICITY: 220 volts AC, 50Hz. Two-pin plugs are widely used; adaptors recommended.
COMMUNICATIONS: Telephone: Full IDD is available. Country code: 33. Outgoing international code: 00. Card-only telephones are common, with pre-paid cards bought from post offices and *tabacs*; coin boxes are being phased out throughout the country. International calls are cheaper between Mon-Fri 1900-0800 and all day from Sat-Sun. Calls can be received from all phone boxes showing the sign of a blue bell. **Mobile telephones:** GSM 900 and 1800 networks cover most areas. The use of mobile telephones is prohibited at petrol stations. **Fax:** Services are widely available; many hotels and all post offices have facilities. **Internet:** Public access is available at Internet cafes. There are numerous local ISPs including *wanadoo* (website: www.wanadoo.fr). **Post:** Stamps can be purchased at post offices and *tabacs*. Post normally takes a couple of days to reach its destination within Europe. Post office hours: Mon-Fri 0800-1900, Sat 0800-1200. **Press:** There are many daily newspapers, the most prominent being *Le Monde, Libération, France-Soir* and *Le Figaro*. The main English language daily is the *International Herald Tribune*. Outside the Ile-de-France, however, these newspapers are not as popular as the provincial press. International newspapers and magazines are widely available, particularly in the larger cities.
Radio: BBC World Service (website: www.bbc.co.uk/worldservice) and Voice of America (website: www.voa.gov) can be received. From time to time the frequencies change and the most up-to-date can be found online.

Passport/Visa

	Passport Required?	Visa Required?	Return Ticket Required?
Full British	1	No	No
Australian	Yes	No	Yes
Canadian	Yes	No	Yes
USA	Yes	No	Yes
Other EU	1	No	Yes
Japanese	Yes	No	Yes

Note: Regulations and requirements may be subject to change at short notice, and you are advised to contact the appropriate diplomatic or consular authority before finalising travel arrangements. Details of these may be found at the head of this country's entry. Any numbers in the chart refer to the footnotes below.

Note: France is a signatory to the 1995 **Schengen Agreement**. For further details about passport/visa regulations within the Schengen area, see the introductory section, *How to Use this Guide*.
PASSPORTS: Passport valid for three months beyond length of stay required by all, except:
1. nationals of EU countries, Andorra, Liechtenstein, Monaco, San Marino and Switzerland holding valid national ID cards.
VISAS: Required by all except the following for a period not exceeding three months:
(a) nationals of countries referred to in the chart and under passport exemptions above;
(b) nationals of Argentina, Bermuda, Bolivia, Brazil, Brunei, Bulgaria, Chile, Costa Rica, Croatia, El Salvador, Guatemala, Honduras, Hong Kong (SAR; blue passport holders only), Iceland, Israel, Korea (Dem Rep), Malaysia, Mexico, New Zealand, Norway, Panama, Paraguay, Romania, Singapore, Uruguay, Vatican City and Venezuela;
(c) transit passengers continuing their journey by the same or first connecting aircraft, provided holding valid onward or return documentation and not leaving the airport. The following nationals always require an airport transit visa when not leaving the airport, unless they are permanent residents in the UK, EU, Andorra, Canada, Iceland, Japan, Liechtenstein, Monaco, Norway, San Marino, Switzerland or the USA: Afghanistan, Albania, Angola, Bangladesh, Burkina Faso, Cameroon, Congo (Rep), Côte D'Ivoire, Eritrea, Ethiopia, Ghana, Guinea, Haiti, India, Iran, Iraq, Liberia, Libya, Mali, Nigeria, Pakistan, Senegal, Sierra Leone, Somalia, Sri Lanka, Sudan, Syrian Arab Republic and holders of Palestinian refugee travel documents issued by the Egyptian, Lebanese or Syrian authorities.
Note: (a) Pupils travelling on a school trip may also be exempt from visa regulations if their names are entered on a 'List of Travellers' obtainable from the British Council (tel: (0161) 957 7755), for those resident in the UK. (b) Nationals of Bermuda, although visa-exempt when entering France, may still require visas to enter other Schengen countries. (c) Visa-exempt nationals may still be required to produce proofs of financial means of support, hotel bookings or a return ticket to country of residence, either at borders of entry or within the Schengen area.
Types of visa and cost: A uniform *Schengen* visa, is issued for *Short-stay* visits (tourist, business and students),

Airport transit, *Transit* and *Long-validity* (circulation) visits. Visa application fees must be paid at the time of application. No visa application fee can be refunded, whatever the result of the application.
All Schengen visa applications are now charged at €35, irrespective of the duration of stay requested. The fee remains payable in Pounds Sterling only, approximately £22-26.
Note: (a) Prices change with the prevalent exchange rate, so visitors are advised to check the exact price before travelling. Payment is by cash or by credit/debit card (excluding American Express and Diners), and in Pounds Sterling only. (b) Spouses and children of EU nationals can obtain a visa free of charge on presentation of relevant documentation.
Validity: Short-stay visas are valid for a maximum of six months from date of issue for single or multiple entries of maximum 90 days in total. Transit visas are valid for single or double entries of maximum five days per entry, including the day of arrival. Long-stay visas are valid for up to three years for a maximum stay of 90 days in every six-month period. Visas cannot be extended; a new application must be made each time.
Application to: All persons wishing to apply must make an appointment by telephone before attending and submitting their documents in person at the consulate. An automated telephone appointment booking service is available; see *Contact Addresses* section. Travellers visiting just one Schengen country should apply to the Consulate of that country; travellers visiting more than one Schengen country should apply to the Consulate of the country chosen as the main destination *or* the country they will enter first (if they have no main destination).
Application requirements: (a) Passport valid for at least three months longer than validity of the visa with blank pages to affix visa stamp. If British, the British Residence permit must exceed the validity of the requested visa by more than three months. An exception will be made (one month) for those returning permanently to their country on presentation of travel tickets. (b) One completed application form. (c) Two passport-size photos. (d) Evidence of sufficient funds for stay (eg a recent bank statement of less than one month or traveller's cheques; a minimum of £40 per day spent in France is required). (e) Proof of occupation with letter from employer, accountant, school or university (less than one month old), or last three payslips. (f) Return ticket to country of residence, and visa for next destination if required, or confirmed booking from travel agent. (g) Evidence of hotel reservations, a certificate of board and lodging to be obtained by your French host from the local town hall, means of support or proof of official invitation from host or company. (h) Evidence of medical insurance (including repatriation and covering the duration of the requested visa). (i) Fee; payable by cash or credit/debit card. (j) For business travellers: a letter of invitation from a French company. (k) For student trips: a letter from school stating dates of trip, address in France and name of persons responsible for student.
Note: Postal applications are only acceptable for certain nationals; consult the Consulate (*or* website: www.frenchembassy.org.uk) for further information.
Working days required: 24 hours to several weeks, depending on nationality. Six to eight weeks for group visas.
Temporary residence: A Work Permit may have to be obtained in France. For full details, contact the long stay visa section of the Consulate General; see *Contact Addresses* section.

Money

Single European currency (Euro): The Euro is now the official currency of 12 EU member states (including France). The first Euro coins and notes were introduced in January 2002; the French Franc was still in circulation until 17 February 2002, when it was completely replaced by the Euro. Euro (€) = 100 cents. Notes are in denominations of €500, 200, 100, 50, 20, 10 and 5. Coins are in denominations of €2 and 1, and 50, 20, 10, 5, 2 and 1 cents.
Currency exchange: Some first-class hotels are authorised to exchange foreign currency. Visitors should also look for the 'Crédit Mutuel' or 'Crédit Agricole', which have longer opening hours. Shops and hotels are prohibited from accepting foreign currency by law. Many UK banks offer differing exchange rates depending on the denominations of currency being bought or sold. Travellers should check with their banks for details and current rates.
Credit & debit cards: American Express, Diners Club, MasterCard and Visa are widely accepted. Check with your credit or debit card company for details of merchant acceptability and other services which may be available.
Travellers cheques: In 2002, the Banque de France stopped dealing in foreign currencies and therefore no longer handles travellers cheques.
Currency restrictions: The import and export of local and foreign currency is unrestricted. Amounts over €7622 must be declared.
Exchange rate indicators: The following figures are included as a guide to the movements of the Euro against Sterling and the US Dollar:

Date	Feb '04	May '04	Aug '04	Nov '04
£1.00=	1.46	1.50	1.49	1.43
$1.00=	0.80	0.84	0.81	0.75

Banking hours: Mon-Fri 0900-1200 and 1400-1630. Some banks close Monday and some are open Saturday. Banks close early (1200) on the day before a bank holiday; in rare cases, they may also close for all or part of the day after. Some banks in Paris are open Mon-Fri 1000-1700.

Duty Free

The following goods may be imported into France without incurring customs duty by passengers aged 17 years of age or older arriving from non-EU countries:
200 cigarettes or 50 cigars or 100 cigarillos or 250g of tobacco; 1l of spirits more than 22 per cent or 2l of alcoholic beverage up to 22 per cent; 2l of wine; 50g of perfume and 250ml of eau de toilette; goods up to the value of €175 (€90 per person under 15 years of age); caviar up to 250g.
Restricted items: (a) Plants and plant products. (b) Meat and meat products from Africa. (c) Pharmaceutical products (except those needed for personal use). (d) Works of art. (e) Collectors' items and antiques.
Abolition of duty free goods within the EU: On 30 June 1999, the sale of duty-free alcohol and tobacco at airports and at sea was abolished in all of the original 15 EU member states. Of the 10 new member states that joined the EU on May 1st 2004, these rules already apply to Cyprus and Malta. There are transitional rules in place for visitors returning to one of the original 15 EU countries from one of the other new EU countries. But for the original 15, plus Cyprus and Malta, there are now no limits imposed on importing tobacco and alcohol products from one EU country to another (with the exceptions of Denmark, Finland and Sweden, where limits *are* imposed). Travellers should note that they may be required to prove at customs that the goods purchased are for personal use *only*.

A B C D E F G H I J K L M N O P Q R S T U V W X Y Z

Public Holidays

2005: Jan 1 New Year's Day. **Mar 28** Easter Monday. **May 1** Labour Day. **May 5** Ascension. **May 8** 1945 Victory Day. **May 16** Whit Monday. **Jul 14** Bastille Day. **Aug 15** Assumption. **Nov 1** All Saints' Day. **Nov 11** Remembrance Day. **Dec 25** Christmas Day.
2006: Jan 1 New Year's Day. **Apr 17** Easter Monday. **May 1** Labour Day. **May 8** 1945 Victory Day. **May 25** Ascension. **Jun 5** Whit Monday. **Jul 14** Bastille Day. **Aug 15** Assumption. **Nov 1** All Saints' Day. **Nov 11** Remembrance Day. **Dec 25** Christmas Day.
Note: In France, the months of July and August are traditionally when the French take their holidays. For this reason, the less touristic parts of France are quiet during these months, while coastal resorts, especially in the south, are very crowded.

Health

	Special Precautions?	Certificate Required?
Yellow Fever	No	1
Cholera	No	No
Typhoid & Polio	No	N/A
Malaria	No	N/A

Note: Regulations and requirements may be subject to change at short notice, and you are advised to contact your doctor well in advance of your intended date of departure. Any numbers in the chart refer to the footnotes below.

1: A yellow fever certificate is required for travellers coming from South American and African countries.
Other risks: Visitors to forested areas should consider vaccination for *tick-borne encephalitis*.
Rabies is present. For those at high risk, vaccination before arrival should be considered. If you are bitten, seek medical advice without delay. For more information, consult the *Health* appendix.
Health care: There is a reciprocal health agreement with the UK. On presentation of Form E111 (which must not be more than 12 months old to avoid the possibility of bureaucratic non-acceptance) at an office of the *Caisse Primaire d'Assurance Maladie* (Sickness Insurance Office), UK citizens are entitled to a refund of 75 per cent or more of charges incurred for dental and medical (including hospital) treatments and around 35 to 65 per cent of charges incurred for prescribed medicines. Application forms for Form E111 are obtainable from post offices. The standard of medical facilities and practitioners in France is very high but so are the fees, and health insurance is recommended – even for UK citizens.

Travel - International

AIR: The national airline is *Air France (AF)* (website: www.airfrance.com). Many airlines operate to France, including an increasing number of low-cost airlines from the UK.
Approximate flight times: From Paris to *London* is one hour five minutes; from Nice and Marseille is two hours. From Paris to *Los Angeles* is 15 hours five minutes; to *New York* is eight hours; to *Singapore* is 15 hours five minutes; and to *Sydney* is 25 hours five minutes.
International airports: *Paris-Charles de Gaulle (CDG)*, also known as *Roissy-Charles de Gaulle*, (website: www.adp.fr) is 23km (14 miles) northeast of the city (travel time – 40 minutes). There are coaches to the city at least every 20 minutes. Taxis are readily available and journeys to the centre cost around €38. An airport limousine service can also be hired for approximately €90. *Roissybus* services operate from the airport to Place de l'Opéra between 0545-2300 every 15 minutes. Fare is approximately €8 and takes approximately 60 minutes. *Air France* coaches run from Étoile via Porte Maillot, from Montparnasse via Gare de Lyon and from Orly Airport to Roissy-Charles de Gaulle. Services run every 12 to 20 minutes and take 40 to 50 minutes. Fares are approximately €11. The airport is also easily accessible by train on the RER B line or SNCF with connecting ADP shuttle bus.
Paris-Orly (ORY) (website: www.adp.fr) is 14km (9 miles) south of the city. Coaches and buses run to the city every 12 minutes (travel time – 25 minutes) from outside Orly Ouest. Taxis are available. RER B and C trains run every 15 minutes via Saint-Michel (travel time – 30 minutes).
Bordeaux (BOD) (Merignac) (website: www.bordeaux.aeroport.fr) is 12km (8 miles) west of the city. There are coaches, buses and taxis to the city.
Lille (LIL) (Lesquin) (website: www.lille.aeroport.fr) is 12km (8 miles) southeast of the city. Coaches and taxis are available to the city.
Lyon (LYS) (Lyon-Saint-Exupéry) (website: www.lyon.aeroport.fr) is 25km (15 miles) east of the city. Coaches or taxis are available to the city.
Marseille (MRS) (Marseille-Marignane) (website: www.marseille-provence.aeroport.fr) is 30km (19 miles) northwest of the city. A coach service departs to the city and taxis are available.
Nice (NCE) (Nice-Côte d'Azur) (website: www.nice.aeroport.fr) is 6km (4 miles) west of the city. Buses depart every 20 minutes. Taxis to the city are available.
Nantes (NTE) (website: www.nantes.aeroport.fr) is 15km (9 miles) south of the city. Trains and buses depart frequently to the city.
Strasbourg (SXB) (website: www.strasbourg.aeroport.fr) is 16km (10 miles) southwest of the city (travel time – 15 to 30 minutes). Trams and taxis are available to the city.
Toulouse (TLS) (Blagnac) (website: www.toulouse.aeroport.fr) is 10km (6 miles) northwest of the city. Buses to the city depart every 20 minutes. Taxis are available to the city.
Facilities at the airports listed above are all of a high international standard and include bank/bureaux de change, duty-free shops, restaurants and bars. There are also small airports with some international flights at *Biarritz*, *Caen*, *Deauville (St Gatien)*, *Le Havre*, *Montpellier*, *Morlaix*, *Rennes* and *Quimper*.
Departure tax: None.
SEA: The following companies run regular cross-channel services:
P&O Stena Line (tel: (08705) 202 020; website: www.poferries.com) from Dover to Calais (travel time – 1 hour 15 minutes);
P&O Portsmouth (tel: (08705) 202 020; website: www.poferries.com) from Portsmouth to Le Havre (travel time – five hours 30 minutes during the day and eight hours at night) and from Portsmouth to Cherbourg (travel time – five hours during the day and eight hours at night);
Seafrance (tel: (08705) 711 711; website: www.seafrance.com) from Dover to Calais (travel time – one hour 30 minutes); *Hoverspeed Fast Ferries* (tel: (0870) 240 8070; e-mail: reservations@hoverspeed.co.uk; website: www.hoverspeed.co.uk) from Dover to Calais (travel time – 50 minutes by seacat) and from Newhaven to Dieppe (travel time – two hours 15 minutes by seacat); *Brittany Ferries* (tel: (08703) 665 333; website: www.brittany-ferries.com) from Plymouth to Roscoff (travel time – six hours), from Portsmouth to St Malo (travel time – eight hours 45 minutes to the UK, 11 hours to France), from Portsmouth to Caen (travel time – six hours) and from Poole to Cherbourg (travel time – four hours 15 minutes by ferry or, in the high season, two hours 15 minutes by seacat); *Condor Ferries* (tel: (01202) 207 207; website: www.condorferries.co.uk) from Poole and Weymouth to St Malo (via Guernsey and Jersey) (travel time – four hours 30 minutes and five hours 30 minutes respectively), from Guernsey to St Malo (travel time – two hours 40 minutes) and from Jersey to St Malo (travel time – one hour 10 minutes).
These companies offer a variety of promotional fares and inclusive holidays for short breaks and shopping trips.
Passenger and roll-on/roll-off ferry links to and from North Africa, Corsica and Sardinia are provided by *Southern Ferries/Société Nationale Maritime Corse-Mediterranée (SNCM)* (website: www.sncm.fr) (see *Travel – Internal* section).
RAIL: International trains run from the channel ports and Paris to destinations throughout Europe. For up-to-date routes and timetables, contact *French Railways (SNCF)* (tel: (1) 5342 0000; website: www.sncf.com) *or* in the UK, *Rail Europe* (tel: (08705) 848 848; website: www.raileurope.co.uk). **The Channel Tunnel:** *Eurostar* is a service provided by the railways of Belgium, the UK and France, operating direct high-speed trains from London (*Waterloo International*) to Paris (*Gare du Nord*) and to Brussels (*Midi/Zuid*). It takes three hours from London to Paris (via Lille). When the high-speed rail link from London through Kent to the tunnel is fully operational (January 2007), the travel time between the two capitals will be reduced to two hours 15 minutes. The Eurostar trains are equipped with standard-class and first-class seating, buffet, bar and telephones, and are staffed by multilingual, highly-trained personnel. Pricing is competitive with the airlines, and seats range from *Premium First* and *Business* to *Standard*. Children aged between four and 11 years benefit from a special fare in first class as well as in standard class. Children under four years old travel free but cannot be guaranteed a seat. Wheelchair users and blind passengers together with one companion get a special fare. For further information and reservations, contact *Eurostar* (tel: (0870) 600 0792 (travel agents) *or* (08705) 186 186 (public; within the UK) or +44 (1233) 617 575 (public; outside the UK); website: www.eurostar.com); *or* Rail Europe (tel: (08705) 848 848; website: www.raileurope.co.uk). Travel agents can obtain refunds for unused tickets from Eurostar Trade Refunds, 2nd Floor, Kent House, 81 Station Road, Ashford, Kent TN23 1PD. Complaints and comments may be sent to Eurostar Customer Relations, Eurostar House, Waterloo Station, London SE1 8SE (tel: (020) 7928 5163; e-mail: new.comments@eurostar.co.uk). General enquiries and information requests must be made by telephone.
ROAD: There are numerous and excellent road links with all neighbouring countries. *Eurolines* (52 Grosvenor Gardens, London SW1W 0AU; tel: (08705) 143 219; website: www.eurolines.com) and *National Express* (Ensign Court, 4 Vicarage Road, Edgbaston, Birmingham B15 3ES; tel: (08705) 808 080; website: www.nationalexpress.com) run regular **coach** services to France from the UK. For **documentation** and **traffic regulations**, see the *Travel - Internal* section. **The Channel Tunnel:** All road vehicles are carried through the tunnel in shuttle trains running between the two terminals, one near Folkestone in Kent, with direct road access from the M20, and one just outside Calais with links to the A16/A26 motorway (Exit 13). Each shuttle is made up of 12 single- and 12 double-deck carriages, and vehicles are directed to carriages depending on their height. There are facilities for cars and motorcycles, coaches, minibuses, caravans, campervans and other vehicles over 1.85m (6.07ft). Bicycles are provided for. Passengers generally travel with their vehicles. Heavy goods vehicles are carried on special shuttles with a separate passenger coach for the drivers. Terminals and shuttles are well-equipped for disabled passengers. Passenger Terminal buildings contain a variety of shops, restaurants, bureaux de change and other amenities. The journey takes about 35 minutes from platform to platform and around one hour from motorway to motorway. Eurotunnel runs up to four passenger shuttles per hour at peak times, 24 hours per day. Services run every day of the year. For further information about departure times of shuttles at the French terminal, contact *Eurotunnel Customer Information* in Coquelle (tel: France (3) 2100 6543). Motorists pass through customs and immigration before they board, with no further checks on arrival. Fares are charged according to length of stay and time of year and whether or not you have a reservation. The price applies to the car, regardless of the number of passengers or size of the car. Promotional deals are frequently available, especially outside the peak holiday seasons. Tickets may be purchased in advance from travel agents, or from Eurotunnel Customer Services in France or the UK with a credit card. For further information, brochures and reservations, contact *Eurotunnel Customer Services UK*, Customer Relations Department, Saint Martin's Plain, Cheriton, Folkestone, Kent CT19 4QD (tel: (08705) 353 535; website: www.eurotunnel.co.uk).

Travel - Internal

AIR: *Air France* flies between Paris (from both Orly and Charles de Gaulle airports) and around 45 cities and towns. It also connects regional airports. For information, contact *Air France* (tel: (08) 2082 0820 (omit the 0 when dialling from abroad) or (0845) 359 1000 (within the UK only); website: www.airfrance.com). Details of independent airlines may be obtained from the French Government Tourist Office (see *Contact Addresses* section).
SEA/RIVER: There are almost 9000km (5600 miles) of navigable waterways in France, and all of these present excellent opportunities for holidays. The main canal areas are the north (north and northeast of Paris) where most of the navigable rivers are connected with canals; the Seine (from Auxerre to Le Havre, but sharing space with commercial traffic); the east, where the Rhine and Moselle and their tributaries are connected by canals; in Burgundy, where the Saône and many old and picturesque canals crisscross the region; the Rhône (a pilot is recommended below Avignon); the Midi (including the Canal du Midi, connecting the Atlantic with the Mediterranean); and Brittany and the Loire on the rivers Vilaine, Loire, Mayenne and Sarthe and the connecting canals. Each of these waterways offers a magnificent variety of scenery, a means of visiting many historic towns, villages and sites and, because of the slow pace (8kph/5mph), an opportunity to learn much about rural France.
Cruising boats may be chartered with or without crews, ranging in size from the smallest cabin cruiser up to converted commercial barges (*péniches*), which can accommodate up to 24 people and require a crew of eight. Hotel boats, large converted barges with accommodation and restaurant, are also available in some areas, with a wide choice of price and comfort. For further information, contact the national or regional tourist board.
State-run car ferries known as '*BACs*' connect the larger islands on the Atlantic coast with the mainland; they also sail regularly across the mouth of the Gironde. The island of Corsica is served by ferries operated by the *Société Nationale Maritime Corse-Mediterranée (SNCM)*, BP 90, 13472 Marseille Cedex 2 (tel: (0891) 701 801; fax: (4) 9156 3586; e-mail: corso@sncm.fr; website: www.sncm.fr). Services run from Marseille, Toulon and Nice to Ajaccio, Propriano, Porto Vecchio and Bastia on the island.
RAIL: *French Railways (SNCF)* operate a nationwide network with 34,200km (21,250 miles) of line, over 12,000km (7500 miles) of which has been electrified. The *TGV (Train à grande vitesse)* runs from Paris to Brittany

and southwest France at 300kph (186mph) and to Lyon and the southeast at 270kph (168mph).
The *SNCF* is divided into five systems (East, North, West, Southeast and Southwest). The transport in and around Paris is the responsibility of a separate body, the *RATP*, at 54 quai de la Rapée, 75599 Paris (tel: (1) 4468 2020; website: www.ratp.fr). This organisation provides a fully integrated bus, rail and *métro* network for the capital.
Rail tickets: There are various kinds of tickets (including Family and Young Person's Tickets) offering reductions which can usually be bought in France. In general, the fares charged will depend on what day of the week and what time of the day one is travelling; timetables giving further details are available from *SNCF* offices. It is essential to validate (*composter*) tickets bought in France by using the orange automatic date-stamping machine at the platform entrance.
There is a range of special tickets on offer to foreign visitors; they usually have to be bought before entering France and some are only available in North America; others are unique to Australia and New Zealand. There are also special European *Rail and Drive* packages. For more information, contact your local French Government Tourist Office (see *Contact Addresses* section).
Motorail (car sleeper): Services are operated from Boulogne, Calais, Dieppe and Paris to all main holiday areas in both summer and winter. Motorail information and booking is available from *Rail Europe* (tel: (08705) 848 848; website: www.frenchmotorail.com); see *Travel - International* section.
ROAD: Traffic drives on the right. France has over 9000km (5600 miles) of motorways (*autoroutes*), some of which are free whilst others are toll-roads (*autoroutes à péage*). Prices vary depending on the route, and caravans are extra. There are more than 28,500km (17,700 miles) of national roads (*routes nationales*). Motorways bear the prefix 'A' and national roads 'N'. Minor roads (marked in yellow on the Michelin road maps) are maintained by the *départements* rather than by the Government and are classed as 'D' roads. It is a good idea to avoid travelling any distance by road on the last few days of July/first few days of August and the last few days of August/first few days of September as, during this time, the bulk of the holiday travel takes place and the roads can be jammed for miles. A sign bearing the words *Sans Plomb* on a petrol pump shows that it dispenses unleaded petrol. The *Bison Futé* map provides practical information and is available from the French Government Tourist Office. **Bus:** Information on services may be obtained from local tourist offices. Local services outside the towns and cities are generally adequate. **Car hire:** A list of agencies can be obtained at local tourist offices (*Syndicats d'Initiative* or *Offices de Tourisme*). Fly-drive arrangements are available through all major airlines. *French Railways (SNCF)* also offer reduced train/car hire rates. **Caravans:** These may be imported for stays of up to six months. There are special requirements for cars towing caravans which must be observed; eg cars towing caravans are prohibited to drive within the boundaries of the *périphérique* (the Paris ring road). Contact the French Government Tourist Office for details. **Regulations:** The minimum age for hiring a car in France ranges from 21 to 25 depending on the company; some companies may also include additional charges for drivers under 25. The maximum age limit is generally 70. Speed limits are 50kph (31mph) in built-up areas, 90kph (56mph) outside built-up areas, 110kph (68mph) on dual carriageways separated by a central reservation, and 130kph (81mph) on motorways. Visitors who have held a driving licence for less than two years may *not* travel faster than 80kph (56mph) on normal roads, 100kph (62mph) on dual carriageways and 110kph (68mph) on motorways. The police in France can - and do - fine motorists on the spot for driving offences such as speeding. Random breath tests for drinking and driving are common. Seat belts must be worn by all front- and rear-seat passengers. Under-10s may not travel in the front seat. *Priorité à droite*: particularly in built-up areas, the driver must give way to anyone coming out of a side-turning on the right. The priorité rule no longer applies at most roundabouts - the driver should now give way to cars which are already on the roundabout with the signs *vous n'avez pas la priorité* or *cedez le passage*; but watch for signs and still exercise great caution. All roads of any significance outside built-up areas have right of way, known as *Passage Protégé*, and will normally be marked by signs consisting either of an 'X' on a triangular background with the words 'Passage Protégé' underneath, or a broad arrow, or a yellow diamond. A red warning triangle must be carried for use in the event of a breakdown. All headlamp beams must be adjusted for rightside driving by use of beam deflectors or (on some cars) by tilting the headlamp bulbholder. For further details on driving in France, a brochure called The *Traveller in France* is available from French Government Tourist Offices and must be ordered by telephone (see *Contact Addresses* section). It contains a section on motoring.
Documentation: A national driving licence is acceptable.

Credit: © Office de Tourisme de Bordeaux

An international sign, distinguishing your country of origin (eg GB sticker or plate), should be positioned clearly on the vehicle. EU nationals taking their own cars to France are *strongly advised* to obtain a Green Card. Without it, insurance cover is limited to the minimum legal cover in France; the Green Card tops this up to the level of cover provided by the car owner's domestic policy. The car's registration document must also be carried.
URBAN: Urban public transport is excellent. There are comprehensive bus systems in all the larger towns. There are also tramways, trolleybuses and an underground in Marseille; trolleybuses, an underground and a funicular in Lyon; and automated driverless trains in Lille, where there is also a tramway. There are tramway services in St Etienne and Nantes and trolleybuses in Grenoble, Limoges and Nancy. The systems are easy to use, with pre-purchase tickets and passes. Good publicity material and maps are usually available.
Paris: The RATP (*Régie Autonome des Transports Parisiens*) controls the underground (*métro*), rail (RER) and bus services in and around Paris. The public transport network is split into several different fare zones and a single ticket will allow travel on any of the systems within that zone (although interchange is only permitted on the métro and RER, and not on buses). Other useful transport links provided by the RATP include: *Orlybus* and *Roissybus* (special buses operating to Orly airport and Roissy Charles de Gaulle airport), *Orlyval* (rail service linking RER stations of Antony and Orly airport) and *Montmartre funicular* (special railway connecting the foot of Montmartre to the top, near the Sacré-Coeur church). **Métro:** This was built during the Paris Exhibition in 1900. Its dense network of 14 lines in the central area makes the *métro* the ideal way to get about in Paris. Trains run from approximately 0530-0115. **Rail:** *RER* (fast suburban services) operate five main lines connecting most areas of the capital. There is also an extensive network of conventional suburban services run by French Railways (SNCF), with fare structure and ticketing integrated with the other modes of public transport. **Bus:** A comprehensive network operates within the city. Services include *PC* buses that run around the outskirts of Paris; *Noctambus* services which run through the night; *Balabus* services which run between La Défense and the Gare du Lyon, navigating around La Seine and major tourist attractions; *Monmatrobus* services that run from Pigalle to Mairie du XVIII Jules Joffrin via Montmartre; sightseeing tourist buses, *l'Opentour* (website: www.paris-opentour.com) and *Paris Trip* (website: www.paris-trip.com). **Special tickets:** *Disneyland Passeport* offers a combined ticket price of RER travel and entrance fee to the theme park at a reduced rate. *Paris Visite Pass* offers superb value for money with a choice of unlimited travel on the entire RATP network (métro, RER, bus etc) for a period of one to five days. A variety of discounts are available wih the pass such as reduced prices at certain museums, cinemas, restaurants and shops. Paris transport tickets can be bought in the UK from *Allo France* (tel: (08702) 405 903; website: www.allofrance.co.uk). All other tickets can be purchased from the RATP Tourist Office at 54 quai de la Rapée, 75599 Paris (tel: (1) 4468 2020 *or* (08) 9268 7714 (within France only); website: www.ratp.fr) or from 50 of the *métro* stations, all mainline railway stations and certain banks. Children under four years of age travel free on buses and underground, while children between four and 11 years travel half price. **Taxi:** Day and night rates are shown inside each cab. There are extra charges on journeys to and from racecourses, stations and airports and for luggage. **Private car:** Parking is now prohibited in many areas of the centre. Otherwise there are parking meters or parking time is restricted (*zone bleue*). Car parks charging a fee are plentiful all over Paris and on the outskirts.

Accommodation

HOTELS: Room and all meals, ie full-board or pension terms, are usually offered for a stay of three days or longer. Half-board or *demi-pension* (room, breakfast and one meal) terms are usually available outside the peak holiday period. They are not expensive but adhere to strict standards of comfort. Hotels charge around 30 per cent extra for a third bed in a double room. For children under 12, many chains will provide another bed in the room of the parents for free. *Logis de France* are small- or medium-sized, inexpensive and often family-run hotels which provide good, clean, basic and comfortable accommodation with a restaurant attached. Further information can be obtained from the Fédération Nationale des Logis de France, 83 avenue d'Italie, 75013 Paris (tel: (1) 4584 8384; fax: (1) 4583 5966; e-mail: service-generaux@logis-de-france.fr; website: www.logis-de-france.fr). *Relais-Châteaux* are châteaux hotels. More details on all types of hotel accommodation can be obtained from the Union des Métiers et des Industries de l'Hôtellerie, 22 rue d'Anjou, 75008 Paris (tel: (1) 4494 1994; fax: (1) 4742 1520; website: www.umih.fr). **Hotels in Paris:** Hotel bookings can be made in person through tourist offices at stations or at the Paris Tourist Office, 127 avenue des Champs-Elysées, 75008 Paris (tel: (8) 9268 3112; fax: (1) 4952 5300; e-mail: question@paris-touristoffice.com; website: www.parisinfo.com) *or* free of charge at www.paris-on-line.com.
Guides: Regional lists or hotels are available, as well as the *Logis de France* guide and various chain/association guides from the French Government Tourist Office and bookshops. The Tourist Office publishes guides to hotels in Paris and the Ile-de-France, available free of charge. **Grading:** *Hôtels de Tourisme* are officially graded into five categories according to the quality of the accommodation, which are fixed by government regulation and checked by the *Préfecture of the Départements*: **4-star:** Deluxe. **3-star:** First class. **2-star:** Standard. **1-star:** Budget. *Logis de France* are subject to a specific code usually above basic requirements for their grade and are inspected regularly to ensure that they conform to the standards laid down.
SELF CATERING: *Gîtes de France* are holiday homes (often old farmhouses) in the country, all of which conform to standards regulated by the non-profitmaking National Federation. Contact the Fédération Nationale des Gîtes de France, 59 rue de St Lazare, 75439 Paris (tel: (1) 4970 7575; fax: (1) 4281 2853; e-mail: info@gites-de-france.fr; website: www.gites-de-france.fr).

Villas, Houses and Apartments Rental: Villas and houses can be rented on the spot. Local *Syndicats d'Initiative* can supply a complete list of addresses of local rental agencies. Tourists staying in France for over one month may prefer to live in an apartment, rather than in a hotel. For information about apartments to rent, apply to: Fédération Nationale de l'Immobilier, 129 rue du Faubourg St-Honoré, 75439 Paris (tel: (1) 4420 7700; fax: (1) 4225 8084; website: www.fnaim.fr).
CHATEAUX HOLIDAYS: An association, *Château-Accueil* (25 rue Jean Giraudoux, 75116 Paris; tel: (1) 4720 1827; fax: (1) 4723 3756; e-mail: rp@chateauxcountry.com; website: www.chateau-accueil.com), publishes a list of châteaux offering accommodation suitable for families. Contact the French Government Tourist Office for further information.
CAMPING/CARAVANNING: There are 7000 campsites throughout France. A few have tents and caravans for hire. Prices vary according to location, season and facilities. All graded campsites will provide water, toilet and washing facilities. Touring caravans may be imported for stays of up to six consecutive months. Contact the Fédération Française de Camping et Caravaning, 78 rue de Rivoli, 75004 Paris (tel: (1) 4272 8408; fax: (1) 4272 7021; e-mail: info@ffcc.fr; website: www.ffcc.fr) for more information. There are 100 British companies offering camping holidays in France. The French Government Tourist Office has a full list of tour operators who run all types of tours, including camping and special interest holidays.
YOUTH HOSTELS: There are hundreds of these in France, offering very simple accommodation at very low prices. There are hostels in all major towns. Stays are usually limited to three or four nights or a week in Paris. Hostels are open to all members of the National Youth Hostel Association upon presentation of a membership card. Lists are available from national youth hostel organisations. For further information, contact the French Youth Hostels Federation (FUAJ) FUAJ Centre National, 27 rue Pajal, 75018 Paris (tel: (1) 4489 8727; fax: (1) 4489 8749; e-mail: centre-national@fuaj.org; website: www.fuaj.org) *or* the French Government Tourist Office (see *Contact Addresses* section).

Resorts & Excursions

As the world's most popular tourist destination, France manages to be all things to all people. For city slickers, Paris is one of the world's truly great cities, with a myriad of attractions and diverse eating and drinking experiences. The large cities of Lyon and Marseille are not far behind Paris with their own bountiful charms, both offering alternatives and complements to the Parisian experience. Outside of the big three, there are many more cities worth exploring and every town and village seems to have something to offer, with even the smallest town usually boasting a couple of worthwhile churches and a civic museum, as well as the copious culinary traditions that the country is rightly famed for. Beyond urban France, there is a diverse range of scenery, with everything from towering Alpine peaks in the southeast and rugged sea cliffs on the Atlantic coast, through to sweeping beaches in the west and south and some of Europe's wildest areas, like the wild Camargue in the south. Any list of French attractions is, by virtue of the country's rich and eclectic nature, bound to be incomplete.
Note: The enclave of Monaco has its own section in the *World Travel Guide*, as do the French Overseas Departments and many of the other French Overseas Possessions; see the relevant sections for details.

PARIS & ILE-DE-FRANCE

PARIS: Paris is one of the world's great cities: with a practically endless amount of things to do, it rewards repeated and extended visits. Despite the massive size of the city, Paris is also an easily navigable destination as the city centre itself is relatively compact and all areas of Paris are connected by a highly efficient public transport system, with the famous **Paris Metro** being an attraction in itself. Paris boasts more than 80 museums and around 200 art galleries. *La Carte* is a pass providing free admission to about 60 national and municipal museums in the Paris area. The *périphérique* and *boulevard circulaire* ring roads roughly follow the line of the 19th-century city walls and within them are most of the well-known sights, shops and entertainments. Beyond the ring roads is an industrial and commercial belt, then a broad ring of suburbs, mostly of recent construction. Central Paris contains fine architecture from every period in a long and rich history, together with every amenity known to science and every entertainment yet devised. The oldest neighbourhood is the **Île-de-la-Cité**, an island on a bend in the Seine where the *Parisii*, a Celtic tribe, settled in about the third century BC. The river was an effective defensive moat and the *Parisii* dominated the area for several centuries before being displaced by the Romans in about 52 BC. The island is today dominated by the newly renovated cathedral of **Notre-Dame**. Beneath it is the **Crypte Archéologique**, housing well-mounted displays of Paris' early history. Having sacked the Celtic city, the Gallo-Romans abandoned the island and settled on the heights along the **Rive Gauche** (Left Bank), in the area now known as the **Latin Quarter** (Boulevards St Michel and St Germain). The naming of this district owes nothing to the Roman city: when the university was moved from the Cité to the left bank in the 13th century, Latin was the common language among the 10,000 students who gathered there from all over the known world. The Latin Quarter remains the focus of most student acivity (the **Sorbonne** is here) and there are many fine bookshops and commercial art galleries. The **Cluny Museum** houses some of the finest medieval European tapestries to be found anywhere, including 'The Field of the Cloth of Gold'. At the western end of the Boulevard St Germain is the **Orsay Museum**, a superb collection of 19th- and early-20th-century art located in a beautifully restored railway station. Other Left Bank attractions include the **Panthéon**, the **Basilica of St Séverin**, the **Palais** and **Jardin du Luxembourg**, the **Hôtel des Invalides** (containing Napoleon's tomb), the **Musée Rodin** and **St-Germain-des-Prés**. Continuing westwards from the Quai d'Orsay past the **Eiffel Tower** and across the Seine onto the Right Bank, the visitor encounters collection of museums and galleries known as the **Trocadéro**, a popular meeting place for young Parisians. A short walk to the north is the **Place Charles de Gaulle**, known to Parisians as the **Étoile**, and to tourists as the site of the **Arc de Triomphe**. It is also at the western end of that most elegant of avenues, the **Champs-Élysées** (Elysian Fields), which is once again famous for its cafes, commercial art galleries and sumptuous shops, rather than the dowdy airline offices and fast-food joints that took it over for much of the 1980s and early 1990s. At the other end of the avenue, the powerful axis is continued by the **Place de la Concorde**, the **Jardin des Tuileries** and, finally, the **Louvre**.

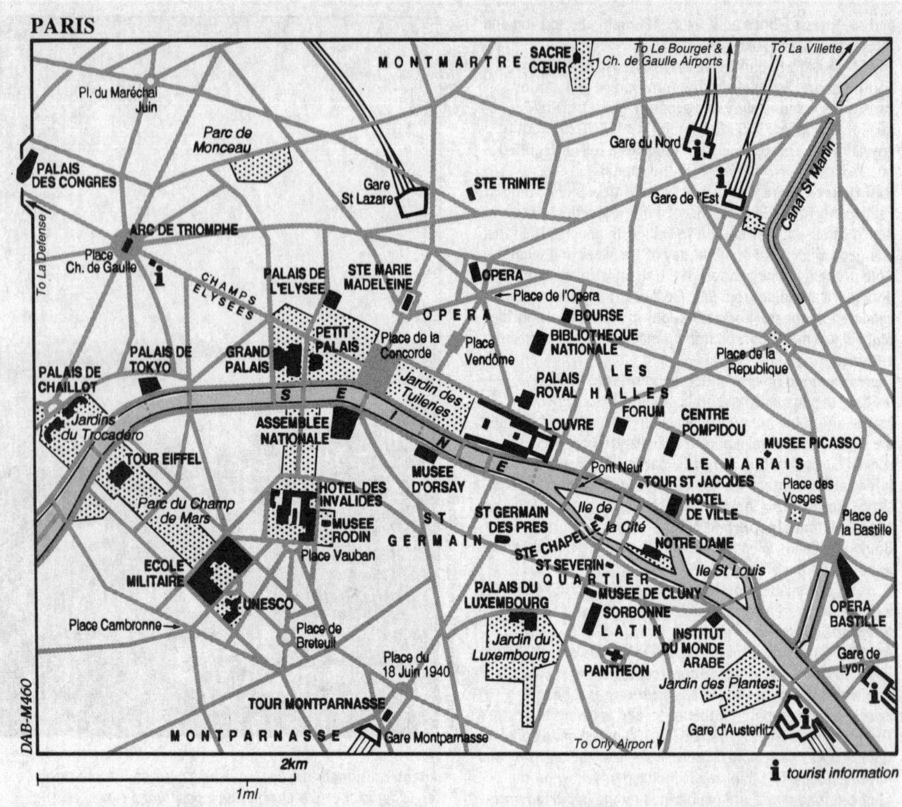

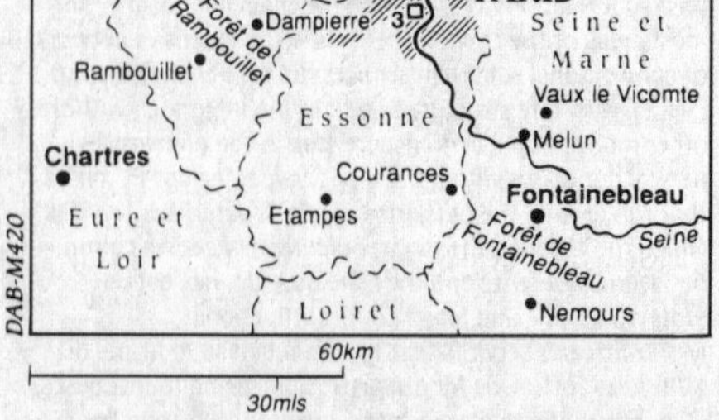

The **Palais du Louvre** has been extensively reorganised and reconstructed, the most controversial addition to the old palace being a pyramid with 673 panes of glass, which juxtaposes the ultra-modern with the classical facade of the palace. The best time to see the pyramid is after dark, when it is illuminated. The Richelieu Wing of the palace was inaugurated in 1993, marking the completion of the second stage of the redevelopment programme. In 1996, a labyrinth of subterranean galleries, providing display areas, a conference and exhibition centre, design shops and restaurants was opened.
North of the Louvre are the **Palais Royal**, the **Madeleine** and **l'Opéra**. To the east is **Les Halles**, a shopping and commercial complex built on the site of the old food market. It is at the intersection of several métro lines and is a good starting point for a tour of the city. There are scores of restaurants in the maze of small streets around Les Halles; every culinary style is available at prices to suit every pocket. Further east, beyond the Boulevard Sébastopol, is the postmodern **Georges Pompidou Centre of Modern Art** (also known as the 'Beaubourg'). It provides a steady stream of surprises in its temporary exhibition spaces (which, informally, include the pavement outside where lively and often bizarre street-performers gather) and houses a permanent collection of 20th-century art. East again, in the Marais district, are the **Carnavalet** and **Picasso Museums**, housed in magnificent town houses dating from the 16th and 18th centuries, respectively. Still further east, the magnificent **Bibliothèque François Mitterrand**, one of the world's most spectacular libraries, can be reached via a new *métro* connection (*ligne 14*) whose beautiful high-tech trains alone (they are constructed mainly of glass) are worth the trip. One of the best-known districts in Paris, **Montmartre**, became almost unbearably popular and crowded after the success in 2001 of the Hollywood blockbuster, *Moulin Rouge*. A funicular railway operates on the steepest part of the Montmartre hill, taking people to the outlandish **Sacré-Coeur**: a love-it or hate-it chocolate box architectural creation. Local entrepreneurs have long capitalised on Montmartre's romantic reputation as an artist's colony and if visitors today are disappointed to find it a well-run tourist attraction, they should bear in mind that it has been exactly that since it first climbed out of poverty in the 1890s. The legend of Montmartre as a dissolute cradle of talent was carefully stage-managed by Toulouse-Lautrec and others to fill their pockets and it rapidly transformed a notorious slum into an equally notorious circus. An earlier Montmartre legend concerns **St Denis**. After his martyrdom, he is said to have walked headless down the hill. The world's first Gothic cathedral, St Denis, was constructed on the spot where he collapsed. Just north of **Belleville** (a working-class district that produced Edith Piaf

and Maurice Chevalier) at **La Villette**, is one of Paris' newer attractions, the **City of Science and Technology**. The most modern presentation techniques are used to illustrate both the history and the possible future of man's inventiveness; season tickets are available. One of the great pleasures of Paris is the great number of sidewalk cafes, now glass-enclosed in wintertime, which extends people-watching to a year-round sport in any part of the city. There are as many Vietnamese and Chinese restaurants as there are French cafes. North African eating places also abound, and dozens of American Tex-Mex eateries are scattered throughout the city. Bric-a-brac or *brocante* is found in a number of flea markets (*marché aux puces*) on the outskirts of town, notably at the Porte de Clignancourt. There are several antique centres (**Louvre des Antiquaires**, **Village Suisse**, etc) where genuine antique furniture and other objects are on sale. Amongst the larger department stores are the **Printemps** and the **Galeries Lafayette** near the Opéra, the **Bazar Hôtel de Ville (BHV)** and the **Samaritaine** on the Right Bank and the **Bon Marché** on the Left Bank. The remains of the great forests of the **Île-de-France** (the area surrounding Paris) can still be seen at the magnificent châteaux of **Versailles**, **Rambouillet** and **Fontainebleau** on the outskirts of Paris. The capital's nightlife has never looked healthier. The 'beautiful people' may have moved on to **Menilmontant**, but the bustling streets of **Bastille** are still a nocturnal playground for far more than just tourists. Menilmontant itself rewards visitors prepared to venture beyond the guidebooks to discover the vibrant, hip, twenty-something scene.

Disneyland Resort Paris: The Disneyland Resort Paris, now open year-round, lies to the east of the capital, a complete vacation destination located at **Marne-la-Vallée**, 32km (20 miles) from Paris. Disney's first European venture has become one of the continent's most popular attractions. The site has an area of 1943 hectares (5000 acres), one-fifth the size of Paris, and includes hotels, restaurants, a campsite, shops and a golf course, and has as its star attractions the **Disneyland Paris Theme Park** and **Walt Disney Studios**. Inspired by previous theme parks, Euro Disneyland features all the famous Disney characters plus some new attractions especially produced to blend with its European home. The site is easily accessible by motorway, regional and high-speed rail services, and by air.

Credit: © Office de Tourisme de Bordeaux

BRITTANY

Brittany is a region of France that boasts a fiercely independent culture that dates back to its Celtic past. Brittany comprises the *départements* of Côtes d'Armor, Finistère, Ille-et-Villaine and Morbihan. Fishing has long been the most important industry and the rocky Atlantic coastline, high tides and strong, treacherous currents demand high standards of seamanship. At Finistère (*finis terrea* or Land's End), the Atlantic swell can drive spouts of water up to 30m (100ft) into the air. The coastal scenery is particularly spectacular at **Pointe du Raz** and **Perros-Guirec**. The Gauls arrived on the peninsula in about 600 BC. Little is known about their way of life or why they constructed the countless stone monuments to be found throughout Brittany – cromlechs, altars, menhirs and dolmens (**Carnac** is the supreme example of this). They were displaced by the Romans during the reign of Julius Caesar who, in turn, were displaced by Celts arriving from Britain in AD 460. The Celts named their new land **Brittanica Minor** and divided it into the coastal area, *l'Ar Mor* (the country of the sea), and the inland highlands, *l'Ar Coat* (the country of the woods). The two areas in Brittany are still referred to as **l'Armor** and **l'Argoat**. The Celts were master stonemasons, as may be seen by the many surviving *calvaires*, or elaborately carved stone crosses. Brittany emerged from the Dark Ages as an independent duchy. A series of royal marriages eventually brought Brittany into France and, by 1532, the perpetual union of the Duchy of Brittany with France was proclaimed. Despite the rugged coastline, it is possible to enjoy a conventional beach holiday in Brittany. The **Emerald Coast**, a region of northern Brittany centred on **Dinard**, has many fine bathing beaches. The beach resorts are often named after little-known saints: **St Enogat**, **St Laumore**, **St Brill**, **St Jacut**, **St Cast**, and so on. There are also bathing beaches in the bay of **St Brieuc**, including **Val André**, **Etables** and **St Quay**. Brittany's main attractions are her wild beauty and the unique Bretn culture. In general, coastal areas have retained a more characteristically Breton way of life than the hills inland, though much of the coastline is blighted by the holiday homes which seem to occupy every possible space. Elaborate Breton head-dresses are still worn in some parts, the style varying slightly from village to village. Breton religious processions and the ceremonies of the *pardons* that take place in a number of communities at various times of the year may have changed little since Celtic times. In the region around **Plouha**, many of the inhabitants still speak Breton, a language evolved from Celtic dialects, and Celtic music and cultural performances are also popular. The coast from **Paimpol** consists of colossal chunks of rock, perilous to shipping, as the many lighthouses suggest. The very pleasant villages and beaches of **Perros-Guirec**, **Trégastel** or **Trébeurden** contrast with the wild and rocky shoreline.

Near the base of the peninsula, at **Aber Vrac'h** and **Aber Benoit**, the ocean is caught and churned up in deep, winding chasms penetrating far inland. Further along the coast is the huge and sprawling port of **Brest**, possessing one of Europe's finest natural harbours which has a 13th-century castle. The canal running from Brest to **Nantes** makes a very pleasant journey either by hired boat or walking or on horseback, although not all of the route is navigable by water. The interior consists of wooded hills and farms, *buttes* (knolls) with fine views, short rivers and narrow valleys. Many of the so-called mountains are merely undulating verdant dunes, barely 300m (1000ft) high. They are nonetheless remnants of the oldest mountain chain on the planet. Breton architecture is perhaps more humble than in other parts of France, being more akin to that of a village in England or Wales. Inland, there are several impressive castles and many walled towns and villages. The churches are small and simple. For the most part, Brittany benefits from the warmth of the Gulf Stream all year round, but the tourist season runs from June to September. The countryside blazes with flowers in the spring, attracting many varieties of birdlife. The city of **Rennes**, the ancient capital of Brittany, is a good base from which to explore the highlands; sights include the **Palais de Justice**, the castle, the **Musée des Beaux-Arts** and the **Musée de Bretagne**, which seeks to preserve and foster all things Breton. Some of Brittany's most productive farms are close to the northern shore. Fertilised with seaweed, they produce fine potatoes, cabbage, cauliflower, artichokes, peas, string beans and strawberries. The quality of locally produced ingredients lends itself to the simple Breton cuisine, which brings out natural flavours rather than concealing them with elaborate sauces. Raw shellfish (including oysters), lobster, lamb and partridge are particularly good. The salt meadows of lower Brittany add a distinctive flavour to Breton livestock and game. *Crêpes* (pancakes) are a regional speciality and there are two distinct varieties: a sweet dessert crêpe served with sugar, honey, jam, jelly or a combination (eg *suzette*); and the savoury *sarrasin* variety, made from buckwheat flour and served with eggs, cheese, bacon or a combination of several of these (the *crêpe* is folded over the ingredients and reheated). They can be bought ready-made in the local shops. Little or no cheese is produced in Brittany, but some of the finest butter in the world comes from here – it is slightly salted, unlike the butter from the other regions of France. Cider is frequently drunk with food, as well as wine. The popular wine, *Muscadet*, comes from the extreme southern point of Brittany, at the head of the Loire Estuary, near Nantes. It is a dry, fruity white wine that goes very well with shellfish, especially oysters.

NORMANDY

Normandy is a region dominated by farming, with mile upon mile of unbroken farmland, which eventually gives way in the west to the waters of the English Channel. Normandy contains five *départements*: Seine Maritime, Calvados, Manche, Eure and Orne, with all but the last two touching on the sea. Its southern border is the **River Couesnon** which has, over the years, shifted its course as it flows over almost flat country, gradually moving south of Mont-Saint-Michel, one of Europe's best-known architectural curiosities. **Mont-Saint-Michel** and its bay are on UNESCO's World Heritage List. The tides are phenomenal: at their peak, there is a difference of about 15m (50ft) between the ebb and the flow, the height of a five-storey building. The sands in the bay are flat and, when the tides are at their highest, the sea runs in over a distance of some 24km (15 miles), forming a wave about 70cm (2ft) deep. The sandbank changes from tide to tide and, if the legend of the sea entering the bay at the speed of a galloping horse is perhaps a slight exaggeration, the danger of quicksand is real enough. The present **Abbey of Saint-Michel** was built in the eighth century by Bishop Aubert; his skull bears the mark of the finger of Saint Michel, the archangel Michael. **Cabourg** is the Balbec in Proust's novels. Maupassant and Flaubert included Norman scenes in their novels and Monet, Sisley and Pissarro painted scenes of the coast and the countryside. **Deauville** – with its beach, casino, golf course and race track – is the social capital of the area. **Bayeux** is worth a visit for the fantastic tapestry – there is nothing like it in the world. The landing beaches and World War II battlefields are remembered by excellent small museums in **Arromanches** (the landings) and Bayeux (battle of Normandy). There is also a **peace museum** in **Caen**, with its beautiful Romanesque church and ruins of an enormous castle, founded by William the Conqueror. Other monuments worth visiting include the 14th-century **Church of St-Etienne**, the **Church of St-Pierre** (Renaissance) and the **Abbaye aux Dames**. There is also a museum of local crafts from the Gallo-Roman period to the present.

The cross-Channel terminus and port of **Dieppe** has attractive winding streets and a 15th-century castle, housing the **Musée de Dieppe**. There are some beautiful châteaux in Normandy, particularly along the route between Paris and Rouen. They include the **Boury-en-Vexin**, **Bizy-Vernon**, **Gaillon**, **Gaillard-les-Andelys**, **Vascoeuil** and **Martinville**. Along the same route are found a number of other sites classed *monument historique*; the **Claude Monet House** and garden in **Giverny**, the **Abbey de Mortemer** (Lisors) and the village of **Lyon-la-Fôret**. All of these merit a detour. The ancient capital of **Rouen** features restored ancient streets and houses, including the **Vieille Maison of 1466** and the **place du Vieux-Marché**, where Jeanne d'Arc was burnt in 1432. There is a magnificent 13th-century cathedral (the subject of a series of paintings by Monet), as well as many fine museums and churches, including **St Ouen** and **St Maclou**. The cloister of St Maclou was a cemetery for victims of the Great Plague. The old port of **Honfleur**, with its well-preserved 18th-century waterfront houses, is also well worth a visit.

Normandy is a land of farmers and fishermen and is one of the finest gastronomic regions of France. Exquisite butter, thick fresh cream and excellent cheeses, including the world-famous *camembert*, *pont l'evêque* and *liverot*, are all produced here. Both crustaceans and saltwater fish abound; *sole Normande* is one of the greatest dishes known to the gastronomic world. There is also lobster from Barfleur, shrimp from Cherbourg and oysters from Dive-sur-Mur. Inland one finds duck from Rouen and Nantes, lamb from the salt meadows near Mont-Saint-Michel, cream from **Isigny**, chicken and veal from the **Cotentin**, and cider and *calvados* (apple brandy) from the **Pays d'Auge**.

NORD, PAS DE CALAIS & PICARDY

Northern France is made up of the *départements* of Nord/Pas de Calais (French Flanders) and Somme-Oise Aisne (Picardy). **Amiens**, the principal town of Picardy, has a beautiful 13th-century cathedral, which is one of

Credit: © Jean-Pierre Duplan / Light Motiv

the largest in France. The choirstalls are unique. The nearby **Quartier Saint-Leu** is an ancient canal-side neighbourhood. **Beauvais** is famous for its Gothic **Cathedral of St-Pierre** (incorporating a ninth-century Carolingian church) which would have been the biggest Gothic church in the world, if it had been completed. Its 13th-century, stained-glass windows are particularly impressive. There is also a fine museum of tapestry.
Compiègne is famous for its **Royal Palace**, which has been a retreat for the French aristocracy from the 14th century onwards, and where Napoleon himself lived with his second wife, Marie-Louise. There are over 1000 rooms within the palace and the bedrooms of Napoleon and his wife, preserved with their original decorations, are well worth viewing for their ostentatiously lavish style. Surrounding the town and palace is the **Forest of Compiègne**, where the 1918 Armistice was signed, and which has been a hunting ground for the aristocracy for hundreds of years – a wander through its dark and tranquil interior is an exceptionally pleasant experience. The town also has a fine **Hôtel de Ville** (town hall) and a **Carriage Museum** is attached to the Palace.
The château of **Chantilly** now houses the **Musée Condé** and there are impressive Baroque gardens to walk around, as well as a 17th-century stable with a 'live' **Horse Museum**. The town of **Arras**, on the **River Scarpe**, has beautiful 13th- and 14th-century houses and the lovely **Abbey of Saint Waast**. There are pretty old towns at **Hesdin** and **Montreuil** (with its ramparts and citadel). **Boulogne** is best entered by way of the lower town with the 13th-century ramparts of the upper town in the background; the castle next to the **Basilica of Notre Dame** is impressive.
Le Touquet is a pleasant all-year-round coastal resort town with 10km (6 miles) of sandy beaches. The port of **Calais**, of great strategic importance in the Middle Ages, is today noted for the manufacture of tulle and lace, as well as being a busy cross-Channel ferry terminus. Calais and its surrounds are also very popular for their large shopping malls, which are particularly popular with British visitors, who often travel across the English Channel specifically for a shopping trip. The further north one goes, the more *beer* is drunk and used in the kitchen, especially in soup and *ragoûts*. Wild rabbit is cooked with prunes or grapes. There is also a thick Flemish soup called *hochepot* which has virtually everything in it but the kitchen sink. The cuisine is often, not surprisingly, sea-based – *matelotes* of conger eel and *caudière* (fish soup). Shellfish known as *coques*, 'the poor man's oyster', are popular too. The *marolles* cheese from Picardy is made from whole milk, salted and washed down with beer. Flanders, although it has a very short coastline, has many herring dishes, *croquelots* or *bouffis*, which are lightly salted and smoked. *Harengs salés* and *harengs fumés* are famous and known locally as *gendarmes* ('policemen').

CHAMPAGNE & ARDENNES

The chalky and rolling fields of Champagne might have remained unsung and unvisited, had it not been for an accident of history. Towards the end of the 17th century, a blind monk, tending the bottles of mediocre wine in the cellars of his abbey at Hautviliers, discovered that cork made a fine stopper for ageing his wine. After the first fermentation, cork kept air - the enemy of ageing wine - from his brew. But it also trapped the carbon dioxide in the bottle and when he pulled the cork it 'popped'. At that moment, some say, the world changed for the better. 'I am drinking the stars,' he is said to have murmured as he took the first sip of *champagne* the world had ever known. This northeastern slice of France is composed of the *départements* of Ardennes, Marne, Aube and Haute Marne. On these rolling plains, many of the great battles of European history have been fought, including many in World Wars I and II. The Ardennes was once known as the 'woody country' where Charlemagne hunted deer, wild boar, small birds and game in the now vanished forests. The area has three main waterways: the **Seine**, the **Aube** and the **Marne**. The **Marne Valley** between Ferté-sous-Jouarre and Epernay is one of the prettiest in France. Forests of beech, birch, oak and elm cover the high ground, vines and fruit trees sprawl across the slopes, and corn and sunflowers wave in the little protected valleys. The valleys form a long, fresh and green oasis, dotted with red-roofed villages. In 496, Clovis, the first king of France, was baptised in the cathedral in **Rheims**. From Louis VII to Charles X, the kings of France made it a point of honour to be crowned in the city where the history of the country really began. Rheims and its cathedral have been destroyed, razed, and rebuilt many times over the centuries. The **Church of St-Rémi**, even older than the cathedral, is half Romanesque, half Gothic in style. The most remarkable feature is its great size, comparable to that of Notre-Dame-de-Paris. Beneath the town and its suburbs, there are endless caves for campagne. **Epernay** is the real capital of champagne, the drink. Here, 115km (72 miles) of underground galleries in the chalk beneath the city store the wine for the delicate operations required to make champagne. These include the blending of vintages, one of the most important tasks in the creation of champagne. It is left to age for at least three years. Aside from champagne as the world knows it, there is an excellent *blanc de blanc champagne* nature, an unbubbly white wine with a slight bite and many of the characteristics of champagne. The perfect Gothic style of the **Cathedral of St-Étienne** in **Châlons-sur-Marne** has preserved the pure lines of its 12th-century tower. Nearby, the little town of **St-Ménéhould**, almost destroyed in 1940, has contributed to the gastronomic world recipes for pigs' feet and carp but, historically, it is known for the fact that the postmaster, in 1791, recognised Louis XVI fleeing from Paris with his family and reported him. Before the annexation of Franche-Comté and Lorraine, **Langres** was a fortified town. Its Gallo-Roman monuments, its 15th- and 17th-century mansions and its religious architecture make it well worth a visit. **Troyes**, ancient capital of the Champagne area, has a beautifully preserved city centre with a Gothic cathedral, dozens of churches and 15th-century houses and a system of boulevards shaped like a champagne cork. The city also boasts the **Musée d'Art Moderne** in the old Bishops' Palace – a private collection of modern art. Troyes is becoming increasingly popular as a base for exploring **Aube en Champagne**, an area that is less saturated with tourists than the more popular champagne areas around Rheims and Epernay. There are beautiful lakes in the Champagne-Ardenne region, the largest being **Lac du Der-Chantecoq**. The **Fôret d'Orient** has a famous bird sanctuary. There is no school of cooking founded on the use of champagne, but locally there are a few interesting dishes that include the wine. **Châlons-sur-Marne** has a dish that involves cooking chicken in champagne. It goes well in a sauce for the local trout; kidneys and pike have also been fried in champagne.

LORRAINE, VOSGES & ALSACE

This part of France is made up of two historic territories, **Alsace** and **Lorraine**, in which there are six *départements*: Vosges, Meurthe-et-Moselle, Meuse, Moselle, Bas-Rhin, Haut-Rhin and the territory of Belfort. These territories have see-sawed from French to German control during conflicts between the two countries for centuries. The major cities of the area are Strasbourg, Metz, Nancy and Colmar.
Strasbourg, by far the largest and most important, has been for centuries what its name suggests: a city on a highway; the highway being the east-west trade (and invasion) route and the north-south river for commerce. Today, it is the headquarters of the European Parliament and the European Court of Human Rights, but it is rich in historic monuments and architecture and possesses a magnificent cathedral.
Metz, a Gallo-Roman city, is situated in a strategic position as a defence point and is also a crossroads of trade routes. It contains some elegant medieval walls, arches and public buildings, but its pride is the **Cathedral of St-Étienne**.
Nancy is best known for its perfectly proportioned **Place Stanislas**, gracefully surrounded with elegant wrought-iron gates. The history of Lorraine is excellently documented in the town's museum. A visit to **Colmar** can be a pleasant glimpse into the Middle Ages, and it is one of the most agreeable cities in Alsace, as well as being capital of the Alsatian wine country. The narrow, winding, cobbled streets are flanked by half-timbered houses, painstakingly restored by the burghers of the city. The 13th-century **Dominican Convent of Unterlinden**, now a museum, contains some important works from the 15th and 16th centuries, including the exquisite **Grünewald triptych**.
Colmar is a perfect place from which to set out along the *Route du Vin* (Wine Route) stopping at many of the appealing towns along the way to taste the local wine. **Turckheim**, just outside Colmar, has some of the best-preserved array of 15th- and 16th-century houses in the district and a town crier takes visitors through the streets at night to recall the atmosphere of old. The town of **Eguisheim**, with its Renaissance fountain and monument in the village square, is also a charming Alsatian town with many historic houses and wine cellars open to the public for wine-tasting. **Kayersberg** (the birthplace of Dr Albert Schweitzer, whose house has been turned into a museum with mementos of his work and life) also has some castle ruins on a hill overlooking the town and a picturesque stream that meanders through the town. A particularly popular town with tourists is **Riquewihr**, with its 13th- and 14th-century fortifications and belfry tower and its many medieval houses and courtyards. **St Hippolyte** is another picturesque wine-tasting town at the foot of the **Haut-Koenigsbourg Castle**, a sprawling and impressive medieval castle where Jean Renoir filmed *La Grande Illusion*. Self-steer boats are readily available for canal cruising in a number of locations. There are also regularly scheduled **Rhine** river and canal tours daily all summer; several hotel boats ply these waterways as well. Sightseeing helicopters and balloons make regular flights, weather permitting. Several ancient steam trains make regular circuits including **Rosheim/Ottrat** (on the wine route); at **Andolsheim**, a steam train runs along the **Canal d'Alsace** between Cernay and Soultz. Throughout Alsace there are artisans' workshops, including glass and wood painting at **Wimmenau** and pottery in **Betschdorf** where studios and shops are open to the public. Organised walking tours that include overnight stops and meals enroute are arranged from Colmar and **Mulhouse**. Bicycle trails are marked along the Rhine, where bicycles are readily available for hire. **Belfort**, a major fortress town since the 17th century, commands the **Belfort Gap**, or **Burgundy Gate**, between the **Vosges** and the **Jura** mountains. Dominating the routes from Germany and Switzerland, it became famous during the Franco-Prussian war of 1870-71 when it withstood a 108-day siege. This is commemorated by a huge stone statue, the **Lion of Belfort**, by Bartholdi, the creator of the Statue of Liberty. The 'route du vin' lies between the Rhine and a low range of pine-covered mountains called the **Vosges**. The flat, peaceful plain is covered with orchards and vineyards. Lovely, rural villages dot the landscape, their church spires piercing the horizon. The wines of Alsace have a long history; the Alsatian grapes were planted before the arrival of the Romans. It has never been clearly understood where they originated; unlike other French wines, these depend more on grape type than soil or processing. Almost exclusively white with a fruity and dry flavour, they make an excellent accompaniment to the local food. Beer also goes well with Alsatian food, and as might be expected, good beer is brewed in both the Alsace and the Lorraine areas. There are famous and popular mineral water sources in **Contréxeville** and **Vittel** (also a spa town). They were well known and appreciated by the Romans and today are the most popular in France. One of the food specialities of Alsace is *truite bleue*, blue trout, which is simply boiled so fresh as to be almost alive when tossed into the water. The swift rivers provide gamey trout and they can be fished by visitors if permits are obtained (at any city hall). The cooking is peppery and hearty and quite unlike that of any other

French region. *Munster*, a strong winter cheese, is usually served with caraway seeds. Lorraine and Alsatian tarts are made with the excellent local fruits: *mirabelles* (small, yellow plums), cherries, pears, and so on. Each of these fruits also makes a world-renowned *eau-de-vie*, a strong white alcohol liqueur drunk as a digestive after a heavy meal. Lorraine is famous for *quiche lorraine* made only in the classical manner: with cream, eggs and bacon. Nancy has *boudin* (blood sausage), although this is found in all parts of France.

BURGUNDY & FRANCHE-COMTÉ

Burgundy begins near **Auxerre**, a small medieval town with a beautiful Gothic cathedral, and extends southward to the hills of Beaujolais just north of Lyon. The *départements* are the Yonne, Côte d'Or, Nièvre and the Saône-et-Loire. Driving through this region, one seems to be traversing a huge *carte des vins*: Mersault, Volnay, Beaune, Aloxe Corton, Nuits-Saint-Georges, Vosne-Romanée and Gevrey-Chambertin. This vast domain of great wines was an independent kingdom for 600 years, at times as strong as France itself, enjoying its heyday in the 15th century. Throughout a stormy history, however, Burgundy's vineyards survived thanks in large part to the knowledge, diligence and good taste of its monks. Several of the orders owned extensive vineyards throughout the region, among them the Knights of Malta, Carthusians, Carmelites and, most importantly, the Benedictines and Cistercians. As a result, the 210km (130 mile) length of Burgundy is peppered with abbeys, monasteries and a score of fine Romanesque churches, notably in **Fontenay**, **Vézelay**, **Tournus** and **Cluny**. There are also many fortified châteaux. **Dijon**, an important political and religious centre during the 15th century, has several fine museums and art galleries, as well as the **Palais des Ducs**, once the home of the Dukes of Burgundy. There are also elegant restored town houses to be visited, dating from the 15th to the 18th century, and a 13th-century cathedral. The towns of **Sens** and **Macon** both possess fine churches dating from the 12th century.
The region of Franche-Comté is shaped like a fat boomerang and is made up of the *départements* of Doubs, Jura, Haute Saône and Territoire de Belfort. The high French **Jura Mountains**, rising in steps from 245 to 1785m (805-5856ft), run north-south along the French-Swiss border. To the west is the forested Jura plateau, the vine-clad hills and eventually the fertile plain of northern Bresse, called the **Finage**. The heights and valleys of the Jura are readily accessible and, in the summertime, beautifully green, providing pasture land for the many milk cows used in the production of one of the great mountain cheeses: *Comté*. There are many lovely (and romantically named) rivers in this region – **Semouse**, **Allance**, **Gugeotte**, **Lanterne**, Barquotte, **Durgeon**, **Colombine**, **Dougeonne**, **Rigotte** and **Romaine** (named by Julius Caesar). They weave and twist, now and then disappearing underground to reappear again some miles away. All these physical characteristics combine to make Franche-Comté an excellent region for summer vacations and winter sports.

VAL DE LOIRE

One of France's most famous regions is the Loire Valley, the former playground of the French monarchs, whose traces and grand palaces attract visitors today. The 'centre' of France from Chartres to Châteauroux and from Tours to Bourges includes the *départements* of Eure-et-Loir, Loiret, Loir-et-Cher, Indre, Indre-et-Loire and Cher. The Central Loire includes the famous *Châteaux* country, perhaps the region most visited by foreign tourists to France. Through it flows a part of the **Loire River**, the longest river in France, and considered to be its most capricious, often reducing to a mere trickle of water in a bed of sand. It has been called a 'useless' great river, because it drives no turbines or mill wheels and offers few navigable waterways. It could be said that the Loire serves only beauty and each of its tributaries has its own character. The **Cher** is a quiet, slow-moving river, flowing calmly through grassy meadows and mature forests. The château of **Chenonceaux** stands quite literally on the river; a working mill in the early medieval period when the Cher flowed more vigorously, it was transformed into perhaps the most graceful of all French châteaux, its court rooms running clear from one bank to the other on a row of delicate arches. Chenonceaux's development owed much to a succession of beautiful and powerful noblewomen, and its charm is of an undeniably feminine nature. The **Indre** is a river of calm reflections. Lilies abound and weeping willows sway on its banks. The château at **Azay-le-Rideau** was designed to make full use of these qualities and stands beside several small manmade lakes, each reflecting a different aspect of the building. Water is moved to and from the river and between the lakes through a series of gurgling channels. The water gardens and its reflections of the intricately carved exterior more than compensate for the rather dull interior. The **Vienne** is essentially a broad stream. It glides gracefully beneath the weathered walls of old **Chinon**, where several important chapters in French history were acted out. The château of

Credit: © Office de Tourisme de Bordeaux

Blois, which is - architecturally speaking - one of the finest, is certainly the most interesting in terms of history. It stands in the centre of the ancient town of the same name, towering over the battered stone houses clustered beneath its walls. **Chambord**, several miles south of the Loire, is the most substantial of the great châteaux. Standing in a moat in the centre of a vast lawn bordered by forests, the body of the building possesses a majestic symmetry. In contrast, the roofscape is a mad jumble of eccentric chimneys and apartments. Some have attributed the bizarre double-helix staircase to Leonardo da Vinci. The five châteaux described above are generally ranked highest amongst the Loire châteaux and form the core of most organised tours. There are, of course, dozens more that can be visited and it is even possible to stay overnight in several of them. The Loire Valley is very warm and crowded with tourists in summer.
Besides châteaux, there is much else of interest in the Loire Valley and surrounding districts. There are magnificent 13th-century cathedrals in **Chartres** and **Tours**, as well as abbeys and mansions and charming riverside towns and villages. Other places of outstanding interest include **Orléans**, famous for its associations with Jeanne d'Arc, with a beautiful cathedral, the **Musée des Beaux Arts** and 16th-century **Hôtel de Ville**; and **Bourges**, a 15th-century town complete with old houses, museums and the **Cathedral of St-Étienne**. The charming little town of Loches, southeast of Tours, has a fine château and an interesting walled medieval quarter. It was in the heartland of the **Touraine** that the true cuisine of France developed (Touraine was given the name 'the garden of France').

WESTERN LOIRE

The region of the Western Loire comprises the *départements* of Loire-Atlantique, Maine et Loire, Mayenne, Sarthe and the Vendée. The Vendée and the Loire-Atlantique share a beautiful and wild coastline with Brittany. There are 305km (190 miles) of sandy beaches. Inland, the mild climate makes for beautiful mature pastures, often made more attractive by clumps of wild camelias and roses.
In the Western Loire, **La Baule**, a summer resort with a fine, seemingly endless beach, is a pleasant town with winding streets and giant pines, excellent hotels, restaurants and a casino. It has an unusually mild microclimate and is exceptionally warm for the region. **Le Mans**, famous for its racetrack, is an historic old town built on a hill overlooking the west bank of the **Sarthe**. The 12th-century choir in the **Cathedral of Saint-Julian** is one of the most remarkable in France. The magnificent 13th- and 14th-century stained glass is also impressive. Most of the Sarthe Valley consists of beautifully wooded hills, divided by the thick hedges that are seasonally draped with wild roses, honeysuckle, or large juicy blackberries. In May or early June, the apple and pear blossoms blend with the hawthorn; the orchards are in bloom and the fields and forests are rich and green. These two months are most attractive and the weather at that time is usually favourable; the autumn is less dry but usually remains pleasant through October.
Nantes, on the coast of the Loire-Atlantique, is a thriving commercial and industrial centre. There is a medieval castle, which also houses the **Musée d'Art Populaire**, a display of Breton costumes; a 15th-century cathedral; and a naval museum. **St-Nazaire**, along the coast from Nantes, boasts the **Escal Atlantic**, a replica of an ocean liner containing interactive exhibits evoking the golden age of ocean travel. Upstream from Nantes, the town of **Angers** contains some spectacular tapestries. In the castle can be seen **St John's Vision of the Apocalypse** (14th century) and in the **Hôpital St-Jean**, Jean Lurcat's **Chant du Monde** (20th century). The Hôpital itself is very beautiful and there are several museums and art galleries in the town worth a visit, as well as the magnificent castle/fortress and the cathedral. The regional cuisine has the advantages of excellent vineyards, an abundance and variety of fish from the Loire and its tributaries, plentiful butter and cheese, fruits and vegetables and easily available game from the forests. In general, the wines of the Loire all have a clean refreshing taste that makes them ideal for light lunches or as an *apéritif*.

AQUITAINE & POITOU-CHARENTES

This area of sunshine and Atlantic air in the southwest of France includes the *départements* of Deux Sèvres, Vienne, Charente-Maritime, Charente, Gironde, Dordogne, Lot-et-Garonne, Landes and Pyrénées Atlantiques, the latter on the Spanish border. The coastline has 270km (170 miles) of beaches and the 30km (20 miles) or so from **Hossegor** to **Hendaye** fall within the Basque area and offer some of the best surfing in Europe.
North of Bordeaux the region of **Guyenne** is sometimes referred to as 'west-centre' as if it were a clearly defined part of France, yet a diversity of landscapes and an extraordinary mixing and mingling of races exists here – Celts, Iberians, Dutch and Anglo Saxons, to name a few. The linguistic frontier between the **langue d'oïl** and **langue d'oc** runs between **Poitiers** (former capital of the Duchy of Aquitaine) and **Limoges**, creating a dialect which developed from both. These people have in common the great north–south highway, the important line of communication between the Parisian basin and the Aquitaine basin. Throughout the centuries it was the route of many invaders: Romans, Visigoths, Alemanni, Huns, Arabs,

Normans, English, Huguenots and Catholics all moved along it. Not far from Poitiers is **Futuroscope**, which is the domestic answer to Disneyland Resort Paris, offering a huge theme park containing interactive and cinematic exhibits, as well as rides and other entertainment. **Biarritz** and **Bayonne** are both resorts on the **Aquitaine/Basque coast**, close to the Spanish border. Biarritz has been famous as a cosmopolitan spa town since the 19th century, when it was popular with the European aristocracy. There are several sheltered beaches, as well as a casino. Bayonne, a few kilometres up the coast but slightly inland, is a typical Basque town that is worth a visit. There is a 13th-century cathedral and two museums (one of them devoted to Basque culture). **Bordeaux** is on the **Garonne River** just above where it joins the Dordogne, the two streams forming an estuary called the **Gironde** which forms a natural sheltered inland harbour. It is flanked on both sides by vineyards as far as the eye can see. The combination of great wines and great wealth made Bordeaux one of the gastronomic cities of France and the city offers an impressive sight from its stone bridge with 17 arches that crowns the enormous golden horn which forms the harbour. The second-largest city of France in area, the fourth in population, the fifth port, it was described by Victor Hugo with the words: 'Take Versailles, add Antwerp to it, and you have Bordeaux'. The city is the commercial and cultural centre for all of the southwest. Its nightlife scene is fuelled by the large local student community, which, along with its eating and drinking scene and the new budget airline route to Bordeaux, is bringing more and more city-breakers into the city. South of Bordeaux along the coast is a strip of long sandy beaches backed by lagoons, some communicating with the sea, some shut off from it. Just at the back of this is the **Landes**, covered with growths of scrubby pine. Here in the marshes, the shepherds walk on stilts. The hilly region between the **Adour** and **Garonne** rivers comprises the inland part of Gascony, first known as **Aquitania Propria** and later as **Novem Populena**. It was inhabited by Vascones, or Basques who, since prehistoric times, had lived in this area and south of the Pyrénées. In the south, the Basque language has survived to this day, but the northern part of the area became known as Vasconia and then **Gascony**, a name made famous by the swashbuckling Gascons of literature: Cyrano de Bergerac, d'Artagnan of 'The Three Musketeers' and *le vert gallant* – Henri IV. In the centre of Gascony is the old countship of **Armagnac** which, like Cognac, provides the world with a magnificent brandy that bears the name of the region. The difference between the two stems from several factors: the type of grape used, the soil, the climate, the method of distilling the wine and the variety of wood used in the maturing casks. Armagnac is still made by local artisans and small farmers. The quality and taste varies much more than Cognac, but it inevitably retains its fine flavour. The **Dordogne** (and neighbouring **Lot**) is the area where traces of prehistoric (Cro-Magnon) man abound. The **Dordogne River** itself, one of the most beautiful of all French rivers, flows swiftly through the region, its banks crowded with old castles and walled towns. In **Montignac**, the fabulous painted caves of **Lascaux** are reproduced in the exact proportions and colours of the original, a few miles away. The reproduction was necessary as the original deteriorated rapidly when exposed to the heat and humidity of visitors. A highly interesting and informative museum and zoo of prehistoric artefacts and animals has been created in **Le Thot** a few miles from **Agen**. The area around **Périgueux** is a country of rivers and castles – very different from those on the Loire as these are older and, for the most part, fortified defence points against medieval invaders. There are facilities for renting horse and gypsy wagons (*roulotte à chevaux*) for slow-moving tours of the region. Along with hiking treks, river boating and bicycling tours, it offers a relaxed way to explore this beautiful land.

It is possible in Aquitaine and Poitou-Charentes to find pleasant hotels and *auberges* for an overnight or few days' stay. They range from *gîtes* and *chambre d'hôtes* – a farm bed & breakfast programme – to *châteaux hôtels* with elegant restaurants. There are no less than 150 *chambres d'hôtes* stopovers in the Poitou-Charentes region alone, including many on the coast, near beaches and pleasure ports. The area of Poitou-Charentes has lovely mature woodland and an attractive coast where oysters are cultivated. The **Charente-Maritime** is known as 'the Jade Coast', with **Royan** to the south (a fine modern resort with 13km/8 miles of fine sand beaches) and **La Rochelle** to the north. The centre of the *département* of Charente, amid low, rolling hills covered with copses of trees and vineyards, is a little town of only 22,000 inhabitants, whose name is known all over the world. Here, in an area of some 150,000 acres, the only brandy that can be called *Cognac* is produced. Use of the name is forbidden for brandy made elsewhere or from other than one of the seven officially accepted varieties of grape. The **Valois Château** located here is the birthplace of Francis I. The ancient port of **La Rochelle**, from which many pioneers left to explore the new world, is today a popular vacation and sailing port. La Rochelle is becoming more and more popular, thanks in no small part to the budget airline route to the city from London. The rivers of the region offer quiet scenic walks or boating trips. Close by, the offshore islands of **Oléron** and **Ré** are both connected to the mainland by bridges.

AUVERGNE & LIMOUSIN

West of the Rhône are the volcanic highlands of the **Massif Central**, historically known as Auvergne and consisting today of the *départements* of Haute-Loire, Cantal, Pays-de-Dôme and Allier. The Limousin region to the west comprises Haute-Vienne, Creuse and Corrèze. Architecturally, Auvergne is rich in châteaux and churches (especially in the Allier and Loire gorges) and is noted for its colourful, rich and mysterious nature. The **National Park** here offers magnificent walking country – a land of water, mountains, plains and extinct volcanoes (the Cantal crater may once have been 30km/20 miles wide). There are 10 spa resorts within its boundaries, as well as many lakes, rivers and forests. The high plateaux of **Combrailles**, **Forez** and **Bourbonnais** are very beautiful. **Clermont-Ferrand**, which is the political and economic nucleus for the whole of the Massif Central, is a lively and sprawling town and the birthplace of the Michelin tyre empire. Much of the town's architecture (especially in the older parts of the Clermont area) is black, because of the local black volcanic rock. There is a 13th-century Gothic cathedral and a 14th-century Romanesque basilica, as well as several museums. The town makes a very good base for exploring the beautiful areas around it.

There are plenty of good hôtels, *gîtes d'hôtes*, and *gîtes de France* throughout the region. The cuisine is splendid, including *cornet de Murat* (pastries), *pounti*, *truffades* and the St Nectaire cheeses. At nearby **Saint-Ours-les-Roches** is the **European Volcano Centre**, **Vulcania**, a specially designed exhibition and entertainment centre.

The 2000-year-old regional capital of Limousin, **Limoges**, is an important rail and route crossroad, famous for the production of extremely fine porcelain. The nearby city of **Aubusson** is noted for its tapestries (a local tradition dating back to the 8th century). Both cities are also famous for their enamel.

LANGUEDOC-ROUSSILLON

The combined territories of Languedoc and Roussillon include five *départements*: Aude, Gard, Hérault, Lozère and Pyrénées-Oriental. The area has been French since the 13th century and the name *languedoc* comes from *langue d'oc*, or language in which 'yes' is *oc* (as opposed to langue *d'oïl* the language in which 'yes' is *oui*). This ancient language is still heard throughout the south of France, on both sides of the Rhône. The Mediterranean coast between **Perpignan** (the ancient capital of the Kings of Mallorca) and **Montpellier** now has one of the most modern holiday complexes in Europe, including the resorts of **La Grande Motte**, **Port Leucate** and **Port Bacarès**. Montpellier itself is the city that surveys show most French people would like to live in. With its grand civic spaces, cutting-edge architecture and state-of-the-art tram system, the city offers a vision into the future of urban living. Other attractions include some excellent museums, galleries and a string of fine, good value restaurants. More wine is produced in Languedoc-Roussillon than any other place in the world. The vineyards, started in the Roman era and producing red, white and rosé wine, begin in the **Narbonne** area, run past **Béziers** (the wine marketing centre for the region) and on to Montpellier. Once an important seaport which imported spices (its name derives from 'the Mount of Spice Merchants'), the city is an important intellectual and university centre with five fine museums, impressive 17th- and 18th-century architecture and a superb summer music festival. There is a great variety of other attractions in this warm southland. The Roman (and some Gallic) ruins are often magnificent; the **Maison Carré**, **Diana's Temple** and the **Roman Arena** in **Nimes**, the Rome of the Gauls, are among the finest examples of Greco-Roman architecture to be found today. The 2000-year-old **Pont de Gard** is one of humanity's greatest architectural accomplishments and certainly merits a special trip. There is the medieval city of **Aigues-Mortes** which would still be recognisable to St Louis and his crusaders, for it was from here they embarked for the east; and the crenellated walled city of **Carcassonne** and towers of **Uzès** are unmissable. On the coast, **Sete** is Mediterranean France's largest fishing port and boasts an attractive town centre, complete with canals, beaches and bountiful restaurants and cafes. Nearby, **Agde** is a smaller fishing port whose main attraction is **Le Cap d'Agde**, with its wide expanse of unspoiled beaches and large nudist colony.

The **Canal du Midi**, ideal for cruise holidays, is a tranquil waterway, largely abandoned by commerce, that connects the Atlantic with the Mediterranean. It runs through the sleepy village of *Castelnaudary*, famous for its *cassoulet*, past the citadel of Carcassonne and on through Montpellier.

RHÔNE, SAVOIE & DAUPHINY

This region includes the French Alps and their foothills, and the vast long valleys of the Rhône and Saône rivers. The *départements* are Loire, Rhône, Ain, Ardèche, Drôme, Isère, Savoie and Haute-Savoie. **Lyon**, in the deepest part of the Rhône valley, has a proud gastronomic tradition. More and more city-breakers are flocking to the city on gastronomic trips, exploring the city's myriad of eating and drinking opportunities, opportunities that many locals and visiting foodies argue more than match those of Paris. France's second city, Lyon is a major cultural, artistic, financial and industrial centre, with international festivals and trade fairs. The **Cathedral of St Jean** is well worth a visit, as are the Roman remains of the city and the **Musée de la Civilisation Gallo-Romaine**. The French Alps stretch across Savoie and Dauphiny on the border with Italy. Napoleon came this way after escaping from Elba in 1815. Landing with 100 men near Cannes, he intended to march along the coast to Marseille and up the Rhône Valley to Lyon and Paris, but he received reports that the population on that route was hostile and was forced instead to head inland through the mountains. They reached **Gap** (150km/93 miles) from the coast) in four days, **Grenoble** a few days after and arrived in Paris (1152km/715 miles) from Cannes) in 20 days with a large and loyal army in tow. It is possible to retrace his route, which passes through much beautiful scenery; each stopping place is clearly marked. The Alps have demanded much of France's engineers and some of the roads and railways are themselves tourist attractions. Notable examples include the 9km (6 mile) steam locomotive run from **La Rochette** to **Poncharra** (about 40km/24 miles from Grenoble); and the 32km (19 mile) track (electrified in 1903) from **Saint-Georges-de-Commiers** to **la Mira** (near Grenoble), with 133 curves, 18 tunnels and 12 viaducts. As in most mountainous regions of the world, white-water boating (*randonnées nautiques*) can be enjoyed on many of the Alpine rivers. Hiking is popular and well organised, utilising the GR (*grandes randonnées* or main trails) maps that show where the official marked trails pass. The rivers racing from the Alpine heights into the Rhône provide a great deal of electrical power and good opportunities for trout fishing. The *Fédération des associations agréées de Pêche et de Pisciculture de la Drôme* in Valence can lead a fisherman to the right spot (HQ in Valence, but branches in 36 cities). Skiing, however, is the principal sport in the French Alps. The best skiing is found, for the most part, west of Grenoble and south of Lake Geneva. All the resorts are well equipped, and provide warm, comfortable lodgings and good food. Some specialise in skiing all year round, but almost all have summer seasons with facilities such as golf courses, tennis courts, swimming pools and natural lakes. At the lake resort of **Annecy**, there is an unusual **Bell Museum** with a very fine restaurant attached; international festivals of gastronomy are held throughout the year.

MIDI-PYRÉNÉES

The Midi-Pyrénées area, with its magnificent mountain scenery, lies between Aquitaine to the west and Languedoc-Roussillon to the east. It encompasses part of the Causses, the high plateau country and most of Gascony. Included in it are the *départements* of Lot, Aveyron, Tarn-et-Garonne, Tarn, Gers, Haut-Garonne, Ariège and Hautes Pyrénées. This is a land of plains dotted with hillocks, sandy stretches, moors and pine woods, desolate plateaux cleft by magical grottos, and little valleys covered with impenetrable forests. The northeastern section is a rough, mountainous land, known as the *Rouergue*. It is situated on the frontier of Aquitaine, formed by the plateau of the *Causse*, where game and wild birds feed on the thyme and juniper growing wild in the chalky soil. As a result, these little animals and birds develop a delicious and individual flavour. The principal town, **Rodez**, is severe and beautiful. The crenelated summit of its red tower, one of the marvels of French Gothic architecture, rises above a confusion of narrow streets and small squares. From here, there are views of the high plateaux beyond the Aveyron, a majestically stark landscape of granite outcrops and steep ravines. The villages and farmhouses, built of local rock, often mimic the rock formations to the extent that they are all but invisible to outsiders.

To the southeast is **Millau**, gateway to the Tarn gorges, and to the south lies **Roquefort** with its windy caves that store the famous ewe's-milk cheese. These damp cold winds are the secret that has created the 'cheese of kings and the king of cheeses'. **Auch** was the ancient metropole of the Roman **Novem Populena**, one of the most important towns in Gaul, long rivalling *Burdigala* (Bordeaux) in importance. The cathedral has two Jesuit towers, choirstalls carved in solid oak and a 16th-century stained glass window. The people of Auch have erected a statue to *le vrai d'Artagnan* ('the real d'Artagnan'), the famous Gascon musketeer immortalised by Dumas. **Cahors**, situated on a peninsula formed by the **River Lot**, has a famous bridge, **Pont Valentré**, with its six pointed arches and three defensive towers rising 40m (130ft) above the river. It is the most magnificent fortified river span that has survived in Europe and was begun in 1308. Legend has it that the construction work was plagued with problems and the bridge still remained unfinished after 50 years. Then one of the architects made a pact with the devil and the bridge was finished without another hitch. A small figure of the devil is still visible on the central tower. A fine, very dark red wine bears the name *Cahors*. It is made from grapes of the Amina variety brought in from Italy in Roman times. **Toulouse**, one of the most interesting cities of France, is an agricultural market centre, an important university town, an aero-research centre and one of the great cities of French art (it has seven fine museums). After the Middle Ages, the stone quarries in the region were exhausted so the city was built with a soft red brick which seems to absorb the light. As a result, it is called the **Ville Rose** and is described as 'pink in the light of dawn, red in broad daylight and mauve by twilight'. There are many beautiful public buildings and private dwellings, like the 16th-century Renaissance **Hôtel d'Assezat** and one known as the **Capitole**, now used as a city hall. The finest Romansque church in southern France is here. The first Gothic church west of the Rhône was built in Toulouse, the **Church of the Jacobins**; and the first Dominican monastery was founded in Toulouse by Saint Dominic himself. Toulouse is a vibrant city with much activity, with its long rue Alsace-Lorraine being its axis. It is here in the early evenings that Toulousians and visitors alike sit for an apéritif at one of the large sidewalk cafes. The region was an important part of the Roman Empire, subjected for 800 years to Arabic influence (the Moors holding substantial parts of Spain just across the Pyrénées) and the cuisine has therefore developed from both Roman and Arabic. Toulouse sausage, a long fat soft sausage whose filling must be chopped by hand, is one of the ingredients of the local *cassoulet* as well as a very popular dish in its own right. **Albi** is another red-brick city, smaller but no less interesting than Toulouse, located on the **River Tarn**. The first extraordinary thing about Albi is its brick church. Albi was the centre of violent religious wars (the Albigensian Heretics resisted the Catholic crusaders for decades). The mammoth red-brick **Cathedral of Saint-Cécile**, towering above all the other buildings of the town, was built as a fortress to protect the cruel bishop who imposed the church on the populace. Inside is a vast hall, subdivided by exquisite stonework embellished with statues. The nearby 13th-century **Palace of the Archbishop** (also fortified) is now a museum containing the largest single collection of the works of Toulouse-Lautrec. The town of **Lourdes** has acted as a magnet for the sick in need of miracle cures, ever since the visions of Bernadette Soubirous in the mid 19th century. Apart from the famous grotto, there is a castle and a museum.

PROVENCE

Spectacular weather is one of the major attractions of *Provence*, whose *départements* comprise Hautes Alpes, Alpes de Haute Provence, Var, Vaucluse and Bouches du Rhône. The deep blue skies of summer are seldom clouded, although there is some rain in spring and autumn. The only inhospitable element is the *mistral*, a wind that sometimes roars down the Rhône Valley, often unrelenting for three or four days. When the Romans arrived in Gaul, they were so delighted with the climate of the Bouches du Rhône that they made it a province rather than a colony, which was more usual. The varied flora that has taken root in this land has given it the hues of pewter, bronze, dark green and vibrant green. The sun has baked the dwellings to shades of ochre and rose while the deep red soil has provided tiles that remain red, defying the searing rays of the Midi sunshine. The towns, their architecture, stones and tiles all blend subtly throughout Provence with the majestic plane trees in the streets and squares. Their long heavy trunks of mottled greys and the graceful vaulting of the heavily leafed branches create a peculiar atmosphere not found anywhere else. These are the principal adornments of most of the cities, market towns and villages, casting a deep blue shade on the inhabitants, the mossy fountains, cafe terraces and games of *pétanque*. The eras of Greek and Roman domination of Provence have left monuments scattered across the countryside. They include walled hill towns, triumphal arches, theatres, colosseums, arenas, bridges and aqueducts. Christianity brought the **Palace of the Popes** in **Avignon**, many churches and hundreds of roadside shrines or 'oratories' which have given the name *oradour* to many communities along the Rhône. Near Avignon is **Orange** with its stunning **Roman ampitheatre** and Roman ruins. Christian art of the highest quality is scattered throughout the area from **Notre-Dame-des-Doms** in Avignon to **Notre-Dame-du-Bourg** in **Digne** in the centre of the lower alps. The pilgrims throughout the territory built wonderful churches typified by graceful semi-circular arches, round rose windows, statues of Christ surrounded by evangelists, saints, the damned in chains and processions of the faithful. These are carved in stone, so worn by the sun and wind they almost have the quality of flesh. Many of the towns and villages are marked by fortified castles and watchtowers to guard against the coming of the Saracens, the Corsairs of the Rhône and marauding bands. For this was the invasion route, by land from the north and by sea from the south. **Tarascon**, **Beauclair**, **Villeneuve**, **Gourdon**, **Entrevaux**, **Sisteron** and many others had their 'close' and tower situated high above the river or overlooking the sea. **Marseille** was founded by the Greeks (they called it Massalia) and used as a base for their colonisation of the Rhône Valley. Today, it is France's most important commercial port on the Mediterranean and consequently many people, often who have never been, dismiss it is an ugly port city. This does Marseille no justice at all as it actually offers a mass of things to do, a vibrant cosmopolitan ambience and some top-class culinary experiences. Marseille is France's most energetic city: a living, throbbing mass of cultures – far more melting pot than salad bowl – unlike many of the country's other major cities. The TGV Sud line from Paris, and a regular budget airline route from London have both helped to bring the city the recognition it has long deserved. There are many sites of interest – the old port, the hilltop church of **Notre-Dame-de-la-Garde**, several museums, **Le Corbusier's Unité d'Habitation**, the **Hospice de la Vieille Charité** and, of course, the **Château d'If**, one of the most notorious of France's historic island fortresses. Vast oil refineries and depots dominate the sparsely populated salt flats and marshes to the north and west of the city, but the land is not yet dead. It is the perfect habitat for several species of birds found in only a few other places in Eastern Europe, including bustards and nightjars. On the far side of the Rhône is the wild, marshy area known as the **Camargue**, long used for the breeding of beef cattle and horses, for the evaporation of sea water to make salt and, more recently, for growing rice. The cattle breeders, or cowboys, are armed with lances instead of lassos. Vast flocks of waterbirds nest here in a national bird reserve, among them pink flamingos and snow-white egrets. When, in 123 BC, Consul Sextias Calvinus established a camp beside some warm springs in the broad lower Rhône Valley, it was named Aquae Sextiae – today known as **Aix-en-Provence**. Other interesting ancient sites are the ruined Roman aqueduct at Pont du Gard and the amphitheatre in Arles. This whole region is also fascinating since it was frequently painted by the great Post-Impressionist painters Cézanne and Van Gogh. The combination of gentle light and breathtaking scenery finds echoes throughout the art galleries of the world. Near Arles is **Les Baux**, a haunting medieval hilltop village. The many olive trees found throughout Provence provide a popular fruit and one of the important staples of the local cuisine, a fine olive oil used extensively in the cooking of local food. Garlic, though not exclusively associated with Provence, is used more here than in any other part of France. It is sometimes called 'the truffle of Provence'. A third element, the tomato, seems to get into most of the delicious Provençal concoctions as well. The cooking here varies from region to region. In the Camargue a characteristic dish is *estouffade de boeuf*. Marseille is noted for a dish called *pieds et paquets* ('feet and packages') which consists of sheep's tripe stuffed with salt pork and cooked overnight in white wine with onions, garlic and parsley. *Trie à la Niçoise* is similar, but nonetheless unique. Perhaps the most typical dish, and one found in most parts of Provence, is *tomates provençales*, a heavenly concoction with all the Provençal specialities: olive oil, garlic and parsley baked in and on a tomato. This combination can also be applied to courgettes and aubergines. All of these vegetables, along with sweet peppers, are found in the most famous Provençal vegetable *ragoût* known, for some long lost reason, as *ratatouille*, this too being well laced with garlic and, of course, cooked in olive oil. Mayonnaise, also, well mixed with Provençal garlic, becomes *aioli*, which is served with boiled vegetables and/or fish. *Gigot* (leg of lamb) is a more common local speciality. Surviving into the era of *nouvelle cuisine* and still the pride of the Provençal coast is the famous fish stew called *bouillabaisse*. Like *cassoulet* in Languedoc, there are several versions, each claiming to be the 'authentic' one. The ingredients are not vastly different – having to do with the amount of saffron or the inclusion or exclusion of certain fish. Few wines are grown in Provence, although some are quite good, especially those originating in the Lubéron. The four districts that have been granted recognition are best known for their rosé wines: *Cassis*, *Bandol*, *Bellet* and *la Palette*. They are all on the coast, except la Palette, which is near Aix.

CÔTE D'AZUR

The **Côte d'Azur**, or French Riviera, is in the *département* of the Alpes-Maritimes. It runs along the coast from the Italian border, through Monaco, and continues to a point just beyond Cannes and reaches more than 50km (30 miles) northward into the steep slopes of the Alps, connecting the balmy coastal region with the ideal ski resorts of the lower Alps. This part of the Mediterranean coast has more visitors each year during July and August than any other part of France, although many of the summer visitors are French. The two most famous French resorts, Cannes and Nice, are to be found here, and the area is one of the most renowned resort spots in the world. Over the centuries, it has attracted a lot more than tourists, with artists like Matisse, Picasso, Chagall and Dufy heading here. There is an abundance of

palm trees, blue sea and beautiful beaches; sparkling cities and villages are set against backdrops of high green mountains. The weather is wonderful with long, hot and sunny summers. There is plenty of diversion here, especially in the spring, summer and early autumn months. The coastal resort towns include: **Cannes**, made popular as a resort by Lord Brougham in the 19th century when, because of a plague in Nice, he was forced to stop here; **Nice**, itself, the largest metropolis on the coast, a thriving commercial city as well as a year-round resort (the annual carnival and battle of roses perhaps date back to 350 BC); **Napoule Plage**, a small and exclusive resort with several sandy beaches, a marina and a splendid view of the rolling green **Maure Mountains**; **Golfe-Juan**, now a popular resort town with many expensive mansions and hotels; **Juan-les-Pins**, with a neat harbour, beaches and pine forests in the hills which protect the village from the winds in both summer and winter; **Antibes** and **Cap d'Antibes**, very popular but expensive resorts; **Villefranche-sur-Mer**, a deep-water port which has been used by pleasure yachts and navies for centuries; **St-Jean-Cap-Ferrat**, an exclusive and expensive resort consisting of great private mansions and seaside estates; **Beaulieu**, much less exclusive, yet a fine resort town; and **Menton** (near the Principality of Monaco), once a fishing village and citrus-fruit-producing area, now a pleasant vacation resort. Despite their reputations, there is no denying that the beaches at Cannes and Nice are poor, and many savvy travellers choose to base themselves at better spots like Antibes, which offers a combination of historic town centre and accessible, good-quality beaches. The Côte d'Azur is an extraordinary playground with every kind of amusement. There are excellent museums, historic places dating from the pre-Christian era to the present day, hills, mountains, lakes and rivers, gorges and alpine skiing trails. The entire area has a generous supply of good, comfortable hotels as well as luxury châteaux, restaurants with every sort of food, and good bars everywhere. One of the greatest museums in the world, the **Maeght Foundation**, is located in **St-Paul-de-Vence**. Picasso, Braque, Matisse and Léger museums also feature and there is plenty of beautiful foothill countryside to explore. Resorts further along the coast from Cannes include **St-Tropez**, a terribly crowded, hard to reach yet fashionable village (popular with the international jet set and their outrageously expensive yachts) and **Port Grimaud**. The 'Port', as many residents call it, sums up many of the worst parts of the Riviera with ostentatious wealth not making up for a lack of any local input, a dearth of nightlife beyond 'British' pubs and a largely ex-patriate population. Nearby are **St-Raphael**, at one time a Roman resort, and now a comfortable middle-class vacation town, and its twin resort of **Frejus**. **Grasse**, just north of Cannes, is a charming hilltop town famed for its perfume.

CORSICA

The island of Corsica is made up of two French *départements*: **Haute Corse** (upper Corsica) and **Corse du Sud** (south Corsica). The 8720 sq km (3367 sq miles) are inhabited by not many more than 250,000 people. It is one of the very few places left in Europe that is not invaded by campers and trailers during the vacation season and its charm lies in this unspoiled and rugged atmosphere. The name Corsica, or *Corse*, is a modernisation of *Korsai*, believed to be a Phoenician word meaning 'covered with forests'. The Phoenician Greeks landed here 560 years before the Christian era to disturb inhabitants who had probably originated in Liguria. From that time on, Corsica has been fought for, or over, creating a bloody history probably unparalleled for such a small area. The Greeks were followed by the Romans, then the Vandals, Byzantines, Moors and Lombards. In 1768, Genoa sold Corsica to France and its 2500 years of disputed ownership ended. In spite of its

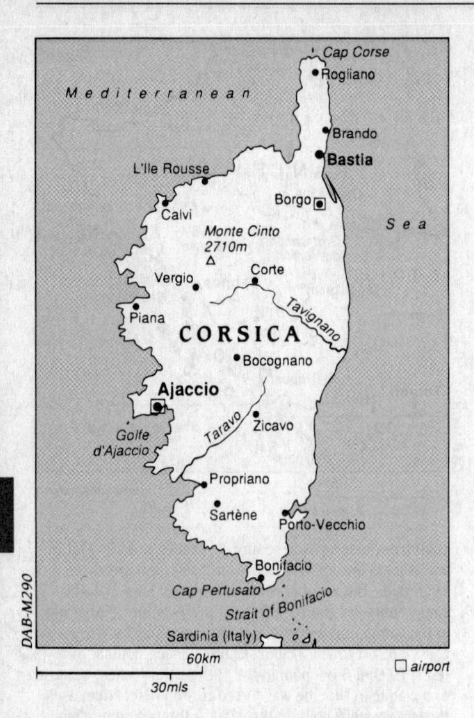

extensive and colourful history, it is of course best known as the birthplace of Napoléon Bonaparte. The island has been described as 'a mountain in the sea', for when approached by sea that is exactly what it looks like. A strange land, the mountains rise abruptly from the western shore where the coast is indescribably beautiful with a series of capes and isolated beachless bays; along its entire length rock and water meet with savage impact. The coastline, unfolded, is about 992km (620 miles) long. Corsica consists of heaths, forests, granite, snow, sand beaches and orange trees. This combination has produced a strange, fiery, lucidly intellectual and music-loving race of people, both superstitious and pious at the same time. The interior is quite undeveloped, with mountains, and dry scrubby land overgrown with brush called *maquis* (from the local *maccia* which means 'brush'). It is a dry wilderness of hardy shrubs – arbutus, mastic, thorn, myrtle, juniper, rosemary, rock rose, agave, pistachio, fennel, heather, wild mint and ashphodel, 'the flower of hell'. During the Geman occupation of France (1940-44), resistance fighters were given the name *maquis* from the association of the wild country in which they hid, much as the savage backlands of Corsica provided at one time comparatively safe shelter for the island bandits. There is a desolate grandeur about the *maquis*, while, on the other hand, the rugged beauty of Corsica's magnificent mountain scenery is anything but desolate. A considerable amount of forested area remains, although, since discovered by the Greeks, it has been frequently raided for its fine, straight and tall *laricio* pine that seems to thrive only here. They have been known to grow as high as 60m (200ft), perfect for use as masts and are still used as such. Corsica is also rich in cork oaks, chestnuts and olives. There is a **Regional Nature Conservation Park** on the island. North of the eastern plain are the lowlands, principally olive groves, known as **La Balagne**, the hinterland of **Calvi** and **l'Ile Rousse**. To the south is the dazzling white city of **Ajaccio**, full of Napoleonic memorabilia. The town runs in a semicircle on the calm bay, set against a backdrop of wooded hills.

At the foot of the cape at the northern end of the island is the commercial, but none the less picturesque, town of **Bastia**, with its historic citadel towering over the headland. The old town has preserved its streets in the form of steps connected by vaulted passages, converging on the **Vieux Port**. The port itself, with a polyglot population, is busy all year round. A little further north, the terraced **St Nicholas Beach**, shaded by palm trees and covered with parasols and cafe tables, separates the old port from the new. The new port, just beyond, is the real commercial port of the island.

Corsican cuisine is essentially simple, with the sea providing the most dependable source of food, including its famous lobster. Freshwater fish abound in the interior and, as is to be expected, the *maquis* is game country. The aromatic herbs and berries add a particularly piquant flavour to the meat. Among the game available, *sanglier* and *marcassin* – young and older wild boar – turn up in season either roasted, stewed in a *daube* of red wine, or with a highly spiced local *pibronata* sauce. Sheep and goats are plentiful. Pigs, fed on chestnuts, are common at the Corsican table and they make an unusually flavoured ham. The extremes of the Corsican climate limit the variety of vegetables available. The Corsicans like hot and strong flavours that use even more herbs than are used in Provence. They like to shock with hot peppers and strong spices. A fish soup called *dziminu*, like *bouillabaise* but much hotter, is made with peppers and pimentos. Inland freshwater fish is usually grilled and the local eels, called *capone*, are cut up and grilled on a spit over a charcoal fire. A peppered and smoked ham, called *prizzutu*, resembles the Italian *prosciutto*, but with an added chestnut flavour. A favourite between-meal snack is *figatelli*, a sausage made of dried and spiced pork with liver. Placed between slices of a special bread, these are grilled over a wood fire. Red wine is available in abundance, but white and rosé are also produced on the island.

Sport & Activities

Watersports: France has over 3000km (1880 miles) of coastline, ranging from the rugged English Channel and Atlantic coasts in the north and west to the sunny shores of the French Riviera (*Côte d'Azur*) along the Mediterranean in the south. All types of watersports are available, although the warm climate of the Mediterranean provides obvious advantages, with **swimming** in the sea possible practically all year round. **Diving** and **snorkelling** are popular in Porquerolles and Corsica. The colder English Channel and Atlantic waters are popular with **sailing** enthusiasts, and Biarritz is renowned for good **surfing**. The Côte d'Azur offers the possibility of sailing to Corsica.

Canal cruises: France is criss-crossed by some 8500km (5313 miles) of canals and rivers, and **houseboats** can be rented easily. Popular itineraries include the Lorient-Redon route (along the former route of the Brittany invasions); Marne-Strasbourg (through the vineyards of Champagne to the Alsace-Lorraine canals); the Burgundy Canal (a popular wine route); and Bordeaux-Sète (a 500km/313 mile-journey from the Atlantic to the Mediterranean along the Canal du Midi). Boats can be rented from numerous private operators who can also arrange the necessary permits. Most vessels sleep between two and 12 people. The return journey is usually via the same route; one-way trips are possible but involve extra costs.

Fishing: Good fishing regions include Brittany (salmon and trout), Franche-Comté (which has many lakes), Languedoc-Roussillon (mountain fishing), and Midi-Pyrénées (famous for the *fario* trout). Trips with local fishermen are possible along the Atlantic coast. Popular catches include crayfish, lobster, scallops and, at low tide, crabs, shrimps and mussels. Deep-sea-fishing trips are widely available on the Côte d'Azur. Permits for river fishing can be obtained from local city halls.

Skiing: The French Alps offer excellent skiing with some of the world's best-known resorts. There are over 480km (300 miles) of ski *pistes*, over 150 ski lifts, innumerable ski schools and quality resort facilities. All the major resorts offer skiing package holidays. The season runs from early December to the end of April. The height of the season is during February and March, which is reflected in the higher prices. SNCF, in association with the French Association of Resorts and Sports Goods Retailers (AFMASS), organises skiing holidays. Packages are only marketed in France; contact SNCF on arrival.

Hiking: There are thousands of miles of carefully marked trails in France. These are known as *Sentiers de Grande Randonnée*, and are generally marked on maps as well as being recognisable by a red and white logo marked *GR*. The hiking routes are complemented by an extensive network of *gîtes* and mountain refuges providing inexpensive but comfortable accommodation. A *Guide des Gîtes de France* is available from bookshops.

Cycling: French towns and cities are actively promoting the use of bicycles. There are some 28,000km (17,500 miles) of marked cycling paths throughout the country. Bicycles can be hired from many local tourist offices, and French Railways (SNCF) also offers bicycles for hire at some 30 stations. There is an extensive network of *pistes cyclables* (cycling paths) along the Atlantic coast, all the way down to the Spanish border.

Horseriding: Although popular and available countrywide, one of France's favourite destinations for horseriding is the Camargue where even inexperienced riders can gallop along sandy beaches and through the characteristic marshland. Horses can be hired from numerous stables.

Golf: There are over 200 golf courses. A number of companies are offering themed golf holidays which combine golfing with other activities as well as sightseeing. Popular destinations include the Loire Valley, Burgundy and the French Alps.

Spectator sports: The most popular are **rugby** and **football**, which the French follow passionately. Emotions exploded to fever pitch when France won the football World Cup in 1998. The *Tour de France* **cycling** race during summer is one of the world's most prestigious cycling races and a favourite spectator event. The French Open at *Roland Garros* near Paris is one of the four Grand Slam **tennis** tournaments and attracts all the world's top players as well as drawing huge crowds. Another notable event on the French sports calendar is the 24-hour **motor race** at Le Mans. The highlight of the **horse racing** calendar is the *Prix de l'Arc de Triomphe* held on the first Sunday in October each year. It takes place in Longchamp close to the Bois de Boulogne.

Traditional sports: Traditional **boules** (also called *pétanque*), requiring as much dexterity as social skill, is frequently played in public squares. Visitors wishing to join in may find it easier if they speak French.

Wine tours: Tailor-made tours to France's numerous wine-producing regions and *domaines* (estates) are widely available. There are 10 principal wine regions, each with its own identity based on grape varieties and *terroir* (soil). Highlights on the wine calendar include the annual appearance of *Beaujolais Nouveau* (released fresh from the cellars on the third Thursday of November); the *Vendanges* (grape harvest) festivals in Burgundy during autumn; and champagne tasting in Champagne (with many producers in Rheims and Epernay offering free samples). The wines' origins and quality are guaranteed by strict *appellation contrôlée* laws. In various regions, the most famous wine routes (*routes du vin*), as well as special sales and auctions, are signposted. Wine tours are frequently combined with **cheese tasting**. Like the wines, France's 365 cheeses vary according to region and climate. For further information, see *Food & Drink* in the *Social Profile* section. An illustrated map with details of cheeses, wines and regional dishes is available from the French National Tourist Office.

For information and detailed brochures/guides on all the sports and activities listed above, contact the French National Tourist Office (see *Contact Addresses* section) or see online (website: www.franceguide.com). Further details on regional attractions, cultural sites and major tourist resorts can be found in the *Resorts & Excursions* section.

Social Profile

FOOD & DRINK: With the exception of China, France has a more varied and developed cuisine than any other country. The simple, delicious cooking for which France is famous is found in the old-fashioned bistro and restaurant. There are two distinct styles of eating in France. One is, of course, 'gastronomy' (*haute cuisine*), widely known and honoured as a cult with rituals, rules and taboos. It is rarely practised in daily life, partly because of the cost and the time which must be devoted to it. The other is family-style cooking, often just as delicious as its celebrated counterpart. Almost all restaurants offer two types of meal: *à la carte* (extensive choice for each course and more expensive) and *le menu* (a set meal at a fixed price with dishes selected from the full *à la carte* menu). At simple restaurants, the same cutlery will be used for all courses. The bill (*l'addition*) will not be presented until it is asked for, even if clients sit and talk for half an hour after they have finished eating. Many restaurants close for a month during the summer, and one day a week. It is always wise to check that a restaurant is open, particularly on Sunday. Generally speaking, mealtimes in France are strictly observed. Lunch is, as a rule, served from 1200 to 1330, dinner usually from 2000-2130, but the larger the city, the later the dining hour. Dishes include: *tournedos* (small steaks ringed with bacon); *châteaubriand*; *entrecôte* (rib steak) served with *béarnaise* (tarragon-flavoured sauce with egg base); and *gigot de présalé* (leg of lamb roasted or broiled) served with *flageolets* (light green beans) or *pommes dauphines* (deep-fried mashed potato puffs). Other dishes include: *brochettes* (combinations of cubed meat or seafood on skewers, alternating with mushrooms, onions or tomatoes); *ratatouille niçoise* (stew of courgettes, tomatoes and aubergines, braised with garlic in olive oil); *pot-au-feu* (beef boiled with vegetables and served with coarse salt); and *blanquette de veau* (veal stew with mushrooms in a white wine/cream sauce). In the north of France (Nord/Pas de Calais and Picardy), fish and shellfish are the star features in menus – oysters, *moules* (mussels), *coques* (cockles) and *crevettes* (shrimps) are extremely popular. In Picardy, duck pâtés and *ficelle picarde* (ham and mushroom pancake) are popular. In the Champagne-Ardenne region, there are the hams of Rheims and *sanglier* (wild boar). Among the fish specialities in this area are *écrevisses* (crayfish) and *brochets* (pike). Alsace and Lorraine are the lands of *choucroute* (sauerkraut) and *kugelhof* (a special cake), *quiche lorraine* and *tarte flambée* (onion tart). Spicy and distinctive sauces are the hallmark of Breton food, and shellfish is a speciality of the region, particularly *homard à l'armoricaine* (lobster with cream sauce). Lyon, the main city of the Rhône Valley, is the heartland of French cuisine, though the food is often more rich than elaborate. A speciality of this area is *quenelles de brochet* (pounded pike formed into sausage shapes and usually served with a rich crayfish sauce). Bordeaux rivals Lyon as gastronomic capital of France. Aquitaine cuisine (in the south-west of France) is based on goosefat. A reference to 'Périgord' will indicate a dish containing truffles. Basque chickens are specially reared. In the Pyrénées, especially around Toulouse,

A B C D E F G H I J K L M N O P Q R S T U V W X Y Z

visitors will find salmon and *cassoulet*, a hearty dish with beans and preserved meat. General de Gaulle once asked, with a certain amount of pride, how it was possible to rule a country which produced 365 different kinds of cheese; some of the better known are Camembert, Brie, Roquefort, Reblochon and blue cheeses from Auvergne and Bresse. Desserts include: *soufflé grand-marnier*; *oeufs à la neige* (meringues floating on custard); *mille feuilles* (layers of flaky pastry and custard cream); *Paris-Brest* (a large puff-pastry with hazelnut cream); *ganache* (chocolate cream biscuit); and fruit tarts and flans.
For more information on the specialities from the various regions of France, consult the regional entries in the *Resorts & Excursions* section. The tourist office publishes a guide to restaurants in Paris and the Île-de-France.
Wine is by far the most popular alcoholic drink in France, and the choice will vary according to region. Cheap wine (*vin ordinaire*) can either be very palatable or undrinkable, but there is no certain way of establishing which this is likely to be before drinking. Wines are classified into AC (*Appellation Contrôlée*), VDQS (*Vin delimité de qualité superieure*), *Vin de Pays* and *Vin de Table*. There are several wine-producing regions in the country; some of the more notable are Bordeaux, Burgundy, Loire, Rhône and Champagne. In elegant restaurants, the wine list will be separate from the main menu but, in less opulent establishments, will be printed on the back or along the side of the *carte*. The waiter will usually be glad to advise an appropriate choice. In expensive restaurants, this will be handled by a sommelier or wine steward. If in doubt, try the house wine; this will usually be less expensive and will always be the owner's pride. Coffee is always served after the meal, and will always be black, in small cups, unless a *café au lait* (or *crème*) is requested. Liqueurs such as Chartreuse, Framboise and Genepi (an unusual liqueur made from an aromatic plant) are available. Many of these liqueurs, such as *eau de vie* and *calvados* (apple brandy) are very strong and should be treated with respect, particularly after a few glasses of wine. A good rule of thumb is to look around and see what the locals are drinking. Spirit measures are usually doubles unless a baby is specifically asked for. There is also a huge variety of apéritifs available. A typically French drink is *pastis*, such as Ricard or Pernod. The region of Nord/Pas de Calais and Picardy does not produce wine, but brews beer and cider. Alsace is said to brew the best beer in France but fruity white wines, such as Riesling, Traminer and Sylvaner, and fine fruit liqueurs, such as Kirsch and Framboise, are also produced in this area. The wines from the Champagne region of the Montagne de Rheims district are firm and delicate (Vevenay Verzy), or full-bodied and ful-flavoured (Bouzy and Ambonnay).
The legal age for drinking alcohol in a bar/cafe is 18. Minors are allowed to go into bars if accompanied by an adult but they will not be served alcohol. Hours of opening depend on the proprietor but, generally, bars in major towns and resorts are open throughout the day; some may still be open at 0200. Smaller towns tend to shut earlier. There are also all-night bars and cafes.
NIGHTLIFE: In major cities such as Paris, Lyon or Marseille, there are lively nightclubs that sometimes charge no entry fee, although drinks are likely to be more expensive. Alternatively, the entrance price sometimes includes a *consommation* of one drink. As an alternative to a nightclub, there are many late-night bars and cafes. Tourist offices publish an annual and monthly diary of events available free of charge. Several guides are also available which give information about entertainments and sightseeing in the capital. In the provinces, the French generally spend the night eating and drinking, although in the more popular tourist areas, there will be discos and dances. All weekend festivals in summer in the rural areas are a good form of evening entertainment. There are over 130 public casinos in the country.
SHOPPING: Special purchases include lace, crystal glass, cheeses, coffee and, of course, wines, spirits and liqueurs. Arques, the home of Crystal D'Arques, is situated between St Omer and Calais, enroute to most southern destinations. Lille, the main town of French Flanders, is known for its textiles, particularly fine lace. Most towns have fruit and vegetable markets on Saturday. Hypermarkets, enormous supermarkets which sell everything from foodstuffs and clothes to hi-fi equipment and furniture, are widespread in France. They tend to be situated just outside of town and all have parking facilities. **Shopping hours:** Department stores are open Mon-Sat 0900-1830. Some shops are closed between 1200-1430. Food shops are open 0700-1830/1930. Some food shops (particularly bakers) are open Sunday mornings, in which case, they will probably close Monday. Many shops close all day or Monday afternoon. Hypermarkets are normally open until 2100 or 2200.
SPECIAL EVENTS: For details of events and festivals throughout France, contact the French Tourist Office (website: www.franceguide.com). The following is a selection of special events occurring in France in 2005:
Until Feb 3 *Nativity*, Notre-Dame Cathedral, Paris. **Jan 8-9** *Kandahar - Alpine Skiing World Cup*. **Jan 15-Mar 8** *Dunkerque Carnival*. **Jan 28-Feb 5** *International Film Festival*. **Feb 12-27** *Nice Carnival*. **Apr 10** *Marathon*, Paris. **May** *Jazz Under the Apple Trees* (one of Normandy's most important annual music events), Coutances. **May 21-22** *Monaco Grand Prix*. **Jun 21** *Summer Solstice and Music Festivals*, countrywide. **Jul** *Tour de France*. **Jul 13-14** *Bastille Day Celebrations*. **Sep 27-Oct 10** *International Festival of Theatre, Music and Literature*, Limosin.
SOCIAL CONVENTIONS: Handshaking and, more familiarly, kissing both cheeks, are the usual forms of greeting. The form of personal address is simply *Monsieur* or *Madame* without a surname and it may take time to get on first-name terms. At more formal dinners, it is the most important guest or host who gives the signal to start eating. Mealtimes are often a long, leisurely experience. Casual wear is common but the French are renowned for their stylish sportswear and dress sense. Social functions, some clubs, casinos and exclusive restaurants warrant more formal attire. Evening wear is normally specified where required. Topless sunbathing is tolerated on most beaches but naturism is restricted to certain beaches – local tourist offices will advise where these are. Smoking is prohibited on public transport and in cinemas and theatres. Tobacconists display a red sign in the form of a double cone. A limited choice of brands can be found in restaurants and bars.
Tipping: A 12 to 15 per cent service charge is normally added to the bill in hotels, restaurants and bars, but it is customary to leave small change with the payment; more if the service has been exceptional. Other services such as washroom attendants, beauticians, hairdressers and cinema ushers expect tips. Taxi drivers expect 10 to 15 per cent of the meter fare.

Business Profile

ECONOMY: France has the fourth-largest economy in the world, after the USA, Japan and Germany, and has an annual per capita income of US$23,000. It has a wide industrial and commercial base, covering everything from agriculture to light and heavy industrial concerns, the most advanced technology and a burgeoning service sector. France is also Western Europe's leading agricultural nation with over half of the country's land area devoted to farming. Wheat is the most important crop; maize, sugar beet and barley are also produced in large quantities. The country is self-sufficient in these (which are produced in sufficient surplus for major exports) and the majority of other common crops. The livestock industry is also expanding rapidly. France is famously one of the world's leading wine producers. Despite the widespread belief in some quarters (not least the UK) that French agriculture is inefficient, the sector has regularly turned in good profit margins and a sound export performance. French companies are prominent in many industries, particularly steel, motor vehicles, aircraft, mechanical and electrical engineering, textiles, chemicals and food processing. In advanced industrial sectors, France has one of the world's largest nuclear power industries, which meets nearly three-quarters of the country's energy requirements (coal mining, once important, is in terminal decline), and is a world leader in computing and telecommunications. The service sector is dominated by tourism, which has long been a major foreign currency earner, although financial services have grown rapidly since the early 1990s.
Recent economic policy has been characterised by a gradual relinquishing of state holdings in 'strategic' industries and a steady reduction in government spending. Economic growth has been sluggish for the last two and a half years, and is still below 1 per cent. France also suffers from a relatively high unemployment rate of 10 per cent, which is climbing again after several years of decline. France was a founder member of the European Community and has benefited greatly from its participation. It was also a founder member of the European Monetary Union and adopted the euro upon its inception. The EU – especially Germany, Belgium, Italy, Spain and the UK – accounts for the bulk of French trade. Outside the EU, the USA and Japan are its principal trading partners.
BUSINESS: Businesspeople should wear conservative clothes. Prior appointments are expected and the use of calling cards is usual. While a knowledge of French is a distinct advantage in business dealings, it is considered impolite to start a conversation in French and then have to revert to English. Business meetings tend to be formal and business decisions are taken only after lengthy discussion, with many facts and figures to back up sales presentations. Business entertaining is usually in restaurants. Avoid the holiday period of mid-July to mid-September for business visits. **Office hours:** Generally Mon-Fri 0900-1200, 1400-1800.
COMMERCIAL INFORMATION: The following organisations can offer advice: Chambre de Commerce et d'Industrie de Paris, 27 Avenue de Friedland, 75382 Paris, Cedex 08 (tel: (1) 5565 5565; fax: (1) 5565 7668; e-mail: del-paris@ccip.fr; website: www.ccip.fr); *or* Centre de Renseignements des Douanes, 84 rue d'Hauteville, 75498 Paris (tel: (0825) 308 263; fax: (1) 5324 6830; e-mail: crd-ile-de-france@douane.finances.gouv.fr; website: www.douane.gouv.fr); *or* Assemblée des Chambres Francaises de Commerce et d'Industrie, 45 Avenue d'iena, 75116 Paris, Cedex 16 (tel: (1) 4069 3700; fax: (1) 4720 6128; e-mail: contactsweb@acfci.cci.fr; website: www.acfci.cci.fr).
CONFERENCES/CONVENTIONS: Paris is the world's leading conference city, with the total amount of seating available (over 100,000 seats) exceeding that of any rival city. Also in demand are the Riviera towns of Nice and Cannes (the Acropolis Centre in Nice being the largest single venue in Europe); other centres are Lyon, Strasbourg and Marseille. The Business Travel Club (CFTAR) is a government-sponsored association of cities, departments, hotels, convention centres and other organisations interested in providing meeting facilities and incentives; it has over 80 members. Enquiries should be made through the French Government Tourist Office which, in several cities, has a special department for business travel; these include London, Frankfurt/M, Düsseldorf, Milan, Madrid and Chicago. The following organisation can offer advice: Maison de la France, Conference and Incentive Department, 178 Piccadilly, London W1J 9AL (tel: (020) 7399 3521; fax: (020) 7493 6594; e-mail: rachel.sobel@franceguide.com; website: www.franceguide.com).

Climate

A temperate climate in the north; northeastern areas have a more continental climate with warm summers and colder winters. Rainfall is distributed throughout the year with some snow likely in winter. The Jura Mountains have an alpine climate. Lorraine, sheltered by bordering hills, has a relatively mild climate.
Mediterranean climate in the south; mountains are cooler with heavy snow in winter.
The Atlantic influences the climate of the western coastal areas from the Loire to the Basque region; the weather is temperate and relatively mild with rainfall distributed throughout the year. Summers can be very hot and sunny. Inland areas are also mild and the French slopes of the Pyrénées are reputed for their sunshine record.
Mediterranean climate exists on the Riviera, and in Provence and Roussillon. Weather in the French Alps is variable. Continental weather is present in Auvergne, Burgundy and the Rhône Valley. Very strong winds (such as the *mistral*) can occur throughout the entire region.
Required clothing: European, according to season.

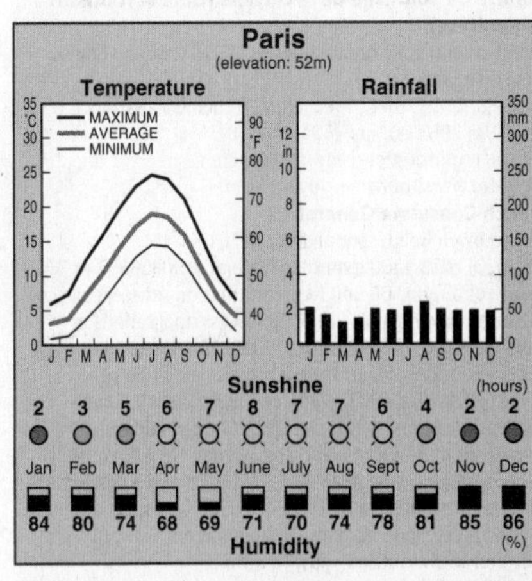

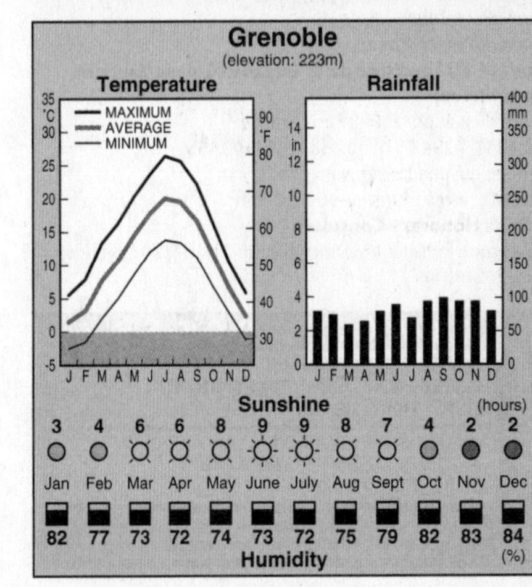

French Guiana

LATEST TRAVEL ADVICE CONTACTS

British Foreign and Commonwealth Office
Tel: (0870) 606 0290 Website: www.fco.gov.uk
US Department of State
Website: http://travel.state.gov/travel
Canadian Department of Foreign Affairs and Int'l Trade
Tel: (1 800) 267 8376 Website: www.dfait-maeci.gc.ca

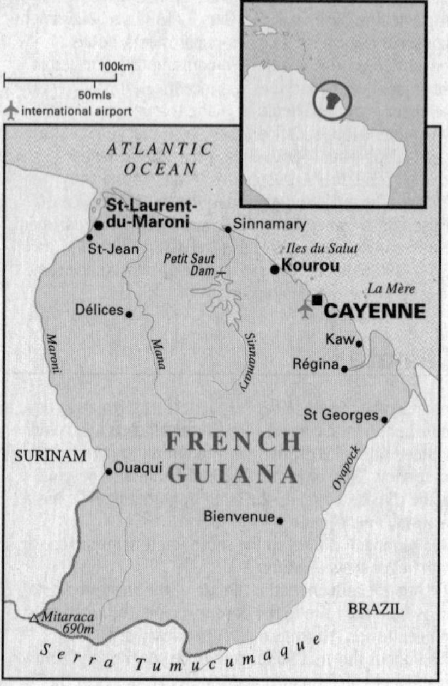

Location: South America, northeast coast.

Country dialling code: 594.

Diplomatic representation
French Guiana is an Overseas Department of the Republic of France, and is represented abroad by French Embassies – see *France* section.
Comité du Tourisme de la Guyane (Guiana Tourism Committee)
Street address: 12 rue Lallouette, 97338 Cayenne Cédex, French Guiana
Postal address: BP 801, Cayenne, French Guiana
Tel: (594) 296 500. Fax: (594) 296 501.
E-mail: ctginfo@tourisme-guyane.com
Website: www.tourisme-guyane.com
French Consulate General
21 Cromwell Road, London SW7 2EN, UK
Tel: (020) 7073 1200 (consular section) *or* (09065) 540 700 (visa section) *or* 508 940 (visa information service; calls cost £1 per minute) *or* (020) 7073 1295 (visa applications in progress; 1500-1700 only) *or* (09065) 266 654 (24-hour visa application form request service; calls cost £1.50 per minute). Fax: (020) 7073 1201 *or* (09001) 669 932 (visa application forms by fax; calls cost 60p per minute).
Visa section: 6A Cromwell Place, London SW7 2EW, UK
Opening hours: Mon-Wed 0845-1500, Thurs-Fri 0845-1200 (general enquiries); Mon-Fri 0845-1130 (visa applications).
E-mail: presse.londres-amba@diplomatie.fr
Website: www.tourisme-guyane.com *or* www.ambafrance-uk.org
Consulate General in: Edinburgh.
Comité du Tourisme de la Guyane (Guiana Tourism Committee)
1 rue Clapeyron, 75008 Paris, France
Tel: (331) 4294 1516. Fax: (331) 4294 1465.
E-mail: guyanaparis@wanadoo.fr
Website: www.tourisme-guyane.com
British Honorary Consulate
16 avenue Président Monnerville, BP 211, 97324 Cayenne, French Guiana
Tel: (594) 311 034. Fax: (594) 304 094.
The US Embassy in Paramaribo deals with enquiries relating to French Guiana (see *Surinam* section).
The Canadian High Commission in Georgetown deals with enquiries relating to French Guiana (see *Guyana* section).

TIMATIC CODES

Health	AMADEUS: **TI-DFT/JIB/HE** GALILEO/WORLDSPAN: **TI-DFT/JIB/HE** SABRE: **TIDFT/JIB/HE**
Visa	AMADEUS: **TI-DFT/JIB/VI** GALILEO/WORLDSPAN: **TI-DFT/JIB/VI** SABRE: **TIDFT/JIB/VI**

To access TIMATIC country information on Health and Visa regulations through the Computer Reservations System (CRS), type in the appropriate command line listed above.

General Information

AREA: 83,534 sq km (32,253 sq miles).
POPULATION: 156,790 (1999).
POPULATION DENSITY: 1.9 per sq km.
CAPITAL: Cayenne. **Population:** 50,594 (1999).
GEOGRAPHY: French Guiana is situated on the northeast coast of South America and is bordered by Brazil to the south and the east and by Surinam to the west. The southern Serra Tumucumaque Mountains are part of the eastern frontier, whilst the rest is formed by the River Oyapock. Surinam is to the west along the rivers Maroni-Itani and to the north is the Atlantic coastline. Along the coast runs a belt of flat marshy land behind which the land rises to higher slopes and plains or savannah. The interior is comprised of equatorial jungle. Off the rugged coast lie the Iles du Salut and Devil's Island. Cayenne, the capital and chief port, is on the island of the same name at the mouth of the Cayenne River.
GOVERNMENT: French Guiana is an Overseas Department of France and, as such, is an integral part of the French Republic. **Head of State:** President Jacques Chirac since 1995, represented locally by Prefect Ange Mancini since 2002.
LANGUAGE: The official language is French, though most of the population speak a Creole *patois*. English is also widely spoken.
RELIGION: Roman Catholic majority, although there are other Christian churches.
TIME: GMT - 3.
ELECTRICITY: 220/127 volts AC, 50Hz.
COMMUNICATIONS: Telephone: IDD available. Country code: 594. Outgoing international code: 00. **Mobile telephone:** GSM 900 network is operated by *France Caraïbe Mobiles*, and covers coastal areas and some of the interior. Handsets can be hired locally. **Fax:** Facilities are widely available, including in hotels. **Internet:** Local ISPs include *Wanadoo* (website: www.wanadoo.fr). There are Internet cafes in Cayenne. **Telegram:** Telegrams can be sent locally. A Telex service links Cayenne and Europe. **Post:** Postal services are reliable in Cayenne (where the central post office is located on route Baduel); post takes around seven days to reach western Europe. Post office hours: Mon-Fri 0730-1330. **Press:** The daily newspapers include *France-Guyane* and *La Presse de Guyane*. There are no English-language newspapers.
Radio: BBC World Service (website: www.bbc.co.uk/worldservice) and Voice of America (website: www.voa.gov) can be received. From time to time the frequencies change and the most up-to-date can be found online.

Passport/Visa

	Passport Required?	Visa Required?	Return Ticket Required?
Full British	Yes	No	Yes
Australian	Yes	No	Yes
Canadian	Yes	No/2	Yes
USA	Yes	No/2/3	Yes
Other EU	Yes/1	No/2	Yes
Japanese	Yes	No/2	Yes

Note: *Regulations and requirements may be subject to change at short notice, and you are advised to contact the appropriate diplomatic or consular authority before finalising travel arrangements. Details of these may be found at the head of this country's entry. Any numbers in the chart refer to the footnotes below.*

PASSPORTS: Passport valid for at least three months beyond applicant's last day of stay required by all except the following:
1. nationals of Belgium, France, Germany, Greece, Italy, Luxembourg, Monaco, The Netherlands, Portugal, Spain and Switzerland, who are holders of national identity cards.
VISAS: Required by all except the following:
(a) nationals of countries referred to in the chart above for stays of up to three months;
(b) nationals of Andorra, Argentina, Bolivia, Brunei, Bulgaria, Chile, Costa Rica, Croatia, El Salvador, Guatemala, Holy See, Honduras, Hong Kong (SAR), Iceland, Korea (Rep), Liechtenstein, Macau (SAR), Malaysia, Mexico, Monaco, New Zealand, Nicaragua, Norway, Panama, Paraguay, San Marino, Singapore, Switzerland, Uruguay and Venezuela for stays of up to three months;
(c) transit passengers continuing their journey by the same or first connecting aircraft, provided holding valid onward or return documentation and not leaving the airport.
Note: (a) Nationals of the EU and EEE, and of the Holy See, Liechtenstein and Monaco do not need a a long stay visa (trips exceeding three months). **2.** (b) Nationals of Canada, Cyprus, Japan, Korea (Rep), Malaysia, Malta, Mexico, Singapore, USA and Venezuela should apply for a visa if they are to receive a salary, even if their trip is a short stay. **3.** (c) US nationals need a visa if they are crew members, or journalists on assignments, or students enrolled at schools and universities in any of the French Overseas Departments.
Types of visa and cost: All visas, regardless of duration of stay and number of entries permitted, cost €35. In most circumstances, no fee applies to students, recipients of government fellowships and citizens of the EU and their family members.
Validity: *Short-stay* (up to 30 days): valid for two months (single- and multiple-entry). *Short-stay* (31 to 90 days and double- or multiple-entry): valid for a maximum of six months from date of issue. *Transit*: valid for single- or multiple-entries of maximum five days per entry, including the day of arrival.
Application to: French Consulate General (for personal visas), or Consular section at Embassy (for diplomatic or service visas); see *Contact Addresses* section for France. All applications must be made in person.
Application requirements: (a) Valid passport with blank page to affix the visa. Minors travelling alone must submit notarised parental authorisation, signed by both parents, plus one copy. (b) Up to two completed application forms. (c) One passport-size photo on each form. (d) Fee, to be paid in cash only if paying by person. If not, fee should be paid by cheque or postal order. (e) Evidence of sufficient funds for stay (two last bank statements, plus copy, or other proof of funds equivalent to US$100 for each day of trip). (f) Letter from employer, or proof of stay in country of residence. (g) Proof of address. (h) Medical insurance. (i) Return ticket and travel documents for remaining journey. (j) Proof of accommodation during stay. (k) Registered self-addressed envelope, if applying by post. (l) Detailed itinerary, including reservations and round-trip airline tickets (only required when visa is issued), plus one copy. (m) Proof of employment (eg last payslip or letter from employer). (n) Proof of valid health/travel insurance with worldwide coverage, plus copy. *Business*: (a)-(n) and, (o) Business invitation guaranteeing payment of travel expenses, plus one copy.
Working days required: One day to three weeks, depending on nationality.
Temporary residence: If intending to work or stay for longer than 90 days, nationals should contact the long stay visa section of the Consulate General or Embassy (tel: (020) 7073 1248).

Money

Currency: Since 1 January 1999, the Euro, which was introduced in January 2002, has been the official currency for the French Overseas Departments (*Départements d'Outre-Mer*) French Guiana, Guadeloupe, Martinique and Réunion. For further details, exchange rates and currency restrictions, see *France* section.
Currency exchange: There is a bureau de change at Rochambeau airport and three bureaux de change in Cayenne (*Change Caraïbes*, *Change Minas* and *Guyane Change*). They will exchange money every day except Saturday.
Credit & debit cards: American Express, *Carte Bleue*, Eurocard, MasterCard and Visa are accepted. Check with your credit or debit card company for details of merchant acceptability and other services which may be available.
Travellers cheques: These are accepted in a few places in Cayenne and Kourou. To avoid additional exchange rate charges, travellers are advised to take travellers cheques in Euros, US Dollars or Pounds Sterling.
Currency restrictions: For details of currency restrictions, see *France* section.
Banking hours: Mon-Fri 0745-1130, 1500-1700.

Duty Free

See *France* section.

Public Holidays

2005: Jan 1 New Year's Day. **Feb 8** Mardi Gras. **Feb 9** Ash Wednesday. **Mar 25-28** Easter. **May 1** Labour Day. **May 5** Ascension. **May 8** VE Day. **May 16** Whit Monday. **Jun 10** Abolition of Slavery. **Jul 14** Bastille Day. **Aug 15** Assumption. **Oct 15** Cayenne Festival. **Nov 1** All Saints' Day. **Nov 2** All Souls' Day. **Nov 11** Remembrance Day. **Dec 25** Christmas Day.
2006: Jan 1 New Year's Day. **Mar 1** Ash Wednesday. **Mar 6** Mardi Gras. **Apr 14-17** Easter. **May 1** Labour Day. **May 8** VE Day. **May 25** Ascension. **Jun 5** Whit Monday. **Jun 10** Abolition of Slavery. **Jul 14** Bastille Day. **Aug 15** Assumption. **Oct 15** Cayenne Festival. **Nov 1** All Saints' Day. **Nov 2** All Souls' Day. **Nov 11** Remembrance Day. **Dec 25** Christmas Day.

Health

	Special Precautions?	Certificate Required?
Yellow Fever	Yes	1
Cholera	No	No
Typhoid & Polio	2	N/A
Malaria	3	N/A

Note: *Regulations and requirements may be subject to change at short notice, and you are advised to contact your doctor well in advance of your intended date of departure. Any numbers in the chart refer to the footnotes below.*

1: A yellow fever vaccination certificate is required from travellers over one year of age coming from all countries, except for transit passengers remaining in the airport.
2: Immunisation against typhoid and polio is sometimes advised.
3: Malaria risk, predominantly in the malignant *falciparum* form, is high throughout the year in the nine municipalities of French Guiana bordering Brazil (Oiapoque river valley) and Surinam (Maroni river valley). In the other 13 municipalities, the transmission risk is low or negligible. High level of multi-resistant *falciparum* reported in areas influenced by Brazilian migration.
Food & drink: Mains water is normally heavily chlorinated and, whilst relatively safe, may cause mild abdominal upsets. Bottled water is available and is advised for the first few weeks of the stay. Drinking water outside main cities and towns is likely to be contaminated and sterilisation is considered essential. Milk is unpasteurised and should be boiled. Powdered or tinned milk is available and is advised, but make sure that it is reconstituted with pure water. Avoid dairy products which are likely to have been made from unboiled milk. Local meat, poultry, seafood, fruit and vegetables are generally considered safe to eat.
Other risks: *Hepatitis A* is common. *Hepatitis B* and *D* are highly endemic. *American trypanosomiasis* (*Chagas disease*) and *cutaneous* and *mucocutaneous leishmaniasis* occcur. *Brucellosis* is common.
There is a slight risk of *rabies* if in contact with wild animals. For those at high risk, vaccination before arrival should be considered. If you are bitten, seek medical advice without delay. For more information, consult the *Health* appendix.
Health care: There are medical facilities in Cayenne but very few elsewhere. Medical insurance is advisable.

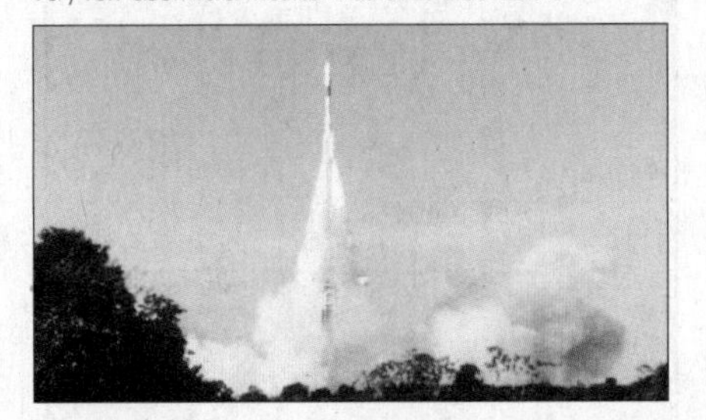

Travel - International

AIR: French Guiana's national airline is *Air Guyane (GG)* (website: www.airguyane.com) but it only offers internal services. *Air France* operates six flights a week to Cayenne from Paris. Other airlines serving the country include *Air Canada* and *Surinam Airways*.
Approximate flight times: From Cayenne to *London* (via Paris) is 11 hours 30 minutes.
International airports: *Cayenne (CAY)* (Rochambeau) is 15km (9 miles) southwest of the city. Taxis are available to the city or hotel (travel time - 25 minutes). Airport facilities include air conditioning, bars, banks/bureaux de change, newsagents and car hire (*Avis* and *Hertz*).
Departure tax: None.
RIVER: There are ferries across the Maroni River from St Laurent du Moroni to Albina (Surinam), from where there is a road to Paramaribo. Services also operate from St Georges to Oiapoque (Brazil) across the Oiapoque River.
ROAD: A road runs along the coast from Guyana through Surinam to French Guiana. There is an all-weather road connecting Cayenne with St Laurent, but it may be impassable in the rainy season. It is possible to drive from Cayenne to Paramaribo (Surinam), but it is safer to leave one's car at St Laurent and take public transport (minibus) to Paramaribo. The Cayenne district is served by a good road system.

Travel - Internal

AIR: *Air Guyane* serves the interior of the country from Cayenne, including Maripasoula, St Georges de l'Oyapock and Saül et Régina.
SEA/RIVER: There are numerous coastal and river transport services. Contact local authorities for information.
ROAD: There is a road along the coast from Cayenne to

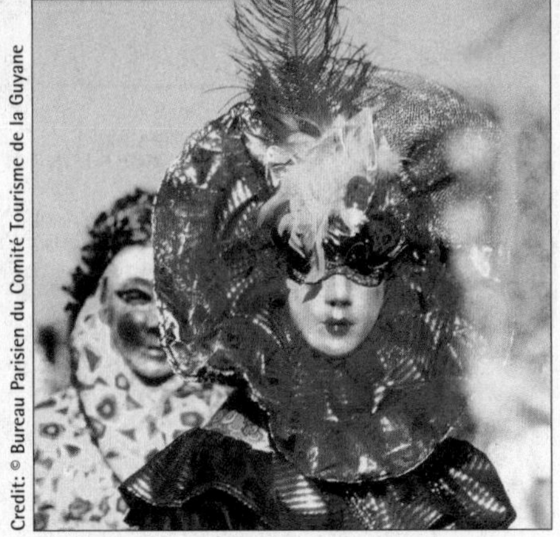

Credit: © Bureau Parisien du Comité Tourisme de la Guyane

Kourou and beyond. Traffic drives on the right. **Bus:** There is a daily service from Cayenne to St Laurent du Maroni. Faster minibuses follow the same route. Bus services also operate along the coast. **Taxi:** Available in Cayenne. **Car hire:** Available at the airport or in Cayenne, Kourou and St Laurent. **Documentation:** An International Driving Permit is recommended, although it is not legally required.

Accommodation

HOTELS: Since French Guiana was chosen as a site for European space development, a number of well-appointed air-conditioned hotels have been built. Prices are the highest on the continent. Cayenne, Kourou, Sinnamary and St Laurent du Maroni all offer excellent accommodation. Guest houses and *gites* (cottages) are cheaper alternatives. For further details, contact the *Comité du Tourisme de la Guyane* (see *Contact Addresses* section).
CAMPING/CARAVANNING: Inland camping is available, sleeping on hammocks strung from the walls of a *carbet* (a jungle version of a shack). It is also possible to hire a camping-car. For further details, contact the *Comité du Tourisme de la Guyane* (see *Contact Addresses* section).

Resorts & Excursions

Cayenne: French Guiana's atmospheric capital and chief port offers a number of attractive sights. Points of interest include the Jesuit-built residence of the Prefect in the **Place de Grenoble**, the **Canal Laussat** (built in 1777) and the **Botanical Gardens**. In the centre of town, the **Musée Départamental** and the **Musée des Cultures Guyanaises** feature good exhibits on indigenous peoples and the notorious penal settlements on Devil's Island. Lively cafes and market stalls are to be found in the **Place des Palmistes**. **Montjoly**, the city's best beach, is a short drive away.
Kourou: The main **French Space Centre** was built here which makes Kourou something of a European enclave. Ultra-modern buildings now dominate the city and there are several restaurants and two good hotels. Tourist attractions include tours of the space centres, bathing, fishing and the **Sporting and Aero Club**.
Iles du Salut: These islands include the infamous **Devil's Island** where political prisoners were held. There is a hotel (an ex-mess hall for the prison warders) on **Ile Royale**.
Haut-Maroni and Haut-Oyapoc: Visits to Amerindian villages in these areas are restricted; permission must be obtained from the *Préfecture* in Cayenne before arrival in the country.

Sport & Activities

Sea-fishing: This is popular, and can be undertaken from rocks, as well as from boats. Fishing for sharks and other big fish can be done in the open sea. **Fresh-water fishing** and **fly-fishing** are also popular.
Other: French Guiana is an expensive destination for adventure travellers. There are **river trips** and **treks** into the interior, and jungle shelters are available for overnight stops. A special permit is necessary from the *Préfecture* in Cayenne. There are **tennis** courts in Cayenne and some hotels also have courts. **Canoeing**, **horseriding**, and **sailing** can also be arranged. **Swimming** is safe around Ile de Cayenne and some hotels have pools. Facilities for **water-skiing** are available in Kourou and Montjoly.

Social Profile

FOOD & DRINK: There is a fairly good selection of restaurants and hotel dining rooms offering a number of different cuisines. The majority of them are in Cayenne, although French, Continental, Vietnamese, Chinese, Creole and Indonesian restaurants can be found elsewhere. A local speciality is the *bouillon d'aoura*, a dish of smoked fish, crab, prawns, vegetables and chicken, served with aoura, the fruit of savana trees.
NIGHTLIFE: There are nightclubs in Cayenne, Kourou and St Laurent du Maroni. Cayenne also has one cinema featuring French-language films. Cinemas can also be found in Kourou and St Laurent.
SHOPPING: Within the past few years, a great many new boutiques have opened offering a wide range of merchandise. Good buys are basketry, hammocks, pottery, wood sculpture and gold jewellery. **Shopping hours:** Mon-Sat 0900-1230, 1600-1830.
SPECIAL EVENTS: For a full list of special events in 2005, contact the Comité du Tourisme de la Guyane (see *Contact Addresses* section). The main event, which takes place every year from Epiphany to Ash Wednesday, is the *Carnival*. The dates for 2005 are **Jan 6-Feb 9**. The following is a selection of other special events celebrated annually in French Guiana: **Jun** *Montsinéry-Tonnégrande*. **Aug** *Maripasoula*; *Saül*. **Sep** *Sinnamary*. **Oct 15** *Cayenne*. **Nov** *Kourou*; *Kaw*. **Dec** *Régina*.
SOCIAL CONVENTIONS: Conservative casual wear is suitable almost everywhere. On beaches, modest beachwear is preferred. Normal social courtesies should be adhered to.
Tipping: In hotels and restaurants, a 10 per cent tip is usual. Taxi drivers are not tipped.

Business Profile

ECONOMY: French Guiana's economy is heavily dependent on that of France. Most of the workforce is engaged in agriculture, principally forestry and fisheries. Vegetables and rice are the principal crops, most of which are consumed domestically. Exploitation of French Guiana's mineral resources, which, in addition to timber from the country's extensive forests, include gold, bauxite and kaolin, is steadily growing. Gold production continues to flourish, with actual production levels and sales suspected to be far higher than official estimates. Exploration activity expanded in the mid-1990s, following the construction of a major new road allowing access to the interior. Development of the service sector, particularly tourism (and the promising field of ecotourism), had previously been hampered by poor infrastructure. The country's other notable economic asset, acquired by virtue of its position close to the equator, is the European Space Agency's satellite launch facility at Kourou. French Guiana runs a huge trade deficit, with exports less than 10 per cent of imports. In common with most French Overseas Territories, French Guiana has a high unemployment level of about 22 per cent. Other than France, Guadeloupe and Martinique, the USA, Trinidad & Tobago and Italy are the country's major trading partners.
BUSINESS: Lightweight suits are required. English will be understood by practically everyone, although a working knowledge of French may be of assistance. The best time to visit is August to November. **Office hours:** Mon-Fri 0800-1300, 1500-1800.
COMMERCIAL INFORMATION: The following organisation can offer advice: Chambre de Commerce et d'Industrie de la Guyane, BP 49, Hôtel Consulaire, place de l'Esplanade, 97321 Cayenne (tel: 299 600; fax: 299 634 or 299 645; e-mail: contact@guyane.cci.fr; website: www.guyane.cci.fr).

Climate

Tropical. Dry season is August to December; rainy season is December and January and April to July. Hot all year round, with cooler nights. Average temperature is 27°C (85°F).
Required clothing: Tropical lightweights and rainwear.

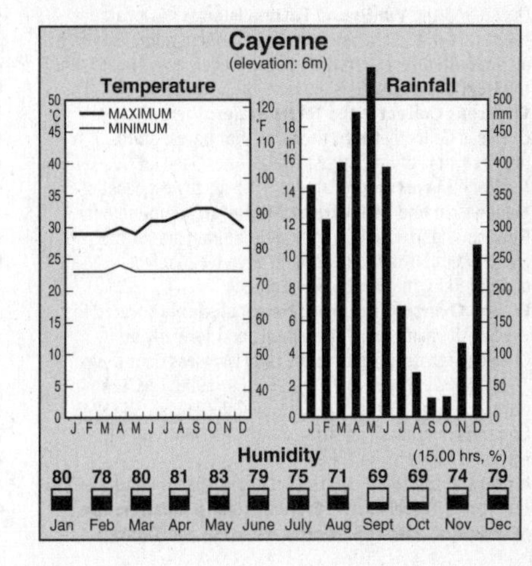

French Overseas Possessions

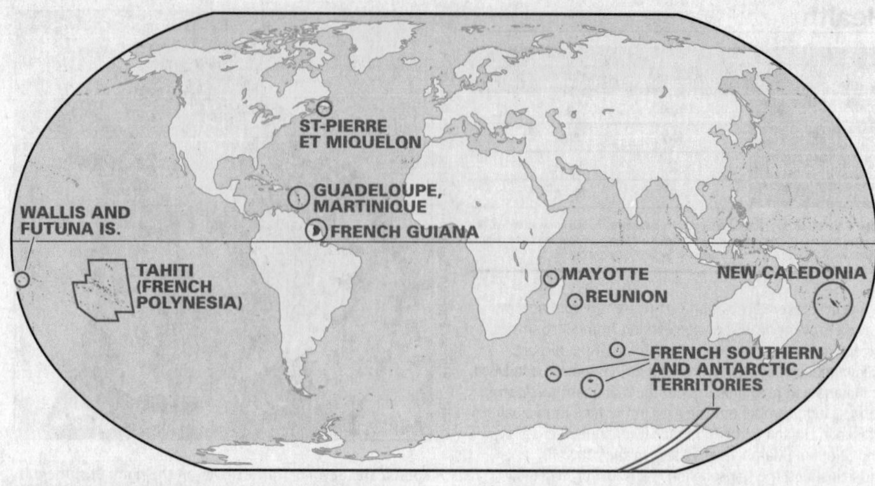

LATEST TRAVEL ADVICE CONTACTS

British Foreign and Commonwealth Office
Tel: (0870) 606 0290 Website: www.fco.gov.uk

US Department of State
Website: http://travel.state.gov/travel

Canadian Department of Foreign Affairs and Int'l Trade
Tel: (1 800) 267 8376 Website: www.dfait-maeci.gc.ca

Scattered throughout the world are several French *Départements d'Outre-Mer* (overseas departments), *Territoires d'Outre-Mer* (overseas territories), *Collectivités Territoriales* and one overseas country (New Caledonia). Most of these have their own sections in the *World Travel Guide*, but basic information is given here on the others. Further information on all of the French Overseas Possessions can be obtained from French embassies; see *France* section.

Direction du Tourisme (Department of Tourism)
23 Place Catalogne, 75014 Paris, France
Tel: (1) 4437 3600. Fax: (1) 4437 3636
Email: cnt@tourisme.gouv.fr
Website: www.tourisme.gouv.fr

Maison de la France (French Government Tourist Office)
20 avenue de l'Opéra, 75001 Paris, France
Tel: (1) 4296 7000. Fax: (1) 4292 7011.
Website: www.franceguide.com

Maison de la France (French Government Tourist Office)
178 Piccadilly, London W1J 9AL, UK
Tel: (09068) 244 123 (France information line; calls cost 60p per minute) *or* (020) 7399 3520 (travel trade only).
Fax: (020) 7493 6594.
E-mail: info.uk@franceguide.com
Website: www.franceguide.com

French Government Tourist Office
444 Madison Avenue, 16th Floor, New York, NY 10022, USA
Tel: (212) 838 7800 *or* (514) 288 1904 (public information service) *or* 6989 (travel trade only). Fax: (212) 838 7855.
E-mail: info.us@franceguide.com
Website: www.franceguide.com

French Government Tourist Office
1981 Avenue McGill College, Suite 490, Montréal, Québec H3A 2W9, Canada
Tel: (514) 876 9881. Fax: (514) 845 4868.
E-mail: canada@franceguide.com
Website: www.franceguide.com

Resorts & Excursions

French Overseas Departments: There are four *Départements d'Outre-Mer*, each one an integral part of the French Republic. **Guadeloupe** (also including the islands of St Martin and St Barthélemy) and **Martinique** are in the Caribbean. **French Guiana** is on the northwest coast of South America. **Réunion** is in the Indian Ocean. Despite the greater autonomy achieved with the formation of their own individual Regional Councils in 1974, each French Overseas Department still returns elected representatives to the Senate and National Assembly in Paris, as well as to the European Parliament in Strasbourg.
French Overseas Territories: Like the French Overseas Departments, the three *Territoires d'Outre-Mer* are integral parts of the French Republic. **Tahiti (French Polynesia)** is in the central South Pacific. **French Southern and Antarctic Territories** are located in the Southern Indian Ocean and the **Wallis and Futuna Islands** are located in the southwest Pacific. However, each one is administered by an appointed representative of the French government, and the level of autonomy is restricted.
Overseas Collectivités Territoriales: There are two Overseas Collectivités Territoriales that have a status in between that of an Overseas Department and an Overseas Territory. **Mayotte** is located off the northwest coast of Madagascar and **St-Pierre et Miquelon** are found near Newfoundland, Canada. They are integral parts of the French Republic and are administered by a Prefect appointed by the French Government.
French Overseas Country: New Caledonia, located in the South Pacific, east of Australia and formerly an Overseas Territory, became the only Overseas Country in 1999 following the Nouméa Accord in 1998. The French government is represented in New Caledonia by the High Commissioner and two deputies are also elected to the National Assembly in Paris.
Note: The following countries all have their own sections in the *World Travel Guide*: **French Guiana**, **Guadeloupe**, **Martinique**, **New Caledonia**, **Réunion** and **Tahiti**.

FRENCH SOUTHERN AND ANTARCTIC TERRITORIES

The territories consist of a thin slice of Antarctic mainland and a few small islands located in the Southern Indian Ocean. The Kerguelen archipelago, which is only slightly smaller than Corsica, is a notable exception. The total area is 439,822 sq km (161,815 sq miles). The territory is used mainly for scientific purposes, although fishing in the area is important.

WALLIS AND FUTUNA ISLANDS

For more information, see online (e-mail: webmaster@wall-islands.com.
Location: Southwest Pacific between Fiji, Samoa and Tonga. **Area:** 160.5 sq km (99.5 sq miles). **Population:** 14,600 (2000). **Population density:** 91.0 per sq km. **Capital:** Mata-Utu (Wallis Island). **Population:** 1137 (1996). **Religion:** Roman Catholic. **Time:** GMT + 12. **Visa:** The passport and visa requirements for persons visiting the Wallis and Futuna Islands are the same as for New Caledonia. For further details, see the *New Caledonia* section. **Health:** Vaccinations against typhoid and tetanus are advised. Precautions should also be taken against *hepatitis B*. There are two hospitals, one on Wallis and one on Futuna, and three dispensaries. Mains water is suitable for drinking on Wallis but not on Futuna. **Travel:** The main airport (Hihifo) is on Wallis Island, 5km (3 miles) from Mata-Utu. Approximate flight time from *London* is 25 hours. There is also an airport in Alo in the southeastern part of Futuna Island. *Air Calédonie (TY)* is the main airline serving the Islands. There are one or two weekly flights from Wallis Island to Nouméa (New Caledonia), and services three or four times a week from Wallis to Futuna. Boat services no longer operate from New Caledonia; however, a fast ferry service is being planned between Wallis and Futuna. Minibus services operate on Futuna and car hire is available. However, the only surfaced roads are in Mata-Utu. **Accommodation:** There are a small number of hotels on the islands; for details of booking accommodation and other information, contact the French Government Tourist Office (see *Contact Addresses* section) *or* the Wallis and Futuna Hotel Association (website: www.wallis-and-futuna.com).

MAYOTTE

For more information on Mayotte, contact the *Comité du Tourisme de Mayotte*, BP 1169, Rue de la Pompe, Mamoudzou, 97600 Mayotte (tel: 610 909; fax: 610 346; e-mail: contact@mayotte-tourisme.com *or* info@mayotte-tourisme.com; website: www.mayotte-tourisme.com).
Location: Part of the Comoro archipelago off the northwest corner of Madagascar. **Area:** 374 sq km (144 sq miles). **Population:** 160,265 (2002). **Population density:** 428.5 per sq km. **Capital:** Dzaoudzi. **Population:** 12,308 (2002). **Time:** GMT + 3. Country dialling code: 269. **Visa:** The passport and visa requirements for persons visiting Mayotte are the same as for New Caledonia. For further details, see the *New Caledonia* section. **Health:** There are no vaccination requirements for any international traveller, although precautions against malaria are advised. Although mains water is chlorinated, bottled water should be drunk for the first few weeks of the stay. Medical services are available free of charge. The island is divided into six sections, each of which has a medical professional. Full medical insurance is advised. **Travel:** The main airport is *Pamandzi* on the island of Petite Terre; services are available from Paris (via Réunion), the Comoros Islands, Madagascar, the Seychelles and Kenya. There is a regular boat service to Grande Terre. There are approximately 90km (55 miles) of roads on the island. **Accommodation:** There is a small number of hotels on the islands; contact the French Government Tourist Office for details of booking accommodation. **History:** The island is claimed by the Federal Islamic Republic of the Comoros (which declared independence from France in 1975), although residents have maintained that they wish to retain their close links with France. Various attempts have been made by international organisations, including the United Nations, to resolve the situation, although both the islanders and the French government are in favour of maintaining Mayotte's special status.

ST-PIERRE ET MIQUELON
10km
5mls
international airport
Le Cap
Miquelon
Miquelon Lagoon
Mirande Lagoon
Miquelon (Grande Miquelon)
Grande Barachois
Langlade Isthmus
Green I. (Canada)
Langlade (Petite Miquelon)
Plate Point
West Point
La Baie
Grand Colombier
St-Pierre I.
ST-PIERRE
Gulf of St Lawrence

ST PIERRE ET MIQUELON

For more information on St-Pierre et Miquelon, contact the Agence Régionale du Tourisme, BP 4274, place du Général de Gaulle, 97500 St-Pierre (tel: 410 222 *or* 410 202; fax: 413 355; e-mail: tourispm@cheznoo.net).
Location: This small group of small islands lies off the southern coast of Newfoundland, Canada. **Area:** 242 sq km (93.4 sq miles). **Population:** 6316 (1999). **Population density:** 26.1 per sq km. **Capital:** St Pierre. **Population:** 5683 (1990); almost all of the population live in the capital or elsewhere on the small island of the same name. **Time:** GMT - 3 (GMT - 2 from first Sunday in April to Saturday before last Sunday in October). Country dialling code: 508. **Visa:** The passport and visa requirements for persons visiting St-Pierre et Miquelon are the same as for French Guiana, Guadeloupe, Martinique and Réunion. For further details, see any of these separate sections. **Health:** No special precautions are required. There are no reciprocal agreements with the UK or USA but visitors have the right to be treated and charges are made. Medical insurance is recommended. **Travel:** The islands' airport is *St-Pierre*, which has international flights from Paris via Montréal, Halifax or St John's; and from London via Paris and St John's (stopovers are generally not permitted). St-Pierre is served by *Air Saint Pierre (PJ)*. Boat services operate between the islands and (in the high season) to Fortune, Newfoundland (travel time – 1 hour). Buses, taxis and hire cars are available. **Accommodation:** Hotels and guest houses are available on the island. **History:** Previously enjoying Departmental status, the islands have, since 1955, been a part of the *collectivités territoriales*, partly as a result of a dispute with Canada over fishing and mineral rights in the area.

Gabon

LATEST TRAVEL ADVICE CONTACTS

British Foreign and Commonwealth Office
Tel: (0870) 606 0290 Website: www.fco.gov.uk

US Department of State
Website: http://travel.state.gov/travel

Canadian Department of Foreign Affairs and Int'l Trade
Tel: (1 800) 267 8376 Website: www.dfait-maeci.gc.ca

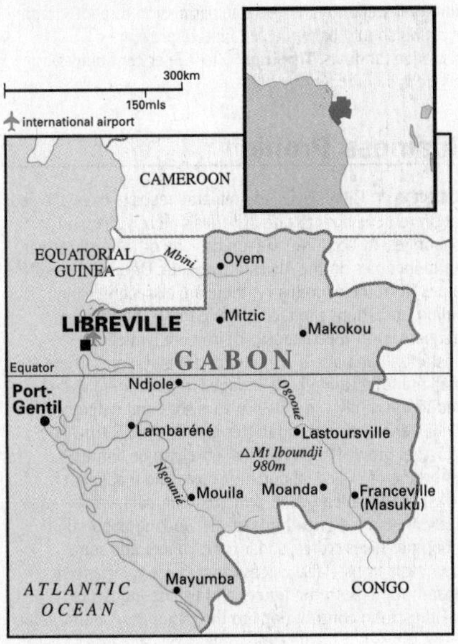

Location: West Coast of Central Africa.

Country dialling code: 241.

Centre Gabonais de Promotion Touristique (GABONTOUR)
Street address: 622 Avenue du Colonel Parant, Centre Ville, Libreville, Gabon
Postal address: BP 2085, Libreville, Gabon
Tel: 728 504 *or* 723 949. Fax: 728 503.
E-mail: gabontour@internetgabon.com
Website: www.gabontour.ga

Embassy of the Gabonese Republic
27 Elvaston Place, London SW7 5NL, UK
Tel: (020) 7823 9986. Fax: (020) 7584 0047.
E-mail: armellepambou@hotmail.com
Website: http://gabon.embassyhomepage.com
Opening hours: Mon-Fri 0900-1500.

British Consulate
PO Box 486, Libreville, Gabon
Tel: 762 200 *or* 742 041. Fax: 765 789.

Embassy of the Gabonese Republic
2034 20th Street, NW, Washington, DC 20009, USA
Tel: (202) 797 1000. Fax: (202) 332 0668.
E-mail: info@ambagabonusa.net
Consulate in: New York.

Embassy of the United States of America
BP 4000, Boulevard Bord de la Mer, Libreville, Gabon
Tel: 762 003/4. Fax: 745 507.

Embassy of the Gabonese Republic
Street address: 4 Range Road, Ottawa, Ontario K1N 8J5, Canada
Postal address: PO Box 368, Ottawa, Ontario K1N 8J5 Canada
Tel: (613) 232 5301/2. Fax: (613) 232 6916.
E-mail: ambgabon@sprint.ca

Canadian Embassy
Street address: Quartier Batterie IV, Libreville, Gabon
Postal address: BP 4037, Libreville, Gabon
Tel: 737 354. Fax: 737 388.
E-mail: lbrve@dfait-maeci.gc.ca
Website: www.dfait-maeci.gc.ca/gabon

TIMATIC CODES

Health	AMADEUS: **TI-DFT/LBV/HE** GALILEO/WORLDSPAN: **TI-DFT/LBV/HE** SABRE: **TIDFT/LBV/HE**
Visa	AMADEUS: **TI-DFT/LBV/VI** GALILEO/WORLDSPAN: **TI-DFT/LBV/VI** SABRE: **TIDFT/LBV/VI**

To access TIMATIC country information on Health and Visa regulations through the Computer Reservations System (CRS), type in the appropriate command line listed above.

General Information

AREA: 267,667 sq km (103,347 sq miles).
POPULATION: 1,329,000 (official estimate 2003).
POPULATION DENSITY: 5 per sq km.
CAPITAL: Libreville. **Population:** 573,000 (official estimate 2003).
GEOGRAPHY: Gabon is bordered to the west by the Atlantic Ocean, to the north by Equatorial Guinea and Cameroon, and to the east and south by the Congo. The 800km- (500 mile-) long sandy coastal strip is a series of palm-fringed bays, lagoons and estuaries. The lush tropical vegetation (which covers about 82 per cent of the interior) gives way in parts to the savannah. There are many rivers and they remain the main communication routes along which settlements have grown. Of the 40 or so Bantu tribes, the largest are the Fang, Eshira, Mbele and Okande. Only a small percentage of native Gabonese live in the towns, as the population is concentrated in the coastal areas and the villages along the banks of the many rivers, following a more traditional rural style of life.
GOVERNMENT: Republic. Gained independence from France in 1960. **Head of State:** President El Hadj Omar Bongo since 1967. **Head of Government:** Prime Minister Jean François Ntoutoume Emane since 1999.
LANGUAGE: The official language is French. The principal African language is Fang. Eshira is spoken by a tenth of the population. Bantu dialects include Bapounou, Miene and Bateke.
RELIGION: About 60 per cent Christian (mainly Roman Catholic), the remainder follow Muslim and animist beliefs.
TIME: GMT + 1.
ELECTRICITY: 220 volts AC, 50Hz.
COMMUNICATIONS: Telephone: IDD is available. Country code: 241. No area codes required. Outgoing international code: 00. **Mobile telephone:** GSM 900. Network operators include *Telecel Gabon* (website: www.telecel.co.ga), *Celtel* (website: www.msi-cellular.com) and *Libertis*. **Internet:** ISPs include *Internetgabon* (website: www.internetgabon.com). There is a growing number of Internet cafes in Libreville. **Post:** Airmail from Gabon takes at least one week to Western Europe. Urgent letters should be sent by special delivery to ensure their safe arrival. Post office hours: 0800-1200 and Mon-Fri 1430-1800. **Press:** The two daily newspapers are *Gabon Matin* and *L'Union*, published in French. There are several periodicals, published mainly on the topics of the Government and the economy. Official bulletins are published in French and have a limited circulation.
Radio: BBC World Service (website: www.bbc.co.uk/worldservice) and Voice of America (website: www.voa.gov) can be received. From time to time the frequencies change and the most up-to-date can be found online.

Passport/Visa

	Passport Required?	Visa Required?	Return Ticket Required?
Full British	Yes	Yes	Yes
Australian	Yes	Yes	Yes
Canadian	Yes	Yes	Yes
USA	Yes	Yes	Yes
Other EU	Yes	Yes	Yes
Japanese	Yes	Yes	Yes

Note: *Regulations and requirements may be subject to change at short notice, and you are advised to contact the appropriate diplomatic or consular authority before finalising travel arrangements. Details of these may be found at the head of this country's entry. Any numbers in the chart refer to the footnotes below.*

PASSPORTS: Passport valid for more than six months required by all.
VISAS: Required by all.
Types of visa and cost:
Single-entry: £50 (Tourist or Transit); £70 (Business).
Double-entry: £100 (Tourist or Transit); £140 (Business).
Multiple-entry: £280 (Tourist, Transit or Business).
Validity: *Single-entry*: three months from date of issue.
Application to: Consulate (or Consular section at Embassy); see *Contact Addresses* section.
Application requirements: (a) One passport-size photo. (b) One application form. (c) Fee, payable in cash or by cheque only. (d) Valid passport. (e) Registered stamped, self-addressed special delivery envelope for postal applications. *Tourist*: (a)-(e) and, (f) Hotel reservation, or invitation from resident of Gabon legalised in the town hall. *Business*: (a)-(e) and, (f) Letter from the company stating the date of departure and the reasons for the visit.
Note: (a) While possession of references is not an official requirement when applying for a tourist visa, they may help speed up the application process. (b) Both yellow fever, tropical disease and cholera vaccination certificates may be required to enter Gabon but are not necessary when applying for a visa. However, it is best to check with the Embassy prior to travel.

Working days required: Minimum four days.

Money

Currency: CFA (*Communauté Financiaire Africaine*) Franc (CFAfr *or* XAF) = 100 centimes. Notes are in denominations of CFAfr10,000, 5000, 2000, 1000 and 500. Coins are in denominations of CFAfr500, 100, 50, 25, 10, 5 and 1. Only currency issued by the *Banque des États de l'Afrique Centrale* (Bank of Central African States) is valid; currency issued by the *Banque des États de l'Afrique de l'Ouest* (Bank of West African States) is not. The CFA Franc is tied to the Euro.
Currency exchange: Gabon is part of the French Monetary Area.
Credit & debit cards: Limited use of American Express, MasterCard and Visa. In general, the use of credit cards in Gabon remains relatively limited. Check with your credit or debit card company for merchant acceptability and other facilities which may be available.
Travellers cheques: To avoid additional exchange rate charges, travellers are advised to take travellers cheques in Euros.
Currency restrictions: The import of local and foreign currency is unlimited, subject to declaration. The export of local and foreign currency is limited to CFAfr200,000.
Exchange rate indicators: The following figures are included as a guide to the movements of the CFA Franc against Sterling and the US Dollar:

Date	Feb '04	May '04	Aug '04	Nov '04
£1.00=	961.13	983.76	978.35	936.79
$1.00=	528.01	550.79	531.03	494.69

Banking hours: Mon-Fri 0730-1130, 1430-1630.

Duty Free

The following goods may be imported into Gabon by persons of 17 and over without incurring customs duty:
200 cigarettes/cigarillos or 50 cigars or 250g of tobacco (women – cigarettes only); 2l of alcoholic beverage; 50g of perfume; gifts up to CFAfr5000.
Restricted items: Guns and ammunition require a licence from the Ministry of Home Affairs in Libreville.

Public Holidays

2005: Jan 1 New Year's Day. **Jan 21** Eid al-Adha (Feast of the Sacrifice). **Mar 28** Easter Monday. **May 1** Labour Day. **May 6** Martyrs' Day. **May 16** Whit Monday. **Aug 15** Assumption. **Aug 16** Independence Day. **Nov 1** All Saints' Day. **Nov 3-5** Eid al-Fitr (End of Ramadan). **Dec 25** Christmas Day.
2006: Jan 1: New Year's Day. **Jan 10** Eid al-Adha (Feast of the Sacrifice). **Apr 17** Easter Monday. **May 1** Labour Day. **May 6** Martyrs' Day. **Jun 5** Whit Monday. **Aug 15** Assumption. **Aug 16** Independence Day. **Nov 1** All Saints' Day. **Oct 22-24** Eid al-Fitr (End of Ramadan). **Dec 25** Christmas Day.
Note: Muslim festivals are timed according to local sightings of various phases of the moon and the dates given above are approximations. During the lunar month of Ramadan that precedes Eid al-Fitr, Muslims fast during the day and feast at night and normal business patterns may be interrupted. Some disruption may continue into Eid al-Fitr itself. Eid al-Fitr and Eid al-Adha may last anything from two to 10 days, depending on the region. For more information see the *World of Islam* appendix.

Health

	Special Precautions?	Certificate Required?
Yellow Fever	Yes	1
Cholera	Yes	2
Typhoid & Polio	3	N/A
Malaria	4	N/A

Note: *Regulations and requirements may be subject to change at short notice, and you are advised to contact your doctor well in advance of your intended date of departure. Any numbers in the chart refer to the footnotes below.*

1: A yellow fever vaccination certificate is required from all travellers over one year of age. Yellow fever risk is particularly high in Ogooue-Ivindo province.
2: Following WHO guidelines issued in 1973, a cholera vaccination certificate is not a condition of entry to Gabon. However, cholera is a serious risk in this country and precautions are essential. Up-to-date advice should be sought before deciding whether these precautions should include vaccination as medical opinion is divided over its effectiveness; see the *Health* appendix for more information.
3: Immunisation against typhoid and poliomyelitis is often recommended.

A B C D E F G H I J K L M N O P Q R S T U V W X Y Z

4: Malaria risk, predominantly in the malignant *falciparum* form, exists all year throughout the country. Resistance to chloroquine has been reported.
Food & drink: All water should be regarded as potentially contaminated. Water used for drinking, brushing teeth or making ice should have first been boiled or otherwise sterilised. Milk is unpasteurised and should be boiled. Powdered or tinned milk is available and is advised, but make sure that it is reconstituted with pure water. Avoid dairy products which are likely to have been made from unboiled milk. Only eat well-cooked meat and fish, preferably served hot. Pork, salad and mayonnaise may carry increased risk. Vegetables should be cooked and fruit peeled.
Other risks: *Diarrhoeal diseases*, including *giardiasis*, and *typhoid fevers* are common. *Hepatitis A* and *E* are widespread. *Hepatitis B* is hyperendemic. *Bilharzia* (schistosomiasis) is present. Avoid swimming and paddling in fresh water; swimming pools which are well-chlorinated and maintained are safe. *Onchocerciasis* (river blindness) and *trypanosomiasis* (sleeping sickness) are present. Epidemics of *meningococcal disease* may occur, particularly in the savannah areas and during the dry season. Immunisation against *diphtheria* is sometimes recommended. *Oriental lung fluke* has been reported. *Rabies* is present. For those at high risk, vaccination before arrival should be considered. If you are bitten, seek medical advice without delay. For more information, consult the *Health* appendix.
Health care: Travellers in rural areas should take a first-aid kit with anti-tetanus and anti-venom serums. Medical facilities are limited. Full health insurance is essential.

Travel - International

AIR: Gabon's national airline is *Air Gabon (GN)*, which operates direct flights from Paris and London to Libreville. *Air France* operates four flights a week from London to Gabon, with a stopover in Paris. Other airlines serving Gabon include *Air Afrique*, *Cameroon Airlines*, *Nigeria Airways*, *Royal Air Maroc* and *Swiss*.
Approximate flight times: From Libreville to *London* is approximately 10 hours (including stopovers).
International airports: *Libreville (LBV)* is 12km (7 miles) north of the city. Taxis are available to the city (travel time - 10 minutes). Airport facilities include bureaux de change, shops, tourist information, left luggage, car hire (*Avis*, *Eurafrique*, *Europcar* and *Hertz*), hotel reservation desk and duty-free shops.
Departure tax: None.
SEA: Ferries depart quite regularly from Libreville to São Tomé. Freight ships to Cameroon may take passengers; enquire locally for details.
ROAD: There are roads to Bitam and Ambam (Cameroon), Bata via Cocobeach (Equatorial Guinea) and the Congo.

Travel - Internal

AIR: *Air Gabon (GN)* operates regular flights from Lambaréné, Libreville, Mitzic, Oyem and other cities. Gabon has a total of nearly 200 airstrips. There are local airports at *Franceville (MVB)* and *Port Gentil (POG)*.
SEA: Ferries run regularly along the coast from Libreville to Port Gentil (travel time - four hours).
RIVER: Riverboats ply the Ogoué River between Port Gentil and Lambaréné (travel time - 10 - 24 hours). Some boats continue on to Ndjolé.
RAIL: The *Trans-Gabon Railway* connects Libreville (Owendo station, 10km (6 miles) from the city centre) with Lastoursville, Booué and Franceville, with extensions under construction to Belinga in the north. Children under four years travel free. Children aged from four to 11 years pay half fare.
ROAD: Traffic drives on the right. There are nearly 7518km (4672 miles) of road, but only 614km (382 miles) are tarred. Most of the country consists of impenetrable rainforest and the roads are generally of a poor standard. Road travel in the rainy season is inadvisable. There is no road connection between the second largest city of Port Gentil or any other part of the country. **Bus:** Inter-urban travel is mainly by minibus or pick-up truck. Daily minibus services run from Libreville to Lambaréné, Mouila, Oyem and Bitam (the last two usually involving night stops). Seats for these and other less frequent routes can be obtained in Libreville. However, this is not normally necessary for the main routes as seats will be readily available in the 'bus station' near the central market (0600-0800). There are also conventional buses on the Mouila route and other services out of Mouila. **Car hire:** Cars may be hired from main hotels and airports, although they tend to be expensive. **Documentation:** International Driving Permit and international insurance are required.
URBAN: There are extensive share-taxis. There are bus services in Port Gentil and Masuku (Franceville), and share-taxis in other centres. Taxi rates vary.

Accommodation

HOTELS: There are a few high-class hotels in Libreville and also first-class hotels in Koulamoutou, Lambaréné, Makokou, Masuku (Franceville), Mouila, Oyem, Port Gentil and Tchibanga but, like most of the accommodation in Gabon, they are expensive. Tourist facilities, including comfortable accommodation, are being expanded throughout the country, especially along the coast and in towns close to the National Parks. There are hotels in other major cities and towns. These hotels will accept most major credit cards. For further information, contact GABONTOUR (see *Contact Addresses* section).
CAMPING: Free but limited. Caution should be used as to where camp is made.

Resorts & Excursions

LIBREVILLE:
Located beside the ocean, Gabon's capital is lively and charming. Its white buildings contrast with the green of the nearby equatorial forest. Sights include the art-craft village (**Village des Artisans**) and the **National Museum**, which contains some of the most beautiful woodcarvings in Africa, especially the indigenous Fang style of carving which influenced Picasso's figures and busts. Visitors can also enjoy the delightful **Peyrie Gardens**, in the heart of the city; the popular quarters of Akebe and Nombakele, the harbour, the **Cathedral of St Michael** and the **Mount Bouet Market**.
ELSEWHERE: The main cities in Gabon are **Port Gentil**, **Lambaréné**, **Moanda**, **Oyem**, **Mouila** and **Franceville**. A route winds through a forest of giant trees from Libreville to the beach of **Cap Estérias**, where the rocks abound with sea urchins, oysters and lobsters. This is a good place to swim. It is possible to go to the **Kinguele Falls** on **M'Bei River** or to Lambaréné, the town made famous by Doctor Albert Schweitzer, the tropical disease specialist and musician. Now in its 70th year, Schweitzer's hospital is open to visitors and a tour on **Evaro Lake** can be organised. Trips are available down the rapids of the **Okanda** region. Further south, the villages of **M'Bigou** and **Eteke** are famous for their local crafts and gold mines and, to the west, the enchanting **Mayumba** set between sea and lake. Eastwards, the region of **Bateke Plateau** comprises savannah and forest galleries, and tumultuous rivers spanned by liana bridges, such as the one at Poubara. Game and wildlife include forest elephants, buffaloes, sitatunga, river hogs, gorillas, panthers, crocodiles, monkeys and parrots. In the **Sette-Cama**, **Iguela** and **N'Dende** zones, hunters going on safari can hire guides experienced in tracking and approaching the game. For those armed only with camera and video-camera, there is the **Lope reserve** and two national parks, **Wonga-Wongue** and **Moukalaba**.

Sport & Activities

Watersports: The beaches on the Atlantic coast offer ideal **bathing**. Port Gentil at the mouth of the *River Ogooué* and Libreville have beaches with facilities for **water-skiing** and other watersports. *Mayumba* in the south and *Cap Estérias*, 35km (22 miles) from Libreville, are popular watersports centres at weekends. *Perroquet* and *Pointe Denis* both offer good **skindiving**.
Many of the rivers offer excellent **fishing**; equipment can be hired at Port Gentil. Fish abound in Gabonese rivers and lakes, but the local fishermen can find the largest variety along the coast and in the numerous lagoons located at the mouth of the Ogooué.
Safaris: Gabon's national parks are rich in wildlife. The largest is the *Lopé-Okanda Reserve*, near La Lopé in the centre of the country. The landscape is a mixture of savannah and dense forest. Gorillas, chimpanzees and elephants are all present, as well as a variety of other primates, large mammals such as buffalo and around 350 species of bird. Details can be obtained from GABONTOUR (see *Contact Addresses* section).

Social Profile

FOOD & DRINK: Most hotels and restaurants serve French and continental-style food and are expensive. Gabonese food is distinctive and delicious, but not always readily available, as most restaurants serve Senegalese, Cameroonian and Congolese food.
Licensing hours are similar to those in France.
NIGHTLIFE: There are nightclubs in Libreville with music and bars. Food is often served, although this can be expensive. There are also casinos at several hotels.
SHOPPING: In Libreville there are two bustling markets at Akebe-Plaine, Nkembo and Mon-Bouet. Stone carvings can be bought on the outskirts of both, fashioned by a group of carvers who have adapted traditional skills for the tourist market. Crafts from local villages can also be bought from stalls in the streets or from the villagers themselves. African (Fang) mask carvings, figurines, clay pots and traditional musical instruments can also be bought. **Shopping hours:** Mon-Sat 0800-1200 and 1500-1900. Some shops close Monday.
SPECIAL EVENTS: The following is a special event celebrated annually in Gabon:
Aug 16 *Independence Day* (the biggest celebration in Gabon).
Other events are celebrated on Muslim holy days.
SOCIAL CONVENTIONS: Dance, song, poetry and myths remain an important part of traditional Gabonese life.
Photography: It is absolutely forbidden to photograph military installations. In general, permission to photograph anything should be requested first, to prevent misunderstandings. **Tipping:** 10 to 15 per cent unless service is included in the bill.

Business Profile

ECONOMY: Oil reserves and mineral deposits have allowed Gabon to develop into one of Africa's more successful economies. At US$3200, Gabon has one of the highest per capita incomes on the African continent. One-third of GDP comes from the oil industry; there are also significant mining operations producing manganese and uranium. There are confirmed deposits of iron ore (which are substantial) and also a number of rare metal ores. There is a small manufacturing base engaged in oil refining and the production of plywood, paints, varnishes and detergents, dry batteries, cement, cigarettes and textiles. Future industrial growth in this sector is likely to be limited by a shortage of skilled labour, high costs and inadequate infrastructure. Meanwhile, agriculture remains important, as it still employs two-thirds of the working population. Gabon produces coffee, sugar cane, rubber and some other cash crops – also cassava and maize for domestic consumption. Both the timber and fishing industries, while making strong contributions to the national economy, may be the subject of future expansion as export earners, although timber production is likely to be limited by environmental concerns. Like all primary producers, Gabon remains vulnerable to fluctuations in commodity prices. Gabon is a member of the Central African Customs and Economic Union (CEEAC) and of the CFA Franc Zone. In June 1996, Gabon announced its withdrawal from OPEC, after 23 years' membership. The country's main trading partners are in the industrialised West, with the USA the largest, followed by France, Japan and Germany.
BUSINESS: Tropical suits are required. French is the principal language used in business circles. Translators and interpreters are available through the Embassy. Strong business ties remain with France despite competition from the USA and Japan. **Office hours:** Mon-Fri 0730-1200 and 1430-1800.
COMMERCIAL INFORMATION: The following organisations can offer advice: Chambre de Commerce, d'Agriculture, d'Industrie et des Mines du Gabon, BP 2234, Libreville (tel: 722 064; fax: 741 220).
CONFERENCES/CONVENTIONS: Further information can be obtained from the Chambre de Commerce, d'Agriculture, d'Industrie et des Mines du Gabon (address as above).

Climate

Equatorial with high humidity. The dry season is from June to August, and the main rainy season is from October to May.
Required clothing: Lightweight tropical, with raincoat advised during the rainy season.

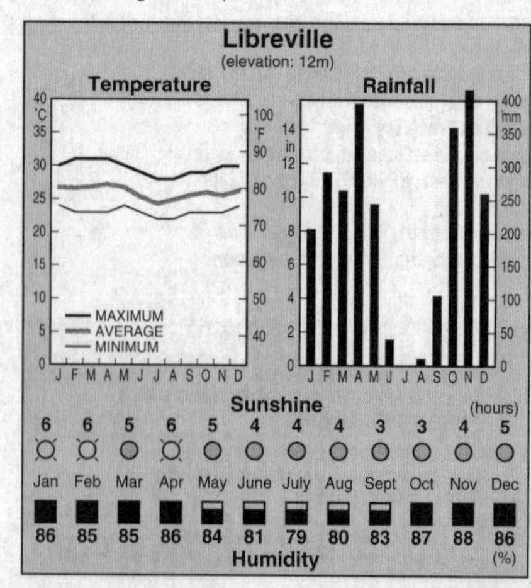

The Gambia

LATEST TRAVEL ADVICE CONTACTS

British Foreign and Commonwealth Office
Tel: (0870) 606 0290 Website: www.fco.gov.uk
US Department of State
Website: http://travel.state.gov/travel
Canadian Department of Foreign Affairs and Int'l Trade
Tel: (1 800) 267 8376 Website: www.dfait-maeci.gc.ca

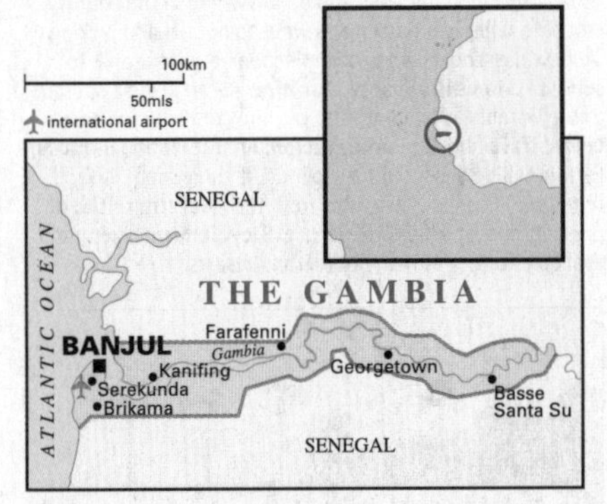

Location: West Africa.

Country dialling code: 220.

The Gambia Tourism Authority
Kololi, PO Box 4085, Bakau, The Gambia
Tel: 446 2491/3. Fax: 446 2487.
E-mail: info@gta.gm
Website: www.visitthegambia.gm
High Commission of the Republic of The Gambia
57 Kensington Court, London W8 5DG, UK
Tel: (020) 7937 6316. Fax: (020) 7937 9095.
E-mail: gambia@gamhighcom.fsnet.co.uk
Opening hours: Mon-Thurs 1000-1600, Fri 1000-1200.
The Gambia Tourism Authority, UK
Address as for High Commission.
Tel: (020) 7376 0093. Fax: (020) 7938 3644.
E-mail: office@ukgta.fsnet.co.uk
Website: www.visitthegambia.gm
British High Commission
Street address: 48 Atlantic Road, Fajara, Banjul, The Gambia
Postal address: PO Box 507, Fajara, Banjul, The Gambia
Tel: 449 5133/4 *or* 7590 (visa section).
Fax: 449 6134 *or* 7583 (visa section).
E-mail: bhcbanjul@gamtel.gm
Website: www.britishhighcommission.gov.uk/thegambia
Embassy of the Republic of The Gambia
Suite 905, 1156 15th Street, NW, Washington, DC 20005, USA
Tel: (202) 785 1399 *or* 1425. Fax: (202) 785 1430.
E-mail: gambiaembassy1@aol.com
Also deals with enquiries from Canada.
Embassy of the United States of America
Street address: 92 Kairaba Avenue, Fajara, Banjul, The Gambia
Postal address: PO Box 19, Fajara, Banjul, The Gambia
Tel: 439 2856 *or* 437 6169 *or* 6170. Fax: 439 2475.
E-mail: consularbanjul@state.gov
Website: www.usembassybanjul.gm
The Canadian High Commission in Dakar deals with enquiries relating to The Gambia (see *Senegal* section).

TIMATIC CODES

Health	AMADEUS: **TI-DFT/BJL/HE** GALILEO/WORLDSPAN: **TI-DFT/BJL/HE** SABRE: **TIDFT/BJL/HE**
Visa	AMADEUS: **TI-DFT/BJL/VI** GALILEO/WORLDSPAN: **TI-DFT/BJL/VI** SABRE: **TIDFT/BJL/VI**

To access TIMATIC country information on Health and Visa regulations through the Computer Reservations System (CRS), type in the appropriate command line listed above.

General Information

AREA: 11,295 sq km (4361 sq miles).
POPULATION: 1,364,507 (official estimate 2003).
POPULATION DENSITY: 120.8 per sq km.
CAPITAL: Banjul. **Population:** 42,326 (1993).
GEOGRAPHY: The Gambia is situated on the Atlantic coast at the bulge of Africa. The country consists of a thin ribbon of land, at no point wider than 50km (30 miles), running east-west on both banks of the River Gambia. The Gambia is bordered to the west by the Atlantic Ocean and on all other sides by Senegal. It is also the smallest and westernmost African nation. The country mainly consists of a low plateau, which decreases in height as it nears the Atlantic coast. The plain is broken in a few places by low flat-topped hills and by the river and its tributaries. The area extending from MacCarthy Island, where Georgetown is located, to the eastern end of the country, is enclosed by low rocky hills. The coast and river banks are backed mainly by mangrove swamps, while the lower part of the river has steep red ironstone banks which are covered with tropical forest and bamboo. Away from the river, the landscape consists of wooded, park-like savannah, with large areas covered by a variety of trees such as mahogany, rosewood, oil palm and rubber. On the coast, the river meets the Atlantic with impressive sand cliffs and 50km (30 miles) of broad, unspoiled beaches, palm-fringed and strewn with shells.

Credit: © Juliet Highet Brimah

GOVERNMENT: Republic. Gained independence from the UK in 1965. **Head of State and Government:** President Yahya Jammeh since 1994.
LANGUAGE: The official language is English. Local languages are Creole, Fula, Jola, Mandinka, Manjango, Serahule, Serere and Wolof.
RELIGION: Over 85 per cent Muslim, with the remainder holding either Christian or animist beliefs.
TIME: GMT.
ELECTRICITY: 230 volts AC, 50Hz. Plugs are either round three-pin or square three-pin (15 or 13 amps).
COMMUNICATIONS: Telephone: IDD is available. Country code: 220. Outgoing international code: 00. The country has an automatic telephone system. **Mobile telephone:** GSM 900; providers include *Africell* (website: www.africell.gm) and *Gamcell* (website: www.gamtel.gm). **Fax:** There are nine *GAMTEL* offices in Banjul offering fax services, some on a 24-hour basis. **Internet:** Main ISPs include *GAMTEL* (website: www.gamtel.gm) and *Quantumnet* (website: www.qanet.gm). E-mail can be accessed in Internet cafes in major towns. **Telegram:** Services are run by *GAMTEL*, 3 Nelson Mandela Street, Banjul. **Post:** Post office hours: Mon-Fri 0800-1300 and 1400-1700, Sat 0800-1100. **Press:** Newspapers are English-language and include *The Daily Observer*, *The Gambia Daily*, *The Gambian*, *The Independent* and *The Point*.
Radio: BBC World Service (website: www.bbc.co.uk/worldservice) and Voice of America (website: www.voa.gov) can be received. From time to time the frequencies change and the most up-to-date can be found online.

Passport/Visa

	Passport Required?	Visa Required?	Return Ticket Required?
Full British	Yes	No	Yes
Australian	Yes	No	Yes
Canadian	Yes	Yes/1	Yes
USA	Yes	Yes/1	Yes
Other EU	Yes	No/1	Yes
Japanese	Yes	Yes/1	Yes

Note: *Regulations and requirements may be subject to change at short notice, and you are advised to contact the appropriate diplomatic or consular authority before finalising travel arrangements. Details of these may be found at the head of this country's entry. Any numbers in the chart refer to the footnotes below.*

PASSPORTS: Passport valid for at least three months after date of return required by all.
VISAS: Required by all except the following for a maximum stay of three months:
(a) nationals of countries referred to in the chart above, except **1.** nationals of Austria, Canada, Cyprus, Czech Republic, Estonia, France, Hungary, Japan, Latvia, Lithuania, Malta, Poland, Portugal, Slovak Republic, Slovenia, Spain and the USA who *do* need a visa;
(b) nationals of ECOWAS countries;
(c) nationals of The Bahamas, Botswana, Iceland, India, Jamaica, Kenya, Malawi, New Zealand, Norway, San Marino, Tanzania, Tunisia, Turkey, Uganda, Zambia and Zimbabwe;
(d) transit passengers continuing their journey by the same or first connecting aircraft within two hours provided holding valid onward or return documentation and not leaving the airport.
Note: (a)* These nationals do not require a visa, but *do* require clearance from the Embassy/High Commission. (b) Nationals of some countries always require a transit visa; enquire with airline for details. (c) All visitors must hold return or onward tickets, all documents for their next destination and sufficient funds for their stay.
Types of visa and cost: *Tourist* and *Business*: £20 (single-entry); £40 (multiple-entry).
Validity: Single-entry visas are valid for six months. Multiple-entry visas are valid for 12 months. Extensions are possible and should be applied for at the Immigration Office in The Gambia.
Application to: Consulate (or Consular section at Embassy); see *Contact Addresses* section.
Application requirements: (a) Valid passport. (b) One application form. (c) One passport-size photo. (d) Fee, payable in cash, cheque or postal order only. (e) Stamped, self-addressed envelope (by registered post).
Working days required: 48 hours in person. At least one week by post.
Temporary residence: Enquiries should be referred to The Gambian Embassy, High Commission or Consulate (see *Contact Addresses* section).

Money

Currency: Gambian Dalasi (D) = 100 bututs. Notes are in denominations of D100, 50, 25, 10 and 5. Coins are in denominations of D1, and 50, 25, 10, 5 and 1 bututs.
Currency exchange: There is a bank/bureau de change (Meridien Bank) at the airport operating during scheduled flights. The capital, Banjul, also has a number of banks where foreign currencies can be exchanged. Some hotels and tourist resorts also offer foreign exchange facilities, but tend to charge high commissions. ATMs are available in large urban areas.
Credit & debit cards: American Express, MasterCard and Visa are accepted in most hotels if arranged at the beginning of the stay. Check with your credit or debit card company for details of merchant acceptability and other services which may be available.
Travellers cheques: To avoid additional exchange rate charges, travellers are advised to take travellers cheques in Pounds Sterling or US Dollars.
Currency restrictions: The thriving black market for hard currency is officially discouraged, and visitors must complete a currency declaration form on arrival. Currency from Algeria, Ghana, Guinea, Mali, Morocco, Nigeria, Sierra Leone and Tunisia is neither accepted nor exchanged. There are no restrictions on the import of local or other foreign currencies. Export of local or other foreign currencies is up to the amount imported. CFA Francs are accepted. Local currency may be difficult to exchange outside the country but there are no restrictions on its import and export.
Exchange rate indicators: The following figures are included as a guide to the movements of the Dalasi against Sterling and the US Dollar:

Date	Feb '04	May '04	Aug '04	Nov '04
£1.00=	54.15	52.24	54.81	55.90
$1.00=	29.75	29.25	29.75	29.50

Banking hours: Mon-Thurs 0800-1330, Fri 0800-1100.

THE GAMBIA

Credit: © Juliet Highet Brimah

Some banks open on Saturday and opening hours may vary from place to place.

Duty Free

The following goods may be imported into The Gambia without incurring customs duty:
200 cigarettes or 50 cigars or 250g of tobacco (or mixed to the same total weight); *1l of spirits*; *1l of wine*; *goods up to a value of D1000 (members of families travelling together may aggregate their individual allowances provided no single article exceeds D1000 in value)*.

Public Holidays

2005: Jan 1 New Year's Day. **Jan 21** Tabaski (Feast of the Sacrifice). **Feb 18** Independence Day. **Mar 25** Good Friday. **Mar 28** Easter Monday. **Apr 21** Milad al-Nabi (Birth of the Prophet). **May 1** Labour Day. **Jul 22** Revolution Day. **Aug 15** Assumption. **Nov 3-5** Koriteh (End of Ramadan). **Dec 25** Christmas.
2006: Jan 1 New Year's Day. **Jan 13** Tabaski (Feast of the Sacrifice). **Feb 18** Independence Day. **Apr 14** Good Friday. **Apr 17** Easter Monday. **May 1** Labour Day. **May 2** Milad al-Nabi (Birth of the Prophet). **Jul 22** Revolution Day. **Aug 15** Assumption. **Oct 22** Koriteh (End of Ramadan). **Dec 25** Christmas.
Note: Muslim festivals are timed according to local sightings of various phases of the moon and the dates given above are approximations. During the lunar month of Ramadan that precedes Koriteh, Muslims fast during the day and feast at night and normal business patterns may be interrupted in a few instances. For more information, see the *World of Islam* appendix.

Health

	Special Precautions?	Certificate Required?
Yellow Fever	Yes	1
Cholera	Yes	2
Typhoid & Polio	3	N/A
Malaria	4	N/A

Note: *Regulations and requirements may be subject to change at short notice, and you are advised to contact your doctor well in advance of your intended date of departure. Any numbers in the chart refer to the footnotes below.*

1: A yellow fever vaccination certificate is required from all travellers over one year of age arriving from endemic or infected areas. Travellers arriving from non-endemic zones should note that vaccination is strongly recommended for travel outside the urban areas, even if an outbreak of the disease has not been reported and they would not normally require a vaccination certificate to enter the country.
2: Following WHO guidelines issued in 1973, a cholera vaccination certificate is no longer a condition of entry to The Gambia. However, cholera is a risk in this country and precautions are necessary. Up-to-date advice should be sought before deciding whether these precautions should include vaccination as medical opinion is divided over its effectiveness; see the *Health* appendix for more information.
3: Immunisation against typhoid and poliomyelitis is often advised.
4: Malaria risk, predominantly in the malignant falciparum form, exists all year throughout the country. Chloroquine resistance has been reported.
Food & drink: All water should be regarded as being potentially contaminated. Water used for drinking, brushing teeth or making ice should have first been boiled or otherwise sterilised. Milk is unpasteurised and should be boiled. Powdered or tinned milk is available and is advised, but make sure that it is reconstituted with pure water. Avoid dairy products that are likely to have been made from unboiled milk. Only eat well-cooked meat and fish, preferably served hot. Pork, salad and mayonnaise may carry increased risk. Vegetables should be cooked and fruit peeled.
Other risks: *Diarrhoeal diseases*, including *giardiasis*, and *typhoid fevers* are common. *Bilharzia* (schistosomiasis) is present. Avoid swimming and paddling in fresh water; swimming pools that are well chlorinated and maintained are safe. *Hepatitis A* and *E* are widespread. *Hepatitis B* is endemic. Epidemics of *meningococcal disease* may occur throughout tropical Africa, particularly in the savannah areas and during the dry season. Immunisation against *diphtheria* is sometimes recommended.
Rabies is present. For those at high risk, vaccination before arrival should be considered. If you are bitten, seek medical advice without delay. For more information, consult the *Health* appendix.
Health care: Visitors are advised to bring good supplies of sunscreen, insect repellent and indigestion/diarrhoea medicines; all of these may be needed and they can prove expensive or, in some cases, impossible to buy in The Gambia. The Government provides both therapeutic and preventative medical and health services, and plays a dominant role in health services. Health insurance is strongly advised.

Travel - International

AIR: The main airlines to serve The Gambia are *Air Senegal*, *Gambia International Airlines*, *Ghana Airways* and *Nigeria Airways*. There are also many charter services.
Approximate flight times: From Banjul to *London* is approximately five hours 30 minutes (direct).
International airports: *Banjul (BJL)* (Yundum International) is 20km (11 miles) southwest of the city. Taxis are available to the city (travel time – approximately 30 minutes). During 1989, NASA built new airport facilities to enable it to serve as an emergency space-shuttle landing site. Airport facilities include banks/bureaux de change, bars, restaurants, duty-free shops, post office and car hire (*Hertz*).
Departure tax: None.
Tourist tax: A tourist tax applies for all tourists arriving at Banjul International Airport, no matter from which country. Travellers can pay in Euros (€ 10), Sterling (£5) or US Dollars (US$10).
RIVER: There is no longer any ferry service between Banjul and Dakar or Zighinchor in Senegal.
ROAD: Taxis can be hired between Dakar (Senegal) and Barra. Buses also travel between Senegal and The Gambia.

Travel - Internal

Note: Visitors should not travel by road from The Gambia to Casamance in southern Senegal because of the risk of armed banditry. Crime against tourists is rare, but sensible precautions must be taken and vigilance maintained. Care should be taken when driving or walking on roads, particularly at night, due to unpredictable driving standards and lack of street lighting.
RIVER: There are no longer any scheduled services along the River Gambia, although private charters are available. There is a ferry link between Banjul and Barra on the other side of the river. Day cruises along the river with lunch or in the evening with dinner and a live band are popular.
ROAD: Traffic drives on the right. There are 2700km (1675 miles) of roads in the country, about 32 per cent of which are paved. Roads in and around Banjul are mostly bituminised, but unsealed roads often become impassable in the rainy season. Extensive road improvements are underway; the latest additions are the Kombo coastal roads which have improved access to the airport and other popular sights and attractions. **Bus:** Local buses operate between Banjul and a number of towns and villages throughout the country. The services are fairly reliable, but buses tend to be overcrowded. **Taxis:** There are three types of taxis: *Tourist Taxis* are usually painted green and are licensed by the Gambian Tourist Authority. They operate a queue system outside hotels and resort areas and have a published tariff for set distances inside the taxi; *General Purpose Taxis* are usually painted yellow with green stripes – these are usually four person shared taxis which are usually used for short distances; *Collective 'Bush' Taxis* are usually seven-seater vans and go anywhere in the country, stopping wherever passengers want to get off and picking up new passengers when there is room. It is advisable to settle taxi fares in advance. **Car hire:** *AB* and *Hertz* operate in the Gambia; check with the car hire company for details before travelling. **Documentation:** An International Driving Permit will be accepted for a period of three months. A temporary licence is available from the local authorities on presentation of a valid UK licence. **Bicycle hire:** Bikes are available to rent at many hotels and resorts.

Credit: © Juliet Highet Brimah

Accommodation

By African standards, The Gambia has a fairly developed tourist industry, with many hotels geared primarily to package tours. During the tourist season (November to May), accommodation is often booked up and confirmation of advance booking is advised. Most of the hotels are self-contained complexes offering a wealth of tourist facilities, including swimming pools, bars, restaurants, shops, sporting facilities and spacious gardens. Bedrooms will not always be air conditioned. The number of hotels has increased greatly in recent years and this is expected to continue; today there are over 24 hotels with 6000 beds, both in Banjul and along the coast. Around 75 per cent of establishments belong to The Gambia Hotel Association, which can be contacted c/o PO Box 2637, The Bungalow Beach Hotel, Serrekunda, Kotu (tel: 465 288; fax: 466 180; e-mail: bbhotel@qanet.gm). There are about a dozen camps, lodges and motels in rural areas which provide basic but comfortable accommodation and meals. The most luxurious of these is Sindola Safari Lodge located at Kanilai, the home of the President of The Gambia. There are others along the Atlantic coast line and they are a great place for boat rides and birdwatching trips - a boon for ecotourists. For further information on different types of accommodation, contact The Gambia Tourism Authority (see *Contact Addresses* section).

Resorts & Excursions

Although The Gambia is Africa's smallest nation, it offers landscapes and attractions of great diversity, ranging from broad, sandy beaches on the Atlantic to lush tropical forests, swamps, marshes and large areas of wooded savannah.

BANJUL & THE COAST

The River Gambia is several miles wide at its mouth near **Cape St Mary**. It narrows to 5km (3 miles) at Banjul (known as Bathurst in pre-independence days), which is situated on **St Mary's Island** and has a deep and sheltered harbour.

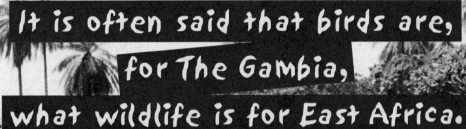

BANJUL: The only sizeable town in the country, Banjul is also the seat of government. There is an interesting **National Museum**. The area around **MacCarthy Square** has a colonial atmosphere, with pleasant 19th-century architecture. Nearby is the craft market. Souvenirs and local handicrafts can also be bought at various *bengdulala* (meaning a 'meeting place' in the Mandinka language); shopping areas consisting of African-style stalls, usually built near hotels.
Resorts: The Atlantic coast to the south of Banjul boasts some of the finest beaches in all of Africa with no less than 15 hotels in the **Banjul**, **Kombo** and **St Mary** area. They are served by the international airport at Yundum, 15 miles southwest of the capital.

Credit: © Juliet Highet Brimah

THE RIVER GAMBIA
This is the dominant feature of the country and is the major method of irrigation, as well as providing opportunities for fishing, boating and sailing. It is possible to take boat trips up the river. Most remarkable is the abundance and variety of birdlife along the shores.
WILDLIFE PARKS: The **Abuko Nature Reserve**, which has crocodiles, monkeys, birds and antelopes, is worth visiting. Details of cruises can be found on hotel noticeboards. The **Kiang West National Park** also has a rich birdlife as well as other animal species; tourist facilities in the park are well developed. Banjul is the starting point for coach and river trips to all parts of the country and coastline. The whole river and the numerous creeks (known locally as *bolongs*) which join it, are fascinating to both the bird lover and the student of nature.
THE RIVERMOUTH: Fort Bullen at **Barra Point** was built by the British 200 years ago to cover the approaches to Banjul and the river, succeeding **James Island Fortress** (destroyed by the French) as the main point of defence in the colony. It can be reached by direct ferry from the capital. **Oyster Creek** is the centre of an area of creeks and waterways which can be visited from Banjul.
UPRIVER FROM BANJUL: Albreda was the main French trading post before they withdrew from The Gambia. Nearby is the village of **Juffure**, the alleged home of the ancestors of black American writer Alex Haley, author of *Roots*. However, the authenticity of his account has been questioned over the years. Visitors who want to see more of the countryside may cross by ferry from Banjul to Barra and travel by road to Juffure and Albreda (the journey lasts about 50 minutes), and then by canoe to **James Island** in the calm waters of the River Gambia. The Niokolo-Koba National Park in the Upper Casamance regions is a World Heritage site of outstanding beauty. The popular tourist destination of **Tendaba** is 160km (100 miles) from Banjul by river or road. Further upriver, the fascinating circles of standing stones around **Wassau** have now been identified as burial grounds more than 1200 years old. **Georgetown** was the 'second city' of colonial days, and is still the administrative and trading centre of the region. **Basse Santa Su** is the major trading centre for the upper reaches of the Gambia River. Handsome trading houses built at the turn of the century can be seen there. By the riverside at **Perai Tenda** can be found a multitude of abandoned shops formerly operated by European, Gambian and Lebanese merchants in the days when upriver commerce offered substantial profits for private traders.

Sport & Activities

Watersports: Atlantic resorts cater for **waterskiing**, **windsurfing** and **surfing**. **Sailing** is possible at The Gambia Sailing Club at Banjul, which welcomes visitors. A notable event is the race to *Dog Island*. Additional regattas are organised on special occasions. Both sea and river **fishing** is good all year round, particularly line-fishing from the beaches. Several sport-fishing boats are available for sea-angling trips. The estuary of the *River Gambia* on the Atlantic coast provides miles of magnificent beaches with warm seas throughout the year for **swimming**. Due to strong currents, caution is necessary when swimming, but the beach at *Cape St Mary* is safe for both children and adults.
Spectator sports: The Banjul Golf Club has an 18-hole **golf** course at Fajara near the Atlantic coast. International meetings are organised every year. **Wrestling** is the traditional national sport; contests can be watched in most towns and villages. **Bouts** (a traditional sport) can be seen on most weekends in Banjul and its suburbs, Serekunda and Bakau. Inter-club **cricket** is played in league matches organised by The Gambia Cricket Association, which also organises international matches. A league **football** championship is organised by The Gambia Football Association.
Birdwatching: This is very popular and the country has one of the largest concentrations of bird species per square mile in the world.

Social Profile

FOOD & DRINK: Western food is available at most tourist hotels and restaurants, and some also serve Gambian food. Recommended dishes include *benachin* (also called 'Jollof Rice', a mixture of spiced meat and rice with tomato puree and vegetables), *base nyebe* (rich stew of chicken or beef with green beans and other vegetables), *chere* (steamed millet flour balls), *domodah* (meat stewed in groundnut puree and served with rice), *plasas* (meat and smoked fish cooked in palm oil with green vegetables) served with *fu-fu* or mashed *cassava chura-gertek* (a sweet porridge consisting of pounded groundnuts, rice and milk). Local fruits like mangoes, bananas, grapefruit, papayas and oranges are delicious and are available in the markets.
A good selection of spirits, beers and wines is available. *Jul Brew* is the local speciality beer. Local fresh fruit juice is delicious.
NIGHTLIFE: In general the nightlife is subdued, although there are nightclubs in Bakau, Banjul, Farjara and Serrekunda. There are organised performances of Gambian ballet, drumming and dancing, and also fire-eating displays.
SHOPPING: Souvenirs can be bought in Banjul at the craft market across from MacCarthy Square and at *bengdulalu* (see *Resorts & Excursions* section). One of the most popular purchases is the Gambishirt, made of printed and embroidered cotton cloth, mostly in bright colours. Some of the souvenirs are gaudy, others exceedingly attractive. Woodcarvings, beaded belts, silver and gold jewellery and ladies' handbags are also popular items. Other West African handicrafts made of straw, beads, leather, cloth or metal can be purchased here. **Shopping hours:** Mon-Thurs 0900-1200 and 1430-1800, Fri-Sat 0900-1300. Some shops may stay open until 2200.
SPECIAL EVENTS: Dance or acrobatic street shows can be seen at any time of the year; for further details, enquire at The Gambia National Tourist Office (see *Contact Addresses* section). The following is a selection of special events celebrated annually in The Gambia:
Feb *Tabaski* (Feast of the Sacrifice); *Ras-as-Sana* (Islamic New Year). **Apr** *Grand Magal*. **Jun-Jul** *International Roots Festival* (a celebration aimed at getting Americans and Europeans of African descent back in touch with Africa).
Oct-Nov *Ramadan*. **Nov** *Koriteh* (end of Ramadan). **Dec** *Christmas*.
SOCIAL CONVENTIONS: Handshaking is a common form of greeting; *Nanga def* ('How are you?') is the traditional greeting. Gambians are extremely friendly and welcoming and visitors should not be afraid to accept their hospitality. Many Gambians are Muslim and their religious customs and beliefs should be respected by guests; however, most understand the English customs and language. Visitors should remember that the right hand must only be used for the giving or receiving of food or objects. Casual wear is suitable, although beachwear should only be worn on the beach or at the poolside. Only the most exclusive dining rooms encourage guests to dress for dinner. Despite the effects of tourism, traditional culture in music, dancing and craftsmanship still flourishes in the many villages on both banks of the River Gambia. **Tipping:** 10 per cent service charge is sometimes included in hotel and restaurant bills.

Business Profile

ECONOMY: The economy of The Gambia is basically agricultural, with groundnuts (in the form of nuts, oil and cattle cake) accounting for 50 per cent of total exports. Cotton and citrus fruits are also cultivated for export. Forestry and fishing are also important. Rice, millet and maize are the main staples, but The Gambia must import large quantities of rice along with various other foodstuffs and petroleum products. There are no viable mineral deposits although surveys have located some oil deposits. The small industrial sector is dominated by agro-industrial activities; drinks and construction materials are produced for the domestic market. After a disastrous spell following the 1994 coup, tourism is once again a viable generator of foreign exchange, and has performed relatively well since then. Principal markets for exports are Belgium, Luxembourg, Japan and Guinea. Government economic strategy aims to position The Gambia as a regional hub for trade, based on an important re-export trade (mostly of Senegalese goods) as well as finance and telecommunications: the strategy has had mixed success in the last few years. Overall, the economy has performed fairly well, achieving annual growth of 3 per cent in 2004. Substantial infrastructural progress has been made (such as the construction of schools and hospitals, a new airport terminal and modernised port facilities). In 1998, the government, unusually, renationalised the groundnut industry, which had been privatised four years earlier but performed poorly under private ownership. International aid remains essential to the health of The Gambia's economy.
BUSINESS: Businessmen wear jackets and ties for business meetings. A personal approach is important in Gambian business circles. Punctuality is appreciated and it is advisable to take business cards, although their use is not widespread. **Office hours**: Mon-Thurs 0800-1600, Fri 0800-1230.
COMMERCIAL INFORMATION: The following organisation can offer advice: The Gambia Chamber of Commerce and Industry, 55 Kairaba Avenue, PO Box 3382, Serrekunda, Banjul (tel: 4378 929; fax: 4378 936; e-mail: gcci@qanet.gm; website: www.gambiachamber.gm *or* www.gcci.gm) *or* The Gambia Investment Promotion and Free Zones Agency (GIPFZA), GIPFZA House, 48 Kairaba Avenue, PO Box 757, SerreKunda, Banjul (tel: 4377 377/8; fax: 4377 379; e-mail: info.gipfza@qanet.gm; website: www.gipfza.gm).

Climate

The Gambia is generally recognised to have the most agreeable climate in West Africa. The weather is subtropical with distinct dry and rainy seasons. From mid-November to mid-May, coastal areas are dry, while the rainy season lasts from June to October. Inland the cool season is shorter and daytime temperatures are very high between March and June. Sunny periods occur on most days even during the rainy season.
Required clothing: Lightweight or tropical for most of the year with rainwear for the rainy season.

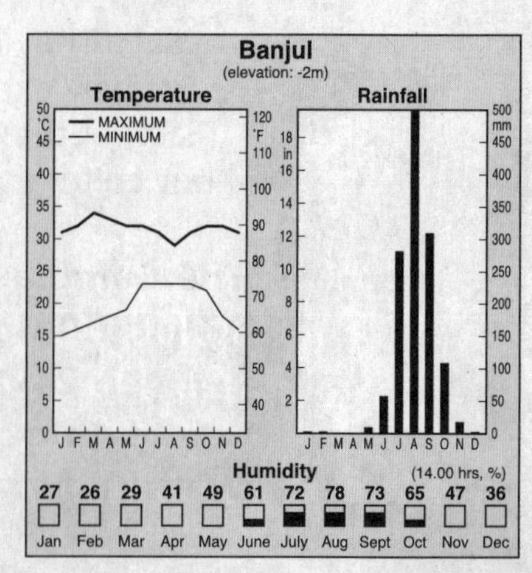

Great Hotels in the Gambia

www.visitthegambia.gm email: info@gta.gm

(The international country code for The Gambia is +220)

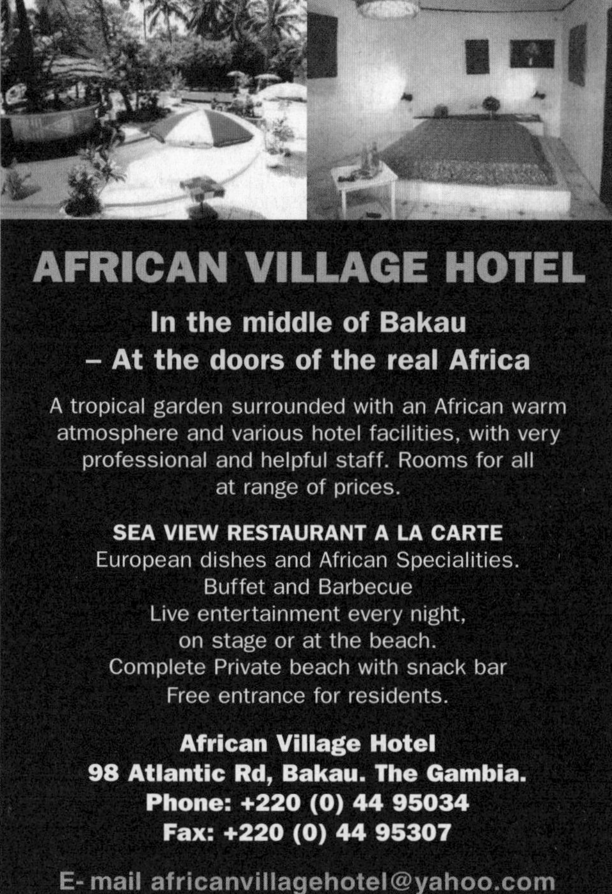

PALM BEACH HOTEL

The star of the 3 stars Gambian Hotels.

Perfectly located on the sandy shores of the Atlantic, within the green belt and tourism area called the Bird Watchers Road where you can bird watch from your balcony.

Photography: Luis Alda

160 rooms, 24 with sea view. A la Carte restaurant – Chinese Restaurant – Beach Bar and Grill – Piano Bar – Conference room for up to 300 Pax – Internet Café – Souvenir Shop – Excursions arranged.
Ideal base for business travellers and holiday makers.

PALM BEACH HOTEL
PMB 467, Serrekunda, Kotu Stream,
The Gambia
Tel: (220) 4462111 Fax: 00 (220) 4463836
E-mail: info@palmbeachhotel.gm
Website: www.palmbeachhotel.gm

Georgia

LATEST TRAVEL ADVICE CONTACTS

British Foreign and Commonwealth Office
Tel: (0870) 606 0290 Website: www.fco.gov.uk
US Department of State
Website: http://travel.state.gov/travel
Canadian Department of Foreign Affairs and Int'l Trade
Tel: (1 800) 267 8376 Website: www.dfait-maeci.gc.ca

Location: Caucasus, north of Turkey.

Country dialling code: 995.

State Department of Tourism and Resorts
80 Chavchavadze Avenue, 0162 Tbilisi, Georgia
Tel: (32) 226 125. Fax: (32) 294 052.
E-mail: info@tourism.gov.ge *or* georgia@tourism.gov.ge
Website: www.tourism.gov.ge *or* www.parliament.ge
Embassy of Georgia
4 Russell Gardens, London W14 8EZ, UK
Tel: (020) 7603 7799.
Fax: (020) 7603 6682 *or* (09065) 540 827 (visa application forms by fax; calls cost 60p per minute).
E-mail: embassy@geoemb.plus.com *or* consular@geoemb.plus.com
Website: www.geoemb.org.uk
Opening hours: Mon-Fri 1000-1800; 1000-1300 (visa lodging and collection), except Wednesdays (closed for consular information but not general enquiries).
British Embassy
20 Telavi Street, Sheraton Metechi Palace Hotel, 0103 Tbilisi, Georgia
Tel: (32) 955 497. Fax: (32) 001 065.
E-mail: british.embassy@caucasus.net
Website: www.britishembassy.gov.uk/georgia
Embassy of the Georgian Republic
1101 15th Street, Suite 602, NW, Washington DC 20005, USA
Tel: (202) 387 2390 *or* 9150 (consular section).
Fax: (202) 393 4537.
E-mail: embgeorgiausa@yahoo.com
Website: www.georgiaemb.org
Also deals with enquiries from Canada and Mexico.
Embassy of the United States of America
25 Atoneli Street, 0105 Tbilisi, Georgia
Tel: (32) 989 967.
Fax: (32) 933 759 *or* 922 953 (consular section).
E-mail: consulate-tbilisi@state.gov
Website: http://georgia.usembassy.gov
The Canadian Embassy in Ankara deals with enquiries relating to Georgia (see *Turkey* **section).**

General Information

AREA: 69,700 sq km (26,911 sq miles).
POPULATION: 5,177,000 (official estimate 2002).
POPULATION DENSITY: 74.3 per sq km.
CAPITAL: Tbilisi. **Population:** 1,081,700 (official estimate 2002).

TIMATIC CODES

Health	AMADEUS: **TI-DFT/JIB/HE** GALILEO/WORLDSPAN: **TI-DFT/JIB/HE** SABRE: **TIDFT/JIB/HE**
Visa	AMADEUS: **TI-DFT/JIB/VI** GALILEO/WORLDSPAN: **TI-DFT/JIB/VI** SABRE: **TIDFT/JIB/VI**

To access TIMATIC country information on Health and Visa regulations through the Computer Reservations System (CRS), type in the appropriate command line listed above.

GEOGRAPHY: Georgia is a mountainous country bordered by the Russian Federation in the north, Turkey in the southeast, Armenia in the south, Azerbaijan in the east and by the Black Sea in the west, which forms a 330km- (206 mile-) long coastline. It includes the two autonomous republics Abkhazia and Ajaria. The state is crossed by the ranges of the Greater Caucasus (highest peak: Mt Kazbek, 5047m/16,554ft). Enclosed high valleys, wide basins, health spas with famous mineral waters, caves and waterfalls combine in this land of varied landscapes and striking beauty.
GOVERNMENT: Republic. Gained independence from the Soviet Union in 1991. **Head of State and Government:** President Mickheil Saakashvili was elected in 2004.
LANGUAGE: The official language is Georgian, the only language in the Ibera Caucasian family written in ancient script, with its own unique alphabet. Russian, Ossetian and Abkhazian are also spoken.
RELIGION: Christian majority, mainly Georgian Orthodox church. Also Eastern Orthodox, Muslim, Jewish and other Christian denomination minorities.
TIME: GMT + 4.
ELECTRICITY: 220 volts AC, 50 Hz. European-type, two-pin plugs are used. The supply of electricity can be intermittent between November and March, and visitors are advised to bring a torch with them.
COMMUNICATIONS: Telephone: IDD is, in theory, available. Country code: 995. Some outgoing calls from Georgia, except to other parts of the CIS, must be made through the operator and long waits can occur. It is possible for visitors to set up an account with the local telecom company that enables them to make direct long-distance calls without the operator's assistance. Many businesspeople and journalists now use satellite links to overcome the considerable problems of ordinary telephone communication. The Metekhi Palace Hotel is equipped with its own satellite phones. **Mobile telephone:** GSM 900 and 1800 networks. Main operators include *Geocell Ltd* (website: www.geocell.com.ge) and *Magti Com* (website: www.magtigsm.com). Coverage extends around the capital and along the coast. **Fax:** Facilities are available at the Central Post Office in Tbilisi, 38 Rustaveli Avenue. Fees for outgoing faxes are charged per page. **Internet:** Local ISPs include *Sanet* (website: www.sanet.ge). **Post:** International postal services can be severely disrupted. Long delays may occur and parcels should be registered or delivered through courier services such as *Air Express* and *DHL*, based locally. It is advisable to post letters in central post offices rather than using the post boxes in the street. **Press:** The principal dailies are *Droni* and *Respublika*. *Georgian Times* is the English-language daily and there are two weekly publications, *Tbilisi Times* and *Weekly Post*. Foreign newspapers are available.
Radio: BBC World Service (website: www.bbc.co.uk/worldservice) and Voice of America (website: www.voa.gov) can be received. From time to time the frequencies change and the most up-to-date can be found online.

Passport/Visa

	Passport Required?	Visa Required?	Return Ticket Required?
Full British	Yes	Yes	No
Australian	Yes	Yes	No
Canadian	Yes	Yes	No
USA	Yes	Yes	No
Other EU	Yes	Yes	No
Japanese	Yes	Yes	No

Note: *Regulations and requirements may be subject to change at short notice, and you are advised to contact the appropriate diplomatic or consular authority before finalising travel arrangements. Details of these may be found at the head of this country's entry. Any numbers in the chart refer to the footnotes below.*

PASSPORTS: Passport valid for at least six months required by all.
VISAS: Required by all except nationals of CIS (except nationals of Russian Federation and Turkmenistan who *do* require a visa).
Note: All visitors must register with the police within three days of arrival.
Types of visa and cost: *Ordinary*: £8 (one month); £23 (three months); £4 (transit). *Double-entry*: £12 (one month); £35 (three months); £8 (transit visa). *Multiple-entry*: £77 (one year). For all other types of visa, contact the Embassy directly.
Validity: Tourist visas are valid from one to three months from date of issue. Multiple-entry visas are valid for 12 months from date of issue for stays of up to three months each. Transit visas are normally valid for a maximum of three days (provided transit passengers are also holding valid onward or return documentation).
Application to: *Individual* travellers should apply to the Embassy (or Consular section at Embassy); see *Contact Addresses* section. Nationals of countries where there is no Georgian diplomatic representation may obtain visas for US$10 at Tbilisi international airport, where a 24-hour service is provided by the Visa Branch of the Consular Department of the Ministry of Foreign Affairs. Visitors should note that this service is only applicable for short-stay visits (maximum 30 days). It is also recommended that the Consular Department of the Ministry of Foreign Affairs be informed in advance of the visitor's planned visit by the inviting party.
Tourist travellers must submit all documentation to the tour operator making the travel arrangements.
Application requirements: (a) Completed application form. (b) One recent passport-size photo. (c) Valid passport. (d) Fee (cheques and postal orders are accepted). (e) Stamped, self-addressed envelope for postal applications. *Business*: (a)-(e) and, (f) Letter of invitation from the inviting company. (g) Letter of introduction from the employer. *Transit*: (a)-(e), and (f) Visa for country of destination (if applicable). (g) Photocopy of confirmed return air ticket to Georgia (if applicable). (h) An official letter from an employer may also be required for the processing of transit visas (if applicable).
Working days required: Two to 10 for personal applications; up to one month for multiple-entry visas; longer for postal applications. If urgent, single- and double-entry visas can be processed the next working day during opening hours. Multiple-entry visas can also be processed, if urgent, within two weeks. An additional fee is required to process visas urgently.

Money

Currency: Lari (GEL) = 100 tetri. Notes are in denominations of GEL500, 100, 50, 20, 10, 5, 2 and 1. Coins are in denominations of 50, 20, 10 and 5 tetri.
Currency exchange: Euros, Roubles or US Dollars can be exchanged at special exchange shops, while other currencies must be exchanged in banks. Cash is the preferred method of payment, and visitors are advised to carry notes in small denominations. There is unlikely to be a substantial difference between rates offered by banks or bureaux de change.
Credit & debit cards: Credit cards are accepted in certain hotels. Check with your credit or debit card company for details of merchant acceptability and other services which may be available.
Travellers cheques: Euros or US Dollars are recommended.
Currency restrictions: The import and export of local currency is unrestricted. The import of foreign currency is permitted. The export of foreign currency is limited to US$500 or equivalent.
Exchange rate indicators: The following table is a guide to the movement of the Lari against Sterling and the US Dollar:

Date	Feb '04	May '04	Aug '04	Nov '04
£1.00=	3.83	3.49	3.37	3.36
$1.00=	2.10	1.96	1.83	1.77

Banking hours: Mon-Fri 0930-1700.

Duty Free

The following goods may be imported into Georgia without incurring customs duty:
200 cigarettes; 3l of wine or 10l of beer; personal goods up to the weight of 100kg.
Note: On entering the country, tourists are advised to complete a customs declaration form, which they should retain until departure. This allows for the import of articles intended for personal use, including currency and valuables (such as jewellery, cameras, computers, etc) which must be registered on the declaration form. Customs inspections are detailed.
Prohibited imports: Military weapons and ammunition, narcotics and drug paraphernalia, pornography, loose pearls and anything owned by a third party that is to be carried in for that third party.
Prohibited exports: Works of art and antiques (unless permission has been granted by the Ministry of Culture). In this case, the passenger should also hold a photo of the work of art or antique.

Public Holidays

2005: Jan 1 New Year's Day. **Jan 7** Orthodox Christmas. **Jan 19** Orthodox Epiphany/Baptism. **Mar 3** Mothers' Day. **Mar 8** Women's Day. **Apr 9** National Day. **May 9** National Holiday. **May 12** National Holiday. **May 26** Independence Day. **Jun 1** Orthodox Easter. **Jun 2** Orthodox Easter Monday. **Aug 28** Mariamoba (Assumption). **Oct 14** Svetitskhovloba (Georgian Orthodox Festival). **Nov 23** Giorgoba (St George's Day).
2006: Jan 1 New Year's Day. **Jan 7** Orthodox Christmas. **Jan 19** Orthodox Epiphany/Baptism. **Mar 3** Mothers' Day. **Mar 8** Women's Day. **Apr 9** National Day. **Apr 14** Orthodox Easter. **Apr 17** Orthodox Easter Monday. **May 9** National Holiday. **May 12** National Holiday. **May 26** Independence Day. **Aug 28** Mariamoba (Assumption). **Oct 14** Svetitskhovloba (Georgian Orthodox Festival). **Nov 23** Giorgoba (St George's Day).

Health

	Special Precautions?	Certificate Required?
Yellow Fever	No	No
Cholera	No	No
Typhoid & Polio	1	N/A
Malaria	2	N/A

Note: *Regulations and requirements may be subject to change at short notice, and you are advised to contact your doctor well in advance of your intended date of departure. Any numbers in the chart refer to the footnotes below.*

1: Immunisation against poliomyelitis and typhoid is sometimes recommended.
2: Malaria risk in the benign *vivax* form exists from July to October in some villages in the southeastern part of the country.
Food & drink: All water should be regarded as being a potential health risk. Boiled water is readily available and should be used. Milk is pasteurised and dairy products are safe for consumption. Only eat well-cooked meat and fish, preferably served hot. Pork, salad and mayonnaise may carry increased risk. Vegetables should be cooked and fruit peeled.
Other risks: *Hepatitis A* occurs. Immunisation against *hepatitis B* should be considered. Outbreaks of *diphtheria* and *anthrax* have been reported.
Rabies is present. For those at high risk, vaccination before arrival should be considered. If you are bitten, seek medical advice without delay. For more information, consult the *Health* appendix. Travellers staying for more than one month must present a medical certificate proving they are *HIV*-negative. If not holding the required documentation, they will be subject to a compulsory *AIDS* test on arrival.
Health care: The health service provides free medical treatment for all citizens in principle. A reciprocal health agreement for urgent medical treatment exists with the UK. In order to obtain treatment, some proof of UK residence will be required. Small sums may have to be paid for medicines and hospital treatment. If a longer stay than originally planned becomes necessary because of the illness, the visitor has to pay for all further treatment. Owing to the present state of medical services, emergency evacuation travel insurance is recommended for all travellers. It is also advisable to take a supply of those medicines that are likely to be required (but check first that they may be legally imported) as medicines can prove very difficult to get hold of.

Travel - International

Note: All travel to the breakaway regions of South Ossetia, Abkhazia, the Pankisi gorge beyond Akhmeta and the Svaneti region (northwest Georgia) should be avoided because of the heightened military and police tensions in these regions. On 1 February 2005 there was a car bomb explosion in the city of Gori, between Tbilisi and South Ossetia. The motive is unknown. Travelling alone in Georgia should be avoided and all precautions against the high levels of crime, including kidnapping, should be undertaken. However, travel to Ajara is possible since tensions have eased.
AIR: *Airzena Georgian Airlines (A9)* (website: www.airzena.com), the national airline, operates regular flights from Athens, Frankfurt/M, Kiev, Moscow, Paris, Prague, Tel Aviv and Vienna. For further information, contact their offices in Paris (tel: (1) 4801 6724; fax: (1) 4801 6758). *British Mediterranean*, a franchise partner of *British Airways*, operates two direct scheduled flights per week to Tbilisi from London Heathrow; contact British Airways for details of flights (tel: (0870) 551 1155). Other airlines serving Georgia include *Aeroflot*, *Air Ukraine*, *Austrian Airlines*, *Swiss* and *Turkish Airlines*.
Approximate flight times: From Tbilisi to *London* is six hours 45 minutes; to *New York* is 15 hours (both times include stopovers); and to *Paris* is four hours 45 minutes.
International airports: *Tbilisi (TBS)* is 16km (9 miles) east of Tbilisi city centre. Buses and taxis are available to the city centre (travel time – 30 minutes). Airport facilities include banks/bureaux de change, bars, restaurants, duty-free shops, first aid and left luggage. In winter, power failures may affect the airport.
Departure tax: None.
SEA: The main ports are Batumi, Poti and Sukhumi. Batumi and Poti provide international connections with the Black Sea ports of Istanbul, Odessa, Sochi and Trabzon and the Mediterranean ports of Genoa and Piraeus.
RAIL: The Transcaucasian railway operates services between Baku (Azerbaijan) and Yerevan (Armenia). The main line runs towards the Russian Federation through Georgia along the Black Sea coast. War in the breakaway region of Abkhazia has adversely affected Georgia's rail link with Russia and it is mainly used for transportation of cargo.
ROAD: Highways connect Georgia with the Russian Federation in the north via the Caucasian Road Tunnel (currently closed) and the Georgian Military Highway which runs south through Turkey, Armenia and Azerbaijan via the Dariali Gorge. At present, visitors are advised not to cross the Georgia–Russia border in either direction.

Travel - Internal

AIR: Domestic flights operated by *Airzena Georgian Airlines* run between Tbilisi and Butani, Kutaisi and Senaki.
RAIL: In total, Georgia has almost 1600km (987 miles) of railway. The Government has now restored order on the railway, which had suffered from fuel shortages, armed attacks on trains, sabotage of track and bridges, and there is now a fundamentally sound infrastructure. However, rail travel in the north and west is very difficult owing to the conflict in Abkhazia and visitors are advised not to undertake long-distance rail travel. Rail passengers are advised to store their valuables in the compartment under the seat/bed and not to leave the compartment unattended. It is also a good idea to ensure the compartment door is secure from the inside by tying it closed with wire or strong cord. Reservations are required for all trains. There are two classes of trains, primarily distinguished by the comfort of the seats. Children under five years of age travel free and children from five to nine years of age pay half fare.
ROAD: Traffic drives on the right. Georgia has approximately 20,000km (12,428 miles) of asphalted roads, and there is an ambitious project to construct a motorway connecting the Black Sea ports to the border with Azerbaijan, passing through Tbilisi. Travellers attempting to drive around Georgia independently should be aware that it is difficult to buy fuel without highly specialised local knowledge and that an adequate supply of fuel should be obtained in Tbilisi beforehand. Also, reliable road maps or signposts do not exist. **Buses** provide a reliable if uncomfortable service between towns within the republic. **Documentation:** An International Driving Permit is required to hire a vehicle.
URBAN: Tbilisi is served by buses, trolleybuses, cable cars and a small underground system. It is common practice to flag down official taxis, but fares should always be negotiated in advance, bearing in mind the likelihood that rates set for foreigners will be unreasonably high. In view of the rising crime rate, foreigners should take precautions before getting into a car, and it is generally safer to use officially marked taxis which should not be shared with strangers. It is inadvisable to take a ride if there is already more than one person in the car.

Accommodation

Under the former Soviet Government, hotels in Georgia were mainly state-owned. Much has changed recently, with many hotels now privatised and standards of tourist facilities far higher than in previous years. Tbilisi has luxury hotels with correspondingly high prices, one of which also houses the British Embassy. There are also a number of good hotels in Batumi and Kutaisi. Some of the large public hotels now provide temporary accommodation for refugees from Abkhazia and do not serve tourists. Most of the accommodation facilities currently available in Georgia are bed & breakfast-type smaller hotels and guest houses typically serving eight to 16 guests, often with shared bathroom facilities. In rural areas, visitors can stay as guests in private houses.

Resorts & Excursions

TBILISI

The capital of Georgia stands on the banks of the **River Mtkvari**, in a valley surrounded by hills. The name for the city derives from the word *tbili* (warm). It is best seen from the top of **Mount Mtatsminda**. With its warm climate, stone houses built around vine-draped courtyards, and winding streets, the city has a lively, Mediterranean atmosphere which was even present during the Soviet period. The old city, spreading out from the south bank of the river, has numerous frescoed churches (the most noteworthy being the sixth-century **Sioni Cathedral**), 19th-century houses with arcaded open galleries on the upper floors, a castle and a surprising number of cafes and enticing tourist shops selling locally produced arts and crafts. **Prospekt Rustaveli**, Tbilisi's main thoroughfare, features an assortment of stylish public buildings testifying to the city's prosperity at the turn of the century. The **Georgian State Museum** on Prospekt Rustaveli houses a collection of icons, frescoes and porcelain, as well as an outstanding display of jewellery discovered in pre-Christian Georgian tombs. The **Georgian Museum of Arts**, in the centre of town, includes many works by the much-loved 19th-century 'primitive' artist, Niko Pirosmani. The **Narikala Fortress**, first established by the Persians in the fourth century AD and most recently rebuilt in the 17th century, is a good vantage point for views over the old city. Visitors can still experiment with health-giving sulphur baths in a domed, oriental-style 19th-century bath house just north of the Metekhi Bridge. Popular with visitors today, Georgian sulphur baths were also frequented by writers such as Pushkin and Tolstoy. The open-air **Museum of Ethnography**, located in a western suburb, has interesting examples of rural buildings and artefacts. Davit Aghmashenebeli Prospekt is the base for the **Georgian State Philharmonic Orchestra** and the internationally known **Georgian National Dance Troupe**.

THE CAUCASUS

MTSKHETA: Located 20km (12 miles) to the northwest of Tbilisi, this town, which has been declared a UNESCO World Heritage Site, predated Tbilisi as the capital of Ibera until the fifth century AD, and remained the centre of Georgian Christianity until the 12th century. The 15th-century **Svetitskhoveli Cathedral** (Pillar of Life), standing at the confluence of the **Mtkvari** and **Aragvi** rivers, was the holiest place in old Georgia. According to legend, the church is built on the spot where Christ's crucifixion robe was dropped to the ground in AD 328, having been brought from Jerusalem by a local Jew, and fragments of the robe are said to be kept inside the cathedral. The existing church has some impressive royal tombs, a fine icon stand and distinctive carved decoration, including bulls' heads and semi-pagan fertility symbols. Also of interest are the **Samtavro Monastery** (still functioning although founded in the 11th century, it is famous as the burial place for the first Christian king, Mirian and his wife Nana) and the sixth-century **Jvari Cathedral**, the design of which became a prototype for Georgian ecclesiastical architecture.
GEORGIAN MILITARY HIGHWAY: Leading 220km (137 miles) from Tbilisi to **Vladikavkaz** (formerly Ordzhonikidze) in North Ossetia (now part of the Russian Federation), this route was built by the Russians in the 19th century to help them control their conquered Georgian territories. The road winds through the dramatic mountain scenery of the high Caucasus, apparently little changed since the 19th-century novelist Lermontov described the route in *A Hero of our Time*. Sites of interest along the road include the 14th-century **Tsminda Sameba Church** (Holy Trinity), overlooking the mountain town of **Kazbegi**, and the city of Mtskheta (see above).
GORI: The birthplace of Iosif Dzhugashvili, better known to the world as Stalin, lies 95km (59 miles) west of Tbilisi. The town has the last surviving public statue of Stalin in the former USSR, as well as a park and a museum devoted to Stalinist hagiography. The latter has been 'temporarily' closed for several years, ostensibly for renovation, but more probably to give the curators pause to decide how to display their exhibition in view of prevailing attitudes to the local hero. It also contains the ruins of a 12th-century fortress and a 16th-century church dedicated to St George.
EXCURSIONS: Some 10km (6 miles) east of Gori is **Uplistsikhe** (Fortress of God), a large complex of natural caves. Inhabited from the sixth century BC to the 14th century AD, the caves were gradually transformed into increasingly sophisticated dwellings, shops and public buildings, including the most ancient theatre in Georgia, dungeons and enormous wine cellars. The **Ateni Sioni Church**, 10km (6 miles) south of Gori, stands in a beautiful setting and is highly prized for its 11th-century stonecarvings and frescoes.
TORI: The spa town of **Bordzhomi**, 150km (93 miles) west of Tbilisi in the Tori region, produces much acclaimed mineral water. It is possible to hike in the surrounding hills. **Bakuriani** is located 29km (18 miles) southeast of Bordzhomi at an altitude of 1700m (5580ft). Before the current breakdown of order, Georgian tourist authorities were working to promote the *studarui* on the Georgian Military Highway as an international ski resort, proclaiming its clean air, uncrowded slopes and marvellous setting. There is a luxury hotel complex run by the same company that owns the Metekhi Palace in Tbilisi. 10km (6 miles) from Bakuriani, heading towards Bordzhomi, is the 12th-century **Daba Monastery**, and nearby a 60m (197ft) waterfall. During the summer it is also possible to visit **Lake Tabatskuri**, sunk into a hollow high in the mountains.

BLACK SEA COAST

BATUMI: A seaside resort and port in the southwest of the republic, Batumi is the capital of the Ajarian Autonomous Republic. Close to the Turkish border (20km/12.5 miles), the town has a decidedly Turkish character, with a mosque and 19th-century bath house. However, its charm lies less in any particular sights than in its lush, subtropical setting, among citrus groves and tea plantations, with mountains rising up from the edge of the sea. The **Ajarian Museum** (with its superb national costume collection), the circus, park, **Botanical Garden** and the theatre are also well worth visiting.
SUKHUMI: The capital of Abkhazia, in the far northwest of Georgia, was until recently a relaxed, sunny port/resort, renowned for its beaches fringed with palms and eucalyptus trees, lively open-air cafes and cosmopolitan population. The ruined 11th-century **Castle of the Georgian Bagratid King**, the **Botanical Gardens**, **Shroma Cave** with its amazing stalactites and stalagmites, and the

monkey-breeding farm were particular favourites among visitors. Abkhaz, Georgians, Greeks, Russians, Turks and others lived here in apparent harmony until recent years when the city was overtaken by civil war and thousands of refugees fled.

Sport & Activities

Formerly the holiday haunt of the privileged elite of the Soviet Union, Georgia is blessed with stunning scenery, a balmy climate and a rich variety of flora and fauna.
Trekking and mountain activities: The mountains to the north and south of the country offer opportunities for a range of trips, from strenuous trekking in the heights of the Caucasus to gentle walking in the lower pastures. It should be noted that political unrest makes certain areas inaccessible and dangerous, notably the breakaway regions of Abkhazia (in the far northwest) and South Ossetia. Areas bordering these regions are also best avoided. The country's infrastructure can also present problems to those attempting to reach remote areas without their own transport. For these reasons, it is best to arrange trips through a specialist operator. A guide is usually necessary for visits to the mountains, and porters may be hired. Given these restrictions however, the country is a rewarding destination for serious **trekkers**. The area around *Mount Kazbek* (or *Mkinvartsveri*, meaning 'ice top'), the third-highest peak in the Caucasus at 16,504 feet (5033m), offers challenging treks. Accommodation is available in two meteorological stations along the way, and special equipment is necessary to attempt the summit. Further east, the *Roshka Valley*, with its glaciers, and the *Chaukhi Mountains* also offer strenuous wilderness treks and stark mountain scenery.
Lowland walks are possible in both the north and the south of the country. The area around the ski resort of *Gudauri* (120km/75 miles north of Tbilisi) makes a good starting point for summer walks through mountain meadows full of flowers. Even in the lowland areas, eagles soar overhead and spectacular views can be had. The mountains in the south and east can offer more gentle walks. These regions are also suitable for **horse-riding** and **mountain biking**, and there are numerous mountain roads and tracks. Special Caucasian horses bred for their endurance and beauty, such as the *Kabardo* and the *Tusheti*, are the traditional means of transport in this area. Trips can be started at the mountain resort of *Bakuriani*. Gentler rides can be done along the Black Sea coast.
Birdwatching: This is another of Georgia's attractions. Approximately 360 species can be found, depending on the season, and the number of birds increases considerably during the spring and autumn migrations. Raptors including the bearded vulture, the long-legged buzzard and the white-tailed eagle can be seen in the Caucasus in summer. In the autumn, the wetlands and mountain steppes in the south near the Armenian border harbour white pelicans, white storks, cranes and Caspian snowcocks.
Wintersports: These include **skiing**, **ski touring**, **heli-skiing** and **snowboarding**. The country's main resorts are *Gudauri* and *Bakuriani*, the latter of which used to be the Soviet Union's most popular ski resort. Both resorts are suitable for skiiers of all abilities. International competitions are held. **Ski mountaineering** trips can also be arranged.
Wine tasting: The *Kakheti* province in the far east of the country is Georgia's wine-growing region. Apart from being an ancient tradition, drinking wine is also a social skill, with the traditional toast (or *Tamada*) being the prerogative of the most powerful male at the table. Other age-old rituals surround the harvesting, preparation and consumption of wine, which is usually of high quality. Georgian food is also very good. For further details of specialities, see the *Social Profile* section.

Social Profile

FOOD & DRINK: According to Georgian legend, when God was distributing land among the peoples of the world, the Georgians were so busy eating and drinking that they lost their place in the queue and there was no land left for them. But when they invited God to join the party, he enjoyed himself so immensely he gave them all the choicest bits of land he had been saving for himself. Georgians pride themselves, with some justification, on being the *bons viveurs* of the former Soviet Union, and their culinary tradition has survived better than most the dead hand of Soviet mass-catering. The cuisine makes extensive use of walnuts, which are used to thicken soups and sauces (anything including the word *satsivi* will be served in a rich sauce flavoured with herbs, garlic, walnuts and egg). Walnuts also feature as desserts, coated in caramelised sugar (*gozinaki*), or in *churchkhela*, when they are threaded on string then dipped in thickened, sweetened grape juice which is subsequently dried into chewy, flavoursome 'candles'. There is less emphasis on lamb to the exclusion of other kinds of meat than in other parts of the Caucasus. Roast suckling pig is often served, and beef and chicken are grilled or casseroled in various sauces, one of the commonest forms being *chakhokhbili*, a stew involving herbs, tomatoes and paprika. Meals usually start with an array of hot and cold dishes which may include spicy grilled liver and other offal, *lobio* (a bean and walnut salad), marinated aubergines, *pkhali* (made from young spinach leaves pounded together with spices), *khachapuri* (consisting of layers of flat bread alternated with melting cheese), and assorted fresh and pickled vegetables and cured meat (*basturma*). Cafes, restaurants and street-food traditions are all better established in Georgia than in many of the other former Soviet republics, and the markets are full of locally grown fruit and vegetables. Privately run restaurants, cafes and bars, which began to thrive during the Gorbachev period, were badly hit by the post-independence breakdown of civil order, but in recent times have begun to bounce back. The future looks bright.
Both red and white wine is produced in Georgia. *Kindzmareuli*, a fruity, red wine, is reputed to have been Stalin's favourite tipple. *Akhasheni* and *Teliani* are two of the commoner red wines, fruity and dry respectively. *Tsinandali* is a dry white wine, as is *Gurdzhaani*.
NIGHTLIFE: Nightlife in the republic is to be found primarily in international hotels. The *Georgian State Dancers* are highly praised but only occasionally to be glimpsed in Tbilisi, being almost constantly on tour. The *Rustaveli Georgian Drama Theatre* also has a good reputation and is particularly renowned for its Shakespeare productions.
SHOPPING: Georgian ceramics, embroidery and jewellery are all distinctive, and may be bought in art salons or special tourist shops. Visitors may also develop a liking for locally produced wines and brandies. Antiques such as rugs and icons attract a heavy export duty and must be licensed for export by the Ministry of Culture. Goods acquired in markets or from private individuals will not come with an export licence, whereas official tourist shops usually take responsibility for certification.
SPECIAL EVENTS: It is traditional in Georgia to mark the anniversaries of the founding of cities and towns. For a complete list, consult the Embassy of Georgia (see *Contact Addresses* section). The following is a special event celebrated annually in Georgia:
Oct 30 *Tbilisoba*, the largest annual celebration in Georgia, commemorating the founding of Tbilisi.
SOCIAL CONVENTIONS: Georgians pride themselves on their reputation for gregariousness and hospitality. Visitors sitting in restaurants are likely to be offered drinks by complete strangers. They will then be invited to raise (and empty) their glasses in response to an endless string of elaborate toasts, preferably interpolating a few suitably enthusiastic toasts of their own into the sequence. Smoking is widespread. Visitors may also be entertained in private homes. On such occasions, gifts such as chocolates, flowers or alcohol are well received. On social occasions foreign women will find themselves the object of immense flattery. Those finding such attentions oppressive should avoid giving any hint of encouragement. Appropriate clothing should be worn when entering a church; visitors should ensure they are not wearing shorts and women should cover their heads. Visitors should also be aware that street crime is far from uncommon. Anyone travelling in the republic should be cautious when venturing out after dark, carry as few valuables as possible, and beware of the risk of being robbed and possibly attacked. **Tipping:** For service in restaurants, cafes or taxis, the bill is usually rounded up.

Business Profile

ECONOMY: Georgia has experienced considerable economic difficulties during the last decade and is one of the poorest of the former Soviet republics with an annual per capita income of US$600. Disruption of the centrally organised Soviet trade and supply networks, plus civil war and political instability produced hyper-inflation and a slump in production. Major structural reforms, centring on the transfer of almost all small-scale enterprises to private ownership and a parallel reduction in the economic role of the state, were instituted. The measures have since contributed to strong annual growth for most of the post-Soviet period (it is currently 5 per cent) and a manageable rate of inflation. Unemployment, however, remains high, as does widespread poverty. A new national currency, the Lari, was introduced in 1995.
The agricultural sector, which accounts for about one-third of total output, produces fruit, tobacco, grain and sugar beet; sheep and goats are widely farmed. There is some heavy industry, notably shipbuilding, but most of Georgia's industry is light and engaged in food processing and production of fertiliser. Coal and manganese are mined in commercial quantities. The Government aims to establish the main ports of Poti and Batumi as regional transport and re-export hubs, which will also be able to handle oil refining and transhipment. (Part of this plan involves the laying of a set of pipelines running east-west across the entire country, linking the oil and gas fields of central Asia to the Turkish Mediterranean port of Ceyhan.) Further reforms, including the privatisation of major industries such as energy, are planned but the government has so far moved cautiously.
In 1992, Georgia joined the IMF, which has been centrally involved in the economic reform programme, the World Bank and the European Bank for Reconstruction and Development as a 'Country of Operation'. It has also acquired membership of the World Trade Organization. Turkey is now Georgia's principal trading partner, followed by Russia, Turkmenistan and Azerbaijan.
COMMERCIAL INFORMATION: The following organisation can offer advice: Chamber of Commerce and Industry of Georgia, Prospekt Chavchavadze 11, 380079 Tbilisi (tel: (32) 230 045; fax: (32) 235 760; e-mail: ggci@access.sanet.ge).

Climate

Hot summers with mild winters, particularly in the southwest. Low temperatures are common in alpine areas. Heaviest rainfall exists in the subtropical southwest.

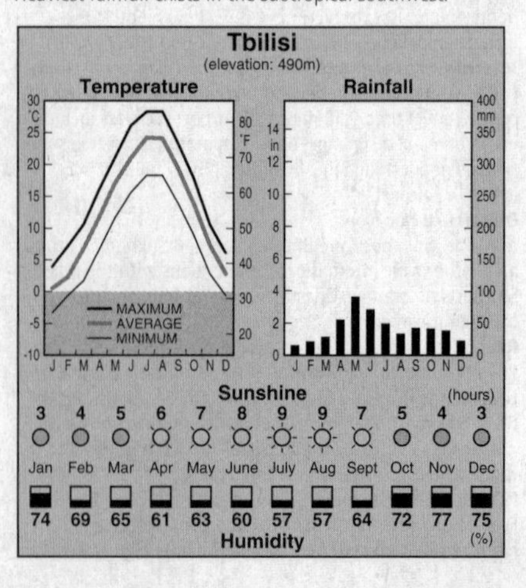

Germany

LATEST TRAVEL ADVICE CONTACTS

British Foreign and Commonwealth Office
Tel: (0870) 606 0290 Website: www.fco.gov.uk
US Department of State
Website: http://travel.state.gov/travel
Canadian Department of Foreign Affairs and Int'l Trade
Tel: (1 800) 267 8376 Website: www.dfait-maeci.gc.ca

Location: Western/Central Europe.

Country dialling code: 49.

Deutsche Zentrale für Tourismus e.V. (DZT) (German National Tourist Board)
Beethovenstrasse 69, 60325 Frankfurt/M, Germany
Tel: (69) 974 640. Fax: (69) 751 903.
E-mail: info@d-z-t.com
Website: www.germany-tourism.de
Embassy of the Federal Republic of Germany
23 Belgrave Square, London SW1X 8PZ, UK
Tel: (020) 7824 1300. Fax: (020) 7824 1449.
E-mail: info@german-embassy.org.uk
Website: www.german-embassy.org.uk
Opening hours: 0830-1700.
Consular section: 1-6 Chesham Place, Belgrave Mews West, London SW1X 8PZ, UK
Tel: (08705) 100 420 (recorded passport information; calls cost 60p per minute) *or* (09065) 508 922 (recorded visa information; calls cost £1 per minute) *or* 540 470 (24-hour automated visa appointment booking service; calls cost £1 per minute) *or* (020) 7823 2854 (consular emergencies only).
Fax: (020) 7824 1449.
E-mail: consular@german-embassy.org.uk
Opening hours: Mon-Fri 0900-1200; Mon-Thur 1400-1600, Fri 1400-1500 (telephone enquiries only).
Consulate General of the Federal Republic of Germany
16 Eglinton Crescent, Edinburgh EH12 5DG, UK
Tel: (0131) 337 2323. Fax: (0131) 346 1578.
E-mail: german.consulate@btconnect.com
Opening hours: Mon-Fri 0900-1200.
German National Tourist Office
PO Box 2695, London W1A 3TN, UK
Tel: (020) 7317 0908 *or* (09001) 600 100 (recorded information and brochure request line; calls cost 60p per minute).

TIMATIC CODES

Health	AMADEUS: **TI-DFT/FRA/HE** GALILEO/WORLDSPAN: **TI-DFT/FRA/HE** SABRE: **TIDFT/FRA/HE**
Visa	AMADEUS: **TI-DFT/FRA/VI** GALILEO/WORLDSPAN: **TI-DFT/FRA/VI** SABRE: **TIDFT/FRA/VI**

To access TIMATIC country information on Health and Visa regulations through the Computer Reservations System (CRS), type in the appropriate command line listed above.

Credit: © German National Tourist Board

Fax: (020) 7317 0917.
E-mail: gntolon@d-z-t.com
Website: www.germany-tourism.co.uk
British Embassy
Wilhelmstrasse 70-71, 10117 Berlin, Germany
Tel: (30) 204 570.
Fax: (30) 2045 7579.
E-mail: info@berlin.mail.fco.gov.uk (information department) *or* consular.berlin@fco.gov.uk
Website: www.britischebotschaft.de
Consulates General in: Dusseldorf, Frankfurt, Hamburg, Munich and Stuttgart.
Embassy of the Federal Republic of Germany
4645 Reservoir Road, NW, Washington, DC 20007, USA
Tel: (202) 298 4000. Fax: (202) 298 4249.
E-mail: ge-embus@ix.netcom.com
Website: www.germany-info.org *or* www.germany.info
Consulates General in: Atlanta, Boston, Chicago, Houston, Los Angeles, Miami, New York and San Francisco.
German National Tourist Office
20th Floor, 122 East 42nd Street, New York, NY 10168, USA
Tel: (212) 661 7200 *or* (800) 651 7010 (toll free).
Fax: (212) 661 7174.
E-mail: gntonyc@d-z-t.com
Website: www.cometogermany.com
Embassy of the United States of America
Neustädtische Kirchstrasse 4-5, 10117 Berlin, Germany
Tel: (30) 238 5174. Fax: (30) 238 6290.
Website: www.usembassy.de
Consulates in: Dusseldorf, Frankfurt/M, Hamburg, Leipzig and Munich.
Embassy of the Federal Republic of Germany
1 Waverley Street, Ottawa, Ontario K2P 0T8, Canada
Tel: (613) 232 1101. Fax: (613) 594 9330.
E-mail: germanembassyottawa@on.aibn.com
Website: www.ottawa.diplo.de
Consulates General in: Montréal, Toronto and Vancouver.
German National Tourist Office
480 University Avenue, Suite 1410, Toronto, Ontario M5G 1V2, Canada
Tel: (416) 968 1685. Fax: (416) 968 0562.
E-mail: info@gnto.ca
Website: www.cometogermany.com
Canadian Embassy
Friedrichstrasse 95, 10117 Berlin, Federal Republic of Germany
Tel: (30) 203 120 *or* 2031 2470 (consular section).
Fax: (30) 2031 2590 *or* 2457 (consular section).
E-mail: brlin@international.gc.ca *or* brlin-cs@international.gc.ca (consular section).
Website: www.canada.de
Consulates in: Düsseldorf, Hamburg, Munich and Stuttgart.

General Information

AREA: 357,027 sq km (137,849 sq miles).
POPULATION: 82,536,680 (official estimate 2002).
POPULATION DENSITY: 231.2 per sq km.
CAPITAL: Berlin. **Population:** 3,392,000 (2002).
GEOGRAPHY: The Federal Republic of Germany shares frontiers with Austria, Belgium, Czech Republic, Denmark, France, Luxembourg, The Netherlands, Poland and Switzerland. The northwest of the country has a coastline on the North Sea with islands known for their health resorts, while the Baltic coastline in the northeast stretches from the Danish to the Polish border. The country is divided into 16 states (*Bundesländer*), including the formerly divided city of Berlin. The landscape is exceedingly varied, with the Rhine, Bavaria and the Black Forest being probably the three most famous features of western Germany. In eastern Germany, the country is lake-studded with undulating lowlands which give way to the hills and mountains of the Lausitzer Bergland, the Saxon Hills in the Elbe Valley and the Erzgebirge, whilst the once divided areas of the Thuringian and Harz ranges in the central part of the country are now whole regions again. River basins extend over a large percentage of the eastern part of Germany, the most important being the Elbe, Saale, Havel, Spree and Oder. Northern Germany includes the states of Lower Saxony (Niedersachsen), Schleswig-Holstein, Mecklenburg-West Pomerania and the city states of Bremen and Hamburg. The western area of the country consists of the Rhineland, the industrial sprawl of the Ruhr, Westphalia (Westfalen), Hesse (Hessen), the Rhineland-Palatinate (Rheinland-Pfalz) and the Saarland. In the southern area of the country are the two largest states, Baden-Württemberg and Bavaria (Bayern), which contain the Black Forest (Schwarzwald), Lake Constance (Bodensee) and the Bavarian Alps. Munich (München), Stuttgart and Nuremberg (Nürnberg) are the major cities. The eastern part of the country is made up of the states of Thuringia, Saxony, Brandenburg, Saxony-Anhalt and Berlin. The major cities in eastern Germany are Dresden, Leipzig, Erfurt, Halle, Potsdam, Schwerin and Rostock. Apart from Leipzig and Rostock, these are also all recently reconstituted state capitals.
GOVERNMENT: Federal Republic. **Head of State:** President Horst Köehler since 2004. **Head of Government:** Chancellor Gerhard Schröder since 1998.
LANGUAGE: German. English is widely spoken and French is also spoken, particularly in the Saarland. In the north of Schleswig-Holstein, Danish is spoken by the Danish minority and taught in schools. In Brandenburg and Saxony, Sorbic is spoken by the ethnic minority called the Sorbs and is also taught in about 50 schools. Regional dialects often differ markedly from standard German.
RELIGION: Approximately 34 per cent Protestant, 34 per cent Roman Catholic, with Jewish, Muslim and other non-Christian minorities.
TIME: GMT + 1 (GMT + 2 from last Sunday in March to Saturday before last Sunday in October).
ELECTRICITY: 230 volts AC, 50Hz. European-style round two-pin plugs are in use. Lamp fittings are screw type.
COMMUNICATIONS: Telephone: Full IDD is available. Country code: 49. Outgoing international code: 00. National and international calls can be made from coin- or card-operated telephone booths. Calls can be made from post offices. Cheap rate applies Mon-Fri 1800-0800 and all day Saturday and Sunday. Discount phonecards from private companies can be bought from shops and kiosks. **Mobile**

telephone: GSM 900 and 1800 networks cover the whole country. It is illegal to use a hand-held mobile telephone while driving. **Fax:** Facilities are readily available. **Internet:** There are many Internet cafes all over the country. Large Internet access centres exist in most main cities. Hotels also provide facilities. ISPs include *Data Online* (website: www.d-online.com). **Telegram:** These can be sent during opening hours from all post offices. **Post:** Stamps are available from hotels, slot machines and post offices. A five-figure postal code is used on all internal addresses. *Poste Restante* mail should be addressed as follows: recipient's name, Postlagernd, Hauptpostamt, post code, name of town. Post office hours: Mon-Fri 0900-1800, Sat 0900-1200. Smaller branches may close for lunch. **Press:** The most influential dailies include the *Die Welt*, *Frankfurter Allgemeine Zeitung* and the *Süddeutsche Zeitung*. The most widely read of the weekly publications are *Der Spiegel* and *Die Zeit*. Some new or revamped newspapers, such as *Berliner Kurier*, have emerged out of eastern Germany and are competing well with western German papers. Most major English newspapers and international magazines are also available in Germany.
Radio: BBC World Service (website: www.bbc.co.uk/worldservice) and Voice of America (website: www.voa.gov) can be received. From time to time the frequencies change and the most up-to-date can be found online.

Passport/Visa

	Passport Required?	Visa Required?	Return Ticket Required?
Full British	Yes	No	No
Australian	Yes	No	No
Canadian	Yes	No	No
USA	Yes	No	No
Other EU	1	No	No
Japanese	Yes	No	No

Note: Regulations and requirements may be subject to change at short notice, and you are advised to contact the appropriate diplomatic or consular authority before finalising travel arrangements. Details of these may be found at the head of this country's entry. Any numbers in the chart refer to the footnotes below.

Note: Germany is a signatory to the 1995 **Schengen Agreement**. For further details about passport/visa regulations within the Schengen area, see the introductory section, *How to Use this Guide*.
PASSPORTS: Passport valid for at least three months beyond length of stay required by all except:
1. EU nationals, and nationals of Iceland, Liechtenstein, Norway and Switzerland, holding a valid national ID card.
VISAS: Required by all except the following for periods not exceeding three months and for non-business (paid work) purposes:
(a) nationals referred to in the chart and under passport exemptions above;
(b) nationals of Andorra, Argentina, Bolivia, Brazil, Bulgaria, Chile, Costa Rica, Croatia, El Salvador, Guatemala, Honduras, Hong Kong (SAR), Israel, Korea (Rep), Macau (SAR), Malaysia, Mexico, Monaco, New Zealand, Nicaragua, Niue, Panama, Paraguay, Romania, San Marino, Singapore, Uruguay, Vatican City and Venezuela;
(c) passengers continuing their journey by the same or first connecting aircraft, provided holding confirmed onward tickets and travel documents. However, the following nationals always need a visa even if transiting by the same aircraft*: Afghanistan, Angola, Bangladesh, Congo (Dem Rep), Eritrea, Ethiopia, The Gambia, Ghana, India, Iran, Iraq, Jordan, Lebanon, Nigeria, Pakistan, Somalia, Sri Lanka, Sudan, Syrian Arab Republic and Turkey. Visitors should check with the Embassy (or Consular section at Embassy).
Note: *A transit visa is not required by some of these nationals if in possession of a residence permit or visa for an EU country, or they possess a "Leave to remain in the UK for an indefinite period" or a "Certificate of entitlement to the right of abode"; contact nearest German Embassy or Consulate for more information.
Types of visa and cost: *Tourist*: Single-entry (up to 30 days): £18 (adults); £9 (minors under 18 years); (up to 90 days): £21; £11. Multiple-entry (up to 90 days): £25; £13. Multiple-entry (for one year up to 90 days): £35; £18. *Transit*: £7; £4.
Note: Spouses and children of EU nationals (providing spouse's passport and the original marriage certificate is produced) and nationals of some other countries receive their visas free of charge (enquire at Embassy for details). Diplomatic missions in the UK and spouses of German nationals may pre-book an appointment by telephoning (020) 7823 2854.
Validity: *Short-stay* (single- and multiple-entry): valid for six months from date of issue for stays of maximum 90 days per entry or for one year from date of entry for stays of maximum 90 days in one half-year. *Transit* (single- and multiple-entry): valid for a maximum of five days per entry, including the day of arrival. Visas cannot be extended and a new application must be made each time.
Application to: Consulate or Consular section at Embassy (see *Contact Addresses* section). Travellers visiting just one Schengen country should apply to the Consulate of that country; travellers visiting more than one Schengen country should apply to the Consulate of the country chosen as the main destination *or* the country they will enter first (if they have no main destination). All first-time applicants must apply in person. Due to the high volume of visa applications, the Embassy has introduced a number system and only the first 100 applicants are guaranteed to be seen on the same day.
Application requirements: (a) Passport with at least three months' validity beyond period of visa, with at least one blank page. (b) Application form(s). (c) Colour passport-size photo(s). (d) Proof of health insurance, covering at least £20 per day. (e) Fee (payable in cash only). *Visitors*: (a)-(e) and, (f) Formal obligation from host in Germany. *Tourist*: (a)-(e) and, (f) Proof of purpose of visit and/or a hotel reservation. (g) Proof of adequate means of support during stay (eg bank statement or travellers cheques). (h) Evidence of occupation or, if studying in Germany, a letter from place of study. *Business*: (a)-(e) and, (f) A letter from employer, or official invitation by fax, from overseas business associate explaining nature and duration of stay, plus guarantee of payment of costs incurred during stay. If self-employed, a letter from a solicitor, accountant, bank manager or local Chamber of Commerce.
Note: (a) Applicants under 18 years of age must also submit a letter from their parents/guardian authorising the visit and appointing the person who will be responsible for them. (b) If individual has obtained a German *Schengen* visa from the USA within the 12 months previous to the visa application, the individual may apply for a German Schengen visa this time by post. A self-addressed 'Special Delivery' envelope must be supplied and the visa paid for by postal order. (c) Nationals of Afghanistan, Algeria, Bahrain, Colombia, Congo (Dem Rep), Egypt, Indonesia, Iran, Iraq, Jordan, Korea (Dem Rep), Kuwait, Lebanon, Libya, Oman, Pakistan, The Philippines, Qatar, Saudi Arabia, Somalia, Sudan, Surinam, Syrian Arab Republic, United Arab Emirates and Yemen, must, in addition to the required visa documents, supply an extra application form and passport-size photo, a copy of their passport data page and provide the full address (including postcode) of a reference in Germany. (d) Minors under 18 must produce a declaration from both parents authorising their travel and stay in a Schengen country, and appointing the person responsible for the minor's welfare in their absence.
Working days required: For UK residents applying in the UK, visas will normally be issued within two days; however, applications from some nationals can take up to 14 days to process. If the stay is likely to be for more than three months, applications should be made at least 10 weeks in advance of the intended date of departure. Visa applications by non-residents have to be referred to the German Embassy in the applicant's home country, and may take several days or weeks to be issued. Applications by post take up to eight days, although the process may take longer on occasion.
Temporary residence: Nationals of EU and EFTA countries (Iceland, Liechtenstein, Norway and Switzerland) and nationals of Australia, Canada, Israel, Japan, New Zealand and the USA may apply for a permit from the local immigration office in Germany, no later than three months after entry. For further details on temporary residence in Germany, enquire at the Consulate (or Consular section at Embassy).
Work permits: EU nationals do not need a visa or work permit to work in Germany. A residence permit must, however, be obtained for stays of over three months (see above). Non-EU nationals must obtain a visa/residence permit before entering Germany. An information sheet, *Working and Living in Germany*, is obtainable from the German Embassy (see *Contact Addresses* section).

Money

Single European currency (Euro): The Euro is now the official currency of 12 EU member states (including Germany). The first Euro coins and notes were introduced in January 2002 and completely replaced the Deutschmark on 28 February 2002. Euro (€) = 100 cents. Notes are in denominations of €500, 200, 100, 50, 20, 10 and 5. Coins are in denominations of €2 and 1, and 50, 20, 10, 5, 2 and 1 cents.
Note: Eurocheques are no longer guaranteed and can no longer be accepted for encashments. However, they may still be used for payments without the guarantee in certain places.
Currency exchange: Foreign currencies and travellers cheques can be exchanged at banks, bureaux de change, post offices, airports, railway stations, ports and major hotels at the official exchange rates.
Credit & debit cards: These are accepted in approximately 60 per cent of all shops, petrol stations, restaurants and hotels. Nationals of other Western European countries, Canada and the USA, will find less credit card availability than they are used to in their own countries and it is advisable to carry cash or a Eurocheque card as well. All major credit cards are accepted. Check with your credit or debit card company for details of merchant acceptability and other services which may be available.
Travellers cheques: Generally provide the best rate of exchange. To avoid additional exchange rate charges, travellers are advised to take travellers cheques in Euros, Pounds Sterling or US Dollars.
Currency restrictions: There are no restrictions on the import or export of either local or foreign currency.
Exchange rate indicators: The following figures are included as a guide to the movements of the Euro against Sterling and the US Dollar:

Date	Feb '04	May '04	Aug '04	Nov '04
£1.00=	1.46	1.50	1.49	1.42
$1.00=	0.80	0.84	0.81	0.75

Banking hours: Generally Mon, Tues, Wed and Fri 0830-1300 and 1430-1600, Thurs 0830-1300 and 1430-1800 in main cities. Main branches do not close for lunch.

Duty Free

The following goods may be imported into the Federal Republic of Germany without incurring customs duty by visitors arriving from countries outside the EU:
200 cigarettes or 100 cigarillos or 50 cigars or 250g of tobacco; 1l of spirits with an alcohol content exceeding 22 per cent by volume or 2l of spirits or liqueurs with an alcohol content not exceeding 22 per cent by volume or 2l of sparkling or liqueur wine; 2l of any other wine; 50g of perfume or 250ml of eau de toilette; 500g of coffee or 200g of coffee extracts; personal goods to the value of €175.00.
Note: (a) The tobacco and alcohol allowances are granted only to those over 17 years of age. (b) Wine in excess of the above allowances imported for personal consumption and valued at less than €128 will be taxed at an overall rate of 16 per cent.
Abolition of duty free goods within the EU: On June 30 1999, the sale of duty free alcohol and tobacco at airports and at sea was abolished in all of the original 15 EU member states. Of the 10 new member states that joined the EU on May 1 2004, these rules already apply to Cyprus and Malta. There are transitional rules in place for visitors returning to one of the original 15 EU countries from one of the other new EU countries. But for the original 15, plus Cyprus and Malta, there are now no limits imposed on importing tobacco and alcohol products from one EU country to another (with the exceptions of Denmark, Finland and Sweden, where limits *are* imposed). Travellers should note that they may be required to prove at customs that the goods purchased are for personal use *only*.

Public Holidays

2005: Jan 1 New Year's Day. **Jan 6*** Epiphany. **Mar 25** Good Friday. **Mar 28** Easter Monday. **May 1** Labour Day. **May 5** Ascension. **May 16** Whit Monday. **Jun 10*** Corpus Christi. **Aug 15*** Assumption. **Oct 3** Day of Unity. **Oct 31*** Day of Reformation. **Nov 1*** All Saints' Day. **Nov 17*** Day of Prayer and Repentance. **Dec 25-26** Christmas.
2006: Jan 1 New Year's Day. **Jan 6*** Epiphany. **Apr 14** Good Friday. **Apr 17** Easter Monday. **May 1** Labour Day. **May 25** Ascension. **Jun 5** Whit Monday. **Jun 15*** Corpus Christi. **Aug 15*** Assumption. **Oct 3** Day of Unity. **Oct 31*** Day of Reformation. **Nov 1*** All Saints' Day. **Nov 17*** Day of Prayer and Repentance. **Dec 25-26** Christmas.
Note: *Epiphany, Corpus Christi, Assumption, Day of Reformation, All Saints' Day and Day of Prayer and Repentance are not observed in all areas. Consult the German National Tourist Office for details (see *Contact Addresses* section).

Health

	Special Precautions?	Certificate Required?
Yellow Fever	No	No
Cholera	No	No
Typhoid & Polio	No	N/A
Malaria	No	N/A

Note: Regulations and requirements may be subject to change at short notice, and you are advised to contact your doctor well in advance of your intended date of departure. Any numbers in the chart refer to the footnotes below.

Other risks: *Tick-borne encephalitis* is present in forested areas of southern Germany. Vaccination is advisable.

HIV testing is required for foreigners staying more than 180 days in Bavaria. Foreign tests are not accepted.
Rabies is present; look out for 'Tollwut' signs. For those at high risk, vaccination before arrival should be considered. If you are bitten, seek medical advice without delay. For more information, consult the *Health* appendix.
Health care: There is a reciprocal health agreement with the UK. On presentation of the form E111 (obtainable from post offices in the UK), UK citizens are entitled to free medical and dental treatment. Prescribed medicines may, in some cases, have to be paid for. The cost of treatment in public hospitals (on referral from a doctor, unless in emergencies) is covered by public health authorities, except for a small daily charge from the start of hospital treatment up to a maximum of 14 days. Private insurance is recommended for specialist medical treatment outside the German National Health Service, which can be very expensive. Surgery hours are generally 1000-1200 and 1600-1800 (not Wednesday afternoon, Saturday or Sunday). The emergency telephone number is 112; additionally, there is an emergency call-out service out of surgery hours (1800-0700). Chemists are open Mon-Fri 0900-1800, Sat 0900-1200. All chemists give alternative addresses of services available outside the normal opening hours. There are 350 officially recognised medical spas and watering places with modern equipment providing therapeutic treatment and recreational facilities for visitors seeking rest and relaxation. A list of the spas and health resorts and various treatments can be ordered from the German National Tourist Office, *or* directly from Deutscher Heilbäderverband e.V. (German Spas Association), Schumannstrasse 111, 53113 Bonn (tel: (228) 201 200; fax: (228) 201 2041; e-mail: info@dhv-bonn.de; website: www.deutscher-heilbaederverband.de).

Travel - International

AIR: The national airline is *Lufthansa (LH)* (website: www.lufthansa.com). Many other airlines serve the country, including an increasing number of low-cost airlines (such as *Easyjet* and *Ryanair*) operating from the UK.
Approximate flight times: From Bremen, Hamburg or Hannover to *London* is one hour 20 minutes; from Cologne/ Bonn to *London* is one hour 10 minutes; from Frankfurt/M to *London* is one hour 25 minutes; from Nuremberg to *London* is two hours 30 minutes (with one stop); and from Munich to *London* is one hour 40 minutes. From Frankfurt/M to *Los Angeles* is 11 hours 20 minutes, to *New York* is eight hours 20 minutes, to *Singapore* is 13 hours and to *Sydney* is 23 hours.
International airports: *Berlin-Tegel (TXL)* (Otto Lilienthal) (website: www.berlin-airport.de) is located 8km (5 miles) northwest of the city (travel time – 20 minutes). Bus nos. 109, 128 and X9 go to the city every five to 10 minutes from 0500-2400; return is from Bahnhof Zoo, Budapester Strasse, Charlottenburg station or Kurfürstendamm underground station. Airport facilities include duty free shop, banks/bureaux de change, left luggage, 24-hour medical facilities, post office, restaurant, bars, snack bar, shops, tourist information, conference rooms, hotel reservation and car hire.
Berlin-Schönefeld (SXF) (website: www.berlin-airport.de) is 20km (12 miles) southeast of the city (travel time – one hour). The *AirportExpress* train departs for the city centre every 30 minutes (0430-2300). S-Bahn no. S9 departs for the city (to *Westkreuz*) via Alexanderplatz and Bahnhof Zoo; S45 departs every 20 minutes to Westend. Further connections with the regional train services R1, R2 and R12 are available at the same tariff as the S-Bahn. Bus no. 171 runs between U-Bahn station Rudow (Line 7) and the airport. Taxi service is available to the city 24 hours. Airport facilities include duty free shop, banks/bureaux de change, post office, restaurant, left luggage, medical facilities, nursery, snack bar, hotel reservation, tourist information and car hire. The mainline railway station is a 10 minute walk from the airport; connections to major German cities and to Basle, Budapest, Prague and Vienna are possible from here. A free shuttle bus is available from the airport to the station.
Berlin-Tempelhof (THF) (website: www.berlin-airport.de) is 6km (4 miles) southeast of the city centre (travel time – 20 minutes). Bus no. 119 departs every 10 minutes to the city. The underground lines 6 and 7 run every two to 10 minutes (travel time – 15 minutes). Taxis are available. Airport facilities include duty free shop, left luggage, 24-hour medical facilities, banks/bureaux de change, snack bar, other shops and car hire.
Bremen (BRE) (Neuenland) (website: www.airport-bremen.de) is 3.5km (2 miles) from the city (travel time – 10 minutes). Tram no. 6 takes approximately 17 minutes to the city centre (main railway station). Services run Mon-Sat every five to 15 minutes, and Sun every 15 to 30 minutes. There is a 24-hour taxi service. Airport facilities include a duty free shop, bank, bureau de change, conference centre, car hire and hotel reservation.
Cologne (Köln/Bonn) (CGN) (Konrad Adenauer) (website: www.airport-cgn.de) is 14km (9 miles) southeast of Cologne, and 21km (13 miles) northeast of Bonn (travel time – 25 and 35 minutes respectively). Express bus no. 170 goes to Cologne every 15 to 30 minutes. Express bus no. 670 goes to Bonn every 20 minutes; return is from the bus stop near the main railway station (stadthaltestelle am hauptbahnhof). There is a 24-hour taxi service at the airport. Airport facilities include a duty free shop, tourist information, conference centre, car hire, restaurant, bar, bank/building society and shops.
Dresden (DRS) (Klotsche) (website: www.dresden-airport.de) is 9km (6 miles) northeast of Dresden (travel time – 25 minutes). Daily bus services are available to the city. Airport facilities include left luggage, bank/bureau de change, car hire, bars, restaurants, shops and tourist information.
Düsseldorf (DUS) (Rhein-Ruhr) (website: www.duesseldorf-international.de) is 8km (5 miles) north of the city. Trains depart to the city every 20 minutes (the airport station is under the arrival hall). Return is from Hauptbahnhof (main railway station) every 30 minutes. An S-Bahn connection (S7) every 20 to 30 minutes and bus services are also available. Taxis run a 24-hour service to Düsseldorf. Airport facilities include a duty free shop, bank, medical facilities, post office, restaurant, bars, snack bar, tourist information, car hire and conference rooms.
Frankfurt/M (FRA) (Rhein/Main) (website: www.frankfurt-airport.de) is 13km (8 miles) southwest of the city. Travel to and from the city is by buses no. 61 and 62 every 20 minutes, returning from Hauptbahnhof (main railway station). Lines S8 and S9 go to the city (the station is underneath the arrival hall). S-Bahn S8 also goes directly to Mainz and Wiesbaden (travel time – 40 minutes). There is a 24-hour taxi service to Frankfurt. The airport has its own InterCity railway station which also offers international services (Austria, Hungary and Switzerland). The *Lufthansa Courtesy Airport Bus* connects with Mannheim (travel time – one hour) and Heidelberg (travel time – one hour 30 minutes). Long-distance bus services from the airport include the T271 to Ostrava in the Czech Republic (travel time – four hours) and the CHECK LINE bus to Strasbourg in France (travel time – three hours). Airport facilities include left luggage, medical facilities, duty free shops, banks, restaurants, bars, snack bars, shops, Airport Conference Centre (23 conference rooms), post office, tourist information and car hire.
Hamburg (HAM) (Hamburg-Fuhlsbüttel) (website: www.ham.airport.de) is 9km (5 miles) north of the city centre (travel time – 25 minutes). Coaches go to the city every 20 minutes, returning from Zentral Omnibus Bahnhof Kirchenallee. The Airport City Line bus runs every 20 minutes to the railway station from 0500-2300. Express bus no. 110 runs every 10 minutes to Ohlsdorf Station (travel time – 10 minutes). A taxi service is available. Airport facilities include duty free shop, banks, shops, restaurants, snack bar, post office, tourist information and car hire.
Hannover (HAJ) (Langenhagen) (website: www.hannover-airport.de) is 11km (7 miles) north of the city (travel time – 30 minutes). S-Bahn S5 runs between the airport and the main railway station every 30 minutes (travel time - 12 minutes). A 24-hour taxi service runs to Hannover. Airport facilities include a duty free shop, luggage lockers, medical facilities, banks/bureau de change, bars, snack bar, post office, restaurants, tourist information and car hire.
Leipzig/Halle (LEJ) (website: www.leipzig-halle-airport.de) is 12km (7 miles) northwest of the city (travel time – 30 minutes). Coaches and trains depart to the city. Return is from the main railway station and major hotels. 24-hour taxi services are available to the city. Airport facilities include duty free shop, conference centre, bank, post office, snack bar, medical facilities, tourist information and restaurant.
Munich (MUC) (Franz Joseph Strauss) (website: www.munich-airport.de) is 28.5km (18 miles) northeast of the city (travel time – 38 minutes). Direct links with the S-Bahn S8 and S1 run every 10 minutes from Hauptbahnhof (main railway station) (0313-0042; return 0355-0115). The Airport City Bus runs every 20 minutes from 0650-1930 to the Hauptbahnhof and every 30 minutes from 0755-2055; further bus services are available. Coach Oberbayern runs every 10 minutes to the city centre. Airport facilities include duty free shop, left luggage, 24-hour medical facilities, snack bar, restaurants, post office, banks, conference centre, car hire and bars. The airport also has a Visitors' Park. Attractions include Dimension M (interactive information centre), Viewing Hill (a vantage point to view airport activity), a display of historical aircraft, an aircraft simulator, movie theatre, a play area and restaurant.
Münster-Osnabrück (FMO) (website: www.airport-fmo.de) is 25km (16 miles) from the city. Buses go to Münster (travel time – 30 minutes) and Osnabrück (travel time – 35 minutes). Taxis take 40 minutes. Airport facilities include a duty free shop.
Nuremberg (NUE) (website: www.airport-nuernberg.de) is 7km (4 miles) north of the city centre. Underground U2 runs to the Hauptbahnhof (travel time - 12 minutes). There is a 24-hour taxi service. Bus no. 32 goes to Thon with interchanging bus no. 30 to Erlangen (travel time – 20 minutes) as well as trams no. 4 and 9. Taxis are available. Airport facilities include a duty free shop, luggage lockers, business centre, 24-hour medical facilities, bars, snack bar, post office, restaurants and car hire. *Saarbrücken (SCN)* (Ensheim) is 16km (10 miles) from the city centre. There is an hourly bus service (27) to the city, and taxis are also available.

Credit: © German National Tourist Board

Stuttgart (STR) (Echterdingen) (website: www.stuttgartairport.com) is 14km (9 miles) south of the city (travel time – 35 minutes). An S-Bahn link (lines S2 and S3) is available with trains running at 10-minute intervals. There is a 24-hour taxi service to Stuttgart. Airport facilities include duty free shops, luggage lockers, conference centre, 24-hour medical facilities, bank/bureau de change, bars, post office, restaurant and car hire.
Departure Tax: None.
SEA: The following shipping lines serve routes to Germany from the UK:
DFDS Seaways: Harwich–Cuxhaven.
Stena Line: Harwich–Hook of Holland.
P&O Ferries: Dover–Calais; Hull–Rotterdam; Hull–Zeebrugge.
Hoverspeed: Dover–Calais; Dover–Ostend.
Ferry connections also exist from Germany to Denmark, Finland, Latvia, Lithuania, The Netherlands, Norway, the Russian Federation and Sweden.
RAIL: The Channel Tunnel: The quickest route by train from the UK is through the Channel Tunnel with connections from Brussels or Paris to Austria. *Eurostar* operates direct high-speed trains through the Channel Tunnel from London (*Waterloo International*) to Paris (*Gare du Nord*) and to Brussels (*Midi/Zuid*). From London to Paris, travel time is three hours; from London to Brussels, travel time is two hours 40 minutes. From Brussels, there is a night train to Vienna leaving at 1910 and taking approximately 14 hours; from Paris (*Gare de l'Est*), there are two trains to Vienna, one at 0749 and another at 1749, taking approximately 15 hours. There are also connections from Brussels or Paris to Munich. For further information and reservations, contact *Eurostar* (tel: (0870) 6000 792 (travel agents) *or* (08705) 186 186 (public; within the UK) *or* +44 (1233) 617 575 (public; outside the UK); website: www.eurostar.com); or *Rail Europe* (tel: (08705) 848 848; website: www.raileurope.co.uk). Travel agents can obtain refunds for unused tickets from Eurostar Trade Refunds, 2nd Floor, Kent House, 81 Station Road, Ashford, Kent TN23 1PD. Complaints and comments may be sent to Eurostar Customer Relations, Eurostar House, Waterloo Station, London SE1 8SE (tel: (020) 7928 5163; e-mail: new-comments@eurostar.co.uk). General enquiries and information requests *must* be made by telephone.
There are excellent connections between the Federal Republic of Germany and other main European cities. In 1998, *Deutsche Bahn* extended their international network eastwards and it now connects with 13 European countries, including Croatia, Hungary and Slovenia. For more information, contact *Deutsche Bahn* in the UK at Passenger Services, UK Booking Centre, PO Box 687A, Surbiton, Surrey KT6 6UB, UK (tel: (0870) 243 5363; fax: (020) 8339 4700; e-mail: sales@deutsche-bahn.co.uk; website: www.bahn.de).
A number of scenic rail journeys begin in Germany and go to Austria or Switzerland, such as the routes through the Black Forest: Frankfurt/M–Offenburg–Singen– Schaffhausen and Würzburg–Zürich.
ROAD: Germany is connected to all surrounding countries by a first-class network of motorways and trunk roads. **The Channel Tunnel:** *Eurotunnel* operates trains 24 hours per day through the Channel Tunnel between Folkestone in Kent (with direct access from the M20) and Calais in France. All vehicles, from motorcycles to campers, can be accommodated. Eurotunnel operates three to four passenger trains per hour at peak times. The journey takes approximately 35 minutes. For further information, contact *Eurotunnel Reservations* (tel: (08705) 353 535; e-mail: callcentre@eurotunnel.com; website: www.eurotunnel.co.uk). **Coach:** For regular coach services from the UK to Berlin, Cologne, Dortmund,

Frankfurt/M, Hannover, Munich and other destinations in the Federal Republic of Germany, contact: *Eurolines* (52 Grosvenor Gardens, London, SW1W 0AU; tel: (08705) 143 219; website: www.eurolines.com). Agents in the UK are *National Express* (tel: (08705) 808 080 *or* (08701) 595 959 (holiday reservations); fax: (0121) 456 1397; website: www.nationalexpress.com).
In every major city, there are *Mitfahrerzentralen* (car-sharing agencies, see *Yellow Pages*) which offer shared car travelling to all European cities on the basis of shared costs; an agency fee is charged. See *Travel - Internal* section for information on documentation and traffic regulations.

Travel - Internal

AIR: Internal services are operated by *Lufthansa* and several regional airlines. Frankfurt/M is the focal point of internal air services and all airports in the Federal Republic of Germany can be reached in an average of 50 minutes' flying time. There are several airports in the country apart from those listed above which offer internal air services. Helgoland, Sylt and some other Friesian Islands are served by seasonal services operated by regional airlines or air taxi services. Connections by air are run daily from Berlin, Bremen, Cologne/Bonn, Düsseldorf, Frankfurt/M, Hamburg, Hannover, Munich, Nuremberg, Stuttgart and Westerland/Sylt (summer only). The majority of western airports offer daily flights to Leipzig and several flights a week to Dresden.
SEA/RIVER: Regular scheduled boat services operate on most rivers, lakes and coastal waters, including the Danube, Main, Moselle, Neckar, Rhine and the Weser, and also on Ammer See, Chiemsee, Königssee and Lake Constance. Ferry services are operated on Kiel Fjord and from Cuxhaven to Helgoland and to the East and North Friesian Islands as well as to Scandinavian destinations. Besides these scheduled services, special excursions are available on all navigable waters. The *KD German Rhine Line* covers the Rhine, Main and Moselle rivers, and has comfortable ships which operate daily from April to late October. Tours with entertainment on board and excursions are arranged as well as cruises between The Netherlands and Switzerland and on the Moselle. In conjunction with the *'White Fleet' Dresden*, the KD also organises cabin cruises on the Elbe between Dresden and Hamburg. The 'White Fleet' offers 30 scheduled services and short trips around Berlin. Further routes include the rivers Saale and Elbe, several lakes and the Mecklenburger Lake District. *Hapag-Lloyd* (website: www.hlag.de) operates cruises of seven to 21 days from Bremerhaven, Hamburg and Kiel in summer. Lake Constance (Europe's third-largest inland lake) is served by regular steamers, pleasure boats and car ferries between the German, Swiss and Austrian shores. The *Bodensee Pass* gives 50 per cent reductions to visitors throughout the Lake Constance area. This includes scheduled ferry services offered by the German, Swiss and Austrian railways as well as some bus, local train and mountain railway routes. The pass is valid for either seven or 15 days. Children up to six years of age travel free. In addition to the pass, there is a Family Ticket which is available free of charge and allows children between six and 16 years of age free travel; unmarried young persons between 16 and 26 years of age pay half price. In both cases they have to be accompanied by a parent. The Family Ticket is only valid on boats together with the Bodensee Pass.
RAIL: Several InterCity and ICE connections are on offer running every one to two hours on the following routes: Berlin–Frankfurt/M–Karlsruhe, Berlin–Cologne–Basel, Munich–Frankfurt/M–Berlin and Hamburg–Berlin–Dresden with direct links to Prague. The *ICE-Business-Sprinter* runs non-stop on the following routes: Frankfurt/M–Hannover, Wiesbaden–Hannover, Frankfurt/M–Hamburg, Wiesbaden–Hamburg, Mannheim–Hamburg, Karlsruhe–Hamburg and Frankfurt/M–Munich. Seats on these services have to be booked in advance; yearly ticket holders can use the Sprinters without surcharge. Generally, reservations are advised on all services. Children under six years of age travel free of charge; those aged six to 11 pay half fare; young people aged 12 to 26 pay 75 per cent of the standard fare. For latest information leaflets, contact German Rail in the UK (see *Travel – International* section).
German National Railways (*Deutsche Bahn*) operates some 32,684 passenger trains each day over a 40,800km- (25,500-mile) network and many international through services. Work on the 3200km- (2000 mile-) fast-train network has already started and should be completed by 2010. The network does not radiate around the capital as the federal structure provides an integrated system to serve the many regional centres. *EuroCity*, *InterCity*, *InterCity Express* and *InterRegio* departure and arrival times are coordinated with each other. More than 50 cities, including Berlin, Erfurt, Dresden and Leipzig, are served hourly by *InterCity* trains – and increasingly by *InterCity Express* trains; regional centres are connected every two hours (west Germany), or every two to four hours in the eastern part of the country, through the *InterRegio* system. Details of up-to-date prices, and where tickets can be bought, are available from *German Rail* (website: www.bahn.co.uk) *or* the Tourist Office.
Deutsche Bahn and Lufthansa have introduced an innovative project aimed at replacing internal German flights with more environmentally friendly rail transport. For travellers using Frankfurt airport wanting to transfer to or from Stuttgart or Cologne, train and flight timetables will be coordinated; one ticket will cover the whole journey and check in/check out will take place at Stuttgart Station. Boarding the train with just hand luggage, the travellers can pick up their luggage at the flight destination or Stuttgart Station. This offer is currently available for every airport Lufthansa flies to from Frankfurt (except Tel Aviv).
With a railway network as complex, modern and sophisticated as that in the western part of the Federal Republic of Germany, it is obviously impossible to give all the details of the main routes, facilities, timetables, fares and reductions which are available. The following section gives brief descriptions of the major special fares and tickets which are currently on offer. Some of these can only be obtained in Germany. Other new schemes, or modifications to existing ones, may be introduced in the future.
The introduction of the high-speed *InterCity Express*, travelling at 280kph (175mph), reduced travel times between the major centres immensely. The service is operating hourly only on some connections at the moment, but this number is increasing; a supplement is payable. The extensive *InterCity* network (300 trains per day) connects the major centres at hourly intervals, and ensures swift interchange between trains. A supplement is charged for first- or second-class on *EuroCity* and *InterCity* trains. Smaller towns are linked by the 26 *InterRegio* lines at 2-hour intervals. Supplementing the system of these longer-distance trains are several commuter networks in larger cities. **Facilities and services:** Buffet cars with some seating for light refreshments and drinks are provided on *InterRegio* (*IR*) trains. Most *EuroCity* and *InterCity* trains carry a 48-seat restaurant, offering a menu and drinks throughout the journey. The newer generation *InterCity Express* trains combine both of the above-mentioned facilities, offering a selection of snacks and menu in their restaurant cars. First-class passengers are provided with 'at-your-seat' service. The *InterCity Express* also provides a service car with conference compartment, card telephones and fully equipped office (photocopier, fax, etc). **Sleeping cars:** Many have showers, and air conditioning is provided on most long-distance overnight trains. Beds can be booked in advance. Some trains provide couchettes instead. Sleeping-car attendants serve refreshments. Seat reservations should be made for all long-distance trains well in advance. When reserving a seat on *EuroCity*, *InterCity* and *InterCity Express* trains, specify *Grossraumwagen*, which is a carriage with adjustable seats and without compartments, or *Abteilwagen*, which is made up of compartments. **Bicycles:** At approximately 260 stations in areas suited for cycle tours, the DB operates a bicycle hire service (ticket holders have special reduced rates). It is also possible to carry your bike on the train but you may need to pre-book a space for it so check prior to travel. **Mountain railways:** Cable cars, chairlifts or cogwheel railways serve all popular mountain sites.
Rail passes: The following is a selection of rail passes available on German railways. Details may change and travellers are advised to check with Deutsche Bahn. Because of the large range of promotions available at any one time, it is not possible to list them all, so visit www.bahn.co.uk for the latest information and offers. Some passes can only be purchased outside Germany (see **Note** below).
Saverticket: Available for a return journey on one weekend or within one month.
Supersaverticket: Available for a return journey on a Saturday or within one month (not valid Friday, Sunday and during peak days).
Twenticket: Available for second-class single or return journeys for regional and long-distance travel between the ages of 12 and 25. Valid for up to two months, the ticket gives up to 20 per cent discount on the regular fare.
Happy Weekend Ticket: Available for up to five persons travelling together at a weekend, from Sat to Mon (0300). Valid on all local trains, second-class only.
Euro Domino: These tickets enable holders to make flexible travel arrangements and are valid in 27 European countries, including the ferry service from Brindisi (Italy) to Igoumenitsa (Greece). They have to be bought in the country of residence for which a valid passport or other form of ID has to be shown. First- and second-class tickets are available for travellers over 26 years of age; for passengers under 26, only second-class is available. The tickets for travellers over 26 years of age are also valid for any three, five or eight days within a month (travel days do not have to be consecutive). They also entitle holders to a discount of 25 per cent on rail travel in the country of origin or in all countries which comply with the system. Discounted Euro Domino tickets are on offer for persons under 26 years of age. Children between four and 11 years get a 50 per cent discount; children under four travel free. The German variety of the ED-ticket is valid on the complete network of the *Deutsche Bahn*; all *InterCity* trains, including the *InterCity Express*, can be used without paying a supplement. Motorail is exempt. Where seat reservation is required, a reduced fee is charged; the usual rates apply for couchette and sleeping-cars.
Inter-Rail: Available to all, but for those aged over 26, tickets are approximately 40 per cent more expensive. Four different tickets are available. Europe is split into 8 zones (A-H) and the pass is valid for an unlimited number of train journeys in the zones chosen, which now include Bulgaria, Macedonia (Former Yugoslav Republic of), Romania and Serbia & Montenegro. The *Global Pass* is valid for one month in all eight zones (32 countries, including Morocco, Turkey and the ferry connection Brindisi-Patras). Other tickets cover just one zone (two to seven countries, 15 days' validity), two zones (six to 10 countries, 22 days' validity) and three zones (nine to 15 countries, one month's validity). Reductions of 50 per cent are offered in the country of residence for travel to the border and back as well as transit journeys. The Inter-Rail ticket is only available for second-class travel and does not include the use of certain services such as the *X2000* in Sweden, the *Pendolino* in Italy or the *AVE* in Spain. Certain other trains incur supplements.
BahnCard: The BahnCard ticket offers half-price rail travel with a choice of first- or second-class travel and is valid for one year. In addition, there are reduced versions for married couples, families, senior citizens, young people and children.
Good Evening Ticket: This ticket is available only in Germany. It offers travel on nearly all routes within Germany for a flat fare between 1900-0300 daily except Christmas, Easter and other major travelling dates. The ticket has to be bought at the station of departure.
Motorail: The German Railway has a fully integrated motorail network, connecting with the rest of the European motorail network. Trains run mostly during the summer and at other holiday periods; most have sleeper, couchette and restaurant/buffet cars; for details see online (website: www.dbautozug.de).
Note: Conditions may apply to some of these tickets. There are certain discount rail passes that can only be purchased outside Germany. The following rail passes can only be purchased through German Rail offices and travel agencies outside Europe: *German Railpass* (valid for five, 10 or 15 days for either first- or second-class travel); *German Rail Youthpass* (second-class travel for travellers under 26 years of age); and *German Rail Twinpass* (for two persons travelling together, first- or second-class, for five, 10 or 15 days).
ROAD: Traffic drives on the right. The Federal Republic of Germany is covered by a modern network of motorways (*Autobahnen*). There are over 487,000km (303,000 miles) of roads in all, and every part of the country can be reached by motorists. Use of the network is free at present, but the introduction of a road toll is being discussed and charges have been levied on some sightseeing roads in Bavaria. Lead-free petrol is obtainable everywhere. The breakdown service of the *German Automobile Association* (*ADAC*) is available throughout the country, though in the eastern part of the country, the *Auto Club Europa (ACE)* and the *Allgemeiner Deutscher Motorsportverband (ADMV)* also provide a service. Help is given free of charge to members of affiliated motoring organisations, such as the AA, and only parts have to be paid for. Breakdown services, including a helicopter rescue service, are operated by the ADAC. In the event of a breakdown, use emergency telephones located along the motorway. When using these telephones, ask expressly for road service assistance, (*Strassenwachthilfe*). In almost all cases, the number to dial for emergency services is 110; if in doubt, dial the fire brigade, 112. Although motorways in eastern Germany are of a reasonable standard, many secondary roads are still being improved to match West German standards.
Bus: Buses serve villages and small towns, especially those without railway stations. Operated by the Post, German Railways or private firms, they only tend to run between or to small places and there are few long-distance services. *Europabus/Deutsche Touring* runs services on special scenic routes such as the *Romantic Road* (Wiesbaden/Frankfurt to Munich/Füssen) and the *Castle Road* (between Mannheim/Heidelberg to Rothenburg and Nuremberg).
Taxi: These are available everywhere. Visitors should watch out for waiting-period charges and surcharges. All taxis are metered.
Car hire: Self-drive cars (companies include *Avis*, *Europcar*, *Hertz* and *Sixt*) are available at most towns and at over 40 railway stations. Chauffeur-driven cars are available in all large towns. Rates depend on the type of car. Some firms offer weekly rates including unlimited mileage. VAT at 16 per cent is payable on all rental charges. On request, cars will be supplied at airports, stations and hotels. Several airlines, including *Lufthansa*, offer 'Fly-drive'. Contact the National Tourist Office for details (see *Contact Addresses* section).

Credit: © German National Tourist Board

Motoring organisations: The *Allgemeiner Deutscher Automobil Club (ADAC)* (website: www.adac.de) based in Munich and the *Automobilclub von Deutschland (AvD)* (website: www.avd.de) based in Frankfurt/M have offices at all major frontier crossings and in the larger towns. They will be able to assist foreign motorists, particularly those belonging to affiliated motoring organisations. They also publish maps and guidebooks, which are available at their offices. German Automobile Association (*ADAC*) operates an emergency service to relay radio messages to motorists. In both winter and summer, there are constant radio reports on road conditions and traffic.

Regulations: Traffic signs are international. Speed limits in western Germany are 50kph (31mph) in built-up areas and 100kph (62mph) on all roads outside built-up areas. Motorways (*Autobahnen*) and dual carriageways have a recommended speed limit of 130kph (81mph). Speed limits in eastern Germany vary according to the condition of the road. Although officially the same as in western Germany, some motorways and dual carriageways carry varying speed limits and are signposted. Children under 12 must travel in a special child seat in the back. Seat belts must be worn in the front and back. All visitors' cars must display vehicle nationality plates. Fines can be imposed for running out of petrol on a motorway. The warning triangle and a first-aid box are compulsory. The nationwide alcohol limit is 0.5 per cent. Disabled drivers should be warned that, although Germany is well-organised for disabled travellers, an orange badge as used in the UK will not entitle the disabled motorist to park freely in Germany.

Documentation: Foreign travellers may drive their cars for up to one year if in possession of a national licence or International Driving Permit and car registration papers. Insurance is legally required. EU nationals taking their own cars are strongly advised to obtain a Green Card. Without it, insurance cover is limited to the minimum legal cover; the Green Card tops this up to the level of cover provided by the car owner's domestic policy.

URBAN: A high standard of public transport services is available in all towns. All urban areas have highly efficient and well-established bus services. These are supplemented in a number of larger cities by underground and suburban railway trains. In many towns, block tickets for several journeys can be purchased at reduced rates and unlimited daily travel tickets are available. In many larger cities, tickets for a local transport journey have to be purchased from ticket machines before boarding the suburban train (*S-Bahn*), underground (*U-Bahn*), bus or tram. There are numerous sophisticated vending machines which service all the main boarding points and a wide range of relevant maps and leaflets is available to travellers. Although there is often no conductor on trams and underground trains, inspections are frequent and passengers without valid tickets will be fined on the spot. Timetables and brochures are available at stations.

Berlin: The city's excellent public transport includes an extensive network of buses, underground and S-Bahn. In the eastern part of the city, tram services and the ferries of the Berliner Verkehrs-Betriebe, BVG (Berlin Public Transport; website: www.bvg.de), in conjunction with east Berlin's 'White Fleet', provide further services. The underground lines 1 and 9 run a 24-hour service Friday night to Saturday and Saturday night to Sunday. The Berlin-Ticket is valid for 24 hours for unlimited travel on bus, underground, S-Bahn and the BVG ferries. The special BVG-excursion coaches are exempt. Holders of the Combined Day-Ticket enjoy unlimited travel with bus, underground and S-Bahn, as well as on the complete ferry network of either organisation. A special Weekly Ticket with a validity of seven days can only be obtained at *Zoo* station. Further details are available from BVG (see above).

Note: Pedestrians should be aware that it is an offence to cross a road when the pedestrian crossing lights are red, even if there is no traffic on the road. On-the-spot fines for offenders are common.

(1): The following chart gives approximate travel times (in hours and minutes) from **Berlin** to other major cities and towns in the Federal Republic of Germany.

	Air	Road	Rail
Hamburg	0.45	4.00	2.25
Cologne	1.05	7.00	4.00
Frankfurt	1.10	6.30	4.00
Munich	1.20	7.00	6.20
Dresden	-	2.30	2.00
Leipzig	-	2.00	1.45
Erfurt	-	4.30	3.20
Rostock	-	2.30	3.00

(2): The following chart gives approximate travel times (in hours and minutes) from **Bonn** to other major cities and towns in the Federal Republic of Germany.

	Air	Road	Rail	River
Hamburg	0.55	4.00	4.00	-
Hannover	-	3.00	3.15	-
Frankfurt	0.40	2.20	2.00	[a]
Düsseldorf	-	2.20	1.00	-
Cologne	-	0.20	0.15	0.40
Stuttgart	0.50	4.00	3.00	-
Munich	1.00	7.00	5.30	-
Berlin	1.05	8.00	5.00	-
Leipzig	-	7.00	6.30	-
Dresden	1.45	8.00	7.00	-

[a]: There is a hydrofoil service (not daily) between Cologne and Mainz via Koblenz and Bonn which takes about three hours 30 minutes.

Note: All the above times are average times by the fastest and most direct route, by motorways in the case of road journeys, and by the quickest hydrofoil service for the time by river. The slow boat from Bonn to Cologne, for instance, takes three hours.

Accommodation

HOTELS: There is a good selection of hotels in the Federal Republic of Germany and comprehensive guides can be found at the German National Tourist Office. They can also provide the *German Hotel Association Guide*, published by the Deutscher Hotel- und Gaststättenverband (DEHOGA), Am Weidendamm 1A, 10873 Berlin (tel: (30) 726 252/0; fax: (30) 726 252/42; e-mail: info@dehoga.de; website: www.dehoga.de). Approximately 50 per cent of establishments offering accommodation in the Federal Republic of Germany belong to the association, which can supply further information on accommodation. A special accommodation guide for the disabled, *Hilfe für Behinderte*, is available through Bundesverband Selbsthilfe Körperbehinderter e.V (BSK), Altkrautheimer Strasse 20, 74238 Krautheim (tel: (6294) 42810; fax: (6294) 428 179; website: www.bsk-ev.de). Some hotels are situated in old castles, palaces and monasteries. Alongside these are modern, comfortable hotels on well-planned and purpose-built premises. Examples of accommodation for a family on holiday is a country inn offering bed, breakfast and meals. More demanding visitors are also well catered for with medium to luxury hotels. The German hotel trade is extremely well equipped with facilities from swimming pools and saunas to exercise gyms. When touring the country with no fixed itinerary, it is obviously often difficult to make reservations in advance. Watch out for *Zimmer frei* (vacancies) notices by the roadside, or go to the local Tourist Office (usually called *Verkehrsamt*). Visitors should try to get to the town where they want to stay the night by 1600, particularly in summer. **Grading:** DEHOGA (website: www.hotelsterne.de) introduced a hotel grading system, which follows the usual grading of **1 to 5 stars**.

Gasthof: A 'Gasthof' (inn) must provide the same facilities as a hotel except for the common rooms such as a lounge, etc. Thirty per cent of establishments fall into this category.

Pension: A 'Pension' must provide accommodation and food only for guests. It does not have to provide a restaurant for non-residents, nor common rooms. Sixteen per cent of establishments fall into this category.

Hotel Garni: Provides accommodation and breakfast only for guests. Twenty-seven per cent of establishments fall into this category.

HISTORIC HOLIDAYS: Information about holidays in castles, stately mansions and historic hostelries may be obtained by contacting the German National Tourist Office.

SELF-CATERING: All-in self-catering deals are available that include sea travel to a German or other Channel port, and accommodation at the resort. The latter might be in anything from a farmhouse to a castle. Details are available from the German National Tourist Office (see *Contact Addresses* section).

FARMHOUSES: The booklet *Urlaub auf dem Bauernhof* (*Holidays on the Farm*) is published in conjunction with the German Agricultural Society and can be obtained from *DLG*-Agrartour GmbH, Eschborner Landstrasse 122, 60489 Frankfurt/M (tel: (69) 2478 8305; fax: (69) 2478 8495; e-mail: dlg-verlag@dlg-frankfurt.de; website: www.dlg-verlag.de). Regional guides on most tourist regions can also be obtained from the GermVerlag, Eschborner Landstrasse 122, 60489 Frankfurt/M (tel: (69) 2478 8451; fax: (69) 2478 8484; e-mail: dlg-verlag@dlg-frankfurt.de; website: www.dlg-verlag.de *or* www.landtourismus.de); *Agrartour GmbH* offers agricultural studies. For more information, contact the German National Tourist Office. All aforementioned booklets are published in German only. A basic knowledge of German will be required for such a holiday. A catalogue with addresses for the whole of the country can be ordered from Landschriften-Verlag GmbH, Landferien Tourist Center, Zentrale für den Landurlaub, Heerstrasse 73, 53111 Bonn (tel: (228) 963 020; fax: (228) 963 0233; e-mail: info@bauernhofurlaub.com; website: www.bauernhofurlaub.com).

YOUTH HOSTELS: There are over 600 youth hostels throughout both eastern and western Germany. They are open to members of any Youth Hostel Association affiliated to the International Youth Hostel Association. Membership can be obtained from the YHA or *Deutsches Jugendherbergswerk* (German Youth Hostel Organisation), Bismarckstrasse 8, 32756 Detmold (tel: (5231) 74010; fax: (5231) 740 149; e-mail: service@djh.de; website: www.djh.de). Reservation is advised during the high season (and throughout the year in major cities).

CAMPING/CARAVANNING: There are well over 2500 campsites in the Federal Republic of Germany. They are generally open from April to October, but 400 sites, mostly in winter sports areas, stay open in the winter and have all necessary facilities. Campsites in the eastern part of the country are of a very basic standard. The permission of the proprietor and/or the local police must always be sought before camp is pitched anywhere other than a recognised campsite. It is not normally possible to make advance reservations on campsites. A free map/folder giving details of several hundred selected campsites throughout the country is available from the German National Tourist Board. The German Camping Club publishes a camping guide of the best sites in Germany; contact *Deutscher Camping-Club (DCC)*, Mandlstrasse 28, 80802 Munich (tel: (89) 380 1420; fax: (89) 334 737; e-mail: info@camping-club.de; website: www.camping-club.de). The *AA Guide to Camping and Caravanning on the Continent* lists nearly 2000 European campsites, including a large section on Germany.

Resorts & Excursions

Situated at the crossroads of Europe, the country consists of 16 states (*Bundesländer*), which are divided for the purposes of this section as follows: **Berlin**, **Baden-Württemburg**, **Bavaria**, **Brandenburg**, **Hesse**, **Mecklenburg-Western Pomerania**, **Northwest Germany** (the states of Lower Saxony, Schleswig-Holstein, Hamburg and Bremen), **Rhineland** (North Rhine-Westphalia, Rhineland Palatinate and Saarland), **Saxony**, **Saxony-Anhalt**, **Thuringia**. **Northwest Germany** includes the **North Sea** coast and the **East Friesian Islands**, **Schleswig-Holstein** and the city-states of **Hamburg** and **Bremen**, along with the **Weser Valley**, **Lüneburg Heath** and part of the **Harz Mountains**.

The **Rhineland** region incorporates the industrial sprawl of the **Ruhr**, the varied landscapes of **Westphalia**, the wine-producing region of **Rhineland-Palatinate**, and **Saarland**.

The state of **Hesse** with its 'fairytale road', also includes the major financial centre of **Frankfurt-am-Main**.

The **Black Forest** is in the southwest, and forms part of the state of **Baden-Württemberg**. Other areas of interest in this state include the **Neckar Valley**, **Swabia** and **Lake Constance**.

Munich (*München*) is the capital of **Bavaria**, whose main tourist regions are the **Bavarian Forest** to the east, **Franconia** to the north, **Upper Bavaria** and the **Alps** to the south and the **Allgäu** region of the southwest. Bavaria is the most popular tourist destination for both Germans and overseas visitors alike.

The states of **Brandenburg** (which surrounds Berlin), **Mecklenburg-Western Pomerania** (on the **Baltic** coast), **Saxony**, **Saxony-Anhalt**, **Thuringia** and, of course,

eastern **Berlin** itself, constituted the former East Germany (GDR) prior to re-unification in 1990. The Baltic coast with its resorts is the major holiday region in the former east, followed in importance by the **Thuringian Forest**, the northern lakes, the **Saxon Hills**, the **Harz Mountains** and the **Zittauer Gebirge**.

The scenery of Germany is enormously varied, ranging from sandy beaches to towering mountains, forests, lakes, medieval villages and some of Europe's greatest cities. Every area has its distinct regional foods, and it offers a huge choice of local wines and beers.

BERLIN

Berlin is the largest city in Germany. It is also the country's capital and seat of Government. The recently renovated **German Parliament** (**Reichstag**), designed by British architect Norman Foster, testifies to the construction boom currently taking place in the German capital. Since November 1989 when the Wall came down, nearly 100 streets have been reconnected, disused 'ghost' railway stations have sprung back to life and the watchtowers, dogs and barbed wire that divided the city, the country and indeed the continent for 28 years have virtually disappeared. Nevertheless, there is often stark contrast between the two parts of the city, partly due to economic contrasts between East and West, but also because they have never been of a uniform character.

The east contains the densely populated working-class quarters of **Mitte**, **Pankow**, **Prenzlauer Berg** and **Friedrichshain**, which inspired the theatre of Erwin Piscator and Bertolt Brecht. West Berlin also had its poorer areas like **Wedding**, **Neukölln** and **Kreuzberg** (the latter known for its pubs and the high proportion of Turkish-owned shops in its streets).

In comparison, the green and leafy areas of **Charlottenburg** and **Zehlendorf** have a more affluent atmosphere. After the city was occupied by the four post-war victorious powers, the two halves diverged even more as West Berliners broke away from their past and embraced the idea of a new, intensely western, Americanised city. At the same time, their eastern counterparts chose to retain what remained of the old Berlin instead. This is why the eastern half of the city probably gives a more accurate image of what Berlin was like in the 1920s and 30s. To find areas retaining the pre-war atmosphere, visitors must move away from the city centre. **Alexanderplatz** was one of the main centres of 1920s Berlin as well as of post-war East Berlin. It is now re-emerging as an important focal point in the newly united city. Relentless modernisation, however, has changed the character of the Alexanderplatz, which is now a bustling if faceless area of cafes, hotels and the 365m- (1190ft-) high **Television Tower** (**Fernsehturm**) which dominates the skyline of the city. The oldest church in Berlin, the **Nikolai Church** (13th century) lent its name to the surrounding district, the **Nikolaiviertel**. This part of the city suffered tremendously during the war. Rebuilding consists partly of historic details, partly of modern facades. Sweeping westwards away from Alexanderplatz is **Unter den Linden**, which Frederick the Great saw as the centrepiece of his royal capital and which changed from one of the premier thoroughfares of the old unified city to the showpiece of the German Democratic Republic.

Restored monumental buildings, and diplomatic missions to the former GDR capital now line it. However, for nearly 30 years it was a dead-end, cut off by the Wall. At its western end, the **Brandenburg Gate** (**Brandenburger Tor**) has been the supreme symbol of the city of Berlin since it was built in 1791. The Wall once partly obscured the view of the Gate from the West, so it became a potent symbol of European division. Now it is again accessible from both East and West. The **Berlin Wall** has all but gone and walkers and cyclists now roam along what was once nicknamed *'Todesstreifen'* or Death Strip. Quite a few tourists bought their 'own' piece of the Wall – museums also display pieces. There is a **Berlin Wall Museum** situated at the former **Checkpoint Charlie** in Friedrichstrasse. Designed by Daniel Libeskind, the innovative Jewish Museum that opened in 2001 is an incredibly moving experience (website: www.jmberlin.de).

Berlin is not just an industrial city but also a cultural and scientific capital with several universities. It houses three opera houses, 53 theatres, more than 100 cinemas, and no less than 170 museums and galleries. It is worth noting that most foreign films are dubbed into German; look for the 'O.m.U.' indicator for the original language versions shown with German subtitles. East Berlin has a rich array of museums, most of which can be found on **Museumsinsel** (**Museum Island**) in a fork of the **River Spree**.

The most famous is the **Pergamon Museum** which houses works of classical antiquity such as the **Pergamon Altar** and art of the Near East, Islam and the Orient. Among the many museums in the west are the **Ägyptisches Museum** (**Egyptian Museum**) in Charlottenburg, which contains the world-famous bust of Queen Nefertiti; the museums at **Dahlem** housing the major part of the Prussian State art collections; and the **Berlin Museum** in the old Supreme Court Building in Kreuzberg.

The restored **Martin-Gropius-Bau** houses changing art exhibitions and the Berlin Gallery, with exhibits of the Jewish collection of the Berlin Museum and 20th-century paintings. Nearby is the **Prinz Albrecht** area where the Gestapo headquarters, later the **Reichssicherheitshauptamt**, stood. The **Topography of Terror** exhibition documents this part of its history. The **Kulturforum Art Gallery** (opened in 1998) stands alongside the **National Gallery**, the **Philharmonic**, the **Chamber Music Hall** and other museums, and serves as a new cultural centre for the city. The **Hamburger Bahnhof**, *Invalidenstrasse*, a restored railway station, contains a collection of modern art. **Potsdamerplatz** is under development as another recreational centre with shops and an IMAX cinema.

One of the main cultural attractions of the eastern part of Berlin is the **Deutsche Staatsoper** (**German State Opera**), staging performances in a refurbished classical setting.

Three times a day, visitors can enjoy the carillon of the **French Cathedral** bell-tower. The **German Cathedral** on **Gendarmenmarkt** now contains an exhibition called *Fragen an die Deutsche Geschichte* (Questioning German History).

The heart of West Berlin is the **Kurfürstendamm**, popularly referred to as the 'Ku'damm'. As with so many features of this once divided city, it is all too easy to attribute symbolic significance to the 'Ku'damm', for, in a sense, it is the embodiment of the glitzy materialistic West. Pulsating with traffic and people 24 hours a day and lined with cafes and shops, despite unification, it still seems a thousand miles away from the bleak Alexanderplatz in the other half of the city. Strolling eastwards along the Ku'damm one will come to the **Kaiser-Wilhelm-Gedächtniskirche**. Preserved as a ruin after World War II, it is a stark reminder of the city's wartime bombardment.

Not far from here is the **Europa Center**, containing shops, nightlife and a rooftop cafe with a splendid view of the whole city and the **KaDeWe** (short for **Kaufhaus des Westens**) department store.

Other attractions in the western half of the city include: the **Siegessäule** (**Victory Column**), built at the order of Kaiser Wilhelm I two years after victory in the Franco-Prussian War of 1871; and the **Tiergarten**, an English-style park in the heart of the city. **Schloss Charlottenburg**, the splendid Baroque and Rococo palace of Frederick the Great, was the former summer home of the king outside Berlin. The Palace Park is ideal for long walks. The **Gedenkstätte Plötzensee** is a memorial to more than 2500 members of the Resistance who were executed here and generally to German resistance during the Nazi regime.

It is easy to find diversion from city life, as the city boundaries include numerous recreational areas, such as the **Pfaueninsel** (peacock island), now a nature reserve, the **Spandau** and **Tegel** Forests and the **Grünewald**. The **People's Park Friederichshain** in the eastern part of the city is the largest and oldest park in east Berlin.

BADEN-WÜRTTEMBERG

The **Neckar Valley**, in the north of the state, is a major wine-growing region, with vineyards located around castles such as **Gutenberg**, **Hornberg** and **Hirschhorn**, each of which offers splendid views of the surrounding landscape. To the east of the romantic university town of **Heidelberg**, another scenic route begins, the 280km- (175-mile) long **Castle Road**, which leads to **Nuremberg** in Bavaria. This route follows the river, branching off at **Heilbronn** and continuing east to medieval places such as **Rothenburg** and **Ansbach**, also across the state border in Bavaria. Further to the south is the **Swabian Jura**, a limestone plateau between the Black Forest and Europe's longest river, the **Danube**. Places to visit here include **Hohenzollern Castle** near **Hechingen**, **Beuren Abbey** and the **Bären Caves**. Picturesque towns include **Urach** and **Kirchheim-unter-Teck**.

Einstein's birthplace, **Ulm**, houses the world's tallest cathedral spire (161m/528ft). Following the road from Ulm, one reaches **Reutlingen** and **Blaubeuren**, with its fine abbey. **Zwiefalten** has another remarkable Baroque church. In the southwestern corner of the state, the **Rhine** acts as a natural border between France, Germany and Switzerland. To the east of the river lies the **Black Forest** (Schwarzwald) where fine mountain scenery and beautifully situated lakeside resorts like **Titisee-Neustadt** and **Schluchsee** combine to make the area popular year-round – with walkers in summer and skiers in winter. The historical character of the area is preserved in the **Black Forest Open Air Museum** at **Gutach**.

The Romans first recognised the therapeutic powers of the Black Forest's springs. In addition to the region's best-known spa town, **Baden-Baden**, there are many other charming villages and resorts in the surrounding area, principally **Freudenstadt**, which claims to have more hours of sunshine than any other German town. The climatic spa of **Triberg** has 162m- (531ft-) high waterfalls and a swimming pool surrounded by evergreens.

BADEN-BADEN: The Black Forest's chief spa, Baden-Baden, was the summer capital of Europe during the last century. Travellers still flock to this delightful town to 'take the waters', which may be inhaled as a vapour, bathed in or simply drunk. Fortified by the water's therapeutic powers, one can take advantage of the town's many sporting facilities. For the less energetic, the evening could be spent playing roulette or baccarat in a casino which Marlene Dietrich herself regarded as the most elegant in the world. Other attractions include the Baroque **Kleines Theater**, **National Art Gallery**, the **Friedrichsbad** Romano-Irish temple and baths, the **Margravial Palace** (museum), 15th-century **Collegiate Church**, **Russian Church**, **Romanesque Chapel**, parks and gardens, **Lichtentaler Allee**, tennis, riding, 18-hole golf course, winter sports, international horse-racing weeks at **Iffezheim** and a modern congress hall.

CONSTANCE (KONSTANZ): Constance is a German university and cathedral town on the **Bodensee** (Lake Constance) which has shores in Austria, Switzerland and the Germany. Constance (Konstanz) is a frontier anomaly, a German town on the Swiss side of the lake, completely surrounded by Swiss territory except for a strip on the waterfront. Attractions include the **Konzilsgebäude** (14th century); Renaissance **Town Hall** (16th century); historic old **Insel Hotel** (14th century); **Barbarossa-Haus** (12th century); **Hus-Haus** (15th century); and the old town fortifications **Rheintorturm**, **Pulverturm** and **Schnetztor**. The town has theatres, concert halls, a casino and hosts an international music festival as well as the **Seenachtfest**, a lake festival. **Reichenau**, an island with a famous monastery and the island of **Mainau**, with stilted buildings, make an interesting day trip.

EXCURSIONS: The Bavarian town of **Lindau** is a former free imperial city on an island in Lake Constance. It has a medieval town centre and an old **Town Hall** (1422-35). Other attractions include **Brigand's Tower**, **Mang Tower** (old lighthouse), **Cavazzen House** (art collection), **Heidenmauer** (wall), **St Peter's** with Holbein frescoes; harbour entry (new lighthouse); international casino; and boat trips. Opposite the town of Constance (Konstanz) is **Meersburg**, an old town with two castles. Here is also the **German Newspaper Museum** which covers the history of the German-language press on its three floors. The museum is only open during the summer. As an area, Lake Constance is the focal point of a delightful holiday district, rich in art treasures and facilities for outdoor activities. The **Rheinfall** (Rhine Falls) at **Schaffhausen**, a Swiss town on the north shore of the lake, are a spectacular draw just over the border.

FREIBURG: Freiburg is the gateway to the Black Forest, an archepiscopal see and an old university town. The Gothic **Cathedral** (12th to 15th centuries) has a magnificent tower (116m/380ft) and is a much lauded architectural masterpiece. Views from the top are reward indeed for the climb. Other attractions include the historic red **Kaufhaus** on the Cathedral Square (1550); Germany's oldest inn, **Zum Roten Bären**; and many excellent wine taverns. The city is famous for its trout and game dishes and environmental innovation – for which it has earned the title of 'green capital' of Germany. Museums include **Zinnfigurenklause** (pewter figures) and the **Augustinemuseum** housing Upper Rhine art. The **Wentzingerhaus** hosts the **City History Museum**. The nearby **Schauinsland Mountain** (1284m/4213ft) is accessible by cable car.
EXCURSIONS: Nearby **Todtnauberg** in the Upper Black Forest is the highest resort in the Black Forest (1006m/3300ft) and a perfect observation point is the **Belchen** summit nearby. The highest mountain is the **Feldberg**, with its popular winter skiing slopes.
HEIDELBERG: The most famous place on the **Neckar River** is Germany's oldest university town, Heidelberg, dominated by the ruins of its famous 14th-century castle. Other attractions include more than 10 museums; the 'Giant Cask' in the cellar holding 220,000 litres (48,422 gallons); **Church of the Holy Ghost**; **St Peter's Church**; **Karlstor** (gate); and wine taverns. The castle is partly Renaissance, partly Gothic and Baroque in style, and serenade concerts take place during the summer in the courtyard. Another highlight is the **German Museum of Pharmacy**.
HEILBRONN: Heilbronn is a former imperial city, surrounded by vineyards and situated on the **Castle Road**. The **Renaissance Town Hall** has an outside staircase, clock, gable and astronomical clock. Other attractions include the 16th-century **Käthchen House**, the **Gothic Kilian Church** with its 62m- (203ft-) high tower (1513-29), and the **Shipping Museum**. The town is also a good base for excursions into the **Neckar Valley**.
KARLSRUHE: The prime reasons for visiting Karlsruhe are the town's **Schloss** and surrounding **Schlossgarten** parkland. It also offers the **ZKM Centre for Art and Media museum**.
MANNHEIM: Mannheim is a commercial, industrial and cultural centre on the confluence of the rivers **Rhine** and **Neckar**. Attractions include the former **Electors' Palace**, now the university; the **Kunsthalle** fine arts museum; the **Barockschloss** castle; **Municipal Art Gallery**; **Reiss Museum** in the old arsenal; the old **Town Hall** and **Market Square**; and the **National (Schiller) Theatre**.
STUTTGART: The state capital is a green and open city surrounded by trees and vineyards with only a quarter of its area built on. Two of its major industries are car manufacture and the publishing industry. Attractions include the modern **Staatsgalerie**; the **Prinzenbau** and **Alte Kanzlei** on the **Schillerplatz**; the **Neues Schloss**, a vast palace now accommodating the **State Museum**, which served as the residence for the kings of Württemberg and has been painstakingly restored after 1945; **Württemberg Regional Museum**; 15th-century **Collegiate Church**; **TV Tower** (217m/711ft high); **Killesberg Park**; **Ludwigsburg Palace**; **Wilhelma Zoo**; botanical gardens; theatre (ballet); and mineral-water swimming pools. The *Stuttgart Ballet and Chamber Orchestra* enjoy worldwide renown. There are **Mercedes** and **Porsche** museums, a covered **Markthalle** (Market Hall), and wine and beer museums. The city is also home to the **Carl Zeiss Planetarium**.
TÜBINGEN: Tübingen, south of Stuttgart, is a world-famous romantic university town on the **River Neckar**. The old town centre is unspoilt. Attractions include the **Castle of the Count Palatine** (1078); late Gothic **Collegiate Church** (1470) with royal burial place; **Market Square** with **Town Hall** (1453); picturesque Neckar front; **Hölderlin Tower**; former student dungeons (1514); old and new lecture theatres (*Aula*) of the university; **Bebenhausen Abbey** and the **Schloss Hohentübingen** museum.
ULM: Ulm is famous above all for its soaring Gothic **Cathedral** (768 steps in the 161m/528ft tower; choir stalls by J Syrlin). Other attractions include the beautiful **Town Hall** with famous astronomical clock; **Corn Exchange** (1594); **Schuhaus** (1536); **Schwörhaus** (1613); old town and fishermen's quarter with city wall and **Metzgerturm** (butchers' tower); **Wiblingen Abbey**; **Baroque library**; **German Bread Museum**; and the **Municipal Museum** with local works of art.

BAVARIA

Bavaria consists of four main tourist areas: the Bavarian Forest and East Bavaria; Swabia and the Allgäu in the southwest; Upper Bavaria in the south; and Franconia to the north. The state offers varying landscapes – towering mountains in the Alpine south, lakes, forests and many resorts.
UPPER BAVARIA: In the Upper Bavaria region, the best-known places include **Garmisch-Partenkirchen**, **Berchtesgaden**, **Mittenwald** and **Oberammergau**, home of the Passion Play. One of the most spectacular feats of architecture, epitomising the fairytale landscape of Bavaria, is **Neuschwanstein Castle**, built by Ludwig II. Constructed on the ridge of a mountain valley surrounded by snow-capped peaks, it is a vision from fairyland, while at night it changes into the perfect home for Count Dracula.
BAVARIAN FOREST: The vast Bavarian Forest is in the east, bordering the Czech Republic, and contains the first German national park. This unspoiled and peaceful region offers outdoor activities, especially walking. Historic towns such as the three-river town of **Passau** and 2000-year-old **Regensburg** provide interesting contrasts to the nature reserves. The northern part of Bavaria, Franconia, is rich in art treasures. Its main attractions include medieval and historic old towns such as **Coburg**, home of Prince Albert (consort of Queen Victoria); the cathedral town of **Bamberg**; **Bayreuth**, which stages the annual *Wagner Opera Festival*; and **Würzburg**, with its world-famous Baroque palace, set on the River Main among the Franconian vineyards. **Nuremberg** (*Nürnberg*), the main city in this region, is a modern metropolis, yet the centre of the town has retained its traditional style. The many valleys, forests, lakes and castles of the 'Swiss' Franconian area and the **Fichtel Mountains**, combined with the nature reserves in the **Altmühl Valley**, make Franconia a popular holiday centre.
THE ROMANTIC ROAD: Connecting the northern area of Bavaria with the south is the most famous of all the German scenic roads – the **Romantic Road**. The towns along the way give visitors an excellent insight into the region's history, art and culture. Places of particular interest are **Würzburg**; medieval **Rothenburg**, **Dinkelsbühl** and **Nördlingen**; **Augsburg**, founded in 15BC by the Romans; the pilgrimage church **Wieskirche** in the meadows; **Steingaden Abbey**; and the most popular site of all, **Neuschwanstein Castle**, near the village of **Schwangau**.
MUNICH: The Bavarian capital, Munich (*München*), is the third-largest German city with 1.3 million inhabitants, and is a major international arts and business centre. The 800-year-old city has numerous museums and several fine Baroque and Renaissance churches.
The **Alte Pinakothek** is home to the largest collection of Rubens paintings in the world; directly opposite is the **Neue Pinakothek** with a collection of modern paintings. Two other galleries of note are **Pinakothek der Moderne**, and the **Museum der Fantasie**. The **German Museum** (natural science and technology) with planetarium, a life-size coal mine and the **German Transport Centre** extension, is also interesting for children.
Elsewhere in the city, motoring enthusiasts will find the **BMW (Bayerische Motorwerke) Museum** dedicated to the famous marque manufactured in Munich.
The **Lenbach Gallery** is located in the impressive villa of the Munich 'Painter Viscount'. Only a short walk away is the **Glyptothek** on the Königsplatz, housing Greek and Roman sculptures. Other attractions include the **Royal Palace** and **Royal Treasury**; **Bavarian National Museum** and others; the **Church of Our Lady** (**Frauenkirche**); the **Theatinerkirche** and **Asamkirche**; and the **Church of St Michael**. The New and Old Town Halls, and the restored **Mariensäule** surround the **Marienplatz**. Thrice daily a large group gathers here to witness a glockenspiel carillon depicting the *Schäfflertanz*.
The **Olympia Park** with its stadium (home of Bayern Munich) is now a recreational area. Site of the 1972 Olympic Games, city residents now use its facilities. Munich hosts the best-known of all German events, the *Oktoberfest* beer festival. This had its origins in 1810 when Crown Prince Ludwig of Bavaria married Princess Therese von Sachsen-Hildburghausen. The people liked the festival so much that it became a regular feature and now takes place annually for two weeks – the first Sunday in October is always the last day of the festival. Munich's nine breweries all have their own beer tents at the festival, but the city has many famous permanent beer cellars, including the **Hofbräuhaus**.
The city's artists' colony is in the district of **Schwabing** which also features shops, cafes, small theatres and market stalls along its **Leopoldstrasse**.
The Englischer Garten, one of the largest parks in Europe, offers an escape from the city bustle. Right in the middle stands the **Chinese Tower**, surrounded by beer gardens. The many theatres include the **National Theatre** (opera house), the Rococo theatre built by Cuvilliés and the **Schauspielhaus** (playhouse). The **Nymphenburg Palace** is home to a portrait gallery and a famous collection of china. The **Fasching** (carnival) season reaches its peak during February with several balls and other festivities; but the **Auer Dult**, a funfair and flea market, takes place three times a year.
AUGSBURG: Founded in AD 15 by the Romans, Augsburg lies northwest of Munich and was once the financial centre of Europe. It was also the home of the Fuggers, a famous medieval aristocratic family and great patrons of the arts. Here, in 1555, German religious conflict during the

Credit: © German National Tourist Board

Reformation ended following the signing of a Peace Treaty. It also boasts the **Fuggerei** – the oldest 'council' housing in the world, dating back to 1519. Other attractions include the **Cathedral** (807 Romanesque/1320 Gothic) with 12th-century stained-glass windows and 11th-century bronze door; **St Anna's Church** (16th-century Luther memorial); **Town Hall** (1615); **Perlach Tower**; Baroque fountains (16th to 17th centuries); **City Gates** (14th to 16th centuries); **Schaezler Palace** and Rococo banquet hall (18th century) with German Baroque gallery and an Old German gallery with paintings by Holbein and Dürer; **Maximilian Museum**; **Roman Museum**; and **Mozart's House**.
BAMBERG: An old imperial town and bishopric, Bamberg stands on seven hills, and has many medieval and Baroque buildings. Attractions include the **Imperial Cathedral** (13th century) with famous 'Bamberger Reiter' sculpture, reliefs, royal tombs and Veit Stoss altar; the old **Town Hall**; picturesque fishermen's dwellings ('**Little Venice**'); the **Franconian Beer Museum**; **Old Royal Palace**; **New Palace** (picture gallery) and rose garden; and **Michaelsberg Monastery**.
BAYREUTH: Bayreuth is mainly famous for its *Wagner Opera Festival* which takes place every year from late July to August. Other attractions, many of which are connected with the life and works of the composer, include the **Festival Theatre** (1872-1876); **Villa Wahnfried** (Wagner's home, now a museum); **Wagner Memorial** ('Chiming Museum'); **Freemasons' Museum**, Wagner's grave in the **Court Gardens**; the **Old** and the **New Palace**, the former residence of the Margraves; **Margraves Opera House** (largest European Baroque stage); **Eremitage** (park); and the parish church. The city is also a convenient base for excursions into the **Fichtel Mountains**, **Oberpfälzer Woods** and the 'Franconian Switzerland'.
COBURG: Coburg Castle (13th to 16th centuries), one of the largest fortified sites in Germany, towers over this former ducal capital. A one-time refuge of Martin Luther, it now houses valuable collections of art, weaponry and copperplate engravings. **Ehrenburg Palace** overlooks the palace square and faces the **Coburg State Theatre** which provides a centre for cultural events. Other attractions include **St Maurice's Church** (14th to 16th centuries), the **Natural Science Museum** and **Doll Museum**. Nearby countryside offers **Banz Monastery**, the game park at **Tambach Castle** and the **Rodach Thermal Spa**.
INGOLSTADT: Among its fine architecture dating from the 14th and 15th centuries (the Old Town dates from the early ninth century), Ingolstadt also numbers the **Neues Schloss**, now home of the **Bavarian Army Museum**, among its attractions. **Alte Anatomie** offers more offbeat diversions, containing the **German Museum of Medical History**. The town hosts a major annual international jazz festival each November.
KEMPTEN: In the heart of the Allgäu holiday region to the southwest of Bavaria, Kempten is a former Celtic and Roman settlement – the **Cambodunum Archaeological Park**, with its partial reconstruction on the original site, highlights this heritage. Two more recent buildings, the **St Lorenz Basilica** and the **Residenz Palace**, feature notable interiors. Museums include the **Allgäu Folk Museum** and the **Alpine Museum**.
NUREMBERG: A mainly modern city, Nuremberg (Nürnberg) has nevertheless managed to retain much of its medieval centre. The region's typical red sandstone forms the fabric of the churches of **St Lawrence** and **St Sebald**. Attractions include the **Kaiserburg Imperial Castle** with its old stables today used as a youth hostel; the **City Wall**

(over 5km/3 miles long) with 80 watchtowers; **Dürer's House**; **Museum of Toys**; **Fembohaus** (municipal museum); the **Post and Communications Museum** (with more than 200,000 stamps); **Germanic National Museum**; **German Railway Museum**; **Town Hall**; and the **'Schöne Brunnen' Fountain** with mechanical clock. The international toy fair and the famous Christmas Fair, **Christkindlmarkt**, also attract many visitors.

PASSAU: On the Austrian border at the confluence of the **Danube**, **Inn** and **Ilz** rivers, Passau's attractions include a Baroque **Cathedral**, with the world's largest church organ; **Bishop's Palace** with Rococo staircase; **Oberhaus** and **Niederhaus** fortresses (13th to 14th centuries); and **Inn Quay** with Italianesque architecture.

REGENSBERG: Situated about 80km (50 miles) northeast of Munich, this city can trace its roots back to the first century AD. Attractions of the old episcopal city include the **Cathedral** (with its famous 'Regensburger Domspatzen' choir); **St Emmeram's Church** (with many crypts and tombs); the **'Scottish Church'** (with its Romanesque portal); **Old Chapel**; **Palace Niedermünster** (excavations); **Porta Praetoria** (North Gate); 12th-century stone bridge (the oldest in Germany); boat trips on the Danube; **Old Town Hall** with the **Imperial Chamber**; **Palace of the Princes of Thurn and Taxis**; and museums.

WÜRZBURG: The northern Bavarian town of Würzburg, about halfway between Frankfurt/M and Nuremberg, nestles between vineyards famous for their **Bocksbeutel** (specially formed bottle). The **Festung Marienberg** (fortress) offers a spectacular view over the city and its numerous spires. From the 15th-century **Old Main Bridge**, with its statues of the Franconian apostles of Lilian, Totnan and Kolonat, the Romanesque **Cathedral** dominates the view.

Attractions include the **Mainfränkisches Museum**, housed in the former arsenal with examples of the work of Riemenschneider (1460-1531), and the **Marienkirche**, built in AD 706 and one of the oldest churches in the country. The Baroque Castle-Palace (*Residenz*), former home of the powerful Prince Bishops, was designed by Balthasar Neumann taking Versailles as a model, is a UNESCO World Heritage Site.

Candlelit Mozart concerts take place during the summer months in the **Emperor's Hall** and the **Hofgarten**. The town library and tourist information are in the **Haus zum Falken** (Falcon House), which has an impressive Rococo facade.

Numerous wine bars, cafes and restaurants provide relaxation and diversion. Almost the entire city centre is a pedestrian zone, only disturbed by the passage of trams.

BRANDENBURG

The 'March' of Brandenburg surrounding Berlin is a region of birch and pine forests.

The picturesque **Spreewald** lies south of Berlin and offers numerous waterways for exploration by boat, and tranquil hamlets such as **Bückchen**. Flat-bottomed barges are still the main means of transport in the heart of this region, as they have been for centuries.

POTSDAM: Potsdam's major new family attraction is the high-tech **Babelsberg Film Theme Park**. There are also several fine 18th-century buildings preserved in the city, which boasts three large parks. The **Neuer Garten** contains the marble palace and **Schloss Cecilienhof**, where Stalin, Truman and Churchill drafted peace treaties in July and August 1945 during the Potsdam Conference. **Sanssouci** has the spectacular **Sanssouci Palace**, which was Frederick the Great's favourite residence, and a gilded teahouse. The picture gallery next door to the palace contains many old masters. The city's **Dutch Quarter** is an attraction in itself, as is the famous **Potsdam Bridge**, where East and West exchanged spies in all the best espionage films of the Cold War era.

ELSEWHERE: Traces of Frederick the Great are also evident at **Rheinsberg**, which was immortalised by Kurt Tucholsky's tale of the same name. The interior of the beautifully situated castle is still undergoing restoration, but visits are possible. One of the towers houses a Tucholsky Memorial. The music academy at **Cavalier House** concentrates on period music as played at the court of Crown Prince Frederick. The **Schorfheide** is an area of forest north of Berlin. Beavers, otters and eagles have claimed this picturesque area as their own. In the centre of this landscape of birches and pines lies the **Werbellin Lake**. Summer concerts at the former Cistercian **Monastery of Chorin** are another Brandenburg highlight, as is **Lehde**, where there is an open-air museum with original houses and farm buildings, complete with interiors. There are also several examples of the culture of the *Sorbs*, a resident Slavic minority.

HESSEN

Hessen's capital is the city of **Wiesbaden**. The northern part of the state – **Kurhesse-Waldeck** – boasts lakes, forests and state-recognised health resorts. Hessen has many rural villages with half-timbered houses and still-observed ancient customs.

The **German Fairy Tale Road** leads through some of these towns. **Schwalmstadt**, home of *Little Red Riding Hood*, is a town where people still wear traditional costumes to church on Sunday and at folk festivals. In the **Reinhardswald**, **Sababurg** – now a castle-hotel – inspired the Brothers Grimm to write *Sleeping Beauty*.

The romantic scenery of the **Lahn**, a tributary of the Rhine, draws many visitors to **Nassau**, **Wetzlar**, **Limburg** and the **Schaumburg Castle**. Also on this river is the historic university town of **Marburg**.

In the far south of Hessen is the rolling hill country of the **Odenwald**, a region rich in legend and folklore and excellent for hiking. The **Bergstrasse** traverses the western slopes. The region has a particularly mild climate, permitting cultivation of a wide range of flowers and fruit. Two routes are available for exploring the Odenwald; the **Nibelungenstrasse** and the **Siegfriedstrasse**.

Erbach, which has a Baroque palace and a medieval watchtower; **Michelstadt** with its half-timbered **Town Hall** and basilica; the resort of **Lindenfels**; and the spa town of **Bad König**, are prime attractions. Northwest of Frankfurt and north of Wiesbaden is the wooded hill country of the **Taunus**, a ski centre during the winter. Resorts here include the old town of **Oberursel**, the spa town of **Bad Homburg** and, nearby, the preserved Roman fort of **Saalburg**, situated on the line marking the frontier of the Roman Empire.

Northeast of Frankfurt is the Baroque town of **Fulda**, gateway to the Rhön region. Some of the buildings here date back to the ninth century. Further north is **Kassel**, home of the **Grimm Brothers Museum** and the **Wilhelmshöhe Palace** with its magnificent grounds.

DARMSTADT: Darmstadt lies a few miles east of the Rhine. Attractions include the **Palace** (16th and 17th centuries); **Prince George Palace** (18th century) with a porcelain collection; **Hesse Regional Museum**; an artists' colony on **Mathildenhöhe**; **'Wedding Tower'** and **Russian Chapel**; **National Theatre** on the **Marienplatz**; and **Kranichstein Hunting Lodge** with hunting museum and hotel.

FRANKFURT-AM-MAIN: The city of Frankfurt-am-Main is Germany's major financial and commercial centre. Its soaring skyline has led to its nickname of 'Mainhattan'. Much of the city suffered destruction in 1944, but extensive restoration has preserved many Old Town buildings, including the *Römer*, town hall and coronation place of German emperors since 1562. Some ancient buildings survived the war, including part of the cathedral and the 13th-century chapel that once adjoined **Frederick Barbarossa's Palace**. In the **City Museum** there is a perfect scale model of the old town and also the astonishing city silver. The stark **Paulus Church** was home to the first German parliament in 1848. Other attractions in the city include the zoo; the birthplace of Goethe; the **Opera House**; the suburbs of **Sachsenhausen** and **Hoechst**, both formerly towns in their own right; and the **Messe**, the exhibition halls complex. The **Städel Art Institute** houses a large collection of European paintings. The **Senckenberg Natural History Museum**, **Jewish Museum** and the **Museum of Post and Communication** offer more specialised diversion.

WIESBADEN: Wiesbaden is the capital of the state of Hesse. It is an international spa and congress centre in the Taunus and on the Rhine; the spas specialise in the treatment of rheumatism. Attractions include the **Kurhaus** and casino; the **Wilhelmstrasse**, with elegant shops and cafes; **Hesse State Theatre**; the **Greek Chapel**; international riding and jumping championships in the grounds of **Biebrich Palace** at **Whitsun**; boat trips on the Rhine; and woodland walks.

MECKLENBURG-WESTERN POMERANIA

The state of **Mecklenburg-West Pomerania** contains a long stretch of Baltic coast, on which lies the former Hanseatic port of **Rostock**. It is primarily a rural state, with numerous lakes in the **Mecklenburgische Seenplatte** region to the south, and is popular for water-based and cycling holidays, as well as its beaches.

ROSTOCK: The **University**, founded in 1419, was the first in Northern Europe. Attractions in the city include the elegant burghers' houses in **Thälmann Square**, the 15th-century **Town Hall**, the late-Gothic **St Mary's Church** with its 15th-century astronomical clock and Baroque organ and the district of **Warnemünde** with its fishing harbour and seaside resort. The **Schifffahrtsmuseum** (Museum of Navigation) tells the story of seafaring from Viking times. **Kröpelin Gate** houses the **City History Museum**.

SCHWERIN: State capital, founded in 1160 and still a charming town. **Schwerin Castle**, on the lake of the same name and surrounded by a terraced garden crossed by a canal, was for many decades the residence of the Dukes of Mecklenburg and is one of the finest examples of German Gothic architecture. In the historic old quarter of the city are the well-preserved Gothic **Cathedral**, the **Town Hall** and an interesting museum with collections of French, German and Dutch paintings from the 17th, 18th and 19th centuries. There is a fine baroque opera house.

ELSEWHERE: Greifswald, a small university town east of Rostock, has original 15th-century burghers' houses and is part of a medieval fishing village. Birthplace of painter Caspar David Friedrich, radical alterations to the city's appearance resulted from construction of new residential areas and industrial zones in the post-war period. The 'White Fleet' of passenger boats serves all the coastal ports, and calls at **Hiddensee Island**, an island with no cars and a large protected bird colony. The island of **Rügen**, with its nature reserve and famous chalk cliffs, is Germany's largest and a popular holiday destination. From **Bad Doberan**, 9 miles west of Rostock, it is possible to take the 'Molli' narrow-gauge railway to Germany's oldest seaside resort, **Heiligendamm**. Notable at **Wismar** is the huge market square, covering 10,000 sq m (12,000 sq yards).

NORTHWEST GERMANY

Undiscovered by many holidaymakers, the northern region, although relatively flat, offers pleasant scenery with gently rolling hills, lake country and fine sandy beaches and dunes in the state of Schleswig-Holstein, bordering on Denmark.

HAMBURG: Hamburg is the second-largest city in Germany with a population of 1.8 million people. It is a city-state, forming with Lübeck, Bremen and Rostock and other European ports the medieval **Hanseatic League**.

A sightseeing tour, starting at the **Hauptbahnhof** (main station) gives a good overall impression of the city. The Baroque **Church of St Michael** (der Michel), the **Town Hall** with its distinctive green roof, the elegant **Hanseviertel**, the **Alster Arcades** and the **Alster Lake**, the biggest lake inside a European city, are principal sights, along with the **Arts Mile**, location of most important museums and galleries.

Museums of interest include the domed **Hamburg Art Gallery** (**Kunsthalle**), the **Historical Museum**, the

FRANKFURT am Main

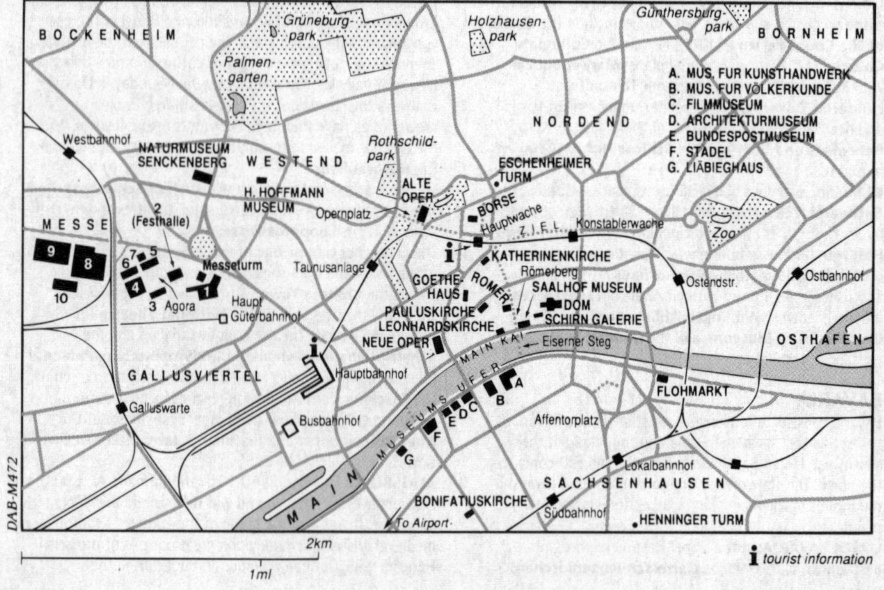

Decorative Arts and Crafts Museum and the **Altonaer Museum**. Hamburg has many theatres, including the **Hamburg State Opera** (**Hamburgische Staatsoper**); Germany's oldest opera house, **John Neumeier Hamburg Ballet**; the **German Theatre** (**Deutsches Schauspielhaus**); and the **Ohnsorgtheater**, which performs plays in the Low German dialect (*plattdeutsch*).
In the city's heart is the **Planten und Blomen** park near the Congress Centrum Hamburg, with its spectacular fountain displays during the summer. During a daytime visit to the park, the **Television Tower** is a highlight. For a small charge, visitors take the lift to the top platform and enjoy a view of the city, the harbour, the northern districts and the surrounding countryside. Just below is a restaurant, which turns full circle in the course of an hour, enabling diners to enjoy every vantage point at their leisure.
Not far from the Television Tower, next to the Feldstrasse underground station, the large **Dom** funfair takes place several times a year. From Feldstrasse, it is not far to the famous St Pauli district, which includes the notorious **Reeperbahn**, with its various 'adult' entertainments. After dark this area comes alive with neon lights, music, crowds, theatres and door staff trying to attract people into their establishments. After a long night out, revellers congregate at the **Fischmarkt**, which opens at 0630, and sells fruit and vegetables as well as fish. A wide range of harbour trips are available, and the **Speicherstadt** historic Warehouse Quarter is a must. Hamburg enjoys unrivalled shopping, with pedestrianised shopping streets, elegant arcades, fine department stores and street cafes concentrated in the area between the main railway station and the **Gänsemarkt**.
Refuge from a hectic day's shopping can be sought by hiring a rowing boat or a paddleboat and exploring the Alster and the intricate network of canals (Hamburg has more bridges than Venice) which extends throughout the city. On Sundays, a stroll on the banks of the River Elbe or a visit to the **Museum Harbour** at **Övelgönne** is a favourite pastime. The numerous cafes and restaurants make sure that nobody overdoes the walking.
BREMEN: Bremen, also a city-state, with over half a million inhabitants, is the oldest German maritime city, having been a market town since AD 965. For all its history, though, it boasts two of the country's most modern high-tech visitor attractions: the interactive **Universum Science Centre** and the **Space Travel Visitor Centre**.
Historic Bremen clusters around the marketplace, featuring the **Gothic Town Hall** (1405-1410), in front of which stands the **Roland**, the statue of a medieval knight and symbol of the city. The extensive pedestrian zone includes a sculpture of the **Bremer Stadtmusikanten** (Musicians of Bremen), made famous in the fairy tale by Grimm. Also part of this is the **Schnoorviertel**, a district full of medieval charm, with narrow cobbled streets now housing art galleries and exclusive shops. The nearby port of **Bremerhaven** is home to the **German Maritime Museum**.
SCHLESWIG-HOLSTEIN: In Schleswig-Holstein is Germany's 'Little Switzerland' and the dukedom of Lauenburg, an area of quiet meadows and wooded hills. Glistening among them are the blue waters of innumerable lakes and fjords reaching deep into the interior of this state. A trip could also include visits to tiny undiscovered towns such as **Ratzeburg** and **Mölln**, or to one of a string of Baltic resorts such as **Timmendorfer Strand**, **Grömitz** and **Schönhagen**, whose golden, sandy beaches attract summer crowds. **Lübeck**, whose picturesque oval-shaped old town, ringed by water, still has many reminders of the city's medieval golden age and is a UNESCO World Heritage Site, claims to be the most beautiful town in northern Germany. The **Holsten Gate**, the **Rathaus** and the many examples of northern red brick town houses are part of the historic heritage. Thomas Mann set his famous novel, *Buddenbrooks*, here. **Buddenbrook House** contains the Heinrich and Thomas Mann Centre, giving information on the life and works of both authors.
Flensburg, the most northerly town in Germany, has architecture dating back to the 16th century and for many years of its history was part of Denmark. Just south of Flensburg is **Kappeln an der Schlei**, a picturesque small town between the **Fjord** and the Baltic. Every hour during the summer the traffic comes to a halt when the rotating bridge allows sail and fishing boats to pass. At the beginning of the season in May, the **Heringstage** lure visitors to taste the town's speciality: herring.
Along the Schlei lies the old Viking town of **Haithabu**, with its interesting museum.
Further south, still on Schleswig-Holstein's east coast, is state capital **Kiel**, a modern city with a large university. It stands on the Nord-Ostsee (Kiel) Canal, which connects the **North Sea** with the Baltic. In June, yachting and sailing enthusiasts flock to the **Kiel Week**. One of Germany's biggest passenger ports, Kiel's highlights include a **Maritime Museum**, the **Molfsee Open Air Museum** and the **Oceanographic Institute Aquarium**.
Large systems of dykes protect the low-lying western coast of Schleswig-Holstein from constant pounding by waves. Sea breezes, a wealth of bird species and nature reserves make the **North Friesian Islands** of **Sylt**, **Föhr** and **Amrum** a favourite for nature holidays. Ferries connect with the numerous *Halligen*, small flat islets off the coast.
WESTPHALIA: Westphalia extends from the Rhine to the Weser Valley. For many, Westphalia conjures up images of the industrial Ruhr Valley (see below), but the region is also one of outstanding natural beauty and historical interest. Highlights include the **Teutoburger Forest** with its nature reserves; the ancient episcopal see of **Münster** (whose attractions include the newly opened **Pablo Picasso Graphics Museum** containing nearly 800 original lithographs); and the **Sauerland Region**, an area of lakes, forests and hills, providing good skiing in winter and walks at any time. Major cities along the Rhine in the west of the state are described in the *Rhineland* section.
THE RUHR VALLEY: South of Münster is the heavily industrialised Ruhr. Made up of several large cities merging to form one huge conurbation, the **Ruhrgebiet** is, however, also a vibrant centre of culture with many museums, theatres, art galleries and opera houses. The region also has a large number of parks providing refuge from the industrial landscape. Many older buildings survive from the days when this was an agricultural area dotted with small towns.
The main cities of the Ruhr are (from west to east): **Krefeld**; **Duisburg**, Germany's largest internal port; **Mühlheim**; **Essen** (in the heart of the region, and home to Germany's newest UNESCO World Heritage Site, the **Zollverein Coke Plant**); **Bochum**; and **Dortmund**, centre of Germany's brewing industry. South of the Ruhr and bordering the beautiful Siegerland and Sauerland regions is **Wuppertal**, which, stretched out along its own valley, is home to a unique suspension railway urban transit system, the **Schwebebahn**.
LOWER SAXONY: East Friesland, on the North Sea coast of Lower Saxony, consists of a wide plain interspersed by ranges of tree-covered hills known for their health resorts and modern spa facilities, as well as their fine sandy beaches. The car-free **East Friesian Islands** also offer relaxing health-oriented holidays. Sea air and scenery along the coast guarantee a happy and restful holiday atmosphere.
In contrast is the large nature reserve between the rivers **Elbe** and **Aller** further inland. The countryside comprises moorland with wide expanses of heather, grazing sheep, clumps of green birch trees and junipers. Of interest in this area are the half-timbered houses of **Celle** and **Lüneburg**, historic centre of Germany's salt industry.
Further west is the town of **Oldenburg**, economic and cultural centre of the region between the **Ems** and the **Weser**; to the north is the spa town of **Wilhelmshaven**, which has relaxing and therapeutic mud baths as its speciality. It is also the starting point for many tours along the East Friesland coast and the off-lying islands.
Romantic Germany can be found in the **Weser Valley**, near **Hanover** (see below), where there are fairytale towns such as **Hameln** (Hamlyn), famed for the tale of the Pied Piper. A play about the infamous piper is re-enacted during the summer months every Sunday at noon. The town has several buildings in Weser Renaissance style. Here is also the romantic area of the **Weserbergland** with numerous hill ranges and deep forests.
In the east of the state is **Wolfsburg**, home of Volkswagen cars. **Autostadt** (Car City), an unusual and major new visitor attraction dedicated to cars, opened recently on a 10 hectare (25 acre) site in the heart of the city.
HANOVER: The state capital of Lower Saxony hosts the renowned Hanover Trade Fair. The 'Big City in the Park' is also an important tourist draw, with many interesting sights. Attractions, linked for visitors' benefit by a 4.2km (2.5 mile) route marked by a red line on the pavements, include the **Herrenhausen Castle** with its baroque gardens incorporating a new rainforest house. The annual music and theatre festival, which is performed on open-air stages within the garden, attracts many visitors each summer. The city also has a 14th-century market church, the **Marienkirche**, several museums and a 15th-century town hall with the famous gable. There are also numerous museums, such as the **Sprengel Museum** near the Masch Lake, which is becoming an important centre for modern art.

RHINELAND

Rhineland is Germany's oldest cultural centre. Names such as Cologne, Aachen and Mainz are synonymous with soaring Gothic architecture and with the history and lives of many of the great names of Western Europe. However, the area consists of more than a series of riverside cities. Here too are the vast plains of the Lower Rhine farmlands, the strange volcanic crater lakes of the **Eifel Hills**, the **Bergische Land** with its lakes and **Altenberg Cathedral** and the **Siebengebirge**. Rhineland and the **Moselle Valley** attract visitors not only for their beauty and romanticism, but also for the convivial atmosphere engendered by wine and song.
Like most of its tributaries, vineyards line the Rhine wherever the slopes face the sun. Alternating with the

Credit: © German National Tourist Board

vineyards are extensive orchards, which are heavy with blossom in spring.
The **Ahr Valley** in the Eifel region is particularly renowned for its lush scenery and its red wine; nearby is the famous **Nürburgring** racing circuit. **Trier**, the oldest German town close to the Luxembourg border, stands on the River Moselle. The city houses the most important Roman ruins north of the Alps. Following the River Moselle eastwards towards Koblenz are several towns well known among wine connoisseurs – **Bernkastel-Kues**, **Kröv**, **Beilstein** and **Cochem**.
The Rhine Valley between Cologne and Mainz is also world famous for its wines and wine festivals during the autumn. **Eltz Castle** is located deep in the woods near the Elzbach River. The Rhine Gorge's numerous castles include **Stolzenfels**, **Marksburg Castle**, **Rheinfels** at **St Goar** and the **Schönburg Castle** at **Oberwesel**.
Along the Cologne–Mainz route, the *KD German Rhine Line* operates boats between Good Friday and the end of October enabling the passenger to enjoy the view of both sides of the river with vineyards and picturesque villages lining the banks. Spectacular **Rhein in Flammen** (Rhine in Flames) fireworks and *son et lumière* events take place at various venues along the river throughout each summer.
DÜSSELDORF: One of the great cities of the industrial north, this important commercial and cultural centre is the state capital of **North Rhine-Westphalia** (*Nordrhein-Westfalen*). The city developed over 700 years from small fishing village at the mouth of the **Düssel River** to the country's leading foreign trade centre. It is extremely prosperous, with a fine opera house as well as many concert halls, galleries and art exhibitions. There are over 20 theatres and 17 museums, including the **State Art Gallery of North Rhine-Westphalia**, the **Kunsthalle** (City Exhibition Hall) and the late-Baroque **Benrath Palace**. The major exhibition centre is to the north of **Hofgarten**, which has been staging trade fairs since Napoleonic times. The heart of the city is the **Königsallee** or 'Kö', a wide boulevard bisected by a waterway and lined with trees, cafes, fashionable shops and modern shopping arcades. Nearby are the botanical gardens, the **Hofgarten**, the Baroque **Jägerhof Castle** and the state legislature. Other attractions

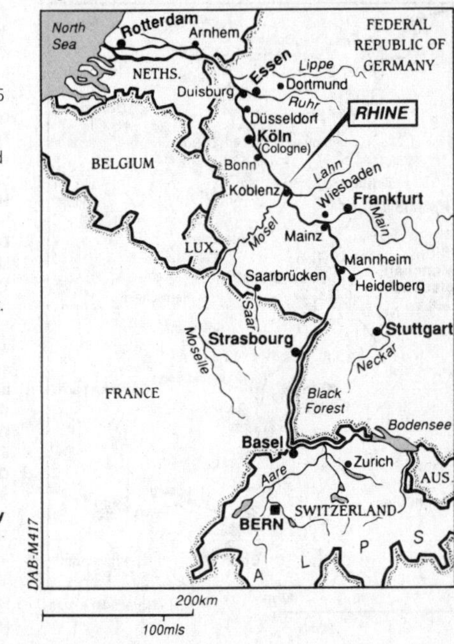

include the ruined 13th-century castle, **St Lambertus Church**, the rebuilt 16th-century **Town Hall**, **Benrath Palace** in southern Düsseldorf and the **Hetjens Museum**, a shrine to ceramics and pottery.

COLOGNE: An old Roman city, Cologne (*Köln*) is an important cultural and commercial centre holding many trade fairs each year. Germany's biggest indoor arena opened in the city recently. Principal attractions include the **Cathedral of St Peter and St Mary** (13th to 19th centuries); the golden reliquary of the Three Magi; the Romanesque churches of **St Pantaleon**, **St George**, **St Apostein**, **St Gereon** and **St Kunibert**, the Gothic churches of **St Andreas** and the **Minoritenkirche** and **Antoniterkirche**; the medieval city wall and the **Roman-Germanic Museum**. There are several examples of preserved Roman art, among them the Dionysus mosaic, the **Praetorium**, the sewage system and the catacombs. The **Wallraf-Richartz Museum** (paintings) is located in a controversial modern building next to the main railway station and the river. The **Schnütgen Museum** contains medieval ecclesiastical art. The **Zoo**, the **Chocolate Museum** and the **Rhine Park** with its 'dancing fountains' are further attractions. The city is a major starting point for boat trips on the Rhine. It also has a famous carnival. The lovingly reconstructed **Altstadt** (Old Town) is enjoyable on foot as is the extensive pedestrian shopping zone. Near the town of **Brühl**, just southwest of Cologne, is the popular theme park, **Phantasialand**.

AACHEN: The beautiful spa town of Aachen (Aix-la-Chapelle) was capital of the empire of Charlemagne. It is not actually on the Rhine, standing 50km (30 miles) west of Cologne on the borders of three countries – Germany, Belgium and The Netherlands – and nearby is a point where a person can stand in all three at once. Attractions in Aachen include the Cathedral (**Kaiserdom**); Charlemagne's marble throne; the **Octagonal Chapel**; the **Town Hall** built between 1333 and 1370 on the ruins of the imperial palace; **Suermond Museum** (paintings, sculptures); and the elegant fountains of sulphurous water, bearing witness to the spa statues of the city. Each July, Aachen hosts an international horse-riding, jumping and driving tournament.

BONN: Until the end of 2000, when the Government moved to Berlin, Bonn was administrative capital of Germany. In the south of the city is the former spa of **Bad Godesberg**, which is also the embassy district and offers a good selection of international restaurants and shops. Attractions include the **Cathedral** (11th to 13th centuries) and cloisters; **Kreuzberg Chapel**, approached by a flight of 'holy steps'; **Schwarzrheindorf Church** (1151); **Town Hall** (1737) and market square; art collections in the **Godesberg** (1210); **Redoute** (1792); **Poppelsdorf Palace** (1715-40) and botanical garden; the **Beethoven Birthplace Museum** and much general theatrical and musical activity associated with his life; **Pützchens Market** (September); the **University** (1725) and **Hofgarten**. Excursion possibilities include the **Siebengebirge**, the **Ahr Valley**, **Brühl Castle** and the **Nürburgring**. The city also has many parkland areas, such as the **Kottenforst**, **Venusberg** and **Rhine Promenade**.

KOBLENZ: Koblenz lies at the confluence of the **Rhine** and the **Moselle**. From the **Ehrenbreitstein Fortress** (1816-32) visitors have a spectacular view over the **Deutsches Eck Monument** to German unity (of 1870) and the confluence of the Rhine and Moselle rivers. Other attractions include the **Old Town**; the **Weindorf** (Wine Village); **Monastery Church** (12th to 13th centuries); former **Electors' Palace**; **Collegiate Church of St Florin** (12th century with a 14th-century chancel); and **Church of Our Lady** (12th century with a 15th-century chancel). Ehrenbreitstein also houses a **Beethoven Museum**.

RÜDESHEIM: On the Rhine south of Koblenz, Rüdesheim is famous for its **Drosselgasse**, a narrow lane with many little wine bars and pubs, some serving the delicious *Rüdesheimer Kaffee* (locally produced brandy with coffee). The **Asbach Distillery** is open to visitors, and there is also the unusual **Museum of Mechanical Musical Instruments**. A cable car from Rüdesheim takes visitors up to the beautiful **Niederwald Castle**, a starting point for walks in the **Taunus** hills. It is also a popular starting point for many of the Rhine cruises. Almost midway between Rüdesheim and Koblenz is the Rhine's symbol, **Lorelei Rock**, which has provided the inspiration for many songs about its legendary siren.

TRIER: On the banks of the Moselle, a Rhine tributary, Trier is near the Luxembourg frontier, about 100km (60 miles) southwest of Koblenz. It is the oldest city in Germany, a Roman imperial capital in the third and fourth centuries AD, and a UNESCO World Heritage Site. Attractions include **The Porta Nigra** (city gate, second century); **Roman Imperial Baths**; **Basilica**; **Amphitheatre**; **Cathedral** (fourth century); **Gothic Church of Our Lady**; **Simeonsstift** with 11th-century cloisters; **Church of St Matthew** (Apostle's grave); **Church of St Paulinus** (designed by Balthasar Neumann); **Regional Museum**; **Episcopal Museum**; **Municipal Museum**; **Municipal Library** (with notable manuscripts); and the birthplace of Karl Marx.

SAARBRÜCKEN: Saarbrücken is mainly a modern industrial city, and capital of the state of **Saarland**, sandwiched between the Rhineland and the French and Luxembourg frontiers. The city lies on the **River Saar**, a Moselle tributary. Saarbrücken is a modern industrial city. Attractions include the **Church of St Ludwig and Ludwigsplatz** (1762-75); the **Collegiate Church of St Arnual** (13th and 14th centuries); a palace with grounds and a Gothic church; and a Franco-German garden with a miniature town (**Gulliver's Miniature World**). Close to Saarbrücken, at **Völklingen**, is the **Hütte Steelworks** UNESCO World Heritage Site.

MAINZ: State capital of **Rhineland-Palatinate** (*Rheinland-Pfalz*), this university town and episcopal see dating back 2000 years is situated on the rivers **Rhine** and **Main**. Attractions include the international museum of printing **Gutenberg Museum**; the 1000-year-old **Cathedral**; **Electors' Palace**; **Roman Jupiter Column** (AD 67); **'Sparkling Hock' Museum**; **Citadel** with monument to General Nero Claudius Drusus; old half-timbered houses; **Mainzer Fassenacht** (carnival); and the **Wine Market** (late August and early September). The sunny slopes of the **Rhinegau Hills** are centre of one of the world's most famous wine-producing regions.

SAXONY

Best-known of the former GDR states, Saxony (*Sachsen*) is famous for cities like **Dresden**, **Leipzig**, and of course, the pottery town **Meissen**.

The **Erzgebirge** region near **Dresden** lies on the border with the Czech Republic. Its mountainous wooded landscape makes it ideal for walkers in the summer and skiers in the winter. **Sächsische Schweiz** (**Saxon Switzerland**) is now a national park, its sandstone mountains attracting many visitors. **Chemnitz** (formerly Karl-Marx-Stadt) is the main town in this region. It was heavily bombed during the war and only a few of its historic buildings remain, such as the **Old Town Hall** (16th century) and the 800-year-old **Red Tower**; others are **Freiberg**, **Kuchwald**, with its open-air theatre, and **Seifen** with its toy museum. **Zwickau** was birthplace of Robert Schumann and is home to a late Gothic **Cathedral**, a **Town Hall** dating back to 1403 and numerous old burghers' houses.

DRESDEN: With over 500,000 inhabitants, this is one of the largest cities in southeast Germany. Its heyday was during the 17th and 18th centuries when August the Strong and subsequently his son August III ruled Saxony. The most famous building in the city is the restored **Zwinger Palace**, which contains many old masters in its picture gallery, among them the *Sistine Madonna* by Raphael. Allied bombings destroyed much of the Baroque magnificence of the city, once known as the 'Florence of the Elbe' during World War II. However, some of the finest buildings, such as the Catholic **Hofkirche**, the **Palace Church**, the **Semper Opera** and the **Green Vault** treasure chamber of the Saxon Princes, either survived the bombings or have been restored in the intervening period. The **Frauenkirche**, since 1945 a chilling reminder of wartime horrors, is currently under reconstruction (due for completion in 2006). Other attractions include the **Arsenal**, which has a vast collection of armour and weapons from the Middle Ages to the present day, the fountains in the **Pragerstrasse**, the old market, the Philharmonic Orchestra and the **Kreuz** Choir. The Dresden district is home to the minority *Sorbs*, a Slavic people who settled there in the sixth century. Sorb-language newspapers and broadcasts combine with teaching in local schools to preserve the culture.

LEIPZIG: Leipzig has a fascinating history. Lenin printed the first issues of his Marxist newspaper here. Lessing, Jean-Paul Sartre and Goethe all studied at the university. Music and books are important – there are no less than 38 publishers in the city, and it is Wagner's birthplace. The **German Museum of Books** claims to be the world's oldest of its kind. Mendelssohn was director of music, and Bach was choirmaster, at the now completely restored **St Thomas' Church**, between 1723 and 1750. There are museums dedicated to both composers in the city. Bach's church choir still exists and is of an excellent standard, as is the city's **Gewandhaus Orchestra**. The old **University** (1407), the famous **Auerbach's Cellar** and the **Kaffeebaum**, the most famous of the city's cafes, are further attractions in the city. Today Leipzig stages major international trade fairs.

MEISSEN: Meissen is the oldest china manufacturing town in Europe, famous for its fine Meissen china. Visitors can tour the factory. The narrow streets of old Meissen retain their historic charm. The **Albrechtsburg Cathedral** (1485) and the **Bishop's Castle** tower above the city. Meissen is also the centre of a wine-growing region.

SAXONY-ANHALT

Saxony-Anhalt (*Sachsen-Anhalt*) boasts no less than four UNESCO World Heritage Sites. **Martin Luther's Birthplace** at **Eisleben**, the **Old Town of Quedlinberg**, the **Castle** at **Wittenberg**, and **Dessau's Bauhausstätten**. Among the towering scenery of the **Harz Mountains**, a region ideal for walking and winter sports holidays and dotted with villages with attractive carved timber-fronted houses, lies the town of **Wernigerode** whose castle and 16th-century **Town Hall** endow it with a fairytale air. There is a museum of church relics here. On a walk the visitor can see half-timbered houses of six centuries, among them the **Crooked House**. The Harz is also one of the most beautiful hiking areas in Germany; since December 1989, hikers have been able to enjoy the **Brocken** (highest point of the Harz) again. Half-timbered houses characterise **Stolberg**, 'Pearl of the South Harz region', where the **Town Hall**, dating back to 1492, contains no inner staircase. Just to the south lies the city of **Halle**, birthplace of Handel, and where Martin Luther often preached in the **Marienkirche** in the **Market Square**.

South of Halle lies the historic town of **Naumburg** with its beautiful late Romanesque/early Gothic **Cathedral of St Peter and St Paul**. A recommended excursion from here takes in the old Hanseatic towns of **Salzwedel**, **Stendal** and **Tangermünde** to see the medieval fortifications.

MAGDEBURG: Located on the banks of the **Elbe** to the southwest of Berlin, Magdeburg is state capital. It has a busy arts scene. One of its most popular attractions is the **Elbauenpark** on the river, with the tallest wooden tower in the world, the **Millennium Tower**. The tower contains an exhibition on 6000 years of human development. **Cathedral Square**, with its Gothic church surrounded by Baroque buildings, stands at the heart of the old city centre, with the **Old Market Square** (site of the **Magdeburg Knight** monument) and the **Town Hall**.

DESSAU: 'Second home' of the **Bauhaus Architectural School**, which moved from Weimar in the mid-1920s, and whose building, the **Bauhausstätten**, designed by Walter Gropius, is a designated World Heritage Site.

QUEDLINBURG: 55km (34 miles) southwest of Magdeburg, this town has many 16th-century half-timbered houses such as the **Finkenherd** and a Renaissance **Town Hall**, all restored to their original condition.

WITTENBERG: One of the most famous Reformation towns, where Martin Luther nailed his '95 Theses Against Indulgences' to the door of the castle church in 1517. Numerous magnificent buildings from the 16th century – **Luther's House**, the **Melanchton House**, the **Castle Church** and the buildings of the former **University** bear witness to the town's historical significance.

THURINGIA

Thuringia (*Thüringen*) lies between Saxony and Hesse, and is the most westerly of the old 'East' German states. Major centres include **Erfurt**, **Jena** and **Weimar**. The wooded heights and slate mountains of the **Thuringian Forest** make the region an ideal area for walking. The best-known hiking route is the **Rennsteig** which stretches for over 168km (105 miles). The entire region of the Rennsteig is a protected zone and is therefore immune to any industrial or urban development.

A flourishing craft industry and winter sports facilities centred in **Suhl** also draw visitors to the state. **Eisenach**, birthplace of Johann Sebastian Bach, contains the oldest **Town Gate** in Thuringia and the Romanesque **Nikolai Church**. **Wartburg Castle**, where Martin Luther sought refuge and translated the New Testament into German, dominates the town. The small town of **Rudolstadt** was

known for its cultural life during the Renaissance, hosting plays of the Weimar Court Theatre, directed by Goethe, and founding a renowned court orchestra in 1635 which attracted many of the best classical musicians. It is now a popular stop along Thuringia's **Classic Road**. **Arnstadt**, where the young Bach was an organist at the local church, is the 'Gateway' to the Thuringia Forest, with its lush hiking trails and magnificent views.
Other noteworthy sites in the region include **Gera** with its Renaissance **Town Hall** and fine **Burghers' Houses**, the castle ruins at **Friedrichsroda**, the imperial city **Nordhausen** with its late Gothic Cathedral and Renaissance **Town Hall** and the picturesque town of **Mühlhausen**.
ERFURT: The cultural centre of Thuringia, and state capital. Formerly a rich trading centre, its well-preserved, medieval city centre contains a wealth of churches, cloisters and old merchants' houses. Dating from 1392, the university is one of northern Europe's oldest. Martin Luther lived as a monk in the city's **Augustinian Monastery**, which displays exhibits relating to his life. Erfurt's museums contain valuable collections of medieval treasures.
JENA: Famous for its optical industry, Jena also offers the world's oldest **Planetarium**, nowadays equipped with the latest laser technology. The **Optics Museum** contains extensive collections of spectacles and *Zeiss* microscopes. **Collegium Jenense**, the original 16th-century university building, is also open to visitors. For children, the interactive **Imaginata** interpretation centre encourages exploration of a variety of topics.
WEIMAR: The southern 1000-year-old town of Weimar was home to many great men, including Luther, Bach, Liszt, Wagner and Schiller. An important cultural centre of the past, the city experienced its golden age in the 18th and 19th centuries. Johann Wolfgang von Goethe lived here for 50 years and was a major influence as a civil servant, theatre director and poet. His house is now the **Goethe National Museum**. Literature enthusiasts should not miss the **Goethe and Schiller Archive**. Bach was Court Organist and Court Concertmaster, Liszt and Richard Strauss were both directors of music. There is documentation of their private and public lives kept in hotels and museums in the town. Weimar was also the original home of the Bauhaus architectural school before it moved to Dessau (see the *Saxony-Anhalt* section). The modern **Weimar House** multimedia presentation tells the full story of the city. A few kilometres from Weimar, a museum occupies the former site of the **Buchenwald** concentration camp.

Credit: © German National Tourist Board

Sport & Activities

Walking: The Harz Mountains, Black Forest and the Bavarian Forest are some of the best areas for walking. The network of marked trails amounts to some 132,000km (82,500 miles). The District of Templin in the March of Brandenburg provides 480km (300 miles) of paths. The German Alps Club (*Deutscher Alpenverein*) maintains several huts in the Alps and the other ranges. It also organises tours and courses in **rock climbing**. The Saxon Hills between Dresden and Bad Schandau, with more than 1000 prepared routes, provide good training for aspiring climbers. Excellent facilities can also be found in Oberhof.
Spectator sports: There are extensive sports facilities, with a sports field or stadium in all larger towns. League **football** matches take place between Friday and Sunday. International matches also take place regularly: the national team were world champions in 1990, a title they previously won in 1954 and 1974, as well as having been runners-up in 1966 (to England), 1982, 1986 and 2002, and quarter finalists in 1998.
Wintersports: Resorts are mainly in the Suhl area in the south of the country. The main resort is Oberhof, which offers excellent **ski-jumping** and **tobogganing**. **Ice hockey** and **skating** are both popular. In Bavaria, **skiing** is available at resorts such as *Berchtesgaden*, *Garmisch-Partenkirchen*, *Inzell*, *Oberstdorf*, *Reit im Winkl*, as well as in the southern mountains. Other areas are the Bavarian Forest, the Black Forest and the Harz Mountains. The season runs from November to April. **Curling** is especially popular in Upper Bavaria.
Cycling: This is increasingly popular and cycling paths ensure that, even in cities, cycling is a safe form of transport. Bicycles can be hired from certain railway stations, a list of which is available through the German National Railways (*Deutsche Bahn*) (see also *Travel – International* and *Travel – Internal* sections) *or* the German National Tourist Office (see *Contact Addresses* section). Further information is available from the German Cycling Club (*Allgemeiner Deutscher Fahrrad-Club*) e.V. (ADFC), Postfach 107747, 28077 Bremen (tel: (421) 346 290; fax: (421) 346 2950; e-mail: kontakt@adfc.de; website: www.adfc.de).
Watersports: The northern coastline and the extensive rivers and lakes provide **sailing**, **swimming**, **windsurfing** and both sea and river **fishing**. A fishing permit is needed. Fishing is particularly good on inland waterways; fishing and sailing are also popular at the Bay of Lietzow on the Baltic coast. The Baltic coast has many beaches.
Horse-riding: Hotels with horse-riding facilities are located in all tourist regions. **Racecourses** can be found at Baden-Baden, Frankfurt/M, Hamburg and Munich.
Wine tasting: German wine country has many small vineyards which welcome visitors. The main wine-growing regions are around the rivers Rhine, Moselle and Neckar in the west of the country and, further east, near the Saale, Unstrut and Elbe rivers. For motorists, there is a signposted 'wine road' (*Weinstrasse*) running through each area. The majority of German wines are white and light, with such varieties as Riesling and Silvaner. Wines are officially classified by the Government as either *Tafelwein/ Landwein* (table wine/country wine) or *Qualitätswein* (higher-quality wine from a specified area). *Qualitätswein mit Prädikat* is the highest category. Within this last category, the wine is classed according to ripeness and quality: *Kabinett* for example is a light, low-alcohol wine made from fully ripened grapes, while *Trockenbeerenauslese* is a sweet wine made from grapes which have shrivelled almost to raisins. For a list of private vineyards open to the public, contact the German National Tourist Office (see *Contact Addresses* section) *or* the German Wine Institute, PO Box 1660, 55116 Mainz (tel: (6131) 28290; fax: (6131) 282 920; e-mail: info@deutscheweine.de; website: www.deutscheweine.de).
Spas: Germany has over 300 spas and health resorts which offer a wide range of traditional and modern treatments. All are strictly regulated by the Government, and promise beneficial results for such conditions as rheumatism, respiratory problems, nervous disorders or stress. Spa stays are very popular with Germans, not only because they are a national tradition, but because they offer holistic treatment combined with relaxation. Under medical supervision, visitors can take the waters or undergo treatments involving mud and peat. Many spas are situated on the North Sea and Baltic coasts. For further information about spa stays, contact the Deutscher Bäderverband (for address, see *Health* section).
Language courses: There are many opportunities to pursue courses in German language and culture. Often these are subsidised by the Government. For further information contact the Goethe Institut, 50 Princes Gate, Exhibition Road, London SW7 2PH, UK (tel: (020) 7596 4000; fax: (020) 7594 0240; e-mail: mail@london.goethe.org; website: www.goethe.de/london).

Social Profile

FOOD & DRINK: The main meal of the day in Germany tends to be lunch with a light snack eaten at about seven in the evening. Breakfast served in homes and hotels usually consists of a boiled egg, bread rolls with jam, honey, cold cuts and cheese slices. Available from snack bars, butcher shops, bakers and cafes are grilled, fried or boiled sausages (*Wurst*) with a crusty bread roll or potato salad. There are also bread rolls filled with all kinds of sausage slices, hot meat filling (such as *Leberkäse*), pickled herring, gherkins and onion rings or cheese. In bakeries, *Strudel* with the traditional apple filling, a variety of fruits and *fromage frais* is available. There is also an astonishingly wide variety of breads. A set menu meal in a simple *Gasthof* or cafe usually includes three courses: soup is the most popular starter. The main meal consists of vegetables or a salad, potatoes, meat and gravy. For pudding, there is often a sweet such as a *blancmange*, fruit or ice cream. Restaurants often serve either beer or wine. Cakes and pastries are normally reserved for the afternoon with Kaffee und Kuchen ('coffee and cakes') taken at home or in a cafe. Cafes serving *Kaffee und Kuchen* are not only to be found in cities, towns and villages but also at or near popular excursion and tourist spots. International speciality restaurants, such as Chinese, Greek, Turkish and others, can be found everywhere in the western part of the country. Waiter or waitress service is normal although self-service restaurants are available. Bakeries and dairy shops specialise in lighter meals if preferred. *Local regional specialities* cover an enormous range:
Frankfurt and Hesse: *Rippchen mit Sauerkraut* (spare ribs) and of course *Frankfurter* sausages, *Ochsenbrust* with green sauce, *Zwiebelkuchen* (onion flan), and *Frankfurter Kranz* cream cake.
Westphalia and Northern Rhineland: *Rheinischer Sauerbraten* (beef marinaded in onions, sultanas, pimento, etc), *Reibekuchen* (potato fritters), *Pfeffer-Potthast* (spiced beef with bay leaves) and *Moselhecht* (Moselle pike with creamy cheese sauce). Westphalia is also famous for its smoked ham, sausages and bread such as *Pumpernickel*.
Stuttgart and Baden: *Schlachtplatte* (sauerkraut, liver sausage and boiled pork). A variety of pastas are served such as *Maultaschen* (a type of ravioli) and *Spätzle* (noodles), as well as *Eingemachtes Kalbfleisch* (veal stew with white sauce and capers) and *Schwarzwälder Kirschtorte* (Black Forest gateau).
Munich and Bavaria: *Leberkäs* (pork and beef loaf), as well as a variety of dumplings, *Spanferkel* (suckling pig), the famous *Weisswurst* (white sausages), *Strudel*, *Leberknödelsuppe* (liver dumplings soup), *Nürnberger Lebkuchen* (gingerbread) and, from the same town, grilled *Rostbratwurst* sausages.
Hamburg and Northern Germany: *Hamburger Aalsuppe* (eel/lobster/crayfish soup), *Labskaus* (hotpot with fried eggs), *Rote Grütze mit Sahne oder Vanillesosse* (fruit compote served with cream or custard), smoked eel, *Rumtopf* (fruit marinated in rum), *Lübeck marzipan*, *Heidschnuckenbraten* (Lüneburg Heath mutton), fish with green sauce, *Bauernfrühstück* (omelette with fried potatoes, tomatoes and onions) and bread rolls filled with fish or prawns as a snack.
Bremen: *Kohl und Pinkel* (kale and sausages), *Matjes Hering* (white herring), eel soup and *Hannoversches Blindhuhn* (hotpot with bacon, potatoes, vegetables and fruit).
Berlin: *Eisbein mit Sauerkraut* (leg of pork) and mashed potatoes, *Bouletten* (hamburgers), *Kartoffelpuffer* (potato fritters), *Eierpfannkuchen* (pancakes), *Berliner Pfannkuchen* (doughnut), and *Berliner Weisse mit Schuss* (beer with a dash of something – usually raspberry syrup).
March of Brandenburg: *Teltower Rübchen* (swedes), *Mohnprielen* and *Mohnstriezel* (pastries with poppy seeds), *Morchelgerichte* (mushroom dishes), *Oder* crabs, *Eberswalder Spritzkuchen* (doughnuts), *Schwarzsauer mit Backpflaumen und Klößen* (black pudding with prunes and dumplings).
Saxony: *Leipziger Allerlei* (vegetables in white sauce), *Dresdner Stollen* (German christmas cake) and *Speckkuchen* (bacon flan).
Saxony-Anhalt: *Lehm und Stroh* (sauerkraut with mushy peas), *Köhlersuppe* (croutons, suet, onions and mushrooms), *Speckkuchen mit Eiern und Kümmel* (bacon flan with eggs and caraway seeds), *Zerbster Brägenwurst* (sausage) with *Bitterbier*, and *Baumkuchen* (literally tree cake, the thin layers of pastry are like the rings of trees).

A B C D E F G H I J K L M N O P Q R S T U V W X Y Z

Credit: © German National Tourist Board

Thuringia: *Thüringer Rostbratwürste* (grilled sausages), *Hefeplinsen* (pancakes with raisins) with sugar or jam. Apple, plum, poppy seed, *fromage frais* or onion crumbles. There are numerous mushroom dishes, which are called *Schwämm*.
Mecklenburg-West Pomerania: *Plum'n un Klüt* (plums and dumplings), *Spickbost* (smoked goose breast).
Bars can either have table service and/or counter service, although customers will often find that the drinks bought are simply marked down on a beer mat to be paid for on leaving. The legal age for drinking alcohol in a bar or cafe is 18. Minors are allowed to go into a bar if accompanied by an adult but they will not be served alcohol. Opening hours depend on the proprietor but, generally, bars in major towns and resorts are open all day and close around midnight or later. Exceptions are Berlin and Hamburg where every pub can open for 24 hours. The national drink is **beer** in its many forms. Regional flavours vary from light *pilsner*-type lagers to heavy stouts. Three of particular note are *Bayrisches G'frornes* (frozen beer) and *Weizenbier* from Bavaria, and *Mumme* (bittersweet beer without hops) to be found in Hannover.
German **wines** are among the finest in the world. Some of the most famous are grown in the Rhine and the Moselle Valley but also in the Ahr region, Nahe, Franconia and Baden area. Worth trying are *Äppelwoi* (cider) in Frankfurt/M, *Cannstatter* (white wine) in Stuttgart, *Kirschwasser* (cherry schnapps) in Baden, and *Würzburger* (dry white wine) in Würzburg.
NIGHTLIFE: In all larger towns and cities in western Germany and also in the major eastern cities, visitors will have the choice between theatre, opera (*Deutsche Oper Berlin*, *Hamburgische Staatsoper* and the *National Theatre* in Munich are some of the most famous names), nightclubs, bars with live music and discos catering for all tastes. Berlin, in particular, is famous for its large selection of after-hours venues. Traditional folk music is found mostly in rural areas. There are *Bierkellers* in the south and wine is drunk in small wine cellars in the Rhineland Palatinate, Franconia and Baden region.
SHOPPING: Special purchases include precision optical equipment such as binoculars and cameras, porcelain, handmade crystal, silver, steelware, Solingen knives, leatherwear, sports equipment, toys from Nuremberg and Bavarian *Loden* cloth. Special purchases in eastern Germany include musical instruments, wooden carved toys from the Erzgebirge Mountains, and Meissen china (the workshops in Meissen are open to the public). **Shopping hours:** Shops can regulate their own opening hours within these times Mon-Fri 0600-2000, Sat 0600-1600. Smaller shops may close 1300-1500 for lunch. All shops, except a few bakeries, are closed on Sunday.
SPECIAL EVENTS: Hundreds of annual festivals and special events are celebrated throughout the country. Full details can be obtained from the Deutsche Zentrale für Tourismus e.V (German National Tourist Board; see *Contact Addresses* section). The following is a selection of special events occurring in Germany in 2005:
Feb 3-9 *Carnival*, Rhineland. **Mar 19-Apr 18/Jul 23-Aug 22/Nov 5-Dec 5** *Hamburger DOM Festival*. **Apr 28-30** *European Grand Prix*, the Nürburgring, Eifel. **Jul 23-25** *German Grand Prix*, Hockenheim Ring. **Jul 25-Aug 28** *Richard Wagner Festival*, Bayreuth. **Aug 16-21** *20th World Youth Day*, Cologne. **Sep 18-Oct 3** *Munich's Oktoberfest: Bavaria's National Beer Festival*. **Dec** *Christmas Markets*.
SOCIAL CONVENTIONS: Handshaking is customary. Normal courtesies should be observed and it is common to be offered food and refreshments when visiting someone's home. Before eating, it is normal to say *Guten Appetit* to the other people at the table to which the correct reply is *Ebenfalls*. It is customary to present the hostess with unwrapped flowers (according to tradition, one should always give an uneven number and it is worth noting that red roses are exclusively a lover's gift). Courtesy dictates that when entering a shop, restaurant or similar venue, visitors should utter a greeting such as *Guten Tag* (or *Grüss Gott* in Bavaria) before saying what it is that they want; to leave without saying *Auf Wiedersehen* can also cause offence. Similarly, when making a telephone call, asking for the person you want to speak to without stating first who you are is considered rude. Casual wear is widely acceptable, but more formal dress is required for some restaurants, the opera, theatre, casinos and important social functions. Evening wear is worn when requested. Smoking is prohibited where notified and on public transport and in some public buildings. Visitors should be prepared for an early start to the day with businesses, schools, etc opening at 0800 or earlier. It is very common practice to take a mid-afternoon stroll on Sunday; town and city centres at this time are often very animated places, in stark comparison with Saturday afternoons when, owing to the early closing of shops, town centres can seem almost deserted. **Tipping:** It is customary to tip taxi drivers, hairdressers, cloakroom attendants, bar and restaurant staff; a 10 per cent tip in standard.

Business Profile

ECONOMY: From the ruins of the Third Reich, both halves of divided post-war Germany emerged over the next two decades as the economic powerhouses of their respective European blocs. The unified German economy is now the fifth-largest in the world. The bulk of its production is in the West (the pre-unification Federal Republic). The Western economy has large chemical and car manufacturing plants, mechanical, electrical and electronic engineering, and rapidly growing advanced technology and service sectors in computing, biotechnology, information processing and media. The East's (former Democratic Republic's) economy never dominated COMECON, the Soviet bloc Council for Mutual Economic Assistance, in the way that the West's did the EU, but it consistently recorded the highest growth and per capita income within the bloc.
Reunification illustrated starkly how far the East had fallen behind the West. After initial difficulties, and much pessimistic forecasting, the Eastern economy was absorbed fairly painlessly into the West albeit at considerable financial cost. Among the benefits was a head start for German companies entering the new markets of Eastern Europe. Nonetheless, Germany's most important trading partners are its fellow members of the EU, plus the USA, Switzerland and Japan. Trade with China is on a similar scale to that with several Eastern European nations. The huge expenditure incurred as a result of unification – estimated at US$100 billion – had a knock-on effect on the speed of the German pursuit of economic and political union in Europe as the Government needed to ensure that Germany met the economic criteria (budget deficit, total debt) for entry into European Monetary Union (EMU) and the introduction of the single currency. The high cost of unification and long-term structural problems in the economy (especially the stagnation of key industrial sectors) have put the German economy under pressure since the late 1990s. Entry into EMU has demanded further fiscal discipline and, in 2004, the economy was minus 0.1 per cent while unemployment remained close to 11 per cent.
BUSINESS: Businesspeople are expected to dress smartly. English is spoken by many local businesspeople, but it is an advantage to have a working knowledge of German, or an interpreter. Appointments should be made well in advance, particularly in the summer. Appointments may be suggested slightly earlier in the day than is often the custom in the UK. Once made, appointment times should be strictly adhered to. Some firms may close early Friday afternoon. Always use titles such as *Herr Doktor* or *Frau Doktor* when addressing business contacts. Punctuality is essential for business visits. **Office hours:** Mon-Fri 0900-1700 (many close earlier on Fridays).
COMMERCIAL INFORMATION: The following organisations can offer advice: German-British Chamber of Industry and Commerce, Mecklenburg House, 16 Buckingham Gate, London SW1E 6LB, UK (tel: (020) 7976 4100; fax: (020) 7976 4101; e-mail: mail@ahk-london.co.uk; website: www.ahk-london.co.uk *or* www.germanbritishchamber.co.uk). This organisation also has branch offices in most major Western European capitals; *or* Deutscher Industrie und Handelstag (Association of German Chambers of Industry and Commerce), Breite Strasse 29, 10178 Berlin (tel: (30) 203 080; fax: (30) 2030 81000; e-mail: dihk@berlin.dihk.de; website: www.diht.de). The organisation is affiliated with 83 Chambers of Industry and Commerce. There are also Chambers of Industry and Commerce in all major German towns and a regional Chamber of Commerce for each of the states.
CONFERENCES/CONVENTIONS: The western part of Germany can offer a highly developed and well-equipped network of conference destinations. For information, contact the German Convention Bureau (Deutsches Kongressbüro) (website: www.gcb.de), which has branches in Frankfurt/M and New York. Frankfurt/M: Münchner Strasse 48, 60329 Frankfurt/M (tel: (69) 242 9300; fax: (69) 2429 3026; e-mail: info@gcb.de); New York: 122 East 42nd Street, 52nd Floor, New York, NY 10168-0072, USA (tel: (212) 661 4582; fax: (212) 661 6192; e-mail: gcbny@gcb.de). Founded in 1973, the Bureau is a non-profitmaking organisation sponsored by Germany's major convention cities, hotels, travel agents and carriers, as well as the country's leading travel and tourist associations, including the German National Tourist Board, Lufthansa and the German Railways.

Climate

Temperate throughout the country with warm summers and cold winters, but prolonged periods of frost or snow are rare. Rain falls throughout the year.
Required clothing: European clothes with light- to mediumweights in summer, medium- to heavyweights in winter. Waterproofs are needed throughout the year.

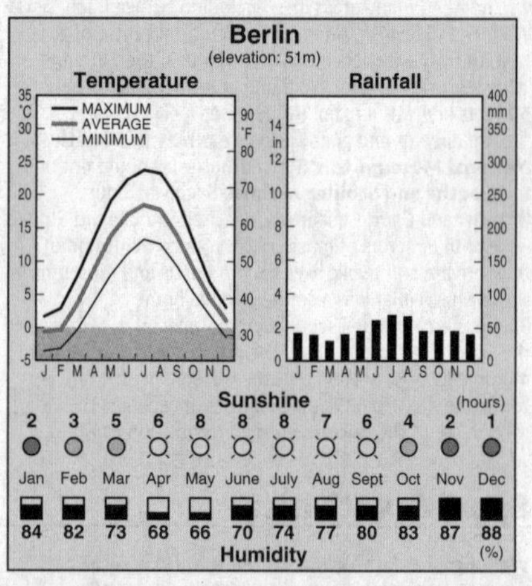

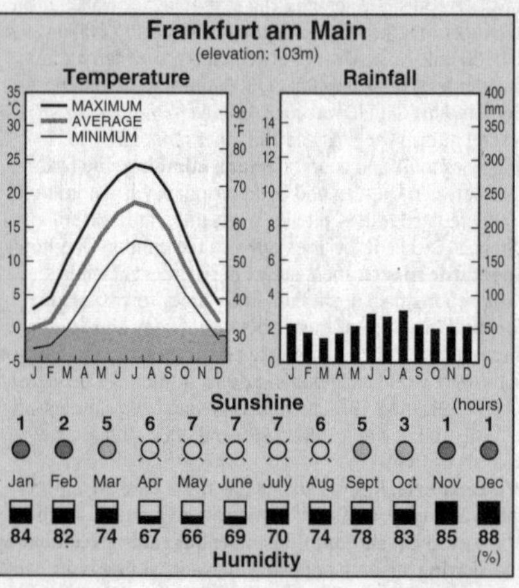

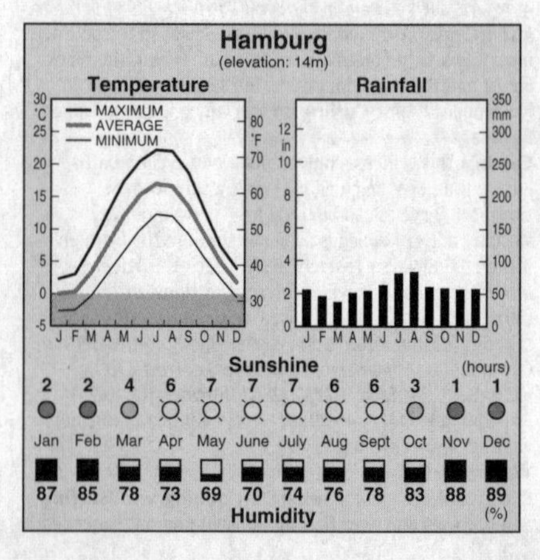

Ghana

LATEST TRAVEL ADVICE CONTACTS

British Foreign and Commonwealth Office
Tel: (0870) 606 0290 Website: www.fco.gov.uk

US Department of State
Website: http://travel.state.gov/travel

Canadian Department of Foreign Affairs and Int'l Trade
Tel: (1 800) 267 8376 Website: www.dfait-maeci.gc.ca

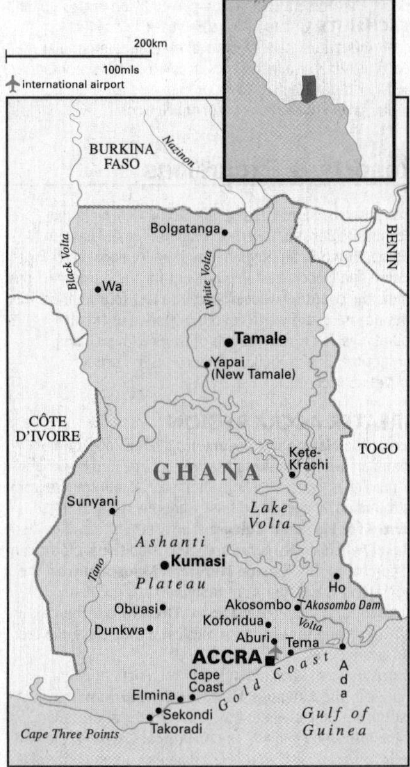

Location: West Africa.

Country dialling code: 233.

Ministry of Tourism
PO Box 4386, Accra, Ghana
Tel: (21) 666 701. Fax: (21) 666 182.
Website: www.ghanatourism.gov.gh

Ghana High Commission (Education, Visas and Trade)
104 Highgate Hill, London N6 5HE, UK
Tel: (020) 8342 7501 *or* 7580. Fax: (020) 8342 8570 (visa section) *or* 8560 (education section).
E-mail: enquiries@ghana-com.co.uk
Website: www.ghana-com.co.uk
Consulate opening hours: Mon-Fri 0930-1300 (visa collection).

Ghana High Commission (Information and Admin)
13 Belgrave Square, London SW1X 8PN, UK
Tel: (020) 7201 5919. Fax: (020) 7245 9552.
E-mail: enquiries@ghana-com.co.uk
Website: www.ghana-com.co.uk
Opening hours: Mon-Fri 0930-1730.

British High Commission
Street address: 2 Osu Link, off Gamel Abdul Nasser Road, Osu Ara, Accra, Ghana
Postal address: PO Box 296, Accra, Ghana
Tel: (21) 701 0650 *or* 0721 (visa section).
Fax: (21) 701 0655 *or* 221 715 (visa section).
E-mail: high.commission.accra@fco.gov.uk
Website: www.britishhighcommission.gov.uk/ghana

Embassy of the Republic of Ghana
3512 International Drive, NW, Washington, DC 20008, USA
Tel: (202) 686 4520. Fax: (202) 686 4527.
E-mail: ghtrade@cais.com
Website: www.ghanaembassy.org

TIMATIC CODES

Health	AMADEUS: **TI-DFT/ACC/HE** GALILEO/WORLDSPAN: **TI-DFT/ACC/HE** SABRE: **TIDFT/ACC/HE**
Visa	AMADEUS: **TI-DFT/ACC/VI** GALILEO/WORLDSPAN: **TI-DFT/ACC/VI** SABRE: **TIDFT/ACC/VI**

To access TIMATIC country information on Health and Visa regulations through the Computer Reservations System (CRS), type in the appropriate command line listed above.

Consulate General of Ghana (Visas and Tourist Information)
19 East 47th Street, New York, NY 10017, USA
Tel: (212) 832 1300. Fax: (212) 751 6743.
E-mail: ghanaperm@aol.com
Website: www.ghanaweb.com

Embassy of the United States of America
Ring Road East, PO Box 194, Accra, Ghana
Tel: (21) 775 348. Fax: (21) 776 008.
Website: http://accra.usembassy.gov
Consular section: 6th and 10th Lanes, Osu, Accra, Ghana
Tel: (21) 776 601. Fax: (21) 701 1831 *or* 0165.
E-mail: consulateaccra@state.gov

High Commission for the Republic of Ghana
1 Clemow Avenue, Ottawa, Ontario K1S 2A9, Canada
Tel: (613) 236 0871. Fax: (613) 236 0874.
E-mail: ghanacom@ghanahighcommission-canada.com
Website: www.ghanahighcommission-canada.com

Canadian High Commission
Street address: 42 Independence Avenue, Accra, Ghana
Postal address: PO Box 1639, Accra, Ghana
Tel: (21) 228 555. Fax: (21) 773 792.
E-mail: accra@dfait-maeci.gc.ca
Website: www.dfait-maeci.gc.ca/accra

Credit: © Ghana Tourist Board

General Information

AREA: 238,537 sq km (92,100 sq miles).
POPULATION: 18,845,265 (official estimate 2000).
POPULATION DENSITY: 79.0 per sq km.
CAPITAL: Accra. **Population:** 1,925,000 (official estimate 2001).
GEOGRAPHY: Ghana is situated in West Africa and is a rectangular-shaped country bordered to the north by Burkina Faso, the east by Togo, the south by the Atlantic Ocean and the west by Côte d'Ivoire. A narrow grassy plain stretches inland from the coast, widening in the east, while the south and west are covered by dense rainforest. To the north are forested hills, beyond which is dry savannah and open woodland. In the far north is a plateau averaging 500m (1600ft) in height. In the east the Akuapim Togo hills run inland from the coast along the Togo border. The Black and White Volta rivers enter Ghana from Burkina Faso, merging into the largest manmade lake in the world, Lake Volta. Ghana's coastline is dotted with sandy palm-fringed beaches and lagoons.
GOVERNMENT: Republic. Gained independence from the UK in 1957. **Head of State:** President John Agyekum Kufuor since 2000.
LANGUAGE: The official language is English. Local Ghanaian languages are widely spoken, including Akan, Ewe, Fante, Ga, Moshi-Dagomba and Twi.
RELIGION: Christian (69 per cent), Muslim and traditional beliefs. All forms of religion have a strong influence on Ghanaian life.
TIME: GMT.
ELECTRICITY: 220 volts AC, 50Hz; usually three-pin plugs. Single phase three-pin plugs are used in larger buildings. Older buildings have two-pin plugs. Light bulbs are of the bayonet type.
COMMUNICATIONS: Telephone: IDD service is available in most parts of the country. Country code: 233. Outgoing international code: 00. **Mobile telephone:** GSM 900 network. Coverage is patchy outside the capital and larger towns. Operators include *Ghana Telecommunications Company Ltd* (website: www.ghanatel.net), *Millicom Ghana Ltd* and *Spacefon* (website: www.spacefon.com). **Fax:** There is a 24-hour fax service in Accra. **Internet:** ISPs include *Ghana.com* (website: www.ghana.com). **Telegram:** Services are available from Ghana Telecom, High Street, Accra and Stewart Avenue, Kumasi. There are three charge rates. **Post:** Airmail letters to Europe may take two weeks or more to arrive. **Press:** Daily and weekly newspapers are available in English and include *Daily Graphic, The Ghanaian Times* (both daily), *Business and Financial Times, New Nation, The Mirror* and *Weekly Spectator* (all weekly). **Radio:** BBC World Service (website: www.bbc.co.uk/worldservice) and Voice of America (website: www.voa.gov) can be received. From time to time the frequencies change and the most up-to-date can be found online.

Passport/Visa

	Passport Required?	Visa Required?	Return Ticket Required?
Full British	Yes	Yes	Yes
Australian	Yes	Yes	Yes
Canadian	Yes	Yes	Yes
USA	Yes	Yes	Yes
Other EU	Yes	Yes	Yes
Japanese	Yes	Yes	Yes

Note: *Regulations and requirements may be subject to change at short notice, and you are advised to contact the appropriate diplomatic or consular authority before finalising travel arrangements. Details of these may be found at the head of this country's entry. Any numbers in the chart refer to the footnotes below.*

PASSPORTS: Passport valid for three months required by all except nationals of ECOWAS countries who will be allowed entry with a valid travel certificate.
VISAS: Required by all except the following for stays of up to three months:
(a) nationals of ECOWAS countries;
(b) nationals of Egypt, Hong Kong (SAR), Kenya, Mauritius, Singapore and Zimbabwe;
(c) those in transit to a third country travelling within 24 hours, as long as they hold onward tickets with reserved seats and do not leave the airport.
Note: The following nationals may obtain visas upon arrival at the port of entry: Botswana, Lesotho, Malawi, Swaziland, Tanzania, Uganda and Zambia.
Types of visa and cost: *Tourist/Business*: £30 (single-entry); £40 (multiple-entry; six months); £60 (multiple-entry; one year); £70 (multiple-entry; two years). *Transit*: £10.
Validity: Valid for three months from the date of issue. However, length of stay is at the discretion of airport officials and only one month is guaranteed. Visas may be extended when in Ghana. Visas for one year may be granted for specific purposes.
Application to: Consulate (or Consular section at Embassy or High Commission); see *Contact Addresses* section for details.
Application requirements: (a) Valid passport. (b) Completed entry permit application form (this must be copied two times if downloaded from the Internet). (c) Two passport-size photos. (d) For postal applications, registered or recorded self-addressed envelope. (e) Fee (payable by cash, postal order or bankers' draft made payable to the High Commission; cash is not valid for postal applications). (f) Evidence of onward/return ticket. (g) Evidence of sufficient funds. (h) If travelling at invitation of host in Ghana, a letter of invitation should be submitted. (i) Valid certificate of inoculation against Yellow Fever, if applicable. *Business*: (a)-(i) and, (j) Letter of guarantee from a company in support of the application (the letter should explain the nature of business the applicant will be conducting in Ghana).
Working days required: Four for personal, 10 for postal applications.
Temporary residence: Application with sufficient notice to be made to High Commission or Embassy.

Money

Currency: Cedi (¢) = 100 pesewas. Notes are in denominations of ¢20,000, 10,000, 5000, 2000, 1000, 500 and 200. Coins are in denominations of 500, 200, 100 and 50 pesewas.
Currency exchange: The exchange rate system has been liberalised and foreign currency is freely available through authorised dealers including banks and Forex Bureaux. Cash is exchanged at a more preferential rate than travellers cheques.
Credit & debit cards: Credit cards are accepted by leading hotels, restaurants, banks and businesses. Check with your credit or debit card company for details of merchant acceptability and other services which may be available. Some banks may give cash advances against leading cards.
Travellers cheques: To avoid additional exchange rate charges, travellers are advised to take travellers cheques in US Dollars or Pounds Sterling.
Currency restrictions: The import of local currency is limited to amounts which have previously been permitted to be taken out of the country and this must be noted in the passport/travel documents; it must also be declared. Unused local currency can be re-exchanged on proof of authorised exchange, and visitors are advised to retain all currency exchange receipts. The export of local currency is limited to ¢5000. The import of foreign currency is unlimited, subject to declaration (on exchange control form T5 which must be retained to record transactions). The export of foreign currency is limited to US$5000.
Exchange rate indicators: The following figures are

included as a guide to the movements of the Cedi against Sterling and the US Dollar:

Date	Feb '04	May '04	Aug '04	Nov '04
£1.00=	16154.7	16092.8	16627.2	17090.7
$1.00=	8875.00	9010.00	9025.00	9025.00

Note: The Cedi is pegged to the US Dollar at an adjustable rate.
Banking hours: Mon-Thurs 0830-1400, Fri 0830-1500.

Duty Free

The following goods may be imported into Ghana by persons aged 16 and over without incurring customs duty:
400 cigarettes or 100 cigars or 454g of tobacco; 750ml of spirits or 750ml of wine; 227ml of perfume.
Note: Duty must be paid on gifts.
Restricted items: Animals, firearms, ammunition and explosives.

Credit: © Ghana Tourist Board

Public Holidays

2005: Jan 1 New Year's Day. **Jan 21** Eid al-Adha (Feast of the Sacrifice). **Mar 6** Independence Day. **Mar 25** Good Friday. **Mar 28** Easter Monday. **May 1** Labour Day. **Jun 4** Anniversary of the 1979 Coup. **Jul 1** Republic Day. **Nov 3-5** Eid al-Fitr (End of Ramadan). **Dec 6** National Farmers' Day. **Dec 25-26** Christmas. **Dec 31** Revolution Day.
2006: Jan 1 New Year's Day. **Jan 10** Eid al-Adha (Feast of the Sacrifice). **Mar 6** Independence Day. **Apr 14** Good Friday. **Apr 17** Easter Monday. **May 1** Labour Day. **Jun 4** Anniversary of the 1979 Coup. **Jul 1** Republic Day. **Oct 22-24** Eid al-Fitr (End of Ramadan). **Dec 6** National Farmers' Day. **Dec 25-26** Christmas. **Dec 31** Revolution Day.

Health

	Special Precautions?	Certificate Required?
Yellow Fever	Yes	1
Cholera	Yes	2
Typhoid & Polio	3	N/A
Malaria	4	N/A

Note: *Regulations and requirements may be subject to change at short notice, and you are advised to contact your doctor well in advance of your intended date of departure. Any numbers in the chart refer to the footnotes below.*

1: A yellow fever vaccination certificate is required by all nationals entering the country.
2: Following WHO guidelines issued in 1973, a cholera vaccination certificate is no longer a condition of entry to Ghana. However, cholera is a serious risk in this country and precautions are essential. Up-to-date advice should be sought before deciding whether these precautions should include vaccination as medical opinion is divided over its effectiveness; see the Health *appendix*.
3: Immunisation against typhoid is usually advised.
4: Malaria risk, predominantly in the malignant *falciparum* form, exists all year throughout the country. Resistance to chloroquine is reported.
Food & drink: According to the Ghanaian High Commission in London, tap water in cities is safe to drink. Other water sources should be regarded as being potentially contaminated, and water used for drinking, brushing teeth or making ice should have first been boiled or otherwise sterilised. Milk is unpasteurised and should be boiled. Powdered or tinned milk is available and is advised, but make sure that it is reconstituted with pure water. Avoid dairy products which are likely to have been made from unboiled milk. Only eat well-cooked meat and fish, preferably served hot. Pork, salad and mayonnaise may carry increased risk. Vegetables should be cooked and fruit peeled.
Other risks: *Diarrhoeal diseases*, including *giardiasis*, and *typhoid fevers* are common. *Bilharzia* (*schistosomiasis*) is present. Avoid swimming and paddling in fresh water; swimming pools that are well chlorinated and maintained are safe. *Hepatitis A* and *E* are widespread. *Hepatitis B* is endemic. *Hepatitis C* occurs, as do *dengue fever* and *TB*. Epidemics of *meningitis* and *meningococcal disease* may occur throughout tropical Africa, particularly in the savannah areas and during the dry season. Immunisation against *diphtheria* is sometimes recommended.
Rabies is present. For those at high risk, vaccination before arrival should be considered. If you are bitten, seek medical advice without delay. For more information, consult the *Health* appendix.
Health care: Health insurance is essential, preferably with cover for emergency evacuation. Medical facilities exist in all the regional capitals as well as in most towns and villages.

Travel - International

Note: The Government of Ghana has lifted the state of emergency that had been in place in the Tamale municipality and Yendi District of the Northern Region of Ghana for the last two years. But visitors considering travelling to the Northern Region should still be alert to potential outbreaks of fighting. Whilst travelling in most regions of Ghana is trouble-free, a high level of vigilance in public areas - and when travelling by road - should be exercised.
AIR: Following safety concerns in 2004, the Ghanaian Government took full control of the national airline, *Ghana Airways*, and is in the process of launching its replacement, *Ghana International Airlines*. Commercial operations are set to begin in late 2005. Several airlines fly from Accra to London and New York, including *Alitalia, British Airways, FlyJet, KLM, Lufthansa, Northwest Airlines, South African Airways, Swiss* and *United Airlines*.
Approximate flight times: From *London* to Accra is six hours 30 minutes (direct) or eight hours 25 minutes (with stopover in Kano). From *New York* is nine hours 30 minutes (direct).
International airports: *Accra (ACC)* (Kotoka), 10km (6 miles) north of Accra (travel time – 20 minutes). Taxis to the city are available. Airport facilities include banks/bureaux de change, car hire, duty free shops, restaurants and tourist information.
Departure Tax: US$20.
SEA: Ghana has two deep-water ports, one at Takoradi, the other at Tema. Ships run between Tema and Nigeria, Côte d'Ivoire, Cameroon and South Africa.
ROAD: A coast road links Lagos (Nigeria), Cotonou (Benin) and Lomé (Togo) to Accra. The best internal road from Abidjan (Côte d'Ivoire) runs inland through Kumasi. The main north–south route is also in good condition. Buses and taxis run between Burkina Faso, Côte d'Ivoire, Togo and Ghana. The road from Burkina Faso crosses the border at Navrongo. Long-distance taxis operate between Ghana and neighbouring countries. See *Travel – Internal* for information on documentation.

Travel - Internal

AIR: There are domestic services between Accra, Kumasi and Tamale.
Departure tax: ¢1000.
LAKE: A lake steamer runs regularly across Lake Volta between Akosombo and Yeji. Ferries connect at Yeji for Buipe and Makongo, from both of which it is possible to arrange onward transportation to Tamale.
RAIL: The rail network is limited to a 1000km- (600 mile-) loop by the coast connecting the cities Accra, Takoradi and Kumasi and several intervening towns. Trains run at least twice a day on all three legs of this single-track triangle. There are two classes of ticket. Passenger cars are not air conditioned. Children under three years of age travel free; half-fare is charged for children aged three to 11.
ROAD: There are 38,940km (24,196 miles) of roads, generally in good condition, although the stretch between Kamasi and Tamale may be prone to pot-holes. Traffic drives on the right. **Car hire:** Available but extremely expensive, with or without driver. **Coach:** State-run and private coach services connect all major towns. **Documentation:** An International Driving Permit is recommended, although it is not legally required. A British driving licence is valid for 90 days.
URBAN: Roads in the major towns have undergone massive renovation to improve traffic flow. Accra has extensive **bus** and **taxi** services operated by the private sector. There are over 300,000 conventional taxis. Drivers do not generally expect tips. Other ways of getting around, for the more adventurous traveller, are *tro-tros* (minibuses) and *mammy wagons* (converted pick-up trucks).

Accommodation

HOTELS: There are a few international chain hotels in Ghana, all located in the capital. In addition to these there are international-standard hotels, hostels and guest houses throughout the country, although they are mainly concentrated in the urban centres. Budget accommodation is available at university campuses in Accra, Cape Coast and Kumasi during the student holidays (Christmas, Easter and summer; June to September). **Grading:** Hotels, hostels and guest houses are star-graded and licensed by the Ghana Tourist Board.
CAMPING: Camping in national parks is possible, but only for the very adventurous, as it can be dangerous. In game reserves, visitors must be accompanied by an armed guide.
BEACH HUTS: Ghana offers some basic beach hut accommodation, made from local materials, in popular beach resorts. For a list of such accommodation, contact the Ministry of Tourism (see *Contact Addresses* section) *or* Ghanaweb (website: www.ghanaweb.com).

Resorts & Excursions

Ghana is divided into 10 regions (Accra, Central Region, Western Region, Volta Region, Ashanti Region, Eastern Region, Brong Ahafo Region, Northern Region, Upper East Region and Upper West Region), but for the purpose of this guide, the country has been split into just four regions. This does not necessarily reflect administrative or tribal boundaries. For further details of tours within Ghana, contact the Ghana High Commission (see *Contact Addresses* section).

GREATER ACCRA REGION

Accra: The **National Museum** has a large collection of Ghanaian art. The **Makola Market**, a large and busy open-air market, is located on Kojo Thompson Road. Traders from surrounding villages bring their wares every day. The **Centre for National Culture** is an arts centre and crafts market, where crafts, *kente* and other traditional cloths can be purchased. The **Kwame Nkrumah Mausoleum** on the High Street is a magnificent monument to the first President of Ghana. The **National Theatre** is a Chinese showpiece and the venue for musical shows, plays, dances and conferences.
Aburi: Located 38km (24 miles) to the north of Accra, Aburi is in the **Akwapim Hills**. The **Sanatorium** (now a rest house), built there in the 19th century, is indicative of the refreshing climate. The **Botanical Gardens**, planted by British naturalists in colonial days, has a comprehensive array of subtropical plants and trees.
Ada: A popular resort at the mouth of the Volta, this is where Ghanaians and tourists go for watersports. A luxury hotel has been built here. Swimming is safe in the river mouth. Anglers have the opportunity to catch barracuda and Nile perch. Nearby are the salt marshes of the **Songow Lagoon**, famous for their birdlife.
Shai Hills Game Reserve: A comparatively small reserve some 50km (30 miles) by road from Accra. Horses may be hired here to explore the park.

CENTRAL AND WESTERN REGION

The central region of Ghana borders the Gulf of Guinea and is home to ancient castles and forts that were often used during the slave trade as holding areas for human cargo. **Cape Coast Castle**, built in the 16th-century and later reconstructed and enlarged, served as the seat of British administration in the then Gold Coast until 1877 (when administration moved to Christiansborg Castle in Accra).
Further west is the **Castle of Elmina** ('the mine'). Elmina was the first Portuguese settlement in Ghana. This huge 15th-century fort, that largely remains intact, is the location of one of the first Catholic churches in sub-Saharan Africa. **Fort St Jago** was primarily used as a military base and stands on a hill commanding fabulous views of both Elmina and the Atlantic Ocean. Cultural shows are often performed at the castles and guided tours are available. Fort St Jago and Cape Coast Castle have both been declared World Heritage Monuments by UNESCO.
Kakum National Park: Located 20km from Cape Coast, the park is a protected conservation area. Wildlife that can be seen includes elephants, bongo antelopes, monkeys, over 800 species of rare birds, butterflies, amphibians and reptiles. Visitors can view wildlife at tree canopy level from the 333m tree-top walkway.
West Coast: There are many popular beach resorts along the western coast. At **Dixcove** there is a fish market and a 17th-century British fort. Nearby **Busua** is a tropical beach with palms and spectacular Atlantic breakers. However, as with much of the Ghanaian coast, swimming is unsafe due to the treacherous undertow of the waves. In this area there are to be found small rocky inlets that are safe for swimming.

VOLTA AND ASHANTI REGION

The Volta region is dominated by **Volta Lake**, the largest manmade lake on earth. The waterway stretches for two-thirds of the length of the country. A round trip on the car ferry to **Kete-Krachi** takes one day; alternatively, take the three-day trip to the northern capital of **New Tamale** at the head of the lake. There are facilities for sailing, water-skiing and other watersports. Ferry links across the lake now make the region more accessible (see *Travel – Internal* section). Akosombo, centre to the important **Akosombo** irrigation dam, is developing as a holiday resort, particularly for watersports.

Kumasi: This is the historic capital of the Ashanti civilisation, where ruins of the **Manhyia Palace** and the **Royal Mausoleum** burnt down by Lord Baden-Powell may be examined. The **Cultural Centre** is a complex comprising a museum, library and outdoor auditorium largely devoted to the Ashanti. There is also a **'Living Museum'**, a farm and reconstituted village, where craftspeople such as potters, goldsmiths and sculptors can be seen at work using traditional methods. Of particular interest are weavers making the vividly coloured *kente cloth*, the ceremonial dress of the region.

Owabi Wildlife Sanctuary: Located to the west, close to Kumasi. Further to the northeast is the **Boufom Wildlife Sanctuary**, containing the spectacular **Banfabiri Falls**. To the south is the pleasant gold-mining city of **Obuasi**.

NORTHERN REGION

The northern region is characterised by high plains and a central plateau rising between 150m and 300m. West of the region's main town, **Tamale**, lies **Mole National Park**, which is one of the best-equipped nature reserves in Ghana. Visitors can go either on foot or hire a four-wheel-drive vehicle, but must always be accompanied by a guide. Routes are planned to take in species of antelope, monkeys, buffalo, warthog and - more rarely - lions and elephants which have been introduced into the region. Unlike in many other African game reserves, visitors are allowed to camp and explore the area at will rather than being confined to a car on a set route. Tourist facilities exist at the entrance to the park; these include a motel with restaurant. Situated five miles north of Mole National Park, the **Larabanga Mosque** is well worth visiting. Built in the style of former Western Sudanese Empires, it houses a holy Koran and is believed by locals to be a 'God-built mosque'.

Sport & Activities

Wildlife: Compared to other African countries, Ghana's national parks and game reserves are small, and relatively few tourists visit them. The country's newest national park is the *Kakum Nature Reserve* which, in addition to animal species such as monkeys, antelopes and water buffalo, has an aerial walkway built through the rainforest canopy offering treetop views. Guided tours leave twice daily.

Safaris are available in all of Ghana's game reserves, including the *Owabi Wildlife Sanctuary*, the *Bia National Park*, the *Bui National Park* and the *Mole Game Reserve*, all of which are also good options for hiking and exploring the savannah and rainforest. For further information, see the *Resorts & Excursions* section.

Watersports: Although Ghana's coast offers miles of sandy beaches, strong currents and tides can make bathing quite dangerous. Near Accra there are three **swimming** pools within yards of the surf. Ada, at the mouth of the *River Volta*, also offers safe swimming, although it is not advisable to swim upstream. Visitors should also make enquiries locally as there may be some risk of bilharzia. For those in search of **sailing** or **water-skiing**, there are numerous centres with good facilities, particularly on **Lake Volta**. Another exhilarating experience is to be taken out over the surf in a local **fishing** boat. Sport fishing for barracuda is popular. The best spots for **surfing** are at Fete, Dixcove (both west of Accra) and Kokrobite (16km/10 miles from Accra).

Other: Ghanaians are keen **footballers**, **tennis players** and **boxers**. Another popular sport is **horse racing**, which takes place at the Accra racecourse every Saturday. There are **golf** courses at Accra, Achimota, Kumasi and Tema.

Social Profile

FOOD & DRINK: International food is available in most large hotels and many restaurants serve a range of local traditional foods. On the coast, prawns and other seafood are popular. Dishes include traditional soups (palmnut, groundnut), *Kontomere* and *Okro* (stews) accompanied by *fufu* (pounded cassava), *kenkey* or *gari*. In Accra there are also restaurants serving Middle Eastern, Chinese, French and other European cuisine. Local beer (which is similar to lager) and spirits are readily available.

NIGHTLIFE: In Accra and other major centres, there are

Credit: © Ghana Tourist Board

nightclubs with Western popular music and Afro beat. Concerts can be seen at the national theatre in Accra. The School of Performing Arts, University of Ghana, Legon often hosts drama, poetry and cultural dancing shows. Foreign and Ghanaian films can be seen at the Ghana Film Theatre and Executive Film House in Accra.

SHOPPING: Almost all commodities, including luxury items, can be found in the shops and markets. Artefacts from the Ashanti region and northern Ghana can be bought along with attractive handmade gold and silver jewellery. Modern and old African art is also available (although prices are high); in particular, Ashanti stools and brass weights formerly used to measure gold. In all the northern markets, earthenware pots, leatherwork, locally woven shirts and *Bolgatanga* baskets woven from multi-coloured raffia are sold. **Shopping hours:** Mon-Tue, Thurs-Fri 0800-1200 and 1400-1730, Wed-Sat 0800-1300.

SPECIAL EVENTS: Ghanaian festivals are well worth seeing, with drumming, dancing and feasting. Every part of the country has its own annual festivals for the affirmation of tribal values, the remembrance of ancestors and past leaders, and the purification of the state in preparation for another year. The following is a selection of special events celebrated annually in Ghana; for more information and exact dates, contact the tourist office (see *Contact Addresses* section):

Jan *Edina Buronya* (New Year), Elmina. **Feb** *DipoKrobo*, Odumase. **Mar** *Gologo*, Talensi, Tong-Zuf. **Jul 5** *Bakatue*, Elmina. **Aug** *Akwambo*, Agona Nyakrom, Agona Swedru. **Sep** *Odwira, Akropong*; *Kobine*, Lowra. **Nov** *Mmoaninko*, Ofinso. **Nov 5** *Hogbetsotso*, Anloga. **Dec** *Fiok*, Centime.

SOCIAL CONVENTIONS: Ghanaians should always be addressed by their formal titles unless they specifically request otherwise. Handshaking is the usual form of greeting. It is customary in much of West Africa not to use the left hand for touching food. **Photography:** Permission should be sought before photographing military installations, government buildings or airports. **Tipping:** When a service charge is not included, a 10 per cent tip is usual.

Business Profile

ECONOMY: Agriculture occupies most of the working population, producing both subsistence and cash crops. The most important of the latter is cocoa, of which Ghana is one of the world's major producers. Coffee and various fruit are the other main crops. Fishing has grown in importance since the acquisition of modern vessels. The country's main industry is mining, particularly for diamonds and gold (produced at the famous Ashanti gold field), and this is both a major employer and an important foreign currency earner. Although recent mineral exploration failed to discover anticipated oil and gas deposits, new bauxite and manganese deposits have been identified. Manufacturing is concentrated in food processing, textiles, vehicles and chemicals. The country's energy needs are met by hydroelectric projects; these produce a surplus which Ghana sells to its neighbours.

As a primary commodity producer, Ghana has suffered from consistently low-world prices for its main products throughout much of the last 20 years. Since the late 1980s, Ghana has been something of a laboratory for a new regime for less developed countries devised by the International Monetary Fund and known as a Structural Adjustment programme. Customised for each state, the IMF, in conjunction with the World Bank, offers steady financial support to the national exchequer in exchange for government undertakings to implement agreed economic policies. The latter are based on liberalisation of the economy, the removal of trade barriers, privatisation of state-owned assets and firm budgetary control (leading invariably to cuts in social and welfare spending). Despite the notable lack of tangible benefits to the population as a whole, the Ghana programme has been judged a qualified success and the country has since been regularly cited as a role model for the developing world. Current growth is around five per cent. Ghana is a member of the Economic Community of West African States (ECOWAS). The UK, Switzerland, Nigeria, the USA, Germany, Japan and The Netherlands are Ghana's principal trading partners.

BUSINESS: Appointments are customary and visitors should always be punctual for meetings. Best time for business visits is from September to April. **Office hours:** Mon-Fri 0800-1200 and 1400-1700, Sat 0830-1200.

COMMERCIAL INFORMATION: The following organisation can offer advice: Ghana National Chamber of Commerce, PO Box 2325, Accra (tel: (21) 662 427; fax: (21) 662 210; e-mail: gncc@ncs.com; website: www.g77tin.org/gncchp.html).

Climate

A tropical climate, hot and humid in the north and in the forest land of Ashanti and southwest plains. There are two rainy seasons in Ghana: from March to July and from September to October.

Required clothing: Tropical lightweight clothing. Sunglasses are advisable.

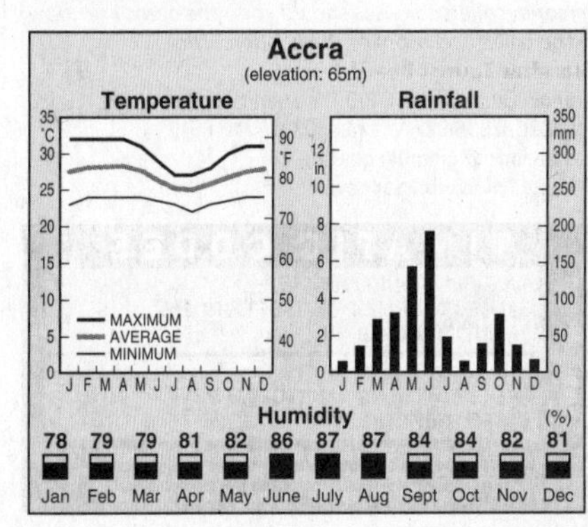

Gibraltar

LATEST TRAVEL ADVICE CONTACTS

British Foreign and Commonwealth Office
Tel: (0870) 606 0290 Website: www.fco.gov.uk
US Department of State
Website: http://travel.state.gov/travel
Canadian Department of Foreign Affairs and Int'l Trade
Tel: (1 800) 267 8376 Website: www.dfait-maeci.gc.ca

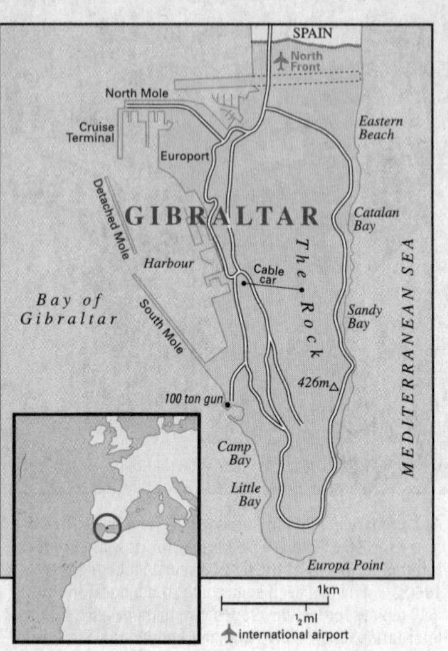

Location: Western entrance to the Mediterranean, southern tip of Europe.

Country dialling code: 350.

Gibraltar is a British Crown Colony, and is represented abroad by British Embassies – see *United Kingdom* section.
Gibraltar Tourist Board
Duke of Kent House, Cathedral Square, Gibraltar
Tel: 74950. Fax: 74943.
E-mail: tourism@gibraltar.gi
Website: www.gibraltar.gov.gi
UK Foreign and Commonwealth Office
Overseas Territories Department, King Charles Street, London SW1A 2AH, UK
Tel: (020) 7008 1500 (general enquiries) *or* (020) 7008 8438 (visa enquiries) *or* 0117 (services for Britons overseas) *or* (0870) 606 0290 (travel advice).
Fax: (020) 7008 0155 (travel advice) *or* 8359 (visa enquiries).
E-mail: consular.fco@gtnet.gov.uk (travel advice only) or otdenquiries@fco.gov.uk
Website: www.fco.gov.uk
Handles Gibraltar's foreign affairs. All other enquiries should be made to the Gibraltar Tourist Board.
The UK Passport Service
London Passport Office, Globe House,
89 Ecclestone Square, London SW1V 1PN, UK
Tel: (0870) 521 0410 (24-hour national advice line) *or* (020) 7901 2150 (visa enquiries for British Overseas Territories).
Fax: (020) 7271 8403.
E-mail: info@passport.gov.uk *or* london@ukpa.gov.uk
Website: www.passport.gov.uk *or* www.ukpa.gov.uk
Opening hours: Mon-Fri 0730-1900; Sat 0900-1600.
Regional offices in: Belfast, Durham, Glasgow, Liverpool, Newport and Peterborough.
Personal callers for visas should go to the agency window in the collection room of the London office.
Gibraltar Tourist Board
Arundel Great Court, 178/9 The Strand, London WC2R 1EL, UK
Tel: (020) 7836 0777. Fax: (020) 7240 6612.
E-mail: info@gibraltar.gov.uk
Website: www.gibraltar.gov.uk

TIMATIC CODES

Health
AMADEUS: **TI-DFT/JIB/HE**
GALILEO/WORLDSPAN: **TI-DFT/JIB/HE**
SABRE: **TIDFT/JIB/HE**

Visa
AMADEUS: **TI-DFT/JIB/VI**
GALILEO/WORLDSPAN: **TI-DFT/JIB/VI**
SABRE: **TIDFT/JIB/VI**

To access TIMATIC country information on Health and Visa regulations through the Computer Reservations System (CRS), type in the appropriate command line listed above.

Gibraltar Government Office
1156 15th Street, NW, Suite 1100, Washington, DC 20005, USA
Tel: (202) 452 1108. Fax: (202) 452 1109.
E-mail: gibraltargov@msn.com
Website: www.gibraltar.gov.gi

General Information

AREA: 6.5 sq km (2.5 sq miles).
POPULATION: 28,231 (2001).
POPULATION DENSITY: 4343.23 per sq km.
CAPITAL: Gibraltar.
GEOGRAPHY: Gibraltar is a large promontory of jurassic limestone, situated in the western entrance to the Mediterranean. The 5km- (3 mile-) long rock contains 143 caves, over 48km (30 miles) of road and as many miles of tunnels. The highest point of the Rock is 426m (1400ft) above sea level. An internal self-governing British Crown Colony, Gibraltar has given its name to the Bay and the Straits, which it overlooks. Spain is to the north and west, and Morocco is 26km (16 miles) to the south.
GOVERNMENT: British Crown Colony since 1713. **Head of State:** HM Queen Elizabeth II, represented locally by Governor Sir Francis Richards since 2003. **Head of Government:** Prime Minister Peter Caruana QC since 1996.
LANGUAGE: English is the official language. Most Gibraltarians are bilingual in English and Spanish.
RELIGION: Roman Catholic majority, also Church of England, Church of Scotland, Jewish, Hindu and other minorities.
TIME: GMT + 1 (GMT + 2 from last Sunday in March to Saturday before last Sunday in October).
ELECTRICITY: 220/240 volts AC, 50Hz. UK-style three-pin plugs are in use.
COMMUNICATIONS: Telephone: IDD is available. Country code: 350. Outgoing international code: 00. **Fax:** Facilities are available in some hotels. **Mobile telephone:** GSM 900 network is operated by *Gibtel*. Coverage spans the whole of Gibraltar and a large part of the sea around. Handsets can be hired from Gibtel, at 25 South Barracks Road. **Internet:** There is at least one Internet cafe – *Cyber World*, Ocean Heights Gallery, Queensway. ISPs include *Gibnet* (website: www.gibnet.gi). **Telegram:** Enquire at *Gibtel*, 60 Main Street; or after office hours at Mount Pleasant, 25 South Barracks Road. **Post:** Airmail within Europe takes one to five days. Airmail flights are usually daily. There is a *Poste Restante* facility at the main post office in Main Street. Post office hours: Mon-Fri 0900-1630 (0900-1415 in summer), Sat 1000-1300. **Press:** Newspapers are in English; some have Spanish sections. *The New People*, *Panorama* and *Vox* are published weekly. *The Gibraltar Chronicle* (est. 1801) is the only daily.
Radio: BBC World Service (website: www.bbc.co.uk/worldservice) and Voice of America (website: www.voa.gov) can be received. From time to time the frequencies change and the most up-to-date can be found online.

Passport/Visa

	Passport Required?	Visa Required?	Return Ticket Required?
Full British	Yes	No	No
Australian	Yes	No	No
Canadian	Yes	No	No
USA	Yes	No	No
Other EU	1	No	No
Japanese	Yes	No	No

Note: Regulations and requirements may be subject to change at short notice, and you are advised to contact the appropriate diplomatic or consular authority before finalising travel arrangements. Details of these may be found at the head of this country's entry. Any numbers in the chart refer to the footnotes below.

PASSPORTS: Required by all except: **1.** EU nationals in possession of a valid national identity card.
VISAS: Required by all except the following:
(a) nationals of countries referred to in the chart above;
(b) nationals of Commonwealth countries (except nationals of Bangladesh, Cameroon, Fiji, Guyana, India, Jamaica, Kenya, Mozambique, Nigeria, Pakistan, Sierra Leone, Sri Lanka, Tanzania, Uganda and Zambia);
(c) nationals of Andorra, Argentina, Bolivia, Chile, Costa Rica, East Timor, El Salvador, Federated States of Micronesia, Guatemala, Honduras, Iceland, Israel, Korea (Rep), Liechtenstein, Marshall Islands, Mexico, Monaco, Nicaragua, Norway, Panama, Paraguay, San Marino, Switzerland, Uruguay and Venezuela.
Note: Transit visas are not required by passengers continuing their journey by the same or first connecting aircraft, provided holding valid onward or return documentation and not leaving the airport.
Types of visa and cost: *Tourist*, *Business* and *Transit*. All visas cost £28.
Application to: Any British visa-issuing post abroad or in the UK, or the visa section of the UK Passport Agency in London (see *Contact Addresses* section).
Application requirements: (a) One application form. (b) Valid passport. (c) Proof of hotel reservation. (d) Fee. (e) Return ticket.
Working days required: Applications are referred to Gibraltar and are normally processed within 20 days.
Note: (a) Holders of multiple-entry UK visas valid for a period of one year or more, and persons with indefinite leave to remain who do not require separate UK entry clearance, do not require separate visas to enter Gibraltar. All other nationals who require a visa to enter the UK need a separate visa to enter Gibraltar. (b) Visa requirements for other nationals wishing to visit Gibraltar are subject to frequent change at short notice and travellers should contact the UK Passport Agency (see *Contact Addresses* section) for up-to-date information.
Temporary residence: Prior permission must be obtained from the Ministry of Employment in New Harbours, Gibraltar if seeking employment (nationals of EU countries are exempt).

Money

Currency: Gibraltar Pound (Gib£) = 100 new pence. The Gibraltar government issues banknotes of Gib£50, 20, 10 and 5 for local use only. Coinage is the UK coinage with a different reverse design. The Gibraltar government also issues its own coins in denominations of Gib£5, 2 and 1, and 50, 20, 10, 5, 2 and 1 pence. All UK notes are accepted. For exchange rates, see *United Kingdom* section.
Currency exchange: Tourists from the UK are strongly advised to change their unspent Gibraltar pounds into UK currency at parity in Gibraltar before departure as UK banks charge for exchanging the Gibraltar Pound.
Credit & debit cards: All major cards accepted. Check with your credit or debit card company for details of merchant acceptability and other services which may be available.
Travellers cheques: Widely accepted. To avoid additional exchange rate charges, travellers are advised to take travellers cheques in Pounds Sterling.
Currency restrictions: There are no restrictions on the import or export of either local or foreign currency.
Banking hours: Mon-Thur 0900-1530, Fri 0900-1600.

Duty Free

The following goods may be taken into Gibraltar without incurring customs duty:
A reasonable quantity of tobacco products, alcoholic beverages and perfume for personal use.

Public Holidays

2005: Jan 1 New Year's Day. **Mar 8** Commonwealth Day. **Mar 25** Good Friday. **Mar 28** Easter Monday. **May 1** May Day. **May 2** May Bank Holiday. **Jun 11** Queen's Birthday. **Aug 29** Late Summer Bank Holiday. **Sep 10** Gibraltar National Day. **Dec 25-26** Christmas.
2006: Jan 1 New Year's Day. **Mar 8** Commonwealth Day. **Apr 14** Good Friday. **Apr 17** Easter Monday. **May 1** May Day. **May 29** May Bank Holiday. **Jun 12** Queen's Birthday. **Aug 28** Late Summer Bank Holiday. **Sep 10** Gibraltar National Day. **Dec 25-26** Christmas.

Health

	Special Precautions?	Certificate Required?
Yellow Fever	No	No
Cholera	No	No
Typhoid & Polio	No	N/A
Malaria	No	N/A

Note: Regulations and requirements may be subject to change at short notice, and you are advised to contact your doctor well in advance of your intended date of departure. Any numbers in the chart refer to the footnotes below.

Food & drink: Mains water is normally chlorinated. Bottled water is available and is advised for the first few weeks of the stay. Milk is pasteurised and dairy products are safe for consumption. Local meat, poultry, seafood, fruit and vegetables are generally considered safe to eat.
Other risks: Visitors to forested areas should consider vaccination for *tick-borne encephalitis*.
Health care: Gibraltar is a British Crown Colony and UK citizens are entitled to free treatment in public wards at St Bernard's Hospital and at Casemates Health Centre on presentation of a UK passport during stays of up to 30 days in the colony. Other EU nationals are similarly entitled on presentation of Form E111. Medical treatment elsewhere and prescribed medicines must be paid for. Dental treatment must also be paid for but extractions are

undertaken for a nominal charge at St Bernard's Hospital during normal weekday working hours.
Note: Passengers travelling from Gibraltar to Spain or Morocco are advised to refer to the *Health* sections for those countries.

Travel - International

AIR: *British Airways (BA)* and *Monarch Airlines (ZB)* operate daily direct services from the UK.
Approximate flight times: From Gibraltar to *London* is two hours 30 minutes.
International airports: *Gibraltar (GIB)* (North Front) is 1km (0.6 miles) north of the town centre. A bus to the centre departs every 15 minutes from 0800-2030. Return is from the Market Place bus stop. Bus no. 3, which runs every 30 minutes, also goes to the airport. Taxis and courtesy coaches are available. Airport facilities include restaurants, banks/bureaux de change, tourist information, duty free shops and car hire (*Avis*, *Budget*, *Europcar* and *Hertz*).
SEA: International cruises are run by *BI*, *Costa Norwegian American*, *CTC*, *Norwegian Cruises/Union Lloyd*, *P&O*, *Polish Ocean* and *TVI Cruises*. There is a regular ferry service to Tangier, Morocco as well as a catamaran service running from the new ferry terminal to Tangier (travel time – 75 minutes).
ROAD: The only international land access is the frontier with Spain at La Linea.

Travel - Internal

ROAD: Traffic drives on the right. The speed limit is 50kph (31mph), except where otherwise indicated. It is compulsory to drive with dipped headlights at night. **Bus:** There are good local bus services operating at frequent intervals. **Taxi:** There are plenty of taxis and the driver is required by law to carry and produce on demand a copy of the taxi fares. **Car hire:** Both self-drive and chauffeur-driven cars are available. Touring outside Gibraltar can also be arranged. **Documentation:** Third Party insurance is compulsory. Valid national driving licences are accepted.
Travel times: The following chart gives approximate travel times (in hours and minutes) from **Gibraltar** to major foreign cities.

	Air	Road	Rail	Sea
London	2.30	-	-	-
Tangier	0.20	-	-	2.00
Malaga	-	2.00	-	-
Madrid	-	12.00	10.00	-

Accommodation

HOTELS: Hotels range from luxury establishments with lounges, terrace shops, bars and swimming pools, to more modest hotels. Summer rates are in force from 1 April to 31 October. More information may be obtained from the Gibraltar Tourist Board on request (see *Contact Addresses* section).
CAMPING/CARAVANNING: Camping is not permitted; however, beach tents or beach umbrellas may be rented at Catalan Bay. These will include two deck chairs. There are no caravan sites in Gibraltar, and there are strict regulations concerning caravans and trailers. Sleeping in vehicles is not permitted. There are several campsites with excellent facilities over the border in Spain.

Resorts & Excursions

The town of Gibraltar is an 18th-century British Regency town built on a 15th-century Spanish town which was, in turn, built on a 12th-century Moorish town. The principal tourist sites and places of interest include **St Michael's Cave**, situated 300m (1000ft) above sea level. This was known to the Romans for its spectacular stalactites and stalagmites. It is part of a complex series of interlinked caves including Leonora's Cave and Lower St Michael's Cave. Today, it is used for concerts and ballet. The Upper Galleries, hewn by hand from the Rock in 1782, house old cannons and tableaux evoking the Great Siege (1779-1783). The **Apes' Den** is the home of the famous Barbary apes, which are in fact not apes but Macaque monkeys without tails. The **Gibraltar Museum** contains caveman tools and ornaments excavated from the Rock's caves, including a replica of the Gibraltar Skull, the first Neanderthal skull found in Europe (1848). There are also exhibits from the Phoenician, Greek, Roman, Moorish, Spanish and British periods of the Rock's history; a comprehensive collection of prints and lithographs; a collection of weapons from 1727 to 1800; a large-scale model of the Rock made in 1865; and displays of fauna and flora. The museum itself was built above a spectacular and complete 14th-century **Moorish Bath House**.
Other sites of interest are: the 14th-century keep of the much rebuilt **Moorish Castle**; the **Shrine of Our Lady of Europe**, a mosque before conversion to a Christian chapel in 1462, housing the 15th-century image of the Patroness of Gibraltar; the **Lighthouse** and new **Mosque**, beautifully designed blending classic Islamic designs with modern facilities, situated within a few yards of the **Shrine of Our Lady of Europe**; the ancient **Nun's Well**, a Moorish cistern; **Parson's Lodge Battery** (1865), above Rosia Bay; the **Rock Buster**, a 100-ton gun; the 18th-century **Garrison Library**; **Trafalgar Cemetery**; **Alameda Gardens**; **Europa Point**, just 26km (16 miles) from Africa; the almost-complete **city walls**, dating in part from the Moorish occupation.
Some popular tourist activities in Gibraltar are: the cable-car trip to the top of the Rock, stopping at the Apes' Den on the way up; the **Convent**, residence of the Governor, and formerly a 16th-century Franciscan Monastic house; the **Guided Walking Tour of Places of Worship**, every Wednesday at 1000, including visits to Gibraltar's two cathedrals, a synagogue, the Garrison chapel, the Presbyterian church and the Methodist chapel – all buildings of historical interest; the guided walking tour around the city walls, every Friday at 1030; and the **Mediterranean Steps Walk** which starts at **O'Hara's Battery** (the highest point in Gibraltar), snakes down the eastern cliff and around the southern slopes to the western side of the Rock. **Marina Quay** and **Queensway Quay** (two modern marina developments) provide visitors with the chance to indulge in some serious people watching while sampling delicious seafood in one of the many attractive harbourside restaurants.
Beaches: Gibraltar has five beaches. On the east side are **Eastern Beach**, **Catalan Bay** and, towards the south, **Sandy Bay**, where the Rock is very sheer and parking difficult. **Little Bay**, a pebble beach, and **Camp Bay/Keys Promenade** are on the western coast.
EXCURSIONS: Day trips to Ronda, Malaga and Jerez in Andalucia (the Spanish province) can be arranged from Gibraltar (see the *Spain* section for further information on Andalucia), as can day trips by air to Tangier and other Moroccan cities (see the *Morocco* section).

Sport & Activities

Watersports: Pier **fishing** facilities are available and there are charter boats for hire, although deep-sea fishing (for blue shark and swordfish) is not always available at short notice. **Scuba-diving** is a popular activity. **Parasailing** and **water-skiing** can also be practised here.
Wildlife: The Bay of Gibraltar is home to a large population of **dolphins** and **whales**, and tourists can take boat trips to view these fascinating creatures. The Barbary apes, living high on the rock, are the only wild primates in Europe. **Birdwatching** can be undertaken in spring and autumn, when thousands of migrating birds on their way between their breeding grounds in northern Europe and their wintering areas in Africa stop at the Rock. Owls, eagles, harriers, hoopoes, buzzards and black kytes join resident species such as Peregrine falcons and Barbary partridge. A large area of the upper rock has been declared a nature reserve, and there are plans for a botanical garden.

Social Profile

FOOD & DRINK: There are bars and bistros throughout the town and at the two marinas, operating under Mediterranean licensing hours and selling British beer. Restaurants cover the whole price range. Gibraltar's geographical location and its history as a British colony means that it can offer a large selection of British dishes as well as French, Spanish, American, Moroccan, Italian, Chinese and Indian cuisine.
Spirits and tobacco are substantially cheaper than in the UK for identical brands. All types of alcoholic drinks are served, including draught beer.
NIGHTLIFE: Gibraltar has a number of discos and nightspots open until the early hours of the morning. The casino complex includes a restaurant, nightclub, roof restaurant (summer) and gaming rooms, and is open from 0900 to the early hours.
SHOPPING: All goods are sold in Gibraltar at reduced-tax prices and free of VAT. The majority of shops are in or near Main Street. Silk, linen, cashmere, jewellery, glassware, porcelain, perfumes, carvings, radios, leatherwork, electronic and photographic equipment and watches can be bought. **Shopping hours:** Mon-Fri 0930-1930, Sat 1000-1300. Some shops open Sunday.
SPECIAL EVENTS: The following is a selection of special events occurring in Gibraltar in 2005; for a complete list with exact dates, contact the Gibraltar Tourist Board:
Jan 25-Feb 3 *3rd Gibtelecom International Chess Festival*. **May 29** *International Mountain Race*. **Sep** *Ceremony of the Keys*, Casemates Square. **Oct** *Trafalgar Festival*.

Credit: © Gibraltar Tourist Board

SOCIAL CONVENTIONS: Gibraltar is a strongly traditional society with an attractive blend of British and Mediterranean customs. **Tipping:** Normally 10 to 15 per cent.

Business Profile

ECONOMY: The main sources of income are tourism and offshore financial services, principally banking, insurance and shipping-related services. The industrial economy is based on ship repair, construction and small-scale manufacturing. The British armed forces – historically the main source of revenue through their base facilities on the Rock – sharply reduced their presence from 1994 onwards and now provide less than 10 per cent of GDP. Since then, concessionary tax and corporate facilities for foreign companies have boosted the financial services sector. Since 1998, a substantial gambling industry has developed, servicing punters from throughout Europe – again the consequence of a favourable tax regime – and it now makes a significant contribution to employment and government revenue. The economy as a whole is sensitive to the state of relations with Spain and, in particular, restrictions on border crossings since a significant number of Spaniards have jobs on the Rock. The UK is naturally the largest source of imports. Gibraltar is not an exporter as such but earns foreign exchange through re-export, mainly into Spain.
BUSINESS: English is normally used for business, but Spanish may be used for business connected with Spain. **Office hours:** Mon-Fri 0900-1700; 0800-1400 in summer. **Government office hours:** Generally Mon-Fri 0845-1315 and 1415-1730, but hours vary according to department and season.
COMMERCIAL INFORMATION: The following organisation can offer advice: Gibraltar Chamber of Commerce, PO Box 29, Watergate House, 2-6 Casements (tel: 78376; fax: 78403; e-mail: gichacom@gibnet.gi; website: www.gibraltarchamberofcommerce.com). Information is also available from the Gibraltar Government Office (tel: (020) 7836 0777; fax: (020) 7240 6612; e-mail: info@gibraltar.gov.uk; website: www.gibraltar.gov.uk).
CONFERENCES/CONVENTIONS: Europort Gibraltar, an 82,000 sq metre (212,000 sq ft) financial complex, offers extensive office and conference facilities in addition to Gibraltar's recently refurbished hotels. St Michael's Cave (see *Resorts & Excursions* section) offers an absolutely unique and scenic location for meetings. For further information contact the Gibraltar Tourist Board, Conference and Incentive Division (tel: (020) 7836 0777; fax: (020) 7240 6612; e-mail: info@gibraltar.gov.uk).

Climate

Warm throughout the year, with hot summers and mild winters. Summer (May to September) can be very hot and humid.
Required clothing: Lightweights for summer and mediumweights for winter months.

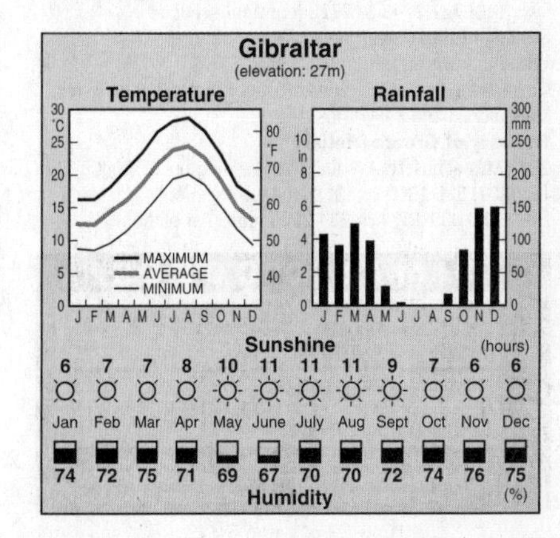

Greece

LATEST TRAVEL ADVICE CONTACTS

British Foreign and Commonwealth Office
Tel: (0870) 606 0290 Website: www.fco.gov.uk
US Department of State
Website: http://travel.state.gov/travel
Canadian Department of Foreign Affairs and Int'l Trade
Tel: (1 800) 267 8376 Website: www.dfait-maeci.gc.ca

Location: Southeast Europe.

Country dialling code: 30.

Ellinikos Organismos Tourismou-EOT (Greek/Hellenic National Tourism Organisation)
26A Annalies Street, 105 57 Athens, Greece
Tel: (210) 3310 392. Fax: (210) 3310 640.
E-mail: infodesk@gnto.gr
Website: www.gnto.gr
Embassy of Greece (Hellas)
1A Holland Park, London W11 3TP, UK
Tel: (020) 7229 3850 *or* 7221 6467 (visa section) *or* 7313 5600 (visa help line) *or* (09065) 540 744 (visa appointment booking line).
Fax: (020) 7229 7221 *or* 7243 3202 (visa section).
E-mail: political@greekembassy.org.uk *or* consulategeneral@greekembassy.org.uk
Website: www.greekembassy.org.uk
Opening hours: Mon-Fri 0900-1600.
Greek/Hellenic National Tourism Organisation (GNTO)
4 Conduit Street, London W1S 2DJ, UK
Tel: (020) 7495 9300. Fax: (020) 7287 1369.
E-mail: info@gnto.co.uk
Website: www.gnto.co.uk
Also deals with enquiries regarding conferences and conventions.
British Embassy
1 Ploutarchou Street, 106 75 Athens, Greece
Tel: (210) 727 2600.
Fax: (210) 727 2743 *or* 2720 (consular section).
E-mail: information.athens@fco.gov.uk
Website: www.british-embassy.gr
Consulates in: Corfu, Heraklion, Kos, Patras, Rhodes, Syros, Thessaloniki and Zakynthos.
Embassy of Greece (Hellas)
2221 Massachusetts Avenue, NW, Washington, DC 20008, USA
Tel: (202) 939 1300 *or* 1318 (consular section).
Fax: (202) 939 1324 *or* 234 2803 (consular section).

TIMATIC CODES

Health	AMADEUS: **TI-DFT/ATH/HE** GALILEO/WORLDSPAN: **TI-DFT/ATH/HE** SABRE: **TIDFT/ATH/HE**
Visa	AMADEUS: **TI-DFT/ATH/VI** GALILEO/WORLDSPAN: **TI-DFT/ATH/VI** SABRE: **TIDFT/ATH/VI**

To access TIMATIC country information on Health and Visa regulations through the Computer Reservations System (CRS), type in the appropriate command line listed above.

E-mail: greece@greekembassy.org *or* consulate@greekembassy.org
Website: www.greekembassy.org
Consulates in: Atlanta, Boston, Chicago, Houston, Los Angeles, New Orleans, New York and San Francisco.
Greek/Hellenic National Tourism Organisation (GNTO)
Olympic Tower, 645 Fifth Avenue, 9th Floor, Suite 903, New York, NY 10022, USA
Tel: (212) 421 5777. Fax: (212) 826 6940.
E-mail: info@greektourism.com
Website: www.greektourism.com *or* www.gnto.gr
Embassy of the United States of America
91 Vasilissis Sophias Avenue, 101 60 Athens, Greece
Tel: (210) 721 2951 *or* 720 2442 (consular department) *or* 363 8114/7740 (press and information).
Fax: (210) 364 2986 (press department).
E-mail: usembassy@usembassy.gr *or* athensconsul@state.gov *or* ircathens@usembassy.gr (press and information) *or* athensamemb@state.gov
Website: www.usembassy.gr
Consulate in: Thessaloniki.
Embassy of Greece (Hellas)
80 MacLaren Street, Ottawa, Ontario K2P 0K6, Canada
Tel: (613) 238 6271. Fax: (613) 238 5676.
E-mail: embassy@greekembassy.ca
Website: www.greekembassy.ca
Consulate General of Greece
1170 place du Frère André, Suite 300, Montréal, Québec H3B 3C6, Canada
Tel: (514) 875 2119. Fax: (514) 875 8781.
Website: www.grconsulatemtl.net
Consulates also in: Toronto and Vancouver.
Greek/Hellenic National Tourism Organisation (GNTO)
91 Scollard Street, 2nd Floor, Toronto, Ontario M5R 1G4, Canada
Tel: (416) 968 2220. Fax: (416) 968 6533.
E-mail: grnto.tor@on.aibn.com
Canadian Embassy
Odos Ioannou Ghennadiou 4, 115 21 Athens, Greece
Tel: (210) 727 3400. Fax: (210) 727 3480.
E-mail: athns@international.gc.ca *or* athns-cs@international.gc.ca (consular section).
Website: www.athens.gc.ca
Consulate in: Thessaloniki.

General Information

AREA: 131,957 sq km (50,949 sq miles).
POPULATION: 11,018,400 (official estimate 2003).
POPULATION DENSITY: 83.5 per sq km.
CAPITAL: Athens. **Population:** 745, 514 (2001); Greater Athens 3,192,606 (2001).
GEOGRAPHY: Greece is situated in southeast Europe on the Mediterranean. The mainland consists of the following regions: Central Greece, Peloponnese, Thessaly (east/central), Epirus (west), Macedonia (north/northwest) and Thrace (northwest). Euboea, the second-largest of the Greek islands, lying to the east of the central region, is also considered to be part of the mainland region. The Peloponnese peninsula is separated from the northern mainland by the Isthmus of Corinth. The northern mainland is dissected by high mountains (such as the Pindus) that extend southwards towards a landscape of fertile plains, pine-forested uplands and craggy, scrub-covered foothills. The islands account for one-fifth of the land area of the country. The majority are thickly clustered in the Aegean between the Greek and Turkish coasts. The Ionian Islands are the exception; they are scattered along the west coast in the Ionian Sea. The Aegean archipelago includes the Dodecanese, lying off the Turkish coast, of which Rhodes is the best known; the Northeast Aegean group, including Chios, Ikaria, Lemnos, Lesvos and Samos; the Sporades, off the central mainland; and the Cyclades, comprising 39 islands (of which only 24 are inhabited). Crete, the largest island, is not included in any formal grouping. For fuller descriptions of these regions and islands, see the *Resorts & Excursions* section.
GOVERNMENT: Republic. **Head of State:** President Konstantinos Stefanopoulos since 1995. **Head of Government:** Prime Minister Costas Karamanlis since March 2004.
LANGUAGE: Greek (Ellenika). Most people connected with tourism and those of a younger generation will speak some English, French, German or Italian.
RELIGION: 97 per cent Greek Orthodox, with Muslim, Roman Catholic and Jewish minorities.
TIME: GMT + 2 (GMT + 3 from last Sunday in March to last Sunday in October).
ELECTRICITY: 220 volts AC, 50Hz. Round two-pin plugs are used.
COMMUNICATIONS: Telephone: IDD is available throughout the mainland and islands. The Greek telecommunication network supplier is *Organismos Telepikinonion Ellados (OTE)*. Country code: 30, followed by (2100) for Athens, (2310) for Thessaloniki and (2810) for Heraklion (all area codes are prefixed with 2 and end with 0). Outgoing international code: 00. **Mobile telephone:** GSM 900 and 1800 networks exist. Coverage is good around the major towns on the mainland and on many islands. Main operators include *Cosmote* (website: www.cosmote.gr), *Q-Telecom* (www.quest.gr), *Stet Hellas* (website: www.tim.com.gr) and *Vodafone* (website: www.vodafone.gr). **Fax:** Main post offices and large hotels have facilities. **Telegram:** There are telegram facilities in main post offices and large hotels in all Greek cities and the major islands. **Internet:** Internet cafes are available in the main cities, including Athens, Thessaloniki and the islands Crete, Kos, Mykonos, Rhodes and Skiathos. ISPs include *Cosmote, Hellas Online* (website: www.hol.gr), *Panafon* and *STET*. **Post:** All letters, postcards, newspapers and periodicals will automatically be sent by airmail. There are *Poste Restante* facilities at most post offices throughout the country. Advance notice is required at all Athens branches except for the central office at 180 Eolou Street. A passport must be shown on collection. Post office hours: Mon-Fri 0800-1400, Sat 0800-1330. **Press:** There are numerous daily newspapers in Athens including *Eleftherotypia, Kathimerini* and *Ta Nea. Athens Daily Post* and *Athens News* are both published daily in English.
Radio: BBC World Service (website: www.bbc.co.uk/worldservice) and Voice of America (website: www.voa.gov) can be received. From time to time the frequencies change and the most up-to-date can be found online.

Passport/Visa

	Passport Required?	Visa Required?	Return Ticket Required?
Full British	Yes	No	No
Australian	Yes	No	Yes
Canadian	Yes	No	Yes
USA	Yes	No	Yes
Other EU	1/2/3	No	No
Japanese	Yes	No	Yes

Note: *Regulations and requirements may be subject to change at short notice, and you are advised to contact the appropriate diplomatic or consular authority before finalising travel arrangements. Details of these may be found at the head of this country's entry. Any numbers in the chart refer to the footnotes below.*

Note: Greece is a signatory to the 1995 **Schengen Agreement**. For further details about passport/visa regulations within the Schengen area, see the introductory section, *How to Use this Guide*.
Entry restrictions: (a) Greece refuses admission and transit to holders of passports issued by Bophutatswana, Ciskei, Transkei and Venda; holders of travel documents issued by Macedonia (Former Yugoslav Republic), unless accompanied by a special visa form; holders of Somalian passports issued or extended after 31 January 1991; Norwegian Fremmedpass or Reisbevis; Ethiopian emergency passports; holders of travel documents issued by the area of Cyprus not controlled by the government of Cyprus; holders of UN laissez-passers; and holders of Turkish travel documents with visas or stamps indicating previous or planned visits to Cyprus. (b) Some nationals may have to register with the Aliens Department of the nearest police station within 48 hours of arrival. It is advised to contact the nearest Embassy/Consulate to determine whether this is necessary prior to travel.
PASSPORTS: Passport valid for at least three months after period of intended stay required by all except:
(a) **1.** EU/EEA nationals with a valid national ID card and with sufficient funds for their length of stay;
(b) **2.** nationals of EU states, Monaco and Switzerland with valid national ID cards;
(c) **3.** nationals of EU countries and Switzerland with passports valid for period of intended stay.
VISAS: Required by all except the following:
(a) nationals of the countries referred to in the chart above for stays of up to 90 days;
(b) nationals of Andorra, Argentina, Bolivia, Brazil, Brunei, Bulgaria, Chile, Costa Rica, Croatia, El Salvador, Honduras, Hong Kong (SAR) (blue and red passport holders), Iceland, Israel, Korea (Rep), Liechtenstein, Macau (SAR), Malaysia, Mexico, Monaco, New Zealand, Nicaragua, Panama, Paraguay, Romania, San Marino, Singapore, Switzerland, Uruguay, Vatican City and Venezuela for stays of up to 90 days;
(c) those continuing their journey to a third country within 48 hours, provided holding tickets with reserved seats and other documents for their onward journey except: nationals of Afghanistan, Angola, Bangladesh, Congo (Dem Rep), Eritrea, Ethiopia, Ghana, India, Iran, Iraq, Nigeria, Pakistan, Somalia, Sri Lanka, Sudan, Syrian Arab Republic and Turkey who always need a visa, even if transiting by the same aircraft.
Types of visa and cost: A uniform type of visa, the *Schengen* visa, is issued for tourist, business and private visits. There are three types of *Schengen* visa. *Short-stay, Transit* and *Airport Transit*: £22.50. Prices depend on

exchange rates. Contact the Consulate/Consular section at Embassy for further details.
Note: Spouses and children of EU nationals (providing spouse's passport and the original marriage certificate, or child's original birth certificate (with certified translation into English, if applicable), are produced), and nationals of some other countries, receive their visas free of charge (enquire at Embassy for details). Minors under 18 years should be accompanied by both parents. Otherwise, a letter from both parents or legal guardians is needed, authorising the minor to travel and stay in Greece, appointing a person responsible for the minor during stay (authenticated by man of law *or* consular officer of applicant's nationality), parents' passports, birth certificate of the minor and proof of legal guardianship enclosed.
Validity: Depends on nationality.
Application to: Consulate (or Consular section at Embassy); see *Contact Addresses* section. Travellers visiting just one Schengen country should apply to the Consulate of that country; travellers visiting more than one Schengen country should apply to the Consulate of the country chosen as the main destination *or* the country they will enter first (if they have no main destination).
Application requirements: (a) Passport or travel document valid for at least three months after expiry date of visa, with blank pages to affix visa, showing valid Residence Permit. (b) Completed application form (signed by legal guardian in case of minors). (c) Two recent passport-size photos. (d) Fee (payable in cash or postal order only). (e) Return or onward ticket (necessary for transit and airport transit visas, which also require a visa for onward country to be submitted, if applicable) or proof of booking/itinerary from travel agent. If visiting friends or relatives, a letter duly certified by a police station in Greece must be submitted. (f) Proof of sufficient funds to cover stay (bank statement or travellers cheques). (g) Proof of reason for visit; a letter of reference from employer detailing wages, and letter of invitation from Greek company for business trips; a letter from school for school trip. If self-employed, a letter from a solicitor or an accountant. (h) Original and photocopy of proof of travel insurance to cover intended stay in Greece. (i) Transport documentation, eg air ticket, confirmed ferry booking or, if driving, registration document, proof of legal ownership of vehicle and insurance certificate. (j) Those who claim visas in the UK and live more than 200 miles from London do not have to collect their visas in person at the London Embassy but may supply a Special Delivery self-addressed envelope instead.
Note: Applications can be made in person only. Appointments must be made through the automated booking service for those residing in the UK and in the vicinity of London (tel: (09065) 540 744). A limited number of visas are issued each day on a first-come, first-served basis. All documents must be submitted both in their original form and with photocopy.
Working days required: At least three weeks.
Note: Nationals from the following countries should allow several weeks from the date of appointment for the processing of their application: Afghanistan, Algeria, Armenia, Bahrain, Belarus, Burundi, China (PR), Colombia, Egypt, Georgia, Guinea, Indonesia, Iran, Iraq, Jordan, Kazakhstan, Korea (Dem Rep), Kuwait, Lebanon, Libya, Moldova, Oman, Palestinian Authority passport holders, Pakistan, The Philippines, Qatar, Russian Federation, Rwanda, Saudi Arabia, Somalia, Sudan, Surinam, Syrian Arab Republic, Taiwan (China), Ukraine, United Arab Emirates and Yemen.
Temporary residence: Apply to the Aliens Department in Athens.
Important note: Persons arriving in and departing from Greece on a charter flight risk having the return portion of their ticket invalidated by the authorities if, at any time during their stay, they leave Greece and remain overnight or longer in another country.

Money

Single European currency (Euro): The Euro is now the official currency of 12 EU member states (including Greece). The first Euro coins and notes were introduced in January 2002; the Greek Drachma was in circulation until 28 February 2002, when it was completely replaced by the Euro. Euro (€) = 100 cents. Notes are in denominations of €500, 200, 100, 50, 20, 10 and 5. Coins are in denominations of €2, 1 and 50, 20, 10, 5, 2 and 1 cents.
Currency exchange: Foreign currency can be exchanged at all banks, savings banks and bureaux de change. Exchange rates can fluctuate from one bank to another. Many UK banks offer differing exchange rates depending on the denominations of currency being bought or sold. Check with banks for details and current rates.
Credit & debit cards: American Express, Diners Club, MasterCard, Visa and other major credit cards are widely accepted (although less so in petrol stations), as well as Eurocheque cards. Check with your credit or debit card company for details of merchant acceptability and other services which may be available.
Travellers cheques: All major currencies are widely accepted and can be exchanged easily at banks. Generally, banks in Greece charge a commission of 2 per cent with a minimum of €0.15 and a maximum of €13.21 on the encashment of travellers cheques. To avoid additional exchange rate charges, travellers are advised to take travellers cheques in Euros, Pounds Sterling or US Dollars.
Currency restrictions: The import of local and foreign currency is not restricted provided any amount exceeding €10,000 is declared on arrival. The export of local and foreign currency is allowed although amounts over €2000 require an Import Currency Declaration Form issued on arrival, and amounts over €10,000 require a Certificate of Tax Clearance or Currency Declaration Form (on import).
Exchange rate indicators: The following figures are included as a guide to the movements of the Euro against Sterling and the US Dollar:

Date	Feb '04	May '04	Aug '04	Nov '04
£1.00=	1.46	1.50	1.49	1.42
$1.00=	0.80	0.84	0.81	0.75

Banking hours: Mon-Thurs 0800-1430, Fri 0800-1400. Banks on the larger islands tend to stay open in the afternoon and some during the evening to offer currency exchange facilities during the tourist season. The GNTO bureau in Athens can give full details.

Duty Free

The following goods may be imported into Greece by visitors without incurring customs duty by:
(a) Passengers arriving from within the EU:
800 cigarettes or 200 cigars or 400 cigarillos or 1kg of tobacco; 10l of alcoholic beverage or 90l of wine and 110l of beer; there is no limit for perfume.
(b) Passengers arriving from non-EU countries within Europe:
200 cigarettes or 50 cigars or 100 cigarillos or 250g of tobacco; 1l of alcoholic beverage over 22 per cent or 2l of alcohol beverages of 22 per cent or less and 2l of wine and liquers; 50g of perfume and 250ml of eau de cologne; gifts up to a value of €175 per person and €90 if under 15.
(c) Passengers arriving from outside Europe:
400 cigarettes or 100 cigars or 200 cigarillos or 500g of tobacco; 1l of alcoholic beverage over 22 per cent or 2l of alcohol beverages of 22 per cent or less and 2l of wine and 2l of still table wine; 50g of perfume and 250ml of eau de cologne.
Note: The tobacco and alcohol allowances listed above are not available to passengers under the age of 18.
Restricted items: It is forbidden to bring in plants with soil. One windsurfboard per person may be imported/exported duty free, if registered in the passport on arrival. The export of antiquities is prohibited without the express permission of the Archaeological Service in Athens; those who ignore this will be prosecuted.
Abolition of duty free goods within the EU: On 30 June 1999, the sale of duty free alcohol and tobacco at airports and at sea was abolished in all of the original 15 EU member states. Of the 10 new member states that joined the EU on May 1st 2004, these rules already apply to Cyprus and Malta. There are transitional rules in place for visitors returning to one of the original 15 EU countries from one of the other new EU countries. But for the original 15, plus Cyprus and Malta, there are now no limits imposed on importing tobacco and alcohol products from one EU country to another (with the exceptions of Denmark, Finland and Sweden, where limits *are* imposed). Travellers should note that they may be required to prove at customs that the goods purchased are for personal use *only*.

Public Holidays

2005: Jan 1 New Year's Day. **Jan 6** Epiphany. **Mar 14** Orthodox Shrove Monday. **Mar 25** Independence Day. **Apr 29** Orthodox Good Friday. **May 1** Labour Day. **May 2** Orthodox Easter

Monday. **Jun 20** Day of the Holy Spirit. **Aug 15** Assumption. **Oct 28** Ochi Day. **Dec 25** Christmas Day. **Dec 26** Boxing Day. **2006: Jan 1** New Year's Day. **Jan 6** Epiphany. **Feb 27** Orthodox Shrove Monday. **Mar 25** Independence Day. **Apr 14** Orthodox Good Friday. **Apr 17** Orthodox Easter Monday. **May 1** Labour Day. **Jun 5** Day of the Holy Spirit. **Aug 15** Assumption. **Oct 28** Ochi Day. **Dec 25** Christmas Day **Dec 26** Boxing Day.

Health

	Special Precautions?	Certificate Required?
Yellow Fever	No	1
Cholera	No	No
Typhoid & Polio	No	N/A
Malaria	No	N/A

Note: *Regulations and requirements may be subject to change at short notice, and you are advised to contact your doctor well in advance of your intended date of departure. Any numbers in the chart refer to the footnotes below.*

1: A yellow fever vaccination certificate is required from all travellers over one year of age coming from infected areas.
Food & drink: Water quality varies from area to area, depending on the source, but in most regions is excellent. Bottled water is available and is advised for the first few weeks of the stay. Milk is pasteurised and dairy products are safe for consumption. Local meat, poultry, seafood, fruit and vegetables are considered safe to eat.
Other risks: Visitors to forested areas should consider vaccination for *tick-borne encephalitis*.
Health care: There is a reciprocal health agreement with the United Kingdom, but it is poorly implemented and it is an essential precaution to take out holiday insurance. Refunds for medical treatment are theoretically available from the Greek Social Insurance Foundation on presentation of form E111 (see the *Health* appendix).
Local chemists can diagnose and supply a wide selection of drugs. There are often long waits for treatment at public hospitals. Hospital facilities on outlying islands are sometimes sparse, although many ambulances without adequate facilities have air-ambulance backup. For emergencies, ring 166 (public ambulance).

Travel - International

AIR: Greece's national airline is *Olympic Airlines (OA)* (website: www.olympic-airways.com). *British Airways* make scheduled flights to Greece. *Delta Airlines* operate daily flights from New York to Athens.
Approximate flight times: From Athens to *London* is five hours; from Rhodes is five hours 15 minutes; from Corfu is four hours; from Heraklion is eight hours; and from Skiathos is six hours (all flight times include a stopover). From Athens to *Los Angeles* is 15 hours; to *New York* is 13 hours; to *Singapore* is 13 hours; to *Sydney* is 24 hours 30 minutes.
International airports: *Athens (ATH)* (*Elfetherios Veniselos*) (website: www.aia.gr) has been newly constructed, replacing all air traffic from the old airport. Located 27km (17 miles) northeast of the city, there is a six-lane motorway linking the two, and regular airport buses running 24 hours from the centre and the port of Piraeus. Airport facilities include duty free shops, car hire (*Avis, Budget, Hertz, Europcar* and *Sixt*), banks, cash machines, bureaux de change, bar and restaurant facilities, post office, business centre and hotel.
Heraklion (HER) (Crete) is 5km (3 miles) from the city. Bus and taxi services are available. Airport facilities include a cafe, bureaux de change, bar and restaurant facilities, hotel reservations and a duty free shop.
Thessaloniki (SKG) (Macedonia) is 16km (10 miles) from the city. Regular coach and taxi services are available. Airport facilities include duty free shops, restaurants, bars, banks/bureaux de change, car hire (*Alamo, Avis* and *Hertz*) and a post office.
Corfu (CFU) (Kerkira) is 3km (2 miles) from the city. Regular coach and taxi services are available. There is a duty free shop, cafe and bar.
Rhodes (RHO) (Paradisi) is 16km (10 miles) from the city. Coach and taxi services are available. Airport facilities include a duty free shop, car hire (*Avis, Rent-a-car*), bank, bureau de change, cafe and bar.
There are also international airports at *Chania (CHQ), Kalamata (KLX), Karpathos (AOK), Kavala (KVA), Kefalonia (EFL), Kos (KGS), Lesbos (Mytilini)* (MJT), *Mykonos (JMK), Preveza (Lefkos)* (PVK), *Samos (SMI), Skiathos (JSI), Thessaloniki (SKG), Thira* (Santorini) *(JTR)* and *Zakynthos (ZTH)*, most of which serve predominantly summer traffic.
Departure tax: €12,15.
SEA: The major Greek ports are Corfu, Heraklion, Igoumenitsa, Patras, Piraeus (Athens), Rhodes, Thessaloniki and Volos. Shipping and ferryboat lines link these ports with Italy, Croatia, Cyprus, Russia and Turkey. Greek ports are used by a number of cruise lines including *Celebrity Cruises, Costa Cruises, Crystal Cruises, Festival Cruises, Holland America Line, Princess Cruises, Silversea* and *Swan Hellenic*. The Greek/Hellenic National Tourism Organisation can give full details (see *Contact Addresses* section). A car ferry links the Italian ports of Brindisi, Venice, Trieste and Ancona with Corfu, Igoumenitsa, Patras and Piraeus. There are also services from Corfu to Bari, Brindisi and Trieste; and from Rhodes to Marmaris (Turkey). During the summer months there are also services from Ithaca and from Cephalonia to Brindisi.
RAIL: The national railway company is *Hellenic Railways Organisation Ltd (OSE)* (website: www.osenet.gr). A good way to travel from the UK is to take the *Eurostar* through the channel tunnel, from London to either Brussels or Paris, both of which have onward connections to Greece. For further information and reservations contact *Eurostar* (tel: (0870) 6000 792 (travel agents) *or* (08705) 186 186 (public; within the UK) *or* +44 1233 617 575 (public; outside the UK); website: www.eurostar.com); *or* Rail Europe (tel: (08705) 848 848; website: www.raileurope.co.uk). Travel agents can obtain refunds for unused tickets from Eurostar Trade Refunds, 2nd Floor, Kent House, 81 Station Road, Ashford, Kent TN23 1PD, UK. Complaints and comments may be sent to Eurostar Customer Relations, Eurostar House, Waterloo Station, London SE1 8SE, UK (tel: (020) 7928 5168; e-mail: new-comments@eurostar.co.uk). General enquiries and information requests *must* be made by telephone. **Rail passes:** *Inter-Rail* tickets, for those aged 26 and under, include rail travel within Greece, but a supplement will be added for couchettes; the ticket does not include the cost of ferries between the mainland, other countries or islands, but certain shipping lines offer a discount to ticket holders. Prices for those aged over 26 are approximately 40 per cent higher. For passengers wishing to make multiple train journeys within Europe, the *EuroDomino* travel card offers reduced prices on various journeys to the destination of their choice. Other discount fares include air or ferry journeys with rail travel packages. Contact Rail Europe for further information.
ROAD: It is possible to ferry cars and caravans across to one of the major ports of entry or to enter overland. Points of overland entry are from the Macedonia (Former Yugoslav Republic of) via Evzoni, and Niki; from Bulgaria via Promahonas or Kastanies and Kipi. From Serbia & Montenegro, the route is via Italy (Trieste), Austria (Graz) and Belgrade. The journey from northern France to Athens is over 3200km (2000 miles). For car-ferry information, see details under *Sea* above. **Bus:** There are routes from Athens via Thessaloniki to Dortmund, Istanbul, Paris and Sofia. Information and bookings are available from terminals in Athens at 6 Sina Street (tel: (210) 362 4402; 1 Karolou Street (tel: (210) 529 7777) and 17 Filellinon Street (tel: (210) 323 6747); also at Thessaloniki rail station.

Travel - Internal

AIR: The national airline, *Olympic Airlines*, flies from *Athens* to Alexandroupolis, Astypalaia, Chania (Crete), Chios, Heraklion, Ikaria, Ioannina, Karpathos, Kassos, Kastellorizo, Kastoria, Kavala, Kefaloniá, Kerkira (Corfu), Kithira, Kos, Kozani, Lemnos, Leros, Milos, Mykonos, Mytilini, Paros, Preveza, Rhodes, Samos, Santorini (Thira), Siros, Sitia, Skiathos, Skiros, Thessaloniki and Zakinthos; from Rhodes to Heraklion, Karpathos, Kassos, Kastellorizo, Kos, Mykonos, and Santorini (Thira); from *Chios* to Mykonos, Samos and Thessaloniki; from *Heraklion* to Santorini (Thira), Mykonos and Paros; from *Karpathos* to Kassos and Sitia; from *Kefaloniá* to Zakinthos; from *Kos* to Leros and Samos; from *Mykonos* to Mytilini; and from *Thessaloniki* to Chania, Heraklion, Ioannina, Kavala Kerkira, Kos, Larissa, Lemnos, Mykonos, Mytilini, Rhodes, Samos and Santorini. There are also regular services to the Greek Aegean Islands (including *Cyclades, Dodecanissa, North Aegean Sea* and the *Sporades*).
Departure tax: €8,51.
SEA: It is both cheap and easy to travel around the islands. There are ferry services on many routes, with sailings most frequent during the summer. The main ports are Attica, Piraeus and Rafina, although there are regular sailings to the islands from the smaller ports of Alexandroupolis, Igoumenitsa, Kavala, Kyllini, Patras, Thessaloniki and Volos. Tickets can be bought from the shipping lines' offices located around the quaysides. In major ports the larger lines have offices in the city centre. There are two classes of ticket (First Class and Economy Class) which offer varying degrees of comfort; couchette cabins can be booked for the longer voyages or those wishing to avoid the sun. Most ships have restaurant facilities. During high season it is wise to buy tickets in advance, as inter-island travel is very popular. **Routes from Piraeus:** There are regular sailings to the following ports: *Dodecanese*: Astipalaia, Chalki, Kalymnos, Karpathos, Kassos, Kastelorizo, Kos, Leros, Lipsi, Nissiros, Patmos, Rhodes, Symi and Tilos. *Cyclades*: Aegiali and Katapola (both on Amorgos), Anafi, Donoussa, Folegandros, Heraklia, Ios, Kimolos, Koufonissia, Kythnos, Milos, Mykonos, Naxos, Paros, Santorini, Schinoussa, Serifos, Sifnos, Sikinos, Siros and Tinos. *Peloponnese*: Gytheion, Hermioni, Kithira, Methana, Monemvassia and Porto Heli. *Saronic Gulf Islands*: Aegina, Hydra, Poros and Spetses. *Crete*: Agios Nikolaos, Chania, Heraklion, Kastelli, Rethymnon and Sitia. *Samos*: Karlovassi and Vathi. *North Eastern Aegean Islands*: Agios Kirykos (Ikaria), Chios, Evdilos (Ikaria), Limnos, Mitilini (Lesvos) and Psara. *Northern Greece*: Kavala and Thessaloniki. Check sailing times either with individual lines, the Greek/Hellenic National Tourist Organisation, or in Piraeus upon arrival in Greece. **Routes from Rafina:** There are local services from Rafina (near Athens) to: Agios Efstratios, Amorgos, Andros, Chalkida (summer only), Chios, Donoussa, Heraklia, Karistos (Evia), Kavala, Koufonissi, Kythnos, Limnos, Marmari (Evia), Milos, Mykonos, Naxos, Paros, Schinoussa, Serifos, Sifnos, Syros, Thessaloniki and Tinos. **Other routes:** These include Agia Marina–Nea Styra; Perama–Salamis; Rio–Antirio; Aedipsos–Arkitsa; Eretria–Oropos; Glifa–Agiokambos; Patras–Ithaca; Patras–Kefalonia (Sami); Patras–Corfu; Patras–Paxi; Preveza–Aktion; Igoumenitsa–Corfu; Corfu–Paxi; Kyllini–Zante; Kyllini–Cephalonia (Poros); Kavala–Thassos (Limenas); Kavala–Thassos (Prinos); Keramoti–Thassos; Alexandroupolis–Samothrace and Lavrion–Kea. **Hydrofoil:** A hydrofoil service (also called the Flying Dolphins) offers a fast and efficient service from Piraeus, travelling to many of the nearby islands. Although this is somewhat more expensive than travelling by ferry, journey times are cut drastically. There are also fast hydrofoil services from Agios, Gytheion, Kimi (Evia), Konstandinos, Lavrion, Thessaloniki, Volos and Zea Marina (Piraeus). For further information on various ferry and hydrofoil timetables, visit www.gtp.gr. **Yachts:** Numerous types of yachts and sailing vessels can be chartered or hired with or without crews. 'Flotilla holidays' are popular, and the *Greek/Hellenic National Tourism Organisation* (see *Contact Addresses* section) has a full list of companies running this type of holiday.
RAIL: The two main railway stations in Athens are Larissa (with trains to northern Greece, Evia and Europe) and Peloponnissos (with trains to the Peloponnese). Train information and tickets are available from the *Hellenic Railways Organisation (OSE)* in Athens (tel: (210) 529 7313 *or* 529 7777) *or* in Thessaloniki (tel: (310) 599 143; website: www.osenet.gr). Travelling north, there are regular daily trains from Athens to Thessaloniki, Livadia, Paleofarsala, Larissa, Plati, Edessa, Florina, Seres, Drama, Komotini and Alexandroupolis (connections from Thessaloniki and Larissa). Travelling south, there are regular daily trains from Athens to Kiato, Xylokastra, Diakofto, Patras, Olympia, Argos, Tripoli, Megalopolis and Kalamata.
Cheap fares: Current promotional offers include:
Inter Rail Cards are open to all European residents for unlimited rail travel in second class in several European countries. Passes are valid for 16 or 22 days or one month.
Euro Domino Cards are open to passengers of all ages and offer rail travel in either first or second class travel in one or more European countries of the holders choice. Passes are valid for three to eight days and do not have to be taken consecutively.
Vergina Flexipass offers unlimited rail travel in Greece for three or five or 10 days within one month or two months in either first or second class depending on the choice of ticket.
Greek Flexipass offers unlimited rail travel in Greece for three or five days within one month in first class.
Students may be entitled to a 25 per cent reduction in the price of domestic rail fares. Travel is restricted to certain routes and times. For further information on the above schemes, contact the *Hellenic Railways Organisation (OSE)*.
ROAD: Greece has a good road network on the whole, totalling approximately 116,150km (72,174 miles), mostly paved. Traffic drives on the right. Examples of some distances from Athens: to Thessaloniki, 511km (318 miles); to Corinth, 85km (53 miles); to Igoumenitsa, 587km (365 miles); and to Delphi, 165km (103 miles). **Bus:** Buses link Athens and all main towns in Attica, northern Greece and the Peloponnese. Service on the islands depends on demand, and timetables should be checked carefully. Some islands do not allow any kind of motorised transport, in which case islanders use boats, or donkeys and carts to travel around. Fares are low. The Greek/Hellenic Railways Organisation Ltd (OSE) runs bus services to northern Greece from the Karolou Street terminus and to the Peloponnese from the Sina Street station. **Bus information:** There are two long-distance bus terminals in Athens: Terminal A and Terminal B. For information on long-distance buses, run by KTEL, from Athens to the provinces, enquire at Terminal A, 100 Kifissou Street, Athens (tel: (210) 512 4910) *or* Terminal B, 260 Liossion Street, Athens. Further information can be obtained from KTEL offices (website: www.ktel.org). **Taxi:** Rates are per km and are very reasonable, with extra charge for fares to/from stations, ports and airports. Taxis run on a share basis, so do not be surprised if the taxi picks up other passengers for the journey. There is an additional charge from 0100-0600, with double fare from 0200-0400.
Car hire: Most car hire firms operate throughout Greece. For details, contact the Greek/Hellenic National Tourism Organisation (see *Contact Addresses* section). Reservations

can be made by writing or telephoning the car hire agency direct. **Regulations:** The minimum age for driving is l8. Children under 10 must sit in the back seat. Seat belts must be worn. There are fines for breaking traffic regulations. The maximum speed limit is 120kph (70mph) on motorways, 110kph (60mph) outside built-up areas and 50kph (31mph) in built-up areas. There are slightly different speed limits for motorbikes. It is illegal to carry spare petrol in the vehicle. EU nationals may import a foreign-registered car, caravan, motorcycle, boat or trailer for a maximum of six months. This period may be extended to 15 months for a fee and further paperwork. **Documentation:** A national driving licence is acceptable for EU nationals. EU nationals taking their own cars to Greece are advised to obtain a Green Card, to top up the insurance cover to that provided by the car owner's domestic policy. It is no longer a legal requirement for visits of less than three months, but without it insurance cover is limited to the minimum legal cover in Greece. The car registration documents have to be carried at all times. Nationals of non-EU countries may need an International Driving Permit and should contact *ELPA* (Automobile and Touring Club of Greece). **Road assistance:** A breakdown service is available on main roads, conditions of which have vastly improved. For details, contact ELPA, Athens Tower, Messogion 2-4, 115 27 Athens (tel: (210) 779 1615; fax: (210) 778 6642; e-mail: elpa@techlink.gr; website: www.elpa.gr). Emergency breakdown services can be contacted toll-free by dialling 104. There are good repair shops in big towns and petrol is easily obtainable.

URBAN: Buses: There are several services around Athens and Attica. The terminal at Mauromateon Street, Areos Park, Athens has regular services to *Amfiaraio*, *Marathonas*, *Nea Makri*, *Porto Rafti*, *Ramnous* and *Sounio*. Trolley buses (ILPAP) and regular buses (ETHEL) have frequent links to tourist attractions and places of interest. Tickets for buses and trolley buses can be purchased from the Athens Urban Transport Organisation (*OASA*) at various booths and kiosks situated around the city. For further information contact OASA at 15 Metsovou Street, 106 82 Athens (tel: (210) 883 6076; fax: (210) 821 2219; e-mail: oasa@oasa.gr; website: www.oasa.gr). **Metro**: Athens has a reliable underground system (ISAP) that consists of three major lines. The old line runs north–south between Athens (suburb of Kifissia) and Piraeus daily 0500-0015. There are also two new lines: Line 2 runs between Aghios Antonios and Aghios Dimitrios and line 3 runs between Monastiraki and the airport. Tickets can be purchased at every Metro and ISAP station. Information on timetables and schedules can be found from Athens Metro (website: www.ametro.gr) *or OASA* (see address details above). **Tram**: A new tram system in Athens cuts through the city from Syntagma Square right through to the coast and runs a pleasant route from Peace and Friendship Stadium all the way to the most southern point of Glyfada. Tickets can be booked at all stations and trams connect with the Metro at Neos Kosmos and Neo Faliro (website: www.tramsa.gr).

Travel times: The following chart gives approximate travel times (in hours and minutes) from **Athens** to other major cities/islands in Greece.

	Air	Road	Sea
Corfu	**0.50**	**11.00***	**-**
Crete	**0.50**	**-**	**6-12.00**
Mykonos	**0.45**	**-**	**3.45-5.00**
Rhodes	**0.55**	**-**	**14.00**
Thessaloniki	**0.50**	**8.00**	**14.00**
Thira	**0.40**	**-**	**4.30-8.00**

Note: *The travel time by road to Corfu includes a sea crossing from Patras.

Accommodation

HOTELS: The range of hotels can vary greatly both among the islands and on the mainland, from high class on larger islands and the mainland to small seasonal chalets. Booking for the high season is essential. Xenia hotels are owned and often run by the Greek/Hellenic National Tourism Organisation. Small family hotels are a friendly alternative to the hotel chains. Hotel reservations can be made by writing directly to the hotels, through a travel agent, or through writing, faxing or phoning the Hellenic Chamber of Hotels, 24 Stadiou Street, 105 64 Athens (tel: (210) 331 0022; fax: (210) 322 5449; e-mail: grhotels@otenet.gr; website: www.grhotels.gr). **Grading:** Hotels are all officially classified as **Luxury** or rated on a scale from **A** to **E**. The category denotes what facilities must be offered and the price range that the hotelier is allowed to charge.

SELF-CATERING: Furnished rooms in private houses, service flats, apartments and villas are available. On most of the Greek islands, rooms in private homes are an extremely popular form of accommodation and can usually be arranged on the spot. All types of accommodation can be arranged through tour operators in this country. The Greek/Hellenic National Tourism Organisation can provide further information on request.

TRADITIONAL SETTLEMENTS: Known also as *paradosiakoi oikismoi* in Greek, these traditional hostels can be found throughout the country, notably in Areopolis (Mani), Gythion (Peloponnese), Ia (Santorini), Koriskades (Central Greece), Makrinitsa (Pilion), Mesta (Chios), Milies (Pilion), Monemvasia (Peloponnese), Papingo (Epirus), Psara Island, Vathia (Mani), and Vizitsa (Pilion). This type of accommodation normally offers single, double or triple bedrooms with shower, or a four-bed house.

CAMPING/CARAVANNING: There is a wide network of official campsites (website: www.panhellenic-camping-union.gr). For details, contact the Greek/Hellenic National Tourism Organisation (see *Contact Addresses* section). **Note:** It is not permitted to camp anywhere except registered sites.

YOUTH HOSTELS: Greece has only one youth hostel recognised by the International Youth Hostel Federation, which is located in Athens, 16 Victor Hugo Street, 104 38 Athens (tel/fax: (210) 523 2540; e-mail: info@athenshostel.com; website: www.interland.gr/athenshostel). A number of youth hostels belong to the Greek Youth Hostels Association, whose main office is in 75 Damareos Street, Athens (tel: (210) 751 9530; fax: (210) 751 0616; e-mail: y-hostels@otenet.gr). Other youth hostels exist in Crete, the Cyclades and the Peloponnese. For further details, contact the Greek Youth Hostel Association.

Credit: © Greek National Tourist Office

Resorts & Excursions

For the purposes of clarity, information on *Resorts & Excursions* within Greece has been divided into mainland Greece, in the first part of the section (with five regional sections plus Athens), and the Greek islands, in the latter part of the section (with six island groups plus Crete). These do not necessarily reflect administrative boundaries.

Note: (a) Following an initiative by the Greek government, opening hours and fees for major museums and archaeological sites are now uniform throughout the country. Archaeological sites with adjoining museums charge a single admission fee, allowing entry to both at no extra cost. Visitors have access to these attractions Tues-Sun 0830-1500. (b) Tourist police in the main tourist destinations are trained to assist visitors with accommodation, maps, timetables, details of places to visit and special events. All wear flag badges denoting which language(s) they speak. English and German are fairly common. Do not hesitate to ask them for help.

ATHENS

Capital of Greece and the country's largest city, Athens is dominated by the flat-topped hill of the **Acropolis**, site of the 2400-year-old **Parthenon**, one of the most famous classical monuments in the world. Close by lie the **Theatre of Dionysus** and the restored **Odeon of Herodes Atticus**, a superb theatre in which open-air performances of the *International Athens Festival* are held from June to September. The ruins of the civic, political and commercial centre of the **Ancient Agora** can be visited, as can the reconstructed **Hellenistic Stoa of Attalos**, which houses the **Agora Museum**. Most artefacts are displayed in the **National Archaeological Museum** on Patission Street. The old quarter of the town, **Plaka**, which spreads around the Acropolis, is picturesque with its famed flea market, small tavernas, craft shops and narrow winding alleys. The excavations of the **Library of Hadrian** can be observed from Pandrossou Street. The centre of modern Athens, most notably the chic area of Kolonaki, has many designer boutiques, smart restaurants and international-class hotels. The city has a thriving nightlife, with most bars and clubs staying open until at least 0300.

PIRAEUS: Lying at the innermost point of the Saronic Gulf just outside Athens, and connected to the centre by metro, Piraeus is the city's main port. From here, ferries leave regularly for the Islands (see the information on the Greek Islands).

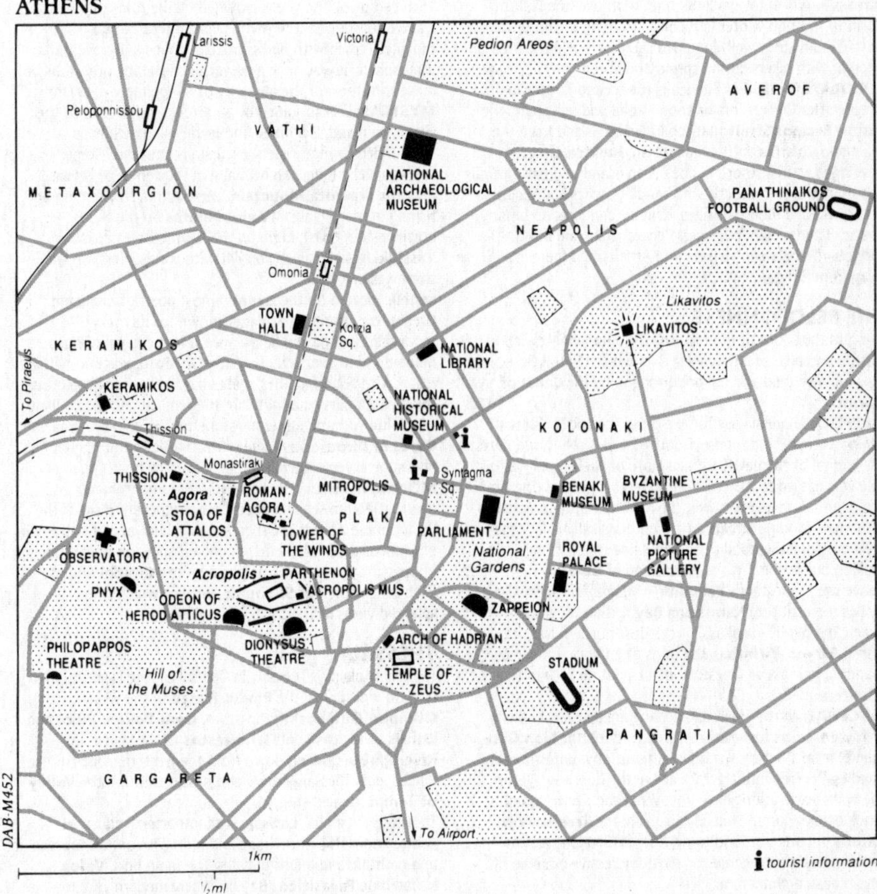

A B C D E F G H I J K L M N O P Q R S T U V W X Y Z

CENTRAL GREECE WITH EUBOEA

The area surrounding Athens, known as Attica, is characterised by calm beaches, and the pinewoods and thyme-covered slopes of **Mount Parnes**, **Hymettus** and **Pentelico**. As one travels northwest, towards the interior, the landscape combines fertile plains planted with tobacco and cotton, and rugged mountains with unspoilt villages and winter ski resorts.

CAPE SOUNIO: 69km (43 miles) east of Athens, crowning Cape Sounio is a towering promontory which dominates the landscape for miles around. Here stand the superb ruins of the **Temple of Poseidon**, built in the fourth century BC, commanding spectacular views over the sea and islands. The **Apollo Coast**, a highly developed tourist area stretching from Piraeus to Cape Sounio, is dotted with exclusive resorts such as **Glifada** (17km/11 miles from Athens) and **Vouliagmeni** (24km/15 miles from Athens), offering marinas, well-kept beaches, modern hotel complexes, seafood tavernas and luxury-class restaurants and nightclubs. North of Cape Sounio lies **Rafina**, Athens' second port, with ferry connections to Euboea and some of the Greek Islands.

OSSIOS LOUKAS: Northwest of Athens, close to the town of Livadia, stands the magnificent monastery of **Ossios Loukas**. Within the monastery complex one can visit the 11th-century **Church of St Luke**, noted for its marvellous Byzantine mosaics, and the 13th-century **Church of the Virgin**, built by Cistercian monks who occupied the monastery during the Middle Ages. **Livadia**, built into the foothills of **Mount Helikon**, was famous in ancient times for the **Oracle of Trophonios Zeus** and the **Springs of Forgetfulness** (**Lethe**) and **Memory** (**Mnemosyne**) to the north of the town.

DELPHI: Lying 176km (109 miles) northwest of Athens, Delphi can be reached by road via Livadia and Arahova. This is the site of the famous **Oracle**, where rulers of ancient Greece came for many centuries for political and moral guidance. The complex of treasury buildings, plinths and the foundations for the fourth-century BC **Temple of Apollo** are set on the steep rocky hillside, overlooking olive groves and the **Sanctuary of Athena**, known as the **Marmaria** (marbles). A steep uphill climb from the Temple brings one to the theatre, offering stunning views over the entire site, and further uphill still lies the ancient stadium. The **Delphi Museum** contains a superb collection of finds from the site. Many visitors to Delphi stay overnight in nearby **Arahova**, a pretty hillside town renowned for its cheese, *formaela*. Alternatively, a short distance southwest of Delfi, on the northern coast of the Gulf of Corinthia, lie the seaside towns of **Itea** and **Galaxidi**, offering hotels, restaurants and beaches. A regular bus connects Athens and Itea, passing through Arahova and Delphi enroute.

MOUNT PARNASSUS: Close to Arahova, on the main road from Athens to Delphi, lie the southern slopes of Mount Parnassus, which towers 2457m (8061ft) over the Gulf of Corinth. Through winter (December to April) the mountain hosts a number of well-equipped ski resorts, and the area is popular with hikers during spring and autumn.

EUBOEA: The island of Euboea is the second-largest in Greece after Crete. A major bridge (road and rail) spans the narrow **Evripos Strait** that separates the island from the mainland, to arrive in the main town, **Halkida**, a well-developed tourist resort. Euboea is an island of great natural beauty and scenic variety, with sandy beaches and secluded coves, wooded mountainsides ideal for climbing, and many peaceful and unspoilt villages. Regular train and bus services run between Halkida and Athens, and there is a ferry from Rafina.

THE PELOPONNESE

Lying to the south of the country, the Peloponnese, rich in history and diverse landscapes, is joined to Central Greece by a massive road and rail bridge spanning the **Canal of Corinth**.

NAFPLIO: An ideal base for exploring the ancient sites of the northeast Peloponnese, from 1824 to 1834, Nafplio was the capital of the newly formed state of Greece, before this role was passed to Athens. Considered by many as one of the country's loveliest towns, the historic centre is made up of narrow winding streets with Neo-classical and Ottoman-style buildings. Seafood restaurants line the seafront, looking out to the tiny fortified island of **Bourdzi**. High above the town stands **Palamidi**, a Venetian fortress. Close by lies the beautiful **Karathona Bay**, with a wide sand beach, backed by eucalyptus trees. Just north of Nafplio stands **Tiryns** (**Tirintha**), the ruins of an ancient fortress made up of massive limestone blocks, dating back to the 13th century BC.

MYCENAE: North of Nafplio lies the ancient fortified city of Mycenae. The fortress is entered through the **Lion Gate**, named after the two magnificent lions (now unfortunately headless) carved into the rock above the doorway. Within the walls, excavations have uncovered the palace complex, while close by on the hill of Panagitsa, the **Treasury of Atreus** (an underground tomb, 36m (118ft) long and 6m (20ft) wide) is considered the most impressive example of Mycenaean architecture.

CORINTH: North of Mycenae lies Corinth. The modern city, despite its beautiful location, is unremarkable, having been destroyed by an earthquake in 1858, rebuilt but destroyed again in 1928. However, 8km (5 miles) away, on the northern slopes of **Akrokorinthos Hill**, are the ruins of **Ancient Corinth** (**Arhea Korinthos**), where the remains of the **Temple of Apollo** are still to be seen. On the hilltop stands **Acrocorinth** (**Akrokorinthos**), with a medieval fortress built upon an ancient site. From the highest point, once the **Temple of Afrodite**, one can enjoy a magnificent panorama.

EPIDAURUS: East of Nafplio stands the impressive open-air **Epidaurus Theatre**, dating back to the fourth century BC. The acoustics are perfect, and there is seating for 14,000. From July to August, each weekend, the *Epidaurus Festival* offers performances of ancient Greek dramas in this magical setting.

East of Epidaurus, jutting out from the Peloponnese peninsula, lies **Methana**, an important spa town since ancient times, with sulphuric waters and modernised hydrotherapy installations.

PATRAS: Patras is a thriving commercial and industrial port, and the third most important town in Greece. From here, daily ferry services connect the country to Italy and the Ionian islands. Southwest of Patras, at **Kyllini** there are mineral springs, hydropathic installations, new hotels and a public beach. The stretch of coast south of Kyllini as far as **Kiparissia** offers plenty of good beaches and seaside resorts. East of Patras, one can travel through the deep **Vouraikos Gorge**, taking a spectacular train journey from **Diakofto** to **Kalavrita**.

OLYMPIA: Olympia, the original site of the Olympic Games, which begun in 776 BC, and the site where the Olympic Flame is still lit today, can be reached by train or by the mountain road from Kalavrita, or along the coast, via Patras and Pyrgos. The site is a mass of marble inscriptions, restored temples and civic buildings, including the **Temple of Zeus**, which once housed the colossal gold and ivory statue of Zeus, one of the 'Seven Wonders of the Ancient World' (later taken to Constantinople and destroyed in a fire). There is also a good **Archaeological Museum** on the site, and a **Museum of the Olympic Games** located in the modern town of Olympia. Southeast of Olympia at **Bassae** (**Vasses**) is the well-preserved monumental **Temple of Apollo Epicurius**, dating back to the fourth century BC.

PILOS: Northeast of Pilos, at **Mystra**, lie the ruins of a fortified Byzantine city, once inhabited by 42,000 citizens but now home to just a small number of nuns. In the lower town, which was the religious centre, stand the 13th-century frescoed **Cathedral** and several interesting churches and monasteries. In the Upper Town, where the aristocrats lived, stand numerous *palazzi* (palaces), notably the **Palace of the Despots**, built between the 13th and 15th centuries. The site is crowned by the ruins of a hilltop **Kastro** (Castle). East of Mytras lies **Sparta**. Now a provincial town with parks, broad avenues and a pleasant atmosphere, it was once a powerful city-state, notorious in ancient history for the austerity of its regime.

MYSTRAS: Levkas, joined by a narrow strip of land to the Greek mainland, is a green and fertile island which is surrounded by many islets. Excursions, involving some mountain climbing, can be made in the centre of Levkas, near the **Stavrota Mountain**. There is good swimming and fishing in the villages of **Agios Nikitas** on the northwestern coast, **Ligia** on the southeastern coast or **Vassiliki** (which is also popular with windsurfers) on the southwestern coast.

MANI: Located on the southernmost point of mainland Greece, the Mani peninsular is known for its rocky mountains and barren landscapes, and medieval villages made up of towers and churches. **Githio**, a peaceful holiday resort with good facilities, makes a good base for exploring the area. Of particular note are the semi-abandoned village of **Vathia** with its numerous stone towers, and the amazing **Caves of Dirou**, a vast network with underground channels and huge caverns, which can be visited by boat.

MONEMVASSIA: Built into a rocky promontory overlooking the sea, almost on the southeastern tip of the Peloponnese, stands the spectacular medieval fortified town of Monemvassia. Made up of cobbled alleys and old stone houses, the town is crowned by a hilltop **Citadel** and the Byzantine church of **St Sophia**, both of which offer splendid views of the town and gulf below.

THESSALY

The fertile plain of Thessaly in Central Greece is surrounded by high mountains: the **Pindus Range** to the west, **Olimpus** (**Olimbos**) to the north, **Ossa**, **Pelion** (**Pilio**) and **Othris** to the east, and **Trimfrestos** to the south. The **River Pinios**, flowing down from the western slopes of the Pindus, cuts Thessaly in two and passes through the **Valley of Tempi** to meet the sea.

The region's capital, **Larissa**, is an important industrial centre and traffic node (road and rail), with good shopping and nightlife and plentiful cafes. The main port, **Volos**, situated on **Pagasiticos Bay**, is largely modern, due to repeated destruction by earthquakes. However, there is a pleasant seafront with cafes and restaurants, and frequent ferry services for the **Sporades** (see the information on the Greek islands). Close by, on the slopes of **Mount Pelion**, stand the pretty villages of **Makrinitsa** and **Vizitsa**, noted for their traditional architecture, and the winter sports centre of **Hania**.

Mount Olympus, home of Zeus and the immortal gods and land of the Centaurs, is Greece's highest mountain, standing 2917m (9570ft). Walking tours depart from the village of **Litohoro**, where one finds hostels, hotels and *tavernas*.

To the west, above the Pinios Valley and the town of **Kalambaka**, just as the Pindus Range begins to form, stand the incredible cliff-top monasteries of the **Meteora**. Perched upon bizarre vertical rock formations of up to 300m (984ft) high, a total of 24 monasteries, some with beautiful Byzantine frescoes, were founded here during the 15th-century. Several are open to the public (accessed by a series of steep steps carved into the rocks), notably **Megalo Meteoro** and **Varlaam Monastery**.

EPIRUS

Lying between the Ionic Sea and Thessaly, in the northwest corner of the Greek peninsula, Epirus is the most mountainous region in Greece. Due to its isolation, locals here have retained many of their traditions: costumes, dances and handicrafts.

The chief settlement, **Ioannina**, overlooking **Ioannina Lake**, reached its peak during the 18th century under the Ottomans when it was an important administrative centre and home to the notorious Ali Pascia, Istanbul's local representative at that time. The town has conserved a marked eastern atmosphere, thanks to a bazaar and several mosques, notably **Aslan Pacha Mosque**, which now houses the **Museum of Popular Art**.

North of town lies the spectacular **Perama Cave**, filled with stalactites, stalagmites and running waters. Further north still, one enters the mountainous area of **Zagoria**, noted for its dense pine forests, wildlife (wolves and bears) and picturesque stone villages. Here, contained within the **Vikos-Aoos National Park** lies the dramatic **Vikos Gorge**, a canyon formed by the **River Aoos**, popular with hikers. South of Ioannina lie the archaeological remains of **Dodoni**, notably the well-conserved theatre dating back to the third century BC, where open-air performances are held during summer. On the coast, built around a bay, the pretty town of **Parga** is backed by pine woods, olive groves and orchards. Here one finds a 16th-century Venetian fortress, whitewashed houses, hotels and an excellent sandy beach.

MACEDONIA

Bordering onto Albania, Macedonia (Former Yugoslav Republic of) and Bulgaria, Macedonia stands slightly apart from the rest of the country; its scenery and climate have more in common with the adjoining Balkans, the mountains being bitterly cold in winter. Though little known by foreign tourists, this is still a particularly beautiful part of Greece, rich in historical monuments and archaeological sites. The region's capital, **Thessaloniki**, is the second-largest city in Greece. A modern industrial port, partly protected by impressive city walls, it is home to the superb **Archaeological Museum**, housing the 'Treasures of Ancient Macedonia'. On the seafront, the imposing 16th-century **White Tower**, built by the Ottomans as part of the city's defence system, houses an excellent Byzantine Art Collection. Churches of note include the fourth-century **Rotonda** (also known as St George's), **Agios Dimitrios** with its seventh-century mosaics, and the eighth-century **Agia Sofia**, converted into a mosque during Ottoman rule. The main ancient sites are the **Arch of Galerius** built in AD 297, and the ruins of the **Roman Agora**.

Southeast of Thessaloniki are the three mountainous peninsulas of **Halkidiki**: Kassandra, Sithonia and Agio Oros (Mount Athos). Kassandra and Sithonia shelter Northern Greece's best beaches and are both popular holiday resorts. However, **Mount Athos**, with its renowned monasteries, is undoubtedly the region's highlight. The first religious community, **Megistis Lavras**, was founded here in AD 963. Between the 13th and 16th centuries, the number of monasteries multiplied, until there were about 30,000 monks living in the area. Today, about 1500 monks remain (predominantly Greeks, but also some Russians, Bulgarians and Serbs), housed in 20 monasteries. Women (and female animals) are refused entry, but men can gain a special permit by proving religious or scholarly interests. For further information, contact: The Ministry of Foreign Affairs, Directorate of Churches, Zalokosta 2, Athens (tel: (210) 368 1000/2000/2311/3000/4000; website: www.mfa.gr), *or* the Ministry of Macedonia and Thrace, Directorate of Political Affairs, Plateia Diikitiriou, 541 23 Thessaloniki (tel: (2023) 103 7900; website: www.mathra.gr). East along the coast, **Kavala** is a modern, commercial seaside port with hotels, beaches, museums, restaurants and tavernas. The old town retains many traditional features, notably the aqueduct and Byzantine fortress. There are some good sand beaches, and facilities for fishing, water-skiing and sailing. From here one can reach the island of **Thassos**, another popular summer retreat with fine beaches, hotels, and some interesting ancient ruins. North of Kavala, **Filippoi** is one of Macedonia's most extensive archaeological sites. Named after the father of Alexander the Great, it is where Caesar's murderers, Brutus and Cassius, were defeated by Octavius in 42 BC, and is believed to be the site of St Paul's first recorded preaching in Greece.

West of Thessaloniki, at **Vergina** (Aigai), findings from the monumental fourth-century BC 'royal tombs' are displayed in an excellent museum, housed underground, within one of the former burial mounds.

Further west still, overlooking **Kastoria Lake**, lies the beautiful town of **Kastoria**, home to some exquisite frescoed Byzantine churches and an important fur coat industry. From Kastoria, driving north to the border with Albania and Macedonia (Former Yugoslav Republic of), are the **Prespa Lakes** (**Limnes Prespes**) contained within the **Prespa Lakes National Park**.

THRACE: Going east from Macedonia, the towns and villages become more oriental in style. **Xanthi** is an attractive small town clinging to the hilly sides of the **Remma Valley**. Southwest of Xanthi is **Avdira**. Nearby **Lagos**, built on the narrow strip of land in the lagoon, is rich in wildfowl. One of the best northern beaches is 8km (5 miles) east of **Fanari**. The main road dips down to the coast before going inland again to **Komotini**, further east, then follows the coast via **Nea Hili** to **Alexandroupolis**, which has an archaeological museum of local finds. North from here is **Soufli**, famous for its silks. East from here lies the **River Evros**, marking the natural boundary with **Turkey**.

SARONIC ISLANDS

Lying south of Athens and to the east of the Peloponnese, these islands are within easy reach of the capital, with regular ferry and hydrofoil services running from the port of Piraeus. Aegina, Hydra, Poros, Salamis and Spetses are the most popular islands, with Hydra as the indisputable highlight.

SALAMIS: (Perama, 1 nautical mile.) Closest to the mainland, Salamis (Salamina) can be reached from both Piraeus and Perama. There are reasonable sandy beaches at **Iliakti**, **Kanakia**, **Moulki** and **Peristeria**, though the island's natural beauty is somewhat spoilt by the proximity of heavy industry. The island has good roads and a network of bus and taxi services.

AEGINA: (Piraeus, 17.5 nautical miles.) Famed for pistachios and ceramics, Aegina (Egina) makes a perfect daytrip from Athens, thanks to its excellent beaches, clear seas and proximity to Piraeus. Boats arrive at the main port, **Aegina Town**. East from here, on top of a wooded hill offering panoramic views, stands the **Temple of Aphaia** made up of 22 Doric columns erected in the fifth century BC. On the coast, below the temple, **Agia Marina** is the island's most popular resort, thanks to its long sandy beach. South of Aegina Town lies **Perdika**, a pretty fishing village with a good sandy beach and boat trips running to the small wooded islands of **Angistri** and **Moni**. Aegina is relatively flat. Bicycles are available for hire, and it is possible to take a ride in a horsedrawn carriage. The island is also served by buses and taxis.

POROS: (Piraeus, 35 nautical miles.) Poros is a thickly wooded island separated from the Peloponnese by a very narrow channel. Regular boats cross the channel from **Galatas**, on the Peloponnese mainland. There is also a service from Piraeus. The island was formed through the union of two smaller islands, **Kalavria** and **Sphaeria**. The chief settlement, **Poros Town**, is known for its white buildings with blue woodwork, typical of Greek island architecture. Close by lie the remains of the **Sanctuary of Poseidon**, built in the sixth century BC. The best sand beaches lie at **Askeli** and **Neorio**.

HYDRA: (Piraeus, 42 nautical miles.) A barren, rocky, car-free island, Hydra (Idra) is popular with artists and jet-setters, primarily for the beauty of its chief settlement and port, **Hydra Town**. Built into the hill overlooking the harbour, Hydra Town is a labyrinth of steep cobbled streets, filled with chic bars, restaurants and art galleries. 500m (1640ft) above town stands a monastery, offering fantastic views out over the sea. There are a number of small hotels and private rooms to rent, though visitors should make reservations well in advance as Hydra is extremely busy through high season. Being so rocky, there are few good beaches, but it is possible to swim south of town at **Kaminia**, **Molos** and **Vlichos**, and north of town at **Mandraki**.

SPETSES: (Piraeus, 35 nautical miles.) Located at the southern extremity of the Saronic Gulf, Spetses has long been a popular holiday retreat for wealthy Athenians, who are attracted here by good beaches, beautiful pine woods and fresh air. Cars are forbidden, except to residents. Bicycles are available for rent, and the island is served by buses and taxis. There are plenty of good hotels and entertainment facilities in the chief settlement, **Spetses Town**. The best beaches lie at **Agia Anangiri** and **Agia Pasaskevi**.

Credit: © Greek National Tourist Office

IONIAN ISLANDS

Located off the west coast of mainland Greece, the seven Ionian Islands (Cephalonia, Corfu, Ithaki, Kythira, Lefkada, Paxi and Zakinthos) are comparatively isolated from one another. Consequently, through the centuries each one has developed its own identity. The most popular islands are Cephalonia, Corfu and Kythira. Ferry connections to each destination are given within their relative section.

CORFU: (Igoumenitsa, 18 nautical miles.) The northernmost island of western Greece, Corfu is the best-known, busiest and most cosmopolitan of the Ionian islands. Although its natural beauty has led to rampant commercialisation along parts of the coast, visitors who arrive during spring or autumn will still find idyllic beaches, romantic landscapes studded with cypresses and olive groves, and unspoilt inland villages.

The capital, **Corfu Town**, is presided over by two imposing Venetian fortresses and gives onto a series of pretty harbours and bays. With Italian, French and English influences evident in its architecture, it is made up of wide avenues and large squares, among them the graceful **Spianada** or esplanade, cobbled alleyways, arches and colonnades. Worth visiting are the **Archaeological Museum**, which houses finds from local excavations; the **Byzantine Museum**, with a fine collection of icons; and the **Museum of Asiatic Art**. The **Town Hall**, a splendid example of 17th-century Venetian architecture, and the 12th-century Byzantine **Church of St Jason and Sosipater** and the **Church of St Spyridon** are also of interest. At **Kanoni**, on the tip of a small peninsular south of the town centre, a narrow causeway leads to the much photographed **Monastery of Vlacherna**. From here, it is possible to take a boat to the tiny island of **Pondikonissi**, crowned by a 13th-century church.

South of Corfu Town, at **Gastouri**, stands the 19th-century **Achillion**, the summer palace of Empress Elizabeth of Austria, surrounded by beautiful Italian-style gardens. West of town, built into a rocky hill, lies the village of **Pelekas**, reputedly the best place to watch the sunset. Close by, the **Ropa Valley** (**Livaditou Ropa**) is home to the excellent **Corfu Golf Club**. North of town lie the popular seaside resorts of **Ipsos**, **Kassiopi** and **Sidari**, the latter known for its unique rock formations and beaches, which have unfortunately been somewhat spoilt by commercial development. Northwest of Corfu Town, the fortunately unspoilt resort of **Paleokastritsa** offers crystal clear seawater and two delightful sandy coves for bathing. Close by stands **Angelokastro**, a 13th-century Byzantine fortress. Corfu can be reached by ferry from either Patras (see *Peloponnese* section) or Igoumenitsa (on the northwest coast of mainland Greece, just south of Albania), and there are direct ferries from Italy in summer. The island's airport offers direct flights to Athens and several other European cities.

CEPHALONIA: (Patras, 53 nautical miles.) Best known as the setting of Louis de Bernières *Captain Corelli's Mandolin*, Cephalonia is the biggest Ionian island. The mountainous scenery, culminating with the 1600m (5250ft) **Mount Enos**, is dramatic and the island has a good network of roads.

The chief settlement, **Argostoli**, was largely destroyed in the disastrous 1953 earthquake. However, the **Archaeological Museum** and **Folk Art Museum** are both worth visiting, and the nearby beaches of **Makris** and **Platis Gialos** are perfect for bathing. Inland, close to **Perata**, stands the 16th-century **St George's Castle** (**Agios Georgios**), built by the Venetians. **Lixouri** is peaceful and old-fashioned, and a little south from here lie some of the island's best beaches. On the northwest coast, the village of **Assos** is known for its picturesque castle. **Fiskardo**, the northernmost harbour, is unspoilt and has some good beaches. On the east coast, the **Cave of Melissani**, noted for its extraordinary colours caused by the reflection of the sun's rays through the sea, can be visited by boat. Cephalonia can be reached by ferry from Patras. The island's airport offers direct flights to Athens.

KYTHERA: (Piraeus, 28 nautical miles.) Lying at the southeastern tip of the Peloponnese, Kythera is the southernmost Ionian island. Much loved by artists such as Watteau, it was often portrayed as a 'Garden of Paradise' and has some beautiful sand beaches.

The capital, **Kythera Town**, is a neat settlement overlooking the sea, close to the main port of **Kapsali**. The second port, **Agia Pelagia**, is the main tourist centre. At **Milopotamos** stand the ruins of a Byzantine town and the **Cave of St Sophia**, formerly used as a chapel and adorned with frescoes, stalagmites and stalactites. Kythera can be reached by ferry from Piraeus and Monemvassia. During summer there are also direct flights from Athens.

THE CYCLADES

Lying east of the Peloponnese and southeast of the coast of Attica in the Aegean, a total of 30 islands make up the Cyclades, the best-known being Mykonos and Santorini. Other popular islands are Andros, Delos, Naxos, Paros and Tinos, while the small islands of the eastern Cyclades are less visited and offer only basic amenities. All can be reached by ferry from Piraeus, and several have small airports with daily fights to Athens through summer.

ANDROS: (Piraeus, 89 nautical miles.) Most northerly of the Cyclades, Andros is a green mountainous island planted with olive groves, vineyards and pine trees. Its capital, **Andros Town**, is made up of typical white cottages, plus a number of neoclassical-style town houses and the remains of a 13th-century Venetian castle. Worth visiting are the **Archaeological Museum**, displaying a rich collection of finds from the excavations on the island; the **Museum of Modern Art**, staging exhibitions of contemporary Greek artists; and the **Maritime Museum**.

There are many fine beaches, the largest being at **Batsi**, which also has several small hotels. Other places of interest are **Paleopolis**, the island's ancient port, much of which now lies below the sea, though some ruins can still be seen; **Panachrantou Monastery** at **Falika**; and the **Byzantine Church of Taxiarchon** in **Messaria**. **Apikia** is known for its mineral springs. The principal port is **Gavrio**, west of Andros Town.

TINOS: (Piraeus, 86 nautical miles.) The island's largest settlement, **Tinos Town**, is best known as a pilgrimage site. Each year believers gather here to pay their respect to an icon of *Our Lady* (said to perform miracles) kept in the **Church of the Annunciate Virgin** (**Evangelistria**). The town's second attraction is the **Archaeological Museum**, exhibiting finds from the ancient **Temple of Poseidon**. Remains of the temple itself can be seen at **Kionia**, northeast of town, where there is also a good beach. Buses connect Tinos Town to the island's numerous villages, the most interesting being **Pirgos**, noted for its sculpture school and marble workshops, plus another pleasant beach.

MYKONOS: (Piraeus, 95 nautical miles.) The most visited and most expensive of all the Greek islands, Mykonos is known for its lively nightlife and some of Greece's best discos. It is now especially popular among the international gay community. **Mykonos Town** (also known as **Hora**) comprises a modern harbour, whitewashed houses and churches, shops selling local arts and crafts, small tavernas and cafes, and is backed by a hill with five thatched windmills. The **Paraportiani Church**, a complex of four chapels, is considered to be an architectural masterpiece. The **Archaeological Museum** exhibits finds excavated from the necropolis on the nearby islet of **Rhenia**. There is also a **Folklore Museum**. Interesting excursions can be made to the monasteries of **Agios Panteleimon**, close to Mykonos Town, and the **Tourliani Monastery**, close to the old fishing village of **Ano Mera**. Beaches range from cosmopolitan to secluded, the most popular being **Agios Stefanos** and **Platis Gialos**. On the south side of the island lie several unspoilt nudist beaches, the best known being **Paradise** and **Super Paradise**, which can be reached by boat from Plati Gialos. It is also possible to visit the uninhabited island of **Delos** (see *Delos* section) by boat from Mykonos Town.

Through summer, there are daily flights from Mykonos to Athens.

DELOS: (Mykonos, 6 nautical miles.) The religious and political centre of the Aegean in ancient times, the tiny island of Delos is said to have been the birthplace of Apollo and Artemis. Today uninhabited, it is possible to visit this superb archaeological site, arriving by boat from Mykonos. Star attractions include the **Avenue of the Lions**, featuring five crouching stone lions, guardians of the Sacred Lake, and the **Sanctuary of Apollo**, made up of three temples. The **Archaeological Museum** exhibits archaic, Classical, Hellenistic and Roman sculptures, including the **Archaic Sphinx of the Naxians** and **Acroteria** (**Victories**) from the **Temple of the Athenians**, found in excavations on the site.

PAROS: (Piraeus, 95 nautical miles.) The island's hinterland has undulating hills that contain the famous Parian marble. It is becoming an increasingly popular tourist destination, thanks to its sand beaches, unspoilt fishing villages, reasonably priced hotels and lively nightlife. **Parikia**, the island's picturesque capital and main port, is built on the site of the ancient city. There is a ruined Venetian castle and close to the port stands the impressive sixth-century Byzantine church of **Ekatondapiliani** (Church of a Hundred Doors). A number of good beaches lie near **Naousia**, the island's second port, notably **Kolimbithres**, where the rugged coast forms inlets with golden sands. Of the island's monasteries, **Zoodohos Pigi Longovarda** and **Christou Tou Dassous** are the most significant.

Antiparos is separated from Paros by a narrow channel. The main attraction on this small island is its famous cave with stalactites. There are also several hotels and a number of good sand beaches. Through summer, there are daily flights from Paros to Athens.

NAXOS: (Piraeus, 103 nautical miles.) The largest and most fertile island in the Cyclades islands, Naxos lies almost in the centre of the Aegean. The capital and main port, **Naxos Town** (also known as **Hora**) is crowned by the ruins of a Venetian castle. A little way out of town, the **Pirgos Bellonia** (Bellonian Tower) was built under Venetian rule (note the Lion of St Mark emblem) as a refuge from pirates. The island is particularly noted for its numerous sand beaches, and just south of Naxos Town lie the bathing areas of **Agia Anna**, **Agios Georgios** and **Agios Prokopios**. The island's second town and port, **Apolonas**, also has an excellent beach. The inland village of **Halki** has a medieval fortress and several Byzantine churches.

Through summer, there are daily flights from Naxos to Athens.

SANTORINI: (Piraeus, 127 nautical miles.) Considered by many as the most dramatically beautiful of all the Greek islands, Santorini (also known as Thira) was formed by the eruption of a now dormant volcano around 1600 BC. Arrival by ferry brings one to the west side of the island, with the whitewashed cliff top villages of **Fira** (the capital) and **Ia** (the Aegean's most photographed town) overlooking the circular *caldera* (a huge depression created by a volcanic explosion). A steep winding path leads up from the harbour of **Skala** to **Fira**, where one finds many excellent hotels, chic restaurants and bars, and a vibrant nightlife. The **Archaeology Museum**, displaying finds from the excavations at **Akrotiri**, is worth a visit. From Fira, a mountain path leads along the cliff edge to Ia, noted for its beautiful white buildings with blue domes. On the east side of the island lie the archaeological remains of **Ancient Thira**, a Dorian city dating back to the ninth century BC. Akrotiri is also of great interest for the relics of the Minoan civilisation which were buried under lava following the eruption of 1600 BC: about 40 buildings have been uncovered to date. The 18th-century **Monastery of Profitas Ilias** on the island's summit and the swimming beaches of **Perissa** and **Kamari** are other attractions. Through summer, there are daily flights from Santorini to Athens.

KEA: (Piraeus, 42 nautical miles.) Kea is dotted with small cultivated valleys, sandy beaches, fruit orchards, clusters of whitewashed houses, several windmills and a large number of churches. A short distance inland from the port of **Korissia** lies the chief settlement **Hora** (also known as Kea Town). The **Convent of Panagia Kastriani**, overlooking **Otzia Bay**, is worth visiting. At **Koundouro** and **Pisses**, there are good swimming beaches.

KITHNOS: (Piraeus, 54 nautical miles.) A small island, the harsh landscape of Kithnos is softened by vineyards and fig trees. Most hotels are found in the small port towns of **Loutra** (noted for its warm medical springs) and **Merihas**. The main town, **Hora** (also known as **Messaria**), is built into a barren hillside. White Cycladic cottages, churches with frescoes and icons and the islanders' hospitality combine to make Kithnos increasingly popular with visitors in search of beauty and quiet.

SERIFOS: (Piraeus, 70 nautical miles.) Ships calling at the island anchor at **Livadi**, which is surrounded by gardens and orchards. From here the road climbs up to Hora (the chief settlement), where narrow paved alleys are lined by typical Cycladic houses and churches. Higher still stands the old Venetian fortress. Attractive beaches are to be found at **Mega Livadi** and **Koutalas**.

SIROS: (Piraeus, 80 nautical miles.) Siros lies at the heart of the Cycladic complex. Its capital and main port, **Ermoupolis**, has many notable neoclassical buildings, such as the **Town Hall** and the **Apollo Municipal Theatre** (which is a miniature copy of *La Scala* in Milan), plus spacious public squares and impressive churches. Upper Siros retains a strong medieval flavour with city walls, narrow cobbled streets and arcades.

SIFNOS: (Piraeus, 78 nautical miles.) Sifnos is the most popular of the western Cyclades. An attractive drive inland from the port of **Kamares** leads to the main settlement, **Apollonia**, made up of distinctive Cycladic houses, a number of notable churches, and the **Museum of Folklore**. Other places to see are the atmospheric medieval town of **Kastro**, and the village of **Artemonas**, built on gently undulating hills surrounded by picturesque windmills. There are good beaches at **Faros** and **Vathy**.

MILOS: (Piraeus, 82 nautical miles.) This beautiful island has been inseparably associated with Venus since a statue of the goddess of love, which is now in the Louvre in Paris, was found here during the 19th century. A copy of the statue can be seen in the **Archaeological Museum** in the chief settlement, **Plaka**. Also of interest in Plaka are the remains of a hilltop Frankish castle and the 13th-century Byzantine **Church of Thalassitras**. Close to Plaka, at **Tripiti**, there are extensive early-Christian **catacombs**. The best beaches and accommodation are found at **Apollonia** and **Adamas** (the island's port), and a number of sea caves, notably **Sikia** (also known as the *Blue Cave*) and **Kleftiko**, can be visited by boat.

IOS: (Piraeus, 114 nautical miles.) The chief settlement of this extremely popular island, **Hora** (also known as **Ios Town**), stands above the small harbour of **Ormos** and the attractive swimming beaches of **Milopotas** and **Yalos**. Hora boasts whitewashed cottages, a number of interesting churches and the ruins of a 15th-century hilltop fortress. Each year, thanks to a steady influx of visitors, numerous summer discos open up in Hora.

NORTHEAST AEGEAN ISLANDS

The four most popular islands of this group are Chios, Lemnos, Lesbos and Samos, all of which lie fairly far apart in the waters of the northeast Aegean, close to Turkey. It is possible to reach each of these islands by ferry from Piraeus.

CHIOS: (Piraeus, 153 nautical miles.) Lying just 8km from Turkey, this surprisingly unexploited island offers excellent beaches, unspoilt medieval towns and stunning landscapes. The north side of the island is dominated by **Pelinio**, a 1297m- (4255ft-) high mountain of volcanic origin. The capital and main port, **Chios Town**, lies on the eastern shore. Several of the town's churches, which date back to Byzantine times, were converted into mosques by the Turks, but have since resumed their Christian function. The **Byzantine Museum** is housed in a former 19th-century mosque. In the hills east of town lies the splendid 12th-century monastery of **Nea Moni**, one of the country's finest Byzantine monuments, with a beautiful octagonal church adorned with golden mosaics. The inland villages on the south side of the island have conserved a medieval appearance, the best examples being **Pirgi** and **Mesta**. Pirgi is unique in that all the building facades are decorated with grey and white geometric designs, known as *xista*. The settlement of Mesta is made up of narrow winding streets and traditional cottages, many of which offer tourist accommodation, plus a fine Byzantine church.

There is an airport, providing daily flights to and from Athens.

SAMOS: (Piraeus, 174 nautical miles.) Separated from Turkey by a narrow strait, Samos is an island of forested hills, olive groves, vineyards and meadows. **Samos Town**, the island's capital, is divided into two parts: the new quarter, which developed during the 19th century; and the old quarter, **Ano Vathi**, on a hill above the port. The **Archaeological Museum** displays finds from **Heraion**, an ancient sanctuary located on the southeast coast. **Pythagorio**, a lively fishing port and tourist resort, was known as Tigani until 1955, when it was renamed in honour of its best known citizen, the philosopher and mathematician, Pythagoras. From Samos Town a good asphalt road runs the length of the northern coast to **Potami**, passing through the picturesque villages of **Kokari**, **Tsamadou** and **Avlakia**, each of which have good beaches close by, and Karlovassi, renowned for its excellent sweet wine.

There is an airport, providing daily flights to and from Athens.

LESBOS: (Piraeus, 118 nautical miles.) Lesbos, home of the ancient poet Sappho, is the largest island in this group, with vast olive groves, shady pinewoods, good beaches and picturesque monasteries. The capital, **Mitilini**, is dominated by a 14th-century castle, and has a nearby beach with good facilities. There are more good beaches at **Agios Issidoros**, **Petra**, **Skala Eftalou** and **Vateron** and along the **Gulf of Kaloni** on the south coast of the island. At **Loutropoli Thermis**, there are therapeutic springs which have been known since antiquity. **Mithimna** (**Molivos**), on the north of the island, is popular with artists and has a fine pebble beach.

There is an airport, providing daily flights to and from Athens.

LEMNOS: (Piraeus, 188 nautical miles.) Lemnos is still relatively unknown to mainstream tourism. **Mirina**, its capital, is built on the site of an ancient city of the same name and has an **Archaeological Museum** housing exhibits from around the island. The hilltop castle, extended successively by the Venetians, Genovese and Turks, offers wonderful views. North of the town, close to the village of **Kaspakas**, lies **Kaspakas Bay** with several excellent sand beaches. Likewise, south of town, close to the village of **Plati**, lies the **Bay of Plati** and another large sand beach. To the east of the island, ancient ruins are found at **Poliohni** and **Ifestia**.

There is an airport, providing daily flights to and from Athens.

SPORADES ISLANDS

East of the Thessaly region on mainland Greece lie the four islands of the Sporades – Alonissos, Skiathos, Skiros and Skopelos. They are becoming very popular and it is advisable to book early, especially in the high season. It is possible to reach these islands by either ferry or hydrofoil from Volos on the mainland, and from Kimi on Euboea. Skiathos and Skiros can also be reached by plane from Athens.

SKIATHOS: (Volos, 41 nautical miles.) Planted with pine trees and olive groves, Skiathos is a popular tourist destination, thanks to its indented coast with numerous sandy coves. The capital, **Skiathos Town**, was built in 1830 on two low hills. The seafront is lined with cafes and seafood restaurants, and there is a good marina. Numerous hotels, villas and private rooms provide seasonal accommodation, and the town's bars and discos ensure a vibrant nightlife through summer. Boat trips take tourists around the island to visit the **Blue Cave**, the ruins of the medieval walled town of **Kastro** on the south coast, and the pebble beach of **Lalaria**. From Skiathos Town, a good road follows the southern coast with its many bays, to arrive at the renowned pine grove beach of **Koukounaries**.

There is an airport, providing daily flights to and from Athens the year round.

SKOPELOS: (Volos, 58 nautical miles.) This island has small bays, golden sands and slopes covered with pine forests, olive groves and plum trees (prunes are a local speciality). Less busy than Skiathos, it is known for its traditional architecture and tiny white chapels. The main settlement, **Skopelos Town**, is made up of narrow cobbled streets, whitewashed houses and the Venetian **Kastro** (fortress). The island has numerous beaches, both of sand and pebble, and shallow waters safe for children.

There is an airport, providing daily flights to and from Athens during summer.

ALONISSOS: (Volos, 62 nautical miles.) The most distant and least populated island of the Sporades, the hills of

Alonissos are covered with unspoilt woods. There are limited tourist facilities – a number of small hotels and private rooms to let. With only 10km (6 miles) of roads, the best way of getting about is by motorboat, sharing the fare. There are a number of good beaches, but as the coast has been declared a Marine Conservation Park, building development is forbidden.
SKIROS: (Kimi, 25 nautical miles; Piraeus, 118 nautical miles.) The largest of the Sporades, Skiros lies far out from Volos and is most easily accessed from Kimi on Euboea. Tourist facilities are not particularly developed, though there are some beautiful sand beaches, good tavernas serving authentic seafood and local cheeses, and interesting craft shops. The main settlement, **Skiros Town** (also known as **Horio**), is made up of whitewashed cottages and narrow winding alleys, crowned by the hilltop Venetian **Kastro** (fortress). The **Folklore Museum** gives an excellent presentation of local handicrafts, and includes a reconstruction of a traditional house. Close to town lies the large sand beach of **Magazia**.

DODECANESE ISLANDS

This cluster of 12 (*dodeca*) islands lies east of Peloponnese, closer to Turkey than to mainland Greece. All the islands can be reached by ferry from Piraeus, and distances between them are fairly small, so visitors can easily hop from one to another, swapping the relative sophistication of Rhodes and Kos for the calmer and simpler life on Tilos or Astipalaia.
RHODES: (Piraeus, 267 nautical miles.) One of the most popular and best-developed islands in the Mediterranean, Rhodes offers international-class hotels, varied nightlife and good sports facilities. It has 370km (230 miles) of coastline and a good, well-surfaced road network, with bus services linking most of the towns and villages. Travel agents organise daily sightseeing trips to the archaeological sites and beauty spots.
The capital, **Rhodes Town**, lies almost at the northern tip of the island. It is made up of two distinct parts – an old town and a new town. The old town, contained within the walls of a medieval fortress, centres of the **Avenue of the Knights**, lined with magnificent medieval buildings, including the monumental 14th-century **Palace of the Grand Masters**. The 15th-century **Knight's Hospital** now houses the **Archaeological Museum**. 2km (1.2 miles) west of the town walls lies the **Acropolis of Ancient Rhodes**. Many impressive ruins can still be seen, including the **Temple of Apollo**, and a theatre and stadium dating back to the second century BC.
Just out of town lie the main tourist complexes of **Faliraki** on the east coast, and **Ixia** and **Ialissos** (also known as **Trianda**) on the west coast, all with numerous hotels and good beaches. At **Filerimos**, 15km (9 miles) from Rhodes Town, lie the ruins of ancient **Ialisos**, and 25km (16 miles) southwest from here stand the remains of ancient **Kameiros**. 56km (35 miles) southeast of the capital stands the delightful town of **Lindos**, made up of winding streets and whitewashed buildings, crowned by a 15th-century hilltop fortress standing aside an imposing ancient **Acropolis**. Rhodes can be reached by ferry from Piraeus. There are regular flights to Athens and several other Greek islands, plus a number of European cities.
KOS: (Piraeus, 201 nautical miles.) This fertile island boasts sandy beaches (some of black volcanic sand) and ample hotel accommodation. Most places of historical and sightseeing interest lie in or close to the main settlement, **Kos Town**, and can be visited on foot or bicycle (available for hire). Activity centres on **Platia tou Platanou**, a piazza named after the **Plane Tree of Hippocrates**, a massive tree (12m (39ft) in circumference), beneath which the philosopher Hippocrates is said to have taught his students.
Close by, the 15th-century **Castle of the Knights of St John** is accessed across a drawbridge. There are also some interesting ancient Greek and Roman archaeological sites. From Kos Town, a road traverses the length of the island all the way to **Kefalos**, a town on the southwest coast with an old **Fortress** and a splendid beach. Also of note is **Kardamena**, a pretty fishing village and well-developed resort with many hotels and beautiful sand beaches.
Kos can be reached by ferry from Piraeus and Rhodes. There are regular flights to Athens and Rhodes.
SIMI: (Piraeus, 235 nautical miles.) A lovely mountainous island with several good beaches, Simi offers limited hotels and tourist facilities. The chief settlement, **Simi Town**, is divided between Ano Simi (upper town) and Kato Poli (lower town). The lower town, also known as **Yialos**, is made up of charming pastel-coloured, neoclassical mansions built close to the port, while the upper town is capped by the ruins of a castle, built by the Knights of St John. On the southwest coast stands the 18th-century **Monastery of St Michel of Panormitis**.
Simi can be reached by ferry from both Piraeus and Rhodes.
KARPATHOS: (Piraeus, 227 nautical miles.) Karpathos, a mountainous island with fertile valleys and several good beaches, lies between Rhodes and Crete. The main settlement and port, **Karpathos Town** (also known as **Pigadia**), sits in a bay on the southeast coast. It was built primarily from funds sent home by immigrants to the USA and does not reflect the traditional style found in the older villages, but has good tourist facilities and numerous hotels. From the island's second port, **Diafani**, on the northern coast, a road leads to **Olimbos**, an isolated but well-preserved medieval village where local customs are very much alive.
Karpathos can be reached by ferry from both Piraeus and Rhodes. There are regular flights to Athens and Rhodes.
KASSOS: (Piraeus, 255 nautical miles.) Kassos, the most southern of the Dodecanese lies just 3 nautical miles from Karpathos. **Emborios**, the port, and **Fri**, the principal town, are picturesque settlements, both with good beaches. **Selai**, a cave to the west of the village of **Agia Marina**, is filled with impressive stalactites.
Kassos can be reached by ferry from Piraeus.

PATMOS: (Piraeus, 140 nautical miles.) St John is said to have been exiled to Patmos and was inspired to write his *Revelations* here. During the 11th century, the massive fortified **Monastery of St John the Divine** was built above the capital, **Patmos Town** (also known as **Hora**), to honour the saint. The monastery is worth visiting for its church and chapels, displaying Byzantine icons, and also for the panoramic view it affords out to sea. The island's main tourist resorts are **Skala** and **Grikos**. Skala, made up of whitewashed houses, bars and tavernas, is also the principal port, and lies 2km (1.2 miles) from Hora Town. Grikos is built overlooking **Grikos Bay** and has a fine beach nearby.
Patmos can be reached by ferry from Piraeus.
KALIMNOS: (Piraeus, 180 nautical miles.) Kalimnos is famous for its sponge fishing – a tradition which is expressed in many folk songs and local dances. Along the northwest coast of the island there are several resorts with lovely beaches, notably **Mirties** and **Massouri**. Good hotels can also be found in the chief settlement, **Pothia**, a cheerful port town with brightly coloured houses, founded in 1850. Close to Pothia lies **Therma**, a well-equipped spa with therapeutic bathing installations and overnight accommodation. The old capital, **Horio**, stands below the remains of a medieval castle. Kalimnos can be reached by ferry from Piraeus.
LEROS: (Piraeus, 169 nautical miles.) Leros is an island of fertile valleys, green hills and unspoilt beaches. The chief settlement, **Agia Marina**, is made up of steep winding alleyways, whitewashed houses, and several neoclassical buildings, and crowned by a 14th-century Byzantine fortress. Most hotels are found in **Laki** (one of the Mediterranean's largest natural harbours) and **Alinda**, both of which have fine beaches.
Leros can be reached by ferry from Piraeus and by plane from Athens.
TILOS: (Piraeus, 290 nautical miles.) Little known by tourists, Tilos is a hilly island with many isolated and unspoilt beaches. The main settlements are the inland town of **Megalo Horio**, crowned by a medieval castle, and **Livadia**, the island's port. Close to Megalo Horio it is possible to visit the monastery of **Agios Antonios**.
Tilos can be reached by ferry from Piraeus.
NISSIROS: (Piraeus, 200 nautical miles.) This small volcanic island lies between Kos and Tilos. The capital and port, **Mandraki**, is built below a medieval castle. Close by at

Credit: © Greek National Tourist Office

Loutra lie the renowned hot springs, while in the centre of the island one can visit the vast smouldering crater, formed in 1522 by a massive volcanic explosion.
Nissiros can be reached by ferry from Kos, Piraeus and Rhodes.
HALKI: (Piraeus, 302 nautical miles.) Halki is a small hilly island, little known by tourists. From the main settlement and port, **Nimborio** (also known as Halki), **Potamo** is the only beach accessible on foot, though many other beautiful unspoilt beaches can be reached by boat. The island's second town and former capital, **Horio**, was built inland to avoid pirate attacks. Halki can be reached by ferry from Piraeus.
ASTIPALAIA: (Piraeus, 165 nautical miles.) The westernmost of the Dodecanese, Astipalaia is mountainous but fertile, and little discovered by tourists. The capital, also called Astipalaia, is built on a steep hill and dominated by an austere Venetian castle. The most beautiful part of the island is around **Livadia**, where there is a fine sandy beach. **Astipalaia** can be reached by ferry from Piraeus and by plane from Athens.

CRETE

(Piraeus, 174 nautical miles.) Crete is the largest and most southerly Greek island. Despite a busy tourist industry concentrated along the north coast, Crete has preserved its unspoilt nature, local traditions and ancient monuments. The Minoan culture, Europe's first advanced civilisation, developed here between 2800 and 1000 BC. When Constantinople fell to the Ottomans in 1453, many artists took refuge on the island, founding the renowned 'Cretan School' of painters.
The capital and main port, **Heraklion** (**Iraklio**), offers a variety of cafes, restaurants, nightlife and sightseeing opportunities. The old town lies within the 16th-century Venetian city walls, while the harbour is protected by **Koules**, an imposing Venetian Fortress. The **National Archaeological Museum** is one of the country's top museums, displaying finds from the Minoan era, and the **History Museum** tells the island's story from Byzantine times up to the present day. Close to town stand three wonderful Minoan sites – **Knossos**, **Malia** and **Phaestos**. The palace at Knossos, founded in 2000 BC, was a vast city of 50,000 inhabitants, destroyed around 1600 BC by earth movements provoked by the volcanic eruption on Santorini. The highlights here are the frescoed sanctuary and the royal apartments. Another palace, built on an identical plan around a central courtyard, can be seen at Phaestos, though the frescoes here are not so well preserved. The remains of yet a third palace can be seen at Malia.
East of Heraklion, **Agios Nikolaos**, one of the island's best-known holiday resorts, overlooks the **Gulf of Mirambello** and several fine beaches. East from here stands **Sitia**, another popular resort with bars, restaurants, hotels and a Venetian fortress. West of Heraklion, the well-preserved port town of **Rethimno** is made up of narrow winding alleys conserving a number of 16th-century Venetian stone buildings and 19th-century Turkish houses with traditional wooden balconies. At the western end of the island, **Hania** has a mixture of modern, neoclassical and Venetian architecture, plus a **Naval Museum** and good beaches. South of Hania, the beautiful **Samaria Gorge**, declared a **National Park**, is the longest gorge in Europe. Keen hikers will be able to walk the 18km (11.2 miles) length in a day, while the less sporting can join an organised tour, departing from Hania.
The only major resort on the south side of the island is the small port of **Matala**, offering good sandy beaches and excellent fish restaurants.
Crete can be reached by ferry from Piraeus. There are airports at Hania, Iraklio and Sitia, with regular flights to Athens and several other Greek islands, plus a number of European cities.

AEGEAN SEA
Rhodes
Ixia
Kremasti
Ialisos
Kalithia
Faliraki
Kameiros
Afandou
Alimnia
Kritinia
Profitis Elias
Ataviros 1215m
Arkhangelos
RHODES
Lindos
Cape Lardhos
Genadi
Katavia
Prasonisi
DAB-M292
30km
15mls
international airport

Sport & Activities

Watersports: There are excellent facilities along all coastlines of the mainland and particularly in the islands. Most major hotels can help with arrangements. **Water-skiing** is especially popular and there are over 30 water-ski schools in Greece with restaurants and child-care facilities. **Speed boats** are also available for hire. Independent **scuba-diving** is strictly forbidden, in order to guard against the pilfering of underwater antiquities. Divers may only venture out under the auspices of a recognised diving school. **Snorkelling** is permitted, however, and is possible practically anywhere. For further information, contact the Hellenic Federation of Underwater Activities, West Terminal Post Office, Agios Cosmos, 166 04 Hellenikon, Athens (tel: (210) 981 9961; fax: (210) 981 7558; website: www.sportsnet.gr *or* www.finswimming.org.gr
Fishing: Greek waters offer good fishing, particularly during the summer and autumn. Boats and equipment can be found in most villages.
Mountaineering: This is becoming increasingly popular and there is scope for **hill walking** and **climbing**. There are well-maintained trails in the most popular areas, supplemented by donkey and goat tracks connecting villages and leading over mountains. The best areas for walking include the *Peloponnese*, the *Pindos Mountains* and the south and west of *Crete*.
Other: Sites of **archaeological interest** abound, and the visitor can often come across ancient ruins and traces of lost civilisations. It is often advisable to use a guide when visiting the more remote regions. There are over 7000 **karstic cave formations** in the country, the majority in Crete. Further information on these caves is available from the Hellenic Speleological Society, 32 Sina Street, 106 72 Athens (tel: (210) 361 7824; fax: (210) 364 3476; e-mail:ellspe@otenet.gr; website: http://web.otenet.gr/ellspe). There are some **horse-riding** clubs in Greece (in Attica, Crete, Corfu and Thessaloniki).

Social Profile

FOOD & DRINK: Restaurant and taverna food tends to be very simple, rarely involving sauces but with full use of local olive oil and charcoal grills. Dishes like *dolmades* (stuffed vine leaves), *moussaka* (aubergine casserole with minced lamb, cinnamon, red wine and olive oil), *kebabs* and *avgolemono* (chicken broth with rice, eggs, salt and lemon juice) can be found everywhere. *Taramasalata* (a dip made from fish roe, bread, onion, olive oil and lemon juice) and a variety of seafood dishes, especially squid (*kalamari*) or octopus, are excellent. Greek menus typically include a selection of *meze* (appetisers), such as *keftedes* (hot spicy meatballs) or *tzatziki* (a dip made from yoghurt, olive oil, garlic, shredded cucumber and dill). Salads are excellent and often made with the local *feta* cheese, tomato, cucumber and fresh olive oil. Other vegetarian specialities include *gigantes* (large white beans) and *kolokithakia* (small boiled courgette with oil and lemon). Olives are cheap and plentiful. Deserts, such as *baklavas* (filo pastry filled with almonds and topped with honey, vanilla and sugar) or *loukoumades* (honey-drenched pastry puffs) are sweet and filling. All restaurants have a standard menu which includes the availability and price of each dish. A good proportion of the restaurants will serve international dishes. Hours are normally 1200-1500 for lunch and 2000-2400 for dinner. Waiter service is usual.
One of the best-known Greek drinks is *retsina* wine, made with pine-needle resin. Local spirits include *ouzo*, an aniseed-based clear spirit to which water is added and very similar to the French pastis. Local brandy is sharp and fiery. Greek coffee is served thick and strong, and sugared according to taste. Greek beer is a light *Pilsner* type. Opening hours vary according to the region and local laws.
NIGHTLIFE: This is centred in main towns and resorts with concerts and discos. Athens offers many local tavernas, particularly in the Plaka area, and *ouzeris* (typical Greek bars). Regular concerts and evening shows are also held at the Odeion of Herodes in Attica. Nightclubs featuring Greek *bouzouki* music are extremely popular. There are some casinos in Greece, such as the Mount Parnes Casino in Athens, the Corfu Casino in Corfu and the Casino at the Grand Hotel Astir in Rhodes.
SHOPPING: Special purchases include lace, jewellery, metalwork, pottery, garments and knitwear, furs, rugs, leather goods, local wines and spirits. Athens is the centre for luxury goods and local handicrafts. The flea markets in Monastiraki and Plaka, below the Acropolis, are all crowded in high season. Regional specialities include silver from Ioannina, ceramics from Sifnos and Skopelos, embroidery and lace from Crete, the Ionian Islands, Rhodes and Skiros, fur from Kastoria, alabaster from Crete and *flokati* rugs from the Epirus region. **Note:** (a) Visitors should be aware that many 'antiques' sold to tourists are fake; it is illegal to export any item of real antiquity without a special permit from the Export Department of the Ministry of Culture.
(b) Non-EU citizens can get a refund on Greek VAT (4 per cent on books and 18 per cent on nearly everything else); the process is fairly complex, but well worth it. Non-EU visitors may buy goods from certain shops bearing the sign 'Member of the Tax-Free Club' and have the VAT refunded, in cash, at special refund points at the airport. Ask store owners and tourist information offices for details.
SHOPPING HOURS: These vary according to the season, location and type of shop, but a rough guide follows: Mon, Wed, and Sat 0800-1430, Tues, Thurs and Fri 0800-1400 and 1730-2030.
Note: Most holiday resort shops stay open late in the evening.
SPECIAL EVENTS: For a complete list, contact the Greek/Hellenic National Tourism Organisation (see *Contact Addresses* section). The following is a selection of special events occurring in Greece in 2005:
Jan *Feast of St Basil* (the New Year's Cake is sliced, and the person whose slice contains a coin is said to have good luck for the coming year), nationwide; *The Gynaecocratia* (celebrates matriarchy with men and women reversing roles for the day), Kilkis, Komotini, Serres and Xanthi. **Jan 6** *Epiphany* (a cross is thrown into rivers, lakes and seas as the blessing of the waters takes place), nationwide. **Feb 7** *Shrove Monday* (the first day of Lent is welcomed with picnics in the country, kite flying and other special celebrations reflecting the local traditions of the villages), nationwide. **Mar** *Carnival* (a national celebration marked by pageantry and partying, fancy dress, masked figures, practical jokes and processions of Carnival chariots), nationwide; *Easter* (celebrated with feasts of spit-roasted lamb, red-dyed eggs and folk-dancing), nationwide, and especially at Livadia, Metsovo, Patras, Trapeza and Tripolis. **Mar 25** *Independence Day and Feast of the Annunciation* (the anniversary of Greek independence is marked with military parades in cities and larger towns, with Athens having the most spectacular celebrations). **May** *Anastenaria* (traditional fire-walking ritual), Serres and Thessaloniki. **May 1** *Labour Day and Flower Festival* (celebrated by country picnics), nationwide. **Jun** *Rally Acropolis* (drivers from throughout the world take part in auto race competition), Athens. **Jun 23-26** *AthFest* (music and arts festival). **Jul** *International Sailing Regatta*, Athens. **Jul-Aug** *Wine Festivals*, Alexandroupolis, Daphni, Patras and Rethymnon. **Aug** *Hippokrateia* (ancient drama performances, musical evenings, a flower show and a re-enactment of the Hippocratic Oath), Kos. **Oct-May** *Winter Cultural Season* (performances of opera, ballet and concerts), Greek National Opera House in Athens. **Oct-Nov** *Demetria Festival* (performances in music, dance, opera, theatre and art), Thessaloniki. **Oct 28** *Ochi! Day* (commemorates Greece's refusal to allow Mussolini's troops to enter the country), nationwide. **Nov** *International Marathon*, (retracing the original marathon route taken by a young warrior in 490 BC to announce the Athenian victory over the invading Persians), Athens. **Dec 6** *St Nikolas Day* (Christmas celebrations in Greece begin on this day, when children make their rounds singing carols, and continue until the end of the year), nationwide.
SOCIAL CONVENTIONS: Visitors to Greece will find the Greeks to be well aware of a strong historical and cultural heritage. Traditions and customs differ throughout Greece, but overall a strong sense of unity prevails. The Greek Orthodox Church has a strong traditional influence on the Greek way of life, especially in more rural areas. The throwing back of the head is a negative gesture. Dress is generally casual. Smoking is prohibited on public transport and in public buildings.
Tipping: 12 to 15 per cent is usual.

Business Profile

ECONOMY: Traditionally agricultural, accession to the EU gave a new impetus to the Greek economy, particularly the industrial sectors of textiles, clothing and shoes, cement, mining and metals, chemicals, steel and processed agricultural products. Nonetheless, 20 per cent of the working population still work the land – a very high proportion by EU standards. Tourism, the most important service industry, has boomed since the 1980s, with upwards of 10 million tourists now visiting the country annually. Shipping is also an important source of income: Greece has one of the largest merchant fleets in the world. Greek enterprises have consistently encountered difficulty penetrating European markets, however, because of the comparatively small size of the majority of businesses and high transport costs (owing to its geographical position). Nonetheless, the country exports large quantities of wheat, barley, maize, tobacco and fruit to the rest of the EU and elsewhere. The Greeks have benefited substantially from transfers of funds within the EU and support for its large public-sector debt. Growth is steady at around 5 per cent, with inflation at nearly 4 per cent. Unemployment has finally retreated from double figures, at 9.4 per cent in 2004. Greece's huge public-sector deficit prevented it from meeting the convergence criteria for the European single currency and the country entered the Euro zone in January 2001. The EU accounts for about 65 per cent of Greek trade. Outside the EU, Saudi Arabia (oil), Japan and the USA are the country's major trading partners.
BUSINESS: Formal suits are expected. French, German and English are often spoken as well as Greek.
COMMERCIAL INFORMATION: The following organisation can offer advice: Athens Chamber of Commerce & Industry (ACCI), 7 Akademias Street, 106 71 Athens (tel: (210) 362 5342; fax: (210) 361 8810; e-mail: info@acci.gr; website: www.acci.gr).
CONFERENCES/CONVENTIONS: Greece has many convention centres and hotels with conference facilities, in locations ideal for post-conference tours, eg Athens, Corfu, Crete, Halkidiki, Metsovo (Epirus) and Rhodes. It also has ships equipped for 'floating conferences', sailing between the islands. For further enquiries, contact the Greek/Hellenic National Tourism Organisation (see *Contact Addresses* section).

Climate

Greece has a warm Mediterranean climate. In summer, dry hot days are often relieved by stiff breezes, especially in the north and coastal areas. Athens can be stiflingly hot, so visitors should allow time to acclimatise. The evenings are cool. Winters are mild in the south but much colder in the north. November to March is the rainy season.
Required clothing: Lightweight clothes during summer months, including protection from the midday sun. Light sweaters are needed for evenings. Rainproofs are advised for autumn. Winter months can be quite cold, especially in the northern mainland, so normal winter wear will be required.

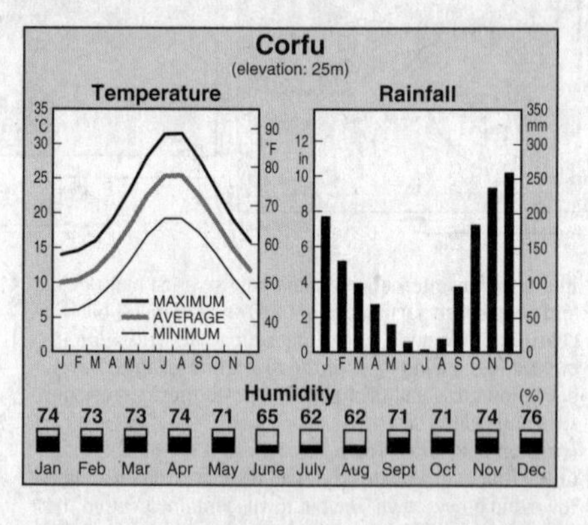

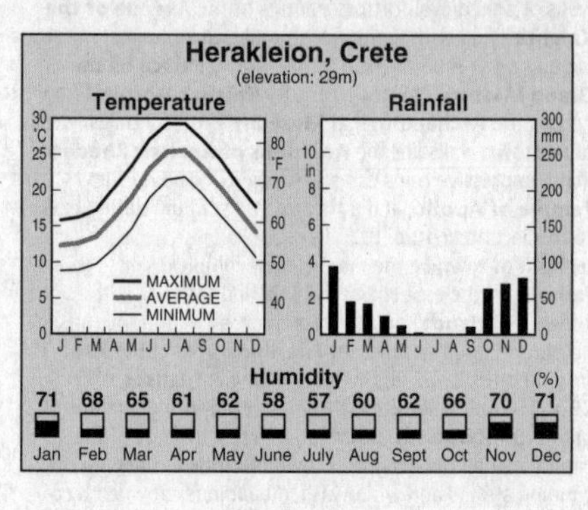

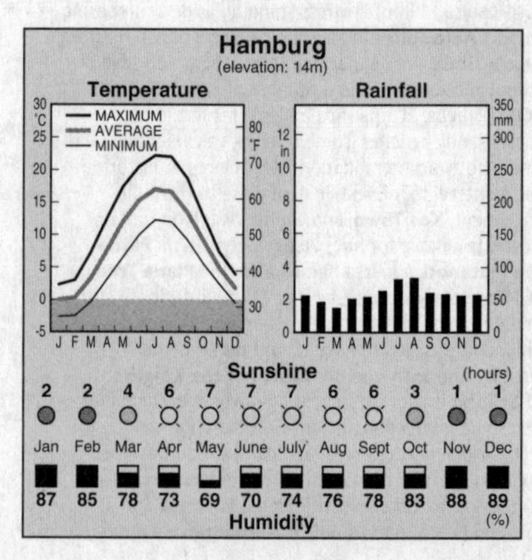

Greenland

LATEST TRAVEL ADVICE CONTACTS

British Foreign and Commonwealth Office
Tel: (0870) 606 0290 Website: www.fco.gov.uk
US Department of State
Website: http://travel.state.gov/travel
Canadian Department of Foreign Affairs and Int'l Trade
Tel: (1 800) 267 8376 Website: www.dfait-maeci.gc.ca

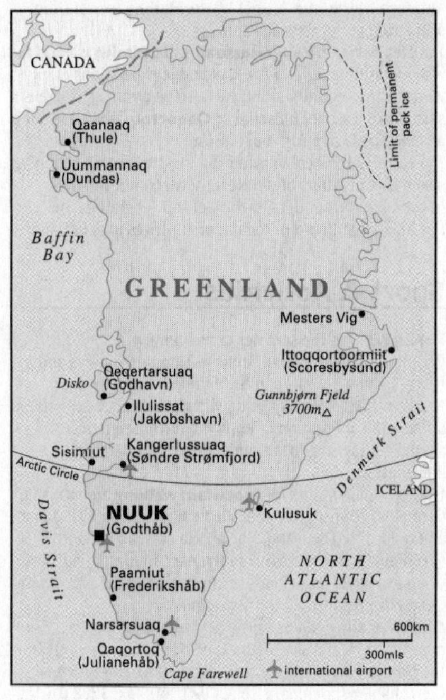

Location: South Arctic/North Atlantic.

Country dialling code: 299.

Greenland is part of the Kingdom of Denmark, and is represented abroad by Danish Embassies – see *Denmark* section.

Greenland Tourism
Head Office: PO Box 1615, Hans Egedesvej 29, DK-3900 Nuuk, Greenland
Tel: 342 820. Fax: 322 877.
E-mail: info@visitgreenland.com
Website: www.greenland.com

Grønlands Hjemmestyre (Greenland Home Rule Government)
PO Box 1015, DK-3900 Nuuk, Greenland
Tel: 345 000. Fax: 358 602.
E-mail: info@gh.gl
Website: www.nanoq.gl

Greenland Tourism – The National Board of Greenland
PO Box 1139, Strandgade 91, DK-1010 Copenhagen K, Denmark
Tel: 3283 3880. Fax: 3283 3889.
E-mail: info@greenland.com
Website: www.greenland.com

Danish Tourist Board
55 Sloane Street, London SW1X 9SY, UK
Tel: (020) 7259 5959 (Mon, Wed and Fri 1000-1300).
Fax: (020) 7259 5955.
E-mail: dtb.london@dt.dk
Website: www.visitdenmark.com

The British Embassy and US Embassy in Copenhagen deal with enquiries related to Greenland (see *Denmark* section).

Danish Tourist Board
PO Box 4649, Grand Central Station, New York, NY 10163, USA
Tel: (212) 885 9700. Fax: (212) 885 9710.
E-mail: info@goscandinavia.com
Website: www.goscandinavia.com

TIMATIC CODES

Health	AMADEUS: **TI-DFT/SFJ/HE** GALILEO/WORLDSPAN: **TI-DFT/SFJ/HE** SABRE: **TIDFT/SFJ/HE**
Visa	AMADEUS: **TI-DFT/SFJ/VI** GALILEO/WORLDSPAN: **TI-DFT/SFJ/VI** SABRE: **TIDFT/SFJ/VI**

To access TIMATIC country information on Health and Visa regulations through the Computer Reservations System (CRS), type in the appropriate command line listed above.

Also deals with enquiries relating to Canada. Not open to personal callers.

Canadian Consulate
Postal address: PO Box 1012, 3900 Nuuk, Greenland
Tel: 343 430. Fax: 320 288.

General Information

AREA: 2,166,086 sq km (836,330 sq miles).
POPULATION: 56,676 (2003).
POPULATION DENSITY: 0.026 per sq km.
CAPITAL: Nuuk (Godthåb). **Population:** 13,85 (2003).
GEOGRAPHY: Greenland is the world's biggest island. The surrounding seas are either permanently frozen or chilled by the mainly cold currents caused by the meeting of the Arctic and the North Atlantic oceans. The inland area is covered with ice, stretching 2500km (1500 miles) north-south and 1000km (600 miles) east-west. In the centre, the ice can be up to 3km (2 miles) thick. The ice-free coastal region, which is sometimes as wide as 200km (120 miles), covers a total of 410,449 sq km (158,475 sq miles), and is where all of the population is to be found. This region is intersected by deep fjords which connect the inland ice area with the sea. The Midnight Sun can be seen north of the Arctic Circle; the further north you are, the longer the period of the Midnight Sun. The arctic night in the winter results in a continuous twilight and, in the far north of the country, complete darkness. The Northern Lights can be seen during the autumn, winter and early spring.
GOVERNMENT: Part of the Kingdom of Denmark. **Head of State:** HM Queen Margarethe II since 1972. **Head of Government:** Prime Minister Hans Enoksen since 2002.
LANGUAGE: The official languages are Greenlandic, an Inuit (Eskimo) language and Danish. Greenlanders connected with tourism will normally speak English.
RELIGION: Evangelical Lutheran Church of Denmark majority, with small groups of Roman Catholics and other Protestant denominations.
TIME: Scoresby Sound: GMT - 1 (GMT from last Sunday in March to Saturday before last Sunday in September).
Ammassalik and west coast: GMT - 3 (summer and winter).
Thule area: GMT - 4 (GMT - 3 from April to October).
ELECTRICITY: 220 volts AC, 50Hz.
COMMUNICATIONS: Telephone: IDD is available. Country code: 299. There are no area codes. Outgoing international code: 009. There are no telephone boxes in Greenland, but calls can be made from hotels. **Mobile telephone:** GSM 900 network covers all 18 cities. Network operator is *TELE Greenland* (website: www.tele.gl). Handsets can be hired at *TELE Greenland* shops (in all cities). A deposit of DKr10,000 is required. There is also an analogue NMT network. **Fax:** Services are available in telegraph stations and hotels. **Internet:** The only ISP is *TELE Greenland* (website: www.tele.gl). At present, there are Internet cafes in Aasiaat, Itilleq, Nuuk and Sismut. Access is available in some public libraries. **Telegram:** All towns have a telegraph station. **Post:** Greenland produces its own stamps which are popular among collectors. Post from Greenland takes about four to five days to reach Europe. Post office hours: Mon-Fri 0900-1500. **Press:** There are no daily newspapers in Greenland, but *Atuagagdliutit/Gronlandsposten* is published twice a week, *Sermitsiaq* is the main weekly publication and *Niviarsiaq* is published monthly. There are no English language newspapers.
Radio: BBC World Service (website: www.bbc.co.uk/worldservice) and Voice of America (website: www.voa.gov) can be received. From time to time the frequencies change and the most up-to-date can be found online.

Passport/Visa

The regulations for Tourist and Business visas are the same as for Denmark (see *Passport/Visa* in the *Denmark* section). Visitors should specify that they wish to visit Greenland when they make their application. Special permits are necessary for persons wishing to transit in Pittuffik (Thule Airbase), as it is a North Atlantic Territory. Further information and application requirements may be obtained from the Nordic Countries, Faroe Islands and Greenland Office at the Ministry of Foreign Affairs, Asiatisk Plads 2, DK-1448 Copenhagen (tel: 3392 0000; fax: 3254 0533; e-mail: um@um.dk; website: www.um.dk). Visitors who wish to explore the glaciers and mountains or visit the National Park also require a special permit. Applications should be made to the Danish Polar Centre, Strandgade 100H, DK-1401 Copenhagen (tel: 3288 0100; fax: 3288 0101, e-mail: dpc@dpc.dk; website: www.dpc.dk).

Money

Currency: Danish Krone (DKr) = 100 øre. Notes are in denominations of DKr1000, 500, 200, 100 and 50. Coins are

Credit: © Greenland Tourism

in denominations of DKr20, 10, 5, 2 and 1, and 50 and 25 øre.
Note: There is no banking service in Søndre Strømfjord at present.
Currency exchange: Cheques drawn on Danish banks or on Eurocheque cards can be cashed at banks and cash can also be exchanged. There are two banks in Greenland; *Grønlandsbanken* (PO Box 1033, DK-3900 Nuuk) and *Nuna Bank* (PO Box 1031, DK-3900 Nuuk). *Nuna Bank* has branches in Nuuk, Sisimiut, Oaqortoq, Ilulissat and Maniitsoq. *KNI* represents the banks in other towns and villages.
Credit & debit cards: Diners, Eurocard and Visa are accepted in most restaurants, shops and hotels. Check with your credit or debit card company for details of merchant acceptability and other services which may be available. Most larger towns now have ATMs.
Travellers cheques: Cheques in major currencies may be exchanged as indicated in the currency exchange section above. To avoid additional exchange rate charges, travellers are advised to take travellers cheques in Pounds Sterling or US Dollars.
Currency restrictions: The import of local currency is unlimited; export of more than DKr50,000 is allowed provided it can be proved this amount was imported or obtained by changing imported foreign currencies. The import and export of foreign currencies is unlimited. All amounts (either for import or export) greater than € 15,000 must be declared to Danish Customs Authorities.
Exchange rate indicators: The following figures are included as a guide to the movements of the Danish Krone against Sterling and the US Dollar:

Date	Feb '04	May '04	Aug '04	Nov '04
£1.00=	10.91	11.16	11.09	10.60
$1.00=	5.99	6.25	6.02	5.60

Banking hours: Mon-Wed and Fri 1000-1600, Thurs 1000-1800.

Duty Free

The following goods may be imported into Greenland without incurring customs duty:
200 cigarettes or 100 cigarillos or 50 cigars or 250g of tobacco; 1l of alcoholic beverages over 22 per cent volume or 2l of fortified wine between 15 and 22 per cent volume; 2.25 litres of table wine; 50g perfume and 250ml toilet water; goods up to a value of DKr700; 1k of coffee or tea; up to 2k of chocolate or sweets.
Note: These goods must be carried by the traveller personally. Alcohol allowances are for travellers aged over 18 only.
Prohibited items: (a) Fresh food. (b) Pistols, fully- or semi-automatic weapons. A permit is required from the carrying airline to bring a hunting rifle to Greenland, but hunting is only permitted on special hunting trips organised by a tour operator who has been authorised by the Home Rule Government to do so. (c) Narcotics.
Note: Special permission is needed to export souvenirs of whales' teeth and walrus tusks. Authorisation forms are available from shops and tourist offices in Greenland.

Public Holidays

2005: Jan 1 New Year's Day. **Jan 6** Epiphany. **Mar 24** Maundy Thursday. **Mar 25** Good Friday. **Mar 28** Easter Monday. **Apr 22** Great Prayer Day. **May 5** Ascension. **May 16** Whit Monday. **Jun 21** National Day. **Dec 24-26** Christmas. **Dec 31** New Year's Eve.
2006: Jan 1 New Year's Day. **Jan 6** Epiphany. **Apr 13** Maundy Thursday. **Apr 14** Good Friday. **Apr 17** Easter Monday. **May 12** Great Prayer Day. **May 25** Ascension. **Jun 5** Whit Monday. **Jun 21** National Day. **Dec 24-26** Christmas. **Dec 31** New Year's Eve.

Credit: © Greenland Tourism

Health

	Special Precautions?	Certificate Required?
Yellow Fever	No	No
Cholera	No	No
Typhoid & Polio	No	N/A
Malaria	No	N/A

Note: Regulations and requirements may be subject to change at short notice, and you are advised to contact your doctor well in advance of your intended date of departure. Any numbers in the chart refer to the footnotes below.

Other risks: *Hepatitis A* occurs. *Hepatitis B* is endemic. *TB* may occur. Extreme cold during the winter months is another potential risk to travellers.
Rabies is present. For those at high risk, vaccination before arrival should be considered. If you are bitten, seek medical advice without delay. For more information, consult the *Health* appendix.
Health care: There are hospitals and dentists in all towns. Although medical services are generally free, medical insurance is advisable, particularly as charges are made for dental treatment. Travellers are also advised to bring their own medicines and prescribed drugs, as these can often be difficult to obtain in Greenland.

Travel - International

Note: The arctic weather conditions in Greenland may cause delays and interruptions in transport services or changes to planned itineraries. Visitors are advised to leave enough time for possible disruptions to flights and check with their airline or tour operator before flying.
AIR: Flying to Greenland by scheduled services will usually involve a stopover in Iceland or Denmark; contact *Air Greenland (GL)* or *SAS Scandinavian Airlines (SK)*. Other airlines serving Greenland include *Air Iceland (NY)* and *FirstAir* (7F from Ottawa).
Approximate flight times: From Greenland to *London* is five hours 30 minutes (including stopover in Copenhagen).
International airports: There are international airports at:
Kangerlussuaq (*Søndre Strømfjord*) (*SFJ*), served from Copenhagen by *SAS* and *Air Greenland* and from Canada by *First Air*;
Kulusuk (KUS), served from Iceland by *Air Greenland* and *Air Iceland*;
Narsarsuaq (UAK), served from Copenhagen by *Air Greenland* and from Iceland by *Air Greenland* and *Air Iceland*;
Nuuk (GOH), served from Canada/Frobisher Bay by *First Air*. Services are generally more frequent during the summer months.
Other international airports include *Neerlerit Inaat (CNP)* and *Pituffik (THU)*.
Departure Tax: None.

Travel - Internal

AIR: *Air Greenland* (website: www.airgreenland.gl) serves all towns on the west coast, from Nanortalik in the south to Thule/Qaanaq in the north. The frequency of departure on all routes is variable, and it is advisable to make reservations well in advance. Reservations made outside Greenland will take some time to confirm. Many routes are served by helicopters or charter planes.
SEA: *Arctic Umiaq Line* operates services along the west coast between Nanortalik and Upernavik. In addition, all villages are served by local boats connecting them with the nearest town, but space may be limited. Boats in some towns may be available for hire, with a skipper. *Coastal Cruise Greenland* offers cruises with all-inclusive flights. For further information, contact Arctic Umiaq Line A/S, PO Box 608, 3900 Nuuk (tel: 349 900; fax: 349 949; e-mail: aul@aul.gl; website: www.aul.gl) *or* Greenland Tourism (see *Contact Addresses* section).
ROAD: The only places that are connected by road are Ivituut and Kangilinnguit. The harsh landscape and weather conditions make road building elsewhere a virtually impossible task. Air and sea travel are the recommended ways of getting around.
RAIL: There are no railways between towns in Greenland.
DOG SLEDGES: These can be hired for the day, or for longer periods. Sledging is possible in all towns on the east coast and on the west coast north of the polar circle. Note: It is important to remember that sledge dogs are usually only semi-tame. This is just one reason why dog sledges should be given right of way at all times. Take particular care, as they are almost totally silent.
Travel times: The following chart gives approximate travel times (in hours and minutes) from **Kangerlussuaq** to other regions in Greenland:

	Air
Disko Bay	0.50
South Greenland	1.30
East Greenland	1.10

Accommodation

HOTELS: There are hotels in the major towns, but only those in Ammassalik, Ilulissat, Maniitsoq, Narsaq, Narsarsuaq, Nuuk, Qaqortoq, Qasigiannguit, Sisimiut, Søndre, Strømfjord and Ummannaq approach European standards. There is no public accommodation in Scoresbysund, Thule or Upernavik. All reservations should be made in advance; contact Greenland Tourism *or* Greenland Tourism in Copenhagen (see *Contact Addresses* section) for information. **Grading:** A star-grading system is in place. Hotels are classified by Greenland Tourism, and gradings are roughly equivalent to those in Denmark.
CAMPING: There are no official campsites, but most places have specific areas for pitching tents. Camping is permitted everywhere except on ruins and on cultivated land in south Greenland. Local tourist offices have the latest information and will be able to advise on the nearest site.
IGLOOS: An 'igloo hotel' is constructed in winter each year in Kangerlussuaq. A large central igloo is connected to four to six smaller ones via ice tunnels. The complex features a bar, decorative ice sculptures and ice furniture.
YOUTH HOSTELS: Youth hostel accommodation is available in several towns, although they may not quite be of the same style or standard as those in the rest of Europe. Elsewhere in south Greenland it is possible to stay overnight in seamens' houses or mountain huts – contact Greenland Tourism in Copenhagen for more information (see *Contact Addresses* section).

Resorts & Excursions

Organised excursions can be arranged from every town in Greenland. However, the Disko Bay region and South Greenland are the most visited places and offer the widest selection of tours. For information on all-inclusive tours/package tours, hiking and hotels, contact Greenland Tourism in Copenhagen for a list of tour operators (see *Contact Addresses* section).
Greenland is not a country for those seeking an ordinary holiday. It is a place of wild and rugged scenery and clear, clean air. The region may be seen on foot, by boat, by plane, by helicopter or by dog sledge according to the season and the terrain.
Note: (a) By far the most common, and recommended, method of visiting Greenland is with a tour operator. Stories of people travelling independently and subsequently finding themselves in trouble are not uncommon. Only travellers already familiar with the country are advised to make the journey by themselves. (b) No finds may be removed from ancient monuments, which are all protected areas.
ILULISSAT (JAKOBSHAVN): In west Greenland, Ilulissat is one of the country's growth areas and the gateway to **Disko Bay** and the whole of northern Greenland. Originally named Jakobshavn in honour of its Danish founder Jakob Sverin (1691-1753), the Greendlandic name Ilulissat (meaning iceberg) is now more commonly used. Local history, however, dates much further back than the founding of Jakobshavn. **Sermermiut**, a settlement situated a few kilometres southwest of the town, shows traces of habitation as early as 2000 BC. With a population of approximately 4700, Ilulissat boasts many modern as well as traditional buildings surrounded by breathtaking scenery. The famous explorer Knud Rasmussen was born here in 1879 and the house where he grew up has been transformed into the interesting **Knud Rasmussen Museum**. Motor-trips to nearby trading stations can sometimes be arranged.
SOUTH GREENLAND: In addition to Ilulissat, the main tourist centres are in South Greenland. **Nuuk**, the capital, with a population of 13,889, overlooked by **Sermitsiaq Mountain**, is a popular destination for visitors. One of the major attractions is the **Greenland National Museum**. It is situated near the entrance to a large fjord complex with steep mountains, lush valleys and a few small villages.
Narsarsuaq and **Qassiarsuk** in southern Greenland was the area first settled by the Viking Eric the Red 1000 years ago. Many ruins from this epoch of Greenland's history still survive.
Qaqortoq is the largest town in South Greenland and the area's administrative centre. The town has several houses of historical interest and a museum. Excursions can be arranged by the local tourist office. **Narsaq** tourist office also arranges regular excursions.
The area between **Kangerlussuaq** and **Sisimiut** is good for walking in summer and for dog-sledge expeditions in winter. Cross-country skiing can also be arranged. There is a small *Inuit* (Eskimo) museum at **Qaqortoq**, which includes an exact copy of a turf-built house.
There are minor local museums in most towns. The country also has many ruins of old Norse settlements and Inuit houses. For further details, contact tour operators, the Danish Tourist Board *or* local tourist offices in Greenland.

Sport & Activities

Fishing: During the summer period anglers come to Greenland for the superb Arctic fishing in the rivers and fjords. Fishing permits can be obtained from the local tourist offices. Persons fishing without a licence are liable to a fine and confiscation of equipment. Those interested should contact the local tourist offices for detailed information.
Hiking: Guided tours for **mountain walking** are available. Greenland Tourism has published colour-coded hiking maps and guides for Qaqortoq, Narsaq, Narsarsuaq in South Greenland and Ammassalik in the east. Mountain huts are often available, particularly in the region of the *Narsaq* and *Qaqortoq* peninsulas and *Vatnahverfi*.
Glacier scaling can be performed by experienced mountaineers and skiers. All expeditions need a permit from the Danish Polar Centre, Strandgade 100H, DK-1401 Copenhagen K, Denmark (tel: 3288 0100; fax: 3288 0101; e-mail: dpc@dpc.dk; website: www.dpc.dk). The centre also provides information about organising expeditions and stays in the National Park area. Greenland also offers excellent opportunities for those interested in activities such as **geology**, **botany** and **birdwatching**. Maps of the coastal area (scale 1:250,000) can be purchased from the Kort og Matrikelstyrelsen, Proviantgaarden, Rigsdagsgaarden 7, DK-1218 Copenhagen K.
Ice golf: This can be played among the ice hills on metre-thick ice in Uummannaq. Greenland's first **grass golf** course has recently been inaugurated, and is situated in the countryside near Nuuq. This 9-hole course features hillocks and waterholes as obstacles. There is also a golf course among the sandy riverbanks of Kangerlussuaq.
Cruises: It is becoming increasingly popular to take **cruises** along Greenland's coast, with most following the west coast, from Nuuk to Thule. Highlights include fjords, mountains, islands and icebergs. There are abundant opportunities to view wildlife including several species of whale, seals and birds. Greenland's quality of light, one of the reasons tourists visit the country, can be especially appreciated at sea. Aspiring photographers should remember to use a UV filter or a sunlight filter and lens hood when capturing the many sights. From mid-May to mid-August, the Midnight Sun can be experienced in the north.

Social Profile

FOOD & DRINK: Most hotels have restaurants of a good standard, where Danish food and Greenland specialities are served. Reindeer meat (caribou), seal and whale meat, musk ox, fowl, shrimps and fish are the most popular local food. Prices are similar to Denmark.
SHOPPING: The range of goods available is similar to that in an ordinary Danish provincial town, but prices are, in general, slightly higher. Alcohol, tobacco, fruit and vegetables are expensive. Special purchases include bone and soapstone carvings, skin products and beadwork. The Greenland Home Rule Administration can provide information on claiming tax back on items purchased in Greenland. **Shopping hours:** Mon-Thurs 1000-1730, Fri 1000-1800 and Sat 0900-1300. These will vary from region to region.
SPECIAL EVENTS: For further details, contact Greenland Tourism in Copenhagen (see *Contact Addresses* section). The following is a selection of special events occurring in Greenland in 2005:
Mar 10-17 *Greenland Shark Challenge*. **Apr 8-10** *Arctic*

Circle Race, starts and finishes in Sisimiut. **Jul 14-27** *Arctic Team Challenge*. **Aug 6** *Arctic Marathon*. **Sep** *Greenland Adventure Race*. **Oct 8** *Polar Circle Marathon*.
SOCIAL CONVENTIONS: Life is generally conducted at a more relaxed pace than is usual in northern Europe, as exemplified by the frequent use of the word *immaqa* – 'maybe'. Until recently, foreign visitors were very rare. The name of the country in Greenlandic is *Kalaallit Nunaat*, meaning 'Land of the People'. **Photography:** Throughout the country there is a ban on taking photographs inside churches or church halls during services. A UV or skylight filter and a lens shade should always be used. In winter, the camera must be polar-oiled. It is advisable to bring your own films. Film cannot always be developed in Greenland. **Tipping:** Service charge is usually added to the bill. Tips are not expected.

Business Profile

ECONOMY: Fish and fish products, especially shrimps, are the territory's most valuable exports. Greenland withdrew from the European Community (now the European Union) in February 1985 over the issue of the fisheries policy. EU member states are allowed to fish within Greenland's maritime exclusion zone in exchange for an annual cash payment; this compensates, in part, for the loss of development aid which Greenland would otherwise have received. It also enjoys preferential access to EU markets. Although there are plans to develop the island's mineral deposits of iron ore, uranium, zinc, lead and coal, the economy ultimately depends on large subsidies from the Danish central government. Denmark retained a monopoly on trade with Greenland until 1950 and continues to dominate its trading patterns. The KNI – Royal Greenland Trade Department – organises transport, supplies and production in the country. Germany, Norway, the USA and France are the territory's other significant trading partners.
BUSINESS: Suits should be worn. A knowledge of Danish is extremely useful. **Office hours:** Mon-Fri 0900-1700 or 0800-1600.
CONFERENCES/CONVENTIONS: The Cultural Conference Centre in Katuaq is Greenland's principal conference site, hosting many national and international events. Contact Katuaq, PO Box 1622, DK-3900 Nuuk, Greenland. Several hotels in Greenland also have the facilities to host conferences and conventions. For further information on conferences and conventions, contact Greenland Tourism (see *Contact Addresses* section).

Climate

Greenland has an Arctic climate, but owing to the size of the country there are great variations in the weather. As the climate graph shows, winters can be severe and the summers comparatively mild, particularly in areas which are sheltered from the prevailing winds. Precipitation, mostly snow, is moderately heavy around the coast. The north of the country, and much of the interior, enjoys true Arctic weather, with the temperature only rising above freezing for brief periods in the summer.
Note: Conditions in all parts of the country can become hazardous when there is a combination of a low temperature and a strong wind. Local advice concerning weather conditions should be followed very carefully. Nevertheless, the summer months are suitable for a wide range of outdoor activities.
Required clothing: Good-quality windproof and waterproof clothes, warm layers and moulded sole shoes at all times of the year; also some slightly thinner clothes – it is important to be able to change clothing during a day's climbing as temperatures can vary greatly during one day. Sunglasses and protective sun lotion are strongly advised. In July and August, mosquitoes can be a problem, especially inside the fjords and so a mosquito net can prove indispensable. Extra warm clothes are necessary for those contemplating dog-sledge expeditions. Extra clothes are not always available for hire in Greenland.

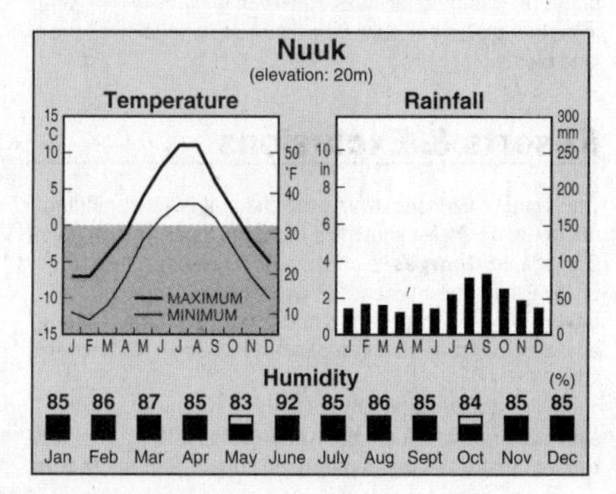

Grenada

LATEST TRAVEL ADVICE CONTACTS

British Foreign and Commonwealth Office
Tel: (0870) 606 0290 Website: www.fco.gov.uk
US Department of State
Website: http://travel.state.gov/travel
Canadian Department of Foreign Affairs and Int'l Trade
Tel: (1 800) 267 8376 Website: www.dfait-maeci.gc.ca

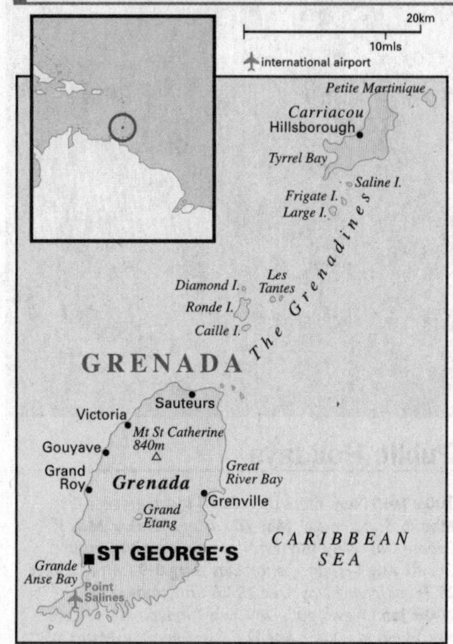

Location: Caribbean, Windward Islands.

Country dialling code: 1 473.

Grenada Board of Tourism
PO Box 293, Burns Point, St George's, Grenada
Tel: 440 2001 *or* 440 2279.
Fax: 440 6637.
E-mail: gbt@caribsurf.com
Website: www.grenadagrenadines.com
Grenada High Commission
5 Chandos Street, London W1G 9DG, UK
Tel: (020) 7631 4277.
Fax: (020) 7631 4274.
E-mail: grenada@high-commission.demon.co.uk
Opening hours: Mon-Fri 0900-1700; 1000-1400 (consular).
Grenada Board of Tourism
c/o Representation Plus, 11 Blades Court, 121 Deodar Road, London SW15 2NU, UK
Tel: (020) 8877 4516.
Fax: (020) 8874 4219.
E-mail: grenada@representationplus.co.uk
Website: www.grenadagrenadines.com
British High Commission
PO Box 56, Netherlands Building, Grand Anse, St George's, Grenada
Tel: 440 3222 *or* 440 3536.
Fax: 440 4939.
E-mail: bhcgrenada@caribsurf.com
Embassy of Grenada
1701 New Hampshire Avenue, NW, Washington, DC 20009, USA
Tel: (202) 265 2561. Fax: (202) 265 2468.
E-mail: grenada@oas.org
Website: www.grenadaconsulate.org *or* www.grenadaembassyusa.org
Grenada Board of Tourism
PO Box 1668, Lake Worth, FL 33460, USA
Tel: (561) 588 8176. Fax: (561) 588 7267.
E-mail: cnoel@grenadagrenadines.com
Website: www.grenadagrenadines.com
Embassy of the United States of America
Street address: Lance aux Epines, St George's, Grenada
Postal address: PO Box 54, St George's, Grenada

TIMATIC CODES

Health
AMADEUS: **TI-DFT/GND/HE**
GALILEO/WORLDSPAN: **TI-DFT/GND/HE**
SABRE: **TIDFT/GND/HE**

Visa
AMADEUS: **TI-DFT/GND/VI**
GALILEO/WORLDSPAN: **TI-DFT/GND/VI**
SABRE: **TIDFT/GND/VI**

To access TIMATIC country information on Health and Visa regulations through the Computer Reservations System (CRS), type in the appropriate command line listed above.

Tel: 444 1173-6. Fax: 444 4820.
E-mail: usemb_gd@caribsurf.com
Website: www.spiceisle.com *or* www.grenadaexplorer.com
High Commission for the Eastern Caribbean States
130 Albert Street, Suite 700, Ottawa, Ontario K1P 5G4, Canada
Tel: (613) 236 8952. Fax: (613) 236 3042.
E-mail: echcc@travel-net.com
Website: www.oecs.org/ottawa
Consulate General of Grenada/Grenada Board of Tourism
439 University Avenue, Suite 930, Toronto, Ontario M5G 1Y8, Canada
Tel: (416) 595 1339 (tourist office) *or* 1343 (consulate general).
Fax: (416) 595 8278.
E-mail: info@grenadaconsulate.com *or* tourism@grenadaconsulate.com
Website: www.grenadaconsulate.com *or* www.grenadagrenadines.com
The Canadian High Commission in Bridgetown deals with enquiries relating to Grenada (see *Barbados* **section).**

General Information

AREA: 344.5 sq km (133 sq miles).
POPULATION: 100,895 (2001).
POPULATION DENSITY: 292.9 per sq km.
CAPITAL: St George's. **Population:** 3,908 (2001).
GEOGRAPHY: Grenada is located in the Caribbean. The island is of volcanic origin and is divided by a central mountain range. It is the most southerly of the Windward Islands. Agriculture is based on nutmeg, cocoa, sugar cane and bananas. Tropical rainforests, gorges and the stunning beauty of dormant volcanoes make this a fascinating and diverse landscape with some of the finest beaches in the world. Carriacou and some of the other small islands of the Grenadines are also part of Grenada.
GOVERNMENT: Constitutional monarchy. **Head of State:** HM Queen Elizabeth II, represented locally by Governor-General Sir Daniel Williams since 1996. **Head of Government:** Prime Minister Keith Mitchell since 1995.
LANGUAGE: English.
RELIGION: Roman Catholic 64 per cent, Anglican 22 per cent, as well as other smaller Protestant denominations.
TIME: GMT - 4.
ELECTRICITY: 220/240 volts AC, 50Hz.
COMMUNICATIONS: Telephone: Full IDD service. Country code: 1 473. No area codes are in use. Coin and telephone card payphones are available. Telephone cards can be purchased at the offices of *Cable & Wireless Grenada* and from other agents. **Mobile telephone:** A GSM 900/1900 network provides good coverage of most of the island. Network providers include *Cable & Wireless Caribbean Cellular* (website: www.caribcell.com), Trans-World Telecom Caribbean (www.transworldtel.net), Digicel Grenada and Grenada Wireless Holdings Ltd. Handsets can be hired for the duration of your stay. **Fax:** *Cable & Wireless Grenada* provide a service in St George's. Many hotels also offer fax services. **Internet:** Internet is widely available throughout Grenada. Main ISPs include *Caribsurf* (website: www.caribsurf.com). **Telegram:** *Cable & Wireless Grenada* offer telegraphic services. **Post:** The post office in St George's (at Burns Point) is open Mon-Thurs 0800-1530, Fri 0800-1630 (closed weekends). **Press:** All newspapers are in English, and are printed weekly or monthly. They include *Grenada Times*, *Grenada Today* and *The Grenadian Voice*.
Radio: BBC World Service (website: www.bbc.co.uk/worldservice) and Voice of America (website: www.voa.gov) can be received. From time to time the frequencies change and the most up-to-date can be found online.

Passport/Visa

	Passport Required?	Visa Required?	Return Ticket Required?
Full British	Yes	No	Yes
Australian	Yes	No	Yes
Canadian	Yes	No	Yes
USA	Yes	No	Yes
Other EU	Yes	No	Yes
Japanese	Yes	No	Yes

Note: *Regulations and requirements may be subject to change at short notice, and you are advised to contact the appropriate diplomatic or consular authority before finalising travel arrangements. Details of these may be found at the head of this country's entry. Any numbers in the chart refer to the footnotes below.*

PASSPORTS: Passport valid for six months from date of departure from Grenada required by all.
VISAS: Required by all except the following:
(a) nationals of countries shown in the chart above including Australian External Territories, French Overseas

A B C D E F G H I J K L M N O P Q R S T U V W X Y Z

Credit: © Grenada Board of Tourism

Dependencies and Netherlands Associated Territories;
(b) nationals of Commonwealth countries, British Dependent Territories and New Zealand Associated and Dependent Territories;
(c) nationals of Argentina, Bulgaria, Chile, China (PR), CIS countries, Cuba, Iceland, Israel, Korea (Rep), Liechtenstein, Norway, Romania and Venezuela.
Note: Visitors may be required to deposit an amount equal to the fare of their return passage.
Types of visa and cost: *Visitor*: £35.
Validity: Up to three months.
Application to: Consulate (or Consular section at Embassy or High Commission) well in advance of intended day of departure; see *Contact Addresses* section for details.
Application requirements: (a) Valid passport. (b) Completed application form. (c) Two passport-size photos. (d) Return or onward ticket. (e) Fee payable by cash or postal order (to include additional £4 fee to cover postage). (f) For postal applications, a recorded delivery envelope. (g) Confirmation of hotel reservation. (h) For Business visas, letter from contact in Grenada.
Working days required: One to three.

Money

Currency: East Caribbean Dollar (EC$) = 100 cents. Notes are in denominations of EC$100, 50, 20, 10 and 5. Coins are in denominations of EC$1, and 50, 25, 10, 5, 2 and 1 cents.
Note: The East Caribbean Dollar is tied to the US Dollar.
Note: The East Caribbean Dollar is tied to the US Dollar.
Currency exchange: Barclays Bank, Grenada Bank of Commerce, Grenada Co-operative Bank, National Commercial Bank and Scotia Bank are all found on the island.
Credit & debit cards: American Express, Diners Club, MasterCard and Visa and other major cards are accepted by most shops, car hire companies and hotels. Check with your credit or debit card company for details of merchant acceptability and other services which may be available.
Travellers cheques: Widely accepted. To avoid additional exchange rate charges, travellers are advised to take travellers cheques in US Dollars.
Currency restrictions: No restrictions on the import or export of local or foreign currency.
Exchange rate indicators: The following figures are included as a guide to the movements of the Eastern Caribbean Dollar against Sterling and the US Dollar:

Date	Feb '04	May '04	Aug '04	Nov '04
£1.00=	4.91	4.82	4.97	5.11
$1.00=	2.70	2.70	2.70	2.70

Banking hours: Mon-Thurs 0800-1500, Fri 0800-1700.

Duty Free

The following goods may be imported into Grenada without incurring customs duty:
200 cigarettes or 50 cigars or 250g of tobacco; 1l of wine or spirits.
Prohibited items: Narcotics; arms and ammunition; fruit and vegetables.
Note: Licensed firearms must be declared. A local licence can be obtained from the police.

Public Holidays

2005: Jan 1 *New Year's Day*. **Feb 7** *Independence Day*. **Mar 25** *Good Friday*. **Mar 28** *Easter Monday*. **May 1** *Labour Day*. **May 16** *Whit Monday*. **May 26** *Corpus Christi*. **Aug 1** *Emancipation Day*. **Aug 8-9** *Carnival*. **Oct 25** *Thanksgiving Day*. **Dec 25-26** *Christmas*.
2006: Jan 1 *New Year's Day*. **Feb 7** *Independence Day*. **Apr 14** *Good Friday*. **Apr 17** *Easter Monday*. **May 1** *Labour Day*. **Jun 5** *Whit Monday*. **Jun 15** *Corpus Christi*. **Aug 7** *Emancipation Day*. **Aug 14-15** *Carnival*. **Oct 25** *Thanksgiving Day*. **Dec 25-26** *Christmas*.

Health

	Special Precautions?	Certificate Required?
Yellow Fever	No	1
Cholera	No	No
Typhoid & Polio	No	N/A
Malaria	No	N/A

Note: Regulations and requirements may be subject to change at short notice, and you are advised to contact your doctor well in advance of your intended date of departure. Any numbers in the chart refer to the footnotes below.

1: A yellow fever vaccination certificate is required from all travellers over one year of age coming from infected areas.
Food & drink: Mains water is normally chlorinated and relatively safe, but there is still some risk of diarrhoea, particularly in rural areas. Bottled water is available. Milk is pasteurised and dairy products are safe for consumption. Local meat, poultry, seafood, fruit and vegetables are generally considered safe to eat.
Other risks: Immunisation against *hepatitis A, B* and *diphtheria* is sometimes recommended.
Rabies is present. For those at high risk, vaccination before arrival should be considered. If you are bitten, seek medical advice without delay. See the *Health* appendix for further details.
Health care: There is a general hospital in St George's and small hospitals in Mirabeau and Carriacou. Health insurance is advised.

Travel - International

Note: In September 2004 Hurricane Ivan ripped through the island causing devastation and severely affecting much of the country's infrastructure. Many buildings, including the main airport in the capital at St George's, were damaged. Repair work is ongoing but travellers should seek specific advice for individual areas prior to travel.
AIR: The main airlines serving Grenada are *British Airways (BA)* which offers a direct flight from London thrice weekly; *Virgin Airlines* which flies direct from London once a week; *Excel Airways* which flies twice-weekly from London on Sunday and Monday; *BWIA International* which offers daily flights from London via Port of Spain (Trinidad) with connections to Grenada; and *Air Jamaica, American Airlines, Caribbean Star, LIAT, SVG* Air, *TIA* and *US Airways* which offer connections with Grenada from other Caribbean islands.
Approximate flight times: From Grenada to *London* is 10 hours, to *Los Angeles* is 11 hours and to *New York* is seven hours (including stopovers).
International airports: *Grenada International Airport (Point Salines) (GND)* is 11km (8 miles) south of St George's. Taxis and buses are available. Facilities include duty-free shops, bureaux de change, car hire (*Dollar*), handicraft shops, snack bars, boutiques and tourist information.
Departure tax: EC$50 per adult, payable in cash. EC$25 for children five to 12 years of age. Children under five are exempt.
SEA: St George's, considered the most picturesque port in the Caribbean, is a port of call for many cruise lines, including *Costa, Cunard* and *Royal Viking*. *Geest Line* (website: www.geestline.co.uk) sails from the UK via Martinique, Antigua, St Lucia and Barbados. Around 70 per cent of tourist arrivals are cruise-ship passengers. An inter-island ferry service sails to Carriacou, Petit Martinique and Isle de Ronde up to four times weekly. There are also daily shuttle boat services between Grenada and Carriacou. Check at a local tourist office for times and fares.

Travel - Internal

SEA: Water-taxis are available from St George's across the Carenage to the Esplanade or Grand Anse Beach. A large number of yachts and boats are available to charter. Arrangements can be made via the Grenada Board of Tourism (see *Contact Addresses* section).
ROAD: There is a network of approximately 1046km (650 miles) of paved roads. Most main roads are in good condition but they are narrow and winding. Traffic drives on the left. **Bus:** These are cheap but slow. The main bus terminal is located at the west end of Granby Street. Minibuses run between Hillsborough, Windward and Tyrell Bay. **Taxi:** Taxis are the most efficient means of transport. They are available from the airport, the Carenage and most hotels. **Car hire:** A large range of vehicles are available in St George's or St Andrew's. Credit cards are not always accepted by car hire companies. To hire a vehicle drivers must be over the age of 21. Some rental firms have a minimum rental period of three days during peak periods.
Documentation: A temporary licence to drive is available from local authorities on presentation of a valid driving licence. The cost is approximately EC$30. An International Driving Permit is recommended, although it is not legally required.
Travel times: The following chart gives approximate travel times (in hours and minutes) from **St George's** to other towns/islands in Grenada.

	Air	Road	Sea
Grenville	-	0.35	-
Carriacou	0.20	-	1.30

Accommodation

HOTELS: Grenada offers a variety of modern, luxurious hotels. Pre-booking is essential. An 8 per cent government tax is added to all hotel and restaurant bills, and a 10 per cent service charge is added to the bill by many hotels and restaurants. Contact the Board of Tourism for details and exact price listings (see *Contact Addresses* section). Further information is available from the Grenada Hotel Association, 16 Le Marquis Complex, Grande Anse, St George's (tel: 444 1353; fax: 444 4847; e-mail: grenhota@caribsurf.com; website: www.grenadahotelsinfo.com).
GUEST HOUSES: There are several guest houses, some of which offer self-catering facilities.
SELF-CATERING: There are a growing number of apartments and villas available for hire. Contact the Grenada Board of Tourism for details (see *Contact Addresses* section).
CAMPING: Camping is not encouraged because there are no proper camping facilities. However, it is possible to camp in certain places but only with the prior permission of the land owner.

Resorts & Excursions

The island of Grenada dwarfs the chain of islands spinning off to the northeast known as the Grenadines. The capital of Grenada, **St George's**, is on the southwest coast near one of the island's best beaches at **Grand Anse**; another is at **Levera Bay** near the island's northern tip. At **Grand Etang**, an extinct volcano cradles a beautiful 30 acre- (12 hectare-) lake.
There are several waterfalls in Grenada, the most spectacular of which are the **Annandale Falls**, a 15m (50ft) cascade that flows into a mountain stream, and the **Mount**

Carmel Waterfall, the island's highest waterfall, which has two falls cascading over 21m (70ft) to clear pools below.
St George's: The **Carenage**, a picturesque inner harbour with 18th-century warehouses and restaurants, and **Fort George** (built by the French in 1705) are both worth a visit. See also the outer harbour, **St Andrew's Presbyterian Church** and **Fort Frederick**.
Spice Country: On the way here, north from the capital, visitors pass through some of the prettiest fishing villages on the island. Hidden among the red roofs of **Gouyave** is the factory where spices are sorted, dried and milled. The **Dougaldston Estate** is a traditional plantation in the centre of the nutmeg- and cocoa-growing region.
Sauteurs/Morne des Sauteurs: From these rocks, the last of the island's Carib Indians plummeted to their deaths in 1650.
Carriacou: In 'the Grenadines of Grenada', this island is a yachtsman's paradise. The **Carriacou Museum** in **Hillsborough** has an impressive collection of Amerindian artefacts and mementoes dating back to occupation by the French and British.

Sport & Activities

Watersports: Grenada's best-known white-sand beach, the *Grand Anse*, is complemented by several others, notably those on neighbouring *Morne Rouge*, the deserted beaches on the southern coast and *Levera Bay*, which is also a favourite **surfing** spot. Apart from in the sea, **swimming** is also possible at several of the islands' rainforest pools and lakes, many of which are formed by waterfalls, such as the *Annandale Falls* and the *Concord Falls*. **Diving** and **snorkelling** can be practised widely, with the Grand Anse beach being the starting point for many diving trips to the nearby reefs and islands. Most dive sites are easily accessible from the coast. Some of the best are *Molinière Reef*, located approximately 5km (3 miles) from St George's; *Martin's Bay*, close to Grand Anse, also a popular snorkelling spot; and *Channel Reef*. The neighbouring island of *Carricou*, part of the Grenadines, is known as the 'island of coral reefs' and offers ideal diving conditions, with a rich marine life. **Yachting** is also extremely popular and a number of major yacht races and regattas are held throughout the year, notably the *January Sailing Festival* (lasting five days) and the sailing regatta in *Tyrell Bay* on Carricou. Particularly popular sailing destinations in the area include the Grenadine islands *Sugar Loaf*, *Green Island* and *Sandy Island*. A variety of small and large craft may be hired. Contact the Grenada Board of Tourism for details. Visitors can also make **boat trips** on traditional wooden schooners, which is a popular way to cross the 5km- (3-mile) distance between the islands of Carricou and Petit Martinique.
Walking: The *Grand Etang National Park and Forest Reserve* contains numerous marked trails. The road to the park passes by the northwestern edge of *Mount Sinai* (703m/2306ft), with its beautiful crater lake, the *Grand Etang*. The park contains a wealth of interesting flora and fauna, and there are spectacular flower displays depending on the season. Another volcanic crater lake, *Lake Antoine*, is located in the *Levara National Park*, a well known destination for **birdwatching**. The *La Sagesse Nature Reserve*, located in the south, is a protected bird sanctuary with several rivers, mangroves and salt lakes.

Social Profile

FOOD & DRINK: Local specialities include seafood and vegetables, *calaloo soup*, crabs, conches (lambi) and nutmeg ice-cream. Most hotels and restaurants offer international cuisine, serving a large variety of tropical fish and English, Continental, American and exotic West Indian food. A local company supplies a wide variety of local fruit juices and nectars. The local rum and beer, *Carib*, is excellent. Bars are stocked with most popular wines and spirits, including various brands of whisky, rum and brandy.
NIGHTLIFE: Home to the vibrant calypso and reggae music, Grenada offers a good mix of local and international restaurants and bars. Many resorts provide night time entertainment, such as discos, organised shows and cabarets. The Regal Cinema has recently been refurbished and hosts many multi-cultural events as well as showing films.
SHOPPING: Special purchases include leather crafts, jewellery, spices, straw goods, printed cottons and other fabrics. There are a number of duty free shops selling quality goods from all over the world. A vendors market has now opened close to the Grand Anse Beach with 82 vendors offering various goods and services. **Shopping hours:** Mon-Fri 0800-1600, Sat 0800-1300. Supermarkets are usually open Mon-Sat 0900-1900.
SPECIAL EVENTS: Grenada's annual carnival in August involves colourful street parties, steel bands and calypso competitions. There are several yachting and fishing events throughout the year; in addition, public holidays are usually accompanied by some form of special celebration. For full details of events, contact the Grenada Board of Tourism (see *Contact Addresses* section). The following is a selection of special events occurring in Grenada in 2005:
Jan 21-5 *Spice Island Billfish Tournament*. **Jan 28-Feb 2** *Grenada La Source Sailing Festival*, Grand Anse Beach. **Feb 7-9** *Carriacou Carnival*. **Mar 17** *St Patrick's Day Festival*. **Mar 24-29** *Grenada Round-the-Island Easter Regatta*. **Apr 11-20** *Grenada Classics Festival*, cricket festival. **May 14** *Whitsuntide Athletic Games*. **Jun 29** *Fishermans' Birthday Celebrations*. **Jul/Aug** *Carnival 2005*. **Jul 29-Aug 1** *Carriacou Regatta*. **Dec** *Carriacou Parang Festival*.
SOCIAL CONVENTIONS: Local culture reflects the island's history of British and French colonial rule and, of course, the African cultures imported with the slaves – African influence is especially noticeable on the island of Carriacou in the Big Drum and in Grenada with the Shango dance. The Roman Catholic Church also exerts a strong influence on the way of life. Local people are generally friendly and courteous. Dress is casual and informal but beachwear is not welcome in town. **Tipping:** A 10 per cent service charge is added by most hotels and restaurants. If no charge is added, it is customary to leave a 10 per cent tip.

Business Profile

ECONOMY: Grenada's agricultural economy is centred on the production of spices. The principal exports are nutmeg, cocoa, bananas and sugar cane. There are extensive timber reserves but exploitation is being strictly controlled to prevent deforestation. The fishing industry has grown in recent years and now generates one-sixth of export earnings. There are thought to be some oil and gas deposits off the southern coast of Grenada, and attempts to locate them continue. Industry is confined to production of nutmeg oil and rum, as well as drinks, paint and paper. Tourism (particularly stopover and cruise-ship visitors) has developed gradually since the mid-1980s but the industry is now the island's leading foreign exchange earner. This has, to some extent, eased the depressed condition of the economy which has suffered from the general low level of world commodity prices during the last 10 years or so. Grenada has also developed a sizeable financial services industry in recent years, but has fallen foul of global efforts to tighten regulation.
The other main source of income for the island has been remittances from the estimated 100,000 Grenadians working abroad, mainly in the USA, Canada and Europe. Grenada also relies on foreign aid from the USA, the UK, Canada and the EU. This has declined in recent years and the Government has been looking elsewhere (including Libya) for financial support. The UK and the USA are the island's main trading partners. Grenada is a member of the Caribbean trade bloc, CARICOM (website: www.caricom.org), and the Organisation of East Caribbean States (website: www.oecs.org).
BUSINESS: All correspondence and trade literature is in English. **Office hours:** Mon-Fri 0800-1200 and 1300-1600.
COMMERCIAL INFORMATION: The following organisation can offer advice: Grenada Chamber of Industry and Commerce, PO Box 129, Decaul Building, Mount Gay, St George's (tel: 440 2937 *or* 440 8858; fax: 440 6627; e-mail: gcic@caribsurf.com; website: www.spiceisle.com).
CONFERENCES/CONVENTIONS: Eight hotels offer meeting facilities, seating from 25 to 300 persons. For details, contact Grenada Board of Tourism (see *Contact Addresses* section).

Climate

Tropical. The dry season runs from January to May. The rainy season runs from June to December. The average temperature is 28°C (82°F).
Required clothing: Tropical lightweights and cool summer clothing.

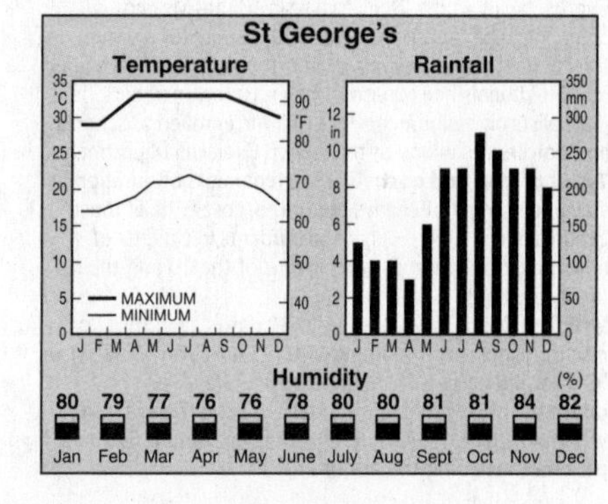

Guadeloupe

LATEST TRAVEL ADVICE CONTACTS

British Foreign and Commonwealth Office
Tel: (0870) 606 0290 Website: www.fco.gov.uk
US Department of State
Website: http://travel.state.gov/travel
Canadian Department of Foreign Affairs and Int'l Trade
Tel: (1 800) 267 8376 Website: www.dfait-maeci.gc.ca

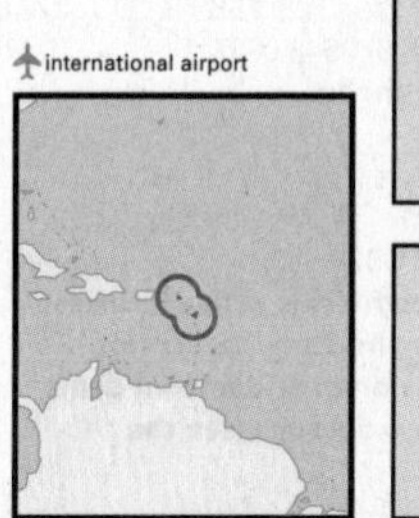

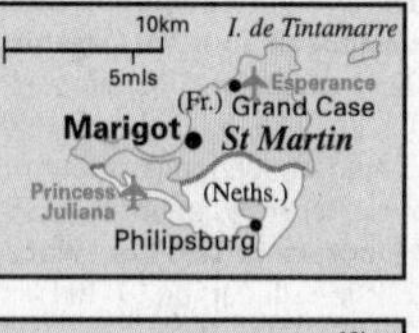

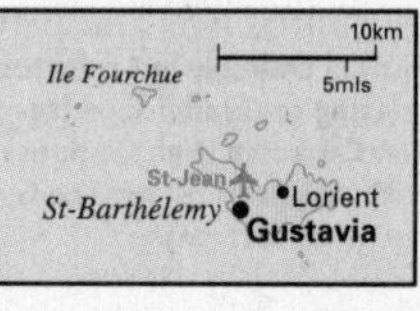

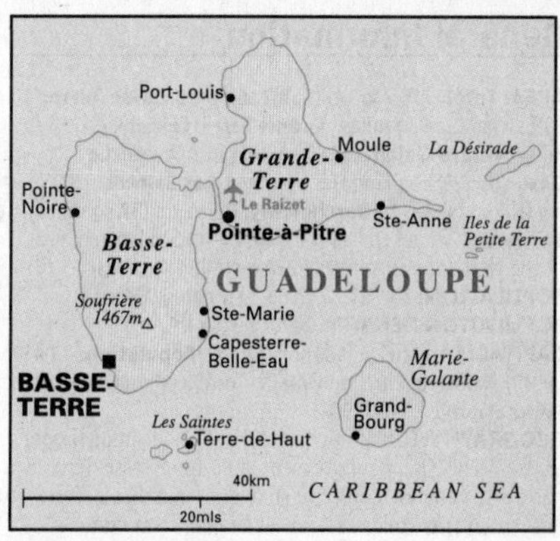

Location: Caribbean, at the arc of the Leeward group of islands of the Lesser Antilles.

Country dialling code: 590.

Guadeloupe is an Overseas Department of the Republic of France, and is represented abroad by French Embassies – see *France* section.

Office du Tourisme
5 square de la Banque, 97166 Pointe-à-Pitre, Guadeloupe
Tel: (590) 820 930. Fax: (590) 838 922.
E-mail: office.tourisme.guadeloupe@wanadoo.fr *or* info@lesilesdeguadeloupe.com
Website: www.lesilesdeguadeloupe.com

St Barthélemy Office du Tourisme
Quai du Général de Gaulle, Gustavia, St Barthélemy, Guadeloupe.
Tel: (590) 278 727. Fax: (590) 277 447.
E-mail: odtsb@wanadoo.fr
Website: www.st-barths.com

St Martin Tourist Office
Route Sandy Ground, Marigot, 97150 St Martin, Guadeloupe
Tel: (590) 875 721. Fax: (590) 875 643.
E-mail: sxmto@aol.com
Website: www.st-martin.org

French Consulate General
21 Cromwell Road, London SW7 2EN, UK
Visa section: 6A Cromwell Place, London SW7 2EW, UK
Tel: (020) 7073 1200 (consular section) *or* 7073 1250 (visa section) *or* (09065) 508 940 (visa information service; calls cost £1 per minute) *or* (020) 7073 1295 (visa applications in progress; 1500-1700 only) *or* (09065) 266 654 (24-hour visa application form request service; calls cost £1.50 per minute) *or* (09065) 540 700 (24-hour automated visa appointment booking service).

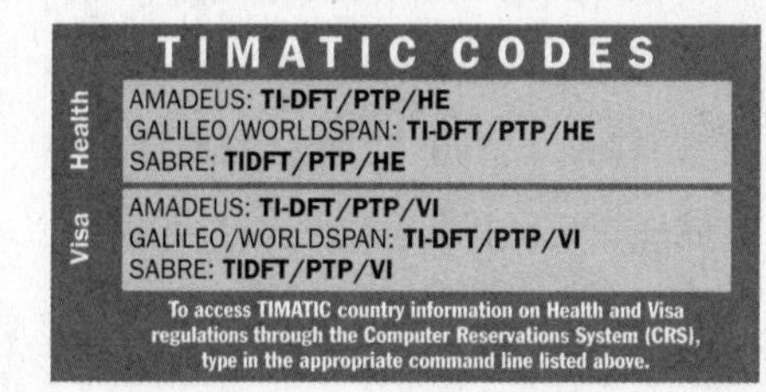
TIMATIC CODES

Health
AMADEUS: **TI-DFT/PTP/HE**
GALILEO/WORLDSPAN: **TI-DFT/PTP/HE**
SABRE: **TIDFT/PTP/HE**

Visa
AMADEUS: **TI-DFT/PTP/VI**
GALILEO/WORLDSPAN: **TI-DFT/PTP/VI**
SABRE: **TIDFT/PTP/VI**

To access TIMATIC country information on Health and Visa regulations through the Computer Reservations System (CRS), type in the appropriate command line listed above.

Fax: (020) 7073 1201 *or* (09001) 669 932 (visa application forms by fax; calls cost 60p per minute).
Opening hours: Mon-Wed 0845-1500, Thurs and Fri 0845-1200 (general enquiries); Mon-Fri 0845-1130 (visa applications).
E-mail: presse.londres-amba@diplomatie.fr (information).
Website: www.ambafrance-uk.org *or* www.consulfrance-londres.org
Consulate General also in: Edinburgh.

Maison de la France (French Government Tourist Office)
178 Piccadilly, London W1J 9AL, UK
Tel: (09068) 244 123 (information line; calls cost 60p per minute) *or* (020) 7399 3520 (travel trade only).
Fax: (020) 7493 6594.
E-mail: info.uk@franceguide.com
Website: www.franceguide.com

Caribbean Tourism Organisation
22 The Quadrant, Richmond, Surrey, TW9 1BP, UK
Tel: (020) 8948 0057. Fax: (020) 8948 0067.
E-mail: ctolondon@caribtourism.com
Website: www.caribbean.co.uk

Honorary British Consulate
23 rue Sadi Carnot, 97110 Pointe-à-Pitre, Guadeloupe
Tel: (590) 825 757. Fax: (590) 828 933.

The US Embassy in Bridgetown deals with enquiries relating to Guadeloupe (see the *Barbados* **section).**
The Canadian High Commission in Bridgetown deals with enquiries relating to Guadeloupe (see the *Barbados* **section).**

General Information

AREA: Total: 1705 sq km (658.3 sq miles). **Basse-Terre:** 839 sq km (324 sq miles). **Grand-Terre:** 564 sq km (218 sq miles). **Marie-Galante:** 150 sq km (58 sq miles). **La Désirade:** 29.7 sq km (11.5 sq miles). **Les Saintes:** 13.9 sq km (5.4 sq miles). **St-Barthélemy:** 95 sq km (37 sq miles). **St-Martin** (which shares the island with St Maarten, part of the Netherlands Antilles): 88 sq km (34 sq miles).
POPULATION: 444,515 (official estimate 2004).
POPULATION DENSITY: 247.8 per sq km.
CAPITAL: Basse-Terre (administrative). **Population:** 12,410 (1999). Pointe-à-Pitre, on Grande-Terre (commercial centre). **Population:** 20,948 (1999).
GEOGRAPHY: Guadeloupe comprises Guadeloupe proper (Basse-Terre), Grande-Terre (separated from Basse-Terre by a narrow sea channel) and five smaller islands. Basse-Terre has a rough volcanic relief whilst Grande Terre features rolling hills and flat plains. All the islands have beautiful white- or black-sand palm-fringed beaches. There are also many lush mountainous areas with stunning and unspoiled tropical scenery.
GOVERNMENT: Guadeloupe is an Overseas Department of France and as such is an integral part of the French Republic. **Head of State:** President Jacques Chirac since 1995, represented locally by Prefect Dominique Vian since 2002.
LANGUAGE: The official language is French. The *lingua franca* is Creole.
TIME: GMT - 4.
RELIGION: The majority are Roman Catholic, with a minority of predominantly Evangelical protestant groups.
ELECTRICITY: 220 volts AC, 50Hz.
COMMUNICATIONS: Telephone: IDD is available. Country code: 590. Good internal network. There are no area codes. Phonecards (*télécartes*) are necessary to make calls from public telephones. **Mobile telephone:** GSM 900 network. Handsets can be hired at the airport. Network providers include *Améris* and *France Télécom*. Coverage extends throughout the French West Indies and in French Guiana. St-Martin and St-Barthélemy also have digital analogue networks, system B, operated by *St-Martin Mobiles* (website: www.stmartinmobiles.com). These analogue networks are compatible with most US handsets, which can be activated on the island by dialling 0 or by registering online. **Internet:** Local ISPs include *wanadoo* (website: www.wanadoo.fr), *Antilles-net* (website: www.antilles-net.com) and *MediaServ* (website: www.mediaserv.net). There are Internet cafes at Saint-Francois, Sainte Anne, Mare-Gaillard and Pointe-a-Pitre; there are also terminals in some larger post offices and public buildings. **Post:** Airmail takes about one week to reach Europe. **Press:** Newspapers are all in French. The main daily is *France-Antilles*.
Radio: BBC World Service (website: www.bbc.co.uk/worldservice) and Voice of America (website: www.voa.gov) can be received. From time to time the frequencies change and the most up-to-date can be found online.

Passport/Visa

	Passport Required?	Visa Required?	Return Ticket Required?
Full British	Yes	No	Yes
Australian	Yes	No	Yes
Canadian	Yes	No	Yes
USA	Yes	No	Yes
Other EU	Yes/1	No	Yes
Japanese	Yes	No	Yes

Note: *Regulations and requirements may be subject to change at short notice, and you are advised to contact the appropriate diplomatic or consular authority before finalising travel arrangements. Details of these may be found at the head of this country's entry. Any numbers in the chart refer to the footnotes below.*

PASSPORTS: Passport valid for at least three months beyond applicant's last day of stay required by all except the following:
1. nationals of Belgium, France, Germany, Greece, Italy, Luxembourg, Monaco, The Netherlands, Portugal, Spain and Switzerland, who are holders of national identity cards.
VISAS: Required by all except the following:
(a) nationals of countries referred to in the chart above for stays of up to three months;
(b) nationals of Andorra, Argentina, Bolivia, Brunei, Bulgaria, Chile, Costa Rica, Croatia, El Salvador, Guatemala, Honduras, Hong Kong (SAR), Iceland, Korea (Rep), Liechtenstein, Macau (SAR), Malaysia, Mexico, Monaco, New Zealand, Nicaragua, Norway, Panama, Paraguay, San Marino, Singapore, Switzerland, Uruguay, Vatican City and Venezuela for stays of up to three months;
(c) transit passengers continuing their journey by the same or first connecting aircraft provided holding valid onward or return documentation and not leaving the airport.
Note: (a) Nationals of the EU and EEE, and of the Holy See, Liechtenstein and Monaco do not need a a Long Stay visa (trips exceeding three months). (b) Nationals of Canada, Cyprus, Japan, Korea (Rep), Malaysia, Malta, Mexico, Singapore, USA and Venezuela should apply for a visa if they are to receive a salary, even if their trip is a Short Stay. (c) US nationals need a visa if they are crew members, or journalists on assignments, or students enrolled at schools and universities in any of the French Overseas Departments.
Types of visa and cost: All visas, regardless of duration of stay and number of entries permitted, cost €35. In most circumstances, no fee applies to students, recipients of government fellowships and citizens of the EU and their family members.
Validity: *Short-stay* visas (up to 30 days): valid for two months (single- and multiple-entry). *Short stay* visas (31 to 90 days and double- or multiple-entry): valid for a maximum of six months from date of issue. *Transit* visas: valid for single- or multiple-entries of maximum five days per entry, including the day of arrival.
Application to: French Consulate General (for personal visas), or Consular section at Embassy (for diplomatic or service visas); see *Contact Addresses* section for France. All applications must be made in person.
Application requirements: (a) Valid passport with blank page to affix the visa. Minors travelling alone must submit notarised parental authorisation, signed by both parents, plus one copy. (b) Up to two completed application forms. (c) One passport-size photo on each form. (d) Fee, to be paid in cash only if paying by person. If not, fee should be paid by cheque or postal order. (e) Evidence of sufficient funds for stay (two last bank statements, plus copy, or other proof of funds equivalent to US$100 for each day of trip). (f) Letter from employer, or proof of stay in country of residence. (g) Proof of address. (h) Medical insurance. (i) Return ticket and travel documents for remaining journey. (j) Proof of accommodation during stay. (k) Registered self-addressed envelope, if applying by post. (l) Detailed itinerary, including reservations and round trip airline tickets (only required when visa is issued), plus one copy. (m) Proof of employment (eg last payslip or letter from employer). (n) Proof of valid health/travel insurance with worldwide coverage, plus copy. *Business*: (a)-(n) and, (o) Business invitation guaranteeing payment of travel expenses, plus one copy.
Working days required: One day to three weeks depending on nationality.
Temporary residence: If intending to work or stay for longer than 90 days, nationals should contact the Long Stay visa section of the Consulate General or Embassy (tel: (020) 7073 1248).

Money

Currency: Since January 2002 the Euro has been the official currency for the French Overseas Departments, French Guiana, Guadeloupe, Martinique and Réunion. For further details, exchange rates and currency restrictions, see *France* section.
Currency exchange: All the major French banks are represented on the island. ATMs are available.
Credit & debit cards: American Express, Diners Club, MasterCard and Visa are accepted. Check with your credit or debit card company for details of merchant acceptability and other services that may be available.
Travellers cheques: Accepted in most places. Their use may qualify visitors for discounts on luxury items. To avoid additional exchange rate charges, travellers are advised to take travellers cheques in Euros. US and Canadian Dollar cheques are also accepted in some places.
Banking hours: Mon-Fri 0800-1200 and 1400-1600, Sat 0800-1200 (closed Wednesday afternoons).

Duty Free

Guadeloupe is an Overseas Department of France, and the duty free allowances are the same as for France.
Note: Plants and vegetables of any sort are prohibited, as are animals and food of animal origin from Haiti.

Public Holidays

2005: Jan 1 New Year's Day. **Mar 28** Easter Monday. **May 1** Labour Day. **May 5** Ascension. **May 8** Victory Day. **May 16** Whit Monday. **Jul 14** Bastille Day. **Aug 15** Assumption. **Nov 1** All Saints' Day. **Nov 11** Remembrance Day. **Dec 25** Christmas Day.
2006: Jan 1 New Year's Day. **Apr 17** Easter Monday. **May 1** Labour Day. **May 8** Victory Day. **May 25** Ascension. **Jun 5** Whit Monday. **Jul 14** Bastille Day. **Aug 15** Assumption. **Nov 1** All Saints' Day. **Nov 11** Remembrance Day. **Dec 25** Christmas Day.

Health

	Special Precautions?	Certificate Required?
Yellow Fever	No	1
Cholera	No	No
Typhoid & Polio	2	N/A
Malaria	No	N/A

Note: *Regulations and requirements may be subject to change at short notice, and you are advised to contact your doctor well in advance of your intended date of departure. Any numbers in the chart refer to the footnotes below.*

1: A yellow fever vaccination certificate is required by travellers over one year of age arriving from an infected or endemic zone within six days.
2: Vaccination against typhoid and polio is recommended.
Food & drink: Mains water is chlorinated and whilst relatively safe, may cause mild abdominal upsets. Bottled water is available and is advised for the first few weeks of

stay. Drinking water outside main cities and towns may be contaminated and sterilisation is advised. Milk is pasteurised and dairy products are safe for consumption. Local meat, poultry, seafoods and fruit are generally considered safe to eat.

Other risks: *Bilharzia* (schistosomiasis) is present. Avoid swimming and paddling in fresh water; swimming pools that are well maintained and chlorinated are safe. *Hepatitis A* can occur.

The sap of the manchineel tree is toxic and causes burns to the skin. Travellers should avoid contact with its leaves and fruit, and should not stand under the tree when it is raining. These trees, which look similar to apple trees, are often marked with a red sign on the trunk.

Health care: Health care is of a good standard, but health insurance is advisable to cover costs as the reciprocal health agreement between the UK and France may not apply in Guadeloupe.

Travel - International

AIR: Guadeloupe's national airline is *Air Caraïbes (TX)* (website: www.aircaraibes.com). Air France operates at least one flight a day to Pointe-à-Pitre from Paris. Other airlines serving Guadeloupe include *Air Canada*, *Air Liberté AOM*, *American Airlines* and *LIAT*.

Approximate flight times: From Guadeloupe to *London* is 12 hours 40 minutes (including a stopover time of one hour in Paris), to *Los Angeles* is nine hours and to *New York* is six hours.

International airports: *Pointe-à-Pitre (PTP)* (Le Raizet) (website: www.guadeloupe.aeroport.fr), 3km (2 miles) from Pointe-à-Pitre. Buses and taxis to the city are available. The airport has two international terminals: *Guadeloupe Pôle Caraibes* and *le Raizet*. Airport facilities include banks/bureaux de change, ATM, duty free shops, restaurants/bars and tourist information.

Departure tax: None.

SEA: Guadeloupe is a point of call for the following international cruise operators: *Cunard*, *Holland America*, *Royal Caribbean*, *Royal Olympic* and *Princess Cruises*. Many ships ply between Guadeloupe and Martinique, and also connect with Miami and San Juan (Puerto Rico). Ferries and catamarans sail regularly from Pointe-à-Pitre to Dominica, Martinique and St Lucia. *Compagnie Générale Maritime* has weekly 'banana boats' carrying passengers between Guadeloupe and Martinique, Dominica and St Lucia.

Travel - Internal

AIR: *Air Caraïbe*, *Air Guadeloupe*, *Air Martinique*, *Air St Barth*, *Air St Martin* and *LIAT* connect Guadeloupe with the smaller islands in the group. *Air France* also offers a limited inter-island service. There are domestic airports on the islands of La Désirade, Marie-Galante, St-Barthélemy and St-Martin.

Domestic airports: *St-Martin (SFG)* (*Espérance*) is 4km (3 miles) from Marigot. Buses and taxis are available. The airport is served by *Air Caraïbes*. Facilities include a bar. *St-Barthélemy (SBH)* is 2km (1 mile) from Gustavia. Taxis are available.

SEA: Regular ferry services ply around the islands.

ROAD: There is a good public **bus** service, **taxi** services and many **car** and **van rental** companies. Driving is on the right. Buses depart from Pointe-à-Pitre and Basse-Terre to all towns and villages. **Documentation:** National driving licence is sufficient, but at least one year's driving experience is required. An International Driving Permit is advised.

Accommodation

HOTELS: There is a good selection of hotels on Guadeloupe, ranging from first-class beach resorts to country inns. Visitors can also stay in traditional small hotels known as *Relais Créoles*. Most accommodation is to be found on the south coast of Grande-Terre. Accommodation on the outlying islands can be interesting, but may be very basic. At present there are over 4000 rooms throughout the group. The tax on hotel rates is usually inclusive. A standard charge of US$1.50 per day is levied by many hotels. Additional service charges can range between 15 and 30 per cent depending on the time of year. The Relais de la Guadeloupe provides a central booking service.

Grading: 3- and 4-star hotels offer sporting and cultural activities in addition to board and lodging. There are also two particular categories of hotel: Hibiscus (H) and Alamandas (A). Hibiscus hotels are 2- or 3-star establishments usually run as a family affair. Alamandas hotels are sophisticated 1- or 2-star establishments. Many hotels in the Caribbean offer accommodation according to one of a number of plans: **FAP** is Full American Plan; room with all meals (including afternoon tea, supper, etc). **AP** is American Plan; room with three meals. **MAP** is Modified American Plan; breakfast and dinner included with the price of the room, plus in some places British-style afternoon tea. **CP** is Continental Plan; room and breakfast only. **EP** is European Plan; room only.

SELF-CATERING: Villas and cottages may be rented. It is also possible for visitors to stay in traditional accommodation, known as *gîtes ruraux*, which are small furnished apartments or villas located away from major resorts owned by Guadeloupe hosts. Further information can be obtained from the Office du Tourisme (see *Contact Addresses* section).

CAMPING: There is only one campsite in Guadeloupe at present. For further details contact the Guadeloupe Office du Tourisme (see *Contact Addresses* section).

Resorts & Excursions

GRANDE-TERRE: Pointe-à-Pitre, the commercial capital of Guadeloupe, is situated on the island of Grande-Terre. This gracious town has a pleasant square at its core, the **Place de la Victoire**, which is surrounded by a busy market and, further out, the docks. It is an active, lively port with many narrow streets to explore. The **Pavillion d'Exposition de Bergevin** and the **Centre Cultural Rémy Nainsouta** are two interesting museums in the town. At **Fort Fleur d'Épée**, there are some fascinating underground caves and to the north of these is the old sugar town of **Sainte-Anne**.

BASSE-TERRE: Highlights include **Sainte-Marie de Capesterre** and the Hindu temple to its south, where it may be possible to see religious ceremonies taking place. The small town of **Trois Rivières** has a collection of interesting Indian relics which could easily be visited on the way to the **National Park of Guadeloupe** near **St-Claude**. This 74,000-acre park, of great natural beauty, is situated at the base of **La Soufrière**, a dormant volcano. In the rainforests there are some good walking and picnic areas which make a pleasant alternative to lying on the islands' fine beaches. The town of **Basse-Terre** itself is a beautiful old French colonial town, situated at the foot of La Soufrière. The **St-Charles Fort** is of French military architecture, built in 1605 and now restored and converted into a museum. The cathedral and market place are also worth seeing.

OUTLYING ISLANDS: The other islands of **Marie-Galante**, **La Désirade** and **Les Saintes** are visited less frequently and are best suited to the resourceful traveller. La Désirade, quiet and undeveloped, is known for its seafood. Les Saintes are a string of tiny islands, only two of which are inhabited, **Terre-de-Haut** and **Terre-de-Bas**. These are both very attractive and have a selection of modestly priced hotels. Marie-Galante has a number of good hotels and beaches. Its old and crumbling mills are reminders of its history as a major sugar plantation.

Sport & Activities

Watersports: Guadeloupe's beaches are good for **swimming**, and the sand varies depending on the area: Grande-Terre has white sand, and the sand on the leeward coast is brown, while black-sand beaches can be found on the western end of Basse-Terre. Nude and topless sunbathing is restricted to just a few beaches. **Snorkelling** and **diving** can be practised widely, and there are several commercial operators offering equipment hire, courses and diving trips. Snorkellers can usually access coral reefs directly from the beaches. Divers should note that harpoons and artificial lights are strictly prohibited. Glass-bottomed boats operate at several marine nature reserves on Petite-Terre and Basse-Terre. Marine species such as lobsters and sea turtles are protected, and visitors should familiarise themselves with Guadeloupe's conservation policies upon arrival. There are good facilities (such as boat charters and equipment hire) for **fishing**, including deep-sea fishing. In maritime reserves fishing is either forbidden or strongly regulated; visitors should enquire locally. **Small-boat sailing** and **water-skiing** are both popular. Guadeloupe hosts a number of regional and international sailing competitions and there are sailing schools throughout the islands. Pleasure sailing boats do not require a licence.

Walking: The National Park of Guadeloupe provides around 300km (188 miles) of marked trails leading into the rainforest, where visitors can observe many tropical animals and plants. The scenery on these walks often includes waterfalls (such as the Cascade aux Ecrevisses) or lakes (such as the Grand Etang). On Grande-Terre, hiking trails lead through the mangrove or along the cliffs of the Atlantic coast. For further information, contact the Office du Tourisme (see *Contact Addresses* section).

Other: Horse riding and **mountain climbing** are also possible. There is a well-known 18-hole **golf** course, the Sainte-Françoise, designed by Robert Trent Jones.

Social Profile

FOOD & DRINK: Predominantly seafood, cooked in French, Creole, African or South-East Asian styles. Dishes include lobster, turtle, red snapper, conch and sea urchin. Island specialities include stuffed crab, stewed conch, roast wild goat, jugged rabbit and broiled dove. The spicy flavour of Creole cuisine is unique. The more formal restaurants will require appropriate dress. Drinks include a great supply of French wines, champagnes, liqueurs and local rum. A local speciality, *Rum Punch* (a brew of rum, lime, bitter and syrup), is a must. There are no licensing restrictions.

NIGHTLIFE: There are plenty of restaurants, bars and discos, with displays of local dancing and music. The famous dance of the island is called the *Biguine*, where colourful and ornate Creole costumes are still worn.

SHOPPING: Worthwhile purchases are French imports, including perfume, wine, liqueurs and Lalique crystal. Local items include fine-flavoured rum, straw goods, bamboo hats, voodoo dolls, and objects of aromatic Vetevier root. Travellers cheques give a 20 per cent discount in some shops. **Shopping hours:** Mon-Fri 0830-1800, Sat 0830-1300.

SPECIAL EVENTS: There are many local festivals and special events, both Roman Catholic and Creole. For details, contact the Office du Tourisme (see *Contact Addresses* section). The following special event is occurring in Guadeloupe in 2005:

Aug 10 *Festival of the Women Cooks* (a culinary nirvana proclaimed as one of Guadeloupe's most spectacular events), Pointe-à-Pitre.

SOCIAL CONVENTIONS: The atmosphere is relaxed and informal. Casual dress is accepted everywhere, but formal dress is needed for dining out and in nightclubs. **Tipping:** 10 per cent is normal.

Business Profile

ECONOMY: Guadeloupe's economy is relatively diverse by regional standards – with agriculture, light industry and tourism as its main components – but remains heavily dependent on French aid and is vulnerable to the vagaries of the Caribbean climate. Bananas and sugar are the main export commodities, accounting for over one-third of total foreign earnings (although the banana trade is threatened by a World Trade Organization ruling preventing preferential access to European markets). Coffee, cocoa and vanilla are the other important cash crops. Industry is largely devoted to processing agricultural products and light manufactured goods such as boats. Tourism is a key and fast-growing sector; mainly ecotourism and a growing market for cruise ship stopovers. France supplies most of the island's imports and takes three-quarters of its exports.

BUSINESS: Lightweight suits, safari suits, and shirt and tie are recommended for business meetings. Best times to visit are January to March and June to September. Much of the island's business is connected to France. **Office hours:** Mon-Fri 0800-1200 and 1400-1800.

COMMERCIAL INFORMATION: The following organisations can offer advice: Chambre de Commerce et d'Industrie de Pointe-à-Pitre, rue Félix Eboué, 97159 Pointe-à-Pitre (tel: (590) 937 600; fax: (590) 902 187; e-mail: contacts@cci-pap.org; website: www.cci-pap.org); *or* Chambre de Commerce, 6 Rue Victor Hugues, 97100 Basse-Terre (tel: (590) 994 444; fax: (590) 812 117; e-mail: cci-basse-terre@wanadoo.fr; website: www.basseterre.cci.fr).

Climate

Warm weather throughout the year with the main rainy season occurring from June to October. Showers can, however, occur at any time although they are usually brief. The humidity can be exceedingly high at times.

Required clothing: Lightweights with warmer top layers for the evenings; showerproofs are advisable.

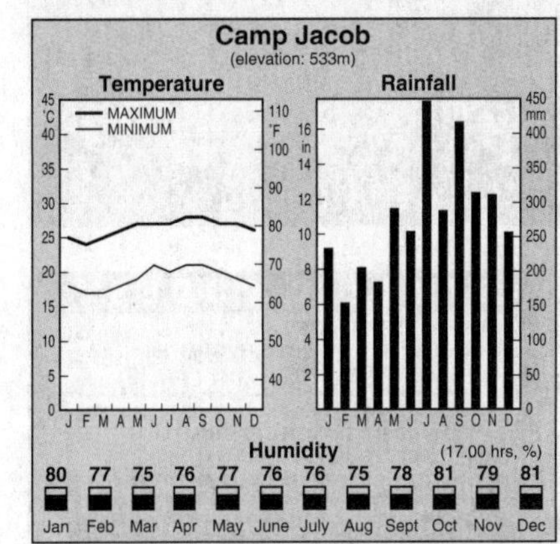

Guam

LATEST TRAVEL ADVICE CONTACTS

British Foreign and Commonwealth Office
Tel: (0870) 606 0290 Website: www.fco.gov.uk

US Department of State
Website: http://travel.state.gov/travel

Canadian Department of Foreign Affairs and Int'l Trade
Tel: (1 800) 267 8376 Website: www.dfait-maeci.gc.ca

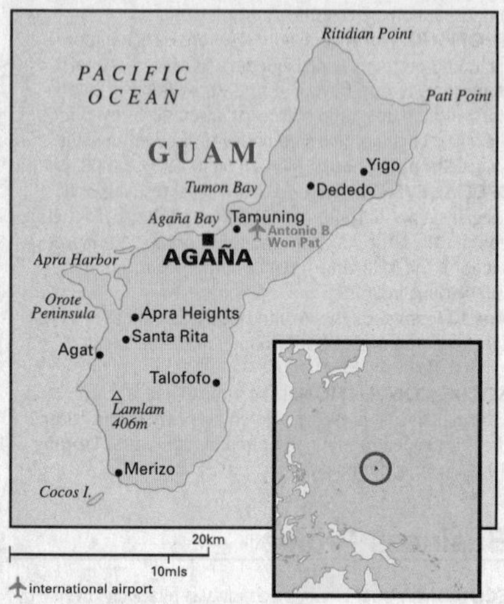

Location: Western Pacific, Micronesia.

Country dialling code: 671.

Guam is an External Territory of the United States of America and is represented abroad by US Embassies – see *USA* section.

Guam Visitors Bureau
401 Pale San Vitores Road, Tamuning, GU 96913, Guam
Tel: 646 5278/9. Fax: 646 8861.
E-mail: guaminfo@visitguam.org
Website: www.visitguam.org

Guam Visitors Bureau
Aviso Inc, 1301 Marina Village Parkway, Suite 210, Alameda, CA 94501, USA
Tel: (510) 865 1756 *or* (800) 873 4826 (toll-free in USA).
Fax: (510) 865 5165.
E-mail: guam@avisoinc.com
Website: www.visitguam.org

Credit: © Guam Visitors Bureau

TIMATIC CODES

Health
AMADEUS: **TI-DFT/GUM/HE**
GALILEO/WORLDSPAN: **TI-DFT/GUM/HE**
SABRE: **TIDFT/GUM/HE**

Visa
AMADEUS: **TI-DFT/GUM/VI**
GALILEO/WORLDSPAN: **TI-DFT/GUM/VI**
SABRE: **TIDFT/GUM/VI**

To access TIMATIC country information on Health and Visa regulations through the Computer Reservations System (CRS), type in the appropriate command line listed above.

General Information

AREA: 549 sq km (212 sq miles).
POPULATION: 159,547 (official estimate 2002).
POPULATION DENSITY: 290.6 per sq km.
CAPITAL: Hagåtña. Tamuning is the commercial centre. **Population:** 1122 (2000) in Hagåtña and 10,833 in Tamuning.
GEOGRAPHY: Guam is the largest and most southerly island of the Marianas archipelago. It is a predominantly hilly island and its northern end is a plateau of rolling hills and cliffs rising 152m (500ft) above sea level. The cliffs are tunnelled with caves. The island narrows in the middle, with the southern half widening into a land of mountains and valleys cut by streams and waterfalls. The most sheltered beaches are on the western coast.
GOVERNMENT: US External Territory (Unincorporated). Gained internal autonomy in 1982. **Head of State:** George W Bush since 2001. **Head of Government:** Governor Felix Camacho since 2003.
LANGUAGE: English is the official language; Chamorro is the local language. Japanese is also spoken – particularly by the older generation who were alive during the Japanese occupation.
RELIGION: Christian; 90 per cent Roman Catholic.
TIME: GMT + 10.
ELECTRICITY: 120 volts AC, 60Hz.
COMMUNICATIONS: Telephone: Overseas telecommunications facilities are available in Hagåtña. Country code: 671. Outgoing international code: 001. **Mobile telephone:** GSM 1900 network exists. Main provider is *Guam Wireless Co LLC* (website: www.hafatel.com). **Fax:** Many hotels have facilities. **Internet:** Main ISPs are *Guam.Net* (website: www.guam.net) and *IT&E* (website: www.ite.net). **Post:** The Hagåtña and Tamuning branches are open Mon-Fri 0800-1600, Sat 0930-1200. The Guam Main Facility branch is open Mon-Fri 0930-1700, Sat 1300-1600. **Press:** The English-language daily newspaper is *The Pacific Daily News*.
Radio: BBC World Service (website: www.bbc.co.uk/worldservice) and Voice of America (website: www.voa.gov) can be received. From time to time the frequencies change and the most up-to-date can be found online.

Passport/Visa

Note: Visa requirements for Guam are the same as for mainland USA; travellers require a visa or, if qualified, may travel visa free under the US Visa Waiver Program. If applying for a visa, application procedures are also the same (see *Passport/Visa* in *US* section). However, there is also a Visa Waiver Program specifically for Guam, the regulations for which are printed in this section.

	Passport Required?	Visa Required?	Return Ticket Required?
Full British	Yes	No/1	Yes
Australian	Yes	No/1	Yes
Canadian	Yes	Yes	Yes
USA	1	No	No
Other EU	Yes	Yes/1	Yes
Japanese	Yes	No/1	Yes

Note: Regulations and requirements may be subject to change at short notice, and you are advised to contact the appropriate diplomatic or consular authority before finalising travel arrangements. Details of these may be found at the head of this country's entry. Any numbers in the chart refer to the footnotes below.

Restricted entry: The following are not eligible to receive a USA entry visa:
(a) people afflicted with certain serious communicable diseases or disorders deemed threatening to the property, safety or welfare of others;
(b) anyone who has been arrested (except for very minor driving offences) or who has a criminal record;
(c) narcotics addicts or abusers and drug traffickers;
(d) anyone who has been deported from or denied admission to the USA.
Note: Those who are ineligible may be eligible for a waiver of ineligibility.
PASSPORTS: Required by all except **1.** US citizens entering Guam from the US mainland or a US territory, provided they hold proof of citizenship and valid photo ID card.
Note: All visitors must now hold a machine-readable passport (MRP).
VISAS: A US visitor visa is required by all except the following for stays of up to 15 days:
1. Citizens of Andorra, Australia, Austria, Belgium, Brunei, Denmark, Finland, France, Germany, Hong Kong, Iceland, Ireland, Italy, Indonesia, Japan, Korea (Rep.), Liechtenstein, Luxembourg, Malaysia, Monaco, Nauru, Netherlands, New Zealand, Norway, Papua New Guinea, Portugal, San Marino, Singapore, Slovenia, Solomon Islands, Spain, Sweden, Switzerland, Taiwan*, United Kingdom, Vanuatu, or Western Samoa.
* Taiwanese nationals are only visa exempt if in possession of a Taiwanese National ID card and they begin their journey in Taiwan and travel directly to Guam.
Note: The nationals listed above are declared visa-exempt under the Guam Visa Waiver Program on the following conditions: (a) Purpose of visit is for business, touristic or transit purposes only. (b) The air carrier is a participant in the Guam visa waiver programme. (c) All visitors are in possession of a completed and signed visa waiver form, I-736 (obtainable from the airline).
Note: Travellers who enter Guam visa free are not eligible to travel onward to the USA.
Types of visa and cost: *Non-immigrant* (business or tourist): £67. There are several other types of visa; enquire at local US Consulate (or Consular Section at Embassy); see *Contact Addresses* section. Some nationals may also have to pay a reciprocal visa issuance fee – details are available from the State Department (website: www.travel.state.gov).
Validity: Validity varies but visas have a maximum validity of 10 years. The Embassy no longer issues visas "indefinitely".
Application to: US Consulate (or Consular Section at Embassy). See *Contact Addresses* in *USA* section.
Application requirements: (a) Completed visa application form DS-156. (b) Passport valid six months after visit and with at least one blank page. (c) One passport-size colour photo. (d) Fee, payable by bank paying in slip only, which must be payed and endorsed by the bank prior to application. (e) Documentation of intent to return to country of residence. (f) Supporting documents (such as purpose of visit), where relevant. (g) Self-addressed, special delivery envelope.
Note: (a) Most non-immigrant visa applicants are required to schedule an appointment for a visa interview with a consular officer, and may have to undergo a medical examination, for which there is an additional fee. (b) The six month requirement does not apply to United Kingdom passports. (c) Nationals of China (PR), Cuba, Russian Federation and Vietnam are also required to complete two DS-156 application forms and provide two colour passport-size photos. Male applicants aged 16-45 and nationals of Cuba, Iran, Iraq, Korea (DPR), Libya, Northern Cyprus, Somalia, Sudan and the Syrian Arab Republic are required to complete one DS-157 application form. Nationals of Northern Cyprus are also required to provide four colour passport-size photos.
Please note that requirements are subject to change at short notice and any applicant should check with the US Embassy (website: www.usembassy.org.uk).
Working days required: At least 10 days, but up to several weeks. Applications lodged during the peak travel season may take longer.
Temporary residence: The individual must obtain a work or immigrant visa or be petitioned by a US citizen. Contact the US Consulate (or Consular section at Embassy).

Money

Currency: US Dollar (US$) = 100 cents. Notes are in denominations of US$100, 50, 20, 10, 5, 2 and 1. Coins are in denominations of US$1, and 50, 25, 10, 5 and 1 cents. For exchange rates and currency restrictions, see the *USA* section.
Currency exchange: There are numerous US and international banks on the island. ATMs are available.
Credit & debit cards: Most major credit and charge cards are widely accepted on Guam. Check with your credit or debit card company for details of merchant acceptability and other services which may be available.
Travellers cheques: To avoid additional exchange rate charges, travellers are advised to take travellers cheques in US Dollars.
Banking hours: Mon-Thurs 1000-1500, Fri 1000-1800, Sat 0900-1200 (Bank of Guam only). Hours may vary slightly.

Duty Free

The following may be imported into Guam without incurring customs duty:
200 cigarettes or 50 cigars or 200g of tobacco (or a combination of the three); three bottles of spirits; a reasonable amount of perfume for personal use; goods up to the value of US$1000.
Restricted items: Fruit, vegetables, flowers and plants; livestock and meat products; narcotics; items in breach of US copyright law.

Public Holidays

2005: Jan 1 New Year's Day. **Jan 17** Martin Luther King Day. **Feb 14** President's Day. **Mar 7** Guam Discovery Day. **Mar 25** Good Friday. **May 30** Memorial Day. **Jul 4** Independence Day. **Jul 21** Liberation Day. **Sep 5** Labour Day. **Oct 10** Columbus Day. **Nov 2** All Souls' Day. **Nov 11** Veterans Day. **Nov 24** Thanksgiving Day. **Dec 8** Lady of Camarin Day. **Dec 25** Christmas Day.

2006: Jan 1 New Year's Day. **Jan 16** Martin Luther King Day. **Feb 13** President's Day. **Mar 6** Guam Discovery Day. **Apr 14** Good Friday. **May 29** Memorial Day. **Jul 4** Independence Day. **Jul 21** Liberation Day. **Sep 4** Labour Day. **Oct 9** Columbus Day. **Nov 2** All Souls' Day. **Nov 11** Veterans Day. **Nov 23** Thanksgiving Day. **Dec 8** Lady of Camarin Day. **Dec 25** Christmas Day.

Health

	Special Precautions?	Certificate Required?
Yellow Fever	No	No
Cholera	No	No
Typhoid & Polio	1	N/A
Malaria	No	N/A

Note: *Regulations and requirements may be subject to change at short notice, and you are advised to contact your doctor well in advance of your intended date of departure. Any numbers in the chart refer to the footnotes below.*

1: Poliomyelitis has not been reported for more than six years, although precautions should be taken against typhoid fever.

Food & drink: Mains water is normally chlorinated, and whilst relatively safe may cause mild abdominal upsets. Bottled water is available. Milk is pasteurised and dairy products are safe for consumption. Local meat, poultry, seafood, fruit and vegetables are generally considered safe to eat. There is, however, a risk of biointoxication from raw or cooked fish or shellfish.

Other risks: *Hepatitis B* is endemic, *Hepatitis A* and *TB* also occur. *Dengue fever* and *Japanese encephalitis* can occur in epidemics. Jellyfish might also pose some threat.

Health care: Health insurance is strongly advised, owing to the high cost of health care. There is one civilian hospital, the Guam Memorial Hospital, and a number of private clinics, as well as some medical facilities run for US military personnel.

Travel - International

AIR: *Virgin Atlantic* flies regularly to Narita (Tokyo, Japan), where passengers can connect with a *Continental Micronesia* flight to Guam. Other airlines serving Guam include *Air Japan, All Nippon Airways, Asiana Airlines, Continental Micronesia, Korean Air, Northwest Airlines* and *Philippine Airlines*.

Approximate flight times: From Guam to *London* is 14 hours 30 minutes.

International airports: *Antonio B Won Pat International Airport (GUM)* (website: www.airport.guam.net) is 11km (7 miles) from the city. Taxis are available. Airport facilities include a bureau de change, duty free shop, car hire, restaurant and coffee shop. The terminal has recently been renovated to improve cargo and passenger facilities and there are plans to add a further runway.

Departure tax: None.

SEA: Apra Harbour is the principal port in Micronesia and a port of call for the following shipping lines: *American President, Austfreight, Daiwa, Kyowa, Micronesia Transport* and *Sea-Land Services*.

ROAD: Bus: The *Guam Mass Transit Authority* operates buses on nine routes, connecting nearly all the villages on the island. Buses do not run on Sundays or public holidays. Discount fares are available for senior citizens, disabled people and students. **Taxi:** Fares are metered. Taxis are available near major shopping centres and at hotels. **Car hire:** Available through most major companies. Charges are based on time and mileage plus insurance.

Documentation: An International Driving Permit is required.

Accommodation

HOTELS: Over the past few years tourism has been growing rapidly and, to cater for this, numerous hotels have been built offering a good range of facilities to suit most tastes and pockets. Many hotels cater almost exclusively for Japanese tourists. There is now a good range of accommodation on offer. For more details, contact the Guam Hotel & Restaurant Association, PO Box 8565, Tamuning 96931 (tel: 649 1447; e-mail: ghra@ghra.org; website: www.ghra.org) *or* the Guam Visitors Bureau (see *Contact Addresses* section).

CAMPING: Camping is permitted on some beaches and parks; but not all places are suitable so you should seek advice first. Information can be obtained from the Guam Visitors Bureau (see *Contact Addresses* section).

Resorts & Excursions

Guam is the largest island in Micronesia and, owing to the large US Naval presence, the most cosmopolitan and energetic. Spain ruled the islands for 333 years and **Hagåtña**, the capital, has many historic buildings dating from this era. Also of interest are buildings from the Spanish colonial period and the relics of the Chamorro period (a culture which remains alive today, albeit much modified, in about 55,000 persons). Many attractions are geared towards US GIs at the local US military base. For other visitors to Guam, there are many outdoor and water recreation activities to enjoy.

Tumon Bay, just up the coast from Hagåtña, is the main tourist centre. There are fine coral reefs around the coast. The interior is mountainous, particularly in the south. There are several spectacular cliffs on the north coast. There are three botanical gardens in Guam: the **Inarajan Shore Botanical Garden** by the sea in the southern part of the island; the **Nano Fall Botanical Gardens** in **Agat**, where swimming can be enjoyed in the Nano River under rushing cascades; and the **Pineapple Plantation** in **Yigo**. There are also many parks in Guam, some dedicated to the war years. The **South Pacific Memorial Park** in Yigo commemorates those killed in World War II, and the **War in the Pacific National Historical Park** is the location of five World War II battle sites with a museum of war photos and relics. Guam has another small museum with sections dedicated to Chamorro culture, natural history and the Japanese soldier who hid in the interior until 1972, unaware that the war was over. As most tourists to Guam are Japanese, many sites commemorate the war. Other parks include **Latte Park**, located at the bottom of Kasamata Hill; and **Merizo Pier Park**, with recreational facilities for watersports and the location of the annual *Merizo Water Festival*, is a one acre resort surrounded by a clear lagoon and accessible by speedboat. Beach parks include **Talofofo Bay Beach Park**, located at the mouth of the Talofofo River and a surfers' paradise; and **Ipao Beach Park**, once the location of an ancient Chamorro settlement, later a penal and leper colony, and now one of Guam's most popular recreational areas.

Sport & Activities

Watersports: Local **dive** shops offer daily charters to the popular sites. Attractions for divers include World War II wrecks, reefs and a variety of marine flora and fauna. A type of dolphin, the spinner dolphin, inhabits the island's shallow bays. A number of creatures which hide in the corals during the day can be seen on night dives. Fully-equipped boats may be chartered for **skindiving** and **snorkelling**. **Surfing** facilities are available at coastal resorts. Most hotels have **swimming** pools, and there is a public pool in Hagåtña; the west coast offers safe bathing.

Fishing: Reef fishing with net and rod is popular, as is spearfishing for groupers and skipjacks and deep-sea fishing for marlin, tuna, wahoo, barracuda, bonito and sailfish.

Golf: There are several 18-hole courses. The *Windward Hills Course* has a clubhouse and pool, as does the *Country Club of the Pacific*. Visitors are welcome at both.

Other: Cycling and **hiking** are increasing in popularity and it is possible to take such trips through Guam's jungle. **Greyhound races** are held three times a week.

Social Profile

FOOD & DRINK: Guamanian cooking is very similar to Spanish cuisine. Typical Guamanian dishes include red rice, shrimp patties and *kelagven* (a dish of chopped chicken, lemon juice, grated coconut and hot peppers). The wide selection of restaurants features American, Chinese, European, Filipino, Indonesian, Japanese, Korean and Mexican food.

NIGHTLIFE: A range of nightclubs feature music and dancing. Major hotels frequently stage shows with musicians from the US mainland, or local performers including the *Guam Symphony & Choral Society*. There are a number of cinemas in Tamuning, including at least one 14-screen cinema, most showing recent US films. Dance shows and dinner cruises are also available.

SHOPPING: There are many shopping centres in Agaña, Tumon, Tamuning and Dededo that offer an array of retail items. The main malls include the *Hagåtña* and *Gibson's Shopping Centers* – the former with a 14-screen multiplex cinema. *Micronesia Mall* has recently undergone expansion and has the distinction of being the island's first indoor mall. Good buys in Guam include watches, perfume, jewellery, alcohol, china, stereo equipment and cameras.

Shopping hours: Generally Mon-Sat 1000-2100, Sun 1200-1800 but hours do vary from centre to centre.

SPECIAL EVENTS: Each village has its own fiesta to celebrate its patron saint. They are celebrated on the weekend closest to the Saint's Day and show the strong Spanish influence on local culture. The following is a selection of special events celebrated annually in Guam:

May *Malojloj Festival* (the most famous of the patron Saint's days), Inarajan. **Jul** *Island Carnival*, Y'pao Beach Park. **Jul 21** *Liberation Day* (celebrated with fireworks, feasts and one of the year's most impressive parades).

Credit: © Guam Visitors Bureau

Aug *Merizo Water Festival* (various watersports events). **Dec 8** *Immaculate Conception* (celebrated with an impressive parade).

SOCIAL CONVENTIONS: Western customs are well understood – for the visiting Westerner it is quite likely that it will not be the customs of the locals that have to be observed, but those of the visiting Japanese who make up around 90 per cent of the island's tourists. The most evident Chamorro legacy is the Chamorro language and a range of facial expressions, called 'Eyebrow', which virtually constitutes a language of its own. **Tipping:** 10-15 per cent is standard for taxi drivers, in restaurants and hotels. Where a 10 per cent service charge has already been added to the bill, tipping is optional.

Business Profile

ECONOMY: The main components of Guam's economy are tourism and the US military for whom the island is a vital staging post for operations through the Pacific region. Tourism has expanded rapidly despite the island's remote location and small size: Guam now receives over one million visitors annually, of whom 90 per cent come from Japan. A range of crops, including maize, cassava, bananas and coconuts, are grown for domestic consumption. Exports include copra, fish and handmade goods. Industry is limited to a petroleum refinery and a handful of light manufacturing operations. Guam is also an important re-export centre for distribution of goods throughout the Pacific, particularly to Micronesia, and this provides a large proportion of its export income.

Government policy presently concentrates on attracting foreign investment, principally from Asia, and has been examining the country's potential as an offshore financial centre. However, the development of the latter is not favoured by the extensive competition in the Pacific and Guam's tax laws.

COMMERCIAL INFORMATION: The following organisation can offer advice: Guam Chamber of Commerce, 173 Aspinall Avenue, Ada Plaza Center, Suite 101, Hagåtña, GU 96910 (tel: 472 6311 *or* 472 8001; fax: 472 6202; e-mail: gchamber@guamchamber.com.gu; website: www.guamchamber.com.gu).

Climate

Tropical, with dry and rainy seasons. The hottest months precede the rainy season, which is July to November. The temperature ranges from 26-30°C (75-86°F).

Required clothing: Casual lightweight clothing, with waterproof wear needed for the rainy season.

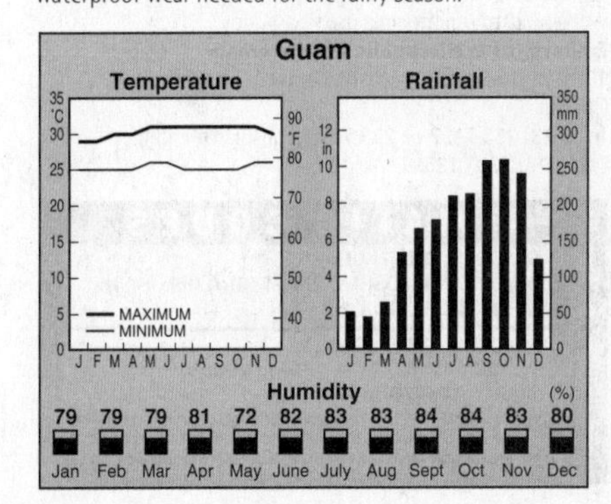

Guatemala

LATEST TRAVEL ADVICE CONTACTS

British Foreign and Commonwealth Office
Tel: (0870) 606 0290 Website: www.fco.gov.uk

US Department of State
Website: http://travel.state.gov/travel

Canadian Department of Foreign Affairs and Int'l Trade
Tel: (1 800) 267 8376 Website: www.dfait-maeci.gc.ca

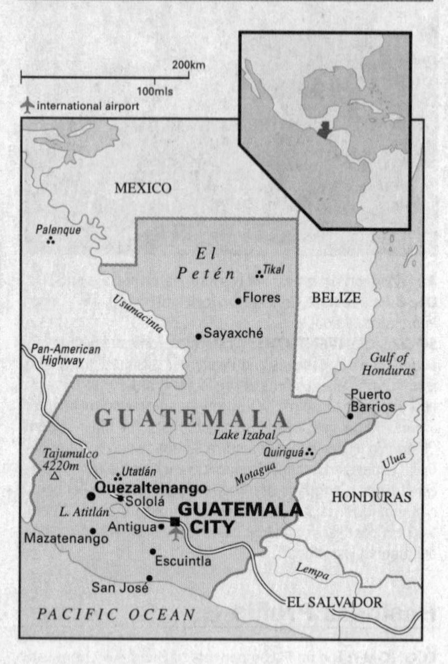

Location: Central America.

Country dialling code: 502.

Guatemala Tourist Commission (INGUAT)
Centro Cívico, 7A Avenida 1-17, Zona 4, Guatemala City 01004, Guatemala
Tel: 2421 0000 *or* (888) 464 8281 (24-hour toll-free number in USA) *or* (801) 464 8281 (24-hour toll-free number in Guatemala). Fax: 2421 2879.
E-mail: informacion@inguat.gob.gt *or* info@inguat.gob.gt
Website: www.mayaspirit.com.gt

Embassy of the Republic of Guatemala
13 Fawcett Street, London SW10 9HN, UK
Tel: (020) 7351 3042. Fax: (020) 7376 5708.
E-mail: embaguate.gtm@btconnect.com
Opening hours: Mon-Fri 0900-1800; 1000-1300 only for walk in queries (consular section).
The Embassy also handles tourism queries.

British Embassy
Avenida la Reforma 16-00, Zona 10, Edificio Torre Internacional, Nivel 11, Guatemala City, Guatemala
Tel: 2367 5425-9. Fax: 2367 5430.
E-mail: embassy@intelnett.com

Embassy of the Republic of Guatemala
2220 R Street, NW, Washington, DC 20008, USA
Tel: (202) 745 4952. Fax: (202) 745 1908.
E-mail: info@guatemala-embassy.org (general) *or* consulate@guatemala-embassy.org (consular section).
Website: www.guatemala-embassy.org

Embassy of the United States of America
Avenida de la Reforma 7-01, Zona 10, Guatemala City, Guatemala
Tel: 2326 4000. Fax: 2334 8477.
Website: http://guatemala.usembassy.gov

Embassy of the Republic of Guatemala
130 Albert Street, Suite 1010, Ottawa, Ontario K1P 5G4, Canada
Tel: (613) 233 7237 *or* 233 7188 (consular section).
Fax: (613) 233 0135.
E-mail: embassy1@embaguate-canada.com
Website: www.embaguate-canada.com

Canadian Embassy
Street address: 13 Calle 8-44, Zona 10, Edyma Plaza, Piso 8, Guatemala City, CA, 1010, Guatemala
Postal address: PO Box 400, Guatemala City, Guatemala
Tel: 2363 4348.
Fax: 2365 1214 (visa section) *or* 2365 1211 (general enquiries).
E-mail: gtmla@international.gc.ca
Website: www.guatemala.gc.ca

TIMATIC CODES

Health
AMADEUS: **TI-DFT/GUA/HE**
GALILEO/WORLDSPAN: **TI-DFT/GUA/HE**
SABRE: **TIDFT/GUA/HE**

Visa
AMADEUS: **TI-DFT/GUA/VI**
GALILEO/WORLDSPAN: **TI-DFT/GUA/VI**
SABRE: **TIDFT/GUA/VI**

To access TIMATIC country information on Health and Visa regulations through the Computer Reservations System (CRS), type in the appropriate command line listed above.

General Information

AREA: 108,889 sq km (42,042 sq miles).
POPULATION: 11,237,196 (official census 2002).
POPULATION DENSITY: 103.2 per sq km
CAPITAL: Guatemala City. **Population:** 1,022,000 (official estimate 2001).
GEOGRAPHY: Guatemala is located in Central America and shares borders to the north and west with Mexico, to the southeast with El Salvador and Honduras, to the northeast with Belize and the Caribbean sea and to the south with the Pacific ocean. The landscape is predominantly mountainous and heavily forested. A string of volcanoes rises above the southern highlands along the Pacific, three of which are still active. Within this volcanic area are basins of varying sizes which hold the majority of the country's population. The region is drained by rivers flowing into both the Pacific and the Caribbean. One basin west of the capital has no river outlet and thus has formed Lake Atitlán, which is ringed by volcanoes. To the northwest, bordering on Belize and Mexico, lies the low undulating tableland of El Petén, 36,300 sq km (14,000 sq miles) of almost inaccessible wilderness covered with dense hardwood forest. This area covers approximately one-third of the national territory, yet contains only 40,000 people.
GOVERNMENT: Republic. Gained independence from Spain in 1821. **Head of State and Government:** President Oscar Berger Perdomo since 2004.
LANGUAGE: The official language is Spanish. English is widely spoken in tourist areas and major hotels and restaurants. 23 indigenous languages are also spoken.
RELIGION: The constitution guarantees freedom of worship, but Catholicism is the most widespread religion with a 10 per cent Protestant minority. Some indigenous communities hold services combining Catholicism with pre-Columbian rites.
TIME: GMT - 6.
ELECTRICITY: 115-125 volts AC, 60Hz. There are some regional variations.
COMMUNICATIONS: Telephone: IDD is available. Country code: 502. Outgoing international code: 00. Telephone calls to Europe are slightly cheaper between 1900 and 0700. **Mobile telephone:** GSM 860/1900 is available. Handsets can be hired from *Ruracel* and other companies. Operators include *Comcel* (website: www.comcel.com.gt), *Sercom S.A.* (website: www.pcsdigital.com.gt) and *Telefonica Centroamerica Guatemala* (website: www.telefonica.com.gt). Some hotels also supply them. Coverage is increasing in Guatemala; consult network operator for details. **Fax:** Most hotels have facilities. **Internet:** There are several Internet cafes in Guatemala City and the main tourist areas. ISPs include *GuateNet* (website: www.guate.net). **Telegram:** Local telegrams can be sent from the central post office. Urgent telegrams are charged at double the ordinary rate. **Post:** Regular airmail to Europe takes 12 days. **Press:** Publications include *Diario Centroamérica, El Periódico, La Hora, Prensa Libre* and *Siglo Veintiuno*. English-language publications include *Central America Report, Guatemala Weekly, Siglo News* and *The Review*.
Radio: BBC World Service (website: www.bbc.co.uk/worldservice) and Voice of America (website: www.voa.gov) can be received. From time to time the frequencies change and the most up-to-date can be found online.

Passport/Visa

	Passport Required?	Visa Required?	Return Ticket Required?
Full British	Yes	No	No
Australian	Yes	No	No
Canadian	Yes	No	No
USA	Yes	No	No
Other EU	Yes	No/1	No
Japanese	Yes	No/1	No

Note: *Regulations and requirements may be subject to change at short notice, and you are advised to contact the appropriate diplomatic or consular authority before finalising travel arrangements. Details of these may be found at the head of this country's entry. Any numbers in the chart refer to the footnotes below.*

Restricted entry: Entry and transit is refused to deportees of other countries who are not nationals of Guatemala. Nationals of some countries require special authorisation from the Department of Immigration in Guatemala before they are granted a visa; nationals of these countries will need to make their application in Guatemala, through a person, company or institution that will be responsible for that person's stay in Guatemala. Authorisation from Guatemala will take two to five weeks and applicants are also required to attend an interview at the Consulate. For an up-to-date list of nationalities, enquire at the nearest Consulate (or Consular section at Embassy).
PASSPORTS: Passport valid for at least six months required by all.
VISAS: Required by all except the following:
(a) nationals of countries referred to in the chart above and nationals of their overseas territories;
(b) nationals of Andorra, Antigua & Barbuda, Argentina, Bahamas, Bahrain, Barbados, Belize, Brazil, Brunei, Bulgaria, Chile, Costa Rica, Croatia, El Salvador, Honduras, Hong Kong (SAR), Iceland, Israel, Korea (Rep), Kuwait, Liechtenstein, Macedonia (Former Yugoslav Republic of), Madagascar, Malaysia, Marshall Islands, Mexico, Monaco, New Zealand, Nicaragua, Norway, Panama, Paraguay, Qatar, Romania, St Kitts and Nevis, St Lucia, St Vincent & the Grenadines, San Marino, São Tomé e Príncipe, Singapore, Solomon Islands, South Africa, Switzerland, Taiwan (China), Trinidad & Tobago, Turkey, Tuvalu, Uruguay, Vanuatu, Vatican City and Venezuela;
(c) transit passengers continuing their journey to a third country by the same or first connecting aircraft within eight hours, provided holding tickets with confirmed onward reservations and not leaving the transit area.
Note: 1. Nationals of Andorra, Argentina, Austria, Belgium, Chile, Denmark, Finland, Germany, Israel, Italy, Japan, Liechtenstein, Luxembourg, Monaco, The Netherlands, Norway, Sweden, Switzerland and Uruguay may extend their visit to three months by written agreement.
Types of visa and cost: *Visitor/Tourist*: £25 (single-entry); £50 (multiple-entry). *Business*: £50 (multiple-entry). *Transit*: £10.
Validity: *Visitor/Tourist*: 90 days from date of entry. *Business*: 180 days from date of entry. Visas must be used within 30 days of issue.
Application to: Consulate (or Consular section at Embassy); see *Contact Addresses* section.
Application requirements: *Visitor/Tourist*: (a) Two application forms. (b) Two passport-size photos. (c) Valid passport. (d) Onward or return ticket. (e) Stamped, self-addressed, registered envelope (if applying by post). (f) Bank or Credit Card statements for at least three months.
Business: (a)-(e) and, (f) Letter from applicant's company in duplicate, indicating the nature and status of the company as well as the applicant's planned activities.
Working days required: Two to three.

Money

Currency: Quetzal (Q) = 100 centavos. Notes are in denominations of Q100, 50, 20, 10 and 5. Coins are in denominations of Q1, and 50, 25, 10, 5 and 1 centavos. The US Dollar also became an official currency in 2001.
Currency exchange: The Quetzal is extremely difficult to obtain outside Guatemala or exchange after leaving Guatemala, and visitors are strongly advised to exchange local currency before departure. It may be difficult to negotiate notes which are torn. Unused local currency can be exchanged at the bank at the airport (opening hours: Mon-Fri 0800-2000). ATMs are common throughout the country.
Credit & debit cards: American Express and Visa are accepted, whilst Diners Club and MasterCard have a more limited acceptance. Check with your credit or debit card company for details of merchant acceptability and other services that may be available.
Travellers cheques: Accepted by most banks and good hotels, although visitors may experience occasional problems. To avoid additional exchange rate charges, travellers are advised to take travellers cheques in US Dollars.
Currency restrictions: The import and export of local currency is prohibited. The import and export of foreign currency is unlimited.
Exchange rate indicators: The following figures are included as a guide to the movements of the Quetzal against Sterling and the US Dollar (official rates):

Date	Feb '04	May '04	Aug '04	Nov '04
£1.00=	14.80	14.29	14.61	14.68
$1.00=	8.13	8.00	7.93	7.75

Banking hours: Mon-Fri 0830-1230 and 1430-1630 (certain branches 0900-2000), Sat 0900-1230.

Duty Free

The following goods may be imported into Guatemala by persons over 18 years of age without incurring customs duty:
80 cigarettes or 100g of tobacco; 1.5l of alcoholic beverages; two bottles of perfume.

Public Holidays

2005: Jan 1 New Year's Day. **Mar 24-27** Holy Week. **May 1** Labour Day. **Jun 30** Army Day. **Aug 15** Assumption (Guatemala City only). **Sep 15** Independence Day. **Oct 20** Revolution Day. **Nov 1** All Saints' Day. **Dec 24** Christmas Eve (afternoon only). **Dec 25** Christmas Day. **Dec 31** New Year's Eve (afternoon only).
2006: Jan 1 New Year's Day. **Apr 13-16** Holy Week. **May 1** Labour Day. **Jun 30** Army Day. **Aug 15** Assumption (Guatemala City only). **Sep 15** Independence Day. **Oct 20** Revolution Day. **Nov 1** All Saints' Day. **Dec 24** Christmas Eve (afternoon only). **Dec 25** Christmas Day. **Dec 31** New Year's Eve (afternoon only).

Health

	Special Precautions?	Certificate Required?
Yellow Fever	No	1
Cholera	Yes	2
Typhoid & Polio	3	N/A
Malaria	4	N/A

***Note:** Regulations and requirements may be subject to change at short notice, and you are advised to contact your doctor well in advance of your intended date of departure. Any numbers in the chart refer to the footnotes below.*

1: A yellow fever vaccination certificate is required from travellers over one year of age coming from countries with infected areas.
2: Following WHO guidelines issued in 1973, a cholera vaccination certificate is no longer a condition of entry into Guatemala. However, cases of cholera were reported in 1996 and precautions are essential. Up-to-date advice should be sought before deciding whether these precautions should include vaccination as medical opinion is divided over its effectiveness. See the *Health* appendix for further information.
3: Typhoid occurs.
4: Malaria risk exists throughout the year below 1500m (4921ft), especially in Alta Verapaz, Baja Verapan, Ixcan, Petén and San Marcos. Chloroquine is the recommended prophylaxis.
Food & drink: Bottled water is available everywhere. Other water sources may be contaminated, and water used for drinking, brushing teeth or making ice should have first been boiled or otherwise sterilised. Milk may be unpasteurised and should be boiled. Powdered or tinned milk is available and is advised, but make sure that it is reconstituted with pure water. Avoid dairy products which are likely to have been made from unboiled milk. Only eat well-cooked meat and fish, preferably served hot. Pork, salad and mayonnaise may carry increased risk. Vegetables should be cooked and fruit peeled.
Other risks: *Onchocerciasis* (river blindness) occurs in localised foci in rural areas. *Dengue fever* may occur. *Dysentery* and *diarrhoeal diseases* are common. *Visceral, cutaneous* and *mucocutaneous leishmaniasis* also occur. *Hepatitis A* occurs and inoculation is recommended. *Altitude sickness* may be experienced in higher places such as volcanoes and mountains, and exertion should be avoided.
Rabies occurs. For those at high risk, vaccination before arrival should be considered. If you are bitten, seek medical advice without delay. For more information, consult the *Health* appendix.
Health care: There are both public and private medical facilities in Guatemala City, but insurance is strongly advised. Some hotels offer doctor's services to their guests.

Travel - International

AIR: Guatemala's national airline is *Grupo TACA* (website: www.grupotaca.com). *American Airlines* operates daily flights to Guatemala, via Miami or Dallas. Other airlines serving Guatemala include *Aeroméxico, Continental Airlines, Iberia Airlines* (regular flights from London via Madrid), *Lufthansa* and *United Airlines.*
Approximate flight times: From Guatemala to *London* is 11 hours (plus stopover time in USA or Madrid), to *Los Angeles* is six hours, to *New York* is six hours and to *Miami* is two hours 30 minutes.
International airports: *Guatemala City (GUA)* (la Aurora) is 6km (4 miles) south of the city. Airport facilities include car hire (*Avis, Budget, Dollar* and *Hertz*), duty-free shop, bar, buffet, post office, restaurant, bank, tourist information, telephones and bureaux de change. A bus to the city runs every 30 minutes (travel time – 30 minutes). Taxi services to Guatemala City are available (travel time – 20 minutes).
Departure tax: US$30. 24-hour transit passengers are exempt.
SEA: There are several international passenger services from North America, the Far East and Europe to Santo Tomás de Castilla and Puerto Quetzal. Cargo services run to the Pacific ports of San José and Champerico. There are also seven direct lines linking Guatemala with the Far East.
RAIL: There is no rail service at present. The national railway company is currently being transferred to the private sector.
ROAD: The Pan-American Highway runs through Guatemala from Mexico in the north and El Salvador in the south covering 511km (318 miles). Access is also possible from Belize. **Bus:** There are bus services from Mexico and El Salvador, Nicaragua, Costa Rica and Panama. Border crossings can be subject to considerable delays. The buses used by some companies are comfortable and air conditioned, but it is vital to book as far in advance as possible for every stage of the journey.

Travel - Internal

AIR: Air transport is by far the most efficient means of internal travel since there are over 380 airstrips. *Aerocaribe* and *Tikal Jets* run daily flights from Guatemala City to El Petén. Inter, a subsidiary of Grupo TACA, runs scheduled flights to several towns. Private charter flights are available.
ROAD: Traffic drives on the right. There is an extensive road network but less than a third of the roads are all-weather. Many of the roads are made from volcanic ash, and therefore very muddy during the rains. There are, however, about 13,000km (8000 miles) of first- and second-class roads in the country with paved highways from Guatemala City to the principal towns in the interior and to both the Atlantic and Pacific ports. **Bus:** The network of regular bus services between major towns is cheap but crowded. Slightly more expensive air-conditioned services are available. **Taxi:** Flat rate for short or long runs within the city although prices tend to be high. Cars can also be hired by the hour. Vehicles may be summoned by phone or in the street. There are ranks at the main international hotels. Tipping is discretionary (5 to 10 per cent). **Car hire:** *Budget, National* and local firms provide services in Guatemala City. Rates are low, but insurance is extra. It is possible to hire a car for up to 30 days with either an International Driving Permit or national licence. It is also possible to hire motorcycles. Regulations may vary from company to company. **Documentation:** A local licence will be issued on production of the visitor's own national driving licence.
URBAN: Guatemala City and major towns have limited, but cheap and regular, bus services. New circulating taxi services have been introduced in the capital.

Accommodation

HOTELS: There are many first-class hotels in Guatemala City and throughout the country. Many offer excellent service in restaurants, bars and nightclubs. La Antigua Guatemala (the capital until largely destroyed by earthquakes in 1773, a fate which also befell the present capital in 1976) also has a good choice of hotels. Chichicastenango, Cobán, Panajachel (near Lake Atitlán), Puerto Barrios, and Quetzaltenango also have a reasonable selection of hotels, although elsewhere accommodation is more limited. Throughout the country standards are inconsistent. Registered hotels are required to display room rates; the Tourist Office in Guatemala City will deal with complaints. **Tipping:** 10 per cent is normal in hotels where service has not been included. Most hotels charge a 20 per cent room tax.
PENSIONS & GUEST HOUSES: Most large towns have guest houses and boarding houses offering inexpensive accommodation.
CAMPING: There are a few campsites dotted around the country but facilities are usually basic. A popular excursion is to stay overnight in camping grounds on the still active Pacaya volcano to see the glow of the ashes and lava from the volcano's eruptions. Around Lake Atitlán, camping is permitted only in designated areas.

Resorts & Excursions

For travellers, Guatemala represents an intriguing mix. It is a diverse country with landscape that ranges from lush tropical rainforest in the northern lowlands, where some of the most spectacular Mayan archaeological sites (including Tikal) are found, to the pineforested hills of the Highlands, which are home to Mayan communities that still wear their traditional weavings. Guatemala has around 21 different ethnic groups, such as the Cakchiquels, Mams, Quichés and Tzutujils speaking some 23 languages (21 of Mayan origin; the other two are Garifuna and Xinca).
While the country's political heart is found in the capital, Guatemala City, more attractive still is the former colonial capital, Antigua Guatemala, which is saturated with the ruins of old convents and churches and surrounded by majestic volcanoes – some still active – that are good for hiking and climbing. The Caribbean (with its fishing communities of Afro-Caribbean heritage) and Pacific coastlines offer good fishing, swimming and boating opportunities, as do the beautiful lakes of Atitlán and Izabal. Guatemala also has unspoiled tracts of virgin rainforest (protected in a network of national parks), spectacular waterfalls and underground caves (such as those in the Verapaz region).
For the purposes of this section, the country has been divided into seven regions: Central Guatemala, Petén, Verapaz Region, Caribbean Coast, Eastern Guatemala, Pacific Coast and the Highlands.

CENTRAL GUATEMALA

Those visitors from overseas not landing at the international airport at Flores (for connections to Tikal) land at la Aurora International Airport in Guatemala City. Other than being the primary urban centre in the country, Guatemala City is ideally positioned for visitors wishing to make the short journey by road to la Antigua Guatemala, situated 45km (28 miles away).
GUATEMALA CITY: There were three attempts to establish a capital before Guatemala City was founded in 1775. The first colonial settlement, called **Santiago de los Caballeros Guatemala**, was built in 1524 by the conquistador Pedro de Alvarado close to the Cakchiquel settlement of Iximché (near the present day town of **Tecpán** – see **Iximché** under *The Highlands* section). After continuing battles with the Cakchiquel warriors, the capital was relocated in 1527 to the **Almolonga Valley**, near present-day **San Miguel Escobar**, between the volcanoes **Agua** and **Fuego** until an earthquake destroyed it in 1541. A third capital was then established just a few kilometres away on the present site of **la Antigua Guatemala** in the **Panchoy Valley** (see the *Antigua* section below). Established as the new city in 1543, it was decided to retain the name of Santiago while the former (second) capital was referred to as **Ciudad Vieja**, or Old City. The new capital grew in wealth, size and prestige, surviving a number of earthquakes until 1773, when it was hit by a huge earthquake and eventually abandoned. The capital moved to its present location while the former capital was thereafter known as **la Antigua Guatemala** or Old Guatemala.
The capital, Guatemala City lies at the edge of a plateau cut by deep ravines in the **Valley of the Hermitage**. Few colonial buildings remain but the old quarter, with its low colonial houses, is situated in the northern part of the city. The main plaza, **Parque Central** lies at its heart and is bordered by the **National Palace**, the **Cathedral**, the **National Library** and an arcade of shops. In the south of the city, close to the airport and the national racecourse, are **Parque la Aurora**, which contains the zoo, the **Museum of Archaeology and Ethnology** and the **Ixchel Museum**, housing a good collection of handwoven textiles. Other museums with fine collections include the **Popol Vuh Museum** (a private collection of Mayan and Spanish colonial art) and the **National Museum of Modern Art**. Some of the most interesting religious buildings (mainly either neo-classical or Baroque) include the 17th-century **Hermitage of El Carmen** and the churches of **La Merced**, **Santo Domingo**, **Santuario Expiatorio**, **Las Capuchinas**, **Santa Rosa** and **Capilla de Yurrita** (built in the first half of the 20th century).
LA ANTIGUA GUATEMALA: The former capital (originally called **Santiago de los Caballeros Guatemala**), Antigua is situated southwest of Guatemala City, and was considered to be one of the most splendid cities in Central America before its partial destruction in the earthquake of 1773. Further devastation to many buildings was wreaked in the massive earthquake in 1976 and the town is now a UNESCO Cultural Heritage Site. Despite the damage of countless earthquakes, floods and fires, Antigua is a beautiful place of multi-coloured, single-storey buildings, tropical gardens, plazas, fountains and cobbled streets. A popular tourist centre, it has several good hotels, restaurants and bookshops with a fairly lively nightlife. Monuments, former palaces, convents and churches that have survived in varying degrees of intactness include the **Main Square**, **Cathedral**, **Palace of the General Captains**, **University of San Carlos** (containing the **Museum of Colonial Art**), and the churches of **La Merced**, **Santa Clara**, **Las Capuchinas**, **La Recolección** and **San Francisco**. The **Casa Santa Domingo** is a former convent that is now a smart hotel with two small but fine collections housed in the **Colonial** and **Archaeological** museums. The town is particularly busy at Easter time where locals and visitors flock to see the spectacular Easter processions when huge litters bearing religious icons are carried over carpets of flowers and coloured sawdust. Antigua is also one of the main centres for Spanish-language schools in Guatemala.
Beyond Antigua: Just outside the town is a coffee plantation, which now houses the small but interesting **Coffee Museum** (**Museo del Café**) and **Music Museum** (**Casa K'ojom**). (*K'ojom* means music in the Cakchiquel language.) Three nearby volcanoes, **Acatenango**, **Agua** and **Fuego**, all offer incomparable views of the city and surrounding countryside. **Santa María de Jesús** is the

starting point for climbing to the crater of the Agua Volcano. Two towns worth visiting for their fine crafts are **Jocotenango** (a centre for ceramics, as well as the site of a lively fiesta held to celebrate the feast day of the Virgin of the Ascension on 15 August) and **San Antonio Aguascalientes** (for beautiful handwoven textiles). The Day of the Dead festival (on 1 November) is a celebrated ritual in **Santiago Sacatepéguez** when hundreds of multi-coloured circular or hexagonal kites, made from bamboo or tissue paper (increasingly polyester or plastic) are flown in honour of the dead.

A B C D E F G H I J K L M N O P Q R S T U V W X Y Z

PETÉN

The vast tropical lowland jungles of the Petén department share borders with Belize to the east and Mexico to the north and west. It is home to most of the major Mayan sites in Guatemala and many visitors exploring the Mayan sites in all three countries tend to fly direct from either Mexico or Belize into the international airport at **Flores**. Most of the major Mayan sites are located in this department.

FLORES: This former Mayan ceremonial centre is built on an island in the middle of **Lake Petén Itza**. None of the Mayan structures survived the arrival of the conquistadors who built their main plaza, church and government building on the top of the hill in the centre of the island. The town's hotels, restaurants and shops are laid out below. A causeway connects Flores to the mainland town of **Santa Elena**, where the banks and main shops are located. Buses run throughout the day from both Santa Elena and Flores to Tikal, passing through the pleasant village of **El Remate**, which has a couple of lakeside restaurants, lodgings and language schools. Also accessible from Flores is the **Cerro Cahuí Biosphere** – a 600-hectare (1482-acre) nature reserve that contains cedar, sapodilla, indigo and mahogany trees, orchids and ferns as well as fauna such as white-tailed deer, armadillos, spider monkeys, hawks, parrots and toucans. From October to April, hundreds of migratory birds settle in the reserve.

TIKAL: The spectacular Mayan ruins of Tikal (City of Voices) encompass vast pyramidal temples, ball courts, causeways, plazas and public buildings that extend over some 16 sq km (6 sq miles). While there are about 3000 known structures, many more lie buried under dense jungle vegetation. First occupied in about 800 BC, this great city was eventually abandoned around 1000 years later. Copies of some of the more elaborate friezes, stelae, sculptures and bas-reliefs are found in the **Sylvanus Morley Museum**, which is near the entrance. At least two days are recommended to see all of the archaeological sites. Visitors can stay in the park lodges, in Flores, Santa Elena or El Remate, and guided tours around the ruins can be arranged both for the evening and at sunrise. The site is located in the heart of **Tikal National Park**, where there are over 50,587 hectares (125,000 acres) of rare forest (kapoka, breadnut, mahogany and cedar) and tropical vegetation. Wildlife that can be seen there includes howler monkeys, tropical birds, reptiles, red coates, racoons and white-tailed deer. Tikal National Park is itself situated in the much larger **Mayan Biosphere Reserve**.

Other Mayan sites in north Petén: Several Mayan sites are currently under excavation, one of the most impressive of which is **El Mirador**, about 4km (2.5 miles) from the Mexican border. Also in the northern part of the department, **Uaxactún** (Eight Stones) shows how developed the Mayan civilisation had become by the ninth century AD. Building E-VII-B was used for determining the precise dates of the equinoxes and the solstices. **Ixlú** was an important lake port, situated in between the **Petén Itza** and **Salpetén** lagoons. Further east, on the edge of the **Yaxhá Lagoon**, **Yaxhá** (Green Water) is an extensive Mayan site of terraces, plazas and causeways. North from here are the smaller sites of **Nakum** and **Naranjo**.

SAYAXCHÉ: This town in the southern part of the Petén department provides a good starting point for exploring other major Mayan sites. **Ceibal**, southeast of Sayaxché, has a small observatory that was designed to pinpoint the location of galaxies, planets and stars. It is also where some of the finest post-Classical stelae (AD 900 to 1523), carved with large anthropomorphous clay figures, were recovered. Other impressive stelae representing battle scenes were found at **Dos Pilas**. Southeast from here, the post-Classical site of **Aguateca** was once an important ceremonial centre.

VERAPAZ REGION

This region is made up of the two departments of Alta (high) and Baja (Low) Verapaz, which are located in the north-central part of Guatemala. While many of the towns and villages retain their folklore, traditional handcrafts and religious feast days, the region is also a prime destination for whitewater rafting, caving and other outdoor activities. As access may be difficult or remote, many of the national parks and rivers need to be visited with registered guides and 4-wheel drive vehicles, either arranged privately or as part of a package offered by tour operators.

COBÁN: This is the capital of the Alta Verapaz department that, along with Antigua, produces some of the best coffee in Guatemala. Situated on the banks of the **Cahabón River**, the town's colonial past is reflected in its architecture, such as that of the **El Calvario** church. It is also a centre for the production of many fine silver handicrafts. Celebrations to mark the ancient Mayan feast of Paabanc are still held in Cobán and **San Pedro Carchá** to the east. Some of the region's most colourful handwoven clothes can be seen in towns and villages such as **Tactic**, **San Juan Chamelco** and **Lanquín**. One of the highlights of the region are the **Semuc Champey Waterfalls**, which are formed as the Cahabón River falls some 300m (985ft) across rocks and ledges. Around 10km (6 miles) further on, the river enters the **Languin Caves**, parts of which can be explored with a guide, either on foot or by boat. Some 200km (124 miles) from Cobán is the **National Park of Lanchúa**, which is a very humid, subtropical rainforest teeming with many species of mammals and amphibians. Visitors to the park will need a guide and full camping equipment. From the **Lanchuá Lagoon**, it is possible to take a boat to explore parts of the **Caves of Candelaria**. These ancient caves were considered sacred by the Maya and remnants of ceremonial altars and pots have been found here.

SALAMÁ: The attractive departmental capital of Baja Verapaz is a good place to buy souvenirs handcrafted from silver, clay and leather. The nearby town of **Purulhá** is the location for the **Mario Dary Rivera Nature Reserve**, which was set up to protect the quetzal, Guatemala's national bird and a symbol of liberty. Two walking trails cut through the cloudforest, where visitors can see about 50 different types of trees and a variety of tropical birds such as toucans, hummingbirds and macaws.

CARIBBEAN COAST

Caribbean Guatemala is less developed than some other parts of the country in terms of tourism infrastructure. As a result, the villages along the coast, inland and around **Lake Izabal**, Guatemala's largest, remain unspoiled. The coast has strong Afro-Caribbean influences as black Afro-Guatemalans known as *Garífunas*, the descendants of former African slaves who intermarried with the indigenous Maya, settled here. Caribbean traditions remain evident in the area's music, festivals and cooking (in dishes such as *tapado* – made with fresh fish, coconut milk and green bananas). Sailing, fishing, swimming and scuba-diving are all popular activities and trips to the **Belize Keys** (such as the **Cayos Sapodillas**) are possible.

PUERTO BARRIOS: The main port, **Puerto Barrios** is the capital of the Izabal department. It is a safe harbour for yachts and the starting point for trips up the inland waterways and rivers that crisscross the region. Southeast of Puerto Barrios is the remarkable UNESCO Cultural Heritage Site of **Quiriguá**. The Maya carved stelae and altars with intricate details that reveal much of their beliefs, animal deities, battles, the feats of their kings and cosmology. Stela E, at 11m high (36ft), is one of the tallest that has been recovered across the former Mayan Empire.

LIVINGSTON: Accessible from Puerto Barrios, this small town of brightly painted wooden houses and balconies is located in the jungle among coconut groves. Formerly the departure point for coffee farmed in the plantations of the Verapaz region, it still has a small fishing economy. Celebrations during *Easter Week* and on 12 December (*Feast day of the Virgin of Guadalupe*) are particularly colourful. From Livingston, boat trips can be taken along the **Río Dulce**, a jungle river that has its source in **Lake Izabal** and winds its way between steep cliffs and dense vegetation, through the lake of **El Golfete**, to flow into the **Amatique Bay**. Along the river, near **Fronteras**, is the fort of **San Felipe**, which was constructed by the Spanish in the 17th century as a defence against pirate attacks. The waterways of the river also pass through the mangrove swamps and lagoons of the **Chocón Machacas Biosphere**. This is a habitat for the endangered manatee (sea cow), which is Guatemala's largest aquatic mammal. North of Livingston is the **Siete Altares**, a series of waterfalls and pools, which have been formed where the Río Dulce empties into the Caribbean.

EASTERN GUATEMALA

Encompassing parts of the El Progreso, Zacapa, Jalapa, Chiquimula, Santa Rosa and Jutiapa departments, this is one of the most varied regions in the country – both geographically and culturally. Visitors can tour fine colonial churches, small local museums, coffee plantations and buy excellent handcrafted souvenirs while travelling through a changing landscape of subtropical forests, past volcanic peaks and sulphurous lakes.

EL PROGRESO & ZACAPA DEPARTMENTS: Two of the finest examples of 16th-century Baroque architecture can be found about 90km (56 miles) from Guatemala City in the parish churches of **San Agustín Acasaguastlán** and **San Cristóbal Acasaguastlán** in El Progreso. The departmental capital of **Zacapa** is well known for its distinctive handwoven cloth and for its small **Museum of Paleontology, Archaeology and Geology**. Nearby **Estanzuela** also has a **Paleontology Museum**.

CHIQUIMULA & JALAPA DEPARTMENTS: The town of **Esquipulas** in the Chiquimula Department is one of the most significant in Central America. Second only in importance to the shrine of the Virgin of Guadalupe outside Mexico City is the **Basilica of Esquipulas** with its **Icon of the Black Christ** that dates back to 1595. Pilgrims from all over Central America gather here on the feast day of 15 January. Esquipulas is also the seat of the Central American Parliament and, given its location just a short distance from the borders with Honduras and El Salvador, it has also been the place where several important peace agreements have been signed. Other attractions include the **Franciscan Sanctuary**, **Belén Convent** and colonial **Little Bridge** (*Puente Chiquito*). **Montecristo National Park** (the Tri-State Park) is located nearby and extends over the borders of all three countries. Over half of its 12,000 hectares (29,652 acres) of humid and subtropical forest are in Guatemala. The villages, forests and mountains of **Mataquescuintla** are home to the Pocomam Indians who produce some outstanding textiles and ceramics. Under the *Spanish Rural Tourism Plan*, visitors can travel on horseback, by bicycle, on foot or by 4-wheel drive vehicle from **Quetzaltepeque**, through **San Luis Jiltepeque** to the attractive departmental capital of **Jalapa**, staying in family homes en route.

SANTA ROSA DEPARTMENT: Located near **Pueblo Nuevo Viñas** and surrounded by mountains and forests is sulphurous **Lake Ixpaco**, which is the site of many springs that are believed to have healing properties. Northwest through a landscape of pine forests and low subtropical mountains is **Ayarza Lagoon**, also slightly sulphurous but with shoals of tilapias and mojarras.

PACIFIC COAST

The Pacific coastline stretches some 250km (155 miles) from the Mexican border in the west to the border with El Salvador to the east and includes parts of six administrative departments. The region is characterised by black volcanic sand beaches on the coast; mangrove swamps irrigated by numerous rivers behind and lush, subtropical forests further inland. Agriculture is the prime industry, with extensive coffee, sugar cane, cardamom, cotton and banana plantations. As well as enjoying watersports and swimming on the coast and exploring the rainforests and swamps with their unique habitats, visitors can tour several important Olmec archaeological sites.

SAN JOSÉ: After Puerto Barrios on the Caribbean, **San José** is the country's second-largest port, which is connected to Guatemala City in the north by Highway CA9 (more commonly known as the Pan American Highway). There are several seaside resorts on either side of San José where a variety of watersports are available. The waters here have abundant marine life (such as red snapper, tarpon, bass and sailfish) and the sea fishing is rated very highly. To the west, an interesting journey can be taken by launch from the old Spanish port of **Iztapa** through the **Chiquimulilla Canal**, which runs through mangrove swamps rich with plant life such as water lilies and irises. This canal is part of the **Monterrico Nature Reserve**, which was created to conserve coastal wildlife such as the green iguana, marine turtle and crocodile.

ESCUINTLA DEPARTMENT: Guatemala has 33 volcanoes, three of which are still active. Although not the highest, one of the most dramatic is the **Pacaya Volcano** (2252m/7388ft), which is located about halfway between Guatemala City and **Escuintla**. During periods of activity, guided tours are organised to watch the eruptions and the lava flows. When inactive, an ascent of the volcano can be made by a marked route from **San Francisco de Sales**. Northwest of Escuintla are the sugarcane fields of **Santa Lucía Cotzumalguapa**. The remains of great stone heads and other carved reliefs are dotted throughout the fields belonging to three *fincas* (plantations) – **Bilbao**, **El Baúl** and **las Ilusiones**. South from here is the site of **La Democracia**, which contains dramatic basalt sculptures of heads with closed eyes and furrowed brows.

RETALHULEU DEPARTMENT: North of **Retalhuleu** is **El Asintal** and the site of **Abaj Takalik** ('standing stone' in the Quiché language). This is one of the few sites that has remnants of terraces, carved stones, inscribed altars and calendars from two civilisations: the Mayan and the Olmec, who preceded the Mayas. A little further east in **San Martín Zapotitlán** is the **Xocomil Aquatic Park** – a theme park with pools and waterslides built around replica Mayan temples, palaces and sanctuaries.

THE HIGHLANDS

Known in Spanish as **El Altiplano**, the highlands region is one of the most popular for visitors to Guatemala. The towns and villages there are inhabited by the greatest number of modern day, indigenous Mayan groups – many of whom still speak the languages and uphold the sacred rituals of their ancestors. Although this practice is gradually dying out, many of the villagers in more remote areas still wear traditional handwoven garments and market days or fiesta celebrations are the best times for visitors to appreciate their vibrant colours. While the main towns are connected with paved highways, some of the outlying villages are accessible only by 4-wheel vehicles. Tourism

infrastructure, however, is developing all the time.
HUEHUETENANGO: The departmental capital of **Huehuetenango** makes a good base for exploring as it has more accommodation options and facilities than some of the smaller villages surrounding it. To the west is the small post-Classical site of **Zaculeu** (*White Land* in the Quiché language). A number of tombs containing objects carved from pyrite and ceramic vessels have been found here. North of Huehuetenango is **Chintla** whose church contains the silver **Virgin of La Candelaria**, which draws many worshippers. A beautiful drive into the mountains further north in the region lies the isolated village of **Todos Santos Cuchumatán**. The men's traditional costumes of high-necked red shirts, red and white-striped trousers, black capes and red fabric tied under straw hats are particularly smart. One of the best times to visit is during the annual fiesta between 31 October - 5 November. On the *Day of the Dead* (*All Souls' Day*) on 1 November, a traditional horse race takes place in the village. Fuelled by *quetzalteca* (the local sugar cane spirit), the riders in traditional costume race up and down a dirt track at the far end of the village. The winner is the last man still on his horse.
SANTA CRUZ DEL QUICHÉ: The Spanish used the carved stones from the ancient Mayan Quiché capital they had destroyed to build the church in **Santa Cruz**. The town has a good market but even more famous are the market days held every Thursday and Saturday in the small hill village of **Chichicastenango**, 19km (12 miles) to the south. Mayan traders from outlying villages spread their traditional food, cloth and wooden masks on stalls around the steps of the **Church of St Thomas** in a wonderfully colourful spectacle. Many others come to burn *copal* (incense) and pray on the church steps, combining ancient Mayan and Catholic rituals. On the south side of the main square, the **Regional Museum** houses a fine collection of jade and ceramic pieces and incense burners. Located on a hilltop above the town is the Mayan stone idol of **Pascual Abaj**.
TOTONICAPAN: The regional capital, **Totonicapán** is a thriving industrial town. One of the best times to visit is during the week celebrating the feast days of *San Miguel Arcangel* (24-30 September) when traditional dances (*morerías*) are held here with descriptive titles such as *Mexicans* and *The Deer and the Monkey*. To the west is **San Cristóbal Totonicapán**, whose market day on Thursday is the best time to purchase outstanding ceramics. It is also an important centre for textiles. **Momostenango** (City of Altars), in the north, is the centre for traditional handwoven ponchos.
QUETZALTENANGO: After the capital, this is the second most important city in Guatemala, set amongst a group of high mountains and volcanoes. Although Quetzaltenago (often referred to as Xela) is quite modern, it also contains narrow colonial streets, broad avenues, fine public buildings such as the neoclassical **City Hall**, **Municipal Theatre** and **Natural History Museum**, and a magnificent central plaza. It is also an important centre for language schools. Other places to visit outside the city are the hot sulphur springs at **Fuentes Georginas**, **Aguas Amargas** and **Los Vahos**. Several picturesque towns include **Salcajá** with the 16th-century **Church of San Jacinto**, **Zunil**, dominated by the ornate façade of its church and one of the places where Maximón is still worshipped actively (see **Santiago Atitlán** below), **San Andrés Xecul** and **San Francisco El Alto**.
SOLOLA: The road through **Solola** winds down to the beautiful, volcanic **Lake Atitlán**, much praised by Aldous Huxley, and is surrounded by purple highlands, olive-green mountains and three distinctive volcanoes – **Tolimán**, **Atitlán** and **San Pedro**. Although there are some small hotels around the edge of the lake, most visitors stay at **Panajachel**, the key tourist centre with a long strip of guest houses, restaurants, bookshops, cafes and banks. Water-skiing, swimming and boating are all available on the lake, which is 19km (12 miles) in length and between 6.5km (4 miles) and 12km (7.5 miles) wide. Around the lake are several villages, each of whose inhabitants wear differently coloured, densely embroidered clothes. **Santiago Atitlán** is the largest of these. *Easter Week* is famous for combining two traditions – the Catholic Easter procession and the rival procession conducted by the *cofradía* (religious brotherhood). Their idol is Maximón – a black-suited figure with a moustache that combines physical characteristics and attributes of St Simón, Mam (a Mayan god), Alvarado (the Guatemalan conquistador) and Judas Iscariot. Inside the church, a little Maximón figure is carved into the altar, as is a scene showing the feast day of the *cofradía*. Some of the women in Santiago still wear traditional headdresses that are made from long lengths of cloth wound repeatedly around the back of the head (a visual reference to *Ixchel*, the snake goddess of weaving). In **San Antonio Palopó**, the women weave on long rectangular backstrap looms. The men use the standing loom introduced by the Spanish and wear a type of wrap-around brown and white kilt. Both men and women in **San Catarina Palopó** wear shirts, *huipiles* (blouses), skirts and trousers embroidered with colourful geometric designs.
CHIMALTENANGO: Northwest of **Chimaltenango** is the important fortified hilltop site of **Iximché**. Having conquered the Cakchiquel warriors, the Spanish conquistadors established their first capital near here in 1524. Today, there are well-preserved ruins of the former ball court, four main plazas and a temple. Almost on the border with the Quiché department is the site of **Mixco Viejo** (*Pocomán*), which was also a fortified city like Iximché. A shrine to San Simon (Maximón) is also found at **San Andreas Iztapa**.

Sport & Activities

Mountaineering: This is practised on and around Guatemala's volcanoes. At 4200m (13,776ft) above sea level, the *Tajumulco* in the San Marcos region is the highest volcano in Central America. In spite of this, it is technically an easy climb. Those requiring something more challenging can try the *Tolimán*, with its 3158m- (10,358ft-) twin peak summit. An easier climb is the *San Pedro* volcano, whose summit can be reached in about six hours. One of the most visited volcanoes, given its proximity to Guatemala City, is *Pacaya* at 2252m (7386ft). Excursions to this constantly erupting volcano must be made in a group and with a guide. The ascent of the *Agua* (or *Hunapu*) volcano at 3776m (1233ft) gives the opportunity to spend the night in the crater where there is a refuge for 30 people. Aktun Kan, Jobtzinaj, Lanquín and La Candelaria are principal locations for **caving**.
Watersports: *Río Dulce* and *Lakes Izabal* and *Atitlán* are good for **windsurfing**, with *Lake Atitlán* also popular for **diving**. Guatemala's fast-moving rivers, including *El Cahabón*, *El Chiquibul*, *El Motagua*, *La Pasión* and *El Usamacinta* are ideal for boating and rapids shooting. Lakes and rivers suitable for fishing include *El Lago de Izabal*, *El Petén*, *Río Dulce* and the rivers of *Alta Verepaz*. The Pacific Coast is one of the best places worldwide for **sports fishing**. **Birdwatching** is also recommended at these locations.
Other: There are around six 18-hole **golf** courses in Guatemala, with others currently under construction. Facilities at the *Guatemala Country Club* and the *San Isidro* courses, 8 km (5 miles) and 10km (5.5 miles) from the city respectively, are open to members only. The course at the *Hacienda Nueva Country Club* is open to the public. Other courses are at the *Alta Vista Country Club* in San José Pinula, which also had other sporting facilities, and *Mayan Golf* in Villa Nueva. *Green Place* in Guatemala City has a 9-hole course.
Cycling is popular in la Antigua Guatemala, Izabál, the Guatemalan Altiplano, Panajachel, Santa Catarina Palopó and the plains of El Petén.

Social Profile

FOOD & DRINK: There is a variety of restaurants and cafes serving a wide selection of cooking styles including American, Argentinian, Chinese, French, Italian, Japanese, Mexican and Spanish. There are many fast-food chains and continental-style cafes. The visitor should note that food usually varies in price rather than quality and some of the cheap eateries are amongst the best.
NIGHTLIFE: In Guatemala City in particular, there are nightclubs and discos with modern music and dance, featuring national and international artists. Guatemala is the home of *marimba* music, which can be heard at several venues. In the cities, the *marimba* is a huge elaborate xylophone with large drum sticks played by four to nine players. In rural areas the sounding boxes are made of different shaped gourds (*marimbas de tecomates*). There are regular concerts throughout Guatemala. There are also theatres and numerous plays in English and other cultural performances. Films with English and Spanish subtitles are often shown in major towns. The most important museums and art galleries are found in Guatemala City, la Antigua Guatemala and Tikal National Park.
SHOPPING: Special purchases include textiles, handicrafts, jewellery, jade carvings, leather goods, ceramics and basketry. Markets are best for local products and bargaining is necessary. Ceramics can be purchased cheaply in many places including Villa de Chinautla, San Luis Jilotepeque and Rabinal. Cobán is the cheapest place to buy silverware. The Central Market in Guatemala City and the Craft Market provide a range of crafts combining traditional and modern styles. Guatemala City contains many modern shopping centres and malls. Gran Centro Comercial Los Proceres, Galerias La Pradera, Plaza Cemaco and Geminis International Mall are all located in Zone 10. In addition, visitors may make use of the facilities at Tikal Futura, Peri-Roosevelt Shopping Mall and the Century Shopping Centre. **Shopping hours:** Mon-Sat 0930-1930. Malls are also open on Sunday.
SPECIAL EVENTS: For further details, contact the Guatemala Tourist Commission (see *Contact Addresses*). The following is a selection of special events occurring in Guatemala in 2005:
Mar *Easter Processions*, Antigua; *Easter Week Celebrations*, Livingston. **Aug 15** *Virgin of the Ascension Fiesta*, Socolenango. **Oct-Nov** *Todos Santos Cuchumatán Fiesta*. **Nov 1** *Day of the Dead Kite Festival*, Santiago Sacatepequez. **Nov 1-2** *Day of the Dead* (celebrations and horse racing), Todos Santos. **Dec 7** *La Quema del Diablo* (burning of the devil), Antigua. **Dec 12** *Feast Day of the Virgin of Guadalupe*, Livingston. **Dec 21** *Festival de San Tomás* (festival of Saint Thomas), Chichicastenango.
SOCIAL CONVENTIONS: Guatemala is the most populated of the Central American republics and is the only one which is predominantly Indian, although the Spanish have had a strong influence on the way of life. Full names should be used when addressing acquaintances, particularly in business. Dress is conservative and casual wear is suitable except in the smartest dining rooms and clubs. **Tipping:** 10 per cent is normal in restaurants where service has not been included..

Business Profile

ECONOMY: Coffee is the leading export in this largely agricultural economy, accounting for about one-third of foreign earnings. Other major crops are sugar cane, bananas, cardamom and cotton. In the fishing industry, shrimps are a significant export earner. Guatemala boasts the largest manufacturing sector in Central America, accounting for 20 per cent of GDP, and produces processed foods, textiles, paper, pharmaceuticals and rubber goods. Oil deposits, first discovered in the mid-1970s, are being exploited by French and American concerns but the country remains a marginal producer and continues to rely heavily on imported oil. There is a small mining industry producing marble, copper, lead, zinc and other metals.
Although Guatemala has received solid support from the USA and international institutions such as the Inter-American Development Bank and the IMF, its economic development in the last 25 years has been undermined by chronic internal conflict, exacerbated by several major natural disasters and low prices for Guatemala's main export commodities. Nonetheless, the economy has grown steadily in the last few years and is currently 4 per cent. The USA is substantially Guatemala's largest trading partner, followed by El Salvador, Honduras, Mexico and some EU countries, notably Germany and Italy. Guatemala is a member of the Central American Common Market.
BUSINESS: Guatemalan businesspeople tend to be rather formal and conservative. Normal courtesies should be observed and appointments should be made. Punctuality is appreciated and calling cards can be useful. **Office hours:** Mon-Fri 0800-1800, Sat 0800-1200.
COMMERCIAL INFORMATION: The following organisation can offer advice: Cámara de Comercio de Guatemala (Chamber of Commerce), 10A Calle 3-80, Zona 1, Guatemala City (tel: 253 5353; fax: 220 9393; e-mail: info@camaradecomercio.org.gt; website: www.negociosenguatemala.com); *or* Cámara de Industria (Chamber of Industry), Ruta 6 9-21, Zona 4, Edificio Cámara de Industria, 01004 Guatemala City (tel: 334 0850; fax: 334 1090; e-mail: cig@industriaguate.com; website: www.industriaguate.com).
CONFERENCES/CONVENTIONS: Guatemala has the facilities and hotel infrastructure for conventions, conferences and business meetings. The Centro Cultural Miguel Angel Asturias and other modern conference centres are available for such events, often quite close, or accessible to Guatemala's beauty spots. For further information regarding conference facilities, contact Guatemala Tourist Commission (see *Contact Addresses* section).

Climate

Guatemala's climate varies according to altitude. The coastal regions and the northeast are hot throughout the year with an average temperature of 20°C (68°F) sometimes rising to 37°C (99°F). Generally, nights are clear all year round. In higher climes, near the centre of the country, the rainy season, running from May to September, is characterised by clear skies after abundant rainfall in the afternoons and evenings. Temperatures fall sharply at night.
Required clothing: Lightweight tropical clothing. Jacket or light woollens for the evening.

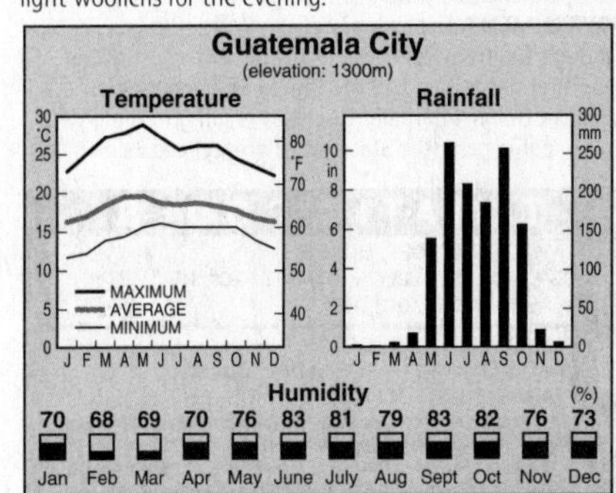

Guernsey

LATEST TRAVEL ADVICE CONTACTS

British Foreign and Commonwealth Office
Tel: (0870) 606 0290 Website: www.fco.gov.uk
US Department of State
Website: http://travel.state.gov/travel
Canadian Department of Foreign Affairs and Int'l Trade
Tel: (1 800) 267 8376 Website: www.dfait-maeci.gc.ca

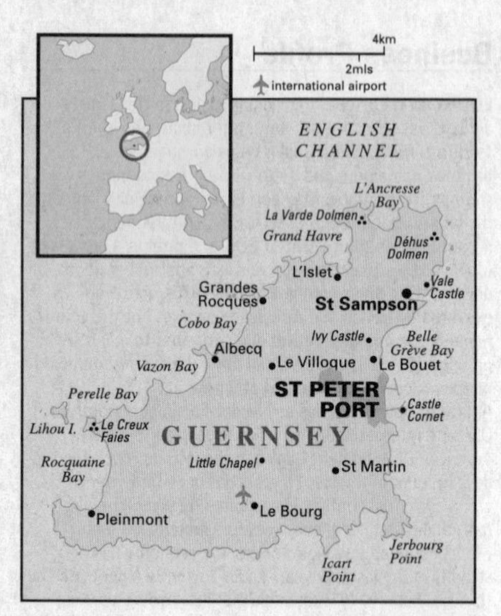

Location: English Channel, off the northern coast of France.

Country dialling code: 44.

Guernsey is a Dependency of the British Crown represented abroad by British Embassies – see *United Kingdom* section.

Visit Guernsey
PO Box 23, St Peter Port, Guernsey,
Channel Islands GY1 3AN, UK
Tel: (01481) 723 552. Fax: (01481) 714 951.
E-mail: enquiries@visitguernsey.com
Website: www.visitgurensey.com

Guernsey Government
States of Guernsey, Sir Charles Frossard House, St Peter Port, Guernsey, Channel Islands GY1 1FH, UK
Website: www.gov.gg

PR Representation for Guernsey
c/o Charisma PR Cromwell House, 20 New Road,
Brighton BN1 1UF, UK
Tel: (01273) 698 988. Fax: (01273) 699 051.
E-mail: info@charismapr.co.uk
Website: www.charismapr.co.uk
Only deals with PR enquiries.

General Information

AREA: 63.1 sq km (24.3 sq miles).
POPULATION: 59,807 (2001).
POPULATION DENSITY: 947.8 per sq km.
CAPITAL: St Peter Port.
GEOGRAPHY: Guernsey is situated in the Gulf of St Malo, 50km (30 miles) from the coast of France and 130km (80 miles) from the south coast of England. The cliffs on the south coast rise to 80m (270ft), from which the land slopes away gradually to the north. Guernsey is an ideal centre for excursions to the other Channel Islands and France. The islands of Alderney, Brecqhou, Herm, Jethou, Lihou and Sark are dependencies of Guernsey.
GOVERNMENT: Dependency of the British Crown. Although Guernsey is British, its history and constitution mean that it is not part of the United Kingdom or the European Union. Internally, Guernsey is self governing with its own parliament (the States of Guernsey) and its own laws. Only foreign affairs and defence are handled by the UK, although there are arrangements by which Guernsey laws are approved by the crown. **Head of State:** HM Queen Elizabeth II, represented locally by Lieutenant-Governor Sir John Foley since 2000. **Head of Government:** Bailiff De Vic Graham Carey since 1999.
LANGUAGE: English is the official language. Norman *patois* is spoken in some parishes.
RELIGION: Church of England, Presbyterian, Baptist, Congregational and Methodist.
TIME: GMT (GMT + 1 from March to October).
ELECTRICITY: 240 volts AC, 50Hz. Three-pin plugs in use.
COMMUNICATIONS: Telephone: Country code: 44, followed by (0)1481. Outgoing international code: 00. **Mobile telephone:** GSM 900. Main network operator is *Cable & Wireless Guernsey* (website: www.cwguernsey.com). Some single and triple band handsets will function. Roaming agreements are in operation. Handsets can also be hired. **Fax:** Services are available in hotels and fax bureaux. **Internet:** Public access is available at Internet cafes and in libraries. Local ISPs include *Cable & Wireless Guernsey*. **Post:** Only Guernsey stamps will be accepted on outgoing mail. The main post office is at Smith Street, St Peter Port. Post boxes are painted blue. **Press:** The local newspapers are *The Guernsey Press* and *Star* and *The Guernsey Weekly Press*. English, French, German, Dutch and Italian newspapers are also available at newsagents. All the main British newspapers are available in Guernsey on the day of publication.

TIMATIC CODES

Health	AMADEUS: **TI-DFT/GCI/HE** GALILEO/WORLDSPAN: **TI-DFT/GCI/HE** SABRE: **TIDFT/GCI/HE**
Visa	AMADEUS: **TI-DFT/GCI/VI** GALILEO/WORLDSPAN: **TI-DFT/GCI/VI** SABRE: **TIDFT/GCI/VI**

To access TIMATIC country information on Health and Visa regulations through the Computer Reservations System (CRS), type in the appropriate command line listed above.

Credit: © States of Guernsey Tourist Board

Passport/Visa

Passport and Visa requirements are the same as those for the rest of the UK; see the *United Kingdom* section for further information.

Money

Currency: Guernsey has its own currency but all UK notes and coins are legal tender, and circulate with the Channel Islands issue. Pound Sterling (£) = 100 pence. Notes are in denominations of £50, 20, 10, 5 and 1. Coins are in denominations of £2 (special issue) and 1, and 50, 20, 10, 5, 2 and 1 pence.
Note: (a) Guernsey still has its own £1 note. (b) Channel Islands notes and coins are not accepted in the UK, although they can be reconverted at parity in UK banks.
Currency exchange: Foreign currencies can be exchanged at bureaux de change, in banks and at many hotels.
Credit & debit cards: American Express, Diners Club, MasterCard and Visa are all widely accepted. Check with your credit or debit card company for details of merchant acceptability and other services which may be available.
Travellers cheques: Widely accepted.
Exchange rates: See the *United Kingdom* section.
Banking hours: Mon-Fri 0930-1530. Some banks are open earlier and close later on weekdays.

Duty Free

The following goods may be imported into Guernsey by persons of 18 years or over without incurring customs duty:
200 cigarettes or 100 cigarillos or 50 cigars or 250g of tobacco; 2l of still table wine; 1l of alcoholic beverages over 22 per cent proof or 2l of fortified wine/sparkling wine/liqueurs or an additional 2l of still table wine; other goods to a value of £145.
Note: (a) Certain animals may be imported into the Channel Islands under the 'Pet Passport' scheme. For further details, contact an official source. (b) Commercial goods, prohibited and restricted goods, or goods in excess of the personal allowance must be declared. (c) Guernsey is not part of the EU and therefore normal restrictions apply.
Prohibited goods: Unlicensed drugs; offensive weapons; obscene or pornographic material; counterfeit goods.
Restricted items: Firearms, explosives and ammunition; animals and birds; uncooked meats and poultry; certain plants.

Public Holidays

Public holidays are as for the rest of the UK (see *United Kingdom* section) with the following date also observed:
May 9 Liberation Day (commemorating the arrival of the British Forces at the end of World War II).

Health

	Special Precautions?	Certificate Required?
Yellow Fever	No	No
Cholera	No	No
Typhoid & Polio	No	N/A
Malaria	No	N/A

Note: Regulations and requirements may be subject to change at short notice, and you are advised to contact your doctor well in advance of your intended date of departure. Any numbers in the chart refer to the footnotes below.

Health care: Most doctors and dentists are in private practice and patients are required to pay for any treatment by a GP. This can be at a surgery, at a temporary residence or in the Accident and Emergency Department at the Princess Elizabeth Hospital (PEH) which is operated by the Board of Health, as these services are provided by GPs in private practice. However, the Reciprocal Health Agreement only provides for immediately necessary treatment, such as urgently needed treatment for conditions which may arise during a stay. Hospital accommodation and medical services are provided free of charge to UK visitors under the act. There is also a charge for the ambulance service. Medical insurance is strongly recommended.

Travel - International

AIR: Guernsey can be reached all year round from various locations on mainland Britain, Dinard, Zurich and Amsterdam and at weekends during the summer from Rotterdam, Dortmund and Hanover. Airlines serving Guernsey include *Aurigny Air Services, British Airways Express, Flybe and Swiss.*
Approximate flight times: From Guernsey to *London* is one hour.
International airports: *Guernsey (GCI)*, 6km (4 miles) from St Peter Port. Bus and taxi services are available to the town (travel time – 15 minutes). Airport facilities include ATM, car hire, tourist information, first aid room, shops (including duty-free shop in departure lounge) and light refreshments.
Departure tax: None.
SEA: *Condor Ferries* operates car/passenger catamaran services to Guernsey from Poole (travel time – two hours 30 minutes), Weymouth (travel time – two hours) and St Malo (travel time – two hours). A car ferry operates to Portsmouth (travel time – 10 hours 30 minutes). Services also operate from Jersey. *Emeraude Lines* operates from St Malo, Jersey and Sark. Day excursions are available daily to Herm, Jersey and Sark by boat. Inter-island services are also available from *Aurigny Air Services, Condor Ferries* and *Emeraude Lines.*

Travel - Internal

ROAD: Bus: A comprehensive bus service has recently been revised and serves all parts of the island. A variety of island tours are also available during the summer. **Car hire:** There are many car hire companies available on Guernsey, with rates that compare favourably with the UK. There is an unlimited mileage allowance. Coach hire for large parties is also available. **Bicycle hire:** Available from various firms for daily or weekly hire. **Regulations:** Driving is on the left. Maximum speed limit is 35mph (56kph). Parking is free, although time limits are imposed. If these are exceeded, fines are levied. **Documentation:** A full national driving licence is required.

Travel times: The following chart gives approximate travel times (in hours and minutes) from **St Peter Port** to the neighbouring Channel Islands.

	Air	Sea
Alderney	**0.15**	**-**
Herm Island	**-**	**0.20**
Jersey	**0.15**	**1.00**
Sark Island	**-**	**0.40**

Accommodation

A full-colour brochure of all accommodation is available from the Guernsey Tourist Board (see *Contact Addresses* section). The Guernsey Government has a scheme for the compulsory inspection and grading of hotels to ensure standards of accommodation are maintained and improved. It is advised to book accommodation in advance during the summer months.
HOTELS: A large selection of well-maintained hotels, offering facilities for the single or group visitor, is available. Over 94 per cent of rooms have en suite facilities. All have at least a washbasin and hot and cold running water. Advance booking is advisable during the summer period. For the brochure mentioned above, contact the Guernsey Tourist Board *or* the Guernsey Hotel and Tourism Association (GHATA), c/o Guernsey Chamber of Commerce, Suite 3, 16 Glategny Esplanade, St Peter Port GY1 1WN (tel: (01481) 713 583; fax: (01481) 710 755; e-mail: info@ghata.guernsey.net; website: www.ghata.com).
Grading: All hotels are graded, being given a number of stars (with 5 stars given as the highest grade) according to the facilities offered. Some registered hotels have either not been awarded any stars or are awaiting their assessment. **5-star:** The highest classification, with an extensive range of facilities and services, including excellent staff, high-quality service and a luxurious standard of decor, furnishings and fittings. All rooms have en suite facilities which include baths fitted with overhead showers, bath robes and bath sheets. All colour TVs offer cable and satellite channels, along with video channels. Additional fax and computer points may be provided; **4-star:** Includes hotels with extensive accommodation and smaller luxury hotels, which provide high standards of service and a wide range of facilities. These include a dry cleaning service and a superior standard of decor, furnishings and fittings in all bedrooms. All en suite/private facilities will include baths with overhead showers. At least one restaurant will be open daily to residents and non-residents, for all meals. A full lunch service will be available in a restaurant, brasserie or similar; **3-star:** The range of facilities includes a laundry service and more emphasis is placed on the quality and comfort of bedrooms, including remote-control TVs. Staffing levels and quality are of a good standard. Full dinner service, light snacks and lunches are available to residents and non-residents; **2-star:** Accommodation offering extensive facilities including colour TV and private/en suite facilities in all bedrooms, a lunch availability option and a restaurant serving evening meals; **1-star:** Clean and comfortable accommodation, with a minimum of six bedrooms, three-quarters of which will have en suite/private facilities. Range of facilities will include a lounge area, alcohol licence, lunch availability option and dining facilities for evening meals.
GUEST HOUSES: These are normally family-run establishments, providing a good standard of accommodation in a homely atmosphere. This can be based on full-board, half-board or bed & breakfast, according to the visitor's requirements. A number of these have residential liquor licences.
Grading: All are graded under the Diamond Scheme with 5 diamonds offering the best service and 1 diamond offering basic comfort.
SELF-CATERING: Units are graded 5 stars to 1 star according to size, number of persons accommodated, standards and amenities offered.
CAMPING/CARAVANNING: There are four official campsites at various locations around the island. Full details are available from the Tourist Office. Visitors are not permitted to bring caravans into Guernsey.

Resorts & Excursions

Guernsey has a quieter charm than Jersey, with fewer of the trappings of mass tourism, and is a tranquil alternative to its larger neighbour to the southeast. Like Jersey, though, it has a strong culture of annual special events like the Battle of Flowers floral carnival which takes place each August.
ST PETER PORT: The island's capital retains much of the character of a traditional fishing village. The church dates in part from the 12th century, while the 17th-century oldest house, now a National Trust shop, stands in Cornet Street. The **Priaulx Library** contains a large browsable collection of historical records. Nearby, **Castle Cornet** overlooks the harbour. Built during the reign of King Stephen, it bears influences from many eras, through to the German occupation of World War II. It also contains the **Royal Guernsey Militia Museum**, a **Maritime Museum** and attractive gardens.
Hauteville House, on the south side of St Peter Port at the top of the hill, was once the home of Victor Hugo. It was here that he wrote *The Toilers of the Sea* (which is set in **St Sampson**). His statue stands in **Candie Gardens**, as does the main **Island Museum**, and a small **botanical gardens**.
THE COAST: Guernsey has an extensive array of beaches ranged all around its coastline. Within walking distance of **St Peter Port** are those of **Havelet Bay** and **Belle Grève Bay**. On the West Coast lies **Fortress Rousse**, an 18th-century tower now open to the public. Fortifications are scattered all around the coast – among them are **Ivy Castle** near **Le Bouet**, a Norman stronghold, and **Vale Castle** at **St Sampson**.
In the north of the island are **L'Ancresse Bay** and **Grande Havre**, both with big sandy beaches. Further afield, and popular with surfers, is the northwest-facing **Vazon Bay**, with its huge sweeping sands. At the western end lies **Roquaine Bay**, which boasts two beaches as well as the **Fort Grey Maritime Museum**, focusing on the many shipwrecks that have occurred off Guernsey. At the northern end of the bay, **Lihou Island** is home to flocks of seabirds, and is accessible to walkers at low tide. On the south coast, steep steps reach the beach at **Petit Bôt**, and **Moulin Huet Bay** is a sheltered location for sunbathers. The cliff paths around the island make for interesting walks. The **Water Lanes** leading to the shore, particularly at **Moulin Huet** and **Petit Bôt**, are highlights among these. **Dolmens** (neolithic tombs) are common on Guernsey. Among them are **Déhus Dolmen**, near the yacht marina in the **Vale**, and **La Catioroc**, on a mound overlooking **Perelle Bay** (reputedly once a witches' meeting place).
INLAND: In the north of the island at **Sausmarez Park**, the **Folk Museum** has an extensive collection of old farming equipment and Victorian domestic furniture. The wartime **German Underground Hospital** at **St Andrew** is now a tourist attraction, and the **German Occupation Museum** at **Forest** gives an insight into island life during World War II German occupation. Also located in German tunnels is the island's **Aquarium**. The **Little Chapel** at **Les Vauxbelets** is thought to be the smallest church in the world, with space for a priest and a congregation of two.
Guernsey's only stately home open to the public is **Sausmarez Manor** at **St Martin**.

Sport & Activities

Watersports: Guernsey's location and mild climate provide good opportunities for beach holidays and water sports, particularly **swimming** and **sailing**. Amongst the best beaches are *l'Ancresse, Cobo, Petit Bôt* and *Vazon Bay*. **Fishing** tours on chartered boats are also available. **Diving** excursions and courses are offered by the Guernsey School of Diving/Sarnia Skin Divers (tel: (01481) 722 884) and other organisations; contact the Guernsey Tourist Board for details (see *Contact Addresses* section).
Golf: Guernsey has two 18-hole golf courses and one 9-hole course. The 18-hole course at *La Grand De Mare* was designed by Fred Hawtree and is particularly suitable for beginners and intermediate players. Visitors wishing to play must have a handicap certificate from a recognised club. Guernsey's second 18-hole course is at the *Royal Guernsey/L'Ancresse Golf Club* in the north; a current handicap certificate from a recognised club is required. *St Pierre Park*'s 9-hole course is good for putting practice; a handicap is not required.
Other: Due to its small size, **cycling** holidays are popular in Guernsey. Excursions to the neighbouring islands of Herm and Sark as well as to France are possible via frequent ferry links. **Walking** tours can be organised throughout the Channel Islands, with trails along the cliffs providing dramatic scenery and beautiful views. Contact the Guernsey Tourist Board for details (see *Contact Addresses* section).

Social Profile

FOOD & DRINK: Guernsey is famous for its food and the island has a wide variety of restaurants ranging from traditional French and English cuisine to Italian, Indian and Chinese. The local speciality is shellfish, with freshly caught lobsters, crabs and scallops forming the basis of many dishes. Other Guernsey specialities include *Guernsey Gâche* - pronounced 'gosh' (a fruit loaf usually served with local butter) and *Gâche Melée* (a local apple cake). Table service is normal in restaurants, with counter service in bars. There are two self-service restaurants in St Peter Port. A wide variety of alcoholic beverages are available and spirits, beers and wines are relatively cheap compared to the mainland. Eating out is also excellent value for money as there is no VAT. After a recent change in the licensing laws, pubs in Guernsey are now able to stay open until 0045 seven nights a week.
NIGHTLIFE: Discos are located in St Peter Port, whilst live music and cabarets are organised by some hotels during the summer season. The Beau Sejour Leisure Centre at St Peter Port contains a cinema, theatre, bars and cafe.
SHOPPING: There is no VAT but a Guernsey Bailiwick tax is imposed on certain goods such as spirits, wines, beers and tobacco. Prices of luxury goods are cheaper than in the UK, although the overall cost of foodstuffs is higher. Special purchases include Guernsey's local pottery, knitted sweaters, crafts, gold and silver jewellery and candles. **Shopping hours:** Mon-Sat 0900-1730 (there may be limited Sunday opening).
SPECIAL EVENTS: For full details and exact dates, contact the Guernsey Tourist Board (see *Contact Addresses* section). The following is a selection of special events occurring in Guernsey in 2005:
Jan 24-Mar 20 *Guernsey Eisteddfod Society 75th Annual Festival.* **Mar 25-28** *Alderney Easter Weekend/Easter Runs.* **Apr 1-3** *Guernsey Blues Festival.* **Apr 8-10** *14th Open International Guernsey Masters Swim Meet.* **May 1-16** *Alderney Seafood Festival.* **May 21-29** *Spring Walking Week.* **Jun 9-11** *Floral Guernsey Show.* **Jun 24** *Harbour Carnival*, St Peter Port. **Jul 1-30** *Seafood Festival & Fair.* **Jul 23-31** *St Peter Port Carnival.* **Jul 30-Aug 7** *Alderney Week.* **Aug 24-25** *North Show and Battle of Flowers* (finale of summer shows), Saumarez Park, Castel. **Sep 3-18** *St Peter Ale & Food Festival.* **Sep 9-11** *34th Guernsey International Air Rally.* **Sep 10-18** *Autumn Walking Week.* **Sep 30-Oct 2** *Guernsey Jazz Festival.* **Oct 1-Nov 11** *Tennerfest.*
SOCIAL CONVENTIONS: Handshaking is the customary form of greeting and normal social courtesies should be observed when visiting someone's home. It is not usual to start eating until everyone is served. If invited to someone's home, a small present such as flowers or chocolates is appreciated. Casual wear is acceptable in most places. Smoking is not allowed on buses. **Tipping:** 10 to 12 per cent is normal, except where a service charge is included.

Business Profile

ECONOMY: Finance, tourism and light industry are the main components of Guernsey's economy. The island has gradually been developed as an offshore financial centre and the financial sector now accounts for 60 per cent of government revenues. Various institutions are incorporated on the island to take advantage of its favourable tax and corporate disclosure requirements. However, along with Jersey, the island's government agreed in 2002 to join an EU-wide campaign to improve international financial transparency and stamp out tax evasion.
Flowers and tomatoes are the main horticultural exports and enjoy international recognition. Tourism's relative importance has been far outstripped by the financial sector.
BUSINESS: Businesspeople are generally expected to dress smartly, with a suit and tie for men. Appointments should be made and business cards are customary. Business is conducted in English. **Office hours:** Mon-Fri 0900-1700.
COMMERCIAL INFORMATION: The following organisation can offer advice: Guernsey Chamber of Commerce, Suite 3, 16 Glategny Esplanade, St Peter Port GY1 1WN (tel: (01481) 727 483; fax: (01481) 710 755; e-mail: director@chamber.guernsey.net; website: www.chamber.guernsey.net).
CONFERENCES/CONVENTIONS: Guernsey's main conference venue, the Beau Sejour Centre, has a maximum seating capacity of 1500 with 2646 sq m (28,482 sq ft) of exhibition space and banqueting for 900 people or a reception area for 2000 people. Many hotels also offer conference space. More information can be obtained from Conference Guernsey (tel: (0118) 934 5542; e-mail: info@conferenceguernsey.gg; website: www.conferenceguernsey.gg).

Climate

The most popular holiday season is from Easter to October, with temperatures averaging 20-21°C (68-70°F). These months give an average of 200 and 260 hours of sunshine. Rainfall is mainly during the cooler months. The sea is 17°C (63°F) on average during the summer.
Required clothing: Normal beach and holiday wear for summer, with some warmer clothing as there are often sea breezes. Warm winter wear and rainwear are advised.

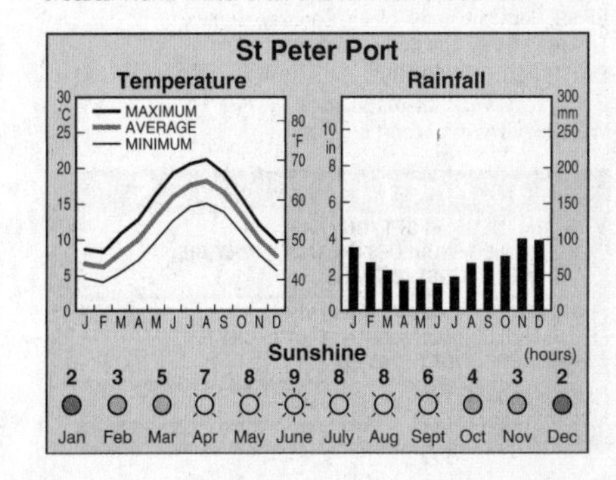

Guinea Republic

LATEST TRAVEL ADVICE CONTACTS

British Foreign and Commonwealth Office
Tel: (0870) 606 0290 Website: www.fco.gov.uk
US Department of State
Website: http://travel.state.gov/travel
Canadian Department of Foreign Affairs and Int'l Trade
Tel: (1 800) 267 8376 Website: www.dfait-maeci.gc.ca

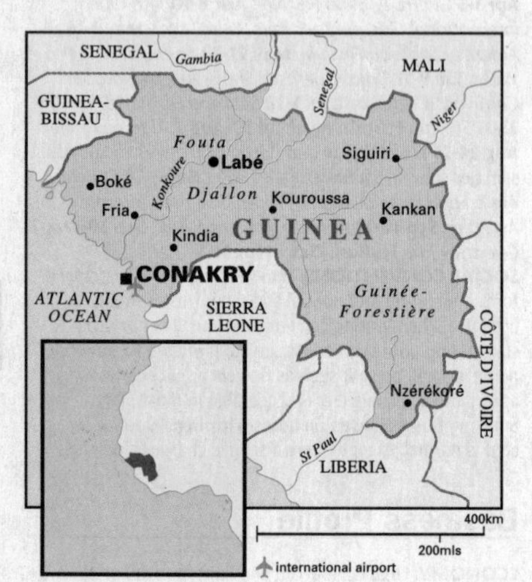

Location: West Africa

Country dialling code: 224.

Office National du Tourisme
BP 1275, 6 Avenue de la République, Immeuble Al-Iman, Conakry, Guinea
Tel: 455 163. Fax: 455 164.
E-mail: ontour@leland-gn.org
Website: www.guinee.gov.gn *or* www.mirinet.net.gn/ont

Consulate General of the Republic of Guinea
83 Victoria Street, London, SW1H 0HW, UK
Tel: (020) 7078 6087
Fax: (020) 7078 6086
E-mail: genevieverippon@guineaconsuluk.freeserve.co.uk

Embassy of the Republic of Guinea
51 Rue de la Faisanderie, 75016 Paris, France
Tel: (1) 4704 8148.
Fax: (1) 4704 5765.
Opening hours: Mon-Fri 0900-1600.

British Embassy
BP 6729, Conakry, Guinea
Tel: 455 807. Fax: 456 020
E-mail: britcon.oury@biasy.net
Public access is restricted and interviews are strictly by appointment only.
The British Embassy in Dakar deals with most enquiries relating to Guinea (see *Senegal* section).

Embassy of the Republic of Guinea
2112 Leroy Place, NW, Washington, DC 20008, USA
Tel: (202) 986 4300. Fax: (202) 986 4800.

Embassy of the United States of America
Street address: Second Boulevard and Ninth Avenue, Conakry, Guinea
Postal address: BP 603, Conakry, Guinea
Tel: 411 520/1/3. Fax: 411 522.
Website: http://conakry.usembassy.gov

Embassy of the Republic of Guinea
483 Wilbrod Street, Ottawa, Ontario K1N 6N1, Canada
Tel: (613) 789 8444. Fax: (613) 789 7560.
E-mail: ambassadedeguinee@bellnet.ca

Canadian Embassy
BP 99, Corniche Sud, Coleah, Conakry, Guinea
Tel: 462 395 *or* 464 448 *or* 463 732.
Fax: 464 235 *or* 409 198.
E-mail: cnaky@dfait-maeci.gc.ca
Website: www.infoexport.gc.ca/gn

TIMATIC CODES

Health
AMADEUS: **TI-DFT/CKY/HE**
GALILEO/WORLDSPAN: **TI-DFT/CKY/HE**
SABRE: **TIDFT/CKY/HE**

Visa
AMADEUS: **TI-DFT/CKY/VI**
GALILEO/WORLDSPAN: **TI-DFT/CKY/VI**
SABRE: **TIDFT/CKY/VI**

To access TIMATIC country information on Health and Visa regulations through the Computer Reservations System (CRS), type in the appropriate command line listed above.

General Information

AREA: 245,857 sq km (94,926 sq miles).
POPULATION: 8,359,000 (2002).
POPULATION DENSITY: 34.0 per sq km.
CAPITAL: Conakry. **Population:** 1,092,936 (1996 census).
GEOGRAPHY: The Republic of Guinea is located in West Africa and bordered to the northwest by Guinea-Bissau, the north by Senegal and Mali, the east by Côte d'Ivoire, the south by Liberia and the southwest by Sierra Leone. Guinea's many rivers supply water to much of West Africa. The River Niger flows north from the southern highlands into Mali before turning south again through Niger and Nigeria. The coastal plain is made up of mangrove swamps, while inland are the Fouta Djalon hills which form several distinct ranges and plateaux over the whole of western Guinea. In the northeast, savannah plains of the Sahel region stretch into Mali. To the south are mountains known as the Guinea Highlands.
GOVERNMENT: Republic since 1958. Gained independence from France in 1958. **Head of State:** President Lansana Conté since 1984. **Head of Government:** Francois Loseny Fall became Prime Minister in February 2004 but then left the country and resigned in April 2004 claiming his life would be in danger if he returned. He is currently living in exile and the position has not been reappointed.
LANGUAGE: French is the official language. Susu, Malinké and Fula are local languages.
RELIGION: The majority of the population are Muslim, with animist and Roman Catholic minorities.
TIME: GMT.
ELECTRICITY: 220 volts, 50Hz.
COMMUNICATIONS: Telephone: IDD service is available. Country code: 224. The communication is relatively poor and outgoing international calls must be made through the operator. Limited telephone and fax lines are usually available 1800-0600. **Mobile telephone:** GSM 900 networks covering main inhabited areas are operated by *Celtel Guinea* (website: www.msi-cellular.com), *Sotelgui*, *Spacetel Guinee* and *Telecel Guinee SARL*. **Post:** There are numerous post offices in the capital. **Internet:** ISPs include *ETI-Bull* and *BINNTA*. **Press:** Newspapers include *Horoya* (official, daily), *Le Lynx* (satirical, weekly), *L'Indépendant* and *La Lance* (weekly), *Journal Officiel de Guinée* (official, fortnightly) and *L'Evénement de Guinée* (monthly).
Radio: BBC World Service (website: www.bbc.co.uk/worldservice) and Voice of America (website: www.voa.gov) can be received. From time to time the frequencies change and the most up-to-date can be found online. www.voaa.gov

Passport/Visa

	Passport Required?	Visa Required?	Return Ticket Required?
Full British	Yes	Yes	No
Australian	Yes	Yes	No
Canadian	Yes	Yes	No
USA	Yes	Yes	No
Other EU	Yes	Yes	No
Japanese	Yes	Yes	No

Note: *Regulations and requirements may be subject to change at short notice, and you are advised to contact the appropriate diplomatic or consular authority before finalising travel arrangements. Details of these may be found at the head of this country's entry. Any numbers in the chart refer to the footnotes below.*

PASSPORTS: Passports valid for a minimum of six months beyond date of departure required by all.
VISAS: Required by all.
Types of visa and cost: *Tourist* and *Business*: £65 (single-entry for a stay of up to one month); £90 (multiple-entry for a stay of up to three months)
Application to: Consulate (or Consular section at Embassy). UK nationals may apply to the Chancery Consulate General of the Republic of Guinea in London (see *Contact Addresses* section).
Application requirements: (a) Two application forms. (b) Two passport-size photos. (c) Passport with a remaining validity of six months after intended length of stay. (d) Proof of sufficient funds and letter of invitation or hotel reservation. (e) Proof of funds. *Business:* (a)-(e) and (f) Letter from the applicant's company. (g) Letter from the sponsoring company in Guinea
Working days required: Two.

Money

Currency: Guinea Franc (FG) = 100 centimes. Notes are in denominations of FG5000, 1000 and 500. Coins are in denominations of FG25, 10, 5 and 1.
Currency exchange: Hotels will accept some foreign currencies in payment. Inter-bank fund transfers are frequently difficult, if not impossible, to accomplish.
Credit & debit cards: Limited acceptance. Check with your credit or debit card company for details of merchant acceptability and other services which may be available.
Travellers cheques: To avoid additional exchange rates charges, travellers are advised to take travellers cheques in US Dollars or Euros.
Currency restrictions: It is possible to import up to 1,000 guinea Francs providing you have a valid export declaration for that amount. Import of foreign currency is unlimited, provided declared on arrival; export is limited to the amount declared on arrival.
Note: It is compulsory to exchange a certain amount of foreign currency. The amount depends on the length of stay specified in the visa, and is at the discretion of the immigration authorities. Unused currency can sometimes be re-exchanged – again at the discretion of the authorities. Travellers are advised to check that the amounts exchanged have been entered correctly onto the declaration form.
Exchange rate indicators: The following figures are included as a guide to the movements of the Guinea Franc against Sterling and the US Dollar:

Date	Feb '04	May '04	Aug '04	Nov '04
£1.00=	3649.60	3594.53	4679.57	5169.80
$1.00=	2005.00	2012.50	2540.00	2730.00

Banking hours: Mon-Fri 0830-1230 and 1430-1630.

Duty Free

The following goods may be imported into Guinea without incurring customs duty:
1000 cigarettes or 250 cigars or 1kg of tobacco; one bottle of alcoholic beverage (opened); a reasonable quantity of perfume.

Public Holidays

2005: Jan 1 New Year's Day. **Jan 21** Eid al-Adha (Feast of the Sacrifice). **Mar 28** Easter Monday. **Apr 21** Mouloud (Birth of the Prophet). **May 1** Labour Day. **May 5** Ascension. **Aug 15** Assumption. **Aug 27** Anniversary of Women's Revolt. **Sep 28** Referendum Day. **Oct 2** Republic Day. **Nov** Laila toul Kadir (day after the night's vigil); Day of 1970 Invasion. **Nov 1** All Saints' Day. **Nov 3-5** Eid al-Fitr (End of Ramadan). **Dec 25** Christmas Day.
2006: Jan 1 New Year's Day. **Jan 10** Eid al-Adha (Feast of the Sacrifice). **Apr 14** Easter Monday. **May 1** Labour Day. **Apr 11** Mouloud (Birth of the Prophet). **May 25** Ascension. **Aug 15** Assumption. **Aug 27** Anniversary of Women's Revolt. **Sep 28** Referendum Day. **Oct 2** Republic Day. **Oct 22-24** Eid al-Fitr (End of Ramadan). **Nov 1** All Saints' Day. **Nov** Laila toul Kadir (day after the night's vigil)/Day of 1970 Invasion. **Dec 25** Christmas Day.
Note: Muslim festivals are timed according to local sightings of various phases of the moon and the dates given above are approximations. During the lunar month of Ramadan that precedes Eid al-Fitr, Muslims fast during the day and feast at night and normal business patterns may be interrupted. Many restaurants are closed during the day and there may be restrictions on smoking and drinking. Some disruption may continue into Eid al-Fitr itself. Eid al-Fitr may last anything from two to 10 days, depending on the region. For more information, see the *World of Islam* appendix.

Health

	Special Precautions?	Certificate Required?
Yellow Fever	Yes	1
Cholera	2	No
Typhoid & Polio	3	N/A
Malaria	4	N/A

Note: *Regulations and requirements may be subject to change at short notice, and you are advised to contact your doctor well in advance of your intended date of departure. Any numbers in the chart refer to the footnotes below.*

1: A yellow fever vaccination certificate is required from travellers over one year of age coming from infected areas. Travellers arriving from non-endemic zones should note that vaccination is strongly recommended for travel outside the urban areas, even if an outbreak of the disease has not been reported and they would normally not require a vaccination certificate to enter the country.
2: Following WHO guidelines issued in 1973, a cholera vaccination certificate is no longer a condition of entry to Guinea. However, cholera is a serious risk in this country and precautions are essential. Up-to-date advice should be sought before deciding whether these precautions should include vaccination as medical opinion is divided over its effectiveness. See the *Health* appendix for more information.

3: Immunisation against typhoid and poliomyelitis is often recommended.
4: A malaria risk, predominantly in the malignant *falciparum* form, exists all year throughout the country. Resistance to chloroquine has been reported.
Food & drink: All water should be regarded as being potentially contaminated. Water used for drinking, brushing teeth or making ice should have first been boiled or otherwise sterilised. Only eat well-cooked meat and fish, preferably served hot. Pork, salad and mayonnaise may carry increased risk. Vegetables should be cooked and fruit peeled.
Other risks: *Diarrhoeal diseases*, including *giardiasis*, and *typhoid fevers* are common. *Bilharzia* (schistosomiasis) is present. Avoid swimming and paddling in fresh water; swimming pools which are well chlorinated and maintained are safe. *Onchocerciasis* (river blindness) and *trypanosomiasis* (sleeping sickness) are present. *Hepatitis A, C* and *E* are widespread. *Hepatitis B* is hyperendemic. Epidemics of *meningococcal disease* may occur, particularly in the savannah areas and during the dry season. *Dengue fever* and *TB* both occur. Immunisation against *diphtheria* is sometimes recommended.
Rabies is present. For those at high risk, vaccination before arrival should be considered. If you are bitten, seek medical advice without delay. For more information, consult the *Health* appendix.
Health care: Health insurance is essential. There are rudimentary medical, dental and optical facilities in Conakry. Doctors and hospitals expect immediate cash payment for health services.

Travel - International

Note: Visitors are strongly recommended not to travel to the borders with Côte d'Ivoire and Liberia. The civil war in neighbouring Sierra Leone ended in 2002 and is now largely peaceful, but travellers should stay in touch with any local developments. Travel to Nzerekore is advised against due to violence between different ethnic groups. For further information, contact a local government advice department.
AIR: *Air France* flies regularly from London to Conakry, via Paris. *Aeroflot*, *KLM* and *Sabena* also fly direct from Europe. *Air Afrique* operates from New York to Dakar, from where connecting flights to Guinea are available. Other airlines serving Guinea include *Ghana Airways*.
Approximate flight times: From Conakry to *London* is 11 hours (including a stopover time in Paris or Brussels of up to three hours).
International airports: *Conakry (CKY)* is 13km (8 miles) southwest of the city. Taxis are available to the city.
Note: Foreigners at Conakry Airport are particular targets for pickpockets and persons posing as officials who will offer assistance and then make off with bags, purses and wallets. Being met at the airport by travel agents, business contacts, family members or friends lessens the risk of this.
Departure tax: None.
SEA/RIVER: There is a fast hydrofoil service along the coast from Conakry to Freetown in Sierra Leone. There is also a ferry to Mali which operates when the river is high enough.
ROAD: There are road links with Danané (Côte d'Ivoire), Bamako (Mali), Tambacounda (Senegal) and Freetown (Sierra Leone). Bus services are available to the neighbouring countries - including Sierra Leone since the end of the civil war in 2002 - but services can be unreliable and timetables may be purely theoretical (see also *Travel – Internal* section). Visitors should also note that political instability is persisting in some neighbouring countries - notably in Guinea-Bissau. Check with an embassy or relevant organisation for up-to-date travel advice.

Travel - Internal

AIR: *Guinee Airlines* operates internal services to some of the main towns, such as Boké, Conakry, Labé, Kankan, Kissidougou, Macenta, Nzérékoré and Siguiri. Schedules are erratic.
RAIL: Despite the existence of rail lines and plans to upgrade them, there are currently no rail services in Guinea.
ROAD: Many roads are in poor condition and the minor roads are often overgrown with bush. Travel by road is often impossible in the rainy season (May-Oct). The roads between Conakry (via Kindia) and Kissidougou and from Boké to Kamsar are both paved, as is the road to Freetown. Traffic drives on the right. In an effort to counter urban crime, the Guinean Government maintains roadblocks from 0000-0600. **Bus:** The government bus company, *SOGETRAG*, operates services from Conakry to most other towns. The buses are fairly comfortable and good value.
Taxi: These are available, although fares should be negotiated in advance. Bush taxis usually cover smaller distances than buses and can take up to seven passengers.
URBAN: Buses and taxis operate cheaply within Conakry. It is not usual to tip taxi drivers.

Accommodation

HOTELS: In Conakry there are a few fairly expensive hotels of a good standard. In addition, the city centre also has a number of good-value hotels with basic, but adequate, facilities. Outside the city centre, accommodation gets sparser, but there are hotels available, for instance in Labé, Kindia and Dalaba. Visitors are advised to book in advance and obtain written confirmation.
REST HOUSES: These are available in most of the major towns; enquire locally.

Resorts & Excursions

In 1958, when it declared independence from France and voted in a staunchly socialist one-party government, Guinea became an isolated and secretive country. However, after the death of the dictator Sekou Touré in 1984, Guinea began, slowly, to allow tourists through its once stubbornly closed doors. Even so, it is still one of the least visited countries in Africa and it can be difficult, despite declarations to the contrary, to acquire visas. Guinea's main attraction to tourists is its relatively undisturbed countryside. Its landscape varies from mountains to plains and from savannah to forest, and the three great rivers of West Africa – the Gambia, the Senegal and the Niger – all originate here. The capital, **Conakry**, is located on the island of Tumbo and is connected to the Kaloum Peninsula by a 300m-long (984ft) pier. The city is well laid-out, its alleys shaded by mangrove and coconut palm trees. The **Cathedral**, built in the 1930s and located in the town centre, is well worth viewing. There is also a **National Museum**. The **Kakimbon Caves** in the village of Ratoma, now a suburb of Conakry, are the source of many interesting legends and are bestowed with great religious significance by the local Baga people. The **Îles de Los**, off the Kaloum Peninsula some 10km (6 miles) southwest of Conakry, are recommended as a tourist destination and are easily accessible from Conakry. Good beaches can also be found at the **Île de Roume** and **Île de Kassa**, the latter being accessible via a public boat service. Approximately 150km (93 miles) outside Conakry is the picturesque **le Voile de la Mariée**, nestled at the bottom of a 70m-high (230ft) rock from which the **River Sabende** plunges, amidst lush vegetation, into a deep pond. In **Pita**, located between Dalaba and Labé, the **Kinkon Falls** can be found which produce 150m (492ft) of cascading water. Known as the land of waters, fruit, faith and freedom, the **Fouta Djalon** highlands are renowned for their picturesque hills, offering superb views, and the rolling valleys and waterfalls, which are all presided over by the mostly Muslim population of Fula herders and farmers. In the eastern region of Guinea lie many historical towns with echoes and remnants of medieval empires. Along a road following the **Nimba Range**, which stretches from Guinea to the Côte d'Ivoire, small groups of round houses nestle in traditional African villages. In the south is the **Guinée Forestière**, a highland area of rainforest and old pre-Islamic tribes. There are no national parks in Guinea, but wildlife can be best seen in the northeast savannahs between the **Tinkisso River** and the Mali border, in the foothills of the Fouta Djalon highlands and in the southeast.

Sport & Activities

In Landreah is the *28 September Stadium* where numerous sporting events are held. **Football** is the most popular sport and the national team is of a good standard. The best beaches for **swimming** are on the *Îles de Los* (which lie just off the coast near Conakry), the *Île de Roume* and the *Île de Kassa*, but currents can be strong and swimmers are advised to exercise care and follow local advice. Hiking is possible in the attractive *Fouta Djalon* region.

Social Profile

FOOD & DRINK: Restaurants, except in the capital where Western-style food is available, generally serve local dishes including *jollof rice*, stuffed chicken with groundnuts, and fish dishes. These are usually served with rice and may be spicy. Staples are cassava, yams and maize. Guineans are fond of very hot maize soup, served from calabashes. Main hotels, mostly in the capital, have reasonable restaurants where a wide variety of alcoholic beverages is served, including good West African brands of beer. This is also available in local bars.
NIGHTLIFE: Although there are theatres, nightclubs and cinemas, Guineans prefer to make their own entertainment. In the streets people can often be seen gathered together to dance, sing and play traditional musical instruments or home-made guitars. Conakry is a dynamic centre for music and the singing of the Kindia people is renowned.
SHOPPING: Although department stores in the major cities are poorly stocked, local markets sell a unique display of goods. Special purchases include brightly coloured, distinctive Guinean clothes, woodcarvings, leather rugs in bold black-and-white designs, skins, locally produced records, calabashes and jewellery. **Shopping hours:** Mon-Sat 0900-1800.
SPECIAL EVENTS: The main events celebrated in Guinea are Muslim holy days and feasts. The following is a selection of special events celebrated annually in Guinea Republic:
Feb *Tabaski* (Feast of the Sacrifice). **May** *Mouloud* (Prophet's Anniversary). **Nov** *Eid al-Fitr* (End of Ramadan).
SOCIAL CONVENTIONS: Although Muslim customs are less strict than in the Arab world, beliefs and traditions should be respected by tourists. Casual dress is acceptable. Street crime is relatively common. It is important to greet people and ask them how they are before starting a conversation. Guineans always use titles when addressing others, so the visitor should do likewise (Monsieur, Madame, Mademoiselle etc). **Photography:** A permit (applied for in advance) has to be obtained from the *Ministère de l'Intérieur et de la Sécurité* when photographing government buildings, military and transportation facilities or public works. It is inadvisable to photograph buildings at present, and visitors should always ask local people if they want to photograph them. **Tipping:** A 5 per cent service charge will usually be included in the bill.

Business Profile

ECONOMY: Given its resources, Guinea should not be suffering its current impoverished condition in which the annual per capita income is just over US$1000. The majority of the population is engaged in subsistence agriculture, producing cassava and rice as staples, plus fruit, palm, groundnuts and sometimes coffee as cash crops. Fisheries have undergone major growth in the last 10 years. The main part of the industrial economy is mining. Guinea has huge reserves of bauxite (perhaps one-quarter of the world's total) which account for more than 90 per cent of export earnings; there are also substantial diamond deposits. Guinea also boasts massive hydroelectric power potential, some of which has been tapped. The country's economic progress has, however, been hampered by the absence of the necessary legal, corporate and governmental machinery, allied to corruption and maladministration. For the time being, Guinea will continue to depend on substantial foreign aid, principally from France, although it is also deriving growing benefit from burgeoning regional co-operation: Cameroon, for example, processes much Guinean bauxite ore to produce aluminium. Guinea is a member of both the Mano River Union (with Liberia and Sierra Leone) and of the Gambia River Development Organisation (with The Gambia and Senegal). The country is also a member of the West African economic community, ECOWAS. France (the main recipient of Guinea's exports) and the USA are the country's main trading partners.
BUSINESS: Appointments should be made in advance. Tropical-weight suits and ties are worn by some business visitors, but these are not essential. A knowledge of French is helpful. **Office hours:** Mon-Thurs 0800-1630, Fri 0800-1300.
COMMERCIAL INFORMATION: The following organisation can offer advice: Chambre de Commerce, d'Industrie et d'Agriculture de Guinée, BP 545, Conakry (tel: 454 516; fax: 454 517).

Climate

The climate is tropical and humid with a wet and a dry season. Guinea is one of the wettest countries in West Africa. The wet season lasts from May to October; dry season lasts from November to April.
Required clothing: Tropical or washable cottons throughout the year. A light raincoat or umbrella is needed during the rainy season.

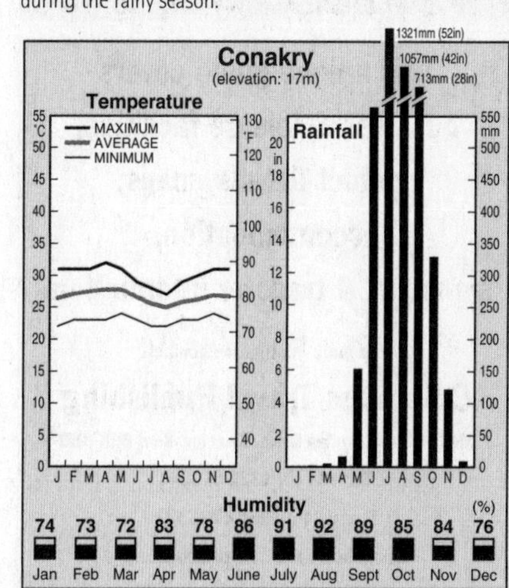

Guinea-Bissau

LATEST TRAVEL ADVICE CONTACTS

British Foreign and Commonwealth Office
Tel: (0870) 606 0290 Website: www.fco.gov.uk
US Department of State
Website: http://travel.state.gov/travel
Canadian Department of Foreign Affairs and Int'l Trade
Tel: (1 800) 267 8376 Website: www.dfait-maeci.gc.ca

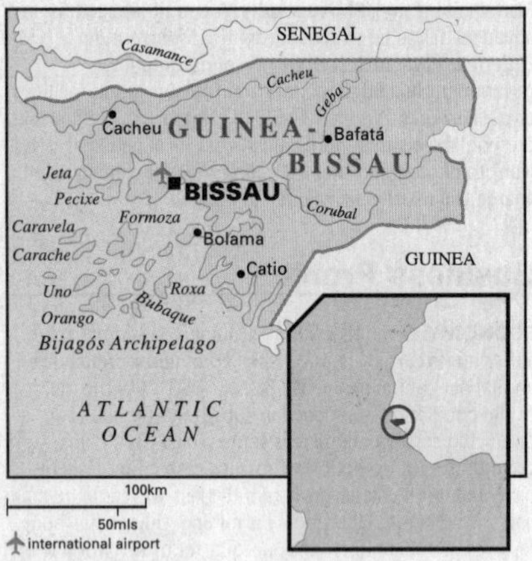

Location: West Africa.

Country dialling code: 245.

All Embassies in Guinea-Bissau are now closed. The British, US and Canadian Embassies in Dakar, Senegal deal with enquiries relating to Guinea-Bissau (see *Senegal* **section).**

Centro de Informação e Turismo
CP 294, Bissau, Guinea-Bissau
Tel: 213 905 *or* 212 844 (government office).

British Consulate
CP 100, Bissau, Guinea-Bissau
Tel: 201 224 *or* 201 216. Fax: 201 265.
E-mail: mavegro@gtelecom.gw *or* mavegro@hotmail.com
The Consulate can only provide limited assistance.

Embassy of Guinea-Bissau
94 Rue St Lazare, 75009 Paris, France
Tel: (1) 4526 1851. Fax: (1) 4526 6059.

TIMATIC CODES

Health	AMADEUS: **TI-DFT/OXB/HE** GALILEO/WORLDSPAN: **TI-DFT/OXB/HE** SABRE: **TIDFT/OXB/HE**
Visa	AMADEUS: **TI-DFT/OXB/VI** GALILEO/WORLDSPAN: **TI-DFT/OXB/VI** SABRE: **TIDFT/OXB/VI**

To access TIMATIC country information on Health and Visa regulations through the Computer Reservations System (CRS), type in the appropriate command line listed above.

Embassy of Guinea-Bissau
15929 Yukon Lane, Rockville, MD 20855, USA
Tel/Fax: (301) 947 3958.
Also deals with Canadian enquiries.

General Information

AREA: 36,125 sq km (13,948 sq miles).
POPULATION: 1,449,000 (official estimate 2002).
POPULATION DENSITY: 40.1 per sq km.
CAPITAL: Bissau. **Population:** 197,610 (1991).
GEOGRAPHY: Guinea-Bissau (formerly Portuguese Guinea) is located in West Africa, and is bordered to the north by Senegal and to the south and east by the Republic of Guinea. It encompasses the adjacent Bijagós Islands and the island of Bolama. The country rises from a coastal plain broken up by numerous inlets through a transitional plateau to mountains on the border with Guinea. Thick forest and mangrove swamp cover the area nearest to the Atlantic Ocean. Savannah covers the inland areas.
GOVERNMENT: Republic. Gained independence from Portugal in 1973. **Head of State:** Interim President Henrique Pereira since 2003. **Head of Government:** Prime Minister Carlos Gomes Junior since May 2004.
LANGUAGE: Official language is Portuguese. The majority of the population speak Guinean Creole. Balante and Fulani languages are also spoken.
RELIGION: Mainly animist and Muslim. There is a small minority of Roman Catholics and other Christians.
TIME: GMT.
ELECTRICITY: Limited electricity supply on 220 volts AC, 50Hz.
COMMUNICATIONS: Telephone: IDD is available. Country code: 245. Outgoing international calls must go through the operator. It is difficult to find public telephones or to receive international calls. Telephone services are also expensive. **Press:** There are no English-language papers. *Journal Nô Pintcha* is published daily and *Banobero*, *Correio-Bissau* and *Fraskera* weekly.
Radio: BBC World Service (website: www.bbc.co.uk/worldservice) and Voice of America (website: www.voa.gov) can be received. From time to time the frequencies change and the most up-to-date can be found online.

Passport/Visa

	Passport Required?	Visa Required?	Return Ticket Required?
Full British	Yes	Yes	Yes
Australian	Yes	Yes	Yes
Canadian	Yes	Yes	Yes
USA	Yes	Yes	Yes
Other EU	Yes	Yes	Yes
Japanese	Yes	Yes	Yes

Note: Regulations and requirements may be subject to change at short notice, and you are advised to contact the appropriate diplomatic or consular authority before finalising travel arrangements. Details of these may be found at the head of this country's entry. Any numbers in the chart refer to the footnotes below.

PASSPORTS: Passport valid for six months required by all.
VISAS: Required by all except the following:
(a) nationals of ECOWAS member countries for a maximum stay of one month (exceptions are possible, check with nearest Consulate);
(b) transit passengers continuing their journey by the same or first connecting aircraft provided holding valid onward or return documentation and not leaving the airport.
Types of visa and cost: *Tourist*, *Business*: €45 (single-entry). Multiple-entry and *Transit* only available on request. An extra €5 is needed for postal applications.
Validity: Single-entry visas are normally valid for up to 45 days; multiple-entry visas are valid for up to 90 days within a period of six months. *Transit* visas are valid for up to five days. Extensions are then granted at the discretion of the Immigration Authorities.
Application to: Consulate (or Consular section at Embassy); see *Contact Addresses* section.
Application requirements: (a) Two completed application forms. (b) Two passport-size photos. (c) Valid passport. (d) Return ticket. (e) Fee. Business: (a)-(e) and, (f) Confirmation of a job placement.
Working days required: Five. Urgent visas can be handled within 24-48 hours.

Money

Currency: CFA (*Communauté Financiaire Africaine*) Franc (CFAfr) = 100 centimes. Notes are in denominations of CFAfr10,000, 5000, 2500, 1000 and 500. Coins are in denominations of CFAfr250, 100, 50, 25, 10 and 5. Guinea-Bissau is part of the French Monetary Area. Only currency issued by the *Banque des Etats de l'Afrique de l'Ouest* (Bank of West African States) is valid; currency issued by the *Banque des Etats de l'Afrique Centrale* (Bank of Central African States) is not. The CFA Franc is tied to the Euro.
Currency exchange: US currency in small denominations is the most useful for exchange. Inter-bank fund transfers are frequently difficult and time-consuming to accomplish.
Credit & debit cards: Very limited use. Check with your credit or debit card company for details of merchant acceptability and other services which may be available.
Travellers cheques: These are rarely accepted. They can sometimes be cashed at banks. There is a fixed rate of commission on all transactions.
Currency restrictions: Import and export of local currency is prohibited. Import of foreign currency is unlimited, provided declared on arrival; export of foreign currency is limited to the amount declared on arrival.
Exchange rate indicators: The following figures are included as a guide to the movements of the CFA Franc against Sterling and the US Dollar:

Date	Feb '04	May '04	Aug '04	Nov '04
£1.00=	961.13	983.76	978.35	936.79
$1.00=	528.01	550.79	531.03	494.69

Banking hours: Mon-Fri 0730-1430.

Duty Free

The following goods can be imported into Guinea-Bissau without incurring customs duty:
A reasonable quantity of tobacco products; 2.5l of alcoholic beverages (non-Muslims only); and a reasonable quantity of perfume in opened bottles.

Public Holidays

2005: Jan 1 New Year's Day. **Jan 20** Death of Amílcar Cabral. **Jan 21** Tabaski (Feast of the Sacrifice). **Mar 8** International Women's Day. **May 1** Labour Day. **Aug 3** Anniversary of the Killing of Pidjiguoiti. **Sep 24** National Day. **Nov** Korité (end of Ramadan). **Dec 25** Christmas Day.
2006: Jan 1 New Year's Day. **Jan 10** Tabaski (Feast of the Sacrifice). **Jan 20** Death of Amílcar Cabral. **Mar 8** International Women's Day. **May 1** Labour Day. **Aug 3** Anniversary of the Killing of Pidjiguoiti. **Sep 24** National Day. **Oct 22-24** Korité (end of Ramadan). **Dec 25** Christmas Day.
Note: Muslim festivals are timed according to local sightings of various phases of the moon and the dates given above are approximations. During the lunar month of Ramadan that precedes Korité, Muslims fast during the day and feast at night and normal business patterns may be interrupted. Many restaurants are closed during the day and there may be restrictions on smoking and drinking. Some disruption may continue into Korité itself. Korité and Tabaski may last anything from two to 10 days, depending on the region. For more information, see the *World of Islam* appendix.

Health

	Special Precautions?	Certificate Required?
Yellow Fever	Yes	1
Cholera	Yes	2
Typhoid & Polio	3	N/A
Malaria	4	N/A

Note: Regulations and requirements may be subject to change at short notice, and you are advised to contact your doctor well in advance of your intended date of departure. Any numbers in the chart refer to the footnotes below.

1: A yellow fever vaccination certificate is required from travellers over one year of age coming from infected areas (contact the nearest Embassy for latest details). Travellers arriving from non-endemic zones should note that a vaccination is strongly recommended for travel outside the urban areas, even if an outbreak of the disease has not been reported and they would normally not require a vaccination certificate to enter the country.
2: Following WHO guidelines issued in 1973, a cholera vaccination certificate is no longer a condition of entry to Guinea-Bissau. However, cholera is a serious risk in this country and precautions are essential. Up-to-date advice should be sought before deciding whether these precautions should include vaccination as medical opinion is divided over its effectiveness. See the *Health* appendix for more information.
3: Immunisation against typhoid and poliomyelitis is often advised.
4: Malaria risk, predominantly in the malignant *falciparum* form, exists all year throughout the country. Resistance to chloroquine has been reported.
Food & drink: All water should be regarded as being potentially contaminated. Water used for drinking, brushing

teeth or making ice should have first been boiled or otherwise sterilised. Only eat well-cooked meat and fish, preferably served hot. Pork, salad and mayonnaise may carry increased risk. Vegetables should be cooked and fruit peeled.
Other risks: *Diarrhoeal* diseases, including *giardiasis*, and *typhoid fevers* are common. *Bilharzia* (schistosomiasis) is present. Avoid swimming and paddling in fresh water; swimming pools which are well chlorinated and maintained are safe. *Onchocerciasis* (river blindness) and *trypanosomiasis* (sleeping sickness) are present. *Hepatitis A* and *E* are widespread. *Hepatitis B* is hyperendemic. *TB* occurs. Epidemics of *meningococcal disease* may occur, particularly in the savannah areas and during the dry season. Immunisation against *diphtheria* is sometimes recommended.
Rabies is present. For those at high risk, vaccination before arrival should be considered. If you are bitten, seek medical advice without delay. For more information, consult the *Health* appendix.
Health care: Medical facilities are extremely limited and medicines often unavailable. Doctors and hospitals often expect immediate cash payment for health services. Health insurance is essential. Most doctors work in the public service and have their private clinic in the afternoon and evening. There are few specialists. Several foreign aid agencies have their own doctor and medical facilities, including the French Mission and the Swedish Embassy. There is also a UN clinic. All these clinics will receive visitors in an emergency, but none of them have surgical facilities.

Travel - International

Note: All travel to the northwest border area should be avoided because of insecurity in the area. Additionally, although Guinea-Bissau is currently peaceful, the economic and social situation remains fragile.
AIR: Guinea-Bissau's national airline is *Guiné Bissau Airlines (G6)*. Other airlines that fly direct to Bissau include *Aeroflot* and *TAP Air Portugal*.
Approximate flight times: From Bissau to *London* is 10 hours 20 minutes (including stopover of one hour 30 minutes, usually in Lisbon). There are daily flights to *Lisbon*.
International airports: *Bissau (OXB)* (Bissalanca), 11km (7 miles) from the city. Taxi service is available to the city (travel time – 30 minutes).
Departure tax: None.
SEA/RIVER: Ferries running between coastal and inland ports form an important part of the transport system, especially as roads are often impassable (see *Sea/River* in *Travel – Internal* section). The main port is Bissau. This and four inland ports are currently being expanded and upgraded. A new commercial river port is being constructed at N'Pungda.
ROAD: Travellers should check that overland entry is allowed and travelling is safe before embarking (the usual route of entry is by plane from Conakry in Guinea Republic); entry from Senegal is not recommended.

Travel - Internal

AIR: There are 10 small internal airports. The national airline provides internal flights, including to the outlying islands.
SEA/RIVER: Most towns are accessible by ship. Riverboats can reach almost all areas; there are ferries from Bissau to Bolama (often irregular owing to tides) and Bissau to Bafatá, calling at smaller towns en route. Coast-hopping ferries go from the north coast to Bissau.
ROAD: There are about 4150km (2578 miles) of roads, one-fifth tarred and a similar proportion improved for all-weather use. Improvements are planned. There are local and long-distance **taxis** and **buses** (the latter offer limited services). Traffic drives on the right. **Documentation:** An International Driving Permit is recommended, although it is not legally required. A temporary driving licence is available from local authorities on presentation of a valid UK driving licence.

Accommodation

HOTELS: A range of hotels is on offer, some of international standard and others that are small and inexpensive. Accommodation should be booked in advance. Tariffs are liable to change at any time, therefore confirmation of booking is essential.
CAMPING: With the exception of Bolama, there are no designated campsites and camping is not recommended.

Resorts & Excursions

Until recently, Guinea-Bissau was well off the tourist route, but efforts have been made to encourage visitors to this beautiful and largely unspoilt country.
Bissau: The capital is a relaxed and pleasant town of approximately 200,000 inhabitants. The **Museum of African Artefacts** is a treasure trove of traditional sculpture, pottery, weaving and basketware. Nearby, the covered central market features colourful stalls and a lively ambience.
Bijagós Archipelago: This archipelago comprises a group of small islands, several of which are uninhabited, and most of which are very rarely visited by foreigners. The easiest ones to reach are Bolama and Bubaque. **Bolama**, the original capital of Guinea-Bissau, is now a rather attractive ruin, and the island is worth seeing, with several good beaches. There is no accommodation, but camping is an option. The unspoilt island of **Bubaque** is easily accessible from Bissau and offers accommodation in the town.

Social Profile

FOOD & DRINK: Guinea-Bissau's few hotels and restaurants offer excellent food, though some places are expensive. Local specialities include *jollof rice*, chicken and fish dishes. Staples are cassava, yams and maize.
SHOPPING: Locally-made artefacts and carvings can be found in the markets. There are also some modern shops in Bissau. **Shopping hours:** Mon-Fri 0730-1230 and 1430-1830.
SPECIAL EVENTS: The following is a selection of special events celebrated annually in Guinea-Bissau:
Jan *or* **Feb** *Tabaski* (Feast of the Sacrifice). **Feb** *Bissau Carnival* (Guinea-Bissau's largest annual event, a Latin-esque carnival). **Oct** *or* **Nov** *Korite* (End of Ramadan).
SOCIAL CONVENTIONS: Casual wear is widely accepted. Social customs should be respected, particularly in Muslim areas. Petty thievery and pickpocketing are increasingly common, particularly at the airport, in markets and at public gatherings. **Photography:** Visitors should request permission from security personnel before photographing military or police installations. **Tipping:** 10 per cent is an acceptable amount, although not encouraged.

Business Profile

ECONOMY: Rice is the staple food in this poor, largely subsistence economy. The main cash crops are groundnuts, cashew nuts and palm kernels. Timber is the only significant industry. An attempt to revive cotton production has received EU assistance; sugar refining and fishing have also undergone major development. Planned developments of oil and bauxite deposits have not progressed as far as had been hoped. Guinea-Bissau is a member of the West African Economic Community (ECOWAS) and joined the CFA Franc Zone in May 1997. Since then, the country has been recovering from internal conflicts which cut economic output by up to one-third and damaged much of the country's already limited infrastructure. In the short term, Guinea-Bissau will continue to rely on large quantities of foreign aid, of which it is among the highest per capita recipients in the world. France, Portugal, Italy and Thailand are Guinea-Bissau's largest trading partners.
BUSINESS: Businesspeople wear safari suits (bush jackets without a tie). A knowledge of Portuguese is useful as only a few executives speak English. Visits during Ramadan should be avoided. **Office hours:** Mon-Fri 0730-1400.
COMMERCIAL INFORMATION: For further information contact the Embassy (or Consular section at Embassy); see *Contact Addresses* section.

Climate

The climate is tropical, with a wet season from June to October. The dry season is from December to April, with hot winds from the interior. Humidity is high from July to September. Temperatures vary with altitude and distance from the coast.
Required clothing: Tropical lightweight cotton clothes and raincoat for the rainy season.

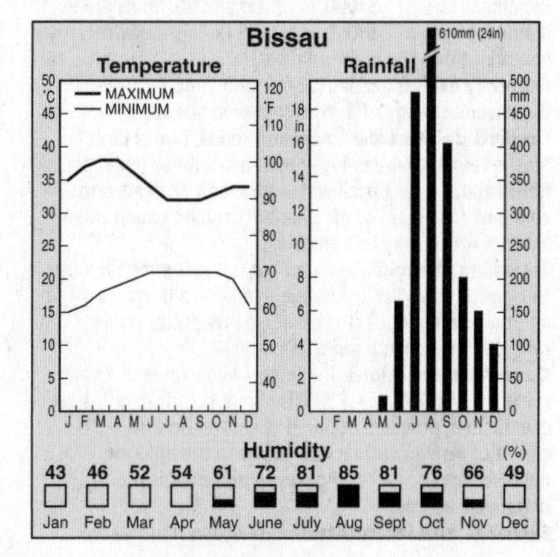

Guyana

LATEST TRAVEL ADVICE CONTACTS

British Foreign and Commonwealth Office
Tel: (0870) 606 0290 Website: www.fco.gov.uk
US Department of State
Website: http://travel.state.gov/travel
Canadian Department of Foreign Affairs and Int'l Trade
Tel: (1 800) 267 8376 Website: www.dfait-maeci.gc.ca

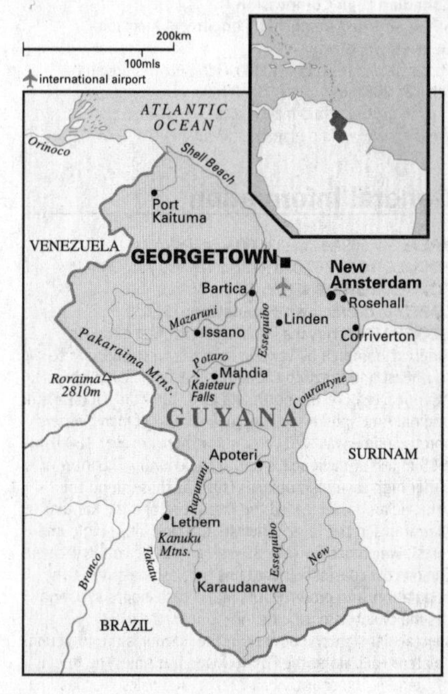

Location: South America, northeast coast.

Country dialling code: 592.

Guyana Tourism Authority
National Exhibition Centre, Sophia, Greater Georgetown, Guyana
Tel: 223 6351/2. Fax: 231 6672.
Website: www.guyana-tourism.com
Tourism & Hospitality Association of Guyana
157 Waterloo Street, North Cummingsburg, Georgetown, Guyana
Tel: 225 0807 *or* 225 6699. Fax: 225 0817.
E-mail: thag@networksgy.com
Website: www.exploreguyana.com
Guyana High Commission
3 Palace Court, Bayswater Road, London W2 4LP, UK
Tel: (020) 7229 7684. Fax: (020) 7727 9809.
E-mail: ghc.1@ic24.net
Opening hours: Mon-Fri 0930-1730 (except national and UK holidays); Mon-Fri 0930-1430 (consular enquiries).
Caribbean Tourism Organisation
22 The Quadrant, Richmond, Surrey, TW9 1BP, UK
Tel: (020) 8948 0057. Fax: (020) 8948 0067.
E-mail: ctolondon@caribtourism.com
Website: www.caribbean.co.uk
British High Commission
Street address: 44 Main Street, Georgetown, Guyana
Postal address: PO Box 10849, Georgetown, Guyana
Tel: 226 5881-4.
Fax: 225 3555 *or* 225 0671 (consular section).
E-mail: enquiries@britain-in-guyana.org
Website: www.britain-in-guyana.org
Embassy of the Republic of Guyana
2490 Tracy Place, NW, Washington, DC 20008, USA
Tel: (202) 265 6900/1. Fax: (202) 232 1297.
E-mail: guyanaembassydc@hotmail.com
Website: www.guyana.org
Consulate General in: New York.

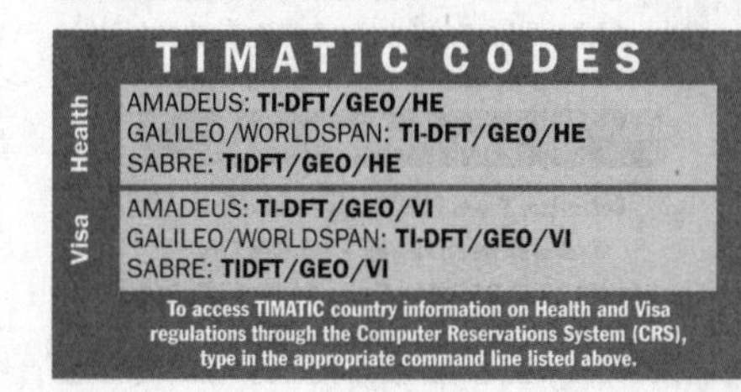
TIMATIC CODES

Health
AMADEUS: **TI-DFT/GEO/HE**
GALILEO/WORLDSPAN: **TI-DFT/GEO/HE**
SABRE: **TIDFT/GEO/HE**

Visa
AMADEUS: **TI-DFT/GEO/VI**
GALILEO/WORLDSPAN: **TI-DFT/GEO/VI**
SABRE: **TIDFT/GEO/VI**

To access TIMATIC country information on Health and Visa regulations through the Computer Reservations System (CRS), type in the appropriate command line listed above.

Embassy of the United States of America
Street address: 99-100 Young and Duke Streets, Kingston, Georgetown, Guyana
Postal address: PO Box 10507, Georgetown, Guyana
Tel: 225 4900-9. Fax: 225 8497.
E-mail: visageorge@state.gov
Website: www.georgetown.usembassy.gov
High Commission for the Republic of Guyana
Burnside Building, 151 Slater Street, Suite 309, Ottawa, Ontario K1P 5H3, Canada
Tel: (613) 235 7240/49. Fax: (613) 235 1447.
E-mail: guyanahcott@travel-net.com
Website: www.guyanamissionott.org
Consulate in: Toronto.
Canadian High Commission
Street address: Young and High Streets, Kingston, Georgetown, Guyana
Postal address: PO Box 10880, Georgetown, Guyana
Tel: 227 2081-5. Fax: 225 8380.
E-mail: grgtn@dfait-maeci.gc.ca
Website: www.dfait-maeci.gc.ca/guyana

General Information

AREA: 214,969 sq km (83,000 sq miles).
POPULATION: 767,000 (official UN estimate 2004).
POPULATION DENSITY: 3.6 per sq km.
CAPITAL: Georgetown. **Population:** 151,679.
GEOGRAPHY: Guyana lies in the northeast of South America, bordered by Venezuela to the west, Surinam to the southeast and Brazil to the south. It is bordered by the Atlantic Ocean to the north and east. The word 'Guiana' (the original Amerindian spelling) means 'land of many waters' and the name was well chosen, for there are over 1600km (965 miles) of navigable rivers in the country. The interior is either high savannah uplands (such as those along the Venezuelan border, called the Rupununi, and the Kanuku Mountains in the far southwest), or thick, hilly jungle and forest, which occupy over 83 per cent of the country's area. The narrow coastal belt contains the vast majority of the population, and produces the major cash crop, sugar, and the major subsistence crop, rice. One of the most spectacular sights to be seen in the interior is the towering Kaieteur Falls along the Potaro River, five times the height of Niagara. The country has 322km (206 miles) of coastline. More than 25 per cent of the population lives in or near Georgetown.
GOVERNMENT: Republic. **Head of State:** President Bharrat Jagdeo since 1999. **Head of Government:** Prime Minister Samuel A Hinds since 1997.
LANGUAGE: English is the official language, but Creole, Hindi, Urdu and Amerindian dialects are also spoken.
RELIGION: 50 per cent Christian, 33 per cent Hindu, less than 10 per cent Muslim.
TIME: GMT - 4.
ELECTRICITY: 110 and 220 volts AC, 60Hz.
COMMUNICATIONS: Telephone: IDD is available to main towns and cities. Country code: 592. Outgoing international code: 001. **Mobile telephone:** GSM 900 network in use. Network providers include *Cel Star Guyana Inc* and *Guyana Telephone and Telegraph Company* (GT&T) (website: www.gtt.co.gy). Mobile phones can be hired from *GT&T*. **Fax:** Facilities are available at the GT&T, the Bank of Guyana Building in Georgetown and hotels. **Telegram:** Available at the GT&T and Bank of Guyana Building. Certain hotels also have facilities. **Internet:** Internet cafes are available in Georgetown. *ISPs* include *GT&T* and *GuyanaNet* (website: www.guyana.net.gy).
Press: The daily state-owned newspaper is *The Guyana Chronicle*. The independent *Stabroek News* and the *Kaieteur News* are published weekdays. On weekends, there are also *The Mirror*, *The Sunday Chronicle* and *The Sunday Stabroek*.
Radio: BBC World Service (website: www.bbc.co.uk/worldservice) and Voice of America (website: www.voa.gov) can be received. From time to time the frequencies change and the most up-to-date can be found online.

Passport/Visa

	Passport Required?	Visa Required?	Return Ticket Required?
Full British	Yes	No	Yes
Australian	Yes	No	Yes
Canadian	Yes	No	Yes
USA	Yes	No	Yes
Other EU	Yes	No/1	Yes
Japanese	Yes	No	Yes

Note: *Regulations and requirements may be subject to change at short notice, and you are advised to contact the appropriate diplomatic or consular authority before finalising travel arrangements. Details of these may be found at the head of this country's entry. Any numbers in the chart refer to the footnotes below.*

PASSPORTS: Passport valid for at least six months beyond intended stay required by all.
VISAS: Required by all except the following:
(a) **1.** nationals mentioned in the chart above for stays of up to 90 days (except nationals of Austria, Cyprus, the Czech Republic, Estonia, Hungary, Latvia, Lithuania, Malta, Poland, Slovak Republic and Slovenia who *do* need a visa);
(b) persons of Guyanese birth with foreign passports provided their passports clearly indicate place of birth or they have other satisfactory documentary evidence;
(c) nationals of Antigua & Barbuda, The Bahamas, Barbados, Belize, Dominica, Grenada, Jamaica, Korea (Dem Rep), Korea (Rep), Montserrat, New Zealand, Norway, St Kitts & Nevis, St Lucia, St Vincent & the Grenadines, South Africa, Surinam, Switzerland and Trinidad & Tobago, provided they hold onward or return tickets and sufficient funds for the duration of stay;
(d) transit passengers continuing their journey to a third country by the same aircraft or by first connecting aircraft within seven hours, without leaving the airport.
Note: Those with Guyanese parentage may enter Guyana visa-free, provided they can submit original birth certificate, and birth certificate/passport of Guyanese parent(s). This will also have to be submitted to the Immigration Officer upon arrival.
Types of visa and cost: *Tourist*: £20. *Business*: £20 (single-entry); £25 (one-year multiple-entry). *Courtesy* visas are issued free of charge to spouses or close relatives of Guyanese citizens, provided they supply documentary proof.
Validity: Visas are valid for three months from the date of issue. Length of stay and extension is at the discretion of the Immigration Office.
Application to: Consulate (or Consular section at Embassy or High Commission); see *Contact Addresses* section.
Application requirements: (a) Two application forms. (b) Two passport-size photos. (c) Evidence of sufficient funds to cover length of stay or proof of other satisfactory arrangement for support while in Guyana, in the form of a letter of invitation from Guyana, a recent bank statement, a letter from employer, or a business letter with a certificate from the Chamber of Commerce. (d) Passport valid for at least six months prior to travel. (e) Return or onward ticket. (f) Fee. *Business*: (a)-(f) and, (g) Letter of approval from the Minister of Home Affairs, Guyana, or other appropriate evidence.
Working days required: Applicants should contact Embassy or High Commission at least one week in advance of travel to Guyana. If passport is to be returned by a courier service, pre-paid arrangements (making sure to include own account number) must be made by the applicant.
Temporary residence: Permission must be obtained from the Minister of Home Affairs, Guyana.

Money

Currency: Guyanese Dollar (G$) = 100 cents. Notes are in denominations of G$1000, 500, 100 and 20. Coins are in denominations of G$10, 5 and 1. US Dollars are widely accepted throughout Guyana.
Currency exchange: Banks offer exchange facilities. Bureaux de change offer free conversion of currencies.
Credit & debit cards: American Express, Diners Club, MasterCard and Visa enjoy limited acceptance (eg at certain hotels and shops). Check with your credit or debit card company for details of merchant acceptability and other services which may be available.
Travellers cheques: Accepted but not recommended for those who may wish to change money in a hurry. To avoid additional exchange rate charges, travellers are advised to take travellers cheques in US Dollars.
Currency restrictions: The import and export of local currency is limited to G$200. The import of foreign currency is unlimited, provided declared in writing on arrival. The export of foreign currency is limited to the amount imported and declared. The Guyanese Dollar is not negotiable abroad.
Exchange rate indicators: The following figures are included as a guide to the movements of the Guyanese Dollar against Sterling and the US Dollar:

Date	Feb '04	May '04	Aug '04	Nov '04
£1.00=	325.82	319.71	329.78	338.97
$1.00=	179.00	170.00	179.00	179.00

Banking hours: Mon-Fri 0800-1430; some banks stay open later on a Friday afternoon.

Duty Free

The following goods can be imported into Guyana by travellers aged 16 years or over without incurring customs duty:
200 cigarettes or 50 cigars or 225g of tobacco; spirits not exceeding 750ml; wine not exceeding 750ml; a reasonable amount of perfume for personal use.

Public Holidays

2005: Jan 1 New Year's Day. **Jan 21** Eid ul-Azha (Feast of the Sacrifice). **Feb 23** Republic Day (Mashramani). **Mar 25** Good Friday/Phagwah (Holi). **Mar 28** Easter Monday. **May** You-Man-Nabi (Birth of the Prophet). **May 1** Labour Day. **May 26** Independence Day. **Jul 4** Caricom Day. **Aug 1** Freedom Day. **Nov 1** Deepavali (Hindu Festival of Light). **Dec 25-26** Christmas.
2006: Jan 1 New Year's Day. **Jan 10** Eid ul-Azha (Feast of the Sacrifice). **Feb 23** Republic Day (Mashramani). **Mar 15** Phagwah (Holi). **Apr 14** Good Friday. **Apr 17** Easter Monday. **May 1** Labour Day. **Apr 11** Yum an-Nabi (Birth of the Prophet). **May 26** Independence Day. **Jul 3** Caricom Day. **Aug 7** Freedom Day. **Oct 21** Deepavali (Hindu Festival of Light). **Dec 25-26** Christmas.
Note: (a) Muslim festivals are timed according to local sightings of various phases of the moon and the dates given above are approximations. For more information, see the *World of Islam* appendix. (b) Hindu festivals are declared according to local astronomical observations and it is only possible to forecast the month of their occurrence.

Health

	Special Precautions?	Certificate Required?
Yellow Fever	Yes	1
Cholera	No	No
Typhoid & Polio	2	N/A
Malaria	3	N/A

Note: *Regulations and requirements may be subject to change at short notice, and you are advised to contact your doctor well in advance of your intended date of departure. Any numbers in the chart refer to the footnotes below.*

1: A yellow fever vaccination certificate is required from travellers over one year of age coming from infected areas and from the following countries: Angola, Benin, Burkina Faso, Burundi, Cameroon, Central African Republic, Chad, Congo (Dem Rep), Congo (Rep), Côte d'Ivoire, Gabon, The Gambia, Ghana, Guinea, Guinea-Bissau, Kenya, Liberia, Mali, Niger, Nigeria, Rwanda, São Tomé e Príncipé, Senegal, Sierra Leone, Somalia, Tanzania, Togo and Uganda; and in Latin America: Belize, Bolivia, Brazil, Colombia, Costa Rica, Ecuador, French Guiana, Guatemala, Honduras, Nicaragua, Panama, Peru, Surinam and Venezuela. Travellers arriving from non-endemic zones should note that vaccination is strongly recommended for travel outside the urban areas, even if an outbreak of the disease has not been reported and they would normally not require a vaccination certificate to enter the country.
2: Typhoid is a risk.
3: Malaria risk exists throughout the year in the northwest region, areas along the Pomeroon River and in all parts of the interior. Chloroquine-resistant *falciparum* is reported. The recommended prophylaxis is mefloquine unless contra-indicated, in which case use chloroquine plus proguanil plus protection against mosquito bites.
Food & drink: Mains water is normally chlorinated in main cities, and whilst relatively safe may cause mild abdominal upsets. Bottled water is readily available and is advised for the first few weeks of the stay. Milk is unpasteurised and should be boiled. Powdered or tinned milk is available and is advised, but make sure that it is reconstituted with pure water. Avoid dairy products that are likely to have been made from unboiled milk. Local meat, poultry, seafood, fruit and vegetables are generally considered safe to eat.
Other risks: *Hepatitis A* is common. *Hepatitis B* and *D* are highly endemic in the Amazon basin and precautions should be taken. *Bancroftian filariasis* is endemic in certain parts and *mucocutaneous leishmaniasis* occurs. *TB* occurs. *Jungle yellow fever* may be found in forest areas. *Dengue fever* may occur.
Rabies occurs. For those at high risk, vaccination before arrival should be considered. If you are bitten, seek medical advice without delay.
Health care: Health insurance is recommended. Hospital treatment in Georgetown is free, but doctors will charge for

an appointment. Medical care and prescription drugs are limited and sanitary conditions are poor in many medical facilities. Travellers are advised to bring prescription medicines sufficient for their length of stay.

Travel - International

AIR: *Air France (AF)* operates a daily flight to Cayenne in French Guiana. There are no direct flights from Europe. Other airlines serving Trinidad & Tobago, from where connecting flights can be made, include *BWIA (British West Indies Airways)*.
Approximate flight times: From Georgetown to *London* is 10 hours (via Antigua, Barbados or Trinidad & Tobago). There are no direct flights.
International airports: *Georgetown (GEO)* (Cheddi Jagan International) is 40km (26 miles) from the city (travel time – 45 minutes). An irregular and crowded bus service to the city is available. Taxis meet every plane (fare: approximately G$3500). Airport facilities include duty free, restaurants, bars, post office and a bank.
Departure tax: G$4000 or equivalent in US Dollars; transit passengers and children under seven years of age are exempt. Note: Tax is sometimes paid at the point of ticket sale.
SEA/RIVER: Numerous schooners sail between Guyana and the Caribbean islands, but schedules are erratic. For details, contact local ports. Cargo vessels run by the *Guyana National Shipping Corporation* ply from Miami to Georgetown and vessels run by the *Demerara Shipping Company* ply between European ports and Georgetown weekly. Cruise lines serving Guyana include *American Canadian Caribbean Line*, *Cunard* and *Royal Carribean Cruise Line*. Following recent improvements in relations with Surinam, a ferry service across the Courantyne River now links the two countries.
RAIL: There are no passenger rail services.
ROAD: There is a soft road from Georgetown via Kurupukari to Lethem to Brazil. The journey will take at least 12 hours in a 4-wheel drive vehicle. Improvements have been made to many roads in recent years and travel during the rainy season is now possible - although care should still be taken to avoid potholes. Buses travel from Boa Vista in Brazil to Lethem and then onwards to Georgetown. There is still no reliable route to Venezuela.

Travel - Internal

AIR: The only reliable means of travelling into the interior is by air. A number of different airlines and charter companies offer flights to most destinations; enquire locally for details.
SEA/RIVER: Guyana has 1077km (607 miles) of navigable inland waterways, the most notable being the Mazaruni, Essequibo, Potaro, Demerara and Berbice rivers. Government steamers communicate with the interior up the Essequibo and Berbice rivers, but services can be irregular owing to flooding. The Government also runs a coast-hopping service from Georgetown to several northern ports. Smaller craft operate where there is sufficient demand throughout the country.
RAIL: Mining concerns operate railways, but there are no scheduled passenger services.
ROAD: Traffic drives on the left. All-weather roads are concentrated in the eastern coastal strip, although there is now a road inland as far as the Brazilian border and a bridge linking to the two countries is nearing completion. The coastal road linking Georgetown, Rosignol, New Amsterdam and Crabwood Creek (Corentyne) is fairly good, but generally road conditions are poor. Because of Guyana's many rivers, most journeys of more than a few miles outside the capital will involve ferries and the attendant delays. **Bus:** Georgetown's Stabroek Market is the terminus for minibuses. These are regular but generally crowded. Buses run to all areas, departing whenever they are full. The first buses leave at around 0500, and services continue until about 2100. Within Georgetown, buses run all night. Services from Vreed-en-Hoop to Parika operate in conjunction with the passenger-ferry service across the Demerara to Georgetown; services from New Amsterdam to Crabwood Creek operate in conjunction with ferries across the Berbice River. **Taxi:** At night, it is advisable to travel by taxi. Vehicles are plentiful. There is a standard fare for intercity travel; night fares are extra. For longer trips, fares should be agreed before departure. A 10 per cent tip is usual in taxis. **Car hire:** Limited availability from local firms in Georgetown as well as *Hertz*. **Documentation:** Foreign licence or International Driving Permit is accepted.

Accommodation

HOTELS: Hotels in Georgetown range from good to reasonable. There are no high-season charges. Nature lovers can stay in cabins at the interior resorts and camps. As power cuts are common, it is advisable to take a torch.
GUEST HOUSES: There is a variety of nature resorts, ranches and lodges which offer unusual accommodation. There are also numerous camps, for instance Maparri Wilderness Camp which overlooks the crystal clear river and waterfall, and the Shell Beach Camp at Almond Beach where turtles nest between April and August. Contact *Wilderness Explorers* for further information (Cara Suites, 176 Middle Street, Georgetown, Guyana; tel: 227 7698; fax: 226 2085; e-mail: info@wilderness-explorers.com; website: www.wilderness-explorers.com).

Resorts & Excursions

GEORGETOWN: The 19th-century wooden houses supported on stilts and charming green boulevards laid out along the lines of the old Dutch canals give the capital a unique character. Some of the more impressive wooden buildings dating from the colonial past include the city hall, **St George's Cathedral**, the **Law Courts** and the **State House**. The **Botanical Gardens**, covering 120 acres (48.6 hectares), have a fine collection of palms, orchids and lotus lilies; nearby is the new **Cultural Centre**, which contains what is probably the best theatre in the Caribbean. Also worth visiting are the **Natural History Museum**, which contains an up-to-date display of all aspects of Guyanese life and culture, and the **Walter Roth Anthropological Museum**.
ELSEWHERE: At the junction of the **Essequibo** and **Mazaruni** rivers, **Bartica** is the 'take-off' town for the gold and diamond fields, **Kaieteur Falls** and the rest of the interior. A visit to the Kaieteur Falls in the **Kaieteur National Park** is particularly recommended; situated on the **Potaro River**, it ranks with Iquazú, Niagara and Victoria in majesty and beauty. There are numerous beaches in Guyana; these include **Almond Beach**, **Shell Beach**, **No 63 Beach** and **Saxacalli Beach**. There are rainforests in **Iwokrama** with a **Canopy Walkway** and the **Pakaraima** mountains. **Surama**, set in savannah surrounded by forest-covered mountains, is home to the Amerindian community of the Macushi tribe, which welcomes tourists. **Rupununi** is the oasis in the desert with the **Rockview Nature Resort** and the ranches of **North** and **South Rupunini**, **Karanambo** and **Dadanawa**.

Sport & Activities

Fishing: The rivers and the interior abound in game fish, the best known of which is the man-eating piranha (called locally *perai*). The most sought after by the sportsman is the *lucanni*, a fish similar to the large-mouth bass. Most of the interior rivers are difficult for the more casual visitor to get to, but those who book in advance can reach them by air. Some of the coastal rivers within reach of Georgetown are also good for fishing, although it is wise to stay overnight in the fishing grounds, as the best are four to five hours' drive from the city. Fishing licences are required.
Other: Camping treks, **hiking** and **whitewater rafting** have become increasingly popular over recent years. **Horse riding** is available at Manari Ranch in the Rupununi Savannahs. **Cricket** and **hockey** are both popular, and the Bourda is one of the most attractive cricket grounds in the area. **Birdwatching** is also very good in some parts of the country.

Social Profile

FOOD & DRINK: The food in hotels and restaurants reflects the range of influences on Guyanese society. From India came curries - especially mutton, prawn or chicken - and Africa contributed dishes such as *foo-foo* (plantains made into cakes) and *metamgee* (dumplings made from cornflour, eddews, yams, cassava and plantains cooked in coconut milk and grated coconut). Portuguese garlic pork and Amerindian pepperpot are specialities. On the menus of most restaurants you will often find chicken, pork and steak and, most of the time, shrimp. The best Chinese food in the country can be found in Georgetown. It is best to drink bottled water in Guyana. Local rum, Demerara Rum, is well worth trying, while the local beer is *Banks*.
NIGHTLIFE: There are numerous nightclubs and bars in Georgetown.
SHOPPING: Hibiscus Plaza outside the Post Office in Georgetown has a wide variety of local arts and crafts including straw hats, baskets, clay goblets and jewellery. Other shops sell Amerindian bows and arrows, hammocks, pottery and salad bowls. Government-run shops sell magnificent jewellery, utilising local gold, silver, precious and semi-precious stones. Prices are very reasonable for the quality of the goods. It is absolutely essential to ensure that receipts and correct documentation are retained, otherwise visitors may experience difficulty when clearing customs. **Shopping hours:** Mon-Fri 0800-1200 and 1300-1630, Sat 0800-1200.
SPECIAL EVENTS: The following is a selection of special events occurring in Guyana in 2005:
Jan *Mashramani Jamboree*. **Feb 23** *Annual Carnival*, celebrations coincide with Mashramani (Republic Day). **Jun 5** *Environmental Day*. **Jul** *Jamzone Pageant*. **Aug** *Bartica Summer Regatta*. **Oct 16** *World Food Day*. **Nov** *Guyana Open Golf Tournament*. **Nov 17-22** *Home & Garden Show*, National Exhibition Centre. **Dec 27** *Main Big Lime*, Georgetown.
For more information about events in Guyana contact the Tourism & Hospitality Association of Guyana (see *Contact Addresses* section).
SOCIAL CONVENTIONS: Hospitality is important to the Guyanese and it is quite common for the visitor to be invited to their homes. Informal wear is widely acceptable, but men should avoid wearing shorts. **Tipping:** 10 per cent at hotels and restaurants.

Business Profile

ECONOMY: Agriculture allows Guyana to be self-sufficient in sugar, rice, vegetables, fruit, meat and poultry, as well as to make major export earnings from the first two. Although 80 per cent of the land area is covered by forest, timber has only very recently assumed any economic significance (subject to internationally backed restrictions on logging). Bauxite mining is the main industry, and responsible for one-third of export earnings. The mining sector also produces gold and diamonds, almost all of which are exported. Gold production has increased sharply since the opening of a new mining complex in 1992. Imported oil meets most of the country's energy requirements, although Guyana and Surinam have begun joint exploration projects. Guyana has been a beneficiary of a debt write-off which has saved more than £100 million annually in debt-servicing payments, following the Government's implementation of a major economic reform programme. Since 1997, many formerly state-owned assets and industries have been sold, and deregulation measures introduced, as part of that programme. A major obstacle to Guyana's future economic progress is a shortage of trained personnel, especially in the fields of management and technical expertise; the emigration rate remains high, and only serves to compound this long-term problem. Guyana is a founder member of the regional trading bloc CARICOM. The country's main export markets are the UK, the USA, Canada, Germany, Indonesia and Trinidad & Tobago.
BUSINESS: Appointments should be made and punctuality is appreciated. Calling cards are useful. The pace of business and general attitudes are very Caribbean-orientated. It is, however, wise to bear in mind that the country is very much part of South America, the ties with the Caribbean being more a hangover from British colonial days than a reflection of Guyanese popular consciousness. **Office hours:** Mon-Fri 0800-1200 and 1300-1630.
COMMERCIAL INFORMATION: The following organisations can offer advice: Guyana Manufacturer's Association, National Exhibition Centre, Sophia, Georgetown (tel: (22) 74295; fax: (22) 75615; e-mail: gma_guyana@yahoo.com); *or* Georgetown Chamber of Commerce and Industry, PO Box 10110, 156 Waterloo Street, North Cummingsburg, Georgetown (tel: (22) 55846; tel/fax: (22) 63519; e-mail: info@georgetownchamberofcommerce.org; website: www.georgetownchamberofcommerce.org); *or* Ministry of Tourism, Industry and Commerce, 229 South Road, Georgetown (tel: 226 2505; fax: 225 4370; e-mail: permsect@mintic.gov.gy; website: www.mintic.gov.gy).

Climate

Guyana's climate is warm and tropical throughout the year. The rainfall is generally high for most of the year, as is the humidity. December to January and May to June are the rainy seasons, while in coastal areas the climate is tempered by sea breezes.

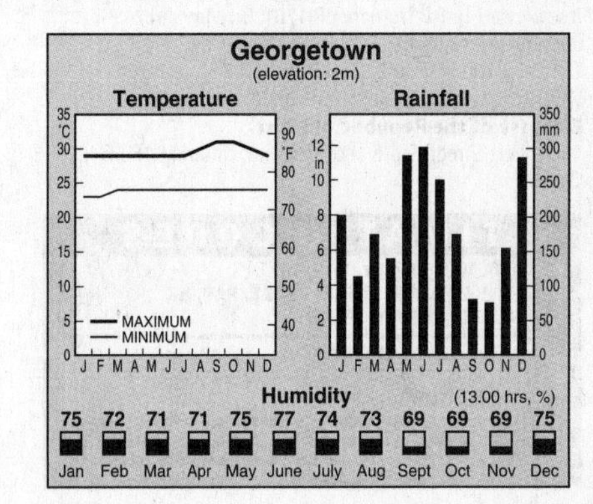

Haiti

LATEST TRAVEL ADVICE CONTACTS

British Foreign and Commonwealth Office
Tel: (0870) 606 0290 Website: www.fco.gov.uk
US Department of State
Website: http://travel.state.gov/travel
Canadian Department of Foreign Affairs and Int'l Trade
Tel: (1 800) 267 8376 Website: www.dfait-maeci.gc.ca

Location: Caribbean, island of Hispaniola.

Country dialling code: 509.

Ministere du Tourisme
8 rue Légitime, Port-au-Prince, HT 6112, Haiti
Tel: 223 5631. Fax: 221 3613 *or* 223 5359.
Website: www.haititourisme.org
Embassy of the Republic of Haiti and Tourist Office
10 rue Théodule Ribot, BP275, Cedex 28, 75017 Paris, France
Tel: (1) 4763 4778. Fax: (1) 4227 0205.
E-mail: haiti01@francophonie.org
Opening hours: Mon-Thurs 1000-1300 and 1400-1700; Fri 1000-1600.
Consulates in: Cayenne and Pointe-à-Pitre.
Embassy of the Republic of Haiti
139 Chaussée de Charleroi, B-1060, Brussels, Belgium
Tel: (2) 649 7381. Fax: (2) 640 6080.
Opening hours: Mon-Fri 1000-1630.
Accredited to the UK and The Netherlands.
British Consulate
Street address: Apartment 6, Hotel Montana, Rue de F Cardozo, Bourdon, Port-au-Prince, Haiti
Postal address: PO Box 1302, Port-au-Prince, Haiti
Tel: 257 3969. Fax: 257 4048.
E-mail: britcon@transnethaiti.com
Embassy of the Republic of Haiti
2311 Massachusetts Avenue, NW, Washington, DC 20008, USA
Tel: (202) 332 4090. Fax: (202) 745 7215.
E-mail: embassy@haiti.org
Website: www.haiti.org
Consulate General of Haiti
271 Madison Avenue, 5th Floor, New York, NY 10016, USA
Tel: (212) 697 9767. Fax: (212) 681 6991.
E-mail: info@haitianconsulate-nyc.org
Consulates also in: Boston, Chicago and Miami.
Embassy of the United States of America
5 boulevard Harry Truman, BP 1761, Bicentenaire, Port-au-Prince, Haiti
Tel: 222 0200. Fax: 223 9038 *or* 1641.
Website: http://usembassy.state.gov/haiti
Embassy of the Republic of Haiti
130 Albert Street, Suite 1409, Ottawa, Ontario K1P 5G4, Canada

TIMATIC CODES

Health	AMADEUS: **TI-DFT/PAP/HE** GALILEO/WORLDSPAN: **TI-DFT/PAP/HE** SABRE: **TIDFT/PAP/HE**
Visa	AMADEUS: **TI-DFT/PAP/VI** GALILEO/WORLDSPAN: **TI-DFT/PAP/VI** SABRE: **TIDFT/PAP/VI**

To access TIMATIC country information on Health and Visa regulations through the Computer Reservations System (CRS), type in the appropriate command line listed above.

Tel: (613) 238 1628. Fax: (613) 238 2986.
E-mail: bohio@bellnet.ca
Consulate General of Haiti
1801 avenue McGill College, Suite 1335, Montréal H3A 2N4, Canada
Tel: (514) 499 1919. Fax: (514) 499 1818.
E-mail: consgen@haiti-montreal.org
Website: www.haiti-montreal.org
Canadian Embassy
Delmas, between Delmas 75 and 71, Port-au-Prince, Haiti
Tel: 249 900 *or* 8000. Fax: 249 9920 *or* 9928.
E-mail: prnce@international.gc.ca
Website: www.dfait-maeci.gc.ca/haiti

General Information

AREA: 27,750 sq km (10,714 sq miles).
POPULATION: 8,132,000 (official estimate 2001).
POPULATION DENSITY: 293 per sq km.
CAPITAL: Port-au-Prince. **Population:** 917,112 (official estimate 1997).
GEOGRAPHY: Haiti is situated in the Caribbean and comprises the forested mountainous western end of the island of Hispaniola, which it shares with the Dominican Republic. Its area includes the Île de la Gonâve, in the Gulf of the same name; among other islands is La Tortue off the north peninsula. Haiti's coastline is dotted with magnificent beaches, between which stretches lush subtropical vegetation, even covering the slopes which lead down to the shore. Port-au-Prince is a magnificent natural harbour at the end of a deep horseshoe bay.
GOVERNMENT: Republic. Gained independence from France in 1804. **Head of State:** Interim President Boniface Alexandre sworn in in 2004. **Head of Government:** Prime Minister Gerard Latortue.
LANGUAGE: The official languages are French and Creole. English is spoken in tourist areas.
RELIGION: The official religions are Roman Catholicism (75 per cent) and Voodooism (70 per cent); most Haitians practise both. Voodooism is a polytheistic folk religion, manifested by a series of complex ritual drawings, songs and dances. It is an African religion, and not incompatible with a shared belief in Christianity. There are Protestant minorities.
TIME: GMT - 5.
ELECTRICITY: 110 volts AC, 60Hz.
COMMUNICATIONS: Telephone: IDD available. Country code: 509. There are no area codes. The internal service, operated by *Telecommunications d'Haïti (Teleco)*, is reasonable. There are telephone booths in the towns which take cards. **Mobile telephone:** The GSM network is run by *Haïtel*. Handsets can be hired locally. **Internet:** Internet cafes can be found in towns and cities. ISPs include *Compa*, *Hintelfocus* and *Netcom*. **Post:** Airmail to Europe takes up to one week. The main post office in Port-au-Prince, Cité de l'Exposition, is in place d'Italie. Post office hours: Mon-Fri 0800-2000, Sat 0830-1200. Letters posted after 0900 will not be despatched until the following working day. **Press:** The two main dailies, *Le Matin* and *Le Nouvelliste*, are published in French. *Haiti Progres*, also in French, is published weekly.
Radio: BBC World Service (website: www.bbc.co.uk/worldservice) and Voice of America (website: www.voa.gov) can be received. From time to time the frequencies change and the most up-to-date can be found online.

Passport/Visa

	Passport Required?	Visa Required?	Return Ticket Required?
Full British	Yes	No	Yes
Australian	Yes	No	Yes
Canadian	Yes	No	Yes
USA	Yes	No	Yes
Other EU	Yes	No	Yes
Japanese	Yes	No	Yes

Note: Regulations and requirements may be subject to change at short notice, and you are advised to contact the appropriate diplomatic or consular authority before finalising travel arrangements. Details of these may be found at the head of this country's entry. Any numbers in the chart refer to the footnotes below.

PASSPORTS: Passport valid for six months from date of entry required by all.
VISAS: Not required for touristic stays of up to six months except for nationals of China (PR), Colombia, Dominican Republic and Panama who *do* require a tourist visa.
Types of visa and cost: *Visitor Visa*: €46.
Note: It is possible for visas to be extended under certain circumstances; contact the nearest Consulate/Embassy for further information.
Application to: The Consulate or Consular section at the Embassy (see *Contact Addresses* section).
Application requirements: (a) Valid passport. (b) One completed application form. (c) One passport-size photo. (d) Fee, payable by postal order only. (e) Self-addressed, stamped and registered envelope, if applying by post.
Working days required: One week.
Temporary residence: Contact the Consulate (or Consular section at Embassy).

Money

Currency: Gourde = 100 centimes. Notes are in denominations of Gourde 500, 250, 100, 50, 25, 10, 5, 2 and 1. Coins are in denominations of Gourde 5 and 1, and 50, 20, 10 and 5 centimes. US currency also circulates.
Currency exchange: US Dollars are accepted and exchanged everywhere. Other foreign currencies are accepted for exchange only by some banks.
Credit & debit cards: American Express is widely accepted; Diners Club has more limited use. Check with your credit or debit card company for details of merchant acceptability and other services which may be available.
Travellers cheques: Accepted by most major shops and banks. To avoid additional exchange rate charges, travellers are advised to take travellers cheques in US Dollars.
Currency restrictions: There are no restrictions on the import and export of foreign or local currency. However, amounts in excess of Gourde 200,000 or equivalent must be declared.
Exchange rate indicators: The following figures are included as a guide to the movements of the Gourde against Sterling and the US Dollar:

Date	Feb '04	May '04	Aug '04	Nov '04
£1.00=	77.81	66.53	64.94	68.17
$1.00=	42.75	37.25	35.25	36.00

Banking hours: Mon-Fri 0900-1630. Some banks open in the afternoons and Sat 0900-1300.

Duty Free

The following goods can be imported into Haiti without incurring customs duty:
200 cigarettes or 50 cigars or 1kg of tobacco; 1l of spirits; small quantity of perfume or eau de toilette for personal use.
Note: In addition, Haitian nationals and foreign residents may bring in, once a year and for their personal use, new goods with a total value not exceeding US$200.
Prohibited items: Coffee, matches, methylated spirits, pork, all meat products from Brazil and the Dominican Republic, drugs and firearms (except sporting rifles with relevant permit).

Public Holidays

2005: Jan 1 Independence Day. **Jan 2** Ancestors' Day. **Mar 21** Carnival. **Mar 25** Good Friday. **Apr 14** Pan-American Day/Bastilla's Day. **May 1** Labour Day. **May 5** Ascension. **May 18** Flag and University Day. **May 26** Corpus Christi. **Aug 15** Assumption. **Oct 17** Anniversary of the Death of Dessalines. **Oct 24** United Nations Day. **Nov 1** All Saints' Day. **Nov 2** All Souls' Day. **Nov 18** Battle of Vertiérès Day. **Dec 25** Christmas Day.
2006: Jan 1 Independence Day. **Jan 2** Ancestors' Day. **Feb/Mar** Carnival. **Apr 14** Good Friday; Pan-American Day/Bastilla's Day. **May 1** Labour Day. **May 18** Flag and University Day. **May 25** Ascension. **Jun 15** Corpus Christi. **Aug 15** Assumption. **Oct 17** Anniversary of the Death of Dessalines. **Oct 24** United Nations Day. **Nov 1** All Saints' Day. **Nov 2** All Souls' Day. **Nov 18** Battle of Vertiérès Day. **Dec 25** Christmas Day.

Health

	Special Precautions?	Certificate Required?
Yellow Fever	Yes	1
Cholera	No	No
Typhoid & Polio	2	N/A
Malaria	3	N/A

Note: Regulations and requirements may be subject to change at short notice, and you are advised to contact your doctor well in advance of your intended date of departure. Any numbers in the chart refer to the footnotes below.

1: A yellow fever vaccination certificate is required from travellers arriving within six days from infected areas.
2: Typhoid occurs in rural areas.
3: Malaria risk, in the malignant *falciparum* form, exists throughout the year in certain forest areas in Chantal, Gros Morne, Hinche, Jacmel and Maissade and all other areas below 300m. In the other cantons, risk is estimated to be low. Chloroquine is the recommended prophylaxis.
Food & drink: All water should be regarded as being potentially contaminated. Water used for drinking, brushing teeth or making ice should have first been boiled or

otherwise sterilised. Milk is unpasteurised and should be boiled. Powdered or tinned milk is available and is advised, but make sure that it is reconstituted with pure water. Avoid dairy products which are likely to have been made from unboiled milk. Only eat well-cooked meat and fish, preferably served hot. Pork, salad and mayonnaise may carry increased risk. Vegetables should be cooked and fruit peeled.
Other risks: *Hepatitis A* and *Bancroftian filariasis* occur. *Tularaemia* and seasonal *meningococcal meningitis* have been reported. Outbreaks of *dengue fever* occur in the area. *Rabies* is present. For those at high risk, vaccination before arrival should be considered. If you are bitten, seek medical advice without delay. For more information, consult the *Health* appendix.
Health care: Health insurance providing cover for repatriation in the event of serious illness is strongly recommended. Medical facilities are fairly good. The local herb tea is said to be good for stomach upsets.

Travel - International

Note: Owing to the current political climate, non-essential travel is not recommended. A Multination Interim Force (MIF) is currently deployed in Haiti to ensure peace after months of violence and turmoil.
AIR: There are good connections with the USA, the French West Indies and France. *American Airlines* (website: www.aa.com) operates daily flights from London to Port-au-Prince via New York. *Air Canada* (website: www.aircanada.ca) operates flights from London to Port-au-Prince via Montréal at weekends.
Approximate flight times: From Port-au-Prince to *London* is 11 hours (not including overnight stop in New York), to *Los Angeles* is 10 hours, to *New York* is four hours, to *Miami* is two hours and to *Singapore* is 33 hours (with good connections).
International airports: *Port-au-Prince (PAP)* (Mais Gaté) is 13km (8 miles) from the city. There is a snack bar, duty free shop, bank, bar and car hire facilities. Taxis are available to the city.
Cap-Haïtien (CAP) is Haiti's second international airport and is approximately 10km (6 miles) from the town.
Departure tax: US$30 plus Gourde 10 (security charge); transit passengers and children under two years of age are exempt.
SEA: Labadee is a port of call for several cruise lines, including *Royal Caribbean*.
ROAD: There are bus services from the Dominican Republic.

Travel - Internal

AIR: There are scheduled routes, operated by *Caribintair*, between Port-au-Prince and Cap-Haïtien, Hinche and Jérémie. Reservations should be double-checked as delays and cancellations are common. Planes may be chartered.
SEA: Sailing trips can be arranged from Port-au-Prince to beaches around the island. Glass-bottomed boat trips over Sand Cay Reef are available. Cargo ships operating between Jérémie, Cap-Haïtien and Port-au-Prince can take passengers between these ports.
ROAD: During the 1980s, all-weather roads were constructed from Port-au-Prince to Cap-Haïtien and Jacmel. Driving is on the right. **Bus:** Services depart from Port-au-Prince to Cap-Haïtien, Les Cayes, Jacmel, Jérémie, Hinche and Port-de-Paix on an unscheduled basis. **Taxi:** Station-wagons (*camionettes*) run between Port-au-Prince and Pétionville, as well as some other towns. **Car hire:** Available independently in Port-au-Prince and Pétionville, or through hotels and the airport. Petrol can be very scarce outside Port-au-Prince. All hired cars' registration numbers begin with 'L'. **Documentation:** An International Driving Permit is required.
URBAN: Bus: *Tap-taps*, which run within Port-au-Prince with a standard rate for any journey, are colourful but crowded. **Taxi:** Unmetered, with fixed route prices, otherwise fares agreed in advance. Taxi licence plates begin with the letter 'P'. Shared taxis (*publiques*) are the cheapest form of taxi service in the towns. Drivers can be hired for tours by the hour or the day with price negotiated.

Accommodation

Accommodation is limited in Haiti. Existing facilities include modest small inns, guest houses and palatial-style hotels. The majority of accommodation is in Port-au-Prince and Pétionville, while the beach hotels are north of the capital on the road to St Marc or west towards Petit-Gonâve. Accommodation is also to be found in Cap-Haïtien, Les Cayes, the Gonâve Bay area, Jacmel and the Petit-Gonâve beach area. Swimming pools and air conditioning are essential in central hotels where the heat can become severe. All resorts offer substantial reductions between 16 April and 15 December. A 10 per cent room tax is added to all hotel bills. For more information, contact the Ministère du Tourisme (see *Contact Addresses* section).
Note: It is vital to make reservations well in advance for the *Carnival* period (see *Special Events* in the *Social Profile* section).

Resorts & Excursions

Port-au-Prince: The capital is a bustling city with a population of almost 1 million. Places to visit include the busy **Iron Market**, the two cathedrals, the **Museum of Haitian Art**, the **Statue of the Unknown Slave**, the **Gingerbread Houses** and the **Defly Mansion**. The hillside suburb of **Pétionville** offers a calmer respite and some of the city's best dining, gallery-hopping and nightlife. For views over Port-au-Prince and the Gulf of Gonâve, visitors should head for the suburb of **Boutillier**, high in the mountains.
Cap-Haïtien and the North coast: On Christmas Eve 1492, Columbus ràn aground on the north coast of Hispaniola near the present-day site of Cap-Haïtien. The wreck of the **Santa Maria** lies nearby. Today, communications in the region are more convenient, and Cap-Haïtien is only 40 minutes by plane from the capital. Nestling at the foot of lush green mountains and surrounded by several fine beaches, the town has a more laid-back air than the capital and features many fine Spanish-style buildings. Haiti's beautiful **Citadelle**, built by Henri Christophe after the French were overthrown, is not to be missed – a remarkable fortress in the mountains, 40km (25 miles) south of Cap-Haïtien, and the nearby ruins of **Sans Souci Palace**. A half-hour drive leads to the village of **Milot**, gateway to the Citadelle and site of the palace ruins. Versailles was the model for **Sans Souci**, and the ruins still suggest a link.
Jacmel and the South coast: Since the completion of the well-marked road over the mountains, the drive to Jacmel is a pleasant two hours or less through spectacular scenery. Jacmel itself is an elegant town of Victorian stuccoed palaces adorned with filigree balconies. It is an important centre for voodoo and there are several interesting temples to visit. Artists come from all over Europe, America and the Caribbean to work in Jacmel, providing a lively Arts scene that is further enhanced at Carnival time, when dancers in *papier maché* costumes parade the streets and a host of street theatre performances take place. There are several beaches in this region. High in the mountains, south of the capital, is the town of **Kenscoff**, much favoured by Haitians as a summer resort. **Parc Macaya** is perhaps Haiti's most famous national park, offering the visitor trails through spectacular mountain scenery covered in lush rainforest. 12 km outside Jacmel lie the **Bassins Bleus**, a series of three pools joined by waterfalls; the best way to reach the pools is on horseback from Jacmel.

Sport & Activities

Watersports: *Kyona* and *Ibo* beaches (Ibo is on Cacique Isle) are best for **swimming**, **snorkelling**, **spearfishing**, **sailing**, **boomba racing** in dugout canoes and **water-skiing**. *La Gonâve* is a popular location for **fishing**.
Spectator sports: Football is the favourite national sport, followed by **basketball**.
Other: There is a 9-hole **golf** course at the *Pétionville Club*. **Tennis** courts can be found at the *Club Med* in Montraus, *El Rancho*, *Habitation Le Clerc*, *Ibo Beach*, *Ibo Lake*, *Kaloa Beach*, *Pétionville Club* and *Royal Haitian* hotels. The national parks of *La Visite* and *Parc Macaya* offer excellent hiking opportunities.

Social Profile

FOOD & DRINK: The French cuisine is good and the Creole specialities combine French, tropical and African influences. Dishes include Guinea hen with sour orange sauce, *tassot de dinde* (dried turkey), *grillot* (fried island pork), *diri et djondjon* (rice and black mushrooms), *riz et pois* (rice and peas), *langouste flambé* (local lobster), *ti malice* (sauce of onions and herbs), *piment oiseau* (hot sauce) and *grillot et banane pese* (pork chops and island bananas). Sweets include sweet potato pudding, mango pie, fresh coconut ice cream, cashew nuts and island fruits. French wine is available in the better restaurants. The island drink is rum and the best is probably 'Barbancourt', made by a branch of Haiti's oldest family of rum and brandy distillers.
NIGHTLIFE: There is plenty of choice ranging from casinos to African drum music and modern Western music and dance. There is something happening in at least one major hotel every evening with the main attraction being folkloric groups and voodoo performances. On Saturday nights, *bamboche*, a peasant-style dance, can be seen in one of the open-air dance halls. Hotels often have the most up-to-date information on local nightlife.
SHOPPING: Bargaining is recommended at the Iron Market, where both good- and bad-quality local items can be bought, including carvings, printed fabrics, leatherwork, paintings (particularly in the *naïf* style, for which Haiti is famous), straw hats, seed necklaces and jewellery, cigars and foodstuffs. Port-au-Prince has a good selection of shops and boutiques selling a wide range of local and imported items. Bargaining is an accepted practice. **Shopping hours:** Mon-Fri 0800-1200 and 1300-1600, Sat 0800-1200.
SPECIAL EVENTS: For a complete list of carnivals and festivals, contact the Ministère du Tourisme (see *Contact Addresses*). The following is a selection of special events occurring in Haiti in 2005:
Mar 21 *Carnival*, throughout Haiti. **Feb-Mar** *Rara*, Leogane. **Apr** *Pan-American Day*. **Jul/Aug** Local traditional and religious festivals, many towns including Limonade, Petit Goaves, Plaine du Nord and Ouanaminthe. **Jul** *Saut d'Eau*, Ville-Bonheur; *Feast of St. Anne*, Limonade. **Nov** *Gede* (or *Fétdemó*). **Dec** *Discovery Day* (celebrations to commemorate Columbus' landing on the north coast in 1492).
SOCIAL CONVENTIONS: Informal wear is acceptable, although scanty beachwear should be confined to the beach or poolside. Only the most elegant dining-rooms encourage guests to dress for dinner. **Tipping:** 10 per cent service charge is added to hotel and restaurant bills. Taxi drivers do not expect tips.

Business Profile

ECONOMY: Haiti's average annual income of about US$500 per head is the lowest in the western hemisphere; moreover, vast disparities exist between the incomes of rich and poor. The World Bank estimates that 85 per cent of the people live below the absolute poverty line. Two-thirds of the employed population work in agriculture, mainly in the coffee plantations, which generate 25 per cent of Haiti's export earnings, although these have suffered from periodic droughts and persistently low world prices. Sugar cane, sweet potatoes, cocoa and sisal are also grown for export. The mining industry extracts marble, limestone and clay; there are also unexploited deposits of copper, silver and gold. The rest of the manufacturing sector involves food processing, metal products and textiles. Tourism, once promising, has all but vanished thanks to the country's chronic political instability. Haiti's problems are so intractable that even after repeated, large injections of foreign aid and an IMF-approved economic plan, the economy remains stubbornly inert. The appalling state of the country's infrastructure has much to do with this. Haiti's major trading partners are the USA followed by Japan, France, Italy and Belgium. Haiti joined the Caribbean trading bloc CARICOM as a provisional member in 1997 and became a full member in 2002.
BUSINESS: It is usual to wear a suit for initial or formal calls. The British Trade Correspondent can put visitors in touch with a reliable English-French translator if required. Business visitors are generally entertained to lunch or dinner by their agents or important customers and should return invitations either at their hotel or a restaurant. Best time to visit is November to March. **Office hours:** Mon-Fri 0800-1600.
COMMERCIAL INFORMATION: The following organisations can offer advice: Chambre Haïtienne de Commerce et d'Industrie, BP 982, Boulevard Harry Truman, Port-au-Prince (tel: 223 0786 *or* 222 8661; fax: 220 0281); *or* Chambre Franco-Haïtienne de Commerce et d'Industrie, Le Plaza, 10 rue Capois, Champs-de-Mars, Port-au-Prince (tel: 223 8424; fax: 223 8131; e-mail: ccih@compa.net).

Climate

Tropical, with intermittent rain throughout the year. Much cooler temperatures exist in hill resorts and there is a high coastal humidity.
Required clothing: Tropical lightweights with rainwear and warm clothing for hill regions.

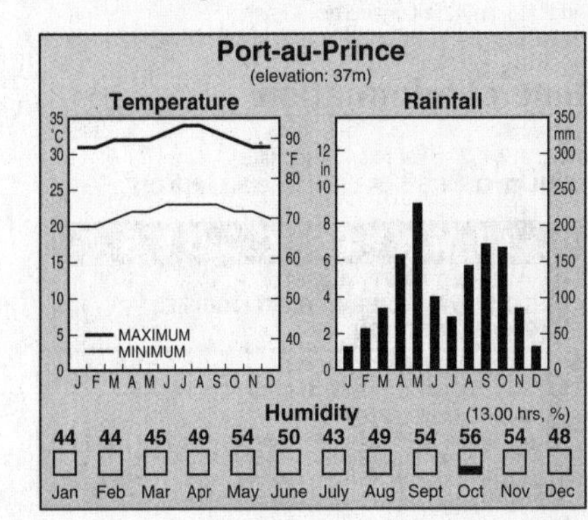

Honduras

LATEST TRAVEL ADVICE CONTACTS

British Foreign and Commonwealth Office
Tel: (0870) 606 0290 Website: www.fco.gov.uk

US Department of State
Website: http://travel.state.gov/travel

Canadian Department of Foreign Affairs and Int'l Trade
Tel: (1 800) 267 8376 Website: www.dfait-maeci.gc.ca

Location: Central America.

Country dialling code: 504.

Instituto Hondureño de Turismo
Apartardo Postal 3261, Edificio Europa, Colonia San Carlos, Tegucigalpa, Honduras
Tel: 222 2124 ext. 502 *or* 503. Fax: 222 2124 ext. 507.
E-mail: tourisminfo@iht.hn
Website: www.letsgohonduras.com

The British Embassy in Guatemala City deals with enquiries relating to Honduras (see *Guatemala* **Section).**

Embassy of the Republic of Honduras and Consulate General
115 Gloucester Place, London W1U 6JT, UK
Tel: (020) 7486 4880. Fax: (020) 7486 4550.
E-mail: hondurasuk@lineone.net
Opening hours: Mon-Fri 1000-1600.

Embassy of the Republic of Honduras
3007 Tilden Street, NW, Suite 4M, Washington, DC 20008, USA
Tel: (202) 966 7702. Fax: (202) 966 9751.
E-mail: embassy@hondurasemb.org
Website: www.hondurasemb.org

Embassy of the United States of America
Avenida La Paz, Apartardo 3453, Tegucigalpa, Honduras
Tel: 238 5114 *or* 236 9320. Fax: 236 9037.
Website: http://honduras.usembassy.gov

Embassy of the Republic of Honduras
151 Slater Street, Suite 805, Ottawa, Ontario K1P 5H3, Canada
Tel: (613) 233 8900. Fax: (613) 232 0193.
E-mail: embhonca@embassyhonduras.ca
Website: www.embassyhonduras.ca
Consulate General in: Montréal.

Canadian Consulate
Street address: 1st Floor, Centro Financero Banexpo, Boulevard San Juan Bosco, Colonia Payaqui, Tegucigalpa, Honduras
Postal address: PO Box 3552, Tegucigalpa, Honduras
Tel: 232 4551 ext. 3301 (consular section) *or* 3201 (general enquiries). Fax: 239 7767.
E-mail: tglpa@dfait-maeci.gc

General Information

AREA: 112,492 sq km (43,433 sq miles).
POPULATION: 6,535,344 (official estimate 2001).

TIMATIC CODES

Health	AMADEUS: **TI-DFT/TGU/HE** GALILEO/WORLDSPAN: **TI-DFT/TGU/HE** SABRE: **TIDFT/TGU/HE**
Visa	AMADEUS: **TI-DFT/TGU/VI** GALILEO/WORLDSPAN: **TI-DFT/TGU/VI** SABRE: **TIDFT/TGU/VI**

To access TIMATIC country information on Health and Visa regulations through the Computer Reservations System (CRS), type in the appropriate command line listed above.

POPULATION DENSITY: 58.1 per sq km.
CAPITAL: Tegucigalpa. **Population:** 1,089,200 (official estimate 2001).
GEOGRAPHY: Honduras shares borders in the southeast with Nicaragua, in the west with Guatemala, and in the southwest with El Salvador. To the north lies the Caribbean and to the south the Pacific Ocean. The interior of the country comprises a central mountain system running from east to west, cut by rivers flowing into both the Caribbean and Pacific. The lowlands in the south form a plain along the Pacific coast. The Gulf of Fonseca in the southwest contains many islands which have volcanic peaks. The large fertile valleys of the northern Caribbean lowlands are cultivated with banana plantations. However, large areas of land in Honduras are unsuitable for cultivation. The majority of the population lives in the western half of the country, while the second-largest concentration of people is in the Cortés area which extends northwards from Lake Yojoa towards the Caribbean.
GOVERNMENT: Republic. **Head of State and Government:** President Ricardo Maduro since 2002.
LANGUAGE: The official language is Spanish. English is widely spoken by the West Indian settlers in the north and on the Bay Islands off the Caribbean coast.
RELIGION: Roman Catholic majority.
TIME: GMT - 6.
ELECTRICITY: 110/120/220 volts AC, 60Hz.
COMMUNICATIONS: Telephone: IDD is available. Country code: 504. Outgoing international code: 00. **Mobile telephone:** GSM 850/1900 networks are available. *Celtel* is the main network provider (website: www.celtel.net). *Alo* is another (website: www.alo.hn). **Fax:** *Empresa Hondureña de Telecomunicaciones (HONDUTEL)* offers a service. **Internet:** ISPs include *NetSys* (website: www.netsys.hn). Internet cafes exist in major towns. **Telegram:** Ordinary and letter telegrams (minimum 22 words) may be sent. **Post:** Airmail to Western Europe takes between four and seven days. Post office hours: Mon-Sat 0800-1200 and 1400-1800. **Press:** Daily newspapers are in Spanish, and include *El Heraldo*, *La Prensa*, *El Tiempo* and *La Tribuna*. The weekly *Honduras This Week* is published in English.
Radio: BBC World Service (website: www.bbc.co.uk/worldservice) and Voice of America (website: www.voa.gov) can be received. From time to time the frequencies change and the most up-to-date can be found online.

Passport/Visa

	Passport Required?	Visa Required?	Return Ticket Required?
Full British	Yes	No	No
Australian	Yes	No	No
Canadian	Yes	No	No
USA	Yes	No	No
Other EU	Yes	No/1	No
Japanese	Yes	No	No

Note: *Regulations and requirements may be subject to change at short notice, and you are advised to contact the appropriate diplomatic or consular authority before finalising travel arrangements. Details of these may be found at the head of this country's entry. Any numbers in the chart refer to the footnotes below.*

PASSPORTS: Passport valid for six months from date of arrival required by all.
Note: It is advisable to have a return ticket but not obligatory. However, visitors may be asked to prove how they plan to leave the country.
VISAS: Required by all except the following:
(a) nationals of countries referred to in the chart above, and of their overseas territories, except **1.** nationals of Cyprus, Estonia, Latvia, Lithuania and the Slovak Republic who *do* need a visa;
(b) nationals of Antigua & Barbuda, Argentina, The Bahamas, Bahrain, Barbados, Belize, Brazil, Brunei, Chile, Costa Rica, El Salvador, Guatemala, Iceland, Kuwait, Liechtenstein, Malaysia, Mexico, Monaco, New Zealand, Nicaragua, Norway, Panama, Paraguay, Qatar, Romania, St Lucia, San Marino, Saudi Arabia, Singapore, Switzerland, Turkey, United Arab Emirates, Uruguay and Vatican City;
(c) those in transit continuing their journey within 48 hours, except for those nationals who require special authorisation.
Note: For certain nationalities, authorisation will have to be obtained from Honduras before a visa can be issued.
Types of visa and cost: *Tourist* and *Business:* £10 (single-entry); £50 (multiple-entry).
Validity: Single-entry: up to 90 days. Multiple-entry: up to one year. A visa extension may be obtained in Honduras at the Immigration Authorities for both tourism and business.
Application to: Consulate (or Consular section at Embassy); see *Contact Addresses* section for details.
Application requirements: (a) One passport-size photo.

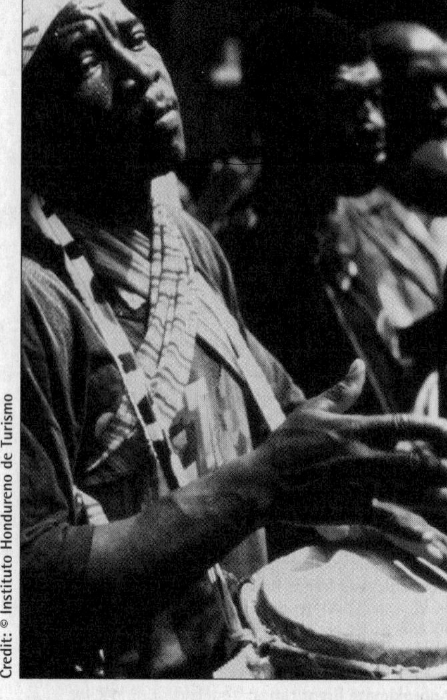
Credit: © Instituto Hondureno de Turismo

(b) Valid passport. (c) Completed application form. (d) Fee, payable by cash or cheque, but the visa will only be issued after the cheque has cleared. (e) For postal applications, a self addressed, pre-paid courier envelope. *Tourist*: (a)-(e) and where possible, (f) Return tickets and travel itinerary. (g) Bank statements. *Business*: (a)-(e) and, (f) Company letters giving purpose of visit and confirming financial responsibility for the applicant.
Working days required: One to two, unless approval is needed from the Ministry of Foreign Affairs in Honduras, which can take up to 10 days.

Money

Currency: Lempira (La) = 100 centavos. Notes are in denominations of La500, 100, 50, 20, 10, 5, 2 and 1. Coins are in denominations of 50, 20, 10, 5, 2 and 1 centavos. A real is one-eighth of a Lempira, and is used colloquially, though there is no such coin.
Currency exchange: Sterling cannot normally be exchanged, except at branches of Lloyds Bank; visitors should therefore take US Dollars.
Credit & debit cards: American Express, Diners Club, MasterCard and Visa are accepted. Check with your credit or debit card company for details of merchant acceptability and other services which may be available.
Travellers cheques: To avoid additional exchange rate charges, travellers are advised to take travellers cheques in US Dollars.
Currency restrictions: There are no restrictions on the import and export of local or foreign currency, but it is advisable to declare US Dollars.
Exchange rate indicators: The following figures are included as a guide to the movements of the Lempira against Sterling and the US Dollar:

Date	Feb '04	May '04	Aug '04	Nov '04
£1.00=	32.41	32.29	33.77	35.15
$1.00=	17.81	18.08	18.33	18.56

Banking hours: Mon-Fri 0900-1500 (some banks open until 1800). Some branches open Sat 0900-1200.

Duty Free

The following goods may be imported into Honduras without incurring customs duty:
200 cigarettes or 100 cigars or 450g of tobacco; two bottles of alcoholic beverages; a reasonable amount of perfume for personal use; gifts up to a total value of US$50.

Public Holidays

2005: Jan 1 New Year's Day. **Mar 24** Maundy Thursday. **Mar 25** Good Friday. **Apr 14** Day of the Americas. **May 1** Labour Day. **Sep 15** Independence Day. **Oct 3** Soldier's Day. **Oct 12** Americas Day. **Oct 21** Armed Forces Day. **Dec 25** Christmas.
2006: Jan 1 New Year's Day. **Apr 13** Maundy Thursday. **Apr 14** Good Friday; Day of the Americas. **May 1** Labour Day. **Sep 15** Independence Day. **Oct 3** Soldier's Day. **Oct 12** Americas Day. **Oct 21** Armed Forces Day. **Dec 25** Christmas Day.

Health

	Special Precautions?	Certificate Required?
Yellow Fever	Yes	1
Cholera	2	No
Typhoid & Polio	3	N/A
Malaria	4	N/A

***Note:** Regulations and requirements may be subject to change at short notice, and you are advised to contact your doctor well in advance of your intended date of departure. Any numbers in the chart refer to the footnotes below.*

1: A yellow fever vaccination certificate is required from all travellers arriving withing six days from infected areas.
2: Following WHO guidelines issued in 1973, a cholera vaccination certificate is no longer a condition of entry into Honduras. However, cases of cholera were reported in 1996 and 1999 and precautions are essential. Up-to-date advice should be sought before deciding whether these precautions should include vaccination as medical opinion is divided over its effectiveness.
3: Typhoid may be a risk in rural areas.
4: Malaria risk, in the benign *vivax* form, exists throughout the year in 80 per cent of the municipalities, especially the rural areas. Transmission risk is low in the remainder, which includes the cities of Tegucigalpa and San Pedro Sula.
Food & drink: All water should be regarded as being potentially contaminated. Water used for drinking, brushing teeth or making ice should first be boiled or otherwise sterilised. Milk is unpasteurised in rural areas and should be boiled. Powdered or tinned milk is available and is advised, but make sure that it is reconstituted with pure water. Avoid dairy products that are likely to have been made from unboiled milk. Only eat well-cooked meat and fish, preferably served hot. Pork, salad and mayonnaise may carry increased risk. Vegetables should be cooked and fruit peeled.
Other risks: *Visceral, cutaneous* and *mucocutaneous leishmaniasis* and *hepatitis A* all occur. *Dengue fever* may also occur. *Paragonimiasis* (oriental lung fluke) has been reported.
Rabies is present. For those at high risk, vaccination before arrival should be considered. If you are bitten, seek medical advice without delay. For more information, consult the *Health* appendix.
Health care: Health insurance is recommended. There are hospitals in Tegucigalpa and all the large towns. Mosquito nets are recommended for coastal areas.

Travel - International

AIR: *American Airlines* operates daily flights to Honduras with a one-night stopover in Miami. Other airlines serving Honduras include *Continental Airlines*, *Copa Airlines* and *Taca International Airlines*. A sales tax of 10 per cent is payable on international bookings for tickets issued in Honduras.
Approximate flight times: From Tegucigalpa to *London* is 15 hours. (There are no direct flights to London; connections are generally via Miami, Houston or Los Angeles.) From Tegucigalpa to *New York* is eight hours (not including stopovers).
International airports: *Tegucigalpa (TGU)* (Toncontín) is 5km (3 miles) southeast of the city. Taxis and buses are available to the city. Airport facilities include bar, restaurant, duty free shop, bank, car hire (*Avis*, *Budget*, *Hertz* and *Thrifty*), post office and first-aid facilities.
There are also international airports at *San Pedro Sula (SAP)* (Dr Ramón Villeda Morales), at *La Ceiba (LCE)* (Golosón) and at *Roatán (RTB)* (Dr Juan Manuel Galvez).
Departure tax: US$25 is levied on all passengers aged 12 years of age and over.
SEA: The principal ports on the Caribbean coastline are La Ceiba, Puerto Cortés, Tela and Trujillo. There is a ferry service between Port Isabel in Texas and Puerto Cortés. The principal ports on the Pacific coastline are Amapala and El Henecan. Ships operated by *Carol Line*, *Cie Generale Transatlantique*, *Hapag-Lloyd*, *Harrison Line*, *The Royal Netherlands Steamship Company* and vessels owned or chartered by the *Standard Fruit Company* and *United Fruit Company* sometimes have limited passenger accommodation.
RAIL: There are no rail services between Honduras and neighbouring countries.
ROAD: Road routes run from El Salvador and Nicaragua via the Pan-American Highway, and from Guatemala on the Western Highway. Visas must be obtained before the journey is undertaken. Border crossings can be fraught with long delays. **Bus:** The *Ticabus* company (website: www.ticabus.com) runs international services to all Central American capitals, but these comfortable coaches are often booked days in advance.

Credit: © Instituto Hondureno de Turismo

Travel - Internal

AIR: The three local airlines (*Isleña Airlines*, *Rollins Air* and *Sosa Airlines*) operate daily services which link Tegucigalpa and other principal towns. *Isleña Airlines* and *Sosa Airlines* run services to Utila, the cheapest Bay Island (off the Caribbean coast). Over 30 small airfields handle light aircraft and commercial aviation.
Departure tax: There is an airport tax on internal journeys of $1.30.
SEA: Ferries operate between ports on the Pacific and Caribbean coastlines. For details, contact local port authorities. There are sailings from La Ceiba and Puerto Cortés to the Bay Islands several times a week. Arrangements must be made with local boat owners.
RAIL: There are only three railways, confined to the northern coastal region and mainly used for transport between banana plantations. Visitors can, however, take a trip from San Pedro Sula on a banana train, and from La Ceiba on a tourist train.
ROAD: Traffic drives on the right. There is a total of 14,600km (9052 miles) of roads of which 8364km (5228 miles) are all-weather, and 2543km (1586 miles) are paved. However, internal air transport is much more convenient for business visitors. An all-weather road exists from Tegucigalpa to San Pedro Sula, Puerto Cortés, La Ceiba and towns along the Caribbean coast, as well as to the towns around the Gulf of Fonseca in the south. **Bus:** Local lines run regular services to most large towns, but the services are well used and booking in advance is essential. On the whole, the services are very cheap. **Taxi:** Not metered, and run on a flat rate within cities. For other journeys, fares should be agreed before commencing journey. **Car hire:** Self-drive cars are available at the airport.
Documentation: Both international and foreign driving licences are accepted.
Travel Times: The following chart gives approximate travel times (in hours and minutes) from **Tegucigalpa** to other major cities/towns in Honduras.

	Air	Road
Comayagua	-	1.00
Siguatepeque	-	2.30
San Pedro S.	0.25	3.30
Choluteca	-	2.30
La Ceiba	0.35	5.00
Bay Islands	0.40	7.00*
Sta Rosa de Copán	6.00	-
Puerto Cortés	-	4.00

Note: *Includes sea crossing of two hours.

Accommodation

HOTELS: Reasonable hotels are available in both Tegucigalpa and San Pedro Sula (where the rates are lower, but standards equivalent to those in the capital are maintained). Elsewhere both rates and standards of comfort are somewhat lower. The Instituto Hondureño de Turismo (see *Contact Addresses* section) can supply lists of hotels with accommodation details. **Grading:** Hotels are split into three categories (upper, middle and lower) according to standard.

Resorts & Excursions

Note: In 1998 Hurricane Mitch devastated much of the island. Despite initial forecasts which put the island's full recovery at 50 years, an international effort quickly rebuilt much of the country's infrastructure. But there has been a long-term effect on the economy, which is still very weak. Many people live in poverty and, as a result, crime levels have soared since the hurricane. Cocaine trafficking controlled by violent gangs has become a major economic force in the country. Incidents of violent crime, including sexual assault and car hijacking, have increased, and caution should be exercised. Road travel is best avoided at night.
TEGUCIGALPA: The capital was originally founded as a mining camp in 1524. Unlike so many of Central America's cities, Tegucigalpa has never been subjected to the disasters of earthquake or fire and so retains many traditional features. The city's impressive parks, particularly **Concordia**, where models of Copan's Mayan architecture were displayed, was badly affected by the hurricane. The **United Nations Park** provides a spectacular view of the city, although caution is advised due to an increase in violent crime in the park. Also recommended is a visit to neighbouring **Comayagua**, former capital of Honduras and now a colonial masterpiece of cobbled streets, tiny plazas and whitewashed houses.
SAN PEDRO SULA: A fast-growing banana, sugar manufacturing and distribution centre for the entire north coast, today San Pedro Sula boasts a new airport, first-class hotels and several excellent restaurants.
COPÁN: The ancient city of Copán is 171km (106 miles) from San Pedro Sula. The **Copán Ruins Archaeological Park** in western Honduras is the best remaining testament to the culture of the Mayan Indians. Among the best of the ruins are the magnificent Acropolis composed of courts and temples, the **Great Plaza**, a huge amphitheatre, and the **Court of the Hieroglyphic Stairway**. Near the **Great Acropolis**, recent archaeological work has brought to light invaluable excavations. The majority of the site's original sculptures are on display at the **Copán Sculpture Museum**, the four-storey centrepiece of which is the **Rosalita** temple, a full-scale replica of a temple recently excavated beneath the Acropolis.
THE CARIBBEAN COAST: Two coastal towns are important to tourists and commercial visitors: La Ceiba and Trujillo. **La Ceiba**, which lies at the foot of the towering 1500m (5000ft) **Pico Bonito**, still a major banana port, now looks to tourism (particularly ecotourism) as a future major industry. There are good hotels and beaches, and an international airport – one of the city's major assets. The nearby **Pico Bonito National Park** is a protected rainforest area where high rainfall and steep slopes combine to form numerous waterfalls and spectacular scenery.
Trujillo was once a thriving port and the old capital of colonial Honduras. Trujillo is today home to many old Spanish buildings, a fascinating pirate history and superb tropical beaches. New resorts and subdivisions are now opening in the Trujillo area.
BAY ISLANDS: 50km (30 miles) off the Caribbean coast of Honduras lies the exotic archipelago of the Bay Islands. Consisting of three major islands (Guanaja, Roatan and Utila) and several smaller islands, the Bay Islands have a

history that spans the ancient Mayan civilisation, early Spanish exploration, colonial buccaneers and the British Empire. **Guanaja** and **Roatán** are hilly, tropical islands, protected by a great coral reef that provides fine diving. **Utila** offers wide expanses of sandy beach and is ringed by tiny cays surrounded by palm trees.

Credit: © Instituto Hondureno de Turismo

Sport & Activities

Ecotourism: The exciting, unspoilt landscape of Honduras and the multitude of flora and fauna that can be found there offer much interest to nature lovers. There are wildlife refuges and national parks all over the country. Cloud forests, mountains, dry forests, pine forests and huge rivers are among the natural features to be enjoyed. The coastal wetlands are home to monkeys and manatees, and visitors can take boat rides through the swamps to view these animals. Toucans and orchids are amongst the attractions of the cloud forests. The centre for activities focusing on ecotourism is La Ceiba and, particularly, the nearby *Pico Bonito National Park*, which offers excellent opportunities

Credit: © Instituto Hondureno de Turismo

for **hiking** through the rainforest. For **birdwatching**, the premier destination is *Lake Yojoa* in the west of the country. **Wildlife** enthusiasts can also take **boat trips** along the winding canals of the *Cuero y Salado Wildlife Refuge*, which provides a habitat for numerous animal species (including monkeys, alligators and manatees) and dozens of waterbirds.
Watersports: There is excellent **diving** in the clear waters of the *Bay Islands*, teeming with coral and tropical fish. The gateway to these islands is La Ceiba, which has gained an excellent reputation amongst the many diving destinations in the Caribbean. Some hotels include hire of equipment in their price. Safe **swimming** can be enjoyed on both seaboards, where beautiful sandy beaches are found. There is good **fishing** on both coasts and Lake Yojoa offers some of the best bass fishing in the world. **Whitewater rafting** is popular on the *Río Cangrejal* in Pico Bonito National Park and day trips can be arranged from La Ceiba.
Other: Golf is an increasingly popular sport, with courses available in most major populated areas. **Football** is the most popular spectator sport. A new popular activity is **canopy touring**; a series of cables are fixed from tree to tree, and attached to a pully while wearing a harness, one can 'fly' through the canopy of the rainforest (contact Junglas Tropicales's Jungle Canopy Tours in La Ceiba: tel: (504) 440 1268).

Social Profile

FOOD & DRINK: There is a wide variety of restaurants and bars in Tegucigalpa and the main cities. Typical dishes include *curiles* (seafood), *tortillas, frijoles, enchiladas, tamales de elote* (corn tamales), *nacatamales, tapado, yuca con chicharrón* and *mondongo*. Typical tropical fruits include mangoes, papayas, pineapples, avocados and bananas.
NIGHTLIFE: There are cinemas and discos in the main cities.
SHOPPING: Local craftsmanship is excellent and inexpensive. Typical items include woodcarvings, cigars, leather goods, straw hats and bags, seed necklaces and baskets. **Shopping hours:** Mon-Fri 0800-1200 and 1330-1800, Sat 0800-1700.
SPECIAL EVENTS: A great many religious celebrations and local festivals take place throughout the year in Honduras; for a full list, contact the Embassy of Honduras (see *Contact Addresses* section). The following is a selection of special events occurring in Honduras in 2005:
May *Fiesta de San Isidro* (carnival festivities), La Ceiba. **Jun** *Fiesta de San Antonio*, Tela; *Fiesta de San Juan Batista*, Trujillo. **Sep 15** *Independence Day Celebrations*, nationwide. **Oct** *Morazan Day* (Soldiers Day), nationwide.
SOCIAL CONVENTIONS: There are strong Spanish influences, but the majority of the population is *mestizo*, mainly leading an agricultural way of life with a low standard of living. Many rural communities can still be found living a relatively unchanged, traditional lifestyle. Social courtesies should be observed. It is customary for a guest at dinner or someone's home to send flowers to the hostess, either before or afterwards. Conservative casual wear is widely acceptable with dress tending to be less conservative in coastal areas. Beachwear and shorts should not be worn away from the beach or poolside. Men are required to wear dinner jackets for formal social occasions. Hotels, restaurants and shops include a 12 per cent sales tax on all purchases. **Tipping:** Service is included in most restaurant bills. In hotels, cafes and restaurants, 10 per cent of the bill is customary where service is not included. Porters and cab drivers should be tipped when helping with the luggage (La0.50 to La1). Hotels, travel agencies and tour operators charge an extra 4 per cent for tourism services.

Business Profile

ECONOMY: The economy of Honduras, which is one of the poorest nations in the western hemisphere, relies on agriculture and timber. The main agricultural products are bananas, beans, coffee, cotton, maize, rice, sorghum and sugar; there is also some dairy and beef farming, and a trade in shellfish. Apart from wood and wood products, light industries produce a variety of consumer goods. There is a small mining industry which produces lead, zinc and silver for export. The economy draws heavily on various forms of US-sponsored aid – both direct and multilateral (through the IMF, Inter-American Development Bank and others). Export earnings have been badly hit in recent years by low world prices and slack demand within the Central American Common Market, of which Honduras is a member. To compound its difficulties further, Honduras was badly affected by Hurricane Mitch in 1998, which caused an estimated US$3 billion worth of damage. In 2004, the economy contracted by about 3 per cent. The USA is the principal market for exports, followed by Germany, Belgium and the UK.
BUSINESS: It is customary to address a professional person by his or her title, particularly on first meeting or during early acquaintance. Businesspeople are generally expected to dress smartly and some dining rooms require men to wear a jacket. There are very few local interpreter or translation services available. Though many businesspeople throughout the country also speak English, correspondence should be in Spanish. **Office hours:** Mon-Fri 0800-1200 and 1400-1700, Sat 0800-1100. Government offices: Mon-Fri 0830-1200 and 1300-1630.
COMMERCIAL INFORMATION: The following organisations can offer advice: Cámara de Comercio Hondureño-Americana, Sección Comercial Hotel Honduras Maya, Apdo 1838, Tegucigalpa (tel: 232 7043; fax: 232 2031; e-mail: amcham@t.hn2.com; website: www.amcham.hn2.com); *or* Cámara de Comercio e Industrias de Tegucigalpa, Bulevar Centroamérica, Apdo 3444, Tegucigalpa (tel: 232 4200; fax: 232 0159; e-mail: ccit@ccit.hn; website: www.ccit.hn).

Climate

The climate is tropical with cooler, more temperate weather in the mountains. The north coast is very hot with rain throughout the year, and though the offshore breezes temper the climate, the sun is very strong. The dry season is from November to April and the wet season runs from May to October.
Required clothing: Lightweight cottons and linens; warmer clothes are recommended between November and February and in the mountains. Waterproofs are needed for the wet season.

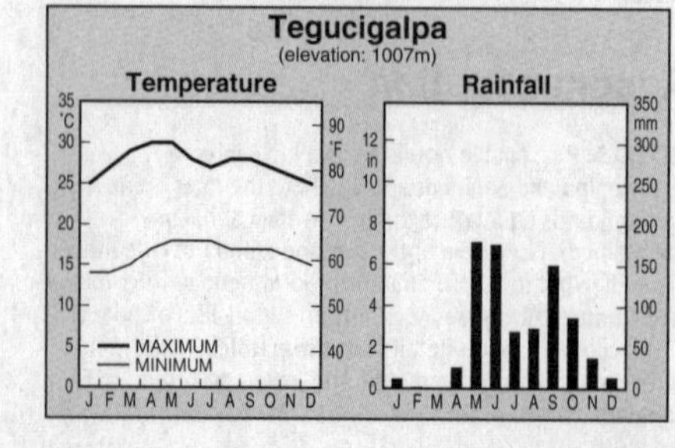

Hungary

LATEST TRAVEL ADVICE CONTACTS

British Foreign and Commonwealth Office
Tel: (0870) 606 0290 Website: www.fco.gov.uk
US Department of State
Website: http://travel.state.gov/travel
Canadian Department of Foreign Affairs and Int'l Trade
Tel: (1 800) 267 8376 Website: www.dfait-maeci.gc.ca

Location: Central Europe.

Country dialling code: 36.

Hungarian National Tourist Office (HNTO)
Vérmezo Street 4, 1012 Budapest, Hungary
Tel: (1) 488 8700. Fax: (1) 488 8600.
E-mail: mtrt@hungarytourism.hu *or* htbudapest@hungarytourism.hu
Website: www.hungary.com *or* www.tourinform.hu
Embassy of the Republic of Hungary
35 Eaton Place, London SW1X 8BY, UK
Tel: (020) 7235 5218. Fax: (020) 7823 1348.
Consular section: Tel: (020) 7235 2664 *or* (09065) 508 936 (visa enquiries; calls are charged at the rate of £1 per minute).
E-mail: office@huemblon.org.uk
Website: www.huemblon.org.uk
Opening hours: Mon-Fri 0930-1200.
Hungarian National Tourist Office (HNTO)
46 Eaton Place, London SW1X 8AL, UK
Tel: (020) 7823 1032 *or* 1055 *or* (09001) 171 200 (recorded information; calls cost 60p per minute).
Fax: (020) 7823 1459.
E-mail: htlondon@hungarytourism.hu
Website: www.hungary.com *or* www.hungarywelcomesbritain.com
British Embassy
Harmincad utca 6, 1051 Budapest, Hungary
Tel: (1) 266 2888. Fax: (1) 266 0907 *or* 429 6360 (consular section).
E-mail: info@britemb.hu
Website: www.britishembassy.hu
Embassy of the Republic of Hungary
3910 Shoemaker Street, NW, Washington, DC 20008, USA
Tel: (202) 362 6730. Fax: (202) 966 8135.
E-mail: office@huembwas.org
Website: www.huembwas.org
Hungarian National Tourist Office (HNTO)
150 East 58th Street, 33rd Floor, New York, NY 10155, USA
Tel: (212) 355 0240. Fax: (212) 207 4103.
E-mail: info@gotohungary.com *or* hnto@gotohungary.com
Website: www.gotohungary.com
Embassy of the United States of America
Szabadság tér 12, 1054 Budapest, Hungary
Tel: (1) 475 4400. Fax: (1) 475 4764
E-mail: usconsular.budapest@state.gov
Website: www.usembassy.hu

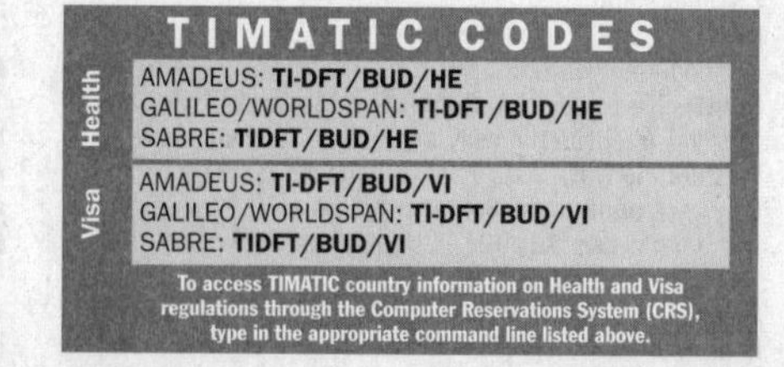

TIMATIC CODES

Health	AMADEUS: **TI-DFT/BUD/HE** GALILEO/WORLDSPAN: **TI-DFT/BUD/HE** SABRE: **TIDFT/BUD/HE**
Visa	AMADEUS: **TI-DFT/BUD/VI** GALILEO/WORLDSPAN: **TI-DFT/BUD/VI** SABRE: **TIDFT/BUD/VI**

To access TIMATIC country information on Health and Visa regulations through the Computer Reservations System (CRS), type in the appropriate command line listed above.

Take me to Budapest, please!

Embassy of the Republic of Hungary
299 Waverley Street, Ottawa, Ontario K2P 0V9, Canada
Consular section: 302 Metcalfe Street (mailing address is the same as for the Embassy).
Tel: (613) 230 2717. Fax: (613) 230 7560 *or* 8887 (consular section).
E-mail: sysadmin@huembott.org
Website: www.docuweb.ca/Hungary
Consulates General in: Montréal and Toronto.
Honorary Consulates in: Calgary and Vancouver.
Canadian Embassy
Zugligeti út 51-53, 1121 Budapest, Hungary
Tel: (1) 392 3360. Fax: (1) 392 3390.
E-mail: bpest@international.gc.ca
Website: www.canada.hu

General Information

AREA: 93,030 sq km (35,919 sq miles).
POPULATION: 10,142,000 (official estimate 2002).
POPULATION DENSITY: 109 per sq km.
CAPITAL: Budapest. **Population:** 1,759,569 (2002).
GEOGRAPHY: Hungary is situated in Central Europe, sharing borders to the north with the Slovak Republic, to the northeast with Ukraine, to the east with Romania, to the south with Croatia and Serbia and to the west with Austria and Slovenia. There are several ranges of hills, chiefly in the north and west. The Great Plain (*Nagyalföld*) stretches east from the Danube to the foothills of the Carpathian Mountains in the CIS, to the mountains of Transylvania in Romania, and south to the Fruska Gora range in Croatia. Lake Balaton is the largest unbroken stretch of inland water in Central Europe.
GOVERNMENT: Republic. **Head of State:** President Ferenc Mádl since 2000. **Head of Government:** Prime Minister Ferenc Gyurcsany since 2004.
LANGUAGE: Hungarian (Magyar) is the official language. German and English are widely spoken. Some French is also spoken, mainly in western Hungary.
RELIGION: 62 per cent Roman Catholic, 20 per cent Calvinist, 5 per cent Lutheran. Eastern Orthodox and Jewish minorities. There is no official national religion.
TIME: GMT + 1 (GMT + 2 from last Sunday in March to Saturday before last Sunday in October).
ELECTRICITY: 220 volts AC, 50Hz. European-style two-pin plugs are used.
COMMUNICATIONS: Telephone: IDD available. Country code: 36. Outgoing international code: 00. Public telephones are operated by Ft100, Ft50, Ft20 and Ft10 coins or by telephone cards. **Mobile telephone:** GSM dual band 900/1800, coverage throughout the country. Network operators include *Pannon GSM Telecoms* (website: www.pannongsm.com), *T-Mobile* (website: www.t-mobile.hu) and *Vodafone* (website: www.vodafone.hu). **Fax/Telegram:** Services are available at main post offices all over the country and at the Telecommunications Information and Service Office, Petöfi Sándor u., Budapest. **Internet:** ISPs include *Matáv* (website: www.matav.hu). There are Internet cafes in larger towns. **Post:** Airmail takes three days to one week to reach other European destinations. In addition to the main post office, the offices at West and East railway stations in Budapest are open daily 0700-2100. Stamps are available from tobacconists as well as post offices. Post office hours: Mon-Fri 0800-1800, Sat 0700-1400. **Press:** National dailies include *Magyar Hírlap*, *Népszabadság* and *Népszava*. English-language newspapers include the *Budapest Business Journal, Budapest Week, Courier Diplomatique, The Budapest Sun, The Hungarian Economy, The Hungarian Observer* and *The Hungarian Quarterly*.
Radio: BBC World Service (website: www.bbc.co.uk/worldservice) and Voice of America (website: www.voa.gov) can be received. From time to time the frequencies change and the most up-to-date can be found online.

Passport/Visa

	Passport Required?	Visa Required?	Return Ticket Required?
Full British	Yes	No	Yes
Australian	Yes	No	Yes
Canadian	Yes	No	Yes
USA	Yes	No	Yes
Other EU	1/2	No	Yes
Japanese	Yes	No	Yes

Note: *Regulations and requirements may be subject to change at short notice, and you are advised to contact the appropriate diplomatic or consular authority before finalising travel arrangements. Details of these may be found at the head of this country's entry. Any numbers in the chart refer to the footnotes below.*

PASSPORTS: Passport valid for at least six months required by all, except:
(a) **1.** nationals of Austria, Belgium, Cyprus, Czech Republic, Estonia, Finland, France, Germany, Greece, Italy, Liechtenstein, Lithuania, Luxembourg, Malta, The Netherlands, Poland, Portugal, Slovak Republic and Spain holding a national identity card;
(b) **2.** nationals of Croatia, Slovenia and Switzerland holding valid ID cards but *only* when staying for up to 90 days for touristic purposes, with return ticket and proof of sufficient funds.
VISAS: Required by all except the following:
(a) nationals of countries referred to in the chart above for stays of up to 90 days (nationals of the UK and Ireland for stays of up to six months, and nationals of Cyprus, Latvia, Malta and Slovenia for stays of up to 30 days);
(b) nationals of Andorra, Argentina, Bolivia, Brazil, Brunei, Bulgaria, Chile, Costa Rica, Croatia, El Salvador, Guatemala, Honduras, Hong Kong (SAR), Iceland, Israel, Korea (Rep), Liechtenstein, Macau (SAR), Malaysia, Mexico, Monaco, New Zealand, Norway, Panama, Paraguay, Switzerland, Uruguay, Vatican City and Venezuela (tourist visits only) for stays of up to 90 days;
(c) nationals of Bosnia & Herzegovina, Nicaragua, Romania, San Marino and Singapore for stays of up to 30 days;
(d) persons continuing their journey to a third country within 24 hours, provided not leaving the airport and holding valid onward tickets and documentation. However, nationals who are not eligible for visa exemptions and are non-residents of the UK may need to acquire an *airport transit* visa in all circumstances; contact nearest Embassy/Consulate for further details.
Note: The length of stay which nationals of the exempted countries are allowed is subject to frequent change; contact the embassy for more information.
Types of visa and cost: All visas, regardless of type and duration of stay allocated, cost £25. However, long-term visas cost £35. Multiple-entry visas are only valid for business travellers and for those possessing a long-term visa.
Note: (a) Nationals of Serbia & Montenegro and Ukraine, and family members of UK nationals (eg husband/wife and children under 21 years), can obtain visas free-of-charge.
(b) If the visa has to be issued on a separate sheet (because there is no free page in the passport), an additional fee is payable of £17.
Validity: *Single-entry* (*tourist* and *business*): Valid for 90-day stay within six months of the date of issue. *Double-entry*: Valid for 90-day stay taken *twice* within six months from date of issue. *Multiple-entry*: Valid for multiple 90-day stays in Hungary within one year from the date of issue. Validity subject to frequent change according to nationality. *Transit*: Valid for five days within six months from date of issue. *Double-transit*: Maximum of five days *twice* within six months from date of issue.
Application to: Consulate (or Consular section at Embassy; see *Contact Addresses* section). Visas are not issued at road border points or at Budapest Airport.
Application requirements: (a) Passport valid for at least six months (with at least one blank page). (b) Completed application form. (c) One passport-size photo. (d) Fee (non reimbursable), payable in cash (personal applications) or postal order only. (e) Return ticket or ticket reservation and travel insurance. (f) For postal applications, a pre-paid special delivery return envelope. (g) Confirmation of accommodation in Hungary, or letter of invitation from friends or relatives living in Hungary (copy of the ID cards of the inviting party must be attached; if travelling on a travel document and not a passport, nationals must seek endorsement from the local Hungarian migration authority). (h) Recent bank statement or payslip. *Business* (or just for business purposes, eg a trip to attend a conference): (a)-(h) and, (i) Written invitation from host organisation or company. *Transit*: (a)-(h) and, (i) Valid visa for country of destination.
Working days required: Two, or seven for postal applications and if applicant is applying with a travel document and not a passport.

Money

Currency: Hungarian Forint (Ft) = 100 fillér. Notes are in denominations of Ft20,000, Ft10,000, 5000, 2000, 1000, 500 and 200. Coins are in denominations of Ft100, 50, 20, 10, 5, 2 and 1. A large number of commemorative coins in circulation are legal tender.
Currency exchange: Currency can be exchanged at hotels, banks, bureaux de change, airports, railway stations, travel agencies and some restaurants throughout the country. Automatic exchange machines are available in Budapest and other main tourist centres. Credit and debit cards can be used to withdraw money from ATMs. Visitors should retain all exchange receipts, as it is illegal to change money on the black market.
Credit & debit cards: It is possible to withdraw cash by credit card at more than 3200 post offices. American Express, Cirrus, Diners Club, MasterCard and Visa are accepted. Check with your credit or debit card company for details of merchant acceptability and other services which may be available.
Travellers cheques: Widely accepted in stores and banks. To avoid additional exchange rate charges, travellers are advised to take travellers cheques in US Dollars or Pounds Sterling.
Currency restrictions: The import of local currency is limited to Ft200,000, provided the amount is declared on arrival. The export of local currency is limited to Ft200,000 and must be declared. The import of foreign currency is unlimited, provided amounts greater than Ft50,000 are declared. The export of foreign currency is limited to the amount declared on import and should be made no longer than three months after import. There is no compulsory money exchange. Hungarian currency can be re-exchanged for up to 50 per cent of the officially exchanged sum (but not more than US$450) at any authorised office or branch of the National Savings Bank.
Exchange rate indicators: The following figures are included as a guide to the movements of the Forint against Sterling and the US Dollar:

Date	Feb '04	May '04	Aug '04	Nov '04
£1.00=	386.60	379.06	370.19	350.72
$1.00=	212.38	212.23	200.93	185.20

Banking hours: Mon-Fri 0800-1600. Some banks are open on Saturdays.

Duty Free

The following may be imported into Hungary by persons over 16 years of age without incurring customs duty:
200 cigarettes or 100 cigars or 250g of tobacco; 1l of spirits, 1l of wine and 5l of beer; gifts to the value of Ft29,500; up to 1kg each of coffee, tea, cocoa and other spices (excluding paprika and paprika mixtures).
Abolition of duty free goods within the EU: On June 30 1999, the sale of duty free alcohol and tobacco at airports and at sea was abolished in all of the original 15 EU member states. Of the 10 new member states that joined the EU on May 1 2004, these rules already apply to Cyprus and Malta. There are transitional rules in place for visitors returning to one of the original 15 EU countries from one of the other new EU countries. But for the original 15, plus Cyprus and Malta, there are now no limits imposed on importing tobacco and alcohol products from one EU country to another (with the exceptions of Denmark, Finland and Sweden, where limits *are* imposed). Travellers should note that they may be required to prove at customs that the goods purchased are for personal use *only*.

Public Holidays

2005: Jan 1 New Year's Day. **Mar 15** Anniversary of 1848 uprising against Austrian rule. **Mar 28** Easter Monday. **May 1** Labour Day. **May 16** Whit Monday. **Aug 15** Assumption. **Aug 20** National Day (Feast of St Stephen). **Oct 23** Republic Day (Anniversary of 1956). **Nov 1** All Saints' Day. **Dec 25-26** Christmas. **Dec 31** New Year's Eve.
2006: Jan 1 New Year's Day. **Mar 15** Anniversary of 1848 uprising against Austrian rule. **Apr 17** Easter Monday. **May 1** Labour Day. **Jun 5** Whit Monday. **Aug 15** Assumption. **Aug 20** National Day (Feast of St Stephen). **Oct 23** Republic Day (Anniversary of 1956). **Nov 1** All Saints' Day. **Dec 25-26** Christmas. **Dec 31** New Year's Eve.

Health

	Special Precautions?	Certificate Required?
Yellow Fever	No	No
Cholera	No	No
Typhoid & Polio	No	N/A
Malaria	No	N/A

Note: *Regulations and requirements may be subject to change at short notice, and you are advised to contact your doctor well in advance of your intended date of departure. Any numbers in the chart refer to the footnotes below.*

Food & drink: Mains water is normally chlorinated and, whilst relatively safe, may cause mild abdominal upsets. Bottled water is available and is advised for the first few weeks of the stay. Milk is pasteurised and dairy products are safe for consumption. Local meat, poultry, seafood, fruit and vegetables are generally considered safe to eat.
Other risks: *Hepatitis A* occurs. *Tick-borne encephalitis* occurs in forested areas. Vaccination is advisable.
Rabies, although on the decrease, is present. For those at high risk, vaccination before arrival should be considered. If you are bitten, seek medical advice without delay.
For more information, consult the *Health* appendix.

Health care: There is a reciprocal health agreement with the UK. On presentation of a UK passport, treatment is free at hospitals, 'poly-clinics' and doctor's surgeries. For emergencies, call 104. Charges will be made for dental and ophthalmic treatment and for prescribed medicines. Chemists are generally open from 0800-1800. There are chemists with a 24-hour emergency service open in every district.

Travel - International

AIR: The national airline is *Malév (MA)*, operating flights to more than 40 cities. For further information, contact Malév Hungarian Airlines (tel: 0870 9090 577; website: www.malev.com). Other airlines serving Budapest include *Aeroflot, Air France, British Airways, easyJet, KLM, Lufthansa, Sky Europe, Swiss, United Airlines* and *Wizz Air*.
Approximate flight times: From London to *Budapest* is two hours 20 minutes.
International airports: *Budapest Ferihegy (BUD)*, 16km (10 miles) from the city (travel time - 45 minutes). There are now two passenger terminals - A and B. Facilities include a duty free shop, florist, newsagent, restaurants and bar, bureaux de change, banks, tourist information centre, gift shop and post office. Regular coach and bus services are available to the city, costing around Ft800 for the centrum bus and approximately Ft2100 or Ft3600 return for the airport minibus, which runs to and from any address in the city. The 93 bus runs an express service between the underground terminus at Kobánya-Kispest and the Ferihegy terminals, however you need a pre-purchased or season ticket. Taxis are available at all times. The major car hire companies are represented.
Departure tax: None.
RIVER: From April to October there is a daily hydrofoil service run by *MAHART* between Vienna, Bratislava and Budapest. The journey costs approximately €75 for a single and takes six hours. Reservations must be made in advance. 20kg of luggage may be carried free of charge. Passengers arriving by boat are advised to reserve a taxi through the shipping line, as none are readily available on the dock. For further details contact MAHART at Belgrád rakpart, 1056 Budapest (tel: (1) 484 4013; fax: (1) 266 4201; e-mail: passnave@mahartpassnave.hu; website: www.mahartpassnave.hu).
RAIL: Direct rail links connect Hungary to 16 European cities and there are 47 international trains daily to Budapest. Inter-Rail, Eurotrain and RES concessions are valid on the Hungarian State Railways (MÁV). Between Dresden and Budapest there is a car transport system. The *Wiener Waltzer* from Basel travels via Zurich, Salzburg and Vienna to Budapest. First- and second-class day carriages run from Basel through to Budapest and both sleeping cars and couchettes (the latter is second-class only) as far as Vienna. There is a minibar service in Switzerland and Austria, and a dining car in Hungary. There are two main routes from London: via Paris or Brussels (*Eurostar* connection from London) to Vienna (including a Paris-Vienna EuroNight service), where several direct trains run daily to Budapest-Keleti; or via Brussels (Eurostar connection from London) to Munich, where several direct trains run daily to Budapest-Keleti (including a EuroNight service). **Luggage allowances:** 35kg for adults, 15kg for children.
Note: Travellers leaving Hungary by train must pay their fare in convertible currency. Most generally recognised international concessionary tickets are accepted in Hungary. For further details, contact MÁV at Budapest VI, Andrássy út 35 (tel: (1) 461 5500 (international timetables) or (1) 461 5400 (internal timetables); website: www.mav.hu). Seat reservations are strongly advised for all services.
ROAD: Route via The Netherlands, Belgium and Austria and from Vienna via the E5 Transcontinental Highway which passes near Bratislava (Slovak Republic). Bus connections are available from most major European cities, check for further details with Volanbusz (website: www.volanbusz.hu). Eurolines, departing from Victoria Coach Station in London, serves destinations in Hungary. For further information, contact *Eurolines*, 52 Grosvenor Gardens, London, SW1V 0AU (tel: (08705) 143 219; website: www.eurolines.com).
The Channel Tunnel: Eurotunnel operates trains 24 hours per day through the Channel Tunnel between Folkestone in Kent (with direct access from the M20) and Calais in France. All vehicles from motorcycles to campers can be accommodated. Eurotunnel operates three to four passenger trains per hour at peak times. The journey takes approximately 35 minutes. For further information contact Eurotunnel Reservations (tel: (08705) 353 535; e-mail: callcentre@eurotunnel.com; website: www.eurotunnel.co.uk).

Travel - Internal

AIR: There are currently no scheduled internal air services in Hungary. Some are planned for the near future, however.
RIVER/LAKE: There are regular services on the Danube and Lake Balaton from spring to late autumn. *MAHART* and the *Budapest Travel Company (BKV)* (website: www.bkv.hu) also operate ferries in the city centre, the Roman Embankment (*Római Part*) and at some crossing points. Due to the opening of the bridge between Esztergom and Párkány (Sturovo) in 2001, the former ferry service on the Danube is no longer available. On Lake Balaton, a ferry operates during the summer at 40-minute intervals daily between Tihanyrév and Szántódrév; and between Révfülöp and Balatonboglér 0620-0000; at other times of the year the service runs 0630-1930. Contact *MAHART* for further details (see *Travel – International* section for contact details).

Credit: © Hungarian National Tourist Office

RAIL: Services are operated by *MÁV*. All main cities are linked by efficient services but facilities are often inadequate. Supplements are payable on IC and express trains. Reservations are compulsory for IC trains and recommended for express trains, particularly in summer. Tickets can be bought 60 days in advance on domestic railway lines, as can seat reservations. The most popular tourist rail routes are: Budapest-Kecskemet-Szeged-Budapest and Budapest-Siofok-Lake Balaton.
Rail-bus services are available between the main railway stations within Budapest at fixed rates (tel: (1) 353 2722; fax: (1) 353 2187; website: www.mav.hu). There are also narrow-gauge railways in operation in many parts of the country. The website www.elvita.hu houses up-to-date travel information and timetables.
Cheap fares: Concessions are available for groups (minimum of 10 persons), children, families and pensioners. Children under six travel free. Children aged six to 12 pay approximately a third of the full fare. Balaton and Tourist Season Tickets (seven to 10 days) are also available. Contact *MÁV* for details (see *Travel – International* section for contact details). The *Hungarian Flexipass*, sold by travel agents worldwide and by Rail Europe, offers unlimited first-class train travel for five days in a 15-day period or for 10 days in a 30-day period. The *Hungarian Tourist Card* offers discounts on rail, bus, taxi and ship services, as well as accommodation, restaurants and museums. The Hungarian National Tourist Office can provide further information (see *Contact Addresses* section).
ROAD: Traffic drives on the right. There are eight arterial roads in the country: all but the M8 start from central Budapest. Tolls are payable on some roads and all motorways. Season tickets can be purchased. From Budapest, the two main highways are the M1 from Györ to Vienna and the M7 along Lake Balaton. The M3 connects Budapest with eastern Hungary. Generally the road system is good. **Bus:** Budapest is linked with major provincial towns. Tickets are available from *Volán* long-distance bus terminal, Budapest, and at *Volán* offices throughout the country. A bus season ticket is also available. **Car hire:** Available at Ferihegy Airport or at Volán and Budapest tourist offices, as well as at major hotels. **Regulations:** Speed limits are 50kph (31mph) in built-up areas, 90kph (50mph) on main roads, 110kph (62mph) on highways and 130kph (75mph) on motorways. Seat belts are compulsory. Petrol stations are frequent and there are no special tourist petrol coupons. There is a total alcohol ban when driving; severe fines are imposed for infringements. It is obligatory to keep headlights dipped at all times when on the open road. Mobile phones are allowed only with headsets. Child seats are compulsory. **Breakdowns:** The Hungarian Automobile Club operates a breakdown service on main roads at weekends and a 24-hour service on motorways. For further details, contact the Hungarian Automobile Club, Rómer Flóris utca 4/A, H-1024 Budapest (tel: (1) 345 1800 *or* 345 1755 (24-hour emergency helpline); e-mail: info@autoklub.hu; website: www.autoklub.hu).
Documentation: Pink format EU licence accepted but International Driving Permit required if green licence held.
URBAN: There is good public transport in all the main towns. Budapest has bus, trolleybus, tramway, suburban railway (*HEV*), a three-line metro and boat services. The metro has ticket barriers at all stations. The bus-trolleybus-tramway system has pre-purchase flat fares with ticket puncher on board. Day passes are available for all the transport modes in the city. Trams and buses generally run from about 0430-2300. Some night services also operate. The metro runs from 0430-2310 and stations can be identified by a large 'M'. There is also a cogwheel railway (Városmajor-Széchenyi Hill), a Childrens' Railway (Hüvösvölgy-Széchenyi Hill), a chairlift and a funicular. There are tramways in some of the other towns, or else good bus services. Day passes and season tickets are available in Budapest.
Travel Times: The following chart gives approximate travel times (in hours and minutes) from **Budapest** to other major cities/towns in Hungary.

	Road	Rail
Sopron	3.00	2.25
Miskolc	2.30	1.55
Pécs	3.00	2.45
Szeged	2.30	2.20
Szentendre	0.30	0.50
Lake Balaton	2.00	2.30

Accommodation

Note: The *Hungarian Tourist Card* provides discounts on accommodation including hotels, guest houses and youth hostels (the Hungarian National Tourist Office can provide further information or visit the website www.budapestinfo.hu).
HOTELS: In all classes of hotel, visitors from the West can expect to be made very welcome and service will usually be friendly and smooth. In addition to hotels, there are Tourist Hostels, which provide simple accommodation usually in rooms with four or more beds. For information, contact the Hungarian Hotel Association, Secretariat, Novotel Budapest Convention Centre, Jagello-u 1-3, 1123 Budapest (tel: (1) 466 9462; tel/fax: (1) 322 3854; e-mail: hah@axelero.hu; website: www.hah.hu). The HNTO also issues a brochure with listings of hotels, guest houses and tourist hotels.
Grading: Hungarian hotels are classified by use of a star rating system: **5-** and **4-star** hotels are luxury class and are generally extremely comfortable; **3-star** hotels are comfortable but less luxurious and offer good value for money; and **2-** and **1-star** hotels are generally adequate and clean.
GUEST HOUSES: Available almost everywhere. Paying-guest accommodation is an inexpensive and excellent way of getting to know the people. Renting often includes a bathroom but not breakfast. Such accommodation should be reserved well in advance. Further information can be obtained from the Hungarian National Tourist Office (see *Contact Addresses* section).
SELF-CATERING: Bungalows with two rooms, fully equipped, can be rented at a large number of resorts. Full details and rates can be obtained from the Hungarian National Tourist Office (see *Contact Addresses* section).
CAMPING/CARAVANNING: Camping is forbidden except in specially designated areas. Booking is through the Hungarian Camping and Caravanning Club, Mária u., 34. II floor, 4apt, H-1085 Budapest (tel: (1) 267 5255 *or* 5256; fax: (1) 267 5254). Further information can also be obtained in a special catalogue published by the Hungarian National Tourist Office (see *Contact Addresses* section) and there is an online booking facility (website: www.travelport.hu). Most

of the sites cater only for campers bringing in their own equipment. Caravans are permitted in all sites that have power points; a parking charge is made. There is no charge for children under the age of six and young people between six and 16 years of age pay half price.
Grading: There are four categories of site, designated **I**, **II**, **III** and **IV**, according to the amenities provided, and most are open from May to September.
YOUTH HOSTELS: There are 10 in Budapest and 14 in other towns. Hostels are open all day and beds cost around US$6. For further information, contact Express Travel Bureau, Semmelweis U. 4, 1052 Budapest (tel: (1) 266 6188; fax: (1) 266 6191; e-mail: info@express-travel.hu; website: www.express-travel.hu); *or* Hungarian Youth Hostel Association (MISZSZ), 1077 Almassy ter 6, Budapest (tel: (1) 413 2065; e-mail: info@youthhostels.hu; website: www.youthhostels.hu).

Resorts & Excursions

Hungary does not regard itself as a Balkan or a Slavic country, and the Magyars who settled there from central Asia have always identified with western values. The country has survived the devastations of the Tartars, Turks, Habsburgs and Russians, retaining its unique language and culture. In Hungary, admitting that you're a tourist is positive and people will often want to meet, talk and help visitors to enjoy their country.
For the purpose of this guide, the country has been divided into six regions: Budapest, The Danube, The West & Lake Balaton, The Great Plain Area, Southern Hungary and The Northern Highlands.

BUDAPEST

The capital city was originally two cities on each side of one of the most beautiful stretches of the Danube river – **Buda**, the older, more graceful part, with cobbled streets and medieval buildings, and **Pest**, the commercial centre. The 'Pearl of the Danube' is a lively city which has long been a haven for writers, artists and musicians.
BUDA: In Buda, **Gellért Hill** gives a wonderful view of the city, river and mountains. On the hill is the **Citadella**, a fort built after the unsuccessful 1848 uprising, and a number of thermal baths, including the great **Gellért Baths** adjoining the hotel of that name. The **Royal Palace**, fully reconstructed after being bombed during World War II, houses the **National Gallery**, with collections of fine Gothic sculpture and modern Hungarian art, and the **Historical Museum of Budapest**, containing archaeological remains of the old city as well as furnishings, glass and ceramics from the 15th century. Also on this side of the Danube is the rampart of **Halászbástya** (**Fisherman's Bastion**), so called because it was the duty of the city's fishermen to protect the northern side of the

Credit: © Hungarian National Tourist Office

Palace during the Middle Ages, and the great **Mátyás templon** (**church**) with its multicoloured tiled roof.
PEST: On the Pest side are the **Parliament**; the **Hungarian National Museum**, containing remarkable treasures ranging from the oldest skull found in Europe to Franz Liszt's gold baton; the **Belvárosi Templom**, Hungary's oldest church, dating from the 12th century, the **Museum of Fine Arts** housing European paintings and the **Ethnographic Museum**. **Margaret Island**, connected to both Buda and Pest by bridges, is a park with a sports stadium, swimming pool, spas, a rose garden and fountains. Budapest has about 100 hot springs.

THE DANUBE

The Danube Bend upstream from Budapest has long been a favourite summer retreat from the humid heat of the capital. Three historic towns draw most of the visitors. A few miles further up river, **Szentendre** is an old market town originally inhabited by Serbian refugees fleeing from the Turks. Churches had to face east regardless of their position on the streets, producing unusual layouts, and the Serbian house styles added greatly to the village's charm. Due to trade restrictions and floods, the town was abandoned, only to be rediscovered and settled by Hungarian artists in the 1920s. The **Margit Kovács Musuem** has a remarkable display of the work of Hungary's greatest ceramicist. The **Béla Czóbel Museum** shows paintings from the 1890s and the **Károly Ferenczy Museum** contains historical, archaeological and ethnographic collections as well as paintings. The **Serbian Museum for Ecclesiastical History** contains many fine examples of ecclesiastical art from the 14th to the 18th centuries. The **Ethnographic Museum** (**skanzen**) is a large open-air addition from the 1960s, still being added to, of reconstructed folk villages from all over the country.
VISEGRAD: A few miles further upriver, Visegrád was once a royal stronghold, but is now a rather sleepy tourist resort with spectacular views over the Danube. The 15th-century **summer palace** has been excavated and restored, and the **Mátyás Museum** in the **Salamon Tower** displays many archaeological discoveries.
ESZTERGOM: Originally a Roman outpost, Esztergom later became the country's capital from the 11th to the 14th centuries and remains at the heart of the country's Catholicism. Hungary's largest Basilica, the Palace ruins, the **Museum of the Stronghold of Esztergom** and the **Christian Museum of Esztergom**, containing some of Hungary's finest art collections, are all important attractions.

THE WEST & LAKE BALATON

Sopron, close to the Austrian frontier, is built on old Roman foundations, and reminders of the region's history are still very much in evidence in the town's 240 listed buildings. Among the sights here are the **Firewatch Tower**, **Storno House** showing Roman, Celtic and Avar relics, as well as mementos of Franz Liszt, the **Gothic Goat Church** and the gargoyled **Church of St Michael**.
ELSEWHERE: 27km (17 miles) away is the Baroque **Esterházy Palace** at **Fertöd**, designed to rival Versailles; Josef Haydn was music master here at the end of the 18th century. Nearby is the spa town of **Balf**. The walled town of **Köszeg** and the riverside town of **Györ**, on the main Budapest–Vienna highway, **Szombathely** (which claims to be the oldest town in Hungary and has some excellent Romanesque stonework) and **Zalaegerszeg** are also attractive towns to visit. Located between Budapest and Lake Balaton, **Székesfehérvár** boasts a **Baroque Town Hall**, as well as the **Zichy Palace** and the **Garden of Ruins** – an open-air museum. **Fertö-Hanság National Park**, the main areas of which are **Lake Fertö**, the westernmost steppe lake in Eurasia, and the **Hanság**, an area of wetlands, adjoins the **Austrian National Park Neusiedlersee-Seewinkel**. Birdwatching, cycling and hiking are popular, and there is a permanent wildlife and ethnographic museum at **Öntésmajor**.
LAKE BALATON: Lake Balaton is a popular holiday region because of its sandy beaches (*strands*) and shallow waters. The surrounding countryside consists mainly of fertile plains dotted with old villages. **Siófok**, on the south shore of the lake, has some of the sandiest beaches and best facilities for tourists. **Keszthely** is a pleasant old town – the Balaton's best – including the **Festetics Palace** with its **Helicon Library**, and the **Balaton Museum**. **Hévíz**, Europe's largest thermal lake, is a short bus ride away. **Balatonfüred** is a well-known health resort with 11 medicinal springs. **Tihany's Benedictine Abbey** was founded in 1055; **Belsö-tó Lake** and the **Aranyház geyser** cones are nearby. **Veszprém**, 10km (6 miles) north of Lake Balaton, is a pretty town with cobbled streets, built on five hills. It is the home of the **Var Museum**, an **Episcopal Palace** and the 13th-century **Gizella Chapel**.

THE GREAT PLAIN AREA

This region covers more than half the country and contains thousands of acres of vineyards, orchards and farmland. **Kecskemét**, 85km (53 miles) southeast of the capital, is the home town of the composer Zoltán Kodály. Although an industrial town in many respects, there is still an artists' colony and a centre for folk music there. It also has some fine examples of peasant architecture and of crafts in the **Native Artists and Katona Jozsef Museum**. Outside the town, the **Kiskunság National Park** preserves parts of the **Danube Tisza Floodplain** of Central Hungary in seven disconnected areas, including swamps, alkali plateaus and lakes. The famous **Bugac Puszta** stretches out here as well. **Szeged** is the economic and cultural centre of this region, housing Hungary's finest Greek Orthodox (Serbian) church. **Baja** is a small, picturesque town on the banks of both the **Danube** and **Sugovica** rivers, with many small islands, old churches and an artists' colony. Further east is the **Hortobágy National Park**, the 'Hungarian Puszta', the alkali plains which begin the Asian steppes.

SOUTHERN HUNGARY

Pécs, one of Transdanubia's largest towns, was colonised by the Romans, and has the fifth-oldest university in Europe (1367) and the finest Hungarian examples of Ottoman architecture from Turkish occupancy (1543-1686). Important tourist sites include the **Cathedral**, the **Mosque of Gazi Kasim Pasha**, and the **Archaeological Museum**. The **Danube-Drava National Park** encompases the area between these two rivers and includes **Mohács** on the **Danube**, with the battlefield – now a memorial park – where, in 1526, the Turks gained control of the country, and **Kalocsa**, noted for its folk museums. South of the town is the attractive **Forest of Gemenc** which can be explored by boat or narrow-gauge train.

THE NORTHERN HIGHLANDS

Miskolc, Hungary's second-largest city, is situated near the Slovak border. Primarily industrial, the city nevertheless has several points of interest, including medieval architecture and the warren of manmade caves in the **Avas Hills** near the city centre. Nearby are the beautiful forested **Bükk National Park**, part of the Northern Hill Range, which is also an area of karst topography, including the country's deepest caves at **Lillafüred**; many traces of Neanderthal man have been found here. North of Bükk, the **Aggtelek National Park** is part of the **Gömör Torna Karst** area of cave systems which extends into the Slovak Republic. Caving, fishing and riding are popular, and there are many cultural monuments, masterpieces of folk architecture, ruins recalling the atmosphere of the Middle Ages, old churches, graveyards and locally surviving farming techniques. **Eger**, one of the country's oldest and most colourful cities, has nearly 200 historical monuments, including its 14-sided **Minaret**; just west of the town are the vineyards of the **Szépasszony Valley**, where visitors can sample the famous *Bikavér* (Bull's Blood) wine. Due east is **Tokaj**, the equivalent of Champagne as a wine-producing area. Halfway between Tokaj and the Slovak border is the spectacular Sárospatak Castle, one of Hungary's greatest historical monuments.

Sport & Activities

Wildlife: Hungary has nine national parks and nearly 1000 protected areas. **Hikers** can head for the mountains in the north and northwest of the country. The *Börzsöny*, *Mátra* and *Pilis* ranges not far to the north of Budapest are popular, with the *Mátra* mountains containing Hungary's highest peak, *Kékesetö* (1015m/3329ft). Less strenuous walking is possible around *Lake Balaton* and in the hills in the south of the country. Hungary's many wetlands, rivers and lakes attract large numbers of water birds, and **birdwatching** is popular. A particularly good area for this is *Hortobágy National Park* in the Great Plain in the east of the country, where different types of storks, warblers, eagles and herons can be seen. A guide is required for visits to some parts of the park, and motor vehicles are not permitted. Other wildlife to be found in the country includes rare wild cats and lake bats, while species such as boar, otter and deer are common.
Fishing: The *River Tisza*, by the Kisköre reservoir, is regarded by many as Europe's second-best angling area (after the Danube Delta). Accommodation for anglers is readily available, and guides can be hired if required. Species such as carp, bream, pike, trout and tench are abundant. There are rules and regulations governing fishing seasons and licences; for further information, contact the Hungarian National Tourist Office (see *Contact Addresses* section).
Spa stays: Budapest alone has over 100 thermal springs and around 50 swimming pools and medicinal baths. The culture of bathing has been established since Roman times and, today, a wide variety of therapeutic treatments, both ancient and modern, is on offer. Some of Hungary's bath houses are also of great architectural interest: the *Király Medicinal Baths*, for example, date from the Middle Ages, while the *Rudas Medicinal Baths* feature a fine dome dating from the 16th century. Outside Budapest, notable spa resorts include *Debrecen* in the far east; *Hévíz*, near Lake Balaton; *Harkány* in the south; and *Eger*, northwest of Budapest. Treatment is cheaper than in western Europe or North America, and many foreign insurers will pay part of the cost.
Other: With its long tradition of equestrianism, **horse-riding** is particularly good in Hungary. Long-distance riding in areas such as the *Great Plain* with its wide open spaces is popular, and riders are well catered for. Hungary is the only European country, apart from Ireland, which places no restrictions on riders. There are many riding schools all over the country which can organise all types of excursions. The Great Plain contains several famous stud farms, and horse

Credit: © Hungarian National Tourist Office

shows take place regularly. **Carriage driving** is also popular, and tourists can arrange to have tuition in this art through riding schools. **Cycling** is a good way to see the country. Local tourist offices can assist in the organisation of cycling tours by providing bicycles, transporting luggage and arranging picnics and sightseeing. Although bicycles can be hired in many places, those planning to do longer tours should bring their own.

Social Profile

FOOD & DRINK: A good range of restaurants is available. Table service is common, although there are many inexpensive self-service restaurants. A typical menu offers two or three courses at inexpensive rates. Fine dairy and pastry shops (*cukrászda*) offer light meals. Specialities include *halászlé* (fish soups) with pasta and Goulash *gulyás* soup. Western goulash is called *pörkölt* or *tokány*. Stuffed vegetables, sweet cakes, *gundel palacsinta* (pancake) and pastries are also popular.
Eszpresszó coffee bars and *Drink* bars offer refreshments. *Gerbeaud's* is probably Budapest's most famous coffee-house. *Tokaji* (strong dessert wine) or *Bull's Blood* (strong red wine) are recommended. *Pálinka* or *barack* (apricot brandy) is a typical liqueur. Imported beers and soft drinks are also available. There are no licensing hours, but the legal age for drinking in a bar is 18 years. Minors are allowed to go into bars but will not be served alcohol.
NIGHTLIFE: Budapest has many nightclubs, bars and discos. There are two casinos in Budapest: one next to the Sofitel Hotel (formerly Hyatt Regency), and one near Buda castle. Cinemas in major towns show many English-language films. During the summer months the popular Lake Balaton resort has a lively nightlife. Western Hungary in particular has a lot of very good wine cellars. Visitors would do well to search out traditional folk music and dancing, as the gypsy music which is so common in restaurants is not considered the 'true' folk tradition of the country. The magnificent Budapest Opera House stages regular performances, and seats are (by Western standards) exceedingly cheap.
SHOPPING: Special purchases include embroideries, Herend and Zsolnay porcelain and national dolls. **Shopping hours:** Department stores are open from Mon-Wed and Fri 1000-1800, Thurs 1000-2000, Sat 0900-1300. Food shops are open from Mon-Fri 0700-1900, Sat 0700-1400.
SPECIAL EVENTS: For a detailed list of festivals and special events celebrated, contact the Hungarian National Tourist Office (see *Contact Addresses* section) or see online (website: www.fesztivalvaros.hu/english). The following is a selection of special events occurring in Hungary in 2005:
Jan 28-30 *Mini Festival.* **Mar 18-Apr 3** *25th Anniversary of the Budapest Spring Festival.* **May 29-Jun 8** *Budapest Early Music Festival.* **Jun 17-Jul 17** *Ferencváros Summer Festival.* **Jun 25-26** *Budapest Fair.* **Oct 1-10** *Music of Our Age.* **Oct 14-23** *Autumn Festivals.*
SOCIAL CONVENTIONS: Most Hungarians enjoy modern music and dance, although older people still preserve their traditions and culture, particularly in small villages. Handshaking is customary. Both Christian name and surname should be used. Normal courtesies should be observed. At a meal, toasts are usually made and should be returned. A useful word is *egészségünkre* (pronounced ay-gash-ay-gun-gre), meaning 'your health'. Few people speak English outside hotels, big restaurants and tourist offices. A knowledge of German is very useful. Gifts are acceptable for hosts as a token of thanks, particularly when invited for a meal. Casual wear is acceptable in most places, with the exception of expensive restaurants and bars. Formal attire should be worn for important social functions, but it is not common practice to specify dress on invitations. Smoking is prohibited on public transport in towns and public buildings. Travellers may smoke on long-distance trains.
Photography: Military installations should not be photographed; other restrictions are usually signposted.

Tipping: 10 to 15 per cent is expected for nearly all services in restaurants, bars, clubs, taxis and so on.

Business Profile

ECONOMY: Hungary is poor in natural resources other than bauxite, natural gas and some oil. For this reason, it relies heavily on foreign trade, which accounts for half of its GDP. The country has a fairly well-developed industrial economy concentrated in chemicals, plastics, pharmaceuticals, fertilisers, computers and telecommunications, mining, construction and aluminium (from bauxite deposits). It has also traditionally been an exporter of agricultural produce, particularly fruit and vegetables, maize and wheat, sugar beet, potatoes and livestock.
Before the political upheaval in Eastern Europe during 1989, Hungary had gone the furthest of all the socialist-bloc countries towards decentralising and deregulating the economy. In the 1990s, it eschewed the Polish-style 'big bang' road to capitalism and opted for a more gradual transition. Price controls were removed, and a programme of privatisation was implemented, starting with the retail and property sectors. By 1995, small business privatisation was more or less complete, while sales of the larger state-owned concerns proceeded apace. Current estimates put 85 per cent of the economy under private ownership.
Hungary's economic performance is currently steady: growth is 3 per cent, and inflation nearly 5 per cent. Foreign investment has picked up, largely as a result of the liberalisation of trade through agreements with the EU, EFTA and the Visegrad mechanism, although in recent years there has been a mild backlash against the extent to which foreign companies have penetrated the Hungarian economy. EU membership was a high priority for the Hungarian government and, since signing an Association Agreement in 1998, the country has secured a place in the 'first wave' of new members. Hungary became a full member of the EU, along with nine other countries, on May 1 2004. The country's principal trading partners are Germany, Austria, Italy, the Russian Federation and the Czech Republic. Outside Europe, there are important links with the USA, Japan and Brazil.
BUSINESS: Businesspeople are expected to dress smartly. Local businesspeople are generally friendly and hospitable and it is usual for visitors to be invited to lunch or dinner in a restaurant. Business cards are widely distributed and visitors are well advised to have a supply available in Hungarian. Best months for business visits are September to May. Appointments should always be made. Interpreter and translation services may be booked through travel agents.
Office hours: Mon-Thurs 0800-1630, Fri 0800-1400.
COMMERCIAL INFORMATION: The following organisation can offer advice: Budapest Kereskedelmi és Iparkamara (Budapest Chamber of Commerce and Industry), Krisztina Krt 99, H-1016 Budapest (tel (1) 488 2173; fax: (1) 488 2180; website: www.bkik.hu); *or* ITD Hungary, 46 Eaton Place, London SW1X 8AL, UK (tel: (020) 7235 8767; fax: (020) 7235 4319; e-mail: itdlondon@btconnect.com *or* info@hungarytrade.co.uk; website: www.itd.hu *or* www.hungarytrade.co.uk).
CONFERENCES/CONVENTIONS: The following organisation can offer advice: Hungarian Convention Bureau, Vérmező út. 4, 1012 Budapest (tel: (1) 488 8642; fax: (1) 488 8641; e-mail: hcb@hungarytourism.hu; website: www.hcb.hu).

Climate

There are four seasons, with a very warm summer from June to August. Spring and autumn are mild, while winters are very cold. Rainfall is distributed throughout the year with snowfalls in winter.

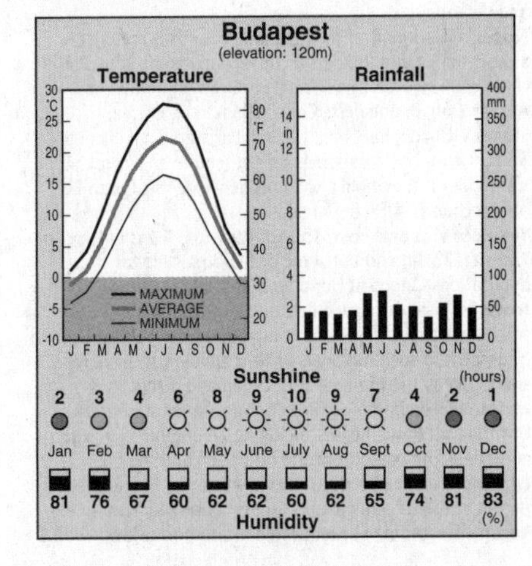

Iceland

LATEST TRAVEL ADVICE CONTACTS

British Foreign and Commonwealth Office
Tel: (0870) 606 0290 Website: www.fco.gov.uk
US Department of State
Website: http://travel.state.gov/travel
Canadian Department of Foreign Affairs and Int'l Trade
Tel: (1 800) 267 8376 Website: www.dfait-maeci.gc.ca

Note: Icelandic consulates no longer issue visas. For visa information, contact the Royal Danish Embassy (see *Denmark* section).

Location: North Atlantic, close to Arctic Circle.

Country dialling code: 354.

Icelandic Tourist Board
Laekjargata 3, 101 Reykjavík, Iceland
Tel: 535 5500. Fax: 535 5501.
E-mail: info@icetourist.is
Website: www.icetourist.is
Embassy of Iceland
2A Hans Street, London SW1X 0JE, UK
Tel: (020) 7259 3999 *or* (0906) 554 0755 (for visa appointments via the Danish embassy).
Fax: (020) 7245 9649.
E-mail: icemb.london@utn.stjr.is
Website: www.iceland.org/uk
Opening hours: Mon-Fri 0930-1600.
There is currently no Icelandic Tourist Board in the UK, but the office in Iceland can deal with all enquiries.
British Embassy
Street address: Laufásvegur 31, 101 Reykjavík, Iceland
Postal address: PO Box 460, 121 Reykjavík, Iceland
Tel: 550 5100. Fax: 550 5105.
E-mail: britemb@centrum.is
Website: www.britishembassy.is
Vice-Consulate in: Akureyri.
Embassy of Iceland
1156 15th Street, NW, Suite 1200, Washington, DC 20005, USA
Tel: (202) 265 6653. Fax: (202) 265 6656.
E-mail: icemb.wash@utn.stjr.is
Website: www.iceland.org/us
Icelandic Tourist Board
c/o The Scandinavian Tourist Board, 655 Third Avenue, New York, NY 10017, USA
Tel: (212) 885 9700. Fax: (212) 885 9710.
E-mail: usa@icetourist.is
Website: www.icelandtouristboard.com *or* www.goscandinavia.com
Embassy of the United States of America
Laufásvegur 21, 101 Reykjavík, Iceland
Tel: 562 9100. Fax: 562 9110.
E-mail: consularreykja@state.gov
Website: www.usa.is

TIMATIC CODES

Health	AMADEUS: **TI-DFT/REK/HE** GALILEO/WORLDSPAN: **TI-DFT/REK/HE** SABRE: **TIDFT/REK/HE**
Visa	AMADEUS: **TI-DFT/REK/VI** GALILEO/WORLDSPAN: **TI-DFT/REK/VI** SABRE: **TIDFT/REK/VI**

To access TIMATIC country information on Health and Visa regulations through the Computer Reservations System (CRS), type in the appropriate command line listed above.

Credit: © Icelandic Tourist Board

Embassy of Iceland
360 Albert Street, Suite 710, Ottawa, Ontario K1R 7X7, Canada
Tel: (613) 482 1944. Fax: (613) 482 1945.
E-mail: icemb.ottawa@utn.stjr.is
Website: www.iceland.org/ca
Consulates also in: Calgary, Edmonton, Halifax, Montréal, Regina, St John's, Toronto, Vancouver and Winnipeg.
Canadian Embassy
Street address: Túngata 14, 101 Reykjavík, Iceland
Postal address: PO Box 1510, 121 Reykjavík, Iceland
Tel: 575 6500. Fax: 575 6501.
E-mail: rkjvk@international.gc.ca
Website: www.canada.is

General Information

AREA: 103,000 sq km (39,769 sq miles).
POPULATION: 288,471 (2002).
POPULATION DENSITY: 2.8 per sq km.
CAPITAL: Reykjavík. **Population:** 112,554 (2002).
GEOGRAPHY: Iceland is a large island in the North Atlantic close to the Arctic Circle and includes islands to the north and south. The landscape is wild, rugged and colourful, with black lava, red sulphur, hot blue geysers, grey and white rivers with waterfalls and green valleys, its coastline richly indented with bays and fjords. The whole of the central highland plateau of the island is a beautiful but barren and uninhabitable moonscape - so much so that the first American astronauts were sent there for pre-mission training. Five-sixths of Iceland is uninhabited, the population being concentrated on the coast, in the valleys and in the plains of the southwest and southeast of the country. More than half the population live in or around Reykjavík, the capital. Iceland is one of the most volcanically active countries in the world. Hekla, in the south of Iceland, is the most famous and magnificent volcano of them all. It has erupted no fewer than 16 times since Iceland was settled, and throughout the Middle Ages was considered by European clergymen as one of the gateways to Hell itself. Another volcano, Snæfellsnes, fired Jules Verne's imagination to use its crater as the point of entry for his epic tale, *Journey to the Centre of the Earth*. Iceland's highest and most extensive glacier is Vatnajökull; at 8500 sq km (3280 sq miles), it is the largest in Europe, although it is now reported to be melting.
GOVERNMENT: Republic. Gained full independence from Denmark in 1944. **Head of State:** President Ólafur Ragnar Grímsson since 1996. **Head of Government:** Prime Minister Halldór Ásgrímsson since 2004. Iceland's Parliament (the Althing) is the oldest in the world.
LANGUAGE: The official language is Icelandic, which has remained virtually unchanged since the Vikings settled Iceland in the ninth and 10th centuries. The Icelandic language refuses to accept foreign words, preferring instead to coin new words from ancient Viking roots. The word for computer thus becomes *tölva*, a hybrid made up of the old words for 'number' and 'prophetess'. English (which is taught in schools) and Danish are widely spoken.
RELIGION: Lutheran, with a Catholic minority.
TIME: GMT.
ELECTRICITY: 220 volts AC, 50Hz. Plug fittings are normally two-pin with round section pins 4mm in diameter with centres 2cm apart. Lamp fittings are screw-type. Power is generated by a mix of geothermal and hydroelectric stations.
COMMUNICATIONS: Telephone: Full IDD service is available. Country code: 354. Outgoing international code: 00. **Mobile telephone:** GSM 900 and 1800 networks exist, serving Reykjavík and coastal towns. Network operators include *Iceland Telecom* (website: www.simi.is), *Og Vodaphone* (website: www.ogvodafone.is) and *Viking Wireless*. **Fax:** Public facilities are available at the main telephone headquarters in Austurvoll Square and in most hotels and offices. **Internet:** Internet cafes provide public access to e-mail and Internet services. ISPs include *Hringidan/Vortex Inc* (website: www.vortex.is) and *Vodafone* (website: www.itn.is). **Telegram:** There is a 24-hour telegram service from the Telegraph Office in Reykjavík. **Post:** There is an efficient airmail service to Europe. Post office hours: Mon-Fri 0830-1630. The post office at Austurstræti is also open Sat 1000-1400 from June to September. **Press:** The most popular newspapers are *DV*, *Frettabladid* and *Morgunblaoio*. International English-language newspapers and magazines are available.
Radio: BBC World Service (website: www.bbc.co.uk/worldservice) and Voice of America (website: www.voa.gov) can be received. From time to time the frequencies change and the most up-to-date can be found online.

Passport/Visa

	Passport Required?	Visa Required?	Return Ticket Required?
Full British	Yes	No	No
Australian	Yes	No	Yes
Canadian	Yes	No	Yes
USA	Yes	No	Yes
Other EU	Yes	No	No
Japanese	Yes	No	Yes

Note: Regulations and requirements may be subject to change at short notice, and you are advised to contact the appropriate diplomatic or consular authority before finalising travel arrangements. Details of these may be found at the head of this country's entry. Any numbers in the chart refer to the footnotes below.

Note: Iceland is a signatory to the 1995 **Schengen Agreement**. For further details about passport/visa regulations within the Schengen area, see the introductory section *How to Use this Guide*.
PASSPORTS: Passport valid for at least three months after intended date of departure required by all. Certain nationals may be permitted to enter Iceland with a travel document valid for at least six months after intended date of departure; please consult the nearest Danish embassy for further details.
VISAS: Required by all except the following for stays of up to three months:
(a) nationals of countries referred to in the chart above;
(b) nationals of Andorra, Argentina, Bolivia, Brazil, British Overseas Territories, Bulgaria, Chile, Costa Rica, Croatia, El Salvador, Guatemala, Honduras, Israel, Korea (Rep), Liechtenstein, Malaysia, Mexico, Monaco, New Zealand, Nicaragua, Norway, Panama, Paraguay, Romania, San Marino, Singapore, Switzerland, Uruguay, Vatican City and Venezuela.
Note: (a) Nationals of the following countries require an airport transit visa (holders of travel documents issued by these countries are also subject to such requirements): Afghanistan, Bangladesh, Congo (Dem Rep), Eritrea, Ethiopia, Ghana, Iran, Iraq, Nigeria, Pakistan, Somalia and Sri Lanka. (b) These nationals do not require an airport transit visa if they hold a valid residence permit for an EU or EEA country, USA or Canada.
Types of visa and cost: *Tourist*, *Business*, *Transit*, *Airport Transit*: £23. An additional fee of £11 is payable for applications lodged at Honorary Consulates.
Note: (a) Visas are issued free of charge to spouses of EU or EEA nationals, or persons related in direct line of ascent or descent to such nationals or their spouses, if they are supported by the national in question and if they have legal residence in the UK. Relevant documentation must be produced in such cases, including an original marriage certificate, the passport of the EU citizen and the EU citizen's residence permit and evidence of an EEA residence permit in the UK, plus proof of joint household. Further documentation may be requested in addition to this.
Validity: Up to three months. For extensions, apply to the Immigration authority in Iceland.
Application to: Royal Danish Embassy; see *Denmark* section. Applications cannot be made by post. Appointments must be made in advance by calling (09065) 540 7555 (automated; 24-hour). Travellers visiting just one Schengen country should apply to the Consulate of that country; travellers visiting more than one Schengen country should apply to the Consulate of the country chosen as the main destination *or* the country they will enter first (if they have no main destination).
Application requirements: (a) Completed visa application form. (b) One colour passport-size photo on a light background. (c) Valid passport or travel document, if applicable, with a blank page to affix the visa. (d) Fee, payable by cash or cheque (non-refundable). (e) Proof of purpose of visit and accommodation such as a letter of invitation from relatives or a hotel reservation. (f) Evidence of sufficient funds to cover the duration of stay, such as bank statements travellers cheques or credit card statements. (g) A pre-paid self-addressed envelope for registered post, if you would like your visa to be sent to your home address. (h) Evidence of occupation/student status, eg an original letter from an employer or solicitor; if unemployed, a social benefit booklet; if a student, an original letter from the appropriate school/university.
(i) Valid health insurance. *Business*: (a)-(i) and, (j) Letter of invitation from a business contact in Iceland stating nature and duration of stay, type of visa and accommodation.
Working days required: Varies according to nationality; may take several weeks.
Temporary residence: Enquire at Embassy of the Republic of Iceland.

Money

Currency: Icelandic Krona (Ikr) = 100 aurar. Notes are in denominations of Ikr5000, 2000, 1000 and 500. Coins are in denominations of IKr100, 50, 10, 5 and 1.
Currency exchange: Foreign currencies can be exchanged in all major banks, some of which (such as the Landesbanki at Keflavik airport) are open 24 hours. Most hotels also provide their guests with exchange services. Exchange services are also available from The Change Group, which has offices at Keflavik airport, the Tourist Information Centre and in central Reykjavík. ATMs are also available throughout the country, especially Reykjavík.
Credit & debit cards: American Express, Diners Club, Europay, MasterCard and Visa are widely accepted. Check with your credit or debit card company for details of merchant acceptability and other services which may be available.
Travellers cheques: Widely used. To avoid additional exchange rate charges, travellers are advised to take travellers cheques in US Dollars.
Currency restrictions: The import and export of local currency is limited to Ikr8000; the import of foreign currency is unlimited and the export of foreign currency is limited to the amount imported.
Exchange rate indicators: The following figures are included as a guide to the movements of the Krona against Sterling and the US Dollar:

Date	Feb '04	May '04	Aug '04	Nov '04
£1.00=	126.52	132.02	129.82	123.74
$1.00=	69.50	73.92	70.46	65.35

Banking hours: Mon-Fri 0915-1600.

Duty Free

The following goods may be imported into Iceland by passengers aged 18 years and over (tobacco products) or aged 20 and over (alcoholic beverages) without incurring customs duty:
200 cigarettes or 250g of tobacco products; 1l of spirits or 1l of wine or 12 bottles of beer (or a combination of two of these quantities).
Note: All fishing equipment, including waders and rubber boots, must be disinfected and a certificate of disinfection issued by an official veterinary authority should be presented on arrival.
Prohibited items: Drugs, firearms, unpasteurised milk and dairy products, poultry, eggs and uncooked meats.

Public Holidays

2005: Jan 1 New Year's Day. **Mar 24** Maundy Thursday. **Mar 25** Good Friday. **Mar 28** Easter Monday. **Apr 21** First Day of Summer. **May 1** Labour Day. **May 5** Ascension. **May 16** Whit Monday. **Jun 17** National Day. **Aug 1** Commerce Day. **Dec 24-26** Christmas. **Dec 31** New Year's Eve (from noon).
2006: Jan 1 New Year's Day. **Apr 13** Maundy Thursday. **Apr 14** Good Friday. **Apr 17** Easter Monday. **Apr 20**

Credit: © Icelandic Tourist Board

First Day of Summer. **May 1** Labour Day. **May 25** Ascension. **Jun 5** Whit Monday. **Jun 17** National Day. **Aug 7** Commerce Day. **Dec 24-26** Christmas. **Dec 31** New Year's Eve (from noon).

Health

	Special Precautions?	Certificate Required?
Yellow Fever	No	No
Cholera	No	No
Typhoid & Polio	No	N/A
Malaria	No	N/A

Note: *Regulations and requirements may be subject to change at short notice, and you are advised to contact your doctor well in advance of your intended date of departure. Any numbers in the chart refer to the footnotes below.*

Other risks: Care should be taken as *hypothermia* is a real risk.
Health care: All hospitals have excellent standards of medical service. There is a reciprocal health agreement with the UK. On presentation of a UK passport or NHS card, all in-patient treatment at hospitals and emergency dental treatment for children aged six to 15 is free. Citizens of EU countries, Liechtenstein and Norway get free medical treatment in hospital on presentation of an E-111 form. For others, medical and dental treatment, prescribed medicines and travel by ambulance must be paid for. If wrongly charged, one can apply for a refund by presenting any receipts to the State Social Security Institute, Laugavegur 114, 150 Reykjavík (tel: 560 4400). There are medical centres and hospitals in all major towns and cities. The emergency number for medical assistance is 112 (open 24 hours).

Travel - International

AIR: The national airline, *Icelandair (FI)* (website: www.icelandair.net), operates direct flights all-year-round to Reykjavík (Keflavík) from Amsterdam, Baltimore, Boston, Copenhagen, Frankfurt, Glasgow, Halifax, London, Minneapolis, Orlando, Oslo, Paris, Stockholm and Washington, plus other destinations in the summertime only. Airlines include *Air Greenland* (website: www.airgreenland.gl) and *Iceland Express* (website: www.icelandexpress.com). Other, predominantly Scandinavian, carriers also operate services. Some airlines, such as *Condor* and *Corsair*, operate flights during the summertime. Flights are operated to the Faroe Islands and Greenland during the summer months.
Approximate flight times: From Iceland to *London* is three hours; to *Paris* is three hours and 25 minutes; to *Frankfurt* is three hours and 45 minutes and to *New York* is five hours and 30 minutes.
International airports: *Reykjavík (Keflavík) (REK/KEF)* is 51km (32 miles) southwest of Reykjavík (travel time - 45 minutes). Airport facilities include bus services, departing after the arrival of each flight; taxi services; a duty free shop; banking and exchange facilities, open on arrival of all scheduled services; restaurants and bars and car hire (*Avis*, *Europcar* and *Hertz*).
Departure tax: None.
SEA: There is no longer a direct service between the UK and Iceland. Sea passengers must travel from Aberdeen, with a three-day stopover in the Faroe Islands on the return journey. This is a costly and aggravating route, not recommended by travel agents. A few ferry companies also operate services to Iceland from Denmark, Germany and Norway. Although most of these are mainly cargo ships, they have comfortable and modern facilities for passengers. *Smyril Line*, the Faroe Island's ferry service, runs a weekly passenger and car ferry service between the Shetland Islands, Denmark, Norway and Seyoisfjördur in Iceland during the summer months. Many cruises also stop at Iceland. Operators include *Crystal*, *Cunard*, *Holland America*, *Orient Cruises*, *Princess*, *Royal Caribbean International*, *Seabourn* and *Silversea*.

Travel - Internal

AIR: *Air Iceland* (formed through merging with *Icelandair Domestic* and *Norlandair*) runs domestic services throughout the island to 10 major destinations which link up with regional carriers in the west, north and east of the country. For further details, contact the local office or check online (website: www.airiceland.is).
Departure tax: None.
SEA: Ferry services serve all coastal ports in summer, although weather curtails timetables in winter. There is a tunnel between Reykjavík and Akranes.
RAIL: There is no railway system in Iceland.
ROAD: Roads serve all settlements. The 12,000km (7500 miles) of roads are mostly gravel rather than tarred. The Ring Road is approximately 1430km (894 miles) long, of which 80 per cent is tarred. Traffic drives on the right. It is obligatory to use headlights at all times of the day and night and to wear safety belts, both in the front and back seats. The Icelandic Tourist Board publishes a useful brochure, *The Art of Driving on Icelandic Roads*.
Bus: Services are efficient and cheap, connecting all parts of the island during the summer. In winter, buses operate to a limited number of destinations. Holiday tickets (*Omnibus Passport*) and *Air/Bus Rovers* are valid for unlimited travel by scheduled bus services; also *Full-Circle Passports* are available, valid for circular trips around Iceland (without any time limit). **Taxi:** Available from all hotels and airports.
Car hire: Car rental services are available from Reykjavík, Akureyri and many other towns. **Documentation:** Drivers must be over 20 years of age. An International Driving Permit is recommended, although it is not legally required. A temporary driving licence is available from local authorities on presentation of a valid UK driving licence.
Travel Times: The following chart gives approximate travel times (in hours and minutes) from **Reykjavík** to other major cities/towns in Iceland.

	Air	Road	
Sealsafjördur	0.50	9.00	-
Saudakrokur	0.45	3.30	-
Akureyri	0.55	5.00	-
Husavik	1.00	6.00	-
Höfn	0.65	9.30	-
Westmann Is.	0.30*	1.00	6.00
Egilsstadir	0.70	14.00	-

Note: *To Thorlakshofn, then sea crossing.

Accommodation

HOTELS: The most deluxe hotels are in the capital Reykjavík and some of them also have hairdressers, shops and beauty parlours. Hotel or hostel accommodation is available in most areas. **Grading:** All accommodation is classified from **5 star** (luxurious) to **1 star** (basic) and is managed by the Icelandic Tourist Board. Visitors should look for the blue and red sign near the entrance to a hotel for the current grading. For a complete list of classified accommodation, contact the Icelandic Tourist Board (see *Contact Addresses* section).
PENSIONS & GUEST HOUSES: These are available in the larger towns. Rooms are also available in private houses with breakfast included in the cost.
FARMHOUSE HOLIDAYS: Fairly widely available; contact the Icelandic Tourist Board for details. Full board (three meals daily) is included. Reductions are available for children. Further information is available from Icelandic Farm Holidays, Sidumúli 13, 15-08 Reykjavík (tel: 570 2700; fax: 570 2799; e-mail: ifh@farmholidays.is; website: www.farmholidays.is).
CAMPING/CARAVANNING: There are approximately 125 registered camping sites. Due to unpredictable weather conditions, camping grounds are normally open between June and late August or mid-September. The best-equipped camping grounds are to be found in Akureyri, Eglisstadir, Husafell, Isafjördur, Jokulsargljufur, Laugarvatn, Myvatn, Reykjavík, Skaftafell, Thingvellir and Varmahlid. In some places, camping is restricted to certain specially marked areas. Prices are approximately US$5-7 and it is also possible to camp in National Parks that are supervised by the Convention Council. Campers, however, must request permission from the local farmer to camp on any fenced and/or cultivated land. For further information, contact the Icelandic Tourist Board (see *Contact Addresses* section).
YOUTH HOSTELS: A total of 24 youth and family hostels are open, including Fossholl, Hrauneyjar, Leirubakki, Njardvik, Reykholt, Reykjavík, Stafafell and Stykkisholmur. Many country hostels provide overnight accommodation for travellers bringing their own sleeping bags or bedrolls for a fee. In uninhabited areas there are a number of huts where travellers can stay overnight. They must observe regulations posted in the huts and bring their own sleeping bags and food. For more information, contact the Icelandic Youth Hostel Association, Sundlaugavegi 34, 105 Reykjavík (tel: 553 8110; fax: 588 9201; e-mail: info@hostel.is; website: www.hostel.is). The Youth Hostel Association also offers a travel service to help with bookings, tours and travel arrangements.

Resorts & Excursions

Only the coastal regions of Iceland are inhabited. Probably the best way to enjoy the tourist attractions is to take one of the coach tours arranged all over the island and use the coastal towns as a base. The main fjord areas are in the far northwest and southeast, while along the southern coastline are sandy beaches, farmlands, waterfalls and glaciers. The central region consists of spectacular highland plateaux, volcanoes, glaciers and mountains. Waterfalls abound in Iceland and, with the many glacial streams and rivers in the country, are among the largest in Europe. **Gullfoss** - the 'Golden Waterfall' - near **Geysir**, is one of the prime tourist destinations.

REYKJAVÍK: Reykjavík is the world's most northerly capital (although Nuuk in Greenland runs a close second). The city was named after a geothermal stream and actually means 'Smoky Bay'. It is set on a broad bay, surrounded by mountains, and is in an area of geothermal hot springs providing it with a natural central heating system and pollution-free environment. The city has a wonderful mix of natural beauty and lively sophistication. There are plenty of parks and wild outdoor areas for hiking, walking and exploring, but enough nightlife, shopping and museums to keep the chic city-dweller happy. Reykjavík is a busy city of around 100,000 inhabitants, with a combination of old-fashioned wooden architecture and modern buildings. There are many nightclubs, cafes, art galleries and museums, as well as numerous bookshops selling books in English, German and Icelandic. Icelanders are said to be among the most prolific readers and writers in the world, and literature plays an important part in Icelandic culture and history. The *Icelandic Sagas*, the oldest of which was written in AD 930 as a chronicle of Iceland's history, are still very much alive in Iceland today. The language used over 1000 years ago in the sagas remains virtually unchanged.
THE SOUTH: 50km outside Reykjavík, the **Blue Lagoon** is a unique natural pool of mineral-rich geothermal water located in the middle of a lava field in the Icelandic wilderness. Known for its special properties and beneficial effect on the skin, the warm waters of the lagoon - approximately 35°C (90°F) all year round - are one of Iceland's most popular tourist attractions. Another natural spring is **Krysuvik**. Flights can be booked to visit the **Westmann Islands** (**Vestmannæyjar**) off the south coast, and **Heimæy**. This is a great place for birdwatchers (see *Sport & Activities* section). There are also trips to the hot springs and geysers close to the capital. Also to be found in the south of Iceland is **Thingvellir National Park**, **Gullfoss** (Golden Falls) and **Geysir**, with its geothermal fields and views of the active volcano **Mount Hekla**. There are also charming villages in the south, such as **Stokkseyri** and **Eyrarbakki**, where visitors can see beautifully preserved old houses and the village of **Vik**, which is a base for cruises through **Dyrholæy** cliff. A number of companies operate daily excursions from Reykjavík throughout the southwestern part of Iceland as well as city sightseeing tours and special itineraries. For further details, contact the Icelandic Tourist Board (see *Contact Addresses* section).
THE WESTERN FJORDS: There are coach trips from Reykjavík to visit the small fishing villages and towns along the fjords in the northwest: **Holmavik**, **Isafjördur**, **Kroksfardarnes**, **Korksfjardarnes** and **Orlygshofn**. This area of Iceland is full of lava formations and geothermal activity. There is some fine woodland, lakes and rivers, as well as breathtaking chasms and waterfalls, overlooked by glaciers. Iceland's highest waterfall, **Glymir**, is found here. A replica Viking Age farmstead is located in **Eiriksstadir** - birthplace of Leif the Lucky, who discovered America in AD 1000. **Isafjördur** is the region's main town and it has plenty of social and cultural facilities, as well as being a starting

point for tours of the region. Travelling around this area, the road takes you over mountain passes between each new fjord, stopping at Iceland's only whaling station, the **Museum of Farm Implements and Fishing Equipment** between Orlygshofn and Isafjördur and the **Dynjandi Waterfall**. Accommodation on these trips is in community centres and schools for those with sleeping bags.

THE CENTRAL HIGHLANDS: A number of Icelandic tour companies operate 'safaris' in specially constructed overland buses into the mountainous interior. These are camping tours, and tents are provided. Sleeping bags can be bought or hired. Visitors are advised to take warm clothing, hiking shoes, rubber boots and swimsuits for bathing in the warm pools. The tours go through lava beds, sandy deserts and barren wilderness, passing glacial lakes with floating icebergs, glaciers, vast icefields, mountain ranges, crevasses and extinct volcanoes, and the **Skaftafell National Park**.

AKUREYRI AND THE NORTH: Akureyri is the country's second most important town and is the commercial centre of a mainly agricultural region. There are museums of folklore and natural history in the town itself and coach tours to visit **Lake Myvatn**, an important bird sanctuary with many rare species, surrounded by lava formations, volcanoes and craters. It has been designated as Iceland's winter sports centre (see *Sport & Activities* section). *Nordair* offers a midnight sun trip flight to **Grimsey**, an offshore island which is within the Arctic Circle. Other places within easy reach of Akureyri include **Dimmuborgir**, the **Dettifoss** and **Godafoss** waterfalls and the **Myvatn** district, where there are hot pools for bathing. The temperature of some of these pools is now too high for bathing, but others are still usable. On **Skjalfandi Bay** lies the town of **Husavik**, which is becoming Europe's main whale watching centre. The district of **Skagafjordur** is an area of outstanding natural beauty, with glacial rivers, highlands, lush green valleys and mountains. It is, not surprisingly, a very popular area for river rafting (see *Sport & Activities* section). The main town in this region is **Sauoarkrokur**.

HÖFN AND THE SOUTHEAST: This is an area of increasing tourist development. From **Höfn**, a fishing village on the southeast coast, sightseeing trips leave for **Jokullon**, a river lake at the mouth of the largest glacier in Europe, **Vatnajökull**. Höfn is the main starting point for trips to the nearby glacier and visitors can indulge in ice-climbing, skiing, riding snow scooters and hiking. Höfn's multimedia **Glacier Centre** gives information about the geology, formation, history and potential of glaciers. Also on the edge of this region is the scenically stunning **Skaftafell National Park** (see *Central Highlands* section above). It is made up of woodlands and black mountains and a sheer white glacier lying in the shadow of **Hvannadalshnukur**, the country's highest peak.

Sport & Activities

Hiking: Few places in Iceland have marked walking paths. The Iceland Touring Association, Ferdafelag Islands, Morkin 6, 108 Reykjavik (tel: 568 2533; fax: 568 2535; e-mail: fi@fi.is) operates walking tours all year round. During winter, these are mostly day or weekend tours, but longer tours are organised during summer.

Glacier tours: A number of travel agencies and tour operators can organise trips to Iceland's glaciers, which cover 11 per cent of the country. Transport is by 4-wheel-drive vehicles, snow cats or – the most popular option – snowmobiles (also called *skidoos*). The best time for skidooing is between January and March when the snow is fresh and plentiful. The most visited glaciers are *Drangajökull*, *Gleràdalsjökull*, *Snæfellsjökull* and *Vindheimajökull*.

A list of tour operators can be obtained from the Icelandic Tourist Board (see *Contact Addresses* section).

Skiing: This is a year-round activity and Iceland's most popular winter sport. Ski resorts offering both downhill skiing and cross-country skiing can be found throughout the country. Several Alpine-style resorts are located near *Akureyri* (Hlítharfjall), *Ísafjördur* and *Reykjavík* (Bláfjöll). These resorts are equipped with standard lifts and facilities. Many good ski slopes are just 30 minutes' drive from Reykjavík. The main skiing season is normally from January until May or June. Summer skiing is possible on the glaciers. *Myrdalsjökull* has a ski lift which is open throughout summer.

Swimming: This is very popular in Iceland since there are many natural and manmade pools such as the *Blue Lagoon* near Reykjavík, heated by geothermal springs (see also *Resorts & Excursions* section). Most towns and cities have outdoor and indoor pools filled with water from natural hot springs (water temperature in the pools averages around 29°C/85°F). Many places also have saunas, jacuzzis and hot pots with water temperatures of up to 44°C/112°F.

Fishing: Iceland is famous for its trout and, particularly, salmon fishing, for which it is reputed to be among the best locations in the world. The main salmon fishing season is from around 20 June to mid-September. Permits must be reserved well in advance from the National Angling Association, Bolholt Six, IS-105 Reykjavík (website: www.angling.is). The trout fishing season varies from one river to the next, but is generally from April/May until late September/October. Permits can be obtained at short notice, often the same day. Fishing boats and gear can be rented in towns around the coast.

Golf: There are approximately 55 courses in Iceland, all of which are open to visitors. During the Midnight Sun period (end of May to the beginning of August), it is possible to play golf at night. The *Akureyri Golf Club* in the north hosts the yearly *Arctic Open*, an international competition at the end of June which climaxes with a tee-off at midnight, continuing until the early morning hours. For further information, contact the Icelandic Tourist Board.

Wildlife: One of Iceland's most popular special interest activities is **birdwatching**. Many tours, often involving a boat trip, are available. The *Westmann Islands* are particularly good for spotting seabirds as well as being home to the world's largest puffin population. *Lake Myvatn* in northern Iceland is apparently the most fertile spot on the globe at that latitude and is a favourite breeding ground for many species of birdlife, particularly waterfowl. Southern Iceland is known for its great skua colony living on the sands. Nearly as popular as birdwatching is **whale watching** and tours to the best spots around the coast are widely available. It is also possible to see **dolphins**. The Icelandic Tourist Board can provide further details.

Icelandic horse trekking: When the Vikings created Iceland's (and the world's) first Parliament in 930, one of their acts was to prohibit further import of horses. More than 10 centuries later, the Icelandic horse breed remains pure. This small but sturdy and sure-footed horse is reputed for its friendliness and willingness to carry riders over even the roughest terrain. Horses are available for hire near most towns, with experienced guides if required. Longer expeditions, including camping, can be arranged by tour operators.

Running: The *Reykjavík Marathon* takes places every year in August and attracts thousands of runners. Participants are offered a choice of a full or half marathon ('fun run'). Pollution levels in Reykjavík are very low.

Geothermal attractions: Icleand is still relatively young in geothermal terms and a popular activity is to visit the naturally occurring springs for bathing.
River rafting: Because of the wide variety of rivers and beautiful scenery to be found in Iceland, river rafting is a very popular activity.

Social Profile

FOOD & DRINK: Icelandic food in general is based on fish and lamb, as well as owing much to Scandinavian and European influences. The salmon of Iceland is a great delicacy, served in many forms, one of the most popular being *gravlax*, a form of marinating. Fishing is Iceland's most important export, accounting for some 80 per cent of the country's Gross National Product. There is also a heavy emphasis on vegetables grown in greenhouses heated by the natural steam from geysers. Specialities include *hangikjot* (smoked lamb), *harofiskur* (dried fish), *skyr* (curds) and *Icelandic sild* (herring marinated in various flavours). There have been some welcome additions to the selection of eating places in Reykjavik and there is now a small but attractive choice of restaurants to cater for all pockets with new tourist menus.
Bars have table and/or counter service, and will serve coffee as well as alcohol. Beer was prohibited in Iceland for 75 years and was finally legalised in March 1989. Alcohol is generally expensive (a large beer costs approximately US$8, a small one US$4.70). In coffee shops you pay for the first cup then help yourself to subsequent cups. There is a wide selection of European spirits and wines. *Brennivin* (a potent variation of aquavit made from potatoes) is a local drink.
NIGHTLIFE: There are plenty of nightclubs, bars, cafes and cinemas in Iceland, most of them in the capital. Icelandic nightlife is particularly vibrant from June to August when there is nearly 24 hours of perpetual daylight (Icelanders call this period the 'White Nights'). Leading theatres are the National Theatre and the Reykjavík City Theatre, closed in summer, but during the tourist season there is an attractive light entertainment show in English called 'Light Nights' with traditional Icelandic stories and folk songs. The *Iceland Symphony Orchestra* gives concerts every two weeks at the University Theatre during the season (September to June). Iceland has a vibrant music scene which has produced, amongst others, the internationally acclaimed artist Björk. This has, in turn, attracted a number of British and American pop stars to Iceland, such as Damon Albarn from the British band Blur, who opened his own cafe, the *Kaffibarinn*, in Reykjavík.
SHOPPING: Fluffy, earth-coloured *Lopi* wool blankets and coats, jackets, hats and handknits are synonymous with Iceland. Several local potters handthrow earthenware containers in natural colours. Crushed lava is a common addition to highly glazed ceramic pieces, which are popular as souvenirs. The duty free shop at Keflavik Airport sells all of these products, as does the Icelandic Tourist Bureau souvenir shop in Reyjkavík. **Shopping hours:** Mon-Fri 1000-1800, Sat 1000-1400, with variations from shop to shop. Shopping malls are open Mon-Thurs 1000-1830, Fri 1000-1900, Sat 1000-1600 and Sun 1300-1600.
SPECIAL EVENTS: For a full list, contact the Icelandic Tourist Board (see *Contact Addresses* section). The following is a selection of special events occurring in Iceland in 2005:
Jan-Mar *Thorrablot Feast* (pagan midwinter feast), Reykjavík. **Jan 21-Feb 19** *Thorri* (Viking celebrations), cnationwide. **Mar 1** *Beer Day* (celebration of the end of beer probation in 1989), nationwide. **Apr 20** *First Day of Summer* (ancient holiday), nationwide. **May** *Reykjavík Arts Festival*. **Jun** *International Viking Festival*, Hafnarfjördur; *Summer Solstice*; *Arctic Open International Golf Tournament*, Akureyri; **Jun 17** *National Independence Day* (commemoration of birth of Jón Sigurdsson), nationwide. **Aug** *Reykjavík Marathon*; *Verslunnarmannahelgi*, Labour Day weekend (big festivals take place mainly in the Westmann Islands but also around the country); *Gay Pride Festival*, Reykjavík. **Sep** *Annual Sheep & Horse Round-up*. **Oct** *Reykjavík Jazz Festival*; *Iceland Airwaves Festival*, Reykjavík. **Dec-Jan 2006** *Christmas Traditions in Iceland*, various locations.
SOCIAL CONVENTIONS: Visitors will find Iceland is a classless society with a strong literary tradition. Handshaking is the normal form of greeting. An Icelander is called by his first name because his surname is made up of his father's Christian name plus 'son' or 'daughter' (eg John, the son of Magnus, would be called John Magnusson, while John's sister, Mary, would be known as Mary Magnusdóttir). People are addressed as *Fru* (Mrs) and *Herra* (Mr). Visitors will often be invited to homes especially if on business and normal courtesies should be observed. Icelanders pay careful attention to their appearance and, as for most Western countries, casual wear is widely acceptable although unsuitable for smart and social functions.
Tipping: Service charges are included in most bills and extra tips are not expected.

Business Profile

ECONOMY: Iceland is short of indigenous raw materials and thus relies heavily on foreign trade to keep its relatively successful economy ticking over. Exports of goods and services account for more than one-third of GNP. The largest proportion of these derives from fisheries and related products such as fishmeal and oil. The economy is thus particularly susceptible to fluctuating world prices in this commodity and maintains a broad fisheries exclusion zone (320km/200 miles) to protect its earnings. As several European governments (including the British) have discovered to their cost, the Icelanders are fiercely determined and quite capable of defending their perceived territorial rights. Other sources of revenue come from the sale of minerals such as aluminium, ferro-silicon, cement and nitrates used in fertilisers, although these have lately been affected by low demand. Light industry produces knitwear, blankets, textiles and paint. There is a burgeoning advanced technology sector involved in software and biotechnology, and an embryonic financial services industry. Accession to the European Economic Area (an amalgam of the EU and the European Free Trade Association; Iceland belongs to the latter) effected a wholesale liberalisation of trade among the member states and caused some disruption to the Icelandic economy. This highlighted the fact that Iceland's economy is too dependent on its fishing industry and needs to diversify in areas that will allow it to compete in international markets. Iceland's principal import suppliers are, in order of importance, Norway, Germany and the UK. The UK, the USA and Germany are the country's main trading partners.
BUSINESS: Businesspeople are expected to dress smartly. Local businesspeople are conservative but very friendly and most speak English. Previous appointments are not generally necessary, but visits between May and September should be planned in advance as many local businesspeople travel abroad at this time. The telephone directory is listed by Christian name. **Office hours:** Mon-Fri 0800-1600 (summer) and 0900-1700 (winter). Most offices are closed Saturday. Some firms close down completely for an annual three-week holiday, usually in July.
COMMERCIAL INFORMATION: The following organisation can offer advice: Iceland Chamber of Commerce, Kringlan 7, 103 Reykjavík (tel: 510 7100; fax: 568 6564; e-mail: info@chamber.is; website: www.chamber.is).
CONFERENCES/CONVENTIONS: There are several large hotels in Reykjavík equipped for conferences and business meetings, while smaller conferences may be held at venues outside the capital. For further information, contact the Iceland Convention & Incentive Bureau, Laekjargata 3, 101 Reykjavik (tel: 562 6070; fax: 562 6073; e-mail: info@icelandconvention.com; website: www.icelandconvention.com).

Climate

Iceland's climate is tempered by the Gulf Stream. Summers are mild and winters rather cold. The colourful Aurora Borealis (Northern Lights) appear from the end of August. From the end of May to the beginning of August, there are nearly 24 hours of perpetual daylight in Reykjavík, while in the northern part of the country, the sun barely sets at all. Winds can be strong and gusty at times and there is the occasional dust storm in the interior. Snow is not as common as the name of the country would seem to suggest and, in any case, does not lie for long in Reykjavík; it is only in northern Iceland that skiing conditions are reasonably certain. However, the weather is very changeable at all times of the year and, in Reykjavík, there may be rain, sunshine, drizzle and snow in the same day. The air is clean and free of pollution.
Required clothing: Lightweights in warmer months, with extra woollens for walking and the cooler evenings. Medium- to heavyweights are advised in winter. Waterproofing is recommended throughout the year.

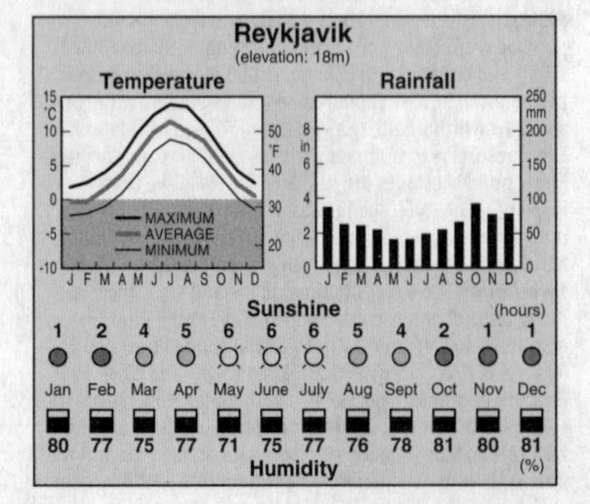

India

LATEST TRAVEL ADVICE CONTACTS

British Foreign and Commonwealth Office
Tel: (0870) 606 0290 Website: www.fco.gov.uk
US Department of State
Website: http://travel.state.gov/travel
Canadian Department of Foreign Affairs and Int'l Trade
Tel: (1 800) 267 8376 Website: www.dfait-maeci.gc.ca

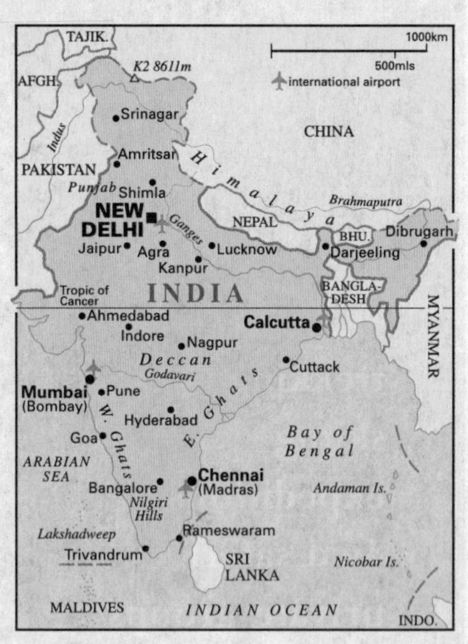

Location: South Asia.

Country dialling code: 91.

Incredible India
Ministry of Tourism, Transport Bhavan, Parliament Street, New Delhi 110 001, India
Tel: (11) 2371 5084. Fax: (11) 2371 0518.
E-mail: contactus@incredibleindia.org
Website: www.TourismOfIndia.com
India Tourism Development Corporation Ltd (ITDC)
SCOPE Complex, Core 8, 6th Floor, 7 Lodhi Road, New Delhi 110 003, India
Tel: (11) 2436 0303. Fax: (11) 2436 0233.
Website: www.theashokgroup.com
Office of the High Commissioner for India
India House, Aldwych, London WC2B 4NA, UK
Tel: (020) 7836 8484. Fax: (020) 7836 4331.
E-mail: fc.office@hcilondon.net
Website: www.hcilondon.net
Opening hours: Mon-Fri 0830-1200 (visa enquiries); 0915-1730 (visa applications and collections; telephone enquiries).
Consulate General of India
20 Augusta Street, Jewellery Quarter, Hockley, Birmingham B18 6JL, UK
Tel: (0121) 212 2782. Fax: (0121) 212 2786.
E-mail: cgi@congend.demon.co.uk
Website: www.cgibirmingham.org
Opening hours: Mon-Fri 0930-1300 and 1330-1730.
Consulate General of India
17 Rutland Square, Edinburgh EH1 2BB, UK
Tel: (0131) 229 2144.
Fax: (0131) 229 2155.
E-mail: indianconsulate@btconnect.com *or* indian@consulate.fsnet.co.uk
Website: www.cgiedinburgh.org
Opening hours: Mon-Fri 0915-1745.
Incredible India (UK)
7 Cork Street, London W1S 3LH, UK
Tel: (020) 7437 3677 *or* (0870) 010 2183 (brochure request line).
Fax: (020) 7494 1048.
E-mail: info@indiatouristoffice.org
Website: www.incredibleindia.org

TIMATIC CODES

Health	AMADEUS: **TI-DFT/DEL/HE** GALILEO/WORLDSPAN: **TI-DFT/DEL/HE** SABRE: **TIDFT/DEL/HE**
Visa	AMADEUS: **TI-DFT/DEL/VI** GALILEO/WORLDSPAN: **TI-DFT/DEL/VI** SABRE: **TIDFT/DEL/VI**

To access TIMATIC country information on Health and Visa regulations through the Computer Reservations System (CRS), type in the appropriate command line listed above.

British High Commission
Shanti Path, Chanakyapuri, New Delhi 110 021, India
Tel: (11) 2687 2161. Fax: (11) 2687 0065.
E-mail: Postmaster.NewDelhi@fco.gov.uk
Website: www.ukinindia.org
Deputy High Commissions in: Chennai, Kolkata and Mumbai.

Embassy of India
Chancery: 2107 Massachusetts Avenue, NW, Washington, DC 20008, USA
Consulate: 2536 Massachusetts Avenue, NW, Washington, DC 20008, USA
Tel: (202) 939 7000 *or* 9806 (consular section).
Fax: (202) 265 4351 *or* 797 4693 (consular section).
E-mail: info2@indiagov.org
Website: www.indianembassy.org

Consulate General of India
3 East 64th Street, New York, NY 10021, USA
Tel: (212) 774 0600. Fax: (212) 861 3788.
Website: www.indiacgny.org

Incredible India (USA)
Suite 1808, 1270 Avenue of the Americas, New York, NY 10020, USA
Tel: (212) 586 4901. Fax: (212) 582 3274.
E-mail: ny@itonyc.com
Website: www.incredibleindia.org
Office also in: Los Angeles.

Embassy of the United States of America
1 Shantipath, Chanakyapuri, New Delhi 110 021, India
Tel: (11) 2419 8000. Fax: (11) 2419 0017.
E-mail: ndcentral@state.gov
Website: http://newdelhi.usembassy.gov
Consulates General in: Chennai, Kolkata and Mumbai.

High Commission for India
10 Springfield Road, Ottawa, Ontario K1M 1C9, Canada
Tel: (613) 744 3751/3.
Fax: (613) 744 0913.
E-mail: hicomind@hciottawa.ca
Website: www.hciottawa.ca
Consulates in: Toronto and Vancouver.

India Tourism
Suite 1003, 60 Bloor Street West, Toronto, Ontario M4W 3B8, Canada
Tel: (416) 962 3787/8.
Fax: (416) 962 6279.
E-mail: indiatourism@bellnet.ca *or* india@istar.ca
Website: www.incredibleindia.org

Canadian High Commission
7/8 Shantipath, PO Box 5207, Chanakyapuri, New Delhi 110 021, India
Tel: (11) 5178 2000. Fax: (11) 5178 2020.
E-mail: delhi@international.gc.ca
Website: www.dfait-maeci.gc.ca/new-delhi
Consulates in: Chandigarh, Chennai and Mumbai.
Honorary Consulate in: Kolkata.

General Information

AREA: 3,166,414 sq km (1,222,582 sq miles).
POPULATION: 1,049,000,000 (official estimate 2003).
POPULATION DENSITY: 331 per sq km.
CAPITAL: New Delhi. **Population:** 19,817,439 (2001).
GEOGRAPHY: India shares borders to the northwest with Pakistan, to the north with China, Nepal and Bhutan, and to the east with Bangladesh and Myanmar. To the west lies the Arabian Sea, to the east the Bay of Bengal and to the south the Indian Ocean. Sri Lanka lies off the southeast coast, and the Maldives off the southwest coast. The far northeastern states and territories are all but separated from the rest of India by Bangladesh as it extends northwards from the Bay of Bengal towards Bhutan. The Himalayan mountain range to the north and the Indus River (west) and Ganges River (east) form a physical barrier between India and the rest of Asia. The country can be divided into five regions: Western, Central, Northern (including Kashmir and Rajasthan), Eastern and Southern.
GOVERNMENT: Republic since 1947. **Head of State:** President APJ Abdul Kalam since 2002. **Head of Government:** Prime Minister Manmohan Singh since 2004.
LANGUAGE: The official language is Hindi which is spoken by about 30 per cent of the population; English is also often used for official or commercial purposes. In addition, 17 regional languages are recognised by the Constitution. These include Bengali, Gujarati, Oriya and Punjabi which are widely used in the north, and Tamil and Telegu, which are common in the south. Other regional languages are Kannada, Malayalam and Marathi. The Muslim population largely speak Urdu.
RELIGION: About 82 per cent Hindu, 11 per cent Muslim with Sikh, Christian, Jain and Buddhist minorities.
TIME: GMT + 5.5.
ELECTRICITY: Usually 220 volts AC, 50Hz. Some areas have a DC supply. Plugs used are of the round two- and three-pin type.
COMMUNICATIONS: Telephone: IDD service is widely available all over India. Otherwise calls must be placed through the international operator. Country code: 91. Outgoing international code: 00. **Mobile telephone:** GSM 900 networks. Network operators include *Aircel LTD* (website: www.aircel.com), *BPL Mobile* (website: www.bplmobile.com, *CellOne* (website: www.bsnl.co.in) and *SPICE* (website: www.spiceindia.com). Coverage is limited to major towns. **Fax:** 24-hour facilities are available in most large hotels and some offices of the Overseas Communication Service in large cities. **Internet:** ISPs include *Narmada* and *VSLnet* (website: www.vsnl.net.in). E-mail can be accessed from Internet cafes across the country. **Telegram:** International 24-hour service from large hotels and telegraphic offices in major cities. **Post:** Airmail service to Western Europe takes up to one week. Stamps are often sold at hotels. **Press:** There are numerous local dailies published in several languages. Many newspapers are in English, the most important include *The Economic Times*, *The Hindu*, *Hindustan*, *Hindustan Times*, *Indian Express*, *Navbharat Times*, *Punjab Kesari*, *The Statesman* and *The Times of India*.
Radio: BBC World Service (website: www.bbc.co.uk/worldservice) and Voice of America (website: www.voa.gov) can be received. From time to time the frequencies change and the most up-to-date can be found online.

Passport/Visa

	Passport Required?	Visa Required?	Return Ticket Required?
Full British	Yes	Yes	No
Australian	Yes	Yes	No
Canadian	Yes	Yes	No
USA	Yes	Yes	No
Other EU	Yes	Yes	No
Japanese	Yes	Yes	No

Note: *Regulations and requirements may be subject to change at short notice, and you are advised to contact the appropriate diplomatic or consular authority before finalising travel arrangements. Details of these may be found at the head of this country's entry. Any numbers in the chart refer to the footnotes below.*

A B C D E F G H I J K L M N O P Q R S T U V W X Y Z

PASSPORTS: Passport valid for at least six months required by all.
VISAS: Required by all.
Types of visa and cost: The following prices are for UK nationals only; prices for other nationals vary. *Tourist:* £30. *Business:* £30 (three/six months, single- and multiple-entry [which permits up to two years' validity]); £50 (one year); £90 (up to two years). *Transit:* £8 (up to 72 hours, single- or double-entry; stay in India can not exceed 15 days from date of arrival). *Student:* £30 (up to six months); £50 (up to one year); £55 (more than five years). *Journalist, Employment* and *Conference* visas are also available (contact the Embassy or High Commission for details). Visas for restricted/protected areas entail an additional fee of £20, and the need for a special permit.
Some nationals are exempt from visa fees.
Note: (a) The High Commission in London reserves the right to decide on the duration of the visa notwithstanding the minimum fee. (b) Non-UK nationals applying in the UK need to pay an additional £10 (amounts charged may also vary according to nationality and type of passport held) unless holding proof of at least one-year residence in the UK. (c) A £1 fee may be required for postal applications, depending on Consulate. (d) When visas are issued for a duration exceeding six months, registration with the Foreigners Regional Registration Office (FRRO) must be made within 14 days of arrival.
Validity: From date of issue. Validity of transit visas is three months from date of issue for a single entry.
Application to: Embassy or High Commission (or Consular section at Embassy or High Commission); see *Contact Addresses* section.
Application requirements: (a) Passport valid for up to six months with at least two blank pages. (b) Completed application form. Nationals of Bangladesh and Pakistan must complete special application forms. Personal interviews in some cases may also be necessary. (c) Two passport-size photos. Nationals of Pakistan will require five. (d) Fee (bank draft or postal orders only; company cheques accepted for business visas). (e) Stamped, addressed, special-delivery envelope. *Business:* (a)-(e) and, (f) Letter from employer stating the reason for visit and an invitation from the company in India and a letter of introduction from UK company addressed to the Embassy. *Transit:* (a)-(e) and, (f) Proof of onward travel. *Student:* (a)-(e) and, (f) Proof of admission to appropriate university/educational institution with duration of course.
Working days required: Personal applications can normally be processed the same day. Postal applications may take up to 15 working days or longer (early September to February). Those requiring an additional fee may need a minimum of seven working days for their visa application to be processed.
For British nationals with dual nationality and other special cases, authorisation from India is required and the time taken to process the visa will vary according to individual cases: an estimation is two weeks to six months.
Nationals of Bangladesh, Pakistan and Sri Lanka may find their visa's processing time requires longer than a working week.
Care should be taken not to apply too late (to avoid unforeseen delays) or too early, since visas are issued on receipt of passport and are valid from date of issue and not date of travel.
Temporary residence: Prior permission should be sought before entry into India.
Restricted and protected areas: Certain parts of the country have been designated protected or restricted areas that require special permits and, in some cases, prior government authorisation, which is easily obtained. Intent to visit a specific restricted region should be indicated when applying for a visa and a permit will be granted to visit that region only. Passengers are advised to check with India Tourism for up-to-date information before departure.
The following states are subject to some restrictions: Andaman & Nicobar Islands, Assam, Manipur, Meghalaya, Sikkim and West Bengal.

Money

Currency: Rupee (Rs) = 100 paise. Notes are in denominations of Rs1000, 500, 100, 50, 20, 10, and 5. Coins are in denominations of Rs5, 2 and 1, and 50, 25, and 10 paise. **Note**: 1 and 2 Rupee notes and 5 paise coins may still be in circulation but are no longer being produced.
Currency exchange: Currency can be changed at banks, airports or authorised money changers. It is illegal to exchange money through unauthorised money changers. US Dollars and Pounds Sterling are the easiest currencies to exchange.
Credit & debit cards: American Express, Diners Club, MasterCard and Visa are accepted. Check with your credit or debit card company for details of merchant acceptability and other services which may be available.
Travellers cheques: These are widely accepted and may be changed at banks. To avoid additional exchange rate charges, travellers are advised to take travellers cheques in US Dollars or Pounds Sterling. Some banks may refuse to change certain brands of travellers cheques which others exchange quite happily.
Currency restrictions: Import of local currency is prohibited. Export of local currency is also prohibited, except for passengers proceeding to Nepal (excluding notes of denominations of Rs100 or higher), Bangladesh, Pakistan or Sri Lanka (up to Rs20 per person). Foreign currency may be exported up to the amount imported and declared. All foreign currency must be declared on arrival if value is over US$5000, and when exchanged, the currency declaration form should be endorsed, or a certificate issued. The form and certificates must be produced on departure to enable reconversion into foreign currency. Changing money with unauthorised money changers is not, therefore, advisable.
Exchange rate indicators: The following figures are included as a guide to the movements of the Rupee against Sterling and the US Dollar:

Date	Feb '04	May '04	Aug '04	Nov '04
£1.00=	82.44	79.70	85.22	85.15
$1.00=	45.29	44.62	46.26	44.97

Banking hours: Mon-Fri 1000-1400, Sat 1000-1200.

Duty Free

Note: Import by non-residents is only permitted if the national has entered India for a stay of not less than 24 hours and not more than six months, provided they visit not more than once a month.
The following goods may be imported into India by passengers over 17 years of age without incurring customs duty:
200 cigarettes or 50 cigars or 250g of tobacco; *1 bottle of alcoholic beverage (0.95l)*; *60ml of perfume and 250ml of eau de toilette*; *goods for personal use*; *travel souvenirs (differing amounts according to nationality and duration of stay)*; *reasonable quantities of medicines.*
Prohibited items: Livestock (bird and bird products, including feathers and eggs, etc) and pigs and pig meat products.

Public Holidays

2005: Jan 21 Idu'z Zuha/Bakrid (Feast of the Sacrifice). **Jan 26** Republic Day. **Feb 10** Muharram (Islamic New Year). **Mar 8** Mahavir Jayanthi. **Mar 25** Holi; Good Friday. **Apr 18** Sri Rama Navami (Birthday of Sri Rama). **May 23** Buddha Purnima. **Aug 15** Independence Day. **Oct 2** Mahatma Gandhi's Birthday. **Oct 12** Vijaya Dasami/Dussera. **Nov 1** Diwali. **Nov 3-5** Eid al-Fitr (End of Ramadan). **Nov 26** Guru Nanak's Birthday. **Dec 25** Christmas Day.
2006: Jan 10 Idu'z Zuha/Bakrid (Feast of the Sacrifice). **Jan 26** Republic Day. **Jan 31** Muharram (Islamic New Year). **Feb 26** Mahavir Jayanthi. **Mar 15** Holi. **Apr 6** Sri Rama Navami (Birthday of Sri Rama). **Apr 11** Milad-Un-Nabi (Birth of the Prophet). **Apr 14** Good Friday. **May 13** Buddha Purnima. **Aug 15** Independence Day. **Sep 2** Vijaya Dasami/Dussera. **Oct 2** Mahatma Gandhi's Birthday. **Oct 21** Diwali. **Oct 22-24** Eid al-Fitr (End of Ramadan). **Nov 26** Guru Nanak's Birthday. **Dec 25** Christmas Day.
Notes: (a) Public holidays in India tend to be observed on a strictly regional basis. Only the secular holidays of Republic Day, Independence Day and Mahatma Gandhi's Birthday are universally observed. The above dates are Government of India holidays, when government offices will be closed nationwide. In addition, there are numerous festivals and fairs which are also observed in some States as holidays, the dates of which change from year to year. For more details, contact Incredible India (see *Contact Addresses* section). See also under the heading *Special Events* in the *Social Profile* section. (b) Muslim festivals are timed according to local sightings of various phases of the moon and the dates given above are approximations. During the lunar month of Ramadan that precedes Eid al-Fitr, Muslims fast during the day and feast at night and normal business patterns may be interrupted. Many restaurants are closed during the day and there may be restrictions on smoking and drinking. For more information, see the *World of Islam* appendix.

Health

	Special Precautions?	Certificate Required?
Yellow Fever	Yes	1
Cholera	Yes	2
Typhoid & Polio	3	N/A
Malaria	4	N/A

Note: *Regulations and requirements may be subject to change at short notice, and you are advised to contact your doctor well in advance of your intended date of departure. Any numbers in the chart refer to the footnotes below.*

1: Any person (including infants over six months old) arriving by air or sea from an infected country must obtain a yellow fever certificate. Otherwise, isolated detainment may occur for up to six days. Those countries that are considered infected are all African countries (except Algeria, Botswana, Djibouti, Egypt, Eritrea, Lesotho, Libya, Malawi, Mauritania, Morocco, Mozambique, Namibia, South Africa, Swaziland, Tunisia and Zimbabwe) and all South American countries (except Argentina, Chile, Paraguay and Uruguay). When a case of yellow fever is reported from any country, that country is regarded by the government of India as being infected.
2: Following WHO guidelines issued in 1973, a cholera vaccination certificate is not a condition of entry to India. However, cholera is a serious risk in this country and precautions are essential. Up-to-date advice should be sought before deciding whether these precautions should include vaccination, as medical opinion is divided over its effectiveness.
3: Poliomyelitis is widespread. Immunisation is generally recommended.
4: Malaria risk exists, mainly in the benign *vivax* form, throughout the year in the whole country below 2000m excluding parts of the states of Himachal Pradesh, Jammu and Kashmir and Sikkim. High resistance to chloroquine and sulfadoxine-pyrimethamine is reported in the malignant *falciparum* form. The recommended prophylaxis is chloroquine plus proguanil in risk areas and mefloquine in Assam.
Food & drink: All water should be regarded as being potentially contaminated. Well water near the Ganges and in West Bengal may contain traces of arsenic chemical. Water used for drinking, brushing teeth or making ice should have first been boiled or otherwise sterilised. Milk is unpasteurised and should be boiled. Powdered or tinned milk is available and is advised, but make sure that it is reconstituted with pure water. Avoid dairy products that are likely to have been made from unboiled milk. Only eat well-cooked meat and fish, preferably served hot. Pork, salad and mayonnaise may carry increased risk. Vegetables should be cooked and fruit peeled.
Other risks: *Visceral leishmaniasis* occurs in rural areas of eastern India. *Cutaneous leishmaniasis* occurs in Rajasthan. *Filariasis* is common throughout India and sandfly fever is increasing. An outbreak of *plague* occurred in 1994 and was contained by adequate government measures. *Tick-borne relapsing* fever is reported, as is *typhus*, and outbreaks of *haemorrhagic dengue fever* have occurred in eastern India. *Tick-borne haemorrhagic fever* has been reported in the forest areas in Karnataka State. *Hepatitis A* and *E* are common. *Hepatitis B* is endemic. Outbreaks of *Japanese encephalitis* occur, particularly in eastern coastal areas. *Meningococcal meningitis* is present in Delhi from November to May. Vaccination is advisable.
Rabies is present. For those at high risk, vaccination before arrival should be considered. If you are bitten, seek medical advice without delay. For more information, consult the *Health* appendix.
Note: All visitors aged between 18 and 70 years of age who are wishing to extend their visa for one year or more are required to take an AIDS test.
Health care: Health care facilities are limited and travellers are strongly advised to take out full medical insurance before departing for India. It is advisable to bring specific medicines from the UK. There are state-operated facilities in all towns and cities and private consultants and specialists in urban areas.
On leaving India: Visitors leaving for countries which impose health restrictions on arrivals from India are required to be in possession of a valid certificate of inoculation and vaccination.

Travel - International

Note: Visitors are strongly advised not to travel to Jammu and Kashmir (with the exceptions of Ladakh via Manali or air to Leh), all travel in the immediate vicinity of the border with Pakistan and the Line of Control (excepting Amritsar and Jaisalmer and for those travelling overland to Pakistan through the Wagah border crossing), and all travel to Manipur and Tripura. Tidal waves caused by the south-east Asia earthquake on 26 December 2004 hit the southern coast of India. For further information, visitors should seek official advice.
AIR: India's national airline is *Air India (AI)* (website: www.airindia.com). *British Airways* and *Virgin Atlantic* fly to India from the UK; *Delta Airlines* and *United Airlines* fly from the USA.
Approximate flight times: From *London* to Delhi is nine hours, to Kolkata (Calcutta) is 12 hours, to Chennai is 12 hours 30 minutes and to Mumbai is nine hours. From *Los Angeles* to Delhi is 25 hours 30 minutes. From *New York* to Delhi is 18 hours. From *Singapore* to Delhi is five hours. From *Sydney* to Delhi is 10 hours.
International airports: All the airports mentioned below

have money exchange facilities, tourist information offices and hotel reservation services:
New Delhi (DEL) (Indira Gandhi International) is 23km (14 miles) south of the city (travel time - 45 minutes). There are coach, bus and taxi services to the city. There are duty free shops, banks/bureaux de change, post office, restaurants and car hire.
Mumbai (BOM) (Chhatrapati Shivayi International) is 29km (18 miles) north of the city (travel time - 50 to 75 minutes). Taxi services go to the city. Taxi fares should have fixed rates from the airport to the city. Public transport is also available in the form of the EATS bus service and local buses. There is also a railway system connecting with the Metro rail system. Facilities include a bank/bureau de change, post office, nursery, restaurant and shops.
Kolkata (Calcutta) *(CCU)* is 13km (8 miles) northeast of the city (travel time - 40 to 70 minutes). There is a 24-hour coach service to Indian Airlines city office and major hotels. A bus goes every 10 minutes, 0530-2200. Taxi services go to the city. There is a post office, bank, bars, duty free shops and restaurants available.
Chennai (MAA) is 14km (9 miles) southwest of the city (travel time - 20 minutes). A coach meets all flight arrivals 0900-2300. There is a train every 20 to 30 minutes from 0500-2300. Bus 18A runs every 25 minutes from 0500-2200. Taxi services go to the city.
Amritsar (ATQ) is 11km (7 miles) from the city. Car hire, taxis and hotel pick ups can be arranged from the airport.
Departure tax: £10. (£8 for neighbouring countries only.)
SEA: The main passenger ports are Calicut, Chennai, Kochi, Kolkata (Calcutta), Mumbai, Panaji (Goa) and Rameswaram (the main departure point for the sea crossing to Sri Lanka; passenger services are presently suspended owing to the political situation in Sri Lanka). Indian ports are also served by several international shipping companies and several cruise lines. There are, however, no regular passenger liners operating to South-East Asia.
Departure tax: Seaports levy the following departure tax: RS150 (for journeys to Afghanistan, Bangladesh, Bhutan, Maldives, Myanmar, Nepal, Pakistan and Sri Lanka). RS500 (all other destinations).
RAIL: This section gives details of the major overland routes to neighbouring countries (where frontiers are open); in most cases, these will involve road as well as rail travel. Details should be checked with Incredible India as they may be subject to change (see *Contact Addresses* section).
Connections to Pakistan: Currently only possible between Amritsar and Lahore (New Delhi–Amritsar–Lahore–Hyderabad–Karachi).
Connections to Nepal: The most practical and popular route to Nepal is by train to Raxaul (Bihar) and then by bus to Kathmandu or by train to Gorakphur (or by bus if coming from Varanasi) and then by bus to Kathmandu crossing the border at Sunauli; also, by train to Nantanwa (UP) and then by bus to Kathmandu/Pokhara, or Bhairawa to Lumbini for Pokhara. It is also possible to make the crossing from Darjeeling by bus to Kathmandu across the southern lowlands.
Connections to Bhutan: The best way of reaching Bhutan is by train to Siliguri, then bus to Phuntsholing. There is also an airlink from Kolkata (Calcutta) to Paro by *Druk Air*.
Connections to Bangladesh: The best route to Bangladesh is Kolkata (Calcutta) to Bongaon (West Bengal) by train, rickshaw across the border to Benapol, with connections via Khulna or Jessore to Dhaka. Another route is from Darjeeling via Siliguri, then train or bus from Jalpaiguri to Haldibari.
Currently, no land frontiers are open between India and Myanmar or India and China (PR).
ROAD: Of late, the overland route from Europe to India has become very popular, but travellers should have accurate information about border crossings, visa requirements and political situations enroute. The most popular border crossings into India are Sunauli (for Delhi and northwest India), Birganj (for Kolkata (Calcutta) and east India) and Kakarbhitta (for Darjeeling). Amritsar is now open for overland crossings into Lahore (Pakistan). Several 'adventure holiday' companies arrange overland tours and buses to India. A **bus** service between New Delhi and Lahore (Pakistan) has recently been launched (the first one in 50 years). The journey takes roughly 10 hours and there are four weekly return trips available. For information on this and other overland routes to neighbouring countries, contact India Tourism (see *Contact Addresses* section).

Travel - Internal

AIR: The domestic airline is *Indian Airlines (IC)* (website: www.indian-airlines.nic.in). The network connects over 70 cities. Indian Airlines also operates regular flights to the neighbouring countries of Bangladesh, Malaysia, the Maldives, Myanmar, Nepal, Pakistan, Singapore, Sri Lanka, Thailand and the Middle East. Domestic airlines include *Alliance Airlines (3A)*, a subsidiary of *Indian Airlines*, *Jet Airways (9W)* and *Sahara Airlines (S2)*.
Special fares: There are various special *Indian Airlines* fares available to foreign nationals and Indian nationals residing abroad. All are available throughout the year, and may be purchased either abroad or in India, where payment is made in a foreign convertible currency (such as US Dollars or Pounds Sterling). With the exception of the Youth Fare India (see below), discounts of 90 per cent are available for children under two years of age, and of 50 per cent for children aged two to 12. Full details of all the special fares are contained in the *India* brochure, available from Incredible India. A summary of each is given below. Group discounts of up to 30 per cent are also available.

Credit: © Incredible India

Discover India: There are two types of ticket available; a 21-day ticket costs US$750 and a 15-day ticket costs US$500. These offer unlimited economy-class travel on all domestic *Indian Airlines* services. No stop may be visited more than once, except for transfer.
Youth Fare India: This is valid for three months, offering a 25 per cent discount on the normal US Dollar fare. It is available to those aged 12 to 30 at the commencement of travel for journeys on economy/executive class of domestic air services and Indo-Nepal services.
India Wonderfares (North, South, East and West): Cost US$300 and are valid for seven days, offering unlimited economy-class travel within the north, south, east or western regions of India. No town may be visited more than once, except for transfer. Details of the main air centres included in the deal can be obtained from *Indian Airways* offices.
Departure tax: £8.
SEA/RIVER: There are ships from Kolkata (Calcutta), Vishakapatnam and Chennai to Port Blair in the Andaman Islands, and from Kochi and Calicut to the Lakshadweep Islands. Services are often seasonal, and are generally suspended during the monsoon. One particularly attractive boat journey is the 'backwaters' excursion in the vicinity of Kochi in Kerala. Several local tours are available.
RAIL: The Indian internal railway system is state-run by *Indian Railways* (website: www.indianrail.gov.in). It is the largest rail system in Asia and the second-largest in the world. There are over 62,000km of track, over 7000 stations and over 11,000 locomotives, including 5000 steam engines. Its trains carry over 12 million passengers every day. The network covers much of the country and is a quintessential part of the fabric of India, as well as being relatively inexpensive. Express services link all the main cities and local services link most other parts of the country. Buses connect with trains to serve parts of the country not on the rail network. Children five to 11 years old pay half price, children under five travel free. There are six classes of travel: first-class air conditioned, first-class sleeper, second-class air conditioned, second-class sleeper, third-class air conditioned and air conditioned chair car. Major trains carry restaurant cars.
Indrail Pass: This special pass consists of a single non-transferable ticket which enables a visitor to travel on any train without restriction within the period of validity. First-class sleeper tickets are: US$135 for seven days; US$185 for 15 days; US$198 for 21 days; US$248 for 30 days; US$400 for 60 days and US$530 for 90 days. A/C tickets are twice as much and second-class tickets are much cheaper. Children under five travel free; children aged five to 12 are entitled to half-price fares. It is sold only to foreign nationals and Indians residing abroad holding a valid passport, and replaces all other concessional tickets. Payment is accepted only in foreign currency (US Dollars or Pounds Sterling). Refunds can be given only if cancellation is made before the starting date. Validity period is from the date of commencement of the first journey up to midnight of the date on which validity expires. A ticket can be used within one year of its issue. Advance reservation is essential, particularly on overnight journeys, arranged through travel agents. Reservations are on a first-come, first-served basis. Indrail passes can be reserved in the UK from *SD Enterprises Ltd* (tel: (020) 8903 3411; fax: (020) 8903 0392; e-mail: info@indiarail.co.uk; website: www.indiarail.co.uk). The passes can also be purchased in India at all the main railway stations and authorised agents.
Special trains: The **Palace on Wheels** is an expensively decorated Edwardian-style luxury steam train with 14 coaches, which travels to Rajasthan. Each coach consists of a saloon, four sleeping compartments with upper and lower berth, bathroom, shower, toilet and small kitchen. Room service is available. There is a dining car, a bar, an observation car and a fully-equipped first aid centre. Modern amenities include air conditioning, four-channel music and telephone intercom throughout the train. Tariff includes cost of travel; full catering; elephant, camel and boat rides; conducted sightseeing tours; and entrance fees. *Itinerary:* Delhi–Jaipur–Chittaurgarh–Udaipur–Jaisalmer–Jodhpur–Bharatpur–Agra–Delhi. *Bookings:* Several tour operators/travel agents organise escorted tour facilities which include the Palace on Wheels. **Royal Orient Express:** This luxury train journeys through Gujarat and Rajasthan taking in the sights of Chittargarh, Udaipur, Palitana, Ahmedabad and Jaipur. The trip takes eight days and accommodation is in furnished carriages with lounge, minibar and kitchenette. Multi-cuisine restaurants and a library are also available. Contact *Indian Railways* for further information. **Hill Trains:** Narrow-gauge rail lines completed in the 19th century linking numerous hill stations and various mountain landscapes. For example, the Kolkata (Calcutta)-Darjeeling route takes eight hours, crosses over 500 bridges and offers ample opportunity for photos as the pace is leisurely.
Other trains: The **Rajdhani Express** trains are deluxe super-fast trains connecting Delhi with Mumbai, Kolkata (Calcutta), Chennai, Bangalore, Bhubhaneswar, Guwahati, Jammu Tawi, Secunderabad, Thiruvananthapuram, Ahmedabad, Ajmer and many others. **Shatabdi Express:** Super-fast trains connecting major and secondary city centres. Visitors can travel chair-car or executive class. Snacks and meals are provided. **Konkan Express:** This connects the states of Marharshtra, Goa, Karnataka and Kerala along the coast of the Arabian sea. The route includes 72 tunnels and many bridges often crossing ravines of over 50m deep.
ROAD: Traffic drives on the left. An extensive network of **bus** services connects all parts of the country, and is particularly useful for the mountainous regions where there are no rail services. However, public transport is often crowded and can be uncomfortable. Details of routes may be obtained from the local tourist office. **Tourist cars:** There are a large number of chauffeur-driven tourist cars (some air conditioned) available in the main tourist centres. These unmetered tourist cars run at a slightly higher rate than the ordinary taxis, and are approved by Incredible India. Self-drive cars are not generally available. Driving around India is not recommended due to the erratic nature of Indian driving standards. **Documentation:** An International Driving Permit is required.
URBAN: Taxis and **auto rickshaws** are available in large cities and fares should be charged by the kilometre. They do not always have meters but, where they do, visitors should insist on the meter being flagged in their presence. Fares change from time to time and therefore do not always conform to the reading on the meter, but drivers should always have a copy of the latest fare chart available for inspection. Kolkata (Calcutta) has a 16.45km (10 mile) underground railway.
Travel times: The following chart gives approximate travel times (in hours and minutes) from **Delhi** to other major cities/towns in India.

	Air	Road	Rail	Sea
Mumbai	1.50	28.00	17.30a	-
Kolkata	2.00	30.00	18.00b	-
Chennai	3.00	45.00	32.00	-
Hyd'bad	1.55	40.00	24.00	-
Agra	0.40	4.30	3.15	-
Jaipur	0.40	6.00	5.15	-
Jammu	1.50	14.45	16.00	-
Triv'rum	5.00c	62.00	60.00	-
Patna	1.30	22.00	16.00	-
Port Blair	5.05	c	-	d

Note:
a. Time by express (not daily); normal train takes 23 hours.
b. Time by express (not daily); normal train takes 25 hours.
c. Does not include stopover in Chennai.
d. Boat journey from Chennai takes three to four days.
Note: Further information (including route maps, times of express trains and more detailed travel-time charts) may be found in the official India brochure, available free from Incredible India (see *Contact Addresses* section).

Credit: © Incredible India

Accommodation

For all sections, contact India Tourism for detailed information (see *Contact Addresses* section).
HOTELS: Modern Western-style hotels are available in all large cities and at popular tourist centres. Usually they offer a choice of first-class Western and Indian cuisine. The well-known Taj Group offers accommodation in either eight grand luxe hotels or in its many superb business hotels. Several beach resorts, so-called palace hotels, garden retreats and hotels in areas of cultural significance are also part of the international group. Hotel charges in India are moderate compared to those in many other countries. Hotel bills may be subject to a 10 per cent expenditure tax, 7 to 15 per cent luxury tax and a variable service charge.
A full list of government-approved Hotels, Palace Hotels and *ITDC* (Ashok) Travellers' Lodges is available from India Tourism; *or* contact the Federation of Hotel and Restaurant Associations of India, B-82, 8th Floor, Himalaya House, 23 Kasturba Gandhi Marg, Connaught Place, New Delhi 110001 (tel: (11) 2331 8781/2 *or* 2332 2634 *or* 3770; fax: (11) 2332 2645; e-mail: fhrai@vsnl.com; website: www.fhrai.com).
Grading: Hotels range from old palace buildings that have been converted into **Heritage Hotels**, **5-star deluxe**, **5-** and **4-star** hotels, which are fully air conditioned with all luxury features, **3-star** hotels, which are functional and have air conditioned rooms, to **2-** and **1-star** hotels, which offer basic amenities.
TOURIST BUNGALOWS: There are tourist bungalows (known as holiday homes in Maharashtra and Gujarat, and tourist lodges in West Bengal) at almost every tourist centre in the country, under the control of the respective State Government Tourist Development Corporation, except in the metropolitan cities of Delhi, Kolkata (Calcutta), Chennai, Mumbai (Bombay) and Bangalore. These include a clean single, double and family room, most with a bath and general canteen. At holiday homes and certain tourist cottages there are kitchen facilities. Bookings should be made (a deposit will be required) with the managing director of the respective corporation, or with the manager of the bungalow.
CAMPSITES: These are to be found throughout India. Full addresses may be obtained from Incredible India.
YOUTH HOSTELS: These provide a convenient and cheap base for organised tours, trekking, hiking or mountaineering. The Department of Tourism has set up several hostels, spread throughout every region, ideally placed for exploring both the plains and the hill stations. Each has a capacity for about 40 beds or more, segregated roughly half and half into male and female dormitories. Beds with mattresses, bedsheets, blankets, wardrobe with locks, electric light points, member kitchen utensils and parking areas are available at each hostel. For further details, contact the Youth Hostels Association of India, 5 Nyaya Marg, Chanakyapuri, New Delhi 110 021, (tel: (11) 2611 0250; fax: (11) 2611 3469; e-mail: yhostel@del2.vsnl.net.in; website: www.yhai.org).

Resorts & Excursions

India has a rich history and the palaces, temples and great cities of its ancient cultures cannot fail to grip the imagination. In the spring, particularly, the big cities come alive with concerts, plays, parties and exhibitions. Among the most spectacular hill stations (mountain resorts which make ideal destinations in summer) are **Shimla** (once the Imperial summer capital), **Mussoorie**, **Ranikhet** and **Nainital** (within reach of Delhi), and West Bengal's magnificent resort, **Darjeeling**, which offers a breathtaking view of the whole Kanchenjunga range. Along the fabled coasts of **Malabar** and **Coromandel**, unspoiled sandy beaches stretch for miles. Skiing is possible in the silent snowbound heights of **Gulmarg** and **Kufri** in the Himalayas.

THE NORTH

DELHI: Delhi has two parts: **New Delhi**, India's capital and the seat of government, is a modern city, offering wide tree-lined boulevards, spacious parks and the distinctive style of Lutyens' architectural design; **'Old' Delhi**, on the other hand, is a city several centuries old, teeming with narrow winding streets, temples, mosques and bazaars. Must sees include the **Red Fort** and the nearby **Jama Masjid** (India's largest mosque) both built in the mid-17th century at the height of the Moghul Empire. Also of note is the **Qutab Minar's** soaring tower built in 1193 by Qutab-ud-din immediately after the defeat of Delhi's last Hindu kingdom. At the base of the tower is the **Quwwat-ul-Islam Mosque**, built in the same period using stone from demolished Hindu temples. Delhi attracts the finest musicians and dancers, offering an ideal opportunity to hear the *sitar*, *sarod* and the subtle rhythm of the *tabla*, and to see an enthralling variety of dance forms, each with its own costumes and elaborate language of gestures. Theatres and cinemas show films from all over India, and the city has some of the country's finest restaurants offering many styles of regional cuisine.
UTTAR PRADESH: To the east of Delhi is the state of Uttar Pradesh, through which flows the sacred **River Ganges**. Built along its bank is the wondrous city of **Varanasi**, India's holiest Hindu location. The town itself is a maze of winding streets, dotted with temples and shrines. Lining the river are a series of ghats which, at dawn, are thronged with pilgrims and holy men performing ritual ablutions and prayers.
Delhi lies at the apex of the 'Golden Triangle' – an area filled with ancient sites and monuments. In the southeast lies **Agra**, city of the fabled **Taj Mahal**. This magnificent mausoleum was built by Shah Jahan as a monument to his love for his wife, Mumtaz, who died in childbirth in 1631. Shah Jehan was later imprisoned by his own son in the nearby **Red Fort**, another major attraction whose massive red sandstone walls rise over 65 feet and measure 1.5 miles in circumference. Other important landmarks are **Akbar's Palace**, the **Jahangir Mahal**, the octagonal tower **Mussumman Burj** and the **Pearl Mosque**. An hour outside Agra is **Fatehpur Sikri**, the town Akbar built as his new capital but abandoned after only a few years. This town is now no more than a ghost town but is definitely worth seeing if you have time.
RAJASTHAN: The southwestern pivot of the triangle is **Jaipur**, gateway to the desert state of Rajasthan. Known as the 'Pink City' because of the distinctive colour of its buildings painted in preparation for the visit of Britain's Prince of Wales in 1853, Jaipur is a town of broad, open avenues and many palaces. The **Amber Palace**, just outside the city is spectacular and the facade of the **Palace of the Winds** within the city walls is an essential photo stop. Also worth seeing is Jai Singh's **City Palace** and the **Jantar Mantar Observatory**. To the southwest is the most romantic city in Rajasthan, **Udaipur**, built around the lovely **Lake Pichola** and famed for its **Lake Palace Hotel**, it has been dubbed the 'Venice of the East'. To the north, in the centre of the Rajasthan desert, is **Jodhpur**, with its colourful, winding lanes and towering fortress. Near **Ajmer** is the small lakeside town of **Pushkar**. It is a site of religious importance for Hindus and it is here that every November the fascinating *Camel Fair* is held. **Jaisalmer** is a charming oasis town, once a resting place on the old caravan route to Persia. Among its attractions are the camel treks out into the surrounding desert.
MADHYA PRADESH: To the south of the 'Golden Triangle' is the huge state of Madhya Pradesh. Its greatest attractions lie close to the northern frontier. Less than 160km (100 miles) from Agra is the great ruined fortress at **Gwalior**. To the east lies **Khajuraho** with its famous temples and friezes of sensuously depicted figures – a must for any visitor.
HIMACHAL PRADESH: Less than 320km (200 miles) to the north of Delhi is **Shimla**, the greatest of all hill stations, surrounded by finely scented pine forests and the rich beauty of the **Kulu Valley**.
JAMMU AND KASHMIR: In the far north, reaching into Central Asia, is the extensive mountain region of Kashmir, formerly a popular summer resort (visitors are now advised to consult government advice before visiting this area), and the valley of the **River Jhelum**. The gateway to the region is **Jammu**, a town surrounded by lakes and hills. The temples of **Rambireshwar** and **Raghunath** number among its most impressive sights. Jammu is the railhead for **Srinagar**, the ancient capital of Kashmir, and favourite resort of the Mughal emperors. It was they who built the many waterways and gardens around **Lake Dal**, complementing the natural beauty of the area. Among the attractions are the houseboats where visitors can live on the lakes surrounded by scenery so beautiful it is known as 'paradise on earth'. Srinagar is also a convenient base for trips to **Gulmarg** and **Pahalgam**. Gulmarg offers fine trout fishing, and enjoys the distinction of having the highest golf course in the world. From here there are good views of **Nanga Parbat**, one of the highest mountains in the world. It is well placed as a starting point for treks into the hills and mountains. Pahalgam is another popular hill resort and base for pilgrimages to the sacred cave of **Amarnath**. More exotic, though less accessible, is the region of **Ladakh**, beyond the Kashmir Valley. It is a mountainous land on the edge of the Tibetan Plateau which is still largely Tibetan in character. The capital, **Leh**, is situated high in the **Karakouram** mountain range, through which passed the old **Silk Road** from China to India and Europe.

THE WEST

MUMBAI (BOMBAY): The principal metropolis of Western India is Mumbai, the capital of the state of Maharashtra, a bustling port and commercial centre, with plate-glass skyscrapers and modern industry jostling alongside bazaars and a hectic streetlife. Many of the country's films are made in the famous Mumbai studios. The city also boasts one of the finest race tracks in India, the **Mahalaxmi** course. There is a pleasant seafront with a palm-lined promenade and attractive beaches such as **Juhu**, **Versova**, **Marve**, **Madh** and **Manori**. On the waterfront is Mumbai's best-known landmark, the **Gateway to India**, whence boats leave on the 10km (6 mile) journey across the busy harbour to the **Elephanta Island**. The island is famous for the eight-century cave temples, on whose walls are large rock carvings, the finest of which is the three-faced **Maheshmurti**, the great Lord.
MAHARASHTRA: To the east of Mumbai is **Aurangabad**, the starting point for visits to two of the world's most outstanding rock-cut temples. The Buddhist cave temples at **Ajanta** date back at least 2000 years. Cut into the steep face of a deep rock gorge, the 30 caves contain exquisite paintings depicting daily life at that time.
The caves at **Ellora** depict religious stories and are Hindu, Buddhist and Jain in origin. The **Temple of Kailasa** is the biggest hewn monolith temple in the world. Southeast of Mumbai are several fine hill stations, notably **Matheran** with its narrow gauge trains, and Mahabaleshwar. The thriving city of **Pune** with its peaceful **Bund Gardens** and its cultural attractions is also in this area.
GUJARAT: To the north of Mumbai lies the state of Gujarat, renowned for its silks, as the birthplace of Mahatma Gandhi, and as the last refuge of the Asian lion, found deep in the **Gir Forest**. **Ahmedabad**, in the east of the state, is the principal textile city of India, producing silks which are famous throughout the world. Ahmadabad is also the site of **Sabarmati Ashram**, founded by Mahatma Gandhi, from where his ideology of non-violence is still promoted. Gandhi's birthplace is some 320km (200 miles) to the west, in the fishing village of **Porbandar**.
GOA: To the south of Maharashtra lies Goa. The 100km- (60 mile-) long coastline offers some of the finest beaches in the subcontinent. Goa was Portuguese until 1961, and there is also a charming blend of Latin and Indian cultures. **Panaji**, the state capital, is one of the most relaxed and elegant of India's cities. The town is dominated by the huge **Cathedral of the Immaculate Conception**, but the shops, bars and pleasant streets are its main attraction. 'Old Goa', only a bus ride away from Panaji, displays a bewildering variety of architectural styles. Buildings of note include the **Basilica** and the **Convent and Church of St Francis of Assisi**. In nearby **Ponda** is the 400-year-old **Temple of Shri Mangesh**, which is said to be the oldest Hindu shrine.
Goa's infamous hippies are being replaced by backpackers, Indian visitors and package tourists. Full moon parties still take place in **Anjuna** but are smaller and less authentic than in the heady days of the 1960s. Anjuna is also famous throughout Goa for its Wednesday flea market. If you are looking for beautiful, quiet beaches head for the South between **Benaulim** and **Palolem**. Accommodation in the region includes the luxury resort of Aguada, the Taj holiday village and the **Aguada** hermitage. There are also good, simple hotels and cottages for rent in villages along the coastline, notably **Calangute**, **Baga** and **Colva**.
Goa also has several wildlife sanctuaries, including **Bondla** in the hills of western **Ghats**, where wild boar and sambar can be seen in their natural habitat. The region is famous for its food – an array of dishes, both Indian and Portuguese – as well as for its colourful festivals, including the spectacular *Carnival* held on the three days leading up to Ash Wednesday.

THE SOUTH

The south is the part of India least affected by incursions of foreign cultures through the centuries. It is here that Indian

heritage has survived in its purest form.
CHENNAI: The regional capital is Chennai (formerly Madras), India's fourth-largest city and capital of the state of Tamil Nadu. Chennai is the cradle of the ancient Dravidian civilisation, one of the oldest articulate cultures in the world. It is also home of the classical style of Indian dancing and a notable centre of temple sculpture art. Sprawling over 130 sq km (50 sq miles), the metropolis has few tall buildings and enjoys the relaxed ambience of a market town rather than the bustle of a huge city. From **Chennai Lighthouse** there is a fine view of the city that includes many churches which tell of the city's strong Christian influence, first introduced in AD 78 when the apostle St Thomas was martyred here.
Chennai, however, is largely a commercial city and the centre of the area's rail, air and road networks, and serves as a good starting point from which to explore the south.
TAMIL NADU: Within the state are several important religious centres, notably **Kanchipuram**, which has an abundance of temples, and whose striking *gopurams*, or gateways, are decorated with sculptures of gods and goddesses. Inland is **Madurai**, with a large and bustling temple, and **Thanjavur**. Also worth visiting is **Tiruchirappalli**, which has a fortress built atop a strange boulder-shaped hill that dominates the town.
Further south, along the coast, is **Pondicherry**, an attractive town with a distinctive French style, and beyond, **Rameswaram**, once the ferry link to Sri Lanka.
KERALA: To the west lies the state of Kerala, where many of India's major coastal resorts are to be found. Among the finest is **Kovalam**, offering unspoilt beaches with increasingly modern amenities, including luxury bungalows and a number of hotels (some including a swimming pool). Only a few miles away is **Trivandrum**, the state capital with its famous **Padmanabhaswamy Temple**. Further inland is the **Periyar Game Sanctuary** which has a rich and varied wildlife. Other resorts include **Cranganorre**, **Alleppey** and **Kochi**.
KARNATAKA: Further to the north is the state of Karnataka, which has fine, unexplored beaches at **Karwar**, **Mahe** and **Udupi**. The state's capital is **Bangalore**, an affluent city which is the centre of electronics and engineering industries, but has many charming parks and gardens. To the southwest lies **Mysore**, where incense is manufactured.
Karnataka has a number of important religious and historical sites, including the ruins at **Hampi** to the north of Bangalore, and the vast statue of Lord Bahubali at **Sravanabelagola**, north of Mysore.
ANDHRA PRADESH: To the east of Karnataka is the state of Andhra Pradesh, with its capital at **Hyderabad**, offering a well-stocked one-man museum. **Visakhapatnam**, the fourth-largest port, is 220km (350 miles) to the east.
ANDAMAN ISLANDS: Far away to the east across the **Bay of Bengal** are the **Andaman Islands**, a lushly forested archipelago which has exotic plant life and a wide variety of corals and tropical fish, making it a major attraction for snorkelling enthusiasts. The islands' capital, **Port Blair**, can be reached from Chennai and Kolkata (Calcutta) by boat or air. Visitors should note that the islands are subject to special entry restrictions and a Restricted Area Permit may be required; see the *Passport/Visa* section for details.

THE EAST

KOLKATA (CALCUTTA): The largest city in India and hub of the east is Kolkata, the capital of West Bengal. Established as a British trading post in the 17th century, it grew rapidly into a vibrant centre. Its colonial heritage is reflected in the buildings of **Chowringhee Street** and **Clive Street**, now **Jawaharlal Nehru Road** and **Netaji Subhash Road**. The city is filled with life and energy. It is a major business centre and offers fine markets and bazaars. It is also the centre of much of the country's creative and intellectual activity, including the subcontinent's best film-makers. Central Kolkata (Calcutta) is best viewed from the **Maidan**, the central area of parkland where early morning yoga sessions take place. The city's **Indian Museum** is one of the finest in Asia. Other attractions include the white marble **Victoria Memorial**, the **Ochterlony Monument** (Sahid Minar) and the headquarters of the Rama Krishna movement. Across the river are the **Kali Temple of Dakshineshwasar** (Belur Math headquarters of Ramakrishna Movement) and the **Botanical Gardens**.
BIHAR AND ORISSA: To the west is the state of **Bihar**, with the religious centre of **Bodhgaya**, a sacred place for both Hindus and Buddhists. To the south, in the state of **Orissa**, are three temple cities. Foremost is **Bhubaneswar**, a town in which there once stood no less than 7000 temples, 500 of which have survived. Largest of these is the great *Lingaraja Temple*, dedicated to Lord Shiva. A short journey away to the south of Bhubaneswar lies **Puri**, one of the four holiest cities in India, now being developed as a beach resort. In June and July, Puri stages one of India's most spectacular festivals, the *Rath Yatra* or *'Car Festival'*, at which pilgrims pay homage to images of gods drawn on massive wooden chariots. A short distance along the coast to the north is **Konarak**, known for its 'Black Pagoda' – a huge solitary temple to the sun god in the form of a chariot drawn by horses. The sculpture has a sensuous nature similar to that of Khajuraho, and is counted amongst the finest in India.
DARJEELING: To the north of Kolkata (Calcutta) is one of the great railway journeys of the world, the 'Toy Train' to Darjeeling. The last part of the line runs through jungle, tea gardens and pine forests. Darjeeling straddles a mountain slope which drops steeply to the valley below, and commands fine views of **Kanchenjunga** (8586m/28,169ft), the third-highest mountain in the world. It is the headquarters of the Indian Mountaineering Institute, as well as the birthplace of Sherpa Tenzing. It is also a world-renowned tea-growing centre.
A bus journey of two-and-a-half hours takes one to **Kalimpong**, a bazaar town at the foot of the Himalayas. From here, a number of treks can be made to places offering fine panoramas of the mountains.
SIKKIM: Further north is the mountain state of Sikkim. The capital, **Gangtok**, lies in the southwest. The main activity for visitors is trekking, although it is still in its infancy and facilities are minimal. At the moment, travel for non-Indian residents is limited. Trekking is allowed only in groups, while individuals may only visit Gangtok, **Rumtek** and **Phodom**. The nearest railheads are Darjeeling and Siliguri, on the slow but spectacular line of India's northeast frontier railway.
ASSAM AND MEGHALAYA: Even further to the east are the states of Assam and Meghalaya. **Assam** is famous for tea and wildlife reserves, and can be reached from the state capital of **Guwahati**. The tiger reserve of **Manas** is also rich in other varieties of wildlife, while in **Kaziranga** it is possible to see the one-horned rhinoceros of India.
Shillong, the capital of **Meghalaya**, is the home of the Khasi people. The region is filled with pine groves, waterfalls and brooks and is described as the 'Scotland of the East'.

BEACH RESORTS

India's coast has some of the most beautiful beaches in the world. Below are listed both well-known resorts, such as Goa, and several lesser-known beaches. Hotel facilities and accommodation are also indicated. Further information may be obtained by consulting the main *Resorts & Excursions* sections. Major beaches include:
Goa: Baga Beach, Calangute and Colva Beach. *5-star hotels with private beaches:* Cidade de Goa, Fort Aguada Beach Resort and Oberoi Bogmalo Beach. It has reasonably priced hotels, tourist cottages, a tourist resort and youth hostels.
Mumbai: Juhu Beach; crowded 5-star hotel complex.
Kovalam: Ashok Beach resort. 5-star hotel complex, including beach cottages, Halcyon Castle and Kovalam Palace Hotel. Hotel Samudra, Kerala Tourism Development Corporation, is reasonably priced. Kovalam Beach gets crowded during the peak tourist season (November to March).
Chennai Region: Fisherman's Cove at Covelong beach resort; shore cottages by the shore temples at **Mamallapuram** (which also has a beach resort).
Puri: 3- and 4-star hotels, tourist bungalows, youth hostels. Major Hindu pilgrim centre.
Lesser-known beaches: These include: **Andhra Pradesh:** Bheemunipatnam, Machilipatnam, Maipadu and Mangiripundi. **Goa:** Ankola, Bhatkal, Gokarna, Honnavar and Karwar. **Gujarat:** Chorwad, Dahanu, Daman (UT), Diu (UT), Dwarka, Hajira, Tithal and Ubhrat. Cheap hotels, holiday homes. **Karnataka:** Mahe (UT), Mangalore, Udupi (Hindu pilgrim centre) and Ullal (smaller beach resort, Summer Sands, cottages). **Kerala:** Cannanore, Quilon, Varkala. **Maharashtra:** Off Mumbai – Madh, Manori and Marve. Cheap hotels – Murud Janjira. Holiday homes – Erangal. **Orissa:** Golpalpur on Sea, Oberoi Hotel. **Tamil Nadu:** Kanya Kumari, Karikal (UT), Pondicherry (UT), Rameswaram and Tiruchendur. **West Bengal:** Digha – reasonably priced hotels, tourist bungalows.
Note: UT = Union Territory.

HILL STATIONS

Hill stations have long been popular among Indians and foreign visitors alike for providing a relaxing and salubrious retreat from the heat of the plains. Further information on some of the places mentioned here may be found by consulting the information above.
Popular hill stations: These include: **Kashmir:** Leh in Ladakh, Pahalgam, Srinagar and Gulmarg for lakes, houseboats, good hotels, tourist reception centres.
Himachal Pradesh: Shimla (various types of hotels, tourist bungalows), nearby Kufri (winter sports centre, skating rink, skiing facilities), Kulu, Manali (reasonably priced hotels, log huts, travellers lodges and tourist bungalows). **Uttar Pradesh:** Nainital boasts a lake boat club, Almora, Mussoorie, Ranikhet (reasonably priced hotels, tourist bungalows, clubs, youth hostels), Ropeway (hotels and tourist bungalows). **West Bengal:** Darjeeling, RA, Kalimpong for mountaineering. **Maharashtra:** Khandala, Lonavla, Mahabaleshwar, Matheran, and Panchgani. **Meghalaya:** Shillong. **Sikkim:** Gangkok (RA, hotels). **Tamil Nadu:** Ootacamund, Udagamandalam, Kodaikanal and Silvery Lake – hotels, tourist bungalows.
Lesser-known hill stations: These include: **Himachal Pradesh:** Chamba, Dalhousie, Dharamsala, Kangra, Keylong, Nahan and Paonta Saheb. **Kashmir:** Batote and Sonamarg. **Uttar Pradesh:** Dehra Dun and Lansdown. **West Bengal:** Mirik. **Madhya Pradesh:** Pachmarhi. **Maharashtra:** Panhala. **Gujarat:** Saputara. **Rajasthan:** Mount Abu. **Tamil Nadu:** Coonoor, Kotagiri and Yercaud. **Kerala:** Munnar, Periyar and Ponmundi. **Karnataka:** Mercara. **Andhra Pradesh:** Horseley Hills. **Bihar:** Netarhat. **Assam:** Haflong.

TREKKING

Below is a description of the most important trekking areas in India. For further practical details on trekking, see the *Sport & Activities* section.
JAMMU AND KASHMIR: Jammu and Kashmir is India's northernmost state, and the one which is best-known for trekking. It is an extravagantly beautiful land of forests, icy mountain peaks and clear streams and rivers. The capital, **Srinagar**, is the base for many treks, notably to the blue **Zabarwan Hills** and **Shankaracharya Hill**. The three other main bases in Jammu and Kashmir are **Pahalgam** (100km/62 miles from Srinigar) in the **Lidder Valley**, the base for treks to sacred **Amarnath**, **Aru**, **Lidderwat** and the glacial lakes of **Tarsar** and **Tulian**; **Gulmarg** (51km/32 miles from Srinagar), from which treks can be made to the crystal tarns of **Apharwat** and **Alpather**, the upland lakes of **Vishansar** and **Gangabal** and the **Thajiwas Glacier**; and **Sonamarg**, in the **Sindh Valley**, the base for treks into the surrounding mountains.
Srinagar is also the roadhead for trips into the arid plateau of **Ladakh**, a country of perpetual drought, the home of wild asses and yaks and with high ranges that have some of the largest glaciers in the world outside the polar regions. **Leh**, the divisional capital, lies on an ancient Silk Road and is the base for spectacular treks across this remarkable landscape.
Further south, excellent trekking may be had in the vicinity of Jammu, the railhead to the **Kashmir Valley**. The three main centres are **Kishtwar**, **Doda** and **Poonch**.
HIMACHAL PRADESH: The landscape of this province ranges from the barren rocks and raging torrents of the valleys of **Spiti** and **Lahaul** in the north to the southern orchard country of **Kangra** and **Chamba**. Treks from **Manali** include the **Bhaga River** to **Keylong**, and then on to the **Bara Shigri** glacier or over the **Baralacha Pass** to Leh (see above). **Kullu**, in the centre of the province, is set in a narrow valley between the towering Himalayas and the **River Beas**, and is famous for its temples and religious festivals. Treks from here traverse terraced paddy fields and on to remoter regions of snow and ice. The view from the **Rohtang Pass** is particularly spectacular. The town of **Dharamsala**, in the **Kangra Valley** area, is the base for treks into the **Bharmaur Valley** over the **Indrahar Pass**, and on to other still higher passes beyond. **Chamba**, situated on a mountain above the **Ravi River**, is named after the fragrant trees which flourish around its richly carved temples. Treks from the nearby town of **Dalhousie** lead to the glacial lake of **Khajjiar** and to the passes of **Sach** and **Chini**. **Shimla**, once the summer capital of the British, is a high hill station and the base for treks into **Kullu Valley** via the **Jalori Pass** and on to the **Kalpur** and **Kinnaur valleys**.
GARHWAL: Set high in the **Garhwal Himalayas**, this region (which is sometimes referred to as the Uttarakhand) abounds in myths and legends of the Indian gods. It is also where the source of the life-giving 'Ganga' is to be found; indeed, many of the great rivers of northern India have their headwaters in this land of lush valleys and towering snow-ridged peaks. **Mussoorie**, a hill station much used by the British to escape the searing heat of the plains, is an excellent base for treks into the **Gangotri** and **Yamounotri** valleys. The source of the Ganga at **Gaumukh** can also be reached from here. Another hill station, **Rishikesh**, is situated just north of the sacred city of **Hardwar**, and is the base for treks to another holy shrine, **Badrinath**.
A particularly rewarding stop enroute to Badrinath is the breathtaking **Valley of Flowers**, which is in full bloom in August. Other destinations include **Hemkund Lake**, **Mandakini Valley** and **Kedarnath**, one of the 12 Jyotirlings of Lord Shiva with a beautiful temple.
KUMAON: This region, which stretches from the Himalayas in the north to the green foothills of Terai and Bhabar in the south, consists of the three northeastern Himalayan districts of Uttar Pradesh, all of which are particularly rich in wildlife. One of the major trekking centres is **Almora**, an ideal base for treks into pine and rhododendron forests with dramatic views of stark, snow-capped mountains. The **Pindiri Glacier** and the valley of **Someshwar** can be reached from here. Another base is **Nanital**, a charming, orchard-rich hill station. It is the base for short treks to **Bhimtal**, **Khurpatal** and **Binayak Forest**. **Ranikhet**, with a magnificent view of the central Himalayas, is the base for treks to **Kausani**. The view from here is one of the most spectacular in India, and inspired Mahatma Gandhi to pen his commentary on the Gita-Anashakti Yoga.

DARJEELING AND SIKKIM: Dominated by the five summits of mighty **Kanchenjunga**, the Darjeeling and Sikkim area of the Eastern Himalayas is also a region of gentle hills and dales, pine forests, turquoise lakes and babbling streams. One of the best ways of arriving in the area is by the 'Toy Train' from New Jalpaiguri. The town of **Darjeeling** is the home of the Everest-climber Tenzing Norgay and also of the Himalayan Mountaineering Institute, and is the base for both low- and high-level treks. Destinations include **Tiger Hill** (offering a breathtaking view of the Himalayas), and the peaks of **Phalut**, **Sandakphu**, **Singalila** and **Tanglu**. To the north, Sikkim is a wonderland of ferns and flowers, birds and butterflies, orchids and bamboo, forests of cherry, oak and pine, all set among slowly flowing rivers, terraced paddy fields and blazing rhododendrons. Deep in the interior are Sikkim's famous monasteries, their white prayer flags fluttering against a deep blue sky. The capital is **Gangtok**, a convenient base for treks into the mysterious north and east of the region, to sacred **Yaksum**, **Pemayangtse** and the mountains near **Bakkhim** and **Dzongri**.
ARAVALLI HILLS: The Aravallis, remnants of the oldest mountain range in the subcontinent, resemble outcroppings of rocks rather than mountains and are virtually barren except for thorny acacias and date palm groves found near the oases. The main resort in the region, **Mount Abu**, stands on an isolated plateau surrounded by rich green forest. A variety of one-day treks are available from here, all of which afford the opportunity to visit some of the remarkable temples in the region, notably **Arbuda Devi Temple**, carved out of the rock face and offering spectacular views across the hills. **Guru Shikhar**, **Gaumukh** and **Achalgarh Fort** can all be reached during one-day treks from Mount Abu.
SATPURA RANGE: This range straddles central India and forms the northern border of the **Deccan**. The main hill station is **Pachmarhi**, a beautiful resort of green forest glades and deep ravines overlooking red sandstone hills. Short treks can be had from here to the **Mahadeo** and **Dhupgarh** peaks.
WESTERN GHATS: The Western Ghats run parallel to the west coast of India from the River Tapti to the southernmost tip of the subcontinent. The mountains are lush and thickly forested and although they cannot claim to have the awesome majesty of the great Himalayas, the region has many features of great natural beauty. The hill station of **Mahabaleshwar**, in the north of the range, is the highest in the area and is considered an ideal base for trekkers. Other popular bases and trekking destinations include **Lonavala**, **Khandala**, **Matheran** and **Bhor Ghat**, a picturesque region of waterfalls, lakes and woods. Further south in Karnataka is **Coorg**, perched on a green hilltop and surrounded by mountainous countryside. **Madikeri** is a take-off point for treks in this region. The **Upper Palani** hills in Tamil Nadu are an offshoot of the Ghats, covered in rolling downs and coarse grass. **Kodaikanal** is the attractive base for two short treks to **Pilar Rock** and **Green Valley View**. **Courtallam**, also in Tamil Nadu, is surrounded by dense vegetation and coffee and spice plantations; rich in wildlife, it is also one of the most beautiful areas of the Western Ghats.
NILGIRIS: The gentle heights of southern India, a world away from the daunting Himalayas, are friendly and approachable with treks made simple by moderate altitudes and a pleasant climate. Sometimes known as the **Blue Mountains** because of their lilac hue, they are noted for their orange orchards, tea gardens, wooded slopes and tranquil lakes. There are three major trekking centres here: **Ootacamund** (popularly known as Ooty) is the base for walks to the **Wenlock Downs**, the **Kalahatti Falls** and **Mudumali Game Sanctuary**; **Coonoor**, conveniently situated for **Drogg's Peak** and **Lamb's Rock**; and **Kotagiri**, the oldest of the three, whose sheltered position enables it to offer many shaded treks to explore the tranquillity of the Nilgiris.

WILDLIFE

The Indian peninsula is a continent in itself, the geographical diversity of which has resulted in a vast range of wildlife, with over 350 species of mammals and 1200 species of birds in the country. There are 90 national parks and 411 wildlife sanctuaries in the country. Each region has something special to offer: the **hangul** is restricted to the valley of Kashmir in northern India, the **rhino** is found in isolated pockets along the Brahmaputra River in the east, the **black langur** in the Western Ghats, and Western India is the home of the last remaining **Asiatic lions**. Two of India's most impressive animals, the **Bengal** (or Indian) **tiger** and the **Asiatic elephant** are still found in most regions, though their population has shrunk drastically. Most of India's wildlife finds refuge in over 200 sanctuaries and parks around the country. The following list refers to some of the more important of these. Accommodation often needs to be booked in advance, either by direct application or through the local State ITDC or the controlling authority of the respective park.
NORTHERN INDIA: Dachigam Wildlife Sanctuary (Kashmir): Broad valley; mountain slopes; rare hangul deer, black and brown bear, leopard; heronry.
Govind Sagar Bird Sanctuary (Himachal Pradesh): Bird sanctuary with crane, duck, goose and teal.
Corbett National Park (Uttar Pradesh): Himalayan foothills near Dhikala; Sal forest and plains; tiger, elephant, leopard and rich birdlife. Excellent fishing in Ramganga River.

Credit: © Incredible India

Dudhwa National Park (Uttar Pradesh): Nepal border; tiger, sloth bear and panther.
Valley of Flowers National Park (Uttar Pradesh): When in bloom this 'roof garden' at 3500m (11,500ft) is a glorious blaze of colour. Permits are required to enter.
Sariska National Park (Rajasthan): About 200km (125 miles) from Delhi. Forest and open plains; sambar (largest Indian deer), cheetal (spotted deer), nilgai (Indian antelope), black buck, leopard and tiger; good night-viewing.
Ranthambhor (Sawai Madhopur – Rajasthan): Hill forest, plains and lakes; sambar, chinkara (Indian gazelle), tiger, sloth bear, crocodiles and migratory water-birds.
Bharatpur National Park (Keoloadeo Ghana Bird Sanctuary) (Rajasthan): India's most outstanding bird sanctuary; many indigenous water-birds; huge migration from Siberia and China; crane, goose, stork, heron, snakes, birds, etc.
Bandhavgarh National Park (Madhya Pradesh): Situated in the Vindhyan Mountains, this park has a wide variety of wildlife including panther, sambar and gaur.
Kanha National Park (Madhya Pradesh): Sal forest and grassland; only home of barasingha (swamp deer), tiger, cheetal and gaur.
Shivpuri National Park (Madhya Pradesh): Open forest and lake; chinkara, chowsingha (four-horned antelope), nilgai, tiger, leopard and water-birds.
WESTERN INDIA: Krishnagiri Upavan National Park (Maharashtra): Formerly known as Borivli, this park protects an important scenic area close to Mumbai (Bombay). Kanheri Caves and Vihar, Tulsi and Powai lakes; water-birds and smaller types of wildlife. Lion Safari Park nearby.
Tadoba National Park (Maharashtra): Teak forests and lake; tiger, leopard, nilgai and gaur. Night-viewing.
Sasan Gir National Park (Gujarat): Forested plains and lake; only home of Asiatic lion, sambar, chowsingha, nilgai, leopard, chinkara and wild boar.
Nal Sarovar Bird Sanctuary (Gujarat): Lake; migratory water-birds; indigenous birds include flamingo.
Little Rann of Kutch Wildlife Sanctuary (Gujarat): Desert; herds of khur (Indian wild ass), wolf and caracal.
Velavadar National Park (Gujarat): New Delta grasslands; large concentration of black buck.
SOUTHERN INDIA: Periyar Wildlife Sanctuary (Kerala): Large artificial lake; elephant, gaur, wild dog, black langur, otters, tortoises and rich birdlife including hornbill and fishing owl. Viewing by boat.
Vedanthangal Water Birds Sanctuary (Tamil Nadu): One of the most spectacular breeding grounds in India. Cormorant, heron, stork, pelican, grebe and many others.
Point Calimere Bird Sanctuary (Tamil Nadu): Particularly noted for its flamingo, also for heron, teal, curlew and plover, black buck and wild pig.
Pulicat Bird Sanctuary (Andhra Pradesh): Flamingo, grey pelican, heron and tern.
Dandeli National Park (Karnataka): Park with bison, panther, tiger and sambar. Easily accessible from Goa.
Jawahar National Park (includes **Bandipur** and **Nagarhole National Parks** (Karnataka), and the Wildlife Sanctuaries of **Mudumalai** (Tamil Nadu) and **Wayanad** (Kerala): Extensive mixed forest; largest elephant population in India, leopard, gaur, sambar, muntjac and giant squirrel. Birds include racquet-tailed drongo, trogon and barbet.
EASTERN INDIA: Kaziranga National Park (Assam): Elephant grass and swamps; one-horned Indian rhinoceros, water buffalo, tiger, leopard, elephant, deer and rich birdlife. Elephant transport is available within the park.
Manas Wildlife Sanctuary (Assam): On the Bhutan border, rainforest, grassland and river banks; rhino, water buffalo, tiger, elephant, golden langur and water-birds; fishing permitted.
Nameri National Park (Assam): Tiger and water-birds; fishing permitted.
Palamau Tiger Reserve (Bihar): Rolling, forested hills; tiger, leopard, elephant, sambar, jungle cat, rhesus macaque (monkey) and, occasionally, wolf.
Hazaribagh National Park (Bihar): Sal forested hills; sambar, nilgai, cheetal, tiger, leopard and occasionally muntjac (larger barking deer).
Sundarbans Tiger Reserve (West Bengal): Mangrove forests; tiger, fishing cat, deer, crocodile, dolphin and rich birdlife. Access and travel by chartered boat.
Jaldapara Wildlife Sanctuary (West Bengal): Tropical forest and grassland; rhino, elephant and rich birdlife.
Similipal Tiger Reserve (Orissa): Immense Sal forest; tiger, elephant, leopard, sambar, cheetal, muntjac and chevrotain.
Chilika Wildlife (Bird) Sanctuary (Orissa): Migratory birds, flamingo, Siberian ducks, heron and Teal Comorant.

Sport & Activities

Trekking: India is the ideal destination for a trekking holiday, offering everything from short and easy excursions to the long challenges of the snowy peaks. The highest mountain range on earth – the Himalayas – forms 3500km (2200 miles) of India's northern and eastern frontiers. The spectacle of the snow-capped peaks, glaciers, pine-forested slopes, rivers and lush meadows of wild flowers cannot be equalled. Peninsular India offers natural beauty of another kind, clothed in green woodland and fragrant orchards. (For further details on the main trekking areas, see Trekking in the *Resorts & Excursions* section.) No system of issuing trekking permits exists in India. Trekkers are, however, reminded that it is forbidden to enter Restricted and Protected Areas without the correct documentation. Consult Incredible India before departure or local tourist offices on arrival in India to ascertain what restrictions may apply and what documentation may be required. The trekking season varies from region to region; check with Incredible India for further information (see *Contact Addresses* section). In general, it runs from April to June and September to November. It is possible to undertake treks in the valleys of Lahaul, Pangi and Zanskar and in Ladakh during the rainy season (June to August), as these areas receive minimal precipitation.
Board and lodging accommodation is available on all trekking routes. Essential equipment includes a tent, sleeping bag, foam/inflatable mattress, rucksack, umbrella (doubles as a walking stick), sun-hat, dark glasses, toilet requirements. The best clothing is a windproof jacket, trousers, shirts, woollen pullover, woollen underwear (for high altitudes), and gloves. Be sure to take a light, flexible and comfortable pair of trekking boots (two pairs should be taken for longer treks) and at least three pairs of woollen socks. Use talc to keep feet dry. A first-aid kit is recommended, as are anti-sunburn cream, morphia salt tablets to avoid cramps, a torch, thermos/water bottle, insect repellent, mirror, cold cream, lip-salve, walking stick, spare boot laces, sewing kit, tinned and dehydrated food.
Watersports: India has some of the most beautiful beaches in the world, the most popular ones being in the southern states of Goa and Kerala. But though the beaches are stunning, the waters, particularly in the south, can be quite treacherous, with big waves and strong currents creating hazardous conditions for inexperienced swimmers. To make up for the rough seas, most large hotels now have swimming pools, and there are facilities for a wide range of watersports including **sailing**, **rowing** and **water-skiing**. (For further details on beach resorts, see *Beach Resorts* in the *Resorts & Excursions* section.) The Andaman Islands and Lakshadweep Islands off the southern coast are noted for their white-sand, deserted beaches and excellent swimming and **scuba-diving** (but visitors should note that they may require a special permit to visit; see *Passport/Visa* section).
Whitewater rafting is a young sport in India; the snow-fed mountain rivers of the northern Himalayas place them among the best regions in the world for this sport.
Fishing is also available, particularly in the Kangra Valley and Shimla, in Darjeeling and Orissa and throughout the Himalayas. Tackle can often be hired from local fishing authorities. Check with the local tourist office for details of seasons and licences.
Outdoor activities: Camel safaris can be taken in the Thar desert and range from one to 15 days' duration; an ideal way to visit this fascinating region. Delhi is the country's centre for **rock climbing**, also available in the Aravalli Hills and the Western Ghats. Permission for **mountaineering** *must* be obtained from the Indian Mountaineering Foundation, 6 Benito Juarez Road, New Delhi 110 021 (tel: (11) 2467 1211; fax: (11) 2688 3412; e-mail: indmount@vsnl.com; website: www.indmount.org).
Hang gliding, **ballooning** and **gliding** are also becoming more widely available for those who wish to obtain a bird's-eye view of some of the landscape. **Skiing** is fast becoming a popular sport, and facilities are offered by some resorts in the north of the country (including Gulmarg and Kufri), set in some of the most beautiful mountain

landscape in the world. **Horse-riding** is available in hill stations.
Spectator sports: One of the great Indian sports is **cricket**. Interest in the game reaches almost fever pitch, particularly during the winter test season when the country's national team is in action in all the major cities. Club matches can also be seen in almost every town. Other popular spectator sports include **polo** and **hockey**, sports at which the Indians have long excelled, winning many Olympic gold medals in the latter. Interest in **football** is increasing.
Golf: Enthusiasts will find many courses open to visitors throughout India; enquire at major hotels for details of temporary membership. *Calcutta Amateur Golf Championships* attract large numbers of serious golfers in the east; the standards are high and, for those interested, temporary membership is available from the *Royal Kolkata (Calcutta) Golf Club*. Gulmarg and Srinagar have good courses and hold tournaments in the spring and autumn, with Gulmarg enjoying the reputation of being the highest golf course in the world. The course at Shillong is widely regarded as being one of the most beautiful in the world.

Credit: © Incredible India

Social Profile

FOOD & DRINK: The unforgettable aroma of India is not just the heavy scent of jasmine and roses on the warm air. It is also the fragrance of spices so important to Indian cooking – especially to preparing curry. The word 'curry' is an English derivative of *kari*, meaning spice sauce, but curry does not, in India, come as a powder. It is the subtle and delicate blending of spices such as turmeric, cardamom, ginger, coriander, nutmeg and poppy seed. Like an artist's palette of oil paints, the Indian cook has some 25 spices (freshly ground as required) with which to mix the recognised combinations or *masalas*. Many of these spices are also noted for their medicinal properties and, like the basic ingredients, vary from region to region. Although not all Hindus are vegetarians, vegetable dishes are more common than in Europe, particularly in southern India. Broadly speaking, meat dishes are more common in the north, notably, *Rogan Josh* (curried lamb), *Gushtaba* (spicy meat balls in yoghurt) and the delicious *Biryani* (chicken or lamb in orange-flavoured rice, sprinkled with sugar and rose water). Mughlai cuisine is rich, creamy, deliciously spiced and liberally sprinkled with nuts and saffron. The ever-popular *Tandoori* cooking (chicken, meat or fish marinated in herbs and baked in a clay oven) and kebabs are also northern cuisine. In the south, curries are mainly vegetable and inclined to be hotter. Specialities to look out for are *Bhujia* (vegetable curry), *Dosa*, *Idli* and *Samba* (rice pancakes, dumplings with pickles, and vegetable and lentil curry), and *Raitas* (yoghurt with grated cucumber and mint). Coconut is a major ingredient of southern Indian cooking. On the west coast there is a wide choice of fish and shellfish: *Mumbai duck* (curried or fried bombloe fish) and *pomfret* (Indian salmon) are just two. Another speciality is the *Parsi Dhan Sak* (lamb or chicken cooked with curried lentils) and *Vindaloo*. Fish is also a feature of Bengali cooking as in *Dahi Maach* (curried fish in yoghurt flavoured with turmeric and ginger) and *Malai* (curried prawn with coconut). One regional distinction is that, whereas in the south, rice is the staple food, in the north this is supplemented and sometimes substituted by a wide range of flat breads, such as *Pooris*, *Chapatis* and *Nan*. Common throughout India is *Dal* (crushed lentil soup with various additional vegetables), and *Dahi*, the curd or yoghurt which accompanies the curry. Besides being tasty, it is a good 'cooler'; more effective than liquids when things get too hot.
Sweets are principally milk-based puddings, pastries and pancakes. Available throughout India is *Kulfi*, the Indian ice cream, *Rasgullas* (cream cheese balls flavoured with rose water), *Gulab Jamuns* (flour, yoghurt and ground almonds), and *Jalebi* (pancakes in syrup). Besides a splendid choice of sweets and sweetmeats, there is an abundance of fruit, both tropical – mangoes, pomegranates and melons – and temperate – apricots, apples and strawberries. Western confectionery is available in major centres. It is common to finish the meal by chewing *Pan* as a digestive. *Pan* is a betel leaf in which are wrapped spices such as aniseed and cardamom.
Besides the main dishes, there are also countless irresistible snacks available on every street corner, such as *Dosa*, *Fritters*, *Samosa* and *Vada*. For the more conservative visitor, Western cooking can always be found. Indeed, the best styles of cooking from throughout the world can be experienced in the major centres in India.
Tea (or *chai*) is India's favourite drink and many of the varieties are enjoyed throughout the world. It will often come ready-brewed with milk and sugar unless 'tray tea' is specified. Coffee is increasingly popular. *Nimbu Pani* (lemon drink), *Lassi* (iced buttermilk) and coconut milk straight from the nut are cool and refreshing. Soft drinks (usually sweet) and bottled water are widely available, as are Western alcoholic drinks. There is a huge variety of excellent Indian beer. There is also good Indian-made gin, rum, brandy and wine. Bottled water, essential for visitors, is sold everywhere in India, but make sure the bottles are properly sealed.
Restaurants have table service and, depending on area and establishment, will serve alcohol with meals. Most Western-style hotels have licensed bars. Visitors will be issued All India Liquor Permits on request by Indian Embassies/High Commissions, Missions or Tourist Offices. Various states impose prohibition but this may change; check with the Tourist Office for up-to-date information. In almost all big cities in India, certain days in the week are observed as dry days when the sale of liquor is not permitted. Tourists may check with the nearest local tourist office for the prohibition laws/rules prevailing in any given state where they happen to be travelling or intend to travel.
NIGHTLIFE: India has generally little nightlife as the term is understood in the West, although in major cities, a few Western-style shows, clubs and discos are being developed. In most places, the main attraction will be cultural shows featuring performances of Indian dance and music. The Indian film industry is the largest in the world, now producing three times as many full-length feature films as the USA. Mumbai (Bombay) and Kolkata (Calcutta) are the country's two 'Hollywoods'. Almost every large town will have a cinema, some of which will show films in English. Music and dancing are an important part of Indian cinema, combining with many other influences to produce a rich variety of film art. Larger cities may have theatres staging productions of English-language plays.
SHOPPING: Indian crafts have been perfected over the centuries, from traditions and techniques passed on from generation to generation. Each region has its own specialities, each town its own local craftspeople and its own particular skills. Silks, spices, jewellery and many other Indian products have long been acclaimed and are widely sought after; merchants would travel thousands of miles, enduring the hardships and privations of the long journey, in order to make their purchases. Nowadays, the marketplaces of the subcontinent are only eight hours away, and for fabrics, silverware, carpets, leatherwork and antiques, India is a shopper's paradise. Bargaining is expected, and the visitor can check for reasonable prices at state-run emporia. **Fabrics:** One of India's main industries is textiles; its silks, cottons, and wools rank amongst the best in the world. Of the *silks*, the brocades from Varanasi are among the most famous; other major centres include Kanchipuram, Murshidabad, Patna and Surat. Rajasthan cotton with its distinctive 'tie and dye' design is usually brilliantly colourful, while Chennai cotton is known for its attractive 'bleeding' effect after a few washes. Throughout the country may be found the *himroo* cloth, a mixture of silk and cotton, often decorated with patterns. Kashmir sells beautiful *woollens*, particularly shawls. **Carpets:** India has one of the world's largest carpet industries, and many examples of this ancient and beautiful craft can be seen in museums throughout the world. Each region will have its own speciality, such as the distinctive, brightly coloured Tibetan rugs, available mainly in Darjeeling. **Clothes:** Clothes are cheap, and can be quickly tailor-made in some shops. Cloth includes silks, cottons, *himroos*, brocades, chiffons and *chingnons*. **Jewellery:** This is traditionally heavy and elaborate. Indian silverwork is world-famous. Gems include diamonds, lapis lazuli, Indian star rubies, star sapphires, moonstones and aquamarines. Hyderabad is a leading pearl centre. **Handicrafts and leatherwork:** Each area has its speciality; the range includes bronzes, brasswork (often inlaid with silver), canework and pottery. Woven rugs and *papier mâché* (some decorated in gold leaf) are a characteristic Kashmir product. Inlaid marble and alabaster are specialities of Agra. Rajasthan is known for its colourful fabrics and silks. Leatherwork includes open Indian sandals and slippers. **Woodwork:** Sandalwood carvings from Karnataka, rosewood from Kerala and Chennai. **Other goods:** Pickles, spices, Indian tea, perfumes, soap, handmade paper, Orissan playing cards and musical instruments. **Shopping hours:** Mon-Sat 0930-1700 in most large stores.
Note: There is a veto on the export of antiques, art objects over 100 years old, animal skins and objects made from skins.
SPECIAL EVENTS: For further information, contact the Government of India Tourist Office (see *Contact Addresses*). The following is a selection of special events occurring in India in 2005:
Jan *Dalai Lama's Kalachakra Initiation* (religious ceremony), Bodh Gaya; *Bikaner Camel Festival*. **Feb** *Goa Carnival*; *Desert Festival*, Jaisalmer. **Mar** *Holla Mohalla* (ancient Sikh festival), all over the Punjab. **Apr 6** *Ramnavami* (anniversary of Lord Rama's birth), nationwide. **May 23** *Buddha Purnima* (celebration of the birth of Lord Buddha), nationwide. **Jun** *Summer Festival*, Mount Abu. **Jul** *Birthday of the Dalai Lama*, Dharamsala. **Aug-Sep** *Gogamedi Fair*. **Sep** *Ganesh Chaturthi* (festival of the elephant God Ganesh), nationwide. **Sep-Oct** *Navarati* (Hindu festival of dancing), Mumbai. **Oct** *Dussehra* (Hindu festival), nationwide. **Nov** *Ganga Mahotsava* (washing in the Ganges River), Varanasi; *Pushkar Camel Fair*, Ajmer; **Nov 1** *Deepvali* (Hindu festival of lights), nationwide. **Dec 24-Jan 3 2006** *Christmas Parties* (beach parties), Goa.
Note: Besides the above festivals, there are hundreds of festivals and fairs which are of regional significance, celebrated with equal pomp and colour. The most authentic of these are the following: the Temple Festivals in southern India, a list of which is often available from Incredible India; festivals at Ladakh in Kashmir and Rajasthan; a visitor will be unlucky to visit Rajasthan at a time when a festival of some kind is not either in progress or about to take place. The visitor may also be lucky enough to witness dancing at a village festival or a private wedding.
SOCIAL CONVENTIONS: The Indian Hindu greeting is to fold the hands and tilt the head forward to *namaste*. Indian women prefer not to shake hands. All visitors are asked to remove footwear when entering places of religious worship. The majority of Indians remove their footwear when entering their houses. Because of strict religious and social customs, visitors must show particular respect when visiting someone's home. Many Hindus are vegetarian and many, especially women, do not drink alcohol. Sikhs and Parsees do not smoke. Small gifts are acceptable as tokens of gratitude for hospitality. Women are expected to dress modestly. Short skirts and tight or revealing clothing should not be worn, even on beaches. Businesspeople are not expected to dress formally except for meetings and social functions. English-speaking guides are available at fixed charges at all important tourist centres. Guides speaking French, German, Italian, Japanese, Russian or Spanish are available in some cities. Consult the nearest Incredible India office. Unapproved guides are not permitted to enter protected monuments. Tourists are advised to ask for guides with certificates from the Ministry of Tourism or Incredible India (see *Contact Addresses* section). **Photography:** Formalities mainly concern protected monuments and the wildlife sanctuaries. Special permission of the Archaeological Survey of India, New Delhi, is necessary for the use of tripod and artificial light to photograph monuments. Photography at many places is allowed on payment of a prescribed fee, which varies. Contact the nearest Government of India Tourist Office. **Tipping:** Taxis and restaurants do not expect to be tipped, however, hotel and airport porters should be tipped around Rs20, and guides and drivers Rs100 per day where service is not included (equalling roughly 10 per cent where appropriate).

Business Profile

ECONOMY: India's industrial economy, which has invested much in advanced technology initiatives such as digital communications and space research, contrasts with the poverty that persists, particularly in rural areas. The country ranks among the top dozen in the world by gross national product. Roughly two-thirds of the population are involved in agriculture, both subsistence – mainly cereals – and cash crops including tea, rubber, coffee, cotton, jute, sugar, oil seeds and tobacco. Growth in this sector has been steady despite frequent damage through drought and flooding. India's energy requirements are met by oil, most of which is imported despite the growth of indigenous production, and hydroelectric schemes, mostly based amid the powerful northern rivers. Mining is a relatively small sector, but does produce iron ore and cut diamonds for export. India's main industrial development has been in engineering, especially transport equipment (a major export earner), iron and steel, chemicals, electronics and textiles. Economic reforms were put into effect throughout the 1990s, under which trade has been liberalised, the sprawling public sector cut back, and state-owned industries sold off. The plan was approved with the IMF, which supplied substantial credits to the Indian treasury.

After the hiatus following the 1997 Asian financial crisis, the economy has resumed its healthy growth rate, currently just over 8 per cent per annum, while inflation is just under 4 per cent. Indian colleges and universities are turning out large numbers of graduates with advanced technology skills who are now the target of employers in Europe and North America (where there is a shortage of qualified IT workers): the Indian economy is as yet not sufficiently developed to absorb this resource. Further reforms, especially improvements to the national infrastructure and basic services, are now seen as the priority for central and regional governments. Foreign direct investment has reached an all-time peak of over US$4 billion annually and is set to continue rising. Japan and the Russian Federation are India's major trading partners, among a wide range of extensive bilateral economic relations stretching from Australia and the Pacific Basin through Western Europe to the USA, Canada and Brazil.

BUSINESS: English is widely used in commercial circles, so there is little need for interpreter and translation services. Business cards are usually exchanged and should be presented with both hands. When introduced to someone, wait to see if your host greets you with a *Namaste*, the traditional Indian greeting in which hands are clasped as if in prayer in front of the chest accompanied by a little bow, or offers the hand. When eating, visitors should wait to see if their host uses fingers or cutlery, and follow suit (it is essential that only the right hand is used for eating). All weights and measures should be expressed in metric terms. Indian businesspeople welcome visitors and are very hospitable. Entertaining usually takes place in private clubs. The best months for business visits are October to March, and accommodation should be booked in advance.

Office hours: Mon-Fri 0930-1700, Sat 0930-1300.

COMMERCIAL INFORMATION: The following organisations can offer advice: Ministry of External Affairs, South Block, New Delhi 110 011 (tel: (11) 2301 2318 *or* 1165; fax: (11) 2379 3062; website: http://meaindia.nic.in) *or* Associated Chambers of Commerce and Industry of India (ASSOCHAM), 147B Gautam Nagar, Gulmohar Enclave, New Delhi 110 049 (tel: (11) 2651 2477-9; fax: (11) 2651 2154; e-mail: assocham@nic.in; website: www.assocham.org); *or* Federation of Indian Chambers of Commerce and Industry (FICCI), Federation House, Tansen Marg, New Delhi 110 001 (tel: (11) 2373 8760-70; fax: (11) 2332 0714 *or* 2372 1504; e-mail: ficci@ficci.com; website: www.ficci.com).

CONFERENCES/CONVENTIONS: The main congress and exhibition centres in the country are Agra, Bangalore, Bhubeneswar, Chennai, Delhi, Hyderabad, Jaipur, Kolkata (Calcutta), Mumbai, Panaji, Udaipur and Varanasi. In addition, top-class hotels and auditoria with convention and conference facilities are found throughout the country. *Air India*, *Indian Airlines* and leading hoteliers and travel agents are members of the International Congress and Conference Association (ICCA) and together they provide all the services required for an international event, including the organising of pre- and post-conference tours. There is a particularly useful booklet which gives information on India in general, and in particular on conference facilities, called *India: A Convention Planner*, available from Incredible India (see *Contact Addresses* section).

Climate

Hot tropical weather with variations from region to region. Coolest weather lasts from December to February, with cool, fresh mornings and evenings and dry, sunny days. Really hot weather, when it is dry, dusty and unpleasant, is between March and May. Monsoon rains occur in most regions in summer between June and September.

Western Himalayas: Srinagar is best from March to October; July to August can be unpleasant; cold and damp in winter. Simla is higher and therefore colder in winter. Places like Gulmarg, Manali and Pahalgam are usually under several feet of snow (December to March) and temperatures in Ladakh can be extremely cold. The road to Leh is open from June to October.

Required clothing: Light- to mediumweights are advised from March to October, with warmer wear for winter. Weather can change rapidly in the mountains and therefore it is important to be suitably equipped. Waterproofing is advisable.

Northern Plains: Extreme climate, warm inland from April to mid-June, falling to almost freezing at night in winter between November and February. Summers are hot with monsoons between June and September.

Required clothing: Lightweight cottons and linens in summer with warmer clothes in winter and on cooler evenings. Waterproofing is essential during monsoons.

Central India: Madhya Pradesh State escapes the very worst of the hot season, but monsoons are heavy between July and September. Temperatures fall at night in winter.

Required clothing: Lightweights are worn most of the year with warmer clothes during evenings, particularly in winter. Waterproofed clothing is advised during monsoon rains.

Western India: November to February is most comfortable, although evenings can be fairly cold. Summers can be extremely hot with monsoon rainfall between mid-June and mid-September.

Required clothing: Lightweight cottons and linens are worn most of the year with warmer clothes for cooler winters, and waterproofing is essential during the monsoon.

Southwest: Tamil Nadu experiences a northeast monsoon between October and December and temperatures and humidity are high all year. Hills can be cold in winter. Hyderabad is hot, but less humid in summer and much cooler in winter.

Required clothing: Lightweight cottons and linens. Waterproofing is necessary during the monsoon. Warmer clothes are worn in the winter, particularly in the hills.

Southeast: Tamil Nadu experiences a northeast monsoon between October and December and temperatures and humidity are high all year. Hills can be cold in winter. Hyderabad is hot, but less humid in summer and much cooler in winter.

Required clothing: Lightweight cottons and linens. Waterproofing is necessary during the monsoon. Warmer clothes are worn in the winter, particularly in the hills.

Northeast: March to June and September to November are the driest and most pleasant periods. The rest of the year has extremely heavy monsoon rainfall and it is recommended that the area is avoided.

Required clothing: Lightweight cottons and linens. Waterproofing is advisable throughout the year and essential in monsoons, usually from mid-June to mid-October. Warmer clothes are useful for cooler evenings.

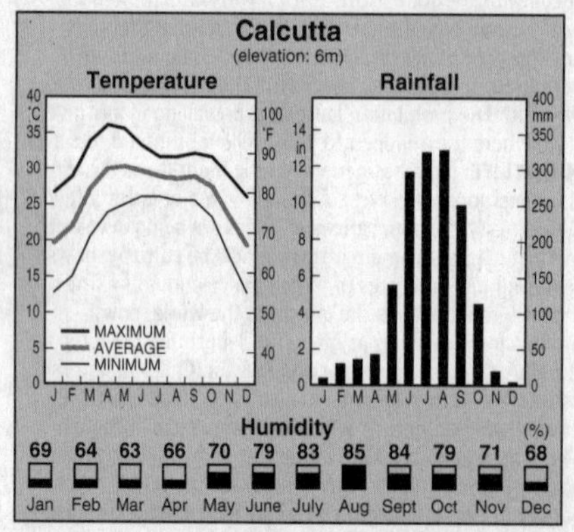

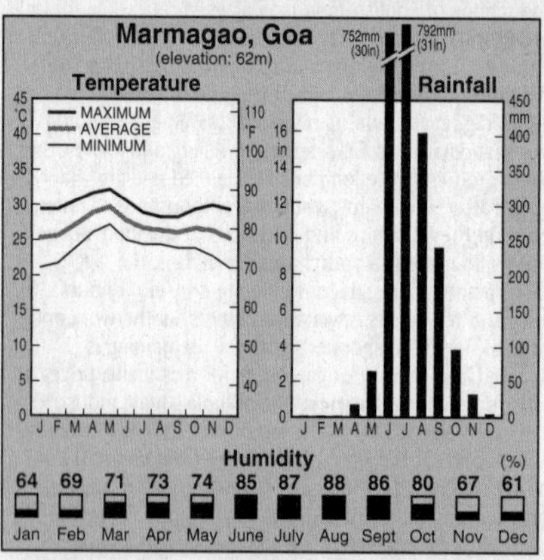

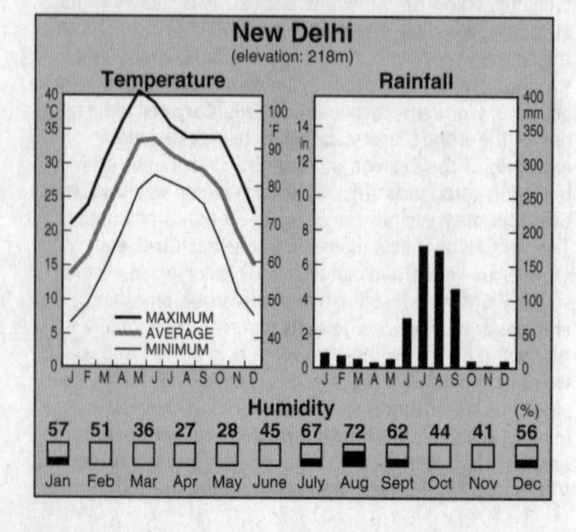

Indonesia

LATEST TRAVEL ADVICE CONTACTS

British Foreign and Commonwealth Office
Tel: (0870) 606 0290 Website: www.fco.gov.uk

US Department of State
Website: http://travel.state.gov/travel

Canadian Department of Foreign Affairs and Int'l Trade
Tel: (1 800) 267 8376 Website: www.dfait-maeci.gc.ca

Location: South-East Asia.

Country dialling code: 62.

Indonesia Culture and Tourism Board
Data and Information Centre, Sapta Pesona Building, 21st Floor, Jalal Medan Merdeka Barat 17, Jakarta 10110, Indonesia
Tel: (21) 383 8717. Fax: (21) 345 2006.
E-mail: pusdatin@budpar.go.id
Website: www.budpar.go.id

Indonesia Tourism Promotion Board (ITPB)
Wisma Nugra Santana Building, 9th Floor, Jalan Jend Sudirman Kav 7-8, Jakarta 10220, Indonesia
Tel: (21) 570 4879. Fax: (21) 570 4855.
Website: www.tourismindonesia.com

Embassy of the Republic of Indonesia
38 Grosvenor Square, London W1K 2HW, UK
Consular section: 38A Adam's Row, London W1X 9AD, UK
All post should be addressed to 38 Grosvenor Square.
Tel: (020) 7499 7661. Fax: (020) 7491 4993.
E-mail: kbri@btconnect.com
Website: www.indonesianembassy.org.uk
Opening hours: Mon-Fri 0900-1700 (general and tourist enquiries); 1000-1300 (visa applications) and 1430-1600 (visa collections).

British Embassy
Jalan M H Thamrin 75, Jakarta 10310, Indonesia
Tel: (21) 315 6264. Fax: (21) 3190 1344 (press and public affairs section).
Website: www.britain-in-indonesia.or.id

British Consulate General
Deutsche Bank Building, 19th Floor, Jalan Imam Bonjol 80, Jakarta 10310, Indonesia
Tel: (21) 390 7484-7. Fax: (21) 316 0858.
Website: www.britain-in-indonesia.or.id
Honorary Consulates in: Bali and Medan.

Embassy of the Republic of Indonesia
2020 Massachusetts Avenue, NW, Washington, DC 20036, USA
Tel: (202) 775 5200. Fax: (202) 775 5365.
E-mail: information@embassyofindonesia.org
Website: www.embassyofindonesia.org

Consulate General of Indonesia
5 East 68th Street, New York, NY 10021, USA
Tel: (212) 879 0600. Fax: (212) 570 6202.
E-mail: kjriny@ix.netcom.com
Website: www.indony.org
Consulates General in: Chicago, Houston, Los Angeles and San Francisco.

Embassy of the United States of America
Jalan Medan Merdeka Selatan 4-5, Jakarta 10110, Indonesia
Tel: (21) 3435 9000. Fax: (21) 3435 9922.
Website: http://jakarta.usembassy.gov
Consulates General in: Surabaya. *Consular Agency in:* Bali.

Embassy of the Republic of Indonesia
55 Parkdale Avenue, Ottawa, Ontario K1Y 1E5, Canada
Tel: (613) 724 1100.
Fax: (613) 724 1105 *or* 4959.
E-mail: kbri@indonesia-ottawa.org *or* info@indonesia-ottawa.org
Website: www.indonesia-ottawa.org
Consulates General in: Toronto and Vancouver.

Canadian Embassy
Street address: 6th Floor, World Trade Centre, Jalan Jendral Sudirman Kav. 29-31, Jakarta 12920, Indonesia
Postal address: PO Box 8324/JKS.MP, Jakarta 12920, Indonesia
Tel: (21) 2550 7800. Fax: (21) 2550 7811.
E-mail: canadianembassy.jkrta@dfait-maeci.gc.ca
Website: www.dfait-maeci.gc.ca/jakarta
Honorary Consulate in: Surabaya.

TIMATIC CODES
Health
AMADEUS: TI-DFT/CGK/HE
GALILEO/WORLDSPAN: TI-DFT/CGK/HE
SABRE: TIDFT/CGK/HE
Visa
AMADEUS: TI-DFT/CGK/VI
GALILEO/WORLDSPAN: TI-DFT/CGK/VI
SABRE: TIDFT/CGK/VI
To access TIMATIC country information on Health and Visa regulations through the Computer Reservations System (CRS), type in the appropriate command line listed above.

General Information

AREA: 1,922,570 sq km (742,308 sq miles).
POPULATION: 217,131,000 (UN estimate 2002).
POPULATION DENSITY: 112.9 per sq km.
CAPITAL: Jakarta (Java). **Population:** 11,429,400 (UN estimate 2001).
GEOGRAPHY: Indonesia lies between the mainland of South-East Asia and Australia in the Indian and Pacific oceans. It is the world's largest archipelago state. Indonesia is made up of five main islands – Sumatra, Java, Sulawesi, Kalimantan (part of the island of Borneo) and Irian Jaya (the western half of New Guinea) – and 30 smaller archipelagos. In total, the Indonesian archipelago consists of about 17,500 islands; 6000 of these are inhabited and stretch over 4828km (3000 miles), most lying in a volcanic belt with more than 300 volcanoes, the great majority of which are extinct. The landscape varies from island to island, ranging from high mountains and plateaux to coastal lowlands and alluvial belts.
GOVERNMENT: Republic. Declared independence from the Netherlands in 1945. **Head of State and Government:** President Susilo Bambang Yudhoyono since 2004.
LANGUAGE: Bahasa Indonesia is the official national language. It is similar to Malay and written in the Roman alphabet. All together, there are an estimated 583 languages and dialects spoken in the archipelago. Many local languages are further divided by special forms of address depending on social status, and all languages are spoken in a variety of local dialects. English is the most widely used foreign language for business and tourism, and many people in the more remote areas have a basic command of English. The older generation still speaks Dutch as a second language and French is spoken at some of the better hotels and restaurants.
RELIGION: There is a Muslim majority of approximately 90 per cent, with Christian, Hindu (mainly in Bali) and Buddhist minorities. Animist beliefs are held in remote areas.
TIME: Indonesia spans three time zones:
Bangka, Balitung, Java, West and Central Kalimantan, Madura and Sumatra: GMT + 7 (West), GMT + 8 (Central), GMT + 9 (East).
Bali, Flores, South and East Kalimantan, Lombok, Sulawesi, Sumba, Sumbawa and Timor: GMT + 8.
Aru, Irian Jaya, Kai, Moluccas and Tanimbar: GMT + 9.
ELECTRICITY: Generally 220 volts AC, 50Hz, but 127 volts AC, 50Hz, in some rural areas.
COMMUNICATIONS: Telephone: IDD is available to main cities. Country code: 62 (followed by 22 for Bandung, 21 for Jakarta, 61 for Medan and 31 for Surabaya). Outgoing international code: 00. Many hotel lobbies have public phones which take credit cards and phone cards. State-operated phone booths (WARTEL), which work on a pay-as-you-leave basis, can be found throughout the country. For emergencies, dial 110 (police) or 118 (ambulance for traffic accidents) *or* 119 (ambulance for general health) *or* 113 (fire department). **Mobile telephone:** GSM 900 and 1800 networks. Main operators include *Excelcom* (website: www.excelcom.co.id), *Lippo Telecom* (website: www.lippotel.com) and *Telkomsel* (website: www.telkomsel.com). Coverage may be limited to main towns and cities. **Fax:** Faxes can be sent and received from WARTEL shops. **Internet:** ISPs include *Indobiz* (website: www.indobiz.com) and *Indosat* (website: www.indosatm2.com). There are Internet cafes in all major cities and tourist destinations. **Telegram:** These can be sent from any telegraphic office; in Jakarta, facilities are available 24 hours a day, but services outside Jakarta are less efficient. **Post:** Airmail to Western Europe takes up to 10 days. Internal mail is fast and generally reliable by the express service (*Pos KILAT*), but mail to the outer islands can be subject to considerable delays. **Press:** There are several English-language newspapers in Jakarta and on the other islands, notably *Bali Post*, *Indonesian Observer*, *Jakarta Post* and *The Indonesia Times*.
Radio: BBC World Service (website: www.bbc.co.uk/worldservice) and Voice of America (website: www.voa.gov) can be received. From time to time the frequencies change and the most up-to-date can be found online.

Passport/Visa

	Passport Required?	Visa Required?	Return Ticket Required?
Full British	Yes	Yes/1	Yes
Australian	Yes	Yes/1	Yes
Canadian	Yes	Yes/1	Yes
USA	Yes	Yes/1	Yes
Other EU	Yes	Yes/1	Yes
Japanese	Yes	Yes/1	Yes

Note: *Regulations and requirements may be subject to change at short notice, and you are advised to contact the appropriate diplomatic or consular authority before finalising travel arrangements. Details of these may be found at the head of this country's entry. Any numbers in the chart refer to the footnotes below.*

Restricted entry: (a) Nationals of Israel will be refused entry unless they have applied to the Immigration Office in Indonesia, prior to travelling, to obtain a special permit.
PASSPORTS: Passport valid for at least six months from date of entry required by all.
VISAS: Required by all except nationals of Brunei, Chile, Hong Kong (SAR), Macau (SAR), Malaysia, Morocco, Peru, The Philippines, Singapore, Thailand and Vietnam, provided that they enter through one of the authorised airports, seaports or Etikong overland port for touristic stays of up to 30 days.
Note: 1. Nationals of Argentina, Australia, Brazil, Canada, Denmark, Finland, France, Germany, Hungary, Italy, Japan, Korea (Rep), New Zealand, Norway, Poland, South Africa, Switzerland, Taiwan (China), United Arab Emirates, UK and USA can apply for a *Tourist* visa, valid for 30 days (non-extendable), on arrival, provided that they enter through one of the authorised airports or seaports.
Warning: Visitors who exceed their visa-free stay will be given severe fines and possibly deported or imprisoned.
Types of visa and cost: *Single-entry*: £35. *Multiple-entry*: £125 (*business* only). *Transit*: £15. Fees are non-refundable.
Validity: *Single-entry*: Three months from date of issue for a maximum stay of 60 days. *Multiple-entry*: One year, with each stay lasting no longer than 60 days. The first entry must be within three months of date of issue. *Transit*: Three months from the date of issue for a maximum stay of 14 days.
Application to: Visa section at Embassy; see *Contact Addresses* section. All visitors are advised to process their visas at the visa section at the Embassy before entry to Indonesia.
Application requirements: (a) Passport valid for at least six months from date of entry. (b) One (double-sided) application form (the original not a photocopy, signed by the applicant). (c) One recent colour passport-size photo. (d) Proof of sufficient funds (£1000 for touristic stays), for instance bank statement less than one month old or travellers cheques. (e) Fee, payable in cash or by postal order only. (f) For postal applications, a pre-paid special delivery envelope. *Tourist*: (a)-(f) and, (g) Travel itinerary. (h) Hotel reservation. (j) Letter, less than one month old from applicant's employer, certifying the applicant's obligation to return (if self-employed, from solicitor, accountant or bank manager; if a student, from school, college or university). *Business*: (a)-(f) and, (g) Letter from the applicant's company in home country and the sponsor/counterpart in Indonesia, stating the reason and duration of the visit and guarantee of financial responsibility and responsibility for arrangement of accommodation. *Social Visit*: (a)-(f) and, (g) Letter of invitation from the applicant's family, friends or relatives in Indonesia, stating the reason and duration of the visit and details of accommodation, and a photocopy of their passport/ID.
Working days required: Five to six. Applications for multiple-entry business visas and applications from nationals of certain countries will need to be referred to the authorities in Indonesia and may take two months or more. There is an additional £5 fee in this case.
Temporary residence: People wishing to stay and work in Indonesia must apply directly to the Immigration Office in Indonesia for a temporary stay visa.

Money

Currency: Rupiah (Rp) = 100 sen. Notes are in denominations of Rp100,000, 50,000, 20,000, 10,000, 5000, 1000, 500 and 100. Coins are in denominations of Rp1000, 500, 100, 50 and 25.
Currency exchange: Although there should be no difficulty exchanging major currencies in the main tourist centres, problems may occur elsewhere. The easiest currency to exchange is the US Dollar.
Credit & debit cards: American Express, MasterCard and Visa are widely accepted in Jakarta and the main tourist areas. In more remote areas, it is best to carry cash in small denominations. Check with your credit or debit card company for details of merchant acceptability and other services which may be available.
Travellers cheques: Limited merchant acceptance but can be easily exchanged at banks and larger hotels. To avoid additional exchange rate charges, travellers are advised to take travellers cheques in US Dollars or Pounds Sterling.
Currency restrictions: There are no restrictions on the import or export of foreign currency. The import and export of local currency is limited to Rp5,000,000 which must be declared; more than Rp10,000,000 needs authorisation. Failure to declare amounts in excess of Rp10,000,000 may result in heavy fines. Local currency may be exchanged on departure.
Exchange rate indicators: The following figures are included as a guide to the movements of the Rupiah against Sterling and the US Dollar:

Date	Feb '04	May '04	Aug '04	Nov '04
£1.00=	15396.60	15600.7	17041.7	17043.3
$1.00=	8458.50	8734.50	9250.00	9000.00

Banking hours: Mon-Fri 0800-1500.

Credit: © Bali Tourism Authority

Duty Free

The following goods may be imported into Indonesia by travellers over 18 years of age without incurring customs duty:
200 cigarettes or 50 cigars or 100g of tobacco; *1l of alcohol (opened)*; *a reasonable quantity of perfume*; *gifts up to a value of US$250 per person or US$1000 per family*.
Note: Cameras must be declared on arrival. Video cameras, radio cassette recorders, binoculars and sport equipment may be imported provided exported on departure. Motion-picture film, video tapes, video laser discs, records and computer software must be screened by the censor board.
Prohibited items: Weapons, firearms and ammunition, non-prescribed drugs, narcotics, television sets, cordless telephones and other electronic equipment, fresh fruit, Chinese publications and medicines, pornography, and any commercial or merchandised goods as part of baggage (infringements will be charged Rp25,000 per piece).

A B C D E F G H I J K L M N O P Q R S T U V W X Y Z

Public Holidays

2005: Jan 1 New Year's Day. **Jan 21** Eid al-Adha (Feast of the Sacrifice). **Feb 9-11** Chinese New Year. **Feb 10** Muharram (Islamic New Year). **Mar 25** Good Friday. **Apr 9** Nyepi (Hindu New Year). **Apr 21** Mouloud (Birth of the Prophet). **May 5** Ascension. **May 23** Waisak Day (Buddha's Birthday). **Aug 17** Indonesian Independence Day. **Sep 1** Lailat al Miraj (Ascension of the Prophet). **Nov 3-5** Eid al-Fitr (End of Ramadan). **Dec 25** Christmas Day.
2006: Jan 1 New Year's Day. **Jan 13** Eid al-Adha (Feast of the Sacrifice). **Jan 29** Chinese New Year. **Jan 31** Muharram (Islamic New Year). **Mar 30** Nyepi (Hindu New Year). **Apr 11** Mouloud (Birth of the Prophet). **Apr 14** Good Friday. **May 13** Waisak Day (Buddha's Birthday). **May 25** Ascension. **Aug 17** Indonesian Independence Day. **Aug 22** Lailat al Miraj (Ascension of the Prophet). **Oct 22-24** Eid al-Fitr (End of Ramadan). **Dec 25** Christmas Day.
Note: (a) Muslim festivals are timed according to local sightings of various phases of the moon and the dates given above are approximations. During the lunar month of Ramadan that precedes Eid al-Fitr, Muslims fast during the day and feast at night and normal business patterns may be interrupted. Many restaurants are closed during the day and there may be restrictions on smoking and drinking. Some disruption may continue into Eid al-Fitr itself. Eid al-Fitr and Eid al-Adha may last anything from two to 10 days, depending on the region. For more information, see the *World of Islam* appendix. (b) Buddhist festivals are also timed according to phases of the moon and variations may occur.

Health

	Special Precautions?	Certificate Required?
Yellow Fever	No	1
Cholera	Yes	2
Typhoid & Polio	3	N/A
Malaria	4	N/A

Note: Regulations and requirements may be subject to change at short notice, and you are advised to contact your doctor well in advance of your intended date of departure. Any numbers in the chart refer to the footnotes below.

1: A yellow fever vaccination certificate is required from travellers coming from infected areas. The countries and areas included in the yellow fever endemic zones are considered by Indonesia as infected areas. For a map of yellow fever endemic zones, see the *Health* appendix.
2: Following WHO guidelines issued in 1973, a cholera vaccination certificate is no longer a condition of entry to Indonesia. However, cholera is a serious risk in this country and precautions are essential. Up-to-date advice should be sought before deciding whether these precautions should include vaccination as medical opinion is divided over its effectiveness; see the *Health* appendix.
3: Typhoid occurs. Poliomyelitis transmission has been interrupted in Indonesia.
4: Malaria risk exists throughout the year everywhere except in the main tourist resorts of Java and Bali, Jakarta municipality and other big cities where risk is only slight. The malignant form *falciparum* is reported to be highly resistant to chloroquine and sulfadoxine-pyrimethane. The benign form *vivax* is reported to be resistant to chloroquine. The recommended prophylaxis in risk areas is mefloquine.
Food & drink: All water should be regarded as a potential health risk. Water used for drinking, brushing teeth or making ice should have first been boiled or otherwise sterilised. Milk is unpasteurised and should be boiled. Powdered or tinned milk is available and is advised, but make sure that it is reconstituted with pure water. Avoid dairy products that are likely to have been made from unboiled milk. Only eat well-cooked meat and fish, preferably served hot. Salad and mayonnaise may carry increased risk. Vegetables should be cooked and fruit peeled.
Other risks: *Amoebic* and *bacillary dysenteries* occur. *Hepatitis A* and *E* occur and *hepatitis B* is highly endemic. *Dengue fever*, *giardiasis*, *Japanese Encephalitis* and *Parityphoid* can occur. *Tuberculosis* and *diphtheria* vaccinations are sometimes recommended. *Bilharzia* (schistosomiasis) is present in central Sulawesi. Avoid swimming and paddling in fresh water; swimming pools which are well chlorinated and maintained are safe. *Rabies* is present. For those at high risk, vaccination before arrival should be considered. If you are bitten, seek medical advice without delay. For more information, consult the *Health* appendix.
Health care: Health insurance to include emergency repatriation cover is strongly advised. Adequate routine medical care is available in all major cities, but emergency services are generally inadequate outside major cities. Fees must be paid before leaving the hospital. Although medical costs are relatively cheap, drugs can be expensive.

Travel - International

Note: Travellers are forewarned of continual reports of threats of terrorist activity against westerners and western interests in Indonesia. All travel to Aceh is advised against (except for those involved in humanitarian operations), and also some parts of Maluku (especially Ambon) and Sulawesi, due to high levels of civilian unrest. For further advice, visitors should contact their local government travel advice department.
AIR: Indonesia's national airlines are *Garuda Indonesia (GA)* (website: www.garuda-indonesia.com) and *Merpati Nusantara Airlines (MZ)*. Other major airlines that serve Indonesia include *Air France*, *Air India*, *Cathay Pacific*, *Emirates*, *Gulf Air*, *Japan Airlines*, *KLM*, *Lufthansa*, *Qantas*, *Singapore Airlines* and *Thai Airways International*.
Approximate flight times: From *London* to Jakarta is 20 hours 20 minutes and to Bali is 22 hours 15 minutes (with a good connection in Jakarta). From *Los Angeles* to Jakarta is 24 hours 20 minutes. From *New York* to Jakarta is 30 hours via Europe or 31 hours via Los Angeles. From *Singapore* to Jakarta is one hour 35 minutes. From *Sydney* to Jakarta is seven hours 55 minutes.
International airports: *Jakarta (CGK)* (Soekarno-Hatta) is 20km (12 miles) northwest of the city (travel time - 45 minutes). Airport facilities include banks/bureaux de change, a post office, duty free shops, gift shops, restaurants, snack bars, car hire and medical/vaccination facilities. A bus goes to the city every hour. Buses leave Jakarta from Gambir railway station and from Rawamangun and Blok M bus stations. Taxis are also available to the city centre. A regular bus shuttle goes to Jakarta's second airport, *Halim Perdana Kusuma (HLP)*, 13km (8 miles) southeast of the city (travel time - 45 minutes).
Denpasar (DPS) (Ngurah Rai), 13km (8 miles) southwest of the city, is the main airport on Bali (travel time - 30 minutes). There are duty free facilities at the airport. A bus goes to the city centre. Taxis are available to the city and to Kuta, Logian, Nusadua and Sanur.
Departure tax: Rp100,000; infants under the age of two are exempt.
Note: For a list of the air- and seaports which may be used to enter and exit Indonesia, see the *Passport/Visa* section.
SEA: International ports are listed at the end of the *Passport/Visa* section. High-speed ferries run between Sumatra and Malaysia. Routes are either Medan–Penang or Dumai–Melaka. There are also services between Mandalo (Sulawesi) and The Philippines. **Cruise Lines:** *Crystal Cruises*, *Cunard*, *Norwegian*, *Orient Lines*, *P&O*, *Radisson Seven Seas* and *Royal Caribbean*.
RAIL: There is a daily sea and rail service between Belawan and Penang (West Malaysia), operated by *National Railroad of Indonesia*.
ROAD: Indonesia's international land borders are between Kalimantan and the Malaysian states of Sarawak and Sabah on the island of Borneo, and Irian Jaya and Papua New Guinea. There are no road links with Sabah and the few (poorly maintained) roads to Sarawak are not recognised as gateways to Indonesia.

Travel - Internal

AIR: Indonesia has a good internal air system linking most of the larger towns to Jakarta. Domestic flights from Jakarta depart from Terminal 1 at *Soekarno-Hatta International Airport* (except *Garuda Airlines* flights, which leave from Terminal 2). Domestic operators include: *Bouraq Indonesia Airlines (BO)*, *Garuda Indonesia (GA)* and *Merpati Nusantara Airlines (MZ)*.
Cheap fares: The *Asean Air Pass* offers special fares on domestic flights and gives access to varying numbers of cities depending on the ticket bought. Passes must be bought at Garuda Indonesia offices in Australia, Europe, Japan or the USA (not available inside Indonesia). For prices and further information, contact *Garuda Indonesia* (tel: (020) 7467 8600; fax: (020) 7467 8601); e-mail: enquiries@garuda-indonesia.co.uk; website: www.garuda-indonesia.com).
Departure tax: Rp8-20,000, depending on airport of departure; infants under the age of two are exempt.
SEA: *PELINI*, the state-owned shipping company, has six modern ferries serving all the main ports across the archipelago. Foreign cruise liners also operate on an irregular basis. Luxury cruise ships offer trips to various destinations, including the eastern islands (leaving from Bali). For further details, contact the Indonesia Tourism Promotion Office (see *Contact Addresses* section).
RAIL: Children under three travel free. Children aged three to seven pay half fare. There are nearly 7000km (4350 miles) of track on Java, Madura and Sumatra. In Sumatra, trains connect Belawan, Medan and Tanjong Balai/Rantu Prapet (two or three trains daily) in the north, and Palembang and Panjang (three trains daily) in the south. An extensive rail network runs throughout Java. The *Bima Express*, which has sleeping and restaurant cars, links Jakarta and Surabaya; there are also other express services. There are three classes of travel, but first-class exists only on principal expresses. There is some air-conditioned accommodation.
ROAD: Traffic drives on the left. There are over 378,000km (234,360 miles) of roads in the country, of which about 28,500km (17,670 miles) are main or national roads and 200km (125 miles) are motorway. Nearly half of the network is paved. There are good road communications within Java and, to a lesser extent, on Bali and Sumatra. The other islands have poor road systems, although conditions are improving with tourism becoming more important. Road tolls are in operation on some major city roads and need to be paid for by visitors if using a taxi. Chauffeur-driven cars are widely available, with rates varying according to the type of destination. **Bus:** There are regular services between most towns. Bus trips can be made from Jakarta to Bali (two days). Indonesia is the land of *jam karet* (literally, 'rubber time') and complicated journeys involving more than a single change should not be attempted in a day. Bus fares are about the same as third-class rail. Vehicles can be extremely crowded, although many of them are air conditioned. The crew includes three conductors who also act as touts. There are 'Bis Malam' night buses on a number of routes, running in competition with the railways. Pre-booking is essential. Special 'travel minibuses' offering a door-to-door service are also available in cities and major tourist areas. Visitors should note that Indonesian bus drivers are notorious for reckless driving.
Taxi: Widely available in most large cities and some smaller towns. Metered taxis are usually only found in the main cities and major tourist areas. Taxi drivers do not always know how to get to the desired destination and passengers may have to tell them. Like all public transport vehicles, taxis have yellow number plates (for private and rented vehicles, the number plates are black, while government vehicles have red plates). **Car hire:** Available from a number of companies and from taxi firms, some of which also provide a limousine service. **Documentation:** An International Driving Permit is required.
Alternative transport: There are two forms of tricycle **rickshaws** available in Indonesia: the motorised version is called *bajaj* (pronounced 'baj-eye'), which is a bright orange colour and seats two passengers, with the driver in front; and the *becak* (pronounced 'be-chak') is pedal-powered by a rider sitting behind a maximum of two passengers. Fares should be negotiated in advance. Rickshaws are an extremely popular and cheap form of transport and can be hired almost everywhere (though becaks have now been banned from Jakarta city centre). **Motorcycles** and **bicycles** can be rented on a daily or weekly basis; for motorcycles, an International Driving Licence is recommended and a helmet should be worn. **Bemos** and **Colts** are small buses, seating up to 10 people, and can be chartered on a daily or weekly basis for travel away from the city centres; fares should be negotiated in advance. **Horse carts** may still be hired in rural areas (though they are no longer available in Jakarta).
URBAN: Jakarta is the only city with an established conventional bus service of any size. Double-deckers are operated.

Accommodation

International hotels are found only in major towns and tourist areas. Several of these have business centres with a variety of services. High hotel taxes are charged (10 per cent service, plus 11 per cent government tax). However, hotels of all grades from deluxe to standard can be found in most towns around the country. Resort hotels on Bali vary from international class, luxury hotels to beach cottages along the shore. Most hotels have pools and can supply most leisure equipment. **Grading:** All hotels are graded according to facilities. For more information, contact the Indonesian Hotel & Restaurant Association, JL RP Soeroso no. 27 GHI, Jakarta 10350 (tel: (21) 310 2922; fax: (21) 3190 7407; e-mail: phri-bpp@ihra.co.id; website: www.ihra.co.id).

Resorts & Excursions

JAVA

JAKARTA: The capital city of Jakarta retains much from the colonial Dutch and British periods, with many fine colonial-style buildings and the recently restored 'old quarter'. The **National Monument** towers 140m (450ft) above the Merdeka Square and is crowned with a 'flame' plated in pure gold. The **Central Museum** has a fine ethnological collection, including statues dating from the pre-Hindu era. Worth visiting is the **Portuguese Church**, completed by the Dutch in 1695, which houses a magnificent and immense Dutch pump organ. The modern **Istiqlal Mosque** in the city centre is one of the largest in the world. There is an antiques market on Jalan Surabaya and batik factories in the Karet. Throughout the island, puppet shows are staged in which traditional *wayang golak*

and *wayang kulit* marionettes act out stories based on well-known legends; performances can sometimes last all night.
ELSEWHERE ON JAVA: Around 13km (8 miles) from Yogyakarta is the **Prambanan** temple complex, built in honour of the Hindu gods Brahma, Shiva and Vishnu, which includes the 10th-century **Temple of Loro Jonggrang** and said to be the most perfectly proportioned Hindu temple in Indonesia. At the temple there are also open-air performances of Ramayana ballet which involve hundreds of dancers, singers and *gamelan* musicians. Perched on a hill to the west of Yogyakarta is **Borobudur**, probably the largest Buddhist sanctuary in the world, which contains more than 5km (3 miles) of relief carvings. The **Royal Mangkunegaran Palace** in Surakarta is now used as a museum and has displays of dance ornaments, jewellery and 19th-century carriages used for royal occasions. **Mount Bromo** in the east of Java is still very active, and horseback treks to the crater's edge can be made from nearby Surabaya. During August and September, **Madura** is a venue for a series of bullock races which culminate in a 48-hour non-stop carnival celebration in the town of **Pamekasan**.

SULAWESI

Unofficially known as 'Orchid Island', Sulawesi is a land of high mountains, misty valleys and lakes. In the south is **Bantimurung Nature Reserve** which has thousands of exotic butterflies. The island has geysers and hot springs, the most celebrated of which are at Karumengan, Kinilow, Lahendong, Leilem and Makule. **Torajaland** is known as the 'Land of the Heavenly Kings' and its people are noted for their richly ornamented houses and custom of burying the dead in vertical cliffside tombs. **Ujung Pandang**, formerly Makassar, is celebrated for the **Pinsa Harbour**, where wooden schooners of the famous Buganese seafarers are moored. **Fort Rotterdam**, built by Sultan Ala in 1660 to protect the town from pirates, is now being restored. Racing is a popular island activity; there is horse racing and bullock-racing and, at **Ranomuut**, there are races with traditional horse-drawn carts (*bendi*).

SUMATRA

Sumatra is the second-largest island in Indonesia, straddling the Equator, with a volcanic mountain range, hot springs, unexplored jungle and vast plantations. There are many reserves established to protect the indigenous wildlife from extinction. **Bengkulu**, **Gedung Wani** and **Mount Loeser Reserve** organise supervised safaris enabling visitors to see tigers, elephants, tapirs and rhinos at close hand. **Lake Toba**, once a volcanic crater, is 900m (3000ft) above sea level and has an inhabited island in the middle. **Lingga** village near **Medan** is a traditional Karonese settlement with stilted wooden houses which have changed little through the centuries. At **Bukittinggi** is the old fortress of **Fort de Kock** and nearby a zoo, market, a renovated rice barn and the **Bundo Kandung Museum**. The best beaches are on the east coast.

BALI

The landscape of Bali, 'Island of the Gods', is made up of volcanic mountains, lakes and rivers, terraced ricefields, giant banyans and palm groves and, on the coast, bays ringed with white sandy beaches. The island lies a short distance from the eastern coast of Java, across the Strait of Bali. Although its total area is only 2095 sq km (1309 sq miles), the island supports a population of approximately 2.5 million. Unlike the rest of Indonesia, the predominant religious faith is Hinduism, though in a special form known as 'Agama-Hindu'. Stretching east to west across the island is a volcanic chain of mountains, dominated by the mighty **Gunung Agung** (Holy Mountain), whose conical peak soars more than 3170m (10,400ft) into the sky. North of the mountains, where the fertility of the terrain permits, is an area devoted to the production of vegetables and copra. The fertile rice-growing region lies on the central plains.
The tourist areas are in the south, around **Sanur Beach** and at **Kuta**, which lies on the other side of a narrow isthmus. Nearby **Nusa Dusa** is also a popular tourist area and has a number of reasonably priced resorts and hotels.
The island has thousands of temples – the exact number has never been counted – ranging from the great 'Holy Temple' at **Besakih** to small village places of worship. Of the many festivals, most are held twice a year and involve splendid processions, dances and daily offerings of food and flowers made to the gods. Cremations are also held in great style, though their cost is often almost prohibitive for the average Balinese family.
Denpasar is the island's capital. Sights include the **Museum**, a new art centre and the internationally recognised **Konservatori Kerawitan**, one of the major centres of Balinese dancing. The **Sea Temple of Tanah Lot** on the west coast (a short drive from Kediri) is one of the most breathtaking sights of Bali. **Goa Gajah** (Elephant Cave) near Bedulu is a huge cavern with an entrance carved in a fantastic design of demonical shapes, animals and plants, crowned by a monstrous gargoyle-like head. The **Holy Springs of Tampaksiring** are believed to possess curative properties and attract thousands of visitors each year. **Serangan Island** is also known as Turtle Island because of the turtles kept there in special pens. The island lies south of Sanur and can be reached by sail boat or, at low tide, on foot. Every six months, the island becomes the scene of a great thanksgiving ceremony in which tens of thousands take part.
The sacred monkey forest at **Sangeh** is a forest reserve which, as well as being the home of a variety of exotic apes, also has a temple. **Penelokan** is a splendid vantage point for views of the black lava streams from **Mount Batur**. It is also possible to sail across the nearby **Lake Batur** to Trunyan for a closer look at the crater. North of Kintamani, at an altitude of 1745m (5725ft), lies the highest temple on the island, **Penulisan**. **Pura Besakih**, a temple which dates back originally to the 10th century, stands high on the volcanic slopes of **Gunung Agung**. Nowadays, it is a massive complex of more than 30 temples, and the setting for great ceremonial splendour on festival days. **Padangbai** is a beautiful tropical coastal village, where lush vegetation backs a curving stretch of white, sandy beach. It is also the island's port of call for giant cruise liners. **Goa Lawah** lives up to its name ('bat cave' in the local tongue), a safe and holy haven for thousands of bats which line every inch of space on its walls and roof. Non bat-lovers should avoid moonlight strolls in the area, as the animals leave for food sorties at night. **Kusambe** is a fishing village with a black sand beach. **Lake Bratan** is reached via a winding road from Budugul. The shimmering cool beauty of the lake and its pine-forested hillsides is an unusual sight in a tropical landscape.
Art centres: The village of **Ubud** is the centre of Bali's considerable art colony and contains the galleries of the most successful painters, including those of artists of foreign extraction who have settled on the island. Set in a hilltop garden is the **Museam Puri Lukistan** (Palace of Fine Arts) with its fine display of sculpture and paintings in both old and contemporary styles. **Kamasan**, near Klungkung, is another centre, but the painting style of the artists is predominantly *wayang* (highly stylised). Other artistic centres include *Celuk* (gold and silver working), *Denpasar* (woodworking and painting) and *Batubulan* (stone carving).

LOMBOK

Only a 15-minute flight (or ferry trip) away is Lombok, an unspoilt island whose name means 'chilli pepper'. Its area is 1285 sq km (803 sq miles). The island possesses one of the highest volcanic mountains in the Indonesian archipelago, **Mount Rindjani**, whose cloud-piercing peak soars to 3745m (12,290ft). The population of about 750,000 is a mixture of Islamic Sasaks, Hindu Balinese and others of Malay origin. The two main towns are **Mataram**, the capital, and the busy port of **Ampenan**; both are interesting to explore. The south coast is rocky. The west, with shimmering rice terraces, banana and coconut groves and fertile plains, looks like an extension of Bali. The east is dry, barren and desert-like in appearance. The north, the region dominated by **Mount Rindjani**, offers thick forests and dramatic vistas. There are also some glorious beaches, some of white sand, others, such as those near Ampenan, of black sand.
At **Narmada**, reached by an excellent east-west highway, is a huge complex of palace dwellings, complete with a well containing 'rejuvenating waters', built for a former Balinese king. At **Pamenang**, visitors can hire a boat and go skindiving, entering a clear-water world of brilliantly coloured coral and inquisitive tropical fish.

EASTERN INDONESIA

The wildest and least visited of Indonesia's 17,000 islands are in the east, gathered in two great archipelagos north and south of the treacherous Banda Sea.
MOLUCCAN ARCHIPELAGO: Also known as the Maluku Archipelago, it is made up of 1000 islands, many uninhabited and the rest so isolated from each other and (since the decline of the spice trade) from the outside world that each has its own culture and very often its own language.
Halmahera is the largest island in the Moluccan group and one of the most diverse. On the coast are relic populations of all the great powers who competed for domination of the Spice Trade – Arabs, Dutch, Gujuratis, Malays and Portuguese – whilst inland the people speak a unique language that has little or nothing in common even with other unique, but related, languages on the more remote islands. **Morotai**, to the north, was the site of a Japanese air base during World War II, but is now engaged in the production of copra and cocoa products.
Ternate and **Tidore**, tiny volcanic islands off the west coast of Halmahera, were once the world's most important source of cloves and consequently amassed far more wealth and power than their size would seem to merit. The Sultanate of Ternate was an independent military power of considerable muscle before the arrival of the Portuguese, exerting influence over much of South-East Asia. Both islands are littered with the remains of this and the equally strident colonial era, and draw more tourists than their larger neighbour.
Further south, **Ambon** was another important centre of the clove trade, and has over 40 old Dutch fortresses dating from the early 17th century. **Banda**, in the middle of the Banda Sea, is often referred to as the original 'Spice Island' and is famous as a nutmeg-growing centre.
NUSA TENGARA ARCHIPELAGO: Nusa Penida was at one time a penal colony but now attracts visitors to its dramatic seascapes and beaches. **Komodo** is home to the world's largest and rarest species of monitor lizard, while **Sumba** is noted for its beautiful *Ikat* cloth. **Mount Keli Mutu** is one of Indonesia's most spectacular natural sights, famous for its three crater lakes, whose striking colours change with the light of the day.
The islands north of **Timor** – including Adonara, Alor, Lembata, Pantar, Solor and Wetar – are rarely visited by tourists; there are many old fortresses on the islands and from here seafarers used to set sail on whale hunts. Timor itself is out of bounds to tourists because of the bloody and protracted war with freedom fighters in the east of the island. The cultures on **Roti**, **Ndau** and **Sawu** have apparently changed little since the Bronze Age, yet the islands' inhabitants are renowned as musicians and palm weavers.
The **Terawangan Islands** is a small group with beautiful beaches and coral gardens. **Lucipara** has excellent waters for snorkelling. **Bone Rate**, **Kangean**, **Tenggaya** and **Tukang Besi** is a group of isolated atolls in the Flores and Banda seas, epitomising a tropical paradise.
IRIAN JAYA: The western part of the island of New Guinea, this is one of the last great unexplored areas of the world. Even today, visiting ships are often greeted by flotillas of warriors in war canoes. All those intending to visit Irian Jaya must obtain special permits from State Police Headquarters in Jakarta. Travellers are advised to avoid this area at present.

Credit: © Bali Tourism Authority

Sport & Activities

Surfing: The Indonesian archipelago is one of the world's top surfing destinations. The best time to surf is from April to September with the best waves generally found on islands facing south and southwest, including Bali, Flores, Java, Lombok, Sumatra, Sumba and Sumbawa. Some well-known surfing beaches, such as *Ulu Watu* on Bali, tend to get overcrowded, but organised trips to isolated areas are widely available. Surf camps such as those at *Cempi Bay* (Sumbawa) or *Lagundri Bay* (Nias) offer basic accommodation and simple food. **Windsurfing** is particularly popular on *Bintan Island* and *Sanur* and *Nusa Dua* beaches on Bali.
Diving: There are approximately 80,000km (50,000 miles) of coastline, reputed to contain 15 per cent of the world's coral reefs. In spite of the obvious opportunities, Indonesia's diving industry is still relatively young, though the number of companies offering courses and excursions is rising rapidly.

Credit: © Bali Tourism Authority

On Java island, the best diving is on the west coast, where three volcanic islands mark the remains of the *Krakatoa* volcano (which last erupted in 1883). Bali's tourist stronghold in the *Kuta*, *Nusa Dua* and *Suar* triangle offers easy and moderate diving, with easily accessible reefs. Tours to more remote (and less busy) areas are available. On the northern tip of Sulawesi island, the *Taman Nasional Laut Bunaken Manado Tua* is a national marine reserve with particularly steep coral walls; international air connections to the island facilitate access. Further north, the lesser-known *Sanggihe-Talaud* and *Togian* islands are reached by live-aboard dive boats. In the south, *Take Bone Rate* is the world's third-largest atoll, while the *Tukang Besi* islands have featured extensively in the films by the French underwater explorer Jacques Cousteau. Nusa Tenggara's most popular sites are the three *Gili* islands near Lombok, whose calm shallow waters are ideal for beginners. *Maluku* consists of approximately 1000 islands and has only recently been discovered as a top diving destination. Southeast of Ambon, the *Bandana* islands are accessible by air and offer a number of sites suitable for beginners and experienced divers. The major resort in the Sumatra and Riau islands is Bintan, easily accessible from Singapore. The clearest and most colourful dive sites are in *Pulau Sikuai* off the Padang coast (western Sumatra) and *Pulau Weh off Banda Aceh* (northern Sumatra). Irian Jaya also offers good diving around the famous *Mapia Atoll* (where dolphins and killer whales can sometimes be spotted) and the waters of *Cenderawasih Bay* off the western end of Bird's Head peninsula.
Climbing: The island of Sumatra is perhaps the best location. *Gunung Padang*, near the island's capital, Padang, is a small black basalt cliff reached via a river-paddling trip followed by a trek through rainforest. Further inland, *Bukittinggi* offers challenging cliffs overlooking rice paddies. The dramatic canyon rocks in nearby *Harau National Park* are still largely unexplored and should only be attempted by experienced climbers.
Caving: Indonesia's most accessible caves are on the island of Java and include *Luweng Jaran*, stretching over 20km (125 miles) beneath the Gunung Seuw mountain range; *Gua Barat*, which has the longest underground river system in the southern hemisphere; and *Gombong*, whose stone towers rise spectacularly to some 40m (132ft) above sea level. On Kalimantan island, *Mangkalihat* offers a rarely visited underground world of giant limestone corridors. Even less explored are the isolated caves near *Wamena* on the remote Bird's Head peninsula in Irian Jaya.
Sailing: The majority of companies offering **whitewater rafting** are located in Bali, where several rivers – including the Ayung, Balian, Telega, Ubaya and Unda – are commercially rafted. Spectacular rapids can also be found on the Citartik River (western Java), the Sadan River (Sulawesi) and the Alas River (Sumatra). Rapids are generally at their strongest between November and March. **River tours** up the great *Mahakam River* on the island of Kalimantan, which is dissected by a network of rivers running from the mountainous interior to the coasts, are billed as a trip into the 'heart of darkness'. Starting from the port city Samarinda, such tours last for several days (with onboard accommodation available) and continue deep into the upper jungle reaches, where tribal communities have largely preserved their traditions.
Trekking: Indonesia has some 120 active volcanoes and numerous **volcano treks** are possible: on Java island, popular volcanic destinations include *Krakatoa* (reached by a five-hour boat trip, followed by a 30-minute climb), *Mount Bromo* (the most visited of Indonesia's volcanoes) and *Kawah Ijen* (whose crater is filled by a turquoise-blue lake). Those preferring dormant volcanoes may head to *Gunung Agung* in Bali (known as the 'Navel of the World'), *Gunung Rinjani* on Lombok island (which has hot springs at the top and is revered for its mystical qualities) and *Keli Mutu* on Nusa Tenggara Barat (whose crater contains three spectacular mineral lakes). For **jungle trekking** through the Indonesian rainforest, the islands of Irian Jaya, Kalimantan and Sumatra offer the most remote and untouched terrain. The best trails include trips to *Bukit Barisan National Park*, a remote and beautiful peninsula in Sumatra (with routes leading through tropical rainforest onto a beach inhabited by turtles); the *Muller Mountain* on Kalimantan (with a trail following the traditional jungle route used by the native Iban people); and *Lake Habbema* on Irian Jaya (a week-long trek to remote villages and mountains).
Ecotourism: Having been criticised in the past for the destruction of large areas of its rainforest through forest exploitation, the Indonesian government is now keen to encourage an environmentally friendly tourism policy. The growing trend for back-to-nature holidays means that numerous types of eco-tours are available. In the Tukangbeshi archipelago near Sulawesi, tourists have the opportunity to participate in coral reef preservation projects by helping to collect scientific data.

Social Profile

FOOD & DRINK: The staple diet for most Indonesians is rice (*nasi*), which is replaced on some islands with corn, sago, cassava and sweet potatoes. Rice dishes include *nais campur*, *nasi uduk* and *rasirames*. Indonesia's spices make its local cuisine unique. Specialities include: *rijstafel* (a Dutch concoction consisting of a variety of meats, fish, vegetables and curries), *sate* (chunks of beef, fish, pork, chicken or lamb cooked on hot coals and dipped in peanut sauce). Almost every type of international cuisine is available in Jakarta, the most popular being Chinese, French, Italian, Japanese and Korean *sate ajam* (broiled, skewered marinated chicken), *ajam ungkap* (Central Java; deep-fried, marinated chicken), *sate lileh* (Bali; broiled, skewered fish sticks), *ikan acar kuning* (Jakarta; lightly marinated fried fish served in a sauce of pickled spices and palm sugar), *soto* (a soup dish with dumpling, chicken and vegetables), *gado-gado* (Java; a salad of raw and cooked vegetables with peanut and coconut milk sauce), *babi guling* (Bali; roast suckling pig) and *opor ajam* (boiled chicken in coconut milk and light spices). Indonesians like their food highly spiced and the visitor should always bear this in mind. In particular, look out for the tiny, fiery hot, red and green peppers often included in salads and vegetable dishes. Seafood is excellent and features highly on menus everywhere (with salt and fresh-water fish, lobsters, oysters, prawns, shrimp, squid, shark and crab all available). Coconuts, which are found everywhere, are often used for cooking. Vegetables and fresh fruit, such as bananas, papaya, pineapple and oranges, are available throughout the year; some tropical fruit such as mango, watermelon and papaya are seasonal. A feature of Jakarta are the many *warungs* (street stalls). Each specialises in its own dish or drink, but travellers are probably best advised not to try them without the advice of an Indonesian resident. There are restaurants in the hotels which, along with many others, serve European, Chinese and Indian food.
Indonesia is a major producer and exporter of coffee and tea, which is available on almost every street corner. Bali produces a delicious rice wine called *brem*, while in Tana Toraja (southern Sulawesi), visitors may wish to sample a *Tuak*, a famously potent local brew. Local *pilsner* beer is also available.
NIGHTLIFE: Jakarta nightclubs feature international singers and bands and are open until 0400 during weekends. Jakarta has over 40 cinemas and some English-language and subtitled films are shown. There are also casinos, and theatres providing cultural performances. Dancing is considered an art, encouraged and practised from very early childhood. The extensive repertoire is based on ancient legends and stories from religious epics. Performances are given in village halls and squares, and also in many of the leading hotels by professional touring groups. The dances vary enormously, both in style and number of performers. Some of the more notable are the *Legong*, a slow, graceful dance of divine nymphs; the *Baris*, a fast moving, noisy demonstration of male, warlike behaviour; and the *Jauk*, a riveting solo offering by a masked and richly costumed demon. Many consider the most dramatic of all to be the famous *Cecak* (Monkey Dance), which calls for 100 or more very agile participants. Many of the larger hotels, particularly in Bali, put on dance shows accompanied by the uniquely Indonesian Gamelan Orchestras.
Throughout the year, many local moonlight festivals occur; tourists should check locally. Indonesian puppets are world famous and shows for visitors are staged in various locations.
SHOPPING: Favourite buys are batik cloth, woodcarvings and sculpture, silverwork, woven baskets and hats, bamboo articles, *krises* (small daggers), paintings and woven cloth. At small shops, bartering might be necessary. **Shopping hours:** Mon-Sun 1000-2100. Most local markets open either very early in the morning or at dusk.
SPECIAL EVENTS: There are numerous festivals which take place during the year, the dates of which often vary according to the Hindu or Buddhist calendars. Bali stages some magnificent festivals all year round. Festival calendars can be obtained on arrival. The Sultan's birthday in mid-December is celebrated by a fair and festival in Yogyakarta, Java. For a full list of festivals and special events, contact the Indonesia Tourism Promotion Board or a representative ITPO office (see *Contact Addresses*). The following is a selection of special events occurring in Indonesia in 2005:
Jan *Lomban Festival* (fishermen's festival), Jepara. **Apr** *Nyepi* (Day of Silence), Bali and Tenggara. **Jun-Jul** *Bali Arts Festival*, Denpasar. **Aug-Sep** *Kerapan Sapi* (bull races), Madura Island. **Sep 24** *Dugderran* (festival for the start of Ramadan), various towns/venues. **Oct 24** *Idul Fitri* (Eid al-Fitr), marking the end of Ramadan, Kebumen. **Dec** *Pukul Sapu*.
SOCIAL CONVENTIONS: Indonesia encompasses at least 583 separate languages and dialects, many of them as different from each other as Welsh is from English. Since independence, many people have developed a strong sense of national pride, and maintain traditions of dance, painting, woodcarving and stonecarving. Social courtesies are often fairly formal. In particular, when drink or food is served, it should not be touched until the host invites the guest to do so. Never pass or accept anything with the left hand. Public displays of affection between men and women are frowned upon and kissing in public will attract a great deal of unwanted attention. Touching a stranger of the same sex while in conversation is very common. Pointing is considered impolite and patting children on the head should be avoided. Indonesians are polite and will extend endless courtesies to visitors whom they trust and like. Smiling is a cultural tradition and Indonesians smile frequently, even in an uncomfortable or difficult situation. Visitors should avoid the temptation of losing their temper. When invited home, a gift is appreciated (as long as it is given with the right hand). Informality is normal, but a few smart establishments encourage guests to dress for dinner. Safari suits are acceptable on formal occasions and for business wear. Muslim customs, especially those concerning female clothes, should be observed. **Tipping:** Tipping is normal and 10 per cent is customary, except where a service charge is included in the bill. Taxi fees should be rounded up to the nearest number. Small change is rarely given and visitors should carry a supply of their own.

Business Profile

ECONOMY: 'The most dramatic economic collapse anywhere in the past five decades' is how one World Bank official described the calamitous disintegration of the Indonesian economy in the autumn of 1997. In 1998, economic output in Indonesia declined by more than 12 per cent and the national currency, the Rupiah, lost 80 per cent of its value. The crash occurred after more than a decade of uninterrupted growth at between eight and 10 per cent annually. In January 1998, the IMF was forced into arranging its largest-ever financial rescue package, totalling US$43 billion, in order to prevent total economic collapse. During 1999, the economy stabilised and, since 2000, has resumed steady annual growth of around four per cent. Inflation has now stabilised at around seven per cent; unemployment remains relatively high at about nine per cent of the workforce. The value of the Rupiah has also settled down. Nonetheless, only limited measures have been taken to deal with the structural problems which previously blighted the economy. The Suharto era's system of 'crony capitalism' still prevails, and essential reforms to the country's financial system have yet to be effected.
Thirty years earlier, as Indonesia's economic expansion began in earnest after the upheavals of the mid-60s, the country was far less developed than many of its neighbours. However, it was able to exploit its considerable mineral resources as a foundation on which to build an industrial economy. Oil and natural gas are the most important raw materials produced by Indonesia; it is still one of the largest exporters of liquefied natural gas. The country is also the second-largest producer of tin and extracts substantial quantities of other metals and metal ores (bauxite, copper, silver, gold and nickel) as well as coal and rubber. Much of the processing of these products is now done within the country. The agricultural sector (including fishing and forestry) remains important but more as a source of employment – it accounts for half the work force – than for its contribution to the economy. The service sector grew rapidly from the beginning of the 1980s onwards. Tourism has become a major industry and a vital source of foreign exchange (though likely to suffer in the wake of the Bali bomb attacks). Transport and communications, financial services and international freight traffic also made important contributions. However, it was the manufacturing industry, which developed from virtual non-existence in 1965 to its mid-90s position of providing one-quarter of economic output, which received most attention from the Government (as well as outsiders) and announced Indonesia's arrival as a fully fledged 'Asian Tiger' economy. Despite the high profile of the vehicle, aerospace and electronics industries, Indonesia's manufacturing success was rooted in less glamorous areas such as textiles, food processing, tobacco and timber products. The bulk of Indonesia's trade is conducted within the region, especially with Japan (which accounts for approximately

one-quarter of total trade), Singapore, Korea, Australia and China (including Hong Kong). Outside the region, the USA and Germany are its major trading partners.
BUSINESS: Business dealings should be conducted through an agent and tend to be slow. Visiting cards are widely used. It is conventional to shake hands and give a slight bow with the head on meeting and taking leave. Literature should be in English, but prices should be quoted in US Dollars as well as Pounds Sterling. **Private office hours:** Mon-Fri 0800-1600 or 0900-1700. **Government office hours:** Mon-Thurs 0800-1430, Fri 0800-1200.
COMMERCIAL INFORMATION: The following organisation can offer advice: Kamar Dagang dan Industri Indonesia (KADIN) (Indonesian Chamber of Commerce and Industry), 3rd-5th Floors, Chandra Building, Jalan M H Thamrin 20, Jakarta 10350 (tel: (21) 324 000; fax: (21) 315 0241).
CONFERENCES/CONVENTIONS: The Balai Sidang Jakarta Convention Centre has the capacity for up to 5000 people. For information or assistance in organising a conference or convention in Indonesia, contact the Directorate-General of Tourism *or* the Indonesia Tourism Promotion Board *or* a representative IPTO office (see *Contact Addresses* section).

Climate

Tropical climate varying from area to area. The eastern monsoon brings the driest weather (June to September), while the western monsoon brings the main rains (December to March). Rainstorms occur all year. Higher regions are cooler.
Required clothing: Lightweights with rainwear. Warmer clothes are needed for cool evenings and upland areas. Smart clothes such as jackets are required for formal occasions, and it is regarded inappropriate to wear halter-neck tops and shorts anywhere other than the beach or at sports facilities.

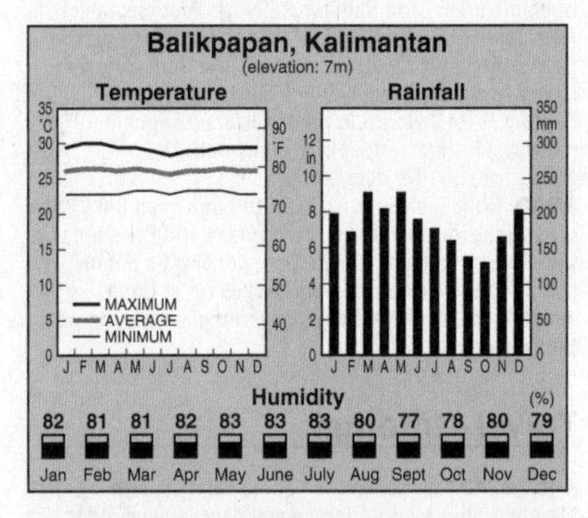

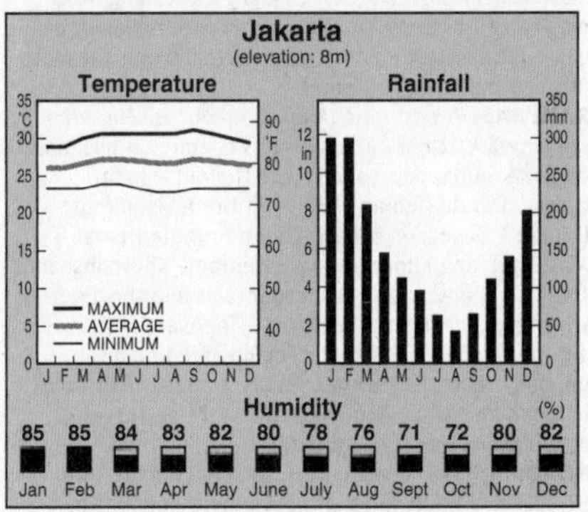

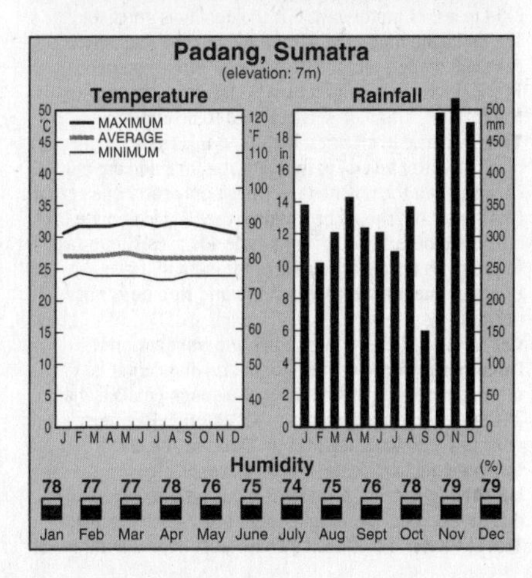

Iran

LATEST TRAVEL ADVICE CONTACTS

British Foreign and Commonwealth Office
Tel: (0870) 606 0290 Website: www.fco.gov.uk
US Department of State
Website: http://travel.state.gov/travel
Canadian Department of Foreign Affairs and Int'l Trade
Tel: (1 800) 267 8376 Website: www.dfait-maeci.gc.ca

Location: Middle East.

Country dialling code: 98.

Iran Touring and Tourism Organisation (ITTO)
238 Sindokht Street, Fatemi Avenue, Tehran, Iran
Tel: (21) 643 5650. Fax: (21) 643 5689.
E-mail: info@itto.org
Website: www.itto.org
Iran Tourist Company
257 Ostad Motahari Avenue, Ghaem Magham Farahni Street, Cross Road, Tehran, Iran
Tel: (21) 873 9819 *or* 6762-5.
Fax: (21) 873 6158 *or* 874 7860.
E-mail: info@irantouristco.com
Website: www.irantouristco.com
Embassy of the Islamic Republic of Iran
16 Prince's Gate, London SW7 1PT, UK
Tel: (020) 7225 3000. Fax: (020) 7589 4440.
E-mail: info@iran-embassy.org.uk
Website: www.iran-embassy.org.uk
Opening hours: Mon-Fri 0900-1700.
Iranian Consulate
50 Kensington Court, Kensington High Street, London W8 5DB, UK
Tel: (020) 7937 5225 *or* (0906) 302 0600 (visa section).
Fax: (020) 7938 1615.
E-mail: consulate@iran-embassy.org.uk
Website: www.iran-embassy.org.uk
Opening hours: Mon-Thurs 0900-1300, Fri 0900-1200.
British Embassy
Street address: 198 Ferdowsi Avenue, Tehran 11316-91144, Iran
Postal address: PO Box 11365-4474, Tehran, Iran
Tel: (21) 670 5011-7. Fax: (21) 670 8021 (commercial section) *or* 0720 (visa section).
E-mail: BritishEmbassyTehran@fco.gov.uk *or* visaenquiries.Tehran@fco.gov.uk
Website: www.britishembassy.gov.uk/iran
Permanent Mission of the Islamic Republic of Iran to the United Nations
622 Third Avenue, 34th Floor, New York, NY 10017, USA
Tel: (212) 687 2020. Fax: (212) 867 7086.

TIMATIC CODES

Health
AMADEUS: **TI-DFT/THR/HE**
GALILEO/WORLDSPAN: **TI-DFT/THR/HE**
SABRE: **TIDFT/THR/HE**

Visa
AMADEUS: **TI-DFT/THR/VI**
GALILEO/WORLDSPAN: **TI-DFT/THR/VI**
SABRE: **TIDFT/THR/VI**

To access TIMATIC country information on Health and Visa regulations through the Computer Reservations System (CRS), type in the appropriate command line listed above.

E-mail: iran@un.int
Website: www.un.int/iran
Interests Section of the Islamic Republic of Iran
c/o The Embassy of Pakistan, 2209 Wisconsin Avenue, NW, Washington, DC 20007, USA
Tel: (202) 965 4990. Fax: (202) 965 1073.
E-mail: requests@daftar.org
Website: www.daftar.org
Embassy of the Islamic Republic of Iran
245 Metcalfe Street, Ottawa, Ontario K2P 2K2, Canada
Tel: (613) 235 4726 *or* 233 4726 (consular section).
Fax: (613) 232 5712 *or* 236 4726 (consular section).
E-mail: iranemb@salamiran.org *or* consulate@salamiran.org
Website: www.salamiran.org
Canadian Embassy
Street address: 57 Shahid Javad-e-Sarfaraz Street, Ostad Motahari Avenue, Tehran 15868, Iran
Postal address: PO Box 11365-4647, Tehran, Iran
Tel: (21) 873 2623-6. Fax: (21) 873 3202 *or* 875 7054 (visa section).
E-mail: teran@dfait-maeci.gc.ca

General Information

AREA: 1,648,043 sq km (636,313 sq miles).
POPULATION: 66,479,838 (official estimate 2003).
POPULATION DENSITY: 40.3 per sq km.
CAPITAL: Tehran. **Population:** 7,038,000 (UN estimate, including suburbs, 2001).
GEOGRAPHY: Iran is located in the Middle East, bordered to the north by Turkmenistan and the Caspian Sea, the east by Afghanistan and Pakistan, the south by the Persian Gulf and the Gulf of Oman, and the west by Iraq and Turkey. The centre and east of the country are largely barren undulating desert, punctured by *qanats* (irrigation canals) and green oases, but there are mountainous regions in the west along the Turkish and Iraqi borders and in the north where the Elburz Mountains rise steeply from a fertile belt around the Caspian Sea.
GOVERNMENT: Islamic Republic since 1979. **Head of State:** Supreme Leader (Rahbar-e Moazam) Seyyed Ali Khameni since 1989. **Head of Government:** President Mohammad Khatami since 2001.
LANGUAGE: Persian (*Farsi*) is the most widely spoken language. Arabic is spoken in Khuzestan in the southwest, and Turkish in the northwest around Tabriz. English, French and (to a lesser extent) German are spoken by many businesspeople and officials.
RELIGION: Predominantly Islamic; mostly Shi'ite, with a minority of Sunnis. The 1976 census recorded 300,000 Christians, 80,000 Jews and 30,000 Zoroastrians.
TIME: GMT + 3.5 (GMT + 4.5 from 20 March to 21 September).
ELECTRICITY: 230 volts AC, 50Hz. Plugs are of the round two-pin type.
COMMUNICATIONS: Telephone: IDD service available. Country code: 98. Outgoing international code: 00. Telephone booths are yellow. **Mobile telephone:** GSM 900 network. Main network operators include *MTCE* (website: www.mtce.ir), *TCI* and *TKC* (website: www.tkckish.com). **Fax/telegram:** Facilities are available at main post offices. There are three charge bands. There are also fax facilities at the major hotels. **Internet:** ISPs include *Pishgaman Kavir Yazd* and *Tehran Web* (website: www.mz3.com). There are Internet cafes in Tehran and other cities. **Post:** Airmail to Western Europe can take at least two weeks. There are 10 main post offices in Tehran. Post boxes are yellow. Stamps can be bought at some cigarette kiosks. Post office hours: Generally Sat-Thurs 0730-1500, but some main post offices stay open until 2100. **Press:** The main English-language papers are the *Iran News*, *Kayhan International* and *Tehran Times*.
Radio: BBC World Service (website: www.bbc.co.uk/worldservice) and Voice of America (website: www.voa.gov) can be received. From time to time the frequencies change and the most up-to-date can be found online.

Passport/Visa

	Passport Required?	Visa Required?	Return Ticket Required?
Full British	Yes	Yes	No
Australian	Yes	Yes	No
Canadian	Yes	Yes	No
USA	Yes	Yes	No
Other EU	Yes	Yes	No
Japanese	Yes	Yes	No

Note: *Regulations and requirements may be subject to change at short notice, and you are advised to contact the appropriate diplomatic or consular authority before finalising travel arrangements. Details of these may be found at the head of this country's entry. Any numbers in the chart refer to the footnotes below.*

Restricted entry: Nationals of Israel or holders of passports containing a visa for Israel (either valid or expired) will be refused entry under all circumstances. Women judged to be dressed immodestly will be refused entry.
PASSPORTS: Passport valid for six months beyond stay required by all.
VISAS: Required by all except the following:
(a) nationals of Turkey for stays of up to three months;
(b) nationals of Malaysia and Singapore may obtain a visa on arrival, free of charge, for stays of up to two weeks;
(c) transit passengers continuing their journey within 12 hours, provided holding valid onward or return documentation and not leaving the airport. Transit passengers continuing their journey within 48 hours (under the above conditions) can obtain a transit visa on arrival against a fee of US$40, or within 72 hours for US$30.
Types of visa and cost: *Tourist/Business/Pilgrimage*: £61 (single-entry); £68 (double-entry). *Business* (multiple-entry): £79 (three months); £90 (six months); £90 (one year). *Transit*: £61. The above prices are for UK nationals; fees vary according to nationality of applicant.
Validity: *Tourist*, *Business* and *Pilgrimage* visas are issued for stays of up to one month and are valid for three months from date of authorisation. *Transit* visas are valid for five days. Applications for renewal or extension should be made to the Iranian Embassy.
Application to: Consulate (or Consular section at Embassy); see *Contact Addresses* section for details.
Application requirements: (a) Valid passport with a minimum of two blank pages to affix visa. (b) Two application forms. (c) Two passport-size photos (women should be photographed wearing the *hejab* – Islamic head dress). (d) For postal applications, self-addressed, registered delivery envelope. (e) Proof of fee payment (payable by postal order or banker's draft to the 'Embassy of the Islamic Republic of Iran', *or* by direct payment into the Embassy bank account at Melli Bank plc, 98A Kensington High Street, London W8 4SG, UK, or by credit card, form to be filled in and sent with application). *Pilgrimage*: (a)-(e) and, (f) Letter of introduction signed by the Head of an Islamic Centre. *Business*: (a)-(e) and, (f) Letter of invitation from the sponsoring company in Iran, authorised and given a reference number by the Iranian Ministry of Foreign Affairs. The applicant should allow five working days before contacting the appropriate Embassy/Consulate with this reference number.
Working days required: A minimum of four weeks.
A *pilgrimage* visa may only take two weeks to process.
Temporary residence: All visitors wishing to stay for more than three months must obtain a residence permit. Application must be made within eight days of arrival to Police Headquarters or the Ministry of Foreign Affairs in Tehran.

Money

Currency: Iranian Rial (IR) = 100 dinars. Notes are in denominations of IR10,000, 5000, 2000 and 1000. Coins are in denominations of IR250, 100, 50, 20, 10 and 5.
Currency exchange: It is advisable to bring hard currency for exchange purposes.
Credit & debit cards: MasterCard is accepted in some places, but credit cards should not be relied on as the sole means of payment. Be aware that if the card was issued in the USA, it may not be usable due to the US trade embargo.
Travellers cheques: It is not possible to change travellers cheques.
Currency restrictions: The import and export of local currency is limited to IR500,000. Any amount larger than this requires authorisation from the Central Bank. The import of foreign currency is unlimited, provided declared on arrival (there is a special form). The export of foreign currency is limited to the amount declared on arrival. There are no ATMs.
Exchange rate indicators: The following figures are included as a guide to the movements of the Iranian Rial against Sterling and the US Dollar:

Date	Feb '04	May '04	Aug '04	Nov '04
£1.00=	15242.80	15280.1	16062.5	16653.2
$1.00=	8374.00	8555.00	8718.50	8794.00

Banking hours: Sat-Wed 0800-1600; some branches are open 0800-2000. Most banks are closed Thurs-Fri.

Duty Free

The following goods may be imported into Iran without incurring customs duty:
A reasonable quantity of cigarettes; a reasonable quantity of perfume for personal use; gifts on which the import duty/tax does not exceed US$80.
Prohibited items: Alcoholic beverages; all horticultural and agricultural goods, including seeds and soil; living (or collection): bacteria, fungi, insects, nematodes or viruses; old books or magazines; live birds, animals and their products.
Penalties for being in possession of narcotics are very severe.

Public Holidays

2005: Jan 21 Eid al-Adha (Feast of the Sacrifice). **Feb 10** Islamic New Year. **Feb 11** Victory of the 1979 Islamic Revolution. **Feb 19** Ashoura. **Mar 20** Oil Nationalisation Day. **Mar 21** Nowrooz (Iranian New Year). **Apr 1** Islamic Republic Day, and Arba'in-e Hosseini. **Apr 2** Sizdah-Bedar (Public Outing Day to end Nowrooz). **Apr 7** Death of the Prophet and Martyrdom of Imam Hassan. **Apr 21** Prophet's Birthday and Imam Sadeq. **Jun 4** Death of Imam Khomeini. **Jun 5** Anniversary of Uprising Against the Shah. **Aug 17** Birthday of Iman Ali. **Sep 1** Leilat al-Meiraj (Ascension of the Prophet). **Sep 18** Birthday of Imam Mahdi. **Sep 22** Martyrdom of Imam Ali. **Nov 1** Quds Day. **Nov 3-5** Eid al-Fitr (End of Ramadan). **Nov 27** Martyrdom of Imam Sadeq. **Dec 23** Birthday of Imam Reza.
2006: Jan 13 Eid al-Adha (Feast of the Sacrifice). **Jan 31** Islamic New Year. **Feb 9** Ashoura. **Feb 11** Victory of the 1979 Islamic Revolution. **Mar 20** Oil Nationalisation Day. **Mar 21** Nowrooz (Iranian New Year). **Apr 1** Islamic Republic Day. **Apr 2** Sizdah-Bedar (Public Outing Day to end Nowrooz). **Apr 11** Prophet's Birthday and Imam Sadeq. **Jun 4** Death of Imam Khomeini. **Jun 5** Anniversary of Uprising Against the Shah. **Aug 22** Leilat al-Meiraj (Ascension of the Prophet). **Oct 22-24** Eid al-Fitr (End of Ramadan).
* Note: Some extra dates in 2006 to be confirmed.
Note: Muslim festivals are timed according to local sightings of various phases of the moon and the dates given above are approximations. During the lunar month of Ramadan that precedes Eid al-Fitr, Muslims fast during the day and feast at night and normal business patterns may be interrupted. Many restaurants are closed during the day and there may be restrictions on smoking and drinking. Some disruption may continue into Eid al-Fitr itself. Eid al-Fitr and Eid al-Adha may last anything from two to 10 days, depending on the region. For more information, see the *World of Islam* appendix.

Health

	Special Precautions?	Certificate Required?
Yellow Fever	Yes	1
Cholera	2	No
Typhoid & Polio	3	N/A
Malaria	4	N/A

Note: *Regulations and requirements may be subject to change at short notice, and you are advised to contact your doctor well in advance of your intended date of departure. Any numbers in the chart refer to the footnotes below.*

1: A yellow fever vaccination certificate is required from all travellers coming from infected areas.
2: Following WHO guidelines issued in 1973, a cholera vaccination certificate is no longer a condition of entry to Iran. However, cholera is a serious risk in this country and precautions are essential. Up-to-date advice should be sought before deciding whether these precautions should include vaccination as medical opinion is divided over its effectiveness; see the *Health* appendix for further information.
3: Immunisation against typhoid is advised.
4: Limited malaria risk exists from March to November in rural areas of the provinces of Sistan-Baluchestan, Hormozgan and Kerman (tropical part); in some areas north of the Zagros mountains and in western and southwestern regions during the summer months. Resistance to chloroquine and sulfadoxine-pyrimethamine has been reported in the malignant *falciparum* strain. The recommended prophylaxis is chloroquine in the *vivax* risk areas; chloroquine plus proguanil in the *falciparum* risk areas.
Food & drink: Mains water is normally chlorinated and, whilst relatively safe, may cause mild abdominal upsets. Bottled water is available and is advised for the first few weeks of the stay. Pasteurised milk is available; unpasteurised milk should be boiled. Powdered or tinned milk is available and is advised, but make sure that it is reconstituted with pure water. Avoid dairy products which are likely to have been made from unboiled milk. Only eat well-cooked meat and fish, preferably served hot. Salad and mayonnaise may carry increased risk. Vegetables should be cooked and fruit peeled.
Other risks: *Bilharzia* (schistosomiasis) is present in southwestern Iran. Avoid swimming and paddling in stagnant water; swimming pools which are well chlorinated and maintained are safe. *Diarrhoeal diseases* such as *dysentery*, *giardiasis* and *typhoid fever* are common. *Tick-borne relapsing fever*, *cutaneaous leishmaniasis* and *hepatitis A* and *B* occur. *Trachoma* is reported to be common.
Rabies is present. For those at high risk, vaccination before arrival should be considered. If you are bitten, seek medical advice without delay. For more information, consult the *Health* appendix.
Health care: Health facilities are limited in remote areas. Medical insurance is essential.

Travel - International

Note: All travel to the border areas with Afghanistan, Pakistan and Iraq is strongly advised against. Westerners have been the target of kidnaps by armed gangs in southeast Iran. All overland travel to Pakistan is highly inadvisable. Since 2002, there have been several violent attacks on, and violent demonstrations outside, British Embassy compounds in Tehran, and the possibility of further incidents cannot be dismissed. Demonstrations and similar large gatherings in public places should be especially avoided.
AIR: Iran's national airline is *Iran Air (IR)* (website: www.iranair.com), which operates three/four direct flights per week to Tehran from London (Heathrow). *British Mediterranean* (a franchise partner *of British Airways*) operates four services a week from London to Tehran. Other airlines serving Iran include *Emirates*, *Gulf Air*, *KLM*, *Lufthansa* and *Turkish Airlines*.
Approximate flight times: From Tehran to *London* is six hours.
International airports: *Tehran (THR)* (Mehrabad) is 5km (3 miles) west of the city. Airline buses are available to the city (travel time – 45 minutes) for approximately IR200-500. Taxis are also available to the city centre for approximately IR10,000 (travel time – 30 minutes). Airport facilities include a bank, post office, restaurants and snack bar, duty free shop, gift shops, tourist information and first aid/vaccination facilities.
Departure tax: IR70,000.
SEA: The main port was Khorramshahr until its destruction during the war with Iraq. It is currently under reconstruction. The ports of Abbas and Bushehr are to be found in the Persian Gulf and Nowshahr and Anzelli on the Caspian Sea. *P&O Ferries* connects Iranian ports with Persian Gulf States and Karachi.
RAIL: *RAJA Trains* (part of *Iranian Islamic Republic Railways*) operates passenger services from Tehran to Isanbul (Turkey) and Damascus (Syrian Arab Republic); from Tabiz to Djolfa (for the CIS) and Van (Turkey); and from Zahedan to Quetta (Pakistan). The Qom-Zahedan Line, when completed, will link Europe with India. Contact *RAJA Trains* (c/o Iranian Islamic Republic Railways) (e-mail: info@irirw.com; website: www.irirw.com) for details.
ROAD: No reliable international through-road links. There are various routes possible from Turkey and Pakistan, but these are not recommended. Cars can also be put on boats at Venice or Brindisi and picked up at Ezmir. For details of political conditions governing access, contact the Embassy.

Travel - Internal

AIR: *Iran Air* runs services to Ahwaz, Esfahan, Kish, Mashhad, Shiraz, Tabriz, Tehran and Zahedan and other major cities. *Aseman Air* also runs services to the major cities. The vast size of Iran makes internal flights the most practical method of transport.
RAIL: *RAJA Trains* run a fairly comprehensive internal rail network. Major intercity trains operate on five main regional routes: Azarbaijan route (Tehran – Jolfa); Golestan route (Tehran – Gorgan); Hormozgan route (Tehran – Bandar-e-Abbas); Khorasan route (Tehran – Mashhad); and Khozetan route (Tehran – Khorramshahr). There are many areas in the mountains and the desert which can only be reached by rail. There are some air-conditioned trains, and sleeping and dining cars on many trains. For further details, contact RAJA Trains (c/o Iranian Islamic Republic Railways) (see *Travel – International* section) for details.
ROAD: The road network is extensive, with more than 51,300km (31,800 miles) of paved roads and 490km (304 miles) of motorways, but the quality is unreliable. The two main roads, the A1 and A2, link the Iraqi and Pakistani borders and the Afghan and Turkish borders. Traffic drives on the right. **Bus:** Widespread, cheap and comfortable, although services tend to be erratic.
Taxi: Available in all cities. The urban taxis (orange or blue) will carry several passengers at a time and are much cheaper than the private taxis, which only carry one person. Unofficial taxis should be avoided; use only legitimate taxis or those ordered through legitimate agencies. Group taxis for up to 10 people are available for intercity travel. Prices are negotiated beforehand and tipping is not necessary.
Car hire: Available in most cities and from airports.
Documentation: An International Driving Permit is recommended but it is not a legal requirement. Personal insurance is required. All motorists entering Iran must possess a *Carnet de Passage en Douane* and an International Certificate of Vehicle ownership.
URBAN: Tehran has an extensive bus system, including double-deckers. Tickets are bought in advance at kiosks.
Travel times: The following chart gives approximate travel

times (in hours and minutes) from Tehran to other major cities/towns in Iran.

	Air	Road	Rail
Ahvaz	**1.30**	**17.00**	**19.00**
B. Abbas	**1.55**	**28.00**	**-**
Esfahan	**1.00**	**8.00**	**9.00**
Kerman	**1.30**	**20.00**	**18.00**
Mashhad	**1.30**	**14.00**	**15.00**
Shiraz	**1.30**	**15.00**	**-**
Tabriz	**1.20**	**12.00**	**11.00**

Accommodation

HOTELS: A number of hotels are available and there is a fair range of accommodation. Student accommodation is available in small hotels. Schools and private houses also offer accommodation. For more information, contact the Iran Tourist Company *or* the Iran Touring and Tourism Organisation (ITTO) (see *Contact Addresses* section).
CAMPING/CARAVANNING: There are limited camping facilities and off-site camping is discouraged. Registration with the police is required if camping.

Resorts & Excursions

TEHRAN: The capital is essentially a modern city, but the best of the old has been preserved. The **Shahid Motahari Mosque** has eight minarets, from which the city can be viewed. The **Bazaar** (open every day except Friday and religious holidays) is one of the world's largest; another bazaar, catering mainly for local communities, can be found in the **Tajrish** suburb. Located in the north of the capital, an endless maze of vaulted alleys, everything from fine carpets to silver- and copperware to exotic aromatic spices can be found here. There is a separate section for each trade practised and craftspeople can be seen at their work.
Tehran has several good museums, including the **Abgineh Museum of Iranian Pottery**; the **Rea Abbasi Muesum**, housing a rare collection of Iranian calligraphy and paintings; the **National Museum of Iran (Iran Bastan Museum)**, which displays mostly archaeological and anthropological exhibits; the **Rassam Cultural and Art Foundation of Carpet**, which includes a carpet museum and carpet weaving school; the **Carpet Museum**, whose oldest carpet is 450 years old; and the **Anthropological Museums** in Golestan Place and Saad Abad. Iran's capital also has a number of cultural centres (including Azadi, Bahman and Khavaran) as well as a **National Library**, a **City Theatre**, a **Zoo** and a **University**.
EXCURSIONS: The **Alborz** mountain chain is a popular destination for excursions from Tehran. There are numerous mountain resorts offering cable car facilities as well as skiing slopes (the season running from January to March). Within easy reach of Tehran are the towns of **Rey**, **Varamin**, **Qazvin** and **Shemshak**, which have preserved much of their original character.
NORTHWESTERN IRAN: The country's second-largest city, **Tabriz**, has a ruined but restored fine blue mosque built in 1465. The covered **Qaisariyeh Bazaar** dates back to the 15th century. About 22km (14 miles) from the salt lake is the town of **Uromieh**, which claims to be the birthplace of Zoroaster. Other towns worth visiting include **Ardabil**, **Astara**, **Bandar-e Anzali** and **Rasht**.
THE GOLDEN TRIANGLE: The Golden Triangle is the name popularly given to the region enclosed by the ancient cities of Hamadan, Kermanshah and Khorramabad. This is a part of Iran which is particularly rich in historical associations; for many centuries the **Silk Road** passed through the pleasant rolling countryside of the region, and there are several indications of settlements dating back over 6000 years. **Hamadan** was the summer capital of the Persian Emperors, although one of the few easily visible signs of the city's antiquity is the **Stone Lion**, dating back to the time of Alexander the Great. **Kermanshah** is a good base for visiting the **Taghe Bostan Grottoes**, which have several excellent bas-relief carvings. The site of the **Seleucid Temple of Artemis** is in **Kangavar**; it consists of massive fallen columns and is now being reconstructed.
ESFAHAN: Esfahan is the former capital of Persia and has been designated by UNESCO as a World Heritage Site. The city's most remarkable feature is its magnificent central square which is roughly seven times larger than San Marco in Venice. The mosques, palaces, bridges and gardens also deserve a visit. The **Friday Mosque** (Masjid-e Jomeh) is one of Iran's finest buildings. The **Shaikh Lotfullah Mosque** is famous for the stalactite effect of its northern entrance. There are also several good bazaars.
ELSEWHERE: Shiraz is the capital of the Fars Province, and another of the country's ancient cities. Several of the buildings date back to the ninth century, and there are many excellent parks and gardens. About 50km (30 miles) away is **Persepolis**, also on the UNESCO World Heritage list, and famous for the Ceremonial Seat of Darius, built on an enormous platform carved out of the Kuhe Rahmat.
Another UNESCO-listed archaeological site can be found at **Changha Zanbil**, 40km (25 miles) southeast of **Susa**.
Khorasan is a large province in the east where a great revival of learning occurred in the early Middle Ages.
Mashhad, a former trading post on the Silk Road, is the capital of the region.
The city of **Kerman** in the southern desert region has several stunning mosques and a ruined citadel, although visitors are advised to exercise caution and only travel on tours organised through Iranian government-approved tourist organisations.

Sport & Activities

Watersports: Water-skiing facilities are available at the Karadj Dam near Tehran. Hotel **swimming** pools are open to non-residents and an entrance fee is charged. **Fishing:** Many streams are well stocked with trout, including the Djaje-Rud, the Karadje and the Lar. The dammed lakes of the Karadje River and the Sefid Rud are also filled with fish. The Caspian Sea is another good choice, with large numbers of bream, mullet, salmon and sturgeon.
Wintersports: The skiing season is from January to March in the Alborz Mountains. Resorts include Abe Ali, 62km (38 miles) east of Tehran; the Noor Slope, 71km (44 miles) from the capital; Shemshak, 59km (37 miles) from Tehran, and Dizine near the town of Gatchsar. Equipment for hire and all the usual winter sports facilities are available.
Other: Horse racing meetings are held at the Park-e-Mellat, Tehran. **Polo** matches are played at the polo grounds on the Karadj road out of Tehran. *Iran Air* operate **trekking** and **climbing** package holidays, which can be booked at any of their offices throughout the world. Some hotels have **tennis** courts and instruction is available at the *Amjadieh Sports Centre* in Tehran. There are several **horse-riding** clubs, particularly in Tehran. There is an 18-hole **golf** course in Tehran affiliated to the Hilton Hotel on Valiye Asr Avenue.

Social Profile

FOOD & DRINK: Rice is the staple food and the Iranians cook it superbly. Most Iranian meals are eaten with a spoon and fork, but visitors may choose a Western dish and eat with a knife and fork.
Fruit and vegetable juices are popular, as are sparkling mineral waters. Tea is also popular and drunk in the many tea-houses (*ghahve khane*). The consumption of alcohol is strictly forbidden.
SHOPPING: While the shops offer a wide selection of quality goods, local items can be bought in the many bazaars. Purchases include hand-carved, inlaid woodwork, carpets, rugs, silks, leather goods, mats, tablecloths, gold, silver, glass and ceramics. Bargaining is customary. There are restrictions on which items may be taken out of the country; see *Duty Free* section for details. **Shopping hours:** Generally 0900-1300 and 1500-2000.
SPECIAL EVENTS: For a complete list of special events, contact the Iran Touring and Tourism Organisation (ITTO) (see *Contact Addresses* section). The following is a special event occurring in Iran in 2005:
Mar *Chahar Shanbeh Suri*, usually the first Wednesday before the Spring Equinox; bonfires are lit in the streets for people to jump through in order to exorcise the old year and bring about the regeneration of the world through the new one; various towns.
SOCIAL CONVENTIONS: Feelings about certain countries (such as the USA and the UK) run high, so the visitor should avoid contentious subjects. The Westernisation of the Iranian way of life has been arrested since the fall of the Shah, and Koranic law exercises a much more traditional influence over much of the populace. In general, Western influences are now discouraged. Handshaking is customary, but not with members of the opposite sex. It must be remembered that intimate relations between non-Muslim men and Muslim women is illegal, and may incur imprisonment. Visitors should address hosts by their surname or title. Iranians are very hospitable and like to entertain. It is also customary to be offered tea, and guests are expected to accept such offers of hospitality. Because of Islamic customs, dress should be conservative and discreet, especially women's. This has been especially enforced of late; women should cover their heads when in the public sphere, wear loose-fitted clothing, and ensure that their arms and legs are also concealed. Businesspeople are expected to wear a suit and more formal attire is also needed in smart dining rooms and for important social functions. During Ramadan, smoking, eating and drinking in public are prohibited between sunrise and sunset; however, facilities are always available in major hotels. **Tipping:** In large hotels, a 10 to 15 per cent service charge is added to the bill. In restaurants (*chelokababis*), it is usual to leave some small change. Tipping is not expected in small hotels.

Business Profile

ECONOMY: Iran's main sources of income are its huge oil and gas deposits, which are among the world's largest. The agricultural sector is important for the numbers employed, although output has been depressed by drought and migration of rural labour to the cities. Both subsistence crops, mainly wheat, barley and sugar, and cash crops are grown. The manufacturing sector, which accounts for about one-sixth of total output, produces textiles, food-processing and transport equipment. Apart from hydrocarbons, Iran also has viable deposits of coal, magnesium ores and gypsum. Government policy has sought to promote the agricultural and light industry in order to reduce the economy's dependence on oil and increase the influence of the private sector – about 80 per cent of economic activity is state controlled. The economy is performing fairly steadily at present: annual growth is about five per cent and inflation is 12 to 15 per cent. As in other areas, economic policy is dominated by fundamental difference of approach between the elected government and the ruling clergy. On the trade front, Iran has developed important new links with the newly independent states of central Asia, as well as Turkey and China but, more importantly, existing trade with traditional partners in Europe, Japan and the Middle East have been restored. Bilateral trade with the US remains, not surprisingly, at a low level.
BUSINESS: Most Iranian businesspeople speak English and are polite and conservative in manner and expect an appropriate response from visitors. Exchanging calling cards is normally restricted to senior people. Appointments should be made and punctuality is expected for business meetings. Business gifts are quite acceptable. **Office hours:** Sat to Wed 0800-1600, Thurs 0900-1200 (some offices may close all day).
COMMERCIAL INFORMATION: The following organisation can offer advice: Export Promotion Centre, PO Box 1148, Tadjrish, Dr Chamran Highway, Tehran (tel: (21) 21911; fax: (21) 204 2858 *or* 204 5733; website: www.iran-export.com); *or* Iranian Trade Association, PO Box 927743, San Diego, California 92192, USA (tel: (619) 368 6790; e-mail: info@iraniantrade.org; website: www.iraniantrade.org).

Climate

Dry and hot in summer, harsh in winter. Low annual rainfall. Iran is highly prone to earthquakes and tremors.
Required clothing: Tropical attire is worn from April to October. Mediumweights are advised from November to March.

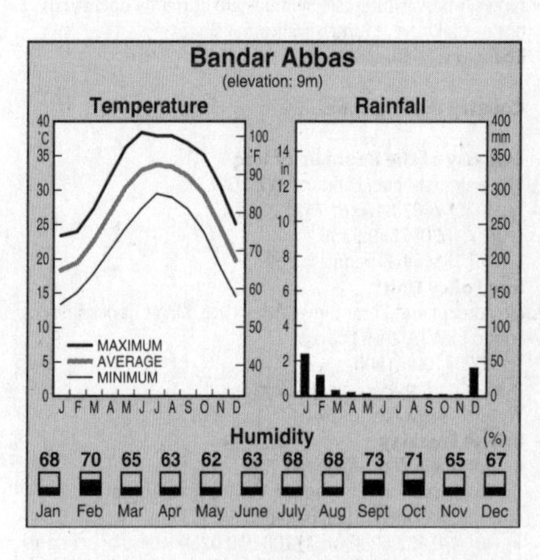

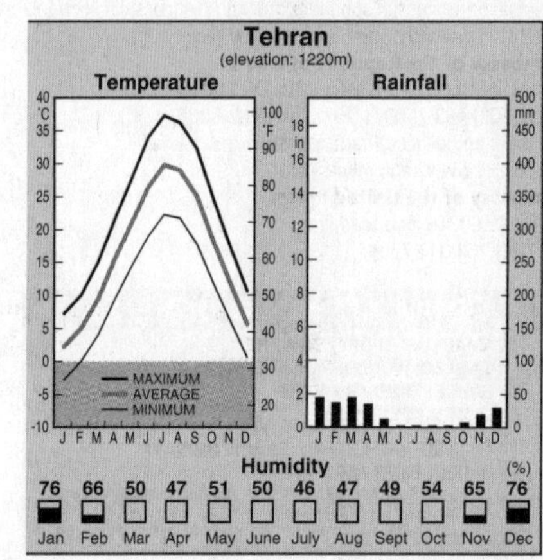

Iraq

LATEST TRAVEL ADVICE CONTACTS

British Foreign and Commonwealth Office
Tel: (0870) 606 0290 Website: www.fco.gov.uk

US Department of State
Website: http://travel.state.gov/travel

Canadian Department of Foreign Affairs and Int'l Trade
Tel: (1 800) 267 8376 Website: www.dfait-maeci.gc.ca

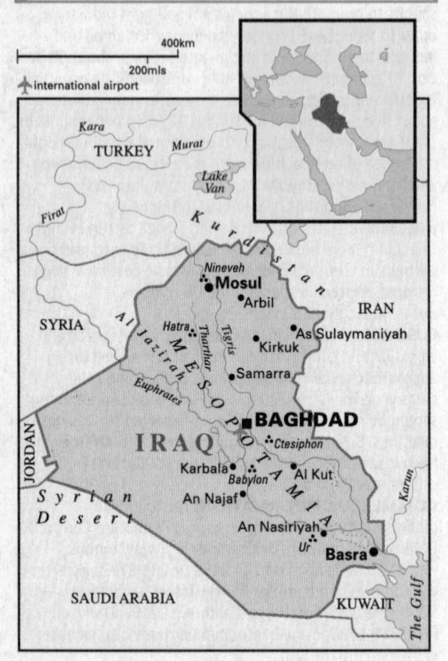

Iraq continues to undergo a period of transition following the US-led war against Saddam Hussein's regime in March/April 2003. Most of the country's political, social, physical and economic infrastructures have, by and large, been destroyed and need to be rebuilt. The USA formed the Office of Reconstruction and Humanitarian Assistance (ORHA) to provide humanitarian aid and rebuild infrastructure. The new Iraqi interim government is still developing these cursory measurements. Some diplomatic representatives/Interests Sections are currently operating, but not all have returned to normal since.
Location: Middle East.

Country dialling code: 964.

Embassy of the Republic of Iraq
169 Knightsbridge, London SW7 1DW, UK
Tel: (020) 7602 8456 or 7581 2264.
Tel/Fax: (020) 7589 3356.
E-mail: lonemb@iraqmofa.net
Iraq Policy Unit
c/o Foreign and Commonwealth Office, King Charles Street, London SW1A 2AH, UK.
Tel: (020) 7008 1500.
E-mail: iraqtraveladvice@fco.gov.uk
Website: www.fco.gov.uk
British Embassy
International Zone, Baghdad, Iraq
Consular section: Convention Centre (Iraqi Forum), opposite Rasheed Hotel, Baghdad, Iraq
Tel: (0) 790 192 6280 *or* (1) 703 270 0254 (consular section).
E-mail: britishconsulbaghdad@gtnet.gov.uk (consular section).
Website: www.britishembassy.gov.uk/iraq
Embassy of the Republic of Iraq
1801 P Street, NW, Washington, DC 20036, USA
Tel: (202) 483 7500. Fax: (202) 462 5066.
E-mail: amboffice@iraqiembassy.org
Website: www.iraqiembassy.org
Embassy of the United States
APO AE 09316, Baghdad, Iraq
Tel: (1) 703 343 7604.

TIMATIC CODES

Health	AMADEUS: **TI-DFT/BGW/HE** GALILEO/WORLDSPAN: **TI-DFT/BGW/HE** SABRE: **TIDFT/BGW/HE**
Visa	AMADEUS: **TI-DFT/BGW/VI** GALILEO/WORLDSPAN: **TI-DFT/BGW/VI** SABRE: **TIDFT/BGW/VI**

To access TIMATIC country information on Health and Visa regulations through the Computer Reservations System (CRS), type in the appropriate command line listed above.

General Information

AREA: 438,317 sq km (169,235 sq miles).
POPULATION: 24,510,000 (UN estimate 2002).
POPULATION DENSITY: 55.9 per sq km.
CAPITAL: Baghdad. **Population:** 4,958,000 (UN estimate 2001).
GEOGRAPHY: Iraq shares borders with Turkey, Iran, the Gulf of Oman, Kuwait, Saudi Arabia, Jordan and the Syrian Arab Republic. There is also a neutral zone between Iraq and Saudi Arabia administered jointly by the two countries. Iraq's portion covers 3522 sq km (1360 sq miles). The country's main topographical features are the two rivers, the Euphrates and the Tigris, which flow from the Turkish and Syrian Arab Republic borders in the north to the Gulf in the south. The northeast is mountainous, while the country in the west is arid desert. The land surrounding the two rivers is fertile plain, but the lack of effective irrigation has resulted in flooding and areas of marshland.
GOVERNMENT: Interim government. **Head of State:** President Ghazi Mashal Ajil a-Yawer since 2004. **Head of Government:** Prime Minister Iyad Allawi since 2004.
LANGUAGE: 80 per cent Arabic, 15 per cent Kurdish. Assyrian and Armenian may also be spoken.
RELIGION: More than 50 per cent Shia Muslim, with the remaining Sunni Muslim, and Druze and Christian minorities.
TIME: GMT + 3 (GMT + 4 from 1 May to 30 September).
ELECTRICITY: 230 volts AC, 50Hz. Various two- and three-pin plugs are in use. Electricity supplies were severely affected in the recent conflict.
COMMUNICATIONS: Telephone: IDD service available, but services were severely disrupted following the conflict and only gradually returning. Country code: 964. Outgoing international code: 00. **Mobile telephone:** Extremely limited coverage. GSM 900 operates through the following companies: *Asia Cell* (website: www.wataniya.com), *Atheer* (website: www.mtc-vodafone.com), *Iraqna* and *SanaTel* (website: www.sanamobile.com). **Telegram/Fax:** There are facilities in Baghdad. Telegrams can be sent from the telegraph office next to the post office in Rashid Street. Services are also available at major hotels. **Internet:** There are no ISPs in Iraq at present. However, although connectivity within the home is rare, Internet access is sprouting everywhere via cafes and hotels, mainly in Baghdad. **Post:** All mail may take several weeks to process and is inadvisable. **Press:** Newspapers published in Arabic include *Al-Mannarah*, *Al-Mu'tamar* and *Tariq ash-Shaab*. Periodicals are also published. The main English-language daily is the *As-Sabah* (Morning).
Radio: BBC World Service (website: www.bbc.co.uk/worldservice) and Voice of America (website: www.voa.gov) can be received. From time to time the frequencies change and the most up-to-date can be found online.

Passport/Visa

Note: Iraq continues to undergo a period of transition following the end of the US-led war against Saddam Hussein's regime in March/April 2003. Most of the country's political, social, physical and economic infrastructures have, by and large, been destroyed and need to be rebuilt, are in the process of being so, or have only just initiated recovery. As a result of the uncertain situation, some of the following information may be unreliable or inaccurate. All travel to Iraq is ill-advised unless for relief purposes.

	Passport Required?	Visa Required?	Return Ticket Required?
Full British	Yes	Yes	Yes
Australian	Yes	Yes	Yes
Canadian	Yes	Yes	Yes
USA	Yes	Yes	Yes
Other EU	Yes	Yes	Yes
Japanese	Yes	Yes	Yes

Note: Regulations and requirements may be subject to change at short notice, and you are advised to contact the appropriate diplomatic or consular authority before finalising travel arrangements. Details of these may be found at the head of this country's entry. Any numbers in the chart refer to the footnotes below.

PASSPORTS: Passport valid for at least six months from date of issue of visa required by all.
VISAS: Required by all.
Types of visa and cost: *General*: £25.
Validity: Three months.
Application to: Consulate (or Consular section at Embassy); see *Contact Addresses* section for details.
Application requirements: (a) Valid passport. (b) Two passport-size photos. (c) One application form. (d) Fee. (e) Letter explaining purpose of visit from company for whom the applicant will be working in Iraq.
Working days required: One week from receipt of approval from Baghdad (which may take one month or more).

Money

Currency: The new Iraqi Dinar was introduced in October 2003. Iraqi Dinar (ID) = 20 dirhams = 1000 fils. Notes are in denominations of ID25,000, 10,000, 5000 and 500. There are plans to introduce ID 100, 50 and 25 denomination notes. Because the cost of scrap metal rose higher than the actual value of the coins, the central bank of Iraq withdrew all coins tendering a bid to sell the coins for scrap metal. This information is subject to frequent change in the current conditions.
Currency exchange: Foreign currency can be used at special duty free shops in Baghdad up to a value of US$200. To obtain this concession, goods must be purchased within 20 days of arrival and passports must be produced.
Credit & debit cards: Not widely used.
Travellers cheques: These are not generally accepted.
Currency restrictions: The import of local currency is allowed up to ID25 and export up to ID5. The import of foreign currency is unlimited, provided declared on arrival. The export of foreign currency is limited to the amount imported and declared.
Exchange rate indicators: The following figures are included as a guide to the movements of the Iraqi Dinar (new Iraqi Dinar values from May '04) against Sterling and the US Dollar:

Date	Feb '04	May '04	Aug '04	Nov '04
£1.00=	0.56	2621.10	2694.44	2769.53
$1.00=	0.31	1467.50	1462.50	1462.50

Banking hours: Sat-Wed 0800-1200, Thurs 0800-1100. Banks close at 1000 during Ramadan.

Duty Free

The following goods may be imported into Iraq without incurring customs duty:
200 cigarettes or 50 cigars or 250g tobacco; one bottle of wine and one bottle of spirits with a total volume of not more than 1l; 500ml of perfume (two small opened bottles); gifts to the value of ID10.
Note: (a) The total value of the above goods may not exceed ID100. (b) Travellers who have not left the country within 120 days must report to customs.
Prohibited items: Electrical appliances other than personal effects, souvenirs in quantities considered to have commercial value, many types of fruits and plants.

Public Holidays

2005: Jan Eid al-Adha (Feast of the Sacrifice). **Jan 1** New Year's Day. **Jan 6** Army Day. **Feb 8** Ramadan Revolution. **Feb 10** Islamic New Year. **Feb 20** Ashoura. **Apr 17** FAO Day. **Apr 21** Mouloud (Birth of the Prophet Muhammad). **May 1** Labour Day. **Jul 14** National Day. **Jul 17** Republic Day. **Aug 8** Ceasefire Day (End of Iran-Iraq War). **Nov** Eid al-Fitr (End of Ramadan).
2006: Jan 1 New Year's Day. **Jan 6** Army Day. **Jan 13** Eid al-Adha (Feast of the Sacrifice). **Jan 31** Islamic New Year. **Feb 8** Ramadan Revolution. **Feb 9** Ashoura. **Apr 11** Mouloud (Birth of the Prophet Muhammad). **Apr 17** FAO Day. **May 1** Labour Day. **Jul 14** National Day. **Jul 17** Republic Day. **Aug 8** Ceasefire Day (End of Iran-Iraq War). **Oct 22-24** Eid al-Fitr (End of Ramadan).
Note: Muslim festivals are timed according to local sightings of various phases of the moon and the dates given above are approximations. During the lunar month of Ramadan that precedes Eid al-Fitr, Muslims fast during the day and feast at night and normal business patterns may be interrupted. Many restaurants are closed during the day and there may be restrictions on smoking and drinking. Some disruption may continue into Eid al-Fitr itself. Eid al-Fitr and Eid al-Adha may last anything from two to 10 days, depending on the region. For more information, see the *World of Islam* appendix.

Health

	Special Precautions?	Certificate Required?
Yellow Fever	No	1
Cholera	No	No
Typhoid & Polio	2	N/A
Malaria	3	N/A

Note: Regulations and requirements may be subject to change at short notice, and you are advised to contact your doctor well in advance of your intended date of departure. Any numbers in the chart refer to the footnotes below.

1: A yellow fever vaccination certificate is required from travellers coming from infected areas.
2: Vaccination against typhoid is advised.
3: Malaria risk is almost entirely in the benign *vivax* form and exists from May to November, principally in areas in

the north below 1500m (4920ft) – Basrah, Duhok, Erbil, Ninawa, Sulaimaniya and Ta'min Province.
The recommended prophylaxis is chloroquine.
Food & drink: All water should be regarded as being potentially contaminated. Water used for drinking, brushing teeth or making ice should have first been boiled or otherwise sterilised. Milk is unpasteurised and should be boiled. Powdered or tinned milk is available and is advised, but make sure that it is reconstituted with pure water. Avoid dairy products which are likely to have been made from unboiled milk. Only eat well-cooked meat and fish, preferably served hot. Pork, salad and mayonnaise may carry increased risk. Vegetables should be cooked and fruit peeled.
Other risks: *Bilharzia* (schistosomiasis) is present. Avoid swimming and paddling in fresh water; swimming pools which are well chlorinated and maintained are safe.
Diarrhoeal diseases, including *giardiasis*, *dysentery* and *typhoid fever* are common. *Hepatitis B* is endemic and *hepatitis A* is widespread. *Visceral leishmaniasis* is common in central Iraq. *Cutaneous leishmaniasis* is reported.
Crimean-Congo haemorrhagic fever has been reported.
Tick-borne relapsing fever may occur.
Rabies is present. For those at high risk, vaccination before arrival should be considered. If you are bitten, seek medical advice without delay. For more information, consult the *Health* appendix.
Health care: Health insurance including emergency repatriation cover is essential. Basic modern medical care and medicines may not be available. Doctors and hospitals often expect immediate cash payment for services.

Travel - International

Travel Warning: All travel to Iraq is advised against. The security situation is dangerous and there continues to be widespread outbreaks of violence. Even the most essential of travel to Iraq should be delayed, if possible. There has been a steady increase in the number of attacks against non-Iraqi civilians, including British nationals. Since the beginning of March 2004, a number of British nationals have been killed and many more have been seriously injured in terrorist incidents. If in Iraq, security arrangements should be carefully reviewed. Terrorists are actively targeting British, international and other interests in Iraq. Targets include hotels where UK and other nationals may stay, as well as civilian vehicles and aircraft. Attacks have often involved the use of firearms and explosives. There is a continuing threat from kidnapping. There have been numerous kidnappings of non-Iraqi civilians, particularly in the region surrounding Fallujah and Al Ramadi and on the Baghdad-Amman highway. However, this threat applies to all nationals. There are curfews in Baghdad (2230-0400), Fallujah and Al Ramadi.
AIR: Iraq's national airline is *Iraqi Airways (IA)*. At present, there is extremely limited access into Iraq by air. *Royal Jordanian Airlines* operate some flights between Baghdad and Amman (Jordan), and flights between Baghdad and Damascus (Syrian Arab Republic). *Qatar Airways* (website: www.qatarairways.com) may operate some flights to Iraq.
Approximate flight times: From Baghdad to *London* is six hours.
International airports: *Baghdad (BGW)* is 18km (11 miles) south of the city (travel time – 20 minutes). Taxi services go to the city with rates negotiable for shared taxis. There is a surcharge after 2200. Airport facilities include banks, bureaux de change, post office, duty free shops and bars. Car hire is also available. Coach service is available to the city. Visitors should note that the airport has repeatedly been targeted by rocket and mortar attacks.
Departure tax: ID2000.
SEA: At present, all ports in Iraq are closed.
RAIL: There is a rail journey between Istanbul (Turkey) and Baghdad. All other overland routes may not be accessible to foreigners.
ROAD: At present, only the borders from Turkey and Jordan are open to road travel. Before the Gulf War, principal international routes ran through Jordan, Syrian Arab Republic and Turkey. Work on the Express Highway, an attempt to link Iraq with Jordan, Kuwait and Syrian Arab Republic has been suspended for the time being.

Travel - Internal

AIR: Aircraft are not normally allowed into Baghdad. However, before sanctions, there were regular flights between Baghdad, Al Basrah and Mosul.
RAIL: Rail services are operated by the *State Enterprise for Iraqi Railways*. The country has over 2000km (1242 miles) of track, most of which is standard gauge. A further 300km (200 miles) or so is under construction. The principal route is from the Syrian Arab Republic border at Tel-Kotchek to Mosul, Baghdad and Al Basrah. Trains also run from Baghdad to Kirkuk and Arbil. A service operates three times daily between Baghdad and Al Basrah. Some sleeping cars, restaurants and air-conditioned coaches are available.
Note: Many tracks were destroyed during the fighting and it is uncertain if any passenger services are running at all.
ROAD: Travel by road is not wholly recommended at present, due to the continuing threat of car-jacking, robbery and random attacks; these have often occurred on the Baghdad-Amman highway, in particular. Road closures must also be expected. Traffic drives on the right. There are 36,500km (22,680 miles) of road. Principal routes are from Baghdad to Kirkuk, Arbil and Zakho; Baghdad to the Jordanian frontier; Baghdad to Kanaquin (Iranian border); Baghdad to Hilla and Kerbela; and Baghdad to Al Basrah and Safwan (Kuwait border). **Bus:** Services run from Baghdad and other main cities. **Taxi:** Services are available both in cities and for transit. Fares should be negotiated in advance. Metered taxis charge twice the amount shown on the meter. Tipping is not necessary. **Car hire:** Available at the airport and in Baghdad. **Documentation:** International Driving Permit required. Third Party insurance is necessary.
URBAN: Baghdad has an extensive bus system with double-deckers, and also private minibuses and share-taxis. Bus tickets should be pre-purchased at kiosks. A metro is under construction.

Accommodation

Accommodation is mainly for business travellers. Hotel accommodation is limited and bookings should be made in advance. Small hotels are also available for low budgets, but with a lower standard of facilities. Hotel bills are payable in foreign currency but operate on a cash-only basis. A 10 per cent service charge is usually added to the bill.

Resorts & Excursions

BAGHDAD: In the capital, there is a striking contrast between the new buildings and the shabbier back streets. The aim is to preserve the city's Islamic character by protecting the ruins of historic buildings such as the **Ike Abbasid Palace**. Long-established markets still trade. The museums of **Iraqi Folklore** and **Modern Art** are well worth visiting. The **River Tigris** is a central feature of the city.
Excursions: South of the capital is **Babylon**, the great city once ruled by the Semitic King Hammirabi. The city and, particularly, the famous **Hanging Gardens** are being restored.
NORTHERN/KURDISH REGION: This is a mountainous and forested area. **Mosul** is the main northern town, with the 13th-century **Palace of Qara Sariai** and the old **Mosque of Nabi Jirjis**. **Nineveh** is an ancient and rich archaeological site near Mosul. **Arbil** is probably the oldest continuously inhabited city in the world. **Kirkuk** has assumed importance since the discovery of oil. It is famous for 'Eternal Fires' - the endless burning of gas seepage.

Social Profile

FOOD & DRINK: Restaurants serve both Middle Eastern and European dishes. Popular Iraqi dishes are *kubba*, *dolma* (vine leaves, cabbage, lettuce, onions, aubergine, marrow or cucumbers stuffed with rice, meat and spices), *tikka* (small chunks of mutton on skewers grilled on a charcoal fire), *quozi* (small lamb boiled whole and grilled, stuffed with rice, minced meat and spices and served on rice) and *masgouf* (fish from the Tigris, cooked on the river bank). Waiter service is usual.
There is strict adherence to Islamic laws on the consumption of alcohol, which is available within the limits of religious laws. A permit for alcohol may be necessary, although this may only be valid at international hotels. Certain hotels prohibit the consumption of alcohol by visitors. During the lunar month of Ramadan, smoking and drinking in public is not permitted.
NIGHTLIFE: Baghdad has nightclubs with cabaret, music and dancing, as do other main towns. There are also cinemas, theatres and bars.
SHOPPING: The long-established town markets sell copperware, silver, spices, carpets and brightly coloured rugs. In Baghdad, the copper market is a centre of noisy activity with coppersmiths beating their pots into shape.
Shopping hours: Sat-Thurs 0830-1300 and 1700-1900.
SOCIAL CONVENTIONS: Owing to a long and varied history, Iraq is a culturally rich country. Today, traditional Islamic culture predominates, with Koranic law playing an active role in the day-to-day life of the country, and visitors should be careful to respect this and act accordingly. Visitors should always address their hosts by full name and title. Traditional Arab hospitality is followed as a rule, in accordance with religious law. Conservative and discreet dress should be worn in observance of local Islamic laws.
Photography: The summary execution of journalist Farzad Bazoft exemplifies the need for extreme caution when photographing anything of a sensitive nature. This includes photographs of local people (the Muslim religion does not allow the representation of human or animal images in any form); and, most importantly, any government installations, buildings or indeed anything else that may be considered off-limits to visitors. If in any doubt, do not take a photo.
Tipping: Normal limit is 10 to 15 per cent. Taxi drivers need not be tipped since the fare is agreed before the journey.

Business Profile

ECONOMY: With proven deposits of over 110 billion barrels – about 10 per cent of the total – Iraq has the world's second-largest oil reserves. Oil income drove Iraq's rapid post-war development until the end of the 1970s. However, the Iran-Iraq war, which lasted from 1980 until 1988, brought Iraq's growth to a halt. Now Iraq's US-led occupation has formally ended and the transferral of power to a new Iraqi government has been instigated, perhaps a glimmer of economic optimism can be permitted, although the situation remains perilous and eminently unstable. As reconstruction progresses, the country's economic momentum should recover, although the scale of destruction and dilapidation is such that this continues to be a lengthy process.
The agricultural sector by contrast fared relatively well, at least during the early sanctions period as Iraq sought to grow more food in order to compensate for the absence of imported produce. However, light industry, which the government originally promoted as part of an import substitution programme, operated far below the levels of the 1980s. The all-important oil industry, meanwhile, was constrained by limits imposed by the UN sanctions. But gradually, the Iraqis developed an extensive network of smuggling routes and 'illicit' markets; indeed, the scale of these was such that by 2001, the Iraqis announced that they were no longer prepared to abide by the agreement with the UN and withdrew entirely from the international market.
But there was no disguising the decline which the Iraqi economy had undergone, especially during the previous 10 years. Accurate figures about the Iraqi economy are inevitably hard to come by. There were several bouts of hyperinflation during the 1990s, and the economy contracted at an estimated average annual rate of five per cent during the same period. Iraq also has a vast external debt in the region of US$200 billion, the majority of which is owed to Kuwait and Saudi Arabia. Hopes that the economy might grow in 2003 were dashed by both the extent of the rehabilitation needed by the oil industry and the consequences of the US-led war against Iraq in the early part of that year.
BUSINESS: Formal courtesies are common and expected. Visiting cards are regularly exchanged and these are often printed in Arabic and English. Meetings may not always be on a person-to-person basis and it is often difficult to confine items to the business in progress as many topics may be discussed in order to assess the character of colleagues or traders. **Office hours:** Sat-Wed 0800-1400; Thurs 0800-1300. Friday is the weekly day of rest when offices tend to be closed.

COMMERCIAL INFORMATION: For information or advice, contact the Federation of Iraqi Chambers of Commerce, PO Box 11348, Mustansir Street, Baghdad (tel: (1) 888 8850; fax: (1) 888 2305) *or* the Baghdad Chamber of Commerce, PO Box 24168 Almsarif, Baghdad Almustansir Street, Baghdad (tel: (1) 887 6211/1; fax: (1) 887 9563).

Climate

Summers are very hot and dry. Winters are warm with some rain.
Required clothing: Tropical attire is worn in summer months. Mediumweights are advised during the winter.

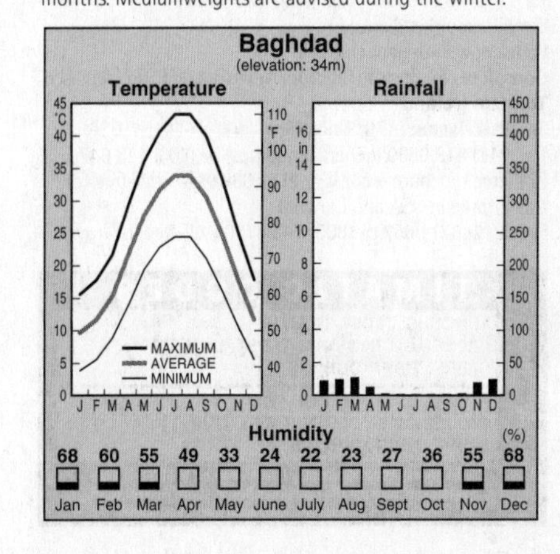

Ireland

LATEST TRAVEL ADVICE CONTACTS

British Foreign and Commonwealth Office
Tel: (0870) 606 0290 Website: www.fco.gov.uk
US Department of State
Website: http://travel.state.gov/travel
Canadian Department of Foreign Affairs and Int'l Trade
Tel: (1 800) 267 8376 Website: www.dfait-maeci.gc.ca

Location: Europe, off the west coast of Great Britain.

Country dialling code: 353.

Fáilte Ireland
Baggot Street Bridge, Baggot Street, Dublin 2, Ireland
Tel: (1) 602 4000. Fax: (1) 855 6821.
E-mail: info@failteireland.ie
Website: www.ireland.ie *or* www.failteireland.ie
Embassy of the Republic of Ireland
17 Grosvenor Place, London SW1X 7HR, UK
Tel: (020) 7235 2171. Fax: (020) 7245 6961.
Opening hours: Mon-Fri 0930-1700.
Passport and Visa office: Montpelier House, 106 Brompton Road, London SW3 1JJ, UK
Tel: (020) 7225 7700. Fax: (020) 7225 7777.
Opening hours: Mon-Fri 0930-1630.
Tourism Ireland
Nations House, 103 Wigmore Street, London W1U 1QS, UK
Tel: (0800) 039 7000 (travel enquiries) *or* (020) 7518 0800 (trade enquiries). Fax: (020) 7493 9065.
E-mail: info.gb@tourismireland.com
Website: www.tourismireland.com
British Embassy
29 Merrion Road, Ballsbridge, Dublin 4, Ireland
Tel: (1) 205 3700. Fax: (1) 205 3890 (consular section).
E-mail: britishembassy@abtran.com (visa section) *or* consular.dubli@fco.gov.uk
Website: www.britishembassy.ie
Embassy of the Republic of Ireland
2234 Massachusetts Avenue, NW, Washington, DC 20008, USA
Tel: (202) 462 3939. Fax: (202) 232 5993.
E-mail: embirlus@aol.com
Website: www.irelandemb.org
Consulates in: Boston, Chicago, New York and San Francisco.
Tourism Ireland
345 Park Avenue, 17th Floor, New York, NY 10154, USA
Tel: (212) 418 0800 (general enquiries) *or* (800) 223 6470 (toll-free brochure request line) *or* 669 9967 (toll-free for travel trade in USA and Canada).
Fax: (212) 371 9052 *or* (800) 748 3730 (toll-free for travel trade in USA and Canada).
E-mail: info@shamrock.org
Website: www.tourismireland.com
Embassy of the United States of America
42 Elgin Road, Ballsbridge, Dublin 4, Ireland
Tel: (1) 668 8777. Fax: (1) 668 9946.
Website: http://dublin.usembassy.gov
Embassy of the Republic of Ireland
130 Albert Street, Suite 1105, Ottawa, Ontario K1P 5G4, Canada
Tel: (613) 233 6281. Fax: (613) 233 5835.
E-mail: embassyofireland@rogers.com
Website: www.irishembassyottawa.com
Canadian Embassy
65 St Stephen's Green, Dublin 2, Ireland
Tel: (1) 417 4100. Fax: (1) 417 4101.
E-mail: cdnembsy@iol.ie
Website: www.canada.ie
Tourism Ireland
2 Bloor Street West, Suite 3403, Toronto, Ontario M4W 3E2, Canada
Tel: (416) 925 6368 *or* (800) 223 6470 (consumers) *or* (866) 477 7717 (travel trade). Fax: (416) 925 6033.
E-mail: info.ca@tourismireland.com
Website: www.tourismireland.com

TIMATIC CODES

Health	AMADEUS: **TI-DFT/DUB/HE** GALILEO/WORLDSPAN: **TI-DFT/DUB/HE** SABRE: **TIDFT/DUB/HE**
Visa	AMADEUS: **TI-DFT/DUB/VI** GALILEO/WORLDSPAN: **TI-DFT/DUB/VI** SABRE: **TIDFT/DUB/VI**

To access TIMATIC country information on Health and Visa regulations through the Computer Reservations System (CRS), type in the appropriate command line listed above.

General Information

AREA: 70,182 sq km (27,097 sq miles).
POPULATION: 4,048,800 (2004).
POPULATION DENSITY: 56.7 per sq km.
CAPITAL: Dublin. **Population:** 1,144,400 (2004).
GEOGRAPHY: The Republic of Ireland lies in the north Atlantic Ocean and is separated from Britain by the Irish Sea to the east. The northeastern part of the island (Northern Ireland) is part of the United Kingdom. The country has a central plain surrounded by a rim of mountains and hills offering some of the most varied and unspoilt scenery in Europe – quiet sandy beaches, semi-tropical bays warmed by the Gulf Stream, and rugged cliffs make up the 5600km (3500 miles) of coastline.
GOVERNMENT: Republic. **Head of State:** President Mary McAleese since 1997. **Head of Government:** Prime Minister Bertie Ahern since 1997.
LANGUAGE: Irish (Gaelic) is the official language, spoken as a first language by about 55,000 people (mostly in the west). The majority speak English. Official documents are printed in both languages.
RELIGION: Roman Catholic 77 per cent, the remainder being Protestant, with Jewish and Islamic minorities.
TIME: GMT (GMT + 1 from last Sunday in March to Saturday before the last Sunday in October).
ELECTRICITY: 220 volts AC, 50Hz. Three-pin plugs are in use.
COMMUNICATIONS: Telephone: IDD is available. Country code: 353 followed by the area code, omitting the initial zero. Outgoing international code: 00. **Mobile telephone:** GSM 900 networks cover the whole country. GSM 900/1800 networks operated by *O2 Communications* (Ireland) *Ltd*, *Meteor* (website: www.meteor.ie) and *Vodafone* (website: www.vodafone.ie). Handsets can be hired. **Fax:** Facilities are widely available. **Internet:** Public access is available free in libraries. Internet cafes exist in nearly every town. ISPs include *Ireland On-Line* (website: http://home.iol.ie). **Post:** Post office hours: Mon-Fri 0900-1730/1800, Sat 0900-1300. Sub-post offices close at 1300 one day a week. The Central Post Office is in O'Connell Street, Dublin. **Press:** There are several daily newspapers published in Dublin including *Evening Herald*, the *Irish Independent* and *The Irish Times*; and two in Cork (*Evening Echo* and *Irish Examiner*). British dailies and Sunday papers are available.
Radio: BBC World Service (website: www.bbc.co.uk/worldservice) and Voice of America (website: www.voa.gov) can be received. From time to time the frequencies change and the most up-to-date can be found online.

Passport/Visa

	Passport Required?	Visa Required?	Return Ticket Required?
Full British	1	No	No
Australian	Yes	No	No
Canadian	Yes	No	No
USA	Yes	No	No
Other EU	2	No	No
Japanese	Yes	No	No

Note: *Regulations and requirements may be subject to change at short notice, and you are advised to contact the appropriate diplomatic or consular authority before finalising travel arrangements. Details of these may be found at the head of this country's entry. Any numbers in the chart refer to the footnotes below.*

PASSPORTS: Valid passport required by all except:
(a) **1.** persons born in the UK travelling direct from the UK (applicable to British passport holders only);
(b) **2.** nationals of Belgium, France, Germany, Luxembourg and The Netherlands holding a valid national photo identity card (it is, however, advisable to bring a valid passport).
Note: Whilst UK citizens do not require a passport or visa to enter Ireland, most carriers by air or sea now require some form of identification with photograph, usually a passport or driving license with photo. Visitors are advised to check what form of ID is required with the individual airline, ferry company or travel agent before travelling.
VISAS: Required by all except the following for stays of up to 90 days:
(a) nationals of countries referred to in the chart above;
(b) nationals of Andorra, Antigua & Barbuda, Argentina, The Bahamas, Barbados, Belize, Bolivia, Botswana, Brazil, British Dependent Territories*, Brunei, Chile, Costa Rica, Croatia, Dominica, El Salvador, Fiji, Grenada, Guatemala, Guyana, Honduras, Hong Kong (SAR), Iceland, Israel, Kiribati, Korea (Rep), Lesotho, Liechtenstein, Macau (SAR), Malawi, Malaysia, The Maldives, Mauritius, Mexico, Monaco, Nauru, New Zealand, Nicaragua, Norway, Panama, St Kitts & Nevis, St Lucia, St Vincent & the Grenadines, San Marino, Seychelles, Singapore, Solomon Islands, South Africa, Swaziland, Switzerland, Tonga, Trinidad & Tobago, Tuvalu, Uruguay, Vanuatu, Vatican City, Venezuela and Western Samoa;
(c) transit passengers continuing their journey within 24 hours by the same or first connecting flight provided holding valid onward or return documentation and not leaving the airport. However, the following nationals *do* always require a transit visa: Afghanistan, Albania, Bulgaria, Cuba, Congo (Dem Rep), Eritrea, Ethiopia, Ghana, Iran, Iraq, Lebanon, Moldova, Nigeria, Romania, Serbia & Montenegro, Somalia, Sri Lanka and Zimbabwe.
Types of visa and cost: *Single-entry*: €60. *Multiple-entry*: €100. *Transit*: €25. Nationals of some countries receive visas free of charge. Enquire at Consulate/Consular Section of Embassy for further details (see *Contact Addresses* section).
Application to: Consulate (or Consular section at Embassy); see *Contact Addresses* section for details.
Application requirements: (a) Valid passport. (b) One completed application form. (c) Fee. (d) Letters of reference to substantiate purpose of visit or confirmation of hotel booking containing dates of proposed stay. (e) Three passport-size photos. (f) Evidence that applicant is obliged to return to country of residence, eg letter from current employer stating when applicant is due to return to work. (g) Evidence of sufficient funds or letter of reference resident in Ireland claiming full financial support of applicant, with proof they have sufficient funds to do so (eg bank statement). *Student*: (a)-(g) and, (h) Letter of acceptance from place of study (must be full-time and at least 15 hours' study time per week). (i) Proof of paid fees and sufficient funds for duration of course. (j) Copies of educational qualifications. *Business*: (a)-(g) and, (h) Letter of invitation from company in Ireland/conference host.
Working days required: Six to eight weeks.

Money

Single European currency (Euro): The Euro is now the official currency of 12 EU member states (including Ireland). The first Euro coins and notes were introduced in January 2002; the Irish Punt was completely replaced by the Euro on 9 February 2002. Euro (€) = 100 cents. Notes are in denominations of €500, 200, 100, 50, 20, 10 and 5. Coins are in denominations of €2 and 1, and 50, 20, 10, 5, 2 and 1 cents.
Currency exchange: Available in banks, airports and in bureaux de change. ATMs are widely available, catering for Cirrus and Mastero symbols.
Credit & debit cards: American Express, Diners Club, MasterCard and Visa are all widely accepted, as well as Eurocheque cards. Check with your credit and debit card company for details of merchant acceptability and other services which may be available.
Travellers cheques: Accepted throughout Ireland. To avoid additional exchange rate charges, travellers are advised to take travellers cheques in Euros, Pounds Sterling or US Dollars.
Currency restrictions: There are no restrictions on the import of local and foreign currencies. The export of local currency is restricted to €190.46 and of foreign currency notes up to €634.87 or up to amount imported.
Exchange rate indicators: The following figures are included as a guide to the movements of the Euro against Sterling and the US Dollar:

Date	Feb '04	May '04	Aug '04	Nov '04
£1.00=	1.46	1.50	1.49	1.43
$1.00=	0.85	0.84	0.80	0.75

Banking hours: Mon-Fri 1000-1600. In Dublin, banks stay open Thurs until 1700; there are also late opening nights in other parts of the country, but the day will vary.

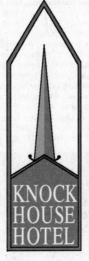

Duty Free

The following goods may be imported by persons over 17 years of age without incurring customs duty if obtained duty and/or tax-free outside the EU:
200 cigarettes or 100 cigarillos or 50 cigars or 250g of tobacco; 1l of spirits and distilled beverages (more than 22 per cent) or 2l of other alcoholic beverages with an alcoholic strength not exceeding 22 per cent, including sparkling or fortified wine, plus 2l of table wine; 50g of perfume and 250ml of eau de toilette; other dutiable goods to the value of €40.63, or €20.32 if under 15 years old.
Prohibited items: Meat, poultry, dairy products (even if in tins); raw vegetables.
Abolition of duty free goods within the EU: On June 30 1999, the sale of duty free alcohol and tobacco at airports and at sea was abolished in all of the original 15 EU member states. Of the 10 new member states that joined the EU on May 1 2004, these rules already apply to Cyprus and Malta. There are transitional rules in place for visitors returning to one of the original 15 EU countries from one of the other new EU countries. But for the original 15, plus Cyprus and Malta, there are now no limits imposed on importing tobacco and alcohol products from one EU country to another (with the exceptions of Denmark, Finland and Sweden, where limits *are* imposed). Travellers should note that they may be required to prove at customs that the goods purchased are for personal use *only*.

Public Holidays

2005: Jan 1 New Year's Day. **Mar 17** St Patrick's Day. **Mar 25** Good Friday. **Mar 28** Easter Monday. **May 2** Bank Holiday. **Jun 6** Bank Holiday. **Aug 7** Summer Bank Holiday. **Oct 31** Halloween Bank Holiday. **Dec 25** Christmas Day. **Dec 26** St Stephen's Day.
2006: Jan 1 New Year's Day. **Mar 17** St Patrick's Day. **Apr 14** Good Friday. **Apr 17** Easter Monday. **May 1** Bank Holiday. **Jun 5** Bank Holiday. **Aug 7** Summer Bank Holiday. **Oct 30** Halloween Bank Holiday. **Dec 25** Christmas Day. **Dec 26** St Stephen's Day.

Health

	Special Precautions?	Certificate Required?
Yellow Fever	No	No
Cholera	No	No
Typhoid & Polio	No	N/A
Malaria	No	N/A

Note: *Regulations and requirements may be subject to change at short notice, and you are advised to contact your doctor well in advance of your intended date of departure. Any numbers in the chart refer to the footnotes below.*

Health care: There is a reciprocal health agreement with the UK. However, health care in Ireland is not normally free and health insurance is advisable. Local Health Boards arrange consultations with doctors and dentists. Evidence of residence in the UK is required to take advantage of the agreement - for example, an NHS medical card or a driving licence. Visitors should make it clear before treatment that they wish to be treated under the EU's social security regulations; it may be necessary to complete a simple statement to this effect. Visitors from other EU and EEA member states are entitled to urgent medical treatment without charge, provided that they present form E111, which should be obtained before departure.

Travel - International

AIR: The Republic of Ireland's national airline is *Aer Lingus (EI)* (website: www.aerlingus.com). *Aer Lingus* provides a service from Los Angeles and New York's JFK to Shannon and Dublin. *Delta Air Lines* operates a service from New York's JFK Airport to Shannon and Dublin. Services to London are frequent and moderately priced. There is a wide range of promotional air fares to Ireland from main cities in the UK, and an ever-increasing number of airlines connect regional UK airports with Ireland.
Approximate flight times: From Dublin to *London* is one hour 15 minutes, to *New York* is seven hours 30 minutes.
International airports: *Dublin Airport (DUB)* (website: www.dublin-airport.com) is 10km (6 miles) north of the city. Bus no. 41A leaves Abbey Street at regular intervals (travel time – 35 minutes). Bus no. 747 runs to O'Connell Street, the central bus station and onto Parnell Square. Airport express coaches and taxis are available to the city centre. Airport facilities include airside duty free shop, car hire, bank, bureau de change, bars, restaurants, tourist information centre and chemist.
Shannon Airport (SNN) (website: www.shannonairport.com) is 24km (15 miles) west of Limerick (travel time – 25 minutes). Bus services are available to and from both Limerick and Clare, approximately every hour. A daily express coach travels between Limerick and Shannon and between Galway and Shannon, plus to Ennis bus station. Taxi service is available to Limerick. Airport facilities include outgoing duty free shop, bank, bureau de change, bar, restaurant and tourist information centre.
Cork Airport (ORK) (website: www.corkairport.com) is 8km (5 miles) southwest of the city. Buses travel between the city centre and airport (travel time – 15 minutes). Airport facilities include outgoing duty free shop, car hire, bar and restaurant.
Knock International Airport (NOC) (www.knockairport.com) is 11km (7 miles) north of Claremorris (Co Mayo) and receives international flights from the UK only: Ryanair from London, Stansted, mytravellite from Birmingham and British Airways from Manchester. Taxi services are available to Claremorris, where onward rail and bus connections are available to the rest of the country. Airport facilities include duty free shop, bar, restaurant and car hire (pre-booking advised).
Departure tax: None.
SEA: In addition to conventional ferry crossings, many ferry companies now offer high-speed services as well as upgraded, state-of-the-art craft on many Irish sea routes. Fares will vary by season and promotional offers are available. Routes from Britain and France include:
From England: *Liverpool–Dublin* (travel time - eight hours); *Fleetwood–Larne* (Northern Ireland, travel time - eight hours). From the Isle of Man: Douglas–Dublin (travel time - two hours 45 minutes, summer only, or four hours

A B C D E F G H I J K L M N O P Q R S T U V W X Y Z

45 minutes on conventional ferries); *Douglas–Belfast* (Northern Ireland, travel time - two hours 45 minutes).
From Scotland: *Cairnryan–Larne* (Northern Ireland, travel time - one hour on fast ferries and one hour 45 minutes on conventional ferries); *Troon–Belfast* (Northern Ireland, travel time - two hours 35 minutes); *Stranraer–Belfast* (travel time - one hour 45 minutes on fast ferries and three hours 15 minutes on conventional ferries).
From Wales: *Holyhead (Isle of Anglesey)–Dublin* (travel time - one hour 50 minutes on fast ferries and minimum three hours 15 minutes on conventional ferries); *Holyhead (Isle of Anglesey)–Dun Laoghaire* (travel time - one hour 40 minutes on fast ferries); *Fishguard–Rosslare* (travel time - one hour 40 minutes on fast ferries and three hours 30 minutes on conventional ferries); *Swansea–Cork* (seasonal, travel time - 10 hours); *Pembroke–Rosslare* (travel time - three hours 45 minutes).
From France: Irish Ferries operate at least four direct ferry crossings a day between France and Ireland. The routes are *Cherbourg–Rosslare* (travel time - 19 hours); *Roscoff– Rosslare* (travel time - 18 hours). For information on routes, fares and reservations, contact one of the following: *Brittany Ferries* (tel: (08705) 360 360; website: www.brittany-ferries.com); *Irish Ferries* (tel: (08705) 171 717 (UK office) *or* (1) 638 3333 (Dublin office); website: www.irishferries.com); *Isle of Man Steam Packet* (tel: (01624) 661 661; website: www.steam-packet.com); *P&O Irish Sea* (tel: (0870) 242 4777; website: www.poirishsea.com); *Stena Line* (tel: (08705) 707 070; website: www.stenaline.co.uk); and *Swansea-Cork Ferries* (tel: (01792) 456 116; website: www.swansea-cork.ie).
Most ferry companies now also offer an online booking facility on their website.
RAIL: Rail links serve Ireland from all the above ferry ports, as well as from Northern Ireland.

Travel - Internal

AIR: *Aer Lingus* (as well as several other carriers) operates services throughout the country. Charter flights are also available. The Aran Islands are served by *Aer Arann* via a 15-minute flight from Connemara Regional Airport (located 27km/17 miles west of Galway city).
Domestic airports: *Galway (GWY)* is approximately 8km (5 miles) from the city centre. Bus and taxi services are available into Galway centre.
Sligo (SXL) is 8km (5 miles) from Sligo. Essential facilities only. Taxis need prior booking. Bus and taxi services are available into Sligo.
Carrickfinn (CFN) is in Co Donegal.
Kerry (Farranfore) (KIR) in Co Kerry is 19km (12 miles) from both Killarney and Tralee. Taxi services are available to both these towns and to the nearby railway station. Car hire is also available. As well as the airports listed above (and in *Travel – International*), there are various small licensed airstrips which receive passenger services; enquire at Fáilte Ireland for details of operators and routes (see *Contact Addresses* section).
SEA: Ferry services run to the various west coast islands; enquiries should be made locally.
RAIL: Rail services in the Republic are owned by *Iarnród Eireann (Irish Rail)* (website: www.irishrail.ie) and express trains run between the main cities. There are two classes of accommodation, with restaurant and buffet cars on some trains. Children under five travel free. Children aged five to 15 pay half fare. A range of rail-only and combined rail and bus tickets are available for unlimited travel within the Republic of Ireland. The *Britrail* and *Eurorail* card systems are valid in Ireland.
ROAD: The network links all parts of Ireland; road signs are international. Traffic drives on the left. **Bus:** Internal bus services are run by *Bus Eireann (Irish Bus)* (website: www.buseireann.ie), which has a nationwide network of buses serving all the major cities and most towns and villages outside the Dublin area. Bus services in remote areas are infrequent. An 'Expressway' coach network complements rail services. The central bus station is in Store Street, Dublin. A variety of special passes are available, including the *Irish Rambler*, which offers unlimited travel for three, eight or 15 days. Several independent bus companies, which are often cheaper, faster and more frequent than Bus Eireann, operate regular, scheduled services to and from Dublin. Further information can be found in local papers. **Coach tours:** Many companies offer coach tours, varying in length and itinerary. Full-day and half-day guided tours are organised from the larger towns and cities. These run from May to October. Full details are available from *Bus Eireann* and *CIE Tours International*.
Taxi: Service is available in major cities. Cruising taxis are infrequent. Places to get taxis are at hotels, rail and bus stations or taxi stands. **Car hire:** Available from all air- and seaports as well as major hotels. All international hire companies are represented in Ireland, as well as local operators. Age requirements vary from a minimum of 21 to a maximum of 75 years. A full licence from the driver's home country is required, and the driver will normally be required to have had at least two years' experience.
Bicycle hire: Ask for a Tourist Board leaflet.
Documentation: EU nationals taking cars into the Republic require: motor registration book (or owner's authority in writing); full EU driving licence or International Driving Permit; nationality coding stickers; and insurance cover valid for the Republic. A Green Card is strongly recommended, as without it, insurance cover is limited to the minimum legal requirement in Ireland - the Green Card tops this up to the cover provided by the visitor's domestic policy.
URBAN: Extensive bus services operate in Dublin. There is a new, fast suburban rail service (*DART*), connecting Howth and Bray, including a link to Dun Laoghaire (the ferry port). The *Dublin Explorer* ticket is valid for four days on all Dublin buses and *DART* suburban trains. This ticket may not be used before 0945, but there are no evening restrictions.

Credit: © Fáilte Ireland

This links LUCAS Sandyford to St Stephens Green, and Tallaght to Connolly Station.
Travel Times: The following chart gives approximate travel times (in hours and minutes) from **Dublin** to other major cities/towns in Ireland.

	Air	Road	Rail
Cork	0.40	3.00	2.40
Galway	0.35	2.45	2.40
Limerick	-	3.30	2.10
Shannon Airport	0.35	3.00	-
Waterford	0.30	2.30	2.40
Kilkenny	-	2.00	1.45
Killarney	-	3.00	3.50

Accommodation

Note: Fáilte Ireland can provide information on published accommodation guides, although it no longer publishes its own. For details, apply to Fáilte Ireland; see *Contact Addresses* section.
HOTELS: There are 849 hotels inspected, approved and graded by Fáilte Ireland and prices are fixed by Fáilte Ireland. Most hotels belong to the Irish Hotels Federation, 13 Northbrook Road, Dublin 6 (tel: (1) 497 6459; fax: (1) 497 4613; e-mail: info@ihf.ie; website: www.irelandhotels.com). A selection of some of the finest hotels in Ireland is available (website: www.distinctionworld.com). **Grading:** Fáilte Ireland registers and grades hotels as follows: **5-star:** Top grade of hotel. All rooms have private bathroom, many have suites. Dining facilities include top-class à la carte. **4-star:** All provide a high standard of comfort and service. All have private bathrooms. **3-star:** Medium-priced. Comfortable accommodation and good service. All have private bathrooms. **2-star:** Likely to be family operated with a limited but satisfactory standard of food and comfort. Most rooms will have a private bathroom. **1-star:** Hotels that are clean and comfortable with satisfactory accommodation and service.
GUEST HOUSES: Guest houses are smaller, more intimate establishments often under family management. There are over 490 guest houses registered and inspected by Fáilte Ireland. These range from converted country houses to purpose-built accommodation. Meals range from bed & breakfast to full board. The minimum number of bedrooms is five and the availability of meals is not a requirement.
Grading: Fáilte Ireland registers and grades guest houses as follows: **4-star:** guest houses which provide a very high standard of comfort and personal service. In most cases, 4-star guest houses provide a good-quality evening meal, hot and cold running water in all bedrooms. All premises have rooms with private baths; **3-star:** guest houses which provide a high standard of comfort and personal service. Hot and cold running water in all bedrooms. All premises have rooms with private baths; **2-star:** guest houses that are well furnished, offering very comfortable accommodation with limited, but good standard of food and service. Hot and cold running water in all bedrooms; **1-star:** guest houses that are clean and comfortable. Hot and cold running water in all bedrooms. Adequate bathroom and toilet facilities; **Ungraded premises:** Hotels and guest houses not sufficiently long in operation are left ungraded.
FARMHOUSES/TOWN & COUNTRY HOMES: There are 3229 town or country homes and 562 farmhouses offering bed & breakfast on a daily or weekly basis with other meals often provided. This informal type of accommodation gives visitors the opportunity to share in the life of an Irish family in an urban or country setting. They may live in a Georgian residence, a modern bungalow or a traditional cottage. A farmhouse holiday again gives scope for meeting people and is especially suitable for children. Visitors can forget about city life and enjoy the everyday life of the farm. Either way, it will be a relaxing and friendly holiday.
All homes and farmhouses that have been inspected and approved by Fáilte Ireland are listed in the official guide, available from the Tourist Board. In addition to this, the Town and Country Homes Association and Fáilte Tuaithe (pronounced Foil-tya Too-ha), the Irish Farmhouse Association, produce their own annual guides to their members' houses. These are also available from Tourism Ireland in Britain and from tourist information offices throughout Ireland. For more information, contact Fáilte Tuaithe (Irish Farm Holidays), 2 Michael Street, Limerick (tel: (61) 400 700; fax: (61) 400 771; e-mail: info@irishfarmholidays.com; website: www.irishfarmholidays.com); *or* the Town and Country Homes Association, Belleek Road, Ballyshannon, Co Donegal (tel: (71) 982 2222; fax: (71) 982 2207; e-mail: admin@townandcountry.ie; website: www.townandcountry.ie).
SELF-CATERING: There are over 2432 self-catering establishments scattered throughout Ireland, listed by Fáilte Ireland. Self-catering holidays are available for those who like to come and go as they please without any restrictions. There is self-catering accommodation to suit all tastes, including houses, self-contained apartments, cottages and caravans. There are even traditional-style thatched cottages which are fully equipped and located in carefully selected beauty spots. Further details can be obtained from Irish Cottage Holiday Homes, Central Reservations Office, Bracken Court, Bracken Road, Sandyford, Dublin 18 (tel: (1) 205 2777; fax: (1) 293 3025; e-mail: info@irishcottageholidays.com; website: www.irishcottageholidays.com).
CAMPING/CARAVANNING: Ireland's caravan and camping parks are inspected by Fáilte Ireland. Those that meet minimum requirements are identified by a special sign and listed in an official guide which shows the facilities at each park. Firms offering touring caravans, tents and camping equipment for hire are included in the listing. There are 135 caravan and campsites. The majority are open from May to September. Further details are available from the Irish Caravan and Camping Council, PO Box 4443, Dublin 2 (fax: (98) 28237; e-mail: info@camping-ireland.ie; website: www.camping-ireland.ie).
YOUTH HOSTELS: A total of 32 youth hostels are operated by *An Oige* (Irish Youth Hostel Association), 61 Mountjoy Street, Dublin 7 (tel: (1) 830 4555; fax: (1) 830 5808; e-mail: mailbox@anoige.ie; website: www.irelandyha.org *or* www.anoige.ie). They provide simple dormitory accommodation with comfortable beds and facilities for cooking meals. Usage is confined to members of *An Oige* or other youth organisations affiliated to the International Youth Hostel Federation. Non-members can buy stamps at hostels entitling them to further hostel use.
HOLIDAY HOSTELS: There are 177 registered holiday hostels offering privately owned accommodation at reasonable prices. Dormitory-style sleeping accommodation and/or private bedrooms are available, with fully equipped kitchens. No membership is required. Some provide meals, others breakfast only. For further information, contact Fáilte Ireland (see *Contact Addresses* section).
HOLIDAY CENTRES: These centres offer a comprehensive holiday with a wide variety of amenities and facilities including self-catering units, indoor heated swimming pool and restaurant facilities. The centres are registered with Fáilte Ireland.

Resorts & Excursions

The 3500km (2200 miles) of Ireland's coastline embrace a remarkable diversity of scenery and conditions from long, gently sloping strands (beaches) and rocky sea cliffs and headlands to raised bogs, outstanding mountains, attractive villages and towns, prehistoric and religious sites - and a laid-back approach to life that is without equal. The shape and comparatively small size of Ireland means that nowhere is very far from the sea. But beware, many of Ireland's roads are narrow, and the through routes are heavily used. Resorts and beaches in Ireland are uncrowded, and the tourism infrastructure is underpinned by a network of more than 50 tourist information offices offering help, advice, accommodation and suggestions on all aspects of travel. Most tourist offices are open Mon-Fri 0900-1800, closing on Saturday at 1300, but times vary, with offices at seaports and airports generally open longer during the summer months.

In this review, the country has been divided into six arbitrary regions embracing a number of counties within each:

Dublin and the East Coast: Counties Louth, Meath, Kildare and Wicklow.

The southeast: Counties Waterford, Wexford, Tipperary and Kilkenny.

The Midlands: Counties Monaghan, Cavan, Longford, Westmeath, Offaly and Laios.

The southwest: Counties Cork, Kerry and Limerick.

The west: Counties Clare, Galway, Roscommon and Mayo.

The northwest: Counties Sligo, Leitrim and Donegal.

DUBLIN AND THE EAST COAST

DUBLIN: The capital city of Ireland sprawls across the Liffey valley, reaching in a great sweep from the headlands of **Howth** in the north to **Dalkey**. Dublin is a complex city of almost dual personality, divided by the **Liffey** into the heavily populated north and more genteel south. This is a city with a quirky sense of humour, ideal to explore on foot. The historic heart of the city lies south of the Liffey, unaltered in appearance since Georgian times, though the last decade of the 20th century saw major urban regeneration that makes the place buzz with excitement, especially around **Temple Bar**. This upbeat part of the city got its name from Sir William Temple, the Provost of Trinity College. Today, the area boasts fashionable pubs, good places to eat, discos and inordinate *joie de vivre*. Founded during the reign of Elizabeth I, **Trinity College**, the city's most famous landmark, was a symbol of English dominance to which, until 1873, admission was restricted to Protestants. Many of the college's students have achieved a measure of fame, notably Oscar Wilde, Bram Stoker, Samuel Beckett and Jonathan Swift. The **Old Library** houses a number of important manuscripts in its **Treasury**, among which the *Book of Kells* is the best known. West of Trinity College stands **Dublin Castle**, the seat of British rule in Ireland, and worth a visit for its beautiful state apartments. On the corner of Suffolk Street and the popular shopping area, **Grafton Street**, stands the statue of Molly Malone, the Dublin beauty. **Merrion Square** is the city's most elegant place, lined with classical Georgian houses with stunning doorways, canopies and fanlights. Oscar Wilde lived at 1 Merrion Square, Daniel O'Connell at 58, with WB Yeats only a few doors higher, at 82. **St Stephen's Green** is an important 24.8 acre (10 hectare) open space, popular with office workers and a delightful place to soak up the atmosphere. The **National Gallery** houses one of the finest collections in Europe, and includes works by Gainsborough, Reynolds and Hogarth.

When the Normans invaded Dublin, in the process they forced the Vikings to the lands north of the Liffey, where they established Oxmanstown. The south continued to prosper, but the northern part of the city only became urbanised in the 18th century. Today, this is a less well-known area of busy pedestrianised streets, shopping centres and the popular **Moore Street Market**. In the 18th century, O'Connell Street was known as **Gardener's Mall**, a fashionable area, renamed in honour of Daniel O'Connell. Worth seeking out here are the **National Wax Museum** at the corner of Dorset Street and Granby Row, and the **James Joyce Centre** in North Great George's Street.

To the northwest, **Phoenix Park** is the largest city park in Europe, and a good place to watch the city going about its business. **Dublin Zoo** is in the southeast corner of the park.

EXCURSIONS: Dun Laoghaire (pronounced Dun Leery) has attractive Victorian buildings, castles and a fine seafront. The **James Joyce Tower and Museum**, at **Sandycove**, is housed in a Martello Tower built in the early 1800s. Many personal effects of James Joyce are gathered here, including a first edition of *Ulysses*. Three castles at **Dalkey** survive from the 15th and 16th centuries: **Bullock Castle** (not open to the public), **Archbold's Castle**, now the town hall, and **Goat Castle**, housing the **Dalkey Heritage Centre**. **Malahide Castle**, north of the city, was built in the 12th century and houses some lovely furniture and a portrait gallery with paintings by Irish and British artists.

Castletown House, west of Dublin is a stunning Palladian building, among the best in Europe. It was built for the Speaker of the Irish House of Commons, William Connolly, who contrived to become the richest man in Ireland.

COUNTIES LOUTH AND MEATH: These two counties have much in common: outstanding Neolithic, Celtic and early-Christian history; extensive settlement by Normans; and a wealth of castles, monasteries, and rich farmland. They also share the **River Boyne**; wide, gentle and very beautiful, and famous for the Battle of the Boyne in 1690, when James II sought to regain the English throne, but was outmanoeuvred by William of Orange.

Astride the Boyne, **Drogheda**, the harbour town of Co Louth, holds an important place in the history of medieval Ireland. It was besieged by Oliver Cromwell in 1649, who massacred or transported most of the inhabitants. Today, it is a useful centre for exploring the **Boyne Valley**, which fashions a meandering course between Trim and Drogheda, hallmarked by an extensive list of prehistoric sites.

The prehistoric burial sites of **Brú na Bóinne**, west of Drogheda, number more than 40 and predate the pyramids. Among these, **Newgrange** is western Europe's most outstanding chambered tomb, built around 5000 years ago. **Monasterboice** was formerly a sixth-century monastery; in the cemetery stand three of the finest **High Crosses** in the country.

Dundalk is an industrial, harbour township, founded in the 12th century but largely rebuilt during Georgian times. Bordering Northern Ireland, the **Cooley Peninsula** forms a huge upland covered by heather, megaliths and pine plantations. The best way to see the peninsula is on foot, following parts of the Táin Way, a circular walk from Carlingford and **Omeath**.

Famed for its oysters, **Carlingford** looks across the lough to the **Mourne Mountains**. Historical links are found in **King John's Castle**, a small stronghold overlooking the sea, and **Taaffe's Castle**, one of many fortified residences in the area dating from the 16th century.

COUNTY KILDARE: Bounded by the **Liffey** and the **Wicklow Mountains**, County Kildare lies between the built-up area around Dublin and the boglands of The Midlands. The county has an enviable reputation, founded on the luxuriant turf of the Curragh, for the breeding and exercising of thoroughbred horses.

Kildare Town is built around **St Brigid's Cathedral**, which contains a number of Renaissance tombs and a splendid timber roof shaped like the hull of a ship. Close by is the **round tower**, the only one in Ireland to have an external staircase.

Peatland World, at **Lullymore**, 25km (15 miles) north of Kildare, tells all there is to know about peat. The **National Stud** at **Tully**, just outside Kildare Town, was started by Colonel Hall-Walker (to become Lord Wavertree), and its importance in the racing world is immense; open for guided tours, it includes a **Horse Museum**.

Naas (pronounced Nace) is a small industrial town on the edge of the Wicklow Mountains. Once the seat of the kings of the Province of Leinster, Naas was the heart of the ancient Irish kingdom of **Ui Dunlainge**. Today, it is a good shopping centre, and very much a hunting and horse racing locality.

On the banks of the huge **Poulaphouca Reservoir**, 20km (12.5 miles) southeast of Naas, **Russborough House** is a stunningly elegant Palladian mansion begun in 1741, built in Wicklow granite. On show here are works of art by European masters like Murillo, Poussin, Reynolds and Rubens.

COUNTY WICKLOW: The beauty of **Wicklow** is renowned far and wide. This land of mountains, forests, waterfalls and lakes takes its name from the tiny county town and the adjacent mountain range. Wicklow lies sandwiched between the heavily urban areas of Dublin and Wexford, and has the Irish Sea to the east. For centuries, the county was a stronghold of Celtic Christianity, with a focal point around **Glendalough**.

At the northern end of the county, **Bray** is a lively seaside resort with an air of Victorian charm, now rather faded and heavily reliant on daytrippers from Dublin. A fine beach, backed by amusement arcades and the **National Sea-Life Centre**, continues to make Bray popular. **Killruddery House Gardens**, offer splendid formal gardens, lakes and canals. Glencormac Gardens, southwest of Bray, were created by James Jameson of the famous distilling family. The fine 18th-century house at **Powerscourt**, west of Bray, is hugely popular, as are its formal gardens. A pleasant footpath leads to the **Powerscourt Waterfall**, the highest falls in Ireland, formed by the **Dargle River** which drops over cliffs 122m (400ft) high.

The county town of Wicklow is a delightfully sleepy place bordering a shingle bay. The main attraction in the town is the **Wicklow Historic Gaol**, which recounts the grim events and unsavoury personalities of Irish history. The luxurious displays of **Mount Usher Gardens** were set up in the 1860s by a Dublin linen manufacturer, Edward Walpole, and are a plant-lover's paradise. **Glendalough**, the glen of the two lakes, is a place of holiness among the hills and a place of pilgrimage, where St Kevin founded a monastery in AD 570. The tall **round tower** is a familiar landmark, variously used as a look-out post, a grain store and a belfry. The **cathedral** is now in ruins, but is no less evocative for that. Down towards the river is **St Kevin's Church**, a modest building with a chimney-shaped belfry. The little village of **Avoca** achieved fame as *Ballykissangel* in the television drama of that name.

THE SOUTHEAST

COUNTY WEXFORD: Lying in the southeast corner of Ireland, Co Wexford has an enviable sunshine record,

Credit: © Fáilte Ireland

beautiful countryside and a string of delightful harbour towns and sandy beaches. The climate is milder than elsewhere and produces a number of stunning gardens, open to the public by arrangement.

Built close to the mouth of the **River Slaney**, **Wexford** is a busy commercial and fishing town named by Vikings. Shops, pubs and an atmospheric charm make Wexford an appealing place to visit; that and its internationally renowned week-long *Opera Festival*, held in October.

The **Irish National Heritage Park** at **Ferrycarrig**, northwest of Wexford comprises 17 sites linking Ireland's history from prehistoric times to medieval. The mudflats of the **Slaney Estuary** (known as 'slobs') make up the **Wexford Wildfowl Reserve**, at its best between October and April when wildfowl are here. Kilmore Quay is an attractive fishing village with fine sandy beaches, thatched cottages, pubs and a maritime museum. A short distance offshore, the uninhabited **Saltee Islands**, one of Ireland's most important bird sanctuaries, are worth visiting. More easily accessed from Waterford, there is a beautiful drive down from **Arthurstown** to **Hook Head Peninsula**, which boasts many lovely sandy beaches and clifftops that are ideal for walking, cycling and horse-riding.

Surrounded by farmland and stretched out along the **River Slaney**, **Enniscorthy's** moment of fame arrived in 1798 in the form of the Battle of Vinegar Hill, when the United Irishmen made their last stand against the British. The thriving market town, by far the most attractive in Co Wexford, was established by the Normans – it is still dominated by the Norman castle and the much later **St Aidan's Cathedral**. The castle houses the **Wexford County Museum**.

Well inland for an old port, **New Ross**, perched along the **River Barrow**, was the original family base of the American Kennedy family and remains devoted to the US President. The **John Fitzgerald Kennedy Park and Arboretum**, south of New Ross, is dedicated to his memory and was opened in 1968 and is a popular place for easy walks. **Kilmokea Gardens** are arguably the most beautiful gardens in the southeast of Ireland, and not to be missed.

COUNTY WATERFORD: Bordered by the sea and divided by two upland ranges – the **Comeragh** and the **Monavullagh** – Waterford has both rugged beauty and an attractive coastline of fishing villages, holidays resorts and beaches.

Tightly compressed into a curve of the **River Suir**, **Waterford** was founded by Vikings in order to control shipping entering the rivers Suir and **Barrow**. Above the quayside, **Reginald's Tower and Museum**, built in 1003, is a forceful reminder of a turbulent past – Waterford was one of the few places to successfully oppose Cromwell's forces. Organised tours of **Waterford Crystal Glass Factory** illustrate the comprehensive story of crystal manufacture. **Dunmore East**, southeast of Waterford, is a charming village close to safe bathing beaches and attractive coves, including **Lady Cove**, a neat sandy bay popular with local people and tourists. **Tramore**, south of Waterford is one of Ireland's main holiday resorts. It has a racecourse, plenty of pubs, a large amusement park, miniature railway, boating lake and a 4.8km- (3 mile-) sandy beach caressed by the Gulf Stream.

The small harbour town of **Dungarvan** is found where the **River Colligan** flushes into **Dungarvan Harbour**. It provides a good base from which to explore the clifftops of **Helvick Head**. Nearby, **Ardmore** is renowned for its long, fine beach set against high cliffs and its place in Irish history as an important ecclesiastical site based on a

Credit: © Fáilte Ireland

seventh-century monastic settlement founded by St Declan.
COUNTY CARLOW: The second-smallest of Ireland's counties, **Carlow**, sandwiched between the rivers Barrow and Slaney, is mostly flat acres of rich farmland that edge along the base of hill country to the south, east and west. This is an unspoilt part of Ireland, a place of sleepy villages and lush countryside. **Carlow Town** used to be an Anglo-Norman stronghold, but these days it is largely concerned with the manufacture of sugar beet. It was the southernmost outpost of the area controlled by the English Crown and, as a result, heavily fortified. **Carlow County Museum** is in the town hall on Centaur Street.
COUNTY KILKENNY: This is a busy agricultural county, a place of lush, well-tended countryside, neat, attractive villages, homely cottages and dramatic castles along the river valleys of the **Nore** and the **Barrow**. Fishing, horse racing, riding and golf are the main activities in this manicured landscape.
Kilkenny is named after St Canice, who established a monastery here. **Kilkenny Castle** continues to dominate the town, a blend of Gothic, Classical and Tudor styles. Built on a hilltop site in the sixth century, **St Canice's Cathedral** dates mostly from the 13th century.
Dunmore Cave, north of Kilkenny is one of the most famous in Ireland, notably for its great beauty. In the past, people took refuge here from the Vikings, not always successfully. **Kells Priory**, south of Kilkenny, the site of an Augustinian priory, is little known in Ireland, but is one of the most beautiful and finest ruins in the country. **Jerpoint Abbey**, south of **Thomastown** is a remarkable Cistercian ruin, famed for the carvings on its tombs. It dates from 1158, but was embraced by Henry VIII's dissolution of the monasteries.
COUNTY TIPPERARY: The lack of a coastline does not affect the beauty of this county in any way, as a walk to the top of **Slievenamon** (the mountain of the fairies), north of Clonmel, will reveal. Northwards, amid farmlands, rises the limestone **Rock of Cashel**, to the south are the **Comeragh Mountains**. The countryside of Tipperary is dotted with Norman castles and churches, and Stone and Iron Age sites. The town of **Clonmel** sits on the banks of the **River Suir**, and dates from the 10th century, but there is considerable evidence all around of occupation from prehistoric times. Today, Clonmel is the most important town in the county. The **County Museum** in Parnell Street has a diverse collection of artefacts, including Roman coins and prehistoric items.
The **Comeragh** and **Knockmealdown** mountain ranges are vast uplands of forest and bog, but easy to explore either by car or on foot. **Ballymacarbry** on the **River Nier** is also a good base for walking.
Carrick-on-Suir, a thriving market town east of Clonmel is today best known for Sean Kelly the cyclist who had noted success in the *Tour de France*. **Ormond Castle**, just outside the town, is a fortified Elizabethan mansion and well worth visiting.

THE MIDLANDS

COUNTY MONAGHAN: This county lies between **Fermanagh** to the west and **Armagh** to the east, and has a delightful landscape of low, rolling hills. Lakes abound too, making this a popular place with coarse fishermen. The central part of the county is hilly but intensively farmed.
Monaghan is a market town, built on a monastic site, with some excellent architecture. The **Monaghan County Museum** on Market Street contains the Clogher Cross among its treasures, a sample of early Christian metalwork.
Castleblaney lies at the head of **Lough Muckno**, the county's largest lake and a source of excellent coarse fishing. **Carrickmacross**, south of **Ballybay**, is famed for its handmade lace. To the north stands **Mannan Castle**, a 12th-century motte and bailey.
COUNTY CAVAN: Known to anglers as a place of lakes and rivers and the very best in coarse fishing. Non-anglers scarcely know it at all for Cavan is an undiscovered county, peaceful and unspoilt, an attractive countryside dotted with woodlands and folded into wild glens that rise to the summit of Cuilcagh at 665m (2182ft), which it shares with Co Fermanagh.
Cavan, the county town, is uninspiring, but nearby **Clough Oughter**, a circular tower castle, tells of a time when this was the stronghold of the O'Reillys, the princes of Breffni. A short way out of Cavan, is a group of standing stones, **Finn MacCool's Fingers**, said to be the place where the princes were crowned. West of the town, **Lough Oughter** is the name given to a collection of lakes, part of the **River Erne** system, and a major coarse fishing area.
COUNTY LONGFORD: Like Co Cavan, **Longford** holds great appeal for anglers. It sits in the middle of Ireland, and lies in the catchment of the **River Shannon**. Lakes abound, notably **Lough Gowna** in the north and **Lough Kinale** in the east. Today, Co Longford is primarily given to farming. Perched on the **River Camlin**, **Longford Town** grew up around a fortress of the O'Farrells. The towers of the **Cathedral of St Mel** dominate the town. A few miles west, **Cloondara** is worth a visit: an attractive village on the **Royal Canal**. During the summer months, Irish music is performed in the *teach cheoil* (Irish music house).
Ballymahon is famed for Oliver Goldsmith, author of *She Stoops to Conquer* and the classic poem *The Deserted Village*. He was born at **Pallas**, a few miles to the east.
COUNTY WESTMEATH: This county has an air of quiet beauty, being a place of lakes and wooded countryside, and a huge slice of untamed bogland, producing a unique habitat for flora and fauna. Old-fashioned pubs and ruins dot the landscape, and make Westmeath a fascinating place to explore. The former garrison town of **Mullingar** is now an important centre for angling and one of the most agreeable market towns in Ireland, with an atmosphere that is lacking in other towns in The Midlands. Hunting, shooting and fishing are the main pursuits here.
In **Crookedwood** village, at the foot of **Lough Derravaragh**, stands **St Munna's Church**, the stuff of fairytales, complete with 15th-century tower and battlements and a lakeside setting. At **Castlepollard** are the beautiful grounds of **Tullynally Castle**, the family seat of the earls of Longford.
COUNTIES OFFALY AND LAIOS: Sharing almost the same identity - of remote, unspoilt boglands unaffected by mass tourism - the counties of Offaly and Laios lie at the heart of The Midlands. Co Offaly is bordered to the west by the River Shannon, which offers cruising tours, as does the **Grand Canal** that runs through the middle of the county. Co Laios (pronounced Leash) is a place of attractive villages with fine houses. Co Offaly shares with Co Laios the beautiful glens of the **Slieve Bloom Mountains** which, in spite of a low elevation and a distinctly boggy feel about them, nevertheless convey a sense of grandeur and remoteness.
One of Ireland's most holy places, **Clonmacnoise**, was founded in AD 548 by St Ciaran at a strategic crossing point of the Shannon. During medieval times, it developed into a great seat of learning, acknowledged by kings.
Using a former trackbed built for the transportation of peat, the **Clonmacnoise and West Offaly Railway** is the key to the natural history of bogs, as it fashions an 8.8km- (5.5 mile-) course around the **Blackwater Bog**.
Birr is an attractive town of Georgian streets and buildings. The grounds of **Birr Castle** are superb, though the castle itself is not open to the public. Here, too, is the **Historic Science Centre**, housing a large reflecting telescope - the largest in the world in its day.
There is little of interest in **Portlaoise** itself, though there is a defensive fort, the **Rock of Dunamase**, just outside the town, and a **Steam Traction Museum** at **Stradbally**.
Emo Court, west of Kildare, is an elegant neoclassical building constructed in 1792. Not far from **Mountrath** is **Roundwood House**, a lovely Palladian mansion, now a guest house.

THE SOUTHWEST

COUNTY CORK: This is Ireland's largest county, combining rich agricultural land, an important sea port, glorious coastal and mountain scenery, gentle bays and romantic castles. Tourism and related activities form a major part of Cork's economy, but instead of brashness and tackiness, the county has become more discerning and produced a wide range of quality shops, pubs, hotels and restaurants.
Although the county extends northwards to Limerick, its most dramatic landscapes are in the southwest, where long fingers of land probe the **Atlantic Ocean**, making for stunning car tours and breathtaking excursions on foot. Ferries reach out to the offshore **Sherkin Island**, **Bear Island** and **Cape Clear Island**.
The name *Corcaigh* means 'swamp', a reminder that **Cork** is built on the marshy ground flanking the River Lee. The city is lively, buzzing with industry, academia and, invariably, the sound of impromptu music recitals, making this a delightful place to amble through the streets or sample Irish pub hospitality. The main part of the city is squashed onto an elongated island linked by elegant bridges. The **English Market**, at the rear of St Patrick Street, is a wacky place to wander around, not dissimilar in atmosphere to the open-air flea market on Cornmarket Street. North of St Patrick lies Paul Street, the trendy part of Cork, a place of pedestrianised streets, buskers and high-quality shops. Other places worth taking in are the tower of **St Anne's Shandon**, the **Butter Exchange** which houses the **Shandon Craft Centre**, **Cork City Gaol**, **Elizabeth Fort** (now a Garda station), the **Cork Public Museum** in **Fitzgerald Park** and **St Fin Barre's Cathedral**.
Blarney Castle is renowned far and wide for the **Blarney Stone**, a kiss on which endows 'the gift of the gab'. While in Blarney, the **Woollen Mills** and **Blarney House** are both worth seeking out.
Cobh (pronounced Cove) is Ireland's main trans-Atlantic port, grown out of a former fishing village. The town centre is dominated by **St Colman's Cathedral**. The history of the port and its luxury liners (which included the *Titanic*) is told in **Cobh Heritage Centre**.
Along the coast: Kinsale, an attractive seaside town at the mouth of **Bandon River**, has superb restaurants and fine buildings. Each October sees a gourmet festival here. **Kilbrittain**, **Timoleague** and **Courtmacsherry** are all unspoilt in lovely settings around the bay. **Clonakilty** is famed as a centre for Gaelic culture and music.
Castletownhead is another charming Georgian village, while nearby **Skibbereen** is a small market town renowned for its opinionated local newspaper, the *Skibbereen Eagle*. The isolated fishing village of **Baltimore** lies at the far end of one of the peninsulas, the place from which to visit the islands. **Bantry** is ideal for exploring **Bantry Bay** and the **Sheep's Head Peninsula**. **Bantry Bay House** deserves a quick visit, with its glorious view and some important French tapestries.
COUNTY KERRY: The county is blessed with the finest scenery in Ireland, from the tranquil beauty of **Killarney Lake** to the majestic crags of **MacGillycuddy's Reeks** and the highest mountain in Ireland, **Carrantoohill**. The **Iveragh Peninsula** is without equal and is circled by the **Ring of Kerry**. The **Beargha Peninsula** is less well known, and relatively unexplored.
Set against a backdrop of mountains, **Kenmare** is a busy market town at the meeting of three rivers - the **Roughty**, **Finihy** and **Sheen**. The town has craft shops, restaurants, pubs and **Kenmare Heritage Centre**. **St Mary's Holy Well** is reputed to have healing properties.
The Ring of Kerry is a stunning, 180km- (112 mile-) scenic drive around the Iveragh Peninsula, with numerous diversions along coastal roads and out to islands like **Skellig Michael**. A drive through the hills via **Ballaghbearna Gap** and the **Ballaghisheen Pass**, promises rugged landscapes studded with lakes and carved by rivers. The resort town of **Killarney** spreads itself in the shadow of **MacGillycuddy's Reeks**, the finest ridge walk in Ireland. A traverse of the ridge is not for the faint-hearted, nor is the climb to the top of Carrantoohill an easy stroll. The town bustles to the needs of visitors, but its best feature is undoubtedly **St Mary's Cathedral**, which boasts an untypically tall spire.
Killarney National Park embraces three lakes all linked by a river. A good starting point is **Muckross House and Gardens**, a neo-Tudor building with rooms furnished in the Victorian style. **Torc Waterfalls** are modest, but lie in a beautiful woodland setting. A nearby stairway of over 170 steps climbs to a fine viewpoint. The **Dingle Peninsula** has lovely beaches and the fine town of Dingle itself, the westernmost town in Europe. It is a slim peninsula with a spectacular coastal road and numerous diversions. Not to be missed is **Brandon Mountain** and **Brandon Bay**. **Ventry** has a lovely white-sand strand, on which legend claims the King of the Other World landed to subjugate Ireland.
COUNTY LIMERICK: It was Edward Lear who popularised the five-line limerick of nonsense verse that is forever associated with this lovely Irish county. Today a farming region, Limerick has hundreds of castle ruins that tell of more troubled times. Astride the **River Shannon** and fringed by hills and mountains, the county has a long history of monastic settlement.
Limerick stands on both banks of the Shannon and the **Abbey River**. It is Georgian in character and has a grid pattern of streets. Limerick is still undergoing a renaissance in its culture, music, drama and self-esteem. Mass tourism has yet to discover Limerick, and it remains an agreeable base for exploration. **King John's Castle** is a weighty Norman stronghold built on the site of a Viking settlement. The **English Town** and **Irish Town** are the more interesting areas to explore. The **Hunt Museum** in the old custom house is the finest museum outside Dublin, containing artefacts collected by John Hunt, a specialist in Celtic culture.
Adare is picture-postcard country, a place of thatched cottages. **Loch Gur**, hidden in the hills, is surrounded by archaeological remains - including stone circles and dolmens - and guarded by the remains of two castles. Murroe lies among the foothills of the **Slievefelim**

Mountains. The village is dominated by the **Mansion of Glenstal**, now a Benedictine monastery. The gardens are especially beautiful in spring and early summer.

THE WEST

COUNTY CLARE: More than 2000 stone forts litter the landscape of Co Clare, a county that would be virtually unknown were it not for **The Burren**, a beautiful limestone district overlooking **Galway Bay** and formed around an ancient barony of that name. More than three-quarters of the county is fringed by water and the main activities are farming, fishing and tourism.

Ennis sits on a bend in the **River Fergus**, a place of narrow, winding streets and the ruins of **Ennis Friary**. The spectacular **Cliffs of Moher** are one of Ireland's most dramatic sights, extending for 8km (5 miles) and rising to more than 200m (650ft) above the sea, hosting huge colonies of seabirds. The **Burren Coast** is for those interested in geology and outstanding landscapes. Here, limestone pavements shelter unique flora that develop in their fissures. The **Burren Display Centre** is at **Kilfenora**.

COUNTY GALWAY: If one place typifies the visitor's image of Ireland it is Co Galway, a place of contrasts from prime bogland and rich farming, to mountains, loughs and stone cottages. Long, lonely valleys, sublime hills and vast golden beaches are the hallmarks of the county, which reaches from the banks of the Shannon to the wild region in the west known as **Connemara**.

Galway stretches along the **Corrib River**, divided by it into the traditional fisherman's village of **Claddagh** and the medieval town of ancient streets and quaysides. This is a bustling, vibrant city and the centre of trade for this part of Ireland for centuries. Today, it is one of the fastest developing towns in Europe, with a fascinating blend of modernity and Celtic culture.

The **Aran Islands** are great swathes of limestone defending the approach to Galway. Legend has it that they were inhabited by a tribe expelled from the mainland, and they certainly have been inhabited for centuries. **Clifden** lies at the western edge of the beautiful region known as Connemara, a place of bogs, lakes, mountains and moors, and a coastline etched by deep bays and inlets. **Letterfrack** is a tidy village laid out by Quakers, one of a number of mission settlements along the coast. **Connemara National Park Visitor Centre** is close by.

COUNTY ROSCOMMON: Green and fertile **Roscommon** has numerous lakes and rivers, its eastern boundary formed by the Shannon, largely in the shape of **Lough Ree**. The centre of the county is given to sheep and cattle farming, the east and west runs to bogland. There are numerous archaeological sites. **Lough Key Forest Park** is laid out with trails and gardens.

The small town of Roscommon is dominated by the ruins of its Norman castle. Nearby are the remains of a **Dominican Friary**. **Strokestown Park House** is a fine Palladian mansion with original 18th-century furniture.

COUNTY MAYO: Land of wide sandy beaches and high mountains, Mayo is a quieter version of Connemara, rising to the sacred mountain of **Croagh Patrick**, an annual place of pilgrimage. Mayo is one of Ireland's loveliest counties, extending round **Clew Bay** to the **Corraun Peninsula** and **Achill Island**, and beyond to the windswept corners of the **Mullet Peninsula**. This northern part of Mayo is virtually unknown.

A delightful little town, **Westport** contrasts remarkably with the wild countryside all around. Ideal for walkers visiting Croagh Patrick, Westport lounges along the **Carrowbeg River**, exuding a busy air from the elegance of its Georgian designs. The annual *Westport Sea Angling Festival* and the *Horse Fair* are great attractions. The sea angling in Clew Bay is reputedly the finest in Europe.

Achill Island, linked by a bridge, is best explored on foot, from the high cliffs at **Achill Head**, to the lovely beaches at **Keem Strand** and **Trawmore Strand**. The **Atlantic Drive** is the finest way to view the island by car and begins from the village of **Mulrany**. Along the north Mayo coast is the archaeological site known as the **Céide Fields**, supported by an imaginative visitor centre that explains the 5000 years of settlement in this part of Ireland.

In the southeast of the county, the small town of **Knock** has an internationally recognised **Marian shrine**. Approximately 1.5 million pilgrims visit the shrine annually.

THE NORTHWEST

COUNTY SLIGO: This county owes a good deal of its fame to WB Yeats, the Nobel Prize winner, who used to visit here with his artist brother, Jack. *Crannogs* (lake dwellings) were once a common feature here, and their remains can still be found.

The town of **Sligo** grew in prosperity, trading on beer, spirits, rope and linen, and was one of the main ports sailing to the USA. This is the largest town in northwest Ireland, built around bridges spanning the **River Garavogue**. **Sligo Abbey** is a ruined Dominican priory, founded in 1252, but destroyed by Cromwell's forces; it is the town's oldest building. The **Municipal Art Gallery** and **Sligo County Museum** have a good deal about the Yeats brothers. **Doorly Park** and **Sligo Racecourse** have some lovely walks.

Carrowmore is an important prehistoric site with a vast number of stone circles and dolmens. The **Arigna Scenic Drive** gives good views of **Lough Key**. **Benbulben** is a distinctive mountain to the north of Sligo; the climb is steep but not especially demanding, and the view worth the effort.

COUNTY LEITRIM: The county of Leitrim is a perfect place for a peaceful holiday; with its foothold on the Atlantic coast, and forming a long and narrow county divided by hills and rivers, and the beauty of **Lough Allen**. The main pursuit here is angling, though walkers will find solitude among the **Manorhamilton Hills**.

To the south of the county, **Carrick-on-Shannon** was always an important crossroads and meeting place. Today, it is the centre of river cruising on the Shannon, and heavily geared up to all aquatic pursuits, with over 40 lakes where fishing is unrestricted. **Costelloe Memorial Chapel** claims to be the second-smallest chapel in the world.

COUNTY DONEGAL: All Ireland is represented in Donegal, from the heather moors, mountains and bogs of the **Gaeltacht** in the west, to the rich farmlands and towns of the east. Taking the full force of Atlantic gales, much of Donegal's beauty is fashioned by the sea. The coastal cliffs around **Slieve League** are stunning as is the great arc of **Donegal Bay**. But the county is primarily one of rocky landscapes and hauntingly beautiful moorlands.

Donegal has an air of charm about it, in spite of being busy and often crowded. **Donegal Castle** was once the stronghold of the O'Donnells.

St John's Point sticks out on a limb; **Slieve League** is outstanding, from the cliffs of Bunglass to the glorious sands of **Silver Strand**. **Glencolumbkille** is named after St Columba, who founded a monastery here. The **Northern Peninsulas** and their islands are a world apart, stretching northwards from **The Rosses** through **Gweedore**, **Cloghaneely** and across **Lough Swilly** to **Inishowen**. Inland, **Glenveagh National Park** is a region of undulating peat hills that embrace **Glenveagh Castle and Gardens**.

Sport & Activities

Horse-riding: Equestrianism is one of Ireland's principal tourist attractions and facilities for horse-riding are found all over the country. A full list of stables and riding holidays is available from Fáilte Ireland (see *Contact Addresses* section). The principal **racecourses** are at Leopardstown, Fairyhouse (*Irish Grand National* every year), The Curragh (*Irish Sweeps Derby*) and Punchestown (an international cross-country and three-day-event riding course).

Hiking: Ireland's sparsely populated countryside makes it ideal for walkers of all levels. The mild climate means that the mountains are accessible all year round. The more mountainous areas are towards the coast, which makes for dramatic seascapes, especially by the Atlantic Ocean. More adventurous walkers may want to tackle Ireland's highest peak, *Carrauntoohil* (1041m/3415ft) in Macgillycuddy's Reeks, in the far southwest of the country. Other notable mountains include *Croagh Patrick* (765m/2510ft) near Westport in Co Mayo, a holy mountain and, on the last Sunday in July, a place of pilgrimage. Its distinctive conical summit is silhouetted against the horizon for miles, acting as a beacon to pilgrims. St Patrick is supposed to have driven all the snakes out of Ireland from this mountain. The 12 Bens in Connemara offer lovely hill walking, with views over towards the jagged coastline. The beautiful scenery of the *Wicklow Mountains* is barely one hour's drive from Dublin. There are 28 national waymarked ways in the country, including the Kerry Way, the Beara Way and the Wicklow Way. Tailor-made tours with a local guide can be arranged through Walking Cycling Ireland (e-mail: info@irelandwalkingcycling.com; website: www.irelandwalkingcycling.com). There are many gentle walks for the less energetic.

Cycling: Although some of Ireland's coastal parts are mountainous, the sheltered valleys and the gently undulating central plain are excellent for easy cycling. Roads are well maintained and most are very quiet. Inland, the landscape is dotted with small farms, and one is never too far away from some form of civilisation if one requires it. There is a surprisingly high number of pre-celtic monuments in lonely places; owing to old Irish superstitions, these were not cleared away when the land was farmed. The Boyne Valley alone contains over 300.

Fishing: Being blessed with miles of rivers and streams and over 5500km (3500 miles) of coastline, Ireland offers excellent fishing. There is no closed season for **freshwater angling**, but March to October are the most suitable months for bream, rudd, roach, dace and perch. For **coarse angling**, there are new regulations regarding share certificates; further details can be obtained from Fáilte Ireland (see *Contact Addresses* section). **Game fishing** requires a licence and, generally, also a permit. The brown

Credit: © Fáilte Ireland

trout season is usually from mid-February or March until 30 September. Open salmon season is 1 January to 7 September, according to district. The best sea trout period is from June to 30 September or 12 October in some areas. Salmon licences/permits also cover sea trout. Along the Atlantic coast, **sea angling** is possible from piers, rocks, in the surf or during a day's boat fishing excursion (which can be organised locally).

Golf: There are 350 golf courses run by the Golfing Union of Ireland, and many people come to Ireland specifically for a golfing holiday, where the course rates are relatively cheap compared with the UK. The courses are set both by the sea and inland – two-thirds are 18-hole.

Other: For those travelling in pursuit of culture or in order to discover their roots, Ireland has much to offer. There are **summer schools** all over the country, where it is possible to learn Gaelic and to pursue other courses in Irish culture. Courses available include archaeological walks around Celtic sites, classes in traditional Irish music, courses on literary figures such as Oscar Wilde, WB Yeats and Gerard Manley Hopkins, and on popular culture and storytelling. A list is available from Fáilte Ireland.

Accommodation can be arranged with local families, and programmes of entertainment are laid on for the evening. These courses attract participants from all over the world.

Genealogical centres exist widely, and will help those who come to trace their family history. Fáilte Ireland (see *Contact Addresses* section) publishes a free booklet called *Tracing your Ancestors*. They can put visitors in touch with the appropriate centre. The National Library of Ireland offers a free genealogy advisory service run by a panel of genealogists and an expert member of staff, which provides visitors with an overview of genealogical records and gives advice on specific family research. Further information is available (tel: (1) 603 0200; fax: (1) 676 6690; e-mail: info@nli.ie; website: www.nli.ie).

Pilgrimages to and within Ireland are burgeoning and visits to religious sites such as the *Knock Marian Shrine* in Co Mayo are increasing in popularity. The national sports are **Gaelic football** and **hurling**.

Social Profile

FOOD & DRINK: Ireland is a farming country noted for its meat, bacon, poultry and dairy produce. The surrounding sea, inland lakes and rivers offer fresh fish including salmon, trout, lobster, Dublin Bay prawns, oysters (served with Guinness and wholemeal bread), mussels and periwinkles. Dublin has a wide selection of restaurants and eating places to suit every pocket, as do the other major towns. Table and self-service are both common. The most typical Irish dishes will usually be found in a country restaurant, and include corned beef and carrots, boiled bacon and cabbage and Irish stew. Other local delicacies are *crubeens* (pigs' trotters), *colcannon* (a mixture of potatoes and cabbage cooked together), soda bread and a soufflé made with *carrageen* (a variety of seaweed). Visitors should note that 'tea' is often almost a full meal with sandwiches and cakes. Pubs, of which Ireland has plenty, are sometimes called 'lounges' or 'bars' and there is often a worded sign outside the premises rather than the traditional painted boards found in Britain. Pubs and bars have counter service. The measure used in Ireland for spirits is larger than that used in Britain, for example an Irish double is equal to a triple in Britain. *Irish coffee* is popular (a glass of strong black coffee, brown sugar and whiskey with cream). Almost any drink is imported but the two most internationally distinctive products are *whiskey* (spelt with an 'e') and *stout*. *Guinness*, one of the most famous, popular and distinctive drinks in the world, is found everywhere, and *Murphy's* is almost as widely available. One of the most popular of lighter ales is

Smithwick's or *Harp Lager*, also available everywhere. Irish whiskey has a uniquely characteristic flavour and is matured in a wooden barrel for a minimum of seven years. Amongst the most popular brands are *Jamesons* and *John Powers Gold Label*, but others include *Hewitts, Midleton, Old Bushmills, Paddy, Reserve* and *Tullamore Dew*. Certainly as popular as whiskey is stout, which is bottled or served from the tap. Liqueurs such as *Bailey's* and *Irish Mist* are both made from a base of Irish whiskey. **Licensing hours:** Mon-Wed 1030-2330, Thurs-Sat 1030-0030 and Sun 1030-2300. **Legal drinking age:** 18, although some bars will insist that patrons are over 21 and carry ID. Children under 18 years must leave establishments by 2100.

Credit: © Fáilte Ireland

NIGHTLIFE: Most towns in Ireland have clubs, bars and pubs with live music. It is quite common to find pubs holding *seisun*, playing traditional Irish music with traditional instruments. The dancehalls and discos of previous eras have now been replaced with clubs similar to those found throughout the UK and Western Europe. Special events and themed nights often take place at special attractions such as the medieval banquet at Bunratty Castle. There is still a good choice of theatres and cinemas.

SHOPPING: Special purchases include hand-woven tweed, hand-crocheted woollens and cottons, sheepskin goods, gold and silver jewellery, Aran knitwear, linen, pottery, Irish crystal and basketry. **Shopping hours:** Mon-Sat 0900-1730/1800. Many towns have a late night opening on Thursday or Friday until 2000/2100 and smaller towns may have one early closing day a week.

Note: Under the 'Retail Export Scheme', it is possible to claim VAT back on goods bought in Ireland on leaving the EU. For further information, contact the VAT Administration Branch, Stamping Building, Dublin Castle, Dublin 2 (tel: (1) 674 8858; fax: (1) 657 5000; e-mail: vatinfo@revenue.ie; website: www.revenue.ie).

SPECIAL EVENTS: For full details, contact Fáilte Ireland (see Contact Addresses). The following is a selection of special events occurring in Ireland in 2005:

Jan 1 *Lord Mayor's New Year's Day Parade*, Dublin. **Feb 9-13** *Chinatown Festival*, Dublin. **Feb 25-Mar 5** *North Cork Drama Festival*. **Mar 11-17** *St Patrick's Week Celebrations*, nationwide. **Mar 29-Apr 3** *Pan Celtic International Festival*, Kerry. **Apr 12-17** *Wexford Book Festival*. **Apr 17** *Sliabh Beagh Walking Festivals*. **Apr 29-May 1** *Bray Jazz Festival*, Wicklow. **May 5-8** *Bantry Mussel Fair*, Cork. **Jun 2-6** *The Murphy's Cat Laughs Festival*, Kilkenny. **Jul 1-15** *Ballyheigue Summer Festival*, Kerry. **Aug 10-12** *Puck Fair*, Kerry. **Sep 22-24** *36th Ryder Cup Golf Tournament*, Kildare. **Oct 7-10** *Harvest Moon Festival*, Tyrone. **Nov 16-20** *Darklight Film Festival*, Dublin.

SOCIAL CONVENTIONS: The Irish are gregarious people, and everywhere animated *craic* (talk) can be heard. Oscar Fingal O'Flahertie Wills (better known as Oscar Wilde) once claimed: 'We are the greatest talkers since the Greeks.' Close community contact is very much part of the Irish way of life and almost everywhere there is an intimate small-town atmosphere. Pubs are often the heart of a community's social life. Visitors will find the people very friendly and welcoming no matter where one finds oneself in the country. A meal in an Irish home is usually a substantial affair and guests will eat well. Dinner is the main meal of the day and is now eaten in the evening. Even in cities there is less formal wear than in most European countries and casual dress is widely acceptable as in keeping with a largely agricultural community. Women, however, often dress up for smart restaurants and social functions. Handshaking is usual, and modes of address will often be informal. Smoking is banned in all public enclosed/working spaces, including pubs, bars and restaurants. **Tipping:** The customary tip in Ireland is 10 to 12 per cent. Many hotels and restaurants add this in the form of a service charge indicated on the menu or bill. It is not customary to tip in bars unless you have table service when a small tip is advised. Tipping porters, taxi drivers, hairdressers etc is customary but not obligatory.

Business Profile

ECONOMY: Ireland's recent economic history is characterised by what is now the cliché of the 'Celtic Tiger'. Fuelled by EU membership and effective investment promotion policies, the Irish economy has been transformed over a period of two decades from a European backwater into the fastest growing economy in the EU.

Hitherto Ireland had not been industrialised to the same degree as the rest of Europe, and only recently has agriculture been overtaken as the largest single contributor to the national product. It remains a key sector, and the Government is seeking to consolidate its role within the economy by modernisation and expansion of food-processing industries. Beef and dairy dominate the sector, but there is also large-scale production of potatoes, barley and wheat. Ireland's recent industrial development has been achieved by a deliberate policy of promoting export-led and advanced technology businesses, partly by offering attractive packages for foreign investors. Textiles, chemicals and electronics have performed particularly strongly. Most of Ireland's economic development in the 1990s, however, was in the service sector. Banking and finance have grown to the extent that Dublin now supports a sizeable international financial centre, while tourism has become a substantial foreign exchange earner.

The statistics of Ireland's remarkable development are average GDP growth between 7 and 10 per cent since the mid-1990s, while inflation and unemployment were kept consistently below 5 per cent. However, there has been a slowdown of late, with GDP growth in 2004 being 1.4 per cent. The Irish are famously enthusiastic about Europe and there is little of the scepticism so prevalent in Britain. Ireland joined EMU with the majority of EU members in the first wave at the beginning of 1999, despite some concern about the consequences of Britain's non-membership. Trade with the UK, which provides 30 per cent of total imports and takes 20 per cent of Ireland's exports, remains important but the proportion is declining gradually as other EU countries assume greater significance.

BUSINESS: Businesspeople should wear formal clothes for meetings. Local businesspeople are very friendly and an informal business approach is most successful. However, it is advisable to make prior appointments and to allow enough time to complete business matters. Avoid business visits in the first week of May, during July, August and at Christmas or New Year.

COMMERCIAL INFORMATION: The following organisation can offer advice: Chambers of Commerce of Ireland, 17 Merrion Square, Dublin 2 (tel: (1) 661 2888; fax: (1) 661 2811; e-mail: info@chambersireland.ie; website: www.chambersireland.ie).

CONFERENCES/CONVENTIONS: For more information, contact Fáilte Ireland, Bord Fáilte, Baggot Street Bridge, Dublin 2 (tel: (1) 602 4000; fax: (1) 602 4336; e-mail: cbi@failteireland.ie; website: www.conference-ireland.ie).

Climate

The temperate climate is due to mild southwesterly winds and the Gulf Stream. Summers are warm, while temperatures during winter are much cooler. Spring and autumn are very mild. Rain falls all year.

Required clothing: Lightweights during summer with warmer mediumweights for the winter. Rainwear is advisable throughout the year.

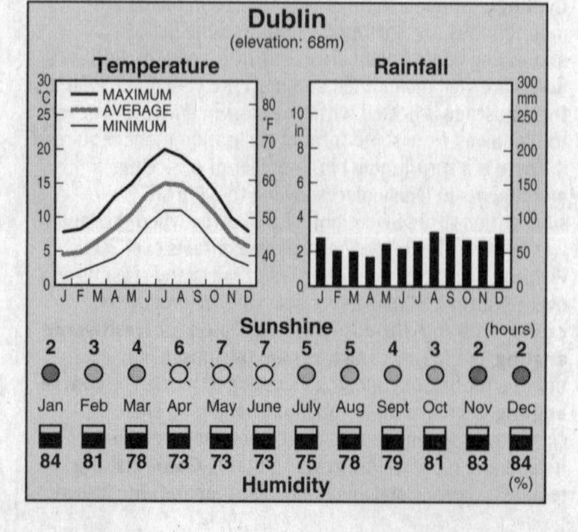

Israel

LATEST TRAVEL ADVICE CONTACTS

British Foreign and Commonwealth Office
Tel: (0870) 606 0290 Website: www.fco.gov.uk
US Department of State
Website: http://travel.state.gov/travel
Canadian Department of Foreign Affairs and Int'l Trade
Tel: (1 800) 267 8376 Website: www.dfait-maeci.gc.ca

Location: Eastern Mediterranean.

Country dialling code: 972.

Ministry of Tourism
5 Bank Israel Street, B Genri Building, Jerusalem 91009, Israel
Tel: (2) 666 4200. Fax: (2) 666 4402.
Website: www.tourism.gov.il

Palestinian Ministry of Tourism and Antiquities
PO Box 534, Manger Street, Bethlehem, Palestine
Tel: (2) 274 1581/2/3. Fax: (2) 274 3753.
E-mail: mota@visit-palestine.com
Website: www.visit-palestine.com
Offices also in: Gaza, Hebron, Jericho, Nablus and Ramallah.

Embassy of Israel
2 Palace Green, London W8 4QB, UK
Tel: (020) 7957 9500. Fax: (020) 7957 9555.
E-mail: info-assist@london.mfa.gov.il
Website: http://london.mfa.gov.il
Opening hours: Mon-Thurs 0900-1730, Fri 0830-1330.
Consular Section: 15a Old Court Palace, London W8 4QB, UK
Tel: (020) 7957 9576/9627/9680. Fax: (020) 7957 9577.
E-mail: cons-sec@london.mfa.gov.il
Opening hours: Mon-Thurs 1000-1330, Fri 1000-1230.

Israel Government Tourist Office
UK House, 180 Oxford Street, London W1D 1NN, UK
Tel: (020) 7299 1100/10/11. Fax: (020) 7299 1112.
E-mail: info@igto.co.uk
Website: www.go-israel.org

British Embassy
192 Hayarkon Street, Tel Aviv 63405, Israel
Tel: (3) 725 1222. Fax: (3) 527 8574.
E-mail: webmaster.telaviv@fco.gov.uk
Website: www.britemb.org.il
Consular section: 6th Floor, Migdal Or Building,

TIMATIC CODES

Health
AMADEUS: **TI-DFT/TLV/HE**
GALILEO/WORLDSPAN: **TI-DFT/TLV/HE**
SABRE: **TIDFT/TLV/HE**

Visa
AMADEUS: **TI-DFT/TLV/VI**
GALILEO/WORLDSPAN: **TI-DFT/TLV/VI**
SABRE: **TIDFT/TLV/VI**

To access TIMATIC country information on Health and Visa regulations through the Computer Reservations System (CRS), type in the appropriate command line listed above.

1 Ben Yehuda Street, Tel Aviv 63801, Israel
Tel: (3) 510 0166 *or* 0497. Fax: (3) 510 1167.
E-mail: bricontv@netvision.net.il
Consulates in: Eilat and Jerusalem.
Embassy of Israel
3514 International Drive, NW, Washington, DC 20008, USA
Tel: (202) 364 5500 *or* 5527 (consular section).
Fax: (202) 364 5607 *or* 5429 (consular section).
E-mail: ask@israelemb.org *or* info@washington.mfa.gov.il
Website: www.israelemb.org
Consulates in: Atlanta, Boston, Chicago, Houston, Los Angeles, Miami, New York, Philadelphia and San Francisco.
Israel Government Tourist Office
800 Second Avenue, 16th Floor, New York, NY 10017, USA
Tel: (212) 499 5660 *or* (888) 77 477 235 (toll-free in USA and Canada). Fax: (212) 499 5665.
E-mail: info@goisrael.com Website: www.goisrael.com
Offices also in: Los Angeles.
Embassy of the United States of America
71 Hayarkon Street, Tel Aviv 63903, Israel
Tel: (3) 519 7575 *or* 7617 (visa section).
Fax: (3) 519 7619 (visa section).
E-mail: ac5@bezegint.net *or* nivtelaviv@state.gov (visa section).
Website: www.usembassy-israel.org.il
Consulate General in: Jerusalem.
Embassy of Israel
50 O'Connor Street, Suite 1005, Ottawa, Ontario K1P 6L2, Canada
Tel: (613) 567 6450. Fax: (613) 567 9878.
E-mail: ottawa@israel.org
Website: www.embassyofisrael.ca
Consulates in: Montréal and Toronto.
Israel Government Tourist Office
Suite 700, 180 Bloor Street West, Toronto, Ontario M5S 2V6, Canada
Tel: (416) 964 3784. Fax: (416) 964 2420.
E-mail: info@igto.ca
Canadian Embassy
Street address: 3/5 Nirim Street, 4th Floor, Tel Aviv 67060, Israel
Postal address: PO Box 9442, Tel Aviv 67060, Israel
Tel: (3) 636 3300. Fax: (3) 636 3380.
E-mail: taviv@dfait-maeci.gc.ca
Website: www.dfait-maeci.gc.ca/telaviv
The main Palestinian National Authority Region (on the West Bank) and part of the Gaza strip are administered by the Palestine National Authority.

Credit: © Israel Government Tourism Office

General Information

AREA: 22,145 sq km (8550 sq miles; includes East Jerusalem and the Golan sub-district).
POPULATION: 6,631,000 (official estimate 2002).
POPULATION DENSITY: 306.0 per sq km.
CAPITAL: Jerusalem. **Population:** (including East Jerusalem) 680,400 (2002). The Israeli government has designated Jerusalem as the capital, although this is not recognised by the UN, and most foreign embassies are based in Tel Aviv.
GEOGRAPHY: Israel is on the eastern Mediterranean, bordered by Lebanon and the Syrian Arab Republic to the north, Jordan to the east, and Egypt to the south. The autonomous Palestinian Authority Region lies mostly on the west bank of the River Jordan. Part of the Gaza strip, in the south of the country, is also administered by the Palestinians. The country stretches southwards through the Negev Desert to Eilat, a resort town on the Red Sea. The fertile Plain of Sharon runs along the coast, while inland, parallel to the coast, is a range of hills and uplands with fertile valleys to the west and arid desert to the east. The Great Rift Valley begins beyond the sources of the River Jordan and extends south through the Dead Sea (the lowest point in the world), into the Red Sea, continuing on into Eastern Africa.
GOVERNMENT: Republic. The state of Israel was founded in 1948. **Head of State:** Moshe Katzav since 2000. **Head of Government:** Prime Minister Ariel Sharon since 2001.
LANGUAGE: Hebrew is the official language, spoken by about two-thirds of the population. Arabic is spoken by around 15 per cent of the population. English is spoken in most places and other languages, including French, German, Hungarian, Polish, Romanian, Russian, Spanish and Yiddish are widely used.
RELIGION: 77 per cent Jewish, 15 per cent Muslim, with Christian, Druze and other minorities.
TIME: GMT + 2 (GMT + 3 from March to September).
ELECTRICITY: 230 volts AC, 50Hz. Three-pin plugs are standard; if needed, adaptors can be purchased in Israel.
COMMUNICATIONS: Telephone: Full IDD service. Country code: 972. Outgoing international code: 00. Local telephone directories are in Hebrew, but there is a special English-language version for tourists. **Mobile telephone:** GSM 1800 and 900 network operated by *Partner Communications (Orange)* (website: www.orange.co.il), *Cellcom* (website: www.cellcom.co.il) and *Cellcom Israel Ltd* provide coverage practically all over the country, including over parts of the sea. Visitors should note that it is illegal to drive whilst holding a mobile telephone. **Fax:** This service is widely available. **Internet:** ISPs include *Internet Gold* (website: http://zahav.msn.co.il) and *PalNet* (website: www.palnet.com). There are many Internet cafes. **Telegram:** Facilities are available to guests in most deluxe hotels in Jerusalem and Tel Aviv, and in main post offices. **Post:** Airmail to Europe takes up to one week. There are *Poste Restante* facilities in Jerusalem and Tel Aviv. Post office hours: May vary but are generally Sun-Tues and Thurs 0800-1200 and 1530-1830, Wed 0800-1330 and Fri 0800-1200. All post offices are closed on Shabbat (Saturday) and holy days, although central telegraph offices are open throughout the year. **Press:** The main dailies are *Ha'aretz*, *Ma'ariv* and *Yedioth Aharonoth*. Newspapers are printed in a variety of languages, including English. Political and religious affiliations are common. The English-language daily is the *Jerusalem Post*. The *Jerusalem Post International Edition* is published weekly and goes out to 95 countries.
Radio: BBC World Service (website: www.bbc.co.uk/worldservice) and Voice of America (website: www.voa.gov) can be received. From time to time the frequencies change and the most up-to-date can be found online.

Passport/Visa

	Passport Required?	Visa Required?	Return Ticket Required?
Full British	Yes	No	Yes
Australian	Yes	No	Yes
Canadian	Yes	No	Yes
USA	Yes	No	Yes
Other EU	Yes	1	Yes
Japanese	Yes	No	Yes

Note: Regulations and requirements may be subject to change at short notice, and you are advised to contact the appropriate diplomatic or consular authority before finalising travel arrangements. Details of these may be found at the head of this country's entry. Any numbers in the chart refer to the footnotes below.

PASSPORTS: Passport valid for a minimum of six months beyond intended date of arrival required by all.
Note: (a) Persons wishing to proceed to an Arab country other than Egypt or Jordan after visiting Israel should ensure their passport does not contain an Israeli visa or stamp. However, persons permitted to stay in Israel for a period of three months or more will be required to have an extension stamped in their passport. (b) Former nationals of Israel holding a foreign passport must have written proof of having given up Israeli identity, otherwise, they may be required to obtain a new Israeli passport or renew their original one.
VISAS: All nationals require a stamp on arrival. Visas are required by all except the following:
(a) **1.** nationals of countries mentioned in the chart above (*except* nationals of Estonia and Germany if born before 1 January 1928 who *do* require a visa);
(b) nationals of Argentina, The Bahamas, Barbados, Bolivia, Brazil, Central African Republic, Chile, Colombia, Costa Rica, Croatia, Dominican Republic, Ecuador, El Salvador, Fiji, Gibraltar, Guatemala, Haiti, Hong Kong (SAR), Iceland, Jamaica, Korea (Rep), Lesotho, Liechtenstein, Malawi, Mauritius, Mexico, Micronesia (Federated States of), Monaco, Mongolia, New Zealand, Norway, Panama, Paraguay, The Philippines, St Kitts & Nevis, San Marino, South Africa, Surinam, Swaziland, Switzerland, Trinidad & Tobago, Uruguay and Vanuatu;
(c) transit passengers continuing their journey within 24 hours by the same or first connecting flight, provided holding valid onward or return documentation and not leaving the airport.
Note: It is advisable to check with nearest Consulate (or Consular section at Embassy) for visa requirements before travelling to Israel as requirements may vary for some nationals.
Types of visa: *Tourist/Entry*: £11 (cash only, or £12 postal order). These fees are for UK nationals; prices vary according to nationality. Cruise ship passengers visiting Israel will be issued *Landing Cards*, allowing them to remain in the country for as long as the ship is in port. No visa applications are required.
Validity: Three months but varies according to nationality. Visas may be extended (for a nominal fee) at offices of the Ministry of the Interior in the following locations: Afula, Akko (Acre), Ashqelon, Be'ersheba, Eilat, Hadera, Haifa, Herzrelia, Holon, Jerusalem, Nazareth, Netanya, Petah Tiqva, Ramat Gan, Ramla, Rehovot, Safed, Tel Aviv and Tiberias.
Application to: Consulate (or Consular section at Embassy); see *Contact Addresses* section for details.
Application requirements: (a) Valid passport. (b) Application form. (c) One passport-size photo. (d) Return ticket. (e) A copy of tenancy agreement or mortgage arrangements. (f) Bank statement for last three months. (g) Self-addressed envelope. (h) Invitation from company/friends/contact in Israel *or* letter from travel agent confirming reservation of return ticket, hotel and medical insurance. (i) Letter from employer/university specifying period of time you have worked with them and that you will be returning after trip. (j) Fee, payable by postal order or cash.
Note: Different application requirements, and advice on crossing the border, will almost certainly apply to those travelling on to Egypt or Jordan; it is essential that the Embassy/Consulate be consulted beforehand.
Working days required: Depends on nationality. Some visas will require authorisation from Israel and so it is advisable to contact the Embassy before booking travel tickets.
Temporary residence: Apply to the Ministry of the Interior in Israel.
Note: As a concession to travellers intending to travel at a later date to countries with entry restrictions for visitors to Israel, entry stamps will, on request, be entered only on the entry form AL-17 and not on the passport. This facility is not available to those required to obtain their Israeli visas in advance.

Money

Currency: New Shekel (IS) = 100 agorot (singular, agora). Notes are in denominations of IS200, 100, 50, and 20. Coins are in denominations of IS10, 5 and 1, and 50 and 10 agorot.
Currency exchange: Foreign currency can only be exchanged at authorised banks, hotels and bureaux de

change. It is advisable to leave Israel with the minimum of Israeli currency. Payment in foreign currency exempts tourists from VAT on certain purchases and services. A maximum of US$500 worth of new shekels can be reconverted to foreign currency by travellers leaving Israel.
Credit & debit cards: All major credit cards are accepted.
Travellers cheques: These are widely accepted. To avoid additional exchange rate charges, travellers are advised to take travellers cheques in US Dollars.
Currency restrictions: There are no restrictions on the import of local or foreign currency. Travellers planning to export local currency should apply to a local bank before departure from Israel. The export of foreign currency is limited to the amount imported.
Exchange rate indicators: The following figures are included as a guide to the movements of the New Israel Shekel against Sterling and the US Dollar:

Date	Feb '04	May '04	Aug '04	Nov '04
£1.00=	8.16	8.20	8.37	8.27
$1.00=	4.48	4.59	4.54	4.37

Banking hours: Sun-Fri 0830-1200 and Sun, Tues, Thurs 1600-1800.

Duty Free

The following goods may be imported into Israel without incurring customs duty (alcohol and tobacco can only be imported by persons aged 17 years and over):
250 cigarettes or 250g of tobacco products; 1l of spirits and 2l of wine; 250ml of eau de cologne or perfume; gifts up to the value of US$150.
Note: Provided for personal use and re-exported, one video camera, one photographic camera, one movie camera, one tape recorder and up to a value of US$250 in film and video cassettes may be imported; subject to high deposits paid in cash or VISA credit card only. For flowers, plants and seeds, a health certificate is required.
Prohibited: Fresh meat, bananas and pineapples; fruit and vegetables from the African continent, especially South Africa; and dogs and cats aged under three months.

Public Holidays

2005: Mar 25 Purim. **Apr 24-30*** Pesach (Passover). **May 14** Yom Ha'Atzmaut (Israel Independence Day). **Jun 13** Shavu'ot (Pentecost). **Oct 4-5** Rosh Hashana (New Year). **Oct 13** Yom Kippur (Day of Atonement). **Oct 17-24** Sukkot (Tabernacles). **Oct 25** Shemini Atzeret (Celebration of Renewal and Thanksgiving). **Dec 28-Jan 2** Chanukah (Feast of the Lights).
2006: Mar 14 Purim. **Apr 12-19*** Pesach (Passover). **May 3** Yom Ha'Atzmaut (Israel Independence Day). **Jun 2** Shavu'ot (Pentecost). **Sep 24-25** Rosh Hashana (New Year). **Oct 2** Yom Kippur (Day of Atonement). **Oct 6-13*** Sukkot (Tabernacles). **Oct 14** Shemini Atzeret (Celebration of Renewal and Thanksgiving). **Dec 14-16** Chanukah (Feast of the Lights).
Note: *Only the first and last days of Passover and Sukkot are officially recognised as national holidays, but there may be some disruption on intermediate dates; many shops and businesses may open but close early. Jewish festivals commence on the evenings before the dates given above. The Jewish religious day is Saturday – *Shabbat* – and begins at nightfall on Friday until nightfall on Saturday. Most public services and shops close early on Friday as a result. Muslim and Christian holidays are also observed by the respective populations. Thus, depending on the district, the day of rest falls on Friday, Saturday or Sunday.

Health

	Special Precautions?	Certificate Required?
Yellow Fever	No	No
Cholera	No	No
Typhoid & Polio	1	N/A
Malaria	No	N/A

Note: Regulations and requirements may be subject to change at short notice, and you are advised to contact your doctor well in advance of your intended date of departure. Any numbers in the chart refer to the footnotes below.

1: Immunisation against typhoid and poliomyelitis is sometimes recommended.
Food & drink: Mains water is normally chlorinated and, whilst relatively safe, may cause mild abdominal upsets. Bottled water is available and is advised for the first few weeks of the stay. Drinking water outside main cities and towns may be contaminated and sterilisation is advisable. Milk is pasteurised and dairy products are safe for consumption. Local meat, poultry, seafood, fruit and vegetables are generally considered safe to eat.
Other risks: *Hepatitis A* and *B* occur. *Tick-borne relapsing fever* may occur.
Rabies is present. For those at high risk, vaccination before arrival should be considered. If you are bitten, seek medical advice without delay. For more information, consult the *Health* appendix.
Health care: Israel has excellent medical facilities and tourists may go to all emergency departments and first-aid centres. However, any medical form of treatment can be expensive. Health centres are marked by the red Star of David on a white background. Medical insurance is recommended.

Travel - International

Note: Travel along Israel's border with Lebanon, and close to the Israeli side of the Israel/Gaza Strip border, is advised against. Care should be taken at crossing points between Israel and Jordan. All travel to the Gaza Strip outside Gaza City is advised against, plus all travel to the West Bank and the Gaza Strip at night. There is a high threat from terrorism and military activity in Israel and in the Occupied Territories. If planning to travel to Israel or the Occupied Territories, nationals should be very careful about personal security arrangements. Because of current travel and other restrictions, there are limits to the level of consular assistance provided in the West Bank and Gaza Strip for most nationals. UK/Palestinian dual nationals are subject to complex Israeli travel restrictions. Crime is generally not a problem in Israel or the Occupied Territories, but sensible precautions should be taken.
AIR: Israel's national airline is *El Al Israel Airlines (LY)* (website: www.elal.co.il). Other airlines serving Israel include *Air Canada, Air France, British Airways, Continental Airlines, Iberia, KLM, Lufthansa, South African Airways* and *United Airlines.*
Approximate flight times: From *London* to Tel Aviv is four hours 30 minutes and to Eilat is five hours. From *Los Angeles* to Tel Aviv is 17 hours, from *New York* is 11 hours, from *Singapore* is 10 hours 55 minutes and from *Sydney* is 14 hours 35 minutes.
International airports: *Tel Aviv (TLV)* (Ben Gurion International) is 20km (12 miles) southeast of the city. An *EGGED* bus runs every 30 minutes between 0500-2300 (travel time – 25 minutes), and *United Tours* shuttle bus no. 222 runs hourly 0400-0000 to Tel Aviv railway station, before stopping at all hotels along Hayarkon St. There is also a taxi service (travel time – 20 minutes). A shared *sherut* (taxi service) is available, charging a fixed rate per passenger. The *El Al* airline bus goes to the airport terminal in Tel Aviv. Departure depends on *El Al* flights. The best way to travel to Jerusalem, which is 50km (31 miles) away, is by *sherut*. Airport facilities include banks, restaurants, duty free shops, general shops and tourist information.
Eilat Central Airport (ETH) is 20 minutes from the city. The airport bus departs every 15 minutes, and taxis are available to the city (travel time – 15 minutes). Airport facilities include a duty free shop, light refreshments and a souvenir shop.
Departure tax: None.
SEA: Principal international passenger ports are Ashdod and Haifa. Foreign yachts sailing to Israel may use these ports of entry as well as Eilat and the marinas of Ashkelon, Herzliya and Tel-Aviv. There are regular sailings of car/ passenger ferries from Greece (Piraeus) and Cyprus to Haifa. Cruise lines run to Haifa and Ashdod from Venice and other Mediterranean ports. These cruise companies include *The Cruise People, Louis* and *Viamare Travel LTD* (website: www.viamare.com).
ROAD: On the whole, road access to Israel is somewhat limited. There are two crossing points from Egypt into Israel. Travellers are permitted to cross the border on foot, by bus or in privately owned cars only; taxis and hired cars may not cross. Rafiah (Rafah), the main point of entry, is located some 50km (31 miles) southwest of Ashqelon (open 0900-1700). Four bus companies maintain services between Cairo and Tel Aviv and Jerusalem via Rafiah. *EGGED* Bus no. 362 leaves Tel Aviv for the Rafiah terminal daily and Rafiah for Tel Aviv at Taba, just south of Eilat, is open 24 hours a day. A regular bus service is available between Taba, Santa Katerina (Sinai) and Cairo.
It is possible to enter Jordan via the Allenby Bridge near Jericho, about 40km (25 miles) from Jerusalem. The Allenby Bridge border opening hours are Sun-Thurs 0800-0000, Fri 0800-1500. *EGGED* buses and taxi services are also available to the bridge. At present, every tourist passing through here must obtain an entry visa to and an exit visa from Jordan. Exit fees are only payable on leaving for Jordan. Nationals of countries who are required to obtain an Israeli visa in advance should do so before visiting Jordan, as such visas cannot be obtained at the Allenby Bridge.
The Arava Checkpoint crossing is situated 4km (3 miles) north of Eilat. It is possible to cross the border in both directions. Nationals should check whether visas are required for this crossing with their local embassy. The opening hours for the Arava border checkpoint are Sun-Thurs 0630-2230, Fri-Sat 0800-2000 (closed on *Yom Kippur* and the Muslim festival of *Eid al-Adha*).
The Jordan River Crossing (Sheikh Hussein Bridge) can be crossed by holders of UK passports valid for at least six months from the date of entry and persons with dual nationality as individuals or in groups.
Entry visas for Jordan or Israel can either be organised through travel agents who will make the necessary arrangements or can be provided on arrival for all those who have organised pre-arranged visas (except for Israeli passport holders who must make arrangements through travel agents). Travel agents are requested to coordinate the arrival time of buses with the management of the crossing point. All UN cars (on official business or not) and vehicles with foreign registration will be permitted to cross freely without paying any fees; however, Israeli cars with diplomatic plates will not be permitted to cross the border.
Transfer of passengers between the Israeli and Jordanian checkpoints will be carried out by shuttle service. Transfers on foot will not be permitted. The Jordan River (Sheikh Hussein) border crossing hours are Sun-Thurs 0630-2200, Fri-Sat 0800-2000 (closed on Yom Kippur and the Jordanian festival on the first day of the Hijirah Calendar). There is no access to the Syrian Arab Republic and Lebanon. Mobile telephones are not allowed on buses crossing the border.

Travel - Internal

AIR: A comprehensive service linking Tel Aviv with Eilat and all major cities is run by *Arkia/Israel Inland Airways (IZ)* (website: www.arkia.co.il) and by *Israir (6H)* (website: www.israirairlines.com).
SEA/LAKE: Ferries run across the Lake Tiberias (Sea of Galilee) from Tiberias on the west side to Ein Gev kibbutz on the eastern shore. Coastal ferries serve all ports. For details, contact local port authorities.
RAIL: *Israel Railways* (website: www.israrail.org.il) provides regular services between Tel Aviv and Herzliya, Netanya, Hadera, Haifa, Akko (Acre) and Nahariya, as well as a daily train between Tel Aviv and Jerusalem, which follows a particularly scenic route. Reserved seats may be ordered in advance. There is no railway service on *Shabbat* (Saturday) and major holidays.
ROAD: Traffic drives on the right. An excellent system of roads connects all towns. However, driving is erratic and there are frequent accidents. Radar speed traps operate and fees for speeding are high. Distances by road from Jerusalem to other cities are as follows: Tel Aviv 62km (39 miles), Tiberias 157km (97 miles), Eilat 312km (194 miles), Netanya 93km (58 miles), Dead Sea 104km (65 miles), Zefat 192km (120 miles) and Haifa 159km (99 miles).
Bus: Two national bus systems, run by the *DAN* and *EGGED* cooperatives, provide extensive services. The service is fast and efficient as well as cheap. With a few exceptions, services are suspended on religious holidays, and between sunset on Friday and sunset on Saturday.
Taxi: Services are either run by companies or by individuals. There are both shared taxis (*sheruts*) and ordinary taxis. Taxi drivers are required by law to operate a meter and are recommended for short journeys only.
Car hire: Available in major cities. Hire fees are not cheap.
Documentation: Full driving licence and insurance are required. An International Driving Permit is recommended.
URBAN: *DAN* and *EGGED* provide good local bus services in the main towns. Taxis are available.

Accommodation

Ranging from small, simple guest houses to deluxe hotels, Israel offers a wide choice and high standards of accommodation. For a holiday with a difference, unique to Israel, there are *kibbutz country inns* in all parts of the country where one can find relaxed informality in delightful rural surroundings. Kibbutz Fly-Drive holidays are very popular and so are discovery tours by air-conditioned coach, staying at different hotels and kibbutzim to see the whole country.
HOTELS: There are over 300 hotels listed for visitors by the Ministry of Tourism. Prices vary according to season and region. It is best to book months in advance for Israel's high season (usually July to August, though this varies according to the region) and for religious holiday seasons. 380 hotels are members of the Israel Hotel Association, PO Box 50066, 29 Hamered Street, Tel Aviv 61500 (tel: (3) 517 0131; fax: (3) 510 0197; e-mail: infotel@israelhotels.org.il; website: www.israelhotels.org.il).
HOLIDAY/RECREATION VILLAGES: Located on the Mediterranean or the Red Sea Gulf, these villages provide accommodation usually in the form of small two-bed cabins and bungalows. The standard fittings often include full air conditioning and facilities. Most are only open between April and October and the emphasis is on casual living.

SELF-CATERING: Apartments and individual rooms are available on a rental basis throughout the country.
KIBBUTZ GUEST HOUSES: All are clean and comfortable with modern dining rooms. Most have swimming pools (though it is wise to check that this facility is open to visitors) and provide a valuable insight into the style and aims of kibbutz life. Approximately 130 out of the 280 kibbutzim have guest houses and each is located in a rural or scenic part of the country and is usually open all year. Further information is available from the Israel Government Tourist Office.
CHRISTIAN HOSPICES: Throughout the country, some 30 Christian hospices (operated by a variety of denominations) provide rooms and board at low rates. Although preference is given to pilgrimage groups, most will accommodate general tourists. They vary greatly in size and standards but all offer tourists basic accommodation in situations where hotels are full. Details are available from the Israel Government Tourist Office.
CAMPING/CARAVANNING: The fine climate means Israel is a good country for camping, with campsites providing a touring base for each region. They offer full sanitary facilities, electric current, a restaurant and/or store, telephone, postal services, first-aid facilities, shaded picnic and campfire areas and day and night watchmen. They can be reached by bus, but all are open to cars and caravans. Most have tents and cabins, as well as a wide range of equipment for hire. All sites have swimming facilities either on-site or within easy reach. Hitchhiking is not recommended.
YOUTH HOSTELS: Hostels in Israel can be dormitory, family bungalows, guest house standard rooms, huts or modern cubicles and they are scattered all over the country in both urban and rural areas. For further details, write to the IYHA, Binyanei Ha'mah, PO Box 6001, Jerusalem 91060 (tel: (2) 655 8400/6; fax: (2) 655 8432; e-mail: iyha@iyha.org.il; website: www.youth-hostels.org.il). Information is also available from the Israel Government Tourist Office.

Resorts & Excursions

Note: Visitors should check official government advice before travelling to the Palestinian National Authority Region or to Jerusalem, as these areas may be dangerous owing to political tension.
Israel is a remarkable, fascinating and controversial country. For many it is, above all, the Holy Land. Religious attractions include the walk along the **Via Dolorosa** to the **Church of the Holy Sepulchre** in **Jerusalem** (the Holy City and cradle of Christianity, Islam and Judaism); the **Church of the Annunciation** in **Nazareth**; the serenity of **Galilee** and the ride across the **River Jordan**, the river in which Jesus was baptised.
JERUSALEM: For Christians, Jews and Muslims, this is one of the most revered cities on earth. Attractions range from religious emblems and relics of antiquity to modern items of interest. Religious tours are available from West Jerusalem and include **Mount Zion** and the **Tomb of David**. Other sites are the **Tomb of Judges**; **Yad Vashem**, the memorial to the six million Jews who died in the Holocaust; and **Mea Shearim** ('the hundred gates'). Visitors in East Jerusalem may follow the **Way of the Cross**, enter the **Church of the Holy Sepulchre**, see the **Wailing Wall**, the **Dome of the Rock** and the **Jaffa** and **Damascus gates**. The **Israel Museum** in Jerusalem houses the *Dead Sea Scrolls* and is worth visiting.
Excursions: Three important excursions are to the **Abu Ghush**, **En Karem** and the **Hill of Rachel**.
TEL AVIV: An exciting city offering commerce, culture, nightlife and sandy beaches. The *Israeli Philharmonic Orchestra* draws audiences from all over the world. The **Museum of the Diaspora** is internationally famous. The bustling **Carmel Market** is a popular place to visit. In 1950, **Jaffa** was united with Tel Aviv; situated a mile from the city, this is one of the oldest ports in the world. It has archaeological finds reaching back to the third century BC, a beach, lively nightlife in **Old Jaffa** and a flea market.
THE NEGEV: This area, once largely desert, is now being irrigated and farmed in a settlement movement started by, amongst others, David Ben Gurion. **Beersheba** and **Dimona** are both of interest, but **Eilat**, in particular, is the place for tourists. Eilat is the best-equipped seaside resort in the Middle East, and a paradise for underwater enthusiasts. There are several attractive places nearby; these include the **Timna Valley National Park** (near Eilat).
GALILEE AND THE NORTH: Places of interest are **Lake Tiberias** (the **Sea of Galilee**) itself, **Nazareth**, the **Bet She'arim Catacombs**, **Megiddo**, **Tiberias** and the **Mount of Beatitudes**. The Tourist Office, together with a consortium of interested parties, is actively promoting Galilee as a tourist destination. Emphasis is being placed on the environment, sports, culture, history and health, with spa resorts (which have been used since Roman times) especially featured. The **Museum of Mediterranean**

Credit: © Israel Government Tourism Office

Archaeology celebrates many finds in the region. **Haifa**, on the coast and Israel's leading seaport, is both an industrial town and an ancient fortress. Further south, notable attractions include the artists' colony of **En Hod** and the Roman ruins at **Caesarea**.
THE DEAD SEA: 60km (41 miles) long and 17km (11 miles) wide, the Dead Sea is an inland lake lying 400m (1320ft) below sea level in the lower part of the **Jordan Valley**, flanked by the **Judean Mountains** to the west and the **Moab Mountains** to the east. It has more minerals and salt than any other body of water in the world and is renowned for its rejuvenating and health-giving properties. There are a number of health spas and resorts in the area. A range of cosmetic and therapeutic products, containing Dead Sea minerals, are available worldwide. Spas are found in the Dead Sea region offering a variety of treatments, including mud packs, salt massages and salt water pools.
Masada (**Mezada**), on the left bank of the Dead Sea, is where the once luxurious palace of King Herod still stands (and site of the famous seige), perched on a clifftop. It can be reached by cable car or a winding footpath and there is a breathtaking view of the Dead Sea and the pink mountains of Moab from here.
Other interesting sights around the Dead Sea include **Mount Sodom**, a 13km- (8 mile-) long mountain range made up of pure salt which has many caves with extraordinary hanging salt formations, and **Qumran**, where the *Dead Sea Scrolls*, written by Essene scribes, were discovered in ancient pottery jars. The discovery of the Scrolls was made in 1947 by an Arab shepherd looking for a stray goat. Seven scrolls were found, the most famous being the scroll of Isaiah, which is 1 foot wide and 24 feet long. Excavations at the site found more than 900 pieces of scrolls in more than 30 caves. Except for two scrolls written on copper, all the scrolls were written on leather and papyrus.
THE PALESTINE NATIONAL AUTHORITY REGION: For further information about the Palestinian National Authority Region, contact the Palestinian Ministry of Tourism (see *Contact Addresses* section).
Bethlehem: The city lies 750m (2500ft) above sea level, on the ancient caravan route, 10km (6.2 miles) south of Jerusalem. Bethlehem is, of course, most famous for being the birthplace of Christ, although it is also well known for olive woodcarving and mother-of-pearl jewellery, which, today, has developed into a modern industry.
Jericho: One of the prime sites of interest in the region for historians and visitors alike is the ancient town of Jericho, which dates back more than 10,000 years and lies 260m (853ft) below sea level, 36km (22.5 miles) east of Jerusalem. Known as the 'City of Palms', Jericho is one of the world's oldest continuously inhabited sites. The walls and towers of Jericho are 4000 years older than the pyramids of Egypt, and the domestication of animals took place 1000 years earlier in Jericho than in Mesopotamia and Egypt. Other sites worth visiting in the area include **Deir Qurunta**l and **Mt Temptation**, where Jesus spent 40 days and nights fasting and meditating and where a monastery was later built. Deir Quruntal can be reached on a steep and fairly difficult path.
Elsewhere: The city of **Hebron** lies in the mountainous region south of Jerusalem, at an altitude of 1000m (3280ft). Hebron is an unspoiled town, with many narrow and winding streets, flat-roofed stone houses and old bazaars. Other places worth visiting in the area include **Nablus**, the major commercial, industrial and agricultural centre in the northern West Bank and renowned for olive oil soap, wrought gold and *Kenafa*, a tasty oriental pastry; **Rammallah**, whose cool climate makes it a popular summer resort, with many restaurants and an international feel; **Samaria** and **Gaza**, located on the western Mediterranean coast, 32km (22.4 miles) north of the Egyptian border and, owing to its strategic location, a long-established economic regional centre for trade in citrus fruits and other goods.

Sport & Activities

Watersports: Fishing, **sailing**, **surfing**, **swimming**, **water-skiing** and **yachting** are all available. There are marinas in Akko, Eilat, Jaffa and Tel Aviv. All the large hotels have swimming pools. **Skindiving** and **aqualung diving** are especially popular in Eilat on the Red Sea coast with an excellent underwater observatory descending to the floor of the coral reef near the town. Eilat is a particularly good destination for winter sun for visitors from Western Europe.
Note: The Red Sea coastline has been designated a preservation area and any tourists found with 'souvenirs' such as coral will suffer severe fines from both the Israeli and Egyptian authorities.
Other: To many people's surprise, there is a full **skiing** season at Mount Hermon, on the northern border. Among annual sports events are the *Tel Aviv Marathon* and the *Kinereth Swimming Gala*. **Basketball** and **football** are popular and many hotels have **tennis** courts. There is a fine 18-hole **golf** course at Caesarea. **Horse-riding** is available throughout the country. There is also the opportunity to take **camel rides**; contact the Israel Government Tourist Office for further details. **Bicycling** is also popular. There are excellent facilities at kibbutz sportsgrounds and in cities. The Israel Government Tourist Office (see *Contact Addresses* section) can provide further information.

Social Profile

FOOD & DRINK: Restaurants in Israel offer a combination of Oriental and Western cuisine, in addition to the local dishes. Some restaurants are expensive, though a high price does not necessarily mean a high standard. Table service is usual. There are many snack bars. Restaurants, bars and cafes catering to tourists usually have menus in two languages (Hebrew, plus French or English). Israeli cuisine is essentially a combination of Oriental and Western cuisine, plus an additional distinct flavour brought by the many and varied nationalities which make up the Israelis. Dishes such as Hungarian *goulash*, Russian *bortsch*, Viennese *schnitzel* or German *braten* are found next to Middle Eastern items such as *falafel*, *humus*, *tahini*, *shishlik*, *kebabs* and Turkish coffee, as well as traditional Jewish dishes such as *gefilte fish*, chopped liver and chicken soup. **Kosher food:** The Hebrew word *kosher* means food conforming to Jewish religious dietary laws. Milk, cream or cheese may not be served together with meat in the same meal. Pork and shellfish are officially prohibited, but it is possible to find them on many menus in non-kosher restaurants.
The wines of Israel range from light white to dry red and sweet rosé. Israeli beers are *Gold Star* and *Maccabee*. There is also a good choice of local brandies and liqueurs. Liqueurs include *Arak* (an anise drink), *Hard Nut* (a walnut concoction of Eliaz winery) and *Sabra* (chocolate and orange). A centre for liqueurs is the monastery at Latrun on the road between Jerusalem and Tel Aviv.
NIGHTLIFE: There are nightclubs and discos in most cities. Tel Aviv has a wealth of entertainment to divert the visitor and there are rock, jazz, folk and pop music clubs in all the main cities and resorts. Israeli folklore and dance shows can be seen everywhere, especially in the kibbutzim. The Israeli Philharmonic Orchestra can be heard at the ICC Binaynei Ha'uma Hall in Jerusalem during the winter. A summer attraction is the *Israel Festival of International Music*. Cinema is popular in Israel and many cinemas screen three daily shows of international and local films (all Hebrew films are subtitled in English and French). Tickets for all events and even films can be bought in advance from ticket agencies and sometimes from hotels and tourist offices.
SHOPPING: There is a wide choice for shoppers in Israel; and in certain shops, especially in Arab markets, visitors can - and should - bargain. Tourists who buy leather goods at shops listed by the Ministry of Tourism and pay for them in foreign currency are exempt from VAT and receive a 25 per

cent discount on leather goods if these are delivered to them at the port of departure. Special purchases include jewellery, diamonds and other precious stones, ceramics, embroidery, glassware, wines, religious articles and holy books. 'Cashback' on purchased items can be claimed from the Customs Office at the airport. **Shopping hours:** Sun-Fri 0800-1900; some shops close 1300-1600 and some early on Friday. Remember that the shopping facilities are both Israeli and Arabic, and are therefore governed by two different sets of opening hours and methods of business. Jewish stores observe closing time near sunset Friday evenings before *Shabbat* (Saturday), and Arabic stores close Friday. It takes a while to realise that Sunday is a normal working day unlike in Western countries. For shoppers, the Jewish stores are therefore open Friday, Arab markets Saturday and both are open Sunday when Christian stores close. Shops in the hotels are often open until midnight.

SPECIAL EVENTS: For a complete list of special events, contact the Israel Government Tourist Office (see *Contact Addresses* section). The following is a selection of special events occurring in Israel in 2005:

Mar 20-26 *Holy Week in Jerusalem.* **Mar 25** *Purim* (Jewish festival), nationwide. **Apr** *The Haifa International Theatre Festival for Children and Youth.* **May 5** *Holocaust Martyrs and Heroes Remembrance Day*, Yad Vashem, Jerusalem. **May 26-Jun 16** *Israel Festival*, Jerusalem. **Aug 18-28** *Jerusalem World Pride* (gay and lesbian festival). **Oct** *Israel Fringe Theatre Festival*, Acre; *Sukkot - The Festival of Shelter*, nationwide. **Oct 13** *Yom Kippur* (Day of Atonement), nationwide. **Dec** *Hanukkah*, celebration of the Jewish equivalent to Christmas.

SOCIAL CONVENTIONS: Israelis are usually very informal but in keeping with the European style of hospitality. Visitors should observe normal courtesies when visiting someone's home and should not be afraid to ask questions about the country as most Israelis are happy to talk about their homeland, religion and politics. Often the expression *shalom* ('peace') is used for hello and goodbye. Dress is casual, but in Christian, Jewish and Muslim holy places, modest attire is worn. For places such as the Wailing Wall, male visitors are given a smart cardboard *yarmulke* (scull cap) to respect the religious importance of the site. Businesspeople are expected to dress smartly, while plush restaurants, nightclubs and hotel dining rooms may require guests to dress for dinner. Formal evening wear is usually specified on invitations. It is considered a violation of the *Shabbat* to smoke in certain restaurants and many hotels. There is usually a sign to remind the visitor, and to disregard this warning would be regarded as discourteous to Orthodox Jews. **Tipping:** Less evident than in many other countries. A 15 per cent service charge is added to restaurant, cafe and hotel bills by law.

Business Profile

ECONOMY: Israel has a diverse and sophisticated manufacturing economy that, in many respects, rivals that of western Europe (this much is recognised by the IMF, which in 1997, reclassified Israel's economy as 'industrial' rather than 'developing'). Agriculture is relatively small – about 4.2 per cent of GDP – with citrus fruit as the main commodity and export earner. The industrial sector is concentrated on engineering, aircraft, electronics, chemicals, construction materials, textiles and food-processing. Mining is also small but set to expand through production of potash and bromine. There is a small indigenous oil industry. The infrastructure is well developed and tourism, in which there has been considerable investment, has become an important sector of the economy.

Israel's economic difficulties, which were particularly serious during the 1970s and 1980s, were largely the product of political circumstances: specifically very heavy defence expenditure (estimated at around 40 per cent of GDP) and the cost of resettling Jewish arrivals. Other important factors are a large and relatively inefficient state sector and a substantial annual aid package from the USA, estimated at around US$10 billion per year. Israel is the single largest recipient of US aid, which accounts for about 10 per cent of GDP. The economy performed relatively well during the 1990s in the wake of economic reforms introduced at the beginning of the decade, including deregulation and some privatisation. However, Israel was experiencing serious recession by 2000. This lasted until 2002 when the economy contracted by 1 per cent; since then a mild recovery has been under way: growth for 2003 was 1.3 per cent. Under the Sharon government, economic reforms have continued unevenly. Israel has free-trade agreements with the EU and the USA: the latter is its largest trading partner, followed by Belgium/Luxembourg, Germany and the UK.

The areas under the control of the Palestinian Authority have not shared in Israeli prosperity; economic development under the Palestinian Authority was managed in a haphazard and often corrupt manner, especially regarding the use of foreign aid. Since the Sharon administration came to power in Israel, the Palestinian areas have been effectively sealed off; the wall currently under construction around the West Bank (at huge cost) merely confirms that strategic decision. Large areas under nominal Palestinian control have been completely destroyed and those remaining are barely able to function economically. Equally damaging, Palestinians with jobs in the Israeli territory have been unable to pursue them properly through punitive security measures. Much of the population now relies on assistance from aid organisations.

BUSINESS: Business can be frustrating, as in many instances it is difficult to get a direct reply to a question. Appointments are usual, as is the use of business cards. Normal courtesies should be observed, although business meetings tend to be less formal than in Britain. **Office hours:** Business hours vary owing to the different religions practised. Some offices are open half a day on Friday.

COMMERCIAL INFORMATION: The following organisation can offer advice: Federation of Israeli Chambers of Commerce, PO Box 20027, 84 Haashmonaim Street, Tel Aviv 67132 (tel: (3) 563 1010; fax: (3) 561 9027; e-mail: chamber@chamber.org.il; website: www.chamber.org.il).

CONFERENCES/CONVENTIONS: The Ministry of Tourism's brochure, *Israel Conventions & Congresses 1996-2000*, states that "about 2000 years ago, some of the greatest conventions were held near Tiberias where it was recorded that 5000 were amply catered for". Israel's record as a contemporary international conference centre began in 1963, and the country now attracts about 150 international meetings a year with 50,000 delegates; scientific and academic meetings account for about half the meetings, though religious and sporting events are on the increase. In 1992, 55 per cent of meetings were held in Jerusalem. Apart from hotels and the convention centres in Jerusalem, Eliat and Tel Aviv, opportunities exist to hold meetings in kibbutzim. For further information, contact the International Conventions Department at the Ministry of Tourism (see *Contact Addresses* section); *or* the Jerusalem International Convention Centre (JICC), Binyaney Ha'ooma, PO Box 6001, Jerusalem 91060 (tel: (2) 655 8558; fax: (2) 538 3064; e-mail: infoicc@iccjer.co.il; website: www.iccjer.co.il).

Climate

Mediterranean, with a pleasant spring and autumn. Winters in the north can be cool. Rain in winter is widespread, particularly in Jerusalem. Snow is rare. Summers can be very hot, especially in the south. The Red Sea resort of Eilat has a good climate for beach holidays all the year round.

Required clothing: Lightweight cottons and linens for warmer months are required. Mediumweights are recommended for winters, although on the Red Sea coast they are unlikely to be necessary during the day.

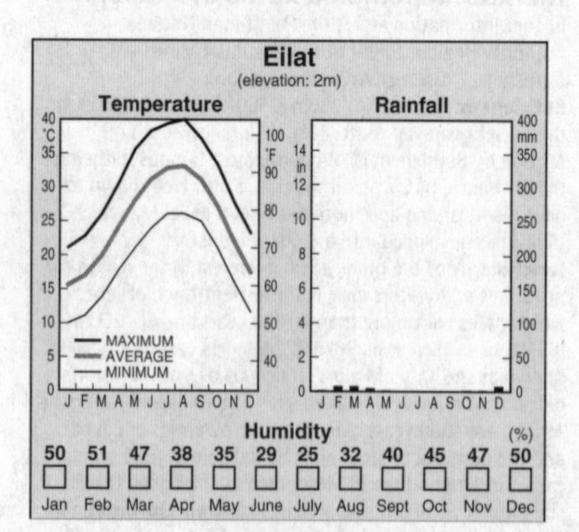

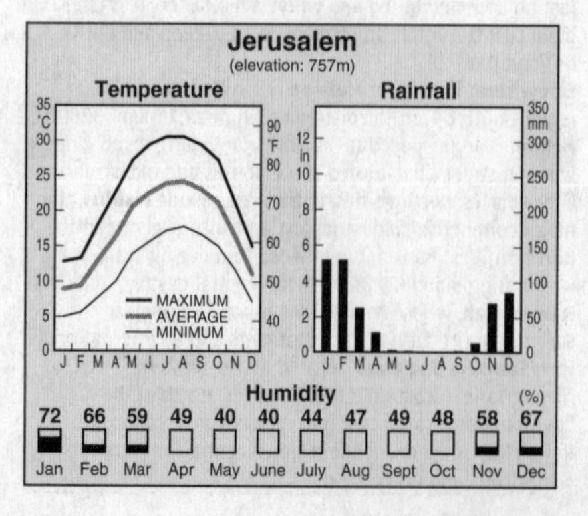

Italy

LATEST TRAVEL ADVICE CONTACTS

British Foreign and Commonwealth Office
Tel: (0870) 606 0290 Website: www.fco.gov.uk

US Department of State
Website: http://travel.state.gov/travel

Canadian Department of Foreign Affairs and Int'l Trade
Tel: (1 800) 267 8376 Website: www.dfait-maeci.gc.ca

Location: Western Europe.

Country dialling code: 39. The 0 preceding the area code should not be omitted.

Ente Nazionale Italiano per il Turismo (ENIT) (Italian State Tourist Board)
Via Marghera 2, 00185 Rome, Italy
Tel: (06) 49711. Fax: (06) 446 3379.
E-mail: sedecentrale@enit.it
Website: www.enit.it

Italian Embassy
14 Three Kings Yard, London W1K 4EH, UK
Tel: (020) 7312 2200. Fax: (020) 7312 2230.
E-mail: italianembassy@btconnect.com
Website: www.embitaly.org.uk
Political enquiries only.

Italian Consulate General
136 Buckingham Palace Road, London SW1W 9SA, UK
Tel: (020) 7235 9371 *or* 7823 6519 (visa section) *or* (09001) 600 340 (recorded visa information; calls cost 60p per minute). Fax: (020) 7823 1609 *or* 4449 (visa section).
E-mail: consolato.londra@esteri.it *or* visti.londra@esteri.it
Website: www.embitaly.org.uk
Opening hours: Mon-Fri 0900-1200.
Consulate General in: Edinburgh.
Consulate in: Manchester. *Vice-Consulate in:* Bedford.

Italian State Tourist Board (ENIT)
1 Princes Street, London W1B 2AY, UK
Tel: (020) 7408 1254 *or* 7399 3550 (brochure request).
Fax: (020) 7399 3567.
E-mail: italy@italiantouristboard.co.uk
Website: www.enit.it

British Embassy
Via XX Settembre 80/A, 00187 Rome, Italy
Tel: (06) 4220 0001 *or* 2600 (consular section).
Fax: (06) 4220 2347 *or* 2334 (consular section).
E-mail: inforome@fco.gov.uk *or* consularrome@fco.gov.uk
Website: www.britain.it

British Consulate
Lungarno Corsini 2, 50123 Florence, Italy
Tel: (055) 284 133. Fax: (055) 219 112.
E-mail: Consular.Florence@fco.gov.uk *or* Commercial.Florence@fco.gov.uk

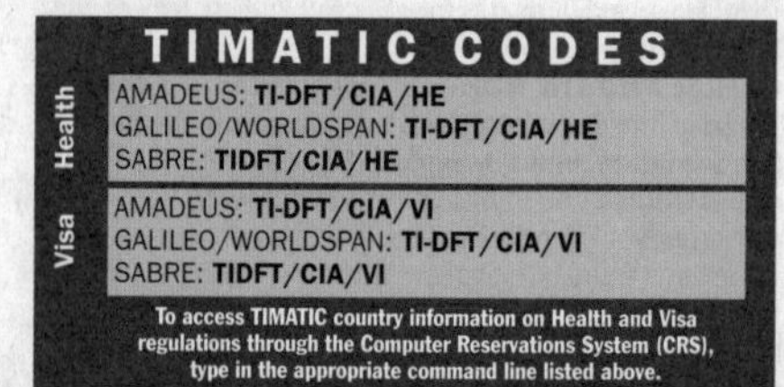
TIMATIC CODES

Health
AMADEUS: **TI-DFT/CIA/HE**
GALILEO/WORLDSPAN: **TI-DFT/CIA/HE**
SABRE: **TIDFT/CIA/HE**

Visa
AMADEUS: **TI-DFT/CIA/VI**
GALILEO/WORLDSPAN: **TI-DFT/CIA/VI**
SABRE: **TIDFT/CIA/VI**

To access TIMATIC country information on Health and Visa regulations through the Computer Reservations System (CRS), type in the appropriate command line listed above.

Website: www.britain.it
Consulates also in: Bari, Cagliari, Catania, Milan, Naples, Palermo, Rome, Trieste, Turin and Venice.
Embassy of the Italian Republic
3000 Whitehaven Street, NW, Washington, DC 20008, USA
Tel: (202) 612 4400 *or* 4405/7 (visa section).
Fax: (202) 518 2154 *or* 2142 (consular section).
E-mail: stampa@itwash.org *or* visti.washington@itwash.org (consular section).
Website: www.italyemb.org
Consulate General of Italy
690 Park Avenue, New York, NY 10021, USA
Tel: (212) 439 8600.
Fax: (212) 249 4945 *or* 439 8649 (visa section).
E-mail: info@italconsulnyc.org
Website: www.italconsulnyc.org
Consulates General in: Boston, Chicago, Detroit, Houston, Los Angeles, Miami, Philadelphia and San Francisco.
Italian Government Tourist Board (ENIT)
630 Fifth Avenue, Suite 1565, New York, NY 10111, USA
Tel: (212) 245 5618. Fax: (212) 586 9249.
E-mail: enitny@italiantourism.com
Website: www.italiantourism.com
Embassy of the United States of America
Via Vittorio Veneto 119/A, 00187 Rome, Italy
Tel: (06) 46741. Fax: (06) 4882 672 *or* 4674 2356.
Website: www.usembassy.it
US Consulate General
Lungarno Vespucci 38, 50123 Florence, Italy
Tel: (055) 266 951. Fax: (055) 284 088.
E-mail: visaflorence@state.gov
This office does not deal with visas or give out information regarding visas.
Embassy of the Italian Republic
275 Slater Street, 21st Floor, Ottawa, Ontario K1P 5H9, Canada
Tel: (613) 232 2401. Fax: (613) 233 1484.
E-mail: ambital@italyincanada.com
Website: www.italyincanada.com
Consulates in: Edmonton, Montréal, Toronto and Vancouver.
Honorary Consulate in: Calgary.
Italian Government Tourist Board (ENIT)
175 Bloor Street East, Suite 907, South Tower, Toronto, Ontario M4W 3R8, Canada
Tel: (416) 925 4882. Fax: (416) 925 4799.
E-mail: enitto@italiantourism.com
Website: www.italiantourism.com
Canadian Embassy
Via G B de Rossi 27, 00161 Rome, Italy
Tel: (06) 445 981. Fax: (06) 4459 83750 (general section).
Consular section: Via Zara 30, 00198 Rome, Italy
Tel: (06) 4459 83937 (automated information service).
Fax: (06) 4459 82905.
E-mail: rome@international.gc.ca *or* roma-cs@international.gc.ca (consular section).
Website: www.canada.it

General Information

AREA: 301,338 sq km (116,346 sq miles).
POPULATION: 58,145,360 (official estimate 2004).
POPULATION DENSITY: 193 per sq km.
CAPITAL: Rome. **Population:** 2,546,804 (2001).
GEOGRAPHY: Italy is situated in Europe and attached in the north to the European mainland. To the north, the Alps separate Italy from France, Switzerland, Austria and Slovenia. **Northern Italy:** The Alpine regions, the Po Plain and the Ligurian-Etruscan Appennines. Piedmont and Val d'Aosta contain some of the highest mountains in Europe and are good areas for winter sports. Many rivers flow down from the mountains towards the Po Basin, passing through the beautiful Italian Lake District (Maggiore, Como, Garda). The Po Basin, which extends as far south as the bare slopes of the Appennines, is covered with gravel terraces and rich alluvial soil and has long been one of Italy's most prosperous regions. To the east, where the River Po flows into the Adriatic Sea, the plains are a little higher than the river itself; artificial (and occasionally natural) embankments prevent flooding. **Central Italy:** The northern part of the Italian peninsula. Tuscany (Toscana) has a diverse landscape with snow-capped mountains (the Tuscan Appennines), lush countryside, hills and a long sandy coastline with offshore islands. Le Marche, lying between the Appennines and the Adriatic coast, is a region of mountains, rivers and small fertile plains. The even more mountainous regioni (administrative districts) of Abruzzo and Molise are bordered by Marche to the north and Puglia to the south, and are separated from the Tyrrhenian Sea and to the west by Lazio and Campania. Umbria is known as the 'green heart of Italy'; hilly with broad plains, olive groves and pines. Further south lies Rome, Italy's capital and largest city. Within its precincts is the Vatican City. **Southern Italy:** Campania consists of flat coastal plains and low mountains, stretching from Baia Domizia to the Bay of Naples and along a rocky coast to the Calabria border. Inland, the Appennines are lower, mellowing into the rolling countryside around Sorrento. The islands of Capri, Ischia and Procida in the Tyrrhenian Sea are also part of Campania. The south is wilder than the norh, with mile upon mile of olive trees, cool forests and rolling hills. Puglia, the 'heel of the boot', is a landscape of volcanic hills and isolated marshes. Calabria, the 'toe', is heavily forested and thinly populated. The Calabrian hills are home to bears and wolves. **The Islands:** Sicily (Sicilia), visible across a 3km- (2 mile-) strait from mainland Italy, is fertile but mountainous with volcanoes (including the famous landmark of Mount Etna) and lava fields, and several offshore islands. Sardinia (Sardegna) has a mountainous landscape, fine sandy beaches and rocky offshore islands. For more information on each region, see the *Resorts & Excursions* section.
GOVERNMENT: Unification in 1861. Republic since 1946.
Head of State: President Carlo Azeglio Ciampi since 1999.
Head of Government: Prime Minister Silvio Berlusconi since 2001.
LANGUAGE: Italian is the official language. Dialects are spoken in different regions. German and Ladin are spoken in the South Tyrol region (bordering Austria). French is spoken in all the border areas from the Riviera to the area north of Milan (border with France and Switzerland). German is spoken around the Austrian border. English, French and German are also spoken in the biggest cities and in tourism and business circles.
RELIGION: 90 per cent Roman Catholic with Protestant minorities.
TIME: GMT + 1 (GMT + 2 from last Sunday in March to Saturday before last Sunday in September).
ELECTRICITY: 230 volts AC, 50Hz.
COMMUNICATIONS: Telephone: Full IDD service available. Country code: 390 (followed by 6 for Rome, 2 for Milan, 11 for Turin, 81 for Naples, 41 for Venice and 55 for Florence). Outgoing international code: 00. Telephone kiosks now only accept phonecards, which can be purchased at post offices, tobacconists and certain newsagents. **Mobile telephone:** GSM 900 and 1800 networks. Network operators are *H3G* (website: www.h3g.it), *Telecom Italia Mobile (TIM)* (website: www.tim.it), *Vodafone Omnitel* (website: www.vodafone.it) and *Wind* (website: www.wind.it). **Fax:** Some hotels have facilities. **Internet:** ISPs include *Freenet* (website: www.freenet.it), *Telecom Italia Net* (website: www.tin.it), *Tiscali* (website: www.tiscali.it) and *Virgilio* (website: www.virgilio.it). Public access is available in Internet Corner Kiosks operated by *Telecom Italia*. Kiosks have been installed at airports, major hotels and in other public places. There are also Internet cafes in all main towns. **Telegram:** Both internal and overseas telegrams may be dictated over the telephone. **Post:** The Italian postal system tends to be subject to
delays. Letters between Italy and other European countries usually take seven to 10 days to arrive. Letters intended for *Poste Restante* collection should be addressed to Fermo Posta and the town. Stamps are sold in post offices and tobacconists. Post office hours: Mon-Fri 0800/0830-1200/1230 and 1400/1430-1730/1800, Saturday mornings only. **Press:** The main towns publish a weekly booklet with entertainment programmes, sports events, restaurants, nightclubs, etc. There are several English-language publications: monthly magazines *Enigma Roma* (Rome), *Grapevine* (on the Lucca area) and *Hello Milano* (Milan), as well as *Wanted In Rome* (website: www.wantedinrome.com), published twice monthly. Among the most important Italian dailies are *Corriere della Sera* (Milan), *Il Messaggero* (Rome), *La Repubblica* (Rome) and *La Stampa* (Turin). *The Informer* (website: www.informer.it) is a useful English-language online guide for expatriates living in Italy.
Radio: BBC World Service (website: www.bbc.co.uk/worldservice) and Voice of America (website: www.voa.gov) can be received. From time to time the frequencies change and the most up-to-date can be found online.

Passport/Visa

	Passport Required?	Visa Required?	Return Ticket Required?
Full British	Yes	No	No
Australian	Yes	No	No
Canadian	Yes	No	No
USA	Yes	No	No
Other EU	1	No	No
Japanese	Yes	No	No

Note: *Regulations and requirements may be subject to change at short notice, and you are advised to contact the appropriate diplomatic or consular authority before finalising travel arrangements. Details of these may be found at the head of this country's entry. Any numbers in the chart refer to the footnotes below.*

Credit: © Agento per il Turismo Firenze

Note: (a) Italy is a signatory to the **1995 Schengen Agreement**. For further details about passport/visa regulations within the Schengen area, see the introductory section, *How to Use this Guide*. (b) The regulations stated below also apply to San Marino and the Vatican City.
PASSPORTS: Passport valid for three months beyond the validity of the visa required by all except **1.** nationals of Austria, Belgium, Croatia, Finland, France, Germany, Greece, Liechtenstein, Luxembourg, Malta, Monaco, The Netherlands, Portugal, San Marino, Slovenia, Spain, Sweden and Switzerland, who only require a valid national ID card.
VISAS: Required by all except the following for stays of up to 90 days:
(a) nationals of countries referred to in the chart above;
(b) nationals of Andorra, Argentina, Bolivia, Brazil, Brunei, Bulgaria, Chile, Costa Rica, Croatia, El Salvador, Guatemala, Honduras, Hong Kong (SAR), Israel, Korea (Rep), Macau (SAR), Malaysia, Mexico, Monaco, New Zealand, Nicaragua, Panama, Paraguay, Romania, San Marino, Singapore, Switzerland, Uruguay, Vatican City and Venezuela;
(c) airport transit passengers continuing their journey to a third country by the same or connecting aircraft within 48 hours, provided holding tickets with reserved seats and valid documents for onward travel (except nationals of Afghanistan, Bangladesh, Congo (Dem Rep), Ethiopia, Ghana, Iran, Iraq, Nigeria, Pakistan, Senegal, Somalia and Sri Lanka, who *always* require a visa, unless granted indefinite leave to remain in the UK). As the preceding list is liable to change at short notice, visitors are advised to check transit regulations with the relevant Embassy or Consulate before travelling.
Types of visa and cost: The visa administration fee ranges from £23.60; this must be paid in advance on presentation of the application and is non-refundable even if the visa is not issued.
There are three types of *Schengen* visa: *Airport transit* and *Transit*: £6.70; *Short-stay* (for tourism, business and study purposes); £16.80 (for up to 30 days); £23.50 (for over 30 days). Prices are approximate and are subject to frequent

change with exchange rates. Visitors are advised to check with the Consulate (or Consular section at Embassy); see *Contact Addresses* section.
Note: Spouses and children of EU nationals (providing spouse's passport and the original marriage certificate is produced), and nationals of some other countries, receive their visas free of charge (enquire at Embassy for details).
Validity: *Short-stay* (single- and multiple-entry): valid for six months from date of issue for stays of maximum three months per entry. *Transit* (single- and multiple-entry): valid for five days with up to two entries. Visas cannot be extended and a new application must be made each time.
Application to: Consulate (or Consular section at your nearest Embassy - Bedford, Edinburgh, Manchester and London); see *Contact Addresses* section. Postal applications are not accepted. Because of the high volume of visa applications an appointment system has been introduced. Appointments must be made via the 24-hour call line 09065 540 707 (call charged at £1 per minute). Admission without an appointment is not permitted. Travellers visiting just one Schengen country should apply to the Consulate of that country; travellers visiting more than one Schengen country should apply to the Consulate of the country chosen as the main destination *or* the country they will enter first (if they have no main destination).
Application requirements: *Tourism*: (a) Passport valid for at least three months longer than the validity of the requested visa, with one blank page to affix the visa. (b) Completed application form. (c) One passport-size photograph. (d) UK residence permit valid for at least three months beyond the expiry date (for UK applicants). (e) Proof of sufficient funds to cover duration of stay (credit cards will only be accepted as proof of financial means if accompanied by recent statement; sufficient funds for students applying for a visa means no less than £700 per month). (f) Proof of accommodation. (g) Proof of occupation, eg letter from employer, solicitor or Chamber of Commerce. *Business*: (a)-(d) and, (e) Letter from employer addressed to the Italian Consulate General explaining the purpose and duration of the visit. If self-employed, a letter from an accountant, company secretary, solicitor or local Chamber of Commerce. Applicants in the UK should also arrange for an invitation from the host Italian company or firm to be faxed directly to the Italian Consulate General in London (fax: (020) 7823 1609) at least 48 hours before submitting an application. *Student*: (a)-(e) and, (f) Full medical insurance to cover period of stay. (g) Letter from Italian university addressed to the Italian Consulate General confirming acceptance of the application, explaining details of the course (duration, programme etc). (h) Letter of reference from UK university confirming applicant's status. *Transit*: (a)-(e) and, (f) Proof of travel arrangements. (g) Visa for the onward destination country, if required.
Note: (a) Minors under 18 years of age not travelling with their parents require a declaration from both parents or their legal guardian authorising their travel. (b) Visa officers may also ask for additional documents. Supplying the documents listed above does not, in itself, guarantee the issue of a visa to the applicant.
Working days required: Usually two. No visas are issued within 24 hours. Nationals of the following countries should allow 14 to 21 days from the date of appointment for the processing of their application: Afghanistan, Algeria, Bahrain, Colombia, Congo (Dem Rep), Egypt, Indonesia, Iran, Iraq, Jordan, Kuwait, Lebanon, Libya, Nigeria, Oman, Palestinian Authority Region, Pakistan, The Philippines, Qatar, Saudi Arabia, Somalia, Sri Lanka, Surinam, Sudan, Syrian Arab Republic, United Arab Emirates, Vietnam and Yemen. This list is subject to change; check with the Consular section at Embassy for details.
Temporary residence: Enquire at Consulate (or Consular section at Embassy); see *Contact Addresses* section.

Money

Single European currency (Euro): The Euro is now the official currency of 12 EU member states (including Italy). The first Euro coins and notes were introduced in January 2002; the Italian Lira was still in circulation until 28 February 2002, when it was completely replaced by the Euro. Euro (€) = 100 cents. Notes are in denominations of €500, 200, 100, 50, 20, 10 and 5. Coins are in denominations of €2 and 1, and 50, 20, 10, 5, 2 and 1 cents.
Currency exchange: Travellers cheques, cheques and foreign money can be changed at banks, railway stations and airports, and very often at major hotels (generally at a less convenient rate). Many UK banks offer differing exchange rates depending on the denominations of currency being bought or sold. Check with banks for details and current rates.
Credit & debit cards: Diners Club, MasterCard and Visa are widely accepted, as well as Eurocheque cards. Check with your credit or debit card company for merchant acceptability and other facilities that may be available.
Travellers cheques: Travellers cheques are accepted almost everywhere. To avoid additional exchange rate charges, travellers are advised to take travellers cheques in Euros, Pounds Sterling or US Dollars.
Currency restrictions: Check with the Embassy before departure. Import and export of both local and foreign currency is limited to €10,329.14. If it is intended to import or export amounts greater than this, the amount should be declared and validated in Italy on form V2.
Exchange rate indicators: The following figures are included as a guide to the movements of the Euro against Sterling and the US Dollar:

Date	Feb '04	May '04	Aug '04	Nov '04
£1.00=	1.46	1.50	1.49	1.43
$1.00=	0.80	0.84	0.80	0.75

Banking hours: These vary from city to city but, in general, Mon-Fri 0830-1330 and 1500-1600, Sat 0830-1300, although many banks are closed on Saturdays and Sundays.

Duty Free

The following goods may be imported into Italy without incurring customs duty by passengers over 17 years of age arriving from countries outside the EU with goods bought duty free:
200 cigarettes or 50 cigars or 100 cigarillos or 250g of tobacco; 2l of wine and 1l of spirits (over 22 per cent) or 2l of fortified or sparkling wine; 50g of perfume and 250ml of eau de toilette; 500g of coffee or 200g of coffee extract (if over 15 years of age); 100g of tea or 40g of tea extract; gifts not exceeding €89.96 (if entering from an EU country), €174.82 (if entering from a non-EU country).
Abolition of duty free goods within the EU: On June 30 1999, the sale of duty free alcohol and tobacco at airports and at sea was abolished in all of the original 15 EU member states. Of the 10 new member states that joined the EU on May 1 2004, these rules already apply to Cyprus and Malta. There are transitional rules in place for visitors returning to one of the original 15 EU countries from one of the other new EU countries. But for the original 15, plus Cyprus and Malta, there are now no limits imposed on importing tobacco and alcohol products from one EU country to another (with the exceptions of Denmark, Finland and Sweden, where limits *are* imposed). Travellers should note that they may be required to prove at customs that the goods purchased are for personal use *only*.

Public Holidays

2005: Jan 1 New Year's Day. **Jan 6** Epiphany. **Mar 28** Easter Monday. **Apr 25** Liberation Day. **May 1** Labour Day. **Jun 2** Anniversary of the Republic. **Aug 15** Assumption. **Nov 1** All Saints' Day. **Nov 7** World War 1 Victory Anniversary Day. **Dec 8** Immaculate Conception. **Dec 25** Christmas Day. **Dec 26** St Stephen's Day.
2006: Jan 1 New Year's Day. **Jan 6** Epiphany. **Apr 17** Easter Monday. **Apr 25** Liberation Day. **May 1** Labour Day. **Jun 2** Anniversary of the Republic. **Aug 15** Assumption. **Nov 1** All Saints' Day. **Nov 7** World War I Victory Anniversary Day. **Dec 8** Immaculate Conception. **Dec 25** Christmas Day. **Dec 26** St Stephen's Day.
Note: In addition, local feast days are held in honour of town patron saints, generally without closure of shops and offices. These include:
Turin/Genoa/Florence: Jun 24 (St John the Baptist). **Milan:** Dec 7 (St Ambrose). **Siena:** Jul 2 and Aug 16, Palio horserace. **Venice:** Apr 25 (St Mark). **Bologna:** Oct 4 (St Petronius). **Naples:** Sep 19 (St Gennaro). **Bari:** Dec 6 (St Nicholas). **Palermo:** Jul 15 (St Rosalia). **Rome:** Jun 29 (St Peter). **Trieste:** Nov 3.

Health

	Special Precautions?	Certificate Required?
Yellow Fever	No	No
Cholera	No	No
Typhoid & Polio	No	N/A
Malaria	No	N/A

Note: *Regulations and requirements may be subject to change at short notice, and you are advised to contact your doctor well in advance of your intended date of departure. Any numbers in the chart refer to the footnotes below.*

Food & drink: Tap water is generally safe to drink. Bottled water is available. The inscription 'Acqua Non Potabile' means water is not drinkable. Milk is pasteurised and dairy products are safe for consumption. Local meat, poultry, seafood, fruit and vegetables are considered safe to eat.
Other risks: *Leishmaniasis* (*cutaneous* and *visceral*), *sandfly fever*, *typhus* and *West Nile virus*, though rare, may occur along the Mediterranean coast. *Echinococcosis* and *brucellosis* also occur, although rarely.
Rabies is present. For those at high risk, vaccination before arrival should be considered. If you are bitten, seek medical advice without delay. For further information, see the *Health* appendix.
Health care: A reciprocal health agreement with the rest of the EU, Iceland, Liechtenstein and Norway allows reduced-cost dental and medical (including hospital) treatment on presentation of form E111; a fee must be paid, plus part of the cost of any prescribed medicines. Insurance is advised for specialist treatment. Italy is well endowed with health spas, some famous since the Roman era. The most important and best-equipped health resorts in Italy are Abano Terme and Montegrotto Terme (Veneto), Acqui Terme (Piedmont), Chianciano Terme and Montecatini Terme (Tuscany), Fiuggi (Lazio), Porretta Terme and Salsomaggiore Terme (Emilia-Romagna), Sciacca Terme (Sicily) and Sirmione (Lombardy). At Merano (Alto Adige), it is possible to have a special grape-diet treatment. More information on health spas in Italy is available from *La Federterme* (Italian Federation of Thermal Industries and Curative Mineral Waters; website: www.federterme.it).

Travel - International

AIR: Italy's national airline is *Alitalia (AZ)* (website: www.alitalia.it). A great number of major international airlines operate direct flights to various destinations in Italy from Australia, Canada, Europe and the USA. Owing to the number of flights available, ticket prices vary greatly and there is a wide range of discount fares and special tickets available. Further information can be obtained from the airline or a travel agent.
Approximate flight times: From Rome to *London* is two hours 30 minutes, to *Los Angeles* is 15 hours 35 minutes, to *New York* is nine hours 45 minutes, to *Singapore* is 13 hours 55 minutes and to *Sydney* is 24 hours 50 minutes.
International airports: *Rome (FCO)* (Fiumicino) (website: www.adr.it), 26km (16 miles) southwest of the city (travel time – 30 to 55 minutes). Airport facilities include outgoing duty free shop, car hire, bank and bureau de change and bar/restaurant. There is a direct rail link to Termini Station in central Rome and a bus service every 15 minutes. Taxis are also available to the city.
Rome (CIA) (Ciampino) (website: www.adr.it), 32km (15 miles) from the city (travel time – 60 minutes). Airport facilities include a bank/bureau de change, duty free shop and souvenir shop and cafe. Buses are available to the underground station Anagnina. Taxis are also available.
Bologna (BLQ) (G Marconi) (website: www.bologna-airport.it), 6km (4 miles) northwest of the city (travel time – 20 minutes) has good airport facilities. Buses and taxis are available to the city.
Florence (FLR) (Amerigo Vespucci) (website: www.aeroporto.firenze.it), 4km (2.4 miles) north of the city (travel time – 20 minutes) has banks, bureaux de change, left luggage, bars and restaurants and duty free facilities. Buses and taxis are available to the city.
Genoa (GOA) (Cristoforo Colombo, Sestri) (website: www.airport.genova.it), 6km (4 miles) west of the city (travel time – 20 minutes) has duty free facilities. Buses are available to the city.
Milan (MXP) (Malpensa) (website: www.sea-aeroportimilano.it) is 45km (29 miles) northwest of the city (travel time – 30 minutes) and has duty free facilities.
Milan (LIN) (Linate) (website: www.sea-aeroportimilano.it) is 10km (6 miles) east of the city (travel time – 30 minutes). Airport facilities include outgoing duty free facilities, car hire, bank/bureau de change and bar/restaurant. Taxis and buses are available to the city.
Bergamo (BGY) (Milano Orio al Serio) (website: www.sacbo.it) is 45km (28 miles) east of Milan. Taxis and buses are available to both Milan and Bergamo.
Naples (NAP) (Capodichino) (website: www.gesac.it) is 7km (4.5 miles) north of the city (travel time – 20-30 minutes) and has good airport facilities. Buses and taxis operate to the city centre.
Pisa (PSA) (Galileo Galilei) (website: www.pisa-airport.com) is 2km (1.5 miles) northeast of the city (travel time – 10 minutes) and has duty free facilities.
Palermo (PMO) (Punta Raisi) (website: www.gesap.it) is 30km (19 miles) west of the city (travel time – 40 minutes).
Turin (TRN) (Citta di Torino) (website: www.airport.turin.it) is 16km (10 miles) northeast of the city (travel time – 35 minutes). Airport facilities include bureaux de change, left luggage, restaurants, bars and duty free shopping. Buses, trains and taxis all run to the city centre.
Venice (VCE) (Marco Polo) (website: www.veniceairport.it) is 10km (6 miles) northwest of the city (travel time – 20 minutes) has good airport facilities. Buses and taxi services run to Piazzale Roma and the railway station. Water taxis operate to San Marco.
Note: People travelling to Florence can fly to Pisa and then take the new train service directly from Pisa Airport to Florence (travel time – 60 minutes). The railway station in

Pisa is practically inside the airport. Rail services connect with arrivals and departures of all international flights and major domestic services.
Departure tax: None.
SEA: International sailings to Italy run from Albania, Croatia, the Far East, France, Greece, Libya, Malta, Portugal, South America, Spain, Tunisia, Turkey and West Africa. For details, contact shipping agents direct. The quickest route from the UK is via France. The following companies run regular cross-channel ferries from the UK to France: *Brittany Ferries* from Plymouth to Roscoff, from Portsmouth to St Malo and Caen, and from Poole to Cherbourg; *Condor Ferries* from Jersey, Guernsey, Poole, Portsmouth and Weymouth to Cherbourg and St Malo; *Hoverspeed* from Dover to Calais, and from Newhaven to Dieppe; *SeaFrance* from Dover to Calais; *P&O Stena Line* from Dover to Calais; and *P&O Portsmouth* from Portsmouth to Cherbourg and Le Havre. These companies offer a variety of promotional fares and inclusive holidays for short breaks and shopping trips.
RAIL: Travelling from the UK, the quickest way is to travel by *Eurostar* through the Channel Tunnel to Paris (travel time - 3 hours) and, from there, to Italy. For further information and reservations, contact: *Eurostar* (tel: (0870) 600 0792 (travel agents) *or* (08705) 186 186 (public; within the UK) *or* (1233) 617 575 (public; outside the UK); website: www.eurostar.com); *or Rail Europe* (tel: 08705 848 848). Travel agents can obtain refunds for unused tickets from Eurostar Trade Refunds, 2nd Floor, Kent House, 81 Station Road, Ashford, Kent TN23 1PD. Complaints and comments may be sent to Eurostar Customer Relations, Eurostar House, Waterloo Station, London SE1 8SE (tel: (020) 7928 5163). General enquiries and information requests *must* be made by telephone. Rail travellers not using the Channel Tunnel link need to make some form of sea crossing, usually by ferry or catamaran; for details on sea crossings, see *Sea* section above. The cost of the crossing is usually included in the price of the rail ticket. For information and reservations, contact Rail Europe (tel: (08705) 848 848). The main rail connections from London (Victoria) and Paris to Italy are: *Artesia* (Paris, Lyon, Turin, Milan and Rome); and *Simplon Express* (Paris, Lausanne, Brigue, Domodossola, Milan, Venice and Trieste).
ROAD: Travelling by car from the UK, the quickest way is via *Eurotunnel* trains, which carry all types of vehicles through the channel tunnel (travel time - 35 minutes). For further details, see *also Travel - International* in the *France* section. For information and reservations, contact Eurotunnel in the UK (tel: (08705) 353 535; website: www.eurotunnel.com). Routes from the UK to Italy run through Austria, France, Slovenia and Switzerland and most routes use the tunnels under the Alps and Apennines. *Italian State Railways* run regular daily services called *autotreni* (trains carrying cars), especially during the summer holiday season. The main routes covered are: Milan–Genoa–Naples–Villa San Giovanni; Bologna–Naples–Villa San Giovanni; Milan–Rome–Naples–Villa San Giovanni; Turin–Bolzano–Bari; and Bologna–Catania. These services operate from special railway stations and are generally bookable at the departure station. Owners must travel on the same train. The documents required are the log-book, valid driving licence with Italian translation, Green Card insurance and national identity plate fixed to the rear of the vehicle. For more information on routes, contact the Italian State Tourist Board (see *Contact Addresses* section). For more information on required documentation and traffic regulations in Italy, see *Travel – Internal* section.
Coach: *Eurolines* run coach services from the UK to the following destinations: Ancona, Bologna, Cattolica, Florence, Genoa, L'Aquila, Mestre, Milan, Montecatini, Naples, Padua, Parma, Pesaro, Pisa, Riccione, Rimini, Rome, Siena, Teramo, Turin, Venice and Verona. For information on timetables and fares, contact Eurolines, 4 Cardiff Road, Luton, Bedfordshire L41 1PP, UK (tel: (08705) 143 219; fax: (01582) 400 694; website: www.eurolines.com *or* www.nationalexpress.com).

Travel - Internal

AIR: *Alitalia (AZ)* and other airlines run services to all the major cities. There are over 30 airports. For details, contact the airlines direct or *ENIT*, the Italian State Tourist Office (see *Contact Addresses* section).
SEA: Italy's principal ports are Ancona, Bari, Brindisi, Cagliari, Catania, Civitavecchia, Genoa, Livorno, Messina, Naples, Palermo, Pescara, La Spezia, Trieste and Venice. A number of car and passenger ferries operate throughout the year linking Italian ports. **Ferries:** Regular boat and hydrofoil services run to the islands of Capri, Elba, Giglio, Sardinia, Sicily and the Aeolian Islands. There are also some links along the coast.
RAIL: There are nearly 16,000km (9400 miles) of track in the country, of which more than half is electrified. The *Italian State Railways (FS)* (website: www.fs-on-line.com) runs a nationwide network at very reasonable fares, calculated on the distance travelled, and there are a number of excellent reductions.
A new rail pass, the *Trenitalia Pass*, is now the only pass available to people resident outside of Italy (it supersedes the old Italy Flexicard, Railcard and Kilometric ticket). This allows from four to 10 days of unlimited travel within a two-month period. Any train in Italy can be used, although a small supplement is payable on Eurostar Italia services. The pass also entitles the holder to discounts on some Italy-Greece ferry routes, hotels and other special offers. Both first- and second-class passes are available. Children aged from four to 11 pay half the adult fare, and there is a reduced-rate Youth Pass for travellers aged under 26. For further information, contact *Trenitalia* (website: www.trenitalia.com) *or Railchoice* (tel: (020) 8659 7300; fax: (020) 8659 7466; e-mail: sales@railchoice.co.uk; website: www.railchoice.co.uk); *or Freedom Rail* (tel: (0870) 757 9898; fax: (01253) 595 151; e-mail: sales@freedomrail.com; website: www.freedomrail.com).
ROAD: There are more than 300,000km (185,500 miles) of roads in Italy, including over 6000km (3700 miles) of motorway (*autostrada*) which link all parts of the country. Tolls are charged at varying distances and scales, except for the Salerno–Reggio Calabria, Palermo–Catania and Palermo–Mazara Del Vallo stretches, which are toll-free. Secondary roads are also excellent and require no tolls. Road signs are international. Many petrol stations are closed 1200-1500. Visitors are advised to check locally about exact opening times. More information on the Italian motorway network is available from the *Società Autostrade* (website: www.autostrade.it).
Traffic regulations: Traffic drives on the right. Speed limits are 50kph (30mph) in urban areas, 90/110kph (55/65mph) on country roads, 130kph (80mph) on motorways. Undipped headlights are prohibited in towns and cities, but are compulsory when passing through tunnels. All vehicles must carry a red warning triangle, available at border posts. **Note:** Fines for speeding and other driving offences are on-the-spot and particularly heavy. **Breakdown service:** In case of breakdown on any Italian road, dial 116 at the nearest telephone box. Tell the operator where you are, your plate number and type of car and the nearest *Automobile Club of Italy (ACI)* office will be informed for immediate assistance.
Customs regulations: Visitors must carry their log-book, which must either be in their name as owner, or have the owner's written permission to drive the vehicle. Customs documents for the temporary importation of motor vehicles (also aircraft and pleasure-boats) have been abolished.
Bus: Good coach services run between towns and cities and there are also extensive local buses, including good services on Sicily and Sardinia. In more remote areas, buses will usually connect with rail services. **Taxi:** Services are available in and between all cities. **Car hire:** Self-drive hire is available in most cities and resorts. Many international and Italian firms operate this service with different rates and conditions. With the larger firms, it is possible to book from other countries through the car hire companies, their agents or through the air companies. Generally, small local firms offer cheaper rates, but cars can only be booked locally. Many car hire agencies have booths at the airport or information in hotels. *Avis* has offices in Rome at 38 Via Sardegna (tel: (06) 4282 4728; fax: (06) 4201 0282) *or* 1231 Via Tiburtina (tel: (06) 413 1414 *or* 0812; fax: (06) 413 1778). *Hertz* are located at Ciampino Airport (tel: (06) 7934 0616; fax: (06) 7934 0095). Many special-rate fly/drive deals are available for Italy.
Documentation: Visitors must either carry an international Green Card for their car or motor vehicle (also for boats) or other insurance. A UK driving licence and EU pink format licences are valid in Italy but green-coloured licences must be accompanied by an International Driving Permit. Motorcycles no longer require customs documents, but refer to the customs regulations above. A driving licence or a motorcycle driving licence is required for motorcycles over 49cc. Passengers are required by law to wear seat belts.
URBAN: All the big towns and cities (Genoa, Milan, Naples, Rome, Turin and Venice) have good public transport networks. **Underground:** In Rome there are two underground lines – Metropolitana A from Via Ottaviano via Termini station to Via Anagnina and also connecting with the new Ottaviano-San Pietro link; and Metropolitana B, which runs between Termini Station, via Exhibition City (EUR) (Via Laurentina) and then onwards to Rebibbia. Both day and monthly passes are available. Line B was expanded considerably at the beginning of the 1990s, when 10 new stations were added to its network. Line A has been expanded much more recently to include five new stations via the Ottaviano-San Pietro connection. Milan also has a three-line underground system, with tickets useable on both underground and bus. **Tram:** There is a 28km- (17-mile) network consisting of eight routes in Rome; Milan, Naples and Turin also have tram services. **Bus:** Services operate in all main cities and towns; in Rome, the network is extensive and complements the underground and tram systems. The fare structure is integrated between the various modes. Flat-fare tickets and weekly passes can be bought in advance from roadside or station machines or

Credit: © Venezia - Azienda di Promozione Turistica

from tobacconists (*tabacchi*). Information is available from the ATAC booth in front of the Termini station. Trolleybuses also run in a number of other towns. In larger cities, fares are generally pre-purchased from machines or tobacconists (*tabacchi*). Bus fares – generally at a standard rate per run – can be bought in packets of five or multiples and are fed into a stamping machine on boarding the bus.
Taxi: Available in all towns and cities. Government-regulated taxis are either white or yellow. Visitors should avoid taxis that are not metered. In Rome, they are relatively expensive, with extra charges for night service, luggage and taxis called by telephone. All charges are listed on a rate card displayed in the cab with an English translation. Taxis can only be hailed at strategically located stands or booked by telephone. A 10 per cent tip is expected by taxi drivers and this is sometimes added to the fare for foreigners.
City tours: *Rome:* Run by many travel agencies, these tours allow first-time visitors to get a general impression of the main sights and enable them to plan further sightseeing. Information is available from the local tourist office. Horse-drawn carriages are available in Rome. Charges are high. *Venice:* Privately hired boats and gondolas are available, as well as a public ferry service.
Travel times: The following chart gives approximate travel times (in hours and minutes) from **Rome** to other major cities/towns in Italy.

	Air	Road	Rail
Florence	0.45	2.30	2.30
Milan	0.65	6.00	6.00
Venice	0.65	6.00	6.30
Naples	0.45	2.00	2.30
Palermo	0.60	10.00	14.30
Cagliari	0.55	-	-

Accommodation

HOTELS: There are about 40,000 hotels throughout the country. Every hotel has its fixed charges agreed with the provincial tourist board. Charges vary according to class, season, services available and locality. The Italian State Tourist Board publishes the official list of all Italian hotels and pensions (*Annuario Alberghi*) every year, which can be consulted through a travel agent or ENIT, the Italian State Tourist Board (see *Contact Addresses* section). In all hotels and pensions, service charges are included in the rates. VAT (IVA in Italy) operates in all hotels at 10 per cent (19 per cent in deluxe hotels) on room charges only. Visitors are now required by law to obtain an official receipt when staying at hotels. Rome is well provided with hotels, but it is advisable to book in advance. Rates are high with added extras. To obtain complete prices, ask for quotations of inclusive rates. Many luxury hotels are available. Cheap hotels, which usually provide basic board (room plus shower), offer an economical form of accommodation throughout Italy, and there is a wide choice in the cities. Again, especially in the main cities, it is wise to book in advance (bookings should always be made through travel agents or hotel representatives). There are many regional

ROME

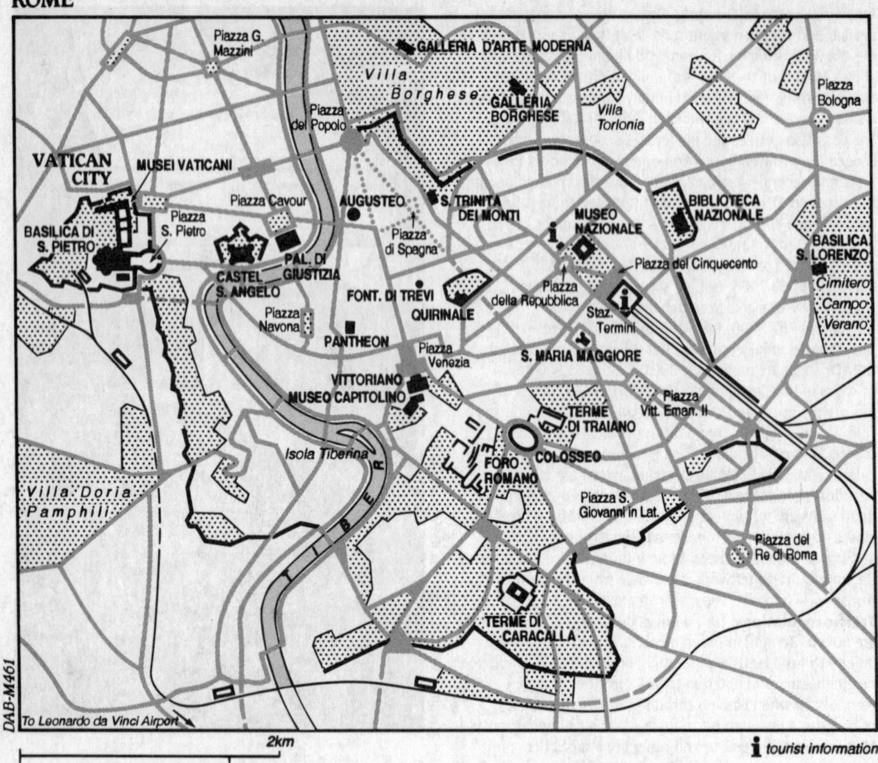

hotel associations in Italy; the principal national organisation is Federalberghi, Via Toscana 1, 00187 Rome (tel: (06) 4274 1151; fax: (06) 4287 1197; e-mail: info@italyhotels.it; website: www.italyhotels.it).

GRADING: Hotels are graded on a scale of **1** to **5 stars**.

MOTELS: Located on motorways and main roads.

SELF-CATERING: Villas, flats and chalets are available for rent at most Italian resorts. Information is available through daily newspapers and agencies in the UK and from the Italian State Tourist Office or the Tourist Office (*Azienda Autonoma di Soggiorno*) of the locality concerned. The latter are also able to advise about boarding with Italian families.

TOURIST VILLAGES: These consist of bungalows and apartments, usually built in or near popular resorts. The bungalows vary in size but usually accommodate four people and have restaurant facilities.

CAMPING/CARAVANNING: Camping is very popular in Italy. The local Tourist Office in the nearest town will give information and particulars of the most suitable sites. On the larger campsites, it is possible to rent tents/caravans. There are over 2100 campsites and full details of the sites can be obtained in the publication *Campeggi e Villaggi Turistici In Italia*, published by the Touring Club Italiano (TCI) and Federcampeggio. An abridged list of sites with location map, *Carta d'Italia Parchi Campeggio*, can be obtained free of charge by writing to the Italian Confederation of Campers, via Vittorio Emanuele 11, 50041 Calenzano (Firenze) (tel: (055) 882 391; fax: (055) 882 5918; e-mail: federcampeggio@tin.it; website: www.federcampeggio.it). The Italian State Tourist Office (ENIT) may also be able to supply information.

The tariffs at Italian campsites vary according to the area and the type of campsite. There are discounts for members of the AIT, FICC and FIA. Usually there is no charge for children under three years of age. The Touring Club Italiano offers campsites already equipped with fixed tents, restaurants, etc. For details, contact Touring Club Italiano, Corso Italia 10, 20122 Milano (tel: (02) 85261; fax: (02) 852 6406; e-mail: viaggi@touringclub.it *or* info@touringclub.it; website: www.touringclub.it). To book places in advance on campsites belonging to the International Campsite Booking Centre, it is necessary to write to Centro Internazionale Prenotazioni Campeggio, Casella Postale 23, 50041 Calenzano (Firenze), asking for a list of the campsites with the booking form.

YOUTH HOSTELS: There are 54 youth hostels run by the Italian Youth Hostels Association (*Associazione Italiana Alberghi per la Gioventù*), Via Cavour 44, 00184 Rome (tel: (06) 487 1152; fax: (06) 488 0492; e-mail: aig@uni.net; website: www.ostellionline.org). Listings and opening dates can be obtained from the Rome Tourist Office, Via Parigi 11, 00185 Rome (tel: (06) 488 991; fax: (06) 481 9316; e-mail: info@aptroma.com; website: www.romaturismo.it). During the summer season in the major cities, reservations are essential and must be applied for directly from the hostel at least 15 days in advance, specifying dates and numbers. There are also student hostels in several towns.

Resorts & Excursions

For ease and speed of reference, the country has been divided into the following areas:

Rome; Northern Italy (including the regions of Valle d'Aosta, Piedmont, Lombardy, Liguria, Trentino & Alto Aldige, Veneto, Friuli-Venezia Giulia and Emilia-Romagna and the cities of Turin, Milan, Genoa, Venice, Trieste and Bologna); Central Italy (including the regions of Tuscany, Umbria, Marche, Abruzzo, Molise and Lazio and the cities of Florence, Siena, Pisa, Perugia and Ancona); Southern Italy (including the regions of Campania, Puglia, Basilicata and Calabria and the city of Naples and the Amalfi Coast); and The Islands (Sicily and Sardinia). Main holiday resorts are included in each section, as well as important religious sites, business centres and a brief mention of the region's art history.

ROME

Capital of Italy and the country's largest city, Rome, littered with relics of over 2000 years of history, exerts an enduring fascination over its countless visitors. The monuments of ancient times and the splendours of the Baroque are the backdrop to the hectic buzz of swarming scooters, bellowing motorists and animated street cafes.

The streets contain reminders of all the eras in Rome's rich history – the **Colosseum** and the **Forum** are the most famous from the classical period and ancient basilicas bear witness to the early Christian era. The influence of the 17th century can be seen through the work of architects such as Bernini, Borromini and Maderno. Magnificent squares and flamboyant façades mask a wealth of painting and sculpture by some of the greatest High Renaissance and Baroque artists – Caracci, Caravaggio, Michelangelo and Raphael, to name but a few.

Via del Corso, Rome's main thoroughfare, cuts through the length of the city centre from **Piazza Venezia** in the south, with the vast marble **Vittorio Emanuele Monument** (erected to commemorate the unification of Italy and honour her first king), to emerge in **Piazza del Popolo** in the north, beyond which lies the cool green refuge of the **Villa Borghese**. East of Via del Corso lie the elegant shopping streets, including **Via Borgognona** and **Via Condotti**, which lead up to **Piazza di Spagna** (the famous Spanish Steps). At the nearby **Trevi Fountain**, visitors guarantee their return to Rome by throwing a coin into the waters. West of Via del Corso, a maze of narrow streets winds its way down to the **River Tiber**. It is here, in the historic centre of Rome, that the most complete ancient Roman structure is found: the **Pantheon**, on **Piazza della Rotonda**, built by Emperor Hadrian and completed in AD 125. Monumental in scale, the diameter of the dome and its height are precisely equal, while the interior is illuminated by sunlight entering through a 9m (30ft) hole in the dome's roof. Just beyond the Pantheon lies **Piazza Navona**, a long thin square, on a classical site, rebuilt in the 17th century in High Baroque style.

Across the River Tiber is the Vatican City (see below). Close by stands the circular hulk of **Castel Sant'Angelo**, burial place of Emperor Hadrian and the papal city's main fortified defence in later times. Moving south, the district of **Trastevere** is the city's alternative focus and is home to numerous bars, restaurants and nightclubs.

There is a useful tourist information line providing general information on the city of Rome from multilingual personnel (tel: (06) 3600 4399).

VATICAN CITY: On the west bank of the Tiber, the Vatican City is an independent sovereign state, best known for the magnificent **St Peter's Basilica**. The Basilica is approached through the 17th-century **St Peter's Square**, a superb creation by Bernini, enclosed by two semi-circular colonnades, with an Egyptian obelisk in the centre. To the right of St Peter's stands the **Vatican Palace**, the Pope's residence. Among the principal features of the Palace are the **Sistine Chapel** and the **Vatican Museum**. The **Vatican Gardens** can be visited only by those on guided tours. For further information, see the separate *Vatican City* country section.

VALLE D'AOSTA

A ruggedly scenic region, sitting at the foot of Europe's highest mountains – **Cervino** (Matterhorn), **Gran Paradiso**, **Mont Blanc** and **Monte Rosa** – bordering France and Switzerland, Valle d'Aosta is politically autonomous and to some extent culturally distinct from the rest of Italy; French is spoken as a first language by most of the inhabitants. The picturesque ruins of countless castles (some of which are open to the public, eg **Fenis** and **Issogne**) testify to the region's immense strategic significance before the era of air travel, it being the gateway to two of the most important routes through the Alps, the Little and Great St Bernard Passes. However, the **Mont Blanc Tunnel** has largely superseded the St Bernard Passes as a major overland freight route.

The **Gran Paradiso National Park**, home to wildlife including the chamois and ibex, is a popular destination for hillwalkers and climbers. There are several fine ski resorts in the area, most notably **Breuil-Cervinia** and **Courmayeur**. One of Italy's few casinos is found at **St Vincent**.

AOSTA: The principal city of Valle d'Aosta has many well-preserved Roman and Medieval buildings. The massive Roman city walls remain mostly intact and, within them, the old town retains the grid-iron street plan characteristic of all such military townships. An impressive gateway, the **Porta Pretoria**, formed the main entrance into the old Roman town. During the Middle Ages a noble family lived in the gatehouse tower, which now houses temporary exhibitions. Further ancient Roman sites include the **Teatro Romano**, where theatrical performances are still staged throughout summer, and the **Arco di Augusto**, erected in 25 BC to honour Emperor Augustus, after whom the city is named (Aosta being a corruption of Augustus).

PIEDMONT

The densely populated **Upper Po Basin**, a vast plain dotted with gargantuan factories and crisscrossed by motorways, is the site of Italy's most important heavy industries. By contrast, the mountains to the west, on the border with France, are sparsely populated and have an economy based on agriculture and winter tourism (the main ski resorts being **Bardonecchia**, **Sansicario** and **Sestriere**).

The wine region of **Le Langhe** offers a landscape of terraced vineyards, old hilltop towns and, owing to the small number of visitors, is a quiet and peaceful region to stay. The region produces several noted wines, the best known being the sweet, sparkling white, *Asti Spumante*, from **Asti**, and the bold red, *Barolo*, from **Alba**.

TURIN: Turin (Torino) is the largest city in the region and the fourth-largest in the country. Through the early years of the 20th century, it was the automobile capital of the world. It was here that the Futurists became so excited with the potential of mechanised transport that they declared Time dead – henceforth, they naïvely declared, everything would be measured in terms of speed alone. The city still remains the focus of Italy's automobile industry. **Fiat** offer guided tours of their headquarters, where a full-scale test track may be found on the roof, while the **Museo dell'Automobile** (Automobile Museum), traces the history of the car on an international level. Turin does, of course, add up to far more than an infatuation with motor cars. The inhabitants boast that, with its broad, tree-lined avenues flanked by tall, handsome townhouses, it is *La Parigi d'Italia* (the Italian Paris). Uptown Turin is centred on the main shopping street, **Via Roma**, which links the city's favourite square, the **Piazza San Carlo**, with its most dramatic building, the **Baroque Palazzo Madama**, which houses the **Museum of Ancient Art**, one of several nationally important museums in the city, and the **Egyptian Museum**, the second-largest in the world after Cairo.

The famous **Turin Shroud** may be viewed in the 15th-century white marble Cathedral.

LOMBARDY

A prosperous region with fertile soil, a temperate climate and, for the tourist, the spectacular lakes of **Como**, **Garda**, **Maggiore** (shared with Piedmont) and **Lugano**. As in

Piedmont, the Po Valley is the site of much heavy industry. High mountains in the north, marking Italy's frontier with Switzerland, provide excellent skiing and climbing. Lombardy's most famous culinary inventions are *minestrone* soup and *osso buco* – literally, ox knuckles.

MILAN: Italy's most sophisticated city, Milan (Milano) is a financial and commercial centre of world importance and a rival to Paris in the spheres of modern art and fashion. Its international character is marked by a concentration of skyscrapers found nowhere else in Italy, contrasting and competing with the landmarks of historic Milan, but built in the same boastful spirit of civic pride that, 500 years ago, gave the city its splendid Gothic **Duomo** (Cathedral). Even today, this is one of the world's largest churches, yet despite its size, it creates an impression of delicate and ethereal beauty due to its pale colour and the fine intricate carving that covers its exterior. The whole fabric of the city – its many palaces, piazzas and churches – speaks of centuries of continuous prosperity. The **Castello Sforzesco**, in the west of the city, is a massive fortified castle, which now houses a number of museums. The **Pinacoteca di Brera** displays some of the city's most valuable artistic treasures, while the **Museo Poldi-Pezzoli** houses a private collection of paintings, ancient jewellery and Persian carpets. Leonardo da Vinci's masterpiece, *The Last Supper*, may be viewed at the convent of **Santa Maria della Grazie**. The **Teatro della Scala** (Scala Theatre) remains the undisputed world capital of opera and is well worth viewing for its magnificent opulence.

PAVIA: Just south of Milan, the town of Pavia is home to several interesting churches and the 14th-century **Castello**, housing an art gallery, archaeology museum and sculpture museum.

The **Certosa di Pavia**, 10km (6 miles) outside of town, is a monastery famous for its lavish design. Originating as the family mausoleum of the Visconti family, it later became the dwelling of a Carthusian order of monks sworn to deep contemplation and silence. However, a chosen few are allowed to give visitors a guided tour and tell the story behind their palatial surroundings.

CREMONA: The birthplace of the Stradivarius violin is a charming haven of historic architecture. A walk around the Medieval **Piazza del Comune** offers various architectural treats: the **Torazzo**, one of Italy's tallest Medieval towers; the **Cathedral**, with its magnificent astronomical clock; and the **Loggia dei Militia**, the former headquarters of the town's Medieval army. There are also two interesting museums: the **Museo Stradivariano**, housing a wealth of Stradivarius musical instruments, and the **Museo Civico**, displaying mosaics and relics from the Romanesque period.

MANTUA: Mantua (Mantova) is the birthplace of a number of renowned Italians, ranging from Virgil (a statue of whom overlooks the square facing the **Broletto**, the Medieval town hall) to Tazio Nuvolari, one of Italy's most famous racing drivers (a small museum pays tribute to his accomplishments). Its churches, **Sant'Andrea** (designed by Alberti and the burial place of Mantua's famous court painter, Mantegna) and the Baroque **Cathedral** in the **Piazza Sordello** are both important works of architecture. However, the most famous sites of Mantua are its two palaces: the **Palazzo Ducale** and the **Palazzo del Te**. The Palazzo Ducale, once the largest in Europe, was the home of the Gonzaga family, and has a number of impressive paintings by artists such as Mantegna and Rubens. The Palazzo del Te was built as a Renaissance pleasure palace for Frederico Gonzaga (known as a playboy) and his mistress, Isabella. The decorations by Giulio Romano are outstanding and well worth viewing.

BERGAMO: Nestled at the foot of the Bergamese Alps, Bergamo is made up of two cities – the old and once Venetian-ruled Upper Bergamo (*Bergamo Alta*) and the modern Lower Bergamo (*Bergamo Bassa*). The old city is well appreciated for its ancient Venetian fortifications, palaces, towers and churches, including the 12th-century **Palazzo della Ragione**, the **Torre del Comune**, the **Cathedral**, the **Colleoni Chapel** and the **Church of Santa Maria Maggiore**. The modern city's main attraction is the **Accademia Carrara**, one of Italy's largest art collections, with paintings by Bellini, Botticelli, Canaletto, Carpaccio, Lotto and Mantegna, amongst others. The two cities are connected by a funicular railway.

THE LAKES: The great northern lakes lie in a series of long, deep valleys running down onto the plains from the Alps. **Lake Como** is perhaps the most attractive, **Lake Maggiore** the most elegant (and populous) and **Lake Garda** the wildest and most spectacular. On the south shore of Lake Garda lies the peninsula of **Sirmione**, renowned for its mild, Mediterranean climate, its beautiful countryside and the **Caves of Catullo**, an archaeological site of a former Roman villa situated on the tip of the peninsula. The **Sirmione Spa**, the largest privately owned thermal treatment centre in Italy, whose sulphurous waters originate from the depths of **Lake Garda**, has long been one of Sirmione's main attractions. There is plenty of accommodation available as well as frequent boat services to other lakeside towns and villages.

Credit: © Venezia – Azienda di Promozione Turistica

LIGURIA

This is a region of 320km (200 miles) of rocky, wooded coastline running from France to Tuscany, where the Italian 'boot' begins. This is the **Riviera**, Italy's answer to the Côte d'Azur, and there are ample facilities for tourists even in the smallest of ports. The coastal hills are less developed.

GENOA: Genoa (Genova), capital of Liguria, has long been an important commercial and military port. Ferries depart daily from the port for **Sardinia**. The Medieval district of the city holds many treasures, such as the **Church of Sant'Agostino** (next to the **Museo dell'Architettura e Scultura Ligure**), the beautiful **Church of San Donato**, the 12th-century **Church of Santa Maria di Castello**, the **Gothic Cathedral** of San Lorenzo and the **Porta Soprana** (the old stone entrance gate to the city). Outside the Medieval district, **Via Garibaldi**, where many of the city's richest inhabitants built their palaces, is a beautiful walk, with **Palazzo Bianco** (now an art gallery with paintings by Rubens and Van Dyck), **Palazzo Podesta** and the magnificently decorated **Palazzo Rosso** (adjacent to **Palazzo Bianco** and housing paintings by Caravaggio, Dürer and Titian). The **Acquario** (Aquarium) presents underwater ocean life, with 1000 species housed in 50 vast tanks, making it the largest centre of its kind in Europe.

THE RIVIERA: This narrow strip of coastline is divided into two sections: the **Riviera di Ponente** (to the west), from Ventimiglia to Genoa, and the **Riviera di Levante** (to the east), from Genoa to La Spezia. The former includes wide sandy beaches and the rather commercial seaside resorts of **San Remo** and **Bordighera**, while the latter boasts small bays backed by rocky cliffs and more exclusive retreats such as **Portofino** and **Cinque Terre**. Portofino is the best known, with its small picturesque harbour full of sleek yachts, its luxury clothes shops, its romantic villas owned by the rich and famous perched on the hillside and the **Castello di San Giorgio**, sitting high up on a promontory with magnificent views of the Portofino harbour and bay. The beach at **Santa Margherita Ligure**, just 5km (3 miles) south of Portofino, is an excellent place to swim, with a magical view of the surrounding cliffs and villas from the warm and crystal-clear aquamarine water. Nearby **Rapallo**, 8km (5 miles) south of Portofino, is less fashionable and subsequently less expensive. At the southern tip of the Riviera di Levante lie **Cinque Terre**, a series of five picturesque fishing villages linked by scenic mountainside paths and surrounded by vineyards and olive groves. Here one finds the region's least exploited beaches.

TRENTINO & ALTO ALDIGE

These wholly mountainous regions on the Swiss border straddle the valley of the **River Isarco**, which flows from the **Brenner Pass**, into the **River Adige** and thence into the Mediterranean. Germanic and Italian cultures blend here to the extent that, towards the north, German is increasingly found as the first language. The **Dolomites** to the east are a range of distinctively craggy mountains, isolated to such an extent from both Italy and Switzerland that, in the more remote valleys, the inhabitants speak Ladin, an ancient Romance language not much different from Latin. The area is traversed by clearly marked mountain paths and served by numerous hostels, making it ideal for hiking and climbing.

TRENTINO: The principal town of Trentino is **Trento**, worth visiting for its wealth of art works, gathered by the dynasty of princes who ruled the area between the 10th and 18th centuries. Many of these artistic acquisitions are viewable in the town's museums, which include the **Castello di Buonconsiglio**, **Museo Diocesano Trentino** and the **Museo Provinciale d'Arte**.

ALTO ADIGE: Bolzano is the principal town of Alto Aldige, further north. A somewhat austere commercial town, it appears as an unlikely portal to one of the most extraordinary panoramic drives in Italy – the mountain route through the Dolomites to Cortina d'Ampezzo called **La Grande Strada delle Dolomiti**. Upon entering the **Val d'Ega**, at the beginning of the route, the scenery is suddenly lush with foliage and rocks as the light seeps through the forest trees. About 20km (12 miles) from the beginning of the route is **Lake Carezza**, a beautiful limpid pool of bright green water reflecting the trees and mountains around it. This is just the beginning of an awe-inspiring passage through the Dolomites and its small alpine towns, ski resorts and endless panoramas of craggy peaks and tree-clad mountainsides. One of the most famous mountain resorts and the second-largest town in this region is **Merano**, 28km (17 miles) north of Bolzano. Popular for its spas, thermal waters and moderate climate (the temperature tends to remain above freezing all winter, despite its close proximity to a range of snow-laden ski slopes), it is also visually rewarding, with extensive landscaped gardens and a charming mixture of architectural styles, from Gothic to Art Nouveau. The **Merano Valley** is dotted with historic castles, several of which have been transformed into charming castle hotels.

VENETO

Veneto comprises the **Lower Po Valley**, the eastern bank of Lake Garda and the eastern Dolomites, occupying what was once the Republic of Venice. On the Adriatic coast lie several rather commercial seaside resorts, such as **Jesolo**, while high in the Dolomites, the chic town of **Cortina d'Ampezzo** is probably Italy's best-known (but not most challenging) ski resort. The Winter Olympics were held here in 1956. It makes a fine base for exploring the Dolomites in summer.

VENICE: Venice (Venezia) stands upon a series of islands in a lagoon at the northern end of the **Adriatic Sea**, a position which gave it unique economic and defensive advantages over its trading rivals. Much of the wealth generated was, of course, invested in the construction of monuments to the glory of both God and the merchants, and Venice must be counted as one of the highlights of any tour of Italy.

The city's main monuments – **St Mark's Basilica** and the **Doge's Palace** overlooking **St Mark's Square** – have gained fame through innumerable paintings by such artists as Canaletto, but the whole city is in many ways a work of art. The city's most important thoroughfare is the **Grand Canal**, lined with fine Gothic and Renaissance *palazzi* (buildings) and crossed by the bustling **Ponte di Rialto** (Rialto Bridge) and the wooden **Ponte dell'Accademia** (Academy Bridge). Nearby, the **Galleria dell'Accademia** displays hundreds of Venetian paintings dating from between the 14th and 18th centuries, while the **Collezione Peggy Guggenheim** exhibits international 20th-century art, including works by Picasso, Giacometti and Ernst.

Away from the main thoroughfares, Venice is characterised by narrow canals, small squares (often containing remarkable Gothic churches) and, above all, since it contains no motor traffic, by serenity – the city's ancient name was '*La Serenissima*'.

The Venetian islands of **Burano** (famous for lacemaking), **Murano** (famous for glassmaking) and **Torcello** (noted for the magnificent Byzantine **Basilica of Santa Maria Assunta**) can be visited by boat.

Note: The city is linked to **Mestre**, on the mainland, by a causeway which can be crossed by road or rail. Although there is a large car park in Venice, at the end of the causeway, it is easier and cheaper to park in Mestre and continue by train.

Credit: © Venezia – Azienda di Promozione Turistica

PADUA: The city of Padua (Padova) is famous for the great, seven-domed 13th-century **Basilica of St Anthony**; St Anthony was buried here and it is an important pilgrimage site. Inside, the bronzes on the main altar are by Donatello, as is the equestrian statue in front of the entrance. Padua's other main attraction is the tiny **Scrovegni Chapel**, decorated with a stunning cycle of 14th-century biblical frescoes by Giotto. Padua's other delights include **Prato della Valle**, a vast square with a central green space, and the **Orto Botanico**, botanical gardens dating back to 1545, making it the oldest place of its kind in Europe.

VICENZA: Dating back to Roman times, Vicenza is best known for the 16th-century works of Andrea Palladio, whose published analyses of ancient architecture did much to spread the Renaissance throughout Europe. His buildings here include the monumental **Basilica Palladiana**, the **Teatro Olimpico** with its brilliantly painted stage-set, and the **Palazzo Chiericati**, home to the **Museo Civico**. A short distance out of town stands one of Palladio's finest villas, **La Rotonda**, a model of Renaissance architecture, based on a square plan with four identical façades.

VERONA: A graceful city built upon the banks of the **River Adige**, Verona was the setting of Shakespeare's *Romeo and Juliet*. The **Casa di Giulietta** (Juliet's House), a small Medieval home with a balcony and courtyard, attracts thousands of visitors each year. The other big attraction is the well-preserved **Roman Arena**, built in AD 290 and able to accommodate over 20,000 spectators. An opera festival, with open-air night-time performances, is staged here throughout summer. The 14th-century red-brick **Castelvecchio**, next to the river, houses an extensive art museum, with important Renaissance paintings and sculpture from northern Italy. The city's most noted church is the lovely Romanesque **San Zeno**.

RIVIERA DEL BRENTA: During the 16th century, the banks of this waterway linking Venice and Padua became a popular place for aristocrats and wealthy merchants to build their 'country' villas. From March to October, daily boat trips run from Venice to Padua, with stops enroute to admire several of the villas, such as **Villa Foscari** at **Malcontenta**, designed by Palladio, and the 18th-century **Villa Pisani** at **Stra**.

FRIULI-VENEZIA GIULIA

This region in the northeastern corner of Italy bordering Austria and Slovenia has changed hands many times over the centuries and Friulian society is a complex mix of cultures. Half of the population speak Friulian, a language closely allied to Latin.

TRIESTE: In the 18th century, Austro-Hungary commissioned the construction of a deep-water port at Trieste and so ended Venice's long domination of the **Adriatic Sea**. Following the collapse of the Austro-Hungarian Empire after World War I, Trieste was ceded to Italy. The city's most prominent buildings date from the Hapsburg era, the most beautiful being **Miramare Castle** which is set amid beautifully landscaped gardens overloooking the sea, and is open to the public.

ELSEWHERE: The coast west of Trieste has several popular beach resorts, such as **Grado**. The area inland from Trieste is known for its Karst landscape and caves. The **Grotta Gigante** (Giant Grotto) is listed in the *Guinness Book of Records* as the largest accessible cave in the world.
Inland are **Pordenone** and **Udine**, agricultural centres on the fertile Friuli plain. Further north are the foothills of the eastern **Dolomites** and the **Julian Alps** (part of Slovenia), where ski resorts are now being developed. The road from Udine to Villach in Austria is an important overland freight route; it winds up the dramatic valley of the **Isonzo**, a river rendered an astonishing shade of blue by minerals leached from the Julian Alps.

EMILIA-ROMAGNA

A region of gentle hills between the **River Po** and the **Appennines**. As elsewhere in the Po Basin, intensive agriculture is pursued alongside heavy industry. The region is famed for culinary delights such as bolognese sauce and *mortadella* (a specially prepared type of sausage) from Bologna, and Parmesan cheese and Parma ham from Parma.

BOLOGNA: One of the oldest cities in Italy and the site of Europe's oldest university. Often overlooked as a tourist destination, it nevertheless possesses a distinctive charm, due largely to the imaginative use of brickwork. A total 45km (28 miles) of arcades flank many of the streets, and a 3.6km- (2.3 mile-) stretch leads all the way out of town to the hilltop **Basilica di San Luca**. The main square, **Piazza Maggiore**, is dominated by the huge Gothic **Church of San Petronio**, while on **Piazza di Porta Ravegnana**, the **Torre degli Asinelli** and the leaning **Torre Garisenda** are the only survivors of numerous towers that were built across the city in Medieval times.

RAVENNA: Sometimes referred to as the 'Capital of Mosaics', between the sixth and eighth centuries, Ravenna was the principal centre of Byzantine civilisation in Italy. The city's former importance is recorded by a profusion of early Byzantine and Christian monuments decorated with stunning mosaics, notably the splendid **Mausoleum of Galla Placidia**, the octagonal **Basilica di San Vitale**, and the churches of **San Apollonare Nuovo** and **Sant'Apollinare** in **Classe**, all of which are UNESCO-listed World Heritage Sites.

ELSEWHERE: Parma boasts a fine Romanesque cathedral and baptistry, and an opera house with strong connections with Verdi, who lived at nearby **Sant'Agata**. **Faenza** (known to the French as 'Faience') is famed for its majolica pottery. Other cities in Emilia-Romagna include **Modena** and **Ferrara**, both with many fine palaces associated with the Este family; and **Reggio**, the old provincial capital. The seaside resort of **Rimini** is renowned for its lively party scene, with numerous nightclubs on the beach throughout summer.

TUSCANY

This fertile region lies between the northern **Appennines** and the **Mediterranean Sea**. The landscape of Tuscany is, typically, one of vine-covered hills, cypress woods, fields of sunflowers and remote hilltop villages. *Chianti*, the best-known Italian wine, is made in the area north of Siena, and several wine cellars are open to the public. There are a number of **volcanic spas**, most notably **Monsummano Terme** and **Montecatini Terme**. Regarding the coast, the **Versalia**, to the north, offers a 30km- (18-mile) stretch of organised bathing establishments, while the beaches to the south are less exploited.

FLORENCE: The principal Tuscan city, Florence (Firenze) is the world's most celebrated storehouse of Renaissance art and architecture. Set on the banks of the **Arno** below the wooded foothills of the Appennines, this beautiful city has long been the focus of Italian arts and letters. Alberti, Boccaccio, Botticelli, Brunelleschi, Dante, Donatello, Fra Angelico, Giotto, Leonardo da Vinci, Masaccio, Michelangelo, Petrarch and Vasari are among the many associated with establishing the pre-eminence of the city. Brunelleschi's revolutionary design for the dome of the **Duomo** (Cathedral) is generally accepted as the first expression of Renaissance ideas in architecture. This dome still dominates the city's roofscape, just as the great **Piazza del Duomo** at its feet dominates life at street level. The square is ringed with cafes and is a popular meeting point. Between there and the river are many of the best-loved *palazzi* (palaces), whilst close by to the north are the churches of **San Lorenzo** and **Santa Maria Novella**. The shop-lined **Ponte Vecchio** bridge scans the river to arrive at **Palazzo Pitti** and the **Boboli Gardens**.
The **Uffizi Gallery** houses one of the world's most celebrated art collections including masterpieces such as Botticelli's *Birth Of Venus*, Caravaggio's *Young Bacchus*, Leonardo da Vinci's *Annunciation*, Michelangelo's *Holy Family* and Titian's *Urbino Venus*. Some of the country's most important sculptures are found within the **Museo Nazionale del Bargello**, notably works by Michelangelo and Donatello. Michelangelo's famous statue of *David* may be viewed at the **Accademia di Belle Arti** near the University.

SIENA: Siena's most prosperous era pre-dated the Renaissance and consequently much of the fabric of the city is in the older Gothic and Romanesque styles. While most buildings are of reddish-brown brick (hence the colour 'burnt sienna'), the stunning **Cathedral** is constructed of alternating stripes of black and white marble, and is said to be one of the best examples of Italian Gothic architecture. The labyrinth of narrow cobbled streets that make up the historic centre converge at **Piazza del Campo**. Overlooked by the giant *campanile* of the **Palazzo Pubblico**, this is possibly the most complete Medieval piazza in Italy. Twice a year, on July 2 and August 16, a notorious bareback horse race known as the *Palio* is held here. It has been a special event since the 13th century and attracts crowds from all over the world. The 700-year-old university holds a summer school in Italian.

PISA: Located north of Siena, Pisa is famous for its **Leaning Tower**, a free-standing *campanile* or bell tower. Closed to the public since 1990, the tower has now reopened following a lengthy restoration project to reduce its tilt. Next to the tower, on **Campo dei Miracoli**, stand the elegant 11th-century Gothic **Cathedral** and the **Baptistry**. Nearby, the 13th-century **Camposanto** is a cemetery contained within a unique collonaded courtyard, said to have been built to enclose earth brought from Jerusalem by the Crusaders.

AREZZO: Arezzo is made up of an old upper town and a modern lower town, and is an important centre for the production of gold jewellery. Within the old town lie the **Duomo**, decorated with 16th-century stained glass windows, and the **Basilica di San Francesco**, containing a highly esteemed cycle of frescoes by Piero della Francesca depicting the *Legend of the True Cross*. The **Piazza Grande** is a wonderful Medieval square, famous for its regular antiques market, overlooked by several impressive historic buildings, notably the church of **Santa Maria della Pieve** and the **Loggiato del Vasari**, the home Vasari built for himself in 1540.

LUCCA: The peaceful walled town of Lucca is famed for its elaborate churches, which include the **Cathedral of San Martino** with its asymmetric facade and campanile, the striking **San Frediano** decorated with colourful mosaics, and San Michele in Foro, built on the site of the Roman forum. The main shopping street, **Fillungo**, is noted for a number of early-20th-century, Liberty-style facades.

SAN GIMIGNANO: Known as the 'city of beautiful towers', San Gimignano is one of the best-preserved Medieval towns in Italy. During the Middle Ages, when the height of one's tower was a symbol of prestige, families vied to build the tallest structure. Today, 14 of the original 76 towers remain, creating a truly unforgettable skyline.

THE TUSCAN ARCHIPELAGO: The Tuscan Archipelago is a group of scattered islands lying between Tuscany and Corsica. The best known is **Elba**, which is linked to **Piombino** on the mainland by regular hydrofoil and ferry services. Famous as the place where Napoleon was briefly exiled before his final defeat at Waterloo, it has lovely beaches and campsites shaded by pines. Napoleon's two homes, **Palazzina Napoleonica dei Mulini** (created out of two windmills) and **Villa Napoleonica di San Martino** are both open to the public.

ELSEWHERE: Other places of note in Tuscany are **Volterra**, a beautifully preserved Medieval hilltown; **Livorno**, the principal commercial port; and **Carrara**, where high-grade white marble has been quarried since Etruscan times.

UMBRIA

Sometimes referred to as 'the green heart of Italy', Umbria is a small, hilly and fairly untouched region between Tuscany and Marche, with little industry and few towns of any great size. The landscape is similar to that of Tuscany and combines austere Medieval architecture and stone farmhouses with gently rolling hills and rivers. **Lake Trasimeno** is contained within the **Trasimeno Regional Park**, and serves as a seasonal home to many species of migrating birds, while the **River Nera Regional Park** contains the **Marmore Waterfalls**, the highest falls in Italy. Umbria's rich history is still very much in evidence: traces of Umbri, Etruscan and Roman cultures exist alongside Medieval and Renaissance architecture in towns such as **Assisi**, **Orvieto**, **Perugia** and **Spoleto**.

PERUGIA: Umbria's capital has been continuously inhabited for more than 25 centuries and contains many Etruscan and Roman remains. Particularly notable are the ancient **Etruscan city walls**, the **Piazza IV Novembre** with the Cathedral, and the **Fontana Maggiore** (Great Fountain). On the top floor of the 14th-century **Palazzo dei Priori**, the **Galleria Nazionale dell'Umbria** contains one of the world's finest collections of Renaissance paintings, with works by Piero della Francesca, Perugino, Beato Angelico and others. The state-funded **Università per Stranieri** (University for Foreigners) offers courses for foreigners wishing to study Italian language and civilisation. Perugia is less than two hours by car from Florence and Rome, and one hour from Siena.

ASSISI: A picturesque Medieval hilltown to the east of Perugia, Assisi is famous as the birthplace of St Francis, founder of the Franciscan order of monks. The life of St Francis is commemorated in frescoes by Giotto in the 13th-century **Basilica di San Francesco**, one of Italy's best-loved and most-visited churches. Other interesting sites include the **Basilica di Santa Maria degli Angeli** and the **Roman Temple of Minerva**.

ORVIETO: Orvieto is a Medieval city perched on a volcanic outcrop. The well-preserved city centre has a number of sites and buildings dating from the Etruscan period. Orvieto's most memorable monument is the **Duomo** (Cathedral), which cleverly mixes Romanesque and Gothic styles.

SPOLETO: The peaceful streets of the romantic hilltown of Spoleto come alive each year for the world-renowned *Summer Festival*, featuring music, theatre and a range of other cultural events. The town has several interesting Roman monuments, including the classical **Arch of Druso** and the **Roman Theatre**, plus the Medieval **Ponte delle Torri** bridge and a number of delightful Romanesque churches.
GUBBIO & TODI: Other important Umbrian towns include **Gubbio**, a well-preserved Medieval town situated at the foot of Mount Ingino and home to the famous **Gubbio Tablets** – the oldest surviving record of the Umbrian people; and **Todi**, overlooking the Tiber valley, whose beautiful Medieval square is surrounded by a wealth of historic buildings, including the 13th-century **Palazzo del Popolo**, the **Palazzo del Capitano** and the **Cathedral**.

MARCHE, ABRUZZO & MOLISE

MARCHE: A mountainous agricultural region on the central Adriatic coast, south of **San Marino**. The regional capital is **Ancona**, an important naval and commercial port, with daily ferry services to Albania, Croatia, Greece and Montenegro. The city is also home to several well-preserved Roman remains such as the **Arco di Traiano** and the **Anfiteatro Romano**. The majestic hilltop **Basilica di San Ciriaco**, built in the 11th century, combines Romanesque style with Byzantine elements. Out of town, along the coast, lie several highly organised beach resorts, with sunbeds and umbrellas laid out in neat lines. A more informal beach is found below the spectacular **Costa Conero** cliffs, a few miles south of Ancona.
Urbino was once Italy's greatest seat of learning and is now a pleasant Renaissance hilltown, its skyline a soaring vista of domes and towers. Also the birthplace of Raphael, several of his works may be viewed in the art gallery at the **Ducal Palace**, along with works by Piero della Francesca and Titian. Raphael's childhood home is also open for viewing. **Loreto**, said to be the site of the house of the Virgin Mary, attracts many pilgrims from around the world. According to legend, the house was carrried here from Nazareth by angels, and is now enclosed in the elaborate Gothic **Santuario della Santa Casa**. The *Madonna of Loreto* was elected patron saint of airmen in 1920.
ABRUZZO: This region encompasses the highest parts of the great Apennine chain. The northern mountains are generally too desolate for agriculture and much of the land is sparsely populated. The southern uplands are covered with a great forest of beech, which has been designated the **National Park of Abruzzo**. Marsican brown bears (unique to Italy), wolves, chamois and eagles may be seen here.
L'Aquila, the principal city, contains an imposing castle; other noteworthy monuments include the **Fontana delle 99 Cannelle**, a fountain with 99 spouts (one for each of the villages that founded the city) and the pink and white marble **Basilica di Santa Maria di Collemaggio**. **Pescara** is, as its name implies, primarily a fishing port.
MOLISE: One of the poorest parts of mainland Italy, this area is mountainous with poor soil and a scattered population. It does, however, possess its own rugged beauty. The **Matese mountain range** is still the haven of wolves and various birds of prey. It also offers some excellent skiing resorts and tends not to be too crowded. The region's capital, **Campobasso**, is home to **Castello Monforte** and the Romanesque churches of **San Bartolomeo** and **San Giorgino**.

LAZIO

On the western side of the Italian 'boot', this is a region of volcanic hills, lakes and fine beaches that are easily reached from Rome.
HILL TOWNS: Inland from Rome are the hill towns known as the **Castelli Romani**, which are popular for excursions. **Tivoli**, just 40km (25 miles) east of Rome, was once the haven of the rich, first in Roman times and later during the Renaissance. It is well known for its magnificent villas and gardens, such as **Villa d'Este** and **Villa Adriana**. The pleasant town of **Frascati**, only 20km (12.5 miles) south of Rome, is famous for its *Frascati* wine, a light, delicate, dry white which has an international reputation.
Castelgandolfo overlooks the spectacular **Lake Albano**, and is dominated by the **Palazzo Pontificio**, the Pope's summer retreat.
THE COAST: Ostia Lido, close to **Ostia Antica**, the ancient port of Rome, is a well-organised but not particularly attractive beach resort. **Terracina**, further south, is noted for its soft, white-sand beaches. The old town, up on a hill above the sea, is home to a Cathedral and the Roman **Temple of Jupiter Anxurus**, believed to have been built in the first century BC. Further south, the most exclusive seaside resort is **Sperlonga**. The town itself is reminiscent of a Greek island village; seemingly endless steps wind up and around through white arches, offering unexpected but spectacular views of the sea and cliffs. Down below lies a beautiful small beach; 30km (20 miles) offshore is the unspoilt island of **Ponza**. Still further south, the resorts of **San Felice**, **Circeo** and **Sabaudia** are known for clean seawater and wide, sandy beaches.
Northwest of Rome, **Civitavecchia** is an important naval and merchant port, with regular ferries to Sardinia.

CAMPANIA

Called *Campania Felix* ('blessed country') by the Romans because of its fertile soil, mild climate and (by southern Italian standards) plentiful water. Citrus fruits, tobacco, wheat and vegetables are grown, and the region is known for excellent wines, notably the white *Greco di Tufo*.
The **Amalfi Coast**, running along a peninsula just south of Naples, is one of the most popular regions in Italy for holidaymakers, especially those in search of sun and sand. But the added bonus for many is the extraordinary beauty of the region: sheer craggy cliffs rise over the shimmering blue-green Mediterranean waters, and everywhere there are views of hills and sea. History and culture are also present in abundance and it is easy to understand the persistent attraction of the area for visitors.
NAPLES: The third-largest Italian city, Naples is famous as the place where pizza was invented. Set on the **Bay of Naples** and overshadowed by **Mount Vesuvius**, the city occupies one of the most beautiful natural settings of any city in Europe. Frequently criticised for urban decay and delinquency, it is a city where splendid churches and palaces stand aside squalid tenement blocks, and where street markets sell high-quality food produce, plus counterfeit designer goods. Notable monuments include the 17th-century **Palazzo Reale**, built by the Bourbons, the massive stone **Castel Nuovo**, overlooking the sea, and the **San Carlo Opera House**. The impressive **Museo Archeologico Nazionale** houses an excellent collection of Greco-Roman artefacts, including mosaics from Pompeii and Herculaneum. The **Museo di Capodimonte** displays porcelain and majolica pieces, plus paintings by Dutch, Italian and Spanish masters.
MOUNT VESUVIUS: Above Naples is the bare cone of Mount Vesuvius, an active volcano, and beside it the broad sweep of the **Bay of Naples** and the **Tyrrhennian Sea**. A toll-road leads most of the way up to the summit of Vesuvius (it is the local Lover's Lane; people also gather mushrooms here when the conditions are right); the final few hundred yards involve an easy hike up a well-maintained bare pumice track. The viewing platform is right on the rim of the caldera and provides a good view of both the steam-filled abyss and the whole of the Bay of Naples and Pompeii below. Nearby, the remains of **Pompeii** and **Herculaneum**, engulfed in the great eruption of AD 79, are a unique record of how ordinary first-century Romans lived their daily lives. Moulds of people and animals found well-preserved, buried under the burning ash, can be seen at Pompeii, and the decoration in some of the excavated villas is amazingly intact, including numerous wall paintings of gods and humans in scenes ranging from the heroic to the erotic.
SORRENTO: Sorrento, now a rather commercial resort, has attracted artists for centuries. Gorky, Nietzsche and Wagner spent time here and Ibsen wrote *The Ghosts* while in Sorrento. The **Museo Correale** is an attractive 18th-century villa with a collection of decorative arts and paintings belonging to the Correale family. Outside, a walk through the gardens and vineyards brings one to a promontory overlooking the bay, offering a spectacular view of the harbour and the surrounding towns and cliffs.
CAPRI: Capri, one of Italy's most lovely and most visited islands, can be reached by ferry or hydrofoil from Amalfi, Naples, Positano and Sorrento. Upon arrival at the **Marina Grande**, it is possible to take a boat trip to the island's main tourist attraction, the **Blue Grotto**. A strenuous 45-minute uphill trek brings one to the ruins of **Villa Tiberio**, built as the Roman Emperor Tiberius's luxurious retirement home. The **Garden of Augustus**, south of the town of Capri, is pretty but often very crowded. From here, a winding road brings one down to the sea, where it is possible to swim off the rocks.
THE AMALFI COAST: The Amalfi Coast, running from Sorrento to Salerno, is one of Europe's most beautiful coastlines. Departing from Sorrento, the first port of call is **Positano**, a small exclusive resort of great beauty. Heaped high above the coast, its brightly painted houses and bougainvillaea have inspired a thousand picture postcards and draw crowds of visitors every summer. There is an excellent beach and clean seawater for bathing. **Amalfi** is perhaps the most well known of the region's resort towns. However, the town still has an authentic air about it, despite its popularity with tourists. The Romanesque **Cathedral** with its 13th-century bell tower, located in the main square, looks entirely untouched by the contemporary hustle and bustle around it. The **Cloister of Paradise**, just to the right of the cathedral, also makes good viewing. There are some excellent restaurants and the local wine, **Sammarco**, bottled in Amalfi, is superb and inexpensive. Perched high above Amalfi, 'closer to the sky than the seashore', as André Gide wrote, is the former independent republic of **Ravello**. From here, the most spectacular views of the Amalfi Coast can be had, above all from the **Villa Cimbrone** where marble statues line a belvedere that is perched on the very edge of the cliff, 335m (1100ft) up.
ELSEWHERE: The city of Caserta to the north of Naples was the country seat of the Kings of Naples. The Baroque Royal Palace owes much to Versailles, and the surrounding gardens are magificent. South along the coast, past Salerno, the imposing Greek temples at **Paestum** are among the country's best-preserved ancient relics.
Ischia, an island on the west side of the Bay of Naples, is easily accessible from Sorrento or from Naples. Although larger than Capri, it is not quite so popular with tourists, but well visited by the locals who appreciate it more for its calm and scenic beauty.

PUGLIA, BASILICATA & CALABRIA

PUGLIA: The southeastern region of Puglia (Apulia) encompasses the forested crags of the **Gargano Peninsular** (home to **Gargano National Park**), the mostly flat **Salentine peninsula** (the 'heel' of Italy) and, between them, the **Murgia**, a limestone plateau riddled with caves. With the exception of **Bari** and **Taranto**, both large industrial ports, the Apulian economy is wholly agricultural. The main products are almonds, grapes, olives, tobacco and vegetables. There are fine beaches on the Adriatic coast between Barletta and Bari. Puglia was important in Roman times as the gateway to the eastern Mediterranean. The port of **Brindisi**, now eclipsed by Bari in commercial terms, was the terminus of the **Via Appia**, along which Eastern produce was conveyed to Rome and beyond. The **Museo Archeologico Provinciale** houses many relics from this prosperous era. Virgil died in Brindisi in 19 BC.
On the **Murgia** plateau, in **Alberobello**, one can visit a number of extraordinary stone dwellings known as trulli. Circular with conical roofs (also of stone), they are similar to the *nuraghi* of Sardinia. Also in this area stands a unique octagonal castle, the **Castel del Monte**, built as a hunting lodge in the 13th century by the Holy Roman Emperor Frederick II (the self-styled Stupor Mundi, 'Wonder of the World'). Both are now UNESCO-listed World Heritage Sites.
BASILICATA: A remote and mainly mountainous region between Puglia and Calabria, Basilicata is heavily forested in the north around **Monte Vulture**, a large extinct volcano; elsewhere, the hills are flinty and barren. Many rivers flow down from the southern Appennines into the **Gulf of Taranto**, irrigating the fertile coastal plain behind **Metaponto** (birthplace of Pythagoras). The population is small. The principal town, **Potenza**, was almost entirely rebuilt after a severe earthquake in 1857, only to suffer a similar scale of destruction in World War II. In **Matera**, one can visit the extraordinary **Sassi**, a vast troglodyte settlement of houses and churches carved into tufa rock. Home to 15,000 residents until the 1950s, this is now a UNESCO-listed World Heritage Site.
CALABRIA: The toe of the 'boot', a spectacularly beautiful region of high mountains, dense forests and relatively empty beaches. Beech, chestnut, oak and pine cover almost half of Calabria and are a rich hunting ground for mushroom enthusiasts. *Porcini* (boletus edulis), fresh, dried and pickled, naturally adorn the shelves of all the speciality shops of the region. Higher up in the mountains the land only sustains light grazing, but the meadows bloom with a multitude of wild flowers each spring. It is only on isolated patches of reclaimed land on the marshy coast that agriculture is possible and consequently the inhabitants are among the poorest in Italy. They are further tormented by frequent earthquakes. Some wolves still survive in the mountains, particularly in the central **Sila Massifs**. **Catanzaro**, **Cosenza** and **Reggio Calabria**, on the straits of Messina, are the major towns.
Calabria's best beaches are on the west coast, where one finds long stretches of sand, punctuated by rocky outcrops and secluded coves. The beaches on the east coast are rockier, more rugged and less explored.

SICILY

Strategically situated between Italy and North Africa and with fertile soil and rich coastal fishing grounds, Sicily has suffered an almost continuous round of invasion for as long as history has been recorded. The Greeks, Carthaginians, Romans, Byzantines, Arabs, Normans, Angevins, Aragonese, Bourbons and, most recently, the Germans (and the Allies) during World War II – all have left their mark on this unique island, the most populous in the Mediterranean. The economy is based on the production of citrus fruit, almonds, olives, vegetables, wine (including *Marsala*), wheat and beans, together with mining, fishing (anchovies, tuna, cuttlefish and swordfish) and the raising of sheep and goats.
PALERMO: The capital, Palermo, is a splendid city in a grand style, opulent, vital and full of remarkable architecture, particularly Norman and Baroque. Notable buildings include the **Cathedral**, the **Martorana**, the **Palazzo dei Normanni**, **San Cataldo**, **San Giuseppe dei Teatini** and **Santa Maria di Gesù** churches. The catacombs at the **Capuchin Monastery** contain thousands of mummified bodies.

A B C D E F G H I J K L M N O P Q R S T U V W X Y Z

THE EAST COAST: Catania is a spacious city dating mostly from the 18th century, having been rebuilt following a succession of earthquakes. Europe's largest and most active volcano, **Mount Etna**, stands nearby and with its fine beaches the city attracts many tourists. **Taormina**, further up the coast, is a picturesque and immensely popular resort town. Perched on a cliff within sight of Mount Etna, it has fine beaches, a well-preserved **Greek Theatre**, a **Castle** and a **Cathedral**, as well as a plethora of chic bars and restaurants.

HISTORIC SITES: Sicily is littered with the remains of successive invading cultures and a full listing of important sites is beyond the scope of this entry. The most important ancient Greek sites are: the temples of the **Valle dei Templi** at **Agrigénto**, said to be better preserved than any in Greece itself; the **Greek Theatre** at **Syracuse** (where there is also a Roman Amphitheatre); and the vast **Temple of Apollo** at **Selinunte**. Other notable monuments include the **Norman Cathedral at Monreale**, containing 1.5 acres of dazzling mosaics, and the Byzantine cliff dwellings at **Cava d'Ispica** near **Modica**.

AEOLIAN ISLANDS: This group of attractive small islands is popular for its crystal clear waters ideal for diving and underwater fishing, and stunning beaches of hot black sand and rocky outcrops. **Lipari** is the largest and most 'touristy' island. **Panarea** is smart but unspoilt. **Vulcano**, the closest island, and **Stromboli**, the most distant, are both active volcanoes. Accommodation is generally simple, although there are some excellent hotels.

SARDINIA

This is the second-largest island in the Mediterranean. Much of Sardinia away from the coasts is an almost lunar landscape of crags and chasms and is largely uninhabited. The coastline is jagged and rocky, interspersed with marvellous beaches of very fine sand. In recent years there has been much investment in tourist infrastructure, particularly in the northern area known as the **Costa Smeralda** (Emerald Coast), which has become a favourite retreat of Italian celebrities, and on the west coast near **Alghero**. This is the only region in Italy without motorways. The Sardinian language is closer to Latin than modern Italian is.

CAGLIARI: The capital stands in a marshy valley at the south of the island. It was founded by the Phoenicians and subsequently expanded by the Romans, who knew it as **Carales**. It is today a busy commercial port and site of most of the island's heavy industry

ELSEWHERE: The only other towns of any size are **Sassari**, in the northwest near the resort area of Alghero; **Nuoro**, an agricultural town on the edge of the central massif, a good base from which to explore the interior; and **Olbia**, a fishing port and car-ferry terminus on the edge of the **Costa Smeralda**.

There are numerous Bronze Age remains throughout the islands, the best known being the *nuraghi* – circular (sometimes conical) stone dwellings. The largest collection of these may be found at **Su Nuraxi**, about 80km (50 miles) north of Cagliari.

Sport & Activities

Watersports: Italy has some 8500km (5345 miles) of coastline and remains one of Europe's favourite destinations for beach holidays. Facilities such as sun loungers and deckchairs (which are common on Italian beaches) usually attract a small charge. All types of watersports are available at major resorts. The enduring appeal of the Italian Riviera in Liguria (a 350 km-/219 mile-stretch from France to Tuscany), or of the Adriatic and Amalfi coasts, the latter known for its steeply terraced villages clinging to a rocky coastline, is witnessed by the ever-growing number of visitors. Less busy are the beaches on the islands, in Sicily, which has large sandy stretches on the southern coast, and in Sardinia, much of which is still relatively untouched. Many of Italy's best **dive** sites are located in Sardinia, and Italy's first **surfing** school is based in Mauro. Diving courses and equipment hire are also available on the Tremiti Islands (Puglia) in the Adriatic and along the coasts of Tuscany and Liguria. **Fishing** is excellent throughout Sardinian and Sicilian waters (also renowned for their healthy lobster population), while the rivers in northern Italy, Umbria and Tuscany can offer particularly scenic fishing holidays. For sea fishing, private or chartered boats can be rented. Genoa has frequent **yachting** regattas, as does Santa Margherita Ligura, where a canoe and small boat regatta is held in July. **Sailing** is popular on Italy's five major lakes near the Alps in the north – Como, Garda, Iseo, Lugano and Maggiore.

Wintersports: The **skiing** infrastructure has been greatly improved in recent years, and the facilities at resorts in the Italian Alps now rival those in neighbouring Austria, France and Switzerland. Ski resorts can be broadly split into four geographical areas. To the west of Turin, in the Piedmont region, major resorts include Bardonechia, Sauze d'Oulx and Sestriere. Further north, the Aosta Valley and its main resorts, such as Cervinia, Courmayeur and La Thuile, are easily reached from France (via the Mont Blanc tunnel from Chamonix) or from Switzerland (via the St Bernard tunnel). To the east, the region across the Swiss border is fairly isolated and accessible via long, winding roads which can be treacherous in bad weather. Driving can be equally difficult in the Dolomites, still further east, but the beautiful scenery more than makes up for it, helping to make this one of Italy's prime skiing destinations; major resorts include Cortina D'Ampezzo (Italy's most upmarket resort), Madonna di Campiglio and Selva/Sella Ronda. Skiing is also possible in Central Italy, in resorts such as Abetone (Tuscany), Campo Imperatore (Abruzzo), and in several other places in Abruzzo, down to Mount Etna in Sicily.

Horse-riding: The biennial *Palio* bareback horse race in Siena, held on July 2 and August 16, draws thousands of spectators and has been a special event since the 14th century. One of Rome's most prestigious events is its international horse show held in May. There is also flat racing in February at the Capanelle track. Each of the three seasons lasts two months, the second starting in May and the third in September. Trotting races take place at the *Villa Gloria* track in February, June to November.

Cultural holidays: Italian **language** and **art** courses are available throughout Italy. Language courses are often complemented by subjects such as **cooking** or **architecture**. Well-known institutions offering a range of art courses include the *Palazzo Spinelli* and *Università Internazionale dell'Arte* in Florence; the *Accademia Italia* in Rome; the *Centro Internazionale degli Studi per l'Insegnamento del Mosaico* in Ravenna for **mosaic making**; and, for **music** courses, the *Accademia Chigiana* in Siena. Further information can be obtained from the Italian Cultural Institute in London (tel: (020) 7235 1461; fax: (020) 7235 4618; e-mail: ici@italcultur.org.uk; website: www.italcultur.org.uk) *or* the Italian State Tourist Board (see *Contact Addresses* section).

Other: There are first-class **golf** courses all over Italy, from Lombardy and Trentino in the north, through Tuscany and Lazio, down to Calabria and Sardinia where the golf season is very long, owing to the mild climate.

Italy's most popular spectator sport is **football** (the national team won the *World Cup* in 1934, 1938 and 1982, and hosted the 1990 event, in which they finished third). The *Giro d'Italia* is an internationally renowned **cycling** race through Italy, attracting the world's top cyclists. **Motor-racing** is held at the Monza autodrome near Milan (Lombardy). **Bocce bowling** is as traditional in Italy as it is in France, especially in small villages where it is played on Sunday after High Mass.

Social Profile

FOOD & DRINK: Table service is most common in restaurants and bars. There are no licensing laws.

Pasta plays a substantial part in Italian recipes, but nearly all regions have developed their own special dishes. Examples of dishes from each region are listed below. Italy has over 20 major wine regions, from Valle d'Aosta on the French border to Sardinia and Sicily in the south.

Wines are named after grape varieties or after their village or area of origin. The most widespread is the *Chianti* group of vineyards, governed by the Chianti Classico quality controls (denoted by a black cockerel on the neck of each bottle). The Chianti area is the only area in Italy with such quality controls. *Denominazione di origine controllata* wines come from officially recognised wine-growing areas (similar to *Appellation Contrôlée* in France), while wines designated *Denominazione controllata e garantita* are wines of fine quality. Vermouths from Piemonte vary from dry and light pink to dark-coloured and sweet. Aperitifs such as *Campari* and *Punt e Mes* are excellent appetisers, while Italian liqueurs include *Amaretto*, *Galliano*, *Sambuca* and *Strega*. Examples of wine from each region are listed below.

Rome: Food: *abbacchio* (suckling lamb in white wine flavoured with rosemary), *cannelloni* (pasta stuffed with meat, calves' brains, spinach, egg and cheese), *broccoli romani* (broccoli in white wine), *salsa romana* (sweet-sour brown sauce with raisins, chestnut and lentil purée served with game) and *gnocchi alla romana* (semolina dumplings). Of Rome's cheeses, the best include *mozzarella*, *caciotta romana* (semi-hard, sweet sheep cheese), *pecorino* (hard, sharp sheep's milk cheese) and *gorgonzola*. **Wines:** *Albano*, *Frascati*, *Grottaferrata*, *Marino*, *Montefiascone* and *Velletri* (whites); *Cesanese*, *Marino* and *Piglio* (reds).

Piemonte: Food: *Bagna caoda* (a traditional anchovy soup, served with vegetables), *fritto misto piemontese* (fried meat, vegetables and fruit), *bonet* (a chocolate cake made with coffee and local biscuits).

Valle d'Aosta: Food: *Fonduta* (a hot dip with Fontina cheese, milk and egg yolks sprinkled with truffles and white pepper), *lepre piemontese* (hare cooked in Barbera wine and sprinkled with herbs and bitter chocolate), *zabaglione* (hot dessert with beaten egg and Marsala wine). **Wines:** *Barolo*, *Barbera*, *Barbaresco*, *Gattinara* and *Grignolino*.

Lombardy: Food: *Risotto alla milanese* (rice with saffron and white wine), *zuppa pavese* (tasty clear soup with poached eggs), *minestrone* (thick soup with chopped vegetables), *osso buco* (shin of veal cooked in tomato sauce served with rice), *panettone* (Christmas cake with sultanas and candied fruit). **Wines:** *Grumello*, *Inferno*, *Sassella* and *Valtellina*.

Trentino and Alto Adige: Food: Some excellent sausages and hams come from these regions. **Wines:** *Lago di Caldaro* and *Santa Maddalena*.

Veneto: Food: *Fegato alla veneziana* (calves' liver thinly sliced and cooked in butter with onions), *baccalà alla vicentina* (salt cod simmered in milk), *radicchio rosso di treviso* (wild red chicory with a bitter taste). **Wines:** *Bardolino*, *Soave* and *Valpolicella*.

Friuli-Venezia Giulia: Food: *Pasta e fagioli* (pasta and beans), *prosciutto di San Daniele* (raw ham). **Wines:** *Malvasia*, *Pinot Bianco*, *Pinot Grigio* and *Tokai* (whites); *Cabernet*, *Merlot* and *Pinot Nero* (reds).

Liguria: Food: *Pesto* (sauce made of basil, garlic, pine nuts and pecorino cheese with pasta), *cima genovese* (cold veal stuffed with calves' brains, onions and herbs), *pandolce* (sweet cake with orange flavour). **Wine:** *Sciacchettra*.

Emilia-Romagna: Food: *Parmigiano* (parmesan cheese), *prosciutto di Parma* (Parma ham), *pasta con salsa bolognese* (sauce of meat, cheese and tomato served with pasta), *vitello alla bolognese* (veal cutlet cooked with Parma ham and cheese), *cotechino e zampone* (pigs' trotters stuffed with pork and sausages). **Wines:** *Albana*, *Lambrusco*, *Sangiovese* and *Trebbiano*.

Tuscany: Food: *Bistecca alla fiorentina* (thick T-bone steak grilled over charcoal, sprinkled with freshly ground black pepper and olive oil), *minestrone alla fiorentina* (tasty vegetable soup with slices of country bread), *pappardelle alla lepre* (pasta with hare sauce), *tortina di carciofi* (baked artichoke pie), *cinghiale di maremma* (wild boar from Maremma region near Grosseto) and dishes of ham, sausages and steaks. Sweets include *panforte di Siena* (confection of honey, candied fruits, almonds and cloves), *castagnaccio* (chestnut cake with nuts and sultanas) and *ricciarelli* (delicate biscuit of honey and almonds from Siena). **Wines:** *Aleatico*, *Brunello di Montalcino*, *Chianti* and *Vernaccia*.

Marche: Food: *Brodetto* (a thick soup made from many varieties of fish, similar to chowder), *pasticciata* (pasta baked in oven, a method preferred by Marches). **Wine:** *Verdicchio*.

Abruzzo-Molise: Food: The favourite pasta in this region is known as *maccheroni alla chitarra* because it is cut in thin strips. Lamb is a favourite ingredient in many dishes. Desserts include *parrozzo* (rich chocolate cake) and *zeppole* (sweetened pasta). **Wines:** *Cerasolo di Abruzzo, Montepulciano d'Abruzzo* (red), *Trebbiano d'Abruzzo* (dry white). The district is also home of a strong liqueur known as *Centerbe*.

Umbria: Food: Extra virgin olive oil, black and white truffles, spaghetti, *porchetta alla perugina* (suckling pig), *carne ai capperi e acciughe* (veal with caper and herb sauce) and good-quality local sausages, salami and prosciutto famous throughout Italy. Local ingredients used in Umbrian cooking include pork and beef, cheeses, lentils from the Valerina, fish from Lake Trasimeno and the River Nera, mushrooms and potatoes from Colfiorito. **Wine:** *Orvieto* (white, sweet or dry) and numerous red and white wines (including *Rubesco* from Torgiano and wines from Montefalco and Sagrantino).

Campania: Food: *Pizza* (the culinary pride of Campania) served in a great variety of recipes, *bistecca alla pizzaiola* (steak with sauce made from tomatoes, garlic and oregano), *sfogliatelle* (sweet ricotta cheese turnovers) and *mozzarella* cheese (originally made with buffalo milk). **Wines:** These come from the islands of Capri and Ischia.

Puglia: Food: *Coniglio ai capperi* (rabbit cooked with capers) and *ostriche* (fresh oysters baked with bread crumbs). **Wines:** *Aleatico di Puglia, Sansevero, Santo Stefano*.

Calabria and Basilicata: Food: *Sagne chine* (lasagne with artichoke and meat balls), *zuppa di cipolle* (onion soup with Italian brandy), *sarde* (fresh sardines with olive oil and oregano), *alici al limone* (fresh anchovies baked with lemon juice), *melanzane Sott'Olio* (pickled aubergines), *mostaccioli* (chocolate biscuits) or *cannariculi* (fried honey biscuits). **Wines:** *Agliatico* and *Cirò*.

Sicily: Food: *Pesce spada* (swordfish stuffed with brandy, mozzarella and herbs, grilled on charcoal), *pasta con le sarde* (pasta with fresh sardines), *caponata* (rich dish of olives, anchovies and aubergines), *pizza siciliana* (pizza with olives and capers) and *triglie alla siciliana* (grilled mullet with orange peel and white wine). Excellent sweets are *cassata* (ice cream of various flavours with candied fruit and bitter chocolate) and *frutti di marturana* (marzipan fruits). **Wines:** *Corvo di Salaparuta* (both red and white, a highly aromatic wine ideal for fish), *Marsala* and *Regaleali*.

Sardinia: Food: The coastline offers a wide selection of fish, including lobster which is served in soup, stews and grills. Main dishes include *burrida* (fish stew with dogfish and skate) and *calamaretti alla sarda* (stuffed baby squid). **Wines:** *Cannonau, Malvasia, Oliena, Piani* and *Vernaccia*.

NIGHTLIFE: Nightclubs, discos, restaurants and bars with dancing can be found in most major towns and tourist resorts. In the capital, English-language films can be found at the Pasquine Cinema, *Vicolo della Paglia*, just off Santa Maria in Trastevere. Restaurants and cafes throughout Italy will invariably have tables outside: in Rome, the *Massimo D'Azeglio* is a hotel restaurant famous for its classic food. Open-air concerts in summer are organised by the *Academy of St Cecilia* and the *Opera House*, while there is open-air theatre at the *Baths of Caracalla*. Jazz, rock, folk and country music can all be heard at various venues.

SHOPPING: Many Italian products are world-famous for their style and quality. Care should be taken when buying antiques since Italy is renowned for skilled imitators. Prices are generally fixed and bargaining is not general practice, although a discount may be given on a large purchase. Florence, Milan and Rome are famous as important fashion centres, but smaller towns also offer good scope for shopping. It is advisable to avoid hawkers or sellers on the beaches. Some places are known for particular products, eg Carrara (Tuscany) for marble, Como (Lombardy) for silk, Deruta (Umbria) and Faenza (Emilia-Romagna) for pottery, Empoli (Tuscany) for the production of bottles and glasses in green glass and Prato (Tuscany) for textiles. Alghero (Sardinia) and Torre Annunziata (Campania) are centres for handicraft products in coral, and in several parts of Sardinia, business cards and writing paper made of cork are produced. Cremona (Lombardy) is famous for its handmade violins. Castelfidardo (Marche) is famous for its accordion factories, and for its production of guitars and organs. Two small towns concentrate on producing their speciality: Valenza (Piedmont), which has a large number of goldsmith artisans, and Sulmona (Abruzzo), which produces 'confetti', sugar-coated almonds used all over Italy for wedding celebrations. Vietri sul Mare (Campania) is one of the most important centres of ceramic paving-tiles, and Ravenna (Emilia-Romagna) is famous for mosaics. Main shopping areas are listed below.

ROME: offers a wide choice of shops and markets. Every shop in the fashionable Via Condotti–Via Sistina area offers a choice of styles, colours and designs rarely matched, but at very high prices. Equally expensive are shops along Via Vittorio Veneto, a street famous for its outdoor cafes. Old books and prints can be bought from bookstalls of Piazza Borghese. Rome's flea market is at Porta Portese in Trastevere on Sunday mornings, selling everything from secondhand shoes to 'genuine antiques'.

MILAN: the city's industrial wealth is reflected in the chic, elegant shops of Via Montenapoleone. Prices tend to be higher than in other major cities.

VENICE: is still famous for its glassware and there is a great deal of both good and bad glass; that made on the island of Murano, where there are also art dealers and skilful goldsmiths, has a reputation for quality. Venetian lace is also exquisite and expensive; however, most of the lace sold is no longer made locally (only lace made on the island of Burano may properly be called Venetian lace).

FLORENCE: boasts some of the finest goldsmiths, selling from shops largely concentrated along both sides of the Ponte Vecchio bridge. Florentine jewellery has a particular quality of satin finish called *satinato*. Much filigree jewellery can also be found. Cameos are another speciality of Florence, carved from exotic shells.

SOUTHERN ITALY: in the south, there are still families handmaking the same local products as their ancestors: pottery and carpets in each region; filigree jewellery and products of wrought iron and brass in Abruzzo; products in wood in Calabria; corals and cameos in Campania; a variety of textiles, including tablecloths, in Sicily and Sardinia. In Cagliari, it is possible to find artistic copies of bronze statuettes from the Nuraghe period of the Sardinian Bronze Age. In the larger towns, such as Bari, Cagliari, Calabria, Naples, Palermo and Reggio, there are elegant shops with a whole range of Italian products. Many smaller towns have outdoor markets, but souvenirs sold there are sometimes of very low quality, probably mass-produced elsewhere.

SHOPPING HOURS: Mon-Sat 0830-1230 and 1530-1930, with some variations in northern Italy where the lunch break is shorter and the shops close earlier. Food shops are often closed on Wednesday afternoons.

SPECIAL EVENTS: Traditional festivals are celebrated in most towns and villages in commemoration of local historical or religious events. For further details, contact ENIT, the Italian State Tourist Board (see *Contact Addresses*). The following is a selection of special events occurring in Italy in 2005:

Jan-Mar *Ivrea Carnival*. **Jan 6** *Epiphany Celebrations*, nationwide (particularly Piana degli Albanesi and Bordonaro). **Jan 23** *Viareggio Carnival* (famous for its puppets); *Ravel Evening*, Milan. **Jan 28-Feb 8** *Venice Carnival* (traditional masked balls and elaborate costumes). **Feb 15-24** *Carnival in Acireale*. **Feb** *Baroque Carnival*, Palermo; *Mandorlo in Fiore* (spring festival), Agrigento. **Mar 13** *Rome Marathon*. **Mar 20-26** *Holy Week*, Rome. **Apr 20** *Birth of Rome Celebrations*. **May 15** *Vogalonga* (boat race), Venice. **Jun** *Heineken Jamin Festival* (rock festival), Imola. **Jul** *Festino di Santa Rosalia* (parades, processions and fireworks), Palermo. **Aug-Sep** *San Rocco Music Festival* (Baroque music), Venice. **Sep** *International Urban Theatre Festival*, Rome. **Oct** *Autumn Festival*, Abbadia San Salvatore. **Dec** *Christmas Markets*, nationwide; *Feast of St Nicholas*, nationwide. **Dec 26-Feb 24** *Putignano Carnival*.

SOCIAL CONVENTIONS: The social structure is heavily influenced by the Roman Catholic church and, generally speaking, family ties are stronger than in most other countries in Western Europe. Normal social courtesies should be observed. Dress is casual in most places, though beachwear should be confined to the beach. Conservative clothes are expected when visiting religious buildings and smaller, traditional communities. Formal wear is usually indicated on invitations. Smoking is prohibited in some public buildings, transport and cinemas. Visitors are warned to take precautions against theft, particularly in the cities.

Tipping: Service charges and state taxes are included in all hotel bills. It is customary to give up to 10 per cent in addition if service has been particularly good.

Business Profile

ECONOMY: Traditionally agricultural, Italy industrialised rapidly after 1945, particularly in manufacturing and engineering, to the point where less than 5 per cent of the population is now engaged in agriculture. The majority of these live in the south of Italy, which is substantially poorer than the centre and north of the country. The principal crops are sugar beet, wheat, maize, tomatoes and grapes (many are used for wine, of which Italy is a leading producer). As with most Western European economies, the tourism industry now enjoys a major position in the economy alongside other service industries such as financial services and communications media. Italy continues to rely heavily on the export of manufactured goods, particularly of industrial machinery, vehicles, aircraft, chemicals, electronics, textiles and clothing. Its particular strengths are in advanced manufacturing techniques and systems, high-quality design and precision engineering.

Italy's historic trade performance has been all the more impressive given the dearth of raw materials, in particular the fact that all of the country's oil and many of its raw materials must be imported.

The economy has been sluggish since the turn of the millennium with growth in 2004 less than 1 per cent. Inflation is just under 3 per cent; unemployment has fallen slightly to just under 9 per cent. In Europe, despite some doubts about the size of its budget deficit, Italy was among the founding members of the Euro-zone in 1999. The current Berlusconi government is trying to implement a programme of tax cuts and labour reform which are intended to boost economic performance but it has been hamstrung by political difficulties. The bulk of Italy's trade is conducted with its EU partners, but it also has important trade links with the USA, Canada, Russian Federation, parts of Latin America, Saudi Arabia and Libya.

BUSINESS: A knowledge of Italian is a distinct advantage. Prior appointments are essential. Visitors should remember that ministries and most public offices close at 1345 and, except by special appointment, it is not possible to see officials in the afternoon. Genoa, Milan and Turin form the industrial triangle of Italy; Bologna, Florence, Padua, Rome, Verona and Vicenza also have important business centres. In all the above cities, major trade fairs take place throughout the year. See the relevant cities in the *Resorts & Excursions* section. **Office hours:** Mon-Fri 0900-1700.

COMMERCIAL INFORMATION: The following organisation can offer advice: Unione Italiana delle Camere di Commercio, Industria, Artigianato e Agricoltura (Italian Union of Chambers of Commerce, Industry, Crafts and Agriculture), Piazza Sallustio 21, 00187 Rome (tel: (06) 47041; fax: (06) 470 4240; e-mail: segreteria.generale@unioncamere.it; website: www.unioncamere.it).

CONFERENCES/CONVENTIONS: There are many hotels with facilities. Further information can be obtained from Italian State Tourist Board (see *Contact Addresses* section).

Climate

Summer is hot, especially in the south. Spring and autumn are mild with fine, sunny weather. Winter in the south is much drier and warmer than in northern and central areas. Mountain regions are colder with heavy winter snowfalls.

Required clothing: Lightweight cottons and linens are worn during the summer, except in the mountains. Light- to mediumweights are worn in the south during winter, while warmer clothes are worn elsewhere. Alpine wear is advised for winter mountain resorts.

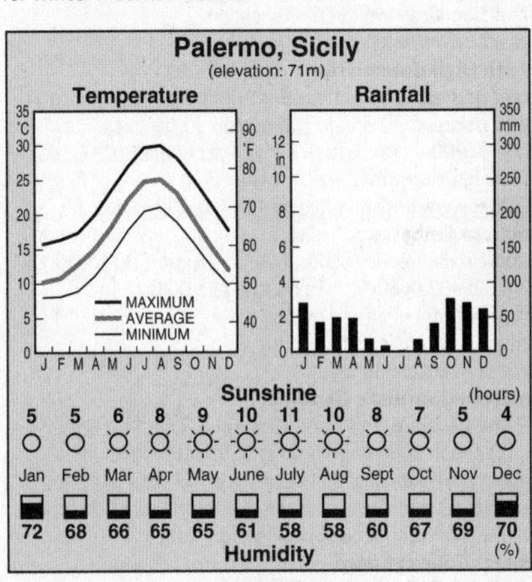

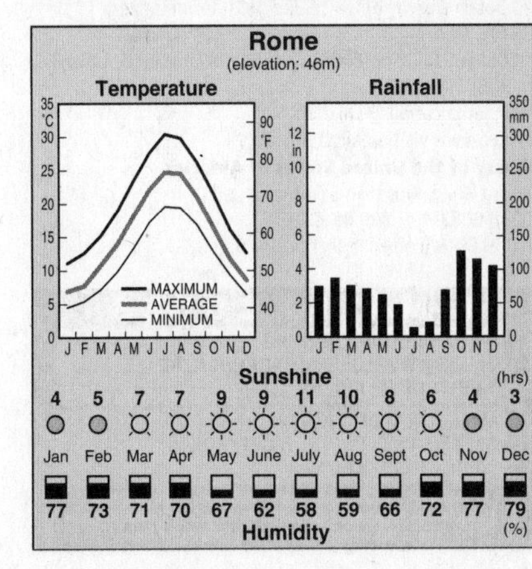

Jamaica

LATEST TRAVEL ADVICE CONTACTS

British Foreign and Commonwealth Office
Tel: (0870) 606 0290 Website: www.fco.gov.uk

US Department of State
Website: http://travel.state.gov/travel

Canadian Department of Foreign Affairs and Int'l Trade
Tel: (1 800) 267 8376 Website: www.dfait-maeci.gc.ca

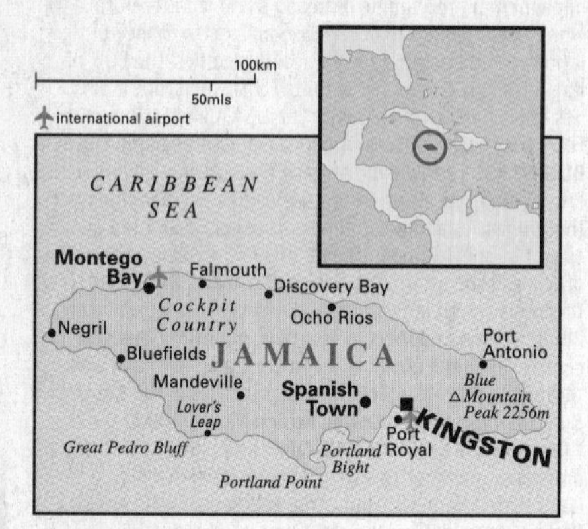

Location: Caribbean.

Country dialling code: 1 876.

Jamaica Tourist Board (JTB)
64 Knutsford Boulevard, Kingston 5, Jamaica
Tel: 929 9200-19. Fax: 929 9375.
E-mail: info@visitjamaica.com
Website: www.visitjamaica.com

Jamaica High Commission
1-2 Prince Consort Road, London SW7 2BZ, UK
Tel: (020) 7823 9911. Fax: (020) 7589 5154.
E-mail: jamhigh@jhcuk.com
Website: www.jhcuk.com
Opening hours: Mon-Thurs 0900-1700, Fri 0900-1600 (High Commission); Mon-Fri 1000-1530 (Consulate).

Jamaica Tourist Board
Address as above.
Tel: (020) 7224 0505. Fax: (020) 7224 0551.
E-mail: jamaicatravel@btconnect.com
Website: www.visitjamaica.com

British High Commission
Street address: 28 Trafalgar Road, Kingston 10, Jamaica
Postal address: PO Box 575, Kingston 10, Jamaica
Tel: 510 0700. Fax: 510 0738 (visa section) *or* 0737.
E-mail: bhckingston@mail.infochan.com
Website: www.britishhighcommission.gov.uk/jamaica

Jamaican Embassy
1520 New Hampshire Avenue, NW, Washington, DC 20036, USA
Tel: (202) 452 0660-9. Fax: (202) 452 0081.
E-mail: info@emjamusa.org *or* contactus@jamaicaembassy.org
Website: www.emjamusa.org

Jamaican Consulate General
767 Third Avenue, 2nd Floor, New York, NY 10017, USA
Tel: (212) 935 9000. Fax: (212) 935 7507.
E-mail: registry@congenjamaica-ny.org (general enquiries) *or* passport@congenjamaica-ny.org (passport/visa information).
Website: www.congenjamaica-ny.org

Jamaica Tourist Board
1320 South Dixie Highway, Suite 1101, Coral Gables, FL 33146, USA
Tel: (305) 665 0557 *or* (800) 233 4582 (toll-free in the US only).
Fax: (305) 666 7239.
E-mail: jamaicatrv1@aol.com
Website: www.visitjamaica.com

Embassy of the United States of America
2 Oxford Road, Kingston 5, Jamaica
Tel: 935 6053/4 *or* 929 4850-9.
Fax: 935 6019 (consular section) *or* 929 3637.
E-mail: opakgn@state.gov
Website: http://kingston.usembassy.gov

Jamaica High Commission
275 Slater Street, Suite 800, Ottawa, Ontario K1P 5H9, Canada
Tel: (613) 233 9311. Fax: (613) 233 0611.
E-mail: hc@jhcottawa.ca *or* info@jhcottawa.ca
Website: www.jhcottawa.ca
Consulates in: Edmonton, Toronto and Winnipeg.

Jamaica Tourist Board
303 Eglington Avenue East, Suite 200, Toronto, Ontario M4P 1L3, Canada
Tel: (416) 482 7850 *or* (800) 465 2624 (toll-free in Canada only).
Fax: (416) 482 1730.
E-mail: jtb@jtbcanada.com
Website: www.visitjamaica.com

Canadian High Commission
Street address: 3 West Kings House, Waterloo Road Entrance, Kingston 10, Jamaica
Postal address: PO Box 1500, Kingston 10, Jamaica
Tel: 926 1500. Fax: 511 3494 *or* 511 3480 (consular section).
E-mail: kngtn@dfait-maeci.gc.ca
Website: www.dfait-maeci.gc.ca/jamaica

TIMATIC CODES

Health
AMADEUS: **TI-DFT/KIN/HE**
GALILEO/WORLDSPAN: **TI-DFT/KIN/HE**
SABRE: **TIDFT/KIN/HE**

Visa
AMADEUS: **TI-DFT/KIN/VI**
GALILEO/WORLDSPAN: **TI-DFT/KIN/VI**
SABRE: **TIDFT/KIN/VI**

To access TIMATIC country information on Health and Visa regulations through the Computer Reservations System (CRS), type in the appropriate command line listed above.

General Information

AREA: 10,991 sq km (4244 sq miles).
POPULATION: 2,624,700 (2002).
POPULATION DENSITY: 238.8 per sq km (2002).

Credit: © Jamaica Tourist Board

CAPITAL: Kingston. **Population**: 697,000 (1994).
GEOGRAPHY: Jamaica is the third-largest island in the West Indies and is a narrow outcrop of a submerged mountain range. The island is crossed by a range of mountains reaching 2256m (7402ft) at the Blue Mountain Peak in the east, and descending towards the west with a series of spurs and forested gullies running north and south. Most of the best beaches are on the north and west coasts. The island's luxuriant tropical and subtropical vegetation is probably unsurpassed anywhere in the Caribbean.
GOVERNMENT: Constitutional monarchy. Gained independence from the UK in 1962. **Head of State**: HM Queen Elizabeth II, represented locally by Governor General Howard Cooke since 1991. **Head of Government**: Prime Minister Percival J Patterson since 1992.
LANGUAGE: The official language is English. Local *patois* is also spoken.
RELIGION: Protestant majority (Anglican, Baptist, Church of God and Methodist) with Roman Catholic, Jewish, Muslim, Hindu and Bahai communities. Rastafarianism, a religion based on belief in the divinity of the late Emperor of Ethiopia, Haile Selassie (Ras Tafari), is also widely practised.
TIME: GMT - 6.
ELECTRICITY: 110 volts AC, 60Hz, single phase. American two-pin plugs are standard, but many hotels offer, in addition, 220 volts AC, 50Hz, single phase, from three-pin sockets.
COMMUNICATIONS: Telephone: Full IDD is available. Country code: 1 876. There are no area codes. Outgoing international code: 011. **Mobile telephone:** As of 2003, GSM 1900 network. TDMA network, non-GSM compatible. The networks are *Digicel* (website: www.digiceljamaica.com) and *Cable & Wireless Jamaica LTD*. **Fax:** This service is available daily from 0700-1000 at the *Cable & Wireless* office in Kingston. Widely available in most hotels and offices. **Internet:** There are several free Internet kiosks at shopping centres in Kingston. Internet cafes exist mainly in the Kingston area. Internet is also available in many hotels and parish libraries. ISPs include *Cable & Wireless* (website: www.cwjamaica.com), *Infochannel Ltd* (website: www.infochan.com) and *Jamaica Online* (website: www.jol.com.jm). **Telegram:** Facilities are widely available. **Post:** Airmail to Europe takes up to four days. Post office hours: Mon-Fri 0830-1630. **Press:** Daily papers are *The Daily Gleaner, The Daily Star* and *The Jamaica Observer*. **Radio:** BBC World Service (website: www.bbc.co.uk/worldservice) and Voice of America (website: www.voa.gov) can be received. From time to time the frequencies change and the most up-to-date can be found online.

Passport/Visa

	Passport Required?	Visa Required?	Return Ticket Required?
Full British	Yes	No	Yes
Australian	Yes	No	Yes
Canadian	Yes	No	Yes
USA	No/1	No	Yes
Other EU	Yes	No/2	Yes
Japanese	Yes	No	Yes

Note: *Regulations and requirements may be subject to change at short notice, and you are advised to contact the appropriate diplomatic or consular authority before finalising travel arrangements. Details of these may be found at the head of this country's entry. Any numbers in the chart refer to the footnotes below.*

Restricted entry: Jamaica does not recognise passports issued by the Palestinian Government.
PASSPORTS: Passport valid for at least six months required by all except the following:
(a) **1.** nationals of the USA holding a certified copy of a birth certificate and photo identification (eg driver's licence or student ID).
VISAS: Required by all except the following:
(a) nationals of countries referred to in the chart above, except **2.** nationals of Czech Republic, Estonia, Hungary, Latvia, Lithuania, Poland, Slovak Republic and Slovenia who can obtain their visas on arrival;
(b) nationals of Commonwealth countries, except nationals of Nigeria, Pakistan and Sri Lanka who *do* need visas;
(c) nationals of Argentina, Brazil, Chile, Costa Rica, Ecuador, Iceland, Israel, Korea (Rep), Liechtenstein, Mexico, Norway, San Marino, Surinam, Switzerland, Turkey, Uruguay, Venezuela and Zimbabwe for stays not exceeding 90 days.
Note: (a) All of the above *must* have evidence of sufficient funds and a return or onward-bound ticket for their next destination. (b) Except for persons in certain categories, a Work Permit is required for a business visit. The Consulate (or Consular section at Embassy or High Commission) can advise. (c) Nationals of the following countries can obtain a visa on arrival, provided holding valid onward or return tickets and evidence of sufficient funds: Albania, Andorra, Bosnia & Herzegovina, Bulgaria, CIS, Croatia, Macedonia (Former Yugoslav Republic of), Monaco, Romania, Serbia & Montenegro and Taiwan. These visas cost US$20.
Types of visa and cost: *Entry* and *Transit*: £25.
Application to: Consulate (or Consular section at Embassy or High Commission); see *Contact Addresses* section.
Application requirements: (a) One passport-size photo. (b) Valid passport. (c) Completed application form. (d) Fee, payable in cash or postal orders only. (e) For postal applications, £5 for return postage. (f) Travel itinerary. *Business*: (a)-(f) and, (g) Letter from company.
Working days required: 48 hours, but longer in cases where applications are referred to Immigration Authorities in Kingston.
Temporary residence: Enquire at High Commission.

Money

Currency: Jamaican Dollar (J$) = 100 cents. Notes are in denominations of J$1000, 500, 100 and 50. Coins are in denominations of J$20, 10, 5, 2 and 1, and 25 and 10 cents.
Currency exchange: Money can be exchanged at the airport as well as at banks, hotels and bureaux de change. Receipts must be retained, as changing money on the black market is illegal. There are ATMs all over the island.
Credit & debit cards: American Express, Diners Club, MasterCard and Visa are all widely accepted. Check with your credit or debit card company for details of merchant acceptability and other services which may be available.
Travellers cheques: To avoid additional exchange rate charges, travellers are advised to take travellers cheques in US Dollars.
Currency restrictions: The import and export of local currency is prohibited; that of foreign currency is unrestricted, subject to declaration.
Exchange rate indicators: The following figures are included as a guide to the movements of the Jamaican Dollar against Sterling and the US Dollar:

Date	Feb '04	May '04	Aug '04	Nov '04
£1.00=	109.47	106.99	112.47	116.12
$1.00=	60.14	59.90	61.05	61.32

Banking hours: Mon-Thurs 0900-1400, Fri 0900-1200 and 1430-1700.

Duty Free

The following goods may be imported into Jamaica without incurring customs duty:
200 cigarettes or 50 cigars or 225g of tobacco; 1l of spirits (excluding rum) and 1l of wine and 1l of other alcoholic beverages (for passengers aged over 18 years); 150g of

perfume; personal and household effects up to a value of J$500.
Prohibited items: Fur-bearing goatskin products (unless properly shaven, cured and cleaned); birds imported from the USA unless accompanied by the required health certificate.

Public Holidays

2005: Jan 1 New Year's Day. **Feb 9** Ash Wednesday. **Mar 25** Good Friday. **Mar 28** Easter Monday. **May 23** Labour Day. **Aug 1** Emancipation Day. **Aug 6** Independence Day. **Oct 17** National Heroes' Day. **Dec 25-26** Christmas.
2006: Jan 1 New Year's Day. **Feb 9** Ash Wednesday. **Apr 14** Good Friday. **Apr 17** Easter Monday. **May 22** Labour Day. **Aug 1** Emancipation Day. **Aug 6** Independence Day. **Oct 16** National Heroes' Day. **Dec 25-26** Christmas.

Health

	Special Precautions?	Certificate Required?
Yellow Fever	No	1
Cholera	No	No
Typhoid & Polio	No	N/A
Malaria	No	N/A

Note: Regulations and requirements may be subject to change at short notice, and you are advised to contact your doctor well in advance of your intended date of departure. Any numbers in the chart refer to the footnotes below.

1: A yellow fever vaccination certificate is required from travellers over one year of age coming from infected areas.
Food & drink: Mains water is normally chlorinated and, whilst relatively safe, may cause mild abdominal upsets. Bottled water is available. Milk is pasteurised and dairy products are safe for consumption. Local meat, poultry, seafood, fruit and vegetables are generally considered safe to eat.
Other risks: *Hepatitis A* occurs. There is a high prevalence of HIV/AIDS and precautions should be undertaken to avoid exposure.
Health care: Health insurance is recommended, since medical treatment can be expensive. There are 16 public and six private hospitals. Standards vary hugely.

Travel - International

Note: Most visits to Jamaica are trouble-free, but there are high levels of crime, particularly in the Kingston area and tourists should avoid certain routes.
AIR: Jamaica's national airline is *Air Jamaica (JM)* (website: www.airjamaica.com). *British Airways* operates three flights a week non-stop from London to Kingston. Other airlines serving Jamaica include *Air Canada, American Airlines, BWIA* and *Continental Airlines.*
Approximate flight times: From Kingston or Montego Bay to *London* is 10 hours (direct flight), to *Los Angeles* is six hours 30 minutes and to *New York* is four hours 20 minutes.
International airports: *Norman Manley International (KIN)* (Kingston) is 18km (11 miles) southeast of the city. Coach, bus and taxis depart to the city (travel time – 30 to 60 minutes). Airport facilities include banks/bureaux de change, bars, restaurants, shops and duty free facilites, and car hire (including *Avis, Budget* and *Hertz*).
Montego Bay (MBJ) (International) is 3km (2 miles) north of the city. Duty free facilities are available. *Air Jamaica Express* runs shuttle services between the airports.
Departure tax: None.
SEA: Both Montego Bay and Ocho Rios are ports of call for the following cruise lines: *Carnival Cruise, Celebrity, Costa Cruise Line, Holland America, P&O Cruises, Princess Cruises* and *Royal Caribbean.* Other passenger/freight lines (Geest) sail from North, South and Central American ports. *Lauro Lines* sails to Kingston from the Mediterranean.

Travel - Internal

AIR: The new *Air Jamaica Express* (formerly *Trans-Jamaica Airlines*) runs services to and from Kingston, Montego Bay, Negril, Ocho Rios and Port Antonio. During the winter season, there are frequent daily flights. For more information, contact the airline (tel: 922 4661 or (888) 359 2475; toll-free in North America and the Caribbean).
SEA: There are a number of local operators running yacht tours around the island, as well as cruises. Boats and yachts can also be hired on a daily or weekly basis. Contact the Jamaica Tourist Board for details (see *Contact Addresses* section).
RAIL: Since 1994, the service has been suspended with no immediate plans to resume a daily scheduled service.
ROAD: There is a 17,000km- (11,000mile-) road network, one-third tarred. Traffic in Jamaica drives on the left. Speed limits are 30mph (48kph) in towns and 50mph (80kph) on highways. **Bus**: Reliable service in Kingston and Montego Bay; less reliable for trans-island travel. Coach and minibus tours are bookable at most hotels. *JUTA* (tel: 952 0813; fax 952 5355) is the main provider of scheduled and unscheduled bus/minibus and vehicle charter services. **Taxi**: These have red plates marked PPV (Public Passenger Vehicle). They charge fixed rates, and it is best to check standard charges prior to embarkation. A 10 per cent tip is usual. It is recommended that only taxis authorised by the Jamaica Union of Travellers Association and ordered from hotels (unshared) should be used. **Car hire**: Most major towns, as well as airports, have hire facilities, both local and international. Hire can also be arranged via hotels. Drivers must be aged 25 or over. There is a general consumption tax of 15 per cent on all car hire transactions.
Documentation: A full UK driving licence is valid for up to six months.
URBAN: Most transport in the capital is now by private minibus.
TRAVEL TIMES: The following chart gives approximate travel times (in hours and minutes) from **Montego Bay** to other major cities/towns in Jamaica.

	Air	Road	Rail
Kingston	0.30	3.00	4.00
Negril	0.20	1.30	-
Ocho Rios	0.30	2.00	-
Port Antonio	0.40	4.30	-

Accommodation

HOTELS: There are over 144 hotels and guest houses throughout the island; all are subject to 15 per cent general consumption tax. Around 90 per cent of all hotels belong to the Jamaica Hotel & Tourist Association, 2 Ardenne Road, Kingston 10 (tel: 926 3635 *or* 920 3482; fax: 929 1054; e-mail: info@jhta.org; website: www.jhta.org). There is an annual 'Spring Break' over March/April, during which students holidaying in Jamaica are offered discount rates at selected hotels. Contact the Jamaica Tourist Board for details (see *Contact Addresses* section). **Grading**: Hotels are government-controlled in four categories: **A**, **B**, **C** and **D**. The categories are based on rates charged. Many of the hotels offer accommodation according to one of a number of 'Plans' widely used in the Caribbean; these include Modified American Plan (MAP), which consists of room, breakfast and dinner, and European Plan (EP), which consists of room only.
SELF-CATERING: There are over 837 cottages for rent on the island. Information is available from the Jamaica Tourist Board (see *Contact Addresses* section). The properties range from small apartments to houses with several bedrooms. Some tour operators can arrange villa accommodation including car hire and tours, as well as travel to and from the villa. Information is also available from the Jamaican Association of Villas & Apartments Ltd (JAVA), PO Box 298, 11A Pineapple Place, Ocho Rios, St Ann (tel: 974 2508 or 974 2763; e-mail: java-jam-villas@cwjamaica.com; website: www.villasinjamaica.com).
CAMPING/CARAVANNING: The island has many campsites, including the well-known Strawberry Fields, which offers all types of facilities, including the hiring of tents and ancillary equipment.

Resorts & Excursions

Jamaica is a tropical island of lush green vegetation, waterfalls and dazzling white beaches. Columbus was in the habit of declaring that each new island he chanced upon was more beautiful than the last, but he seems to have maintained a lifelong enthusiasm for the beauty of Jamaica, despite having been marooned there for a year on his last voyage. One of the larger islands of the Caribbean, it offers excellent tourist facilities and superb beaches and scenery. For the purpose of this guide, the main resorts in Jamaica have been divided into the following sections: Kingston and the South (including Mandeville and Spanish Town); Montego Bay (including the northwest coast resort of Negril); and the North Coast Resorts (including Falmouth, Ocho Rios and Port Antonio).

KINGSTON AND THE SOUTH

KINGSTON: Kingston is Jamaica's capital city and cultural centre. With the largest natural harbour in the Caribbean (and seventh-largest in the world), Kingston is also an industrial centre where Georgian architecture mixes with modern office blocks while, on the outskirts, spreading suburbs house the hundreds of thousands who increasingly work in the city. Although most tourists head for the beaches and resorts, Kingston has much to offer in the way of sightseeing.
The **National Gallery of Art** has a colourful display of modern art and is recommended. **Hope Botanical Gardens** contain a wide variety of trees and plants and are particularly famous for orchids. A band plays here on Sunday afternoons. There is a **Crafts Market** on King Street and the **Port Royal**, on top of the peninsula bordering **Kingston Harbour**, is a museum to the time when Port Royal (Jamaica's ancient capital city that was submerged under the sea after an earthquake in 1692) was known as the 'richest and wickedest city on earth' under the domination of Captain Morgan and his buccaneers. The **White Marl Arawak Museum** is also worth visiting; here visitors can see artefacts and relics of the ancient culture of the Arawak Indians. The grounds of the **University of the West Indies**, built on what was once a sugar plantation, are open to the public. **Caymanas Park** is a popular racetrack, where you can bet on the horses every Wednesday and Saturday and also during public holidays.
SPANISH TOWN: A short drive to the west of Kingston, Spanish Town is the former capital of Jamaica. The **Spanish Town Square** is said to be one of the finest examples of Georgian architecture in the Western hemisphere. The Spanish **Cathedral of St Jago de la Vega** is the oldest in the West Indies.
MANDEVILLE: Mandeville is set amid beautiful gardens and fruits, at the heart of Jamaica's citrus industry, 600m (2000ft) above sea level and the highest town on the island. Mandeville offers cool relief from the heat of the coast, and has a golf course, tennis and horse-riding facilities. The town is the centre of the bauxite industry, and is a good starting point for trips to the surrounding areas.
SOUTH COAST: On the south coast are **Milk River Spa**, a naturally radioactive mineral bath with waters at a temperature of 33°C (86°F); **Lover's Leap** in the **Santa Cruz Mountains**, a sheer 18m (60ft) cliff overhanging the sea; **Treasure Beach** and the resort of **Bluefields**.

MONTEGO BAY AND THE WEST

MONTEGO BAY: Montego Bay (or Mo'Bay, as it is more colloquially called) is the capital of Jamaican tourism and market town for a large part of western Jamaica. Dating back to 1492, Montego Bay is Jamaica's second-largest city and one of the most modern in the Caribbean. From Gloucester and Kent Avenues, there are superb views onto the clear Caribbean waters and the long reef protecting the bay. Most of the hotels are found on a strip of coastline about 2.4km (1.5miles) long. There are three main beaches: **Doctor's Cave Beach** (so named because it was once owned by a Dr McCatty and had a cave that has since eroded away) which has beautiful white sand, and where the exceptionally clear water is believed to be fed by mineral springs; **Walter Fletcher Beach**, nearest the centre and a short walk from the Upper Deck Hotel; and **Cornwall Beach**, which is a few yards from the local Tourist Board Office. A short way inland from the Bay is **Rose Hall**, a restored Great House on a sugar plantation.
Excursions: Rocklands Feeding Station is home to some of the most exotic birds in the world, such as the mango hummingbird, orange quit and the national bird of Jamaica, the Doctor Bird. Visitors are allowed to feed the birds at certain times of the day. Very popular is a motor coach ride through thick mountain forests into the interior, passing through banana and coconut plantations and **Ipswich Caves** (a series of deep limestone recesses) to the sugar estate of the famous **Appleton Rum Factory** and onwards to **Catadupa**, where shirts and dresses are made to measure.
NEGRIL: Negril is 80km (50 miles) west of Montego Bay and has a beach stretching for 11km (7 miles) which offers sailing, water-skiing, deep-sea fishing, scuba diving, parasailing and windsurfing. First coming to attention as an artists' centre, and later as a focus of 'alternative' culture in the 1960s, it is becoming increasingly popular as a holiday destination which seems likely to preserve much of its original character – indeed, the law requires all buildings to be of modest proportions. Along the street, entrepreneurial Jamaicans sell a variety of craft goods from the many shanty-like shops in Negril. There is also a hectic nightlife in the many clubs that have, over the years, proliferated along the beach. **Rick's Café**, located at **West Point** (which is as far west as Jamaica goes), is a favourite haunt both for Jamaicans and visitors and is famous as the place from which to observe the sun going down.

NORTH COAST RESORTS

FALMOUTH: Falmouth is a delightful harbour resort, 42km (26 miles) east of Montego Bay. From here, you can visit **Rafters Village** for rafting on the **Martha Brae**, and a fascinating crocodile farm called **Jamaica Swamp Safaris**. There is also a plantation mansion, **Greenwood Great House**, once owned by the Barrett Brownings. The **Church of St Paul** has Sunday services, where visitors can listen to the choir singing.
OCHO RIOS: Ocho Rios lies roughly 108km (67 miles) east of Montego Bay. The name is said to have come from the old Spanish word for *roaring river* or, in modern Spanish, *eight rivers*. Ocho Rios was once a sleepy fishing village,

and although there are now resort facilities, international hotels and restaurants offering a variety of cuisines, the town has kept something of the sleepy atmosphere of small-town Jamaica. One of the most stunning sights in Jamaica is **Dunn's River Falls**, a crystal water stairway which leads to the nearby botanical gardens. Ocho Rios is known as the garden-lover's paradise, and the **Shaw Park Botanical Gardens** exhibit the fascinating variety of the area's exotic flora, for which the town is celebrated. Not surprisingly, two of the most popular tours available are to working plantations at **Brimmer Hall** and **Prospect** where sugar, bananas and spices are still grown and harvested, using many of the traditional skills handed down through generations. Any sightseeing itinerary should include a drive along **Fern Gully**, a road running along an old river-bed that winds through a 6.5km (4 mile) valley of ferns. Another tour is the **Jamaica Night** on the **White River**, a canoe ride up the torchlit river to the sound of drums. Dinner and an open-air bar is available on the riverbank (Sunday evenings).

Excursions: Columbus Park, at **Discovery Bay**, commemorates Columbus' arrival in Jamaica with a museum and 24-hour open-air park exhibiting relics of Jamaican history. Other tours include **Runaway Bay**, which has fine beaches, excellent scuba diving and horse-riding; and the **Runaway Caves** nearby, which offer a boat ride 35m (120ft) below ground on a lake in the limestone **Green Grotto**.

PORT ANTONIO: Set on one of the Caribbean's most beautiful bays, Port Antonio is surrounded by the **Blue Mountains**. The town dates back to the 16th century, and sights include **Mitchell's Folly**, a two-storey mansion built by the American millionaire Dan Mitchell in 1905, and the ruins of the 60-room **Great House**. The surrounding sea is rich in game fish, such as kingfish, yellowtail, wahoo and bonito. Blue marlin, however, are the great prize and there is an annual *Blue Marlin Tournament* run alongside the *Jamaican International Fishing Tournament* in Port Antonio every autumn. Rafting is available on the **Rio Grande**, comprising two-hour trips on two passenger bamboo rafts, which begin high in the Blue Mountains at **Berrydale**, sail past plantations of bananas and sugar cane, and end up at **Margaret's Bay**. The scenic **Somerset Falls** nearby are a popular picnic spot. Beaches in the Port Antonio area include **San San** and **Boston** (where the Jamaican 'jerk pork' is found), while the **Blue Lagoon** is a salt-water cove offering fishing, swimming and water-skiing and is considered one of the finest coves in the Caribbean.

Sport & Activities

Watersports: Many hotels have **swimming** pools and beaches. The best beaches for bathing are mainly on the northern coast. **Surfing** is also best on the north coast, east of Port Antonio, where long lines of breakers roll into Boston Bay. Most beach hotels have sunfish, sailfish and/or windsurfing boards for hire. To charter larger boats, contact the Royal Jamaica Yacht Club. Facilities for **water-skiing** are offered at most beach hotels and at the Kingston Ski Club at Morgan's Harbour.

Diving: Jamaica has many attractions for divers, including close-to-shore wrecks, sponge forests, underwater caves and coral reefs. In some areas, visibility is exceptional, reaching 30.5m (100ft). Popular dive sites include the *Throne Room* near Negril, where it is possible to see corals, sponges, nurse sharks and cubera snapper; *Ricky's Reef*, with brightly coloured fish; and the wreck of the *Kathryn*. There are many professional dive operators on the island; contact the Tourist Board for a list of licensed operators. Shops are equipped for rentals and offer guided snorkel and scuba trips.

Fishing: Fresh- and sea-water fishing are popular. Mountain mullet, hognose mullet, drummer and small snook are caught in rivers. Deep-sea fishing charters can be arranged through hotels in main resorts. Spearfishing is permitted among the reefs. No licence is needed. Entry forms are available for the *Blue Marlin Tournament* held in Port Antonio during September.

Golf: Jamaica has developed some of the Caribbean's most beautiful and challenging golf courses. Montego Bay is the best area and it is not necessary to be resident at a hotel to play on its three courses. Other golf courses include *Caymanas Golf Course* (which hosts the *Jamaica Open* and *Pro-Am* every November) and *Constant Spring* near Kingston.

Other: For those keen on **mountain climbing** and **hiking**, the Blue Mountains, which reach above 2134m (7000ft), offer unspoilt scenery and a variety of flora and fauna. It is best to go hiking with a guide. Some stables for **horse-riding** are open all year, others run schedules during the winter season and most arrangements can be made through hotels. **Cricket** is the 'national obsession' and matches are played from January to August in Sabina Park, Kingston and other locations throughout the island. Probably the second most popular sport is **football**, which is played throughout the year. There are plenty of **tennis** courts, and most hotels without their own court have access to those nearby. **Polo** has a tradition going back over a century; matches are played all year round in Kingston. Matches at Kingston and at Drax Hall, near Ocho Rios, are played every week. **Horse races** are held at *Caymanas Race Track*, Kingston.

Social Profile

FOOD & DRINK: Jamaican food is full of fire, taking advantage of pungent spices and peppers. Jamaican dishes include 'rice and peas', a tasty dish with no peas at all but with kidney beans, white rice, coconut milk, scallions (spring onions) and coconut oil. Another dish is salt fish (dried cod) and *ackee* (the cooked fruit of the ackee tree), curried goat and rice (spicy and strong), Jamaican pepperpot soup (salt pork, salt beef, *okra* and Indian kale known as *callaloo*), chicken fricassé Jamaican-style (a rich chicken stew with carrots, scallions, yams, onions, tomatoes and peppers prepared in unrefined coconut oil) and roast suckling pig (a three-month-old piglet which is boned and stuffed with rice, peppers, diced yam and thyme mixed with shredded coconut and corn meal). *Patties* are the staple snack of Jamaica (pastries filled with ground beef and bread crumbs) and can be found everywhere, but vary in price and filling. Waiter service is usually available in catering establishments. Jamaican rum is world famous, especially *Gold Label* and *Appleton*. *Rumona* is a delicious rum cordial. *Red Stripe* beer is excellent, as is *Tia Maria* (a Blue Mountain coffee and chocolate liqueur). Fresh fruit juice is also recommended, as is Blue Mountain coffee, an excellent variety. Bars have table and/or counter service. There are no licensing hours and alcohol can be bought all day.

NIGHTLIFE: There is no shortage of night-time entertainment on the island that is the home of reggae music. Every town or village has some sort of nightlife, and there are regular street dances. Folkloric shows at larger resort hotels are held and steel bands often play. At least once a week, there is a torchlit, steel band show with limbo dancing and fire-eating demonstrations. Nightclubs feature jazz, soca, reggae and other music. For details of events, visitors should consult local newspapers. The Jamaica Tourist Board arranges 'Meet the People' evenings in various scenic locations throughout the island. Contact the Tourist Board in Kingston, Montego Bay, Ocho Rios or Port Antonio.

SHOPPING: Special purchases are locally-made items and duty free bargains. Crafts include hand-loomed fabrics, embroidery, silk screening, woodcarvings, oil paintings, woven straw items and sandalmaking. Custom-made rugs and reproductions of pewter and china from the 17th-century ruins of the ancient submerged city of Port Royal can be bought in the In-Craft workshop. At *Highgate Village* in the mountains, Quakers run a workshop specialising in wicker and wood furniture, floor mats and other tropical furnishings. Jamaican rum, the *Rumona* liqueur (the world's only rum-based liqueur, hard to find outside the island) and *Ian Sangsters Rum Cream* are unique purchases. Other local specialities are *Pepper Jellies*, jams and spices. There are shops offering facilities for 'in-bond' shopping, which allows visitors to purchase a range of international goods free of tax or duty at very competitive prices. These goods are sealed (hence the 'bond') and, because goods are tax or duty free, can only be opened once away from Jamaican waters or territory. All goods must be paid for in Jamaican currency. **Shopping hours**: Mon-Sat 0900-1700. Some shops close half day Wednesday in Kingston, and Thursday in the rest of the island.

SPECIAL EVENTS: The following is a selection of special events occurring in Jamaica in 2005; for a complete list, contact the Jamaica Tourist Board (see *Contact Addresses* section):

Jan 26-29 *Air Jamaica Jazz & Blues*, Montego Bay. **Feb 21-Apr 18** *Negril Spring Break*. **May 27** *Calabash International Literary Festival*. **Jun 8-15** *Caribbean Fashionweek*. **Jul 1** *International Reggae Day*. **Jul 17** *Portland Jerk Festival*.

SOCIAL CONVENTIONS: Handshaking is the customary form of greeting. As tourism is a major industry in Jamaica, the visitor is well catered for, and hotel and restaurant staff are generally friendly and efficient. Outside Kingston, the pace of life is relaxed and people are welcoming and hospitable. Normal codes of practice should be observed when visiting someone's home. It may be common to see signs on the island referring to 'Jah lives', Jah being the name given to God by the Rastafarians. Casual wear is suitable during the day, but shorts and swimsuits must be confined to beaches and poolsides. Evening dress varies from very casual in Negril to quite formal during the season in other resorts, where some hotels and restaurants require men to wear jackets and ties at dinner. Possession of marijuana may lead to imprisonment and deportation.

Tipping: Most Jamaican hotels and restaurants add a service charge of 10 per cent; otherwise 10 to 15 per cent is expected. Chambermaids, waiters, hotel bellboys and airport porters all expect tips. Taxi drivers receive 10 per cent of the fare.

Business Profile

ECONOMY: Jamaica is one of the world's largest producers of bauxite, which accounts for half of the country's export earnings, but, despite expanding production, low world prices and falling demand have kept revenues static. After a period of rapid expansion in the mid-1970s, tourism has become the major source of foreign exchange. Agriculture (principally sugar cane, bananas, coffee and cocoa) has also been largely stagnant, with improved efficiency and production methods offset by climatic conditions and the state of the world markets. The manufacturing sector produces cement, textiles, tobacco and other consumer goods among its products. Imported oil and gas account for the bulk of the island's energy requirements.

Economic policy has pursued a familiar course of privatisation of state-owned enterprises, deregulation, tight budgetary controls, and reform of the tax and banking systems. The process was supervised by the IMF and aimed principally at reducing Jamaica's large debt burden. These measures improved Jamaica's financial position, but with little benefit to the population who still suffer from high inflation and unemployment. The economy as a whole has contracted by an average of 1 per cent annually since the mid-1990s. However, in the last few years this trend has been reversed and the economy is now growing slowly. The USA dominates Jamaica's trade, providing half the country's imports and taking more than 30 per cent of exports (followed by the UK, Canada and Norway). Jamaica is a member of the Caribbean trading bloc, CARICOM, and of the Inter-American Development Bank.

BUSINESS: The traditional 'shirtjac' (jacket without a tie), also known locally as a *kareba*, which was popular until the 1970s, has been replaced by a suit, jacket and tie. Usual formalities are required and appointments and business cards are normal. All trade samples now need an import licence which can be obtained from the Trade Board Ltd, 107 Constant Spring Road, Kingston 10 (tel: 969 0883/3228/2785; fax: 925 6513 *or* 6526; e-mail: tbldata@cwjamaica.com; website: www.tradeboard.gov.jm). Samples of non-commercial value are allowed into the country without a licence prior to arrival, although it may still be necessary to visit the office of the Trade Administrator to exchange the licence copy for a clearance copy, which the customs authorities demand before clearing the goods. **Office hours**: Mon-Fri 0830-1700.

COMMERCIAL INFORMATION: The following organisation can offer advice: Jamaica Chamber of Commerce and Associated Chambers of Commerce of Jamaica, 7-8 East Parade, Kingston (tel: 922 0150; fax: 924 9056; e-mail: jamcham@cwjamaica.com; website: www.jcc.org.jm).

CONFERENCES/CONVENTIONS: The Jamaican Conference Centre in Kingston was opened by HM Queen Elizabeth II in 1983. There are also several hotels in Jamaica with dedicated conference facilities. Seating is available for up to 1000 persons at some centres. The Jamaica Tourist Board (see *Contact Addresses* section) can supply information.

Climate

Tropical all year. Temperature in mountain areas. The rainy months are May and October, but showers may occur at any time. Hurricanes are prone during the rainy season, between June and November. Jamaica also lies within the earthquake zone. Cooler evenings.

Required clothing: Lightweight cottons and linens; light woollens are advised for evenings. Avoid synthetics. Waterproofing is necessary all year round.

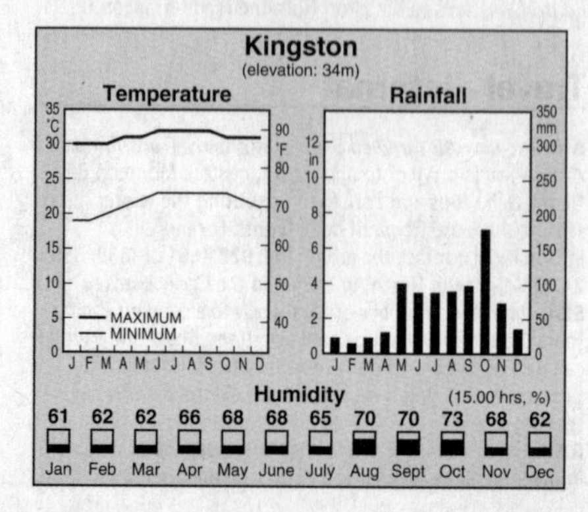

Japan

LATEST TRAVEL ADVICE CONTACTS

British Foreign and Commonwealth Office
Tel: (0870) 606 0290 Website: www.fco.gov.uk
US Department of State
Website: http://travel.state.gov/travel
Canadian Department of Foreign Affairs and Int'l Trade
Tel: (1 800) 267 8376 Website: www.dfait-maeci.gc.ca

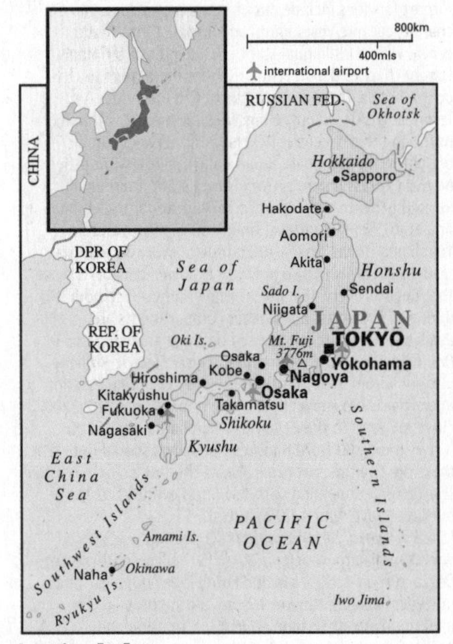

Location: Far East.

Country dialling code: 81.

Japan National Tourist Organisation (JNTO)
Tokyo Kotsu Kaikan Building, 10th Floor, 2-10-1 Yuraku-Cho, Chiyodaku, Tokyo 100-0006, Japan
Tel: (3) 3201 3331. Fax: (3) 3201 3347.
Website: www.jnto.go.jp
Tourist Information Centre
Contact details as above.
Embassy of Japan
101-104 Piccadilly, London W1J 7JT, UK
Tel: (020) 7465 6500 *or* 7465 6565 (visa section).
Fax: (020) 7491 9347.
E-mail: info@jpembassy.org.uk
Website: www.uk.emb-japan.go.jp
Opening hours: Mon-Fri 0930-1300 and 1430-1730; 0930-1330 and 1430-1630 (consular section).
Consulate in: Edinburgh.
Japan National Tourist Organisation (JNTO)
Heathcoat House, 20 Saville Row, London W1S 3PR, UK
Tel: (020) 7734 9638. Fax: (020) 7734 4290.
E-mail: info@jnto.co.uk
Website: www.seejapan.co.uk
Japan External Trade Organisation (JETRO)
Leconfield House, Curzon Street, London W1J 5HZ, UK
Tel: (020) 7470 4700. Fax: (020) 7491 7570.
Website: www.jetro.co.uk
British Embassy
No 1 Ichiban-cho, Chiyoda-ku, Tokyo 102-8381, Japan
Tel: (3) 5211 1100. Fax: (3) 5275 3164.
Website: www.uknow.or.jp/be_e
Consulate General in: Osaka.
Honorary Consulates in: Fukuoka, Hiroshima and Sapporo.
Embassy of Japan
2520 Massachusetts Avenue, NW, Washington, DC 20008, USA
Tel: (202) 238 6700. Fax: (202) 328 2187.
E-mail: eojjicc@erols.com
Website: www.us.emb-japan.go.jp
Consulates in: Anchorage, Atlanta, Boston, Chicago, Denver, Detroit, Guam, Hawaii, Honolulu, Houston, Kansas City, Los Angeles, Miami, New Orleans, New York, Portland, San Francisco and Seattle.
Japan Information and Culture Center
Lafayette Center III, 1155 21st Street, NW, Washington, DC 20036, USA
Tel: (202) 238 6949. Fax: (202) 822 6524.
E-mail: jicc@embjapan.org
Website: www.us.emb-japan.go.jp/jicc
Provides general information to the public in the Washington, DC area. Enquiries from those living elsewhere should be directed to their local Japanese Consulate.
Japan National Tourist Organisation (JNTO)
1 Rockefeller Plaza, Suite 1250, New York, NY 10020, USA
Tel: (212) 757 5640. Fax: (212) 307 6754.
E-mail: info@jntonyc.org
Website: www.japantravelinfo.com
Offices also in: Los Angeles and San Francisco.
Embassy of the United States of America
1-10-5, Akasaka, Minato-ku, Tokyo 107-8420, Japan
Tel: (3) 3224 5000 *or* 5354 4033 (visa enquiries).
Fax: (3) 3505 1862.
Website: http://tokyo.usembassy.gov
Consulates in: Fukuoka, Nagoya, Naha, Osaka and Sapporo.
Embassy of Japan
255 Sussex Drive, Ottawa, Ontario K1N 9E6, Canada
Tel: (613) 241 8541. Fax: (613) 241 7415.
E-mail: infocul@embjapan.ca
Website: www.ca.emb-japan.go.jp
Consulates in: Calgary, Montréal, Toronto and Vancouver.
Japan National Tourist Organisation

Credit: © JNTO

165 University Avenue, 4th Floor, Toronto, Ontario M5H 3B8, Canada
Tel: (416) 366 7140. Fax: (416) 366 4530.
Website: www.jnto.go.jp
Canadian Embassy
7-3-38 Akasaka, Minato-ku, Tokyo 107-8503, Japan
Tel: (3) 5412 6200. Fax: (3) 5412 6247.
Website: www.dfait-maeci.gc.ca/ni-ka
Consulates in: Fukuoka and Nagoya.
Consulate General in: Osaka.

TIMATIC CODES

Health
AMADEUS: **TI-DFT/TYO/HE**
GALILEO/WORLDSPAN: **TI-DFT/TYO/HE**
SABRE: **TIDFT/TYO/HE**

Visa
AMADEUS: **TI-DFT/TYO/VI**
GALILEO/WORLDSPAN: **TI-DFT/TYO/VI**
SABRE: **TIDFT/TYO/VI**

To access TIMATIC country information on Health and Visa regulations through the Computer Reservations System (CRS), type in the appropriate command line listed above.

General Information

AREA: 377,864 sq km (145,894 sq miles).
POPULATION: 127,450,000 (official estimate 2002).
POPULATION DENSITY: 337.3 per sq km.
CAPITAL: Tokyo. **Population**: 8,130,408 (2000).
GEOGRAPHY: Japan is separated from the Asian mainland by 160km (100 miles) of sea. About 70 per cent of the country is covered by hills and mountains, a number of which are active or dormant volcanoes. A series of mountain ranges runs from northern Hokkaido to southern Kyushu. The Japanese Alps (the most prominent range) run in a north–south direction through central Honshu. The highest mountain is Mount Fuji at 3776m (12,388ft). Lowlands and plains are small and scattered, mostly lying along the coast and composed of alluvial lowlands and diluvial uplands. The coastline is very long in relation to the land area, and has very varied features. The deeply indented bays with good natural harbours tend to be adjacent to mountainous terrain.
GOVERNMENT: Constitutional monarchy. **Head of State**: Emperor Akihito since 1989. **Head of Government**: Prime Minister Koizumi Junichiro since 2001.
LANGUAGE: Japanese is the official language. Some English is spoken in major cities.
RELIGION: Shintoism and Buddhism (most Japanese follow both religions) with a Christian minority. In Okinawa, however, people believe in Niraikanai, the realm of the dead beyond the sea.
TIME: GMT + 9.
ELECTRICITY: 100 volts AC, 60Hz in the west (Osaka); 100 volts AC, 50Hz in eastern Japan and Tokyo. Plugs are flat two-pin and light bulbs are screw-type.
COMMUNICATIONS: Telephone: Full IDD service. Country code: 81. Outgoing international code: Variable; 0051 through the operator. Three companies provide international communications services: KDDI, IDC and ISD, each possessing their own international access number (001 010, 0061 and 0041, respectively). Credit cards can also be used directly in some phoneboxes. **Mobile telephone:** The Japanese mobile network uses PDC (Personal Digital Cellular System) technology, which is not compatible with GSM or other mobile services. Visitors can hire handsets from companies such as *NTT*, Mover Rental Centre, 2-2-1 Marunouchi, Chiyoda-ku, Tokyo 100-8019 (tel: (3) 3282 0100) or *Sony Finance*, Rental Sales Department, Minamiaoyama, Minato-ku, Tokyo (tel: (3) 3475 5721). For UK travellers, mobiles can also be hired before departure from *Adam Phones* (tel: (0800) 123 000), *Cellhire PLC* (tel: (0800) 610 610; e-mail: london@cellhire.com) or *Mobell Communications* (tel: (01543) 426 999). **Fax:** Sending and receiving can be arranged at any hour at major hotels. KDDI offers facilities in Nagoya, Osaka, Tokyo and Yokohama. **Internet:** There are many Internet cafes in Tokyo and in the main cities in Japan. The main ISPs include *ASCII* (website: www.ascii.co.jp), *Jeton* and *Starnet*. Some hotel telephones and the new grey telephones have modular sockets for computer network access. **Telegram:** These can be sent from the main hotels and from the above company, also from larger post offices in major cities. Two rates are available. Overseas telegrams can also be sent from the Central Post Office in Tokyo until midnight. **Post:** Letters can be taken to the Central Post Office in front of Tokyo Station or the International Post Office, near exit A-2 Otemachi subway station, which provide English-speaking personnel. Airmail to Europe takes four to six days. All main post offices have *Poste Restante* facilities and will hold mail for up to 10 days. Post office hours: Mon-Fri 0900-1700. The International Post Office and Central Post Office are open weekdays until 1900, and Saturday until 1700. **Press:** The English-language daily newspapers in Tokyo include *Daily Sports, The Daily Yomiuri, The Japan Times* and *The Mainichi Daily News*.
Radio: BBC World Service (website: www.bbc.co.uk/worldservice) and Voice of America (website: www.voa.gov) can be received. From time to time the frequencies change and the most up-to-date can be found online.

Passport/Visa

	Passport Required?	Visa Required?	Return Ticket Required?
Full British	Yes	1	Yes
Australian	Yes	3	Yes
Canadian	Yes	2	Yes
USA	Yes	3	Yes
Other EU	Yes	1/2/3	Yes

Note: Regulations and requirements may be subject to change at short notice, and you are advised to contact the appropriate diplomatic or consular authority before finalising travel arrangements. Details of these may be found at the head of this country's entry. Any numbers in the chart refer to the footnotes below.

PASSPORTS: Passport valid for the duration of intended stay in Japan required by all.
Note: Whether or not they hold a visa, visitors who do not possess visible means of support for their stay, onward or return tickets, or other documents for their next destination, may be refused entry.
VISAS: Required by all except the following for tourism, short-term business meetings or to attend a conference:
(a) **1.** nationals of Austria, Germany, Ireland, Liechtenstein, Mexico, Switzerland and the UK for stays of up to six months*;
(b) **2.** nationals of Argentina, The Bahamas, Belgium, Canada, Chile, Costa Rica, Croatia, Cyprus, Denmark, Dominican Republic, El Salvador, Finland, France, Greece, Guatemala, Honduras, Iceland, Israel, Italy, Lesotho, Luxembourg, Macedonia, Malta, Mauritius, Netherlands, Norway, Portugal, San Marino, Singapore, Slovenia, Spain, Suriname, Sweden, Tunisia, Turkey and Uruguay for stays of up to three months;
(c) **3.** nationals of Andorra, Australia, Barbados, Czech Republic, Estonia, Hungary, Hong Kong (SAR and British National Overseas), Latvia, Lithuania, Monaco, New Zealand, Poland, Slovak Republic and the USA for stays of up to 90 days;
(d) nationals of Brunei for stays of up to 14 days.
Note: *Nationals who are permitted to stay for six months will initially be granted a stay of up to 90 days and may then apply, while in Japan, to the local Immigration Department for an extension of up to a further 90 days. Such extensions are at the discretion of the Immigration authorities in Japan. For further information, contact the

A B C D E F G H I J K L M N O P Q R S T U V W X Y Z

Consulate (or Consular section at Embassy); see *Contact Addresses* section.
Types of visa and cost: *Temporary Visitor*, *Working*, *General/Student* and *Transit*. Prices vary greatly according to nationality, the exchange rate and nature of intended visit. Visas for many nationals are issued free of charge. Contact the Consulate (or Consular section at Embassy) for further details.
Validity: Varies greatly according to nationality and purpose of visit. Most single-entry visas are valid for three months (extensions for another three months granted at the discretion of Immigration Department in Japan); double-entry and multiple-entry visas for 12 months. Enquire at the Consulate (or Consular section at Embassy) for further details.
Application to: Consulate (or Consular section at Embassy); see *Contact Addresses* section. Applications for all visas must be made in person.
Application requirements: *Temporary Visitor*: (a) Valid passport. (b) Two completed application forms. (c) Two passport-size photos. (d) Return air/sea ticket or copy. (e) Fee (cash only). (f) Proof of sufficient funds for stay (eg recent bank statement). (g) Proof of accommodation or travel itinerary. *Working and General/Student*: (a)-(f) and, (g) A letter of invitation from person or company in Japan may also be requested. Various other requirements are specified depending on what type of job or educational activity will be undertaken in the country. (h) A Certificate of Eligibility (original and photocopy), endorsed by the Ministry of Justice prior to application for the visa itself, is highly recommended in order to speed up the visa processing time. For more information, check with the Consulate (or Consular section at Embassy). (i) Pre-paid self-addressed envelope for return of passport by post (see *Note* below).
Note: All visas must be applied for in person by each applicant. Once a visa has been issued, passports may be returned via post if a pre-paid, self-addressed, special delivery envelope is submitted.
Working days required: Five working days for applications that do not need referral to the Ministry of Foreign Affairs in Tokyo. Up to four weeks if referral is needed. For those nationals that possess a Certificate of Eligibility, the processing time will be reduced to three days. Some types of visa may take three months or longer. Contact the nearest Consulate (or Consular section of the Embassy) for more information.
Temporary residence: Contact the nearest Consulate (or Consular section of the Embassy) for more information.

Credit: © JNTO

Money

Note: Japan has a strong cash culture, and it is usual to see people carrying large amounts of cash with them because of the low crime rate. It is only recently that credit cards have begun to become more popular. However, travellers may still encounter difficulties with foreign credit cards.
Currency: Japanese Yen (¥). Notes are in denominations of ¥10,000, 5000 2000 and 1000. Coins are in denominations of ¥500, 100, 50, 10, 5 and 1.
Currency exchange: All money must be exchanged at an authorised bank or money changer.
Credit & debit cards: American Express, Diners Club, MasterCard and Visa other major credit cards are widely used. Check with your credit or debit card company for merchant acceptability. ATMs are widely available although many do not accept foreign credit or debit cards. They only operate during normal banking hours and weekend services can be restricted to Saturday morning. A wide selection of foreign credit and debit cards are accepted, however, at over 21,000 post office ATMs, which are generally open Mon-Fri 0700-2300, Sat-Sun 0900-1900. *Citibank* machines also accept foreign credit cards and are often open 24 hours.
Travellers cheques: These can be exchanged at most major banks, larger hotels and some duty free shops. To avoid additional exchange rate charges, travellers are advised to take travellers cheques in Japanese Yen or US dollars.
Currency restrictions: The import and export of local and foreign currency is unrestricted, subject to declaration of amounts equivalent to ¥1,000,000 or above.
Exchange rate indicators: The following figures are included as a guide to the movements of the Japanese Yen against Sterling and the US Dollar:

Date	Feb '04	May '04	Aug '04	Nov '04
£1.00=	192.67	199.93	203.99	194.53
$1.00=	105.85	111.94	110.72	102.73

Banking hours: Mon-Fri 0900-1500.

Duty Free

The following goods may be imported into Japan without incurring customs duty:
400 cigarettes or 100 cigars or 500g of tobacco or 500g of a combination of these; 3 bottles (approximately 0.75l each) of spirits; 57ml of perfume; gifts up to the value of ¥200,000.
Note: Tobacco and alcohol allowances are for those aged 20 or over. Oral declaration is necessary on arrival at customs.
Prohibited items: Counterfeit, altered or imitated coins, paper money, banknotes or securities; all plants with soil; most meats and fruits (prohibited meats include eggs, bones, horns etc of cows, goats, sheep, bees, chickens, dogs, ducks, geese, horses, rabbits and turkeys); animals without health certificates; firearms and ammunition; narcotics; obscene articles and publications (including films).

Public Holidays

2005: Jan 1 New Year's Day. **Jan 2** Bank Holiday. **Jan 3** Bank Holiday. **Jan 10** Coming of Age Day. **Feb 11** National Foundation Day. **Mar 20** Vernal Equinox. **Apr 29** Greenery Day. **May 3** Constitution Memorial Day. **May 5** Children's Day. **Jul 18** Maritime Day. **Aug 6** Hiroshima Peace Festival (Hiroshima only). **Aug 9** Nagasaki Memorial Day (Nagasaki only). **Sep 19** Respect for the Aged Day. **Sep 23** Autumnal Equinox. **Oct 10** Health and Sports Day. **Nov 3** Culture Day. **Nov 23** Labour Thanksgiving Day. **Dec 23** Birthday of the Emperor. **Dec 31** Bank Holiday.
2006: Jan 1 New Year's Day. **Jan 2** Bank Holiday. **Jan 3** Bank Holiday. **Jan 9** Coming of Age Day. **Feb 11** National Foundation Day. **Mar 20** Vernal Equinox. **Apr 29** Greenery Day. **May 3** Constitution Memorial Day; Children's Day. **Jul 24** Maritime Day. **Aug 6** Hiroshima Peace Festival (Hiroshima only). **Aug 9** Nagasaki Memorial Day (Nagasaki only). **Sep 25** Respect for the Aged Day. **Sep 23** Autumnal Equinox. **Oct 9** Health and Sports Day. **Nov 3** Culture Day. **Nov 23** Labour Thanksgiving Day. **Dec 23** Birthday of the Emperor. **Dec 31** Bank Holiday.
Note: (a) With the exception of New Year Bank Holidays, if a holiday falls on a Sunday, the following day is treated as a holiday instead. (b) When there is a single day between two national holidays, it is also taken as a holiday. (c) Between 29 December and 3 January government offices and many shops and offices are closed.

Health

	Special Precautions?	Certificate Required?
Yellow Fever	No	No
Cholera	No	No
Typhoid & Polio	1	N/A
Malaria	No	N/A

Note: *Regulations and requirements may be subject to change at short notice, and you are advised to contact your doctor well in advance of your intended date of departure. Any numbers in the chart refer to the footnotes below.*

1: It is sometimes recommended to be vaccinated against typhoid.
Food & drink: Food and drink are generally considered safe but there is risk of parasitic infection and toxins from raw seafood.
Other risks: Vaccination against *Hepatitis A* is sometimes recommended; *hepatitis C* also occurs. *Typhus* occurs in some river valleys. *Japanese encephalitis* may occur and *paragonimiasis* has been reported. *TB* occurs.
Health care: Health insurance is strongly recommended, owing to the high cost of treatment. The International Association for Medical Assistance to Travellers provides English-speaking doctors. There are hospitals in all major cities.

Travel - International

AIR: Japan's largest international airline is *Japan Airlines (JL)* (website: www.jal.co.jp). Many international airlines fly to Japan including: *Air Canada*, *Air France*, *Air New Zealand*, *American Airlines*, *Austrian Airlines*, *British Airways*, *Cathay Pacific Airways*, *Finnair*, *Garuda Indonesia*, *IBERIA*, *KLM*, *Korean Air*, *Lufthansa*, *Malaysia Airlines*, *Qantas Airways*, *SAS*, *Singapore Airlines*, *SWISS*, *United Airlines* and *Virgin Atlantic*.
Approximate flight times: From Tokyo to *London* is 12 hours; to *New York* is 12 hours 30 minutes; to *Los Angeles* is nine hours 30 minutes; to *Hong Kong* is five hours; to *Sydney* is nine hours 30 minutes.
International airports: *Tokyo Narita Airport (NRT)* (Narita City) (website: www.narita-airport.or.jp) is 65km (40 miles) east of Tokyo (travel time - one hour 10 minutes). Airport facilities include duty free shops, bank/bureau de change, car hire, restaurants and a tourist information centre with multilingual staff located in both terminals. Luxury coaches depart regularly from the airport to city-centre hotels. There is also a bus to the Tokyo City Air Terminal (TCAT). A shuttle bus links the airport with major hotels in the city centre. Tickets for all services can be bought in the terminals. Japan Railways' reservation-only *Narita Express* line runs from Narita station terminal located beneath the airport to Tokyo station (travel time - one hour), Shinjuku (travel time - 90 minutes) and Yokohama (travel time - 105 minutes) every 30 minutes from 0745-2145. *JR* also operates a slower, cheaper service that departs every 45 minutes (travel time - one hour 20 minutes). First-class and private compartments are available. *JR Passes* can be used on these trains; see under *Rail* below for more information. *Keisei Electric Railway* also runs from the airport terminal to Keisei Ueno station in central Tokyo (travel time - one hour) from 0920-2200. There are taxis to the city, with a surcharge after 2200 (travel time - 60 to 70 minutes). Travellers should note that these are five times as expensive as the trains. There is a free shuttle bus connecting both terminals every 10 to 15 minutes (travel time - 10 minutes).
(Osaka) Kansai International (KIX) (Kansai) (website: www.kansai-airport.or.jp) is 50km (31 miles) southwest of Osaka. Airport facilities include duty-free shops, car hire (includes Japaren, Nippon, Nissan and Toyota), banks/bureaux de change, tourist information and bar/restaurant. There is a bus to the city every 30 minutes from 0800-2120 (travel time - one hour). The Nankai RR service goes to Namba station every 15 minutes (travel time - 30 minutes). The JR West service goes to JR Osaka station every 30 minutes (travel time - 70 minutes). Taxis are available to the city (travel time - one hour), although a surcharge may be imposed after 2200. It is also possible to take the jetfoil from Kansai Airport to Kobe's Port Island (travel time - 32 minutes).
Fukuoka International (FUK) is 20 minutes' travel time from Fukuoka City. Airport facilities include an outgoing duty-free shop, car hire, bank/bureau de change and bar/restaurant.
Nagoya International (NGO) is 10km (6 miles) north of the city and has flights to 29 international destinations including: Bangkok, Brisbane, Frankfurt/M, Hong Kong City, Honolulu, Melbourne, Paris, Seoul, Singapore, Sydney and Taipei.
Departure tax: Depends on airport; ¥2040 from Narita Airport. Children under 12 are charged half price; children under two are exempt. Departure tax is usually paid when purchasing tickets and not at the airport.
SEA: Japan is easily accessible by sea, and passenger ships include the major ports on their schedules. Ferries operate daily from Osaka and Kobe to Shanghai (China) and weekly from Kobe to Tanggu (near Tianjin, China). For Taiwan, ferries depart from Okinawa. The Shimonoseki-Busan ferry runs nightly across the Sea of Japan to Korea (Rep). Links to the Russian Federation include weekly services between Yokohama and Nakhoda (near Vladivostok). Alternatively, there is a twice-weekly service to Wakkanai in Hokkaido from Korsakov in the Russian Federation. There are cruises between the Japanese islands en route to Shanghai and Hong Kong. Cruise lines that call at Japan include *Clipper Cruise Lines*, *Crystal Cruises*, *Cunard*, *Norwegian Cruise Lines*, *Princess Cruises* and *Silversea Cruises*.
RAIL: The Trans-Siberian route to Japan is an interesting and very well organised, if lengthy, trip. Connections can be made daily from London (Liverpool Street) via Harwich or London (Victoria) via Dover through Europe to Moscow. There are sleeping cars four times a week from Hook of Holland to Moscow, and twice a week from Ostend to Moscow. The Trans-Siberian railway departs regularly from Moscow (see *Russian Federation* section).

Travel - Internal

AIR: *All Nippon Airways (ANA)*, *Japan Air Systems (JAS)* and *Japan Airlines (JAL)* and several other airlines maintain an extensive network covering Japan proper and its islands. Tokyo's domestic airport is *Haneda (HND)*. A monorail service runs from Hamamatsu-cho to Haneda. One international airline, *China Airlines*, serves Haneda. Other international flights to and from Haneda are made via Fukuoka, Nagoya, Osaka or Tokyo airports. Main routes are Tokyo–Sapporo; Tokyo–Fukuoka; Tokyo–Osaka; and Tokyo–Naha. Tickets can be purchased at automatic machines at Tokyo International Airport's domestic departure counter, and at Osaka International Airport.

SEA: There are frequent services by high-speed boat, ferry or hydrofoil to Japan's islands. Popular routes include Tokoyo–Hokkaido (in the north) and Tokyo–Okinawa (in the south). Major sea routes include Awaji Island: Akashi-Iwaya; Shodo Island: Himeji–Fukuda, Okayama–Tonosho and Takamatsu–Tonosho; Shiraishijima and Manabejima Islands: Kasaoka–Shiraishijima–Manabejima; Ikuchijima and Omishama Islands: Mihara–Setoda. Bullet train services travel frequently to ports.

RAIL: The *Japan Railways Group (JR)* runs one of the best rail networks in the world, and is widely used for both business and pleasure. Express and 'limited express' trains are best for intercity travel. Very frequent services run on the main routes. *Shinkansen*, the 'Bullet Train', are the fastest, with compartments for wheelchair passengers, diners and buffet facilities. Supplements are payable on the three classes of express train and in 'Green' (first-class) cars of principal trains, for which reservations must be made. Other types of train include *Kyuko* (Express), *Tokkyu* (Limited Express), *Kaisoku* (Rapid Train) and *Futsu* (Local Train). For short-distance trains, tickets can only be bought at vending machines outside train stations. For route maps, timetables, fares and reservations, see online (website: www.japanrail.com).

Discount fares: The *Japan Rail Pass*, an economical pass for foreign tourists which must be purchased before arrival in Japan, can be obtained from *Japan Airlines* (*JL* users only) or authorised travel agents and agencies. It can be used on all trains except the new Nozomi super express trains, and also on Japan Rail buses and Japan Rail ferries. A *Japan Rail Pass* brochure is available from the Japan National Tourist Organisation (see *Contact Addresses* section). A seven-day basic pass currently costs ¥28,300. For travellers without a Japan Rail Pass, there are various other discount schemes in operation including a 10 per cent discount at any JR Group Hotel. Other rail passes include the *JR East Pass*, *JR Kyushu Rail Pass*, *JR West Rail Pass*, *Kansai Area Pass* and the *Sanyo Area Pass*. For details of other discount fares, contact the Japan Railways Group (website: www.japanrail.com).

ROAD: Driving in Japan is complicated for those who cannot read the language as it will be a problem to understand the road signs. Traffic in cities is often congested. Traffic drives on the left. The Keiyo Highway, Meishin Expressway, Tohoku Expressway and the Tomei Expressway link Japan's major Pacific coastal cities, passing through excellent scenery. **Documentation**: An International Driving Permit is required.

URBAN: Public transport is well developed, efficient and crowded. The underground systems and privately run suburban rail services, which serve all the main cities, are very convenient but best avoided in rush hours. Tokyo also has a good network of trams. **Bus**: These can be confusing and are best used with someone who knows the system. Otherwise visitors should get exact details of their destination from the hotel. Fare systems are highly automated, but passes may be available. On buses, payment may be made on leaving. **Metro**: All of Japan's largest cities have subway systems. Tokyo has two underground systems: the Teito Rapid Transit Authority (TRTA) runs the Eidan Subway with eight lines, and the Tokyo Metropolitan Government (TBTMG) operates four lines. A variety of tickets can be bought including a monthly open pass, one-day open ticket, 14 tickets for the price of 10, and a Tokyo Combination ticket; this can be bought six months in advance and entitles the passenger to unlimited travel on the subway, JR rail and Toei buses for one day within the six months. Kyoto also has its own subway system with two major lines: the Karasuma and Tozai lines. Kyoto Sightseeing Passes can be bought enabling unlimited rides on buses and the underground. **Taxi**: These can be expensive, particularly in rush hour (0730-0930 and 1700-1800). There is a minimum charge for the first 2km (1.2 miles) and there is a time charge in slow traffic. It is advisable for visitors to have prepared in advance the name and address of their destination in Japanese writing, together with the name of some nearby landmark; a map may also help. Hotels can provide this service.

Travel times: The following chart gives approximate travel times (in hours and minutes) from **Tokyo** to other major cities/towns in Japan.

	Air	Road	Rail	Sea
Nagoya	-	4.00	2.00	-
Kagoshima	1.50	26.00	10.00	48.00
Fukuoka	1.45	13.00	6.30	-
Nagasaki	1.40	18.00	9.00	-
Okinawa	2.30	-	-	60.00
Osaka	1.00	6.00	3.15	-
Sapporo	1.25	-	14.00	-

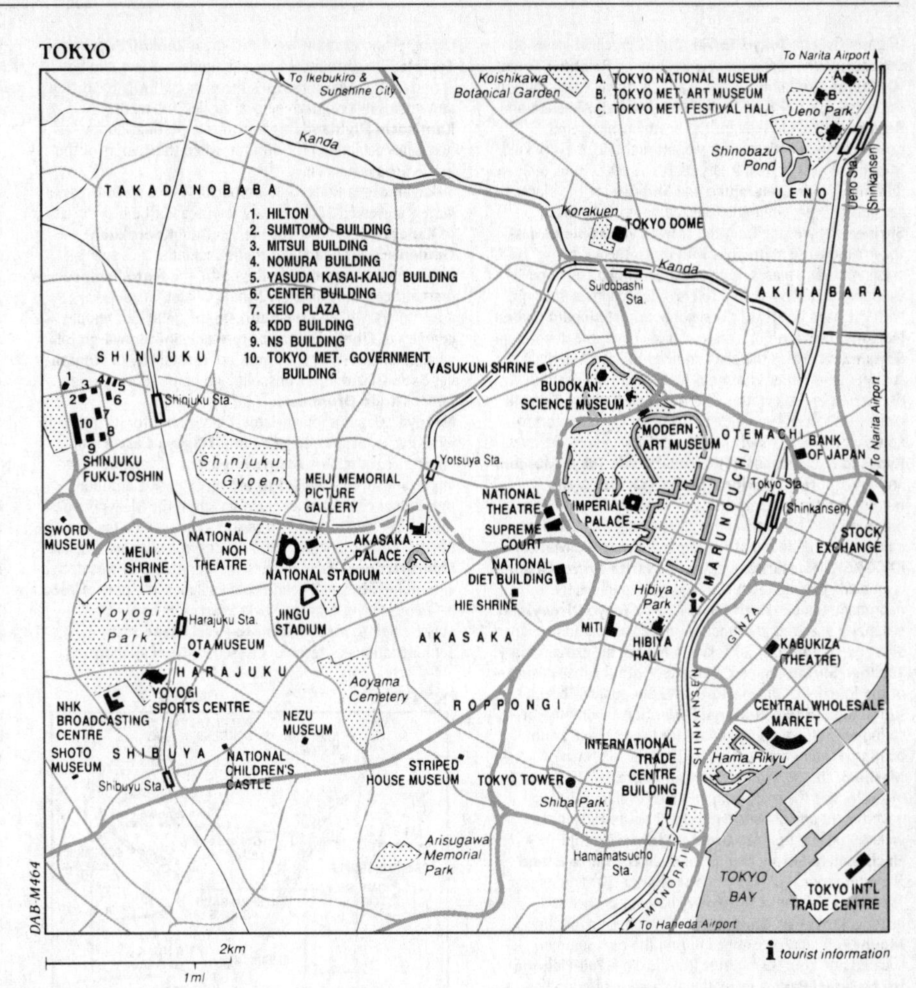

Accommodation

Note: The *Welcome Card* (Culture Card) offers reductions for foreign visitors on accommodation, meals, shopping and entertainment. It is available free of charge at JNTO's Tokyo Tourist Information Centres, or for ¥700 from information centres at Kansai International Airport, Kobe City Information Centre, Kyoto City Information Centre and Kyoto Prefectural Information Centre.

HOTELS: Hotels are 'Western' or 'Japanese' style. Western-style accommodation (ranging from deluxe hotels to pensions) are much like any modern US or European hotel. Japanese-style hotels (*ryokan*) provide exciting new experiences: guests receive kimonos and wooden clogs and rooms come equipped with Japanese bathtubs and paper sliding doors. Many non-obligatory extras are available. Service charges of 10 to 20 per cent are added to the bill. For more details contact the Japan Ryokan Association (website: www.ryokan.or.jp). Further information about other Japanese accommodation can be obtained by contacting the Japan Hotel Association, Shin Otemachi Building, 2-2-1 Otemachi, Chiyoda-ku, Tokyo 100-0004 (tel: (3) 3279 2706; fax: (3) 3274 5375; website: www.j-hotel.or.jp); *or* Japan Hotel Network, Akae Machi, Hanagashima Cho, Miyazaki City 880-0036 (fax: (985) 833 479; e-mail: jhn@japanhotel.net; website: www.japanhotel.net); *or* the Japan National Tourist Organisation (see *Contact Addresses* section). For Tokyo Hotels specifically, contact the Tokyu Hotel Chain Co Ltd, 10-3 Nagata-Cho, 2-Chome, Chiyoda-Ku, Tokyo 100-0014, Japan (tel: (3) 3581 8655; fax: (3) 3264 0225; website: www.tokyuhotelsjapan.com). **Grading**: No accommodation grading system operates in Japan.

GUEST-HOUSES: *Minshuku*, often found in resorts and vacation spots, are the Japanese equivalent of guest home-type lodging. Rates are moderate, and visitors should expect considerably fewer amenities than *ryokan* or western-style hotels. Visitors are expected to fold up their bedding in the morning and stow it away in a closet, and towels are usually not provided. No shoes are worn in the house as slippers are provided. Small gifts or a five per cent tip may be given with the bill.

YOUTH HOSTELS: There are roughly 400 youth hostels throughout Japan. Many require visitors to be a member of the International Youth Hostel Federation, although a guest card can be bought in advance at the Tokyo National Headquarters. Contact Japan Youth Hostels Inc, 2-20-7 Misaki-Cho, Chiyoda-ku, Tokyo 100-0006 (tel: (3) 3288 1417; fax: (3) 3288 1248; e-mail: info@jyh.jp; website: www.jyh.or.jp).

PENSIONS: These are 'Bed & Breakfast' style lodges which offer a comfortable atmosphere. They are often located near ski resorts, lakesides or in more rural areas. For further information contact the Japan National Tourist Organisation (see *Contact Addresses* section).

SHUKUBO: Some temples offer temple lodging (Shukubo). Guests may have to join in the routines of the monks (getting up early, chanting, doing chores etc) and facilities may be basic. The JNTO can provide a list (see *Contact Addresses* section).

Accommodation tax: The Tokyo Metropolitan Government enforces an 'Accommodation Tax' on hotels and inns around the city that charge over ¥10,000 per room. The tax is ¥100 on rooms costing between ¥10,000 and ¥14,999 per night, and ¥200 for rooms costing ¥15,000 and over. For more information check online (website: www.tax.metro.tokyo.jp).

Resorts & Excursions

The Japanese archipelago stretches over 3000km (1900 miles) from the temperate, northernmost island of **Hokkaido** to the subtropical islands of **Okinawa** in the south. Both **Tokyo** and **Kyoto** are located on **Honshu**, the largest and economically and culturally most important of the four major islands. **Shikoku** and **Kyushu** lie to the southwest. Much of the archipelago is mountainous and only a small percentage of land is available for agriculture and development. Thus large areas remain forested while towns and cities tend to be densely populated. The coastline is indented with numerous bays, inlets and small islands.

Note: A volunteer 'Goodwill Guide' service is available in Kyoto, Nara and other popular destinations such as Himeji and Hiroshima. Call the Tourist Information Centre in the areas visited for more information (Kyoto 075 371 5641; Osaka 072 456 6025; Tokyo 033 201 3331; see *Contact Addresses* section).

TOKYO

Japan's capital and centre of business and finance, Tokyo offers a surprising blend of futuristic cityscapes, historic sights and cultural entertainments. A vast conglomeration of districts, each boasts its own characteristic attractions. The **Ginza** is one of Asia's shopping paradises. Prices are high but the selection and presentation are superb. Nearby is the **Kabukiza Theatre** and the **Imperial Palace** (closed to the public) with its impressive moat and **East Garden**

(Higashi Gyoen). **Tokyo Tower** affords excellent views of the bay and the space age architecture on **Rainbow Town** (**O-daiba**), a reclaimed island. Early risers will enjoy touring the massive waterfront **Tsukiji Fish Market**. **Akasaka** and **Roppongi**, playgrounds for the nearby banking and governmental districts, offer vibrant nightlife of every kind, from geisha tea houses to discos. For youth culture, fashion and trendy dining, **Harajuku** and **Shibuya** are the places to see and be seen, while the forested oasis of the **Meiji Shrine** offers respite from the crowds. **West Shinjuku** is Tokyo's high-rise metropolis with its 'Gothem City' skyscrapers and plazas. To the east, **Shinjuku**'s bustling shopping and neon-lit nightlife districts contrast strongly with the calm beauty of the neighbouring **Shinjuku Gyoen National Garden**. For a taste of 'Old Tokyo', the downtown **Shitamachi** area is the place to head for, particularly in the summer when three enormous festivals attract vast crowds of revellers and spectators. The **Asakusa-Kannon Temple** is the area's main tourist draw, a vibrant Buddhist complex approached via a colourful shopping lane. Across the river, **Ryogoku** is the location of the excellent **Edo-Tokyo Museum** and the renowned **National Sumo Stadium**. **Ueno** is famous for its large park containing several important art museums and cultural venues. Cheap eats and bargains galore are to be found at the raucous **Ameyoko Market**.
EXCURSIONS: Narita, location of **Narita Tokyo Airport**, is an attractive old town with a large and impressive pilgrimage temple, **Narita-san**. Nearby **Tokyo Disneyland** is a major year-round attraction for Japanese and foreigners alike. Two hours north of Tokyo in **Nikko**, the extraordinary **Toshogu Shrine** complex is situated with the mausoleum of the founder of Japan's Tokugawa Shogunate. The surrounding **Nikko National Park** offers mountain hot spring resorts and opportunities for hiking, fishing and boating. Pottery fans will enjoy the rural kiln town of **Mashiko**. The coastal town of **Kamakura**, one hour south of Tokyo, was the seat of Japan's medieval feudal government and abounds in historic sights. Highlights include the giant bronze **Great Buddha**, colourful **Hachimangu Shrine** and picturesque **Enoshima Island**. The international port city of **Yokohama**, 30 minutes from Tokyo, has a vibrant **Chinatown**, harbour district and historic **Sankei-en Garden**. Japan's highest mountain, **Mount Fuji**, may be climbed during the high summer. Located one hour 30 minutes from Tokyo is **Fuji-Hakone-Izu National Park**, a recreational paradise offering hot spring resorts, golf courses and facilities for fishing, camping, hiking, swimming and boating. At **Hakone**, cable cars carry visitors over volcanic landscapes of boiling mud, sightseeing boats ply scenic **Lake Ashi** and there is an **Open Air Sculpture Museum**, a **Porsche Museum** and several sights of historical interest.

NORTHERN HONSHU & HOKKAIDO

Northern Honshu, known as **Tohoku**, offers wonderful natural scenery spread over three national parks plus numerous lesser-known cultural and historical treasures. **Sendai** is a lively, modern city, home of the famous August *Tanabata Star Festival* and gateway to the Tohoku region. Nearby **Matsushima** boasts a famously scenic bay. The pleasant city of **Aizu-Wakamatsu** is known for its lacquerware, historic **Tsurugaoka Castle** and fascinating **Buke-yashiki** samurai residence. The volcanic landscapes of the adjacent **Bandai-Asahi National Park** are a favourite with hikers, as is the dramatic **Dewa Sanzan** area and **Mount Zao**, which transforms into one of Japan's top ski resorts in winter. Historic **Hiraizumi** is of interest for the fabulously ornate **Chusonji Temple** and **Hirosaki** is an attractive castle town. To the very north of Honshu, the stunning volcanic crater of **Lake Towada** is surrounded by the alpine landscapes of the **Towada-Hachimantai National Park**, also known for its hot springs and ski resorts. Hokkaido was for a long time Japan's 'Wild West' and still retains a distinct pioneer feel. The island is home to the last of Japan's indigenous *Ainu* people, and the remnants of their distinct culture are a major attraction. Large parts of Hokkaido are protected as National Parks: areas of fantastic volcanic scenery, 'bottomless' crater lakes, hot springs and numerous mountain and ski resorts.
Furano, in particular, is renowned for its summer flower fields and winter skiing. During the winter visitors flock to see two of Hokkaido's outstanding natural phenomena: 'dancing' cranes and hot-spring-bathing monkeys.
Sapporo, Hokkaido's vibrant capital, is famous for its great nightlife and the extraordinary *Snow Festival* in February. To the south, the port city of **Hakodate** was one of the first of Japan's ports to open to foreign trade. Known for its historic **Goryokaku Fort** and gorgeous night views, the city displays a notable Russian influence.

THE JAPANESE ALPS & CENTRAL JAPAN

The Japanese Alps run through the centre of **Honshu Island**, an area known as 'the Roof of Japan'. A popular natural playground for hikers, climbers and sightseers in all seasons, much of the area is protected as a National Park. **Nagano**, the prefectural capital, hosted the 1998 Winter Olympics and is renowned for its great **Zenkoji Pilgrimage Temple**. The surrounding area abounds in skiing and hot spring resorts. **Matsumoto** is the main gateway to the Alps and retains its original medieval castle. The nearby **Kamikochi Highlands** are a favourite destination for hikers, particularly in the autumn when the colours of the leaves are spectacular.
Takayama is famous for its colourful festivals and boasts a largely preserved 17th-century townscape. The historic city of **Kanazawa** is known for the beautiful **Kenrokuen Garden** and for a range of traditional industries such as silk-dying and ceramics. To the north, the **Noto Peninsula**'s dramatic coastline and tiny fishing villages attract adventurers, while to the south are the great Zen temple complex of **Eiheiji** and the picturesque **Shirakawa-go** folk villages. One hour by boat from the coastal city of **Niigata** lies **Sado Island:** rural, unspoilt, and home to the world-famous **Kodo Drummers**.
Nagoya is Japan's fourth-largest city, noted for its porcelain industry, textile and lacquer crafts. **Nagoya Castle** is an impressive sight, as is **Atsuta Jingu**, one of Japan's most important shrines. **Meiji Mura** is an extensive outdoor museum of characteristic buildings from the Meiji period. Japan's pre-eminent Shinto shrine is the revered **Ise Grand Shrine**, located one hour 30 minutes from Nagoya. The **Ise Shima National Park** protects the scenic coastal area dotted with numerous small pearl fishing villages. The port of **Toba** is famous for its 'Married Rocks', two islets linked by a massive Shinto rope. **Mikimoto Pearl Island** features demonstrations of techniques used in the pearl industry.

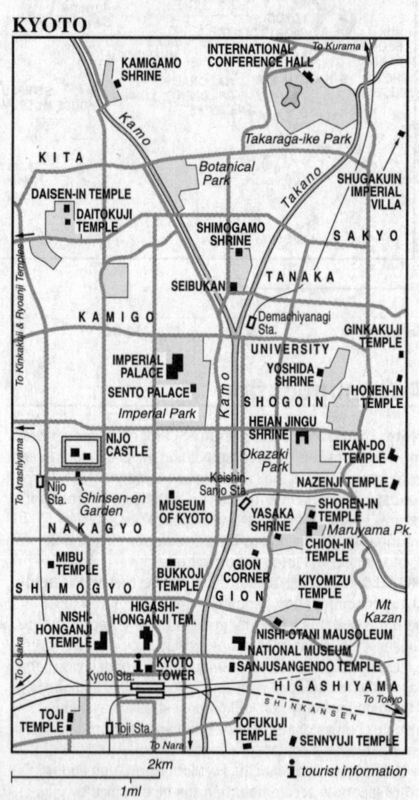

KYOTO, NARA & OSAKA

Located in the Kansai area of central Honshu, these three famous cities are all major tourist destinations, each having contributed distinctive elements towards Japanese history and culture. Capital of Japan for over 1000 years, **Kyoto** remains Japan's star attraction. Founded in AD 794, the city's vast number of temples, shrines, museums and historical sites acts as a textbook to Japanese history, while her arts, crafts and cuisine rank among the country's finest. 'Must see' sights include the **Golden Pavilion** (Kinkakuji), the minimalist Zen rock garden of **Ryoanji**, impressive **Kiyomizu Temple** and the Imperial gardens and villas of **Katsura** and **Shugakuin** (permit required). The splendid medieval **Nijo Castle**, the vermilion-lacquered **Heian Shrine** and the Buddhist art treasures of **Sanjusangendo Temple** are also well worth visiting. The city's many historical neighbourhoods, such as the rural temples of **Arashiyama**, the textile workshops of **Nishijin** and the **Gion** geisha district, are best explored on foot. Kyoto hosts three major traditional summer events: the colourful *Aoi, Gion* and *Jidai Festivals*.
Nara, one hour south of Kyoto, is a major Buddhist centre and acted as Japan's capital during the eighth century AD. Visitors flock to see the famous 'great Buddha' of **Todaiji Temple**, the world's largest wooden structure, ancient **Kasuga Shrine** and the Buddhist sculptures of **Kofukuji Temple**. The beautiful expanses of **Nara Park** are home to hundreds of sacred deer. Nearby, the venerable **Horyuji Temple** dates back to the seventh century AD.
One of Japan's largest cities, prosperous and commercial **Osaka** is renowned for its abundance of excellent restaurants, historic **Osaka Castle** and the performing arts of Kabuki and Bunraku. The city also boasts an impressive aquarium and superb **Museum of Oriental Ceramics**. The city's busy **Namba** and **Umeda** districts are renowned for their nightlife and the **Dotonburi** area is particularly vibrant after dark. **Universal Studios Japan**, a 140-acre theme park in Osaka, is enormously popular.
EXCURSIONS: The historic town of **Uji**, between Kyoto and Nara, is famous for the graceful **Byodoin Temple** which is featured on Japan's ¥10 coin. Pilgrims and tourists are welcomed by the many temples and monasteries on scenic **Mount Koya**, two hours from Osaka, where overnight temple lodgings and Buddhist vegetarian cuisine are offered at reasonable prices. The port city of **Kobe** has an international flavour and is famous for its old foreign-style houses and buildings dating from the Meiji era.

WESTERN HONSHU

The main attractions of Western Honshu are to be found along the coasts, namely the **Inland Sea Coast** (Sanyo) and the **Japan Sea Coast** (Sanin). The gleaming white walls of **Himeji Castle** dominate the city of **Himeji**. Known as the 'White Heron Castle', it is the best-preserved and most beautiful castle in Japan. The pleasant city of **Okayama** is known for its **black castle** and the **Korakuen Stroll Garden**, considered one of the three most beautiful in the country. Nearby is the pottery town of **Bizen** and wonderfully preserved **Kurashiki** with its historic merchants' quarter, now housing numerous museums and craft galleries. Further west, **Hiroshima** was the target of the world's first atomic bomb during World War II but has risen from the ashes to become a thriving modern city. The bombing is commemorated by the **Peace Memorial Park and Museum**. Nearby is the beautiful island of **Miyajima**, its famous red **Shinto torii gateway** seemingly floating on the sea at high tide. **Itsukushima Shrine**, the cable car up the central mountain for panoramic views and the tame deer are all major attractions. **Iwakuni** is known for its five-arched bridge while **Hagi**, on the western Japan Sea Coast, is famous for its pottery and will appeal to history buffs. The sand dunes of **Tottori**, ancient **Izumo Taisha Shrine** and the famous coastal panorama of **Amanohashidate** are the most famous attractions along this northern coastline.

SHIKOKU

The smallest of Japan's four main islands, Shikoku is linked to Honshu by two major bridges and numerous ferries which crisscross the beautiful island-studded waters of the **Inland Sea**. Protected as the **Inland Sea National Park**, many of the 600 islands are popular summer beach destinations. Facing these placid waters, the attractive city of **Takamatsu**, on the northern coast of Shikoku, is the main gateway to the island. The historic **Ritsurin Park** is considered among the most beautiful in Japan and the mountaintop **Kotohira Shrine**, about one hour away, is extremely impressive. To the east is **Tokushima**, a city famous for its coastal **Naruto Whirlpools** and massive summer **Awa Odori** dance festival. **Matsuyama**, on the western coast of Shikoku, boasts one of Japan's best-preserved medieval castles. The nearby **Dogo Spa** is famous as being among the oldest in Japan. Located on Shikoku's rugged Pacific southern coast, **Kochi** is also noted for its castle. The mountainous interior of the island remains wild and largely unspoilt. Shikoku is famous for its **pilgrimage circuit** of 88 temples dedicated to **Kannon**, the Goddess of Mercy.

KYUSHU

The southernmost of Japan's four main islands, Kyushu is best known for its mild climate, volcanic landscape, excellent hot springs and ceramics. The gateway to Kyushu, **Fukuoka** (**Hakata**) is known for its traditional textile and doll-making industries, its delicious food and for the nearby **Dazaifu Tenmangu Shrine**, a very active place of worship where students go to pray to the god of learning. On Kyushu's west coast, **Nagasaki** was one of Japan's earliest designated foreign ports and is famous for *Arita* and *Imari* ceramics and for the **Peace Park** that commemorates the devastation caused by the second nuclear bomb of World War II. Other major sights include **Chinatown**, the **Chinese Temple** and **Glover House**, said to be the setting that inspired Puccini's opera *Madame Butterfly*. Nearby **Mount Unzen**, an active volcano, is also a well-known hot spring resort. **Kumamoto** is an old castle town and gateway to the scenic wonders of the **Mount Aso National Park**. To the south of the island, the seaport of **Kagoshima** is overshadowed by the dramatic smoking cone of **Sakurajima** volcanic island. Nearby **Ibusuki Spa**, on the southern tip of Kyushu, boasts some of the most famous hot springs in Japan and is renowned for its hot-sand saunas. Summer whale- and dolphin-watching tours depart from the town of **Kasasa**. Beyond **Kagoshima** lies the beautiful, mountainous island of **Yakushima**, a National Park renowned for its primeval cedar forests and hiking trails. **Miyazaki**, situated on Kyushu's southeastern coast, is a prosperous modern city famous for its palm trees, golf courses and ancient burial mounds. The **Beppu** hot spring resort, near the city of **Oita**, is great fun despite its slightly sleazy atmosphere. Dozens of hotel and bathing complexes compete for customers by offering everything from amusement parks and sports facilities to museums, gardens and shopping arcades.

OKINAWA

The 161 islands that make up Okinawa lie to the far south of Japan, like stepping stones between Kyushu and Taiwan. The subtropical climate, clear turquoise seas and many fine beaches mean that the islands have long been a holiday favourite among the Japanese. Recently, however, several of the islands have also started to become well known as eco-destinations. Numerous coral reefs offer excellent diving opportunities, with many resorts catering to enthusiasts. **Okinawa Island**, the main island of the group, has a number of famous resorts such as **Manza Beach** and **Onna Beach**, offering white sands and watersports. The fantastic formations of the **Gyokusendo Caves** are also a popular attraction. **Naha**, the relaxed Okinawan capital, is famous for its pottery and textiles and impressive **Shuri Castle**, former seat of the Ryukyu kings. The large US bases nearby help to fuel its lively nightlife. The island retains many reminders of the fierce fighting that took place there during World War II, and the southern coastline is dotted with **war memorials**. **Ishigaki Island** has great diving, snorkelling and folkcrafts and is a good base from which to explore the remoter islands. **Iriomote Island** is known for its mangrove swamps, jungle interior and rare wildlife such as the Iriomote Wildcat, while tiny **Taketomi** retains its rural charm. Occurring throughout the islands, Okinawa's ancient Ryukyu festivals are some of Japan's most colourful and feature distinctive performing arts.

Sport & Activities

Martial arts: Japanese ceremonial wrestling, sumo and judo are Japan's national sports, both drawing huge crowds. There are six **sumo** tournaments a year, each of which lasts for 15 days. Three of them are held in Tokyo, and the others take place in Fukuoka, Nagoya and Osaka. Matches by senior wrestlers begin at 1500. Sumo training sessions can be observed between 0500 and 1030 at Kasungo Stable in Tokyo (tel: (3) 3631 1871). **Judo** enthusiasts can visit the Kodokan Judo Hall, 1-16-30, Kasuga, Bunkyo-ku, Tokyo (tel: (3) 3818 4172), where there is a spectators' gallery. There are opportunities for the visitor to purchase a costume and learn some of the techniques. There are separate classes for men and women and English is spoken in most large schools. More information can be obtained from the All Japan Judo Federation (website: www.judo.or.jp). **Karate**, the art of self-defence, is taught at schools in Japan and has become a very popular sport since it was introduced into the country in 1922. For further information, contact the Japan Karatedo Federation (website: www.karatedo.co.jp). **Kendo**, Japanese fencing, is practised in numerous clubs and college halls. In December, the All-Japan Championships are held in Tokyo. **Kyudo**, Japanese archery, is one of the oldest martial arts. It is closely associated with Zen Buddhism. Unlike many martial arts, it is pursued by almost as many female students as males. **Yabusame**, or archery on horseback, which was originally performed by courtiers or imperial guards in the seventh century, is today a Shinto rite for ensuring peace and good harvests. It is staged by horse riders in colourful costumes who gallop down a narrow 250m course shooting at small wooden targets set up at 80m intervals. The best-known events are at Tsurugaoka Hachmagu shrine in Kamakura on the third Sunday in April and on 16 September and at the Shimogano Shrine in Kyoto on 3 May.

Wintersports: These are very popular and there are over 50 major ski resorts, especially in the Japanese Alps and on the northern island of Hokkaido. One of the great attractions is the prevalence of hot springs in the **skiing** areas. Various resorts at Nagana in Central Honshu offer facilities for night-skiing. The southernmost natural ski slope in Japan is the *Gokase Highland Ski*, in the north Miyazaki prefecture, which offers grass skiing out of season between late April and late November. Transport connections are very good, and there are sometimes railway stations within a few minutes walk of the slopes. During the ski season, it is necessary to reserve seats on trains and buses. Although equipment is easy to hire, it can sometimes be a problem to obtain ski boots in larger sizes; skiers should telephone the resort in advance in order to check on availability.

Both **diving** and **snorkelling** are popular around the Kerama Islands near Okinawa, which is one of the world's clearest sea areas. Between January and March, it is also an area for **whale watching**.

All kinds of **fishing** are practised, and there are many keen anglers in Japan. Freshwater fish include trout, *funa* (silver carp) and *ayu* (sweetfish). Given the shape of the country, fishing locations are never far away. Travellers might like to try *ukai* or **cormorant fishing**, a type of fishing where cormorants are used to catch fish. The cormorants and the crew do the work while the passengers watch. Food and drink are provided. Expeditions go out at night and can be arranged through hotels and tourist boards in the Kyoto area.

Cycling: This is popular in April and May during the cherry blossom season and also in October and November when autumnal colours adorn Japan. Owing to snow and ice, cycling in Hokkaido and in the northern area of the main island, Honshu, is not recommended between December and March. Cyclists must keep to the left and should be careful at all times because of heavy traffic, especially on the national highways. There are numerous interesting paths routed through Toyko.

Football: Japan co-hosted the *2002 World Cup* with Korea (Rep). Football has taken off in a big way in Japan in recent years with the introduction of the Japanese soccer *J-League* and the participation of the Japanese national team in the World Cup of 1998 and 2002.

Golf: Courses in and around Tokyo are considered by some to be among the most challenging in the world. However, membership or an invitation is sometimes required. Some courses have the additional attraction of hot spring baths and *mahjhong* rooms. For further information, contact the Japan Golf Association (tel: (3) 3566 0003; fax: (3) 3566 0101; website: www.jga.or.jp).

Cultural activities: Among the traditional entertainments on offer is *bunraku*, a unique form of **puppet theatre**. This can be seen in major towns, as *can noh drama* and *kabuki*, **traditional Japanese drama** forms, with participants attired in medieval costumes. The most fascinating and colourful of Japan's **religious festivals** takes place in Kyoto, the old imperial capital. The *Gion Festival* reaches its climax on 16-17 July. A street parade takes place with the participants dressed in fine costumes and carrying portable shrines. The large floats depict ancient themes. The *Aoi* (or hollyhock) *Festival* on 15 May dates back to the sixth century. The procession, consisting of imperial messengers in oxcarts followed by a retinue of 600 people dressed in traditional costume, leaves at around 1000 from the imperial palace and heads for the Shimogamo-jinja shrine where ceremonies take place. It then proceeds to Kamigamo-jinja shrine. The *Jidai Festival* (Festival of the Ages) is of more recent origin, though still splendid to watch. More than 2000 people parade through the town dressed in costumes dating from different periods. For dates of other festivals, see Special Events in the *Social Profile* section. Those wishing to see the **Japanese tea ceremony** can arrange to do so through the tourist information centres in Kyoto and Tokyo (see *Contact Addresses* section). If visitors are interested in **eastern religions** they can arrange to stay at a *shukubo* (temple lodging). The tourist office will have a full list of temples offering this service. Sometimes it is possible to participate in meditation sessions.

Social Profile

FOOD & DRINK: Japanese cuisine, now popular in the West, involves very sensitive flavours, fresh crisp vegetables and an absence of richness. Specialities include *teriyaki* (marinated beef/chicken/fish seared on a hot plate), *sukiyaki* (thin slices of beef, tofu and vegetables cooked in soy sauce and then dipped in egg), *tempura* (deep fried seafood and vegetables), sushi (slices of raw seafood placed on lightly vinegared rice balls – very tasty and refreshing) and *sashimi* (slices of raw seafood dipped in soy sauce). The best place to try sushi is a *Kaiten Sushi Bar*, where many varieties pass the customer on a conveyor belt allowing complete choice over which delicacies to try, at more reasonable prices than a traditional Sushi Bar. Fine Oriental food (Korean – very hot – and Chinese) is served in restaurants. An amazing number and variety of international restaurants are also available, catering for every possible taste and budget, from French and Italian to Chinese, Indian and Thai. Western dishes in expensive places are good, but cheaper restaurants may be disappointing. Restaurants have table service and in some places it is customary to remove footwear.

Green tea is by far the most popular bevarage amongst the Japanese. The quality of the tea varies greatly from *houjicha* (a common brown-coloured tea) to *matcha* (a bitter green tea used in tea ceremonies). *Sake*, rice wine served hot or cold according to the season, is strong and distinctively fresh tasting. *Shochu*, a strong aquavit, is an acquired taste. Japanese wines are worth trying once, and beer – similar to lager – is recommended. Popular brands are *Asahi*, *Kirin*, *Sapporo* and *Suntory*. Waiter service is common in bars. The Japanese are very fond of original Scotch whisky, but this is both very expensive and highly sought after, therefore Japanese versions of this drink are often served. There are no licensing hours. Drinking is subject to long-standing rituals of politeness. The hostess will pour a drink for the visitor, and will insist on the visitor's glass being full. It is also appreciated if the visitor pours drinks for the host, but it is bad manners for a visitor to pour one for himself.

NIGHTLIFE: Tokyo has an abundance of cinemas, theatres, bars, coffee shops, discos and nightclubs. A wide range of bars are available, from the upmarket and stylish to cheap street stalls. In the summer, rooftop beer gardens are popular. Some clubs have hostesses who expect to be bought drinks and snacks. In bigger nightclubs and bars, a basic hostess charge is levied. However, there are thousands of other bars and clubs. In Tokyo there are concerts of all styles of music almost every night. Foreign opera companies, ballet companies, orchestras and rock/pop stars visit Japan all year round. Some live jazz houses are also available. For those who would like to try the traditional Japanese performing arts, there is *Kabuki* and *Noh* theatre in Tokyo. *Play Guide* ticket offices are situated in major department stores. It is advisable to purchase the tickets in advance because shows are quickly sold out. *Karaoke* bars are a very popular form of entertainment in Japan.

SHOPPING: A blend of Oriental goods and Western sales techniques confronts the shopper, particularly at the big department stores, which are more like exhibitions than shops. Playgrounds for children are available. Special purchases include *kimonos*, *mingei* (local crafts including kites and folk toys); *Kyoto* silks, fans, screens, dolls; religious articles such as Shinto and Buddhist artefacts; paper lanterns; lacquerware; hi-fi equipment, cameras, televisions and other electronic equipment. Bargaining is not usual. **Tax exemptions**: These are available in authorised tax-free stores. Certain items costing more than ¥10,000 are exempt from tax. **Shopping hours**: 1000-1900/2000 every day of the week and on public holidays.

SPECIAL EVENTS: A large number of festivals are held in Japan throughout the year in different parts of the country. Some are hugely spectacular, some are religious in orientation. For full details of events and festivals, contact the Japan National Tourist Organisation (see *Contact Addresses* section). The following is a selection of special events occurring in Japan in 2005:

Dec 31 2004-Jan 3 *O-Shogatsu* (New Year's celebrations), nationwide. **Jan 2** *Ippan Sanga* (Imperial Palace Celebrations, palace opens to public), Tokyo. **Jan 8-10** *Toka Ebisu* (Festival of Imamiya Ebisu Shrine), Osaka. **Jan 20** *Niramekko Obisha Festival*, Ichikawa. **Feb 7-13** *Sapporo Snow Festival*. **Mar** *Cherry Blossom Viewing*, nationwide. **Mar 1-14** *Omizutori* (Water-drawing Festival), Nara. **Mar 3** *Hinamatsuri Doll Festival*, nationwide. **May** *Sanja Festival*, Tokyo. **Jul 7** *Tanabata* (Star Festival), nationwide. **Aug** *Daimonji*, Kyoto. **Aug 9** *Nagasaki Memorial Day*. **Sep 7-8** *Tokyo Gay & Lesbian Pride*. **Oct** *Jidai Matsuri* (Festival of Eras), Kyoto. **Nov 15** *Shichi-go-san* (Children's Shrine Visiting Day), nationwide. **Dec** *Chichibu Yo-matsuri* (All-night Festival), Chichibu City. **Dec 31-Jan 3 2006** *O-Shogatsu* (New Year's celebrations), nationwide.

SOCIAL CONVENTIONS: Japanese manners and customs are vastly different from those of Western people. A strict code of behaviour and politeness is recognised and followed by almost all Japanese. However, they are aware of the difference between themselves and the West and therefore do not expect visitors to be familiar with all their customs but expect them to behave formally and politely. A straightforward refusal does not form part of Japanese etiquette. A vague 'yes' does not really mean 'yes' but the visitor may be comforted to know that confusion caused by non-committal replies occurs between the Japanese themselves. Entertaining guests at home is not as customary as in the West, as it is an enterprise not taken lightly and the full red-carpet treatment is given. Japanese men are also sensitive lest their wives be embarrassed and feel that their hospitality is inadequate by Western standards; for instance, by the inconvenience to a foreign guest of the custom of sitting on the floor. Bowing is the customary greeting but handshaking is becoming more common for business meetings with Westerners. The honorific suffix *san* should be used when addressing all men and women; for instance Mr Yamada would be addressed as *Yamada-san*. When entering a Japanese home or restaurant it is customary to remove shoes. Table manners are very important, although the Japanese host will be very tolerant towards a visitor. However, it is best if visitors familiarise themselves with basic table etiquette and use chopsticks. It is customary for a guest to bring a small gift when visiting someone's home. Exchange of gifts is also a common business practice and may take the form of souvenir items such as company pens, ties or high-quality spirits. Smoking is only restricted where notified. **Tipping**: Tips are never expected since a 10 to 20 per cent service charge is added to the bill at hotels, ryokan and restaurants; where a visitor wishes to show particular appreciation of a service, money should not be given in the form of loose change but rather as a small financial gift. Special printed envelopes can be bought for financial gifts of this type.

Business Profile

ECONOMY: After suffering massive destruction during World War II, Japan was the economic phenomenon of the late 20th century. At $4,000 billion, the country's GDP ranks second in the world after the USA. This has been achieved through several decades of sustained growth (although this period has now ended – see below) driven by judicious application of import controls and consistently high domestic investment, coupled with an aggressive export drive orchestrated by the powerful Ministry of International Trade and Industry (MITI). The structure of the Japanese domestic economy revolves around a group of large multi-product corporations (many of which have since become global household names), linked in loose alliances (known as *keiretsu*) with banks and finance houses. The corporations are serviced with components and raw materials by a plethora of small firms with low overheads and labour costs, and a well-honed distribution system (many of these lower-level processes are now carried out in the 'tiger economies' of the Pacific Basin).

The model worked superbly until the early 1990s, when competition from abroad and excessive lending by the banks began to put the Japanese economy under a set of pressures to which it has proved quite unable to respond. The extent of the problem became apparent initially with the 1991 property crash and, more spectacularly, with the 1997 Asian financial crisis. Since then, the economy has stagnated, often struggling to reach 1 per cent growth annually. Unemployment, a comparative novelty in a country where jobs were typically guaranteed for life, has now reached 6 per cent. Successive governments have made little more than token efforts at structural reform. The financial sector continues to operate much as before. The Koizumi government has tabled a set of proposals, which include deregulation and much-needed reform as well as a package designed to kick-start the economy and create 5 million jobs. Unfortunately, its plans are being undermined by the government's poor fiscal position (government debt is 150 per cent of GDP – by way of comparison, conditions for Eurozone countries require that the figure not exceed 60 per cent).

Agriculture is the only sector of the economy that does not measure up to Western standards in terms of technology and management, and remains relatively inefficient and heavily protected by the government. (This is a quirk of the Japanese electoral system, which affords a disproportionate number of parliamentary seats to rural areas.) Rice, potatoes, sugar and citrus fruits are the main crops. The manufacturing industry is still important, particularly vehicles and electronic goods, although traditional industries such as coal mining, shipbuilding and steel are also sizeable and, unlike many of their Western counterparts, profitable. Overall, industry contributes 35 per cent of economic output – a larger proportion than the world's other leading economies. The service sector grew rapidly in the 1980s as the economy matured and Japan became a major force in the international economy. The emphasis in Japanese trade thus switched from manufactured goods to export of services and 'invisibles', such as finance and insurance. Japan's major trading partner is still the US but China (PR) has overtaken Korea (Rep), Taiwan (China), Indonesia and various Middle Eastern oil producers in importance. In the international arena, Japan is a leading member of the Organisation of Economic Co-operation and Development (OECD) and the Asia-Pacific Economic Co-operation (APEC) forum.

BUSINESS: A large supply of visiting cards printed in English and Japanese is essential. Cards can be quickly printed on arrival with Japanese translation on the reverse side. Appointments should be made in advance and, because of the formality, visits should consist of more than a few days. Punctuality is important. Business discussions are often preceded by tea and are usually very formal.

Office hours: Mon-Fri 0900-1700. Some offices are open Sat 0900-1200.

COMMERCIAL INFORMATION: The following organisations can offer advice: Japanese Chamber of Commerce, Salisbury House, 29 Finsbury Circus, London EC2M 5QQ, UK (tel: (020) 7628 0069; fax: (020) 7374 2280); *or* Nippon Shoko Kaigi-sho (The Japan Chamber of Commerce and Industry), 2-2 Marunouchi 3 Chome, Chiyoda-ku, Tokyo 100-0005 (tel: (3) 3283 7824; fax: (3) 3211 4859; e-mail: info@jcci.or.jp; website: www.jcci.or.jp); *or* JETRO (Japan External Trade Organisation), 2-2-5 Toranomon, Minato-ku, Tokyo 105-8466 (tel: (3) 3582 5511; fax: (3) 3587 0219; website: www.jetro.go.jp).

CONFERENCES/CONVENTIONS: The Japan Convention Bureau is a division of the Japan National Tourist Organisation (see *Contact Addresses* section); its *Convention Planner's Guide to Japan* lists 35 cities with conference facilities including Hiroshima, Kyoto, Nagasaki, Osaka, Tokyo and Yokohama. Kyoto has proved to be one of the most popular locations for international meetings over the last few years. For further information, contact the Japan Convention Bureau, 2-10-1 Yuraku-cho, Chiyoda-ku, Tokyo 100-0006 (tel: (3) 3216 2905; fax: (3) 3216 1978; e-mail: tsato@jnto.go.jp; website: www.jnto.go.jp).

Climate

Except for the Hokkaido area and the subtropical Okinawa region, the weather is mostly temperate, with four seasons. Winters are cool and sunny in the south, cold and sunny around Tokyo (which occasionally has snow), and very cold around Hokkaido, which is covered in snow for up to four months a year. Summer, between June and September, ranges from warm to very hot, while spring and autumn are generally mild throughout the country. Rain falls throughout the year but June and early July is the main rainy season. Hokkaido, however, is much drier than the Tokyo area. Rainfall is intermittent with sunshine. Typhoons are only likely to occur in September or October but rarely last more than a day.

Required clothing: Lightweight cottons and linens are required throughout summer in most areas. There is much less rainfall than in Western Europe. Light- to mediumweights during spring and autumn; medium- to heavyweights for winter months, according to region. Much warmer clothes will be needed in the mountains all year round.

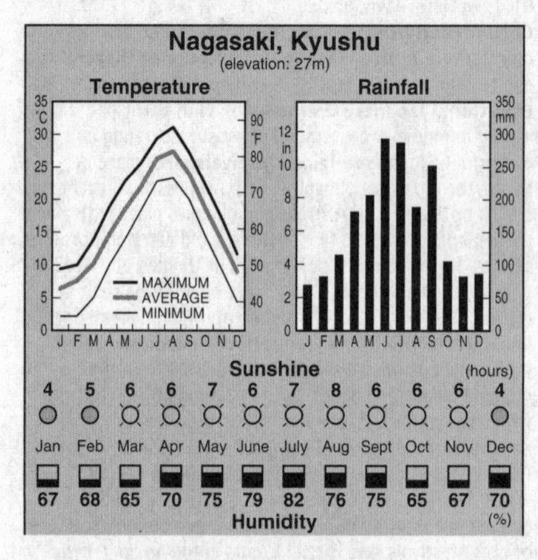

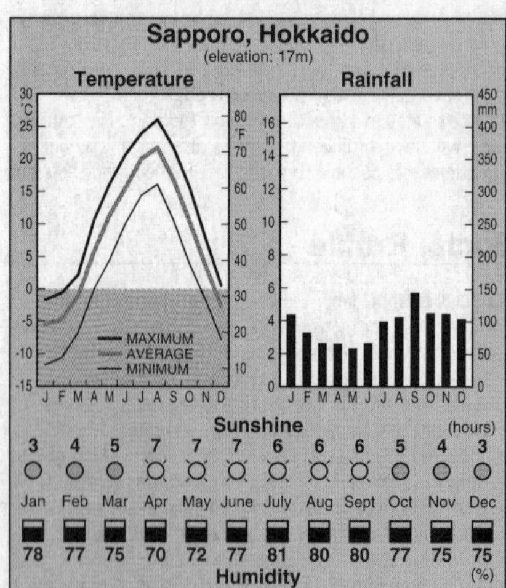

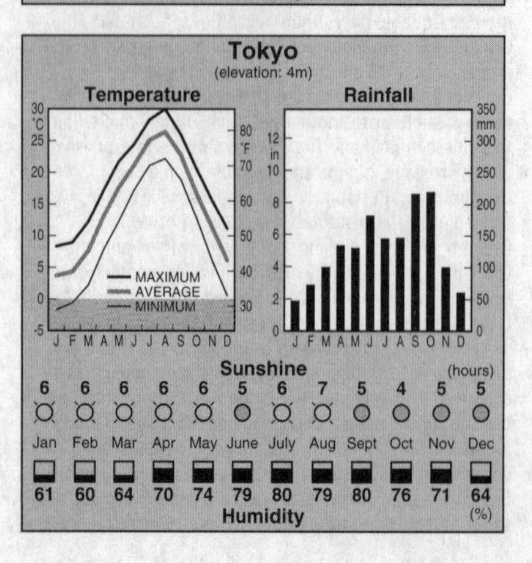

Jersey

LATEST TRAVEL ADVICE CONTACTS

British Foreign and Commonwealth Office
Tel: (0870) 606 0290 Website: www.fco.gov.uk

US Department of State
Website: http://travel.state.gov/travel

Canadian Department of Foreign Affairs and Int'l Trade
Tel: (1 800) 267 8376 Website: www.dfait-maeci.gc.ca

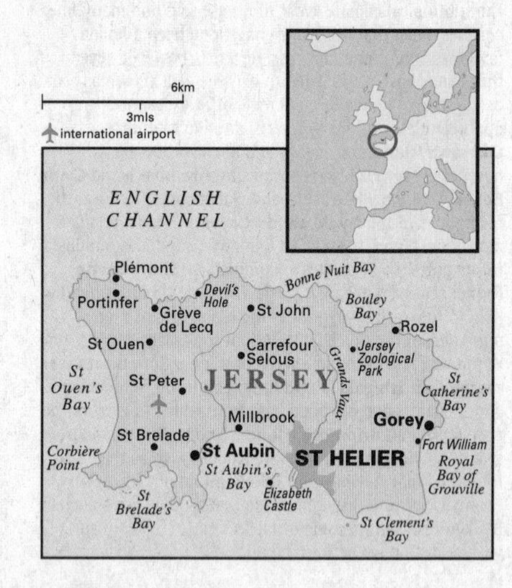

Location: English Channel, off the northern coast of France.

Country dialling code: 44.

Jersey is a Dependency of the British Crown represented abroad by British Embassies – see *United Kingdom* section.

Jersey Tourism
Liberation Square, St Helier, Jersey JE1 1BB, Channel Islands
Tel: (01534) 500 700 *or* 500 777 (general visitor enquiries) *or* 500 800 (brochure line) *or* 500 888 (accommodation reservations). Fax: (01534) 500 808.
E-mail: info@jersey.com *or* David.deCarteret@Jersey.com
Website: www.jersey.com

Jersey Tourism (Trade Information Office)
7 Lower Grosvenor Place, London SW1W 0EN, UK
Tel: (020) 7233 7474. Fax: (020) 7630 0747.
E-mail: trade@jersey.com
Website: www.jersey.com

VisitBritain (USA)
551 Fifth Avenue, 7th Floor, Suite 701, New York, NY 10176, USA
Tel: (1-800) 462 2748 (toll-free in the US only) *or* (212) 986 2266 (PR and trade enquiries only). Fax: (212) 986 1188.
E-mail: info@visitbritain.org *or* travelinfo@bta.org.uk
Website: www.jersey.com

General Information

AREA: 116.2 sq km (44.9 sq miles).
POPULATION: 87,186 (2001).
POPULATION DENSITY: 750.3 per sq km.
CAPITAL: St Helier. **Population**: 28,310 (2001).
GEOGRAPHY: Jersey is the largest of the Channel Islands, lying approximately 160km (100 miles) south of the coast of England and 23km (14 miles) from the coast of Normandy in France. The island is roughly 14.5km (9 miles) by 8km (5 miles). It slopes from north to south and often appears to visitors to be largely composed of pink granite. Jersey has over 20 bays, many small harbours and magnificent beaches bathed by the warm waters of the Gulf Stream.
GOVERNMENT: Dependency of the British Crown.
Head of State: Queen Elizabeth II, represented locally by the Lieutenant-Governor Michael Wilkes. **Head of Government**: Bailiff Sir Philip Bailhache since 1995.

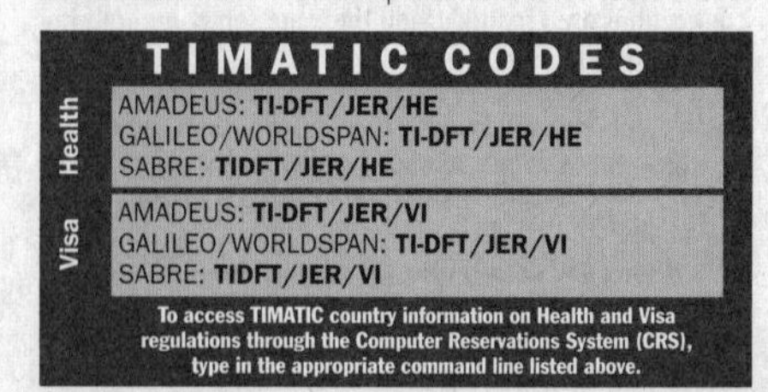

LANGUAGE: English is the official language. A dialect of Norman-French is still spoken by some people. French is still used in courts.
RELIGION: Each of Jersey's parishes has its own Anglican church, but some parishes, particularly St Helier, have been subdivided to provide more than one centre for Church of England worship. There are 12 Roman Catholic and 18 Methodist churches, as well as a wide range of free churches.
TIME: GMT (GMT + 1 from last Sunday in March to Saturday before last Sunday in October).
ELECTRICITY: 240 volts AC, 50Hz.
COMMUNICATIONS: Telephone: Country code: 44 (not necessary when dialling from the UK), followed by (0)1534. Outgoing international code: 00. **Mobile telephone:** GSM network 900/1800 operated by *Jersey Telecom* (website: www.jerseytelecom.com). Triple band and some single band handsets also function. Handsets can be hired for a minimum of three days (cost: £30-100). Most mobile phone networks will work in Jersey but require a roaming facility. 'Pay As You Go' phones will *not* work in Jersey. **Fax:** Facilities are available for business guests in a few hotels and at fax bureaux in St Helier. **Internet:** Public access is available at Internet cafes and libraries. Roaming agreements exist. Local ISPs include *Jtsurf* (website: www.jerseytelecoms.com), *Localdial* and *PSInet*. **Post:** There is a standard one-price rate to the UK, which is, in general, as good as a first class UK service, although the prices are lower than UK first class. There is also one rate for internal mail. UK stamps are not valid in Jersey. The main post office is in Broad Street, St Helier. Post office hours: Mon-Fri 0900-1730, Sat 0900-1230. **Press:** Newspapers published in Jersey are the *Jersey Evening Post* and *Jersey Weekly Post*.

Passport/Visa

Passport and Visa requirements are the same as those for the rest of the UK. See the *United Kingdom* section for further information.

Money

Currency: Jersey has its own currency but all UK notes and coins are legal tender, and circulate with the Channel Islands issue. Pound Sterling (£) = 100 pence. Notes are in denominations of £50, 20, 10 and 1. Coins are in denominations of 50, 20, 10, 5, 2 and 1 pence.
Note: Channel Islands notes and coins are not accepted in the UK, although they can be reconverted at parity in UK banks.
Exchange rates: For exchange rates and currency restrictions, see the *United Kingdom* section.
Currency exchange: Foreign currencies can be exchanged at bureaux de change, in banks and at many hotels. ATMs are available.
Credit & debit cards: American Express, Diners Club, MasterCard and Visa are all widely accepted. Check with your credit or debit card company for details of merchant acceptability and other services which may be available.
Travellers cheques: Widely accepted.
Banking hours: Mon-Fri 0930-1530. Some banks are open later on weekdays and Saturday mornings.

Duty Free

The Channel Islands are a low-duty zone. The following goods may be imported into Jersey by persons over 17 years of age without incurring customs duty:
200 cigarettes or 50 cigars or 100 cigarillos or 250g of tobacco; 2l of still table wine; 1l of spirits or 2l of alcoholic beverages under 22 per cent or 2l of sparkling or fortified wine; 50g (2 fl oz) perfume and 250ml eau de toilette; other goods to a value of £145.

Public Holidays

Public holidays are as for the rest of the UK (see *United Kingdom* section) with the following date also observed:
May 9: Liberation Day (commemorating the arrival of the British Forces at the end of World War II).

Health

	Special Precautions?	Certificate Required?
Yellow Fever	No	No
Cholera	No	No
Typhoid & Polio	No	N/A
Malaria	No	N/A

***Note:** Regulations and requirements may be subject to change at short notice, and you are advised to contact your doctor well in advance of your intended date of departure. Any numbers in the chart refer to the footnotes below.*

Health care: There is a reciprocal health agreement with the UK. On presenting proof of UK residence (driving licence, NHS card, etc), free in- and out-patient treatment is available at the General Hospital, Gloucester Street, St Helier (tel: (01534) 622 000) and at the Morning Medical Centre, Woodville Avenue, St Helier (tel: (01534) 616 833). The agreement does not cover the costs of medical treatment at a doctor's surgery (but there is a free GP-style surgery most mornings in Newgate Street, St Helier), prescribed medicines, or dental treatment, but travel by ambulance is free. Despite the agreement, private medical insurance is advised for UK residents on long visits in case emergency repatriation is necessary and to cover the cost of prescribed medicines and dental treatment. All visitors should bring the name and address of their family doctor in case of a serious accident or illness.

Travel - International

AIR: Jersey can be reached by air from London and most other major cities in the UK. There are also direct flights to Jersey from Antwerp and Zurich. Major airlines operating to Jersey include *British Airways*, *British Midland* and *Flybe.com* (from London and major UK cities), *VLM* (from London) and *Swiss* (from Zurich). Airlines operating to Jersey from the French coast include *Aurigny Air Services* (from Dinan).
Approximate flight times: From Jersey to *London* is 50 minutes.
International airports: *St Peters (JER)* is 8km (5 miles) from St Helier. Facilities include low-tariff shopping, restaurant and bar, car hire, ATMs, business facilities and provision for the disabled. Taxis are available and the local bus leaves for St Helier centre every 20 minutes.
Departure tax: None.
SEA: There are several sea routes to Jersey from abroad:
From the UK: Crossings are by catamaran (car/passenger) from Poole (travel time - three hours 45 minutes) and Weymouth (travel time - three hours 30 minutes). Catamarans for foot passengers only operate to St Malo (travel time - one hour 10 minutes). A car ferry operates from Portsmouth (travel time - 10 hours 30 minutes). Crossings are more frequent between April and October. For further information, contact Condor Ferries (tel: (0845) 345 2000; e-mail: reservations@condorferries.co.uk; website: www.condorferries.co.uk).

Credit: © Jersey Tourism & Stuart Abraham

From France: From St Malo: car/passenger and passenger crossings with *Emeraude Lines*; passenger crossings with *Condor Ferries*. From Granville: passenger crossings with *Emeraude Lines* and *Granville Island Sea*. From Carteret: *Alizés Côtes des Iles* and *Emeraude Lines*.
From Guernsey: *Condor Ferries* and *Emeraude Lines* operate between Jersey and Guernsey. Services are also available from the other Channel Islands.
Visitors bringing speedboats, surfboards or sailboards into Jersey *must* register at the Harbour Office on arrival. Third party insurance is required.

Travel - Internal

ROAD: Traffic drives on the left. There are over 800km (500 miles) of roads and lanes crisscrossing the island. There is a speed limit of 64kph (40mph). **Bus**: These operate throughout the island; the network centres on the bus and coach station at Weighbridge, St Helier. Explorer tickets are valid for one, three, five and seven days (prices range from £5.75 to £23.95), available from *Connex* in St Helier, and cannot be purchased prior to arrival. **Car hire**: This is generally very cheap, and so is petrol. There are over 30 car hire firms, mostly in St Helier. Persons wishing to hire a car must: (a) be over 21 years of age; (b) have had a full licence for at least one year; and (c) have a valid full licence with no endorsements or disqualifications for dangerous driving or driving over the alcohol limit within the previous five years. **Bicycle hire:** Available from over 10 firms; mainly in St Helier, one in Millbrook and one in St Ouen. **Mopeds:** Can also be hired from a number of companies in St Helier. Crash helmets must be worn. Addresses and telephone numbers of all these companies can be obtained from Jersey Tourism (see *Contact Addresses* section). **Documentation**: Visitors who wish to drive must have a valid Certificate of Insurance or an International Green Card, and a valid driving licence or International (not UK International) Driving Permit (not photocopies). Nationality plates must be displayed. **Motor caravans** and **trailers** may not be imported.

Accommodation

The booklet *Jersey – Open House*, available from Jersey Tourism (see *Contact Addresses* section), gives comprehensive information on all types of accommodation on the island. Short-break and longer-stay holidays are available throughout the year. The most popular season is from May until September.
HOTELS: The official consumer information pack, compiled by the Jersey Hospitality Association, la rue le Masurier, St Helier, Jersey JE2 4YE (tel: (01534) 721 421; fax: (01534) 722 496; e-mail: hospitality@jerseyhols.com; website: www.jerseyhols.com) is available from Jersey Tourism (see Contact Addresses section).
Disabled visitors should contact the Maison des Landes Hotel, St Ouen, Jersey JE3 2AA (tel: (01534) 481 683; fax: (01534) 485 327; e-mail: maisonlandes@localdial.com; website: http://mdl.2000net.com) for information. This offers accommodation for up to 40 disabled visitors and family/friends. All rooms have en suite bathrooms and there is a heated swimming pool. It is open between early April and late October.
Grading: Jersey has its own hotel and guest house grading scheme. Hotels are graded from **1 to 5 suns** and guest houses are graded from **1 to 3 diamonds**. The greater the number of suns or diamonds, the higher the grade achieved. All hotels are inspected and graded annually.
GUEST-HOUSES: There are more than 200 guest houses on the island, some offering bed, breakfast and evening meals, others just bed and breakfast. Despite the large number of establishments, advance booking is recommended as many guest houses are not open throughout the whole year.
SELF-CATERING: There is limited self-catering accommodation registered with the Tourism Department. Premises taking less than six people do not have to register and are not inspected. This type of accommodation is available through a number of handling agents. Furnished flats, bungalows, chalets and villas are not generally available, owing to the acute shortage of housing for permanent residents. Some units do, however, become available at various times and advertisements can be placed in the local newspaper. Contact the *Jersey Evening Post*, Advertisement Department, PO Box 582, Five Oaks, St Saviour, Jersey JE4 8XQ (tel: (01534) 611 611; fax: (01534) 611 704; e-mail: advertising@jerseyeveningpost.com; website: www.thisisjersey.com) for details.
CAMPING: Camping is only permitted on recognised

campsites, of which there are four. Owing to limited capacity, advance booking is essential. There are no caravan sites on Jersey.
YOUTH HOSTELS: There are no youth hostels on Jersey.

Credit: © Jersey Tourism & Stuart Abraham

Resorts & Excursions

The largest of the Channel Islands, Jersey is highly developed for tourism. It boasts a formidable array, for its small size, of modern attractions and special events catering for its huge number of visitors. The island does not neglect its natural and historical heritage though – there is plenty of historical interest as well as many beautiful scenic attractions.
ST HELIER: Two historic fortifications overlook the capital, by far the biggest town on the island. **Elizabeth Castle** stands on an island on the bay, accessible by causeway at low tide. This imposing fortress withstood Cromwell's forces for seven weeks in 1651, and housed occupying Germans during World War II. On an outcrop above the town, **Fort Regent** is now a leisure complex with sports and conference facilities. The former castle's ramparts offer excellent views across the town and the bay. Highlights in the town centre include the award-winning **Jersey Museum**, the **Maritime Museum** and the **Occupation Tapestry Gallery**.
THE COAST: Jersey is known for its **Points**, clifftop headlands overlooking the sea and offering fine views. Most of these are on the northern side of the island, notably those at **Grosnez** and **Plemont** on the northwest corner. Further east are **Belle Hougue**, **Ronez**, **Sorel** and **Vicard Points**, while on the southwest tip, **Corbière Point** is another popular sightseeing port of call. Visitor attractions dotted around the coastline include mighty **Mont Orgueil** castle at **Gorey**, as well as a number of restored military bunkers in various locations. The **Jersey Zoological Park**, in **Trinity**, is the headquarters of the **Jersey Wildlife Preservation Trust**, founded by the late Gerald Durrell. The Trust is a sanctuary for many endangered species of animals and is close to **Bouley Bay**. At **La Grève de Lecq**, there is the **British Army Barracks Museum**, while a **Flower Centre** with tropical gardens and trout pond and the **Kempt Tower Interpretation Centre** are in **St Ouen's Bay**.
On the south side of the island, and on either side of St Helier, extensive beaches stretch 5km (3 miles) west around **St Aubin's Bay**, and east to **La Roque Point**. **Portelet**, a secluded sandy bay; **St Brelade's Bay**, regarded as one of the island's most beautiful beaches and popular for windsurfing and water-skiing; and **Beauport**, a small bay flanked by towering rocks of pink granite, are situated to the west of **St Aubin**.
Both east and west seaboards are dominated by long, sweeping beaches - the **Royal Bay of Grouville** and **St Catherine's Bay** flanking the town of **Gorey** to the east, and the 8km- (5mile-) beach on **St Ouen's Bay**, which forms almost the entirety of the west coast. This area is particularly good for surfers. There are fewer beaches on the north coast, but **Plémont**, with its rock pools and caves, is particularly attractive. **Bouley Bay** is popular with sub-aqua enthusiasts and anglers; and **Rozel**, on the northeast coast, is a fishing harbour with an old fort and a small sandy beach.
INLAND: Traditional crafts are a feature of the island, and many of the workshops are open to visitors. Leatherwork at **L'Etacq** (**St Ouen**) and stoneground flour from locally grown corn at **Le Moulin de Quetivel**, **St Peter's Valley**, are among these, while in **Grouville** at **Jersey Pottery**, also renowned for its restaurant and gardens, one is able to visit the workshops and retail area.
La Mare Vineyards, close to **Devil's Hole**, has vineyards set in the grounds of an 18th-century farmhouse. There are displays from the local cider industry and homemade products are on sale.
St Peter is the home of the 24-lane **Jersey Bowl** bowling centre, and the award-winning **Living Legend Village** attraction. There is also a museum in **St Ouen**, displaying floats entered in the **Battle of Flowers**, a festival held on the second Thursday in August each year. At **La Hougue Bie** in **Grouville**, a museum housed in a massive neolithic tomb dating back 5000 years has exhibitions on the agriculture, archaeology, geology and history of the island. **Howard Davis Park** in **St Saviour** is an attractive public garden with many subtropical plants flourishing in the mild climate. In the **St Lawrence** parish, St Peter's Valley, is the **German Military Underground Hospital**, which contains displays of photographs and documents, and a collection of firearms, daggers and memorabilia from the World War II occupation.

Sport & Activities

Outdoor pursuits: The best way of seeing the island is to walk or cycle round it. The north has the highest land and the most rugged scenery, but gentler **walks** are possible inland and in the south. One suggested route follows the line of the old Jersey Railway – now a traffic-free public path – which runs from St Aubin to the lighthouse at Corbière on the island's southwestern tip. Jersey's network of 'Green Lanes', which have a 24kph (15mph) speed limit, are ideal for cyclists; free organised **cycling** and walking tours are available.
Swimming: This is a popular leisure activity, and there are many bays and beaches offering excellent bathing (for information on the best beaches, see the *Resorts & Excursions* section). Bathers should beware, however, as Jersey has some of the largest tidal movements in the world, with as much as 12m (40ft) between low and high tide, causing very strong currents. Some beaches are patrolled by beach guards and have safe areas marked with flags. On the western coast (St Ouen's Bay), the strong waves can also prove hazardous. There are open-air swimming pools at Havre des Pas and West Park, and two indoor pools, one at Fort Regent and one at Quennevais, St Brelade.
Watersports: Waters around the island support a rich and varied marine life and there are good facilities for **divers**. Boat dives, skindiving and equipment hire are available from specialist operators. The best area for **surfing** is around St Ouen's Bay. There are surfing schools and equipment-hire facilities. **Windsurfing** races are held during the summer and there are several windsurfing schools. **Water-skiing** facilities and tuition are available. There are two **sailing** clubs on the island: The Royal Channel Islands Yacht Club, St Aubin, and The St Helier Yacht Club. There is also a canoeing school in St Helier. **Angling** is very popular, particularly during the summer, and there are a number of sea-fishing clubs which run shore and boat festivals during the summer. Boating and fishing trips operate from St Helier. Warning: Fishing from rocks should not be attempted until the visitor has obtained information about local tides, currents and weather conditions. Fly fishing is available at the Val de la Mar and the St Catherine Reservoirs; temporary membership can be obtained.
Other: Jersey has two 18-hole **golf** courses open to visitors who are members of a recognised golf club. Both courses are well known throughout the golfing world: **La Moye** in St Brelade and **Royal Jersey** in Grouville (website: www.royaljersey.com); both courses require proof of handicap or membership. Golfers who do not belong to a club can play at the 18-hole *Les Mielles* or *Les Ormes* courses and either of the two nine-hole courses at *Wheatlands* or *Greve D'Azette*, where no handicap is needed. For further details, contact Jersey Tourism (see *Contact Addresses* section). Several schools provide **horse-riding** tuition and escorted hacks. Temporary membership of the island's two **squash** clubs is available; contact Jersey Squash Club and the Lido Squash and Social Club. There are also courts at the Fort Regent Leisure Centre. Pottery and other **crafts** are popular in Jersey and courses (for pottery, candle-making or leatherwork) are available.

Social Profile

FOOD & DRINK: Jersey has an excellent range of restaurants to cater for every taste. Seafood is very popular and a wide selection of home-grown produce is available; scallops, oysters, spider crabs and lobster are particularly good. Fresh seafood can be bought from the local fish market. Jersey cows are renowned for their rich and creamy milk; cream tea with strawberries is a speciality and available in Jersey's many tea rooms. The island has an enviable reputation for good cuisine whether in small pubs, wine bars or high-class restaurants.
Licensing hours: Daily 0900-2300.
SHOPPING: The island is a low-duty area and there is no VAT. As well as St Helier (where there are two covered markets), there are shopping areas such as Red Houses, St Brelade and Gorey, St Martin. Luxury items such as spirits, cigarettes, jewellery and perfumes are popular buys. Local products such as knitwear, pottery, woodcrafts and even flowers are good value. **Shopping hours**: Mon-Sat 0900-1730. The markets and some shops are closed on Thursday afternoons. During the summer months, many shops are open in the evenings.
SPECIAL EVENTS: For a complete list and further dates, contact Jersey Tourism (see *Contact Addresses* section). The following is a selection of special events occurring in Jersey in 2005:
Feb 13-19 *Chess Festival*. **Apr 2-3** *Spring Flower Show*. **Apr 2-10** *Spring Garden Festival*. **Apr 16-24** *Island Flavours - A Taste of Jersey in Springtime*. **May 2-Jun 6** *Jersey Festival of Motoring*. **May 9** *60th Anniversary of Liberation Day*. **May 14** *Gorey Fete de la Mer*. **May 28-30** *La Fête Nouormande*. **Jun 18-19** *Early Summer Rose and Flower Festival*. **Jun 24-26** *Out of the Blue Maritime Festival*. **Jul 16-17** *Gorey Regatta*. **Jul 17** *Jazz in the Park*. **Jul 17-24** *Jersey in Bloom*. **Aug 11-12** *Jersey Battle of Flowers*. **Aug 13-19** *Jersey Film Festival*. **Aug 20-21** *Summer Flower Show*. **Aug 27-Sep 3** *Jersey Open Shore Angling Festival*. **Sep 3** *Jersey Live Music Festival*. **Oct 1-Nov 12** *Tennerfest*. **Oct 7-9** *Autumn Fruit and Flower Festival*. **Nov 26-Dec 11** *La Fête de Noué Christmas Festival*.
SOCIAL CONVENTIONS: Similar to the rest of the UK, with French influences (see the *United Kingdom* section).
Tipping: In general, this follows UK practice.

Business Profile

ECONOMY: Although agriculture is still important as a source of employment and prestige – Jersey cows are renowned throughout the world – offshore banking and tourism are the mainstays of the economy: the former because of the island's exemption from the UK tax system and the latter through continental influence and a benign climate. Finance and banking account for more than half of the GDP and are largely responsible for Jersey's unemployment rate of less than 1 per cent. New and highly regulated legislation designed to tighten up some of the less salubrious aspects of Jersey's financial environment should serve to strengthen its reputation in an era when offshore finance is coming under growing political pressure through its implication in money-laundering. In the last few years Jersey has signed up to several international initiatives designed to tackle the problem while improving financial transparency.
BUSINESS: Businesspeople are generally expected to dress smartly (suits are usual apart from Fridays when office workers generally 'dress down'). Appointments should be made and the exchange of business cards is customary. A knowledge of English is essential. **Office hours**: Mon-Fri 0900/0930-1700/1730.
COMMERCIAL INFORMATION: The following organisation can offer advice: Jersey Chamber of Commerce, Chamber House, 25 Pier Road, St Helier, Jersey JE1 4HF (tel: (01534) 871 031 or 724 536; fax: (01534) 734 942; e-mail: admin@jersey-chamber.co.uk; website: www.jerseychamber.com).
CONFERENCES/CONVENTIONS: Jersey plays host each year to a large number of conferences; the main period is from October to May. For further details, contact the Jersey Conference Bureau, Liberation Square, St Helier, Jersey JE1 1BB (tel: (01534) 733 449; e-mail: jcb@jersey.com; website: www.jerseyconferences.co.uk).

Climate

The most popular holiday season is from May until the end of September, with temperatures averaging 20-21°C (68-70°F). Rainfall averages 33 inches a year, most of which falls during the cooler months. Sea temperatures average over 17°C (63°F) in deep water during the summer.
Required clothing: Normal beach and holidaywear for summer, with a jumper or similar as there are often sea breezes. Warm winterwear and rainwear are advised.

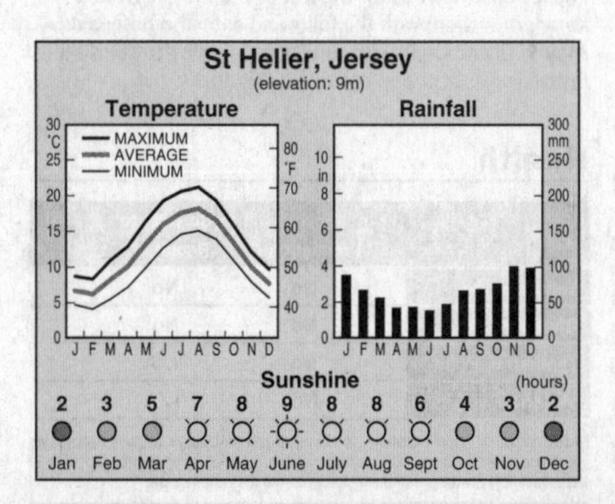

Jordan

LATEST TRAVEL ADVICE CONTACTS

British Foreign and Commonwealth Office
Tel: (0870) 606 0290 Website: www.fco.gov.uk

US Department of State
Website: http://travel.state.gov/travel

Canadian Department of Foreign Affairs and Int'l Trade
Tel: (1 800) 267 8376 Website: www.dfait-maeci.gc.ca

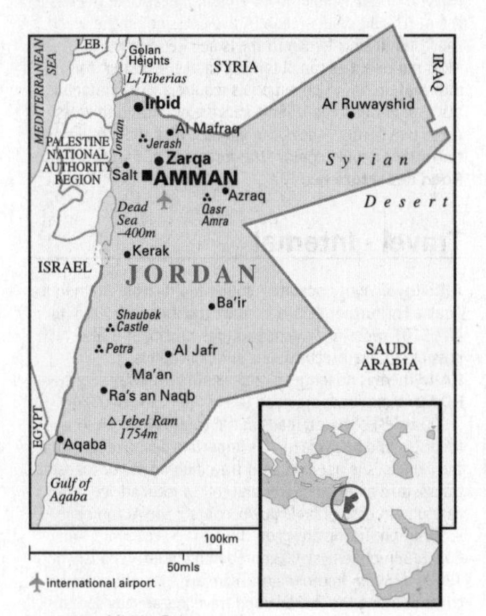

Location: Middle East.

Country dialling code: 962.

Ministry of Tourism & Antiquities
PO Box 224, Amman 11118, Jordan
Tel: (6) 460 3360. Fax: (6) 464 8465.
E-mail: contacts@tourism.jo

Jordan Tourism Board
PO Box 830688, Amman 11183, Jordan
Tel: (6) 567 8294. Fax: (6) 567 8295.
E-mail: jtb@nets.com.jo
Website: www.see-jordan.com

Embassy of the Hashemite Kingdom of Jordan
6 Upper Phillimore Gardens, London W8 7HB, UK
Tel: (020) 7937 3685. Fax: (020) 7937 8795.
E-mail: info@jordanembassyuk.org
Website: www.jordanembassyuk.org
Opening hours: Mon-Fri 0900-1200 (consulate enquiries); 1400-1500 (visa collection).

Jordan Tourism Board
Kennedy House, 1st Floor, 115 Hammersmith Road, London W14 0QH, UK
Tel: (020) 7371 6496. Fax: (020) 7603 2424.
E-mail: info@jordantourismboard.co.uk
Website: www.see-jordan.com

Jordan Information Service
6 Upper Phillimore Gardens, London W8 7HA, UK
Tel: (020) 7937 9499. Fax: (020) 7937 6741.
E-mail: info@jiblondon.com
Opening hours: Mon-Fri 0900-1500.
Media enquiries only.

British Embassy
PO Box 87, Amman 11118, Jordan
Tel: (6) 592 3100. Fax: (6) 592 3759.
E-mail: info@britain.org.jo
Website: www.britain.org.jo

Embassy of the Hashemite Kingdom of Jordan
3504 International Drive, NW, Washington, DC 20008, USA
Tel: (202) 966 2664 *or* 966 2861 (consular section).
Fax: (202) 966 3110 *or* 686 4491 (consular section).
E-mail: HKJEmbassyDC@aol.com *or* HKJConsular@aol.com (consular section).
Website: www.jordanembassyus.org

TIMATIC CODES

Health	AMADEUS: **TI-DFT/AMM/HE** GALILEO/WORLDSPAN: **TI-DFT/AMM/HE** SABRE: **TIDFT/AMM/HE**
Visa	AMADEUS: **TI-DFT/AMM/VI** GALILEO/WORLDSPAN: **TI-DFT/AMM/VI** SABRE: **TIDFT/AMM/VI**

To access TIMATIC country information on Health and Visa regulations through the Computer Reservations System (CRS), type in the appropriate command line listed above.

Jordan Tourism Board
6867 Elm Street, Suite 102, Mclean, VA 22101, USA
Tel: (703) 243 7404/5 *or* (877) 733 5673 (toll-free in USA and Canada). Fax: (703) 243 7406.
E-mail: info@seejordan.org
Website: www.seejordan.org

Embassy of the United States of America
PO Box 354, Abdoun, Amman 11118, Jordan
Tel: (6) 590 6000. Fax: (6) 592 0121.
E-mail: ResponseAmman@state.gov (visa- and travel-related enquiries).
Website: http://amman.usembassy.gov

Embassy of the Hashemite Kingdom of Jordan
100 Bronson Avenue, Suite 701, Ottawa, Ontario K1R 6G8, Canada
Tel: (613) 238 8091. Fax: (613) 232 3341.

Canadian Embassy
Street address: Pearl of Shmeisani Building, Abdalhameed Shoman Street, Shmeisani, Amman 11180, Jordan
Postal address: PO Box 815403, Amman 11180, Jordan
Tel: (6) 566 6124. Fax: (6) 568 9227.
E-mail: amman@dfait-maeci.gc.ca
Website: www.dfait-maeci.gc.ca/world/embassies/jordan

Credit: © Jordan Tourism Board

General Information

AREA: 89,342 sq km (34,495 sq miles; not including West Bank).
POPULATION: 5,329,000 (2002). The West Bank is now administered by the Palestinian National Authority; see *Israel* section for details of area and population.
POPULATION DENSITY: 59.6 per sq km.
CAPITAL: Amman. **Population**: 2,027,685 (2002).
GEOGRAPHY: Jordan shares borders with Israel, the Syrian Arab Republic, Iraq and Saudi Arabia. The Dead Sea is to the northwest and the Red Sea to the southwest. A high plateau extends 324km (201 miles) from the Syrian Arab Republic to Ras en Naqab in the south with the capital of Amman at a height of 800m (2625ft). Northwest of the capital are undulating hills, some forested, others cultivated. The Dead Sea depression, 400m (1300ft) below sea level in the west, is the lowest point on earth. The River Jordan connects the Dead Sea with Lake Tiberias (Israel). To the west of Jordan is the Palestinian National Authority Region. The east of the country is mainly desert. Jordan has a tiny stretch of Red Sea coast, centred on Aqaba.
GOVERNMENT: Constitutional Monarchy since 1952.
Head of State: King Abdullah Ibn al-Hussein al-Hashimi since 1999. **Head of Government**: Prime Minister Faisal al-Fayez since 2003.
LANGUAGE: Arabic is the official language. English is widely spoken in the cities. French, German, Italian and Spanish are also spoken.
RELIGION: Over 90 per cent Sunni Muslim, with Christian and Shi'i Muslim minorities.
TIME: GMT + 2 (GMT + 3 from April to September).
ELECTRICITY: 230 volts AC, 50Hz. Lamp sockets are screw-type, and there is a wide range of wall sockets.
COMMUNICATIONS: Telephone: IDD service is available within cities, with direct dialling to most countries. Country code: 962 (followed by 6 for Amman). Outgoing international code: 00. There are telephone and facsimile connections to Israel from Jordan. **Mobile telephone:** GSM 900 network in use. Network providers include *Jordan MTS* (website: www.fastlink.com.jo) and *MobileCom* (website: www.mobilecom.jo). **Fax:** The use of fax is increasing. Most good hotels have facilities and the main post office in Amman also provides a fax service. **Telegram:** The overseas telegram service is reasonably good. Telegrams may be sent from the Central Telegraph Office; Post Office, First Circle, Jebel Amman; Post Office, Jordan Intercontinental, Jebel Amman; or from major hotels and post offices. **Internet:** There are Internet cafes in Amman, Aqabam Jerash and Jordan. The main ISP is *Jordan Data Communications* (website: www.wanadoo.jo). **Post:** Packages should be left opened for customs officials. Airmail to Western Europe takes three to five days. For a higher charge, there is a rapid service guaranteeing delivery within 24 hours to around 22 countries. Post office hours: Sat-Thurs 0800-1800, closed Friday (except for the downtown post office on Prince Mohammed Street in Amman which is open on Fridays). **Press:** The English-language newspapers are *Arab Daily*, *The Jordan Times* (daily) and *The Star* (weekly). **Radio:** BBC World Service (website: www.bbc.co.uk/worldservice) and Voice of America (website: www.voa.gov) can be received. From time to time the frequencies change and the most up-to-date can be found online.

Passport/Visa

	Passport Required?	Visa Required?	Return Ticket Required?
Full British	Yes	Yes/1	No
Australian	Yes	Yes/1	No
Canadian	Yes	Yes/1	No
USA	Yes	Yes/1	No
Other EU	Yes	Yes/1	No
Japanese	Yes	Yes/1	No

Note: *Regulations and requirements may be subject to change at short notice, and you are advised to contact the appropriate diplomatic or consular authority before finalising travel arrangements. Details of these may be found at the head of this country's entry. Any numbers in the chart refer to the footnotes below.*

PASSPORTS: Passport valid for six months required by all.
VISAS: Required by all except the following:
(a) nationals of Bahrain, Egypt, Iraq, Kuwait, Oman, Qatar, Saudi Arabia, Syrian Arab Republic, United Arab Emirates and Yemen for maximum stays of one month (extensions may be obtained at the nearest police station);
(b) transit passengers continuing their journey to another country by the same or first connecting aircraft within 24 hours provided holding valid onward or return documentation and not leaving the airport. Some nationalities may obtain a seven-day transit visa upon arrival if travelling from a neighbouring Arab country. Transit visas can only be issued at Jordanian airports/airlines and not at embassies or consulates.
Note: 1. (a) Nationals of certain countries – including all Western European countries, Australia, Canada, Japan, New Zealand and the USA – can obtain visas on arrival at the airport in Jordan. Multiple-entry visas can only be obtained at the nearest Embassy/Consulate. (b) For information about land border crossings, see the *Travel - International* section or contact the Embassy.
Types of visa and cost: *Tourist*, *Transit* and *Business*: £11 (single-entry); £21 (multiple-entry).
Validity: Validity varies according to nationality. For Australian, Canadian, UK and US nationals, visas are valid as follows: *Tourist*: Three months for single-entry, six months for multiple-entry; *Business*: Three months. After the first two weeks of stay, all visitors holding a visa must report to the nearest police station.
Application to: Consulate (or Consular section at Embassy); see *Contact Addresses* section.
Application requirements: (a) Completed application form. (b) Passport valid for at least six months with at least one blank page. (c) One recent passport-size photo. (d) Stamped, self-addressed, recorded or registered envelope if applying by post. (e) Fee (only cash or postal orders are accepted). *Business* (a)-(e) and, (f) Company letter supporting application.
Working days required: Two if applying in person; two weeks by post once application has been received.
Note: Nationals of Afghanistan, Albania, Angola, Bangladesh, Belize, Benin, Bosnia & Herzegovina, Botswana, Burkina Faso, Burundi, Cambodia, Cameroon, Central African Republic, Chad, Congo (Dem Rep), Congo (Rep), Colombia, Côte d'Ivoire, Cuba, Djibouti, Eritrea, Ethiopia, Gabon, Gambia, Ghana, Guinea, Guinea-Bissau, Guyana, India, Iran, Laos, Lebanon, Liberia, Macedonia (Former Yugoslav Republic of), Madagascar, Mali, Mauritania, Mongolia, Mozambique, Namibia, Niger, Nigeria, Pakistan, Papua New Guinea, The Philippines, Russian Federation, Senegal, Sierra Leone, Somalia, Sri Lanka, Sudan, Tanzania, Togo, Uganda, Vietnam and Zambia are required to seek approval from the Ministry of Interior in order to obtain a visa and therefore should allow two to four weeks for their

applications to be processed. Contact the Embassy for further information (see *Contact Addresses* section).
Temporary residence: Apply to Embassy; see *Contact Addresses* section.

Money

Currency: Dinar (JD) = 1000 fils. Notes are in denominations of JD50, 20, 10, 5 and 1, and 500 fils. Coins are in denominations of 1000, 500, 250, 100, 50, 25, 10 and 5 fils.
Currency exchange: Foreign currencies can be exchanged easily in banks and bureaux de change. Most hotels also provide exchange facilities. The daily exchange rates are published in local newspapers.
Credit & debit cards: American Express and Visa are widely accepted, whilst Diners Club and MasterCard have more limited use. Check with your credit and debit card company for details of merchant acceptability and other services which may be available.
Travellers cheques: Those issued by UK banks are accepted by licensed banks and bureaux de change. To avoid additional exchange rate charges, travellers are advised to take travellers cheques in US Dollars.
Currency restrictions: The import of local currency is unlimited. The export of local currency is restricted to JD300. The import of foreign currency is unrestricted provided declared on arrival. Export of foreign currency is up to the amount imported and declared.
Exchange rate indicators: The following figures are included as a guide to the movements of the Dinar against Sterling and the US Dollar:

Date	Feb '04	May '04	Aug '04	Nov '04
£1.00=	1.29	1.27	1.30	1.34
$1.00=	0.71	0.71	0.70	0.70

Banking hours: Sat-Thurs 0830-1500. Hours during Ramadan are 0830-1000, although some banks open in the afternoon.

Credit: © Jordan Tourism Board

Duty Free

The following goods may be imported into Jordan by people 18 years of age and older without incurring customs duty: *200 cigarettes or 25 cigars or 200g of tobacco (a charge of JD3.75 for each additional 200 cigarettes, up to a maximum of 2000); 1l of alcohol (a charge of JD2.91 for each additional litre, up to a maximum of 4l); one or two opened bottles of perfume and reasonable amount of eau-de-cologne or lotion in opened bottles for personal use only; gifts up to the value of JD50 or the equivalent of US$150.*
Prohibited items: Narcotics.
Restricted items: Firearms, sporting guns and other weapons require prior approval from both country of origin and destination. They may be carried as checked baggage only.

Public Holidays

2005: Jan 1 New Year's Day. **Jan 21** Eid al-Adha (Feast of the Sacrifice). **Feb 10** Islamic New Year. **Mar 25** Good Friday. **Mar 28** Easter Monday. **Apr 21** Eid al-Mawlid al-Nawabi (Birth of the Prophet). **May 1** Labour Day. **May 25** Independence Day. **Jun 9** Accession of HM King Abdullah. **Jun 10** Army Day. **Sep 12** Isra wa al-Miraj (Prophet's Night Journey). **Nov 4-6** Eid al-Fitr (End of Ramadan). **Nov 14** King Hussein Remembrance Day. **Dec 25** Christmas. **Dec 31** New Year's Eve.
2006: Jan 1 New Year's Day. **Jan 10** Eid al-Adha (Feast of the Sacrifice). **Feb 31** Islamic New Year. **Apr 11** Eid al-Mawlid al-Nawabi (Birth of the Prophet). **Apr 14** Good Friday. **Apr 17** Easter Monday. **May 1** Labour Day. **May 25** Independence Day. **Jun 9** Accession of HM King Abdullah. **Jun 10** Army Day. **Sep 12** Isra wa al-Miraj (Prophet's Night Journey). **Nov 14** King Hussein Remembrance Day. **Oct 22-24** Eid al-Fitr (End of Ramadan). **Dec 25** Christmas. **Dec 31** New Year's Eve.
Note: (a) Christmas and Easter holidays are only observed by Christian business establishments. (b) Muslim festivals are timed according to local sightings of various phases of the moon and the dates given above are approximations. During the lunar month of Ramadan that precedes Eid al-Fitr, Muslims fast during the day and feast at night and normal business patterns may be interrupted. Many restaurants are closed during the day and there may be restrictions on smoking and drinking. Some disruption may continue into Eid al-Fitr itself. Eid al-Fitr and Eid al-Adha may last anything from two to 10 days, depending on the region. For more information, see the *World of Islam* appendix.

Health

	Special Precautions?	Certificate Required?
Yellow Fever	No	1
Cholera	No	No
Typhoid & Polio	2	N/A
Malaria	No	N/A

Note: Regulations and requirements may be subject to change at short notice, and you are advised to contact your doctor well in advance of your intended date of departure. Any numbers in the chart refer to the footnotes below.

1: A yellow fever vaccination certificate is required from travellers over one year of age coming from infected areas.
2: Immunisation against typhoid and poliomyelitis is often recommended.
Food & drink: Water that is not bottled should never be drunk unless it has first been boiled or otherwise sterilised. Milk should not be consumed unless bought in a container stating that it has been pasteurised. Avoid dairy products which are likely to have been made from unboiled milk. Food and water in rural areas may carry increased risk. Only eat well-cooked meat and fish, preferably served hot. Salad and mayonnaise may carry increased risk. Vegetables should be cooked and fruit peeled.
Other risks: *Hepatitis A* may occur, *hepatitis B* is endemic. *Heat* and *dehydration* may become a health hazard for pilgrims on their way to Mecca and Medina. Precautions should be taken.
Rabies is present. For those at high risk, vaccination before arrival should be considered. If you are bitten, seek medical advice without delay. For more information, consult the *Health* appendix.
Health care: Health insurance is recommended. There are excellent hospitals in large towns and cities, with clinics in many villages.
Notes: An HIV test is mandatory for anyone planning to stay longer than three months.

Travel - International

Note: Following the military action in Iraq, there is a high risk of terrorism in Jordan and vigilance is necessary. The Jordanian security forces foiled several possible terrorist attacks in 2004. Extra care should be taken at the crossing points between Jordan and Israel.
AIR: The national airline is *Royal Jordanian Airlines (RJ)* (website: www.rja.com.jo). *British Mediterranean* (a franchise partner of *British Airways*) operates daily services from London to Amman. Other airlines serving Jordan include *Aeroflot Russian Airlines, Air Canada, Air France, Arkia Israeli Airlines, Delta Air Lines, Emirates, Gulf Air, KLM Royal Dutch Airlines, Lufthansa* and *United Airlines.*
Approximate flight times: From *London* to Amman is five hours.
International airports: *Queen Alia International (AMM)* is 35km (22 miles) southeast of the capital, to which it is connected by a good highway (travel time - approximately 40 minutes). There is a regular bus service to Amman every 30 minutes (travel time - approximately 50 minutes), and taxis are also available. Facilities include duty free shops, bank/bureau de change, eating and shopping facilities, and car hire (*Avis* and *Hertz*).
Departure tax: JD5 for individual tourists, JD25 for Jordanian nationals on international departures. Transit passengers are exempt.
SEA: The only port is Aqaba, which is on the cruise itineraries for *Cunard, P&O* and *Swan Hellenic.* Car and passenger ferries from Aqaba to Cairo and Aqaba to Nuweiba operate twice-daily and there is also a high-speed hydrofoil service. There is a weekly passenger service to Suez and Jeddah. Contact *Telstar Maritime Agencies* (tel: (6) 464 0168; e-mail: amman@telstarmaritime.com; website: www.telstarmaritime.com).
Departure tax: JD6.
RAIL: The Hijaz Railway operates on the old Ottoman track between Amman and Damascus (Syrian Arab Republic).
ROAD: There are roads into the Syrian Arab Republic via Ramtha or Jaber. The route to/from the Syrian Arab Republic to Western Europe is through Turkey. Driving time from Amman to Damascus is four hours. From Egypt, there is a ferry connection from Nuweiba to Aqaba (visa should be obtained in advance). Multiple-entry visas may be needed. A coach service runs from Damascus to Irbid or Amman. There is a share-taxi service from Amman to Damascus. Public buses and coaches run from Amman to Damascus and Baghdad daily, as well as to Allenby Bridge for the crossing to the Palestinian National Authority Region. To cross, a visa is required, and it should be obtained in advance. Further border crossings to Israel are at Sheikh Hussein Bridge (Jordan River Crossing) near Lake Tiberias in the north and Wadi Arabah (Arava Crossing) in the south, the latter linking Jordan to the Israeli Red Sea resort of Eilat. Most nationalities can obtain a visa at the border; for information on which nationals require a visa, contact a travel agent in Jordan. Some cars are permitted to cross these two borders, subject to various rules and regulations; for further details, contact the Jordanian authorities.
Road departure tax: JD4.

Travel - Internal

AIR: *Royal Wings* operates regular flights from Amman to Aqaba. For further details, contact the following: (tel: (6) 487 5201; website: www.royalwings.com.jo). It is also possible to hire executive jets and helicopters.
RAIL: There is no longer a reliable public railway service.
ROAD: Main roads are good (there are nearly 3000km (1900 miles) of paved roads in the country), but desert tracks should be avoided. It is important to make sure that the vehicle is in good repair if travelling on minor roads or tracks. Take plenty of water and follow local advice carefully. In case of breakdown, contact the Automobile Association. Traffic drives on the right. Speed limits are 60kph/38mph (cities), 80 kph/50mph (country roads) and 120kph/75mph (motorways). There are frequent passport controls along the Red Sea and travellers are advised to have their papers ready. **Bus**: Services are efficient and cheap. *Alpha, JETT* and *Petra* all operate modern, air-conditioned fleets. **Taxi**: Share-taxi service to all towns on fixed routes is also available for private hire. Share-taxis to Petra should be booked in advance owing to demand. **Car hire**: *Avis* and four national companies operate services in the main towns, including Amman and Aqaba, available also from hotels and travel agents. Drivers are available for the day. **Documentation**: National driving licences are accepted if they have been issued at least one year before travel. However, an International Driving Permit is recommended. Visitors are not allowed to drive a vehicle with normal Jordanian plates unless they have a Jordanian driving licence.
Note: When using routes which go near the Israeli border (and even when sailing or swimming in the Red Sea without a guide), the traveller should always have all papers in order and within reach.
URBAN: There are conventional buses and extensive fixed-route 'Servis' (share-taxis, most seating up to seven) in Amman. The 'Servis' are licensed, with a standard fare scale, but there are no fixed pick-up or set-down points. Vehicles often fill up at central or outer terminal points and then run non-stop.

Accommodation

There are several high-standard hotels throughout the country, most of which are run by well-known international chains. Amman and Aqaba, in particular, have a good choice of hotels. Hotels are fully booked during business periods so reservations are advised. Winter and summer rates are the same. All rates are subject to 20 per cent tax and service. There are serviced apartments available. **Grading**: Hotels are graded from **5- to 1-star**. 5- and 4-star hotels have discos and nightclubs with live music. Prices are fixed by the Ministry of Tourism, which can also deal with complaints. For further information, contact the Ministry of Tourism or the Jordan Tourism Board (see *Contact Addresses* section).

Resorts & Excursions

AMMAN & THE NORTH

AMMAN: The capital since 1921, Amman contains about one-third of the population. It was formerly the Ammonite capital of Rabbath-Ammon and later the Graeco-Roman city of Philadelphia. Often referred to as the 'white city', Amman was originally, like Rome, built on seven hills which still form its natural focal points. With extensive modern building projects, Amman is now very well equipped with excellent hotels and tourist facilities, especially in the *jabal* (hill) areas. The central market (*souk*) is lively and interesting and provides a taste of a more traditional city.

Remains from Roman, Greek and Ottoman Turk occupations are dotted around the city, the main attraction being the Roman amphitheatre from the second century AD in the centre of the city. There is also the **Jebel el Qalat** (citadel) which houses the **Archaeological Museum**; the **National Gallery of Fine Arts** and the **Popular Museum of Costume and Jewellery**.
Owing to Jordan's small size, any destination within the country may be reached by road from the capital, Amman, in one day.
SALT: Once the Biblical 'Gilead', Salt is now a small town set in the fertile landscape west of Amman, retaining much of its old character as a former leading city of **Transjordan**. Filled with the character, sights, sounds and aromas of an old Arab town with its narrow market (*souk*), its innumerable flights of steps, and its donkeys and coffee houses, it has a tolerant, friendly, oriental atmosphere. 24km (15 miles) from Amman is **Iraq al-Amir**, the only Hellenistic palace still to be seen in the Middle East.
JERASH: Less than one hour's drive north of Amman through the picturesque hills of ancient **Gilead** is Jerash. A magnificent Graeco-Roman city on an ancient site, beautifully preserved by the desert sands, Jerash is justly famous for the **Triumphal Arch**, the **Hippodrome**, the great elliptical forum, the theatres, baths and gateways, the Roman bridge and the wide street of columns that lead to the **Temple of Artemis.** *Son et lumière* programmes run in four different languages (Arabic, English, French and German). Other languages can be catered for upon request. For information on festivals in Jerash, see Special Events in the *Social Profile* section.
UMM QAIS: In the far north of the country, Umm Qais, the Biblical '**Gadara**', dominates the area around **Lake Tiberias** (Sea of Galilee). Once a city favoured by the Romans for its hot springs and theatres, it had declined to a small village by the time of the Islamic conquests. Its ruins, however, are still impressive: the **Acropolis** built in 218 BC, the forum, the colonnaded street with still-visible chariot tracks and the **Nymphaeum** and remains of a large basilica.
ELSEWHERE IN THE NORTH: Irbid, to the southeast of Umm Qais, is 77km (49 miles) from Amman and is a city of Roman tombs and statues, and narrow streets with close-packed shops and arched entrances.
Alternatively, return along the northwest border from Umm Qais to Jerash through the lush scenery of the **Jordan River Valley**, stopping at the town of **Al Hammeh**, in sight of the Israeli-occupied **Golan Heights**, a town known for its hot springs and mineral waters. Visitors can also stop at **Pella**, once a city of the **Roman Decapolis**, now being excavated, and the hilltop castle of **Qalaat al-Rabadh** built by the Arabs in defence against the crusaders. The scenery in this surprisingly fertile part of Jordan is often very beautiful, especially in the spring when the Jordan Valley and surrounding area is covered in flowers.
EAST OF AMMAN: Towards **Azraq** and beyond is the vast desert which makes up so much of Jordan. Within this arid landscape are the fertile oases of the **Shaumari** and **Azraq Wetland Parks**, now run with the help of the World Wide Fund for Nature. Wild animals once native to Jordan, such as the oryx and gazelle, are being re-introduced, while the wetlands are visited by thousands of migratory birds each year. The Shaumari was opened in October 1983 in an attempt to protect the country's dwindling oryx population. There are plans to open a further 10 wildlife reserves which will cover more than 4100 sq km (1580 sq miles). The project is being organised by the Jordanian Royal Society for the Conservation of Nature, a body which has recently stepped up its efforts to protect the country's wildlife and to prevent pollution affecting the very busy port of Aqaba. Severe fines are imposed on anyone contravening Jordan's strict laws on these matters.
Also in the east are the desert **Umayyad** castles (Qasr) of **Al-Kharanah** and **Amra**. Built as hunting lodges and to protect caravan routes, they are well preserved with frescoes and beautiful vaulted rooms.

THE SOUTH

THE DEAD SEA: The Dead Sea, 392m (1286ft) below sea level and the lowest point on earth, glistens by day and night in an eerie, dry landscape. The Biblical cities of Sodom and Gomorrah are thought to be beneath its waters. Supporting no life and having no outlet, even the non-swimmer can float freely in the rich salt water. The Dead Sea at the end of the **River Jordan** is the natural barrier between Jordan and the Palestinian National Authority Region.
THE KING'S HIGHWAY: There are three routes from Amman to Aqaba, the most picturesque being the **King's Highway**, the whole length of which is dotted with places of interest. **Madaba** and nearby **Mount Nebo**, where Moses is said to have struck the rock, were both flourishing Byzantine towns and have churches and well-preserved mosaics. In Madaba, there are also ancient maps of sixth-century Palestine, a museum and an old family carpet-making industry which uses ancient looms. Off the Highway is **Mukawir**, a small village near the ruins of **Machaerus of Herod Antipas**, where Salome performed her fateful dance. From the summit of nearby **Qasr al-Meshneque**, where St John was beheaded, is a magnificent view of the Dead Sea, and sometimes even of Jerusalem and the **Mount of Olives**. Nearby, **Zarqa Main** has hot mineral water springs. Rugged scenery characterises this area: deep gorges, waterfalls, white rocks, small oases, birds and wild flowers. Further south on the Highway is **Kerak**, a beautiful medieval town surrounded by high walls and with a castle. Other places of historical, scenic or religious interest along the route before Petra include **Mazar** and **Mutah**, **Edomite Qasr Buseirah**, **Tafila** and the magnificent crusader hill fortress, **Shaubek Castle**.
PETRA: Petra is one of the wonders of the Middle-Eastern world: a gigantic natural amphitheatre hidden in the rocks out of which a delicately coloured city with immense facades has been carved; it was lost for hundreds of years and only rediscovered in 1812. The temples and caves of Petra rest high up above a chasm, with huge white rocks forming the *Bab*, or gate, of the *Siq*, the narrow entrance which towers over 21m (70ft) high. Until recently, the rock caves were still inhabited by Bedouins. Most of this unique city was built by the Nabatean Arabs in the fifth and sixth centuries BC as an important link in the caravan routes. It was added to by the Romans who carved out a huge theatre and, possibly, the spectacular classical facade of the **Khazneh** (treasury). Away from the road, it is only possible to reach Petra on horseback. This city of rock stairs, rock streets, rock-carved tombs and dwellings and temples has among its other attractions the **Qasr al-Bint** castle shrine and the **Al-Habis** caves and museums; while a short distance away from the more commercialised site of Petra is **Al-Barid** where a number of tombs lie in solitude and tranquility among the rocks. There is a rest house in Petra built against the rock wall near the beginning of the Siq, where it is advisable to book early in season, but is bitterly cold in winter. A variety of hotels offer accommodation. The last stop south before Aqaba is **Wadi Rum**, about five hours from Amman by road. A Beau Geste-type fort run by the colourful Desert Patrol (Camel Corps), it was built to defend the valley in a great plain of escarpments and desert wilderness, and is a place strongly associated with TE Lawrence (Lawrence of Arabia). Many Bedouins, of a tribe thought to be descended from Muhammad, still live in the valley in tents. Some tours will arrange trips into the desert to stay with a Bedouin tribe or camping in the valley, a round-trip entailing 97km (60 miles).
AQABA: At the northeast end of the Gulf of Aqaba is Jordan's only port, which can be reached from Amman by road or air. It has grown considerably over the past few years, both as a port and as a tourist centre, due in part to its excellent beach and watersports facilities, and its low humidity and hot climate. The town has a variety of small shops and several good restaurants, and it leaves most of the other tourist facilities to be provided for by the hotels. These include windsurfing, scuba diving, sailing and fishing. Most hotels have swimming pools, and will offer continental and some traditional cuisine. Some provide business and conference facilities and excursions to Amman, Petra and Wadi Rum. **Aqaba's Church**, which was destroyed by an earthquake in 363 AD, was recently excavated and is one of the oldest buildings in the world.

Sport & Activities

Watersports: The coast south of Aqaba, on the shores of the Gulf of Aqaba, is teeming with tropical fish and coral and is renowned for its excellent year-round **diving** and **snorkelling**. The coral reefs are often very close to shore and the water temperature rarely falls below 20°C (68°F). There are several dive centres at Aqaba offering PADI courses, equipment rental and boat tours. It is forbidden to remove coral or shells, or to use harpoon guns and fishing spears. Aqaba's beaches, notably the *Aquamarine* or *Holiday Beach*, offer good **swimming**. **Dolphin-**, **shark-** and **whale-watching** trips can also be arranged.
Hiking: One of the best destinations is *Wadi Rum*, a vast area of dry riverbeds, mountains, black hills and sand dunes, located some 50km (30 miles) northeast of Aqaba, and a location for the film *Lawrence of Arabia*. **Camel treks** and **jeep trips** into the desert are also available, as are **hot-air balloon trips** over Wadi Rum's *Valley of the Moon*. Limited hiking equipment and supplies can be rented in the village of Rum; the nearest town is Quweirah.
Wildlife: There are 10 designated wildlife reserves in Jordan, the best being the *Azraq Wetland Wildlife Reserve* (whose oasis is home to over 300 species of birds), and the *Shaumari Wildlife Reserve*. Both can be visited on day trips from Amman. Animals that can be seen include hyenas, red wolves, jerboas, gazelles, ostriches and Arabian oryxes.

Social Profile

FOOD & DRINK: The cuisine varies, although most restaurants have a mixed menu which includes both Arabic and European dishes. Dishes include *meze* (small starters such as *fool*, *humus*, *kube* and *tabouleh*); a variety of *kebabs*; *Mahshi Waraq 'inab* (vine leaves stuffed with rice, minced meat and spices); *musakhan* (chicken in olive oil and onion sauce roasted on Arab bread); and the Jordanian speciality *mensaf* (stewed lamb in a yogurt sauce served on a bed of rice), a dish which is normally eaten with the hand. Sweets are very popular and include: *baklava* (pastry filled with nuts or honey); *kanafa* (pastry filled with nuts or goats cheese); *ataif* (small fried pancakes filled with nuts or cheese and traditionally eaten during Ramadan); and *mohallabiya* (milk-based pudding perfumed with rose water or orange). Drinking Arabic coffee is a ritual. Coffee tends to be very strong and is served in small cups (with plenty of coffee grounds at the bottom). Local beer, wine and other types of alcohol are served in most restaurants and bars, except during the fasting month of Ramadan (non-Arabic nationals can drink alcohol only in hotels during Ramadan).

Credit: © Jordan Tourism Board

NIGHTLIFE: There are nightclubs, theatres and cinemas in Amman, while some other major towns have cinemas. Often clubs will only admit couples or mixed groups. Many of the 4- and 5-star hotels have popular clubs and bars.
SHOPPING: Every town will have a *souk* (market), and there are also many good craft and jewellery shops. There is a particularly good gold and jewellery market in Amman. Special items include: Hebron glass; mother-of-pearl boxes; pottery; backgammon sets; embroidered tablecloths; jewelled rosaries and worry beads; nativity sets made of olive wood; leather hassocks; old and new brass and copper items; and caftans hand-embroidered with silver and gold thread. Jordan is famous for its gold and silver; the centre of Amman has a gold *souk* with over 50 shops. Necklaces with a small golden coffee pot (*dalleh*) – a national symbol – are popular and widely available. **Shopping hours**: Sat-Thurs 0900-1300 and 1500-2000 (closed Friday).
SPECIAL EVENTS: For a complete list, consult the Jordan Tourism Office (see *Contact Addresses*). The following is a selection of special events occurring in Jordan in 2005: **Apr 3-7** *Amman International Motor Show*. **Apr 8-15** *Amman International Theatre Festival*. **Apr 15** *Dead Sea Ultra Marathon*. **Jul 24-26** *Jordan International Rally*.
SOCIAL CONVENTIONS: Handshaking is the customary form of greeting. Jordanians are proud of their Arab culture, and hospitality here is a matter of great importance. Visitors are made to feel very welcome and Jordanians are happy to act as hosts and guides, and are keen to inform tourists about their traditions and culture. Islam always plays an important role in society and it is essential that Muslim beliefs are respected (see the *World of Islam* appendix). Arabic coffee will normally be served continuously during social occasions. To signal that no more is wanted, slightly tilt the cup when handing it back, otherwise it will be refilled. A small gift is quite acceptable in return for hospitality. Women are expected to dress modestly and beachwear must only be worn at the beach or poolside.

Photography: It is polite to ask permission to take photographs of people and livestock; in some places photography is forbidden. **Tipping**: 10 to 12 per cent service charge is generally added in hotels and restaurants, and extra tips are discretionary. Porters' and drivers' tips are about 8 per cent.

Business Profile

ECONOMY: Jordan's agricultural sector has never recovered from the loss of the West Bank after the 1967 Middle East war, which deprived Jordan of 80 per cent of its fruit-growing area and a proportionate amount of export revenue. Tomatoes, citrus fruit, cucumbers, watermelons, aubergines and wheat are the principal commodities grown in the remaining, mostly desert area. Phosphate mining and potash extraction from the Dead Sea area are the longest established industries; to these, oil refining, chemical manufacturing, food processing, and the production of metals and minerals have since been added. Other commercial enterprises include paints, plastics and cement production. The ongoing search for exploitable oil deposits - unsuccessful thus far - continues, and attempts have been made to develop alternative sources of power.
The service sector, which accounts for around two-thirds of total output, covers wholesale and retail trading, finance, transport and tourism. This sector has been especially badly hit by events in Iraq, Jordan's eastern neighbour, which accounted for some 20 per cent of Jordan's total pre-sanctions trade. UN sanctions against Iraq curtailed much Iraqi transit trade that would otherwise have come through the Jordanian port of Aqaba. Cheap oil supplies from Iraq have been made up, but only in part, by shipments from other Arab countries.
During the latter years of King Hussein's rule, some economic reforms based on the customary package of deregulation and privatisation were instituted. These brought the country's rampant inflation under control but failed to dent the country's massive unemployment problem. These reforms have, by and large, continued under King Abdullah. Many Jordanian workers have moved abroad in search of employment and their remittances are an essential means of support for many families. Jordan is a member of various pan-Arab economic bodies, notably the Council of Arab Economic Co-operation and the Arab Monetary Fund. Jordan joined the World Trade Organization in 2000. Apart from other Arab states, some of which also provide financial aid, other major trading partners include Germany, India, Saudi Arabia and the USA (which is also an aid donor).
BUSINESS: English is widely spoken in business circles. Avoid Friday appointments. A good supply of visiting cards is essential. Formality in dress is important and men should wear a suit and tie for business meetings. **Office hours**: Sat-Thurs 0800-1800 (with one- or two-hour lunch breaks). **Government office hours**: Sun-Thurs 0800-1500. During the month of Ramadan, working hours are greatly reduced (see *Public Holidays* section).
COMMERCIAL INFORMATION: The following organisation can offer advice: Amman Chamber of Industry (ACI), 2nd Circle, Amman (tel: (6) 464 3001; fax: (6) 464 7852; e-mail: aci@aci.org.jo; website: www.aci.org.jo); *or* Federation of Jordanian Chambers of Commerce (FJCC), PO Box 7029, Amman 11118 (tel: (6) 566 5492 or 567 4495; fax: (6) 568 5997; e-mail: fjcc@go.com.jo; website: www.jocc.org.jo).

Climate

Hot and dry summers with cool evenings. The Jordan Valley below sea level is warm during winter and extremely hot in summer. Rain falls between November and March, while colder weather conditions occur in December/January.
Required clothing: Lightweight cottons and linens are advised between May and September. Warmer clothes are necessary for winter and cool summer evenings. Rainwear is needed from November to April.

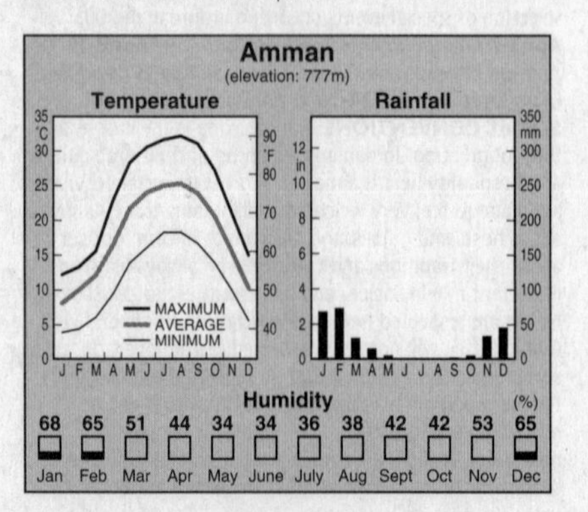

Kazakhstan

LATEST TRAVEL ADVICE CONTACTS

British Foreign and Commonwealth Office
Tel: (0870) 606 0290 Website: www.fco.gov.uk
US Department of State
Website: http://travel.state.gov/travel
Canadian Department of Foreign Affairs and Int'l Trade
Tel: (1 800) 267 8376 Website: www.dfait-maeci.gc.ca

Location: Central Asia, north of Uzbekistan.

Country dialling code: 7.

State Agency for Tourism and Sport
473000 Astana, Mukhtar Auezor 126, Kazakhstan
Tel: (3272) 396 638. Fax: (3272) 396 468.
E-mail: turlykhanov@kazsport.kz
Website: www.kazsport.kz
Hotel Complex Otrar and Travel & Air Agency
ul Gogolya 73, Hotel Otrar, Almaty 480002, Kazakhstan
Tel: (3272) 506 806/40 *or* 848. Fax: (3272) 506 809/11.
E-mail: otrar@group.kz
Website: www.group.kz
Embassy of the Republic of Kazakhstan
33 Thurloe Square, London SW7 2SD, UK
Tel: (020) 7581 4646 (ext 207/8 for visa section) *or* (09065) 508 978 (recorded visa information; calls cost £1 per minute).
Fax: (020) 7584 8481 *or* 9905 (consular section).
E-mail: london@kazakhstan-embassy.org.uk *or* consulate@kazakhstan-embassy.org.uk (consular section).
Website: www.kazakhstanembassy.org.uk
Opening hours: Mon-Fri 0830-1830; Mon-Fri 0900-1200 (consular section, closed Wednesdays except for nationals of Kazakhstan).
British Embassy
ul Furmanova 173, Almaty 480062, Kazakhstan
Tel: (573) 150 2200 *or* (3272) 506 260.
Fax: (573) 150 2212.
E-mail: british-embassy@nursat.kz
Website: www.britishembassy.gov.uk/kazakhstan
Consular section: ul Panfilova 158, Almaty 480064, Kazakhstan
Tel: (3272) 506 191. Fax: (3272) 507 432.
E-mail: visa-british-embassy@nursat.kz
Embassy of the Republic of Kazakhstan
1401 16th Street, NW, Washington, DC 20036, USA
Tel: (202) 232 5488. Fax: (202) 232 5845.
E-mail: kazakh.embusa@verizon.net *or* kazakh.consul@verizon.net
Website: www.kazakhembus.com
Also deals with enquiries from Canada.
Consulate in: New York (tel: (212) 888 3024).

TIMATIC CODES

Health
AMADEUS: **TI-DFT/ALA/HE**
GALILEO/WORLDSPAN: **TI-DFT/ALA/HE**
SABRE: **TIDFT/ALA/HE**

Visa
AMADEUS: **TI-DFT/ALA/VI**
GALILEO/WORLDSPAN: **TI-DFT/ALA/VI**
SABRE: **TIDFT/ALA/VI**

To access TIMATIC country information on Health and Visa regulations through the Computer Reservations System (CRS), type in the appropriate command line listed above.

Embassy of the United States of America
97 Zholdasbekova, Samal-2, Almaty 480099, Kazakhstan
Tel: (3272) 504 802 (consular section) *or* 940.
Fax: (3272) 504 884 (consular section) *or* 867.
E-mail: ConsularAlmaty@state.gov (consular section) *or* usembassy@freenet.kz.
Website: www.usembassy-kazakhstan.freenet.kz
Canadian Embassy
ul Karasai Batyr 34, Almaty 480100, Kazakhstan
Tel: (3272) 501 151-3.
Fax: (3272) 582 493.
E-mail: almat@dfait-maeci.gc.ca
Website: www.dfait-maeci.gc.ca/canadaeuropa/kazakhstan

General Information

AREA: 2,717,300 sq km (1,049,150 sq miles).
POPULATION: 14,862,700 (2002).
POPULATION DENSITY: 5.5 per sq km.
CAPITAL: Astana (formerly called Akmola). **Population:** 328,000 (UN estimate 2001).
GEOGRAPHY: Five times the size of France and half the size of the USA, Kazakhstan is the second largest state in the Commonwealth of Independent States, and is bordered by the Russian Federation to the north and west, the Caspian Sea, Turkmenistan and Uzbekistan to the southwest, Kyrgyzstan to the south and China to the southeast. 90 per cent of the country is made up of steppe, the sand massives of the Kara Kum and the vast desert of Kizilkum, while in the southeast of the country the mountains of the Tian Shan and the Altai form a great natural frontier with tens of thousands of lakes and rivers. The Aral Sea and Lake Balkhash are the country's largest expanses of water.
GOVERNMENT: Republic. **Head of State:** President Nursultan A Nazarbayev since 1991. **Head of Government:** Prime Minister Daniyal Akhmetov since 2003.
LANGUAGE: The official language is Kazakh, a Turkic language closely related to Uzbek, Kyrgyz, Turkmen and Turkish. The Government has begun to replace the Russian Cyrillic alphabet with the Turkish version of the Roman alphabet. Meanwhile, the Cyrillic alphabet is in general use and most people in the cities can speak Russian, whereas country people tend to only speak Kazakh. English is usually spoken by those involved in tourism. Uygur and other regional languages and dialects are also spoken.
RELIGION: Mainly Sunni Muslim. There are Russian Orthodox and Jewish minorities. There are 10 independent denominations of Christianity. The Kazakhs do not express their religious feelings fervently – Kazakhstan is an outlying district of the Muslim world and a meeting point of Russian, Chinese and Central Asian civilisations. Islam plays a minor role in policy and there are no significant Islamic political organisations in the country.
TIME: Kazakhstan is divided into three time zones:
GMT + 6 (GMT + 7 from 28 March to 26 October).
GMT + 5 (GMT + 6 from 28 March to 26 October).
GMT + 4 (GMT + 5 from 28 March to 26 October).
ELECTRICITY: 220 volts AC, 50Hz. Round two-pin continental plugs are standard.
COMMUNICATIONS: Telephone: Country code: 7. Area code for Almaty: 3272. International calls can be made at a reduced rate from 2000-0800 local time. International calls should be made from a telephone office; these are usually attached to post offices. **Mobile telephone:** Dual band 900 networks in use. Coverage is good around the main cities. Network providers include *K'CELL* (website:

www.kcell.kz) and *K-MOBILE* (website: www.k-mobile.kz/ru). **Telegram:** Facilities available from any post office. **Internet:** ISPs include *Astel* (website: www.astel.kz) and *Parasang* (website: www.ricc.kz). There are Internet cafes in most towns and cities. **Post:** Full postal facilities are available at main post offices in the cities, which are open 24 hours a day, seven days a week. The main post office in Almaty is located on Ulitsa Kurmangazy. International postal communication is undertaken by the firms *Blitz-Pochta*, *International Press* (e-mail: mpress87@hotmail.com) and *Press Limited*. Delivery within the republic takes three to five days. Post to Western Europe and the USA takes between two to three weeks. Mail addresses should be laid out in the following order: country, postcode, city, street, house number and, lastly, the person's name. Post office hours: Mon-Fri 0900-1800. Visitors can also use post offices located within major hotels. **Press:** There are 70 newspapers and 50 magazines in German, Kazakh, Korean, Russian and Uygur published in the country. The most popular dailies are *Ekspress K*, *Kazakhstanskaya Pravda* and *Yegemen Kazakhstan*.
Radio: BBC World Service (website: www.bbc.co.uk/worldservice) and Voice of America (website: www.voa.gov) can be received. From time to time the frequencies change and the most up-to-date can be found online.

Passport/Visa

	Passport Required?	Visa Required?	Return Ticket Required?
Full British	Yes	Yes	No
Australian	Yes	Yes	No
Canadian	Yes	Yes	No
USA	Yes	Yes	No
Other EU	Yes	Yes	No
Japanese	Yes	Yes	No

Note: *Regulations and requirements may be subject to change at short notice, and you are advised to contact the appropriate diplomatic or consular authority before finalising travel arrangements. Details of these may be found at the head of this country's entry. Any numbers in the chart refer to the footnotes below.*

PASSPORTS: Passport valid for at least six months required by all.
VISAS: Required by all except the following:
(a) nationals of CIS holding passports, and holders of valid passports issued by the former Soviet Union and registered in the CIS (nationals of Ukraine do not require a visa for stays of up to three months; nationals of Turkmenistan *always* require a visa);
(b) nationals of Turkey for stays of up to one month.
Note: Nationals of the following countries may apply for a single-entry tourist visa without obtaining an invitation letter validated by the Kazakhstan Ministry of Interior: nationals of countries referred to in the chart above (except nationals of Cyprus, Czech Republic, Estonia, Hungary, Latvia, Lithuania, Malta, Poland, Slovak Republic and Slovenia) and nationals of Iceland, Korea (rep), Liechtenstein, Malaysia, Monaco, New Zealand, Norway, Singapore, and Switzerland, who must instead provide a letter of introduction explaining the purpose of the visit.
Types of visa and cost: *Tourist*: £23 (single-entry); £33 (double-entry). *Business and Private*: £33 (single-entry); £43 (double-entry); £73 (triple-entry); £133 (multiple-entry, up to one year); £263 (multiple-entry, up to two years). *Transit*: £13.
Validity: *Tourist*: one month (single-entry); two months (double-entry). *Business and Private*: three months (single-, double- and triple-entry); one or two years (multiple-entry). *Transit*: five days
Application to: The Consulate (or Consular section at Embassy), see *Contact Addresses* section.
Application requirements: (a) Completed application form. (b) Valid passport with one blank page to affix visa. (c) One recent passport-size photo. (d) Letter of invitation with reference number, validated by the Kazakhstan Ministry of Interior (not required by certain nationals - see note above). (e) Fee, payable by personal cheque or postal order (not cash). (f) Self-addressed, stamped registered envelope, if applying by post. *Business*: (a)-(f) and, (g) Letter of invitation from host organisation in Kazakhstan with registration number approved by the Ministry of Foreign Affairs in Kazakhstan. (h) Letter from own business company with details of the purpose of the visit and name and address of partner organisation. *Transit*: (a)-(f) and, (g) Valid visa for country of final destination. (h) Air or railway ticket to third country.
Note: (a) All nationals staying longer than five days must register with an OVIR office and pay a registration charge. Failure to do so will result in penalties on departure.
Working days required: One day.
Temporary Residence: Enquire at Embassy.

Money

Currency: Tenge (T) = 100 tiyin. Notes are in denominations of T5000, 2000, 1000, 500, 200, 100, 50, 20, 10, 5, 2 and 1, and 20, 10, 5, 3 and 1 tiyin. Coins are in denominations of T100, 50, 20, 10 and 1.
Currency exchange: The national currency, the Tenge, may only be obtained within Kazakhstan. Conversion of the Tenge back into hard currency may prove difficult. Foreign currency should only be exchanged at official bureaux and all transactions must be recorded on the currency declaration form that is issued on arrival. It is wise to retain all exchange receipts, although they are seldom inspected. Unless travelling with a licensed tourist company (in which case, accommodation, transport and meals are paid before departure), money should be brought in US Dollars cash and exchanged when necessary.
Credit & debit cards: Major European and international credit cards, including Diners Club and Visa, are accepted in the larger hotels in Almaty and in major shops and restaurants. Facilities exist for credit card cash withdrawals in Kazakhstan.
Travellers cheques: To avoid additional exchange rate charges, travellers are advised to take travellers cheques in US Dollars.
Currency restrictions: The import and export of local currency and import of foreign currency is unlimited provided declared on arrival. The export of foreign currency is limited to the amount imported. Special bank permission is required for all amounts exceeding this.
Exchange rate indicators: The following figures are included as a guide to the movements of the Tenge against Sterling and the US Dollar.

Date	Feb '04	May '04	Aug '04	Nov '04
£1.00=	254.03	245.32	249.39	246.09
$1.00=	139.56	137.35	135.37	129.95

Banking hours: Mon-Fri 0930-1730. Banks close for lunch 1300-1400. All banks are closed Sat-Sun.

Duty Free

The following goods may be imported into Kazakhstan by persons over 16 years of age without incurring customs duty:
1000 cigarettes or 1kg of tobacco products; 2l of spirits or 2l of wine; a reasonable quantity of perfume for personal use; gifts up to the value of US$500 for personal use only.
Note: On entering the country, tourists must complete a customs declaration form, which must be retained until departure. This allows the import of articles intended for personal use, including currency and valuables, which must be registered on the declaration form. They must be exported at the end of the stay. Customs inspection can be long and detailed. It is advisable to keep receipts for items bought in Kazakhstan in order to avoid difficulties at customs on departure.
Prohibited imports: Military weapons and ammunition; narcotics; pornography; live animals (unless with special permit); photographs or other printed materials aimed against Kazakhstan; pigeons; loose pearls; anything owned by a third party that is to be carried in for that third party.
Prohibited exports: As prohibited imports, as well as annulled securities, state loan certificates, lottery tickets, works of art and antiques (unless permission has been granted by the Ministry of Culture), saiga horns, Siberian stag, punctuate and red deer antlers (unless on organised hunting trip), and punctuate deer skins.

Public Holidays

2005: Jan 1 New Year's Day. **Mar 8** International Women's Day. **Mar 21** Nauryz Meyrami (Traditional Spring Holiday). **May 1** Kazakhstan People's Unity Day. **May 9** Victory Day. **Aug 30** Constitution Day. **Oct 25** Republic Day. **Dec 16** Independence Day.
2006: Jan 1 New Year's Day. **Mar 8** International Women's Day. **Mar 21** Nauryz Meyrami (Traditional Spring Holiday). **May 1** Kazakhstan People's Unity Day. **May 9** Victory Day. **Aug 30** Constitution Day. **Oct 25** Republic Day. **Dec 16** Independence Day.

Health

	Special Precautions?	Certificate Required?
Yellow Fever	Yes	1
Cholera	Yes	2
Typhoid & Polio	Yes	N/A
Malaria	No	N/A

Note: *Regulations and requirements may be subject to change at short notice, and you are advised to contact your doctor well in advance of your intended date of departure. Any numbers in the chart refer to the footnotes below.*

1: A yellow fever vaccination certificate is required from travellers arriving within six days from infected areas (children under one year are exempt).
2: Following WHO guidelines issued in 1973, a cholera vaccination certificate is no longer a condition of entry to Kazakhstan. However, cholera is a serious risk in this country and precautions are essential. Up-to-date advice should be sought before deciding whether these precautions should include vaccination as medical opinion is divided over its effectiveness; see the *Health* appendix for further information.

Credit: © MTA

Food & drink: All water should be regarded as being a potential health risk. Water used for drinking, brushing teeth or making ice should have first been boiled or otherwise sterilised. Milk is pasteurised and dairy products are safe for consumption. Only eat well-cooked meat and fish, preferably served hot. Pork, salad and mayonnaise may carry increased risk. Vegetables should be cooked and fruit peeled.
Other risks: *Hepatitis A*, *B* and *E* occur. *Diphtheria* outbreaks have been reported in the area. *Giardiasis*, *echinococcosis*, *typhus* (tick-borne), *Crimean-Congo haemorrhagic fever*, *trechinellosis*, *leishmaniasis* and *brucellosis* can also occur. Although rare, foci of *plague* exist. *Tuberculosis* and *typhoid* are increasing throughout. Increased cases of *meningitis* and *encephalitis* have also been reported in Almaty.
There is some presence of *Rabies*. For those at high risk, vaccination before arrival should be considered. If you are bitten, seek medical advice without delay. For more information, consult the *Health* appendix.
Note: Foreign visitors (except nationals of CIS countries) staying in Kazakhstan for longer than three months may be required to take an AIDS test.
Health care: There is a large network of hospitals, emergency centres and pharmacies. The largest include the Central Hospital, the Maternity and Childhood Institute Clinic and the Medical Teaching Institute Clinic in Almaty, and the Spinal Centre and Hospital of Rehabilitation Treatment in Karaganda. However, standards within the public healthcare system have declined significantly since the Soviet era. It is hard to ascertain the level of expertise of the doctors, and visitors cannot rely on the availability of western medicines. Medical insurance is strongly recommended and should include medevac insurance.

Travel - International

AIR: Almaty is rapidly gaining importance as an international hub. It has air links with many cities in the CIS. *British Airways* flies direct from London to Almaty three times a week. Connections from London can also be made on *Austrian Airlines* (via Vienna), *KLM* (via Amsterdam), *Lufthansa* (via Frankfurt/M) and *Turkish Airlines* (via Istanbul). There are no direct flights from Australia or the USA. Further connections are offered by *Aeroflot* from Almaty to Urumchi (China), from where there are connections to Beijing. New direct routes from Almaty to Delhi, Tehran and Tel Aviv are planned.
Approximate flight times: From *London* to Almaty is eight hours, from *Istanbul* is six hours, from *Ulgi* (Mongolia) is four hours and from *Hanover* and *Frankfurt/M* is 10 hours.
International airports: *Almaty (ALA)* is located 10km (6 miles) northeast of the city. Bus nos. 38, 446 and 492 connect the airport with the city centre (travel time – 20 minutes). Taxis are also available at the airport for transport into the city centre. Airport facilities include car hire, duty free shops, restaurant and post office.
Departure Tax: None.
SEA: Freight is carried on the Caspian Sea to Iran and the Russian Federation.
RAIL: There are international rail connections with China, the Russian Federation, Turkmenistan and Uzbekistan. Services run regularly from Almaty to Urumchi in China and daily to Moscow (travel time – three days) and connect with the entire Russian Federation railway network. The *Tashkent–Novosibirsk Express* passes through Almaty each day in both directions. The lines from Almaty in the north connect with the *Trans-Siberian Railway* running west to Chimkent and finally to Orenburg in the Russian Federation. A new railway line is being built to connect Kazakhstan to Iran and Turkey. Foreign visitors should exercise caution when using trains other than the Almaty–Moscow train; violent crime against westerners is on the increase.
ROAD: There are good road connections into the Russian Federation, the other Central Asian states and China. **Bus:** Buses leave Chimkent for Tashkent every 25 minutes 0700-1925. The journey is 160km (100 miles) (travel time – three hours). There are also buses from Chimkent to Bishkek.

Credit: © MTA

Travel - Internal

AIR: There are frequent flights from Almaty to Astana, Chimkent (four times a day), Dzhambul, Karaganda, Kzil-Orda, Pavlodar, Semipalatinsk and Ust-Kamenogorsk. Flights also leave Chimkent for Almaty, Karaganda and Semipalatinsk. Travellers should note that maintenance procedures for aircraft operating internally may not conform to internationally accepted standards
Domestic airports: *Chimkent* has an airport offering mostly domestic flights. However, there are also services to Moscow (four times a week) and Novosibirsk (Russian Federation), and to Tashkent (Uzbekistan) (daily). Bus no. 12 runs from the city centre to the airport.
Semipalatinsk has a domestic airport with flights to Almaty, Chimkent, Dzhambul, Karaganda and Ust-Kamenogorsk. However, it also receives flights from Bishkek, Krasnoyarsk, Moscow (four times a week), Omsk, Tashkent and Tomsk.
The airport at *Ust-Kamenogorsk* receives flights from Almaty and a few other Kazakh cities, as well as from Moscow, Novosibirsk and a few other Siberian cities. Bus no. 12 runs to the Hotel Ust-Kamenogorsk in the city centre.
RIVER: River trips can be taken in Semipalatinsk on the River Irtysh.
RAIL: There are two *TurkSib* trains leaving Chimkent daily, one to Tashkent (Uzbekistan) and the other to Novosibirsk (Russian Federation), stopping at destinations in between. The cost of rail travel in Kazakhstan is minimal in comparison with Western Europe and there are regular connections between all the main centres. Queues at stations to buy a ticket can be long and passengers should bring their own food and drink for the journey. It may be advisable for foreign visitors to travel by bus between cities, owing to an increase in robberies on trains.
ROAD: Traffic drives on the right. There is a reasonable network of roads in Kazakhstan connecting all the towns and regional centres. Petrol supplies are reasonably reliable in comparison with other Central Asian republics. **Bus:** There are regular bus connections between all the main cities of Kazakhstan. **Taxi:** These are available in all Kazakh cities. **Car hire:** Available in Almaty and Astana and at the airports. **Documentation:** An International Driving Permit is required.
URBAN: Almaty is served by trolleybuses and buses.

Accommodation

HOTELS: Most towns in Kazakhstan have a limited supply of reasonable accommodation. It is advisable to make reservations in advance, either directly or through a travel agency. Most hotels deliver a basic level of comfort, although Western standards should not be expected.
Grading: A star-grading system is in use. There are at least two 5-star hotels in Almaty, as well as numerous new hotels of a reasonable standard. Classification of tourist hotels and campsites is carried out by the Department of Tourism (see *Contact Addresses* section); classification of other forms of accommodation is carried out by the local authorities.
TURBAZAS: These 'tourist bases' are an alternative to hotel accommodation. For a small fee, visitors have access to basic bungalow accommodation and three meals a day.
CAMPING: The only designated campsites are the permanent base camps from which the high peaks of Kazakhstan are climbed. Travellers pitch their tents in other localities at their own risk, although there are no regulations against it.

Credit: © MTA

Resorts & Excursions

Note: It is advisable to visit the country as part of an organised tour. Although independent travel is increasing, bureaucratic difficulties may still be encountered. For further information, contact the Embassy (see Contact Addresses section).
Nine-tenths of Kazakhstan is made up of steppe. For centuries, these vast plains were home only to nomads and they are still virtually empty. Most settlements are concentrated in the southeast and the east of the republic where the plains give way to the mountains of the **Altai** and the **Tien Shan**.
THE SPAS: Kazakhstan has a wide range of spas offering various treatments. There are 98 sanatoria holiday hotels and 115 preventative medicine sanatoria. Most are located in areas with much to interest the tourist, such as sports, cultural events, historical and archaeological sites, and offer developed excursion facilities. The most internationally renowned resorts include **Sari Agach** (in the south), **Mujaldi** (in the Pavlodar region), **Arasan-Kapal** (in the Taldikorgan region), **Jani-Kurgan** (in the Kzil-Orda region), **Kokshetau** and **Zerenda** (in the Kokshetau region) and those located in **Zaili Alatau**.

THE SOUTH

South Kazakhstan is a focus of Central Asian history and culture and there are many famous monuments in the region. It is a scenically diverse region in which all four seasons can be experienced in the space of a day, as the snow-capped peaks, lakes and glaciers of the **Tien Shan** range give way to steppe and desert land which stretches for thousands of kilometres. The mountains serve as a centre for mountaineering and skiing and there are resorts offering a wide variety of winter sports. The desert is home to the **Singing Barkhan** – a sand dune 80m (260ft) high and 3km (2 miles) long, which, as it crumbles and shifts, produces a peculiar sound reminiscent of loud singing.
ALMATY: Almaty (formerly *Alma Ata*) enjoys a beautiful setting between mountains and plains. It is a city of modern architecture, wide streets, cool fountains, parks and squares and spectacular mountain views and, particularly in spring and autumn, is an attractive place despite the inevitable legacy of Soviet architecture. Attractions in the city include the **Panfilov Park**, which is dominated by one of the world's tallest wooden buildings, built at the turn of the 20th century without using a single nail, and the **Zenkov Cathedral**. This served in Soviet times as a concert and exhibition hall, but is currently standing empty, whilst the Christians of Almaty worship at **St Nicholas Cathedral**. Other sights include **New Square**, which is usually the location for national ceremonies and parades and is overlooked by the **City Hall** (the President's official residence) and the **Obelisk of Independence**. Almaty boasts several fine museums including the **Museum of Kazakh National Instruments**, the **Central State Museum** and the **State Art Museum** which has, among its exhibits, traditional Kazakh rugs, jewellery and clothing. The **Arasan Baths**, in the western area of **Panfilov Park**, have Eastern, Finnish and Russian saunas.
THE MOUNTAINS: The 4000m- (1310ft-) high **Zaili Alatau Mountains** near Almaty offer numerous opportunities all year round for sports and recreation. The **Medeu ice rink** is situated 15km (9 miles) outside the city in a stunning gorge (see *Sports and Activities* section). There are large areas of unspoilt nature among the mountains which attract many walkers and climbers to the region in summer and skiers in the winter.
The **Tien Shan Mountains** in the southeast of Kazakhstan stretch for more than 1500km (932 miles). The highest peaks are **Pobeda Peak** (7439m/24,406ft) and **Khan-Tengri Peak** (7010m/23,000ft), a snow-white, marble-like pyramid. The huge **Inylchek Glacier**, reaching almost 60km (37 miles) in length, splits the summits and the beautiful **Mertzbakher Lake** lies at its centre. The **Kolsai Lakes** are three blue mountain lakes, known as the 'pearls of the northern Tien-Shan', that lie within the ridges of the **Kungei Alatau** range at heights of up to 2700m (8858ft) above sea level. The **Khan-Tengri International Mountaineering Camp** provides experienced mountain guides to take visitors on organised climbing and trekking programmes. Other facilities include horse-riding, a souvenir shop and bar.
ELSEWHERE: The city of **Chimkent** is an industrial city, producing the largest amount of lead in the CIS. 160km (100 miles) away (travel time – two hours 30 minutes) is the 14th-century **Kodja Ahmed Yasavi Mausoleum** in **Turkestan**; built under Tamerlane, this mausoleum has the largest dome in Central Asia. **Dzhambul**, too, is an industrial city in the region with some reproductions of ancient remains from when it was known as **Taraz** – these are housed in the **Karakhan** and the **Daudbek Shahmansur Mausoleums**. The nearby village of **Golovachovka**, 18km (11 miles) to the west, has authentic remains from Taraz, including the 11th-century **Babadzi-Khatun Mausoleum** and the 12th-century **Mausoleum Aisha Bibi**. Another ancient historical centre is **Taldikorgan**. Much of this region was crossed by the **Great Silk Road**.

THE REST OF THE COUNTRY

CENTRAL KAZAKHSTAN: Central Kazakhstan has one of the largest lakes in the world. The unique **Lake Balkhash** is half saline, half fresh water. Some archaeological and ethnographic sites have been preserved in central Kazakhstan. There are Bronze Age and Early Iron Age sites and New Stone Age and Bronze Age settlements in the **Karkarala Oasis**. The **Bayan-Aul National Park** has rock drawings, stone sculptures, clean, sparkling lakes and pines clinging to the rocks. The **Baikonur Cosmodrome**, located 5km (3 miles) from the garrison city of **Leninsk** and 230km (143 miles) from **Kzil-Orda**, is the Central Asian answer to Cape Canaveral – tours are available, during which visitors can witness space launches. It was from here, on 12 April 1961, that Yuri Gagarin, the world's first cosmonaut, took off, and it is still a point of departure for space launches.
THE WEST: West Kazakhstan marks the southern convergence of Europe and Asia in the basin of the Caspian Sea. The region's **Karagie Depression**, 132m (433ft) below sea level, is the lowest point in the world after the Dead Sea in Sinai. There are many architectural heritage sites in this region, including the subterranean cross-shaped **Shakpak-Ata Mosque** (12th-14th century) which is hewn out of rock.
THE NORTH: **Astana** was made Kazakhstan's new capital in 1997, as its location was thought to be more accessible to the Russian Federation and less earthquake-prone than Almaty (the former capital), where foreign embassies and consulates are still based. Although a small and friendly town and an important centre for the production of grain, it has little else to recommend it. The nature reserve of **Kurgaldjino** in the north of Kazakhstan houses the most northerly settlement of pink flamingoes in the world, while another nature reserve, **Naurzum**, offers a rich landscape of geographical contrasts – salt lakes ringed by forests, the remains of ancient pines strewn amongst sand dunes, pine forests growing out of salt-marsh beds, vast meadows, and rare animals such as hisser swans and grave eagles.
THE EAST: East Kazakhstan offers a colourful landscape of snow-capped mountain peaks, plunging forested canyons and picturesque cedar forests. **Lake Marakol** rivals Baikal in beauty. It is 35km (22 miles) long and 19km (12 miles) wide and lies 1449m (4754ft) above sea level. The city of **Semipalatinsk**, 30km (19 miles) from Siberia, was a Russian place of exile; Dostoyevsky was exiled here from

1857-1859 and his house is preserved as a museum – exhibits include notes for *Crime and Punishment* and *The Idiot*. Other museums in the city include the **Abai Kununbaev Museum**, commemorating the Kazakh poet, and the **History Museum**. Nuclear tests were carried out southwest of Semipalatinsk until 1990, although background radiation today is easily within reach of internationally accepted levels. The town of **Ust-Kamenogorsk** is a mining and smelting town and is the gateway to the **Altai Mountains**. Occupying the central point of the continent, these gentle mountains are covered with meadows and woods and stretch for 1000km (620 miles) into Mongolia. **Rakhmanovski** in the Altai Mountains offers a *turbaza* (see *Accommodation* section) and is renowned for its cross-country skiing.

Nature Reserves:

Aksu-Jabagli: A UNESCO biosphere reserve in southern Kazakhstan, situated 1000 to 4000m (3280 to 3120ft) above sea level, and home to 238 species of birds, 42 species of animals and 1300 species of plants.

Almaty: Located in the southern Tian Shan Mountains and home to snow leopards, jeirans, gazelles, arkhars and the unique Tjan-Shan fir tree.

Barsa Kelmes: Translated as 'the land of no return', this island, off the northwestern Aral Sea coast, is the home of the rarest hoofed animal in the world – the kulan.

The West-Altai: Situated in the Altai Mountains and home to 16 types of forest, 30 species of mammals and 120 species of birds.

Kurgaldjino: Located in central Kazakhstan, this A-class nature reserve is of international importance, and its feather-grass steppe is home to 300 types of plant and the most northerly settlement of flamingos in the world.

Marakol: Home to 232 species of bird, 50 species of animal and 1000 types of plant, the reserve is set in the southern foothills of the Altai Mountains.

Naurzum: Located in northern Kazakhstan and home to such rare animals as white herons, jack-bustards, hisser swans and grave eagles.

Ustiurt: Situated in west Kazakhstan in the Karagie Depression, 132m (433ft) below sea level, this chalk-cliffed reserve is the largest in the country.

Bayan-Aul National Nature Park: Known as 'the museum of nature', the reserve is located in central Kazakhstan.

Credit: © MTA

Sport & Activities

Hiking and trekking: Due to the country's rugged landscape and incredible mountain ranges, **mountain climbing** and trekking are becoming increasingly popular with visitors. The best season for trekking is between June and September. **Horse-riding** is also popular in Kazakhstan. Visitors may either take part in or view competitions of the many Kazakh equestrian sports, such as *baiga*, *kiz-kuu* and *kokpar*.

Wintersports: Near Almaty, 12km (7 miles) from the city centre, surrounded by mountains, the Medeu ice-skating rink is the largest speed-skating rink in the world and is very popular with all the inhabitants of the capital. Over 120 world records in **ice skating** and ice hockey have been set at Medeu. A comfortable hotel, restaurant and cafe are located nearby. **Ice hockey** games can be viewed at the rink in Ust-Kamenogorsk. On a spur of Zaili Alatau, 7km (4 miles) to the south, the wintersports complex of Chimbulak offers some of the finest **skiing** in the CIS and many ski competitions take place here. Skis and boots can be hired, but they are not up to Western European or US standards. Costs are minimal. Shymbulak is a popular ski resort, located near Medeu ice rink, with a 1.6km- (1mile-) long chair lift.

Watersports: All the regional centres boast sport complexes, **swimming** pools and training halls. **Rafting** and **canoeing** can be easily arranged through local travel agents. The Ili river between Lake Qapshaghay and Lake Balhash is a good place for this.

Social Profile

FOOD & DRINK: Kazakh dishes include *kazi*, *chuzhuk*, *suret* and *besbarmak* (made from horse meat or mutton). *Shashlyk* (skewered chunks of mutton barbecued over charcoal) and *lepeshka* (round unleavened bread) are often sold on street corners and make an appetising meal. *Plov* is made up of scraps of mutton, shredded yellow turnip and rice, and is a staple dish in all the Central Asian republics. Other mutton dishes such as *laghman* and *beshbermak* include long thick noodles garnished with a spicy meat sauce. *Manty* (boiled noodle sacks of meat and vegetables), *samsa* (samosas) and *chiburekki* (deep-fried dough cakes) are all popular as snacks. Almaty is renowned for its apples – indeed the city was named after them.

Kazakh tea or chai is very popular and there are national cafes called *Chai-Khana* (tea-rooms) where visitors may sip this Kazakh speciality. It is drunk very strong with cream. Beer, vodka, brandy and sparkling wines are available in many restaurants. The national speciality is *kumis*, fermented mare's milk. Cafes where this can be ordered are called Kumis-Khana. Refusing it when offered may cause offence. In the steppe and desert regions where camels are bred, the camel's milk, called *shubat*, is offered to guests.

NIGHTLIFE: There are a number of nightclubs and casinos in Almaty and several other cities. Many restaurants play music after 2000. Kazakhstan's most reknowned concert halls and theatres are all located in Almaty.

SHOPPING: Located north of Panfilov Park, Almaty has a bazaar, where a diverse range of items can be bought.

Shopping hours: Mon-Sat 0900-2000.

SPECIAL EVENTS: The following is a selection of special events occurring in Kazakhstan in 2005:

Jan 10 *Eid-ul-Azha* (Feast of the Sacrifice). **Aug** *Voice of Asia Festival* (international song contest with folk festivals attracting people from all over the south of the country, during which national music, songs, dance, sports, national costumes and dishes can be experienced), Almaty; *Khan Tengri Mountain Festival* (extreme sports climbing competition), Khan Tengri. **Oct 22-24** *Eid al-Fitr* (End of Ramadan).

SOCIAL CONVENTIONS: Kazakhs are very hospitable. When greeting a guest, the host gives him/her both hands as if showing that he/she is unarmed. When addressing a guest or elder, a Kazakh may address him/her with a shortened form of the guest's or elder's name and the suffix 'ke'. For example, Abkhan may be called Abeke, Nursultan can be called Nureke. This should be regarded as indicating a high level of respect for the visitor. At a Kazakh home, the most honoured guest, usually the oldest, is traditionally offered a boiled sheep's head on a beautiful dish as a further sign of respect. National customs forbid young people whose parents are still alive from cutting the sheep's head. They must pass the dish to the other guests for cutting. Inside mosques, women observe their own ritual in a separate room, and must cover their heads and their arms (see the *World of Islam* appendix for more information). Formal dress is often required when visiting the theatre, or attending a dinner party. Shorts should not be worn except on the sports ground. **Tipping:** This is not customary at restaurants and cafes, but is increasingly common in international hotels. A service charge is included in hotel and restaurant bills. There is also a fixed charge in taxi and railway transport.

Credit: © MTA

Business Profile

ECONOMY: Kazakhstan has enormous natural deposits: iron, nickel, zinc, manganese, coal, chromium, copper, lead, gold and silver are presently being mined. The coalfields of the Karaganda are some of the largest in Asia. There are substantial oil and gas deposits, many of which have only recently been located and the Kazakh government has signed joint production deals with US and European consortia. New pipeline projects agreed with the Russian Federation and Oman will offer further outlets for Kazakh oil and boost national revenues. The rapid increase in the size of the sector mainly accounts for the country's recent healthy growth, which saw GDP increase by around 10 per cent annually since 2000 (9.5 per cent in 2002). Inflation and unemployment in the same year were 6 and 9 per cent respectively. The government's economic policy has limited the involvement of foreign investors (the oil and gas industry apart). A privatisation programme has seen the bulk of the country's commercial enterprises transferred to the domestic private sector. The government has established a strong financial position, albeit at the

Credit: © MTA

expense of much-needed investment in Kazakhstan's decaying infrastructure.

Other than oil and gas, stone, such as marble and granite, is produced in large quantities. The country's industries are predominantly concerned with processing these raw materials. Domestic production also fulfils Kazakhstan's own energy needs. Agriculture still accounts for half of economic output. The main commodities are wheat, meat products, wool and a variety of crops: sugar beet, potatoes, cereals, cotton, fruit and vegetables. Livestock rearing is also important in this very arid region. However, one of the consequences of extensive cultivation has been heavy demand on water supplies, most particularly the rivers of Kazakhstan and its neighbour Uzbekistan: this was the major cause of one of the greatest ecological disasters of recent times – the shrinking of the Aral Sea.

Since independence, Kazakhstan has joined the IMF, World Bank and the European Bank for Reconstruction and Development, and has signed a partnership and co-operation agreement with the EU. It also belongs to the main regional economic co-operation venture, the Central Asian Economic Union (ECO). Since the dissolution of the Soviet Union, the Kazakhs have sought economic independence from the Russian Federation but find that they are still affected by developments in their larger neighbour. The Russian Federation remains Kazakhstan's largest trading partner, followed by China (PR), Germany, the US and Italy. In 1993, the Kazakh exchequer introduced a new currency, the *tenge*, to replace the rouble.

COMMERCIAL INFORMATION: The following organisations can offer advice: Trading House of the Republic of Kazakhstan, 58 Ribblesdale Avenue, London N11 3BQ, UK (tel: (020) 8368 4348; fax: (020) 8368 6886; e-mail: thrk@dircon.co.uk); *or* the Ministry of Economy and Trade, Ministry House, Astana 47330 (tel: (3172) 117 511 *or* 118 146; tel/fax: (3172) 118 145); *or* the Union of Chambers of Commerce and Industry of the Republic of Kazakhstan, Masanchi Street 26, Almaty 480091 (tel: (3272) 920 052; fax: (3272) 507 729; e-mail: tpprkaz@online.ru; website: www.ccikaz.kz).

CONFERENCES/CONVENTIONS: Many international business events, by such organisations as UNESCO, ICF and others, are held in the Alatau Winter Resort near Almaty. There is an annual International Exhibition Fair called *Karkara* held at the Exhibition Complex of the Business Cooperation Centre in Almaty every September. Businesspeople from all over the world meet here to make contacts and conclude business contracts. Other large industrial towns, such as Chimkent, Karaganda and Pavlodar have conference and convention facilities and other industrial exhibitions and fairs are held here.

Climate

Continental climate with cold winters and hot summers. Although Kazakhstan has some of the highest peaks in the CIS, the climate is fairly dry. The hottest month is July (August in mountain regions).

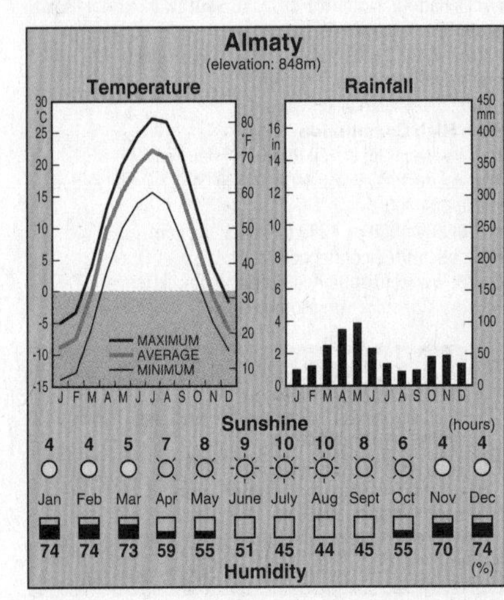

A B C D E F G H I J K L M N O P Q R S T U V W X Y Z

Kenya

LATEST TRAVEL ADVICE CONTACTS

British Foreign and Commonwealth Office
Tel: (0870) 606 0290 Website: www.fco.gov.uk

US Department of State
Website: http://travel.state.gov/travel

Canadian Department of Foreign Affairs and Int'l Trade
Tel: (1 800) 267 8376 Website: www.dfait-maeci.gc.ca

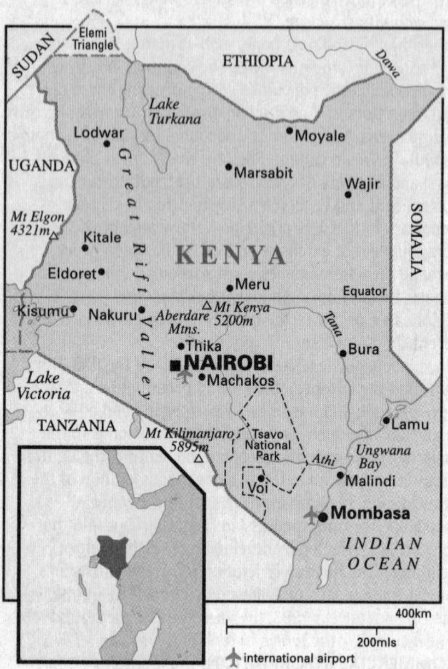

Location: East Africa.

Country dialling code: 254.

Kenya Tourist Development Corporation
PO Box 42013, Utalii House, Uhuru Highway, Nairobi-00100, Kenya
Tel: (20) 229 751 *or* 311 474. Fax: (20) 227 815 *or* 222 661.
E-mail: info@ktdc.co.ke

Kenya Tourist Board
Street address: Kenya-Re Tower, 7th Floor, Ragati Road, Upper Hill, Nairobi, Kenya
Postal address: PO Box 30630, Nairobi, 00100 Kenya
Tel: (202) 711 262. Fax: (202) 719 925.
E-mail: info@kenyatourism.org
Website: www.magicalkenya.com

Kenya Wildlife Service
PO Box 40241, Nairobi, Kenya
Tel: (20) 600 800. Fax: (20) 603 792.
E-mail: kws@kws.org
Website: www.kws.org

Kenya High Commission
45 Portland Place, London W1B 1AS, UK
Tel: (020) 7636 2371/5. Fax: (020) 7323 6717.
E-mail: info@kenyahighcommission.com *or* consular@kenyahighcommission.com (consular section).
Website: www.kenyahighcommission.com
Opening hours: Mon-Fri 0930-1200 and 1400-1530.

Kenya Tourist Board, UK
c/o Hills Balfour, Notcutt House, 36 Southwark Bridge Road, London SE1 9EU, UK
Tel: (020) 7202 6373 (dial 1). Fax: (020) 7928 0722.
E-mail: kenya@hillsbalfour.com
Website: www.magicalkenya.com

British High Commission
Street address: Upper Hill Road, Nairobi, Kenya
Postal address: PO Box 30465-00100 GPO, Nairobi, Kenya
Tel: (20) 284 4000.
Fax: (20) 284 4088 *or* 4239 (consular section).
E-mail: bhcinfo@iconnect.co.ke
Website: www.britishhighcommission.gov.uk/kenya
Honorary Consulate in: Mombasa.

TIMATIC CODES

Health	AMADEUS: **TI-DFT/NBO/HE** GALILEO/WORLDSPAN: **TI-DFT/NBO/HE** SABRE: **TIDFT/NBO/HE**
Visa	AMADEUS: **TI-DFT/NBO/VI** GALILEO/WORLDSPAN: **TI-DFT/NBO/VI** SABRE: **TIDFT/NBO/VI**

To access TIMATIC country information on Health and Visa regulations through the Computer Reservations System (CRS), type in the appropriate command line listed above.

Kenya Embassy
2249 R Street, NW, Washington, DC 20008, USA
Tel: (202) 387 6101. Fax: (202) 462 3829.
E-mail: info@kenyaembassy.com
Website: www.kenyaembassy.com

Embassy of the United States of America
Street address: United Nations Avenue, Village Market 00621, Nairobi, Kenya
Postal address: PO Box 606, 00621-Nairobi, Kenya
Tel: (20) 363 6000 *or* 375 3700 (consular section).
Fax: (20) 363 6410 (consular section) *or* 6353.
E-mail: consularnairob@state.gov (consular section) *or* ircnairobi@state.gov .
Website: http://nairobi.usembassy.gov

Kenya High Commission
415 Laurier Avenue East, Ottawa, Ontario K1N 6R4, Canada
Tel: (613) 563 1773-6. Fax: (613) 233 6599.
E-mail: kenrep@on.aibn.com
Website: www.kenyahighcommission.ca

Canadian High Commission
Street address: Limuru Road, Gigiri, Nairobi, Kenya
Postal address: Immigration Section, PO Box 1013, 00621-Nairobi, Kenya
Tel: (20) 366 3000.
Fax: (20) 366 3900 *or* 366 3914 (consular section).
E-mail: nrobi@dfait-maeci.gc.ca
Website: www.dfait-maeci.gc.ca/nairobi

General Information

AREA: 580,367 sq km (224,081 sq miles).
POPULATION: 30,493,792 (official estimate 2001).
POPULATION DENSITY: 52.5 per sq km.
CAPITAL: Nairobi. **Population:** 2,143,020 (1999).
GEOGRAPHY: Kenya shares borders with Ethiopia in the north, Sudan in the northwest, Uganda in the west, Tanzania in the south and Somalia in the northeast. To the east lies the Indian Ocean. The country is divided into four regions: the arid deserts of the north; the savannah lands of the south; the fertile lowlands along the coast and around the shores of Lake Victoria; and highlands in the west, where the capital Nairobi is situated. Northwest of Nairobi runs the Rift Valley, containing the town of Nakuru and Aberdare National Park, overlooked by Mount Kenya (5200m/17,000ft), which also has a national park. In the far northwest is Lake Turkana (formerly Lake Rudolph). Kenya is a multicultural society; in the north live Somalis and the nomadic Hamitic peoples (Rendille, Samburu and Turkana), in the south and eastern lowlands are Kamba and Masai and the Luo live around Lake Victoria. The largest group is the Kikuyu who live in the central highlands and have traditionally been dominant in commerce and politics, although this is now changing. There are many other smaller groups and although Kenya emphasises nationalism, tribal and cultural identity is a factor. A small European settler population remains in the highlands, involved in farming and commerce.
GOVERNMENT: Republic. Gained independence from the UK in 1963. **Head of State and Government:** President Emilio Mwai Kibaki since December 2002.
LANGUAGE: Swahili is the national language and English is the official language. There are over 42 ethnic languages spoken, including Kikuyu and Luo.
RELIGION: Mostly traditional but there is a sizeable Christian population (both Catholic and Protestant) and a small Muslim community.
TIME: GMT + 3 (Winter), GMT + 2 (Summer).
ELECTRICITY: 220/240 volts AC, 50Hz. Plugs are UK-type square three-pin. Bayonet-type light sockets exist in Kenya.
COMMUNICATIONS: Telephone: IDD service is available to the main cities. Country code: 254 (followed by 20 for Nairobi, 41 for Mombasa and 51 for Nakuru). Outgoing international code: 000. International calls can sometimes be made direct or operator-assisted by dialling 0196. Public telephones work with coins or with phone cards (which may be purchased from post offices or from international call services in major towns); coin-operated phone booths are painted red, card-operated booths are painted blue. Major hotels also offer a phone service, but they usually charge up to 100 per cent more. For local calls, it is useful to have plenty of small change available. **Mobile telephone:** GSM 900. The main network providers are *Celtel* (website: www.celtel.com) and *Safaricom* (website: www.safaricom.co.ke). **Fax:** This service is available to the public at the Main Post Office, the Kenyatta International Conference Centre in Nairobi, and at major hotels. **Telegram:** Overseas telegrams can be sent from all post and telegraphic offices and private telephones. Nairobi GPO is open 24 hours. **Internet:** There are over 30 ISPs in Kenya: *JamboNet* and 19 of the other ISPs belong to *The East African Internet Association*. There are Internet cafes in major cities and hotels. **Post:** Post offices are identified by Telkom Kenya (Kenya Posts & Telecommunications Corporation). Post boxes are red. Stamps can usually be bought at post offices, stationers, souvenir shops and hotels. Airmail to Western Europe takes up to four days, and the service is generally reliable. Post office hours: Mon-Fri 0800-1700, Sat 0900-1200 (main post offices). **Press:** The main dailies (all published in English) include *Daily Nation*, *The East African Standard*, *Kenya Times* and *The People*. Nairobi is the main publishing centre.
Radio: BBC World Service (website: www.bbc.co.uk/worldservice) and Voice of America (website: www.voa.gov) can be received. From time to time the frequencies change and the most up-to-date can be found online.

Passport/Visa

	Passport Required?	Visa Required?	Return Ticket Required?
Full British	Yes	Yes	Yes
Australian	Yes	Yes	Yes
Canadian	Yes	Yes	Yes
USA	Yes	Yes	Yes
Other EU	Yes	Yes	Yes
Japanese	Yes	Yes	Yes

Note: *Regulations and requirements may be subject to change at short notice, and you are advised to contact the appropriate diplomatic or consular authority before finalising travel arrangements. Details of these may be found at the head of this country's entry. Any numbers in the chart refer to the footnotes below.*

PASSPORTS: Passport valid for three months from date of entry required by all.
VISAS: Required by all except nationals of the following:
(a) nationals of Commonwealth countries for stays of up to three months *except* those nationals listed in the chart above, and nationals of Antigua & Barbuda, Bangladesh, Belize, Cameroon, Guyana, India, New Zealand, Nigeria, Pakistan, Sri Lanka, St Kitts & Nevis and Trinidad & Tobago who *do* require a visa;
(b) nationals of Ethiopia, San Marino, Turkey and Uruguay;
(c) nationals of Malaysia if staying less than 30 days;
(d) all holders of a re-entry pass to Kenya;
(e) transit passengers continuing their journey by the same or first connecting aircraft provided holding valid onward or return documentation and not leaving the airport.
Types of visa and cost: *Entry*: £30(single-entry); £60 (multiple-entry). *Transit*: £10.
Note: If the application is referred to Immigration in Nairobi, an additional £7 will be payable.
Validity: *Single-entry*: up to three months from date of issue; *Multiple-entry*: up to 12 months from date of issue. Renewals (up to six months) or extensions can be made at Immigration in Nyayo House, Uhuru Highway, Nairobi or at Kisumu and Mombasa. The period of stay in Kenya can be given at the port of entry (maximum three months).
Note: Multiple-entry visas may only be issued to nationals of the United Kingdom.
Application to: Consulate (or Consular section at Embassy or High Commission); see *Contact Addresses* section.
Application requirements: (a) Valid passport with at least one blank page. (b) Completed application form. (c) One recent passport-size photo. (d) Fee, payable by postal order, bank draft, building society cheque, or cash if applying in person. (e) Holiday itinerary or business letter. (f) For postal applications, include a self-addressed stamped and registered envelope for return of passport.
Working days required: Three (applying in person) or five (postal applications). If the visa has to be referred to Nairobi it will take at least eight weeks.
Note: The following nationals will automatically be referred to the Principal Immigration Officer in Nairobi before a visa can be granted: nationals of Afghanistan, Armenia, Azerbaijan, Iran, Iraq, Jordan, Korea (Dem Rep), Lebanon, Libya, Mali, Nigeria, Senegal, Somalia, Sudan and the Syrian Arab Republic.
Temporary residence: Apply to Principal Immigration Officer, PO Box 30191, Nairobi.

Money

Currency: Kenyan Shilling (KSh) = 100 cents. Notes are in denominations of KSh1000, 500, 200, 100 and 50. Coins are in denominations of KSh20, 10 and 5.
Currency exchange: Currency can be exchanged at the major banks. There are over 140 ATMs. Barclays has the largest network, with more than 65 ATMs located in Nairobi and Mombasa and all other major towns. Standard Chartered Bank's computerised network allows access to 62 ATMs countrywide. International visitors with Visa cards can access their own bank or credit card account through any Standard Chartered dispenser, 24 hours a day.
Credit & debit cards: American Express, Diners Club, MasterCard and Visa are all widely accepted. Major hotels now also accept payment by credit card, as do major safari companies, travel agencies and restaurants. Check with your

credit or debit card company for details of merchant acceptability and other services which may be available.
Travellers cheques: These can be changed at banks, and are widely accepted. To avoid additional exchange rate charges, travellers are advised to take travellers cheques in US Dollars or Pounds Sterling.
Currency restrictions: There is no restriction on the import and export of local or foreign currency. However, authorisation from the Central Bank is required for amounts of 500,000 KSh and above.
Exchange rate indicators: The following figures are included as a guide to the movements of the Kenyan Shilling against Sterling and the US Dollar:

Date	Feb '04	May '04	Aug '04	Nov '04
£1.00=	139.34	140.57	149.13	153.86
$1.00=	76.50	78.70	80.95	81.25

Banking hours: Mon-Fri 0900-1500; 0900-1100 on the first and last Saturday of each month. National and international banks have branches in Mombasa, Nairobi, Kisumu, Thika, Eldoret, Kericho, Nyeri and in most other major towns. Banks in Mombasa and the coastal areas open and close half an hour earlier. Many of the banks and bureaux de change at the international airports open 24 hours every day.

Duty Free

The following goods may be imported into Kenya by passengers over 16 years of age without incurring customs duty:
200 cigarettes or 50 cigars or 225g of tobacco; one bottle of alcoholic beverages; 568 ml of perfume.
Note: Firearms and ammunition require a police permit. Pets require a good health certificate, a rabies certificate and an import permit.
Prohibited items: The import of fruit, plants, seeds, children's toys and imitation firearms. The export of gold, diamonds and wildlife skins or game trophies not obtained from the authorised Kenyan government department is also prohibited.

Public Holidays

2005: Jan 1 New Year's Day. **Mar 25** Good Friday. **Mar 28** Easter Monday. **May 1** Labour Day. **Jun 1** Madaraka Day. **Oct 10** Moi Day. **Oct 20** Kenyatta Day. **Nov 3-5** Eid al-Fitr (End of Ramadan). **Dec 12** Independence Day. **Dec 25-26** Christmas.
2006: Jan 1 New Year's Day. **Apr 14** Good Friday. **Apr 17** Easter Monday. **May 1** Labour Day. **Jun 1** Madaraka Day. **Oct 10** Moi Day. **Oct 20** Kenyatta Day. **Oct 22-24** Eid al-Fitr (End of Ramadan). **Dec 12** Independence Day. **Dec 25-26** Christmas.
Note: (a) Holidays falling on a Sunday are observed the following Monday. (b) Muslim festivals are timed according to local sightings of various phases of the moon and the dates given above are approximations. During the lunar month of Ramadan that precedes Eid al-Fitr, Muslims fast during the day and feast at night and normal business patterns may be interrupted. Many restaurants are closed during the day and there may be restrictions on smoking and drinking. Some disruption may continue into Eid al-Fitr itself. Eid al-Fitr may last anything from two to 10 days, depending on the region. For more information, see the *World of Islam* appendix.

Health

	Special Precautions?	Certificate Required?
Yellow Fever	Yes	1
Cholera	Yes	2
Typhoid & Polio	3	N/A
Malaria	4	N/A

Note: Regulations and requirements may be subject to change at short notice, and you are advised to contact your doctor well in advance of your intended date of departure. Any numbers in the chart refer to the footnotes below.

1: A yellow fever vaccination certificate is required from travellers over one year of age arriving from infected areas; those countries formerly classified as endemic zones are considered to be still infected by the Kenyan authorities. Travellers arriving from non-endemic zones should note that vaccination is strongly recommended for travel outside the urban areas, even if an outbreak of the disease has not been reported and they would normally not require a vaccination certificate to enter the country.
2: Following WHO guidelines issued in 1973, a cholera vaccination certificate is no longer a condition of entry to Kenya. However, cholera is a serious risk in this country and precautions are essential. Up-to-date advice should be sought before deciding whether these precautions should

Credit: © Kenya Tourist Board

include vaccination, as medical opinion is divided over its effectiveness; see the *Health* appendix for further information.
3: Immunisation against typhoid and poliomyelitis is recommended.
4: Malaria risk exists throughout the year in the whole country. There is usually less risk in Nairobi and in the highlands (above 2500m/8200ft) of the Central, Eastern Nyanza, Rift Valley and Western Provinces. The predominant *falciparum* strain has been reported as highly resistant to chloroquine and resistant to sulfadoxine/pyrimethamine. Mefloquine is the recommended prophylaxis.
Food & drink: Mains water is normally chlorinated and relatively safe. Bottled water is available and is advised for the first few weeks of the stay. Drinking water outside main cities and towns is likely to be contaminated and sterilisation is considered essential. Milk is pasteurised and dairy products are safe for consumption. Local meat, poultry, seafood, fruit and vegetables are generally considered safe to eat.
Other risks: *Dysenteries* and *diarrhoeal diseases* are common. *Hepatitis B* is hyperendemic; *hepatitis A* and *E* are widespread. *Meningococcal meningitis* is a risk, particularly in the savannah in the dry season; long-staying visitors and backpackers should consider vaccination. *Bilharzia* (schistosomiasis) is present. Avoid swimming and paddling in fresh water; swimming pools which are well chlorinated and maintained are safe. *Dengue fever* is present, as are *leishmaniasis*, *trypanosomiasis* (sleeping sickness) and *filariasis*. Avoid sandfly, mosquito and tsetse fly bites, and wear shoes to protect against hookworm. *Relapsing fever* and *typhus* are present. In June 2004, there were 141 suspected cases, including six deaths, of *Leptospirosis* in a high school in the Bungoma district. A nearby primary school also reported two deaths. Travellers should be aware of these developments when within the Bungoma district.
Rabies is present. For those at high risk, vaccination before arrival should be considered. If you are bitten, seek medical advice without delay. See the *Health* appendix for further information.
Note: There is a risk of contracting *AIDS* if the necessary precautions are not taken. It is advisable to take a kit of sterilised syringe needles for any possible injections needed, as well as drip needles for emergencies.
Health care: Health insurance is essential. *East African Flying Doctor Services* have introduced a special Tourist Membership which guarantees that any member injured or ill while on safari can call on a flying doctor for free air transport. There are good medical facilities in Mombasa and Nairobi. The Kenya Tourism Federation (KTF) safety communication centre (24 hour) help tourists in difficulty (tel: (20) 604 767; e-mail: safetour@wananchi.com).

Travel - International

Note: Kenya shares with neighbouring countries a high threat from terrorism. Previous attacks have been against civilian or visibly Western targets where foreigners have been present, as demonstrated by the bomb attacks on a hotel and an unsuccessful attempt to bring down a civilian airliner in Mombasa in November 2002. Muggings and armed attacks are prevalent, particularly in Nairobi and Mombasa.
AIR: Kenya's national airline is *Kenya Airways (KQ)*. Kenya is served by a large number of airlines from all over the world, particularly from Asia, Europe and the rest of Africa. These include *British Airways* and *KLM*.
Approximate flight times: From Nairobi to *London* is nine hours 30 minutes; to *New York* is 18 hours; to *Los Angeles* is 20 hours; to *Singapore* is 21 hours; and to *Sydney* is 25 hours.
International airports: *Nairobi (NBO)* (Jomo Kenyatta International) is 16km (10 miles) southeast of the city. A *Kenyan Bus Services* bus and a *Kenyan Airways* bus leave every 20 minutes (travel time - 40 minutes). Taxis are readily available, but the fare should be established before getting into the vehicle (travel time - 15 minutes). The state-controlled *Kenacto* taxis work on a fixed rate as do the British-style black cabs, and *Dial a Cab*, which are legally required to charge per kilometre. Airport facilities include an outgoing duty free shop, hotel reservation, bank/bureau de change, post office, restaurant/bar and car hire.
Mombasa (MBA) (Moi International) is 13km (8 miles) west of the city. There is a regular bus service by *Kenya Airways* to their city centre office in Mombasa (travel time - 20 minutes). Taxis are also available. Fares should be negotiated in advance. State-controlled *Kenacto* taxis and British-style black cabs work on a fixed rate. Airport facilities include an outgoing duty-free shop, bank, restaurant/bar, tourist information and car hire (*Avis, City Car Hire* and *Hertz*).
Note: Immigration procedures in Kenyan airports are likely to be extremely slow, so it is advisable to arrive early.
Departure tax: None.
SEA/LAKE: Short-distance ships sail between Mombasa, Mauritius, the Seychelles and Zanzibar. Passenger and cruise lines that run to Kenya are *Barwil Shipping Company, Inchcape Shipping Company* and *Seaforth Shipping Company*. The ports in the Lake Victoria passenger service include Homa Bay, Mfangano and Port Victoria/Kisumu. The ferries in Lake Victoria connect Kisumu in Kenya to Mwanza, Musoma and Bukoba in Tanzania. Fares are paid for in the currency of the port of embarkation. It is also possible to get ferries from Mombasa to Pemba and Zanzibar in Tanzania, and also to Chiamboni in Somalia. Enquire locally for details.
RAIL: Train services operate between Voi and Moshi (Tanzania) and between Nairobi and Kampala (Uganda). Travellers should check beforehand as these rail services may be subject to disruption. For more information contact Kenya Railways, PO Box 30121, Nairobi (tel: (20) 221 211; fax: (20) 340 049).
ROAD: The main crossing points from Tanzania are at Lunga Lunga and Namanga, with smaller posts at Isebania and Taveta. Some direct coach services operate. From Uganda there are crossing points at Buisa and Malaba. Note that at Malaba, the Kenyan and Ugandan customs posts are about 1km (0.6 miles) apart and no transport between them is available. For all road frontier crossings, it is advisable to contact the Kenya AA, PO Box 40087, Embakasi, Nairobi (tel: (20) 825 060-6; fax: (20) 825 068/119) prior to departure from the country of origin for up-to-date information concerning insurance requirements and conditions.

Travel - Internal

AIR: *Kenya Airways* operates an extensive network of flights, which includes scheduled services to Eldoret, Kisumu (on the shore of Lake Victoria), Lamu Island, Lockichogio, Malindi and Mombasa. *Air Kenya* offers scheduled flights from Nairobi to Amboseli, Kiwayu, Lamu, Malindi, Masai

Mara, Mombasa, Nanyuki and Samburu. Air Kenya also operates into all of Kenya's game parks. *Regional Air* also operates from Nairobi. There are also private airlines operating light aircraft to small airstrips. Planes can be chartered and are useful for transport into game parks.
Departure tax: None.
SEA: Local ferries run between Mombasa, Malindi and Lamu. For details, contact local authorities and tour operators. It is also possible to hire a traditional Kenyan sailing boat (*dhow*) in Lamu, Malindi and Mombasa. This is a very basic form of sea travel which requires travellers to take their own food and drinking water.
RAIL: *Kenya Railways Corporation* runs passenger trains between Mombasa and Nairobi; trains generally leave in the evening and arrive the following morning after a journey of around 13 to 14 hours. There are also branches connecting Taveta and Kisumu to the passenger network. There is a daily train in each direction on the Nairobi–Kisumu route, and also an overnight service (travel time - approximately 14 hours). Trains are sometimes delayed, but most of the rolling stock is modern and comfortable, and most trains have restaurant cars. There are three classes: first class is excellent, with two-berth compartments, wardrobe, etc; second class is more basic but comfortable; third is basic. The dining-car service on the Nairobi–Mombasa route is very highly regarded. Sleeping compartments should be booked in advance. Sexes are separated in first and second class. Children under three years of age travel free. Children between three and 15 years of age pay half fare. For further information contact Kenya Railways (see address in *Travel – International* section).

Credit: © Kenya Tourist Board

ROAD: Traffic drives on the left. All major roads are paved and many of the others have been improved, particularly in the southwest, although vast areas of the north still suffer from very poor communications. Care should be taken when leaving trunk roads as the surfaces of the lesser roads vary greatly in quality, particularly during the rainy season. There are petrol stations on most highways. The Kilifi Bridge linking Mombasa to Malindi has opened, serving as an alternative to the Kilifi ferry, and easing traffic flows to the northern circuit. **Bus:** City buses operate in Nairobi and Mombasa at reasonable prices. Peak hours should be avoided as buses get very crowded. Fares are paid to the conductor. There is a network of regular buses and shared minibuses (*Matatu*); the fares do not vary greatly, but buses tend to be the safer method of transport. All bus companies are privately run. In some towns the different bus services and the *matatu* share the same terminus. **Taxi**: Kenya is very well served by long-distance taxis, carrying up to seven passengers. The best services are between the capital and Mombasa and Nakuru. Taxis and minibuses are a convenient method of travel on the coast. **Car hire:** Self-drive and chauffeur-driven cars may be hired from a number of travel agents in Malindi, Mombasa and Nairobi. This can be expensive, and rates - particularly the mileage charges - can vary a good deal. Most companies insist that only 4-wheel-drive vehicles should be rented. **Tours and safaris:** Many tour companies in Nairobi offer package arrangements for visits to the game parks and other attractions. Before booking it is very important to know exactly what the all-in price provides. For further information contact Kenya Association of Tour Operators (KATO), PO Box 48461, 00100 Nairobi (tel: (20) 713 348 *or* 713 386; e-mail: info@katokenya.org; website: www.katokenya.org). **Documentation:** Visitors bringing in vehicles with registration other than Ugandan or Tanzanian must obtain an 'International Circulation Permit' from the Licensing Officer in Nairobi. This will be issued free of charge on production of a permit of customs duty receipt and a certificate of insurance. A full British driving licence is valid, otherwise an International Driving Permit is required. For further details, apply to the Registrar of Motor Vehicles in Nairobi.
URBAN: Bus: Nairobi and Mombasa have efficient bus systems. Single tickets are sold (by conductors), but monthly bus passes are also available from the Kenya Bus Offices in the city centre. There are also unregulated *Matatu*, 12- to 25-seat light pick-ups and minibuses. These are often severely overloaded and badly driven and therefore should be used with caution. **Taxi:** *Dial a Cab*, *Jatco* and *Kenatco* run fleets of taxis and these are usually very reliable. The older yellow-band taxis do not have meters, so fares should be agreed in advance. A 10 per cent tip is expected. Taxis cannot be hailed in the street.
Travel times: The following chart gives approximate travel times (in hours and minutes) from **Nairobi** to other major cities/towns in Kenya.

	Air	Road	Rail
Kisumu	1.05	7.00	14.00
Malindi	0.45	8.00	-
Mombasa	1.00	6.00	14.00
Lamu	1.30	13.00*	-
Diani	1.30	7.00	-
Nakuru	0.30	3.00	5.00
Eldoret	1.15	7.00	9.00
Masai Mara	0.30	5.00	-
Amboseli	0.30	3.00	-

Note: *Travel to Lamu by road is not recommended.

Accommodation

HOTELS: Many of Nairobi's hotels are of top international standards, and some of them are still in the colonial style. Cheaper hotels are also available. Hotel bills must be paid in foreign currency or Kenyan Shillings. **Grading:** Accommodation in Kenya is divided into groups: town hotels, vacation hotels, lodges and country hotels. Within each group, grading is according to amenities and variety of facilities. The rating is subject to the fulfilment of strict requirements concerning technical equipment, comfort, services, sanitation and security. For further information, contact the Kenya Association of Hotel Keepers & Caterers, PO Box 46406, Nairobi (tel: (20) 726 640/2; fax: (20) 714 401).
CAMPING/CARAVANNING: There are no restrictions on camping in Kenya. However, visitors should be aware that camping in remote regions can be dangerous, owing to wild animals and to *shifta* (armed bandits); the latter are a hazard particularly in the far north. Visitors intending to camp in remote areas should contact the Kenya Association of Tour Operators (see *Travel – Internal* section) *or* Kenya Wildlife Service (KWS) (see *Contact Addresses* section).
GAME LODGES/SAFARI TENTS: The type of accommodation available on a safari depends on the type of safari booked. Upmarket safaris offer overnight stays in luxurious game lodges and luxury tented camps. These are often situated in beautiful or dramatic surroundings, with animals sometimes roaming around the grounds freely. Camping safaris are also available - but only travellers willing to live without luxuries such as running water or flushing toilets should consider this. For further information, contact the Kenya National Tourist Office, the Kenya Wildlife Service (see *Contact Addresses* section) *or* KATO (see *Travel – Internal* section).
YOUTH HOSTELS: There are youth hostels in all major towns. For further information, contact the Kenya Youth Hostels Association, Ralph Bunche Road, PO Box 48661, Nairobi (tel: (20) 723 012 *or* 720 353; fax: (20) 724 862; e-mail: kyha@africaonline.co.ke).
COUNTRY BUSH HOMES: The KWS recently completed the rehabilitation of selected self-catering *bandas* (cabins) in various national parks. These are privately owned country bush homes usually in spectacular locations, major cities or on main tour circuits. Most travel agents in Nairobi can arrange stays. Contact the Kenya Wildlife Service (KWS) for more information (see *Contact Addresses* section).
SELF CATERING: Apartments ranging from luxury villas to basic beach cottages can be rented. Assistance with domestic chores can also be arranged.

Resorts & Excursions

Kenya, regarded by many as the 'jewel of East Africa', has some of the continent's finest beaches, most magnificent wildlife and scenery and an incredibly sophisticated tourism infrastructure. It is a startlingly beautiful land, from the coral reefs and white sand beaches of the coast to the summit of Mount Kenya, crowned with clouds and bejewelled by strange giant alpine plants. Between these two extremes is the rolling savannah that is home to game parks such as Amboseli, the Masai Mara, Samburu and Tsavo; the lush, agricultural highlands with their sleek green coat of coffee and tea plantations; and the most spectacular stretch of the Great Rift Valley, the giant scar across the face of Africa. One-tenth of all land in Kenya is designated as national parks and reserves. Over 50 parks and reserves cover all habitats from desert to mountain forest, and there are even six marine parks in the Indian Ocean. Tourist facilities are extremely good. There are many organised safaris, but visitors with the time and money may choose to hire their own vehicle and camping equipment.
Kenya also has a fascinatingly diverse population with around 40 different tribes, all with their own (often related) languages and cultures. The major tribes include the Kikuyu from the central highlands, the Luyia in the northwest, and the Luo around Lake Victoria. Of them all, however, the most famous are the tall, proud, beautiful red-clad Masai, who still lead a traditional semi-nomadic lifestyle of cattle-herding along the southern border.
Kenya does have its downside as a tourist destination. Rampant corruption means that many of the roads are in poor condition and driving can be a chore. Urban crime is high and continuing inter-tribal skirmishes and banditry are a threat in some areas of the North. More prosaically, the tourist trade has taught people there to think of foreigners as open wallets. Prices for everything from park fees to hotel rooms are set way above the local level. There is enormous pressure to buy anything and everything, often at ridiculously inflated prices, and even taking a photograph in the local market is likely to incur a cost.

THE COAST

MOMBASSA: The second-largest city in Kenya, 500km (300 miles) from Nairobi, Mombasa town actually sits on an island. Until the ascendancy of the Western powers in the Indian Ocean, Mombasa was second only to Zanzibar as a centre for trade with Arabia, India and the Far East - slaves and ivory were exchanged for spices and small goods, and later for gold dollars. Mombasa is still an important port, prospering from its position at the head of the only railway into the Kenyan interior, but visitors are likely to find the rakish grey forms of foreign warships to be more typical of modern Mombasa than the flotillas of Arab *dhows* that still collect in the **Old Harbour**. Mombasa is the headquarters for Kenya's coastal tourist trade, but has none of the fine beaches to be found to the north and south. There are, however, several places of interest: the **Old Town** retains a strongly Arab flavour, with narrow, crowded streets and street vendors selling all manner of local and imported craftwork; **Fort Jesus**, built by the Portuguese in 1593 and taken by the Omani Arabs in 1698 after a 33-month seige, is now a museum and worth visiting (open 0830-1830 every day of the year, including son-et-lumière shows); the **Old Harbour** is an interesting place for early morning and late afternoon strolls, and is often filled with sailing dhows from the Yemen and Persian Gulf. For those who want to go shopping with atmosphere, **Biashara Street** is probably the best place to go to buy kikoi and khanga cloths; the main city market is the **Makupa Market**, off Mwembe Tayari and there is a floating market at **Tudor Creek**, to the north of the city. There are plenty of dhow trips here, and around the harbour if you fancy a spell on the water. The tourist office is on Moi Avenue near the Giant Tusks (Mon-Fri 0800-1700, Sat 0800-1200; tel: (11) 315 922 *or* 223 465). Staff are very helpful. Alternatively, there is also excellent information about the city online (website: www.mombasaonline.com).
RESORTS: Most of the beach resorts which are actually listed as Mombasa are some way out of town, along a 120km- (70 mile-) stretch of coast. To the north of the city, resorts such as **Bamburi Beach**, **Casuarina Beach**, **Kenya Beach** and **Nyali Beach** are amongst the older developments with easy access to the city centre and activities, restaurants and clubs. The **Kenya Marineland and Snake Park**, **Bamburi Quarry Nature Trail**, which also has a butterfly farm, the **Mamba Crocodile Village** in **Freretown**, and the **Ngomongo Villages** cultural park, showing off the lifestyle of 11 different Kenyan tribes, are entertaining for children and adults alike. Serious souvenir shoppers should head for **Bombolulu Workshops** and **Cultural Village**, where 260 disabled men and women produce high-quality leatherwork, jewellery and other crafts. There is some good diving on the somewhat damaged coral reef of the **Mombasa Marine National Park**, off the **Nyali** headland.
The best beaches, such as **Likoni** and **Tiwi** (popular with backpackers), stretch out for some distance along the South Coast, reached only by ferry from the city centre. The best and most famous of them all is the 10km long, dazzlingly white **Diani Beach**, some 40km (24 miles) south of the city, lined by a string of large resort hotels. A short way inland, the 192 sq km **Shimba Hills National Reserve** is the most accessible place to see big game for those staying on the coast, although the wooded vegetation does not always make it easy. It does, however, boast a lot of leopard and Kenya's only population of sable antelope. In the far south, little **Shimoni** is an increasingly popular centre for diving and deep sea fishing, with three small marine parks, **Kisite Marine National Park**, **Mpunguti National Reserve** and **Wasini Marine National Park** within easy boat-trip distance. The coral reefs around here are spectacular and there are dhow trips to go dolphin-watching.
MALINDI: Malindi, 125km (80 miles) north of Mombasa,

was once the centre of a powerful kingdom. Today it is a small, somewhat tatty resort town, but the **Malindi** and **Watamu Marine National Parks** are nearby. Here the coral reef is close enough to the white sand beach to walk out at low tide and you can snorkel, dive or watch the technicolour fish through a glass-bottomed boat. There are also several operators running deep-sea fishing charters. A small white cross on the bay marks the arrival in 1499 of Vasco da Gama, the first European ever to visit the Kenyan coast. Close to **Watamu**, the **Gedi National Park** protects the well-preserved ruins of a Swahili city, founded in the 13th century and destroyed by Somali raiders in the 17th century. The **Arabuko-Sokoke Forest**, south of Watamu, and the little village of **Mambrui**, north of Malindi, are also worth a visit.

LAMU ISLAND: Lamu Island, 200km (125 miles) north of Malindi, is an exceptionally beautiful place with fine, white sandy beaches, sailing dhows and a fascinating town. No motorised vehicles are allowed on the island and the streets are so narrow that donkeys and hand-carts are the only vehicles that can negotiate them. The area is strongly Muslim and the only places on the island to buy alcohol are in a couple of the larger tourist hotels.

Lamu Town was founded in the ninth century and is one of a handful of Swahili towns whose many mosques and fine old Arab houses with impressive carved wooden doors have survived intact. There are a couple of excellent museums; the **Lamu Museum** and the **Swahili House Museum**. The **Fortress** is also open to the public. Other attractions in the city include the **Hindu Temple** in Mwagogo Road, off Treasury Square, and the bazaars. The best beaches are about 2km (1.2 miles) south of the town at **Shela**, or on the nearby islands.

Excursions: Fishing trips may be taken by dhow, and day trips to the 14th- and 15th-century ruins on the nearby islands of **Manda** and **Pate** can be arranged with local boat owners. On the Prophet's Birthday there is a week-long festival with dancing, singing and other celebrations. Many Muslims come to Lamu from all along the coast to enjoy this celebration. The best time to visit the island is outside the main tourist season (April to November).

THE SOUTHEAST

Southeastern Kenya is low, dry, flat savannah country, much of it taken up by the vast Tsavo National Park, a collection of privately owned game ranches in the Taita Hills and the smaller Amboseli National Park, on the Tanzanian border.

TSAVO NATIONAL PARK: The largest park in Kenya, Tsavo covers a mammoth 21,000 sq km (8000 sq miles). It is actually managed as two separate parks - Tsavo East, most of which is closed to the public, and Tsavo West. Between the two, the **Taita Hills** are the setting for most of the local game lodges, all of which stand on private concessions run as part of the same ecosystem as the park itself. Despite a drastic fall in the elephant population, caused by massive poaching in the 1970s and 80s, numbers are again on the increase and it is possible to see large herds. Much of the land is open savannah and bush woodland inhabited by buffaloes, a few rhinos, lions, antelopes, gazelles, giraffes and zebras. Crocodiles and hippos can be seen at **Mzima Springs** in the northwest of the park. Nearby, the **Shetani Lava Flow** is a 50 sq km lava bed formed by an eruption in the **Chyulu Hills**. As well as being rich in wildlife, **Tsavo** has a wealth of birds, with over 440 species recorded.

AMBOSELI NATIONAL PARK: A small park by Kenyan standards, covering 329 sq km, Amboseli lies on the Tanzanian border 220km (140 miles) from Nairobi. The fine view it affords of snow-capped **Mount Kilimanjaro**, Africa's highest mountain (5895m/19,340ft), draws many visitors, but the park itself has seen better days. The once-lush savannah is now largely a dust-bowl and most animals have retreated into areas of scrub forest and marshland.

CENTRAL HIGHLANDS

NAIROBI: The 'Green City in the Sun' is an attractive city with wide tree-lined streets and spacious parkland suburbs. Its pleasant nature together with judicious investment in facilities such as the **Kenyatta Conference Centre** have made Nairobi an important centre for international business and conference activities. However, despite the capital's appearance, urban crime is on the increase and visitors are advised to take precautions such as avoiding certain areas, or walking anywhere at night (travellers are advised against walking alone through **Uhuru Park** at any time). There is a full range of shopping opportunities, from purpose-built American-style malls to African markets, and a variety of restaurants and nightclubs. There are open-air swimming pools at the Boulevard, Jacaranda and Serena hotels – non-residents may pay to swim.

Other places of interest in or near Nairobi include the **Bomas of Kenya**, a short distance outside the city centre, where displays of traditional dancing are put on for visitors; the **Kenya National Museum** with its particularly good ethnographic and archaeological exhibits (this is where many of the earliest human remains, discovered by the Leakeys at Olduvai, Koobi Fora and other well-known prehistoric sites, are displayed); and the **Snake Park**, opposite the museum, which houses snakes indigenous to East Africa and a few from other parts of the world. Adjacent to Snake Park is a collection of traditional mud and thatch huts and granaries containing tools characteristic of different tribes. In the suburb of Karen, the **Karen Blixen Museum** occupies the farmhouse made famous by the author's book, *Out of Africa*.

Excursions: Although it is just 8km (5 miles) from Nairobi city centre, **Nairobi National Park** still seems a savage and lonely place during the week (carloads of city-dwellers invade at the weekend). It was Kenya's first national park and today still looks much as it did in the early photographs – wild, undulating pasture dotted with every kind of East African plain-dwelling animal except elephants. At the gates to the park is the **Animal Orphanage** where young, sick and wounded animals are cared for. Also near here, the **Langata Giraffe Centre** offers the enchanting opportunity of hand-feeding the resident Rothschild giraffes.

North of Nairobi, the road climbs steadily through the suburb of **Thika** and rich agricultural lands, offering excellent views of the **Great Rift Valley**. The eastern wall of the Rift is made up by the **Aberdare Mountains**, while further east still looms the vast bulk of **Mount Kenya**. Between the two are several attractive small towns such as **Nyeri**; **Nyahururu**, home of the **Thomson's Falls**; **Muranga'a**, whose cathedral tells the story of the Mau Mau rebellions in a series of colourful murals; **Nanyuki** and **Naro Moru**, both acting as starting points for those wishing to climb the mountain.

ABERDARE NATIONAL PARK: The park is set amidst a densely wooded mountain range rising to over 4000m (13,000ft), adjacent to Mount Kenya. It is possible to see elephants, rhinos, dik-dik, leopards, lions and monkeys as well as rare forest antelopes such as the bongo. However, the thick vegetation and misty alpine climate hides most wildlife from the inexpert observer, the exceptions being giant forest pigs, baboons and buffaloes, which often sleep or feed beside the many dirt tracks. Most visitors prefer to watch for animals from the comfort of the park's two lodges, 'Treetops' and 'Ark', both built on platforms overlooking clearings which are floodlit at night. On the higher slopes, giant alpine plants sprout from an almost perpetual fog. There are many waterfalls, the greatest being **Guru Falls**, which drops over 300m (1000ft). The western face of the mountain range is the sheer **Mau Escarpment**, which falls dramatically to the floor of the **Great Rift Valley**.

MOUNT KENYA NATIONAL PARK: Conical **Mount Kenya**, an extinct volcano, is the second-highest mountain in Africa, at 4986m (16,358ft) above sea level. The national park covers 600 sq km (230 sq miles) of forest and bare rock straddling the equator, all above 1800m (6000ft). The mountain may be climbed without special equipment, but it is advisable to take time so as to avoid altitude sickness. The ascent is very beautiful with the vegetation ranging from farmland to thick forest, bamboo forest, open moorland, giant alpine vegetation, sheer rock and finally, at the summit, year-round snow fields. The lower slopes are one of the last haunts of the black leopard and the black and white colobus monkey. Climbers should be accompanied by a guide. Porters are also available and there are huts to stay in along the way. Plenty of warm clothes are required as well as one's own food supplies. *A Rockclimber's Guide to Mount Kenya and Mount Kilimanjaro* can be bought from the Mountain Club of Kenya, PO Box 45741, Nairobi (tel: (20) 602 330; e-mail: MCKenya@iname.com; website: www.mck.or.ke).

THE GREAT RIFT VALLEY

About 20 million years ago, a vast seismic scar was torn across the face of Africa, stretching for nearly 6000km (3600 miles), from the **Red Sea** to the **Drakensberg** in South Africa. Known today as the Great Rift Valley, it is at its most dramatic and visible in central Kenya where escarpment walls 2000m high plunge to the flat-bottomed valley floor, decorated by a small string of volcanoes and brackish soda lakes.

Driving down into the valley from Nairobi, the first landmark on the valley floor is the almost perfect cone of **Mount Longonot**, a dormant volcano (2885m/9466ft), that has recently been gazetted as a national park. The walk up is hard, but worth it both for the wildlife and the final spectacular views of the crater and along the Rift.

Known for the abundance and variety of its birdlife and spectacular views, freshwater **Lake Naivasha**, is one hour's drive from the capital, and the centre of a booming horticultural industry. The south shore is lined by hotels and guest houses, popular as a weekend retreat from Nairobi, with the option of boat trips to little **Crescent Island**. Also on the south shore is **Elsamere**, home of Joy and George Adamson and the real setting of *Born Free*, their effort to return the lioness, Elsa, to the wild. It is now a small museum, guest house and conservation centre. Nearby, **Crater Lake** is another small volcanic crater and **Hell's Gate National Park**, both of which allow you to walk amongst the wildlife. **Happy Valley**, centre of the 'White Mischief' scandal is a short distance north of Naivasha, in the foothills of the Aberdares. Much of the socialising in the 1920s took place in the mansions surrounding Lake Naivasha, notably the **Djinn Palace** (still there, but closed to the public).

Lake Elementeita is the first of the brackish soda lakes in the string. There is a small game reserve on its shores and excellent birdwatching. Also nearby is a small but fascinating prehistoric site, **Kariandusi**.

Kenya's third-largest city, **Nakuru** is situated a little further north still, about 230km (140 miles) west of Nairobi. A vibrant town, with a huge central market, it is a good place to hunt down souvenirs (keep an eye on wallets and bags).

Lake Nakuru National Park was once said to be home to half the world's total population of pink flamingos and, even today, visitors in winter will encounter these ungainly birds in vast numbers, along with around 450 other species of bird. Although tiny, this gem of a park has huge concentrations of game (everything except elephant). Above all, it is one of Kenya's rhino sanctuaries, and it is possible to see up to 15 of these magnificent animals in one game drive. Also near Nakuru are **Hyrax Hill**, another important prehistoric settlement, and the **Menengai Crater**, an extinct volcano with a vast caldera. You can drive right up to the rim.

Lake Bogoria National Park, about 70km (42 miles) north of Nakuru, surrounds a long thin soda lake, dramatically set at the foot of the 600m-high **Laikipia Escarpment**. It also has good game-viewing and giant flocks of flamingos, and area of belching geysers and hot springs lie in one corner of the park, which have dyed the surrounding rocks a kaleidoscope of colours.

Of the most northerly of the string of lakes (approximately 118km (65 miles) north of Nakuru), **Lake Baringo** is a large, beautiful freshwater lake with excellent birdlife. There is a permanent tented camp on the island at the lake's centre where boats may be hired to cruise through the reeds at the northern end, a habitat rich in water fowl, egrets, giant herons and fish eagles. With village tours on offer and a huge variety of local tribes, this is one of the best places in Kenya to explore the rich human culture of the country.

WESTERN KENYA

With the exception of the magnificent Masai Mara, Western Kenya is rarely visited by tourists and there are fewer hotels and lodges of international standard. On the plus side, the area is stunningly beautiful, culturally diverse and offers a real chance to explore the country away from the crowds.

MASAI MARA NATIONAL RESERVE: Situated 390km (240 miles) from Nairobi in the southwest corner of the country, this reserve, owned by the local Masai Council but operated as a national park by Kenya Wildlife Services, is a slice of Africa as seen by Hollywood (much of the film *Out of Africa* was shot here) – a vast rolling plain beneath the **Oloololo escarpment** that forms part of the vast **Serengeti plains** in neighbouring Tanzania. Each year, this is the spectacular setting for the great migration, the constant clockwise motion of an estimated two million wildebeests and zebra who arrive in the Mara from late June onwards, heading south again in September. Continually harried by predators, thick columns of exhausted animals eventually converge at one spot on the **Mara River** and wait nervously to cross. A panic anywhere within the herd is transmitted flank-to-flank until it reaches those by the river, who fall 6m (20ft) into water already bloodied and bobbing with bloated carcasses. The inelegant beasts must swim past crocodiles, hippos and flapping vultures to join the sparse but growing herd on the other side. The stench is unimaginable and while it is undoubtedly fascinating, also requires a strong stomach to watch the immense distress.

During the migration season (July/August), the reserve's resident lions lounge prominently in the sun, fat and seemingly placid, and apparently indifferent to tourists.

Other animals to be seen, at any time of the year, include elephants, cheetahs, baboons, gazelles, giraffes, jackals, hyenas, water buffaloes, ostriches and several types of antelope. There are numerous lodges and tented camps both within the park and on its immediate borders. *Mara Serena Lodge*, *Mara Sopa Lodge* and *Keekorok Lodge* are the best known of the hotel-style properties. *Governor's Camp* is the largest of the camps. For true luxury, try *Bateleur's Camp* or *Cottars 1920s Safari Camp*. Most of the small lodges and camps have their own airstrips. A highlight for any visitor is the hot air balloon trips which operate from *Governor's Camp*, *Sarova Camp* and *Fig Tree Camp*. Masai tribespeople live on the reserve's fringes. They are very keen to sell traditional bead necklaces and decorated gourds to tourists, or to pose for tourist cameras in return for a fee.

LAKE VICTORIA: West of the Mara, on the Ugandan border, Lake Victoria is the largest lake in Africa, a vast inland sea that is also the source of the fabled **Nile River**. **Kisumu**, Kenya's fourth city, made its reputation as the inland end of the Lunatic Line railway and a trading centre with Tanzania and Uganda. These days, the lake steamer and trade have gone and the city struggles to survive on the few tourists who head over to the lake. Three islands, a

little further south, near **Homa Bay – Rusinga Island**, **Mfangano Island** and **Takawiri Island** – have luxury lodges which provide excellent fishing and birdwatching. In the far south, tiny **Ruma National Park** (painfully reached by an appalling road) protects several rare species such as the roan antelope and Rothschild giraffe.
Inland, **Kisii** is the centre of production for most of Kenya's trademark pink and white soapstone, while the area around **Kericho** and the **Nandi Hills** is tea country, with vast estates flowing across rolling hills.
The **Kakamega Forest Reserve** is Kenya's last surviving patch of primeval rainforest, a wonderful cool green cave of soaring trees and tangled vines, with hundreds of species of birds, around 60 of which are found nowhere else in the country.
THE NORTHWEST: The northwest of the country is largely agricultural, its steep hills patchworked by terraces and villages. The two main towns of Eldoret and Kitale act as jumping off points for many stunning scenic tours. The most important attraction in the region is **Mount Elgon National Park**, the Kenyan half of a giant forested volcano (4321m/14,178ft), famous for its mountain flora and fauna, its wonderful birdlife and for the elephants who scratch salt from the walls of **Kitum Cave**. To the north, the **Cherengani Hills** offer excellent mountain hiking and the tiny **Saiwa Swamp National Park**. To the east, bordering the Rift Valley, are the **Tugen Hills** and the dramatic escarpments of the **Kerio Valley**.

NORTHERN KENYA

Due north of the Central Highlands is a belt of savannah which provides a home to several game-rich, if less visited, national parks, including Samburu, Meru and Kora, plus a whole host of small game reserves, few of which have any tourist facilities. The far north of Kenya is largely desert, difficult to travel, remote and wild. Unfortunately, much of the area is also troubled by inter-tribal violence and banditry and tourists should take local advice before travelling in the region. It is possible to fly up to Lake Turkana, the largest of the Kenyan soda lakes, on the Sudan border.
MERU AND KORA NATIONAL PARKS: Located 400km (250 miles) from Nairobi, **Meru National Park** remains one of the more unspoilt parks, an oasis within the parched land all round, with 13 rivers lined with Doum palms and mountain-fed streams watering richly tangled woodlands on the slopes of the **Nyambene Mountain Range**. To the east, the park is adjoined by **Kora National Reserve**, a largely dry area bisected by the great **Tana River**. Both areas have plenty of game but were badly affected by poaching in the 1970s and 80s. Security has been strengthened these days and there are three lodges and several campsites in Meru, all operating happily. However, security is still a concern in less well-trodden areas.
SAMBURU GAME PARK: An area of semi-desert halfway between Nairobi and Lake Turkana (see below) that provides a rare chance to see the oryx, gerenuk, reticulated giraffe and Grevy's zebra. Ostriches and elephants are easily spotted in this open habitat. There are two lodges, *Samburu Lodge* and *River Lodge*, both of which hang out bait to attract leopards for the guests to study whilst sitting at the bar. The park takes its name from the Samburu people, distantly related to the Masai.
LAKE TURKANA: There are several parks and reserves in the far north of Kenya, gathered around Lake Turkana (formerly Lake Rudolph). This extraordinary lake has recently been designated a UNESCO World Heritage Site. Running for several hundred miles through windswept and largely uninhabited deserts, the lake contains many unique species of fish and marine plants and has recently gained a reputation as a fishing resort. Several lodges have sprung up on the eastern shore to cater for this trade and, consequently, general tourism is expected to increase. Despite the harsh climate, many of Kenya's better known animals manage to survive here, as do the tiny people of the El Molo tribe, who fish the eastern waters. There are two large volcanic islands in the lake. The flooded crater of the southernmost island has a resident population of unnaturally large crocodiles. The lake is subject to violent storms that disturb algae to produce remarkable colour changes in the water. Those who wish to visit Turkana are advised to fly. The road takes two days, crosses immensely harsh landscape and there is danger of violence.

Sport & Activities

Wildlife safaris: The most common way to see Kenya's rich wildlife is by organised tours in small vans (which typically carry six to eight people). Private drives and walking safaris are also possible, although both require armed guides. Aeroplane or hot-air balloon trips are available at the Masai Mara National Reserve. **Camel safaris** can be organised in the *Samburu* and *Turkana* areas between Isiolo and Lake Turkana. Each park or game reserve offers different types of animals and vegetation. For further details, see the *Resorts & Excursions section or* contact the Kenya Wildlife Service (see *Contact Addresses* section). A list of safari tour operators can be obtained from the Kenya Association of Tour Operators, KATO (see *Travel - Internal* section).
Watersports: The coastal resorts on Kenya's Coral Coast, north and south of Mombasa, have fine sandy beaches and there are several coral reefs. The most popular resorts include *Bamburi*, *Kikambala*, *Kilifi*, *Malindi*, *Nyali*, *Shanzu*, and *Wasini Island*. A wide range of watersports is available, including **scuba diving**, **snorkelling**, **sailing**, **water-skiing**, **swimming** and **surfing**. The coast around Malindi is renowned for **game fishing**. **Trout fishing** in the lakes (notably at *Lake Naivasha* and *Lake Victoria*) is particularly good between November and March. **Deep-sea fishing** is good along the coast between July and April. Sailfish, marlin, wahoo, swordfish, kingfish, barracuda and tuna are all available. **Whitewater rafting** is popular on the *Athi/Galana River*.
Other: Kenya has a total of 39 **golf** courses ranging from minigolf to 18-hole courses. The most popular destination for **trekking** is *Mount Kenya*, although the trails tend to get fairly busy. Other trekking destinations include *Mount Elgon* (on the border with Uganda) and the *Ngong Hills* (near Nairobi). **Tennis**, **squash**, **bowls**, **horse-riding** and **polo** are all popular. Kenya also has good **athletics** facilities and the Kenyans have a fine record in world competitions. Sports clubs accept visitors.

Social Profile

FOOD & DRINK: Kenya's national dishes appear on most hotel menus. The country's beef, chicken, lamb and pork are outstandingly good, as is the wide variety of tropical fruits. Local trout, Nile perch and lobster, shrimps and Mombasa oysters are included on menus in season. Indian and Middle Eastern food is available in most areas. Some game-park lodges serve game, including buffalo steaks marinated in local liqueurs and berries, often garnished with wild honey and cream. Most Kenyans eat maize, beans and maize meal. At the small 'hotels', *chai* (tea boiled with milk and sugar) and *mandazi* (doughnuts) are popular. There is a wide range of restaurants in Nairobi and Mombasa, otherwise hotels in smaller towns offer restaurant service.
Locally brewed beer (*Tusker* and *White Cap*) and bottled sodas may be found throughout the country. *Kenya Cane* (spirit distilled from sugar cane) and *Kenya Gold* (a coffee liqueur) are produced in Kenya. Traditional beer made with honey (*uki*) and locally made spirit distilled from maize (*changaa*) may sometimes be found.
NIGHTLIFE: Most of the major hotels in Nairobi and the tourist resorts have dancing with live bands or discos each evening. There are also a few nightclubs. There is a large selection of cinemas in Nairobi which show mainly British, European and US films.
SHOPPING: *Khanga*, *kitenge* and *kikoi* cloths may be bought in markets and the Bishara Streets of Nairobi, Mombasa and the Masai market held in Nairobi city centre on Tuesdays. There is a particularly good cooperative shop in Machakos which sells *kiondos*, bags stained with natural dyes and with strong leather straps. *Makonde* woodcarvings are sold throughout the country, and young Kamba and Masai men sell carvings and necklaces on the beaches of the south coast. **Shopping hours:** Mon-Sat 0830-1230 and 1400-1730.
Note: The sale of souvenirs made of wildlife skins (this includes reptiles) and shells is forbidden.
SPECIAL EVENTS: For a complete list of special events, contact the Kenya National Tourist Office (see *Contact Addresses*). The following is a selection of special events occurring in Kenya in 2005:
Feb 16-Mar 6 *Kijani Kenya International Festival*. **May** *The Dugong Festival and the Lamu Donkey Racing*. **Jun** *Maulidi Festival*. **Jun 26** *Safaricom Marathon*. **Jul** *Ferodo Councours d'Elegance*. **Jul-Oct** *Wildebeest Migration to the Masai Mara*. **Aug 7** *15th Annual Maralal Camel Derby*. **Oct 20** Kenyatta Day. **Nov** Mombasa Carnival. **Dec 1-10** *East African Safari Rally*.
SOCIAL CONVENTIONS: Western European habits prevail throughout Kenya as a result of British influences in the country. Kenyans are generally very friendly. Dress is informal, and casual lightweight clothes are accepted for all but the smartest social occasions. **Tipping:** This is not required. Most hotels include a 10 per cent service charge to the bill. If the service charge has not been included, a KSh20 tip is usual, although the amount is entirely at the visitor's discretion.

Business Profile

ECONOMY: The Kenyan economy is largely agricultural – 75 per cent of the population work on the land, contributing around 30 per cent of national output. The main cash crops are tea and coffee, although pyrethrum, sisal, sugar and cotton are also important. Kenya is one of the few African countries with a significant dairy industry. Hydroelectric plants meet 80 per cent of the country's energy requirements. The remainder comes from imported oil, which is also used for one of the country's principal industries, the manufacture of petroleum-based products such as plastic and chemicals. Kenya, which has one of Africa's largest manufacturing sectors, also produces cement, paper, drinks, tobacco, textiles, rubber and metal products, ceramics, and electrical and transport equipment. The mining industry, however, is very small. In the service sector, tourism is the largest industry and the country's principal source of foreign exchange.
Like many African countries, Kenya signed up to an IMF-imposed Structural Adjustment Programme in the mid-1990s but it lapsed following policy disagreements between the Fund and the Kenyan government. Further concerns, mainly concerning political reform and widespread corruption, disrupted Kenyan relations with its other major Western aid donors. The IMF and World Bank withdrew support entirely in January 2000. However, following introduction of anti-corruption measures and the privatisation of several major state-owned enterprises, the IMF is now expected to resume its support by the end of 2003. In addition, for the first time, foreign investors have been allowed to take controlling stakes in Kenyan companies. Recent economic performance has been moderate. An estimated two million Kenyans are unemployed and the new government, elected in 2003, plans to create 500,000 new jobs. The UK is Kenya's major trading partner, followed by Germany, Japan and the United Arab Emirates. In Africa, Uganda is Kenya's most important export market and source of imports. Along with Tanzania, Kenya and Uganda have explored plans to establish a customs union as the first step towards an east African regional trading bloc (a previous effort collapsed in 1977).
BUSINESS: Lightweight suits are recommended for all occasions. Prior appointments are necessary. Although Swahili is the national language, English is the official language and is widely spoken. **Office hours:** Mon-Fri 0800-1300 and 1400-1700. In Mombasa, offices usually open and close 30 minutes earlier.
COMMERCIAL INFORMATION: The following organisations can offer advice: Kenya National Chamber of Commerce and Industry, PO Box 47024, Ufanisi House, Hailé Sélassie Avenue, Nairobi (tel: (20) 220 867; e-mail: kncci@swiftkenya.com); *or* Investment Promotion Centre, PO Box 55704, 8th Floor, National Bank Building, Harambee Avenue, Kenya City Square 00200, Nairobi (tel: (20) 221 401-4; fax: (20) 336 663; e-mail: info@investmentkenya.com; website: www.investmentkenya.com).
CONFERENCES/CONVENTIONS: Main urban centres, such as Mombassa and Nairobi, and most international hotels have conference facilities available. The Kenyatta International Conference Centre, PO Box 30510, Nairobi (tel: (20) 332 383; fax: (20) 252 779) offers facilities, as does the Kenya College of Communication and Technology. For further information, contact Kenya Tourist Board (see *Contact Addresses* section).

Climate

The coastal areas are tropical, but tempered by monsoon winds. The lowlands are hot but mainly dry, while the highlands are more temperate with four seasons. Nairobi has a very pleasant climate throughout the year due to its altitude. Near Lake Victoria, the temperatures are much higher and rainfall can be heavy.
Required clothing: Lightweight cottons and linens with rainwear are advised for the coast and lakeside. Warmer clothing is needed in June and July and for the cooler mornings on the coast. Lightweights are needed for much of the year in the highlands. Rainwear is advisable between March and June and October and December.

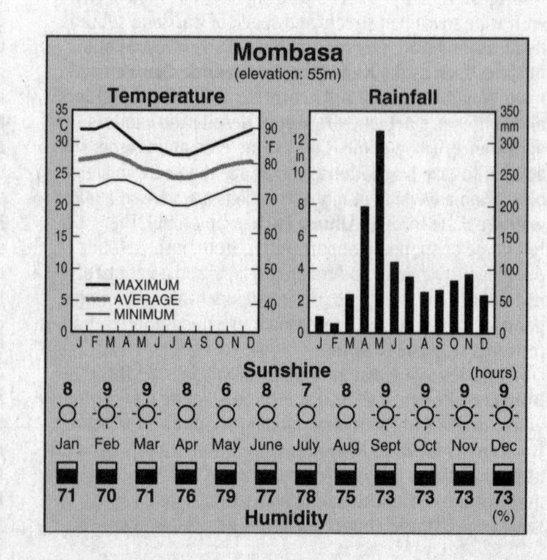

Kiribati

LATEST TRAVEL ADVICE CONTACTS

British Foreign and Commonwealth Office
Tel: (0870) 606 0290 Website: www.fco.gov.uk

US Department of State
Website: http://travel.state.gov/travel

Canadian Department of Foreign Affairs and Int'l Trade
Tel: (1 800) 267 8376 Website: www.dfait-maeci.gc.ca

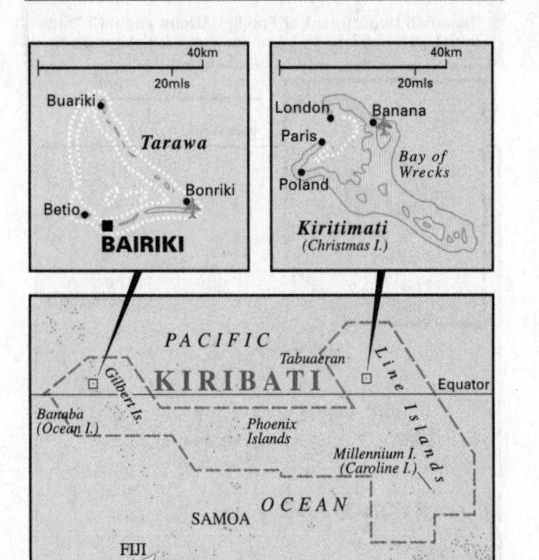

Location: South Pacific, Micronesia.

Country dialling code: 686.

Ministry of Commerce, Industry and Tourism
PO Box 510, Betio, Tarawa, Republic of Kiribati
Tel: 26157/8. Fax: 26233.
E-mail: commerce@tskl.net.ki

South Pacific Tourism Organisation
Street address: Level 3 FNPF Place, 343-359 Victoria Parade, Suva, Fiji
Postal address: PO Box 13119, Suva, Fiji
Tel: 330 4177. Fax: 330 1995.
Website: www.tcsp.com

Honorary Consulate of Kiribati
The Great House, Llanddewi Rhydderch, Monmouthshire NP7 9UY, UK
Tel/Fax: (01873) 840 375.
E-mail: michael.walsh@sema.co.uk
Visas issued by appointment only.

Commonwealth Resource Centre
The British Empire and Commonwealth Museum Resource Library, The British Empire and Commonwealth Museum, Clock Tower Yard, Temple Meads, Bristol BS1 6QH, UK
Tel: (0117) 925 4980. Fax: (0117) 925 4983.
E-mail: resources@empiremuseum.co.uk (archives).
Website: www.empiremuseum.co.uk
Provides information on Kiribati.

The US Embassy in Pohnpei deals with enquiries relating to Kiribati (see *Federated States of Micronesia – Marshall Islands* **section).**

General Information

AREA: 810.5 sq km (312.9 sq miles).
POPULATION: 87,400 (official estimate 2002).
POPULATION DENSITY: 104.2 per sq km.
CAPITAL: South Tarawa atoll (including Bairiki, the capital town). **Population:** 36,717,000 (2000).
GEOGRAPHY: Kiribati (pronounced 'Kiribass', formerly the Gilbert Islands) consists of three groups in the central Pacific: Kiribati (including Banaba, formerly Ocean Island), the Line Islands and the Phoenix Islands. The 33 islands, scattered across 2 million square miles of the central Pacific, are low-lying coral atolls with coastal lagoons. The exception is Banaba, which is a coral formation rising to 80m (265ft). The soil is generally poor, apart from Banaba, and rainfall is variable. Coconut palms and pandanus trees comprise the main vegetation. There are no hills or streams throughout the group. Water is obtained from storage tanks or wells.
GOVERNMENT: Republic. Gained independence from the UK in 1979. **Head of State and Government:** President Anote Tong since July 2003.
LANGUAGE: Kiribati and English.
RELIGION: Christianity (53.4 per cent Roman Catholic and 39.2 per cent Kiribati Protestant), the Bahai Faith and Islam.
TIME: GMT + 12, except as follows:**Canton Island, Enderbury Island:** GMT +13; **Christmas Island:** GMT +14.
ELECTRICITY: 240 volts AC, 50Hz.
COMMUNICATIONS: The Government provides radio and postal services to all inhabited islands.**Telephone:** Country code: 686. Outgoing international code: 0. Most international calls from Kiribati have to go through the operator. IDD is available throughout urban Tarawa. Radio telephone calls can be arranged to most outer islands. **Mobile telephone:** GSM 900 network in use. Network provider is *Telecom Services Kiribati Ltd* (website: www.tskl.net.ki). **Fax:** This is available at the local Telecoms Office. **Telegram:** Available in Betio Mon-Fri 0800-1900 and on outer islands Mon-Fri 0800-1600. Telegrams may take several days to reach Europe. **Internet:** ISPs include *VPM Internet Services*. There are currently no Internet cafes in Kiribati. **Post:** Airmail to Western Europe takes up to two weeks. There is a weekly postal service for overseas mail. Post office hours: Mon-Fri 0900-1500. **Press:** The weekly papers are *Kiribati Newstar* and *Te Uekera*, published in English and Kiribati. *Kiribati Business Link* is published in English. **Radio:** BBC World Service (website: www.bbc.co.uk/worldservice) and Voice of America (website: www.voa.gov) can be received. From time to time the frequencies change and the most up-to-date can be found online.

TIMATIC CODES

Health	AMADEUS: **TI-DFT/TRW/HE** GALILEO/WORLDSPAN: **TI-DFT/TRW/HE** SABRE: **TIDFT/TRW/HE**
Visa	AMADEUS: **TI-DFT/TRW/VI** GALILEO/WORLDSPAN: **TI-DFT/TRW/VI** SABRE: **TIDFT/TRW/VI**

To access TIMATIC country information on Health and Visa regulations through the Computer Reservations System (CRS), type in the appropriate command line listed above.

Passport/Visa

	Passport Required?	Visa Required?	Return Ticket Required?
Full British	Yes	1	Yes
Australian	Yes	Yes	Yes
Canadian	Yes	2	Yes
USA	Yes	Yes	Yes
Other EU	Yes	1	Yes
Japanese	Yes	Yes	Yes

Note: Regulations and requirements may be subject to change at short notice, and you are advised to contact the appropriate diplomatic or consular authority before finalising travel arrangements. Details of these may be found at the head of this country's entry. Any numbers in the chart refer to the footnotes below.

PASSPORTS: Passport valid for six months required by all.
VISAS: Required by all except the following:
(a) **1.** nationals of Spain, Sweden and the UK (irrespective of endorsement in passport regarding national status) for stays of up to 28 days; all other EU nationals *do* require a visa;
(b) **2.** nationals of Canada for stays of up to 28 days;
(c) nationals of Antigua & Barbuda, The Bahamas, Barbados, Botswana, Cyprus, Fiji, Grenada, Guyana, Hong Kong (SAR), Iceland, India, Jamaica, Kenya, Lesotho, Liechtenstein, Malaysia, Malta, New Zealand, Norway, St Kitts & Nevis, St Lucia, Samoa, San Marino, Seychelles, Sierra Leone, Singapore, Solomon Islands, Switzerland, Tonga, Trinidad & Tobago, Tunisia, Tuvalu, Uruguay, Vanuatu and Zimbabwe for up to 28 days;
(d) nationals of Korea (Rep) and Nauru for up to 30 days;
(e) nationals of the The Philippines for up to 21 days;
(f) nationals of American Samoa, Ecuador, Guam, Marshall Islands, Pacific Islands of Micronesia and Palau for up to 20 days;
(g) transit passengers continuing their journey by the same or first connecting aircraft, provided holding onward or return documentation and not leaving the airport (some nationalities *always* require a transit visa; enquire at the Consulate).
Note: (a) Nationals of the following countries require permission to enter the country from the Principal Immigration Officer: Albania, Algeria, Bahrain, Bosnia & Herzegovina, Bulgaria, Cambodia, China (PR), CIS (except nationals of Belarus), Croatia, Cuba, Czech Republic, Egypt, Hungary, Iraq, Jordan, Korea (Dem Rep), Kuwait, Laos, Lebanon, Libya, Macedonia (Former Yugoslav Republic of), Mongolia, Morocco, Poland, Saudi Arabia, Serbia & Montenegro, Slovak Republic, Slovenia, South Africa, Sudan, Syrian Arab Republic, United Arab Emirates, Vietnam and Yemen. Visa application will take an additional two weeks. The nationals of some countries require references along with their visas; check details with the Consulate. (b) On arrival, visitors may apply for a Visitor's Permit to stay for a maximum of four months; a visa, return or onward travel tickets and sufficient funds for the duration of stay are required.
Types of visa and cost: *Tourist* and *Business*: A$50 (single- and multiple-entry).
Validity: From 20 days to four months depending on nationality. Enquire at nearest Consulate.
Application to: The Honorary Consulate or Consular section at the Embassy (see *Contact Addresses* section).
Application requirements: (a) Completed application form. (b) Passport. (c) Travel itinerary. (d) Stamped and self-addressed envelope. (e) Appropriate letters from company/sponsors if on business. (f) Fee.
Working days required: Allow three weeks for postal applications. An additional two weeks is required when permission needs to be obtained from the Principal Immigration Officer in Tarawa.

Money

Currency: Australian Dollar (A$) = 100 cents. Notes are in denominations of A$100, 50, 20, 10 and 5. Coins are in denominations of A$2 and 1, and 50, 20, 10 and 5 cents.
Currency exchange: Currency may be exchanged at the Bank of Kiribati Ltd or local hotels. There are ATMs at branches of the Bank of Kiribati/ANZ in Betio, Bairiki and Bikenibeu (all on Tarawa atoll).
Credit & debit cards: MasterCard and Visa have very limited acceptance. Check with your credit or debit card company for details of services which may be available.
Travellers cheques: Accepted in hotels, some shops and at the Bank of Kiribati Ltd. To avoid additional exchange rate charges, travellers are advised to take travellers cheques in Australian Dollars.
Currency restrictions: There are no restrictions on the import or export of either local or foreign currency.
Exchange rate indicators: The following figures are included as a guide to the movements of the Australian Dollar against Sterling and the US Dollar:

Date	Feb '04	May '04	Aug '04	Nov '04
£1.00=	2.39	2.53	2.57	2.40
$1.00=	1.31	1.42	1.39	1.26

Banking hours: Mon-Fri 0930-1500. The Bikenibeu branch is open 0900-1400.

Duty Free

The following goods may be imported into Kiribati without incurring customs duty:
200 cigarettes or 225g tobacco or cigars; 1l of spirits and 1l of wine (only if aged 21 years and older); a reasonable amount of perfume for personal use (subject to declaration); one pair of binoculars, one camera and six rolls of film, one cine camera and 200m of film, one radio, one broadcast receiver, one tape recorder, one typewriter (subject to declaration); reasonable quantity of sports equipment for personal use (subject to declaration).

Public Holidays

2005: Jan 1 New Year's Day. **Mar 25** Good Friday. **Apr 18** Health Day. **Jul 12** Independence Day. **Aug 7** Youth Day. **Dec 25-26** Christmas.
2006: Jan 1 New Year's Day. **Apr 14** Good Friday. **Apr 18** Health Day. **Jul 12** Independence Day. **Aug 7** Youth Day. **Dec 25-26** Christmas.

Health

	Special Precautions?	Certificate Required?
Yellow Fever	No	1
Cholera	No	No
Typhoid & Polio	2	N/A
Malaria	No	N/A

Note: Regulations and requirements may be subject to change at short notice, and you are advised to contact your doctor well in advance of your intended date of departure. Any numbers in the chart refer to the footnotes below.

1: A yellow fever vaccination certificate is required from travellers over one year of age arriving within six days from infected areas.
2: Immunisation against typhoid and poliomyelitis is often recommended.
Food & drink: All water should be regarded as a potential health risk. Water used for drinking, brushing teeth or making ice should have first been boiled or otherwise sterilised. Only eat well-cooked meat and fish, preferably served hot. Pork, salad and mayonnaise may carry increased risk. Vegetables should be cooked and fruit peeled.
Other risks: *Hepatitis A* and B are reported. *Diarrhoeal diseases* are common. *Dengue fever*, including its haemorrhagic form, occurs in epidemics. *Diphtheria* and *tuberculosis* may all occur.
Health care: Health insurance is strongly recommended.

Tungaru Central Hospital on Tarawa provides medical service to all the islands. Government dispensaries on all islands are equipped to handle minor ailments and injuries. Visitors should bring their own supply of basic medicines with them.

Travel - International

AIR: Kiribati is mainly served by *Air Fiji*, *Air Marshall Islands* and *Air Nauru*. The national airline is *Air Kiribati*. *Air Kiribati* flies to Honolulu (Hawaii) and Fiji and provides a weekly connection between Christmas Island and Honolulu.
Approximate flight times: From *London* to Tarawa via Sydney and Nauru is 30 hours 30 minutes.
International airports: *Tarawa (Bonriki)* (TRW) lies 11km (7 miles) northeast of Bikenibeu. Buses operate every three to four minutes from the airport to the capital. Other airports include *Christmas Island (CXI)*.
Departure tax: A$20; children under two years of age and transit passengers are exempt.
SEA: International ports are Banaba, Christmas Island and Tarawa. Kiribati is served by *Norwegian Cruise Lines*, which call at Fanning Island.

Travel - Internal

AIR: *Air Kiribati* operates an internal scheduled service to nearly all outer islands, linking them with Tarawa.
SEA: Several passenger ferries run between the smaller islands. Boats are available for hire.
ROAD: Traffic drives on the left. All-weather roads are limited to urban Tarawa and Christmas Island. Privately owned **buses** and **taxis** are available on urban Tarawa only. Buses are fairly cheap (A$15 is the maximum fare), but taxis are expensive (A$25 for a journey from the airport to urban Tarawa). **Car hire**: Available on urban Tarawa and Christmas Island only. **Documentation**: International Driving Permit required.

Accommodation

HOTELS: There are few hotels in Kiribati, the major ones being on Tarawa, Christmas Island and Abemama. The small island of Kirimati also has a few hotels.
Most accommodation is quite basic, but there are plans to build a luxury 150-room hotel on Christmas Island.
A 10 per cent service charge is added to all hotel bills. Further information is available from the South Pacific Tourism Organisation or the Honorary Consulate (see *Contact Addresses* section).
REST HOUSES: Inexpensive rest houses can be found on all the other islands. However, cooking facilities are limited and visitors should take what they need with them.

Resorts & Excursions

Kiribati is remote and tourism is very much in its infancy, but it is moving further into the tourist spotlight. The islands boast superb white sandy beaches and crystal-clear lagoon waters. There are excellent facilities for snorkelling and deep-sea fishing. It is also possible to charter boats for sailing across the **Tarawa Lagoon**. The capital of Kiribati, **Tarawa** is fast becoming one of the most densely populated areas in the Pacific, being similar in density to Hong Kong. **The President's Office**, **Parliament** building and International Airport are all situated on **Bonriki**. A number of war relics can be seen on **Betio** and visits to World War II battlegrounds and natural history expeditions can be organised.
Stretching for almost half the land mass of Kiribati, **Christmas Island** is covered in lakes and ponds and boasts some of the largest colonies of birds. Trips with studies of the local birdlife are available. The main towns are **London**, **Paris** and **Banana**. Game fishing is extremely popular.
There are also trips to see outrigger canoe races and dancing contests. Or visit the *maneaba*, a community meeting house, where you may enjoy traditional dancing, singing and storytelling. A fine way to get the whole picture of Kiribati is to take a 'flight-seeing' trip on board frighteningly small planes. Tours take in the islands of **Abaiang**, **Abemama**, **Maiana** and **Tarawa** – other islands can be visited on request.

Sport & Activities

Hotels offer **canoeing**, **fishing** and **snorkelling** facilities. **Scuba divers** are advised to bring their own equipment. **Birdwatching** is popular, especially on Christmas Island. **Game fishing** on Christmas Island is also popular. A fishing licence is unnecessary and charters are easily available. Numerous beaches offer safe bathing. **Golf** can also be played on *Ambo Island* (part of *Tarawa*) where the green of the golf course is actually rolled sand. However, **swimming** in south Tarawa Lagoon is not advisable due to the extent of its pollution, and extreme caution is recommended on oceanside reefs.

Social Profile

FOOD & DRINK: Restaurants are few in number and are situated mainly in the larger towns. Local specialities in the southern islands include the boiled fruit of *pandanus* (screwpine), sliced thinly and spread with coconut cream. A Kiribati delicacy is *palu sami*, which is coconut cream with sliced onion and curry powder, wrapped in taro leaves and pressure cooked in an earth-oven packed with seaweed.
NIGHTLIFE: There are 'Island Nights' which feature traditional Polynesian music and dancing, film shows and feasts in *maneabas* (local meeting houses), which can be found throughout the islands.
SHOPPING: Handicrafts include baskets, table mats, fans and cups made from pandanus leaves, coconut leaves, coconut shells and sea shells. Sea-shell necklaces are popular, as are models of Gilbertese canoes and houses. A prized item is the Kiribati shark-tooth sword made of polished coconut wood with shark teeth, filed to razor sharpness, lashed to the two edges. These days, most examples are modern reproductions. **Shopping hours**: Mon-Sat 0800-1900 (some shops open until 2030), Sun 0800-1900 (most small shops).
SPECIAL EVENTS: Special events that take place in Kiribati are usually Christian festivals, or celebrations on public holidays. The following is a selection of special events celebrated annually in Kiribati:
Jan 1 *New Year; New Year Sunrise*. **Mar 8** *Womens Day*. **Mar 25-27** *Easter*. **Jul** *National Churches Day*. **Jul 12** *Independence Day*. **Aug 7** *Youth Day*.
SOCIAL CONVENTIONS: Like the other Pacific islanders, the people are very friendly and hospitable and retain much of their traditional culture and lifestyle. In this casual atmosphere, European customs still prevail alongside local traditions. Although in official correspondence the Western convention of signing names with initials is adopted, it is more polite (and customary) to address people by their first name. Bikinis should not be worn except on the beach. Nudity and overly scant swimming costumes are forbidden by local law. **Tipping**: Not expected.

Business Profile

ECONOMY: The main agricultural crop is coconut, from which copra, the principal export commodity, is derived. Bananas, breadfruit and papayas are also produced, largely for domestic consumption. The local fishing industry has declined drastically, especially after the closure of the state fishing company, but the sale of licences to foreign fleets is an important source of government revenue. Despite its remoteness, Kiribati has developed a tourism industry which now accounts for about one-fifth of GDP. Kiribati remains heavily dependent on foreign aid and remittances from the many islanders of working age employed overseas.
Kiribati is a member of the Pacific Community, the South Pacific Forum and the Asian Development Bank. Kiribati is also involved with various regional initiatives to promote economic development. Most trade takes place with Australia, New Zealand, the UK, Japan, the USA, Papua New Guinea and Fiji. Kiribati is also one of the 14 signatories to the Pacific Islands Countries Trade Agreement, agreed in 2001, which plans measures to boost regional trade.
BUSINESS: Shirt and smart trousers or skirt will suffice most of the time; ties need only be worn for formal occasions. **Office hours**: Mon-Fri 0800-1230 and 1330-1615.

Climate

Maritime equatorial in the central islands of the group. The islands to the north and south are more tropical. The trade winds blow between March and October, making this the most pleasant time of the year, while the highest rainfall (December to May) is concentrated on the northern islands. November to February is more wet and humid than the rest of the year.

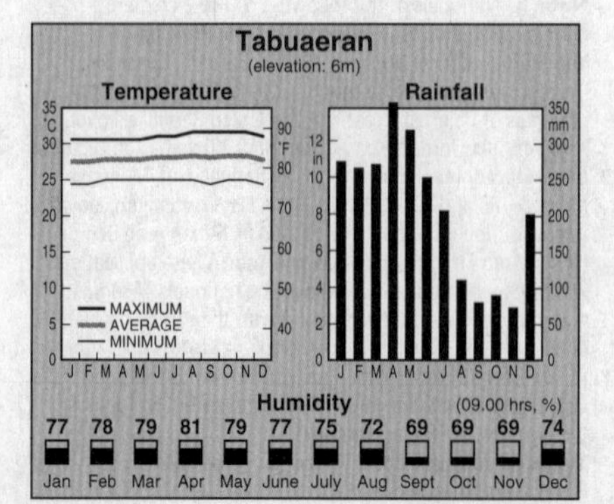

Korea (Democratic People's Republic of)

LATEST TRAVEL ADVICE CONTACTS

British Foreign and Commonwealth Office
Tel: (0870) 606 0290 Website: www.fco.gov.uk
US Department of State
Website: http://travel.state.gov/travel
Canadian Department of Foreign Affairs and Int'l Trade
Tel: (1 800) 267 8376 Website: www.dfait-maeci.gc.ca

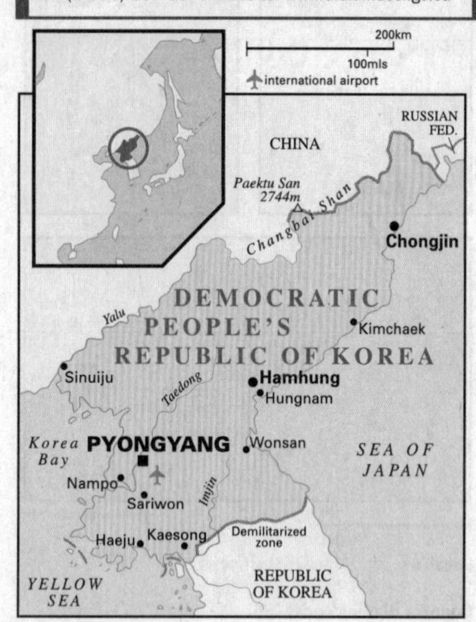

Location: Far East.

Country dialling code: 850.

The National Tourism Administration of the DPRK
Central District, Pyongyang, Korea (Dem Rep)
Tel: (2) 381 8901. Fax: (2) 381 4547.
E-mail: nta@silibank.com
Kumgangsan International Tourist Company
Central District, Pyongyang, Korea (Dem Rep)
Tel: (2) 31562. Fax: (2) 381 2100.
British Embassy
Munsu-dong Diplomatic Compound, Pyongyang, Korea (Dem Rep)
Tel: (2) 381 7980. Fax: (2) 381 7985.
E-mail: postmaster.PYONX@fco.gov.uk
Embassy of the Democratic People's Republic of Korea
73 Gunnersbury Avenue, Ealing, London W5 4LP, UK
Tel: (020) 8992 4965. Fax: (020) 8992 2053.
General Delegation of the DPRK
3 rue Asseline, 75014 Paris, France
Tel: (1) 5654 2603. Fax: (1) 4047 9754.
E-mail: delegationcoree@wanadoo.fr
The US Embassy in Beijing deals with enquiries relating to the Democratic People's Republic of Korea (see *China* section).

General Information

AREA: 122,762 sq km (47,399 sq miles).
POPULATION: 22,541,000 (UN estimate 2002).
POPULATION DENSITY: 183.6 per sq km.
CAPITAL: Pyongyang. **Population**: 2,741,260 (1993).
GEOGRAPHY: The Democratic People's Republic of Korea shares borders in the north with China, in the east with the Sea of Japan, in the west with the Yellow Sea, and in the south with the demilitarised zone (separating it from the Republic of Korea). Most of the land consists of hills and low mountains and only a small area is cultivable. Intensive water and soil conservation programmes, including land reclamation from the sea, are given high priority. The eastern coast is rocky and steep with mountains rising from

TIMATIC CODES

Health	AMADEUS: **TI-DFT/FNJ/HE** GALILEO/WORLDSPAN: **TI-DFT/FNJ/HE** SABRE: **TIDFT/FNJ/HE**
Visa	AMADEUS: **TI-DFT/FNJ/VI** GALILEO/WORLDSPAN: **TI-DFT/FNJ/VI** SABRE: **TIDFT/FNJ/VI**

To access TIMATIC country information on Health and Visa regulations through the Computer Reservations System (CRS), type in the appropriate command line listed above.

the water and this area contains most of the waterways.
GOVERNMENT: Communist Republic. **Head of State**: President Kim Jong-Il since 1994. **Head of Government**: Prime Minister Hong Song-nam since 1997.
LANGUAGE: Korean.
RELIGION: Buddhism, Christianity and Chundo Kyo are officially cited as the main religions.
TIME: GMT + 9.
ELECTRICITY: 110/220 volts AC, 60Hz.
COMMUNICATIONS: Telephone: IDD to the country is available, although there is a very sparse internal network. Some hotels in Pyongyang provide direct international calls although this may be expensive. Country code: 850. **Mobile telephone:** Limited GSM 900 network. *SUNNET* is the only network provider. **Internet:** Access to the Internet is unavailable. **Telegram:** Services available in all Pyongyang hotels. **Post:** Services are extremely slow and limited outside the capital. Airmail takes about 10 days to reach Western Europe. Post office hours: Mon-Sat 0900-2100. **Press:** Major daily newspapers include *Minju Choson*, *Pyongyang Sinmun*, *Rodong Sinmun* and *Sonyon Sinmun*. *The Pyongyang Times* is published weekly in English, French and Spanish. There are also several monthly English-language magazines.
Radio: BBC World Service (website: www.bbc.co.uk/worldservice) and Voice of America (website: www.voa.gov) can be received. From time to time the frequencies change and the most up-to-date can be found online.

Passport/Visa

	Passport Required?	Visa Required?	Return Ticket Required?
Full British	Yes	Yes	Yes
Australian	Yes	Yes	Yes
Canadian	Yes	Yes	Yes
USA	Yes	Yes	Yes
Other EU	Yes	Yes	Yes
Japanese	Yes	Yes	Yes

Note: *Regulations and requirements may be subject to change at short notice, and you are advised to contact the appropriate diplomatic or consular authority before finalising travel arrangements. Details of these may be found at the head of this country's entry. Any numbers in the chart refer to the footnotes below.*

Note: Tourism in Korea (Dem Rep) is currently permitted only in officially organised groups of minimum one person. Visas can be obtained through officially recognised travel companies or the nearest Korea (Dem Rep) embassy.
Passports: Valid passport required by all, including nationals of Korea (Dem Rep).
VISAS: Required by all, including nationals of Korea (Dem Rep).
Types of visa and cost: *Ordinary* and *Tourist*: £30.
Application to: Consular section of the General Delegation of the DPRK or of the nearest Korean (Dem Rep) Embassy. Applications should be made by an officially recognised tour operator.
Application requirements: (a) Valid passport. (b) One passport-size photo. (c) One completed application form. (d) Tour confirmation from recognised travel company. (e) Proof of sufficient funds to cover stay. (f) Copy of applicant's passport.
Working days required: Approximately 20 days.
Note: For stays of over 24 hours registration with the MFA is required, although most hotels and travel agents will automatically do this for the visitor. It is advisable to contact the nearest embassy prior to departure for further details.

Money

Currency: Won (Won) = 100 chon. Notes are in denominations of Won100, 50, 10, 5 and 1. Coins are in denominations of Won1, and 50, 10, 5 and 1 chon.
Note: Hotels tend to only accept cash payments in local currency whilst shops prefer US Dollars.
Currency exchange: Currencies may be changed at the Trade Bank (Mon-Sat 0900-1200 and 1400-1700) or at some hotels. Convertible currencies include Australian, Hong Kong and US Dollars, Euros, Pounds Sterling and Yen.
Credit & debit cards: Main hotels in Pyongyang will accept credit and debit cards such as Mastercard and Visa. However, American Express is not usually accepted.
Travellers cheques: Generally not accepted. However, US Dollars are often accepted as an alternative method of payment.
Currency restrictions: The import and export of local currency is prohibited. The import and export of foreign currency is unrestricted, subject to declaration on arrival.
Exchange rate indicators: The following figures are included as a guide to the movements of the Won against Sterling and the US Dollar:

Date	Feb '04	May '04	Aug '04	Nov '04
£1.00=	4.00	3.93	4.05	4.16
$1.00=	2.20	2.20	2.20	2.20

Duty Free

The following goods may be imported into Korea (Dem Rep) without incurring customs duty:
A reasonable amount of tobacco and alcoholic beverages.
Prohibited items: Binoculars, arms, ammunition, explosives, drugs, any books or literature in Korean language, and seeds. Animals, plants and all groceries require certificates of entry.
Note: Gifts, precious metals and personal items such as cameras, watches and tape recorders must be declared.

Public Holidays

2005: Jan 1 New Year's Day. **Feb 16** Kim Jong Il's Birthday. **Apr 15** Day of the Sun/Kim Il Sung's Birthday. **Apr 25** Foundation of the People's Army. **May 1** International Workers' Day. **Jul 27** Victory Day. **Aug 15** Anniversary of Liberation. **Sep 9** Independence Day. **Sep 17-19** Ch'usok (Harvest Moon Festival). **Oct 10** Foundation of the Korean Workers' Party. **Dec 27** Constitution Day.
2006: Jan 1 New Year's Day. **Feb 16** Kim Jong Il's Birthday. **Apr 15** Day of the Sun/Kim Il Sung's Birthday. **Apr 25** Foundation of the People's Army. **May 1** International Workers' Day. **Jul 27** Victory Day. **Aug 15** Anniversary of Liberation. **Sep 9** Independence Day. **Sep 23-25** Ch'usok (Harvest Moon Festival). **Oct 10** Foundation of the Korean Workers' Party. **Dec 27** Constitution Day.

Health

	Special Precautions?	Certificate Required?
Yellow Fever	No	No
Cholera	1	No
Typhoid & Polio	2	N/A
Malaria	3	N/A

Note: *Regulations and requirements may be subject to change at short notice, and you are advised to contact your doctor well in advance of your intended date of departure. Any numbers in the chart refer to the footnotes below.*

1: Following WHO guidelines issued in 1973, a cholera vaccination certificate is not a condition of entry to the Democratic People's Republic of Korea. However, cholera is a risk and precautions are essential. Up-to-date advice should be sought before deciding whether these precautions should include a vaccination, as medical opinion is divided over its effectiveness; see the *Health* appendix.
2: Immunisation against typhoid is highly recommended, and against poliomyelitis is generally advised.
3: Malaria risk is low; mainly in the benign vivax form.
Food & drink: All water should be regarded as a potential health risk. Water used for drinking, brushing teeth or making ice should have first been boiled or otherwise sterilised. Bottled water is widely available and considered fine to drink. Milk is unpasteurised and should be boiled. Powdered or tinned milk is available and is advised, but make sure that it is reconstituted with pure water. Avoid dairy products which are likely to have been made from unboiled milk. Only eat well-cooked meat and fish, preferably served hot. Pork, salad and mayonnaise may carry increased risk. Vegetables should be cooked and fruit peeled.
Other risks: Diarrhoeal diseases including *giardiasis*, *dysentery* and *typhoid fever* are common. *Hepatitis B* is endemic in the area. *Hepatitis A* and *E* also occur along with tuberculosis. Epidemics of *Japanese encephalitis* and *dengue fever* may occur.
Rabies is present. For those at high risk, vaccination before arrival should be considered. If you are bitten, seek medical advice without delay.
Health care: 'People's Hospitals' and clinics are found throughout the country, but resources can be limited and basic. At present, emergency medical flights are not permitted into the country. International travellers are strongly advised to take out health insurance.

Travel - International

AIR: The national airline is *Air Koryo (JS)*. During the summer months *China Northern Airlines (CJ)* also serves Korea (Dem Rep). Direct flights run four times a week from Beijing (China) with both airlines, and *Air Koryo* also operates weekly flights to Beijing and Shenyang (China), Bangkok (Thailand), Macau (SAR) and Moscow and Vladivostok (Russian Federation).
Approximate flight times: From Pyongyang to *London* is 13 hours.
International airports: *Pyongyang (FNJ)* (Sunan) is 24km (15 miles) from the city (travel time – 45 minutes). Facilities include bars, restaurants and duty-free shops.
Departure tax: None.
SEA: Main international ports are Chongjin, Haeju, Hungnam, Kimchaek, Kosong, Najin, Sinuiju, Sonbong, Songnim, Unsang, Wonsan and Nampo, the port of Pyongyang.
RAIL: The country has a relatively good rail network with connections to China and the Russian Federation. The *Trans Mongolian Railway* and *Trans China Railway* runs between Shineuiju and China. Namyang connects with the *Trans Manchurian Railway* and the *Trans Siberia Railway* links Rajin with the Russian Federation. There are no routes to the Republic of Korea, although it is hoped that these may open sometime in the future, following negotiations between the two countries.
ROAD: There are roads from Dandong, Lu-ta, Liaoyang, Jilin and Changchun in China and Vladivostock in the Russian Federation, but foreigners are only permitted to enter the country by rail or by air.

Travel - Internal

AIR: There are flights from Chongjin, Hamhung, Kaesong, Kanggye, Kiliju, Pyongyang, Sinuiju and Wonsan, although foreigners are not allowed to use these.
RAIL: The extensive rail network built by the Japanese during World War II has been broken by the separation of North and South Korea, but the main passenger routes run from Pyongyang to Sinuiju, Haeju and Chongjin. Service, however, is slow. Timetables are not published and it is advised to purchase tickets through a travel agent.
ROAD: Traffic drives on the right. The quality of major roads is good; many are dual carriageways. All roads leading out of Pyongyang have police security checkpoints where identity documents must be shown. There are no buses between cities. There are very few road signs. International driving licences are not accepted and in order to drive within the country it is necessary to sit a local driving test and obtain a local licence.
URBAN: Pyongyang has a two-line metro and regular bus services.

Accommodation

Pyongyang has a few first-class hotels where foreign visitors stay, although groups cannot know in advance which one will be used. All other towns have at least one first-class hotel for use by groups. Visitors must stay in designated tourist hotels (rather than in local yogwan). These are generally of reasonable standard, and are graded as deluxe, first, second and third class.

Resorts & Excursions

Note: Only travel companies officially recognised by the North Korean Authorities are permitted to bring groups of tourists to Korea (Dem Rep). Independent tourism is not permitted, and foreigners must be accompanied by a guide at all times.
PYONGYANG: Korea (Dem Rep)'s capital, Pyongyang, was completely rebuilt after the Korean War as a city of wide avenues, neatly designed parks and enormous marble public buildings, leading to its alternative name of the 'youthful city'. The **Palace of Culture**, the **Grand Theatre**, the **Juche Tower** and the **Ongrui Restaurant** epitomise the Korean variant of Communist architecture. The **Gates of Pyongyang** and the **Arch of Triumph** (built in honour of Kim Il Sung's 70th birthday) are particularly impressive, while **Morangborg Park** and **Taesongsan Recreation Ground** (with its fairground attractions) offer relaxation. For the (mainly communist) *13th World Festival of Youth and Students* in 1989, a 150,000-seat stadium was built in Pyongyang.
Mangyongdae, Kim Il Sung's birthplace, is a national shrine. His family's thatched cottage, now a museum, overlooks the **Taedong River** and the capital.
ELSEWHERE: Many ancient buildings in **Kaesong** (six hours from the capital by train), bear witness to Korea's 500-year imperial history. The town is surrounded by beautiful pine-clad hills. **Kumgangsan** is the country's largest national park, consisting of a range of mountains (known as 'the Diamond Mountains') along the east coast of the country. Its unspoilt, diverse environment is popular with birdwatchers, photographers and botanists.
Myohyangsan, whose name means 'exotic fragrant mountain', offers pleasant walks and climbs through a contrasting scenery of waterfalls, woods and Buddhist pagodas, just 120km (75 miles) northeast of the capital. The **Exhibition Centre**, with its imposing 4-tonne bronze doors, houses thousands of gifts presented by foreigners to Kim Il Sung and his son.

Social Profile

FOOD & DRINK: Reasonable restaurants can be found in the main towns and cooking is usually based on the staple food: rice. In hotels and restaurants it is better to stick to the Chinese, Japanese or Korean items on the menu as

experience of Western and Russian cooking is limited. Eating out is arranged by the guide.
NIGHTLIFE: A night at the revolutionary opera provides a unique experience. There are also circuses and musical events of a high quality.
SPECIAL EVENTS: The following is a selection of special events celebrated annually in the Democratic People's Republic of Korea; for further information contact the National Tourism Administration of the DPRK (see *Contact Addresses* section):
May 1 *May Day*. **Aug 15** *Liberation Day*, with parades in Pyongyang.
SOCIAL CONVENTIONS: Discretion and a low political profile are advised. **Photography**: It is strongly advised to ask permission before taking a photo. Photographs of Korean officials or guarded buildings should be avoided.
Tipping: Officially frowned upon although some hotel staff may expect a tip.

Business Profile

ECONOMY: The Democratic People's Republic of Korea has a Soviet-style command economy based on heavy industry. The country has rich mineral deposits, including most of the major base metals, as well as gold, silver and tungsten. Since the main industrial infrastructure was developed in the 1950s, development resources have gradually shifted to light industry and latterly concentrated on automation and modernisation. Most trade is conducted with the Russian Federation, Japan and China, where a number of joint industrial ventures have been set up. These measures have only partially compensated, however, for the serious loss of trade with the former Soviet Union, which precipitated Korea (Dem Rep)'s economic decline during the 1990s. Estimated at 4 per cent per annum, this contraction has been compounded by a series of serious floods. Although most evidence is anecdotal – in the absence of detailed official information – it is clear that the North Korean people have recently suffered severe shortages and, in some areas, starvation.
The North Koreans have yet to adopt political or economic reforms on the scale seen in China, the Russian Federation and Eastern Europe. China is the most likely model, but so far Korea (Dem Rep) has gone no further than devaluing the won (a largely artificial measure since the won is not convertible) and cutting the subsidies on some basic goods. Pyongyang has pinned its hopes on an improvement of relations with the South. There is $300 million of trade between the two countries, conducted at present through intermediaries. In August 2003, an economic and trade agreement was signed under which South Korean companies manufacture products in the North (where labour costs are much lower). The major obstacle is political: Washington is still hostile to Korea (Dem Rep)'s nuclear ambitions.
BUSINESS: Suits are required. Business transactions will take place outside the office, generally in the evening, as visitors are not allowed to enter offices.
COMMERCIAL INFORMATION: The following organisation can offer advice: The DPRK Committee for the Promotion of External Economic Cooperation, Jungsongdong, Central District, Pyongyang (tel: (2) 381 6163; fax: (2) 381 4498).

Climate

Moderate with four distinct seasons. The hottest time is July to August, which is also the rainy season; coldest is from December to January, winters in the far north can be very severe. Spring and autumn are mild and mainly dry.
Required clothing: Lightweight cottons and linens are worn during the summer. Light- to mediumweights are advised in the spring and autumn, and medium- to heavyweights in the winter. Waterproofs are advisable during the rainy season.

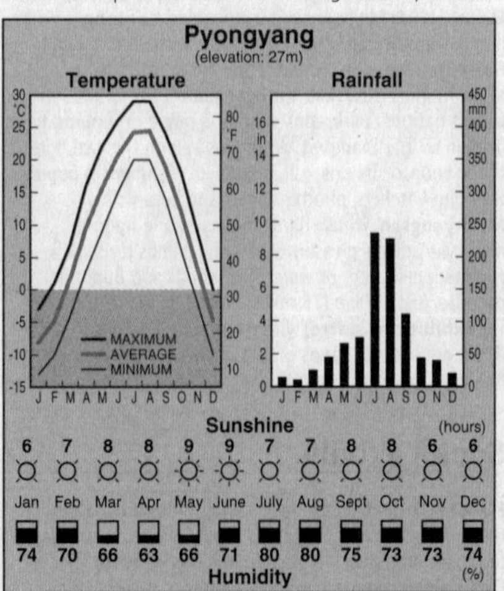

Korea (Republic of)

LATEST TRAVEL ADVICE CONTACTS

British Foreign and Commonwealth Office
Tel: (0870) 606 0290 Website: www.fco.gov.uk
US Department of State
Website: http://travel.state.gov/travel
Canadian Department of Foreign Affairs and Int'l Trade
Tel: (1 800) 267 8376 Website: www.dfait-maeci.gc.ca

Location: Far East.

Country dialling code: 82.

Korea National Tourism Organization (KNTO)
10 Da-dong, Jung-gu, Seoul 100-180, Republic of Korea
Tel: (2) 729 9600. Fax: (2) 757 5997.
E-mail: einfo@mail.knto.or.kr
Website: www.tour2korea.com *or* www.knto.or.kr
KNTO Tourist Phone Service: tel: 1330 *or* 080 757 2000 (toll-free within the Republic of Korea); these numbers will automatically connect users to the nearest KNTO tourist office.
Embassy of the Republic of Korea
60 Buckingham Gate, London SW1E 6AJ, UK
Tel: (020) 7227 5500 *or* 7227 5505 (consular section).
Fax: (020) 7227 5504 (consular section).
E-mail: koreanembinuk@mofat.go.kr
Website: www.mofat.go.kr
Opening hours: Mon-Fri 1000-1200 and 1400-1600 (visa section).
Korea National Tourism Organization (KNTO)
3rd Floor, New Zealand House, Haymarket, London SW1Y 4TE, UK
Tel: (020) 7321 2535. Fax: (020) 7321 0876.
E-mail: london@mail.knto.or.kr
Website: www.tour2korea.com
British Embassy
Taepyung-ro 40, 4 Chung-dong, Choong-gu, Seoul 100-120, Republic of Korea
Tel: (2) 3210 5500 (embassy).
Fax: (2) 725 1738 *or* 3210 5653 (consular section).
E-mail: bembassy@britain.or.kr *or* consular.seoul@fco.gov.uk
Website: www.britishembassy.or.kr
Embassy of the Republic of Korea
2450 Massachusetts Avenue, NW, Washington, DC 20008, USA
Consular section: 2320 Massachusetts Avenue, NW, Washington, DC 20008, USA
Tel: (202) 939 5600 *or* 939 5661-3 (consular section).
Fax: (202) 797 0595 *or* 342 1597 (consular section).

TIMATIC CODES

Health	AMADEUS: **TI-DFT/SEL/HE** GALILEO/WORLDSPAN: **TI-DFT/SEL/HE** SABRE: **TIDFT/SEL/HE**
Visa	AMADEUS: **TI-DFT/SEL/VI** GALILEO/WORLDSPAN: **TI-DFT/SEL/VI** SABRE: **TIDFT/SEL/VI**

To access TIMATIC country information on Health and Visa regulations through the Computer Reservations System (CRS), type in the appropriate command line listed above.

E-mail: consular_usa@mofat.go.kr (consular section).
Consulates General in: Atlanta, Boston, Chicago, Honolulu, Houston, Los Angeles, New York, San Francisco and Seattle.
Korea National Tourism Organization (KNTO)
1 Executive Drive, Suite 100, Fort Lee, NJ 07024, USA
Tel: (201) 585 0909 *or* (800) 868 7567 (toll-free in USA).
Fax: (201) 585 9041.
E-mail: ny@kntoamerica.com
Website: http://english.tour2korea.com/newyork
Offices also in: Chicago and Los Angeles.
Embassy of the United States of America
32 Sejongno, Jongno-gu, Seoul 110-710, Republic of Korea
Tel: (2) 397 4114.
Fax: (2) 397 4101 *or* 725 6843 (visa enquiries).
E-mail: seoul_acs@state.gov *or* seoulniv@state.gov *or* seoulgoldteam@state.gov (both visa enquiries).
Website: http://seoul.usembassy.gov
Embassy of the Republic of Korea
150 Boteler Street, Ottawa, Ontario K1N 5A6, Canada
Tel: (613) 244 5010. Fax: (613) 244 5043.
E-mail: manager@emb-korea.ottawa.on.ca
Website: www.emb-korea.ottawa.on.ca
Consulate General of the Republic of Korea
555 Avenue Road, Toronto, Ontario M4V 2J7, Canada
Tel: (416) 920 3809. Fax: (416) 924 7305.
E-mail: toronto@mofat.go.kr
Website: www.consulatekorea-tor.org
Consulates also in: Montréal and Vancouver.
Korea National Tourism Organization (KNTO)
700 Bay Street, Suite 1903, Toronto, Ontario M5G 1Z6, Canada
Tel: (416) 348 9056 *or* (800) 868 7567 (toll-free in USA and Canada). Fax: (416) 348 9058.
E-mail: toronto@knto.ca
Website: http://english.tour2korea.com/toronto
Canadian Embassy
Street address: 9th Floor, Kolon Building, 45 Mukyo-dong, Chung-ku, Seoul 100-170, Republic of Korea
Postal address: CPO Box 6299, Seoul 100-170, Republic of Korea
Tel: (2) 3455 6000.
Fax: (2) 755 0686 *or* 776 0974 (visa enquiries only).
Website: www.korea.gc.ca
Consulate in: Busan.

General Information

AREA: 99,313 sq km (38,345 sq miles, excluding demilitarised zone).
POPULATION: 47,925,318 (official estimate 2003).
POPULATION DENSITY: 482.6 per sq km.
CAPITAL: Seoul. **Population**: 9,853,972 (2000).
GEOGRAPHY: The Republic of Korea (South Korea) shares borders to the north with the demilitarised zone (separating it from the Democratic People's Republic of Korea), to the east with the Sea of Japan (East Sea), to the south with the Korea Strait (separating it from Japan), and to the west with the Yellow Sea. There are many islands, bays and peninsulas in the Korea Strait. The volcanic island of Cheju-do lies off the southwest coast. Most of the country consists of hills and mountains and the 30 per cent of flat plain contains the majority of the population and cultivation. Most rivers rise in the mountains to the east, flowing west and south to the Yellow Sea. The Naktong River flows into the Korea Strait near the southern port of Busan. The eastern coast is rocky and steep with mountains rising from the sea.
GOVERNMENT: Republic since 1945. **Head of State**: President Roh Moo-Hyun since 2002. **Head of Government**: Prime Minister Lee Hai-Chan since 2004
LANGUAGE: Korean.
RELIGION: Mahayana Buddhism with a large Christian minority. Also Confucianism and Chundo Kyo, which is peculiar to Korea and combines elements of Shamanist, Buddhist and Christian doctrines.
TIME: GMT + 9.
ELECTRICITY: 110/220 volts AC, 60Hz. Government policy is to phase out the 110 volt supply and many hotels now have a 220 volt supply.
COMMUNICATIONS: Telephone: IDD is available to Seoul and other major cities. Country code: 82. Outgoing international code: 001 *or* 002. **Mobile telephone:** *SK Telecom* is the main network provider (website: www.sktelecom.co.kr). It is possible to rent a handset to use whilst in Korea (Rep) (contact *SK Telecom*, as above). A new 3G network, KT ICOM (website: www.ktf.com), is also available. **Fax:** Available at major hotels and business centres. **Internet:** ISPs include *Korea-Afis* (website: www.korea-afis.co.kr), *Korea Telecom* (website: www.kornet.net) and *Shinbiro* (http://english.shinbiro.com). There are Internet cafes available in Seoul, and one in Taejon. **Telegram:** There is a service at all main hotels. Korea International Telecommunications Services at 1, Choongmo-ro, Chung-gu, Seoul provides a 24-hour public service. **Post:** Airmail to Western Europe takes up to 10 days. Post offices hours: Mon-Fri 0900-1700, Sat 0900-

1300. **Press:** English-language national dailies are *Korea Daily News, The Korea Herald* and *The Korea Times.*
Radio: BBC World Service (website: www.bbc.co.uk/worldservice) and Voice of America (website: www.voa.gov) can be received. From time to time the frequencies change and the most up-to-date can be found online.

Passport/Visa

	Passport Required?	Visa Required?	Return Ticket Required?
Full British			
Australian	Yes	No	Yes
Canadian	Yes	No	Yes
USA	Yes	No	Yes
Other EU	Yes	No/1	Yes
Japanese	Yes	No	Yes

Note: *Regulations and requirements may be subject to change at short notice, and you are advised to contact the appropriate diplomatic or consular authority before finalising travel arrangements. Details of these may be found at the head of this country's entry. Any numbers in the chart refer to the footnotes below.*

PASSPORTS: Passport valid for a minimum of three months required by all.
VISAS: Required by all except the following:
(a) nationals countries referred to in the table above except **1.** nationals of Latvia, who *do* need a visa;
(b) nationals of Albania, Andorra, Argentina, Antigua & Barbuda, The Bahamas, Bangladesh, Barbados, Brazil, Brunei, Bulgaria, Chile, Colombia, Costa Rica, Croatia, Dominica, Dominican Republic, Egypt, El Salvador, Federated States of Micronesia, Fiji, Grenada, Guam, Guatemala, Haiti, Honduras, Hong Kong (SAR), Iceland, Israel, Jamaica, Kiribati, Kuwait, Lesotho, Liberia, Liechtenstein, Macau (SAR), Malaysia, Marshall Islands, Mexico, Monaco, Morocco, Nauru, New Caledonia, New Zealand, Nicaragua, Norway, Oman, Palau, Panama, Paraguay, Peru, Qatar, Romania, St Kitts & Nevis, St Lucia, St Vincent & the Grenadines, San Marino, Saudi Arabia, Singapore, Solomon Islands, South Africa, Surinam, Swaziland, Switzerland, Taiwan, Thailand, Trinidad & Tobago, Tunisia, Turkey United Arab Emirates, Uruguay, Vatican City, Venezuala and Yemen.
Types of visa and cost: *Single-entry* (up to 90 days): £16.20. *Single-entry* (more than 90 days): £27. *Multiple-entry*: £43. The same fees apply for both business and tourist visas. Nationals of Italy, Japan, Spain, Sweden, Taiwan (China), Thailand and UK can obtain a visa valid up to six months free of charge.
Validity: Up to three months from date of issue, although this may vary.
Application to: Consulate (or Consular section at Embassy); see *Contact Addresses* section for details.
Application requirements: These may vary according to visa required and nationality of applicant. (a) Valid passport. (b) Completed application form. (c) One recent passport-size colour photo. (d) Fee, payable by cash or postal order (but not cheque). (e) Stamped, self-addressed envelope, if applicable. (f) Proof of sufficient funds (a bank statement for £1000 if not working in the UK and a company letter if working in the UK). *Short-term business*: (a)-(f) and, (g) Substantiating documents for the activity of the applicant, eg letter of invitation from the host company in the Republic of Korea, business-related documents etc. *Private visit*: (a)-(f) and, (g) A certificate for confirmation of visa issuance, obtained by the person in Korea with whom the applicant will be staying. *Student*: (a)-(f) and, (g) Standard admission letter for students, substantiating the educational ability and coverage of the expense of the applicant, issued by the president or a dean of the University. (h) Substantiating documents for researchers, including a reference, if applicable.
Note: (a) For a national who cannot fulfill the necessary requirements and entry conditions (such as the expiration of passport validity) due to unavoidable circumstances, or is required for further review before a visa can be issued, a conditional entry permit may be granted with a validity of up to 72 hours. In regards to this permit, the chief of a district or branch office may impose conditions such as a reference, financial guarantee, restrictions on duration of stay, a duty to obey summons or other necessary conditions, and, if deemed necessary, a monetary deposit not exceeding 10 million won (US$10,000). (b) When a short-term visitor or unregistered national who visited Korea (DPR) re-enters the Republic of Korea, an immigration officer shall issue the same visa which was granted, minus the duration of stay in Korea (DPR). If a national's duration of stay on the visa expired whilst in Korea (DPR), or remaining period is less than 30 days, a new visa may have to be granted. (c) A national who wishes to enter the Republic of Korea via Korea (DPR) must carry a valid passport and visa. If the national has a visa waiver agreement with the Republic of Korea, they must present a passport, a written paper outlining the reason for visiting Korea (DPR) and E/D Card (Immigration Card) to the Immigration officer at an inspection counter.

Credit: © KNTO

Working days required: Five.
Temporary residence: Applications for a residence certificate or for a stay of more than 90 days should be made to the Immigration Office in Seoul. For details contact the Consulate (or Consular section at Embassy); see *Contact Addresses* section.

Money

Currency: Won (W). Notes are in denominations of W10,000, 5000 and 1000. W1000 is called Chon Won in Korean (*chon* means 'one thousand'). Coins are in denominations of W500, 100, 50 and 10.
Currency exchange: Foreign banknotes and travellers cheques can be exchanged at foreign exchange banks and other authorised money changers. ATMs are available in all major cities, but all instructions are in Korean.
Credit & debit cards: American Express, Diners Club, MasterCard and Visa are widely accepted at major hotels, shops and restaurants in the larger cities. Check with your credit or debit card company for details of merchant acceptability and other services which may be available.
Travellers cheques: Accepted, but may be difficult to change in smaller towns. To avoid additional exchange rate charges, travellers are advised to take travellers cheques in US Dollars.
T2K Card: The Shinhan Bank and Tour2Korea.com have consolidated in order to issue the T2K Card, only available to foreign tourists or residents. This card provides discounts on currency charges, accommodation and entertainment performances, etc. The card can be received at Shinhan Bank's currency exchange booths at Incheon International Airport.
Currency restrictions: The import and export of local currency is allowed up to W8,000,000. The import of foreign currency is unlimited, provided amounts greater than US$10,000 (including travellers cheques) are declared on arrival. Export of foreign currency is limited to the amount declared on arrival.
Exchange rate indicators: The following figures are included as a guide to the movements of the Won against Sterling and the US Dollar:

Date	Feb '04	May '04	Aug '04	Nov '04
£1.00=	2136.06	2092.42	2141.64	1981.76
$1.00=	1173.50	1171.50	1162.45	1046.50

Banking hours: Mon-Fri 0930-1630, Sat 0930-1330.

Duty Free

The following goods may be imported into the Republic of Korea by persons aged 19 and over without incurring customs duty:
200 cigarettes or 50 cigars or 250g of other tobacco products; 57g of perfume; gifts up to the value of KRW400,000.
The following goods may be imported into the Republic of Korea by persons aged 20 and over, in addition to the aforementioned goods, without incurring customs duty:
one bottle (not exceeding 1l) of alcoholic beverage.
Prohibited items: Narcotics, drugs, fruit, hay, seeds; printed material, films, records or cassettes considered by the authorities to be subversive, obscene or harmful to national security or public interests; products originating from communist countries.
Restricted items: Firearms, explosives and other weapons and ammunition, even for sporting purposes, unless prior police permission is obtained, and item(s) is/are declared on arrival; plants and and plant products require a phytosanitary certificate issued by the plant quarantine office of the country of origin.

Public Holidays

2005: Jan 1 New Year. **Feb 8-10** Sollal (Lunar New Year). **Mar 1** Independence Movement Day. **Apr 5** Arbor Day. **May 5** Children's Day. **May 15** Birth of Buddha. **Jun 6** Memorial Day. **Jul 17** Constitution Day. **Aug 15** Liberation Day. **Sep 17-19** Harvest Moon (Chusok). **Oct 3** National Foundation Day. **Dec 25** Christmas Day.
2006: Jan 1 New Year. **Feb 8-10** Sollal (Lunar New Year). **Mar 1** Independence Movement Day. **Apr 5** Arbor Day. **May 5** Children's Day. **May 26** Birth of Buddha. **Jun 6** Memorial Day. **Jul 17** Constitution Day. **Aug 15** Liberation Day. **Sep 26-28** Harvest Moon (Chusok). **Oct 3** National Foundation Day. **Dec 25** Christmas Day.

Health

	Special Precautions?	Certificate Required?
Yellow Fever	Yes	No
Cholera	No	1
Typhoid & Polio	No	N/A
Malaria	2	N/A

Note: *Regulations and requirements may be subject to change at short notice, and you are advised to contact your doctor well in advance of your intended date of departure. Any numbers in the chart refer to the footnotes below.*

1: Following WHO guidelines issued in 1973, a cholera vaccination certificate is not a condition of entry to the Republic of Korea. However, cholera may be a risk in this country and precautions are essential. Up-to-date advice should be sought before deciding whether these precautions should include a vaccination, as medical opinion is divided over its effectiveness; see the *Health* appendix.
2: Limited malaria risk, exclusively in the benign vivax form, exists mainly in the northern areas of the Kyunggi Do and Gangwon Do provinces.
Food & drink: Mains water is normally chlorinated and, whilst relatively safe, may cause mild abdominal upsets. Bottled water is available and is advised for the first few weeks of stay. Powdered or tinned milk is available and is advised, but make sure that it is reconstituted with pure water. Avoid

A B C D E F G H I J K L M N O P Q R S T U V W X Y Z

dairy products which are likely to have been made from unboiled milk. Only eat well-cooked meat and fish, preferably served hot. Vegetables should be cooked and fruit peeled.
Other risks: *Japanese encephalitis* may be transmitted by mosquitoes between June and the end of October in rural areas. A vaccine is available, and travellers are advised to consult their doctor prior to departure. *Hepatitis A* is common; *B* is highly endemic, as is *Korean haemorrhagic fever*. TB occurs.
Rabies may be present. For those at high risk, vaccination should be considered. If you are bitten, seek medical advice without delay. For more information consult the *Health* appendix.
Note: Travellers wishing to stay for more than three months may need to supply a certificate showing they have tested HIV negative, issued within one month before their arrival in Korea. Ask at the Consulate (or Consular section at Embassy) for details.
Health care: Health insurance is recommended. There are facilities in all tourist areas, and hotels will recommend a local doctor. Almost all hospitals require payment and registration prior to treatment. Most nurses and receptionists do not speak English; writing words out on paper can help in an emergency.

Travel - International

AIR: The Republic of Korea's national airlines are *Asiana Airlines (OZ)* (website: http://us.flyasiana.com) and *Korean Air (KE)* (website: www.koreanair.com). Other major airlines which serve Korea (Rep) include *Air Canada*, *Air China*, *Air France*, *American Airlines*, *Cathay Pacific Airlines*, *Garuda Indonesia Airlines*, *Japan Airlines*, *KLM*, *Lufthansa*, *Malaysia Airlines*, *Qantas Airways*, *Singapore Airlines*, *Thai Airways*, *United Airlines* and *Vietnam Airlines*.
Approximate flight times: From Seoul to *London* is 11 hours; add one hour if flying to any other main European city. From Seoul to *New York* is 17 hours 40 minutes (including stopover in Anchorage). From Seoul to *Los Angeles* is 10 hours 30 minutes. From Seoul to *Sydney* is nine hours.
International airports: *Seoul (SEL) Incheon International Airport (ICN)* (website: www.airport.or.kr) is located 40km (25 miles) west of Seoul on Yongion. Limousine buses, taxis and coaches operate regular routes between the main urban area (travel time - 90 minutes). A ferry service operates a daily service every 20 to 30 minutes between the airport ferry pier and Wolmido/Yuldo on the coast of Incheon city (travel time - 15 to 20 minutes). The Korea Train Express (KTX) has two lines (the Honam line, running from Seoul to destinations such as Cheonana, Iksan and Mokpo; and the Gyeongbu line, running from Seoul to destinations such as Gwangmyeong, Dongdaegu and Busan) to transport people from the airport. Airport facilities include left luggage, banks/bureaux de change, chemist, duty free shops, post office, restaurants and tourist information.
Busan (PUS) (Kimhae) is 27km (17 miles) from Busan (in the far south). The airport receives flights from Fukuoka, Osaka and Tokyo. There are bus, coach and taxi services to the town. Airport facilities include currency exchange, post office, duty free shop, snack bar, gift shop, restaurant, travel information service and car hire.
Jeju (CJU) (Jeju), located on the island of Jeju, is 4km (2.5 miles) from the town centre. Buses and coaches are available to the town and leave every 10 to 15 minutes (0610-2230). Airport facilities include currency exchange, post office, duty free shop, snack bar, gift shop and travel information service.
Note: *Seoul (SEL) Gimpo (GMP)* airport is the main domestic airport, although a few international flights (mainly to Hong Kong) do still depart from there (see *Travel Internal* section).
Departure tax: W10,000. Transit passengers and infants under two years old are exempt.
SEA: International ports are Busan (in the far south) and Incheon (due west of Seoul). Passenger lines that sail to Japan are *Bugwan Ferry*, *Korea Ferry* and *Korea Marine Express*. *Jinchon Ferry* and *Weidong Ferry* sail regularly to China. Cargo/passenger lines include *American Mail* and *American President*. Weekly trips from the USA are offered by *American President Lines* and *Lykes Lines*.
Under an agreement reached between Korea (Dem Rep) and Korea (Rep) tour operators, groups of tourists are now allowed to travel to Korea (Dem Rep) on cruise ships leaving from the port of Tonghae, in Korea (Rep), and sailing to the port of Changjon. For further details contact Korea National Tourist Organisation (see *Contact Addresses* section).
RAIL/ROAD: The Republic of Korea's only land frontier with Korea (Dem Rep) remains closed, although a limited number of tourists are now allowed to travel to the north via certain cruise ships (see *Sea* above).
Discount tickets: The *Korea-China Through-ticket* and *Korea-Japan Through-ticket* provide discounts on travel between the countries, including transport by ferry and train. For more information, contact KNTO (see *Contact Addresses* section).

Travel - Internal

AIR: *Asiana Air* and *Korean Air* run frequent services between Seoul and Busan, Taegu, Cheju, Ulsan and Kwangju, linking the Republic of Korea's 16 major cities. The main domestic airport is *Seoul Gimpo (GMP)*, located 17km (10 miles) from the city. Airport Limousine Buses depart to the city every five to 10 minutes from 0700-2215 (travel time - 40 minutes). Airport Express buses depart every 12 minutes. A subway line 5 runs to the city centre (travel time - 40 minutes). Taxis to the city are also available. Airport facilities include currency exchange, pharmacy, children's restroom, post office, gift shop, duty-free shop, car hire, local products shop, restaurant and travel information desk.
Departure tax: W3000-5000.
SEA/RIVER: A steamer service runs along the scenic south coast between Mokpo and Busan twice daily. A hydrofoil service links Busan and Yosu via Ch'ungmu five times a day (*Angel Line*). Ferries connect Busan with Cheju-do Island once a day. Car ferries run three times a week. *Semo Cruise Company* operates a cruise service on the Han-Gang River in Seoul, which runs through the centre of the capital. Children pay half fare and night cruises are available.
RAIL: *Korean National Railroads* connect major destinations. There are three classes of trains: Super-Express, Express and Local. Super-Express trains operate on Seoul–Mokpo, Seoul–Busan, Seoul–Chungju–Yosu, Seoul–Incheon (particularly scenic) and Seoul–Onyang (second-class only) routes. Some have air conditioning and restaurant cars. A supplement is payable for better-quality accommodation on some trains. Station signs in English are common and English translations of timetables are usually available. Children under six travel free and children six to 12 years old pay half fare. Timetables and fares are accessible online (website: http://app.korail.go.kr).
Korea Rail Pass: The Korea Rail Pass allows visitors free travel with reserved seats on any KR train (except subways) within a three-, five-, seven- or 10-day period. Saver passes are available for groups of between two and five people and for people aged between 13 and 25 years old. A Korea Rail Pass voucher can be purchased at certain offices and travel agencies abroad and exchanged for the actual pass at Korean railway stations. The voucher must be exchanged within 60 days from the date of purchase. For further details, contact the Korea National Tourist Organisation (see *Contact Addresses* section).
ROAD: Cars drive on the right. The network extends over more than 60,000km (37,300 miles) of roads; over half of it is paved. Excellent motorways link all major cities, but minor roads are often badly maintained. Road signs are usually written in both Korean and English. **Bus**: Local and express buses are inexpensive, though local buses within cities are often crowded and make no allowances for English-speakers. Hotel staff will be able to assist in choosing the correct bus and stop. Air-conditioned city-express buses, called *Chwasok* buses in Korean and much more comfortable than local buses, operate in competition with trains for connections to major cities. Towns and villages are linked by local bus services. Fares are paid in change into the coin box to the right of the driver upon boarding. To stop the bus at your destination, push one of the stop buttons located along the length of the bus. **Taxi**: Cheap and a good way to travel. There are also deluxe-taxis (mobom taxis) that are black with a yellow sign on top. **Car hire**: There are numerous car hire companies operating, including the major international ones. Some hotels and travel agents also provide a car hire service. For details about driving in the Republic of Korea, contact the Korea Car Rental Union (tel: (2) 552 8772). **Documentation**: International Driving Permit required. Drivers must have more than one year's driving experience, be in possession of a valid passport and be over 21 years of age.
URBAN: Seoul has underground and suburban railways and well-developed bus services, all of which are very crowded during the rush hour. Underground station names, ticket counters and transfer signs are clearly marked in English as well as Korean. Underground lines are colour-coded, and all trains have multilingual announcements. Fares are relatively cheap, but do vary with service areas. Taxis are widely available. Good bus services also operate in other cities.
Travel times: The following chart gives approximate travel times (in hours and minutes) from **Seoul** to other major cities/towns in the Republic of Korea.

	Air	Road	Rail
Busan	0.50	5.30	4.10
Taegu	0.40	3.50	4.10
Kwangju	0.50	3.55	4.20
Ulsan	0.50	4.40	4.00
Chonju	1.10	3.00	3.20
Cheju	0.55	-	-
Kyongju	-	4.40	3.30

Additional times: From Busan to Cheju by sea is 11 hours (three hours 30 minutes via the super-express ferry). From Mokpo to Cheju by sea is five hours 30 minutes. From Busan to Kyongju is one hour by road and 40 minutes by rail.

Accommodation

HOTELS: There are many modern tourist hotels in the major cities and tourist areas. All of these are registered with the Government. Most rooms have private baths as well as heating and cooling systems. Facilities in most tourist hotels include dining rooms, convention halls, bars, souvenir shops, cocktail lounges, barber and beauty shops and recreation areas. For further information and reservations, contact the Korea National Tourism Organisation (see *Contact Addresses* section) *or* the Korea Hotel Reservation Center, PO Box 1099, Fort Lee, NJ 07024, USA (tel: (845) 426 7335; fax: (845) 426 7338; e-mail: philip@khrc.com; website: www.khrc.com). A service charge of 10 per cent and 10 per cent VAT are included in hotel bills; tipping is not necessary. **Grading**: All registered hotels are classified according to their standard and quality of service. Hotels range from **5-Star** (super deluxe) to **1-Star** (third class). For further information, contact Korea National Tourism Organisation (see *Contact Addresses* section).
YOGWANS: These are Korean inns, very reasonable and considered by many travellers as the 'only place to stay'. Sleeping arrangements consist of a small mattress and a firm pillow on the *ondol*, the hot floor-heating system which is traditional in Korea. There are also Western-style rooms. Korea National Tourism Organisation can provide a list of yogwans throughout Korea (see *Contact Addresses* section).
SELF-CATERING: Cottages are available for rent at seaside resorts, but fees are high and few services are provided.
HOMESTAY PROGRAMME: Programme supported by the Korea National Tourism Organisation, offering visitors the chance to stay with a host family in Korea. For more information, contact the KNTO (see *Contact Addresses* section).
CAMPING: Campsites are located throughout the country. Contact Korea National Tourism Organisation for details.
YOUTH HOSTELS: At present there are 51 youth hostels in Korea (Rep), mainly located in Busan, Kyongju, Puyo, Seoul, Sokcho and vicinities. For more information and reservations, contact the Korean Youth Hostels Association, Room 409, Jeokseon Hyundai Building, 80 Jeokseon-dong, Jongno-gu, Seoul (tel: (2) 725 3031; fax: (2) 725 3113; e-mail: sjlee@kyha.or.kr; website: http://yh.kyha.or.kr).
TEMPLE STAYS: There is also a Temple Stay Programme where visitors can, as the name suggests, stay in temples and see what goes on. Further information can be obtained online (website: www.templestaykorea.com) *or* from KNTO (see *Contact Addresses* section).

Resorts & Excursions

Note: The Korea National Tourism Organisation offers a special English language Travel Phone service for overseas visitors. The number is 1330 and can be called from all over the country (daily 0900-1800). If calling from overseas the number is (0082) 2 1330.
A 'Goodwill Guide' service is also available (website: www.goodwillguide.com), by which registered volunteers provide free interpretation services, guided tours of sights and festivals and advice about making the most of your trip to the Republic of Korea. To take advantage of this service overseas visitors must register at least seven days in advance.
Korea (Rep) is a mountainous peninsular which divides the Chinese Yellow Sea from the Sea of Japan. Alpine to the north, the southern Island of Cheju basks in an almost subtropical climate. The country has several dozen National and Provincial Parks and a ruggedly scenic coastline. Despite some moves towards a political thaw, the border with Korea (Dem Rep) is closed and is likely to remain so for the foreseeable future.

SEOUL

Seoul's many attractions and excellent transport links make it the Republic of Korea's number one destination for foreign visitors and the logical place from which to embark on a tour of the country. The capital since 1394, it is a bustling, sophisticated commercial centre, which nevertheless retains numerous reminders of its rich heritage. Seoul's greatest attractions are perhaps the royal residences, several of which are UNESCO-listed.
Changdokkung Palace is surrounded by the picturesque **Secret Gardens**, while the nearby **Chongmyo Shrine**, set in wooded grounds, contains the ancestral tablets of the Kings of the Joseon Dynasty. A colourful Confucian ceremony takes place here annually on the first Sunday in May. The **Museum of Modern Arts** is within the grounds of **Toksukung Palace**, a former royal villa which presents

an interesting contrast with the surrounding skyscrapers. **Kyongbokkung Palace**, the most impressive of the palaces, dates in part to 1394 and has the excellent **National Folk Museum** and temporary displays of treasures from the fantastic collection of the **National Museum of Korea** within its grounds. The symbol of Seoul, the **Great South Gate** (Namdaemun) was the main gate in the city's 15th-century defences. **Pagoda Park** (Tapkol Park) commemorates the 1919 Korean Declaration of Independence and is a good place for people-watching. For fine city panoramas it is worth ascending **Seoul Tower**, which sits atop landscaped **Namsan Mountain** in the heart of the city. The **War Memorial and Museum** on **Yongsan-gu** military base traces the history of conflict on the Korean Peninsular. Seoul is a great place to see performances of Korea's vibrant performing arts. For those interested in finding a unique souvenir, the traditional shopping area of **Insadong** offers everything from antiques to calligraphy brushes. Bargain hunters will enjoy the city's huge markets such as the daily **East Gate** (Dongdaemun) **Market**, while for fashion shopping and nightlife the **Itaewon** district is the place to head for. **Lotte World** is a massive entertainment complex featuring everything from a major theme park to sports facilities and a luxury hotel.

Excursions: Just north of the capital, the forests and cliff-top temples of **Pukansan National Park** offer great hiking and recreational facilities. One hour from Seoul, on the border with **North Korea**, is the truce village of **Panmunjom**, where the 1953 armistice negotiations took place. Access is possible only on an official tour, but many will find the sight of the North Korean landscape and soldiers well worth it. The **Everland leisure complex**, one hour from Seoul, features a huge theme park, a zoo and a speedway-racing track. Also part of the complex, the superb treasures of the **Hoam Art Museum** will appeal to anyone interested in Korean art. South of Seoul is the **Suwon Korean Folk Village**, a functioning rural community and wonderful reconstruction of the past. Craftspeople can be observed at their trades and there are daily performances of traditional folk dances and entertainments. The impressively preserved city walls and defences of nearby **Suwon City** are UNESCO-listed. Southeast of Seoul, Icheon is a traditional centre of Korea's ceramics industry. Attractions include the **Haegang Ceramics Museum** and nearby hot springs. **Incheon**, the location of South Korea's new **International Airport**, is a major seaport and famous for the 1950 'Incheon Landings' of UN troops during the Korean War. These days visitors flock to the many shopping malls and the amusement park and waterfront attractions of the **Wolmido** area.

THE EAST

Eastern Korea provides breathtaking mountain and coastal scenery, a blaze of colour in autumn and a fine setting for wintersports with modern, fully-equipped ski centres. The mountains run down to the sea along much of the 390km- (240 mile-) east coast but are interspersed by harbours, fishing villages and long, sandy beaches, such as the popular resort of **Hwajinpo**. The beautiful beaches of the **Samchok** area range from tiny, undiscovered coves to large resorts. The incredibly scenic volcanic island of **Ullungdo** lies 130km (80 miles) off the coast and is accessible by ferry. Three of Korea's National Parks, **Soraksan**, **Odaesan** and **Chuwangsan**, are accessible from the East Coast highway. **Soraksan National Park**, the northernmost, is widely considered to offer the most beautiful scenery in Korea with its rugged peaks, waterfalls, forests and temples. Excellent tourist facilities range from hiking trails and campsites to the **Osaek Springs** luxury hot spring resorts. The resort village of **Soarkdong** is a popular starting point for climbing expeditions and a cable car runs from the village to the ancient **Kwongumsong Fortress** from where there are spectacular views. For wintersports, the nearby **Alps Ski Resort** is well known. **Odaesan National Park** is famous for its ski resorts, as is the **Dragon Valley** (Yongpyong) area further south. Rock climbers will enjoy the challenges of the Chiaksan area.

Towards the centre of the country, **Songnisan National Park** is another area renowned for its natural beauty. The famous **Popchusa Temple** dates back to AD 553 and has an impressive pagoda, and a number of art treasures such as an immense standing Buddha. Rural **Andong** district retains much of its traditional culture and the **Musil Folk Village and Museum** is well worth visiting. The nearby **Hahoe Folk Village** is particularly known for its mask makers and dancers. The annual *Andong Folk Festival and Masked Dance Festival* takes place in October.

KYONGJU: Known as Korea's 'museum without walls', Kyongju is a repository of ancient Korean history and Buddhist culture and has been designated by UNESCO as one of the world's 10 most historically significant sites. Capital of the *Shilla* Kingdom from 57 BC to AD 935, many traces of the temples, palaces and monuments of that era still remain. The most impressive structure to survive is undoubtedly the seventh-century **Chomsongdae**, an observatory that ranks amongst the oldest in Asia. Nearby

Credit: © KNTO

Tumuli Park contains 20 tomb mounds of Shilla Royalty, one of which, the **Heavenly Horse Tomb**, can be entered. Many treasures of the area, including golden crowns excavated from the tombs, can be seen in the **Kyongju National Museum**. The **Anapji Pond and Gardens** are a reconstructed pleasure garden complete with pavilions. The surrounding hills are dotted with ancient monuments and temples and laced with scenic hiking trails.

Excursions: Within easy reach of Kyongju is the **Pomun Lake Resort**, a complex of hotels, a convention centre, golf courses, sports facilities, a casino, marina and shopping centres. Nearby **Pulguksa Temple** is one of the country's most famous and a major tourist draw. This large wooden temple is beautifully painted and very atmospheric and the stone foundations and pagodas date back to the eighth century. High on the mountain above **Pulguksa** is the fascinating **Sokkuram Grotto**, an ancient and highly complex cave-like structure containing a large granite Buddha and wall carvings of guardian deities, all of great artistic importance.

50km west of **Taegu City** is the **Kayasan National Park**, at the centre of which is **Haeinsa**, Korea's best-known temple. Built in AD 802, it houses the extraordinary **Tripitaka Koreana**, a set of over 80,000 wooden printing blocks engraved with the complete Buddhist scriptures. Completed in 1252 after 16 years of work, they are still in perfect condition.

THE SOUTH

Busan, on South Korea's southeastern coast, is the country's largest sea port. There are great views from the **Busan Tower**, and the city's attractions include **Pomosa Temple**, **Kumjongsansong Fortress** and the large, busy fish market. The nearby coast boasts two major beach resorts, **Haeundae** and **Songjong**. Haeundae is the more popular and has a long, sandy beach with a good range of hotels and restaurants. Additional attractions are sightseeing boat tours and the nearby medicinal hot springs. Another hot-spring resort in the area is **Tongnae**, while **Kumgang Park** features unusual rock formations and historic monuments, including a pagoda and several temples. The superb **Ulsukdo Bird Sanctuary** offers world-class birdwatching. **Chirisan National Park** is known as a fine hiking and mountaineering destination. Located on the flank of **Mount Chirisan**, **Hwaeomsa Temple** is famous for its ancient pagodas and annual lantern festival.

Korea's southwestern area offers dramatic coastal scenery, most notably the 1000-plus islands that make up the **Tadohae Haesang Marine National Park**. Of the islands that offer accommodation and facilities for visitors, scenic **Hongdo** and craggy **Huksando** are two of the most popular. The area is famous for its beautiful sunsets. The coastal town of **Mokpo** is the location of the excellent new **National Maritime Museum** and departure point for ferries to many of the National Park's islands and also for Cheju-do Island.

CHEJU-DO ISLAND: Lying off the southwest coast of the Republic of Korea, the scenic resort island of Cheju-do is dominated by **Mount Halla**, Korea's highest mountain at 1950m (6400ft). Just a one-hour flight from Seoul, the island's warm, sunny climate and myriad leisure facilities mean that it is the country's most popular honeymoon destination. Hikers will enjoy following the trail to the summit of Mount Halla while those in search of a beach holiday will find sandy beaches, warm waters and sports facilities. The **Chungmun** tourist complex offers watersports, a golf course and a 'Pacific'-themed leisure centre. A major amusement park, *Cheju World*, provides fun for lovers of thrills and rides. Numerous natural attractions include the **Samsonghyol Caves**, three spectacular waterfalls and the volcanic scenery of **Songsanilchulbong Park**. Tours of the many tangerine orchards and visits to **Songup Folk Village** are also popular. Cheju-do is famous for its seafood, some of which is still harvested by traditional *haenyeo* women divers.

THE WEST

South of Seoul, South Korea's western area is known for its jagged scenic coastline and numerous National and Provincial Parks. Particularly notable is the **Kyeryongsan National Park** which includes the two beautiful temples of **Kapsa** and **Dongkaksa**. 35km (20 miles) apart, both **Kongju** and **Puyo** were once capital of the ancient **Paekche** kingdom. Today, numerous burial mounds are still to be found in the area and both towns boast branches of the **National Museum** featuring fine displays of artefacts dating back over 1000 years. The **Kongju National Museum** also houses the crowns and other treasures excavated from the tomb of King Muryeon. Nearby, a reconstruction of the tomb is open to visitors. Not far from **Puyo**, the **Nakhwaam Rock** is renowned for the tragic suicide of 3000 women of the *Paekche* court during the last days of the *Paekche* dynasty in the seventh century AD. Further south, **Teogyusan National Park** has numerous waterfalls and is famous as the southernmost skiing area in Korea (Rep). The temple of **Tapsa**, located at the base of **Mount Maisan**, is renowned for its 80 unique pagodas, built with thousands of small stones by a Buddhist hermit.

Sport & Activities

The Republic of Korea has considerable experience in hosting major international sporting events, notably the 1986 Asian Games, the 1988 Olympic Games in Seoul, the 2002 Asian Games and the 2002 FIFA World Cup, which it co-hosted together with Japan – the first time this major sporting event has taken place in an Asian country. Sports facilities are therefore generally of a high standard, particularly in Seoul and in the larger cities.

Watersports: Visitors will find plenty of facilities for watersports along the southern coast and islands. The best time is from June to November, but **swimming**, **paragliding** and **whitewater rafting** are possible year-round. There are numerous **scuba diving** centres along the coast, with diving classes, equipment rental and air tanks all provided. Cheju-do Island (one hour by plane from Seoul) is the most popular destination for scuba diving enthusiasts; the waters surrounding the island are also considered exceptionally good for **deep-sea fishing**, and a number of hotels and companies offer organised fishing trips. Standard facilities for **windsurfing**, **water-skiing** and **boating** are widely available in all coastal resorts. (For further details on the most important beach resorts, see the *Resorts & Excursions* section.) Following a massive clean-up during the 1980s, Seoul's *Han-gang River* now provides a range of watersports facilities and is a popular destination for those wishing to escape a busy city life.

Golf: There are more than 181 golf courses in Korea, the best ones located near Seoul, Kyongju and Chejudo. Many of them can be reached within one hour by car. Facilities for accommodation and other sports (such as swimming pools) are often also integrated within the golf complex. Reservations (which should be made at least one week in advance) can be made directly to the golf course or through a travel agent. Players should note that personal golf clubs must be declared to customs officials upon entering the country. For details of membership and fees, contact the Korea National Tourism Organisation (see *Contact Addresses* section).

Skiing: There are 13 ski resorts all within four or five hours of Seoul. The principal ones are the *Yongpyong Ski Resort*

(Dragon Valley International Ski Resort) at Tackwallyong Area and *Chonmasan Ski Resort* near Seoul.
Traditional sports: T'aekwondo is the main martial art practised in Korea. The traditional Korean sport, **Ssirum** (Korean wrestling), is similar to Sumo wrestling and is a big spectator sport in Korea. **Kite-flying** and **archery** are also popular traditional games.
Festivals: Korea's rich cultural, historic and religious heritage is celebrated throughout the year in the myriad festivals, some in honour of religious figures (such as Buddha's birthday), others focusing on nature (eg the changing seasons). For dates of festivals and special events, see the *Public Holidays* and *Social Profile* sections. A full and detailed list can be obtained from the Korea National Tourism Organisation (see *Contact Addresses* section). The KNTO also organises a variety of theme tours, focusing on history, religion, shopping and crafts as well as nature and health.
Historical and cultural tours: A variety of these are available, with particular focus on Korea's Buddhist heritage. The country has over 10,000 temples and 20,000 monks. Given the increasing worldwide interest in Buddhism, Korean monks are now opening their temples and monasteries to tourists. Ceremonies, traditional dining rituals and tea parties are organised to cater for spiritual tourism, while more dedicated seekers can enrol in Buddhist retreats to practise silence, meditation and prayer for periods lasting anything from three weeks to several years.
Souvenir tours: More material-minded visitors may go on one of Korea's souvenir tours, which are based on the country's reputation as a shoppers' paradise, with many shops providing special duty free prices for foreigners. (For further details on shopping, see the *Social Profile* section.) Fashion, antiques, medicine, herbs and spices, electronics and wedding clothes feature highly on Korea's shopping itinerary; organised tours often combine souvenir and bargain hunting with sightseeing. The best shopping districts and markets are in the capital, Seoul, and include *Namdaemun* (Korea's largest general wholesale market); *Tongdaemun* (one of Seoul's oldest markets, good for bargains); *Myong-dong* (Korea's fashion district); *Insa-dong* (antiques and art); and *Changanp'yong* (one of the largest antiques markets in the Far East); *Itaewon* (modern shopping district particularly popular with foreign tourists); *Noryargjin* (fish market); *Yongsan Electronics Market* (largest electronics and computer market in Korea); *Koyndang* (Oriental medicine, spices and herbs market); *Hwangkhak-dong* (flea market, good for second-hand shopping); *Ahyon-dong* (the 'wedding street', featuring over 120 wedding boutiques); and *Shinch'on* (a shopping street popular with young people, good for accessories and fashion).
Pottery and ceramics centres: Organised tours to Korea's pottery and ceramics centres (such as the Yoju ceramic art village and the Kangjin Koryo Celadon kiln site) are also available, offering visitors the opportunity to participate in ancient pottery-making techniques.
Nature tours: Focusing on seasonal changes and festivals, the most popular itineraries for nature tours include the cherry blossom trails, Korea's flower villages, mountain trips and birdwatching.

Social Profile

FOOD & DRINK: Korea has its own cuisine, quite different from Chinese or Japanese. Rice is the staple food and a typical Korean meal consists of rice, soup, rice water and eight to 20 side dishes of vegetables, fish, poultry, eggs, bean-curd and sea plants. Most Korean soups and side dishes are heavily laced with red pepper. Dishes include *kimchi* (Korean national dish, highly spiced pickle of Chinese cabbage or white radish with turnips, onions, salt, fish, chestnuts and red pepper), soups (based on beef, pork, oxtail, other meat, fish, chicken and cabbage, almost all spiced), *pulgogi* (marinated, charcoal-broiled beef barbecue), *Genghis Khan* (thin slices of beef and vegetables boiled at the table) or *sinsollo* (meat, fish, eggs and vegetables such as chestnuts and pinenuts cooked in a brazier chafing dish at the table). Other examples of local cuisine are *sanjok* (strips of steak with onions and mushrooms), *kalbichim* (steamed beef ribs), fresh abalone and shrimps (from Chejudo Island, served with mustard, soy or chilli sauces) and Korean seaweed (prized throughout the Far East). There is waiter as well as counter service. Most major hotels will offer a selection of restaurants, serving Korean, Japanese and Chinese cuisine or more Western-style food. For more information about Korean food, a brochure called *The Wonderful World of Korean Food* is available from Korea National Tourism Organisation's Tourist Information Centres (see *Contact Addresses* section).
Local drinks are mostly made from fermented rice or wheat and include *jungjong* (expensive variant of rice wine), *soju* (like vodka and made from potatoes or grain) or *yakju/takju* (cloudy and light tan-coloured) known together as *makkoli*. There are many brands of Korean beer, including *Cass*, *Hite* and *OB*. *Ginseng* wine is strong and sweet, similar to brandy, but varies in taste according to the basic ingredient used. The most common type of drinking establishment is the *Suljip* (wine bar), but there are also beer houses serving well-known European brands.
NIGHTLIFE: Korea's nightlife successfully blends the traditional with increasing external influences. Yong-Dong and Itaewon are areas of Seoul with nightclubs catering largely to visitors, many with cabaret evenings. Some hotels also have nightclubs but these tend to be expensive. Larger hotels have their own private theatre restaurants; *Korea House* provides local food in a Korean setting, followed by traditional Korean dancing and music. Beer halls, many decorated along a European theme, are popular places to drink and meet friends. Visitors are expected to eat as well as drink. There are also many cinemas. Operas, concerts and recitals can be seen at the *National Theatre* and performances of Korean classical music, dances and plays can be seen at *Korea House* and the *Drama Centre*. For daily listings of events, consult Korea's English-language papers. Several licensed state-of-the-art casinos operate at various locations throughout the country.
SHOPPING: Favourite buys to look for are hand-tailored clothes, sweaters (plain, embroidered or beaded), silks, brocades, handbags, leatherwork, gold jewellery, topaz, amethyst, amber, jade and silver, ginseng, paintings, costume dolls, musical instruments, brassware, lacquerware, woodcarvings, baskets, scrolls and screens. Prices are fixed in department stores, but may be negotiated in arcades and markets. Major cities have foreigners' duty free shops where people can use foreign currency with a valid passport. Hotels will be able to tell guests the location (see *Sports & Activities* section for further information). **Shopping hours**: Mon-Fri 1030-1930 (department stores); 1030-2030 (markets and smaller shops).
Note: For visitors who purchase goods worth more than W50,000 at stores with 'Tax Free Shopping' signs or goods over W30,000 at outlets with 'Tax Refund Shopping' signs, 70 to 80 per cent of the paid VAT (Value Added Tax) and SET (Special Excise Tax) will be refunded in cash at the airport. Purchases and receipts may need to be shown to the customs officer.
SPECIAL EVENTS: Korea (Rep) celebrates many annual festivals throughout the year. The most significant festival is Buddha's Birthday, during which the 'Feast of Lanterns' is performed in the Republic of Korea's streets. Of great importance are the annual village rituals which are nationally recognised. At these festivals, mountain spirits, great generals and royalty of the past are remembered and celebrated. There are also festivals that mark the changing seasons and festivals of prayer for a good harvest. All are characterised by processions, by masked and costumed local people, music, dancing, battles and sports, to recreate the original historic event or to conjure up good spirits. For more details and exact dates, contact the Korea National Tourism Organisation (see *Contact Addresses* section). The following is a selection of special events occurring in Korea (Rep) in 2005:
Jan 1 *Seongsan Ilchul Festival* (New Year's sunrise). **Jan 27-30** *Daegwallyeong Snow Flower Festival*, Gangwon-do/*Inje Pond Smelt Fishing* (ice fishing competition and festivities), Soyangho Lake. **Feb 17-19** *First Full Moon Field Fire Festival* (burning of dry grass), Jeju-do. **Mar 15-23** *Cheongdo Bullfighting Festival*, Gyeongsangbuk-do. **Apr 2-5** *Yeongam Wang-in Cultural Festival*, Jeollanam-do. **Jul 14-23** *Bucheon-si Puchon International Fantastic Film Festival*, Goyang-si. **Aug 8-10** *Yeosu International Youth Festival*.
SOCIAL CONVENTIONS: Shoes should be removed before entering a Korean home. Entertainment is usually lavish and Koreans may sometimes be offended if their hospitality is refused. Customs are similar to those in the West. Small gifts are customary and traditional etiquette requires the use of the right hand for giving and receiving. Dress should be casual and practical clothes are suitable. Traditional costume, or *hanbok*, is mainly worn on holidays and special occasions. For men it consists of a short jacket and loose trousers, called *baji*, that are tied at the ankles. Womens' hanboks comprise a wrap-around skirt and a bolero-style jacket and is often called a *chima-jeogori*. Both ensembles may be topped by a long coat called a *durumagi*. **Tipping**: Although not a Korean custom, most hotels and other tourist facilities add a 10 per cent service charge to bills. Taxi drivers are not tipped unless they help with the luggage.

Business Profile

ECONOMY: Korea (Rep) is one of the so-called 'tiger economies' of the Pacific Rim, which underwent rapid growth and industrialisation from the 1960s onwards and forged a major presence in world export markets. The Republic of Korea's strength came from four main areas: shipbuilding, steel, consumer goods and construction. The agricultural sector, dominated by rice-growing and fisheries, is an important export earner as well as meeting domestic demand. Tourism dominates the service sector, which is still relatively small but received a boost from the success of the 2002 World Cup football competition, which Korea (Rep) co-hosted. Compared with the North, which has extensive coal and mineral deposits, the South is relatively poor in natural resources, although there have been recent offshore discoveries of natural gas which should help to reduce South Korea's dependence on imported energy. The financial crisis which struck Asia in the autumn of 1997 had a very serious effect on the South Korean economy and raised major concerns about the long-term viability of the chaebol – the large conglomerates that form the foundations of Korea (Rep)'s industrial economy – and the stability of the finance sector, which had assumed increasing importance. The economy was saved from further damage at the beginning of 1998 by a US$60 billion financial rescue package put together by the IMF which kick-started a strong recovery by the South Korean economy. After settling down, the economy is now accelerating again: growth in 2002 increased to 6.3 per cent on the back of an increase in exports and investment, although a partial slowdown is expected in 2003/4. Inflation and unemployment for 2002 were 2.8 and 3.1 per cent. The government has successfully dealt with important structural weaknesses in the financial sector, but has yet to tackle the chaebol. The USA, Japan, China, Hong Kong and Saudi Arabia are Korea (Rep)'s main trading partners. The slow thaw in relations with the North has also seen a growth of economic links between th two parts of Korea.
BUSINESS: Businessmen are expected to wear a suit and tie. English is widely spoken in commercial and official circles. Prior appointments are necessary and business cards are widely used. The use of the right hand when giving and receiving particularly applies to business cards. Best months for business visits are February to June. **Office hours**: Mon-Fri 0900-1800, Sat 0900-1300.
COMMERCIAL INFORMATION: The following organisations can offer advice: Korean Chamber of Commerce and Industry (KCCI), PO Box 25, 45 4-ga, Namdaemun-ro, Chung-gu, Seoul 100-743 (tel: (2) 316 3114; fax: (2) 771 3267; e-mail: trade@kcci.or.kr; website: www.kcci.or.kr); *or* Korea Trade Centre, 5th Floor, 39 St James's Street, London SW1A 1JD, UK (tel: (020) 7491 8057; fax: (020) 7491 7913; e-mail: kotra@kotra.co.uk; website: www.kotra.or.kr/london).
CONFERENCES/CONVENTIONS: The following organisations can offer advice: Korea Exhibition Centre (COEX), World Trade Center, 159 Samsong-dong, Kangnam-ku, Seoul 135-731 (tel: (2) 6000 0114; fax: (2) 6000 1302; website: www.coex.co.kr); *or* Korea Convention and Coordinating Committee, PO Box 903, c/o Korea National Tourism Organisation (see *Contact Addresses* section), which can also offer advice and information on meeting facilities in the Republic of Korea. There is also a new convention centre, the International Convention Centre Jeju, in the island of Jeju (2700 Jungmun-dong, Seoguipo City, 697-120 Jeju, Korea; e-mail: webmaster@iccjeju.co.kr; website: www.iccjeju.co.kr).

Climate

Moderate climate with four seasons. The hottest part of the year is during the rainy season between July and August, and the coldest is December to February. Spring and autumn are mild and mainly dry and are generally considered the best times to visit.
Required clothing: Lightweight cottons and linens are worn during summer, with light- to mediumweights in spring and autumn. Medium- to heavyweights are advised during the winter.

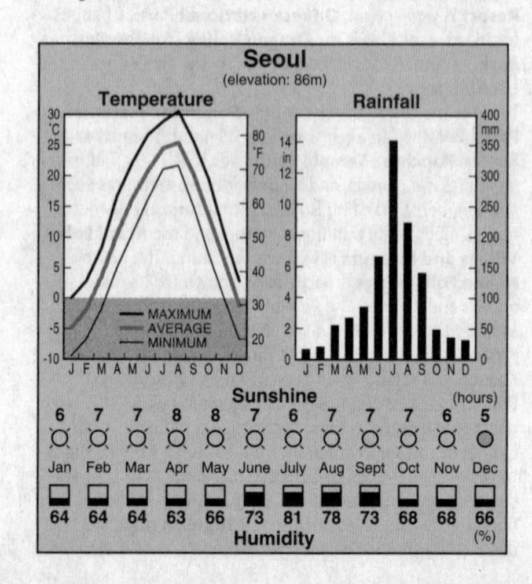

Kuwait

LATEST TRAVEL ADVICE CONTACTS

British Foreign and Commonwealth Office
Tel: (0870) 606 0290 Website: www.fco.gov.uk

US Department of State
Website: http://travel.state.gov/travel

Canadian Department of Foreign Affairs and Int'l Trade
Tel: (1 800) 267 8376 Website: www.dfait-maeci.gc.ca

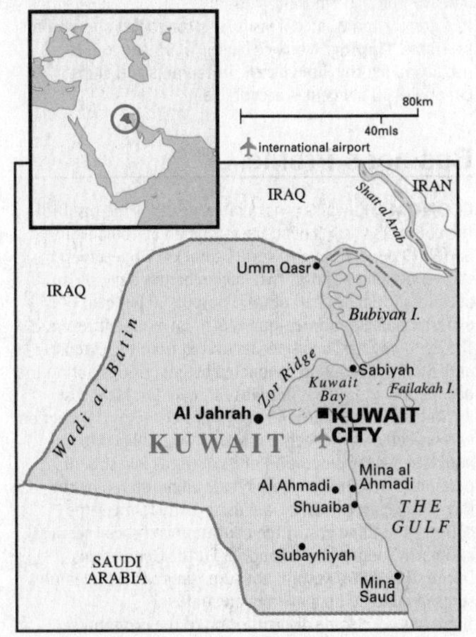

Location: Middle East.

Country dialling code: 965.

Touristic Enterprises Company of Kuwait
PO Box 23310, Safat 13094, Kuwait City, Kuwait
Tel: 565 3771 *or* 2775. Fax: 565 2367.
E-mail: tec@tec.com.kw
Website: www.kuwaittourism.com

Embassy of the State of Kuwait
2 Albert Gate, London SW1X 7JU, UK
Tel: (020) 7590 3400. Fax: (020) 7823 1712.
E-mail: kuwait@dircon.co.uk
Website: www.kuwaitinfo.org.uk
Opening hours: Mon-Fri 0900-1230 and 1400-1600 (visa collection only).

Kuwait Information Centre
Hyde Park House, 60/60A Knightsbridge, London SW1X 7JX, UK
Tel: (020) 7235 1787. Fax: (020) 7235 6912.
E-mail: kuwait@dircon.co.uk
Website: www.kuwaitinfo.org.uk

British Embassy
Street address: Arabian Gulf Street, Dasman, Kuwait City, Kuwait
Postal address: PO Box 2, Safat 13001, Kuwait City, Kuwait
Tel: 240 3335/6. Fax: 242 6799.
E-mail: kuwaitinfo/PPA.Kuwait@fco.gov.uk *or* VisaSection.Kuwait@fco.gov.uk
Website: www.britishembassy-kuwait.org

Embassy of the State of Kuwait
2940 Tilden Street, NW, Washington, DC 20008, USA
Tel: (202) 966 0702. Fax: (202) 966 0517.

Embassy of the United States of America
Street address: Area 14, al-Masjad al-Aqsa Street, Bayan, Kuwait
Postal address: PO Box 77, Safat 13001, Kuwait City, Kuwait
Tel: 539 5307/8. Fax: 538 0282.
E-mail: PASKuwaitM@state.gov
Website: http://usembassy.state.gov/kuwait/

Embassy of the State of Kuwait
333 Sussex Drive, Ottawa, Ontario K1M 1J9, Canada
Tel: (613) 780 9999. Fax: (613) 780 9905.
E-mail: emailcanada@embassyofkuwait.ca
Website: http://embassyofkuwait.ca

TIMATIC CODES

Health
AMADEUS: **TI-DFT/KWI/HE**
GALILEO/WORLDSPAN: **TI-DFT/KWI/HE**
SABRE: **TIDFT/KWI/HE**

Visa
AMADEUS: **TI-DFT/KWI/VI**
GALILEO/WORLDSPAN: **TI-DFT/KWI/VI**
SABRE: **TIDFT/KWI/VI**

To access TIMATIC country information on Health and Visa regulations through the Computer Reservations System (CRS), type in the appropriate command line listed above.

Canadian Embassy
Street address: Block 4, 24 Al-Mutawakkel Street, Da'aiyah, Area 4, Kuwait City, Kuwait
Postal address: PO Box 25281, Safat 13113, Kuwait City, Kuwait
Tel: 256 3025 *or* 251 9603 (visa enquiries). Fax: 256 0173.
E-mail: kwait@dfait-maeci.gc.ca
Website: www.dfait-maeci.gc.ca/kuwait

General Information

AREA: 17,818 sq km (6880 sq miles).
POPULATION: 2,419,900 (official estimate 2002).
POPULATION DENSITY: 135.8 per sq km.
CAPITAL: Kuwait City. **Population**: 28,747 (1995).
GEOGRAPHY: Kuwait shares borders with Iraq and Saudi Arabia. To the southeast lies the Persian Gulf, where Kuwait has sovereignty over nine small islands (the largest is Bubiyan and the most populous is Failaka). The landscape is predominantly desert plateau with a lower, more fertile coastal belt.
GOVERNMENT: Traditional Arab monarchy. Gained full independence from the UK in 1961. **Head of State**: Jabir Al Ahmad Al Jabir Al Sabah since 1978. **Head of Government**: Sabah Al Ahmad Al Jabir Al Sabah since 2003.
LANGUAGE: Arabic, but English is widely understood, especially in commerce and industry.
RELIGION: 95 per cent Muslim (mostly of the Sunni sect), with Christian and Hindu minorities.
TIME: GMT + 3.
ELECTRICITY: 240 volts AC, 50Hz; single phase. UK-type flat three-pin plugs are used.
COMMUNICATIONS: Telephone: Full IDD is available. Country code: 965. Outgoing international code: 00. **Mobile telephone:** GSM 900 and 1800 networks. Network operators include *Mobile Telecom* (website: www.mtc-vodafone.com) and *National Mobile Telecom* (website: www.wataniya.com). **Fax:** Most hotels have facilities. **Internet:** Internet cafes throughout Kuwait provide public access to e-mail and Internet services. ISPs include *Gulfnet International* (website: www.zajil.com) and *QualityNet*. **Telegram:** Telegram services are available 24-hours at the Ministry of Post and Telegraph Offices, Abdullah Al Salem Square, Kuwait City, but must be handed to the post office. **Post:** Airmail to Western Europe takes about five days. Post office hours: Sat-Wed 0700-1400, Thurs 0700-1200. **Press:** The English-language newspapers are the *Arab Times* and the *Kuwait Times*. Although remaining loyal to the ruling family, the press enjoys a fair degree of freedom.
Radio: BBC World Service (website: www.bbc.co.uk/worldservice) and Voice of America (website: www.voa.gov) can be received. From time to time the frequencies change and the most up-to-date can be found online.

Passport/Visa

	Passport Required?	Visa Required?	Return Ticket Required?
Full British	Yes	Yes	No
Australian	Yes	Yes	No
Canadian	Yes	Yes	No
USA	Yes	Yes	No
Other EU	Yes	Yes	No
Japanese	Yes	Yes	No

Note: *Regulations and requirements may be subject to change at short notice, and you are advised to contact the appropriate diplomatic or consular authority before finalising travel arrangements. Details of these may be found at the head of this country's entry. Any numbers in the chart refer to the footnotes below.*

PASSPORTS: Passport valid for at least six months required by all.
Note: Married women and children (except nationals of Iran and Iraq) may travel on the passport of their husband or father.
VISAS: Required by all except nationals of Bahrain, Oman, Qatar, Saudi Arabia and the United Arab Emirates for an unlimited period.
Types of visa and cost: *Business*, *Visitor* and *Transit*. Transit visas are not required provided passengers hold onward tickets and do not leave the airport. The fee for a visa depends on the applicant's nationality. For UK nationals the fees are as follows: *Single-entry*: £30 (for three months); £48 (for six months). *Multiple-entry*: £66 (for six months); £75 (for one year); £96 (for two years); £135 (for five years).
Validity: Depends on nationality and purpose of visit. Validity of the visa is usually three months from date of issue. Enquire at Consulate (or Consular section at Embassy) for further details.
Application to: Consulate (or Consular section at Embassy); see *Contact Addresses* section for details.
Note: Nationals of Andorra, Australia, Brunei, Canada, China (PR), nationals of the EU (except nationals of Cyprus, Czech Republic, Estonia, Hungary, Ireland, Latvia, Lithuania, Malta, Poland, Slovak Republic and Slovenia), Hong Kong (SAR), Iceland, Japan, Korea (Rep), Liechtenstein, Malaysia, Monaco, New Zealand, Norway, San Marino, Singapore, Switzerland, USA and the Vatican City can now obtain visas for entry into Kuwait upon arrival at the port of entry.
Application requirements: (a) Valid passport. (b) One completed application form. (c) One passport-size photo. (d) Fax or other confirmation of invitation from sponsor/contact in Kuwait. This should be faxed directly to the Embassy; see *Contact Addresses* section for fax numbers (not required for visa on arrival - see above). (e) Covering letter from employer in home country detailing evidence of position and status within company, purpose of visit, length of stay. (f) Registered, self-addressed envelope if applying by post. (g) Fee.
Working days required: 10.
Temporary residence: Enquire at Embassy. Note that UK nationals who wish to take up employment will eventually require a *Residence Permit*. This must be obtained before arrival in Kuwait as it is not possible to transfer status from 'visitor' to 'temporary resident' without first leaving Kuwait.

Money

Currency: Kuwait Dinar (KD) = 1000 fils. Notes are in denominations of KD20, 10, 5 and 1, and 500 and 250 fils. Coins are in denominations of 100, 50, 20, 10, 5 and 1 fils.
Credit & debit cards: American Express, Diners Club, MasterCard and Visa are accepted. Check with your credit or debit card company for details of merchant acceptability and other services which may be available.
Travellers cheques: Widely accepted. To avoid additional exchange rate charges, travellers are advised to take travellers cheques in US Dollars or Pounds Sterling.
Currency restrictions: The import and export of local and foreign currency is not restricted.
Exchange rate indicators: The following figures are included as a guide to the movements of the Kuwait Dinar against Sterling and the US Dollar:

Date	Feb '04	May '04	Aug '04	Nov '04
£1.00 =	0.54	0.53	0.54	0.55
$1.00 =	0.30	0.30	0.29	0.29

Banking hours: Sun-Thurs 0800-1200.

Duty Free

The following goods may be imported into Kuwait without incurring customs duty:
500 cigarettes or 2lb of tobacco.
Prohibited items: Alcohol, narcotics, unsealed milk products, unsealed salty fish, unsealed olives and pickles, food prepared abroad, fresh vegetables, shellfish and its products, fresh figs and mineral water. Penalties for attempting to smuggle restricted items are severe.

Public Holidays

2005: Jan 1 New Year's Day. **Jan 21** Eid al-Adha (Feast of the Sacrifice). **Feb 10** Islamic New Year. **Feb 25** National Day. **Feb 26** Liberation Day. **Apr 21** Mouloud (Birth of the Prophet). **Sep 1** Al-Esra Wa Al-Meraj (Ascension of the Prophet). **Nov 3-5** Eid al-Fitr (End of Ramadan).
2006: Jan 1 New Year's Day. **Jan 10** Eid al-Adha (Feast of the Sacrifice). **Jan 31** Islamic New Year. **Feb 25** National Day. **Feb 26** Liberation Day. **Apr 11** Mouloud (Birth of the Prophet). **Aug 22** Al-Esra Wa Al-Meraj (Ascension of the Prophet). **Oct 22-24** Eid al-Fitr (End of Ramadan).
Note: (a) Muslim festivals are timed according to local sightings of various phases of the moon and the dates given above are approximations. During the lunar month of Ramadan that precedes Eid al-Fitr, Muslims fast during the day and feast at night and normal business patterns may be interrupted. Many restaurants are closed during the day and there may be restrictions on smoking and drinking. Some disruption may continue into Eid al-Fitr itself. Eid al-Fitr and Eid al-Adha may last anything from two to 10 days, depending on the region. For more information see the appendix *World of Islam*.
(b) If a holiday falls on a Friday, a day is given in lieu.

Health

	Special Precautions?	Certificate Required?
Yellow Fever	No	No
Cholera	No	No
Typhoid & Polio	1	N/A
Malaria	No	N/A

Note: *Regulations and requirements may be subject to change at short notice, and you are advised to contact your doctor well in advance of your intended date of departure. Any numbers in the chart refer to the footnotes below.*

1: Vaccination against typhoid and poliomyelitis is sometimes advised.
Food & drink: Mains water is normally chlorinated and, whilst relatively safe, may cause mild abdominal upsets. Bottled water is available and is advised for the first few weeks of the stay. Milk is pasteurised and dairy products are safe for consumption. Local meat, poultry, seafood, fruit and vegetables are generally considered safe to eat.
Other risks: *Diarrhoeal diseases* such as *giardiasis*, *dysentery* and *typhoid fever* are common. *Hepatitis A* occurs and *hepatitis B* is endemic in the region. *Cutaneous leishmaniasis* is reported. *Tick-borne relapsing fever* may occur.
Rabies is present. For those at high risk, vaccination before arrival should be considered. If you are bitten, seek medical advice without delay. For more information, consult the *Health* appendix.
Health care: Medical insurance is essential. Both private and government health services are available.

Travel - International

Note: Following the military action in Iraq, there is an increased risk of terrorism in Kuwait. For further advice visitors should contact the relevant local government travel advice department.
AIR: Kuwait's national airline, *Kuwait Airways (KU)* (website: www.kuwait-airways.com), operates daily non-stop flights to Kuwait from London. Other airlines serving Kuwait include *Air France*, *British Airways*, *Emirates*, *Gulf Air*, *KLM*, *Lufthansa*and *United Airlines*.
Approximate flight times: From Kuwait to *London* is seven hours 30 minutes, to *New York* is 15 hours, to *Los Angeles* is 19 hours, to *Singapore* is eight hours 30 minutes and to *Sydney* is 27 hours.
International airports: *Kuwait (KWI)* (website: www.kuwait-airport.com.kw) lies 16km (10 miles) south of Kuwait City (travel time – 20 minutes). Reliable transport to and from the city is available, including a bus (travel time – 30 minutes) departing every 45 minutes (0600-2300), and taxi service costing KWD4. Airport facilities include restaurants, shops, cafe, bank/bureau de change, car hire (*Al Mulla*, *Avis*, *Budget*, *Europcar*, *Hertz*, *National*, *Thrifty* and *Sixt*), conference room and post office.
Departure tax: KD2; transit passengers not leaving the airport transit area and children under 12 are exempt.
SEA: More than 30 shipping lines call regularly at Kuwait City, Kuwait's major port. Most traffic is commercial.
ROAD: All road links with Iraq, and therefore through to the Syrian Arab Republic and Jordan, are advised against due to political instability within Iraq. It is also wise to check with the embassy before considering travelling to Lebanon. There are **bus** services between Kuwait City and Cairo (Egypt), via Aqaba in Jordan and Nuweiba in Egypt. Buses also operate to Damman in Saudi Arabia. The main land route into Saudi Arabia is Beirut–Damascus–Amman–Kuwait, which follows the Trans-Arabian Pipeline (TAP line) through Saudi Arabia.

Travel - Internal

SEA: *Dhows* and other small craft may be chartered for trips to the offshore islands.
ROAD: There is a good road network between cities. Driving is on the right. **Bus**: *Kuwait Transport Company* operates a nationwide service which is both reliable and inexpensive.
Taxi: These are recognisable by red licence plates and may be hired by the day, in which case fares should be agreed beforehand. Share-taxis are also available. Taxis can be phoned and this service is popular and reliable. A standard rate is applicable in most taxis, but those at hotel ranks are more expensive. Tipping is not expected. **Car hire**: Self-drive is available. If you produce an International Driving Permit, the rental company will, within five days, grant a temporary local licence valid for one month.
Documentation: International Driving Permit required. A temporary driving licence is available from local authorities on presentation of a valid British or Northern Ireland driving licence. Insurance must be arranged with the Gulf Insurance Company or the Kuwait Insurance Company.

Accommodation

Hotels range from deluxe to first and second class.
Many top hotels in Kuwait City feature sport complexes, restaurants and shopping malls. Serviced apartments, some with hotel-style room service, are also available. Prices are generally high. All rates are subject to a 15 per cent service charge.

Resorts & Excursions

KUWAIT CITY: Kuwait City is a bustling metropolis of high-rise office buildings, luxury hotels, wide boulevards and well-tended parks and gardens. Its seaport is used by oil tankers, cargo ships and many pleasure craft. Its most dominant landmark is **Kuwait Towers**, and its oldest is **Seif Palace**, built in 1896, the interior of which features original Islamic mosaic tilework, though these suffered badly during the Iraqi occupation. The **Kuwait National Museum** was also stripped of many artefacts – part of it has been renovated and is now open to the public. The **Sadu House**, near the museum, is made of coral and gypsum and is used as a cultural museum to protect the arts and crafts of Bedouin society. It is an ideal place to purchase Bedouin goods. The huge **Grand Mosque** in the centre is also worth visiting.
ELSEWHERE: A port with many old *dhows*, **Failakai Island** can be reached by regular ferry services. There are also some Bronze Age and Greek archaeological sites well worth viewing, including the island's Greek temple. Traditional-style *boums* and *sambuks* (boats) are still built in **Al Jahrah**, although, nowadays, vessels are destined to work as pleasure boats rather than pearl fishing or trading vessels.
Mina Al Ahmadi, lying 12 miles south of Kuwait City, is an oil port with immense jetties for supertanker traffic. The **Oil Display Centre** pays homage to the work of the Kuwait Oil Company.

Sport & Activities

Swimming, **sailing** and **scuba diving** are available.
Powerboating is a Kuwaiti passion. **Horse-riding** clubs flourish in the winter. There are numerous **tennis** courts in the capital, usually owned by hotels. **Football** is popular.

Social Profile

FOOD & DRINK: There is a good choice of restaurants serving a wide choice of international and Arab cuisine, prices are reasonable. Typical middle-eastern food includes *hummus*, *falafel* and *foul*. Everything is eaten with *aish* (Arabic flat bread).
Alcohol is totally prohibited in Kuwait.
NIGHTLIFE: Several cinemas in Kuwait City show recent films. Two theatres often put on very good amateur productions.
SHOPPING: Numerous large shopping complexes have recently been built. The *Souk Sharp Complex* is an extensive centre near the waterfront in Kuwait City, and contains Western chain stores as well as Kuwaiti shops. Other centres include the *Al-Fanar Shopping Centre* and the *Leila Gallery*. Boutiques and small general stores in Kuwait City sell all the basic and most luxury goods.
Shopping hours: Sat-Thurs 0830-1230 and 1630-2100, Fri 1530-2030.
SPECIAL EVENTS: Major events celebrated are Muslim holidays, namely *Ramadan*, *Eid al-Fitr* (End of Ramadan), *Rabi-ol-Avval* (birthday of Mohammad), and *Ghadir-é Khom* (commemoration of the day the Prophet Mohammad appointed his successor).
SOCIAL CONVENTIONS: Handshaking is the customary form of greeting. It is quite likely that a visitor will be invited to a Kuwaiti's home, but entertaining is also conducted in hotels and restaurants. A small gift promoting the company, or representing your own country, is always welcome. The visitor will notice that most Kuwaitis wear the national dress of long white *dishdashes* and white headcloths, and that many women wear *yashmaks*. It is important for women to dress modestly according to Islamic law. Men do not usually wear shorts in public and should not go shirtless. All other Islamic rules and customs must be respected. Convicted users of narcotics can expect to receive a sentence of up to five years' imprisonment, plus a heavy fine. 'No Smoking' signs are posted in many shops. It is greatly appreciated if visitors learn at least a few words of Arabic. **Tipping**: A service charge of 15 per cent is usually added to bills in hotels, restaurants and clubs. Otherwise 10 per cent is acceptable.

Business Profile

ECONOMY: Kuwait's considerable wealth is the result of the country's vast oil deposits, estimated at 100 billion barrels (9 per cent of the world's total known reserves). With production of over two million barrels daily, oil now accounts for about half of total output, 90 per cent of export income and three-quarters of government revenue. The economy has long since recovered from the extensive and systematic looting conducted by Iraqi troops during the occupation of 1990-1. This was estimated to have cost Kuwait US$170 billion, and the extent of the reconstruction was reflected in the fact that Kuwait was obliged to liquidate a large proportion of its overseas investment portfolio. These holdings, which are administered by the Kuwait Investment Office, are used partly to meet the country's running costs (free education and social services) and partly lodged in the Fund for Future Generations. During the 1990s, Kuwait, not surprisingly, invested large sums in building up a military apparatus.
There has been some diversification of the economy, promoted and funded by the government. Heavy industrial projects have been eschewed in favour of light manufacturing industries such as paper and cement production. There is a small fishing industry and some agriculture. The government has tabled a privatisation programme both as a means to raise revenue and as an instrument of economic policy. A free-trade zone has also been established. Kuwait is a member of OPEC and of the Gulf Co-operation Council. The re-emergence of OPEC as a major influence appears to have triggered some disputes inside the Kuwaiti government over oil production and pricing policy. Japan, The Netherlands and Italy are the main markets for Kuwaiti oil. The principal exporters to Kuwait are Japan, the USA, Germany and the UK.
BUSINESS: Men are expected to wear suits and ties for business and formal social occasions. English is widely spoken in business circles, although a few words or phrases of Arabic are always well received. Visiting cards are widely used. Some of the bigger hotels have translation and bilingual secretarial services. **Government office hours**: Sat-Wed 0700-1300 (winter); 0730-1330 (summer). **Office hours**: Sat-Wed 0730-1230 and 1600-1900.
COMMERCIAL INFORMATION: The following organisation can offer advice: Kuwait Chamber of Commerce and Industry, PO Box 775, Safat 13008, Kuwait City (tel: 805 580 ext. 555; fax: 246 0693; e-mail: kcci@kcci.org.kw; website: www.kcci.org.kw).

Climate

Kuwait shares European weather patterns but is hotter and drier. Summers (April to October) are hot and humid with very little rain. Winters (November to March) are cool with limited rain. Springs are cool and pleasant.

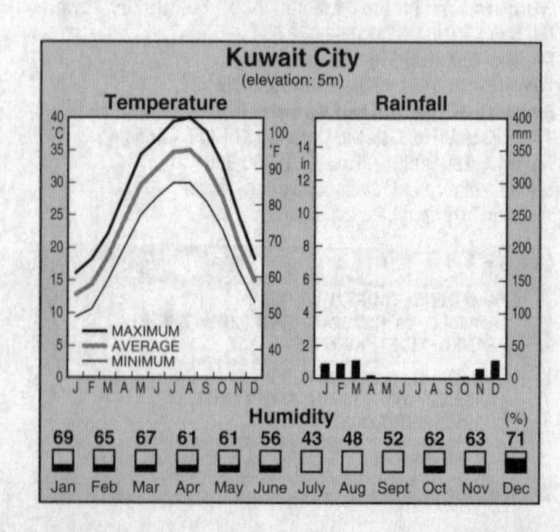

Kyrgyzstan

LATEST TRAVEL ADVICE CONTACTS

British Foreign and Commonwealth Office
Tel: (0870) 606 0290 Website: www.fco.gov.uk

US Department of State
Website: http://travel.state.gov/travel

Canadian Department of Foreign Affairs and Int'l Trade
Tel: (1 800) 267 8376 Website: www.dfait-maeci.gc.ca

Location: Central Asia, north of Afghanistan and Tajikistan.

Country dialling code: 996.

Ministry of Tourism
ul Togolok Moldo 17, 720033 Bishkek, Kyrgyzstan
Tel: (312) 220 657. Fax: (312) 212 845.
E-mail: gatiskr@bishkek.gov.kr

Embassy of the Kyrgyz Republic
Ascot House, 119 Crawford Street, London W1U 6BJ, UK
Tel: (020) 7935 1462. Fax: (020) 7935 7449.
E-mail: mail@kyrgyz-embassy.org.uk
Website: www.kyrgyz-embassy.org.uk
Opening hours: Mon-Fri 0900-1800; 0930-1230 (visa section).

Regent Holidays (UK) Limited
15 John Street, Bristol BS1 2HR, UK
Tel: (0117) 921 1711. Fax: (0117) 925 4866.
E-mail: regent@regent-holidays.co.uk
Website: www.regent-holidays.co.uk

British Honorary Consul
Street address: Osoo Fatboys, 104 Prospekt Chui, Bishkek, Kyrgyzstan
Postal address: PO Box 153, 93 Toktogula Street, Bishkek 720040, Kyrgyzstan
Tel: (312) 680 815 *or* 584 245 (mobile). Fax: (312) 287 360.
E-mail: fatboys@ekat.kg

Embassy of the Kyrgyz Republic
1732 Wisconsin Avenue, NW, Washington, DC 20007, USA
Tel: (202) 338 5141. Fax: (202) 338 5139.
E-mail: embassy@kyrgyzstan.org
Website: www.kyrgyzstan.org
Also deals with enquiries from Canada.

Embassy of the United States of America
Prospekt Mira 171, 720016 Bishkek, Kyrgyzstan
Tel: (312) 551 241. Fax: (312) 551 264.
Website: http://bishkek.usembassy.gov

The Canadian Embassy in Almaty deals with enquiries relating to Kyrgyzstan (see *Kazakhstan* section).

General Information

AREA: 199,900 sq km (77,182 sq miles).
POPULATION: 5,067,000 (UN estimate 2002).
POPULATION DENSITY: 25.3 per sq km.
CAPITAL: Bishkek (called Frunze from 1926 to 1991).
Population: 736,000 (UN estimate 2001).
GEOGRAPHY: Kyrgyzstan is bordered by Kazakhstan, Uzbekistan, Tajikistan and China. The majestic Tian Shan (Heavenly Mountains) range occupies the greater part of the area. Its highest peak is Pik Pobedy at 7439m (24,406ft).

TIMATIC CODES

Health	AMADEUS: **TI-DFT/FRU/HE** GALILEO/WORLDSPAN: **TI-DFT/FRU/HE** SABRE: **TIDFT/FRU/HE**
Visa	AMADEUS: **TI-DFT/FRU/VI** GALILEO/WORLDSPAN: **TI-DFT/FRU/VI** SABRE: **TIDFT/FRU/VI**

To access TIMATIC country information on Health and Visa regulations through the Computer Reservations System (CRS), type in the appropriate command line listed above.

GOVERNMENT: Republic. Gained independence from the Soviet Union in 1991. **Head of State and Government**: President Askar Akajev since 1990. **Prime Minister**: Nikolaj Tanajev since May 2002.
LANGUAGE: The official language is Kyrgyz, a Turkic language closely related to Uzbek, Kazakh, Turkmen and Turkish. Any attempt by a foreigner to speak Kyrgyz will be greatly appreciated. In deference to the large Russian population of Kyrgyzstan, Russian is also protected under law. In 1993, the Government undertook to replace the Russian Cyrillic Alphabet with the Turkish version of the Roman alphabet. Meanwhile, most people can speak Russian, and do so, especially in the north. English is widely spoken by those involved in tourism. Uzbek, Kazakh, Tajik and various other regional languages and dialects are also spoken.
RELIGION: The major religion is Islam with the majority of Kyrgyz being Sunni Muslim with Christian and Russian Orthodox minorities.
TIME: GMT + 5 (GMT + 6 from second Sunday in April to Saturday before last Sunday in September).
ELECTRICITY: 220 volts AC, 50Hz. Round two-pin continental plugs are standard.
COMMUNICATIONS: Telephone: Country code: 996 (312 for Bishkek). International calls should be made from a telephone office which will usually be found attached to a post office; they can also be made from some hotels by asking at reception. All international calls from Kyrgyzstan have to go through the operator. Local calls (within the city) are free of charge if made from private telephones; hotels sometimes levy a small charge. Direct-dial calls within the CIS are obtained by dialling 8 and waiting for another dial tone and then dialling the city code followed by the number. **Mobile telephone:** GSM 900 network in use. The main provider is *Bitel Ltd* (website: www.bitel.kg). **Fax:** Services are available in main hotels for residents only. **Telegram:** Services are available from post offices in large towns. **Internet:** ISPs include *Asiainfo* (website: www.asiainfo.kg), *ElCat* (website: www.elcat.kg) and *Intra Net* (website: www.intranet.kg). There are two Internet cafes on ul Sovetskaya in Bishkek, amongst others. **Post:** Letters to and from Western Europe and the USA can take anything between two weeks and two months. Stamped envelopes can be bought from post offices. Mail to recipients within Kyrgyzstan should be addressed in the following order: country, postcode, city, street, house number and, lastly, the person's name. Visitors can also use post offices located within some major hotels. Post office hours: Mon-Fri 0900-1800. **Press:** The *Bishkek Observer*, *Kyrgyzstan Chronicle*, *Times of Central Asia* and *Zaman Kyrgyzstan* are published weekly in English. The main dailies are published in Bishkek and include *Kyrgyz Tuusu* (both in Kyrgyz), and *Delo No*, *Slovo Kyrgyzstana* and *Vechernii Bishkek* (in Russian).
Radio: BBC World Service (website: www.bbc.co.uk/worldservice) and Voice of America (website: www.voa.gov) can be received. From time to time the frequencies change and the most up-to-date can be found online.

Passport/Visa

	Passport Required?	Visa Required?	Return Ticket Required?
Full British	Yes	Yes	No
Australian	Yes	Yes	No
Canadian	Yes	Yes	No
USA	Yes	Yes	No
Other EU	Yes	Yes/1	No
Japanese	Yes	No	No

Note: *Regulations and requirements may be subject to change at short notice, and you are advised to contact the appropriate diplomatic or consular authority before finalising travel arrangements. Details of these may be found at the head of this country's entry. Any numbers in the chart refer to the footnotes below.*

PASSPORTS: Passport required by all.
VISAS: Required by all except the following:
(a) nationals of CIS countries (except Turkmenistan and Uzbekistan who *do* require a visa), provided residing in country of nationality;
(b) nationals of Malaysia and Turkey for stays of up to 30 days;
(c) **1.** nationals of Albania, Bosnia & Herzegovina, Bulgaria, Croatia, Cuba, Czech Republic, Japan, Korea (Dem Rep), Macedonia, Mongolia, Poland, Romania, Serbia & Montenegro, Slovak Republic, Slovenia and Vietnam travelling as tourists (provided they are permanent residents of their country);
(d) transit passengers continuing their journey by the same or first connecting aircraft within 48 hours, provided holding onward or return documentation and not leaving the airport
Note: Nationals of the following countries may apply for a visa valid for one month or less without providing a letter of support from Kyrgyzstan: nationals of countries referred to in the chart above (except countries who do not require a visa, as listed above, and nationals of Estonia, Hungary, Latvia and Lithuania, who do need to provide an invitation letter), and nationals of Iceland, Israel, Korea (Rep), Liechtenstein, Monaco, New Zealand and Norway.
Types of visa and cost: *Business*, *Private Trip*, *Tourist* and *Transit*. *Single-entry*: £40 (one month). *Multiple-entry*: £100 (six months); £125 (one year). *Transit*: £20 (one week). *Express*: double the price. Multiple-entry visas can only be issued with authorisation from the Ministry of Foreign Affairs of the Kyrgyz Republic.
Validity: Up to three months from date of issue. Multiple-entry visas are valid for six months.
Application to: Consulate (or Consular section at Embassy); see *Contact Addresses* section. Those resident in the UK can also obtain visas from Russia House (for address, see *Russian Federation* section).
Application requirements: (a) Completed application form. (b) One passport-size photo. (c) Valid passport (must be an original, not a photocopy) with one blank page to affix visa. (d) Stamped self-addressed, registered envelope. (e) Fee, payable by cash, cheque or bank transfer. (f) Letter of support from Kyrgyzstan, authorised by the Ministry of Foreign Affairs (not required by certain nationals - see note above).
Working days required: Five; one for Express visa applications.
Temporary residence: Enquire at Embassy for details (see *Contact Addresses* section).

Money

Currency: Som (KS) = 100 Tyin. Notes are in denominations of KS1000, 500, 200, 100, 50, 20, 10, 5 and 1, and 50, 10 and 1 Tyin.
Currency exchange: Foreign currencies can be exchanged at commercial banks and at authorised bureaux de change. The US Dollar is the easiest currency to exchange.
Credit & debit cards: Credit cards are accepted in some of the larger hotels in Bishkek and can also be used at banks to withdraw cash from the counter. Check with your credit or debit card company for merchant acceptability and other services which may be available.
Travellers cheques: There is limited acceptance of these, but some banks in Bishkek accept travellers cheques, with US Dollars probably the best option; commission charges are high. Cash is recommended.
Currency restrictions: There are no restrictions on the import or export of foreign currency, provided declared on arrival. The import and export of local currency is unlimited for Kyrgyz residents only.
Exchange rate indicators: The following figures are included as a guide to the movements of the Som against Sterling and the US Dollar.

Date	Feb '04	May '04	Aug '04	Nov '04
£1.00=	76.06	78.30	76.84	78.45
$1.00=	41.78	43.84	41.71	41.43

Banking hours: Usually Mon-Fri 0930-1730.

Duty Free

The following goods may be imported into Kyrgyzstan by travellers of 16 years or over without incurring customs duty: *1000 cigarettes or 1000g of tobacco products; 1.5l of alcoholic beverages and 2l of wine; a reasonable quantity of perfume for personal use.*
Note: On entering the country, tourists must complete a customs declaration form which must be retained until departure, and then handed over on the international flight leaving any CIS country. This allows the import of articles intended for personal use, including currency and valuables which must be registered on the declaration form. Customs inspection can be long and detailed.
Prohibited imports: Military weapons and ammunition (subject to special permit); narcotics; fruit and vegetables; live animals (subject to special permit); photographs and printed matter directed against Kyrgyzstan; anything owned by a third party that is to be carried in for that third party. If there are any queries regarding items that may be imported, an information sheet is available on request from Intourist.
Prohibited exports: As prohibited imports, as well as precious metals and articles, works of art and antiques (unless permission has been granted by the Ministry of Culture), furs.

Public Holidays

2005: Jan 1 New Year's Day. **Jan 7** Russian Orthodox Christmas. **Jan 21** Kurban Ait (Feast of the Sacrifice). **Mar 8** International Women's Day. **Mar 21** Nooruz (Kyrgyz New Year). **May 1** Labour Day. **May 5** Constitution Day. **May 9** Victory Day. **Aug 31** Independence Day. **Nov 3-5** Eid al-Fitr (End of Ramadan).

2006: Jan 1 New Year's Day. **Jan 7** Russian Orthodox Christmas. **Jan 10** Kurban Ait (Feast of the Sacrifice). **Mar 8** International Women's Day. **Mar 21** Nooruz (Kyrgyz New Year). **May 1** Labour Day. **May 5** Constitution Day. **May 9** Victory Day. **Aug 31** Independence Day. **Oct 22-24** Eid al-Fitr (End of Ramadan).

Health

	Special Precautions?	Certificate Required?
Yellow Fever	No	No
Cholera	Yes	1
Typhoid & Polio	2	N/A
Malaria	3	N/A

Note: *Regulations and requirements may be subject to change at short notice, and you are advised to contact your doctor well in advance of your intended date of departure. Any numbers in the chart refer to the footnotes below.*

1: Following WHO guidelines issued in 1973, a cholera vaccination certificate is not a condition of entry to Kyrgyzstan. However, cholera is common in this country and precautions are essential. Up-to-date advice should be sought before deciding whether these precautions should include vaccination, as medical opinion is divided over its effectiveness. For more information, see the *Health* appendix.

2: Typhoid is common in rural areas. Polio eradication is underway, rapidly reducing the risk of infection with the disease.

3: A Malaria risk, exclusively in the *vivax* form, exists from June to September in some southern and western parts of the country - mainly in Batken, Osh amd Zhele-Abudskaya provinces, in areas bordering Tajikistan and Uzbekistan.

Food & drink: The water has been tested by the US-based Center for Diseases Control and found to be generally bacteria-free; however, it does have a high metal content. Milk is pasteurised and dairy products are safe for consumption. Only eat well-cooked meat and fish, preferably served hot. Pork, salad and mayonnaise may carry increased risk. Vegetables should be cooked and fruit peeled. Owing to the difficulty of obtaining a balanced diet in some parts of Kyrgyzstan, visitors are recommended to take vitamin supplements.

Other risks: *Diphtheria* outbreaks have been reported in the area. *Hepatitis A* and *E* are common. *Hepatitis B* is endemic. *Rabies* is present. For those at high risk, vaccination before arrival should be considered. If you are bitten, seek medical advice without delay. For more information, consult the *Health* appendix.

Note: HIV testing is required for visits of over one month.

Health care: There is no reciprocal health agreement with the UK. Medical services offered to foreigners, except emergency care, require immediate cash payment and are somewhat limited. There is a severe shortage of basic medical supplies, including disposable needles, anaesthetics and antibiotics, and travellers are advised to bring any necessary medication or equipment. Elderly travellers and those with existing health problems may be at risk owing to inadequate medical facilities. The US Embassy maintains a list of English-speaking physicians in the area. Medical insurance is strongly recommended.

Travel - International

Note: All but essential travel to the south and west of Osh and to the Ferghana Valley region is advised against, due to the history of terrorist activity and armed violence, and to the threat of landmines in the Batken region and along the Kyrgyz-Uzbek border that Kyrgyzstan shares with other countries in Central Asia. However, this should not deter travel since most visits to Kyrgyzstan are trouble-free.

AIR: The national airline is *Kyrgyzstan Airlines (R8)*, which operates direct flights to Bishkek from Germany, India, Russian Federation and Turkey (Istanbul). *British Airways* operates a direct flight from London to Bishkek. *British Mediterranean* (a franchise partner of British Airways) operates services three times a week from London to Bishkek. *Turkish Airlines* also flies to Bishkek from London, with a stopover in Istanbul. In addition, there is a number of direct flights from Europe to Almaty, in neighbouring Kazakhstan. The connection from there to Kyrgyzstan is via frequent bus services to Bishkek (travel time - four hours). Other European airlines flying direct to Almaty include *KLM* (from Amsterdam) and *Lufthansa* (five weekly flights from Frankfurt/M). There are also direct flights to Bishkek from Moscow and St Petersburg (Russian Federation) and from Tashkent (Uzbekistan).

Approximate flight times: From *London* to Bishkek is nine hours. From *London* to Almaty (Kazakhstan) is six hours 30 minutes; from *Istanbul* to Almaty is five hours 30 minutes and from *Frankfurt/M* to Almaty is seven hours.

International airports: *Bishkek Manas Airport (FRU)* is 30km (18 miles) north of Bishkek. There is a minibus shuttle service to the city centre when the airport is open (travel time - 30 minutes). Taxis are available 24 hours. There is also the bus service 153 every 30 minutes (travel time - 45 minutes). Airport facilities include left luggage, crèche, bars, restaurant, chemist, bank and bureau de change.

Departure Tax: US$10.

RAIL: There are rail connections with the Russian Federation (travel time to Moscow is three days) and with other Central Asian Republics. However, tourists are advised that robberies on trains have been reported.

ROAD: The main international road links are with Kazakhstan and there is presently one crossing point into China (PR); visitors should note that the Chinese authorities normally require proof of an invitation by a Chinese tour operator as a condition of entry. There are regular **bus** links from Bishkek to Tashkent (Uzbekistan) (travel time - 10 to 12 hours) and Almaty (Kazakhstan) (travel time - six hours); services leave the long-distance (*zapadni*) bus station in Bishkek. There is also a direct service to Osh from Tashkent (Uzbekistan) via the Fergana Valley, but road conditions are very poor on this route (see also *Uzbekistan* section). Generally, roads can be affected by landslides (especially during spring in the mountain areas), while winter may cause hazardous conditions on a number of roads (especially on mountain passes, some of which may be closed during certain periods); visitors should also note that garage services are very limited.

Travel - Internal

AIR: There are internal connections from Bishkek to Cholpan-Ata, Kara-Kol, Naryn and Osh. Travellers should note that maintenance procedures for aircraft operating internally may not conform to internationally accepted standards. Access to the Central Tien-Shan region is via helicopter, which takes climbers up the Inylchek Valley.

RAIL: There is only one railway line, which runs from Bishkek to Balikchi at the western end of Lake Issyk-Kul. Osh, in the south of the country, can be reached by rail vią Tashkent (Uzbekistan). A new North-South railway is currently planned. Travellers are advised that robberies on trains have been reported.

ROAD: Kyrgyzstan has 28,400km (17,400 miles) of roads. Traffic drives on the right. Visitors should note that roads are poorly maintained and badly signposted. **Bus:** There are regular bus connections to all parts of Kyrgyzstan. Buses are crowded. The FCO currently advises against the use of local buses/minibuses due to their commonly poor maintenance. **Taxi:** Taxis can be found in all major towns. Many are unlicensed, and fares should be agreed in advance. As many of the street names, particularly in the capital, have changed since independence, visitors are advised to ask for both the old and the new names when seeking directions. **Car hire:** Car hire is not available. It is possible to hire cars with drivers for long-distance journeys, but because of the shortage of petrol, it is generally an expensive option. Foreigners are generally expected to pay in US Dollars. **Documentation:** Licences for long-stay residents intending to buy or import a car can be obtained from the Protocol Department of the Foreign Ministry. An International Driving Permit and two photos are required.

URBAN: There are bus and trolleybus services around the capital.

Travel times: The following chart gives approximate travel times from **Bishkek** (in hours and minutes) to other towns in Kyrgyzstan.

	Road
Osh	12.00
Tokmak	1.00
Balikchi	2.30
Kara-Kol	5.30

Accommodation

HOTELS: Accommodation is limited outside the capital and visitors should not expect Western standards of comfort (although hotels are generally clean). Hotels charge considerably higher prices for individual tourists from non-CIS countries. Foreign tour operators booking for their clients are usually offered a preferential rate. Some hotels in more remote areas may still be wary of accepting foreigners travelling independently.

TURBAZAS: These 'tourist bases' are an alternative to hotel accommodation. For a dollar or two in local currency, visitors have access to basic bungalow accommodation and three meals a day. Homestays are also possible throughout the country as are stays in camps made of *yurts* - the traditional Kyrgyz nomadic tents.

SANATORIA: Since the break-up of the Soviet Union, the sanatoria on the shores of Lake Issyk-Kul - originally built by cooperatives and trade unions for fatigued workers - have started to take in tourists, but the atmosphere may not be to everyone's taste.

MOUNTAINEERING CAMPS: Various private companies run a number of camps for mountaineers attempting to climb the many peaks in Kyrgyzstan's mountains. For further details, contact the State Committee for Tourism, Sport and Youth Policy *or* Regent Holidays (see *Contact Addresses* section).

Resorts & Excursions

The main attraction of Kyrgyzstan lies in the breathtaking landscape of mountains, glaciers and lakes; their isolation ensures that they have been almost forgotten by the crowds. The lakes and mountainous terrain provide excellent opportunities for trekking, skiing, climbing, sailing and swimming.

For more ambitious travellers, it is possible to follow the route of the old **Silk Road** to Kashgar in China, crossing the border at the **Torugart Pass**, near Lake Chatyr-Kul. Trekking tours and adventure holidays in this region are offered by a growing number of companies.

BISHKEK: The capital was founded in 1878 on the site of a clay fort built by the Khan of Kokand and destroyed by the

Russians, and sits at the foot of the *Tian Shan* mountain range. A largely Soviet-built city, it has a similar spacious atmosphere to its Kazakh neighbour, Almaty. **Ulitsa Sovietskaya**, the broad tree-lined road between the railway station and the city centre, houses the **Kyrgyz State Opera and Ballet Theatre**, the **Chernyshevsky Public Library** and the **State Art Museum**. Other attractions include the **History Museum** in the Old Square (*Stary Ploshad*), the **Lenin Museum**, the **Zoological Museum** and the **Kyrgyz Drama Theatre**. The Government plans to redevelop the former **General Frunze Museum** on Frunze Street – which commemorated the Kyrgyz-born Russian general who subdued Central Asia for the Bolsheviks – into a celebration of the ethnic diversity that is found in Kyrgyzstan. A section on Jewish culture has already been opened.

EXCURSIONS: Less than one hour's drive from Bishkek, the **Ala-Archa Nature Reserve** offers spectacular scenery for trekking and skiing. A further 50 minutes east from the city, the **Burana Tower** is a 25m- (82ft-) high minaret which dates from the 11th century and is all that remains of the ancient city of **Balasagun**.

LAKE ISSYK-KUL: Still further east lies the jewel in the crown of the republic. Lying 1600m (5249ft) above sea level, the saltwater Lake Issyk-Kul was closed to foreigners during the Soviet era. Both its Kyrgyz name and Chinese name (Ze-Hai) mean warm sea, as it never freezes over, despite the altitude. Surrounded by snow-capped mountains and ringed with sandy beaches, the lake has a pristine and outstanding beauty. On the north shore, the town of **Cholpan-Alta** is a spa town which was a former retreat for the Communist Party elite. The resort of Issyk-kul is now open to anyone, although it is very busy during the summer season and visitors are advised to book in advance. In the **Kungay Ala-Too Mountains** behind it, four trekking routes start, leading eventually to Medeo, outside Almaty (Kazakhstan), four to six days away. For scuba-diving enthusiasts, there is spectacularly clear water and a 12th-century town that lies 2 to 3m (6 to 10ft) below the surface of the lake near **Ulan**, 18km (11 miles) from Balikchi. At the southeast end of the lake is the town of **Kara-Kol**, with its attractive houses and tree-lined streets, and behind it are the **Terskay Ala-Too Mountains**, an unspoilt wilderness populated only by nomadic shepherds, and only then during the summer. There are few roads and little accommodation. Around 16km (10 miles) outside Kara-Kol is the health resort of **Ak-Soo** with hot mineral springs.

OSH: Kyrgyzstan's second city is in the south, on the Uzbek border. Although it is 2500 years old, few traces of its ancient history remain. Since the 10th century, pilgrims have come to visit the **Suleiman Gora**, a hill in the middle of the city where legend has it that the Prophet once prayed. Childless women come here in the hope that they may conceive (the hill is supposed to look like a pregnant woman lying on her back). Other attractions include the **Museum of Local Studies** and the bazaar.

EXCURSIONS: North of Osh is the town of **Uzgen** where there is a mausoleum that is supposed to have contained the body of the Kyrgyz hero Manas. East of Osh is the **Sary-Chelek Nature Reserve**, which includes the stunning **Lake Sary-Chelek**.

THE SILK ROAD

This ancient trading route was used by silk merchants from the second century AD until its decline in the 14th century, and is open in parts to tourists, stretching from northern China through bleak and foreboding desert and mountainous terrain to the ports on either the Caspian Sea or Mediterranean Sea. For further details of the route, see the *Silk Road* in the China section.

The main attraction of the route in Kyrgyzstan is the amazing alpine scenery including the **Kyrgyz Altau** and **Tian Shan** mountain ranges and **Issyk Kul Lake** (the world's second-largest alpine lake). The difficult but exhilarating journey between Bishek and Kashgar (China) via the **Torugart Pass** is a popular trekking route.

Travel along the Silk Road can be quite difficult due to the terrain, harsh climate and lack of developed infrastructure. Visitors to the region are advised to travel with an organised tour company or travel agent.

Sport & Activities

Hiking and trekking: Kyrgyzstan's reputation as a trekking and climbing destination has improved considerably in recent years and a growing number of tour operators now offer walking, mountaineering and heli-skiing tours throughout Kyrgyzstan and the neighbouring republics; these companies can also arrange entry formalities for border crossings into China and other CIS countries where visas may be required. Mountaineering camps are available: the *Ala-Archa camp*, 40km (25 miles) from Bishkek, offers over 160 routes and is the base for attempts to climb the Kyrgyz range (highest point: 4876m/15,997ft). In the south, the *Pamir camp* offers opportunities on the peaks of the *Pamir Mountains*.

Horse-riding: The national sports reflect the importance of the horse in Kyrgyz culture. *Ulak Tartysh* is a team game in which the two mounted teams attempt to deliver the carcass of a goat weighing 30 to 40kg over the opposition's goal line. Players are allowed to wrestle the goat from an opponent, but physical assault is frowned upon. Each game is 15 minutes long. **Aht Chabysh** are horse races held over distances varying between 4 and 50km (2.5 to 31 miles). Competitors under 13 years of age are barred from entering. *Udarysh* is a competition on horseback in which two riders or two teams of riders attempt to wrestle each other, and frequently their mounts, to the ground.

Other: Increasingly, sports such as **football**, **skiing** and **swimming** , are also popular.

Social Profile

FOOD & DRINK: Kyrgyz food shows the effect of its location and history; befitting a nation descended from nomadic herdspeople, mutton is the staple meat, enlivened with Chinese influences. *Shashlyk* (skewered chunks of mutton barbecued over charcoal) and *lipioshka* (round unleavened bread) are often sold on street corners. *Plov*, rice fried with shredded turnip and scraps of mutton, served with bread, is a Central Asian staple. *Laghman* is a noodle soup with mutton and vegetables that was originally imported from Chinese Turkestan. *Beshbarmak* is noodles with shredded, boiled meat in bouillon. Around Lake Issyk-Kul, the noodles are sometimes served with jellied potato starch rather than meat. *Shorpur* is a meat soup with potatoes and other vegetables. *Manty* (steamed noodle sacks of meat and vegetables), *samsa* (samosas) and *chiburekki* (deep-fried dough cakes) are all popular as snacks. The Kyrgyz and the Kazakhs are almost alone among Central Asian people in eating horse meat; only young mares are used and they are fed on the Alpine grasses, which are thought to impart a particularly good flavour. Restaurants in the capital tend to stop serving at 2200.

Black or green tea is the most popular drink. *Koumys* (fermented mares' milk) is mildly alcoholic and can still be found in the countryside; refusing an offer of *koumys* may cause offence. Other local specialities include *dzarma* (fermented barley flour) and *boso* (fermented millet, resembling beer). During the summer, *chai khanas* (open-air tea houses) are popular. Beer, vodka and local brandy are all widely available in restaurants.

NIGHTLIFE: There are performances of both Russian and European operas and ballets in the State Opera House in Bishkek. Local music and theatre has enjoyed a strong revival since independence and excerpts from the *Manas*, the Kyrgyz national epic about the eponymous warrior that runs to some 500,000 lines, play to packed houses. The *Manas* was originally handed down orally, but was written down in the early part of the 19th century.

SHOPPING: In Bishkek, Osh and Al-Medin bazaars are popular for food and handicrafts. There is also a shop in the Art Gallery that sells paintings and traditional Kyrgyz products. Particularly popular are embroidered Kyrgyz felt hats (*kalpak*), felt carpets and chess sets with traditional Kyrgyz figures. **Shopping hours**: Mon-Sat 0900-1700.

SPECIAL EVENTS: Special events in Kyrgyzstan usually reflect Muslim holy days, such as *Ramadan*, *Eid al-Fitr* (End of Ramadan), and *Eid ul-Azha* (Feast of the Sacrifice). The Spring festival of *Navrus* (New Days) is also celebrated. Dates of these events vary according to the lunar calendar.

SOCIAL CONVENTIONS: Tipping: This is becoming more customary, especially in international hotels.

Business Profile

ECONOMY: Like the other central Asian States, the government of Kyrgyzstan inherited a seriously unbalanced and dysfunctional economy from the Soviet Union. It chose a policy of rapid change, including privatisation and a freely floating and convertible currency (the Som, introduced in 1993) which has, by and large, been reasonably successful in ensuring steady economic growth. This was also an important factor in attracting foreign aid and investment, which has done much to bolster the economy.

Despite the relatively small area of fertile land, agriculture remains the largest employer, occupying almost half of the working population and contributing a similar proportion of GDP. Half of the irrigated agricultural land is devoted to livestock, which is the mainstay of the farming sector. Other agricultural products include grain, potatoes, fruit and vegetables, cotton and tobacco. Kyrgyzstan's economic potential lies in its mineral resources: there are known deposits of iron ore, copper, lead, zinc, mercury, antimony, tin, bismuth, vanadium, bauxite, molybdenum, manganese, silver and gold. Oil reserves, provisionally thought to be sufficient to cover domestic needs for 20 years, were located in 2001. There are also large amounts of stones such as marble, granite and limestone.

The industrial sector was the main casualty of the post-Soviet era and output of metal goods, machinery, electronics and textiles has declined over the last decade. In the service sector, tourism has future potential but, given the dearth of necessary infrastructure, this must be considered a long-term objective. Finance grew quickly during the late 1990s following reform of the banking industry. In November 2000, the privatisation of several major state enterprises (including telecommunications, air transport and energy) was agreed by the government despite serious domestic opposition. Kyrgyzstan belongs to the Central Asian Economic Union (ECO) which aims to promote regional economic co-operation and trade among the former Soviet republics and their neighbours. Kyrgyzstan is a member of the World Bank, the IMF (which in October 2001 agreed a US$100 million loan), the European Bank for Reconstruction and Development (as a 'country of operation') and the Asian Development Bank. The United Nations Development Programme has also been active in Kyrgyzstan.

BUSINESS: Kyrgyzstan is actively seeking overseas partners to modernise its industry and introduce new technology. To this end, it has enacted a number of laws to encourage and protect foreign investors; the law on property extends to all foreign investors the rights granted to Kyrgyz citizens with respect to ownership; foreigners are allowed to purchase businesses and buildings to carry out their activities, but the Government reserves the exclusive right to own land, natural resources, water, agriculture and livestock. There are significant tax holidays for foreign investors. In order to invest in Kyrgyzstan, foreigners must be registered with the Ministry of Economy and Finance. Applications to set up in Kyrgyzstan should be sent in the first instance to the State Committee on Foreign Investments and Economic Assistance (Goskominvest). The Government is particularly interested in encouraging investment in mining, industry (including electronics, light agricultural machinery and pharmaceuticals), petroleum, hydroelectricity and agriculture. **Office hours**: Mon-Fri 0900-1800, Sat 0900-1300 (Mar-Oct). **Government office hours**: Mon-Fri 0900-1700, Sat 0900-1300 (Nov-Feb).

COMMERCIAL INFORMATION: The following organisations can offer advice: State Technical Committee of the Kyrgyz Republic on Foreign Investments and Economic Development, Room 210, ul Erkindik 58A, 720040 Bishkek (tel: (312) 223 292; fax: (312) 661 075); *or* Ministry of Finance, Prospekt Erkindik 58, 720040 Bishkek (tel: (312) 228 922; fax: (312) 227 404); *or* Kyrgyz Chamber of Commerce and Industry, Foreign Affairs Department, Kievskaya 107, 720001 Bishkek (tel: (312) 210 565; fax: (312) 210 575; e-mail: cci-kr@totel.kg; website: www.ihk-kg.de). Information can also be obtained from the US Department of Commerce International Trade Administration, USA Trade Centre, 1401 Constitution Avenue, Washington, DC 20230, USA (tel (202) 482 4655; fax: (202) 482 2293; e-mail: bisnis@ita.doc.gov; website: www.bisnis.doc.gov).

Climate

Kyrgyzstan has a continental climate with relatively little rainfall. It averages 247 sunny days a year. In the summer, in the mountains, the mornings are generally fine and the afternoons hazy with occasional rain. In the lowlands, the temperature ranges between -4° and -6°C (21-24°F) in January to 16 and 24°C (61-75°F) in July. In the highlands, the temperatures range from -14° and -20°C (6.8° and -4°F in January to 8-12°C (46-54°F) in July. There are heavy snowfalls during winter.

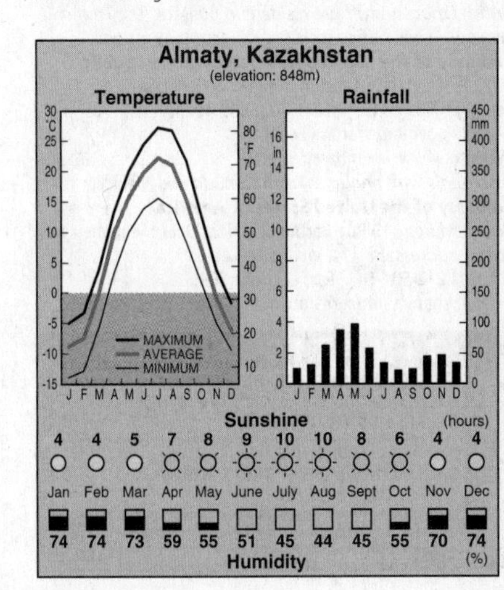

Laos

LATEST TRAVEL ADVICE CONTACTS

British Foreign and Commonwealth Office
Tel: (0870) 606 0290 Website: www.fco.gov.uk

US Department of State
Website: http://travel.state.gov/travel

Canadian Department of Foreign Affairs and Int'l Trade
Tel: (1 800) 267 8376 Website: www.dfait-maeci.gc.ca

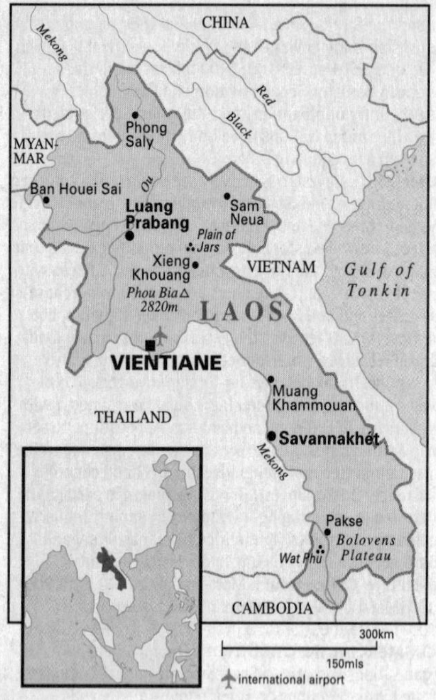

Location: South-East Asia.

Country dialling code: 856.

Lao National Tourism Authority (LNTA)
PO Box 3556, Lane Xang Avenue, Hadsady, Chanthaboury, Vientiane, Laos
Tel: (21) 222 971. Fax: (21) 212 251.
E-mail: info@visit-mekong.com
Website: www.visit-mekong.com/laos

Embassy of the Lao People's Democratic Republic
74 Avenue Raymond Poincaré, 75116 Paris, France
Tel: (1) 4553 0298. Fax: (1) 4727 5789.
E-mail: ambalaoparis@wanadoo.fr
Website: www.laoparis.com

Adventure World Ltd
Street Address: 179 Progress Drive, Bibra Lake, 6163 Western Australia, Australia
Postal Address: PO Box 1186, Bibra Lake, 6965 WA, Australia
Tel: (8) 5417 9666. Fax: (8) 9417 3132.
E-mail: fun@adventureworld.net.au
Website: www.adventureworld.net.au

British Embassy
PO Box 6626, Vientiane, Laos
Tel: (21) 413 606. Fax: (21) 413 607.
British Embassy staff are resident in Bangkok (see Thailand section). Trade Office staff are resident in Vientiane.

Embassy of the Lao People's Democratic Republic
2222 S Street, NW, Washington, DC 20008, USA
Tel: (202) 332 6416. Fax: (202) 332 4923.
E-mail: laoemb@starpower.net
Website: www.laoembassy.com
Also deals with enquiries from Canada and Mexico.

Embassy of the United States of America
Street address: 19 Rue Bartholonie, That Dam, Vientiane, Laos
Postal address: BP 114, Vientiane, Laos
Tel: (21) 212 581-9. Fax: (21) 212 584.
E-mail: khammanhpx@state.gov
Website: http://usembassy.state.gov/laos

The Canadian Embassy in Bangkok deals with enquiries relating to Laos (see *Thailand* section).

TIMATIC CODES

Health	AMADEUS: **TI-DFT/VTE/HE** GALILEO/WORLDSPAN: **TI-DFT/VTE/HE** SABRE: **TIDFT/VTE/HE**
Visa	AMADEUS: **TI-DFT/VTE/VI** GALILEO/WORLDSPAN: **TI-DFT/VTE/VI** SABRE: **TIDFT/VTE/VI**

To access TIMATIC country information on Health and Visa regulations through the Computer Reservations System (CRS), type in the appropriate command line listed above.

General Information

AREA: 236,800 sq km (91,400 sq miles).
POPULATION: 5,529,000 (2002).
POPULATION DENSITY: 23.3 per sq km (2002).
CAPITAL: Vientiane. **Population:** 663,000 (UN estimate 2001).
GEOGRAPHY: Laos is a landlocked country bordered to the north by China, to the east by Vietnam, to the south by Cambodia, and to the west by Thailand and Myanmar. Apart from the Mekong River plains, along the border of Thailand the country is mountainous, particularly in the north, and in places is densely forested.
GOVERNMENT: People's Republic since 1975. Gained independence from France in 1953. **Head of State:** Khamtai Siphandon since 1998. **Head of Government:** Prime Minister Boungnang Vorachith since 2001.
LANGUAGE: The official language is Lao, however, many tribal languages are also spoken. French, Vietnamese and some English are also spoken.
RELIGION: The Laos-Lum (Valley Laos) people follow the *Hinayana* (Theravada) form of Buddhism. The religions of the Laos-Theung (Laos of the mountain tops) range from traditional Confucianism to animism and Christianity.
TIME: GMT + 7.
ELECTRICITY: 230 volts AC, 50Hz.
COMMUNICATIONS: Telephone: Restricted IDD available. Country code: 856. Outgoing international code: 00. **Mobile telephone:** GSM 900 network operator is Lao Telecommunications (website: www.laotel.com). Coverage is sporadic and mainly, though not exclusively, situated around Vientiane. GSM 900/1800 network is available through Millicom Lao Co Ltd. **Fax:** Facilities may be available in large hotels in urban areas. **Internet:** Internet cafes are located in the major towns. **Press:** English-language newspapers in Laos include the *Vientiane Times*.
Radio: BBC World Service (website: www.bbc.co.uk/worldservice) and Voice of America (website: www.voa.gov) can be received. From time to time the frequencies change and the most up-to-date can be found online.

Passport/Visa

	Passport Required?	Visa Required?	Return Ticket Required?
Full British	Yes	Yes	Yes
Australian	Yes	Yes	Yes
Canadian	Yes	Yes	Yes
USA	Yes	Yes	Yes
Other EU	Yes	Yes	Yes
Japanese	Yes	Yes	Yes

Note: *Regulations and requirements may be subject to change at short notice, and you are advised to contact the appropriate diplomatic or consular authority before finalising travel arrangements. Details of these may be found at the head of this country's entry. Any numbers in the chart refer to the footnotes below.*

PASSPORTS: Passport with at least six months remaining validity required by all.
VISAS: Required by all.
Types of visa and cost: *Tourist, Business*: US$50 (including service and document fees). Families may only be charged US$50 per family if all living at the same address, and same surname is indicated on passports.
Validity: Validity starts from day of entry into Laos. *Tourist/Business*: 30 days (can be extended in Vientiane for 30 days twice). Visas must be used within three months of being issued.
Application to: Consulate (or Consular section at Embassy) or an officially recognised tour operator. A visa valid for Laos can also be obtained from travel agencies in Bangkok (Thailand) or on arrival (see above). Visas are issued on arrival at 14 international checkpoints throughout Laos, including Luang Prabang Airport, Pakse Airport and (Wattay) Vientiane International Airport for stays of 15 days and costs US$30. For further details, contact the nearest Embassy.
Application requirements: (a) One passport-size photo. (b) One signed and completed application form. (c) Valid passport. (d) Fee payable by cash or cheque. (e) Postal applications should include an additional US$5 (inside France) or US$10 (international), to cover postage. *Business*: (a)-(e) and, (f) Letter from sponsor in Laos.
Working days required: Three.
Temporary residence: Enquire at nearest Embassy or Consulate. For extension of visa, consult the Immigration Office (tel: (21) 512 012); neglecting to do so will result in a fine of US$10 per day until leaving the country.

Money

Currency: Lao Kip (Kip) = 100 cents. Notes are in denominations of Kip5000, 2000, 1000, 500 and 100.
Currency exchange: Thai Baht and US Dollars are the easiest currencies to exchange. They are also widely accepted in shops, markets and hotels in Vientiane and Luang Prabang.
Credit & debit cards: Major credit cards are accepted in the more upmarket hotels and restaurants. Check with your credit or debit card company for details of merchant acceptability and other services which may be available.
Travellers cheques: Limited acceptance. To avoid additional exchange rate charges, travellers are advised to take travellers cheques in US Dollars or Thai Baht.
Currency restrictions: The import and export of local currency is prohibited. There are no restrictions on the import or export of foreign currency, but amounts greater than US$2000 must be declared.
Exchange rate indicators: The following figures are included as a guide to the movements of the Lao Kip against Sterling and the US Dollar:

Date	Feb '04	May '04	Aug '04	Nov '04
£1.00=	14347.2	14078.0	14447.7	14848.5
$1.00=	7882.00	7882.00	7842.00	7841.00

Banking hours: Mon-Fri 0800-1200 and 1330-1730.

Duty Free

The following goods may be imported into Laos, from countries not bordering Laos, without incurring customs duty:
500 cigarettes or 100 cigars or 500g of tobacco; one bottle of alcoholic beverage and two bottles of wine; personal jewellery up to 500g.

Public Holidays

2005: Jan 1 New Year's Day. **Jan 6** Pathet Lao Day. **Jan 20** Army Day. **Feb 1** Chinese New Year. **Mar 8** International Women's Day. **Mar 22** Day of the People's Party. **Apr 13-15*** Lao New Year (Pi Mai). **Apr 21** Birth of Buddha. **May 1** Labour Day. **Jun 1** Children's Day. **Jun 21** Khao Pansa (Buddhist Fast begins). **Aug 13** Lao Issara (Day of the Free Laos). **Sep 11** Bouk ok Pansa (Buddhist Fast ends). **Oct 12** Day of Liberation. **Dec 2** National Day.
2006: Jan 1 New Year's Day. **Jan 6** Pathet Lao Day. **Jan 20** Army Day. **Jan 29** Chinese New Year. **Mar 8** International Women's Day. **Mar 22** Day of the People's Party. **Apr 13-15*** Lao New Year (Pi Mai). **May 1** Labour Day. **May 13** Birth of Buddha. **Jun/Jul** Khao Pansa (Buddhist Fast begins). **Jun 1** Children's Day. **Aug 13** Lao Issara (Day of the Free Laos). **Sep** Bouk ok Pansa (Buddhist Fast ends). **Oct 12** Day of Liberation. **Dec 2** National Day.
Note: *Variations may occur.

Health

	Special Precautions?	Certificate Required?
Yellow Fever	No	1
Cholera	Yes	2
Typhoid & Polio	3	N/A
Malaria	4	N/A

Note: *Regulations and requirements may be subject to change at short notice, and you are advised to contact your doctor well in advance of your intended date of departure. Any numbers in the chart refer to the footnotes below.*

1: A yellow fever vaccination certificate is required from travellers arriving from infected areas.
2: Following WHO guidelines issued in 1973, a cholera vaccination certificate is not a condition of entry to Laos. However, cholera is a serious risk in this country and precautions are essential. Up-to-date advice should be sought before deciding whether these precautions should include vaccination, as medical opinion is divided over its effectiveness; see the *Health* appendix.
3: Typhoid may occur. Poliovirus transmission has been interrupted, but complete eradication is not yet certain.
4: Malaria risk exists throughout the year in the whole country, except in Vientiane. The malignant *falciparum* form is prevalent and is reported to be highly resistant to chloroquine. The recommended prophylaxis is mefloquine.
Food & drink: All water should be regarded as being potentially contaminated. Water used for drinking, brushing teeth or making ice should have first been boiled or otherwise sterilised. Milk is unpasteurised and should be boiled. Powdered or tinned milk is available and is advised, but make sure that it is reconstituted with pure water. Avoid dairy products that are likely to have been made from unboiled milk. Only eat well-cooked meat and fish, preferably served hot. Pork, salad and mayonnaise

may carry increased risk. Vegetables should be cooked and fruit peeled.
Other risks: *Hepatitis A* and *E* occur; *hepatitis B* is highly endemic. *Dengue fever, diphtheria, tuberculosis* and *Japanese encephalitis* occur. Some vaccinations may be advised. *Liver fluke* (opisthorchiasis) is present; travellers should avoid eating raw or undercooked fish.
Rabies is present. For those at high risk, vaccination before arrival should be considered. If you are bitten, seek medical advice without delay. For more information, consult the *Health* appendix.
Health care: Any treatment must generally be paid for in cash. Health insurance is essential and should include cover for air evacuation.

Travel - International

Note: Penalties for illegal drug importation and use are severe and can include the death penalty. Over the past year there have been explosions in the capital Vientiane and attacks on buses, resulting in injury and death. There are also reports of banditry in rural areas and unexploded ordnance is an ongoing danger. It is illegal not to carry an ID document or a passport, and fines for not having one for presentation on demand can be high. The Lao Government prohibits sexual relationships, including sexual contact between foreign citizens and Lao nationals, except when the two parties have been married in accordance with Lao family law. Penalties for failing to register a relationship range from fines to imprisonment. Most visits to Laos are trouble-free.
AIR: The national airline of Laos is *Lao Aviation (QV)* which serves the international routes from Vientiane to Hanoi and Ho Chi Minh City (Vietnam), Bangkok and Chiang Mai (Thailand), Phnom Penh (Cambodia) and Kunming (China). *Thai Airways International* (website: www.thaiair.com) flies from Bangkok; *Vietnam Airlines* (website: www.vietnamairlines.com) flies from Hanoi.
International airports: *Vientiane (VTE)* (Wattay) is 3km (2 miles) from the city (travel time – 20 minutes). Taxis cost US$5, on average. Facilities include bank/bureaux de change, bars, post office, restaurants and car hire.
Departure tax: US$10; children under two years of age and transit passengers are exempt.
RAIL: There are no railways in Laos, but the Thai system stretches from Bangkok via Nakhon Ratchasima to Nong Khai on the Laos/Thailand border. A ferry and a bridge link the Lao side of the Mekong, 19km (12 miles) east of Vientiane.
ROAD: It is possible to enter Laos from Thailand at Nong Khai over the Friendship Bridge. Other border crossings include Chiang Kong (Thailand)–Houei Xay (Laos) in the north; Mukdahan (Thailand)–Savannakhet (Laos); Chong Mek (between Pakse and Ubon Ratchathani); Nakorn Phanom (Thailand)–Tha Kek (Laos) and Jouay Kone (Thailand)–Xaingnabouri (Laos). It is possible to enter Laos by road from Vietnam either at Lao Bao or at the new border post of Lak Xao near Vinh. Laos can also be entered from China, from Mengla in Yunnan province to Luang Nam Tha. Overland travel to Cambodia and Myanmar is not feasible owing to security risks. Internally, the road link between Vientiane and Luang Prabang to the north has been upgraded.

Travel - Internal

AIR: Domestic air services run from Vientiane to Houayxai, Luang Nmatha, Luang Prabang, Oudomxai, Sam Neua and Sayabouti in the north *and* Pakse and Savanakhet in the south. Private charter flights are also available through *Westcoast Helicopters*.
RIVER: The Mekong and other rivers are a vital part of the country's transport system. The choice is between irregular (and very basic) slow ferries and exciting but noisy and hazardous speedboats. Both services run from Vientiane to Luang Prabang and Luang Prabang to Huay Xai. Ferries often depart early in the mornings and can take several days, whilst speedboats run more regularly and take approximately eight hours for each leg of the journey. Times and prices alter according to demand. Private jet boats can be hired from *Lao River Exploration Services*. For further details, contact Lao National Tourism Authority (see *Contact Addresses* section).
ROAD: Traffic drives on the right. Many of the roads have been paved in recent years, including the main highway from the Thai border at Savannakhet to the Vietnamese border. However, few main roads are suitable for all-weather driving. In the north of the country, there is a road link between Vientiane and Luang Prabang, and from Vientiane to Nam Dong and Tran Ninh. **Bus:** Services link all major towns and cities. Buses can vary from the more traditional type to the converted pick-up truck. **Car hire:** It is not recommended to hire cars in Laos as driving standards are low. However, it is possible to hire cars with a driver through hotels or tourist agencies. *Asia Vehicle Rental Co Ltd* in Vientiane can help visitors with all their rental needs (tel: (21) 217 493 (and fax) *or* 223 867; e-mail: avr@loxinfo.co.th; website: www.avr.laopdr.com). **Documentation:** International Driving Permit recommended, although it is not legally required.
URBAN: There is a mixture of old and metered taxis in Vientiane that can usually be located at Wattay Airport, the Friendship bridge and the Morning market. Taxis can also be hired for approximately US$20 per day. Converted motorcycles, known as *tuk-tuks* or *jumbos*, are available in all major towns and cities and are perfect for shorter journeys around town. Bargaining is expected. Motorcycles and bicycles can be hired for the day in Vientiane and Luang Prabang.
Note: Travel outside Vientiane should be prearranged with a tour company.

Accommodation

HOTELS: There are good hotels and guest houses in Luang Prabang, Vang Vieng and Vientiane, but facilities are sparse elsewhere. Local village hostels are available, but with few amenities. For more details of prices and location, contact a tour company with experience in Laos.
CAMPING: There are no facilities for camping in Laos.
ECOLODGES: Laos is eager to promote ecotourism and visitors can stay in specially constructed ecolodges in either **Laopako**, one hour 30 minutes from Vientiane on the **Nam Mgum river**, or the Boat Landing in **Luang Namtha** province.

Resorts & Excursions

Until 1988 tourists were not allowed access to Laos, but the country has now opened up and it is perfectly feasible to travel all over the country, preferably with a recognised tour company. The number of tourists is expected to continue increasing over the next few years.

VIENTIANE & NORTHERN LAOS

VIENTIANE: One of Asia's most relaxed and quiet capital cities, Vientiane is nestled in fertile plains on the banks of the **Mekong River**. Many buildings reflect the country's past links with Europe, such as the old French colonial houses and the capital's **Victory Monument**, which bears a striking, if somewhat *rococo*, similarity to the *Arc de Triomphe* in Paris. An important national monument is the 16th-century **That Luang** (Royal Stupa) that symbolises Buddhist and Lao union. Other interesting sights include the **Lao Revolutionary Museum**; **Wat Ho Prakeo**, a former royal temple; **Wat Sisaket**, one of the capital's oldest temples; **Wat Xieng Khouang** (Buddha Park), situated 24km (15 miles) south of the city and displaying fascinating Buddhist and Hindu structures.
XIANG KHOUANG: Xiang Khouang province in the northeast of the country is characterised by lush green mountains and Karst limestone. The capital, **Phonsavan**, enjoys a favourable climate being at an altitude of 1200m (3937ft). The unusual **Plain of Jars** is accessible from the city and offers the mysterious sight of hundreds of stone jars, some weighing up to 6 tonnes, scattered over the landscape. The jars are over 2000 years old and legend says that they were used to ferment rice wine in the sixth century in order to celebrate a victory in battle. Some 52km (32 miles) north of Phonsavan, visitors can enjoy bathing in two hot springs: **Bo Noi** and **Bo Yai**.
LUANG PRABANG: This ancient royal city has been a UNESCO World Heritage Site since 1995. Located between the Mekong and **Khan River**, it is the cultural and religious centre of the country, boasting 32 large temple complexes. **Wat Xieng Thong** is one of the most impressive temples, decorated with coloured glass and gold. Testament to the fact that it had been the royal capital until 1975, the royal palace there contains fine artwork and gifts made for former kings. Nearby, in the town centre, visitors can ascend **Mount Phousi** for a panoramic view of the city and surrounding rivers. Also worth seeing is the **Palace Museum** (the former royal palace), easily recognisable by its golden-spired stupa, which houses an impressive collection of artefacts from old rulers of the Kingdom of **Lane Xang**.
Excursions: Close by is **Ban Phanom Village**, famous for its weavings, which offers the opportunity to visit a traditional community and to purchase bargain-priced silk and embroideries. Around 25km (16 miles) along the Mekong river lie the fascinating **Pak Ou Caves**, that can be easily reached by speedboat from Luang Prabang. The two caves, **Tham Ting** and **Tham Phun**, are full of Buddha images that have been left there over hundreds of years by worshippers. Further downriver is the small village of **Ban Xang Hai**, famous for its production of rice whisky. Also worth seeing are the **Kuang Si Waterfalls**, situated 30km (19 miles) from Luang Prabang. Visitors can swim in the lower pools.
LUANG NAMTHA: Situated in the far northwest of Laos, Luang Namtha province is a mountainous region, with areas of tropical rainforest and over 39 ethnic minority groups. An ecotourism project for the region has been proposed by UNESCO. **Muang Xing** is a small town on the river plains which used to be an outpost for an ancient southern Chinese empire. A number of guest houses can offer hiking trips starting from here.

SOUTHERN LAOS

KHAMMOUANE: Khammouane province is accessible from Vientiane by bus. The region is currently being explored for its potential as a place for ecotourism, and its amazing limestone formations, caves, rivers and jungle make it a unique environment. Its capital, **Tha Kek**, is a good place to reach other sights, such as the **Tham Xieng Lap Caves** and the **That Skihotabang**, a stunning stupa built by King Nanthasen in around the 10th century.
SAVANNAKHET: Within easy reach by bus from Khammouane is Savannakhet province. Positioned between Thailand and Vietnam, the province acts as a useful trading junction between the two. Most of the town's architecture is French colonial, including a large Catholic church, although there are several buddhist temple buildings worth seeing, such as **Wat Sainyaphum**. It is possible to walk the **Ho Chi Minh Trail**, a former clandestine route used by the North Vietnamese Army to transport military gear to South Vietnam. The trail was bombed by the USA during the Vietnam war and parts of this devastation can still be viewed. However, the trail *must* be seen with a guide as large parts of the route still contain unexploded bombs.
CHAMPASSAK: Pakse, capital of Champassak province, is easily reached by air from Vientiane. Pakse is home to many ethnic minority groups, much of the **Bolaven Plateau** and the famous, although relatively unvisited, Wat Phu temple. **Wat Phu** was constructed around the fifth century on a mountain top near fresh spring water by the Khmer Hindus, who went on to settle their empire at its former capital – *Ankor Wat* (Cambodia). There are breathtaking views across the Mekong valley from the temple. The complex can be reached by chartered boat along the Mekong river. Other excursions worth making are to the Bolaven Plateau, where visitors can enjoy elephant riding and trekking, and to **Sii Pan Dan** (Four Thousand Islands), where islands are formed during the rainy season on the Mekong river. There is the opportunity to see spectacular waterfalls and the endangered *irriwaddy* dolphins.

Sport & Activities

Wildlife: Laos's pristine landscape hosts a variety of flora and fauna, including rare primates, mammals and birds. Freshwater dolphins can be found in the Mekong river. There is still some unexploded ordnance in the countryside, and official advice should be taken about which areas to avoid.
Trekking: Travellers can head to the hills independently or take part in locally organised guided tours.
Mountain biking: The lack of cars makes cycling a good proposition. Terrain can be difficult, however, and there are not many roads. Visitors are advised to bring their own bicycles, though there are some for hire in the larger towns.

Social Profile

FOOD & DRINK: Rice, especially sticky rice, is the staple food and dishes will be Indo-Chinese in flavour and presentation. Lao food can be found on the stalls in the markets. There are several fairly good French restaurants in Vientiane, catering mainly for the diplomatic community. Baguettes and croissants are normally eaten for breakfast. Rice whisky, *lao lao*, is popular and there are two brands available. The beer is also good.
NIGHTLIFE: There are several discos in Vientiane that tend to have live Lao bands. Most large hotels will have their own nightclubs.
SHOPPING: The markets in Vientiane and Luang Prabang (about 40 minutes by air from Vientiane) are worth visiting. Silk, silver jewellery and handmade shirts are good buys. Although the majority of shops have fixed prices, bartering is still advisable for antiques and other art objects.
Shopping hours: Mon-Fri 0800-1600; Mon-Sat 0900-2100 (private shops).
SPECIAL EVENTS: The majority of festivals are linked to Buddhist holidays. The following is a selection of special events occurring in Laos in 2005:
Jan *Têt* (Chinese New Year). **Feb** *Magha Puja* (anniversary

of a speech held by the Buddha), nationwide. **Apr 13-15** *Pi Mai* (celebrations for the new lunar year), nationwide. **May** *Visakha Bu-saa* (Buddha's birth, enlightenment and death), nationwide; *Bun Bang Fai* (Rocket Festival), nationwide. **Sep** *Haw Khao Padap Din* (Festival of the Dead) nationwide. **Oct 2-21** *Ok Phansa Boat Race Festival*, Vientiane. **Nov** *Pha That Luang Festival* (processions of monks receiving alms and floral votives; fireworks and music), Vientiane.
SOCIAL CONVENTIONS: Religious beliefs should be respected. Lao people should not be touched on the head. Handshaking is not that usual; Lao people greet each other with their palms together and a slight bowing of the head. Take care when discussing politics and related subjects in conversation so as not to cause offence. Shorts or revealing clothes are not always acceptable. **Tipping:** Practised modestly in hotels and restaurants.

Business Profile

ECONOMY: Laos is one of the world's poorest countries, and its predominantly agricultural economy operates almost entirely at subsistence level. Rice, the main crop, is grown in several different varieties; other crops include maize, cassava, pulses, groundnuts, fruits, sugar cane, tobacco and coffee. Though little known outside the region, Laotian coffee is highly rated among connoisseurs and is now the country's single largest export commodity. The country has considerable, though largely untapped, reserves of tin, lead and zinc, as well as iron ore, coal and timber. Industry is mostly concerned with processing raw materials, principally timber and food; textiles and basic consumer goods are also produced. Despite its relative obscurity and secretive nature, a tourism industry has developed which is now Laos' single largest source of income. Development is hampered by chronic shortages of skilled labour and foreign exchange, and the Laotian economy relies heavily on foreign aid (80 per cent of public sector investment is financed by aid) from Japan and Scandinavia, and more recently Thailand, Taiwan and Australia.
Economic reforms began in the early 1990s and included an extensive programme of privatisation. These initially attracted the support of the IMF but the government's failure to meet successive financial targets led to a withdrawal of the Fund's support in 1998. Compounded by the regional financial crisis, the economy was in serious difficulties by the beginning of 1999 with 100 per cent annual inflation, a collapsed currency value and a desperate shortage of foreign and domestic currency. Since then, something of a recovery has taken place: the economy is now growing at around 6 per cent annually while inflation has been cut to a more manageable 25 per cent.
Nonetheless, the country's economic prospects are uncertain. Laos is a member of the Asian Development Bank and the Colombo Plan, which promotes economic and social development in Asia and the Pacific.
BUSINESS: Punctuality is appreciated. Lightweight suits, shirt and tie should be worn. English is not spoken by all officials and a knowledge of French is useful. Business cards should have a Laotian translation on the reverse. Best time to visit is during the dry season, from November to April.
Office hours: Mon-Fri 0800-1200 and 1330-1730.
COMMERCIAL INFORMATION: The following organisations can offer advice: Lao National Chamber of Commerce and Industry, BP 4596, Sihom Road, Ban Haisok, Vientiane (tel/fax: (21) 219 223; e-mail: ccilcciv@laotel.com); *or* Ministry of Finance, Luang Prabang Road, Ban Phonxang, Vientiane (tel: (21) 412 401; fax: (21) 412 415).

Climate

Throughout most of the country, the climate is hot and tropical, with the rainy season between May and October when temperatures are at their highest. The dry season runs from November to April.
Required clothing: Lightweights and rainwear, with a sweater for winter and upland areas.

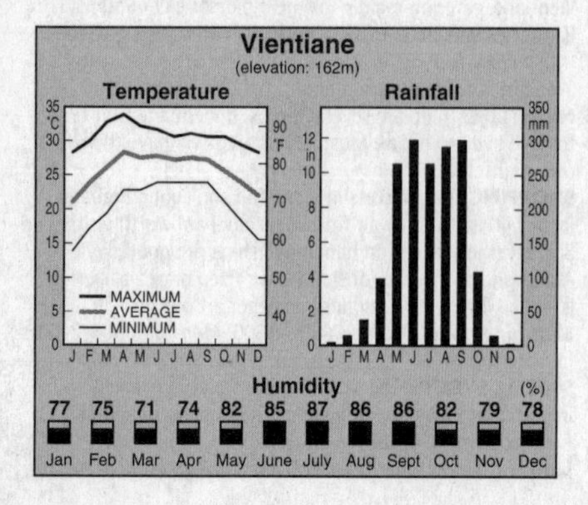

Latvia

LATEST TRAVEL ADVICE CONTACTS

British Foreign and Commonwealth Office
Tel: (0870) 606 0290 Website: www.fco.gov.uk
US Department of State
Website: http://travel.state.gov/travel
Canadian Department of Foreign Affairs and Int'l Trade
Tel: (1 800) 267 8376 Website: www.dfait-maeci.gc.ca

Location: Northern Europe.

Country dialling code: 371.

Latvia Tourism Development Agency
Pils Lauqums 4, LV-1050 Riga, Latvia
Tel: 722 9945. Fax: 708 5393.
E-mail: tda@latviatourism.lv
Website: www.latviatourism.lv
Embassy of Latvia
45 Nottingham Place, London W1U 5LY, UK
Tel: (020) 7312 0040. Fax: (020) 7312 0042.
E-mail: embassy.uk@mfa.gov.lv
Website: www.london.am.gov.lv
Opening hours: Mon-Fri 0830-1700; 1000-1300 (consular section).
British Embassy
J. Alunana Street 5, LV-1010 Riga, Latvia
Tel: 777 4700. Fax: 777 4707.
E-mail: british.embassy@apollo.lv
Website: www.britain.lv
Embassy of Latvia
4325 17th Street, NW, Washington, DC 20011, USA
Tel: (202) 726 8213. Fax: (202) 726 6785.
E-mail: Embassy@Latvia-USA.org *or* visa@Latvia-USA.org (consular section).
Website: www.latvia-usa.org
Embassy of the United States of America
Raina Blvd. 7, LV-1510 Riga, Latvia
Tel: 703 6200. Fax: 782 0047.
E-mail: pas@usembassy.lv (public affairs section) *or* AskConsular@USRiga.lv (consular section) *or* ambassador-riga@state.gov
Website: www.usembassy.lv
Embassy of Latvia
280 Albert Street, Suite 300, Ottawa, Ontario K1P 5G8, Canada
Tel: (613) 238 6014 *or* 238 6868 (consulate).
Fax: (613) 238 7044.
E-mail: embassy.canada@mfa.gov.lv *or* consulate.canada@mfa.gov.lv (consular section).
Website: www.ottawa.mfa.gov.lv
Canadian Embassy
20/22 Baznicas Street, 6th Floor, LV-1010 Riga, Latvia
Tel: 781 3945 *or* 3961 (visa section). Fax: 781 3960.
E-mail: riga@dfait-maeci.gc.ca
Website: www.dfait-maeci.gc.ca/canadaeuropa/baltics

TIMATIC CODES

Health
AMADEUS: **TI-DFT/RIX/HE**
GALILEO/WORLDSPAN: **TI-DFT/RIX/HE**
SABRE: **TIDFT/RIX/HE**

Visa
AMADEUS: **TI-DFT/RIX/VI**
GALILEO/WORLDSPAN: **TI-DFT/RIX/VI**
SABRE: **TIDFT/RIX/VI**

To access TIMATIC country information on Health and Visa regulations through the Computer Reservations System (CRS), type in the appropriate command line listed above.

General Information

AREA: 64,589 sq km (24,938 sq miles).
POPULATION: 2,311,480 (official estimate 2003).
POPULATION DENSITY: 35.8 per sq km.
CAPITAL: Riga. **Population:** 739,232 (2003).
GEOGRAPHY: Latvia is situated on the Baltic coast and borders Estonia in the north, Lithuania in the south, the Russian Federation in the east and Belarus in the southeast. The coastal plain is mostly flat but, inland to the east, the land is hilly with forests and lakes. There are about 12,000 rivers in Latvia, the biggest being the River Daugava. The ports of Riga, Liepaja and Ventspils often freeze over during the winter.
GOVERNMENT: Republic. Gained independence from the Soviet Union in 1991. **Head of State:** President Vaira Vike-Freiberga since 1999. **Head of Government:** Prime Minister Indulis Emsis since 2004.
LANGUAGE: Latvian is the official language. It is an Indo-European, non-Slavic and non-Germanic language and is similar only to Lithuanian. Russian is the mother tongue of over 30 per cent of the population and is understood by most people. English and German may also be understood.
RELIGION: Predominantly Protestant (Lutheran) with 19 per cent of the population being Roman Catholic. There is also a Russian Orthodox minority.
TIME: GMT + 2. (GMT + 3 from last Sunday in March to Saturday before last Sunday in October.)
ELECTRICITY: 220 volts AC, 50Hz. European-style two-pin plugs are in use.
COMMUNICATIONS: Telephone: IDD is available. Country code: 371. Outgoing international code: 00. Directory enquiries: 09. International calls can be made from telephone booths. Payphones are operated by phonecards which can be purchased at kiosks, post offices and in some shops. **Mobile telephone:** GSM 900 and 1800 networks operated by *LMT GSM* (website: www.lmt.lv) and *Tele2* (website: www.tele2.lv). Roaming agreements exist. It is illegal to use a mobile telephone while driving. **Fax:** Facilities are available in the main post office in Riga (for address, see below). **Internet:** Main ISPs include *Apollo*. There are many Internet cafes in Riga and some in other towns. **Telegram:** Services are available from all post offices and the hotel service bureau. For services from public phones, dial 06. **Post:** The main post office is at Brivibas bulvaris 19 (open 24 hours). Postboxes are yellow. Airmail to Western Europe takes five to seven days. Post office hours: Mon-Fri 0900-1800 and Sat 0900-1300. **Press:** There are Latvian and Russian newspapers – *Diena, Neatkariga Rita Avize* and *Vakara Zinas* being the most popular Latvian titles. *The Baltic Times* is an English-language paper published weekly. *Rigas Balss* is a popular daily, available in both Latvian *and* Russian.
Radio: BBC World Service (website: www.bbc.co.uk/worldservice) and Voice of America (website: www.voa.gov) can be received. From time to time the frequencies change and the most up-to-date can be found online.

Passport/Visa

	Passport Required?	Visa Required?	Return Ticket Required?
Full British	Yes	No	No
Australian	Yes	No	No
Canadian	Yes	No	No
USA	Yes	No	No
Other EU	1	No	No
Japanese	Yes	No	No

Note: *Regulations and requirements may be subject to change at short notice, and you are advised to contact the appropriate diplomatic or consular authority before finalising travel arrangements. Details of these may be found at the head of this country's entry. Any numbers in the chart refer to the footnotes below.*

PASSPORTS: Passport valid for three months after expiry date of visa or date of intended departure required by all except:
1. EU nationals, and nationals of Iceland, Liechtenstein and Norway with valid national ID cards.
VISAS: Required by all except the following for a stay of up to 90 days within any six-month period:
(a) nationals of countries mentioned in the table and under passport exemptions above;
(b) nationals of Andorra, Argentina, Bolivia, Brazil, Brunei, Bulgaria, Chile, Costa Rica, Croatia, El Salvador, Guatemala, Honduras, Hong Kong (SAR), Israel, Korea (Rep), Macau (SAR), Malaysia, Mexico, Monaco, New Zealand, Nicaragua, Panama, Paraguay, Romania, San Marino, Singapore, Switzerland, Uruguay, Vatican City and Venezuela;
(c) transit passengers continuing their journey by the same or first connecting aircraft, provided holding onward or return documentation and not leaving the airport, except citizens of: Afghanistan, Bangladesh, Congo (Dem Rep), Eritrea, Ethiopia, Ghana, Iran, Iraq, Nigeria, Pakistan, Somalia

and Sri Lanka who must obtain an airport transit visa issued prior to arrival.
Note: Nationals of countries who require an airport transit visa can cross the transit zone without one provided that they: (a) hold a valid residence permit, entry visa or transit visa for Latvia; (b) hold a valid entry visa or residence permit issued by a member of the EU or Schengen Agreement; (c) hold a valid residence permit issued by Andorra, Canada, Japan, Liechtenstein, Monaco, San Marino, Switzerland, USA and the Vatican City, guaranteeing the right to return; (d) the national is a crew member of an aeroplane or citizen of a country which is a member of the December 7th 1944 International Civil Aviation Convention.
Types of visa and cost: *Short-term*: £23 (single- and double-entry); £40 (multiple-entry).
Note: There is no separate category for a 'Business' visa. If travelling to Latvia for business purposes, please consult the requirements and cost of a tourist visa.
Validity: *Short-term*: from one day to 12 months. *Transit*: Three days.
Application to: Consulate (or Consular section at Embassy); see *Contact Addresses* section.
Application requirements: (a) Passport valid for at least three months beyond expiry of visa, with at least two blank pages. (b) One completed application form. (c) One passport-size photo. (d) Valid travel health insurance policy guaranteeing coverage of costs associated with health care (except for nationals of Estonia, Finland, Sweden and Ukraine). (e) Fee. *Short-term*: (a)-(e) and, (f) An invitation to visit Latvia, approved by the Office of Citizenship and Migration Affairs at the Ministry of Interior in Riga (see below for address). *Transit* and *Airport Transit*: (a)-(e) and, (f) Valid visa for the country to be entered after Latvia, if required.
Note: (a) Additional documents, such as return or onward tickets, confirmed hotel reservation and proof of sufficient funds, may also be requested. (b) All invitations must be registered by the Office of Citizenship and Migration Affairs, Alunāna Str. 1, Riga LV-1050 (tel: 721 9656; fax: 721 9655; e-mail: aad@pmlp.gov.lv *or* pmlp@pmlp.gov.lv; website: www.pmlp.gov.lv).
Working days required: Seven, but in some cases may take up to 30.

Money

Currency: Latvian Lat (Ls) = 100 santims. Notes are in denominations of Ls500, 100, 50, 20, 10 and 5. Coins are in denominations of Ls2 and 1, and 50, 20, 10, 5, 2 and 1 santims.
Currency exchange: Bureaux de change are found all over main towns, including inside shops, hotels, post offices and train stations. These tend to close at 1900. Currency may also be obtained at ATMs in towns and cities. The most convenient currencies to exchange are German DM and the US Dollar.
Credit & debit cards: American Express, Diners Club, Eurocard, JCB, MasterCard and Visa are accepted by most hotels and petrol stations. Some shops in Riga also accept credit cards. Check with your credit or debit card company for details of merchant acceptability and other services which may be available.
Travellers cheques: To avoid additional exchange rate charges, travellers are advised to take travellers cheques in US Dollars or Pounds Sterling.
Currency restrictions: There are no restrictions on the import and export of either local or foreign currency.
Exchange rate indicators: The following figures are included as a guide to the movements of the Lat against Sterling and the US Dollar:

Date	Feb '04	May '04	Aug '04	Nov '04
£1.00=	0.97	0.98	0.98	0.98
$1.00=	0.53	0.55	0.53	0.53

Banking hours: Mon-Fri 0900-1700. Some banks are open Sat 0900-1300.

Duty Free

The following goods may be imported into Latvia without incurring customs duty by travellers aged 18 years or older: *200 cigarettes or 20 cigars or 200g of tobacco; 1l of alcoholic beverages in their original packaging, up to 2l of wine and 5l of beer; up to 1kg of coffee; up to Ls15 of food or foodstuff with equal designation up to a maximum of three pieces; up to Ls150 of new goods.*
Prohibited items: Narcotics; guns and ammunition (without a police import permit).
Note: (a) It is advisable to declare expensive items such as jewellery and furs. (b) A certificate must be obtained from the Latvian authorities in order to export pieces of art over 50 years old.
Abolition of duty free goods within the EU: On June 30 1999, the sale of duty free alcohol and tobacco at airports and at sea was abolished in all of the original 15 EU member states. Of the 10 new member states that joined the EU on May 1 2004, these rules already apply to Cyprus and Malta. There are transitional rules in place for visitors returning to one of the original 15 EU countries from one of the other new EU countries. But for the original 15, plus Cyprus and Malta, there are now no limits imposed on importing tobacco and alcohol products from one EU country to another (with the exceptions of Denmark, Finland and Sweden, where limits *are* imposed). Travellers should note that they may be required to prove at customs that the goods purchased are for personal use *only*.

Credit: © Latvian Tourism Development Agency and Latvia Tourism Bureau

Public Holidays

2005: Jan 1 New Year's Day. **Mar 25** Good Friday. **Mar 28** Easter Monday. **May 1** May Day. **Jun 23** Ligo Day. **Jun 24** St John's Day (Summer Solstice). **Nov 18** National Day (Proclamation of the Republic). **Dec 25-26** Christmas (Winter Solstice). **Dec 31** New Year's Eve.
2006: Jan 1 New Year's Day. **Apr 14** Good Friday. **Apr 17** Easter Monday. **May 1** May Day. **Jun 23** Ligo Day. **Jun 24** St John's Day (Summer Solstice). **Nov 18** National Day (Proclamation of the Republic). **Dec 25-26** Christmas (Winter Solstice). **Dec 31** New Year's Eve.

Health

	Special Precautions?	Certificate Required?
Yellow Fever	No	No
Cholera	No	No
Typhoid & Polio	No	N/A
Malaria	No	N/A

Note: *Regulations and requirements may be subject to change at short notice, and you are advised to contact your doctor well in advance of your intended date of departure. Any numbers in the chart refer to the footnotes below.*

Food & drink: Water used for drinking, brushing teeth or making ice should have first been boiled or otherwise sterilised.
Other risks: *Tick-borne encephalitis* is present, particularly in forested areas. Campers and trekkers should wear protective clothing; immunisation is strongly advisable as reported cases have increased in recent years. *Diphtheria* and *hepatitis A* have been reported in the area. *Diphyllobothriasis* (fish tapeworm) can be ingested from freshwater fish caught around the Baltic Sea area. *Tuberculosis* has been reported and precautions are necessary.
Rabies is present. For those at high risk, vaccination before arrival should be considered. If you are bitten, seek medical advice without delay. For more information, consult the *Health* appendix.
Health care: The dental surgery at Stabu iela 9 has an emergency service from 2000-0800 and the reception of the City Clinical Hospital No 1 at Bruninieku iela 8 is open 24 hours. Health insurance is advised. A full range of medicines is available at pharmacies; however, it is advisable to bring any medicines necessary, as instructions on the packet are in Latvian, and familiar brands may not be available.

Travel - International

AIR: Airlines serving Riga are *Aeroflot, Air Baltic , Austrian Airlines, British Airways, Czech Airlines, Finnair, LOT Polish Airlines, Lufthansa, Malev Hungarian* and *SAS*.
Approximate flight times: From Riga to *Frankfurt/M* is two hours 10 minutes, to *London* is two hours 30 minutes, and to *New York* is approximately 14 hours (via Helsinki).
International airports: *Riga (RIX)* (Spilve) is 8km (5 miles) from the city. Bus no. 22 runs every 20 to 30 minutes to the city centre (0545-2240), costing LVL 0.20 (travel time - 30 minutes). An express bus service goes to various hotels in the city upon request. Taxis are also available, costing LVL 0.35 (travel time - 15 minutes). Airport facilities include duty free shop, car hire (*Avis, Budget, Europcar, Hertz, National* and *Sixt*), restaurant, bar/cafe and post office. There is an international airport at *Liepaja (LPX)*, with flights to Copenhagen and Moscow.
Departure tax: None.
SEA: There are ferry connections from Riga to Stockholm with *Monolines* (travel time - 18 hours). There are direct ferries from Travemunde in Germany and Stockholm in Sweden. There are also connections from Liepaja to Rostock and to Karlshamm in Sweden. Several shipping lines run cruises on the Baltic Sea calling at Riga.
RAIL: Latvia has links with Belarus, the Russian Federation, Estonia to the north, and Lithuania to the south. The main route into Western Europe runs from Riga to Berlin via Warsaw and Vilnius.
ROAD: The road network is relatively well developed and there are good routes through to Belarus and to the neighbouring two Baltic Republics. Entry by car is possible from the Russian Federation, Estonia, Belarus or Lithuania. Border posts between Poland and Lithuania: Ogrodniki-Lazdijai; between Poland and Belarus: Terespol-Brest. Recent changes in Eastern Europe have opened a new highway through the Baltic countries, known as the *Via Baltica*. To drive along the Via Baltica is to discover places that were closed to Western tourists for decades. Services along this highly attractive route are improving all the time. Both the road network and signposting are being modernised; the service station network is represented by both local and foreign companies (many of which are open 24 hours). *Eurolines*, departing from Victoria Coach Station in London, serves destinations in Latvia. For further information, contact *Eurolines* (website: www.eurolines.com *or* www.gobycoach.com).

Travel - Internal

RAIL: Latvia's reasonably well-developed rail network includes routes from Riga to all other major towns in the country. The railway terminal is at Stacijas laukums. For information about trains, contact LDZ (tel: 723 4940 *or* 4208;

Credit: © Latvian Tourism Development Agency and Latvia Tourism Bureau

fax: 782 0231; e-mail: info@ldz.lv *or* webmaster@ldz.lv; website: www.ldz.lv).
ROAD: There are reasonable connections to all parts of the country from Riga. Traffic drives on the right. **Bus:** A better form of transport than trains in Latvia. The Central Bus Station is at Pragas iela 1. **Car hire:** Available through hotels and directly from car hire companies, reservations are recommended. Drivers can also be hired. **Traffic regulations:** Seat belts must be worn. Speed limits on country lanes are 90kph (56mph) and 50kph (32mph) in cities. It is compulsory to drive with headlights on 24 hours a day all year round. The consumption of alcohol by drivers is strictly forbidden as is the use of mobile telephones while driving. **Documentation:** European nationals should be in possession of an EU pink format licence, otherwise an International Driving Permit is required.
URBAN: Public transport in Riga runs from 0530-0000. Taxis in Riga are cheap, but prices are rising. All taxis are now privately run and all have meters. There is a 50 per cent surcharge at night. All parts of the city can also be reached by bus, tram and trolleybus. Tickets should be bought on board from the conductor and retained for inspection. Share-taxis (*taksobussi*) also operate but are slightly more expensive than ordinary buses. Fines for fare dodging are common.

Accommodation

HOTELS: Owing to the present level of bed capacity, early reservation is absolutely necessary. Since independence, there has been a scramble from Western firms to turn the old state-run hotels into modern Western-standard enterprises. Several of the main hotels in Riga have been renovated in joint ventures with Western firms. A number of newer hotels, including representatives of the major international chain hotels, have recently opened. Many more such joint ventures with firms from all over Western Europe and the USA have ensured that the standard of accommodation in Latvia has reached Western European levels. Outside Riga, which for the time being is the main location of the current expansion in hotel accommodation, Latvia enjoys a good range of modest accommodation, left over from the pre-independence days, including large hotels and smaller pension-type establishments. Accommodation listings for Latvia are available online (website: www.allhotels.lv). **Grading:** A star-grading system has recently been introduced. For more details, contact AllHotels.lv, 1 Kengaraga Street, Riga, Latvia LV-1063 (fax: 718 7457; e-mail: info@allhotels.lv).
RURAL ACCOMMODATION: Advice on farm holidays, bed & breakfast and self-catering cottages may be obtained from the Latvian Country Tourism Association, Kugu iela 11, LV-1048 Riga (tel: 761 7600; fax: 783 0041; e-mail: lauku@celotajs.lv; website: www.celotajs.lv).
CAMPING: Most of Latvia's campsites are located along main highways and the Gulf of Riga, especially the resort of Jurmala. For more details, contact the Latvian Embassy or the Tourist Office (see *Contact Addresses* section).
YOUTH HOSTELS: There are 10 hostels in the network. Information on youth accommodation is available from Hostelling Latvia (tel: 921 8560; fax: 751 7006; e-mail: info@hostellinglatvia.com; website: www.hostellinglatvia.com).

Resorts & Excursions

RIGA: Situated on a sandy plain 15km (9 miles) from the mouth of the River Daugava, Riga is the capital of Latvia and is one of the most beautiful of the Baltic cities. According to legend, once every 100 years the devil rears his head from the waters of the **River Daugava** and asks whether Riga is 'ready' yet. If the answer were 'yes', the now nearly 900-year-old city would be doomed to sink into the Daugava. The Latvian capital is a major tourist attraction, and has excellent air, train and road connections. It is rich in history and culture with remarkable Gothic, Baroque, Classical and Art Nouveau buildings. The centre of the city is considered to contain the finest concentration of Art Nouveau buildings in Europe and has been declared a UNESCO World Heritage Site. **Old Riga** contains a remarkable diversity of architectural styles, perhaps best epitomised by the **Dome Cathedral**. Begun in 1211, the building has been added to throughout the centuries, resulting in a fascinating blend of Romanesque, Gothic, Renaissance, Baroque and Classical styles. The cathedral's organ, with nearly 7000 pipes, is recognised as one of the world's greatest musical instruments and concerts are regularly performed here. The numerous other historical buildings in Riga bear witness to Latvia's chequered history. Since its restoration after World War I, the old quarter of the city has been a protected area. The one surviving town gate is the so-called **Sweden Gate**, whilst the symbol of Riga, the 137m- (450ft-) high tower of **St Peter's Church**, rises above the city. The **St John's Church** of the former Dominican monastery was built in the 14th century and is one of several interesting churches in this former Episcopal seat. Most of the structure dates back to the 15th century and was constructed in a mixture of Romanesque and Gothic styles. The Catholic **St Jacob's Church** was built in 1226 and is a fine example of Gothic architecture. The delightful **Viestura Garden** is ideal for relaxation. Its foundations were laid by Peter the Great who planted the first tree, an event commemorated by a flagstone in the park. **Alexander Gate**, the entrance to the park, was erected to mark the Russian victory over Napoleon's army. It was in this park that the first Latvian Song Festival was held in 1873. At the end of the 18th century, Katharina II built the **Peter and Paul Church** north of the castle. Merchants' houses from the Middle Ages such as the **Three Brothers** and the 24 warehouses in the old quarter are also picturesque examples of Latvian architecture. The residence of Peter I near the Cathedral has been dramatically altered and rebuilt. Riga has several museums including the **Historical Museum of Latvia** (founded in 1896), housed in the castle, and the **Latvian Museum of Medicine**, as well as two art galleries – the **Museum of Foreign Art**, which contains Flemish masterpieces, and the state **Art Gallery of Latvia**. The **Riga Motor Museum** displays the history of motor-car engineering, with veteran cars including rarities such as Stalin's and Brezhnev's private cars. In central Riga, the **Freedom Monument** (*Brivibas Piemineklis*) is a very significant site for Latvians. Built in 1935, the monument is a striking obelisk crowned by a female figure with upstretched arms holding three stars which represent the three historic regions of Latvia: Kurzeme, Latgale and Vidzeme. Reminiscent of the famous Statue of Liberty in New York, though much smaller at 42m (138ft), the statue ranks among the most distinguished monuments in Europe. Another place of interest is the **Warriors' Cemetery** which was designed by the sculptor Zale, the architect Birznieks and the landscape gardener Zeidaks. Approximately 2000 graves from World War I are divided into three sections.
Not far from the city is the open-air **Latvian Ethnographic Museum**. With buildings from all over the country, ranging from wooden churches to windmills, it covers traditional rural architecture from the 16th to the 19th centuries.
ELSEWHERE: Some 17km (11 miles) from the Latvian capital, the Baltic resort of **Jurmala** – consisting of 12 small villages – extends over 30km (19 miles) along the **Gulf of Riga** at the mouth of the River Lielupe. Fresh pine forest-scented air, sun and endless sandy beaches make this stretch of coast a particularly attractive holiday destination for all age groups. Drivers entering Jurmala need to purchase a special ticket; the fee is used to sponsor ecological programmes in the area. The area is connected by roads and the commuter railway, which takes about 15 minutes from Riga.
Another Latvian health resort is **Sigulda**, about 53km (33 miles) from Riga. Situated on the picturesque banks of the **River Gauja**, the town has been established since the 13th century and attractions here include the ruins of the castle and local caves. In the **National Park** that is situated here, **Turaida Castle** (13th century) and its museum can be visited, as well as a sculpture park where Latvian folk poetry has been captured in stone. There is good downhill skiing in winter, and Sigulda is a popular boating spot in summer.
The most important Baroque building is the **Palace** in **Pilsrundale**, about 77km (48 miles) south of Riga, near the Lithuanian border. This fine summer residence of the Dukes of Courland was designed by the Italian architect Rastrelli, who also designed the Winter Palace in St Petersburg – an outstanding blend of Baroque architecture and Rococo decorative art, with gardens modelled on those of Versailles. The surrounding park is excellent for long walks.
Nature enthusiasts will enjoy the rich flora and fauna in the regions of **Kurzeme**, **Latgale** and **Vidzeme**, which are also favourites with hikers. Throughout the country, the landscape is dotted with picturesque villages such as **Bauska**, **Cesis**, **Kolka** and **Talsi**, where life generally follows a very relaxed pace amidst beautiful countryside. Nearby **Kuldiga**, situated on the banks of the River Venta, is Latvia's highest waterfall and a favourite picnic spot.

Sport & Activities

Hiking: With approximately 10 per cent of its area below sea level, Latvia is characterised by wetlands, rivers and forests. Its highest point, in the Vidzeme Uplands, is only 311m (1020ft). The largely unspoilt landscape offers good opportunities for outdoor activities. In summer, **hikers** can take to the trails in the national parks and protected areas. *Gauja National Park*, located 32km (20 miles) north of Riga between Sigulda and Valmiera, is the country's biggest. Covering an area of nearly 94km (58 miles) around the River Gauja, it features caves, rocks and dense woods. Wildlife includes elk, deer, brown bears and wolves. There are special nature trails to introduce walkers to the plants and animals. *Kemeri National Park* is also rich in flora and fauna. Other hiking trails include the *Amber Trail* along the western coast of Courland.
Birdwatching: Latvia's wetlands and traditionally cultivated farmland attract significant populations of interesting and rare birds. The country's many meadows and pastures are a prime habitat for the corncrake, now rare in other parts of Europe. White storks are common in agricultural areas near wetlands. Northern European birds such as red-throated and black-throated divers and Slavonian grebes breed in the open water. Reed marshes harbour bitterns and marsh harriers, while ospreys and the large white-tailed eagle can be seen by lakes and rivers. The forests contain a variety of birds including hazelhens, black storks, pygmy owls and three-toed woodpeckers. Local operators can arrange birdwatching trips. For more information, contact the Latvian Ornithological Society, AK 1010, Riga 1050 (tel: 722 1580; fax: 760 3100; e-mail: putni@lob.lv; website: www.lob.lv).
Watersports: These are widely practised on the rivers and lakes and on the coast. The *River Gauja* is a popular location for boating, with facilities available for accommodation and mooring. **Canoeing** is very popular on the *Abava*, *Gauja* and *Salaca* rivers, and in the *Latgale* lakes region. Along the coast, there are **yacht** harbours. Freshwater and sea **fishing** are very popular. Catches include perch, pike, salmon, eel and herring.

Social Profile

FOOD & DRINK: Hors d'oeuvres are very good and often the best part of the meal. Local specialities include *kotletes* (meat patties), *skabu kapostu zupa* (cabbage soup), *Alexander Torte* (raspberry- or cranberry-filled pastry strips), smoked fish (including salmon or trout), sweetbread soup with dried fruit, *piragi* (pastry filled with bacon and onions) and sorrel soup with boiled pork, onions, potatoes and barley. Potatoes feature regularly on the menu prepared in a variety of ways. There is also a large selection of excellent dairy products on offer, such as *skabs krejums* (sour cream).
Riga's *Black Balsam* is a thick, black alcoholic liquid which has been produced since 1700. The exact recipe is a closely guarded secret, but some of the ingredients include ginger, oak bark, bitter orange peel and cognac. It is drunk either with coffee or mixed with vodka. There are several good local beers, including the dark beer *bauskas Tumsais* and the pale *Gaisais*. *Kvass* is a refreshing summer drink. Sparkling wine is also popular.
NIGHTLIFE: Riga has a good range of excellent restaurants, bars and cafes.
SHOPPING: Amber is of high quality and a good buy. Other purchases include folk art, wicker work and earthenware. **Shopping hours:** Mon-Fri 0900/1000-1800/1900, Sat 0900/1000-1600/1700. Some smaller shops may be closed 1400-1500 for lunch. Food shops open 0800/0900-2000/2100. Some shops are open 24 hours.
SPECIAL EVENTS: For a complete list of events, contact the National Tourist Board *or* local Embassy (see *Contact Addresses* section). The following is a selection of special events occurring in Latvia in 2005:
Jan 7 *14th Festival of Ancient Music*, Valmiera.
Feb 5-6 *International Festival of Ice Sculptures*, Jelgava.
Feb 18-20 *International Festival of Music Traditions*, Riga. **Mar** *380th Anniversary of Liepaja City*. **Mar 11-13** *Riga Fashion Week*. **May 7** *May Fair*, Riga. **Jun 7-12** *and* **15-19** *8th Riga Opera Festival*. **Jun 19** *Enchanting of John's Day*, Riga. **Aug 5-7** *City Festival*, Ventspils.
Sep 25 *Fair of Autumn Solstice*, Riga. **Dec 18** *Traditional Latvian Christmas Celebrations*. **Dec 26** *Winter Party*, Riga.
SOCIAL CONVENTIONS: Handshaking is customary. Normal courtesies should be observed. The Latvians are somewhat reserved and formal, but nevertheless very hospitable. They are proud of their culture and visitors should take care to respect this sense of national identity. **Tipping:** Taxi fares and restaurant bills usually include a tip. It is customary to give a little extra for good service.

Business Profile

ECONOMY: With few raw materials, the Latvian economy is principally dependent on producing manufactured goods from imported materials. Key industries include vehicle and railway rolling stock manufacture, electronics, and the production of fertilisers, chemicals, timber and wood products, light machinery and food processing, which draws on Latvia's own dairy and fisheries products as well as imported raw materials from the Russian Federation. The infrastructure is, in common with the other Baltic States, comparatively well developed. Latvia relies on power supplies from its Baltic neighbours and on imported fuel from the Russian Federation to meet its energy needs; energy imports account for one-third of Latvia's total import bill. Through the Ventsplils Nafta terminal on the Baltic coast, Latvia is one of the major outlets for Russian oil exports. In the service sector, Riga is now an important regional financial centre. Latvia has pursued economic reform in a gradual manner. The government's reform programme during the 1990s was limited by political opposition which prevented, for example, the sale of major state enterprises. The economy performed steadily during most of the 1990s, although the effects of the immediate post-Soviet period and the 1998 Russian economic crisis meant there was an overall contraction between 1990 and 2000 of about 20 per cent. Since 2000 annual growth has accelerated to its current level of about 8 per cent, possibly conferring on Latvia the status of a 'Baltic tiger'. The country introduced its own currency, the Lat, in 1993: this is now the sole legal tender. The following year, a free trade zone was established with Estonia and Lithuania. In June 1995, Latvia signed an Association Agreement with the European Union, as the first stage on the path towards joining the EU – a major objective of successive governments since independence. Negotiations proceeded more rapidly and successfully than had been expected, and Latvia was able to join the EU, along with nine other countries (including both of Latvia's Baltic neighbours) on May 1 2004. Latvia had previously been admitted to the European Bank for Reconstruction and Development in 1991, then in 1996 to the World Bank and IMF (which in 2001 provided a loan of US$40 million to finance structural reforms). The EU – especially Germany, Sweden and Finland – now accounts for half of total Latvian trade; the Russian Federation and the other Baltic states are the other main trade partners.
BUSINESS: Business cards are exchanged. Appointments should be arranged in advance. In general, business is conducted in a fairly formal manner. **Office hours:** Mon-Fri 0830-1730.
COMMERCIAL INFORMATION: The following organisations can offer advice: Latvian Chamber of Commerce and Industry, Valdemara Street 35, Riga LV-1010 (tel: 722 5595; fax: 782 0092; e-mail: info@chamber.lv; website: www.chamber.lv); *or* Latvian Development Agency, Perses iela 2, Riga LV-1042 (tel: 703 9400; fax: 703 9401; e-mail: invest@lda.gov.lv).
CONFERENCES/CONVENTIONS: Information can be obtained from The Association of Latvian Travel Agents, PO Box 59, Riga LV-1012 (tel/fax: 721 0065; e-mail: alta.assoc@apollo.lv).

Climate

Temperate climate, but with considerable temperature variations. Summer is warm with relatively mild weather in spring and autumn. Winter, which lasts from November to mid-March, can be very cold. Rainfall is distributed throughout the year with the heaviest rainfall in August. Snowfall is common in the winter months.
Required clothing: Light- to mediumweights are worn during summer months. Medium- to heavyweights are needed during winter. Rainwear is advisable all year.

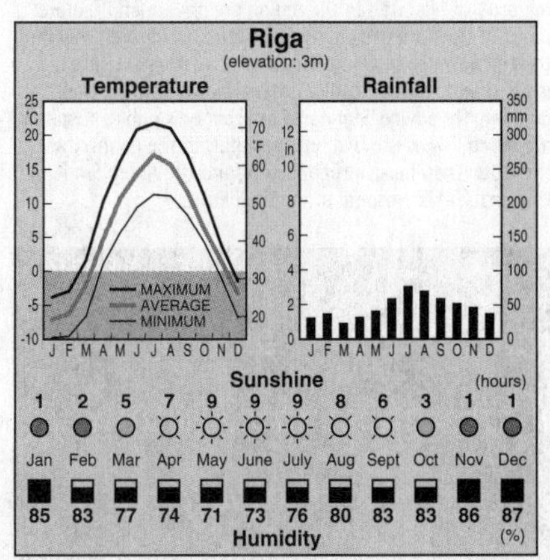

Lebanon

LATEST TRAVEL ADVICE CONTACTS

British Foreign and Commonwealth Office
Tel: (0870) 606 0290 Website: www.fco.gov.uk
US Department of State
Website: http://travel.state.gov/travel
Canadian Department of Foreign Affairs and Int'l Trade
Tel: (1 800) 267 8376 Website: www.dfait-maeci.gc.ca

Location: Middle East.

Country dialling code: 961.

Ministry of Tourism
Street address: 550 rue de la Banque Centrale, Hamra, Beirut, Lebanon
Postal address: PO Box 11-5344, Beirut, Lebanon
Tel: (1) 340 940-4. Fax: (1) 340 945.
E-mail: mot@inco.com.lb
Website: www.destinationlebanon.com
Embassy of the Republic of Lebanon
21 Palace Gardens Mews, London W8 4QM, UK
Tel: (020) 7727 6696 *or* 7229 7265 (consular section).
Fax: (020) 7243 1699.
E-mail: emb_leb@btinternet.com
Opening hours: Mon-Fri 0930-1230 (visa applications); 1400-1500 (visa collection).
Also deals with tourism enquiries.
British Embassy
Street address: Embassies Complex, Army Street, Zkak Al-Blat, Serail Hill, Beirut Central District, Lebanon
Postal address: PO Box 11-471, Beirut, Lebanon
Tel: (1) 990 400. Fax: (1) 990 420.
E-mail: chancery@cyberia.net.lb *or* ConsularEnquiries.BEI@fco.gov.uk
Website: www.britishembassy.gov.uk/lebanon
Consulate in: Tripoli.
Embassy of the Republic of Lebanon
2560 28th Street, NW, Washington, DC 20008, USA
Tel: (202) 939 6300. Fax: (202) 939 6324.
E-mail: info@lebanonembassyus.org
Website: www.lebanonembassyus.org
Consulates General in: Los Angeles, Michigan and New York.
Honorary Consulates in: Florida, Miami and Texas.
Consulate General of the Republic of Lebanon
9 East 76th Street, New York, NY 10021, USA
Tel: (212) 744 7905/6.
Fax: (212) 794 1510.
E-mail: lebconsny@aol.com
Website: www.lebconsny.org

TIMATIC CODES

Health	AMADEUS: **TI-DFT/BEY/HE** GALILEO/WORLDSPAN: **TI-DFT/BEY/HE** SABRE: **TIDFT/BEY/HE**
Visa	AMADEUS: **TI-DFT/BEY/VI** GALILEO/WORLDSPAN: **TI-DFT/BEY/VI** SABRE: **TIDFT/BEY/VI**

To access TIMATIC country information on Health and Visa regulations through the Computer Reservations System (CRS), type in the appropriate command line listed above.

Embassy of the United States of America
PO Box 70-840, Antelias, Beirut, Lebanon
Tel: (4) 542 600 *or* 543 600. Fax: (4) 544 136.
E-mail: BeirutNIV@state.gov (non-immigrant visa section).
Website: www.usembassy.gov.lb
Embassy of the Republic of Lebanon
640 Lyon Street, Ottawa, Ontario K1S 3Z5, Canada
Tel: (613) 236 5825/55. Fax: (613) 232 1609.
E-mail: info@lebanonembassy.ca
Website: www.lebanonembassy.ca
Embassy of Canada
Street address: 434 Jal Al-Dib Highway, 1st Floor, Coolrite Building, Jal Al-Dib, Beirut, Lebanon
Postal address: PO Box 60163, Jal el Dib, Beirut, Lebanon
Tel: (4) 713 900 *or* 710 591. Fax: (4) 710 595/3.
E-mail: berut.webmaster@dfait-maeci.gc.ca *or* berut-td@dfait-maeci.gc.ca (trade enquiries).
Website: www.dfait-maeci.gc.ca/beirut

Credit: © Ministry of Tourism, Lebanon

General Information

AREA: 10,452 sq km (4036 sq miles).
POPULATION: 3,700,000 (2003).
POPULATION DENSITY: 344 per sq km.
CAPITAL: Beirut. **Population:** 1,171,000 (2003).
GEOGRAPHY: Lebanon lies to the east of the Mediterranean, sharing borders to the north and east with the Syrian Arab Republic, and to the south with Israel/Palestinian Territory. It is a mountainous country and between the two mountain ranges of Jebel Lubnan (Mount Lebanon), Mount Hermon and the Anti-Lebanon range lies the fertile Bekaa Valley. Approximately half of the country lies at an altitude of over 900m (3000ft). Into this small country is packed such a variety of scenery that there are few places to equal it in beauty and choice. The famous cedar trees grow high in the mountains, while the lower slopes bear grapes, apricots, plums, peaches, figs, olives and barley, often on terraces painstakingly cut out from the mountainsides. On the coastal plain, citrus fruit, bananas and vegetables are cultivated, with radishes and beans grown in tiny patches.
GOVERNMENT: Republic. **Head of State:** President Emil Jamil Lahoud since 1998. His term of presidency was set to end in November 2004 but was controversially extended by another term (lasting three years) when the constitution was amended to allow Lahoud to remain in office. **Head of Government:** Prime Minister Rafiq al-Hariri since 2000.
LANGUAGE: The official language is Arabic, followed by French as the second language; English is widely spoken. Armenian is spoken by a small percentage of the population.
RELIGION: Islam and Christianity are the main religions. Islam (predominantly Shi'ite) accounts for approximately 40 per cent of the population's beliefs. Christian denominations, mainly Greek Orthodox, Maronite, Armenian and Protestant account for another 40 per cent. Other religions account for the remaining 20 per cent (including a very small Jewish community).
TIME: GMT + 2 (GMT + 3 from April to September).
ELECTRICITY: 230 volts AC, 50Hz.
COMMUNICATIONS: Telephone: IDD is available. Country code: 961. Outgoing international code: 00. Cellular phones are widely used and are available for hire to visitors. **Mobile telephone:** GSM 900 network in use. Network providers are *Faldete* (website: www.faldete.com.lb) and *MTC* (website: www.mtc.com.lb). **Fax:** International facilities available. Faxes can be sent from *centrales* (state telephone bureaux) in major towns and from most hotels (which often add 25 per cent to the official rates). **Internet:** The main ISPs are *Cyberia* (website: www.thisiscyberia.com), *IDM* (website: www.idm.net.lb) and *Terranet* (website: www.terra.net.lb). There are Internet cafes in Beirut, Tripoli and most major towns. **Post:** Post to Europe usually takes two to four days, and between four to seven days to the USA. **Press:** There are more than 30 daily newspapers published in Arabic, Armenian and French and over 100 publications appear on a weekly or monthly basis. *Beirut Times* and *The Daily Star* are published in English and there are several English-language weeklies, primarily Monday Morning. The best-selling Arabic dailies are *Al Anwar*, *Al Dyar*, *Al Liwa'*, *An Nahar* and *Al Safir*. The most

important daily in French is *L'Orient-le Jour*.
Radio: BBC World Service (website: www.bbc.co.uk/worldservice) and Voice of America (website: www.voa.gov) can be received. From time to time the frequencies change and the most up-to-date can be found online.

Passport/Visa

	Passport Required?	Visa Required?	Return Ticket Required?
Full British	Yes	Yes/1	Yes
Australian	Yes	Yes/1	Yes
Canadian	Yes	Yes/1	Yes
USA	Yes	Yes/1	Yes
Other EU	Yes	Yes/1	Yes
Japanese	Yes	Yes/1	Yes

Note: *Regulations and requirements may be subject to change at short notice, and you are advised to contact the appropriate diplomatic or consular authority before finalising travel arrangements. Details of these may be found at the head of this country's entry. Any numbers in the chart refer to the footnotes below.*

Credit: © Ministry of Tourism, Lebanon

Restricted entry: The Government of Lebanon refuses entry to holders of Israeli and Palestinian passports, holders of passports containing a visa for Israel, valid or expired, used or unused and passports with entry stamps to Israel.
PASSPORTS: Passport valid for six months required by all except nationals of the Syrian Arab Republic arriving from their country with a valid national ID.
VISAS: Required by all except the following:
(a) nationals of the Syrian Arab Republic for unlimited stays, provided arriving directly from the Syrian Arab Republic (check with Embassy for current regulations);
(b) nationals of Bahrain, Kuwait, Oman, Qatar, Saudi Arabia and the United Arab Emirates for stays of up to three months;
(c) transit passengers continuing their journey by the same or first connecting aircraft, provided holding onward or return documentation and not spending the night at, or leaving, the airport.
Note: 1. The following can obtain their visas on arrival at Beirut International Airport or any other port of entry at the Lebanese border, providing passport holders do not possess an Israeli stamp, and they hold return or onward tickets:
(a) nationals of countries listed in the chart above, except nationals of Czech Republic, Estonia, Hungary, Latvia, Lithuania, Poland, Slovak Republic and Slovenia who must obtain a visa prior to arrival;
(b) nationals of Andorra, Argentina, Brazil, Chile, China (PR), Costa Rica, Hong Kong (SAR), Iceland, Liechtenstein, Malaysia, Mexico, Monaco, New Zealand, Norway, Panama, Peru, Singapore, Switzerland and Venezuela. The above list is subject to frequent changes. All visitors requiring a visa should contact the Consulate (or Consular section at Embassy) before leaving for details about where to obtain their visa; see *Contact Addresses* section.
Types of visa and cost: *Visitor* and *Business*: £25 (single-entry); £50 (multiple-entry). *Transit* (available at the border): US$25.
Validity: Visitor visas are generally issued for stays of up to three months.
Application to: Consulate (or Consular section at Embassy); see *Contact Addresses* section.
Application requirements: (a) Valid passport. (b) Two completed application forms. (c) Two passport-size photos. (d) Fee payable by cash or postal order only. (e) For *Visitor* visas, a letter of invitation from Lebanese host or confirmation of accommodation booking from travel agent. (f) For *Business visas*, a letter of invitation from the Lebanese host company and/or the applicant's company in country of origin. (g) Stamped, self-addressed, registered envelope for postal applications.
Note: Children under 18 years old require written consent from their parents/guardian before their visa can be processed.
Working days required: One to two days.
Temporary residence: Formalities for temporary residence will be arranged in Lebanon. For details of student and employment visas, enquire at Consulate (or Consular section at Embassy); see *Contact Addresses* section.

Money

Currency: Lebanese Pound (L£) = 100 piastres. Notes are in denominations of L£100,000, 50,000, 20,000, 10,000, 5000, 1000, 500, 250 and 100. Coins are in denominations of L£500, 250, 100 and 50.
Currency exchange: There are a large number of banks in Beirut where international currencies can be exchanged. Numerous licensed exchange shops also operate and some hotels offer exchange services. US Dollars are best and do not need to be exchanged as they are accepted even in small shops.
Credit & debit cards: All major credit cards are widely accepted. Check with your credit or debit card company for details of merchant acceptability and other services which may be available.
Travellers cheques: Limited acceptance, as major banks only accept certain types of travellers cheques. Travellers cheques also require up to two weeks to clear and are therefore generally not recommended.
Currency restrictions: There are no restrictions on the import or export of local or foreign currency.
Exchange rate indicators: The following figures are included as a guide to the movements of the Lebanese Pound against Sterling and the US Dollar:

Date	Feb '04	May '04	Aug '04	Nov '04
£1.00=	2757.68	2705.05	2789.32	2789.32
$1.00=	1515.00	1514.50	1514.00	1514.00

Banking hours: Mon-Fri 0800-1400, Sat 0800-1230. Some banks stay open until 1700.

Duty Free

The following goods may be imported into Lebanon by residents and non-residents over 18 years of age without incurring customs duty:
800 cigarettes or 50 cigars or 100 cigarillos or 1000g of tobacco; 2l of champagne, whisky or cognac or a maximum of 4l of other alcoholic beverages; 1l of eau de cologne and 100g of perfume; personal belongings not exceeding L£2,000,000; prescribed dosages for medicine.
Note: Those aged under 18 years are permitted half the specified quantities for duty free except tobacco and alcoholic beverages, which are forbidden.
Restricted items: A valid import licence is required for any arms or ammunition.
Prohibited: Antiques without an export license.

Public Holidays

2005: Jan 1 New Year's Day. **Jan 6** Orthodox Armenian Christmas. **Jan 21** Eid al-Adha (Feast of the Sacrifice). **Feb 9** Feast of St Maroun. **Feb 10** Islamic New Year. **Feb 19** Ashoura. **Mar 25** Good Friday. **Mar 27** Easter Sunday. **Apr 21** Mawlid (Prophet's Birthday). **Apr 29** Orthodox Good Friday. **May 1** Labour Day; Orthodox Easter Sunday. **May 6** Martyrs' Day. **May 25** Liberation of the South. **Aug 15** Assumption. **Nov 1** All Saints' Day. **Nov 3** Eid al-Fitr (End of Ramadan). **Nov 22** Independence Day. **Dec 25** Christmas Day.
2006: Jan 1 New Year's Day. **Jan 6** Orthodox Armenian Christmas. **Jan 10** Eid al-Adha (Feast of the Sacrifice). **Jan 31** Islamic New Year. **Feb 9** Feast of St Maroun/Ashoura. **Apr 11** Mawlid (Prophet's Birthday). **Apr 14** Good Friday (including Orthodox). **Apr 17** Easter Sunday (including Orthodox). **May 1** Labour Day. **May 6** Martyrs' Day. **May 25** Liberation of the South. **Aug 15** Assumption. **Nov 1** All Saints' Day. **Oct 22-24** Eid al-Fitr (End of Ramadan). **Nov 22** Independence Day. **Dec 25** Christmas Day.
Note: Muslim feasts are timed according to local sightings of various phases of the moon and the dates given above are approximations. During the lunar month of Ramadan that precedes Eid al-Fitr, Muslims fast during the day and feast at night and normal business patterns may be interrupted. Many restaurants are closed during the day and there may be restrictions on smoking and drinking. Some disruption may continue into Eid al-Fitr itself. Eid al-Fitr and Eid al-Adha may last anything from two to 10 days, depending on the region. For more information, see the *World of Islam* appendix.

Health

	Special Precautions?	Certificate Required?
Yellow Fever	No	1
Cholera	No	No
Typhoid & Polio	2	N/A
Malaria	No	N/A

Note: *Regulations and requirements may be subject to change at short notice, and you are advised to contact your doctor well in advance of your intended date of departure. Any numbers in the chart refer to the footnotes below.*

1: A yellow fever vaccination certificate is required from travellers from infected areas.
2: Typhoid occurs in rural areas.
Food & drink: Mains water is normally chlorinated and, whilst relatively safe, may cause mild abdominal upsets. Bottled water is available and is advised for the first few weeks of the stay. Drinking water outside main towns and cities is likely to be contaminated and sterilisation is considered essential. Milk is pasteurised and dairy products are safe for consumption. Local meat, poultry, seafood, fruit and vegetables are generally considered safe to eat.
Other risks: *Hepatitis A* and *B* are present but rare. Rabies is present. For those at high risk, vaccination before arrival should be considered. If you are bitten, seek medical advice without delay. For more information, consult the *Health* appendix.
Health care: Health insurance is essential. Lebanese hospitals are very modern and well equipped and many doctors are highly qualified, reputed to be among the best in the world. All doctors speak either English or French. The majority of hospitals in the region are private and require proof of the patient's ability to pay the bill before providing treatment (even in emergency cases). Visitors who are not insured and require hospitalisation should contact their Embassy for advice. Standards at Lebanon's public hospitals are much lower. The two best hospitals in the country are the Hôtel Dieu in Achrafieh, Beirut, and the American University/AUB Hospital in Hamra, Beirut.

Travel - International

Travel Warning: All but essential travel is advised to the northern Beka'a Valley and areas of South Lebanon close to the Israeli border. There continues to be a high risk of terrorist attacks throughout the Middle East, including in Lebanon. All visitors should be particularly vigilant in public places - such as tourist sites - and avoid military sites and Palestinian refugee camps.
AIR: The national airline is *Middle East Airlines (MEA)* (website: www.mea.com.lb), which operates nine direct flights per week from London to Beirut. Further information can be obtained from the Middle East Airlines office in the UK (tel: (020) 7467 8010; reservations). *British Mediterranean* (a franchise partner of *British Airways*) operates daily non-stop services from London to Beirut. *Air France* also operates direct flights to Beirut.
International airports: *Beirut International (BEY)* (Khaldeh) is 8km (5 miles) south of the city (travel time - 20 minutes). A bus service operates to the city centre (0600-2000) leaving every 30 minutes. Taxis are also available (*Allô Taxi*, *New Taxi* or *Premier Taxi*). Airport facilities include a tourist information desk, duty free shops, post office, restaurants, bars, hotel reservations and bank/bureau de change. Facilities also include a VIP lounge.
Departure Tax: L£100,000 for first class; L£75,000 for business class; and L£50,000 for economy class.
SEA: Main international ports are Beirut, Jounieh, Tripoli, Sidon and Tyre. Cruise ships are available from Jounieh. Cruise lines operating to Lebanon include *First European*, *Fred Olsen* and *Louis Cruise Lines*. The sea connection between the Cypriot port of Larnaca and Jounieh in Lebanon may be closed and travellers considering that route are advised to check with the Ministry of Tourism or the Embassy.
RAIL: There are no passenger services operating at present..
ROAD: Best international routes are via Turkey and Aleppo-Homs and Lattakia in the Syrian Arab Republic along the north-south coastal road, and also the Beirut-Damascus trunk road. Bus services are available from Europe. For details, contact the Ministry of Tourism *or* the Embassy (see *Contact Addresses* section).

Travel - Internal

AIR: There are no internal flights.
SEA: Ports are served by coastal passenger ferries. For details, contact the Embassy (see *Contact Addresses* section).
ROAD: Traffic drives on the right. Speed limit signs, traffic police and traffic lights are present but may not always be respected and driving, particularly in Beirut, can be quite unpredictable. As public transport is limited, roads in Beirut are over-congested. The worst times for traffic jams are 0730-0930 and 1630-1900. **Bus:** Intercity buses run by private companies are cheap and efficient. Many hotels also offer complimentary bus and other transport services. **Taxi:** Intercity taxis operate throughout Beirut and Lebanon. Travel is normally shared. Prices are negotiated in advance. Town taxis have red licence plates and an official tariff. There is a surcharge of 50 per cent after 2200. **Car hire:** Self-drive cars are available, but chauffeur-driven vehicles are recommended: check with the Ministry of Tourism. It should be noted that the price of petrol is very expensive in Lebanon. **Documentation:** An International Driving Permit and Green Card are required.
URBAN: Public bus services are available in Beirut, where bus services have recently been expanded, although service taxis remain the most widely used option.

Accommodation

HOTELS: Following the large-scale destruction during the civil war, Beirut's hotels have now all been rebuilt, and a number of new ones added. Lebanon today offers accommodation to suit all budgets and the Ministry of Tourism publishes an annual hotel guide which lists most of the hotels in the country. Outside Beirut, however, hotels are few and far between, particularly in the South. Visitors are advised to check reservations through a Lebanese representative at home before departing. Winter and summer rates are the same. Accommodation rates are normally subject to a 15 per cent service charge.
Grading: Hotels are classified from **1** to **4** stars (**A** and **B** within each class) and **luxury**. Prices are usually quoted in US Dollars and only hotels with rooms costing more than US$50 tend to accept credit cards. For further information, contact the Lebanese Hotels Owners Association, Sodeco Street, PO Box 166011, Beirut (tel: (1) 202 059 *or* 329 095/6; fax: (1) 201 002; e-mail: synhotlb@cyberia.net.lb) *or* the Ministry of Tourism (see *Contact Addresses* section).
GUEST HOUSES: Local hostels are available in coastal villages at reasonable prices.
SELF-CATERING: Furnished and other apartments are available for rent.
CAMPING/YOUTH HOSTELS: There are a number of campsites throughout Lebanon, notably in Amchite, near Byblos, and particularly in mountainous regions, such as Barouk and Chouk. For further information on campsites, cheap rooms, youth hostels and work camps, contact the Ministry of Tourism (see *Contact Addresses* section).

Resorts & Excursions

BEIRUT: Once known as the 'Paris of the East', Beirut commands a magnificent position, thrust into the Mediterranean. Behind the city are towering mountains, visible when the traffic haze settles down. The Corniche seafront boasts beaches, restaurants, theatres and a dazzling variety of shops and restaurants. Beirut suffered greatly from Lebanon's 16-year civil war, but following an impressive and ongoing process of reconstruction, the city is once again one of the most popular tourist and business destinations in the Middle East. The so-called 'Green Line' which, during the war, divided the city into East and West, has now gone, and two competing centres have grown up several kilometres apart. One is Hamra in West Beirut, where the **American University** is located along with the majority of hotels. The other is Achrafieh in East Beirut, home to the **Université St Joseph** and an increasing number of smart shops and expensive restaurants. Beirut's Central District, known as *Solidere* (the company in charge of the reconstruction programme), is seeing a spectacular number of modern buildings and office blocks springing up everywhere. After massive landfill, two new marinas, a new seaside promenade and a green park are also planned. While many of the new buildings look very modern, Beirut's old *souks* (covered markets) are being reconstructed in an authentic way. The **Turkish bath** at **Al-Nouzha** provides another glimpse of the old Beirut. Lebanon's only museum, the **Beirut National Museum**, has been rehabilitated and is constantly updating its interesting collection. On the western tip of Beirut, **Raouche** is an increasingly popular district with a lively seaside promenade. Its famous landmark, the Pigeon Rocks, are huge formations standing like sentinels off the coast.
Excursions: Around 20km (13 miles) north of Beirut, the spectacular **Jeita caverns** are a popular tourist attraction. The caverns are on two levels, and the lower gallery includes an underground waterway which can be visited by boat (but may be closed during winter).
TRIPOLI: The country's second city, Tripoli is Lebanon's most Arabian city and retains much of its provincial charm. Its history dates back to the eighth century BC, and the town centre, though surrounded by modern housing developments and beach resorts, has preserved its character. There are two parts - the port area and the city proper - which are divided by acres of fragrant orange plantations. Tripoli's old medieval centre at the foot of the **Crusader castle** has a number of interesting mosques, including the **Al-Muallaq Burtasiyat Madrassa**, **Al-Qartâwiyat Madrassa**, **Great Mosque** and **Taynâl**. The old *souks* (covered markets) provide interesting shopping. Tripoli is famous for its sweets and traditional olive oil-based soap. The port area, known as **Al Mina**, has numerous seafood restaurants and fish markets; most hotels can be found in the modern beach resorts along the coast.
Excursions: Just off Tripoli, numerous small islands can be visited, the largest of which, the **Island of Palm Trees**, has been listed by UNESCO as a nature reserve for green turtles and rare birds.
TYRE: Tyre was founded at the start of the third millennium BC and still bears impressive traces of its ancient origins today. Tyre's archaeological sites are divided into three areas: area one is located on what was the Phoenician Island and contains ruins of the large district of civic buildings, public baths and mosaic streets; area two contains an extensive network of Romano-Byzantine roads and other installations; area three is most notable for containing one of the largest Roman hippodromes ever found.
BYBLOS: Byblos is reputed to be the oldest town in the world, with excavations unearthing artefacts dating back to Neolithic times as well as from Canaanite, Phoenician, Hellenistic, Roman and Crusader periods. Fishing boats and pleasure craft ply the old harbour. Today, Byblos is a thriving modern town, with the old town centre being the most interesting part for the visitor to explore.
ELSEWHERE: A small port city between Beirut and Tyre, **Sidon** has a sea castle built of stone from Roman remains and it offers well-stocked markets.
Beiteddine, in the **Chouf Mountains**, is the site of the palace built by the Amir Basheer in the 19th century. The courtyard and state rooms are well worth a visit. Near the Syrian border, **Baalbek** contains one of the best-preserved temple areas of the Roman world still in existence. It is, in fact, a complex of several temples behind which soar the columns of the **Temple of Jupiter**.
Besharre, to the northwest, is best known as the birthplace of the famous Lebanese poet Khalil Gibran, author of *The Prophet*, and there is a **Gibran museum**. The town is also a gateway to the mountainous region, famous for its many cedar trees.

Sport & Activities

Golf: Lebanon has four golf courses, the best and most popular of which is *The Golf Club of Lebanon*. Situated on the outskirts of Beirut, the club offers an 18-hole 72 par course, with scenic views of the mountains on one side and the Mediterranean sea on the other. The club offers guest membership to visitors. Caddies and club rentals are available and special group green fees may be arranged. The course is playable all year. The club also includes a sport and leisure complex with facilities for tennis, squash, swimming and snooker as well as dining areas.
Watersports: Scuba diving and **snorkelling** are available. The waters near the ancient city of Tyre offer some interesting underwater archaelogical ruins, which divers may explore. **Swimming** is generally popular and many beaches offer full facilities, with guest memberships and freshwater pools provided to supplement the sea. Other watersports that can be practised in Lebanon incude **water-skiing** and **sailing**. Boats may be rented by **anglers** along the coast, but most local anglers prefer to fish in the deep waters by the shore.
Other: Despite its Mediterranean setting, **skiing** is possible in Lebanon and is actually quite popular. Mountain resorts such as *Bakish*, *The Cedars*, *Faqra*, *Faraya*, *Laklouk* and *Zarour* offer excellent accommodation and facilities. These mountains and gorges also present excellent terrain for **hiking**. There is a wide selection of **tennis** courts in major towns and resorts. **Horse riding** is also popular, and Lebanon's Equestrian Federation now includes six riding clubs with excellent Arab horses available.

Social Profile

FOOD & DRINK: Lebanese cuisine is widely acknowledged to be the finest in the Middle East. The country's gastronomic tradition is characterised by the use of an extremely wide variety of locally-produced, and therefore extremely fresh, vegetables served in all forms and shapes with an abundance of fresh herbs (mostly coriander, parsley and mint). Excellent Lebanese food is available everywhere. A dish unique to Lebanon is *kebbeh*, made of lamb pounded to a fine paste, with *burghul* or cracked wheat, and served raw or baked in flat trays or rolled into balls and fried. Also recommended is the traditional Lebanese *mezza*, a range of up to 40 small dishes served as hors d'oeuvres with *arak*. Main courses are likely to include Lebanese staple ingredients of vegetables, rice and mutton. *Lahm mishwi* (pieces of mutton with onions, peppers and tomato) is popular. Other typical dishes are *tabbouli*, *houmos* and *mtabbal*. Lebanese palates also favour pastries with local varieties of baked doughs flavoured with nuts, cream and syrup. A meal is always concluded with a wide range of fresh fruit, including melon, apples, oranges, persimmon, tangerines, cactus fruit, grapes and figs, which are all grown locally. Beirut also offers a large choice of international restaurants which offer dishes from all over the world. Bars have table and/or counter service. Alcohol is not prohibited.
NIGHTLIFE: Nightclubs spice up the evenings in Beirut and mountain resorts. Entertainment ranges from solo guitarists to orchestras and floor shows. Some British-style pubs can be found in Beirut. There are many cinemas presenting the latest films from all over the world. The internationally renowned Casino du Liban in Maameltain (22km/14 miles north of Beirut) is equipped with lavish gambling halls, luxurious restaurants and a cabaret.
SHOPPING: Lebanon's traditional *souks* or markets are found all over the country offering decorative and precious handmade items at very low prices. Special purchases include traditional pottery and glassware, as well as cutlery made of tempered steel or copper with ram or buffalo bone handles shaped in the form of beautiful and colourful birds' heads. Brass and copper goods include braziers, bowls, fluted jugs, ashtrays, swords and doorstops, all attractively designed and hand engraved. Cloth, silk and wool kaftans, *abayas* (embroidered nightwear) and table linen are popular, as are handworked gold and silver. Shops sell the latest Western goods including clothes, cosmetics, furniture and electrical appliances. **Shopping hours:** Mon-Sat 0800-1900.
SPECIAL EVENTS: For a complete list of special events taking place in Lebanon, contact the Ministry of Tourism (see *Contact Addresses* section). The following is a selection of special events occurring in Lebanon in 2005: **Jan 10** *Eid al-Adha* (Feast of the Sacrifice). **Feb 6-10** *International Weddings Exhibition*. **Feb 15-Mar 20** *Al Bustan Festival* **Jul-Aug** *Baalbeck International Festival*; *Beiteddine Festival*. **Sep 4-21** *Freikeh Festival*, Beit-Chabab. **Sep 8-12** *Ayloul Festival Forum*, Beirut. **Oct 2-9** *Beirut Film Festival*.
SOCIAL CONVENTIONS: Lebanese people are known for their hospitality. Handshaking is the normal form of greeting. It is acceptable to give a small gift, particularly if invited home for a meal. As far as dress is concerned, casual dress is suitable for daytime wear, except in main towns where dress tends to be rather formal. Smarter hotels and restaurants often require guests to dress for dinner. Since Lebanon is almost evenly divided between those adhering to the Muslim faith, and those adhering to the Christian

faith, visitors should dress according to the custom of the majority in the individual places being visited. Smoking is common and acceptable unless specified otherwise.
Tipping: In hotels and restaurants, a tip of between 5 and 10 per cent of the bill is expected. It is not necessary to tip taxi drivers.

Business Profile

ECONOMY: The 15-year civil war from 1976 to 1991 all but completely destroyed the economy; Beirut's position as a major financial and commercial centre for the Middle East was lost. Since then, both Lebanon and its capital have gone a long way to re-establishing themselves. Agriculture now accounts for about 10 per cent of GDP, with citrus fruit, olives and cereals as the main products. Light industries include textiles, processed foods and industrial machinery. There are no significant mineral resources, but the manufacturing industry is growing rapidly. In the all-important service sector, the two main components, banking and transit trade (both of which were almost wiped out during the civil war) have recovered reasonably well. Essential reconstruction, financed by expatriate capital, international aid and foreign investment, began with infrastructural projects. However, by the late-1990s, the government's failure to control the budget deficit and external debt was causing serious difficulties. Annual growth had fallen from an average 4 per cent during most of the 1990s to just over 1 per cent by 2000. At the end of 2000, the government introduced a major reform programme based on privatisation and promotion of foreign investment. However, it was at pains to do so outside the normal channels of the IMF and World Bank which, the government felt, imposed unacceptable constraints on its freedom of manoeuvre on economic policy-making. To that end, in November 2002, Lebanon successfully raised a $4 billion loan package from a consortium including a dozen governments (notably excluding the US) and a number of investment banks and multinational funds. Earlier in the year, Lebanon concluded a major bilateral trade deal with the EU. Besides the EU, Saudi Arabia, the Syrian Arab Republic, the United Arab Emirates and Kuwait are Lebanon's principal trading partners.
BUSINESS: Businesspeople usually wear a jacket and tie. English is spoken by many local businesspeople and normal courtesies are observed. Appointments and business cards are used. **Office hours:** Mon-Fri 0800-1330 and 1500-1800. **Government office hours:** Mon-Thurs 0800-1400, Fri 0800-1100, Sat 0800-1300.
COMMERCIAL INFORMATION: The following organisations can offer advice: Chamber of Commerce, Industry and Agriculture of Beirut and Mount Lebanon, PO Box 11-1801, Rue Sanayeh, Sanayeh, Beirut (tel: (1) 353 390 or 744 160; fax: (1) 353 395; e-mail: tradeinfo@ccib.org.lb; website: www.ccib.org.lb); *or* Ministry of Economy and Trade, Artois Street, Hamra, Beirut (tel: (1) 340 504/5; fax: (1) 354 640; website: www.economy.gov.lb); *or* Euro Info Correspondence Centre (EICC), PO Box 11-1801, 1 Rue Justinien, Sanayeh, Beirut (tel: (1) 744 163; fax: (1) 341 039; website: www.euroinfocentre.net).
CONFERENCES/CONVENTIONS: Beirut is an increasingly popular business destination and a number of companies offer extensive conference and exhibition facilities. For further details, contact the Ministry of Tourism (see *Contact Addresses* section).

Climate

There are four seasons. Summer (June to September) is hot on the coast and cooler in the mountains. Spring and autumn are warm and pleasant. Winter (December to mid-March) is mostly rainy, with snow in the mountains.

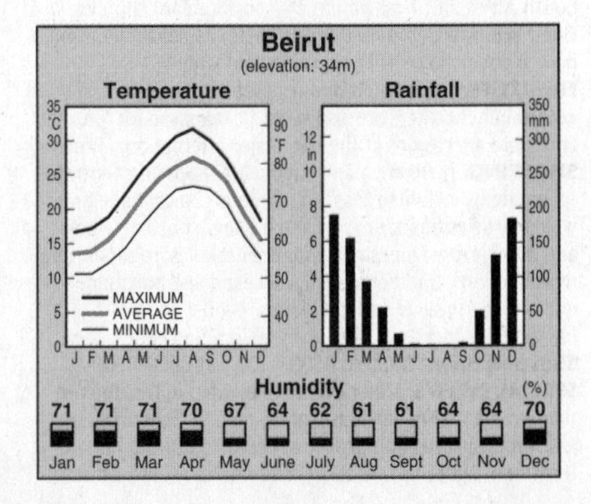

Lesotho

LATEST TRAVEL ADVICE CONTACTS

British Foreign and Commonwealth Office
Tel: (0870) 606 0290 Website: www.fco.gov.uk
US Department of State
Website: http://travel.state.gov/travel
Canadian Department of Foreign Affairs and Int'l Trade
Tel: (1 800) 267 8376 Website: www.dfait-maeci.gc.ca

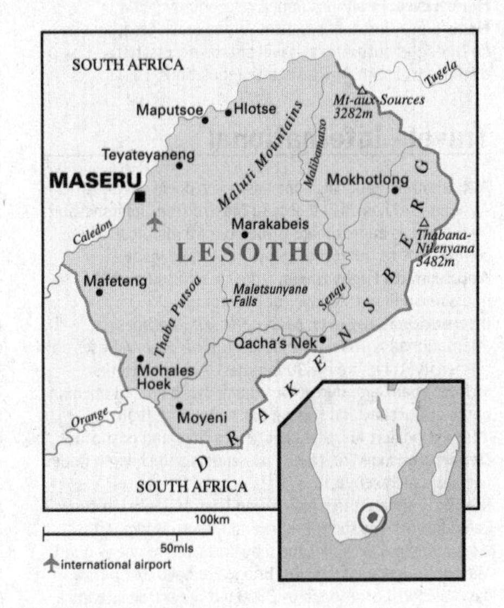

Location: Southern Africa.

Country dialling code: 266.

Ministry of Tourism, Sports and Culture
PO Box 52, Maseru 100, Lesotho
Tel: (22) 313 034. Fax: (22) 310 194 *or* 711.
Website: www.lesotho.gov.ls
Lesotho High Commission
7 Chesham Place, Belgravia, London SW1 8HN, UK
Tel: (020) 7235 5686. Fax: (020) 7235 5023.
E-mail: lhc@lesotholondon.org.uk
Website: www.lesotholondon.org.uk
British High Commission
PO Box 521, Maseru 100, Lesotho
Tel: (22) 313 961. Fax: (22) 310 120.
Embassy of the Kingdom of Lesotho
2511 Massachusetts Avenue, NW, Washington, DC 20008, USA
Tel: (202) 797 5533. Fax: (202) 234 6815.
E-mail: lesothoembassy@verizon.net
Website: www.lesothoemb-usa.gov.ls
Also deals with enquiries from Canada.
Embassy of the United States of America
Street address: 254 Kingsway Road, Maseru 100, Lesotho
Postal address: PO Box 333, Maseru 100, Lesotho
Tel: (22) 312 666. Fax: (22) 310 116.
E-mail: infomaseru@state.gov
Website: http://maseru.usembassy.gov
Consulate of Canada
Street address: LNDC Development House Building, Kingsway Road, Block D, 5th Floor, Maseru, Lesotho
Postal address: PO Box 1191, Maseru 100, Lesotho
Tel: (22) 316 435. Tel/Fax: (22) 314 187.
E-mail: canada@lesoff.co.za

General Information

AREA: 30,355 sq km (11,720 sq miles).
POPULATION: 2,200,000 (official estimate 2002).
POPULATION DENSITY: 67.0 per sq km.
CAPITAL: Maseru. **Population:** 271,000 (UN estimate 2001, including suburbs).
GEOGRAPHY: Lesotho is a landlocked country surrounded

TIMATIC CODES

Health
AMADEUS: **TI-DFT/MSU/HE**
GALILEO/WORLDSPAN: **TI-DFT/MSU/HE**
SABRE: **TIDFT/MSU/HE**

Visa
AMADEUS: **TI-DFT/MSU/VI**
GALILEO/WORLDSPAN: **TI-DFT/MSU/VI**
SABRE: **TIDFT/MSU/VI**

To access TIMATIC country information on Health and Visa regulations through the Computer Reservations System (CRS), type in the appropriate command line listed above.

on all sides by South Africa. It is a mountainous kingdom situated at the highest part of the Drakensberg escarpment on the eastern rim of the South African plateau. Its mountainous terrain is cut by countless valleys and ravines, making it a country of great beauty. To the west, the land descends through a foothill zone of rolling hills to a lowland belt along the border where two-thirds of the population live. Three large rivers, the Caledon, the Orange, and the Tugela, rise in the mountains.
GOVERNMENT: Kingdom. Gained independence from the UK in 1966. **Head of State:** King Letsie III since 1996. **Head of Government:** Prime Minister Bethuel Pakalitha Mosisili since 1998.
LANGUAGE: Sesotho and English.
RELIGION: 90 per cent Christian; mainly Anglican, Roman Catholic and Lesotho Evangelical. The remainder belong to other denominations, including Islam.
TIME: GMT + 2.
ELECTRICITY: 220 volts AC, 50Hz.
COMMUNICATIONS: Telephone: IDD is available to some cities. Country code: 266 (no area codes). Outgoing international code: 00. There is a limited internal telephone network. **Mobile telephone:** GSM 900 networks operated by *Econet Ezi-Cel* and *Vodacom Lesotho*. Coverage is limited to main urban areas. **Internet:** There are Internet cafes in Maseru. ISPs include *LEO Internet Services* (website: www.lesoff.co.za). **Telegram:** Limited facilities exist in main post offices and hotels. For charges, contact the High Commission or Embassy. **Post:** Post office hours: Mon-Fri 0800-1300 and 1400-1630, Sat 0800-1200. **Press:** *Lesotho Today*, *Public Eye* and *The Sun* are the major English-language newspapers.
Radio: BBC World Service (website: www.bbc.co.uk/worldservice) and Voice of America (website: www.voa.gov) can be received. From time to time the frequencies change and the most up-to-date can be found online.

Passport/Visa

	Passport Required?	Visa Required?	Return Ticket Required?
Full British	Yes	No	Yes
Australian	Yes	No	Yes
Canadian	Yes	No	Yes
USA	Yes	No	Yes
Other EU	Yes	No/1	Yes
Japanese	Yes	No	Yes

Note: Regulations and requirements may be subject to change at short notice, and you are advised to contact the appropriate diplomatic or consular authority before finalising travel arrangements. Details of these may be found at the head of this country's entry. Any numbers in the chart refer to the footnotes below.

Note: Visitors travelling via South Africa will need to comply with South African passport/visa regulations.
PASSPORTS: Required by all.
VISAS: Required by all except the following for stays of up to three months:
(a) nationals referred to in the chart above except:
1. nationals of Czech Republic, Estonia, Hungary, Latvia, Lithuania, Poland, Slovak Republic and Slovenia who *do* need a visa;
(b) nationals of Commonwealth countries, except for nationals of Bangladesh, Cameroon, Fiji, Ghana, India, Mozambique, Nigeria, Pakistan and Sri Lanka who *do* require a visa;
(c) nationals of Iceland, Israel, Madagascar, Norway, Switzerland and Zimbabwe.
Types of visa and cost: *Tourist/Business*: £30 (single-entry); £50 (multiple-entry).
Validity: *Single-entry*: up to three months. *Multiple-entry*: up to six months.
Application to: Consulate (or Consular section at Embassy or High Commission); see *Contact Addresses* section.
Application requirements: (a) Valid passport. (b) Two application forms. (c) Two passport-size photos. (d) Return ticket. (e) Fee. *Business*: (a)-(e) and, (f) Letter from sponsor.
Working days required: One.
Temporary residence: Apply to the Ministry of Home Affairs, Maseru. Enquire at Embassy for details.

Money

Currency: Loti (M) = 100 lisente. Notes are in denominations of M200, 100, 50, 20 and 10. Coins are in denominations of 500, 200, 100, 50, 25, 10, 5, 2 and 1 lisente. The plural of 'loti' is 'maloti' and the singular of 'lisente' is 'sente'. The South African Rand is accepted as legal currency on a par with the Loti (Rand R1 = 100 cents).
Credit & debit cards: Limited acceptance of Diners Club, MasterCard and Visa. Check with your credit or debit card company for details of merchant acceptability and other services which may be available.

Travellers cheques: These are widely accepted. To avoid additional exchange rate charges, travellers are advised to take travellers cheques in US Dollars or Pounds Sterling.
Currency restrictions: The import and export of local and foreign currency is unrestricted.
Exchange rate indicators: The following figures are included as a guide to the movements of the Loti against Sterling and the US Dollar:

Date	Feb '04	May '04	Aug '04	Nov '04
£1.00=	12.87	12.51	11.90	11.05
$1.00=	7.07	7.00	6.46	5.83

Banking hours: Mon-Tues and Thurs-Fri 0830-1530, Wed 0830-1300, Sat 0830-1100.

Duty Free

The following goods may be imported into Lesotho without incurring customs duty:
400 cigarettes and 50 cigars and 250g of tobacco; 1l of spirits and 2l of wine (irrespective of age); 50ml of perfume and 250ml of eau de toilette; gifts up to value of M500.
Note: (a) Goods with serial numbers must be declared. (b) No alcohol may be imported by South African nationals.

Public Holidays

2005: Jan 1 New Year's Day. **Mar 11** Moshoeshoe Day. **Mar 25** Good Friday. **Mar 28** Easter Monday. **Apr 4** Heroes' Day. **May 1** Workers' Day. **May 5** Ascension. **Jul 17** King Letsie III's Birthday. **Oct 4** Independence Day. **Dec 25-26** Christmas.
2006: Jan 1 New Year's Day. **Mar 11** Moshoeshoe Day. **Apr 4** Heroes' Day. **Apr 14** Good Friday. **Apr 17** Easter Monday. **May 1** Workers' Day. **May 25** Ascension. **Jul 17** King Letsie III's Birthday. **Oct 4** Independence Day. **Dec 25-26** Christmas.

Health

	Special Precautions?	Certificate Required?
Yellow Fever	Yes	1
Cholera	No	No
Typhoid & Polio	2	N/A
Malaria	No	N/A

***Note:** Regulations and requirements may be subject to change at short notice, and you are advised to contact your doctor well in advance of your intended date of departure. Any numbers in the chart refer to the footnotes below.*

1: A yellow fever vaccination certificate is required from all travellers arriving from infected areas, even if they do not leave the airport.
2: Typhoid fever is common in some areas. Poliomyelitis has very nearly been eradicated, so risk of infection is very low.
Food & drink: Tap water is considered safe to drink. However, drinking water outside main cities and towns may be contaminated and sterilisation is advisable. Milk is pasteurised and dairy products are safe for consumption. Local meat, poultry, seafood, fruit and vegetables are generally considered safe to eat.
Other risks: *Hepatitis A* and *B* occur. Lesotho is free of *bilharzia* (schistosomiasis) and people may swim in fresh water without danger. There is a high incidence of HIV/AIDS.
Health care: Health insurance is recommended.
Note: Since the most practical way to reach Lesotho is to go through South Africa, it will also be necessary to conform to South African health regulations.

Travel - International

AIR: Lesotho's national airline has closed down. *South African Airways (SA)* has daily flights to Maseru from Johannesburg (flight time is approximately one hour 10 minutes), where connections to the rest of the world can be made.
Approximate flight times: From Maseru to *London* is 14 hours (including a stopover of two hours).
International airports: *Maseru (MSU)* (Moshoeshoe International) is 18km (11 miles) south of Maseru. Buses go to the city (travel time - 30 minutes). Airport facilities include a bank and bureau de change (with limited opening hours on Tuesday and Friday), bar, restaurant, flight information, left luggage facilities, car hire and post office.
Departure tax: M20; transit passengers and children under five years are exempt.
ROAD: There are three major road links to South Africa: at Caledonsport, Ficksburg Bridge and Maseru Bridge. Other crossing points exist, but the road surfaces are not as good. Maseru Bridge and Ficksburg Bridge are open 24 hours a day. Caledonsport is open by 0800 but may close as early as 1600. **Bus:** Minibuses run regularly between Maseru and Johannesburg.
Road tax: M5, payable by all travellers leaving Lesotho by road.
RAIL: Lesotho is linked with the South African railway system by a short line (2.6km/1.6 miles) from Maseru to Marseilles, on the Bloemfontein/Natal main line. However, this is only used for goods trains at present.

Travel - Internal

ROAD: Traffic drives on the left. The road system is underdeveloped and few roads are paved. The main road which runs through the towns from the north to the western and southern borders is tarred, but other roads can be impassable during the rainy season. There are **minibuses** in the lowlands. **Car hire** is available in Maseru. It is advised not to drive in rural areas at night (or even walk around Maseru at night). There have been incidents of mugging and vehicle hijacking. **Documentation:** An International Driving Permit is recommended. National driving licences are normally valid, providing that they are either in English or accompanied by a certified translation. Enquire at the High Commission or Embassy for details.
Travel times: The following chart gives travel times (in hours and minutes) from **Maseru** to other towns in Lesotho.

	Road
Teyateyaneng	-
Leribe	1.00
Butha-Buthe	
Mokhotlong	7.00
Qachas Nek	8.00
Thabatseka	5.00
Mohales Hoek	1.30
Quthing	3.00
Mafeteng	1.00

Accommodation

HOTELS: There are hotels of varying quality in the main towns and mountain lodges giving access to the wilder regions. There are several hotels in Maseru of international standard. Further information can be obtained from the Lesotho Tourist Board (see *Contact Addresses* section).
LODGES: Commercial concerns have built several lodges (mostly self-catering) providing bungalow accommodation.

Resorts & Excursions

Note: Civil unrest throughout 1999 caused some destruction in most of the town centres and the country is still in the process of rebuilding.

MASERU: Lesotho's capital is the obvious stepping-off point for a holiday. There are local highlights to visit such as the historic cemetery and the fascinating architecture of the **King's Palace** and the **Prime Minister's Residence**. From Maseru, you can take many day trips, either independently or by luxury minibus, visiting surrounding points of interest.
Near Maseru, the **Ha Khotso Bushmen Rock Paintings** make an interesting visit. Also nearby is **Thaba Bosiu**, a flat-topped hill where the Basotho made a last heroic stand against the Boers. Many of their chiefs are buried here.
THE SOUTH: The southern region of Lesotho is being promoted for tourism, with hotels at **Moyeni** and **Mohales Hoek** offering facilities for horse riding, mountain climbing and hiking. Worth visiting in the district are the **Motlejoeng Caves**, 2km (1.2 miles) south of Mahale's Hoek; the dinosaur footprints at **Moyeni**; the **Masitise Cave House** and the petrified forest on the mountain of **Thaba-Ts'oeu**. In the southeast, in the region bordering South Africa, is one of the most beautiful parts of Lesotho - if not southern Africa. It is ideal for trekking. Places of most interest include **Ramanbanta**, **Semonkong** (where the **Maletsunyane Waterfalls** can be visited) and the **Sehlabathebe National Park**.

Sport & Activities

Pony trekking: At the moment three treks are on offer, two of them covering the great falls at *Ribaneng*, *Ketane* and *Maletsunyane*, the latter being particularly noteworthy as it is the highest single-drop fall in southern Africa. There is a choice of return, once Semonkong has been reached, between going back to Maseru by road on the fourth day or continuing the pony ride for another two days to Ha Ramabanta, where motor transport is available for the return to Maseru. The other route is the *Molimo Nthuse* circular trip, starting at the *Molimo Nthuse* ('God Help Me') *Centre* (the actual base for the Basotho Pony Trekking Centre) and going over *Thaba Putsoa* ('Blue Mountain') *Pass* to reach Ha Marakabei-Senqunyane Lodge on the second day. The return trip via Molikaliko and *Qiloane Falls* reaches Molimo Nthuse from a different direction on the fifth day. Unlike the three falls of the first trip, Qiloane is a wide fall with several smaller drops. Overnight stops are usually made in the rural areas in the huts of the remote Basotho where a taste of real Basotho life is experienced. All the routes pass through magnificent countryside.
Skiing: In conjunction with a private company, the Lesotho government has developed a modern ski resort in the heart of the Lesotho highlands. Just four-and-a-half hours' drive from Johannesburg, the resort aims to attract skiers from both Southern Africa and Europe (website: www.afriski.co.za).
Mountain climbing: Mountain climbing is a popular and ideal way of seeing the rugged beauty of the land.
Birdwatching: As many as 279 species of birds have been recorded and keen birdwatchers should take a trip along the Mountain Road to see birds rare to southern Africa.
Fishing: Lesotho's dams and rivers contain local and imported fish. Brown and rainbow trout and carp provide satisfying sport for anglers.
Other: Horseracing is a popular sport and meetings take place throughout the country. **Football** is Lesotho's national game and matches are played most Saturdays and Sundays. Maseru has high-standard **tennis** courts. For **swimming**, bilharzia-free rivers and lakes and hotel pools are available for bathing.

Social Profile

FOOD & DRINK: The main hotels in Maseru serve international food, but there are also some interesting places to dine in the main towns. Hotels and restaurants in Lesotho cater for all nationaljties. There are *halal* foods and seafood. Cooking styles include French, Italian, Continental and Chinese in Maseru. Much food has to be imported from South Africa, but freshwater fish is in abundant supply. Good beer is widely available and better establishments will have a good choice of beers, spirits and wines.
NIGHTLIFE: Some hotels and restaurants have live entertainment. There are also several cinemas in Maseru and there are casinos at the two major international hotels.
SHOPPING: There are many handicraft shops and centres selling items including Lesotho's famous conical hats; grass-woven articles (mats, brooms and baskets); pottery; wool and mohair rugs; tapestries and other textiles; rock painting reproductions; traditional seed, clay bead and porcupine quill jewellery; silver and gold items; copper work (particularly chess sets of African design) and ebony items.
Shopping hours: Mon-Fri 0800-1700, Sat 0800-1500.
SPECIAL EVENTS: Major events celebrated in Lesotho are the two main Christian feasts of Easter and Christmas. The following is a selection of special events occurring in Lesotho in 2005:

Mar 11 *Moshoeshoe Day*. **Jul 17** *King's Birthday*. **Oct 4** *National Independence Day*.
SOCIAL CONVENTIONS: If spending some time in rural villages, it is polite to inform the Head Chief. It is likely that he will be very helpful. Normal social courtesies and a friendly, warm approach will be greatly appreciated. Dress should be practical and casual but local customs should be respected (including those regarding modesty in dress). Religion plays an important part in daily life.
Photography: Photographs must not be taken of the following: the palace, police establishments, government offices, the airport or monetary authority buildings.
Tipping: It is customary in restaurants and hotels to give a tip as a reward for good service.

Business Profile

ECONOMY: The earnings of the estimated 150,000 Lesotho nationals working in South Africa account for a substantial proportion of the country's income. Inside the country, 40 per cent of the workforce are engaged in agriculture, farming maize, wheat and other crops. Wool, mohair and hides are important exports. Nonetheless, Lesotho's vulnerability to drought means that over half the country's food must be imported from South Africa: this was particularly apparent during mid-2002, when large-scale famine was narrowly averted. There are reserves of ores and minerals, including diamonds, uranium, lead and iron ore, but little exploitation has taken place. Light manufacturing, meanwhile, has grown steadily with food, drink and textiles as the main products. Tourism is a major source of foreign exchange. Lesotho's government has historically relied on foreign aid, particularly for infrastructure programmes (large parts of which were destroyed during a major civil insurrection in 1998). The most important infrastructure project of recent years has been Lesotho Highlands Water Project, which aims to deliver water to South Africa and provide 60 per cent of Lesotho's electricity supply. South Africa is Lesotho's major trading partner and the Southern African Customs Union provides over 95 per cent of the country's imports. Unfortunately, Lesotho and South Africa also share the scourge of the region, HIV/AIDS, which has infected over one-third of Lesotho's productive labour force.
BUSINESS: Lightweight suit, shirt and tie should be worn for business meetings. English will be spoken by most businesspeople. Usual business formalities should be observed, but expect a casual atmosphere and pace.
Office hours: Mon-Fri 0800-1245 and 1400-1630, Sat 0800-1300.
Government office hours: Mon-Fri 0800-1245 and 1400-1630.
COMMERCIAL INFORMATION: The following organisations can offer advice: Ministry of Trade, Industry and Marketing, PO Box 747, Maseru 100 (tel: 312 938); *or* Lesotho National Development Corporation, Private Bag A96, Development House, Block A, Kingsway Street, Maseru 100 (tel: 312 012; fax: 310 038; e-mail: info@lndc.org.ls; website: www.lndc.org.ls); *or* Lesotho Chamber of Commerce and Industry, PO Box 79, Kingsway Avenue, Maseru 100 (tel: 323 482; fax: 310 417).
CONFERENCES/CONVENTIONS: The Lesotho Tourist Board can provide advice (see *Contact Addresses* section).

Climate

Temperate climate with well-marked seasons. Summer is the rainy season; 85 per cent of rainfall occurs from October to April, especially in the mountains. Snow occurs in the highlands from May to September. The hottest period is from January to February. Lesotho is a land of clear blue skies and more than 300 days of sunshine a year.
Required clothing: During the summer, lightweight cottons with warmer wear for the evenings is needed. In winter, medium- to heavyweight clothes are advised. Waterproofing is necessary during the rainy season.

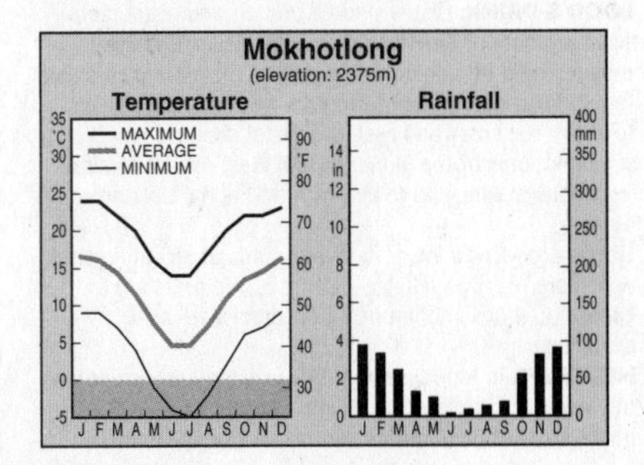

Liberia

LATEST TRAVEL ADVICE CONTACTS

British Foreign and Commonwealth Office
Tel: (0870) 606 0290 Website: www.fco.gov.uk
US Department of State
Website: http://travel.state.gov/travel
Canadian Department of Foreign Affairs and Int'l Trade
Tel: (1 800) 267 8376 Website: www.dfait-maeci.gc.ca

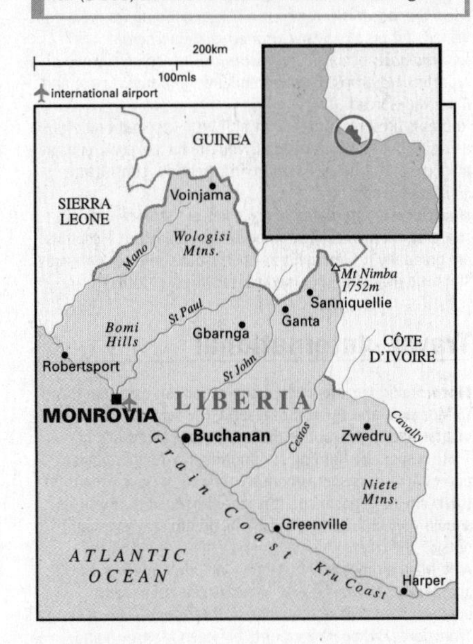

Location: West Africa.

Country dialling code: 231.

Ministry of Information, Cultural Affairs and Tourism (MICAT)
110 United Nations Drive, PO Box 10-9021, Capitol Hill, 1000 Monrovia, Liberia Tel: 226 269. Fax: 226 069.
Embassy of the Republic of Liberia
23 Fitzroy Square, London W1 6EW, UK
Tel: (020) 7388 5489. Fax: (020) 7380 1593.
Opening hours: Mon-Fri 1300-1600; Mon-Thurs 1030-1500 (visa section).
Also deals with tourism enquiries.
The British High Commission in Freetown deals with enquiries relating to Liberia (see *Sierra Leone* **section).**
British Consulate
Street address: c/o UMARCO, Clara Town, Bush Rod Island, Monrovia, Liberia
Postal address: PO Box 1196, Monrovia, Liberia
Tel: 226 056 *or* 6516 973 (mobile telephone number for use outside consular hours). Fax: 226 061.
E-mail: chalkleyroy@aol.com
Embassy of the Republic of Liberia
5201 16th Street, NW, Washington, DC 20011, USA
Tel: (202) 723 0437. Fax: (202) 723 0436.
E-mail: info@embassyofliberia.org
Website: www.embassyofliberia.org
Also deals with enquiries from Canada.
Embassy of the United States of America
Street address: 111 United Nations Drive, Mamba Point, 1000 Monrovia, Liberia
Postal address: PO Box 10-0098, 1000 Monrovia, Liberia
Tel: 226 370/80. Fax: 226 1490/93 (consular section).
E-mail: mrveduconsular@state.gov (consular section).
Website: http://monrovia.usembassy.gov
Embassy may close temporarily due to regular reviews of its security policy.
Consulate General of the Republic of Liberia
1441 Ontario Street, Burlington, Ontario L7S 1G5, Canada.
Tel: (905) 333 4000/1. Fax: (905) 632 4000.
The Canadian High Commission in Abidjan deals with enquiries relating to Liberia (see *Côte d'Ivoire* **section).**

TIMATIC CODES

Health	AMADEUS: **TI-DFT/MLW/HE** GALILEO/WORLDSPAN: **TI-DFT/MLW/HE** SABRE: **TIDFT/MLW/HE**
Visa	AMADEUS: **TI-DFT/MLW/VI** GALILEO/WORLDSPAN: **TI-DFT/MLW/VI** SABRE: **TIDFT/MLW/VI**

To access TIMATIC country information on Health and Visa regulations through the Computer Reservations System (CRS), type in the appropriate command line listed above.

General Information

Foreigners are advised against all but essential travel to Monrovia and the rest of Liberia: the security situation is volatile and flights out of the country are intermittent. There is sporadic fighting and looting. For further advice, potential visitors should contact their local government travel advice department.
AREA: 97,754 sq km (37,743 sq miles).
POPULATION: 3,239,000 (2003).
POPULATION DENSITY: 33.1 per sq km.
CAPITAL: Monrovia. **Population:** 550,200 (2003).
GEOGRAPHY: Liberia borders Sierra Leone, Guinea Republic and Côte d'Ivoire. The Atlantic coastline to the west is 560km (348 miles) long, of which over half is sandy beach. Lying parallel to the shore are three distinct belts. The low coastal belt is well watered by shallow lagoons, tidal creeks and mangrove swamps, behind which rises a gently undulating plateau, 500 to 800m (1640 to 2625ft) high, partly covered with dense forests. Inland and to the north is the mountain region which includes Mount Nimba at 1752m (5748ft) and Waulo Mountain at 1400m (4593ft). About half of the country's population are rural dwellers.
GOVERNMENT: Republic. Declared independence in 1847.
Acting Head of State and Government: President Charles Gyude Bryant since 2003, who replaced Taylor after international pressure and a civil war ousted him - a new government has yet to be formed.
LANGUAGE: English is the official language. The main local languages are Bassa, Dan (Gio), Kpelleh, Kru, Lorma and Mano. There are 16 major languages and dialects.
RELIGION: Officially a Christian state, with more than 30 denominations represented; Islam is practised in the north and traditional animist beliefs exist throughout the country.
TIME: GMT.
ELECTRICITY: 110 volts AC, 60Hz.
COMMUNICATIONS: Telephone: IDD service to some cities. Country code: 231 (no area codes). Outgoing international code: 00. The internal network in Monrovia is gradually being extended over the country. **Mobile telephone:** GSM 900 networks operated by *Comium* (website: www.comium.com), *Libercell* and *LonestarCell*. **Internet:** There are a few Internet cafes in Monrovia. ISPs include *Africalink* (website: www.africalink.com). **Post:** Airmail to Europe takes up to one month. **Press:** The Liberian press is in English; the main papers are the *Inquirer* and the *Monrovia Guardian*.
Radio: BBC World Service (website: www.bbc.co.uk/worldservice) and Voice of America (website: www.voa.gov) can be received. From time to time the frequencies change and the most up-to-date can be found online.

Passport/Visa

	Passport Required?	Visa Required?	Return Ticket Required?
Full British	Yes	Yes	No
Australian	Yes	Yes	No
Canadian	Yes	Yes	No
USA	Yes	Yes	No
Other EU	Yes	Yes	No
Japanese	Yes	Yes	No

Note: *Regulations and requirements may be subject to change at short notice, and you are advised to contact the appropriate diplomatic or consular authority before finalising travel arrangements. Details of these may be found at the head of this country's entry. Any numbers in the chart refer to the footnotes below.*

PASSPORTS: Passport valid for a minimum of six months from date of entry required by all.
VISAS: Required by all except the following:
(a) nationals of ECOWAS countries, Israel, Korea (Rep) and Thailand;
(b) transit passengers continuing their journey by the same or first connecting aircraft within 48 hours, provided holding onward or return documentation and not leaving the airport.
Types of visa and cost: *Tourist/Business*: £30 (single-entry); £60 (multiple-entry).
Validity: *Single-entry*: three months from date of issue; *multiple-entry*: six months from date of issue. Visas may be extended at the Immigration office in Monrovia.
Application to: Consulate (or Consular section at Embassy); see *Contact Addresses* section.
Application requirements: (a) Valid passport. (b) Completed application form. (c) Two passport-size photos attached to each form. (d) International yellow fever vaccination certificate. (e) Letter stating purpose of visit and name of contact in Liberia. Applicants must produce proof of financial status while in the country. (f) For business trips, a letter from company, or statement giving purpose of visit.
Working days required: One.
Temporary residence: Application should be made prior

to arrival to the Ministry of Foreign Affairs, Monrovia.
Note: All visitors holding a visa issued abroad and intending to stay in Liberia for more than 15 days must report within 48 hours of their arrival to the Immigration Office, Broad Street, Monrovia. Two passport-size photos must be submitted.

Money

Currency: Liberian Dollar (L$) = 100 cents. Notes are in denominations of L$100, 50, 20, 10 and 5. US Dollar notes are in circulation in the following denominations: US$100, 50, 20, 10, 5 and 1.
Note: The Liberian Dollar is tied to the US Dollar.
Currency exchange: Money can be exchanged at the Liberia Bank for Development and Investment (LBDI), on the corner of Randall and Ashmun Streets in Monrovia. LBDI also incorporates a Western Union office, which can receive urgent money transfers from abroad (though the procedure is lengthy and will take approximately one day).
Credit & debit cards: Not generally accepted.
Travellers cheques: These are generally not accepted.
Currency restrictions: There are no restrictions on the import or export of local currency. The import of foreign currency over the equivalent of US$10,000 should be declared or heavy fines may be imposed. The export of foreign currency is permitted up to US$7500; more may be exported only as bank drafts, travellers cheques or money orders.
Exchange rate indicators: The following figures are included as a guide to the movements of the Liberian Dollar against Sterling and the US Dollar:

Date	Feb '04	May '04	Aug '04	Nov '04
£1.00=	1.82	94.66	103.17	89.00
$1.00=	1.00	53.00	56.00	47.00

Banking hours: Mon-Thurs 0900-1200, Fri 0800-1400. Some banks may open on Saturday.

Duty Free

The following goods may be imported into Liberia without incurring customs duty:
200 cigarettes or 25 cigars or 250g tobacco products; 1l of spirits and 1l of wine; 100g of perfume and 1l of eau-de-toilette; goods to the value of US$125.

Public Holidays

2005: Jan 1 New Year's Day. **Feb 11** Armed Forces Day. **Mar 8** Decoration Day. **Mar 15** J J Roberts' Birthday. **Apr 12** National Redemption Day. **Apr 14** Fast and Prayer Day. **May 6** Samuel K Doe's Birthday. **May 14** National Unification Day. **May 25** Africa Day. **Jul 26** Independence Day. **Aug 24** Flag Day. **Oct 29** Youth Day. **Nov 24** Thanksgiving Day. **Nov 29** President Tubman's Birthday. **Dec 25** Christmas Day.
2006: Jan 1 New Year's Day. **Feb 11** Armed Forces Day. **Mar 8** Decoration Day. **Mar 15** J J Roberts' Birthday. **Apr 12** National Redemption Day. **Apr 14** Fast and Prayer Day. **May 6** Samuel K Doe's Birthday. **May 14** National Unification Day. **May 25** Africa Day. **Jul 26** Independence Day. **Aug 24** Flag Day. **Oct 29** Youth Day. **Nov 25** Thanksgiving Day. **Nov 29** President Tubman's Birthday. **Dec 25** Christmas Day.

Health

	Special Precautions?	Certificate Required?
Yellow Fever	Yes	1
Cholera	2	No
Typhoid & Polio	3	N/A
Malaria	4	N/A

Note: Regulations and requirements may be subject to change at short notice, and you are advised to contact your doctor well in advance of your intended date of departure. Any numbers in the chart refer to the footnotes below.

1: A yellow fever vaccination certificate is required from all travellers over one year of age. Note that the certificate must be presented with all visa applications.
2: Following WHO guidelines issued in 1973, a cholera vaccination certificate is not a condition of entry to Liberia. However, cholera is a serious risk in this country and precautions are essential. Up-to-date advice should be sought before deciding whether these precautions should include vaccination, as medical opinion is divided over its effectiveness; see the *Health* appendix.
3: Typhoid is widespread and poliomyelitis is still endemic.
4: Malaria risk, predominantly in the malignant *falciparum* form, exists all year throughout the country. High resistance to chloroquine and resistance to sulfadoxine-pyrimethamine has been reported. The recommended prophylaxis is mefloquine.

Food & drink: All water should be regarded as being potentially contaminated. Water used for drinking, brushing teeth or making ice should have first been boiled or otherwise sterilised. Milk is unpasteurised and should be boiled. Powdered or tinned milk is available and is advised, but make sure that it is reconstituted with pure water. Avoid dairy products which are likely to have been made from unboiled milk. Only eat well-cooked meat and fish, preferably served hot. Pork, salad and mayonnaise may carry increased risk. Vegetables should be cooked and fruit peeled.
Other risks: *Bilharzia* (schistosomiasis) is present. Avoid swimming and paddling in fresh water; swimming pools which are well chlorinated and maintained are safe.
Meningococcal meningitis is a risk, depending on the area visited and time of year. *Cutaneous* and *visceral leishmaniasis* occur. *Trypanosomiasis* (sleeping sickness) is reported. *Hepatitis B* is hyperendemic, and *hepatitis A* and *E* are widespread.
Rabies is present. For those at high risk, vaccination before arrival should be considered. If you are bitten, seek medical advice without delay. For more information, consult the *Health* appendix.
Health care: International travellers are strongly advised to take out full medical insurance before departure. Hospitals are gradually re-emerging in Liberia, but some patients may still need evacuation to medical facilities in Côte d'Ivoire.

Travel - International

Note: Foreigners are advised against all but essential travel to Monrovia and the rest of Liberia; the security situation is volatile and flights out of the country are intermittent. There is sporadic fighting and looting. For further advice, potential visitors should contact their local government travel advice department. It is recommended that visitors, should they choose to visit Liberia, do not stay overnight outside the city.
AIR: Main airlines serving Liberia include *Air Afrique (RK)* and *Ghana Airways (GH)*. *Air Ivoire* operates flights between Monrovia and Abidjan (Côte d'Ivoire). *Weasua Air Transport (XA)* operates flights between Monrovia and Freetown (Sierra Leone) (tel: 275 440; fax: 226 067).
Approximate flight times: From Monrovia to *New York* (via Dakar) is nine hours; to *London* (via Brussels) is 11 hours.
International airports: *Monrovia (ROB)* (Roberts International) is 60km (36 miles) southeast of the city. There are bus services and taxis to and from the city. Airport facilities are limited, but include restaurant and first aid facilities.
No airlines currently land at *Spriggs Payne Airport (MLW)* which is in the city itself.
Departure tax: None.
SEA: There are unscheduled freighter services with passenger accommodation from European ports. The main Liberian ports are Monrovia, Buchanan, Greenville, Harper and Robertsport. The port in Monrovia is being expanded.
ROAD: Best routes to Liberia are through Guinea Republic and Côte d'Ivoire, but they are impassable during the rainy season. The northeastern route to Sierra Leone (via Kolahun and Kailahun) is currently closed.

Travel - Internal

AIR: There are 60 airfields for small aircraft.
SEA/RIVER: There is a passenger service between Monrovia and Buchanan. There is also a boat service which runs weekly between Harper and Greenville. Unscheduled coastal steamers may sometimes take passengers. Small craft are used for local transportation on Liberia's many rivers. **Canoe safaris:** Between December and March, specialist companies arrange canoe trips upriver from Greenville, a small seaport 200km (125 miles) southeast of Monrovia. Contact the Ministry of Information, Culture and Tourism for further details (see *Contact Addresses* section).
RAIL: No service at present.
ROAD: Traffic drives on the right. Difficulties in bypassing lagoons and bridging river estuaries often result in long detours and delays along the coast. Main roads are from Monrovia to Buchanan and from Monrovia to Sanniquellie with branches to Ganta and Harper. Many of the smaller roads are still untarred. Vehicle transport is limited. **Bus:** No services between main towns at present. **Car hire:** Self-drive or chauffeured cars may be hired in Monrovia.
Documentation: An International Driving Permit is recommended, although it is not legally required. A temporary licence to drive is available from local authorities on presentation of a valid British, Northern Ireland or US driving licence and is valid for up to 30 days.
URBAN: Taxis are available and tipping is unnecessary.

Accommodation

HOTELS: Hotel accommodation can be quite expensive, but is not extortionate by international standards. It is advisable to book well in advance, whatever the category of accommodation. There are a few air-conditioned hotels of international standard and a range of inexpensive hotels and motels. The top hotels charge from US$110 a night. Hotels in the mid-range charge from US$60 and tend to provide the bare minimum.
GUEST HOUSES: There are several mission guest houses with both cooking and laundry facilities about 4km (2 miles) from the city centre.
CAMPING: There are few official sites. Camping is free but caution should be exercised when choosing where to camp. Specialist operators run sites near national parks; contact the Ministry of Tourism or West African Safaris for details (see *Contact Addresses* section).
YOUTH HOSTELS: The YMCA is cheap, but often full, and is located on the corner of Broad and McDonald Streets.

Resorts & Excursions

The most evocative description of Liberia can be found in Graham Greene's *Journey without Maps*, an account of his overland trip across the country in 1935. Although it can now hardly pretend to be an up-to-date guide book, the descriptions and the atmosphere of the country it creates – particularly when dealing with the mysterious and jungle-rich interior – make the book a valuable and entertaining introduction for anyone planning to visit the country.
MONROVIA: The capital is a sprawling city on the coast divided by inlets, lagoons and rocky headlands. The city has several nightclubs, restaurants and bars, centred on the area around Gurley Street. There are several good sandy beaches near the capital.
Excursions: Around 80km (50 miles) from the capital is **Lake Piso**, ideal for fishing and watersports. Conducted tours of the **Firestone Rubber Plantation**, one of the largest in the world, make an interesting day excursion, situated only 50km (30 miles) from Monrovia. Some of the country's most beautiful beaches can be found at **Robertsport**. The **Kpa-Tawe Waterfalls** are four hours 30 minutes' drive away from Monrovia (a 4 wheel drive vehicle is recommended).
SAPO NATIONAL PARK: For wildlife and nature enthusiasts, the Sapo National Park has much to offer: located in Sinoe County, this pristine forest wilderness is home to a great variety of plants and animal species (including elephant, leopard, giant forest hog and the rare pygmy hippo). The park is only accessible on foot (there are no roads) and consists largely of rainforest, which has never been logged, and hence makes it Western Africa's largest untouched tract of rainforest. The park's western boundary is formed by the **Sinoe River**.

Sport & Activities

Safaris: The *Sapo National Park* (see *Resorts & Excursions* section) is West Africa's largest untouched tract of rainforest and offers excellent opportunities for safaris and jungle treks. West African Safaris, a company in the USA, offers comprehensive and exclusive safari packages that include transport to the park, accommodation in luxury safari tents as well as experienced local guides. River trips on the Sinoe River are also available. For further information, contact the Ministry of Information, Culture and Tourism (see *Contact Addresses* section).
Watersports: Swimming and **boating** are popular at Liberia's many sandy beaches. These include *Bernard's Beach, Caesar's Beach, Cedar Beach, Cooper's Beach, Elwa Beach, Kendaje Beach, Kenema Beach* and *Sugar Beach*, all of which charge a small entrance fee. *Lake Piso* is also ideal for watersports. The skindiving season is from December to May, when the sea is at its clearest. There is good **fishing** in the *Mesurado* and *Saint Paul* rivers, along the coast and at Lake Piso, where there are traditional fishing villages.
Other: There is a private **golf** club in Monrovia. **Football** is the Liberian national sport.

Social Profile

FOOD & DRINK: Liberia's hotels, motels and restaurants serve a variety of American, European, Asian, Chinese, Lebanese and African dishes, as well as the more predictable fare of hotel dining rooms. Here, as well as in the smaller towns of the north and east, the visitor should enjoy sampling some of the more unusual West African foods in 'cookhouses' which serve rice with traditional Liberian dishes.
Liberia produces a lot of its own brands of alcoholic drink, which are readily available – some of the beers are excellent; wines and imported beverages are also available.
NIGHTLIFE: In Monrovia, nightlife is extensive with dozens of crowded nightclubs, discos and bars open until the early hours. Most of the nightlife centres on Gurley Street.

Providence Island has a bandstand and an amphitheatre where performances of traditional African music and dance are staged.

SHOPPING: Monrovia's sidestreets are crowded with tailors selling brightly coloured tie-dyed and embroidered cloth which they will make up immediately into African or European styles. Monrovia offers the shopper elegant boutiques and shops as well as modern, air-conditioned supermarkets which compete with old-fashioned stores. Liberian handicrafts include carvings in sapwood, camwood, ebony and mahogany, stone items, soapstone carvings (such as fertility symbols from the Kissi), ritual masks, metal jewellery and figurines and reed dolls of the Loma. **Shopping hours:** Mon-Sat 0800-1300 and 1500-1800.

SOCIAL CONVENTIONS: In Muslim areas, the visitor should respect the conventions of dress and the food laws, since failure to do so will be taken as an insult. Dress is casual and must be practical, but smarter dress will be expected in hotel dining rooms and for important social functions. The visitor should be aware that the cost of living is high. Sending flowers or chocolates to hosts is inappropriate; a letter of thanks is all that is required.

Tipping: There is no need to tip taxi drivers, but other tips are normally around 10 per cent.

Business Profile

ECONOMY: The civil war caused severe damage to the economy and, following the peace settlement, reconstruction has been the highest priority. 70 per cent of the population work the land, producing rice and cassava as staple foods and palm oil, coffee and cocoa as cash crops. The country's principal export commodities are iron ore and rubber. Some gold and diamonds are also mined. The manufacturing industry – still operating far below capacity – produces cement and other building materials, chemicals, drinks and tobacco and consumer products. Liberia operates one of the longest established open registry (flag of convenience) merchant shipping fleets. This continues to be an essential source of foreign exchange and government revenue. Liberia relies heavily on international aid and financial support. It is a member of the West African trading bloc ECOWAS. The USA is Liberia's largest trading partner, followed by Germany, Belgium, France and Italy.

BUSINESS: Business dress is informal – normally a shirt and tie is acceptable. The language used in business circles is English. **Office hours:** Mon-Fri 0800-1200 and 1400-1700.

COMMERCIAL INFORMATION: The following organisation can offer advice: Liberia Chamber of Commerce, PO Box 92, Monrovia (tel: 222 040 *or* 223 738).

Climate

Hot, tropical climate with little variation in temperature. The wet season runs from May to October. The dry *harmattan* wind blows from December to March, making the coastal belt particularly arid.

Required clothing: Lightweight cottons and linens are worn throughout the year, with waterproofing advised during the wet season.

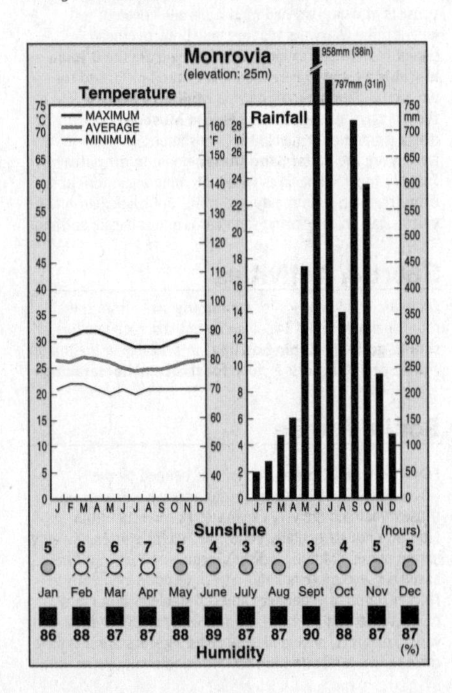

Libya

LATEST TRAVEL ADVICE CONTACTS

British Foreign and Commonwealth Office
Tel: (0870) 606 0290 Website: www.fco.gov.uk

US Department of State
Website: http://travel.state.gov/travel

Canadian Department of Foreign Affairs and Int'l Trade
Tel: (1 800) 267 8376 Website: www.dfait-maeci.gc.ca

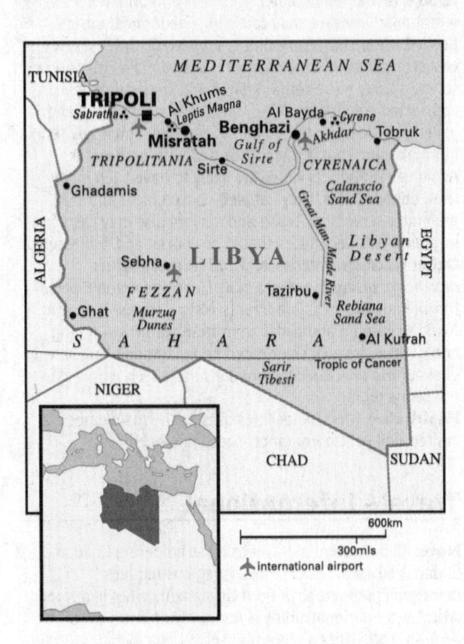

Location: North Africa.

Country dialling code: 218.

Embassy of the Socialist People's Libyan Arab Jamahiriya
2 Rue Charles-Lamoureux, Paris 75116, France
Tel: (1) 4704 7160. Fax: (1) 4755 9625.

Libyan People's Bureau
61-62 Ennismore Gardens, London SW7 1NH, UK
Tel: (020) 7589 6120. Fax: (020) 7589 6087 *or* 9137 (consular section).
Opening hours: Mon-Wed 1000-1100 (visa application); Thurs 1400-1500 (visa collection).

British Embassy
PO Box 4206, Tripoli, Libya
Tel: (21) 335 1422 (consular section) *or* 1419.
Fax: (21) 335 1425 (consular and management section) *or* 1427 (visa section) *or* 340 3648 (chancery).
E-mail: trade.libya@fco.gov.uk (commercial section) *or* belibya@hotmail.com *or* visa.libya@fco.gov.uk (visa section).
Website: www.britain-in-libya.org

US Liaison Office
Street address: c/o Embassy of Belgium, Tower 4, Dhat al-Emad Towers Complex, 5th Floor, Tripoli, Libya
Postal address: PO Box 91650, Tripoli, Libya
Tel: (21) 335 1990 (ask for room 1050) *or* 0936 (consular section). Fax: (21) 335 0937/0118.
E-mail: consulartripoli@yahoo.com

Canadian Embassy
Street address: Great Al-Fateh Tower 1, 7th Floor, Tripoli, Libya
Postal address: PO Box 93392, Al-Fateh Tower Post Office, Tripoli, Libya
Tel: (21) 335 1633. Fax: (21) 335 1630.
E-mail: trpli@dfait-maeci.gc.ca
Website: www.dfait-maeci.gc.ca/libya

Permanent Mission of the Great Socialist People's Libyan Arab Jamahiriya to the United Nations
309-315 East 48th Street, New York, NY 10017, USA
Tel: (212) 752 5775. Fax: (212) 593 4787.
E-mail: info@libya-un.org

TIMATIC CODES

Health
AMADEUS: **TI-DFT/TIP/HE**
GALILEO/WORLDSPAN: **TI-DFT/TIP/HE**
SABRE: **TIDFT/TIP/HE**

Visa
AMADEUS: **TI-DFT/TIP/VI**
GALILEO/WORLDSPAN: **TI-DFT/TIP/VI**
SABRE: **TIDFT/TIP/VI**

To access TIMATIC country information on Health and Visa regulations through the Computer Reservations System (CRS), type in the appropriate command line listed above.

Website: www.libya-un.org
Also deals with enquiries from Canada.

Embassy of the Great Socialist People's Libyan Arab Jamahiriya
81 Metcalfe Street, Suite 1000, Ottawa, Ontario K1P 6K7, Canada
Tel: (613) 230 0919. Fax: (613) 230 0683.
E-mail: info@libya-canada.org
Website: www.libya-canada.org

General Information

AREA: 1,775,500 sq km (685,520 sq miles).
POPULATION: 5,678,484 (2003).
POPULATION DENSITY: 3.2 per sq km.
CAPITAL: Tripoli (Tarabulus). **Population:** 1,149,957 (2003).
GEOGRAPHY: Libya consists mostly of huge areas of desert. It shares borders with Tunisia and Algeria in the west and Egypt in the east, while the Sahara extends across the southern frontiers with Niger, Chad and the Sudan. There are almost 2000km (1250 miles) of Mediterranean coast, with a low plain extending from the Tunisian border to the Jebel Akhdar (Green Mountain) area in the east. Inland the terrain becomes more hilly. With the exception of the 'Sand Sea' of the Sarir Calanscio, and the Saharan mountains of the Sarir Tibesti, there are oases scattered throughout the country.
GOVERNMENT: Jamahiriya (state of the masses). Gained independence from Italy in 1951. **Head of State:** Muammar al-Qadhafi (Leader of the Revolution) since 1969. **Head of Government:** Mubarak Abdullah al-Shamikh (Secretary of the General People's Committee) since 2000.
LANGUAGE: Arabic (which must be used for all official purposes), with some English or Italian. All road, shop and other signs are in Arabic. English is normally understood by people working in hotels, restaurants and shops.
RELIGION: Sunni Muslim.
TIME: GMT + 2.
ELECTRICITY: 220 volts AC, 40Hz. All services may be intermittently disrupted by power cuts.
COMMUNICATIONS: Telephone: IDD service is available. Country code: 218. Outgoing international code: 00. **Mobile telephone:** GSM 900 and 1800 networks in use. Network providers include *General Post* and *Telecommunications Company*, *El Madar* and *Orbit*. **Internet:** ISPs include *Libya Telecom* and *Technology* (website: www.lttnet.com). There are Internet cafes in Tripoli and some other towns. **Post:** Postal services are available in all main towns, but services are generally poor and erratic, and mail may be subject to censorship. Airmail to Europe takes approximately two weeks. **Press:** There are several newspapers and periodicals, but none are published in English. The main dailies are *Al-Fajir al-Jadid* and *Az-zahf al-Akhdar*.
Radio: BBC World Service (website: www.bbc.co.uk/worldservice) and Voice of America (website: www.voa.gov) can be received. From time to time the frequencies change and the most up-to-date can be found online.

Passport/Visa

	Passport Required?	Visa Required?	Return Ticket Required?
Full British	Yes	Yes	Yes
Australian	Yes	Yes	Yes
Canadian	Yes	Yes	Yes
USA	Yes	Yes	Yes
Other EU	Yes	Yes	Yes
Japanese	Yes	Yes	Yes

Note: *Regulations and requirements may be subject to change at short notice, and you are advised to contact the appropriate diplomatic or consular authority before finalising travel arrangements. Details of these may be found at the head of this country's entry. Any numbers in the chart refer to the footnotes below.*

Restricted entry: (a) Holders of Israeli passports, or holders of passports containing a valid or expired visa for Israel will be refused entry or transit. (b) Children of nationals of Arab League countries will be refused entry if they are travelling alone, unless they are met at the airport by their husband/father or unless they are holding a 'No Objection Certificate', issued by the Libyan Immigration Department, and are met at the airport by the resident relative who made the application.

PASSPORTS: Passport valid for a minimum of six months required by all except Algeria, Bahrain, Egypt, Kuwait, Mauritania, Morocco, Oman, Qatar, Saudi Arabia, Tunisia and United Arab Emirates holding valid ID cards.

VISAS: Required by all except the following:
(a) nationals of Algeria, Bahrain, Egypt, Kuwait, Mauritania, Morocco, Oman, Qatar, Saudi Arabia, Sudan, Tunisia and United Arab Emirates ;
(b) nationals of Jordan and the Syrian Arab Republic, provided arriving from their country of origin;
(c) transit passengers continuing their journey by the same

or first connecting aircraft within 24 hours provided holding valid onward or return documentation and not leaving the airport.
Types of visa and cost: *Tourist/Business*: £20.
Validity: 45 days.
Application to: Any of Libya's diplomatic representatives in the relevant country or abroad (such as the Libyan People's Bureau in London; see *Contact Addresses* section). Nationals of Germany must obtain their visas in Bonn/Berlin. Nationals of Canada *must* obtain their visas in Brussels, Belgium.
Application requirements: (a) One completed visa application form. (b) Four recent passport-sized photos. (c) Valid passport. (d) Visa authorisation telex/invitation with reference number from Libya or travel agent. *Business*: (a)-(d) and, (e) Proof that they are sponsored by a Libyan company which will organise the issue of the visa.
Working days required: Two to three.

Money

Currency: Libyan Dinar (LD) = 1000 dirhams. Notes are in denominations of LD10, 5 and 1, and 500 and 250 dirhams. Coins are in denominations of 100, 50, 20, 10, 5 and 1 dirhams.
Credit & debit cards: Limited acceptance of Diners Club and Visa. Check with your credit or debit card company for details of merchant acceptability and other services which may be available.
Travellers cheques: Travellers cheques are generally not accepted, owing to US government sanctions.
Currency restrictions: Free import of foreign currency, subject to declaration. Export of foreign currency is limited to the amount declared on arrival. The import and export of local currency is prohibited.
Exchange rate indicators: The following figures are included as a guide to the movements of the Libyan Dinar against Sterling and the US Dollar:

Date	Feb '04	May '04	Aug '04	Nov '04
£1.00=	2.36	2.36	2.42	2.40
$1.00=	1.29	1.32	1.31	1.27

Banking hours: Sat-Wed 0800-1200 (winter); Sat-Thurs 0800-1200 and Sat-Wed 1600-1700 (summer).

Duty Free

The following goods may be imported into Libya without incurring customs duty:
200 cigarettes or 250g of tobacco or 250g cigars; 250ml of perfume.
Prohibited items: All alcohol is prohibited, as is the import of obscene literature, pork, pork products and any kind of food (including tinned). All goods made in Israel or manufactured by companies that do business with Israel are prohibited.

Public Holidays

2005: Jan 21 Eid al-Adha (Feast of the Sacrifice). **Feb 10** Islamic New Year. **Feb 19** Ashoura. **Mar 3** Declaration of the Authority's Power. **Mar 28** British Evacuation Day. **Apr 21** Mouloud (Prophet's Birthday). **Jun 11** Evacuation Day. **Jul 23** Revolution Day. **Sep 1** National Day. **Oct 7** Italian Evacuation Day. **Nov 3-5** Eid al-Fitr (End of Ramadan).
2006: Jan 10 Eid al-Adha (Feast of the Sacrifice). **Jan 31** Islamic New Year. **Mar 3** Declaration of the Authority's Power. **Mar 9** Ashoura. **Mar 28** British Evacuation Day. **Apr 11** Mouloud (Prophet's Birthday). **Jun 11** Evacuation Day. **Jul 23** Revolution Day. **Sep 1** National Day. **Oct 7** Italian Evacuation Day. **Oct 22-24** Eid al-Fitr (End of Ramadan).
Note: Muslim festivals are timed according to local sightings of various phases of the moon and the dates given above are approximations. During the lunar month of Ramadan that precedes Eid al-Fitr, Muslims fast during the day and feast at night and normal business patterns may be interrupted. Many restaurants are closed during the day and there may be restrictions on smoking and drinking. Some disruption may continue into Eid al-Fitr itself. Eid al-Fitr and Eid al-Adha may last anything from two to 10 days, depending on the region. For more information see the *World of Islam* appendix.

Health

	Special Precautions?	Certificate Required?
Yellow Fever	No	1
Cholera	2	No
Typhoid & Polio	3	N/A
Malaria	4	N/A

Note: *Regulations and requirements may be subject to change at short notice, and you are advised to contact your doctor well in advance of your intended date of departure. Any numbers in the chart refer to the footnotes below.*

1: A yellow fever vaccination certificate is required from travellers arriving from infected areas.
2: Following WHO guidelines issued in 1973, a cholera vaccination certificate is not a condition of entry to Libya. However, cholera is a risk in this country and precautions are essential. Up-to-date advice should be sought before deciding whether these precautions should include vaccination, as medical opinion is divided over its effectiveness; see the *Health* appendix.
3: Immunisation against typhoid and poliomyelitis is often recommended.
4: A very limited malaria risk exists in the southwest of the country from February to August.
Food & drink: Mains water is normally chlorinated and, whilst relatively safe, may cause mild abdominal upsets. Bottled water is available and is advised for the first few weeks of the stay. Drinking water outside main cities and towns is likely to be contaminated and sterilisation is considered essential. Milk is unpasteurised and should be boiled. Powdered or tinned milk is available and is advised, but make sure that it is reconstituted with pure water. Avoid dairy products which are likely to have been made from unboiled milk. Only eat well-cooked meat and fish, preferably served hot. Salad and mayonnaise may carry increased risk. Vegetables should be cooked and fruit peeled.
Other risks: *Dysenteries*, *typhoid fever* and other *diarrhoeal diseases* are common. *Hepatitis A* and *E* occur throughout the area. *Bilharzia* (schistosomiasis) is present. Avoid swimming and paddling in fresh water; swimming pools which are well chlorinated and maintained are safe. Cases of *meningococcal meningitis* have been reported in the Sebha region.
Health care: Medical facilities outside the main cities are limited. Full health insurance is recommended.

Travel - International

Note: All but essential travel to areas bordering Chad and Sudan is advised. Travel to desert regions requires permission (a desert pass) from Libyan authorities in advance.
AIR: Libya's national airline is *Jamahiriya Libyan Arab Airlines (LN)*. Other airlines that serve Libya include *Alitalia*, *British Airways*, *Lufthansa* and *Royal Jordanian*.
Approximate flight times: From Tripoli to *London* is four hours.
International airports: *Tripoli International (TIP)* is 35km (22 miles) south of the city. Bus and taxi services are available to the city (travel time – 40 minutes). Airport facilities include chemist, post office, light refreshments, duty free shops, banks, restaurants and shops.
Benghazi International (BEN) is 19km (12 miles) from Benghazi city centre.
Sebha (SEB) is 11km (7 miles) from the town.
Departure tax: LD6; children under two years of age and transit passengers, provided not leaving the airport and departing within 24 hours, are exempt.
SEA: The main ports are as-Sider, Benghazi, Darna, Mersa Brega, Misurata, El Mina and Tripoli. Several shipping lines operate services from Europe to Libya. A car ferry operated by the Libyan government shipping line sails regularly from Tripoli to Malta and several Italian ports. Italian lines *Grimaldi* and *Tirrenia* run similar services from Genoa, Trapani and Naples to Tripoli and Benghazi. Other cruise lines include *P&O* and *Swan Hellenic*.
RAIL: There is no passenger rail system.
ROAD: Main routes to Libya are from Algeria, Chad, Egypt, Niger and Tunisia. The most popular routes are via Tunisia or Egypt. Several buses and taxis operate on these routes.

Travel - Internal

AIR: *Jamahiriya Libyan Arab Airlines (LN)* provides fast and frequent internal services between Tripoli, Benghazi, Sebha, Al Bayda, Mersa Brega, Tobruk, Misratah, Ghadamis and Al Khufrah. They also offer an hourly shuttle between Tripoli and Benghazi.
Departure tax: LD3; children under two years of age and transit passengers, provided not leaving the airport and departing within 24 hours, are exempt.
ROAD: The main through-road follows the coast from west to east. Petrol is available throughout Libya and is very reasonably priced. There are no reliable town maps. Spare parts are often difficult to obtain: in particular, automatic transmissions can prove almost impossible to repair. The quality of servicing is generally poor by European standards, as is the standard of driving. Traffic drives on the right. **Bus & taxi:** There are bus services between Tripoli and Benghazi and other major urban areas. A minibus service operates from Benghazi to Tobruk. Taxi fares can be quite expensive and should be agreed in advance. **Car hire:** Self-drive cars are available in Tripoli and Benghazi. **Documentation:** National driving licence valid for three months. After this time, a Libyan licence must be obtained.
URBAN: A substantial publicly owned bus system operates in Tripoli. Fares are charged on a three-zone basis. There is a similar system in operation in Benghazi. Services are generally irregular and overcrowded.

Accommodation

Tripoli and Benghazi have several comfortable modern hotels. There are hotels in Al Bayda, Cyrene (Shahat), Derna, Ghadamès, Homs, Sabha and Tobruk.

Resorts & Excursions

TRIPOLI

Libya's capital has retained much of its historical heritage; Tripoli's old walled city is a picturesque African jumble of narrow alleyways leading to traditional mosques, houses and *khans* (public houses). The architecture is a fusion of the country's many rulers and includes Turkish, Spanish, Maltese and Italian influences. Worth seeing is the ancient **Marcus Aurelian Arch**, the **Al Nagha** and **Ahmed Pash** mosques, and some of the many vibrant souqs (markets) in the heart of **Medina** (Tripoli's centre).
Situated on a promontory above the city is **Assai al-Hamra** (Red Castle); a spectacular fortress stretching over an area of approximately 13,000 sq metres, that houses a maze of courtyards and buildings. Next to the castle on the **Green Square** is the **Jamahiriya Museum** that was designed in conjunction with UNESCO. Classical artefacts such as ancient mosaics and statues are among the extensive collection displayed here. Visitors to the city can also enjoy a number of beautiful Mediterranean beaches.
LEPTIS MAGNA: This historical town lies 120km (75 miles) east of Tripoli overlooking the Mediterranean. This incredible archaeological site was originally a port, built by the Phoenicians in the first millennium BC. Since then it became a Roman settlement and today many of the ruins from that time remain preserved. Among the things to see are the **Severan Arch** (erected in honour of Emperor Septimus Severus), the marble- and granite-lined **Hadrianic Baths**, a detailed basilica and an amphitheatre.

BEYOND TRIPOLI

EASTERN REGION: Benghazi is Libya's second-largest city, located on the Eastern edge of the Gulf of Sirt. Far more commercial and less aesthetically pleasing then Tripoli, **Benghazi** is nevertheless a popular tourist spot due to its close proximity to a number of beautiful beaches. **Ras Alteen** is a nearby beach with pristine white sands. It has recently been the location of an amazing archaeological discovery where Greek and Byzantine graves from a colossal underwater city were recovered. Other historical sites include the battlefield of **Tobruk**, 140km east of Ras Alteen, and the town of **Cyrene**, 245km east of Benghazi. The lush forested range of the Green Mountains is easily reached from Benghazi and Ras Alteen and is a great area for walking. A suspended cave named after the apostle Mark, who was thought to have been raised in the **Green Mountains**, can be found in the **Marcus Valley**.
WESTERN REGION: Ghadames, known as the 'Pearl of the Desert', is a unique desert oasis town 800km (500 miles) southwest of Tripoli. The old town's unique architecture consists of white-washed mud walls and covered labyrinthine walkways that are only lit by overhead skylights and open squares. Worth seeing are the **D'jmaa al-Kabir** mosque, where the minaret can be climbed for a wonderful panorama of the city; **Mulberry Square**, site of the old slave market; and the **House Museum**, that displays traditional mercantile furnishings.
Nearby are the **Zallaf Sand Dunes**, home to the native Tuareng tribe. Saline lakes with high mineral content and palm trees surround the dunes. In this unusual environment visitors can enjoy relaxing sand baths and salt-lake bathing.

Sport & Activities

There are good beaches for **swimming** away from the municipal beaches of Tripoli and Benghazi. Facilities for **tennis**, **golf** and **10-pin bowling** are available in the major cities. Spectator sports include **football** and **horseracing**.

Social Profile

FOOD & DRINK: Since alcohol was banned by the Government in 1969, many restaurants have closed, and those remaining are very expensive. Hotel restaurants, although not particularly good, are therefore often the only eating places. Traditional dishes include *couscous*, a dish based on savoury semolina that can be combined with chicken, lamb or vegetables and is a staple dish in many northern African countries; and *ruuz*, a rice dish with a variety of spices, meat and vegetables. Most restaurants have table service, and although food is traditionally eaten with

the right hand only, knives and forks will generally be available.
NIGHTLIFE: All nightclubs and bars have been closed. There are several cinemas in major towns, some showing foreign films. There are no theatres or concert halls.
SHOPPING: *Souks* in the main towns are the workplaces of many weavers, copper-, gold- and silversmiths and leatherworkers. There are numerous other stalls selling a variety of items including spices, metal engravings and various pieces of jewellery.
SPECIAL EVENTS: Special events celebrated in Libya are generally Muslim holy days and festivals. The following is a selection of special events celebrated annually in Libya:
Jul 23 *Revolution Day*. **Oct** *Date Harvest Festival*.
SOCIAL CONVENTIONS: Life in Libya is regulated fairly strictly along socialist/Islamic principles; in general, Arab courtesies and social customs prevail and should be respected. Women do not generally attend typical Arab gatherings; see the *World of Islam* appendix for further information. In religious buildings and small towns, women should dress modestly. Beachwear must only be worn on the beach. Smoking is common and codes of practice concerning smoking are the same as in Europe.
Photography: It is unwise to use or carry cameras.
Tipping: A tip of 10 to 20 per cent is usually included in hotel and restaurant bills.

Business Profile

ECONOMY: Oil- and gas-related industries account for the bulk of Libya's economy; 95 per cent of export earnings come from oil. The high quality of Libyan oil has produced strong demand from consumers so that, despite relatively small reserves, Libya has been able to sustain high production levels of around 1.5 million barrels per day. The recent discovery of large deposits is a further bonus. Oil revenues have enabled the government to build up the country's economic infrastructure virtually from scratch since the early 1970s. However, low world oil prices and UN sanctions brought the economy to a virtual standstill during the 1990s, undermining economic development and forcing the cancellation of a number of large projects. By 2003 though, the Libyan government's rapprochement with the international community, and more favourable conditions in the world oil market, had allowed the resumption of economic growth. Outside the oil and gas industry, agriculture is almost entirely geared to domestic consumption: animal husbandry is the most important part of this, but crops including barley and wheat are also grown in the country's few fertile areas. An industrial sector producing petrochemicals, iron, steel and aluminium has also been developed. Libya is a member of the Arab Development Bank, the Union of the Arab Maghreb and various other pan-Arab economic organisations. It is also a member of the Organisation of Petroleum Exporting Countries (OPEC). Italy and Germany are Libya's major trading partners.
BUSINESS: Shirt sleeves are acceptable business wear in hot weather. Suits and ties are worn for more formal occasions. Most business dealings take place with state organisations and English is often understood. It is, however, government policy for official documents to be in Arabic (or translated into Arabic) and for official business to be conducted in Arabic. Business visitors need to be fully prepared for this. Appointments are necessary and business cards are useful, though not widely used. Hours for businesses and government offices fluctuate, but the working day starts early. **Office hours:** Generally Sat-Wed 0700-1400.
COMMERCIAL INFORMATION: The following organisation can offer advice: Tripoli Chamber of Commerce, Industry and Agriculture, PO Box 2321, Tripoli (tel: (21) 333 3755; fax: (21) 333 2655).

Climate

Summers are very hot and dry: winters are mild with cooler evenings. The desert has hot days and cold nights.

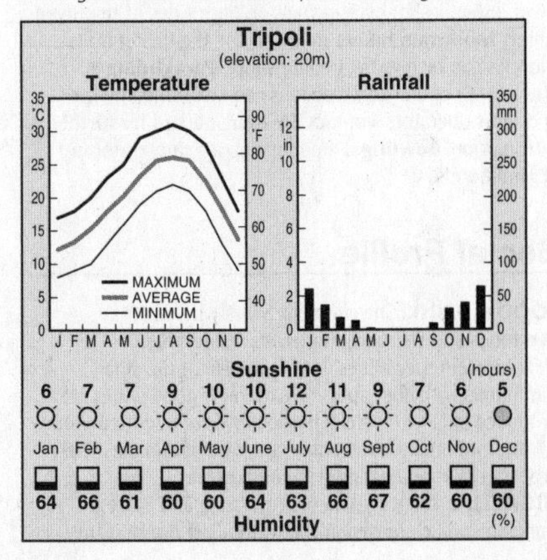

Liechtenstein

LATEST TRAVEL ADVICE CONTACTS

British Foreign and Commonwealth Office
Tel: (0870) 606 0290 Website: www.fco.gov.uk
US Department of State
Website: http://travel.state.gov/travel
Canadian Department of Foreign Affairs and Int'l Trade
Tel: (1 800) 267 8376 Website: www.dfait-maeci.gc.ca

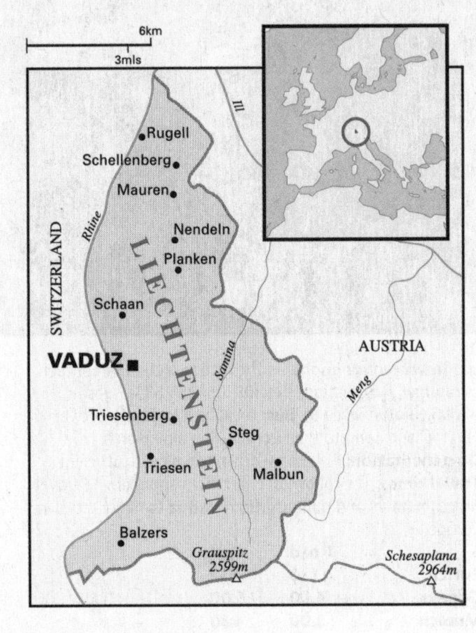

Location: Western Europe.

Country dialling code: 423 (Liechtenstein); 41 (Switzerland).

Diplomatic representation
Liechtenstein maintains very few overseas missions and is generally represented by Switzerland. For addresses, see *Switzerland* section.
Liechtenstein Tourismus (National Tourist Office)
Städtle 37, PO Box 139, FL-9490 Vaduz, Liechtenstein
Tel: 239 6300. Fax: 239 6301.
E-mail: info@tourismus.li
Website: www.tourismus.li *or* www.liechtenstein.li
Switzerland Tourism
30 Bedford Street, London WC2E 9ED, UK
Tel: (00800) 1002 0030 (toll-free in Europe) *or* (020) 7420 4900.
Fax: (00800) 1002 0031 (toll-free in Europe) *or* (020) 7292 1599 *or* 7851 1720 (marketing and press only).
E-mail: info.uk@myswitzerland.com *or* res.uk@switzerland.com
Website: http://uk.myswitzerland.com
Opening hours: Mon-Fri 0900-1700; Thurs 1000-1700.
British Consulate General
37-39 Rue de Vermont, 6th Floor, CH-1211 Geneva 20, Switzerland
Tel: (22) 918 2400. Fax: (22) 918 2322.
Website: www.britain-in-switzerland.ch
The British Embassy in Berne deals with enquiries relating to Liechtenstein (tel: (31) 359 7700; fax: (31) 359 7701; e-mail: info@britain-in-switzerland.com), *with the Ambassador resident there.*
Vice Consulates also in: Basle, Montreux/Vevey, Ticino, Valais and Zurich.
Switzerland Tourism
608 Fifth Avenue, New York, NY 10020, USA
Tel: (212) 757 5944 *or* (877) 794 8037 (toll-free in USA) *or* (011800) 1002 0030 (toll-free international) *or* (800) 794 7763 (travel trade). Fax: (212) 262 6116.
E-mail: info.usa@myswitzerland.com
Website: www.myswitzerland.com
The US Embassy in Berne deals with enquiries relating to Liechtenstein (see *Switzerland* section).

TIMATIC CODES

Health
AMADEUS: **TI-DFT/ZRH/HE**
GALILEO/WORLDSPAN: **TI-DFT/ZRH/HE**
SABRE: **TIDFT/ZRH/HE**

Visa
AMADEUS: **TI-DFT/ZRH/VI**
GALILEO/WORLDSPAN: **TI-DFT/ZRH/VI**
SABRE: **TIDFT/ZRH/VI**

To access TIMATIC country information on Health and Visa regulations through the Computer Reservations System (CRS), type in the appropriate command line listed above.

Switzerland Tourism
926 The East Mall, Toronto, Ontario M9B 6K1, Canada
Tel: (416) 695 3496 (media enquires) *or* (800) 1002 0030 (toll-free in USA and Canada) *or* (800) 1002 0033 (for French Canadians) *or* (416) 695 2605 (trade enquiries).
Fax: (416) 695 2774.
E-mail: ursula.beamish@switzerland.com (media enquiries).
Website: www.myswitzerland.com
The Canadian Embassy in Berne deals with enquiries relating to Liechtenstein (see *Switzerland* section).

General Information

AREA: 160 sq km (61.8 sq miles).
POPULATION: 34,294 (2004).
POPULATION DENSITY: 211.6 per sq km.
CAPITAL: Vaduz. **Population:** 5,038 (2002).
GEOGRAPHY: Liechtenstein shares borders with Austria and Switzerland and lies between the upper reaches of the Rhine Valley and the Austrian Alps. The principality is noted for its fine vineyards.
GOVERNMENT: Imperial Principality with a hereditary constitutional monarchy. Principality established in 1719. **Head of State:** Prince Hans Adam II since 1989. **Head of Government:** Prime Minister Otmar Hasler since 2001.
LANGUAGE: German; a dialect of Alemannish is widely spoken. English is also widely spoken.
RELIGION: Christian, predominantly Roman Catholic (78 per cent).
TIME: GMT + 1 (GMT + 2 from last Sunday in March to Saturday before last Sunday in October).
ELECTRICITY: 230 volts AC, 50Hz. European two-pin plugs are used.
COMMUNICATIONS: Telephone: Full IDD service. Country code: 423. Outgoing international code: 00. **Mobile telephone:** GSM 900/1800 network. Handsets can be hired at the Telecom shop in Vaduz. Main network operators include *Mobilkom* (website: www.mobilkom.li), *Orange*, *Swisscom Mobile* (website: www.swisscom-mobile.ch) and *Tele2* (website: www.tele2.li). **Fax:** Most hotels have facilities. **Internet:** Internet access is available in phone booths operated by Swisscom. Charges are payable by phonecard or credit card. Public access is also available at the Telecom shop in Vaduz. ISPs include *LIE-NET* (website: www.lie-net.li). **Telegram:** Telecommunications are available from post offices and hotels. Service is reliable and efficient. **Post:** Post office hours: Mon-Fri 0730-1200 and 1345-1830, Sat 0800-1100, (Mon-Fri 0745-1800, Sat 0800-1100 in Vaduz). Post to European destinations takes three to four days. **Press:** There are two daily newspapers, *Liechtensteiner Vaterland* and *Liechtensteiner Volksblatt*, and two weekly papers, *Apotheke und Marketing* and *Liechtensteiner Wochenzeitung*. All are published in German. **Radio:** BBC World Service (website: www.bbc.co.uk/worldservice) and Voice of America (website: www.voa.gov) can be received. From time to time the frequencies change and the most up-to-date can be found online.

Passport/Visa

The passport and visa requirements for persons visiting Liechtenstein are the same as for Switzerland. For further details, see the *Switzerland* section.

Money

Currency: Swiss Franc (sfr) = 100 centimes. For further information on currency, currency exchange, credit cards, travellers cheques, exchange rates and currency restrictions, see the *Switzerland* section.
Banking hours: Mon-Fri 0830-1630.

Duty Free

The customs regulations for persons visiting Liechtenstein are the same as for Switzerland. For further details, see the *Switzerland* section.

Public Holidays

2005: Jan 1 New Year's Day. **Jan 2** St Berchtold's Day. **Jan 6** Epiphany. **Feb 2** Candlemas. **Feb 8** Shrove Tuesday. **Mar 19** Feast of St Joseph. **Mar 25** Good Friday. **Mar 28** Easter Monday. **May 1** Labour Day. **May 5** Ascension. **May 16** Whit Monday. **May 26** Corpus Christi. **Aug 15** Assumption. **Sep 8** Nativity of Our Lady. **Nov 1** All Saints' Day. **Dec 8** Immaculate Conception. **Dec 25** Christmas Day. **Dec 26** St Stephen's Day. **Dec 31** New Year's Eve.
2006: Jan 1 New Year's Day. **Jan 2** St Berchtold's Day. **Jan 6** Epiphany. **Feb 2** Candlemas. **Feb 28** Shrove Tuesday. **Mar 19** Feast of St Joseph. **Apr 14** Good Friday. **Apr 17** Easter

Credit: © Liechtenstein Tourism

Monday. **May 1** Labour Day. **May 25** Ascension. **Jun 5** Whit Monday. **Jun 15** Corpus Christi. **Aug 15** Assumption. **Sep 8** Nativity of Our Lady. **Nov 1** All Saints' Day. **Dec 8** Immaculate Conception. **Dec 25** Christmas Day. **Dec 26** St Stephen's Day. **Dec 31** New Year's Eve.

Health

	Special Precautions?	Certificate Required?
Yellow Fever	No	No
Cholera	No	No
Typhoid & Polio	No	N/A
Malaria	No	N/A

Note: Regulations and requirements may be subject to change at short notice, and you are advised to contact your doctor well in advance of your intended date of departure. Any numbers in the chart refer to the footnotes below.

Other risks: *Rabies* is present in some animals although risk is low. For those at high risk, vaccination before arrival should be considered. If you are bitten, seek medical advice without delay. Post-exposure treatment should be readily available. For more information, consult the *Health* appendix.
Health care: There is only one hospital in Liechtenstein, but the standard of medical facilities is very good. A reciprocal health agreement exists with the UK and other EEA member countries. To obtain emergency medical treatment, form E111 and a passport are required and a standard fee may be charged. Medical bills and form E111 should be sent to the National Office of the Economy for refunds. Dental treatment is not part of the state insurance scheme so must be paid for in full. All other international travellers are strongly advised to take out full medical insurance before departure.

Travel - International

AIR: The nearest international airport (and the most convenient for travel from the UK) is Zurich. For details of airlines serving the airport, see *Switzerland* section.
Approximate flight times: From Zurich to *London* is one hour 30 minutes.
International airports: *Zurich (ZRH)* (Kloten) (website: www.zurich-airport.com) is approximately 130km (81 miles) from Vaduz. Travel to Liechtenstein from Zurich can be continued by rail, bus or road. An autoroute connects the city with Liechtenstein (first exit: Balzers; further exits: Vaduz, Schaan, Bendern and Ruggell). Cars can be hired through agencies at the airport for this journey, and in Liechtenstein.
Departure Tax: None.
RAIL: The best rail access is via the Swiss border stations at Buchs (SG) or Sargans (easier and closer when coming from Zurich) or the Austrian station at Feldkirch. All are well served by express trains and connected with Vaduz by bus. From Buchs it takes only 15 minutes by bus or 10 minutes by taxi.
ROAD: An autoroute (N13) runs along Liechtenstein's Rhine frontier to Lake Constance, Austria and Germany in the north, and southwards past Chur towards St Moritz. To the west, there are autoroutes to Zurich, Berne and Basel. Traffic drives on the right. *Eurotunnel* operates trains 24 hours per day through the Channel Tunnel between Folkestone in Kent (with direct access from the M20) and Calais in France, from where you can drive to Liechtenstein. For further information, see *Travel - International* in the France section or contact Eurotunnel Reservations (tel: (08705) 353 535; website: www3.eurotunnel.com). **Bus:** Local buses operate between all 11 villages, and to the Liechtenstein alpine area.
Documentation: A national driving licence is sufficient.
Travel times: The following chart gives approximate travel times (in hours and minutes) from **Vaduz** to major cities in Europe.

	Road	Rail
Zurich	1.30	1.30
Geneva	4.00	5.00
Munich	3.00	4.30
Frankfurt/M	6.30	5.30
Milan	4.30	5.30
Paris	10.00	9.00

Accommodation

HOTELS/GUEST HOUSES: Until recently, with few notable exceptions, the best hotels (although none of deluxe standard) were in or near Vaduz, but new establishments have now been built along the Rhine Valley and in the mountains. There are 44 hotels and guest houses in Liechtenstein, with approximately 1300 beds in total. Eight hotels have an indoor swimming pool. In the alpine region, there are around 40 chalets and other self-catering establishments. Around 165 establishments belong to Gastronomie Liechtenstein (website: www.hotels.li).
INNS: A Liechtenstein speciality is the mountain inn. All are at least 1200m (4000ft) up, but easily accessible by car. They are ideal for those seeking peace and quiet and clean air. Some of these inns have recently been enlarged and modernised.
ALPINE HUTS: There are alpine huts at Gafadura, 1428m (4284ft) high, which accommodates 47, Bettlerjoch Pfälzer-Hütte, 2111m (6333ft) high, which accommodates 80, and at Triesenberg-Malbun which sleeps 45; check online (website: www.alpenverein.li).
CAMPING: Campsites exist at Mittagspitze, FL-9495 Triesen (tel: 392 2311 *or* 392 3677; fax: 392 3680) and Bendern, FL-9487 Bendern.
HOLIDAY APARTMENTS/CHALETS: Contact the local tourist offices in Malbun, Triesenberg or Vaduz for information.
YOUTH HOSTELS: Liechtenstein's only youth hostel, Youth Hostel Schaan-Vaduz, is between Schaan and Vaduz, 500m (1640ft) away from the main road. It has sleeping accommodation for 110 in a variety of room sizes.

Resorts & Excursions

The Principality of Liechtenstein covers both lowlands – including part of the fertile Rhine Valley and the steep western slope of the Three Sisters massif – and mountains. The latter are in the eastern part of the country and are accessible through three high valleys, the best known being that of Malbun, Liechtenstein's premier ski resort (see below). In summer, hikers and ramblers may wish to explore Liechtenstein's vineyards, forests and nature reserves. The principality's mountains attract climbers of all abilities. For the less energetic, there are several tourist sites of interest. For further information about attractions within the country, contact Liechtenstein Tourismus (see *Contact Addresses* section).
VADUZ: In the capital, Vaduz, the **Postage Stamp Museum** (**Postal Museum**), the **National Library**, the **Ski Museum**, and the **National Museum** are worth visiting. The **Liechtenstein Art Museum**, housed in a specially designed building, contains the treasures of the Prince's collection, including works by Rembrandt, Rubens and Van Dyck, as well as modern art from the former Liechtenstein State Art Collection. Wine tasting groups of 10 or more people are welcome in the **Prince's Wine Cellars** in Vaduz, subject to reservation (tel: 232 1018; fax: 233 1145; e-mail: office@hofkellerei.li; website: www.hofkellerei.li). A 'City Train' will take visitors around the sights on a 30-minute tour.
ELSEWHERE: There are local museums in **Triesenberg** (the **Walser Museum**) and **Schellenberg-Ruggell**. **Schaan** is noted for its theatre, its Roman excavations, the **St Maria zum Trost Chapel** and **DoMus – Museum and Gallery of the Community of Schaan**. Also of interest are the **Gutenberg Castle** and **St Peter's Chapel** at Balzers; the **St Mamerten** and **Maria Chapels** and the old part of the village in **Triesen**; the **Chapel of St Joseph** in **Planken**; the Roman excavations at **Eschen-Nendeln**; the parish churches in **Bendern**, **Mauren** and **Ruggell**; and the ruins of the upper and lower **Burg Schellenberg**.
Resorts: The winter sports area is concentrated around **Malbun** at 1600m (5250ft) and **Steg** at 1300m (4250ft). At Malbun, there are two chair lifts, four ski lifts and a natural ice rink. Steg has become famous for its popular cross-country skiing loop with three distances – 4km (2.5 miles), 12km (7 miles), 12.5km (7.8 miles) – which is also equipped for use at night. Steg also has a ski lift and sledge-run.

Sport & Activities

Wintersports: Like neighbouring Austria and Switzerland, Liechtenstein has excellent wintersports facilities (though on a comparatively small scale). The main **ski** resorts include *Malbun* and *Steg* (see *Resorts & Excursions* section). Malbun is popular on the international skiing circuit for its varied facilities, and is a particularly good resort for beginners. Steg is renowned for excellent **cross-country skiing**.
Other: In the summer, all the resorts are good starting points for **walking** tours. Gaflei at 1500m (4920ft) is the starting point for the *Fürstensteig*, a path along the high ridge dividing the Rhine and Samina valleys. **Cycling** is possible in the valleys and lower-lying areas, and there are 96km (56 miles) of cycling trails on both sides of the River Rhine. **Mountain bikers** may also use the hiking trails. Bicycles can be hired at cycling shops. **Paragliding** is gaining in popularity. Excursions can be arranged with specialist operators; contact the tourist board for further information. **Bowling** is a popular sport, catered for in several hotels.

Social Profile

FOOD & DRINK: The cuisine is Swiss with Austrian overtones and there are numerous restaurants. Liechtenstein specialities include *Käseknöpfle*, small dumplings with cheese. Some extremely good wines are produced in Liechtenstein, particularly *Vaduzer* (red wine). All internationally known beverages are obtainable. There are strict laws against drinking and driving.
NIGHTLIFE: There are cinemas at Vaduz and Balzers. Dancing can be enjoyed at the *Maschlina-Bar* and the

Hubraum in Triesen; *Tiffany* in Eschen; *Derby* in Schaanwald; and *Pacha* and *Schlosshof* at Balzers.
SHOPPING: Prices and the range of goods are the same as in Switzerland. Specialist buys include handmade ceramics, pottery and Liechtenstein postage stamps. **Shopping hours:** Generally Mon-Fri 0800-1200 and 1330-1830, Sat 0800-1600. From April to October, souvenir stores in Vaduz are open Sunday and holidays.
SPECIAL EVENTS: For a full list of events, contact Liechtenstein Tourism or Switzerland Tourism (see *Contact Addresses* section). The following is a selection of special events occurring in Liechtenstein in 2005:
Jun 24-26 *Verbandsmusikfest* (band music festival), Eschen. **Jul 1-2** *Liechtensteinisches Verbandsmusikfest.* **Jul 4-17** *Internationale Meisterkurse und Jazztage*, Vaduz.
SOCIAL CONVENTIONS: Similar to northwest Europe. Regulations concerning smoking are becoming increasingly strict. **Tipping:** A service charge will be included in most bills.

Business Profile

ECONOMY: The population of Liechtenstein is amongst the world's most prosperous. Dairy and arable farming account for the bulk of agriculture. The manufacturing industry processes and recycles metals, producing machine tools and precision instruments. Financial services are the main component of the economy: over 75,000 foreign corporations have taken advantage of the principality's banking secrecy laws to establish nominee companies which pay low taxes on both income and profits. Fees from these companies provide about one-third of government revenues.
Since the mid-1990s, Liechtenstein has come under sustained pressure to deal with money laundering and other financial malpractice. In April 2002, Liechtenstein was strongly condemned by the Organisation for Economic Co-operation and Development (the 24-strong club of industrialised nations) as one of seven countries worldwide which had refused to cooperate properly and continually faces economic sanctions.
With a very small domestic market, Liechtenstein has a large balance of payments surplus. The country has vital economic links with Switzerland, based upon a customs union, and uses the Swiss franc as currency. Liechtenstein joined the European Free Trade Association (EFTA) in 1991 and the European Economic Area (EEA), the body established by amalgamating the EU and EFTA, in May 1995. Other than Switzerland, most of Liechtenstein's trade is conducted with members of the EU.
BUSINESS: Personal visits and the following of all business formalities are very important. Times to avoid business visits include the Easter holiday, the second half of July and August, and the week after Christmas. **Office hours:** Generally Mon-Fri 0800-1200 and 1400-1700.
COMMERCIAL INFORMATION: The following organisation can offer advice: Liechtensteinische Industrie- und Handelskammer (Chamber of Industry and Commerce), Josef Rheinberger-Strasse 11, FL-9490 Vaduz (tel: 237 5511; fax: 237 5512; e-mail: info@lcci.li; website: www.lihk.li).
CONFERENCES/CONVENTIONS: Although there is no conference association in Liechtenstein, a number of hotels have conference facilities and can organise conventions: Löwen in Vaduz, Schaanerhof in Schaan, Meierhof in Triesen, Kulm in Triesenberg, Gorfion and Malbuner-Hof in Malbun/Triesenberg.

Climate

Liechtenstein has a temperate, alpine climate, with warm, wet summers and mild winters.
Required clothing: Mediumweights with some lightweight clothing is advised for summer. Warmer heavyweights are worn in winter. Waterproofs are needed throughout the year.

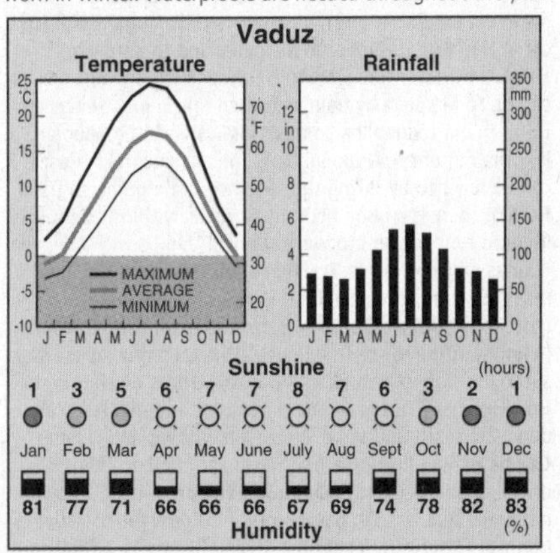

Lithuania

LATEST TRAVEL ADVICE CONTACTS

British Foreign and Commonwealth Office
Tel: (0870) 606 0290 Website: www.fco.gov.uk
US Department of State
Website: http://travel.state.gov/travel
Canadian Department of Foreign Affairs and Int'l Trade
Tel: (1 800) 267 8376 Website: www.dfait-maeci.gc.ca

Location: Northern Europe.

Country dialling code: 370.

Lithuanian State Department of Tourism
Juozapavicius Street 13, 09311 Vilnius, Lithuania
Tel: (5) 210 8796. Fax: (5) 210 8753.
E-mail: vtd@tourism.lt *or* info@tourism.lt
Website: www.tourism.lt
Embassy of the Republic of Lithuania
84 Gloucester Place, London W1U 6AU, UK
Tel: (020) 7486 6401 *or* 6404 (visa section).
Fax: (020) 7486 6403.
E-mail: chancery@lithuanianembassy.co.uk *or* consular@lithuanianembassy.co.uk
Website: http://amb.urm.lt/jk
Opening hours: Mon-Fri 0930-1300 (consular section); Mon, Wed & Fri 1500-1600 (visa section).
British Embassy
2 Antakalnio Street, 10308 Vilnius, Lithuania
Tel: (5) 246 2900. Fax: (5) 246 2901.
E-mail: be-vilnius@britain.lt
Website: www.britain.lt
Embassy of the Republic of Lithuania
2622 16th Street, NW, Washington, DC 20009, USA
Tel: (202) 234 5860. Fax: (202) 328 0466.
E-mail: info@ltembassyus.org
Website: www.ltembassyus.org
Consulates General in: Chicago and New York.
Honorary Consulate Generals in: Chicago, Cleveland and Los Angeles.
Embassy of the United States of America
Akmenu 6, 2600 Vilnius, Lithuania
Tel: (5) 266 5500. Fax: (5) 266 5510.
E-mail: WebMailVilnius@state.gov
Website: www.usembassy.lt
Embassy of the Republic of Lithuania
130 Albert Street, Suite 204, Ottawa, Ontario K1P 5G4, Canada
Tel: (613) 567 5458. Fax: (613) 567 5315.
E-mail: litemb@storm.ca *or* zelniene@storm.ca (trade section).
Website: www.lithuanianembassy.ca
Honorary Consulates in: Calgary, Montréal, Toronto and Vancouver.
Office of the Canadian Embassy
Jogailos St 4, 7th Floor, 11116 Vilnius, Lithuania
Tel: (5) 249 0950. Fax: (5) 249 7865.
E-mail: vilnius@canada.lt
Website: www.dfait-maeci.gc.ca/canadaeuropa/baltics

TIMATIC CODES

Health
AMADEUS: **TI-DFT/VNO/HE**
GALILEO/WORLDSPAN: **TI-DFT/VNO/HE**
SABRE: **TIDFT/VNO/HE**

Visa
AMADEUS: **TI-DFT/VNO/VI**
GALILEO/WORLDSPAN: **TI-DFT/VNO/VI**
SABRE: **TIDFT/VNO/VI**

To access TIMATIC country information on Health and Visa regulations through the Computer Reservations System (CRS), type in the appropriate command line listed above.

General Information

AREA: 65,300 sq km (25,212 sq miles).
POPULATION: 3,462,553 (official estimate 2003).
POPULATION DENSITY: 53 per sq km.
CAPITAL: Vilnius. **Population:** 553,373 (official estimate 2002).
GEOGRAPHY: Lithuania is situated on the eastern Baltic coast and borders Latvia in the north, the Kaliningrad region of the Russian Federation and Poland in the southwest, and Belarus in the southwest and east. The geometrical centre of Europe lies in eastern Lithuania near the village of Bernotai, 25km (16 miles) north of Vilnius. The landscape alternates between lowland plains and hilly uplands and has a dense, intricate network of rivers, including the Nemunas and the Neris. 1.5 per cent of the country's territory is made up of lakes, of which there are over 2800. The majority of these lie in the east of the country and include Lake Druksiai and Lake Tauragnas.
GOVERNMENT: Republic. Gained independence from Russia/Germany 1918-1940, and then from the Soviet Union in 1990. **Head of State:** President Valdas Adamkus since 2004. **Head of Government:** Prime Minister Algirdas Mykolas Brazauskas since 2001.
LANGUAGE: Lithuanian is the official language. Lithuania has a large number of dialects for such a small territory, including High Lithuanian (*Aukstaiciai*) and Low Lithuanian (*Zemaiciai*).
RELIGION: Predominantly Roman Catholic with Evangelical Lutheran, Evangelical Reformist, Russian Orthodox, Baptist, Muslim and Jewish minorities.
TIME: GMT + 2 (daylight saving time GMT + 3 from 29 Mar to 26 Sep).
ELECTRICITY: 220 volts AC, 50Hz. European two-pin plugs are in use.

Credit: © Lithuania Commercial Attache

COMMUNICATIONS: Telephone: IDD is available. Country code: 370. City codes: 2 for Vilnius, 7 for Kaunas, 6 for Klaipeda. Outgoing international code: 810. There are two kinds of payphone: rectangular telephones which take magnetic strip cards and rounded telephones which take chip cards. Phonecards are sold at kiosks and post offices. Plans are underway to introduce one type of phonecard, compatible with both phones. **Mobile telephone:** GSM 900 and 1800 networks in use. Network operators include *Bite* (website: www.bite.lt), *Omnitel* (website: www.omnitel.lt) and *Tele2* (website: www.tele2.lt). Coverage extends all over the country. Roaming agreements are in operation. **Fax:** Services in Vilnius are available in large hotels, at the Central Post Office, Gedimino 7, and at Faxsav and at a few other fax bureaux. **Internet:** Public access is available at the Lithuanian National Library and increasingly at Internet centres and cafes in main cities and towns. ISPs include *Aiva* (website: www.aiva.lt) and *Omnitel* (website: www.omnitel.net). **Telegram:** There are telegram facilities in main post offices in each town. **Post:** Post to Western Europe takes up to six days. There is a variety of private companies offering express mail services. **Press:** Newspapers are published in Lithuanian and some in Russian or Polish. The major dailies are *Kauno Diena*, *Lietuvos Rytas*, *Respublika* and *Vakaro Zinios*, plus the twice-weekly *Valstieciu Laikrastis*.
Radio: BBC World Service (website: www.bbc.co.uk/worldservice) and Voice of America (website: www.voa.gov) can be received. From time to time the frequencies change and the most up-to-date can be found online.

Passport/Visa

	Passport Required?	Visa Required?	Return Ticket Required?
Full British	Yes	No	No
Australian	Yes	No	No
Canadian	Yes	No	No
USA	Yes	No	No
Other EU	Yes	No	No
Japanese	Yes	No	No

Note: *Regulations and requirements may be subject to change at short notice, and you are advised to contact the appropriate diplomatic or consular authority before finalising travel arrangements. Details of these may be found at the head of this country's entry. Any numbers in the chart refer to the footnotes below.*

PASSPORTS: Passport valid for a minimum of three months after expiry of visa, required by all.
Note: There is now a new application form that those seeking visas must fill out, consistent with the visa forms of other European Union member states, which Lithuania joined on May 1 2004. At present, the Lithuanian visa will only be valid for travelling to Lithuania but will become valid for travelling to other *Schengen* countries once Lithuania joins the *Schengen* area.
VISAS: Required by all except the following:
(a) nationals listed in the chart above for tourist stays of up to 90 days;
(b) nationals of Andorra, Argentina, Armenia, Bolivia, Brazil, Brunei, Bulgaria, Chile, Costa Rica, Croatia, El Salvador, Guatemala, Honduras, Hong Kong (SAR), Iceland, Israel, Korea (Rep), Liechtenstein, Macau (SAR), Malaysia, Mexico, Monaco, New Zealand, Nicaragua, Norway, Panama, Paraguay, Romania, San Marino, Singapore, Switzerland, Uruguay, Vatican City and Venezuela for tourist stays of up to 90 days.
Note: (a) Nationals of South Africa holding valid Estonian or Latvian visas *do not* need a separate visa for Lithuania. (b) Nationals of the following countries may apply for a Lithuanian visa without first obtaining an invitation endorsed by the Lithuanian Migration Authorities: The Bahamas, Bahrain, Belarus, Bermuda, Ecuador, Kazakhstan, Moldova, Russian Federation, South Africa, Taiwan, Tunisia, Ukraine and United Arab Emirates. The length of stay permitted without this requirement varies according to the applicant's nationality. All of the above nationals are required to present proof of sufficient funds (minimum €40 or £27 per day), via traveller's cheques, credit cards and bank statements. Enquire at the Consulate/Embassy for details.
Types of visa and cost: *Single-entry*: £14/€20. *Multiple-entry*: €35. *Special-entry* (for employment or studies): €60. *Transit/Airport Transit*: €10 (single-entry); €25 (double-entry). *Group single-entry* (five to 30 members with appointed guide and on the condition that group have same purpose of visit, follow same travel itinerary with same arrivals, departures and locations): €15 per person; *group transit*: €10 per person; *group double-entry transit*: €25 per person. Consular fees are waived in certain circumstances; consult Embassy/Consulate for details. There is no consular fee for members for certain charity missions, official delegations, those aged under 16 years, and Lithuanians travelling with foreign passports.
Validity: *Single-* and *Multiple-entry*: Three months. In some cases, a multiple-entry visa may be issued for up to one or even five years. Documents must be submitted that prove the need for a multiple-entry visa and warrant amount of validity allocated. *Transit*: No more than five days each stay. *Airport Transit*: 48 hours.
Application to: Consulate (or Consular section at Embassy); see *Contact Addresses* section.
Application requirements: (a) Passport valid for at least three months after expiry of visa. (b) One passport-size photo. (c) Completed application form. (d) Letter of invitation endorsed by the Lithuanian Migration Authorities (not required by certain nationals – see note above). (e) Fee. (f) Other documents, such as hotel reservations, tickets, right to return country form/right to travel to onward country, documents certifying payment of consular fee, and bank statements may be required. (g) Valid health and travel insurance. *Transit* and *Airport Transit*: (a)-(g) and, (h) Visa and/or other documents granting right to enter country of destination.
Working days required: Five. Visas can be obtained within 24 or 72 hours for an additional charge. This service is not available to all nationalities/passport holders.

Money

Currency: Litas (Lt) = 100 centas. Notes are in denominations of Lt500, 200, 100, 50, 20, 10, 5, 2 and 1. Coins are in denominations of Lt5, 2 and 1, and the worthless 50, 20, 10, 5, 2 and 1 centas.
Currency exchange: Currency can be exchanged at banks and bureaux de change. ATMs are available in most cities. There are 24-hour exchange bureaux at Gelezinkelio 6, near the main railway station and at Lietuvos Taupomasis Bankas, Savanoriu 15A in Vilnius.
Credit & debit cards: Most major credit cards are accepted in the main hotels, restaurants, shops and in some petrol stations. Check with your credit and debit card company for details of merchant acceptability and other services which may be available.
Travellers cheques: Not accepted by retailers and can only be exchanged at a few outlets. To avoid additional exchange rate charges, travellers are advised to take travellers cheques in US Dollars.
Currency restrictions: The import of local and foreign currency is unlimited. The export of local currency is limited to Lt5000. The export of foreign currency is unlimited. Any amount exceeding Lt40,000 or equivalent must be declared.
Exchange rate indicators: The following figures are included as a guide to the movements of the Litas against Sterling and the US Dollar:

Date	Feb '04	May '04	Aug '04	Nov '04
£1.00=	5.05	5.18	5.14	4.93
$1.00=	2.77	2.90	2.79	2.60

Banking hours: Mon-Fri 0900-1700. Some banks also open Sat 0900-1300.

Duty Free

The following goods may be imported into Lithuania by persons 18 years of age and over without incurring customs duty:
200 cigarettes or 250g of tobacco or combination, provided amount does not exceed 250g; 1l of spirits and 2l of wine and champagne and 3l of beer; 0.5kg of chocolate or foodstuffs containing cocoa; 1kg of coffee; 1kg of foodstuffs containing sugar; 50g of jewellery; goods for personal use; two individually packed items of perfume or cosmetics of same trade name for individual use.
Prohibited: Ethyl alcohol and homemade alcoholic beverages; meat, meat products, meat sub-products, dairy products and eggs; military weapons, hunting guns, ammunition, electric fishing equipment, drugs and psychotropic substances, radioelectronic equipment, colour photocopying equipment (all require a permit).
Abolition of duty free goods within the EU: On June 30 1999, the sale of duty free alcohol and tobacco at airports and at sea was abolished in all of the original 15 EU member states. Of the 10 new member states that joined the EU on May 1 2004, these rules already apply to Cyprus and Malta. There are transitional rules in place for visitors returning to one of the original 15 EU countries from one of the other new EU countries. But for the original 15, plus Cyprus and Malta, there are now no limits imposed on importing tobacco and alcohol products from one EU country to another (with the exceptions of Denmark, Finland and Sweden, where limits *are* imposed). Travellers should note that they may be required to prove at customs that the goods purchased are for personal use *only*.

Public Holidays

2005: Jan 1 New Year's Day. **Feb 16** Independence Day. **Mar 11** Restoration of Lithuania's Statehood. **Mar 28** Easter Monday. **Jul 6** Anniversary of the Coronation of King Mindaugas. **Aug 15** Assumption. **Nov 1** All Saints' Day. **Dec 25-26** Christmas.
2006: Jan 1 New Year's Day. **Feb 16** Independence Day. **Mar 11** Restoration of Lithuania's Statehood. **Apr 17** Easter Monday. **Jul 6** Anniversary of the Coronation of King Mindaugas. **Aug 15** Assumption. **Nov 1** All Saints' Day. **Dec 25-26** Christmas.

Health

	Special Precautions?	Certificate Required?
Yellow Fever	No	No
Cholera	No	No
Typhoid & Polio	No	N/A
Malaria	No	N/A

Note: *Regulations and requirements may be subject to change at short notice, and you are advised to contact your doctor well in advance of your intended date of departure. Any numbers in the chart refer to the footnotes below.*

Food & drink: Water supplies are generally reliable in cities, though it has a high mineral content and can be cloudy. Bottled or filtered water is preferable for these reasons. If travelling in rural areas, drink only bottled water. Milk is pasteurised and dairy products are generally safe for consumption. Local meat, poultry, seafood, fruit and vegetables are generally considered safe to eat, although there is some risk of fish tapeworm from freshwater fish. Exercise food and drink hygiene precautions, especially in rural areas.
Other risks: *Hepatitis A* and *B*, and *diphtheria* are present. *TB* may be a threat. *Tick-borne encephalitis* occurs in forested areas, and vaccination is strongly advisable. *Rabies* is present. For those at high risk, vaccination before arrival should be considered. If you are bitten, seek medical advice without delay. For more information, consult the *Health* appendix.
Health care: Health insurance is recommended. Although emergency treatment for foreign tourists is provided free of charge, all other medical services incur a charge.

Travel - International

AIR: The national airline, *Lithuanian Airlines (TE)* (website: www.lal.lt), flies from Vilnius to Amsterdam, Berlin, Copenhagen, Frankfurt/M, Helsinki, Kiev, London, Moscow, Paris, Stockholm, Tallinn and Warsaw. Other airlines offering connections to Vilnius include *Aeroflot*, *Air Baltic*, *Austrian Airlines*, *British Airways*, *Estonian Air*, *Finnair*, *LOT Polish Airlines*, *Lufthansa* and *SAS*. For further information, contact *Lithuanian Airlines* in the UK (tel: (01293) 579 900); or *Air Lithuania* in Kaunas (tel: (37) 229 706; website: www.airlithuania.lt). *Air Lithuania* offers flights from Kaunas and Palanga to Billund, Cologne, Hamburg, Kristianstad, Moscow and Oslo.
Approximate flight times: From Vilnius to *London* is three hours, to *Copenhagen* is one hour 30 minutes and to *Berlin* is one hour 20 minutes.
International airports: *Vilnius Airport (VNO)* (website: www.vilnius-airport.lt) is situated approximately 6km (3.5 miles) southeast of the city centre. There are taxi and bus services to the city (travel time – 10 minutes). Airport facilities include duty free shop, banks/bureaux de change, refreshments and tourist information. There are also international airports in *Kaunas (KUN)* and *Palanga (PLQ)*; the latter serves the whole of the Baltic coast.
Departure tax: Lt60.
SEA: Klaipeda is connected by trade routes with 200 foreign ports. There are ferry services to Denmark, Germany and Sweden. For information on ferry services from Klaipeda, contact Krantas Shipping (tel: (6) 395 111; fax: (6) 395 222; e-mail: travel@krantas.lt; website: www.krantas.lt). At present, there are services to Karlshamm in Sweden; Aarhus and Aabenraa in Denmark; and to Kiel and Sassnitz in Germany.
RAIL: Lithuania has a well-developed rail network and Vilnius is the focal point for rail connections in the region. Major routes go to Kaliningrad, Lviv (Ukraine), Minsk, Moscow, Riga, Sczecin, St Petersburg and Warsaw. Vilnius has passenger train connections with Berlin, Budapest, Prague, Sofia through Belarus and a direct connection with Suwalki (Poland).
ROAD: Lithuania has a good network of roads connecting the country with all neighbouring states. The crossing points on the Lithuanian-Polish border are Ogrodniki (Poland)–Lazdijai (Lithuania) and for trucks at Kalvarija (Lithuania). There are numerous crossing points with Latvia, Belarus and the Kaliningrad region of the Russian Federation. The international road Via Baltica goes from Tallinn to Warsaw through Latvia and Lithuania, thus connecting Scandinavia with Western Europe. **Coach:** There are passenger coaches from Vilnius to cities including Berlin, Gdansk, Kaliningrad, Minsk, Moscow, Prague, Riga, Tallinn, Vienna and Warsaw. Charter buses go to all Western European countries. *Eurolines*, departing from Victoria Coach Station in London, serves destinations in Lithuania. For further information, contact *Eurolines* (52 Grosvenor Gardens, London SW1; tel: (08705) 143 219; website: www.eurolines.com *or* www.nationalexpress.com).

Travel - Internal

AIR: There are domestic airports at Kaunas, Palanga and Siauliai. There are not many domestic flights.
RAIL: There are good connections from Vilnius to Kaunas, Klaipeda and Siauliai. Twice-daily passenger trains (including a sleeper train) connect Vilnius with the Baltic coast. Though the train does not stop in Palanga, the major resort on the Baltic coast, passengers to Palanga usually get off at Kretinga station or in Klaipeda, and then reach Palanga by bus. Passengers to Neringa (Nida, Juodkrante) can go to Klaipeda by train, and then take a bus. Suburban trains going to Ignalina connect Vilnius with the popular lake district of the National Park. The ancient Trakai Castle can be reached by taking the suburban train going to Trakai.
ROAD: There is a good network of roads within the country. Modern four-lane motorways connect Vilnius with Klaipeda, Kaunas and Panevezys. **Traffic regulations:** Seat belts must be worn. The speed limit is 110kph (68mph) on motorways, 90kph (56mph) on country roads and 60kph (44mph) inside towns. The Vilnius-Kaunas highway has a speed limit of 100kph (60mph). Traffic drives on the right. **Bus:** Generally, buses are more frequent and quicker than domestic trains and serve almost every town and village. **Car hire:** *Avis*, *Europcar* and *Hertz* can provide chauffeur-driven or self-drive cars. **Documentation:** Most European nationals should be in possession of EU pink format driving licences. Otherwise, a national driving licence is sufficient, if

supported by photograph-bearing ID.
URBAN: Public transport in urban districts includes **buses** and **trolleybuses**, which usually run from 0600-0100. Transport coupons can be bought either at news kiosks before boarding or from the driver. Minibuses are less crowded but more expensive. **Taxi:** These display illuminated *Taksi* signs and can be hailed in the street, found at taxi ranks or ordered by phone.

Accommodation

HOTELS: Since independence, western-style hotels and motels have been built in Lithuania in cooperation with foreign firms. Vilnius and the other major centres in the country enjoy an adequate range of good accommodation including large hotels and smaller pensions. A star grading system is in force. For further details, contact the Lithuanian State Department of Tourism (see *Contact Addresses* section) *or* the Lithuanian Hotel and Restaurant Association, Jasinsjio 16, Vilnius (tel/fax: (5) 249 7478; e-mail: lvra@mail.lt; website: www.lvra.lt).
PRIVATE ROOMS: Travel agencies can arrange rental of rooms in private homes as well as houses. This is especially popular in resort regions.
Self-catering apartments in Vilnius can also be rented (tel: (6) 824 1569 *or* 987 1344; website: www.oldtown-apartments.com).
CAMPING: Campsites are not numerous. The majority of them are located in the most picturesque regions: Palanga (on the shore of the Baltic Sea), Trakai (lake district) and near larger towns. There are three sites in close proximity to Vilnius. Pitching a tent is permitted at the majority of Lithuanian lakes and rivers (including the National Park) for a small fee, but almost no other facilities are provided at these sites.
YOUTH HOSTELS: There are currently about five hostels in Lithuania. For further information, contact Lithuanian Youth Hostels, Ausros Vartu 20-15, 2001 Vilnius (tel: (5) 262 5357; e-mail: booking@lithuanianhostels.org; website: www.lithuanianhostels.org).

Resorts & Excursions

VILNIUS: The historic city of Vilnius (founded in 1323) is the capital of Lithuania. Surrounded on three sides by wooded hills and situated in a picturesque valley formed by the rivers Neris and Vilnia, the ancient yet modern centre of the city lies on the southern or left bank of the river. Unlike Riga and Tallinn in the other Baltic Republics, Vilnius is not of Germanic origin, although like these other cities it has a large old quarter which is gradually being restored. Almost all major European architectural styles are represented, although ultimately it was the Baroque which came to dominate. The heart of the capital is the beautiful and spacious **Gediminas Square**, the main feature of which is the **Cathedral** built in the Classical style. Other interesting churches are the Gothic **St Ann's Church** and the **St Peter and St Paul's Church**, which houses the body of St Casimieras, one of the most revered of Lithuania's dukes. It also includes some fine sculptures. Any itinerary of the city should include the historic **University of Vilnius**, which was granted its charter in 1579, the Golden Age in the city's history. The university is among the oldest in Central Europe and has a distinctly Renaissance feel with its inner courtyards and arcades. To enjoy a view of the whole city, visitors should climb the tower of **Gediminas Castle**. High on a hill in the centre of the city, it rises above Vilnius and is the symbol of the Lithuanian capital.
EXCURSIONS: About 25km (18 miles) from Vilnius lies **Trakai**, an ancient capital of Lithuania. Situated on the shore of the picturesque **Lake Galve**, on which boat rides are available, the city has a castle dating from the 14th century. Further to the west is the spa of **Birstonas**, renowned for its mineral waters and tranquility.
KAUNAS: To the west of Vilnius lies the industrial and cultural centre of Kaunas, Lithuania's second city. Also known as the 'city of museums', it boasts, amongst others, the **Museum of Devil's Sculptures** and a memorial to those who suffered during the Nazi occupation. The most famous museum is dedicated to the works of the Lithuanian painter Ciurlionis. Kaunas also numbers three theatres, some 11th-century castle ruins and the old **City Hall** among its attractions.
ELSEWHERE: Other places of interest in Lithuania include the small riverside spa resort of **Druskininkai**, situated 135km (84 miles) from Vilnius, and the small town of **Rumsiskes**, 80km (50 miles) from Vilnius and 20km (12.5 miles) from Kaunas, with its open-air museum of wooden architecture exhibiting farmhouses from all the various regions of the country. Popular seaside resorts include **Palanga** and **Kursiu Nerija** (with the settlements of **Nida** and **Juodkrante**), which are famous for their clean white sand beaches, natural sand dunes and pine forests. Palanga also boasts the **Amber Museum** and an interesting botanical park. Nida is the last village on the Lithuanian half of the spit surrounded by endless stretches of clean white sand. A lighthouse from 1874 can be visited here, as can the **Thomas Mann Museum**, situated in the house where the German writer spent his holidays between 1930 and 1932. To the south lies the city of **Klaipeda**, an important seaport as well as the main centre for ferry connections from Lithuania. The two main towns in the north of the country are **Siauliai**, an important industrial centre with the famous **Hill of Crosses** about 10km (6 miles) from the city, and **Panevezys** with its famous **Drama Theatre**.

Sport & Activities

Hiking: Lithuania is a predominantly flat country, a quarter of which is covered by forests. There are five national parks and numerous other conservation areas. Hiking trails can be found all over the country. One of the highlights is the *Curonian Spit National Park*. Rare flora and fauna are to be found here. *Trakai National Park* contains many lakes while *Aukstaitija* and *Zemaitija National Parks* feature hills, lakes and uplands.
Watersports: A range of watersports is practised on Lithuania's many lakes and rivers, and equipment can be hired locally. **Fishing** is very popular. Licences, which are compulsory, are issued by the Department of Water Resources, Juozapaviciaus 9, Vilnius (tel: (5) 272 3786). **Sailing** and **windsurfing** are popular on the lakes near Trakai, at Kursiu marios (a lagoon at the Baltic) and at Kauno marios near Kaunas.
Other: Wintersports include **ice-fishing**, **cross-country skiing** and **skating**. Lithuania has extensive sporting facilities including the 15,000-seat *Zalgiris* stadium in Vilnius and facilities for **swimming**, **football**, **handball**, **basketball** (the most popular sport), **tennis** and **hockey**. **Cycling** is also popular.

Social Profile

FOOD & DRINK: Local specialities include *skilandis* (smoked meat), *salti barsciai* (cold soup) and *bulviniai blynai* (potato pancakes). Smoked eel is a famous Baltic delicacy. Waiter service is the norm in restaurants and cafes.
Local brands of beer and imported drinks are popular. A famous Lithuanian spirit is *midus*, a mild alcoholic beverage made from honey.
NIGHTLIFE: Cinemas can be found in all towns. Lithuanian theatres, most of which are concentrated in the capital, are also renowned. The Jaunimo *teatras* in Vilnius are famous throughout the country. Opera and ballet are staged in the city at the Vilnius Opera Theatre and Kaunas has a Musical Theatre. Puppet shows are staged for children in Vilnius and Kaunas. There are restaurants with live music as well as numerous discos and nightclubs with variety shows in the larger towns.
SHOPPING: Amber, linen goods and local crafts are good buys. National artists sell their works in specialised art galleries in major towns. **Shopping hours:** Grocery shops open Mon-Fri 0800-2000.
SPECIAL EVENTS: For full details, contact the Lithuanian State Department of Tourism (see *Contact Addresses* section). The following is a selection of special events occurring in Lithuania in 2005:
Jan 6 *Epiphany Procession* (*The Three Magi*), Vilnius. **Feb 5** *SARTAI 2005*, Dusetos, Zarasai Region. **Feb 10-13** *Vilnius Book Fair*. **Mar 4-6** *Kaziukas Fair*. **Mar 11** *Day of Restoration of Independence of Lithuania*. **Mar 25-Apr 1** *Cinema Festival 'Vilniaus Pavasaris'*. **Apr** *International Contemporary Dance Festival*, Vilnius. **May 26-29** *32nd International Folklore Festival*, Vilnius. **Jun-Jul** *Vilnius Festival*. **Jun-Aug** *Vilnius Carnival*. **Jun 3-5** *XII Jazz Festival at Klaipeda Castle*. **Jun 23** *Feast of St John*, nationwide. **Jul** *Wine Festival*, Anyksèiai; *Cucumber Festival*. **Jul 1-Aug 1** *St Christopher's Summer Festival*. **Jul 9-16** *International Thom Mann's Festival*. **Jul 19-24** *Sea Festival*, Klaipeda. **Aug 1-23** *VIII International Opera & Symphony Festival*, Klaipeda. **Sep 10-18** *The Days of the Capital - Vilnius 2005*. **Sep 15-18** *International Festival - Vilnius Jazz 2005*. **Oct 21-23** *International Festival of Singing Poetry*, Vilnius. **Dec-Jan 2006** *Christmas Festivities*.
SOCIAL CONVENTIONS: Handshaking is customary. Normal courtesies should be observed. The Lithuanians are proud of their culture and their national heritage and visitors should take care to respect this sense of national identity. **Tipping:** Taxi fares and restaurant bills include a tip. Otherwise, tips are discretionary.

Business Profile

ECONOMY: Lithuania has historically been the least developed of the Baltic republics, with a smaller industrial base and greater dependence on agriculture, prior to rapid industrialisation during the Soviet era. Sugar beet, cereals, potatoes and vegetables are the main crops. Electrical, electronic and optical goods and light machinery are the main industrial products. Food processing is also an important industry, with an ample supply of agricultural products from Lithuania's own farming and fisheries sector and more recently from Russia. Timber production has expanded on the back of growing trade links with Scandinavia. Lithuania's other major economic asset is the Baltic's only naturally ice-free port (other than Kaliningrad) at Klaipeda. Lithuania is a founder member of the regional cooperation organisation for Baltic littoral states, the Council of Baltic Sea States. The government has largely completed the dismantling of the old Soviet-style command economy, introducing a market system and liberalising foreign trade. Domestic political factors stalled some parts of the otherwise rapid privatisation programme, especially the key energy industries as well as the finance and banking sector. Action in the energy field is further complicated by the fact that 80 per cent of Lithuania's energy comes from nuclear power (the highest figure of any country in the world): the government plans to reduce the percentage but faces major problems regarding waste disposal and alternative energy sources. Further privatisations of state assets, principally in the banking and transport sectors were completed in 2002. Lithuania's trade patterns have gradually shifted during the 1990s towards the West, and the European Union now accounts for just under half of all Lithuanian trade. Some 30 per cent of import trade and 20 per cent of export trade is conducted with partners in the former Soviet Union, principally the Russian Federation and Latvia. Lithuania has recovered from the serious knock-on effects of the 1998 Russian financial crisis and is now growing fairly quickly at around 6 per cent annually. The country joined the IMF and World Bank in 1992, as well as the European Bank for Reconstruction and Development as a Country of Operation. A convertible currency, the Litas, was introduced in 1993. Membership of the European Union has been a high priority for Lithuania since independence. Accession negotiations began in October 1999 and progressed well. Following a 90 per cent endorsement in a national referendum held in May 2003, Lithuania – along with nine other countries, including both its Baltic neighbours – joined the EU on May 1 2004.
BUSINESS: Business is conducted in a fairly formal manner and a smart appearance is important. Appointments should be made in advance. English is used for international commerce. A knowledge of German, Russian or Polish may also be useful. **Office hours:** Mon-Fri 0900-1300 and 1400-1800.
COMMERCIAL INFORMATION: The following organisations can offer advice: Association of Lithuanian Chambers of Commerce, Industry and Crafts, J Tumo-Vaizganto 9/1-63A, 01108 Vilnius (tel: (5) 261 2102; fax: (5) 261 2112; e-mail: info@chambers.lt; website: www.chambers.lt); *or* European Committee of the Government of the Republic of Lithuania, Gedimino ave 11, 01103 Vilnius (tel: (5) 266 3827; fax: (5) 266 3745; e-mail: euro@lrvk.lt; website: www.euro.lt).
CONFERENCES/CONVENTIONS: A number of hotels in Vilnius have conference facilities and can organise conventions. Some rest homes in Palanga also provide facilities during the low season. For further information, contact the Lithuanian State Department of Tourism (see *Contact Addresses* section), the Lithuanian Hotel and Restaurant Association (see *Accommodation* section) *or* LITEXPO, Laisves pr 5, LT 04215 Vilnius (tel: (5) 245 1800; fax: (5) 245 4511; e-mail: info@litexpo.lt; website: www.litexpo.lt).

Climate

Temperate climate, but with considerable temperature variations. Summer is warm with relatively mild weather in spring and autumn. Winter, which lasts from November to mid-March, can be very cold. Rainfall is distributed throughout the year with the heaviest rainfall in August. Heavy snowfalls are common in the winter months.

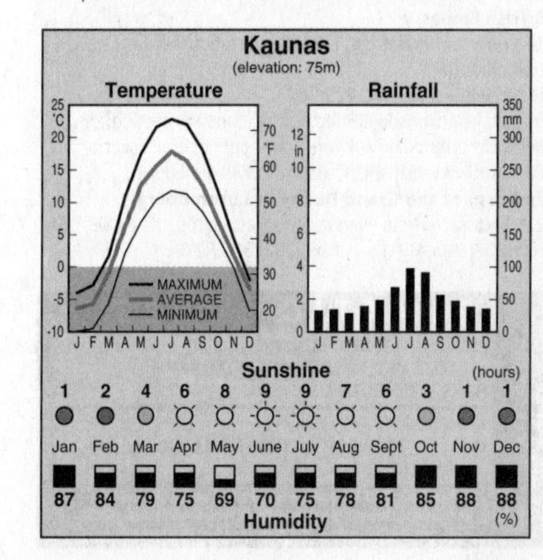

Luxembourg

LATEST TRAVEL ADVICE CONTACTS

British Foreign and Commonwealth Office
Tel: (0870) 606 0290 Website: www.fco.gov.uk

US Department of State
Website: http://travel.state.gov/travel

Canadian Department of Foreign Affairs and Int'l Trade
Tel: (1 800) 267 8376 Website: www.dfait-maeci.gc.ca

Credit: © eu2005.lu & ONT

Location: Western Europe.

Country dialling code: 352.

Office National du Tourisme (ONT) (National Tourist Office)
Gare Central, BP 1001, L-1010 Luxembourg-Ville, Luxembourg
Tel: 4282 821. Fax: 4282 8238.
E-mail: info@ont.lu
Website: www.ont.lu
ONT tourist offices also in each main town.

Luxembourg City Tourist Office
Street address: Place d'Armes, L-2011 Luxembourg-Ville, Luxembourg
Postal address: PO Box 181, Luxembourg-Ville, Luxembourg
Tel: 222 809. Fax: 467 070.
E-mail: touristinfo@lcto.lu
Website: www.lcto.lu

Embassy of the Grand Duchy of Luxembourg
27 Wilton Crescent, London SW1X 8SD, UK
Tel: (020) 7235 6961. Fax: (020) 7235 9734.
E-mail: amb.lux@virgin.net
Opening hours: Mon-Fri 0900-1230 and 1330-1700; 1000-1145 (visa section; applications).

Luxembourg National Tourist Office
122 Regent Street, London W1B 5SA, UK
Tel: (020) 7434 2800. Fax: (020) 7734 1205.
E-mail: tourism@luxembourg.co.uk
Website: www.luxembourg.co.uk
Opening hours: Mon-Fri 1000-1700.

British Embassy
14 Boulevard Roosevelt, L-2450 Luxembourg-Ville, Luxembourg
Tel: 229 864-6. Fax: 229 867.
E-mail: jason.lonsdale@fco.gov.uk (consular section) *or* petra.kiefer@fco.gov.uk (press and public affairs section).
Website: www.britishembassy.gov.uk/luxembourg

Embassy of the Grand Duchy of Luxembourg
2200 Massachusetts Avenue, NW, Washington, DC 20008, USA
Tel: (202) 265 4171/2. Fax: (202) 328 8270.
E-mail: washington.info@mae.etat.lu
Website: www.luxembourg-usa.org
Consulates in: Atlanta, Chicago, Cleveland, Fort Worth, Indianapolis, Kansas City (Missouri), New Orleans, New York, San Francisco, Seattle and Washington. (New York and San Francisco process visas.)

Luxembourg National Tourist Office
17 Beekman Place, New York, NY 10022, USA
Tel: (212) 935 8888. Fax: (212) 935 5896.
E-mail: info@visitluxembourg.com
Website: www.visitluxembourg.com

Embassy of the United States of America
22 Boulevard Emmanuel-Servais, L-2535 Luxembourg-Ville, Luxembourg
Tel: 460 123. Fax: 461 401.
E-mail: LuxembourgConsular@state.gov (consular section).
Website: www.amembassy.lu

Honorary Consul of Canada
15 Rue Guillaume Schneider, L-2522 Luxembourg-Ville, Luxembourg
Tel: 2627 0570. Fax: 2627 0670.
E-mail: canada@pt.lu
Website: www.canada.lu

TIMATIC CODES

Health	AMADEUS: **TI-DFT/LUX/HE** GALILEO/WORLDSPAN: **TI-DFT/LUX/HE** SABRE: **TIDFT/LUX/HE**
Visa	AMADEUS: **TI-DFT/LUX/VI** GALILEO/WORLDSPAN: **TI-DFT/LUX/VI** SABRE: **TIDFT/LUX/VI**

To access TIMATIC country information on Health and Visa regulations through the Computer Reservations System (CRS), type in the appropriate command line listed above.

General Information

AREA: 2586 sq km (999 sq miles).
POPULATION: 448,300 (official estimate 2003).
POPULATION DENSITY: 173.4 per sq km.
CAPITAL: Luxembourg-Ville. **Population:** 78,300 (official estimate 2003).
GEOGRAPHY: The Grand Duchy of Luxembourg shares borders to the north and west with Belgium, to the south with France and to the east with Germany. One-third of the country is made up of the hills and forests of the Ardennes, while the rest is wooded farmland. In the southeast is the rich wine-growing valley of Moselle. The capital, Luxembourg-Ville, is built on a rock overlooking the Alzette and Petrusse valleys.
GOVERNMENT: Constitutional monarchy. Luxembourg is a founding member of the European Union and the only Grand Duchy in the world. **Head of State:** Grand Duke Henri since 2000. **Head of Government:** Prime Minister Jean-Claude Juncker since 1994.
LANGUAGE: Lëtzeburgesch, a German-Moselle-Frankish dialect, became the officially recognised national language in 1984. French and German are generally used for administrative and commercial purposes. Many Luxembourgers also speak English.
RELIGION: Around 88 per cent Roman Catholic, with Protestant, Anglican and Jewish minorities.
TIME: GMT + 1 (GMT + 2 from last Sunday in March to Saturday before last Sunday in October).
ELECTRICITY: 220 volts AC, 50Hz.
COMMUNICATIONS: Telephone: Full IDD is available. Country code: 352 (no area codes). Outgoing international code: 00. International phones have a yellow sign showing a telephone dial with a receiver in the centre. **Mobile telephone:** GSM 900 and 1800 networks. Network operators are *P & T Luxembourg* (website: www.luxgsm.lu), *Tango SA* (website: www.tango.lu) and *Vox Mobile* (website: www.vox.lu). **Fax:** There is a fax booth at the Luxembourg-Ville main post office. Faxes may be sent to a central number (491 175) for delivery by express mail within Luxembourg. **Internet:** Internet and e-mail services are available in Internet cafes. ISPs include *Visual Online Sarl* (website: www.vo.lu). **Telegram:** There are facilities at the post office at 25 rue Aldringen, Luxembourg-Ville, and in all major towns. Hotels often allow guests to use their facilities. **Post:** Post to other European destinations takes two to four days. There are *poste restante* facilities throughout the country. Prospective recipients must first register for a PO Box. Mail will be held for up to one month. Post office hours: Mon-Fri 0800-1200 and 1330-1700. The Luxembourg-Ville main office (opposite the railway station) is open Mon-Fri 0600-1900, Sat 0600-1200. Smaller offices may open for only a few hours. Telephone 49911 for details.
Press: There are several daily newspapers including the *Lëtzebuerger Journal*, *Luxemburger Wort*, *Tageblatt/Zeitung fir Letzebuerg* and *Zeitung vum Lëtzebuerger Vollek*. There is one weekly English-language newspaper, *The Luxembourg News*.
Radio: BBC World Service (website: www.bbc.co.uk/worldservice) and Voice of America (website: www.voa.gov) can be received. From time to time the frequencies change and the most up-to-date can be found online.

Passport/Visa

	Passport Required?	Visa Required?	Return Ticket Required?
Full British	Yes	No	No
Australian	Yes	No	2
Canadian	Yes	No	2
USA	Yes	No	2
Other EU	1	No	No
Japanese	Yes	No	2

Note: *Regulations and requirements may be subject to change at short notice, and you are advised to contact the appropriate diplomatic or consular authority before finalising travel arrangements. Details of these may be found at the head of this country's entry. Any numbers in the chart refer to the footnotes below.*

Note: Luxembourg is a signatory to the **1995 Schengen Agreement**. For further details about passport and visa regulations in the Schengen area see the introductory section *How to Use This Guide*.
PASSPORTS: Passport valid for three months beyond length of stay required by all except:
(a) **1.** nationals of EU countries who hold a valid national ID card;
(b) nationals of Andorra, Liechtenstein, Monaco, San Marino and Switzerland, providing they hold a valid national ID card.
Note: 2. It is advisable to have a return ticket, but not obligatory. If a visitor is not in possession of a return ticket, proof of sufficient means of support may be required.
VISAS: Required by all except the following nationals for periods not exceeding three months and as long as the passport is still valid for three months beyond length of stay:
(a) nationals referred to in the chart above;
(b) nationals mentioned under passport exemptions above;
(c) nationals of Argentina, Bolivia, Brazil, Brunei, Bulgaria, Chile, Costa Rica, Croatia, El Salvador, Guatemala, Honduras, Hong Kong (SAR), Iceland, Israel, Korea (Rep), Macau (SAR), Malaysia, Mexico, New Zealand, Nicaragua, Norway, Panama, Paraguay, Romania, Singapore, Uruguay, Vatican City and Venezuela;
(d) passengers continuing their journey by the same or first connecting aircraft within 72 hours provided holding valid onward or return documentation and not leaving the airport (except nationals of certain countries who *always* need an airport transit visa). Please contact the Consulate for details.
Types of visa and cost: A uniform type of visa, the *Schengen* visa, is issued for tourist, business and private visits. All *Schengen* visas, regardless of the duration of stay and whether single- or multiple-entry, are available for approximately £27, although prices are subject to change.
Note: Spouses and children of EU nationals (providing spouse's passport and the original marriage certificate is produced) receive their visas free of charge (enquire at Embassy for details).
Validity: Short-stay visas are valid for up to six months from date of issue for single- or multiple-entries of maximum 90 days in total. Transit visas are valid for single- or multiple-entries of maximum five days per entry, including the day of arrival. Long-stay visas are valid for up to one year. Visas cannot be extended; a new application must be made each time.
Application to: Applications must be made in person to the Consulate (or Consular section at Embassy) of the Benelux country which the applicant will enter first.
Application requirements: (a) One completed application form. (b) One passport-size photo. (c) Passport valid for at least three months longer than the validity of the visa (with a blank page to affix visa stamp). (d) Proof of the purpose of visit (official letter of invitation/confirmed hotel booking; onward or return ticket). (e) Evidence of sufficient funds to cover the duration of stay. (f) Evidence of medical coverage for the Schengen countries (eg form E111). (g) Fee.
Working days required: Two days to three weeks depending on purpose of visit and nationality.
Temporary residence: Enquire about special application procedures at Consulate (or Consular section at Embassy); see *Contact Addresses* section.

Money

Single European currency (Euro): Single European currency (Euro): The Euro is now the official currency of 12 EU member states (including Luxembourg). The first Euro coins and notes were introduced in January 2002; the Luxembourg Franc was completely replaced by the Euro on 28 February 2002. Euro (€) = 100 cents. Notes are in denominations of €500, 200, 100, 50, 20, 10 and 5. Coins are in denominations of €2 and 1, and 50, 20, 10, 5, 2 and 1 cents.
Currency exchange: Foreign currencies, travellers cheques and cheques can be exchanged at banks, bureaux de change, the airport, railway stations, the post office and major hotels (generally at a less advantageous rate).
Credit & debit cards: American Express, Diners Club, MasterCard, Visa and others are all widely accepted, as well as Eurocheque cards. Many retailers require a minimum (eg €10 to 25) before accepting credit/debit cards. Check with your credit or debit card company for details of merchant acceptability and other services which may be available.
Travellers cheques: Widely accepted. To avoid additional exchange rate charges, travellers are advised to take travellers cheques in Euros, Pounds Sterling or US Dollars.
Currency restrictions: There are no restrictions on the import and export of either local or foreign currency.
Exchange rate indicators: The following figures are included as a guide to the movements of the Euro against Sterling and the US Dollar:

Date	Feb '04	May '04	Aug '04	Nov '04
£1.00	1.46	1.50	1.49	1.42
$1.00	0.80	0.84	0.80	0.75

Banking hours: Generally Mon-Fri 0900-1200 and 1400-1600, but may vary greatly.

Duty Free

The following goods may be imported into Luxembourg without incurring customs duty by travellers arriving from countries outside the EU:
200 cigarettes or 100 cigarillos or 50 cigars or 250g of tobacco; 1l of spirits or 2l of sparkling wine or 2l of liqueur wine and 2l of non-sparkling wine; 50g of perfume and 250ml of eau de toilette; 500g of coffee and 200g of coffee extract; 100g of tea and 40g of tea extract; other goods to the value of €64.45 for passengers over 15 years and €24.79 for passengers under 15.
Note: Alcohol and tobacco products are only available to passengers of 17 years of age or over.
Abolition of duty free goods within the EU: On June 30 1999, the sale of duty free alcohol and tobacco at airports and at sea was abolished in all of the original 15 EU member states. Of the 10 new member states that joined the EU on May 1 2004, these rules already apply to Cyprus and Malta. There are transitional rules in place for visitors returning to one of the original 15 EU countries from one of the other new EU countries. But for the original 15, plus Cyprus and Malta, there are now no limits imposed on importing tobacco and alcohol products from one EU country to another (with the exceptions of Denmark, Finland and Sweden, where limits *are* imposed). Travellers should note that they may be required to prove at customs that the goods purchased are for personal use *only*.

Public Holidays

2005: Jan 1 New Year's Day. **Feb 7** Carnival. **Mar 28** Easter Monday. **May 1** May Day. **May 5** Ascension. **May 16** Whit Monday. **Jun 23** National Day. **Aug 15** Assumption. **Sep 1*** Luxembourg City Kermesse. **Nov 1** All Saints' Day. **Dec 25** Christmas Day. **Dec 26** St Stephen's Day.
2006: Jan 1 New Year's Day. **Feb 27** Carnival. **Apr 17** Easter Monday. **May 1** May Day. **May 25** Ascension. **Jun 5** Whit Monday. **Jun 23** National Day. **Aug 15** Assumption. **Sep 4*** Luxembourg City Kermesse. **Nov 1** All Saints' Day. **Dec 25** Christmas Day. **Dec 26** St Stephen's Day.
Note: (a) *Applies to the City of Luxembourg only. (b) Official public holidays falling on a Sunday may be deferred to the following Monday, for a maximum of two holidays. Exact details should be confirmed with the National Tourist Office or the Embassy (see *Contact Addresses* section).

Health

	Special Precautions?	Certificate Required?
Yellow Fever	No	No
Cholera	No	No
Typhoid & Polio	No	N/A
Malaria	No	N/A

Note: *Regulations and requirements may be subject to change at short notice, and you are advised to contact your doctor well in advance of your intended date of departure. Any numbers in the chart refer to the footnotes below.*

Food & drink: Tap water is considered safe to drink. Milk is pasteurised and dairy products are safe for consumption. Local meat, poultry, seafood, fruit and vegetables are generally considered safe to eat.
Other risks: *Rabies* may be present in wildlife. For those at high risk, vaccination before arrival should be considered. If you are bitten, seek medical advice without delay. For more information, consult the *Health* appendix.
Health care: There are reciprocal health agreements with all other EU member states. UK citizens should obtain form E111 from the Department of Health before travelling. Hospital treatment is normally free on presentation of the E111 but patients must pay a standard daily fee which is not refunded. For health information, contact the *Caisse Nationale d'Assurance Maladie des Ouvriers*.

Travel - International

AIR: Luxembourg's national airline is *Luxair (LG)* (website: www.luxair.lu), which offers regular services to a number of European destinations (including Austria, Greece, Italy, Portugal, Spain, Sweden and the UK) as well as flights to Africa (Morocco and Tunisia) and Turkey. *Luxair* recently introduced a direct connection between Luxembourg and the USA (New York) and there are weekly flights to Newark Airport. Luxair flies daily from Luxembourg to London Heathrow, London Stansted and Manchester. *British Airways* flies daily from London Heathrow and London Gatwick. There are also flights to London City Airport by *VLM UK*.
Approximate flight times: From *London* to Luxembourg is one hour. From *New York* to Luxembourg is approximately eight hours.
International airports: *Luxembourg (LUX)* (Findel) is 5km (3.5 miles) northeast of the city (travel time - 20 minutes). Coaches and buses run regular services to the city. Buses cost about €1.20. Taxis are also available (travel time - 10 minutes), costing between €15-25. Airport facilities include an outgoing duty-free shop, car hire, bank/bureau de change and a tourist information office.
Departure tax: None.
RAIL: *Eurostar* is a service provided by the railways of Belgium, the United Kingdom and France, operating direct high-speed trains from London (*Waterloo International*) to Paris (*Gare du Nord*) and to Brussels (*Midi/Zuid*). It takes two hours 40 minutes from London to Brussels with onward connections to Luxembourg. Total travelling time from London to Luxembourg is approximately six hours 30 minutes. Trains depart up to eight times a day from Waterloo to Brussels. When work on the UK section of the high-speed line is completed, the transit times between London St Pancras and Brussels will be just two hours, and two hours 15 minutes between London St Pancras and Paris. The Eurostar trains are equipped with standard-class and first-class seating, buffet, bar and are staffed by multi-lingual, highly trained personnel. Pricing is competitive with the airlines, and there is a large range of different tickets and prices. Children aged between four to 11 years benefit from a special fare in first class as well as in standard class. Children under four years old travel free but cannot be guaranteed a seat. Wheelchair users and blind passengers together with one companion get a special fare. For further information and reservations, contact *Eurostar* (tel: (0870) 600 0792 (travel agents) *or* (08705) 186 186 (public; within the UK) *or* (+44 (1233) 617 575 (public; outside the UK only); website: www.eurostar.com); *or Rail Europe* (tel: (08705) 848 848; website: www.raileurope.com). Travel agents can obtain refunds for unused tickets from Eurostar Trade Refunds, 2nd Floor, Kent House, 81 Station Road, Ashford, Kent TN23 1PD. Complaints and comments may be sent to Eurostar Customer Relations, Eurostar House, Waterloo Station, London SE1 8SE (tel: (020) 7928 5163). General enquiries and information requests must be made by telephone. Enquiries in France should be made to Eurostar in Paris (tel: (8) 3635 3539; only available from within France). Information about package deals, inclusive of accommodation and travel on Eurostar can be obtained from Eurostar Holidays Direct (tel: (0870) 167 6767).
Another daily rail connection is London (Charing Cross)–Ostend–Brussels–Luxembourg, taking approximately 11 hours, including the channel crossing by Catamaran from Dover Hoverport. There are direct train links with principal cities in neighbouring countries. Inter-Rail and Eurailpass are valid.
ROAD: Luxembourg is easily reached within one day from the UK, via Belgium or France. The quickest way to cross the channel is by driving the car onto *Eurotunnel* trains. All road vehicles are carried through the tunnel in *Eurotunnel* shuttles running between the two terminals, one near Folkestone in Kent, with direct road access from the M20, and one just outside Calais, with links to the A16/A26 motorway (Exit 13). Each shuttle is made up of 12 single- and 12 double-deck carriages, and vehicles are directed to single- or double-deck carriages depending on their height. There are facilities for cars and motorcycles, coaches, minibuses, caravans, campervans and other vehicles over 1.85m (6.07ft). Bicycles are provided for. Passengers generally travel with their vehicles. Heavy goods vehicles are carried on special shuttles and drivers travel in a separate carriage. Terminals and shuttles are well equipped for disabled passengers, and Passenger Terminal buildings contain a variety of shops, restaurants, bureaux de change and other amenities. The journey takes about 35 minutes from platform to platform and about one hour from motorway to motorway. Services run every day of the year, and there are between two and five an hour, depending on the time of day. There is a reservation system and a turn-up-and-go service. Motorists pass through customs and immigration before they board the shuttle without further checks on arrival. Fares vary according to length of stay, time of day and time of year and whether you have a reservation or not. The price applies to the car, regardless of the number of passengers or its size. The fare may be paid in cash, by cheque or by credit card. There is a reduction of £2 when booking online. For further information, contact *Eurotunnel Customer Services UK* (tel: (08705) 353 535; website: www.eurotunnel.com).
For drivers not using the shuttle through the channel tunnel, car ferries operate frequently between Dover and Calais (regular ferries and Hovercraft services) and Dover and Ostend (regular ferries as well as Catamaran and Hoverspeed services). Luxembourg-Ville is approximately 320km (200 miles) from Ostend, and 420km (260 miles) from Calais. From Calais, the quickest route is to take the motorway to Brussels via Lille, then head south through Namur along the E411 to Luxembourg; from Ostend, take the E40 motorway to Brussels, then the E411 to Luxembourg. In total, the journey from London (including the ferry crossing) takes approximately eight hours.

Coach: *Eurolines* runs a twice-weekly (Wednesday and Saturday) coach service from London to Luxembourg. Further information can also be obtained by calling Eurolines in the UK (52 Grosvenor Gardens, London SW1; tel: (08705) 143 219; website: www.eurolines.com *or* www.nationalexpress.com).
Travel times: The following chart gives approximate travel times (in hours and minutes) from **Luxembourg-Ville** to other major cities/towns in Europe.

	Air	Road	Rail
Amsterdam	**0.45**	**5.30**	**6.30**
Brussels	**0.45**	**2.00**	**2.30**
Frankfurt/M	**0.50**	**2.30**	**3.30**
Paris	**1.00**	**4.00**	**4.00**
London	**1.00**	***8.00**	****6.30**
Zürich	**1.20**	**5.00**	**5.00**

Note: *Includes ferry crossing from Dover (via Calais or Ostend); **Eurostar via Bruxelles-Midi (Brussels).

Travel - Internal

RAIL: The national railway company, *Chemins de Fer Luxembourgeois (CFL)*, runs an efficient rail service which is fully integrated with the bus network. CFL has recently introduced a so-called *horaire cadencé* schedule, meaning there is now at least one train every hour to every station at the same time in every hour. Reductions are offered for weekend and holiday return tickets. CFL rail services and *CFL/CRL* buses in Luxembourg are covered by the *Benelux Tourrail* rail pass covering Belgium, Luxembourg and The Netherlands. This gives unlimited travel on any five days within a one-month period throughout the year.
Rail/Coach Rover Tickets are valid for both networks. The *Luxembourg Card* gives unlimited travel on public transport for a period of one to three days, with free entrance to up to 40 attractions. There is also an *Öko Pass*, which is a single-day ticket for unlimited travel on all forms of public transport (not valid on sightseeing buses), with concessions for senior citizens. For further information, contact CFL (tel: 49901 *or* 4990 5572; e-mail: info@cfl.lu; website: www.cfl.lu).
ROAD: As in the rest of Western Europe, there is an excellent network of roads and motorways in Luxembourg. Traffic drives on the right. **Bus:** Cross-country buses are punctual and operate between all major towns. For information on passes, see the *Rail* section. **Taxi:** These are metered. There is a minimum charge and a 10 per cent surcharge is applied from 2200-0600. Taxis are plentiful but cannot be hailed in the street. A 10 per cent tip is usual for taxi drivers. **Car hire:** All the main agencies operate in Luxembourg. Traffic regulations: The minimum age for driving is 18. It is obligatory to carry €15 at all times for the payment of on-the-spot fines; there are stiff drinking/driving spot fines. The wearing of seat belts is compulsory in the front seat and in the back, where seat belts are fitted. Children under 12 years of age must travel in the back seats, unless they are 1.5m (5ft) or taller, or if the front seat is fitted with an appropriate ECE-approved child seat. Motorcyclists must use a dipped beam even by day. The speed limit is 50kph (31mph) in built-up areas, 90kph (56mph) outside built-up areas, and 120kph (74mph) on motorways. For more details, contact Automobile Club du Grand-Duché de Luxembourg, 54 route de Longwy, L-8007 Bertrange, Luxembourg-Helfenterbruck (tel: 450 455; e-mail: acl@acl.lu; website: www.acl.lu).
Documentation: Third Party insurance is necessary. A Green Card is not obligatory but is strongly recommended. Without it, visitors have only the minimum legal cover in Luxembourg (if they have motor insurance at home). The Green Card tops this up to the level of cover provided by the visitor's domestic policy. A valid national driving licence is sufficient.
URBAN: Luxembourg-Ville has municipal bus services, for which single-journey flat-fare tickets may be purchased. This 'short distance' ticket is valid for one hour (or for a maximum of 10km/6 miles) from purchase on the whole of Luxembourg's public transport network, and also allows transits between city and country buses and trains. Ten-journey tickets are also available, but must be purchased in advance. There is no underground or tramway service.

Accommodation

HOTELS: For information on hotels in Luxembourg, contact the Luxembourg National Tourist Office (which can supply a free national guide) *or* the National Hotel Association, Horesca (to which all hotels in the Grand Duchy belong) at 7 rue Alcide de Gasperi, PO Box 2524, L-1025 Luxembourg-Kirchberg (tel: 421 351-5; fax: 421 355-299; e-mail: mail@horesca.lu; website: www.horesca.lu).
Grading: Luxembourg has a wide range of hotels, more than half of which are classified according to the Benelux system. Standard of accommodation is indicated by a row of 3-pointed stars from the highest (5 stars) to the minimum (1 star). However, membership of this scheme is voluntary and there may be first-class hotels which do not have a classification. *Benelux* star ratings comply with the following criteria: **5-star (H5)**: Luxury hotels. There are four establishments in this category; **4-star (H4)**: First-class hotels; 80 per cent of rooms have a private bath. Other amenities include night reception and room service. Around 15 per cent of graded hotels in Luxembourg belong to this category. There are 48 in this grouping; **3-star (H3)**: Around 50 per cent of rooms have a private bath. Other amenities include day reception; 29 per cent of graded hotels in Luxembourg belong to this category. There are 81 in this grouping; **2-star (H2)**: Around 25 per cent of rooms have a private bath. Other amenities include a bar; 9 per cent of graded hotels in Luxembourg belong to this category. There are 26 hotels in this grouping; **1-star (H1)**: Simple hotel. No private baths, but hot and cold water in rooms. Breakfast available. Eight graded hotels in Luxembourg belong to this category.
HOLIDAY APARTMENTS: A number of holiday flats and chalets are available throughout the country. A free pamphlet giving location and facilities is published by the National Tourist Office (see *Contact Addresses* section).
CAMPING: There are over 120 campsites throughout the country. According to government regulations, campsites are ranged in three different categories and the tariff in each camp is shown at the entrance. The National Tourist Office publishes a free, comprehensive brochure giving all relevant information concerning campsites.
YOUTH HOSTELS: There are youth hostels at Beaufort, Bourglinster, Echternach, Ettelbruck, Grevenmacher, Hollenfels, Lultzhausen, Luxembourg-Ville, Troisvierges, Vianden and Wiltz. A *Youth Hostel Guide* may be obtained free of charge from the National Tourist Office in London *or* the Centrale des Auberges de Jeunesses Luxembourgeoises, 24-26 place de la Gare, L-616 Luxembourg (tel: 2629 3500; fax: 2629 3504; e-mail: information@youthhostels.lu).

Resorts & Excursions

The capital, Luxembourg-Ville, is split into two districts: the delightful old centre, complete with fortress towers, turrets and winding, cobblestone streets; and the modern downtown area on the plâteau du Krichberg – the Luxembourg version of Wall Street. The city's history goes back to the year 963 AD, when Siegfried, Count of the Ardennes, had a castle named **Lucilinburhuc** built on a rock overlooking the **River Alzette**. It was the famous French fortress builder Vauban who, at the service of Louis XIV, later turned Luxembourg into one of his masterpieces, suitably known as the 'Gibraltar of the North'. At its height, the fortress was girdled by three ring-walls studded with 24 forts and linked underground by a 23km- (15 mile-) network of underground tunnels. It survived until 1867, when it was dismantled according to the provisions of the Treaty of London. But many of the old fortifications remain well preserved to this day and, in 1994, the entire old part of Luxembourg-Ville was declared a World Heritage Site by UNESCO. The Luxembourg City Tourist Office (whose main office is on the Place d'Armes) can provide details and maps for numerous walks taking visitors past the city's medieval remains and historic sites. The underground tunnels, known as *casemates*, can also be visited. A special open-air tourist train called the 'Petrusse Express' offers frequent guided tours through the **Petrusse Valley** (from which many of the remaining fortifications can easily be viewed), giving visitors an insight into life in the former fortress, with commentaries in several languages. The train departs from underneath one of the arches of the **Pont Adolphe** viaduct. Tickets can be bought from the city tourist office. Most of the city's historical sites are easily visited on foot and a walk through the Petrusse and Alzette valleys (which are spanned by several bridges) offers excellent views of the ancient fortifications. The city's main square, the **Place d'Armes**, has a number of outdoor cafes and restaurants although, after redevelopment, the square has lost some of its 'French' charm. In the city centre, the area known as the *Grund*, near the River Alzette, has many lively cafes and restaurants; it can be reached via a lift going down through the ancient rock (with the entrance located on the square **Fëschmaart** above). Other attractions in the city centre include the recently renovated **Palais Grand Ducal**, the official residence of the Grand Duke, where visitors can observe the changing of the guard; the Place Guillaume (also called *Knuedler*) and its twice-weekly market (Wednesday and Saturday); and, near the **Place Guillaume**, the 17th century **Notre Dame Cathedral**. Art lovers will find numerous galleries in the capital. Interesting museums include the **National Museum of Natural History**, the **National Museum of History and Art** and the **Museum of the City of Luxembourg** (whose architecture interestingly combines the 'old' and the 'new' and which displays a very detailed and informative account of Luxembourg's colourful history). The modern district on the plâteau du Kirchberg (reached via the **Pont Grand Duchesse Charlotte** – the most impressive of the many bridges in the capital) is expanding rapidly. Luxembourg's main cinema complex, **Utopolis**, is located here, next to the country's biggest shopping complex. The myriad of new modern office complexes being built on the plateau Kirchberg testify to Luxembourg's reputation as a major international financial centre. The country's geographical position at the 'heart of Europe', its strict banking secrecy laws and fiscal legislation are amongst the reasons why there are some 12,000 holding companies, 1300 investment funds and over 220 banks based in the capital, making Luxembourg the country with the highest banking concentration in Europe. The Kirchberg is also home to numerous European institutions. Proud of its role as a founding member of the EU, Luxembourg sees itself as playing a prominent position in European affairs and there are a number of European Union institutions based in Luxembourg-Ville, including: the **Commission of the European Community** (including the Statistical Office – EUROSTAT – and the Publications Office); the **European Court of Justice**; the **General Secretariat of the European Parliament**; the **European Investment Bank**; the **European Court of Auditors**; and the **Official Publications Office**. The sessions of the European Council of Ministers take place in Luxembourg three months a year.

BEYOND THE CAPITAL

Luxembourg is an attractive country with a green and picturesque landscape and many historical sites within easy reach of one another. The country is divided into five tourist regions. The central and southern part of the country that surrounds the capital, known as 'the Good Land', consists mainly of rolling farmland and woods. To the northeast is the Müllerthal, characterised by sandstone rock formations and forests (website: www.mullerthal.lu), while the northern third of the country is the Ardennes, set in beautiful forested hills and valleys. South of the capital is the Land of the Red Rocks, so named from its 'red earth', rich in iron. The southeast frontier is marked by the Moselle Valley, famous for its wines.
MÜLLERTHAL: Approximately 30km (19 miles) north of the capital, the Müllerthal region is frequently referred to as Luxembourg's 'Little Switzerland'. Hundreds of footpaths through densely wooded forests (many of which have vast expanses of needle trees), crystal-clear brooks and spectacular rock formations combine to make this one of the country's most popular areas for walking and hiking. Coach tours to the Müllerthal, also known as the **Germano-Luxembourg Natural Park**, leave daily from the main bus station in Luxembourg-Ville. The main resorts are **Beaufort** and **Larochette**, both of which also have castles located on a hilltop offering good views. Another well-known resort in the area is **Berdorf**.
Echternach: Further east, the town of Echternach is particularly well known for its religious dancing procession, which takes place annually on Whit Tuesday and attracts pilgrims from all over the world. The town's **Benedectine Abbey** (which was founded in the seventh century by St Willibrord and now also houses a museum) and, in particular, the **St Willibrord Basilica** (with its crypt as a centrepiece) are well worth visiting. Echternach also has a distinctive 15th-century **Town Hall** overlooking the market square.
ARDENNES: Almost one-third of Luxembourg's total land area consists of forest and it is particularly the north (a region known as the Luxembourg Ardennes referred to locally as *Eisléck*) which offers the best natural attractions. The scenic beauty and quiet of this region, which consists of forested plateaux, wooded hills and lush valleys, attracts many nature and outdoor enthusiasts. The towns of **Diekirch** and **Wiltz**, where two of the country's breweries are located, are the gateways into the Luxembourg Ardennes. The small town of **Esch-sur-Sûre** is a well-known regional resort which is entirely surrounded by the natural moat of the **River Sûre** (*Sauer*). A few miles further upstream is the country's drinking water reservoir, where a barrage dam (the *Staudamm*) makes a beautiful lake, used extensively for many types of watersports, and located within the **Upper Sûre National Park**, an area of outstanding natural beauty.
Vianden: The town of Vianden, crossed by the **River Our** and located close to the eastern border with Germany, is well known for its magnificent **castle**, built between the 11th and 14th centuries and one of Luxembourg's major tourist attractions. The castle overlooks the town from a 450m- (1476ft-) elevation that can be reached by the country's only chairlift. Vianden also has a wild boar sanctuary. Another castle can be visited at **Bourscheid** nearby.
Clervaux: Further north, Clervaux is a medieval market town, sunk into a narrow and tortuous valley, surrounded by rugged hills covered with woods. The town's main attraction is the 12th-century **Clervaux Castle**, which now houses the offices of the local government, the

reception of the local tourist office (*syndicat d'initiative*), a small war museum exhibiting weapons and souvenirs from the 1944-1945 Ardennes offensive (the famous 'Battle of the Bulge'), and the renowned collection of documentary art photography, the *Family of Man*, by Edward Steichen.
RED ROCKS: In the extreme south, a number of industrial towns and largely redundant steelworks testify to Luxembourg's once booming steel industry. The south's main city, **Esch**, is also the country's second largest. A number of cultural establishments, notably the *Kulturfabrék*, testify to the city's lively cultural life.
THE MOSELLE VALLEY: In the southeast, the **River Moselle** (a tributary to the Rhine) flows through the lush valleys of Luxembourg's main wine-producing region (referred to as 'the Moselle' or *d'Musel* in Luxembourgish) and forms a 42km- (27 mile-) border between Luxembourg and Germany. **Grevenmacher**, from where a bridge crosses the river into Germany, is the main administrative and commercial centre of the region. The small village of **Schengen** nearby, where the Moselle marks the meeting of three countries (Luxembourg, France and Germany) has become internationally known after the 'Schengen Agreement' was signed there in 1995. It has a picturesque **castle** which was painted by the French writer Victor Hugo while he was in exile in Luxembourg. Many wine cellars in Grevenmacher and in the nearby towns of **Remerschen**, **Remich** and **Wormeldange** offer excellent wine tasting. Boat-cruises on the Moselle are also available. The spa town of **Mondorf-les-Bains** offers extensive thermal health treatments as well as sports and leisure facilities and a casino.

Sport & Activities

Hiking: Although small, Luxembourg has an extensive network of marked hiking and walking routes. Sometimes referred to as 'the green heart of Europe', almost one-third of the country consists of forests. The best areas for walking are in the north where the *Müllerthal* (also known as Luxembourg's 'Little Switzerland') and the Luxembourg Ardennes (known as *Eisléck* in the national language) offer spectacular rock formations, densely wooded forests and lush valleys (see also the *Resorts & Excursions* section). There are 171 official hiking routes (marked by a blue triangle) and 19 national footpaths (*sentiers nationaux*, marked by a yellow sign). The Youth Hostels footpath (marked by a white triangle) links together the country's 12 youth hostels. Maps of footpaths (*circuits autopédestres*) and hiking guides are readily available from bookshops and newsagents. **Rock climbing** is available near Berdorf in the Müllerthal region. Permission is required and can be obtained by writing to Eaux et Forêts, Diekirch, PO Box 30, L-920, Diekirch.
Golf: There are six golf clubs in the country. There are five 18-hole courses: *Golf Club Grand Ducal* (located in Senningerbierg, close to Luxembourg-Ville); *Golf de Clervaux* (located just outside the town of Clervaux, north of the capital, offering good views and golf cars for rent); *Kikuoka Country Club Chant Val* (located at Scheierhaff near the town of Canach); *Golf & Country Club Christnach*; and the *Golf de Luxembourg* (located in Junglinster). A nine-hole course is available at the *Golf Club Eischen*. For all courses, players must be members of an official golf club.
Watersports: Near the town of Esch-sur-Sûre, in the heart of the *Upper Sûre National Park*, the River Sûre was damned up in 1961 to form the *Upper Sûre Lake* (*Staudamm*). The lake provides drinking water, supplies and generates electricity and offers a range of watersports. The protected area for drinking water stretches back some 5km (3 miles) from the main dam. **Swimming** is allowed only in marked areas and the water temperature is usually warm enough from June to September. **Sailing** and **windsurfing** are very popular and there are a number of sailing schools as well as companies hiring out boats and windsurfing boards. The best resorts for sailing and windsurfing are Insenborn, Lultzhausen and Liefrange. Further lakes where waterports can be pursued are at Echternach, Remerschen and Weiswampach. **Water-skiing** is allowed on the *River Moselle* from mid-April to mid-October from dawn to dusk in the sections of the river marked SKI. Luxembourg's many rivers also offer a range of watersports: the rivers *Sûre*, *Moselle* and the mountain rivers *Clerve*, *Wiltz* and *Our* are particularly good for **kayaking** and **canoeing**.
Wine tasting: This is popular in Luxembourg's main wine-growing region in the southeast, the Moselle (*d'Musel*), which is named after the *River Moselle* flowing through it and forming a 42km- (27 mile-) border with Germany. The mild, sunny climate of the Moselle is ideal for wine making. White wines such as Riesland, Rivaner and Elbling are the most popular. Top-quality wines are labelled *Grand Premier Cru*. Wine cellars are happy to receive visitors. For further information, contact the Luxembourg National Tourist

Credit: © eu2005.lu & ONT

Board (see *Contact Addresses* section).
Fishing: This is possible only in designated parts of lakes and rivers throughout the country. Trout is a popular catch. Many country hotels have their own fishing grounds which are open to guests, and where the chef will be pleased to cook the day's catch. Fishing licences are required and issued by the District Commissioners of Luxembourg, Diekirch and Grevenmacher, as well as by different communal administrations.
Cycling: There are over 30 marked cycling routes and it is possible to cycle from the south to the north on car-free routes. Contact the Luxembourg National Tourist Office for details (see *Contact Addresses* section).

Social Profile

FOOD & DRINK: Luxembourg cooking combines German heartiness with Franco-Belgian finesse. Local dishes include *carré de porc fumé* (smoked pork and broad beans or sauerkraut), *cochon de lait en gelée* (jellied suckling pig), and *jambon d'Ardennes* (famous smoked Ardennes ham). The preparation of trout, pike and crayfish is excellent, as are the pastries and cakes. *Tarte aux quetsches* is recommended. Delicious desserts are prepared with local liqueurs and some restaurants will make *omelette soufflée au kirsch*. A dash of *quetsch*, *mirabelle* or *kirsch* will be added to babas or fruit cups. Most aspects of restaurants and bars are similar to the rest of Europe.
Luxembourg's white Moselle wines resemble those of the Rhine, but are drier than the fruitier wines of the French Moselle. Beer is another speciality and is a traditional industry. Best-known brands are *Bofferding*, *Diekirch Mousel* and *Simon*. There are also many local liqueurs and strong spirits such as *Eau de vie* (45 to 50 per cent alcohol). The minimum age for drinking in bars is 17, and anyone younger than 17 must be accompanied by an adult in cafes and bars. Hours are generally from 0700-2400 (weekdays) and until 0300 (weekends and public holidays). Nightclubs are generally open until 0300.
NIGHTLIFE: Visitors to Luxembourg can enjoy a variety of evening entertainment from theatre performances, classical music concerts, opera and ballet, to nightclubs, cinemas and discos. For more information, contact the Luxembourg City Tourist Office (see *Contact Addresses* section).
SHOPPING: Special purchases include beautiful porcelain and crystal. Villeroy & Boch's crystal factories in Septfontaines are open to visitors. A regional speciality is earthenware pottery from Nospelt, where in August there is a fortnight's exhibition of local work. **Shopping hours:** Mon 1400-1800, Tues-Sat 0800-1800.
SPECIAL EVENTS: For a full list of events throughout the year, contact the National Tourist Office (see *Contact Addresses* section). The following is a selection of special events occurring in Luxembourg in 2005:
Mar 28 *Emaischen*. **Apr 17** *Octave Notre-Dame*. **May 1** *Celebration of the 1st Anniversary of Luxembourg's Entry into the EU*. **Jun 22** *Eve of the National Holiday*. **Jul 16** *Blues n' Jazzrallye*. **Jul 30-21** *Anno Domini*. **Aug 14** *Street Anima(RT)tion*. **Oct-Nov** *Festival 'Live at Vauban'*. **Nov 25-Feb 2006** *Winterlights*.
SOCIAL CONVENTIONS: Handshaking is the normal greeting. The code of practice for visiting someone's home is similar to other Western European countries: it is acceptable to give gifts or flowers if invited for a meal. Smart-casual dress is widely acceptable, but some dining rooms, clubs and social functions will demand formal attire. Evening wear, black tie (for men) is usually specified on invitation if required. Smoking is prohibited where notified and is becoming increasingly unacceptable. **Tipping:** Bills generally include service, but a rounding up is often given. Taxi drivers expect 10 per cent of meter charge.

Business Profile

ECONOMY: Luxembourg is one of the most prosperous countries in Western Europe. Two very different industries – banking and steel – have historically been the mainstays of the economy. The steel industry has ceased to be dominant while other industries, notably chemicals, rubber, plastics, metal products and light manufacturing (textiles, paper, electronic equipment), have prospered. The banking and finance sector is also in a healthy condition: companies originally attracted to Luxembourg by favourable banking secrecy laws and low taxation have prospered despite the gradual harmonisation of taxes and tariffs across the EU. There is also a small but healthy agricultural sector mainly producing crops. During 2001 and 2002, the economy grew at around 5 per cent annually – twice the average EU rate, with inflation of 3 per cent. The Luxembourgeois economy has long been linked with that of Belgium, initially through the 1921 economic union, supplemented by a further treaty in 1958 and latterly, by mutual membership of the EU. Luxembourg was an inaugural adopter of the Euro at the beginning of 1999. Belgium is the largest single trading partner, followed by The Netherlands and France.
BUSINESS: Businesspeople are expected to wear suits. It is advisable to make prior appointments and business cards are often used. Avoid business visits during Christmas and New Year, Easter week and July and August. **Office hours:** Generally Mon-Fri 0830-1200 and 1400-1800.
COMMERCIAL INFORMATION: The following organisations can offer advice: Belgium/Luxembourg Chamber of Commerce, Riverside House, 27/29 Vauxhall Grove, London SW8 1SY (tel: (020) 7793 1623 (general) *or* (020) 7820 7839 (members only); fax: (020) 7793 1628; e-mail: info@blcc.co.uk; website: www.blcc.co.uk); *or* Chamber of Commerce, 31 boulevard Konrad Adenauer, L-2981 Luxembourg-Kirchberg (tel: 423 9391; fax: 438 326; e-mail: chamcom@cc.lu; website: www.cc.lu).
CONFERENCES/CONVENTIONS: The location of the Grand Duchy of Luxembourg at the heart of the EU ensures its status as one of the most popular destinations for conferences and conventions in Western Europe. For further information, contact Luxembourg-Congrès, Hémicycle Européen, 1 rue de Fort Thüngen, L-1499 Luxembourg-Ville (tel: 4302 57750-3; fax: 4302 57575; e-mail: info@luxcongress.lu; website: www.luxcongress.lu).

Climate

Warm weather from May to September and snow likely during winter months. The north (the Ardennes region) tends to be wetter and colder than the south.
Required clothing: Waterproofs are advisable at all times of the year.

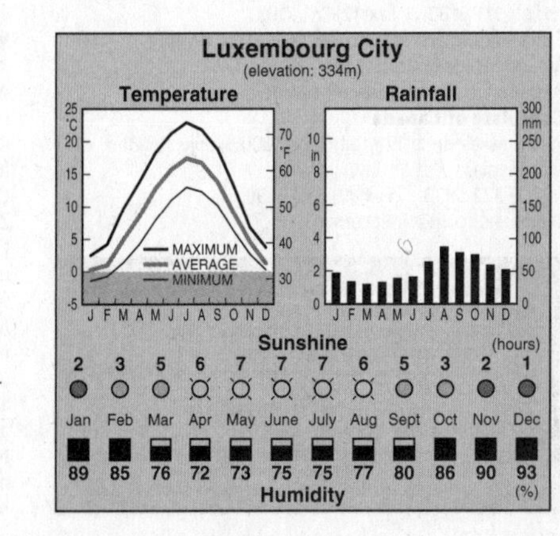

Macedonia

LATEST TRAVEL ADVICE CONTACTS

British Foreign and Commonwealth Office
Tel: (0870) 606 0290 Website: www.fco.gov.uk
US Department of State
Website: http://travel.state.gov/travel
Canadian Department of Foreign Affairs and Int'l Trade
Tel: (1 800) 267 8376 Website: www.dfait-maeci.gc.ca

Location: Former Yugoslav Republic; southeastern Europe.

Country dialling code: 389.

Tourist Association of Skopje
Street address: Dame Gruev Gradski Blok 3, 1000 Skopje, Republic of Macedonia
Postal address: PO Box 399, Skopje, Republic of Macedonia
Tel: (2) 3118 498. Fax: (2) 3230 803.
Embassy of the Republic of Macedonia
Suite 2.1 & 2.2, 2nd Floor, Buckingham Court, Buckingham Gate, London SW1E 6BE, UK
Tel: (020) 7976 0535 *or* 0538 (consular section).
Fax: (020) 7976 0539.
E-mail: info@macedonianembassy.org.uk
Website: www.macedonianembassy.org.uk
Opening hours: Mon-Fri 0930-1730.
British Embassy
2614 Dimitrija Chupovski, 1000 Skopje, Republic of Macedonia
Tel: (2) 329 9299. Fax: (2) 311 7555 *or* 7566 (for consular/visa information).
E-mail: britishembassyskopje@fco.gov.uk *or* Information.Skopj@fco.gov.uk *or* consular.Skopj@fco.gov.uk (consular section) *or* visa.Skopj@fco.gov.uk (visa section).
Website: www.britishembassy.gov.uk/macedonia
Embassy of the Republic of Macedonia
1101 30th Street, Suite 302, NW Washington, DC 20007, USA
Tel: (202) 337 3063.
Fax: (202) 337 3093.
E-mail: rmacedonia@aol.com
Permanent Mission of the Republic of Macedonia to the United Nations
866 UN Plaza, Suite 517, Newark, New York, NY 10017, USA
Tel: (212) 308 8504. Fax: (212) 308 8724.
E-mail: macedonia@ny-int
Embassy of the United States of America
Ilinden bb, 1000 Skopje, Republic of Macedonia
Tel: (2) 311 6180. Fax: (2) 311 7103.
E-mail: consularskopje@state.gov (consular) *or* AmEmbSkopje@mt.net.mk
Website: http://skopje.usembassy.gov
Consulate of Canada
Partizanska odredi 17a, 1st Floor, 1000 Skopje, Republic of Macedonia
Tel: (2) 322 5630. Fax: (2) 322 0596.
E-mail: honcon@unet.com.mk

TIMATIC CODES

Health	AMADEUS: **TI-DFT/SKP/HE** GALILEO/WORLDSPAN: **TI-DFT/SKP/HE** SABRE: **TIDFT/SKP/HE**
Visa	AMADEUS: **TI-DFT/SKP/VI** GALILEO/WORLDSPAN: **TI-DFT/SKP/VI** SABRE: **TIDFT/SKP/VI**

To access TIMATIC country information on Health and Visa regulations through the Computer Reservations System (CRS), type in the appropriate command line listed above.

General Information

AREA: 25,713 sq km (9928 sq miles).
The former Yugoslav republic of 'Macedonia' is only one of three areas of the historical region of 'Macedonia', which includes Pirin Macedonia (Bulgaria) and Aegean Macedonia (Greece), with a total area of 66,600 sq km (25,700 sq miles), most of which is in Greece. In deference to Greek sensibilities, the United Nations and other international organisations have formally recognised Macedonia under the interim name of 'The Former Yugoslav Republic of Macedonia'; however this is gradually reverting to 'The Republic of Macedonia'.
POPULATION: 2,022,547 (official estimate 2002).
POPULATION DENSITY: 79.7 per sq km.
CAPITAL: Skopje. **Population:** 467,257 (2002).
GEOGRAPHY: Roughly rectangular in shape, and on the strategic Vardar Valley north–south communications route, Macedonia (Former Yugoslav Republic) is landlocked, bordering Serbia & Montenegro to the north, Albania to the west, Greece to the south and Bulgaria to the east.
GOVERNMENT: Republic since 1991. Gained independence from Yugoslavia (now Serbia and Montenegro) in 1991. **Head of State:** President Branko Crvenkovski since 2004. **Head of Government:** Premier Hari Kostov since 2004.
LANGUAGE: Macedonian (a slavonic language using the Cyrillic script) is the most widely used language. Albanian, Turkish and Serbo-Croat are also used by ethnic groups. English, French and German are widely spoken.
RELIGION: 67 per cent of the population are Eastern Orthodox Macedonians and around 23 per cent are Muslim Albanians. There are also Muslim Turks and Serbian Orthodox minorities. As elsewhere in the former Yugoslav federation, local politics are now strongly divided along national confessional lines.
TIME: GMT + 1 (GMT + 2 from last Sunday in March to Saturday before last Sunday in October).
ELECTRICITY: 220 volts AC, 50Hz.
COMMUNICATIONS: Telephone: IDD is available. Country code: 389. Outgoing international code: 00. All telecommunications services are generally working normally. **Mobile telephone:** GSM 900 network operated by *Cosmofon* and *Makedonski Telekomunikacii* (website: www.mobimak.com.mk). Coverage is limited to the main towns. **Internet:** ISPs include *Macedonia On-Line* (website: www.mol.com.mk). There are a few Internet cafes in the main towns. **Post:** Services work normally. **Press:** The main daily newspapers are *Dnevnik, Flaka e Vëllazërimit, Nova Makedonija* and *Vecer* (an evening paper). Weekly papers include *Fokus* and *Puls*. The *Macedonian Times* comes out monthly in English and Macedonian.
Radio: BBC World Service (website: www.bbc.co.uk/worldservice) and Voice of America (website: www.voa.gov) can be received. From time to time the frequencies change and the most up-to-date can be found online.

Passport/Visa

	Passport Required?	Visa Required?	Return Ticket Required?
Full British	Yes	No	No
Australian	Yes	Yes	No
Canadian	Yes	Yes	No
USA	Yes	No	No
Other EU	Yes	No/1	No
Japanese	Yes	No	No

Note: Regulations and requirements may be subject to change at short notice, and you are advised to contact the appropriate diplomatic or consular authority before finalising travel arrangements. Details of these may be found at the head of this country's entry. Any numbers in the chart refer to the footnotes below.

PASSPORTS: Passport with at least three to six months' validity (depends on the individual case) required by all.
VISAS: Required by all except the following:
(a) **1.** nationals referred to in the chart above (except Australia, Canada, Czech Republic, Estonia, Hungary, Latvia, Lithuania, Poland, Slovak Republic and Slovenia) for tourist and business stays of up to three months;
(b) nationals of Barbados, Bosnia & Herzegovina, Botswana, Croatia, Cuba, Iceland, Israel, Liechtenstein, Monaco, New Zealand, Norway, San Marino, Switzerland and the Vatican City for tourist and business stays of up to three months;
(c) nationals of Serbia & Montenegro and Turkey for tourist and business stays of up to 60 days;
(d) nationals of Bulgaria and Malaysia for tourist and business stays of up to one month;
(e) nationals of CIS countries, except nationals of Moldova and Uzbekistan, can travel without a visa for purposes such as organized tourism and visiting relatives.
Note: (a) Nationals of the following countries need to obtain official approval from the Ministry of Interior in Macedonia in order to obtain visas: Afghanistan, Algeria, Bangladesh, Burundi, Cameroon, Chile, China (PR), Congo (Rep), Egypt, Ethiopia, Gabon, Ghana, Guatemala, Guinea, Guinea-Bissau, Honduras, Hong Kong (SAR), India, Iran, Iraq, Jordan, Lebanon, Libya, Morocco, Niger, Nigeria, Oman, Pakistan, The Philippines, Rwanda, Saudi Arabia, Senegal, Somalia, Sri Lanka, Sudan, Syrian Arab Republic, Tunisia, United Arab Emirates, Vietnam and Yemen. Their visas must also be issued at an embassy (including for nationals of Czech Republic, although they do not need prior approval). All other nationals require visas, but their applications do not need to be referred to Skopje. (b) Any holders of travel documents other than a passport must also require approval from Macedonia.
Types of visa: *Single-entry*: £13 (£21*); *Double-entry*: £17 (£25*); *Multiple-entry*: £24 (£32*).
* These prices are for those nationals that require approval from the Macedonian authorities. Visas are issued free of charge to nationals of the CIS (except nationals of Moldova and Uzbekistan).
Validity: Valid for 30 days. Transit visas valid for up to five days.
Application to: Nearest Diplomatic or Consular mission (see *Contact Addresses* section).
Application requirements: (a) Valid passport. (b) Application form, which must be submitted in person. (c) One passport-size photo. (d) Fee payable in cash. *Tourist*: (a)-(d) and, (e) Hotel reservation. *Business*: (a)-(d) and, (e) Letter of invitation from Macedonian company. (f) Business letter from the applicant's company. *Transit*: (a)-(d) and, (e) Visa for next country, if required.
Working days required: Usually one to three, although if approval is needed from Macedonia (see above), can take a minimum of 10 days.

Money

Currency: Macedonian Denar (Den) = 100 deni. Notes are in denominations of Den5000, 1000, 500, 100, 50 and 10. Coins are in denominations of Den5, 2 and 1, and 50 deni.
Currency exchange: All major currencies may be exchanged, but Euros are easiest to exchange.
Credit & debit cards: Very limited acceptance. Check with your credit or debit card company for details of merchant acceptability and other services which may be available.
Travellers cheques: To avoid additional exchange rate charges, travellers are advised to take cheques in US Dollars or Euros.
Currency restrictions: There are no restrictions on the import and export of local or foreign currency.
Exchange rate indicators: The following figures are included as a guide to the movements of the Denar against Sterling and the US Dollar:

Date:	Feb '04	May '04	Aug '04	Nov '04
£1.00=	90.58	92.88	92.68	91.51
$1.00=	49.76	52.00	50.31	48.32

Banking hours: Mon-Fri 0700-1900; Sat 0700-1300.

Duty Free

The following goods may be imported into Macedonia (Former Yugoslav Republic of) without incurring customs duty:
One box of cigarettes; one bottle of alcohol; gifts to the value of €30.70.

Public Holidays

2005: Jan 1 New Year's Day. **Jan 6-7** Orthodox Christmas. **Mar 8** International Women's Day. **May 1** May Day. **May 24** St Cyrilus and St Methodius Day. **Aug 2** Ilinden (National Holiday). **Sep 8** Independence Day.
2006: Jan 1 New Year's Day. **Jan 6-7** Orthodox Christmas. **Mar 8** International Women's Day. **May 1** May Day. **May 24** St Cyrilus and St Methodius Day. **Aug 2** Ilinden (National Holiday). **Sep 8** Independence Day.

Health

	Special Precautions?	Certificate Required?
Yellow Fever	No	No
Cholera	No	No
Typhoid & Polio	No/1	N/A
Malaria	No	N/A

Note: Regulations and requirements may be subject to change at short notice, and you are advised to contact your doctor well in advance of your intended date of departure. Any numbers in the chart refer to the footnotes below.

1: An outbreak of poliomyelitis occurred in the region in 1996, and immunisation is advisable. Vaccination against typhoid is also advised.

Food & drink: Mains water is normally chlorinated and, whilst relatively safe, may cause mild abdominal upsets. Bottled water is available and is advised for the first few weeks of the stay. Milk is pasteurised and dairy products are safe for consumption. Local meat, poultry, seafood, fruit and vegetables are generally considered safe to eat.
Other risks: *Hepatitis A* and *brucellosis* are endemic. *Rabies* is present. For those at high risk, vaccination before arrival should be considered. If you are bitten, seek medical advice without delay. For more information, consult the *Health* appendix.
Health care: Prescribed medicines must be paid for. There is a reciprocal health agreement with the UK but health insurance with emergency repatriation is strongly recommended.

Travel - International

Note: Nationals living in, or intending to travel to, the northern and western border regions of Macedonia should exercise caution. Sporadic acts of violence do still occur in Macedonia, particularly in the north, but also including Skopje. However, most visits to Macedonia are trouble-free.
AIR: The national airline is *Macedonian Airlines – MAT (IN)*. Other airlines serving Skopje are *Adria Airways, Austrian Airlines, Croatia Airlines* and *KLM*. Connections are available to Austria, Croatia, Denmark, Germany, The Netherlands, Italy, Serbia & Montenegro, Slovenia, Sweden, Switzerland and Turkey.
Approximate flight times: From Skopje to *London* is approximately four hours.
International airports: *Skopje (SKP)* is 25km (16 miles) from the city. Taxis are available to the city centre (travel time – 25 to 30 minutes). Airport facilities include duty-free shop, bar and restaurant, bank/bureau de change, baggage facilities, post office and car hire (*Avis* and *Hertz*). There is also an airport at *Ohrid*.
Departure tax: None.
RAIL: Intercity trains operate five times a day between Skopje and Belgrade (Serbia) via Nijs. Trains also run twice daily between Skopje and Thessaloniki (Greece).
ROAD: Bus: The international bus station in Skopje serves buses destined for Tirana (Albania), Sofia (Bulgaria), Belgrade (Serbia) and Istanbul (Turkey), which run daily, and buses to Germany, which run twice weekly.

Travel - Internal

AIR: There are no regularly scheduled domestic flights - however, there are occasional flights between Ohrid and Skopje.
RAIL/ROAD: All the main internal road and rail services are operating normally, with links from Skopje to Kumanovo in the north, to Stip in the east, to Veles and Gevgelija in the south, and to Prilep and Bitola in the southwest. **Buses:** The bus network in Macedonia is well developed with frequent services from Skopje to Ohrid and Bitola. Long distance buses need to be booked well in advance.

Accommodation

Macedonia (Former Yugoslav Republic of) has one deluxe/A-class hotel. There are B-class hotels in Skopje and the Ohrid Lake tourist area on the border with Albania and Greece.

Resorts & Excursions

Macedonia (Former Yugoslav Republic) is a mountainous land right at the heart of the Balkans. Its churches and mosques contain many fine examples of art and architecture from the Byzantine and Ottoman periods.
SKOPJE: Macedonia's capital is largely new, owing to an earthquake in 1963. There is, however, plenty to see. **Skopje Old Town** is the most attractive quarter of the city. It is full of shops and restaurants. Here also is the **Church of the Holy Saviour** with its intricately carved *iconostasis* (a screen in orthodox churches on which icons are hung). Also to be found in the Old Town are the **Kursumli An** (16th-century) and the **Suli An** (15th-century) *caravanserais* and the **Daut Pasha Baths** with its two large and 11 small domes. It now houses the **Art Gallery**. There are also a number of mosques dating from the Ottoman period, particularly the 15th-century **Mustafa Pasha Mosque**, as well as the old 10th-century **Kale Fortress** and a magnificent footbridge spanning the **River Vardar**. Near Skopje is the **Nerezi Monastery** with the accompanying 12th-century Church **of St Pantelejmon** housing magnificent Byzantine frescoes.
BITOLA: Located 18km (11 miles) from the Greek border, Bitola is the second-largest town in Macedonia. It was an important centre of Ottoman rule and also has the nearby ruins of the ancient city of **Heraclea**.
OHRID: Situated on **Lake Ohrid**, this is probably the most attractive town in Macedonia. Here St Clement of Ohrid laid the foundations of the first Slav university. In the 10th and 11th centuries, Ohrid became the capital of the Macedonian Tsar Samuil. The walls of his fortress still survive and now provide a venue for summer concerts, operas and plays. Near the old fortress are the remains of a Classical theatre. Dotted around this beautiful town are a number of ancient churches, particularly the **Cathedral of St Sophia** containing some magnificent 11th-century frescoes.

Social Profile

FOOD & DRINK: Macedonian cuisine is similar to that of Turkey and Greece. Different varieties of kebab can be found almost everywhere, as can dishes such as *moussaka* (aubergines and potatoes baked in layers with minced meat). National specialities are *gravce tavce* (beans in a skillet) and the delicious Ohrid trout.
SHOPPING: Shopping hours: Mon-Fri 0800-2000 and Sat 0800-1500.
SPECIAL EVENTS: For full details contact the Embassy (see *Contact Addresses* section). The following is a selection of special events occurring in Macedonia (Former Yugoslav Republic of) in 2005:
Jan 7 *Orthodox Christmas*. **Jan 13** *Old New Year*. **May** *Spring Bazaar*, Skopje. **Jun-Aug** *Skopje Summer Festival*; *Ohrid Summer Festival*. **Jul** *Balkan Festival of Folk Dances & Songs*, Ohrid. **Aug** *International Festival of Poetry*, Struga. **Oct** *Skopje Jazz Festival*. **Nov** *Autumn Bazaar*, Skopje.
SOCIAL CONVENTIONS: Handshaking is the common practice on introduction. Local business protocol is fairly informal, but things go very slowly or not at all owing to the local bureaucracy and the more recent general socio-economic collapse in the Republic.

Business Profile

ECONOMY: As the smallest of the six former Yugoslav republics, Macedonia accounted for just 6 per cent of total Yugoslav output. It was the most dependent on federal government subsidies but these vanished along with guaranteed markets in Yugoslavia (now Serbia & Montenegro) when the old central economic planning system ceased in 1991. Since then the economy has been further undermined by regional strife – the civil war in the neighbouring Serbian province of Kosovo, instability in Albania and, most recently, the conflict between the government and Albanian nationalists – which has also deterred investment from the region. The economy shrank consistently throughout the 1990s; in 2001, it contracted by 5 per cent.
Macedonia has a predominantly agricultural economy in which the main products are rice, wine and wheat (for export), fruit and vegetables, cheese, lamb and tobacco for domestic consumption. Food processing is a major component of the industrial sector, which also produces metal goods, chemicals and textiles. Many families are dependent for their survival on remittances from émigré Macedonians working elsewhere in Europe. Unemployment remains exceptionally high at around 40 per cent, with the result that a thriving black economy – a characteristic of most of the southern Balkans – is operating.
Reconstruction in Macedonia is closely linked to a number of factors: the settlement of the territorial dispute with Greece; the cancellation of old debts from the Yugoslav era; and the resolution of the conflict with Albanian nationalists. All have improved Macedonia's economic prospects. Thus, in the spring of 2002, international donors including the IMF, World Bank and the European Union, were able to authorise a US$500 million aid package which will go a long way in rebuilding the country.
BUSINESS: Suits and ties are correct attire for men, with skirt, blouse and tights the accepted attire for women. English, French and German are spoken in most business circles. **Office hours:** Mon-Fri 0730-1530.
COMMERCIAL INFORMATION: The following organisations can offer advice: National Bank of the Republic of Macedonia, Kompleks Banki bb, PO Box 401, 1000 Skopje (tel: (2) 3108 108; fax: (2) 3108 357; e-mail: governorsoffice@nbrm.gov.mk; website: www.nbrm.gov.mk); *or* Economic Chamber of Macedonia, PO Box 324, St Dimitrie Cupovski br. 13, 1000 Skopje (tel: (2) 3116 543; fax: (2) 3116 210; e-mail: ic@ic.mchamber.org.mk; website: http://info.mchamber.org.mk).

Climate

As a landlocked country, the Republic of Macedonia has a pronounced continental climate, with very cold winters and hot summers.
Required clothing: Mediumweight clothing and very warm overcoats in winter; lightweight clothing and raincoats required for the summer.

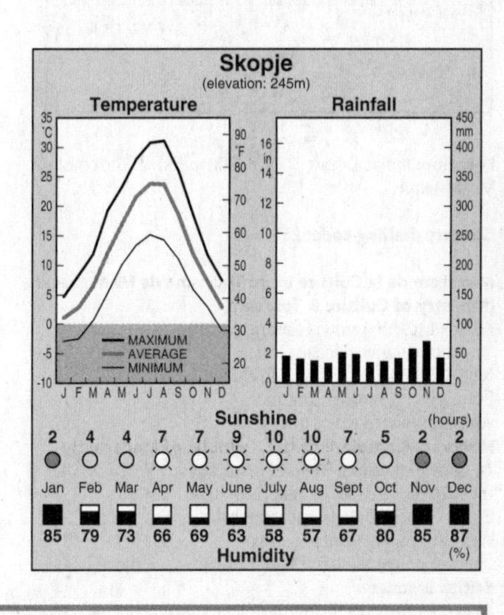

A B C D E F G H I J K L M N O P Q R S T U V W X Y Z

Madagascar

LATEST TRAVEL ADVICE CONTACTS

British Foreign and Commonwealth Office
Tel: (0870) 606 0290 Website: www.fco.gov.uk
US Department of State
Website: http://travel.state.gov/travel
Canadian Department of Foreign Affairs and Int'l Trade
Tel: (1 800) 267 8376 Website: www.dfait-maeci.gc.ca

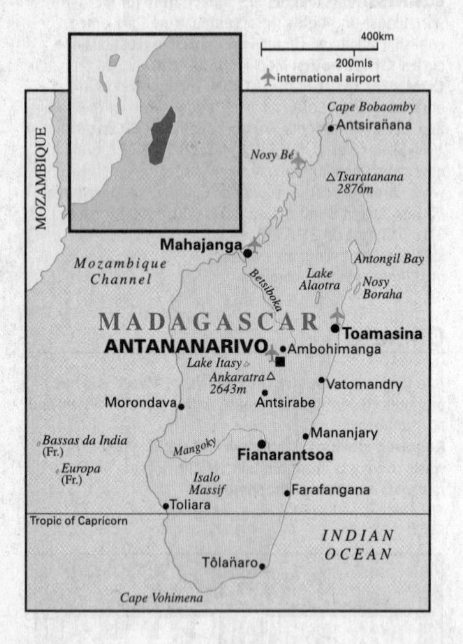

Location: Indian Ocean, 500km (300 miles) off the coast of Mozambique.

Country dialling code: 261.

Ministère de la Culture et du Tourisme de Madagascar (Ministry of Culture & Tourism)
PO Box 610, rue Fernand Kasanga, Tsimbazaza,
101 Antananarivo, Madagascar
Tel: (2022) 66805. Fax: (2022) 78953.
E-mail: mct@tourisme.gov.mg
Website: www.tourisme.gov.mg
Honorary Consulate of the Republic of Madagascar
16 Lanark Mansions, Pennard Road, London W12 8DT, UK
Tel: (020) 8746 0133. Fax: (020) 8746 0134.
E-mail: consul@madagascar.org.uk
Website: www.madagascar.org.uk
Opening hours: Mon-Fri 0930-1300.
British Embassy
Street address: Lot II I 164 Ter Alenrobia, Amboniloa, Madagascar
Postal address: BP 167, 101 Antananarivo, Madagascar
Tel: (20) 224 9378. Fax: (20) 224 9381.
E-mail: ukembant@simicro.mg
Embassy of the Republic of Madagascar
2374 Massachusetts Avenue, NW, Washington, DC 20008, USA
Tel: (202) 265 5525-7. Fax: (202) 265 3034.
E-mail: malagasy.embassy@verizon.net
Consulates in: Pennsylvania and San Diego.
Embassy of the United States of America
Street address: 14 rue Rainitovo, 101 Antananarivo, Madagascar
Postal address: BP 620, Antsahavola, 101 Antananarivo, Madagascar
Tel: (2022) 21273 *or* 20956 *or* 21257. Fax: (2022) 34539.
E-mail: Uswebmaster@wanadoo.mg
Website: www.usmission.mg/embassy/embassy.htm
Embassy of the Republic of Madagascar
200 Catherine Street, Suite 510, Ottawa, Ontario K2P 2K9, Canada
Tel: (613) 567 0505. Fax: (613) 567 2882.
E-mail: ambamadcanada@bellnet.ca
Website: www.madagascar-embassy.ca
Canadian Consulate
Street address: c/o QIT - Madagascar Minerals, Villa 3H Lot II J-169 Ivandry, 101 Antananarivo, Madagascar
Postal address: PO Box 4003, 101 Antananarivo, Madagascar
Tel: (2022) 42559 *or* 42322. Fax: (2022) 42506.
E-mail: consulat.canada@wanadoo.mg

TIMATIC CODES

Health
AMADEUS: **TI-DFT/TNR/HE**
GALILEO/WORLDSPAN: **TI-DFT/TNR/HE**
SABRE: **TIDFT/TNR/HE**

Visa
AMADEUS: **TI-DFT/TNR/VI**
GALILEO/WORLDSPAN: **TI-DFT/TNR/VI**
SABRE: **TIDFT/TNR/VI**

To access TIMATIC country information on Health and Visa regulations through the Computer Reservations System (CRS), type in the appropriate command line listed above.

General Information

AREA: 587,041 sq km (226,658 sq miles).
POPULATION: 15,529,000 (official estimate 2001).
POPULATION DENSITY: 26.5 per sq km.
CAPITAL: Antananarivo (formerly Tananarive). **Population:** 1,111,392 (official estimate 2001).
GEOGRAPHY: Madagascar, the fourth-largest island in the world, lies in the Indian Ocean off the coast of Mozambique. It includes several much smaller islands. A central chain of high mountains, the Hauts Plateaux, occupies more than half of the main island and is responsible for the marked differences – ethnically, climatically and scenically – between the east and west coasts. The narrow strip of lowlands on the east coast, settled from the sixth century by Polynesian seafarers, is largely covered by dense rainforests, whereas the broader west-coast landscape, once covered by dry deciduous forests, is now mostly savannah. The east coast receives the monsoon and, on both coasts, the climate is wetter towards the north. The southern tip of the island is semi-desert, with great forests of cactus-like plants. The capital, Antananarivo, is high up in the Hauts Plateaux near the island's centre. Much of Madagascar's flora and fauna is unique to the island. There are 3000 endemic species of butterfly; the many endemic species of lemurs fill the niches occupied elsewhere by animals as varied as racoons, monkeys, marmots, bushbabies and sloths. There is a similar diversity of reptiles, amphibians and birds (especially ducks), and also all levels of plant life.
GOVERNMENT: Republic since 1992. Gained independence from France in 1960. **Head of State:** President Marc Ravalomanana since 2002. **Head of Government:** Prime Minister Jean-Jacques Rasolondraibe since 2002.
LANGUAGE: The official languages are Malagasy (which is related to Indonesian) and French. Local dialects are also spoken. Very little English is spoken.
RELIGION: 51 per cent follow animist beliefs, about 43 per cent Christian; remainder Muslim.
TIME: GMT + 3.
ELECTRICITY: Mostly 127/220 volts AC, 50Hz. Plugs are generally two-pin.
COMMUNICATIONS: Telephone: IDD is available to major towns. Country code: 261, followed by a two-digit number for an access provider: 20 for *TELMA* (the most reliable), 30 for *Telecel*, 31 for *Sacel*, 32 for *SRR* and 33 for *Madacom*. (A standard dialling code is expected to be introduced soon.) After the international and access codes, numbers should be seven digits including two initial digits for the geographical area. Outgoing international code: 16. **Mobile telephone:** GSM 900 network in use. Main network providers are *Madacom* and *Orange Madagascar* (website: www.orange.mg). Coverage reaches major cities and main roads. **Internet:** Public Internet access exists in large cities; there are a few Internet cafes in Antananarivo. **Telegram:** The main post office (*PTT*) in Antananarivo offers a 24-hour telegram transmission service. **Post:** The *Poste Restante* facilities at main post offices are the most reliable option. Airmail to Europe takes at least seven days and surface mail three to four months. **Press:** There are no English-language newspapers; six dailies are published in French and/or Malagasy. The main papers include *La Gazette de la Grande, Madagascar Tribune* and *Midi Madagasikara*.
Radio: BBC World Service (website: www.bbc.co.uk/worldservice) and Voice of America (website: www.voa.gov) can be received. From time to time the frequencies change and the most up-to-date can be found online.

Passport/Visa

	Passport Required?	Visa Required?	Return Ticket Required?
Full British	Yes	Yes	Yes
Australian	Yes	Yes	Yes
Canadian	Yes	Yes	Yes
USA	Yes	Yes	Yes
Other EU	Yes	Yes	Yes
Japanese	Yes	Yes	Yes

Note: *Regulations and requirements may be subject to change at short notice, and you are advised to contact the appropriate diplomatic or consular authority before finalising travel arrangements. Details of these may be found at the head of this country's entry. Any numbers in the chart refer to the footnotes below.*

Passports: Passports valid for six months after date of entry required by all.
VISAS: Required by all except:
Transit passengers continuing their journey by the same or first connecting aircraft within 24 hours provided holding onward or return documentation and not leaving the airport.
Types of visa and cost: *Tourist*: £40 (single-entry); £50 (multiple-entry). *Business*: £55 (single-entry); £65 (multiple-entry).
Validity: Visas are issued for stays of up to 90 days and are valid for six months from date of issue.
Application to: Consulate (or Consular section at Embassy). Some nationalities are able to get a visa at Antananarivo airport on arrival. Contact the embassy for further information prior to departure.
Application requirements: (a) Valid passport. (b) One application form. (c) Four passport-size photos. (d) Return ticket or confirmation of booking from travel agent. (e) Fee payable by cheque or cash. (f) If applying by post enclose pre-paid, next-day special delivery envelope. *Business*: (a)-(f) and, (g) Letter of recommendation and confirmation of employment on company-headed notepaper with details about the applicant's business activity.
Working days required: Same day (personal applications); up to five days (postal applications).
Temporary residence: Enquire at Consulate (or Consular section at Embassy).

Money

Currency: The pre-colonial Ariary (MGA) has been reintroduced to replace the Malagasy Franc (MGF). Notes are in denominations of MGA10,000, 5000 and 2000. Malagasy Francs are exchangeable at banks only up until the end of 2005.
Currency exchange: Malagasy Francs can be bought only at banks and official bureaux de change in hotels and at the airport in Antananarivo. Hotels have a less favourable exchange rate. A few ATMs have now been installed in Antananarivo.
Credit & debit cards: American Express, Diners Club, MasterCard and Visa are accepted at the capital's Colbert and Hilton hotels. These and other cards have limited use elsewhere in the country. Check with your credit or debit card company for details of merchant acceptability and other services which may be available.
Travellers cheques: These can be exchanged in banks and major hotels. To avoid additional exchange rate charges, travellers are advised to take travellers cheques in Euros or US Dollars.
Currency restrictions: The import of local currency is limited to Mgfr5000. The export of local currency is prohibited to non-residents. The import and export of foreign currency is unlimited, subject to declaration.
Exchange rate indicators: The following figures are included as a guide to the movements of the Malagasy Franc against Sterling and the US Dollar:

Date	Feb '04	May '04	Aug '04	Nov '04
£1.00=	10466.4	15003.2	18607.8	18463.6
$1.00=	5750.00	8400.00	10100.0	9750.00

Banking hours: Mon-Fri 0800-1500.

Duty Free

Duty-Free: The following goods can be imported into Madagascar without incurring customs duty by persons 21 years of age and over:
500 cigarettes or 25 cigars or 500g of tobacco; 1 bottle of alcoholic beverage.
Note: All perfume is subject to duty. All vegetables must be declared and import permit received before travel. Animals need a detailed veterinary certificate. Dogs and cats must be vaccinated against rabies. Arms and ammunition require an exit permit. Tourists should be aware that many items on sale may have been manufactured illegally and may not be taken out of the country, with or without a permit.

Public Holidays

2005: Jan 1 New Year's Day. **Mar 25** Good Friday. **Mar 28** Easter Monday. **Mar 29** Commemoration of the 1947 Rebellion. **May 1** Labour Day. **Jun 26** Independence Day. **Aug 15** Assumption. **Sep 27** St Vincent de Paul's Day. **Nov 1** All Saints' Day. **Dec 25** Christmas Day. **Dec 30** Anniversary of the Republic of Madagascar.
2006: Jan 1 New Year's Day. **Mar 29** Commemoration of the 1947 Rebellion. **Apr 14** Good Friday. **Apr 17** Easter Monday. **May 1** Labour Day. **Jun 26** Independence Day. **Aug 15** Assumption. **Sep 27** St Vincent de Paul's Day. **Nov 1** All Saints' Day. **Dec 25** Christmas Day. **Dec 30** Anniversary of the Republic of Madagascar.

Health

	Special Precautions?	Certificate Required?
Yellow Fever	Yes	1
Cholera	Yes	2
Typhoid & Polio	3	N/A
Malaria	4	N/A

Note: *Regulations and requirements may be subject to change at short notice, and you are advised to contact your doctor well in advance of your intended date of departure. Any numbers in the chart refer to the footnotes below.*

1: A yellow fever vaccination certificate is required from travellers arriving from, or having passed through, an area considered by the Malagasy authorities to be infected within six days; enquire at Embassy.
2: A cholera vaccination certificate is recommended for travellers arriving from, or having passed through, an area considered by the Malagasy authorities to be infected; enquire at Embassy.
3: Immunisation against typhoid and poliomyelitis is often recommended.
4: Malaria risk, predominantly in the malignant *falciparum* form, exists all year throughout the country and is highest in coastal areas. Resistance to chloroquine has been reported. The recommended prophylaxis is mefloquine.
Food & drink: All water should be regarded as being potentially contaminated. Water used for drinking, brushing teeth or making ice should have first been boiled or otherwise sterilised. Milk is unpasteurised and should be boiled. Powdered or tinned milk is available and is advised, but make sure that it is reconstituted with pure water. Avoid dairy products that are likely to have been made from unboiled milk. Only eat well-cooked meat and fish, preferably served hot. Pork, salad and mayonnaise may carry increased risk. Vegetables should be cooked and fruit peeled.
Other risks: *Bilharzia* (schistosomiasis) is present. Avoid swimming and paddling in fresh water; swimming pools which are well chlorinated and maintained are safe. *Hepatitis A, B*, and *E* are endemic and precautions are advised. *Dysenteries* and *diarrhoeal diseases* are common. Many *viral diseases* including severe *haemorrhagic fevers* have been reported. Natural foci of plague occur. *Rabies* is present. For those at high risk, vaccination before arrival should be considered. If you are bitten, seek medical advice without delay. For more information, consult the *Health* appendix.
Health care: Health insurance is strongly recommended; it should include cover for emergency repatriation. Private and public healthcare is available, but public facilities can be very limited. It is highly recommended that visitors bring medication for stomach upsets.

Travel - International

AIR: Madagascar's national airline is *Air Madagascar (MD)* (website: www.airmadagascar.mg).
Approximate flight times: From Antananarivo to *London* is 13 hours 50 minutes (including connection in Paris). There are regular flights from Madagascar to the Comoro Islands, Kenya, Mauritius, Réunion, the Seychelles and Tanzania.
International airports: *Antananarivo (TNR)*, is 17km (11 miles) from the city. Airport facilities include a restaurant and bureau de change. It is linked by a regular bus service to the *Air Madagascar* office and the Hilton Hotel (the centre for Madagascar Airtours). Taxis asking special higher rates are also available at the airport. Further airports are at *Arivonimamo* (international standby airport), which is 45km (28 miles) from the capital, *Mahajanga* (links to East Africa and the Comoro Islands), *Nossi Bé* (links to the Seychelles) and *Toamasina* (links to Mauritius and Réunion islands).
Departure tax: None.
SEA: International tour operators promote Madagascar as a stopping place on extended cruises of the Indian and western Pacific Oceans. Expensive private cruises can be arranged from Europe and the USA. Toamasina is the main port.

Travel - Internal

AIR: Most of Madagascar can be reached by air (there are more than 200 airfields), the exceptions being a few towns in the central highlands. *Air Madagascar* flies to 51 towns and localities in the island and they offer an *Air Tourist Pass* which allows unlimited travel for certain periods.
SEA/RIVER/CANAL: Madagascar has a strong maritime tradition and there are many coastal transport services. Rapids render many of the rivers unnavigable; local tour operators can organise small-boat safaris on the Betsiboka and the Tsiribihina. The Pangalanes Canal runs for almost 600km (370 miles) along the east coast. Much of it is currently too clogged with silt for commercial traffic; the Tourist Board can arrange sailing holidays.
RAIL: The only regular passenger rail service runs from Antananarivo to Moramanga and Lake Alaotra. Services leave every Tuesday, Thursday and Saturday, returning on Wednesday, Friday and Sunday. The Fianarantsoa-Manakara line passes through spectacular rainforests. First-class carriages are air conditioned. Light refreshments are sometimes available. The rail service is intermittent in that trains arrive on one day and return on the following day. Children under four years old travel free. Children aged four to six years old pay half fare.
ROAD: The road network is in need of repair. Tarred roads of varying quality link the main towns in the central highlands and continue to the most populous parts of the east and northwest coasts. There are three main routes, from Antananarivo to Mahajanga (RN4), to Toamasina (RN2), and to Tuléar (RN7). There are isolated sections of tarred road elsewhere, but dirt tracks are more common. Many roads are impassable in the rainy season (November to March). In 1988, the World Bank approved a US$140-million loan to rehabilitate the network. Traffic drives on the right. **Bus:** A flat fare is charged, irrespective of the distance travelled. Services can be unreliable and buses tend to be crowded. **Taxi:** Flat fares apply except in Antananarivo and Fianarantsoa, where fare is calculated according to whether the ride is confined to the 'lower town' or goes on to the 'upper town'. There are two types of taxi: the *taxi-be*, which is quick and comfortable, and the *taxi-brousse* (bush taxi), which is cheaper, slower, makes more stops and generally operates on cross-country routes. Fares should be agreed in advance and tipping is unnecessary. **Rickshaw:** The *pousse-pousse* (rickshaw) takes passengers except where traffic or gradient renders it impractical. Prices are not controlled and vary according to distance. **Stagecoach:** A few covered wagons continue to take passengers in Antananarivo. **Car hire:** This is not widespread and car hire agencies can only be found in the main tourist towns. It is advisable to make enquiries in advance about insurance requirements for car hire. **Motorbike hire:** Available from several companies in Madagascar. **Documentation:** A national driving licence is sufficient.

Accommodation

Since hotel development is in its early stages, some areas are better served than others, notably the capital Antananarivo, Nossi Bé and Toamasina. However, recent projects aimed at increasing the number of international-standard establishments have led to the opening of national tourism centres where good- to medium-standard accommodation is now available at moderate prices. As well as classified or classifiable accommodation, group and youth lodging is available. European-style accommodation is scarce outside the larger towns, and those visiting remote areas should travel with an open mind. Enquiries should be addressed to the Tourism Office in Antananarivo or *Air Madagascar* agencies. The *Guide to Madagascar* by Hilary Bradt provides excellent information on hotels and is available through the Madagascan Consulate in the UK or through bookshops. **Grading:** Hotels are classified from **1** to **5 stars** (5-star being equivalent to an international standard of about 3 stars); a secondary system of **ravinala** (travellers' palms) is used for more 'rustic' accommodation. More information is available from the Ministry of Tourism (see *Contact Addresses* section).

Resorts & Excursions

Note: Those who intend to make their own arrangements should be aware that bandits operate in certain highland regions and that the terrain and climate make surface travel exceedingly difficult (and often impossible) throughout much of the country for much of the year.

The Ministry of Tourism (see *Contact Addresses* section) offers a wide range of tours, some lasting as long as a month.

THE CENTRAL HIGHLANDS

The capital and several other important towns are situated in the central section of the **Hauts Plateaux**, the chain of rugged, ravine-riven mountains that run from north to south down the centre of Madagascar.
ANTANANARIVO: Antananarivo, often abbreviated to **Tana**, has a distinctively French flavour and atmosphere: French is widely spoken, and road as well as shop signs are mostly in French. The city is built on three levels. Dominating the city is the **Queen's Palace** and associated Royal Village or **Rova**. Now a national monument, it was once the residency of the Merina Dynasty which, in the 19th century, united all Madagascar for the first time. On the lowest level is the market of **Analakely**. The **Zuma Market**, claimed to be the second-largest in the world and certainly worth a visit, is busiest on Fridays. The **Tsimbazaza Zoological and Botanical Garden** is open Thursday, Sunday and holidays 0800-1100 and 1400-1700. The Tourist Information Office is nearby. It is wise not to wander too far after dark.
AMBOHIMANGA: The birthplace of the Malagasy state, Ambohimanga is 20km (12 miles) from the capital. Known variously as 'the blue city', 'the holy city' and 'the forbidden city', it is surrounded by forests. The citadel was an important Merina stronghold and retains several structures associated with their ceremonies. Its main gate is an enormous stone disc; 40 men were needed to roll it into position.
ELSEWHERE: Situated 80km (50 miles) from the capital, **Mantasoa** is a popular spot for picnics. The area was landscaped for the Merina Queens by a shipwrecked Frenchman and includes an artificial lake, pine forests and Madagascar's first industrial park.
Ampefy, 90km (60 miles) from the capital, is a volcanic region with spectacular waterfalls and geysers. Dams are used here to catch eels. **Perinet**, 140km (90 miles) from the capital, is a nature reserve, home of the *indri* (a tail-less lemur) and many species of orchid. Also known as *Andasibe*, **Antsirabe**, 170km (110 miles) from the capital, is a thermal spa and Madagascar's main industrial centre. The volcanic hills surrounding the town are dotted with crater lakes. Madagascar's second-highest mountain, **Tsiafajovona**, may be seen to the west of the road from Antananarivo.

THE NORTH

The lush north is dominated by two great mountains. **Tsarantanana**, the island's highest at 2880m (9450ft), is covered with the giant ferns and lichens peculiar to high-altitude rainforests. **Montagne d'Arbre** (1500m/4900ft) is a national park and is famous for its orchids and lemurs. The monsoon falls in the north between December and March.
MAHAJANGA: A provincial capital, Mahajanga stands at the mouth of Madagascar's largest river, the **Betsiboka**. The road to the capital is open between July and October. Boats depart for **Nossi Bé** and several other islands. The beach here is said to be free of sharks. The island's finest grottoes are at **Anjohibe**, 90km (60 miles) inland. There is a nature reserve at **Ankarafantsika**.
NOSSI BÉ: Nossi Bé is Madagascar's most important holiday resort. An island surrounded by smaller islands lying off the northwest coast, it is one hour by air from the capital. Exotic perfume plants such as ylang-ylang, vanilla (Madagascar is the world's largest producer), lemon grass and patchouli are grown here. The main town is **Hell-Ville**. Nearby, there is a ruined 17th-century Indian village.
ANTSERANANA: A provincial capital, Antseranana (formerly Diégo Suarez) is a cosmopolitan seaport overlooking a beautiful gulf at the northernmost tip of the island. There are many lakes, waterfalls and grottoes in the rainforests above the port. Wildlife and flora includes lemurs, crocodiles and orchids. Permission to visit the national park at Montagne d'Arbre nearby must be obtained from the **Ministère des Eaux et des Forêts**, which has an office in the town. Boats may be taken to Nossi Bé. There is a good sandy beach at **Ramena**, but sharks may be a problem. The road southwards to the capital is only open between July and October.
ILE STE-MARIE: Ile Ste-Marie (Nossi Boraha) lies off the east coast, 150km (90 miles) north of *Toamasina*. Its dense vegetation and the difficulty of navigating the lagoons which surround it made it an ideal base for pirates and, later, a colony for convicts. There are many clove plantations and several historic sites, including Madagascar's oldest Catholic church. The island is also known for its beautiful white-sand beaches and coral reefs.
THE EAST COAST: Situated on the northeast coast, **Toamasina** is the country's main port and a provincial capital. It is an eight-hour drive from Antananarivo and, like the capital, it has several busy markets, including the **Bazaar Be**. Around 11km (7 miles) north of the town are the **Ivolina Gardens**, containing every kind of vegetable species from the eastern forests and many varieties of animal life. **Vatomandry**, further south, is a very popular beach resort even though the sharks prevent swimming.

THE SOUTH

The arid south is noted for its many remarkable species of cactus- and baobab-like plants and for the highly developed funerary art of its inhabitants, past and present.
SOUTHERN HIGHLANDS: Fianarantsoa, a provincial capital, is an important centre for wine and rice production and a good base for exploring the southern highlands. Places to visit in the surrounding mountains include **Amabalavao**, said to be the 'home of the departed', where *antemore* paper and *lamba aridrano* silk are made; nearby **Ambondrome** and **Ifandana** crags, where the revered bones of exhumed ancestors may be seen (the latter was the site of a mass suicide in 1811); **Ambositra** and the neighbouring **Zafimaniny** villages, where intricate marquetry products are made; the **Isalo National Park**,

situated in a chain of sandstone mountains (camping is possible but it can only be reached by 4-wheel-drive vehicles or on foot with a guide); and **Ranomafana**, a thermal spa.
THE EAST COAST: Mananjary is a popular beach resort on the east coast (but not for sea-bathing because of sharks). **Taolanaro** (formerly Fort Dauphin), in the southeast corner of the island, is the site of the first French settlement. Parts of the 17th-century fort remain. The city and surrounding area are famous for seafood and for orchids and carnivorous pitcher plants, which can be seen at the **Mandona Agricultural Centre** at **Sainte-Luce Bay**.
THE SOUTHWEST: Western Madagascar was once covered with deciduous forests, but is now mostly savannah. The economy is based around the *zebu*, a species of ox introduced in the eighth century by settlers from South-East Asia. **Toliara**, a provincial capital on the southwest coast, has excellent bathing beaches and opportunities for skindiving, fishing, sailing and other watersports.

NATIONAL PARKS

Spread across 152,000 hectares, the **Tsingy de Bemaraha Strict Nature Reserve** is located 60 to 80km inland from the west coast in the northern sector of the Anstingy region of the **Bemaraha Plateau**, north of the **Manambolo River Gorge**. Undisturbed forests, lakes and mangrove swamps are home to a variety of rare and endangered birds and lemurs. Rocky landscapes and limestone uplands are cut into large peaks with a mass of limestone needles. Rivers flow on the plateau and springs arise on each flank of the **Tsingy**, making this an important water catchment area. Ancient cemeteries can also be found in the Gorge. Visitors are currently restricted to the pinnacle region to the south or to the forests in the north; both of these areas are accessible overnight with guides based at **Antsalova** and **Bekopaka**.

Sport & Activities

Watersports: Many towns have municipal pools. Sea-bathing along the east coast is not advised due to sharks. The main **diving** centres are Nossi Bé (with its neighbouring islands Nossi Mitsio, Nossi Radama and Tanikely), Nossi Lava, Toliara and Ile Ste-Marie (Nossi Boraha). **Scuba-diving** centres are located on the north and west coasts. **Water-skiing** and **sailing** centres are located at Ambohibao (Lake Mantasoa), Antsiralse (on Andraikiba Lake) and Ramona. **River-rafting** can be done in season on the Manambole, from Ankavandra in the west to Bekupaca.
Trekking: Local tour operators can organise a variety of trekking and **hiking** trips in many different parts of the country. They are generally designed to cater for specific interest groups – speleologists, mineralogists, ethnologists, ornithologists, those who wish to see rare orchids or lemurs, etc. **Pony-trekking** is also possible.
Other: For **golf**, there are facilities at Tana. There are numerous **football** pitches and, during the dry season, it has been known for rice fields to be used as pitches. **Basketball** and **volleyball** are very popular and covered stadiums have been built.

Social Profile

FOOD & DRINK: In Madagascar, eating well means eating a lot. Malagasy cooking is based on a large serving of rice with a dressing of sauces, meat, vegetables and seasoning. Dishes include *ro* (a mixture of herbs and leaves with rice); beef and pork marinated in vinegar, water and oil, then cooked with leaves, onion, pickles and other vegetables and seasoned with pimento; *ravitoto* (meat and leaves cooked together); *ramazava* (leaves and pieces of beef and pork browned in oil); *vary amid 'anana* (rice, leaves or herbs, meat and sometimes shrimps), often eaten with *kitoza* (long slices of smoked, cured or fried meat). The people of Madagascar enjoy very hot food and often serve dishes with hot peppers. Local restaurants are often referred to as *hotely*.
The choice of beverages is limited. The national wine is acceptable. Malagasy drinks include *litchel* (an aperitif made from litchis), *betsa* (fermented alcohol) and *toaka gasy* (distilled from cane sugar and rice) and 'Three Horses' lager. Non-alcoholic drinks include *ranon 'apango* or *rano vda* (made from burnt rice) and local mineral waters.
NIGHTLIFE: There are a few discos, sometimes with bands and solo musicians. Casinos can be found at Antananarivo, Toamasina and on Nossi Bé. Most main towns have cinemas and theatres, and touring theatre groups perform local plays throughout the country. Traditional dance troupes can also be seen.
SHOPPING: Handicrafts include *lamba* (traditional squares of cloth in various designs and woven materials); *zafimaniny* marquetry, which is applied to furniture, chessboards and boxes; silverwork such as *mahafaly* crosses and *vangavanga* bracelets; jewellery made from shells and precious stones; items woven from reeds, raffia and straw; *antemore* paper decorated with dried flowers; and embroidery. All products incorporating Malagasy flora or fauna (including dried flowers) often require export permits (see *Duty-Free* section).
Shopping hours: Mon-Fri 0800-1200 and 1400-1800.
SPECIAL EVENTS: There are many customary events and celebrations (see *Social Conventions* below), especially in rural areas. *Mphira gasy* (Malagasy singers) sing and dance theatrically in groups recounting a story and presenting its moral; typically a performance lasts from 30 minutes to an hour. The following is a selection of special events occurring in Madagascar in 2005:
Mar *Alahamady Be* (New Year celebrations). **Mar-Apr** *Internet Festival*. **May** *Rice Harvest*, throughout the country. **May-Jun** *Donia* (traditional music festival), Nosy Be. **Jun** *Fisemana* (ritual purification ceremony of the Antakarana people). **Jun-Sep** *Famadihana* (turning of the bones festival). **Oct-Nov** *Madajazzcar* (jazz festival).
SOCIAL CONVENTIONS: The Madagascans are extremely hospitable and welcoming, although their relaxed attitude to time (public forms of transport, for example, will not generally move until they are full – no matter how long it takes to fill the last seat) may be frustrating. Dress is casual, except for the very smartest hotel and restaurant functions. Visitors are advised not to wear any military-style clothing; locally it is disapproved of and could lead to detention. Entertaining is done in restaurants and bars, and a good degree of acquaintance is necessary before being invited to a family home. Gifts should be offered if staying at a local village, particularly to the village headman, although monetary contributions will be seen as an insult. Respect should be paid to the many local taboos (*fady*) – but as these vary from region to region this is not always easy; however, it is clear that advice should be sought before approaching tombs and graves. It remains the practice in some regions (though it is increasingly rare due to the enormous cost) to invite an ancestor to a village celebration, disinterring the body so that the ancestor may attend physically, and later re-interring the body with new shrouds; this traditional observance (known as *famadihana*) demonstrates the continuing hold of traditional beliefs. Visitors invited to such an occasion should consider it a great honour. **Photography:** Do not photograph military or police establishments. **Tipping:** Not customary, although waiters expect 10 per cent of the bill. In European-style hotels and restaurants, the French system of tipping is followed. One should also tip in Chinese and Vietnamese establishments.

Business Profile

ECONOMY: Madagascar's mainly agricultural economy relies heavily on coffee production to earn foreign exchange, and this has suffered lately from a decline in world demand and prices. Vanilla, cloves, sisal, cocoa and butter beans are the island's other important cash crops. Rice and cassava are produced primarily for domestic staple consumption. Fishing is underdeveloped thus far: the government, which still exercises extensive control over the economy, is hoping to improve its performance. The country has appreciable mineral deposits of chromium ore, bauxite and titanium ore, all of which are being exploited. The recent discovery of oil deposits is set to bring about further development as well as hopefully resolve Madagascar's energy problems. 15 per cent of GDP derives from the manufacturing industry, mainly textiles and food processing. The service sector is relatively underdeveloped at present. The government has been looking at ways of developing the tourism industry, and has focused on the island's abundance of exotic wildlife as a major attraction. Although the Madagascan economy has considerable potential, there are major problems to overcome. There is little that can be done about the climate; Madagascar suffers from frequent cyclones which have done severe damage to agriculture, especially in the last few years. More seriously, the political instability which has afflicted Madagascar throughout 2002 threatens to undermine the economy. In 2001, economic growth rose sharply from near zero to a healthy 6 per cent. The country continues to rely heavily on loans and grants from the EU (especially France) and the World Bank: these were among a consortium of donors which in July 2002 agreed a major aid package worth $2.3 billion over four years. France accounts for about 30 per cent of all Madagascar's trade; the USA and the CIS are other important trading partners.
BUSINESS: Tropical lightweight suits are appropriate wear. If arranged far enough in advance, the Embassy can arrange interpreters for business meetings. **Office hours:** Mon-Fri 0800-1630.
COMMERCIAL INFORMATION: The following organisation can offer advice: Fédération des Chambres de Commerce, d'Industrie et d'Agriculture de Madagascar, BP 258, 101 Antananarivo (tel: (2022) 20211; fax: (2022) 20213).

Climate

Hot and subtropical climate, colder in the mountains. Rainy season: November to March. Dry season: April to October. The south and west regions are hot and dry. Monsoons bring storms and cyclones to the east and north from December to March. The mountains, including Antananarivo, are warm and thundery from November to April and dry, cool and windy the rest of the year.
Required clothing: Lightweights are worn during the summer on high central plateaus and throughout the year in the north and south. Warmer clothes are advised for the evenings and when in moutainous areas. Rainwear is advisable throughout the year.

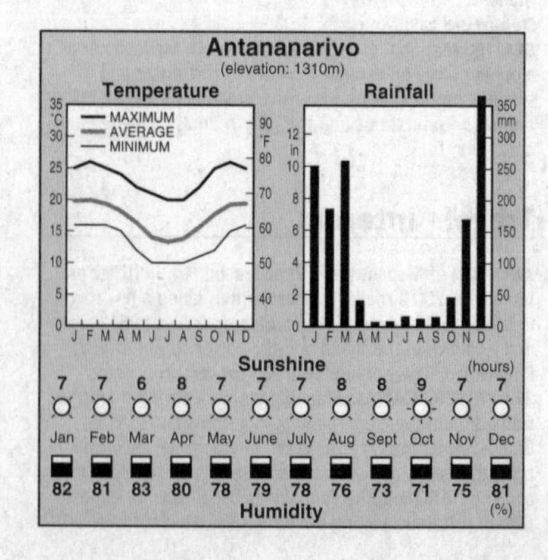

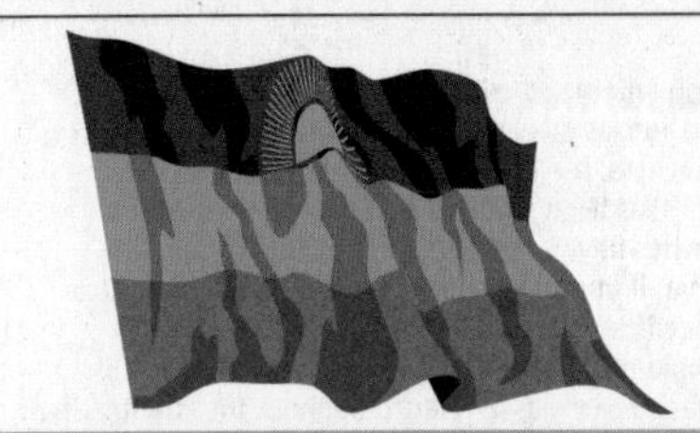

Malawi

LATEST TRAVEL ADVICE CONTACTS

British Foreign and Commonwealth Office
Tel: (0870) 606 0290 Website: www.fco.gov.uk
US Department of State
Website: http://travel.state.gov/travel
Canadian Department of Foreign Affairs and Int'l Trade
Tel: (1 800) 267 8376 Website: www.dfait-maeci.gc.ca

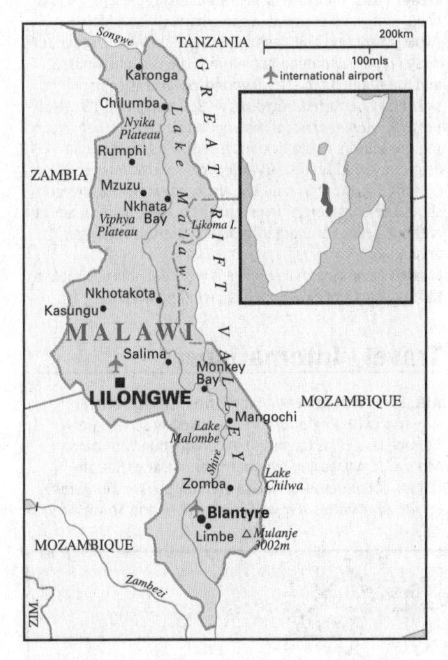

Location: Southeast Africa.

Country dialling code: 265.

Ministry of Tourism, Parks and Wildlife
Street address: Tourism House, off Convention Drive, Lilongwe, Malawi
Postal address: P/Bag 326, Lilongwe 3, Malawi
Tel: (0) 177 1295/5499/2702. Fax: (0) 177 0650/4059.
E-mail: tourism@malawi.net *or* pstourism@globemw.net
Website: www.tourismmalawi.com
High Commission for the Republic of Malawi and Malawi Tourist Office
33 Grosvenor Street, London W1K 4QT, UK
Tel: (020) 7491 4172/7. Fax: (020) 7491 9916.
E-mail: tourism@malawihighcomm.prestel.co.uk (tourism section).
Opening hours: Mon-Fri 0930-1600.
Malawi Tourism Information Service
4 Christian Fields, London SW16 3JZ, UK
Tel: (0115) 982 1903. Fax: (0115) 981 9418.
E-mail: enquiries@malawitourism.com
Website: www.malawitourism.com
The service is supported by the Malawi Tourist Industry and provides information and advice to the public, travel trade and travel media.
British High Commission
PO Box 30042, Lilongwe 3, Malawi
Tel: (0) 177 2400/2683/2701/2182. Fax: (0) 177 2657.
E-mail: bhclilongwe@fco.gov.uk

TIMATIC CODES

Health	AMADEUS: **TI-DFT/LLW/HE** GALILEO/WORLDSPAN: **TI-DFT/LLW/HE** SABRE: **TIDFT/LLW/HE**
Visa	AMADEUS: **TI-DFT/LLW/VI** GALILEO/WORLDSPAN: **TI-DFT/LLW/VI** SABRE: **TIDFT/LLW/VI**

To access TIMATIC country information on Health and Visa regulations through the Computer Reservations System (CRS), type in the appropriate command line listed above.

Credit: © Malawi Tourism Marketing Consortium

Embassy of the Republic of Malawi
1156 15th Atreet, Suite 320, NW, Washington, DC 20005, USA
Tel: (202) 721 0270. Fax: (202) 721 0270.
Embassy of the United States of America
Street address: Area 40, Plot 24, Kenyatta Road, Lilongwe, Malawi
Postal address: PO Box 30016, Lilongwe 3, Malawi
Tel: (0) 177 3166 *or* 3342. Fax: (0) 177 0471.
Website: http://usembassy.state.gov/malawi
High Commission for the Republic of Malawi
7 Clemow Avenue, Ottawa, Ontario K1S 2A9, Canada
Tel: (613) 236 8931. Fax: (613) 236 1054.
E-mail: malawi.highcommission@bellnet.ca
Consulates in: Montréal (tel: (514) 395 8789), Toronto (tel: (416) 234 9333) and Victoria (tel: (250) 478 0237).
Canadian Consulate
Street address: Accord Centre, Masauko Chipembere Highway, Blantyre-Limbe, Malawi
Postal address: PO Box 51146, Blantyre-Limbe, Malawi
Tel: (0) 164 5441 *or* 1612 *or* 3277. Fax: (0) 164 3446.
E-mail: kokhai@malawibiz.com

General Information

AREA: 118,484 sq km (45,747 sq miles).
POPULATION: 11,871,000 (UN estimate 2002).
POPULATION DENSITY: 100.2 per sq km.
CAPITAL: Lilongwe. **Population:** 440,471 including suburbs (1998). Blantyre, with a population of 502,053 (1998), is the largest city in the country.
GEOGRAPHY: Malawi shares borders to the north and northeast with Tanzania, to the south, east and southwest with Mozambique and to the west with Zambia. Lake Malawi, the third largest lake in Africa, is the dominant feature of the country, forming the eastern boundary with Tanzania and Mozambique. The scenery varies in the country's three regions. The Northern Region is mountainous, with the highest peaks reaching over 2500m (8200ft), and features the rolling Nyika Plateau, rugged escarpments, valleys and the thickly forested slopes of the Viphya Plateau. The Central Region is mainly a plateau, over 1000m (3300ft) high, with fine upland scenery. This is the country's main agricultural area. The Southern Region is mostly low-lying except for the 2100m- (6890ft-) high Zomba Plateau south of Lake Malawi and the huge, isolated Mulanje Massif (3000m/10,000ft) in the southeast. The variety of landscape and the wildlife it supports make this relatively unspoilt country particularly attractive to visitors.
GOVERNMENT: Republic since 1966. Gained independence from the UK in 1964. **Head of State and Government:** President Bingu Wa Mutharika since 2004.
LANGUAGE: The national language is the widely spoken Chichewa but the official language, and that of the business community, is English.
RELIGION: 80 per cent are Christian, 13 per cent Muslim, 7 per cent follow traditional beliefs and there is a small Hindu minority.
TIME: GMT + 2.
ELECTRICITY: 230 volts AC, 50Hz. The standard plug is square three-pin.
COMMUNICATIONS: Telephone: IDD is available. Country code: 265 (no area codes). Outgoing international code: 101. The digits 01 were added to the beginning of each land telephone number in 2002; the zero should be omitted when calling from outside Malawi. The number of landlines has doubled in the past three years. **Mobile telephone:** GSM 900 network. Mobile telephone numbers begin (0)8 or (0)9. Network providers include *CelTel Limit*ed (website: www.msi-cellular.com) and *Callpoint 900*. Roaming agreements currently exist with Vodafone. **Fax:** There are facilities for travellers in the main towns, including those in hotel business centres. **Internet:** ISPs include *MalawiNet* (website: www.malawi.net). Services are available in business centres in hotels, and there are a few Internet cafes. **Telegram:** Public facilities for sending telegrams exist at the main post offices. **Post:** Letters take about seven to 10 days to reach Europe by airmail. Post office hours: generally Mon-Fri 0730-1200 and 1300-1700. Post offices in some of the larger towns may be open Sun 0900-1000, but only to sell stamps or to accept telegrams. **Press:** There are two main daily English-language newspapers, *The Daily Times* (Mon-Fri) and *The Monitor*. *The Malawi News* and *The Nation* are published weekly, and a number of other newspapers are published periodically, including the news magazine, *Malawi First*. **Radio:** BBC World Service (website: www.bbc.co.uk/worldservice) and Voice of America (website: www.voa.gov) can be received. From time to time the frequencies change and the most up-to-date can be found online.

Passport/Visa

	Passport Required?	Visa Required?	Return Ticket Required?
Full British	Yes	No	Yes
Australian	Yes	No	Yes
Canadian	Yes	No	Yes
USA	Yes	No	Yes
Other EU	Yes	Yes/1	Yes
Japanese	Yes	No	Yes

Note: *Regulations and requirements may be subject to change at short notice, and you are advised to contact the appropriate diplomatic or consular authority before finalising travel arrangements. Details of these may be found at the head of this country's entry. Any numbers in the chart refer to the footnotes below.*

PASSPORTS: Passport valid for at least six months beyond date of intended departure required by all.
VISAS: Required by all except the following:
(a) nationals of countries referred to in the chart above, except **1.** nationals of Austria, Czech republic, Estonia, Greece, Hungary, Latvia, Lithuania, Poland, Slovak Republic and Slovenia, who *do* need a visa;
(b) nationals of Commonwealth countries (except Cameroon, India, Nigeria and Pakistan who *do* require a visa);
(c) nationals of Iceland, Israel, Madagascar, Norway, San Marino and Zimbabwe;
(d) foreign nationals in transit who are continuing their journey by the same or connecting aircraft to a third country within 24 hours. Permission must be obtained to leave the airport, however.
Types of visa and cost: *Single-entry*: £45. *Multiple-entry*: £70 (up to six months); £90 (up to one year). *Transit*: £32.
Validity: Three months from date of issue.
Application to: Consulate (or Consular section at Embassy or High Commission); see *Contact Addresses* section.
Application requirements: (a) Valid passport. (b) Two

application forms. (c) Two passport-size photos. (d) Fee. (e) Onward or return air ticket. (f) Proof of means of support during residence in country. (g) Confirmed hotel booking or host address of where visitor may stay. (h) Letter from company/sponsor, where required. (i) For postal applications, pre-paid recorded delivery envelope.
Working days required: In most cases, applications will be processed within five working days, but for nationals of India, Nigeria and Pakistan, applications may take two to three weeks.
Temporary residence: Application should be made prior to arrival. Contact the Controller of Immigration Services, PO Box 331, Blantyre, Malawi.

Money

Currency: Kwacha (K) = 100 tambala. Notes are in denominations of K500, 200, 100, 50, 20, 10 and 5. Coins are in denominations of K1 and 50, 20, 10, 5, 2 and 1 tambala.
Currency exchange: US Dollars, Pounds Sterling, Euros or South African Rand are readily exchanged but lesser-known currencies may prove difficult to exchange.
Credit & debit cards: Acceptance of credit and debit cards is very limited, although in Lilongwe and Blantyre and in main hotels, American Express, Diners Club, MasterCard and Visa can be used. Check with your credit or debit card company for details of merchant acceptability and other services which may be available.
Travellers cheques: Travellers cheques can be exchanged in banks, hotels and other institutions. In remote areas, the Treasury Office of Local District Commissioner's offices will cash travellers cheques. To avoid additional exchange rate charges, travellers are advised to take travellers cheques in US Dollars, Euros, Pounds Sterling or South African Rand.
Currency restrictions: The import of local currency is unlimited. The export of local currency is limited to K200. The import of foreign currency is unlimited on arrival. The export of foreign currency is allowed up to the amount imported and declared on entry.
Exchange rate indicators: The following figures are included as a guide to the movements of the Kwacha against Sterling and the US Dollar:

Date	Feb '04	May '04	Aug '04	Nov '04
£1.00=	194.94	194.87	200.81	204.70
$1.00=	107.10	109.10	109.00	108.10

Banking hours: Mon-Fri 0800-1400.

Duty Free

The following goods may be imported into Malawi by passengers without incurring customs duty:
200 cigarettes or 225g of tobacco in any form; for those over 16 years of age, also 1l of spirits and 1l of beer and 1l of wine.
Prohibited items: The import of firearms is prohibited unless a permit has been bought in advance from the Registrar of Firearms, Box 41, Zomba.

Public Holidays

2005: Jan 1 New Year's Day. **Jan 15** John Chilembwe Day. **Mar 3** Martyrs' Day. **Mar 25-28** Easter. **May 1** Labour Day. **Jun 14** Freedom Day. **Jul 6** Republic Day. **Oct 10** Mothers' Day. **Dec 12** Arbor Day. **Dec 25-26** Christmas.
2006: Jan 1 New Year's Day. **Jan 15** John Chilembwe Day. **Mar 3** Martyrs' Day. **Apr 14-17** Easter. **May 1** Labour Day. **Jun 14** Freedom Day. **Jul 6** Republic Day. **Oct 9** Mothers' Day. **Dec 11** Arbor Day. **Dec 25-26** Christmas.
Note: If a public holiday falls on a Saturday, the preceding day will be a holiday; if on a Sunday, the next day will be a holiday. *Ad hoc* public holidays or extensions may also be declared, sometimes at short notice.

Health

	Special Precautions?	Certificate Required?
Yellow Fever	No	1
Cholera	Yes	2
Typhoid & Polio	3	N/A
Malaria	4	N/A

Note: *Regulations and requirements may be subject to change at short notice, and you are advised to contact your doctor well in advance of your intended date of departure. Any numbers in the chart refer to the footnotes below.*

1: A yellow fever vaccination certificate is required from travellers arriving from, or transiting through, infected areas.
2: Following WHO guidelines issued in 1973, a cholera vaccination certificate is not a condition of entry to Malawi. However, cholera is a risk in this country and precautions are essential. Up-to-date advice should be sought before deciding whether these precautions should include vaccination, as medical opinion is divided over its effectiveness; see the *Health* appendix.
Note: It has been reported that cholera vaccination certificates have been demanded at the border with Tanzania; if immunisation is necessary, avoid the use of local needles under all circumstances.
3: Typhoid may occur in rural areas.
4: Malaria risk exists all year throughout the country. The predominant malignant *falciparum* strain is reported to be highly resistant to chloroquine and resistant to sulfadoxine-pyrimethamine. The recommended prophylaxis is mefloquine.
Food & drink: All water should be regarded as being potentially contaminated. Water used for drinking, brushing teeth or making ice should have first been boiled or otherwise sterilised. Milk is unpasteurised and should be boiled. Powdered or tinned milk is available and is advised, but make sure that it is reconstituted with pure water. Avoid dairy products which are likely to have been made from unboiled milk. Only eat well-cooked meat and fish, preferably served hot. Pork, salad and mayonnaise may carry increased risk. Vegetables should be cooked and fruit peeled.
Other risks: *Bilharzia* (schistosomiasis) is present, and has been confirmed to occur in some parts of Lake Malawi. Avoid swimming and paddling in slow-moving or stagnant fresh water; swimming pools which are well chlorinated and maintained are safe. *Trypanosomiasis* (sleeping sickness) is reported. *Hepatitis A, B, C* and *E* and *TB* are all present. *Meningococcal meningitis* can occur, especially in the dry season. Avoid tick and insect bites, as they can result in viral diseases. *HIV* infection is a risk. *Rabies* is present. For those at high risk, vaccination before arrival should be considered. If you are bitten, seek medical advice without delay. For more information consult the *Health* appendix.
Health care: Health insurance is essential. It is advisable to take personal medical supplies, including needles.

Travel - International

AIR: For intercontinental flights from Europe, *British Airways* (with *Regional Air*) has a weekly service via Nairobi, as well as operating in conjunction with *Air Malawi (QM)* via the regional hubs of Dar es Salaam, Harare, Johannesburg, Lusaka and Nairobi. *Air Zimbabwe*, *Ethiopian Airlines*, *Kenya Airways*, *KLM* and *South African*

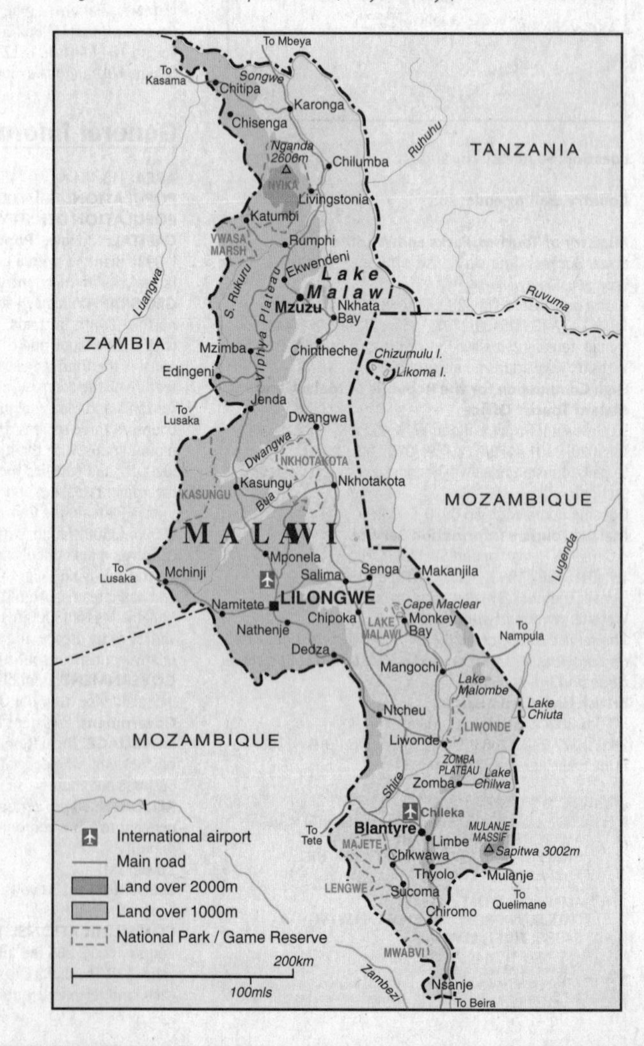

Credit: © Malawi Tourism Marketing Consortium

Airways (five flights a week via Johannesburg) offer similar connecting services. Regional links between Malawi and Kenya, South Africa, Tanzania and Zimbabwe are provided by *Air Malawi* and the various national airlines.
Approximate flight times: From Lilongwe to *London* is approximately 12 hours.
International airports: *Lilongwe (LLW)* (Lilongwe International) is 26km (16 miles) from the city (travel time - 25 to 30 minutes). Taxis and a bus service are available to the city from the airport. Airport facilities include a duty free shop, post office, local travel agents, car hire, bank/bureau de change, restaurant and bar. Blantyre (BLZ) (Chileka) is 13km (8 miles) from the city. There is a coach service to the city. Airport facilities include car hire, restaurant and bar.
Departure tax: A passenger service charge of US$30 (payable in US currency) is levied on all international flights. Malawi passport holders can pay in local currency (K950). Children under two years of age and transit passengers are exempt.
ROAD: There are road connections with Mozambique at Mwanza in southwestern Malawi and at Chiponde in the east; with Tanzania at the Songwe River Bridge in the far northwest of the country; and with Zambia on the main Lilongwe–Lusaka highway near Chipata in the west. A luxury coach service connects Blantyre with Johannesburg (South Africa).

Travel - Internal

AIR: *Air Malawi*'s domestic network provides regular links between Blantyre, Lilongwe, Mzuzu, Club Makokola (southern lakeshore) and Liwonde National Park. *Jakamaka Air Charters* serves the main tourist destinations in the country.
Departure tax: K150 is payable on domestic flights.
LAKE: Cruises on Lake Malawi are available by local steamer. Food and cabins are available. For details contact local travel bureaux.
RAIL: *Malawi Railways* operates the lines in the country. The main route connects Mchinji, Lilongwe, Salima, Chipoka, Blantyre, Limbe and Nsanje. For further information, contact Malawi Railways, PO Box 5144, Limbe (tel: 01 640 844; fax: 01 643 496 *or* 640 683). Trains tend to be slow and crowded and are little used by tourists.
ROAD: Traffic drives on the left. There are over 13,500km (8400 miles) of roads in the country. All major roads are tarmac and most secondary roads are all-weather. **Bus:** There is a good bus system, including an express service, connecting main towns. The journey from Mzuzu to Karonga is particularly spectacular. Luxury coaches connect Blantyre to Lilongwe and Mzuzu. **Car hire:** This is becoming increasingly available, with a number of companies offering a wide choice of vehicles. Standards do vary (even with the internationally franchised chains) so it is worth seeking a recommendation. Nonetheless, cars should be reserved well in advance as they are very much in demand. Chauffeur-driven cars are also available. **Documentation:** An International Driving Permit is required.
URBAN: Bus: There are services in all major cities. **Taxi:** These are in short supply and cannot be hailed on the street. Taxi drivers expect a tip.
Travel times: The following chart gives approximate average travel times (in hours and minutes) from **Lilongwe** to other major cities/towns in Malawi.

	Air	Road
Blantyre	0.40	4.00
Mzuzu	1.00	5.00
Zomba	-	4.00
Karonga	1.30	6.30
Salima	-	1.00
Mangochi	1.00	4.30

Accommodation

HOTELS: There is a range of hotels in the main towns: Lilongwe, Blantyre/Limbe and Mzuzu. The same is true along the lakeshore with a concentration in the south between Monkey Bay, Mangochi and Senga Bay. Zomba Plateau has a luxury hotel. For further information, see the *Resorts & Excursions* section.
REST HOUSES: A programme of privatisation has seen many of the rest houses and forest reserve lodges transformed into luxury or mid-range lodges, the equivalent of established hotels.
LAKESIDE LODGES: There is a scattering of small luxury and mid-market lodges along the western shore of Lake Malawi and on Likoma Island. Most offer the same facilities as the larger hotels with watersports and excellent private beaches. Some accommodation is on islands and lake safaris are catered for.
SAFARI CAMPS/LODGES: Recent years have seen a transformation in four of the parks and reserves: Liwonde, Kasungu, Nyika and Vwasa. Single privately-run safari camps/lodges have replaced government camps in all of these parks. New luxury en-suite accommodation is provided in permanent tents, rondavels, log cabins or bamboo huts. There is also good-quality, mid-price accommodation and camping. Full catering is available. Booking ahead is important especially at weekends and in holiday periods. See also *National Parks* in the *Resorts & Excursions* section.
CAMPING: There are campsites along the lakeshore, often near the hotels, and elsewhere in the resort and forest areas. Most game parks and reserves have campsites. Sites are usually well equipped and camping is excellent during the dry season which runs from April to November.

Resorts & Excursions

THE NORTHERN & CENTRAL REGIONS

MZUZU & THE NORTH: The capital of the northern region, Mzuzu, has one major hotel and several smaller establishments. The town is approached from the south by a road across the rolling hills of the **Viphya Plateau** or by the lakeshore road. There are two game areas in the region: the beautiful and unique plateau of **Nyika National Park** and the **Vwasa Marsh Wildlife Reserve**. Both have new luxury lodges as well as simpler accommodation. Also in the region is the famous **Livingstonia Mission** with its interesting museum. Access is difficult up the escarpment road but the Mission can also be reached from the east via **Rumphi**. Nearby, the **Manchewe Falls** spill off the escarpment.
LILONGWE: Malawi's capital, Lilongwe, is in the central region, 90 minutes' drive inland from **Lake Malawi**. Alongside the traditional Old Town, with its interesting markets, is the modern city and seat of government with its imaginative architecture in a garden setting. There is a wide range of hotels in Lilongwe.
Excursions: Northwest of the capital is the vast **Kasungu National Park** with a variety of wildlife and good accommodation. North of Lilongwe is the famous **Kamuzu Academy** (the 'Eton of Africa'). This is also the region supplying much of the country's important tobacco crop.

THE SOUTHERN REGION

BLANTYRE: Malawi's commercial capital and largest town was established at the end of the 19th century. It is really two towns: Blantyre and **Limbe**, joined by a development corridor. Visits can be made to the **National Museum**, to **St Michael and All Angels Church** (associated with Dr David Livingstone) and to **Mandala House** (the oldest European building in Malawi).
ELSEWHERE: North of Blantyre is the university town and former capital, **Zomba**. Towering above the town is the 2100m- (6890ft-) **Zomba Plateau** with its vast forests and waterfalls. There is a newly rebuilt luxury hotel as well as lodges and two campsites. The views from the plateau are stunning and it is possible to drive around or walk on the plateau top. There is also a trout farm which is now rehabilitated and has a very nice picnic area.
Large tea estates, which offer accommodation, lie to the southeast of Thyolo, overshadowed by the magnificent **Mulanje Massif**, a huge block of mountains of more than 640 sq km (250 sq miles) rising to over 3000m (10,000ft) at its highest point at **Sapitwa**. For the tourist, **Mulanje** offers a wide variety of activities, from rock climbing and mountain walking to the more leisurely pursuit of trout fishing. Much of the massif is accessible and guides can be hired. Forest huts provide simple accommodation. Mulanje is best visited between April and November.
The **Lower Shire Valley** is different from the rest of the country, as it is low lying, hotter, and dominated by the great river which drains Lake Malawi. There are vast sugar plantations at **Sucoma**.

LAKE MALAWI & LAKESHORE REGIONS

LAKE MALAWI: This vast lake stretches from the northern tip of the country to **Mangochi** in the south. The surface area of the lake covers nearly 24,000 sq km (15,000 sq miles), and lies in the deep, trough-like rift valley which runs the length of the country. The shores of the lake are generally sandy and the resort areas are largely bilharzia-free. There are no tides or currents. Most of the hotels provide pleasure craft enabling visitors to enjoy water-skiing, sailing, fishing, snorkelling and windsurfing. Lake Malawi is known to contain more species of fish than any other lake in the world: over 500 and up to a possible 1000 at the latest estimate. Some of the rarest tropical fish in the world are unique to the lake, which is also the home of fish eagles, black eagles, several varieties of kingfisher, tern and many other birds. One of the best ways of seeing lake Malawi is to cruise in the 630-ton *Ilala II*, the lake's mini-liner, which cruises the lake between **Monkey Bay** and **Karonga** in the north of the country. The 1052km (654 mile) voyage gives the passenger the opportunity to visit lake ports and to view the spectacular mountain scenery. Luxury yacht chartering is also available.
THE LAKESHORE: Nkhotakota, on the central lake shore, is one of Africa's oldest market towns and was once a centre of the slave trade. There are mid-range lodges here from which one can visit the nearby wildlife reserve. The beautiful Chintheche Strip has excellent small lodge accommodation.
Further north is **Nkhata Bay**, a busy port and market and a favourite stopping place for visitors. There is plenty of budget accommodation around the bay.
Senga Bay, near the market town of **Salima**, is the main lakeshore resort of the central region. **Lizard Island**, home to many varieties of lizard and eagle, is one of the many off-shore islands.
Cape Maclear, near Monkey Bay, has a beautiful sandy beach and is in the **Lake Malawi National Park**, the world's first freshwater reserve. It is here that the fish-rich lake is seen at its best. There is top-class accommodation at the island camps, and at a new lodge offering sailing in luxury yachts and kayaking and diving are offered from the islands. There are plenty of mid-range and budget lodges and there are plans for a hotel.
LIKOMA ISLAND: Located on the east side of the lake, near the Mozambique shore, Likoma Island is worth a visit - there is excellent swimming off the beaches and a very interesting **Anglican Cathedral**, built by missionaries over 100 years ago. Accommodation is limited but includes a luxury lodge.

NATIONAL PARKS & WILDLIFE RESERVES

Malawi has nine national parks and wildlife reserves but six are especially recommended for visitors. There are also many attractive and accessible forest reserves. All the parks and reserves are uncrowded and give visitors an excellent experience of unspoilt wilderness.
NYIKA NATIONAL PARK: Situated in the far north of the country, the park's unique rolling grassland covers most of the Nyika Plateau, which lies at an altitude of 2500m (8200ft). The whaleback hills are broken by deep valleys and occasional patches of evergreen, natural forest and bubbling streams. Nyika is known to sustain many rare birds and butterflies, game and a multitude of flowers, including an incredible range of orchids. At **Chelinda** there is a variety of accommodation, including new luxury log cabins. The lodges and camps are set high up on the edge of a pine forest, overlooking trout-filled lakes. The enormous plateau has zebra, antelope, leopard and hyena as well as elephants on the lower slopes. A speciality of Chelinda is its horse safaris. There is an airstrip for visitors arriving by air.
VWASA MARSH WILDLIFE RESERVE: Located to the west of Mzuzu. A camp with luxury reed huts has been established, overlooking **Lake Kazuni**. There is a variety of game including elephant, buffalo and hippos, as well as a

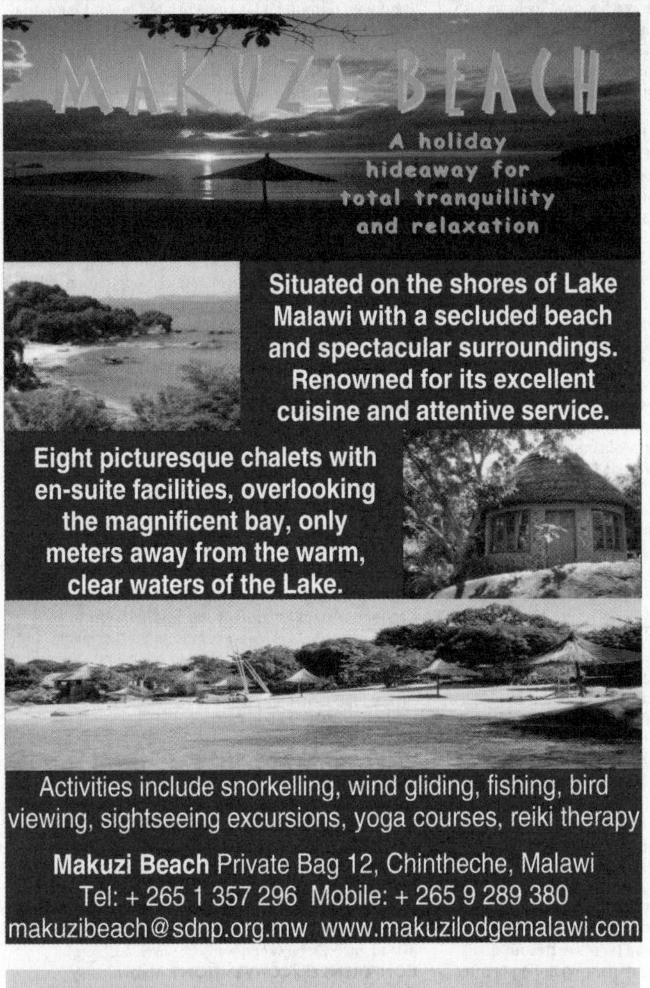

MAKUZI BEACH
A holiday
hideaway for
total tranquillity
and relaxation
Situated on the shores of Lake Malawi with a secluded beach and spectacular surroundings. Renowned for its excellent cuisine and attentive service.
Eight picturesque chalets with en-suite facilities, overlooking the magnificent bay, only meters away from the warm, clear waters of the Lake.
Activities include snorkelling, wind gliding, fishing, bird viewing, sightseeing excursions, yoga courses, reiki therapy
Makuzi Beach Private Bag 12, Chintheche, Malawi
Tel: + 265 1 357 296 Mobile: + 265 9 289 380
makuzibeach@sdnp.org.mw www.makuzilodgemalawi.com

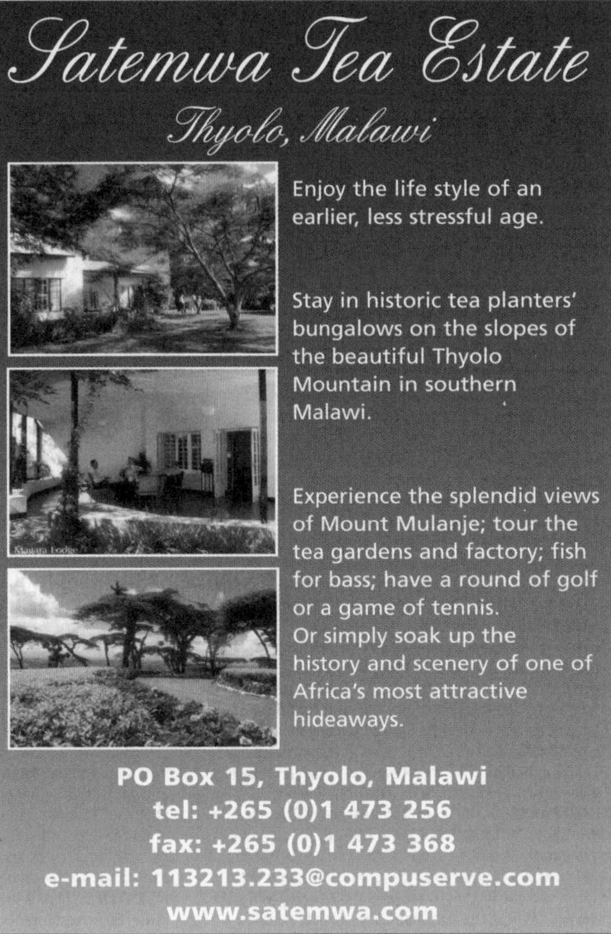

Satemwa Tea Estate
Thyolo, Malawi
Enjoy the life style of an earlier, less stressful age.
Stay in historic tea planters' bungalows on the slopes of the beautiful Thyolo Mountain in southern Malawi.
Experience the splendid views of Mount Mulanje; tour the tea gardens and factory; fish for bass; have a round of golf or a game of tennis.
Or simply soak up the history and scenery of one of Africa's most attractive hideaways.
PO Box 15, Thyolo, Malawi
tel: +265 (0)1 473 256
fax: +265 (0)1 473 368
e-mail: 113213.233@compuserve.com
www.satemwa.com

Korea Garden Lodge
• Convenient location
• A personal service
• Range of room types
• Landscaped gardens
• Conference facilities
• Relaxing Environment
• Great value
Setting standards of excellence in executive accommodation in the Capital City of Malawi
For Reservations: Tel: +265 1 753 467 +265 1 757 854
+265 9 934 433 Fax: +265 1 756 612
P.O.Box 2181 Lilongwe Malawi
e-mail: kgl@malawi.net www.kglodge.net

MALAWI

which appear in the early morning and evening to drink from *dambos* (river channels). The grasslands support large herds of buffalo, as well as varieties of antelope such as kudu and reedbuck. Predators such as lion and leopard may be seen. Accommodation in the park is easily accessed at *Lifupa*, where there are luxury rondavels as well as a separate self-catering camp.

LIWONDE NATIONAL PARK: Situated in the Shire Valley, south of Lake Malawi and north of Zomba, Liwonde is the most popular of the national parks. The River Shire flows along the eastern border of the park allowing for boat safaris. The river is frequented by vast numbers of hippo; elephants and crocodiles can also be seen. There is a wide range of game in the park, including rhino and various antelope. Through introductions, Liwonde now has the 'big five' for visitors to see. The birdlife includes one of the greatest variety of species in Africa. There is accommodation in the park at **Mvuu**, including a luxury lodge and a separate permanent camp and camping site. Walking, boating and driving safaris (in 4-wheel-drive vehicles) are on offer. There is a landing strip for visitors coming by air. A second safari lodge has been opened on a hill site in the southern part of the park.

LAKE MALAWI NATIONAL PARK: Close to **Monkey Bay**, this reserve lies towards the southern extremity of the lake. Opened in 1980, it was the world's first freshwater national park and its setting and attractions are world-renowned. Tropical fish, which can be viewed by snorkelling or scuba-diving, are a speciality of the park, while further inland klipspringer, bushbuck and vervet monkeys may be seen. Access to the park is easy throughout the year. In the past, only budget accommodation was available but there are now excellent camps on two deserted islands in the park, as well as a luxury guest house, which is also linked to an upmarket yachting operation. Many visitors make day-trips from the hotels on the lakeshore south of Monkey Bay.

LENGWE NATIONAL PARK: Lengwe National Park is in the Lower Shire Valley and is only 130 sq km (80 sq miles) large. The park has the distinction of being the farthest point north where the rare Nyala antelope can be found. Also here is the diminutive Livingstone's Suni, one of the smallest of antelopes, as well as the rare Blue or Samango monkey. These and other game can be viewed from concealed hides. New accommodation is being developed here and it is possible to visit the park in a daytrip from Blantyre.

OTHER PARKS: Of the other wildlife reserves, the vast **Nkhotakota Wildlife Reserve** is little developed and lacks drivable tracks. However, there is a good range of game including lion and elephant. Accommodation can be had nearby along the lakeshore. **Majete** and **Mwabvi Wildlife Reserves** are in the Lower Shire Valley. Majete has little viewable game and Mwabvi is difficult to access.

Credit: © Malawi Tourism Marketing Consortium

Sport & Activities

Wildlife: Malawi is becoming well known for the number of activities it can offer visitors. **Wildlife and game viewing** in the national parks are especially attractive to those wanting to experience trekking and viewing in entirely natural surroundings without tarred roads filled with convoys of 4-wheel-drive vehicles. **Birdwatching** is excellent throughout the country, which is something of a birdwatcher's paradise at any time in the year. There are over 650 recorded species.

Watersports: *Lake Malawi* offers a range of watersports along its whole length. **Snorkelling** and **scuba-diving** are increasingly popular in Lake Malawi because of the attraction of seeing the brilliantly coloured fish, the *mbuna*. Instruction in these sports for beginners as well as for experienced practitioners is possible at many resorts. **Swimming**, **water-skiing**, **sailing** and **kayaking** are all available along the lakeshore. The *Lake Malawi 500km Sailing Marathon*, which is the world's longest freshwater sailing race, is held each year in July and attracts an international entry field. The risk of contracting bilharzia when engaging in watersports in Lake Malawi is minimised if sensible precautions are taken: bathers should swim only at the resort areas known to be free of bilharzia, avoiding parts of the lake where there is still water or close human habitation. Many areas of the lake are bilharzia-free. **Fishing** is especially attractive on the southern lakeshore north of *Mangochi* and at *Senga Bay*. Tournaments take place each year and catches include the delicious Sungwa. There are also opportunities to fish for yellow fish, lake salmon and lake tiger. Elsewhere, angling for trout is easily arranged at Chelinda on *Nyika Plateau* and on *Zomba Plateau*. There is also good fishing for lake-salmon (*mpasa*) in the rivers of the *Nkhotakota Game Reserve*.

Trekking and hiking: The Nyika Plateau is popular for trekking and walking. Guides and porters are available for one to six-day wilderness hikes. The same arrangements apply on Mount Mulanje where huts are available for hire. There is excellent walking on the Zomba and Viphya Plateaux. There is plenty of scope for **climbing**. Rising to a height of 3000m (9850ft), *Mount Mulanje* is the highest mountain in central Africa and has proved to be an irresistible lure to climbers. The massif has the longest sheer rock face in Africa. Dedza, south of Lilongwe, and *Michiru*, *Ndirande* and *Chiradzulu*, near Blantyre, also offer challenging slopes.

Other: Horse riding is a speciality on *Nyika Plateau*, where safaris on horseback are popular, and on *Zomba Plateau*, where there is a dressage school. **Cycling** has more recently been added to Malawi's list of activities for tourists and has also attracted the interest of charity organisations. Popular areas include *Nyika*, *Luwawa Forest* and along the lakeshore. **Tennis**, **golf** and **squash** are available at some hotels and at sports clubs in *Lilongwe*, *Blantyre* and *Mzuzu*. A pro-am golf tournament also takes place at Club Makokola on the southern shores of Lake Malawi every June.

Social Profile

FOOD & DRINK: Fresh fish from Lake Malawi is the country's speciality, *chambo* (Tilapia fish) being the main lake delicacy. There are trout from streams on the Zomba, Mulanje and Nyika plateaux. Hotel restaurants and many of those in the cities are of a good standard. They offer a wide choice of dishes including European, Korean and Chinese as well as authentic Malawi dishes and *haute cuisine*. Poultry and dairy produce are plentiful and tropical fruits are abundant in season. The local beer is very good and imported beer and soft drinks are widely available. Malawi gin and tonic is well known and inexpensive, with almost cult status. Wine is imported largely from South Africa.

NIGHTLIFE: There is little nightlife in the European or US sense. Some restaurants have entertainment as do some of the hotels but outside Blantyre and Lilongwe this will usually take the form of a display of dancing during or after dinner at the lakeshore hotels.

SHOPPING: Malawi produces a variety of colourful arts and crafts. Items are invariably handmade and there is no factory production of curios. Purchases include woodcarvings, wood and cane furniture, soapstone carvings, decorated wooden articles, colourful textiles, pottery, beadwork, cane and raffia items. The standard of woodcarving is one of the highest in Africa. The *Mua Mission*, south of Salima, where carvers are trained, has an excellent shop. Traditional musical instruments are also sold throughout Malawi. **Shopping hours:** Mon-Sat 0800-1700. Markets and roadside stalls function every day.

SPECIAL EVENTS: Dance plays a part in most ceremonies in Malawi, an important dance being the *Gule Wamkulu* (performed by the Chewa and Mang'anja), with its heavily carved masks, feathers and skin paint. For further information on events in Malawi, contact the Malawi Tourism Information Service (see *Contact Addresses* section). The following is a selection of special events occurring in Malawi in 2005:

May 1-Jul 31 *Hiking on Mount Mulanje*. **Jul 4-10** *Lake Malawi Sailing Marathon*. **Jul 6** *Malawi Republic Day celebrations*. **Sep 9-11** *Lake of Stars Festival*, music event.

SOCIAL CONVENTIONS: Despite the large number of tribal backgrounds in the Malawi population, integration is well established and the visitor need not be aware of any social differences. The white population is very small in number. There are some religious differences, most noticeable among the Muslim population and especially as far as alcohol consumption is concerned. Malawians place emphasis on the importance of shaking hands on meeting and departing. The special handshake, which includes grasping the thumb and putting the other hand on the forearm, is best avoided unless practised. Children and some women may curtsey as a greeting or if being made a presentation. Offering a soft drink to a visitor is common at meetings. Malawians tend to be conventional rather than casual in their dress, especially in formal gatherings. The strict dress code of Dr Banda's days are gone but modest dress should be worn unless at the beach or playing sport.

Tipping: Generally not expected, but some employees who are very poorly paid might appreciate a small tip for good service.

Business Profile

ECONOMY: The economy is almost entirely agricultural, with both subsistence and cash crops including tobacco, sugar, tea and maize being farmed. The manufacturing industry now accounts for about 15 per cent of economic output, and is concentrated in light industrial import substitution projects such as textiles, chemicals, agricultural implements and processed foodstuffs. Tourism is intended to become a major source of foreign exchange but this will depend on improvements in basic infrastructure and political stability in the region. The overall economy is weak with inflation around 30 per cent and negative growth of 1.5 per cent in 2001. Recent economic policy has followed an orthodox course of privatisation, deregulation and government spending cuts. The latter have had a severe impact on the country's already limited basic services, especially healthcare, which Malawi can ill afford as the HIV/AIDS pandemic continues to devastate the population. Between one-third and one-half of the working population are thought to be infected, with the inevitable economic consequences.

Malawi is normally self-sufficient in food, especially maize, the main staple. But it also has a vast balance of payments deficit and is heavily dependent on foreign aid, both bilateral and from the World Bank. In 2000, in a development which had repercussions across Africa, Malawi was pressurised by international financial institutions due to the surplus from its bumper maize crop to meet debt repayments. Two years later, there was a disastrous harvest, but no reserves to meet the shortfall - and Malawi was forced to call upon emergency food aid. Malawi is a member of the Southern African Development Community and, in 1993, signed the treaty establishing a Common Market for Eastern and Southern Africa (COMESA). The UK is Malawi's most important single trading partner, taking one-third of the country's exports and providing 15 per cent of Malawi's imports. South Africa, Japan, Germany and The Netherlands are Malawi's other important trading partners.

BUSINESS: Suits or a jacket and tie are suitable for business meetings in cities. Similar to the European system, appointments should generally be made and business cards are used. Offices tend to open early in Malawi. Best months for business visits are May to July and September to November. **Office hours:** Mon-Fri 0730-1700.

COMMERCIAL INFORMATION: The following organisation can offer advice: Malawi Confederation of Chambers of Commerce and Industry, PO Box 258, Chichiri Trade Fair Grounds, Blantyre (tel: 167 1988; fax: 167 1147; e-mail: mcci@eomw.net; website: www.mccci.org).

CONFERENCES/CONVENTIONS: Malawi's only dedicated conference centre is the Kwacha International Conference Centre in Blantyre, with seating for up to 500 people. Details of this and hotels with conference facilities can be obtained from the Malawi Tourism Information (see *Contact Addresses* section).

Climate

Varies from cool in the highlands to warm around Lake Malawi. Winter (May to July) is dry and nights can be chilly, particularly in the highlands. The rainy season runs from November to March. Around Lake Malawi, in winter, the climate is particularly dry with pleasant cooling breezes.

Required clothing: Lightweights are worn all year in the Lake Malawi area, with warmer clothes advised in the mountains, particularly during winter and on chilly evenings elsewhere. Visitors to Nyika and Zomba should note that the nights can be cold. Dark or 'natural' coloured clothing should be worn for game viewing.

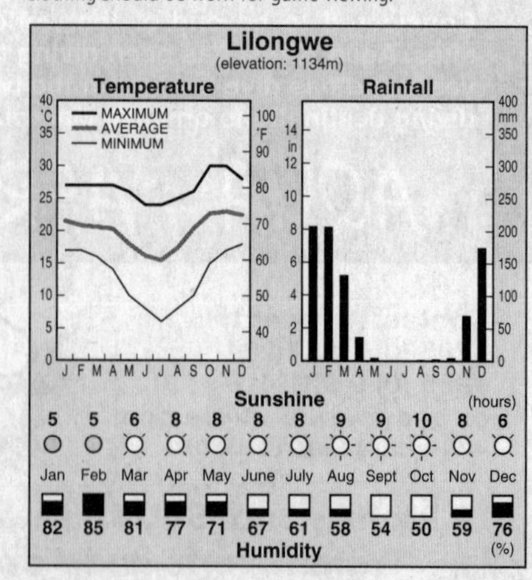

Malaysia

LATEST TRAVEL ADVICE CONTACTS

British Foreign and Commonwealth Office
Tel: (0870) 606 0290 Website: www.fco.gov.uk
US Department of State
Website: http://travel.state.gov/travel
Canadian Department of Foreign Affairs and Int'l Trade
Tel: (1 800) 267 8376 Website: www.dfait-maeci.gc.ca

Location: South-East Asia.

Country dialling code: 60.

Malaysia Tourism Promotion Board
Menara Dato' Onn, 17th Floor, Putra World Trade Centre, 45 Jalan Tun Ismail, 50480 Kuala Lumpur, Malaysia
Tel: (3) 2615 8188.
Fax: (3) 2693 5884 *or* 0207.
E-mail: webmaster@tourism.gov.my
Website: www.tourism.gov.my

Malaysian High Commission
45 Belgrave Square, London SW1X 8QT, UK
Tel: (020) 7235 8033 *or* 7930 7932 (tourist board).
E-mail: mwlondon@btinternet.com
Opening hours: Mon-Fri 0900-1300 and 1400-1700; 0915-1215 (consular section).
Also deals with tourism enquiries.

TIMATIC CODES

Health	AMADEUS: **TI-DFT/KUL/HE** GALILEO/WORLDSPAN: **TI-DFT/KUL/HE** SABRE: **TIDFT/KUL/HE**
Visa	AMADEUS: **TI-DFT/KUL/VI** GALILEO/WORLDSPAN: **TI-DFT/KUL/VI** SABRE: **TIDFT/KUL/VI**

To access TIMATIC country information on Health and Visa regulations through the Computer Reservations System (CRS), type in the appropriate command line listed above.

Tourism Malaysia
Malaysia House, 57 Trafalgar Square, London WC2N 5DU, UK
Tel: (020) 7930 7932.
Fax: (020) 7930 9015.
E-mail: info@tourism-malaysia.co.uk
Website: www.malaysiatrulyasia.co.uk
Opening hours: Mon-Fri 0900-1700.

British High Commission
Street address: 185 Jalan Ampang, 50450 Kuala Lumpur, Malaysia
Postal address: PO Box 11030, 50732 Kuala Lumpur, Malaysia
Tel: (3) 2170 2200 *or* 2345 (consular section) *or* 2164 9323 (visa application section). F
ax: (3) 2170 2370 *or* 2303 *or* 2360 (consular and visa section).
E-mail: consular.kualalumpur@fco.gov.uk (consular services) *or* info@vfs.com.my (visa application services) *or* Political.KualaLumpur@fco.gov.uk
Website: www.britain.org.my
Honorary British Representatives in: Johor Bahru, Kota Kinabalu, Kuching, Miri and Penang.

Embassy of Malaysia
3516 International Court, NW, Washington, DC 20008, USA
Tel: (202) 572 9700.
Fax: (202) 572 9882.
E-mail: malwash@kln.gov.my

Tourism Malaysia
120 East 56th Street, Suite 810, New York, NY 10022, USA
Tel: (212) 754 1113-5.
Fax: (212) 754 1116.
E-mail: mtpb@aol.com
Website: www.tourismmalaysia.gov.my

Tourism Malaysia
818 West Seventh Street, Suite 970, Los Angeles, CA 90017, USA
Tel: (213) 689 9702.
Fax: (213) 689 1530.
E-mail: malaysiainfo@aol.com
Website: www.malaysiamydestination.com

Embassy of the United States of America
376 Jalan Tun Razak, 50400 Kuala Lumpur, Malaysia
Tel: (3) 2168 5000.
Fax: (3) 2142 2207 *or* 2148 5801 (consular section).
E-mail: lrckl@po.jaring.my
Website: http://malaysia.usembassy.gov

High Commission for the Federation of Malaysia
60 Boteler Street, Ottawa, Ontario K1N 8Y7, Canada
Tel: (613) 241 5182.
Fax: (613) 241 5214.
E-mail: malottawa@kln.gov.my
Website: http://home.istar.ca/~mwottawa
Consulate General in: Vancouver (tel: (604) 685 9550).
Honorary Consulate in: Toronto (tel: (416) 364 6800).

Tourism Malaysia
1590-1111 West Georgia Street, Vancouver, British Columbia, Canada
Tel: (604) 689 8899 *or* (1888) 689 6872 (toll-free).
Fax: (604) 689 8804.
E-mail: info@malaysiatourism.ca
Website: www.malaysiatourism.ca

Canadian High Commission
Street address: 17th Floor, Menara Tan and Tan, 207 Jalan Tun Razak, 50400 Kuala Lumpur, Malaysia
Postal address: PO Box 10990, 50732, Kuala Lumpur, Malaysia
Tel: (3) 2718 3333.
Fax: (3) 2718 3399.
E-mail: klmpr-td@dfait-maeci.gc.ca
Website: www.dfait-maeci.gc.ca/kualalumpur
Consulate in: Penang.

General Information

AREA: 329,847 sq km (127,355 sq miles).
POPULATION: 24,530,000 (official estimate 2002).
POPULATION DENSITY: 74.4 per sq km.
CAPITAL: Kuala Lumpur. **Population:** 1,410,000, including suburbs (UN estimate 2002).
GEOGRAPHY: Malaysia is situated in central South-East Asia, bordering on Thailand in the north, with Singapore and Indonesia to the south and The Philippines to the east. It is composed of Peninsular Malaysia and the states of Sabah and Sarawak on the north coast of the island of Borneo, 650 to 950km (404 to 600 miles) across the South China Sea. Peninsular Malaysia is an area of forested mountain ranges running north–south, on either side of which are low-lying coastal plains. The coastline extends some 1900km (1200 miles). The west coast consists of mangrove swamps and mudflats which separate into bays and inlets. In the west, the plains have been cleared and cultivated, while the unsheltered east coast consists of tranquil beaches backed by dense jungle. Sarawak has alluvial and, in places, swampy coastal plains with rivers penetrating the jungle-covered hills and mountains of the interior. Sabah has a narrow coastal plain which gives way to mountains and jungle. Mount Kinabalu, at 4094m (13,432ft), is the highest peak in Malaysia. The major islands are Langkawi (a group of 99 islands), Penang and Pangkor off the west coast; and Tioman, Redang, Kapas, Perhentian and Rawa off the east coast.
GOVERNMENT: Constitutional monarchy since 1963. Gained independence from the UK in 1957. **Head of State:** King Syed Sirrajuddin ibni al-Marhum Syed Putra Jamalullail since 2001. **Head of Government:** Prime Minister Datuk Abdullah Ahmad Badawi since 2003.
LANGUAGE: Bahasa Malaysia is the national and official language, but English is widely spoken. Other languages such as Chinese (Cantonese and Hokkien), Iban and Tamil are spoken by minorities.
RELIGION: Muslim (53 per cent) and Buddhist (19 per cent) majorities. The remainder are Christian, Taoist, Confucianist, Hindu and animist.
TIME: GMT + 8.
ELECTRICITY: 240 volts AC, 50Hz. Square three-pin plugs and bayonet-type light fittings are generally used.
COMMUNICATIONS: Telephone: Full IDD is available. Country code: 60. Outgoing international code: 00. Public coin-operated phones can be found in many areas, such as supermarkets and post offices. Local calls cost 10 sen. Public cardphones can be found throughout the country. Cards can be purchased at airports, petrol stations and some shops for amounts ranging from RM3 to 50. There are currently two types – Kadfon and Unicard – and these can only be used in their appropriate phone booths. **Mobile telephone:** GSM 900 and 1800 networks cover practically the whole country. Network operators include *Celcom* (website: www.celcom.com.my), *DiGi* (website: www.digi.com.my) and *Maxis Mobile*. **Fax:** Centres for public use are located in the main post offices of all large towns. Most main hotels also have facilities. **Internet:** ISPs include *Jaring* (website: www.jaring.net.my) and *TMnet* (website: www.tm.net.my). There are numerous Internet cafes. Hotels and hostels often have facilities. **Telegram:** Telegrams can be sent from any telegraph office. **Post:** There are post offices in the commercial centre of all towns, open Mon-Sat 0800-1700. **Press:** The English-language dailies printed in Peninsular Malaysia are the *Business Times*, *The Edge*, *Malay Mail*, *Malaysiakini*, *New Straits Times*, *The Star* and *The Sun*. There are also several English-language Sunday newspapers and periodicals. English-language newspapers available in Sarawak include the *Borneo Post* and *Sarawak Tribune*. English-language dailies in Sabah include the *Borneo Mail*, *Daily Express* and *Sabah Times*.
Radio: BBC World Service (website: www.bbc.co.uk/worldservice) and Voice of America (website: www.voa.gov) can be received. From time to time the frequencies change and the most up-to-date can be found online.

Passport/Visa

	Passport Required?	Visa Required?	Return Ticket Required?
Full British	Yes	No/3	Yes
Australian	Yes	No/1	Yes
Canadian	Yes	No/1	Yes
USA	Yes	No/2	Yes
Other EU	Yes	No/3/4	Yes
Japanese	Yes	No/5	Yes

Note: *Regulations and requirements may be subject to change at short notice, and you are advised to contact the appropriate diplomatic or consular authority before finalising travel arrangements. Details of these may be found at the head of this country's entry. Any numbers in the chart refer to the footnotes below.*

Restricted entry: (a) Certain nationals have to apply for a visa with a reference/approval from the Immigration Department in Malaysia, rather than through an Overseas Mission in their country of residence. (b) Foreign women who are at least six months pregnant (unless in transit) and people of scruffy appearance may be denied entry. (c) Nationals of Israel and Serbia & Montenegro are banned from entry into Malaysia.
PASSPORTS: A valid passport or other travel documents recognised by the Malaysian government required by all. The former must have enough pages for the embarkation stamp upon arrival and be valid for at least six months at date of entry. The latter should be endorsed with a valid re-entry permit. If not in possession of a passport or travel document, a Document in lieu of Passport must be obtained from any Malaysian Representation Office. Holders of travel documents such as a Certificate of Identity, a Laisser Passer, a Titre de Voyage or a Country's Certificate of Residence must ensure guarantee of return to country that issued the documents or the national's country of residence.
Note: All visitors must also have proof of adequate funds and an onward or return sea or air ticket.
VISAS: Most visitors (including all nationals of countries

listed in the chart) do not require a visa to enter Malaysia if the period is less than one month and the purpose of the visit is business or social (see below for more detailed requirements).
Visas are not required by the following:
(a) **1.** nationals of all Commonwealth countries (except nationals of Bangladesh, India, Pakistan and Sri Lanka who *do* require a visa), and nationals of Liechtenstein, San Marino and Switzerland for all purposes and durations of visits;
(b) **2.** nationals of the USA for social and study-related visits of any duration;
(c) **3.** nationals of EU countries (except nationals of Cyprus, Estonia, Greece, Ireland, Latvia, Lithuania, Malta, Portugal and Slovenia who *do* require a visa) for social visits of up to three months (except **4.** nationals of The Netherlands, who may enter visa-free for all purposes and durations);
(d) **5.** nationals of Albania, Algeria, Argentina, Bahrain, Bosnia & Herzegovina, Brazil, Croatia, Cuba, Egypt, Iceland, Japan, Jordan, Korea (Rep), Kuwait, Kyrgyzstan, Lebanon, Morocco, Norway, Oman, Peru, Qatar, Romania, Saudi Arabia, Tunisia, Turkey, Turkmenistan, United Arab Emirates, Uruguay and Yemen (North) for social visits of up to three months;
(e) nationals of Iran, Iraq, Libya, Sierra Leone, Somalia, the Syrian Arab Republic, Yemen (South) and holders of Portuguese alien passports, Palestinian travel documents or a Macau Travel Permit for social visits of up to 14 days;
(f) nationals of all countries other than those mentioned above for stays of up to one month, except for nationals of Angola, Afghanistan, Bangladesh, Bhutan, Burkina Faso, Burundi, Cameroon, Central African Republic, China (PR), Colombia, Congo (Dem Rep), Congo (Rep), Côte D'Ivoire, Djibouti, Equatorial Guinea, Eritrea, Ethiopia, Ghana, Guinea-Bissau, India, Liberia, Mali, Mozambique, Myanmar, Nepal, Niger, Nigeria, Pakistan, Rwanda, Sri Lanka, Taiwan and Western Sahara who *always* require a visa;
(g) nationals on transit without leaving the airport precincts and who continue their journey to the next destination with the same flight.
Note: Different procedures apply according to nationality. For instance, certain nationals can only enter Malaysia through airports and not seaports. Consult the Embassy/Consulate for further details. Nationals may still require a pass upon arrival, even if they are permitted to enter Malaysia visa-free.
Types of visa and cost: *Single-entry*: £10. Prices are subject to change. *Student*: RM60 per year, available only in Malaysia. Enquire at the Malaysian High Commission for details.
Validity: One to three months from date of issue. Multiple-entry visas are valid for up to three months; in certain cases, validity of up to 12 months may be granted. Extensions are also possible. Enquire at the Malaysian High Commission for further details. Transit: 120 hours. The validity of the visa can also vary from nationality to nationality in accordance with whether a reference from the Immigration Department is obtained.
Application and enquiries to: Malaysian High Commission; see *Contact Addresses* section.
Application requirements: (a) Passport or travel documents valid for at least six months. (b) Three identical passport-size photos. (c) Fee (payable in cash or postal order only). (d) Completed and signed forms (three copies). (e) Proof of sufficient funds (including original and photocopy of most recent bank statement). (f) Onward or return ticket or travel itinerary from travel agent. (g) Compulsory yellow fever vaccination certificate for all visitors coming from infected areas as listed by WHO in the last six months. (h) Letter of introduction (and copy) from applicant's employer, college or university. For the spouse who is not working, a marriage certificate, photocopy of other spouse's passport and a letter of introduction from their spouse's employer must be submitted. (i) Self-addressed envelope (recorded delivery) if applying by post. *Student*: (a)-(i) and, (j) Letter of acceptance from educational institution, two passport-size photos, two copies of valid passport/travel document and two copies of particular student application form. Applications must not be applied directly to the Immigration Department.
Note: (a) Family members of a Student Pass holder should submit proof of family relationship. If person lives in a country with no Malaysian representative, that person may enter on a Visit Pass and then *must* apply to State Immigration Office within one month. (b) Wives of Malaysian nationals must submit photocopy of national's ID card, photocopy of national's Entry Permit, various forms, photocopy of wife and applicant's passport (all pages), national's birth certificate, marriage certificate, letter of Declaration of Marriage certified by the Commissioner of Oaths, two photos of husband and wife, wedding family photo, photocopy of divorce certificate (if divorced prior to marriage; marriage must have been longer than six months) or death certificate (if widowed prior to marriage) and a security bond. (c) Spouses and children of holders of Temporary Employment Visit passes must submit proof of relationship and proof of holder's Temporary Employment Visit pass. (d) Those travelling on transit visas can only enter at certain airports. They must also ensure that they enter and exit at the same Entry/Exit point.
Working days required: Same day – morning submission of the application (0915-1215) and afternoon collection (1530-1630). Times apply to the Malaysian High Commission in London. Applications by post take approximately two weeks. Students who apply for a student pass on arrival will usually obtain one within two weeks.
Temporary residence (Special pass for employment): Those wishing to take up employment should apply for a job in advance. Their prospective employers should then apply on their behalf for a Professional or Employment Pass by contacting the Malaysian Immigration Head Office, Block I, Pusat Bandar Damansara, Bukit Damansutra, 50550 Kuala Lumpur (tel: (3) 2095 5077; fax: (3) 2092 4869; website: www.imi.gov.my). For further details, contact the Malaysian High Commission (see *Contact Addresses* section).

Money

Currency: Ringgit (RM) = 100 sen. Notes are in denominations of RM1000, 500, 100, 50, 10, 5, 2 and 1. The RM1000 and RM500 notes are now being phased out. Coins are in denominations of RM1, and 50, 20, 10, 5 and 1 sen. There are also many commemorative coins in various denominations which are legal tender. The Ringgit is often referred to as the Malaysian Dollar.
Currency exchange: The best currency for exchange is the Pound Sterling, but US Dollars are also widely accepted. Although all major currencies can be exchanged easily in the main tourist centres, problems may occur elsewhere. It is difficult to exchange Malaysian currency outside of Malaysia, Singapore or Indonesia. All visitors need to fill in a Travellers Declaration Form (TDF); see below for details.
Credit & debit cards: American Express, Diners Club, MasterCard and Visa are accepted. Check with your credit or debit card company for details of merchant acceptability and other services which may be available.
Travellers cheques: Accepted by all banks, hotels and large department stores. To avoid additional exchange rate charges, travellers are advised to take travellers cheques in Pounds Sterling, US Dollars or Australian Dollars.
Currency restrictions: All visitors entering Malaysia (including children) must declare amounts over RM1000 that they have in their possession (local and equivalent in foreign currencies) on a Travellers Declaration Form (TDF), which can be obtained at the airport or Malaysian embassies, high commissions and tourist offices. On departure, the TDF has to be filled in prior to immigration clearance.
The import and export of local currency is limited to RM1000. The import of foreign currency is unlimited. The export of foreign currency is limited to the amount imported on arrival.
Exchange rate indicators: The following figures are included as a guide to the movements of the Ringgit against Sterling and the US Dollar:

Date	Feb '04	May '04	Aug '04	Nov '04
£1.00=	6.91	6.79	7.00	7.19
$1.00=	3.80	3.80	3.80	3.80

Banking hours: Mon-Fri 0930-1500, Sat 0930-1130. Banks in Sabah open at 0800 and usually break for lunch (1200-1400).

Duty Free

The following goods may be imported into Malaysia without incurring customs duty:
200 cigarettes or 50 cigars or 225g of tobacco; 1l of spirits or wine or malt liquor; cosmetics, perfumery, soaps and dentifrices up to the total value of RM200; gifts and souvenirs not exceeding a total value of RM200 (except goods from Langkawi and Labuan, up to a value of RM500); 100 matches; a total of RM75 for dutiable food preparations; a maximum of three pieces of new wearing apparel, plus one pair of new footwear; one unit of each portable electrical or battery-operated appliance for personal care and hygiene.
Prohibited items: It is prohibited to import any goods from South Africa and Israel. Non-prescribed drugs, weapons, pornography, any cloth bearing the imprint or reproduction of any verses of The Koran, as well as any imprint or reproduction of any currency note or coin, are prohibited. Drug-smuggling carries the death penalty.

Public Holidays

2005: Jan 1 New Year's Day. **Jan 23** Hari Raya Haji (Feast of the Sacrifice). **Feb 9-11** Chinese New Year. **Feb 10** Hari Raya Tussa (Islamic New Year). **Apr 22** Birth of the Prophet Muhammad. **May 1** Labour Day. **May 23** Vesak Day (Birth of the Buddha). **Jun 4** Official Birthday of HM the Yang di-Pertuan Agong. **Aug 31** National Day. **Nov 1** Deepvali Festival. **Nov 3-5** Hari Raya Puasa (End of Ramadan). **Dec 25** Christmas Day.
2006: Jan 1 New Year's Day. **Jan 10** Hari Raya Haji (Feast of the Sacrifice). **Jan 28-30** Chinese New Year. **Jan 31** Hari Raya Tussa (Islamic New Year). **Apr 11** Birth of the Prophet Muhammad. **May 1** Labour Day. **May 13** Vesak Day (Birth of the Buddha). **Jun 3** Official Birthday of HM the Yang di-Pertuan Agong. **Aug 31** National Day. **Oct 21** Deepvali Festival. **Oct 22-24** Hari Raya Puasa (End of Ramadan). **Dec 25** Christmas Day.
Note: (a) Muslim festivals are timed according to local sightings of various phases of the moon and the dates given above are approximations. During the lunar month of Ramadan that precedes Hari Raya Puasa, Muslims fast during the day and feast at night and normal business patterns may be interrupted. Some restaurants are closed during the day and there may be restrictions on smoking and drinking. Some disruption may continue into Hari Raya Puasa itself and Hari Raja Haji may last anything from two to 10 days, depending on the region. For more information see the *World of Islam* appendix. (b) Buddhist festivals are also timed according to phases of the moon and variations may occur.

Health

	Special Precautions?	Certificate Required?
Yellow Fever	No	1
Cholera	Yes	2
Typhoid & Polio	3	N/A
Malaria	4	N/A

Note: Regulations and requirements may be subject to change at short notice, and you are advised to contact your doctor well in advance of your intended date of departure. Any numbers in the chart refer to the footnotes below.

1: A yellow fever vaccination certificate is required from travellers over 1 year of age arriving within six days from infected areas. Those countries formerly classified as endemic by the WHO are considered by the Malaysian authorities to be infected areas.
2: Following WHO guidelines issued in 1973, a cholera vaccination certificate is not a condition of entry to Malaysia, although it may be required if travelling on to a cholera-infected country. However, outbreaks have been reported in Malaysia in the recent past; see the *Health* appendix.
3: Typhoid risk exists, especially in rural areas.
4: Malaria risk exists only in certain isolated inland regions. Urban and coastal areas are safe. The *falciparum* strain is reported to be highly resistant to chloroquine and resistant to sulfadoxine/pyrimethamine. The recommended prophylaxis is mefloquine.
Food & drink: All water should be regarded as being potentially contaminated. Water used for drinking or making ice should have first been boiled or otherwise sterilised. Milk is unpasteurised and should be boiled. Powdered or tinned milk is available and is advised, but make sure that it is reconstituted with pure water. Avoid dairy products that are likely to have been made from unboiled milk. Only eat well-cooked meat and fish, preferably served hot. Pork, salad and mayonnaise may carry increased risk. Vegetables should be cooked and fruit peeled.
Note: It is generally considered safe to drink water straight from the tap; however, as no authority is absolutely clear on this matter, the above advice is included as it reflects the necessity for caution for visitors who are unused to the Malaysian way of life.
Other risks: *Hepatitis A*, *C* and *E* occur and *hepatitis B* is hyperendemic. Epidemics of *dengue fever* and *Japanese encephalitis* can occur in both urban and rural areas. Immunisation against *tetanus*, *TB*, *diphtheria*, *hepatitis A* and *E* is recommended. Outbreaks of *meningococcal meningitis* can occur.
There may be some risk of *rabies* in certain areas. For those at high risk, vaccination before arrival should be considered. If you are bitten, seek medical advice without delay. For more information, consult the *Health* appendix.
Health care: Health insurance is recommended. Hospitals are found in all the main cities and can deal with all major needs. Private hospitals, some managed and staffed by British-trained doctors and nurses, provide a high standard of medical care and include Gleneagles Intan Medical Centre in Kuala Lumpur and Ampang Puteri Specialist Hospital, Selangor. Smaller towns and rural areas have private clinics. In an emergency, dial 999.

Travel - International

Note: There is suspicion that terrorists operating in Malaysia are harbouring plans to kidnap foreign tourists from the islands and coastal areas of eastern Sabah.

Although most travel to Malaysia is trouble-free, visitors may wish to utilise more cautious safety measures when travelling in these aforementioned areas - or even avoid them altogether.

AIR: The national airline is *Malaysia Airlines (MH)* (website: www.malaysiaairlines.com), which is southeast Asia's biggest airline and flies to over 110 cities across six continents. Further details can be obtained from the London office of *Malaysia Airlines* (tel: (0870) 607 9090). *Singapore Airlines*, *Royal Brunei* and *Thai International* operate flights to certain Malaysian destinations.

Approximate flight times: From Kuala Lumpur to *London* is 14 hours.

International airports: *Kuala Lumpur International Airport (KUL)* (Sepang) (website: www.klia.com.my) is 55 km (34 miles) south from Kuala Lumpur and near Putra Jaya, Malaysia's future administrative capital. It currently handles 25 million passengers a year and is served by all major international airlines. Kuala Lumpur's city centre is accessible via the Kuala Lumpur–Seremban Highway/KLIA interchange and the Shah Alam/North-South Central Link Expressway (travel time - 45 minutes). Taxis must be pre-paid in the Arrivals Area at the airport (travel time - 40 minutes). *KL City Buses* operates a 24-hour Express Bus Service to the Airport Bus Terminal, Hentian Duta, Kuala Lumpur city centre, which leaves every 15 minutes (luxury coach) or every hour (semi-luxury coach). The journey takes approximately one hour. Regular feeder buses travel from Hentian Duta to Lot 10 on Jalan Sultan Ismail in the city centre between 0800 and 2430 (travel time - 30 minutes). The cheapest way to travel to the city is by combined bus and train. The *Stage Bus Service*, which operates 0715-2230, leaves the airport every 30 minutes for Nilai KTM Station (travel time - 30 minutes). From Nilai, trains travel to Kuala Lumpur Railway Station 0644-2244 every 20 to 30 minutes (travel time - 1 hour). The *Express Rail Link (ERL)* runs between Kuala Lumpur (KL Sentral) and the main airport terminal at a speed of 100mph (160km/h) (estimated travel time - 30 minutes). Airport facilities include ATMs, bureaux de change, shopping, duty-free, restaurants, postal services, tourist information, hotel reservations, medical service, left-luggage, prayer rooms and car hire (including *Budget* and *Hertz*). Business facilities include executive lounges, limousine services to the city and business centres, which provide telephone, fax, Internet, teleconferencing, postal and secretarial services.

Penang (PEN) (Bayan Lepas) is 16km (10 miles) south of Georgetown, capital of this small island off the northwest coast of the peninsula. Though not receiving as many international flights as Kuala Lumpur, there are connections from the UK via Hong Kong (SAR), Singapore or Bangkok. Airport facilities include an incoming and outgoing duty-free shop, restaurant and bar, bank/bureau de change and car hire.

Kota Kinabalu (BKI) is 6.5km (4 miles) from the city. Situated on the northern coast of Sabah state (the northeastern part of Borneo Island), this airport is the international gateway to East Malaysia (Sabah and Sarawak) and receives international flights from all over the world. Connections from the UK go via Singapore, Hong Kong and Kuala Lumpur. Airport facilities include bank/bureau de change facilities, restaurant and bar.

Kuching (KCH) is 11km (7 miles) from the city. Situated in the west of Sarawak on the island of Borneo, the airport receives a limited number of international flights.

Departure tax: RM45 for international departures.

SEA: The major international ports are Georgetown (Penang), Port Kelang (for Kuala Lumpur) and, in East Malaysia (for Sabah and Sarawak), Bintulu, Kota Kinabalu, Kuching, Lahad Datu, Rejang, Sandakan and Tawau. Shipping lines with passenger services to Malaysia include *Blue Funnel*, *P&O* and *Straits Shipping*. Cargo/passenger lines are *Austasia*, *Knutsen*, *Lykes*, *Neptune Orient*, *Orient Overseas* and *Straits Shipping*. *Star Cruises* (Singapore) organises luxury cruises from Port Kelang. Other lines that offer cruises from this port include *Coral Princess* and *Gemini*. *Norwegian Cruise Lines*, *Royal Caribbean* and *Seabourn Cruise Lines* also call at Malaysia.

RAIL: Through services operate to and from Singapore via Kuala Lumpur and between Butterworth and Bangkok (Thailand) daily. There is also a 41-hour round trip available from the *Eastern and Oriental Express*, a luxury train service modelled on the famous Orient Express, which leaves from Singapore, journeys through Kuala Lumpur and heads north to Bangkok from where it returns to Singapore.

ROAD: Peninsular Malaysia is linked by good roads to Thailand and (via two causeways) to Singapore. Toll fees are levied on all highways throughout Malaysia. Road connections between the two eastern states, Sarawak and Sabah, and their neighbours on Borneo, Brunei and the Indonesian state of Kalimantan are fairly good.

Travel - Internal

Note: During major festivals (especially *Hari Raya Pusa*, the *Chinese New Year* and *Hari Raya Haji*), internal travel becomes extremely difficult unless tickets have been pre-booked long in advance. Domestic express bus tickets often go on sale up to two months before the festivals and sell out within one or two weeks. Even domestic flights tend to be packed during these periods. For festival dates, see *Social Profile* section *or* contact Tourism Malaysia (see *Contact Addresses* section).

AIR: *Malaysia Airlines (MH)* serves numerous commercial airports in Peninsular Malaysia. In East Malaysia, *Malaysia Airlines* crisscrosses both Sabah and Sarawak and also flies to Brunei. *Transmile Air* offers discounts on domestic flights to Sabah and Sarawak.

Domestic airports: *Kuala Lumpur Subang (KUL)* is 22 km (14 miles) west from the city. Previously the main international airport, it is now mainly used for domestic flights. Most Malaysian states have domestic airports and plans are underway for the further development of several airports.

Departure tax: RM6.

SEA/RIVER: Coastal ferries sail frequently between Penang and Butterworth and there is a scheduled passenger service linking Port Kelang with both Sarawak and Sabah. Small rivercraft often provide the most practical means of getting about in East Malaysia, even in the towns, and they are the only way to reach the more isolated settlements (unless one has access to a helicopter). Boats may easily be chartered and river buses and taxis are plentiful.

RAIL: *Malayan Railway* (Keretapi Tanah Melayu Berhad *or* KTM) at Jalan Sultan Hishamuddin, 50621 Kuala Lumpur (tel: (3) 2263 1111; e-mail: passenger@ktmb.com.my; website: www.ktmb.com.my) operates nearly 2092km (1300 miles) of line. There are three classes of train: Deluxe or First Class (with upholstered seats), Eksekutif or Second Class (with padded leather seats) and Ekonomi or Third Class (with cushioned plastic seats). The fast daytime *Express Rakyat* runs from Singapore to Butterworth, and continues on to Thailand. Express trains are modern, and some have sleeping berths and buffet cars. Some trains are air conditioned. East Malaysia has one railway line, known by travellers as the Jungle Railway, which is the main overland route for the Taman Negara National Park; it runs along the coast from Kota Kinabalu (Sabah), then inland up a steep jungle valley to the small town of Tenom. Other than this line, there are two main lines operated for a passenger service. One runs along the west coast and from Singapore, which runs northwards to Kuala Lumpur and Butterworth, meeting the Thai railways at the border. The other line separates from the west coast line at the town of Gemas and takes a northeastern route to Kota Bharu and Tenom. There is also a passenger service to two of Malaysia's seaports – Penang and Padang Besar on the west coast. The *KTM Komuter*, a commuter service, runs from Kuala Lumpur to Port Klang (west), Rawang (north) and Seremban (south). There are no rail services in Sarawak.

Cheap fares: Children under four travel free; children aged four to 11 pay half fare. For further information on discount fares available to passengers, contact Malayan Railway (see address details above).

Special tickets: The *Malayan Railway Pass* is available in 10- and 30-day tickets, giving unlimited travel on all trains through Peninsular Malaysia and Singapore and can be purchased from train stations in Butterworth, Johor Bahru, Kuala Lumpur, Padang Besar, Port Kelang, Rantau Panjang, Singapore and Wakaf Bharu. However, reservations must be made in advance for seats in first-class, air-conditioned trains and a supplement is charged. Reservations may be made up to three months in advance from the Director of Commerce, Malayan Railway, Jalan Sultan Hishamuddin, Kuala Lumpur. Enquire at Tourism Malaysia for further details.

ROAD: Traffic drives on the left. Most roads in the peninsular states are paved and signs leading to the various destinations are well placed and clear. The north-south highway, spanning 890km (553 miles) from Bukit Kayu Hitam (on the Kedah-Thailand border) to Johor Bahru is fully open to traffic. The dual carriageway will provide shorter travel times between towns. **Bus:** Local bus networks are extensive; there are almost 1000 routes, with regular services in and between all principal cities. 4-wheel-drive buses are used in rural areas of Sabah and Sarawak. **Trishaw:** Available in Penang and Malacca, these are inexpensive for short trips. Fares should be negotiated in advance. **Taxi:** Shared and normal taxis are a fast means of inter-town travel, but delays may be encountered whilst drivers get their passenger load before moving off. Ask drivers to turn the meter on before starting the journey. There is a 50 per cent surcharge for fares between 0000-0600 and an extra RM1 is charged for taxis booked by phone. Taxi coupons providing fixed prices to specific destinations can be purchased at the Kuala Lumpur railway station and the airport. **Car hire:** This is available through several agencies. Some agencies provide cars on an unlimited mileage basis. Cars with driver are also available. **Documentation:** An International Driving Permit is required. For UK citizens, a national driving licence is sufficient, but it has to be endorsed by the Registrar of Motor Vehicles in Malaysia.

URBAN: Parking in the centre of Kuala Lumpur and other towns is restricted to spaces for which a charge is made and a receipt is given. Public transport services in Kuala Lumpur are provided by conventional buses and by 'Bas Mini' fixed-route minibuses, taxis and pedi-cabs (trishaws) licensed by the Government. Bus fares vary, but the 'Bas Mini' have flat rates. These are used for shorter journeys, and tend to be crowded. The *PUTRA Light Rail Transit (LRT)* is a quick way to get around the city and provides links to the eastern and western suburbs of Kuala Lumpur. Routes and timetables are indicated in stations with an LRT logo.

Travel times: The following chart gives approximate travel times (in hours and minutes) from **Kuala Lumpur** to other major centres in Malaysia.

	Air	Road	Rail
Ipoh	**0.30**	**2.00**	**4.30**
Penang	**0.45**	**5.00**	**9.30**
Alor Setar	**0.45**	**7.00**	**7.30**
Kuantan	**0.35**	**4.00**	**-**
Johor Bahru	**0.35**	**3.00**	**6.00**
Singapore	**0.45**	**6.00**	**7.00**

Accommodation

HOTELS: Malaysia has many luxury and economy class hotels. Many new luxury hotels have recently been built in Kuala Lumpur. It is necessary to book well in advance, especially during school and public holidays when the Malaysians take their holidays in the popular resorts, notably Penang, Langkawi and the highlands. The more basic hotels have little in the way of modern washing or bathing facilities, often only a water trough instead of a bath or shower. There is no formal classification system. Government tax of 5 per cent and a service charge of 10 per cent are added to bills. Tips are only expected (on the basis of good service) for room service and porterage. Laundry service is available in most hotels. For further information, contact the Malaysian Association of Hotels, C5-3, Wisma MAH Jalan Ampang Utama 1/1, 1 Ampang Avenue, 68000 Ampang, Kuala Lumpur (tel: (3) 4251 8477; fax: (3) 4252 8477); e-mail: mahotel@po.jaring.my; website: www.hotels.org.my).

GOVERNMENT REST HOUSES: These are subsidised, moderately priced hotels. They are basic, but always clean and comfortable, with full facilities and usually good restaurants. As they are primarily travelling inns they tend to fill up quickly, so it is advisable to telephone and reserve a room.

CAMPING: There are camping facilities in the Taman Negara or national parks. Here jungle lodges provide tents, camp beds, pressure lamps and mosquito nets for trips into the rainforests.

YOUTH HOSTELS: Malaysia is a full member of the International Youth Hostel Federation. There are not many youth hostels, but they are very cheap. Accommodation is in dormitories and meals can be arranged. Visitors must register at the hostel from 1700-2000. Hostels are to be found in Cameron Highlands, Kuala Lumpur, Kuantan, Malacca, Penang and Port Dickson. Further details can be obtained from the Malaysian Youth Hostel Association, Kuala Lumpur International Youth Hostel, 21 Jalan Kg Attap, 50460 Kuala Lumpur, Malaysia (tel: (3) 2273 6870; fax: (3) 2274 1115; e-mail: myha@pd.jaring.my) *or* Tourism Malaysia (see *Contact Addresses* section).

HOMESTAY PROGRAMMES: Increasing in popularity in many states, Malaysian Homestay Programmes combine budget accommodation with the opportunity to experience typical Malaysian life. For further details, contact the Association of Homestay Programme, (tel: (3) 3263 0048; fax: (3) 3263 0049; e-mail: araitu@mapro.or.ja).

Resorts & Excursions

Malaysia today is a complex and richly diverse country that spreads across a network of islands which encompass an eclectic collage of ethnic groups, cultures and religions. The economic and spiritual heart is the impressive capital of Kuala Lumpur on Peninsular Malaysia, while other mainland cities worth visiting include the haunting colonial beauty of Georgetown on the island of Penang and the ramshackle sprawl of Malacca in southern Malaysia. On the western and eastern coasts of Peninsular Malaysia a myriad of islands, many blessed with stunning beaches, recline in the tropical sun and to the east the East Malaysian states of Sabah and Sarawak boast their own charms, including superb beaches and unspoilt wilderness.

KUALA LUMPUR

KL, as it is locally known, is Malaysia's hub; a huge, bustling, cosmopolitan city that is the business heart of the nation. Its very ethnic diversity is part of the attraction with Malays, Chinese, Indian and European cultures melting together on the tropical streets. Often overlooked by many tourists, KL has a wealth of attractions, with the voluminous **Petronas Twin Towers**, at a height of 436m (1453ft), amongst the tallest buildings in the world. From the viewing level of the Towers the city unfolds with its old mosques and ramshackle buildings, contrasting with the gleaming skyscrapers that have sprouted as Malaysia has become one of the regional economic powerhouses. **Merdeka Square** is at the very heart of old Malaysia, with the stunning highlight, the **Sultan Abdul Samad Building**, which bizarrely blends Victorian and Moorish architectural styles. The **Tasek Perdana Lake Gardens** are one of the city's best known natural landmarks, a popular spot for picnics and walking. Within the gardens are **Parliament House** and the **National Monument**. The National Monument, an impressive brass sculpture, is one of the world's largest free-standing sculptures. Close by is the **National Museum**, which houses many historical exhibits. The building incorporates various different Malaysian architectural styles and craftwork from different parts of the nation, making it an embodiment of many aspects of the nation. Near the railway station is the **National Mosque** surrounded by lawns ornamented with fountains. This modern mosque, built in 1965, gleams every bit as brightly as any of Kuala Lumpur's skyscrapers. The main dome is moulded in the shape of an 18-point star to represent the 13 states of Malaysia and the five central Pillars of Islam. The huge main prayer hall can hold up to 10,000 worshippers, although this section of the mosque is closed to non-worshippers. Nearby is the old Chinese clan house of **Chan See Yuen** and the colourful Indian temple of **Sri Mahamariaman**. Shopping and eating are other key attractions with retail opportunities, including everything from huge air-conditioned malls with bargains on many items, through to local handicrafts sold by the people who make them. KL has a smorgasbord of eating opportunities, with fine dining restaurants through to local eateries that showcase the finest culinary delicacies from all over Malaysia. Then there are the **street markets**, with food stalls, where some of the best and cheapest food is to be found for the adventurous. The **Friday Mosque**, situated astride the confluence of the Klang and Gombak Rivers at the point where the first Europeans scrambled ashore, is the most stunning and popular sight in the city. The best time to visit is at sunset or during the muezzin's call to prayer, which echoes around the ornate domes and palm trees, lending the mosque an air of calm amidst the skyscrapers.

Excursions: The **Batu Caves** lie a few miles to the north of the city. These large natural caves, reached by 272 steps, house the Hindu shrine of Lord Subramaniam. Nearby is the **Museum Cave**, a fascinating display of brightly coloured statues and murals from Hindu mythology. **Templar Park**, 22km (14 miles) north of Kuala Lumpur, is a well-preserved tract of primary rainforest, which is rich in scenic beauty. Jungle paths, swimming lagoons and waterfalls all lie within the park boundaries. Malaysia's latest agricultural park, located at **Cherakah** in Shah Alam, **Selangor**, has a large playing area with facilities for skateboarders and rollerskaters. The **Forestry Research Institute**, 15km northwest of KL, is a genuine example of ecotourism in that it is a stretch of jungle that has been protected and is now being used to study how this unique eco-system works. The centre also looks at ways of sustainable development and at ways of protecting this environment. There are a number of low eco impact trails that visitors can explore.

PERAK & PANGKOR

Perak derives its name from the rich silver tin ore deposits once so fruitful in the region. Perak translates as 'silver' in the Malay language. Major towns within Perak include Ipoh, the administration centre and capital, Kuala Kangsar, the royal town and Taiping.

IPOH: Dubbed the 'City of Millionaires' (due to its tin mining wealth) *Ipoh*, Malaysia's third-largest city, offers the ghosts of its grand colonial days with the mixture of colonial and modern architecture; the best example of the former is the Moorish and Victorian pastiche of the train station. The city centre also boasts many colonial-era shops, which retain their original atmosphere today. The **Kuala Gula Bird Sanctuary** in Ipoh is of great interest to all nature lovers. In addition to over 160 different species of birds, lucky visitors may get a chance to see smooth otters, long-tailed macque and ridge-back dolphins. The best time to visit is between September and December when many migratory birds arrive at the sanctuary.

Excursions: 30 minutes' drive from Ipoh, near **Batu Gajah**, stands the impressive **Kellie's Castle**. Surrounded by rubber plantations, the magnificent ruins of the unfinished castle are all that remains of Scotsman William Kellie Smith's nostalgic ambition to recreate an authentic piece of his Scottish homeland. Work halted with the sudden demise of Smith in 1926 and, since his death, the rumours and mystique surrounding the castle have intensified. Reputed to be haunted, the castle is also believed to possess secret rooms and tunnels, undetected to this day.

KUALA KANGSAR: Just north of Ipoh at **Jalan Kuala Kangsar**, **Perak Tong**, a limestone cave temple, houses over 40 statues of Buddha. 385 steps in a cave behind the main altar lead up to a magnificent viewpoint, from where one can survey the surrounding countryside. **Sam Poh Tong** and **Kek Lok Tong**, near **Gunung Rapat**, are impressive cave temples where statues of Buddha stand alongside magical stalactites and rock formations. Both temples have Buddhist vegetarian restaurants in the temple grounds. Kuala Kangsar is the birthplace of the rubber industry. In 1877, nine rubber trees were first planted here and the industry was born. Three of the town's most beautiful buildings include **Istana Iskandariah**, the royal palace, **Istana Kenangan**, the former royal palace now home to the **Perek State Museum**, and the **Ubudiah Mosque**.

TAIPING: Although it may be known as the 'Town of Everlasting Peace', Taiping grew to fame as a raffish tin mining centre, though the importance of the industry has declined since a major slump in the 1980s. Some of the wealth from the tin mining was pumped into Taiping's main attraction, the disused mining pools that were transformed in the late 19th century to become the stunning, carefully landscaped **Lake Gardens**. Taiping is also home to some impressive colonial architecture and the charming **Ling Nam Temple**, which is reputed to be the oldest Chinese temple in Perak. The more sinister history of Taiping emerges in the **old prison**, that was used by the Japanese in World War II, and the **Allied War Cemetery**, the last resting place of hundreds of victims of the Japanese invaders.

PANGKOR ISLAND: No longer is Pangkor Island, about 100km (60 miles) south of Penang Island, unspoilt and seldom-visited. Over recent years it has gained in popularity, which has brought better facilities at the expense of increasing crowds and development of the pristine environment. Since 1996, an internal air link to the island has facilitated access for tourists. Innumerable bays boast excellent sandy beaches and all kinds of watersports.

PENANG & LANGKAWI

PENANG: The island of Penang, eulogised as the 'Pearl of the Orient', lies just off the northwest coast of Peninsular Malaysia. Recently a network of expanded tourist facilities has been created, which have ruined many of the island's main beach charms. Some of the beaches that are popular with resort developers, in particular those around **Batu Feringgi** on the north coast, have become blighted by jet skis, private hotel stretches of sand and various touts and hawkers. Despite this uncontrolled development to the north, much of the rest of the island is still a beautiful tropical oasis of palm trees and sandy beaches, and it is also the main international gateway to northern Malaysia. It was the natural harbour that first attracted the British to Penang in the late 18th century, and the port is still one of the most important in the country today. There is a regular ferry service between the island and the town of Butterworth on the mainland and a spectacular road bridge.

GEORGETOWN: Charming Georgetown is Penang's main settlement, a thriving hub where Malay, Chinese, Thai, Indian and European cultures merge, as does the architecture which, in the space of a few miles, takes in a British colonial-style cricket pitch and a rumble of Chinese stilt houses. The main shopping is on Campbell Street and Canarvon Street. Worth visiting are **Khoo Kongsi**, an old Chinese clan house, **Fort Cornwallis**, a British 18th-century fortress, **Penang Museum and Art Gallery** and the many churches, temples and mosques found throughout the town. The first-class laksas and unique Penang dishes are reason for visiting alone, with many meals enjoyed outside at the ubiquitous food stalls.

REST OF PENANG: Penang has more than just beaches. One of the most unusual attractions is the **Snake Temple**, which swarms with poisonous snakes, but their venomous threat is countered by heavily drugging them with incense. **Wat Chayamangkalaram Temple** contains an enormous gold-plated reclining Buddha which, at 33 metres long, is believed to be the third largest in the world. **Penang Bird Park** is a must for bird lovers' and horticultural enthusiasts alike. The landscaped park in **Seberang Jaya** is home to over 400 species of birds. Specially designed aviaries are placed among manmade islands with beautiful waterfalls and gardens ablaze with ornamental flowers and tropical greenery. A wide variety of orchid and hibiscus can also be seen. Over 100 species of butterflies and insects can be seen in the gardens of **Penang Butterfly Farm** in **Teluk Bahang**. The farm is open daily to visitors. In the centre of the island is **Penang Hill**, with a 700m (2300ft) summit, where tourists who can bear the massive queues to ascend the cable car are rewarded with splendid views and jungle walks.

LANGKAWI: More than 100km (60 miles) north of Penang lie the 104 islands, many of which are just outcrops of coral, that make up Langkawi. The largest, **Langkawi Island**, is the only one with sophisticated tourist facilities (it has been declared a free port and duty-free shopping is available). Several international hotels and resorts have opened as the government and international developers flood into what is set to become Malaysia's premier island beach resort. The island's many coves, lagoons and inlets make it ideal for all kinds of watersports such as swimming, sailing, fishing and scuba diving. Horse riding facilities and golf courses are also available. Travel to Langkawi is by air from Kuala Lumpur, Penang and Alor Setar or by road and sea.

KELANTAN: Bordering Thailand in the north is the state of Kelantan, whose capital **Kota Bharu** is a colourful, vibrant city, very much the archetypal South-East Asian border town. The beaches here are clean and unspoilt and the sea is ideal for swimming, diving and fishing. The state is renowned for its many cultural festivals, some of which are unique to the region. *Puja Umur* (the birthday of the Sultan) is celebrated with a week-long festival, beginning with a parade in Kota Bharu. A form of art unique to Kelantan is the *Ma'yong*, a combination of ballet, opera, romantic drama and comedy, originally a form of court entertainment.

CENTRAL HIGHLANDS HILLS RESORTS

Dotted about the mountain range that runs down the spine of Malaysia are several hill resorts. All are situated more than 1400m (4500ft) above sea level and offer cool, pleasant weather after the humidity of the plain and the cities.

GENTING HIGHLANDS: Less than one hour by road from Kuala Lumpur is Genting Highlands, which boasts Malaysia's only casino (passports required). Genting Highlands can also be reached by regular helicopter service from Kuala Lumpur. Facilities include four hotels, golf courses with a magnificent clubhouse, an artificial lake, a health and sports centre, and an indoor swimming pool.

FRASER HILL: Set in lush jungle 100km (60 miles) north of Kuala Lumpur, Fraser Hill is popular with both holidaymakers and golf enthusiasts. A wide range of other sports are available. There is also a self-contained township, self-catering bungalows and an international-standard hotel.

CAMERON HIGHLANDS: Still further north, about four hours from Kuala Lumpur, are the Cameron Highlands. These are among the best-known mountain resorts in Asia, and consist of three separate townships: **Brinchang**, **Tanah Rata** and **Ringlet**. An international-standard hotel and many bungalows are set around a golf course in lush green surroundings. Tennis, squash, badminton, jungle walks and swimming are available. From here you can visit **Gunung Brinchang**: at 2064m (6773ft) above sea level, it is the highest inhabited point in Peninsular Malaysia and therefore a magnificent viewpoint.

NEGERI SEMBILAN & MALACCA

NEGERI SEMBILAN: The state of Negeri Sembilan is located in the southwest corner of Peninsular Malaysia. It is famed throughout the region for its Minangkabau-style architecture, which reflects the influence of its first inhabitants from Sumatra.

SEREMBAN: Negeri Sembilan's capital is 64km (39 miles) south of Kuala Lumpur. Journey time from Kuala Lumpur by car is about 30 minutes. **Seremban Lake Gardens** is one of the town's most attractive features - it has two beautiful lakes, one of which has a floating stage where cultural shows are performed. The **State Mosque**, which has nine pillars to represent the nine districts of the state, overlooks the tranquil gardens.

The **Cultural Handicraft Complex** at **Labu Spur** houses the **Negeri Sembilan State Museum**. Historical artefacts representative of the state and its inhabitants are on display in this museum, built entirely from wood.

PORT DICKSON: Port Dickson is on the coast, about one-and-a-half hour's travelling time from Kuala Lumpur and 32km (19 miles) from Seremban. Malaysians flock here from the city at weekends, but with 18km (11 miles) of beach, there is always plenty of room. The bays are fine for all kinds of watersports and fishing and there are facilities for water-skiing, motor cruising and deep-sea fishing. The water quality is not always good, though, and the sea around the beaches is often too shallow for decent swimming. The only real tourist attraction apart from the beaches is the **Tanjong Tuan Lighthouse**, where the coastline of Indonesia across the Straits of Malacca can be made out on a clear day.

ELSEWHERE: The **Fort of Raja Jumaat** (a 19th-century Bugis Warrior) is 7km (4 miles) from Port Dickson, in **Kota Lukut**. Remains of an old royal palace and a royal burial ground can be viewed, along with the remains of the fort, built in 1847 to control the tin trade in the vicinity. **Pedas Hot Springs** are 30km (18 miles) south of Seremban. Visitors wanting to take to the restorative waters will find bathing enclosures, dining and recreational facilities.

MALACCA: The city of Malacca may only be two hours by road south of Kuala Lumpur, but it is centuries away in ambience. Old men in fishing boats still cruise up through the centre of the modern city with the catch of the day, which can be enjoyed in the city's excellent restaurants. River cruises that open up the city's history are increasingly popular. Founded in the early 15th century, Malacca remains predominantly a Chinese community, although there are many reminders of periods under Portuguese, Dutch and British rule; some of these can be seen in the **Malacca Museum**. Architectural remains include the **Cheng Hoon Teng Temple** in the centre of the city, the gateway of the **A Formosa** Portuguese fortress, **St Paul's Church** with the grave of St Xavier, the **Stadthuys**, the Dutch **Christ Church** and the **Tranquerah Mosque**, one of the oldest in the country. There are several international hotels in Malacca, augmented by a fully-equipped resort complex 12km (7 miles) outside the city.

JOHOR: In the southern state of Johor, **Johor Bahru** is Malaysia's southernmost gateway, and also the road and rail gateway from Singapore via a 1.5km- (1 mile-) causeway that connects the island to Peninsular Malaysia. Places of interest in the State include **Johor Lama**, the seat of the Johor Sultanate after eviction from Malacca; the **Kota Tinggi Waterfalls**; the **Ayer Hitam** ceramic works; **Muar**, famous throughout the country for its ghazal music and trance-inducing Kuda Kepang dances; the rubber and palm-oil plantations; and **Desaru**, one of Johor's newest resorts. Desaru boasts unspoilt beaches and jungle. All kinds of sports are played here, from swimming, canoeing and snorkelling to pony riding and jungle trekking. Accommodation is in Malaysian-style chalets and hotels, and campers are also welcome.

THE EAST COAST

This part of the country contains many of the finest beaches, including some of the least spoilt in southern Asia. In effect, the whole east coast is one huge beach, backed by jungle. The region, which covers two-thirds of Peninsular Malaysia, comprises the states of **Kelantan**, **Terengganu**, **Pahang** and **Johor**, as well as the islands of **Tioman** and **Rawa**.

PAHANG - THE COAST: Kuantan, the state capital of Pahang, is fast gaining popularity as a beach resort. The region around Kuantan is also well known for village festivals and for the craft of weaving pandanus leaves into mats, hats and baskets. Woodcarving and batik are also traditional crafts in this part of the country. **Telek Chempadek**, just 5km (3 miles) north of Kuantan is another popular beach resort with a wide range of watersports available, including windsurfing, water-skiing and sailing. It has a good selection of restaurants along the seafront. 7km (4 miles) north of Kuantan, **Besarah**, an attractive fishing village, is famed for its shellcraft, batik and crafts modelled from coconuts.

Asia's first Club Mediterranée holiday village is in **Cherating**, about 45km (30 miles) north of Kuantan. The beaches at Cherating are some of the finest on the east coast and conditions are particularly favourable for windsurfing.

PAHANG - THE INTERIOR: Malaysia's answer to Loch Ness is **Lake Chini**, in whose waters mythological monsters are said to lurk, guarding the entrance to a legendary sunken city. **Kenong Rimba Park**, located in the valley of the **Sungai Kenong**, is a must for adventure seekers. Activities available include cave explorations, jungle trekking, fishing and rock climbing.

In the north of the state is Malaysia's largest national park, **Taman Negara**. Surrounded by the world's oldest tropical forest (supposedly 130 million years old), the park has remained virtually untouched and is a favourite haunt for outdoor enthusiasts, especially birdwatchers. The journey to the park headquarters involves travel by train, road and a three-hour boat ride. Accommodation is mostly modest and the more comfortable lodgings are limited.

TIOMAN: The island of Tioman, in the South China Sea off the coast of Pahang, will be familiar to fans of the film *South Pacific*, as it was here that the film-makers found their mythical Bali Hai. The sweeping palm trees and luxuriously white beaches are still there, but fame has come at a price with a rush of development, which on one side has brought the ease of direct flights and express boats from the mainland, but also a raft of accommodations, not all of them of the same quality and aesthetic standards. Tioman is the largest of a group of 64 volcanic islands, and also the largest island on Malaysia's east coast. The three most popular resorts are ABC, Salang and Juara. Tioman is also one of the best destinations in Malaysia for scuba diving and snorkelling. The jungle-clad interior is also popular for trekking, with many swathes of jungle still unspoilt. The cross island trek from Telek to Juara is the most popular trek, with no special equipment needed.

TERENGGANU: The state of Terengganu has 225km (140 miles) of white sandy beaches. Swimming and all forms of watersports are favourite pastimes. There are several turtle-breeding beaches; at **Rantau Abang**, the Visitor Centre can arrange for guests to watch giant turtles laying their eggs.

PERHENTIAN ISLANDS: Many Malays consider the twin islands of **Perhentian Besar** and **Perhentian Kecil** to be the two most beautiful islands in the country. They both boast pristine white beaches, crystal clear waters and are still relatively unexploited. The strict local beliefs mean that alcohol is not common and this has helped deter major companies from setting up here, leaving the islands in their natural state for those who do choose to visit. The islands are popular for scuba diving and snorkelling with easy access to reefs and good visibility.

SABAH

Separated from Peninsular Malaysia by 950km (600 miles) of the South China Sea, Sabah, on the northern tip of Borneo, can be reached by direct flights from Kuala Lumpur and Singapore. Known as 'The Land Below The Wind', Sabah is an adventure playground, home of the world's oldest jungles and one of South-East Asia's highest peaks, **Mount Kinabalu**. Sabah also offers the unique opportunity to see orang-utans in their natural environment.

KOTA KINABALU: The capital and main gateway to Sabah, Kota Kinabalu does little justice to its spectacular natural surroundings. It is a new city built upon the ruins of Jesselton, which was badly damaged during the Second World War, and designed around the gold-domed **State Mosque**. From **Signal Hill** there is a good view of the city and the surrounding mountains and sea.

EXCURSIONS: Just south of Kota Kinabalu is the resort of **Tanjung Aru**, where the recently opened beach complex has been designed with both business traveller and holidaymaker in mind. As well as conference and meeting facilities, there is also a ferry-shuttle service into the town. **Tuaran** is 30 minutes' drive northeast of Kota Kinabalu. The road runs through lush valleys, forested hills and rubber plantations. The town has a good *'Tamu'* (market).

SANDAKAN: Nearly 400km (250 miles) from Kota Kinabalu, Sandakan is the old capital of Borneo. The **Sandakan Orchid House** displays a rare collection of wonderful orchids and is a must for green-fingered enthusiasts. Also of interest is the **Crocodile Farm**, located outside Sandakan along the seventh mile Labuk Road. Over 1000 crocodiles, of varying sizes inhabit the farm at any one time. 24km (15 miles) from the town is the **Sepilok Orang-Utan Rehabilitation Centre**, home of the 'wild men of Borneo', the world's largest orangutan population. The sanctuary is a rehabilitation centre where orangutans reap the benefits of inhabiting virgin rainforest in a protected environment. Now one of Sabah's top tourist attractions, the centre is no flippant tourist site as it actively manages to take in injured

or orphaned orangutans and return them to the wild once they are rehabilitated. There is no guarantee of seeing an orangutan, but they usually turn up for their twice-daily feedings.
TURTLE ISLANDS: 40km (24 miles) north of Sandakan, **Pulau Selingan**, **Pulau Bakungan Kecil** and **Pulau Gulisan** collectively form the **Turtle Islands**. Visitors get the opportunity to witness the amazing sight of Hawksbill and Green turtles coming ashore in the evening to lay their eggs. The islands can be visited all year round but, from July to October, the number of turtles visiting the island increases. Accommodation is available but highly sought after.
TENOM: The Tenom region can be reached from Kota Kinabalu by Sabah's only railway line. A spectacular and thrilling experience, it follows the **Padas River** up through narrow jungle gorges in the **Crocker Range**. Tenom town is renowned for its style of longhouse building, unchanged in centuries, and for the traditional songs and dances performed there.

LABUAN

The island of **Labuan** is 10km (6 miles) off the coast of Sabah, and covers an area of 98 sq km (38 sq miles). It is a duty-free port and operates as Malaysia's offshore financial centre. Excellent duty-free shopping and wide expanses of white sandy beaches throughout the island make Labuan a popular tourist destination. It is also a popular destination for divers and has four established wreck diving sites. The *Cement Wreck* is suitable for beginners, but the *Blue Water Wreck* requires more advanced diving experience. It is possible to penetrate the hull of the Australian and American wrecks, but these dive sights are only accessible to qualified wreck divers with relevant experience. Religious buildings of interest on the island are the **An'nur Jamek Mosque**, **Kwong Fook Kung Temple** and **Lauan Gurdwara Sahib**. The mosque, a place of worship for Labuan's Muslim community, has a progressive futuristic design. The temple, constructed in 1952, is the oldest Chinese temple on the island. The Hokkien community stages a deity procession with trance-like dances and food offerings each year in March. Lauan Gurdwara Sahib, a place of worship for Labuan's Sikh community was built in 1957. The Sikh 'Golden Temple' in Amritsar inspired the design. The **Peace Park** at **Layang-Layangan**, commemorating World War II, is a tranquil retreat. Japanese-inspired pavilions and ponds with stone bridges are dotted throughout beautifully landscaped gardens.
PULAU PAPAN: An island only five minutes by boat from Labuan, Pulau Papan is a popular retreat for weekenders from Brunei. Attractive landscaping throughout the island and a colonial lighthouse enhance Pulau Papan's natural charm. Chalet accommodation is available; the only alternative for anyone wanting to stay overnight on the island is camping.

SARAWAK

The state of Sarawak shares East Malaysia with Sabah but is a vastly different destination to its neighbour with a greater degree of ethnic and tribal diversity leading to a more interesting culture and more varied cuisine. Most people who live in Sarawak use the intricate network of waterways to get about. Visitors are encouraged to do so too, although taxis and hire cars are available in the larger towns for those who prefer more conventional means of transport. Separated from Peninsular Malaysia by 650km (404 miles) by the South China Sea, Sarawak can be reached by direct flights from Kuala Lumpur and Singapore.
KUCHING: Situated on the banks of the River Sarawak, Kuching is a charming historic town, as well as being a gateway to a huge hinterland of dense tropical rainforest and mountain ranges. Villages on stilts still cling precariously to the river banks. Kuching has many places of interest worth visiting. A visit to the **Sarawak Museum** affords valuable insights into the history, wildlife and anthropology of Borneo. The **Court House**, built in 1847, is adorned with local art forms and is regarded as one of the finest buildings in Sarawak. The **Hong San Temple**, built in honour of the God Kuek Seng, dates back to 1895. The Chinese community reveres Kuek Seng, who became a god 1000 years ago. It is supposed that he grants all requests from his devotees. At the heart of Kuching, the splendour of **Sarawak State Mosque**, with its magnificent gilt domes is a majestic sight. Situated at the Junction of Jalan Tunku Abdul Rahman and the Main Bazaar, **Tua Pek Kong Temple** is Kuching's oldest Chinese temple, which dates back to 1876.
EXCURSIONS: Overnight excursions can be made up the **Skrang River**, with accommodation provided in longhouses. There are also downriver trips to Santubong, an ancient trading post on the coast.
The **Bako National Park**, covering an area of approximately 26 sq km (10 sq miles), has interesting wildlife and vegetation, including carnivorous plants, long-nosed monkeys and Sambar deer. Excursions are organised from Kuching.
GUNUNG MULU NATIONAL PARK: Gunung Mulu National Park, a World Heritage Site, has over 3500 different plant species and is home to an abundance of wildlife including exotic birds and butterflies, fish and mammals. Small Borneo gibbons swinging through the trees are a common sight. The magnificent limestone caves in the park are the main tourist attraction, and include **Deer Cave**, **Clearwater Cave** and **The Cave of the Winds**.
NIAH CAVES: Other excursions, often via Miri, can be made to the Niah Caves, which show evidence of human existence dating back to 5000 BC. The caves are also valued for their guano and bird's nests, the latter being used to make soup. Many of the caves – and some are more easily accessible than others – may be visited with a guide.

Sport & Activities

After hosting the 1998 Commonwealth Games, for which Malaysia invested over £300 million, sports facilities have been greatly improved throughout the country. The authorities' initiative to present Malaysia as an international sports venue continued with an unusual bid for the 2008 Olympic Games and the construction of a £44 million Formula One racing circuit in Sepang (located adjacent to Kuala Lumpur International Airport). However, it is Malaysia's beaches and rainforests which endure as the main attraction for activity holidays. A comprehensive list of tour operators offering tailor-made package holidays is available from Tourism Malaysia (see *Contact Addresses* section).
Adventure sports: Sabah, located in northern Borneo, is Malaysia's premier destination for outdoor adventure sports and there is a wide range of sporting and activity events held in the region throughout the year. For further details, contact the Sabah Tourism Promotion Corporation (tel: (88) 212 121; fax: (88) 212 075 *or* 219 311 *or* 222 666; e-mail: info@sabahtourism.com; website: www.sabahtourism.com).
Scuba diving: The tropical waters off peninsular Malaysia and Borneo offer ideal conditions for scuba-diving. Water visibility is often greater than 30m (100ft). The selection below gives a brief overview of some of Malaysia's best dive sites:
Layang Layang: Located northwest of Kota Kinabulu, off the coast of Sabah and accessible by air, this coral atoll consists of 13 coral reefs linked together. Underwater sights include an amazing array of corals, marine life and cliffs that plunge 2000m to the ocean bed.
Miri: Located north of Kuching, off the coast of Sarawak, Borneo. Popular dive sites include 'Sea Fan Garden', 'Atago Maru', a Japanese World War II shipwreck and 'Scubasa Reef', a shallow reef which provides refuge for migrating turtles during August each year.
Pulau Redang: Home to Malaysia's first protected marine park, the Terengganu Marine Park, located north of Kuala Terengganu. The Pulau Redang archipelago contains nine islands. Popular sites include the 'Mini Mount' (good for both day and night dives), the 'Picture Wall' (dotted with sea fans and corals) and 'Cathedral Arches' (canyon network with huge arches). 'Turtle Bay', known for its sea turtles, is at the northern end of the island.
Pulau Sipadan: Located off the northeastern coast of Borneo, Pulau Sipadan is Malaysia's only oceanic island. It is renowned for its wide range of rare marine species.
Pulau Tioman: Located within the Pahang Marine Parks, consisting of eight islands. One of the best dive sites is Tiger Reef, which has a particularly high number of sea fans; divers should note that currents can be very strong.
Tunku Abdul Rahman Park: Close to Kota Kinabulu (15 minutes by boat). One of the most popular sites in this area is Mamutik.
Pulau Tenggol: Popular weekend getaway for Malaysians, located south of Terengganu, accessible by air. The waters are protected by marine park status.
Pulau Paya Marine Park: Located on Peninsular Malaysia, in the south of Langkawi Island (a busy tourist resort) in the north of the Malacca Straits.
Pulau Perhentian: Eastern Malaysia's northernmost island group consisting of Perhentian Besar and Perhentian Kecil, located in the South China Sea, off the coast of Kelantan. Can be reached on a fishing-boat trip from Kuala Besut, a small fishing village on the mainland. It is rich in coral and marine life and is possibly one of the finest tropical islands in Malaysia. It is surrounded by beautiful beaches and has a tropical interor, filled with wildlife, such as monkeys, lizards, flying squirrels and butterflies. A fairly isolated region, praised by divers for the giant soft corals, large schools of pelagic fish and nocturnal shellfish.
Tunku Abdul Rahman Marine Park: Located in Borneo, easily accessible from Kota Kinabalu. Local marine life includes manta rays, lion fish and whale sharks (from December to April).
Labuan Island: Popular wreck-diving destination. Two wrecks from ships sunk in World War II, and one recent Malaysian wreck.
Trekking and caving: Nearly 75 per cent of Malaysia is covered in forests, of which the rainforest is reputedly the world's oldest (130 million years). There are seven national parks and many wildlife reserves and protected areas. Many of the parks offer excellent trails for jungle trekking, particularly at *Taman Negara National Park* (peninsular Malaysia). The best time to visit is between February and September (dry season). Expert guides should be hired from the Wildlife Department at the Taman Negara Resort at Kuala Tahan, the park's headquarters. Kuala Tahan is reached by a three-hour riverboat trip from Kuala Tembeling, but there are also flights from Kuala Lumpur. Treks up *Gunung Tahan* mountain (2187m/7174ft) are also possible; a guide is compulsory and the trip takes several days. In East Malaysia, the best treks are in Sarawak, Borneo and *Gunung Mulu National Park*, which is renowned amongst caving enthusiasts. The recently discovered *Sarawak Chamber* and the 51km- (32 mile-) long *Clearwater Cave* (accessible by boat only) are favourite destinations. Permits for Gunung Mulu National Park must be obtained in Miri, reached either by a short flight or a couple of three-hour boat trips. Adventurous trekkers may wish to explore the *Kelabit Highlands* around nearby Bario, but these are quite demanding and should only be undertaken in the company of a local guide. Another famous trekking destination is the *Kinabalu National Park*, located in the state of Sabah, whose centrepiece, *Mount Kinabulu* (4101m/13,452ft), is South-East Asia's highest peak. Despite its size, Kinabulu is very easy to climb. No skills are required, but a guide and a climbing permit (which can be bought on location) are still compulsory. The climb involves an overnight stay in one of the resthouses along the route. Due to the altitude, people with high blood pressure or heart problems should not attempt the climb.
Golf: Malaysia has nearly 250 golf courses. The locations vary from coast to tropical rainforest or the mountainous highlands. The *Malaysian Open Golf Championships*, held each March, attract top professionals. For further information, contact Tourism Malaysia (see *Contact Addresses* section).
Karate: More than 150 karate training centres offer regular training sessions under black-belt instructors six days a week. Visitors are welcome to receive free karate training for one week in any of the centres. A list can be obtained from the Chief Instructor, Karate Budokan International, Jalan Jubilee, Kuala Lumpur.
Traditional sports: Malaysia has many unusual sports, including **Gasing-top spinning** (called *Main Gasing*), which uses tops fashioned from hardwood and delicately balanced with lead. **Wau-kite flying** is a traditional pastime. **Sepak Takraw** is a game like volleyball, played with a ball made of rattan strips. Players may use their heads, knees and feet but not their hands.
Longhouse visits: Malaysian longhouses, which are common along the rivers in Sarawak and Sabah, are really entire villages housed under one single roof, inhabited by native communities. For some years now, Tourism Malaysia has been promoting these characteristic habitations to tourists who are welcome to stay free of charge (although small gifts as a sign of appreciation are recommended). Visitors should be accompanied by a local guide who can also take them on a jungle walk.
Jungle railway: Malaysia's central railway travels largely through areas of dense jungle. It commences near Kota Bahru and continues via Kuala Krai, Gua Musang, Kuala Lipis and Jerantut to meet the Singapore-KL railway line at Gemas. Owing to extensive road building, this itinerary may change, and travellers are advised to check with Tourism Malaysia (see *Contact Addresses* section).

Social Profile

FOOD & DRINK: In multiracial Malaysia, every type of cooking from South-East Asia can be tasted. Malay food concentrates on subtleties of taste using a blend of spices, ginger, coconut milk and peanuts. *Sambals* (a paste of ground chilli, onion and tamarind) is often used as a side dish. *Blachan* (a dried shrimp paste) is used in many dishes and *ikan bilis* (dried anchovies) are eaten with drinks. Popular Malay dishes include *satay*, which consists of a variety of meats, especially chicken, barbecued on small skewers with a spicy peanut dipping sauce and a salad of cucumber, onion and compressed rice cakes. The best sauce often takes several hours to prepare to attain its subtle flavour. *Gula Malacca* (a firm sago pudding in palm sugar sauce) is also served in restaurants. There are many regional types of Chinese cooking including Cantonese, Peking, Hakka, Sichuan and Taiwanese. Indian food is also popular, with curries ranging from mild to very hot indeed. Vegetarian food, chutneys and Indian breads are also available. Indonesian cuisine also combines the use of dried seafoods and spiced vegetables with the Japanese method of preparation with fresh ingredients cooked to retain the natural flavour. Japanese-style seafood such as *siakaiu beef* (grilled at the table), *tempura* (deep-fried seafood) and *sashimi* (raw fish with salad) are excellent. Korean and Thai

food are available in restaurants. Amongst Malaysia's exotic fruits are starfruit, durian, guavas, mangos, mangosteen and pomelos. Western food is served throughout the country and includes US, Spanish, Italian and French cuisine. Kuala Lumpur has several restaurants which rival the high standards set by established Western restaurants in Singapore and Hong Kong. Table service is normal, and chopsticks are customary in Chinese restaurants. Indian and Malay food is eaten with the fingers. Set lunches, usually with four courses, are excellent value for money.
Although the country is largely Islamic, alcohol is available. Local beers such as *Tiger* and *Anchor* are recommended and the famous *Singapore Gin Sling*. International beers are also available.
NIGHTLIFE: Kuala Lumpur has a selection of reputable nightclubs and discos, most belonging to the big hotels. Nightclubs generally stay open until 0500 or 0600 and usually request a cover charge which includes the first drink free. Many of Kuala Lumpur's bars have a 'Happy Hour', offering two drinks for the price of one, between 1700-2000/2100. *Bintang Walk* is a lively spot and has a good selection of al fresco bars and coffee shops. Penang is also lively at night, larger hotels having cocktail lounges, dining, dancing and cultural shows. There are night markets in most towns, including both Kuala Lumpur and Penang Chinatown. Malay and Chinese films often have English subtitles and there are also English films. The national lottery and Malaysia's only casino at *Genting Highlands* are government-approved and visitors are not supposed to gamble elsewhere. *Keno* and Chinese *Tai Sai*, roulette, baccarat, french bull and blackjack are played at the casino. Dress is relatively formal and visitors must be over 21 years of age.
SHOPPING: Shopping in Malaysia ranges from exclusive department stores to street markets. Bargaining is expected in the markets, unless fixed prices are displayed. Kuala Lumpur is a popular shopping destination, rivalling Singapore and Hong Kong. *Suria KLCC*, a shopping mall with a spectacular fountain, gardens and a beautiful piazza, houses a great selection of leading couture outlets. *Star Hill* and *Lot 10* are popular shopping malls and there were plans underway to develop and finish an additional mall – *Times Square*. The islands of Labuan and Langkawi are duty-free zones. Cameras, pens, watches, cosmetics, perfume and electronic goods are available duty free throughout Malaysia. Malaysian speciality goods include pewterware, silverware and brassware; batik; jewellery; pottery and *songket*. Enquire at Malaysian Royal Customs and Excise about claiming cashback on duty-free goods. **Shopping hours:** Most shops keep their own opening hours, usually within the range of 1000-2200.
SPECIAL EVENTS: Annual Malaysian festivals, which celebrate significant religious events and public holidays are staged throughout the year and are magnificent spectacles, bursting with vibrancy and colour. Each of the different communities has its own customs, traditions and festivals, and to list all the events would take many pages. For details of the many other festivities taking place throughout the year, contact Tourism Malaysia (see *Contact Addresses* section). The following is a selection of special events occurring in Malaysia in 2005:
Jan 25 *Thaipusam* (Hindu day of atonement), Kuala Lumpur, Selangor, Penang and Malacca. **Jan 28-30** *Chinese New Year*, nationwide. **Feb 1** *Federal Territory Day*, Kuala Lumpur. **Mar 18-20** *Petronas Malaysian F1 Grand Prix*, Selangor. **Apr 9-May 7** *Malaysia Water Festival* (aquatic events and festivities), Lumut, Perak. **May 28-Jun 25** *Colours of Malaysia Festival*, nationwide. **Jun 1-2** *Gawai* (Harvest festival celebrated by the Ibans people), Sibu, Sarawak. **Jun 11-12** *26th Annual Penang International Dragon Boat Festival*. **Jul 1-31** *Food & Fruits Fiesta*, nationwide. **Jul 23-Sep 3** *Malaysia Mega Sale Carnival*. **Sep 15** *Lantern & Mooncake Festival*. **Nov 1** *Deepvali* (Hindu 'Festival of Lights'), nationwide. **Nov 4-6** *Hari Raya Puasa* (End of Ramadan), nationwide.
SOCIAL CONVENTIONS: Malaysia's population is a mixture of diverse cultures and characters. In general, the racial groups integrate, but keep to their individual traditions and lifestyles. Malays still form more than half of the total population and lead a calm life governed by the authority of elders and a strong sense of respect and etiquette. The Indian, Pakistani and Sri Lankan members of the population originally came to Malaysia to take up positions in the civil service, police and local government departments, as well as in the new rubber plantations, but many are now among the professional classes. European influences (British, Dutch and Portuguese in particular) are also very marked in Malaysia, although the European section of the population is now small. As far as greetings are concerned, the Malaysian equivalent of 'hello' is the Muslim 'peace be with you'. Malay men are addressed *Encik* (pronounced Enchik) with or without the name; Malay women should be called *Cik* (pronounced Che) if they are single and *Puan* if they are married. Touching the hand to the chest is a sign of respect and a relaxed wrist and gentle touch should be adopted when shaking hands. Chinese and Indians usually use Western forms of address. Hospitality is always warm, lavish and informal. When eating food by hand, only the right hand should be used. Visitors should respect religious beliefs and follow the Malaysian example, such as wearing appropriate clothing. Footwear should be taken off at the door when entering a house or temple. Dress should be informal, but not over-casual. Within towns, smoking has now become the subject of government disapproval and fines are levied in a number of public places,
TIPPING: 10 per cent service charge and 5 per cent government tax are commonly included in bills. Taxi drivers are not tipped.

Business Profile

ECONOMY: A fully fledged 'tiger' economy, from the 1970s onwards Malaysia grew rapidly at around 10 per cent annually. This extraordinary economic development had been achieved through the familiar East Asian combination of a strong state allied to unfettered capitalism. The government plays a central role in guiding the country's economic progress – the New Development Policy was unveiled in 1991 as the country's economic blueprint for the following 20 years. However, in 1997 the Asian financial crisis brought this process to a shuddering halt. Malaysia has recovered reasonably well since then, although the headlong pre-1997 expansion has been replaced by a more measured pace of growth of between 4 and 4.5 per cent per annum in 2002 and 2003. Inflation was a respectable 1.8 per cent in 2002 and Malaysia enjoys a substantial trade surplus ($18 billion in 2002). The government also took the key decision in September 1998 to fix the Malaysian currency, the ringgit, to the price of the US dollar. The manufacturing sector produces electronics, transport equipment, machinery steel and textiles. There are also reserves of oil and natural gas and mineral deposits of tin (of which it is a major producer), bauxite, copper, iron and gold. In the agricultural sector palm oil, of which Malaysia is the world's leading producer, is a major export commodity. Timber production remains important although it has been limited by the introduction of conservation measures in the mid-1990s. Other cash crops include rubber (again, Malaysia is one of the world's top producers), cocoa and pepper. Tourism dominates the service sector.
Malaysia's largest single trading partners are the USA, Japan and Singapore, followed by the EU and China. Malaysia is a member of the Pacific Rim organisation APEC (Asia-Pacific Economic Forum), which is assuming an increasingly important role in the regional economy. The essential stability of Malaysia's financial sector meant that although it suffered short-term damage, it was able to recover quickly. Over the last five years, Malaysia has averaged annual growth of 3 per cent.
BUSINESS: Suits or safari suits are acceptable for business meetings. Business visitors should remember that the Malay population is predominantly Muslim and religious customs should be respected and normal courtesies observed, eg appointments, punctuality and calling cards. **Office hours:** These vary between Peninsular Malaysia and East Malaysia. In general most offices are open by 0830 and close between 1600 and 1730. Almost all close for an hour between 1200 and 1400. Most close at 1200 Saturday.
COMMERCIAL INFORMATION: The following organisations can offer advice: Malaysian Trade Commission, 17 Curzon Street, London W1J 5HR, UK (tel: (020) 7499 5255; fax: (020) 7499 4597); *or* National Chamber of Commerce and Industry of Malaysia, 37 Jalan Kia Peng, 50450 Kuala Lumpur (tel: (3) 241 9600; fax: (3) 241 3775; e-mail: nccim@po.jaring.my); *or* Malaysian International Chamber of Commerce and Industry (MICCI), PO Box 12921, 50792 Kuala Lumpur (tel: (3) 6201 7708; fax: (3) 6201 7705; e-mail: micci@micci.com; website: www.micci.com); *or* Malaysian Industrial Development Authority (MIDA), Block 4, Plaza Sentral, Jalan Stesen Sentral 5, 50470 Kuala Lumpur (tel: (3) 2267 3633; fax: (3) 2274 7970; e-mail: promotion@mida.gov.my; website: www.mida.gov.my).
CONFERENCES/CONVENTIONS: Many conferences and conventions are held in Malaysia each year. Apart from the dedicated facilities at the Putra World Trade Centre in Kuala Lumpur, many hotels have facilities. Further information can be obtained from Tourism Malaysia, Convention Promotion Division (see *Contact Addresses* section).

Climate

Tropical without extremely high temperatures. Days are very warm, while nights are fairly cool. The main rainy season in the east runs between November and February, while August is the wettest period on the west coast. East Malaysia has heavy rains (November to February) in Sabah and in Sarawak. However, it is difficult to generalise about the country's climate, as rainfall differs on the east and west coasts according to the prevailing monsoon winds (northeast or southwest).
Required clothing: Lightweight cottons and linens are worn throughout the year. Waterproofing is advisable all year.

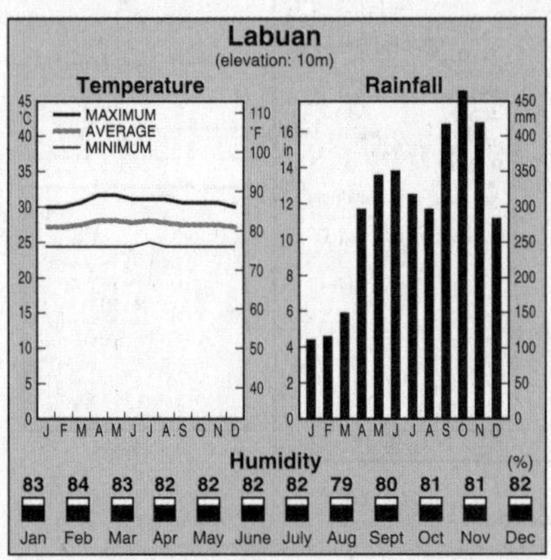

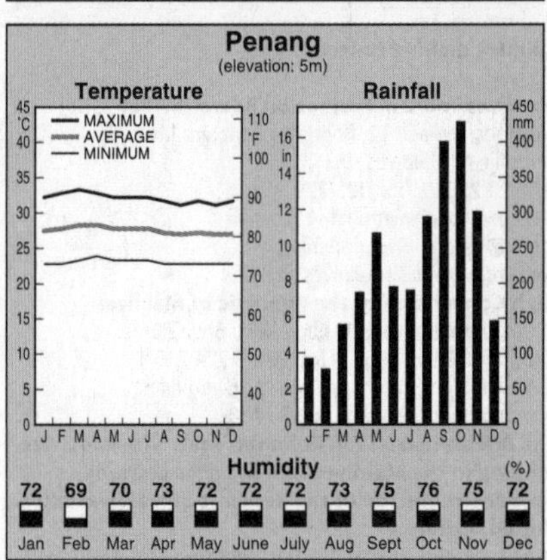

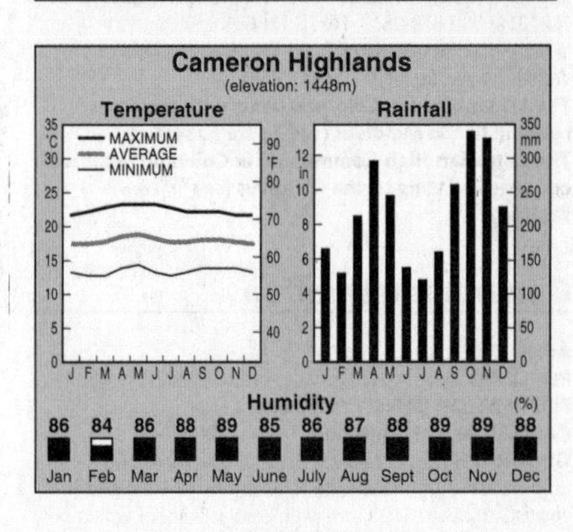

Maldives

LATEST TRAVEL ADVICE CONTACTS

British Foreign and Commonwealth Office
Tel: (0870) 606 0290 Website: www.fco.gov.uk

US Department of State
Website: http://travel.state.gov/travel

Canadian Department of Foreign Affairs and Int'l Trade
Tel: (1 800) 267 8376 Website: www.dfait-maeci.gc.ca

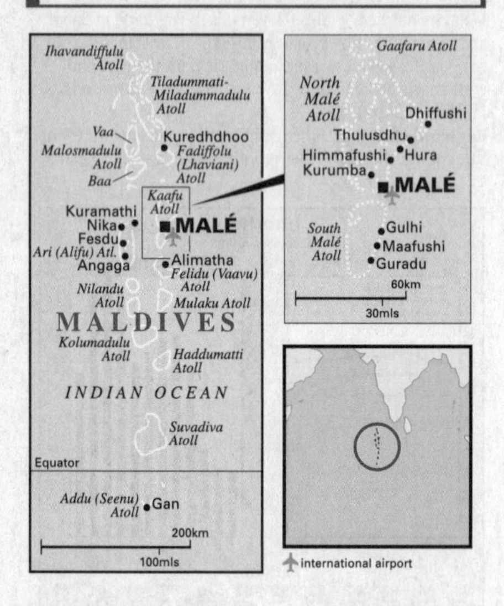

Location: A group of islands in the Indian Ocean, 500km (300 miles) southwest of the southern tip of India.

Country dialling code: 960.

Maldives Tourism Promotion Board (MTPB)
3rd Floor, H. Aage 12, Boduthakurufaanu Magu, Malé, Republic of Maldives
Tel: 323 228. Fax: 323 229.
E-mail: mtpb@visitmaldives.com *or* mtpb@visitmaldives.com.mv
Website: www.visitmaldives.com.mv

High Commission of the Republic of Maldives
22 Nottingham Place, London W1U 5NJ, UK
Tel: (020) 7224 2135. Fax: (020) 7224 2157.
E-mail: maldives.high.commission@virgin.net
Opening hours: Mon-Fri 0930-1730.

The British Embassy in Colombo deals with enquiries relating to the Maldives (see *Sri Lanka* **section).**

Permanent Mission of the Republic of Maldives to the United Nations
800 Second Avenue, Suite 400E, New York, NY 10017, USA
Tel: (212) 599 6194/5. Fax: (212) 661 6405.
E-mail: maldives@un.int
Website: www.un.int/maldives

The US Embassy in Colombo deals with enquiries relating to the Maldives (see *Sri Lanka* **section).**

The Canadian High Commission in Colombo deals with enquiries relating to the Maldives (see *Sri Lanka* **section).**

General Information

AREA: 298 sq km (115 sq miles).
POPULATION: 276,000 (official estimate 2001).
POPULATION DENSITY: 926 per sq km.
CAPITAL: Malé. **Population:** 74,069 (2000).
GEOGRAPHY: The Maldives Republic is located 500km (300 miles) southwest of the southern tip of India and consists of about 1190 low-lying coral islands, of which only 200 are inhabited. Most of the inhabited islands are covered by lush tropical vegetation and palm trees, while the numerous uninhabited islands, some of which are mere sand spits or coral tips, are covered in shrubs. Each island is surrounded by a reef enclosing a shallow lagoon. Hundreds of these islands together with other coral growth form an atoll, surrounding a lagoon. All the islands are low-lying, none more than 2m (7ft) above sea level. The majority of the indigenous population does not mix with the tourist visitors, with the exception of those involved with tourism in the resorts and Malé.
GOVERNMENT: Republic since 1965. Gained independence from the UK in 1965. **Head of State and Government:** President Maumoon Abdul Gayoom since 1978.
LANGUAGE: The national language is Dhivehi. English is widely used as a business language in government offices and the commercial sector. Other languages are widely used within tourist areas.
RELIGION: The indigenous population is almost entirely Sunni Muslim.
TIME: GMT + 5.
ELECTRICITY: 230 volts AC, 50Hz. Round-pin plugs are used, although square-pin plugs are now becoming more common.
COMMUNICATIONS: Telephone: IDD is available. Country code: 960. Outgoing international code: 00. **Mobile telephone:** GSM 900 network operated by the Maldives Telecommunications Company, *DhiMobile* (website: www.dhiraagu.com.mv). Handsets can by hired by the day. **Fax:** Services are available in Malé and the resorts. **Internet:** The Internet can be accessed from most areas of the Maldives. Malé, the capital, has an Internet cafe and almost all resorts facilitate the sending and receiving of e-mails. The islands' ISP is *Dhivehi* (see above). **Telegram:** Telecommunications in the Maldives are good – telegram services are available to and from anywhere in the world from *Dhivehi* in Malé and the resorts. **Post:** Airmail to Western Europe takes about one week. Post office hours: Sat-Thurs 0730-1330 and 1600-1750. **Press:** *The Maldives News Bulletin* is published weekly in English. The other dailies *Aafathis Daily News*, *Haveeru Daily* and *Miadhu News* have English sections. Information about local events is widely available on all the resort islands.
Radio: BBC World Service (website: www.bbc.co.uk/worldservice) and Voice of America (website: www.voa.gov) can be received. From time to time the frequencies change and the most up-to-date can be found online.

Credit: © World Link Travel Private Ltd.

Passport/Visa

	Passport Required?	Visa Required?	Return Ticket Required?
Full British	Yes	1	Yes
Australian	Yes	1	Yes
Canadian	Yes	1	Yes
USA	Yes	1	Yes
Other EU	Yes	1	Yes
Japanese	Yes	1	Yes

Note: *Regulations and requirements may be subject to change at short notice, and you are advised to contact the appropriate diplomatic or consular authority before finalising travel arrangements. Details of these may be found at the head of this country's entry. Any numbers in the chart refer to the footnotes below.*

PASSPORTS: Passport valid for the duration of stay required by all.
VISAS: 1. Tourist visas for 30 days will be issued on arrival only and are free of charge to all visitors in possession of valid travel documents.
Note: Foreign visitors who enter the Maldives must be in possession of return or onward tickets and sufficient funds to cover duration of stay.
Types of visa and cost: Tourist visas can be extended for a minimum of three months for a fee of Rf750 (£45).
Validity: Three months to one year.
Application to: Visas are issued on arrival at the immigration desk at Maldives International Airport.
Application Requirements: (a) Valid passport and travel documents. (b) Fee. (c) Return or onward ticket. (d) Proof of sufficient funds to cover duration of stay.
Working days required: Visa extensions can be requested on arrival at Maldives International Airport, and will be issued immediately provided nationals are holding valid travel documents.

Money

Currency: Maldivian Rufiya (Rf) = 100 laari. Notes are in denominations of Rf500, 100, 50, 20, 10 and 5. Coins are in denominations of Rf2 and 1, and 50, 25, 10, 5, 2 and 1 laari.
Currency exchange: Major currencies can be exchanged at banks, tourist resort islands, hotels and leading shops. Payments in hotels can be made in most hard currencies (particularly US Dollars) in cash, travellers cheques or credit cards.
Credit & debit cards: Most major island resorts, local and souvenir shops will accept American Express, Diners Club, Eurocard, MasterCard and Visa. Arrangements vary from island to island, and it is advisable to check with your credit or debit card company for details of merchant acceptability and other facilities which may be available. There are ATMs at a few places on the Capital Island.
Travellers cheques: These are generally accepted in Sterling and US Dollars. To avoid additional exchange rate charges, travellers are advised to take travellers cheques in US Dollars.
Currency restrictions: There are no restrictions on import or export of either local or foreign currencies.
Exchange rate indicators: The following figures are included as a guide to the movement of the Maldivian Rufiya against Sterling and the US Dollar:

Date	Feb '04	May '04	Aug '04	Nov '04
£1.00=	23.29	22.86	23.58	24.23
$1.00=	12.80	12.80	12.80	12.80

Banking hours: Sun-Thurs 0800-1330.

Duty Free

The following goods may be imported into the Maldives Republic without incurring customs duty:
A reasonable amount of cigarettes, cigars and tobacco; a reasonable number of gifts.
Prohibited items: Pornographic literature; idols of worship; pork products and certain other animal products; explosives and weapons; alcoholic beverages. Drugs are strictly prohibited; the penalty for importing drugs for personal or other use is life imprisonment. Animals require a veterinary certificate.
The following may not be exported in any form: tortoise and turtle shells and products made of turtle shell (the Government has banned the killing of turtles), and black coral in whole form.

Public Holidays

2005: Jan 1 New Year's Day. **Jan 20** Hajj Day. **Jan 21** Eidal Alha (Feast of the Sacrifice). **Feb 10** Islamic New Year. **Apr 21** National Day, and Mouloud (Birth of the Prophet). **Jul 9** Huravee Day. **Jul 26-27** Independence Day. **Sep 4** Martyrs' Day. **Oct 3** Start of Ramadan. **Nov 3** Victory Day. **Nov 3-5** Kuda Eid (End of Ramadan). **Nov 11-12** Republic Day.
2006: Jan 1 New Year's Day. **Jan 10** Hajj Day. **Jan 11** Eidal Alha (Feast of the Sacrifice). **Jan 31** Islamic New Year. **Apr 11** Mouloud (Birth of the Prophet). **Apr 21** National Day. **Jul** Huravee Day. **Jul 26-27** Independence Day. **Sep** Martyrs' Day. **Sep 24** Start of Ramadan. **Oct 22-24** Kuda Eid (End of Ramadan). **Nov 3** Victory Day. **Nov 11-12** Republic Day.
Note: Muslim festivals are timed according to local sightings of various phases of the moon and the dates given above are approximations. During the lunar month of Ramadan that precedes Eid al-Fitr, Muslims fast during the day and feast at night and normal business patterns may be interrupted. Many restaurants are closed during the day and there may be restrictions on drinking in public places. Some disruption may continue into Eid al-Fitr itself, although this is generally unlikely to affect life on the resort islands. Eid al-Fitr and Eid el-Kebir may last anything from two to 10 days, depending on the region. For more information, see the *World of Islam* appendix.

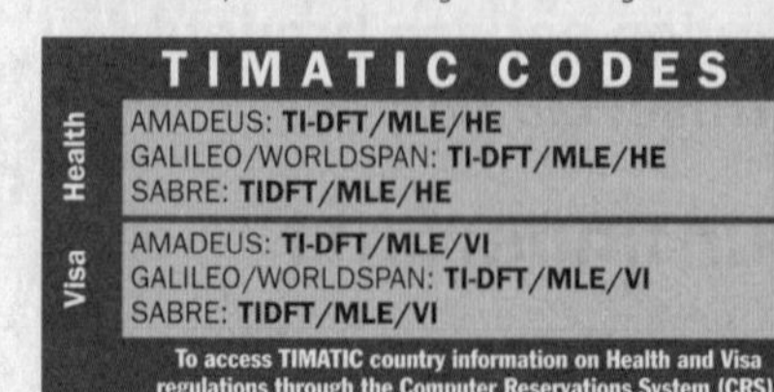
TIMATIC CODES

Health
AMADEUS: **TI-DFT/MLE/HE**
GALILEO/WORLDSPAN: **TI-DFT/MLE/HE**
SABRE: **TIDFT/MLE/HE**

Visa
AMADEUS: **TI-DFT/MLE/VI**
GALILEO/WORLDSPAN: **TI-DFT/MLE/VI**
SABRE: **TIDFT/MLE/VI**

To access TIMATIC country information on Health and Visa regulations through the Computer Reservations System (CRS), type in the appropriate command line listed above.

A B C D E F G H I J K L M N O P Q R S T U V W X Y Z

Health

	Special Precautions?	Certificate Required?
Yellow Fever	Yes	1
Cholera	Yes	2
Typhoid & Polio	3	N/A
Malaria	4	N/A

Note: *Regulations and requirements may be subject to change at short notice, and you are advised to contact your doctor well in advance of your intended date of departure. Any numbers in the chart refer to the footnotes below.*

1: A yellow fever vaccination certificate is required from travellers arriving from infected areas.
2: Following WHO guidelines issued in 1973, a cholera vaccination certificate is not a condition of entry to the Maldives.
3: Typhoid may occur.
4: Malaria is disappearing. The risk of infection is very low.
Food & drink: The water provided in the resort areas is generally safe to drink. In other areas, water of uncertain origin used for drinking, brushing teeth or making ice should have first been boiled or otherwise sterilised. Food in hotels and resorts is usually risk free, although visitors should be cautious elsewhere.
Other risks: *Hepatitis A, B,* and *E* can occur. *Tuberculosis* and *diphtheria* vaccines are sometimes advised. *Dengue fever* occurs.
Rabies may be present although there have been no reported incidences in animals or humans since 1996. For those at high risk, vaccination before arrival should be considered. If you are bitten, seek medical advice without delay. For more information, consult the *Health* appendix.
Health care: There are two hospitals on Malé, the Indhira Gandhi Memorial hospital and the ADK private hospital. First-aid facilities are available on all resort islands. A decompression chamber is accessible from most resorts in case of diving emergencies. Health insurance is recommended.

Travel - International

AIR: The national airline is *Island Aviation Services (Q2).* There are direct flights from Bahrain, Bombay, Bucharest, Colombo, Doha, Dubai, Dusseldorf, Frankfurt, Gatwick, Italy, Karachi, Kuala Lumpur, London, Madrid, Narita, Paris, Rome, Sharjah, Singapore, Trivandrum, Vienna and Zurich. Other airlines running services to Malé include *Austrian Airlines*, *Malaysia Airlines* and *Singapore Airlines*, which operate daily flights into Malé from Singapore.
Approximate flight times: From Malé to *London* is 13 hours (excluding stopover).
International airports: *Hulule International (MLE)* (Malé) (website: www.maldive.com/tour/arrival.html) on Hulule Island is 2km (1.2 miles) from Malé (travel time by boat - 15 minutes). Boats from the various island resorts meet each arriving plane to take visitors to their accommodation. There is no scheduled transfer from Hulule Island to the other islands. If an advance booking has been made, representatives of the resorts will receive tourists at the airport and will take care of all onward transport arrangements. Airport facilities include left luggage, first aid, bank, duty-free shops, snack bar, post office and restaurant.
Departure tax: None if airport tax has been paid before; otherwise, US$12.
SEA: Many cruise ships stop over at the Maldives islands as part of their itinerary. Cruise operators include *Seabourn Cruises* and *Swan Hellenic*.

Travel - Internal

AIR: Internal air services are operated by *Island Aviation Services*, linking Malé with Kaadedhdhoo, Kadhdhoo and Gan. There are also services to Hanimaadhoo in the north, although these islands will not be on most visitors' itineraries.
A number of companies operate twin-otter and float plan services around the Maldives. The transfer from the airport to the resort islands may be an optional extra on the tour. These services are also available for trips around the islands.
SEA: Visitors generally remain on their resort island for the duration of their stay, although island-hopping trips by ferries are widely available. Local charter boats are also easily available for hire. High-speed boats meet arrivals at the airport, supplied by the resort they are booked with, and boats are available for hire at the ferry counter near the jetty area. The speedboats connect the airport with Ari Atoll and some outlying islands. The indigenous inhabitants, however, live a parochial life and tend to visit only Malé, and even then irregularly.
ROAD: Travel on individual islands does not present any problem since few of them take longer than half an hour to cross on foot. In Malé, it is possible to take taxis.

Accommodation

HOTELS: There are four hotels on Malé and one on Gan; there are also a large number of guest houses on Malé, although most visitors stay on resort islands. There are no guest houses or self-catering facilities on any of the resort islands. For more information, contact the Maldives Association of Tourism Industry (MATI), 3rd Floor, Gadhamoo Buliding, Malé (tel: 326 640; fax: 326 641; e-mail: mati@dhivehinet.net.mv).
RESORTS: There are over 90 resorts which vary from extravagantly luxurious to fairly simple. Accommodation almost invariably consists of thatch-roofed coral cabanas with ensuite facilities. Most of the resorts have air-conditioned rooms with mini-bar, although some of the resorts still have fan-cooled rooms. Many resort groups have recently installed desalination plants to provide clean tap water. The resorts are fully integral communities with sport and leisure facilities including scuba diving and snorkelling, restaurants and bars and, in some cases, a shop and/or disco. A few islands have more than one resort and these generally range in size from six to 250 units, with most having 30 to 100 units. There is a shop on every resort island. Different islands tend to attract different nationalities.

Resorts & Excursions

For a long time, the Republic of Maldives was one of the best-kept secrets in the world; a beautiful string of low-lying coral islands in the Indian Ocean, a paradise for scuba divers, watersports enthusiasts and sunseekers alike. All of these attractions are still very much in evidence but, in recent years, the tourism potential of the country has been developed in the form of a large number of island resorts. Several tour operators have added the Maldives to their programmes, and since the introduction of direct flights from Europe, the islands have become an increasingly popular long-haul destination.
The Maldives consist of 26 natural atolls, approximately 1190 islands in all, most of them uninhabited. Most of the resorts are to be found in **Malé (Kaafu) Atoll**. A few are found in **Vaavu**, **Baa** and **Lhaviyani**. **Alifu (Ari) Atoll** has been declared the new Tourism Zone of the Maldives and work to upgrade and build new resorts is progressing in this area. All resorts offer night-fishing trips, superb snorkelling and windsurfing, and most have facilities for scuba diving, catamaran sailing, para-sailing, banana-boating, water-skiing and volleyball. Some offer other sporting facilities, including badminton and tennis.
This guide describes some of the major resort islands in the Maldives. Further information can be obtained from tour operators or by contacting the island resort directly.

KAAFU (MALÉ) ATOLL – NORTH

MALÉ: The capital of the Maldives, Malé, is situated close to the airport on the southern point of the North Malé Atoll. Although accommodation is available, very few foreign visitors stay in the capital; even those doing business normally stay in one of the nearby resort islands and travel to Malé by boat. The capital has several shops which sell examples of local handicrafts and imported goods. Other attractions include the *Mulee-aage*, a former palace; **National Museum**, located in the Sultan's Park with a superb collection of artefacts including Sultanese thrones and palanquins; the fish and vegetable markets; the beautiful 17th-century *Hukuru* (or **Friday Mosque**); and the **Islamic Centre**, with its magnificent golden dome. There are over 20 other mosques scattered around Malé.
Baros: Covering a land area of 60,680 sq m (653,160 sq ft) and with a beach length of 1024m (3360ft), this oval-shaped island is located approximately one hour by boat from the airport. One side of the island is full of corals, within 3 to 6m (10 to 20ft) of the shallow beach, perfect for snorkelling and diving lessons, whilst the other side is a superb beach ideal for swimming and water-skiing.
Bandos: East of Baros is the island of Bandos, one of the larger resorts whose accommodation consists of well-furnished beach bungalows with a view of the beach. There is a particularly good diving school; one of the attractions is a dive down to the aptly-named **Shark Point**.
Hudhuveli: Situated on the east side of the North Malé Atoll, Hudhuveli is, like Bandos and Vaadhu, operated by Deen's Orchid Agency. It is a modern beach resort with single-unit bungalows with straw roofing and freshwater showers.
Ihuru: This small island is exceedingly beautiful and much photographed. The accommodation consists of simple bungalows.
Kurumba: A tiny island covering an area of half a square mile, Kurumba is 15 minutes by boat from the airport and 10 minutes from Malé. There are conference facilities, swimming pools, gymnasia and jacuzzis, as well as five restaurants. Most watersports can be arranged, including scuba diving; the colourful fish in the lagoon will eat out of your hand.
Nakatchafushi: Situated on the west side of the North Malé Atoll and boasting the country's largest lagoon, Nakatchafushi is perhaps one of the most photographed of all the islands. Located on the western side of the Malé Atoll, it is 24km (15 miles) from the airport (travel time - approximately 90 minutes). The lagoon is perfect for watersports and a long strip of sand at the western end of the island is a haven for beachcombers. There is also a swimming pool.
Full Moon (Furana): This resort can be reached in 20 minutes from the airport. The resort's deep lagoon makes it a favourite base for visiting yachts. It also boasts a gymnasium, a business centre and five restaurants.
Giraavaru: The island of Giraavaru lies 11km (7 miles) west of the airport. It can be reached by speed boat (travel time - 15 minutes) or by normal transfer boat (travel time - 45 minutes). The well-appointed rooms face either a tropical garden or have a view of the Indian Ocean.
Reethi Rah: An untouched and beautiful island on the northwest of the North Malé Atoll. Thatched bungalows and 10 water bungalows built on stilts over the lagoon are influenced by local architectural styles without missing any of the modern comforts.
Makunudhoo: This island is reached by a two-hour voyage from the airport. It is one of the most expensive resorts and one that is renowned for its food. The Maldivian-run island probably provides the best anchorage of any resort and always has yachts for charter. It is protected on all sides by a beautiful lagoon. The accommodation consists of individual thatched bungalows situated in coconut groves leading down to the beach.
Kanifinolhu (Kani): The island of Kanifinolhu (Kani) is on the eastern edge of the North Malé Atoll. The seas around the island boast some of the best inside reefs in the country, and the protection provided by the external reef makes diving possible even in the roughest conditions. The style of the accommodation is influenced by local and oriental design and some rooms have air conditioning. The island has a desalination plant for fresh water.
Other resorts: The resorts of **Farukolhufushi** (**Club Med**) and **Thulhaagiri** have superb facilities for watersports. Both have a swimming pool and Thulhaagiri has one windsurfing board for every twin-bedded room. Club Med has a qualified team organising sport and leisure activities during the day and in the evening. **Summer Island Village** offers 93 air-conditioned rooms in an idyllic tropical setting. Other highly regarded North Malé resorts are **Boduhithi** and the neighbouring **Kudahithi** and, closer to the airport, **Lhohifushi**, which has a beautiful lagoon and a wide range of watersport facilities. Kudahithi, one of the most expensive resorts in the Maldives, has only six units - excellent for small, private groups.

KAAFU (MALÉ) ATOLL – SOUTH

Still in the Malé (Kaafu) Atoll, but to the south of the airport, are a further score of resorts. Notable among these are **Biyadhoo** and **Villivaru** which are 33km (21 miles) from the airport. Both are owned and managed by the Taj Group from India.
Coco Island: The nearby Coco Island has only eight two-storey thatched huts, all of which are beautifully furnished. Private groups can rent the entire resort.
Veligandu Huraa (Palm Tree Island) and Dhigufinolhu: To the east of Coco Island, these 'twin' islands are connected by a causeway across the lagoon. The latter is the livlier of the two, with more rooms and more in the way of entertainment: Veligandu Huraa has individual bungalows and a more intimate atmosphere. They are only a gentle stroll away from each other should one feel the need for a change of mood.
Kadooma: South of Coco Island is Kandooma, where flowering shrubs surround chalet-style accommodation. Trips can be arranged to the nearby fishing village.
Bodufinolhu (Fun Island): Located on the south eastern reef of the South Malé Atoll, this island is ringed with a massive lagoon and connected to two uninhabited islets which can be reached on foot at low tide. All rooms are on the beachfront with en suite bathrooms, air conditioning, IDD telephones and hot and cold desalinated water.
Embudu Village: Located 11km (7 miles) from the airport in South Malé Atoll, this resort offers 36 non-air-conditioned bungalows, 72 air-conditioned bungalows and 16 deluxe bungalows built over the lagoon. It boasts a house reef as well as two wrecks, caves and drop offs.
Vaadhu: This diving paradise, on the north tip of the South Malé Atoll and about 45 minutes by taxi boat and 20 minutes by speedboat from the airport, has a fully-equipped diving school. There are 31 cabana-style rooms on this island whose features include freshwater showers, and which reflect the high level of capital investment which has been made in the resort.

OTHER ATOLLS

Most of the other resorts are to be found in the North and South Malé Atolls, but there are also several others, most in the northern island groups (see map).

ALIFU (ARI) ATOLL: Resorts in the Alifu (Ari) Atoll, which is to the west of Malé with 26 resorts, include **Kuramathi**, a relatively large island which has first-class facilities and offers an excellent beach, superb diving, windsurfing, water-skiing, parasailing and night fishing and has three resorts. **Aribeach** is a 121-room resort offering standard and superior accommodation with hot and cold fresh water, air conditioning and a superb range of scuba diving and watersport facilities. **Nika Island** is a small, away-from-it-all, upmarket, 25-room resort offering clients some of the most comfortable boats in the Maldives. **Fesdu** is situated in the heart of the atoll rather than on the periphery. Accommodation consists of 50 thatched round-houses, all of which are close to the beach. **Angaga**, also in Ari Atoll, is small and impressively constructed in traditional Maldivian style and with air-conditioned rooms and fresh hot and cold water. Among other resorts are **Bathala**, **Ellaidoo**, **Gangehi**, **Halaveli**, **Maayaafushi**, **Machchafushi** and **Madoogali**. Several others are under construction or have recently opened and there are now 23 resorts in the Ari Atoll.
BAA ATOLL: The Baa Atoll is about 130km (80 miles) northwest of the capital, one of the few places where traditional arts and crafts are still practised, and now home to five resorts. The atoll's coral reefs are in pristine condition and are famous for the large number of mantas and reef sharks visiting during the southwest monsoon (May to July). The resorts of **Reethi Beach** and **Coco Palm** are both 5-star, each with over 100 rooms divided into three categories of luxurious villas. There are five restaurants, a fully equipped gym and even squash and tennis courts. Unlike other islands, Baa has its own in-house doctor. Transfer is a 30-minute journey by sea plane or helicopter from the airport. The **Soneva Fushi** resort, situated on Kunfunadhoo Island, has 62 villas, all scattered along the beach front on both sides of the island. It is situated 121km (75 miles) north of Malé airport (travel time – 25 to 30 minutes by *Hummingbird Island Airways*). Soneva Fushi has two main restaurants, both offering interior and exterior dining with local and international cuisine. The atoll's other resort is **Royal Island**, which has facilities for a wide range of watersports, a health spa and a professional dive school.
ELSEWHERE: To the north of the North Kaafu Atoll is **Lhaviani Atoll** with the fairly simple 250-bungalow **Kuredhdhoo** resort, essentially a spot for the besotted diver. Immediately south of the South Kaafu Atoll is the **Vaavu Atoll**, with some of the best diving in the entire archipelago. A well established, long-popular resort, especially among visiting Italians, is the 70-bungalow **Alimatha**.
Most tourism is in the northern atolls, but **Seenu**, the southernmost atoll of the archipelago (situated south of the equator), is known to many as the site of a former RAF staging post in **Gan**. It provides tourist accommodation at the Ocean Reef Club. There is a regular, heavily booked domestic flight between Malé and Gan.

Sport & Activities

Watersports: Exceptional and easily accessible underwater life makes the Maldives one of the world's top **diving** and **snorkelling** destinations. All of the resorts have professional dive schools with fully qualified multilingual instructors offering a range of courses, from beginners to full PADI certification. Basic diving equipment is provided in all resorts and some also rent out underwater cameras. Dive schools organise daily dive boat trips to sites around the islands throughout the year. Night dives and special trips for more experienced divers are also available. Most of the resorts also offer reef sightseeing trips on glass-bottomed boats. Below is a selection of the best dive sites in the Maldives:
Maldives Victory Wreck: The wreck of the Maldives Victory (which sank in 1981) lies on the western side of Hulule island at a depth of 35m (115ft). Due to strong currents, this dive is for experienced divers only.
Mushimasmingili Thila (*Shark Thila*): Located in the northern section of the Ari Atoll, close to the islands of Fesdu, Halaveli, Ellaidhu and Maayafushi. Renowned for its abundance in fish, notably grey reef shark, giant snappers and tropical reef fish.
Guraidhoo Corner: Near the islands of Losfushi, Guraidhoo and Kandooma, this reef lies on the east side of the South Malé Atoll. Powerful vertical currents make this suitable for experienced divers only. The reef is particularly known for its large fish, including grey reef sharks, eagle rays, sailfish and large snappers.
Kuda Rah Thila (*Broken Rock*): Located in the southernmost corner of the Ari Atoll, close to the islands of Dhangethi and Dhigurah. Good for less experienced divers as the currents are fairly weak.
Banana Reef: Located on the eastern side of the North Malé Atoll, near the islands of Fullmoon Island, Farukolh, Fushi and Kurumba. Strong currents make for an exceptionally abundant marine life, with reef sharks, bannerfish and oriental sweetlips all present. The large lagoons surrounding most of the islands are ideal for **windsurfing**, a sport extensively catered for in all resorts (with windsurfing schools available in most of them).
Surfing has recently become popular and there are numerous resorts on the atoll edges that have good waves, notably those located in the north of the South Malé atolls. Many resorts offer regular **boat trips** to surf breaks. The best time for surfing is during the northeast monsoon (November to April). A list of the best surfing spots is available from the Maldives Tourism Promotion Board (see *Contact Addresses* section). Most resorts also have **water-skiing** facilities and catamarans for hire. Most of the larger resorts also offer facilities and courses for **parasailing**. In order to allow visitors to see more than one of the Maldives' many islands, several types of **sailing** cruises are available (including diving safaris or relaxing cruises through the atolls). Some boats offer luxury accommodation and all modern amenities, while others offer more basic facilities. Further details can be obtained from the Maldives Tourism Promotion Board (see *Contact Addresses* section).
Note: Visitors should note that the Maldives adhere to a strict reef and marine conservation policy and that severe penalties may be imposed for disrespecting the environment (see also 'Prohibited Items' in the *Duty-Free* section).
Fishing: For the people of the Maldives, fishing has been a lifeline and, with over 99 per cent of the Maldives' total area consisting of water, the country has some of the world's best fishing grounds. Many resorts offer fishing trips on modern speedboats equipped for big game fishing. Night fishing for groupers, snappers, squirrelfish or barracuda is particularly popular. Fishing trips will usually end with a barbecue at the resort with the day's catch being cooked and eaten.
Note: As a conservation measure, sport fishing is confined to the tag and release method. The use of harpoon guns and hunting of marine mammals such as whales and dolphins and large fish such as the whale shark is strictly prohibited. The fishing and collection of the following is also prohibited: turtle, Napolean wrasse, berried and small lobster, conch, giant clam and black coral.
Excursions: Different types of excursions are available. **Island-hopping tours** usually last for a full or half day and frequently combine a visit to a fishing village with a trip to an uninhabited island (where often a beach barbecue will be served). Traditional boats (*dhoni*) or speedboats can be hired privately. There are options for spending a day and night alone on an uninhabited island. **Aerial excursions** usually combine aerial sightseeing with diving. **Photo flights** are also possible. Further details can be obtained from the Maldives Tourism Promotion Board (see *Contact Addresses* section).
Other: Some resorts have facilities for sports such as **tennis**, **football**, **volleyball** and **badminton**.

Social Profile

FOOD & DRINK: Malé, the capital, has a few simple restaurants which serve local and international food. On the other islands, there are a few restaurants in addition to those run by the resorts. Cuisine is international, with all foodstuffs other than seafood imported. The fish is magnificent. Curries and oriental buffets are widely available.
There is a good range of alcoholic and non-alcoholic drink available at the resorts, reflecting the demands of the visitors. There are a few local cocktails, including *The Maldive Lady*, a powerful and delicious concoction, whose composition varies from bar to bar and island to island.
Note: All bars are situated in tourist resorts (no alcohol is available on Malé). All accept cash, but normally add orders onto the total bill. Locals do not drink at all. During the month of Ramadan (see *Public Holidays*), visitors are not allowed to drink alcohol in public except in the tourist resorts.
NIGHTLIFE: There is little or no organised nightlife, although most resorts have informal discos around the bar areas, sometimes featuring live bands playing either traditional or Western music. Beach parties and barbecues are also popular. On some evenings, many resorts have cultural shows and some show videos.
SHOPPING: Local purchases include sea shells (only when bought in official shops; they may not be removed from the beach or from the sea), lacquered wooden boxes and reed mats. Jewellery to purchase includes gold, silver, coral, mother-of-pearl and turtle-shell items. However, there are strict prohibitions against the export of coral and turtle-shell. **Shopping hours:** Sat-Thurs 0830-2300, Fri 1330-2300. Shops officially shut for 15 minutes five times a day in deference to Muslim prayer times; however, this rule is not always strictly adhered to in the tourist areas away from the capital.
SPECIAL EVENTS: For further details on special events and festivals in the Maldives, contact the Maldives Tourism Promotion Board (see *Contact Addresses* section). The following is a selection of special events occurring in the Maldives in 2005:
Jan 1 *New Year Celebrations*. **Jan 21** *Eid al Adha* (Feast of the Sacrifice). **Jul 26-27** *Independence Day Theme Floats* (celebrations with themed floats). **Sep 27** *Tourism Day*. **Nov 4-6** *Kuda Eid* (End of Ramadan).
SOCIAL CONVENTIONS: Dress is informal, but locals who are Muslim will be offended by nudity or scanty clothing in public places, and the Government rigidly enforces these standards. Bikinis and other scanty beachwear are not acceptable in Malé or on any other inhabited island. When entering a mosque, the legs and the body, but not the neck and the face, should be covered. Handshaking is the most common form of greeting. The indigenous population not involved in the tourist trade lives in isolated island communities maintaining almost total privacy. A large number of locals smoke, but smoking and eating during Ramadan is discouraged. **Tipping:** This is officially discouraged.

Business Profile

ECONOMY: Small quantities of cereals, fruit and vegetables are grown on the little fertile land available on the islands. Fishing is far more important: tuna fishing accounts for half of the Maldives' export earnings. The industrial sector has grown substantially since 1980 as a result of major infrastructure investment in desalination plants, refurbished accommodation, generators and air conditioning. Much of this was originally designed for use by the tourism industry, which has also grown rapidly following the decline of shipping, and now accounts for almost one quarter of GDP. Otherwise, there is some light industrial activity, including fish-canning, textiles and boat building, and a small financial services sector which has recently come under scrutiny (along with several dozen other small economies offering 'offshore' services). In general, the islands' economic development has been constrained by their relative isolation and the small size of the domestic market. Hopes that the Maldives might become an oil producer were dashed when a 10-year exploration programme failed to locate deposits in the islands' territorial waters. The Maldives is a member of the Asian Development Bank and the Colombo Plan.
BUSINESS: Since the islands import almost everything, business potential is high, but only on Malé. Most business takes place during the morning. An informal attitude prevails. Appointments should be made well in advance. For business meetings, men normally wear a shirt and tie and a lightweight or tropical suit. Women wear a lightweight suit or equivalent. Handshaking is the customary form of greeting. **Office hours:** Sun-Thurs 0730-1430. Friday and Saturday are official rest days.
COMMERCIAL INFORMATION: The following organisation can offer advice: State Trading Organisation, STO Building, 7 Haveeree Higun, Malé 20-02 (tel: 323 279; fax: 325 218; e-mail: sto@dhivehinet.net.mv).
CONFERENCES/CONVENTIONS: For further information, contact Kurumba Village, Universal Enterprises Ltd, 38 Orchid Magu, Malé (tel: 442 324; fax: 322 678 *or* 320 274); *or* Bandos Island Resort, North Malé Atoll (tel: 440 088; fax: 443 877); *or* Paradise Island, Villa Hotels, STO Trade Centre, Malé (tel: 440 011; fax: 440 022).

Climate

The Maldives have a hot tropical climate. There are two monsoons, the southwest from May to October and the northeast from November to April. Generally the southwest brings more wind and rain in June and July. The temperature rarely falls below 25°C (77°F). The best time to visit is November to Easter.
Required clothing: Lightweight cottons and linens throughout the year. Light waterproofs are advised during the rainy season.

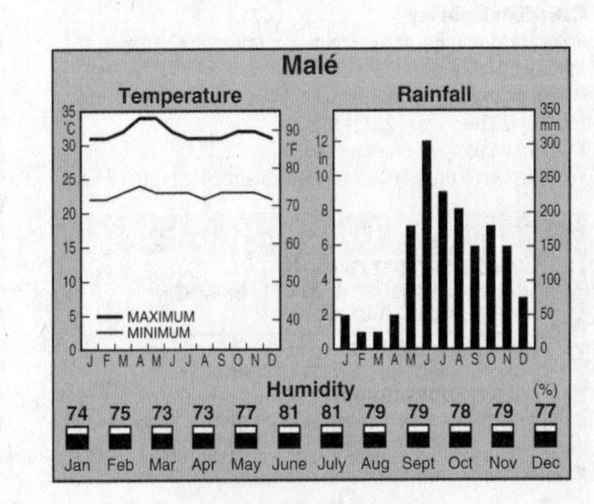

A B C D E F G H I J K L M N O P Q R S T U V W X Y Z

Mali

LATEST TRAVEL ADVICE CONTACTS

British Foreign and Commonwealth Office
Tel: (0870) 606 0290 Website: www.fco.gov.uk
US Department of State
Website: http://travel.state.gov/travel
Canadian Department of Foreign Affairs and Int'l Trade
Tel: (1 800) 267 8376 Website: www.dfait-maeci.gc.ca

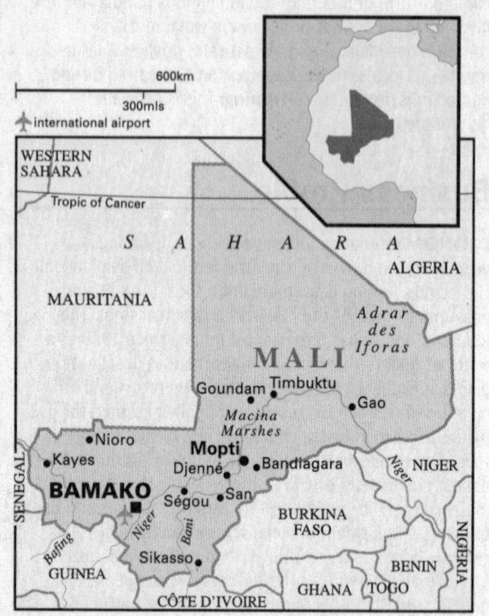

Location: Central West Africa.

Country dialling code: 223.

Office Malien du Tourisme et de l'Hôtellerie (Tourist Office of Mali)
Street address: Rue Mohamed V., Bamako, Mali
Postal address: BP 191, Bamako, Mali
Tel: 222 5673. Fax: 222 5541.
E-mail: info@malitourisme.com
Website: www.malitourisme.com

Embassy of the Republic of Mali
Avenue Molière 487, 1050 Brussels, Belgium
Tel: (2) 345 7432. Fax: (2) 344 5700.

British Embassy Liaison Office
Street address: Canadian Embassy Compound, Hippodrome, Road of Koulikoro, Bamako, Mali *Postal address*: BP 2069, Bamako, Mali
Tel: 674 9077 (mobile) *or* 277 4637. Fax: 221 8377.
E-mail: belo@afribone.net.ml

Embassy of the Republic of Mali
2130 R Street, NW, Washington, DC 20008, USA
Tel: (202) 332 2249. Fax: (202) 332 6603.
E-mail: infos@maliembassy.us
Website: www.maliembassy.us

Embassy of the United States of America
Street address: 3 rue de Rochester NY et rue Mohamed V, Bamako, Mali
Postal address: BP 34, Bamako, Mali
Tel: 222 5663 *or* 222 5470 *or* 222 3678. Fax: 222 3712.
E-mail: ConsularBamako@state.gov (consular section).
Website: www.usa.org.ml

Embassy of the Republic of Mali
50 Goulburn Avenue, Ottawa, Ontario K1N 8C8, Canada
Tel: (613) 232 1501. Fax: (613) 232 7429.
E-mail: Ambassadedumali@rogers.com
Website: www.ambamalicanada.org
Consulate in: Toronto (tel: (416) 489 4849).

Canadian Embassy
Street address: Route de Koulikoro, Immeuble Séméga, Bamako, Mali
Postal address: BP 198, Bamako, Mali
Tel: 221 2236. Fax: 221 4362.
E-mail: bmako@dfait-maeci.gc.ca
Website: www.dfait-maeci.gc.ca/africa/mali-contact-en.asp

TIMATIC CODES

Health
AMADEUS: **TI-DFT/BKO/HE**
GALILEO/WORLDSPAN: **TI-DFT/BKO/HE**
SABRE: **TIDFT/BKO/HE**

Visa
AMADEUS: **TI-DFT/BKO/VI**
GALILEO/WORLDSPAN: **TI-DFT/BKO/VI**
SABRE: **TIDFT/BKO/VI**

To access TIMATIC country information on Health and Visa regulations through the Computer Reservations System (CRS), type in the appropriate command line listed above.

General Information

AREA: 1,240,192 sq km (478,841 sq miles).
POPULATION: 12,623,000 (official estimate 2002).
POPULATION DENSITY: 10.2 per sq km.
CAPITAL: Bamako. **Population:** 1,016,167 (1998).
GEOGRAPHY: Mali is a landlocked republic, sharing borders with Mauritania, Algeria, Burkina Faso, Côte d'Ivoire, Guinea, Niger and Senegal. It is a vast land of flat plains fed by two major rivers, the Senegal on its western edge and the great River Niger. On its journey north the Niger converges with the River Bani, and forms a rich inland delta, the marshlands of the Macina, stretching for some 450km (280 miles) along the river's length, in some places 200km (124 miles) wide. The central part of the country is arid grazing land, called the Sahel, which has suffered great drought. At Timbuktu, the Niger reaches the desert and here it turns first to the east, then to the southeast at Bourem, where it heads for the ocean. In the desert, near the Algerian and Niger borders in the northeast, the Adrar des Iforas massif rises 800m (2625ft). The north of the country is true desert except for the few oases along the ancient trans-Saharan camel routes. Tuaregs still live around these oases and camel routes. Further south live the Peulh cattle-raising nomads. The majority of the population lives in the savannah region in the south. The peoples of this region comprise Songhai, Malinke, Senoufou, Dogon and the Bambara (the largest ethnic group).
GOVERNMENT: Republic. Gained independence from France in 1960. **Head of State:** President Amadou Toumani Touré since 2002. **Head of Government:** Prime Minister Ousmane Issoufi Maïga since 2004.
LANGUAGE: The official language is French. There are a number of local languages.
RELIGION: Muslim (80 per cent), with Animist (18 per cent) and Christian (under 2 per cent) minorities.
TIME: GMT.
ELECTRICITY: 220 volts AC, 50Hz in Bamako. Larger towns in Mali have their own locally-generated supply.
COMMUNICATIONS: Telephone: Limited IDD service. Country code: 223. Outgoing international calls must be made via the international operator. These are expensive and collect calls cannot be made from Mali. **Mobile telephone:** GSM 900 network exists. Operators are *Ikatel* (website: www.ikatel.net) and *Malitel-SA* (website: www.malitel.com). **Internet:** Main ISPs include private companies *Cefib* (website: www.cefib.com), *Datatech* (website: www.datatech.toolnet.org) and *Spider* (website: www.spider.toolnet.org). There is an Internet cafe in Bamako. **Post:** International post is limited to main towns and the central post office. Airmail to Europe takes approximately two weeks. For further details, contact the Embassy. **Press:** There are no English-language newspapers. The other dailies, including *Les Echos*, *L'Essor* (website: www.essor.gov.ml), *Info Matin* and *Le Républicain*, are published in French.
Radio: BBC World Service (website: www.bbc.co.uk/worldservice) and Voice of America (website: www.voa.gov) can be received. From time to time the frequencies change and the most up-to-date can be found online.

Passport/Visa

	Passport Required?	Visa Required?	Return Ticket Required?
Full British	Yes	Yes	Yes
Australian	Yes	Yes	Yes
Canadian	Yes	Yes	Yes
USA	Yes	Yes	Yes
Other EU	Yes	Yes	Yes
Japanese	Yes	Yes	Yes

Note: *Regulations and requirements may be subject to change at short notice, and you are advised to contact the appropriate diplomatic or consular authority before finalising travel arrangements. Details of these may be found at the head of this country's entry. Any numbers in the chart refer to the footnotes below.*

PASSPORTS: Passport valid for at least six months from date of entry required by all except the following in possession of a valid ID card:
(a) nationals of ECOWAS countries;
(b) nationals of Algeria, Andorra, Cameroon, Chad, The Gambia, Monaco, Morocco and Tunisia.
VISAS: Required by all except the following for stays of up to three months:
(a) nationals of the countries referred to under passport exemptions above;
(b) transit passengers continuing their journey by the same or first connecting aircraft within 24 hours provided holding onward or return documentation and not leaving the airport.
Types of visa and cost: *Tourist*, *Business* and *Transit*: *single entry*: US$80 (three months); *multiple entry*: US$110 (three months); US$200 (six months); US$370 (one year).
Validity: One month from the date of entry, although visas can be extended in Mali, either in Bamako at the Immigration Service or at any police station. Visas may be obtained up to three months in advance of travelling to Mali.
Application to: Consulate (or Consular section at Embassy); see *Contact Addresses* section.
Application requirements: (a) Valid passport. (b) Two application forms (must be completed in block capitals and returned to the consulate with several photocopies of the form). (c) Two passport-size photos. (d) Stamped, self-addressed envelope for postal applications (which must be sent by registered post). (e) Fee; payable in cash, company cheque or postal order (personal cheques are not accepted). (f) Copy of airline itinerary or flight ticket(s). (g) Yellow fever certificate, if travelling from an infected area. (h) Proof of hotel reservation. *Business*: (a)-(h) and, (i) Letter of invitation from company, stating purpose of trip. *Transit*: (a)-(h) and, (i) Copies of onward tickets and visas to further destinations.
Working days required: Five. Visas can be issued more quickly (in three days) for an additional fee of US$10.
Temporary residence: Enquire at Embassy.

Money

Currency: CFA (*Communauté Financiaire Africaine*) Franc (CFAfr) = 100 centimes. Notes are in denominations of CFAfr10,000, 5000, 2000 and 1000. Coins are in denominations of CFAfr500, 200, 250, 100, 50, 25, 10 and 5. Mali is part of the French Monetary Area. Only currency issued by the *Banque des Etats de l'Afrique de l'Ouest* (Bank of West African States) is valid; currency issued by the *Banque des Etats de l'Afrique Centrale* (Bank of Central African States) is not. The CFA Franc is tied to the Euro.
Currency exchange: Possible at main banks in Bamako, but exchange rates are often out of date.
Credit & debit cards: Diners Club, MasterCard and Visa are accepted in two hotels in Bamako. Cash advances on credit cards are available at only one bank in Mali, the BMCD Bank in Bamako, and only with a Visa credit card. Check with your credit or debit card company for details of merchant acceptability and other services which may be available.
Travellers cheques: Can be exchanged at banks. To avoid additional exchange rate charges, travellers are advised to take travellers cheques in US Dollars or Euros.
Currency restrictions: The import and export of local currency is unlimited. The import and export of foreign currency is unlimited provided amounts exceeding CFAfr25,000 are declared.
Exchange rate indicators: The following figures are included as a guide to the movements of the CFA Franc against Sterling and the US Dollar:

Date	Feb '04	May '04	Aug '04	Nov '04
$1.00=	961.13	983.76	978.35	936.79
£1.00=	528.01	550.79	531.03	494.69

Banking hours: Mon-Thurs 0730-1200 and 1315-1500, Fri 0730-1230.

Duty Free

The following items may be imported into Mali without incurring customs duty:
1000 cigarettes or 250 cigars or 2kg of tobacco; two bottles of alcoholic beverage; a reasonable amount of perfume for personal use.
Note: (a) Cameras and films must be declared. An import permit is needed for sporting guns. Plants, except fruit and vegetables, need a certificate. (b) Authorisation from the National Museum in Bamako must be obtained when exporting certain Malian archaeological objects, particularly those from the Niger River Valley.

Public Holidays

2005: Jan 1 New Year's Day. **Jan 20** Armed Forces Day. **Jan 21** Tabaski (Feast of the Sacrifice). **Mar 26** Day of Democracy. **Mar 28** Easter Monday. **Apr 21** Mawloud (Prophet's Birthday). **May 1** Labour Day. **May 25** Africa Day. **Sep 22** Independence Day. **Nov 3-5** Korité (End of Ramadan). **Dec 25** Christmas Day.
2006: Jan 1 New Year's Day. **Jan 10** Tabaski (Feast of the Sacrifice). **Jan 20** Armed Forces Day. **Mar 26** Day of Democracy. **Apr 11** Mawloud (Prophet's Birthday). **Apr 17** Easter Monday. **May 1** Labour Day. **May 25** Africa Day. **Sep 22** Independence Day. **Oct 22-24** Korité (End of Ramadan). **Dec 25** Christmas Day.
Note: Muslim festivals are timed according to local sightings of various phases of the moon and the dates given above are approximations. During the lunar month of Ramadan that precedes Korité (Eid al-Fitr), Muslims fast during the day and feast at night and normal business patterns may be interrupted. Many restaurants are closed during the day and there may be restrictions on smoking and drinking. Some disruption may continue into Korité itself. Korité and Tabaski (Eid al-Adha) may last anything from two to 10 days, depending on the region. For more information, see the *World of Islam* appendix.

A B C D E F G H I J K L M N O P Q R S T U V W X Y Z

Health

	Special Precautions?	Certificate Required?
Yellow Fever	Yes	1
Cholera	Yes	2
Typhoid & Polio	3	N/A
Malaria	4	N/A

Note: *Regulations and requirements may be subject to change at short notice, and you are advised to contact your doctor well in advance of your intended date of departure. Any numbers in the chart refer to the footnotes below.*

1: A yellow fever vaccination certificate is required by all travellers over one year of age arriving from all countries.
2: Following WHO guidelines issued in 1973, a cholera vaccination certificate is not a condition of entry to Mali. However, cholera is a serious risk in this country and precautions are essential. There was, for instance, a recent outbreak in the Segou district, central Mali. Up-to-date advice should be sought before deciding whether these precautions should include vaccination, as medical opinion is divided over its effectiveness; see the *Health* appendix for further information.
3: Typhoid is widespread and appropriate precautions should be taken. Polio is endemic.
4: Malaria, mainly in the malignant *falciparum* form, is present all year throughout the country. Resistance to chloroquine and sulfadoxine-pyrimethamine has been reported. The recommended prophylaxis is mefloquine.
Food & drink: All water should be regarded as being potentially contaminated. Water used for drinking, brushing teeth or making ice should have first been boiled or otherwise sterilised. Milk is unpasteurised and should be boiled. Powdered or tinned milk is available and is advised, but make sure that it is reconstituted with pure water. Avoid dairy products which are likely to have been made from unboiled milk. Only eat well-cooked meat and fish, preferably served hot. Pork, salad and mayonnaise may carry increased risk. Vegetables should be cooked and fruit peeled.
Other risks: *Bilharzia* (schistosomiasis) is present. Avoid swimming and paddling in fresh water; swimming pools which are well chlorinated and maintained are safe. The following health risks have been reported from the area: many *viral diseases* (transmitted by mosquitoes, ticks and sandflies), *meningococcal meningitis* (particularly in the savannah areas and during the dry season), *dysenteries, diarrhoeal diseases, diphtheria, tuberculosis, hepatitis A, B* and *E* (all widespread) and *trachoma*.
Rabies is also present. For those at high risk, vaccination before arrival should be considered. If you are bitten, seek medical advice without delay. For more information, consult the *Health* appendix.
Health care: Medical facilities are very limited and inadequate for dealing with emergencies. Health insurance (including adequate medical evacuation) is therefore essential. Many medicines are unavailable, and doctors and hospitals expect immediate cash payment for health care services.

Travel - International

Note: All travel to the north of Timbuktu, the western border area with Mauritania, and the eastern border with Niger, is advised against.
AIR: Mali's national airline is *Air Mali (L9)*. Mali also has a share in the multinational airline, *Air Afrique (RK)*. Airlines operating between Mali and Europe include *Aeroflot* and *Air France*. *Air Afrique* also operates flights between Mali and New York via Dakar (Senegal) or Abidjan (Côte d'Ivoire). There are three weekly flights between Mali and Niger.
Approximate flight times: From Bamako to *London* is 11 hours (including stopover in Brussels or Paris).
International airports: *Bamako (BKO)* is 15km (9 miles) from the city (travel time - 20 minutes). A bus service into the city is available.
Departure tax: CFAfr10,000; for destinations in Africa CFAfr8000. Children under two years are exempt.
RAIL: There is a twice-weekly service from Bamako to Dakar (Senegal) which has air conditioning, sleeper facilities and restaurant cars (travel time - 35 hours). It will also carry cars. There are also plans to extend rail links into Guinea.
ROAD: The best road connections are from Côte d'Ivoire and Burkina Faso. There are also road links with Senegal, Guinea, Niger and Mauritania. The all-weather road follows the Niger as far as Niamey (Niger). Travel via the Algerian border is currently considered dangerous and not recommended. **Bus:** Services operate from Kankan (Guinea) to Bamako, as well as from Bobo Dioulasso (Burkina Faso) to Ségou and Mopti, and Niamey (Niger) to Gao. From Côte d'Ivoire, there are three buses per week (travel time - at least 36 hours). From Niger, the national bus line SNTN operates three weekly buses to Mali.

Travel - Internal

AIR: Some domestic flights are provided by *Air Mali*. Light aircraft can also be chartered from the *Société des Transports Aériens (STA)*.
Departure tax: CFAfr2500.
RIVER: Between July and December, there are weekly services between Bamako and Gao via Timbuktu along the River Niger. However, because of drought in the Sahel desert, services are sometimes suspended. The journey is approximately 1300km (800 miles) and takes five or six days. Between December and March, travel is only possible between Mopti and Gao. Food is available on the boats and first-class cabins can be booked in advance. Motorised and non-motorised *pirogues* and *pinasses* (types of river boat) are available for hire between Timbuktu and Mopti. Since the completion of the Manantali Dam in 1988, work has continued to improve the navigability of the River Senegal.
RAIL: There is a daily service from Bamako to Kayes, enroute to Dakar on the Senegal coast. There are two trains, one Malian and one Senegalese - the Senegalese train is far superior, with air conditioning and buffet car. The railway line is Mali's most important method of transport, over and above the road link. There is also a daily service from Bamako to Koulikoro.
ROAD: Traffic drives on the right. Roads in Mali range from moderate to very bad. Particular care should be taken if driving in Bamako. The main road runs from Sikasso in the south to Bamako, and to Mopti and Gao. The roads from Bamako to Mopti, Douentza, Koutiala, Sikasso and Bougouni, along with a few other roads, are paved. Between Mopti and Gao, travel can be difficult during the rainy season (mid-June to mid-September) when the Niger, at its confluence with the Bani, splits into a network of channels, and floods its banks to form the marshlands of the Macina. Stops at customs and police checkpoints are frequent on major roads and driving is particularly hazardous after dark.
Bus: Services run between the main towns.
Documentation: International Driving Permit recommended, although not legally required. Insurance and a *carnet de passage* are also needed.
Note: Visitors are advised to keep to the main roads, otherwise they should travel in convoy. Caution should be exercised when travelling at night. Visitors should be aware of the recent violent incidents which have occurred in northern Mali and the Mauritanian border.
URBAN: Taxi: Collective taxis in cities are very cheap. The taxis charge a standard fare regardless of the distance travelled. Tipping is not expected.

Accommodation

HOTELS: Only Bamako has hotels that meet international standards, but other main towns have hotels of an adequate standard and some have air conditioning. Accommodation tends to be expensive and difficult to obtain at short notice - advance booking is recommended. Further information can be obtained from the *Office Malien du Tourisme et de l'Hôtellerie* (see *Contact Addresses* section).
LODGES: There are a number of *campements* in the National Park of La Boucle du Baoule. The reserve is 120km (75 miles) from Bamako.

Resorts & Excursions

BAMAKO: The capital is a modern town and the educational and cultural centre of Mali. The main places of interest are the markets, the **Botanical Gardens**, the **Musée National**, the zoo and the craft centre at the **Maison des Artisans**.
DJENNÉ: Known as the 'Jewel of the Niger', Djenné was founded in 1250. It has a beautiful mosque, the **Grande Mosquée**, and it is one of the oldest trading towns along the trans-Saharan caravan routes. **Old Djenné** is located about 5km (3 miles) from Djenné and was founded around 250BC. The town quickly developed into a market centre and important link in the trans-Saharan gold trade. In the 15th and 16th centuries, it became one of the spiritual centres for the dissemination of Islam. Nearly 2000 of its traditional houses, built on hillocks (*toguere*) and adapted to the seasonal floods, have survived. Old Djenné is today listed by UNESCO as a World Heritage Site.
MOPTI: The centre of Mali's tourist industry, Mopti is located at the confluence of the Bani and the Niger and is built on three islands joined by dykes. There is another fine mosque here. The market in the town centre, **Marché des Souvenirs**, and the area surrounding the port are also worth visiting.
BANDIAGARA: Southeast of Mopti is the Bandiagara country, peopled by the Dogons, whose ancient beliefs have remained largely untouched by Islam. Visitors should treat villagers with respect. The **Cliffs of Bandiagara** have been listed by UNESCO as a World Heritage Site. The Dogon people are believed to have been the original inhabitants of the Niger river valley and, for thousands of years, inhabited villages cut into the cliffs of the 200km- (80mile-) long Bandiagara escarpment. Although most of the Dogons have now relocated to the plains, the ancient villages on the cliffs are still standing.
TIMBUKTU: Timbuktu is a name that has passed into English vernacular as a byword for inaccessibility and remoteness. It is, however, neither of these things owing to the magnificent camel caravans (some of them comprising over 3000 animals) which arrive every year from the Taoudenni salt mines to distribute their produce throughout the Sahel. By the 15th century, Timbuktu was the centre of a lucrative trade in salt and gold, straddling the trans-Saharan caravan routes, as well as being a great centre of Islamic learning. Much of this ancient city is in decay, but it is the site of many beautiful mosques (**Djingerebur**, **Sankore** and **Sidi Yahaya** for example) and tombs, some dating back to the 14th century.
ELSEWHERE: Another ancient city which had its heyday in the 15th century is **Gao**. Gao houses the mosque of **Kankan Moussa** and the tombs of the Askia Dynasty. There are also two excellent markets. The city has recently undergone much urban development. **San** and **Ségou** are both interesting towns. The **National Park of La Boucle de Baoule** contains an array of southern Sahelian species of wildlife, including giraffe, leopard, lion, elephant, buffalo and hippo.

Sport & Activities

Trekking: A good area for trekking is the *Bandiagara* escarpment in the Dogon country, with Bandiagara, Bankass and Mopti being the main starting points for trekking trips. Guides are available and recommended; travellers should check that guides have an official identification card.

Social Profile

FOOD & DRINK: Several of the hotels have restaurant and bar facilities of international standard, serving international cuisine, and most towns have small restaurants serving local and north African dishes. Hotel restaurants are open to non-residents. A particular Malian speciality is *La Capitaine Sangha*, a kind of Nile perch served with hot chilli sauce, whole fried bananas and rice. There is a limited choice of restaurants.
Alcohol is available in bars (with very late opening hours), but since the majority is Muslim, there is a good range of fresh fruit juices. Most people tend to drink fruit juice rather than alcohol. Malian tamarind and guava juices are delicious. A traditional drink is Malian tea which should be drunk in three stages; the first is very strong ('as bitter as death'); the second is slightly sweetened ('just like life'); the third is well sugared ('as sweet as love'). Visitors to Mali may be invited to partake in this tea ritual.
NIGHTLIFE: Bamako has a good selection of nightclubs with music and dancing.
SHOPPING: Traditional crafts range from the striking masks of the Bambara, Dogon and Malinko peoples, to woodcarvings, original designs in ebony and bronze, woven cloth, and mats, gold and silver jewellery and copperware. Excellent pottery is made in the Ségou region, while Timbuktu is a good centre for iron and copper articles, including swords, daggers and traditional household utensils.
SPECIAL EVENTS: The following is a selection of special events celebrated annually in Mali:
Jan 10 *Tabaski*, nationwide. **Apr 11** *Mawloud* (Prophet's Birthday), nationwide. **Oct 22-24** *Korité* (End of Ramadan), nationwide. **Dec** *Crossing of the Cattle*, Diafarabé.
SOCIAL CONVENTIONS: Malians are hospitable people and will welcome visitors gracefully into their homes. Visitors must remember that this is a Muslim country and the religious customs and beliefs of the people should be respected. Modesty in dress, particularly for women, is essential. **Photography:** This is no longer restricted, except for military subjects. However, interpretation of what is considered off limits tends to vary. Other subjects may be considered sensitive from a cultural or religious point of view and it is advisable to obtain permission before taking photographs in Mali. **Tipping:** A 10 per cent tip is customary in restaurants and bars, but is not normal for taxi drivers. Porters receive CFAfr100 per piece of luggage.

Business Profile

ECONOMY: Mali is one of the poorest countries in the world with an average per capita annual income of about US$200. The economy is almost entirely agricultural even though less than 2 per cent of the land is cultivable. Livestock and subsistence crops such as millet, sorghum, maize and rice are raised for domestic consumption. The main cash crop is cotton, of which Mali is one of Africa's largest producers and exporters, along with groundnuts, fruit and vegetables. The Malian cotton industry, upon which one-third of the population depend for their livelihood, is in serious difficulty because of exceptionally low world prices, caused in part by subsidies provided to cotton growers in the industrialised world (in 2003, this was the subject of a major dispute at the World Trade Organisation). Local manufacturing has grown steadily, albeit from a very low level, and is mostly concerned with the processing of agricultural produce: food, drinks and tobacco are the main products. Construction materials are also produced locally. There is a small but fast-growing mining sector centred on Mali's recently discovered gold deposits. Mali is now the third-largest gold producer in Africa after South Africa and Ghana, and the growth in this sector largely accounts for the country's rapid 2002 growth rate of 9 per cent. Marble, salt and phosphates are also being exploited; there are also known reserves of iron ore and uranium. Much of the economy has been privatised and deregulated since 1997 under the supervision of the IMF with which Mali presently enjoys good relations. Mali has also been one of the main beneficiaries of the debt cancellation for the poorest countries, and it continues to rely on foreign aid and remittances from émigrés. France is Mali's major trading partner, providing a quarter of imports and taking a similar proportion of exports, followed by Côte d'Ivoire, Senegal, Germany and Switzerland. Mali is a member of ECOWAS and various other West African multinational economic organisations.

BUSINESS: The forms of address are those of France, eg Monsieur le Directeur. Lightweight or tropical suit and tie are advised for only the smartest meetings. Otherwise, a light, open-neck shirt is worn. It is essential to be able to speak French for business purposes. **Office hours:** Mon-Thurs 0730-1230 and 1300-1600, Fri 0730-1230 and 1430-1730.

COMMERCIAL INFORMATION: The following organisation can offer advice: Chambre de Commerce et d'Industrie du Mali, BP 46, place de la Liberté, Bamako (tel: 222 5036 *or* 222 9645; fax: 222 2120).

CONFERENCES/CONVENTIONS: Information can be obtained from the Ministry of Foreign Affairs (Protocol Section), Kounoulba, Bamako (tel: 225 489; fax: 228 559 *or* 225 226).

Climate

Three main seasons which vary according to latitude. Rainy season runs between June and October, diminishing further north. The cooler season (October to February) is followed by extremely hot, dry weather until June.

Required clothing: Lightweight cottons and linens are worn throughout most of the year, though warmer clothing is needed between November and February. Waterproofing is advised during the rainy season.

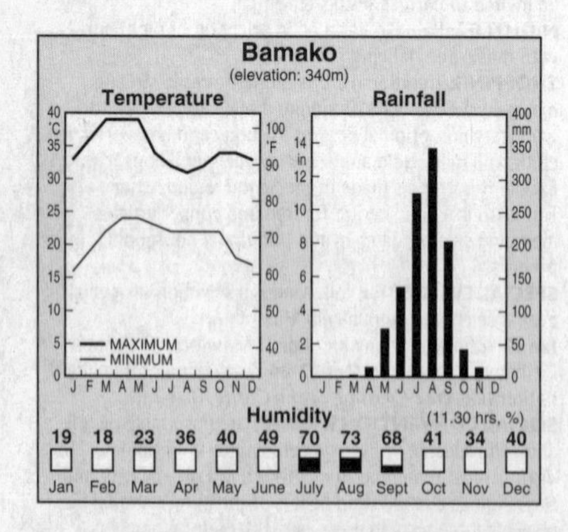

Malta

LATEST TRAVEL ADVICE CONTACTS

British Foreign and Commonwealth Office
Tel: (0870) 606 0290 Website: www.fco.gov.uk

US Department of State
Website: http://travel.state.gov/travel

Canadian Department of Foreign Affairs and Int'l Trade
Tel: (1 800) 267 8376 Website: www.dfait-maeci.gc.ca

Location: Mediterranean, south of Sicily.

Country dialling code: 356.

Malta Tourism Authority
229 Merchants Street, CMR 02, Auberge d'Italie, Malta
Tel: 2291 5000 *or* 2122 4444. Fax: 2291 5893.
E-mail: info@visitmalta.com
Website: www.visitmalta.com

Malta High Commission
Malta House, 36-38 Piccadilly, London W1J 0LE, UK
Tel: (020) 7292 4800. Fax: (020) 7734 1831/2.
E-mail: maltahighcommission.london@gov.mt
Website: www.gov.mt
Opening hours: Mon-Fri 0900-1230 and 1400-1600.

Malta Tourist Office
Unit C, Parkhouse, 14 Northfields, London SW18 1DD, UK
Tel: (020) 8877 6990. Fax: (020) 8874 9416.
E-mail: office.uk@visitmalta.com
Website: www.visitmalta.com

British High Commission
Whitehall Mansions, Ta'Xbiex Seafront, Ta'Xbiex, MSD 11, Malta
Tel: 2323 0000. Fax: 2323 2234.
E-mail: bhc@vol.net.mt
Website: www.britishhighcommission.gov.uk/malta

Embassy of Malta
2017 Connecticut Avenue, NW, Washington, DC 20008, USA
Tel: (202) 462 3611. Fax: (202) 387 5470.
E-mail: maltaembassy.washington@gov.mt
Website: www.gov.mt
Consulates in: Dallas, Detroit, Florida, Houston, Los Angeles, Minnesota, New York, Philadelphia, San Francisco, Seattle and Tennessee.

Embassy of the United States of America
Street address: 3rd Floor, Development House, St Anne Street, Floriana, Valletta VLT 01, Malta
Postal address: PO Box 535, Valletta CMR 01, Malta
Tel: 2561 4000. Fax: 2124 3229.
E-mail: usembmalta@state.gov
Website: http://usembmalta.state.gov/malta

Consulate General of Malta
10th Floor, Suite 3020, Centre Tower, Toronto, Ontario M8X 2X2, Canada
Tel: (416) 207 0922. Fax: (416) 207 0986.

Consulate of Canada
Demajo House, 103 Archbishop Street, Valletta VLT 09, Malta
Tel/Fax: 2552 3233.
E-mail: maltaconsulate.toronto@gov.mt

TIMATIC CODES

Health	AMADEUS: **TI-DFT/JIB/HE** GALILEO/WORLDSPAN: **TI-DFT/JIB/HE** SABRE: **TIDFT/JIB/HE**
Visa	AMADEUS: **TI-DFT/JIB/VI** GALILEO/WORLDSPAN: **TI-DFT/JIB/VI** SABRE: **TIDFT/JIB/VI**

To access TIMATIC country information on Health and Visa regulations through the Computer Reservations System (CRS), type in the appropriate command line listed above.

General Information

AREA: 316 sq km (122 sq miles).
POPULATION: 399,867 (2003).
POPULATION DENSITY: 1224 sq km.
CAPITAL: Valletta. **Population:** 7173 (2002).
GEOGRAPHY: The Maltese archipelago is situated in the middle of the Mediterranean, with the largest inhabited island, Malta, lying 93km (58 miles) south of Sicily and 290km (180 miles) from North Africa. Gozo and Comino are the only other inhabited islands. The landscape of all three is characterised by low hills with terraced fields. Malta has no mountains or rivers. Its coastline is indented with harbours, bays, creeks, sandy beaches and rocky coves. Gozo is connected to Malta by ferry and is more thickly vegetated, with many flat-topped hills and craggy cliffs. Comino, the smallest island, is connected to Malta and Gozo by ferry and is very sparsely populated.
GOVERNMENT: Republic. Gained independence from the UK in 1964. **Head of State:** President Fenech Adami since 2004. **Head of Government:** Prime Minister Lawrence Gonzi since 2004.
LANGUAGE: Maltese (a Semitic language) and English are the official languages. Italian is also widely spoken.
RELIGION: 91 per cent Roman Catholic.
TIME: GMT + 1 (GMT + 2 from last Sunday in March to Saturday before last Sunday in October).
ELECTRICITY: 240 volts AC, 50Hz. UK-style three-pin plug are in use.
COMMUNICATIONS: Telephone: IDD is available. Country code: 356. There are no area codes. Outgoing international code: 00. Public telephone booths are widely available. **Mobile telephone:** GSM 900 and 1800 networks exist, with extensive coverage of land and sea. Network providers include *GoMobile* (website: www.go.com.mt) and *Vodafone Malta* (website: www.vodafonemalta.com.mt). **Fax:** *Maltacom PLC* provides an international service through its offices and branches. Also available at hotels. **Internet:** ISPs include *Maltanet* (website: www.maltanet.net). There are a few Internet cafes. **Telegram:** Can be sent from *Maltacom PLC*, St Georges Road, St Julian's. **Post:** Good postal services exist within the island. **Press:** Maltese dailies include *In-Nazzjon Taghna* and *L'Orizzont*. The daily English-language newspapers published on the island are *The Malta Independent* and *The Times*. *The Malta Business Weekly*, *The Malta Independent on Sunday* and the *Sunday Times* are also available.
Radio: BBC World Service (website: www.bbc.co.uk/worldservice) and Voice of America (website: www.voa.gov) can be received. From time to time the frequencies change and the most up-to-date can be found online.

Passport/Visa

	Passport Required?	Visa Required?	Return Ticket Required?
Full British	Yes	No	Yes
Australian	Yes	No	Yes
Canadian	Yes	No	Yes
USA	Yes	No	Yes
Other EU	1	No	Yes
Japanese	Yes	No	Yes

Note: *Regulations and requirements may be subject to change at short notice, and you are advised to contact the appropriate diplomatic or consular authority before finalising travel arrangements. Details of these may be found at the head of this country's entry. Any numbers in the chart refer to the footnotes below.*

PASSPORTS: Valid passport required by all except the following:
(a) **1.** nationals of Austria, Belgium, France, Germany, Greece, Italy, Liechtenstein, Luxembourg, The Netherlands, Portugal, Slovenia, Spain and Switzerland in possession of valid national ID card who are visiting as tourists for stays of up to three months;
(b) nationals of Germany in possession of a passport that expired within the last year;
(c) nationals of Austria, Belgium, France, Luxembourg, Portugal, Spain and Switzerland in possession of a passport that expired within the last five years.
VISAS: Required by all except the following for stays of up to three months:
(a) nationals of countries referred to in the chart above;
(b) nationals of Andorra, Argentina, Bolivia, Brazil, Brunei, Bulgaria, Chile, Costa Rica, Croatia, Cyprus, Czech Republic, Denmark, El Salvador, Estonia, Finland, Guatemala, Honduras, Hong Kong (SAR), Hungary, Iceland, Ireland, Israel, Korea (Rep), Latvia, Liechtenstein, Lithuania, Malaysia, Mexico, Monaco, New Zealand, Nicaragua, Norway, Panama, Paraguay, Romania, San Marino, Singapore, Slovak Republic, Sweden, Switzerland, Uruguay, Vatican City and Venezuela;
(c) nationals of UK Overseas Territories;
(d) nationals of Macau, provided in possession of passports bearing 'Regio Administrativa Especial de Macao';

(e) transit passengers continuing their journey by the same of first connecting airport within 24 hours provided holding valid onward or return documentation and not leaving the airport.
Note: Citizens of countries who are visa-exempt must still apply for an entry or transit visa before proceeding to Malta.
Types of visa and cost: *Entry*: £23.50 (single-entry); for Algerian and Moroccan nationals: £15.50; for Libyan nationals: £11.50. *Transit*: £17.50. Multiple-entry visas for one year are issued only by the Immigration Police in Malta. Sudanese nationals en route for Libya via Malta require a transit visa and a valid residence permit for Libya.
All visa applicants, except nationals of Tunisia and Turkey (for whom there is no visa processing fee), are subject to an administrative charge of Lm4 (except nationals of Libya who must pay Lm10), even if a visa is not issued.
Note: Visitors requiring an entry visa to Malta and undertaking day trips of less than 24 hours to another country do not need to pay for another entry visa on their return to Malta.
Validity: *Single-entry visa*: one month; *Transit visa*: 24 hours. For renewal, apply to the High Commission or Embassy. For extension, apply to the Principal Immigration Officer at the Immigration Office, Police Headquarters, Floriana, Malta.
Application to: Consulate (or Consular section at Embassy or High Commission); see *Contact Addresses* section. If there is no embassy/consulate in the applicant's country of residence, the applicant must contact either an Honorary Consul or directly contact the Immigration Police in Malta.
Application requirements: (a) Valid passport with at least one blank page. (b) Application form. (c) Two recent passport-size photos. (d) Fee (payable in cash or by postal order only). (e) £3.75 is required to cover postage costs, if not collecting visa in person. These can be handed in at the High Commission or Embassy. (f) Self-addressed envelope for applications by post. (g) Other documents may be required in certain cases, including invitation from host, proof of financial means, proof of means of transport and valid health insurance.
Working days required: 15.
Temporary residence: Apply to Principal Immigration Officer, Immigration Office, Police Headquarters, Floriana, Malta.

Money

Currency: Maltese Lira (Lm) = 100 cents = 1000 mils. Notes are in denominations of Lm20, 10, 5 and 2. Coins are in denominations of Lm1, and 50, 25, 10, 5, 2 and 1 cents. A number of gold and silver coins are also minted.
Currency exchange: Money can be changed at banks, bureaux de change, some hotels, larger shops and restaurants. Automated foreign exchange machines and ATMs are available at various locations on the islands.
Credit & debit cards: American Express, Diners Club, MasterCard and Visa are accepted. Check with your credit or debit card company for details of merchant acceptability and other services which may be available.
Travellers cheques: Exchanged in the normal authorised institutions.
Currency restrictions: The import of local currency is limited to Lm1000. The export of local currency is limited to Lm1000. The import and export of foreign currency is unlimited, subject to declaration if contemplating re-export up to amount imported.
Exchange rate indicators: The following figures are included as a guide to the movements of the Maltese Lira against Sterling and the US Dollar:

Date	Feb '04	May '04	Aug '04	Nov '04
£1.00=	0.62	0.63	0.63	0.61
$1.00=	0.34	0.35	0.34	0.33

Banking hours: Mon-Fri 0830-1230 and 1430-1600, Sat 0830-1130.

Duty Free

The following items may be imported into Malta without incurring customs duty from non-EU countries:
200 cigarettes or 100 cigarillos or 50 cigars or 250g tobacco; 1l of spirits and 1l of wine; 60ml of perfume and 250ml of eau de toilette; gifts to a value not exceeding Lm50.
The following items may be imported into Malta without incurring customs duty from EU countries:
800 cigarettes, 400 cigarillos (cigars not weighing more than 4g each), 200 cigars, 1kg of tobacco; 10l of spirits, 20l of fortified wine, 90l of wine (including a maximum 60l of sparkling wine), 10l of beer; gifts to a value not exceeding Lm50.
Note: It is advisable to declare any larger or unusual items of electrical equipment brought into the island (such as video cameras, portable televisions or video recorders), as this will prevent duty being levied on these items when leaving the country. Those under 17 cannot bring in alcohol or tobacco.
Prohibited items: Firearms and ammunition; counterfeit goods; unlicensed drugs; obscene literature and other media; animals and birds (dead or alive); transmitting aparatus; plants and meat products (without import licence).
Abolition of duty free goods within the EU: On June 30 1999, the sale of duty free alcohol and tobacco at airports and at sea was abolished in all of the original 15 EU member states. Of the 10 new member states that joined the EU on May 1 2004, these rules already apply to Cyprus and Malta. There are transitional rules in place for visitors returning to one of the original 15 EU countries from one of the other new EU countries. But for the original 15, plus Cyprus and Malta, there are now no limits imposed on importing tobacco and alcohol products from one EU country to another (with the exceptions of Denmark, Finland and Sweden, where limits *are* imposed). Travellers should note that they may be required to prove at customs that the goods purchased are for personal use *only*.

Public Holidays

2005: Jan 1 New Year's Day. **Feb 10** Feast of St Paul's Shipwreck. **Mar 19** St Joseph's Day. **Mar 25** Good Friday. **Mar 31** Freedom Day. **May 1** Labour Day. **Jun 7** Sette Giugno (Commemoration of 1919 Riot). **Jun 29** Feast of St Peter and St Paul. **Aug 15** Assumption. **Sep 8** Feast of Our Lady of Victories. **Sep 21** Independence Day. **Dec 8** Immaculate Conception. **Dec 13** Republic Day. **Dec 25** Christmas Day.
2006: Jan 1 New Year's Day. **Feb 10** Feast of St Paul's Shipwreck. **Mar 19** St Joseph's Day. **Mar 31** Freedom Day. **Apr 14** Good Friday. **May 1** Labour Day. **Jun 7** Sette Giugno (Commemoration of 1919 Riot). **Jun 29** Feast of St Peter and St Paul. **Aug 15** Assumption. **Sep 8** Feast of Our Lady of Victories. **Sep 21** Independence Day. **Dec 8** Immaculate Conception. **Dec 13** Republic Day. **Dec 25** Christmas Day.

Health

	Special Precautions?	Certificate Required?
Yellow Fever	No	1
Cholera	No	No
Typhoid & Polio	No	N/A
Malaria	No	N/A

Note: Regulations and requirements may be subject to change at short notice, and you are advised to contact your doctor well in advance of your intended date of departure. Any numbers in the chart refer to the footnotes below.

1: A yellow fever vaccination certificate is required from travellers over nine months of age arriving from infected areas. If indicated on epidemiological grounds, infants under nine months of age are subject to isolation or surveillance if arriving from an infected area.
Food & drink: Mains water is normally chlorinated and, whilst safe, may cause mild abdominal upsets. Bottled water is available and is advised for the first few weeks of the stay. Milk is pasteurised and dairy products are safe for consumption. Local meat, poultry, seafood, fruit and vegetables are generally considered safe to eat.
Health care: There is a UK/Malta reciprocal health agreement. UK passport-holders staying less than 30 days will receive free emergency hospital treatment at a state-run hospital. The principal hospitals are St Luke's, Guardamangia in Malta and Gozo General Hospital in Gozo. Health insurance is nevertheless advised.

Travel - International

AIR: Malta's national airline is *Air Malta (KM)* (website: www.airmalta.com). Other airlines serving Malta include *Aeroflot, Alitalia, Austrian Airlines, British Airways, Emirates, Libyan Arab Airlines, Lufthansa* and *Transavia.*
Approximate flight times: From Luqa to *London* is three hours.
International airports: *Malta International (MLA)* (Luqa) (website: www.maltairport.com), Luqa, 5km (3 miles) south of Valletta (travel time - 15 minutes). Buses depart regularly to and from Valletta City Gate. There is a full taxi service to all parts of Malta, with fares regulated by meter. Airport facilities include incoming and outgoing duty free shops, car hire, bank, bureau de change, left luggage and restaurant/bar.
Departure tax: None.
SEA: The main ports are Valletta, Marsaxlokk and Mgarr/Gozo. Services operate to the Sicilian ports of Catania and Pozzallo. These routes are served by high-speed hydrofoils and catamarans (travel time - one hour 30 minutes) and car ferries (travel time - three hours). There are also sailings to Italy (to Reggio Calabria, Genoa and Salerno).

Travel - Internal

AIR: There is a helicopter service operating all year round between Malta and Gozo. A quick alternative to the ferry service, it takes only 10 to 15 minutes.
SEA: A passenger car ferry operates several times daily between Cirkewwa in Malta and Mgarr in Gozo. Crossing time is about 30 minutes. Services to Comino operate from mid-March to mid-November. For further information, contact the *Gozo Channel Company*, Hay Wharf, Sa Maison, Malta (tel: 2124 3964-6; fax: 2124 8007; e-mail: admin@gozochannel.com; website: www.gozochannel.com).
ROAD: Driving is on the left. Speed limit is 80kph (50mph) on highways and 50kph (30mph) in residential areas. **Bus:** Good local services operate from Valletta and Victoria (Gozo) to all towns. **Taxi:** Identifiable by their all-white livery. Although taxis are under meter charge at government-controlled prices, it is best to agree prices before departure. **Car hire:** A number of car hire firms offer self-drive cars. Both *Avis* and *Hertz* have desks at the airport. Rates on Malta are among the cheapest in Europe. **Documentation:** Valid international driving licence required.

Accommodation

Accommodation in Malta is provided in hotels, holiday complexes, guest houses, hostels or self-catering flats. Many hotels offer substantial reductions, particularly during the low season. For further information, contact the Malta Tourism Authority (see *Contact Addresses* section).
Grading: There is a star classification standard for all hotels in the Maltese islands. All classified hotels are thoroughly inspected before their star grading is allocated and are regularly inspected to ensure that standards are maintained. Gradings range from **2** to **5 stars**, indicating the level of standards, facilities and services offered by the hotel. Gradings are as follows:
5-star: Superior standard, fully air-conditioned accommodation. All rooms with private bath and shower, telephone, radio and TV. Room service available on a 24-hour basis. Other facilities include bar, restaurant and coffee shop, lounge area, dancing facilities, pool and sports facilities, 24-hour reception, laundry, pressing and dry-cleaning; shops and hairdresser; **4-star:** High standard, fully air-conditioned accommodation. All rooms with private bath or shower and internal or external telephone and radio. Room service from breakfast time to midnight. Other facilities include bar, restaurant, pool or service beach facilities, 24-hour reception, laundry, pressing and dry-cleaning, lounge and shops, including hairdresser; **3-star:** Good accommodation. All rooms with private bath or shower and internal or external telephone. Other facilities include bar and restaurant facilities, lounge area, 24-hour reception and laundry, pressing and dry-cleaning service; **2-star:** Modest accommodation. At least 20 per cent of rooms have private bath or shower; all rooms with washbasin and mirror and usually breakfast facilities are offered; telephone or service bell in all rooms. Front office service during the day and at least porter service during the night.
YOUTH HOSTELS: There are five youth hostels in Malta, four of which are located in Malta, and one in Gozo (with a minimum of two hostels open at any time of the year). Further information can be obtained from NSTS, 220 St Paul Street, Valletta VLT 07 (tel: 2124 4983; fax: 2123 0330; e-mail: nsts@nsts.org; website: www.nsts.org).

Resorts & Excursions

The Maltese islands, situated almost at the centre of the Mediterranean, offer the attraction of clear blue waters, secluded bays and sandy beaches while, in the towns, medieval walled citadels and splendid baroque churches and palaces reflect the rich history of the islands.

MALTA

VALLETTA: The town was built at the end of the 16th century by the Knights of St John as the island's new capital and, more importantly, as a fortress commanding an impregnable position over the peninsula. The city developed around what is now **Republic Street**, **Old Bakery Street** and **Merchants Street**, the latter containing some of the finest examples of Maltese-style Baroque architecture in the islands. The **Co-Cathedral of St John** has an austere exterior, but the interior is a sumptuous mixture of gilded tracery, marble mosaic floors and a lapis lazuli altar behind which is a remarkable marble group of the Baptism of Christ. The painting by Caravaggio of the beheading of St John is in the Oratory. The **Grand Master's Palace** in Republic Street was built 500 years ago as the abode of the Grand Master of the Order of St John, and contains a series of paintings depicting the great siege of 1565, painted by a pupil of Michelangelo, and a group of tapestries originally designed for Louis XIV. The palace also houses an armoury which has one of the best collections in existence. The **Manoel Theatre**, named after one of the most popular Grand Masters, is the second-oldest theatre in Europe and stages performances of opera, theatre, music and ballet between October and May. The **National Museum of Fine Art**, housed in an 18th-century palace, has a collection of furniture, paintings and treasures connected with the Knights of St John. The **Church of Our Lady of Victories**, built in 1566, is the oldest church in Valletta and was built to commemorate the victory over the Turks. At the nearby **Auberge de Provence** is the **National Museum of**

A B C D E F G H I J K L M N O P Q R S T U V W X Y Z

Archaeology, which has exhibits from the area dating back to prehistory. The town also has a bustling market in the Floriana suburb on Sunday mornings and another one in Merchants Street from Monday to Saturday.
SLIEMA: Sliema lies facing Valletta. It is a large, modern cosmopolitan town bustling with hotels, shops, cafés, cinemas, restaurants, bars, clubs and discos. The shoreline here is rocky, but is nevertheless good for bathing. The neighbouring **St Julian's** is also a lively and popular resort area.
MDINA: Mdina is perched on a high plateau towering over the rest of the island. It was once Malta's capital and the citadel is one of the finest surviving examples of a medieval walled city. The town is entered by a stone drawbridge which leads to a maze of narrow streets, lined with churches, monasteries and palaces, connected by tiny piazzas. Of particular interest is the Norman-style **Palazzo Falzon** which has a collection of antique weapons and pottery, a cathedral, and a museum that still houses a magnificent collection of art treasures; survivals from the sacking which the town suffered at the hands of the French in the 18th century. From **Bastion Square**, the visitor has a breathtaking view of the surrounding fields and villages, and also of **St Paul's Bay**.
RABAT: Rabat has fine Baroque churches, **St Paul's** and **St Agatha's Catacombs** and the **Roman Villa**. There are many interesting walks within close proximity to the town, such as the **Chadwick Lake**, **Dingli Cliffs** and **Verdala Castle** overlooking **Buskett Gardens**, the only wooded area in Malta. On the southwest shore is the **Blue Grotto** where, legend reports, sirens bewitched seafarers with their songs. Four caves reflect the brilliant colours of the corals and minerals in the limestone. The most spectacular is the Blue Grotto itself, which is best viewed in the early morning with a calm sea. Buses run to an embarkation point in Valletta where a boat can be taken to the caves.
ELSEWHERE: Within close proximity to **Paola** are the archaeological sites of **Tarxien**, with its neolithic temple; **Hypogeum**, a complex of ancient underground burial chambers on three levels dating back 3000 years; and **Ghar Dalam** (Dark Cave) where the remains of now extinct birds and animals such as dwarf hippos and elephants have been found. **Hagar Qim** on the south of the island is a neolithic temple dating back 3000 years and constructed from huge closely-fitting stones decorated in a very ornate style. Typical Maltese fishing communities such as **Marsaxlokk**, **Birzebbugia** and **Marsacala** are sprawled along the coves and inlets at the southernmost tip of Malta. Fishing nets and colourfully painted boats crowd the waterfronts, and each day's fresh catch can be eaten at the family-run tavernas. Also at Marsaxlokk is the recently discovered **Temple of Juno**, which was originally used by the Greeks as a place of worship to the goddess of fertility.
RESORTS: The most popular beach area is along the north coast where sandy beaches are plentiful and the clear waters here are ideal for sailing, skindiving and water-skiing. The best beaches are at **Paradise Bay**, **Golden Bay**, **Mellieha Bay**, **Armier Bay** and **Ghajn Tuffieha Bay**, all of which are very popular during the summer and pleasantly quiet during spring.

GOZO & COMINO

GOZO: Gozo is Malta's sister island and the second-largest of the archipelago. The landscape consists of flat-topped hills, steep valleys and rugged cliffs and villas that nestle among peach, lemon, olive and orange groves. In spring the island comes ablaze with the flowering hibiscus, oleander, mimosa and bougainvillaea. Some of the local crafts (lace and knitwear) are sold from the doorways of houses and on the street.
VICTORIA: The capital of Gozo is Victoria (also known as Rabat), built by the Arabs on **Castle Hill**, which offers the visitor panoramic views of the whole island. The cathedral has no dome, but inside, a *trompe l'oeil* painting on its ceiling gives the illusion of a dome. There is also a cathedral museum. The **Museum of Archaeology** contains Roman remains from a shipwreck on the island and items excavated from the neolithic temple at **Ggantija**.
ELSEWHERE ON GOZO: Other places of interest on Gozo include the **Citadel** ('Gran Castello'), with its historic bastions and old houses (one of them set up as a folk museum). There are alabaster caves at **Xaghra**, with stalactites and stalagmites. These underground caves are known as **Xerri's Grotto** and **Ninu's Grotto**. The basilica at **Ta'Pinu**, near the village of **Gharb**, is one of the most beautiful of Maltese churches and an official Vatican place of pilgrimage. **Xewkija** is a small town with a beautiful new church, built round the old parish **Church of St John the Baptist**.
Resorts: The waters surrounding the island are unpolluted and crystal clear. The most important beaches are **il-Qawra** (better known as the inland sea, with a secluded pebbly bathing pool, crystal clear water and sheer cliffs), an unspoilt sandy beach known as **Ir-Ramla il-Wamra** and **Xlendi Bay**. In summer there are numerous festivals with fireworks and horseracing in the streets. **Marsalforn** is a fishing village on the north coast which has become one of Gozo's most popular seaside resorts.
COMINO: The island of Comino, thick with wild herbs (particularly cumin), lies between Malta and Gozo and is inhabited by probably no more than a dozen farmers. Paths which wind through the unusual rock formations provide the only communication links and the island is ideal for anyone seeking a very quiet holiday. A few sandy coves and small bays, such as **Blue Lagoon**, are the main attractions.

Sport & Activities

There are a number of scenic spots that are only accessible on foot, which makes **walking** – as well as **cycling** – one of the best ways to explore the islands.
Watersports: Most large hotels have their own **swimming** pool and bathing is safe everywhere around the islands. Malta offers good conditions for **scuba diving** and **snorkelling**. The sea temperature never drops below 13°C (55 °F), even in a severe winter, which makes diving possible all-year-round. Diving equipment can be hired at favourable rates, making it unnecessary for divers to bring their own. On the island of Malta, the best dive sites are located around the northern part, the many caves and steep drop-offs, such as *Qawra Point* and *Cirkewwa*, being a particular attraction; also on Malta, *Wied Iz-Zurrieq* is good for night dives. On Gozo island, one of the most spectacular sites is *Dwejra Point*, which features a 35m (115ft) tunnel. On the island of Comino, cold currents support large shoals of sardines and bogue at *Irieqa Point*, while the St Marija Caves offer interesting cave diving. **Rowing** regattas are held in the Grand Harbour during April and September. The *Valletta Yacht Club* is at Couvre Port, Manoel Island, in Marsamxetto Harbour (temporary members accepted). **Windsurfing** has become very popular and many hotels and beach establishments offer equipment.
Spectator sports: National **water polo** competitions are held during summer. A summer league takes place at various water-polo clubs. **Horseraces** are held all Sunday afternoons at the Marsa National Racecourse from the end of October until mid-May. **Clay pigeon/Skeet shooting** is a popular sport in Malta, with regular practice-sessions and competitions being held on Sunday mornings. **Football** matches are played at the Ta'Qali stadium from September to June.
Other: There is an 18-hole **golf** course at the Marsa Sports Club which also has facilities for **tennis**, **squash**, **cricket**, **polo** and **horseracing**. There is a **10-pin bowling** centre at St George's Bay, St Julian's.

Social Profile

FOOD & DRINK: There is a very good choice of restaurants and cafes from deluxe to fast food (hamburgers and fish & chips), including Chinese, fish and beachside bars. Table service is normal, but many bars and cafes have table and/or counter service. Local dishes include *lampuki pie*, *bragoli* and *fenek* (rabbit cooked in wine). Pork and fish dishes are recommended and vegetables are excellent. The best Maltese fruits are oranges and grapes; also delicious are strawberries, melons, mulberries, tangerines, pomegranates and figs.
Maltese beer is excellent, and foreign beers are also available. There is a wide variety of good and inexpensive Maltese wine and foreign wines and spirits. Licensing hours of bars, restaurants and cafes are usually 0900-0100 and beyond. Most hotel bars close between 1300 and 1600 and then reopen after 1800.
NIGHTLIFE: There are several discos, bars and nightclubs. Roulette, baccarat, blackjack and boule can be played at the 'Dragonara' casino, St Julian's or at the Casino de Venezia in Vittoriosa. The Manoel Theatre is one of the oldest in Europe. Cinemas show mainly English and American films.
SHOPPING: Special purchases include Malta weave, pottery, blown glass, ceramics, dolls, lace, copper and brass items. Malta is renowned for its gold and silver filigree work and handmade lace. **Shopping hours:** Mon-Sat 0900-1300 and 1600-1900.
SPECIAL EVENTS: The Malta Tourism Authority can supply full details of events, including a complete list of the various Saint's Days celebrated throughout Malta (see *Contact Addresses* section). The following is a selection of special events occurring in Malta in 2005:
Feb 3-8 *Carnival* (featuring masks, floats and dancing), Valletta. **Feb 27** *Malta Marathon*, Mdina. **Mar 10-13** *Mediterranean Food Festival*, Valetta. **Mar 21-27** *Easter Week*. **Apr-Sep** *Festa Season* (commemoration to the various saints with church services, outdoor festivities and fireworks), various locations. **May 6-7** *Fireworks Festival*, Valletta. **May 21-22** *Maltese Folk Singing Festival*, Floriana. **Jun-Jul** *Victoria International Arts Festival* (classical concerts, vocal ensembles, ballet, jazz and lectures), Gozo. **Jul 5-17** *Malta International Jazz Festival*, Valletta. **Sep 25-26** *Malta International Air Show*, Luqa Airfield. **Oct** *Rolex Middle Sea Race*, Valletta. **Oct 6-16** *Historic Cities Festival*, various locations. **Nov 8-11** *Malta International Choir Festival*, Valletta. **Dec 24-31** *Christmas Entertainment Programme* (carol singing, ethnic dance groups and Santa fun run), Valletta.
SOCIAL CONVENTIONS: The usual European courtesies are expected, but the visitor should also bear in mind the tremendous importance of Roman Catholicism; if visiting a church, for instance, modest dress covering the shoulders and legs will be expected. Smoking is prohibited on public transport and in some public buildings, including cinemas.
Tipping: 10 to 15 per cent is expected in hotels and restaurants when not included in the bill. Taxi drivers are usually tipped 10 per cent of the fare.

Business Profile

ECONOMY: The agricultural sector is small, with potatoes being the only major export commodity. Although Malta is an island, the fishing industry is also relatively insignificant. With few natural resources, governments have sought to develop the economy through tourism and export-dedicated manufacturing. Tourism now accounts for over a quarter of Malta's foreign exchange earnings. The industrial sector includes textiles, footwear and clothing (the most important of the new industries), plastics, printing, electronic components and electrical equipment. The old naval dockyards used by the British have now converted to operate as a commercial shipyard. Malta has developed close economic links with Libya, which has invested heavily in property and commerce on the island as well as supplying the bulk of the oil that meets the island's energy needs. France has become the principal market for exports, followed by the USA, Germany, Singapore, the UK and Italy. The main economic policy issue under debate in Malta is relations with the EU and the country's application for membership. The conservative Nationalist Party (PN) favours joining while the Maltese Labour Party is strongly opposed to membership. After a sudden withdrawal in 1996 of its original application, the PN administration reapplied in 1998. The PN went on to win the 2003 poll, and Malta's membership was endorsed in March 2003 by popular referendum. Negotiations progressed fairly smoothly and Malta joined the EU, along with nine other countries (mostly from eastern Europe), in May 2004.
BUSINESS: English is widely spoken in business circles and, on the whole, Maltese businesspeople have a conservative approach to business protocol. Punctuality is expected and appreciated and dress must be smart. The best months for business visits are October to May. Office hours: Mon-Fri 0830-1245 and 1430-1730, Sat 0830-1200. Some smaller offices close 1300-1600, opening again later.
COMMERCIAL INFORMATION: The following organisations can offer advice: Ministry of Foreign Affairs, Palazzo Parisio, Merchants' Street, Valletta (tel: 2124 2191; e-mail: info.mfa@gov.mt; website: www.foreign.gov.mt); *or* Malta Chamber of Commerce, Exchange Buildings, Republic Street, Valletta VLT05 (tel: 233 873; fax: 245 223; e-mail: admin@chamber.org.mt; website: www.chamber.org.mt).
CONFERENCES/CONVENTIONS: The Conference Division of the Malta Tourism Authority can loan a free promotional video to conference and incentive organisers and is happy to assist with all initial enquiries. For further information, contact the Conference and Incentive Travel Division, 'Auberge d'Italie', Merchants Street, Valletta, CMR 02, Malta (tel: 2291 5204-6; fax: 2291 5898; e-mail: info@maltaconferences.com *or* cit@visitmalta.com; website: www.maltaconferences.com).

Climate

Warm most of the year. The hottest months are between July and September, but the heat is tempered by cooling sea breezes. Rain falls for very short periods, mainly in the cooler winter months.
Required clothing: Lightweight cottons and linens are worn between March and September, although warmer clothes may occasionally be necessary in spring and autumn and on cooler evenings. A light raincoat is advisable for winter

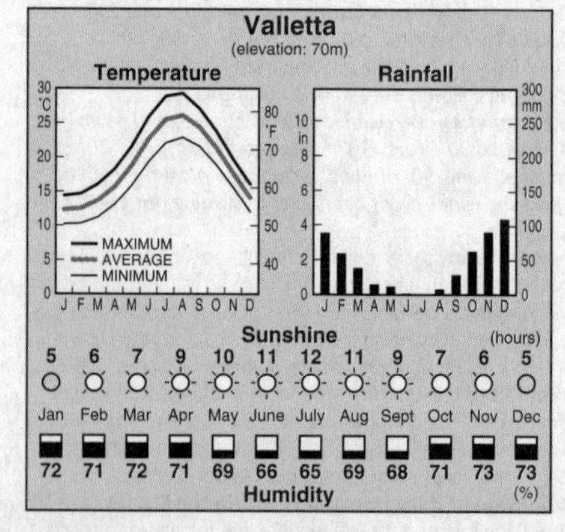

Martinique

LATEST TRAVEL ADVICE CONTACTS

British Foreign and Commonwealth Office
Tel: (0870) 606 0290 Website: www.fco.gov.uk

US Department of State
Website: http://travel.state.gov/travel

Canadian Department of Foreign Affairs and Int'l Trade
Tel: (1 800) 267 8376 Website: www.dfait-maeci.gc.ca

Location: Caribbean, northernmost of the Windward group of islands.

Country dialling code: 596.

Martinique is an Overseas Department of the Republic of France and does not maintain overseas missions. Addresses of French Embassies, Consulates and Tourist Offices may be found in the *France* section.

Office du Tourisme de la Martinique (Martinique Tourist Office)
Immeuble le Beaupré, Pointe de Jaham, 97233 Schoelcher, Martinique
Tel: (596) 616 177. Fax: (596) 612 272.
Website: www.touristmartinique.com

Office du Tourisme de la Martinique (Martinique Tourist Office)
2 rue des Moulins, 75001 Paris, France
Tel: (1) 4477 8600. Fax: (1) 4477 8625.
E-mail: infos@martiniquetourisme.com
Website: www.touristmartinique.com

Maison de la France (French Government Tourist Office)
178 Piccadilly, London W1J 9AL, UK
Tel: (09068) 244 123 (information line; calls cost 60p per minute) *or* (020) 7399 3520 (travel trade only).
Fax: (020) 7493 6594.
E-mail: info.uk@franceguide.com
Website: www.franceguide.com

British Honorary Consul
96 route du Phare, 97200 Fort-de-France, Martinique
Tel: (596) 618 892. Fax: (596) 613 389.

Martinique Promotion Bureau
444 Madison Avenue, 16th Floor, New York, NY 10022, USA
Tel: (212) 838 7800 ext. 228. Fax: (212) 838 7855.
E-mail: info@martinique.org
Website: www.martinique.org

Martinique Tourist Office
1981 Avenue McGill College, Suite 490, Montréal, Québec H3A 2W9, Canada
Tel: (514) 844 8566. Fax: (514) 844 8901.
E-mail: tourist.martiniquemontreal@qc.aira.com
Website: www.touristmartinique.com

The Canadian Embassy in Bridgetown deals with enquiries related to Martinique (see *Barbados* section).

TIMATIC CODES

Health	AMADEUS: **TI-DFT/FDF/HE** GALILEO/WORLDSPAN: **TI-DFT/FDF/HE** SABRE: **TIDFT/FDF/HE**
Visa	AMADEUS: **TI-DFT/FDF/VI** GALILEO/WORLDSPAN: **TI-DFT/FDF/VI** SABRE: **TIDFT/FDF/VI**

To access TIMATIC country information on Health and Visa regulations through the Computer Reservations System (CRS), type in the appropriate command line listed above.

General Information

AREA: 1100 sq km (424.7 sq miles).
POPULATION: 381,427 (1999).
POPULATION DENSITY: 346.8 per sq km.
CAPITAL: Fort-de-France. **Population:** 93,000 (UN estimate 2001).
GEOGRAPHY: The French Overseas Department of Martinique, a volcanic and picturesque island, is the northernmost of the Windward Caribbean group. The island is noticeably more rocky than those of the Leeward group, with beaches (of fine black or white or peppered sand) surrounded by sugar, palm, banana and pineapple plantations. Christopher Columbus called it 'the most beautiful country in the world' and before he named it in honour of St Martin, it was called *Madinina* ('island of flowers') by the native population.
GOVERNMENT: Martinique is an Overseas Department of France and as such is an integral part of the French Republic. **Head of State:** President Jacques Chirac since 1995, represented locally by Prefect Michel Cadot since 2000. **Head of Government:** Claude Lise, President of the General Council since 1992.
LANGUAGE: The official language is French; a Creole patois is widely used.
RELIGION: The majority of the population is Roman Catholic.
TIME: GMT - 4.
ELECTRICITY: 220 volts AC, 50Hz.
COMMUNICATIONS: Telephone: IDD is available. Country code: 596. Outgoing international code: 19. There are both payphones and card phones on the island. *Télécartes* (phonecards) are sold at post offices, newsagents and kiosks. There are only card phones at the airport. **Mobile telephone:** GSM 900/1800 networks in use. Roaming agreements in operation. Network providers include *Bouygues Telecom Caraibe* and *Orange Caraibe* (website: www.orange.gp). Coverage extends throughout the French Antilles and in French Guiana. **Fax:** Available in most hotels. **Internet:** Local ISPs include *Net Antilles* (website: www.antilles-net.com) and *Wanadoo*. **Post:** Letters take about a week to reach Europe. Post office hours: Mon-Fri 0700-1800, and Saturday mornings. **Press:** Newspapers are in French and vary in their political bias. The main dailies are *Carib Hedo* and *France Antilles*.
Radio: BBC World Service (website: www.bbc.co.uk/worldservice) and Voice of America (website: www.voa.gov) can be received. From time to time the frequencies change and the most up-to-date can be found online.

Passport/Visa

	Passport Required?	Visa Required?	Return Ticket Required?
Full British	Yes	No	Yes
Australian	Yes	No	Yes
Canadian	Yes	No	Yes
USA	Yes	No	Yes
Other EU	Yes/1	No	Yes
Japanese	Yes	No	Yes

Note: *Regulations and requirements may be subject to change at short notice, and you are advised to contact the appropriate diplomatic or consular authority before finalising travel arrangements. Details of these may be found at the head of this country's entry. Any numbers in the chart refer to the footnotes below.*

PASSPORTS: Passport valid for at least three months beyond applicant's last day of stay required by all except the following:
1. nationals of Belgium, France, Germany, Greece, Italy, Luxembourg, Monaco, The Netherlands, Portugal, Spain and Switzerland, who are holders of national identity cards.
VISAS: Required by all except the following:
(a) nationals of countries referred to in the chart above for stays of up to three months;
(b) nationals of Andorra, Argentina, Bolivia, Brunei, Bulgaria, Chile, Costa Rica, Croatia, El Salvador, Guatemala, Honduras, Hong Kong (SAR), Iceland, Korea (Rep), Liechtenstein, Macau (SAR), Malaysia, Mexico, Monaco, New Zealand, Nicaragua, Norway, Panama, Paraguay, San Marino, Singapore, Switzerland, Uruguay, Vatican City and Venezuela for stays of up to three months;
(c) transit passengers continuing their journey by the same or first connecting aircraft provided holding valid onward or return documentation and not leaving the airport.
Note: (a) Nationals of Canada, Cyprus, Japan, Korea (Rep), Malaysia, Malta, Mexico, Singapore, USA and Venezuela should apply for a visa if they are to receive a salary, even if their trip is a short stay. (b) US nationals need a visa if they are crew members, or journalists on assignments, or students enrolled at schools and universities in any of the French Overseas Departments.
Types of visa and cost: All visas, regardless of duration of stay and number of entries permitted, cost €35. In most circumstances, no fee applies to students, recipients of government fellowships and citizens of the EU and their family members.
Validity: *Short-stay* visas (up to 30 days): valid for two months (single- and multiple-entry). *Short stay* visas (31 to 90 days and double- or multiple-entry): valid for a maximum of six months from date of issue. *Transit* visas: valid for single- or multiple-entries of maximum five days per entry, including the day of arrival.
Application to: French Consulate General (for personal visas), or Consular section at Embassy (for diplomatic or service visas); see *Contact Addresses* section for France. All applications must be made in person.
Application requirements: (a) Valid passport with blank page to affix the visa. Minors travelling alone must submit notarised parental authorisation, signed by both parents, plus one copy. (b) Up to two completed application forms. (c) One passport-size photo on each form. (d) Fee, to be paid in cash only if paying by person. If not, fee should be paid by cheque or postal order. (e) Evidence of sufficient funds for stay (two last bank statements, plus copy, or other proof of funds equivalent to US$100 for each day of trip). (f) Letter from employer, or proof of stay in country of residence. (g) Proof of address. (h) Medical insurance. (i) Return ticket and travel documents for remaining journey. (j) Proof of accommodation during stay. (k) Registered self-addressed envelope, if applying by post. (l) Detailed itinerary, including reservations and round-trip airline tickets (only required when visa is issued), plus one copy. (m) Proof of employment (eg last payslip or letter from employer). (n) Proof of valid health/travel insurance with worldwide coverage, plus copy. *Business*: (a)-(n) and, (o) Business invitation guaranteeing payment of travel expenses, plus one copy.
Working days required: One day to three weeks depending on nationality.
Temporary residence: If intending to work or stay for longer than 90 days, nationals should contact the Long Stay visa section of the Consulate General or Embassy (tel: (020) 7073 1248).

Money

Currency: Since January 2002 the Euro has been the official currency for the French Overseas Departments (*Départements d'outre-mer*), French Guiana, Guadeloupe, Martinique and Réunion. For further details, exchange rates and currency restrictions, see *France* section. US Dollars are also accepted in some places.
Currency exchange: All major currencies can be exchanged at banks and bureaux de change.
Credit & debit cards: American Express, Diners Club and Visa are accepted. MasterCard has limited acceptance. Cards can also be used in cash dispensers. Check with your credit or debit card company for details of merchant acceptability and other services which may be available.
Travellers cheques: Accepted in most places, and may qualify for discounts on luxury items. To avoid additional exchange rate charges, travellers are advised to take travellers cheques in Euros or US Dollars.
Banking hours: Mon-Fri 0730-1230 and 1430-1630.

Duty Free

The island of Martinique is an Overseas Department of France, and therefore duty-free allowances are the same as those for France; see *France* section.

Public Holidays

As for France (see *France* section) with the following dates also observed:
2005: Feb 6-9 Carnival. **Mar 25** Good Friday. **May 22** Slavery Abolition Day. **Jul 21** Schoelcher Day.
2006: Feb Carnival. **Apr 14** Good Friday. **May 22** Slavery Abolition Day. **Jul 21** Schoelcher Day.

Health

	Special Precautions?	Certificate Required?
Yellow Fever	No	No
Cholera	No	No
Typhoid & Polio	1	N/A
Malaria	No	N/A

Note: *Regulations and requirements may be subject to change at short notice, and you are advised to contact your doctor well in advance of your intended date of departure. Any numbers in the chart refer to the footnotes below.*

Notes: 1: Immunisation against typhoid and poliomyelitis is occasionally recommended.

A B C D E F G H I J K L M N O P Q R S T U V W X Y Z

Food & drink: Mains water is normally chlorinated and, whilst relatively safe, may cause mild abdominal upsets. Bottled water is available and is advised for the first few weeks of the stay. Drinking water outside main cities and towns may be contaminated and sterilisation is advisable. Milk is pasteurised and dairy products are safe for consumption. Local meat, poultry, seafood, fruit and vegetables are generally considered safe to eat.
Other risks: *Bilharzia* (schistosomiasis) is present. Avoid swimming and paddling in fresh water; swimming pools which are well chlorinated and maintained are safe. *Typhoid, hepatitis B, diphtheria* and *tuberculosis* immunisations are occasionally recommended.
Rabies is present, particularly in the mongoose. For those at high risk, vaccination before arrival should be considered. If you are bitten, seek medical advice without delay. For more information, consult the *Health* appendix.
Health care: A reciprocal health agreement exists between France and the UK. However, the benefits which go with this agreement may not be fully available in Martinique. Check with your doctor before departure. Martinique has 18 hospitals and several specialists and clinics.

Travel - International

AIR: Martinique's national airline is *CTA Air Martinique*. Other airlines serving Martinique include *Air France, AOM, KLM* and *LIAT*.
Approximate flight times: From Martinique to *London* is 12 hours (including an average stopover time of one hour in Paris); to *Los Angeles* is nine hours; to *New York* is six hours and to *Singapore* is 25 hours.
International airports: *Fort-de-France (FDF)* (Lamentin) is 11km (7 miles) from the city. Airport facilities include restaurants, banks and bureaux de change, shops, tourist information and car hire.
Departure tax: None.
SEA: The main port is at Fort-de-France. The Pointe Simon cruise dock, nearer the city centre, accommodates larger cruise ships. Regular high-speed catamaran services run to Guadeloupe, St Lucia and Dominica. For more information, contact either *Express des Îles* (tel: (596) 631 211; fax: (596) 633 447; e-mail: info@express-des-iles.com) *or Brudey Frères* (tel: (596) 700 850; fax: (596) 705 375). Other ships sail from Miami and San Juan (Puerto Rico). Martinique is a port of call for the following international cruise lines: *Holland America, Norwegian Cruise Line, Princess Cruises* and *Royal Olympic Cruises*.

Travel - Internal

AIR: Aeroplanes and helicopters may be chartered from *Air Martinique*.
SEA: Scheduled ferries ply between Fort-de-France and the main resorts of Trois Îlets and Sainte-Anne via Anse Mitan, Pointe du Bout, Anse à l'Âne and Anses d'Arlet. Children's tickets are half price.
ROAD: Traffic drives on the right. The road system is well developed and surfaced. **Bus:** A limited although inexpensive service is provided within the communes. Most of Martinique's public transport is served by communal taxis, denoted by the sign TC. TCs depart at frequent intervals from Pointe Simon (by the waterfront in Fort-de-France) to destinations all over the islands, making stops along the way. Fares are fixed and are reasonable. TCs run from early morning until 1800. **Taxi:** Government-controlled, plentiful and reasonably cheap if shared. There is a surcharge at night. Main taxi stands are at major hotels, resorts and the airport. **Car hire:** The island has excellent car hire facilities. Rental agencies include *Avis, Budget, Carib-rent-a-car, Europcar* and *Hertz*. 50cc **mopeds** do not need a licence. Bicycles can also be hired.
Documentation: An International Driving Permit is recommended, but a national driving licence is sufficient, provided the driver has at least one year's experience. The minimum driving age is 21.

Accommodation

HOTELS: There is a good selection of hotels on Martinique; 10 per cent service is charged, sometimes with other government taxes added. The Relais de la Martinique is an association of small hotels, often called *Relais Créoles*, and guest houses offering special reservation and tour facilities. Hotels range from deluxe, to medium- and low-priced. For further information, contact the tourist office, *or Centrale de Réservation Martinique*, Immeuble le Beaupré, Pointe de Jahan 97233 Schoelcher (tel: (596) 616 177; fax: (596) 612 272; website: www.martinique.org); *or* Maison de la France (see *Contact Addresses* section).
SELF-CATERING: *Gites* (furnished apartments or bungalows) are widely available. For rental, contact the *Relais des Gites de France – Martinique*, BP 1122, Maison du Tourisme Vert, 9 boulevard du Général-de-Gaulle, 97248 Fort-de-France (tel: (596) 737 474; fax: (596) 635 592; e-mail: gites@touristofficemartinique.com; website: www.itea.fr/GDF/972).

Resorts & Excursions

The terrain of Martinique varies from the high mountains of the north and centre to the rolling hills around Fort-de-France and the safe, sheltered harbours of the lower west coast. Martinique has a variety of small museums celebrating aspects of the island's culture and history, including the Empress Josephine's connection with the island, the eruption of Montagne Pelée, the rum trade and dolls made from local materials.
FORT-DE-FRANCE: The island's capital is a town of winding streets and colourful markets. In the centre of the town is the park of **La Savanne**. A statue in La Savanne commemorates Napoleon's Empress Josephine, a native of Martinique, whose home, **La Pagerie**, is one of the main tourist attractions. The **Musée Départemental** has remains of the predominantly Arawak and Carib Indian prehistory of the island. There is an interesting **Caribbean Arts Centre**. **Les Trois-Îlets** (Josephine's birthplace) is situated across the bay from Fort-de-France.
ST PIERRE: The 1430m (4700ft) volcanic mountain in the north, **Montagne Pelée**, last erupted in 1902 (in a unique explosion which literally ripped the summit off), destroying the city of St Pierre and its entire population of 30,000. (Only a prisoner in an underground cell, Auguste Ciparis, survived – he was subsequently pardoned and ended his days as a fairground exhibit in the USA.) The remains of St Pierre, once a beautiful and remarkable city known as the 'pearl of the Caribbean', are now a tourist attraction. The **Musée Volcanologique** contains exhibits, photographs and documents that tell the story of the disaster. Today, St Pierre is Martinique's second city and, although run down, still shows some signs of its former glory: the old stone stairways and bridges still exist, and the ruins of the theatre are a prominent feature. Some of the historic buildings are being rebuilt and restored, notably the old customs house by the waterfront. The long grey-sand beach is very popular with local people. It is possible to visit the wrecks of the ships which were in the harbour on the day Montagne Pelée erupted – all but one of them went down in the disaster. Special submarines with glass windows take tourists to view the wrecks and the colourful fish which swim around them. It is also possible to dive to see them.
LE CARBET: Near Le Carbet, where Columbus landed on his fourth voyage in 1502, is the restored plantation of **Leyritz**, which is now visited by many tourists. The **Centre d'Art Paul Gauguin** may be found in Le Carbet itself. It contains exhibits relating to the painter's stay in the area and the work he did while there.
THE SOUTH: In the south of the island is **Pointe du Bout**, Martinique's major resort area. **Ste Anne**, **Le Diamant** and **Les Anses d'Arlets** have some of the island's best bathing beaches. **HMS Diamond Rock**, 4km (2.5 miles) off Diamant, is a rock which was designated a man-of-war by the British during the Napoleonic wars and rates a 12-gun salute from passing British warships.

Sport & Activities

Swimming, **water-skiing**, **small-boat sailing**, **snorkelling** and **spearfishing** are available at many coastal resorts. There are **tennis** courts at many large hotels, and around 40 tennis clubs in Martinique. Visitors can obtain temporary membership and play at night as well as during the day. For further information, contact *La Ligue Régionale de Tennis de la Martinique*, Petit Manoir, 97232 Lamentin (tel: 510 800; fax: 516 560; e-mail: ligue.martinique@fft.fr; website: www.ligue.fft.fr). There is an 18-hole **golf** course at Trois-Ilets. **Horse riding** is a very enjoyable way to see Martinique's lovely countryside. There is also **horseracing** at the Carère track at Lamentin. **Hiking** and **mountain climbing** are also catered for.

Social Profile

FOOD & DRINK: The island's cuisine is characterised by French and Caribbean influences and often features seafood, including lobster, red snapper, conch and sea urchin. Island specialities include stuffed crab, stewed conch, roast wild goat, jugged rabbit and broiled local dove. *Colombo* is a dish of goat, chicken, pork or lamb in a thick curry sauce. Creole cuisine is also widely available and is an original combination of French, Indian and African traditions seasoned with exotic spices. Meals are ended with tropical fruit. There is a great supply of French wines, champagne, liqueurs and local rum. Local specialities are *'ti punch*, a brew of rum, lime juice, bitters and syrup; *shrub*, a Christmas liqueur consisting of rum and orange peel; and *planteur*, made from rum and fruit juice. Guava, soursop, passionfruit, mandarin and sugar-cane juice are all common. There are no licensing restrictions.
NIGHTLIFE: There are plenty of restaurants, bars and discos, a few casinos, and some displays of local dancing and music. The *Ballet Martiniquais* is one of the world's most prestigious traditional ballet companies. Limbo dancers and steel bands often perform at hotels in the evenings. The local music, *zouk*, lively, two-beat music similar to merengue but unique to the French West Indies, can be heard everywhere. Martinicans are very proud of it. The local guide, *Choubouloute*, contains information on local entertainment and is sold at newsagents.
SHOPPING: French imports are worthwhile purchases, especially wines, liqueurs and Lalique crystal. Local items include rum, straw goods, bamboo hats, voodoo dolls, baskets and objects of aromatic vetiver roots. A discount of 20 per cent is given if payment is made by travellers cheques in some tourist shops. **Shopping hours:** Mon-Fri 0900-1300 and 1500-1800, Sat 0900-1300.
SPECIAL EVENTS: Every village celebrates its Saint's Days - there is generally one a month throughout Martinique. For a complete list and location details, contact the Martinique Tourist Office or Promotion Bureau (see *Contact Addresses* section). The following is a selection of special events occurring in Martinique in 2005:
Feb 5-9 *Carnival*. **Mar 12-13** *The 'Rivière-Pilote' Agricultural Trade-Fair*. **Jul 31-Aug 8** *21st Tour of Martinique in Skiffs*.
SOCIAL CONVENTIONS: The atmosphere is generally relaxed and informal. Casual dress is acceptable everywhere, but formal attire is needed for dining out and nightclubs.
Tipping: 10 per cent is acceptable.

Business Profile

ECONOMY: In the agricultural sector, sugar cane and bananas are the main cash crops; a range of fruit is also grown for domestic consumption and export. Cut flowers have also become an important export earner. The processing of agricultural goods and refining of imported oil (which is also the main source of energy) are the island's main industries. The most important part of the economy is tourism, both as a major employer and a vital source of foreign exchange – worth some US$400 million a year to the economy. Martinique also enjoys substantial material benefits from being an integral part of the French nation, receiving financial support both from Paris and the EU. France accounts for more than 75 per cent of Martinique's foreign trade, with the remainder of the import market captured by the major EU economies and the USA.
BUSINESS: Lightweight suits and safari suits are recommended. The best time to visit is January to March and June to September. A command of French is essential, as most of the island's business is connected with France. Office hours: Mon-Fri 0800-1200 and 1400-1800.
COMMERCIAL INFORMATION: The following organisation can offer advice: *Chambre de Commerce et d'Industrie de la Martinique*, BP 478, 50 rue Ernest Deproge, 97241 Fort-de-France Cédex (tel: 552 800; fax: 606 668; e-mail: info@martinique.cci.fr; website: www.martinique.cci.fr).
CONFERENCES/CONVENTIONS: Facilities for business conferences are available at the Palais des Congrès Convention Centre, Schoelcher Commune, Madiana (tel: 721 515-6).

Climate

Warm weather throughout the year, with the main rainy season occurring in the autumn. Showers can occur at other times of the year, but they are usually brief. Cooler in the upland areas.
Required clothing: Lightweight, with waterproof wear advised for the rainy season.

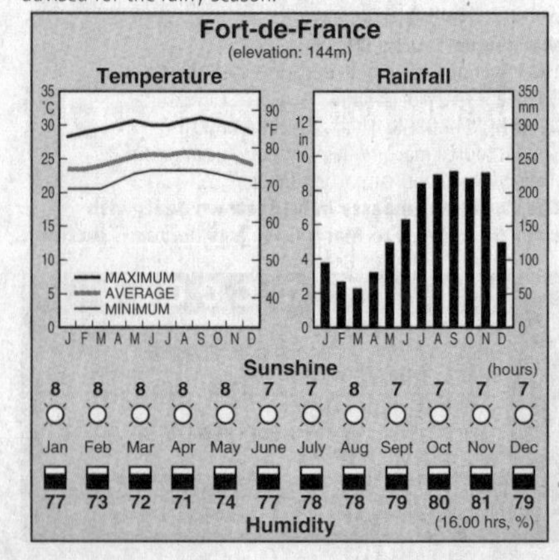

Mauritania

LATEST TRAVEL ADVICE CONTACTS

British Foreign and Commonwealth Office
Tel: (0870) 606 0290 Website: www.fco.gov.uk

US Department of State
Website: http://travel.state.gov/travel

Canadian Department of Foreign Affairs and Int'l Trade
Tel: (1 800) 267 8376 Website: www.dfait-maeci.gc.ca

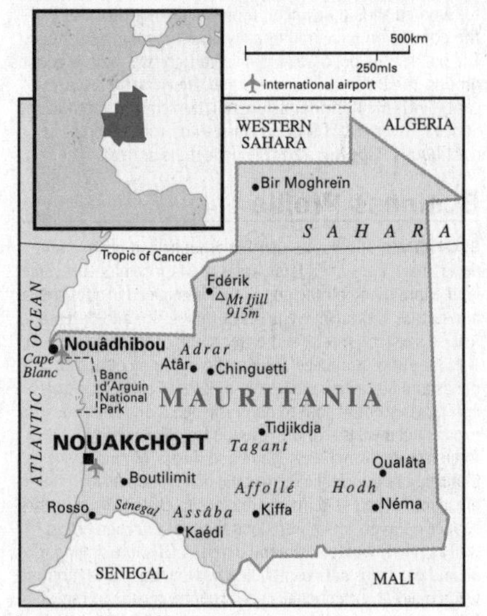

Location: West Africa.

Country dialling code: 222.

Office National du Tourisme
BP 246, Nouakchott, Mauritania
Tel: 525 3572.

Embassy of the Islamic Republic of Mauritania
8 Carlos Place, Mayfair, London W1K 3AS, UK
Tel: (020) 7478 9323. Fax: (020) 7478 9339.
E-mail: ambarim@aol.com
Opening hours: Mon-Fri 0930-1630.

The British Embassy in Rabat deals with enquiries relating to Mauritania (see *Morocco* section).

Embassy of the Islamic Republic of Mauritania
2129 Leroy Place, NW, Washington, DC 20008, USA
Tel: (202) 232 5700. Fax: (202) 319 2623.
E-mail: info@mauritaniembassy-usa.org
Website: www.ambarim-dc.org

Embassy of the United States of America
Street address: 288 rue 41-100 (rue Abdallaye), Nouakchott, Mauritania
Postal address: BP 222, Nouakchott, Mauritania
Tel: 525 2660/63. Fax: 525 1592.
E-mail: ConsularNKC@state.gov (visa section).
Website: http://usembassy.state.gov/mauritania

Embassy of the Islamic Republic of Mauritania
121 Sherwood Drive, Ottawa, Ontario K1Y 3V1, Canada
Tel: (613) 237 3283. Fax: (613) 237 3287.
E-mail: info@mauritania-canada.ca
Website: www.mauritania-canada.ca

The Canadian Embassy in Dakar deals with enquiries relating to Mauritania (see *Senegal* section).

General Information

AREA: 1,030,700 sq km (397,950 sq miles).
POPULATION: 2,807,000 (UN estimate 2004).
POPULATION DENSITY: 2.7 per sq km.
CAPITAL: Nouakchott. **Population:** 611,883 (2001).
GEOGRAPHY: Mauritania is bordered by Algeria, Mali, Western Sahara (Sahrawi Arab Democratic Republic) and Senegal. To the west lies the Atlantic Ocean. Mauritania consists mainly of the vast Saharan plain of sand and scrub. Most of this area is a sea of sand dunes, but in places the land rises to rocky plateaux with deep ravines leaving isolated peaks. The Adrar plateau in the central region rises to 500m (1640ft), and the Tagant further south to 600m (1970ft). The area is scattered with towns, small villages and oases. The northern bank of the Senegal River, which forms the country's southern border, is the only area in the country with any degree of permanent vegetation and it supports a wide variety of wildlife.
GOVERNMENT: Republic. Gained independence from France in 1960. **Head of State:** President Maaouiya Ould Sid'Ahmed Taya since 1984. **Head of Government:** Prime Minister Sghair Ould M'Bareck since 2003.
LANGUAGE: The official language is Arabic. The Moors of Arab/Berber stock, speaking Hassaniya dialects of Arabic, comprise the majority of the people. Other dialects include Soninke, Poular and Wolof. French and English are increasingly spoken.
RELIGION: Islam is the official religion. Despite ethnic and cultural differences among Mauritanians, they are all bound by a common Muslim attachment to the Malekite sect.
TIME: GMT.
ELECTRICITY: 220 volts AC, 50Hz. Round two-pin plugs are normal.
COMMUNICATIONS: Telephone: IDD is available in Nouakchott and Nouadhibou. Country code: 222 (no area codes). Outgoing international calls must go through the operator. **Mobile telephone:** GSM 900 network operaters include *Mattel* and *Mauritel* (website: www.mauritelmobiles.mr). **Internet:** ISPs include *Mauritel* (website: www.mauritel.mr). **Post:** International postal facilities are limited to main cities. Airmail to Europe takes approximately two weeks. **Press:** Newspapers are in French and Arabic. The dailies are *Châab* and *Nouakchott-Info*. The main weeklies include *Le Calame*, *L'Eveil-Hebdo* and *Rajoul Echarée*. **Radio:** BBC World Service (website: www.bbc.co.uk/worldservice) and Voice of America (website: www.voa.gov) can be received. From time to time the frequencies change and the most up-to-date can be found online.

TIMATIC CODES

Health
AMADEUS: **TI-DFT/JIB/HE**
GALILEO/WORLDSPAN: **TI-DFT/JIB/HE**
SABRE: **TIDFT/JIB/HE**

Visa
AMADEUS: **TI-DFT/JIB/VI**
GALILEO/WORLDSPAN: **TI-DFT/JIB/VI**
SABRE: **TIDFT/JIB/VI**

To access TIMATIC country information on Health and Visa regulations through the Computer Reservations System (CRS), type in the appropriate command line listed above.

Passport/Visa

	Passport Required?	Visa Required?	Return Ticket Required?
Full British	Yes	Yes	Yes
Australian	Yes	Yes	Yes
Canadian	Yes	Yes	Yes
USA	Yes	Yes	Yes
Other EU	Yes	Yes	Yes
Japanese	Yes	Yes	Yes

Note: *Regulations and requirements may be subject to change at short notice, and you are advised to contact the appropriate diplomatic or consular authority before finalising travel arrangements. Details of these may be found at the head of this country's entry. Any numbers in the chart refer to the footnotes below.*

PASSPORTS: Valid passports required by all except nationals of some other ECOWAS countries (Burkina Faso, Cape Verde, Côte d'Ivoire, Gambia, Ghana, Guinea, Mali, Niger, Senegal and Sierra Leone) and Cameroon, Central African Republic, Chad, Congo (Rep), Gabon and Madagascar holding a valid national ID card.
VISAS: Required by all except the following:
(a) nationals of Algeria, Benin, Burkina Faso, Cameroon, Cape Verde, Central African Republic, Chad, Congo (Rep), Côte d'Ivoire, Gabon, Gambia, Ghana, Guinea, Guinea-Bissau, Liberia, Libya, Madagascar, Mali, Niger, Nigeria, Romania, Senegal, Sierra Leone, Togo and Tunisia;
(b) transit passengers continuing their journey by the same or first connecting aircraft provided holding onward or return documentation and not leaving the airport.
Types of visa and cost: *Tourist* or *Business*: £42. All visas are multiple-entry.
Validity: Three months.
Application to: Consulate (or Consular section at Embassy); see *Contact Addresses* section.
Application requirements: (a) Valid passport. (b) Application form. (c) Two passport-size photos. (d) Fee. (e) For Business visas, a letter of invitation from sponsor may be required. (f) Stamped, self-addressed envelope if applying by post.
Working days required: Usually takes 72 hours to be processed.
Temporary residence: Applications should be made to the Home Ministry in Mauritania.

Money

Currency: Mauritanian Ouguiya (UM) = 5 khoums. Notes are in denominations of UM1000, 500, 200 and 100. Coins are in denominations of UM20, 10, 5 and 1, and 1 and 0.2 khoums.
Currency exchange: Currency declaration forms are issued on arrival and should be kept. Currencies can be exchanged at the airport or at the main banks in Nouakchott. It is illegal to exchange money on the black market.
Credit & debit cards: Generally not accepted. American Express is accepted in a few hotels in Nouakchott and Nouadhibou. Check with your credit or debit card company for details of merchant acceptability and other services which may be available.
Travellers cheques: Limited use. To avoid additional exchange rate charges, travellers are advised to take travellers cheques in US Dollars.
Currency restrictions: The import and export of local currency is prohibited. There is no restriction on the import of foreign currency provided the amount is declared on arrival. The balance of foreign currency not spent but declared on entry may be exported, but the import declaration must be produced.
Exchange rate indicators: The following figures are included as a guide to the movements of the Ouguiya against Sterling and the US Dollar:

Date	Feb '04	May '04	Aug '04	Nov '04
£1.00=	483.45	475.10	490.06	500.09
$1.00=	265.60	266.00	266.00	264.51

Banking hours: Sun-Thurs 0800-1600.

Duty Free

The following items can be imported into Mauritania by persons of 18 years of age and over without incurring customs duty:
200 cigarettes or 25 cigars or 450g of tobacco (women – cigarettes only); 50g of perfume and 250ml eau de toilette; *one still camera, one cinecamera and one wireless set; one projector (tourists only).*
Note: Sporting guns require an import and gun licence, obtained prior to arrival from the Home Ministry.
Prohibited items: Alcohol.

Public Holidays

2005: Jan 1 New Year's Day. **Jan 21** Tabaski (Feast of the Sacrifice). **Feb 10** Islamic New Year. **Apr 21** Mouloud (Prophet's Birthday). **May 1** Labour Day. **May 25** African Liberation Day (Anniversary of the OAU's Foundation). **Jul 10** Armed Forces Day. **Nov 3-5** Korité (End of Ramadan). **Nov 28** Independence Day.
2006: Jan 1 New Year's Day. **Jan 10** Tabaski (Feast of the Sacrifice). **Jan 31** Islamic New Year. **Apr 11** Mouloud (Prophet's Birthday). **May 1** Labour Day. **May 25** African Liberation Day (Anniversary of the OAU's Foundation). **Jul 10** Armed Forces Day. **Oct 22-24** Korité (End of Ramadan). **Nov 28** Independence Day.
Note: Muslim festivals are timed according to local sightings of various phases of the moon and the dates given above are approximations. During the lunar month of Ramadan that precedes Korité (Eid al-Fitr), Muslims fast during the day and feast at night and normal business patterns may be interrupted. Many restaurants are closed during the day and there may be restrictions on smoking and drinking. Some disruption may continue into Korité itself. Korité and Tabaski (Eid al-Adha) may last anything from two to 10 days, depending on the region. For more information, see the *World of Islam* appendix.

Health

	Special Precautions?	Certificate Required?
Yellow Fever	Yes	1
Cholera	2	No
Typhoid & Polio	3	N/A
Malaria	4	N/A

Note: *Regulations and requirements may be subject to change at short notice, and you are advised to contact your doctor well in advance of your intended date of departure. Any numbers in the chart refer to the footnotes below.*

1: A yellow fever vaccination certificate is required from all travellers over one year of age, except travellers arriving from a non-infected area and staying less than two weeks in the country.
2: Following WHO guidelines issued in 1973, a cholera vaccination certificate is not a condition of entry to Mauritania. However, cholera is a serious risk in this country and precautions are essential. Up-to-date advice should be sought before deciding whether these precautions should include vaccination, as medical opinion is divided over its effectiveness; see the *Health* appendix for further information.
3: Immunisation against typhoid is recommended and vaccination against poliomyelitis is sometimes advised.
4: Malaria risk, mainly in the malignant falciparum form, exists throughout the year except in the northern areas of Dakhlet-Nouadhibou and Tiris-Zemour. In Adrar and Inchiri, there is a malaria risk during the rainy season (July through October). Resistance to chloroquine has been reported. The recommended prophylaxis in these areas is chloroquine plus proguanil.
Food & drink: All water should be regarded as being potentially contaminated. Water used for drinking, brushing teeth or making ice should have first been boiled or otherwise sterilised. Milk is unpasteurised and should be boiled. Powdered or tinned milk is available and is advised, but make sure it is reconstituted with pure water. Avoid dairy

products that are likely to have been made from unboiled milk. Only eat well-cooked meat and fish, preferably served hot. Vegetables should be cooked and fruit peeled.
Other risks: *Bilharzia* (schistosomiasis) exists. Avoid swimming or paddling in fresh water; swimming pools that are well chlorinated and maintained are safe. Also present are *hepatitis A* and *E. Hepatitis B* is hyperendemic. *Rift Valley fever* is present in the Trarza region. Epidemics of *meningococcal meningitis* may occur, particularly in the savannah areas and during the dry season.
Rabies is present. For those at high risk, vaccination before arrival should be considered. If you are bitten, seek medical advice without delay. For more information, consult the *Health* appendix.
Health care: Medical facilities are very limited. Nouakchott boasts the country's best medical facilities with many doctors, most in private practices or clinics, and plenty of chemists stocking most existing French medicines. The hospital in the capital has 450 beds; there are fewer than 100 other beds elsewhere. Health insurance, to include cover for emergency repatriation, is essential.

Travel - International

AIR: Mauritania's national airline is *Air Mauritanie (MR). Air France* operates weekly flights from London to Nouakchott via Paris. Other airlines serving Mauritania include *Air Algerie, Delta Air Lines, Royal Air Maroc* and *Tunis Air*.
Approximate flight times: From Nouakchott to *London* is seven hours (via Paris).
International airports: *Nouakchott (NKC)* is 5km (3 miles) east of the city (travel time - 20 minutes). Taxis are available. Facilities include shops and restaurants.
Nouâdhibou (NDB) is 4km (2.5 miles) from the city. Taxis are available.
Departure tax: UM560 for those departing for countries in Africa. UM860 for all other countries.
SEA: The principal port is Nouadhibou and there is a small port at Nouakchott, while St Louis in Senegal also serves Mauritania.
ROAD: The most reliable way into Mauritania overland is from Senegal. From Dakar, the journey to Nouakchott is along a 575km- (360 mile-) tarred road (travel time - approximately eight hours). The River Senegal has to be crossed by ferry at Rosso. A service operates daily 0730-1200 and 1500-1800. There is also a paved road from Mali. Travellers intending to drive into Mauritania from the north should contact the nearest Mauritanian diplomatic mission for an assessment of political conditions in the Western Sahara; the *Route de Mauritanie* via Algeria and Senegal is out of service. The border with Algeria is currently closed.

Travel - Internal

AIR: *Air Mauritanie (MR)* operates internal flights between Nouakchott and Atâr, Nouâdhibou (daily), Ayoûn el Atroûs, Tidjikja, Kaédi, Néma and Zouérat. It is possible to charter light aircraft.
Departure tax: UM270.
RAIL: The only line runs between Nouâdhibou and Zouérat and is provided by the national mining company, SNIM, to serve the ore mines. Services are free but booking in advance is advisable.
ROAD: Traffic drives on the right. There are adequate roads linking Nouakchott with Rosso in the south of the country, Néma in the southeast and Akjoujt in the north. A paved highway, namely *La Route de l'Espoir*, runs east from Nouakchott to Mali. All other routes are sand tracks necessitating the use of 4-wheel drive vehicles. In some regions during and after the rainy season roads may become impassable. Similarly, in the dry season tracks can be obscured by drifting sand; a guide is highly recommended, if not essential. **Car hire:** Available in Nouakchott, Nouâdhibou and Atâr. 4-wheel drive vehicles with a driver can be hired and are recommended, but they are expensive. **Documentation:** An International Driving Permit is recommended, although it is not legally required. **Note:** Travellers should never attempt any desert journey without a full set of spare parts and essential safety equipment. The Direction du Tourisme in Nouakchott, part of the Ministère du Commerce de l'Artisanat et du Tourisme, can give further information and advice on road travel (see *Contact Addresses* section).
URBAN: Taxis are plentiful but very expensive in the towns (Nouakchott and Nouadhibou). Fares are set, not metered, and a small tip is expected.

Accommodation

HOTELS: Hotel accommodation is very limited in Mauritania and visitors are advised to book well in advance. The larger hotels in Nouakchott are comfortable and have air conditioning but, even in the capital, accommodation is limited and expensive. Bills normally include service and local tax.
REST HOUSES: There are numerous government rest houses throughout the country, bookable through the Ministère du Commerce de l'Artisanat et du Tourisme.

Resorts & Excursions

Much of the land is dry and inhospitable and many locations are difficult to reach without long journeys in 4-wheel drive vehicles. Drawbacks aside, Mauritania is a fascinating country with a colourful, indigenous Moorish population.
NOUAKCHOTT: The capital of Mauritania is a new city created in 1960. It lies near the sea in a desert landscape of low dunes scattered with thorn bushes, on a site adjoining an old Moorish settlement, the **Ksar**. The modern buildings maintain the traditional Berber style of architecture. The following places are worth visiting: the **Plage du Wharf**, the mosque, the Ksar and its market, the African market and the camel market, the crafts centre, the **Maison de la Culture** and the carpet factory.
PARC NATIONAL DU BANC D'ARGUIN: Possibly Mauritania's best attraction, this national park is a vast area of islands and coastline located on the Atlantic desert coast midway between Nouakchott and Nouâdhibou. The park, which was declared a World Heritage Site by UNESCO, is one of the world's largest bird sanctuaries and provides a shelter for over two million migrant birds from northern Europe. There are also several archaeological sites on the islands.
THE COAST: Mauritania's coast is essentially an 800km-(500 mile-) long sandy beach, all but devoid of vegetation but supporting an astonishingly large and varied population of birds. The waters are equally rich in fish and, consequently, despite the shortage of fresh water, some coastal stretches are inhabited by people. A growing port and centre of the fishing industry, Nouâdhibou is situated on a peninsula at the northern end of the **Bay of Levrier**. Inland, the landscape is empty desert.
One tribe, halfway between Nouakchott and **Nouâdhibou**, survives through a symbiotic relationship with wild dolphins: the marine mammals drive fish towards the shore, the tribesmen swim out with nets, and both get their share. Foreign trawlers, however, are rapidly depleting offshore fish stocks.
ADRAR REGION: It is important to check on conditions for travel before setting out for this region as government permission may be necessary. The Adrar is a spectacular massif of pink and brown plateaux gilded with dunes and intersected by deep canyons sheltering palm groves. It lies in the north central part of the country, and begins about 320km (200 miles) northeast of Nouakchott. **Atâr**, capital of the region, is an oasis lying on the route of salt caravans. It is the market centre for the nomads of northern Mauritania and has an old quarter, the **Ksar**, with flat-roofed houses and a fine palm grove. The oasis of **Azoughui** was the Almoravid capital in the 11th and 12th centuries, and remains of fortified buildings from this period can still be seen. A whole-day excursion from Atar leads over the breathtaking mountain pass of **Homogjar** to **Chinguetti**, a holy city of Islam, founded in the 13th century, and now listed by UNESCO as a World Heritage site. The city has a medieval mosque and a library housing ancient manuscripts, but much of the old town is disappearing under the encroaching drifts of sand.
AFFOLÉ AND ASSABA REGIONS: It is worth making a tour of the Affolé and Assaba regions, south and southeast of the Tagant, via **Kiffa**, **Tamchakett** and **Ayoun el Atrous**, to the wild plateaux of **El Agher**. The interesting archaeological sites include **Koumbi Saleh**, once capital of the Ghana Empire, 70km (45 miles) from Timbedra along a good track. Near Tamchakett is **Tagdawst**, which has been identified as 'Aoudaghost', an ancient capital of a Berber empire. **Oualata** lies 100km (60 miles) from **Néma** at the end of a desert track. Declared a World Heritage Site by UNESCO, Oualata was at one time among the greatest caravan *entrepôts* of the Sahara. A fortified medieval town built in terraces up a rocky peak, it has for centuries been a place of refuge for scholars and has a fine library. The Muslim cemetery of **Tirzet** is nearby.

Sport & Activities

Birdwatching: The Parc National du Banc d'Arguin is reputed to be one of Africa's best places for birdwatching. Amongst the many species that can be observed are large colonies of aquatic birds, such as herons, pelicans and flamingos. The park is fairly difficult to access and the entry fee is approximately US$6 per day. The head office is located in Nouâdhibou.
Watersports: There are some good spots for **fishing** and even **surfing** along the coast in the west. **Swimming** is also possible, but travellers should note that pickpocketing and crime is reported to be rife on Mauritania's beaches. Remote and deserted beaches can be found near Nouâdhibou, although travellers should beware of landmines in the area.

Social Profile

FOOD & DRINK: Moroccan, Lebanese, Chinese and French restaurants can be found in the capital, especially in hotels. Local cuisine, based on lamb, goat and rice can be sampled throughout the country. Mauritanian food includes *mechoui* (whole roast lamb), dates, spiced fish and rice with vegetables, fish balls, dried fish, dried meat and *couscous*. Consumption of alcohol is prohibited by the Islamic faith, but alcoholic beverages may be found in hotel bars. *Zrig* (camel's milk) is a common drink, as is sweet Arab tea with mint.
SHOPPING: Handicrafts such as dyed leather cushions and some engraved silver items, rugs and woodcarvings can be bought on the open market. A fine selection of silver jewellery, daggers, wood and silver chests, carpets and decorated nomad tents can be bought in the crafts centre in Nouakchott. Unique to the Tagant region are neolithic arrowheads, awls and pottery, while at Boutilimit in the south is a Marabout centre (Institute of High Islamic Studies) where fine carpets of goat and camel hair are made.
Shopping hours: Sat-Thurs 0800-1200 and 1400-1900.
SPECIAL EVENTS: Special events celebrated in Mauritania are generally Muslim holy days and feasts.
SOCIAL CONVENTIONS: Islam has been the major influence in this country since the seventh and eighth centuries and visitors should respect the religious laws and customs. Dress for women should be uncompromisingly modest. Nearly all the population have traditionally been nomadic herdsmen. The bulk of the population is divided into two main Moorish groups, the Bidan (55 per cent) and the Harattin (20 per cent), with the non-Moorish population concentrated in the Senegal River area. Different classes and tribes tend to be contiguous. **Tipping:** 12 to 15 per cent is normal.

Business Profile

ECONOMY: Successive years of drought and encroaching desert have consumed large areas of Mauritania's cultivable land. More than half the population is engaged in subsistence agriculture, producing vegetables, millet, rice and dates, and rearing livestock, mostly in the area south of the Senegal River. The quantities produced are insufficient to meet domestic needs and Mauritania relies on imports of basic foodstuffs. Fishing is essential both to domestic needs and the country's export income, also for the revenue from licences granted to foreign fleets from Korea, Japan and Russia. Mining is Mauritania's principal industry: the main products are iron ore, gypsum and gold. There are plans to exploit the country's copper reserves, which were long thought uneconomic, as well as newly located diamond deposits. Offshore drilling for oil and gas fields has recently begun. Nonetheless, Mauritania will remain an exceptionally poor country for the foreseeable future and a major aid recipient, with other Arab countries as the main donors. The economy grew by 5 per cent in 2002; inflation was 3 per cent in the same year. The IMF and World Bank have given some economic support in exchange for the standard economic reform programme. Current economic growth is around 5 per cent annually. Nonetheless, Mauritania's financial position remains precarious. Japan and the southern EU countries are the main export markets, while the major exporters to Mauritania are France, Spain, Germany, The Netherlands and the USA. Mauritania is a member of the Union of the Arab Maghreb. It was also a member of the Economic Community of West African States (ECOWAS) until its withdrawal from the organisation in 2000.
BUSINESS: Use forms of address as for France, eg 'Monsieur le Directeur'. It is essential that businesspeople have a sound knowledge of French, as very few executives speak English. Office hours: Sun-Thurs 0800-1500.
COMMERCIAL INFORMATION: The following organisation can offer advice: Chambre de Commerce, d'Agriculture, d'Elevage, d'Industrie et des Mines de Mauritanie, Avenue de la Republique, BP 215, Nouakchott (tel: 252 214; fax: 253 895).

Climate

Most of the country is hot and dry with practically no rain. In the south, however, rainfall is higher with a rainy season which runs from July to September. The coast is tempered by trade winds and is mild with the exception of the hot Nouakchott region (where the rainy season begins a month later). Deserts are cooler and windy in March and April.
Required clothing: Lightweight cottons and linens, with a warm wrap for cool evenings. Waterproofs are necessary for the rainy season.

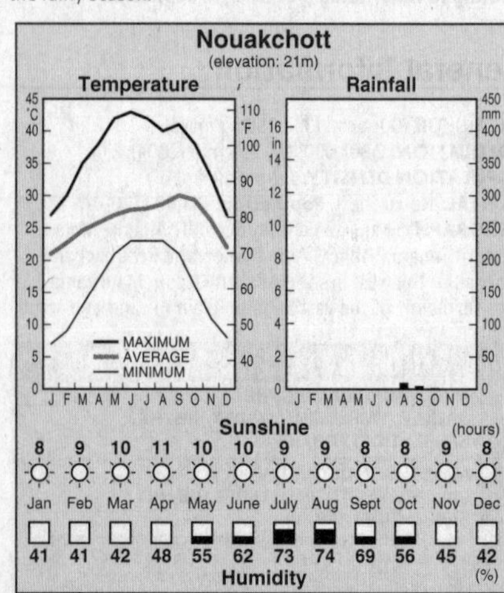

A B C D E F G H I J K L M N O P Q R S T U V W X Y Z

Mauritius

LATEST TRAVEL ADVICE CONTACTS

British Foreign and Commonwealth Office
Tel: (0870) 606 0290 Website: www.fco.gov.uk

US Department of State
Website: http://travel.state.gov/travel

Canadian Department of Foreign Affairs and Int'l Trade
Tel: (1 800) 267 8376 Website: www.dfait-maeci.gc.ca

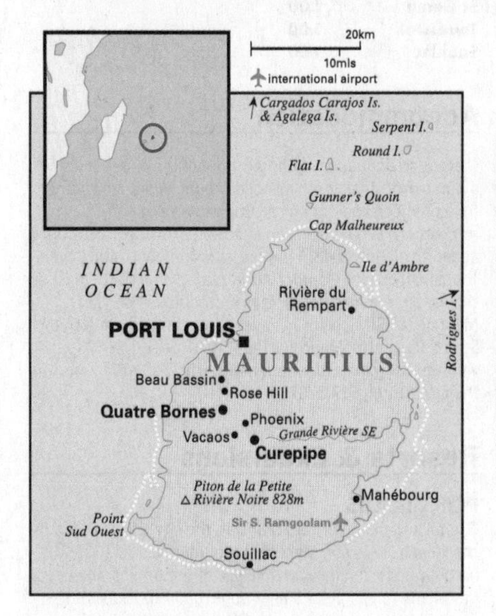

Location: Indian Ocean, off southeast coast of Africa; due east of Madagascar.

Country dialling code: 230.

Mauritius Tourism Promotion Authority
Air Mauritius Building, 11th Floor, President John Kennedy Street, Port Louis, Mauritius
Tel: 210 1545 *or* 208 6397. Fax: 212 5142.
E-mail: mtpa@intnet.mu
Website: www.mauritius.net

Mauritius High Commission
32-33 Elvaston Place, London SW7 5NW, UK
Tel: (020) 7581 0294-8. Fax: (020) 7823 8437.
E-mail: londonmhc@btinternet.com
Opening hours: Mon-Fri 0930-1200 (consular section); 0930-1700 (general enquiries).
Also deals with tourism enquiries.

Mauritius Tourism Promotion Authority
32 Elvaston Place, London SW7 5NW, UK
Tel: (020) 7584 3666. Fax: (020) 7225 1135.
E-mail: mtpa@btinternet.com
Website: www.mauritiustourism.co.uk

British High Commission
Street address: Les Cascades Building, Edith Cavell Street, Port Louis, Mauritius
Postal address: PO Box 1063, Port Louis, Mauritius
Tel: 202 9400.
Fax: 202 9408 *or* 07 (visa and consular section).
E-mail: bhc@intnet.mu

Embassy of Mauritius
4301 Connecticut Avenue, Suite 441, NW, Washington, DC 20008, USA
Tel: (202) 244 1491/2. Fax: (202) 966 0983.
E-mail: mauritius.embassy@prodigy.net
Website: http://ncb.intnet.mu
Also deals with enquiries from Canada.

Embassy of the United States of America
4th Floor, Rogers House, John Kennedy Avenue, Port Louis, Mauritius
Tel: 202 4400. Fax: 208 9534.
E-mail: usembass@intnet.mu
Website: http://mauritius.usembassy.gov

TIMATIC CODES

Health
AMADEUS: **TI-DFT/MRU/HE**
GALILEO/WORLDSPAN: **TI-DFT/MRU/HE**
SABRE: **TIDFT/MRU/HE**

Visa
AMADEUS: **TI-DFT/MRU/VI**
GALILEO/WORLDSPAN: **TI-DFT/MRU/VI**
SABRE: **TIDFT/MRU/VI**

To access TIMATIC country information on Health and Visa regulations through the Computer Reservations System (CRS), type in the appropriate command line listed above.

Credit: © Mauritius Tourism Promotion Authority

Honorary Consulate of Mauritius
606 Cathcart Street, Suite 200, Montréal, Québec H3B 1K9, Canada
Tel: (514) 393 9500. Fax: (514) 393 9324.
E-mail: info@gga-mtl.ca

Canadian Consulate
Street address: 18 Jules Koenig Street, c/o Blanche Birger Co LTD, Port Louis, Mauritius
Postal address: PO Box 209, Port Louis, Mauritius
Tel: 212 5500. Fax: 208 3391.
E-mail: canada@intnet.mu

The Canadian High Commission in Pretoria usually deals with enquiries relating to Mauritius (see *South Africa* **section).**

General Information

AREA: 2040 sq km (788 sq miles).
POPULATION: 1,122,811 (official estimate 2003).
POPULATION DENSITY: 599.4 per sq km.
CAPITAL: Port Louis. **Population:** 144,303 (2000).
GEOGRAPHY: Mauritius, a volcanic and mountainous island in the Indian Ocean, lies 2000km (1240 miles) off the southeastern coast of Africa, due east of Madagascar. The island state stands on what was once a land bridge between Asia and Africa called the Mascarene Archipelago. From the coast, the land rises to form a broad fertile plain on which sugar cane flourishes. Some 500km (310 miles) east is Rodrigues Island, while northeast are the Cargados Carajos Shoals and 900km (560 miles) to the north is Agalega.
GOVERNMENT: Republic. Gained independence from the UK in 1968. **Head of State:** President Anerood Jugnauth since 2003. **Head of Government:** Prime Minister Paul Bérenger since 2003.
LANGUAGE: English is the official language. The most widely spoken languages are French, Creole (36 per cent), Hindi and Bhojpuri (32 per cent). Urdu and Chinese are also among the languages spoken.
RELIGION: 51 per cent Hindu, 30 per cent Christian, 17 per cent Muslim.
TIME: GMT + 4.
ELECTRICITY: 220 volts AC, 50Hz. UK-type three-pin plugs are commonly used in hotels.
COMMUNICATIONS: Telephone: IDD is available. Country code: 230. There are no area codes. Outgoing international code: 00. There are a limited number of public telephone booths, mainly at the airport and in major hotels. **Mobile telephone:** GSM 900 networks, with coverage extending over the whole island. Network operators include *Cellplus Mobile Comms* (website: www.gocellplus.com) and *Emtel* (website: www.emtel-ltd.com). Handsets and SIM cards can be hired. **Fax:** Most hotels have facilities, as well as *Mauritius Telecom* offices in Port Louis and Cassis. **Internet:** There are a number of ISPs in Mauritius; they include *MauriNet*, *Mauritius Network (MNS)*, *Mauritius Telecom* (website: http://mt.intnet.mu) and *Telecom Plus* (website: www.servihoo.com). There are Internet cafes in Phoenix, Vaoas and other main towns. Most hotels offer Internet facilities. **Telegram:** Messages can be sent from the Mauritius Telecommunications Service offices in Cassis and Port Louis. There are also facilities at Overseas Telecoms Services Ltd, Rogers House, John Kennedy Street, Port Louis. **Post:** Airmail to Western Europe usually takes five days; by sea, mail takes four to six weeks. Post office hours: Generally Mon-Fri 0815-1115 and 1200-1600, Sat 0800-1145. **Press:** Of the 10 daily newspapers, two are published in Chinese and the remainder in French and English. *L'Express*, *Le Mauricien* and *Le Quotidien* have the highest circulation.
Radio: BBC World Service (website: www.bbc.co.uk/worldservice) and Voice of America (website: www.voa.gov) can be received. From time to time the frequencies change and the most up-to-date can be found online.

Passport/Visa

	Passport Required?	Visa Required?	Return Ticket Required?
Full British	Yes	No	Yes
Australian	Yes	No	Yes
Canadian	Yes	No	Yes
USA	Yes	No	Yes
Other EU	Yes	No	Yes
Japanese	Yes	No	Yes

Note: Regulations and requirements may be subject to change at short notice, and you are advised to contact the appropriate diplomatic or consular authority before finalising travel arrangements. Details of these may be found at the head of this country's entry. Any numbers in the chart refer to the footnotes below.

PASSPORTS: Passport valid for at least six months from date of entry required by all. Passports issued by the government of Taiwan are not recognised. The holders of such documents can apply for an entry permit to the Passport and Immigration Officer (see address below).
Note: All visitors must hold valid tickets and documents for their onward or return journey and adequate funds for their intended length of stay.
VISAS: Required by all except the following:
(a) nationals of countries referred to in the chart above for stays up to three months;
(b) nationals of Commonwealth countries, except nationals of India (see below) and nationals of Bangladesh, Cameroon, Fiji, India, Nigeria, Pakistan, Sri Lanka and Swaziland, who *do* require a visa for stays of up to three months;
(c) nationals of Bahrain, Hong Kong (SAR), Israel, Kuwait, Liechtenstein, Monaco, Norway, Oman, Qatar, San Marino, Saudi Arabia, Switzerland, Tunisia, Turkey, United Arab Emirates, Vatican City and Zimbabwe for stays of up to three months;
(d) nationals of China (PR), India, Jordan and Lebanon for touristic stays of up to 15 days;
(e) transit passengers continuing their journey to a third country within 24 hours provided holding valid onward or return documentation and not leaving the airport.
Types of visa and cost: *Tourist*, *Business* and *Social*, each

available as single- or multiple-entry. Visas are issued free of charge.
Validity: *Tourist/Business* visas: Up to three months. Applications for extensions should be made to the relevant authority (see below).
Application to: Consulate (or Consular section at Embassy or High Commission); see *Contact Addresses* section for details.
Note: (a) Nationals of Argentina, Brazil, Chile and Paraguay can obtain a visa on arrival for stays of up to three months. (b) Nationals of Korea (Rep) can obtain a visa on arrival for stays of up to 16 days. (c) Nationals of Albania, Bulgaria, CIS, Comoro Islands, Fiji, Madagascar and Romania can obtain a visa on arrival for stays of up to two weeks. Extensions are possible.
These visas can be issued from Sir Seewoosagur Ramgoolam International Airport or the Passport and Immigration Office in Port Louis (see *Contact Addresses* section).
Application requirements: (a) Valid passport. (b) Completed application form. (c) Two passport-size photos. (d) Photocopy of passport page with date of birth. (e) Proof of sufficient funds (at least US$50 per day or equivalent, or at least US$100 per day for some other nationals). (f) Proof of accommodation such as hotel booking or letter of invitation. (g) Self-addressed stamped envelope. (h) Appropriate documents for the next destination, including return or onward tickets.
Working days required: Varies according to nationality of applicant. Most can be issued within seven days but can take up to one month.
Temporary residence: Residence permits are issued by the Passport and Immigration Officer, Sterling House, Lislet Geoffrey Street, Port Louis (tel: 210 9312-9; fax: 210 9322). Work permits are necessary for those taking up employment.

Money

Currency: Mauritian Rupee (MRs) = 100 cents. Notes are in denominations of MRs2000, 1000, 500, 200, 100, 50 and 25. Coins are in denominations of MRs10, 5 and 1, and 50, 20, 10, and 5 cents.
Currency exchange: Available in banks and at bureaux de change. A better rate of exchange can be obtained on travellers cheques than on cash.
Credit & debit cards: American Express, Diners Club, MasterCard and Visa are widely accepted. Check with your credit, or debit, card company for details of merchant acceptability and other services which may be available.
Travellers cheques: May be exchanged at banks, hotels and authorised dealers.
Currency restrictions: There are no limits on the import or export of local or foreign currency.
Exchange rate indicators: The following figures are included as a guide to the movements of the Mauritian Rupee against Sterling and the US Dollar:

Date	Feb '04	May '04	Aug '04	Nov '04
£1.00=	46.50	49.03	52.21	53.83
$1.00=	25.55	27.45	28.34	28.43

Banking hours: Mon-Thurs 0915-1515, Fri 0915-1530, Sat 0915-1115 (except for Bank of Mauritius). Some banks may open Mon-Fri 0900-1700.

Duty Free

The following goods may be imported into Mauritius by persons 18 and over without incurring customs duty:
200 cigarettes or 250g of tobacco products or 50 cigars; *1l of spirits and 2l of wine or beer*; *250ml of eau de toilette and 100ml of perfume for personal use*.
Restricted items: Vegetables, fruit, flowers, plants and seeds must be declared (all require permit from the Ministry of Agriculture), as must firearms and ammunition. Imported animal products also require a permit.
Prohibited items: Sugarcane and related parts thereof, soil micro-organisms and invertebrate animals.

Public Holidays

2005: Jan 1-2 New Year. **Jan 25** Thaipoosam Cavadee. **Feb 1** Abolition of Slavery Day. **Feb 9** Chinese New Year. **Mar 8** Maha Shivaratri. **Mar 12** National Day. **Apr 9** Ougadi. **May 1** Labour Day. **Aug 15** Assumption of the Blessed Virgin Mary. **Sep 8** Ganesh Chaturthi. **Nov 1** Diwali. **Nov 2** Arrival of Indentured Labourers. **Nov 3-4** Eid al-Fitr (End of Ramadan). **Dec 25** Christmas Day.
2006: Jan *or* **Feb** Thaipoosam Cavadee. **Jan 1-2** New Year. **Jan 29** Chinese New Year. **Feb 1** Abolition of Slavery Day. **Feb 26** Maha Shivaratri. **Mar 12** National Day. **Mar 15** Ougadi. **May 1** Labour Day. **Aug 15** Assumption of the Blessed Virgin Mary. **Aug 27** Ganesh Chaturthi. **Nov 2** Arrival of Indentured Labourers. **Oct 21** Diwali. **Oct 22-24** Eid al-Fitr (End of Ramadan). **Dec 25** Christmas Day.
Note: (a) Hindu festivals are timed according to local sightings of various phases of the moon. The dates given above are approximations. (b) There is a diversity of cultures in Mauritius, each with its own set of holidays. (c) Muslim festivals are timed according to local sightings of various phases of the moon and the dates given above are approximations. During the lunar month of Ramadan that precedes Eid al-Fitr, Muslims fast during the day and feast at night and normal business patterns may be interrupted. Some disruption may continue into Eid al-Fitr itself. Eid al-Fitr may last from two to 10 days, depending on the town or region. For more information, see the *World of Islam* appendix. (d) Chinese festivals are declared according to local astronomical observations and it is often only possible to forecast the approximate time of their occurrence.

Health

	Special Precautions?	Certificate Required?
Yellow Fever	No	1
Cholera	No	No
Typhoid & Polio	2	N/A
Malaria	3	N/A

Note: *Regulations and requirements may be subject to change at short notice, and you are advised to contact your doctor well in advance of your intended date of departure. Any numbers in the chart refer to the footnotes below.*

1: A yellow fever vaccination certificate is required of travellers over one year of age arriving from infected areas. The Mauritius government considers those countries and areas classified as yellow fever endemic to be infected.
2: Immunisation against typhoid and poliomyelitis is sometimes advised.
3: Malaria risk, exclusively in the benign *vivax* form, exists throughout the year in northern rural areas, except on Rodrigues Island.
Food & drink: Water used for drinking should have first been boiled or otherwise sterilised. Bottled water is readily available. Milk is unpasteurised and should be boiled. Powdered or tinned milk is available and is advised but make sure that it is reconstituted with pure water. Avoid dairy products which are likely to have been made from unboiled milk. Vegetables should be cooked and fruit peeled.
Other risks: *Diarrhoeal diseases*, *giardiasis*, *dysentery* and *typhoid fever* are common. *Bilharzia* (schistosomiasis) is present. Avoid swimming and paddling in fresh water; swimming pools which are well chlorinated and maintained are safe. *Hepatitis A, B* and *E* occur.
Health care: Public medical facilities are numerous and of a high standard and there are several private clinics. All treatment at state-run hospitals is free for Mauritians but foreign visitors have to pay. There is no reciprocal health agreement with the UK; health insurance is advised.
Note: For travellers applying for a working visa or permanent residence, an HIV test will be required.

Travel - International

AIR: The national airline of Mauritius is *Air Mauritius (MK)* (website: www.airmauritius.com). *Air Austral*, *Air Europe*, *Air France*, *Air India*, *Air Madagascar*, *Air Seychelles*, *Air Zimbabwe*, *Condor*, *Emirates*, *Malaysian Airlines* and *South African Airways* also fly to Mauritius. *British Airways* operates four weekly flights.
Approximate flight times: From Mauritius to *London* is 11 hours 30 minutes (non-stop).
International airports: *Mauritius (MRU)* (Sir Seewoosagur Ramgoolam) is 48km (30 miles) southeast of Port Louis. Taxis are available to the city (travel time – 45 minutes). Airport facilities include duty free shops, banks/bureaux de change, snack bar, post office, shops and car hire (includes *Avis*, *Europcar* and *Hertz*). A new terminal has recently been built.
Departure tax: None.
SEA: Port Louis is the main port. It is primarily commercial but there is a limited passenger service to Réunion and Rodrigues Island.

Travel - Internal

AIR: *Air Mauritius* operates daily flights connecting Plaisance Airport and Rodrigues Island (flight time – one hour 15 minutes).
SEA: *Coraline* sails once a week to Rodrigues Island from Port Louis. Contact Mauritius Shipping, Nova Building, One Military Road, Port Louis (tel: 242 2912 *or* 5255; fax: 242 5245).
ROAD: There is a good network of paved roads covering the island. Traffic drives on the left. **Bus:** There are excellent and numerous bus services to all parts of the island. **Taxi:** These have white registration plates with black figures. Taxis are metered. **Car hire:** There are numerous car hire firms. Most require drivers to be over 23 years old. **Documentation:** International Driving Permit recommended, although a foreign licence is accepted. A temporary driving licence is available from local authorities on presentation of a valid British or Northern Ireland driving licence.
URBAN: Bus and taxi services are available in urban areas. Bicycles and boats are also available to hire.
Travel times: The following chart gives approximate travel times (in hours and minutes) from **Port Louis** to other major cities/towns in Mauritius.

	Road
Curepipe	0.20
Plaisance	1.00
Grand Bay	0.30
St Geran	1.00
Touessrok	1.00
Souillac	1.00

Accommodation

There is an abundance of hotels throughout the island and a number of smaller family holiday bungalows. From June to September, and during the Christmas season, reservations should be made in advance. A 10 per cent tax is added to all hotel bills. For more information, contact the Tourist Office (see *Contact Addresses* section for details) *or* the Association des Hôteliers et Restaurateurs de l'Ile Maurice (AHRIM), Level 7, Travel House, Sir William Newton Street, Port Louis, Mauritius (tel: 211 6105; fax: 211 7359; website: www.mauritius.net/ahrim), who also have a desk at the airport (tel: 637 3782).

Resorts & Excursions

PORT LOUIS

Capital and main port of Mauritius, the city was founded by the French Governor, Mahé de Labourdonnais, in 1735. The harbour is sheltered by a semicircle of mountains. The city has plenty of character and, in some quarters, signs of its past elegance are still evident. Off the main square, the palm-lined **Place d'Armes**, there are some particularly fine French colonial buildings, especially **Government House** (built in 1738) and the **Municipal Theatre**, built around the same time. There are two cathedrals, one Protestant and one Catholic, a fine **Supreme Court Building**, some 18th-century barracks and the **Natural History Museum** (exhibiting Mauritius's most famous bird, the extinct Dodo). On the outskirts of the city, at the foot of the mountains, is the **Champ de Mars**, originally laid out by the French for military parades, and now a racecourse. The splendid **Edward VII Avenue** and **Fort Adelaide**, a citadel fortified in the time of William IV, offer the best views of the racecourse, city and harbour. South of Port Louis is **Le Réduit**, the French colonial residence of the President of Mauritius, set in magnificent gardens. Other places of interest include the **Jummah Mosque** in Royal Street and the **Chinese Pagoda**.
Excursions: The **Domaine Les Pailles** nature park nestling at the foot of the Moka mountain range covers an area of 3000 acres. Among the attractions are a natural spring, a spice garden, a replica of a sugar mill and an old rum distillery. Trips through the park in 4-wheel-drive vehicles, horse-drawn carriages or trains are also possible.

NORTHERN AND WESTERN MAURITIUS

To the north of Port Louis are the **Pamplemousses Gardens**. These, created at the end of the 18th century, are known to naturalists throughout the world for their large collection of indigenous and exotic plants, including the giant *Victoria regia* water lilies and many species of palm trees. Of particular interest is the *talipot* palm, which is said to flower once, after 60 years, and then die. There are also tortoises here, some of them over 100 years old.
Facing the calm water of the lagoon between **Pointe aux Piments** and **Trou aux Biches** is the **Aquarium** populated by 200 species of fish, invertebrates, live coral and sponges, all originating from the waters around the island. An open-circuit seawater cycle of one million litres runs through the 36 tanks every day. The Aquarium offers a unique opportunity to admire the colourful treasures of the Indian Ocean.
The island's main residential town in the west of the country, **Curepipe**, provides good shops and restaurants. Between Curepipe and **Floreal** lies **Trou aux Cerfs**, a dramatic, extinct crater 85m (280ft) deep and more than 180m (600ft) wide, which offers extensive views of the island from its rim.
Open daily, **Casela Bird Park** is set in the district of the **Rivière Noire**, stretches over 20 acres of land and contains more than 140 varieties, amounting to 2500 birds. Specimens from the five continents may be seen there, but the main attraction is the Mauritian Pink Pigeon, which is one of the rarest birds in the world. Other attractions are the fish ponds, tortoises, monkeys and orchids (seasonal).

Trees, streams and small cascades all add to the remarkably peaceful atmosphere.
RODRIGUES ISLAND: Situated 550km (340 miles) northeast of Mauritius, this tiny, rugged, volcanic island is a beautiful and relaxing refuge for travellers. The island is covered in coconut palms, *casuarina* trees and pink-flowered bushes known as *vieilles filles* (spinsters). The capital, **Port Mathurin** is the main port of entry and the 'Mauritius Pride' sails regularly to and from Mauritius.

SOUTHERN MAURITIUS

Domaine des Grands Bois covers over 2000 acres of magnificent parkland, rich in lush and exotic fauna. Ebony, eucalyptus, palm trees and wild orchids provide the backdrop for stags, deer, monkeys and other wildlife.
Near **Souillac**, in the wild south, **La Vanille Crocodile Park** breeds Nile crocodiles imported from Madagascar. The site offers a vast park with a nature walk through luxuriant forest studded with freshwater springs. A small zoo of animals found in the wild in Mauritius is also located here. Situated nearby, the **Rochester Falls** can be reached by a road which crosses a sugar plantation that is open to visitors. Water cascades over spectacular rock formations. Spectacular joints have been formed by the contraction of lava due to sudden cooling. Within a short distance of **Bois Cheri**, **Grand Bassin** rests in the crater of an extinct volcano, this is one of the island's two natural lakes. It is a place of pilgrimage for a large number of Mauritians of the Hindu faith.
To the southwest lies **Plaine Champagne**, the highest part of the central plateau (740m/2430ft), from where there is a superb view of the **Rivière Noire Mountains** and the sea lining the horizon. The forest-clad slopes contain some fine specimens of indigenous timber and interesting plants peculiar to the island. For the keen birdwatcher, the mountains are the habitat of most of the remaining indigenous species.
A twisting, tarred road leads from **Case Noyale** village to **Chamarel**. This is an area of undulating land of seven contrasting layers of coloured dunes: blue, green, red and yellow earth, believed to be the result of weathering. The nearby **Chamarel Waterfall** emerges from the moors and the primeval vegetation and is very beautiful.

BEACHES

Tamarin: Lying in the shadow of the Rivière Noire Mountains, Tamarin has a fine lagoon which is split in two by the Rivière Noire estuary. The bathing at this point is a big attraction, and amenities for surfing in the big ocean swells are available.
Grand Baie: The northern coastline beyond **Baie du Tombeau** has many delightful beaches: Pointe aux Piments, famous for its underwater scenery; **Trou aux Biches**, with its fringe of *filaos* (casuarina) and coconut palms and its splendid Hindu temple; further up the coast, **Choisy**, one of the most popular beaches on the island, offering facilities for safe bathing, sailing, windsurfing and water-skiing; finally, the coastline curves into Grand Baie itself, the main centre for yachting, water-skiing, windsurfing and many other sports.
Péreybère: This delightful little cove is midway on the coast road between Grand Baie and Cap Malheureux. The deep, clear water makes it one of the very best bathing places on the whole island.
Cap Malheureux: This is a fishing village in the extreme north, with a magnificent view of **Flat Island**, **Round Island** and **Gunner's Quoin**, which are islands of volcanic origin, rising from the light-green sea.
Grand Gaube: Further along the coast is another charming fishing village where fishermen have earned a well-deserved reputation for their skill in the making of sailing craft and of deep-sea fishing.
Roches Noires/Poste Lafayette: These are both favoured seaside resorts, especially in the hotter months, because of the fresh prevailing winds that blow almost all the year round from the sea.
Belle Mare: A beautiful white sandy beach with fine bathing is found here. The coast, with its white sweep of sands at **Palmar** and **Trou d'Eau Douce**, stretches out lazily to **Grand Port**, a quaint little village by the sea. There, the beach narrows and the road follows the coastline closely to **Mahébourg**. **Pointe d'Esny**, the adjoining white sandy beach with its string of bungalows, leads to Blue Bay.
Blue Bay: In a semicircle of *filao* trees lies one of the finest bathing spots on the island. Situated on the southeast coast, not far from Mahébourg, Blue Bay offers a fine stretch of white sandy beach, and a deep, clear, light-blue bathing pool. There is also scope for yachting and windsurfing.

Sport & Activities

Watersports: Beaches, lagoons and inlets around the coast offer plenty of opportunity for safe **swimming** (see *Resorts & Excursions* section), supplemented by hotel swimming

Credit: © Mauritius Tourism Promotion Authority

pools. *Grand Baie*, north of Pamplemousses Gardens, is a popular beach for **diving**. Further good dive sites can be found around *Flic-en-Flac* on the west coast of Mauritius, and on *Rodrigues Island*. The Mauritian Scuba Diving Association can provide further information (tel: 454 0011; e-mail: msda@intnet.mu). There is good coastal and inland **fishing** around the island.
Golf: This is becoming increasingly popular on Mauritius, with an annual *Golf Open* held in December. Golf courses offering 18 holes are at *Belle Mare Plage* in the northeast and the *Le Paradis* at the *Le Morne* in the southwest, and the *Ile Aux Cerf* golf course. Smaller rounds can be played at *St Géran Hotel, Trou aux-Biches, La Pirogue, Sugar Beach* and *Maritim* which offer nine holes.
Other: There are many opportunities for **trekking** in the interior of the island. Many of the best walks are in the *Réserve Forrestière Macchabée* and *Rivière Noire National Park*. Rodrigues Island also has some lovely hiking country, with coastal and mountain walks, notably to the island's highest points, *Mount Limon* and *Mount Malartic*. The Hippodrome at the *Champ de Mars* has meetings at the weekends between May and October where spectators can watch **horse racing**.

Social Profile

FOOD & DRINK: Waiter service is normal in restaurants and bars. Standards of cuisine, whether French, Creole, Indian, Chinese or English, are generally very high but fruit, meat, vegetables and even fresh seafood are often in short supply and restaurants must usually depend on imports. Specialities include venison (in season), *camarons* (freshwater prawns) in hot sauces, octopus, creole fish, fresh pineapple with chilli sauce, and rice with curry. *Dholl purri* is a wheat pancake stuffed with *dholl* and dipped in tomato sauce, whilst *samosas* are also very popular.
Rum and beer are staple beverages for Mauritians but there is good imported wine, mineral water, *alouda* (almond drink) and fresh coconut milk.
NIGHTLIFE: In Grand Baie and some towns there are discos and nightclubs with music and dancing. Rivière Noire is a Creole fishermen's district where *sega* dancing is especially lively on Saturday nights. *Sega* troupes give performances at most hotels. Gamblers are lavishly catered for; casinos in the island's hotels are amongst the island's attractions.
SHOPPING: The Central Market in Port Louis is full of beautifully displayed goods, including fruit, vegetables, spices, fish, meat and handicrafts. Island crafts include jewellery, Chinese and Indian jade, silks, basketry and pottery. Shopping centres are located at Quatre-Bornes and Rose-Hill. There is no duty payable on a number of products, including textiles. Shop signs may be in English, French or Chinese. Beside the Museum in Mahébourg, on the southeast coast of the island, is a handicraft village.
Shopping hours: Ranges from Mon-Sat 0930-1930. Some shops are open until 1200 on Sundays and public holidays. There are no shops open on Rose-Hill, Curepipe and Quatre-Bornes on Thursday afternoons.
SPECIAL EVENTS: With origins in three continents and three major religions there is a great diversity of religious and cultural festivals. For a complete list and for exact dates of festivals and events, enquire at the Mauritius Tourism Promotion Authority (see *Contact Addresses* section). The following is a selection of special events occurring in Mauritius in 2005:
Jan 13 *Thai Pongal* (Tamil new year celebrations). **Jan 29** *Chinese Spring Festival* (Chinese New Year). **Feb** *Maha Shivaratree* (celebrated in honour of Lord Shiva). **Mar 25** *Holi* (Hindu Festival of Light). **Sep** *Pere Laval's Day* (celebrated in honour of the missionary), Port Louis.
SOCIAL CONVENTIONS: Handshaking is the customary form of greeting. Visitors should respect the traditions of their hosts, particularly when visiting a private house. The type of hospitality the visitor receives is determined by the religion and social customs of the host, which are closely related. It is appropriate to give a gift as a small token of appreciation if invited for a meal. Dress is normally informal although men will need to wear a suit for particularly formal occasions. **Tipping:** 10 per cent is usual in most hotels and restaurants. Tips are not customary for taxi drivers.

Business Profile

ECONOMY: Sugar dominates Mauritius' agricultural economy: raw and processed sugar accounts for one-quarter of the island's export earnings. Tobacco and tea are the other main cash crops. Since independence in 1968, the government has deliberately sought to develop the industrial and service components of the economy. The island's industrial capacity is centred on a number of Export Processing Zones whose main products are clothing and textiles, consumer and industrial electronics, flowers and jewellery. Mauritius' service economy is based on tourism and financial services. Tourism is well established and now worth over US$500 million annually. The growth of financial services arose from a government initiative implemented in 1989; as a result, the island has since attracted more than US$1 billion of investment, mainly from South Africa and the Indian subcontinent. The overall economy grew at 7 per cent in 2001.
The government's economic policy aims to counter the threat to the two largest sectors of the economy – sugar and textiles – from new regulations introduced by the World Trade Organization. The centrepiece of its strategy is the creation of a custom-built 'cyber-city', based on similar development in India, using high-speed communications links to offer e-commerce and financial transactions.
The island's largest trading partners are France, the USA, Hong Kong, the UK and South Africa. Mauritius is a member of the Indian Ocean Commission, which promotes regional economic cooperation, and of the Southern African Development Community.
BUSINESS: Suits are often worn in business circles. Appointments **Office hours:** Mon-Fri 0930-1600, Sat 0900-1200 (some offices only).
COMMERCIAL INFORMATION: The following organisation can offer advice: Mauritius Chamber of Commerce and Industry, 3 Royal Street, Port Louis (tel: 208 3301; fax: 208 0076; e-mail: mcci@intnet.mu; website: www.mcci.org).

Climate

Warm coastal climate (particularly January to April), with relatively little seasonal variation in temperatures, although they are generally slightly lower inland, with more rain on the plateau around Curepipe. Cyclones may occur between November and February. Sea breezes blow all year, especially on the east coast.
Required clothing: Tropical lightweights, with warmer wear for evenings and winter months (July to September). Rainwear advisable all year round. In the summer months, sun-care products and a hat are advisable.

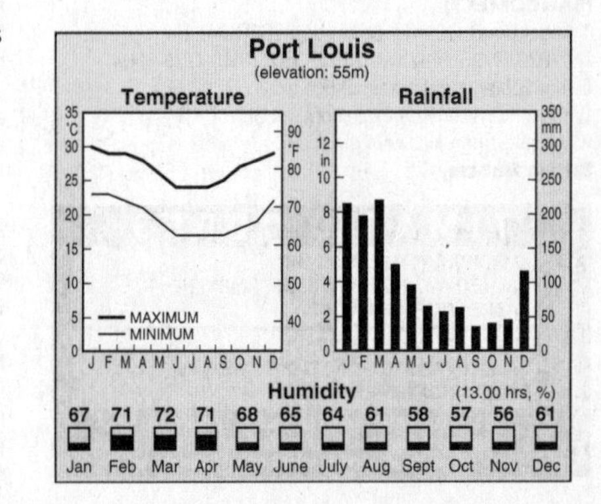

Mexico

LATEST TRAVEL ADVICE CONTACTS

British Foreign and Commonwealth Office
Tel: (0870) 606 0290 Website: www.fco.gov.uk

US Department of State
Website: http://travel.state.gov/travel

Canadian Department of Foreign Affairs and Int'l Trade
Tel: (1 800) 267 8376 Website: www.dfait-maeci.gc.ca

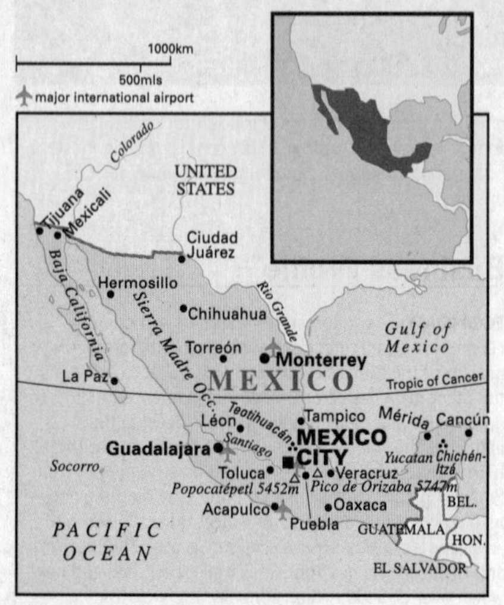

Location: Central America

Country dialling code: 52.

Secretaría de Turismo (SECTUR)
Av. Presidente Masaryk 172, Col. Chapultepec Morales, 11587 México DF, Mexico
Tel: (55) 3002 6300. Fax: (55) 3002 6371.
Website: www.sectur.gob.mx

Fondo Nacional de Fomento al Turismo (FONATUR)
Tecoyotitla No.100, Col. Florida CP 01030 México DF, Mexico
Tel: (55) 5090 4200. Fax: (55) 5687 5058.
Website: www.fonatur.gob.mx

Consejo de Promoción Turística de México
Mariano Escobedo 550, Piso 7, Col Anzures, 11590 México DF, Mexico
Tel: (55) 2581 0941 *or* (800) 929 4555 (toll free).
E-mail: mexicotravelnews@bm.com
Website: www.visitmexico.com

Mexican Embassy
16 St George Street, Hanover Square, London W1S 1LX, UK
Tel: (020) 7499 8586 *or* 7201 0961-3 (visa section).
Fax: (020) 7495 4035.
E-mail: mexuk@easynet.co.uk
Website: www.mexicanembassy.co.uk

Mexican Consulate
8 Halkin Street, London SW1X 7DW, UK
Tel: (020) 7235 6393 *or* (0906) 550 8969 (recorded visa information; calls cost £1 per minute).
Fax: (020) 7235 5480.
E-mail: info@mexicanconsulate.org.uk *or* consularlondon@easynet.co.uk
Website: www.mexicanconsulate.org.uk
Opening hours: Mon-Fri 0930-1300.

Mexican Tourism Promotion Board
Wakefield House, 41 Trinity Square, London EC3N 4DJ, UK
Tel: (020) 7488 9392. Fax: (020) 7265 0704.
E-mail: uk@visitmexico.com
Website: www.visitmexico.com

Trade Commission of the Mexican Embassy (BANCOMEXT)
1 Angel Court, 19th Floor, London EC2R 7HJ, UK
Tel: (020) 7726 4442 ext. 223. Fax: (020) 7726 6004.
E-mail: oblanco@bancomext.co.uk
Website: www.buyinmexico.com.mx *or* www.investinmexico.com.mx

British Embassy
Río Lerma 71, Colonia Cuauhtémoc, CP 06500 México DF, Mexico
Tel: (55) 5242 8500 *or* 5207 2089.
Fax: (55) 5242 8522 *or* 5242 8523 (consular section).
E-mail: consular.mexico@fco.gov.uk (consular section) *or* commsec@embajadabritanica.com.mx
Website: www.britishembassy.gov.uk/mexico
Consulates in: Acapulco, Cancún, Ciudad Juárez, Guadalajara, Monterrey, Oaxaca, Tijuana and Veracruz.

Mexican Embassy
1911 Pennsylvania Avenue, NW, Washington DC 20006
Tel: (202) 728 1600. Fax: (202) 728 1766.
E-mail: mexembusa@sre.gob.mx
Website: http://portal.sre.gob.mx/usa

Mexican Consulate
2827 16th Street, NW, Washington DC 20009, USA
Tel: (202) 736 1000 *or* 736 1002. Fax: (202) 234 4498.
E-mail: consulwas@aol.com
Website: www.embassyofmexico.org

Mexican Government Tourism Office
375 Park Avenue, Floor 19, Suite 1905, New York, NY 10152, USA
Tel: (212) 308 2110. Fax: (212) 308 9060.
E-mail: newyork@visitmexico.com
Website: www.visitmexico.com
Offices also in: Chicago, Coral Gables (Miami), Houston and Los Angeles.

Embassy of the United States of America
Paseo de la Reforma 305, Colonia Cuauhtémoc, 06500 México DF, Mexico
Tel: (55) 5080 2000. Fax: (55) 5511 9980.
E-mail: ccs@usembassy.net.mx *or* visas_mexico@state.gov (visa enquiries).
Website: www.usembassy-mexico.gov
Consulates General in: Ciudad Juárez, Guadalajara, Monterrey and Tijuana.
Consulates in: Hermosillo, Matamoros, Mérida, Nogales and Nuevo Larido.

Mexican Embassy
45 O'Connor Street, Suite 1000, Ottawa, Ontario K1P 1A4, Canada
Tel: (613) 233 8988 *or* 9272 *or* 9917. Fax: (613) 235 9123.
E-mail: fvasquez@embamexcan.com *or* velarde@embamexcan.com (consular section).
Website: www.embamexcan.com
Consulates in: British Colombia, Montréal and Toronto.
Honorary Consulates in: Calgary, Portsmouth, Regina, St Johns and Quebec.

Mexico Tourism Board
2 Bloor Street West, Suite 1502, Toronto, Ontario M4W 3E2, Canada
Tel: (416) 925 0704. Fax: (416) 925 6061.
E-mail: toronto@visitmexico.com
Website: www.visitmexico.com
Offices also in: Montréal and Vancouver.

Canadian Embassy
Street address: Calle Schiller 529, Colonia Polanco, 11580 México DF, Mexico
Postal address: Apartado Postal 105-05, 11580 México DF, Mexico
Tel: (55) 5387 9324 (information).
E-mail: enqserve@dfait-maeci.gc.ca *or* www@canada.org.mx
Website: www.dfait-maeci.gc.ca/mexico-city
Consulates in: Acapulco, Cancún, Guadalajara, Mazatlán, Monterrey, Oaxaca, Puerto Vallarta, San José del Cabo and Tijuana.

TIMATIC CODES

Health
AMADEUS: **TI-DFT/MEX/HE**
GALILEO/WORLDSPAN: **TI-DFT/MEX/HE**
SABRE: **TIDFT/MEX/HE**

Visa
AMADEUS: **TI-DFT/MEX/VI**
GALILEO/WORLDSPAN: **TI-DFT/MEX/VI**
SABRE: **TIDFT/MEX/VI**

To access TIMATIC country information on Health and Visa regulations through the Computer Reservations System (CRS), type in the appropriate command line listed above.

General Information

AREA: 1,959,248 sq km (758,449 sq miles).
POPULATION: 101,965,000 (UN estimate 2002).
POPULATION DENSITY: 51.9 per sq km.
CAPITAL: Mexico City. **Population:** 8,605,239 (2000).
GEOGRAPHY: Mexico is at the southern extremity of North America and is bordered to the north by the USA, northwest by the Gulf of California, west by the Pacific, south by Guatemala and Belize, and east by the Gulf of Mexico and the Caribbean. Mexico's geographical features range from swamp to desert, and from tropical lowland jungle to high alpine vegetation. Over half the country has an altitude above 1000m (3300ft). The central land mass is a plateau flanked by ranges of mountains to the east and west that lie roughly parallel to the coast. The northern area of this plateau is arid and thinly populated, and occupies 40 per cent of the total area of Mexico. The southern area is crossed by a range of volcanic mountains running from Cape Corrientes in the west through the Valley of Mexico to Veracruz in the east, and includes the magnificent volcanoes of Cofre de Perote, Ixtaccíhuatl, Matlalcueyetl, Nevado de Toluca, Orizaba and Popocatépetl. This is the heart of Mexico and where almost half of the population lives. To the south, the land falls away to the sparsely populated Isthmus of Tehuantepec whose slopes and flatlands support both commercial and subsistence agriculture. In the east, the Gulf Coast and the Yucatán peninsula are flat and receive over 75 per cent of Mexico's rain. The most productive agricultural region in Mexico is the northwest, while the Gulf Coast produces most of Mexico's oil and sulphur. Along the northwest coast, opposite the peninsula of Baja California, and to the southeast along the coast of Bahía de Campeche and the Yucatán peninsula, the lowlands are swampy with coastal lagoons.
GOVERNMENT: Republic since 1917. Gained independence from Spain in 1821. **Head of State and Government:** President Vicente Fox Quesada since 2000.
LANGUAGE: Spanish is the official language (spoken by more than 90 per cent). English is widely spoken. 8 per cent speak indigenous languages, of which Nátinate is most widely spoken.
RELIGION: 90 per cent Roman Catholic.
TIME: Mexico spans three different time zones:
South, Central and Eastern Mexico: GMT - 6 (Central Standard Time). (GMT - 5 from first Sunday in April to Saturday before last Sunday in October.)
Nayarit, Sonora, Sinaloa and Baja California Sur: GMT - 7 (Mountain Time). (GMT - 6 from first Sunday in April to Saturday before last Sunday in October.)
Baja California Norte (Pacific Time): GMT - 8 (GMT - 7 from first Sunday in April to Saturday before last Sunday in October).
ELECTRICITY: 110 volts AC, 60Hz. US two-pin (flat) plugs are usual.
COMMUNICATIONS: Telephone: IDD is available. Country code: 52. Outgoing international code: 00. Long-distance calls are very expensive. **Mobile telephone:** AMPS network is operated by IUSACELL. GSM 1900 network operated by *Movistar GSM*. The main network provider is *Telcel* (website: www.telcel.com). Handsets can be hired. **Fax:** Major hotels have facilities. **Internet:** ISPs include *Internet Mexico* (website: www.internet.com.mx) and *Red Internet* (website: www.redinternet.com.mx). Internet cafes exist in all regions, particularly the main tourist areas. **Telegram:** Services are operated by *Telégrafos Nacionales* and international telegrams should be handed in to their offices. **Post:** Airmail to Europe takes about six days. Surface mail is slow. Within the capital, there is an immediate delivery (*Entrega Inmediata*) service, which usually takes two or three days. **Press:** The major daily newspapers published in Spanish are *Esto*, *Excélsior*, *EL Financiero*, *El Heraldo de México*, *Le Jornada*, *La Prensa* and *El Universal*. The English-language papers available are *Mexico City Times*, *New York Times*, *The News* and *USA Today*.
Radio: BBC World Service (website: www.bbc.co.uk/worldservice) and Voice of America (website: www.voa.gov) can be received. From time to time the frequencies change and the most up-to-date can be found online.

Passport/Visa

	Passport Required?	Visa Required?	Return Ticket Required?
Full British	Yes	2	Yes
Australian	Yes	4	Yes
Canadian	1	3	Yes
USA	1	3	Yes
Other EU	Yes	2	Yes
Japanese	Yes	3	Yes

Note: *Regulations and requirements may be subject to change at short notice, and you are advised to contact the appropriate diplomatic or consular authority before finalising travel arrangements. Details of these may be found at the head of this country's entry. Any numbers in the chart refer to the footnotes below.*

Note: No brief account of the complex Mexican Passport/Visa regulations is likely to be fully successful and visitors are advised to use the following information for general guidance only. Non-compliance with visa regulations will result in fines and transportation (at the carrier's expense) to the visitor's country of origin.
PASSPORTS: Passport valid for at least six months after date of entry required by all except the following:
1. nationals of Canada and the USA holding a certified copy of a birth certificate/voter's card and photo identification (eg driver's licence or student ID).
Tourist Cards (FM-T): Available *only* to nationals entering Mexico on holiday, for reasons of health, or to engage in scientific, artistic or sporting activities which are neither remunerative nor lucrative. Valid for the holder only. Other persons (including minors) travelling on the same passport must have their own card. The card is a single-entry document and is issued free of charge.
The following nationals are eligible for a Tourist Card:
(a) **2.** EU countries for stays of up to 180 days (except nationals of Austria, Cyprus, Czech Republic, Estonia, France, Greece, Hungary, Italy, Latvia, Lithuania, Poland, Portugal, Slovak Republic and Slovenia who can stay for up to 90 days);

(b) **3.** Canada, Japan and the USA for stays of up to 180 days;
(c) Andorra, Argentina, Bermuda, Brazil, Chile, Costa Rica, Liechtenstein, New Zealand, Norway, San Marino, Singapore, Switzerland and Uruguay for stays of up to 180 days;
(d) **4.** Australia, Iceland, Israel, Korea (Rep), Monaco and South Africa for up to 90 days;
(e) Venezuela for stays of up to 30 days.

Note: (a) The Consular office retains the right to request further evidence - such as return or onward tickets and proof of financial means - of the applicant's intention to visit Mexico as a tourist whenever such intention has not been established to the Consul's satisfaction. (b) Tourist Cards must be kept by the visitor during the entire length of stay as they will have to be presented and stamped on leaving. (c) Certain nationals who are eligible for tourist cards require either red or blue tourist cards. The colour of the tourist card will determine the exact application requirements.

Application to: Consulate or Consular section at Embassy; see *Contact Addresses* section. Also available on board the plane or at the point of entry in Mexico. However, in some cases personal applications may be required.

Application requirements: (a) Passport valid for at least six months from date of entry. (b) Return or onward ticket. (c) Proof of sufficient funds. (d) If applying by post, a covering letter giving dates of entry and departure. Postal applications must be accompanied by a stamped, self-addressed envelope for recorded return delivery.

VISAS: Required by all except holders of a Tourist Card or visa-replacing document. Nationals of the following countries require special authorisation before a visa can be granted:
Afghanistan, Albania, Algeria, Angola, Armenia, Bahrain, Bangladesh, Bosnia & Herzegovina, Cambodia, China (PR), CIS, Colombia, Congo (Dem Rep), Croatia, Cuba, East Timor, Egypt, Eritrea, Ethiopia, Grenada, Haiti, India, Iran, Iraq, Jordan, Korea (Dem Rep), Lebanon, Liberia, Libya, Macedonia (Former Yugoslav Republic of), Mauritania, Mongolia, Morocco, Nigeria, Oman, Pakistan, Qatar, Saudi Arabia, Serbia & Montenegro, Somalia, Sri Lanka, Sudan, Syrian Arab Republic, Taiwan, Tunisia, Turkey, United Arab Emirates, Vietnam, Yemen and holders of British Travel or Palestinian documents. Authorisation takes approximately three - four weeks. Please note that these nationals are also subject to special application requirements. For further details, contact the Consulate (or Consular section at Embassy); see *Contact Addresses* section.

Types of visa and cost: *Tourist*: £19.60. *Business*: £53 (non-lucrative) *or* £85.90 (lucrative). Visa prices fluctuate according to the exchange rate.

Validity: *Tourist*: One to six months (single-entry but can also be obtained for double and multiple-entry in particular circumstances). *Business Visitor*: Up to a maximum of one year. Each national has 90 days from date of issue to use the visa before it is defunct. Extensions for visas must be submitted 30 days before the expiration of the allocated visa.

Application requirements: *Tourist*: (a) Passport with minimum of six months' validity plus photocopies. (b) Completed application form. (c) One passport-size photo. (d) Original and photocopy of return, or onward, ticket. (e) Fee (payable by cash or postal order only). (f) Proof of sufficient funds to cover length of stay (eg last three bank statements, original work letter stating current salary and period of time working, or original letter from the person who supports the traveller economically with proof of relation, such as birth or marriage certificate. (g) Postal applications must be accompanied by a covering letter specifying the purpose of the trip and the dates of entry and departure. Applications should be made in a stamped, self-addressed envelope with recorded or registered delivery. (h) Letter stating purpose of visit, itinerary, date of departure, intended duration of stay plus a reference letter. *Business Visitors Card*: (a)-(b) and, (c) Two identical passport-size photos. (d) Letter from applicant's employer accepting financial responsibility to cover the applicant's stay, which also states the nature of business to be undertaken. (e) Letter from company in Mexico to be visited, explaining purpose of visit. (f) Fee (payable in cash, postal order or company cheque). (g) Postal applications must be accompanied by a stamped, self-addressed envelope with recorded delivery.

Note: (a) Non-British nationals seeking to visit Mexico on business are advised to check with the Consulate regarding visa requirements and fees. (b) Vaccinations against cholera and yellow fever are required by the Mexican Immigration Office if the visitor has been in an infected area two weeks prior to entry into Mexico. They are not required for transit passengers remaining in the airport.

Application to: Consulate (or Consular section at Embassy); see *Contact Addresses* section.

Working days required: Two in person; one week by post. Applications should be made in good time as it may take up to four weeks for some nationals.

Temporary residence: Application should be made to the Mexican Home Office with proof of sufficient funds to cover length of stay without working. Contact the Consulate (or Consular section at Embassy) for further details; see *Contact Addresses* section.

Credit: © AllMexico TB

Money

Currency: New Peso (peso) = 100 centavos. Notes are in denominations of peso500, 200, 100, 50 and 20. Coins are in denominations of peso20, 10, 5, 2 and 1, and 50, 20, 10 and 5 centavos.

Currency exchange: Currency may only be exchanged at authorised banks. The exchange rate of the Mexican peso against Sterling and other hard currencies has, in recent years, been subject to considerable fluctuation.

Credit & debit cards: American Express, Diners Club, MasterCard and Visa are widely accepted. Check with your credit or debit card company for details of merchant acceptability and other services which may be available. There is a government tax of 6 per cent on such transactions.

Travellers cheques: Travellers cheques or letters of credit in US Dollars issued by well-known banks or travel organisations are readily negotiable in banks and hotels. Sterling travellers cheques are not readily negotiable except at head offices of banks in the capital, and may be subject to a considerable discount. To avoid additional exchange rate charges, travellers are advised to take travellers cheques in US Dollars.

Currency restrictions: Local currency may be imported and exported up to the equivalent of US$10,000; larger amounts must be declared. The import of foreign currency is unlimited, provided declared. Foreign currency may be exported up to the amount imported and declared. The export of gold coins is prohibited.

Exchange rate indicators: The following figures are included as a guide to the movements of the New Peso against Sterling and the US Dollar (free-market rates).

Date	Feb '04	May '04	Aug '04	Nov '04
£1.00=	20.06	20.56	21.02	21.30
$1.00=	11.02	11.51	11.40	11.25

Banking hours: Mon-Fri 0900-1700; some banks are open Saturday afternoon.

Duty Free

The following goods may be imported into Mexico by persons over 18 years of age without incurring customs duty:
400 cigarettes or 50 cigars or 250g of pipe tobacco; 3l of wine, spirits or beer; a reasonable amount of perfume or eau de toilette or lotions for personal use; a photo, movie or video camera for non-residents and up to 12 unexposed rolls of film or video cassettes; goods up to the value of US$300 or equivalent.

Prohibited items: Any uncanned food, pork or pork products; plants, fruits, vegetables, flowers, seeds (except if special permit is obtained prior to arrival) and their products. Canned food is permitted, provided it is not pork or pork products. Firearms and ammunition need an import permit. Archaeological relics may not be exported.

Public Holidays

2005: Jan 1 New Year's Day. **Feb 5** Constitution Day. **Mar 21** Birthday of Benito Juárez. **Mar 25-28** Easter. **May 1** Labour Day. **May 5** Anniversary of Battle of Puebla. **Sep 16** Independence Day. **Oct 12** Día de la Raza (Columbus Day). **Nov 2** Día de los Muertos (Day of the Dead). **Nov 20** Anniversary of the Mexican Revolution of 1910. **Dec 12** Day of Our Lady of Guadalupe. **Dec 25** Christmas Day.

2006: Jan 1 New Year's Day. **Feb 5** Constitution Day. **Mar 21** Birthday of Benito Juárez. **Apr 13-16** Easter. **May 1** Labour Day. **May 5** Anniversary of Battle of Puebla. **Sep 16** Independence Day. **Oct 12** Día de la Raza (Columbus Day). **Nov 2** Día de los Muertos (Day of the Dead). **Nov 20** Anniversary of the Mexican Revolution of 1910. **Dec 12** Day of Our Lady of Guadalupe. **Dec 25** Christmas Day.

Note: (a) In addition there are many local holidays. For details, contact the Mexican Tourist Office. (b) Holidays falling at the weekend are not celebrated on the previous or following weekday.

Health

	Special Precautions?	Certificate Required?
Yellow Fever	No	No
Cholera	No	No
Typhoid & Polio	1	N/A
Malaria	2	N/A

Note: Regulations and requirements may be subject to change at short notice, and you are advised to contact your doctor well in advance of your intended date of departure. Any numbers in the chart refer to the footnotes below.

1: Immunisation against typhoid is sometimes recommended.

2: Malaria risk, almost exclusively in the benign *vivax* form, exists in rural areas of the following states (in decreasing order of risk): Chiapas, Quintano Roo, Sinaloa, Tabasco, Chihuahua, Durango, Nayarit, Oaxaca, Sonora, Campeche, Guerrero, Michoacán and Jalisco. The recommended prophylaxis is chloroquine.

Food & drink: Water supplied in bottles and from taps marked 'drinking/sterilised water' in hotels can be drunk without precautions. All other water should be regarded as being potentially contaminated. Water used for drinking, brushing teeth or making ice should have first been boiled or otherwise sterilised. Milk in major cities, hotels and resorts is pasteurised. Otherwise, milk is unpasteurised and

Credit: © AllMexico TB

should first be boiled. Powdered or tinned milk is available and is advised, but make sure that it is reconstituted with pure water. Avoid dairy products which are likely to have been made from unboiled milk. Only eat well-cooked meat and fish, preferably served hot. Pork, salad and mayonnaise may carry increased risk. Vegetables should be cooked and fruit peeled.

Other risks: *Visceral* and *mucutaneous leishmaniasis* occur. *Dysenteries* and *diarrhoeal diseases* are present. *Hepatitis A* occurs and *hepatitis E* has been reported. *Dengue fever* is predominant in the northern border states. *Rabies* is present. For those at high risk, vaccination before arrival should be considered. If you are bitten, seek medical advice without delay. For more information, consult the *Health* appendix.

Health care: Health insurance is recommended. Medical facilities are very good and there are both private and state-organised hospitals, doctors, clinics and chemists. Medicines are often available without prescriptions, and pharmacists are permitted to diagnose and treat minor ailments. Owing to the high altitude of Mexico City, visitors may take some time to acclimatise to the atmosphere, particularly since its geographical location results in an accumulation of smog. The levels of pollution in Mexico City are extremely high and are considered a health threat, so precautions should be taken.

Travel - International

AIR: Mexico's national airlines are *Aeroméxico (AM)* (website: www.aeromexico.com) and *Mexicana (MX)* (website: www.mexicana.com). *British Airways* operates three direct flights each week from Heathrow to Mexico City.

Approximate flight times: From Mexico City to *London* is 11 hours 25 minutes; to *Los Angeles* is four hours 20 minutes; to *New York* is six hours; to *Singapore* is 22 hours 45 minutes and to *Sydney* is 19 hours.

International airports: *Mexico City (MEX)* (Benito Juárez) is 13km (8 miles) south of the city. Buses run to and from the city at regular intervals (travel time - 35 minutes). Underground trains and taxis are also available. Airport facilities include duty free shops, restaurants, bank/bureau de change, bar, snack bar, chemist, shops, tourist information, left luggage, post office, first aid (with vaccinations for cholera and yellow fever available) and car hire (includes *Avis*, *Budget*, *Dollar* and *Hertz*).

Guadalajara (GDL) (Miguel Hidalgo) is 20km (12 miles) southeast of the city (travel time - 35 minutes). Airport facilities include restaurant, bar, snack bar, bank, post office and shops.

Acapulco (ACA) (General Juan N Alvarez) is 26km (16 miles) southeast of the city (travel time - 35 minutes). Coaches and taxi services run to the city. Airport facilities include restaurant, bank, post office and car hire.

Monterrey (MTY) (General Mariano Escobedo) is 24km (15 miles) northeast of the city (travel time - 45 minutes). Coach and taxi services run to the city. Airport facilities include restaurant, bar, bank, post office, shops and car hire.

Departure tax: Approximately US$23.20; children under two years and transit passengers are exempt. The tax is sometimes included in the price of the ticket.

SEA/RIVER: The major cruise ports in Mexico are Acapulco, Cozumel, Manzanillo, Mazatlán, Puerto Vallarta, Tampico and Zihuatanejo/Ixtapa. Regular passenger ships run from the USA and South America. Principal shipping lines are *Fred Olsen Lines*, *P&O* and *Star Clipper*. There are also riverboat services from Flores and Tikal (Guatemala) to Palenque, Chiapas in Mexico; enquire locally for details.

RAIL: Railway connections with Mexico can be made from any city in the USA or Canada. All trains are provided with pullman sleepers, restaurant cars, lounge observation and club cars. Most trains are air-conditioned.

ROAD: Main points of entry from the USA are Mexicali from San Diego; Nogales from Phoenix/Tucson; El Paso/Ciudad Juárez from Tucson and Alberquerque; Eagle Pass/Piedras Negras from Del Río, San Angelo and El Paso; Laredo/Nuevo Laredo from Houston, San Antonia and Del Río; and Brownsville/Matamoros from Houston and Galveston. From Guatemala, there are two main roads into Mexico. The Pan American Highway crosses into Mexico from Guatemala and continues through Central America and South America. There is also a road border crossing point from Belize near Chetumal and Corozal.

Travel - Internal

Note: Armed groups are still present in parts of the state of Chiapas. Caution should be exercised when visiting the highlands around San Cristobel de las Casas, and municipality of Ocosingo, and the jungle area towards the Guatemalan border.

AIR: There is an excellent network of daily scheduled services between principal commercial centres operated by *Aero California*, *Aeroméxico* and *Mexicana*. Many of the smaller airports also have capacity for large planes and some international flights. Flights between Mexico City and Guadalajara take about 55 minutes, and those between Mexico City and Monterrey about 75 minutes.

Departure tax: US$23.20.

SEA: Steamer ferries operate regularly between Mazatlán and La Paz (Baja California) daily; between Guaymas and Santa Rosalia, across the Gulf of California; between La Paz and Topolobampo three or four times weekly; and from Puerto Vallarta to Cabo San Lucas twice-weekly. Some west coast cruises include Pacific ports such as Mazatlán, Puerto Vallarta and Acapulco. There are also regular ferries from the mainland to the Caribbean Islands of Isla Mujeres and Cozumel.

RAIL: Mexico has a good railway network and trains link all the main towns in the country. A spectacular route is the *Copper Canyon Railway* that runs between Chihuahua and Los Mochis. However, most people travel by bus since it is considerably faster and provides a more extensive service. Children under five travel free, provided they are accompanied by a parent. Children aged five to 11 pay half-fare.

ROAD: Traffic drives on the right. Mexico's road network extends to almost 252,000km (157,500 miles), of which somewhat less than half is paved. A toll is charged for use of the expressways, which are managed by *Caminos y Puentes Federales de Ingresos y Servicios Conexos*. Rest areas at toll sites also provide ambulance and breakdown services. An organisation known as 'Angeles Verdes' (Green Angels) provides breakdown assistance to tourists on the highways free of charge except for petrol, oil and spare parts. Car use in Mexico City is restricted to cut down on pollution. The last digit of the car number plate determines when that car *cannot* be driven. **Bus:** Mexico is linked by a good and very economical bus system. There are first-class and deluxe coaches as well as ordinary buses. Central bus terminals in major cities provide service and information on fares and schedules. **Car hire:** Self-drive cars are available at airports, city centres and resorts. **Documentation:** An International Driving Permit or a full British Driving Licence is required for locally registered vehicles. Minimum driving age is 18. Payment is by credit card. Full car insurance is recommended.

URBAN: There is an excellent and cheap metro system in Mexico City with frequent trains and flat fares. However, it is often crowded and some familiarity with the city is necessary to use it successfully. The metro opens Mon-Sat at 0500 and Sun 0700 and closes at about midnight. There is also a small tramway network, and extensive bus and trolley bus services. The latter system has recently been modernised, and also has a flat fare. There is a state-run bus and trolley bus service in Guadalajara, with trolley buses running in tunnels, and also extensive private bus services.

Taxi: Four different types of taxi operate in Mexico City. Yellow and white taxis (usually volkswagens) are metered, as are orange taxis (*Sitio*), which are available at taxi-stands. These charge slightly more, and it is advisable to agree on the fare before starting the journey. *Turismo* taxis with English-speaking drivers are available outside main hotels. They are not metered and fares should be agreed before starting journey as rates can be excessive. *Peseros* (green and white) are share-taxis travelling on fixed routes, for which fares are charged according to the distance travelled. Tipping is not compulsory for any of the taxi services.

Travel times: The following chart gives approximate travel times (in hours and minutes) from **Mexico City** to other major cities/towns in Mexico.

	Air	Road	Rail
Acapulco	0.35	3.30	-
Cancún	2.15	30.00	-
Oaxaca	0.15	6.00	12.00
Chihuahua	2.15	34.00	40.00
Puerto Vallarta	1.55	14.00	-
Guadalajara	0.55	7.00	12.00
Tijuana	2.45	36.00	-

Accommodation

HOTELS: The enormous growth of tourism in Mexico is reflected in the wide range of hotels from the modern, elegant and expensive to the clean and modest. There are a variety of chain hotels throughout Mexico as well as 'dude' ranches, thermal spas and resorts that feature specific facilities. Reservations should be confirmed by hotels in writing at the time of booking as hotel tariffs are liable to alteration at any time; it is especially important to make reservations when travelling in the high season. There is a wide range of prices with plenty of choice throughout the country; every hotel is required to display officially approved rate schedules, but the visitor should note that most rates do not include meals. There are also a number of more modest guest houses (*casas de huespedes*). Information can be obtained from the Mexican Hotel and Motel Association, CP 11590, Thiers 83, Colonia Anzurez, México DF (tel: (5) 203 0466/6946; fax: (5) 203 7246; e-mail: reservaciones@asociaciondehoteles.com.mx; website: www.hotelesenmexico.com.mx).

Grading: Mexico operates a 5-star grading system similar to that in Europe, with an additional Gran Turismo category. All hotels are covered. The criteria for inclusion in each of the six grades are as follows: **Gran Turismo:** 108 criteria including central air-conditioning, satellite dish and minimum floor area of 32 sq metres (105 sq ft). Shopping area and additional quality services are also required; **5-star:** 96 to 101 criteria, including room service 16 hours a day and minimum floor area of 28 sq metres (92 sq ft). Restaurant, cafe, nightclub, commercial areas, good hygiene and security are also required; **4-star:** 71 to 76 criteria, including adequate furniture and minimum floor area of 25 sq metres (82 sq ft). Some commercial areas and a good standard of maintenance are also required; **3-star:** 47 to 52 criteria, including adequate furniture and minimum floor area of 21.5 sq metres (71 sq ft). Restaurant, cafe, ceiling fan and some complimentary services are required; **2-star:** 33 to 37 criteria, including adequate furniture and minimum floor area of 19 sq metres (62 sq ft). Standards for hygiene and security should be met. First-aid facilities are required; **1-star:** 24 to 27 criteria, including adequate furniture and minimum floor area of 15 sq metres (49 sq ft). Standards for guests' comfort should be met.

CAMPING/CARAVANNING: The national parks in Mexico are officially the only areas where no permits or fees are required for camping and hiking. Camping is allowed anywhere within the park areas. Most camping, however, is outside national parks - the most popular regions being the west coast and Baja California. The western Pacific coast has excellent caravan 'hookups' while Baja California is far more informal and isolated. The number of caravan parks along Mexico's major motorways is growing, and there is no difficulty in locating places to park.

Resorts & Excursions

Mexico, rich in reminders of ancient civilisations, is also a modern developing nation. Temples and cathedrals contrast with futuristic buildings and fully-equipped beach resorts. Elsewhere, elements of the ancient and colonial cultures persist in aspects of rural life. Fêtes and festivals are celebrated with enthusiasm, and the markets in towns and villages are lively and colourful.

MEXICO CITY

The capital of Mexico stands at an altitude of 2240m (7350ft) beneath two snow-capped volcanoes, **Popocatépetl** and **Ixtaccíhuatl**. It is a huge rambling city with a distinctly colonial feel. Many of the buildings are in the exuberant Latin American Baroque style. Despite its pollution and sprawling size, Mexico City - or 'El DF', standing for *Distrito Federal* (Federal District) - is a very attractive city made up of 16 *delegaciones* (districts) and about 400 *colonias* (neighbourhoods), with many green spaces and quiet back streets. Exclusive residential areas, such as **Polanco** and **La Condesa**, have their own village-like centres. The street names in each district have been

given particular themes such as philosophers, European cities, rivers or writers, which lend a certain charm and atmosphere to each area, as well as helping the visitor navigate around the city.
In the centre of the **Centro Histórico** (Historic Centre) is the **Plaza de la Constitución**, more commonly referred to as the **Zócalo** – the Aztec word for 'plinth' or 'pedestal' – all that was actually completed of a monument to independence planned by General Santa Ana. Construction of the square began in 1573 and was finished in the 19th century. Vast in scale, it is surpassed in size only by Red Square in Moscow. Each evening, the enormous Mexican flag that flies in the middle of the square is taken down and folded with great ceremony by the Mexican army. The **Catedral Metropolitana**, on the north side of the square, was begun in 1563 and exhibits a plethora of architectural styles (mainly Gothic, Baroque and Neo-Classical). The highlight of the ornate gilded interior is the **Capilla de los Reyes** (Kings' Chapel) and its altar. Just east of the cathedral is the excavated site of the Aztec **Templo Mayor** (Great Temple), part of the sacred complex of **Tenochtitlán**, which was demolished by the Spaniards in the 1520s. Remains of the temple layout can be viewed from raised walkways. The adjoining museum displays artefacts excavated from the site in the 1970s, including the first artefact to be discovered – a huge votive disk to the goddess of the moon, Coyolxauhqui. On the east side of the zócalo, the **National Palace**, built in 1692 on the ruins of the **Palace of Montezuma**, is now the office of the President of the Republic. Diego Rivera's depiction of Mexican history is illustrated in a dramatic mural that adorns the stairwell leading up to the middle storey of the main courtyard. Other outstanding examples of Rivera's work – and that of Siqueiros, Orozco and Tamayo – can be found in the **Palacio de Bellas Artes** (Palace of Fine Arts) near **Alameda Central** (Central Park). This beautiful arts centre and concert hall, sculptured out of white Carrara marble, was built between 1900-34 in Neo-Classical, Art-Nouveau and Art-Deco styles. The *Ballet Folklórico* perform here every Wednesday and Sunday with a blend of ancient Mayan and Aztecritual, dramatised episodes from Mexican history, as well as current songs and dances from all over Latin America. Another hugely popular and sentimental form of Mexican music can be heard through a late afternoon and evening visit to the **Plaza Garibaldi**, where 'mariachis' from all over Mexico, usually dressed in ornate clothes and giant sombreros, play for the public. With so many sites of architectural, religious and cultural merit, it is not surprising that the capital has museums with world-class collections. In particular, the **Museo Nacional de Antropología**, in **Chapultepec Park** ('Grasshopper Hill' in the Nahuatl language), holds an enormous and absolutely fascinating collection of Pre-Hispanic artefacts within 12 halls on the first floor, including the 24-ton Aztec Sun Stone – the Calendar Stone. Ethnological exhibits on the second floor illustrate life today in Mexico's indigenous communities. Also worth visiting in the park is the **Museo Nacional de Historia**, situated in the former castle of the viceroys. Other museums that contain outstanding collections include: the **Museo del Carmen** (colonial religious paintings and sculpture housed in a former 16th-century Carmelite monastery); **Museo Franz Mayer** (16th to 19th century European, Asian and Mexican fine and applied arts, displayed in a restored 16th-century hospital); **Museo de Arte Moderno** (a collection of some of the major works from 20th-century Mexican and Latin American artists); **Museo Frida Kahlo** (examples of the artist's work, her own art collection and belongings displayed in her former home and studio); and **Museo Anahuacalli** (an extraordinary volcanic stone-clad house, designed by Diego Rivera to house his extensive collection of pre-Hispanic artefacts).
Just to the north of the centre are two places that offer a good insight into Mexican history and architecture, as well as its cultural and religious life today. **Plaza de las Tres Culturas** in Tlatelolco celebrates the three major cultures that have shaped Mexico: there are Aztec ruins, the 17th-century colonial church of San Diego, built in the Baroque style, and several late 20th-century buildings. Another location worth visiting is the **Basilica of Nuestra Señora de Guadalupe**. The shrine that is built around **Tepeyac hill** signifies the spot where the Virgin Mary is said to have appeared to the Indian Juan Diego in 1531. It is also a major pilgrimage site. Each year, on 12 December, millions of devout pilgrims from all over Mexico, many shuffling forward on their knees, congregate at the Basilica to worship their patron saint. Built in 1976, it has a capacity of 10,000 inside plus another 25,000 outside when the 70 surrounding portals are opened.
The oldest university in the Americas, and one of the largest in the world, the **Ciudad Universitaria** (University City), located in **Pedregal Square**, is a remarkable architectural complex dating back to the 1950s. Among its landmark buildings is the library – a tower encased in an astonishing natural stone, glass and tile mural, which was designed by Juan O'Gorman to illustrate key chapters in Mexico's history.

Excursions: Some 20km (14 miles) south of the Zócalo are the floating gardens and tree-lined canals of **Xochimilco**. Engineered by the Aztecs, the gardens are now a weekend haunt of the city's inhabitants who hire brightly painted *trajineras* (gondolas), often accompanied by 'mariachis', to cruise the canals.
Two of Mexico City's prettiest colonial villages on the southern fringes – **Coyoacán** and **San Angel** – are best visited at the weekend, when the attractive squares and cobble-lined streets are alive with students, artists, craftspeople, musicians and other Mexicans out strolling with their families. The **Bazar del Sábado** (Saturday Market) in San Angel's **Plaza San Jacinto** is one of the best places to buy good-quality handicrafts and artworks.

SOUTHCENTRAL MEXICO

TEOTIHUACÁN: The 'City of the Gods', 48km (30 miles) northeast of Mexico City, was built about 2000 years ago. It was the largest pre-Hispanic city in Mexico and, at the height of its power, controlled most of Mexico. Visitors to the site can see the Pyramids of the Sun and Moon, the Citadel with the Temple of Quetzalcoatl (the plumed serpent) and the Palace of Quetzalpapálotl (the plumed butterfly), all found in a mile-long stretch called the Calle de los Muertos (Avenue of the Dead).
TULA: Tula, 95km (59 miles) north of Mexico City, is the former capital of the Toltec empire. Architectural highlights include the four basalt *Atlantes*. These 5m (16ft) tall figures originally supported the roof of the sanctuary on top of the **Templo de Tlahuizcalpantecuhtli** (Temple of the Morning Star), and depict Quetzalcoatl as the morning star, dressed as a heavily armed Toltec warrier.
TEPOTZOTLÁN: Tepotzotlán, 43km (27 miles) from the capital, is notable for its Churrigueresque **Church of San Francisco Javier**, the façade of which is decorated with more than 300 sculptures of angels, saints, plants and people. On a hill nearby, there is an Aztec shrine dedicated to the god of feasting and drinking where annually, on September 8, a fête is held which features Aztec dancing and the performance of an Aztec play. In the town itself, in the third week of December, a different kind of performance takes place. The experiences of Mexican pilgrims en route to Bethlehem are enacted in *pastorellas*.
ACOLMAN: The village of Acolman, 39km (24 miles) north of the capital on the road to Teotihuacán, is centred around the beautiful 16th-century monastery of *San Agustin Acolman*. The building is now a museum containing religious paintings and artefacts.
CUERNAVACA: Cuernavaca, 85km (53 miles) from the capital, is built around two large squares. On one stands the **Palacio de Cortés** (built in 1538), now a museum containing frescoes by Diego Rivera. The Cathedral dates from the 16th century. The town also contains the 18th-century **Borda Gardens** and the Indian market which sells *huaraches* (sandals), leather goods and articles made of straw.
XOCHICALCO: Situated 40km (25 miles) south of Cuernavaca, Xochicalco is one of the country's most interesting ceremonial centres, especially noted for its **Building of the Plumed Serpent**.
TEPOZTLÁN: Tepoztlán (Place of Copper) is an attractive, relaxed town in a spectacular natural setting. Spread out across the valley floor, it is surrounded by steep, jagged cliffs that glow pink in the afternoon sun. It is also the legendary birthplace of Quetzalcóatl, the Aztec serpent god. Set on a cliff, 400m (1312ft) above the town, is a pyramid dedicated to Tepoztécatl, god of the harvest, fertility and *pulque* (a light alcoholic drink). The hour-long climb to the summit is a strenuous one, but well worth it for the extensive views that are afforded over the town, valley and surrounding hills. Dominating the town centre is the fortress-like Dominican church and monastery. From the market side, the entrance to the churchyard has an arch which is decorated with a golden mural depicting local gods and history, and crafted entirely from seeds, stones and other natural products.
TAXCO: Located 160km (100 miles) from Mexico City, Taxco has been classed as a national monument. The town's fortune was made from the silver mines. The selling of silverware and jewellery is a thriving local trade. As well as numerous interesting, narrow and winding cobbled streets, the **Church of Santa Prisca and San Sebastián** is a jewel of Churrigueresque architecture, with a *reredos* decorated with gold leaf and a wealth of statues and ornaments. Residences of the colonial period include the **Casa Humboldt**, **Casa de Borda** and **Casa de Figueroa**. A cable-car runs from **Los Arcos**, at the northern end of the town, to the summit of **Monte Taxco**. The view over the valley and surrounding mountains from the top are spectacular. The **Cacahuamilpa Caves** are to the north of Taxco.
TOLUCA: Toluca, 66km (41 miles) from the capital, lies in a valley dominated by the snow-capped **Nevado de Toluca**, an extinct volcano (its two craters are known as the Sun and the Moon). As well as a fine market, the town has several interesting museums in its **Cultural Centre**,

Credit: © AllMexico TB

dedicated to archaeology, folk and modern art. Nearby are the Indian villages of **Tenancingo**, **Metepec** and **Chiconcuac**. About 8km (5 miles) north of Toluca is **Calixtlahuaca**, an Aztec site of archaeological interest where a circular pyramid is dedicated to the god of wind. The spa town of **Ixtapan de la Sal**, 80km (50 miles) from Toluca, has excellent hot springs and spa facilities. **Valle de Bravo**, 70km (44 miles) southwest of Toluca, is a resort town at an elevation of 1869m (6135ft), set amid pines on a large lake.
PUEBLA: Nestled in the foothills of the **Sierra Madre** is Puebla – originally named **Puebla de los Angeles** (City of the Angels) in 1531. Capital of the state of the same name, it can be reached by a 96km- (60 mile-) drive southwest from Mexico City. It is famous for its colonial architecture with glazed tiles (known as **Talavera** after a town in Spain), which cover most of the church domes and house walls, and for the skilled craftspeople who produce them. Tiles and other ceramics can be purchased in **El Parián** market and in the street leading to **Plazuela de los Sapos**. The **Convention Centre**, a modern building of striking elegance and clean lines, reflects its artistic heritage in its choice of tiles and use of natural materials found within the state. This juxtaposition of ancient and modern is made explicit with a walkway that literally bridges the convention centre and the **Barrio del Artista** (Artists' Quarter). In 1988, UNESCO declared Puebla part of the 'Cultural Heritage of Mankind'. Highlights include the **Cathedral** (one of the oldest in Mexico), which has 14 chapels and is built of blue-grey stone. Its towers, at 69m (226ft), are the highest in Mexico. The building thus dominates the arcade-lined zócalo with its beautiful gardens and **Fuente de San Miguel** (Saint Michael Fountain), the patron saint of the city. Opposite the cathedral is the **Palacio Municipal**, which was remodelled in accordance with the Neo-Classical architectural guidelines issued under the Porfirian dictatorship. The **Church of Santo Domingo** is famous for its **Capilla del Rosario** (Rosary Chapel), a breathtaking masterpiece in goldleaf that was consecrated in 1690. Puebla's colonial heritage is also expressed in the architectural riches of its former monasteries and *casonas* (mansions). Two of the best examples of colonial mansions are the **Casa de los Muñecos** (Dolls' House), the tiles on the façade depicting the Labours of Hercules (the building is now the **University Museum**), and the **Casa del Alfeñique** (Sugar Paste House), which displays craftware and regional costumes. The city has several fine museums, including **Museo Bello** (Pueblan **Talavera** and colonial religious artefacts); **Museo Ampara** (a superb pre-Hispanic collection of artefacts); and the **Ex-Convento de Santa Rosa & Museo de Artesanías** (Pueblan State handicrafts). Now a hotel, the Ex-Convento de la Concepción, is a startling reminder of the wealth of the church during the colonial period, with its beautifully preserved cloisters and wall paintings. From Puebla, it is possible to see the volcanoes of **Popocatépetl**, **Iztaccíhuatl**, **Malinche** and **Citlaltépetl**.
CHOLULA: 10km (6 miles) west from Puebla, Cholula is a pre-Hispanic ceremonial centre that once contained about 400 shrines and temples, most of which were destroyed by Cortés's army and replaced with colonial churches – the Spanish claimed to have constructed 365 here. The

A B C D E F G H I J K L M N O P Q R S T U V W X Y Z

Pyramid of Tepanapa has the largest base of any pyramid in the world and is the most striking feature of the archaeological site; on the summit stands the **Sanctuary of Nuestra Señora de los Remedios**. The plaza in the town centre has three fine churches, the most unusual being the **Capilla Real** (Royal Chapel), which, with its 49 domes, has the appearance of a mosque.

Excursions: Two additional places worth visiting are the churches of **Santa Maria** and **San Francisco** at **Tonantzintla** and **Acatepec** respectively. The painted stucco flowers, birds, saints and devils that cover every surface of the dome of the church at Tonantzintla demonstrate incredible artistry. The town is also noted for its fiestas which include traditional dances and processions on 15 August. The **Church of San Francisco Acatepec**, a few kilometres away, is notable for its exterior, clad in beautiful green, yellow and blue tiles from Puebla, set in an ornate Churriguerresque façade.

OAXACA: Known as the 'Jade City' due to the green tinge in the stone used in the construction of many of its buildings, Oaxaca is a culturally diverse city. It is the capital of a state whose pre-Hispanic, colonial and indigenous roots are vividly expressed through its architecture, craft traditions, Zapotec and Mixtec archaeological sites, gastronomy and festivals – the *Noche de Rábanos* (Night of the Radishes) and the **Guelaguetza** in particular reflect age-old traditions. Within its 95,364 sq km (59,258 miles) live 16 ethnic groups, each with its own dialect or language, making the state one of the most linguistically and culturally varied of any in Mexico. In 1987, UNESCO declared both Oaxaca city and the Zapotec site of Monte Albán, 9km (5.5 miles) away, to be a 'Cultural Heritage of Humanity'. Traditional arts and crafts – hand-woven and hand-embroidered clothing, *alebrijes* (painted wooden figures and fantastical creatures), rugs, gold jewellery and distinctive, shiny black pottery – reflect the vibrancy and skill of modern artists who have built on, and refined, older artistic traditions. Works by Oaxacan artists, particularly those of Rufino Tamayo, Francisco Toledo and Rodolfo Morales, are recognised internationally, and several galleries within the town specialise in modern art; it is also possible to visit artists in their homes to purchase paintings.

Oaxaca's relaxed atmosphere belies its sizeable student and language-school population, both of which have added vibrancy to the town's nightlife. In the bandstand of the central zócalo, the former state marimba band gives free concerts most nights of the week, while local musicians play at the tables of the cafes and restaurants under the arcades that edge the square. Dominating the northwest corner of the square is the Cathedral. Construction commenced in the 16th century but, due to earthquake damage, it was only completed two centuries later. Its Baroque façade is decorated with some fine bas-reliefs. The neoclassical **Palacio de Gobierno**, on the south side, contains murals by Arturo Garciá Bustos that show key moments from Oaxacan history and legend. The pedestrianised **Calle Alcalú** leads to the monumental former monastery and church complex of **Santo Domingo**. The inside of the church is decorated with a profusion of colourful Baroque ornaments, statues and altars. Of particular interest are the family tree of St Domingo de Guzmán, the founder of the order, sculpted as a vine with leaves and tendrils; Old and New Testament scenes on the barrel roof; the main altar; and the adjoining **Capilla del Rosario** (Rosary Chapel). Attached to the church is the former monastery, now the **Museo Regional de Oaxaca**. Among the highlights of the collection are the Zapotec and Mixtec artefacts fashioned from gold, jade, silver, turquoise and quartz that were excavated from Tomb Seven at Monte Albán. Outside, the former monastery gardens are being re-landscaped and planted with Oaxacan flora, including some dramatic cacti. Also well worth a visit are the **Rufino Tamayo** and **Contemporary Art museums**.

Two churches central to the religious life of the area are the **Basílica de Nuestra Señora de la Soledad** with its statue of the Virgin of la Soledad, patron saint of the town, to whom many miracles are ascribed, and **San Juan de Dios**, the oldest church in Oaxaca.

Excursions: Outside Oaxaca, other major Dominican sites of worship are to be found at **Coixtlahuaca**, **Cuilapan**, **Teposcolula**, **Tlacochahuaya**, **Tlaxiaco** and **Yanhuitlán**.

Many of the villages surrounding Oaxaca have weekly markets where food and craft products can be bought, of which the following are the most notable: **Tlaxiaco** (blankets); **Tlacolula** (rugs and ceramics); **Miahuatlán** (*mescal*, leather goods and bread); **Santa Ana del Valle** (a general market); **Etla** (flowers, cheese and meat); **Ejutla** (embroidered clothes and *mescal*); **Ocotlán** (pottery, flowers and textiles); and **Oaxaca** (crafts of all descriptions). Villages where the actual manufacture of local crafts can be seen include the *barro negro brillante* (black, shiny pottery) of **San Bartolo Coyotepec** and the beautiful woven rugs stained with natural dyes at **Teotitlán del Valle**.

MONTE ALBÁN: Situated 14km (9 miles) drive from Oaxaca, Monte Albán was a sacred city in prehistoric times and the religious centre of the Zapotec culture, which flourished 2000 years ago. The remarkable **Central Plaza**, the **Ball Court**, and many of the tombs, are open to the public. It is an amazing complex situated on a levelled mountain top. Aldous Huxley wrote that 'even today this high place of the Zapotecs remains extraordinarily impressive...Monte Albán is the work of men who knew their architectural business consummately well'. The best time to appreciate the spectacular beauty of the buildings in the changing light is either early in the morning or at sunset.

TUXTLA GUTIERREZ: The state capital of Chiapas and the home of Mexico's famed *marimba* music. Set in a thriving coffee-growing region, it is a good base from which to explore the nearby villages where life has changed little since pre-Hispanic times. A short drive away is the impressive **Sumidero Canyon. Mountain** peaks surround the 1829m (6000ft) drop along the 42km- (26 mile-) rift and are an impressive sight.

SAN CRISTOBEL DE LAS CASAS: San Cristobal de las Casas was founded in 1528 by Diego de Mazariegos as the colonial capital of the region. At an altitude of 2195m (7200ft), the two-hour drive from Tuxlta Gutierrez involves a rapid temperature change. It is a cool, white-washed town with an almost alpine atmosphere. During the year, several festivals are held here, making it an important gathering spot for the local craftspeople. In the near vicinity are a number of indigenous villages populated by Tzeltzal, Tzotzil and Chamula people. These can be visited, but the visitor should respect local traditions and sensitivities, especially when taking photographs. San Cristobal is also known as a centre for writers, musicians and poets.

ELSEWHERE: Situated 45km (28 miles) from Oaxaca, the prehistoric site of **Mitla** features numerous Mixtec remains, including the **Hall of Columns** and the **Column of Life**, which visitors are invited to grasp if they wish to determine how long they will live. Also in the village is the **Frisel Museum**. Other key archaeological sites are to be found at **Yagul**, **Lambityeco** and **Dainzú**.

The State of Oaxaca also contains areas of outstanding natural beauty: the 2000-year-old tree at **Santa Maria del Tule**; the **Hierve el Agua** ('boiling water') near San Lorenzo Albarradas; and the lagoons at **Chacahua** and **Manialtepec**. Along the Pacific Coast, the resorts of **Huatulco**, **Puerto Angel** and **Puerto Escondido** also have dramatic natural settings, as well as excellent facilities (see the *Beach Resorts* section for more information).

CENTRAL MEXICO

The central highlands, benefiting from a milder climate, constitute the most populous region of Mexico. Many of the colonial cities of this region include a unique blend of indigenous and Spanish culture; these historic centres have remained virtually intact since the time of the conquest. The conquistadores built very Spanish-looking villages near the silver mines. Today, the main attractions of this region are the architecture, the views, and some very good local cooking. One of the most popular driving circuits is the one following the so-called **Independence Route**, which links all of the major colonial cities in Central Mexico. Beginning in Mexico City, the route takes the traveller north to Querétaro, San Miguel de Allende, Guanajuato, Morelia, Patzcuaro and Guadalajara. Another circuit picks up in Guadalajara, again going north, to Aguascalientes, Zacatecas and San Luis Potosí.

GUADALAJARA: The capital of Jalisco still has a Spanish colonial atmosphere, despite being the agricultural, commercial and industrial centre of the western highlands. The **Cathedral** has 11 altars, 30 columns and a big art collection. There are also a lot of parks: the **Parque Agua Azul** ('Blue Water') is noteworthy for its forest-like atmosphere; the **Parque de las Armas** is where the boys and girls of the town court each other. Around the Cathedral there are two parks, the **Parque de los Laureles** and the **Parque de la Revolución**. The **Plaza de Rotonda** contains columns and statues in honour of Jalisco's past heroes; the **Plaza Libertad** has a market with a wide range of locally-produced goods. During the annual *October Festival*, horsemanship and bullfighting can be seen at the *charreada* (rodeo). The famous 'Mexican Hat Dance' originated in this area - locally, it is called *Jarabe Tapatio*.

GUANAJUATO: Guanajuato is steeped in history, legend and folklore. It is situated on Mexico's famous Independence Route, a road 1400km (875 miles) in length, along which can be traced Mexico's historic struggle for independence. Designated as a UNESCO World Heritage Site, the town preserves a colonial charm in places such as **Hidalgo Street**, an underground street, the **Governor's Palace**, the **Juarez Theatre**, the **University**, the **Basilica of Nuestra Señora de Guanajuato** and the **Valenciana Church**. The parish **Church of Dolores Hidalgo** is of great significance, being the place where, in 1810, Father Miguel Hidalgo raised the 'Grito de Dolores', the cry of rebellion against the Spanish when, with 80,000 armed supporters, he commenced the independence struggle. The town also features several museums, including the **Diego Rivera Museum** (the birthplace of the internationally renowned muralist) and the somewhat bizarre **Mummy Museum**. The **Botanical Gardens of San Miguel de Allende** also provide an eco-tourist feature to visit.

SAN MIGUEL DE ALLENDE: A short distance away from Guanajuato is San Miguel de Allende, which features thermal waters and spas, art and language schools and the laid-back way of life typical of these small colonial cities. The town, founded by a Franciscan friar in 1542, is now classed as a national monument. It is a place of narrow, cobbled streets and squares lined with trees. The houses and patios have elegant colonial architecture and the town is a fitting location for the **Allende Institute**, a school of fine arts named after a hero of the revolution whose name was also added to the name of the town. In 1880, the Indian master mason, Ceferino Gutierez, applied the tools of his trade to the architecture of the **Parroquia de San Miguel**. Its Franciscan starkness was transformed into Gothic. The **Casa de los Perros** (House of Dogs) has sculptured dogs on its balcony. The annual *Posadas* at Christmas-time is one of the fiestas for which the town is noted.

MORELIA: The aristocrat among the colonial cities is Morelia, a city halfway between the capital and Guadalajara. Apart from a few modern buildings, the city retains an atmosphere of old Spain. The **Plaza de los Martires** forms the centre of the city, flanked on one side by the Cathedral, bearing an unusual pink stone façade, with its 61m- (200ft-) high tower. Other sights include the **College of San Nicolas** (founded in 1540), the **Church of Santa Rosa** and the impressive **Aqueduct** built in 1790 to carry water into the city. Between November and February, visitors should go to the **Monarch Butterfly Refuge** near Angangueo, Morelia. Each year these butterflies migrate from Canada and the USA to a mountain bordering the state of Michoacan in Mexico.

QUERÉTARO: Situated 250km (155 miles) northwest of Mexico City and linked to it by a busy six-lane motorway is the town of Querétaro, with a population of around one million. It is here that the Emperor Maximilian was captured, tried and executed, and where the present Mexican constitution was drawn up in 1917. A former San Franciscan monastery is now a local museum, whilst the San Agustin monastery has become the **Federal Palace**. The mansion of the Marquis Villa del Aguila, who ordered the building of the town's aqueduct, can be found in the **Plaza de la Independencia**. The town has excellent hotels and restaurants.

Excursions: The Querétaro region is also noted for its striking juxtaposition of ancient sites with colonial mission towns. **Ranas** is an important example of an ancient ceremonial centre, which scholars have attributed to the Teotihuacán-Toltoec period. Located on a hill top, **Toluquilla** has remains of military fortifications which show the influences of the Huasteca culture. The second architectural tradition, that of strikingly beautiful Mexican Baroque churches, dates back to the life and work of the Franciscan friar, Fray Junipero Serra, who founded five missions in the 18th century at **Concá**, **Jalpan**, **Landa**, **Tancoyol** and **Tilaco**.

AGUASCALIENTES: North of Guadalajara, Aguascalientes has belonged to the Kingdom of Nueva Galicia since 1535. It was a stopping place for travellers on the silver route during the 18th century. Many of the Baroque buildings from this period still remain; the most interesting are the temples of Guadalupe, Encino, San Marcos, San Diego and San José de la Merced; also worth visiting are the government and municipal palaces, the **House of Culture** and **Excedra**, and the Ionian column marking the centre of Mexico.

SAN LUIS POTOSI: The capital of the state of the same name, San Luis Potosí is 351km (218 miles) northeast of Guadalajara and is the centre of a rich mining and agricultural area. Featured throughout the city are colourful, glazed tiles found on churches, plazas and streets. Good examples are the **Church of San Francisco** with its blue-and-white tiled dome and a suspended glass boat in the transept, and **Carmen**, at the Plaza Morelos, with a tiled dome and intricate façade, as well as the **Church of San Miguelito** in the old part of the city. Other sites include the **Palacio de Gobierno** (1770), housing paintings of former governors, and the colonial treasury, the **Antigua Caja Real** (1767).

ZACATECAS: At the time Zacatecas was founded by the Spanish in 1546, the nearby silver mines were among the richest in the country. Much of the revenue was sent to Spain, but enough remained to finance the fine cathedrals and palaces. The **Convent of Guadalupe** houses one of the largest art collections of the Americas and is also an important place for pilgrimages.

NORTHCENTRAL MEXICO

The northcentral part of the country is mostly desert: a vast, high, windswept plateau flanked by the Occidental and Oriental chains of the **Sierra Madre**. Most of the population is gathered in several large cities; parts of the plateau are used for agriculture, but much of the north bears little trace of human habitation.

The remarkable **Copper Canyon Railway** passes through **Chihuahua** on its way from **Ojinaga** on the **Río Grande** to the **Gulf of California**. It is an engineering miracle in itself and also provides a good way of seeing the canyons, mesas and bare peaks of the Sierra Madre Occidental. The view at the **Barranca del Cobre**, where the **Urique River** has cut a 1840m- (6136ft-) deep chasm through the mountains, rivals the Grand Canyon. The journey lasts about 13 hours.

CHIHUAHUA: Chihuahua, capital of the state of the same name (Mexico's largest), is an important industrial and commercial centre. There are many edifices dating from the colonial era, including the 18th-century **Cathedral**, the **Government Palace**, the **City Hall** and **Quinta Luz**, which is the **Villa Museum** (containing Pancho Villa memorabilia). There is a monument to the **División del Norte de Doroteo Arango** (Pancho Villa in the unfamiliar guise of his real name). Entertainments include bullfights, dog and horseraces, nightclubs and restaurants.

CIUDAD JUÁREZ: In the state of Chihuahua, Ciudad Juárez has a commercial and cultural centre with modern buildings based on traditional styles of architecture. The handicrafts section includes *sarapes* (blankets) and glassware. There are bullfights, and horse- and greyhound-racing, along with a good nightlife. Restaurants serve international and Mexican food.

THE WEST COAST

The west coast of Mexico incorportates the **Baja California**; a peninsula 1100km (700 miles) long that extends south from **Tijuana** into the **Pacific Ocean**. It comprises two states, **Baja California Norte** and **Baja California Sur**. The enclosed Gulf is rich in marine life and offers excellent opportunities for experienced divers and anglers (although the currents are treacherous). Baja's Pacific lagoons are an important breeding ground for whales, particularly the gray whale, which is often referred to as the 'Mexican Gray' whale. The estuary of the **Colorado River** lies at the top of the Gulf; only a trickle of fresh water now reaches the sea, most having been diverted for agriculture far upstream. The interior is mountainous desert, for the most part waterless and inhabited by only the hardiest plants and animals.

TIJUANA: Tijuana claims to be 'the world's most visited city', receiving more than 20 million visitors every year, many of them day-trippers from California. With San Diego just a few miles away across the border, it is the land gateway to and from the USA, thriving on the sale of souvenirs.

MEXICALI: The capital of Baja California Norte, Mexicali provides a base for those who wish to explore the surrounding mountains and countryside of **Rumorosa**.

LA PAZ: La Paz, the capital of Baja California Sur, is in a bay on the Gulf of California. Watersports and deep-sea angling are well catered for. The beaches of **Las Hamacas**, **Palmeira**, **El Coromuel** and **Puerto Balandra** provide excellent bases for swimmers and skindivers; the waters are calm and clear. Fish and seafood figure prominently on local menus.

PATZCUARO: Situated in the coastal state of Michoacan, in westcentral Mexico, Patzcuaro is best known for butterfly net fishing for whitefish. Every Friday morning the plaza is covered with numerous market stalls, offering ceramics, woodcarvings, copper and woven goods, laquerware and even furniture for sale. The *Day of the Dead* on November 2 is celebrated on the Island of **Janitzio**, as nowhere else in Mexico.

COLIMA: Colima, the capital of the state of the same name, is located near Mexico's mid-Pacific coast. Founded in the 11th century, when it was known by the Aztec word 'Cajitlán', the city was captured in 1523 by Spanish conquistadors loyal to Cortés. One of its principal sights is the **Cathedral** whose twin towers were constructed out of volcanic stone quarried from the local **Volcán de Colima National Park**, one of whose peaks, the **Volcán del Fuego de Colima**, last erupted in 1991. Colima also hosts a festival, the 'Virgin of the Health' in late January and early February, where amateur toreadors can attempt to overpower a local bull in the *Torre de Once* competition.

BEACH RESORTS

On the Baja Peninsula, **Cabo San Lucas** and **San José del Cabo** are the main tourist destinations, offering miles of excellent beaches. At Cabo San Lucas on the tip of the peninsula, 260km (162 miles) from La Paz, seals may often be seen.

MAZATLÁN: Famed as an angling centre, Mazatlán also has numerous beaches and facilities for surfing, skindiving, tennis, golf, riding and shooting. The name of the town means 'Place of the Deer' in the Nahuatl language, an indication of the town's longstanding association with sporting activities. The *malecón*, which runs along the beachfront, is disguised by a variety of names, being named Avenida Camaron in the north and then proceeding through a number of name changes till it becomes Olas Atlas in the south. In the evening, strollers promenade along this beachfront among the *arañas* (covered carts), 4-wheeled carriages and 3-wheeled taxis. The **Mirador** is a tower on the *malecón* from which divers give a spectacular display twice a day. 'El Faro' on the promontory of Cerro del Creston is one of the highest lighthouses in the world. There are direct flights from Los Angeles as well as from numerous Mexican cities, and a ferry crosses regularly from La Paz in Baja California. The island of **Mexcaltitán** nearby is said to be the original home of the Aztecs.

Credit: © AllMexico TB

PUERTO VALLARTA: Puerto Vallarta is the largest town in the immense Bahía de Banderas resort area (one hour 10 minutes by air from Mexico City). It is situated on the **Bahía de Banderas**, which is the largest natural bay in Mexico. There are a hundred miles of coastline with many sandy beaches and facilities for parasailing, shooting, scuba diving, sailboarding, fishing, golf and tennis. Boat trips provide opportunities to explore the coast. For the visitor who would relish the experience of journeying in a dugout canoe, there is the chance to visit **Yelapa**, a Polynesian-style village which cannot be visited in any other way. The mountains behind the bay may be explored on horseback. **Charreadas**, uniquely Mexican rodeos, are held at certain times of the year. Amongst the smaller resorts are **San Blas**, **Barra de Navidad** and **Zihuatanejo**.

Excursions: Manzanillo, a major seaport, has recently become an important resort. The emphasis is on watersports, but the spacious beaches afford good swimming. Fishing is of a world-class standard. **Ixtapa**, to the south of Manzanillo, is a new resort complex with moorings for yachts and a golf course.

ACAPULCO: Situated on Acapulco Bay, Acapulco is probably the most famous beach resort in Mexico. The town stretches for over 16km (10 miles) round the bay. It has many beaches as well as numerous top-class hotels. The *malecón* (seaside promenade) runs along the beaches. There is a square in the centre of the old town to the west of the Bay. This lively and fashionable resort offers skindiving, angling, parachute sailing, water-skiing, golf, tennis, riding and the unique spectacle of the Quebrada divers. The waters of the Bay are famous for their calmness and safety, though the beach of **La Condesa** has rougher waters and good surf for those who want it. The two beaches nearest the centre of the town are **Playa Caleta** and **Playa Caletilla**; the sun on these is considered to be at its best in the morning. The late afternoon sun is thought to be best on **Playa Hornos**, which is further around the bay to the east. Scuba-diving lessons can be arranged on request. Nearby is **Roqueta Island**, visited regularly by glass-bottomed boats, from which the underwater image of the Virgin of Guadalupe can be seen. The island itself is popular for family trips. **Fort San Diego**, in the middle of the town, is where the last battle of the Mexican War of Independence was fought. Admission is free but it is closed on Thursdays. Behind the town of Acapulco rise the **Sierra Madre Mountains**, a favourite location for photographers who relish the greenery, the rocky cliffs and the breathtaking views over the bay. 16km (10 miles) away is **Pie de la Cuesta** which has a lagoon and several large beaches. The surf is rough.

PUERTO ESCONDIDO AND PUERTO ANGEL: Further down the coast from Acapulco, in Oaxaca state, are the well-known resorts of Puerto Escondido and Puerto Angel. Puerto Escondido (Hidden Port), once an isolated fishing village, has now developed into a well-equipped resort, though it has still retained some of its original character. The string of beaches stretching from the main bay are frequented by bathers, surfers and fishermen. On the hills behind are cheap restaurants and hotels. Puerto Angel, to the west, also a fishing port, is relatively low-key and sleepy. Charming secluded beaches are its main attraction, plus authentic eating places and cheap accommodation. Nearby is the famous beach of **Zipolite**, a 2km- (1.2 mile-) stretch of palm-fringed, white sand, which, although renowned amongst surfers, has treacherous undercurrents; local people rarely swim there.

HUALTULCO: One of Mexico's newest resort areas is at Hualtulco, a group of nine interlocking bays set against rainforest-covered mountains. Until the mid-1980s, this area was a sleepy fishing village with no water or electricity. However, a carefully planned expansion programme has brought luxury hotels and other amenities to the area, while strict regulations conserve its natural beauty. The beaches include **Playa La Entrega** (good for snorkelling with beautiful, calm water) and **Bahía Tangolunda** (where there is an 18-hole golf course). Watersports and other activities are easily arranged.

THE EAST COAST

MONTERREY: In the North, Mexico's industrial powerhouse stands beneath the highest peaks of the **Sierra Madre Oriental** in a setting of great natural beauty. The remnants of Monterrey's more tranquil past (the **Cathedral**, the **Palacio del Gobierno**, the **Obispado**) compete with its present-day preoccupations.

VERACRUZ: The capital, which shares the state's name, is a lively seaport, with excellent seafood cuisine – the visitor will particularly enjoy carnival time in this easy-going city, which is also well-known for its lively nightlife. For centuries, Veracruz was Mexico's main seaport, and it has seen invasions by the French and the Spanish, as well as numerous attacks by pirates. Its colourful history is reflected in its architecture, the highlights of which date from the 17th and 18th centuries. The main square or *zócalo*, said to be the oldest in Mexico, features the **Palacio Municipal** (containing the tourist office) and the **Cathedral**. Street cafes, hotels and bars add to the lively atmosphere. Nearby beaches include **Mocambo** and **Boca del Rio**, 9km (5.6 miles) and 13km (8 miles) to the south respectively. The **Isla de Sacrifios**, accessible by ferry, also has attractive beaches and is the site of a pre-Hispanic shrine. Veracruz is also known for its exceptional seafood cuisine.

EL TAJÍN: Approximately four hours north of Veracruz lie the ruins of the Totonac city of El Tajín, one of Mexico's most impressive ancient sites. Most of the buildings to be seen on this extensive site date from AD 600-700, while the Totonac civilisation was at its height at around AD 600-900. Abandoned around 1200, El Tajín was rediscovered by the Spaniards in 1785. The central edifice is the **Píramide de**

los Nichos, so called because of the 365 square niches on the sides of the building, representing the solar year. Around the pyramid are 11 ball courts whose walls are carved with bas-reliefs depicting human sacrifices, warriors and ball games. Behind this edifice is a network of buildings, **El Tajín Chico**, which is dominated by the **Edificio de las Columnas**, featuring massive columns covered in mosaics. An ancient Totonac ritual is performed daily at about noon by the 'voladores' of Papantla. Five men in traditional dress climb to a small platform at the top of a pole where one of them performs a dance in honour of the sun god, accompanying himself on the drum and whistle. Meanwhile, the other four wrap themselves in rope fastened to a suspended frame. At a given signal, they launch themselves gracefully into space, rotating exactly 13 times, arms outstretched to greet the sun while the rope unwinds. The exact significance of this ritual is unknown, though it is thought to relate to a pre-Hispanic calendar.

THE YUCATÁN PENINSULA

More than 3000 years ago, there emerged a highly sophisticated civilisation, the Mayas, in the diverse landscape of what is now Guatemala, Belize, western Honduras and part of El Salvador, as well as the Mexican states of Yucatan, Quintana Roo, Campeche, Chiapas and Tabasco. The variety of landscape is matched by the abundance of flora and fauna, unrivalled anywhere else in the continent. Birdlife, especially, seems to abound, including toucans, parrots and macaws, hummingbirds and others. The lowland rainforest of Chiapas, Campeche and Quintana Roo is home to such exotic wildlife as ocelots, margays, whitetail deer, anteaters, peccaries, tapirs, howler and spider monkeys and jaguars, the largest wildcats in the Americas. The upland cloud-forests are home to the multicoloured *guacamayas* as well as the resplendent and elusive *quetzal*, an emerald-coloured bird with trailing feathers considered sacred by the Mayan Indians. The coast also supports a wealth of birdlife, as well as alligators and *manatee*, a rare aquatic animal distantly related to the elephant, which can be found in the coastal lagoons. The **Wildlife Reserve of Contoy Island** is the resting and nesting place for hundreds of migrant and resident birds. Even the underwater world can offer a richness of species such as marlin, snapper, grouper, bonito, wahoo, shrimp, lobster, octopus and sailfish, and the beaches are important nesting places for sea turtles during the summer months. At the height of their development (AD 250-900), the Mayans built extraordinary temples and ceremonial centres, many of which are now engulfed by the rainforest. Among the most important archaeological sites to be found in this region are Palenque and Bonampak (Chiapas); La Venta and Comacalco (Tabasco); Edzna, Chicanna and Becan (Campeche); Chichén-Itzá and Uxmal (Yucatán) and Tulum and Coba (Quintana Roo).

MÉRIDA: The capital of Yucatan State is Mérida, the 'White City', founded in 1542 on the site of an ancient Mayan town. It has an air of elegant, faded grandeur, a legacy of its once worldwide importance as a centre of *henequén* (sisal used in the manufacture of rope) production. It is still reckoned to be one of the best places in Latin America to buy fine quality cotton hammocks. There is much to keep the tourist here, including a fine cathedral, the **Casa de Montejo**, and a museum of archaeology, but above all it is a good base for excursions.

PALENQUE: Nestled in the foothills at the edge of the Chiapas rainforest lies Palenque. This small but important Mayan site is one of the most aesthetically appealing sites of the Mayan world, with its exquisite stucco facades. The **Temple of Inscriptions** (above the crypt of a Maya king), the **Multileveled Palace** and the **Temple of the Count** are other highlights. It is easily reached in a couple of hours' drive from **Villahermosa** or **San Cristobal de las Casas**.

BONAMPAK: The site of Bonampak, 150km (90 miles) southeast of Palenque, is famous for the finest Mayan murals ever to be discovered. Housed in the **Temple of Frescoes**, the multicoloured murals depict scenes of Mayan warfare, sacrifice and celebration.

LA VENTA: The museum park of Parque-Museo La Venta not only boasts one of the few extensive collections of Olmec artefacts, but it is also the only archaeological site ever to be completely transplanted. The original Olmec city of La Venta (1500 BC) was situated on the island of Tonala and featured, among other exceptional sculptures, the colossal human heads that now characterise the Olmec civilisation. Originally evacuated in 1925, it was moved to **Villahermosa** in the 1970s because of the fear that nearby oil drilling would damage the site. The museum park contains 30 Olmec sculptures set in a botanical garden.

COMACALCO: About 67km (42 miles) from Villahermosa is Comacalco. This archaeological site of the Maya civilisation dates back to the late Classic period (AD 500-900). Some of the structures resemble those at Palenque though they are still unique in the region. All the buildings here are made from bricks rather than the stone used elsewhere. In fact, Comacalco means 'in the house of bricks'. Sights include the **Great Acropolis** with its detailed stucco masks and the small museum.

EDZNA: Edzna, 65km (40 miles) southeast of Campeche, dates back to 300 BC. Besides the Chenes-style architecture, visitors can also see an extensive network of canals, reservoirs and waterholes. Attractions include the **Great Acropolis**, the **Small Acropolis**, the **Platform of the Knives**, the **Ball Court**, the **Temple of Stone Masks** and the **Nohochna**.

CHICHÉN-ITZÁ: The famous archaeological and UNESCO World Heritage Site of Chichén-Itzá, 120km (75 miles) east of Mérida, contains the **Pyramid of Kukulcan** (**El Castillo**), where one can find the 'Red tiger with jade eyes'. During the spring and autumn equinoxes (March 21-22 and September 21-22), huge crowds gather to see a unique spectacle, when shadows create the illusion of a serpent descending the northern staircase. Of interest are also the snaking columns of the **Temple of the Warriors**, a ball court in perfect condition, **El Caracol** (the observatory), the **Caves of Balankanche** and the **Sacred Cenote** (where bejewelled young girls were thrown into the well as sacrifices to the rain god Chac).

UXMAL: The elaborate stucco work and detailed façades of Uxmal, 80km (50 miles) south of Mérida, have led to a comparison of the city with Rome. Among the fine stonework are the entwined serpents in the **Nun's Quadrangle**, the **House of Pigeons** and the **Ball Court**. Other attractions include the **Pyramid of the Magician** and the **Governor's Palace**.

TULUM: The walled fortress of Tulum, 131km (78 miles) south of **Cancún**, has been described as one of the most dramatic sites of the pre-Hispanic world. Perched atop rugged cliffs on the coast, this last outpost of the Maya civilisation commands a breathtaking view of the Caribbean. Settlement here dates from AD 900-1500 and sights include the **Temple of the Descending God**, **El Castillo** and the **Temple of the Frescoes**.

COBA: Coba, 38km (24 miles) north of Tulum, is possibly the largest archaeological site on the Yucatán peninsula. This town, set amongst dense jungle and marshlands and including four lakes, dates from the classical period and is believed to have been occupied during the time of the conquest. The most significant groupings of sites are the **Coba Group**, **Las Pinturas**, the **Macanxoc Group**, the **Crossroad Pyramid** and the **Chumuc Mul Group**. It also houses the tallest structure in Yucatán, the **Nohoch Mul Pyramid**.

BEACH RESORTS: Cancún, **Cozumel**, and **Isla Mujeres** were once little more than sleepy villages, but now these Caribbean Coast resorts are world renowned for their vacation facilities. The **Isla de Cancún**, made up of some of Mexico's most expensive beachfronts occupies the northeast tip of the Yucatán. The *Punta*, or point of the island, is nestled between the **Bahía de Mujeres** (Bay of Women) and the Caribbean Sea and boasts some of the best areas for sunbathing on the Peninsula. At the tip of the point is **Playa Chac Mool**, a public beach area offering comfortable dining and shopping. Although the beaches of Cancún are known for their powder white sand and exquisite beauty, the waters along the east edge of the island are subject to strong undertow and should be treated with caution. Lifeguards are posted on the beaches fronting most of the major hotels and swimming is encouraged in these areas only. On the west side of the island are the shimmering waters of **Laguna Nichupté** (Nichupté Lagoon) and **Laguna Río Inglés** (English River Lagoon), which are home to 200 species of birds and host a number of watersports. The Ciudad de Cancún borders the west side of the lagoons, and is a good place for shopping. South of the point lies the Zona Arqueológica El Rey, with a small collection of Mayan ruins. The **Isla Mujeres**, once known for its remote jungle and mysterious ambience, attracts visitors who prefer to explore the less developed areas of the Peninsula. Accessible by a 25-minute boat ride from Cancún, the island is home to six different species of endangered turtles, and a marine farm that oversees their protection. The reefs of **Los Manchones**, **Cuevones**, **Chital** and **La Bandera** are prized diving spots, known for their extraordinary marine life and unusual cave structures. South of Cancún is the equally prized beach resort of **Cozumel**, with its extraordinary coral reefs, gentle currents and exceptional diving.

Sport & Activities

Ecotourism: Mexico hosts a wide variety of landscapes and ecosystems within its borders: deserts, swamps, volcanoes and rainforest are all present. There are 58 national parks and biosphere reserves where the abundant flora and fauna receive special protection. The country boasts approximately 176 kinds of orchids and more species of birds than exist in the USA and Canada combined. Guided 'ecotourist excursions' with multilingual professional guides can be arranged. Transportation is via kayak, mountain bike, jeep or on horseback. If visitors care to venture out alone, updated information on protected camping sites and special permits is provided by tourism offices in each state. Those wishing to observe sea life can go to *Guerrero Negro* in Baja California, home to one of Mexco's prime **whale-watching** spots, the *Parque Natural de la Ballena Gris* (Gray Whale National Park), where grey whales breed near the shores of *Scammon's Lagoon* from November through March. The small town of San Ignacio (145 km/90 miles to the southeast) is noted for its nearby *San Ignacio Lagoon*, where whales are reputed to be so 'friendly' that they swim close enough to be petted. *Puerto Lopez Mateos* on *Magdalena Bay* is another good spot for whale watching. Several islands in Baja California host colonies of **sea lions** and **sea birds**. In the central plains, there are high peaks to climb, including the volcanoes *Popocatépetl* and *Nevado de Toluca*, where it is possible to go scuba diving in the crater. **Monarch butterflies** are a must-see in the region of *Michoan*.

Watersports: Mexico has nearly 16,000km (10,000 miles) of coastline and a warm climate. While the Caribbean coast features white-sand beaches and gentle seas, the Pacific coast is characterised by rolling surf and darker sand. The gentlest **swimming** conditions are offered by the waters of the Yucatan coast (Cancún, Rivera Maya and Cozumel) and the Sea of Cortés (Loreto, Guayamas and La Paz). For more information about coastal resorts, see *Beach Resorts* in the *Resorts & Excursions* section. Major city hotels and most hotel resorts have swimming pools and some towns have public baths. Almost all Mexican resorts have facilities for the full range of watersports, including **jet-skiing**, **windsurfing** and **sea kayaking**. **Surfing** can be enjoyed on the pacific breakers and **parasailing** is another exciting sport. Equipment can be hired at hotels or through watersports centres. Acapulco has particularly good facilities for **water-skiing**. Visitors can marvel at the skill of the professional divers that **swallow-dive** from the cliffs at *Acapulco*. All over Mexico, there are excellent facilities for **sailing**, with modern marinas sited around the coasts. Most resort hotels will rent small sailing boats to guests. **Diving** is particularly popular in two areas: the Sea of Cortés and the Yucatan Peninsula's east coast. In these areas, the sea is clear and placid, and facilities are outstanding. The Yucatan Peninsula features the second-largest coral reef in the world. **Snorkelling** enthusiasts may like to head for the Puerto Vallarta area on the Pacific coast, where resorts include Punta Mita, Guayabitos, Mismaloya and Los Arcos. In Zihuatanejo, Playa Las Gatas and Ixtapa Island offer good conditions and in Huatulco, the bays of La Entrega and Tangolunda are very suitable. Mexico's coast offers some of the best **deep-sea fishing** in the world. Every major port has charter boats and fishing gear for hire and even the smallest fishing village is likely to have at least one fishing boat for hire. **Freshwater fishing** for black and striped bass is possible mainly around Hermosillo (Sonora) and El Fuerte, Culiacán and Cosalá (Sinaloa).

Golf: Mexico has around a dozen top-class golf courses and numerous other courses. Many are located in spectacular natural settings, with some specially designed by famous golfers such as Jack Niklaus. In contrast to North American courses, they are usually uncrowded and comparatively reasonably priced.

Language courses: There are many opportunities for visitors to attend courses of study in the Spanish language and in Mexican culture. Summer schools and other institutions are located in a variety of places, from major cities to beach resorts. It is usually possible to stay with a Mexican family, in order to make the visit more rewarding and productive. Further information is available from the tourist board (see *Contact Addresses* section). A detailed directory listing courses and fees can be obtained free of charge from the National Registration Center for Study Abroad, PO Box 1393, Milwaukee, WI 53201, USA (tel: (414) 278 0631; fax: (414) 271 8884; website: www.nrcsa.com).

Spa holidays: The Aztecs, Tarascans and other native peoples used to frequent the countless hot springs which abound in the country, especially in the area around Mexico City. Nowadays, there are many resorts with high-class facilities offering a range of treatments. Visitors can choose from spiritual retreat spas, with a New Age bias and a meditation programme, mineral water spas, hot springs and 'upscale spas', which are mini-resorts offering complete packages based on weight reduction, stress management and body fitness.

Spectator sports: These include **football**, **baseball**, **jai alai** (a very fast game of Basque *pelota* played with a small ball and straw rackets) and **horse racing**.

Social Profile

FOOD & DRINK: Self-service (fast food) is available but table-service is usual. Bars have table- and/or counter-service. There are laws relating to minors and licensing on civic holidays. Mexican cuisine is delicious and varied; there are many specialities, such as *turkey mole*, a sauce containing a score of ingredients including several sorts of chilli, tomatoes, peanuts, chocolate, almonds, onions and garlic. Another sauce, *guacamole*, incorporates avocado pears, red peppers, onions and tomatoes, and often accompanies turkey or chicken with *tortillas* (pancakes made with maize). There are also *enchiladas*, *tacos* (maize pancakes served with pork, chicken, vegetables or cheese and chilli) and *tamales*. Every region of Mexico has its own dishes. International cuisine is available at most hotels in the larger cities, and at most restaurants. There is a wide variety of exotic fruits such as papayas, mangoes, guavas, *zapotes*, pineapples, *mameyes* and *tunas* (juicy prickly pears, fruit of the cactus). Imported spirits are expensive; local spirits probably give better value for money. The best buys are rum and gin. European aperitifs are produced in Mexico and are of excellent quality; and, of course, there is *tequila* (made from *maguey*, a variety of cactus). It is traditionally drunk neat with a pinch of salt and a bite of lemon, and makes an excellent cocktail-base. Mexico's coffee liqueur, *kahlúa*, is world famous. *Hidalgo*, *Domecq* and *Derrasola* are good Mexican white wines, whilst *Los Reyes* and *Calafia* are excellent reds. Mexico is a producer of good beer; both the dark beers and the light beers are worth sampling. All the big supermarkets sell spirits, beer and wine.

NIGHTLIFE: With a range of settings from panoramic restaurants to intimate bars, Mexico City offers excellent music and assorted cuisine, with some of the best bars and restaurants located in hotels. Nightlife is very vibrant and exciting and features a large variety of top-name entertainers, international shows, jazz groups, rock groups, traditional Mexican music and dancing, Spanish flamenco dancers and gypsy violinists. Worth seeing is the impressive light show, with accompanying sound show at the archaeological site of Teotihuacán. The history and mythology of this ancient civilisation are recreated through a gorgeous display of coloured lights, poetic dialogue and music. The season runs from October to May.

SHOPPING: Good buys include silverware, ceramics and locally made pottery, woven wool blankets (*sarapes*), brightly coloured scarves in wool or silk (*rebozos*), richly embroidered charro hats, straw work, blown glass, embossed leather, hard- and semi-precious stones, gold and silver jewellery, finely pleated men's shirts in cotton voile (*guayaberas*), white dresses embroidered with multi-coloured flowers (*huipiles*), which are sold in the markets, and hammocks. The best shopping is in Mexico City, Acapulco, Campeche, Cuernavaca, Guadalajara, Mérida, Oaxaca, San Miguel de Allende and Taxco. **Shopping hours:** Mon-Sat 0900-2000 (Mexico City); Mon-Fri 0900-1400 and 1600-2000 (rest of the country).

SPECIAL EVENTS: Mexicans celebrate more than 120 fêtes and festivals every year; some of them religious, others secular, national or local. Most events provide an occasion for music, dancing, processions and fireworks. For a complete list, contact the Mexican Tourist Office (see *Contact Addresses* section). The following is a selection of special events occurring in Mexico in 2005:

Jan 2-12 *City of Merida Festival*. Jan 19 Ceremony of the Pocho Dance. Feb International Contemporary Film Festival of Mexico City. **Feb 2** *Candlemas*, nationwide. **Feb 3-8** *Carnival*, nationwide. **Mar 4** *Annual Witch Gathering*, Catemaco. **Mar 6** *LALA International Marathon Torreon 2005*. **Mar 11-13** *Corona Rally Mexico*, Guanajuato State. **Apr** *Sardine Fishing Ritual*; *Xalapa Fair*; *San Marcos Fair*. **Apr 16-19** *Annual Mexico City Festival*. **May** *18th Alarconian Theatrical Festival*. **May 15-20** *ROLEX/IGFA Offshore Championship*; *Cancun Jazz Festival 2005*. **May 21-Jun 6** *International Wine and Cheese Festival*, Tequisquiapan, Queretaro. **Jun** *37th Annual Tecate SCORE Baja 500 Race*, Ensenada, Baja California; *Corpus Christi Fair*; *San Pedro Fair*, Tlaquepaque, Jalisco. **Aug 29** *Chile in Walnut Sauce Festival*, Puebla. **Sep** *XXII International Mexico City Marathon*; *Poetry Festival*, San Luis Potosi. **Sep 24** *Running of the Bulls*, San Miguel. **Oct 5-23** *33rd International Cervantine Festival*. **Oct 22-Nov 2** *Festival of Skulls*, Aguascalientes. **Nov** *National Tequilla Fair*. **Nov 1-2** *Day of the Dead*. **Nov 20** *Mexican Revolution Day*.

SOCIAL CONVENTIONS: Handshaking is the most common form of greeting. Casual sportswear is acceptable for daytime dress throughout the country. At beach resorts, dress is very informal for men and women and nowhere are men expected to wear ties. In Mexico City, however, dress tends to be smart in elegant restaurants and hotel dining rooms. Smoking is unrestricted except where notified. Mexicans regard relationships and friendships as the most important thing in life next to religion and they are not afraid to show their emotions. A large Mexican family always seems to find room for one more and a visitor who becomes friends with a Mexican will invariably be made part of the family. Visitors should always remember that local customs and traditions are important. **Tipping:** Service charges are rarely added to hotel, restaurant or bar bills and many of the staff depend on tips for their livelihood. 15 per cent is expected and 20 per cent if the service has been very good. Airport porterage is charged at the equivalent of US$1 per bag.

Credit: © AllMexico TB

Business Profile

ECONOMY: The agricultural sector produces various staple crops, including sorghum, wheat, maize, rice, beans and potatoes largely for domestic consumption; while coffee, sugar cane, fruit and vegetables are grown for export. The contribution made by agriculture (including fishing, which is a major employer in coastal areas) has declined since the 1980s, it now employs about 20 per cent of the workforce and accounts for about 5 per cent of GDP.

Manufacturing has grown considerably during the last 20 years. The main products are vehicles, processed foods, iron and steel, chemicals and machinery. Many companies in this sector are located in so-called *maquiladora* plants, where semi-finished goods or raw materials from the southern USA are shipped across the border into Mexico, completed, and then (for the most part) returned to the USA. The system allows American companies to take advantage of lower wages and running costs, as well as a less stringent regulatory regime. NAFTA (see below) has also contributed substantially to the growth of this part of the Mexican economy. Mexico also has a sizeable mining sector, producing a wide range of minerals including silver, bismuth, arsenic and antimony; there are also smaller deposits of sulphur, lead, zinc and cadmium. However, the largest single natural resource, and the source of much of Mexico's revenue in recent years, is oil. In some respects this has been a mixed blessing: Mexico has suffered several economic crises in which over-reliance on oil income was at least a contributory factor. In the service sector, tourism is the most important single industry, although it suffered a serious downturn in the wake of the '9-11' catastrophe and has yet to fully recover. As for the overall economy, after a mild recession in 2001/02, estimated Mexican GDP growth for 2003 was 1.5 per cent; this is expected to rise to 2.5 per cent in 2004. In 2002, inflation and unemployment were 5 and 2.7 per cent respectively.

Under the statist policies of the PRI, the government was always in firm control of economic policy. However, once the party's stranglehold had been broken, Mexico embarked on the type of reform process familiar throughout the world: privatisation of state-controlled industries, deregulation and removal of tariffs and subsidies, and the opening of the economy to foreign investment. The reform process has been somewhat spasmodic and piecemeal, however, as a result of continuous political disputes. In 1993, Mexico signed the North American Free Trade Agreement (NAFTA), which created a free trade bloc among the USA, Canada and Mexico of a size to rival the EU in both population and economic output. Mexican trade with its fellow NAFTA members increased threefold, and accounts for 80 per cent of the total trade volume. Nor has Mexico neglected trade links with its fellow Latin American countries: there are free-trade agreements with Central America, Colombia and Venezuela. Mexico is also a member of the Inter-American Development Bank, the Association for Latin American Integration (ALADI) and, most recently, the Asian-Pacific Economic Forum (APEC). Outside the American continent, Japan, Germany and Spain are Mexico's other important trading partners. The UK is the largest foreign investor in Mexico after the USA.

BUSINESS: English is widely spoken in business circles although it is preferable for the visitor to be able to speak Spanish. Letters written in Spanish should be replied to in Spanish. Business wear is formal. Mexicans attach much importance to courtesy and the use of titles. Prior appointments are necessary and if in doubt about a correct title it is advisable to use *licenciado* in place of *señor*. Best months for business visits are January to June and September to November. Avoid the two weeks before and after Christmas and Easter. **Office hours:** Vary considerably; usually Mon-Fri 0900-1400 and 1500-1800.

COMMERCIAL INFORMATION: The following organisation can offer advice: Confederación de Cámaras Nacionales de Comercio, Servicios y Turismo (CONCANACO), 3rd Floor, Balderas 144, Col. Centro, 06079 México DF (tel: (55) 5722 9300; e-mail: gerardo@concanacored.com; website: www.concanacored.com).

CONFERENCES/CONVENTIONS: The meetings, conventions, exhibitions and incentives planner's kit issued by the Mexican Ministry of Tourism lists over 70 convention venues in Mexico City, Acapulco, Taxco, Morelia, Puerto Vallarta, Ixtapa, Guadalajara, Mazatlán, Cancún and Mérida. Taxco, Acapulco, Morelia and Cancún have dedicated centres, the largest of which, in Acapulco, can seat up to 8000 people.

Climate

Climate varies according to altitude. Coastal areas and lowlands (*tierra caliente*) are hot and steamy with high humidity, while the central plateau is temperate even in winter. The climate of the inland highlands is mostly mild, but sharp changes in temperature occur between day and night. The cold lands (*tierra fría*) lie above 2000m (6600ft). Rainfall varies greatly from region to region. Only the Sierra Madre Oriental, the Isthmus of Tehuantepec and the state of Chiapas in the far south receive any appreciable amount of rain during the year, with the wet season running between June and September. All other areas have rainless seasons, while the northern and central areas of the central plateau are dry and arid. There is some snow in the north in winter. The dry season runs from October to May.

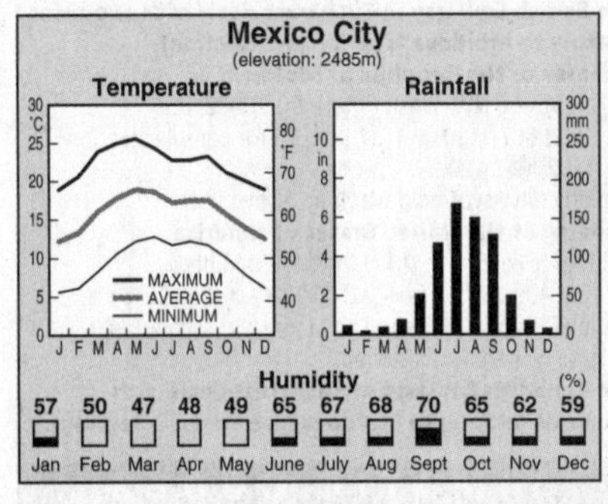

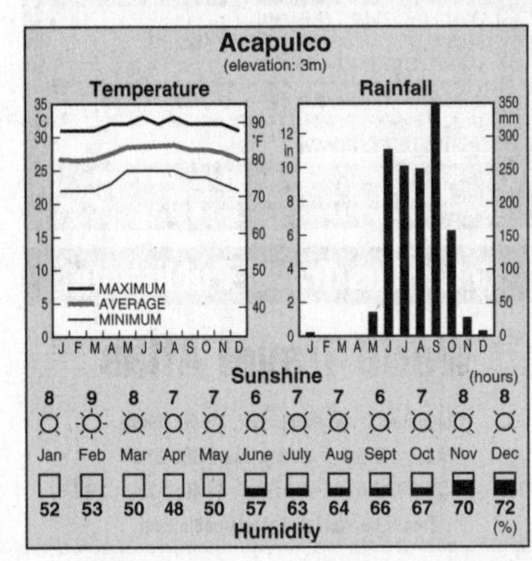

Moldova

LATEST TRAVEL ADVICE CONTACTS

British Foreign and Commonwealth Office
Tel: (0870) 606 0290 Website: www.fco.gov.uk
US Department of State
Website: http://travel.state.gov/travel
Canadian Department of Foreign Affairs and Int'l Trade
Tel: (1 800) 267 8376 Website: www.dfait-maeci.gc.ca

Location: Southeastern Europe.

Country dialling code: 373.

National Tourism Agency
180 Stefan cel Mare Street, Office 901, Chisinau MD 2004, Moldova
Tel: (22) 210 774. Fax: (22) 232 626.
E-mail: dept@turism.md
Website: www.turism.md
Embassy of the Republic of Moldova
5 Dolphin Square, Edensor Road, London W4 2ST, UK
Tel: (020) 8995 6818. Fax: (020) 8995 6927.
E-mail: movilamd@mail.md
The British Embassy in Bucharest deals with enquiries relating to Moldova (see *Romania* **section).**
Embassy of the Republic of Moldova
2101 S Street, NW, Washington, DC 20008, USA
Tel: (202) 667 1130 *or* 1137 (ext. 15 for consular section).
Fax: (202) 667 1204.
E-mail: embassyofmoldova@mcihispeed.net
Embassy of the United States of America
103 Mateevici Street, 2009 Chisinau, Moldova
Tel: (22) 408 300. Fax: (22) 233 044 *or* 226 361.
E-mail: ChisinauCA@state.gov (consular section).
Website: www.usembassy.md
The Canadian Embassy in Bucharest deals with enquiries relating to Moldova (see *Romania* **section).**

TIMATIC CODES

Health
AMADEUS: **TI-DFT/KIV/HE**
GALILEO/WORLDSPAN: **TI-DFT/KIV/HE**
SABRE: **TIDFT/KIV/HE**

Visa
AMADEUS: **TI-DFT/KIV/VI**
GALILEO/WORLDSPAN: **TI-DFT/KIV/VI**
SABRE: **TIDFT/KIV/VI**

To access TIMATIC country information on Health and Visa regulations through the Computer Reservations System (CRS), type in the appropriate command line listed above.

General Information

AREA: 33,800 sq km (13,050 sq miles).
POPULATION: 3,606,800 (official estimate 2004).
POPULATION DENSITY: 106.7 per sq km.
CAPITAL: Chisinau (Kishinev). **Population:** 662,200 (official estimate 2004).
GEOGRAPHY: Moldova is a small landlocked state in southeastern Europe – one of the most highly populated republics of the former USSR. To the north, east and south Moldova, is bound by Ukraine; to the west by Romania. The River Prut constitutes the border with Romania. The country has rich pastures and wooded slopes, ideal for wine-growing.
GOVERNMENT: Republic since 1991. Gained independence from the Soviet Union in 1991. **Head of State:** President Vladimir Voronin since 2001. **Head of Government:** Prime Minister Vasile Tarlev since 2001.
LANGUAGE: The Constitution of 1994 declared the official language as 'Moldovan' although it is considered to be virtually identical to Romanian. In 1940, after Soviet annexation, the Cyrillic script was introduced and was referred to as Moldavian up until 1989 when the Latin alphabet was reintroduced. Russian is still the most widely spoken language. The ethnic and linguistic make-up of Moldova is as follows: Moldovans 64.5 per cent, Ukrainians 13.8 per cent, Russians 13.0 per cent, Gagauz 3.5 per cent, Bulgarians 1.5 per cent, others 3.7 per cent.
RELIGION: Mostly Eastern Orthodox Christian and other Christian denominations. A small amount of the population are Jewish.
TIME: GMT + 2 (GMT + 3 from last Sunday in March to Saturday before last Sunday in October).
ELECTRICITY: 220 volts AC, 50Hz.
COMMUNICATIONS: Telephone: IDD is available to major towns. Country code: 373. For outgoing international calls: dial 0, wait for tone, then dial 0 and the country code. There are two types of payphone: Soviet ones (taking tokens) and modern ones (taking cards). **Mobile telephone:** GSM 900 networks in use. Roaming agreements in operation. Coverage extends over the central area of the country. Network operators include *Moldcell* (website: www.moldcell.md) and *Voxtel* (website: www.voxtel.md). **Internet:** Major commercial ISPs include Moldovan ISP *Dynamic Network Technologies* (website: www.dnt.md), *MegaDat* (website: www.mcc.md), *MoldTelecom* (website: www.moldtelecom.cm) and *Relsoft* (website: www.mldnet.com). **Post:** All mail to and from Moldova may be subject to long delays. The postal and telecommunication systems are being modernised. The main post office is at 73 Stefan cel Mare boulevard, 277012 Chisinau. Post office hours: Mon-Sun 0900-2000. There are express mail services in Chisinau. **Press:** The press is generally uncensored. There are more than a dozen daily newspapers in Moldova, the most popular being *Moldova Suverana* published in Romanian. Other main papers include *Dnestrovskaya Pravda*, *Nezavisimaya Moldova* (published in Russian), *Trudovoi Tiraspol* and *Viata Satului*. English-language publications can sometimes be found at major hotels in Chisinau. Western press deliveries are erratic. **Radio:** BBC World Service (website: www.bbc.co.uk/worldservice) and Voice of America (website: www.voa.gov) can be received. From time to time the frequencies change and the most up-to-date can be found online. Services in Romanian, Russian and English are also available on 68.48MHz (0600-0800 and 1800-2200 local time).

Passport/Visa

	Passport Required?	Visa Required?	Return Ticket Required?
Full British	Yes	Yes	No
Australian	Yes	Yes	No
Canadian	Yes	Yes	No
USA	Yes	Yes	No
Other EU	Yes	Yes/1	No
Japanese	Yes	Yes	No

Note: Regulations and requirements may be subject to change at short notice, and you are advised to contact the appropriate diplomatic or consular authority before finalising travel arrangements. Details of these may be found at the head of this country's entry. Any numbers in the chart refer to the footnotes below.

PASSPORTS: Passport valid for at least six months required by all.
VISAS: Required by all except the following for stays of up to 90 days:
(a) nationals of the CIS, except nationals of Turkmenistan who *do* require a visa;
(b) nationals of **1.** Poland and Romania.
Types of visa and cost: *Tourist*, *Simple*, *Service* (Business) and *Transit*. All may be issued on a single-, double- or multiple-entry basis. Costs vary depending on nationality of applicant and type of visa. Contact Embassy for further details.
Validity: *Tourist*: One month from date of issue.
Application to: Consulate (or Consular section at Embassy); see *Contact Addresses* section.
Application requirements: (a) Passport with blank pages to affix the visa. (b) One application form. (c) One passport-size photo. (d) Fee payable by money order or cheque only. (e) For postal applications, a self-addressed return envelope should also be submitted. (f) Letter of invitation from Moldova, authorised by the Department of Migration in Moldova, or a tourist voucher issued by a Moldovan tourist agency. *Transit*: (a)-(e) and, (f) Entry documents for next country. (g) Onward tickets.
Note: (a) Nationals of EU countries, Bulgaria, Canada, Croatia, Israel, Japan, Norway, Switzerland, Turkey and the USA do not need to submit an invitation to obtain a visa for stays of up to 90 days. (b) All foreign visitors must register with the police within three days of arrival.
Working days required: Five; same day for urgent visas with surcharge of 50 per cent of visa price.
Temporary residence: Apply to the Foreign Ministry in Moldova.

Money

Currency: Leu (MDL) = 100 bani. Notes are in denominations of MDL500, 200, 100, 50, 20, 10, 5 and 1. Coins are in denominations of 50, 25, 10, 5 and 1 bani.
Currency exchange: Foreign currencies can be exchanged in hotels or bureaux de change. Moldova is essentially a cash-only economy. There are three ATMs in Chisinau where local currency can be withdrawn using Visa cards.
Credit & debit cards: Credit cards are only accepted by a few banks. Check with your credit or debit card company for details of merchant acceptability and other services which may be available.
Travellers cheques: Travellers cheques are not generally accepted, though a few banks may exchange them.
Currency restrictions: The import of local and foreign currency is unlimited. The export of local currency is unlimited. The export of foreign currency is limited to amount imported.
Exchange rate indicators: The following figures are included as a guide to the movements of the Moldovan Leu against Sterling and the US Dollar:

Date	Feb '04	May '04	Aug '04	Nov '04
£1.00=	23.58	20.18	22.00	23.51
$1.00=	12.95	11.30	11.94	12.41

Banking hours: Mon-Fri 0930-1730.

Duty Free

The following goods may be imported into Moldova by persons of 18 years of age or older without incurring customs duty:
200 cigarettes; 1l of spirits and/or wine; a reasonable quantity of perfume for personal use.

Public Holidays

2005: Jan 1 New Year's Day. **Jan 7-8** Moldovan Christmas. **Mar 8** International Women's Day. **May 1** Labour Day. **May 2** Easter Monday (Orthodox). **May 8** Memorial Day. **May 9** Victory and Commemoration Day. **Aug 27** Independence Day. **Aug 31** Limba Noastra (National Language Day). **Oct 13-14** National Day of Wine and Wine Festival.
2006: Jan 1 New Year's Day. **Jan 7-8** Moldovan Christmas. **Mar 8** International Women's Day. **Apr 17** Easter Monday (Orthodox). **Apr 18** Memorial Day. **May 1** Labour Day. **May 9** Victory and Commemoration Day. **Aug 27** Independence Day. **Aug 31** Limba Noastra (National Language Day). **Oct 13-14** National Day of Wine and Wine Festival.

Health

	Special Precautions?	Certificate Required?
Yellow Fever	No	No
Cholera	Yes	No
Typhoid & Polio	1	N/A
Malaria	No	N/A

Note: Regulations and requirements may be subject to change at short notice, and you are advised to contact your doctor well in advance of your intended date of departure. Any numbers in the chart refer to the footnotes below.

1: Immunisation against typhoid is sometimes recommended.
Food & drink: Mains water is normally chlorinated but bottled water is available and advised. Local meat, poultry, fruit and vegetables are generally considered safe to eat.
Other risks: There is a small risk of *hepatitis A* in rural areas. Cases of *diphtheria* have also been reported. *Rabies* is present and casual exposure to stray dogs is common

throughout Chisinau. Vaccination before arrival should be considered. If you are bitten, seek medical advice without delay. For more information, consult the *Health* appendix.
Health care: A number of large medical institutions operate in Chisinau, including the Republican Clinical Hospital. Elderly travellers and those with existing health problems may be at risk owing to inadequate medical facilities. There is a reciprocal health agreement with the UK for urgent medical treatment. Otherwise, all services and prescriptions are charged for and doctors and hospitals often expect immediate cash payment; medical insurance is strongly recommended.
Note: Travellers staying longer than three months may be required to produce proof of HIV-negative status.

Travel - International

Note: The threat from terrorism in all parts of Moldova is low. Visitors should be vigilant to petty crime, particularly in Chisinau. Caution is advised if travelling to Transnistria.
AIR: Moldova's national airlines are *Air Moldova (9U)* and *Air Moldova International (RM)*. *Moldovian Airlines*, *Tarom* (Romania's national airline), *Transaero* (Russian airline) and *Tyrolean Airlines* fly regularly to Moldova. There are also charter airlines operating between Chisinau and some major destinations in the CIS, France, Germany, Hungary, Israel, The Netherlands, Romania and Turkey.
Approximate flight times: From *London* to Chisinau is approximately seven hours, with a stopover in Moscow. From *Moscow* to Chisinau is two hours, from *Kiev* is one hour 30 minutes and from *St Petersburg* is three hours.
International airports: *Chisinau International (KIV)* is 14km (8.5 miles) from the city centre (travel time – 15 to 25 minutes). There is a regular bus service to the city. Taxis are also available. *Moldova-Tur* offers a courtesy pick-up by prior arrangement (see *Contact Addresses* section). Facilities include bank, post office, left-luggage and duty free shops.
Departure tax: USD12.
RAIL: There are daily train services between Chisinau and Moscow, Russian Federation (travel time – 22 hours), Odessa, Ukraine (travel time – five hours) and Bucharest, Romania (travel time – 13 hours). Other, less frequent, destinations include Minsk (Belarus) and St Petersburg.
ROAD: Moldova can be entered from Ukraine (although the self-proclaimed 'Republic of Transdniestria' area around Tiraspol should be avoided at present) and also from Romania via the border crossing at Leusheni, Sculeni and Giurgiulesti. From Chisinau to Odessa is 183km (114 miles).

Travel - Internal

RAIL: There is over 1145km (715 miles) of railway track in use in Moldova. Trains run daily to Ocnita, Tighina and Ungheni, and there are connections to most areas of the country. For more details, contact the information service of Moldovan Railways (tel: (22) 252 737/5; website: www.railway.md).
ROAD: The road network covers 13,622km (8500 miles).
Bus: These run between most of the larger towns and cities. For further information, contact either Chisinau Main Bus Station (tel: (22) 542 185) or South East Bus Station (tel: (22) 723 983). **Taxi:** These can be found everywhere. Fares should be negotiated in advance, though drivers prefer to charge per hour. Taxis are requested by calling 900 or 905-8.
Car hire: Self-drive cars can be obtained for self-drive or with an English-speaking driver. *Avis* car hire is represented in Chisinau. **Documentation:** An International Driving Permit is required.
URBAN: Buses, trolleybuses and minibuses are cheap but notoriously crowded and unreliable. They all operate from 0500-2400 with services every 15 minutes. Tickets for buses and trolleybuses can be purchased from kiosks or on board the vehicle. Minibus tickets are bought from the driver.

Accommodation

HOTELS: There is a small selection of hotels in the capital Chisinau, most of which are located close to the railway station and in the city centre. There are some low-grade hotels in other towns.
Grading: From **1-star** (basic facilities) to **4-stars** (larger capacity and greater facilities of a higher standard).

Resorts & Excursions

CHISINAU: The Moldovan capital of Chisinau (formerly Kishinev) stands on the banks of the small **River Byk**. The city was founded around 1470 and the history and life of Moldova through the centuries is best presented in the **History and Regional Lore Museum**, a beautiful Turkish-style complex. The **Fine Arts Museum** houses good examples of Russian, West European and Moldovan paintings, sculpture and applied arts. The **Pushkin House** is the place where the great Russian poet spent his days in exile between 1820-23. The museum is famous as the place where Pushkin began working on his epic poem *Eugene Onegin*. There are also two old cemeteries in Chisinau, the **Armenian Cemetery** and the **Jewish Cemetery**. The latter is famous as the burial place for the victims of the Chisinau Pogrom in 1903; in the 1960s, the lower part of the cemetery was deliberately razed by the authorities. Owing to massive Jewish emigration from Moldova during the 1980s and the beginning of the 1990s, the state of the cemetery has significantly deteriorated. The only working synagogue in Chisinau is situated not far from the city centre, on Habad-Liubavici str. The former Chisinau Choral Synagogue today houses the **Chekhov Drama Theatre**. The **Monument of Stefan cel Mare** (Stefan the Great) is situated at the entrance to the well-tended Pushkin Park. He was Moldova's *Gospodar* (ruler) between 1457-1504 during a time of brief independence, thus securing him a special place in Moldova's history. The monument by the sculptor Plamadeala was unveiled in 1927. In 1990-91, the monument was the focal point of meetings and violent clashes between Moldova's Nationalists and pro-Soviet supporters. Just outside the park is an impressive building housing the largest cinema, **Patria** (Fatherland), which was built in 1947 by German POWs.
Picturesque bathing beaches line the manmade **Chisinau Lake** (formerly Komsomol Lake). Boats can also be hired. There are two parts to the complex: the **Exhibition of Achievements** and the open-air **Green Theatre** with a seating capacity of 7000.
ELSEWHERE: Situated 70km (44 miles) from Chisinau is **Tiraspol**, founded in 1792 on the then Russian border. It now has a population of 200,000 and is one of the main industrial centres of the country. It is also the capital of the self-proclaimed Republic of Transdniestria and travellers are advised to avoid it owing to the unstable political situation. **Benderi** (Tighina) is one of the oldest towns in Moldova. Its beautiful 17th-century fortress, as well as the town itself, were seriously damaged during the recent fighting.
Bâlti, 150km (94 miles) north of the capital is a major industrial centre. The main products from this area are sugar, vegetable oils and fur coats.
Approximately 160km (100 miles) south of Chisinau is **Cahul**. The town is famous for its thermal spas and mud treatments and there is a small hotel in the town. There is also a good local theatre. **Hirjauca** is also a renowned spa in the area. Moldova is a wine-growing country and the vineyards and wine cellars of **Mileshti** and **Krikova-Veki** are famous throughout the region.

Sport & Activities

As Moldova's infrastructure is not very well-developed, there are not yet many opportunities for tourists and travellers to pursue different activities. However, **vineyard tours** are popular, and Moldovan wine has a very good reputation; see *Resorts and Excursions* section for further information.

Social Profile

FOOD & DRINK: There are plenty of small restaurants and coffee shops. The service tends to be slow, but the cuisine is delicious. Local specialities include *mititeyi* (small grilled sausages with onion and pepper) and *mamaliga* (thick, sticky maize pie) which is served with *brinza* (feta cheese). *Tocana* (pork stew) should be tried with sweet-and-sour watermelons and apples. There are more than 100 varieties of excellent wines produced in Moldova. White wines include *Aligote*, *Riesling* and *Sauvignon*. *Moldovan Cabernet* and *Merlot* are noteworthy reds. *Doina* or *Nistru* brandy is an ideal accompaniment with desserts.
NIGHTLIFE: In Chisinau, there is a good selection of theatres and concerts halls, which includes an opera house. The *Eminescu Music and Drama Theatre* specialises in Romanian productions, as does the *Youth Theatre Luceafarul* (Poetic Star). All performances in the Chekhov Drama Theatre are exclusively in Russian (the building used to be the Chisinau Choral Synagogue). The Philharmonia Concert Hall houses *Moldova's Symphony Orchestra*. It is also the base for the folklore *Doina Choir*, the internationally renowned *Zhok National Dance Ensemble* and the *Fluerash Orchestra of National Music*. Russian and Romanian productions can be seen in the puppet theatre Licurici (Glow-worm).
SHOPPING: Good buys are the vividly coloured costumes, handmade carpets and locally produced wines and brandies. The main open-air market or *tolchok* is on Calea Mosilor, about 10 minutes' drive away from central Chisinau. Although crowded, it sells everything and is a good place for bargains. **Shopping hours:** Larger shops open 0800-2000; all others open 0900-1700.
SPECIAL EVENTS: There are few special events celebrated in Moldova. The following is a selection of special events occurring in Moldova in 2005; for a complete listing, contact the National Tourism Agency (see *Contact Addresses* section):
Feb-Mar *International Specialised Exhibition of Sports, Leisure and Tourism*. **Aug 27** *Independence Day*. **Oct 13-14** *Wine Festival*.
SOCIAL CONVENTIONS: Dress should be casual but conservative. For official engagements, men should wear a jacket and tie. The country is famous for its tradition of folk arts and there are many lively musical groups (*Tarafs*), which play a variety of rare folk instruments including the *tsambal* (not unlike a dulcimer), *cimpoi* (bagpipe), *fluier* and *nai*. **Tipping:** 5 to 10 per cent will be gladly accepted.

Business Profile

ECONOMY: Moldova's economy is dominated by agriculture, food processing and related industries which account for over half of total output. The land is very fertile: some 85 per cent is cultivated. The republic was the largest wine-growing region in the former Soviet Union and this is still a major source of revenue. It also grows fruit, vegetables, tobacco and grain, and produces dairy and meat products in large quantities. Other than food and drink processing, Moldova's industrial sector is dominated by metals and machinery, textiles and footwear. The once thriving electronics industry has declined due to the dissolution and/or contraction of its major clients in the Russian space and defence sector. Under the Soviet system of economic planning, Moldova exported much of its output to other Soviet republics in exchange for raw materials and fuel products. The demise of the Soviet system triggered a major collapse which saw Moldovan economic output decline by 15 per cent annually during the early 1990s. This catastrophic decline has been arrested but there are few signs of economic growth, and Moldova is now one of the poorest countries in an already impoverished region. In 1992, Moldova joined the IMF, World Bank and the European Bank for Reconstruction and Development (EBRD) as a 'Country of Operation'. After an uncertain start, a reform programme got under way in Moldova and by 1999 much of the economy had been privatised and deregulated. However, the IMF and World Bank then cut off financial support when the government refused to sell off the key tobacco and wine industries. Following some shifts in policy, the government has since been able to secure funding from the EBRD and occasional small packages from the IMF and World Bank. But relations with the latter pair are still difficult. At the beginning of 2003, the government announced its intention to liberalise the economy further.
The national currency, the Leu, introduced in November 1993, has been reasonably stable apart from the period immediately after the 1998 Russian financial crisis. Russia remains Moldova's largest trading partner, followed by the Belarus, Romania, Ukraine and Germany. In May 2001, Moldova joined the World Trade Organization. Moldova eventually hopes to join the European Union. That aspiration depends on the results of the 2004 expansion and Moldova's own economic performance.
COMMERCIAL INFORMATION: The following organisation can offer advice: Chamber of Commerce and Industry of the Republic of Moldova, 151 Stefan cel Mare st., Chisinau, MD 2004 (tel: (22) 221 552; fax: (22) 234 425; e-mail: camera@chamber.md; website: www.chamber.md).

Climate

Very mild and pleasant. Temperate with warm summers 20-23°C (68-73°F), crisp, sunny autumns and cold, sometimes snowy, winters.
Required clothing: Mediumweights, heavy topcoat and overshoes for winter; lightweights for summer. A light raincoat is useful.

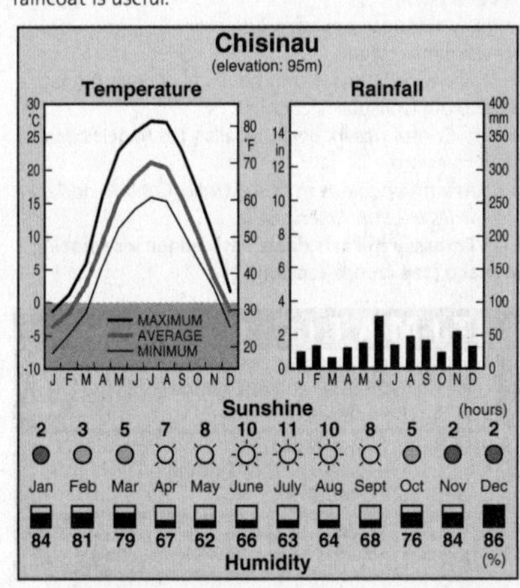

Monaco

LATEST TRAVEL ADVICE CONTACTS

British Foreign and Commonwealth Office
Tel: (0870) 606 0290 Website: www.fco.gov.uk
US Department of State
Website: http://travel.state.gov/travel
Canadian Department of Foreign Affairs and Int'l Trade
Tel: (1 800) 267 8376 Website: www.dfait-maeci.gc.ca

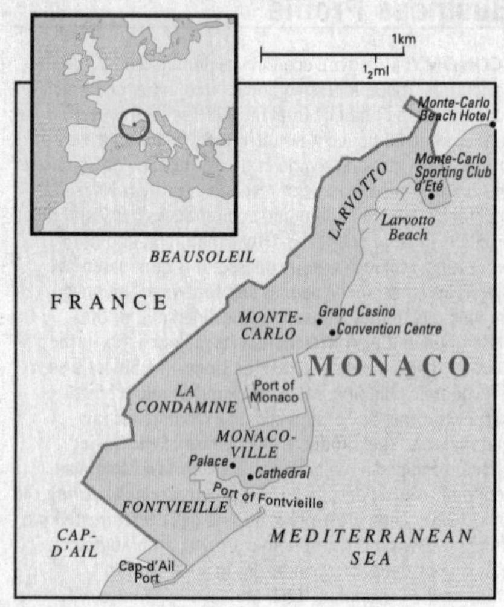

Location: Western Europe.

Country dialling code: 377.

Direction du Tourisme et des Congrès de la Principauté de Monaco
2A boulevard des Moulins, MC 98030 Monaco, Cedex
Tel: 9216 6116. Fax: 9216 6000.
E-mail: dtc@monaco-tourisme.com
Website: www.monaco-tourisme.com
Consulate General of the Principality of Monaco
4 Cromwell Place, London SW7 2JE, UK
Tel: (020) 7225 2679.
Fax: (020) 7581 8161.
E-mail: ivanovic_chiara@onetel.com
Website: www.monacoconsulate.uk.com
Opening hours: Mon-Fri 1000-1200 and 1400-1700.
Monaco Government Tourist & Convention Office
2nd Floor, 206 Harbour Yard, Chelsea Harbour, London SW10 0XD, UK
Tel: (020) 7352 9962 *or* (0500) 006 114 (toll-free in UK).
Fax: (020) 7352 2103.
E-mail: monaco@monaco.co.uk
Website: www.monaco-tourisme.com
British Honorary Consul
Street address: 33 boulevard Princesse Charlotte, MC 98005 Monaco, Cedex
Postal address: BP 265, MC 98005 Monaco, Cedex
Tel: 9350 9954.
Fax: 9770 7200.
Consulate General of the Principality of Monaco and Monaco Government Tourist Office
23rd Floor, 565 Fifth Avenue, New York, NY 10017, USA
Tel: (212) 286 3330 (tourist office) *or* 286 0500 (consular section) *or* (800) 753 9696 (toll-free in USA and Canada).
Fax: (212) 286 9890 (tourist office) *or* (212) 286 1574 (consular section).
E-mail: info@monaco-consulate.com *or* info@visitmonaco.com
Website: www.visitmonaco.com (tourism) *or* www.monaco-consulate.com (consular section).
Honorary Consulates in: Boston, Dallas, Los Angeles, Miami and San Francisco.
Also deals with enquiries from Australia, Canada and all the countries in Latin America.
The US Embassy in Paris deals with enquiries relating to Monaco (see *France* section).

TIMATIC CODES

Health	AMADEUS: **TI-DFT/MCM/HE** GALILEO/WORLDSPAN: **TI-DFT/MCM/HE** SABRE: **TIDFT/MCM/HE**
Visa	AMADEUS: **TI-DFT/MCM/VI** GALILEO/WORLDSPAN: **TI-DFT/MCM/VI** SABRE: **TIDFT/MCM/VI**

To access TIMATIC country information on Health and Visa regulations through the Computer Reservations System (CRS), type in the appropriate command line listed above.

Consulate General of the Principality of Monaco
1 Place Ville-Marie, Suite 3900, Montréal, Québec H3B 4M7, Canada
Tel: (514) 878 5878. Fax: (514) 878 8197.
The Canadian Embassy in Paris deals with enquiries relating to Monaco (see *France* section).

General Information

AREA: 1.95 sq km (0.75 sq miles).
POPULATION: 32,020 (2000).
POPULATION DENSITY: 16,435 per sq km.
CAPITAL: Monaco-Ville. **Population:** 1034 (2000).
GEOGRAPHY: Monaco is second only to the Vatican as the smallest independent state in Europe. Set on the Mediterranean coast of France just a few miles from the Italian border, the principality is a constitutional monarchy and relies largely on foreign currency for an economic base. Its principal industry is tourism. The country is a narrow ribbon of coastline backed by the Alpes-Maritimes foothills, creating a natural amphitheatre overlooking the sea, with the population centred in four districts. Monaco-Ville is set on a rocky promontory dominating the coast. The Palace is the home of the Grimaldi family, the oldest ruling house in Europe. Monaco-Ville also boasts a fine Romanesque cathedral among its other attractions. La Condamine is the area around the Port, while Monte-Carlo is the main centre for business and entertainment. Fontvieille has been set aside as an area for new light industrial and residential development.
GOVERNMENT: Constitutional monarchy. **Head of State:** Prince Rainier III since 1949. **Head of Government:** Minister of State Patrick Leclercq since 2000.
LANGUAGE: French. Monégasque (a mixture of French Provençal and Italian Ligurian), English and Italian are also spoken. Native Monégasques make up only a minority of Monaco's population.
RELIGION: 91 per cent Roman Catholic (Monaco has a Catholic Bishop), with Anglican minorities.
TIME: GMT + 1 (GMT + 2 from last Sunday in March to Saturday before last Sunday in October).
ELECTRICITY: 220 volts AC, 50Hz. Round two-pin plugs are in use.
COMMUNICATIONS: Telephone: Full IDD is available. Country code: 377. Outgoing international code: 00. **Mobile telephone:** GSM 900 network covers the whole principality, operated by *Monaco Telecom*. **Fax:** All hotels have facilities. **Internet:** ISPs include *Monaco Internet* (website: www.monaco.net). There is at least one Internet cafe. **Telegram:** Available at hotels and post offices. Telephones and telegraphic services are open 0800-2100 daily at the main post office (see below). **Post:** Same rates as France. The main post office is at The Scala Palace, Beaumarchais Square. Post office hours: Mon-Fri 0800-1900, Sat 0800-1200. There are special Monégasque stamps. **Press:** The principal regional daily is *Nice-Matin* (which includes two pages on Monaco). The *Monaco Hebdo* covers Monaco's current affairs. The *Journal de Monaco*, an internal government journal, is published weekly. Other newspapers include *Gazette Monaco-Côte d'Azur*, *Monaco Actualité* and *Monte Carlo Méditerranée*. French newspapers are widely available, as are English books and magazines. The *Riviera Reporter*, the only English-language magazine for residents in the French riviera, is published every two months. **Radio:** BBC World Service (website: www.bbc.co.uk/worldservice) and Voice of America (website: www.voa.gov) can be received. From time to time the frequencies change and the most up-to-date can be found online.

Passport/Visa

The passport and visa requirements for persons visiting Monaco as tourists are the same as for France. For further details, see the *France* section. Monaco is not a member of the EU, however, so residency and long-stay requirements differ and are liable to change. For further details, contact any French Consulate (or Consular section at Embassy).

Money

Currency: The first Euro coins and notes were introduced in January 2002. For details of the Euro currency, exchange rates and currency restrictions, see *France* section.
Credit & debit cards: All major credit cards are widely accepted. Check with your credit or debit card company for details of merchant acceptability and other services which may be available.
Travellers cheques: Widely accepted. To avoid additional exchange rate charges, travellers are advised to take travellers cheques in Euros, US Dollars or Pounds Sterling.
Banking hours: Mon-Fri 0900-1200 and 1400-1630.

Duty Free

See *France* section for details.

Public Holidays

2005: Jan 1 New Year's Day. **Jan 27** Saint-Devote's Day. **Mar 28** Easter Monday. **May 1** Labour Day. **May 5** Ascension. **May 16** Whit Monday. **May 26** Corpus Christi. **Aug 15** Assumption. **Nov 1** All Saints' Day. **Nov 19** Monaco National Day. **Dec 8** Immaculate Conception. **Dec 25** Christmas Day.
2006: Jan 1 New Year's Day. **Jan 27** Saint-Devote's Day. **Apr 17** Easter Monday. **May 1** Labour Day. **May 25** Ascension. **Jun 5** Whit Monday. **Jun 15** Corpus Christi. **Aug 1** Assumption. **Nov 1** All Saints' Day. **Nov 19** Monaco National Day. **Dec 8** Immaculate Conception. **Dec 25** Christmas Day.

Health

	Special Precautions?	Certificate Required?
Yellow Fever	No	No
Cholera	No	No
Typhoid & Polio	No	N/A
Malaria	No	N/A

Note: *Regulations and requirements may be subject to change at short notice, and you are advised to contact your doctor well in advance of your intended date of departure. Any numbers in the chart refer to the footnotes below.*

Health care: Health insurance is recommended. There are high standards of medical care.

Travel - International

AIR: There is no airport in Monaco. Helicopter services run by *Héli-Air Monaco (YO)* link the principality with the nearest airport, *Nice* (Nice-Cote d'Azur) (website: www.nice.aeroport.fr), 22km (14 miles) from Monaco. The journey takes seven minutes and costs €135 for a return ticket. *Héli-Air* also serves points along the Côte d'Azur and in Italy. There are free shuttle links from the heliport to hotels in the principality. For more information, contact *Héli-Air Monaco*, Monaco Heliport, Quartier de Fontvieille, 98000 Monaco (tel: 9205 0050; fax: 9205 0051; e-mail: reservations@heliairmonaco.com; website: www.heliairmonaco.com).
Departure tax: None.
SEA: The main harbours are at Condamine (Hercule port) and Fontvieille, which are equipped to handle yachts of all tonnages. Intercontinental liners are able to anchor in the bay of Monaco.
RAIL: An extensive train service, including daily and overnight through-trains, runs through the principality to all neighbouring towns. The *TGV Méditerranée* line runs between Paris and Monaco (travel time – five hours 45 minutes). High-speed trains on this route run through the beautiful Burgundy and Provencal countryside. For more information, contact *Rail Europe* (tel: (0870) 830 2000; website: www.raileurope.co.uk). The *SNCF Métrazur* summer service runs every 30 minutes, stopping at all towns on the Côte d'Azur between Cannes and the Italian frontier at Vintimille, including Monaco. A new station has recently been built underground. For more information, contact *French Railways* (SNCF) (tel: (8) 3635 3535; website: www.sncf.com).
ROAD: Cannes and Nice are 50km (31 miles) and 18km (11 miles) west of Monaco. The French/Italian border and Menton are 12km (7 miles) and 9km (6 miles) east of Monaco. No formalities are required to cross the frontier between France and the Principality of Monaco. **Coach:** There is a direct service from Nice Airport to Monaco, which stops at major hotels. The return journey stops at slightly fewer hotels and takes passengers to Terminals 1 and 2 at Nice airport (travel time – 45 minutes). **Bus:** There are good connections with the surrounding areas, with regular services as outlined. *Nice*: Seaside route with stops at Cap d'Ail, Eze-sur-Mer, Beaulieu-sur-Mer and Villefranche-sur-Mer. Service from 0600-2100 approximately every 30 minutes. Middle Corniche route with stops at Cap d'Ail, Eze-Village and Col de Villefranche. Services from 0600-1815 (Sat-Sun 2000) approximately every hour. *Menton*: Seaside route with stops in Roquebrune and Cap-Martin (service from 0530-2100) approximately every 30 minutes. Service to Saint Roman/Rocher de Monaco, Jardin Exotique/Rocher de Monaco, Gare SNCF/Larvotto Beach and Rocher de Monaco/Parking Touristique Fontvieille. Buses run approximately every five minutes between Monaco-Ville and the Casino, every 10 minutes towards Saint Roman or the Jardin Exotique and between the Railway Station and beaches (Larvotto). **Taxi:** Available from Casino Square, Monaco Monte-Carlo Railway Station, avenue Princesse Grace, Fontvieille, Métropole, Place des Moulins and the Post Office of Monte-Carlo. There is a surcharge after 2200.
Documentation: As for France, a national driving licence will suffice.
Travel Times: The following chart gives approximate travel times (in hours and minutes) from **Monaco** to a

selection of other cities in Europe.

	Air	Road	Rail	Sea
London	1.55	20.00	11.00	-
Paris	1.15	-	-	-
Nice	*0.07	0.45	0.30	0.20
Menton	-	0.35	0.25	-
Geneva	0.50	3.30	4.00	-
Rome	1.00	-	-	-

* Time by helicopter; see above under *Air*.

Accommodation

HOTELS: Some of the most luxurious hotels and conference facilities are centred in Monte-Carlo, and all are equipped with extensive modern amenities. For further information, contact the Association de l'Industrie Hôtelière Monégasque, Hôtel Tulipin, 9 avenue Prince Pierre, MC 98000 (tel/fax: 9205 6491; e-mail: aihm@monte-carlo.mc; website: www.monte-carlo.mc).
Grading: Hotels in Monaco are graded in a **1-**, **2-**, **3-**, **4-star** and **4-star deluxe** system. The principality has over 16 hotels, five of which are in the 4-star deluxe category and three of which are in the 4-star category.
SELF-CATERING: Apartments are available to let. For further details, contact the Monaco Government Tourist & Convention Office (see *Contact Addresses* section).

Credit: © MGTO & Miti Image & DTC

Resorts & Excursions

Monaco forms an enclave into the French *Département* of the **Alpes Maritimes**. The narrow ribbon of coastline is backed by the mountains, which form a protective barrier. This area creates a natural amphitheatre. From the heights of the **Tête de Chien** or **Mont Agel**, or from lower down from the Moyenne-Corniche at the level of the entrance to the **Jardin Exotique**, there are a number of panoramic viewpoints looking out over exceptional scenery. The ancestral Rocher and the promontory of Spélugues border the harbour where pleasure boats are moored. The **Rock of Monaco** has a medieval air. It is a city of bright, clean streets which converge on the **Prince's Palace Square**, where there are museums, boutiques and restaurants. Monaco is well located for exploring Provence and the French Riviera. For a description of the area of France surrounding Monaco, see *Côte d'Azur* in the *France* section.
MONACO-VILLE: Perched on the famous Rock, the Old Town (Monaco-Ville) juts into the sea on Monaco's western flank and offers excellent views of the harbour and its usual armada of luxury yachts below. The city's architectural history, reflected in its medieval houses, palaces and vaulted passageways, is best experienced on foot – either alone or through one of the many organised tours available (which tend to make the city quite crowded during the summer months). The main tourist attraction is the **Prince's Palace and State Apartments** (open daily 0930-1830 (June to September), 1000-1700 (October)). Built around 1215, the palace's focal points are the Throne Room and the Main Courtyard with its horse-shaped marble staircase, adorned with millions of geometric patterns. The Changing of the Palace Guard (admission free) takes place daily, just before noon (1155). For a visit of the palace and apartments, an admission fee is charged. Also worth visiting are the serene and sea-facing **Saint-Martin Gardens**, which inspired the poet Guillaume Apollinaire between 1887 and 1889. There are a number of museums of varying degrees of interest located in the Old Town, including the **Oceanographic Museum and Aquarium**, whose grandiose façade rises spectacularly out of the sea and houses a world-renowned collection of marine fauna and interactive exhibits. Other museums and attractions include the **Museum of Napoleonic Souvenirs and Collection of the Palace's Historic Archives**, which exhibits thousands of objects relating to the First Empire (Napoleon I) and provides a colourful history of Monaco; the **Wax Museum of the Princes of Monaco**, Monaco's answer to London's Madame Tussaud's; the **Monte-Carlo Story**, a multivision show about Monaco's history; and the **Azur Express Tourist Train**, which carries up to 54 visitors and offers commentaries in French, Italian, German and English.
For all tourist attractions and museums (except the Japanese Gardens), an admission fee is charged. Opening hours and prices are seasonal; ask for the relevant brochures from the Direction du Tourisme (see *Contact Addresses* section).
MONTE-CARLO AND MONACO: Monaco is perhaps best known for its glittering array of casinos and gaming rooms, the most famous of which is the **Grand Casino** in Monte-Carlo. The casino is located in Monaco's most famous *quartier* known as the **Golden Square**, where all the most luxurious and fashionable hotels, restaurants and boutiques can also be found (including the famous Hôtel de Paris). The casino was originally built in 1863 and demolished in 1878, but was then replaced six months later by a new structure according to the plans of Charles Garnier, the architect of the Paris Opera House. The style is distinctively grand and luxurious and the casino is linked to the **Salle Garnier Opera House** (closed for refurbishment until 2007) by an impressive atrium lined with 28 Ionic columns made of onyx. Public slot machines open daily from 1400, private gambling rooms from 1500. An admission fee is charged. The minimum age for entering any of Monte Carlo's casinos is 21.
Other attractions in Monte-Carlo and Monaco include the **Japanese Gardens**, right next to the sea; the **National Museum of Dolls and Clockwork Exhibits of Yesteryear**; the **Exotic Garden**; **Observatory Caves and Museum of Prehistoric Anthropology** (located in Moneghetti); and the **Condamine Market**, a covered market next to one of Monaco's best shopping districts (the pedestrianised **Rue Princesse Caroline** and the **Rue Grimaldi**).
MONTE-CARLO BORD DE MER (LARVOTTO): The creation of this new district was made possible by re-routing railway tracks underground. The development has a beach, restaurants, snack bar and shops. This part of Monaco also has extensive sporting facilities at the prestigious Monte-Carlo Beach Hotel where there are restaurants and an olympic-sized swimming pool.

Credit: © MGTO & K Prouin & Miti Image Info

FONTVIEILLE: The main attractions in this area include the **Princess Grace Rose Garden**, a large park containing more than 150 varieties of rose. The **Museum of Stamps and Coins** features rare philatelic items from the postal history of the Principality. The permanent exhibition of **Prince Rainier III's Private Collection of Classic Cars**, with over 100 classic cars, is nearby. The **Naval Museum** and the **Zoological Terraces** are also located in Fontvieille.

Sport & Activities

Racing: Monaco's place on the international sports agenda has been secured for many years by the world-famous *Monaco Grand Prix Formula One* race, which takes place every year in the Principality's narrow winding streets, attracting thousands of spectators. Another favourite is the *Historic Grand Prix*, which is held every other year.
Watersports: Monaco's Mediterranean location and climate also create perfect conditions for all types of watersports, with facilities for **water-skiing**, **skindiving**, **parasailing** and **windsurfing** all provided. **Swimming** in the sea is safe (although the beaches tend to be crowded) and, in addition to hotel swimming pools, there are several heated seawater pools open throughout the year. In the main harbour, expensive luxury yachts and boats, which are a permanent fixture, corroborate Monaco's reputation as a glamorous destination for the rich and famous. The Diving Club of Cap d'Ail (outside Monaco) organises **diving** sessions (tel: (4) 9378 3174). **Sailing** and **yachting** are generally popular and the *Yacht Club de Monaco* offers sailing lessons during July and August, while the harbour also offers extensive facilities.
Golf: This is very popular and the *Monte-Carlo Golf Club (SBM)* has an 18-hole course (nearly 6km/3.8 miles long) where international tournaments are regularly staged. The course is open daily all year round. A handicap is required for non-members wishing to play and the green fees range between €53.36 to 68.60. Holders of SBM *Carte d'Or* get a 50 per cent reduction on green fees. Other facilities include a practice range, equipment hire, a shop, bar and a restaurant. There is also a miniature golf course.
Other: For **tennis** and **squash** enthusiasts, the facilities at the *Monte-Carlo Country Club* are excellent; every year, the club's international championship attracts some of the world's best tennis players. Monaco also has a renowned sports academy, the *Monte-Carlo Sports Academy (MCSA)*, which offers special activity holiday packages to adolescents aged 12 to 17. Their approach combines sport and cultural activities with linguistic workshops (French and English lessons are available) and the package also incorporates the facilities provided by the *Centre Méditerranéen*, a campus set in a large park complete with accommodation facilities and an amphitheatre decorated by the French poet Jean Cocteau.
Perhaps most closely associated with Monaco is the activity of **gambling**, for which the Principality has long been famous. The best-known casino is the *Grand Casino* in Monte-Carlo (see also *Resorts & Excursions* section). At all of Monaco's casinos, the minimum age for entering the gambling rooms is 18. There are also a number of *health spas* and *beauty centres*, the most famous one being the *Thermes Marins de Monte-Carlo*.

Social Profile

FOOD & DRINK: Restaurants in Monaco offer a wide choice of food. Service and standards are excellent. Cuisine is similar to France, with some delicious local specialities.

A B C D E F G H I J K L M N O P Q R S T U V W X Y Z

Credit: © MGTO & JC Vinaj & Miti Image Info

There are many restaurants and bars with late opening hours. Specialities include: *barbagiuan*, a type of pastry filled with rice and pumpkin; *fougasse*, fragrant orange flower water pastries decorated with nuts, almonds and aniseed; *socca*, chick-pea flour pancakes; and *stocafi*, dried cod cooked in a tomato sauce.

NIGHTLIFE: The world-famous Monte-Carlo Casino is a perennial attraction. The building also houses the Casino Cabaret and the *Salle Garnier*, the delightful gilded Opera House offering a winter season of ballet, opera and music. There are further gambling venues in the Monte-Carlo Grand Hotel and the Monte-Carlo Sporting Club and the Café de Paris. There are also numerous nightclubs, cinemas, discos and variety shows.

SHOPPING: Monégasque products include perfume, chocolates, ceramics, clothing, hosiery, shoes, books, jewellery and embroidery. Handcrafted items are sold at Boutique du Rocher, a charity of the late Princess Grace. Monégasque stamps are highly prized by collectors.

Shopping hours: Mon-Sat 0900-1230 and 1500-1830.

SPECIAL EVENTS: For further information concerning events and festivals, contact the Government Tourist & Convention Office (see *Contact Addresses* section).

The following is a selection of special events occurring in Monaco in 2005:

Jan 20-23 *73rd Monte Carlo Automobile Rally*. **Jan 20-28** *28th Monte-Carlo International Circus Festival*, Fontvieille Big Top. **Jan 25-27** *Celebration of Sainte Dévote's Day*. **Jan 28-Feb 2** *8th Monte Carlo Historic Car Rally*. **Mar 25-26** *International Dog Show*. **Apr 1-17** *Spring Arts Festival*, Monte Carlo. **May 19-22** *63rd Formula One Monaco Grand Prix*, Monte Carlo. **Jun 14-15** *23rd Monte Carlo International Swimming Meeting*. **Jul 16-Sep 4** *Summer Exhibition*, Grimaldi Forum. **Jul 30-Aug 15** *10th Monte Carlo Antiquities*, International Antiques Fair. **Sep 3-4** *AAF World Athletics Final*, Louis II Stadium. **Nov 18-19** *Monaco National Day (Monegasque) celebrations*. **Dec 24 2005-Jan 4 2006** *Monte Carlo Ballet*, Grimaldi Forum.

SOCIAL CONVENTIONS: Casual wear is acceptable for daytime and dress is the same as for the rest of the French Riviera. Smart restaurants, dining rooms, clubs and the Casino's private rooms require more formal attire. Handshaking and, more familiarly, kissing both cheeks, are accepted forms of greeting. **Tipping:** Hotel and restaurant bills generally include a 15 per cent service charge; however, where this is not added it is customary to leave a 15 per cent tip. Taxi drivers are usually tipped 15 per cent of the fare.

Business Profile

ECONOMY: Service industries, especially property and financial services, account for the bulk of Monaco's economy. Tourism is also a major source of revenue, contributing about 25 per cent of government revenue, as well as being the mainstay of local retail businesses. There is also a highly successful, custom-built business conference venue. The dearth of land precludes any agriculture, but there is some light industry, the main products of which are pharmaceuticals, plastics, electronics, paper and textiles. Monaco attracts many extremely wealthy individuals as residents, by virtue of its pleasant climate, reputation and environment as well as the absence of income or inheritance tax and lack of financial reporting requirements. Migrant, non-resident labour supplies the menial workforce. Since the late 1990s, concerted international efforts to tackle the global problem of money laundering and tax evasion have been led by the Organisation of Economic Co-operation and Development (the group of 24 leading industrial countries) and its Financial Action Task Force. The FATF has set down a number of criteria covering disclosure which 'offshore' financial centres must meet. Most centres have cooperated with the new FATF regime. Monaco is one of seven which, by the deadline in April 2002, had failed to do so: future developments rely on the actions of Monaco's ruling Grimaldi family (itself implicated in a major fraud inquiry) and the attitude of the French government. Almost all the principality's external trade is conducted with France – and France, along with Italy, supplies the bulk of Monaco's visitors (both as tourists and foreign labour).

BUSINESS: A suit should be worn and prior appointments are necessary. Business meetings are formal. It is considered impolite to begin a conversation in French and then revert to English. **Office hours:** Mon-Fri 0900-1200 and 1400-1700.

COMMERCIAL INFORMATION: The following organisation can offer advice: Conseil Economique et Social (consultative organisation dealing with all aspects of the national economy), 8 rue Louis Notari, MC 98000 (tel: 9330 2082; fax: 9350 0596).

CONFERENCES/CONVENTIONS: Monaco is a year-round leisure and business destination and there are extensive conference facilities. The Forum Grimaldi Cultural and Exhibition Centre, one of Europe's largest venues for conference events, provides three terraced auditoria, the largest with 1900 seats and two massive exhibitions halls. Large parts of the new complex are built under water. For further information, contact the Grimaldi Forum Monaco, BP 2000, 10 avenue de la Princesse Grace, MC 98001 (tel: 9999 2000; fax: 9999 2001; e-mail: contact@grimaldiforum.com; website: www.grimaldiforum.com). Other conference venues include the 1100-capacity Convention Centre and Auditorium (built on land reclaimed from the sea), including technical support and exhibition areas; the International Conference Centre (with a capacity for 450 persons); and the Meridien Beach Plaza Club, which can seat up to 1624 people. For further information, contact the Direction du Tourisme (see *Contact Addresses* section).

Climate

Monaco has a mild climate throughout the year, the hottest months being July and August, and the coolest being January and February. Rain mostly falls during the cooler winter months and there is an average of only 60 days' rain per year.

Required clothing: Lightweights are worn, with a warm wrap for cooler summer evenings. Light- to mediumweights are advised for winter.

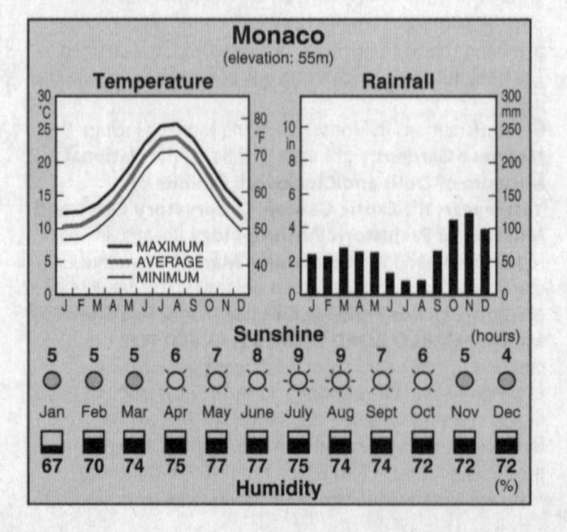

Mongolia

LATEST TRAVEL ADVICE CONTACTS

British Foreign and Commonwealth Office
Tel: (0870) 606 0290 Website: www.fco.gov.uk

US Department of State
Website: http://travel.state.gov/travel

Canadian Department of Foreign Affairs and Int'l Trade
Tel: (1 800) 267 8376 Website: www.dfait-maeci.gc.ca

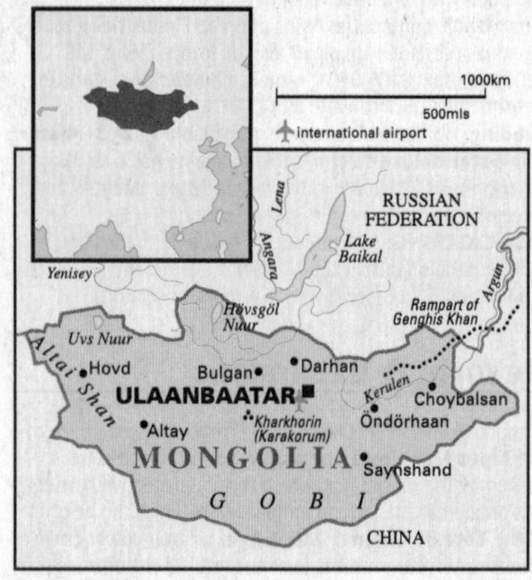

Location: Central Asia.

Country dialling code: 976.

Mongolian Tourism Association
Room 318, Trade Union Building, Sukhbaatar Square-11, Ulaanbaatar - 38, 210628, Mongolia
Tel/Fax: (11) 327 820.
E-mail: info@travelmongolia.org *or* tourismasc@magicnet.mn
Website: www.travelmongolia.org

Embassy of Mongolia
7-8 Kensington Court, London W8 5DL, UK
Tel: (020) 7937 0150 ext. 29 (visa section).
Fax: (020) 7937 1117.
E-mail: office@embassyofmongolia.co.uk
Website: www.embassyofmongolia.co.uk
Opening hours: Mon-Fri 1000-1230 (visa section).

British Embassy
Street address: 30 Enkh Taivny Gudamzh, Ulaanbaatar – 13, Mongolia
Postal address: PO Box 703, Ulaanbaatar – 13, Mongolia
Tel: (11) 458 133. Fax: (11) 458 036.
E-mail: britemb@mongol.net

Embassy of Mongolia
2833 M Street, NW, Washington, DC 20007, USA
Tel: (202) 333 7117. Fax: (202) 298 9227.
E-mail: esyam@mongolianembassy.us
Website: www.mongolianembassy.us

Embassy of the United States of America
PO Box 1021, Ulaanbaatar – 13, Mongolia
Tel: (11) 329 095. Fax: (11) 320 776 *or* 353 788.
E-mail: pao@usembassy.mn *or* cons@usembassy.mn (visa enquiries)
Website: http://us-mongolia.com

Embassy of Mongolia
151 Slater Street, Suite 503, Ottawa, Ontario, K1P 5H3, Canada
Tel: (613) 569 3830 *or* 2623. Fax: (613) 569 3916.
E-mail: mail@mongolembassy.org (general enquiries) *or* consul@mongolembassy.org
Website: www.mongolembassy.org
Honorary Consulates: Alberta, British Columbia, Quebec, Saskatchewan and Toronto.

Canadian Consulate
Street address: Bodi Tower, 7th Floor, Sukhbaater Square, Ulaanbaatar, Mongolia
Postal address: PO Box 1028, Ulaanbaatar 13, Mongolia
Tel: (11) 328 285. Fax: (11) 328 289.
E-mail: can_honcon@mongolnet.mn

TIMATIC CODES

Health	AMADEUS: **TI-DFT/ULN/HE** GALILEO/WORLDSPAN: **TI-DFT/ULN/HE** SABRE: **TIDFT/ULN/HE**
Visa	AMADEUS: **TI-DFT/ULN/VI** GALILEO/WORLDSPAN: **TI-DFT/ULN/VI** SABRE: **TIDFT/ULN/VI**

To access TIMATIC country information on Health and Visa regulations through the Computer Reservations System (CRS), type in the appropriate command line listed above.

General Information

AREA: 1,564,116 sq km (603,909 sq miles).
POPULATION: 2,510,000 (official estimate 2002).
POPULATION DENSITY: 1.6 per sq km.
CAPITAL: Ulaanbaatar. **Population:** 869,900 (2004).
GEOGRAPHY: Mongolia has a 3485km- (2165 mile-) border with the Russian Federation in the north and a 4670km- (2902 mile-) border with China in the south. From north to south, it can be divided into four areas: mountain-forest steppe, mountain steppe and, in the extreme south, semi-desert and desert (the latter being about 3 per cent of the entire territory). The majority of the country has a high elevation, with the principal mountains concentrated in the west. The highest point is the peak of Tavan Bogd, in the Altai Mountains, at 4374m (14,350ft) high. The lowest point, Khukh Nuur lake, in the east, lies at 560m (1820ft). There are several hundred lakes in the country and numerous rivers, of which the Orkhon is the longest at 1124km (698 miles).
GOVERNMENT: Republic. Declared independence from China in 1921. **Head of State:** President Natsagiyn Bagabandi since 1997. **Head of Government:** Prime Minister Tsachiagiyn Elbegdorj since 2004.
LANGUAGE: Khalkh Mongolian is the official language. Kazakh is spoken by 5 per cent of the population. There are also many Mongolian dialects.
RELIGION: Buddhist Lamaism is the main religion, although there is no state religion.
TIME: GMT + 8 (Bayan Ulgii, Uvs & Khovd Aimags in western Mongolia GMT + 7).
ELECTRICITY: 230 volts AC, 50Hz.
COMMUNICATIONS: Telephone: An Asiasat Earth station has provided international telecommunications with Mongolia since 1994. Country code: 976. Area codes: Ulaanbaatar: 11, Darkhan: 01-372, Erdenet: 01-352, Khovd: 01-432. International calls can be made from telephone exchanges in Ulaanbaatar. **Mobile telephone:** GSM 900 network operated by *Mobicom* (website: www.mobicom.mn) covers Altanbulag, Arvaikheer (Uvurkhangai), Darkhan, Erdenet, Nalaikh, Sainshand (Dornogobi), Selenge, Ulaanbaatar, Zamyn-Uud and Zuunkharaa. CDMA network operated by *Skytel Company* covers Bulgan, Darkhan, Selenge, Ulaanbaatar, Uvurkhangai and Zamyn-Uud. **Fax:** Service available at hotels and in the central post office. **Internet:** Access is available in Ulaanbaatar at business centres (often located in hotels), Internet cafes and at the telephone exchange on Suhkbaatar Square. ISPs include *Bodicomputers* (website: www.mongolnet.mn), *MagicNet* (website: www.magicnet.mn) and *Micom* (website: www.micom.com). **Post:** Airmail abroad can be very slow. There is an express mail service available for a limited number of countries.
Press: The main newspapers include *Odriin Sonin*, *Ünen* and *Zuuny Medee*. The English-language papers published in Mongolia include *The Mongol Messenger* and *The UB Post*, both of which are published weekly.
Radio: BBC World Service (website: www.bbc.co.uk/worldservice) and Voice of America (website: www.voa.gov) can be received. From time to time the frequencies change and the most up-to-date can be found online.

Passport/Visa

	Passport Required?	Visa Required?	Return Ticket Required?
Full British	Yes	Yes	No
Australian	Yes	Yes	No
Canadian	Yes	Yes	No
USA	Yes	1	No
Other EU	Yes	Yes	No
Japanese	Yes	Yes	No

Note: Regulations and requirements may be subject to change at short notice, and you are advised to contact the appropriate diplomatic or consular authority before finalising travel arrangements. Details of these may be found at the head of this country's entry. Any numbers in the chart refer to the footnotes below.

PASSPORTS: Passport valid for at least six months required by all.
VISAS: Required by all except the following:
(a) nationals of Kazakhstan for up to three months;
(b) **1.** nationals of the USA, if entering the country as a tourist, for stays of up to three months;
(c) nationals of Cuba, Israel and Malaysia for up to one month;
(d) nationals of The Philippines for up to three weeks;
(e) nationals of Hong Kong and Singapore for up to 14 days.
Types of visa and cost: *Business* and *Ordinary*: *Single-entry/Exit*: £35. *Double-entry/Exit*: £50. *Multiple-entry/Exit*: £65. *Single-transit*: £30. *Double-transit*: £35. *Multiple-transit*: £40.
Validity: Visas are generally valid for 30 days from date of entry (and three months from date of issue) and can be extended in Mongolia by a maximum of 30 days.
Application to: Consulate (or Consular section at Embassy); see *Contact Addresses* section. If travelling on an organised tour, visas can be obtained through tourism companies or travel agencies. A group visa in the name of the tour leader is valid for all tourists on the list attached, providing relevant details (nationality, sex, date of birth, passport numbers, and dates of issue and expiry) are given at the time of application.
Note: All foreign nationals staying in Mongolia for longer than 30 days are required to register with the police within 10 days of arrival.
Application requirements: (a) Valid passport. (b) Application form. (c) One passport-size photo. (d) Fee, payable by cash or cheque; there is an additional £5 fee for postal applications. *Business* (and any visas valid more than one month): (a)-(d) and, (e) Invitation letter from Mongolia.
Working days required: Two to five. An express service is available which costs an additional £10.
Temporary residence/work permit: Enquire at the Mongolian Embassy.

Money

Currency: Tugrug (Tg). Notes are in denominations of Tg10,000, 5000, 1000, 500, 100, 50, 20, 10, 5, 3 and 1. Coins are in denominations of Tg200, 100, 50 and 20.
Currency exchange: Official organisations authorised to exchange foreign currency include commercial banks in Ulaanbaatar and bureaux de change at certain hotels. The easiest currency to exchange is the US Dollar.
Credit & debit cards: Accepted by main commercial banks, large hotels and a few shops and restaurants in Ulaanbaatar. Credit card cash advances can be obtained at the Trade and Development Bank.
Travellers cheques: American Express Travellers Cheques are most widely accepted although Thomas Cook are accepted by the Trade and Development Bank. To avoid additional exchange rate charges, travellers are advised to take travellers cheques in US Dollars. Travellers cheques can be difficult to exchange outside the capital.
Currency restrictions: The import of local currency is limited to Tg815, provided declared on arrival. Bank certificates must be shown. The import of foreign currency is limited to US$2000 or equivalent. The export of local and foreign currency is limited to the amount declared on arrival.
Exchange rate indicators: The following figures are included as a guide to the movements of the Tugrug against Sterling and the US Dollar:

Date	Feb '04	May '04	Aug '04	Nov '04
£1.00=	2126.05	2080.81	2196.08	2080.30
$1.00=	1168.00	1165.00	1192.00	1120.37

Banking hours: Mon-Fri 0930-1230 and 1400-1500.

Duty Free

The following goods may be imported into Mongolia without incurring customs duty:
200 cigarettes or 50 cigars or 250g of tobacco; 1l of vodka and 2l of wine and 3l of beer; personal effects; goods up to a value of US$1000.
Prohibited items: Guns, weapons and ammunition without special permission; explosive items; radioactive substances; narcotics; pornographic publications; any publications, records, films and drawings critical of Mongolia; palaeontological and archaeological findings without special permission; collections of various plants and their seeds; birds and wild or domestic animals; wool, raw skins, hides and furs without permission from the appropriate authorities.
Note: (a) Every tourist must fill in a customs declaration, which should be retained until departure. This allows for the free import and re-export of articles intended for personal use for the duration of stay. (b) Visitors intending to export antiques and fossils must have official permission. Some shops will supply the necessary documents upon purchase; otherwise, permission should be obtained from the Ministry of Enlightenment. (c) Goods to the value of Tg20,000 are allowed to be exported from Mongolia.

Public Holidays

Jan 1 2005 New Year's Day. **Feb 9-11** Tsagaan Sar (Lunar New Year). **Jun 1** Mothers and Children's Day. **Jul 11-13** Naadam. **Nov 26** Independence Day.

Health

	Special Precautions?	Certificate Required?
Yellow Fever	No	No
Cholera	1	No
Typhoid & Polio	2	N/A
Malaria	No	N/A

Note: Regulations and requirements may be subject to change at short notice, and you are advised to contact your doctor well in advance of your intended date of departure. Any numbers in the chart refer to the footnotes below.

1: There may be some risk of cholera; precautions should be considered.
2: Typhoid is a risk.
Food & drink: All water should be regarded as being potentially contaminated. Water used for drinking, brushing teeth or making ice should have first been boiled or otherwise sterilised. Some milk is unpasteurised and should be boiled. Powdered, long-life or tinned milk is available and is advised, but make sure that it is reconstituted with pure water. Avoid dairy products which are likely to have been made from unboiled milk. Only eat well-cooked meat and fish, preferably served hot. Pork, salad and mayonnaise may carry increased risk. Vegetables should be cooked and fruit peeled.
Other risks: Diarrhoeal diseases and outbreaks of *meningococcal meningitis* occur. There is some risk of *plague*. Immunisation against *Hepatitis A* and *TB* is recommended. *Hepatitis B* is highly endemic and *Hepatitis C* also occurs.
Rabies is present. For those at high risk, vaccination before arrival should be considered. If you are bitten, seek medical advice without delay. For more information, see the *Health* appendix.
Health care: There are almost 23,000 hospital beds and over 5000 doctors in Mongolia. However, health-care facilities available to foreigners are limited. All Mongolian hospitals are very short of most medical supplies, including basic care items, drugs and spare parts for medical equipment. Reciprocal agreements with the UK or USA are not available and US medical insurance is not valid in Mongolia. Doctors and hospitals expect immediate cash payment for health services. Visitors are urged to have health insurance including cover for evacuation to Hong Kong and to take with them any regular medication. Emergency care is available at the Russian Hospital, although a translator is essential.

Travel - International

AIR: Mongolia's national airline, *MIAT – Mongolian International Air Transport (OM)* (website: www.miat.com), operates flights to Ulaanbaatar from Beijing, Berlin, Moscow and Seoul all year round, and to and from Hong Kong and Osaka in the summer months. Other airlines serving Mongolia include *Aeroflot*, *Air China* and *Korean Air*.
Approximate flight times: To Ulaanbaatar from *London* is 14 hours including stopovers.
International airports: *Ulaanbaatar (ULN)* (Buyant Ukhaa) is 15km (9 miles) from the city. Buses run to the city centre (travel time – 30 minutes). Taxis are also available (travel time – 15 minutes). Airport facilities include a bank, duty-free shops, car hire, post office and a restaurant.
Departure tax: US$12.
RAIL: Ulaanbaatar is linked to the Russian Federation and China by the *Trans-Mongolian Railway*. An express train runs once a week between Moscow, Ulaanbaatar and Beijing. Trains on international routes have sleeping and restaurant cars. There are also other weekly trains from Ulaanbaatar to Beijing and Ulaanbaatar to Moscow.
Note: At present, there are problems reported on buying train tickets to Ulaanbaatar for the Trans-Mongolia train. Although the trains certainly stop in Ulaanbaatar, tickets are only being sold to Chinese or Russian destinations. Therefore, a passenger wishing to travel from Beijing to Ulaanbaatar will have to pay for a ticket to Ulaan Ude, just over the Russian border. The other trains between Moscow and Ulaanbaatar, and Beijing and Ulaanbaatar are unaffected.
ROAD: There are several international road links; the principal route is via Irkutsk (East Siberia) to Ulaanbaatar. Travellers are not normally allowed to enter Mongolia by road unless they obtain prior permission from the Mongolian authorities.

Travel - Internal

AIR: Internal flights are operated by *MIAT – Mongolian International Air Transport (OM)*. This is the recommended means of travelling to remote areas.
RAIL: There are 1815km (1127 miles) of track. The main line

runs from north to south: Sukhbaatar–Darkhan–Ulaanbaatar–Sainshand. Branch lines serve the principal industrial regions.
ROAD: Paved roads are to be found only in or near major cities. **Bus:** There are frequent bus services between major towns, but the roads are mostly unpaved. **Car hire:** Available through tourism companies (although self drive is not available since most roads are unpaved, maps are poor and there are no road signs). Jeeps, camels or horses are available for hunters, trekkers and special-interest travellers.
URBAN: There are frequent bus and trolleybus services in the city.
Travel times: The following chart gives approximate travel times (in hours and minutes) from **Ulaanbaatar** to other major cities/towns in Mongolia.

	Air	Road
Erdenet	**0.45**	**9.00**
Dalanzadgad	**1.20**	**14.00**
Darkhan	-	**5.00**
Terelj	-	**1.00**
Hovsgol	**1.30**	**17.00 (over 2 days)**
Tsetserleg	**1.00**	**14.00**
Khovd	**4.00**	**4/5 days**
Uvs	**3.50**	**4 days**

Accommodation

HOTELS: There are six major hotels in Ulaanbaatar, offering over 1000 beds. There are also many smaller hotels, guest houses and hostels of varying standards. There is suitable accommodation for backpackers. Outside the capital, hotels are basic and few in number. Most provide full board, daily excursions and entrance fees to museums and the services of a guide or interpreter. Accommodation can be arranged through tourism companies or directly with the hotels.
Grading: There is currently no official grading system for accommodation in Mongolia. For futher information, contact the Mongolian Hotels Association, Children's Palace, Door No 27, Ulaanbaatar (tel: (11) 450 683; fax: (11) 684 595).
RESORT SPAS: There is limited accommodation for visitors. Prices are available on request.
CAMPING: There are now 95 tourist *ger* camps spread throughout the countryside. The accommodation is in *gers* (round felt tents used by nomadic herders). In most cases, there are also restaurants, bars, toilets and showers. *Ger* camps are usually open from May to October. Tourists with their own tents have the opportunity to camp almost anywhere they want although there are restrictions in protected areas and it is advisable to avoid settlements.

Resorts & Excursions

Mongolia is a far-flung, little visited destination, with much to offer in terms of scenery, wildlife, and historic and cultural sites. Outside the main cities, Mongolians continue to live the traditional life of *malchin* (herdsmen), and many are nomadic.
ULAANBAATAR: The capital, Ulaanbaatar, is the country's political, commercial and cultural centre. There are a number of museums in the city, the largest being the **Museum of Natural History**. The palaeontological section has a magnificent display of the skeletons of giant dinosaurs. Others include the **Zanabazar Museum of Fine Arts**, the **National Museum of Mongolian History** and the **Military Museum**. There are also several Buddhist temple museums, and the still-functioning **Gandan Monastery** is worth a visit. Ulaanbaatar also has several theatres and theatre groups, such as the *State Opera and Ballet Theatre*, the *State Drama Theatre* and the *Folk Song and Dance Ensemble*. The Ulaanbaatar **State Public Library** has a unique collection of 11th-century Sanskrit manuscripts.
ELSEWHERE: Every province has its own museums containing examples of local culture. The most popular tour takes the visitor to the **Gobi Desert**, the habitat of several rare animals, including Bactrian wild camels, snow leopards, Prezwalsky horses and Gobi bears. Coaches take parties to the country's tourist camps. The nearest to Ulaanbaatar is **Terelj**, 85km (50 miles) from the capital, where the **Gorki Mountains**, the **Turtle Rock** and the **Terelj River** may be seen. **Khangai** is a mountainous region with more than 20 hot springs renowned for their healing properties. Another therapeutic spring can be found in **Khujirt**, where the ruins of the world-renowned **Kharakhorum**, capital of the Great Mongolian Empire of the 13th century, can also be found.

Sport & Activities

With one of the world's lowest population densities, Mongolia's vast areas of wilderness, desert, lakes and mountains offer plenty of scope for adventurous outdoor enthusiasts. Although independent travel is now becoming more common, travel outside the capital is usually by prior arrangement. For details, contact the Mongolian Embassy (see *Contact Addresses* section). The Mongolian National Tourism Board will be able to put you in touch with Mongolian tour operators that can arrange itineraries and special-interest tours, including visits with nomadic herdsmen and overnight stays in *gers*. Activity tours available include **trekking**, **mountaineering**, **birdwatching**, **horseriding**, **rafting**, **camel riding**, **yak caravan** and overland **motorcycle** tours. Many of these tours focus strongly on **ecology** and **wildlife**, and almost all of them include the *Gobi Desert* as one of their destinations; apart from its numerous native animal species (see also *Resorts & Excursions* section), the desert is famous for its fossilised dinosaur bones and eggs. Mongolia's lakes (notably the huge *Khuvsgul Nuur*) represent another good hiking destination, as do the *Four Holy Peaks* surrounding Ulaanbaatar or the *Gobi Gurvansaikhan National Park*, in the South Gobi. Visitors should note that the weather, although milder than expected, can vary greatly, especially in the mountains and in the Gobi Desert; it is recommended to bring a warm sweater and raincoat for any time of the year. **Skiing** and **cross-country skiing** are possible around Ulaanbaatar.
Outdoor pursuits: For further information about outdoor activities in Mongolia, travellers can contact the Mongolian National Tourism Board (see *Contact Addresses* section); *or* the Mongolian National Ecotourism Society, PO Box 72, Ulaanbaatar 210520 (tel/fax: (11) 318 099; e-mail: ecobund@magicnet.mn; website: www.owc.org.mn/ecobund); *or Runwild*, which organises ecotourism and adventure tours, 40 Miangat Street, Bldg. 68, Sukhbaatar District, Ulaanbaatar (tel/fax: (11) 315 374; email: info@outer-mongolia.com; website: www.runwild.co.uk); *or* the Mongolian Youth Tourism Association, BCC Company, Sukhbaatar Street, Youth Avenue 7/4, PO Box 72, Ulaanbaatar 210520 (tel: (11) 350 615; fax: (11) 325 336; e-mail: aroundworld@hotmail.com).

Social Profile

FOOD & DRINK: Meat is the basis of the diet, primarily beef and mutton. The local cooking is quite distinctive. Traditional meals generally consist of boiled mutton with lots of fat and flour with either rice or dairy products. One local speciality is *Boodog*; this is the whole carcass of a goat roasted from the inside – the entrails and bones are taken out through the throat, the carcass is filled with burning hot stones and the neck tied tightly, and thus the goat is cooked from the inside to the outside. Fish is also beginning to be widely available.
Mongolian tea (*suutei tsai*), meaning salty tea with milk, is very popular. Mongolian vodka is excellent, as is the beer (although it is expensive). Hot and cold beverages are not normally included in meals and many restaurants will add on a 13 per cent sales tax.
NIGHTLIFE: There are evening performances at the *State Opera and Ballet Theatre, State Drama Theatre* and *Puppet Theatre*. The *Folk Song and Dance Ensemble* and *People's Army Song and Dance Ensemble* are in the capital. Other major towns also have theatres. Circus entertainment is also very popular. There is also one cinema featuring English-language films, and large numbers of bars, nightclubs and restaurants that offer dancing or live entertainment (bands).
SHOPPING: In Ulaanbaatar, there are a few duty free shops and restaurants where convertible currencies are accepted. In all other shops, local currency must be used. The best buys include pictures, cashmere garments, camel-wool blankets, national costumes, boots, jewellery, carpets, books and handicrafts. The notorious *black market* on the outskirts of Ulaanbaatar is a large, crowded flea market which sells a huge variety of items. Suitable for the adventurous traveller, it is patronised mainly by local people. Pickpockets can be a problem. **Shopping hours:** Mon-Sun 1000-1800 as a general guide although times and days vary considerably.
SPECIAL EVENTS: For further details of events, contact the Mongolian National Tourism Board (see *Contact Addresses* section).
The following is a selection of special events occurring in Mongolia in 2005:
Jan *Tsagaan Tsar* (spring festival), nationwide. **Feb 24-27** *Camel Festival*, Umnugobi aimag. **Jun 1-30** *Ovoo Worship Festival*. **Jun 29** *Mongolian Sunrise to Sunset International Ultra-Marathon*, Lake Huvusgul National Park. **Jul 11-13** *Naadam Festival* (a centuries-old festival - herdsmen travel from all over the country to take part in large-scale national games, such as wrestling, horseracing and archery), Ulaanbaatar. **Aug 5-6** *Mini Naadam*, Tov.
SOCIAL CONVENTIONS: Religious customs should be respected. Mongolia has a large number of customs and traditions. Further details can be obtained from the Mongolian National Tourism Board (see *Contact Addresses* section). Visitors are requested to familiarise themselves with these customs. **Photography:** Not permitted in temples and monasteries. A fee is payable for photography in protected areas, although this regulation is often not enforced. Caution should be exercised when photographing government buildings, military establishments and border crossings. **Tipping:** Not customary, but this is changing and, if leaving a tip, 10 per cent is the norm.

Business Profile

ECONOMY: The vast bulk of Mongolia's working population is engaged in animal herding. Otherwise, large farms (formerly state owned) produce crops for domestic consumption, principally cereals, potatoes and vegetables. Industrial activity is dominated by production of food, hides and wool, especially high-quality cashmere – much of which is consigned for export – and mining. There are large deposits of coal which meet most of Mongolia's energy requirements, as well as copper, fluorspar, tungsten, tin, gold, lead and molybdenum, a rare metal of which Mongolia is one of the world's largest producers. The output of the copper-molybdenum mine at Erdenet accounts for around half of Mongolia's export earnings. It is likely that there are other large deposits as yet undiscovered. Limited oil production began in 1997, but Mongolia still relies on Russia to meet most of its domestic needs. Textiles and light engineering complete Mongolia's main economic activities. The country suffered badly from the collapse of the former Soviet Union: while Mongolia was not a constituent part of the Soviet Union, its economy was especially dependent on the USSR, with which it did 80 per cent of its trade; most of the rest was with its fellow members of the Council for Mutual Economic Assistance (COMECON). After some initial resistance by the MPRP (Mongolia's historic ruling party), most of the economy has been steadily transferred to the private sector. This process was still underway in 2001 when a diverse collection of two dozen enterprises was earmarked for complete or partial sale.
Unfortunately, structural difficulties and an unprecedented two consecutive years of the *zhud* (a uniquely Mongolian climatic phenomenon associated with very severe winters) have set back the country's economic development. Russia and China are now Mongolia's principal trade partners and South Korea is a major investor. In 1991, Mongolia joined the IMF and World Bank; in 2000, it became a shareholder (but not a 'country of operation') in the European Reconstruction and Development Bank. The EBRD provides support through the Mongolian Co-operation Fund. It is also a member of the Asian Development Bank and receives aid from the EU's technical assistance programme.
BUSINESS: Suits are recommended; mediumweight for summer, and heavyweight for winter. Translator services should be arranged prior to departure for Mongolia, although an increasing number of executives speak English, and Russian is widely spoken. **Office hours:** Mon-Fri 0900-1800.
COMMERCIAL INFORMATION: The following organisation can offer advice: Mongolian Chamber of Commerce and Industry, Freedom Square 1, Democracy Street 1, Ulaanbaatar 210538 (tel: (1) 312 371 *or* 501; fax: (1) 324 620; e-mail: chamber@mongolchamber.mn; website: www.mongolchamber.mn).
CONFERENCES/CONVENTIONS: For further information, contact the Mongolian Chamber of Commerce and Industry (see *Commercial Information* above).

Climate

A dry climate with short, mild summers and long, severe winters (October to April). Some rain falls during summer and there is snow during winter.
Required clothing: Mediumweights are worn during summer, with very warm heavyweights advised for winter.

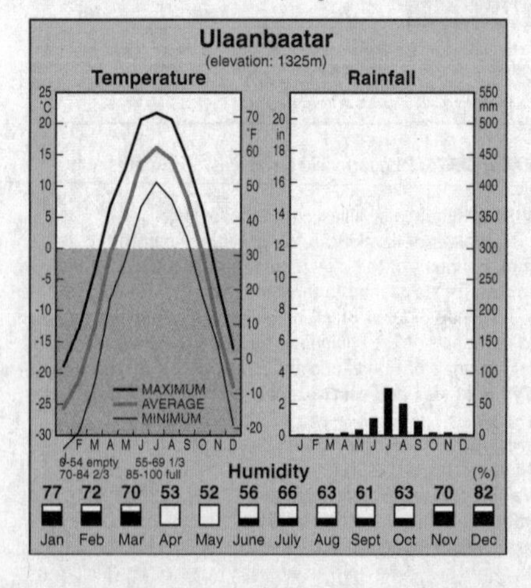

Montserrat

LATEST TRAVEL ADVICE CONTACTS

British Foreign and Commonwealth Office
Tel: (0870) 606 0290 Website: www.fco.gov.uk
US Department of State
Website: http://travel.state.gov/travel
Canadian Department of Foreign Affairs and Int'l Trade
Tel: (1 800) 267 8376 Website: www.dfait-maeci.gc.ca

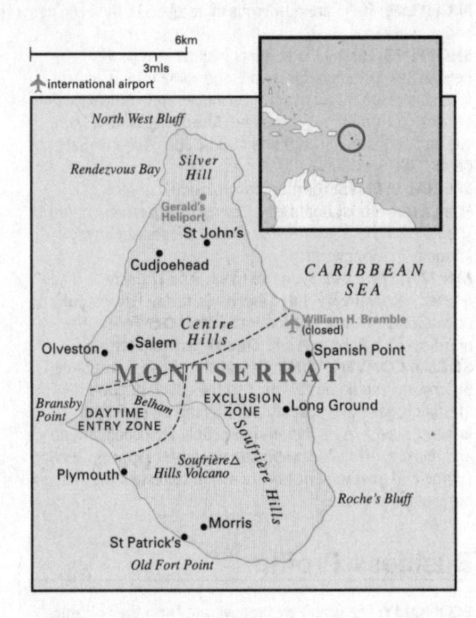

Location: Leeward Islands, Caribbean.

Country dialling code: 1 664.

Montserrat is still experiencing volcanic activity at the Soufrière Hills (which began erupting in 1995), causing the capital, Plymouth, to be closed and the relocation of businesses and residents living on the southern and eastern sides of the island to the northern side. Scientists at the Montserrat Volcano Observatory have advised that the northern part is safe from immediate volcanic activity. Montserrat continues to welcome visitors to the northern part of the island where economic development is now being planned.

Montserrat is a British Overseas Territory, and is represented abroad by British Embassies – see *United Kingdom* section.

Montserrat Tourist Board
PO Box 7, Brades, Montserrat, West Indies
Tel: 491 2230 *or* 491 8730. Fax: 491 7430.
E-mail: mrattouristboard@candw.ag
Website: www.visitmontserrat.com

British Foreign and Commonwealth Office
Overseas Territories Department, King Charles Street, London SW1A 2AH, UK
Tel: (020) 7008 2749. Fax: (020) 7008 1589.
E-mail: otdenquiries@fco.gov.uk
Website: www.fco.gov.uk

The UK Passport Service
London Passport Office, Globe House, 89 Eccleston Square, London SW1V 1PN, UK
Tel: (0870) 521 0410 (24-hour passport advice line).
Website: www.passport.gov.uk *or* www.ukpa.gov.uk
Opening hours: Mon-Fri 0745-1900, Sat 0915-1515 (appointment only).
Regional offices in: Belfast, Durham, Glasgow, Liverpool, Newport and Peterborough.
Personal callers for visas should go to the agency window in the collection room of the London office.

Montserrat Government (UK Office)
7 Portland Place, London W1B 1PP, UK
Tel: (020) 7031 0317. Fax: (020) 7031 0318.
E-mail: j.panton@montserratgov.co.uk
Website: www.montserratfirst.org.uk

TIMATIC CODES

Health	AMADEUS: **TI-DFT/MNI/HE** GALILEO/WORLDSPAN: **TI-DFT/MNI/HE** SABRE: **TIDFT/MNI/HE**
Visa	AMADEUS: **TI-DFT/MNI/VI** GALILEO/WORLDSPAN: **TI-DFT/MNI/VI** SABRE: **TIDFT/MNI/VI**

To access TIMATIC country information on Health and Visa regulations through the Computer Reservations System (CRS), type in the appropriate command line listed above.

Caribbean Tourism Organisation
22 The Quadrant, Richmond, Surrey, TW9 1BP, UK
Tel: (020) 8948 0057. Fax: (020) 8948 0067.
E-mail: ctolondon@carib-tourism.com
Website: www.doitcaribbean.com *or* www.onecaribbean.org
Opening hours: Mon-Fri 0930-1730.

The British High Commission in Bridgetown deals with enquiries relating to Montserrat (see *Barbados* section).

Caribbean Tourism Organisation
32nd Floor, 80 Broad Street, New York, NY 10004, USA
Tel: (212) 635 9530. Fax: (212) 635 9511.
E-mail: ctonewyork@caribtourism.com
Website: www.doitcaribbean.com *or* www.onecaribbean.com

The US Embassy and the Canadian High Commission in Bridgetown deal with enquiries relating to Montserrat (see *Barbados* section).

General Information

AREA: 102 sq km (39.5 sq miles).
POPULATION: 4482 (2001).
POPULATION DENSITY: 43.9 per sq km.
CAPITAL: Plymouth, the former capital, was mostly destroyed by pyroclastic flows in August 1997. Brades is currently the interim capital.
GEOGRAPHY: Montserrat is one of the Leeward Islands group in the Eastern Caribbean. It is a volcanic island with black sandy beaches and lush tropical vegetation. There are three main volcanic mountains on the island and Chances Peak is its highest point at 915m (3002ft). The Soufrière group of hills houses the volcano which began erupting in July 1995 and to date is continuously active. The Great Alps Waterfall, previously one of the most spectacular sights in the West Indies, has been destroyed by the volcano.
GOVERNMENT: British Overseas Territory since 1632. **Head of State:** HM Queen Elizabeth II, represented locally by Governor Deborah Barnes Jones since 2004. **Head of Government:** Chief Minister Dr John A Osborne since 2001.
LANGUAGE: English.
RELIGION: Roman Catholic, Anglican, Methodist and other Christian denominations.
TIME: GMT - 4.
ELECTRICITY: 110/220 volts AC, 60Hz.
COMMUNICATIONS: Telephone: Full IDD is available. Country code: 1 664. Outgoing international code: 011. Phone booths are operated by coins and phonecards. **Mobile telephone:** TDMA network not compatible with GSM handsets. Coverage extends over the northern half of the island. Handsets can be hired from the network provider, *C&W Caribbean Cellular* (website: www.caribcell.com). GSM 850 network operates, provided by *Cable & Wireless West Indies*. **Fax/telegram:** *Cable & Wireless (WI) Ltd* runs international links. **Internet:** Main ISP is *Cable & Wireless* (website: www.cw.com). **Post:** The Main Post Office in Brades is open Mon-Fri 0815-1555 **Press:** *The Montserrat Reporter* and *The Montserrat Times* are both in English and published weekly. **Radio:** BBC World Service (website: www.bbc.co.uk/worldservice) and Voice of America (website: www.voa.gov) can be received. From time to time the frequencies change and the most up-to-date can be found online.

Passport/Visa

	Passport Required?	Visa Required?	Return Ticket Required?
Full British	Yes	No	Yes
Australian	Yes	No	Yes
Canadian	Yes	No	Yes
USA	Yes	No	Yes
Other EU	Yes	No	Yes
Japanese	Yes	No	Yes

Note: *Regulations and requirements may be subject to change at short notice, and you are advised to contact the appropriate diplomatic or consular authority before finalising travel arrangements. Details of these may be found at the head of this country's entry. Any numbers in the chart refer to the footnotes below.*

PASSPORTS: Valid passport required by all.
VISAS: Required by all except the following:
(a) nationals of countries referred to in the chart above, except **1.** nationals of Czech Republic, Estonia, Hungary, Latvia, Lithuania, Slovak Republic and Slovenia who *do* need a visa;
(b) nationals of Commonwealth countries, except nationals of Cameroon and Mozambique who *do* need a visa;
(c) nationals of UK Dependent Territories;
(d) nationals of French Dependent Territories;
(e) nationals of Algeria, Andorra, Argentina, Bahrain, Bolivia, Brazil, Central African Republic, Chile, Colombia, Costa Rica, Côte d'Ivoire, Dominican Republic, Ecuador, El Salvador, Guatemala, Haiti, Honduras, Iceland, Israel, Liechtenstein, Mexico, Monaco, Morocco, Nicaragua, Nigeria, Norway, Panama, Paraguay, Peru, The Philippines, San Marino, Surinam, Tunisia, Turkey, United Arab Emirates, Uruguay, Vatican City and Venezuela.
Types of visa and cost: *Tourist* and *Transit*; £28.
Validity: Three months.
Application to: UK Passport Agency (see *Contact Addresses* section) or nearest British Counsellor.
Application requirements: (a) Completed application form. (b) Valid passport. (c) Evidence of accomodation. (d) Photocopy of travel itinerary. (e) Fee.
Working days required: Three weeks to one month.
Note: All passengers must hold a return or onward ticket to a country to which they have a legal right of entry and sufficient funds to cover the period of their stay. Passengers not in possession of a return or onward ticket may be required to leave a deposit on arrival. Passengers not complying with any of the entry regulations listed above may be deported.
Temporary residence: Enquire at Chief Immigration Officer, Police Headquarters, Brades (tel: 491 2555).

Money

Currency: East Caribbean Dollar (EC$) = 100 cents. Notes are in denominations of EC$100, 50, 20, 10 and 5. Coins are in denominations of EC$1, and 25, 10, 5, 2 and 1 cents. US Dollars are also accepted.
Note: The East Caribbean Dollar is tied to the US Dollar.
Currency exchange: There are three banks on Montserrat.
Credit & debit cards: Major credit and debit cards are accepted.
Travellers cheques: Widely accepted. To avoid additional exchange rate charges, travellers are advised to take travellers cheques in US Dollars.
Currency restrictions: There are no restrictions on the import of local or foreign currency if declared. Export of local and foreign currency is limited to the amount imported and declared.
Exchange rate indicators: The following figures are included as a guide to the movements of the East Caribbean Dollar against Sterling and the US Dollar:

Date	Feb '04	May '04	Aug '04	Nov '04
£1.00=	4.91	4.82	4.97	5.11
$1.00=	2.70	2.70	2.70	2.70

Banking hours: Mon-Thurs 0800-1500, Fri 0800-1500, depending on the bank.

Duty Free

The following goods may be imported into Montserrat without incurring customs duty:
200 cigarettes or 50 cigars; wines and spirits not exceeding 1.14l*; 168g of perfume; gifts up to a value of EC$250 (only once per 12 months).*
Note: * Tobacco products and alcoholic beverages are only available to passengers 17 years of age or over.

Public Holidays

2005: Jan 1 New Year's Day. **Mar 17** St Patrick's Day. **Mar 25-28** Easter. **May 2** Labour Day. **May 16** Whit Monday. **Aug 1** August Monday. **Dec 25-26** Christmas. **Dec 31** Festival Day.
2006: Jan 1 New Year's Day. **Mar 17** St Patrick's Day. **Apr 14-17** Easter. **May 1** Labour Day. **Jun 5** Whit Monday. **Aug 7** August Monday. **Dec 25-26** Christmas. **Dec 31** Festival Day.

Health

	Special Precautions?	Certificate Required?
Yellow Fever	No	No
Cholera	No	1
Typhoid & Polio	No	N/A
Malaria	No	N/A

Note: *Regulations and requirements may be subject to change at short notice, and you are advised to contact your doctor well in advance of your intended date of departure. Any numbers in the chart refer to the footnotes below.*

1: Following WHO guidelines issued in 1973, a cholera vaccination certificate is not normally a requirement of entry to any country. However, Montserratian authorities may require one from travellers arriving from infected areas. See the *Health* appendix for further information about the cholera vaccination.
Food & drink: Mains water is normally chlorinated, and is safe to drink. Bottled water is available. Milk is pasteurised and dairy products are safe for consumption. Local meat, poultry, seafood, fruit and vegetables are generally considered safe to eat.

Other risks: *Bacillary* and *amoebic dysenteries* are common. *Hepatitis A* is present. Outbreaks of *dengue fever* may occur. After an ash fall, the ash-laden air may cause breathing problems for persons suffering from respiratory problems such as asthma.
Health care: There is a well-equipped 30-bed hospital, providing 24-hour casualty service. Montserrat is a UK Dependency and a limited reciprocal health agreement exists with the UK. On presentation of proof of UK residence, free treatment is available at the general hospital and at state-run clinics to those aged over 60 and under 16. Dental treatment is also free for school-age children. Private health insurance is recommended. For specialist treatment, visitors are required to travel to neighbouring islands (eg Antigua or Guadeloupe).

Travel - International

Note: Following a recent lull in volcanic activity, the previously designated Day Time Entry Zone (DTEZ) has been rescinded and these areas are now open for 24-hour occupancy. However, at present, there are no utilities in these areas and roads are in poor condition. Anyone visiting these areas should drive with extreme caution, and the wearing of ash masks is recommended. A small portion of the previously designated Exclusion Zone incorporating St George's Hill has been re-designated a DTEZ, and entry is permitted in this area between the hours of 0600 and 1800, seven days a week. A major part of the island is still a total Exclusion Zone where no entry is permitted. Maps showing the designated zones are available at points of entry and at local police stations. The threat from terrorism is low. Though the crime rate is also very low, visitors should take sensible precautions against petty crime. However, the vast majority of visits to Montserrat remain completely trouble-free.
AIR: The nearest international gateway is Antigua. All information on transport and current timetables can be verified by Montserrat Aviation Services (MAS) (tel: 491 2362; fax: 491 7186).
Approximate flight times: From Montserrat to *London* is eight hours 30 minutes, including an hour's stopover in Antigua; to *Los Angeles* is nine hours; to *New York* is six hours and to *Singapore* is 33 hours.
International airports: *WH Bramble Airport (MNI)* has been closed since August 1997 owing to volcanic activity. A heliport has been established at Gerald's Bottom in the north of the island. *Carib Aviation* and *Montserrat Aviation Services* operate helicopter services to Antigua five days a week, two to four times daily (travel time - 20 minutes). A new airport is to be built by the end of 2004.
There is also a regular helicopter service from UC Bird International Airport in Antigua to the port at Little Bay.
Departure tax: US$10 or equivalent. Children under 12 years of age and transit passengers who continue their journey within 24 hours are exempt.
SEA: A high-speed ferry service operates regular services six days a week between Little Bay, Montserrat and Heritage Quay, Antigua (travel time - one hour).

Travel - Internal

Note: Following a recent lull in volcanic activity, the previously designated Day Time Entry Zone (DTEZ) has been rescinded and these areas are now open for 24-hour occupancy. However, at present, there are no utilities in these areas and roads are in poor condition. Anyone visiting these areas should drive with extreme caution and the wearing of ash masks is recommended. A small portion of the previously designated Exclusion Zone incorporating St George's Hill has been redesignated a DTEZ and entry is permitted in this area between the hours of 06:00 and 18:00, seven days a week. A major part of the island is still a total Exclusion Zone where no entry is permitted. Maps showing the designated zones are available at points of entry and at local police stations.
SEA: Charter yachts are available. The main harbour is at Little Bay where a new jetty has been constructed.
ROAD: Traffic drives on the left. There are good road networks to all towns. Montserrat has 203km (126 miles) of well-paved roads, but driving can be difficult for those not used to winding mountain roads. Speed limits are restricted to 20mph (32 kph). **Bus:** Minibuses are available for sightseeing. A bus service between villages and the town is provided by privately owned minibuses. **Taxi:** There are fixed rates for standard journeys. Drivers can act as guides and a number of different tours can be arranged. **Car hire:** This is available at the heliport and at Little Bay Port.
Documentation: A valid foreign licence can be used to purchase a temporary licence at either the heliport or any police station. This costs EC$50 and the licence is valid for three months.

Accommodation

HOTELS: The Vue Pointe is still operating. An 18-room hotel, the Tropical Mansion Suites, is open. There are a small number of bed & breakfast establishments. Some hotels have had to close due to sporadic volcanic activity. Contact Montserrat Tourist Board for more information (see *Contact Addresses* section).
SELF-CATERING: Villas and apartments are available throughout the island; Montserrat Tourist Board can provide a list. All accommodation bookings must be confirmed with a 20 per cent deposit. A service charge of 10 per cent and a 7 per cent government occupancy tax is added on to all accommodation bills.

Resorts & Excursions

Note: Many of the previously famous sights on Montserrat have been either destroyed by the Soufrière Hills volcano or are currently off-limits. However, there are still opportunities for quiet beach holidays, watersports, ecotourism and volcano viewing. Check with the Montserrat Tourist Board for information.
Introduction: When Catholic-Irish settlers arrived in Montserrat sometime between 1632 and 1633, fleeing from persecution on nearby St Kitts, they nicknamed it 'The Emerald Isle' because of the lush green giant ferns and forests climbing the sides of Montserrat's two volcanoes, and the island's resemblance to Ireland. Place names like Cork Hill and St Patrick's (not to mention Potato Hill) still bear witness to the Irish influence.
THE COAST: Owing to volcanic outbreaks, most of the capital, **Plymouth**, has been destroyed, leaving many tourist attractions off-limits, including the 18th-century **Old Fort** on St George's Hill (300m (1000ft) above the town). However, the island offers diverse and beautiful beaches in a quiet and friendly atmosphere. **Rendezvous Bay** contains the only white (coral) sand beach in Montserrat; sand in the other bays is of volcanic origin and may be grey or black. Several bays offer excellent opportunities for snorkelling and a variety of watersports; others are totally undeveloped (though plans for some of them exist, and those who like their scenery untouched should make the most of current opportunities). The **Sport & Activities** section gives further information about watersports and sports in general.
Pelican Point on the east coast is home to the island's only breeding colony of the spectacular Frigate birds. **Dutchers Studio** in **Olveston** is closed, but is due to reopen soon.
INLAND: Most of the southern part of the island is off-limits, owing to the continuing eruption of the Soufrière Hills volcano. This spectaclar and unusual sight can be seen on helicopter trips (see *Sport & Activities* section for further details). The lush interior of the northern part of the island contains several places of interest, which can be seen on guided scenic walks (see the *Sports & Activities* section).
Montserrat's national bird, the *icterus oberi* (a species of oriole), can be seen at **Centre** and **Silver Hill** in the north of the island.

Sport & Activities

Hiking: The Montserrat Forest rangers offer a wide range of guided walks and hiking tours in the northern part of the island. Popular routes are the *Cot trail* (which runs through an oki banana plantation to a historic family house), *Runaway Ghaut*, the *Centre Hills trail*, and the *Silver Hills trail* (which passes through one of the island's oldest volcanic centres). Trained guides are available to inform hikers about the flora and fauna. Contact Montserrat Tourist Board for further details (see *Contact Addresses* section).
Volcano viewing: Day tours of the volcano area are available. Experienced guides take the visitor to safe vantage points from which they can observe the *Soufrière Hills* volcano. The Montserrat Volcano Observatory can also be visited (tel: (664) 491 5647; fax: (664) 491 2423; e-mail: mvomail@mvo.ms; website: www.mvo.ms). *Caribbean Helicopters* also offer helicopter tours around the volcano (tel: (268) 460 5900 (flight information); fax: (268) 460 5901; e-mail: helicopters@candw.ag; website: www.caribbeanhelicopters.net).
Watersports: Most villas have their own **swimming** pools. Beaches are of 'black' volcanic sand. The surrounding waters are excellent for **scuba-diving**. Both deep and shallow dives are available. Equipment may be hired or purchased on the island. **Snorkelling** equipment is available in resorts. Villa owners or agents can arrange professional instruction, and the tourist board can give details of dive schools. **Sea-fishing** trips can be organised through hotels or directly with specialist operators.
Cricket: This is popular and matches are played from February to June.

Social Profile

FOOD & DRINK: Dining options in Montserrat are varied, with a choice of international or local specialities. The island specialities are fresh seafood and *mountain chicken* - not actually chicken, but the leg from a local species of large frog (Dominica is the only other island where these frogs can be found). Barbecues are popular and other local dishes include pumpkin soup, goat water (comparable to Irish stew), aubergine patties, salt fish, crêpes and dishes made from abundant local fruits. Waiter service is normal. Most bars serve imported beers, spirits and wines. The local rum punch liqueur is *Monserrat Rum Punch*. There is also an abundance of local fruit drinks available.
NIGHTLIFE: There are numerous clubs open in the evenings and at weekends.
SHOPPING: Locally made items include jewellery, needlework, ceramics, glassware and some interesting artefacts made from coconut. Local arts and crafts shops are dotted throughout the island. **Shopping hours:** Mon, Tue and Thurs 0800-1200 and 1300-1600, Wed and Sat 0800-1300, Fri 0800-1700.
SPECIAL EVENTS: For more information, contact Montserrat Tourist Board (see *Contact Addresses* section). The following is a selection of special events celebrated annually in Montserrat:
Mar 17 *St Patrick's Day*, nationwide. **Apr 17** *Easter Monday Road Relay*. **Jun** *Queen's Birthday Parade*. **Jul** *Look Out Day*. **Aug** *Cudjoe Head Day*. **Oct** *Police, Fire and Search & Rescue Week*. **Dec 31** *Festival Day*.
SOCIAL CONVENTIONS: Casual clothes are acceptable. Beachwear should be confined to the beach or poolside. The lifestyle is generally peaceful, combining many English influences with West Indian. The people are usually friendly and relaxed. All visitors are made welcome. **Tipping:** Service charge and government tax are added to restaurant and hotel bills.

Business Profile

ECONOMY: The island was recovering from the volcanic explosion of January 1997, which destroyed much of the island's productive capacity, when it was hit by a new series of eruptions in July 2003. Previously, Montserrat had a diverse if fragile economy. The agricultural sector produced vegetables, cotton and livestock. The industrial sector, which employed one-third of the workforce and earned the bulk of Montserrat's export income, was concentrated in food processing and the assembly of electronic components. In the service sector, e-commerce and financial services were two important growth areas. After the 1997 eruption, the island became largely dependent on foreign aid - in particular, a $125 million aid package from Britain. However, following the latest series of eruptions, Montserrat is reaching the point where the economy is no longer viable.
BUSINESS: A short- or long-sleeved shirt or safari suit is suitable for most business visits. **Office hours:** Mon-Fri 0800-1600.
COMMERCIAL INFORMATION: The following organisation can offer advice: Development Unit, PO Box 292, Brades (tel: 491 2066; fax: 491 4632; e-mail: devunit@candw.ag; website: www.devunit.gov.ms).
CONFERENCES/CONVENTIONS: Contact Montserrat Tourist Board for further details (see *Contact Addresses* section).

Climate

The climate is subtropical, tempered by trade winds. There is little climatic variation throughout the year. The heaviest rainfall occurs between September and November; however, the heavy cloudbursts serve to refresh the atmosphere and once they are over the sun reappears.
Required clothing: Tropical lightweights are worn, with light woollens for cooler evenings. A light raincoat or an umbrella is useful.

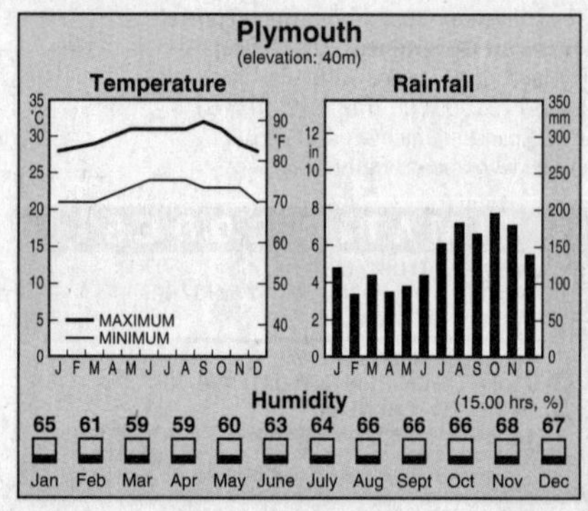

Morocco

LATEST TRAVEL ADVICE CONTACTS

British Foreign and Commonwealth Office
Tel: (0870) 606 0290 Website: www.fco.gov.uk
US Department of State
Website: http://travel.state.gov/travel
Canadian Department of Foreign Affairs and Int'l Trade
Tel: (1 800) 267 8376 Website: www.dfait-maeci.gc.ca

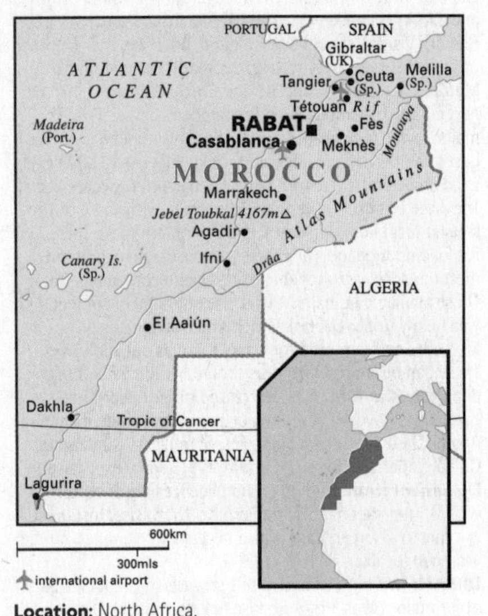

Location: North Africa.

Country dialling code: 212.

Office National Marocain de Tourisme (Moroccan National Tourist Office)
BP 19, Rue Oued Fes, Angle 31, al Abtal, Agdal, Rabat, Morocco
Tel: (37) 673 918. Fax: (37) 674 015.
E-mail: visitmorocco@onmt.org.ma *or* contact@tourisme-marocain.com
Website: www.visitmorocco.com *or* www.tourisme-marocain.com
Embassy of the Kingdom of Morocco
49 Queen's Gate Gardens, London SW7 5NE, UK
Tel: (020) 7581 5001/4. Fax: (020) 7225 3862.
E-mail: mail@sifamaldn.org
Website: www.mincom.gov.ma
Opening hours: Mon-Fri 0930-1700; 1000-1300 (visa section); closed UK and Moroccan national holidays (open until 3pm during Ramadan).
Moroccan Consulate
Diamond House, 97-99 Praed Street, London W2 1NT, UK
Tel: (020) 7724 0624. Fax: (020) 7706 7407.
Opening hours: Mon-Fri 0900-1230.
Moroccan National Tourist Office
205 Regent Street, 2nd Floor, London W1B 4HB, UK
Tel: (020) 7437 0073. Fax: (020) 7734 8172.
E-mail: mnto@morocco-tourism.org.uk *or* info@morocco-tourism.org.uk (general enquiries) *or* media@morocco-tourism.org.uk (media enquiries only).
Website: www.visitmorocco.com
Opening hours: Mon-Fri 0900-1700.
British Embassy
17 boulevard de la Tour Hassan, BP 45 RP, Rabat, Morocco
Tel: (37) 238 600 *or* 729 696. Fax: (37) 704 531.
E-mail: british@mtds.com
Website: www.britain.org.ma
Consulate in: Tangier.
Consulate General in: Casablanca.
Honorary Consulates in: Agadir and Marrakech.
Embassy of the Kingdom of Morocco
1601 21st Street, NW, Washington, DC 20009, USA
Tel: (202) 462 7979. Fax: (202) 462 7643.
E-mail: embassy@embassyofmorocco.us

TIMATIC CODES

Health	AMADEUS: **TI-DFT/RBA/HE** GALILEO/WORLDSPAN: **TI-DFT/RBA/HE** SABRE: **TIDFT/RBA/HE**
Visa	AMADEUS: **TI-DFT/RBA/VI** GALILEO/WORLDSPAN: **TI-DFT/RBA/VI** SABRE: **TIDFT/RBA/VI**

To access TIMATIC country information on Health and Visa regulations through the Computer Reservations System (CRS), type in the appropriate command line listed above.

Moroccan National Tourist Office
20 East 46th Street, Suite 1302, New York, NY 10017, USA
Tel: (212) 557 2520. Fax: (212) 949 8148.
Office also in: Orlando.
Embassy of the United States of America
2 Avenue de Mohamed El Fassi, Rabat, Morocco
Tel: (37) 762 265. Fax: (37) 765 661.
E-mail: ircrabat@usembassy.ma
Website: http://rabat.usembassy.gov
Consulate General in: Casablanca.
Embassy of the Kingdom of Morocco
38 Range Road, Ottawa, Ontario K1N 8J4, Canada
Tel: (613) 236 7391. Fax: (613) 236 6164.
E-mail: info@ambamaroc.ca *or* sifamaot@bellnet.ca
Website: www.ambamaroc.ca
Consulate in: Montréal.
Moroccan National Tourist Office
Suite 2450, 1800 McGill College Avenue, Montréal, Québec H3A 3J6, Canada
Tel: (514) 842 8111. Fax: (514) 842 5316.
E-mail: onmt@qc.aira.com
Website: www.tourismmorocco.ca
Canadian Embassy
Street address: 13 Bis Jaâfa-As-Sadik, Rabat-Agdal, Morocco
Postal address: PO Box 709, Agdal-Rabat, Morocco
Tel: (37) 687 400. Fax: (37) 687 430.
E-mail: rabat@dfait-maeci.gc.ca
Website: www.dfait-maeci.gc.ca/morocco

Credit: © Visit Morocco

General Information

AREA: 710,850 sq km (274,461 sq miles).
POPULATION: 29,631,000 (official estimate 2002).
POPULATION DENSITY: 41.7 per sq km.
CAPITAL: Rabat. **Population:** 1,335,996 (1994).
GEOGRAPHY: Morocco is located on the westernmost tip of north Africa, bordering Algeria to the east and Mauritania to the south and southeast, the Atlantic ocean to the west and the Mediterranean to the north. Running through the middle of the country is the Atlas mountain range, which leads to the fertile plains and sandy beaches of the Atlantic coast. The Middle Atlas range sweeps up from the south, rising to over 3000m (9850ft), covered with woodlands of pine, oak and cedar, open pastureland and small lakes. The Rif Mountains run along the north coast. The ports of Ceuta (Sebta) and Melilla on the north coast are administered by Spain.
GOVERNMENT: Constitutional monarchy since 1956. Gained independence from France in 1956. **Head of State:** King Mohammed VI since 1999. **Head of Government:** Prime Minister Driss Jettou since October 2002.
LANGUAGE: The official language is Arabic, but Berber is spoken by a large minority. French is widely spoken throughout the country, except in the northern regions where Spanish is more predominant. English is also understood, particularly in the north and the main tourist areas.
RELIGION: Predominantly Muslim with Jewish and Christian minorities. Morocco's population and culture stems from a cross-section of origins including Berbers, Arabs, Moors and Jews.
TIME: GMT.
ELECTRICITY: 127/220 volts AC, 50Hz, depending on age and location of building.
COMMUNICATIONS: Telephone: Telephone: IDD is available. Country code: 212. Outgoing international code: 00. **Mobile telephone:** GSM 900 networks. Main operators include *Itissalat Al-Maghrib SA* (website: www.onpt.net.ma) and *Medi Telecom* (website: www.meditel.ma). Coverage is mainly available in the cities in the west of Morocco. **Fax:** Available in hotels. **Telegram:** Facilities are available throughout the country at main post offices. **Internet:** Access is widely available in business centres, hotels and in Internet cafes. ISPs include *Jaweb* (website: www.eljaweb.com) and *Menara* (website: www.casanet.net.ma). **Post:** Airmail to Europe takes up to one week and can be unreliable. Post office hours: Mon-Fri 0830-1200 and 1430-1830, Sat 0830-1400. **Press:** Daily newspapers are published in French and Arabic. The main French newspapers are: *L'Economiste*, *Le Matin du Sahara et du Maghreb* (website: www.lematin.press.ma), *Maroc Soir* and *L'Opinion*. The main Arabic newspapers are *Al Alam* and *Al Maghrib*. The main English-language paper is *Morocco Today*.
Radio: BBC World Service (website: www.bbc.co.uk/worldservice) and Voice of America (website: www.voa.gov) can be received. From time to time the frequencies change and the most up-to-date can be found online.

Passport/Visa

	Passport Required?	Visa Required?	Return Ticket Required?
Full British	Yes	No	Yes
Australian	Yes	No	Yes
Canadian	Yes	No	Yes
USA	Yes	No	Yes
Other EU	Yes	No	Yes
Japanese	Yes	No	Yes

Note: *Regulations and requirements may be subject to change at short notice, and you are advised to contact the appropriate diplomatic or consular authority before finalising travel arrangements. Details of these may be found at the head of this country's entry. Any numbers in the chart refer to the footnotes below.*

PASSPORTS: Passport valid for at least six months from date of entry required by all.
VISAS: Required by all except the following:
(a) nationals of countries shown in the chart above for stays of up to three months;
(b) nationals of Algeria, Andorra, Argentina, Bahrain, Brazil, Chile, Congo (Rep), Côte d'Ivoire, Guinea, Iceland, Indonesia, Korea (Rep), Kuwait, Libya, Liechtenstein, Mali, Mexico, Monaco, New Zealand, Niger, Norway, Oman, Peru, The Philippines, Puerto Rico, Qatar, Romania, Saudi Arabia, Senegal, Singapore, Switzerland, Tunisia, Turkey, United Arab Emirates and Venezuela for stays of up to three months;
(c) transit passengers continuing their journey by the same or first connecting aircraft within 24 hours provided holding onward or return documentation and not leaving the airport.
Types of visa and cost: *Single-entry*: £16; *Double-entry* or *Multiple-entry* (both business only): £25. Prices may fluctuate in accordance with the exchange rate and must be paid by postal order only.
Validity: Entry visas are valid for three months; visitors wishing to stay longer should apply to the local police station within 15 days of arrival. For other visa enquiries, contact the Embassy (see *Contact Addresses* section).
Application to: Consular section at Embassy (*not* the Consulate for those residing in London); see *Contact Addresses* section.
Application requirements: (a) One completed application form. (b) Four passport-size photos taken within the previous six months. (c) Valid passport with at least one blank page, and with a photocopy of the relevant data pages. (d) Fee, payable by postal order only. (e) Photocopy of all flight bookings. (f) Photocopy of hotel reservation. (g) Self-addressed, stamped, registered envelope for postal applications (for those living outside London only).
Working days required: Normally four, upon receipt of all necessary documents. Some nationals should note that their application forms are sent to Morocco for clearance and processing and may take up to two months.

Money

Currency: Moroccan Dirham (Dh) = 100 centimes. Notes are in denominations of Dh200, 100, 50 and 20. Coins are in denominations of Dh10, 5 and 1, and 50, 20, 10 and 5 centimes.
Currency exchange: Moroccan Dirhams can only be obtained in Morocco. National currencies should be exchanged at official bureaux de change only (identified by a golden sign); changing money in the street is illegal. There is no commission charge and visitors will be issued with a receipt which they must keep in order to exchange Moroccan currency back into the original national currency upon departure. Money can be withdrawn in banks with a credit card and a cheque book or directly from an ATM in some larger towns.
Credit & debit cards: Some credit cards are accepted. Check with your credit or debit card company for details of merchant acceptability and other services which may be available.
Travellers cheques: To avoid additional exchange rate charges, travellers are advised to take travellers cheques in Pounds Sterling or US Dollars.
Currency restrictions: The import and export of local currency is prohibited; all local currency must be reconverted prior to departure. The import and export of foreign currency is unlimited but must be declared if in excess of the equivalent of Dh15,000. Upon production of bank vouchers, half the Moroccan currency purchased during a visitor's stay may be re-exchanged for foreign currency (subject to some limitations) and all of it if the stay is less than 48 hours.
Exchange rate indicators: The following figures are included as a guide to the movement of the Moroccan

A B C D E F G H I J K L M N O P Q R S T U V W X Y Z

Dirham against Sterling and the US Dollar:

Date	Feb '04	May '04	Aug '04	Nov '04
£1.00=	16.21	16.41	16.43	15.93
$1.00=	8.90	9.19	8.91	8.41

Banking hours: Mon-Thurs 0815-1215 and 1415-1715; Fri 0815-1115 and 1430-1730; Sat 0900-1300.

Duty Free

The following goods may be imported into Morocco without incurring customs duty:
200 cigarettes or 50 cigars or 400g of tobacco; 1l of spirits and 1l of wine; 5g of perfume.
Restricted items: A special permit is required for sporting guns and ammunition which is obtainable upon arrival from the police authorities if passenger(s) hold a permit from their country of origin.

Public Holidays

2005: Jan 1 New Year's Day. **Jan 11** Manifesto of Independence. **Jan 21** Aïd al-Adha (Feast of the Sacrifice). **Feb 10** Fatih Mouharram (Muslim New Year). **Apr 21** Aïd al-Mawlid (Prophet's Birthday). **May 1** Labour Day. **Jul 30** Feast of the Throne. **Aug 14** Fête Oued Eddahab (Oued Eddahab Allegiance Day). **Aug 20** Révolution du Roi et du Peuple (The King and the People's Revolution Day). **Aug 21** King Mohamed's Birthday. **Nov 3-5** Aïd al-Fitr (End of Ramadan). **Nov 6** Marche Verte (Anniversary of the Green March). **Nov 18** Fête de l'Indépendence (Independence Day).
2006: Jan 1 New Year's Day. **Jan 10** Aïd al-Adha (Feast of the Sacrifice). **Jan 11** Manifesto of Independence. **Jan 31** Fatih Mouharram (Muslim New Year). **Apr 11** Aïd al-Mawlid (Prophet's Birthday). **May 1** Labour Day. **Jul 30** Feast of the Throne. **Aug 14** Fête Oued Eddahab (Oued Eddahab Allegiance Day). **Aug 20** Révolution du Roi et du Peuple (The King and the People's Revolution Day). **Aug 21** King Mohamed's Birthday. **Nov 6** Marche Verte (Anniversary of the Green March). **Oct 22-24** Aïd al-Fitr (End of Ramadan). **Nov 18** Fête de l'Indépendence (Independence Day).
Note: Muslim festivals are timed according to local sightings of various phases of the moon and the dates given above are approximations. During the lunar month of Ramadan that precedes Aïd al-Fitr, Muslims fast during the day and feast at night and normal business patterns may be interrupted. Some disruption may continue into Aïd al-Fitr itself. Aïd al-Fitr and Aïd al-Adha may last anything from two to 10 days, depending on the region. For more information, see the *World of Islam* appendix.

Health

	Special Precautions?	Certificate Required?
Yellow Fever	No	No
Cholera	No	No
Typhoid & Polio	1	N/A
Malaria	2	N/A

Note: Regulations and requirements may be subject to change at short notice, and you are advised to contact your doctor well in advance of your intended date of departure. Any numbers in the chart refer to the footnotes below.

1: Vaccination against polio and typhoid is advised.
2: A minimal malaria risk, exclusively in the benign *vivax* form, exists from May to October in rural areas of the following provinces: Al Hoceima, Taounate and Taza.
Food & drink: Bottled water is available and is advised for the first few weeks of stay. Drinking water outside main cities and towns may be contaminated and sterilisation is advisable. Milk is unpasteurised and should be boiled. Powdered or tinned milk is available and is advised, but make sure that it is reconstituted with pure water. Avoid dairy products which are likely to have been made from unboiled milk. Only eat well-cooked meat and fish, preferably served hot. Salad and mayonnaise may carry increased risk. Vegetables should be cooked and fruit peeled.
Other risks: *Bilharzia* (schistosomiasis) is present in small foci. Avoid swimming and paddling in fresh water; swimming pools which are well chlorinated and maintained are safe. *Soil parasites* are also present; visitors should wear shoes. *Hepatitis A* and *E* also occur. Immunisations are sometimes recommended for *hepatitis B, tuberculosis* and *diphtheria. Tungiasis* and *Lassa fever* also occur, although rarely. *Rabies* is present. For those at high risk, vaccination before arrival should be considered. If you are bitten, seek medical advice without delay. For more information, consult the *Health* appendix.
Health care: There are good medical facilities in all main cities, including emergency pharmacies (sometimes in the Town Hall) outside normal opening hours. Government hospitals provide free or minimal charge emergency treatment. Full health insurance is essential.

Travel - International

Note: Following the series of terrorist attacks that took place in Casablanca on 16 May 2003, all travellers are advised to be vigilant and to avoid crowds and public places crowded with other foreigners. Most visits to Morocco are trouble-free, but violent crime - though not a major problem in Morocco - is on the increase. Visitors to the Western Sahara region should contact their relevant travel advice department for advice prior to arrival.
AIR: Morocco's national airline is *Royal Air Maroc (AT)* (website: www.royalairmaroc.com). Other airlines serving Morocco include *Air France, Alitalia, British Airways, KLM, Lufthansa* and *SWISS*. There are frequent direct flights from all major European cities, from North America and from the Middle East.
Approximate flight times: From Casablanca to *London* is three hours; from Tangier is two hours 30 minutes. From Casablanca to *New York* is six hours 30 minutes.
International airports: *Casablanca (CMN)* (Mohammed V) is 30km (19 miles) south of the city (travel time - 35 minutes). Airport facilities include outgoing duty-free shop, post office, banking and bureau de change facilities, restaurant, bar and car hire facilities (*Avis, Budget, Europcar, InterRent* and *Hertz*). There are taxi services into Casablanca and train services available to Rabat.
Tangier (TNG) (Boukhalef Souahel) is 11km (7 miles) from the city (travel time - 20 minutes). Airport facilities include outgoing duty-free shop, banking and bureau de change facilities, restaurant, bar and car hire facilities (*Avis, Budget, Europcar, Hertz* and *Tourist Car*). Bus and taxi services are available into Tangier.
Other international airports include *Fez (FEZ), Marrakech (RAK)* and *Rabat-Salé (RBA)*.
Departure tax: None.
SEA: Principal ports are Tangier, Casablanca and Ceuta. Lines serving these ports are *Bland Line* (from Spain and Gibraltar), *Comanav* (from France, Spain and Italy), *Compañia Trasmediterránea, Limadet, Polish Ocean Lines* (from Northern Europe) and *Transtour*.
Car/passenger ferries: Ferry operators include *FerriMaroc* (website: www.ferrimaroc.com) and *Trasmediterranea* (website: www.trasmediterranea.com). There are cheap and regular car- and passenger-ferry links between southern Spain and Tangier and the Spanish enclaves on the north Moroccan coast. Most links are roll-on, roll-off car ferries except where shown. The routes are from Algeciras to Ceuta (Sebta) (car ferry); Algeciras to Tangier (hydrofoil and car ferry); Tarifa to Tangier (hydrofoil); Gibraltar to Tangier (hydrofoil and car ferry); Almería to Melilla (car ferry); Málaga to Melilla (car ferry); and Almería to Nador (car ferry).
There are also car ferries between Sète on the French coast (between Béziers and Montpellier on the Golfe du Lyon) and Tangier run by *Compagnie Marocaine de Navigation*.
RAIL: Rail links between Morocco and Algeria are currently suspended. The main international routes are from Oujda to Algiers or from Oran to Algiers.
ROAD: The best road link is from southern Spain or France via passenger/car ferries (see above under *Sea*). The road link on the north Algerian border is currently closed. *Eurolines*, departing from Victoria Coach Station in London, serves destinations in Morocco. For further information, contact *Eurolines* (52 Grosvenor Gardens, London SW1; tel: (08705) 143 219; website: www.eurolines.com *or* www.nationalexpress.com).

Travel - Internal

AIR: *Royal Air Maroc (AT)* operates regular services from Casablanca airport to Agadir, Dakhla, Fès, Marrakech, Ouarzazate, Oujda and Tangier. There are cheaper deals for those under 26 years of age depending on their destination in Morocco. Contact *Royal Air Maroc* for further details. There is also a new airline company, *Regional Airlines (FN)*.
RAIL: The Moroccan rail system is all standard gauge and, run by *Office National des Chemins de Fer (ONCF)* (website: www.oncf.org.ma), provides regular and cheap services with first-class travel available between major centres. Rail fares are amongst the cheapest in the world, although a supplement must be paid for air-conditioned trains. Sleeping cars and restaurant cars are available. The network runs from Oujda in the northeast to Casablanca on the west coast, Tangier on the north coast and Fès and Marrakech in the interior. The main routes include: Marrakech–Casablanca–Rabat–Meknes–Fès–Oujda; Marrakech–Casablanca–Rabat; Marrakech–Casablanca–Meknes–Fès; and Casablanca–Rabat–Tangier. The most useful route is from Fès to Rabat and Casablanca, with five daily and two overnight trains. There are also two daily trains and one overnight train (without sleepers) which run from Casablanca to Marrakech. Also, from Monday to Friday, a train runs every 30 minutes from Kenitra to Rabat.
Cheap fares: Children under four travel free and children from four to 12 may travel for half fare. The European Inter-Rail pass is valid in Morocco; holders may be entitled to a discount on the fare of a ferry ticket - check with the company concerned for details. Discounts of up to 30 per cent are available for groups of more than 10. First- and second-class seats can be reserved in advance. For more information, contact *Rail Europe* (tel: (08705) 848 848; website: www.raileurope.co.uk).
ROAD: Traffic drives on the right. The major Moroccan roads, particularly those covering the north and northwest of the country, are all-weather highways. In the interior, south of the High Atlas Mountains, road travel becomes much more difficult, especially across the Atlas Mountains in winter. **Coach:** The main centres are connected by a wide variety of coach services, many of which are privately run. The two largest firms are *CTM* (covering the whole country) and *SATAS* (between Casablanca, Agadir and south of Agadir). Visitors should bear in mind, however, that Morocco has a poor road safety record; the roads from Agadir to Marrakech, via Imi'n Tanoute and Chichaoua, are particularly hazardous. **Bus:** Connections between most major towns and villages are regular and frequent, although buses can be very crowded and it may be wise to buy tickets in advance and arrive well before departure to secure a seat. The price of tickets is very low, especially with some of the smaller local bus companies. It is customary to tip the guard for loading luggage. For charter purposes, air-conditioned motor coaches are available from several companies. **Taxi:** Those available in major towns, the petits taxis, are metered (see below under *Urban*). Other larger taxis, usually Mercedes cars, are used for travel to areas outside towns. These can be shared, but fares should be agreed before departure. **Car hire:** *Avis, Hertz* and other major hire companies have offices in major towns and cities, including Agadir, Casablanca, Essaouira, Fès, Marrakech, Ouarzazate, Oujda, Rabat and Tangier. Car hire is generally expensive.
Documentation: Foreign driving licences are accepted, as well as International Driving Permits. Third Party insurance is required. A Green Card is also necessary. Insurance can be arranged locally.
URBAN: There are extensive bus services in Casablanca and other main towns. Pre-purchase tickets are sold. Urban area *petits taxis* are plentiful and have metered fares. Taxi drivers expect a 10 per cent tip.
Travel times: The following chart gives approximate travel times (in hours and minutes) from **Casablanca** to other major cities/towns in Morocco.

	Air	Road	Rail
Rabat	0.30	1.30	1.00
Marrakech	0.30	4.00	4.00
Agadir	0.55	9.00	-
Fès	0.40	5.00	5.00
Meknès	-	2.30	4.00
Tangier	0.50	6.00	6.00
Oujda	1.05	12.00	12.00
Laayoune	1.30	20.00	-
Er Rachidia	1.35	12.00	-

Accommodation

HOTELS: Morocco has 100,000 hotel beds to cater for its thriving tourist market. There is quite a wide choice of accommodation in all sizeable centres. The upper end of the market is represented by internationally known hotels in most main towns, notably Agadir, Marrakech and Tangier. For more information, contact the Fédération Nationale de l'Industrie Hôtelière, 320 Bd. Zerktouni, Casablanca 20000 (tel: (22) 267 313/4; fax: (22) 267 273, e-mail: fnih@menara.ma; website: www.fnih.ma).
Grading: Hotels are rated from **1** to **5 stars**.
SELF-CATERING: Self-catering apartments are available in Agadir, Marrakech and Tangier. Full details are available from the Moroccan National Tourist Office (see *Contact Addresses* section).
CAMPING/CARAVANNING: There are established campsites with good facilities in many parts of Morocco. Full details are available in a brochure from the National Tourist Office.
YOUTH HOSTELS: There are hostels in Asni, Azrou, Casablanca, Fès, Ifrane, Meknes and Rabat. Up-to-date information is available from the Fédération Royale Marocaine des Auberges de Jeunes, BP 15998, Casa Principale, Parc de la Ligue Arabe, Casablanca 21000 (tel: (22) 470 952; fax: (22) 227 677). There is also an International Youth Hostel, 6 Place Abmed Al Bidaoui, Ville Ancienne, Casablanca (tel: (22) 220 551; fax: (22) 227 877).

Resorts & Excursions

IMPERIAL CITIES

Fès, Marrakech, Meknes and Rabat are known as the Imperial Cities, each having been the country's capital at some time during its history.
RABAT: Rabat, the present capital of Morocco, was founded in the 12th century. It is a town of trees and

flowers, and many monumental gateways, including the **Gate of the Ambassadors** and the **Oudaias Kasbah Gate**. There is a good selection of hotels and numerous pavement cafes. The nearby **Mamora forest** and the many beaches are popular tourist attractions, particularly during the summer.

Other attractions include **Tour Hassan**, the grandiose minaret of a vast, uncompleted 12th-century mosque; the **Mohammed V Mausoleum**, an outstanding example of traditional Moroccan architecture; the **Royal Palace**; the **Chellah**, with superb monuments, delightful gardens and Roman ruins; the **Oudaias**; the **Archaeological Museum**; the **National Museum of Handicrafts** and the antique Moorish cafe. The battlements surrounding the old town, and part of the new city, date from the mid-12th century. Also worth a visit is **Salé**, Rabat's twin city, at the opposite side of the river, believed to have been founded in the 11th century.

MEKNES: Meknes is protected by 25km (16 miles) of battlements, flanked by towers and bastions. The city reflects the power and the constructive genius of King Moulay Ismail, a contemporary of Louis XIV, who ruled the country for 55 years. The **Michlifen** and **Djebel Habri** are two ski resorts above Meknes. The city boasts a wonderful *souk* (market) and the old town is listed by UNESCO as a World Heritage Site.

EXCURSIONS: About 30km (19 miles) from Meknes, the Roman ruins at **Volubilis** are also on UNESCO's World Heritage list. Excavations and ruins dating back to the third century can be visited for a small admission fee and there is also an interesting archaeological museum.

FÈS: Fès is the most ancient and impressive of the imperial cities. Built in the eighth century, it has more history and mystery than anywhere else in Morocco. Officially encompassing two cities – **El Bali** and **Jadid** – Fès is famous for the **Nejjarine Square** and **Fountain**, the **Er Rsif** and **Andalous** (Al-Andalus) mosques, the **Royal Palace**, the **Kasbah** and **Karaouine** (Al-Qarawiyin) **University**, which is older than Oxford University. The **Dar Bath Museum** is also worth a visit. The old part of the city – **Fès El Bali** – still retains the magical, bustling atmosphere of an ancient time and it is centred around the two famous mosques of **Al-Qarawiyin** and **Al-Andalus**. It is a huge maze of winding streets and covered bazaars where, if one is not careful, it is easy to get lost (it is therefore a good idea to hire an official guide). There are magnificent examples of Hispano-Arabic architecture as well as numerous opportunities to see traditional craftspeople at work. The *medina* (market) in Fès El Bali is one of the largest in the world and is also on UNESCO's World Heritage list. Here, one can buy almost anything. It is particularly good for carpets, rugs and ornate metalwork. As in all of Morocco, the market business is conducted in a leisurely, although deadly earnest way, with the accompaniment of endless glasses of sweet mint tea. Fès is, perhaps, one of the most fascinating cities anywhere in the Middle East or north Africa.

The valley of **Ouergha** to the north is famed for its *souks* and Morocco's most celebrated gathering of riders, which is said to have been attended by Pope Sylvester II prior to his accession in AD 999 and resulted in him introducing Arab mathematics to Europe. Other attractions are the **Karaouine** (Al-Qarawiyin) **Mosque** and **Mesbahai Medersa**, an old school, remarkable for its traditional architecture and late afternoon auctions in the Kissaria, the shopping area.

MARRAKECH: Founded in 1062, Marrakech was once the capital of an empire that stretched from Toledo to Senegal. Called the 'Pink City' because of the colour of the local earth used in its construction, it is a city of labyrinthine alleyways, secluded palaces, museums, mosques and markets. The city's gardens are still supplied with water from 11th-century underground irrigation canals. The **Djemaa el-Fna** (Place of the Dead), the city square, comes alive after nightfall; thronged with dancers, fortune-tellers, musicians, acrobats, storytellers and snake charmers, it is an exciting and occasionally bewildering place – an exotic spectacle that is striking and endlessly surprising. **Koutoubia**, the 12th-century mosque, is as tall as the towers of Nôtre Dame and dominates the Marrakech skyline. The **Ben Youssef Medersa**, with its mosaics, marbles and carved woodwork, is the largest theological site in the Mahgreb. It forms part of Marrakech's UNESCO-listed *medina*, now a World Heritage site, crammed with architectural masterpieces. Other interesting places to see are the sumptuous **Bahia Palace**; the beautiful **Saadian Tombs** housing the remains of rulers of the Saadian Dynasty; the **Dar Sisaid Museum**; the **Menara** and **Aquedal gardens** and the famed camel market.

Excursions: An hour's drive from Marrakech is **Oukaimeden**, Morocco's best ski resort. This trip can be combined with a visit to **Ourika** (which has a donkey market) and **Asni**. The latter is an excellent base for visiting **Jebel Toubkal**, Morocco's highest mountain, set amidst spectacular scenery.

THE COAST

The Mediterranean coast between Tangier and Nador has a string of creeks, bays, sheltered beaches and cliffs along the shore, ideal for swimming, boating and fishing. **Al Hoceima**, **Mdiq**, **Taifor** and **Smir-Restinga** are all new resorts, offering a wide variety of accommodation, from luxury hotels to well-situated bungalows.

The Atlantic coast is often rocky, with some long stretches of fine sand and calm bays.

TANGIER: Tangier, gateway to Africa, is the country's most cosmopolitan town, a place where – surviving from the days when Tangier was a free port – the street signs are in three languages; in fact, no less than 12 nations have occupied the city at one time or another since the fifth century. The city has a picturesque and active market called the **Grand Socco**. Other places worth visiting include the **Mendoubia Gardens**; the **Sidi Bounabib Mosque**; the **Moulay Ismail Mosque**; the **Forbes Museum**; and the **Merinid College**.

EXCURSIONS: Excursions in the region include visits to the mountain town of **Chechaouen**, the fishing village of **Asilah** and the **Caves of Hercules** at **Cape Spartel**. About 40km (25 miles) southeast of Tangier, the city of **Tetouan** has a reputation for minor crime. However, the town is beautifully located on a hillside with a view over the Mediterranean and its *medina* (market) in the old part is a listed UNESCO World Heritage Site.

CASABLANCA: Also on the Atlantic coast is the newer city of Casablanca. Founded at the beginning of the century, it is the country's principal commercial town, the second-largest town in Africa and one of the continent's biggest ports. Here stands the **Hassan II Mosque**, the world's largest mosque with one of the world's tallest minarets.

EXCURSIONS: Just south of Casablanca, in a picturesque location along the banks of the **Oum er-Rbia**, is **Azemmour**, with its abundance of violet bougainvillea and its purple ramparts (which visitors may walk along after agreeing a fee for the guardian to unlock them). Slightly further south is **El Jadida** which has a remarkable Portuguese fortress and one of the most beautiful beaches on the Atlantic coast. It also boasts the **Church of Assumption**, an enormous underground Cistern and the **'Gate on the Sea'** and fortifications.

ELSEWHERE: Travelling further south along the coast brings visitors to **Safi**, a fishing port with a Portuguese palace, pottery shops and a medina.

Agadir is a modern holiday city with superb beaches, excellent resort hotels and self-catering accommodation, which offers all types of sports activities. From here, there are excursions to the towns of **Taroudant**, **Tiznit**, **Tafraout**, **Goulimine** and, of course, the famous **Marrakech**. **Essaouira** is a laid-back fishing port whose narrow streets are lined with whitewashed, blue-shuttered houses. **Mohammedia** is another popular resort in this region.

THE SOUTH

The South is a region rich in folklore and spectacular scenery, dotted with small oasis villages and quiet towns surrounded by orchards and olive groves.

TAFILALT: Erfoud is the centre for excursions to the oasis of **Tafilalt**, kept green and fertile by the underground waters of the **Ziz** and the **Rheris**. **Er Rachidia** is the provincial capital of the Tafilalt region, and has a bustling market on the main square. On the road between Er Rachidia and Erfoud are the 'Blue Springs' at **Meski** and the natural amphitheatre of **Cirque de Jaffar** near **Midelt**. **Tinerhir**, once a garrison of the French Foreign Legion, is worth visiting for its kasbahs. Near Tinerhir is the outstanding scenery of the **Drâa Valley** (famous for its red-earthern kasbahs) and the magnificent **Todra** gorge.

THE DEEP SOUTH: This former French garrison can be reached via a beautifully scenic route from Marrakech over the **Tizi n'Tichka** pass. Ouarzazate is a good starting point for tours to the deep south. Of particular interest is the kasbah of **Taourirt**, the **Museum of Arts and Crafts** and the **Carpet Weavers' Co-operative Shop**. About 30km (19 miles) from Ouarzazate lies the exotic and UNESCO-World-Heritage-listed Ksar of Aït-Ben-Haddou. The Ksar is a traditional pre-Saharan habitat and consists of a group of earthen buildings surrounded by high walls. **Aït-Ben-Haddou** has featured in several films, including *Lawrence of Arabia* and *The Sheltering Sky*. The magnificent ochre-coloured cliffs and rock formations of the **Dadès Gorge**, one of Morocco's highlights, lie approximately 100km (63 miles) east of Ouarzazate. Nearby is the pleasant village of **Boumalne du Dadès** which has several hotels and guest houses offering accommodation.

ZAGORA REGION: From the top of the **Djebel Zagora**, there is a spectacular view of the **Draa Valley** and desert. The oasis of **Tamergroute**, 18km (11 miles) away from Zagora, has a library containing some of the earliest Arabic manuscripts, written nine centuries ago on gazelle skins. They are on display at the **Zaouia Nasseria**. Nearby, **Mhamid** and its palm groves are at the gates of the great sand desert.

ELSEWHERE: South of Agadir, the pink kasbahs of **Tafraoute** perch on spurs of rock, their façades often painted with strange designs in white or ochre. Goulimine is the site of the **Blue Men's** *souk*, held each weekend. A camel market also takes place once a week, on Saturday.

Sport & Activities

Morocco's varied landscapes, which range from a 3500km- (2170 mile-) coastline to the forests, rivers and mountains of the Middle and High Atlas and the Sahara Desert, offer a wide choice of sports and leisure activities.

Golf: This is very popular in Morocco, partly because King Hassan II was an internationally ranked practitioner of the game. Some of the best-known of the country's 16 golf courses are located at the *Royal Dar es Salaam Golf Club* in Rabat, which has three courses and annually hosts the internationally renowned *Hassan II Trophy*. Agadir has three courses: the Agadir Royal Golf Club is a par 36 while the beautiful *Dunes Golf Club* has three 9-hole par 36 courses (designed by a disciple of Robert Trent Jones). The third course, set around lakes, palm trees and eucalyptus, is the 5-star *Golf du Soleil*, which is a 27-hole par 72. The *Marrakech Royal Golf Club* is an 18-hole par 72 course located at the foot of the Atlas mountains. Marrakech has two other 18-hole courses: the *Palmeraie Golf Club*, designed by Robert Trent Jones in a setting with views of the Atlas mountains as well as easy access to the Atlantic beaches nearby; and the *Amelkis Golf Club*. Other 18-hole courses include *Ben Slimane* and *El Jadida* (both near the Atlantic coast), *Mohammedia Royal Golf Club* (near Casablanca) and the *Tangier Royal Golf*. Apart from the *Hassan II Trophy* (see above), the *Moroccan Open* and *Hassan II Challenge* are noteworthy tournaments. The *Mohammed VI Golf Trophy* is held at *Dar es-Salaam Royal Golf Course* in Rabat at the end of March.

Altogether, there are approximately 30 golf courses in the country, including several new ones. A useful golf brochure and information on golfing holidays can be obtained from the Moroccan National Tourist Board (see *Contact Addresses* section).

Hiking and trekking: With its four distinct mountain ranges – the Rif, the Middle Atlas, the High Atlas and the Anti-Atlas – Morocco offers outstanding opportunities for **hiking** and **trekking**. Various trekking tours can be organised through the Moroccan National Tourist Office (see *Contact Addresses* section). Specialist tour operators offer a variety of treks including guided **horse trekking** in the mountains, and **camping** trips. One of the most popular treks in the High Atlas is the ascent of *Jebel Toubkal* (4167m/6668ft), North Africa's highest peak. The Toubkal area is about a one hour drive from Marrakech and the usual starting point for this trek is the picturesque village of Imlil. Official mountain guides with mules are recommended for trips lasting longer than one day; guides are widely available in Imlil. Accommodation is provided in refuges, *gîtes* (resting places) and small hotels along popular trails. Trekking is possible all year round, but the best time is from April to October. The canyons and gorges are best tackled from June to October (in summer, storms can make the gorges impassable).

Watersports: Sandy beaches offer safe **swimming**, although the Atlantic can be cold even in summer. Mohammedia, Agadir, El Jadida, Oualidia, Safi and Essaouira are all good bathing resorts. The Mediterranean coast in the north, opposite Spain, is being developed, and resorts such as Cabonegro (14km/23 miles from Tetouan) offer superb swimming and **diving**. Other dive sites can be found at Agadir and Essaouira. The rivers in the High and Middle Atlas ranges, particularly the Oum-er-Rbia, offer **whitewater rafting** throughout the year (visitors are strongly advised to use experienced guides). **Fishing** permits are necessary for trout streams, lakes and pike lakes, and are issued by the Waters and Forests Department or local clubs. Several ports are equipped for deep-sea fishing, such as Dakhla in the Sahara and Mohammedia near Casablanca.

Skiing: This is possible for several months each year. *Ifrane* in the Middle Atlas and *Oukaïden* in the High Atlas (70km/44 miles from Marrakech) offer skiing facilities. Other ski resorts include *Mischliffen* in the Middle Atlas, on the doorstep of Fès and Meknes. *Mount Tidiquin* in the Ketama district and *Djebel Bou Volane* in the Middle Atlas are popular areas for **expedition-type skiing** and **walking trips** (with few amenities).

Riding: There are **horseriding** clubs in all major towns, notably Agadir, Casablanca, Fès, Marrakech and Rabat. Several clubs organise **pony treks** in the Middle Atlas. The combination of travelling by mule and skiing (known as **mule-skiing**) is characteristic to the High Atlas and can be carried out from February to April. A useful brochure, *The Great Trek through the Moroccan Atlas*, is available from the Moroccan Ministry of Tourism or the Moroccan National Tourist Office (see *Contact Addresses* section). **Camel riding** (*méharrées*) is also available, both in the Atlas mountains and around the Sahara Desert area in the southwest.

Other: Also available throughout Morocco are **4-wheel-drives**, incorporating visits to natural and cultural sights such as the 300m- (984ft-) deep *Gorge of Todra*, the massive sand dunes of *Merzouga* and the Berber region of *Ouarzazate*. Most of these tours feature typical Moroccan feasts and barbecues. The famous *Paris-Dakar* motor rally passes through Morocco every year.

A B C D E F G H I J K L M N O P Q R S T U V W X Y Z

Social Profile

FOOD & DRINK: Morocco's traditional *haute cuisine* dishes are excellent and good value for money. They are often exceedingly elaborate, based on a diet of meat and sweet pastries. Typical specialities include: *harira*, a rich soup, and *pastilla*, a pigeon-meat pastry made from dozens of different layers of thick flaky dough. *Couscous*, a dish based on savoury semolina that can be combined with egg, chicken, lamb or vegetables, is a staple Moroccan dish. *Tajine* is a stew, often rich and fragrant, using marinated lamb or chicken. *Hout* is a fish version of the same stew, while *djaja mahamara* is chicken stuffed with almonds, semolina and raisins. Many of the *souks* have stalls selling kebabs (*brochettes*) often served with a spicy sauce. Most restaurants have waiter service. The national drink is mint tea made with green tea, fresh mint and sugar. It is very refreshing and its consumption is an integral part of Moroccan social courtesy. Coffee is made very strong, except at breakfast. Bars can have either waiter or counter service. Laws on alcohol are fairly liberal (for non-Muslim visitors) and bars in most tourist areas stay open late. Wines, beers and spirits are widely available. Locally produced wines, beers and mineral waters are excellent and good value, but imported drinks tend to be expensive.

NIGHTLIFE: Morocco offers a variety of entertainment from casinos, bars, discos, restaurants and nightclubs, often with belly dancing. There are modern nightclubs in all the cities and resorts around the country. There are casinos in Marrakech, Mohammedia, Tangier and Agadir. Traditional Moroccan entertainment, such as folk dancing, can be seen in every town.

SHOPPING: The co-operative shops of Moroccan craftspeople, *coopartim*, operate under state control selling local handicrafts at fixed prices and issue an authenticity receipt or a certificate of origin for customs when exporting. *Souks* are also worthwhile places to visit for local products. Special buys are leather, tanned and dyed in Fès; copperware; silver; silk or cotton garments; and wool rugs, carpets and blankets. Bargaining is essential, and good buys generally work out at around a third of the asking price. In the south, there are Berber carpet auctions, especially in Marrakech, Taroudannt and Tiznit. Visitors will need a guide to make the best of these occasions. **Shopping hours:** Mon-Thurs 0830-1200 and 1430-1830, and Fri 0830-1100 and 1500-1830; large stores are open Mon-Sat 0900-1300 and 1500-1900; *souks* (traditional markets) are open Mon-Sun 0830-1300 and 1430-1800.

SPECIAL EVENTS: Festivities often mark the seasons and celebrate local resources. Festivals are dedicated to popular art and tradition while *mousseums* are large gatherings paying homage to a holy figure. Events are often organised at the last minute and largely depend on the lunar calendar. For further information, contact the Moroccan National Tourist Office (see *Contact Addresses* section).

The following is a selection of special events celebrated annually in Morocco:

Feb *Almond Tree Blossom Festival*, Tafraout. **Apr** *Sand Marathon*, Ouarzazate. **May** *Wax Candle Feast*, Salé; *Honey Feast*, Immouzzer; *Rose Festival*, Kelaa M'Gouna; *Mousseum of Sidi Mohammad M'a al-Anim*. **Jun** *Desert Symphony Feast*, Ouarzazate; *Guinean Singers and Dancers*, Essaouira; *Cherry Feast*, Séfrou; *Sacred Music Festival*, Fès. **Jul** *Camel Feast*, Guelmim. **Jul 3-6** *Popular Arts Festival*, Marrakech. **Aug** *Asilah Cultural Festival*. **Sep** *Engagement Feast*, Imilchil; *Horse Festival*, Tissa. **Oct** *Date Festival*, Erfoud. **Dec** *Agadir Festival*.

SOCIAL CONVENTIONS: Handshaking is the customary form of greeting. Many of the manners and social customs emulate French manners, particularly amongst the middle class. The visitor may find, in some social situations, that patience and firmness will pay dividends. Often visitors may find themselves the centre of unsolicited attention. In towns, young boys after money will be eager to point out the way, sell goods or simply charge for a photograph, while unofficial guides will always be offering advice or services. The visitor should be courteous but wary of the latter. Normal social courtesies should be observed in someone's home. Casual wear is widely acceptable, although swimsuits and shorts should be confined to the beach or poolside. Women travelling alone, and/or wearing clothes regarded as provocative (eg strappy tops, short skirts, etc) may attract unwanted attention. Sexual relations outside marriage, and homosexual conduct, are punishable by law. Smoking is widespread and it is customary to offer cigarettes. **Tipping:** Service charges are usually included in hotel bills; it is customary to tip hairdressers, cinema usherettes and waiters Dh1-2.

Business Profile

ECONOMY: Agriculture employs one fifth of the working population, the principal crops being cereals, vegetables and citrus fruits (of which Morocco is one of the world's largest exporters), and accounts for about 40 per cent of GDP. Livestock farming produces enough meat to fulfil domestic needs. Fishing is vital to both the domestic and export markets, as well as for the revenue accruing from the sale of licences allowing foreign fleets to fish in Moroccan territorial waters. Mining is the country's principal industry. Morocco is the world's largest exporter of phosphate rock, both in raw and processed form (such as fertilisers), and this is the principal source of export revenue. It has substantial other mineral assets including iron ore, coal, lead, zinc, cobalt, copper, silver and manganese. Morocco has small reserves of oil and gas, but must import the bulk of its needs. The main components of the manufacturing sector are food processing, textiles and the production of leather goods. In the service sector, tourism has grown rapidly and is now worth almost US$2 billion annually. The tourism industry has benefited from Morocco having one of the best infrastructures on the African continent; this is also an important consideration for foreign investors.

Remittances from Moroccan workers abroad (mostly in Europe) are another major source of revenue. During the last 10 years, the government has introduced a series of IMF-sponsored reforms, including trade liberalisation and public expenditure cuts in exchange for successive assistance programmes. This has reduced the size of the public sector and contributed towards easing Morocco's huge foreign debt but at the cost of increased unemployment. Almost half the workforce are officially unemployed. A trade agreement with the EU was signed in 1995 under which all tariff barriers will be removed by 2012. Morocco is also part of a planned Free Trade Zone (including Jordan, Tunisia and Egypt) which will offer preferential access to EU markets. The Moroccan government has been negotiating a free trade agreement with the US, but has encountered difficulties with the EU, which objects to some of its terms. Finally, Morocco is now the largest single recipient of aid from the EU. Morocco is also a member of the African Development Bank, the Islamic Development Bank and a founder member of the Union of the Arab Maghreb. Morocco's main trading partner is France, followed by other EU countries. Spain, Germany and the USA are Morocco's main suppliers. Morocco's principal exports are phosphates, seafood products and fertilisers.

BUSINESS: Businesspeople should be of a smart appearance, although a suit is not necessary in very hot weather. Appointments should be made in advance. Negotiations often involve a great deal of bargaining and a visitor should expect to deal with a number of people. **Office hours:** Mon-Fri 0830-1200 and 1430-1830.

COMMERCIAL INFORMATION: The following organisation can offer advice: La Fédération des Chambres de Commerce et d'Industrie du Maroc, 6 rue d'Erfoud, BP 218, Hassan-Rabat (tel: (37) 767 881 *or* 051; fax: (37) 767 076; e-mail: fccism@ccis.ma).

CONFERENCES/CONVENTIONS: The Pullman Conference Centre in Marrakech provides meeting facilities for up to 5000 people. Additional facilities can be found at the Palais de Congrés. Further information and a special brochure on conferences and conventions, *Morocco, A Feast for the Senses*, can be obtained from the Moroccan National Tourist Office (see *Contact Addresses* section).

Climate

The climate varies from area to area. The coast has a warm, Mediterranean climate tempered on the eastern coast by southwest trade winds. Inland areas have a hotter, drier, continental climate. In the south of the country, the weather is very hot and dry throughout most of the year, with the nights coolest in the months of December and January. Rain falls from November to March in coastal areas. Mostly dry with high temperatures in summer. Cooler climate in the mountains. Marrakech and Agadir enjoy an average temperature of 21°C (70°F) in the winter.

Required clothing: Lightweight cottons and linens are worn during summer, with warm mediumweights for the evenings during winter and in the mountains. Waterproofing is advisable in the wet season, particularly on the coast and in the mountains.

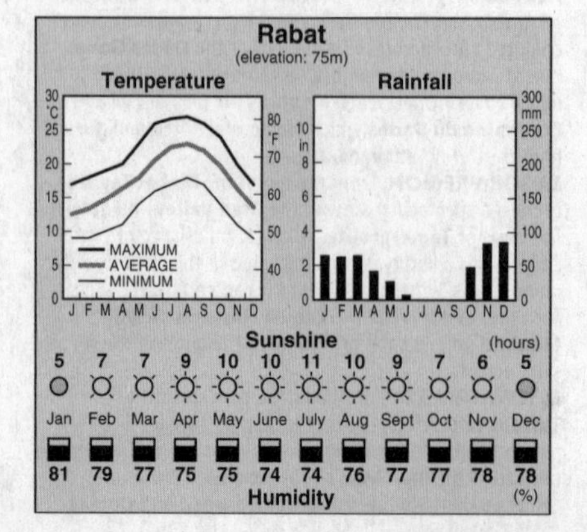

Mozambique

LATEST TRAVEL ADVICE CONTACTS

British Foreign and Commonwealth Office
Tel: (0870) 606 0290 Website: www.fco.gov.uk

US Department of State
Website: http://travel.state.gov/travel

Canadian Department of Foreign Affairs and Int'l Trade
Tel: (1 800) 267 8376 Website: www.dfait-maeci.gc.ca

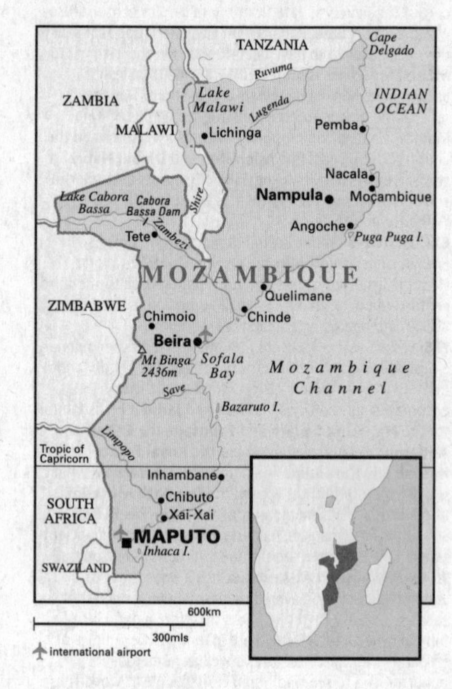

Location: Southeast Africa.

Country dialling code: 258.

Ministry of Tourism
1018 Avenida 25 de Setembro, Maputo, Mozambique
Tel: (1) 310 755. Fax: (1) 306 212.

Fundo Nacional do Turismo (FUTUR) (National Tourism Fund)
Avenida 25 de Setembro 1203, 3rd Floor, CP2758, Maputo, Mozambique
Tel: (1) 307 320. Fax: (1) 307 324.
E-mail: futur@futur.org.mz

Mozambique High Commission
21 Fitzroy Square, London W1T 6EL, UK
Tel: (020) 7383 3800. Fax: (020) 7383 3801.
E-mail: olga@mozambiquehc.co.uk
Website: www.mozambiquehc.org.uk
Opening hours: Mon-Fri 0930-1700; 0930-1600 (consular section).

British High Commission
CP 55, Avenida Vladimir I Lénine 310, Maputo, Mozambique
Tel: (1) 320 111-2/5-7. Fax: (1) 321 666.
E-mail: bhc@virconn.com

Embassy of the Republic of Mozambique
1990 M Street, NW, Suite 570, Washington, DC 20036, USA
Tel: (202) 293 7146/9. Fax: (202) 835 0245.
E-mail: embamoc@aol.com
Website: www.embamoc-usa.org
Also deals with enquiries from Canada.

Embassy of the United States of America
Avenida Kenneth Kaunda 193, CP783, Maputo, Mozambique
Tel: (1) 492 797 *or* 491 659. Fax: (1) 490 114.

Canadian High Commission
No 1128, Avenida Julius Nyerere, Maputo, Mozambique
Tel: (1) 492 623. Fax: (1) 492 667.
E-mail: mputo@dfait-maeci.gc.ca

TIMATIC CODES

Health	AMADEUS: **TI-DFT/MPM/HE** GALILEO/WORLDSPAN: **TI-DFT/MPM/HE** SABRE: **TIDFT/MPM/HE**
Visa	AMADEUS: **TI-DFT/MPM/VI** GALILEO/WORLDSPAN: **TI-DFT/MPM/VI** SABRE: **TIDFT/MPM/VI**

To access TIMATIC country information on Health and Visa regulations through the Computer Reservations System (CRS), type in the appropriate command line listed above.

General Information

AREA: 799,380 sq km (308,641 sq miles).
POPULATION: 18,082,523 (official estimate 2002).
POPULATION DENSITY: 22.6 per sq km.
CAPITAL: Maputo. **Population:** 1,134,837 (UN estimate 2001).
GEOGRAPHY: Mozambique borders Tanzania to the north, Zambia and Malawi to the northwest, Zimbabwe to the west, and South Africa and Swaziland to the southwest. To the east lies the Indian Ocean and a coastline of nearly 2500km (1550 miles) with beaches bordered by lagoons, coral reefs and strings of islands. Behind the coastline, a vast low plateau rising towards mountains in the west and north accounts for nearly half the area of Mozambique. The landscape of the plateau is savannah – more or less dry and open woodlands with tracts of short grass steppe. The western and northern highlands are patched with forest. The Zambezi is the largest and most important of the 25 main rivers which flow through Mozambique into the Indian Ocean. The major concentrations of population (comprising many different ethnic groups) are along the coast and in the fertile and relatively productive river valleys, notably in Zambezia and Gaza provinces. The Makua-Lomwe, who belong to the Central Bantu, live mainly in the area north of Zambezia, Nampula, Niassa and Cabo Delgado provinces. The Tsonga, who are the predominant race in the southern lowlands, provide a great deal of the labour for the South African mines. In the Inhambane coastal district are the Chopi and Tsonga, while in the central area are the Shona. The Makonde inhabit the far north. Mestizos and Asians live in the main populated area along the coast and in the more fertile river valleys.
GOVERNMENT: Republic since 1990. Gained independence from Portugal in 1975. **Head of State:** President Armando Guebuza since 2005. **Head of Government:** Prime Minister Luisa Diogo since 2004.
LANGUAGE: Portuguese is the official language. Many local African languages, such as Tsonga, Sena Nyanja, Makonde and Macua, are also spoken.
RELIGION: Christian (mainly Roman Catholic), Muslim and Hindu. Many also follow traditional beliefs.
TIME: GMT + 2.
ELECTRICITY: 220/240 volts AC, 50Hz.
COMMUNICATIONS: **Telephone:** IDD is available. Country code: 258. Outgoing international calls must go through the operator, although direct dialling is available to South Africa and Swaziland; there may be some delay. **Mobile telephone:** GSM 900/1800 networks with limited roaming agreements. Coverage is expanding to all main cities in most provinces. Network operators include *Mcel* (website: www.mcel.co.mz) and *Vodacom* (website: www.vodacom.co.mz). Handsets cannot be hired for short periods. **Internet:** ISPs include *Teledata* (website: www.teledata.mz). There are at least two Internet cafes in Maputo (one in Avenida Julius Nyerere). **Telegram:** Connections are via South Africa to international telecommunications network. Internal communications exist between most major towns. **Post:** Postal services are available in main centres. Airmail to Europe usually takes five to seven days, but sometimes longer. **Press:** There are no English-language newspapers published in Mozambique. The daily papers are *Correio da Manha*, *Diário de Moçambique* and *Notícias*. *Express da Torde*, *Imparcial Fax* and *Mediafax* are news sheets available by fax.
Radio: BBC World Service (website: www.bbc.co.uk/worldservice) and Voice of America (website: www.voa.gov) can be received. Occasionally frequencies change and the most up-to-date can be found online.

Passport/Visa

	Passport Required?	Visa Required?	Return Ticket Required?
Full British	Yes	Yes	Yes
Australian	Yes	Yes	Yes
Canadian	Yes	Yes	Yes
USA	Yes	Yes	Yes
Other EU	Yes	Yes	Yes
Japanese	Yes	Yes	Yes

Note: *Regulations and requirements may be subject to change at short notice, and you are advised to contact the appropriate diplomatic or consular authority before finalising travel arrangements. Details of these may be found at the head of this country's entry. Any numbers in the chart refer to the footnotes below.*

PASSPORTS: Passport valid for a minimum of six months beyond intended date of departure required by all.
VISAS: Required by all.
Types of visa and cost: *Tourist* and *Business*: £40 (single-entry); £70 (multiple-entry). *Express service*: £50 (single-entry); £100 (multiple-entry). *Same-day express service*: £60 (single-entry); £110 (multiple-entry). *Transit*: £40.
Validity: *Single-entry*: One day to one month from date of entry, renewable to a maximum of three months. *Multiple-entry*: One to six months from date of issue. *Transit*: on request.
Application to: Mozambique Embassies, High Commissions, Consulates; or Empresa Nacional de Turismo (see *Contact Addresses* section).
Note: A visa can sometimes be obtained through a contact living in Mozambique or at the airport although processing is often subject to delay. Apply to nearest High Commission for more information.
Application requirements: (a) Official application form. (b) Two passport-size photos. (c) Valid passport. (d) Return or onward ticket or flight confirmation slip. (e) Evidence of booked hotel/hostel accommodation *or* sufficient financial means. (f) Fee payable in cash or by cheque (made payable to the Mozambique High Commission). (g) Stamped, self-addressed registered envelope for postal applications. *Business*: (a)-(g) and, (h) Letter of invitation to Mozambique and/or introduction from an official or business institution.
Working days required: Three. Visas can be processed within 24 hours (express service) or within 90 minutes (same-day express service) for an additional fee.
Temporary residence: Apply to the Embassy or High Commission (see *Contact Addresses* section).

Money

Currency: Mozambique Metical (MT) = 100 centavos. Notes are in denominations of MT100,000, 50,000, 20,000, 10,000, 5000 and 1000. Coins are in denominations of MT5000, 1000, 500, 100, 50, 20, 10, 5 and 1.
Currency exchange: There are bureaux de change at the airports. Money can also be changed at banks. It is advisable to take US Dollars or South African Rand.
Credit & debit cards: These are rarely used in shops. However, money can be obtained from some ATMs using Visa credit or debit cards.
Travellers cheques: High rates of commission are often charged on these. To avoid additional exchange rate charges, travellers are advised to take travellers cheques in Pounds sterling, US Dollars or South African Rand.
Currency restrictions: The import and export of local currency is prohibited. The import of foreign currency is unlimited, subject to declaration. The export of foreign currency is limited to the amount declared on import.
Exchange rate indicators: The following figures are included as a guide to the movements of the Metical against Sterling and the US Dollar:

Date	Feb '04	May '04	Aug '04	Nov '04
£1.00=	42515.6	41763.5	40604.0	37230.6
$1.00=	23357.0	23382.5	22039.3	19660.2

Banking hours: Mon-Fri 0730-1530.

Duty Free

The following goods may be imported into Mozambique, by persons irrespective of age, without incurring customs duty: *200 cigarettes or 250g of tobacco; 0.75l of spirits; a reasonable quantity of perfume (opened).*
Prohibited/restricted items: Narcotics are prohibited. Firearms require a permit.

Public Holidays

2005: Jan 1 New Year's Day. **Feb 3** Heroes' Day. **Apr 7** Day of the Mozambican Woman. **May 1** Workers' Day. **Jun 25** Independence Day. **Sep 7** Lusaka Agreement Day. **Sep 25** Armed Forces Day. **Dec 25** National Family Day/Christmas Day.
2006: Jan 1 New Year's Day. **Feb 3** Heroes' Day. **Apr 7** Day of the Mozambican Woman. **May 1** Workers' Day. **Jun 25** Independence Day. **Sep 7** Lusaka Agreement Day. **Sep 25** Armed Forces Day. **Dec 25** National Family Day/Christmas Day.

Health

	Special Precautions?	Certificate Required?
Yellow Fever	No	1
Cholera	Yes	2
Typhoid & Polio	3	N/A
Malaria	4	N/A

Note: *Regulations and requirements may be subject to change at short notice, and you are advised to contact your doctor well in advance of your intended date of departure. Any numbers in the chart refer to the footnotes below.*

1: A yellow fever vaccination certificate is required of travellers over one year of age arriving from countries with infected areas.
2: Following WHO guidelines issued in 1973, a cholera vaccination certificate is not a condition of entry to Mozambique. However, cholera is a serious risk in this country and precautions are essential. The last major outbreak was in March 2004. Up-to-date advice should be sought before deciding whether these precautions should include vaccination, as medical opinion is divided over its effectiveness. For more information, see the *Health* appendix.
3: Immunisation against typhoid and poliomyelitis is often advised.
4: Malaria risk exists throughout the year, particularly in the north. The predominant *falciparum* strain is reported to be highly resistant to chloroquine and resistant to sulfadoxine-pyrimethamine. Travellers should bring a mosquito net. The recommended prophylaxis is mefloquine.
Food & drink: All water should be regarded as being potentially contaminated. Water used for drinking, brushing teeth or making ice should have first been boiled or otherwise sterilised. Some milk is unpasteurised and should be boiled. Powdered or tinned milk is available and is advised, but make sure that it is reconstituted with pure water. Avoid dairy products which are likely to have been made from unboiled milk. Only eat well-cooked meat and fish, preferably served hot. Pork, salad and mayonnaise may carry increased risk. Vegetables should be cooked and fruit peeled.
Other risks: *Diarrhoeal diseases, giardiasis, dysentery* and *typhoid fever* are all common. *Bilharzia* (schistosomiasis) is present. Avoid swimming and paddling in fresh water; swimming pools which are well chlorinated and maintained are safe. *Hepatitis A, B* and *E* are present. *Meningococcal meningitis* may occur. *Human trypanosomiasis* (sleeping sickness) has been reported. Plague has been reported in remote areas. Visitors should also be wary of the dangers of *Tetanus*. There is a high level of *HIV/AIDs* reported; travellers should take all necessary precautions.
Rabies is present. For those at high risk, vaccination before arrival should be considered. If you are bitten, seek medical advice without delay. For more information, see the *Health* appendix.
Health care: Full health insurance, preferably including Medevac, is essential. Medical facilities are scarce. Many rural health centres were forced to close during the conflict with the MNR rebels. It is advisable to carry basic medical supplies including medications and sterile syringes.

Travel - International

Note: Visitors should be aware of the risks of violent crime, poor road safety standards and minimal health facilities. Women should not walk alone on any beach in Mozambique.
AIR: Mozambique's national airline is *LAM-Linhas Aéreas de Moçambique (TM)*. Other airlines serving Mozambique include *Air France*, *Air Mauritius*, *Ethiopian Airlines*, *South African Airways* and *TAP Air Portugal*.
Approximate flight times: From Maputo to *London* is 14 hours, including stopover in Johannesburg.
International airports: *Maputo International (MPM)* (Maputo) is 3km (1.8 miles) northwest of the city. Bus and taxi services run to the centre (travel time – 15 minutes). Airport facilities include bank, restaurant, bar, snack bar, car hire (*Avis*, *Hertz* and *Imperial*) and post office.
Beira (BEW) is 13km (8 miles) from the city (travel time – 15 minutes). Beira receives flights from Continental Europe, other African countries and America. Airport facilities include restaurant, shops and a post office.
Departure tax: US$20 if destination is outside Africa; US$10 if destination is within Africa. Infants under two years of age and transit passengers are exempt.
SEA: British, European, American, Japanese and South African cargo vessels call at Maputo and Beira, but there are no regular passenger services.
RAIL: A train runs six times a week from Johannesburg to the Mozambique border at Komatipoort where there is a connection to Maputo (travel time – 15 hours). An overnight train runs regularly from Durban to Maputo. There is a service from Harare to Beira. There are connections from Malawi to Beira (although the border still has to be crossed on foot).
Note: Rail services are sometimes sporadic and unreliable.
ROAD: There are good road links with all neighbouring countries except Tanzania. However, road travel can be dangerous and should only be undertaken in daylight. Highjacking and robberies are rife and travellers should be aware of the possiblilty of unexploded landmines on the lesser-used roads. **Bus:** There is a daily bus service from Maputo to Johannesburg, and there are good bus links to other South African cities. Minibuses run between Maputo and towns in Swaziland, crossing the border at Namaacha. For further information about entry requirements and routes for border crossing, contact the High Commission (see *Contact Addresses* section).

Travel - Internal

Note: All travellers should be aware of the vast quantity of unexploded landmines that perforate Mozambique.
AIR: There are flights linking Maputo with Beira, Blantyre (Malawi), Inhambane, Lichinga, Nampula, Pemba, Quelimane and Tete. Flights depart from Maputo between 0500 and 0730 and are subject to seasonal alterations. Flights are frequently delayed or cancelled and baggage is often lost or tampered with. Air-taxi services are also available, and are the safest means of transport outside the main cities.
Departure tax: US$7.
RAIL: There is no rail connection between Maputo and Beira. There is a rail link between Beira and Tete and lines from the towns of Moçambique and Nacala, via the junction at Monapo, to Nampula and Lichinga. Trains also run from Maputo to Goba and Ressano Garcia, and northwards on the line to Zimbabwe. Most trains have three classes, but there are few sleepers and no dining or air-conditioned cars. For seats and sleepers, it is necessary to book in advance. All train services are subject to disruption.
ROAD: There are an estimated 29,810km (18,631 miles) of roads in Mozambique. Tarred roads connect Maputo with Beira and Beira with Tete. It is now possible to travel by road in southern Mozambique though flood damage can still cause serious delays. Traffic drives on the left. **Bus:** There are regular services covering most of the country. In more rural areas, road passage can only be undertaken by converted passenger trucks known as *chapas*. It is advisable to carry food and water on long journeys. There are occasional controls on the roads to check papers, especially in the north and near the border with Zimbabwe. Bus travel is the cheapest form of transport in the country and is, on the whole, fairly reliable. **Taxi:** Rarely available outside large towns. **Car hire:** Cars can be hired from international and national agencies in Maputo and Beira. Only hard currency is accepted. **Documentation:** International Driving Permit is recommended.

Note: Landmines may make travel by road outside the capital risky, and up-to-date travel advice should be sought. Driving after dark can be hazardous owing to vehicles travelling without headlights. Hijacking occurs.
URBAN: Bus services in Maputo have been improved with the introduction of new vehicles, and there are now fairly extensive services. Taxis are metered. Taxi drivers expect a tip.

Accommodation

HOTELS: Hotels of international standard are found mainly in the cities of Maputo and Beira. Accommodation in smaller towns is generally of a lower standard. More information is available online (website: www.mozambique.mz).
GUEST HOUSES: It is possible to rent holiday cottages, bungalows and *rondavels* cheaply.
CAMPING/CARAVANNING: There are campsites along the beaches, and a rest camp with a restaurant in Gorongosa Game Park. Camping is also permitted at various Catholic and Protestant missions in the country.

Resorts & Excursions

The country is opening up to tourism but, at present, it is mainly in the form of package tours. Independent travellers are relatively few in number. **Beira** has lovely beaches and is the base for trips to Gorongosa National Park (see below). Amongst the numerous beaches in Mozambique are **Ponta do Ouro**, **Malugane** (in the south), **Inhaca Island** (near Maputo), **Inhambane** with its beach resort of **Tofo** (about 400km/250 miles north of the capital), **Xai-Xai**, **Vilankulo**, **São Martino do Bilene** and **Chonguene**. The museum in **Maputo** (the capital) houses paintings and sculptures by well-known local artists. The gallery in the Ministry of Labour building is also worth a visit, as is the market. **Ilha de Moçambique** (Mozambique Island), near Nampula in the north, is a fascinating place, dotted with 17th- and 18th-century buildings, many of them from the colonial Portuguese period. There are also some interesting mosques dating from that period. It has been declared a UNESCO World Heritage Site. Regions that are being promoted as tourist resorts include the **Bazaruto Archipelago** (780km/485 miles north of Maputo), consisting of four islands plus surrounding islets and reefs. This beautiful area features inviting sandy beaches and offers excellent opportunities for game fishing.
NATIONAL PARKS: There are three good national parks in Mozambique. The **Gorongosa National Park** is open from the beginning of May to the end of October. Visits can be booked through the LAM office in Maputo. Access is provided by an airstrip at Chitengo. Guides and cars are available inside the park. The **Maputo Elephant Park** is on the right bank of the Maputo River. The **Marromeu National Park** is at the mouth of the **Zambesi River**.

Sport & Activities

Watersports: There is good **fishing** for marlin, barracuda, sailfish and swordfish. Notable resorts are Inhaca Island near Maputo, the Bazaruto Archipelago and Mozambique Island. There are many beaches and lagoons with safe **bathing**; however, there is a danger of occasional sharks in the warm Indian Ocean. Many hotels have pools. Some resorts have facilities and excellent clear waters full of underwater sights for **divers** or **snorkellers** to explore. Zavora's coral reef is outstanding.
There is also good **hiking** but advice and extreme caution should be taken due to the large amount of leftover landmines in the country. **Birdwatching** is excellent.

Social Profile

FOOD & DRINK: The cuisine is mainly Portuguese with Far Eastern influences. Specialities are *piri-piri* chicken, Zambesi chicken, shellfish, including Delagoa Bay prawns (which are grilled and served with piri-piri sauce), *matapa* (sauce of ground peanuts and cassava leaves) with rice or *wusa* (stiff maize porridge). Restaurants are to be found in main towns, as well as hotel dining rooms.
NIGHTLIFE: Maputo has a lively nightlife, particularly on weekends. *Feira Popular* is the main forum of evening activity with various bars and discos, some with live music. The style of music in clubs varies from typical Mozambican rhythms to Western pop music. The *National Company of Song & Dance* has rehearsals which are open to the public. Most major towns have cinemas.
SHOPPING: Special purchases include basketwork, reed mats, woodcarvings, masks, printed cloth and leather articles. **Shopping hours:** Mon-Fri 0800-1230 and 1400-1730, Sat 0800-1800.
SPECIAL EVENTS: For details of special events in 2005, contact the Mozambique National Tourism Company (see *Contact Addresses* section).

SOCIAL CONVENTIONS: Shaking hands is the customary form of greeting. The courtesies and modes of address customary in Portugal and other Latin countries are still observed. Casual wear is acceptable. Formal dress is seldom required. **Photography:** Visitors should not take photographs of soldiers, airports, bridges or government/public buildings, since this is illegal. Only photos of beaches and other tourist sites may be taken.
Tipping: Not generally expected outside Maputo. In Maputo and other tourist-exposed areas, 5 to 5 per cent of the bill is normal (depending on standards of service and the place itself).

Business Profile

ECONOMY: Agriculture, which employs 80 per cent of the working population, is the mainstay of the economy. Cash crops include cashew nuts (see below), tea, sugar, sisal, maize, cotton, copra, oil seeds and some citrus fruit. Forestry is increasing in importance. Fishing is both an important source of food and a vital export earner. Manufacturing industry produces one quarter of GDP: products include processed foods, textiles, drinks, cement and fertiliser. Mining operations produce coal, salt, bauxite, gemstones and marble. In addition, natural gas is extracted from onshore fields and piped to South Africa.
Following the end of the debilitating civil war in 1994, the Mozambican economy picked up strongly over the next five years, recording annual growth of around 10 per cent (13 per cent in 2001), although at the price of high inflation (around 35 per cent) at times. Mozambique was also deemed eligible for debt relief under the Heavily Indebted Poor Countries (HIPC) initiative, which was agreed by major donors in 1999 and lifted some of the country's substantial debt burden. However, much of Mozambique's fragile economic progress was undone by the devastating floods of 2000. Since then the economy has been further undermined by drought and trade-related disputes over the issue of subsidies to farmers. A number of African countries complain of the international financial community's insistence that they remove subsidies while Western countries continue to support their own agricultural sector. (Mozambique points to the near-collapse of its once thriving cashew nut industry.) In 2002, Mozambique was once again obliged to call upon its aid donors for emergency food aid. Mozambique is a member of the Southern African Development Conference. South Africa, the USA and Portugal are Mozambique's most important trading partners.
BUSINESS: Safari suits are advised for the hot season, while lightweight suits or jackets should be worn for the rest of the year. Prior appointments are recommended. A knowledge of Portuguese is normally necessary for business dealings, although there are translation facilities available in Maputo. January is the main holiday month, so this should be avoided for business trips. **Office hours:** Mon-Fri 0730-1230 and 1400-1730.
COMMERCIAL INFORMATION: The following organisation can offer advice: Câmara de Comércio de Moçambique, CP 1836, Rua Mateus Sansão Mutemba 452, Maputo (tel: (1) 491 970; fax: (1) 490 428).

Climate

Climate varies according to area. Inland is cooler than the coast and rainfall higher as the land rises, with most rain between January and March. Hottest and wettest season is October to March. From April to September the coast has warm, mainly dry weather tempered by sea breezes.
Required clothing: Tropical lightweights, with warmer clothing for evenings. Rainwear advisable all year round.

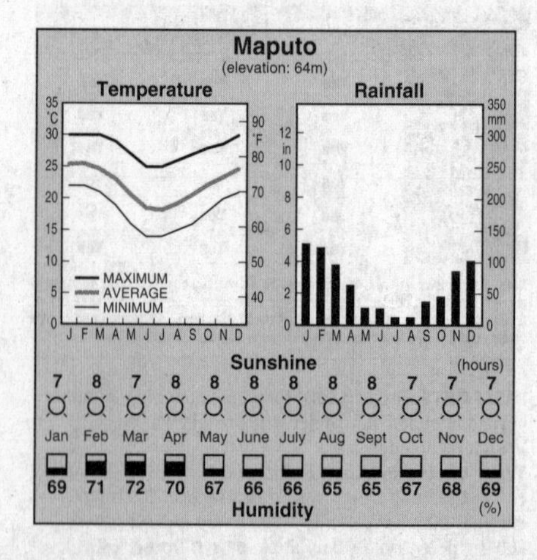

Myanmar

LATEST TRAVEL ADVICE CONTACTS

British Foreign and Commonwealth Office
Tel: (0870) 606 0290 Website: www.fco.gov.uk

US Department of State
Website: http://travel.state.gov/travel

Canadian Department of Foreign Affairs and Int'l Trade
Tel: (1 800) 267 8376 Website: www.dfait-maeci.gc.ca

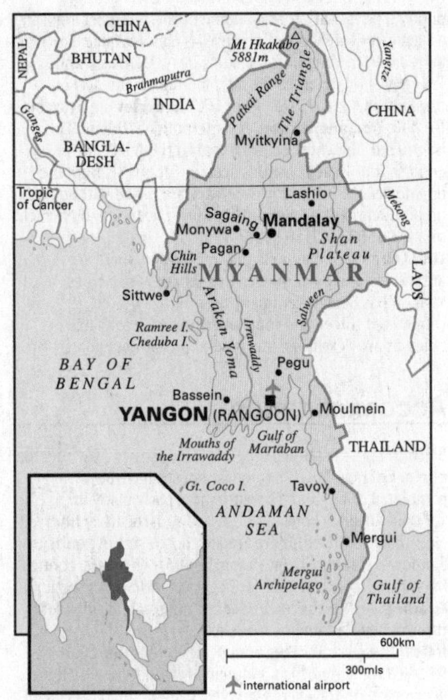

Location: South-East Asia.

Country dialling code: 95.

Myanmar Tourism Promotion Board
c/o Traders Hotel, Level 3, Business Centre, 223 Sule Pagoda Road, Yangon, Myanmar
Tel: (1) 242 828 ext. 6462. Fax: (1) 242 800.
E-mail: mtpb@mptmail.net.mm
Website: www.myanmar-tourism.com

Myanmar Travels and Tours
77-91 Sule Pagoda Road, Yangon, Myanmar
Tel: (1) 252 859 *or* 371 910 *or* 321 927. Fax: (1) 254 417.
E-mail: mtt.mht@mptmail.net.mm
Website: www.myanmars.net/mtt

Embassy of the Union of Myanmar
19A Charles Street, Berkeley Square, London W1J 5DX, UK
Tel: (020) 7499 8841 *or* (0906) 550 8924 (recorded visa and tourism information; calls cost £1 per minute).
Fax: (020) 7629 4169.
E-mail: membloudon@aol.com
Website: www.myanmar.com
Opening hours: Mon-Fri 0930-1630.

British Embassy
80 Strand Road, Box No 638, Yangon, Myanmar
Tel: (1) 370 863. Fax: (1) 370 866.
E-mail: Consular.Rangoon@fco.gov.uk

Embassy of the Union of Myanmar
2300 S Street, NW, Washington, DC 20008, USA
Tel: (202) 332 9044/5. Fax: (202) 332 9046.
E-mail: pyi.thayar@verizon.net
Website: www.mewashingtondc.com *or* www.myanmar.com

Embassy of the United States of America
581 Merchant Street, Yangon, Myanmar
Tel: (1) 379 880/1/3 *or* 370 963-5.
Fax: (1) 538 040 (consular section).
E-mail: consularrangoo@state.gov
Website: http://rangoon.usembassy.gov

TIMATIC CODES

Health
AMADEUS: **TI-DFT/RGN/HE**
GALILEO/WORLDSPAN: **TI-DFT/RGN/HE**
SABRE: **TIDFT/RGN/HE**

Visa
AMADEUS: **TI-DFT/RGN/VI**
GALILEO/WORLDSPAN: **TI-DFT/RGN/VI**
SABRE: **TIDFT/RGN/VI**

To access TIMATIC country information on Health and Visa regulations through the Computer Reservations System (CRS), type in the appropriate command line listed above.

Embassy of the Union of Myanmar
85 Range Road, Suite 902/903, Ottawa, Ontario K1N 8J6, Canada
Tel: (613) 232 6434. Fax: (613) 232 6435.
E-mail: meott@magma.ca Website: www.myanmar.com

The Canadian Embassy in Bangkok deals with enquiries relating to Myanmar (see *Thailand* section).

General Information

AREA: 676,552 sq km (261,218 sq miles).
POPULATION: 48,852,000 (UN estimate 2002).
POPULATION DENSITY: 72.2 per sq km.
CAPITAL: Yangon (Rangoon). **Population:** 4,504,000 (UN estimate 2001).
GEOGRAPHY: Myanmar is a diamond-shaped country extending 925km (575 miles) from east to west and 2100km (1300 miles) from north to south. It is bounded by China, Laos and Thailand in the east, by Bangladesh and India in the north and by the Indian Ocean in the west and south. The Irrawaddy River runs through the centre of the country and fans out to form a delta on the south coast; Yangon stands beside one of its many mouths. North of the delta lies the Irrawaddy basin and central Myanmar, which is protected by a horseshoe of mountains rising to over 3000m (10,000ft), creating profound climatic effects. To the west are the Arakan, Chin and Naga mountains and the Patkai Hills; the Kachin Hills are to the north; to the east lies the Shan Plateau, which extends to the Tenasserim coastal ranges. Intensive irrigated farming is practised throughout central Myanmar, and fruit, vegetables and citrus crops thrive on the Shan Plateau, but much of the land and mountains are covered by subtropical forest.
GOVERNMENT: Socialist Republic since 1974. Power assumed by the army in 1988. **Head of State:** Senior General Than Shwe since 1992. **Head of Government:** Prime Minister Soe Win since 2004.
LANGUAGE: The official language is Myanmar (Burmese). There are over 100 dialects spoken in Myanmar. English is spoken in business circles.
RELIGION: 87 per cent Theravada Buddhist. The remainder are Hindu, Muslim, Christian and Animist.
TIME: GMT + 6.5.
ELECTRICITY: 230 volts AC, 50Hz.
COMMUNICATIONS: Telephone: IDD is available to the main cities. Country code: 95. Outgoing international code: 00. For emergencies, dial 199 (police), 191 (fire) and 192 (ambulance). There is a limited public internal service. Only larger cities can be dialled direct from within Myanmar; smaller towns still use manual switchboards and callers need to ask the operator to connect them to a specific town operator. The *Central Telephone & Telegraph (CTT)* office on the corner of Pansodan and Mahabandoola Streets is the only public place in the country where international telephone calls can be conveniently arranged. The office is open Mon-Fri 0800-1600 and weekends and holidays 0900-1400. **Mobile telephone:** GSM 900 network is operated by *Myanmar Posts and Telecommunications*. Fees are high and coverage limited. Note: All visitors who want to use communication devices such as mobile phones and receivers must first apply for permission from the Government of the Union of Myanmar. Without prior permission granted, mobile phones will be temporarily held by Customs on arrival. **Fax:** May be sent from the Central Telegraph Office on Mahabandoola Street and there are further facilities at the Post and Telecommunications Corporation in Yangon. **Internet:** ISPs include the *Ministry of Post and Telecommunication* (website: www.mpt.net.mm). Set-up fees are high. **Post:** Service to Europe takes up to one week and letter forms are quicker than ordinary letters. To ensure despatch, it is advisable to go to the post office personally to obtain a certificate of posting, for which a small fee is charged. **Press:** The only English-language newspapers are the *Guardian* and the *New Light of Myanmar*. Myanmar Travel & Tours also publishes a tourist publication, *Today*, in English.
Radio: BBC World Service (website: www.bbc.co.uk/worldservice) and Voice of America (website: www.voa.gov) can be received. From time to time the frequencies change and the most up-to-date can be found online.

Passport/Visa

	Passport Required?	Visa Required?	Return Ticket Required?
Full British	Yes	Yes	No
Australian	Yes	Yes	No
Canadian	Yes	Yes	No
USA	Yes	Yes	No
Other EU	Yes	Yes	No
Japanese	Yes	Yes	No

Note: *Regulations and requirements may be subject to change at short notice, and you are advised to contact the appropriate diplomatic or consular authority before finalising travel arrangements. Details of these may be found at the head of this country's entry. Any numbers in the chart refer to the footnotes below.*

Entry restrictions: Holders of passports issued by the government of the Chinese Taipei, if not holding a special affidavit issued by a diplomatic representation of Myanmar abroad.
PASSPORTS: Passport valid for at least six months beyond date of intended departure required by all.
VISAS: Required by all except transit passengers continuing their journey by the same or first connecting aircraft, provided holding valid onward or return documentation and not leaving the airport.
Note: A separate visa is required for each child over seven years of age even if travelling on their parent's passport.
Types of visa and cost: *Tourist* (Foreign Independent Travellers - FIT): £14. *Business* and *Social*: £20.
Validity: Tourist visas are valid for two months from the date of issue for stays of 28 days in Myanmar. This can be extended for an additional 14 days. Business visas are valid for three months from date of issue for stays of 10 weeks, extendable for up to 12 months on an individual basis. Transit visas valid for 24 hours.
Application to: Consulate (or Consular section at Embassy; see *Contact Addresses* section).
Application requirements: (a) One application form. (b) Two passport-size photos. (c) Valid passport. (d) Fee (cash accepted if applying in person; cheque or postal order only if applying by post). (e) Self-addressed, stamped enveloped for postal applications with sufficient postage (registered post is recommended). *Social Visit* (visiting friends or relatives in Myanmar): (a) Two application forms (can be photocopied). (b) Three passport size photos. (c) Valid passport. (d) Fee (cash or postal order). (e) Self-addressed stamped envelope for postal applications with sufficient postage (registered post is recommended). (f) Letter of invitation from friends or relatives in Myanmar. *Business*: (a)-(e) and, (f) Company letter explaining purpose of visit. (g) Letter of invitation from company in Myanmar.
Working days required: Normally three.
Temporary Residence: It is possible to get a stay permit once in Myanmar at the Immigration Department.

Money

Currency: Kyat (Kt) = 100 pyas. Notes are in denominations of Kt1000, 500, 200, 100 and 90 pyas. Coins are in denominations of Kt1, and 50, 25, 10, 5 and 1 pyas. Kt100,000 is known as a *lakh*, and Kt10 million as a *crore*. Kyat is pronounced like the English word 'chat'. To combat the black market and limit the financial power of dissident groups, currency denominations are occasionally declared invalid without prior notice. Limited refunds are usually allowed for certain sectors of the population.
Currency exchange: FECs, which are printed in China, are Myanmar's second legal currency and are issued by the Bank of Myanmar specifically for visiting tourists. They come in denominations equivalent to US$20, 10, 5 and 1. Payment for FECs is *only* accepted in US Dollars. One US Dollar equals one FEC. FECs can be exchanged into Kyats at officially authorised banks, bureaux de change, hotels and Myanmar Travel and Tour offices and can be spent anywhere in the country. Cash payments can also be made in US Dollars, but *only* at establishments (eg hotels, railway stations, airlines) that have an official licence allowing them to accept dollars. Wherever possible, it is advisable to change US Dollars into Kyats rather than FECs, as FECs usually have a poorer exchange rate than Kyats. However, US Dollar travellers cheques can only be exchanged into FECs and not directly into Kyats unlike US Dollar cash. It is also recommended to carry small change as large notes may be difficult to change.
Euros are now also accepted in all banks and currency exchange bureaux. There are no ATMs.
Credit & debit cards: It is unlikely that credit or debit cards will be accepted; it is best to check with your card company prior to travel.
Travellers cheques: Accepted, although probably not by all establishments. To avoid additional exchange rate charges, travellers are advised to take travellers cheques in US Dollars or Pounds Sterling.
Currency restrictions: The import and export of local currency is prohibited. There are no import limits on foreign currencies, but any amounts must be declared on arrival and the declaration certificate kept safe – on departure, foreign currencies are checked with the amounts declared on entry. There are regular customs checks at Yangon airport, aimed at curbing black-market activities; this makes it essential to keep all receipts in order to account for money spent while in the country.
Exchange rate indicators: The following figures are included as a guide to the movements of the Kyat against Sterling and the US Dollar:

Date	Feb '04	May '04	Aug '04	Nov '04
£1.00 =	11.68	11.20	11.82	12.15
$1.00 =	6.42	6.26	6.42	6.42

Banking hours: Mon-Fri 1000-1400.

A B C D E F G H I J K L M N O P Q R S T U V W X Y Z

Duty Free

The following goods may be taken into Myanmar by persons over 17 years of age without incurring customs duty:
200 cigarettes or 50 cigars or 250g tobacco; 1l of alcohol; 0.5l of perfume or eau de cologne.
Prohibited and restricted items: Playing cards, gambling equipment, antiques, archaeological items and pornography are prohibited. Jewellery, electrical goods and cameras must be declared; failure to do so may result in visitors being refused permission to export it on departure. Video cameras will be held in safe custody at the airport and will be returned on departure.
Note: All gems, jewellery and silverware purchased from authorised shops can be taken out of the country.

Public Holidays

2005: Jan 4 Independence Day. **Jan 21** Eid Al Adha (Feast of the Sacrifice). **Feb 12** Union Day. **Feb 24** Full Moon of Tabaung. **Mar 2** Peasants' Day (anniversary of the 1962 coup). **Mar 27** Armed Forces Day. **Apr 13-16** Maha Thingyan (Water Festival). **Apr 17** Myanmar New Year. **Apr 24** Full Moon of Kasone. **May 1** May Day. **May 21** Full Moon of Waso (Beginning of Buddhist Lent). **Jul 19** Martyrs' Day. **Oct 12** Full Moon of Thadingyut (End of Buddhist Lent). **Nov 1** Deepavali. **Nov 14** Tazaungmon Full Moon Day. **Dec 6** National Day. **Dec 23** Kayin New Year. **Dec 25** Christmas Day.
2006: Jan 4 Independence Day. **Jan 10** Eid Al Adha (Feast of the Sacrifice). **Feb** *or* **Mar** Full Moon of Tabaung. **Feb 12** Union Day. **Mar 2** Peasants' Day (anniversary of the 1962 coup). **Mar 27** Armed Forces Day. **Apr** *or* **May** Full Moon of Kasone. **Apr 13-16** Maha Thingyan (Water Festival). **Apr 17** Myanmar New Year. **May 1** May Day. **Jul** *or* **Aug** Full Moon of Waso (Beginning of Buddhist Lent). **Jul 19** Martyrs' Day. **Oct** Full Moon of Thadingyut (End of Buddhist Lent). **Oct 21** Deepavali. **Nov** Tazaungmon Full Moon Day. **Dec 6** National Day. **Dec 23** Kayin New Year. **Dec 25** Christmas Day.
Note: Buddhist holidays are determined according to lunar sightings, and dates given here are approximations only. Other festivals celebrated by minorities include the Islamic observance of Bakri Idd in late November; Christmas and Easter; and the Karen New Year in early January. For further information, contact the Embassy (see *Contact Addresses* section) or see the *World of Buddhism* appendix.

Health

	Special Precautions?	Certificate Required?
Yellow Fever	Yes	1
Cholera	Yes	2
Typhoid & Polio	3	N/A
Malaria	4	N/A

***Note:** Regulations and requirements may be subject to change at short notice, and you are advised to contact your doctor well in advance of your intended date of departure. Any numbers in the chart refer to the footnotes below.*

1: A yellow fever vaccination certificate is required from all travellers arriving from infected areas. Nationals and residents of Myanmar are required to possess certificates of vaccination on their departure to an infected area.
2: Following WHO guidelines issued in 1973, a cholera vaccination certificate is no longer a condition of entry to Myanmar. However, cholera is a serious risk in this country and precautions are essential. Up-to-date advice should be sought before deciding whether these precautions should include vaccination, as medical opinion is divided over its effectiveness. For more information, see the *Health* appendix.
3: Immunisation against typhoid and poliomyelitis is strongly advised.
4: Malaria risk (predominantly in the malignant *falciparum* form) exists below 1000m (3281ft) in the following areas: (a) throughout the year in Karen State; (b) from March to December in Chin, Kachin, Kayah, Mon, Rakhine and Shan States, in Pegu Division, and in Hlegu, Hmawbi and Taikkyi townships of Yangon Division; (c) from April to December in rural areas of Tenasserim Division; (d) from May to December in the Irrawaddy Division and rural areas of Mandalay Division; (e) from June to November in rural areas of Magwe Division and in Sagaing Division. The *falciparum* strain is reported to be highly resistant to chloroquine and resistant to sulfadoxine/pyrimethamine. Mefloquine resistance is reported in the eastern part of the Shan state. Reduced sensitivity to chloroquine in the *vivax* form is reported. The recommended prophylaxis is mefloquine, and doxycycline in the eastern part of the Shan state.
Food & drink: All water should be regarded as being potentially contaminated. Water used for drinking, brushing teeth or making ice should have first been boiled or otherwise sterilised. Milk is unpasteurised and should be boiled. Powdered or tinned milk is available and is advised, but make sure that it is reconstituted with pure water. Avoid dairy products which are likely to have been made from unboiled milk. Only eat well-cooked meat and fish, preferably served hot. Pork, salad and mayonnaise may carry increased risk. Vegetables should be cooked and fruit peeled.
Other risks: *Diarrhoea, amoebic* and *bacillary dysentery* and *typhoid fever* are all common. *Japanese encephalitis* may be caught via mosquito bites, particularly in rural areas between June and October. A vaccine is available, and travellers are advised to consult their doctor prior to departure. *Filariasis, dengue fever, trachoma* and *Hepatitis A, B* and *E* are also present. The WHO advises that foci of plague are present in Myanmar. Further information should be sought from the Department of Health or from any of the hospitals specialising in tropical diseases listed in the *Health* appendix.
Rabies is present. For those at high risk, vaccination before arrival should be considered. If you are bitten, seek medical advice without delay. For more information, see the *Health* appendix.
Health care: Health insurance is strongly recommended. There are hospitals and clinics in cities and larger towns, and regional health centres in outlying areas. It is advisable to carry a remedy against minor enteric upsets.

Travel - International

Note: All travel to the 'Burmese' side of the Myanmar/Thai border should ideally be avoided, especially since a number of bomb explosions have recently occurred in public places, for which no group has claimed responsibility. The political situation in Myanmar remains unsettled and there continues to be stringent restrictions on freedom of movement and speech.
AIR: Myanmar's national airline is *Myanmar Airways International (UB)* (website: www.miaair.com). Yangon has direct air links with Bangkok, Bangladesh, Calcutta, Jakarta, Kunming, Moscow and Singapore. Airlines serving Myanmar include *Air China, Austrian Airlines, Bangladesh Airlines, Indian Airlines, Lufthansa, Silk Air* and *Thai Airways International.*
International airports: *Yangon (RGN)* is 19km (12 miles) from the city. Airport facilities include restaurant, bar, snack bar, bank, post office, duty free shop and tourist information. Buses go to the city (travel time - 30 minutes). Taxis are also available (travel time - 45 minutes).
Departure tax: US$10, payable also in FECs (Foreign Exchange Certificates; see also *Money* section for details). Passengers in direct transit are exempt.
SEA: Cruise ships call at Yangon Port.
ROAD: Overland entry with a border pass is, in theory, permitted at the following border check points: Kyukoke, Namkhan and Muse on the Myanmar-Yunnan (People's Republic of China) border; and Tachileik, Myawaddy and Kawthaung on the Mynamar-Thailand border. Generally speaking, however, foreigners are only allowed to travel as part of an organised group. Owing to continuing political instability, borders may periodically close. Contact the nearest Embassy for up-to-date details.
Note: It is recommended to use only air travel as a means of access into Myanmar.

Travel - Internal

AIR: Air travel is the most efficient way of moving within Myanmar and the only permissible means of transport for independent travellers, but there is a rather limited schedule of flights, and a rather less than perfect safety record. The British Embassy in London bans its staff from using *Myanmar Airways* for this reason; although the staff *do* use *Myanmar Airways International. Air Mandalay* and *Air Yangon* operate internal flights. Internal security can restrict ease of movement. There are daily flights to most towns; charter flights are also available. There are over 60 airstrips in the country. For tickets and information, contact Myanmar Travel and Tours (see *Contact Addresses* section).
Internal flight times: From Yangon to *Mandalay* is two hours 10 minutes; to *Pagan* is one hour 30 minutes; and to *Heho* is one hour 25 minutes.
SEA/RIVER: The best way of seeing Myanmar is by boat, particularly between Bhamo-Mandalay and Mandalay-Pagan. Myanmar has about 8000km (5000 miles) of navigable rivers. Trips can only be arranged as part of an organised tour group. It is generally necessary to provide one's own food.
RAIL: *Myanmar Railways* provide services on several routes, the principal line being Yangon to Mandalay (travel time - 12 to 14 hours). Overnight trains have sleeping cars. There is also a good service from Mandalay-Lashio-Myitkyina. The state-run railway has 4300km (2700 miles) of track and serves most of Myanmar. First class is available but, with the exception of the Yangon to Mandalay line, services are regularly afflicted with delays caused by climatic, technical and bureaucratic difficulties. Tickets must be purchased through Myanmar Travel and Tours as part of an organised tour group. There are regular services from Yangon to Mandalay and from Yangon to Thazi. Visitors should be aware that much railway equipment is decrepit and some accidents are unreported.
ROAD: Traffic drives on the right. There has been some modernisation of Myanmar's once antiquated vehicles. Visitors must remember that, under Burmese law, the driver of a car involved in an accident with a pedestrian is *always* at fault. **Bus:** Buses are generally operated by the state-owned Road Transport Enterprise. Public bus services tend to be unreliable and uncomfortable; visitors may pay using the Kyat currency on certain lines only. Owing to the ongoing privatisation programme of the transport industry, a fleet of privately operated buses is also available. The main lines are from Yangon to Meiktila, Pyay, Mandalay and Taunggyi. Private buses are air conditioned and accept payment in Kyat, US Dollars or FECs. **Bicycles** are available for hire. **Documentation:** An International Driving Permit is required. This must be presented to the police, who will endorse it or issue a visitor's licence. Otherwise, Burmese driving licences, valid for two years, are issued without test on production of a valid British driving licence and payment of a fee of 50 FEC/150 Kyat.
URBAN: Yangon has a circular rail service. There are also antiquated and overcrowded bus services in all cities. Yangon has blue government taxis with set fares. Unmetered three- and four-wheel taxis are available in cities, as are rickshaws; it is wise to pre-arrange fares.

Accommodation

Since the privatisation of the hotel industry in 1993, a large number of new hotels and guest houses have been completed or are under construction, particularly in Yangon. Advance booking is advisable, particularly from November to March. There are also hotels at the resorts of Sandoway, Taunggyi and Pagan. For further details, contact Myanmar Travel and Tour (see *Contact Addresses* section).
Grading: An increasing number of hotels are divided into three categories: luxury, first class and lower.
INNS: These are another option for visitors. Although reserved for state officials in many towns, inns will often accommodate travellers who have been granted official permission. Visitors travelling away from the normal tourist routes should carry sleeping bags or blankets, as pagodas, temples and monasteries will usually only accommodate visitors for a night or two.

Resorts & Excursions

Tourist numbers are steadily rising. Certain areas in Upper and Lower Myanmar are currently out of bounds owing to the past civil war - check with the Embassy or Consulate for the latest information. Tourists should also be aware that foreign nationals are liable to arrest or imprisonment if they criticise the regime in public. Most coastal resorts have now been opened to tourists and Sunday round-trip flights are arranged by Myanmar Travel and Tour to Napali and Sandoway beaches during the dry season. For the purposes of this guide, Myanmar has been divided into three sections: The South (including Yangon); Central Myanmar (including Pagan and Mandalay); The East and The Northwest.

THE SOUTH
YANGON: Yangon (or *Rangoon*), the capital, is a city of Buddhist temples, open-air markets, food stalls and ill-repaired colonial architecture. It has a population of over two million. Although most of the city has been built in the last hundred years, and although it suffered considerable damage during World War II, there are still several examples of a more ancient culture. These include the golden **Shwedragon Pagoda**, one of the most spectacular Buddhist shrines in Asia and reputedly 2500 years old (although rebuilt in 1769); the **Sule Pagoda**, also over 2000 years old; the **Botataung Pagoda**, hollow inside with a mirrored maze; and the **Maha Pasan Guha**, or 'Great Cave'.
Excursions: Outside the capital, places worth visiting include the **Naga-Yone** enclosure near **Myinkaba**, with a Buddha figure entwined and protected by a huge cobra - a combination of Buddhism and Brahman astrology; **Kyaik Tyo** and its 'Golden Rock Pagoda', a 5.5m (18ft) shrine built on a gold-plated boulder atop a cliff; and **Pegu**, founded in 1573, with its golden **Shwemawdaw Pagoda** and market. Just northeast of Pegu is the **Shwethalyaung Buddha**, revered as one of the most beautiful and lifelike of reclining Buddhas, which was lost and totally overgrown by jungle after the destruction of Pegu in 1757. It was rediscovered in the British era, during the construction of the railway line.

A B C D E F G H I J K L M N O P Q R S T U V W X Y Z

CENTRAL MYANMAR

PAGAN: Pagan is one of the greatest historical areas in the country. It is best seen at sunrise or sunset. More than 13,000 pagodas were once spread over this dry plain during the golden age of the 11 great kings (roughly 1044-1287); this came to an end with the threat of invasion by Kublai Khan from China, and this extraordinary area was abandoned. Now there are fewer than 3000 pagodas. The actual village of Pagan has a museum, market and places to eat and stay; within walking distance of Bagan, there are lacquerware workshops and an attractive temple. There are dozens of open temples in the Pagan area (about 40 sq km/15 sq miles), but places of special interest include the **Shwegugyi Temple**, built in 1311 and noted for its fine stucco carvings; the **Gawdawpalin Temple**, badly damaged in the 1975 earthquake, but still one of the most impressive of the Pagan temples; and the **Thatbyinnyu Temple**, which is the highest in Bagan.

MANDALAY: This old royal city is rich in palaces, stupas, temples and pagodas (although the city has suffered several bad fires which have destroyed some buildings), and is the main centre of Buddhism and Burmese arts. There are some excellent craft markets and there are thriving stone-carving workshops and gold-leaf industries. Taking its name from **Mandalay Hill** (rising about 240m/787ft to the northeast of the palace), the city was founded by King Mindon in 1857, the old wooden palace buildings at **Amarapura** being moved and reconstructed. Sights of interest include the huge **Shweyattaw Buddha**, close to the hill, with its outstretched finger pointing towards the city; the **Eindawya Pagoda**, built in 1847 and covered in gold leaf; the **Shwekyimyint Pagoda**, containing the original Buddha image consecrated by Prince Minshinzaw during the Pagan period; and the **Mahumuni Pagoda** or 'Great Pagoda', housing the famous and revered Mahumuni image. Covered in gold leaf over the years by devout Buddhists, this image was brought from Arakan in 1784, although it is thought to be much older. The base, moat and huge walls are virtually all that remain of the once stupendous **Mandalay Palace**, which was an immense walled city (mostly of timber construction) rather than a palace. It was burnt down in 1942. A large-scale model gives an indication of what it must have been like. The **Shwenandaw Kyaung Monastery** was at one time part of the palace complex and was used as an apartment by King Mindon and his chief queen. Like the palace, the wooden building was once beautifully gilded. There are some extraordinary carved panels inside and also a photograph of the **Atumashi Kyaung Monastery**, destroyed by fire in 1890. The ruins can be seen to the south of the **Kuthodaw Pagoda**, called 'the world's biggest book' because of the 729 marble slabs that surround the central pagoda – they are inscribed with the entire Buddhist canon.

Excursions: The area around Mandalay contains several older, abandoned capital cities. **Sagaing** is easily accessible to the visitor, and contains interesting pagodas at **Tupayon**, **Aungmyelawka** and **Kaunghmudaw**. Sagaing was, for a time, the capital of an independent Shan Kingdom. In the 15th century, **Ava** was chosen as the kingdom's new capital and it remained so until well into the 19th century, when the kingdom vanished; the old city walls can still be traced. **Mingun** (a pleasant river trip from Mandalay) possesses the famous **Mingun Bell**, supposedly the largest uncracked hung bell in the world. It was cast in 1790 by King Bodawpaya to be hung in his giant pagoda, which was never finished, due to the king's death in 1819. The base of the pagoda alone is about 50m (165ft) high. **Amarapura**, south of Mandalay, was founded by Bodawpaya in 1783 and the city is famous for its cotton and silk weaving.

THE EAST & THE NORTHWEST

This region of the country offers the visitor opportunities for walking and rock-climbing, and the various hill stations, such as **Kalaw**, provide a pine-forested escape from the heat and humidity of Yangon. The caves and lake at **Pindaya** are famous; the caves contain thousands of Buddha images. Near the village of **Yengan** are the **Padah-Lin Caves**, containing prehistoric paintings. **Inlay Lake** on the Shan Plateau is famous for its floating gardens and leg-rowing fishermen. **Maymyo** is a charming British hill station further north, with attractive waterfalls and a pleasant climate because of its high altitude. Difficult communications usually prevent tourists from visiting the largely tribal Northwest. Many of Myanmar's minority peoples live here.

Sport & Activities

Traditional sports: The national game is **Chinglone**; played in teams of six, the object of the game is to keep a cane ball in the air for as long as possible using any part of the body except the hands.

Burmese boxing is another popular sport; it can appear extremely vicious to the uninitiated spectator. Many Western sports are also played.

A large number of **Buddhist festivals** are held annually in Myanmar and provide an interesting way for visitors to experience local traditions and culture (see also *Special Events* in the *Social Profile* section). For serious practitioners, there are several centres for the study and practice of Theravada Buddhism, the most famous of which is the *Mahasi Meditation Centre* in Yangon. The centre was founded in 1947 by Mahasi Sayadaw, one of Myanmar's greatest meditation teachers. Visitors wishing to participate in Buddhist **retreats** need to obtain a special, long-stay entry visa (allowing stays of up to 12 weeks). The application procedure takes up to 10 weeks. For further details about the necessary application requirements, contact the Embassy or Consular section at the Embassy (see *Contact Addresses* section).

Visitors can also attend performances of Myanmar's traditional popular **theatre**, known as *pwe* (show). Performances take place in a variety of contexts, including religious festivals, weddings, sporting events or even funerals, and sometimes last for an entire night. Of further interest are performances of traditional **dance** forms (*nat pwes*), which pay homage to the spirit world, or **marionette theatre** (*yok-thei pwe*), widely practised during the late-18th century in Mandalay and one of the most characteristic forms of national cultural expression.

Ecotourism: This is encouraged by Myanmar Travels and Tours and there are a number of national parks and wildlife sanctuaries which also offer **trekking** and **safaris**. The best parks are the *Alaungdaw Kathapa National Park* (located northwest of Monywa); *Hlawga National Park* (near Yangon, good for birdwatching); *Popa Mountain Park* (extinct volcano covered in forests in the desert area of central Myanmar); *Lampi Island* (Myeik Archipelago) (which can be reached by boat trips from Myeik and Kawthaung); and *Shwesettaw Wildlife Sanctuary* (located in Minbu).

Other: Swimming and other types of watersports are possible on the following beaches: *Kanthaya Beach* (located on the Rakhine coast); *Maung-ma-gan Beach* (located on the Taninthayi coast in the south and reached from Dawei); *Ngapali Beach* (located on the Rakhine coast); and *Chaung-tha Beach* (located west of Pathein).

Football can be seen at Aung San Stadium in Yangon and on small fields throughout the country.

Social Profile

FOOD & DRINK: The regional food is hot and spicy. Fish, rice, noodles and vegetables spiced with onions, ginger, garlic and chillies are the common local ingredients. Local dishes include *lethok son* (a sort of spicy vegetarian rice salad), *mohinga* (fish soup with noodles) and *oh-no khauk swe* (rice noodles, chicken and coconut milk). The avocados by Inle Lake are very good. Delicious fruits are available in the markets and food stalls appear on the corners of most large towns. Chinese and Indian cuisine is offered in many hotels and restaurants.

Tea is a popular drink; the spices which are added to it can make the tongue turn bright red. Locally produced soft drinks are generally of poor quality and rather expensive. Coffee is not common. Locally produced beer, rum, whisky and gin are generally available.

NIGHTLIFE: Western-style nightlife is almost non existent, although there are occasional performances in Yangon's three theatres as well as a number of rock and pop groups gaining in popularity. Cinemas are popular and seven of Yangon's 50 cinemas regularly show English-language films.

SHOPPING: Souvenirs include handicrafts and jewellery. In Yangon, a good place to shop is Bogyoke Aung San Market, which sells luxury items, handicrafts, food stuffs, clothing, jewellery and consumer goods. It is open from 0800-1800 (except Sunday and public holidays) but the best time to visit is around 1000. Mandalay is a good place for traditional handicrafts which can be purchased at Zegyo Market. Phatahe Bazaar sells Buddhist articles of worship. **Shopping hours:** Mon-Sun 0800-2200.

SPECIAL EVENTS: The Buddhist calendar is full of festivals, many timed to coincide with the full moon. Any visitor would be unlucky not to be able to enjoy at least one during their stay.

The following is a selection of special events celebrated annually in Myanmar:

Jan-Feb *Amanda Pagoda Festival*. **Mar** *Indawgyi Festival*, Hopin; *Pindaya Cave Festival*. **Mar 2** *Peasant's Day*. **Apr** *Maha Thingyan* (New Year). **Jun-Jul** *Thihoshin Pagoda Festival*, Pakkoku. **Jul-Oct** *Buddhist Lent*. **Aug** *Taung Byone Festival*, Matara. **Oct** *Thadingyat Festival* (Festival of Light); *Elephant Dance Festival*, Kyaukse. **Nov** *Tazaaungdaing Festival*; *Fire Balloon Festival*, Taunggyi. **Dec** *Golden Spectacle Pagoda Festival*, Schwetaung.

SOCIAL CONVENTIONS: Handshaking is the normal form of greeting. Full names are used, preceded by *U* (pronounced *oo*) in the case of an older or well-respected man's name, *Aung* for younger men and *Ko* for adult males; a woman's name is preceded by *Daw*. Courtesy and respect for tradition and religion is expected; for instance, shoes and socks must be removed before entering any religious building and it is customary to remove shoes before entering a traditional home (in most modern residences this is no longer observed except in bedrooms). When sitting, avoid displaying the soles of the feet, as this is considered offensive. Small presents are acceptable and appreciated, although never expected. Shorts and mini-skirts should not be worn. Penalties for drug-trafficking range from five years' imprisonment to a death sentence. Homosexuality is illegal. **Tipping:** It is usual to give 5 to 10 per cent on hotel and restaurant bills. Taxi drivers do not expect a tip.

Business Profile

ECONOMY: The largest single sector of Myanmar's economy is agriculture, mainly livestock and fishing, but it continues to rely on traditional non-mechanised methods. Rice, generally the principal export earner, has diminished in importance in line with the continually depressed state of the world market in the commodity. Teak wood is the country's other main export (much of it felled and traded illegally). Other crops include oil seeds, sugar cane, cotton, jute and rubber. Myanmar has significant deposits of tin, copper, zinc, gemstones, silver and coal: commercial exploitation has recently begun. Although Myanmar's oil production, never substantial, has been falling during the last 10 years, there are thought to be large untapped reserves of both oil and gas inland. Domestically produced gas meets about half of the country's energy needs; hydroelectric power covers most of the rest. A wide range of manufactured goods is assembled locally but the majority are imported. Otherwise, Myanmar's industrial sector is mostly concerned with processing domestically produced raw materials. Further significant sources of revenue include opium trafficking and gemstone mining, both of which are largely controlled by the military government and have been mainly used to finance substantial arms purchases. There are few reliable economic statistics for Myanmar; inflation in 2002 was an estimated 26 per cent.

After years of political isolation, Myanmar became a member of ASEAN in July 1997. The government has tried to attract foreign investment by relaxing its previous tight controls over commercial activity. However, many potential investors are deterred by the government's appalling human rights record and the prospect of widespread international opprobrium. Myanmar's economic future depends largely on political developments.

BUSINESS: Lightweight suits are recommended during the day; jackets are needed for top-level meetings. Most commercial business transactions will be conducted in English. Business cards in Burmese script can be useful. The best time to visit is October to February. **Office hours:** Mon-Fri 0930-1630.

COMMERCIAL INFORMATION: There are over 20 Government Corporations dealing with all aspects of business. The Inspection and Agency Corporation in Yangon promotes business with foreign companies. For further information, contact the commercial section of the Embassy (see *Contact Addresses* section).

Climate

A monsoon climate with three main seasons. The hottest period is between February and May, with little or no rain. Rainy season exists from May to October and dry, cooler weather from October to February.

Required clothing: Lightweight cottons and linens throughout most of the year are required. A light raincoat or umbrella is needed during the rainy season. Warmer clothes are advised for coolest period and some evenings.

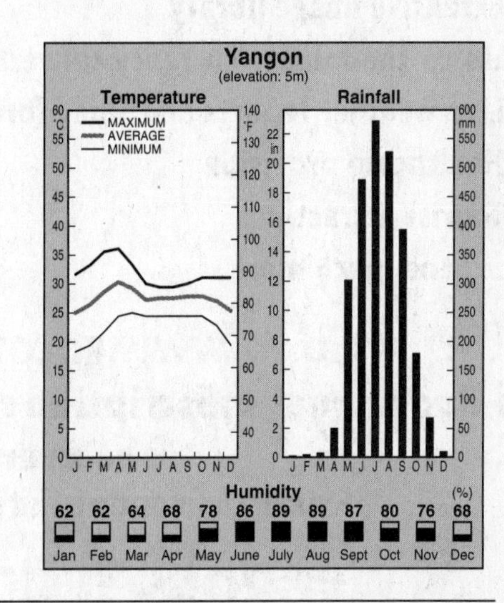

Namibia

LATEST TRAVEL ADVICE CONTACTS

British Foreign and Commonwealth Office
Tel: (0870) 606 0290 Website: www.fco.gov.uk
US Department of State
Website: http://travel.state.gov/travel
Canadian Department of Foreign Affairs and Int'l Trade
Tel: (1 800) 267 8376 Website: www.dfait-maeci.gc.ca

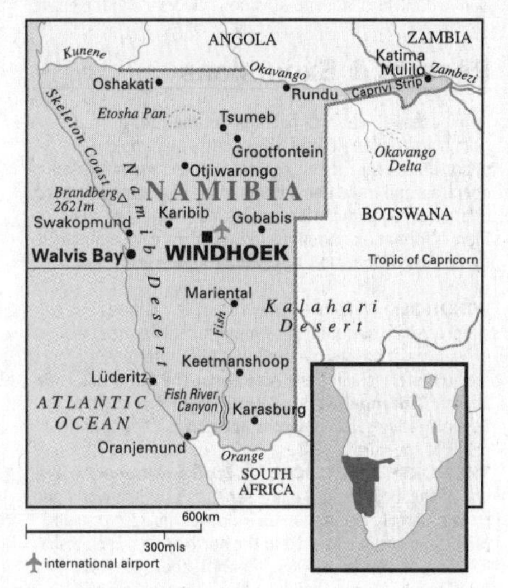

Location: Southwest Africa.

Country dialling code: 264.

Namibia Tourism Board
Ground Floor, Sanlam Centre, corner of Fidel Castro Street, Private Bag 13244, Windhoek, Namibia
Tel: (61) 290 6000. Fax: (61) 254 848.
E-mail: info@namibiatourism.com.na
Website: www.namibiatourism.com.na

High Commission for the Republic of Namibia
6 Chandos Street, London W1G 9LU, UK
Tel: (020) 7636 6244. Fax: (020) 7637 5694.
E-mail: namibia-high-comm@btconnect.com
Opening hours: Mon-Fri 0900-1300 and 1400-1700.

Namibia Tourism
Address as for High Commission.
Tel: (020) 7636 2924 *or* 2928. Fax: (020) 7636 2969.
E-mail: info@namibiatourism.co.uk
Website: www.namibiatourism.com.na

British High Commission
Street address: 116 Robert Mugabe Avenue, Windhoek, Namibia
Postal address: PO Box 22202, Windhoek, Namibia
Tel: (61) 274 800. Fax: (61) 228 895.
E-mail: windhoek.general@fco.gov.uk *or* visa.windhoek@fco.gov.uk
Website: www.britishhighcommission.gov.uk/namibia

Embassy of the Republic of Namibia
1605 New Hampshire Avenue, NW, Washington, DC 20009, USA
Tel: (202) 986 0540. Fax: (202) 986 0443.
E-mail: info@namibianembassyusa.org
Website: www.namibianembassyusa.org
Also deals with enquiries from Canada.

Embassy of the United States of America
Street address: 14 Lossen Street, Windhoek, Namibia
Postal address: Private Bag 12029, Windhoek, Namibia
Tel: (61) 221 601. Fax: (61) 229 792 (consular section).
E-mail: HealyKC2@state.gov *or* Consularwindho@state.gov
Website: www.usembassy.namib.com

The Canadian High Commission in Pretoria deals with enquiries relating to Namibia (see *South Africa* **section).**

TIMATIC CODES

Health
AMADEUS: **TI-DFT/WDH/HE**
GALILEO/WORLDSPAN: **TI-DFT/WDH/HE**
SABRE: **TIDFT/WDH/HE**

Visa
AMADEUS: **TI-DFT/WDH/VI**
GALILEO/WORLDSPAN: **TI-DFT/WDH/VI**
SABRE: **TIDFT/WDH/VI**

To access TIMATIC country information on Health and Visa regulations through the Computer Reservations System (CRS), type in the appropriate command line listed above.

Credit: © Namibia Tourism Board

General Information

AREA: 824,292 sq km (318,261 sq miles).
POPULATION: 1,826,854 (2001).
POPULATION DENSITY: 2.2 per sq km.
CAPITAL: Windhoek. **Population**: 216,000 (UN estimate 2001).
GEOGRAPHY: Namibia is in southwest Africa. It is a large and mainly arid country sharing borders with Angola to the north, Botswana to the east, South Africa to the south and, in the Caprivi Strip, a narrow panhandle of Namibian territory jutting from the northeast corner of the country, with Zambia and Zimbabwe. To the west is 1280km (795 miles) of some of the most desolate and lonely coastline in the world. The port of Walvis Bay, situated roughly halfway down Namibia's coast, was returned by South Africa to Namibian jurisdiction in February 1994. Along its entire length, the vast shifting sand dunes of the Namib Desert spread inland for 80 to 130km (50 to 80 miles). In the interior, the escarpment of a north-south plateau slopes away to the east and north into the vast interior sand basin of the Kalahari. In the far northwest, the 66,000 sq km (25,500 sq miles) of the Kaokoland mountains run along the coast, while further inland lies the Etosha Pan (a dried-out saline lake), surrounded by grasslands and bush which support a large and varied wildlife. The Etosha National Park & Game Reserve is one of the finest in Africa, in that it remains, to a large extent, free of human influence.
GOVERNMENT: Republic. Gained independence from South Africa in 1990. **Head of State:** President Hifikepunye Pohamba since 2005. **Head of Government**: Prime Minister Theo-Ben Gurirab since 2002.
LANGUAGE: English is the official language. Afrikaans is spoken by most people. German, Herero, Kavango, Nama and Ovambo (51 per cent) are also spoken.
RELIGION: Christian majority (90 per cent).
TIME: GMT + 2 (GMT + 1 from April to August).
ELECTRICITY: 220 volts AC, 50hz. Outlets are of the three-pin type.
COMMUNICATIONS: Telephone: IDD is available. Country code: 264. Outgoing international code: 00. **Mobile telephone:** GSM 900/1800 network in use. The main network provider is *MTC* (website: www.mtc.com.na). **Fax:** Most hotels have facilities. **Internet:** ISPs include *IML* (website: www.iml.com.na) and *NCS*. There are Internet cafes in Walvis Bay and Windhoek **Post:** Good postal service. Airmail to Europe takes approximately four days to two weeks. **Press:** Newspapers are printed Monday to Friday. English-language dailies include *The Namibian* and *The Windhoek Advertiser*; weeklies include the *Windhoek Observer*. *New Era* is printed twice weekly.
Radio: BBC World Service (website: www.bbc.co.uk/worldservice) and Voice of America (website: www.voa.gov) can be received. From time to time the frequencies change and the most up-to-date can be found online.

Passport/Visa

	Passport Required?	Visa Required?	Return Ticket Required?
Full British	Yes	No	Yes
Australian	Yes	No	Yes
Canadian	Yes	No	Yes
USA	Yes	No	Yes
Other EU	Yes	1	Yes
Japanese	Yes	No	Yes

Note: *Regulations and requirements may be subject to change at short notice, and you are advised to contact the appropriate diplomatic or consular authority before finalising travel arrangements. Details of these may be found at the head of this country's entry. Any numbers in the chart refer to the footnotes below.*

PASSPORTS: Passport valid for a minimum of six months after the date of departure from Namibia required by all.
VISAS: Required by all except the following for stays of up to 30 days:
(a) **1.** nationals of countries shown in the chart above, except nationals of Cyprus, Czech Republic, Estonia, Greece, Hungary, Latvia, Lithuania, Malta, Poland, Slovak Republic and Slovenia who *do* require a visa;
(b) nationals of Angola, Botswana, Brazil, Cuba, Iceland, Kenya, Lesotho, Liechtenstein, Malawi, Malaysia, Mozambique, New Zealand, Norway, Singapore, South Africa, Swaziland, Switzerland, Tanzania, Zambia and Zimbabwe;
(c) those continuing to a third country and not leaving the airport transit area.
Types of visa and cost: *Tourist*, *Business* and *Transit*: £20
Validity: Valid up to three months from date of issue for stays of up to three months from date of entry. Extensions for a further three months are available from the Ministry of Home Affairs in Windhoek.
Application to: Consulate (or Consular section at High Commission); see *Contact Addresses* section.
Application requirements: (a) Valid passport. (b) Completed application form. (c) Two passport-size photos. (d) Return or onward ticket or proof of accommodation. (e) Fee. *Private* (a)-(e) and, (f) Letter of invitation from Namibian resident, if applicable. *Business*: (a)-(e) and, (f) Company letter. (g) Letter from sponsoring company in Namibia.
Working days required: Three.
Temporary residence: Apply to the High Commission or Embassy; see *Contact Addresses* section.

Money

Currency: The Namibian Dollar (NAD) is in note denominations of NAD200, 100, 50 and 10. Coins are in denominations of NAD5 and 1. It is linked to the South African Rand (R) on a 1:1 basis (South African Rand = 100 cents). The South African Rand is also acceptable as currency in Namibia.
Currency exchange: Available in banks and at bureaux de change. A better rate of exchange can be obtained on travellers cheques than on cash.
Credit & debit cards: American Express, Diners Club, MasterCard and Visa are accepted. Check with your credit or debit card company for details of merchant acceptability and other services which may be available.
Travellers cheques: To avoid additional exchange rate charges, travellers are advised to take travellers cheques in US Dollars or South African Rand.
Currency restrictions: The import and export of local currency is limited to NAD50,000. The import of foreign currency is unlimited, provided declared on arrival. Export of foreign currency is unlimited up to amount imported and declared as long as the departure is within 12 months. No limits exist for travel between Botswana, Lesotho, Namibia, South Africa and Swaziland as these countries are members of the same common monetary area.
Exchange rate indicators: The following figures are included as a guide to the movements of the Namibian Dollar against Sterling and the US Dollar:

Date	Feb '04	May '04	Aug '04	Nov '04
£1.00=	12.87	12.50	11.90	11.05
$1.00=	7.07	7.00	6.46	5.83

Banking hours: Mon-Fri 0900-1530, Sat 0830-1100.

Duty Free

The following may be imported into Namibia by persons over 16 years of age without incurring customs duty:

Credit: © Namibia Tourism Board

400 cigarettes and 50 cigars and 250g of tobacco; 2l of wine and 1l of spirits; 50ml of perfume and 250ml of eau de toilette; gifts to the value of NAD50,000 (including value of imported duty free items).
Restricted items: Hunting rifles need a permit, issued by customs when entering the country. Handguns are not allowed.

Public Holidays

2005: Jan 1 New Year's Day. **Mar 21** Independence Day. **Mar 25-28** Easter. **May 1** Workers' Day. **May 4** Cassinga Day. **May 5** Ascension. **May 25** Africa Day (Anniversary of the OAU's Foundation). **Aug 26** Heroes' Day. **Dec 10** International Human Rights Day. **Dec 25** Christmas Day. **Dec 26** Family Day.
2006: Jan 1 New Year's Day. **Mar 21** Independence Day. **Apr 14-17** Easter. **May 1** Workers' Day. **May 4** Cassinga Day. **May 25** Ascension/Africa Day (Anniversary of the OAU's Foundation). **Aug 26** Heroes' Day. **Dec 10** International Human Rights Day. **Dec 25** Christmas Day. **Dec 26** Family Day.

Health

	Special Precautions?	Certificate Required?
Yellow Fever	Yes	1
Cholera	No	No
Typhoid & Polio	2	N/A
Malaria	3	N/A

Note: *Regulations and requirements may be subject to change at short notice, and you are advised to contact your doctor well in advance of your intended date of departure. Any numbers in the chart refer to the footnotes below.*

1: A yellow fever vaccination certificate is required from travellers arriving from infected areas. Those countries or parts of countries that were included in the endemic zones in Africa and South America are regarded by the Namibian authorities as infected. Travellers on scheduled airlines whose flights have originated outside areas regarded as infected but have passed through such areas in transit are not required to possess a certificate, provided they have remained at the scheduled airport or in the adjacent town during transit. All passengers with unscheduled airlines whose flights originated or passed in transit through an infected area are required to possess a certificate. The certificate is not insisted upon in the case of children under one year of age, but such infants may be subject to surveillance.
2: Typhoid may occur.
3: Malaria risk exists in the northern regions and in Otjozondjupa and Omaheke from November to May/June and along the Kavango and Kunene rivers throughout the year. The predominant *falciparum* strain is reported to be resistant to chloroquine. The recommended prophylaxis is chloroquine plus proguanil.
Food & drink: Mains water is normally chlorinated and, whilst safe, may cause mild abdominal upsets. Bottled water is available and is advised for the first few weeks of the stay. Drinking water outside main cities and towns may be contaminated and sterilisation is advisable. Milk is pasteurised and dairy products are safe for consumption. Local meat, poultry, seafood, fruit and vegetables are generally considered safe to eat.
Other risks: *Bilharzia* (schistosomiasis) is endemic. Avoid swimming and paddling in fresh water (also because of the presence of crocodiles); swimming pools which are well chlorinated and well maintained are safe. *Natural foci* of plague have been reported in Namibia. *Hepatitis A* can occur. *Hepatitis B* is hyperendemic.
Health care: Anti-bite serums for snakes and scorpions are advised. Health insurance is essential.

Travel - International

AIR: Namibia's national airline is *Air Namibia (SW)* (website: www.airnamibia.com), which provides flights from Windhoek to Frankfurt. Other airlines include *LTU International Airways*, *Lufthansa* and *South African Airways*. *British Airways* also flies to Namibia.
Approximate flight times: From *Frankfurt* to Windhoek is nine hours.
International airports: *Windhoek (WDH)* (Windhoek International Airport) is 40km (25 miles) from the city (travel time - 35 minutes). Buses go to the city. Airport facilities include restaurant, bars, snack bar, duty free shops, post office, bureau de change and car hire. Buses return to the airport from the Kalahari Sands Hotel in Windhoek. Taxis are also available (travel time - 40 minutes).
Departure tax: None.
SEA: There is a modern deep-water harbour at Walvis Bay. There is also a small port at Lüderitz.
RAIL: The railway network linking most towns in Namibia to Windhoek is joined to the RSA rail system at Ariamsvlei, Namibia. There is one train per week, with connections from Cape Town and Johannesburg as follows: Johannesburg–De Aar–Keetmanshoop–Windhoek, and Cape Town–Windhoek.
ROAD: A tarred road runs from the south through Upington in South Africa to Grünau, where it connects with the tarred road from Cape Town. The untarred road from the east from Botswana to Gobabis is currently being upgraded as part of a new trans-Kalahari highway. The trans-Caprivi highway runs through the Caprivi strip and via Botswana into Zimbabwe. **Bus:** Overnight services are available from Windhoek to Cape Town and Johannesburg; these depart approximately three times a week. Other services go to Botswana and Zambia.

Travel - Internal

Note: If travelling along the Caprivi Strip, stay on the tarred road. Wildlife and livestock pose a serious hazard, so it is best to avoid driving at night.
AIR: Flying is the quickest and often the most economical way to travel around the country. *Air Namibia (SW)* links all of the major towns in the territory. Planes can also be chartered.
RAIL: The main rail routes in Namibia are Windhoek–Keetmanshoop–De Aar, Walvis Bay–Swakopmund–Windhoek–Tsumeb, and Lüderitz–Keetmanshoop. First- and second-class carriages are available on these routes. Light refreshments are offered on some services. On overnight voyages, seats in first-class compartments convert to four couchettes and those in second class to six couchettes. Local passenger and goods trains run daily. Children under two years of age travel free and children aged two to 11 pay half fare. The *Desert Express*, a luxury train aimed at tourists, runs between Swakopmund and Windhoek. The 19 hour 30 minute journey includes several stops which give travellers the opportunity to watch lions feeding, see the Namib Desert, walk in the sand dunes and admire the stars. A three-course dinner and overnight accommodation are included in the ticket price.
ROAD: Traffic drives on the left. Roads are generally well maintained. There are 64,799km (40,266 miles) of road, of which 7841km (4872 miles) are tarred. **Bus:** Services are not well developed and there is no transport except **taxis** in Windhoek. A luxury bus service exists between Windhoek and all major centres in Namibia and South Africa.
Car hire: Self-drive cars are available at the airport and Windhoek city centre, as well as some other major centres.
Documentation: An International Driving Permit is required.

Accommodation

HOTELS: There are good-quality hotels both in Windhoek and Swakopmund, and some scattered throughout the country. There are a number of 4-star hotels in Windhoek and one in Etosha: all provide modern conference facilities. In Swakopmund, there is one 4-star hotel. Hotel accommodation is limited and visitors are advised to book well in advance. For further information, contact HAN (Hotel Association of Namibia), PO Box 86078, Windhoek (tel/fax: (61) 222 904; e-mail: han@mweb.com.na; website: www.hannamibia.com). **Grading**: Hotels are graded on a scale of **1 to 5 stars**.
LODGES: In the Etosha National Park and other game reserves, there are well-equipped rest camps with comfortable accommodation. Reservations for the national parks can be made with Namibia Wildlife Resorts Ltd. (website: www.nwr.com.na).
CAMPING: Some of the national parks have camping facilities, notably the Etosha National Park & Game Reserve. There is also camping at Ai-Ais, a hot-spring area towards the South African border, Hardap Dam in the south, Gross Barmen near Okahandja, Popa Falls in Kavango, in the Namib-Naukluft Park and at various places along the coast.

Resorts & Excursions

Namibia has 10 national parks, under the control of Namibian Wildlife Resorts. The country has ample opportunities for the self-drive tourist and many local tour operators and travel consultants offer interesting packages or arrange tailor-made tours covering a variety of areas. More information on tours and excursions can be obtained from Namibia Tourism (see *Contact Addresses* section).

WINDHOEK: Windhoek is the attractive capital of the country and is surrounded by mountains. Like other towns in Namibia, it has several examples of German colonial architecture, including the **Alte Feste**, the **Christuskirche** and the **Tintenpalast** (Ink Palace), the former colonial administrative building. **Gross Barmen** is a hot-spring resort to the north.
THE NORTHERN REGION: The **Etosha National Park** is one of the most famous game sanctuaries in the world and remains largely free of human influence. Its 22,270 sq km (8599 sq miles) are located in the north around the Etosha Pan. This depression is 1065m (3494ft) above sea level, forming a huge, salty hollow which is only occasionally filled with water and surrounded by grasslands and bush. There are vast stocks of wildlife, particularly elephants, lions, zebras, giraffes, wildebeest, springboks, kudus, gemsboks or oryxes, hyenas, jackals, leopards and cheetahs. It is open throughout the year. There are well-equipped camps with comfortable rondavel accommodation and camping facilities. **Waterberg Plateau Park**, Namibia's only mountain resort, has striking red sandstone cliffs and is home to many rare and endangered species of game. It is a popular stopover for visitors on their way to Etosha National Park. There are good facilities here for game viewing and a number of hiking trails. Also en route to Etosha is **Lake Otjikoto**, 24km (15 miles) northeast of the mining town of **Tsumeb**. Once fabled to be bottomless, it is now known to be 55m (140ft) deep and contains some rare fish. Northeast of here is **Kaudom Game Reserve** in Kavango, where there are two camping areas and where blue wildebeest, elephant, lion, cheetah, leopard and various species of antelope wander. Further northeast, the **Popa Falls Rest Camp**, where crocodiles and hippos bask in the water, is a popular haven on the banks of the **Okavango River**. About 12km (7 miles) to the south is **Mahango Game Reserve**, catering to day visitors only, with elephants, buffalo and lechwe. Heading still further northeast is **East Caprivi**, bordered by the **Kwando**, **Linyanti**, **Chobe** and **Zambezi** rivers. This region of swamps and flood plains has several safari lodges and offers boat trips, fishing, hiking and game viewing, particularly in the **Mudumu** and **Mamili National Parks**.
The town of **Katima Mulilo**, on the banks of the **Zambezi River**, has an **Arts Centre** where visitors may purchase varous handicrafts such as baskets, bracelets, malachite and soapstone carvings. There are also game-viewing cruises down the Zambezi River on the **Zambezi Queen**, a 56m (142ft) riverboat which departs from Zambezi Lodge. Flights to Victoria Falls, less than one hour's flight away, are available from Katima Mulilo.
THE SOUTHERN REGION: Fish River Canyon is in the south of the country and only second in dimensions to the Grand Canyon. Situated between Seeheim and **Ai-Ais** (a hot spring resort), the gigantic cleft stretches for 150km (93 miles) and is up to 27km (17 miles) wide and up to 550m (1804ft) deep in parts. Trips are best arranged from **Keetsmanshoop**. Situated on the **Fish River** is **Hardap Dam**. The **Kokerboom (Quiver Tree) Forest**, located 14km (9 miles) northeast of Keetmanshoop on Gariganus Farm, features *kokerbooms* , which belong to the aloe family and grow up to 8m (26ft) and were often used by the San people to make quivers for their arrows (thus 'quiver trees'). The trees create a bizarrely elegant effect and are now a protected plant in Namibia.
Lüderitz is a small port in the southern Namib region, with much charm and atmosphere from bygone days of diamond prospecting.
THE NAMIB REGION: The **Namib Desert** appears more like the surface of the moon with its towering sand dunes (some of them 300m/1000ft high), and is believed to be the

oldest desert in the world. **Namib Naukluft Park**, at 49,768 sq km (19,215 sq miles), is the fourth-largest conservation area in the world. There are campsites in the Namib Desert at **Sesriem**, where the **Tsauchab River** disappears down a deep gorge in the plain (leaving pools of water where many animals feed) and in the Naukluft. The nearby **Sossusvlei** area is an ocean of sand dunes up to 300m (762ft) high, stretching as far as the eye can see and is home to countless water birds in the rainy season and oryxes, springbok and ostriches during the dry season.
The delightful little seaside resort of **Swakopmund** is situated in the middle of Namibia's coastline, surrounded by desert and sea. Further north, the **Skeleton Coast** is a strange desert shoreline with massive dunes and treacherous rocks, the name relating to the number of ships wrecked and lost in the vicinity. The cold Benguela current keeps the coastline cool, damp and rain-free for most of the year, with a thick coastal fog.
Inland, the **Brandberg/Twyfelfontein** area has some very ancient rock engravings and paintings, of which the **White Lady of the Brandberg** is the best known. The **Petrified Forest** and the **Welwitschia mirabilis** plant are other attractions.

Sport & Activities

Northwest of Usakos, rising out of the Namib, is the 2000m (6562ft) *Spitzkoppe* where there is good **mountaineering**. Some of the coastal and river areas provide good opportunities for **fishing**, especially in the waters of the northern Caprivi strip. There are several **hiking** trails in the *Fish River Canyon*, the *Naukluft Mountains*, the *Ugab River* and the *Waterberg Plateau Park*. **Sandgliding**, a pastime popular amongst local people, is available in desert areas. **Balloon safaris** are organised by some tour operators. There are excellent opportunities for **birdwatching**. Namibia's flat terrain and vast open spaces provide good **off-road cycling**.

Social Profile

FOOD & DRINK: Restaurants and cafes reflect the German influence on Namibia, and most dining rooms offer a reasonable choice of local and continental cuisine. They are found mainly in the major cities. A speciality of Namibia is game, in all its variations; worth a try are *biltong* (air-dried meat) and *Rauchfleisch* (smoked meat).
NIGHTLIFE: In the central area of Windhoek, there are restaurants, cafes, a cinema and a theatre.
SHOPPING: Windhoek has a selection of fashionable shops. Local crafts can be bought in some specialised shpps and at the Windhoek Street Market, held every second Saturday. Good buys include diamonds and semi-precious stones, *Herero* dolls, hand-carved wooden objects, jewellery, *karosse* rugs, liqueur chocolates made in Windhoek and Swakara garments. **Shopping hours**: Mon-Fri 0900-1700, Sat 0900-1300. Some bigger supermarkets are also open Sun 1100-1300 and 1600-1900.
SPECIAL EVENTS: For a full list of special events occurring in Namibia during 2005, contact Namibia Tourism (see *Contact Addresses* section). The following is a selection of special events celebrated annually in Namibia:
Apr *Windhoek Carnival*. **Aug** *Maherero Day*, Okahandja; *Küste Karnival*, Swakopmund. **Sep** *Windhoek Agricultural, Commercial & Industrial Show*. **Oct** *Oktoberfest*.
SOCIAL CONVENTIONS: Western customs prevail; normal courtesies should be shown when visiting someone's home. **Tipping**: 10 per cent is customary.

Business Profile

ECONOMY: The mining industry is the strongest part of the economy, the kernel of Namibia's export economy, and accounts for about 20 per cent of GDP. Extracted minerals include silver, copper, lead, zinc, tungsten and uranium, and Namibia is also the source of some of the world's highest-quality diamonds. A much larger proportion of the workforce – 45 per cent against 4 per cent engaged in mining – is engaged in agriculture and fishing. Livestock dominates the agricultural sector, although a substantial proportion of the agricultural workforce is engaged in subsistence farming of crops such as wheat, maize and millet. Agriculture is becoming increasingly difficult over time as the desert encroaches on previously fertile soil; it has also suffered chronic damage from the recurrent drought afflicting the whole region. Namibia enjoys exceptionally rich fishing grounds, although stocks of pilchard – the main species in the area – have been depleted by uncontrolled fishing in the period before Namibian independence. Commercial shipping activity has picked up since the return of Walvis Bay, the best deep-water port in Africa on the Atlantic side, to Namibian jurisdiction (the apartheid government in Pretoria tried to

Credit: © Namibia Tourism Board

hang on to the port, even after independence). The establishment of a free-trade zone at Walvis Bay has further enhanced its status as a centre for regional trade. Manufacturing is mainly devoted to processing of raw materials and agricultural produce. Most of the country's trade is with South Africa, essentially involving the exchange of raw materials for manufactured goods. Recent economic policy has seen many former state enterprises transferred to the private sector. The economy has performed reasonably well during the last decade with average annual growth of between 3 and 5 per cent; inflation is currently 7 per cent. Other than South Africa, the UK is the only other significant trading partner, followed far behind by the other larger EU countries, Côte d'Ivoire and the USA.
BUSINESS: Suits should be worn in winter, safari suits in summer. Prior appointments are necessary. English is widely spoken in business circles. The best times for business are February to May and September to November.
Office hours: Mon-Fri 0800-1700.
COMMERCIAL INFORMATION: The following organisations can offer advice: Namibia Chamber of Commerce and Industry, PO Box 9355, Windhoek (tel: (61) 228 809; fax: (61) 228 009; e-mail: info@ncci.na; website: www.ncci.org.na).

Climate

The cold Benguela current keeps the coast of the Namib Desert cool, damp and free of rain for most of the year, with a thick coastal fog. Inland, all the rain falls in summer (November to April). Summer temperatures are high while the altitude means that nights are cool. Winter nights can be fairly cold, but days are generally warm and pleasant.
Required clothing: Light cottons, with slightly heavier cottons or light woollens for evening. Inland, shoes are essential during the day as the ground is very hot.

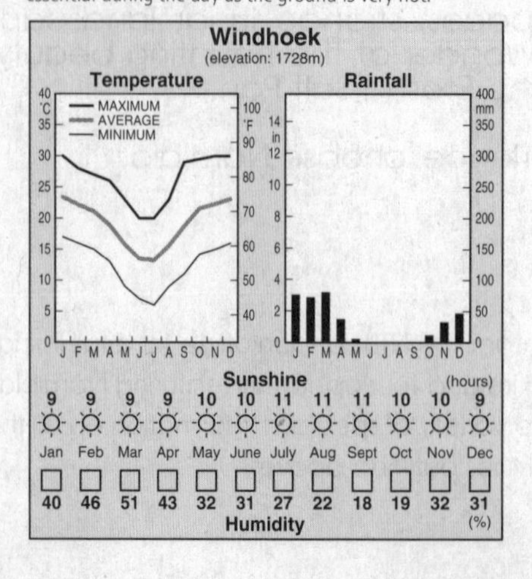

Nauru

LATEST TRAVEL ADVICE CONTACTS

British Foreign and Commonwealth Office
Tel: (0870) 606 0290 Website: www.fco.gov.uk
US Department of State
Website: http://travel.state.gov/travel
Canadian Department of Foreign Affairs and Int'l Trade
Tel: (1 800) 267 8376 Website: www.dfait-maeci.gc.ca

Anna Point
Anabar
Uaboe
Ijuw
Denig
NAURU
Buada Lagoon
Anibare Bay
Aiwo
YAREN
Menang Point
Menang
PACIFIC OCEAN
4km
2mls
international airport

Location: Central Pacific.

Country dialling code: 674.

Consulate General of the Republic of Nauru
Level 7, 128 Exhibition Street, Melbourne, Victoria 3000, Australia
Tel: (3) 9653 5709. Fax: (3) 9654 4738.
E-mail: consulate@nauru.com.au
Website: www.dfat.gov.au/geo/nauru
Customs & Immigration Department of Justice, Government Building, Yaren District, Nauru 4443152
Tel: 444 3152. Fax: 444 3832.
South Pacific Tourism Organisation
Street address: Level 3, FNPF Place, 343-359 Victoria Parade, Suva, Fiji
Postal address: PO Box 13119, Suva, Fiji
Tel: (679) 330 4177. Fax: (679) 330 1995.
Website: www.spto.org
Also deals with enquiries from the UK.
The British Embassy in Suva deals with enquiries relating to Nauru (see *Fiji* section).
The US Embassy in Suva deals with enquiries relating to Nauru (see *Fiji* section).
Nauru Permanent Mission of the Republic of Nauru to the United Nations
800 2nd Avenue, Suite 400D, New York, New York 10017, USA
Tel: (212) 937 0074. Fax: (212) 937 0079.
E-mail: nauru_ny@np1.net
Website: www.un.int/nauru
Canadian High Commission to Nauru
c/o The Canadian High Commission, Commonwealth Avenue, Canberra, ACT 2600, Australia
Tel: (2) 6270 4000 *or* (613) 944 9136. Fax: (2) 6273 3285 *or* 6270 4060/81 (consular section).
E-mail: cnbra@dfait-maeci.gc.ca *or* sydney.immigration@dfait-maeci.gc.ca (visa enquiries only).
Website: www.canada.org.au

General Information

AREA: 21.3 sq km (8.2 sq miles).
POPULATION: 11,845 (official estimate 2000).
POPULATION DENSITY: 556 per sq km.
CAPITAL: Aiwo: 600 (1992).

TIMATIC CODES

Health	AMADEUS: **TI-DFT/INU/HE** GALILEO/WORLDSPAN: **TI-DFT/INU/HE** SABRE: **TIDFT/INU/HE**
Visa	AMADEUS: **TI-DFT/INU/VI** GALILEO/WORLDSPAN: **TI-DFT/INU/VI** SABRE: **TIDFT/INU/VI**

To access TIMATIC country information on Health and Visa regulations through the Computer Reservations System (CRS), type in the appropriate command line listed above.

GEOGRAPHY: Nauru, the world's smallest republic, is an oval-shaped outcrop, situated in the Central Pacific, west of Kiribati, surrounded by a reef which is exposed at low tide. Although there is no deep-water harbour on the island, offshore moorings are reputedly the deepest in the world. A century of phosphate mining has stripped four-fifths of the land area, and has left the central plateau, which rises to 56m (213ft), infertile and unpopulated: a barren terrain of jagged coral pinnacles which stand 15m (49ft) high. The island has a fertile coastal strip 150 to 300m (492 to 984ft) wide, where there are coconut palms, pandanus trees and indigenous hardwoods such as the tomano. On the land surrounding Buada lagoon, bananas, pineapples and some vegetables are grown. Some secondary vegetation grows over the coral pinnacles which intersperse the island's beaches.
GOVERNMENT: Republic. Gained independence from Australia in 1968. **Head of State and Government**: President Ludwig Scotty since 2004.
LANGUAGE: Nauruan and English are spoken.
RELIGION: Christian, mostly Nauruan Protestant Church. There is also a significant Roman Catholic minority.
TIME: GMT + 12.
ELECTRICITY: 240 volts AC, 50Hz.
COMMUNICATIONS: Telephone: IDD is available. Country code: 674. Outgoing international calls must be made through the operator. **Mobile telephone:** Although an AMPS network is in operation, there are no facilities at the moment for travellers to use their handsets on the island. **Fax:** Available from post office and some hotels/shops. **Post:** Airmail to Europe takes up to one week. **Internet:** ISPs include *VPM Internet Services*; there is one Internet cafe on the island, and access to the Internet may be available in hotels. **Press:** The main newspaper is the *Nasero Bulletin*, published fortnightly in Nauruan and English. Others are the *Central Star News* and *The Nauru Chronicle*.
Radio: BBC World Service (website: www.bbc.co.uk/worldservice) and Voice of America (website: www.voa.gov) can be received. From time to time the frequencies change and the most up-to-date can be found online.

Passport/Visa

	Passport Required?	Visa Required?	Return Ticket Required?
Full British	Yes	Yes/1	Yes
Australian	Yes	Yes/1	Yes
Canadian	Yes	Yes/1	Yes
USA	Yes	Yes/1	Yes
Other EU	Yes	Yes/1	Yes
Japanese	Yes	Yes/1	Yes

Note: Regulations and requirements may be subject to change at short notice, and you are advised to contact the appropriate diplomatic or consular authority before finalising travel arrangements. Details of these may be found at the head of this country's entry. Any numbers in the chart refer to the footnotes below.

PASSPORTS: Passport valid for six months from the date of entry required by all.
VISAS: Required by all except the following:
(a) nationals of New Zealand for stays of up to three months and Korea (Rep) for stays of up to 14 days;
(b) transit passengers continuing their journey by the same or first connecting aircraft, provided they hold onward or return documentation and do not leave the airport.
Note: 1. Nationals of the following countries may obtain a tourist visa on arrival for stays of up to 30 days, provided holding valid passport, return or onward tickets, sufficient funds and a confirmed hotel booking: Australia, The Bahamas, Barbados, Canada, Cayman Islands, Fiji, Guam, Ireland, Japan, Korea (Rep), Montserrat, Peru, St Kitts & Nevis, St Lucia, St Vincent & the Grenadines, Sierra Leone, Singapore, Turks & Caicos Islands, the UK and the USA.
Types of visa and cost: *Visitor* and *Business*. Visitor's visas should be organised by the sponsor in Nauru. Passport details should be given so that a visa letter may be sent directly. Visas are issued free of charge.
Validity: 30 days.
Application to: Consulate General.
Application requirements: (a) Letter giving details such as purpose of visit and dates of intended stay. There is no application form. (b) Proof of return or onward ticket and valid documents for next destination. (c) Evidence of prearranged hotel booking or details of other accommodation. (d) Valid passport (should not be sent with application, but presented on arrival). (e) For business visas, letter from Nauruan company or individual.
Working days required: Four to five (tourist visas); five to six (business visas); it is, however, recommended that applications are made at least two weeks prior to date of travel.
Temporary residence: Contact the Principal Immigration Officer in Nauru (tel: (674) 444 3133). A visa can be sent by post; no fee is charged.

Money

Currency: The Australian Dollar (A$) is legal tender. For further information and exchange rates, see *Australia* section.
Currency exchange: Available in banks. There are no ATMs on the island.
Credit & debit cards: American Express, Diners Club and Visa are accepted. Check with your credit or debit card company for details of merchant acceptability and other services which may be available.
Travellers cheques: These can be exchanged in banks and some hotels.
Currency restrictions: The import of local and foreign currency (including travellers cheques) is unlimited, provided declared on arrival. The export of local currency is limited to A$2500; severe penalties can be incurred if this rule is infringed and the proper authority from the Bank of Nauru is not obtained. The export of foreign currency is unlimited.
Banking hours: Mon-Thurs 0900-1600, Fri 0900-1640.

Duty Free

The following goods may be imported into Nauru by those over 16 years of age without incurring customs duty:
400 cigarettes or 50 cigars or 450g of tobacco; three bottles of alcoholic beverage (if visitor is over 21 years of age).
Prohibited items: Explosives, firearms and pornography, drugs and weapons, dangerous drugs, pornographic films and literature.
Restricted exports: Nauruan artefacts may not be exported without a licence.

Public Holidays

2005: Jan 1 New Year's Day. **Jan 31** Independence Day. **Mar 25-28** Easter. **May 17** Constitution Day. **Oct 26** Angam Day. **Dec 25-26** Christmas.
2006: Jan 1 New Year's Day. **Jan 31** Independence Day. **Apr 14-17** Easter. **May 17** Constitution Day. **Oct 26** Angam Day. **Dec 25-26** Christmas.

Health

	Special Precautions?	Certificate Required?
Yellow Fever	No	1
Cholera	No	2
Typhoid & Polio	3	N/A
Malaria	No	N/A

Note: Regulations and requirements may be subject to change at short notice, and you are advised to contact your doctor well in advance of your intended date of departure. Any numbers in the chart refer to the footnotes below.

1: A yellow fever vaccination certificate is required from travellers over one year of age coming from infected areas. (This includes transit passengers not leaving the airport.)
2: Vaccination may be required.
3: Typhoid may occur in rural areas with poor sanitation. Immunisation is advised.
Food & drink: Mains water is normally chlorinated and, whilst relatively safe, may cause mild abdominal upsets. Bottled water is available and is advised for the first few weeks of stay. Drinking water outside main cities and towns may be contaminated and sterilisation is advisable. Local meat, poultry, seafood, fruit and vegetables are generally considered safe to eat.
Other risks: Immunisations are sometimes recommended for *hepatitis A, B, TB* and *diphtheria*. Outbreaks of *Dengue fever* and *Japanese encephalitis* have also been reported. *Sea snakes, poisonous fish* and *corals* may present hazards to the bather.
Health care: Nauru has 14 GPs, all of whom work at either one of the two hospitals – Nauru General Hospital or Nauru Phosphate Corporation Hospital. There are no medical specialists, and serious or complicated cases are sent to Australia for treatment via *Air Nauru*. Travellers are advised to take out full health insurance prior to departure.

Travel - International

AIR: Nauru's national airline is *Air Nauru (ON)*; its destinations include Brisbane and Melbourne in Australia, Guam and Fiji. It also offers charter services to Sydney, Australia and Norfolk Island. There are a number of passes available, including the *Pacific Air Pass* and the *Pacific Wanderer Pass*. *The Visit the South Pacific Pass* is valid for many airlines operating in the South Pacific, including most of the larger ones, such as *Air Caledonie, Air Marshall Islands, Air Nauru, Air Niugingi, Air Pacific, Air Vanuatu, Polynesian Airlines, Qantas, Royal Tongan Airlines* and *Solomon Airlines*. Offering reductions of up to 40 per cent on normal airfares, this sector-based pass allows for flexible island-hopping between the destinations of the Cook Islands, Fiji, Nauru, New Caledonia, Samoa, Tahiti, Tonga, Vanuatu and the more remote Melanesian and Micronesian islands, together with major cities in Australia (Brisbane, Melbourne and Sydney) and New Zealand (Auckland, Christchurch and Wellington). It is only available for people resident outside of the South Pacific. The journey must be started outside the South Pacific and only one stopover in Australia is allowed. A minimum of two sectors must be bought before departure (extra sectors can be purchased en route). There is a maximum of one pass per person, and passes must be used within six months of the first day of travel. Children under 12 years of age pay 75 per cent of the adult fare. For details and conditions, contact the South Pacific Tourist Organisation (see *Contact Addresses* section).
Approximate flight times: From *London* to Nauru Island is 31 hours, including stopovers in Hong Kong, Manila, Guam and Pohnpei.
International airports: *Nauru International Airport (INU)*. There are buses to the town available after every arriving flight, costing approximately A$1. Taxis are also available. Airport facilities include snack bar, gift shops and tourist information.
Departure tax: A$25 per person on departure. Transit passengers and those under 12 years of age are exempt.
SEA: The international port is Nauru. Main sealinks are with Australia, New Zealand and Japan. Coastal hazards force commercial vessels to moor some way offshore.

Travel - Internal

RAIL: There are just over 5km (3 miles) of railway to serve the phosphate mining area.
ROAD: A sealed road, 19km (12 miles) long, circles the island and there are several miles of road running inland to Buada District and the phosphate areas. Traffic drives on the left. The island speed limit is 50kmph (30 mph). **Bus:** Buses run from the hotels. **Car hire:** This is available.
Documentation: A national driving licence will suffice.

Accommodation

There are a few hotels on Nauru situated on both the east and west coasts. Facilities include restaurants and nearby shops. Contact the South Pacific Tourism Organisation for further details (see *Contact Addresses* section).

Resorts & Excursions

Since the extensive phosphate fields were found in the 1900s, the island has been mainly used for the mining of the natural fertiliser. The *Nauru Phosphate Corporation* is the largest employer. The population lives mainly on the coast or on the shore of **Buada Lagoon**, the remainder of the island being used for phosphate extraction. As yet, little is given over purely to tourism, although the situation is slowly changing. In **Yaren**, there are remains of Japanese guns, bunkers and pillboxes left over from World War II. **Anibore Bay** is probably the most beautiful beach on the island, although the sea currents are dangerous.

Sport & Activities

Watersports: Fishing by net or by line is, of course, an essential part of life, and **swimming** is possible at either of the two channels cut into the surrounding reef and in the boat harbour when the ships are not being handled. A coral reef, along with shipwrecks from World War II, provides good **diving**.
Other: The national game is **Australian rules football**, which is played all through Saturday on the sports field just north of Buada Lagoon (in the middle of the island); there is no charge for spectators. The **Frigate bird game** is the most distinctive of the traditional sports, and there are several popular ball games and wrestling games of local origin. In recent years, Nauru's international success in **weightlifting** has created a national interest and many Nauruans are involved in the sport. **Tennis**, **basketball**, **softball** and **volleyball** courts are also available. There is a 9-hole **golf** course. **Snooker** can be played at the *East End Club*.

Social Profile

FOOD & DRINK: Cultivation is difficult on Nauru owing to the poor soil, irregular rainfall and the impact of mining. There are no local fruit or vegetables and most of the available food is canned, refined and imported. Fresh food is limited to a small amount of fish and, very occasionally, beef. The island is, however, very well served with restaurants with a wide range of international dishes, especially Chinese, but little is fresh. The Menen Hotel has a restaurant offering a range of western food. Most international brands of alcohol are available.
NIGHTLIFE: This mostly revolves around the dining rooms and bars. There is one cinema located in the southern part of the island.
SHOPPING: There is a number of shops on the island, although service and goods at government shops tend to be of poor quality. There are numerous supermarkets, the

A B C D E F G H I J K L M N O P Q R S T U V W X Y Z

largest being Capelle's, but visitors should buy essential goods in advance. There are no sales taxes but customs duties are now levied on a range of goods. **Shopping hours**: Mon-Fri 0900-1700, Sat 0900-1300.

SPECIAL EVENTS: The following is a selection of special events celebrated annually in Naura:

Jan 31 *Independence Day*. **May 17** *Constitution Day*.
Oct 26 *Angam Day* (Angam (Homecoming) commemorates the times in Nauru's history when the population returned to 1500, thought to be the minimum number required for survival).

SOCIAL CONVENTIONS: The island has a casual atmosphere, in which diplomacy and tact are always preferable to confrontation; European customs continue alongside local traditions. **Tipping**: Not generally practised.

Business Profile

ECONOMY: Until a few years ago, Nauru's economy depended almost entirely on the extraction and sale of phosphates, over which the Nauru Phosphate Corporation has a monopoly. Much of the revenue was invested in anticipation of the eventual exhaustion of the resource. Now that this has occurred, the Government, in common with a number of other small island states, looked to offshore financial services to sustain the economy. However, the laxity of Nauru's newly established tax and financial disclosure arrangements attracted much foreign money of allegedly uncertain or dubious origin. From 1997 onwards, the OECD (Organisation for Economic Co-operation and Development, the organisation representing the world's richest two dozen economies) took the lead in constructing an international regime to crack down on money-laundering. Most of the several dozen countries loosely described as 'tax havens' have complied with the new system: Nauru is one of the seven which have refused to do so. Accordingly, in April 2002, it was 'named and shamed' and subject to a number of sanctions. There was some hope that a fishing industry could be developed following the completion of a new harbour, but the industry has failed to take off and Nauru accrues more revenue from selling licences to foreign fleets. Nauru has few other strings to its economic bow and in 2004 was facing chaos amid political strife and the collapse of the island's telecommunications system. There is some agriculture, exploiting what little fertile land is available. Although the island has a benign climate and attractive features (those remaining after the damage done during the phosphate mining era), the potential of any tourism industry is limited by Nauru's remoteness and lack of infrastructure. In 2002, Nauru found a novel source of income by accepting asylum seekers (mostly from Iraq and Afghanistan) who had been rejected by Australia. Nauru took 400 of them, and was paid $30 million by Canberra. Australia and New Zealand are the island's main trading partners, and supply almost all basic and capital goods. There are now serious questions about the long-term viability of Nauru's economy.

BUSINESS: Shirt and smart trousers or skirt will suffice; more formal wear is needed only for very special occasions. English and French are widely spoken. The best time to visit is May to October. **Office hours**: Mon-Fri 0800-1200 and 1330-1630.

COMMERCIAL INFORMATION: The following organisation can offer advice: Bank of Nauru, PO Box 289, Civic Centre, Nauru (tel: 444 3238 *or* 3267; fax: 444 3203).

Climate

A maritime, equatorial climate tempered by northeast trade winds from March to October. The wettest period is during the westerly monsoon from November to February. If global warming causes sea levels to rise, the habitable low-lying land areas will be at risk from tidal surges and flooding. **Required clothing:** Lightweight cottons and linens with waterproofing all year.

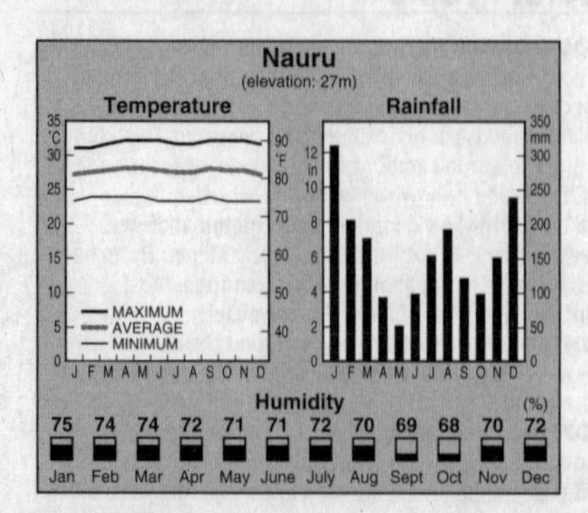

Nepal

LATEST TRAVEL ADVICE CONTACTS

British Foreign and Commonwealth Office
Tel: (0870) 606 0290 Website: www.fco.gov.uk
US Department of State
Website: http://travel.state.gov/travel
Canadian Department of Foreign Affairs and Int'l Trade
Tel: (1 800) 267 8376 Website: www.dfait-maeci.gc.ca

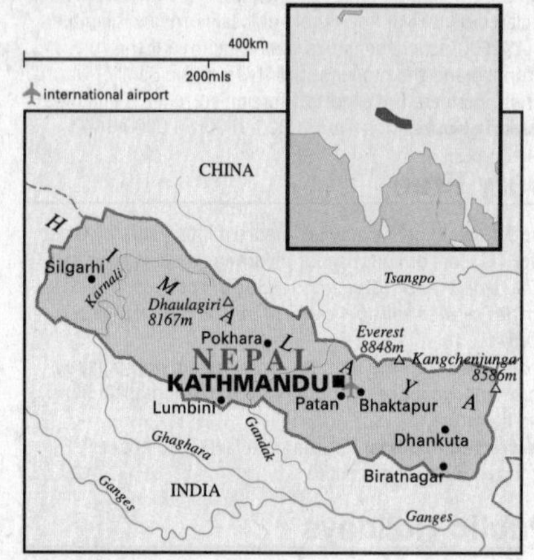

Location: South Asia.

Country dialling code: 977.

Nepal Tourism Board
Bhrikuti Mandap, PO Box 11018, Kathmandu, Nepal
Tel: (1) 425 6909 *or* 6229. Fax: (1) 4256 910.
E-mail: info@ntb.org.np
Website: www.welcomenepal.com

Royal Nepalese Embassy
12A Kensington Palace Gardens, London W8 4QU, UK
Tel: (020) 7229 1594 *or* 6321. Fax: (020) 7792 9861.
E-mail: rnelondon@btconnect.com
Website: www.nepembassy.org.uk
Opening hours: Mon-Fri 0900-1300 and 1400-1700; 1000-1200 (consular section).

British Embassy
PO Box 106, Lainchaur, Kathmandu, Nepal
Tel: (1) 441 0583 (*or* 4588 Fax: (1) 441 1789.
E-mail: britemb@wlink.com.np
Website: www.britishembassy.gov.uk/nepal

Royal Nepalese Embassy
2131 Leroy Place, NW, Washington, DC 20008, USA
Tel: (202) 667 4550. Fax: (202) 667 5534.
E-mail: info@nepalembassyusa.org
Website: www.nepalembassyusa.org

Royal Nepalese Consulate General
820 Second Avenue, Suite 17B, 17th Floor, New York, NY 10017, USA
Tel: (212) 370 3988/9. Fax: (212) 953 2038.
E-mail: nepal@un.int
Consulates also in: Chicago, Marina Del Rey, San Francisco and Sun Valley.

Embassy of the United States of America
PO Box 295, Pani Pokhari, Kathmandu, Nepal
Tel: (1) 441 1179. Fax: (1) 441 9963 *or* 444 4981.
E-mail: consktm@state.gov
Website: www.south-asia.com/USA

Honorary Royal Nepalese Consulate General
c/o Sharma Kanish & Associates Inc, 1200 Bay Street, Suite 1203, Toronto, Ontario M5R 2A5, Canada
Tel: (416) 975 9292 (ext 238 for visa enquiries).
Fax: (416) 975 9275.
E-mail: sharma@sharmakanish-asso.com

Canadian Embassy
c/o Canadian Cooperation Office, PO Box 4574, Lazimpat, Kathmandu, Nepal
Tel: (1) 441 5193 *or* 5861. Fax: (1) 441 0422.
E-mail: cco@cco.org.np
Website: www.cconepal.org.np

TIMATIC CODES

Health
AMADEUS: **TI-DFT/KTM/HE**
GALILEO/WORLDSPAN: **TI-DFT/KTM/HE**
SABRE: **TIDFT/KTM/HE**

Visa
AMADEUS: **TI-DFT/KTM/VI**
GALILEO/WORLDSPAN: **TI-DFT/KTM/VI**
SABRE: **TIDFT/KTM/VI**

To access TIMATIC country information on Health and Visa regulations through the Computer Reservations System (CRS), type in the appropriate command line listed above.

General Information

AREA: 147,181 sq km (56,827 sq miles).
POPULATION: 23,151,423 (2001).
POPULATION DENSITY: 157.3 per sq km (2001).
CAPITAL: Kathmandu. **Population**: 1,081,845 (2001).
GEOGRAPHY: Nepal is a landlocked kingdom sharing borders with Tibet to the north and northwest, and India to the west, south and east. The country can be divided into five zones: the Terai, the Siwaliks, the Mahabharat Lekh, the Midlands or Pahar, and the Himalayas. The greater part of the country lies on the southern slope of the Himalayas, extending down from the highest peaks through hill country to the upper edge of the Ganges Plain. The hilly central area is crossed by the Lower Himalayas, where there are eight of the highest peaks in the world, leading up to Mount Everest. Wildlife in Nepal includes tigers, leopards, gaur, elephants, buffalo, deer and rhinos.
GOVERNMENT: Constitutional monarchy. **Head of State**: King Maharajadhira Gyanendra since 2001. **Head of Government**: Prime Minister Sher Bahadur Deuba since 2004.
LANGUAGE: The official language is Nepali (spoken by 49 per cent). There are many other languages, including Maithili and Bhojpuri. English is spoken in business circles and by people involved in the travel trade.
RELIGION: Mainly Hindu (81 per cent) and Buddhist (11 per cent), with a small Muslim minority (4 per cent).
TIME: GMT + 5.45.
ELECTRICITY: 230 volts AC, 50Hz. There are frequent power cuts.
COMMUNICATIONS: Telephone: IDD is available to all major cities. Country code: 977. Outgoing international code: 00. The Telecommunication Office, Tripureshwar, deals with telephone calls and cables. The International Telephone Office is open Mon-Thurs 0900-1400 and Fri 0900-1330. Hotels and private communication centres provide long-distance telephone services (ISD, STD). **Mobile telephone:** GSM 900 network operated by *Nepal Mobile* (website: www.ntc.net.np), though this offers sporadic and variable coverage. **Fax:** Services are available in most hotels, travel agencies and communications centres. The Nepal Telecommunications Corporation booth at the airport has fax facilities. **Telegram:** The Central Telegraph Office offers a 24-hour international telephone and telegram service seven days a week. **Internet:** ISPs include *World Link* (website: www.wlink.com.np). There are Internet cafes in Kathmandu, Patan and Pokhara. Internet services are also provided by hotels. **Post:** Postal services are available in most centres. Make sure that letters are hand-cancelled
at the post office (post boxes should not be used for important communications). The general post office in Kathmandu (near the Dharahara Tower) is open Sun-Fri 1000-1700. *Poste restante* services are also available from 1000-1600. Express post services are also available. Main hotels will also handle post. **Press:** English-language dailies available in Nepal are *The Commoner Daily News*, *The Himalayan Times*, *Kathmandu Post*, *Motherland* and *Rising Nepal*. *The International Herald Tribune*, *Newsweek* and *Time* can all be found in Kathmandu. *Himal* is a magazine published monthly, devoted to issues throughout the South-Asian region. At certain times of day, there are radio and television news broadcasts in English.
Radio: BBC World Service (website: www.bbc.co.uk/worldservice) and Voice of America (website: www.voa.gov) can be received. From time to time the frequencies change and the most up-to-date can be found online.

Passport/Visa

	Passport Required?	Visa Required?	Return Ticket Required?
Full British	Yes	Yes	No
Australian	Yes	Yes	No
Canadian	Yes	Yes	No
USA	Yes	Yes	No
Other EU	Yes	Yes	No
Japanese	Yes	Yes	No

Note: *Regulations and requirements may be subject to change at short notice, and you are advised to contact the appropriate diplomatic or consular authority before finalising travel arrangements. Details of these may be found at the head of this country's entry. Any numbers in the chart refer to the footnotes below.*

PASSPORTS: Valid passport required by all except nationals of India holding proof of identity and arriving from India. (Acceptable proofs include Voter's Identity Card issued by the Election Commission of India or Photo Identity Card issued by the state or central government of India or Temporary Photo ID issued by the Indian Diplomatic Mission in Nepal.)

Note: Children under 10 years old are not required to produce photo identification.
VISAS: Required by all except the following:
(a) nationals of India;
(b) transit passengers continuing their journey by the same or first connecting aircraft on the same day provided holding valid onward or return documentation and not leaving the airport.
Types of visa and cost: *Tourist*: single-entry £20 (valid for 60 days from date of arrival); multiple-entry £55 (valid for 60 days from date of issue). *Business*: applications can be made on arrival which need to be approved by the Ministry of Industry. Visas valid for 60 days on first visit to Nepal in a visa year are only valid for 30 days when national is visiting Nepal for the second or more time in a visa year (Jan 1-Dec 31).
Note: (a) All nationals may obtain tourist visas on arrival at the airport. Two passport-size photos are required.
(b) Business can be conducted on a Tourist visa for up to 30 days.
Validity: Visas are valid for up to six months from date of issue. They may be extended in Nepal at the Department of Immigration, Kathmandu (tel: 494 273 *or* 337), or the Immigration Office, Pokhara. Maximum stay in Nepal is 150 days in any calendar year. For full conditions on visa extension (including charges and conditions), contact the Consulate (or Consular section at Embassy); see *Contact Addresses* section.
Application to: Consulate (or Consular section at Embassy). Visas can also be obtained on arrival from the Immigration authorities at all entry points (with fees payable in US Dollars) provided travellers are in possession of valid travel documents, two passport photos and the relevant fee. Applications for business visas must be made to the Department of Immigration (see above under *Validity* for address).
Application requirements: (a) One completed application form. (b) Passport valid for at least six months. (c) One passport-size photo. (d) Fee (in cash, postal order or bank draft). (e) For business visas, letter from company explaining purpose of visit, accompanying application made direct to Department of Immigration in Nepal (as above).
(f) A stamped-addressed envelope if applying by post.
Working days required: Minimum 24 hours if applying in person; two weeks if applying by post.

Money

Currency: Nepalese Rupee (NRs) = 100 paisa. Notes are in denominations of NRs1000, 500, 250, 100, 50, 25, 20, 10, 5, 2 and 1. Coins are in denominations of NRs5, 2 and 1, and 50, 25, 10 and 5 paisa.
Note: Visitors should bear in mind that foreign visitors other than Indian nationals are required to pay their airline tickets, trekking permits and hotel bills in foreign currency.
Currency exchange: It is illegal to exchange currency with persons other than authorised dealers in foreign exchange (banks, hotels and licensed money changers). Visitors should obtain Foreign Exchange Encashment Receipts when changing currency and keep them, as these will help in many transactions, including getting visa extensions and trekking permits.
Credit & debit cards: American Express is widely accepted, with MasterCard and Visa in tourist shops, hotels, restaurants and agencies. Check with your credit or debit card company for details of merchant acceptability and other services which may be available.
Travellers cheques: Accepted at banks and major hotels. If trekking, it is important to bear in mind that cash is necessary. To avoid additional exchange rate charges, travellers are advised to take travellers cheques in US Dollars or Pounds Sterling.
Currency restrictions: Import of local and Indian currency is prohibited, except for nationals of Nepal and India. Foreign currency is unlimited but must be declared. Export of local and foreign currency is limited to the amounts declared on arrival. Only 10 per cent of the amount exchanged into local currency will be reconverted into foreign currency on departure and all exchange receipts must be retained.
Exchange rate indicators: The following figures are included as a guide to the movements of the Nepalese Rupee against Sterling and the US Dollar:

Date	Feb '04	May '04	Aug '04	Nov '04
£1.00=	131.92	127.51	136.36	136.24
$1.00=	72.47	71.39	74.01	71.94

Banking hours: Banks in the Kathmandu valley are open Mon-Fri 0900-1430. In other areas, opening hours are usually Sun-Thurs 1000-1430 and Fri 1000-1200. Licensed money changers are open 12 hours a day.

Duty Free

The following goods may be imported into Nepal without incurring customs duty:

Credit: © Nepal Tourism Board

100 cigarettes or equivalent of other tobacco articles; 1l of alcoholic beverages; a reasonable amount of perfume for personal use.
Note: (a) All baggage must be declared on arrival and departure. (b) Certain goods including cameras, videos and electronic goods may only be imported duty free if they are exported on departure. They may not be left in Nepal. (c) It is illegal to export goods over 100 years old. (d) Export certificates need to be obtained from the Department of Archaeology for the export of any metal statues, sacred paintings and similar objects.

Public Holidays

2005: Jan 11 National Unity Day. **Jan 29** Martyrs' Day. **Feb 13** Vasant Panchami. **Feb 19** Rashtriya Prajatantra Divas (National Democracy Day). **Mar 8** Nepalese Women's Day, and Shivaratri (in honour of Lord Shiva). **Mar 9** Ghode Jatra (Festival of Horses). **Mar 18** Chaite Dashain. **Mar 19** Ram Nawami (Birthday of Lord Ram). **Mar 25** Holi. **Apr 14** Navabarsha (New Year's Day). **Apr 21** Buddha Jayanti (Birthday of Lord Buddha). **Aug 19** Rakshya Bandhan (Janai Purnima). **Aug 20** Gai Jatra (Procession of Cows). **Aug 25** Krishna Asthami (Birthday of Lord Krishna). **Sep 6** Teej (Festival of Women). **Oct 10** Dasain (Durga Puja Festival). **Nov 1** Deepawali (Festival of Lights). **Nov 8** Indra Jatra (Festival of Rain God). **Nov 9** Constitution Day. **Dec 29** King Birendra's Birthday.
2006: Jan *or* **Feb** Vasant Panchami. **Jan 11** National Unity Day. **Jan 29** Martyrs' Day. **Feb** *or* **Mar** Shivaratri (in honour of Lord Shiva). **Feb 19** Rashtriya Prajatantra Divas (National Democracy Day). **Mar** Ghode Jatra (Festival of Horses); Chaite Dashain. **Mar** *or* **Apr** Ram Nawami (Birthday of Lord Ram). **Mar 8** Nepalese Women's Day. **Mar 15** Holi. **Apr 14** Navabarsha (New Year's Day). **May 13** Buddha Jayanti (Birthday of Lord Buddha). **Aug** Rakshya Bandhan (Janai Purnima). **Aug** *or* **Sep** Gai Jatra (Procession of Cows); Krishna Asthami (Birthday of Lord Krishna). **Sep** Teej (Festival of Women). **Oct** Dasain (Durga Puja Festival). **Oct** *or* **Nov** Indra Jatra (Festival of Rain God). **Oct 21** Deepawali (Festival of Lights). **Nov 9** Constitution Day. **Dec 29** King Birendra's Birthday.
Note: Some of the above are Hindu festivals, which are declared according to local astronomical observations. It is not possible to predict the exact dates of festivals occuring and the dates published are approximations. Travellers should check locally nearer the time for precise dates.

Health

	Special Precautions?	Certificate Required?
Yellow Fever	No	1
Cholera	Yes	2
Typhoid & Polio	3	N/A
Malaria	4	N/A

Note: Regulations and requirements may be subject to change at short notice, and you are advised to contact your doctor well in advance of your intended date of departure. Any numbers in the chart refer to the footnotes below.

1: A yellow fever vaccination certificate is required of travellers arriving from infected areas.
2: Following WHO guidelines issued in 1973, a cholera vaccination certificate is not a condition of entry to Nepal. However, cholera is a serious risk in this country and precautions are essential. Up-to-date advice should be sought before deciding whether these precautions should include vaccination, as medical opinion is divided over its effectiveness. For more information, see the *Health* appendix.
3: Typhoid is common.
4: Malaria risk, mainly in the benign *vivax* form, exists throughout the year in rural areas of the Terai districts (including forested hills and forest areas) of Bara, Dhanukha, Kapilvastu, Mahotari, Parsa, Rautahat, Rupendehi, Sarlahi, and especially along the Indian border. The malignant *falciparum* form resistant to chloroquine and sulfadoxine-pyrimethamine has been reported. The recommended prophylaxis is chloroquine plus proguanil.
Food & drink: All water should be regarded as being potentially contaminated. Water used for drinking, brushing teeth or making ice should have first been boiled or otherwise sterilised. Milk is unpasteurised and should be boiled. Powdered or tinned milk is available and is advised, but make sure that it is reconstituted with pure water. Avoid dairy products which are likely to have been made from unboiled milk. Only eat well-cooked meat and fish, preferably served hot. Pork, salad and mayonnaise may carry increased risk. Vegetables should be cooked and fruit peeled.
Other risks: *High altitude sickness* is a hazard for trekkers, so it is important to be in good health before travelling. Advice can be obtained from the Himalayan Rescue

Association near the Kathmandu Guest House, Thamel. It is advisable, particularly when in rural areas, to carry a medical kit containing items such as rehydration mixture for the treatment of severe diarrhoea and 'dry spray' for cuts and bruises. Contact the Nepal Tourism Board for advice (see *Contact Addresses* section). *Giardiasis, dysenteries* and *diarrhoeas* are all common. *Japanese encephalitis* occurs in southern lowland, rural areas. *Hepatitis A, B* and *E* occur. *Meningitis* has been reported in some areas. There has been a sharp rise in *visceral leishmaniasis*, and *trachoma* is fairly common.
Rabies is present. For those at high risk, vaccination before arrival should be considered. If you are bitten, seek medical advice without delay. For more information, see the *Health* appendix.
Health care: The most convenient hospital for visitor care is Patan Hospital in Lagankhel. Other hospitals include the Western Regional Hospital and the Manipal Hospital in Pokhara and the Mission Hospital in Tansen. Most hospitals have English-speaking staff and larger hotels have doctors. Pharmacies in Kathmandu, mainly along New Road, offer a wide range of Western drugs at low prices. In Kathmandu, you can get certain vaccinations free of charge at the Infectious Diseases Clinic. Full medical insurance is essential.

Travel - International

Travel Warning: On February 1, 2005, the king dismissed the country's government and assumed direct control, declaring a state of emergency. The mobile phone service is currently suspended. There is a continuing risk that this situation may lead to violent demonstrations in Nepal, especially in Kathmandu and the surrounding valley. Countrywide *bandhs* (strikes) are regularly called which have caused widespread disruption, including to transport. Visitors are advised to travel by air where possible. There is a high threat of terrorism, especially from Maoist rebels. Extreme caution should especially be exercised in Kathmandu.
AIR: Nepal's national airline is *Royal Nepal Airlines (RA)*. It operates flights to Bangalore, Bangkok, Calcutta, Delhi, Frankfurt/M, Hong Kong, Mumbai, Osaka, Paris, London, Shanghai and Singapore. Other airlines operating to Kathmandu include *Biman Bangladesh Airlines, Druk Air, Gulf Air, Indian Airlines, Pakistan International Airlines, Qatar Airways* and *Thai International*.
Approximate flight times: From Kathmandu to *London* is 10 hours 15 minutes.
International airports: *Kathmandu (KTM)* (Tribhuvan) is 6.5km (4 miles) east of the city (travel time - 20 minutes). Buses and taxis to the city are available. Airport facilities include bank/bureau de change, duty free shop, post office, refreshments and tourist information.
Departure tax: NRs1100 for international flights; NRs770 within the Indian sub-continent, eg Bangladesh, Bhutan, India, Maldives, Pakistan and Sri Lanka. Children under two years are exempt.

Note: Foreign nationals must pay for airfares in foreign currency. Only Nepalese and Indian nationals are allowed to pay in Nepalese Rupees for air passage between Nepal and India.
RAIL: Two stretches of the Indian Railway Line run to the border with Nepal, where cycle-rickshaws are available for onward journeys.
ROAD: Kathmandu is connected with India and Tibet by new and picturesque highways through the fertile plains of the Terai. Bus services operate from all border points to Kathmandu. However, during the monsoon season, landslides can often make border points impassable. Visitors are permitted to drive their own cars provided they are in possession of an international carnet. For information on how to obtain an international carnet, visitors should contact their national Automobile Association. See also *Travel - Internal* section for required documentation.
Note: All visitors entering Nepal by land must use one of the following entry points: Belhiya (Bhairahawa), Birgunj, Dhangadi, Kakarbhitta, Mahendra Nagar and Nepalgunj (all on the Nepal-India border); and Kodari (on the Nepal-China border). If entering overland by car, an international carnet is required (enquire at Embassy for details); see *Contact Addresses* section.

Travel - Internal

AIR: There is a network of domestic flights linking major towns, radiating from Kathmandu. Many of these offer spectacular views across the mountains. *Royal Nepal Airlines* operates an extensive range of scheduled flights to around 21 destinations in the interior parts of Nepal. Other domestic airlines, of which there are more than 18, provide regular and charter services to popular destinations. Helicopters can be chartered for various purposes. Nepal's domestic air service is known to be punctual and reliable.
Departure tax: Nrs50 at Bhadrapur, Bharatpur, Biratnagar, Dang, Dhangadi, Janakapur, Kathmandu, Mahendranagar, Nepalgang, Pokhara, Rajbiraj, Siddharthanagar and Simara; Nrs20 for all other airports.
Note: Air fares must be paid in foreign currency by foreign nationals. Only Nepalese and Indian nationals are allowed to pay in Nepalese Rupees.
RAIL: *Nepal Janakpur-Jayanager Railways (NJJR)* operates a freight and passenger service in the eastern Terai.
ROAD: Traffic drives on the left. The interior parts of the country are linked with a number of motorable roads. The road system is of unpredictable quality. **Bus:** There are regular bus services to Kathmandu from all the border points. Tickets may be booked in advance. Buses for the different parts of the country are available at the Gongabu bus terminal, which is located near Balaju. Services are operated by the *Transport Corporation of Nepal* and by private operators. Deluxe tourist buses are available from Kathmandu to Pokhara and Chitwan. Most of them depart at 0700 from near Thamel in the city centre. Visitors should, however, be aware that multiple-fatality accidents on buses are common. **Car hire**: Cars can be hired from the Avis representative, the Hertz representative or *Yeti Travels*, all in Kathmandu. Chauffeur-driven cars can only be hired in the Kathmandu Valley. **Documentation**: An International Driving Permit is valid in Nepal for 15 days, after which a local licence is required. The minimum driving age is 18. A temporary licence to drive is available from local authorities on presentation of a valid national driving licence.
URBAN: There are bus services in the populous areas around Kathmandu, which include the neighbouring cities of Patan and Bhaktapur. A trolleybus route provides frequent journeys over the 11km (7 mile) Kathmandu-Bhaktapur road. Private minibuses feed the trolleybus route from nearby villages. On buses and trolleybuses belonging to the *Transport Corporation of Nepal*, a 4-stage fare system applies, with colour-coded tickets issued by conductors. 'Microbuses' also operate. **Taxi**: Metered taxis are plentiful in Kathmandu; at night, the meter reading plus 50 per cent is standard. Private taxis are more expensive and fares should be agreed before departure. **Tempos**: These are metered 3-wheel scooters, which work out slightly cheaper than taxis. **Rickshaws**: These operate throughout the city. Fares should be negotiated in advance. **Bicycles and motorcycles**: These can be hired from bike-shops or hotels by the hour or day. Motorcyclists require a driving licence. Cyclists should make sure they have a working bell.

Accommodation

HOTELS: Kathmandu has an increasing number of international-class hotels, which are particularly busy during spring and autumn, when it is advisable to book well in advance. Comfortable hotels can also be found in Pokhara, and the Royal Chitwan National Park in the Terai Jungle. A government tax is added to bills, which varies according to the star rating of the hotel. For more information, contact the General Secretary, Hotel Association of Nepal (HAN), PO Box 2151, Kamalpokhari, Kathmandu (tel: (1) 412 705 *or* 410 522; fax: (1) 424 914; e-mail: info@hotelassociation.org.np; website: www.hotelassociation.org.np).
LODGES: Besides the officially recognised hotels, there are a number of lodges or hostels. In Kathmandu, these are located in the old part of the town, in the streets around the Durbar Square or in the Thamel district. Lodges are available outside the main towns, and provide suitable accommodation for mountaineers and trekkers. For a list of approved hostels and lodges, contact the Nepal Tourism Board in Kathmandu or one of their representatives abroad (see *Contact Addresses* section).

Resorts & Excursions

Nepal is known as the abode of the gods. For many years a secret, unknown country, it was, in the 1950s, faced with making a leap from the 11th century to modern times. Visited first by mountaineers and trekkers, it later became the haunt of hippies. In 1989, restrictions barring several areas to tourists were lifted.
The Nepalese Government has set aside more than 35 per cent of the total area of the country as natural sanctuaries. There are now nine National Parks and three wildlife reserves, located both in the mountainous zones as well as in the tropical plains. The Terai lowlands in the south form the richest habitat in the country. Five protected areas are located in the region and many species of wildlife, including the rare Royal Bengal tiger and leopard, can be observed.

KATHMANDU

Kathmandu, the capital and also the cultural, commercial and business hub of the Kingdom, is a magical place. In the centre is **Durbar Square** where there is a wonderful collection of temples and shrines, both Buddhist and Hindu. They are generally built in the pagoda style with a mass of intricate exterior carving. The old **Royal Palace** is in the square, as is the **Statue of Hanuman the Monkey God**, clad in a red cloak. Here also is the house of the living goddess - the *Kumari*. A few kilometres from Kathmandu is the hugely impressive **Bodnath Stupa**. It has become a centre of Tibetan exile culture and is a good place to buy Tibetan handicrafts and artefacts. Climbing upwards from the city one can reach the famous Buddhist stupa of *Swayambhunath*, popularly known as the **Monkey Temple**. There are a great many steps leading up to the temple, which is frequented by an even greater number of monkeys. The monkeys should be treated with some caution since their behaviour can be unpredictable. The monkey temple is noted for its large staring eyes. There are also a number of monasteries. Respect should be shown for local sensitivities when visiting religious sites or temples.
EXCURSIONS: Just 5km (3 miles) west of the city, below the **Nagarjun Forest**, are the **Balaju Water Gardens**, with a reclining statue of Lord Vishnu and a 22-headed sea-dragon fountain. Around 19km (12 miles) south of Kathmandu, and accessible by taxi, are the **Godavari Royal Botanical Gardens** housing trees, shrubs and beautiful orchids in an idyllic setting.

THE KATHMANDU VALLEY

BHAKTAPUR: Kathmandu was once one of three equal cities, the other two being Bhaktapur and Patan. Bhaktapur (also known as the 'temple city') is located some 12km (7.5 miles) from Kathmandu in the eastern part of the valley. The Kathmandu Valley's rich cultural and natural heritage has prompted UNESCO to list seven World Heritage Sites in the area. The **National Art Gallery**, located in the old **Malla Palace**, has unusual, colourful animal paintings on the second floor that are worth a look. Other museums in Bhaktapur are the **National Woodworking Museum**, showing fine examples of Newari woodcarving (for which the city is renowned), and the **Brass and Bronze Museum**, both in Dattatreya Square.
PATAN: Patan is located at the southern end of the Kathmandu Valley and is famous for its bronze and silverware. The city contains many ancient historic and artistic landmarks, including **Patan Durbar Square** (also the location for the interesting **Patan Museum**), **Krishna Mandir**, the **Royal Bath**, the **Kumbheshwor Temple** and the **Golden Temple**. Patan has the **Jawalakhel Zoo**, housing exotic South-Asian animals.
ELSEWHERE: There are shrines for every purpose in the valley, such as the **Shrine of Ganesh the Elephant God**, reputed to bring good luck. There are four Ganesh temples in the valley, each a masterpiece of Nepalese architecture - one in Kathmandu's Durbar Square, one in **Chabahil**, one in **Chobar** and one near Bhaktapur. **Lumbini**, being the birthplace of Lord Buddha, is one of the world's most important pilgrimage sites.
The **Royal Chitwan National Park**, Nepal's first national park, is a jungle overflowing with wildlife. There are many

lodges here offering visitor accommodation, canoeing, white-water rafting and elephant rides. **Nagarkot Village**, situated on rice steppes in magnificent countryside, provides spectacular views of **Mount Everest**, mist permitting. The hill town of **Gorkha** is the ancestral home of the Shah Dynasty and residence of the original Gurkha soldiers. There is a lively bazaar and the **Royal Trek** to **Pokhara** begins here. The secluded town of Pokhara lies 200km (125 miles) west of Kathmandu in the centre of Nepal on **Lake Phewa**. No other place in the world commands such a view of the Himalayas. It is a starting point for mountaineers and trekkers, and was at one time the home of JRR Tolkien.

THE MOUNTAINS

One of the principal reasons for visiting Nepal must be either to see or to climb the mountains, especially **Mount Everest**. Located in **Sagarmatha National Park** in the Khumbu region bordering Tibet, the mountain's appropriate Nepalese name is *Sagarmatha* (Head of the Sky). The Sherpas and Tibetans worship it as *Chomolongma* (Mother Goddess of the Earth). At an altitude of 8848m (29,022ft), Everest is the world's highest peak and has been opened for commercial mountaineering for decades. It is part of the **Great Himalayan Range**, which stretches for some 800km (500 miles) and which includes a further eight peaks above 8000m (26,240ft). The countryside offers an astonishingly varied topography as the snowy mountain peaks give way to intricately green terraced hills, scenic rivers and tropical jungles in the interior.

For walkers and trekkers, Nepal is a true paradise: the picturesque hamlets and mountain villages are linked by hundreds of trails that have been used for centuries, with little change noticeable even today. The practicalities for trekking are now easy to arrange (see *Sport & Activities* section for further details). Numerous temples and Buddhist shrines can be also be discovered en route and visitors should make sure that, when visiting them, they stick to the proper religious protocol (see also *Social Conventions* in the *Social Profile* section).

Sport & Activities

Trekking: The trekking season is generally from September to May, but the best periods are October to December and March to April. The countryside is mostly rugged and the trails are loose, but trekking is by far the best way to enjoy Nepal's spectacular landscape. Different types of trips with varying degrees of difficulty can be arranged. Some foreign travel agencies can book trekking packages in advance in collaboration with the Nepalese trekking agencies. In Kathmandu, there are many local officially registered trekking agencies that can provide a fully organised trek, complete with porters, guide, cook, food tents, sleeping bags, mattresses, transport to and from the starting and finishing points, flight arrangements, permits and insurance. They also provide participants with a choice of itineraries.
Trekking formalities: As of July 1999, trekking permits are no longer required for the general trekking areas designated by the Department of Immigration (such as the Annapurna, the Everest, the Langtang and Rara). For all other areas, a permit is still required and can be obtained from the Department of Immigration located at New Baneshwar, Kathmandu (see *Passport/Visa* section for further details) or trekking agencies and tour operators. Trekking to Dolpa, Kanchanjunga, Makalu and Upper Mustang can only be undertaken through a registered trekking agency. Entrance fees are levied for the national park areas and wildlife reserves; these range from NRs500 to NRs2000 per person per day. Children under 10 are exempt. Higher fees are payable for filming and helicopter landing permits. Further information can be obtained from the Nepal Tourism Board (see *Contact Addresses* section).
Trekking advice: The Nepal Tourism Board gives the following advice to trekkers: use authorised guides and porters only; be careful with matches around wooded or grassy areas as forest fires can cause serious damage; be economical with all fuel, especially local firewood (campfires are not recommended); prioritise tour companies and lodges which do not use firewood; trekkers are strictly forbidden to cut any green forest reserve or kill any wildlife; use washing and toilet facilities provided or, if none are available, make sure to be at least 30 metres away from any water source; use biodegradable items as much as possible; when visiting temples or Buddhist shrines, respect local religious customs (see *Social Conventions* in *Social Profile* section); take necessary precautions when suffering from altitude sickness (for details, see the *Health* section).
Note: In the past, the authorities have discouraged women from trekking on their own. Some Nepalese trekking agencies, however, are now keen to provide a service for female trekkers who can also hire female guides and porters.
Pony treks: Ponies have been a means of transport for people and materials for centuries in Nepal and are today used extensively for trekking. Pony treks follow nearly the same routes as normal treks and are offered mostly in the western region around Pokhara, as well as in the hinterlands of Dolpo and Lo Manthang.
Scenic flights: Most of the domestic airlines arrange flights in light aircraft over Mount Everest. Flights are also available from Pokhara and other locations west of the capital, flying over the spectacular Annapurna range.
Mountaineering: To scale any of the mountain peaks in Nepal, climbing permits are required. They can be obtained from the Ministry of Culture, Tourism and Civil Aviation, Mountaineering Section (MoCTCA) (tel: (1) 247 037 *or* 256 228; fax: (1) 227 281) *or* the Nepal Mountaineering Association (NMA) (tel: (1) 434 525; fax: (1) 434 578; e-mail: office@nma.com.np; website: www.nma.com.np). Further information can also be obtained from the Nepal Tourism Board (see *Contact Addresses* section).
River rafting: Rafting permits are not required for the general areas; however, to raft the Himalayan rivers, a permit must be obtained from the Ministry of Culture, Tourism and Civil Aviation (tel: (1) 247 041; fax: (1) 434 578).
Golf: The popularity of golf is on the increase in Nepal, which has a total of four golf courses, two of which are located in Kathmandu (the *Gokarna Golf Course* and the *Til Ganga Golf Course*). The other two are the *Fulbari Resort Golf Course* and the *Himalayan Golf Course*, both located in Pokhara. For further information, contact the Nepal Tourism Board (see *Contact Addresses* section).
Adventure sports: The tourist potential of adventure sports has not escaped the Nepalese authorities, and the Nepal Tourism Board is now promoting a range of high-adrenalin activities that can be pursued in the country's spectacular landscapes. **Ballooning** and **hang-gliding** are among the newest additions, as Kathmandu has just opened its skies for commercial ballooning, which does provide the opportunity to get excellent aerial views of the city and its panoramic surroundings. Trips over Mount Everest are rare, but also possible. Hang-gliding, which uses an ultra-light, one-person glider system, is popular in Pokhara and in the Langtang region. **Bungee jumping** and **canyoning** are also popular. **Paragliding** and **power paragliding** are available in Pokhara.
The Nepal Yeti: The existence of the famous Nepal Yeti, a giant, gorilla-sized hairy snowman that eats yaks and sheep, remains strongly questionable. Only a few people, including the father of Tenzing Norgay (the first Sherpa to conquer Mount Everest), claim to have seen it. Popular myth recounts that those who did spot the creature got sick and died within a few days. For Yeti enthusiasts wishing to try their luck, the abominable snowman is said to make random appearances around the Khumbu region (in the foothills of Mount Everest).

Social Profile

FOOD & DRINK: Despite its isolation and the variety of its local produce, Nepal has not developed a distinctive style of cooking. Food consists, more often than not, of *Dal Bhat* – lentils and rice. An exception is *Newar* cuisine, which can be very elaborate and spicy. Rice is the staple food. Dishes include *dal* (lentil soup), spiced vegetables, *chapatis* and *tsampa* (eaten by the hill people), which is a raw grain, ground and mixed with milk, tea or water. Sweets and spicy snacks include *jelabi*, *laddus* and *mukdals*. Regional dishes include *gurr*, a Sherpa dish of raw potatoes, pounded with spices, then grilled like pancakes on a hot, flat stone. Tibetan cooking includes *thukba* (thick soup) and *momos* (fried or boiled stuffed dumplings). Meat includes goat, pork, chicken or buffalo, but beef is forbidden. There is a wide selection of restaurants in Kathmandu and Pokhara, although the choice is limited elsewhere. A 12 per cent government tax is added to bills.
The national drink is *chiya* (tea brewed with milk, sugar and spices; in the mountains it is salted with yak butter). Another popular mountain drink is *chang* (beer made from fermented barley, maize, rye or millet). *Arak* (potato alcohol) and *raksi* (wheat or rice spirit) are also drunk. Nepalese beer is available, as is good-quality local rum, vodka and gin. Local whisky is not so palatable, but imported varieties are widely available.
NIGHTLIFE: Kathmandu has a few cinemas featuring mainly Indian films. For Western films, see the programmes of the European and US cultural centres. Most people are asleep by 2200. Nightlife is fairly limited; a few temples and restaurants offer entertainment and some tourist hotels stage Nepalese folk dances and musical shows. There are casinos with baccarat, chemin de fer and roulette, open 24 hours a day, every day, at some 5-star hotels in Kathmandu.
SHOPPING: There are bargains for those careful to avoid fakes and the badly made souvenirs sold by unscrupulous traders. Popular buys include locally made clothes such as lopsided *topis* (caps), knitted mittens and socks, Tibetan dresses, woven shawls, Tibetan multicoloured jackets and men's diagonally fastened shirts; and *pashmina* (fine goat's-wool blankets), *khukri* (the national knife), *saranghi*

Credit: © Nepal Tourism Board

(a small, four-stringed viola played with a horse-hair bow), Tibetan tea bowls, *papier mâché* dance masks, Buddhist statuettes and filigree ornaments, bamboo flutes and other folk objects. **Shopping hours**: Sun-Fri 1000-2000 (some shops stay open on Saturday and holidays).
SPECIAL EVENTS: Nepalese festivals fall into several categories. Most are performed in honour of the gods and goddesses, some mark the seasons or agricultural cycles, and others are simply family celebrations. The usual form of celebration is to take ritual baths in rivers or lakes, visit temples to offer worship, and feasting and ritual fasting. The festivals in Kathmandu Valley are the most rich and spectacular. For a list of special events and festivals in Nepal, send a stamped, self-addressed envelope to the Embassy (see *Contact Addresses* section). The following is a selection of special events celebrated annually in Nepal:
Feb *Losar* (Tibetan New Year), Jawlakhel and Swayambhunath. **Mar** *Maha Shivaratri*, Pashupatinath; *Holi*. **Apr** *Bisket Festival*; *Chaitra Daisan*. **May** *Buddha Jayanti*, Kathmandu. **Aug** *Gai Jantra* (Cow Festival), Kathmandu. **Aug-Sep** *Krishna Jayanti*, Patan. **Sep** *Teej* (Women's Festival). **Oct** *Daisan Festival* (includes the year's largest animal sacrifice). **Nov** *Maini Rimdu*, Solu Khumbu; *Tihar* (Festival of Lights); *Haribodhini Ekadashi* (Hindu Feast), Pashupatinath.
SOCIAL CONVENTIONS: As a foreign visitor, one must be careful to respect local customs in order not to cause offence. The following are some local conventions it is advisable to adhere to: never step over the feet of a person, always walk round; never offer food and drink which is 'polluted', in other words, food that you have tasted or bitten; never offer or accept anything with the left hand, use the right or both hands. It is rude to point at a person or statue with a finger (or even with a foot). Shoes and footwear should be removed when entering houses or shrines. Kitchens and eating areas of houses should also not be entered with footwear, as the hearth of a home is sacred. Do not stand in front of a person who is eating as this means your feet will be next to his food; squat or sit by his side. Local *Chorten* are built to pacify local demons or dead persons and should be passed by in a clockwise direction, as should temples; the earth and universe revolve in this direction. Small flat stones with inscriptions and supplications next to the *Chorten* should not be removed as souvenirs; this is considered sacrilege by the Nepalese. Avoid touching a Nepalese dressed all in white; his dress signifies a death in the family. Shaking hands is not a common form of greeting; the normal greeting is to press the palms together in a prayer-like gesture. A gift given to a host or hostess will probably be laid aside unopened; to open a parcel in the presence of a guest is considered uncivil. Casual wear is suitable except for the most formal meetings or social occasions. Bikinis, shorts, bare shoulders and backs may not be appreciated. Men only remove their shirts when bathing. Overt public displays of affection, especially near religious places, are inappropriate. Nepalese cities are generally safe, but take sensible precautions with personal possessions. **Photography:** Always ask permission first. In general, it is allowed outside temples and at festivals, but not at religious ceremonies or inside temples; however, there is no hard and fast rule and the only way to be sure of not giving offence is to ask first and accept the answer. **Tipping:** Only usual in tourist hotels and restaurants. Taxi drivers need only be tipped when they have been particularly helpful. 10 per cent is sufficient for all three services. Elsewhere, tipping should be avoided.

Business Profile

ECONOMY: Nepal is one of the world's least developed countries with an average annual income of just US$200 per annum. Although little of the land can be cultivated, 90 per cent of the working population finds employment in agriculture and forestry. Foodstuffs and live animals provide about 30 per cent of Nepal's export earnings. The principal crops are maize, rice, barley, wheat, sugar cane, potatoes and fruit. The manufacturing sector is very small and concentrated in light industries such as construction materials, food processing, textiles and carpet-making (the latter being an important export earner).

The country has a considerable hydroelectric potential which would save Nepal from having to import much of its energy requirements, but the sector is as yet underdeveloped. There is some mining of mica and small quantities of lignite, copper, coal and iron ore. The main service industry, tourism, has gone into decline since the late 1990s. In 2002, bad weather and the effects of the Maoist insurgency caused the economy to contract by 0.5 per cent. The sustained expansion of the 1990s has clearly ended and the Nepalese economy is highly vulnerable. It relies on substantial amounts of foreign aid, especially food aid (international donors provide about 30 per cent of the government's budget) and runs a large external debt. India is the main trading partner, although following the 1989/90 dispute which led to the closure of the border between the two countries, Nepal has actively pursued trade links elsewhere. Agreements have also been signed with several other governments, of which that with China (PR) is the most important. Nepal is a member of the Asian Development Bank and the Colombo Plan, both of which aim to promote regional economic cooperation.

BUSINESS: Tropical-weight suits or shirt and tie are recommended. Best time to visit is October to May.

Government office hours: Kathmandu Valley: Mon-Fri 0900-1700 (winter), 0900-1600 (summer). Other areas: Sun-Fri 1000-1700 (winter), 1000-1600 (summer).

Private office hours: Sun-Fri 0930-1700.

COMMERCIAL INFORMATION: The following organisations can offer advice: Nepal Chamber of Commerce, PO Box 198, Kantipath, Kathmandu (tel: (1) 222 890; fax: (1) 229 998; e-mail: chamber@wlink.com.np); *or* Federation of Nepalese Chambers of Commerce and Industry, PO Box 269, Pachali Shahid Shukra, Milan Marg, Teku, Kathmandu (tel: (1) 262 218 *or* 061; fax: (1) 261 022; e-mail: fncci@mos.com.np; website: www.fncci.org); *or* Nepal-Britain Chamber of Commerce & Industry, British Embassy Premises, PO Box 106, Lainchaur, Kathmandu (tel: (1) 410 738 *or* 583; fax: (1) 418 137; e-mail: info@nbcci.org; website: www.nbcci.org).

CONFERENCES/CONVENTIONS: The following organisation can organise these events: Nepal Incentive and Convention Association, PO Box 11034, Kathmandu (tel: (1) 494 411; fax: (1) 473 696; e-mail: nica@mice.mos.com.np; website: www.nica.org.np).

Climate

Nepal's weather is generally predictable and pleasant. There are four climatic seasons: March to May (spring), June to August (summer), September to November (autumn) and December to February (winter). The monsoon is approximately from the end of June to the middle of September. About 80 per cent of the rain falls during that period, so the remainder of the year is dry. Spring and autumn are the most pleasant seasons; winter temperatures drop to freezing with a high level of snowfall in the mountains. Summer and late spring temperatures range from 28°C (83°F) in the hill regions to more than 40°C (104°F) in the Terai. In winter, average maximum and minimum temperatures in the Terai range from a brisk 7°C (45°F) to a mild 23°C (74°F). The central valleys experience a minimum temperature often falling bellow freezing point and a chilly 12°C (54°F) maximum. Much colder temperatures prevail at higher elevations. The Kathmandu Valley, at an altitude of 1310m (4297ft), has a mild climate, ranging from 19-27°C (67-81°F) in summer, and 2-20°C (36-68°F) in winter.

Required clothing: Lightweight and tropical clothes with umbrella are advised for June to August. Between October and March, lightweight clothes are worn in Kathmandu, with a coat for evenings and warm clothing for the mountains.

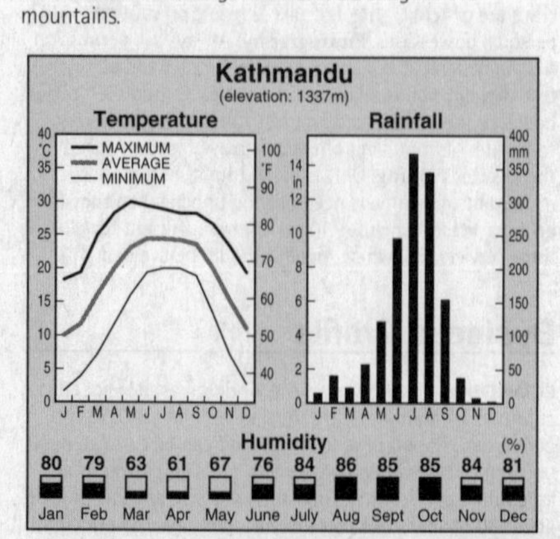

The Netherlands

LATEST TRAVEL ADVICE CONTACTS

British Foreign and Commonwealth Office
Tel: (0870) 606 0290 Website: www.fco.gov.uk

US Department of State
Website: http://travel.state.gov/travel

Canadian Department of Foreign Affairs and Int'l Trade
Tel: (1 800) 267 8376 Website: www.dfait-maeci.gc.ca

Location: Northwest Europe.

Country dialling code: 31.

Nederlands Bureau voor Toerisme & Congressen (Netherlands Board of Tourism & Conventions)
Street address: Vlietweg 15, 2266 KA Leidschendam, The Netherlands
Postal address: PO Box 458, 2260 MG Leidschendam, The Netherlands
Tel: (70) 370 5705. Fax: (70) 320 1654.
E-mail: info@holland.com
Website: www.holland.com

Royal Netherlands Embassy
38 Hyde Park Gate, London SW7 5DP, UK
Tel: (020) 7590 3200 *or* (09065) 508 916 (visa information line; calls cost £1 per minute). Fax: (020) 7225 0947 (general) *or* 7581 3458 (consular section).
E-mail: london@netherlands-embassy.org.uk (general information) *or* consular@netherlands-embassy.org.uk
Website: www.netherlands-embassy.org.uk
Opening hours: Mon-Fri 0900-1700; 0900-1200 (passport and visa section; by appointment only).
Visa applications are on a first-come, first-served basis. The passport and visa section is closed on the first Wednesday of every month.

Netherlands Board of Tourism & Conventions (NBTC)
PO Box 30783, London WC2B 6DH, UK
Tel: (020) 7539 7950 *or* (09068) 717 777 (brochure line; calls cost 60p per minute). Fax: (020) 7539 7953.
E-mail: info-uk@holland.com
Website: www.holland.com/uk

British Embassy
Lange Voorhout 10, 2514 ED The Hague, The Netherlands
Tel: (70) 427 0427. Fax: (70) 427 0348.
E-mail: library@britain.nl
Website: www.britain.nl
For visas and passports, contact the Consulate General.

British Consulate General
Konigslaan 44, PO Box 75488, 1070 AL Amsterdam, The Netherlands
Tel: (20) 676 4343.

TIMATIC CODES

Health	AMADEUS: **TI-DFT/AMS/HE** GALILEO/WORLDSPAN: **TI-DFT/AMS/HE** SABRE: **TIDFT/AMS/HE**
Visa	AMADEUS: **TI-DFT/AMS/VI** GALILEO/WORLDSPAN: **TI-DFT/AMS/VI** SABRE: **TIDFT/AMS/VI**

To access TIMATIC country information on Health and Visa regulations through the Computer Reservations System (CRS), type in the appropriate command line listed above.

Fax: (20) 676 1069 (visa section) *or* 675 8381 (consular section).
E-mail: visaenquiries.amsterdam@fco.gov.uk *or* OtherConsularEnquiries@fco.gov.uk
Website: www.britain.nl

Royal Netherlands Embassy
4200 Linnean Avenue, NW, Washington, DC 20008, USA
Tel: (202) 244 5300. Fax: (202) 362 3430.
E-mail: was-sccscd@embisnbuze.nl
Website: www.netherlands-embassy.org

Consulate General of The Netherlands
1 Rockefeller Plaza, 11th Floor, New York, NY 10020
Tel: (212) 246 1429. Fax: (212) 333 3603.
E-mail: Wanyc@minbuza.nl *or* webmaster@netherlands-embassy.org *or* nyc-visa.passport@minbuza.nl
Website: www.cgny.org
Consulates General also in: Chicago, Houston, Los Angeles and Miami.

Netherlands Board of Tourism & Conventions (NBTC)
355 Lexington Avenue, 19th Floor, New York, NY 10017, USA
Tel: (212) 370 7360. Fax: (212) 370 9507.
E-mail: information@goholland.com
Website: www.holland.com

Embassy of the United States of America
Lange Voorhout 102, 2514 EJ The Hague, The Netherlands
Tel: (70) 310 9209. Fax: (70) 361 4688.
Website: www.usemb.nl

Consulate General of the United States of America
Museumplein 19, 1071 DJ Amsterdam, The Netherlands
Tel: (20) 575 5309. Fax: (20) 575 5310 (visa section).
Website: www.usemb.nl

Royal Netherlands Embassy
350 Albert Street, Suite 2020, Constitution Square Building, Ottawa, Ontario K1R 1A4, Canada
Tel: (613) 237 5030. Fax: (613) 237 6471.
E-mail: nlgovott@netherlandsembassy.ca
Website: www.netherlandsembassy.ca
Consulates in: Calgary, Edmonton, Halifax, Kingston, London, Québec, Regina, Saint John, St John's and Winnipeg.
Consulates General in: Montréal, Toronto and Vancouver.

Netherlands Board of Tourism & Conventions (NBTC)
601 Dundas Street West, Box 24010, Whitby, Ontario L1N 8X8, Canada
Tel: (905) 666 5960. Fax: (905) 666 5391.
E-mail: information@holland.com
Website: www.holland.com/ca

Canadian Embassy
Street address: Sophialaan 7, 2514 JP The Hague, The Netherlands
Postal address: PO Box 30820, 2500 GV The Hague, The Netherlands
Tel: (70) 311 1600. Fax: (70) 311 1620.
E-mail: info@canada.nl
Website: www.canada.nl
Public enquiries should be made by post, fax or e-mail.

General Information

AREA: 41,528 sq km (16,034 sq miles).

POPULATION: 16,254,933 (official estimate 2004).

POPULATION DENSITY: 479.9 per sq km.

CAPITAL: Amsterdam. **Population**: 735,562 (2003). **Seat of Government**: The Hague. **Population**: 463,826 (2003).

GEOGRAPHY: The Netherlands shares borders to the south with Belgium and to the east with Germany, while the North Sea lies to the north and west. Large areas of The Netherlands have been reclaimed from the sea and consequently one-fifth of the country lies below sea level. The country is flat and level and is criss-crossed by rivers and canals. Areas reclaimed from the sea, known as *polders*, are extremely fertile. The landscape is broken by the forest of Arnhem, the bulb fields in the west, the lakes of the central and northern areas, and coastal dunes that are among the most impressive in Europe.

GOVERNMENT: Constitutional monarchy since 1848. **Head of State**: Queen Beatrix Van Oranje Nassau since 1980. **Head of Government**: Prime Minister Jan Peter Balkenende since 2002.

LANGUAGE: Dutch is the official language. English, German and French are widely spoken.

RELIGION: 31 per cent Roman Catholic, 21 per cent Protestant; 40 per cent do not profess any religion.

TIME: GMT + 1 (GMT from last Sunday in March to Saturday before last Sunday in October).

ELECTRICITY: 230 volts AC, 50Hz. Two-pin European-style plugs are in use.

COMMUNICATIONS: Telephone: Full IDD is available. Country code: 31 (followed by 20 for Amsterdam, 10 for Rotterdam and 70 for The Hague). Outgoing international code: 00. Telephone information is given in French, English and German. There is a cheaper rate from Mon-Fri 2000-0800. Calls can be made from public booths or post offices. Most booths only accept cards, which can be bought at post

offices, VVV offices, and shops displaying the *PTT-telephone card* poster; and, sometimes, coins. **Mobile telephone:** GSM 900 and 1800 networks across The Netherlands. Operators are *KPN Mobile* (website: www.kpn.com), *Orange* (website: www.orange.nl), *Telfort* (website: www.telfort.nl) and *T-mobile* (website: www.t-mobile.nl; also provides a 3G service). **Fax:** Services are widely available and are also provided by some hotels. **Internet:** There are many Internet cafes and some Internet access centres. Business centres also provide public access. Using the Internet is very straightforward in Amsterdam, where PCs are available free of charge in libraries and public buildings. **Telegram:** Facilities are available at all main post offices; telegrams can also be sent directly from telephone kiosks. **Post:** Stamps are available from all post offices as well as from tobacconists and kiosks selling postcards and souvenirs. Mail within Europe takes approximately five days. Post office hours: Mon-Fri 0900-1700. Some post offices in major towns are also open on late shopping nights (Thursday or Friday night) and Sat 1000-1300. There are all-night post offices in Amsterdam (Nieuwezijds Voorburgwal, behind the Royal Palace) and Rotterdam (Coolsingel).
Press: The main newspapers are *De Telegraaf*, *De Volkskrant*, *NRC Handelsblad* (an evening paper) and *Trouw*. Foreign newspapers are widely available.
Radio: BBC World Service (website: www.bbc.co.uk/worldservice) and Voice of America (website: www.voa.gov) can be received. From time to time the frequencies change and the most up-to-date can be found online.

Passport/Visa

	Passport Required?	Visa Required?	Return Ticket Required?
Full British	Yes	No	No
Australian	Yes	No	No
Canadian	Yes	No	No
USA	Yes	No	No
Other EU	1	No/2	No
Japanese	Yes	No	No

Note: *Regulations and requirements may be subject to change at short notice, and you are advised to contact the appropriate diplomatic or consular authority before finalising travel arrangements. Details of these may be found at the head of this country's entry. Any numbers in the chart refer to the footnotes below.*

Note: The Netherlands is a signatory to the **1995 Schengen Agreement**. For further details about passport/visa regulations within the Schengen area, see the introductory section in *How to Use this Guide*.
PASSPORTS: Passport valid for at least three months after the last day of the intended visit required by all except:
1. certain nationals of EU countries holding a valid national ID card. Enquire at the nearest Consulate/Embassy for further details.
VISAS: Required by all except the following for stays of up to three months:
(a) nationals referred to in the chart and under passport exemptions above (except **2.** nationals of Latvia who *do* require a visa);
(b) nationals of Andorra, Argentina, Bolivia, Brazil, Brunei, Bulgaria, Chile, Costa Rica, Croatia, El Salvador, Guatemala, Honduras, Iceland, Israel, Korea (Rep), Liechtenstein, Malaysia, Mexico, Monaco, New Zealand, Nicaragua, Norway, Panama, Paraguay, Romania, San Marino, Singapore, Switzerland, Uruguay, Vatican City and Venezuela;
(c) transit passengers continuing their journey to/from other *Schengen* countries within 72 hours by the same or first connecting aircraft, provided holding onward or return documentation and not leaving the airport.
Note: Nationals of Afghanistan, Angola, Bangladesh, Congo (Dem Rep), Eritrea, Ethiopia, The Gambia, Ghana, Guinea, Iran, Iraq, Nigeria, Pakistan, Sierra Leone, Somalia, Sri Lanka, Sudan and the Syrian Arab Republic passing through The Netherlands *always* require an airport transit visa, unless holding a Residence Permit for the USA or EEA countries, UK or temporary residence permit for Canada and the USA, valid on the departure date from The Netherlands, with a confirmed onward ticket and are not leaving the transit lounge. Transit passengers are advised to check transit regulations with the relevant Embassy or Consulate before travelling.
Types of visa and cost: A uniform type of visa, the *Schengen* visa, is issued free of charge for the relevant Schengen member nationals, for tourist, business and private visits. *Short-stay*, *Multiple-entry* and *Transit* visas are available for approximately €35, although prices are subject to change. All visas are subject to a non-refundable visa handling charge of £25, depending on the type of visa and the exchange rate. The Consulate (or Consular section at Embassy) can be contacted for further details.
Note: Spouses and children (under 21 years) and/or dependents of EU nationals (providing spouse's passport and the original marriage/birth certificate, mentioning

Credit: © Netherlands Board of Tourism & Conventions

name of parents with certified translation in English for Embassy in London are produced) receive their visas free of charge (enquire at Embassy or Consulate for details). Nationals of the Dominican Republic, Ghana, India, Nigeria and Pakistan should have their marriage and birth certificates verified and legalised by the relevant Netherlands Embassy or a visa fee will be charged.
Validity: Short-stay visas are valid for up to six months from date of issue for single- or multiple-entries of maximum 90 days per entry. Transit visas are valid for single- or multiple-entries of maximum five days per entry, including the day of arrival. Visas cannot be extended; a new application must be made each time.
Application to: Consulate (or Consular section at Embassy); see *Contact Addresses* section. Applications should be made in person. Travellers visiting just one Schengen country should apply to the Consulate of that country; travellers visiting more than one Schengen country should apply to the Consulate of the country chosen as the main destination *or* the country they will enter first (if they have no main destination).
Application requirements: (a) Passport (valid for at least three months longer than the validity of the visa requested) containing a blank page to affix the visa, or official travel document accepted by *Schengen* countries. If travelling on a new passport, the old one must also be submitted. A residence permit should be endorsed in your current valid passport and must still be valid on departure from the *Schengen* area. (b) Completed application form, listing full address and daytime telephone number. For minors under 18 years, it is necessary to submit approval from both parents or legal guardians, submitting a copy of each parent's/guardian's passport. (c) One passport-size photo. (d) Fee, where applicable (payable in cash or by postal order). (e) Travel insurance policy covering medical expenses, including emergency hotel treatment and repatriation, taken out in the UK, and with a minimum cover of €30 per day. (f) Evidence of sufficient funds for period of stay (eg bank statements or travellers cheques amounting to a minimum of £30 per day). *Business*: (a)-(f) and, (g) An invitation from a Dutch company confirming duration and purpose of stay, and a recent letter from the applicant's employer, solicitor, bank manager or local Chamber of Commerce, plus last payslip. If unemployed, submit a letter from a solicitor, accountant or Company House and Social Security booklet. *Student*: (a)-(f) and, (g) A letter from the applicant's school, college or university. *Tourist/Family Visits*: (a)-(f) and, (g) Original recent letter of guarantee legalised by town hall from sponsor in The Netherlands with a copy of his/her passport, residence permit and pay slips for the last three months, plus proof of accommodation. *Airport Transit*: (a)-(f) and, (g) Confirmed non-refundable and non-endorsable airline ticket.
Note: (a) The number of forms and photos required may vary according to the nationality of the applicant. (b) The applicant may also be asked to provide further relevant documentation in certain cases. (c) Applications must be made in person for those residing in the vicinity of London, UK, and appointments to do so must be made in advance by telephoning the automated telephone appointments booking service (tel: (09065) 540 720; calls cost £1 per minute). For those married to a Dutch national, it is not

A B C D E F G H I J K L M N O P Q R S T U V W X Y Z

Credit: © Netherlands Board of Tourism & Conventions

necessary to telephone the automated booking service. Those married to Dutch nationals may visit the Embassy in London from 0900-1100 on any working day, or visit another of the Dutch consulates in the UK. An original marriage certificate and original passport of Dutch spouse must be submitted. Postal applications are not accepted.
Working days required: Normally within 24 hours, but can take up to three months for certain nationals. It is essential to apply with plenty of time to spare (three weeks at the very least).
Temporary residence: Work permit and residence permit required for non-EU nationals. Enquire at Consulate (or Consular section at Embassy) for further information; see *Contact Addresses* section.

Money

Single European currency (Euro): The Euro is now the official currency of 12 EU member states (including The Netherlands). The first Euro coins and notes were introduced in January 2002; the Dutch Guilder was in circulation until 28 January 2002, when it was completely replaced by the Euro. Euro (€) = 100 cents. Notes are in denominations of €500, 200, 100, 50, 20, 10 and 5. Coins are in denominations of €2 and 1, and 50, 20, 10, 5, 2 and 1 cents.
Currency exchange: Exchange offices are indicated by the letters GWK. GWK is a national organisation with currency exchange offices at major railway stations, at Schiphol Airport and at the border crossings with Germany and Belgium. Hotels tend to charge high commissions. *Verkoopt* means sell, while *Koopt* means buy.
Credit & debit cards: American Express, Diners Club, MasterCard and Visa are accepted, as well as Eurocheque cards. Check with your credit or debit card company for details of merchant acceptability and other services which may be available.
Travellers cheques: Widely accepted. To avoid additional exchange rate charges, travellers are advised to take travellers cheques in Euros, Pounds Sterling or US Dollars.
Currency restrictions: There are no restrictions on the import and export of either local or foreign currency.
Exchange rate indicators: The following figures are included as a guide to the movements of the Euro against Sterling and the US Dollar:

Date	Feb '04	May '04	Aug '04	Nov '04
£1.00=	1.47	1.50	1.49	1.42
$1.00=	0.81	0.84	0.80	0.75

Banking hours: Mon 1300-1600; Tues-Fri 0900-1600. GWK offices are open seven days a week.

Duty Free

The following goods may be imported into The Netherlands without incurring customs duty by travellers from non-EU European countries and countries outside of Europe:
200 cigarettes or 50 cigars or 100 cigarillos or 250g of tobacco; 1l of liquor or 2l of sparkling wine or liqueur wines and 2l of non-sparkling wine; 50g of perfume and 250ml of eau de toilette; 500g of coffee or 200g of coffee extract; 100g of tea or 40g of tea extract; other goods to the value of €56.72 (if bought outside Europe) and €172.44 (if bought inside Europe).
Note: (a) Goods must be purchased in non-EU countries. (b) The above allowances are only for travellers aged 17 years and above. (c) Enquiries concerning current import regulations should be made to the Royal Netherlands Embassy in the country of departure, or to the national Chamber of Commerce. (d) The import of firearms and ammunition requires a licence.
Abolition of duty free goods within the EU: On June 30 1999, the sale of duty free alcohol and tobacco at airports and at sea was abolished in all of the original 15 EU member states. Of the 10 new member states that joined the EU on May 1 2004, these rules already apply to Cyprus and Malta. There are transitional rules in place for visitors returning to one of the original 15 EU countries from one of the other new EU countries. But for the original 15, plus Cyprus and Malta, there are now no limits imposed on importing tobacco and alcohol products from one EU country to another (with the exceptions of Denmark, Finland and Sweden, where limits *are* imposed). Travellers should note that they may be required to prove at customs that the goods purchased are for personal use *only*.

Public Holidays

2005: Jan 1 New Year's Day. **Mar 25-28** Easter. **Apr 30** Queen's Day. **May 5** Ascension/Liberation Day. **May 16** Whit Monday. **Dec 25** Christmas Day. **Dec 26** Boxing Day.
2006: Jan 1 New Year's Day. **Apr 14-17** Easter. **Apr 29** Queen's Day. **May 5** Liberation Day. **May 25** Ascension. **Jun 5** Whit Monday. **Dec 25** Christmas Day. **Dec 26** Boxing Day.

Health

	Special Precautions?	Certificate Required?
Yellow Fever	No	No
Cholera	No	No
Typhoid & Polio	No	N/A
Malaria	No	N/A

Note: *Regulations and requirements may be subject to change at short notice, and you are advised to contact your doctor well in advance of your intended date of departure. Any numbers in the chart refer to the footnotes below.*

Other risks: *Rabies* may be present in animals, although risk to travellers is very rare. For those at high risk, vaccination before arrival should be considered. If you are bitten, seek medical advice without delay. For more information, consult the *Health* appendix.
Health care: The standard of health care (and other social services) is very high, with an unusually high proportion of the national income devoted to public health. There is a reciprocal health agreement with all other EU countries. On presentation of form E111 by UK residents (available from post offices or the Department of Health) medical treatment, including hospital treatment, is free; prescribed medicines and dental treatment must, however, be paid for. Further information can be obtained from The Netherlands General Sickness Insurance Fund (Algemeen Nederlands Onderling Ziekenfonds - ANOZ), at Kaap Hoorndreef 24-28, Utrecht, or the local sickness insurance office. Certain strong medicines can be taken to The Netherlands if they are accompanied by a doctor's prescription. Outside of the EU, The Netherlands has reciprocal health agreements with Cape Verde, Morocco, Serbia & Montenegro, Tunisia and Turkey. All other travellers are advised to take out full medical insurance. For police, fire or ambulance emergencies, dial 112 anywhere in the country.

Travel - International

AIR: The Netherlands' national airline is *KLM-Royal Dutch Airlines (KLM)* (website: www.klm.com). *KLM* flies direct to all major European, North American and Asia-Pacific cities. *KLM Excel* flies between London Stansted and Maastricht. Most major international airlines, and some low-cost carriers fly to Amsterdam.
Approximate flight times: From Amsterdam to *Belfast* is one hour; to *London* is one hour 20 minutes; to *Manchester* is one hour 15 minutes, and to *New York* is seven hours (including stopover in London).
International airports: *Amsterdam (AMS)* (Schiphol) (website: www.schiphol.nl) is 15km (9 miles) southwest of the city (travel time by train - 20 minutes). KLM buses provide a daily service from 0600-0000 departing every 15 to 30 minutes, stopping at a selection of major hotels and returning to Schiphol. There is a direct rail link between the airport and Amsterdam *Centraal Station*, with trains every 15 minutes from 0600-0000 and every hour through the night. Trains to *Zuid Station* (Amsterdam South) run every 15 minutes from 0525-0015; return is from *Zuid Station*, Parnassusweg/ Minervalaan (via tram no. 5 from the city centre) from 0545-0040. There is also a service to the RAI Congress Centre every 15 minutes from 0525-0012. Return is from RAI station (via tram no. 4 from the city centre) from 0545-0040. Plentiful taxis are available to the city. Airport facilities include restaurants, duty free shops, currency exchange machines (able to convert 17 different currencies), banks, an art gallery, baby rooms, showers, a business centre (with fax, personal computer and telephone facilities), conference rooms and car hire.
Rotterdam (RTM) (Zestienhoven) (website: www.rotterdam-airport.nl) is 8km (5 miles) northwest of the city (travel time - 15 minutes). Bus no. 33 departs every 10 minutes. Return is from Central Station (travel time - 20 minutes). Taxis to the city are also available. Airport facilities include restaurant, bank, outgoing duty free shop and car hire.
Eindhoven (EIN) (Welschap) (website: www.eindhovenairport.nl) is 8km (5 miles) from the city. Coaches run every 15 minutes and taxis to the city are also available. Airport facilities include car hire, ATMs, restaurants and outgoing duty free shops.
Maastricht (MST) (Aachen) (website: www.maa.nl) is 8km (5 miles) from the city. Airport facilities include outgoing duty free shop.
Groningen (GRQ) (Eelde) (website: www.groningenairporteelde.nl) is 9km (6 miles) from the city.
Enschede (ENS) (Twente) (website: www.enschede-airport.nl) is 8km (5 miles) from the city.
Departure tax: None.
SEA: The major ferry ports are Hook of Holland (Hoek van Holland), Rotterdam and Vlissingen. Regular car and passenger ferries are operated from the UK to The Netherlands via the following routes and shipping lines:
Stena Line (tel: (08705) 707 070; website: www.stenaline.co.uk): Harwich to Hook of Holland; travel time - three hours 40 minutes (day), six hours 15 minutes (night); two sailings daily.
P&O Ferries (tel: (08705) 202 020; website: www.ponsf.com): Hull to Rotterdam (Europoort); travel time - 12 hours; one sailing nightly.
DFDS Seaways (tel: (08705) 333 000 (within the UK) *or* (01255) 240 240 (outside the UK); website: www.dfdsseaways.co.uk): Newcastle to Amsterdam; travel time - 16 hours.
Note: *Hoverspeed UK* and *P&O European Ferries* run services to The Netherlands via Belgium. French ports also provide connections.
RAIL: Eurostar operates direct high-speed trains from London (*Waterloo International*) to Paris (*Gare du Nord*) and to Brussels (*Midi/Zuid*). It takes three hours from London to Paris and it takes two hours 40 minutes from London to Brussels. Local trains run between Brussels and Amsterdam (travel time - approximately two hours 45 minutes). Eurostar operates eight daily services to Brussels and *Thalys International* runs six daily trains (seven in summer) onwards to Amsterdam and other Dutch destinations.
The Eurostar trains are equipped with standard-class and first-class seating, buffet, bar and are staffed by multilingual, highly trained personnel. Pricing is competitive with the airlines, and there is a large range of different tickets and prices. Children aged between four to 11 years benefit from a special fare in first class as well as in standard class. Children under four years old travel free but cannot be guaranteed a seat. Wheelchair users and blind passengers together with one companion get a special fare. For further information and reservations, contact Eurostar (tel: (0870) 600 0792 (travel agents) or (08705) 186 186 (public; within the UK) *or* (+44 1233) 617 575 (public; outside the UK only); website: www.eurostar.com); *or Rail Europe* (tel: (08705) 848 848). Travel agents can obtain refunds for unused tickets from Eurostar Trade Refunds, 2nd Floor, Kent House, 81 Station Road, Ashford, Kent TN23 1PD, UK. Complaints and comments may be sent to Eurostar Customer Relations, Eurostar House, Waterloo Station, London SE1 8SE, UK (tel: (020) 7928 5163; e-mail: new.comments@eurostar.co.uk). Rail travellers not using the Channel Tunnel link need to make some form of sea crossing, usually by ferry or hovercraft; for details on sea crossings, see also under *Sea* above. The cost of the crossing is usually included in the price of the rail ticket.
There are plenty of rail passes on offer to travellers visiting The Netherlands, including discounts for young and senior citizens. For further details, contact Rail Europe (website: www.raileurope.com).
ROAD: The Netherlands is connected to the rest of Europe by a superb network of motorways. All roads are well signposted with green 'E' symbols indicating international highways, red 'A's indicating national highways, and smaller routes indicated by yellow 'N's. The national speed limit is 120kph (75mph). Although frontier formalities between The

Netherlands, Germany and Belgium have now all but vanished, motorists – particularly on smaller roads – should be prepared to stop when asked to do so by a customs official. The yellow cars of the *ANWB/Wegenwacht* (Royal Dutch Touring Club) (tel: (70) 314 1420) patrol major roads 24 hours a day with qualified mechanics equipped to handle routine repairs. In case of emergencies, assistance is available (tel: 60888 within The Netherlands only).
The Channel Tunnel: All road vehicles are carried through the tunnel in *Eurotunnel* shuttles running between the two terminals, one near Folkestone in Kent, with direct road access from the M20, and one just outside Calais, with links to the A16/A26 motorway (Exit 13). Each shuttle is made up of 12 single- and 12 double-deck carriages, and vehicles are directed to single-deck or double-deck carriages depending on their height. There are facilities for cars and motorcycles, coaches, minibuses, caravans, campervans and other vehicles over 1.85m (6.07ft). Bicycles are provided for. Passengers generally travel with their vehicles. Heavy goods vehicles are carried on special shuttles and drivers travel in a separate carriage. Terminals and shuttles are well equipped for disabled passengers, and Passenger Terminal buildings contain a variety of shops, restaurants, bureaux de change and other amenities. The journey takes about 35 minutes from platform to platform and about one hour from motorway to motorway. Services run every day of the year, and there are between two and five an hour, depending on the time of day. There is a reservation system and a turn-up-and-go service. Motorists pass through customs and immigration before they board the shuttle without further checks on arrival. Fares vary according to length of stay, time of day and time of year and whether you have a reservation or not. The price applies to the car, regardless of the number of passengers or size of the car. The fare may be paid in cash, by cheque or by credit card. For further information, contact *Eurotunnel Customer Services UK* (tel: (08705) 353 535; website: www.eurotunnel.com).
Coach: *Eurolines* run coach services from the UK to The Netherlands and from The Netherlands to various destinations throughout Europe. They have an office in Amsterdam at Julianaplein 5, 1097 DN (tel: (20) 560 8788; fax: (20) 560 8717; e-mail: info@eurolines.nl; website: www.eurolines.nl). Further information can also be obtained by calling Eurolines in the UK (4 Cardiff Road, Luton, Bedfordshire L41 1PP; tel: (08705) 143 219; fax: (01582) 400 694; website: www.eurolines.com *or* www.nationalexpress.com). **Car hire**: Major companies can be found in all the main cities; among them are *Avis, Budget, Europcar* and *Hertz*.

Travel - Internal

AIR: *KLM Cityhopper (WA)* (website: www.klmcityhopper.nl) operates between Amsterdam and Eindhoven. *Transavia Airlines (HV)* (80 per cent of which is owned by *KLM*) also run scheduled flights. *Martinair Holland (MP)* operates passenger and cargo charter services. Enquire at *KLM* offices or at The Netherlands Board of Tourism for further information (see *Contact Addresses* section).
SEA: There are ferry services to the Wadden Islands (Ameland, Schiermonnikoog, Terschilling, Texel and Vlieland) across the Ijsselmeer (former Zuyder Sea) and Schelde Estuary. There is also a service to the Frisian Islands across the Waddenzee. *Boat Tours* runs excursions from Amsterdam, Arnhem, Delft, Giethoorn, Groningen, Maastricht, Rotterdam and Utrecht. *Stena Line* operates a daily service for private cars, freight and trailers.
Wadden Ticket: For travellers wanting to visit any of the five Wadden Islands, the Wadden Ticket allows return travel by bus, train and ferry to an island of choice. The pass is valid for one day of the departure journey and one day of the return journey, although the period between the two must not exceed one year. Contact The Netherlands Board of Tourism for further details (see *Contact Addresses* section).
RAIL: The highly developed rail network, of which about 70 per cent is electrified, is efficient and cheap, and connects all towns. Both Intercity and local trains run at least half-hourly on all principal routes. Rail and bus timetables are integrated, and there is a common fare structure throughout the country. *NV Nederlandse Spoorwegen* (website: www.ns.nl) is the state-owned rail company and operates all lines within the country.
Cheap fares: *Holland Rail Pass* allows unlimited travel in the Netherlands for either three or five days within one month. Reduced rates exist for senior citizens (over 60), travellers under 26 years and children. Every second person travels half-price. Tickets must be purchased from International Rail before travel.
Summer Trip Passes are available between 1 July to 9 September and give two people three days of unlimited travel within a period of 10 days for only a single fare. *Summer Trip Plus Passes* cover unlimited travel on all public transport buses and trams in town and country, and on the underground system in Amsterdam and Rotterdam. Tickets cost between €45 and 72.50.
Euro Passes are available for travel in The Netherlands, or The Netherlands and Belgium. Three- to eight-day passes are available. *The Benelux Tourrail Card* allows unlimited travel for any five days within a one-month period, covering The Netherlands, Belgium and Luxembourg. *Inter-Rail* passes are also valid in The Netherlands.
Children under four years of age travel free on all journeys within The Netherlands. *Child's Railrunner* tickets, which cost €1, are available for children aged between four and 11 years travelling with a fare-paying adult (19 years or older), and include up to three children travelling with any one adult. Contact the Railway Authority of any of the participating countries for prices and further information.
ROAD: There is an excellent road system. Visitors to The Netherlands may use credit cards when obtaining petrol. The motoring association in The Netherlands is the *ANWB* (Royal Dutch Touring Club), PO Box 93200, 2509 BA The Hague (tel: (263) 860 249). **Bus**: Extensive regional bus networks exist. Long-distance coaches also operate between the cities, but costs are generally on a par with trains. **Taxi**: Taxis have an illuminated 'taxi' sign on the roof and there are taxi ranks at railway stations and at various other points in the cities. Rather than hailing taxis in the street, it is more usual in The Netherlands to order a taxi by phone. Taxis should have meters inside to indicate the fare, including the tip. **Car hire**: Available from airports and main hotels. All European car hire companies are represented. **Bicycle hire**: Bicycles can be hired from all main railway stations, but must be returned to the station from which they are hired. A refundable deposit is required.
Driving regulations: Driving is on the right. Drivers should be particularly aware of cyclists; often there are special cycle lanes. There is a chronic shortage of parking space in central Amsterdam, and the rush hours (0700-0900 and 1700-1900) should be avoided throughout the whole country. Parking fines are severe. Headlights should be dipped in built-up areas, but it is prohibited to use sidelights only. Children under 12 years of age should not travel in the front seat. Seat belts are compulsory. Speed limits are 80kph (50mph) on major roads, 120kph (75mph) on motorways and 50kph (30mph) in towns.
Documentation: An International Driving Permit is not required, as long as a driving licence from the country of origin is held. EU pink format licences are accepted. However, it is sometimes advised for non-members of the EU. Trailers and caravans are allowed in without documents. A Green Card is advisable, but not compulsory. Without it, drivers with motor insurance policies in their home country are granted only the minimum legal cover in The Netherlands; the Green Card tops this up to the level of cover provided by the driver's own policy.
URBAN: Public transport is very well developed in the cities and large towns. A *strippenkaart* national fares system exists – strips of 15 tickets each are widely available at railway stations, post offices and some tourist offices. These are accepted anywhere in payment of standard zonal fares. There are also individual and multi-day tickets for the cities. For more detailed information on travel within Amsterdam, The Hague and Rotterdam, see below.
Amsterdam: Amsterdam has an extensive network of buses, trams and underground (*GVB*), with frequent services from early morning to about midnight. There are less frequent services throughout the night at a higher fare. Full information on services (including a map), day tickets and *strippenkaart* (strip-tickets) can be obtained from the GVB office in front of the Central Station (0700-2230 daily) or the GVB Central Office at Prins Hendrikkade 108-114.
Tram: Amsterdam's 17 tram lines provide a fast, frequent and reliable service, making the tram the best way to travel around the capital. Trams operate from Mon-Fri 0600-2400 (from 0630 Saturday and 0730 Sunday). The tram system (as well as the buses and the underground) enables reasonably quick travel even during the busiest periods of the day. Trams leave from Central Station: 1 and 2 traverse the main canals, 19 takes a route to Museumplein and Concertgebouw and 9 and 14 to the Muziektheater and Waterlooplein market. The Circle Tram operates through central Amsterdam, taking in major attractions and hotels.
Underground: Amsterdam's underground lines all originate at the Central Station and serve the southeastern business district and the suburbs. Trains run from Mon-Fri 0600-0015, from Sat 0630 and from Sun 0730. The GVB is easy to use. **Taxi**: These are fairly expensive. Taxis can be ordered by phone or picked up at taxi ranks (Central Station, Leidseplein and Rembrandtplein). Fares are indicated by the meter; a small tip will be appreciated.
Car hire: The major European firms, including *Avis* and *Hertz*, are represented. Cars can also be hired through most hotels. Parking regulations are quite strict and failure to park in prescribed areas or to pay the parking fee can result in a fine and the prospect of the car being clamped or towed away. **Water travel**: Canal Buses (every 25 to 45 minutes between Central Station and Rijksmuseum; children under the age of five travel free); Watertaxis (Mon-Sun 0900-0100, carrying eight to 25 passengers); Museum Boats (departing from Prins endrikkade every 30 minutes in summer and every 45 minutes in winter) and Waterbikes (for two to four people, with a route map provided) are all available. **Boat hire**: Visitors can hire pedalos (also known as canal bikes) and boats to explore the canals.
Bicycle hire: This is an excellent way to travel around Amsterdam, and it seems nearly everyone is doing it. Cycle lanes are clearly marked by white lines – but visitors are advised to watch out for trams, cars and pedestrians. There are numerous companies hiring out bikes.
Rotterdam: The city has excellent bus and tram services and a two-line underground network, which all work on a zonal system. Information is available from the Central Station. **Car hire**: The major European firms, including *Avis, Hertz* and other international agencies are represented.
The Hague: The Hague has bus and tram services. Information is available from the Central Station, Koningin Julianaplein. **Car hire**: *Avis* and *Hertz*, and other international agencies, are represented.
Travel Times: The following chart gives approximate travel times (in hours and minutes) from **Amsterdam** to other major cities in The Netherlands.

	Air	Road	Rail
The Hague	-	0.40	0.44
Rotterdam	-	1.00	1.00
Utrecht	-	0.25	0.30
Groningen	-	2.00	2.20
Arnhem	-	1.10	1.10
Maastricht	0.40	2.30	2.30
Vlissingen	-	2.00	2.45
Eindhoven	0.30	1.30	1.25
Breda	-	1.30	1.50

Accommodation

HOTELS: The Netherlands has a wide range of accommodation, from luxury hotels in big towns to modern motels along motorways. The Netherlands Reservation Centre (NRC) (*Netherlands Reserverings Centrum*) can make reservations throughout the country: Plantsoengracht 2, 1441 DE Purmerend (tel: (299) 689 144; fax: (299) 689 154; e-mail: info@hotelres.nl; website: www.hotelres.nl).
Grading: The Netherlands Board of Tourism issues a shield to all approved hotels by which they can be recognised. This must be affixed to the front of the hotel in a conspicuous position. Hotels which display this sign conform to the official standards set by Dutch law on hotels, which protects the tourist and guarantees certain standards of quality. Hotels are also graded according to the *Benelux* system, in which the standard is indicated by a row of 3-pointed stars from the highest (**5-star**) to the minimum (**1-star**). However, membership of this scheme is voluntary, and there may be first-class hotels that are not classified in this way. *Benelux* star ratings adhere to the following criteria. For further information, contact The Netherlands Board of Tourism (see *Contact Addresses* section).
5-star (H5): This is a new category signifying a luxury hotel. Amenities include private bath and/or shower, toilet, radio and TV in every room; 24-hour room service; fax facilities in reception. **4-star (H4)**: First-class hotels. 80 per cent of rooms have a private bath. Other amenities include night reception and room service. **3-star (H3)**: Half of the rooms have a private bath or shower. Other amenities include day reception and the sale of tobacco products. **2-star (H2)**: A quarter of rooms have a private bath. Other amenities include a bar. **1-star (H1)**: Simple hotel. No private baths, but hot and cold water in rooms; breakfast available. **Cat H**: Hotel with minimal comfort. **Cat O**: Simple accommodation.
GUEST HOUSES: These are called *pensions* and rates vary. Book through local tourist offices.
BED & BREAKFAST: Not as common a form of accommodation as it is in the UK but reservations can be made online (website: www.bedandbreakfast.nl).
SELF-CATERING: Farmhouses for groups can be booked months in advance via the local tourist offices. Holiday chalets, especially in the relatively unknown parts of Zeeland, can be booked through the local tourist office. Bungalow parks throughout the country can be booked through The Netherlands Reserverings Centrum (NRC). Most bungalow resorts offer a full range of recreational facilities including swimming pools, golf and tennis. Prices depend on size, quality of amenities and the time of year. To order a self-catering brochure, call The Netherlands Board of Tourism (see *Contact Addresses* section).
CAMPING/CARAVANNING: There are some 2500 registered campsites in Holland. Only 500 offer advanced booking, the others operate on a first-come, first-served basis. Off-site camping is not permitted. Prices are fairly high and it is often far better value to stay more than one night. A list is available from The Netherlands Board of Tourism (see *Contact Addresses* section) and reservations can be made through the Stichting Vrije Recreatie, Scr Broakseweg 75-77, 4231 VD Meerkerk (tel: (183) 352 741-3; fax: (183) 351 234; website: www.svr.nl).

YOUTH HOSTELS: There are 34 hostels in various surroundings, from castles to modern buildings. People with a Hostelling International card pay approximately €9,00 to 13,60 for an overnight stay including breakfast (non-members pay €2,27 more). Information is obtainable from Stayokay (the Dutch Youth Hostel Association/ tichting Nederlandse Jeugdherberg Centrale) (tel: (10) 264 6064; e-mail: info@stayokay.com; website: www.stayokay.com).

Resorts & Excursions

The Netherlands today has dispelled all images of it being an archaic land of clogs and windmills, with its string of exciting cities, including the cosmopolitan capital, Amsterdam. Elsewhere, Arnhem, Eindhoven, The Hague, Utrecht and the especially buzzing Rotterdam all boast their own charms. Away from the cities, the idyllic land of windmills and tulips does still exist in the bucolic splendour of the countryside, as do a number of coastal towns and resorts, many with fine beaches and similarly interesting heritages to The Netherlands' bigger historical cities.

AMSTERDAM

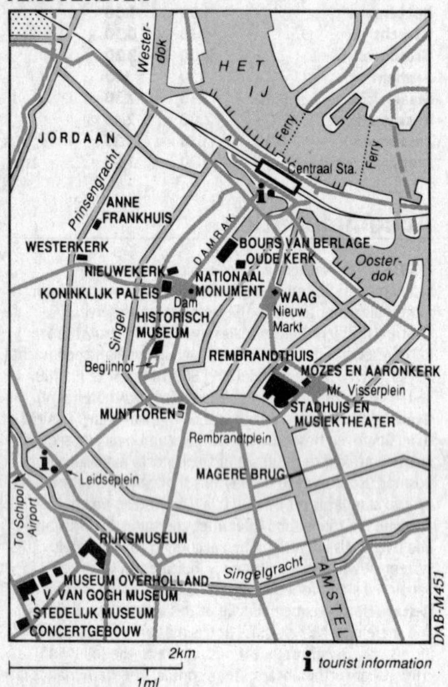

AMSTERDAM

Amsterdam, the capital of The Netherlands (though not the seat of Government) is one of Europe's great destinations, as popular with tourists as it is with businesspeople.
Amsterdam's lifeblood is water, which courses through the city in a concentric network of canals and waterways spanned by more than 1000 bridges. As Amsterdam is inextricably linked with water, one of the most attractive ways of viewing the city is on a canal tour. Many of the houses date back to The Netherlands' golden age in the 17th century. These narrow-fronted merchants' houses are characterised by the traditionally Dutch ornamented gables. The oldest part of the city is **Nieuwmarkt**, located near the first canals – **Herengracht**, **Keizersgracht** and **Prinsengracht** – built to protect the city against invasion. In the 17th century, Amsterdam gained a reputation for religious tolerance, which attracted thousands of Flemish, Walloon and French Protestants, as well as Jewish merchants from Spain, Portugal and Central Europe. The city has also long been a centre for diamond cutting and it is still possible to see diamond cutters at work. Boasting 53 museums, 61 art galleries, 12 concert halls and 20 theatres, Amsterdam has a booming cultural life. A special canal boat (the 'museum boat') links 16 of the major museums. A special Museum Pass entitling holders to free entry to over 400 museums is available from participating museums and local tourist offices.
One of the city's cultural Meccas is the **Rijksmuseum**, a voluminous art gallery that is home to the works of many of the country's artistic luminaries, as well as numerous European masters. The highlight for many visitors is Dutch master Rembrandt's epic *Night Watch*, though the list of the gallery's treasures is almost endless. Fellow Dutch artist Van Gogh is celebrated throughout the city, with the **Rembrandt House Museum**, housed in the historical building where the great artist used to live and work. The **Stedelijk Museum of Modern Art**, a collection of Dutch and international art from 1850 onwards, includes works by Cézanne, Chagall, Monet and Picasso, as well as photography, video, film and industrial design. Amsterdam's most poignant museum is **Anne Frank's House**, where the young Jewish girl hid away from the occupying German forces, who were intent on ridding the city of all Jews and sending them to their cruel fates in the death camps. The museum illuminates the young girl's life and is of interest to everyone, whether they have read her famous diary or not. A more light-hearted attraction is the **Heineken Brewery**. Heineken, the Dutch national brewer, is the world's second-largest brewing empire and this brewery, which operated from 1932-1988, is now a museum. There are daily guided tours, which culminate with ice-cold samples of the famous beer.
Amsterdam is justifiably famous for its nightlife with few other European cities managing to quite satisfy every conceivable taste in the same way as The Netherlands' capital. Within a few blocks, well-heeled couples idle away an evening in a canal-side gourmet restaurant, and a group of backpackers stumble across the cobbles after a night in a cheery pub, as just around the corner the local trendies pose their way through an evening in a new-style bar. Then there is the **Opera House**, the string of concert venues, the football stadium, some of Europe's best nightclubs and the jazz cafes, to name a few other nocturnal pastimes in Amsterdam. And, of course, there are the seedier ways to spend an evening, either exploring the infamous coffee shops of a city where soft drugs are not only allowed, but are sold over the counter, and the **Red Light District**, a nefarious playground where all sorts of low life mingle with the curious and the downright seedy. Wherever tourists spend their evening, there is the same relaxed, live-and-let-live ambience of a city where almost anything goes.
Amsterdam Pass: This offers free admission to many museums, tourist attractions and public transport as well as up to 25 per cent discount on certain other attractions, restaurants and transportation within the city. The pass is available for one day (€26), two days (€36) and three days (€46). Further details about the pass can be obtained from the Amsterdam Tourist Office (tel: (20) 201 8800; fax: (20) 201 8850; e-mail: info@atcb.nl).
AROUND AMSTERDAM: There are numerous possible excursions and day trips available from Amsterdam, with an efficient national rail network that links the surrounding towns and cities to the metropole. **Alkmaar**, where there is a famous cheese market at **Waagplein**, open every Friday from mid-April to mid-September, is a popular day trip. There is also a good bus service from Amsterdam to **Marken** and **Volendam**, both old fishing villages largely built of wood. The former is predominantly Catholic, the latter Protestant and both easily occupy a whole day.
HAARLEM: Located 20km (12 miles) west of Amsterdam, Haarlem is a centre of Dutch tulip growing and the surrounding countryside affords a fine view of the bulb fields from the end of March to mid-May. The town itself has a beautiful 16th- and 17th-century town centre and two fine museums. The **Teyler Museum** was first established in 1784 from its world-famous Oval Room by merchant banker, Pieter Teyler van der Hulst. The museum has a very diverse collection, which includes drawings by Rembrandt, scientific instruments, fossils and coins. The ultramodern new wing offers a striking contrast with the oak-panelled rooms of the original building. The **Frans Hals Museum** houses paintings by the artist. Also worth visiting is **St Bavokerk Cathedral**, containing a 5000-pipe organ, which Mozart is reported to have played.
UTRECHT: The city of Utrecht is a favourite destination with the Dutch, as it offers many of Amsterdam's charms on a smaller scale without the tourist hordes that fill the capital for much of the year. The fourth-largest city in The Netherlands is also one of the oldest cities in the country, the site first having been settled by the Romans. During the Middle Ages, Utrecht was often an imperial residence, and the city's bishops regularly played an important role in the secular affairs of Europe. The city's prosperity allowed the construction of several beautiful churches, particularly the **Cathedral of St Michael** (13th century), **St Pieterskerk** and **St Janskerk** (both 11th century) and **St Jacobkerk** (12th century). Other buildings of note include the **House of the Teutonic Order**, the 14th-century **Huys Oudaen**, the **Hospice of St Bartholomew** and the **Neudeflat**, a more modern construction (built in the 1960s), but one which affords a superb view across the city from its 15th-floor restaurant. The city also has several museums, including the **Central Museum** (which has an excellent Department of Modern Art), the **Archiepiscopal Museum**, the **Railway Museum**, the **Archaeological Collection** and the **Municipal Museum**. The best way to explore Utrecht is by canal boat, which takes visitors on a loop of the city that opens up its different districts. Utrecht's bars and restaurants are also renowned for their quality and good value, and the lively nightlife is propelled by the large local student community.
UTRECHT PROVINCE: The province of Utrecht, in the very heart of The Netherlands, contains numerous country houses, estates and castles set in landscaped parks and beautiful woods. The countryside around Utrecht is very fertile and seems like one large garden.
25km (16 miles) to the northeast of Utrecht is the town of **Amersfoort**, set in a region of heathland and forest. The old town is well preserved, one of the most attractive buildings being the **Church of St George**. Just 8km (5 miles) away is the town of **Soestdijk**, containing the **Royal Palace** and the beautiful parklands of the Queen Mother. Between Soestdijk and **Hilversum** is **Baarn**, a favourite summer resort among the Dutch.
ELSEWHERE: Nearby, the casino at **Zandvoort** (west of Haarlem) is also the site of the annual **Dutch Grand Prix**. There is a famous **Flower Auction in Aalsmeer**; open weekday mornings. Near **Lisse**, south of Haarlem, are the **Keukenhof Gardens**, which have a lily show in late May. The **Frans Roozen Nurseries & Tulip Show** and the bulb fields can also be visited. **Broek op Langedijk** has Europe's oldest vegetable auction hall with a large and interesting exhibition of the land reclamation of the surrounding area. **Enkhuizen** and **Hoorn** are well-known watersports centres. The latter town features the **National Zuyder Zee Museum**, an outdoor museum with ships and reconstructed houses.

THE NORTH

FRIESLAND: The province of Friesland in the northwest of the country has its own language and its own distinct culture. A large part of the marshlands along the North Sea coast have been reclaimed from the sea. Friesian cattle are among the most famous inhabitants of the area. The Friesian lake district in the southern part of the state centres on the town of **Sneek**, and is a good place for watersports, particularly yachting. Near Sneek is the small town of **Bolsward**, which has a magnificent Renaissance **Town Hall**. **Leeuwarden**, the capital of Friesland, has several old buildings and the **Friesian Museum**, probably the most important provincial museum in the country. Some 6km (4 miles) to the west is the village of **Marssum**, which has a 16th-century manor house. There are daily ferry connections with four of the Friesian Islands and a chain of museums on the **Aldfaer's Erf Route**. The **Hollandse and Friesian Islands** (**Ameland**, **Schiermonnikoog**, **Terschelling**, **Texel** and **Vlieland**), on which there are bird sanctuaries and areas of outstanding natural beauty, lie north of the mainland.
GRONINGEN: The agricultural province of Groningen is known for its fortified country houses dating back to the 14th century. The provincial capital, **Groningen**, is commercially the most important town in the north of The Netherlands, as well as being a major cultural centre. The city suffered considerable damage during World War II, but many of the 16th- and 18th-century buildings have now been restored.
DRENTHE: This is a province of extensive cycle paths, prehistoric monuments (particularly in the area of the village of **Havelte**) and Saxon villages. The region is almost entirely agricultural, much of the land being drained by the system of *venns* and *weiks*. The main town, **Assen**, set in an area of woodlands, was an insignificant village until the middle of the last century, and has no historical monuments. The **Provincial Museum** is, however, worth a visit. There are also several Megalithic tombs to be found south and southwest of the town.
THE HAGUE & ZUID-HOLLAND: The Hague (Den Haag, officially known as 's-Gravenhage), the seat of the Dutch government, is home to over 60 foreign embassies, the International Court of Justice and the capital of the province of Zuid-Holland. This has earned the city an unwarranted reputation for being dull and sterile, but in fact The Hague is well worth visiting and boasts a number of attractions. The central part of the Old Town is the **Binnenhof**, an irregular group of buildings surrounding an open space. The seaside resort of **Scheveningen** (which has the country's only pier) is a nearby suburb. Walking around the old parts of town is a joy in itself – the local tourist office publishes a map that opens up the city and also includes most of the 150 antique shops in The Hague. The **Parliament Buildings and Knight's Hall** are 13th-century buildings where there are regular tours and slide shows that illuminate their history, while the **Royal Cabinet of Paintings**, housed in the **Mauritshuis**, is a collection that includes the *Anatomical Lesson of Dr Tulp* by Rembrandt, and other 17th-century Dutch works. Other attractions include the **Gemeentemusem**, a recently renovated municipal museum that houses an interesting collection of modern art as well as interactive displays illustrating a wide range of subjects; the **Puppet Museum**, with its old and new puppets; the antique market at the **Lange Voorhout**; the **Duinoord** district built in the style of old Dutch architecture; the **Haagse Bos** wooded park; the 17th-century **Nieuwe Kerk**; and the **Royal Library**.
On the outskirts of the city is one of Europe's most unusual attractions: **Madurodam Miniature Town** is a playground for the young and not so young alike, a scale model (1:5) of a typical Dutch landscape, complete with houses, motorways and even fire-fighting boats extinguishing real

fires. Adjacent to Madurodam is **Sand World**, a recently opened collection of sand sculptures. Another bizarre local attraction is the **Panorama Mesdag**, the largest panoramic circular painting in the world, create by the artist Mesdag amongst others, and famous for its perfect optical illusion.
ZUID-HOLLAND: About 22km (14 miles) southeast of Rotterdam and about 45km (28 miles) southeast of The Hague is **Kinderdijk**, near **Alblasserdam**, a good place to see windmills. They can be visited during the week. **Delft**, centre of the Dutch pottery industry and world famous for its blue hand-painted ceramics, is roughly midway between Rotterdam and The Hague. **Gouda**, 20km (12 miles) southeast of Rotterdam, is famous for its cheese market and the *Candlelight Festival* in December. The town centre is dominated by the massive late-Gothic **Town Hall**. Nearby is the pretty old town of **Oudewater**, noted for its beautiful 17th-century gabled houses. Northwest of Gouda by 12km (7 miles) is the town of **Boskoop**, renowned for its fruit trees; a visit during the blossom season is a delightful experience. **Dordrecht**, 15km (9 miles) southeast of Rotterdam and about 37km (23 miles) southeast of The Hague, was an important port until a flood in 1421 reduced the economic importance of the town. The museum in the city has a good collection of paintings from the 17th, 18th and 19th centuries, while the most striking building is probably the **Grote Kerk**, begun in about 1305. **Leiden**, 20km (12 miles) northeast of The Hague, 40km (25 miles) north of Rotterdam, the birthplace of Rembrandt, was a famous weaving town during the Middle Ages, and played a large part in the wars of independence against Spain in the 16th century. The university was founded by William the Silent in 1575 in return for the city's loyalty. The Pilgrim Fathers lived here for 10 years (1610-1620) and **The Pilgrim Fathers' Documentation Centre** in **Boisotkade** (Vliet 45) has many artefacts, records and paintings dating from the period of their stay in the city. The town also boasts one of the most charming windmills in the country, set in a park overlooking water.

ROTTERDAM

Rotterdam is no longer content to play second fiddle to Amsterdam and in recent years has rejuvenated its city centre, regenerated much of its dockside and also hosted the European City of Culture. Rotterdam is Europe's largest and, indeed, the world's second-largest port and is the hub of the Dutch economy, but it is now also emerging as a tourist destination in its own right. Much of the city was obliterated during World War II, and only small parts of the old city remain. Historically, the city has been an important manufacturing centre since the 14th century, but its pre-eminence as a port dates only from the early 19th century. The best place to get an idea of the city layout is from the viewing level of the **Euromast & Space Tower**, which at 185m (605ft) is the highest point in The Netherlands. Rotterdam's pride in its maritime heritage is on show at the **Maritiem Museum Prins Hendrik**, where outdoor and indoor exhibits include ships, barges, harbour cranes and marine archaeological artefacts. Regular boat tours also now take tourists around the city's abundance of channels and waterways. Boat tours (*Spido*) through the harbour of Rotterdam are available throughout the year. In the summer, there are excursions to **Europoort**, the **Delta Project** as well as evening tours, and there are also luxury motor cruisers for hire. Rotterdam's cultural scene is also rich with the **Museum Boymans van Beuningen**, a unique collection of paintings, sculptures and *objets d'art* dating from the 14th century to the present day, and the **Museum Voor Volkenkunde**, an ethnological museum, amongst the highlights. For younger visitors, **Dierenpark Blijdorp** (**Zoo**) is an open-plan zoo, beautifully laid out, with a restaurant. The exotic wildlife includes bats, wolves, elephants and rhinos, all amongst tropical forest vegetation. A drive through the harbour of Rotterdam is also possible; the 100 to 150km (60 to 90 mile) journey takes in almost every aspect of this massive harbour. The route passes wharves and warehouses, futuristic grain silos and loading equipment, cranes and bridges, oil refineries, powerstations and lighthouses, all of which create a skyline of awesome beauty, particularly at sunset. The docks, waterways, canals and ports-within-ports are interspersed with some surprising and apparently incongruous features; at one point the route passes a garden city built for shipyard workers, while further on there is a village and, at the harbour's westernmost point, a beach. A visit to Rotterdam harbour is recommended. Other interesting places to visit include the 17th-century houses in the **Delfshaven** quarter of the city; the **Pilgrimskerk**; collections of maps and seacharts at the **Delfshaven Old Town Hall**; many traditional workshops for pottery, watchmaking and woodturning. Rotterdam has also become something of a Mecca for designers and architects, who have flocked to the city to take part in its massive rebuilding programme, and their work is often showcased both in the buildings they create and also in temporary exhibits. Rotterdam's nightlife scene has undergone something of a renaissance over the last decade with myriad new bars, trendy cafes and first-rate restaurants spicing up what was previously an unappealing scene, geared mainly towards itinerant sailors and students. Today, the waterfront is increasingly being transformed into a leisure oasis. The major concert venue is the **De Doelen Concert Hall** (classical music, plays), which has 2000 seats. The local soccer team, **Feyernoord**, play at the impressive **De Kuip Stadium**, which was home to the final of Euro 2000.

THE EAST

The wooded east consists of the provinces of Overijssel, Gelderland and Flevoland.
OVERIJSSEL: The province of Overijssel is a region of great variety. In the little town of **Giethoorn**, small canals take the place of streets, and all transport is by boat. At **Wanneperveen** there is a well-equipped watersports centre. The old Hanseatic towns of **Kampen** and **Zwolle** have splendid quays and historic buildings. There are bird sanctuaries along the **Ijsselmeer**.
GELDERLAND: This is The Netherland's most extensive province, stretching from the rivers of the south to the sand dunes of the north. Gelderland is often referred to as 'the back garden of the west'.
Arnhem: The province's major city was heavily damaged in World War II; indeed, its important position on the Rhine has led to it being captured, stormed and occupied on many occasions during its long history. The old part of the town has, however, been artfully rebuilt. There is a large open-air museum near Arnhem showing a collection of old farms, mills, houses and workshops, all of which have been brought together to form a splendid park. Not far from the town centre, there is a zoo and a safari park.
Hoge Veluwe National Park: Near Arnhem is the Hoge Veluwe National Park, an extensive sandy region and a popular tourist area, which contains a game reserve (in the south), and the **Kroller-Muller Art Gallery and Museum**, with many modern sculptures and paintings (including a Van Gogh collection). One ticket enables the visitor to see all of this, and there are free bicycles available to cycle around the park.
Almost all of the old traditional villages have been converted into holiday resorts. There are no towns of any size in the Veluwe region.
FLEVOLAND: Much of Flevoland was drained for the first time in the 1950-60s, and is in many ways a museum of geography; the southern part of the province is not yet completely ready for cultivation, and visitors can witness the various stages of agricultural preparation. **Lelystad** is the main town of the region, built to a controversial design in the 1960s. Part of the province has also been designated as an overspill area for Randstad Holland. Flevoland's 1100 sq km (425 sq miles) of land includes many large bungalow parks.

THE FAR SOUTH

NORTH BRABANT: This province consists mainly of a plain, rarely more than 30m (100ft) above sea level, and is mostly agricultural. The region is known for its carnival days in February and the **Jazz in Duketown** jazz festival. The capital of the province is the city of **'s-Hertogenbosch** (non-Dutch speaking visitors will welcome the use of 'Den Bosch' as a widely accepted abbreviation) situated at the centre of a region of flat pasture land which floods each winter. **St Jan's Cathedral** is the largest in the country; the provincial museum is also interesting. Other major cities in this large and comparatively densely populated province include **Eindhoven**, an industrial centre which has grown in the last 100 years; **Breda**, an old city with many medieval buildings – it was here that the declaration was signed in 1566 which marked the start of the Dutch War of Independence; and **Tilburg**, an industrial centre which also has a large amusement and recreation park (to the north of the city), whose attractions include a haunted castle. In **Kaatsheuvel** is the **De Efteling Recreation and Adventure Park**, with approximately 50 attractions, including a large fairytale wood and a big dipper.
Overloon is home to the **Dutch National War & Recreation Museum**, which includes displays of heavy armament in a park setting and other exhibits devoted to the history of World War II.
In **Hilvarenbeek** is the **De Beekse Bergen Safari Park**. Safari buses are available (continuous journey).
LIMBURG: The province of Limburg, the most southerly in the country, is bordered by both Belgium and Germany. The rolling hills covered with footpaths make this a good place for walking holidays. It is also famous for its cuisine. In the extreme south of the province is the city of **Maastricht**, and its position at the crossroads of three countries makes it ideal for excursions to such nearby cities as Aachen over the border in Germany. Maastricht itself is one of the oldest towns in the country, and its **Church of St Servatius** is the oldest in The Netherlands. The church treasury is particularly interesting. Further north is the town of **Roermond**, an important cultural and artistic centre dominated by the superb **Munsterkerk**.

THE COAST

There are 280km (175 miles) of beaches and over 50 resorts in The Netherlands, almost all of which are easily accessible from Rotterdam, Amsterdam and The Hague. Large areas have been specially allocated for naturists and the beaches themselves are broad, sandy and gently sloping. There is surf along the coast, and those who wish to swim must be strong enough to withstand the hidden currents. Swimmers should obtain and follow local advice. In the high season, lifeguards are on duty along the more dangerous stretches of the coast.
ZEELAND: The province of Zeeland has several medieval harbour towns where some of the best seafood in Europe can be found. Most of the province lies below sea level and has been reclaimed from the sea. The region also includes several islands and peninsulas in the southwest Netherlands (**Walcheren**, **Goeree-Overflakkee**, **Schouwen-Duiveland**, **Tholen**, **St Filipsland** and **North** and **South Beveland**). The province has become renowned for a massive engineering project of flood barriers designed to protect the mainland and the results of reclamation from the devastating floods that periodically sweep the coastline. The countryside is intensively farmed. The capital of the province is **Middelburg**, a town that has been important since medieval times. The **Town Hall** is widely regarded as being one of the most attractive non-religious Gothic buildings in Europe. The small town of **Veere**, 8km (5 miles) to the north, retains many buildings from its golden age in the early 16th century. The North Sea port of **Flushing** (Vlissingen) is, for many British travellers arriving by boat, their first sight of The Netherlands. It is also the country's first town in another sense; in 1572 it became the first place to fly the free Dutch flag during the War of Independence.

Sport & Activities

Cycling: The Netherlands is rightly known as 'the land of bicycles': around 15 million Dutch people regularly travel by bicycle and there are an estimated 12 million cycles in use. The popularity of cycling is perhaps mainly due to the country's geography: distances between the cities are short and the countryside is almost totally flat, except for a few rolling hills in the east and south (the highest of which is a mere 321m/1053ft). Not surprisingly, cycling facilities are outstanding and there are approximately 17,000km (10,625 miles) of special cycling lanes and paths available. Detailed cycling maps (recommended) can be obtained for every province from local tourist information offices; as well as indicating cycling routes and tracks, the maps provide route descriptions and guides. Cycling lanes are recognisable by a round blue sign with a white bicycle in the middle. Most itineraries are circular routes, starting and ending at the same place. The province of Gelderland has the highest number of marked cycling routes. Landscapes vary from spectacular dunes (on the *Duinroute* in the north of the country) to wilderness and forests (on the route across the *Hoge Veluwe nature reserve* in the Gelderland Valley). Long-distance routes (such as the 270km-/169mile-North Sea route LF1 between the Belgian border and the northern Dutch town of Den Helder) are also available. Bicycles can be hired virtually everywhere and a list of local hire companies is available from The Netherlands Board of Tourism (see *Contact Addresses* section). The Netherlands Railways also offer bike-rental vouchers, which can be bought at railway ticket offices. Vouchers can be used at bicycle depots at over 100 train stations throughout the country. Over 300 stations offer the facility to take bicycles onto the train. The classic Dutch upright single-speed hub-brake bicycle is the most frequent, but other types of bicycles (including mountain bikes, children's bicycles and tandems) are also available.
Walking: In The Netherlands, walking holidays are also very popular; the 300km- (188mile-) long coast has a number of scenic walks through sand dunes and nature reserves. Visitors can obtain maps with walking routes from the Foundation for Long Distance Walks (*Stitching Lange-Afstand-Wandelpadsen*), PO Box 846, 3800 AV Amersfoort (tel: (33) 465 3660; fax: (33) 465 4377). Visitors can also join the annual six-day walking event (beginning of August), where participants walk from Hook of Holland to Den Helder. At *Wadden Sea National Park* (Europe's largest continuous national park), there is also the opportunity to take part in various types of **mud walking** trips on the bottom of the Wadden sea, whose shallows fall dry at low tide.
Watersports: The Dutch coast on the western shore is well suited and well equipped for all types of watersports, including **swimming** and **windsurfing**. **Sailing** is popular on *Friesland Lakes*, the *Ijsselmeer*, *Loosdrechtse Plassen* (south of Amsterdam) and *Veerse Meer*. Boats can be hired without difficulty in most places. Touring Holland's canals and rivers is popular. **Catamaran sailing** and **parachuting** is possible on the islands of *Ameland* and *Texel*.
Water-skiing is not permitted on inland lakes. **Fishing** is

popular throughout the country, but while no licence is needed for sea fishing, inland fishing licences are required and are available at local post offices.
Markets: A visit to one of the famous Dutch **flower markets** is recommended. The best ones are in Amsterdam (where the famous *Bloemenmarkt* along the Singel canal is a major tourist attraction), Delft and Utrecht. Dutch flower bulbs are available for sale but it is essential to make sure the vendor sells them with an official export certificate. The most popular Dutch flowers are tulips and daffodils. There are also various colourful flower parades (*corso*), notably the Bollenstreek flower parade (the country's biggest). Many parades display spectacular flower 'floats' made of hyacinths, daffodils and daliahs. The *Floriade*, held every 10 years in The Netherlands, is one of the world's most famous flower exhibitions. Last held in 2002 (from mid-April to mid-October), the city of Haarlemmermeer hosted this prestigious horticultural event. Visitors may also visit one of the country's unique **flower auctions**, such as the ones in Aalsmeer (easy to reach from Amsterdam) and the 'Flower Auction Holland' near The Hague and Rotterdam in the Westland. The country's traditional **cheese market** is held in Alkmaar, every Friday from 1000-1200, from mid-April to mid-September.

Social Profile

FOOD & DRINK: There are few dishes that can be described as quintessentially Dutch, and those that do fall into this category are a far cry from the elaborate creations of French or Italian cuisine. Almost every large town, however, has a wide range of restaurants specialising in their own brands of international dishes including American, Balkan, British, Chinese, French, German, Italian and Spanish. Indonesian cuisine, a result of the Dutch colonisation of the East Indies, with its use of spices and exotic ingredients, is particularly delicious. A typical Dutch breakfast usually consists of several varieties of bread, thin slices of Dutch cheese, prepared meats and sausage, butter and jam or honey and often a boiled egg. A working lunch would be *koffietafel*, once again with breads, various cold cuts, cheese and conserves. There will often be a side dish of omelette, cottage pie or salad. The most common daytime snack are *broodjes* (sandwiches) and are served in the ubiquitous sandwich bars – *broodjeswinkels*. Filled pancakes are also popular. Lightly salted 'green' herring can be bought from street stalls (they are held by the tail and slipped down into the throat). More substantial dishes are generally reserved by the Dutch themselves for the evening meal: *erwtensoep* (thick pea soup served with smoked sausage, cubes of bacon, pig's knuckle and brown or white bread), *groentensoep* (clear consommé with vegetables, vermicelli and meatballs), *hutspot* (potatoes, carrots and onions), *klapstuk* (an accompaniment of stewed lean beef) and *boerenkool met rookworst* (frost-crisped kale and potatoes served with smoked sausage). Seafood dishes are often excellent, particularly in Amsterdam or Rotterdam, and include *gebakken zeetong* (fried sole), *lekkerbekjes* (fried whiting), royal imperial oysters, shrimps, mussels, lobster and eel (smoked, filleted and served on toast or stewed or fried). Favourite Dutch desserts include *flensjes* or *pannekoeken* (25 varieties of Dutch pancake), *wafels met slagroom* (waffles with whipped cream), *offertje* (small dough balls fried and dusted with sugar) and *spekkoek* (alternate layers of heavy buttered sponge and spices from Indonesia), which translated means 'bacon cake'. Restaurants usually have table service. Bars and cafes generally have the same, though some are self-service.
Coffee, tea, chocolate and fruit juice are drunk at breakfast. The local spirit is *jenever* (Dutch gin), normally taken straight and chilled as a chaser with a glass of beer, but it is sometimes drunk with cola or vermouth; it comes in many varieties depending on the spices used. Favoured brands are *Bols*, *Bokma*, *Claeryn* and *De Kuyper*. Dutch beer is excellent. It is a light, gassy *pils* type beer, always served chilled, generally in small (slightly under half a pint) glasses. The most popular brand in Amsterdam is *Amstel*. Imported beers are also available, as are many other alcoholic beverages. Dutch liqueurs are excellent and include *Curaçao*, *Parfait d'Amour*, *Triple Sec* (similar to Cointreau) and Dutch-made versions of crème de menthe, apricot brandy and anisette. There are no licensing laws and drink can be bought all day. Bars open later and stay open until the early hours of the morning at weekends.
NIGHTLIFE: Large cities have sophisticated nightclubs and discos, but late opening bars and cafes are just as popular in provincial towns. There are theatres and cinemas in all major towns. Amsterdam is a cosmopolitan city, with some of the liveliest nightlife in Europe. There are legal casinos in Amsterdam, Breda, Eindhoven, Den Haag, Groningen, Nymegen, Rotterdam, Scheveningen (which claims to have the largest in Europe), Valkenburg and Zandvoort; all have an age limit of 'over 18' (passports must be shown).
SHOPPING: Special purchases include Delft (between The Hague and Rotterdam) blue pottery and pottery from Makkum and Workum, costume dolls, silverware from Schoonhoven, glass and crystal from Leerdam and diamonds from Amsterdam. **Shopping hours**: Mon 1100-1800; Tues-Fri 0900-1800; Sat 0900-1700. In Amsterdam, Rotterdam and other big cities, supermarkets are open from 0800-2000/2100. In large city centres, shops are open Sun 1200-1700. Shopping malls are also open on Sunday. Some cities also have late-night shopping on Thursdays or Fridays.
Note: Bulbs and plants may not be exported except by commercial growers, or by individuals with a health certificate from the Plant Disease Service.
SPECIAL EVENTS: For a complete list of events and festivals held in The Netherlands, contact the Press and Public Relations Officer at The Royal Netherlands Embassy or The Netherlands Board of Tourism (see *Contact Addresses* section). The following is a selection of special events occurring in The Netherlands in 2005:
Jan 26-Feb 6 *Film Festival Rotterdam*. **Feb 6-9** *Carnaval*, Landelijk (parades throughout the country). **Jun 8-18** *Pasar Malam Besar* (largest Eurasian festival in the world), Den Haag. **Jun 18-24** *Poetry International*, Rotterdam. **Jun 22-25** *Folkloristisch Dansfestival*, Bolsward. **Jul 7-9** *Bospop*, Weert. **Jul 8-10** *North Sea Jazz Festival*, Den Haag. **Jul 23-28** *Kwakoe Zomer Festival* (multicultural festival), Amsterdam. **Aug 3-7** *International Folkloristisch Dansfestival*, Odoorn. **Aug 6-8** *Amsterdam Gay Pride* (and Canal Parade). **Aug 26-Sep 4** *Holland Festival*, Amsterdam. **Oct 16** *Amsterdam Marathon*. **Oct 18-20** *Zuidlaardermarkt* (biggest horse and cattle market in Western Europe), Zuidlaren.
SOCIAL CONVENTIONS: It is customary to shake hands. English is spoken as a second language by many and is willingly used; many Dutch people will also speak German and French. Hospitality is very much the same as for the rest of Europe and the USA. It is customary to take a small gift if invited for a meal. Casual wear is widely acceptable. Men are expected to wear a suit for business and social functions. Formal wear may be required for smart restaurants, bars and clubs. Evening dress (black tie for men) is generally specified on invitation. **Tipping**: All hotels and restaurants include 15 per cent service and VAT. It is customary to leave small change when paying a bill. €0,5-1,00 is usual for porters, doormen and taxi drivers. Hairdressers and barbers have inclusive service prices.

Business Profile

ECONOMY: The Netherlands has a typical developed European economy. It is also the world's third-largest exporter of farm produce (after the USA and France), accounting for 16 per cent of total export earnings. Dairy products, meat, vegetables and flowers are the main products. Industry is concentrated in petrochemicals and plastics, pharmaceuticals, synthetic fibres and food processing. There is also a wide range of light industries, including the manufacturing of electronic goods, although the historically strong textiles has been in long-term decline. By contrast, The Netherlands has developed a strong base in advanced technological industries including computing, telecommunications and biotechnology. Deposits of natural gas (the only mineral resource of any size) meet much of the country's energy needs. Service industries are also important, notably transport through the world's busiest container port at Rotterdam. The Netherlands has derived substantial benefits from its membership of the EU, with whose members the bulk of its trade takes place. It has generally been a strong proponent of further economic integration within Europe and joined the Eurozone upon its inception in January 1999. In 2003, the government was forced to increase taxes and cut spending in order to stay within the limits imposed by Maastricht criteria which govern the operation of the Eurozone. The global economic slow-down which took hold in 2001 reduced annual GDP growth to 1.5 per cent, and in the following year to just 0.2 per cent. In 2003, the Dutch economy was expected to contract by 0.7 per cent. Inflation has declined from 5.1 per cent in 2001 to its present level of 2.7 per cent; unemployment has climbed gently to 4 per cent. Germany is the largest single trading partner, accounting for about 25 per cent of The Netherlands' imports and exports. Belgium/Luxembourg, France and the UK follow. Overall, two-thirds of Dutch trade is with the EU. The Netherlands is a founder member of the Benelux Economic Union and of the European Bank for Reconstruction and Development.
BUSINESS: Appointments are necessary and visiting cards are exchanged. The Dutch expect a certain standard of dress for business occasions. Best months for business visits are March to May and September to November. Practical information can be obtained from the Economic Information Service in The Hague (tel: (70) 379 8933; fax: (70) 379 7878; e-mail: evd@evd.nl; website: www.hollandtrade.com). The majority of Dutch businesspeople speak extremely good English, and promotional literature can be disseminated in English. However, interpreters can be booked through Conference Interpreters, Jan van Goyenkade 11, NL-1075 HP Amsterdam (tel: (20) 625 2535; fax: (20) 626 5642; e-mail: interpreters@conferenceinterpreters.com; website: www.conferenceinterpreters.com). Alternatively, they can be booked through The Netherlands Chamber of Commerce in the country of departure. (There are Netherlands-British Chambers of Commerce in London, Manchester and The Hague, and Netherlands-US Chambers of Commerce in New York and Chicago.) There are also many secretarial agencies in The Netherlands, such as International Secretaries, who will be able to supply short-term help to visiting business travellers. The principal venue for trade fairs is the RAI Exhibition Centre in Amsterdam. **Office hours**: Mon-Fri 0830-1700.
COMMERCIAL INFORMATION: The following organisations can offer advice: The Hague Chamber of Commerce and Industry, Konigskade 30, 2502 LS Gravenhage, The Hague (tel: (70) 328 7100; fax: (70) 326 2010; e-mail: info@denhaag.kvk.nl; website: www.denhaag.kvk.nl); *or* Amsterdam Chamber of Commerce and Industry, De Ruyterkade 5, 1000 CW Amsterdam (tel: (20) 531 4000; fax: (20) 531 4799; e-mail: post@amsterdam.kvk.nl; website: www.amsterdam.kvk.nl); *or* The Netherlands Chamber of Commerce, Imperial House, 15-19 Kingsway, London WC2B 6UN, UK (tel: (020) 7539 7960; fax: (020) 7836 6988; e-mail: info@nbcc.co.uk; website: www.nbcc.co.uk).
CONFERENCES/CONVENTIONS: The largest conference and exhibition centres are RAI in Amsterdam and the Jaarbeurs in Utrecht. There are smaller centres in The Hague, Rotterdam and Maastricht, as well as many hotels with facilities. The fourth-largest conference centre in The Netherlands is Noordwijk, where the largest hotel has a helipad; this small seaside town has won prizes for its clean beaches. Amsterdam and The Hague both have business centres. For further information, contact The Netherlands Board of Tourism in London (see *Contact Addresses* section) *or* The Hague Convention Bureau, PO Box 85456, 2508 CD The Hague (tel: (70) 361 8849; fax: (70) 361 5459; e-mail: conventionbureau@spdh.net.

Climate

Mild, maritime climate. Summers are generally warm with changeable periods, but excessively hot weather is rare. Winters can be fairly cold with the possibility of some snow. Rainfall is prevalent all year.
Required clothing: European according to season, with light- to mediumweights worn in warmer months and medium- to heavyweights in winter. Rainwear is advisable all year.

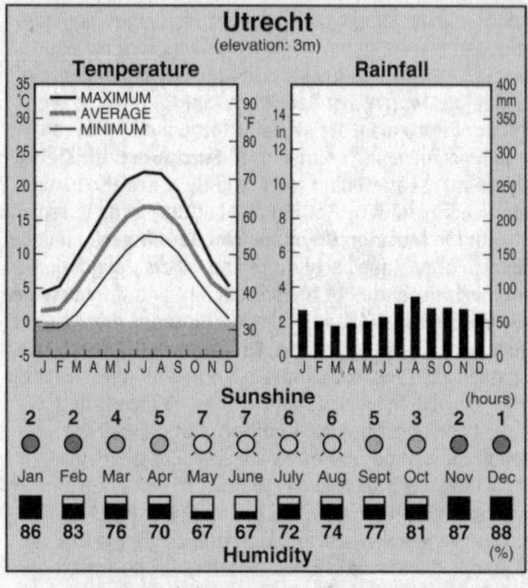

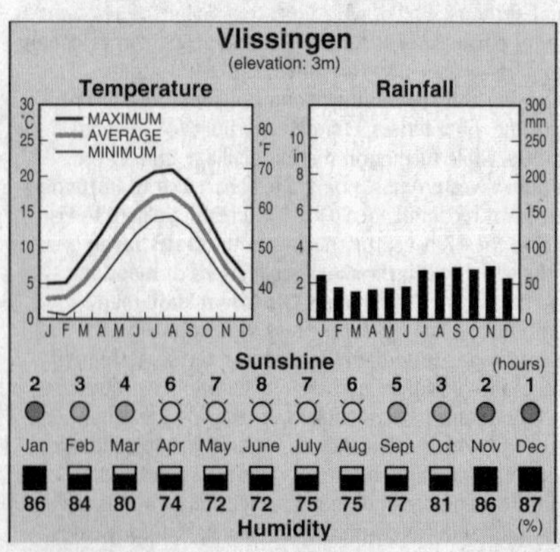

New Caledonia

LATEST TRAVEL ADVICE CONTACTS

British Foreign and Commonwealth Office
Tel: (0870) 606 0290 Website: www.fco.gov.uk
US Department of State
Website: http://travel.state.gov/travel
Canadian Department of Foreign Affairs and Int'l Trade
Tel: (1 800) 267 8376 Website: www.dfait-maeci.gc.ca

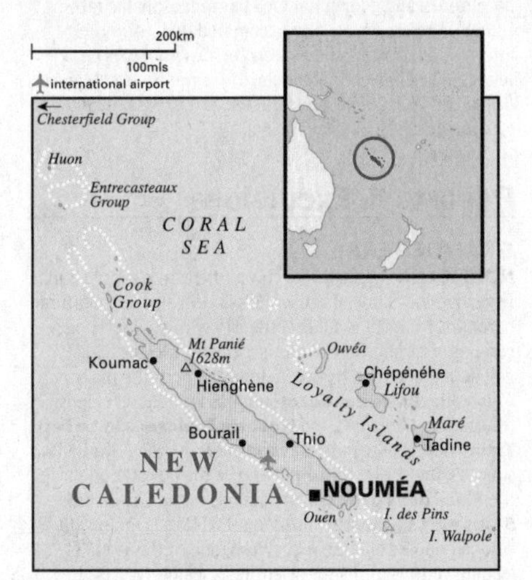

Location: South Pacific.

Country dialling code: 687.

New Caledonia is a French Overseas Territory; addresses of French Embassies, Consulates and Tourist Offices may be found in the *France* section.

New Caledonia Tourism South
Street address: 20 rue Anatole France, Immeuble Nouméa-Centre, Place des Cocotiers, Nouméa, New Caledonia
Postal address: BP 688, 98845 Nouméa Cédex, New Caledonia
Tel: 242 080. Fax: 242 070.
E-mail: info@nctps.com
Website: www.nctps.com

Office of the High Commissioner
Street address: 1 avenue du Maréchal Foch, Nouméa, New Caledonia
Postal address: BP C5, 98848 Nouméa, New Caledonia
Tel: 266 300. Fax: 272 828.
Website: www.etat.nc

South Pacific Tourism Organisation
Street address: Level 3, FNPF Place, 343-359 Victoria Parade, Suva, Fiji
Postal address: PO Box 13119, Suva, Fiji
Tel: (639) 330 4177. Fax: (639) 330 1995.
Website: www.spto.org
Also deals with enquiries from the UK.

New Caledonia Tourism South
7 rue du Général Bertrand, 75007 Paris, France
Tel: (1) 4273 6980. Fax: (1) 4273 6989.
E-mail: info-par@nctps.com
Website: www.nctps.com

British Honorary Consulate
Street address: 14 rue du Général Sarrail Orphelinat, Mont Coffyn, 98800 Nouméa, New Caledonia
Postal address: BP 363, 98845 Nouméa Cedex, New Caledonia
Tel: 282 153. Fax: 285 144.
E-mail: gbconsul@offratel.nc

The US Embassy in Suva deals with enquiries relating to New Caledonia (see *Fiji* **section).**
The Canadian High Commission in Canberra deals with enquiries relating to New Caledonia (see *Australia* **section).**

TIMATIC CODES

Health
AMADEUS: **TI-DFT/NOU/HE**
GALILEO/WORLDSPAN: **TI-DFT/NOU/HE**
SABRE: **TIDFT/NOU/HE**

Visa
AMADEUS: **TI-DFT/NOU/VI**
GALILEO/WORLDSPAN: **TI-DFT/NOU/VI**
SABRE: **TIDFT/NOU/VI**

To access TIMATIC country information on Health and Visa regulations through the Computer Reservations System (CRS), type in the appropriate command line listed above.

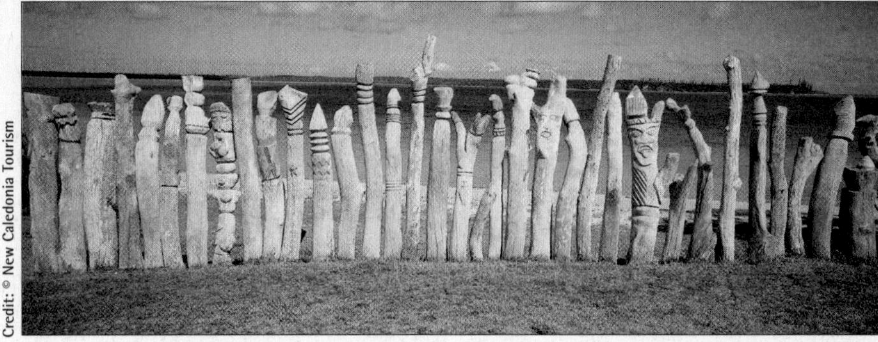
Credit: © New Caledonia Tourism

General Information

AREA: 18,575 sq km (7172 sq miles).
POPULATION: 220,000 (official estimate 2000).
POPULATION DENSITY: 10.6 per sq km.
CAPITAL: Nouméa. **Population**: 196,836 (1996).
GEOGRAPHY: New Caledonia consists of the Mainland, the Isle of Pines to the south of the Mainland, the Loyalty Islands to the east of the Mainland (Maré, Lifou, Tiga and Ouvéa), the Belep Archipelago in the northwest, and numerous islands and islets (Huon & Surprise, Christfield, Walpole, Beautémps-Beaupré, Astrolabe and the Bellona reef); a total surface area of 19,000 sq km (16,372 for the Mainland alone, which is 400km long). The Mainland is divided by a range of mountains (Châine Centrale), the highest points of which are Mount Pancé in the north (1629m) and Mount Humboldt in the south (1618m). Various species of trees can be found here. This unusual relief divides the Grande Terre/Mainland into the East coast (humid and open to trade winds; fertile and exotic with lush tropical vegetation) from the West coast (dry and temperate; filled with *niaouli* trees, cattle and beautiful beaches).
GOVERNMENT: French Overseas Territory since 1957. **Head of State**: President Jacques Chirac, represented locally by High Commissioner Daniel Constantin since 2002.
LANGUAGE: French is the official language, but there are approximately 30 different Melanesian languages. English and Japanese are also widely spoken.
RELIGION: Vast Christian majority, with 59 per cent Roman Catholic.
TIME: GMT + 11 (GMT + 10 in summer).
ELECTRICITY: 220 volts AC, 50Hz. European-style, two-pin plugs are in use.
COMMUNICATIONS: Telephone: IDD is available. Country code: 687. Outgoing international code: 00. There is a 24-hour service for international calls. International calls are bookable at the post office (0745-1115 and 1215-1530) or through hotels. Most hotels have direct dial facilities. **Mobile telephone:** GSM 900 network, operated by *Mobilis* (website: www.opt.nc). Roaming agreements exist (with some countries). **Fax:** Available at most hotels and post offices. **Internet:** ISPs include *Offratel* (website: www.offratel.nc). Public access is available in several Internet cafes and at 'cyber points' (computers available for public use in local businesses/ISPs). **Post:** Airmail to Western Europe takes up to one week. The post office, located on rue Eugène Porcheron, is open Mon-Fri 0745-1115 and 1215-1530. **Press:** Newspapers are published in French and include *Les Nouvelles Calédoniennes* (daily) and *L'Hebdo*, *Les Infos* and *Télé 7 Jours* (weekly).
Radio: BBC World Service (website: www.bbc.co.uk/worldservice) and Voice of America (website: www.voa.gov) can be received. From time to time the frequencies change and the most up-to-date can be found online.

Passport/Visa

	Passport Required?	Visa Required?	Return Ticket Required?
Full British	Yes	No	No
Australian	Yes	No	No
Canadian	Yes	No	No
USA	Yes	No	No
Other EU	Yes/1	No	No
Japanese	Yes	No	No

Note: Regulations and requirements may be subject to change at short notice, and you are advised to contact the appropriate diplomatic or consular authority before finalising travel arrangements. Details of these may be found at the head of this country's entry. Any numbers in the chart refer to the footnotes below.

PASSPORTS: Passport valid for at least six months, except for the following:
1. nationals of Belgium, Germany, Greece, Italy, Luxembourg, Monaco, The Netherlands, Portugal, Spain and Switzerland, who are holders of national identity cards.

VISAS: Required by all except the following:
(a) nationals of the EU (except **1.** nationals of the Czech Republic, Estonia, Latvia and Lithuania who *do* require a visa) and nationals of Andorra, Chile, Iceland, Liechtenstein, New Zealand, Norway, St Maarten, Switzerland and the Vatican City;
(b) nationals of Argentina, Bermuda, Bolivia, Brunei, Bulgaria, Croatia, Guatemala, Honduras, Korea (Dem Rep), Malaysia, Mexico, Monaco, Nicaragua, Panama, San Marino, Singapore, Uruguay and Venezuela for stays of up to one month;
(c) transit passengers continuing their journey by the same or first connecting aircraft provided holding valid onward or return documentation and not leaving the airport.
Types of visa and cost: All visas, regardless of duration of stay and number of entries permitted, cost €35. In most circumstances, no fee applies to students, recipients of government fellowships and citizens of the EU and their family members.
Validity: *Short-stay* (up to 30 days): valid for two months (single- and multiple-entry). *Short stay* (31 to 90 days and double- or multiple-entry): valid for a maximum of six months from date of issue. *Transit*: valid for single- or multiple-entries of maximum five days per entry, including the day of arrival.
Application to: French Consulate General (for personal visas), or Consular section at Embassy (for diplomatic or service visas); see *Contact Addresses* section for France. All applications must be made in person.
Application requirements: (a) Valid passport with blank page to affix the visa. Minors travelling alone must submit notarised parental authorisation, signed by both parents, plus one copy. (b) Up to two completed application forms. (c) One passport-size photo on each form. (d) Fee, to be paid in cash only if paying by person. If not, fee should be paid by cheque or postal order. (e) Evidence of sufficient funds for stay (two last bank statements, plus copy, or other proof of funds equivalent to US$100 for each day of trip). (f) Letter from employer, or proof of stay in country of residence. (g) Proof of address. (h) Medical insurance. (i) Return ticket and travel documents for remaining journey. (j) Proof of accommodation during stay. (k) Registered self-addressed envelope, if applying by post. (l) Detailed itinerary, including reservations and round-trip airline tickets (only required when visa is issued), plus one copy. (m) Proof of employment (eg last payslip or letter from employer). (n) Proof of valid health/travel insurance with worldwide coverage, plus copy. *Business*: (a)-(n) and, (o) Business invitation guaranteeing payment of travel expanses, plus one copy.
Working days required: One day to three weeks, depending on nationality.
Temporary residence: If intending to work or stay for longer than 90 days, nationals should contact the Long Stay visa section of the French Consulate General or Embassy (tel: (020) 7073 1248). Nationals of the EU may gain long-stay in New Caledonia on the condition that they have independent means and self-employed (proof must be submitted).

Money

Currency: French Pacific Franc (FCFP). Notes are in denominations of FCFP10,000, 5000, 1000 and 500. Coins are in denominations of FCFP100, 50, 20, 10, 5, 2 and 1. New Caledonia is part of the French Monetary Area. Australian and New Zealand dollars are widely accepted in shops, hotels and restaurants. The French Pacific Franc is tied to the Euro. For further details on the Euro, see *France* section.
Currency exchange: Exchange facilities are available at the airport and at main branches of banks, but may charge a steep commission. ATMs are available in Nouméa, but sometimes have a maximum weekly withdrawal limit.
Credit & debit cards: American Express and Visa are widely accepted; Diners Club and MasterCard have more limited use. Check with your credit or debit card company for details of merchant acceptability and other services which may be available.

Travellers cheques: To avoid additional exchange rate charges, travellers are advised to take travellers cheques in Euros. There is, however, a charge of FCFP515, including tax, for each transaction.
Currency restrictions: Any amount of money in excess of FCFP909,000, being carried by a person in their baggage, must be declared to customs. This does not engender supplementary costs.
Exchange rate indicators: The following figures are included as a guide to the movement of the French Pacific Franc against Sterling and the US Dollar:

Date	Feb '04	May '04	Aug '04	Nov '04
£1.00=	172.01	175.04	177.85	170.06
$1.00=	94.50	98.00	96.53	89.84

Banking hours: Mon-Fri 0730-1545.

Duty Free

The following goods may be imported into New Caledonia without incurring customs duty:
200 cigarettes or 50 cigars or 100 cigarillos or 250g of tobacco; 2l of wine plus 1l of spirits and liquors not exceeding 22 per cent alcohol content, or 2l of spirits and liquors with 22 per cent alcohol content or less; 50ml of perfume or 250ml of eau-de-toilette; 500g of coffee or 200g of coffee essence; 100g of tea or 50g of tea essence; other goods up to a value of FCFP30,000 per passenger aged 15 years and older, and FCFP15,000 for those aged under 15 years.
Note: Those importing duty free alcohol and tobacco must be aged 18 years and older. If taking personal and everyday goods, such as cameras, tape recorders and radios, it is advised to carry documents providing legal justification of ownership.
Prohibited items: Plants, flowers, seeds and earth (except on import permit); meat and other animal products (except with prescribed sanitary certificate).

Public Holidays

2005: Jan 1 New Year's Day. **Mar 28** Easter Monday. **May 1** Labour Day. **May 8** 1945 Victory Day. **May 9** Whit Monday. **May 20** Ascension. **Jul 14** Bastille Day. **Aug 15** Assumption. **Sep 24** New Caledonia Day. **Nov 1** All Saints' Day. **Nov 11** Armistice Day. **Dec 25** Christmas Day. **Dec 31** New Year's Eve.
2006: Jan 1 New Year's Day. **Mar 28** Easter Monday. **May 1** Labour Day. **May 8** 1945 Victory Day. **May 25** Ascension. **Jul 14** Bastille Day. **Aug 15** Assumption. **Sep 24** New Caledonia Day. **Nov 1** All Saints' Day. **Nov 11** Armistice Day. **Dec 25** Christmas Day. **Dec 31** New Year's Eve.

Health

	Special Precautions?	Certificate Required?
Yellow Fever	No	1
Cholera	No	2
Typhoid & Polio	3	N/A
Malaria	No	N/A

Note: *Regulations and requirements may be subject to change at short notice, and you are advised to contact your doctor well in advance of your intended date of departure. Any numbers in the chart refer to the footnotes below.*

1: A yellow fever vaccination certificate is required from travellers over one year of age arriving from infected areas.
2: Travellers arriving from infected areas do not require cholera vaccination and will not be given chemoprophylaxis. They are required, however, to fill out a form for use by the Health Service.
3: Typhoid is reported. Visitors may wish to ensure up-to-date polio vaccinations have been administered prior to travel.
Food & drink: Mains water is normally chlorinated and generally regarded as safe to drink. Bottled water is available and is advised for the first few weeks of the stay. Milk is pasteurised and dairy products are safe for consumption. Local meat, poultry, seafood, fruit and vegetables are considered safe to eat.
Other risks: *Hepatitis A* and *C* occur and *hepatitis B* is endemic. *Dengue fever* occurs. Immunisations against *diphtheria, tuberculosis* and *tetanus* are advised.
Health care: New Caledonia offers a wide range of efficient medical services in both public and private hospitals, and an adequate selection of chemists. Hotels can generally recommend an English-speaking doctor or dentist. Health insurance is advised.

Travel - International

AIR: New Caledonia's national airline is *Aircalin (Air Calédonie International) (SB)*. Other airlines serving New Caledonia include *Air New Zealand, KLM* and *Qantas*. The *Oceania Pass* is available in Economy class on the *Aircalin* network within the Southwest Pacific, but is limited to non-residents, and must be purchased prior to departure (for details and conditions, see website: www.aircalin.nc). Air travel is by far the easiest and most rapid means of transport to New Caledonia.
Approximate flight times: From Nouméa to *London* is 26 hours, including stopovers, but this may increase to 30 hours, depending on the day of travel; to *Los Angeles* is 18 hours (via Tahiti); to *Sydney* is two hours 30 minutes.
International airports: *Nouméa (NOU)* (La Tontouta), 50km (31 miles) from the city (travel time – 45 minutes). Airport facilities include post office, bureau de change, duty free shops (available for scheduled flights), bar, restaurant and car hire (*Avis, Budget, Discount Location, Hertz, JNJ* and *Visa*). Taxi and coach services are available to the city. It is advisable to book transfers before arrival in New Caledonia.
Departure tax: None.
SEA: International port is Nouméa, served by shipping lines including *CTC, P&O* and *Princess Cruises*.

Travel - Internal

AIR: Domestic flights are run by *Air Calédonie (TY)* (website: www.air-caledonie.nc), maintaining regular services from Nouméa to airfields on the island, and the other smaller islands. The principal local airport is *Magenta Airport*, 6km (4 miles) from Nouméa city centre. From here, *Air Calédonie* operates regular flights to Touho (east coast), Koné, Koumac, Belep (west coast), and to the neighbouring Ile des Pins and the Loyalty Islands: Maré, Ouvéa, Lifou and Tiga. The airport has been extended in order to increase capacity. Light aircraft and helicopters are available from *Air Alizé, Aviazur, Helicocean* and *Helitourisme*.
Approximate flight times: From Nouméa to *Ile des Pins* is 25 minutes; to *Lifou* is 40 minutes; to *Maré* is 40 minutes; to *Ouvéa* is 40 minutes; to *Tiga* is one hour 25 minutes (including stopover); to *Koné* is 45 minutes; to *Touho* is 45 minutes; to *Koumac* is one hour five minutes and to *Belep* is one hour 45 minutes (including stopover).
SEA: An inter-island, high-speed catamaran 'Betico' runs regularly to Ile des Pins and Loyalty Islands from Grande Terre; for further details, contact *Armement Loyaltien*, Quai des Caboteurs, Centre Ville, BP 2217-98845, Nouméa Cedex (tel: 260 100; fax: 289 897). Boats can be hired or chartered to visit smaller islands.
ROAD: The road network consists of 5000km (3125 miles) of paved and unpaved roads. Traffic drives on the right. Petrol costs the same at all petrol stations. **Bus:** Buses are available throughout the island. There are regular services in Nouméa which run every 15 to 30 minutes from 0500-1900. The Green Line travels between Kuendu Beach, the city centre and other beach resorts. The Blue Line travels to Tjibaou Cultural Centre. A tourist day pass can be bought for CFPfr650, which allows the visitor unlimited travel on the buses for one day. **Taxi:** Charges are for time and distance. There is a surcharge after 1900 and on Sundays. **Car hire:** *AB Location, Avis, Budget, Europcar, Hertz, Rent-a-car* and local companies all have representatives in the capital. **Bicycle hire:** Bicycles, motorcycles and motorscooters may also be hired. **Documentation:** International Driving Permit is required. Drivers must be aged 21 or over (in some cases, 25 or over).
Travel Times: The following chart gives approximate travel times (in hours and minutes) from **Nouméa** to other major localities/villages in New Caledonia.

	Air	Road
Bourail	-	2.10
Hienghene	-	5.10
Koné	0.45	3.30
Poindimie	-	4.10
Thio	-	2.00
Tontouta	-	0.45
Touhó	0.45	4.40

Accommodation

There is a very good selection of accommodation available with hotels, country inns and rural lodgings.
HOTELS: Hotels are mostly small and intimate. Prices range from moderate to expensive. Modern **3-** and **5-star** hotels have been built or fully renovated at Anse Vata and there is also bungalow-style accommodation in remoter parts of the main island and in the outer islands. For further information, contact Association des Hôtels de Nouvelle Calédonie, c/o Paillottes de la Ouenghi, 98812 Boulouparis (tel: 351 735; fax: 351 744; e-mail: medefnc@medef.nc; website: www.hotels-nc.com); *or* Association of International Hotel Chains (ACHI), c/o Le Meridien Hotel, PO Box 1915, Nouméa (tel: 265 000; fax: 265 100; e-mail: gm.noumea@meridien.nc).
TRADITIONAL HOMESTAYS: Visitors interested in experiencing the traditional way of life can arrange to stay in Melanesian-style bungalows or huts. Home-cooked meals may be booked in advance. Payment is usually made in cash as credit cards are not accepted. For further information, contact the tourist board (see *Contact Addresses* section).
FARM HOLIDAYS: These are regulated by the Chamber of Agriculture. For further information, contact Chambre d'Agriculture de Nouvelle Calédonie, Antenne de Bourail, BP 847, 98870 Bourail (tel: 442 348; fax: 442 358; e-mail: canc-cd@canl.nc; website: www.bienvenue-a-la-ferme.com).
CAMPING: Major camping sites are in the rural lodging area. Most sites include washrooms, toilets, barbecue facilities and mini-supermarkets. Permission should be sought from landowners before setting up camp.
YOUTH HOSTELS: Situated in Nouméa is a hostel with dormitories and communal facilities at reasonable rates. Non-YHA members are also accommodated. For more information, contact the Association des Auberges de Jeunesse de Nouvelle Calédonie, 51 bis rue Pasteur Marcel Ariege, BP 767, 98845 Nouméa (tel: 275 879; fax: 254 817; e-mail: yha.noumea@lagoon.nc).

Resorts & Excursions

GRANDE TERRE

NOUMÉA: The capital, near the southeastern tip of Grande Terre, overlooks one of the world's largest sheltered natural harbours. Nouméa is a busy little city with a population composed of many racial groups: French, Melanesian, Polynesian and Vietnamese, amongst others. The main square, the **Place des Cocotiers**, has undergone extensive restoration. Minibuses, the **Nouméa Explorer** and **Le Petit Train** are probably the best ways of seeing the city and its suburbs. The centre of the network is the bus station on the **Place des Cocotiers**. Attractions in the city include **St Joseph's Cathedral**, museums, the market, many old colonial houses and the **Aquarium**, one of the world's leading centres of marine scientific research. Nearby, the **South Pacific Commission Building** houses a collection of native handicrafts from all over the South Seas. The **New Caledonia Museum** is open Tuesday to Saturday, and also contains many local handicrafts and ornaments. The new **Museum of Maritime History** (whose exhibits include artefacts from numerous local wrecks) is situated by the port in Nouméa. The **Tjibaou Cultural Centre** in Nouméa is a new venue for concerts, plays and exhibitions celebrating indigenous cultural traditions.
Excursions: Approximately 4km (2.5 miles) from the city centre is the **Botanical and Zoological Gardens**, home to over 700 species of animals. Also near Nouméa is the **Amedée Lighthouse**, constructed in Paris during the reign of Napoleon III and shipped to New Caledonia in pieces. It is located in a coral reef, 18km (11 miles) from the capital. The lagoon, which is the biggest in the world, offers good opportunities for swimming and scuba-diving. East of the capital is **Mont-Dore**, a mountain surrounded by magnificent coastal scenery. On the way, stops can be made at the Melanesian village of **St Louis** and the **Plum Lookout** for a spectacular view across the surrounding reef. The **Blue River Provincial Park** is well worth a visit. Day trips are available from the capital.
THE WEST COAST: Some 170km (105 miles) from Nouméa is **Bourail**, where there are many elaborate and beautiful caves and rock formations shaped by the Pacific breakers. Further north is the ancient site of **Koné**, where decorated pottery dating back to the 10th century BC has been discovered. From the town of **Koumac**, a new road has been constructed which loops round the top of the island. The scenery consists of pure white sand beaches and offshore atolls, backed by dense rainforest.
THE EAST COAST: The new road takes one to **Hienghéne**, which has a lagoon surrounded by 120m- (400ft-) high black cliffs. **Poindimié**, the main town of the east coast, is further south. Nearby is **Touho**, overlooked by a 500m (1640ft) peak. The region is dotted with churches and Melanesian villages, forests, coconut palms and beautiful beaches. At the southern point of this coast is **Yaté**, a village surrounded by lakes, waterfalls and rich wooded countryside.

OUTLYING ISLANDS

ILE DES PINS: Discovered and named the Isle of Pines by Captain Cook in 1774, Ile des Pins lies some 70km (45 miles) off the southeast coast of Grande Terre. This exceedingly beautiful island has many white sand beaches and turquoise lagoons and is lush with rainforests, pines, orchids and ferns. Archaeological excavations have revealed settlements 4000 years old. The island was also briefly used as a convict settlement during the 19th century following the Paris Commune. The ruins of the jail can still be seen amongst the dense vegetation. There are many rural lodges, a luxury hotel and a more modest hotel. Both hotels are situated on or near beaches. Day trips are available from Nouméa to the Ile des Pins.
THE LOYALTY ISLANDS: This archipelago lies 100km (60 miles) off the east coast of New Caledonia, and is widely

regarded as being superb for scuba-diving and spear-fishing. **Maré Island**, the furthest south, has an area of 650 sq km (250 sq miles). Most of the population lives in the village of **Tadine**. **Lifou Island**, the largest of the three with an area of 1150 sq km (445 sq miles), has over 7000 inhabitants. The main village is **Chépénéhé**.
Ouvéa Island is 130 sq km (50 sq miles), but is rarely more than 3 or 4km (2 or 2.5 miles) wide. The lagoon is rich in fish. Almost all of the population lives in **Fayaoué**. There is accommodation on all these islands in the form of either hotels, motels or family lodgings.

Sport & Activities

Watersports: Snorkelling and **diving** are very popular. The New Caledonian authorities have created marine reserves on several islets to protect marine fauna and flora. There are also sunken shipwrecks, which act as artificial reefs. Some of the best dive sites include: around Nouméa, the *Amédée Lighthouse Reserve* (including shark feeding), *La Dieppoise* (shipwreck of a Royal Navy patrol ship sunk in 1988), and *Ilot Maitre*; to the south, the *Prony Needle*; to the north, the *Tenia Horn* (near Boulouparis), the *Fault* (near Bourail) and the *Hienghene Reef*; and *Lifou* in the *Loyalty Islands*. There are many PADI-approved diving centres on the mainland and the outlying islands, all offering beginners' courses, training and certification. Night dives and photo dives are also available. For a list of diving centres, contact New Caledonia Tourism (see *Contact Addresses* section). *The Bay of Anse Vata* and *Côte Blanche*, both in Nouméa, are the favourite locations for **windsurfing**. International competitions such as the *Trophée des Alizés* attract some of the world's top competitors. **Fishing** is one of the locals' favourite pastimes, which visitors can participate in by accompanying them on fishing expeditions to catch tuna, marlin or snapper. Chartered fishing boats can also be hired. The coral barrier reef off the shore of Nouméa is excellent for underwater spearfishing. The main location for freshwater fishing is *Yaté Lake*, which is open from January to October.
Whale watching: From July to September, humpback whales can be spotted during the mating season in the bays of the southern lagoon and Lifou. Excursions are organised from Nouméa and from the south of the mainland to spot them. The whales may also be seen during scuba diving trips.
Boat trips: Excursions in Melanesian **outrigger canoes** are organised at the *Isle of Pines*. Several operators offer trips to the coral reefs in **glass-bottomed boats** from which visitors can observe the marine life. Reservations can be made from *gîtes* or hotels on the islands. **Sailing boats** can be chartered with or without a skipper. **Kayaks** or **canoes** can be rented to explore New Caledonia's network of rivers, streams and lakes.
Hiking: Arrangements can be made in the capital for trips into the interior. Botanical excursions through the forest of *Mount Koghi* (with French- or English-speaking guides) are also available.
Horse-riding: Excursions are organised from Nouméa, Dumbea, La Foa, Bourail, Thio and the Koné villages. These vary from simple rides to major expeditions to the local bush (which involve crossing the mountain range, mustering cattle and camping in the mountains). Advance booking is essential.
Golf: New Caledonia has three 18-hole golf courses plus driving ranges and putting greens. Private lessons, hire of equipment and restaurants are available at the Dumbéa Golf Club, Ouenghi Golf Club and Tina Golf Club.

Social Profile

FOOD & DRINK: The choice of eating places and food on New Caledonia is excellent; costs vary from moderate to expensive. Gourmet restaurants and bistros serve African, Chinese, French, Indonesian, Italian and Spanish cooking. Dishes include Pacific spiny lobsters, prawns, crabs or mangrove oysters and salads of raw fish (marinated in lime juice). An island speciality is *bougna*: fish or chicken wrapped in banana leaves and cooked on hot stones covered with sand. First-class delicatessens and grocers in Nouméa and at Anse Vata Beach provide a wide choice of picnic fare. There is a good selection of French wine available.
NIGHTLIFE: There are plenty of discos and also two casinos, situated in the Anse Vata area. Nightclubs in Nouméa are lively with both European and local floorshows. There are also several cinemas, which show French films.
SHOPPING: In Nouméa, boutiques sell fashionable French clothes, mainly casual but sometimes *haute couture*. Other purchases include luxury French goods such as perfume, jewellery and footwear, and silk scarves, sandals and handbags from France and Italy can also be found. Duty free items are also sold. Local items include curios made of shells, coral, woodcarving, ceramics, hand-painted materials and aloha shirts. **Shopping hours**: Mon-Fri 0730-1100 and 1400-1800, Sat 0730-1100.
SPECIAL EVENTS: For a full list of events, contact New Caledonia Tourism (see *Contact Addresses* section). The following is a selection of special events celebrated annually in New Caledonia:
Mar *The Festival of the Yam*. **Apr** *Nouméa Carnival*. **May** *Avocado Fair*, Nece; *La Regate des Touques*, Nouméa; *Pacific Tempo*, Nouméa (music festival). **Jun** *Music Festival*; *Nouméa Commercial & International Fair*. **Jul** *Gardening and Motorculture Show*. **Jul 14** *Bastille Day Festivities and Fireworks*. **Aug** *Bourail Fair* (country fair with rodeo, cattle, horses etc). **Oct** *Great Nature Festival*. **Oct-Nov** *Sound and Light Show*, Fort Tremba, La Foa. **Dec** *Christmas Celebrations*; *Christmas Show*. **Dec 31** *Fireworks*.
SOCIAL CONVENTIONS: There is a casual atmosphere, and local traditions still prevail alongside European customs. Casual wear is the norm, but smart restaurants require a more formal style of dress. Long trousers are required for men at night in restaurants and casinos. **Tipping**: There is absolutely no tipping.

Business Profile

ECONOMY: The mainstays of the country's economy are mining, tourism and, to a lesser degree, agriculture and fishing. The agricultural sector produces cereals, fruit and vegetables, as well as copra and coffee for export. The fishing industry trawls primarily for shrimp and tuna, the bulk of which is sold to Japan. A small light-industrial sector has grown up in the last two decades, producing building materials, furniture and processed foods, largely for domestic consumption. In the mining sector, New Caledonia is the world's largest producer of nickel after Canada and the USA, and has about one-quarter of the world's known deposits; this generates 90 per cent of the country's export revenue. There are also deposits of cobalt, iron, manganese, lead and zinc. Tourism is the major service industry and remains the most dynamic sector in terms of economic development.
Subventions from France are essential to the territory's economic well-being. And, by virtue of its link with France, New Caledonia is an Associate Member of the EU. France is the largest trading partner, accounting for approximately half of all imports and exports, followed by Australia, Germany, Japan and the USA.
BUSINESS: Appointments should be made. Businesspeople generally work long hours and take long lunch breaks, but business lunches are rare as most businesspeople go home at lunchtime. Prices should be quoted in Euros or French Pacific Francs. The best time to visit is May to October.
Office hours: Mon-Fri 0730-1130 and 1330-1730; Sat 0730-1130.
COMMERCIAL INFORMATION: The following organisation can offer advice: Chambre de Commerce et d'Industrie, BP M3, 15 rue de Verdun, 98849 Nouméa Cédex (tel: 243 100; fax: 243 131; e-mail: cci@cci.nc; website: www.cci.nc).
CONFERENCES/CONVENTIONS: Conferences and conventions take place at major hotels such as Le Meridien, Park Hotel and Novotel Surf Nouméa, as well as at the Chamber of Commerce (for address, see above), the Tjibaou Cultural Centre and the South Pacific Commission, all situated in Nouméa.

Climate

Warm, subtropical climate. The cool season is from April to August and the hottest period is from September to March. The main rains are between January and March. The seasons are less defined on the east coast than the west. Climate is tempered by trade winds.
Required clothing: Tropical lightweights, with jackets and sweatshirts for evenings.

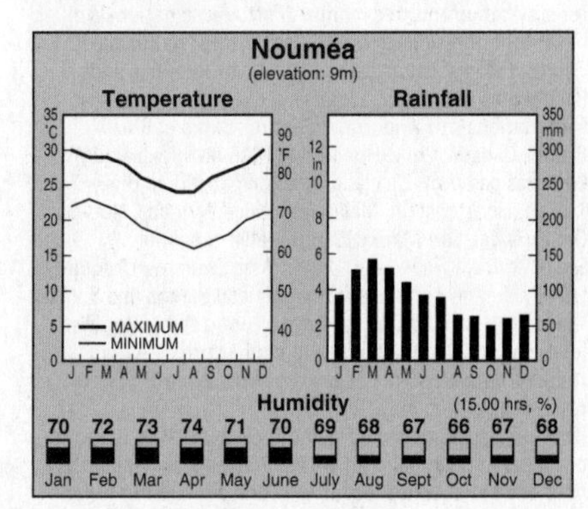

New Zealand

LATEST TRAVEL ADVICE CONTACTS

British Foreign and Commonwealth Office
Tel: (0870) 606 0290 Website: www.fco.gov.uk
US Department of State
Website: http://travel.state.gov/travel
Canadian Department of Foreign Affairs and Int'l Trade
Tel: (1 800) 267 8376 Website: www.dfait-maeci.gc.ca

Location: South Pacific.

Country dialling code: 64.

Tourism New Zealand
Street address: Level 16, 80 The Terrace, Wellington, New Zealand
Postal address: PO Box 95, Wellington, New Zealand
Tel: (4) 917 5400. Fax: (4) 915 3817.
Website: www.newzealand.com *or* www.tourisminfo.govt.nz
Administrative headquarters only. Trade and consumer enquiries should be directed to TNZ's branches around the world.
New Zealand Immigration Service
Mezzanine Floor, New Zealand House, 80 Haymarket, London SW1Y 4TE, UK
Tel: (09069) 100 100 (visa information and immigration service; calls cost £1 per minute). Fax: (020) 7973 0370.
E-mail: info@immigration.govt.nz
Website: www.immigration.govt.nz
Opening hours: Mon-Fri 1000-1545.
New Zealand High Commission
New Zealand House, 80 Haymarket, London SW1Y 4TQ, UK
Tel: (020) 7930 8422. Fax: (020) 7839 4580.
E-mail: aboutnz@newzealandhc.org.nz *or* nzembassy@newzealandhc.org.uk
Website: www.nzembassy.com
Opening hours: Mon-Fri 0900-1700.
Visa and passport enquiries should be made to the New Zealand Immigration Service.
Tourism New Zealand
New Zealand House, 80 Haymarket, London SW1Y 4TQ, UK
Tel: (020) 7930 1662 *or* (09050) 606 060 (recorded information line; calls cost 60p per minute) *or* (09069) 100 100 (immigration). Fax: (020) 7839 8929.
E-mail: enquiries@tnz.govt.nz
Website: www.newzealand.com (consumer information) *or* www.tourisminfo.govt.nz (trade information).
Opening hours: Mon-Fri 0900-1730.
British High Commission
Street address: 44 Hill Street, Thorndon, Wellington, New Zealand

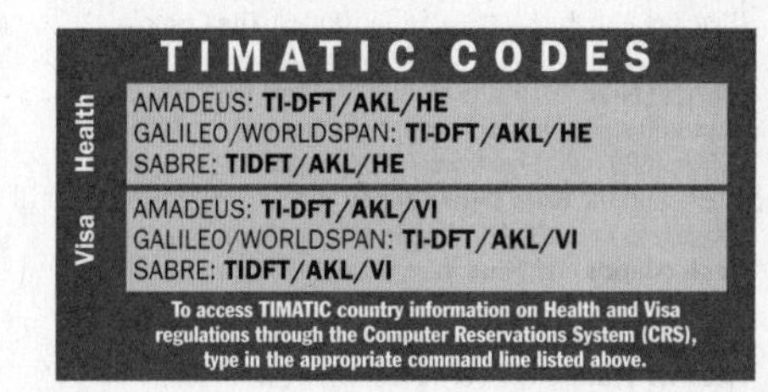

TIMATIC CODES

Health
AMADEUS: **TI-DFT/AKL/HE**
GALILEO/WORLDSPAN: **TI-DFT/AKL/HE**
SABRE: **TIDFT/AKL/HE**

Visa
AMADEUS: **TI-DFT/AKL/VI**
GALILEO/WORLDSPAN: **TI-DFT/AKL/VI**
SABRE: **TIDFT/AKL/VI**

To access TIMATIC country information on Health and Visa regulations through the Computer Reservations System (CRS), type in the appropriate command line listed above.

Postal address: PO Box 1812, Wellington, New Zealand
Tel: (4) 924 2888. Fax: (4) 473 4982.
E-mail: PPA.Mailbox@fco.gov.uk
Website: www.britain.org.nz
Consulate General in: Auckland.

New Zealand Embassy
37 Observatory Circle, NW, Washington, DC 20008, USA
Tel: (202) 328 4800. Fax: (202) 667 5227.
E-mail: nz@nzemb.org
Website: www.nzemb.org
Consulate General in: Los Angeles (tel: (310) 207 1605).

Tourism New Zealand
501 Santa Monica Boulevard, Suite 300, Santa Monica, CA 90401, USA
Tel: (310) 395 7480 *or* (866) 639 9325 (toll-free inside USA only). Fax: (310) 395 5453.
E-mail: laxinfo@tnz.govt.nz
Website: www.newzealand.com *or* www.tourismnfo.govt.nz
Only deals with enquiries from Canada and the USA. All North American Explore applications and business cards should be sent to the Los Angeles office.

Embassy of the United States of America
Street address: 29 Fitzherbert Terrace, Thorndon, Wellington, New Zealand
Postal address: PO Box 1190, Wellington, New Zealand
Tel: (4) 462 6000. Fax: (4) 499 0490.
Website: http://wellington.usembassy.gov
Visa enquiries should be directed to the Consulate General in Auckland.

US Consulate General
Street address: 3rd Floor, Citibank Building, 23 Customs Street, Auckland, New Zealand
Postal address: PO Box 92022, Auckland, New Zealand
Tel: (9) 303 2724. Fax: (9) 366 0870.
Website: http://wellington.usembassy.gov

New Zealand High Commission
99 Bank Street, Suite 727, Ottawa, Ontario K1P 6G3, Canada
Tel: (613) 238 5991. Fax: (613) 238 5707.
E-mail: info@nzhcottawa.org
Website: www.nzhcottawa.org
Consulate General in: Toronto and Vancouver.

Canadian High Commission
Street address: 61 Molesworth Street, Thorndon, Wellington, New Zealand
Postal address: PO Box 12049, Wellington, New Zealand
Tel: (4) 473 9577. Fax: (4) 471 2082.
E-mail: wlgtn@international.gc.ca
Website: www.wellington.gc.ca
Canadian Consulate Trade Office in: Auckland

General Information

AREA: 270,534 sq km (104,454 sq miles).
POPULATION: 4,009,200 (official estimate 2003).
POPULATION DENSITY: 14.8 per sq km.
CAPITAL: Wellington. **Population**: 423,765 (2003). Auckland, with a population of 1,158,891 (2003), is the largest urban area in the country.
GEOGRAPHY: New Zealand is 1930km (1200 miles) southeast of Australia and consists of two major islands, the North Island (116,031 sq km/44,800 sq miles) and the South Island (153,540 sq km/59,283 sq miles), which are separated by Cook Strait. Stewart Island (1750 sq km/676 sq miles) is located immediately south of the South Island, and the Chatham Islands lie 800km (500 miles) to the east of Christchurch. Going from north to south, temperatures decrease. Compared to its huge neighbour Australia, New Zealand's three islands make up a country that is relatively small (about 20 per cent more land mass than the British Isles). Two-thirds of the country is mountainous, a region of swift-flowing rivers, deep alpine lakes and dense subtropical forest. The country's largest city, Auckland, is situated on the peninsula that forms the northern part of the North Island. The southern part of the North Island is characterised by fertile coastal plains rising up to volcanic peaks. Around Rotorua, 240km (149 miles) south of Auckland, there is thermal activity in the form of geysers, pools of boiling mud, springs of hot mineral water, silica terraces, coloured craters and hissing fumaroles, which make Rotorua a world-famous tourist attraction. The South Island is larger, although only about one-third of the population lives there. The Southern Alps extend the whole length of the island, culminating in Mount Cook, the country's highest peak. In the same region are the Franz Josef and Fox glaciers.
There are also four Associated Territories: **The Cook Islands**, about 3500km (2175 miles) northeast of New Zealand; **Niue**, 920km (570 miles) west of the Cook Islands (area 260 sq km/100 sq miles); **Tokelau**, three atolls about 960km (600 miles) northwest of Niue (area 12 sq km/4 sq miles), and the **Ross Dependency**, which consists of over 700,000 sq km (270,270 sq miles) of the Antarctic.
Cook Islands and **Niue** have separate individual sections in the World Travel Guide.
GOVERNMENT: Constitutional monarchy since 1907. **Head of State**: HM Queen Elizabeth II since 1952, represented locally by Governor-General Dame Silvia Cartwright since 2001. **Head of Government**: Prime Minister Helen Clark since 1999.
LANGUAGE: English is the common and everyday language, but other languages are also spoken, including Maori, which is New Zealand's second official language (spoken by the indigenous Maori people who constitute approximately 15 per cent of the population).
RELIGION: 60 per cent Christian: Anglican, Presbyterian, Roman Catholic and Methodist are all represented.
TIME: New Zealand: GMT + 12 (GMT + 13 from the last Sunday in October to the last Sunday in March). **Chatham Island**: GMT + 12.45 (GMT + 13.45 from the last Sunday in October to the last Sunday in March).
ELECTRICITY: 230 volts AC, 50Hz. Most hotels provide 110-volt AC sockets (rated at 20 watts) for electric razors only.
COMMUNICATIONS: Telephone: IDD is available. Country code: 64. Outgoing international code: 00. Most public phones take cards purchased from bookstalls; some also accept credit cards, but very few still accept coins. **Mobile telephone:** Extensive AMPs network operated by *Telecom New Zealand* (website: www.telecom.co.nz). GSM 900 network operated by *Vodafone New Zealand* (website: www.vodafone.co.nz). Handsets can be bought or hired from *Vodafone New Zealand*. There are also mobile telephone shops at Auckland and Christchurch airports. **Fax:** Most hotels provide facilities. **Internet:** ISPs include *Kiwilink* (website: www.kiwilink.co.nz). There are Internet cafes in the city and smaller town central business districts. Travellers may access the Internet at many hotels and youth hostels. **Post:** Post offices are open Mon-Fri 0900-1700. Airmail to Western Europe takes four to five days and to the USA three to 10 days. **Press:** The English-language daily newspapers with the highest circulation include *The Dominion, New Zealand Herald, Otago Daily Times* and *The Press*.
Radio: BBC World Service (website: www.bbc.co.uk/worldservice) and Voice of America (website: www.voa.gov) can be received. From time to time the frequencies change and the most up-to-date can be found online.

Passport/Visa

	Passport Required?	Visa Required?	Return Ticket Required?
Full British	Yes	No/1	Yes
Australian	Yes	No/4	No
Canadian	Yes	No/3	Yes
USA	Yes	No/3	Yes
Other EU	Yes	No/2	Yes
Japanese	Yes	No/3	Yes

Note: *Regulations and requirements may be subject to change at short notice, and you are advised to contact the appropriate diplomatic or consular authority before finalising travel arrangements. Details of these may be found at the head of this country's entry. Any numbers in the chart refer to the footnotes below.*

PASSPORTS: Passport valid for at least three months beyond the intended period of stay required by all. Some governments are not recognised by New Zealand and citizens in doubt should check with the New Zealand Immigration Service (see *Contact Addresses* section).
VISAS: Required by all except the following:
(a) countries referred to in the chart above, including US nationals from American Samoa, Swains Island and nationals of New Zealand Associated Territories (Cook Islands, Niue and Tokelau) for stays of up to three months, although transit visas are required for nationals of the following, provided only holding one-way tickets: Cook Islands, Fiji, Marshall Islands, Samoa, Solomon Islands, Tahiti, Tokelau, Tonga and Vanuatu;
(b) **1**. nationals of the UK and other British passport holders who have evidence of the right to live permanently in the UK for stays of up to six months may be granted a visitors permit on arrival;
(c) **2**. nationals of EU countries (except nationals of the UK) for stays of up to three months (Portuguese nationals must have right of residence in Portugal), except nationals of Cyprus, Estonia, Latvia, Lithuania, Slovak Republic and Poland who *do* require a visa;
(d) **3**. nationals of Andorra, Argentina, Bahrain, Brazil, Brunei, Canada, Chile, Hong Kong (SAR or British Nationals Overseas passports), Iceland, Israel, Japan, Korea (Rep), Kuwait, Liechtenstein, Malaysia, Mexico, Monaco, Norway, Oman, Qatar, San Marino, Saudi Arabia, Singapore, South Africa, Switzerland, United Arab Emirates, Uruguay, USA (including nationals from American Samoa and Swains Island) and Vatican City for stays of up to three months;
(e) **4**. nationals of Australia who hold a current Australian resident return visa or nationals of New Zealand with a residence permit;
(f) transit passengers continuing their journey by the same or first connecting aircraft within 24 hours, providing they hold onward or return documentation and are not leaving the airport (some nationals passing through New Zealand *always* require a transit visa, even when not leaving the transit lounge of the airport; enquire at the New Zealand Immigration Service for details);
(g) nationals travelling on a UN laissez-passer for stays of up to three months.
Note: All nationals listed above must have sufficient funds to cover the duration of stay. This may be NZ$1000 for each person for every month or NZ$400 if the accommodation is already paid for. If travelling on a visa as a student, it is sometimes necessary to submit evidence of NZ$10,000 per year or NZ$1000 per month if staying for less than 36 weeks, as well as submitting an additional form. If national is unable to submit proof of sufficient funds, it is possible to submit guarantee of accommodation and maintenance from a New Zealand citizen/resident who is a friend/relative and is serving as the national's sponsor.
Types of visa and cost: *Visitor*: £50. *Transit*: £65. *Work*: £80. *Student*: £80. For details of special visitor categories, including *Group, Conference* and *Business* visitor visas, contact the New Zealand Immigration Service (see *Contact Addresses* section).
Validity: The maximum period of time most visitors can remain in New Zealand is nine months within an 18-month period. Single-entry visas are usually valid for stays of up to six months. If national has stayed for nine months or more in the last 18 months, it is necessary to leave New Zealand for the same amount of time before returning as a visitor. It is possible to qualify for a three-month extension if national can prove they have financially supported themselves during their stay, or have already lodged an application for residence that is still under consideration at the time of review, or if the national cannot leave New Zealand due to mitigating circumstances that are deemed outside of their control, or the national can prove to be a genuine tourist seeking only three months' additional stay in order to complete an itinerary. If a national has stayed in New Zealand for 12 months out of the last 24 months, they must leave New Zealand for 12 months before being allowed to return as a visitor. Visitors not requiring visas are initially allowed a stay for up to six months with a British passport.
Application to: Consulate (or Consular section at Embassy or Immigration Service at High Commission); see *Contact Addresses* section.
Application requirements: *Visitor*: (a) Completed application form. (b) One recent passport-size photo of each person named in the application. (c) Passport valid for three months beyond the date of departure. (d) Sufficient funds for duration of stay. (e) Onward or return ticket. (f) Fee (payable in cash or by bank/building society cheque, credit card, money order or bank draft). (g) For business trips, a company/sponsor letter. (h) Valid ticket for country the national has right of entry to. *Work*: (a)-(h) and, (i) Valid offer of employment in writing from a New Zealand employer with a full job description and, in many cases, confirmation that the position cannot be filled by a New Zealander. *Student*: (a)-(h) and, (i) Confirmation of placement at an approved educational institution.
Note: Those applying for a visa may also be asked to undergo an interview and/or a medical examination prior to travel, or by the Immigration Officer at port of entry. Anyone applying for residency or temporary entry with a visa allowing a stay of greater than 12 months is required to complete a health declaration form supported by medical records that can be no more than three months old.
Working days required: This may vary depending on type of visa required and nationality of the applicant.
Temporary residence: Enquire at the nearest New Zealand High Commission or Immigration Service for details.

Money

Currency: New Zealand Dollar (NZ$) = 100 cents. Notes are in denominations of NZ$100, 50, 20, 10 and 5. Coins are in denominations of NZ$2 and 1, and 50, 20, 10 and 5 cents.
Currency exchange: Exchange facilities are widely available throughout New Zealand.
Credit & debit cards: American Express, Diners Club, MasterCard and Visa are widely accepted. Check with your credit or debit card company for details of merchant acceptability and other services that might be available.
Travellers cheques: Can be exchanged at official rates at trading banks, large hotels and some shops. To avoid additional exchange rate charges, travellers are advised to take travellers cheques in US Dollars, Pounds Sterling or Australian Dollars.
Currency restrictions: There are no restrictions on the import and export of foreign or local currency.
Exchange rate indicators: The following figures are included as a guide to the movements of the New Zealand Dollar against Sterling and the US Dollar:

Date	Feb '04	May '04	Aug '04	Nov '04
£1.00=	3.26	2.89	2.77	1.42
$1.00=	1.79	1.62	1.50	0.75

Banking hours: Mon-Fri 0900-1630.

Duty Free

The following items may be imported into New Zealand by persons of 17 years of age and over without incurring customs duty:
200 cigarettes or 50 cigars or 250g tobacco or a mixture of all three weighing no more than 250g; 4.5l of wine or beer; 1.125l or 40oz of spirits or liqueurs; goods to a total value of NZ$700.
Prohibited items: Because of the importance of agriculture and horticulture to the New Zealand economy, certain animal products, fruit, plant material or foodstuffs that could contain plant or animal pests may not be allowed into the country. For further information, contact the nearest Embassy, High Commission or Consulate. The import of the following items is also prohibited: firearms and weapons (unless a special permit is obtained from the New Zealand police); ivory in any form; tortoise or turtle shell jewellery and ornaments; medicines using musk, rhinoceros or tiger derivatives; carvings or anything made from whalebone or bone from any other marine animals; cat skins or coats and certain drugs (eg diuretics, depressants, stimulants, heart drugs, tranquillisers, sleeping pills) unless covered by a doctor's prescription.

Public Holidays

2005: Jan 1-2 New Year. **Feb 6** Waitangi Day. **Mar 25-28** Easter. **Apr 25** ANZAC Day. **Jun 16** Queen's Birthday. **Oct 24** Labour Day. **Dec 25** Christmas Day. **Dec 26** Boxing Day.
2006: Jan 1-3 New Year. **Feb 6** Waitangi Day. **Apr 14-17** Easter. **Apr 25** ANZAC Day. **Jun 6** Queen's Birthday. **Oct 23** Labour Day. **Dec 25** Christmas Day. **Dec 26** Boxing Day.
Note: Each region also observes its particular anniversary day as a holiday.

Health

	Special Precautions?	Certificate Required?
Yellow Fever	No	No
Cholera	No	No
Typhoid & Polio	No	N/A
Malaria	No	N/A

Note: *Regulations and requirements may be subject to change at short notice, and you are advised to contact your doctor well in advance of your intended date of departure. Any numbers in the chart refer to the footnotes below.*

Food & drink: Mains water is considered safe to drink. Milk is pasteurised and dairy products are safe for consumption. Local meat, poultry, seafood, fruit and vegetables are generally considered safe to eat.
Other risks: There are no snakes or dangerous wild animals in New Zealand. Sandflies are prevalent in Fiordland, but these can be effectively countered with insect repellent. The only poisonous creature is the very rare katipo spider.
Health care: Medical facilities, both public and private, are of a high standard. Telephone numbers for doctors and hospitals are listed at the front of the white pages of local telephone directories. Should visitors need drugs or pharmaceutical supplies outside normal shopping hours, they should refer to 'Urgent Pharmacies' in the local telephone directory for the location of the nearest pharmacy or check with their hotel. Many hotels have doctors on call. Long-staying visitors with a valid permit to stay for two or more years are entitled to health care services on the same basis as New Zealand citizens. There is a reciprocal health agreement with the UK, which entitles short-term British visitors to publicly funded health treatment. They will receive free treatment as a hospital inpatient, but must pay some charges for any services provided by outpatients and private doctors. Medical insurance is advised to cover any additional charges.

Travel - International

AIR: New Zealand's national airline is *Air New Zealand (NZ)* (website: www.airnz.co.nz).
Approximate flight times: From Auckland to *London* is 25 hours, from Wellington is 27 hours and from Christchurch is 28 hours. From Auckland to *Los Angeles* is 12 hours, to *New York* is 20 hours, to *Singapore* is 10 hours 30 minutes, and to *Sydney* is three hours 30 minutes.
International airports: *Auckland (AKL)* (website: www.auckland-airport.co.nz) is 22.5km (14 miles) south of the city (travel time – 40 minutes). Airbus runs an efficient service between the international terminal to the city centre. These operate from 0600 until the last flight and cost NZ$15/single and NZ$22/return (student and child discounted fares are available). *Eastern Service Buses* operate from 0700-1800 and cost NZ$4 (travel time – approximately 60 minutes). In addition to regular taxis there is a shuttle taxi service which operates 24 hours, the fare is NZ$20-30 depending on the number of passengers. Airport facilities include duty free shopping, banks/bureaux de change, post office, restaurants and cafes, car hire and baggage facilities/left luggage. There is a wide selection of hotels near the airport.
Christchurch (CHC) (website: www.christchurch-airport.co.nz) is 10km (6 miles) northwest of the city (travel time – 20 minutes). Prices vary from the standard buses which cost NZ$2.70 to the more luxurious limousines, which cost around NZ$20. There are good facilities at the airport and hotels within 10km (6 miles).
Wellington (WLG) (website: www.wellington-airport.co.nz) is 8km (5 miles) southeast of the city (travel time – 30 minutes). *Stagecoach Flyer* operates a bus service to the city centre every 30 minutes (fare NZ$4.50). The shuttle service operates on demand (maximum 10 persons) and costs NZ$10-12 accordingly.
Departure tax: Up to NZ$25 (depending on airport) plus NZ$5 security tax; children aged under 12 are exempt (except at Wellington where only passengers under two years of age are exempt and passengers aged two to 11 pay NZ$10). Transit passengers are exempt for 24 hours.
SEA: The principal ports are Auckland, Dunedin, Lyttelton, Opua, Picton and Wellington, which are served by international shipping lines sailing from the USA and from Europe. A few cruise ships visit New Zealand, but there are no regular passenger ship services. For further details, contact Tourism New Zealand (see *Contact Addresses* section).

Travel - Internal

AIR: *Air New Zealand (NZ)* and *Qantas Airways* operate domestic flights between the major airports (see *Travel – International* section). Several smaller airlines, including *Air Nelson, Eagle Air* and *Mount Cook Airlines*, are wholly owned by *Air New Zealand* and have been grouped together as *Air New Zealand Link*. They serve many of the 27 other airports throughout the two islands.
SEA: The North and South Islands are linked by modern ferries operating between Wellington and Picton, carrying passengers and vehicles across Cook Strait. The *Interislander* makes several daily crossings (travel time – three hours) with long-distance train connections from Wellington and Picton railway stations; the faster *Lynx*, a high-speed catamaran, takes two hours 15 minutes, and operates all year round. Reservations on all ferry services are highly recommended, particularly for visitors taking their vehicles. Information can be obtained from Tourism New Zealand (see *Contact Addresses* section) *or* via the Tranz Rail reservation line; see the *Rail* section for further details.
RAIL: *Toll New Zealand* (formerly *Tranz Rail Ltd*) operates a reliable rail service on 4000km (2485 miles) of railway with many routes of great scenic attraction. *Tranz Scenic* operates eight scenic long-distance trains. The *Overlander* runs between Auckland and Wellington (daytime and overnight) with good views of forests, gorges and volcanic peaks. The *Transcoastal* runs between Christchurch and Picton along the east coast between the snow-capped Kaikoura Mountains and past the Kaikoura coast, which is famous for whale-watching. The *TranzAlpine* runs between Christchurch and Greymouth through spectacular landscapes of gorges and river valleys and across the snow-capped Southern Alps. There are buffet cars on all trains, but there are no sleeping cars on overnight services. All services are one-class travel only. For further information, contact *Toll New Zealand* (tel: (4) 498 3000; fax: (4) 498 3259; e-mail: info@tollnz.co.nz; website: www.tollnz.co.nz); or *Tranz Scenic* (tel: (4) 495 0775 *or* (0800) 277 482 (toll free in New Zealand); fax: (4) 472 8903; e-mail: bookings@tranzscenic.co.nz; website: www.tranzscenic.co.nz).
Travel passes: 'Travelpass New Zealand' is a 3-in-1 travel pass which allows unlimited travel on *InterCity* coaches, *Tranz Scenic* trains and *Interislander* ferry services across Cook Strait. It is issued for periods between five days and over eight weeks and can be bought outside New Zealand from any InterCity Coachlines office, Toll New Zealand travel centre or accredited travel agency. The *Best of New Zealand Pass* incorporates all train and ferry services as well as selected coach services and the Taieri Gorge Railway for travel over 180 days. For further information, contact Tourism New Zealand (see *Contact Addresses* section).
ROAD: There are 92,000km (57,200 miles) of roads. Traffic drives on the left. **Coach:** *InterCity Coachlines* (website: www.intercitycoach.co.nz) operates scheduled services throughout the country. *Newmans Coach Lines* (website: www.newmanscoach.co.nz) operates services in both islands. It is advisable to make reservations for seats. Contact an InterCity Travel Centre or Tourism New Zealand for details and information on travel passes (valid for rail, coach and ferries). **Bus:** There are regional bus networks which serve most parts of the country and are on the whole friendly and cheaper than the larger companies. **Taxi:** There are metered taxis throughout the country. **Car hire:** Major international firms and local firms have offices at airports and most major cities and towns. It is recommended to hire vehicles from members of the *New Zealand Vehicle Rental & Leasing Association*. The minimum age for driving a rented car is 21. The legal speed limit is 100kph (60mph) on the open road and 50kph (30mph) in built-up areas. Distances are indicated in kilometres. Both driver and passengers are legally required to wear seat belts at all times. For further information, contact *The New Zealand Automobile Association* (tel: (9) 377 4660 *or* (800) 500 444 (toll free in New Zealand); fax: (9) 309 4563; e-mail: info@aa.co.nz; website: www.aa.co.nz). **Documentation**: All international driving licences are recognised by New Zealand. And, although not compulsory, an International Driving Permit is recommended. For further information, contact Tourism New Zealand (see *Contact Addresses* section).
URBAN: Good local bus services are provided in the main towns; there are also trolley buses in Wellington. Both Auckland and Wellington have zonal fares with pre-purchase tickets and day passes. Rideline (website: www.rideline.co.nz) houses all the bus, train and ferry information about travelling around Auckland.
Travel Times: The following chart gives approximate travel times (in hours and minutes) from **Wellington** to other major cities/towns in New Zealand:

	Air	Road	Rail
Auckland	1.00	9.00	10.00
Rotorua	1.15	5.45	-
Napier	1.00	6.30	-
N. Plymouth	1.00	8.30	-
Palmerston N.	0.30	2.30	2.30
Picton	0.30	-	-
Christchurch	0.45	*7.20	*5.20
Dunedin	1.20	*12.20	-
Queenstown	2.05	*15.40	-
Bay of Islands	2.00	14.00	-
Nelson	0.20	6.00	-
Mt Cook	2.00	10.00	-
Glaciers (west coast)	**1.45	8.20	-

Note: *Plus ferry crossing of three hours. **Plus two hours 30 minutes by road.

Accommodation

MOTELS & HOTELS: New Zealand offers a wide range of top-class hotels, exclusive retreats, motels, moderately priced accommodation and guest houses. Rates on the whole are cheaper in rural areas, while every city and town also offers a choice of budget hotels and motels. Budget accommodation, often with self-catering facilities, is increasingly popular. Further information can be obtained from the Motel Association of New Zealand, PO Box 27-245, 79 Boulcott Street, Wellington (tel: (4) 499 6415; fax: (4) 499 6416; e-mail: motel@manz.co.nz; website: www.nzmotels.co.nz); *or* the Hospitality Association of New Zealand, Level 2, Radio Network House, Corner Abel Smith and Taranaki Streets, PO Box 53 (tel: (4) 385 1369; fax: (4) 384 8044; e-mail: nsc@hanz.org.nz; website: www.hanz.org.nz). **Disabled travellers**: Every new building and every major reconstruction is required by law to provide reasonable and adequate access for people with disabilities. The law specifies that every motel and hotel must provide a certain number of units with accessible facilities. New Zealand is recognised as a world leader in providing accessibility for the disabled. **Grading**: Hotels are graded from **1 to 4 stars**. Motels are graded on a separate scale of **1 to 5 stars**.
GUEST-HOUSES & PRIVATE HOTELS: Usually located in restored, older buildings, guest houses and private hotels offer moderately priced accommodation, often with shared bathroom facilities, but with generally high standards. **Country pubs**: The cheapest type of accommodation and particularly popular on the west coast of the South Island. **Farm and home stays**: A number of established companies can arrange farm holidays, where visitors stay with a family as a guest, sharing bathroom facilities. Many farms are conveniently located for outdoor activities such as fishing, skiing and horse trekking. Prices usually include breakfast and dinner. An independent review of various types of accommodation in New Zealand is offered by Holdsworth (website: www.lodgings.co.nz).
CAMPING/CARAVANNING: There are many campsites throughout New Zealand, which is reputed to have some of the world's best camping grounds. Rates and facilities vary considerably. It is advisable to make advance reservations from December to Easter. **Motorcamps, cabins** and **tourist flats**: These are characteristic of New Zealand. Motorcamps are a combination of camping grounds offering tent and caravan sites (with electricity), simple cabin accommodation and central communal bathroom and cooking facilities. They can be found almost everywhere. Visitors are required to provide their own tents and equipment, which can be hired from a number of companies. Occupants are usually required to supply their own linen, blankets and cutlery. Cabins are ideal for budget travellers and contain only beds and rudimentary furniture (visitors need to bring their own bedding). Tourist flats are

at the top end of the cabin scale and usually offer sheets and bedding as well as fully equipped kitchens. Full details can be obtained from Tourism New Zealand (see *Contact Addresses* section).
YOUTH HOSTELS: The Youth Hostel Association runs 62 hostels throughout the country, and reservations can be made in advance from December to March. The association's address is PO Box 436, Christchurch (tel: (3) 379 9970 *or* (0800) 278 299 (toll free in New Zealand); fax: (3) 365 4476; e-mail: info@yha.org.nz; website: www.yha.org.nz).
BACKPACKER'S HOSTELS: Backpackers' hostels are located all over the country. For further information, contact The Budget Backpacker Hostels (BBH), 99 Titiraupenga Street, Taupo, New Zealand (tel: (7) 377 1568; e-mail: bbh@backpack.co.nz; website: www.backpack.co.nz). BBH also issues a Backpacker card costing NZ$40, which entitles the holder to discounted transport within New Zealand as well as NZ$20 of pre-paid telephone calls.

Resorts & Excursions

New Zealand is the world's best kept secret; it contains six of the seven climatic regions on the planet, boasts a series of unparalleled golden-sand beaches, protected marine parks to explore from on or beneath the surface, safe-but-active volcanic areas, pristine snow-capped Alps to ski and climb, prehistoric forests and unique flora and fauna. It does all this in one easily accessible package without thousands of miles to travel between each destination and it has an enviable reputation as one of the safest destinations in the world, lacking poisonous animals and boasting a low crime rate. It is a country where the only stress is that taken on willfully by the adventure-minded tourist (in the form of bungy jumping, parachuting, white-water rafting etc). You can walk for miles in New Zealand without seeing another soul, accompanied by rustling trees, running water and unusual bird song, but perhaps the country's greatest asset is its warm, friendly and hospitable population. For informed and accurate tourist information, on all of the country's highlights, travellers should contact one of the local *VICs* (Visitor Information Centres) situated all over New Zealand.

NORTH ISLAND

AUCKLAND: Auckland is the country's largest urban and suburban area with a population of over 1.5 million. Even so, it is surrounded by varied and exquisite scenery with attractive harbours and beaches to the east and the rugged **Waitakere Ranges**, the thundering, undeveloped surf beaches and burgeoning vineyards to the west. Known as the 'City of Sails', with more boats per capita than any other city in the world, these days Auckland's reputation as a sailor's Mecca is cemented by repeated successful defences of the *America's Cup*. The city offers excellent shopping, galleries and museums; it has a university and provides a multicultural environment characterised by a blend of European, Asian and Polynesian cultures, particularly on the busy and atmospheric **Karangahape Road**. There is also the distinctive **Sky Tower**, a casino with a glorious circular, glass viewing gallery at its bulbous summit. The views of the city, its beaches and the mountains, the coast and sea beyond are stunning. It is also possible for the particularly brave tourist to abseil down the side of the building to the street, a drop of over 100m (328ft).
An exploration of at least one of the stunning golden-sand islands of the **Hauraki Gulf**, accessible by ferries from **Waitamata Harbour** and also visible from the Sky Tower, is highly recommended. Most of the city centre is walkable but the outlying suburbs of **Devonport**, **Herne Bay**, **Parnell** and **Ponsonby** (with their attractive eateries and well-reputed fashion industry) are brought within easy reach by a reliable public bus network and taxi system.
NORTHLAND: The narrow, predominantly Maori stronghold of Northland, the 'Winterless North' pushes out 350km (217 miles) from Auckland and separates the **Pacific Ocean** from the **Tasman Sea**. It provides the sub-tropical element in the New Zealand equation and is famed for its palms, citrus fruit, avocados, bananas and myriad gorgeous, sandy unspoiled beaches. It also gives tourists the opportunity to begin to understand Maori culture, art and history. On the east coast, the beaches exist between straggling peninsulas and headlands, offering calm bays that are safe for swimming. Perhaps the most famous area is the **Bay of Islands**, intricately sculpted and renowned for excellent diving, boating/sailing and game fishing. The west coast offers enormous dune-backed black-sand beaches that are lashed almost constantly by Tasman breakers, rip tides and biting winds (there is no safe swimming here). The views are fantastic and, just inland, the forests of the **Northland Forest Park**, contain some of the world's oldest trees, including the famous *kauri*, many of which date back centuries. **Cape Karikari**, overlooking **Doubtless Bay** was one of the locations for films such as *From Here to Eternity* and *The Piano*, and offers access to wide, rugged, moody beaches surrounded by steep hills and cliffs, while **Cape Reinga** overlooks the spectacular meeting of the Pacific Ocean and Tasman Sea and the narrow extension of **Ninety-mile Beach** down the west coast back toward Auckland.
PACIFIC COAST HIGHWAY: A spectacular coastal road runs parallel with the intricate filigree of small inlets and beaches around the **Coromandel Peninsula** and the long sweeping bays of the east coast. The journey begins with the ferry from Auckland to **Coromandel**, where the road weaves along the side of the peninsula's tiny, sun-trap inlets before opening out on the long run down from **Hot Water Beach** towards **Tauranga**. The warm water bubbles from beneath the sands overlooking the surf providing a perfect spot from which to watch the tide come in at sunset from your own personally dug hot pool.
The volcanic hills of the Coromandel Peninsula retain much of their original rainforest and the **Coromandel Forest Park Reserve** contains large numbers of giant kauri trees which are famous for their tall straight trunks.
A popular holiday destination in the **Bay of Plenty** is **Tauranga**, with all the amenities of a major tourist city including all levels of accommodation and some wonderful restaurants. The climate here is essentially benign and the sandy beaches attract many visitors while inland there is an abundance of orchards, particularly citrus and kiwi fruit. In **Poverty Bay** lies the city of Gisborne, which sits adjacent to **Hawke's Bay**, a wine growing region of international renown. Around 70 wineries (ranging from large commercial estates to small boutiques) are open for free wine tasting. This area is best known for its red wines, particularly *Pinot Noir*. The reason for the wonderful wine is the high annual sunshine hours which benefit the grapes and visiting tourists to both **Hastings** and **Napier**. **Napier** was razed by an earthquake in 1931 and subsequently rebuilt in the *art deco* style of the time. Today it boasts one of the world's finest collections of lovingly preserved *art deco* buildings. Inland, between Hawke's Bay and the Bay of Plenty, is the UNESCO-listed **Te Urewera National Park**, the largest native forest on the North Island and home of the lovely **Lake Waikaremoana**, 585m (1919ft) above sea level, with its strenuous but rewarding (three- to four-day) circular trail.
CENTRAL NORTH ISLAND: The centre of the North Island is dominated by the geothermal city of **Rotorua**, the extraordinarily picturesque **Lake Taupo** and the UNESCO-listed **Tongariro National Park**. The park is a spectacular mountain area dominated by three peaks, **Ngauruhoe**, **Tongariro** and, the tallest, **Mount Ruapehu** (2797m/9177ft), still an active volcano, and a major ski resort. When **Ruapehu** erupted in 1996, many people took the once-in-a-lifetime opportunity to ski the slopes of a live volcano. **Lake Taupo** presents the less adventurous with an opportunity to enjoy unrivalled brown-trout fishing and a serene expanse of water fed by glacial streams and rivers. **Rotorua** is a good base for exploring the geysers and the large thermal zone of the North Island. It is a lively city full of all the usual tourist prerequisites and has the distinctive sulphurous smell of the surrounding boiling-mud pools. Rotorua is also a major centre for accessible Maori culture – there is an arts centre where young Maori learn the skills of traditional bone, wood and greenstone carving. There is also the opportunity to visit a *Marae* (a Maori meeting house usually forbidden to *pakeha*, foreigners) and enjoy a concert of traditional songs, the *haka* (a Maori challenge usually witnessed before All Black rugby matches) and a *hangi* (a delicious feast cooked in an earth oven).
THE WESTERN NORTH ISLAND: Another area dominated by Maori culture and history which along with Northland provides the best opportunity to pick up authentic souvenirs. This is an atmospheric area with black-sand beaches, rich farm land, natural kaarst limestone architecture, national parks and a spectacular extinct volcano, **Taranaki**. Perhaps one of the most magical areas is the famous water-sculptured limestone caves of **Waitamo** with their glow-worm grottoes. The caves can be explored by punt or by donning a wet-suit and heading underground with an inflated car tyre. This unique New Zealand activity is called 'cave rafting' and provides an opportunity to float through the caverns staring at unusual rock formations and ceilings packed with glow worms, that resemble a star-strewn night sky.
Wanganui, on the west coast of the North Island, lies near the mouth of the **Whanganui River**, New Zealand's longest navigable waterway. Visitors can travel upriver by jetboat or paddle steamer and downriver by kayak or canoe. The UNESCO World Heritage Site **Whanganui National Park** is a green vision of unspoiled native bush where there remains the 'Bridge to Nowhere', a relic of the failed attempt at settlement in the glorious wilderness.
The **Egmont National Park** is also a UNESCO-listed World Heritage area, and provides an excellent though strenuous opportunity, even for the less adventurous, to climb a mountain (*Taranaki*) in a little over eight hours (return). **Mount Taranaki**, at the centre of the national park, is an extinct volcano standing majestically amidst flat areas of lush green dairy farmland. The city of **New Plymouth** (population 50,000) is well known for its parks and gardens and, in particular, its colourful display of rhododendrons and azaleas in the spring.
WELLINGTON: In the south of the North Island, **Wellington**, New Zealand's capital, occupies the flat area surrounding the harbour basin and climbs the surrounding steep hillsides overlooking the water. This makes it a compact metropolis with a thriving and lively heart. The city is a centre of culture, arts, restaurants, theatre, fashion and nightlife. Shopping facilities are excellent and hotels offer splendid views of the bay. Every two years, Wellington hosts the *New Zealand International Festival of the Arts*, the country's main cultural event including street theatre, comedy, music and film festivals, all going under the same umbrella. The spectacular **Te Papa Museum** of New Zealand, on the city's pretty waterfront, combines cultural and historical exhibitions with education, entertainment and leisure activities, including a virtual bungy jump. Wellington is also the departure point for ferries across **Cook Strait** to the **South Island**.
EXCURSIONS: Popular destinations for excursions from **Wellington** include the **Wairarapa** wine region, **Cape Palliser** (whose wild coastline provides a habitat for a large colony of seals) and **Kapiti Island**, home to a bird sanctuary free of introduced predators where *weka*, bellbird and *tui*, to name but a few, show little or no fear and provide photo opportunities of fantastic quality.

SOUTH ISLAND

MARLBOROUGH SOUNDS: To the north of the South Island, the sheltered waterways of the lush and green region known as Marlborough Sounds attract numerous boating, kayaking, sailing and fishing enthusiasts. The Marlborough province is well known for its wine and food, with world-class, new-world wineries such as **Cloudy Bay**, **Le Brun**, **Fromm**, **Highfield**, **Hunters** and **Montana** to name but a few. The best wines from this area tend to be white, sharp *Chardonnay* and crisp *Sauvignon Blanc*. Nearby, **Nelson** is a sunny and busy small city on the coast, where visitors will find pretty gardens, spectacular beaches and a growing arts community. Besides being an interesting place for art and culture lovers, the city is a good starting point for excursions to the three national parks in the vicinity. The UNESCO-listed **Abel Tasman National Park** has a rocky coastline, long golden, crescent-shaped beaches, crystal clear water, a seal colony, an abundance of bird life and a fine coastal track – the **Abel Tasman Track** (three to four days). **Nelson Lakes National Park**, also on the UNESCO World Heritage list, offers skiing and snowboarding during winter and fishing or sub-alpine walking tracks during the summer. The **Kahurangi National Park**, another UNESCO World Heritage area, has a selection of walking tracks that offer an extraordinary range of scenery from mountains and karst tablelands to dramatic black-sand beaches on the west coast. The most famous of these is the tough **Heaphy Track** (four days). The **Kaikoura** coast, further south, is a world-famous conservation area, sitting opposite a deep water trench full of marine life, and is renowned for boat rides at close quarters with various species of whale and the chance to swim with dolphins.
CHRISTCHURCH: To the south, on the edge of the flat patchwork quilt of the **Canterbury Plains**, lies the 'Garden City' of **Christchurch**, the South Island's largest community. The tree-lined **River Avon** meanders through the centre of the city, which with its public school, old university buildings (now a fantastic arts centre) and examples of Neo-Gothic architecture is reminiscent of an old English university town. The central square of the city is occupied by a cathedral which provides a useful landmark for tourists either on foot or using the charming historic trams. About 500m (1640ft) from the square is the vast expanse of **Hagley Park**, on the borders of which are the **Old Canterbury University/Arts Centre**, the **Canterbury Museum**, the **Robert McDougall Art Gallery**, the **botanical gardens** and **Christ's College**. Just a short walk along the river is **St Michael and All Angels Church**; an unusually beautiful wooden Neo-Gothic building combining French and English styles and containing a mixture of Maori and Catholic elements. For excursions from Christchurch, the nearby **Banks Peninsula** provides a hilly alternative to the flat city, with a cable car, beaches, boat trips, pods of Hector's dolphins (unique to New Zealand) and a number of accessible walking tracks. Another alternative is to take a hot air balloon ride and from that vantage point look west across the broad flat plains to the **Southern Alps**, north to the **Kaikoura Ranges** and **Cook Strait** and south down the east coast as far as the historic white-stone city of **Oamaru**.
SOUTHERN ALPS: From Christchurch, a single rail line and road lead to the **Southern Alps**, up over **Arthur's Pass** and down the other side to the wild west coast. This is the route of a breathtaking rail journey which can be completed, there and back, in one day on the **Tranz Alpine Express**. The tiny village of **Arthur's Pass** is a good starting point for climbing, canyoning and trekking trips to the UNESCO-listed **Arthur's Pass National Park** nearby. The Alps themselves, which can be accessed by five main roads from the east coast, are the spine of the South Island pushed up by plate movement in the earth's crust. They are larger than the similarly named mountain range in Europe and the spectacular scenery of snowy peaks and glaciers contains

unique flora and fauna. The area is dominated by the mighty sagging-tent peak of **Mount Cook** (3754m/12,313ft), also known by the Maori name Aoraki (cloud piercer). **Mount Cook National Park** is a UNESCO World Heritage area and contains more than 20 peaks over 3000m (9840ft). Sliding down from one side of Mount Cook is the spectacular **Tasman Glacier**, one of the longest outside the Himalayas. All types of skiing and snowboarding are available along the Alps with many uncrowded ski fields, including heli-skiing, while around Mount Cook there are a number of stunning lone and guided walking and climbing trips of one to five days.

WEST COAST: At the foot of the Southern Alps' western slopes, the thin strip that is the West Coast is one of New Zealand's wildest untouched natural areas. The coast gets about 4m (13ft) of rain a year, and is a sparsely populated region with a dramatic mountain and native forest landscape, with pristine bush-fringed lakes, which provides a home to the **Franz Josef** and **Fox glaciers**. It is possible to take guided 'ice walks' on the glaciers or enjoy the myriad wilderness walking tracks that snake in and out of the forests, round the river valleys and gorges, and into the foothills of the Alps. It is also worth visiting the small communities of **Greymouth** and **Hokitika** where you can purchase carved greenstone, called *pounamu* by the Maori, who use it for decoration and to make weapons. This beautiful, green, hard nephrite jade carved in a traditional shape (each shape carries its own meaning and story) provides the perfect souvenir of a trip to the 'Land of the Long White Cloud'.

FIORDLAND: To the southwest of the South Island is Fiordland, listed by UNESCO as a World Heritage Area, which offers a huge range of walking tracks in the wilderness consisting of numerous lakes, mountains, native forest and a pristine coast. Many scenes from the blockbuster film trilogy *The Lord of the Rings* were filmed in different areas of Fiordland. Nestling beside **Lake Wakatipu** at the foot of the **Remarkables Range**, **Queenstown** is known as New Zealand's 'adventure capital', where tourists can bungy, paraglide, parachute and jet boat (in narrow gorges) until weak at the knees. There are also several world-class walking tracks running out from **Glenorchy** just along the lake shore, including the **Caples**, **Greenstone Tracks** and **Routeburn** (all four to five days). Only 100km (60 miles) or so away is **Te Anau**, on the shores of the gorgeous **Lake Manapouri**, where many more walking trails (from one to six days) wind into the bush, over the saddles and around the fjords, mountains and forests including the famous **Milford Walking Track** (four to five days). From Te Anau travelling north, a beautiful scenic road leads to **Milford Sound** (wrongly named a sound when in fact it is a fjord). Tourist boats carry people out to the sea along the narrow, high-walled, glacially scooped fjord where Fiordland crested penguins, seals and sometimes whales and dolphins take advantage of the abundance of fish due to the unusual conditions. In the fjord, a layer of freshwater, from the mountains, lays on top of the salt water from the ocean refracting light and creating a mini ecosystem teeming with marine life. For those interested in an even more deserted wilderness experience, there are kayak and boat trips into the adjoining **Doubtful Sound**.

SOUTHLAND: The green and fertile province of Southland at the bottom of the South Island is home to the cities of **Invercargill** and **Dunedin** (which is Gaelic for Edinburgh), both of which have strong Scottish roots and retain a distinctive Celtic flavour. In Dunedin, this is perhaps best reflected by the city's streets bearing the same names as those of Edinburgh, and the presence of **Wilson's Whisky Distillery** (reputedly the world's southernmost distillery) and the **Emmerson's** and **Speights breweries**. Unlike Edinburgh, Dunedin also has the **Otago Peninsula**, a glorious natural thumb poking out into the **Pacific**, where it is possible to see rare yellow-eyed penguins (Maori name *hoihoi*, meaning noise maker), enormous yet graceful royal albatross, and basking on the rocks around the peninsula – fur seals. **Invercargill's Sub-Antarctic Audio Visual and Gallery** is a wonderful museum containing, among other interesting exhibits, a number of live tuatara, New Zealand's very rare and prehistoric lizard, while nearby is **Bluff**, home of the famous 'Bluff oysters', a delicacy that should not be missed. Between Invercargill and Dunedin is the **Catlins Forest Park**, with its wild beaches, pods of Hector's Dolphins and the only mainland colony of Hooker sea lions.

STEWART ISLAND: Across the **Foveaux Strait**, New Zealand's third-largest island, Stewart Island, has few inhabitants and can be reached by plane (travel time – 20 minutes), helicopter, or boat ride aboard a motor catamaran from Bluff. The island has various attractions, including a rare chance to see the endangered *kiwi* (New Zealand's national symbol) in the wild. The birds feed in the evenings around **Mason's Beach**, accessible by plane, or by water taxi to **Patterson's Inlet**, followed by a delightful four-hour walk. Another draw card is **Ulva Island**, a predator-free, offshore expanse of bush and beautiful beaches where curious native birds come down to the foreshore to watch tourists clambering off the water taxi.

Sport & Activities

New Zealand's wild coastlines and national parks (two-thirds of the country is mountainous and nearly a quarter is protected as some form of park) create perfect conditions for every kind of outdoor activity. Not surprisingly, some of the world's most cutting-edge adventure activities originated in New Zealand, while more traditional sports, such as sailing, rugby, cricket or golf, continue to be pursued with unwavering passion.

Adventure sports: The **Awesome Foursome** is an adrenaline trip that combines a **helicopter flight**, a **bungy jump**, **high-speed jetboating** and **whitewater rafting** all in one day. **Bungy jumping** was first commercialised by New Zealanders and the country remains the world's prime destination for the sport. Famous jump-off points include the *Kawaru River Bridge*, the *Skippers Bridge*, the *Pipeline*, the *Ledge* (near Queenstown), *Taupo* and *Mangaweka* (in the North Island), *Hanmer Springs* (in the South Island) and the *Bungee Rocket* (at New Brighton Pier). **Rap jumping**, which consists of abseiling headfirst down a cliff, is currently popular in *Auckland*, *Bay of Islands*, *Queenstown* and *Wanaka*. **River sledging** involves riding down a river holding in a polystyrene sled or boogie board and is possible in *Queenstown* (South Island) and on the *Rangitaiki River* near Rotorua (North Island). **Paragliding** (also referred to as 'parapenting') is billed as the closest possible equivalent to flying and is a cross between parachuting and hang-gliding; beginner's courses are available near Queenstown and Wanaka, while experienced paragliders tend to head to Christchurch, the Daney Pass or Wanaka. **Jetboating**, another New Zealand invention, consists of high-speed boat trips in special power boats. It is available to people of all ages and popular on many of the country's best-known rivers. **Surf rafting** invites visitors to accompany experienced rafters through crashing waves while simultaneously being offered a commentary on the coastline nearby. Best locations are the *Otago Peninsula* (near Dunedin, South Island) and *Piha Beach* (near Auckland, North Island). **Zorbing** involves being strapped into an inflatable transparent plastic ball, which is then rolled down a grassy hill or onto a river. Queenstown is generally regarded as New Zealand's 'adventure capital'.

Watersports: New Zealand's coastline stretches for a total of roughly 16,000km (10,000 miles) and the conditions for **swimming** and **diving** are ideal. Many dive spots are easily accessible from the shore, particularly those in *Northland* (North Island). The *Poor Knights Islands* (near Whangarei) are particularly renowned among divers (Jacques Cousteau cited them as one of the world's top diving destinations). Many different types of diving are available, including kelp forests at *Stewart Island* (home to the huge Paua shellfish), black and red coral in the Fiordlands, and wreck-diving, notably at the *Rainbow Warrior*, the famous Greenpeace boat which was sunk off the Bay of Islands. Divers need to bring their diver's certification cards. Many dive stores offer equipment rental and support facilities. A detailed brochure with information on New Zealand's best dive sites can be obtained from New Zealand Underwater, PO Box 875, Auckland (tel: (9) 623 3252; fax: (9) 623 3523; website: www.nzunderwater.org.nz). The long coastlines also offer excellent opportunities for **surfing**, with some of the best breaks located at *Mahia Peninsula* (near Gisborne), *Murawai*, *Palliser Bay* (near Wellington), *Piha* and *Raglan*. **Swimming with dolphins** is possible in the *Bay of Islands* (north of Auckland), the *Coromandel Peninsula*, *Kaikoura* (South Island) and *Whakatane*; numbers are limited and advance booking is recommended. **Whale watching** is possible on the eastern coast of South Island all year round (with the greatest number of sightings in winter, from April to August). For further information and details of prices, contact Whale Watch (website: www.whalewatch.co.nz). **Sailing** and **yachting** are extremely popular and Auckland – 'the city of sails' – is one of the top locations. Charters with a skipper and crew can be hired to sail around the coast or as far as the Pacific Islands. Excursions to the remote maritime reserves in the Bay of Islands, Hauraki Gulf and Marlborough Sounds are also possible. **Whitewater rafting** trips ranging from a couple of hours to five days are available on many rivers, including the *Wairora* (near Tauranga), the *Mohaka* (in Hawke's Bay) and the *Kaituna* (near Rotorua), which also features the world's highest commercially rafted waterfall at 7m (23ft). **Windsurfing** is particularly popular around Wellington, Taupo, Auckland and the Bay of Islands while **kayaking** is widely practised on rivers throughout the country.

Wintersports: New Zealand offers good **skiing** and **snowboarding**, with ideal conditions from June to October. Resorts tend to be less crowded than European ones. On the North Island, the best ski regions are *Whakapapa* and *Turoa* (both located on Mount Ruapehu). Other good ski slopes can be found in the *Southern Lakes region* (particularly Queenstown and Wanaka) and *Mount Hutt* (where the season is from late May to early November). **Heli-skiing** trips are available in Mount Hutt, Queenstown and Wanaka, while **cross-country skiing** is possible on a 26km- (16 mile-) trail through the Pisa range near Wanaka. **Glacier skiing** and **glacier walking** can be enjoyed at the *Fox*, *Franz Josef* and *Tasman glaciers* in the Southern Alps.

Mountaineering: New Zealand has some of the highest peaks in the southern hemisphere. Climbers are advised to hire a commercial guide or contact a local alpine club before setting out.

Caving: The *Waitomo Caves*, whose 'Lost World' cave can be abseiled into through shafts of sunlight, are the most visited. Other ways to explore the country's many underground caves is through **cave rafting** or **tubing**, where participants are kitted out with a wetsuit and helmet (complete with light) and then float through the cave system on custom-made tyres.

Golf: New Zealand has over 400 golf courses. Green fees are relatively low compared to other countries. Most clubs welcome visitors, but it is best to telephone in advance, particularly at weekends. For further information, contact the New Zealand Golf Association, PO Box 11842, Wellington (tel: (4) 385 4330; fax: (4) 385 4331; e-mail: nzga@nzga.co.nz; website: www.nzgolf.org.nz).

Walking: A variety of walks for all ages and levels of fitness is available. Many of the country's footpaths pass through national parks or protected forest areas. Trails are categorised according to four different types: *paths* (easy, suitable for all ages and fitness levels, including wheelchair users), *walking tracks* (easy), *tramping tracks* (more demanding, requiring good fitness) and *routes* (very challenging and for experienced hikers only). The Department of Conservation (DOC) has singled out eight different walks which are generally the best known and most popular, including the *Abel Tasman Coastal Track* (New Zealand's most widely used recreational track), the *Lake Waikaremoana Track* (in Te Urewara National Park), the *Milford Track* (the country's most famous track in World-Heritage-listed Fiordland Park) and the *Rakiura Track* (a remote walk on Stewart Island to New Zealand's southernmost parts). These tracks generally take from one to several days, with accommodation provided en route, either in the form of basic camping and huts or comfortable lodges. A network of remote tramping tracks also exists, but walkers attempting these should be well prepared and able to read maps and use a compass. In most cases, a Great Walks Pass must be obtained from the Department of Conservation, which has local offices throughout the country. For further information, contact the Department of Conservation in Wellington (tel: (4) 471 0726; fax: (4) 471 1082; website: www.doc.govt.nz).

Fishing: Brown and rainbow trout are particularly popular. Salmon fishing is best in the Rakaia, Rangitata, Waimakariri and Waitaki rivers on the East Coast (the season lasts from mid-December to late April). Permits are *only* required for trout and salmon fishing and there is a special Tourist Licence (available only from the Tourism Rotorua Information Office) which allows holders to fish anywhere in the country for a one-month period. For further information, contact the New Zealand Professional Fishing Guides Association, PO Box 16, Motu, Gisborne (tel: (6) 863 5822; fax: (6) 863 5844; e-mail: murphy.motu@xtra.co.nz; website: www.nzpfga.com).

Wildlife: As New Zealand was separated from other land masses some 100 million years ago, many plant and animal species are unique to the country. This is particularly true in the case of birds, which attract **birdwatching** enthusiasts from all over the world. Owing to the lack of predators, many of the country's birds never fully developed wings and, hence, live on the ground. The best-known native bird is the *kiwi*, also the country's unofficial national symbol. Others include the *kea* and *weka*, as well as the endangered *kakapo*, the world's largest parrot. The *emu*, originally from Australia, is also found here; New Zealand's own native equivalent, the *moa*, is now extinct. New Zealand is also home to the world's largest insect, the *weta* (a mouse-sized cricket), and the *tuatara* (a reptile whose lineage stretches back to the dinosaurs). Famous locations for birdwatching include Taiaroa Head (near Dunedin), known for colonies of royal albatrosses and Stewart Island, where kiwis can be observed at night. Cape Kidnappers in Hawkes Bay is the only gannet colony in the world, and is well worth a visit at low tide when it is possible to walk along the beach or take a tractor ride.

Other: Rugby, **netball** and **cricket** are the national sports. Other sports particular to New Zealand include **lawn bowls**, a popular sport played from September to April with greens in most towns, and **sheep dog trials**. Throughout the year, a number of **triathlon** races and endurance events are held. **Bicycles** can be hired easily; special tours offer lifts up to volcano tops (notably at *Mount Ruapehu*, the *Otaga Peninsula* and the *Remarkables Range*). Cycle helmets are compulsory and most buses and trains allow bicycles on board.

Social Profile

FOOD & DRINK: New Zealand has a reputation as a leading producer of meat and dairy produce with lamb, beef and pork on most menus. Venison is also widely available. Locally produced vegetables, such as *kumara* (a natural sweet potato), are good. There is also a wide range of fish available, including snapper, grouper and John Dory. Seasonal delicacies such as whitebait, oysters, crayfish, scallops and game birds are recommended. New Zealand is also establishing a reputation for French-type cheeses: Bleu de Bresse, Brie, Camembert and Montagne Bleu. New Zealand's traditional dessert is *pavlova*, a large round cake with a meringue base, topped with fruit and cream. Many picnic areas with barbecue facilities are provided at roadside sites. Restaurants are usually informal except for very exclusive ones. Waiter service is normal, but self-service and fast-food chains are also available. Some restaurants invite the customer to 'BYO' (bring your own liquor).
New Zealand boasts world-class domestic wines and beers, some of which have won international awards. A wide range of domestic and imported wines, spirits and beers is available from hotel bars, 'liquor stores' and wine shops. Bars have counter service and public bars are very informal. Lounge bars and 'house bars' (for hotel guests only) are sometimes more formal and occasionally have table service. The minimum drinking age in a bar is 18. There is some variation in licensing hours in major cities and some hotel bars open Sunday, providing a meal is eaten. In most hotels and taverns, licensing hours are 1100-2300 except Sunday.
NIGHTLIFE: New Zealand has an active and varied entertainment industry. Theatres offer good entertainment ranging from drama, comedy and musicals to pop concerts and shows. Concert tickets can be booked online (website: www.ticketek.com). In large cities, there are often professional performers or guest artists from overseas. Visitors should check 'What's On' in local papers. There are also cinemas and a small selection of nightclubs in larger cities.
SHOPPING: Special purchases include distinctive jewellery made from New Zealand *greenstone* (a kind of jade) and from the beautiful translucent *paua* shell. Maori arts and crafts are reflected in a number of items such as the carved greenstone *tiki* (a unique Maori charm) and intricate woodcarvings often inlaid with *paua* shell. Other items of note include woollen goods, travel rugs, lambswool rugs, leather and skin products. **Shopping hours**: All shops and businesses are open Mon-Sat 0900-1700, as a minimum; there are local variations but many stores and most malls are also open Sun 1000-1300. In resorts, most shops are also open in the evenings.
SPECIAL EVENTS: For further details and exact dates, contact Tourism New Zealand (see *Contact Addresses* section). The following is just a selection of special events occurring in New Zealand in 2005:
Jan 3-Feb 6 *Global Challenge* yacht race, Wellington. **Jan 10-16** *Heineken Tennis Open*, Auckland. **Feb 5** *Kawhia Traditional Maori Food Festival*. **Feb 4-5** *International Rugby Sevens Tournament*, Wellington. **Feb 5-6** *Harvest Hawkes Bay Wine & Food Festivals*. **Mar 11-13** *Womad International Music Festival*, Taranaki. **Mar 13** *Weka Wildthing Triathalon*, Manawata. **Mar 26-27** *Silverstone Race to the Sky*. **Mar 31-Apr 2** *New Zealand Shearing Championships*, Waikato. **May 6-8** *Savour New Zealand*, food festival. **Jun 4-Jul 9** *British Lions Rugby Tour*. **Jul 22-Aug 7** *International Film Festival*.
SOCIAL CONVENTIONS: Should a visitor be invited to a formal Maori occasion, the *hongi* (pressing of noses) is common. Casual dress is widely acceptable. New Zealanders are generally very relaxed and hospitable. Stiff formality is rarely appreciated and, after introductions, first names are generally used. Smoking is restricted where indicated.
Tipping: Service charges and taxes are not added to hotel or restaurant bills. Tips are not expected.

Business Profile

ECONOMY: New Zealand is primarily thought of as an agricultural country and, although the sector employs less than 10 per cent of the workforce and contributes just 8 per cent of GDP, it accounts for 40 per cent of the country's export income, primarily from wool, meat and dairy, and woods products. Barley, wheat, maize and fruit are the main crops. There is also a sizeable fishing industry. Energy-related natural resources, principally coal but also natural gas, have been heavily developed. There are also deposits of iron, gold and silica. From the late 1970s, a new generation of industrial enterprises centred on these natural resources was established to replace the declining traditional industries.
Between the mid-1980s and mid-1990s, New Zealand underwent one of the most radical economic transformations of any Western industrialised country, with wholesale privatisation, the abolition of subsidies, tariff barriers and corporate regulations, and the dismantling of many welfare systems (although spending has risen sharply of late as the government tackles the pensions crisis afflicting the developed world). The reforms have also meant that New Zealand is much more dependent on foreign trade. Recent economic performance has seen annual growth rise slightly to 3.5 per cent in 2004. Inflation was 1.8 per cent in 2004. Unemployment has hovered around the 5 per cent mark for several years, although much of it is concentrated in particular areas where it remains a major problem.
Australia is New Zealand's largest trading partner, and the two governments have recently established a completely free trading regime between them. Japan, the USA and the UK are the other major trading partners. New Zealand is a member of the Organisation for Economic Co-operation and Development (OECD, the international forum for the world's main industrialised economies), the South Pacific Forum (which aims to promote economic cooperation in the region) and the recently established Asian-Pacific Economic Co-operation (APEC) forum.
BUSINESS: Businesswear is generally conservative and both sexes tend toward tailored suits. Appointments are necessary and punctuality is appreciated. Calling cards are usually exchanged. The business approach is fairly conservative and visitors should avoid the period from Christmas to the end of January. The best months for business visits are February to April and October to November. **Office hours**: Mon-Fri 0900-1700.
COMMERCIAL INFORMATION: The following organisation can offer advice: Wellington Chamber of Commerce and Industry, PO Box 1590, Level 9, 109 Featherson Street, Wellington (tel: (4) 914 6500; fax: (4) 914 6524; e-mail: info@wgtn-chamber.co.nz; website: www.wgtn-chamber.co.nz).
CONFERENCES/CONVENTIONS: The largest centres are in Auckland, Christchurch and Wellington. Many hotels also have facilities. There are over 20 regional convention bureaux in New Zealand, most of which are members of NZ Convention Association (Inc), PO Box 331-202, Suite 3, Level 1, 15 Huron Street, Takapuna, Auckland (tel: (9) 486 4128; fax: (9) 486 4126; e-mail: admin@nzconventions.co.nz; website: www.conventionsnz.com). The organisation is also known as Conventions New Zealand.

Climate

Subtropical in the North and temperate in the South. The North has no extremes of heat or cold but winter can be quite cool in the South, with snow in the mountains. The eastern areas often experience drought conditions in summer; the West, particularly in the South Island, has more rain.
Required clothing: Lightweight cottons and linens are worn in the North Island most of the year and in summer in the South Island. Mediumweights are worn during winter in the South Island. Rainwear is advisable throughout the year, and essential if visiting the South Island's rainforest areas.

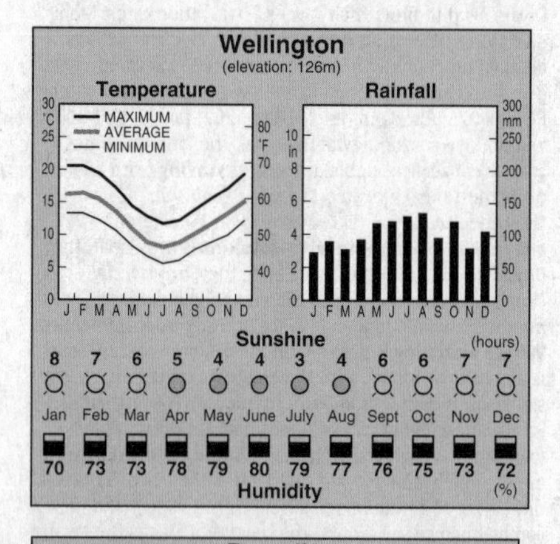

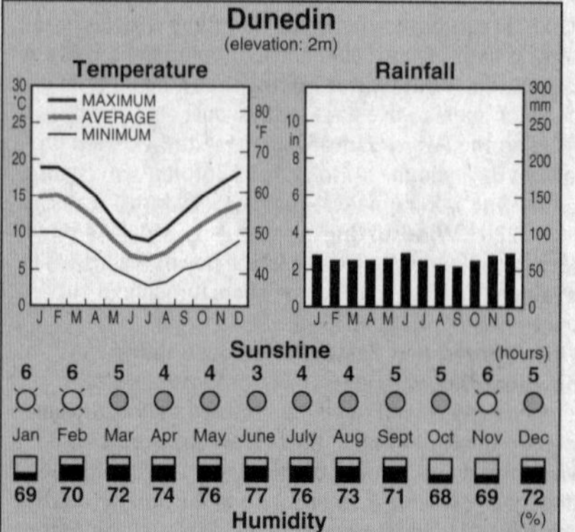

Nicaragua

LATEST TRAVEL ADVICE CONTACTS

British Foreign and Commonwealth Office
Tel: (0870) 606 0290 Website: www.fco.gov.uk
US Department of State
Website: http://travel.state.gov/travel
Canadian Department of Foreign Affairs and Int'l Trade
Tel: (1 800) 267 8376 Website: www.dfait-maeci.gc.ca

Location: Central America.

Country dialling code: 505.

Nicaraguan Institute of Tourism (INTUR)
Hotel Intercontinental, 1 c Sur, 1 c Oeste, Managua, Nicaragua
Tel: 222 3333. Fax: 222 6610.
E-mail: promocion@intur.gob.ni
Website: www.visit-nicaragua.com
Embassy of the Republic of Nicaragua
Vicarage House, Suite 31, 58-60 Kensington Church Street, London W8 4DB, UK
Tel: (020) 7938 2373. Fax: (020) 7937 0952.
E-mail: embanic1@yahoo.co.uk
Website: http://freespace.virgin.net/emb.ofnicaragua
Opening hours: Mon-Fri 0100-1600.
The British Embassy in San José now deals with all enquiries relating to Nicaragua (see *Costa Rica* section).
Embassy of the Republic of Nicaragua
1627 New Hampshire Avenue, NW, Washington, DC 20009, USA
Tel: (202) 939 6570. Fax: (202) 939 6545.
E-mail: haroldrivas@embanic.org (consular section).
Also deals with enquiries from Canada.
Embassy of the United States of America
Apartado 327, Km 4.5 Carretera Sur, Managua, Nicaragua
Tel: 268 0123. Fax: 266 9943.
E-mail: EmbassyInfo@state.gov *or* ConsularManagua@state.gov
Website: http://usembassy.state.gov/managua
Office of the Canadian Embassy
Costado Oriental de la Casa Nasareth, 1 cuadra arriba, Calle El Noval, Managua, Nicaragua
Tel: 268 0433 *or* 3323. Fax: 268 0437.
E-mail: mngua@dfait-maeci.gc.ca
The Canadian Embassy in Costa Rica is now accredited to the Government of Nicaragua.

General Information

AREA: 120,254 sq km (46,430 sq miles).
POPULATION: 5,482,340 (official estimate 2003).
POPULATION DENSITY: 50.3 per sq km.
CAPITAL: Managua. **Population**: 1,374,025 (official estimate 2003).

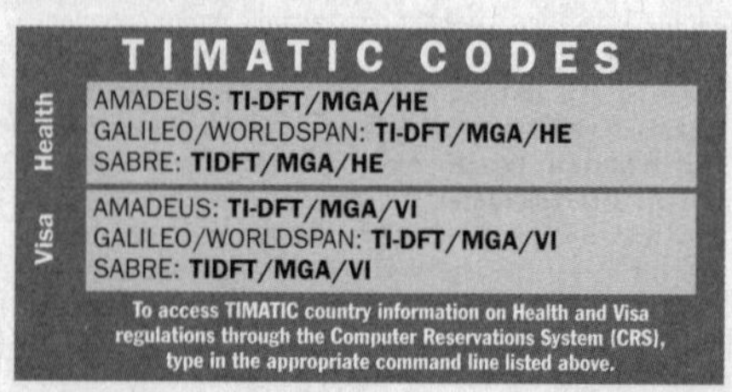
TIMATIC CODES

Health	AMADEUS: **TI-DFT/MGA/HE** GALILEO/WORLDSPAN: **TI-DFT/MGA/HE** SABRE: **TIDFT/MGA/HE**
Visa	AMADEUS: **TI-DFT/MGA/VI** GALILEO/WORLDSPAN: **TI-DFT/MGA/VI** SABRE: **TIDFT/MGA/VI**

To access TIMATIC country information on Health and Visa regulations through the Computer Reservations System (CRS), type in the appropriate command line listed above.

GEOGRAPHY: Nicaragua borders Honduras to the north and Costa Rica to the south. To the east lies the Caribbean, and to the west the Pacific. In the north are the Isabella Mountains, while the country's main feature in the southwest is Lake Nicaragua, 148km (92 miles) long and about 55km (34 miles) at its widest. The island of Ometepe is the largest of the 310 islands on the lake. These islands have a reputation for great beauty and are one of the country's main tourist attractions. Lake Managua is situated to the northwest. Volcanoes, including the famous Momotombo, protrude from the surrounding lowlands northwest of the lakes. The country's main rivers are the San Juan, the lower reaches of which form the border with Costa Rica, and the Rio Grande. The Corn Islands (Islas del Maiz) in the Caribbean are two small beautiful islands fringed with white coral and palms. They are very popular as holiday resorts with both Nicaraguans and tourists. The majority of Nicaragua's population lives and works in the lowland between the Pacific and western shores of Lake Nicaragua, the southwestern shore of Lake Managua and the southwestern sides of the range of volcanoes. It is only in recent years that settlers have taken to coffee growing and cattle farming in the highlands around Matagalpa and Jinotega.
GOVERNMENT: Republic. Gained independence from Spain in 1821. **Head of State and Government**: President Enrique Bolanos Geyer since 2001.
LANGUAGE: Spanish. Along the Mosquito Coast (*Costa de Mosquito*), there are English-speaking communities in which African or mixed African and indigenous Indians predominate.
RELIGION: 85 per cent Roman Catholic; 14 per cent Protestant.
TIME: GMT - 6.
ELECTRICITY: 120 volts AC, 60Hz.
COMMUNICATIONS: Telephone: IDD is available. Country code: 505. Outgoing international calls may be made via the international operator or through direct dialling. **Mobile telephone:** The privatised telecommunications and postal service *ENITEL* (website: www.enitel.com.ni) and *Sercom SA* (website: http://pcsdigital.com.ni) both offer GSM 1900 services but coverage is mainly limited to Managua and the surrounding areas. **Internet:** Internet cafes in Nicaragua provide public access to Internet and e-mail services. ISPs include *IBW Internet Gateway* (website: www.ibw.com.ni).
Fax/Telegram: Facilities in Managua. **Post:** Most larger towns have an Enitel telecommunications and postal office. Airmail to Europe takes up to two weeks. *Poste restante* services are available in Managua. Post office hours: Mon-Sat 0900-1730. **Press:** Main publications include the *Confidencial, Nuevo Diario* and *La Prensa*.
Radio: BBC World Service (website: www.bbc.co.uk/worldservice) and Voice of America (website: www.voa.gov) can be received. From time to time the frequencies change and the most up-to-date can be found online.

Passport/Visa

	Passport Required?	Visa Required?	Return Ticket Required?
Full British	Yes	No/1	Yes
Australian	Yes	No/1	Yes
Canadian	Yes	No/1	Yes
USA	Yes	No/1	Yes
Other EU	Yes	No/1	Yes
Japanese	Yes	No/1	Yes

Note: *Regulations and requirements may be subject to change at short notice, and you are advised to contact the appropriate diplomatic or consular authority before finalising travel arrangements. Details of these may be found at the head of this country's entry. Any numbers in the chart refer to the footnotes below.*

PASSPORTS: Passport valid for at least six months from the date of arrival required by all.
VISAS: Required *only* by nationals of the following countries:
Afghanistan, Albania, Angola, Armenia, Bosnia & Herzegovina, Cameroon, China (PR), Colombia, Cuba, Dominican Republic, Ecuador, Egypt, Ghana, Haiti, India, Iran, Iraq, Jordan, Kenya, Korea (Dem Rep), Lebanon, Liberia, Libya, Mali, Mozambique, Nepal, Nigeria, Pakistan, Palestine National Authority, Peru, Romania, Serbia & Montenegro, Sierra Leone, Somalia, Sri Lanka, Sudan, the Syrian Arab Republic, Ukraine, Vietnam and Yemen.
Note: 1. All other nationals can obtain a **Tourist Card** on arrival for approximately US$10 for touristic stays of one month, provided they are holding valid travel documents and, in the case of business travellers, a letter from their employer and/or company in Nicaragua.
Types of visa and cost: *Tourist* and *Business*: £18.
Validity: One month from date of issue. Visas can be extended for up to 30 more days. Applications should be made to the Immigration Office in Managua.
Application to: Consulate (or Consular section at Embassy); see *Contact Addresses* section. Tourist Cards can be obtained on arrival.
Application requirements: (a) Valid passport and a photocopy of passport required. (b) Completed application form. (c) Two passport-size photos. (d) Fee. (e) Onward or return ticket; including any travel documents needed for previous and next destination.
Working days required: Confirmation for visas takes six to eight weeks as special authorisation from the Nicaraguan Ministry of Foreign Affairs is required.
Temporary residence: Enquire at Embassy.
Note: Applicants need to have lived in Nicaragua for at least one year before applying.

Money

Currency: Nicaraguan Gold Córdoba (C$) = 100 centavos. Notes are in denominations of C$100, 50, 20 and 10, and 50, 25, 10 and 5 centavos.
Note: Frequent adjustments to the traded value of the Nicaraguan Gold Córdoba, and the various exchange systems that have been used, make it impossible to make meaningful comparative assessments over successive years.
Currency exchange: Foreign currencies can be exchanged at the airport, at banks and at official bureaux de change in major cities.
Credit & debit cards: American Express, Diners Club, MasterCard and Visa are accepted on a limited basis. Check with your credit or debit card company for details of merchant acceptability and other services which may be available.
Travellers cheques: Accepted in a number of places.
Currency restrictions: There are no restrictions on the import or export of local or foreign currency.
Exchange rate indicators: The following figures are included as a guide to the movement of the Nicaraguan Gold Córdoba against Sterling and the US Dollar:

Date	Feb '04	May '04	Aug '04	Nov '04
£1.00=	28.23	28.04	29.31	30.58
$1.00=	15.51	15.70	15.91	16.15

Banking hours: Mon-Fri 0830-1700, Sat 0830-1130; some may close for an hour over lunch.

Duty Free

The following items can be imported into Nicaragua without incurring customs duty:
200 cigarettes or 500g of tobacco; 3l of alcoholic beverage; one large bottle or three small bottles of perfume or eau de cologne.
Restricted imports: Canned or uncanned meats, leather and dairy products. A licence is required for firearms.
Prohibited exports: Archaeological items, artefacts of historical or monetary value, and gold.

Public Holidays

2005: Jan 1 New Year's Day. **Mar 24** Holy Thursday. **Mar 25** Good Friday. **May 1** Labour Day. **May 30** Mother's Day. **Jul 19** Liberation Day. **Aug 1** Santo Domingo Day. **Sep 14** Battle of San Jacinto. **Sep 15** Independence Day. **Nov 2** All Souls' Day. **Dec 8** Immaculate Conception. **Dec 25** Christmas Day.
Note: A considerable number of local holidays are also observed.

Health

	Special Precautions?	Certificate Required?
Yellow Fever	No	1
Cholera	2	No
Typhoid & Polio	3	N/A
Malaria	4	N/A

Note: *Regulations and requirements may be subject to change at short notice, and you are advised to contact your doctor well in advance of your intended date of departure. Any numbers in the chart refer to the footnotes below.*

1: A yellow fever vaccination certificate is required from all travellers aged one year and over arriving within six days from infected areas.
2: Following WHO guidelines issued in 1973, a cholera vaccination certificate is not a condition of entry to Nicaragua. However, cholera is a risk in this country, especially after outbreaks in 1999 in Jinotega, Managua, Nueva Segovia and RAAN areas. Precautions are essential. Up-to-date advice should be sought before deciding whether these precautions should include vaccination, as medical opinion is divided over its effectiveness; see the *Health* appendix.
3: Immunisation against typhoid is strongly recommended.
4: Risk of malaria, predominantly in the benign *vivax* form, exists throughout the year in 119 municipalities. In the other 26 municipalities, in the departments of Carazo, Madriz and Masaya, transmission risk is low or negligible. Malaria risk is higher during the rainy season.
Food & drink: All water should be regarded as being potentially contaminated. Water used for drinking, brushing teeth or making ice should have first been boiled or otherwise sterilised. Milk in rural areas may be unpasteurised and should be boiled. Powdered or tinned milk is available and is advised, but make sure that it is reconstituted with pure water. Avoid dairy products which are likely to have been made from unboiled milk. Only eat well-cooked meat and fish, preferably served hot. Pork, salad and mayonnaise may carry increased risk. Vegetables should be cooked and fruit peeled.
Other risks: *Amoebic* and *bacillary dysenteries, diarrhoeal diseases, typhoid fever* and *hepatitis A* are common throughout the country. *Cutaneous* and *visceral leishmaniasis* occur. *Dengue fever* may occur.
Rabies is present. For those at high risk, vaccination before arrival should be considered. If you are bitten, seek medical advice without delay. For more information, consult the *Health* appendix.
Health care: Nicaragua has 27 public hospitals. The Nicaraguan government is currently carrying out a broad programme of renewal and development of the health system, with extensive funding from various development agencies. There is an extensive network of health posts and health centres in rural areas, however, their resources can be limited. International travellers are strongly advised to take out full medical insurance before departure.

Travel - International

Note: Only essential travel to the North Atlantic Autonomous Region (RAAN) should be undertaken. The security situation here is poor and several armed gangs operate.
AIR: Nicaragua's national airline is *Nicaraguenses de Aviación (NICA)*, which is now a member of the *Taca International Airlines (TA)* (website: www.taca.com). Other airlines serving Nicaragua are *Aero Caribbean, American Airlines, Atlantic Airlines, Continental Airlines, Copa Airlines, Iberia* and *Sol Air*. Services are available to Canada, Costa Rica, El Salvador, Guatemala, Honduras, Mexico, Panama, Spain and the USA.
Approximate flight times: From Managua to *London* is 31 hours, including stopovers in Toronto and Miami; to *Madrid* is 13 hours; to *Miami* is two hours 30 minutes.
International airports: *Managua (MGA)* (Augusto Cesar Sandino) is 12km (7 miles) north of the city (travel time – 15 minutes). Bus and taxi services run to the city. Airport facilities include a bank, bars, post office, tourist information, restaurants, duty free shop, refreshments and car hire (*Avis, Budget* and *Hertz*).
Departure tax: US$25 on all departures; children under two years and passengers leaving within eight hours of arrival are exempt.
SEA: Major ports are Corinto, El Bluff, Puerto Cabezas and Puerto Sandino, which are served by shipping lines from Nicaragua, as well as Central American, North American and European countries.
ROAD: The Pan-American Highway runs through Nicaragua via Esteli and Managua. **Bus**: There are daily bus services between Managua and Tegucigalpa (Honduras), San Salvador (El Salvador) and San José (Costa Rica) (travel time – nine hours). Services are provided by *King-Quality, Nicabus, Ticabus* and *Transnica*. Tickets are sold up to five days in advance, and all border documentation must be completed before the ticket is issued.

Travel - Internal

AIR: Given the relative size of the country and the difficulty of some ground travel routes, internal flights are worth considering. *La Costeña* and *Atlantic Airlines* cover a wide range of internal routes.
SEA: A twice-weekly boat service runs between Bluefields and the Corn Islands. It is also possible to visit the 300 or so islands on Lake Nicaragua, which are very beautiful.
RAIL: There is no passenger rail service at present.
ROAD: Lack of road safety is probably the biggest single hazard for travellers in Nicaragua. There is a network of 18,447km (11,463 miles) of roads of which 1749km (1087 miles) are paved. Traffic drives on the right. **Bus**: There is a service to most large towns. Booking seats in Managua in advance is advisable. **Taxi**: Available at the airport or in Managua. Prices should be agreed before departure. A map of each area in the city determines taxi prices.
Car hire: Available in Managua or at the airport. This is often the best way of travelling, as public transport is slow and overcrowded. **Documentation**: National licences are only valid for 30 days.

URBAN: The bus and minibus services in Managua are cheap, but they can be both crowded and confusing.
Travel times: The following chart gives approximate travel times (in hours and minutes) from **Managua** to other major cities/towns in Nicaragua.

	Road
Granada	**1.00**
Masaya	**0.30**
Esteli	**2.15**
Chinandega	**1.30**
Matagalpa	**1.45**
Jinotega	**2.30**
Rivas	**1.30**

Accommodation

Most of the hotels in the capital were destroyed in the earthquake of 1972, but many new hotels have now been opened in Managua. A 15 per cent tax is levied on all hotel bills. There are motels along the Pan-American Highway and modern resort hotels along the west coast, offering a good standard of accommodation. Ecotourism is also developing in the country where some excellent hacienda-style accommodation can be found. **Grading**: Hotels in Managua have been divided into three categories: upper, middle and lower, to provide an indication of price and standard. For more information, contact the Nicaraguan Institute of Tourism (INTUR); see *Contact Addresses* section.

Resorts & Excursions

Nicaragua has three main eco-regions: Pacific, Central and Atlantic; the Pacific region is home to volcanoes, lakes, tropical forests, beaches and mangrove systems; the Central region is home to mountains, rivers and agricultural areas; and the Atlantic region contains rainforests, marine lagoons, mangrove systems and coral reefs. Tourists are well catered for in these areas.
MANAGUA: The centre of the capital was completely destroyed by an earthquake in December 1972 and there was further severe damage during the civil wars of 1978-1979. The Government has now decided that it will rebuild the old centre, adding parks and recreational facilities. In the old centre of Managua, the **National Palace** and the **Cathedral** are excellent examples of colonial architecture. There are several museums of note in Managua, one of the most interesting of which is **Las Huellas de Acahualinca** which houses the site where 9000-year-old footprints were found – testimony to Nicaragua's pre-historic past. There are several volcanic crater lagoons in the environs of Managua – centres of watersports and residential development with boating, fishing and picnicking facilities. **Laguna de Xiloa** is the most popular of these lagoons. Boats can be hired on the shores of **Lake Managua** for visiting the still-smoking **Momotombo** volcano and the shore villages. On **Tiscapa Lagoon**, there is a recreation centre.
LEÓN: This is the intellectual capital of Nicaragua, with a university, religious colleges, the largest cathedral in Central America and several colonial churches. A number of projects are currently underway that will highlight the historical and cultural roots of the city.
GRANADA: Located at the foot of the **Mombacho** volcano, Granada has many beautiful buildings and has faithfully preserved its Castilian traditions. The cathedral has been rebuilt in neo-classical style. Also of interest are the **Church of La Merced**, the **Church of Jalteva** and the fortress-church of **San Francisco**.
RESORTS: One hour's drive from Managua are **Masachapa** and **Pochomil** beaches. **Montelimar Beach Resort** is the largest of its kind in Central America. A visit to the **El Velero** beach is recommended. On the Caribbean coast, there are a number of small ports, the most important of which is **Bluefields**. From here, one can get a boat to the beautiful, coral-fringed **Corn Islands** (Islas del Maiz), the larger of which is a popular Nicaraguan holiday resort with surfing and bathing facilities that make it ideal for tourists. The Pacific coast has a number of fine beaches, including **El Coco**, **Marsella**, **Ocotal**, **San Juan del Sur** and many others which are located in the south of Nicaragua in the department of **Rivas**. These beaches are distinguished by their unique and beautiful surroundings, and a number of touristic developments are underway in this region.

Sport & Activities

Watersports: Beaches on the Pacific coast offer safe **swimming** as do those on the Caribbean, including the popular *Corn Islands*. Often the better beaches have a small entrance charge. Many of the better hotels have pools open to non-residents. In the volcanic crater lagoons, there is also safe swimming. Bathing in *Lake Managua* should be avoided due to contamination,

Credit: © INTUR

although steps to clean up the lake are being taken. Bathing is possible in the *Laguna de Tiscapa*. *El Velero* beach or *Pochomil* on the Pacific coast are ideal for **surfing** as are a number of other beaches along the west coast.
Other: There are a number of good **fishing** spots along the country's waterways and seashores. **Baseball** is the national game.

Social Profile

FOOD & DRINK: Restaurants, particularly in Managua, serve a variety of cooking styles including Chinese, French, Italian, Latin American and Spanish. Local dishes include *gallopinto* (fried rice and pinto beans) and *mondongo* (tripe soup). Plantain is used in many dishes. Other specialities include *nacatamal*, *indio viejo*, *quesillo*, *vigorón* and *roquillas*. Food is often scooped up in *tortillas* instead of using cutlery. Roast corn on the cob is sold on the streets. Seafood is also available. There are a number of cheap but good restaurants/bars (*coreders*) where beer, often the cheap local brand, is available. Imported beverages are available but shortages may occur in some areas. Multicoloured fruit drinks made from fresh tropical fruit are superior to bottled soft drinks. At the other end of the scale, the few plush hotels have sophisticated restaurant/bars with a choice of international cuisine and beverages.
NIGHTLIFE: Managua has several nightclubs, some offering live music. There are also cinemas with English, French and Spanish films. Other cities, such as Granada, Léon, Masaya, Matagalpa and Rivas, also offer nightlife entertainment.
SHOPPING: Local items include goldwork, embroidery, shoes and paintings. Traditional crafts are available, particularly in Masaya, at the handicrafts market. **Shopping hours**: Mon-Fri 0900-1900, Sat 0900-1800.
SPECIAL EVENTS: For a full list of events taking place in 2005, contact the Nicaraguan Institute of Tourism (see *Contact Addresses* section). The following is a selection of special events celebrated annually in Nicaragua:
Feb *Music & Youth Festival*, Managua. **Mar** *Folklore, Gastronomy & Handicraft Festival*, Granada. **May** *'Palo de Mayo' Festival*, Bluefields. **Sep** *Fishing Fair*, San Carlos; *Polkas, Mazarcas & Jamaquellos*, Matagalpa. **Oct** *Music Festival in Jinotega*. **Nov 3-5** *Equestrian Rally*, Ometepe; *Folkloric Festival*, Masaya.
SOCIAL CONVENTIONS: Dress is informal. **Photography**: Avoid photographing military sites or personnel. **Tipping**: 10 per cent of the bill is customary in hotels and restaurants. No tip is necessary for taxi drivers but porters expect a small tip.

Business Profile

ECONOMY: Agriculture is the main component of Nicaragua's economy, with cotton, coffee, sugar, bananas and meat the principal exports. Maize, beans and rice are grown for domestic consumption. The principal manufacturing industries are food, drinks, the production of chemicals and oil refining. There is also a small mining industry working deposits of gold, silver, lead and zinc. Nicaragua's economic travails during the last 20 years have left it one of the poorest countries in the Americas. Some key industrial operations were nationalised following the 1979 Sandinista revolution but the bulk of the economy was left in private hands. Unfortunately, domestic mismanagement, Western economic sanctions and the cost of the civil war against the 'contras' meant that the Sandinista period was one of continuous economic decline. However, the economy has fared little better since then. During the 1990s, Nicaragua implemented a Structural Adjustment programme supervised by the IMF. It also required several injections of emergency aid after a series of major natural disasters – floods and droughts – which caused huge damage to the agricultural economy. Low commodity prices and the pressure of a substantial foreign debt exacerbated the country's economic difficulties. In 2001, Nicaragua was a beneficiary of the Heavily Indebted Poor Countries (HIPC) initiative which wrote off part of the debt, but it remains a significant drain on the economy. Nicaragua's largest trading partners are the USA (over one-third of the total), Germany, Spain, El Salvador and to a lesser extent, Nicaragua's other Central and South American neighbours. Nicaragua is a member of the Central American Common Market and the Inter-American Development Bank.
BUSINESS: Businessmen wear business suits with ties, or long-sleeved shirts and smart trousers; businesswomen wear business dresses. A knowledge of Spanish is an advantage, although some businesspeople speak English. Enquire at the Embassy for interpreter services. The best time to visit is November to March. **Office hours**: Mon-Fri 0800-1700.
COMMERCIAL INFORMATION: The following organisations can offer advice: Cámara de Comercio de Nicaragua, PO Box 135-C-001, Managua (tel: 268 3505 *or* 3514; fax: 268 3600; e-mail: comercio@ibw.com.ni); *or* Servicio de Información Comercial, Centro de Exportaciones e Inversiones, Hotel Intercontinental, 1 cuadra abajo 3 1/2 cuadras al sur 1208, PO Box 5932, Managua (tel: 268 3860; fax: 266 4476; e-mail: cei@cei.org.ni; website: www.cei.org.ni).

Climate

Tropical climate for most of the country. The dry season is from December to May, and the rainy season is from June to November. The northern mountain regions have a much cooler climate.
Required clothing: Lightweight cottons and linens are required throughout the year. Waterproofs are advisable during the rainy season. Warmer clothes are advised for the northern mountains.

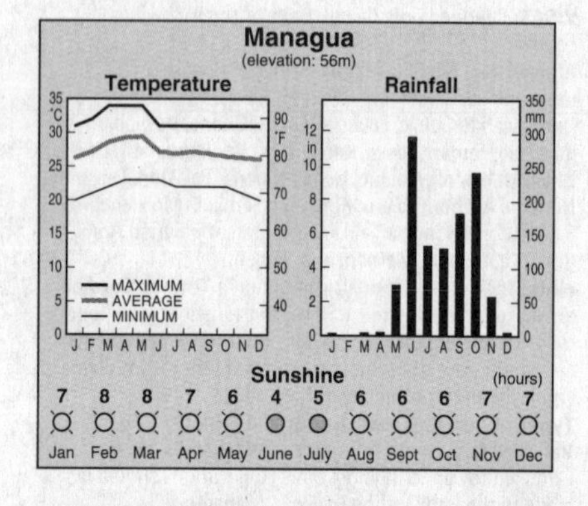

Niger

LATEST TRAVEL ADVICE CONTACTS

British Foreign and Commonwealth Office
Tel: (0870) 606 0290 Website: www.fco.gov.uk
US Department of State
Website: http://travel.state.gov/travel
Canadian Department of Foreign Affairs and Int'l Trade
Tel: (1 800) 267 8376 Website: www.dfait-maeci.gc.ca

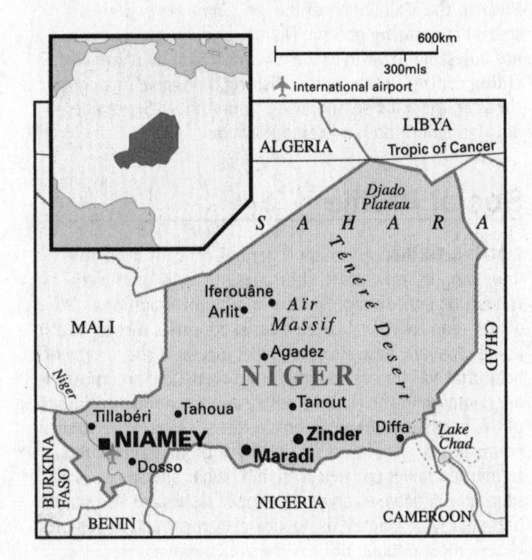

Location: Central Africa.

Country dialling code: 227.

Office National du Tourisme (National Tourist Office)
Avenue du Président H Luebke, BP 612, Niamey, Niger
Tel: 732 447. Fax: 733 940.
Ministère du Tourisme
BP 12130, Niamey, Niger
Tel: 722 831. Fax: 733 685.
Embassy of the Republic of Niger
154 rue du Longchamp, 75116 Paris, France
Tel: (1) 4504 8060. Fax: (1) 4504 7973.
British Honorary Consul
SIL, BP 10151, Niamey, Niger
Tel: 725 046. Fax: 723 860.
There is currently no British Embassy in Niger. The British Embassy in Abidjan deals with enquiries relating to Niger (see *Côte d'Ivoire* section).
Embassy of the Republic of Niger
2204 R Street, NW, Washington, DC 20008, USA
Tel: (202) 483 4224/5/6/7. Fax: (202) 483 3169.
E-mail: ambassadeniger@hotmail.com
Website: www.nigerembassyusa.org
Embassy of the United States of America
Street address: Rue des Ambassades, Niamey, Niger
Postal address: BP 11201, Niamey, Niger
Tel: 733 169. Fax: 735 560.
E-mail: usis@intnet.ne (public affairs).
Website: http://usembassy.state.gov/niamey
Embassy of the Republic of Niger
38 Blackburn Avenue, Ottawa, Ontario K1N 8A3, Canada
Tel: (613) 232 4291. Fax: (613) 230 9808.
Office of the Canadian Embassy
Street address: Mali Béro Boulevard, Niamey, Niger
Postal address: PO Box 362, Niamey, Niger
Tel: 753 686/7. Fax: 753 107.
E-mail: niamy@dfait-maeci.gc.ca

General Information

AREA: 1,267,000 sq km (489,191 sq miles).
POPULATION: 11,544,000 (official estimate 2002).
POPULATION DENSITY: 9.1 per sq km.
CAPITAL: Niamey. **Population**: 550,000 (1988).
GEOGRAPHY: Niger has borders with Libya and Algeria to the north, Chad to the east, Nigeria and Benin to the south, and Mali and Burkina Faso to the west. The capital, Niamey, stands on the north bank of the Niger River and has long been a major trading centre on this important navigable waterway. The river meanders for 500km (300 miles) through the southwestern corner of the country. To the east is a band of semi-arid bush country along the border with Nigeria, shrinking by 20km (12 miles) every year as over-grazing claims more land for the Ténéré Desert, which already occupies over half of Niger. This desert is divided by a range of low mountains, Aïr ou Azbine, in the eastern foothills of which lies the city of Agadez. Surrounded by green valleys and hot springs amid semi-desert, this regional capital is still a major terminus for Saharan caravans. The desert to the west of the mountains is a stony plain hosting seasonal pastures; to the north and west are mostly vast expanses of sand. There is arable land beside Lake Chad in the extreme southeastern corner of the country. The Hausa people live along the border with Nigeria and most are farmers. The Songhai and Djerma people live in the Niger valley and exist by farming and fishing. The nomadic Fulani have spread all over the Sahel. The robed and veiled Tuaregs once dominated the southern cities; the few who remain are camel herders and caravanners on the Saharan routes. The Manga (or Kanun) live near Lake Chad and are well known for their colourful ceremonies in which pipes and drums accompany slow, stately dancing.
GOVERNMENT: Republic since 1960. **Head of State**: President Mamadou Tandja since 1999. **Head of Government**: Prime Minister Hama Amadou since 2000.
LANGUAGE: The official language is French. Also spoken are Hausa (by half of the population), Djerma, Fulani, Manga, Zarma and Tuareg dialects.
RELIGION: Approximately 95 per cent Muslim, with Christian and animist minorities.
TIME: GMT + 1.
ELECTRICITY: 220 volts AC, 50Hz.
COMMUNICATIONS: Telephone: IDD is available. Country code: 227 (no area codes). Outgoing international code: 00. Telephone services are provided by Société Nigérienne des Télécommunications (SONITEL). **Mobile telephone:** GSM 900. Main network providers are *Celtel Niger* (website: www.msi-cellular.com) and *Telecel Niger SA*. **Telegram:** Services are available from the Chief Telegraph Office, Niamey, some hotels and other telegraph offices. There are three rates of charge. **Fax:** Available in large hotels in urban areas. **Internet:** The main ISP is *SONITEL*. Internet access can be found in major urban areas. **Post:** Airmail to Western Europe takes up to two weeks. Post office hours: generally 0730-1230 and 1530-1800. **Press:** All newspapers are published in French; most are weeklies.
Radio: BBC World Service (website: www.bbc.co.uk/worldservice) and Voice of America (website: www.voa.gov) can be received. From time to time the frequencies change and the most up-to-date can be found online.

TIMATIC CODES

Health	AMADEUS: **TI-DFT/NIM/HE** GALILEO/WORLDSPAN: **TI-DFT/NIM/HE** SABRE: **TIDFT/NIM/HE**
Visa	AMADEUS: **TI-DFT/NIM/VI** GALILEO/WORLDSPAN: **TI-DFT/NIM/VI** SABRE: **TIDFT/NIM/VI**

To access TIMATIC country information on Health and Visa regulations through the Computer Reservations System (CRS), type in the appropriate command line listed above.

Passport/Visa

	Passport Required?	Visa Required?	Return Ticket Required?
Full British	Yes	Yes	Yes
Australian	Yes	Yes	Yes
Canadian	Yes	Yes	Yes
USA	Yes	Yes	Yes
Other EU	Yes	1	Yes
Japanese	Yes	Yes	Yes

Note: Regulations and requirements may be subject to change at short notice, and you are advised to contact the appropriate diplomatic or consular authority before finalising travel arrangements. Details of these may be found at the head of this country's entry. Any numbers in the chart refer to the footnotes below.

PASSPORTS: Passport valid for six months required by all, except holders of National ID Cards issued to Benin, Burkina Faso, Côte d'Ivoire, Mali, Mauritania, Nigeria, Senegal and Togo, and holders of a UN laissez-passer.
VISAS: Required by all except the following:
(a) **1.** nationals of Benin, Burkina Faso, Cape Verde, Central African Republic, Chad, Côte d'Ivoire, Denmark, Finland, The Gambia, Ghana, Guinea, Guinea-Bissau, Liberia, Mali, Mauritania, Morocco, Nigeria, Norway, Rwanda, Senegal, Serbia & Montenegro, Sierra Leone, Togo and Tunisia;
(b) alien residents holding a valid 'Permis de Séjour' or 'Visa de Séjour';
(c) transit passengers continuing their journey within 24 hours and who do not leave the airport. Some nationals *do* require a visa for transit. Contact Consular section at Embassy for further information.
Note: Visa exemptions generally apply for periods of up to three months. However, it is advised to contact the nearest Embassy/Consulate for further details as this may vary according to nationality.
Types of visa and cost: *Ordinary*: €50 (up to three-month stay).
Validity: Up to three months, depending on purpose of stay.
Application to: Nearest Consulate (or Consular section at Embassy); see *Contact Addresses* section.
Application requirements: (a) Valid passport. (b) Three completed and signed application forms. (c) Three passport-size photos. (d) A return or onward ticket. (e) Proof of sufficient funds (eg bank letter). (f) Yellow fever vaccination certificate (cholera also required if travelling from a neighbouring country which has reported an outbreak). (g) Postal applications should be accompanied by a stamped, self-addressed, registered envelope. (h) Fee, payable by cash or money order. *Tourist*: (a)-(h) and, (i) Copy of letter from travel agent certifying round-trip ticket has been purchased. (j) Bank statement or proof of at least US$500 (for road travellers). *Transit*: (a)-(i) and, (j) Photocopy of round-trip ticket and/or itinerary.
Working days required: Two. A visa can be processed within 24 hours for an extra fee of €16.
Exit permit: Must be obtained from the Immigration Department in Niamey before departure (except for nationals who do not require an entry visa).
Note: Passports must be presented to the police in each town where an overnight stay is intended. Passports are stamped at each town, so blank pages will be required. It is prohibited to travel by any route other than that stamped in the passport by the police.

Money

Currency: CFA (Communauté Financiaire Africaine) Franc (CFAfr) = 100 centimes. Notes are in denominations of CFAfr10,000, 5000, 2500, 1000 and 500. Coins are in denominations of CFAfr250, 100, 50, 25, 10, 5 and 1. Niger is part of the French Monetary Area. Only currency issued by the Banque des Etats de l'Afrique de l'Ouest (Bank of West African States) is valid; currency issued by the Banque des Etats de l'Afrique Centrale (Bank of Central African States) is not. The CFA Franc is tied to the Euro.
Currency exchange: Currency can be exchanged at the airport as well as at main banks and hotels.
Credit & debit cards: Diners Club and MasterCard are both accepted on a limited basis. Check with your credit or debit card company for details of merchant acceptability and other services which may be available.
Travellers cheques: Accepted by hotels, restaurants, most shops and airline offices. To avoid additional exchange rate charges, travellers are advised to take travellers cheques in Euros.
Currency restrictions: The import of local currency is unrestricted. Export of local currency is limited to CFAfr25,000. The import and export of foreign currency is unlimited.
Exchange rate indicators: The following figures are included as a guide to the movements of the CFA Franc against Sterling and the US Dollar:

Date	Feb '04	May '04	Aug '04	Nov '04
£1.00=	961.13	983.76	978.35	936.79
$1.00=	528.01	550.79	531.03	494.69

Banking hours: Mon-Fri 0800-1100 and 1600-1700.

Duty Free

The following items may be imported into Niger by passengers of 15 years of age or older without incurring customs duty:
200 cigarettes or 100 cigarillos or 25 cigars or 250g of tobacco; one bottle of spirits and one bottle of wine; 500ml of eau de toilette and 250ml of perfume.
Restricted items: A licence is required for sporting guns. Customs must authorise their temporary admission. Digging up or attempting to export ancient artefacts is prohibited. Pornography is prohibited. Apparatus for transmission or reception needs special authorisation (as does photographic equipment, see *Photography* in the *Social Profile* section). Selling cars without permission is prohibited.

Public Holidays

2005: Jan 1 New Year's Day. **Jan 21** Tabaske (Feast of the Sacrifice). **Mar 28** Easter Monday. **Apr 21** Mouloud (Birth of the Prophet Mohammed). **Apr 24** National Concord Day. **May 1** Labour Day. **Aug 3** Independence Day. **Nov 3-5** Eid al-Fitr (End of Ramadan). **Dec 18** Republic Day. **Dec 25** Christmas Day.
2006: Jan 1 New Year's Day. **Jan 10** Tabaske (Feast of the Sacrifice). **Apr 11** Mouloud (Birth of the Prophet Mohammed). **Apr 17** Easter Monday. **Apr 24** National Concord Day. **May 1** Labour Day. **Aug 3** Independence Day. **Oct 22-24** Eid al-Fitr (End of Ramadan). **Dec 18** Republic Day. **Dec 25** Christmas Day.
Note: (a) Muslim festivals are timed according to local sightings of various phases of the moon and the dates given above are approximations. During the lunar month of Ramadan that precedes Eid al-Fitr, Muslims fast during the day and feast at night and normal business patterns may be interrupted. Many restaurants are closed during the day and there may be restrictions on smoking and drinking. Some disruption may continue into Eid al-Fitr itself. Eid al-Fitr and Tabaske may last anything from two to 10 days, depending on the region. For more information, see the *World of Islam*

appendix. (b) Niger's small Christian community also observes Easter, Whitsun, Ascension, Assumption, All Saints' Day and Christmas.

Health

	Special Precautions?	Certificate Required?
Yellow Fever	Yes	1
Cholera	Yes	2
Typhoid & Polio	3	N/A
Malaria	4	N/A

Note: Regulations and requirements may be subject to change at short notice, and you are advised to contact your doctor well in advance of your intended date of departure. Any numbers in the chart refer to the footnotes below.

1: A yellow fever vaccination certificate is required of all travellers over one year of age arriving from all countries: it is also recommended for all travellers leaving Niger.
2: Following WHO guidelines issued in 1973, a cholera vaccination certificate is not a condition of entry to Niger. However, cholera is a serious risk in this country and precautions are essential. Up-to-date advice should be sought before deciding whether these precautions should include vaccination as medical opinion is divided over its effectiveness; see the *Health* appendix for further information.
3: Polio and typhoid both occur.
4: Malaria risk, predominantly in the malignant *falciparum* form, exists all year throughout the country. Chloroquine-resistance has been reported.
Food & drink: All water should be regarded as being potentially contaminated. Water used for drinking, brushing teeth or making ice should have first been boiled or otherwise sterilised. Milk is unpasteurised and should be boiled. Powdered or tinned milk is available and is advised, but make sure that it is reconstituted with pure water. Avoid dairy products which are likely to have been made from unboiled milk. Only eat well-cooked meat and fish, preferably served hot. Pork, salad and mayonnaise may carry increased risk. Vegetables should be cooked and fruit peeled.
Other risks: *Bilharzia* (schistosomiasis) is present; avoid swimming and paddling in fresh water. Swimming pools which are well chlorinated and maintained are safe. *Filariasis, trypanosomiasis* and *leishmaniasis* are also reported; avoid insect bites. Long-staying visitors, particularly backpackers and those living with local people, should consider *meningococcal meningitis, diphtheria* and *hepatitis B* vaccinations. *Hepatitis A, C* and *E* are widespread. *HIV* is a danger and *rabies* may be present. For those at high risk, vaccination before arrival should be considered. If you are bitten, seek medical advice without delay. For more information, consult the *Health* appendix.
Health care: The two main hospitals are in Niamey and Zinder. Only the main centres have reasonable medical facilities. Personal medicines should be brought in as these can be difficult or impossible to obtain in Niger. Full health insurance is essential and should include cover for emergency repatriation.

Travel - International

Travel warning: All travel to the Aïr Massif, Ténéré and Kaouar regions is advised against due to recent clashes between the Nigerien security forces and armed groups. It is possible to travel north from Agadez, as far as the tree of Ténéré and south as far as the Termit Massif. All travel to the Azawagh area, particularly Malian and Algerian borders, and the Nigerien towns of Tahoua and Ingall, and to the east of the Aïr Massif and the area north of Iferouane up to the Algerian border, is advised against. Border areas are generally insecure and it is best to avoid a 200km-deep zone along borders with Mali, Algeria/Libya and Chad. All but essential travel is advised to the Agadez-Arlit road. Terrorists are active in countries neighbouring Niger.
AIR: Most international flights are operated by *Air Afrique (RK)*. Other airlines serving Niger include *Air Algerie, Air France, Royal Air Maroc* and *Sudan Airways*. (There are no direct flights to Niger from the UK.)
Approximate flight times: From *London* to Niamey is six hours, excluding stopover time in Paris.
International airports: *Niamey (NIM)*, 12km (7.5 miles) southeast of the city (travel time – 10 minutes). Airport facilities include bars, shops, post office, currency exchange and car hire. Taxi services are available to the city. Hotels have their own vehicles and provide free transport for their clients between the hotel and the airport.
Departure tax: None.
ROAD: There are main roads from Kano (Nigeria) to Zinder, and from Benin, Burkina Faso and Mali. The principal trans-Sahara desert track runs from Algiers to Asamakka and Arlit, with a paved road to Agadez. Desert driving can be difficult, marker beacons may not always be visible, and petrol is not always available. **Bus**: Services operate from Benin, Burkina Faso and Mali.

Travel - Internal

Note: It is essential that all visitors report to the police station in any town where they are making an overnight stop; see the *Passport/Visa* section.
AIR: *Air Niger* runs services from Niamey to Agadez, Arlit, Maradi and Zinder. Charter flights can be arranged; contact *Air Niger* or *Transniger* in Niamey.
ROAD: Certain roads are permanently closed to tourists without special authorisation. Traffic drives on the right. There are an estimated 13,808km (8580 miles) of classified roads, 3256km (2020 miles) of which are main roads. Principal internal roads are from Niamey to Zinder, Tahoua, Arlit and Gaya. Many tracks are impassable during heavy rain. The best season for road travel is from December to March. Petrol stations are infrequent and garages are extremely expensive. It is prohibited to travel by a different route than the one entered in the passport by the police at the previous town. It is necessary to pay a toll on main routes. **Bus**: There are reasonable services between the main centres, even though many roads have been sealed. Coach services operate from Niamey to Agadez, N'guemi, Tera and Zinder. Elsewhere, it is common practice to pay for rides in cross-country lorries; note that this can be an extremely slow and uncomfortable means of transport and that extra payment is expected of those who wish to ride in the cab.
Car hire: Self-drive and chauffeur-driven cars are available, the latter being compulsory outside the capital. **Note**: Much of the country requires 4-wheel-drive vehicles, guides and full equipment. **Documentation**: An International Driving Permit and a Carnet de Passage are required. Minimum age is 23. Two photos are required.
Travel times: The following chart gives approximate travel times (in hours and minutes) from **Niamey** to other major cities and towns in Niger.

	Air	Road
Zinder	0.45	12.00
Maradi	-	9.00
Tahoua	-	7.00
Dosso	-	1.00
Tillabéri	-	4.50
Agadez	-	17.00

Accommodation

Hotel accommodation is difficult to obtain and reservations for major international hotels should be booked prior to arrival. All reservations should be made well in advance. There are good hotels in Agadez, Ayorou, Maradi, Niamey, La Tapoa and Zinder. There are also 'Encampments' in Agadez, Boubon, Namaro and Tillabéri. Local hotels are available on a first-come, first-served basis. For further information, contact the Ministère du Tourisme et d'Artisanat or the National Tourist Office (see *Contact Addresses* section).

Resorts & Excursions

Niamey: Spread along the northern bank of the **River Niger**, Niamey is a sprawling city with a modern centre and shanty towns on the outskirts. The two markets, the Small and Great markets, are worth a visit. Other places of interest include the **Great Mosque**, the **National Museum** (including a large park with botanical gardens and a zoo, and an artisan/crafts area), the **Franco-Nigerian Cultural Centre** and the **Hippodrome** where horse and camel races often take place on Sundays. Tours of the city are available. Outside Niamey is the famous **'W' National Park**, with its abundant wildlife including buffalos, elephants, lions, hyenas, jackals and baboons. The birdlife is also prolific.
Agadez: This beautiful old Tuareg capital is still a caravan trading city. Beautiful silver and leatherwork can be bought in the back streets and the minaret of the mosque can be climbed at sunset for a spectacular view of the town.
Aïr Mountains: North of Agadez, the Aïr Mountains enjoy slightly more rain than the surrounding semi-desert lowlands and were, until recently, home to many species of animals not generally seen at this latitude, including leopards, lions and giraffes. However, the drought has even taken hold here and the stranded populations are dwindling rapidly. Special permission may be required to visit the region. Expeditions can be arranged through the mountains to the springs at **Igouloulef** and **Tafadek** or the prehistoric site at **Iferouane** and beyond the **Ténéré Desert** and the **Djado Mounta**
Zinder: The town of Zinder was the capital of Niger until 1927. The old part of the town is a compact maze of alleyways, typical of a Hausa town. Near the centre is the **Sultan's Palace** and the mosque, which offers a good view from the minaret. The part of the town known as **Zengou** was formerly a caravan encampment. There is an excellent market here on Thursdays, selling beautiful leatherwork.
Elsewhere: On the route from Niamey to Zinder is the town of **Dosso**, founded in the 13th century by the Zarmas after the fall of Gao. It has an exceptional palace, a lively village square and celebrates many festivals with parades and official ceremonies. Niger's economic centre is **Maradi**, where the people are engaged in various activities from agriculture to diverse crafts. The **Sultanate** and the **Mosque** are well worth viewing.
The **Ayorou** region on the Mali frontier is an old trading station where a market is held every Sunday. In the region around **Tillabéri**, giraffes are often encountered. Two-day tours are available from the capital.

Sport & Activities

Visitors can take **canoes** or **motorboats** along the *Niger River* to the Mali border of the *'W' Game Park*. There are several **swimming** pools in Niamey and Agadez, but it is not advisable to swim in the lakes or rivers. There are two **riding** centres in the capital. **Fishing** is possible throughout the year, the main season being from April to September. Big-game hunting has been outlawed.

Social Profile

FOOD & DRINK: Although Niger has concentrated on improving its agriculture, shortages of locally produced foodstuffs are common, owing to drought. Traditional dishes tend to be less varied than in countries further south and are usually based around millet, rice or *niebé*, a type of bean that has become an important crop. Beef and mutton are common in the Hausa country and the nomadic regions of the north. In both areas, brochettes are sold in the streets. *Foura*, which consists of small balls of ground and slightly fermented millet crushed with milk, sugar and spices, is a speciality. African, Asian and European dishes are also served, particularly in Niamey, using local fish, meat and vegetables. Niger's most popular drink is tea, which is available everywhere from street stalls. There is also a good selection of imported beverages. Alcohol is available, but there are restrictions because of Muslim beliefs and traditions.
NIGHTLIFE: In Niamey, there are several nightclubs with music and dancing. There are also three open-air cinemas in the capital.
SHOPPING: Markets in the main towns, notably Niamey and Agadez, sell a range of local artefacts. The Centre des Métiers d'Art de Niger, close to the National Museum, is worth visiting, as a wide range of local goods can be bought there. Courteous bargaining is expected and items include multicoloured blankets, leather goods, engraved calabashes, silver jewellery, swords and knives. **Shopping hours**: Mon-Fri 0800-1200 and 1600-1900, Sat 0800-1200.
SPECIAL EVENTS: The Peulh people celebrate the end of the rainy season with a lively festival. Also of interest is the *Cure Salée*, when the nomads gather their cattle to lead them to the new pastures; a highlight of this is the *gerewol* festival of the nomadic Wodaabé tribe. The following is a selection of special events celebrated annually in Niger:
Jan *Nwaotam Festival*, Port Harcourt. **Feb** *Durbar Festival; Argungu Fishing & Cultural Festival*, Sokoto River. **Apr** *National Festival Day*. **Jul** *Shango Festival*, Lagos. **Aug** *Pategi Regatta; Oshun Festival at Oshogo*. **Oct 1** *Independence Day celebrations*. **Dec** *Nwaotam Festival*, Port Harcourt.
SOCIAL CONVENTIONS: Handshaking is customary. Casual wear is widely suitable. Women should avoid wearing revealing clothes. Traditional beliefs and Muslim customs should be respected. **Photography**: Permits are required for photography and filming, and can be obtained from police stations. Tour operators and tourist bureaux are often able to make arrangements. Film is expensive and local facilities for processing film are not always good. Ask local people for permission before taking their photographs. Military installations, airports and administrative buildings (including the Presidential Palace) should not be photographed.
Tipping: Expected for most services, usually 10 per cent. Most hotels add a 10 to 15 per cent service charge.

Business Profile

ECONOMY: Niger is one of the world's poorest countries, with a per capita annual income of around US$200. 90 per cent of the country's inhabitants are employed on the land, although less than 5 per cent of the actual land area is cultivated. This already difficult situation is exacerbated by the ever-expanding Saharan desert, drought and problems with pest control. Less than one-tenth of the crops grown are cash crops (cotton and groundnuts), while the rest (sorghum, millet and rice) are staples grown for domestic consumption. Livestock rearing is very important, especially among the country's nomadic population. In a good year, Niger is self-sufficient in basic foodstuffs; otherwise, the country needs food aid. Niger's most valuable commodity is its uranium deposits – the country is one of the world's largest producers. France and Japan buy the bulk of the uranium output but falling demand has reduced Niger's receipts from this mineral. (Alleged attempts by Iraq to procure uranium

from Niger have been the subject of recent controversy). Gypsum, coal and tin ore are also extracted in commercial quantities and there are proven deposits of other minerals, including copper, manganese, lithium, lead and tungsten. Oil deposits are also thought to exist. Niger has a little light industry, which produces food and drinks, textiles and cement. From 1997 onwards the government embarked on a programme of privatisation of the major public utilities at the behest of the IMF and World Bank. The process was delayed by the 1999 coup but several major sales have since gone through, along with an overhaul of the country's financial systems. The following year, Niger was a beneficiary of the Heavily Indebted Poor Countries (HIPC) debt relief programme, while the World Bank and IMF have provided occasional packages of financial support. In the period since 2001, after several years of sluggish performance, the economy has grown, although not achieving such strong growth in 2004, at only 3.8 per cent. Membership of the CFA Franc Zone affords some monetary stability. France is the country's most important trading partner, followed by Nigeria, Côte d'Ivoire, Japan and Germany. Niger is a member of the West African trading bloc, ECOWAS, as well as various other regional bodies concerned with economic cooperation.
BUSINESS: A lightweight suit and tie are generally acceptable. A knowledge of French is essential, as interpreters are not readily available and executives seldom speak English. **Office hours**: Mon-Fri 0730-1230 and 1500-1800, Sat 0730-1230 (winter); Mon-Fri 0730-1230 and 1530-1830, Sat 0730-1230 (summer).
COMMERCIAL INFORMATION: The following organisation can offer advice: Chambre de Commerce, d'Agriculture, d'Industrie et d'Artisanat du Niger, Place de la Concertation, BP 209, Niamey (tel: 732 210; fax: 734 668; website: www.ccaian.org).

Climate

Summers are extremely hot. The dry season is from October to May. Heavy rains with high temperatures are common in July and August.
Required Clothing: Lightweight cottons and linens are required most of the year. Warm clothes during the cool evenings, especially in the north, are essential. Rainwear is advisable.

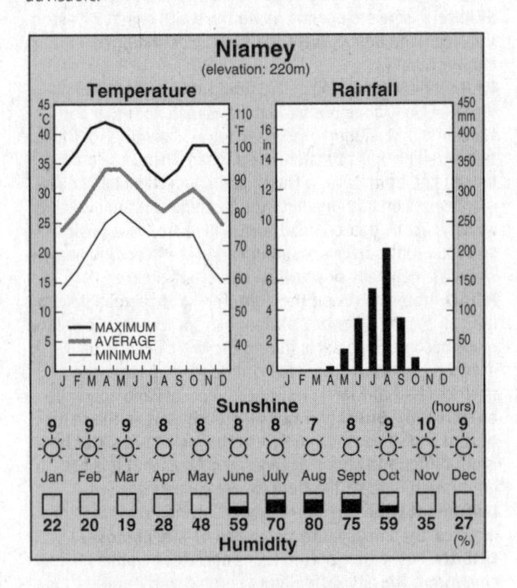

Nigeria

LATEST TRAVEL ADVICE CONTACTS

British Foreign and Commonwealth Office
Tel: (0870) 606 0290 Website: www.fco.gov.uk
US Department of State
Website: http://travel.state.gov/travel
Canadian Department of Foreign Affairs and Int'l Trade
Tel: (1 800) 267 8376 Website: www.dfait-maeci.gc.ca

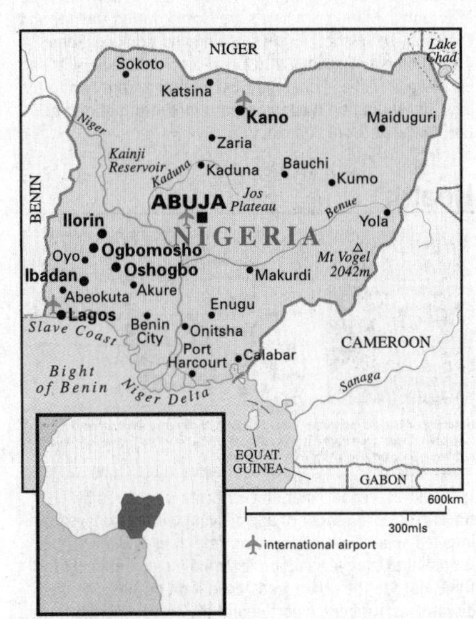

Location: West Africa.

Country dialling code: 234.

Federal Ministry of Culture and Tourism
Old Secretariat, Area 1, Blocks G & H, PMB 88, Garki, Abuja.
Tel: (9) 234 2727
Nigeria Tourism Development Corporation
Old Secretariat, Area 1, Garki, PMB 167, Abuja, Nigeria
Tel: (9) 234 2764. Fax: (9) 234 2775.
E-mail: ntdc@metrong.com
Website: www.nigeriatourism.net
High Commission for the Federal Republic of Nigeria
9 Northumberland Avenue, London WC2N 5BX, UK
Tel: (020) 7839 1244. Fax: (020) 7839 8746.
E-mail: enquiry@nigeriahighcommissionuk.com *or* chancery@nigeriahighcommissionuk.com
Website: www.nigeriahighcommissionuk.com
Opening hours: Mon-Fri 0930-1730; 1000-1300 (visa submission); 1530-1630 (visa collection).
Nigerian Consular Section
56-57 Fleet Street, London EC4 1BT, UK
Tel: (020) 7353 3776. Fax: (020) 7353 2401.
Opening hours: Mon-Fri 0930-1730; 1000-1300 (visa submission); 1530-1630 (visa collection).
British High Commission
Shehu Shangari Way (North), Maitama, Abuja, Nigeria
Tel: (9) 413 2010-1 *or* 0900 (consular section).
Fax: (9) 413 3552 *or* 4565 (consular section).
E-mail: consular@abuja.mail.fco.gov.uk
Embassy of Nigeria
3519 International Court, NW, Washington, DC 20008, USA
Tel: (202) 986 8400 (ext 1005 for consular and immigration section). Fax: (202) 775 1385.
E-mail: babalola@nigeriaembassyusa.org *or* umar@nigeria embassyusa.org (consular and immigration section).
Website: www.nigeriaembassyusa.org
There is no longer a separate Nigerian Information Service Center. All information enquiries must go through the Embassy.
Nigerian Consulate General
828 Second Avenue, 10th Floor, New York, NY 10017, USA
Tel: (212) 850 2200. Fax: (212) 687 8768.
E-mail: info@nigeria-consulate-ny.org
Website: www.nigeria-consulate-ny.org
Embassy of the United States of America
7 Mambilla Street, off Aso Drive Maitama District, Abuja, Nigeria
Tel: (9) 523 0960/0916/5857.
Fax: (9) 523 0353 *or* 2078 (consular section).
E-mail: usabuja@state.gov *or* consularabuja@state.gov
Website: http://usembassy.state.gov/nigeria
US Consulate General
2 Walter Carrington Crescent, Victoria Island, Lagos, Nigeria
Tel: (1) 261 0050/78. Fax: (1) 261 9856.
E-mail: uslagos@state.gov
High Commission for the Federal Republic of Nigeria
295 Metcalfe Street, Ottawa, Ontario K2P 1R9, Canada
Tel: (613) 236 0521-3. Fax: (613) 236 0529.
E-mail: chancery@nigeriahcottawa.com
Website: www.nigeriahcottawa.com
Canadian High Commission
Street address: 3A Bobo Street, Maitama District, Abuja, Nigeria
Postal address: PO Box 5144, Abuja, Nigeria
Tel: (9) 413 9910 *or* 9933. Fax: (9) 413 9911.
E-mail: abuja@dfait-maeci.gc.ca
Website: www.dfait-maeci.gc.ca/nigeria
High Commission also in: Lagos (tel: (1) 262 2512).

TIMATIC CODES

Health
AMADEUS: **TI-DFT/LOS/HE**
GALILEO/WORLDSPAN: **TI-DFT/LOS/HE**
SABRE: **TIDFT/LOS/HE**

Visa
AMADEUS: **TI-DFT/LOS/VI**
GALILEO/WORLDSPAN: **TI-DFT/LOS/VI**
SABRE: **TIDFT/LOS/VI**

To access TIMATIC country information on Health and Visa regulations through the Computer Reservations System (CRS), type in the appropriate command line listed above.

General Information

AREA: 923,768 sq km (356,669 sq miles).
POPULATION: 127,100,000 (UN estimate 2004).
POPULATION DENSITY: 130.9 per sq km.
CAPITAL: Abuja. **Population**: 403,000 (1999).
GEOGRAPHY: Nigeria has borders with Niger to the north, Chad (across Lake Chad) to the northeast, Cameroon to the east and Benin to the west. To the south, the Gulf of Guinea is indented by the Bight of Benin and the Bight of Biafra. The coastal region is a low-lying area of lagoons, sandy beaches and mangrove swamps, which merges into an area of rainforest where palm trees grow to over 30m (100ft). From here, the landscape changes to savannah and open woodland, rising to the Central Jos Plateau at 1800m (6000ft). The northern part of the country is desert and semi-desert, marking the southern extent of the Sahara.
GOVERNMENT: Republic since 1963. Gained independence from the UK in 1960. Military regime from 1983-1999. **Head of State and Government**: President Matthew Olusegun Obasanjo since 1999.
LANGUAGE: The official language is English. A variation of English (Pidgin English) is also spoken. The three main Nigerian languages are Yoruba, Ibo (also spelt Igbo) and Hausa; another 400 languages are also spoken in the country.
RELIGION: 50 per cent Muslim (mainly in the north and west of the country), 40 per cent Christian (mostly in the south) and 10 per cent traditional beliefs.
TIME: GMT + 1.
ELECTRICITY: 240 volts AC, 50Hz. Single phase.
COMMUNICATIONS: Telephone: Full IDD is available. Country code: 234. Outgoing international code: 009. **Mobile telephone:** GSM 900 and 1800 networks. Network operators include *Globacom* (www.gloworld.com), *MTN Nigeria* (www.mtnonline.com), *Nigerian Mobile Telecommunications Limited* and *Vee Networks Nigeria Limited*. **Internet:** Internet and e-mail services are available in Internet cafes in Lagos. ISPs include *Microcom Systems Ltd* (website: www.micro.com.ng). **Fax:** Available in large hotels. **Telegram:** International telegraph services are operated by *Nigerian Telecommunications Limited* (NITEL) in all large cities. **Post:** Airmail to Europe is unreliable and takes up to three weeks. Delivery may be more reliable through international couriers who are represented in major towns. **Press:** English-language newspapers include the *Daily Sketch*, the *Daily Times*, the *Guardian*, the *National Concord*, *New Nigerian*, the *Nigerian Tribune*, the *Post Express*, *This Day* and the *Vanguard*.
Radio: BBC World Service (website: www.bbc.co.uk/ worldservice) and Voice of America (website: www.voa.gov) can be received. From time to time the frequencies change and the most up-to-date can be found online.

Passport/Visa

	Passport Required?	Visa Required?	Return Ticket Required?
Full British	Yes	Yes	Yes
Australian	Yes	Yes	Yes
Canadian	Yes	Yes	Yes
USA	Yes	Yes	Yes
Other EU	Yes	Yes	Yes
Japanese	Yes	Yes	Yes

Note: *Regulations and requirements may be subject to change at short notice, and you are advised to contact the appropriate diplomatic or consular authority before finalising travel arrangements. Details of these may be found at the head of this country's entry. Any numbers in the chart refer to the footnotes below.*

PASSPORTS: Passport valid for a minimum of six months beyond the date of departure required by all.
VISAS: Required by all except the following:
(a) nationals of Benin, Burkina Faso, Cameroon, Cape Verde, Chad, Côte d'Ivoire, The Gambia, Ghana, Guinea, Guinea-Bissau, Liberia, Mali, Mauritania, Morocco, Niger, Senegal, Sierra Leone and Togo for stays of up to 90 days;
(b) transit passengers continuing their journey by the same or first connecting aircraft, provided holding valid onward or return documentation and not leaving the airport, except for nationals of the USA who require a transit visa.
Note: Children under 16 years of age accompanying their parents residing in Nigeria (provided the name of such a child is entered in the passport of one of the parents) do not require visas, but must, however, complete one application form accompanied by a photo. All children holding their own passport must have separate visas or re-entry permits.
Types of visa and cost: *Tourist*, *Business*: £45 (single-entry); £75 (multiple-entry). *Transit*: £45. The prices quoted are for UK nationals; visa costs depend on nationality. Nationals of some African countries receive visas free of charge. Contact High Commission or Consular section at Embassy for further information.
Application to: Consulate (or Consular section at Embassy or High Commission); see *Contact Addresses* section.
Application requirements: (a) One completed application form. (b) Passport. (c) One passport-size photo. (d) Fee, which at present must be paid by postal order. (e) Onward or return ticket for *Tourist* visas. (f) Paid registered post return envelope if applying by post. *Business*: (a)-(f) and, (g) Letter of introduction from a company or a resident of Nigeria, accepting immigration responsibility for applicant; any Nigerian inviting a visitor must attach photocopies of the first five pages of his/her own passport, while a resident must enclose a copy of his/her residence permit.
Working days required: Two if applying in person; seven for postal applications.

Money

Currency: Naira (N) = 100 kobo. Notes are in denominations of N500, 200, 100, 50, 20, 10 and 5. Coins are in denominations of N1 kobo 50, 25, 10 and 1.
Currency exchange: The government of Nigeria has fixed an artificially high rate for local currency (the Naira) in terms of its value in exchange for foreign currencies. However, trading on the black market is extremely dangerous and could lead to arrest. Therefore, visitors are advised to exchange currency at the official rate and at approved exchange facilities, which often include major hotels. Inter-bank transfers are frequently difficult, if not impossible, to accomplish.
Credit & debit cards: American Express, Diners Club, MasterCard and Visa are rarely accepted in Nigeria and, because of the prevalence of credit card fraud, their use is ill-advised.
Travellers cheques: Travellers cheques are generally not recommended.
Currency restrictions: Import of local currency is limited to N20 in notes and must be declared on arrival. Export of local currency is restricted to N20 in notes. Import of foreign currency is unlimited, but it must be declared on arrival; export is limited to the amount declared. Penalties for black market transactions are severe.
Exchange rate indicators: The following figures are included as a guide to the movements of the Naira against Sterling and the US Dollar:

Date	Feb '04	May '04	Aug '04	Nov '04
£1.00=	249.10	243.18	245.68	241.40
$1.00=	136.85	136.15	133.35	130.01

Banking hours: Mon 0800-1500, Tue-Fri 0800-1330. There are over 80 commercial banks. The Government owns 60 per cent of all foreign banks.

Duty Free

The following goods may be imported into Nigeria by persons over 18 years of age without incurring customs duty:
200 cigarettes or 50 cigars or 200g of tobacco; 1l of spirits and 1l of wine; a small amount of perfume; gifts to the value of N300 (excluding jewellery, photographic equipment, electronics and luxury goods).
Note: (a) If more than each of the above is imported, duty will be levied on the whole quantity. Heavy duty will be levied on luxury items such as cameras or radios unless the visitor's stay is temporary. (b) It is forbidden to buy or sell antiques from or to anyone other than the Director of Antiquities or an accredited agent; visitors should obtain a clearance permit from one of the above before presenting antiques, artefacts or curios at the airport.
Prohibited items: Champagne, sparkling wine, beer, mineral water and soft drinks; fruits, vegetables, cereals and eggs, whether fresh or preserved; jewellery and precious metals; textile fabrics and mosquito netting.

Public Holidays

2005: Jan 1 New Year's Day. **Jan 21** Eid al-Kabir (Feast of the Sacrifice). **Mar 25-28** Easter. **Apr 21** Mouloud (Birth of the Prophet). **May 1** Workers' Day. **Oct 1** National Day. **Nov 3-5** Eid al-Fitr (End of Ramadan). **Dec 25-26** Christmas.
2006: Jan 1 New Year's Day. **Jan 13** Eid al-Kabir (Feast of the Sacrifice). **Apr 21** Mouloud (Birth of the Prophet). **Apr 14-17** Easter. **May 1** Workers' Day. **Oct 1** National Day. **Oct 23-25** Eid al-Fitr (End of Ramadan). **Dec 25-26** Christmas.
Note: Muslim festivals are timed according to local sightings of various phases of the moon and the dates given above are approximations. During the lunar month of Ramadan that precedes Eid al-Fitr, Muslims fast during the day and feast at night and normal business patterns may be interrupted. Many restaurants are closed during the day and there may be restrictions on smoking and drinking. Some disruption may continue into Eid al-Fitr itself. Eid al-Fitr and Eid al-Kabir (Eid al-Adha) may last anything from two to ten days, depending on the region. For more information, see the *World of Islam* appendix.

Health

	Special Precautions?	Certificate Required?
Yellow Fever	Yes	1
Cholera	Yes	2
Typhoid & Polio	3	N/A
Malaria	4	N/A

Note: *Regulations and requirements may be subject to change at short notice, and you are advised to contact your doctor well in advance of your intended date of departure. Any numbers in the chart refer to the footnotes below.*

1: A yellow fever vaccination certificate is required by travellers over one year of age arriving within six days from infected areas. Travellers arriving from non-endemic zones should note that vaccination is strongly recommended for travel outside the urban areas, even if an outbreak of the disease has not been reported and they would normally not require a vaccination certificate to enter the country. The risk of contracting yellow fever is highest in Lagos and Kaduna states. Contact Embassy/High Commission for exact details of vaccination requirements prior to travel.
2: Following WHO guidelines issued in 1973, a cholera vaccination certificate is not a condition of entry to Nigeria. However, evidence of cholera vaccination is required by certain nationals before they may enter the country (check with the nearest Nigerian Embassy) and vaccination is therefore advised. Cholera is a serious risk in this country and precautions are essential. Up-to-date advice should be sought before deciding whether these precautions should include vaccination, as medical opinion is divided over its effectiveness; see the *Health* appendix for further information.
3: Polio and typhoid both occur.
4: Malaria risk exists all year throughout the country. The predominant *falciparum* strain has been reported to be resistant to chloroquine.
Food & drink: All water should be regarded as being potentially contaminated. Water used for drinking, brushing teeth or making ice should have first been boiled or otherwise sterilised. Milk is unpasteurised and should be boiled. Powdered or tinned milk is available and is advised, but make sure that it is reconstituted with pure water. Avoid dairy products which are likely to have been made from unboiled milk. Only eat well-cooked meat and fish, preferably served hot. Pork, salad and mayonnaise may carry increased risk. Vegetables should be cooked and fruit peeled.
Other risks: *Bilharzia* (schistosomiasis) is present. Avoid swimming and paddling in fresh water; swimming pools which are well chlorinated and maintained are safe. *Hepatitis A, B, C* and *E* are present; precautions should be taken. *Meningococcal meningitis, leishmaniasis, trypanosomiasis* and *onchocerciasis* (river blindness) occur. *TB* and *Dengue fever* also occur and *HIV* is a risk. *Rabies* is present. For those at high risk, vaccination before arrival should be considered. If you are bitten, seek medical advice without delay. For more information, consult the *Health* appendix.
Health care: The government-provided health care facilities are of a poor standard and are subject to shortages of drugs, equipment, materials and even electricity. It is advisable to take a sufficient supply of drugs or medication to meet personal needs. However, there are some adequate private facilities where the standards approach those of Europe. Doctors and hospitals often expect immediate cash payment for health services. There is no reciprocal health agreement with the UK. Medical insurance is essential.

Travel - International

Note: Travellers are currently advised to avoid the Bakassi Peninsula on the border with Cameroon; plus all but essential travel is advised to Warri, the riverine areas in the Delta State and the southeast Plateau State. Localised outbreaks of civil unrest have been known to occur at short notice, and violent crime is prevalent in the south of the country, including Lagos.
AIR: Nigeria's former national airline, *Nigeria Airways*, has now been liquidated. But several other airlines service the region. Airlines operating between Nigeria, Europe and North America include *Air France, British Airways, KLM Royal Dutch Airlines, Lufthansa, United Airlines* and *Virgin Atlantic*.
Approximate flight times: From Lagos to *London* is seven hours 25 minutes and to *New York* is 12 hours 10 minutes.
International airports: *Lagos (LOS)* (Murtala Muhammed) is 22km (13 miles) north of Lagos (travel time – 40 minutes). Taxis to the city are available. There is a free coach service every 10 minutes. Airport facilities include restaurant, bar, snack bar, bank, post office and car hire.
Kano (KAN) is 8km (5 miles) north of Kano (travel time – 25 minutes). Buses leave for the city every 10 minutes 0600-2200, and taxis are available. Airport facilities include restaurant, bank, post office, duty free shop and car hire. *Abuja (ABV)* is 35km (22 miles) from the city.
Note: Pickpockets and confidence tricksters, some posing as local immigration and other government officials, are especially common at Murtala Muhammed Airport.
Departure tax: None.
SEA: The main ports are Lagos, Port Harcourt and Calabar. Other important ports include Warri and Sepele.
ROAD: Links are with Benin, Cameroon, Chad and Niger. The principal trans-Saharan routes pass through Nigeria from Niger. The principal link with Benin is via the Idoroko border point along the good coast road to Lagos.

Travel - Internal

AIR: The former national carrier, *Nigeria Airways*, has now been liquidated but other airlines offer services between Benin City, Calabar, Enugu, Jos, Kaduna, Kano, Lagos, Maiduguri, Port Harcourt, Sokoto and Yola. Charter facilities are available in Lagos from *Aero Contractors, Delta Air Charter* and *Pan-African Airlines*. It is advisable to book internal flights well in advance. There is often considerable delay in internal air services. Lack of fuel sometimes disrupts internal commercial air travel and flights may be cancelled at short notice.
SEA: Ferry services operate along the south coast and along the Niger and Benue rivers. For timetables and prices, enquire locally.
RAIL: The two main routes are from Lagos to Kano (via Ibadan–Oyo–Ogbombosho–Kaduna–Zaria); and from Port Harcourt to Maiduguri (via Aba–Enugu–Makurdi–Jos). These two lines link up Kaduna and Kafanchan. There is also a branch line from Zaria to Gusau and Kaura Namoda. A daily service runs on both main routes. Sleeping cars are available, which must be booked in advance. There are three classes and some trains have restaurant cars and air conditioning. Trains are generally slower than buses, but cheaper.
ROAD: Traffic drives on the right. The national road system links all the main centres, although in some areas secondary roads become impassable during the rains. Reports of armed robberies in broad daylight on rural roads in the northern half of Nigeria have been reported and appear to be increasing. **Buses** and **taxis** (or 'bush taxis' in the shape of Ford Transit vans) run between the main towns. **Car hire** is not difficult to obtain in Lagos and Abuja, but it is best to go through hotels. Chauffeur-driven cars are advised.
Documentation: An International Driving Permit is required, accompanied by two passport-size photos.
URBAN: Public transport in Lagos operates in rather chaotic conditions. The city suffers from chronic traffic congestion, which makes it impossible for buses and taxis to operate efficiently, especially during the rush hours. There are many private bus companies and several thousand private minibuses. Taxis in Lagos are yellow and both fares and tip should be agreed in advance. A ferry service runs to Lagos Island.

Accommodation

HOTELS: There are first-class hotels in Lagos and in the major towns, but they are heavily booked and advance reservation is essential. Lagos is one of the most congested cities in Africa, and the majority of good hotels are on Lagos Island. Hotels are generally very expensive, but there is a variety of alternative accommodation. Further information can be obtained from the Ministry of Culture and Tourism (see *Contact Addresses* section).
OTHER ACCOMMODATION: Government-run **catering rest-houses** are scattered throughout the country and offer accommodation in colonial-style rest-houses. In many towns, **Christian missions** are able to offer good basic accommodation at a reasonable price. The universities have **guest houses** for visiting academics, but may be able to accommodate other visitors. Most of the big towns have **sporting clubs** which offer cheap accommodation and eating facilities, and can be used by visitors who take temporary

membership. Port Harcourt is the centre of the national oil industry and offers a large selection of accommodation to the industry, which is also available to tourists.

Resorts & Excursions

THE SOUTH

LAGOS: Lagos is a busy and overcrowded city, reputed to be the most expensive in the world. Its commercial and administrative centre is on Lagos Island at the heart of the city, linked to the mainland by two road bridges. **Ikoyi** and **Victoria** islands are also connected to **Lagos Island**, and both have wealthy residential areas and beautiful gardens. The **National Museum** at **Onikan** on Lagos Island houses numerous exhibits of Nigeria's ancient civilisations and has a craft centre which sells examples of Nigerian craft at fixed prices. In the **Jankara Market** on Lagos Island you can bargain for locally dyed cotton and handwoven cloth, herbs and leather goods.

THE SOUTHWEST

Ibadan is famous for its university and its market (one of the biggest in Nigeria). It is a convenient base for trips to the other, more traditional, old towns of the Western State. The large, traditional town of **Oyo** has some old Portuguese-style houses and is the site of the capital of the old Yoruba Empire. **Oshogbo** is the founding centre of the internationally renowned school of Oshogbo art and home of the shrines and grove of Oshun, the Yoruba goddess of fertility. The famous **Oshun Shrine** is to be found here. The **Oshun Festival** takes place towards the end of August each year. *Ile-Ife*, the ancient name of the town of **Ife**, is the cradle of Yoruba culture, and includes the **Ife Museum**, which has many fine bronze and terracotta sculptures dating back to the 13th century. The university here is a centre for batik-dying. **Akure** is a good base from which to explore the seven **Olumirin Waterfalls**.
THE MOUTH OF THE NIGER: Modern **Benin City** is a rapidly developing metropolis, but there are a few reminders of its long Yoruba history. The old city's moat and wall survive in places and the **National Museum** houses an interesting collection of Benin royal art. The **Oba's Palace** is worth visiting, although permission needs to be obtained in Lagos. Many of the villages in **Cross River State** are of interest for their handicrafts and traditions of magic, but may only be accessible by foot or canoe. **Abaraka**, **Auchi**, **Sapele**, **Sapoba** and **Warri** however, can be reached by road. **Calabar** is a pleasant town in a beautiful setting, high on a hill above the Calabar River. **Ikot Ekepne** is the centre for beautiful baskets and carvings, and at **Oron** there is a museum renowned for its exhibits of Ibibio and Efik carvings. **Ikom**, on the road to Cameroon, has curious carved monoliths set in circles.
Port Harcourt has long been an important merchant port and is today the centre of Nigeria's oil industry.

THE NORTH

Abuja, the new federal capital since 1991, is as yet undeveloped for tourism. It has a beautiful setting which gives magnificent views across the savannah.
KANO: Formerly the largest of the ancient Hausa cities, Kano is today Nigeria's third-largest city. The walled old town still remains and gives the city a medieval atmosphere, although the city was founded at least 1000 years ago, being of strategic importance on the trans-Saharan trade routes. **Kurmi Market** has many tourist souvenirs, including the richly embroidered Fulani horse blankets and decorations used at festivals. The famous dye pits (**Kofar Mata**), still in use and apparently some of the oldest in Africa, are interesting, as is the **Grand Mosque**. The **Emir's Palace** is an outstanding example of Hausa architecture. The city has many colonial-style sporting clubs and good restaurants and nightlife.
JOS: Jos is a favourite holiday centre on account of its location (1200m/3900ft above sea level) and pleasant climate. The **Jos Museum** has a large collection of pottery from all over the country, and the nearby **Museum of Traditional Nigerian Architecture** holds a collection of full-size replicas representing different styles of Nigerian architecture, including the **Kano Wall**, **Katsina Palace** and **Zaria Mosque**. There is also a small zoo and easy access to such sights as the **Assob Falls**.
ELSEWHERE: Kaduna is a government town laid out by the British and has fine buildings and modern amenities. The ancient walled city of **Zaria** to the north retains much of its old character and has a fine mosque and **Emir's Palace**. Outside **Katsina**, on the border with Niger, are some old Hausa burial mounds and the city is the site of spectacular *Sallah* festivals (see *Special Events* in the *Social Profile* section).
At **Maiduguri**, the *Sallah* festival is held three months after the festival of *Eid al-Fitr*, during which Borno horsemen demonstrate their equestrian prowess. The town also has a palace, park, zoo and museum.
The area around **Lake Chad** is flat and prone to flooding during and after the rains. The whole region is of special interest to the ornithologist and nature enthusiast. In contrast, some of the most striking and fascinating mountain scenery can be enjoyed around **Biu** and towards the Cameroon border.

Sport & Activities

Watersports: The numerous beaches offer **bathing**, although many have strong currents and bathers should not swim far from the shore, especially in Lagos. Many of the better hotels have pools. Good river and sea **angling** is available throughout the country.
Wildlife: *Yankari National Park* in the eastern half of the country is particularly good for **birdwatching**. Animals which can be viewed here include elephants, crocodiles and monkeys. Nigeria's largest national park, the Gashaka Game Reserve near Yola, also provides opportunities to view birds and animals.

Social Profile

FOOD & DRINK: There are restaurants of all varieties in Lagos and the major towns. European and Oriental food is readily available. Although there are self-service cafes, mainly in department stores, most restaurants have table service. Nigerian food is typical of that found throughout West Africa, and meals will often include yam, sweet potatoes, plantain and pepper soup, with regional variations. In the north, meat is more popular than in other areas; specialities are *suya* (barbecued liver and beef on sticks) and *kilishi* (spiced dried meat), in the east *egussi soup* (stew of meat, dried fish and melon seeds), and in the south goat meat and bush meat, particularly antelope, which is considered a delicacy.
There are many brands of locally brewed and bottled beer which are very good. Spirits are expensive. Larger hotels and clubs have bars and cocktail lounges.
NIGHTLIFE: There are nightclubs in many of the hotels in Lagos and in the Surulere district. Some clubs have live entertainment, details of which are given in the local newspapers. North of Oyo in Ogbomosho, there is a lively market, particularly in the evenings. Local festivals which generally take place in the summer months provide a good opportunity to see dancing, music and traditional costumes.
SHOPPING: Markets are the most interesting places to shop. Special purchases include *adire* (patterned, indigo-dyed cloth), batiks and pottery from the southwest, leatherwork and *kaduna* cotton from the north and carvings from the east. Designs vary greatly, many towns having their own distinctive style. Other purchases include herbs, beadwork, basketry and ceremonial masks such as those of the Ekpo. **Shopping hours**: Mon-Fri 0800-1700, Sat 0800-1630.
SPECIAL EVENTS: In the predominantly Muslim north, the most important festival is *Sallah*, celebrated three months after the feast of *Eid al-Fitr* (End of Ramadan), particularly in the towns of Kano, Katsina, Maiduguri and Zaria. Every family is required to slaughter a ram and festivities last for several days, with horseback processions, musicians and dancers. Featured also in northern communities are *Durbars*, long lines of horsemen led by a band, the horses in quilted armour with the riders wearing quilted coats and wielding ceremonial swords. In the south, there are masquerades and festivals marking events in local religions. In mid- to late **February**, the *Argungu Fishing and Cultural Festival* is held on the banks of the Sokoto River. At Oshogbo, the *Oshun* festival is held at the end of the rainy season (**August** to **September**), attracting thousands of childless women who seek the help of the Yoruba goddess of fertility. Festivals in the western states include masquerades in **June**, the *Oro* festival in **July** and the *Shango* festival in **August**. In **August**, the *Pategi Regatta* takes place half-way between Ibadan and Kaduna. Other festivals are held in **February**, **July** and **August** in the northern town of Ogbomosho. For more information or exact dates, contact the Nigeria Tourism Development Corporation (see *Contact Addresses* section).
SOCIAL CONVENTIONS: Shaking hands with everyone is customary on meeting and departing. In Yorubaland, it is a sign of respect for women to curtsey when introduced and to enquire after relations, even if this is a first meeting. Unless the visitor knows someone well, it is unusual to be invited to a Nigerian's home. Most entertaining, particularly in Lagos, takes place in clubs or restaurants. A small gift of appreciation is always welcome and business souvenirs bearing the company logo are also acceptable. Casual wear is suitable and a lightweight suit and tie are only necessary for businesspeople on formal meetings; on most other occasions men will not need to wear a jacket, although a tie might be expected. Women should dress modestly, and respect local customs regarding dress, particularly in the Muslim north. It is inadvisable for women to wear trousers. There are over 250 tribes in Nigeria, the principal groups being the Hausa in the north, the Ibo (or Igbo) in the southeast and the Yoruba in the southwest. The larger of the minor groups are the Fulani, Idoma, Igala, Igbirra, Kanuri, Tiv and Nupe in the north; the Efik, Ekoi, Ibibio and Ijaw in the east; and the Edo, Itsekiri, Ijaw and Urhobo in the west. A result of this ethnic variety is the diversity of art, dance forms, language, music, customs and crafts. Nigerians have a very strong sense of ethnic allegiance. **Tipping**: Unless a service charge has been included, 10 per cent is expected for most services. Note that for taxi drivers the fare including a tip should be agreed before the journey. Airport porters are usually tipped per case.

Business Profile

ECONOMY: Nigeria is Africa's largest oil producer; the industry earns 90 per cent of the country's export income and has underpinned its economy for decades. Nigeria also has commercially viable quantities of tin, coal, iron ore, zinc and some uranium, plus substantial but as yet largely untapped reserves of natural gas and coal. Agriculture occupies well over half of the population, who produce rice, maize, cassava, sorghum and millet as staples, as well as groundnuts, cocoa, palm oil and rubber as cash crops. Timber and livestock rearing have both developed during the last 20 years. Nonetheless, successive governments have failed to restore Nigeria's one-time self-sufficiency in food. Manufacturing was established during the 1960s, principally with oil money, and now includes food processing and the production of vehicles, textiles, pharmaceuticals, paper and cement. Despite its abundance of natural resources, Nigeria has suffered an almost permanent economic crisis during the last 10 years, due to political instability, mismanagement and corruption. Per capita GDP is just US$300 annually, not much more than that of the world's poorest nations. The country is weighed down by a massive foreign debt. Reduction negotiations have been completed with the 'Paris Club' of leading creditors. As a condition of the rescheduling, the new civilian Government has begun to put into effect economic reforms, including the sale of major state-owned industries. Recent economic performance has been determined mainly by the state of the world oil market. Since government deregulated fuel prices and announced the privatisation of Nigeria's four oil refineries in 2003, GDP rose to 7.1 per cent in 2004. Britain is the largest single exporter to Nigeria. Germany, France, the USA and increasingly Brazil and Spain are other principal sources of imports. The bulk of Nigeria's exports are sold to the USA, Germany, France, Italy and Brazil. Nigeria is the dominant member of the West African economic cooperation organisation, ECOWAS, as well as a leading member of the oil producers' cartel, OPEC.
BUSINESS: English is spoken in business circles. It is common for business meetings to take place without a prior appointment, although these should be made for government visits. Business deals will often progress at a slower pace than is common in Europe. Owing to the prevalence of commercial fraud targeting foreigners, business travellers should contact both their local Nigerian Embassy and Chamber of Commerce before travelling to Nigeria. **Office hours**: Mon-Fri 0730-1530 (government offices); 0830-1700 (private businesses).
COMMERCIAL INFORMATION: Information and advice can be obtained from Nigerian High Commissions and the Nigerian Information Service Center (see *Contact Addresses* section).

Climate

Varies from area to area. The southern coast is hot and humid with a rainy season from March to November. During the dry season, the *Harmattan* wind blows from the Sahara. The north's rainy season is from July to September. Nights can be cold in December and January.
Required clothing: Lightweight cottons and linens are worn, with a warm wrap advisable in the north. Rainwear is essential during the rainy season.

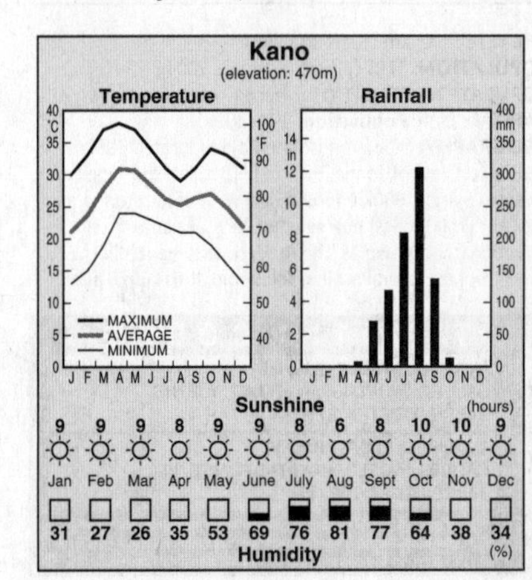

Niue

LATEST TRAVEL ADVICE CONTACTS

British Foreign and Commonwealth Office
Tel: (0870) 606 0290 Website: www.fco.gov.uk
US Department of State
Website: http://travel.state.gov/travel
Canadian Department of Foreign Affairs and Int'l Trade
Tel: (1 800) 267 8376 Website: www.dfait-maeci.gc.ca

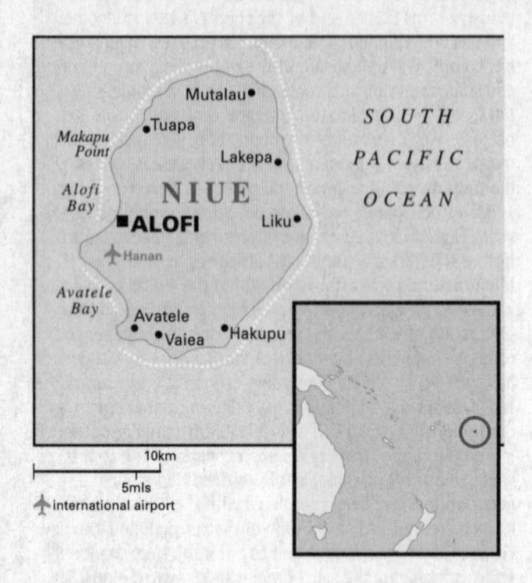

Location: South Pacific.

Country dialling code: 683.

Niue Tourism Office
PO Box 42, Alofi, Niue Island
Tel: 4224 *or* 4394. Fax: 4225.
E-mail: niuetourism@mail.gov.nu *or* infocentre@mail.gov.nu
Website: www.niueisland.com
South Pacific Tourism Organisation
Street address: Level 3, FNPF Place, 343-359 Victoria Parade, Suva, Fiji
Postal address: PO Box 13119, Suva, Fiji
Tel: (679) 330 4177. Fax: (679) 330 1995.
Website: www.spto.org
Also deals with enquiries from the UK.
Niue High Commission
Level 1, Gleneagles Building, 71 The Terrace, Wellington, PO Box 10-123, New Zealand
Tel: (4) 499 4515. Fax: (4) 499 4516.
E-mail: komisina@niuhicom.co.nz
Niue Tourism Office
PO Box 68716, Newton, Auckland, New Zealand
Tel/Fax: (64) 585 1493.
E-mail: niuetourism@clear.net.nz
Website: www.niueisland.com
Niue Tourism Office
Level 3/313 Burwood Road, Hawthorn, Victoria 3122, Australia
Tel: 1300 136 483. Fax: +613 9818 1851.
E-mail: niuetourism@bigpond.com
Website: www.niueisland.com

General Information

AREA: 262.7 sq km (101.4 sq miles).
POPULATION: 1761 (official estimate 2004).
POPULATION DENSITY: 6.7 per sq km.
CAPITAL: Alofi. **Population**: 404 (2004).
GEOGRAPHY: Niue is an isolated island located 480km (298 miles) east of Tonga, 560km (348 miles) southeast of Western Samoa, 980km (609 miles) west of Rarotonga and 2400km (1500 miles) northeast of New Zealand. Affectionately known as 'the rock', Niue is reputedly the largest upraised coral atoll in the world. It has 6178 acres (2500 hectares) of the most undisturbed forests in the world, designated tapu areas by the locals, where no humans were allowed to set foot for centuries. Now all the tapu forests, except the one controlled by Hakupu village, are penetrable. These forests are full of lush undergrowth, coconut palms and some of the oldest-known ebony trees on earth. Light and scattered forest covers approximately 34,594 acres (14,000 hectares). At the edge of the forest, the coast gives way to coral outcrops.
GOVERNMENT: Self-governing state in 'free association' with New Zealand. (New Zealand retains responsibility for external affairs.) **Head of State**: HM Queen Elizabeth II, represented locally by High Commissioner Sandra Lee. **Head of Government**: Premier Young Vivian since 2002.
LANGUAGE: Niuean and English.
RELIGION: Most people belong to the Ekalesia Niue, a Protestant denomination; also Apostolic, Bahaii Faith, Christian Outreach Church, Latter Day Saints (Mormon), Jehovah's Witness, Roman Catholic and Seventh Day Adventist.
TIME: GMT - 11.
ELECTRICITY: 240 volts AC, 50Hz. Plugs are the standard three-pin type.
COMMUNICATIONS: Telephone: IDD and local facilities are available. Country code: 683. International calls can also be made directly from the telephone or with the assistance of an operator. There are telephones in hotels, motels and guest houses. Services are run by the Telecommunications Department located at the Commercial Centre in Alofi, which also provides **fax** facilities, and is open 24 hours a day. Dial 999 for the Police, Fire or Hospital. **Internet:** The island has a wireless Internet service provided by the Niue Internet Users Society. ISPs include *Internet Niue* (website: www.niue.nu). **Post:** The Niue Post Office is open Mon-Fri 0830-1500. **Press:** The *Niue Star* is published weekly in English and Niuean. **Television:** *Television Niue* broadcasts in English and Niuean five evenings a week but other programming is available outside of these times.
Radio: BBC World Service (website: www.bbc.co.uk/worldservice) and Voice of America (website: www.voa.gov) can be received. From time to time the frequencies change and the most up-to-date can be found online.

TIMATIC CODES

Health
AMADEUS: **TI-DFT/IUE/HE**
GALILEO/WORLDSPAN: **TI-DFT/IUE/HE**
SABRE: **TIDFT/IUE/HE**

Visa
AMADEUS: **TI-DFT/IUE/VI**
GALILEO/WORLDSPAN: **TI-DFT/IUE/VI**
SABRE: **TIDFT/IUE/VI**

To access TIMATIC country information on Health and Visa regulations through the Computer Reservations System (CRS), type in the appropriate command line listed above.

Passport/Visa

	Passport Required?	Visa Required?	Return Ticket Required?
Full British	Yes	1	Yes
Australian	Yes	1	Yes
Canadian	Yes	1	Yes
USA	Yes	1	Yes
Other EU	Yes	1	Yes
Japanese	Yes	1	Yes

Note: Regulations and requirements may be subject to change at short notice, and you are advised to contact the appropriate diplomatic or consular authority before finalising travel arrangements. Details of these may be found at the head of this country's entry. Any numbers in the chart refer to the footnotes below.

PASSPORTS: Required by all.
VISAS: Required by all except:
(a) nationals of New Zealand;
(b) **1.** bona fide tourists staying less than 30 days with return or onward tickets, all documents required for the next destination and sufficient funds for length of stay. However an *Entry Permit* is required by all nationals, which is granted on arrival;
(c) those who are in transit, continuing their journey by the first or connecting aircraft and not leaving the airport.
Note: Visas *are* required for all nationals staying for 30 days or longer.
Entry permit requirements: (a) Valid passport. (b) Sufficient funds for duration of stay. (c) Return or onward ticket.
Types of visa: *Ordinary* and *Transit*. Transit visas are not required by nationals of New Zealand or by other nationals continuing their journey by the same or first connecting aircraft, provided they hold valid onward documentation and are not leaving the airport.
Validity: Entry Permit: 30 days. Extensions are available from the Immigration Office, PO Box 69, Alofi, Niue (tel: 4349 *or* 4333; fax: 4336).
Application to: Consulate or High Commission (see *Contact Addresses* section).
Temporary residence: Check with the Immigration Office.

Money

Currency: The New Zealand Dollar (NZ$) is legal tender (see *New Zealand* section). Niue sometimes produces commemorative coins which, when available, may be obtained at the treasury.
Currency exchange: The Bank of the South Pacific in Alofi, the only commercial bank in Niue, can exchange currency.
Credit & debit cards: American Express, Diners Club, MasterCard and Visa are accepted in most hotels and resorts. Contact your credit or debit card company for details of merchant acceptability and other services which may be available.
Currency restrictions: There are no restrictions on the import of local or foreign currency. However, there are restrictions on postal notes, money orders, cheques or promissory notes in New Zealand currency, which must be declared to the Westpac Banking Corporation in Niue. Export of local currency is restricted to NZ$10,000. Export of foreign currency is restricted to the amount declared on arrival and authorisation from a bank is required.
Exchange rate indicators: See *New Zealand* section.
Banking hours: Mon-Thurs 0900-1500, Fri 0830-1500.

Duty Free

The following items can be imported into Niue by persons of 18 years of age or older without incurring customs duty:
400 cigarettes or 50 cigars or 500g of tobacco or a combination of each with a maximum weight of 0.5lb; 3.5l of spirits, liquor or wine; other goods to the value of NZ$250.
Restricted imports: Firearms and ammunition are prohibited unless permission is received from the Chief of Police at the Police Department of Niue. A maximum of one of each of the following: radio, cassette player, tape recorder, typewriter, pair of binoculars, photo or video camera.
Restricted exports: Artefacts, coral and valuable shells.

Public Holidays

2005: Jan 1 New Year's Day. **Jan 4** Takai Commission Holiday. **Feb 6** Waitangi Day. **Mar 25-28** Easter. **Apr 25** ANZAC Day. **Jun 6** Queen's Birthday. **Oct 16-19** Constitution Celebrations. **Oct 17** Peniamina's Day. **Dec 25-26** Christmas. **Dec 27** Christmas Holiday.
2006: Jan 1 New Year's Day. **Jan 4** Takai Commission Holiday. **Feb 6** Waitangi Day. **Apr 14-17** Easter. **Apr 25** ANZAC Day. **Jun 5** Queen's Birthday. **Oct 16-19** Constitution Celebrations. **Oct 17** Peniamina's Day. **Dec 25-26** Christmas.

Health

	Special Precautions?	Certificate Required?
Yellow Fever	Yes	1
Cholera	No	No
Typhoid & Polio	2	N/A
Malaria	Yes	N/A

Note: Regulations and requirements may be subject to change at short notice, and you are advised to contact your doctor well in advance of your intended date of departure. Any numbers in the chart refer to the footnotes below.

1: A yellow fever certificate is required from all travellers over one year of age arriving from infected areas.
2: Typhoid is not currently a concern on the island. However, if coming from an infected area it is advised to take the necessary precautions.
Food & drink: Drinking water is from natural spring and rainwater, but it is also recommended that you boil water prior to drinking. Imported bottled water is also available. There is a low risk of travellers' diarrhoea; exercise moderate food caution. Milk is pasteurised and dairy products are safe for consumption. Local meat, poultry, seafood, fruit and vegetables are generally considered safe to eat.
Other risks: *Hepatitis A* occurs and *hepatitis B* is endemic.
Health care: The Niue Health Centre offers medical and dental treatment. There is a 24-hour on-call emergency service. Patients will be asked for on-the-spot payment. Complicated cases will be sent overseas to New Zealand. International travellers are strongly advised to take out full medical insurance before departure.
Note: Medical charges for overseas patients: Consultation fee: $25; diving certificate: $50; dressings: $10.

Travel - International

AIR: *Polynesian Airlines* (website: www.polynesianairlines.com) flies to Niue from Auckland, New Zealand and from Apia, Samoa.
The *Polypass* (offered by *Polynesian Airlines*) allows the holder to fly between the Southern Pacific destinations of American Samoa, Fiji, Niue, Samoa, Tahiti and Tonga; Honolulu (Hawaii) and Los Angeles in the USA; Brisbane, Melbourne and Sydney in Australia; and Auckland, Christchurch and Wellington in New Zealand. The pass is valid for one year. Once a reservation has been made and travel begun, all travel must be completed within a

A B C D E F G H I J K L M N O P Q R S T U V W X Y Z

maximum of 45 days. Tickets will be issued against the *Polypass* by any *Polynesian Airlines* office (a valid passport is also required). For further information, contact *Polynesian Airlines* (website: www.polynesianairlines.com).
International airports: *Niue International (IUE)* (Hanan) is 7km (4 miles) north of Alofi. Transfer buses are available from the airport to all tourist accommodations. There are some shops at the airport, open for scheduled flights.
Departure tax: NZ$25.
SEA: It is possible to visit Niue by yacht; weekday arrivals are preferred. Moorings and buoys are available.

Travel - Internal

ROAD: There are 123km (76 miles) of paved roads in Niue. Driving is on the left. There is no organised public transport on Niue. **Car hire**: Cars can be hired on the island although it is best to make reservations before arrival. Car hire companies include *Alofi Rentals* and *Niue Rentals*. A limited number of mountain bikes can also be hired on the island. **Documentation**: Along with their national driving licence, visitors must obtain a local licence from the Niue Police Department.

Accommodation

ANAIKI MOTEL: Located next to the Avaiki Caves at Makefu. This accommodation has five units in a long block (single/double/triple), breakfast included. A hot plate is provided for heating up simple meals.
CORAL GARDENS MOTEL: Five self-contained studio-room chalets adjoining Sails Restaurant. Situated near a tropical coral garden close to Alofi and Makefu and in close proximity to popular reefs and swimming pools.
HUVALU FOREST CAMP: Set in the beautiful Huvalu Forest near Hakupu village, this camp offers very basic accommodation with shared bathroom and cooking facilities and bunkhouse-style sleeping arrangements.
KOLOLI'S GUEST-HOUSE: Built in the centre of Alofi, it provides a range of rooms, including a large bedroom suite, a large double bedroom, two double rooms and a twin room with shared bathroom facilities. There is a kitchen and barbecue area, or meals can be provided.
MATAVAI RESORT: Situated on a cliff top, with views overlooking Dolphin Bay and the bays of Avatele and Tamakautoga, this resort is just 10 minutes from Alofi, has 24 rooms and two executive suites. The main building houses a restaurant, two bars, conference facilities and two freshwater swimming pools. They also offer wedding packages.
NAMUKULU MOTEL: With sea and reef views, this motel is situated a 10-minute drive from Alofi and a few minutes walk from Limu. It consists of three self-contained chalets which can sleep up to four people. There is a licensed restaurant and bar nearby, as well as opportunities for snorkelling, swimming and cycling.
PELENI'S GUEST-HOUSE: A former family home in the centre of Alofi, it consists of three bedrooms with shared cooking, bathroom and lounge facilities. Meals can be provided.

Resorts & Excursions

Reputedly the world's largest coral island, Niue's rugged coastline and reef offer excellent fishing, diving and snorkelling opportunities. Parakeets, white-tailed terns, weka and other exotic birds live on this island and butterflies are a common sight darting among the hibiscus and orchids. The island is well off the beaten track but tourist numbers are steadily increasing with 2,758 tourist arrivals by air recorded for 2003 - significantly more than the island's permanent population which continues to decline.
ALOFI: Recommended sites in Alofi include the **Women's Club Town Hall**, with a craft shop featuring various handicrafts for sale; and **Alofi Market** open on Fridays.
Note: The **Huanaki Cultural Centre** and the **Huanaki Museum** were completely destroyed by a Cyclone Heta in January 2004.
THE NORTH: Some 5km (3 miles) north of Alofi, near **Makapu Point**, **Peniamina's Grave**, the resting place of the Niuean who first brought Christianity to the island, can be found in a small clearing on the left side of the road. The **Experimental Farm**, a centre for animal husbandry and plant testing, is another popular destination for visitors. **Opaahi** is the site of Captain Cook's landing where he received a hostile reception from the local people and was almost hit by a spear. There are good swimming holes at **Vaitafe**, 800m (2625ft) south of **Fulala** and 2.5km (1.5 miles) north of **Lakepa**, at **Avaiki**, and at **Limu**, perhaps the most beautiful on the north coast with its colourful coral and its wide variety of marine life (thatched cottages and a barbecue area can also be found here).
THE SOUTH: Avatele Bay is another excellent location for swimming and snorkelling and visitors may watch the many fishermen in their canoes and dinghies who fish the bay's waters for tuna, wahoo and marlin, as well as the spectacular sunsets that set over the bay. An interesting excursion is to the deserted village of **Fatiau Tuai**, 1600m (5249ft) from the main road on the seaward side of **Vaiea Village**. The original inhabitants suffered from an eye disease and the entire population was moved by the Government to Vaiea. The coastline here is stunning for its rough surf crashing against the shore and shooting up through blowholes. Chasms are another of Niue's natural wonders. The amazing **Vaikona Chasm** can be reached by the Namuke sea track from the main road about 4km (2.5 miles) south of **Liku**. **Togo Chasm** is also popular. Located on the eastern side of the island, 4km (2.5 miles) north of **Hakupu**, it is one of Niue's most magnificent scenic areas with a tropical rainforest, towering coral pinnacles and an oasis of white sand, coconut palms and a pond hidden beneath overhanging cliffs (guide recommended). **Matapa Chasm** is another well-known scenic attraction, reached by road from the foot of **Hikutavake Hill**. **Vaotoi Pool**, 3km (2 miles) north of Hakapu, is the scene of the wreck of a Japanese fishing vessel which was beached during a storm in 1967. However, access to many of the chasms and pools are along difficult paths and an experienced guide is usually considered necessary.
CAVES: There are hundreds of caves and grottoes which are excellent for land explorations or dive sites. Various caves are used as repositories for canoes as well as for the bones of dead ancestors. **Avaiki Cave** is reported to be where the first settler's canoe landed. **Talava – The Arches** are a group of extraordinary arches and caverns, many containing stalactites and stalagmites, which may be visited at low tide. Other caves known for their spectacular formations are **Ulupaka Cave**, reached by a track 800m (2625ft) south of Lakepa, and Palaha Caves, 180m (591ft) north of Palaha. **Anatoloa Cave**, 1600m (5249ft) north of Lakepa and a five-minute walk from the main road, is hard to find but is well worth the effort. Niuean mythology cites it as being the home of a dangerous god and human bones have been found within it.

Sport & Activities

Watersports: Surrounded on all sides by the crystal clear and unpolluted waters of the Pacific Ocean, Niue is an ideal destination for **swimming**, **scuba diving** and **snorkelling**. The island's position on top of an undersea mountain and the absence of a fringing lagoon mean that dives are into the open Pacific. Coupled with the lack of rivers or streams on the island, these conditions help to create exceptional visibility (usually a minimum of 50m/164ft). Even in winter, water temperature stays around 25°C/78°F. Snorkellers and divers have the opportunity to encounter humpback whales and dolphins in Niuean waters. For further information as well as bookings of twin-hulled dive boats, scuba and snorkelling gear and PADI certification courses, contact Niue Dive, PO Box 140, Alofi, Niue (tel: 4311; fax: 4360; e-mail: niuedive@dive.nu; website: www.dive.nu).
Below is a selection of the best diving sites in Niue:
Limu (Ana Mahaga): A twin cavern system connected by a tunnel situated approximately a 20-minute boat ride from Alofi wharf. Depth ranges from 8-28m and sightings of lion fish, ribbon eels, white tip reef shark, trevally and midnight sea perch are common.
The Dome: Adventurous divers can swim 30m into a cave system lying under the island before surfacing in a large air filled chamber which has the start of some stalactites and usually a few small uga (coconutcrabs). Once out of the cave system, there are a series of interesting swim-throughs and gullies to explore.
The Chimney: Divers can descend a near vertical shaft into the 'fireplace' - a medium sized cavern with an exit out at the seabed (around 28m) There is a side chamber in the fireplace usually with several painted crayfish inside. Divers pass the wreck of a jeep left there by Cyclone Heta as they exit the cavern.
Bubble Cave: A shallow cave system where sea snakes go to lay their eggs in breeding season. Divers can surface in a small air-filled chamber and see stalactites and possibly small sea snakes.
Egypt: Divers can swim past a series of large columns (like the ruins of temples in Egypt). Turtles, parrotfish and white tipped reef sharks often feature on this dive.
Overhang: A dive over pristine hard coral reef beginning around 5m below the surface, with healthy plate corals extending down to 40m and beyond.
False Beach: Another dive over pristine hard coral reef with a beautiful bommie (large head of coral) covered in fish life. A good selection of reef fish on this dive including lion fish, surgeons and butterflies.
Tamakautoga Drift: A gentle swim over endless coral gardens along the coast at Tamakautoga village. Sightings of dolphins and whales have been known on these dives.
Snake Gully: Generally the most popular of the dive sites, Snake Gully gets its name from the large concentration of sea snakes found in the area. It also features a cave and cavern - one filled with large painted crayfish, the other has streams of light coming in through the many openings to the surface. Marine life often seen here includes maori wrasse, schools of barracuda, white tip reef sharks, ribbon eels and lion fish.
Because of the sheer drops from reefs into deep ocean, land-based game **fishing** is a unique experience here. Red bass, wahoo (also known locally as *paala*), tuna, sailfish and marlin abound. Traditional outrigger canoes and motor boats can be arranged for line-fishing expeditions.
Yachting: There are currently four moorings available at a fee of NZ$5 per day but there are plans to increase this number to 14. A departure fee of NZ$25 per person is also payable to Customs. Visitors travelling to Niue by yacht should avoid arriving at weekends as entry clearance services provided by the Immigration and Port authorities are closed. On arrival, contact ZKN Niue Radio on VHF16; they will contact customs and arrange clearance, which must be gained before coming ashore, and arrange for mooring allocation. There are 18 moorings available which can be hired for NZ$5 per day. For further information, contact the *Niue Yacht Club*, PO Box 129, Alofi, Niue (e-mail: yachtclub@niue.nu; website: www.niueyachtclub.com).
Other: There are excellent opportunities in Niue's numerous caves, notably at Talava - The Arches, and several companies offer caving trips (see also *Resorts & Excursions* section).
At Niue Sport Club, there is a 9-hole **golf** course, with balls, clubs and trundlers for hire, and two **tennis** courts. Traditional Niuean **cricket** is the most popular spectator sport and can be seen in any village when in season. Niue's scenic rainforest areas, particularly around Hakupu and Kikutavake Hill in the east, are popular destinations for **walking** trips. **Cycling** is a good way to see the island along the 170km (106 miles) of bush tracks through scrub and rain forest. A number of companies rent out bicycles, scooters and motorbikes. For further information, contact the Niue Tourism Office or the South Pacific Tourism Organisation (see *Contact Addresses* section).

Social Profile

FOOD & DRINK: Many ceremonies and social events stem from the processing of food. One community ritual is based on the extraction of *nu pia* starch from arrowroot, which is used in traditional dishes and soups and often given as a gift. Another ritualised ceremony surrounds *ti* root, which is made into a sweet drink or eaten as a sweet with coconuts. The *luku* fern is another indigenous plant used in Niuean cooking and is boiled, stir-fried or baked in an earth oven with coconut cream and chicken or corned beef. Other popular foods include taro, kumara, coconuts, pawpaw, bananas, tomatoes, capsicum and many varieties of yam. Restaurants in Niue include the Matavai Resort and Sails Restaurant. Jenna's is open for dinner but bookings are required. Lunch is available at Taki's Cafe and Tavana's Snack Bar. Restaurants do not have service charge or tax.
Note: Some establishments were put out of business by cyclone Heta in 2004. This information is subject to change.
NIGHTLIFE: There are a number of enjoyable nightclubs. Hakupu Village also hosts a traditional cultural night once a week beginning with a tour of the village, followed by a traditional feast with dancing and singing (advance booking is recommended).
SHOPPING: Niuean women are especially regarded for the quality of their weaving, producing hats, baskets, handbags and mats from indigenous plants, such as pandanus, which make excellent buys for the visitor. These are available to visitors at Hinapoto Handcrafts at the Cultural Centre but can also be found at village show days. **Shopping hours**: Mon-Fri 0800-1600, Sat 0800-1600. There are generally one or two small stores in most villages around the island which are open in the evenings and during weekends.
SPECIAL EVENTS: Every month sees a traditional haircutting and ear-piercing ceremony held in various locations in Niue. However, prior permission must be sought. For a complete list of special events, contact Niue Tourism Office (see *Contact Addresses* section). The following is a selection of special events occurring in Niue in 2005:
Jan *Takai Week*; *Show Day*, Alofi South Village. **May** *Makefu Village Show Day*. **Jun** *Hakupu Atua Annual Show Day*; *Queen's Birthday Golf Ambrose Tournament*. **Jul** *Alofi South Show Day*. **Jul/Aug** *Cricket Season*. **Aug** *Lakepa Village Show Day*; *Tamakautoga Show Day*. **Sep** *Tuapa Village Show Day*; *Alofi North Village Annual Show Day*; *Westpac Rally of the Rock*. **Oct** *Annual Constitution Golf Tournament*; *Avatele Village Show Day*; *Mutalau Village Show Day*; *Constitution Day Celebrations*; Sports Expo. **Nov** *Annual Golf Championship*. **Dec 30** *Liku Village Annual Show Day*.
SOCIAL CONVENTIONS: Niuean children are bestowed

with gifts of money or handmade mats and cloths from their relatives upon coming of age, when girls have their ears pierced and boys receive their first haircut. It is polite to ask permission before entering private land. Niueans consider Sunday as a serious day of rest and most attend church both in the morning and afternoon. While many people play golf, go swimming or sightsee, certain activities, such as boating and fishing, are not allowed on Sunday. For further information on Sunday protocol, contact the Niue Tourism Office (see Contact Addresses section). Clothing is usually casual, cool and comfortable but women often wear a hat and cover their shoulders for church and men wear long trousers. Swimming attire is not acceptable in towns or villages. **Tipping**: Not encouraged.

Business Profile

ECONOMY: There is a small amount of agriculture, producing coconuts and honey – some of which is exported – as well as yams, cassava and sweet potatoes for domestic consumption. But the weather is inclement (cyclones are a major problem) and two-thirds of the land surface is unsuitable for cultivation. Some livestock is reared, again for local consumption. Tourism is worth about US$1 million annually and brings in foreign exchange; postage stamps are another valuable source of revenue. However, there is still a budgetary shortfall, which is made up for by aid from New Zealand and, more recently, Australia. In common with other small and remote Pacific island states, Niue has opted for the development of an 'offshore' financial services industry to boost the economy. The necessary legislation was passed by the Assembly in 1994, although little progress has been made, not least due to the intense competition from other Pacific island economies who have adopted the same strategy. Niue continues to suffer a drain on its resources as its younger, educated population leaves for New Zealand in search of work.
BUSINESS: Shaking hands is the usual form of greeting and leaving. Lightweight or tropical suits are recommended for business. Official invitations will always state the dress code required: 'formal' means a jacket and tie for men and 'fiafia' means casual dress is acceptable. **Office hours**: Mon-Fri 0730-1530 or 0800-1600.
CONFERENCES/CONVENTIONS: Matavai Resort conference rooms can seat 50 to 60 people or 120 theatre-style. For further details, contact the Niue Tourism Office (see *Contact Addresses* section) or Matavai Resort, PO Box 133, Alofi, Niue (tel: 4360; fax: 4361; e-mail: matavai@niue.nu).

Climate

Tropical climate bathed by southeast trade winds, Niue has warm days and pleasantly cool nights.
Required clothing: Cotton shorts and shirts (or cotton dresses for women) with a wrap for the evenings.

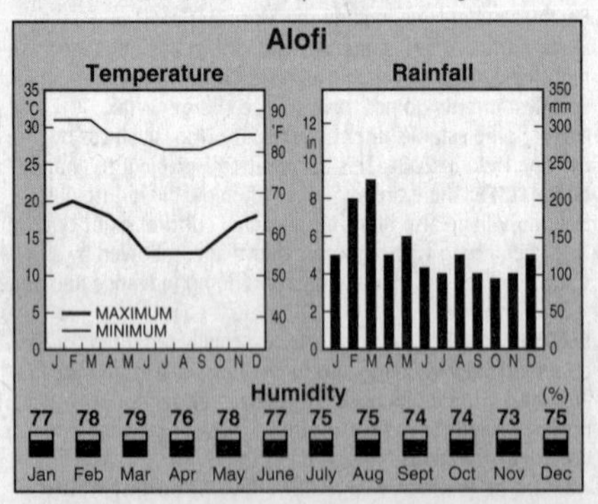

Norway

LATEST TRAVEL ADVICE CONTACTS

British Foreign and Commonwealth Office
Tel: (0870) 606 0290 Website: www.fco.gov.uk
US Department of State
Website: http://travel.state.gov/travel
Canadian Department of Foreign Affairs and Int'l Trade
Tel: (1 800) 267 8376 Website: www.dfait-maeci.gc.ca

Location: Northern Europe, Scandinavia.

Country dialling code: 47.

Innovation Norway
Postboks 448 Sentrum 0104, Oslo, Norway
Tel: 2200 2500. Fax: 2200 2501
E-mail: post@invanor.no
Website: www.invanor.no
Royal Norwegian Embassy
25 Belgrave Square, London SW1X 8QD, UK
Tel: (020) 7591 5500. Fax: (020) 7245 6993.
E-mail: emb.london@mfa.no *or* Konsulat.london@mfa.no (consular section).
Website: www.norway.org.uk
Opening hours: Mon-Fri 0900-1600 (general enquiries); 1000-1200 (visa section), 1330-1500 (visa telephone enquiries).
A full list of regional consulates is available on the website.
Innovation Norway (UK)
Charles House, 5 Lower Regent Street, London SW1 4LR, UK
Tel: (09063) 022 033 (brochure request line) *or* (020) 7389 8800.
Fax: (020) 7839 6014.
E-mail: london@invanor.no
Website: www.visitnorway.com
British Embassy
Thomas Heftyesgate 8, 0244 Oslo, Norway
Tel: 2313 2700. Fax: 2313 2741.
E-mail: britemb@online.no
Website: www.britain.no
Consulates in: Ålesund, Bergen, Bodø, Harstad, Kristiansand (S), Kristiansund (N), Stavanger, Tromsø and Trondheim.
Royal Norwegian Embassy
2720 34th Street, NW, Washington, DC 20008, USA
Tel: (202) 333 6000. Fax: (202) 337 0870.
E-mail: info@norway.org *or* emb.washington@mfa.no
Website: www.norway.org
Consulates General in: Houston, Minneapolis, New York and San Francisco.
Innovation Norway (US)
800 Third Avenue, 23rd Floor, New York, NY 10022, USA
Tel: (212) 421 9210. Fax: (212) 838 0374.
E-mail: new.york.trade@invanor.no
Website: www.invanor.no/usa
Embassy of the United States of America
Drammensveien 18, 0244 Oslo, Norway
Tel: 2244 8550. Fax: 2244 0436.
E-mail: pasoslo@usa.no
Website: www.usa.no
Note: The Embassy is due to move to new premises at Huseby in 2005.
Royal Norwegian Embassy
90 Sparks Street, Suite 532, Ottawa, Ontario K1P 5B4, Canada
Tel: (613) 238 6571. Fax: (613) 238 2765.
E-mail: emb.ottawa@mfa.no
Website: www.emb-norway.ca
Consulates in: Calgary, Edmonton, Halifax, Montreal, Québec, Regina, St John, St John's, Toronto, Vancouver, Victoria, Ville de la Baie and Winnipeg.
Canadian Embassy
Wergelandsveien 7, 0244 Oslo, Norway
Tel: 2299 5300. Fax: 2299 5301.
E-mail: oslo@dfait-maeci.gc.ca
Website: www.canada.no

TIMATIC CODES

Health
AMADEUS: **TI-DFT/OSL/HE**
GALILEO/WORLDSPAN: **TI-DFT/OSL/HE**
SABRE: **TIDFT/OSL/HE**

Visa
AMADEUS: **TI-DFT/OSL/VI**
GALILEO/WORLDSPAN: **TI-DFT/OSL/VI**
SABRE: **TIDFT/OSL/VI**

To access TIMATIC country information on Health and Visa regulations through the Computer Reservations System (CRS), type in the appropriate command line listed above.

General Information

AREA: 323,759 sq km (125,004 sq miles).
POPULATION: 4,552,252 (official estimate 2003).
POPULATION DENSITY: 14.9 per sq km.
CAPITAL: Oslo. **Population**: 517,401 (2003).
GEOGRAPHY: Norway is bordered to the north by the Arctic Ocean, to the east by Finland, the Russian Federation and Sweden, to the south by the Skagerrak (which separates it from Denmark) and to the west by the North Sea. The coastline is 2735km (1700 miles) long, its most outstanding feature being the fjords. Most of them are between 80 to 160km (50 to 100 miles) long, and are often very deep and surrounded by towering mountains. Much of northern Norway lies beyond the Arctic Circle and the landscape is stark. In the south, the landscape consists of forests with many lakes and rivers.
GOVERNMENT: Constitutional monarchy. Declared independence from Sweden in 1905. **Head of State**: King Harald V since 1991. **Head of Government**: Prime Minister Kjell Magne Bondevik since 2001.
LANGUAGE: Norwegian (Bokmål and Nynorsk). Sami is spoken by the Sami population in the north. English is widely spoken.
RELIGION: Approximately 86 per cent Evangelical Lutherans; plus other Christian denominations.
TIME: Norway Mainland: GMT + 1 (GMT + 2 from last Sunday in March to last Saturday before last Sunday in October). **Jan Mayen Islands, Svalbard**: GMT + 1.
ELECTRICITY: 220 volts AC, 50Hz. Plugs are of the European round two-pin type.
COMMUNICATIONS: Telephone: IDD is available. Country code: 47. Outgoing international code: 00. **Mobile telephone:** Most major dual band networks work across Norway. Networks include *Maritime Communications* (website: www.mcpinc.biz), *Net Com GSM* (website: www.netcom.no) and *Telenor Mobil AS* (website: www.telenor.no), which also deals with Internet and telegrams. Mobile phones cannot be hired. **Fax:** This service is available at major hotels. **Internet:** There are many Internet cafes throughout Norway and the Internet can also be accessed via public libraries. **Telegram:** *Telenor*'s headquarters are at Teledirektoratet, Universitetsgt 2. It is easiest to send telegrams by telephone. The telephone directories give instructions in English on page 16. **Post:** Hotel receptions, shops and kiosks selling postcards will sell stamps. Airmail within Europe takes two to four days. There are *Poste Restante* facilities at post offices in all major cities. Post office hours: These vary from place to place but are generally from Mon-Fri 0830-1600, Sat 0800-1300. **Press:** The national newspapers published in Oslo are *Aftenposten*, *Dagbladet* and *Verdens Gang*. There are no English-language newspapers although English newspapers are readily available (one day after publication in the UK).
Radio: BBC World Service (website: www.bbc.co.uk/worldservice) and Voice of America (website: www.voa.gov) can be received. From time to time the frequencies change and the most up-to-date can be found online.

Passport/Visa

	Passport Required?	Visa Required?	Return Ticket Required?
Full British	Yes	No	No
Australian	Yes	No	No
Canadian	Yes	No	No
USA	Yes	No	No
Other EU	Yes/1	No	No
Japanese	Yes	No	No

Note: *Regulations and requirements may be subject to change at short notice, and you are advised to contact the appropriate diplomatic or consular authority before finalising travel arrangements. Details of these may be found at the head of this country's entry. Any numbers in the chart refer to the footnotes below.*

Note: On 25 March 2001 Norway became a signatory to the 1995 **Schengen Agreement**. For further details about passport/visa regulations within the Schengen area see the introductory section *How to Use this Guide*.
PASSPORTS: Passport valid for at least three months beyond the intended period of stay required by all.
Note: In some circumstances, some nationals of EU or EEA countries may travel to Norway for touristic purposes with a valid national ID card *only if issued in their home country*. There are also circumstances when nationals of EU or EEA countries, plus certain other nationals, may travel to Norway with a passport that only needs to be valid during the duration of their stay and not beyond this intended period. However, since regulations are constantly changing, it is advised that all nationals contact their nearest Embassy/Consulate for further details since this passport exemption is not guaranteed and entry may be refused.
VISAS: Required by all except the following for stays of up to three months:
(a) nationals shown in the chart above;
(b) nationals of Andorra, Argentina, Bermuda (only holders of BDTC (Bermuda) passports), Bolivia, Brazil, Brunei, Bulgaria, Chile, Costa Rica, Croatia, El Salvador, Guatemala, Honduras, Hong Kong (SAR), Israel, Korea (Rep), Liechtenstein, Macau (SAR), Malaysia, Mexico, Monaco, New Zealand, Nicaragua, Panama, Paraguay, Romania, San Marino, Singapore, Switzerland, Uruguay, Vatican City and Venezuela;
(c) nationals of Nordic countries (including Årland, Faroe Islands, Greenland and Iceland).
Types of visa and cost: A uniform type of visa, the *Schengen* visa, is issued for tourist, business and private visits. The cost of a visa is £25 but prices are subject to frequent change against the exchange rate. Fee is payable when visa is issued. Enquire at the nearest Embassy for further details.
Note: Spouses and children of EU or EEA nationals (providing spouse's/dependent's passport and the original marriage certificate are produced), and nationals of some other countries, receive their visas free of charge (enquire at Embassy for details).
Validity: Up to three months in any six-month period. For renewal or extension, apply to Embassy.
Application to: Consulate (or Consular section at Embassy); see *Contact Addresses* section. If applying in the UK and living within the London area, all applications *must* be lodged in person at the Embassy. Travellers visiting just one *Schengen* country should apply to the Consulate of that country; travellers visiting more than one *Schengen* country should apply to the Consulate of the country chosen as the main destination or the country they will enter first (if they have no main destination).
Application requirements: (a) Valid passport with at least one blank page (this should not be submitted until the applicant is informed that a visa has been granted). (b) One completed application form. (c) Two recent passport-size photos. (d) Fee, payable in cash (exact money only), cheque supported by a cheque card or postal order (visa fees are non-refundable and payable on submission of the visa application). (e) Further documentation such as a letter of invitation, proof of accommodation or a letter from an employer explaining nature and duration of stay may be required, depending on purpose of visit. (f) Evidence of sufficient funds for stay (recent original bank statement, travellers cheques or credit card with credit limit statement; cash not accepted). (g) Parental consent for minors (under 18 years of age). (h) Evidence of occupation/student status. If unemployed, social security booklet must be submitted.
Working days required: Applicants should usually wait two weeks to receive a response to their application. The total length of processing time depends on individual circumstances. Applications should therefore be lodged several weeks before the proposed journey.
Temporary residence: Apply to Embassy for residence and work permit if the stay exceeds three months.

Money

Currency: Norwegian Krone (NOK) = 100 øre. Notes are in denominations of NOK1000, 500, 200, 100 and 50. Coins are in denominations of NOK20, 10, 5 and 1, and 50 øre.
Currency exchange: Eurocheque cards allow encashment of personal cheques. ATMs are widely available.
Credit & debit cards: All major credit and debit cards are widely accepted. Check with your credit or debit card company for details of merchant acceptability and other services which may be available.
Travellers cheques: Accepted in banks, hotels, shops and by airlines.
Currency restrictions: The import of local and foreign currency is unlimited. The export of local currency is limited to NOK5000. The export of foreign currency is unlimited, provided proof is shown that the currency was imported or obtained by conversion of other currencies.
Exchange rate indicators: The following figures are included as a guide to the movements of the Norwegian Krone against Sterling and the US Dollar:

Date	Feb '04	May '04	Aug '04	Nov '04
£1.00=	12.76	12.16	12.36	11.59
$1.00=	7.01	6.80	6.71	6.23

Banking hours: Mon-Wed and Fri 0815-1530 (1500 in summer), Thurs 0815-1800.

Duty Free

The following items can be imported into Norway without incurring customs duty by:
(a) Residents of European countries:
200 cigarettes or 250g of tobacco products and 200 leaves of cigarette paper (travellers over 18 years of age); 1l of spirits and 1l of wine or 2l of wine and 2l of beer (travellers over 20 years of age); other goods to the value of NOK1200; a small amount of perfume and eau de cologne.
(b) Residents of non-European countries:
400 cigarettes or 500g of tobacco products and 200 leaves of cigarette paper (travellers over 18 years of age); 1l of spirits and 1l of wine or 2l of wine and 2l of beer (travellers over 20 years of age); 50g of perfume and 50cl of eau de cologne; other goods (not to be resold) to the value of NOK3500.
Prohibited items: Spirits over 60 per cent volume (120 per cent proof), certain foodstuffs (including eggs, potatoes, meat, meat products, dairy products and poultry), narcotics, firearms and explosives.

Public Holidays

2005: Jan 1 New Year's Day. **Mar 24** Holy Thursday. **Mar 25** Good Friday. **Mar 28** Easter Monday. **May 1** May Day. **May 5** Ascension. **May 16** Whit Monday. **May 17** Constitution Day. **Dec 25-26** Christmas.
2006: Jan 1 New Year's Day. **Apr 13** Holy Thursday. **Apr 14** Good Friday. **Apr 17** Easter Monday. **May 1** May Day. **May 5** Ascension. **Jun 5** Whit Monday. **May 17** Constitution Day. **Dec 25-26** Christmas.

Health

	Special Precautions?	Certificate Required?
Yellow Fever	No	No
Cholera	No	No
Typhoid & Polio	No	N/A
Malaria	No	N/A

Note: *Regulations and requirements may be subject to change at short notice, and you are advised to contact your doctor well in advance of your intended date of departure. Any numbers in the chart refer to the footnotes below.*

Other risks: *Hepatitis C* may be present. *Rabies* is only present on the islands of Svalbard.
Health care: There are reciprocal health agreements with most European countries. The agreement with the UK allows free hospital in-patient treatment and ambulance travel on presentation of a UK passport. The cost of other treatment (including tooth extractions) may be partially refunded under the Norwegian social insurance scheme. Before leaving Norway, receipts should be presented at the social insurance office (*Trygdekasse*) of the district where treatment was carried out. Chemists are called *Apotek*. Standards of health care are high.

Travel - International

AIR: Norwegian air travel is served by *Braathens SAFE (BU)* (website: www.braathens.no) and *SAS Scandinavian Airlines (SK)* (website: www.sas.se), a Scandinavian airline. *Air France, British Airways, Finnair, Icelandair, KLM, Lufthansa, Northwest Airlines, Norwegian Air Shuttle, Ryanair* and *Swiss* also operate services to Norway.
Approximate flight times: From *London* to Oslo is one hour 45 minutes, to Bergen is one hour 40 minutes and to Stavanger is one hour 30 minutes.
From *New York* to Oslo is 10 hours 45 minutes (including stopover in London).
International airports: *Oslo International Airport (OSL)* (Gardermoen) (website: www.osl.no) is 47km (30 miles) north of Oslo. It is the largest land-based development project in Norway. The high-speed airport express trains *Flytoget* leave every 10 minutes to/from Oslo's central station (travel time - 20 minutes). Buses serving the airport include the *SL buses* and *Busseksspress* which stop in front of the terminal building and take approximately 45 minutes to Oslo. There is a new bus station for regional services located within walking distance of the terminal. Access by car is also facilitated by the construction of new roads (regional no. 174 from Jessheim) and the widening of two others (regional no. 120 from Erpestad and national no. 6 from Tangerud). There is a taxi rank at the terminal building. In addition to regular taxis, there are 'airport taxis', cheaper taxis which must be ordered in advance by groups of up to three people, and wheelchair taxis. Airport facilities include duty free shopping, banks/bureaux de change, restaurants and cafes, car hire, lost luggage, information kiosks as well as laundry/dry cleaning, shoe repair and key-cutting services.
Stavanger (SVG) (Sola) is 14.5km (9 miles) southwest of the city (travel time - 20-30 minutes). Airport facilities include duty free shops, bar, restaurant, snack bar, many shops, tourist information, post office, banks/bureaux de change, left luggage, lockers and car hire (*Avis, Budget, Hertz* and *InterRent/Europcar*). There is a coach to the Royal Atlantic Hotel, Jembaneveien 1. Bus no. 40 goes every 20 minutes (0620-2400) for a fare of approximately NOK21 (travel time - 30 minutes). Taxi services are available to the city with a surcharge after 2200 (travel time - 15 minutes).
Bergen (BGO) (Flesland) is 19km (12 miles) south of the city (travel time - 25 minutes). Airport facilities include left luggage, lockers, banks, bureaux de change, post office, duty free shops, bar, cafes, shops, tourist information, nursery and car hire (*Avis, Budget, Europcar* and *Hertz*). Bus (Flybussen) service leaves for the city every 20 minutes (0645-2130). Return is from various points in the city centre. Taxi services are available to the city for a fare of approximately NOK170 with a surcharge after 2200 (travel time - 25 minutes).
Departure tax: None.
SEA: The main passenger ports are Bergen, Kristiansand, Larvik, Oslo and Stavanger. The main sea routes from the UK, operated by *Fjord Line* and *DFDS Seaways* respectively, are from Newcastle to Bergen (travel time - 25 hours 30 minutes) and to Kristiansand (travel time - 19 hours). Services from Newcastle to Bergen via Stavangar are also operated by *Fjord Line*, a Norwegian line operating a number of fjord cruises within Norway (in UK tel: (0191) 296 1313; website: www.fjordline.co.uk). *Fjord Line* also operates services from Bergen to Hanstholm (Denmark). *Smyril Line* operates services from Bergen to Iceland via the Shetland Islands and the Faroe Islands in the summer (tel: (298) 345 900; fax: (298) 345 950; e-mail: office@smyril-line.no; website: www.smyril-line.no).
RAIL: Connections from the UK are from London via Dover/Ostend (via Denmark, Germany, The Netherlands and Sweden) or Harwich/Hook of Holland, or from Newcastle to Bergen via Stavanger. There are two principal routes to Sweden, with daytime and overnight trains from Copenhagen, Malmö and Stockholm.
Cheap Fares: Reduced fares on rail services have vastly increased the use and range of internal services. *Scanrail* cards allow five or 10 days within two months or 21 consecutive days' unlimited travel in Denmark, Finland, Norway and Sweden on railways and selected ferries, and a 50 per cent reduction on other ferry services. *InterRail* tickets are valid in Norway and are now also available for those aged over 26 years.
ROAD: The only international routes are from Sweden or Finland in the far north. Camping trailers up to 2.3m (7.5ft) wide, with number plates, are permitted on holiday visits. *Eurolines*, departing from Victoria Coach Station in London, serves destinations in Norway. For further information, contact *Eurolines* (tel: (08705) 143 219; fax: (01582) 400 694; website: www.eurolines.com) *or National Express* (tel: (08705) 808 080; website: www.nationalexpress.com).

Travel - Internal

AIR: Domestic flights are run by *Braathens ASA (BU), Norwegian Air Shuttle (DY), SAS Scandinavian Airlines (SK)* and *Widerøe's Flyveselskap (WF)*. A total of 50 airports with scheduled services exist in the fjord country of western Norway and along the remaining coast. Charter sea or land planes are available at most destinations. Reduced airfare tickets are available for families, children under 12 years of age (who pay half price), groups and pensioners. For further information, contact *Widerøe Flyveselskap A/S* (tel: 8100 1200; website: www.wideroe.no).
SEA: All coastal towns are served by ferries, catamarans and hydrofoils. The Hurtigruten (express) from Bergen to Kirkenes (near the Russian border) takes 11 days round trip, leaving daily and stopping at 35 ports on the west coast. Various ferry trips are available (half price in spring and autumn). There are also numerous companies operating cruises on Norway's spectacular fjords, one of which is *Norway Fjord Cruise AS*, Sagnefjordvegen 40, N-6863, Leikanger, Norway (tel: 5765 6999; fax: 5765 6990; e-mail: nfc@fjordcruise.no; website: www.fjordcruise.com).
RAIL: All services are run by *NSB* (*Norwegian State Railways*) (tel: 8150 0888 (dial '4' for an English-speaking operator); website: www.nsb.no). The main internal rail routes are: Oslo-Trondheim (*Dovre Line*); Trondheim-Bodø (*Nordland Railway*); Oslo-Bergen (*Bergen Railway*); and Oslo-Stavanger (*Sorland Railway*). There are also services to Charlottenburg (Stockholm) and Halden (Malmö) on

routes to Sweden. Seats on express trains must be reserved. There are buffet/restaurant cars on some trains, and sleepers on long-distance overnight services. Heavy luggage may be sent in advance. Children under four years of age travel free; children four to 14 years of age pay half fare. The *ScanRail Pass*, valid for all of Scandinavia, offers a substantial reduction. For further information, contact *NSB (Norwegian State Railways)* (telephone number above) or the Norwegian Tourist Board (see *Contact Addresses* section).
ROAD: Traffic drives on the right. The road system is of variable quality (especially under freezing winter conditions in the north), but supplemented by numerous car ferries across the fjords. **Bus**: Principal long-distance internal bus routes are from Bø (in Telemark) to Haugesund (travel time - eight hours); from Ålesund-Molde-Kristiansund to Trondheim (travel time - eight hours); and from Fauske to Kirkenes (travel time - four days) with links to the Bø line in the north. Inter-Nordic runs from Trondheim to Stockholm. There are also extensive regional local bus services, some of which are operated by companies with interests in the ferries. Visitors can contract *NOR-WAY Bussekspress AS* for seat reservations and route information (tel: 8154 4444; fax: 2200 1631; e-mail: ruteinformasjon@nor-way.no; website: www.nor-way.no). The official *Rutehefte* is a must for anyone using public transport, and gives extensive timetable information and maps of all bus, train, ferry and air routes. **Taxi**: In most cases, fares are metered. Taxis can be found at ranks or booked by telephone. **Car hire**: Available in airports and most towns, but costly; in general, problems of cost and parking make public transport more practical and convenient. It is also possible to hire bicycles. **Regulations**: The minimum age for driving is 18. Tolls, ranging from NOK5-50, are charged on certain cross-country roads, underwater tunnels and in certain cities such as Bergen, Oslo and Trondheim. There are severe penalties for drink-driving and illegal parking. Seat belts are compulsory. Children under 12 years of age must travel in the back of the car. It is obligatory for all vehicles to drive with dipped headlights at all times, even on the brightest summer day. This includes motorcycles and mopeds. Carrying spare headlight bulbs is recommended. Speed limits are 80 to 90kph (49 to 56mph) outside built-up areas and 50kph (31mph) in built-up areas. Snow chains or studded winter tyres are advised during the winter. Petrol stations are numerous, although tourist are only able to use credit cards in some of them. The contact for AIT (Alliance Internationale de Tourisme) is the Norwegian Automobile Association (NAF), PO Box 6682 Etterstad, 0609 (tel: 2234 1400; fax: 2233 1372; e-mail: medlemsservice@naf.no; website: www.naf.no). **Documentation**: International Driving Permit or national driving licence and log book are required. A Green Card is strongly recommended (for those with more than Third Party cover on their domestic policy). Without it, visitors with motor insurance in their own countries are allowed the minimum legal cover in Norway; the Green Card tops this up to the level of cover provided by the visitor's own policy. The maximum legal blood to alcohol ratio is 0.5 per cent.
URBAN: Good public transport systems operate in the main towns. Oslo has bus, rail, metro and tramway services. Tickets are pre-purchased and self-cancelled, and there is one hour's free transfer between any of the modes. Meters on taxis are obligatory.
Travel times: The following chart gives approximate travel times (in hours and minutes) from **Oslo** to other major cities/towns in Norway.

	Air	Road	Rail
Bergen	**0.35**	**9.00**	**8.00**
Kristiansand	**0.30**	**5.00**	**5.00**
Lillehammer	**0.20**	**3.00**	**2.30**
Stavanger	**0.35**	**7.00**	**8.00**
Tromsø	**1.40**	**20.00**	**-**
Trondheim	**0.40**	**10.00**	**8.00**

Accommodation

HOTELS: First-class hotels are to be found all over the country. Facilities in all establishments are classified, as hotels must come up to official high standards; for example, there must be a reception service, dining room, and a minimum of 30 rooms, each with full bath or shower. Many hotels are still family-run establishments. Full *en pension* terms are available to guests staying at the same establishment for at least three to five days. Hotels usually allow a reduction on the same *en pension* rate for children according to age. This reduction may only apply when the child concerned occupies an extra bed in the parents' room. There are several schemes which offer visitors reduced rates in selected hotels. A *Fjord Pass* (which covers two adults with special concessions for children under 15 years of age and is available from the Norwegian Tourist Board in the UK) is accepted by 250 hotels in the period one May to 30 September; reductions of 20 per cent or more are possible. The *Nordic Passepartout* is a pan-Scandinavian card accepted by over 50 hotels in Norway in the main summer period and at weekends; the visitor's fifth night is free. A *Scandinavian Bonus Pass* (which covers two adults with special concessions for children under 16 years of age) is accepted by 45 hotels in Norway between 15 May and 1 September and at weekends during winter; a *Scanrail* railway pass will also be accepted. *Scandinavian Hotel Express* is a travel club which enables visitors to have reductions of 50 per cent in certain hotels. Roughly 50 per cent of establishments belong to the Norwegian Hospitality Association, PO Box 5465, Majorstua, 0305 Oslo (tel: (22) 2308 8620; fax: (22) 2308 8621; e-mail: firmapost@rbl.no; website: www.rbl.no). **Grading**: There is no grading system, but establishments designated *turisthotel* or *høyfjellshotell* must meet specified standards.
GUESTHOUSES AND MOUNTAIN LODGES: Guest houses (*pensjonat*) and mountain lodges are generally smaller in size and offer less elaborate facilities than hotels, although many establishments can offer the same standard as those officially listed as hotels. Further information is available from *Bed & Breakfast Norway AS*, PO Box 92, N-6659 Rindal (tel: 9923 7799; fax: 9603 5654; e-mail: rominorg@online.no; website: www.bbnorway.com).
FARMHOUSE HOLIDAYS: These are working farms and anyone who wants to can join in the work, but guests are at liberty to plan their own day, and the hosts will generally be able to suggest tours, excursions and other activities. Contact the Norwegian Tourist Board for further information. The tour operator *Trollsykling* offers many farmhouse holidays, and a programme printed in English, German and Norwegian is available from *Trollsykling A/S*, PO Box 373, Elvegaten 19, 2602 Lillehammer (tel: 6128 9970; fax: 6126 9250; e-mail: info@norske-bygdeopplevelser.no; website: www.norske-bygdeopplevelser.no).
SELF-CATERING: Chalets, log cabins and apartments are available for rent by groups and will generally work out less expensive per head than other kinds of holiday. Most chalets have electric lighting, heating and hot plates; some have kerosene lamps, calor gas for cooking and wood fires, while water will often have to be fetched from a nearby well or stream. Chalets are grouped near a central building which may contain such facilities as a cafe, lounges, TV rooms, sauna, a grocer's shop, and in some cases a swimming pool. All chalets and apartments are regularly inspected by responsible rental firms. Bookings can be made by writing to various firms. *Den Norske Hytteformidling A/S* organises chalet holidays all over Norway, with full board or self-catering. Contact PO Box 309, 0103 Oslo (tel: 8154 4270; e-mail: novasol@novasol.com; website: www.novasol.com). Further information can also be obtained from the *Fjordline* office in the UK (tel: (0191) 296 1313; fax: (0191) 296 1540; e-mail: fjordline.uk@fjordline.com; website: www.fjordline.com); *or* the *Norwegian Hospitality Association* in Norway (tel: 2308 8620; fax: 2308 8621; e-mail: firmapost@rbl.no; website: www.rbl.no).
RORBU HOLIDAYS: A *rorbu* is a hut or shelter used by fishermen during the winter cod-fishing season. Equipped with all the necessary facilities, these are leased to holidaymakers during the summer, providing an inexpensive form of accommodation. They will often be actually over the water. Catching your own fish will further reduce the cost of the holiday. For more information on Rorbu holidays, contact *Destinasjon Lofoten*, PO Box 210, 8301 Svolvær (tel: (76) 069 800; fax: (76) 073 001; e-mail: tourist@lofoten-tourist.no; website: www.lofoten-tourist.no).
CAMPING/CARAVANNING: Offsite camping is permitted in uninhabited areas (not lay-bys), but fires are illegal in field or woodland areas between 15 April and 15 September. Farmers must be asked for permission for farmland camping. Further details and a manual are available from the Norwegian Automobile Association (NAF) (see *Road* section for contact details). **Grading**: There are over 1000 authorised sites in Norway, classified according to standards and amenities from **1-** to **5-star** camps, with charges varying accordingly. Notice of available amenities is posted in each camp.
YOUTH HOSTELS: There are some 100 youth hostels spread all over Norway, some of which are open all year round. Others are in apartment houses attached to schools or universities and are open only during the summer season. Sleeping bags can be hired if necessary. Groups must always make advance bookings. All are welcome, but members of the Norwegian Youth Hostel Association (NUH), or similar associations in other countries, have priority. International membership cards can be bought at most youth hostels. Hostels vary from **1-** to **3-star** establishments. Breakfast is usually NOK50-60. Detailed information can be obtained from the Tourist Board's Camping/YH list, or direct from *Norske Vandrerhjem*, Torggata 1, N-0181 Oslo (tel: 2313 9300; fax: 2313 9350; e-mail: hostels@vandrerhjem.no; website: www.vandrehjem.no).

Resorts & Excursions

Norway's scenery is its main attraction, particularly the fjords of the southwest and the **North Cape** (*Nordkapp*) which is a popular spot from which to observe the Midnight Sun of midsummer. However, the principal cities, among them **Oslo** (the capital), **Bergen** and **Trondheim**, offer a good choice of museums, historical sites and architectural interest for the visitor. The often mountainous inland countryside is ideal for those in search of true wilderness. Unless winter sport is the reason for visiting the country, its appeal is strongest in the months between May and September.
Population is sparse outside the main centres, but Norway is sufficiently large and regionally diverse to warrant geographical division here. There are five defined regions: **Southern Norway** (including Oslo); **Fjordland and the Southwest**; the uplands of **Oppland and Hedmark**; **Central Norway**; and the arctic **North**.

SOUTHERN NORWAY

OSLO: Oslo, which celebrated its millennium in the year 2000, is Norway's most populous district, providing a home for more than one-tenth of the country's inhabitants in a mere 700th of its total area. For all this, urban and industrial development only occupies one-eighth of the land within the city boundaries, the rest consisting mainly of woods, islands in **Oslo Fjord**, and lakes.
The city has a strong arts culture, with a good choice of museums and galleries. The **Munch Museum** is the main draw among these, others include the **National Gallery**; the **Norwegian Museum of Applied Arts**; the **Thor Heyerdahl Kon-Tiki Museum** and the **Norwegian Folk Museum**, both on Bygdøy Island to the west of the city centre; the **Viking Ships Museum**; **Oslo City Museum**; and the **Norwegian Home Front Museum**, which tells the story of the country's occupation during World War II. The **Ibsen Museum** was the playwright's home prior to his death in 1906.
Away from the immediate city centre, the **Holmenkollen ski jumping complex** with its **Museum of Skiing** is popular, as are the 12th-century Cistercian monastery ruins on **Hovedøya**, a short boat trip from the harbour. About 4km (2.5 miles) to the east of the city centre lies **Østensjøvannet**, a lakeside bird sanctuary.
Principal architectural interest in Oslo focuses on the **Kongelige Slott** (Royal Palace), **Stortinget** (Parliament Building), the **Cathedral** and **Åkershus Castle**. Boat trips on the fjord are readily available, and the main shopping area is along **Karl Johansgate**, which runs from the **Central Station** to the Royal Palace. Guided city bus tours operate year round.
Oslo's entertainment centres include the **Norwegian National Theatre**; the **New Theatre**; the **Norwegian Opera House**; **Konserthuset** (the Concert House); and **Oslo Spektrum**, the main rock and pop concert venue. Norway's prime exhibition centre is at **Lillestrøm**, one of the stops with the flytrain to Oslo (website: www.messe.no).
THE OSLO FJORD: Surrounding **Oslo Fjord** are the *Fylker* (counties) of **Åkershus**, **Buskerud**, **Østfold** and **Telemark**, all within a day trip of the capital. These are dotted with historic and prehistoric sites of varying importance, along with manor houses, stone churches (most are built of wood in Norway) and fortifications. Among the principal towns in the region, outside the capital, is **Fredrikstad**, the attractions of which include a picturesque Old Town and 17th-century **Kongsten Fort**. Close to **Lillestrøm**, to the northeast of Oslo, is **Sørumsand**, which boasts the **Tertitten narrow-gauge railway and museum**. The oldest building in the industrialised town of **Drammen** is the **Skoger Old Church**, which dates from 1200. **Kongsberg** is particularly well endowed with museums, among them the **Silver Collection**; the **Royal Mint Museum**; and the **Arms Factory Museum**. The **Saggrenda Silver Mine** is 8km (5 miles) from Kongsberg.
On the western shore of Oslo Fjord lies **Sandefjord**, with its **Whaling Museum** (Norway is one of just three countries worldwide still involved in commercial whaling).
Porsgrunn, near to Sandefjord, has long been a centre of the porcelain industry, the **Town Museum** tells its story, while the **Porcelain Factory** is open to visits by appointment. At nearby **Skien**, birthplace of Ibsen, his childhood home contains a multimedia exhibition about the playwright. The navigable **Telemark Waterway** links Skien with the interior via a system of canals.
South of Oslo, an unusual wooden bridge over the E18 motorway, built to the 1502 design of Leonardo da Vinci and officially unveiled in October 2001, is well worth seeing.

FJORDLAND AND THE SOUTHWEST

Unquestionably, Fjordland and the Southwest is Norway's most important tourist area, due to its scenery. Many visitors arrive on cruise ships working their way north along the coast from **Stavanger** via **Haugesund** to **Bergen** and the best known fjord of all, **Sognefjorden**. **Førdefjorden**, **Hardanger Fjord** and **Nordfjord** are among other notable scenic attractions in the region.
Near **Sogndal**, at the head of Sognefjorden, lies **Urnes**, whose wooden stave-built church is a UNESCO World Heritage Site.
Inland are the **Hardangervidda Mountains**, which rise to over 1700m (5600ft) and incorporate the **National Park** of the same name. To the north of Sognefjorden lies Europe's

biggest glacier, the **Jostedalsbreen**, and its surrounding National Park of the same name. Immediately to the east of this area is the **Jotunheimen National Park**, which contains Norway's highest mountain, **Galdhøpiggen** (2469m/8100ft). Away from the fjords, on the southern holiday coastline of **Vest-Agder**, **Fylke**, is the port of **Kristiansand**, from which ferries serve Denmark and the UK.

BERGEN: Former Hanseatic port and medieval Norwegian capital, the city's appeal centres on the Hanseatic **Bryggen** harbour-side district, a UNESCO World Heritage Site with many buildings dating from the 17th century and earlier. Cable cars take visitors to the summit of **Mount Ulriken**, and a funicular railway climbs **Mount Fløyen** to give outstanding views over the city and coastline. Museums abound, and there is a large aquarium. Additionally, a broad choice of boat excursions plies the waters around the city, which is Norway's busiest tourist destination.

STAVANGER

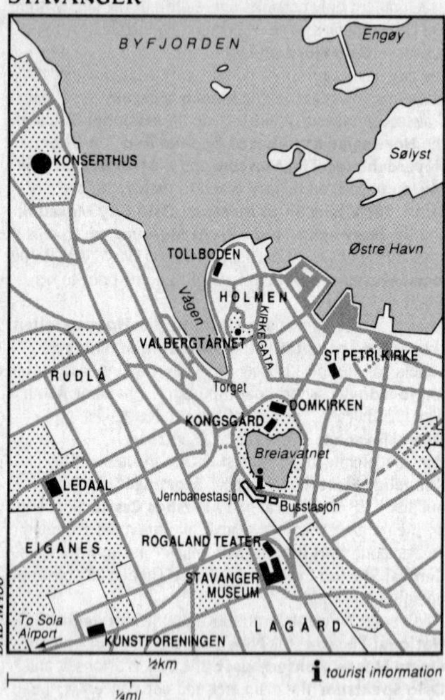

STAVANGER: Centre of the country's North Sea oil industry, Stavanger is Norway's fourth largest city after Oslo, Bergen and Trondheim, with 96,000 inhabitants. **Old Stavanger** is Europe's largest collection of wooden buildings. Other attractions here include the **Norwegian Oil Museum**, the unique **Fish Cannery Museum** (complete with sprat-smokehouse), and the **Rogaland Art Gallery**.

OPPLAND AND HEDMARK

Central southern Norway, comprising Oppland and Hedmark, is a land of mountains, spectacular glacial valleys, including **Gudbrandsdal** (one of Norway's longest and most beautiful), and high plateaux.

Lightly populated throughout, apart from the larger centres of **Elverum**, **Hamar**, **Kongsvinger** and **Lillehammer** (site of the 1994 Winter Olympics), this is a region of small settlements suitable for those seeking solitude and wilderness – or winter sports facilities. Kongsvinger's *Festning* (fortress) dates from the 17th century, but never came under Swedish attack. To the north is the **Dovrefjell National Park** – mythical home of the Mountain King (*Dovregubben*) immortalised by Grieg, and where musk oxen are occasionally spotted roaming wild on the high plateau.

LILLEHAMMER: The country's biggest skiing and winter sports centre, offering both Alpine and Nordic disciplines, Lillehammer stands on the banks of the **Mjøsa Lake**, Norway's largest with an area of 362 sq km (140 sq miles), and which reputedly conceals a 'Loch Ness-type' monster. Among non-winter-specific attractions in the town are the **Norwegian Olympic Museum**, the **Maihaugen Open Air Museum** (which features a collection of over 170 historic buildings from the Gudbrandsdal area), and the **Art Museum**, with its extensive Norwegian collections.

HAMAR: At the northern end of the Mjøsa Lake, Hamar contains the **Hedmark Museum**, dedicated to the medieval period. There is also a **Museum of Holography**, unique in Norway, and the **Olympic Hall**, which staged skating events during the 1994 Winter Olympics. The **Cathedral**, restored in 1954, has origins dating back to the 11th century dawn of Norwegian Christianity.

CENTRAL NORWAY

Like most of the rest of Norway, the central region is largely mountainous, but the peaks do not rise as high as those of the southwest. This is the area where the country narrows on a west to east axis, and the Swedish border is never far away. Mid-Norway consists of three large *Fylker*: **Møre og Romsdal**; **Sør-trøndelag**; and **Nord-trøndelag**, between them home to about one-seventh (635,000) of the Norwegian population. A quarter of them live in and around **Trondheim**, the country's third largest city. It lies on the southern shore of **Trondheimsfjorden**, which although not spectacular scenically when compared to the fjords of the southwest, is one of the largest, stretching more than 70km (44 miles) inland. Other larger towns include **Ålesund**, **Kristiansund**, **Molde** (which stages a major annual summer international jazz festival), **Namsos** and **Steinkjer**.

Outside Trondheim, by far the most important attractions in the region are the former copper-mining town of **Røros** to the east, and the historically significant **Stiklestad**, a short distance south of Steinkjer. It was at the latter that Christianity first came to Norway, when St Olav met his end during a battle in 1030. To the south of Trondheim, the mountain village of **Oppdal** is an important skiing resort.

TRONDHEIM: Founded in 997 AD as *Kaupangr*, and later called *Nidaros*, Norway's early capital has a number of major attractions, not least the **Nidarosdomen Cathedral**, which dates from the late 11th century. Built over St Olav's grave, it has been a centre of pilgrimage since medieval times. Elsewhere, the **Ringve Museum** is famous for its collection of rare historic musical instruments, while the **Trøndelag Folk Museum** incorporates the ruins of a 12th-century castle. **Stiftsgården**, the Trondheim palace of the Norwegian Royal Family, is a fine 18th-century wooden building in the city centre. Across the river stands the **Kristiansten Festning** fortress. The former island monastery of **Munkholmen** in the fjord is a popular boat excursion.

RØROS: One of just four UNESCO World Heritage Sites in Norway, Røros is a small but picturesque mountain town near the Swedish border; from the 17th century until the 1980s it had been a copper mining and smelting settlement. Principal attractions are the **Old Town**, the wooden **church** and the **Mining Museum**. Close to Røros is **Olavsgruve**, an early mine now open to visitors.

THE NORTH

Although encompassing only three *Fylker*, **Finnmark**, **Nordland** and **Troms**, this vast and wild region extends for more than 1200km (750 miles) northwards from **Nord-trøndelag** across the **Arctic Circle** to the **Nordkapp** (North Cape).

Less than 500,000 people inhabit the region, around one-tenth of whom are of the Sami (Lapp) ethnic group. Their 'capital' is at **Karasjok** in Finnmark.

Mo-i-Rana is about 80km (50 miles) south of the Arctic Circle, where there is a visitor centre (**Polarsirkelsenteret**) by the main E6 road. Further north are the coastal cities of **Bodø**, **Hammerfest** and **Tromsø**, while **Alta** (with its nearby UNESCO-listed **prehistoric cave carvings**), and **Kautokeino** (traditionally Norway's coldest town), lie inland. **Kirkenes**, on the Russian border, offers the **Borderland Museum** and a gallery devoted to the work of John Savios, a Sami artist.

The North Cape is a major attraction: people come to observe the summer Midnight Sun. The **North Cape Hall**, built into the side of a mountain, and with panoramic views out to sea, is the main visitor centre here.

TROMSØ: The largest centre in northern Norway, with a population of nearly 50,000, Tromsø spectacularly straddles **Tromsøy Sound**. It boasts the world's most northerly brewery, and even a professional football team. The **Tromsø Museum**, 4km (2.5 miles) from the city centre, features archaeological and historical displays, while the **City Museum** concentrates on development of the settlement. The 43m (140ft) high **Tromsø Bridge** across the Sound affords good views of the surroundings.

BODØ: The **Norwegian National Aviation Centre** is a prime attraction here, as is a climb for the views from **Rønvikfjell Mountain**, which rises 3km (1.9 miles) outside the city centre. The world's most powerful maelstrom, **Saltstraumen**, and a multimedia visitor centre dedicated to the phenomenon, are 33km (21 miles) east of Bodø.

MO-I-RANA: Northern Norway's third largest, and most southerly town of any size is a popular stopping off point for visitors keen to explore the coastline, the mountains and nearby glaciers. It also offers the **Nordland Museum of Nature**.

Sport & Activities

Norway's dramatic scenery and extensive wilderness areas offer scope for a variety of exciting activities.

Hiking: In Norway, hikers are well catered for. The Norwegian Mountain Touring Association (DNT) (tel: 2282 2800; fax: 2282 2801; e-mail: info@turistforeningen.no; website: www.turistforeningen.no) offers guided trips, and maintains more than 300 mountain huts, both staffed and unstaffed. Membership can be bought at a DNT office, a hut or at tourist offices. The DNT also sells maps, and provides information. Glaciers are another attraction for outdoor enthusiasts. The largest mainland glacier in Europe is at *Jostedalsbreen*, near Stryn. Daily **glacier walks** are organised in summer in the company of experienced guides. It is important to remember never to venture onto a glacier without an experienced guide. For information about organised glacier walks, contact the glacier centre at Jostedalsbreen (tel: 5787 7200; fax: 5787 7201; e-mail: post@jostedalsbre.no; website: www.fjordinfo.no *or* www.jostedalsbre.no) *or* consult the following for glacier tours (tel: 5787 6800; website: www.bre.no).

Wintersports: Norway claims to be the birthplace of **skiing**. The country has about 30,000km (18,750 miles) of marked ski trails, winding their way through unspoiled scenery. Both cross-country and downhill skiing are available from November until the end of May. Although skiing is at its best just before Easter, when the days are getting longer, it is possible to ski for long hours in the winter, since many of the tracks are illuminated. In summer, it is possible to go skiing in several parts of Norway. For further information about summer skiing, contact Stryn Sommerskisenter (tel: 5787 4040; e-mail: info@stryneffjellet.com; website: www.strynefjellet.com).

Other: Horseriding holidays are becoming more popular. There are riding schools and clubs throughout the country with horses for hire and instruction provided. Also a number of hotels keep horses. Despite its often mountainous terrain, Norway is a popular destination for **cycling** holidays. Many old roads have been made into cycling routes. For further information, contact Sykkelturisme i Norge, SND, PO Box 3132 Handelstorget, N3706, Skien (fax: 3352 9955; e-mail: info@bike-norway.com; website: www.bike-norway.com). **Fishing** is popular on Norway's many inland waters and surrounding sea. There are over 100 salmon rivers flowing into the fjords, where reasonably priced sport is offered. A national fishing licence is necessary, obtainable from post offices. A permit is required for freshwater fishing. Oslo (Bogstad links), Stokke (between Tønsberg and Sandefjord) and Meland (36km/22 miles north of Bergen in the fjord landscape by the Herdlafjord) all have 18-hole **golf** courses; there are shorter courses in Bergen, Hamar, Kristiansund, Sarpsborg and Trondheim. Altogether, Norway has 25 18-hole golf courses. Most clubs are open to visitors. The Norwegian Golf Federation can provide further information (tel: 2273 6620; fax: 2273 6621; e-mail: golfforbundet@nif.idrett.no; website: www.golfforbundet.no). A number of resort hotels have their own **tennis** courts. A number of hotels, campsites and chalets have **boats** for use by visitors on the coast and inland waters. Hotels and campsites located near stretches of water often hire out equipment for **windsurfing** or **water-skiing** and offer instruction. Norway's coast and inland waters are ideal for **bathing** in warm months. There are several specially designated beaches for **naturists**.

Social Profile

FOOD & DRINK: Breakfasts are often enormous with a variety of fish, meat, cheese and bread served from a cold buffet with coffee and boiled or fried eggs. Many hotels and restaurants serve lunch from a *koldtbord* (cold table), with smoked salmon, fresh lobster, shrimp and hot dishes. Open sandwiches are topped with meat, fish, cheese and salads. Other dishes include roast venison, ptarmigan in cream sauce, wild cranberries, *multer* (a berry with a unique flavour), *lutefisk* (a hot, highly flavoured cod fish) and herring prepared in various ways.

Aquavit (schnapps) is a popular drink, but in general alcohol is limited and expensive, although beer and wine are generally served in restaurants. Bars have table and counter service. Licensing laws are strict and alcohol is sold only by the State through special monopoly. Licensing hours are also enforced.

NIGHTLIFE: Several hotels and restaurants in Oslo stage cabaret programmes and floor shows. Venues change so it is best to check in the local newspaper. Theatres, cinemas, nightclubs and discos are located in major centres. Resorts have dance music, and folk dancing is popular.

SHOPPING: Most towns and resorts have a shop where typical Norwegian handicrafts are on sale. Silversmiths and potteries are numerous and worth visiting. Traditional items include furs, printed textiles, woven articles, knitwear, woodcarving, silver, enamel, pewter, glass and porcelain. Tax-free cheques can be obtained from any of the 2500 shops carrying the sticker 'Tax free for tourists'. These shops save visitors 11 to 18 per cent of the price paid by residents. VAT refunds are paid in cash at airports, ferries, cruise ships and border crossings. **Shopping hours**: Mon-Wed and Fri 0900-1700/1800, Thurs 0900-2000, Sat 0900-1300/1500.

SPECIAL EVENTS: For a full list, contact the Norwegian Tourist Board (see *Contact Addresses* section). The following is a selection of special events occurring in Norway in 2005:

Jan 13-16 *International Film Festival*, Tromsø.

Jan 20-23 *Polarjazz*. **Jan 26-30** *Northern Lights Festival*, Tromsø. **Feb 10-13** *Winter Arts Festival* (music, theatre, art exhibitions), Narvik. **Feb 15-19** *Rorosmartnan*. **Mar 5-12** *Finnmarkslopet*. **Mar 12-13** *Holmenkollen Ski Festival*. **Mar 13-20** *Borealis - Bergen Contemporary Music Festival*. **Mar 20-28** *Easter Festival*. **Apr 4-10** *Snowjam*. **Apr 30** *Svalbard Ski Marathon*. **May 25-Jun 5** *Bergen International Festival*. **Jun 3-13** *Oslo Festival*. **Jun 4** *Norwegian Mountain Marathon*. **Jun 8-11** *The Great Norwegian Humor Festival*. **Jun 8-12** *Viking Festival*. **Jun 17-20** *Norwegian Wood*, music festival. **Jun 18** *Midnight Sun Marathon*, Tromsø. **Jul 29-20** *Cherry Festival*. **Aug 4-14** *Peer Gynt Festival*, Vinstra/Gala. **Aug 5-14** *Nordland Music Festival*. **Aug 11-14** *Mandal Seafood Festival*. **Aug 15-21** *Oslo Jazz Festival*. **Aug 18-26** *Norwegian International Film Festival*. **Aug 24-27** *Norwegian Food Festival*. **Dec 22-31** *Christmas in Lillehammer*.

SOCIAL CONVENTIONS: Normal courtesies should be observed. It is customary for the guest to refrain from drinking until the host toasts their health. Casual dress is normal. Lunch generally takes place between 1200 and 1300 and dinner usually takes place at 1700. It is customary for an invited guest to offer gifts to the host/hostess of a meal. Punctuality is expected if invited out for dinner. Smoking is prohibited in most public buildings and on public transport (although there are often special spaces for smokers to indulge in cafes, bars and restaurants. **Tipping**: It is not customary to tip taxi drivers. Waiters expect a tip of no more than 5 per cent of the bill; porters at airports and railway stations charge per piece of luggage. Hotel porters are tipped NOK5-10 according to the number of pieces of luggage.

Business Profile

ECONOMY: The Norwegian economy is dominated by its oil and gas industry, which accounts for nearly 20 per cent of GDP and 60 per cent of export earnings. There is little cultivable land in Norway, however many farmers breed livestock, combining this with forestry to supply Norway's numerous sawmills. Consequently, wood products and paper are both thriving industries. Offshore fishing has been in decline for some time, although a large number of fish farms have been established, making Norway by far the world's largest supplier of salmon. Heavy engineering industries, principally shipbuilding and machinery, have also declined (although Norway retains a large merchant fleet). Nonetheless, the country has sustained its economic prosperity outside the European Union (see below) through development of an exceptionally strong energy sector. As well as oil and gas, Norway has abundant hydroelectric resources: the development of these has allowed much-reduced overheads for heavy industries such as aluminium production while freeing oil and gas products for export. Norway has been a major oil and gas exporter since the mid-1970s, after discovering large deposits of both in the North Sea. Proven oil reserves are around 11 billion barrels (one-tenth of Saudi reserves and 1 per cent of the world total). Much of the income is invested in a fund, now worth over US$40 billion, for such time (perhaps 15-20 years) as the oil and gas last. The country also has deposits of various iron ores plus copper, lead and zinc, which feed the country's metallurgical and chemical industries. Recent years have seen the emergence of advanced technological industries.

The UK, Germany and Sweden are Norway's principal trading partners. Norway is a member of the European Free Trade Association (EFTA) and hence the so-called 'European Economic Area', which is an amalgam of EU and EFTA members united in a free-trade zone and created in 1991. Concern about the possible effects on the fishing and farming industries lay behind the Norwegians' decision – registered in two referendums, in 1973 and 1994 – to reject EU membership. Nonetheless, with the exception of these two industries, Norway enjoys a wholly liberalised trade regime with EU members, and conducts 70 per cent of its trade with the EU. Recent economic performance has been sluggish. Growth barely reached 1 per cent in 2001 and 2002. Inflation and unemployment in 2002 were 1.3 and 4 per cent respectively.

BUSINESS: Businesspeople are expected to dress smartly. Prior appointments are necessary. Norwegian businesspeople tend to be reserved and formal. English is widely spoken. Punctuality is essential. Calling cards are common. The best months for business visits are February to May and October to December. **Office hours**: Mon-Fri 0800-1600.

COMMERCIAL INFORMATION: The following organisation can offer advice: Innovation Norway, Drammensveien 40, 0104 Oslo (tel: (22) 002 500; fax: (22) 002 501; e-mail: hilde.sannerhaugen@invanor.no; website: www.ntc.no); *or* Innovation Norway, 5th Floor, Charles House, 5 Lower Regent Street, London SW1Y 4LR, UK (tel: (020) 7389 8800; fax: (020) 7973 0189; e-mail: london@ntc.no; website: www.norway.org.uk).

CONFERENCES/CONVENTIONS: Information is available from the Norwegian Tourist Board (see *Contact Addresses* section).

Climate

Coastal areas have a moderate climate owing to the Gulf Stream and North Atlantic Drift. Inland temperatures are more extreme with hot summers and cold winters (November to March). In general, the lowlands of the south experience colder winters and warmer summers than the coastal areas. Rain is distributed throughout the year with frequent inland snowfalls during the winter. The northern part of the country inside the Arctic Circle has continuous daylight at midsummer, and twilight all day during winter.

Required clothing: European according to the season. Light- to mediumweights are worn in summer. Warmer weights are required during the winter. Waterproofing is advisable throughout the year.

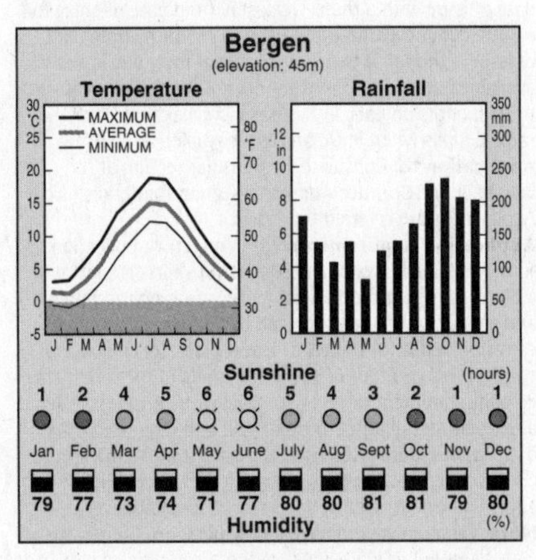

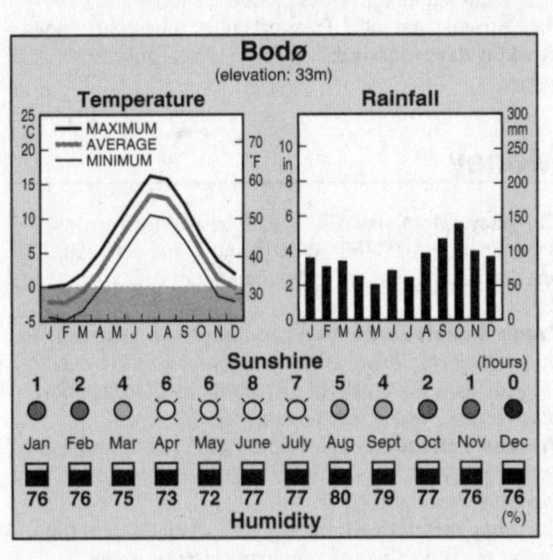

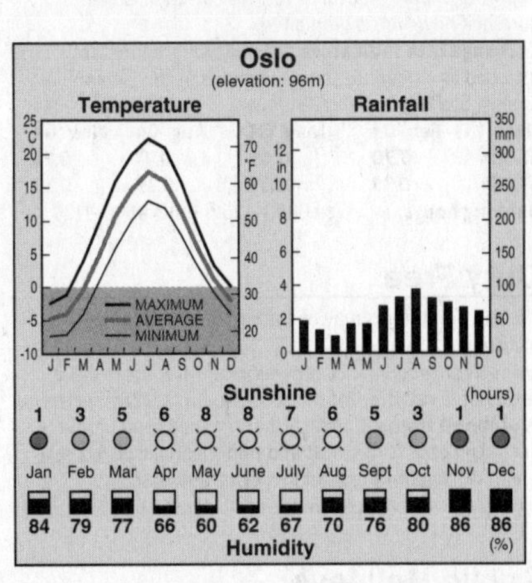

Oman

LATEST TRAVEL ADVICE CONTACTS

British Foreign and Commonwealth Office
Tel: (0870) 606 0290 Website: www.fco.gov.uk

US Department of State
Website: http://travel.state.gov/travel

Canadian Department of Foreign Affairs and Int'l Trade
Tel: (1 800) 267 8376 Website: www.dfait-maeci.gc.ca

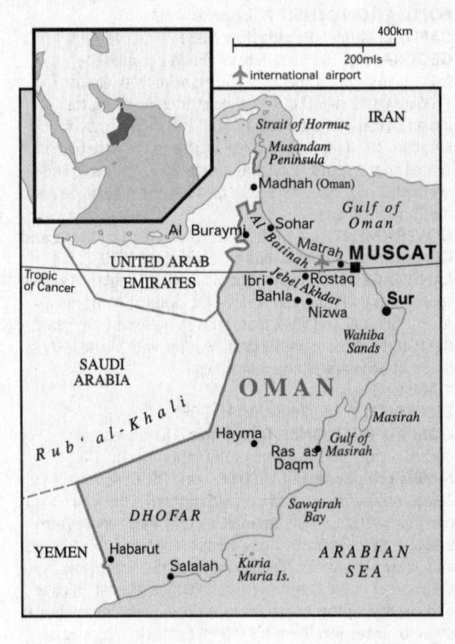

Location: Middle East, southeastern tip of Arabian Peninsula.

Country dialling code: 968.

Directorate General of Tourism
PO Box 550, Muscat, Postal Code 113, Sultanate of Oman
Tel: 771 7085 *or* 774 331/329. Fax: 771 4436/4213.
E-mail: dgt@mocioman.gov.om
Website: www.omantourism.gov.om

Oman Tourism
c/o Representation Plus, 11 Blades Court, 121 Deodar Road, London, SW15 2NU, UK
Tel: 020 8877 424. Fax: 020 8874 4219.
E-mail: oman@representationplus.co.uk
Website: www.omantourism.gov.om

Embassy of the Sultanate of Oman
167 Queen's Gate, London SW7 5HE, UK
Tel: (020) 7225 0001 *or* (0906) 550 8964 (recorded visa information; calls cost £1 a minute).
Fax: (020) 7589 2505 (commercial section).
Opening hours: Mon-Fri 0900-1530; 0900-1200 (visa section).

British Embassy
PO Box 185, Mina Al Fahal PC 116, Muscat, Sultanate of Oman
Tel: 609 000 (main).
Fax: 609 010 (general) *or* 609 012 (trade & investment section) *or* 609 011 (visa and consular section).
E-mail: enquiries.muscat@fco.gov.uk (general) *or* consular.staff@fco.gov.uk (consular).
Website: www.britishembassy.gov.uk/oman

Embassy of the Sultanate of Oman
2535 Belmont Road, NW, Washington, DC 20008, USA
Tel: (202) 387 1980. Fax: (202) 745 4933.
Also deals with enquiries from Canada.

Embassy of the United States of America
Jameat A'Duval Al Arabiya Street, Diplomatic Area of Al Khuwair (Shatti al-Qurum), Muscat, Sultanate of Oman
Tel: 698 989 ext. 203 *or* ext. 216/294 (visa section).
Fax: 699 771 (general enquiries) *or* 699 189 (visa section).
E-mail: aemctira@omantel.net.om
Website: www.usa.gov.om

TIMATIC CODES

Health	AMADEUS: **TI-DFT/MCT/HE** GALILEO/WORLDSPAN: **TI-DFT/MCT/HE** SABRE: **TIDFT/MCT/HE**
Visa	AMADEUS: **TI-DFT/MCT/VI** GALILEO/WORLDSPAN: **TI-DFT/MCT/VI** SABRE: **TIDFT/MCT/VI**

To access TIMATIC country information on Health and Visa regulations through the Computer Reservations System (CRS), type in the appropriate command line listed above.

Consulate of Canada
Street address: Moosa Abdul Rahman Building, Way No. 3109, Bldg No. 475, 2nd Floor, Ruwi, Muscat, Sultanate of Oman
Postal address: PO Box 1275, Muttrah 114, Sultanate of Oman
Tel: 791 738. Fax: 709 091.
E-mail: canada_consulate_oman@hotmail.com
The Canadian Embassy in Riyadh deals with enquiries relating to Oman (see ***Saudi Arabia*** **section).**

General Information

AREA: 309,500 sq km (119,500 sq miles).
POPULATION: 2,538,000 (official estimate 2002).
POPULATION DENSITY: 8.2 per sq km.
CAPITAL: Muscat. **Population**: 685,676 (2001).
GEOGRAPHY: The Sultanate of Oman occupies the southeastern tip of the Arabian Peninsula with almost 1700km (1062 miles) of coastline stretching along the Indian Ocean and the Arabian Gulf. It is bordered by the Kingdom of Saudi Arabia to the west and the Republic of Yemen to the south. The United Arab Emirates lies to the northwest of Oman and to the east lies the Arabian Sea and the Gulf of Oman.
GOVERNMENT: Sultanate since 1744. **Head of State and Government**: Sultan Qabus bin Sa'id since 1970.
LANGUAGE: Arabic is the official language. English is widely spoken. Swahili is also spoken by the population from East Africa. German and French are spoken by some hotel staff.
RELIGION: Predominantly Ibadi Muslim, with Shi'ite Muslim, Sunni Muslim and Hindu minorities.
TIME: GMT + 4.
ELECTRICITY: 220/240 volts AC, 50Hz.
COMMUNICATIONS: Telephone: IDD is available. Country code: 968. Outgoing international code: 00. **Mobile telephone:** GSM 900 network. The *Oman Telecommunications Company (Omantel)* is the local operator (website: www.omantel.net.om). **Fax:** Services are available from Omantel. There are fax facilities in most hotels and in the major cities. **Telegram:** Services are available at the counter in the Central Telegraph Office, Muscat. In case of difficulty, visitors may book calls through the international operator. **Internet:** There are Internet cafes in the cities of Nizwa and Muscat. ISPs include *Omantel* (website: www.omantel.net.om) and *WebOman* (website: www.weboman.com). **Post:** Airmail to Western Europe takes three to four days. **Press:** English-language newspapers include *The Oman Daily Observer* and *The Times of Oman*. **Radio:** BBC World Service (website: www.bbc.co.uk/worldservice) and Voice of America (website: www.voa.gov) can be received. From time to time the frequencies change and the most up-to-date can be found online.

Passport/Visa

	Passport Required?	Visa Required?	Return Ticket Required?
Full British	Yes	Yes/1	Yes
Australian	Yes	Yes/1	Yes
Canadian	Yes	Yes/1	Yes
USA	Yes	Yes/1	Yes
Other EU	Yes	Yes/1	Yes
Japanese	Yes	Yes/1	Yes

Note: *Regulations and requirements may be subject to change at short notice, and you are advised to contact the appropriate diplomatic or consular authority before finalising travel arrangements. Details of these may be found at the head of this country's entry. Any numbers in the chart refer to the footnotes below.*

PASSPORTS: Passport valid for at least six months required by all except the following:
(a) nationals of Bahrain, Kuwait, Qatar, Saudi Arabia and the United Arab Emirates holding national identity cards;
(b) holders of Macau (SAR) Travel Permit.
VISAS: Required by all except nationals of the Gulf Cooperation Council States.
(a) **1**. Nationals of the following countries may apply for a visa (at a cost of 6OR for single-entry visas and 10OR for multiple-entry visas) on arrival at Oman Seeb International Airport for a maximum stay of 14 days: Argentina, Australia, Bolivia, Brazil, Brunei Darussalam, Canada, Chile, Croatia, Ecuador, EU nationals (except Cyprus, Lithuania, Luxembourg, Malta and Slovenia), French Guiana, Iceland, Indonesia, Japan, Korea (Rep), Malaysia, Maldives, New Zealand, Norway, Paraguay, Peru, Seychelles, Singapore, South Africa, Surinam, Switzerland, Thailand, Ukraine, USA, Uruguay and Venezuela.
Note: (a) Any visitor arriving in Oman without a tourist or a sponsored visa will be refused entry. Visitors are not allowed to enter Oman by road unless their visa states such validity and a designated point of entry. A sponsored visa is obtainable from the Royal Oman Police Immigration Department. (b) Travellers who have resided in one of the Gulf Cooperation Council countries for at least one year and who hold a valid residence permit and labour card may obtain a tourist visa on arrival, provided they meet certain conditions regarding professional status. Contact Embassy/Consulate for further details. (c) For minors (under 18 years) travelling unaccompanied, a consent letter is required from one of their parents.
Types of visa and cost: Cost may vary according to nationality, but generally is as follows for tourist/business/sponsored visas: *Single-entry*: £12 (generally for all European and Latin American countries, and the USA; enquire at the Embassy/Consulate for specific details as certain countries may also be/not be eligible); £14 (other countries). *Multiple-entry* (see the list of countries eligible for discounted single-entry): £20. Visitors are advised to contact the embassy. Fees may be paid by cheque if application is made in person.
Validity: Single-entry: three months from date of issue with a one-month stay from date of entry for all European and Latin American countries, plus the USA and possible others (enquire at Embassy/Consulate); one month from date of issue with a three-week stay from date of entry for all other countries. Multiple-entry: 12 months from date of issue, although a two-year multiple-entry visa is also available for UK and USA passport holders, for stays of up to six months on each visit. Visas can be extended for the same periods when in Oman (fees payable).
Application to: Consulate (or Consular section at Embassy); see *Contact Addresses* section for details. Applications are referred to Muscat.
Application requirements: (a) Completed application form (preferably typed) and signed. (b) Valid passport with a blank page to affix the visa. (c) Fee; cash not accepted and cheques must be supported by a cheque guarantee card from bank. (d) Details of travel plans. (e) Evidence of employment or proof of sufficient funds for period of stay, eg bank statement or last two payslips. (f) Business letter, if applicable, detailing purpose of visit and requested travel date. (g) Self-addressed envelope with stamp sufficient to cover cost of posting passport and other documents if applying by post, sent by special or recorded delivery.
Note: Passengers who have a new passport, but whose visa is entered in a previous passport, should also carry their previous passport. Passports must have spare pages.
Working days required: Two fo five. Postal applications take longer.

Money

Currency: Omani Rial (OR) = 1000 baiza. Notes are in denominations of OR50, 20, 10, 5 and 1, and 500, 250, 200 and 100 baiza. Coins are in denominations of 50, 25, 10 and 5 baiza.
Credit & debit cards: American Express is accepted, as are other major credit cards. Check with your credit or debit card company for details of merchant acceptability and other services which may be available.
Travellers cheques: Easily exchanged. To avoid additional exchange rate charges, travellers are advised to take travellers cheques in US Dollars.
Currency restrictions: There are no restrictions on the import or export of local or foreign currency. Israeli currency, however, is prohibited.
Exchange rate indicators: The following figures are included as a guide to the movements of the Omani Rial against Sterling and the US Dollar:

Date	Feb '04	May '04	Aug '04	Nov '04
£1.00=	0.70	0.69	0.71	0.72
$1.00=	0.39	0.39	0.39	0.39

Banking hours: Sat-Wed 0800-1200, Thurs 0800-1130.

Duty Free

The following items may be imported into Oman without incurring customs duty:
Up to 2l of alcoholic beverages (non-Muslims only); a reasonable quantity of tobacco products; 227ml perfume.
Prohibited items: Narcotics, non-canned food products (including vegetables, fruit and non-alcoholic beverages), firearms (including toys and replicas) and obscene films/literature. Videos are subject to censorship.

Public Holidays

2005: Jan 1 New Year's Day. **Jan 21** Eid al-Adha (Feast of the Sacrifice). **Feb 10** Muharram (Islamic New Year). **Apr 21** Mouloud (Birth of the Prophet). **Sep 1** Leilat al-Meiraj (Ascension of the Prophet). **Nov 3-5** Eid al-Fitr (End of Ramadan). **Nov 18** National Day. **Nov 19** Birthday of HM Sultan Qaboos.
2006: Jan 1 New Year's Day. **Jan 13** Eid al-Adha (Feast of the Sacrifice). **Jan 31** Muharram (Islamic New Year). **Apr 11** Mouloud (Birth of the Prophet). **Aug 22** Leilat al-Meiraj (Ascension of the Prophet). **Oct 22-24** Eid al-Fitr (End of Ramadan). **Nov 18** National Day. **Nov 19** Birthday of HM Sultan Qaboos.
Note: Muslim festivals are timed according to local sightings of various phases of the moon and the dates given above are approximations. During the lunar month of Ramadan that precedes Eid al-Fitr, Muslims fast during the day and feast at night and normal business patterns may be interrupted. Many restaurants are closed during the day and there may be restrictions on smoking and drinking. Some disruption may continue into Eid al-Fitr itself. Eid al-Fitr and Eid al-Adha may last anything from two to 10 days, depending on the region. For more information, see the *World of Islam* appendix.

Health

	Special Precautions?	Certificate Required?
Yellow Fever	No	1
Cholera	No	No
Typhoid & Polio	2	N/A
Malaria	3	N/A

Note: *Regulations and requirements may be subject to change at short notice, and you are advised to contact your doctor well in advance of your intended date of departure. Any numbers in the chart refer to the footnotes below.*

1: A yellow fever vaccination certificate is required from travellers arriving within six days from infected areas.
2: Typhoid may occur in rural areas.
3: A limited malaria risk, predominantly in the malignant *falciparum* form, exists throughout the year in the whole country except at altitudes above 2000m and in desert areas. Chloroquine resistance has been reported.
Food & drink: All water outside the capital area should be regarded as being potentially contaminated. Water used for drinking, brushing teeth or making ice should have first been boiled or otherwise sterilised. Bottled water is available and is advised throughout Oman. Food bought in the main supermarkets can be regarded as safe. Outside the capital area, milk may be unpasteurised and if so, should be boiled. Powdered or tinned milk is available and is advised, but make sure that it is reconstituted with pure water. Avoid dairy products which are likely to have been made from unboiled milk. Only eat well-cooked meat and fish, preferably served hot. Salad and mayonnaise may carry increased risk. Vegetables should be cooked and fruit peeled.
Other risks: *Hepatitis A* and *B* occur.
Rabies is present. For those at high risk, vaccination before arrival should be considered. If you are bitten, seek medical advice without delay. For more information, consult the *Health* appendix.
Health care: Oman has an extensive public health service (free to Omani nationals), with approximately 46 hospitals, 86 health centres and 65 preventative health centres. However, costs are high for foreigners and health insurance is essential.

Travel - International

Note: There continues to be a high threat from terrorism. All visitors should remain vigilant, particularly in public places.
AIR: The national airlines of Oman are *Gulf Air (GF)* (website: www.gulfairco.com), which it jointly owns with the governments of Abu Dhabi, Bahrain and Qatar; and *Oman Air (WY)* (website: www.oman-air.com). Other airlines serving Oman include *British Airways*, *Emirates*, *KLM* and *Lufthansa*.
Approximate flight times: From Muscat to *London* is eight hours 10 minutes, to *Singapore* six hours 30 minutes and to *Sydney* 16 hours.
International airports: *Muscat (MCT)* (Seeb International), 40km (25 miles) west of the city (travel time – 15-30 minutes). Airport facilities include bank/bureau de change, duty free shops, bar and light refreshments, restaurants and tourist information as well as post office and car hire (*Avis*, *Budget* and *Hertz*). Taxis and buses to the city are available.
Departure tax: 5OR for all departures (this has usually already been collected at ticket issuance). Children under two years old are exempt.
SEA: The main ports are Mina Raysut and Sultan Qaboos. Traffic is mainly commercial.
ROAD: Travel into Oman by land is only possible with prior government permission. The best route is the north–south road from Muscat to Salalah, a journey of some 10 to 12 hours. Road travel through Saudi Arabia and the United Arab Emirates is extremely limited. There is no access from Yemen.

Travel - Internal

AIR: *Oman Air (WY)* runs domestic flights to Salalah and Khasab from Seeb airport; the approximate flight time to Salalah is 90 minutes.
ROAD: Traffic drives on the right. Principal routes run from east to west, connecting Muscat to Sohor, and from north

to south. **Bus**: The state-owned *Oman National Transport Company* has been developing a network of services in Muscat and north Oman using modern vehicles. There is competition from taxis and pick-up trucks converted for passenger service. **Taxi**: Prices are high and fares should be agreed in advance. Shared taxis are also available. **Car hire**: Available from *Avis* and *Budget* which have offices at hotels throughout the country. Regulations: Heavy penalties are imposed for drinking and driving. It is also forbidden to drive on the beaches. **Documentation**: A local licence must be obtained from the police by presenting a national driving licence or International Driving Permit. Police passes may be required if travelling via the United Arab Emirates.

Accommodation

There is a good selection of hotels to suit all budgets. Smaller hotels are cheaper but facilities are more limited. There are very few hotels in provincial areas but a large hotel-building programme has been initiated. The Shangri-la luxury hotel chain will open the country's first 6-star resort in 2005. Booking well in advance is strongly recommended. All rates are subject to a 10 per cent service charge.

Resorts & Excursions

Note: Entry into mosques is forbidden to non-Muslims.
MUSCAT: Oman's capital is divided into three main districts: Muscat, Mutrah and Ruwi. **Muscat**, the old walled port town, is dominated by the **Sultan's palace**, buildings of the **Royal Court** and government offices. Two well preserved 16th-century Portuguese forts, **Al Jalali** and **Mirani**, guard the entrance to Muscat, and the city walls contain three beautifully carved original gates. The town's old houses and narrow streets are overlooked by the hillside **Mutrah Fort**. The **Ali Mosque** and the **New Mosque** beside the sea add to the district's charm. **Mutrah** port is the capital's commercial centre and its **fish market**, **souk** and many **bazaars** are well worth visiting. **Ruwi** is the capital's business district and has excellent streets for shopping. The **National Museum**, featuring fine displays of Omani silverwork, and the **Sultan's Armed Forces Museum**, which outlines Omani history, are located here.
SALALAH: The capital of the southern region is a city set amongst coconut groves and banana plantations, sprawled along sandy beaches that run the length of its plain. The lush vegetation makes Salalah seem almost tropical, particularly as it is one of the only places in the Arabian peninsular that catches the monsoon. The **Al-Balid** ruins, site of the ancient city of **Zafar**, are a major tourist attraction.
SUR: Situated in the northeastern province of Sharqiya, Sur is a seafaring town, a fishing village and a trading port all rolled into one. Famous for its traditional shipbuilding, Sur started trading along the African coast as early as the sixth century. It is an old town with winding streets, carved wooden doors and old Arabesque buildings. The nearby village of **Tiwi** is also worth a visit.
SOHAR: There is a very large and functional souk (market) here, full of tailors, fruit-sellers and fishermen. An imposing four-storey fort with six towers overlooks the bay.
MATRAH-MUSCAT: Archaeological excavation of the tumuli at the site of **Souks Bausharios** is fascinating.
NIZWA: Now the main town in the interior province, with an immense palm oasis stretching for 13km (8 miles) along the course of two wadis, Nizwa was once the country's capital during the sixth and seventh centuries. Famous for its gold and silver handicrafts, the centre of the town is dominated by the huge circular tower of one of Oman's oldest and largest forts.
JABRIN: The 17th-century fortified palace situated here is notable for its painted wooden ceilings and the splendid view across the desert to the mountains.
BAHLA: Dating back to the third millennium BC, this ancient town has seven miles of ancient defensive walls and is a World Heritage Site. There is a good souk here and the town is known for its pottery. The picturesque village of **Al Hamra** can be found nearby.
JEBEL AKHDAR: Literally 'The Green Mountain', and rising to nearly 3000m (10,000ft), **Jebel Akhdar** is noted for its date palm groves, valleys and terraced villages, including **Bani Habib** and **Sharijah**.
On the northern slopes of the Jebel Akhdar are the fortress of **Al Hazm**, built in 1708, and the oasis town of **Rostaq**, containing the tombs of Oman's early rulers. On the side of a deep wadi on the south slope of the Jebel Akhdar, sits **Misfah**, one of the most picturesque villages in Oman.
QURUM: Encapsulates Oman's archaeology, history and culture. The **National Museum** has a collection of silver, jewellery, weapons and ancient stone artefacts. From here dhows cruise along the palm-fringed coast and there are excellent fishing grounds and beaches.

Sport & Activities

Watersports: There are many sandy beaches offering good **bathing**, **diving** and **sailing** facilities. Many hotels have pools. There are also three private sports clubs with **water-skiing** and **fishing** facilities. The Bander al-Rowdha Marina has a purpose-built watersports complex, with landscaped beach area, swimming pool and restaurants. The *Dubai to Muscat President's Cup Regatta* takes place annually. The waters of the Gulf of Oman and the North Indian Ocean are populated by black marlin, swordfish, tuna and sailfish making them ideal for **game fishing**. A fishing permit is required from the Directorate General of Fisheries, and spearfishing is strictly prohibited. In the southern region, fishing is restricted to between Mughsayl and Taqah. Hunting is completely forbidden.
Caving: This is also popular in Oman. Majlis al-Jhinn is the world's second-largest cave; its long passages, crystal-clear streams, canals and drip curtains extend throughout its 4 million cubic metre expanse.
Other: There are many sports clubs based in Muscat offering facilities for **tennis**, **squash** and **karting**. **Hockey**, **football**, **volleyball** and **basketball** are popular spectator sports and matches are staged at the Wattayah Stadium. Owing to the nature of the terrain and climate, **golf** is not a prominent sport in Oman, although there are a number of sand courses operated by local clubs, as well as plans to build a course at A'Suwadi. **Horseraces** and the more popular **camel races** are held on Fridays and public holidays at a variety of locations.

Social Profile

FOOD & DRINK: Numerous restaurants have opened in recent years, but many people retain the habit of dining at hotels. There is a wide variety of cuisine on offer, including Arabic, Indian, Oriental, European and other international dishes. Coffee houses are popular. Waiter service is usual. Muslim law forbids alcohol, but most hotel bars and restaurants serve alcohol. Visitors are only allowed to drink alcohol in licensed hotels and restaurants. To buy alcohol for home consumption, Western nationals must obtain a licence from their embassy.
NIGHTLIFE: There are a few nightclubs and bars in Muscat, mostly in the hotels. There are three air conditioned cinemas in Ruwi and an open-air cinema at the al-Falaj Hotel showing Arab, Indian and English films.
SHOPPING: The modern shops are mostly in Ruwi and Qurum. The two main *souks* (markets) are located in Matrah and Nizwa. Traditional crafts include silver and gold jewellery, *khanjars* (Omani daggers), coffeepots, saddles, frankincense, handwoven textiles, carpets, baskets and camel straps. Antique khanjars (over 50 years old) may not be exported. It is wise to check with the Ministry of National Heritage and Culture for the necessary documentation before purchasing. **Shopping hours**: Sat-Thurs 0800-1300 and 1600-2000. *Souks* open 0800-1100 and 1600-1900. Many shops close on Friday. Opening hours are one hour later during Ramadan.
SPECIAL EVENTS: Events celebrated in Oman are generally Muslim festivals and feasts. For further information on events in Oman, contact the Directorate General of Tourism (see *Contact Addresses* section).
SOCIAL CONVENTIONS: Shaking hands is the usual form of greeting. A small gift, either promoting your company or country, is well received. As far as dress is concerned, it is important that women dress modestly, ie long skirts or dresses (below the knee) with long sleeves. Tight-fitting clothes must be avoided and although this is not strictly followed by Westerners, it is far better to adopt this practice and avoid causing offence. Shorts should never be worn in public and beachwear is prohibited anywhere except the beach. Collecting sea shells, abalone, corals, crayfish and turtle eggs is also prohibited. Dumping litter is forbidden. It is polite not to smoke in public, but generally no-smoking signs are posted where appropriate. **Photography**: Visitors should ask permission before attempting to photograph people or their property. 'No Photography' signs exist in certain places and must be observed. **Tipping**: Becoming more common and 10 per cent should be given.

Business Profile

ECONOMY: Oman was acutely underdeveloped until the discovery of oil and natural gas in the early 1970s; this now accounts for over 40 per cent of GDP and 80 per cent of the country's export earnings. Agriculture, owing to Oman's desert land, is confined to the coastal plain and a few irrigated areas in the interior. Dates, limes and alfalfa are the main products; some livestock is also bred. There are mineral deposits of copper, chromite, marble, gypsum and limestone, manganese ore and coal. The Government has used some of its oil revenues to develop indigenous industries such as construction, agriculture and tourism,

Credit: © Oman Tourism

and to build up the country's infrastructure; these projects are incorporated in the Vision 2020 economic development programme. In the late 1990s, Oman started to privatise major government-owned parts of the economy and introduce a legislative framework to encourage foreign investment. The economy has been growing at around 4 per cent annually and enjoys low inflation and unemployment. Oman is a member of various pan-Arab political and economic organisations. However, it is not a member of the Organisation of Petroleum Exporting Countries (OPEC) – although its pricing policy tends to follow that of OPEC fairly closely. Oman's principal trading partners are Japan, Korea (Rep), Singapore, the United Arab Emirates and the United Kingdom.
BUSINESS: Men should wear suits and ties for business and formal occasions. English is usually spoken in business circles, but a few words or phrases of Arabic will be useful and welcome. Appointments are essential and punctuality is gradually becoming more important in business circles. Visiting cards are widely used. **Office hours**: Sat-Wed 0800-1300 and 1600-1900, Thurs 0800-1300. Government office hours: Sat-Wed 0730-1430, and sometimes half-day Thursday. All offices are closed Friday. Office hours are shorter during Ramadan.
COMMERCIAL INFORMATION: The following organisations can offer advice: Ministry of Commerce and Industry, PO Box 550, Muscat, Postal Code 113 (tel: 771 7085; fax: 771 4436/4213; e-mail: public@mocioman.gov.om; website: www.mocioman.gov.om); *or* Oman Chamber of Commerce and Industry, PO Box 1400, Postal Code112, Ruwi (tel: 707 674/84/94; fax: 708 497; e-mail: info@chamberoman.com; website: www.chamberoman.com).

Climate

The months between May and August are particularly hot. The climate is best from September through to April. Rainfall varies according to the region. During the period June to September there is a light monsoon rain in Salalah.
Required clothing: Lightweights are worn throughout the year, with a warm wrap for cooler winter evenings. Light rainwear is advisable.

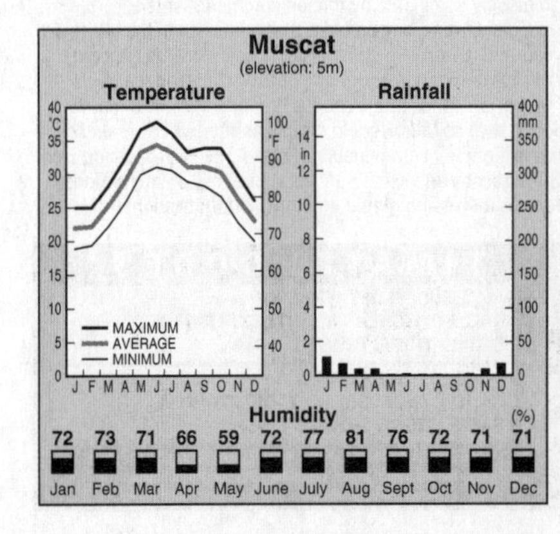

A B C D E F G H I J K L M N O P Q R S T U V W X Y Z

The Pacific

LATEST TRAVEL ADVICE CONTACTS

British Foreign and Commonwealth Office
Tel: (0870) 606 0290 Website: www.fco.gov.uk

US Department of State
Website: http://travel.state.gov/travel

Canadian Department of Foreign Affairs and Int'l Trade
Tel: (1 800) 267 8376 Website: www.dfait-maeci.gc.ca

The Pacific

Most of the countries in the Pacific have their own entries elsewhere; consult the *Contents*.

Pacific Overview

The vast, sparsely populated region of the Pacific Ocean, which covers one-quarter of the Earth's surface, has been the subject of growing interest in the last few years. It is neither easy nor especially useful to make generalisations about the area and the myriad small islands peppered across it. All have unique features of geography, economy and, not least, political history. Some are genuinely independent, some are internally self-governing with foreign and security policies controlled elsewhere, while a handful remain simple colonies. There are, nevertheless, global political and economic trends that are certain to create a substantial impact throughout the Pacific.
A notable feature of the 1970s and 1980s was the growing militarisation of the Pacific. This trend, while yet to be reversed, has at least halted. Its most obvious and damaging manifestation – the nuclear tests run by the French and the Americans – ended in the mid-1990s, at least for the time being. But the region still hosts a large number of airfields, storage depots, port complexes, intelligence-gathering, early-warning and other 'support' facilities. The host governments are often in two minds about their presence – the bases put these small nations in a diplomatic straitjacket, as well as offer a series of targets for hostile forces. On the other hand, they are guaranteed military protection and a steady rental income, plus essential economic aid.
But the islands are well aware that they must develop their own economic systems in order to survive in the long term and have focused on three principal areas in which they hope to progress.
One of these is tourism. Much of the region is currently within reach of the North American traveller but further exploitation of its tourism potential is dependent either on the development of cheaper, faster and perhaps less-polluting forms of long-distance transport to bring the Pacific within reach of Europe, or on a substantial increase in the disposable incomes of the populations of Asia and South America. Neither of these is likely to be realised in the short term.
Another economic asset that might produce more immediate dividends is the Pacific's awe-inspiring wealth of natural resources. Many Pacific nations are just a few score square kilometres of land, however, their boundaries enclose hundreds of thousands of square kilometres of ocean. Commercial fishing, notably by Japan, has long been carried out on a huge scale but has yet to make any real impact on the ocean's deep-sea fish stocks. The region also has enormous mineral potential. Much attention has been given to developing commercially viable methods of harvesting the mineral-rich manganese nodules that cover much of the ocean's abyssal plains, although there are believed to be other mineral deposits of great value. Additionally, the whole Pacific Rim has great potential as an energy source, initially from geothermal installations, later perhaps from deep-sea tidal and temperature gradient devices.
Finally, the islands stand to benefit from the rapidly growing Pacific trade axis as Japan and the Pacific Rim countries link up with the west coast of the Americas. This offers opportunities for developing transit facilities for shipping and 'offshore' financial services of the type that have long been offered by, for example, Jersey and the Cayman Islands. The islands will need more than this type of business to sustain a healthy economy and it remains to be seen whether or not they are able to develop their undoubted assets without becoming excessively dominated by foreign commercial interests.
On a darker note, one problem that has arisen in the last few years and is worrying several Pacific governments, concerns the possible consequences of global warming on sea levels. A number of islands face a serious threat to their land masses. Some, such as Nauru, could disappear altogether – it already has lost one, albeit uninhabited, island. The Pacific islands are consequently an increasingly vocal presence at international forums discussing global environmental questions.

TIMATIC CODES

Health	AMADEUS: **TI-DFT/TRW/HE** GALILEO/WORLDSPAN: **TI-DFT/TRW/HE** SABRE: **TIDFT/TRW/HE**
Visa	AMADEUS: **TI-DFT/TRW/VI** GALILEO/WORLDSPAN: **TI-DFT/TRW/VI** SABRE: **TIDFT/TRW/VI**

To access TIMATIC country information on Health and Visa regulations through the Computer Reservations System (CRS), type in the appropriate command line listed above.

The Pacific Islands of Micronesia

LATEST TRAVEL ADVICE CONTACTS

British Foreign and Commonwealth Office
Tel: (0870) 606 0290 Website: www.fco.gov.uk

US Department of State
Website: http://travel.state.gov/travel

Canadian Department of Foreign Affairs and Int'l Trade
Tel: (1 800) 267 8376 Website: www.dfait-maeci.gc.ca

Location: *This region was administered by the USA on behalf of the United Nations until 1990. It includes the Federated States of Micronesia, the Republic of the Marshall Islands, the Northern Mariana Islands and the Republic of Palau. The Northern Marianas have had US Commonwealth status since 1986. Under the terms of the Compacts of Free Association between the USA and the other former territories, each is a sovereign self-governing state pursuing its foreign policy along agreed guidelines, with the USA retaining responsibility for defence in exchange for economic aid. The Federated States of Micronesia and the Republic of the Marshall Islands became members of the UN in 1991 and Palau became a member in 1994.*
For contact addresses, see individual entries in this section.

General Information

AREA: 7,800,000 sq km (3,000,000 sq miles), of which 1846.3 sq km (721.2 sq miles) is land.
POPULATION: See individual entries.
GEOGRAPHY: Micronesia comprises four archipelagos: the Federated States of Micronesia (Caroline Islands), the Republic of the Marshall Islands, the Northern Mariana Islands and the Republic of Palau. Each archipelago is composed of hundreds of island groups, within which there are many islands varying widely in topography. A more detailed description is given under the individual section for each country. There are three distinct population groups: Malayans who passed through Indonesia and The Philippines; Melanesians coming from the islands of the southwest Pacific; and Polynesians who inhabited the South Pacific.
LANGUAGE: English, Japanese and nine local languages.
RELIGION: Roman Catholic and Protestant with Mormon and Baha'i minorities.
TIME: See individual sections.
ELECTRICITY: 110/120 volts AC, 60Hz. Plugs are the US flat two-pin type.
COMMUNICATIONS: Telephone: IDD is available to any of the islands. See individual entries for country code **Fax:** Available in all the island states. **Internet:** There is basic access and services on the islands. See individual entries. **Telegram:** 24-hour service available in some areas. **Post:** Airmail to Europe takes approximately 10 days. Post offices are located in the centre of each state. **Press:** *The Pacific Daily News* (Guam) is the main English-language daily newspaper in the region and is distributed throughout all the islands. Further information is provided under individual entries.
Radio: BBC World Service (website: www.bbc.co.uk/worldservice) and Voice of America (website: www.voa.gov) can be received. From time to time the frequencies change and the most up-to-date can be found online.

Passport/Visa

Note: (a) Each of the four constitutional governments is responsible for its own tourism policies, and regulations may be subject to change. (b) On many islands, especially the remoter ones, it is not the possession of documents (necessary though they are) that secures access, but the consent of the islanders. For more details, see the individual sections.

TIMATIC CODES

Health	AMADEUS: **TI-DFT/PNI/HE** GALILEO/WORLDSPAN: **TI-DFT/PNI/HE** SABRE: **TIDFT/PNI/HE**
Visa	AMADEUS: **TI-DFT/PNI/VI** GALILEO/WORLDSPAN: **TI-DFT/PNI/VI** SABRE: **TIDFT/PNI/VI**

To access TIMATIC country information on Health and Visa regulations through the Computer Reservations System (CRS), type in the appropriate command line listed above.

Money

Currency: US Dollar (US$) = 100 cents. Notes are in denominations of US$1000, 500, 100, 50, 20, 10, 5, 2 and 1. Coins are in denominations of 50, 25, 10, 5 and 1 cents. Japanese yen are accepted on many islands.
Currency exchange: Foreign exchange services are limited on some islands.
Credit & debit cards: American Express, MasterCard and Visa are accepted in most hotels and tourist-oriented facilities. Check with your credit or debit card company for details of merchant acceptability and other services which may be available.
Travellers cheques: US Dollar travellers cheques are advised.
Currency restrictions: These vary; see individual sections for details.
Exchange rate indicators: The following figures are included as a guide to the movements of the US Dollar against Sterling:

Date	Feb '04	May '04	Aug '04	Nov '04
£1.00=	1.82	1.79	1.84	1.89

Banking hours: Mon-Thurs 1000-1500, Fri 1000-1800. There are some local variations.

Public Holidays

Some US public holidays are observed in addition to regional public holidays, though there are variations from island to island; see individual sections for main holidays in each region.

Health

	Special Precautions?	Certificate Required?
Yellow Fever	1	1
Cholera	2	2
Typhoid & Polio	3	N/A
Malaria	No	N/A

Note: Regulations and requirements may be subject to change at short notice, and you are advised to contact your doctor well in advance of your intended date of departure. Any numbers in the chart refer to the footnotes below.

1: See individual sections for information about yellow fever vaccination requirements.
2: A cholera vaccination is a condition of entry to some of the Pacific Islands of Micronesia; see individual sections for details.
3: Typhoid and para-typhoid vaccinations are strongly recommended.
Food & drink: Mains water is normally chlorinated, and whilst relatively safe may cause mild abdominal upsets. Drinking water outside main towns may be contaminated and sterilisation is advisable. Bottled water is available and is advised for the first few weeks of the stay. Milk is pasteurised and dairy products are safe for consumption. Local meat, poultry, seafood, fruit and vegetables are generally considered safe to eat.
Other risks: *Hepatitis A* and *B* may occur on some islands and precautions should be taken. *Tetanus* vaccination is also advised. *Dengue fever*, including its haemorrhagic form, can occur in epidemics in most islands. Colenterates, poisonous fish and sea snakes can present hazards to bathers.
Health care: Health insurance is recommended. There are nine hospitals in the region.

Travel - International

AIR: The region's major airline is *Continental Micronesia (CS)*. Consult individual entries for further information.
Approximate flight times: Flight durations from London to destinations in the Pacific vary considerably depending on the route taken. The most common route would include stopovers in Los Angeles and Honolulu; eg the flight time from London to Honolulu is 19 hours 30 minutes and from Honolulu to the Marshall Islands four hours 30 minutes.
International airports: *Guam (GUM), Koror Babeldaob (ROR)* and *Saipan (SPN)* when entering from the north and west, *Pohnpei (PNI)* from the south, and *Majuro (MAJ)* from the south and east.
Regional airlines: Scheduled inter-island travel, charters and sightseeing are offered by several local airlines. There is excellent provision for travelling from Guam, Majuro and Saipan to the various islands.
Flights between the islands tend to be rarer. Airlines include: *Air Marshall Islands (CW):* This government-owned airline runs charters, sightseeing tours and point-to-point flights between Majuro and other islands in the Marshalls; also international flights to Fiji, Honolulu, Kiribati and Tuvalu.

Continental Micronesia (CS): Operates between islands in all four groups, and to Guam, Hawaii, Japan and The Philippines. Several smaller airlines fly to Guam.
The *Visit South Pacific Pass* is valid for many airlines operating in the South Pacific, including most of the larger ones, such as *Air Caledonie, Air Marshall Islands, Air Nauru, Air Niugingi, Air Pacific, Air Vanuatu, Polynesian Airlines, Qantas, Royal Tongan Airlines* and *Solomon Airlines*. Offering reductions of up to 40 per cent on normal airfares, this sector-based pass allows for flexible island-hopping between the destinations of the Cook Islands, Fiji, Nauru, New Caledonia, Samoa, Tahiti, Tonga, Vanuatu and the more remote Melanesian and Micronesian islands, together with major cities in Australia (Brisbane, Melbourne and Sydney) and New Zealand (Auckland, Christchurch and Wellington). It is only available for people resident outside of the South Pacific. The journey must be started outside the South Pacific and only one stopover in Australia is allowed. A minimum of two sectors must be bought before departure (extra sectors can be purchased en route). There is a maximum of one pass per person, and passes must be used within six months of the first day of travel. Children under 12 years of age pay 75 per cent of the adult fare. For details and conditions, contact the South Pacific Tourist Organisation (see *Contact Addresses* section).
SEA: The major ports are Koror, Majuro, Pohnpei, Saipan, Tuik and Yap.
The following cargo/passenger lines serve the islands: *Daiwa Navigation Co, Nauru Pacific, Oceania Line Inc, P&O, Royal Shipping Co, Saipan Shipping Co* and *Tiger Line*.
There are numerous boats for touring, ranging from small speed boats to large glass-bottomed boats for fishing, sightseeing, sunset cruising, scuba-diving and short-distance travel. A ferry provides service between Saipan and Tinian. Inter-island vessels provide limited and irregular service between Saipan and the smaller islands. Requests for reservations should be directed to the Office of the Government of the following: Saipan, Commonwealth of the Northern Marianas; Office of Transportation in Majuro, Marshall Islands; Koror, Palau; Kolonia, Pohnpei; Moen, Chuuk and Colonia, Yap. Cabin space is limited, and passengers may be required to sleep on deck (bring own mat). The field trip ships are leased by the governments to private firms, and rates are subject to change.
Cruise lines: *Norwegian American, Princess, Royal Viking* and *Small Ship* currently offer cruises to the islands.

Travel - Internal

ROAD: Good roads are limited to the major island centres. **Bus:** There are no local bus systems other than tourist services. However, public transport is widely available in all the Micronesian district centres in the form of sedans, pickups and *jeepneys*. **Taxi:** Inexpensive taxis are available throughout Micronesia. **Car hire:** Each major centre offers rental cars, either through international or local agents. **Documentation:** A valid national driving licence is required.

Accommodation

Accommodation is extremely varied. Rooms are scarce in some districts and single guests may be required to share twin-bedded rooms with other single guests.

Sport & Activities

There is excellent **fishing**, **hiking** and **watersports**. The islands are particularly appealing for **skindivers**, as the surrounding waters offer unsurpassed underwater scenery and marine life; see individual sections.

Social Profile

FOOD & DRINK: Most hotels serve continental, Chinese, Japanese, Western-style and local cuisine. On some remote islands, the arrival of a stranger calls for a feast of fish, clams, octopus, langusta, sea cucumber and eels. Breadfruit (pounded, boiled, baked or fried), taro, rice and cassava (tapioca) are popular staples. Among the regional delicacies are coconut crabs and mangrove clams. Although some dining rooms serve buffet-style fare, table service is usual and operates at a leisurely pace; see individual sections for further details.
NIGHTLIFE: Some hotels have cocktail lounges with live entertainment. In Saipan there are nightclubs featuring music and dancing. Throughout Micronesia there are cinemas in major areas. However, tourists seek their own entertainment for the most part; see individual sections for further details.
SPECIAL EVENTS: See individual sections.
SOCIAL CONVENTIONS: The Western understanding of private property is alien to many parts of Micronesia and personal possessions should be well looked after, though not necessarily under lock and key; outside main tourist areas, where normal precautions apply, it is usually sufficient just to keep items out of sight. All land, however, does have an owner and before using it, protocol in many areas demands that permission is sought; in places this includes use of footpaths as there is not necessarily immediate right of way. A clearly expressed desire to be courteous will usually see the visitor through; see individual sections for further details.

Business Profile

ECONOMY: In all four territories, subsistence agriculture is a key employer. Copra, coconuts, cassava and sweet potatoes are the major crops: yields are sufficient in some cases to sustain export markets. Fishing is similarly important. The Marshalls and Palau have developed small-scale light industries engaged in food-processing, boat-building and the like. Service economies based on tourism and financial services have generally proved difficult to establish owing to the remoteness of the territories and the lack of infrastructure. Micronesia and the Northern Marianas have gone furthest in their efforts to overcome these obstacles, but the region as a whole continues to rely heavily on foreign aid, mostly from the USA. As members of the Pacific Islands Forum, the islands have agreed to participate in a free trade zone, known as PICTA (Pacific Island Countries Trade Agreement), set up in 2002. Supporters of the Agreement contend that it will bring much-needed trade to the region; critics maintain that the islands are being run over by the globalisation bandwagon and small, fragile economies are being forced to open up before they are ready.
BUSINESS: Lightweight suits or shirt and tie are usually worn. Appointments should be made and calling cards are exchanged. The best time to visit is May to October. **Office hours:** Mon-Fri 0800-1700. **Government office hours:** Mon-Fri 0800-1200 and 1300-1700. There may be some local variations.

Climate

With 2000 islands spread over 7.8 million sq km (3 million sq miles) of the Pacific Ocean, the islands have a variety of weather. The period from autumn to winter (November to April) is the most pleasant time, while May to October is the wet season. The climate can generally be described as tropical in this part of the world, but the cooling sea breezes prevent really extreme temperatures and humidity. For regional climate charts, see under the individual sections.
Required clothing: Lightweight cottons and linens and rainwear.

Federated States of Micronesia

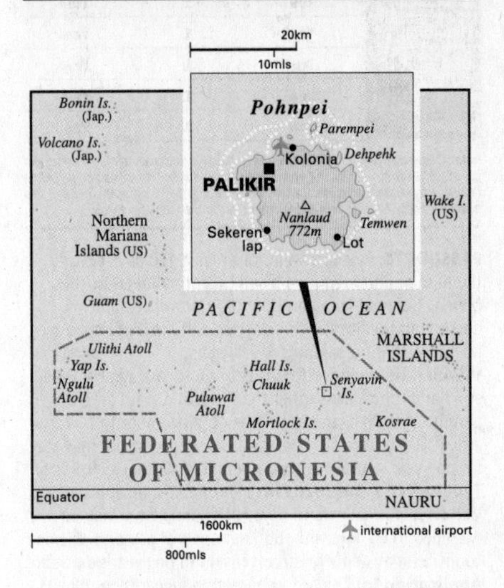

Location: Western Pacific Ocean.

Country dialling code: 691.

FSM Visitors Board
FSM National Government, PO Box PS-12, Palikir, Pohnpei FSM 96941
Tel: 320 5133. Fax: 320 3251.
E-mail: fsminfo@visit-fsm.org *or* Visit_FSM@mail.fm
Website: www.visit-fsm.org
Embassy of the Federated States of Micronesia
1725 N Street, NW, Washington, DC 20036, USA
Tel: (202) 223 4383. Fax: (202) 223 4391.
E-mail: fsm@fsmembassy.org *or* fsmamb@aol.com
Embassy of the United States of America
PO Box 1286, Kolonia, Pohnpei FSM 96941
Tel: 320 2187. Fax: 320 2186.
E-mail: USEmbassy@mail.fm
Website: www.fm/usembassy/

General Information

AREA: Kosrae (five islands) – 110 sq km (42 sq miles); **Pohnpei** (163 islands) – 344 sq km (133 sq miles); **Chuuk** (formerly Truk) (294 islands) – 127 sq km (49 sq miles); **Yap** (145 islands) – 119 sq km (46 sq miles). **Total:** 700 sq km (270.3 sq miles).
POPULATION: 107,008 (2000).
POPULATION DENSITY: 153 per sq km.
CAPITAL: Palikir (Pohnpei). **Population:** 34,486 (Pohnpei; 2000).
GEOGRAPHY: The Federated States of Micronesia lie 3680km (2300 miles) north of Australia and 4000km (2500 miles) west of Hawaii. They comprise 607 islands scattered over 1.6 million sq km (617,761 sq miles), the most widely spread Pacific Islands group. Yap's uplands are covered by dry meadows and scrub growth. Chuuk lagoon is circled by one of the largest barrier reefs in the world, while Pohnpei has mountains rising to over 600m (2000ft).
GOVERNMENT: Federal Republic since 1980. Gained self-governing status (in free association with the USA) in 1986.
Head of State and Government: President Joseph J. Urusemal since 2003.
LANGUAGE: English; Micronesian languages, including Chuukese, Kosrean, Pohnpean and Yapese, are widely spoken.
RELIGION: Mostly Roman Catholic with other Christian denominations.
TIME: Owing to the vast area covered by the islands, Micronesia spans two time zones:
CHUUK AND YAP: GMT + 10.
KOSRAE AND POHNPEI: GMT + 11.
COMMUNICATIONS: Telephone: IDD is available. Country code: 691. Outgoing international code: 00. **Internet:** The main ISP is *FSM Telecom* (website: www.telecom.fm). **Telegram:** Facilities at island capitals and main hotels. **Post:** Post offices are located in Kolonia for Pohnpei, Moen for Chuuk, Lelu for Kosrae and Colonia for Yap. Post office hours: Mon-Fri 0830-1630. **Press:** *Pacific Daily News* (Guam) is the main English-language newspaper in the Federated States of Micronesia. *The Island Tribune* is printed twice weekly.

A B C D E F G H I J K L M N O P Q R S T U V W X Y Z

Passport/Visa

	Passport Required?	Visa Required?	Return Ticket Required?
Full British	Yes	1	Yes
Australian	Yes	1	Yes
Canadian	Yes	1	Yes
USA	No	1	Yes
Other EU	Yes	1	Yes
Japanese	Yes	1	Yes

Note: *Regulations and requirements may be subject to change at short notice, and you are advised to contact the appropriate diplomatic or consular authority before finalising travel arrangements. Details of these may be found at the head of this country's entry. Any numbers in the chart refer to the footnotes below.*

PASSPORTS: Passport valid for at least 120 days beyond the date of entry required by all except nationals of the Marshall Islands, Palau and the USA with acceptable documentation (birth certificate or entry permit issued by Micronesia), if no passport is available.

VISAS: 1. Not required for visits of up to 30 days. For longer stays and for all visits other than touristic visits, an entry permit is required, and should be obtained prior to travel or arrival. Nationals of the passport-exempt countries may stay for one year without an entry permit, if visiting as tourists.

Types of visa and cost: *Entry Permit:* cost on application.

Validity: Normally up to an additional 30 days. May be extended to 60 days, although nationals of passport-exempt countries may apply for an extension of one year's duration.

Application to: Chief of Immigration, Department of Justice, FSM Government Office, PO Box PS 105, Palikir, Pohnpei FSM 96941 (tel: 320 5844 *or* 2605; fax: 320 7250 *or* 6240; e-mail: imhq@mail.fm).

Note: All visitors require proof of adequate funds and return or onward tickets.

Working days required: Must apply by post; applications are dealt with on receipt.

Temporary residence: Apply to Division of Immigration (see address above).

Note: Foreign-owned vessels or aircraft are required to have entry permits (visas) applied for and in their possession prior to entering Micronesia or to apply for one immediately on entry into Micronesia.

Money

Currency: Giant stone money remains in use on Yap, but not for ordinary transactions or any that are likely to involve visitors. For information on convertible currency, see *Money* in the *Pacific Islands of Micronesia* section. The US Dollar is the official currency. There are several US FDIC insured banks operating (although there are no banks on Chuuk) and most major credit cards are welcome at major businesses.

Duty Free

No detailed information was available at time of writing.

Note: Alcohol for passengers over 21 years of age only.

Prohibited items: Firearms and ammunition. Plants and animals must be declared and will be subject to restrictions.

Public Holidays

2005: Jan 1 New Year's Day. **Jan 11*** Kosrae Constitution Day. **Mar 1*** Yap Day. **Mar 25** Good Friday. **Mar 31*** Pohnpei Culture Day. **May 10** Constitution (Federated States of Micronesia) Day. **Sep 8*** Kosrae Liberation Day. **Sep 11*** Pohnpei Liberation Day. **Oct 24** United Nations Day. **Nov 3** National Day. **Nov 8*** Pohnpei Constitution Day. **Nov 24*** Kosrae Thanksgiving Day. **Dec 24*** Yap Constitution Day. **Dec 25** Christmas Day.

2006: Jan 1 New Year's Day. **Jan 11*** Kosrae Constitution Day. **Mar 1*** Yap Day. **Mar 31*** Pohnpei Culture Day. **Apr 14** Good Friday. **May 10** Constitution (Federated States of Micronesia) Day. **Sep 8*** Kosrae Liberation Day. **Sep 11*** Pohnpei Liberation Day. **Oct 24** United Nations Day. **Nov 3** National Day. **Nov 8*** Pohnpei Constitution Day. **Nov 23*** Kosrae Thanksgiving Day. **Dec 24*** Yap Constitution Day. **Dec 25** Christmas Day.

Note: *Variations occur from island to island.

Health

Health care: All the Federated States have good government hospitals in the main cities. There are also dental services and private health clinics throughout the islands. Nevertheless, health insurance is recommended.

No vaccinations are required for entry, but vaccination against *typhoid* and *polio* is advised and *hepatitis A* is present.

Travel - International

AIR: *Palau Micronesia Air* began international flights in 2004 (website: www.palau-air.com). *Continental Micronesia (CS)* flights link the major islands with Guam, Honolulu, Manila and Tokyo. Air Nauru provides weekly services linking Pohnpei to Australia, Fiji, Guam, Manila and Nauru.

The *Visit the South Pacific Pass* is valid for many airlines operating in the South Pacific, including most of the larger ones, such as *Air Caledonie, Air Marshall Islands, Air Nauru, Air Niugini, Air Pacific, Air Vanuatu, Polynesian Airlines, Qantas, Royal Tongan Airlines* and *Solomon Airlines*. Offering reductions of up to 40 per cent on normal airfares, this sector-based pass allows for flexible island-hopping between the destinations of the Cook Islands, Fiji, Nauru, New Caledonia, Samoa, Tahiti, Tonga, Vanuatu and the more remote Melanesian and Micronesian islands, together with major cities in Australia (Brisbane, Melbourne and Sydney) and New Zealand (Auckland, Christchurch and Wellington). It is only available for people resident outside of the South Pacific. The journey must be started outside the South Pacific and only one stopover in Australia is allowed. A minimum of two sectors must be bought before departure (extra sectors can be purchased en route). There is a maximum of one pass per person, and passes must be used within six months of the first day of travel. Children under 12 years of age pay 75 per cent of the adult fare. For details and conditions, contact the South Pacific Tourist Organisation (see *Contact Addresses* section).

Approximate flight times: See *Pacific Islands of Micronesia* section.

International airports: *Pohnpei (PNI)* is 5km (3 miles) from Kolonia. Taxis are available. Facilities include car hire, light snacks and tourist information.

Departure tax: US$10 for Pohnpei; $15 for Chuuk; $10 Kosrae; no departure tax for Yap.

SEA: International ports are Chuuk, Pohnpei and Yap. Inter-island trading ships based in Pohnpei, Yap and Chuuk visit the outlying islands.

ROAD: There are good roads in and around major island centres, although most roads remain unpaved. **Bus:** No scheduled service, although some buses may be available for hire or charter. On Yap, a school bus runs twice daily from Colonia to the villages. **Taxi:** Available throughout Micronesia and inexpensive. **Car hire:** Self-drive cars are available in major towns. **Documentation:** National driving licence or International Driving Permit required.

Accommodation

There are hotels in the various island capitals. Parts of Chuuk, Kosrae and Pohnpei have been developed into beach resorts.

CAMPING: There are no official campsites, but private arrangements can be made with local landowners. For further information, contact the FSM Visitors Board (see *Contact Addresses* section).

Resorts & Excursions

The most important historical sites include **The Spanish Wall** and **Catholic Bell Tower** in **Pohnpei**, the **Japanese Wartime Communication Centre** at Xavier High School in **Chuuk** and the ruins of **INSARU** in **Kosrae**. The **Sokehs Mass Grave** holds the remains of 17 Pohnpeians who were executed by firing squad in 1911 for resisting the German administration. There are also small museums in Chuuk and Kosrae. The **Enpein Marine Park** and ancient ruins of **Nan Madol** in Pohnpei are well worth visiting. Pohnpei has magnificent waterfalls with pools that are ideal for bathing. Two of the most beautiful falls are **Kepirohi** and **Sahwartik**. All States have beautiful white sandy beaches.

Sport & Activities

Diving: Warm water and spectacular underwater scenery attract divers to these islands. Kosrae has over 50 dive sites, each marked with a buoy to prevent improper anchoring. Unspoiled coral reefs close to the shore make the island suitable for both walk-in and boat diving. In neighbouring Pohnpei State, recommended dive sites include the unspoiled *Ant Atoll* and *Pakin Atoll*, both a short boat ride away from the main island. The state of Chuuk contains the famous *Truk Lagoon*, where a whole Japanese fleet was sunk during World War II. More than 50 wrecks can be seen here, with various artefacts still intact. Some of the shallower wrecks are suitable for **snorkellers**. The island of Yap is notable for its schools of manta rays, which can be seen all year round. Tuna, dolphins and reef fish are also abundant. For further information about diving facilities and dive schools, contact the FSM Visitors Board (see *Contact Addresses* section).

Other: There are facilities available for **fishing**, **hiking**, **windsurfing**, **tennis**, **canoeing**, **football**, **basketball**, **volleyball** and **baseball**.

Social Profile

FOOD & DRINK: Local specialities include breadfruit (Chuuk) and thin slices of raw fish dipped in a peppery sauce. Pohnpeians have over 100 words for yams and grow them to massive proportions (it may take several men to carry one); yams occupy a central position in local culture. Although some dining rooms serve buffet-style fare, table service is usual and operates at a leisurely pace.

Sakau, as it is known on Pohnpei, or kava, as it is known throughout the rest of Polynesia, is made from the root of a shrub which yields a mildly narcotic substance when squeezed through hibiscus bark. There are several *sakau* bars where visitors can sample it and watch it being made. Alcohol is prohibited on Chuuk (with the consequence that nearby islands are often used as picnic resorts).

NIGHTLIFE: There are good restaurants and a few cinemas in major island centres. Locals and visitors alike enjoy making their own entertainment. *Sakau* drinking is the most frequent evening activity on Pohnpei. Cultural dances can be arranged through tourist offices or hotels. Most hotels have music, dancing and discos.

SHOPPING: Favourite purchases on Chuuk include love sticks and war clubs. Yap people produce colourful grass skirts, *lava-lavas* woven from hibiscus bark, woven baby cradles, betel-nut pouches and stone money. On Pohnpei, there are elaborate, carefully scaled model canoes and woven items. **Shopping hours:** Mon-Fri 0800-1700. Some stores open Sun 1200-1700.

SPECIAL EVENTS: In Yap, *mitmits* are feasts accompanied by dancing and exchanges of gifts which are given by villages reciprocally, often after a period of years has elapsed. *Liberation Day* (**Sep 11**) in Pohnpei is preceded by a week of sports and traditional events, including canoe racing. Also in Pohnpei, funeral feasts are important events lasting several days. In Kosrae, visitors are invited to participate in Sunday church services.

SOCIAL CONVENTIONS: There are considerable variations of custom and belief. Approximately 95 per cent of Kosreans are Congregationalists with a deeply held respect for Sunday as a day of rest. Pre-European influences are stronger elsewhere and nowhere more so than in Yap where visitors are only allowed with prior permission. Use of islands, paths, beaches etc may also require permission in many areas; it is best to check beforehand. **Photography:** Permission should always be sought. Though people are friendly, and usually accommodating, not to seek prior permission before taking pictures is considered an insult, especially on some of the more remote islands. **Tipping:** Tips are neither encouraged nor expected.

Business Profile

ECONOMY: Subsistence farming and fishing are of declining importance as tourism has come to dominate the domestic economy and fishing is largely pursued by foreign commercial concerns operating under licence. Mineral resources are limited to a few high-grade phosphate deposits. Sales of these licences account for over one-third of national income. Aid from the USA has been a vital source of income: under the Compact of Free Association between the islands and the USA, Micronesia received US$1.3 billion in bilateral aid over the 15-year period up to 2001. Much of this was sunk into infrastructure projects, principally an airport and harbour on each of the main islands. However, the end of this subvention has depressed the economy and, with few other immediate options, Micronesia's economic prospects are at best uncertain. The Federated States of Micronesia is a member of the South Pacific Commission and the South Pacific Forum.

CONFERENCES/CONVENTIONS: For further information, contact FSM Visitors Board (see *Contact Addresses* section); *or* the Pohnpei State Chamber of Commerce, PO Box 405, 96941, Pohnpei, Kolonia (tel: 320 2452; fax: 320 5277).

Climate

Tropical with year-round high humidity.

Required clothing: Lightweight cottons and linens, with light rainwear advisable all year round.

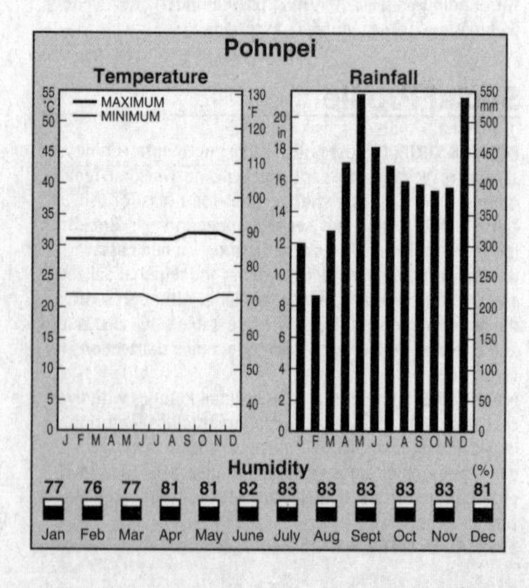

Marshall Islands

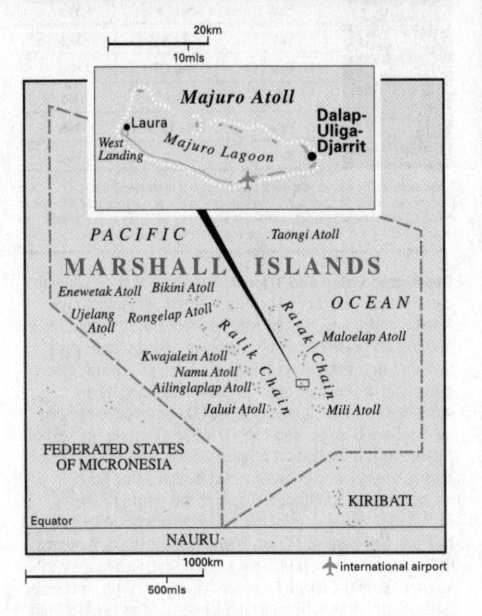

Location: Western Pacific Ocean.

Country dialling code: 692.

Marshall Islands Visitors Authority
PO Box 5, Majuro, Marshall Islands 96960
Tel: 625 6482. Fax: 625 6771.
E-mail: tourism@ntamar.net
Website: www.visitmarshallislands.com

Embassy of the Republic of the Marshall Islands
2433 Massachusetts Avenue, NW, Washington, DC 20008, USA
Tel: (202) 234 5414. Fax: (202) 232 3236.
E-mail: info@rmiembassyus.org
Website: www.rmiembassyus.org

Embassy of the United States of America
PO Box 1379, Ocean Site, Nejen Weto, Long Island, Majuro, Marshall Islands 96960
Tel: 247 4011. Fax: 247 4012.
E-mail: publicmajuro@state.gov
Website: http://usembassy.state.gov/majuro

General Information

AREA: 181.4 sq km (70 sq miles).
POPULATION: 50,848 (1999).
POPULATION DENSITY: 280.3 per sq km.
CAPITAL: Majuro. **Population:** 23,682 (1999).
GEOGRAPHY: The Marshall Islands consist of two almost parallel chains of atolls and islands and lie west of the International Date Line. Majuro Atoll is 2285km (1428 miles) west of Honolulu, 1624km (1015 miles) east of Guam and 2624km (1641 miles) southeast of Tokyo. The eastern *Ratak* (Sunrise) Chain consists of 15 atolls and islands, and the western *Ralik* (Sunset) Chain consists of 16 atolls and islands. Together these two chains comprise 1152 islands and islets dispersed over more than 1,900,000 sq km (500,000 sq miles) of the central Pacific.
GOVERNMENT: Republic since 1990. Gained self-governing status (in free association with the USA) in 1986. **Head of State and Government:** President Kessai H Note (since 2000).
LANGUAGE: Marshallese and English are the official languages.
RELIGION: Christian, mostly Protestant.
TIME: GMT + 12.
ELECTRICITY: 110 volts AC, 60 Hz. Plugs are US two-pin style.
COMMUNICATIONS: Telephone: IDD is available. Country code: 692. Outgoing international code: 00. There are international satellite links. In Majuro, dial 625 3399 *or* 3355 for the hospital; 625 8666 for the fire services; 625 3233 for police; and 625 1411 for general information **Internet:** Main ISPs include *Ntamar* and *VPM* (website: www.vpm.com). Availabilty and reliability are limited. **Telegram:** 24-hour telegram facilities are available in Majuro, near the High School in Rita, and in Ebeye. Opening hours: Mon-Fri 0800-1200 and 1300-1700. **Post:** US post offices are located in Ebeye, Jaluit and Majuro. Post office hours: Mon-Fri 1000-1530, Sat 0900-1545. **Press:** The English/Marshallese-language newspaper is the weekly *Marshall Islands Journal* and the monthly *Marshal Islands Gazette*.

Passport/Visa

	Passport Required?	Visa Required?	Return Ticket Required?
Full British	Yes	Yes	Yes
Australian	Yes	Yes	Yes
Canadian	Yes	Yes	Yes
USA	Yes	No	No
Other EU	Yes	Yes	Yes
Japanese	Yes	Yes	Yes

Note: *Regulations and requirements may be subject to change at short notice, and you are advised to contact the appropriate diplomatic or consular authority before finalising travel arrangements. Details of these may be found at the head of this country's entry. Any numbers in the chart refer to the footnotes below.*

PASSPORTS: Passports valid for at least one year from date of arrival required by all.
VISAS: Required by all except the following:
(a) nationals of the USA;
(b) nationals of the Federated States of Micronesia and the Republic of Palau.
Note: Tourist visas are issued on arrival. It may be necessary to obtain a transit visa for the USA first, as flights to the Marshall Islands are via Guam or Hawaii. Contact an airline such as *Air Marshall Islands* or *Continental Micronesia* for further information. All visitors require proof of adequate funds and return or onward tickets.
Types of visa and cost: *Tourist:* Free (up to 30 days); US$25 (up to 90 days). *Business:* US$50.
Validity: 30 days; extensions for up to 90 days are available upon arrival in the Marshall Islands.
Application to: For stays exceeding 30 days, apply to: Attorney General, Office of the Attorney General, PO Box 890, Majuro, Marshall Islands 96960 (tel: 635 8495; fax: 625 5218).
Application requirements: (a) Valid passport. (b) Completed incoming passenger card (available on board ship/aircraft). (c) Return or onward ticket. (d) Sufficient funds to cover stay. (e) For those intending to stay for more than 30 days, an AIDS certificate is required. Contact the Chief of Immigration for latest information.
Working days required: Applications are dealt with on receipt.
Temporary residence: Apply to Attorney General (address above).

Money

For details of currency, credit & debit cards, traveller's cheques, exchange rate indicators and banking hours, see *Pacific Islands of Micronesia* section.
Currency exchange: The banks of Guam and the Marshall Islands have branches on Majuro; those of the Marshall Islands and Guam have branches on Ebeye; and that of Guam has a branch on Kwajalein.
Currency restrictions: There are no limits on the import and export of local and foreign currency, subject to declaration of amounts exceeding US$5000.

Duty Free

The following items may be imported into the Marshall Islands by passengers without incurring customs duty:
600 cigarettes or 454g of cigars or tobacco; 2l of alcoholic beverages (alcohol for passengers over 21 years of age only).
Prohibited items: Firearms, ammunition, drugs and pornographic materials are not permitted. Birds, animals, fruit and plants need certification from the Quarantine Division of the Ministry of Resources and Development. Coral, turtle shells and certain other natural resources cannot be exported. Any artefacts or objects of historical value cannot be taken out of the country.

Public Holidays

2005: Jan 1 New Year's Day. **Mar 1** Memorial and Nuclear Victims' Remembrance Day. **May 1** Constitution Day. **Jul 1** Fishermen's Day. **Sep 2** Rijerbal (Labour) Day. **Sep 30** Manit (Custom) Day. **Oct 21** Compact Day. **Nov 17** President's Day. **Dec 2** Gospel Day. **Dec 25** Christmas Day.
2006: Jan 1 New Year's Day. **Mar 1** Memorial and Nuclear Victims' Remembrance Day. **May 1** Constitution Day. **Jul 7** Fishermen's Day. **Sep 1** Rijerbal (Labour) Day. **Sep 29** Manit (Custom) Day. **Oct 21** Compact Day. **Nov 17** President's Day. **Dec 1** Gospel Day. **Dec 25** Christmas Day.
Note: Separate holidays occur from island to island.

Health

Yellow fever certificates and *cholera* vaccinations are required by all travellers arriving from infected areas. Vaccination against *Hepatitis A* and *B*, *typhoid*, *tetanus* and *diphtheria* may be advised. HIV testing is required for temporary visitors staying for more than 30 days. Foreign test results are accepted in certain circumstances but you should check prior to travel.
Health care: Majuro has one private clinic and one public hospital. Ebeye has a public hospital. Most outer islands have medical dispensaries.

Travel - International

AIR: *Air Marshall Islands (CW)* provides regular scheduled internal flights to 10 of the atolls in the Marshall Islands and has planes available for charter. Flights are available between Honolulu and the Marshall Islands and to Fiji via Kiribati and Tuvalu. *Continental Micronesia (CS)* stops in Majuro and Kwajalein on its island-hopper service between Guam and Honolulu. *Aloha Airlines* also runs flights to the islands. *Continental Airlines (CO)* also offers weekly flights to and from Guam and Honolulu.
Approximate flight times: From *New York* to Majuro is 14 hours, from *Tokyo* it is 11 hours, from *Guam* it is eight hours and from *Honolulu* it is five hours .
International airports: *Majuro International Airport (MAJ)*. There are taxis and hotel transport from the airport to the town.
Departure tax: US$20 on international flights.
SEA: The international port is Majuro. Shipping lines servicing the Marshalls include *Daiwa Lines*, *Matson Lines*, *Micronesia & Orient Line*, *Nauru Pacific Line*, *Philippine* and *Tiger Lines*.
Four government-owned field ships connect the islands within the Marshalls on a regular schedule. Comfortable passenger cabins are available on these ships and arrangements can be made for charter trips. **Cruise:** *Royal Viking Line* and the *Asuka Cruise Ship* sometimes call at Majuro port, but not on a regular basis. The *Princess Cruise Line* visits Marjuro twice a year. Inter-island cruises are available. Boats can be rented from companies on the islands for sightseeing, diving tours, picnics, game fishing, snorkelling, water-skiing and other boating activities.
ROAD: All the main roads are paved. Driving is on the left. The minimum age is 18. **Taxi:** Plentiful and cheap. Generally used on a seat-sharing basis. **Car hire:** These are usually Japanese sedans. Companies include Deluxe Car Rental, Majuro, MH 96960 (tel: 625 3665; fax: 625 3663).
Documentation: A national driving licence is valid for 30 days.

Accommodation

There is a variety of first-class and budget hotels and some islands have guest houses. Restaurant and bar facilities are available in the more deluxe hotels.
CAMPING: Facilities are available on Majuro and various other islands. For further information, contact the Visitors Authority (see *Contact Addresses* section).

Resorts & Excursions

Many of the atolls are dotted with Flame of the Forest, hibiscus and different-coloured plumeria flowers. There are also at least 160 species of coral surrounding the islands. The uninhabited atolls are noted for their coconut and papaya plantations and for pandanus and breadfruit trees. The first stop in the Marshall Islands should be either **Ebeye** or **Majuro**, although visits to outer islands can be arranged. The former capital **Jaluit** (its name meaning both 'come here' and 'beautiful') boasts some of the best scuba diving and marine life among the islands. There are Sunday day-trips to **Maloelap** or **Mili** atolls where there are opportunities to snorkel over World War II wrecks, eat local food and watch dancing. There are also many historic sites and buildings. The **Alele Museum** ('alele' meaning a traditional Marshallese basket) has preserved the history and local traditions of the Marshallese culture. The Visitors Authority can provide information on various other sites.

Sport & Activities

Watersports: Opportunities for **diving** include drop-offs, coral heads, black coral and World War II wrecks. **Fishing** expeditions can be arranged by local hotels or the Marshalls Billfish Club (tel/fax: 625 7491). The club also organises monthly fishing tournaments. For further information, consult the Marshall Islands Journal *or* the Visitors Authority.

A B C D E F G H I J K L M N O P Q R S T U V W X Y Z

Other: Basketball, **volleyball**, **softball** and **tennis** are the favourite sports. Children play many indigenous games using local materials.

Social Profile

FOOD & DRINK: There are several restaurants in Majuro, serving Chinese, Marshallese, US and Western specialities. Consumption of alcohol is forbidden on some of the islands.
NIGHTLIFE: There are several nightclubs on Majuro and Ebeye and some hotels offer traditional dancing.
SHOPPING: Special purchases include *kili* handbags woven by former residents of Bikini, stick charts (once used to navigate long distances between the region's scattered islands), plaited floor mats, fans, purses, shell necklaces and baskets. There is a 3 per cent sales tax in Majuro. **Shopping hours:** Mon-Fri 0800-1700.
SPECIAL EVENTS: For a full list of special events and festivals taking place in the Marshall Islands, contact the Visitors Authority (see *Contact Addresses*). The following is a selection of special events occurring in the Marshall Islands in 2005:
Jan 1 *Marjuro Block Part*. **May** *Outrigger Marshall Islands Cup Traditional Canoe Race*. **May 1** *Constitution Day Sporting Events and Parade*. **Jul** *Billfish Tournament* (fishing tournament). **Sep** *Mobil All Micronesia Fishing Tournament*. **Nov** *Fishing Tournament*, Majuro. **Dec** *Chamber of Commerce Christmas Parade*.
SOCIAL CONVENTIONS: Informal dress is usual for both business and social occasions. Scanty clothing (including topless bathing) is considered offensive. Use of islands, paths, beaches etc may require permission in many areas; it is best to check locally. **Tipping:** Unnecessary.

Business Profile

ECONOMY: The economy suffers many of the problems faced by the small, remote island states of the Pacific. Aid subventions from the USA remain essential, while repeated and diverse attempts to broaden the base of the economy have met with mixed success. Agriculture is of a subsistence nature, with coconuts, tomatoes, melons and breadfruit as the main products. The fishing industry is dominated by a commercial tuna operation, which includes canning and transhipment. The islands' international shipping registry – a "flag of convenience" – has been a key source of income since the end of the 1980s, when many operators reflagged from Panama. The government had high hopes for a major tourist development, but the plans have been scaled down following the economic downturn in the Asia-Pacific region and may yet be further undermined by the islands' remote location. There is also an important offshore financial services industry. However, in April 2002 the Marshall Islands were one of seven countries 'named and shamed' by the Organisation for Economic Co-operation and Development, which has spearheaded a global assault on money-laundering, for their failure to tackle the issue. The USA provides around US$65 million annually in aid. The Marshall Islands is a member of the South Pacific Commission and the South Pacific Forum.
COMMERCIAL INFORMATION: For further information contact the Majuro Chamber of Commerce, Majuro MH 96960 (tel: 625 2525; fax: 625 2500).

Climate

Tropical, with cooling sea breezes and frequent rain. Trade winds blow steadily from the northeast from December through to March. Wettest months are usually October to November. The average temperature is 27°C (80°F).
Required clothing: Lightweight cottons and linens with rainwear.

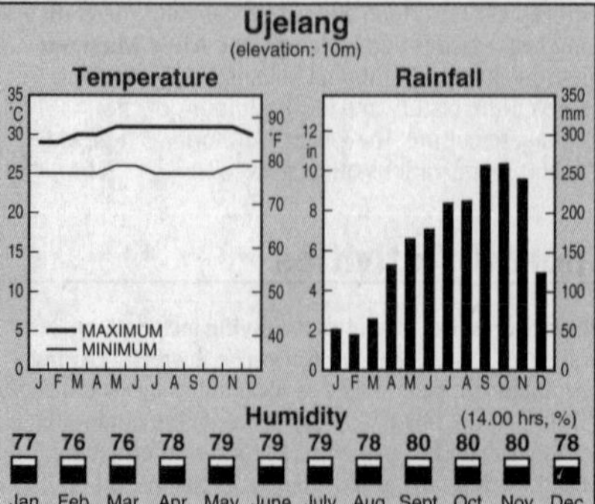

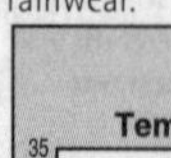

Northern Mariana Islands

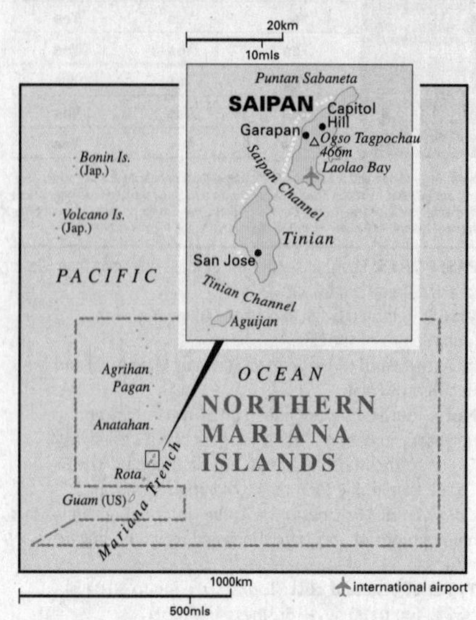

The Northern Mariana Islands include Saipan, Tinian and Rota (formerly the Marianas.)

Location: Western Pacific Ocean.

Country dialling code: 1 670.

Marianas Visitors Authority
PO Box 500861, Saipan MP 96950, Northern Mariana Islands
Tel: 664 3200/1. Fax: 664 3237.
E-mail: mva@saipan.com
Website: www.mymarianas.com
CNMI Division of Immigration
Street address: Afetna Square Building, 2nd Floor, San Antonio, Saipan MP 96950, Northern Mariana Islands
Postal address: PO Box 10007, San Antonio, Saipan MP 96950, Northern Mariana Islands
Tel: 236 0922/23. Fax: 664 3190.
Office of the CNMI Resident Representative to the United States
2121 R Street, NW, Washington, DC 20008, USA
Tel: (202) 673 5869. Fax: (202) 673 5873.
E-mail: rep@resrep.gov.mp
Website: www.resrep.gov.mp

General Information

AREA: 457 sq km (176.5 sq miles).
POPULATION: 74,151 (official estimate 2002).
POPULATION DENSITY: 162 per sq km (official estimate 2002).
CAPITAL: Saipan. **Population:** 67,011 (2002).
GEOGRAPHY: Located to the south of Japan and to the north of Guam, the Northern Mariana Islands comprise 14 islands, the main ones being Rota, Saipan and Tinian. The group is compact, consisting of a single chain 736km (460 miles) long. The islands have high volcanic cones.
GOVERNMENT: Self-governing US Commonwealth Territory (incorporated). Gained internal autonomy in 1986. **Head of State:** President George W Bush since 2000. **Head of Government:** Governor Juan Babauta since 2002.
LANGUAGE: English, Chamorro and Carolinian are the official languages. Japanese and Korean are widely spoken.
RELIGION: Mostly Roman Catholic.
TIME: GMT + 10.
COMMUNICATIONS: Telephone: IDD is available. Country code: 1 670. Outgoing international code: 00. There are payphones in Saipan and most hotels; restaurants and other public facilities have telephones which visitors can use. **Mobile telephone:** A GSM 1900 service is scheduled for launch soon by Wave Runner LLC Mariana Islands. **Fax:** A service is available. **Internet:** Main ISPs include *IT & E*, *MTC* and *Saipan Data Com* (website: www.saipan.com). Availability and reliability is limited. **Telegram:** Telegrams can be sent from Micronesia Telecommunications, PO Box 306, Saipan; opening hours 0800-1700. **Post:** There are post offices on the three main islands, as well as private postal companies in Saipan. US postal rates apply. Post office hours: Mon-Fri 0900-160, Sat 0900-1200. **Press:** The English-language newspapers include the *Pacific Daily News*, *Pacific Star* (weekly), *Saipan Tribune* (twice weekly) and the *Marianas Variety News and Views* (weekdays).

Passport/Visa

	Passport Required?	Visa Required?	Return Ticket Required?
Full British	Yes	No/3	Yes
Australian	Yes	2/3	Yes
Canadian	Yes	Yes/3	Yes
USA	Yes	No	No
Other EU	Yes	No/1/3	Yes
Japanese	Yes	2/3	Yes

Note: *Regulations and requirements may be subject to change at short notice, and you are advised to contact the appropriate diplomatic or consular authority before finalising travel arrangements. Details of these may be found at the head of this country's entry. Any numbers in the chart refer to the footnotes below.*

Restricted Entry and Transit: Nationals of the following countries are 'Excluded Locations' and must apply to the Northern Mariana Islands' Attorney General in Saipan for a preliminary waiver that is issued on a case-by-case basis and that necessitates additional documents (including providing, or having a sponsor provide, a bond by an approved bond company for US$5000 or amount decided by Attorney General, and official letter - bearing the seal of the relevant immigration or governmental authority in the particular excluded country - that declares that such country will unconditionally accept the return of the excluded national without delay): Afghanistan, Algeria, Bahrain, Bangladesh*, Cuba, Egypt, Eritrea, Fujian Province of China, Indonesia, Iran, Iraq, Jordan, Korea (Dem Rep), Kuwait, Lebanon, Libya, Morocco, Myanmar, Oman, Pakistan, Qatar, Saudi Arabia, Somalia, Sri Lanka*, Sudan, Syrian Arab Republic, Tunisia, United Arab Emirates and Yemen, unless having a US Visa in their passport, which should be valid for a minimum of 60 days after entry.
All aforementioned information should be submitted by fax or post at least four weeks prior to the intended date of departure.
Note: Nationals marked * require a letter guaranteeing expedited return in order to gain a preliminary waiver.
PASSPORTS: Passports valid for at least 60 days after date of entry are required by all.
VISAS: Required by all except the following:
(a) nationals of EU countries (except **1.** Cyprus, Czech Republic, Estonia, Greece, Hungary, Latvia, Lithuania, Malta, Poland and Slovak Republic who *do* require a visa as they are not current participants in the US Visa Waiver Program);
(b) **2.** nationals of Andorra, Australia, Brunei, Iceland, Japan, Liechtenstein, Monaco, New Zealand, Norway, San Marino, Singapore and Switzerland.
Note: 3. Nationals of Australia, Canada, Hong Kong (SAR), Ireland, Japan, Korea (Rep) and the UK are exempt from Visitor Entry Permits into the Northern Mariana Islands, although this may be counteracted by individual circumstances.
Types of visa and cost: Various; decided according to individual cases.
Note: All Visitor Entry Permit applications submitted one week or less prior to arrival will be processed at an emergency administrative fee of US$100.
Validity: Various. Visas are generally required for touristic stays of more than 30 days. Stays may be extended by an additional 60 days whilst in the Northern Mariana Islands.
Application to: CNMI Division of Immigration (see *Contact Addresses* section).
Application requirements: *Visitor Entry Permit*: (a) Possession of Authorization Board letter (approved by the Director of Immigration), including full name, permanent address, telephone number(s), purpose of visit, proof of place of employment, date of arrival and departure, airline carrier and flight number (full itinerary), passport (plus photocopy), proof of sufficient funds and address of intended location. A sponsor must submit a notarised Affidavit of Support letter, including copy of passport valid for at least 60 days after entry date, copy of Driver's License (if applicable), copy of entry permit, copy of two latest paycheck stubs, Business License (if applicable), and if sponsor is a company, a copy of the latest Business Gross Revenue (BGR) tax document. (b) Some individuals will need to submit evidence of police clearance, issued within six months of date of embarkation; contact the Division of Immigration for further information. *Visa*: Individuals will need to submit various documents, including some necessary for Visitor Entry Permits. Individuals should prepare by contacting the Division of Immigration well in advance to negotiate what documents are necessary for the individual processing of their visa.
Note: (a) Nationals of Indonesia and Malaysia *always* require Police Clearance for the processing of a Visitor Entry Permit. (b) Nationals of The Philippines *always* require a National Bureau Investigation (NBI) for the processing of a Visitor Entry Permit.
Working days required: By post: applications are dealt with on receipt. In person: subject to the discretion of the Division of Immigration. Generally, documents needed for

Credit: l-r © Larry Lee; © Larry Lee; © Marianas Beach Press

the processing of all Visitor Entry Permits should be submitted at least two weeks prior to arrival.
Temporary residence: Apply to CNMI Division of Immigration (see *Contact Addresses* section).

Money

Currency: The US Dollar is used. For further details of currency, credit & debit cards, traveller's cheques, exchange rate indicators and banking hours, see main *Pacific Islands of Micronesia* section.
Currency exchange: There are several Asian and US banks in the Mariana Islands where currencies from some foreign countries can be exchanged. ATMs are available at most banks and major shopping centres.
Currency restrictions: There are no restrictions on the import and export of local and foreign currency. Amounts exceeding US$10,000, however, must be declared.

Duty Free

The following goods may be imported into the Northern Mariana Islands without incurring customs duty:
600 cigarettes or 454g of cigars or tobacco; 2.3l of alcoholic beverage; 3.8l of wine and Japanese sake; a reasonable quantity of perfume.
Prohibited items: Narcotics and certain cooked and uncooked foods. Enquire at Immigration Office for details (see *Contact Addresses* section). Firearms require a licence.

Public Holidays

2005: Jan 1 New Year's Day. **Jan 9** Commonwealth Day. **Feb 14** President's Day. **Mar 24** Covenant Day. **Mar 25** Good Friday. **May 30** Memorial Day. **Jul 4** US Independence Day. **Sep 5** Labour Day. **Oct 10** Columbus Day. **Nov 4** Citizenship Day. **Nov 11** Veterans Day. **Nov 24** Thanksgiving Day. **Dec 9** Constitution Day. **Dec 25** Christmas Day.
2006: Jan 1 New Year's Day. **Jan 9** Commonwealth Day. **Feb 16** President's Day. **Mar 24** Covenant Day. **Apr 14** Good Friday. **May 29** Memorial Day. **Jul 4** US Independence Day. **Sep 4** Labour Day. **Oct 09** Columbus Day. **Nov 4** Citizenship Day. **Nov 11** Veterans Day. **Nov 23** Thanksgiving Day. **Dec 9** Constitution Day. **Dec 25** Christmas Day.
Note: Variations occur from island to island.

Health

There are no vaccination requirements. *Hepatitis A* and *B*, *dengue fever* and *TB* occur. Rare outbreaks of *Japanese encephalitis* have been reported.
Health care: There is a major, modern hospital on Saipan and routine facilities on Rota and Tinian. Full medical facilities are available but are not free of charge; health insurance is advisable.

Travel - International

AIR: Airlines serving the Northern Mariana Islands include *Asiana Airlines (OZ), China Southern Air (CZ), Continental Airlines (CO), Japan Airlines (JL), Korean Airlines (KE)* and *Northwest Airlines (NW)*.
International airports: International airports: Saipan (SPN), situated 3 miles (5km) south of Chalan Kanoa. Taxis are available to the town (travel time - 15 minutes) and tour buses may meet some flights. Airport facilities include bureau de change, refreshments and car hire (Budget and Hertz). There are smaller airports at Rota (ROP) and Tinian (TIQ).
Departure tax: None.
SEA: The international port of the Northern Mariana Islands is Saipan. The following lines sail there: *Daiwa Navigation Co, Nauru Pacific Line, Oceania Line Inc, P&O, Royal Shipping Co* (PO Box 238, Saipan), *Saipan Shipping Co* and *Tiger Line*.
ROAD: There are good roads in and around major island centres. **Bus:** There is a public shuttle bus service to major shopping facilities from hotels. **Taxi:** Available in all main centres. **Car hire:** Self-drive cars are available in towns; US driving laws are followed. **Documentation:** International Driving Permit or national licence accepted.

Travel - Internal

AIR: Commuter aircraft (from *Pacific Island Aviation* and *Freedom Air*) are available to take visitors from Saipan to Tinian (travel time - 12 minutes) and Rota (travel time - 30 minutes).
SEA: There is a ferry from Tinian to Saipan (travel time - 55 minutes).

Accommodation

Hotels in the Northern Mariana Islands vary in standard from luxury to basic. They cater mainly for Japanese and Korean markets. Contact the Hotel Association of the Northern Mariana Islands (HANMI), PO Box 501983, Saipan, MP 96950 (tel: 234 3455; fax: 234 3411; e-mail: rds@itecnmi.com; website: www.marianashotels.org).

Resorts & Excursions

The Northern Marianas consist of a chain of 14 islands nearly 55 miles in length. Volcanic in origin, they host a variety of scenery including beautiful bays, spectacular cliffs, caves and mountains. Because of their location they played a significant part in World War II, and the many shipwrecks around the coast bear witness to this. These, the numerous coral reefs and the clear water make them particularly good for diving.
Saipan: The largest island, Saipan, is relatively developed, with good amenities and shopping facilities. Its western shore is encircled by a barrier reef, creating a lagoon with white sand beaches. Attractions on Saipan include the last command post of the Japanese Imperial Army known as **Banadero**, with World War II cannons, tanks and artillery preserved in a limestone cave. Japanese and Korean peace memorials commemorate the islands' central role in the war. Spectacular views can be had from the **Puntan Sabaneta** (also known as Banzai Cliff) and **Laderan Banadero** (also known as 'Suicide Cliff' because of the thousands of Japanese soldiers and their families who jumped to their deaths from it in order to avoid capture).
Tinian: The island of Tinian, 3 miles south of Saipan, has a rugged coastline with tiny coves. At **Abbas** on the northern shore, there are blow holes where incoming waves shoot 20ft into the air. The **House of Taga**, a temple or meeting house associated with the legendary chief Taga, consists of magnificent stone pillars, carved in the traditional way and transported from nearby coastal areas.
Rota: Rota is a small and friendly island with a variety of natural attractions. In the main village of **Songsong**, life is conducted at a leisurely pace. Outside Songsong, sights include **Toga Cave**, a huge limestone cavern with stalactites and stalagmites, so large it was used as a wartime hospital. Wedding Cake Mountain, resembling a layered cake, is a fascinating sight. An interesting collection of artefacts can be viewed at the **Rota Cave Museum**, located in a gigantic limestone cave. At the **Taga Stone Quarry**, huge ancient stone remains carved by the Chamorros can be seen.
Elsewhere: Isleta Maigo Fahang (also known as Bird Island) and **Managha Island** are beautiful, unspoilt islands, set aside as nature reserves. The former can be visited in a glass-bottomed boat.

Sport & Activities

Watersports: These are popular, with many suitable **diving** and **snorkelling** locations; **windsurfing** is popular on Saipan. **Parasailing** is available. Local **fishing** competitions are held in several places. Those not wishing to dive to see wrecks and underwater scenery can go on submarine cruises. For details, contact Pacific Subsea Saipan Inc (tel: 322 7746/7; fax: 322 4770; e-mail: submarine@saipan.com; website: www.submarine.co.mp).
Other: San Jose has a **bowling** alley and there are 9- and 18-hole **golf** courses. Good **hiking** is available on all three main islands. **Hunting**, **bird**- and **volcano-watching** may also be possible.

Social Profile

FOOD & DRINK: Local specialities include *kelaguin*, a chewy mixture of diced chicken and shredded coconut and thin slices of raw coconut dipped in a peppery sauce. A wide choice of food is on offer, including Chinese, French, Italian, Japanese, Thai and US.
NIGHTLIFE: There are several popular bars in Garapan and a few nightclubs and discos.
SHOPPING: Special purchases here include wishing dolls, coconut masks, coconut-crab decorations and woodcarvings, plus numerous duty free items.
Shopping hours: Mon-Sun 0800-2100.
SPECIAL EVENTS: Village fiestas in honour of local patron saints are among the principal annual celebrations. For further information on special events in the Northern Marianas contact the Marianas Visitors' Authority (see *Contact Addresses* section), which produces an annual listing. The following is a selection of special events occurring in the Northern Mariana Islands in 2005:
Jan *Half marathon*. **Feb** *5th Annual Pic/Powerade Tennis Championships*, Saipan. **Feb** *Tinian Tropical Triathlon & Reef Swim*. **Mar** *Flame Tree Festival* (a variety of cultural entertainment and exhibitions of local art). **Apr** *5th Rota Blue Ocean Swim*. **Jul-Aug** *Marianas Windsurfing Cup*, Saipan. **Oct** *Festival of San Francisco do Borja*, Rota.
SOCIAL CONVENTIONS: The Chamorro culture of the original inhabitants can still be traced, although it is overlaid by strong American influences. Western conventions are well understood.

Business Profile

ECONOMY: Fruit, vegetables, beef and pork are produced in commercial quantities, with some being exported. Fisheries and copra are other important industries in the agricultural sector. Manufacturing is dominated by textile production. The economy is dominated overall, however, by the service sector, of which tourism is the principal component. The establishment of an air link with Japan gave a major boost to this sector. However, the lack of available workers led to the recruitment of large numbers of foreign workers (which accounts for the huge growth in the islands' population). Bilateral aid from the USA is an important source of income for the Government, particularly monies earmarked for the development of the islands' infrastructure, the poor condition of which is currently holding back further economic growth. The Northern Marianas is a member of the Pacific Community.
COMMERCIAL INFORMATION: For further information contact the Saipan Chamber of Commerce, PO Box 500806 CK, 96950, Saipan MP (tel: 233 7150; fax: 233 7151; e-mail: saipanchamber@saipan.com; website: www.saipanchamber.com).

Credit: © Eran Moore

Climate

Tropical climate, tempered by trade winds. The rainy season is July to November.
Required clothing: Lightweight cottons and linens, with light rainwear advisable all year.

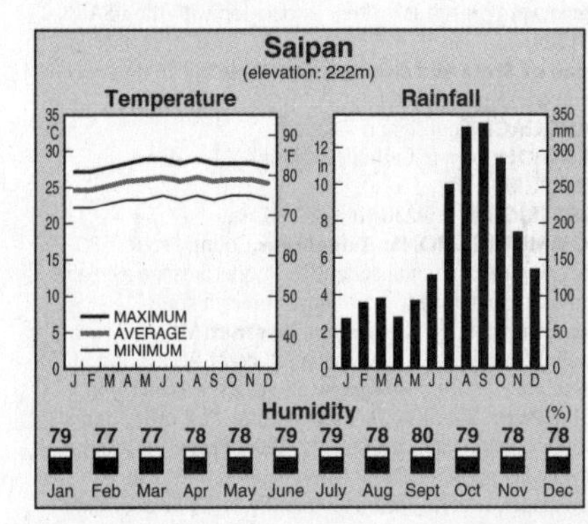

Palua

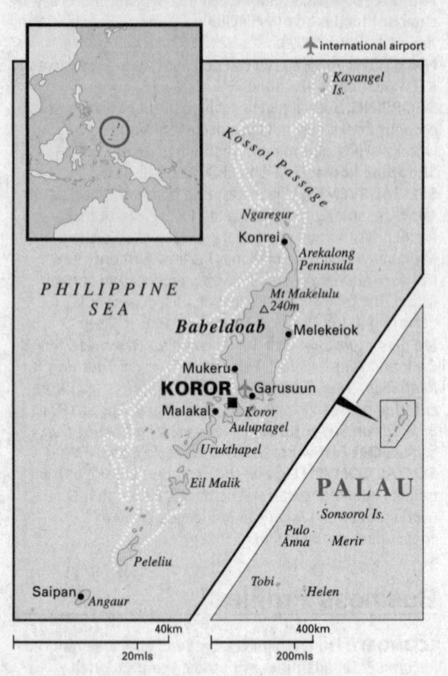

Palau was formerly part of the Caroline Islands.
Location: Western Pacific Ocean.

Country dialling code: 680.

Palau Visitors Authority
PO Box 256, Koror, Palau 96940
Tel: 488 2793/1930. Fax: 488 1453.
E-mail: pva@visit-palau.com
Website: www.visit-palau.com

Embassy of the Republic of Palau
1800K Street, NW 714, Washington, DC 20006, USA
Tel: (202) 452 6814. Fax: (202) 452 6281.
E-mail: info@palauembassy.com
Website: www.palauembassy.com

Embassy of the United States of America
PO Box 6028, Ngermid Hamlet, Koror, Palau 96940
Tel: 488 2920. Fax: 488 2911.
E-mail: usembassy@palaunet.com

General Information

AREA: 508 sq km (196 sq miles), including Babeldaob Island, whose area is 409 sq km (158 sq miles).
POPULATION: 19,129 (2000).
POPULATION DENSITY: 37.7 per sq km.
CAPITAL: Koror. **Population:** 11,560 (1995).
GEOGRAPHY: Palau, the westernmost cluster of the six major island groups that make up the Caroline Islands, lies 1000km (600 miles) east of The Philippines. The archipelago stretches over 650km (400 miles) from the atoll of Kayangel to the islet of Tobi. The Palau islands include more than 200 islands, of which only eight are inhabited. With three exceptions, all of the islands are located within a single barrier reef and represent two geological formations. The largest are volcanic and rugged with interior jungle and large areas of grassed terraces. The Rock Islands, now known as the Floating Garden Islands, are of limestone formation, while Kayangel, at the northernmost tip, is a classic coral atoll.
GOVERNMENT: Republic since 1947. Gained self-governing status (in free association with the USA) in 1994.
Head of State and Government: President Tommy Remengesau since 2001.
LANGUAGE: English and Palauan.
RELIGION: Roman Catholic majority.
TIME: GMT + 9.
ELECTRICITY: 115/230 volts AC, 60 Hz.
COMMUNICATIONS: Telephone: Country code: 680. Outgoing international code: 011. Phonecards are available and calls can be made from most hotels in Koror. **Fax:** Some hotels have facilities. **Internet:** Main ISP is *Paulau Net* (website: www.palaunet.com). Access and reliability is limited. **Telegram:** Services are available in Koror. **Post:** Post office located in Koror. Post office hours: Mon-Fri 0800-1600, Sat 0900 to 1000. **Press:** The main newspaper is *Pacific Daily News* (Guam). The local newspaper, which appears fortnightly, is *Tia Belau*; *Palau Horizon* appears weekly.

Passport/Visa

	Passport Required?	Visa Required?	Return Ticket Required?
Full British	Yes	3	Yes
Australian	Yes	3	Yes
Canadian	Yes	3	Yes
USA	1	2	Yes
Other EU	Yes	3	Yes
Japanese	Yes	3	Yes

Note: *Regulations and requirements may be subject to change at short notice, and you are advised to contact the appropriate diplomatic or consular authority before finalising travel arrangements. Details of these may be found at the head of this country's entry. Any numbers in the chart refer to the footnotes below.*

PASSPORTS: 1. Passports valid for at least 30 days beyond intended period of stay required by all except US nationals holding proof of citizenship accompanied by any other photo ID document.
VISAS: Required by all except:
(a) **2.** nationals of Marshall Islands, Micronesia and the USA for up to one year;
(b) **3.** all other nationals for stays of up to 30 days; Entry Permits are issued on arrival. For longer stays, permission must be granted from the Chief of Immigration.
Types of visa and cost: *Entry Permit*: US$50. Extension is possible for two times 30 days if application is made no less than seven days beyond expiration of visa. *Extension*: US$100.
Validity: Various.
Application to: Chief of Immigration, Bureau of Legal Affairs, Ministry of Justice, PO Box 100, Koror 96940.
Application Requirements: (a) Valid passport. (b) Vaccination certificates from those arriving from infected areas; see the *Health* section for details. (c) Proof of adequate funds (US$200 per week). (d) Return or onward tickets. A bond signed by the chief of Immigration prior to arrival can be accepted instead of return/onward tickets. (e) All visitors must sign a declaration stating that they are HIV-negative. (f) Fee.
Note: These application requirements do not apply to government officials, students and nationals of the Marshall Islands, Micronesia and the USA.
Working days required: Postal applications are dealt with on receipt but visas are usually issued on arrival.
Temporary residence: Apply to Division of Immigration (address above).

Money

Currency: The US Dollar is in use. For further information on currency, currency exchange, credit & debit cards, traveller's cheques, exchange rate indicators and banking hours, see main *Pacific Islands of Micronesia* section.
Currency restrictions: There are no limits on the import and export of local or foreign currency, but amounts of more than US$5000 must be declared.

Duty Free

The following goods may be imported into the Republic of Palau without incurring customs duty:
200 cigarettes or 454g of cigars or tobacco; one bottle of liquor.
Note: Alcohol for passengers over 21 years of age only.
Prohibited items: Narcotics, firearms, shells and natural artefacts.

Public Holidays

2005: Jan 1 New Year's Day. **Mar 15** Youth Day. **May 5** Senior Citizens' Day. **Jun 1** President's Day. **Jul 9** Constitution Day. **Sep 5** Labour Day. **Oct 1** Independence Day. **Oct 24** United Nations Day. **Nov 24** Thanksgiving Day. **Dec 25** Christmas Day.
2006: Jan 1 New Year's Day. **Mar 15** Youth Day. **May 5** Senior Citizens' Day. **Jun 1** President's Day. **Jul 9** Constitution Day. **Sep 4** Labour Day. **Oct 1** Independence Day. **Oct 24** United Nations Day. **Nov 23** Thanksgiving Day. **Dec 25** Christmas Day.

Health

Vaccination certificates for *yellow fever*, *cholera* and *smallpox* are required from all travellers arriving from infected areas. *Hepatitis B* is endemic. *Hepatitis A*, *typhoid fever* and *dengue fever* can occur.
Health care: Palau has two private medical clinics and a public hospital. As health care is not free, health insurance is recommended.

Travel - International

AIR: *Palau Micronesia Air* began international flights in 2004 (website: www.palau-air.com). *Continental Airlines (CO)* operates from Guam. There are twice weekly flights to Manila, from where connections to other destinations can be made. *Japan Airlines (JL)* flies from Nagoya, Japan, and *Far Eastern Airlines (EF)* flies directly from Taipei.
International airports: *Koror Babeldaob (ROR)* on Babeldaob Island, which is near Koror Island, is 12 miles (19km) northeast of Airai. Buses and taxis are available to Airai and Koror. Travel time to Koror is approximately 30 minutes.
Departure tax: US$20.
SEA: International cruise lines seldom call at Palau ports. Visitors who sail privately to Palau will find Naval Oceanographic charts to be most useful. US Naval Chart HO 5500 covers the entire region of Micronesia. Unscheduled inter-island boat services are available to Babeldaob and Kayangel. Anguar and Peleliu have scheduled boat services.
ROAD: The road network is extended beyond Koror to Babeldaob Island with many coral and dirt roads connecting to other states. A 4-wheel-drive car is recommended if you wish to see Babeldaob. Cars can be hired from the airport. Driving is on the right and the speed limit is 40kph (25mph).
Taxi: There are many taxis in Koror offering comfortable travel. They are not metered and fares are fixed.

Accommodation

There is a wide variety of accommodation on Palau and the outlying islands, ranging from first-class luxury resorts with most services, to the mid-priced bungalows and motels. While most resorts are located in Koror, there is quieter and more secluded accommodation available on the southern islands. For more information, contact the Palau Visitors Authority (see *Contact Addresses* section).

Resorts & Excursions

KOROR: The capital, Koror, is the busiest centre in the islands with many gift shops, restaurants and other resort facilities. For an insight into Palau's history, a visit to the **Palau National Museum** is advised, where more than 1000 relics of Palau's past are housed, including shell money and traditional weapons.
BABELDAOB: Palau's biggest island is about 43km (27 miles) long and 24km (15 miles) across at its widest, and is covered in dense foliage. The terrain is varied with steep mountains, freshwater lakes and sand dunes. Palau's first inhabitants settled along the coastline. Today, visitors can explore the 37 stone monoliths known as *Badrulchau* which are concrete examples of the island's early civilisation. Other remnants of Palau's history are located at **Imeungs** in the southwest of the island. These stone foundations and pillars are all that remain of the political and military centre of this part of the island.
ELSEWHERE: For sports lovers, the **Rock Islands** offer endless possibilities for snorkelling, sea kayaking, sailing and fishing. The island of **Peleliu** forms the southern boundary of the Rock Islands. In 1985 it was designated a US National Historic Landmark, owing to the part it played during World War II. Abandoned tanks, helmets and bomb casings are still dotted throughout the island.

Sport & Activities

Snorkelling & diving: Located between Guam, The Philippines and Papua New Guinea, Palau is an archipelago which is more than 640km (400 miles) long and harbours one of the world's greatest concentrations of corals, fish and other marine life. As such, Palau has some of the world's most spectacular snorkelling and diving locations. Palau's coral reefs are home to more than 1500 species of fish and 700 species of corals and sea anemones. Plunging walls, coral gardens and World War II wrecks are all part of the range of diving available. The local marine life is abundant. Palau's most popular dive sites include *Blue Corner*, where Dogtooth tuna, resident Napoleon wrasses, wahoo and other large fish float on the rapid current; *Ngemelis Wall*, commonly referred to as the Big Drop-off, and praised by Jacques Cousteau; the *German Channel*, known for its regular sightings of manta rays; *Siaes Tunnel*, an enormous underwater cavern where white-tip reef sharks can almost always be seen; *Chandelier Cave*, a series of underwater chambers filled with ancient stalactites; and the *Rock Islands*, which are dotted with sunken remains of over 75 World War II ships and seaplanes, which have developed their own ecosystem where fish, corals and other invertebrates not commonly seen along the outer reef systems thrive. Millions of jellyfish inhabit *Jellyfish Lake*, cut off from the rest of the ocean; snorkellers can get up close as they no longer have their stings.
Sea kayaking: Guided tours can be tailored to meet the abilities of an experienced or beginner kayaker. The Rock Islands are one of the most popular kayaking destinations.

Fishing: Palau offers both light-tackle and deep-water fishing, with gamefish such as blue marlin, tuna, snapper, giant trevallies, wahoo and mahi-mahi being among the species that can be caught here.

Social Profile

FOOD & DRINK: Many restaurants offer an eclectic mix of cuisine. Fresh local seafood is the highlight of many menus and there are many exotic local dishes in addition to the ubiquitous pizza.
NIGHTLIFE: There are several open-air cocktail lounges.
SHOPPING: Koror has a range of modern shopping facilities on offer. The Belau National Museum and Ormuul Gift Shop offer authentic handmade local crafts. Palau's best-known art form is the *storyboard*. These are carvings on various lengths of wood. The storyboards depict Palauan stories taken from about 30 popular legends or recorded events. In addition to the storyboards, models of *bais* (men's meeting buses), canoes and sculptured figurines called *dilukai* are also carved. Other gifts include jewellery, etchings and baskets, purses, hats and mats woven from pandanas and palm. The Palau Pacific Resort has a duty free shop. **Shopping hours:** Mon-Sat 0800-2100.
SPECIAL EVENTS: The following is a selection of special events occurring in Palau in 2005:
Mar 16-19 *Underwater Palau International Photo Festival.* **Apr-May** *Annual Fishing Derby* (sports fishing event). **Apr** *Earth Day.* **Jul** *Festival of the Pacific Arts.* **Jul-Aug** *Mini South Pacific Games.* **Oct 1** *Independence Day Celebrations.*
SOCIAL CONVENTIONS: Traditional Palauan society was a complex matriarchal system. The people are now amongst the most enterprising in the region, though a version of traditional beliefs, *Modekngei*, exists alongside the imported Christian beliefs. The political system is modelled on that of the USA, and Western culture is being assimilated – not least because of the many Palauans who continue their education abroad. **Tipping:** Optional.

Business Profile

ECONOMY: Subsistence agriculture is a vital employer, with cassava, coconuts, bananas and sweet potatoes as the main crops. Fishing is valuable mainly through the sale of licences to large foreign fleets allowing them to operate within Palau's 200-mile territorial limit. Industry is limited to small-scale light manufacturing, such as food-processing and boat-building. Foreign aid, mainly from the US, completes the country's principal sources of revenue. Tourism has grown steadily during the last decade despite problems arising from the islands' inaccessibility and a lack of investment, especially in basic infrastructure. Palau is a member of the two main regional economic organisations, the South Pacific Forum and the South Pacific Commission.
COMMERCIAL INFORMATION: For further information contact the Palau Chamber of Commerce, PO Box 1742, Koror 96940 (tel: 488 3400; fax: 488 3401; e-mail: pcoc@palaunet.com).
CONFERENCES/CONVENTIONS: The Airai View Hotel in Koror can provide facilities for up to 150 delegates. For more information, contact the Airai View Hotel, PO Box 8067, Koror, Palau 96940 (tel: 587 3530/1; fax: 587 3533; e-mail: reservation@airaiview.com *or* avh@palaunet.com; website: www.airaiview.com).

Climate

Palau enjoys a pleasantly warm climate all year round, with an annual average temperature of 27°C (82°F). The heaviest rainfall takes place between July and October but typhoons are rare.
Required clothing: Lightweight cottons and linens, with light rainwear advisable all year round.

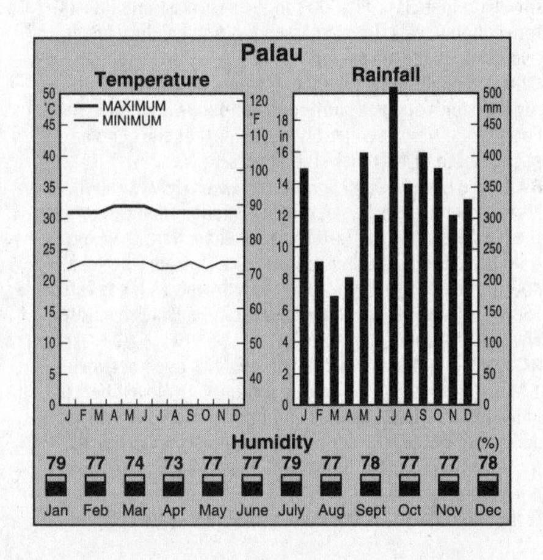

Pakistan

LATEST TRAVEL ADVICE CONTACTS

British Foreign and Commonwealth Office
Tel: (0870) 606 0290 Website: www.fco.gov.uk
US Department of State
Website: http://travel.state.gov/travel
Canadian Department of Foreign Affairs and Int'l Trade
Tel: (1 800) 267 8376 Website: www.dfait-maeci.gc.ca

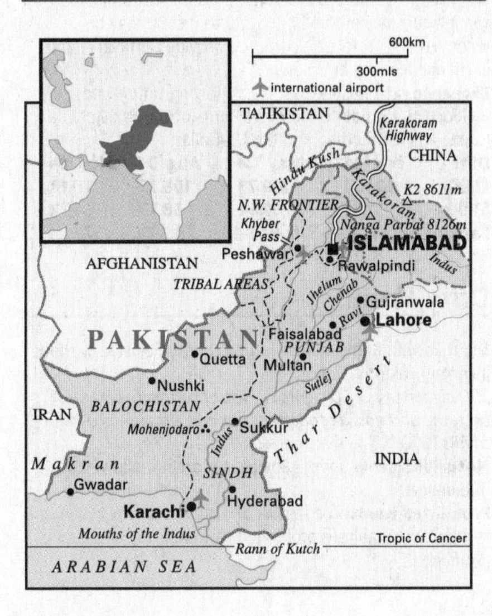

Location: South Asia.

Country dialling code: 92.

Pakistan Tourism Development Corporation (PTDC)
22 Saeed Plaza, Jinnah Avenue, Blue Area, Islamabad 44000, Pakistan
Tel: (51) 921 2722-26.
Fax: (51) 921 9702/08.
E-mail: tourism@isb.comsats.net.pk *or* mdptdc@comsats.net.pk *or* ptdc3@paknet.com.pk
Website: www.tourism.gov.pk
High Commission for the Islamic Republic of Pakistan
34-36 Lowndes Square, London SW1X 9JN, UK
Tel: (020) 7664 9200 (switchboard) *or* 9284 (reception).
Fax: (020) 7664 9224.
E-mail: pareplondon@supanet.com
Website: www.pakmission-uk.gov.pk
Opening hours: Mon-Fri 0930-1300 and 1400-1730; 1000-1300 (visa submission); 1630-1730 (visa collection).
Consulates in: Birmingham (tel: (0121) 233 4123), Bradford (tel: (01274) 661 114), Glasgow (tel: (0141) 429 5335) and Manchester (0161) 225 2005).
British High Commission
Street address: Diplomatic Enclave, Ramna 5, Islamabad, Pakistan
Postal address: PO Box 1122, Islamabad, Pakistan
Tel: (51) 282 4728 *or* 9355.
Fax: (51) 227 9356 (consular section) *or* 9355 (visa section).
E-mail: visqry.islamabad@fco.gov.uk (visa enquiries) *or* Cons.Islamabad@fco.gov.uk (consular enquiries) *or* bhcmedia@dsl.net.pk (all non-visa related enquiries).
Website: www.britishhighcommission.gov.uk/pakistan
Consulate in: Karachi.
Embassy of the Islamic Republic of Pakistan
3517 International Court, NW, Washington, DC 20008, USA
Tel: (202) 243 6500.
Fax: (202) 686 6373 (consular section).
E-mail: info@embassyofpakistan.org
Website: www.embassyofpakistan.org
Consulate General of the Islamic Republic of Pakistan
12 East, 65th Street, New York, NY 10021, USA
Tel: (212) 879 5800 *or* 517 7541. Fax: (212) 517 6987.
E-mail: nyconsulate@embassyofpakistan.org
Website: www.embassyofpakistan.org

TIMATIC CODES

Health	AMADEUS: **TI-DFT/ISB/HE** GALILEO/WORLDSPAN: **TI-DFT/ISB/HE** SABRE: **TIDFT/ISB/HE**
Visa	AMADEUS: **TI-DFT/ISB/VI** GALILEO/WORLDSPAN: **TI-DFT/ISB/VI** SABRE: **TIDFT/ISB/VI**

To access TIMATIC country information on Health and Visa regulations through the Computer Reservations System (CRS), type in the appropriate command line listed above.

Embassy of the United States of America
Street address: Diplomatic Enclave, Ramna 5, Islamabad, Pakistan
Postal address: PO Box 1048, Islamabad, Pakistan
Tel: (51) 2080 0000 *or* 2700 (visa section). Fax: (51) 227 6427 (general) *or* 282 2632 (visa section).
E-mail: paknivinfo@state.gov (non-immigrant visa information).
Website: http://islamabad.usembassy.gov
Consulates in: Karachi, Lahore and Peshawar.
High Commission of the Islamic Republic of Pakistan
10 Range Road, Ottawa, Ontario K1N 8J3, Canada
Tel: (613) 238 7881-2.
Fax: (613) 238 7296.
E-mail: parepottawa@rogers.com
Website: www.pakmission.ca
Consulates in: Montréal (tel: (514) 845 2297) and Toronto (tel: (416) 250 1255).
Canadian High Commission
PO Box 1042, Diplomatic Enclave, Sector G-5, Islamabad, Pakistan
Tel: (51) 227 9100-4.
Fax: (51) 227 9110.
E-mail: isbad@dfait-maeci.gc.ca
Website: www.dfait-maeci.gc.ca/islamabad
Honorary Consulate in: Karachi (tel: (21) 561 0685).

General Information

AREA: 796,095 sq km (307,374 sq miles), excluding data for the disputed territories of Jammu and Kashmir.
POPULATION: 149,030,000 (official estimate 2003).
POPULATION DENSITY: 187.2 per sq km.
CAPITAL: Islamabad. **Population:** 524,500 (1998).
GEOGRAPHY: Pakistan has borders to the north with Afghanistan, to the east with India and to the west with Iran; the Arabian Sea lies to the south. In the northeast is the disputed territory of Jammu and Kashmir, bounded by Afghanistan, China and India. Pakistan comprises distinct regions. The northern highlands – the Hindu Kush – are rugged and mountainous; the Indus Valley is a flat, alluvial plain with five major rivers dominating the upper region, eventually joining the Indus River and flowing south to the Makran coast; Sindh is bounded on the east by the Thar Desert and the Rann of Kutch, and on the west by the Kirthar Range; the Baluchistan Plateau is an arid tableland encircled by mountains.
GOVERNMENT: Federal Islamic Republic since 1973. Gained independence from the UK in 1947. **Head of State:** President Pervez Musharraf since 2001. **Head of Government:** Following a military coup in October 1999, General Pervez Musharraf took over as the leader of the new military regime. Prime Minister: Former finance minister Shaukat Aziz was made prime minister in August 2004.
LANGUAGE: Urdu is the national language. English is widely spoken. Regional languages include Punjabi, which is spoken by 48 per cent of the population (1981), Pushto, Sindhi, Saraiki, and Baluchi. There are numerous local dialects.
RELIGION: 97 per cent Muslim, the remainder are Hindu or Christian.
TIME: GMT + 5.
ELECTRICITY: 220 volts AC, 50Hz. Round two- or three-pin plugs are in use.
COMMUNICATIONS: Telephone: IDD is available. Country code: 92. Outgoing international code: 00.
Mobile Telephone: GSM 900 networks available. Main network providers include *Mobilink* (website: www.mobilinkgsm.com), *Pakistan Communications Mobile Ltd* (website: www.ufonegsm.com), *Paktel Limited* (website: www.paktel.com), *Telenor Pakistan* (website: www.telenor.com/pakistan) and *Warid Telecom.* Coverage is largely limited to main cities. **Fax:** Services are operated by the Pakistani telephone and telegraph department.
Internet: Main ISPs include *Pak Net* (website: www.paknet.com.pk) and *Pakistan Online* (website: www.pol.com.pk). Internet cafes exist in many urban areas. **Telegram:** There are services at post offices, telegraph offices and main hotels. The Central Telegraph Offices provide a 24-hour service. **Post:** Airmail takes four to five days to reach Western Europe. There are *poste restante* facilities in Karachi, Lahore and Rawalpindi. General post offices in major cities offer 24-hour services. Important letters should be registered or insured. **Press:** The English-language press enjoys a great deal of influence in business circles. Dailies include *Business Recorder, Dawn, Financial Post, Frontier Post, Leader, Pakistan Observer, Pakistan Times, Star, The Nation* and *The News.*
Radio: BBC World Service (website: www.bbc.co.uk/worldservice) and Voice of America (website: www.voa.gov) can be received. From time to time the frequencies change and the most up-to-date can be found online.

Passport/Visa

	Passport Required?	Visa Required?	Return Ticket Required?
Full British	Yes	Yes	Yes
Australian	Yes	Yes	Yes
Canadian	Yes	Yes	Yes
USA	Yes	Yes	Yes
Other EU	Yes	Yes	Yes
Japanese	Yes	Yes	Yes

Note: *Regulations and requirements may be subject to change at short notice, and you are advised to contact the appropriate diplomatic or consular authority before finalising travel arrangements. Details of these may be found at the head of this country's entry. Any numbers in the chart refer to the footnotes below.*

Note: Travellers are currently advised against travel to certain areas of Pakistan: All travel to Waziristan is strongly discouraged. All non-essential travel to northern and western Baluchistan and western North West Frontier Province (NWFP) and all border areas is advised against.
Restricted entry and transit: The Government of Pakistan refuses entry to nationals of Israel, even for transit. Nationals of Afghanistan are refused entry if their passports or tickets show evidence of transit or boarding in India. Holders of Taiwan (China) passports are refused entry except in transit or airport transit.
PASSPORTS: Passport valid for six months beyond the intended length of stay required by all.
VISAS: Required by all except the following:
(a) holders of a Pakistan Origin Card (POC) regardless of nationality for unlimited stay;
(b) nationals of Tonga and Trinidad & Tobago for an unlimited period;
(c) nationals of Iceland, Maldives and Zambia for stays of up to a maximum of three months;
(d) nationals of Nepal and Samoa, and holders of Chinese passports issued in Hong Kong (SAR), for stays of up to 30 days;
(e) transit passengers continuing their journey within 24 hours by the same or first connecting aircraft, provided they are holding onward or return documentation and not leaving the airport;
(f) holders of UN laissez-passer.
Note: Nationals of Algeria, Bangladesh, Bhutan, India, Iraq, Israel, Libya, Nigeria, Palestinian Authority passport holders, Serbia & Montenegro, Somalia, Sri Lanka, Sudan, Tanzania, Uganda and Yemen must report to the nearest Foreigners Registration Office for registration, except for those issued *Work* permits/visas in the managerial category. In certain circumstances, this may also be applicable to other nationals and will be indicated on their passports.
Types of visa and cost: Price of visa varies according to nationality. For UK nationals, prices are: *Single-entry:* £40; *Double-entry:* £54; *Multiple-entry:* £74. These prices are identical to those issued for the *Visa for Media Professionals*, which must be routed through the Information Division of the Pakistan High Commission. For Pakistanis holding dual nationality, prices are: *Adult:* £24; *Child* (up to 18 years old): £12; valid for stays of up to one year. Applicants with parents holding Pakistani passports get the same concession, provided they produce the original detailed birth certificate and their parents' Pakistani passports. *Pilgrim (Single-entry)*: £45. This is issued to those wishing to visit holy places (Shrines/Gurdawaras) in Pakistan and is allowed for groups of pilgrims, normally restricted to a specified period. *Business:* £68 (*Single-entry*); £90 (*Double-entry*); £111 (*Multiple-entry*). Certain nationals are issued visas free of charge, but they must be obtained prior to travel. For further information, consult the High Commission or Embassy.
Validity: Single-entry/Double-entry: six months from the date of issue for stays of up to three months. Multiple-entry: six months to one year.
Application to: Consulate (or Consular section at Embassy or High Commission); see *Contact Addresses* section.
Application requirements: (a) Original valid passport, plus one photocopy. (b) One application form. (c) Two passport-size photos. (d) Confirmed return/onward ticket. (e) Proof of sufficient funds for duration of stay. (f) Fee, payable by cash or postal order only. (g) For business trips, a letter of invitation from a company in Pakistan.
Note: There may be slightly different application requirements for Indian nationals and the nearest Consulate/Embassy should be contacted for further information prior to travel.
Working days required: Depends on nationality (in UK, visas are normally granted within 24 to 48 hours). Enquire at the nearest Consulate or Embassy. Pilgrim visas require two months' processing time.

Money

Currency: Pakistani Rupee (PRe, singular; PRs, plural) = 100 paisa. Notes are in denominations of PRs1000, 500, 100, 50, 10 and 5. Coins are in denominations of PRs2 and 1, and 50 and 25 paisa.
Credit & debit cards: American Express is the most widely accepted card. MasterCard and Visa are also good, but Diners Club and other cards have more limited use. Check with your credit or debit card company for details of merchant acceptability and other services which may be available.
Travellers cheques: Generally accepted at most banks, 4- and 5-star hotels and major shops. To avoid additional exchange rate charges, travellers are advised to take travellers cheques in US Dollars or Pounds Sterling.
Currency restrictions: The import and export of local currency is limited to PRs100 in denominations of PRs10 or less (the import of banknotes in denominations of PRs50 and PRs100 or more is prohibited). The import and export of foreign currency are unlimited. Up to Prs500 may be reconverted into foreign currency, provided official exchange receipts are shown.
Exchange rate indicators: The following figures are included as a guide to the movements of the Pakistani Rupee against Sterling and the US Dollar:

Date	Feb '04	May '04	Aug '04	Nov '04
£1.00=	104.51	102.77	108.27	111.81
$1.00=	57.41	57.54	58.77	59.77

Banking hours: Mon-Sat 0900-1330, Fri 0900-1230.

Duty Free

The following items may be imported into Pakistan without incurring customs duty:
*200 cigarettes or 50 cigars or 8oz of tobacco; 250ml of perfume and eau de toilette (opened); gifts up to a value of PRs2000.**
Note: * Residents under 18 years old are not allowed any free import.
Prohibited items: The import of alcohol, matches, plants, fruit and vegetables is prohibited. The export of antiques is prohibited.

Public Holidays

2005: Jan 21 Eid ul-Azha (Feast of the Sacrifice). **Feb 20** Ashoura. **Mar 23** Pakistan Day. **Apr 21** Eid-e-Milad-un-Nabi (Birth of the Prophet). **Aug 14** Independence Day. **Nov 3-5** Eid al-Fitr (End of Ramadan). **Nov 9** Allama Muhammad Iqbal Day. **Dec 25** Quaid-e-Azam's Birthday.
2006: Jan 13 Eid ul-Azha (Feast of the Sacrifice). **Feb 9** Ashoura. **Mar 23** Pakistan Day. **Apr 11** Eid-e-Milad-un-Nabi (Birth of the Prophet). **Aug 14** Independence Day. **Oct 22-24** Eid al-Fitr (End of Ramadan). **Nov 9** Allama Muhammad Iqbal Day. **Dec 25** Quaid-e-Azam's Birthday.
Note: (a) Muslim festivals are timed according to local sightings of various phases of the moon and the dates given above are approximations. During the lunar month of Ramadan that precedes Eid al-Fitr, Muslims fast during the day and feast at night and normal business patterns may be interrupted. Most restaurants are closed during the day and there is a restriction on smoking and drinking in public places. Eid al-Fitr and Eid ul-Azha may last from two to four days, depending on the region. For more information, see the *World of Islam* appendix. (b) Christian holidays are observed by the Christian community only.

Health

	Special Precautions?	Certificate Required?
Yellow Fever	No	1
Cholera	2	No
Typhoid & Polio	3	N/A
Malaria	4	N/A

Note: *Regulations and requirements may be subject to change at short notice, and you are advised to contact your doctor well in advance of your intended date of departure. Any numbers in the chart refer to the footnotes below.*

1: Yellow fever vaccination certificate is required of all travellers arriving within six days from any part of a country in which yellow fever is endemic. Infants under six months of age are exempt if the mother's vaccination certificate shows her to have been vaccinated prior to the child's birth. Countries and areas within the endemic zone are regarded as infected.
2: Following WHO guidelines issued in 1973, a cholera vaccination certificate is no longer a condition of entry to Pakistan. However, cholera is a serious risk in this country and precautions are essential. Up-to-date advice should be sought before deciding whether these precautions should include vaccination, as medical opinion is divided over its effectiveness; see the *Health* appendix.
3: Vaccination against typhoid is advised.
4: Malaria risk exists throughout the year in all areas below 2000m (6560ft). The malignant *falciparum* strain is present and has been reported as chloroquine-resistant.
Food & drink: All water should be regarded as being potentially contaminated. Water used for drinking, brushing teeth or making ice should have first been boiled or otherwise sterilised. Milk is unpasteurised and should be boiled. Powdered or tinned milk is available and is advised, but make sure that it is reconstituted with pure water. Avoid dairy products that are likely to have been made from unboiled milk. Only eat well-cooked meat and fish, preferably served hot. Salad and mayonnaise may carry increased risk. Vegetables should be cooked and fruit peeled.
Other risks: *Hepatitis A* and *E* occur and *hepatitis B* is endemic. *Trachoma* and *typhoid fever* are common. Between June and January, *Japanese encephalitis* is a risk in rural areas. *Dengue fever* may also occur.
Rabies is present. For those at high risk, vaccination before arrival should be considered. If you are bitten, seek medical advice without delay. For more information, consult the *Health* appendix.
Health care: Medical facilities can be very limited. There is no reciprocal health agreement with the UK. Travellers are strongly advised to take out full medical insurance before departure.
Note: A certificate proving the visitor to be HIV-negative is required if planning on staying over one year in the country.

Travel - International

Note: All travel to Waziristan is advised against. It is advised that nationals only undertake essential travel to northern and western Baluchistan and the Sui area, western North West Frontier Province (NWFP), the Federally Administered Tribal Areas and Agencies (FATA) and border areas, except for official crossing points. If visiting Karachi, visitors should take particular care, avoiding travelling on foot and only travelling in vehicles between secure, well-guarded premises. The rural network in Baluchistan should be avoided due to a high incidence of previously planted bombs. There is a high threat from terrorism throughout Pakistan. British nationals of Western origin are particularly likely to be targeted by terrorists, including for kidnap. Everyone is at risk from indiscriminate attacks and from sectarian violence.
AIR: Pakistan's national airline is *Pakistan International Airlines (PK)* (website: www.piac.com.pk) and links Pakistan with 47 destinations around the world. Other airlines serving Pakistan include *British Airways*, *China Xinjiang Airlines*, *Saudia Airlines* and *Thai Airways*.
Approximate flight times: From Karachi to *London* is seven hours 40 minutes, to *Los Angeles* is 22 hours 30 minutes, to *New York* is 21 hours 40 minutes, to *Riyadh* is three hours 35 minutes and to *Singapore* is seven hours 15 minutes.
International airports: *Karachi (KHI)* (Quaid-e-Azam) is 15km (10 miles) northeast of the city (travel time – 30 to 45 minutes). Coaches to the city run every 25 minutes. A bus runs from dusk to dawn every 15 minutes. Taxi services to the city are available. Good airport facilities exist 24 hours, including duty free shops, restaurant, post office, bank and shops.
Lahore (LHE), 18km (5 miles) southeast of the city (travel time – 20 minutes). Coaches and buses leave regularly for the city. Taxi services to the city are also available. Airport facilities include car hire, bank, restaurant and shops.
Islamabad (ISB) (Islamabad International) is 8km (5 miles) southeast of the city (travel time – 20 minutes). Coach and taxi services to the city are available. There are full duty free facilities.
Peshawar (PEW), 4km (2.5 miles) from the city (travel time – 10 minutes). Full bus and taxi services to the city are available.
Departure tax: PRs800 for international passengers travelling first class, PRs600 for business class and PRs400 for economy class. Transit passengers and children under two years of age are exempt.
SEA: The major port is Karachi (Kemari). It is both Afghanistan's and Pakistan's port for goods, together with Port Qasim. No passenger boats or ships for the general public sail to or from Pakistan at present.
RAIL: The Lahore-Delhi *Samjhota Express* leaves Lahore on Mondays and Thursdays. A rail link extends from Quetta (via the border crossing at Taftan) to Zahedan, Iran; the express train (travel time – 27 hours) runs weekly from Quetta, as does the passenger train, which only travels as far as Taftan. For more information, contact Pakistan Railways (website: www.pakrail.com).
ROAD: From China: the Khunjerab Pass is open between 1 May – 31 October for groups and until 15 November for individual tourists. Customs and Immigration posts are open daily from 0830-1100 for outgoing tourists and until 1600 for incoming tourists. Transport includes buses, vans and 4-wheel-drive vehicles.
From India: Wagha is the only land border open between

Pakistan and India (Lahore–Amritsar route). The border post is open daily 0830-1430 from 16 April to 15 October, and 0900-1500 from 16 April to 15 October. A minibus runs from Lahore railway station to Wagha and there are also taxis available (travel time - 30 minutes).
From Iran: travel is only possible via the Quetta–Taftan–Zahedan route. The border is open from 0900-1300 and 1400-1700. Several buses and coaches leave daily from Quetta to Taftan (travel time - 18 hours). There is also a road from Kabul, Afghanistan to Peshawar.
Note: Visitors exiting Pakistan by land routes are subject to a road toll. Travel to the federally administered tribal areas and the border areas with Afghanistan is not recommended. For further information, visitors should seek official advice.

Travel - Internal

Note: Travel to Sindh province and North West Frontier Province, Punjab and Bulchistan should be undertaken with caution. Consult the national foreign affairs department or Consulate before departure (see the *Contact Addresses* section).
AIR: Most domestic services are operated by *Pakistan International Airlines (PK)*. Other airlines are *Aero Asia* and *Bhoja Air*. There are many daily flights between Islamabad, Karachi, Lahore, Multan, Peshawar and Quetta. Air transport is the quickest and most efficient means of travel.
Departure tax: PRs40 for internal flights. Children under two years are exempt.
RIVER: Traffic along the Indus River is almost exclusively commercial. Many goods are carried to Punjab and the north from the main port at Karachi.
RAIL: Much of Pakistan's extensive rail network is a legacy of British rule. The main line, from Karachi to Lahore, Rawalpindi and Peshawar, has several daytime and overnight trains. Most other routes have several daily trains. Even first-class compartments can be hot and crowded. Travel in air-conditioned coaches is advised, as are reservations on long-distance journeys and overnight service. Children under three years of age travel free. Children aged three to 11 years pay half fare. *Pakistan Railways* offer concessions for tourists (on presentation of a certificate issued by PTDC), excluding Indian nationals travelling by rail. A discount of 25 per cent is offered to individuals and groups, and 50 per cent for students. Details are available from railway offices in Pakistan. For more information, contact Pakistan Railways (www.pakrail.com).
Approximate rail times: *Karachi* to Lahore is 16 hours, to Rawalpindi is 28 hours and to Peshawar is 32 hours; and *Lahore* to Rawalpindi is five hours.
ROAD: Traffic drives on the left. The highway network between cities is well-maintained. **Bus:** Regular services run between most towns and villages.
Lahore–Rawalpindi–Peshawar has an hourly service. Air-conditioned coaches/buses are recommended for long distances. Advance booking is advised. **Car hire:** Available in major cities, as well as at Karachi, Lahore and Rawalpindi airports. Most hotels can book cars for guests.
Documentation: An International Driving Permit or own national license is required.
URBAN: Extensive **bus** and **minibus** services operate in Lahore, Karachi and other towns, although services can be crowded. **Taxi:** Reasonably priced and widely available, they are by far the most efficient means of urban travel. Note that they may not operate after sunset during Ramadan. **Auto-rickshaws** are also available.

Accommodation

HOTELS: Pakistan offers a wide range of accommodation. Modern well-equipped hotels can be found in most major towns and offer excellent facilities such as swimming pools and sports facilities. There are also cottages, Dak bungalows and rest houses in all principal hill stations and health resorts. A government room tax of up to 17.5 per cent is added to the cost of accommodation. In all cases it is advisable to book well in advance and check reservations. For further information, contact the Pakistan Hotels Association, Ground Floor, Sha Court, Mereweather Road, Civil Lines, PO Box 7448, Karachi (tel/fax: (21) 568 6407).
PTDC HOTELS & MOTELS: The Pakistan Tourism Development Corporation (PTDC) operates two hotels, *Faletti's* at Lahore and *Flashman's* at Rawalpindi. They also run well-furnished and moderately priced motels at Ayubia, Bahawalpur, Balakot, Bamburet, Barseen (Karakoram Highway), Besham, Chitral, Gilgit, Gupis, Hunza, Kalam, Khaplu, Malam Jabba Ski & Summer Resort, Miandam, Moenjodaro, Naran, Panah Kot (Dir), Saidu Sharif, Satpara, Skardu, Sost (Pakistan-China border), Taftan (Pakistan-Iran border), Taxila, Wagha (Pakistan-India border) and Ziarat. For bookings, please contact PTDC Motels Reservation Office, Block B-4, Markaz F-7, Bhitai Road, Islamabad 44000 (tel: (51) 920 3223; fax: (51) 921 8233; e-mail: tourism@comsats.net.pk).
PAKISTAN TOURS LTD (PVT): A subsidiary of PTDC, operating tours and providing ground handling facilities for domestic and foreign tourists throughout Pakistan. Its Head Office is located in Room 17, Flashman's Hotel, The Mall, Rawalpindi (tel: (51) 556 3038 or 5449; fax: (51) 551 3054).
YOUTH HOSTELS: The Pakistan Youth Hostel Association has 14 hostels throughout the country, available to members of the affiliated International Youth Hostel Federation and young people. Details can be obtained from the Pakistan Youth Hostel Association, Shaheed-e Millat Road, Aabpara, Sector G-6/4, Islamabad (tel: (51) 282 6899; fax: (51) 282 4520; e-mail: pyha@comsats.net.pk).

Resorts & Excursions

KARACHI: Pakistan's former capital and its largest city, Karachi is situated on the shores of the Arabian Sea near the mouth of the Indus. The capital of Sindh Province, it is now a modern industrial city and Pakistan's major port. Though not strictly a tourist centre, there are a number of attractions, such as the fish wharf where brightly coloured boats bring in seafood, one of the country's major foreign exchange earners. There are hundreds of lively street restaurants, tea houses, samosa and juice stalls. Boats can be hired to sail out of the harbour. There are architectural reminders of the former British Imperial presence, especially in the clubs. The most magnificent building, however, is the **Quaid-e-Azam's Mazar**, the mausoleum of the founder of Pakistan, made entirely of white marble with impressive north African arches and magnificent Chinese crystal chandeliers. The changing of the guard, which takes place three times a day, is the best time to visit. Other places to visit are the **National Museum**, parks, the zoo and a beach at **Clifton**.
SINDH: A region known for the remarkable quality of its light, Sindh has two main places of interest: **Mohenjodaro**, a settlement dating back 5000 years, and **Thatta**, notable for its mausoleums and mosques. There are sporting facilities on **Lake Haleji**.
ISLAMABAD: Islamabad, the capital of Pakistan since 1963, and **Rawalpindi** are both located on the **Pothowar Plain**. The decision to build a new capital city in this area transformed the sleepy town of Rawalpindi into a busy counterpart to Islamabad. Rawalpindi now houses many of the civil servants working in the government district. The old part of the town boasts fine examples of local architecture and bazaars crammed into the narrow streets where craftspeople still use traditional methods.
As a planned capital, Islamabad lacks some of the regional flair of other cities, but it houses an interesting variety of modern buildings in the part designated for government offices. The city itself has an air of spaciousness, with parks, gardens and fountains below the silhouette of the **Margalla Hills**. In the midst of these lies **Daman-e-Koh**, a terraced garden with an excellent view over the city. Also in Islamabad is the **Shah Faisal Masjid** (mosque) which can accommodate 100,000 worshippers. The majestic white building comprises four 88m (288ft) minarets and a desert tent-like structure, which is the main prayer chamber.
Excursions: About 8km (5 miles) from the city is **Rawal Lake** with an abundance of leisure facilities for watersports and a picnic area.
THE PUNJAB: Lahore is an historic, bustling city with buildings of pink and white marble. There is plenty to see: bazaars, the **Badshahi Mosque** (one of the largest mosques in the world, and an example of Moghul architecture rivalled only by the Taj Mahal), the beautiful **Shalimar Gardens**, the **National Museum of Archaeology** and the **Gate of Chauburji**. Near **Taxila** are two interesting excavated sites, **Jaulian** and **Sirkap**, dating back to the Buddhist Gandhara period. Other towns in the Punjab include **Attock**, **Bahawalpur**, **Faisalabad** (formerly **Lyallpur**), **Harappa** and **Multan**.
KASHMIR: Some of the highest mountains in the world can be found in this province, such as the famous **Nanga Parbat** and the second-highest mountain in the world, **K2**, also known as **Mount Godwin-Austen**. The **Baltoro Glacier** and the **Batura Glacier** are the largest outside the polar regions. The settlements of **Gilgit** and **Skardu** are well-known stop-offs on the mountaineering trail.
THE KARAKORUM HIGHWAY: In the 1960s and 70s, the Pakistan and Chinese authorities jointly built an asphalt road between Rawalpindi and Islamabad (Pakistan) and Kashgar (Xinjiang province in China). This unique highway follows the ancient silk road (see *China* section) over a breathtaking knot of mountain ranges that incorporates the **Himalaya mountains**, **Hindukush**, **Karakorum**, **Kunlun** and **Pamir**. The trail runs along the **Indus River** and to the beautiful **Gilgit** and **Hunza valleys**. Today the highway is popular with tourists wishing to cycle or trek its length and it is still used by *hajis* (Muslims making a pilgrimage to Mecca). The main attractions of the route are undoubtedly its challenging geography, unusual yet spectacular scenery and hospitable local ethnic groups. The best time to travel here is between September and October, and due to its demanding altitude and difficult terrain, it should be undertaken with an organised tour group or travel agent. For further information, contact the Pakistan Tourism Development Corporation (see *Contact Addresses* section).

Credit: © Pakistan Tourism Development Corporation

NORTH WEST FRONTIER PROVINCE: The capital of the North West Frontier Province, **Peshawar** is surrounded by high walls with 20 entry gates. This is the area of the Pashtuns, or Pathans as they are also known. The lawns and parks reflect the former colonial days. Much of the surrounding area is still under the jurisdiction of tribal law. These areas can only be visited with a permit from the relevant authorities. Many of the tribesmen carry firearms, the normal adornment for a Pathan warrior. In the land of the Afridis is the **Khyber Pass**, the 1067m- (3501ft-) high break in the sheer rock wall separating Afghanistan and Pakistan. North of Peshawar in the Hindu Kush Mountains is the wild and beautiful area of **Chitral**, inhabited by the Kalash people, last of the non-Islamic tribes of Kafiristan. This valley is noted for its hot springs and trout-filled rivers. East of Chitral is the beautiful **Swat Valley**. This is an area (average height 975m) of wild mountains and fantastic alpine scenery. It was, in ancient times, the home of the famous Gandhara school of sculpture, a manifestation of Greek-influenced Buddhist forms. The ruins of great Buddhist stupas, monasteries and statues are found all over Swat. It is now the home to the Swat Pathans and also boasts popular mountain retreats such as **Behrain**, **Kalam**, **Miandam** and **Mingora**, with **Saidu Sharif** its principal town.

Sport & Activities

Watersports: In addition to the beaches, **swimming** pools can be found in various clubs in large towns and in major hotels. Kemari sail or motorboats can be hired at a previously agreed price. Deep-sea night **fishing** is also available and there are a number of freshwater lakes offering good fishing facilities. For permits, enquire at the Pakistan Tourism Development Corporation (see *Contact Addresses* section). **Whitewater rafting** and **canoeing** are increasingly popular on the rivers of the north of the country.
Trekking: Pakistan contains five of the world's highest peaks and several of the world's largest glaciers. The northern areas are the most popular for trekking, with Gilgit and Skardu being good starting points for trips. The Karakorum Highway is also a popular hiking route (see *Resorts & Excursions* section). Trekking areas have been divided into 'open' and 'restricted' zones by the Government. Permits are not required for the open zones, but are necessary if the visitor intends to go to the restricted zones (parts of Baltistan, Chitral and Hunza, including the K2 base camp). They are usually issued within 24 hours. Visitors should check with the authorities before visiting remote areas, as advance permission is sometimes required. In addition, it is wise to consult the travel advice of foreign governments prior to travel, as political tensions can lead to violence, especially in Kashmir.
Golf: Clubs are located in the large cities and visitors are generally allowed to play a course if introduced by a member or if they acquire a temporary membership.
Tennis: Clubs in the large cities have courts. Visitors must be introduced by a member or can often obtain temporary membership through the Pakistan Tourism Development Corporation.
Other: Hockey is Pakistan's national sport; however, it is easily surpassed in popularity by **cricket**, which can be watched in most major towns at many different levels.
Football is fast becoming popular and regular matches can be seen in the stadium at Karachi and at other sports fields all over the country. **Polo** matches can be seen in major cities and most notably in the northern towns of Gilgit and Chitral. **Horse racing** takes place in winter in Karachi and Lahore. There is also a **ski** resort at Malam Jabba in the Karakoram range.

Social Profile

FOOD & DRINK: Pakistani cuisine is based on curry or *masala* (hot and spicy) sauces accompanying chicken, lamb, shrimps and a wide choice of vegetables. Specialities include *brain masala*, *biryani* (seasoned rice with mutton, chicken and yoghurt), *pilao* (similar but less spicy) and *sag gosht* (spinach and lamb curry). Lahore is the centre for Mogul-style cuisine known as *moghlai*. Specialities include *chicken tandoori*, *shish kebabs* (charcoal-grilled meat on skewers), *shami-kebabs* (patties of chopped meat fried in ghee or butter), *tikka-kebabs* (grilled lamb or beef seasoned and spiced) and *chicken tikka* (highly seasoned chicken quarters, charcoal-grilled). Desserts include pastries, *shahi tukray* (slices of fried bread cooked in milk or cream, sweetened with syrup and topped with nuts and saffron), *halwa* (sweetmeat made with eggs, carrots, maize cream, sooji and nuts) and *firni* (similar to vanilla custard). Western and Chinese foods are also widely available.
The national drink is tea, drunk strong with milk and often very sweet. Alcohol may be bought at major hotels by visitors who have been issued a Liquor Permit from the Excise and Taxation Office. Wine is expensive and only available in upscale restaurants. Pakistani-brewed beer is widely available, as are canned carbonated drinks. There are no bars since there are strict laws concerning alcohol, and it is illegal to drink in public. Waiter service is provided in the larger hotels and restaurants. Visitors should avoid drinking water from the tap; bottled water is available everywhere, but it is necessary to make sure it comes in properly sealed plastic bottles.
NIGHTLIFE: Top hotels have bars and dancing but there is little Western-style nightlife. Cinemas in the large cities show international as well as Pakistani films. There are plenty of cultural events featuring traditional music and dance organised by the Pakistani Arts Academy throughout the year. Festivals and annual celebrations are colourful and lively.
SHOPPING: Special purchases include carved wooden tables, trays, screens, silver trinkets, pottery, camel-skin lamps, bamboo decorations, brassware, cane items, conch-shell ornaments, glass bangles, gold ornaments, hand-embroidered shawls, rugs and carpets, silks, cashmere shawls and *saleem shahi* shoes with upturned toes. While some of the major towns have craft centres where handicrafts from different regions are sold, bazaars often provide the most interesting shopping. It is expected that the customer should bargain for goods. **Shopping hours:** Sat-Thurs 0930-1300 and 1500-1830. Bazaars stay open longer.
SPECIAL EVENTS: The following is a selection of special events celebrated annually in Pakistan:
Jan-Feb *Eid ul-Azha* (Feast of the Sacrifice). **Feb** *Sibi Festival* (sport, handicrafts, folk music and dances), Sibi (Balochistan); *Sindh Horse and Cattle Show*, Jacobabad (Sindh). **Mar** *Mela Chiraghan* (Festival of Lamps), Lahore. **May** *Joshi or Chilimjusht* (spring welcoming), Chitral. **Jul** *Utchal* (harvest festival celebrated by the Kalash people), Chitral. **Aug 14** *Independence Day* (processions and rallies), countrywide. **Oct** *Lok Mela* (folk festival), Islamabad. **Oct-Nov** *Eid ul-Fitr* (End of Ramadan). **Nov** *National Horse and Cattle Show*, Lahore.
SOCIAL CONVENTIONS: The right hand is used both for shaking hands (the usual form of greeting) and for passing or receiving things. Mutual hospitality and courtesy are of great importance at all levels, whatever the social standing of the host. Visitors must remember that most Pakistanis are Muslim and should respect their customs and beliefs. Smoking is prohibited in some public places and it is polite to ask permission before lighting a cigarette. It is common for visiting businesspeople to be entertained in hotels and restaurants. If invited to a private home, a gift or national souvenir is welcome. Informal dress is acceptable for most occasions. Women should avoid wearing tight clothing and should ensure that their arms and legs are covered. Pakistani society is divided into classes and within each group there is a subtle social grading. The Koran is the law for Muslims and it influences every aspect of daily life; see the *World of Islam* appendix for more information.
Tipping: Most high-class hotels and restaurants add a 10 per cent service charge. Other tipping is discretionary.

Business Profile

ECONOMY: About half of the Pakistani labour force works in agriculture, where wheat, rice, sugar cane and cotton are the main products. Cotton is by far the country's most important export, accounting for almost 60 per cent of revenues. Textiles and leather goods are significant export earners. Pakistan has some reserves of graphite and limestone, as well as gypsum, silica, coal, copper and manganese. It also has a small oil industry, but most of its needs must be imported: together with chemicals and machinery, this accounts for nearly three-quarters of Pakistan's import expenditure. Established manufacturing industries include textiles, food processing and building materials.
The overriding economic problem for the Pakistani economy is its huge foreign debt burden, which is over 90 per cent of GDP and consumes over half of government revenue to meet interest payments. The situation has been made more difficult by the history of poor relations between Pakistan and the international financial community generally. Sanctions were imposed following Pakistani nuclear tests in 1998, coinciding with the fall-out from the 1997 financial crisis that engulfed the major economies of East Asia. Yet despite these factors, the regional crisis centred on Afghanistan and Iraq, and domestic political instability, the Pakistani economy has performed steadily in the last five years. Both annual economic growth and inflation have been in low single figures for the last few years: the 2004 figures are 5.5 and 2.9 per cent respectively; unemployment is a record 7.7 per cent, but there is a high level of underemployment amongst the workforce. In general, economic policy has been determined by the need to comply with conditions laid down by the IMF. An economic reform programme has gradually been implemented, with several major privatisations in recent years. Pakistan's main trading partners are the USA, Saudi Arabia, Kuwait, Hong Kong (SAR) and the UK.
BUSINESS: Ties should be worn for important business appointments. English is commonly used. Appointments should be made, remembering that businesses are usually closed on Muslim holidays. Visiting cards should be used. **Office hours:** Mon-Thurs and Sat 0900-1700, Fri 0900-1230.
COMMERCIAL INFORMATION: The following organisation can offer advice: Overseas Investors' Chamber of Commerce and Industry, PO Box 4833, Talpur Road, Karachi (tel: (21) 241 0814; fax: (21) 242 7315; e-mail: info@oicci.org; website: www.oicci.org); *or* Federation of Pakistan Chambers of Commerce (FPCCI), PO Box 13875, Federation House, Sharea Firdousi, Main Clifton, Karachi 75600, Pakistan (tel: (21) 587 3691/93-4; fax: (21) 587 4332; e-mail: fpcci@cyber.net.pk *or* info@fpcci.com.pk *or* fpcci@digicom.net.pk; website: www.fpcci.com.pk).

Climate

Pakistan has three seasons: winter (November to March) is warm and cooled by sea breezes on the coast; summer (April to July) has extreme temperatures and the monsoon season (July to September) has the highest rainfall on the hills. Karachi has little rain. The best time to visit southern Pakistan is between November and March, when the days are cool and clear. The best time to visit northern Pakistan is from April to October.
Required clothing: Lightweights, with warmer clothing for upland areas in the winter. Rainwear is advised for the monsoon season.

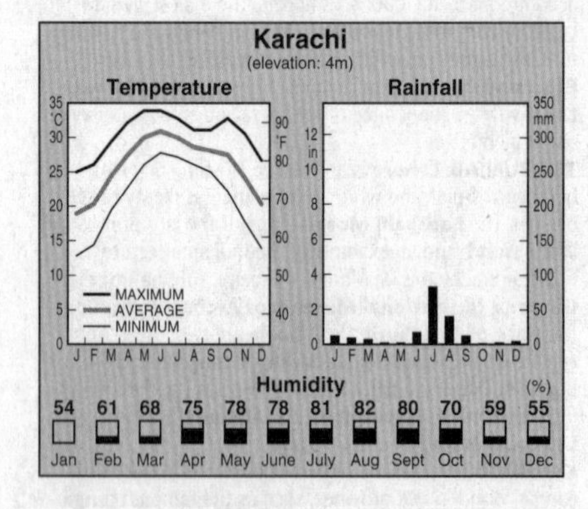

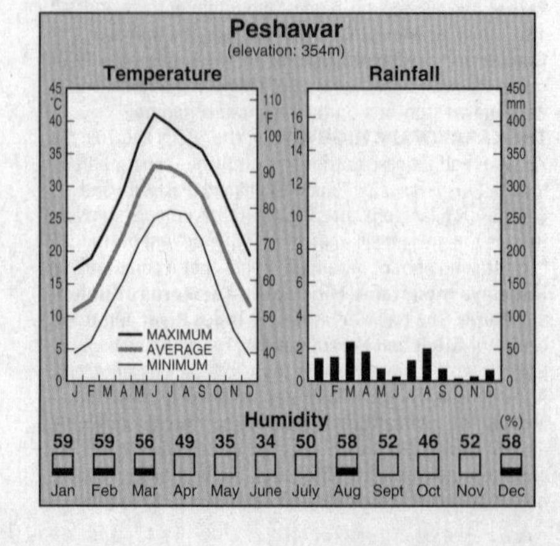

Panama

LATEST TRAVEL ADVICE CONTACTS

British Foreign and Commonwealth Office
Tel: (0870) 606 0290 Website: www.fco.gov.uk
US Department of State
Website: http://travel.state.gov/travel
Canadian Department of Foreign Affairs and Int'l Trade
Tel: (1 800) 267 8376 Website: www.dfait-maeci.gc.ca

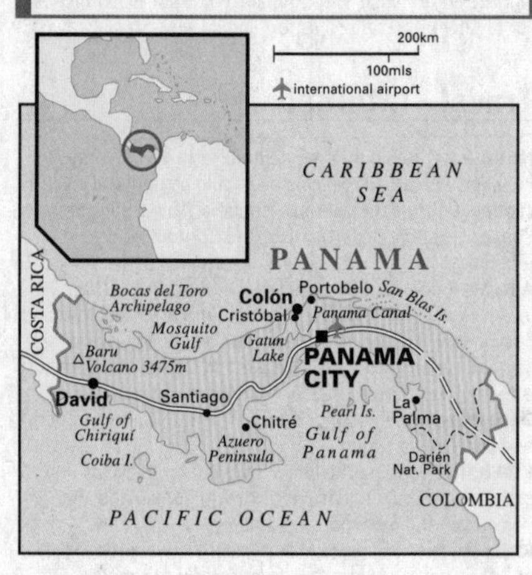

Location: Central America.

Country dialling code: 507.

Instituto Panameño de Turismo (IPAT) (Institute of Tourism)
Apartado 4421, Zone 5, Centro de Convenciones ATLAPA, Via Israel, Republic of Panamá
Tel: 226 7000 *or* 3544. Fax: 226 6856.
E-mail: ggral@ns.ipat.gob.pa (general) *or* infotur@ns.ipat.gob.pa
Website: www.ipat.gob.pa *or* www.visitpanama.com
Consulate of the Republic of Panamá
Panama House, 40 Hertford Street, London W1J 7SH, UK
Tel: (020) 7409 2255. Fax: (020) 7493 4499 *or* 7495 0412.
E-mail: panama@panaconsul.co.uk *or* info@panaconsul.co.uk
Website: www.panaconsul.com
Opening hours: Mon-Fri 0930-1730.
Embassy of the Republic of Panamá
40 Hertford Street, London W1J 7SH, UK
Tel: (020) 7493 4646. Fax: (020) 7493 4333.
E-mail: panama1@btconnect.com
Opening hours: Mon-Fri 1000-1700.
British Embassy
Calle 53, Urbanización Marbella, Swiss Tower, Apartado 889, Zona 1, Panamá City, Republic of Panamá
Tel: 269 0866. Fax: 223 0730.
E-mail: britemb@cwpanama.net *or* britemb@cwp.net.pa
Embassy of the Republic of Panamá
2862 McGill Terrace, NW, Washington, DC 20008, USA
Tel: (202) 483 1407. Fax: (202) 483 8413.
E-mail: iga@panaembadc.org
Consulate General of the Republic of Panamá
Flood Building, 870 Market Street, Suite 551-533, San Francisco, CA 94102, USA
Tel: (415) 391 4268. Fax: (415) 391 4269.
Consulates General in: Atlanta, Houston, Miami, New Orleans, New York, Philadelphia and Tampa.
Embassy of the United States of America
Building 520, Clayton, Apartado 6959, Panamá 5, Republic of Panamá
Tel: 207 7000/30. Fax: 207 7278 *or* 227 1964.
E-mail: panama-acs@state.gov *or* usembisc@cwp.net.pa
Embassy of Panamá
130 Albert Street, Suite 300, Ottawa, Ontario K1P 5G4, Canada
Tel: (613) 236 7177. Fax: (613) 236 5775.
E-mail: pancanem@rapidweb.ca

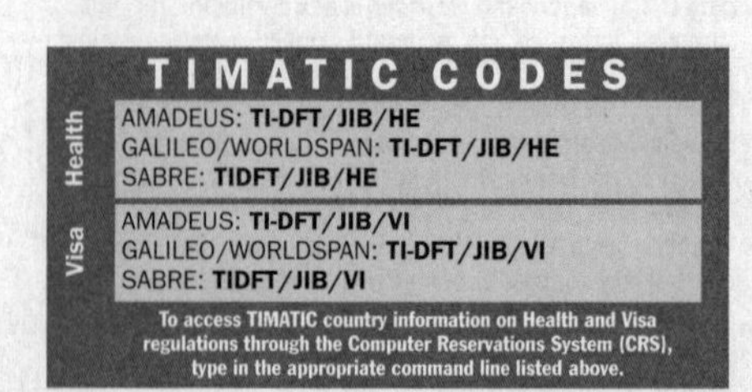
TIMATIC CODES

Health	AMADEUS: **TI-DFT/JIB/HE** GALILEO/WORLDSPAN: **TI-DFT/JIB/HE** SABRE: **TIDFT/JIB/HE**
Visa	AMADEUS: **TI-DFT/JIB/VI** GALILEO/WORLDSPAN: **TI-DFT/JIB/VI** SABRE: **TIDFT/JIB/VI**

To access TIMATIC country information on Health and Visa regulations through the Computer Reservations System (CRS), type in the appropriate command line listed above.

Canadian Embassy
Street address: World Trade Center, 1st Floor, Calle 53 Este Marbella y Calle 5B Sur, Urbanización Marbella, Panamá City, Republic of Panamá
Postal address: Apartado Postal 0832-2446, Estafeta World Trade Center, Panamá City, Republic of Panamá
Tel: 264 9731 *or* 264 7115 *or* 263 7913. Fax: 263 8083.
E-mail: panam@dfait-maeci.gc.ca
Website: www.dfait-maeci.gc.ca/panama

General Information

AREA: 75,517 sq km (29,157 sq miles).
POPULATION: 3,116,000 (2003).
POPULATION DENSITY: 41.3 per sq km.
CAPITAL: Panama City. **Population:** 463,093 (2000).
GEOGRAPHY: Panama forms the land link between the North and South American continents. Panama borders Colombia to the east, Costa Rica to the west, and the Caribbean and the Pacific Ocean to the north and south. The country forms an S-shaped isthmus which runs east-west over a total length of 772km (480 miles) and is 60 to 177km (37 to 110 miles) wide. The landscape is mountainous with lowlands on both coastlines cut by streams, wooded slopes and a wide area of savannah-covered plains and rolling hills called *El Interior* between the Azuero peninsula and the Central Mountains. The Caribbean and the Pacific Ocean are linked by the man-made Panama Canal, cut into a gap between the Cordillera de Talamanca and the San Blas mountain range and stretching for over 65km (40 miles); the length of the Canal is often referred to as 80km (50 miles) as this is the distance between deep-water points of entry. Only about a quarter of the country is inhabited. The majority of the population live either around the Canal and main cities of Panama City and Colón (the two cities which control the entrance and exit of the Canal) or in the Pacific lowlands and the adjacent mountains.
GOVERNMENT: Republic. Gained independence from Colombia in 1903. **Head of State and Government:** President Martin Torrijos since 2004.
LANGUAGE: The official language is Spanish, but English is widely spoken.
RELIGION: Almost all Christian; 86 per cent Roman Catholic.
TIME: GMT - 5.
ELECTRICITY: 120 volts AC, 60Hz. Plugs are the flat two-pin American type.
COMMUNICATIONS: Telephone: IDD is available. Country code: 507. There are no area codes. Outgoing international code: 00. **Mobile telephone:** Roaming agreements exist. The main network provider is *Cable & Wireless* (website: www.cwpanama.com). Coverage is good. **Fax:** Main post offices and hotels have facilities. **Telegram:** Facilities exist in main post offices of Panama City and other major cities and hotels. A tax of 50 cents is levied against each telegram. **Internet:** ISPs include *Inter.net* (website: www.pa.inter.net). Internet cafes exist in main urban areas. **Post:** Airmail to Western Europe takes five to 10 days. Main post offices have *Poste restante* and EMS (Express Mail Services) facilities. Post office hours: Mon-Fri 0800-1600, Sat 0800-1300 **Press:** *Crítica Libre, La Estrella de Panamá, El Matutino, El Panamá América, La Prensa, La República, El Siglo* and *El Universal* (all in Spanish) are the largest daily newspapers.
Radio: BBC World Service (website: www.bbc.co.uk/worldservice) and Voice of America (website: www.voa.gov) can be received. From time to time the frequencies change and the most up-to-date can be found online.

Passport/Visa

	Passport Required?	Visa Required?	Return Ticket Required?
Full British	Yes	1	Yes
Australian	Yes	2	Yes
Canadian	Yes	2	Yes
USA	Yes	2	Yes
Other EU	Yes	1/2/3	Yes
Japanese	Yes	2	Yes

Note: *Regulations and requirements may be subject to change at short notice, and you are advised to contact the appropriate diplomatic or consular authority before finalising travel arrangements. Details of these may be found at the head of this country's entry. Any numbers in the chart refer to the footnotes below.*

Note: (a) No brief account of the complex Panamanian visa regulations is likely to be fully successful as passport and visa regulations are liable to change at short notice.
(b) Panamanian immigration procedures are rigidly enforced and non-compliance with the regulations may result in transportation at carrier's expense to country of origin.
(c) Many nationals requiring visas also require authorisation from the Immigration Authorities in Panama before entry.
PASSPORTS: Passport valid for a minimum of six months required by all.
VISAS: Required by all except the following for stays of up to 90 days (at the discretion of the Immigration Authorities):
1. nationals of Argentina, Austria, Belgium, Chile, Costa Rica, El Salvador, Finland, France, Germany, Guatemala, Honduras, Hungary, Israel, Italy, Luxembourg, Liechtenstein, The Netherlands, Nicaragua, Paraguay, Poland, Portugal, Singapore, Spain, Sweden, Switzerland, Uruguay and the UK (except for UK passports issued in Hong Kong (SAR) to those who were born in Hong Kong).
Note: 2. Nationals of Cyprus, Czech Republic, Dominican Republic, Egypt, Peru and The Philippines may only enter Panama if they have a visa.
Tourist cards: A Tourist Card will be issued in lieu of a visa to the following for stays of up to 30 days (extendable to 90 days at the discretion of the Immigration Authorities):
3. nationals of Antigua & Barbuda, Aruba, Australia, The Bahamas, Barbados, Belize, Bermuda, Bolivia, Brazil, Canada, Colombia, Curacao, Ecuador, Greece, Grenada, Guyana, Jamaica, Japan, Korea (Rep), Malta, Mexico, Monaco, New Zealand, Norway, St Kitts & Nevis, St Lucia, St Vincent & the Grenadines, Samoa, San Marino, São Tomé & Príncipe, Sweden, Surinam, Taiwan, Trinidad & Tobago, USA, Vatican City and Venezuela.
Types of visa and cost: *Tourist:* £20. *Tourist Card:* Prices vary, depending on nationality and also on where the Tourist Card is obtained from (eg prior to departure, on the flight or upon arrival at the airport). Some nationals can obtain the Tourist Card free of charge (including nationals of Colombia, Mexico, Norway, Sweden and the USA). Enquire at the Consulate for details.
Validity: Visas and Tourist Cards are valid within a three-month period from the date of issue and allow stays for up to 30 days (extendable to 90 days at discretion of Immigration Authorities).
Application to: Consulate (or Consular section at Embassy); see *Contact Addresses* section. A Tourist Card can be issued either by the travel agent *or* on the flight *or* at the airport.
Application requirements: (a) Passport valid for at least six months. (b) Two completed application forms. (c) Two passport-size photos. (d) Booking reservation. *For countries requiring special authorisation:* (a)-(c) and, (d) Copies of passport. (e) Copy of return or onward ticket. (f) Letter from the person in Panama taking responsibility for applicant. (g) Proof of financial stability in cash, traveller's cheques or bank statements (at least US$500). (h) Fee, plus postage if necessary.
Working days required: Normally 24 hours if no authorisation is needed; 20 days if authorisation (which depends on nationality) is needed.

Money

Currency: Balboa (B) = 100 centavos. There is no Panamanian paper currency; coins exist in denominations of B10 and 1, and 50, 25, 10, 5 and 1 centavos. US currency was adopted in 1904 and exists alongside the Balboa coinage: B1 = US$1.
Currency exchange: Banks and *cambios* are available for changing currency. There is no need to exchange US Dollars.
Credit cards: MasterCard and Visa are the most commonly used, but American Express and Diners Club are also accepted. Check with your credit or debit card company for details of merchant acceptability and other services which may be available.
Travellers cheques: To avoid additional exchange rate charges, visitors are advised to take travellers cheques in US Dollars.
Currency restrictions: There are no restrictions on the import and export of either foreign or local currency. However, amounts of over US$10,000 must be declared to immigration upon arrival.
Exchange rate indicators: The following figures are included as a guide to the movements of the Balboa against Sterling:

Date	Feb '04	May '04	Aug '04	Nov '04
£1.00=	1.82	1.79	1.84	1.88

Banking hours: Mon-Fri 0800-1500, Sat 0830-1200.

Duty Free

The following items may be imported into Panama without incurring customs duty:
500 cigarettes or 50 cigars or 500g tobacco; three bottles of alcoholic beverage; perfume and eau de cologne in opened bottles for personal use; gifts up to the value of B50.
Prohibited items: Fruit, vegetable and animal products including shrimp.

Public Holidays

2005: Jan 1 New Year's Day. **Jan 10** National Martyrs' Day. **Feb 8** Carnival Tuesday. **Mar 25** Good Friday. **May 2** Labour Day. **Aug 15** Old Panama City Day (Panama City only). **Nov 3** Independence Day (from Colombia). **Nov 5** Independence Day (Colón City only). **Nov 10** First Call for Independence from Spain. **Nov 28** Independence Day (from Spain). **Dec 25** Christmas Day.
2006 Jan 1 New Year's Day. **Jan 9** National Martyrs' Day. **Feb 28** Carnival Tuesday. **Apr 14** Good Friday. **May 1** Labour Day. **Aug 15** Old Panama City Day (Panama City only). **Nov 3** Independence Day (from Colombia). **Nov 5** Independence Day (Colón City only). **Nov 10** First Call for Independence from Spain. **Nov 27** Independence Day (from Spain). **Dec 25** Christmas Day.
Note: For public holidays falling on a Sunday, the following Monday will be observed as a holiday.

Health

	Special Precautions?	Certificate Required?
Yellow Fever	1	No
Cholera	2	No
Typhoid & Polio	3	N/A
Malaria	4	N/A

Note: *Regulations and requirements may be subject to change at short notice, and you are advised to contact your doctor well in advance of your intended date of departure. Any numbers in the chart refer to the footnotes below.*

1: Yellow fever vaccination is recommended for those travelling to Darién. Travellers arriving from non-endemic zones should note that vaccination is strongly recommended for travel outside the urban areas, even if an outbreak of the disease has not been reported and they would normally not require a vaccination certificate to enter the country.
2: Following WHO guidelines issued in 1973, a cholera vaccination certificate is not a condition of entry to Panama. However, cholera may be a slight risk in this country and precautions are essential. Up-to-date advice should be sought before deciding whether these precautions should include vaccination, as medical opinion is divided over its effectiveness; see the *Health* appendix.
3: Typhoid fevers are common, but polio is not present.
4: There is a low malaria risk, predominantly of the *Plasmodium vivax* form in three provinces throughout the year: Bocas de Toro, Darién and San Blas. The risk of transmission in the remaining six provinces is negligible.
Food & drink: Mains water is normally chlorinated and safe. Bottled water is available. Drinking water outside main cities and towns may be contaminated and sterilisation is advised. Milk is pasteurised and dairy products are safe for consumption. Local meat, poultry, seafood, fruit and vegetables are generally considered safe to eat.
Other risks: *Hepatitis A* and *E* occur. *Dengue fever* may occur. *Rabies* is present. For those at high risk, vaccination before arrival should be considered. If you are bitten, seek medical advice without delay. For more information, see the *Health* appendix.
Health care: Modern and reliable private medical services are available. According to current legislation covering sanitary matters, Panama offers healthcare facilities to all nationals and foreign travellers who may require them, independent of any reciprocal agreement with a particular country. International travellers are, however, advised to take out medical insurance.

Travel - International

AIR: Panama's national airline is *Compañía Panameña de Aviación (COPA - CM)* (website: www.copaair.com). *Air France, American Airlines, Continental Airlines, Delta, KLM* and others also fly there.
Approximate flight times: From Panama City to *London* is 14 hours and to *Miami* is two hours 45 minutes.
International airports: *Panamá City (PTY)* (Tocumén) is 27km (17 miles) northeast of the city (travel time - 30 to 60 minutes). Airport services include a bank, car hire, chemist, restaurant and full duty free facilities. Buses and taxis go to the city.
Departure tax: B20. Children under two years of age and passengers in transit to another country not leaving the airport and remaining for under nine hours are exempt.
SEA: The Panama Canal is the major route from the Atlantic to the Pacific Ocean, and Panama (Balboa) is a port of call for many cruise lines and ocean vessels for both passenger and freight. Cruise lines include *Cunard, Delta, Norwegian American, P&O, Princess* and *Royal Caribbean International.*
RAIL: There is currently no rail link betwen Panama and other international destinations.
ROAD: The principal route to Panama is the Pan-American Highway from Costa Rica to Panama City. Visitors are strongly advised not to use the route to Colombia via Darién Gap for personal safety reasons.

Travel - Internal

AIR: Smaller airports for internal flights are: *Aeropuerto Marcos A. Gelabert* in Albrook and *Enrique Malek* in David, Chiriquí. Internal air services operated by *Aeroperlas, Aerotaxi, Ansi, Aviatur* and *Mapiex Aero* include flights from Panama City to all centres in the interior of the country.
RAIL: The *Ferrocarril de Panamá* currently only operates freight trains and is in the process of selling the national rail service. The *Panamá Canal Railway Company (PCRC)* runs a scenic 47-mile passenger route from Panama City to Colón as well as cargo services. Further information can be obtained from the Instituto Panameño de Turismo (see *Contact Addresses* section).
ROAD: The Trans-Isthman Highway links Panama City and Colón. The *Corredor Norte* toll road has reduced the travel time to Colón by 30 minutes. **Bus:** Traffic drives on the right. There are services between most large towns, but they can be very slow. **Taxi:** Not metered, and fares, though varying considerably, are generally very low. Fares should be agreed in advance. **Car hire:** Available in city centres and airport; you must be at least 23 years old to hire a car. **Documentation:** A national driving licence is sufficient.
URBAN: Extensive bus and minibus services run in Panama City. There is a flat fare with coin-operated turnstiles at the entrances of most buses.
Travel times: The following chart gives approximate travel times (in hours and minutes) from **Panama City** to other major cities in Panama.

	Air	Road
Chiriquí	**0.45**	**6.00**
Santiago	**0.30**	**3.00**
Chitre	**0.30**	**3.10**

Accommodation

HOTELS: Panama has embarked on an extensive hotel expansion programme, not only in Panama City, but also in the countryside and in mountain and seaside areas. Accommodation ranges from international standard to inexpensive country inns, very simple hotels and new resort-style hotels. There is a 10 per cent government tax added to hotel bills. For further information, contact Instituto Panameño de Turismo (see *Contact Addresses* section).
CAMPING: There are no official campsites, but it is possible to camp on some beaches, and also in the mountainous areas of Boquete and Volván.

Resorts & Excursions

Panama offers a wide variety of tourist attractions, including excellent shopping. Its position as a crossing point between the Atlantic and the Pacific has naturally made it a major commercial route. Panama City's **Central Avenue**, Colón's **Front Street** and the newer shopping sectors around the hotels, and Tocumen's duty free stores have grown because of this trade.
Note: The *Fiestas* in the various cities are all worth attending, particularly the one at Panama City during the Carnival. This is held on the four days before Ash Wednesday. Others are held to celebrate local patron saints. *Las Balserías*, a Ngöbé-Bugle Indian celebration held in Chiriquí Province every February, includes feasts and a contest in which the young men toss Balsa logs at one another; those who emerge unscathed may choose their partners.
PANAMA CITY: The capital is a curious blend of old Spain, modern America and the bazaar atmosphere of the East. In the old part of the city with its narrow, cobble-stoned streets and colonial buildings, most of the interesting sights are to be found. These include the **Plaza de Francia**, the **Court of Justice Building**, the **Paseo de las Bóvedas** along the massive stone wall, **San José Church** with its magnificent golden Baroque altar and the **Santo Domingo Church**, next to which is the **Museum of Colonial Religious Art**. The old historic city with the **Salón Bolivar** is listed by UNESCO as a World Heritage Site. Overlooking the bay is the **President's Palace**, the most impressive building in the city; further along the waterfront is the colourful public market. The most interesting museum in town is the **Museum of the Panamanian Man** north of the market and near the shopping centres. A worthwhile excursion from the city is a visit to **Panama Viejo** and its ruins including the square tower of the old cathedral, 6km (4 miles) away. This is the original Panama City which – like Fort San Lorenzo – was sacked and looted in 1671 by Henry Morgan, the celebrated Welsh buccaneer who helped to undermine Spanish control of their colonies.
Excursions: An interesting excursion can be made to an easily accessible strip of rainforest within nearby **Soberanía National Park** (40km/25 miles north of the city), particularly renowned for its many bird species.
PANAMA CANAL: The Panama Canal, to the west of the city, is Panama's main tourist attraction and naturally draws many visitors; recommended is a train or bus ride alongside or a boat trip on the Canal itself; the scenery is beautiful, and the mechanics of the Canal equally fascinating. There is a new **Panama Canal Museum** in the Casco Viejo area. The Canal was opened in 1914, and an average transit takes eight hours to complete. On December 31 1999, Panama took over full control of the canal from the USA. Some 50km (30 miles) northwest of the capital lies **Barro Colorado**, the largest island in **Gatun Lake**, a manmade stretch of water created during the construction of the Panama Canal (and one of the world's largest artificial lakes). The island is a biological reserve managed by the **Smithsonian Tropical Research Institute** and reputed to be one of the world's leading natural tropical laboratories. Day trips to the island from Panama City take visitors to the small town of **Gamboa** from where special tours (either on foot or by boat) can be arranged.
BALBOA: A rather Americanised suburb between the Canal quays and **Ancón Hill**. One hour's launch ride away is the island of **Taboga**, where fine beaches and quality hotels abound. The main method of transport is by water taxi, known locally as **panga**. A longer trip by launch is necessary to get to the **Pearl Islands**, which are visited mainly by sea-anglers.
BOCAS DEL TORO: The Bocas del Toro province lies in the northwest of the country and includes an archipelago (of the same name) consisting of seven large islands and hundreds of smaller ones. Many of the islands lie in the **Laguna de Chiriqui**, which is particularly popular with diving enthusiasts. Parts of the province are located in two national parks: the **International Friendship Park**, administered jointly by Panama and Costa Rica; and the **Bastimientos Island Marine Park**, a marine nature reserve located on one of the islands. Small planes from Panama City arrive daily at the town of **Bocas del Toro** and, although the area currently remains fairly undeveloped (with limited accommodation available), it is being targeted for major tourist development.
CHIRIQUI: Located some 450km (270 miles) west of the capital, the Chiriquí province is characterised by volcanic highlands with many waterfalls, rivers and spectacular mountain scenery and is known for its cattle and thoroughbred horses as well as banana and coffee plantations. The province also contains the dormant **Baru Volcano** (3,475m/11,400 ft), located near the popular resort town of **Boquete** and the mountain resort **Cerro Punta**. Also nearby is the **Baru National Park**, famous for its many Quetzal birds. There are several daily flights from Panama City arriving at **David** (travel time – one hour).
COLÓN: The second-biggest city in Panama lies on the Caribbean end of the Canal; visitors should see the **cathedral** and the statues on the promenade known as the **Paseo Centenario**. **Front Street** is famous as a shopping centre for duty free luxuries, though it is now rather run down. The city is bustling and quite rough – most visitors just pass through rather than spend a lot of time here.
DARIÉN GAP: This is a sparsely populated wilderness area linking central and southern America and also the only break in the Pan-American Highway (which runs from Alaska to Argentina). Much of this region lies within the **Darién National Park**, which contains an exceptional variety of habitats, ranging from sandy beaches, rocky coasts, mangroves and swamps to tropical rainforest. The park is also home to two Choco Indian tribes. Trips to the park are available, but visitors are strongly advised to use an experienced guide; the area around the Colombian border, in particular, is a dangerous guerrilla flash point and kidnappings of Western tourists have been reported.
SAN BLAS ISLANDS: An interesting trip can be made from Colón to the San Blas archipelago which comprises 365 islands. It is the home of the Cuna people, the most politically organised of the native groups in Panama, who live on about 40 of the islands and who administer their own autonomous province. The Cuna also operate the region's hotels and can assist visitors in organising trips to nearby villages. There are no roads, but small planes fly to several landing strips. For details on how to organise overnight stays, contact the Panamanian Institute of Tourism (see *Contact Addresses* section).
PORTOBELO: Situated 48km (30 miles) east of Colón, Portobelo was a Spanish garrison town for two centuries with three large stone forts facing the entrance to the harbour. Also in the town are an old Spanish cannon, and the treasure house where gold and silver from Perú and Bolivia were stored before being shipped to Spain. Along the Caribbean coast, between Portobelo and San Lorenzo, are numerous notable 17th- and 18th-century military fortifications.
AZUERO PENINSULA: Much more relaxed and peaceful than Panama's cities is the Pacific Peninsula de Azuero, where charming small colonial towns, quiet villages and near-empty beaches await visitors who do not expect to find big hotels.

Sport & Activities

Ecotourism: The *Gamboa Tropical Rainforest Reserve* and the *Soberania National Park* offer good opportunities for learning about tropical fauna and flora. **Birdwatching** enthusiasts will not be disappointed in Panama: there are about 950 registered species and the country is considered one of the world's best birdwatching spots. The Antón Valley (*El Valle de Antón*), 120km/70 miles west of Panama City, is famous for its orchids and the *El Níspero Botanical Gardens*; one activity on offer here is the **tree canopy adventure**, where participants are fastened into a harness, pulled up to the tree tops and swung from one platform to another in order to enjoy particularly 'green' views. Trips to the famous *Smithsonian Tropical Research Institute* on Barro Colorado Island (which houses a renowned tropical research laboratory) are also possible, although appointments need to be made at least one month in advance.
Boat trips: Boat trips on the Panama Canal are one of Panama's major tourist attractions and there are various types of tours available. Crocodiles, frigate birds and other animals living along the banks and in the surrounding jungle can be observed. Canal tours often aim to provide visitors with a chance to observe one of the many large vessels moving through the canal locks. For further details, contact the Panamanian Institute of Tourism or the Panamanian Embassy (see *Contact Addresses* section).
Watersports: There are some excellent locations for **diving** and **snorkelling** in Panama, the best of which include *Isla Grande* near Portobelo, where there are a number of dive centres offering excursions to the best reefs; the *Bocas del Toro* archipelago; *Taboga Island* (20km/12 miles south of Panama City); and the *San Blás Islands* (off the northeast coast). **Whitewater rafting** is becoming increasingly popular on the *Chiriquí* and *Chiriquí Viejo* rivers (not possible during the rainy season, from April to mid-December). For further details on some of these destinations, see the *Resorts & Excursions* section.
Fishing: Fish are abundant in the Panamanian waters of the Pacific and the Caribbean. Locations include Piñas Bay, Coiba Island, Contadora Island and Taboga on the Pacific side and the San Blas Islands and the Chiriquí Lagoon off the archipelago of Bocas del Toro in the Caribbean.
Golf: There are six golf courses on the isthmus. *Panamá Country Club, Summit* and *Fort Amador's* courses are all open to tourists. Guest cards are needed to play the 18-hole course at *Coronado Beach Country Club*. In addition, *Itoroko*, the former US golf course, has now opened up.
Horseriding: This is popular in the mountainous Chiriquí province, whose wild landscapes provide a natural habitat for cattle and horses. There are numerous horse-breeding farms, some of which can be visited. Horse trips to the Baru Volcano are also available.

Social Profile

FOOD & DRINK: American, French and Spanish food is available in all restaurants and hotels in Panama City and Colón. There is a huge selection of excellent restaurants in Panama City, as well as other main cities. There are also several Oriental restaurants. Native cooking is reminiscent of creole cuisine, hot and spicy. Dishes include *ceviche* (fish marinated in lime juice, onions and peppers), *patacones de plátano* (fried plantain), *sancocho* (Panamanian stew with chicken, meat and vegetables), *tamales* (seasoned pie wrapped in banana leaves), *carimañolas* and *empanadas* (turnovers filled with meat, chicken or cheese). Waiter service is the norm. The choice and availability of wines, spirits and beers in hotels, restaurants and bars is unlimited.
NIGHTLIFE: Panama City, in particular, has a wide range of nightlife from nightclubs and casinos to folk, ballet, belly dancing and classical theatre. Dancing and entertainment are available in all the big hotels, as well as many clubs. Other large towns and resorts have music, dancing, casinos and cinemas. Further details can be found in local papers.
SHOPPING: Panama is a duty free haven and luxury goods from all over the world can be bought at a saving of at least one-third. Local items include leatherware, patterned, beaded necklaces made by Guaymí Indians, native costumes, handicrafts of carved wood, ceramics, *papier mâché* artefacts, macramé and mahogany bowls. **Shopping hours:** Mon-Sat 0800-1900, Sun 1000-1900.
SPECIAL EVENTS: For further information, contact the Instituto Panameño de Turismo (see *Contact Addresses* section). The following is a selection of special events occurring in Panama in 2005:
Jan *Coffee and Flowers Fair*, Boquete; *Festival of San Sebastián*, Ocú. **Feb** *Las Balserías* (Guaymí Indian celebration – see *Resorts & Excursions* section), Chiriquí Province. **Feb 5-8** *Carnaval* (Tues 8 is a national holiday). **Mar** *San José International Fair*. **Apr** *Semana Santa*; *Orchis Fair*, Boquete. **Apr-May** *Azuero Festival*, Villa de los Santos. **Jun** *San Juan Bautista*, Isla Grande, Chitré. **Jul** *Boat Races*, Taboga Island. **Sep** *Feria del Mar*, Bocas del Toro. **Oct** *Black Christ Celebration*, Portobelo.
SOCIAL CONVENTIONS: Handshaking is the normal form of greeting and dress is generally casual. The culture is a vibrant mixture of American and Spanish lifestyles. The

Mestizo majority, which is largely rural, shares many of the characteristics of Mestizo culture found throughout Central America. Only three indigenous tribes have retained their individuality and traditional lifestyles as a result of withdrawing into virtually inaccessible areas.
Tipping: 10 to 15 per cent is customary in hotels (where it is added automatically) and restaurants. Taxi drivers do not expect tips, and rates should be arranged before the trip.

Business Profile

ECONOMY: Panama has a relatively prosperous economy based on agriculture, light industry, revenues from the Panama Canal and the service sector. Over half the land area is given over to agriculture: the main cash crops are sugar cane, coffee and bananas, while the main food crops are rice, maize and beans. Commercial cattle-raising is also prominent. The country has significant reserves of timber, particularly mahogany, and good fishing stocks, shrimp being a major and valuable export earner. Local industries include food processing, clothing, paper and building materials. Panama also exports petroleum refined from imported crude oil. Further revenue is obtained from tolls levied on ships passing through the Panama Canal (which came under full Panamanian control in 2000) and from registration fees for a plethora of 'offshore' companies exploiting Panama's strict banking and commercial secrecy laws (although the Government has recently instituted measures to permit disclosure in suspected cases of money-laundering).
Other important sources of revenue include the Colón Free Trade Zone established near the Canal through which 30 per cent of all Panamanian trade passes, an 'open' shipping registry, and a rapidly growing tourist industry now worth more than US$500 million annually. A major reform programme undertaken during the 1990s saw the privatisation of many state enterprises, reform of the tax and social security systems, and the removal of price controls and import tariffs. Current annual GDP growth is 4 per cent, and inflation is around 1 per cent; the official unemployment rate is 13.8 per cent. Panama is a member of the Inter-American Development Bank. About 40 per cent of two-way trade is with the USA and Japan; Costa Rica and Germany are the country's other important trading partners. Panama is also attracting growing interest from Hong Kong-based commercial concerns.
BUSINESS: Punctuality is appreciated and the exchange of business cards is normal. Suits are necessary for business meetings.
Office hours: Mon-Fri 0800-1700, Mon-Fri 0730-1630 (government offices).
COMMERCIAL INFORMATION: The following organisation can offer advice: Cámara de Comercio, Industrias y Agricultura de Panamá (Chamber of Commerce), Apartado 0816-07517, Avenida Cuba y Ecuador, Calle 34, Edificio 33 A-18, Panamá 1 (tel: 227 1233 *or* 1445; fax: 227 4186; e-mail: infocciap@panacamara.com; website: www.panacamara.com).

Climate

Temperatures are high across the whole country throughout the year, though cooler at high altitudes. The rainy season lasts from May to November. Rainfall is twice as heavy on the Pacific coast as it is on the lowlands of the Caribbean coast.
Required clothing: Lightweight cottons and linens are worn, with rainwear advisable, particularly in the rainy season. Warmer clothes are needed in the highlands.

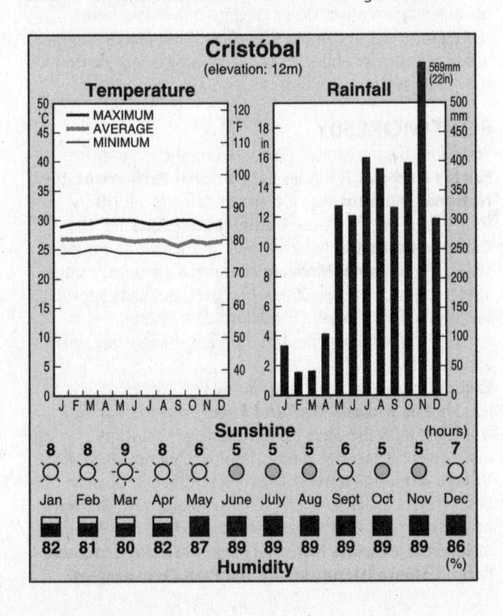

Papua New Guinea

LATEST TRAVEL ADVICE CONTACTS

British Foreign and Commonwealth Office
Tel: (0870) 606 0290 Website: www.fco.gov.uk
US Department of State
Website: http://travel.state.gov/travel
Canadian Department of Foreign Affairs and Int'l Trade
Tel: (1 800) 267 8376 Website: www.dfait-maeci.gc.ca

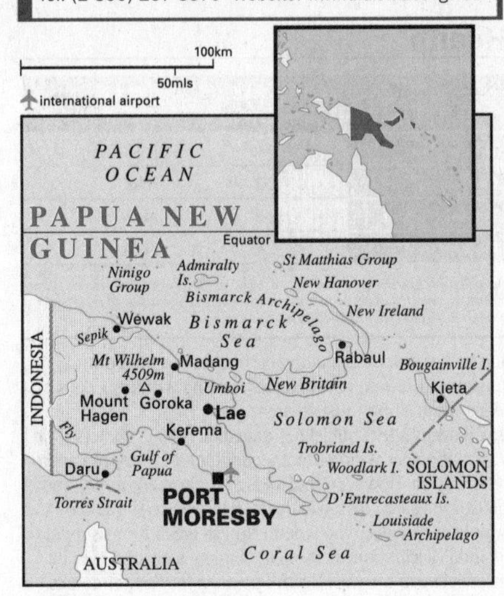

Location: South Pacific.

Country dialling code: 675.

Tourism Promotion Authority
Street address: Level 2, Pacific MMI Building, Champion Parade, Port Moresby, Papua New Guinea
Postal address: PO Box 1291, Port Moresby, Papua New Guinea
Tel: 320 0211. Fax: 320 0223.
E-mail: info@pngtourism.org.pg
Website: www.pngtourism.org.pg
South Pacific Tourism Organisation
Street address: Level 3, FNPF Place, 343-359 Victoria Parade, Suva, Fiji
Postal address: PO Box 13119, Suva, Fiji
Tel: (639) 330 4177. Fax: (639) 330 1995.
Website: www.spto.org *or* www.tcsp.com
Also deals with enquiries from the UK.
Papua New Guinea High Commission
14 Waterloo Place, London SW1Y 4AR, UK
Tel: (020) 7930 0922/7. Fax: (020) 7930 0828.
E-mail: jkekedo@aol.com
Opening hours: Mon-Fri 0900-1300 and 1400-1700.
British High Commission
Street address: Kiroki Street, Port Moresby, Papua New Guinea
Postal address: Locked Bag 212, Waigani, NCD 131, Papua New Guinea
Tel: 325 1677. Fax: 325 3547.
E-mail: bhcpng@datec.net.pg
Website: www.britishhighcommission.gov.uk/papuanewguinea
Papua New Guinea Embassy
1779 Massachusetts Avenue, Suite 805, NW, Washington, DC 20036, USA
Tel: (202) 745 3680. Fax: (202) 745 3679.
E-mail: info@pngembassy.org
Website: www.pngembassy.org
Also deals with enquiries from Canada, Mexico and mid- to South-American continent.
Embassy of the United States of America
Street address: Douglas Street, Port Moresby, Papua New Guinea
Postal address: PO Box 1492, Port Moresby, NCD 121, Papua New Guinea
Tel: 321 1455. Fax: 320 0637.
E-mail: ConsularPortMoresby@state.gov *or* usembassypng@state.gov
Website: http://portmoresby.usembassy.gov

TIMATIC CODES

Health	AMADEUS: **TI-DFT/POM/HE** GALILEO/WORLDSPAN: **TI-DFT/POM/HE** SABRE: **TIDFT/POM/HE**
Visa	AMADEUS: **TI-DFT/POM/VI** GALILEO/WORLDSPAN: **TI-DFT/POM/VI** SABRE: **TIDFT/POM/VI**

To access TIMATIC country information on Health and Visa regulations through the Computer Reservations System (CRS), type in the appropriate command line listed above.

Australian High Commission
Street address: Godwit Road, Waigani NCD, Papua New Guinea
Postal address: PO Box 129, Waigani NCD, Papua New Guinea
Tel: 325 9333. Fax: 325 9183.
Website: www.embassy.gov.au/pg.html
Although the Canadian High Commission in Canberra looks after non-emergency consular issues for Papua New Guinea, under the Canada-Australia Consular Sharing Agreement, the Australian High Commission (see above) now looks after Canadian citizens on the ground in Papua New Guinea.

General Information

AREA: 462,840 sq km (178,704 sq miles).
POPULATION: 5,586,000 (2002).
POPULATION DENSITY: 12.1 per sq km.
CAPITAL: Port Moresby. **Population:** 254,158 (2000).
GEOGRAPHY: Papua New Guinea consists of over 600 islands and lies in the middle of the long chain of islands stretching from mainland South East Asia. It lies in the South Pacific, 160km (100 miles) north of Australia. The country occupies the eastern half of the second-largest non-continental island in the world, as well as the smaller islands of the Bismarck Archipelago (Admiralty Island, Bougainville, New Britain and New Ireland), the D'Entrecasteaux Island group and the three islands of the Louisiade Archipelago. The main island shares a land border with Irian Jaya, a province of Indonesia. The mainland and larger islands are mountainous and rugged, divided by large fertile upland valleys. Fast-flowing rivers from the highlands descend to the coastal plains. A line of active volcanoes stretches along the north coast of the mainland and continues on the island of New Britain. To the north and south of this central mountain range on the main island lie vast stretches of mangrove swamps and coastal river deltas. Volcanoes and thermal pools are also found in the southeast of other islands. Papua New Guinea offers the greatest variety of terrestrial ecosystems in the South Pacific, including five types of lowland rainforest, 13 types of montane rainforest, five varieties of palm and swamp forest and three different mangrove forests. Two-thirds of the world's species of orchids come from Papua New Guinea. Birds include 38 species of the bird-of-paradise, and the megapode and cassowary. Marsupials and mammals include cuscus, tree kangaroos, wallabies, bandicoots, spiny anteaters and, in the coastal waters, the dugong. There are between 170 and 200 species of frog and 450 species of butterfly.
GOVERNMENT: Constitutional monarchy. Gained independence from Australia in 1975. **Head of State:** HM Queen Elizabeth II, represented locally by Governor General Sir Silas Atopare since 1997. **Head of Government:** Prime Minister Sir Michael Somare since 2002.
LANGUAGE: The official language is English, which is widely used in business and government circles. Pidgin English and Hiri Motu are more commonly used (an estimated 742 other languages and dialects are also spoken).
RELIGION: 90 per cent Christian.
TIME: GMT + 10.
ELECTRICITY: 240 volts AC, 50Hz. Australian-style three-pin plugs are in use. Some hotel rooms have 110-volt outlets.
COMMUNICATIONS: Telephone: IDD is available. Country code: 675. Outgoing international code: 05. There are no area codes in Papua New Guinea. **Mobile telephone:** GSM 900 network is in use. The only network provider is *Pacific Mobile Communications* (website: www.pacificmobile.com.pg). Coverage is likely to be limited. **Fax:** Services are available at all major companies and government departments. **Internet:** Main ISPs include *Daltron* (website: www.daltron.com) and *Global* (website: www.global.net.pg). However, services tend to be slow and sometimes unreliable. **Telegram:** Facilities are available in main centres. **Post:** Airmail to Europe takes seven to 10 days. Post office hours: Mon-Fri 0800-1600, Sat 0900-1200. **Press:** Two daily newspapers are published in English: *The National* and *Papua New Guinea Post-Courier*. The most popular daily is *Niugini Nius*.
Radio: BBC World Service (website: www.bbc.co.uk/worldservice) and Voice of America (website: www.voa.gov) can be received. From time to time the frequencies change and the most up-to-date can be found online.

Passport/Visa

	Passport Required?	Visa Required?	Return Ticket Required?
Full British	Yes	Yes	Yes
Australian	Yes	Yes	Yes
Canadian	Yes	Yes	Yes
USA	Yes	Yes	Yes
Other EU	Yes	Yes	Yes
Japanese	Yes	Yes	Yes

Note: *Regulations and requirements may be subject to change at short notice, and you are advised to contact the appropriate diplomatic or consular authority before finalising travel arrangements. Details of these may be found at the head of this country's entry. Any numbers in the chart refer to the footnotes below.*

Note: On receipt of a stamped, self-addressed envelope, the High Commission can supply information sheets on how to apply for visas for Papua New Guinea. The information below should be considered as a guide, as visa requirements may be subject to change at short notice.
PASSPORTS: Passport valid for at least six months after entry required by all.
VISAS: Required by all.
Types of visa and cost: *Tourist:* £7. *Business* (multiple-entry): £175. Costs vary for special categories of visitors (including consultants, yachtsmen and those engaged in medical, research or expedition activities). There will also be charges for extensions and costs incurred in processing documents.
Validity: Up to 60 days for tourists; up to 12 months for business trips with 60 days maximum per stay. Details of renewals or extensions are available from the Embassy or High Commission.
Application to: Consulate (or Consular section at Embassy or High Commission); see *Contact Addresses* section. In emergency cases, Tourist visas can be obtained at Jackson International Airport in Port Moresby *or* at Mount Hagen on arrival, but only for a maximum period of 60 days in any 12-month period, which cannot be extended. However, visitors are strongly advised to obtain visas in advance (which is also the cheaper option).
Application requirements: *Tourist:* (a) Completed application form (one per passport submitted). (b) Two passport-size photos. (c) Passport with minimum one year remaining validity from date of entry. (d) Return ticket. (e) Postal applications should be accompanied by a self-addressed, stamped, registered envelope. (f) Fee, payable by postal order or bank drafts if applying by post or in cash if applying in person. *Business:* (a)-(f) and, (g) Confirmed itinerary from travel agent. (h) Detailed letter in support of application covering curriculum vitae and confirmation of ongoing project in Papua New Guinea. (i) For visas issued at the airport, a letter of guarantee from sponsor must have been sent in advance to the Director of Immigration at the airport. Contact the nearest Papua New Guinea representative office for further information.
Working days required: 48 hours minimum for Business and Tourist visas. Temporary residence visas take up to six weeks or more. It is advisable for visa applications to be made one week or more before departure date, depending on type of visa.
Temporary residence: Available for those entering for employment purposes, usually professional persons or those undertaking research, consultancy, etc. Applications should be made to the nearest High Commission or Embassy in the first instance.

Money

Currency: Kina (Kina) = 100 toea. Notes are in denominations of Kina50, 20, 10, 5 and 2. Coins are in denominations of Kina1, and 50, 20, 10, 5, 2 and 1 toea.
Currency exchange: Exchange facilities are available through trade banks.
Credit cards: American Express is the most widely accepted credit card. Holders of this and other cards should check with their credit or debit card company for details of merchant acceptability and other services which may be available.
Travellers cheques: Accepted by most shops and hotels. To avoid additional exchange rate charges, travellers are advised to take travellers cheques in US Dollars, Pounds Sterling or Australian Dollars.
Currency restrictions: There are no restrictions on the import of local or foreign currency. The export of local currency is restricted to Kina200 and of foreign currency to Kina 10,000; if more, approval is required from the Bank of Papua New Guinea.
Exchange rate indicators: The following figures are included as a guide to the movements of the Kina against Sterling and the US Dollar:

Date	Feb '04	May '04	Aug '04	Nov '04
£1.00=	5.95	5.70	5.70	5.80
$1.00=	3.26	3.19	3.09	3.07

Banking hours: Mon-Thurs 0845-1500, Fri 0845-1600.

Duty Free

The following may be imported into Papua New Guinea by persons over 18 years of age without incurring customs duty:
260 cigarettes or 250g of cigars or tobacco; 1l of alcoholic beverages; a reasonable quantity of perfume; new goods up to a value of Kina200 (Kina100 for persons under 18 years of age), excluding radios, tape recorders, television sets, video cameras, video tapes, record players and associated equipment.
Prohibited items: Plants and soil, uncanned foods of animal origin (unless from Australia or New Zealand), and all pig meat from New Zealand.

Public Holidays

2005: Jan 1 New Year's Day. **Mar 25** Good Friday. **Mar 28** Easter Monday. **Jun 13** Queen's Birthday. **Jul 21** Remembrance Day. **Sep 16** Independence Day; Constitution Day. **Dec 25-26** Christmas.
2006: Jan 1 New Year's Day. **Apr 14** Good Friday. **Apr 17** Easter Monday. **Jun 13** Queen's Birthday. **Jul 21** Remembrance Day. **Sep 16** Independence Day; Constitution Day. **Dec 25-26** Christmas.
Note: In addition, there are various regional festivals throughout the year.

Health

	Special Precautions?	Certificate Required?
Yellow Fever	No	1
Cholera	2	No
Typhoid & Polio	3	N/A
Malaria	4	N/A

Note: *Regulations and requirements may be subject to change at short notice, and you are advised to contact your doctor well in advance of your intended date of departure. Any numbers in the chart refer to the footnotes below.*

1: A yellow fever vaccination certificate is required for travellers over one year of age if arriving within six days of leaving/transiting infected areas.
2: Following WHO guidelines issued in 1973, a cholera vaccination certificate is not a condition of entry to Papua New Guinea. However, cholera is a risk in this country and precautions are advisable. Up-to-date advice should be sought before deciding whether these precautions should include vaccination, as medical opinion is divided over its effectiveness; see the *Health* appendix for further details.
3: Vaccination against typhoid is advised.
4: Malaria risk exists all year throughout the country below 1800m (5760ft). The predominant *falciparum* strain is reported to be highly resistant to chloroquine and resistant to sulfadoxine/pyrimethamine.
Food & drink: All water should be regarded as being potentially contaminated. Water used for drinking, brushing teeth or making ice should have first been boiled or otherwise sterilised. Milk is pasteurised and dairy products are safe for consumption. Only eat well-cooked meat and fish, preferably served hot. Pork, salad and mayonnaise may carry increased risk. Vegetables should be cooked and fruit peeled.
Other risks: *Hepatitis A* and *B* are endemic. *Dengue fever* and *typhoid fever* can occur in epidemics. *Japanese encephalitis* occurs sporadically. Poisonous fish and sea snakes are a hazard to bathers.
Health care: The main hospitals are Port Moresby General (Papuan region), Goroka Base (Highlands) and Angau Memorial. Visitors can use any of the private doctors or public consultation clinics. Doctors and hospitals are not free and often expect immediate payment. Hospitals are poorly equipped and sudden shortages of common medications can sometimes occur; travellers who may need ongoing or routine medical treatment are advised to obtain visas for Australia, where medical facilities are more reliable, before leaving their country of origin. Dental care outside main centres is limited. There is no reciprocal health agreement with the UK. Health insurance is essential and must include evacuation facilities.

Travel - International

Note: Although most visits to Papua New Guinea are trouble-free, law and order remains very poor in many parts of the country. There have been incidents of assaults and robbery in Lae, Port Moresby and Mount Hagen; caution should be exercised when visiting these areas. Outbreaks of tribal fighting may occur without warning in the Highland Provinces and, in particular, the Southern Highlands and Enga Provinces.
AIR: Papua New Guinea's national airline is *Air Niugini (PX)* (website: www.airniugini.com.pg); it is also served by *Qantas (QF)*, amongst others.
Approximate flight times: The total flying time from Port Moresby to *London* is up to 30 hours (using current services and routes), but the journey takes at least two days to complete.
International airports: *Port Moresby (POM)* (Jacksons) is 11km (7 miles) from the city. There are direct flights to Australia and Singapore. Duty free and banking facilities are available at the airport. Buses and taxis are available to the city (travel time – 20 to 60 minutes).
Departure tax: Kina30 is levied on international flights. Children under two years of age and passengers not leaving the airport are exempt.
SEA: The international ports are Alotau, Kieta (North Solomons), Lae, Madang, Momote (Manus), Port Moresby, Rabaul (New Britain) and Wewak (Sepik). Passenger/cruise lines running regular services include *Lindblad, Peter Deilmann, Society Expeditions* and *World Discoverer.* Main cargo/passenger lines include *Austasia* and *Bank Line.*

Travel - Internal

AIR: Services are run by *Air Niugini* to all main centres, but are expensive. Internal services should be booked between November and February. *Air Niugini* flies to over 100 airstrips throughout the country and operates regular services to the 20 major towns of the country. *Air Niugini* also offers reductions for pre-booking excursions. Charter services are also in operation.
SEA: Cruises and excursions are available lasting three to 16 days. These go mainly to the islands and some otherwise inaccessible places on the coast. Cargo/passenger services between Lae and Madang are run by *Lutheran Shipping* with facilities, including passenger cabins, accommodation and meals.
RIVER: For the local people in some regions of the country, rivers, particularly the Sepik, provide the main thoroughfares. In these areas it is possible to hire motorised canoes or obtain passage on a trading boat; however, apart from cruises, there are no regular public transport operators on the rivers; see the *Resorts & Excursions* section.
ROAD: Driving is on the left and is not recommended. Owing to the rugged terrain of Papua New Guinea, road development of the interior has been slow. There are currently 19,736km (12,262 miles) of roads of which 4865km (3023 miles) are highways or trunk roads. There is a network of roads connecting the northern coast towns of Madang and Lae with the major urban centres in the Highlands region. There are few roads connecting the various provinces, however. **Bus:** PMVs (public motor vehicles) operate in the main centres from bus shelters or they can be hailed. **Taxi:** Available in district centres but expensive. Although operated on a metered basis, fares can be negotiated. **Car hire:** *Avis, Budget, Hertz* and the *Travelodge Hotel Cars Service* are available in principal towns. **Documentation:** A national driving licence is sufficient. **RAIL:** There is no railway.

Accommodation

Adequate and comfortable accommodation is available throughout Papua New Guinea. Generally, it is more expensive than in most Australasian states.
HOTELS: There are hotels of international standard in Lae, Madang, Port Moresby and most major centres. Many motels also offer good value accommodation.
LODGES: There is a developing tourist industry and tourist accommodation is increasing in many hitherto inaccessible areas. There are lodges in the Highlands and on the Sepik River, many of which can only be reached by air or river. Generally they consist of bungalows constructed of local materials. Contact the Tourism Promotion Authority for further details (see *Contact Addresses* section).

Resorts & Excursions

The tribal diversity of a country with over 700 languages cannot easily be summarised, although in Papua New Guinea it is the tribal life that is most fascinating to the visitor. Some of the excursions in Papua New Guinea are interestingly different from those offered elsewhere; for example, tourists can be taken to one of the many wrecks of World War II aircraft that lie in the jungle. *Haus Tambarans* ('Spirit Houses') are a feature of many towns and villages in the country, especially in the area of the Sepik River, so only a few of them can be given specific mention. Only initiated men of a tribe can enter (though in places this rule is relaxed for foreigners). They are built in a variety of styles, with massive carved wooden supports being a major feature. Other carvings and masks inside represent spirits. The orator's stools in these places are not used for sitting on; bunches of leaves are slapped down on the stools as the orator makes his points.

PORT MORESBY

Port Moresby, the capital, is situated on the magnificent **Fairfax Harbour**. It houses the **National Parliament**, the **National Museum**, which contains exhibits of pottery from all the provinces, the **Botanical Gardens** and the **Catholic Cathedral** (which is built in the *Haus Tambaran* style). The **National Museum** contains a historical record stretching back over 50,000 years. There are many sporting facilities in Port Moresby, including scuba diving, windsurfing, sailing, game fishing, water-skiing, golf, tennis and squash.
Excursions: Major attractions in the Port Moresby area include **The Kokoda Trail and Sogeri**, 40km (24 miles) from Port Moresby via the Sogeri road, which offers magnificent views and winds through rubber plantations; **Village Arts**, a government-owned artefacts shop with the best artefact collection in the country situated at **Six Mile**, near the airport. Other places of interest near Port Moresby include the **Wairiata National Park**; **Moitaka Crocodile Farm**; **Loloata Island** and the **Sea Park Oceanarium**.

LAE & MOROBE

LAE: Lae, the capital of Morobe province, is Papua New Guinea's second city and an important commercial centre and seaport. The **Botanical Gardens** are among the best in the country. **Mount Lunaman** in the centre of the town was used by the Germans and the Japanese as a lookout point. It gives a magnificent view over the **Huon Gulf** and the **Markham Valley**.
ELSEWHERE: Outside Lae is **Wau**, formerly a gold-mining centre. The **Wau Ecology Institute**, a privately funded organisation, has a small museum and zoo. Visitors can see cassowaries, tree kangaroos, crocodiles, birds of paradise, native butterflies and rhododendrons. Sights near Wau are **McAdam National Park** and **Mount Kaindi**, **Finschhafen** (a very pretty coastal town) and the **Tami Islands**, whose people are renowned for their carved wooden bowls. **Sialum** is an attractive area of coastline known for its coral terraces. White-water rafting on the **Watut River** is an attraction for the adventurous.

MADANG

MADANG: The capital of Madang Province, Madang is an ideal starting place for many of the tours round the islands and up the Sepik River. It has a variety of shops, hotels, restaurants and markets, where storyboards depicting myths and legends can be bought. In nearby **Bilbils** and **Yabobs**, traditional pottery-making can be seen.
ELSEWHERE: There are four main population groupings in the province: island, coastal, river and mountain, each with its own diet, traditions and customs. The **Manam** islanders make houses out of sago trees and toddy palms with leaves and leaf stems tied into each other. The **Ramu River** people make similar houses, but on stilts, and their carving traditions are influenced by the cultures of the Sepik River. The mountain people are physically smaller and grow familiar crops such as lettuce, radishes, cabbages and potatoes. The families of the coastal population place a special value on dog's teeth necklaces, tambu shell headbands and pig tusk amulets. These items are sometimes still used as currency in tribal transactions.

THE SEPIK RIVER

The Sepik River is the longest river in Papua New Guinea and has been for many centuries the trade route into the interior. It winds down from the mountains near the border with Irian Jaya, draining immense tracts of scarcely explored jungle, swamp and grassland until it meets the sea, where it is more than a mile wide. It abounds with meandering waterways, oxbow lakes, tributaries and backwaters, swamps, lagoons, lakes and artificial channels built to short-cut its looping journey. Unusually for a great river, it has no delta system and its waters spew directly into the sea with enormous force. From the many villages along its banks come highly-prized examples of primitive art. The *Haus Tambaran* at **Angoram** possesses a display of art from almost the entire length of the river. At **Kambaramba** village, and elsewhere, houses are built on stilts as a protection against flooding and the dugout canoe is still the main local means of transport. Tourists have the option of being taken on a cruise. Woodcarving is one of the main local crafts and its architectural use in gables and posts in houses is a noteworthy feature as can be seen, for instance, at the village of **Tambanum**. **Timbunke** village is a further example of fine construction techniques, including bridge-building.
The area around the **Chambri Lakes** is home to the diverse species of birds for which Papua New Guinea is famous. These include egrets, pied herons, brahminee kites, whistling kites, jacanas, darters, cormorants and kingfishers. Islands of tangled vegetation and the debris of fallen trees float down the river to the Bismarck Sea. Salt and freshwater crocodiles abound and come out mostly at night. Nightly or early morning excursions into the jungle can be arranged for tourists wishing to experience the unique cacophony of birds preparing for the day's hunting. Tours along the river have a flexible itinerary which is adapted to river conditions and set to coincide with the many local customs and events. Also in the Chambri area can be found a unique pottery-making village, **Aibom**, where clay fireplaces, storage and cooking pots are made by the coil method and fired in the open air by women.
At **Kanganaman**, a *Haus Tambaran* of national cultural importance is being rebuilt, providing an excellent example of the carvings on the immense *Haus Posts*. **Korogo** is famous for its *Mei Masks*.
In the upper reaches of the Sepik, clan representation and art is characterised by insect totems using praying mantis, rhinoceros-beetle motifs and distinctive insect eyes. Canoe prows are extremely elaborate, as are the tops of stepladders leading into dwellings. At **Waskusk**, the drawings on the ceiling of the *Haus Tambaran* depict a clan leader's dream, but conditions on the river sometimes make this village inaccessible. At **Yigei**, Upper Sepik-style *Garamut Drums* ('Slit Gongs') can be seen (and heard); and there are dramatic designs in white and yellow along the waterway in **Swagap Village**, which also has simple, elegant pottery and fireplaces, and often very fine examples of the canoe-builder's craft.

THE HIGHLANDS

The majority of the country's population lives in this least accessible part of Papua New Guinea.
EASTERN HIGHLANDS: This region has the longest history of contact with the West. **Kainantu** is reached from Lae through the **Kassim Pass**. It has a large cultural centre, selling traditional artefacts; it also provides training in print-making and weaving. The largest town is **Goroka**, an agricultural and commercial centre for the entire Highlands region. The **JK McCarthy Museum** has a comprehensive display of regional artefacts; the Leahy wing contains photographs taken by early explorers. In the town centre the **Raun Raun Theatre** company provides contemporary performances of traditional stories and legends. **Bena Bena Village**, 10km (6 miles) from Goroka, is the largest handweaving organisation in the Highlands. Also nearby is **Asaro**, where the men coat themselves with grey mud and re-enact for visitors their historic revenge on a neighbouring village. The legend has it that, having been defeated in battle, the resourceful villagers covered themselves in mud and successfully frightened the opposition, who ran away in fear of being visited by ghosts.
SIMBU PROVINCE: Kundiawa, a small town, is the capital of Simbu Province. Some of the local caves are used as burial places; others are popular with cavers. Rafting down the **Wahgi** and **Purari** rivers is also exciting. **Mount Wilhelm**, 4509m (1480ft), is in Simbu Province and is the highest mountain in Papua New Guinea.
WESTERN HIGHLANDS: In some ways **Mount Hagen** in the Western Highlands resembles a town from the Wild West. Its expansion is only recent and the local population organise a number of *sing-sing* celebrations to mark a diverse variety of events ranging from payment of a bride-price to the opening of a new road. There is also a cultural centre in the town. The **Baiyer River Wildlife Sanctuary** lies 55km (34 miles) north of Mount Hagen and is one of the best places to see the famous birds of paradise. Possums, tree kangaroos, parrots and cassowaries are also part of the natural habitat.
SOUTHERN HIGHLANDS: The **Mendi Valley** of the Southern Highlands is noted for its spectacular scenery and limestone caves. It is home to the *Huli Wigmen* who wear red and yellow face-paint and elaborately decorated wigs made of human hair.
ENGA PROVINCE: Wabang in Enga Province has a large cultural centre with an art gallery and a museum. Young artists can be seen working on sand paintings. War shields, wigs, weapons and other artefacts from all over Papua New Guinea are on display. Enga is the most primitive of the Highland Provinces.

THE ISLANDS

The main islands are New Britain, New Ireland and the Manus group (together comprising the Bismarck Archipelago), the northernmost Solomon Islands of Bougainville and Buka, and an eastern group of islands including the Trobriand and D'Entrecasteaux Islands.
NEW BRITAIN: Rabaul on New Britain is the capital of the island and suffered extensive damage, owing to volcanic activity a few years back. During the eruptions, most of the town was destroyed and the inhabitants were evacuated to other parts of the island. Rabaul used to be renowned for the **Gunantabu** (the remains of Queen Emma's residence) with her private cemetery; the remains of the **German Government House** on **Namanula Hill**; a 576km (360 mile) underground tunnel system left by the Japanese; the **Admirals Bunker**, now a museum; an orchid park; and **Rabaul Market**, which is famous throughout the South Pacific. New Britain is one of the most popular islands for diving and there are many diving boats available.
NEW IRELAND & MANUS: New Ireland and the Manus group of islands are off the general tourist trail. In the northwestern islands of the latter group there are no trees. The islanders have a tradition of making sea-going canoes out of logs that float down the Sepik into the surrounding ocean.
NORTH SOLOMONS: Bougainville and **Buka** are separated by a narrow channel of islets. Before Bougainville was closed to visitors, tourists were well catered for with activities such as scuba diving, snorkelling, game fishing and swimming as well as bushwalking, caving expeditions, a six-hour downhill hike from **Panguna** to **Arawa** and a three-day jungle trek to the summit of **Mount Balbi**, a dormant volcano. For details about visiting this area as well as the nearby **Butterfly Farm** in **Kerei Village**, contact the Tourism Promotion Authority (see Contact Addresses section). Relics of German and Japanese occupation abound throughout Papua New Guinea and visitors will have no trouble finding them. The wreck of Admiral Yamamoto's plane in the rainforest of **Buin** is perhaps one of the most interesting.
MILNE BAY: The islands offshore from Bougainville are lined with white sandy beaches. The **Trobriands** are the most accessible of the groups of islands in Milne Bay Province, but tourists might feel slightly less welcome than in the main tourist areas. As elsewhere in the islands, swimming and snorkelling enthusiasts are well catered for. The harvesting of yams from May to September is accompanied by extended rituals and celebrations which peak in the months of July and August. The mountainous **D'Entrecasteaux Islands** rise out of the sea. In the centre of **Goodenough Island**, there is a large stone decorated with mysterious paintings.

Sport & Activities

Watersports: The beaches and coral reefs around Papua New Guinea offer spectacular **swimming** and **snorkelling** facilities. **Diving** facilities and qualified instructors are available. Madang, Port Moresby and Rabaul offer a wide variety of dives ranging from wrecks to reefs. Diving holidays can also be arranged at locations such as Loloaka and off the island of New Britain, the latter being considered one of the best diving areas in Papua New Guinea. There is an underwater club in Port Moresby which is open to visitors. **Game fish** are plentiful in Lae, Madang, Port Moresby, Rabaul and Wewak. Information is available from Port Moresby Game Fishing Club Gantry, PO Box 154, Boroko (tel: 325 4532; fax: 325 6048; e-mail: kwebber@daltron.com.pg; website: www.pmgfc.org.pg). The Royal Papua Yacht Club (tel: 321 1700; fax: 321 4935; e-mail:rpyc@datec.net.pg website: www.rpyc.com.pg) makes its extensive **sailing** facilities available to visitors; the season begins in late April.
Backpacking and hiking: There are many backpacking and hiking tours are on offer, ranging from simple bush walks to extended tours through the rugged interior.
Other: Golf can be played at *Port Moresby Golf Club*, which has one of the oldest courses in Papua New Guinea, and is open to visitors. Other clubs are at Arowa, Lae, Madang, Minj, Rabaul and Wau. Visitors are welcome to do **horseriding** at Illimo Farm, Port Moresby, where instruction is available in the afternoons and at weekends. **Squash** courts and equipment are available in major centres.

Social Profile

FOOD & DRINK: Hotel dining rooms cater for most visitors and menus in main centres are fairly extensive. The more remote the area, the more likely it is that the menus will be basic. However, increasing use is made of fresh local meat, fish, vegetables and fruit, including pineapples, pawpaws, mangoes, passion fruit and bananas. Traditional cuisine of Papua New Guinea is based on root crops such as taro, kaukau and yams, sago and pig (cooked in the earth on traditional feasts). *Mumu* is a traditional dish combining pork, sweet potatoes, rice and greens. The number of European, Chinese and Indonesian restaurants is rising. Waiter service is usual. Alcohol is readily available and includes Australian and Filipino beers.
NIGHTLIFE: Several hotels in Port Moresby have dancing in the evenings and some organise live entertainment. The Arts Theatre stages regular performances. The local newspaper advertises programmes. *Sing-sings*, tribal events on a smaller scale than the biannual festival, are sometimes held.
SHOPPING: A wide range of crafts is available in shops; alternatively, visitors can buy directly from villagers. Favourite buys include local carvings of ceremonial masks and statuettes from Angoram and the Sepik, *Buka* basketry, arrows, bows and decorated axes, crocodile carvings from the Trobriands, pottery and local art. The many butterfly farms send specimens of unusual species throughout the world. **Shopping hours:** Mon-Fri 0900-1700, Sat 0900-1300 (some open longer and/or Sunday).
SPECIAL EVENTS: National Independence Day and (in some towns) the Chinese New Year are major occasions of celebration. Visitors should not, however, turn down any chances to go to a *sing-sing*, a colourful tribal gathering with dancing, singing and chanting. Colourful flower festivals and traditional feasts also take place throughout the year. For further details, contact the Tourism Promotion Authority (see *Contact Addresses* section). The following is a selection of special events occurring in Papua New Guinea in 2005:
May 14-15 *Papua New Guinea Coffee Festival and Trade* Fair. **May-Jun** *Kula Festival*. **May-Jul** *Milamala Yam Festival*, Kiriwina Island. **Jun** *Port Moresby Show*. **Jul 6-12** *Tolai Warwagira*. **Jul 13-16** *National Mask Festival*, Rabaul. **Sep 2-3** *Garamut and Mambo Festival*. **Sep 16** *Independence Day Celebrations*. **Nov 2-5** *Canoe and Kundu Festival*.
SOCIAL CONVENTIONS: Papua New Guinea's culture still includes elements of a primitive lifestyle. There are universities at Lae (which is a University of Technology with a liberal infusion of Europeans and North Americans) and at Port Moresby. Casual clothes are recommended. Informality

is the order of the day and although shorts are quite acceptable, beachwear is usually best confined to the beach. In the evenings some hotels expect men to wear long trousers but ties are rare. A long dress is appropriate for women on formal occasions. **Tipping:** Not customary and discouraged.

Business Profile

ECONOMY: Although Papua New Guinea has been described as 'a mountain of gold floating on a sea of oil', it is a poor country and most of the population is engaged in subsistence agriculture. The most important commercial cash crops are copra, coffee, cocoa, timber, palm oil, rubber, tea, sugar and peanuts. However, the gradual discovery of exploitable mineral deposits has transformed the country. Papua New Guinea boasts the largest known supply of low-grade copper, the entire production of which is exported to Western Europe and Japan under long-term contract, and accounts for three-quarters of the country's export earnings. Production, though, has been upset by the Bougainville insurgency.
Other identified mineral deposits include gold and chromite. Some oil and natural gas has also been located. Light industry has grown steadily, mostly to meet consumer demands: the construction industry, printing, brewing, bottling and packaging are among these. Papua New Guinea's attempts to develop a tourist industry have been undermined by a lack of basic infrastructure and, more importantly, political stability. The country is always subject to the vagaries of the climate and natural phenomena – in recent years, it has suffered drought, flooding and an earthquake. On top of that, the Asian economic crisis of the previous autumn damaged the PNG economy. During the last five years, the Government has managed to stabilise the economy, cutting the budget deficit, reducing inflation to around 10 per cent and stabilising the currency. However, growth has been stagnant at best and Papua New Guinea is still burdened by an overseas debt of $2.5 billion.
Papua New Guinea belongs to the Asian Development Bank and the South Pacific Commission. Its largest trading partners are Australia, with 50 per cent of the market, followed by Japan, Singapore and the USA.
BUSINESS: Business affairs tend to be conducted in a very informal fashion. A conventional suit will not be required – shirt and tie or safari suit are sufficient. **Office hours:** Mon-Fri 0800-1630. **Government office hours:** Mon-Fri 0800-1600.
COMMERCIAL INFORMATION: The following organisations can offer advice: Papua New Guinea Chamber of Commerce and Industry (tel: 321 3057; fax: 321 0566;
e-mail: pngcci@global.net.pg; website: www.pngcci.org.pg); *or* Investment Promotion Authority, Level 3, Credit Corporation House, Cuthbertson St, Port Moresby (tel: 321 7311; fax: 321 2819; e-mail: iepd@ipa.gov.pg; website: www.ipa.gov.pg).
CONFERENCES/CONVENTIONS: Some hotels provide facilities.

Climate

Hot, tropical climate at sea level, cooling towards the highlands which also cause climatic variation from one area to another, affecting the southeast trade winds and the northwest monsoons. The majority of the rain falls between December and March due to the northwest monsoon, although Port Moresby enjoys a dry season at this time. There is frost and there are occasional snow falls on the highest mountain peaks.
Required clothing: Tropical, lightweights and cottons are recommended. In the highlands, warmer clothing is needed. Rainwear is advised for the monsoon season (December to March).

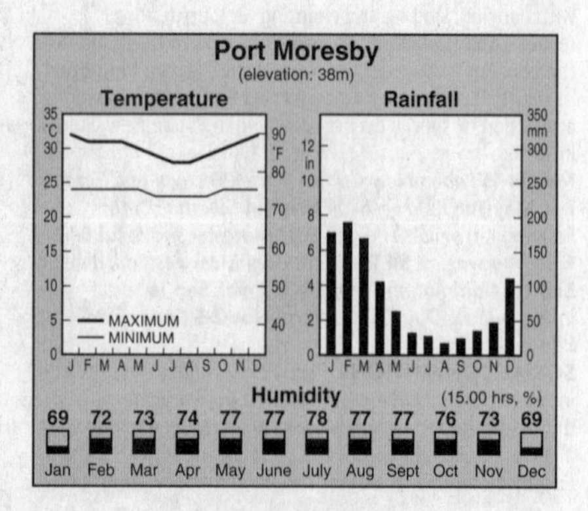

Paraguay

LATEST TRAVEL ADVICE CONTACTS

British Foreign and Commonwealth Office
Tel: (0870) 606 0290 Website: www.fco.gov.uk
US Department of State
Website: http://travel.state.gov/travel
Canadian Department of Foreign Affairs and Int'l Trade
Tel: (1 800) 267 8376 Website: www.dfait-maeci.gc.ca

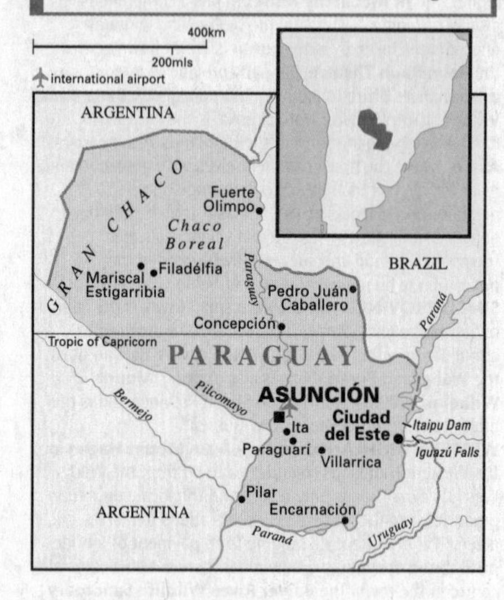

Location: Central South America.

Country Dialling Code: 595.

Secretaría Nacional de Turismo
Palma 468, casi 14 de Mayo, Edificio Central, Asunción, Paraguay
Tel: (21) 441 530 *or* 620. Fax: (21) 491 230 *or* 494 110.
E-mail: infosenatur@senatur.gov.py
Website: www.senatur.gov.py
Embassy of the Republic of Paraguay
344 Kensington High Street, 3rd Floor, London W14 8NS, UK
Tel: (020) 7610 4180. Fax: (020) 7371 4297.
E-mail: embapar@btconnect.com
Website: www.paraguayembassy.co.uk
Opening hours: Mon-Fri 0930-1630.
Embassy of the Republic of Paraguay
2400 Massachusetts Avenue, NW, Washington, DC 20008, USA
Tel: (202) 483 6960. Fax: (202) 234 4508.
E-mail: embapar.usa@verizon.net
Consulates General in: Los Angeles, Miami and New York.
Embassy of the United States of America
Street address: Avenida Mariscal López 1776, Asunción, Paraguay
Postal address: Casilla Postal 402, Asunción, Paraguay
Tel: (21) 213 715. Fax: (21) 213 728.
E-mail: paraguayusembassy@state.gov
Website: http://asuncion.usembassy.gov
Embassy of Paraguay
151 Slater Street, Suite 501, Ottawa, Ontario K1P 5H3, Canada
Tel: (613) 567 1283 *or* 1005. Fax: (613) 567 1679.
E-mail: consularsection@embassyofparaguay.ca
Website: www.embassyofparaguay.ca
Canadian Consulate
Profesor Ramirez, 3 esquina Juan de Salazar, Asunción, Paraguay
Tel: (21) 227 207. Fax: (21) 227 208.
E-mail: honconpy@telesurf.com.py
Website: www.dfait-maeci.gc.ca/argentina/para-en.asp

General Information

AREA: 406,752 sq km (157,048 sq miles).
POPULATION: 5,206,101 (official estimate 2002).
POPULATION DENSITY: 12.8 per sq km.

TIMATIC CODES

Health
AMADEUS: **TI-DFT/ASU/HE**
GALILEO/WORLDSPAN: **TI-DFT/ASU/HE**
SABRE: **TIDFT/ASU/HE**

Visa
AMADEUS: **TI-DFT/ASU/VI**
GALILEO/WORLDSPAN: **TI-DFT/ASU/VI**
SABRE: **TIDFT/ASU/VI**

To access TIMATIC country information on Health and Visa regulations through the Computer Reservations System (CRS), type in the appropriate command line listed above.

CAPITAL: Asunción. **Population:** 513,399 (2000).
GEOGRAPHY: Paraguay is a landlocked country surrounded by Argentina, Bolivia and Brazil, lying some 1440km (900 miles) up the River Paraná from the Atlantic. The River Paraguay, a tributary of the Paraná, divides the country into two sharply contrasting regions. The Oriental zone, which covers 159,800 sq km (61,700 sq miles), consists of undulating country intersected by chains of hills rising to about 600m (2000ft), merging into the Mato Grosso Plateau in the north; the Paraná crosses the area in the east and south. East and southeast of Asunción lie the oldest centres of settlement inhabited by the greater part of the population. This area is bordered to the west by rolling pastures, and to the south by thick primeval forests. The Occidental zone, or Paraguayan Chaco, covers 246,827 sq km (95,300 sq miles). It is a flat alluvial plain, composed mainly of grey clay, which is marked by large areas of permanent swamp in the southern and eastern regions. Apart from a few small settlements, it is sparsely populated.
GOVERNMENT: Republic since 1967. Gained independence from Spain in 1811. **Head of State and Government:** President Óscar Nicanor Duarte Frutos since 2003.
LANGUAGE: The official languages are Spanish and Guaraní; Guaraní is spoken by most of the rural population. Most Paraguayans are bilingual, but prefer to speak Guaraní outside Asunción.
RELIGION: Mostly Roman Catholic.
TIME: GMT - 4 (GMT - 3 from October to March).
ELECTRICITY: 220 volts AC, 50Hz.
COMMUNICATIONS: Telephone: IDD is available. Country code: 595. Outgoing international code: 002. Moderate internal network apart from the main cities.
Mobile Telephone: GSM 1900 network coverage is limited to main urban areas. The local network providers are *Hutchison Telecommunications Paraguay SA* (website: www.porthable.com.py), *Nucleo SA* (website: www.personal.com.py), *Telefonica Celular Del Paraguay* (website: www.telecel.com.py) and *VOX* (website: www.vox.com.py). **Fax:** Some hotels provide facilities.
Internet: ISPs include *Planet* (website: www.pla.net.py). Internet cafes are available in main urban areas. **Telegram:** Many hotels have facilities. Services are also available at *COPACO* (Compañía Paraguaya de Comunicaciones). **Post:** Airmail to Europe takes five days. **Press:** The main newspapers are *ABC Color*, *La Nación*, *Noticias* and *Ultima Hora*. American newspapers are available.
Radio: BBC World Service (website: www.bbc.co.uk/worldservice) and Voice of America (website: www.voa.gov) can be received. From time to time the frequencies change and the most up-to-date can be found online.

Passport/Visa

	Passport Required?	Visa Required?	Return Ticket Required?
Full British	Yes	No	Yes
Australian	Yes	Yes	Yes
Canadian	Yes	Yes	Yes
USA	Yes	Yes	Yes
Other EU	Yes	1	Yes
Japanese	Yes	No	Yes

Note: *Regulations and requirements may be subject to change at short notice, and you are advised to contact the appropriate diplomatic or consular authority before finalising travel arrangements. Details of these may be found at the head of this country's entry. Any numbers in the chart refer to the footnotes below.*

PASSPORTS: Passport valid for six months after the intended length of stay required by all except nationals of Argentina, Bolivia, Brazil, Chile and Uruguay with valid ID cards entering as tourists directly from their own country.
VISAS: Required by all except the following entering as tourists for stays of up to 90 days:
(a) **1.** nationals of EU countries (except nationals of Cyprus, Czech Republic, Estonia, Ireland, Latvia, Lithuania, Malta, Poland, Slovak Republic and Slovenia who *do* require visas);
(b) nationals of Argentina, Bolivia, Brazil, Chile, Colombia, Costa Rica, Ecuador, El Salvador, Israel, Japan, Liechtenstein, Norway, Panama, Peru, South Africa, Switzerland, Uruguay and Venezuela;
(c) transit passengers continuing their journey by the same or first connecting aircraft within six hours provided holding onward or return documentation and not leaving the airport.
Types of visa and cost: *Tourist* and *Business*: *Single-entry*: £36. *Multiple-entry*: £52.
Validity: 90 days from date of issue.
Application to: Consulate (or Consular section at Embassy); see *Contact Addresses* section.
Application requirements: (a) Valid passport (plus two photocopies from page with personal data). (b) Two completed application forms. (c) Two passport-size photos. (d) Self-addressed envelope for postal applications (see

Note below). (e) Fee, payable in cash (or cheque in sterling at the Consulate of Paraguay in London). *The following requirements must be presented with two photocopies:* (f) Proof of adequate funds (bank statement or credit card). (g) Travel tickets and copy of itinerary.
For business visas: (a)-(g) and, (h) A covering letter from employer including name of contact in Paraguay (two photocopies).
Note: Postal applications are accepted only from Australia, Iceland, Ireland and New Zealand and will not be processed until return post is paid or a courier service is arranged. A self-addressed envelope must be included with all postal applications.
Working days required: 24 to 48 hours.
Temporary residence: Apply to Consulate (or Consular section at Embassy); see *Contact Addresses* section.

Money

Currency: Guaraní (G). Notes are in denominations of G100,000, 50,000, 10,000, 5000, 1000 and 500. Coins are in denominations of G500, 100, 50, 10 and 5.
Currency exchange: Paraguay maintains a free monetary exchange policy and the purchase and sale of foreign currencies is not subject to any controls or regulations. There is a bureau de change at the airport. US Dollars, which are more easily negotiable than Sterling, are widely accepted throughout the country. Paraguayan ATMs may not always recognise foreign cards.
Credit & debit cards: American Express, MasterCard and Visa are widely accepted (though not in smaller hotels), while Diners Club has more limited use. Check with your credit or debit card company for details of merchant acceptability and other services which may be available.
Travellers cheques: US Dollar travellers cheques are widely accepted although cheap hotels usually do not exchange travellers cheques.
Currency restrictions: There are no restrictions on the import or export of local or foreign currency.
Exchange rate indicators: The following figures are included as a guide to the movements of the Guaraní against Sterling and the US Dollar:

Date	Feb '04	May '04	Aug '04	Nov '04
£1.00=	11285.60	10216.5	10906.7	11580.0
$1.00=	6200.00	5720.00	5920.00	6115.00

Banking hours: Mon-Fri 0845-1500.

Duty Free

The following items may be imported into Paraguay without incurring customs duty:
A reasonable quantity of tobacco, alcoholic beverages and perfume for personal use; a reasonable quantity of personal and sporting equipment.

Public Holidays

2005: Jan 1 New Year's Day. **Mar 1** Heroes' Day. **Mar 24** Maundy Thursday. **Mar 25** Good Friday. **Mar 27** Easter. **May 1** Labour Day. **May 15** Independence Day. **Jun 12** Peace of Chaco. **Aug 15** Founding of Asunción. **Sep 29** Battle of Boquerón. **Dec 8** Immaculate Conception. **Dec 25** Christmas Day.
2006: Jan 1 New Year's Day. **Mar 1** Heroes' Day. **Apr 13** Maundy Thursday. **Apr 14** Good Friday. **Apr 16** Easter. **May 1** Labour Day. **May 15** Independence Day. **Jun 12** Peace of Chaco. **Aug 15** Founding of Asunción. **Sep 29** Battle of Boquerón. **Dec 8** Immaculate Conception. **Dec 25** Christmas Day.

Health

	Special Precautions?	Certificate Required?
Yellow Fever	No	1
Cholera	No	No
Typhoid & Polio	2	N/A
Malaria	3	N/A

Note: *Regulations and requirements may be subject to change at short notice, and you are advised to contact your doctor well in advance of your intended date of departure. Any numbers in the chart refer to the footnotes below.*

1: A yellow fever vaccination certificate is required from travellers leaving Paraguay to go to endemic areas. A certificate is also required from travellers coming from endemic areas.
2: Typhoid is a risk in rural areas.
3: Malaria risk, almost exclusively in the benign *vivax* form, is moderate in certain municipalities of Alto Paraná, Caaguazú and Canendiyú. In the other 13 departments there is a negligible risk.
Food & drink: Mains water is normally chlorinated, and whilst relatively safe, may cause mild abdominal upsets. Bottled water is available and is advised for the first few weeks of stay. Drinking water outside main cities and towns is likely to be contaminated and sterilisation is considered essential. Milk may be unpasteurised and, if so, should be boiled. Powdered or tinned milk is also available and is advised, but make sure that it is reconstituted with pure water. Avoid dairy products which are likely to have been made from unboiled milk. Only eat well-cooked meat and fish, preferably served hot. Pork, salad and mayonnaise may carry increased risk. Vegetables should be cooked and fruit peeled.
Other risks: *Hepatitis B* and *D* are endemic; *hepatitis A* is common; *hepatitis C* occurs. There have been large epidemics of *dengue fever* across the country in the past few years. *TB* occurs.
Rabies is present. For those at high risk, vaccination before arrival should be considered. If you are bitten, seek medical advice without delay. For more information, consult the *Health* appendix.
Health care: Health insurance is essential. There is no reciprocal health agreement with the UK.

Travel - International

Note: Crime in Paraguay is increasing, so the need to be alert at all times is essential.
AIR: Paraguay's national airline is *Transportes Aéreos del Mercosur (PZ).* Airlines operating direct flights to Asunción include *American Airlines* (from New York). There are currently no direct flights from London. Most major airlines (including *Alitalia, British Airways, Canadian Airlines* and *Lufthansa*) operate connecting flights via Brazil (São Paulo or Rio de Janeiro). There are also a number of scheduled flights to Asunción from other south American cities, notably Buenos Aires, Santa Cruz (Bolivia) and Santiago (Chile).
Approximate flight times: From Asunción to *London* is 15 to 19 hours, depending on the route taken.
International airports: *Asunción (ASU)* (Silvio Pettirossi) is 16km (10 miles) from the city (travel time – 20 minutes). A coach and taxi service runs to the city. Airport facilities include a bureau de change, duty free shopping, restaurants and car hire (*Hertz*).
Air passes: *The Mercosur Airpass:* Valid within Argentina, Brazil, Chile (except Easter Island), Paraguay and Uruguay. Participating airlines include *Aerolíneas Argentinas (AR)* (however, flights on this airline cannot be combined with any others, as it has no agreements and its tickets are not accepted by other airlines), *Austral (AU), LAN-Chile (LA), LAPA (MJ), Pluna (PU), Transbrasil Airlines (TR)* and *VARIG (RG),* with the subsidiary airlines of *Nordeste (JH)* and *Rio Sul (SL).* The pass can only be purchased by passengers who live outside South America, who have a return ticket. Only eight flight coupons are allowed with a maximum of four coupons for each country and is valid from seven to a maximum of 30 days. At least two countries must be visited (to a maximum of five) and the flight route cannot be changed. A maximum of two stopovers is allowed per country.
The Visit South America Pass: Must be bought outside South America in country of residence and allows unlimited travel to 36 cities in the following countries: Argentina, Bolivia, Brazil, Colombia, Chile (except Easter Island), Ecuador, Paraguay, Peru, Uruguay and Venezuela. Participating airlines include *Aer Lingus (EI), American Airlines (AA), British Airways (BA), Cathay Pacific (CX), Finnair (AY), IBERIA (IB), LAN-Chile (LA)* and *Qantas (QF).* A minimum of three flights must be booked, with no maximum; the maximum stay is 60 days, with no minimum, and prices depend on the amount of flight zones covered. Children under 12 years of age are entitled to a 33 per cent discount and infants (under two years old) only pay 10 per cent of the adult fare. For further details, contact one of the participating airlines.
Departure tax: US$18. Transit passengers and children under two years of age are exempt.
RIVER: There are 2500km (1563 miles) of navigable rivers in Paraguay and there are ferry links with Argentina, Bolivia and Brazil. Travellers using the river to travel to Argentina should note that the Posadas (Argentina)–Encarnación (Paraguay) route is 321km (200 miles) shorter than the more traditional route to Buenos Aires. It traverses the Argentine provinces of Misiones and Corrientes and then proceeds across a bridge over the Paraná River to Resistencia. Those who prefer to continue along the left bank of the Paraná River will have to travel to Paraná, provincial capital of Entre Ríos, crossing under the Paraná River in the tunnel between the cities of Paraná and Santa Fé. It is also possible to reach Paraguay by river from Brazil, in boats which connect Asunción with the Brazilian city of Corumba.
RAIL: There is no through service to Argentina, but a weekly train from Asunción serves Posadas in Argentina by means of a train-ferry, with connections to Concordia and Buenos Aires. The rail services are very slow.
ROAD: The roads from Río and São Paulo to Asunción (via the Iguazú Falls) are paved and generally good, as is the one from Buenos Aires. Another road link to Argentina is via the San Roque González de Santa Cruz bridge in Encarnación across the Paraná river. **Bus:** There are daily services from Rio de Janeiro and São Paulo, Buenos Aires (Argentina), Córdoba, Rosario and Santa Fé, and Montevideo (Uruguay).

Travel - Internal

AIR: Air service is run by *LATN (Líneas Aéreas de Transporte Nacional)* and *TAM (Transportes Aéreos del Mercosur).* The most popular visitors' flight is to the Iguazú Falls from Asunción with *Varig Airways (RG).* Air-taxis are popular with those wishing to discover the Paraguayan Chaco (see *Resorts & Excursions* section). Travel agencies offer daily city tours, but services suffer from frequent disruption by weather conditions.
RIVER: River cruises to the main tourist attractions and throughout the Chaco are available. For further details, contact the Dirección de Turismo (see *Contact Addresses* section).
RAIL: A weekly service links Asunción and Encarnación – which are 431km (268 miles) apart – using original steam locomotives. There is also a weekly service from San Salvador to Abay. Services are often unreliable, however, and whole routes may be abandoned for months at a time.
ROAD: Traffic drives on the right. Roads serving the main centres are in good condition. However, unsurfaced roads may be closed in bad weather. Approximately 10 per cent of roads are surfaced. A highway links Asunción with Iguazú Falls, a drive of up to six hours. Some travellers have reported problems with police checks; it is also advisable to lock doors. **Bus:** Often the best and cheapest method of transport within Paraguay. For longer distances, advance booking may be necessary. There are express links to major centres. **Car hire:** Cars can be hired at the airport or through local tourist agencies. **Documentation:** National driving licence or International Driving Permit are both accepted.
URBAN: Bus and minibus services are provided by private companies in Asunción, with two-zone fares collected by conductors. There also remain two routes of the government-operated tramway.
Travel times: The following chart gives approximate travel times (in hours and minutes) from **Asunción** to other major cities in Paraguay.

	Air	Road	Rail	River
Pedro Juan Caballero	1.15	11.00	-	13.00
Concepción	1.00	12.00	-	14.00
Ciudad del Este	1.05	5.00	-	-
Valle Mí	1.30	-	-	15.00
Encarnación	1.10	5.00	14.00	9.00

Accommodation

Outside the capital Asunción, which has approximately 10 hotels of good standard, accommodation is fairly limited. Package tours to national parks in the Chaco or the waterfalls near Ciudad del Este along the Brazilian border include lodgings, but for individual travellers all accommodation must be booked in writing well in advance; details of current prices are available from the Embassy (see *Contact Addresses* section). All hotels in Asunción are likely to be fully booked throughout the tourist season (July and August). Visitors are advised to consult a reputable travel agent for up-to-date information, or to ascertain the rates with hotels when making reservations. For further information, contact the Secretaria Nacional de Turismo (see *Contact Addresses* section).

Resorts & Excursions

ASUNCIÓN: The capital city is situated on the **Bay of Asunción**, an inlet off the **Paraguay River**. Planned on a colonial Spanish grid system, it has many parks and plazas. On the way to the waterfront the visitor enters the old part of town, an area of architectural diversity. A good view of the city can be had from the **Parque Carlos Antonio Lopez** high above Asunción. The **Botanical Gardens** are situated in a former estate of the Lopez family on the Paraguay River. There is also a golf-course and a small zoo. The Lopez Residence has been converted into a natural history museum and library. Package trips can be booked to see the **Iguazú Falls** and the **Salto Crystal Falls**, and river trips to **Villeta** or up the **Pilcomayo River** to the **Chaco**. **Luque**, near the capital, is the home of the famous Paraguayan harps.

THE CENTRAL CIRCUIT: A popular tourist itinerary is the 'Central Circuit', a route of some 200km (125 miles) that takes in some of the country's most interesting sites clustered around the capital. **San Lorenzo** dates from 1775 and is the site of the university halls of residence and an interesting Gothic-style church. Founded in 1539 by Domingo Martínez, **Ita**'s main speciality is handpainted black clay Gallinita hens. **Yaguarón** is set in an orange-growing district, 48km (29 miles) from the capital, and played a part during the Spanish conquest as a base for the Franciscan missions. Their churches date back to 1775.
Situated in the foothills of the **Cordillera de los Altos**, the historic village of **Paraguarí** has several old buildings in colonial style. The holiday centre of **Chololo**, 87km (54 miles) from the capital, has tourist facilities that include bars, restaurants and bungalows for rent.
Piribebuy was the scene of bloody fighting during the war of the triple alliance. The Encaje-yú spindle lace, the 'sixty-stripe' Paraní poncho and other handmade goods are produced here. It is also famous as a place of worship of the 'Virgin of Miracles'. Situated on **Lake Ypacarai**, 47km (29 miles) from the capital, **San Bernardino** is a holiday resort and, owing to its beaches and lake shores, very popular during the summer months. It also has a camping ground, 'Camping 19'.
ALONG THE PARANÁ: On the border with Argentina and Brazil in the northeast of the Chaco, the spectacular **Iguazú Falls** are a major tourist attraction. **Ciudad del Este**, 326km (204 miles) east of the capital, is the fastest-growing town in the country and has a cosmopolitan atmosphere. Situated close to the border with Brazil, the town is also a good starting point for a visit to the majestic **Monday Falls** and Iguazú Falls, which are a 15 to 30 minute drive from the city. Also nearby is the **Italpú Dam**, the largest hydroelectric complex in the world. Stretching over 180km (112 miles), the water reservoir provides a unique ecosystem for wildlife and birds as well as providing tourists with a number of activities, including fishing, watersports, sailing, camping and walking tours.
Well to the south, **Encarnación** has many colonial buildings and a sleepy waterfront area with gauchos and sandy streets. Nearby is the Roque González de Santa Cruz bridge linking Paraguay with Posadas in Argentina across the river Paraná.
THE CHACO: This vast, scarcely populated area, consisting mainly of empty plains and forests, covers 61 per cent of the country's total surface, but is inhabited by only 3 per cent of Paraguay's population. The drive from Asunción leads through the Low Chaco, a land of palm forests and marshes, and reaches the Middle Chaco with its capital **Filadelfia**. Here Mennonites of German descent have set up farms and other agricultural outlets as well as their own schools and are considered to be the only organised community in the whole of the Chaco region. The Chaco is home to Paraguay's major national parks including the **Defensores del Chaco**, **Tifunque**, **Enciso** and **Cerro Cora**. Wildlife and nature enthusiasts can also visit the area's beautiful biological reserves (in **Itabo**, **Limoy**, **Tati Yupi**) or the protected forests in **Mbaracayu** and **Nacunday**, where over 600 species of birds, 200 species of mammals and numerous kinds of reptiles and amphibians live in a natural habitat. The Chaco is, after the Amazon rain forest, the world's second-largest forest area and is a popular location for pursuers of ecotourism.
JESUIT MISSIONS: In the 16th century, the Company of Jesus started the process of converting the Guaraní people to Christianity. As a result, the native Indians eventually agreed to live in *reducciones*, large villages with a fairly rigid socioeconomic structure based on Jesuit principles and values. Skilled in construction and artistic techniques, the Guaranies left behind a heritage of churches, religious sculptures and paintings scattered throughout Argentina, Bolivia, Brazil and Paraguay. Seven of the largest Jesuit missions remain in Paraguay, and those in **Jesús de Taravangue** and **Trinidad del Paraná** have been declared World Heritage Sites by UNESCO. They can be reached either by plane, car/bus or via light river transport.

Sport & Activities

Ecotourism: There are 11 national parks and protected areas, the largest of which are in the *Chaco* region in the north of the country. Birdlife is particularly abundant, and there is also a wide variety of animals, including the Chacoan peccary, once thought to be extinct. Visitors should take plenty of insect repellent with them when visiting remote areas. A good way to view flora and fauna is from boats which run along some of Paraguay's rivers. Trips can sometimes be arranged on cargo vessels if there are no passenger services. The trip along the fast-flowing River Paraguay from Asunción via Concepción passes through fascinating landscapes, eventually leading as far as the huge marshlands in the north and over the Brazilian border. For more information on Paraguayan national parks, contact the Dirección de Parques Nacionales y Vida Silvestre, Madame Lynch 3500, casi Primer Presidente, Asunción (tel/fax: (21) 615 812; e-mail: biodiversidad@seam.gov.py).
Fishing: The *dorado*, found in the Paraguay, Paraná and Tebicuary rivers, can weigh up to 29kg (65lb). International fishing contests are held near Asunción. There are many other smaller fish that are peculiar to Paraguay such as the *surubí, pati, pacu, manguruyus, armados, moncholos* and *bagres*.
Other: The national sport is **football**. There are **tennis** facilities at hotels and in Asunción. The Asunción Golf Club has an 18-hole **golf** course. **Water-skiing** facilities are available in some places. Some large hotels have **swimming** pools.

Social Profile

FOOD & DRINK: Typical local dishes include *chipas* (maize bread flavoured with egg and cheese), *sopa paraguaya* (soup of mashed corn, cheese, milk and onions), *soo-yosopy* (a soup of cornmeal and ground beef), *albóndiga* (meatball soup) and *boribori* (soup of diced meat, vegetables and small maize dumplings mixed with cheese). *Palmitos* (palm hearts), *surubí* (a fish found in the Paraná) and the local beef are excellent. There is a wide choice of restaurants in Asunción, most with table service. The national drink is *caña*, distilled from sugar cane and honey. Sugar cane juice, known as *mosto*, and the national red wine are worth trying, as is *yerba maté*, a refreshing drink popular with nearly all Paraguayans. There are no strict licensing hours and alcohol is widely available.
NIGHTLIFE: In Asunción there are numerous bars, casinos and discos. The *parrilladas* or open-air restaurants offer by far the best atmosphere, especially in Asunción. There is a casino at the border towns of Ciudad del Este and Encarnación. The most popular traditional music in Paraguay is *polcas* and *guaranías*, which have slow and romantic rhythms and which are used as serenades.
SHOPPING: Special purchases include *ñandutí* lace, made by the women of Itagua, and *aopoí* sports shirts, made in a variety of colours and designs. Other items include leather goods, wood handicrafts, silver *yerba maté* cups and native jewellery. **Shopping hours:** Mon-Fri 0800-1200 and 1500-1900, Sat 0730-1300.
SPECIAL EVENTS: The following is a selection of special events celebrated annually in Paraguay; contact the Embassy or Dirección de Turismo for exact dates (see Contact Addresses section):
Feb *San Blas Fiestas*. **Mar/Apr** *Semana Santa* (Holy Week festival). **May** *Día de la Independencia* (Independence day parades and festivities). **Jun** *Verbena de San Juan* (traditional fiesta, including walking on hot embers). **Jul** *Expo Feria de la Industria*; *Nanduti Festival* (traditional folk festival with arts and crafts), Itaugua. **Aug** *Día de la Virgen de la Asunción* and *Aniversario de la Fundación de Asunción* (religious and cultural celebrations). **Sep** *Festival de la Alfalfa*, Sapucai. **Oct** *Encuentro Internacional de Coros* (choir festival), Encarnación. **Nov** *Festival del Poyvi* (arts, crafts and music fair), Carapeguá. **Dec** *Apertura de Temporada* (opening of the tourism season), San Bernadino.
SOCIAL CONVENTIONS: Shaking hands is the usual form of greeting. Smoking is not allowed in cinemas and theatres. Dress tends to be informal and sportswear is popular. **Photography:** Avoid sensitive subjects such as military installations. **Tipping:** 10 to 15 per cent is normally included in hotel, restaurant and bar bills.

Business Profile

ECONOMY: Paraguay's agriculture plays an important part in its economy, supplying one-quarter of GNP and almost all the country's export earnings. Production of Paraguay's principal cash crops, cotton and soya, expanded rapidly during the late 1980s and continues to grow annually. Other crops such as sugar cane, maize and wheat are also grown on a commercial scale. Paraguay also has large timber reserves which feed the country's rapidly expanding wood-based industries. Wood and soya oil are the main export products. The main manufacturing industries are textiles, chemicals, and the production of metal goods and machinery. Recently completed hydroelectric projects, undertaken jointly with Brazil and including the world's largest hydroelectric dam at Itaipu, have made Paraguay self-sufficient in energy. Although since the early 1990s Paraguay has implemented major economic reforms centred on liberalisation and deregulation of the public sector and large private monopolies, as required by its principal external creditors and donors, the economy has performed poorly in recent years. The main reason is persistently low commodity prices, exacerbated by large-scale corruption and structural weaknesses in the banking sector. External factors, notably the economic crises in Argentina and Brazil, have also played an important role. The economy is still in recession; growth is at around 2 per cent, whilst high unemployment (officially at 18.5 per cent but in reality nearer to 40 per cent) has forced much of the workforce into the unregulated 'black' parts of the economy. In July 2002, the IMF offered a US$200 million support package: the Government was unable or unwilling to meet the loan conditions and relations with the IMF are now effectively frozen. The new Government elected in August 2003 faces an urgent task to stimulate the economy.
Paraguay is a member of the 11-strong Latin American Integration Association (*Asociación Latinoamericana de Integración*, ALADI), which seeks to promote free trade and economic development within Latin America, and under which Paraguay, alongside Bolivia, enjoys special tariff concessions. Paraguay is also a founding member to the Mercosur trade bloc of southern Latin American countries. Brazil is Paraguay's largest trading partner, followed by the USA and Argentina.
BUSINESS: For formal occasions or business affairs, men should wear lightweight suits and ties or a dinner jacket in the evening; women a lightweight two-piece suit or equivalent. Most businesspeople are able to conduct a conversation in English, but a knowledge of Spanish will be useful. Appointments and normal business courtesies apply. The best time to visit is from May to September. **Office hours:** Mon-Fri 0800-1200 and 1430-1900, Sat 0800-1200.
COMMERCIAL INFORMATION: The following organisation can offer advice: Cámara Nacional de Comercio y Servicios de Paraguay, Estrella 540-550, Asunción (tel: (21) 493 321/2; fax: (21) 440 817; e-mail: secretaria@ccparaguay.com.py; website: www.ccparaguay.com.py) *or* PROPARAGUAY (Trade & Investment Promotion Agency), Edificio Ayfra, 12th Floor, Asunción (tel: (21) 493 625; fax: (21) 493 862; e-mail: ppy@proparaguay.gov.py; website: www.proparaguay.gov.py); *or* British Paraguayan Chamber of Commerce, Gral Diaz 521, Edificio Internacional Faro, 2nd Floor, Oficina 2a, Asunción (tel/fax: (21) 498 274).

Climate

Subtropical with rapid changes in temperature throughout the year. Summer (December to March) can be very hot. Winter (June to September) is mild with few cold days. Rainfall is heaviest from December to March.
Required clothing: Lightweight cottons and linens are worn in warmer months, with some warm clothes for spring and autumn. Mediumweights are best for winter. Rainwear is advisable throughout the year.

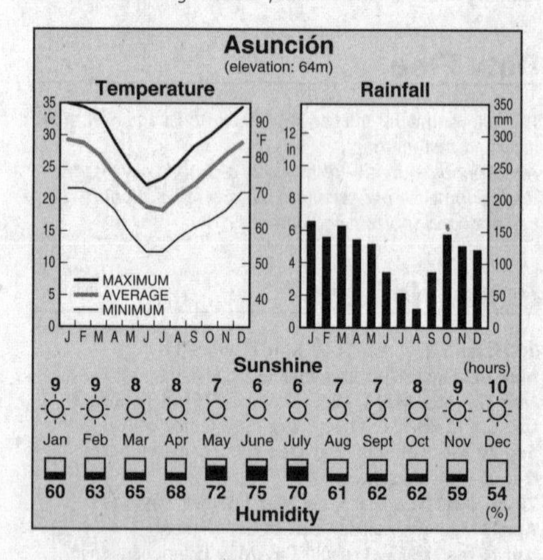

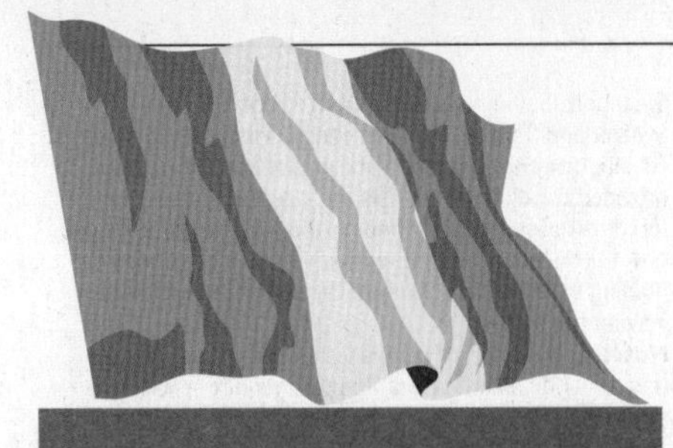

Peru

LATEST TRAVEL ADVICE CONTACTS

British Foreign and Commonwealth Office
Tel: (0870) 606 0290 Website: www.fco.gov.uk

US Department of State
Website: http://travel.state.gov/travel

Canadian Department of Foreign Affairs and Int'l Trade
Tel: (1 800) 267 8376 Website: www.dfait-maeci.gc.ca

Equator
COLOMBIA
ECUADOR
Caquetá
Putumayo
Napo
Tumbes
Talara
Piura
Pongo de Manseriche
Marañón
Iquitos
Amazon
BRAZIL
Juruá
Ucayali
Chiclayo
Cajamarca
Chan Chan
Trujillo
PERU
Pucallpa
△ Huascarán 6768m
Source of the Amazon
PACIFIC OCEAN
Callao
LIMA
Apurímac
Machu Picchu
Puerto Maldonado
Ica
Ayacucho
Cusco
Nasca
Lake Titicaca
Puno
BOLIVIA
Arequipa
Mollendo
Tacna
CHILE
600km
300mls
international airport

Location: Western South America.

Country dialling code: 51.

PromPerú (Commission for the Promotion of Peru)
Calle 1 Oeste 50, Edificio Mincetur, 13th/14th Floor, Urb. Córpac, San Isidro, Lima 27, Peru
Tel: (1) 224 3131. Fax: (1) 224 7134.
E-mail: postmaster@promperu.gob.pe
Website: www.peru.org.pe

Peru's National Chamber of Tourism (CANATUR)
Avenida Pedro Dulanto 103, Barranco, Lima 4, Peru
Tel: (1) 445 2615. Fax: (1) 446 6981.
E-mail: canatur@infonegocio.com.pe
Website: www.go2peru.com

Iperú
Avenida Jorge Basadre 610 San Isidro-Lima
Tel: (1) 421 1627 *or* 574 8000 (24-hour helpline).
Fax: (1) 421 1227.
E-mail: iperulima@promperu.gob.pe
Website: www.peru.org.pe
Provides tourist information and assistance and has 15 offices around Peru in Arequipa, Ayacucho, Chachapoyas, Cuzco, Huaraz, Iquitos, Lima, Puno and Trujillo.

Embassy of the Republic of Peru
52 Sloane Street, London SW1X 9SP, UK
Tel: (020) 7235 1917 *or* 2545.
Fax: (020) 7235 4463.
E-mail: postmaster@peruembassy-uk.com
Website: www.peruembassy-uk.com
Opening hours: Mon-Fri 0930-1700.
Consular section: Tel: (020) 7838 9223. Fax: (020) 7823 2789.
E-mail: consulate@peruembassy-uk.com
Opening hours: Mon-Fri 0930-1300 (general enquiries); 1430-1630 (collection point only).

TIMATIC CODES

Health	AMADEUS: **TI-DFT/LIM/HE** GALILEO/WORLDSPAN: **TI-DFT/LIM/HE** SABRE: **TIDFT/LIM/HE**
Visa	AMADEUS: **TI-DFT/LIM/VI** GALILEO/WORLDSPAN: **TI-DFT/LIM/VI** SABRE: **TIDFT/LIM/VI**

To access TIMATIC country information on Health and Visa regulations through the Computer Reservations System (CRS), type in the appropriate command line listed above.

British Embassy
Torre Parque Mar, Piso 22, Avenida Jose Larco 1301, Miraflores, Lima, Peru
Tel: (1) 617 3000 *or* 50 (consular/visa section).
Fax: (1) 617 3100 *or* 55 (consular/visa section).
E-mail: belima@fco.gov.uk (general section) *or* consvisa.lima@fco.gov.uk (consular section).
Website: www.britemb.org.pe
Honorary Consulates in: Arequipa, Cusco, Iquitos and Trujillo.

Embassy of the Republic of Peru
1700 Massachusetts Avenue, NW, Washington, DC 20036, USA
Tel: (202) 833 9860. Fax: (202) 659 8124.
E-mail: webmaster@embassyofperu.us *or* conpersfco@aol.com
Website: www.peruvianembassy.us

Embassy of the United States of America
Street address: Avenida La Encalada cuadra 17, Surco, Lima 33, Peru
Postal address: PO Box 1995, Lima, Peru
Tel: (1) 434 3000. Fax: (1) 618 2397.
Website: http://usembassy.state.gov/lima

Embassy of the Republic of Peru
130 Albert Street, Suite 1901, Ottawa, Ontario K1P 5G4, Canada
Tel: (613) 238 1777 (embassy) *or* 233 2721 (consulate).
Fax: (613) 232 3062 *or* 233 0835 (cultural office).
E-mail: emperuca@bellnet.ca (embassy) *or* conperottawa@sprint.ca (consular section).
Website: www.embassyofperu.ca
Consulates in: Montréal, Toronto and Vancouver

Canadian Embassy
Street address: Calle Libertad 130, Miraflores, Lima 18, Peru
Postal address: Casilla 18-1126, Correo Miraflores, Lima 18, Peru
Tel: (1) 444 4015. Fax: (1) 444 4347 (trade) *or* 242 4050 (administration).
E-mail: lima@dfait-maeci.gc.ca
Website: www.dfait-maeci.gc.ca/peru

General Information

AREA: 1,285,216 sq km (496,225 sq miles).
POPULATION: 27,148,101 (2003).
POPULATION DENSITY: 21.1 per sq km.

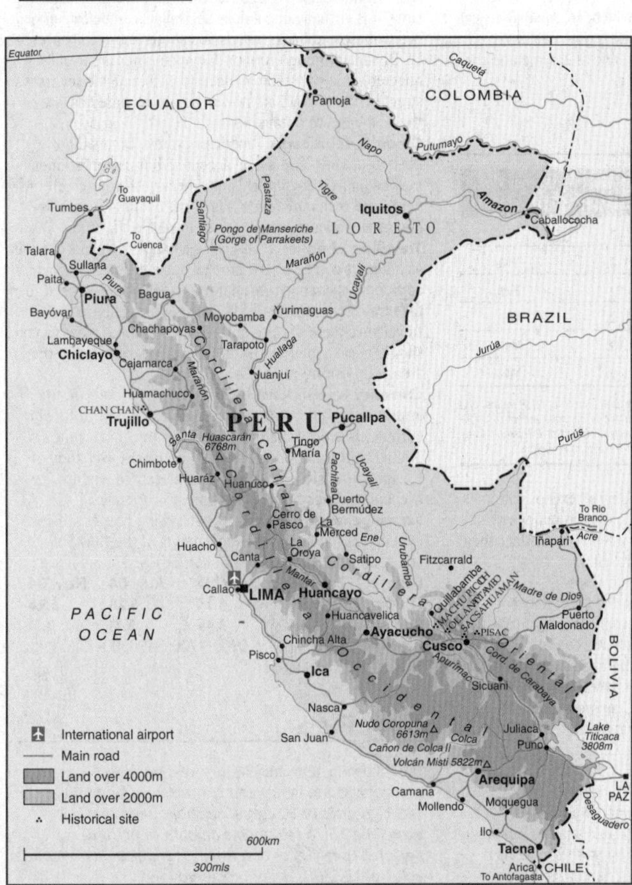

Credit: © PromPeru

CAPITAL: Lima. **Population:** 7,748,528 (2002).
GEOGRAPHY: Peru is a large, mountainous country on the Pacific coast of South America. It has borders with Ecuador and Colombia to the north, Brazil and Bolivia to the east, and Chile to the south. The Pacific Ocean lies to the west. There are three natural zones, running roughly north to south: *Costa* (Coast), *Sierra* (the Highlands) and *Selva* (Amazonian rain forest). The *Costa* region, which contains Lima (the capital), is a narrow coastal plain consisting of large tracts of desert broken by fertile valleys. The cotton, sugar and rice plantations and most of the so-far exploited oil fields lie in this area. The *Sierra* contains the Andes, with peaks over 6000m (20,000ft), most of the country's mineral resources (silver, zinc, lead, copper and gold) and the greater part of its livestock. The *Selva*, an area of fertile, subtropical uplands, lies between the Andes and the border with Brazil. Sections of a proposed international highway are at present being built through it, with some sections already in use. The Amazonian jungle has vast natural resources. The absence of land communications, however, left the area largely uncharted until full-scale oil exploration began in 1973. The population is largely Indian and Mestizo with a noticeable influence from African, Chinese and European (mainly Spanish) settlers.
GOVERNMENT: Republic. Gained independence from Spain in 1824, having declared it in 1821. **Head of State:** President Alejandro Toledo Manrique since 2001.
LANGUAGE: Spanish and Quechua are the official languages. Aymará is spoken in some areas of the region of Puno. Many other dialects exist in the jungle regions. English is spoken in major tourist areas.
RELIGION: 89 per cent Roman Catholic, 7 per cent Evangelical and 4 per cent other denominations.
TIME: GMT - 5.
ELECTRICITY: 220 volts AC, 60Hz. (110 volts AC is available in most 4- and 5-star hotels).
COMMUNICATIONS: Telephone: IDD is available. Country code: 51. Outgoing international code: 00. City code for Amazonas: 41, Arequipa: 54, Ayacucho: 66, Cajamarca: 76, Chiclayo: 74, Cusco: 84, Huaraz: 43, Ica: 56, Iquitos: 65, Lima: 1, Piura: 73, Puerto Maldonado: 82, Puno: 51, Tacna: 52, Tarapoto: 42, Trujillo: 44 and Tumbes: 72. Direct calls are possible from public phones. Telephone cards are available in the main cities. **Mobile telephone:** GSM 1900 network operated by *TIM* (website: www.tim.com.pe). Cellular phones can be rented in Lima and the main cities. **Fax:** *Telefónica del Perú* offers a fax service throughout the country. Small public booths and services are found in commercial areas. The majority of hotels in Lima and the main cities also have facilities. **Internet:** Public Internet booths and Internet cafes are widely available in the main cities. **Telegram:** Facilities are available at Lima and main hotels (for guests), with services run by *Telefónica del Perú*. Their offices are at Pasaje Piura 25, Lima and are open Mon-Sat 0800-2000, Sun 0800-1400. **Post:** Airmail to Western Europe takes up to one week. Postal facilities are limited outside Lima. First-class airmail from Europe or North America addressed to PO boxes in Peru usually takes four days, but may be subject to delay. The main post office (*Correo Central de Lima*) is near the Plaza de Armas. **Press:** Newspapers are in Spanish. Morning dailies include *El Bocón*, *El Comercio*, *Expreso*, *Gestión* and *La República*. The English-language monthly, *Lima Times*, is available in main hotels and bookstores, as are major international newspapers and magazines.
Radio: BBC World Service (website: www.bbc.co.uk/worldservice) and Voice of America (website: www.voa.gov) can be received. From time to time the frequencies change and the most up-to-date can be found online.

Passport/Visa

	Passport Required?	Visa Required?	Return Ticket Required?
Full British	Yes	1	Yes
Australian	Yes	1	Yes
Canadian	Yes	1	Yes
USA	Yes	1	Yes
Other EU	Yes	1	Yes
Japanese	Yes	1	Yes

Note: *Regulations and requirements may be subject to change at short notice, and you are advised to contact the appropriate diplomatic or consular authority before finalising travel arrangements. Details of these may be found at the head of this country's entry. Any numbers in the chart refer to the footnotes below.*

PASSPORTS: Valid passport required by all except nationals of Bolivia, Chile and Ecuador entering certain regions of Peru. Citizens of these countries are advised to contact their nearest Peruvian Consulate before travelling.
VISAS: Required by all except the following:
(a) **1.** nationals of countries shown in the chart above travelling as tourists for stays of up to 90 days with the exception of Malta nationals of which *do* require a visa;
(b) nationals of Andorra, Antigua & Barbuda, Argentina, The Bahamas, Barbados, Belize, Bolivia, Brazil, Brunei, Chile, Colombia, Cook Islands, Costa Rica, Dominica, Dominican Republic, Ecuador, El Salvador, Federated States of Micronesia, Fiji, Grenada, Guatemala, Guyana, Haiti, Honduras, Hong Kong (SAR), Iceland, Indonesia, Israel, Jamaica, Kiribati, Korea (Rep), Liechtenstein, Malaysia, Malta, Marshall Islands, Mexico, Monaco, Nauru, New Zealand, Nicaragua, Niue, Norway, Palau, Panama, Papua New Guinea, Paraguay, The Philippines, St Kitts & Nevis, St Lucia, St Vincent & the Grenadines, Samoa, San Marino, Singapore, Solomon Islands, South Africa, Surinam, Switzerland, Taiwan, Thailand, Tonga, Trinidad & Tobago, Tuvalu, Uruguay, Vanuatu, Vatican City and Venezuela, provided travelling as tourists, for stays of up to 90 days;
(c) transit passengers continuing their journey by the same or first connecting aircraft within 48 hours, provided holding valid onward or return documentation and not leaving the airport.
Note: (a) Nationals of Bangladesh, Cuba, China (PR), Iran, Iraq, Lebanon, Pakistan and Sri Lanka require special authorisation from the Immigration Office in Lima to obtain a visa. This application could take one month (approximately) to be processed. (b) All visitors must hold return tickets or letter of guarantee from travel agency and sufficient funds for their stay.
Types of visa and cost: *Tourist* and *Business*: £19.20. Costs are subject to change according to exchange rates.
Validity: Up to 90 days.
Note: A Business visa is required for all nationals if the purpose of the visit is business. Any business-related unpaid work can be made on a tourist visa. Upon arrival in Peru, the Business visa holder must register at the Dirección General de Contribuciones for taxation purposes. Business visa holders can remain in Peru for 90 days. If wishing to extend the visit, an application must be lodged with the Dirección General de Migraciones.
Application to: Consulate (or Consular section at Embassy); see *Contact Addresses* section for details.
Application requirements: (a) Valid passport. (b) Return or through ticket to show the visitor will be leaving Peru. (c) Two passport-size, colour photos. (d) Fee. (e) Two completed application forms. (f) Proof of economic solvency, such as latest bank statement. (g) For *Business visa*, a company letter specifying the reason for the trip, the length of stay and confirming your employment status. (h) For *Student visa*, a letter from your centre of studies confirming your attendance.
Note: (a) All nationals are advised to check with the Peruvian Consulate prior to departure to obtain current details of any documentation which might be required. Postal visa applications are not accepted unless submitted through a travel agency. (b) Visitors travelling to areas with a tropical climate are advised to have yellow fever, smallpox and malaria vaccinations.
Working days required: At least 24 hours; longer if authorisation from the Immigration Office in Lima is required.

Money

Currency: New Sol (S/.) = 100 céntimos. New Sol notes are in denominations of S/.200, 100, 50, 20 and 10. Coins are in denominations of S/.5, 2 and 1, and 50, 20, 10 and 5 céntimos.
Currency exchange: Only a few bureaux de change in Lima will exchange currencies other than US Dollars. Outside Lima, it is virtually impossible. US Dollars can be exchanged everywhere and banks, hotels and shops also readily accept US Dollars (although torn or damaged notes are usually rejected). It is not recommended to exchange money from street vendors. ATMs are now generally regarded as one of the best ways to obtain money in Peru.
Credit & debit cards: American Express, Diners Club, MasterCard and Visa are all accepted, but usage facilities may be limited outside of Lima. Check with your credit or debit card company for details of merchant acceptability and other services which may be available.
Travellers cheques: Banks will exchange travellers cheques although it can be a slow process outside Lima. To avoid additional exchange rate charges, travellers are advised to take travellers cheques in US Dollars. The ability to use travellers cheques is also quite limited in some areas so you should check whether or not they will be excepted in the area your visiting prior to travel.
Currency restrictions: There are no restrictions on the import and export of local currency. The import of foreign currency is unrestricted. The export of foreign currency is limited to the amount imported. Receipts of exchange of foreign currencies into S/. must be presented when exchanging back from S/. into foreign currency.
Exchange rate indicators: The following figures are included as a guide to the movements of the New Sol against Sterling and the US Dollar:

Date	Feb '04	May '04	Aug '04	Nov '04
£1.00=	6.36	6.24	6.28	6.26
$1.00=	3.49	3.49	3.41	3.31

Banking hours: Mon-Fri 0900-1700, Sat 0900-1300 (may vary during the summer).

Duty Free

The following items may be imported by visitors over 18 years of age into Peru without incurring customs duty:
400 cigarettes or 50 cigars; alcoholic beverages not exceeding 2.5l; a reasonable amount of perfume for personal use; gifts or new articles for personal use up to a value of US$300; 2kg of processed food.

Credit: © PromPeru

Restricted items: If importing sausages, salami, ham or cheese, a sanitary certificate from the manufacturer is required. The export of artistic or cultural articles is prohibited.

Public Holidays

2005: Jan 1 New Year's Day. **Mar 24** Maundy Thursday (half day). **Mar 25** Good Friday. **May 1** Labour Day. **Jun 29** St Peter's and St Paul's Day. **Jul 28-29** Independence Day Celebrations. **Aug 30** St Rosa of Lima Day. **Oct 8** Angamos Battle. **Nov 1** All Saints' Day. **Dec 8** Immaculate Conception. **Dec 24** Christmas Eve (half day). **Dec 25** Christmas Day.
2006: Jan 1 New Year's Day. **Apr 13** Maundy Thursday (half day). **Apr 14** Good Friday. **May 1** Labour Day. **Jun 29** St Peter's and St Paul's Day. **Jul 28-29** Independence Day Celebrations. **Aug 30** St Rosa of Lima Day. **Oct 8** Angamos Battle. **Nov 1** All Saints' Day. **Dec 8** Immaculate Conception. **Dec 24** Christmas Eve (half day). **Dec 25** Christmas Day.

Health

	Special Precautions?	Certificate Required?
Yellow Fever	Yes	1
Cholera	2	No
Typhoid & Polio	3	N/A
Malaria	4	N/A

Note: *Regulations and requirements may be subject to change at short notice, and you are advised to contact your doctor well in advance of your intended date of departure. Any numbers in the chart refer to the footnotes below.*

1: A yellow fever vaccination certificate is required of travellers over six months of age arriving from infected areas. Travellers arriving from non-endemic zones should note that vaccination is strongly recommended for travel to areas within the Amazon Basin, even if an outbreak has not been reported and they would normally not require a vaccination certificate to enter the country.
2: Following WHO guidelines issued in 1973, a cholera vaccination certificate is no longer a condition of entry to Peru. However, autochthonous cases of cholera were reported in 1996. Up-to-date advice should be sought before deciding whether these precautions should include vaccination as medical opinion is divided over its effectiveness; see the Health appendix for more information.
3: Immunisation against typhoid is advised, as the incidence of typhoid is very high.
4: *Falciparum* malaria exists in all areas below 1500m and in the areas of Jaen, Lambayeque, Loreto, Luciano Castillo, Piura, San Martín, Tumbes and Ucayali. All health centres, which are controlled by the Ministry of Health, will provide free information and medication to anyone entering a high risk area.
Food & drink: Drink only bottled water. Pasteurised milk is widely available. Avoid dairy products that are likely to have been made from unboiled milk. Avoid street food vendors and the cheaper restaurants. Only eat well-cooked meat and fish, preferably served hot. Pork, salad and mayonnaise may carry increased risk. Vegetables should be cooked and fruit peeled. Always check the expiry date of processed food.
Other risks: *Hepatitis A* occurs, and *hepatitis B* and *D* are a risk in the Amazon Basin. *Dengue fever* outbreaks are common in the Amazon Basin. The incidence of *typhoid fever* is very high.
Rabies is present. For those at high risk, vaccination before arrival should be considered. If you are bitten, seek medical advice without delay. For more information, consult the *Health* appendix. In the last months of 2004 and first few months of 2005, a number of cases of rabies occurred following bites from vampire bats in the province of Amazonas near the border with Ecuador.
Altitude sickness can be a problem if visiting the highlands. Visitors should take time to acclimatise and avoid doing too much strenuous exercise on the day or arrival.
Insect bites may be a problem in the jungle and the highlands. Insect repellent and long layers for the evening are recommended.
Health care: International travellers are strongly advised to take out full health insurance and should be prepared to pay up front for medical services.

Travel - International

Note: Street crime is a problem, particularly in Lima and Cusco. Street demonstrations, sometimes violent, are a common form of protest in Peru. Visitors should avoid all protests and demonstrations. Domestic terrorism in Peru has largely ended but has not been wholly eradicated. It is advised that visitors to the Huaraz/Huayhuash trekking circuit area contact the tourist police before travel.
AIR: Peru's national airlines are *NuevoContinente (N6)* (website: www.nuevocontinente.com), *Lan Perú (LP)* (website: www.lan.com) and *Taca Perú (TA)* (website: www.taca.com).
Other airlines with regular services to Peru include *Aerolíneas Argentinas, Aeroméxico, AeroPostal, Air Madrid, Alitalia, American Airlines, Avianca, Continental, Copa, Delta Airlines, Iberia, KLM, Lacsa, LAN Chile, Lloyd Aéreo Boliviano, Lufthansa, Servivensa, Transportes Aéreos Militares Ecuatorianos (TAME), United Airlines* and *Varig. Air Canada, Air Plus* and *Cubana* plan to launch services to Peru soon. Many other airlines have representatives in Peru.
Approximate flight times: From Lima to *London* is 15 hours (including stopover in Madrid), to *Los Angeles* is six hours, to *Miami* is five hours and to *New York* is nine hours. Direct flights from Europe take between 12 hours (from Madrid) and 14 hours (from Frankfurt).
International airports: *Lima (LIM)* (Jorge Chávez International; website: www.lap.com.pe) airport is 16km (10 miles) northwest of the city centre (travel time – 25 minutes). Taxis to the city centre are available. Airport facilities include a duty free and handicrafts shop, banks/bureaux de change, left luggage facility, pharmacy, medical centre, Internet cafe, car hire (*Avis, Budget, Hertz, National* and *Thrifty*), coffee shops, bars and restaurants.
Cusco (CUZ), located in the south, receives flights from La Paz (Bolivia).
Vist South America Pass: Vist South America Pass: This must be bought outside South America in country of residence and allows unlimited travel to 36 cities in the following countries: Argentina, Bolivia, Brazil, Colombia, Chile (except Easter Island), Ecuador, Paraguay, Peru, Uruguay and Venezuela. Participating airlines include *Aer Lingus (EI), American Airlines (AA), British Airways (BA), Cathay Pacific (CX), Finnair (AY), IBERIA (IB), LAN-Chile (LA)* and *Qantas (QF)*. A minimum of three flights must be booked, with no maximum; the maximum stay is 60 days, with no minimum, and prices depend on the amount of flight zones covered. Children under 12 years of age are entitled to a 33 per cent discount and infants (under two years old) only pay 10 per cent of the adult fare. For further details, contact one of the participating airlines.
Departure tax: US$28 from Lima's airport. Transit passengers and children under two years of age are exempt. Payment must be paid in cash prior to boarding.
SEA: Some international cruises occasionally call at Callao, the main seaport.
ROAD: The main international highway is the Pan-American Highway running north-south through the coastal desert of Peru from Tumbes to Tacna. Transport from Argentina, Brazil, Chile, Colombia, Ecuador, Paraguay, Uruguay and Venezuela is available through companies like *Bus Tas Choapa Internacional, Empresa Paraguaya de Transporte, Ormeño, El Rápido* and *Rutas de América*. It is also possible to go from La Paz in Bolivia to Puno on Lake Titicaca (south Peru).

Travel - Internal

AIR: *Aerocóndor, Aero Continente, Aviandina, LAN Perú, Star Up, Taca Perú* and *TANS* handle virtually all domestic air traffic linking Lima to Arequipa, Ayacucho, Cajamarca, Chiclayo, Cusco, Iquitos, Juliaca-Puno, Piura, Pucallpa, Puerto Maldonado, Tacna, Tarapoto, Trujillo, Tumbes and other cities. For information on internal flights contact the Peruvian Corporation of Airports (Corpac) (website: www.corpac.gob.pe).
Departure tax: US$5. Children under two years of age are exempt. Payment must be paid in cash prior to boarding.
RIVER: Transportation is available between Pucallpa and Iquitos (approximately five days) and from Iquitos to the border with Brazil and Colombia (two to three days). However, river travel can be long and uncomfortable.
RAIL: A tourist train operates services between Puno and Cusco and from Cusco to Ollantaytambo and Machu Picchu. There is a daytime connection from Puno and Juliaca to Cusco. From Cusco there is a daily train to Machu Picchu, which takes approximately four hours. Always check for revised schedules. For more information, contact Peru Rail in Lima (tel: (01) 444 5020/5; e-mail: reservas@perurail.com; website: www.perurail.com). Fast and comfortable electric *autovagons* operate on some routes. There are no connections between Lima and Cusco.
ROAD: The *Central Highway* connects Lima with La Oroya and Huancayo. From La Oroya there is a road connecting Cerro de Pasco, Huánuco, Tingo María and Pucallpa on the Ucayali River. Landslides are frequent in the rainy season (December to March), making for slow travel. The *Touring y Automóvil Club del Perú* and the *Instituto Geográfico Nacional* sell maps. Travel guides like *Guía Toyota* and *Guía Inca del Perú* include good road maps. Traffic drives on the right. **Bus:** Operated extensively, providing a very cheap means of travel. Greyhound-type buses are operated by *Cruz del Sur, Enlaces, Ittsa, Oltursa, Ormeño, Perú Bus* and many others. Quality of service varies according to prices. **Taxi:** There are taxis at the main hotels and airports. Taxis do not have meters and fares should be agreed before departure (they are relatively inexpensive). There is an extensive and safe taxi service available by telephone in the main cities. **Car hire:** *American, Avis, Budget, Dollar, Mitsui, National, Rentandina* and others have offices in Lima and provide service to all main cities. **Documentation:** Foreign driving permits are valid for 30 days starting the date of arrival. An International Driving Permit is required in case of longer stays. International driving permits in Peru can be obtained through the *Touring y Automóvil Club del Perú*. All foreign vehicles must obtain the appropriate documentation from the National Automobile Association in their own country or on the Peruvian border before entering the country (in this case a 90-day permission will be obtained). You should always carry your driver's licence, a copy of your passport and, if the vehicle is rented, a copy of the rental contract.
URBAN: Public transport in Lima is provided by conventional buses and by minibuses (*combis*). The minimum rate is US$0.30. Wherever possible try to avoid using bus travel late at night.
Travel times: The following chart gives approximate travel times (in hours and minutes) from **Lima** to other major cities/towns in Peru.

	Air	Road
Arequipa	1.25	14.00
Ayacucho	0.35	9.00
Cajamarca	1.00	15.00
Chachapoyas	1.30*	21.00
Chiclayo	1.00	10.00
Cusco	1.00	24.00/26.00
Huancayo	-	6.00
Huánuco	0.50	8.00
Huaraz	0.35*	6.00
Ica	-	4.00
Iquitos	1.30	-
Nazca		6.00
Piura	1.30	16.00
Pucallpa	1.00	20.00
Puerto Maldonado	2.20**	49.00/51.00
Puno (Juliaca)	1.30**	24.00
Tacna	1.30	18.00
Tarapoto	1.00	20.00/24.00
Trujillo	0.45	8.00
Tumbes	1.30	18.00

Note: (a) Approximate travel times are given for travel by bus. (b)* Only charter flights available. (c)** Includes one stopover.

Accommodation

HOTELS: Lima has the largest choice of hotels in Peru. Other cities where 5- and 4-star hotels can be found are Arequipa, Cajamarca, Chiclayo, Cusco, Ica, Iquitos, Puno and Trujillo (the grading does not always match international standards). Throughout Lima and in most major towns, there are many economical *pensiones* (guest houses) to be found. The quality of accommodation in the provinces varies considerably, but hotels are frequently of a good standard. Hotel prices in the provinces are lower than in the capital.
Grading: Hotels are classified by the star system, the highest and most luxurious being 5 stars. The level of comfort, quality of service and general infrastructure are the criteria for inclusion in each grade. Prices vary accordingly. All accommodation prices are subject to 19 per cent tax (IGV). Hotels of the higher categories might also add 1 to 13 per cent service charges. For further information, contact Asociación Peruana de Hoteles, Restaurantes y Afines

(AHORA), Avenida Avenida Benavides 881, Miraflores, Lima 18 (tel: (1) 444 4303). It is advisable to reserve a room during the peak tourist season (June to September).
HOME STAYS: It is possible to arrange a stay in a Peruvian family home. Iperu are able to offer further information (see *Contact Addresses* section).
CAMPING/CARAVANNING: No formal arrangements exist in Peru.
YOUTH HOSTELS: There are 34 youth hostels in the country with dormitory, single or twin rooms. They usually have a bar or cafe and a kitchen. For information contact Asociación Peruana de Albergues Turísticos Juveniles (Peruvian Association of Youth Hostels), Avenida Casimiro Ulloa 328, San Antonio, Miraflores, Lima 18 (tel: (1) 446 5488; fax: (1) 444 8187; e-mail: hostell@terra.com.pe; website: www.limahostell.com.pe).

Resorts & Excursions

Perhaps no other country has more to offer the visitor than Peru; panoramic mountain ranges, vast deserts, beautiful beaches and tropical jungle. All this combined with a rich historical and archaeological past and enduring indigenous cultures. To reflect the importance of tourism to the national economy, PromPerú has set up 15 offices around Peru of *Tourist Information and Assistance* to help visitors solve any problems they may encounter. There is a 24-hour hotline based in Lima (tel: (1) 574 8000). The South American Explorers Club (website: www.saexplorers.org) is another good source of information on the area and has an office in Lima, offering a variety of services to its members such as equipment hire and a safe luggage store. For further information on any of the topics mentioned in this section, please contact the *Tourist Information and Assistance* 24-hour service (tel: (1) 574 8000; e-mail: iperu@promperu.gob.pe).

LIMA

Situated halfway along Peru's desert coastline, Lima is literally stuck between the desert and the deep blue sea. The valley was once dominated by hundreds of pre-Inca temples and palaces. Pizarro chose the palace of local chief Tauri Chusko as the site of the city's inauguration on January 6 1535 and thus began Lima's colonial history, reflected in the opulent mansions with Moorish latticed wooden balconies that grace Lima's plazas. The main square, **Plaza de Armas**, is a UNESCO World Heritage Site, complete with paths, gardens and an elegant bronze fountain. Surrounding the main plaza are the **Cathedral**, **Archbishop's Palace**, the **Town Hall** and the impressive **Palacio de Gobierno** (Government Palace). Located at the northern end of the plaza, the latter is a lavish example of colonial opulence. The sumptuous state rooms are adorned with Carrera marble, cedar and mahogany woodcarvings, French glass and Czech crystal. Highlights are the Grand Salon, modelled on the Versaille Palace's Hall of Mirrors, the dining room adorned with friezes depicting Inca history and the private theatre. Free guided tours operate daily from the visitor's entrance in **Jirón de la Unión**. Outside, visitors can admire the elaborate military uniforms in the Changing of the Guard. The **Baroque Cathedral** has been reconstructed after several earthquakes and its present building is dated around 1758. Visitors should not miss its **Museum of Religious Art and Treasures**, plus the collection of bones believed to be those of Pizarro himself.
One of the few buildings to withstand the 1746 earthquake is the **Church of San Francisco**. Recently renovated with the help of UNESCO, this exquisite church has several highlights, including the extraordinary early 17th-century domed cedarwood roof above the broad staircase leading to the cloisters. The library, in its thin, rectangular two-storey salon with twin delicate wooden spiral staircases, houses a collection of some 20,000 volumes, plus masterpieces by Jordeans, Rubens and Van Dyck. Underneath the church are the catacombs, complete with ghoulish circular displays of the skulls and bones of some 70,000 souls.
The downtown area of Lima also houses historic colonial mansions, some of which still have connections with the original Spanish families who constructed them. Now occupied by the Foreign Ministry, the **Palacio Torre Tagle** (1735) with its Moorish-influenced balconies has particularly interesting *azulejos* (tiles), thought to be the first examples of an artistic fusion between both Native American and European styles. Close by is the striking salmon pink and white stuccoed **Post Office** built in the 1920s. With wrought iron gates and an arcade roof, the **Correo** also houses a **stamp museum** where enthusiasts can buy, trade and sell Peruvian stamps.
Peru's rich cultural heritage is reflected by the variety of museums in the capital. Unmissable for history buffs are the **Museo de Oro del Peru** (Gold Museum), the **Museo de Cultura Peruana** (Museum of Peruvian Culture) and the **Museo de la Inquisición y del Congreso** (Museum of the Inquisition) with its sinister dungeons. Art-lovers should see Goya's etchings at the **Museo Taurino** and the collection of masters at the **National Art Museum**.
On August 30 visitors can marvel at the religious processions held to honour the city's patron saint, Santa Rosa de Lima. Later, on October 18, a purple haze descends upon the city as the faithful don purple robes to march in processions, praising El Señor de los Milagros. Cultural attractions aside, areas such as **Barranco**, **Miraflores** and **San Isidro** have much to offer the visitor in the way of shopping, restaurants and nightlife. Malls and department stores are expanding within the city, and the downtown area, particularly the streets around the **Plaza de Armas**, were remodelled a few years ago. Visitors should not miss the colourful daily market in Lima's Chinatown district. A good place to get a close look at some of Peru's diverse wildlife (such as jaguars and condors) is the **Zoo**, **Parque Zoologico Huachipa** and **Parque de las Leyendas**, landscaped to reflect Peru's three main geographical zones: *costa* (coast); *sierra* (mountains); and *selva* (rainforest).

COSTA

NORTH OF LIMA: Piura and **Tumbes** are the most northerly Peruvian coastal regions and are Peru's most important beach, surfing, sporting and deep-sea fishing centres. There are small resort-type hotels and small fishing villages and beaches.
CHICLAYO: Chiclayo is a northern city with a hot and sunny climate, distinctive cuisine and musical tradition as well as an unparalleled archaeological heritage. Unfortunately, the 26 pyramid complex of **Tucume** (35km/22 miles north of Chiclayo) and **Huaca Rajada** (or the 'Tomb of the Lord of Sipan'), considered to rank among the finest examples of pre-Columbian art, are not yet well restored, thus visitors should hire a local guide. Many of the fascinating ceramics, metal objects and textiles from the region are on view at the **Bruning Museum** in the town of **Lambayeque**, located 11km (6.8 miles) north of Chiclayo. There is a new museum called **Royal Tombs of Sipan**, a modern three-floor pyramid inspired by the Mochica sanctuaries.
TRUJILLO: Known as 'the City of the Eternal Spring', Trujillo's brightly coloured colonial mansions – such as the **Casa Bracamonte** or **Casa del Almirante del Risco** – are well worth visiting. The area's archaeological treasures include **Chan Chan**, the largest pre-Inca mud city (20 sq km/7.7 sq miles) declared a World Heritage Site by UNESCO in 1986 and the *huacas* (religious centres) of the Sun and the Moon (the latter has painted mud walls depicting one of the main deities of the Moche culture). The beautifully restored **Huaca Arco Iris**, located close to the city limits is covered with pre-Inca hieroglyphics. Visitors may be interested in the impressive **Palacio Iturregui** and the **Church of El Carmen** with its **Pinacoteca** (Art Museum). Unmissable is **Casinelli's Musuem** with an impressive collection of pre-Inca pottery and artefacts, collected from local *huaqueros* (native priests). Trujillo's excellent seafood restaurants, coffee shops and bars make this city one of the best places to dine in Peru.
SOUTH OF LIMA: Situated 250km (156 miles) south of Lima via the Pan-American highway, the **Paracas National Reserve** is home to a large concentration of sea fauna and marine birds.
ICA: A pleasant colonial town, famous for its wineries and Pisco distilleries (open to the public all year), Ica is a good point of call on a trip to the **Nazca Lines**. The town's interesting **Museo Regional Adolfo Bermúdez Jenkins** has a striking collection of Paracas, Nazca and Inca artefacts, including a macabre installation of mummies showing the Pre-Inca method of beautifying skulls.
The **Nazca Lines** – located 420km (265 miles) south of Lima – are a set of large geoglyphs thought to be made by three different cultures between 200 BC and AD 600. These spectacular drawings of animals (birds, felines and reptiles), geometric shapes and lines can be seen from an observation tower but are best viewed from the air. Flights are around US$55 and can be booked from Lima or in the town of Nasca. It was declared a World Heritage Site by UNESCO in 1994.

SIERRA

CAJAMARCA: Located in the northern highlands, Cajamarca was the site of the execution of Inca emperor Atahualpa by the Spanish Conquistadors. Visitors can see **Atahualpa's Ransom Room**, allegedly filled with gold to try to buy his release from his Spanish captors. Declared a Historical and Cultural Heritage of the Americas by the Organisation of American States (OAS) in 1986, Cajamarca contains many well-preserved examples of 17th- and 18th-century colonial Spanish buildings and churches and visitors should not miss the **Belén complex** that includes the **Anthropology Museum**. As a highland commercial hub, Cajamarca's central market is a bustling mix of many different native products and people. Cajamarca is also famous for its Carnival celebrations (held four days after Ash Wednesday), undoubtedly the biggest Carnival celebrations in Peru.
HUARAZ: Nicknamed the 'Peruvian Switzerland' for its glacial lakes and snow-capped peaks, Huaraz is the departure point for treks and expeditions to the **Callejón de Huaylas**. Huaraz hosts the annual **Semana del Andinismo**, including international ski events on the **Pastoruri Glacier**. The **Huascarán National Park**, declared a World Heritage Site by UNESCO in 1985, protects the area's biggest indigenous plants, the **Puya Raymondi** (giant bromeliads that grow up to 15m high and live for over 40 years) and is the home of the native *viscacha*, puma, *vicuña* and the rare spectacled bear. The nearby **Chancos thermal baths**, known traditionally as the 'Fountain of Youth', are located 28km north of Huaraz. There are also many archaeological sites nearby, especially remarkable is the pre-Inca stone complex of **Chavín de Huántar**, situated 110km (69 miles) from Huaraz, dating from approximately 1200 BC. It was declared a World Heritage Site by UNESCO in 1985.

Credit: © PromPeru

AYACUCHO: From some city views Ayacucho appears to have more churches than houses and therefore it comes as no surprise that the *Semana Santa* (Holy Week) celebrations are the most important event on the calendar for locals. Semana Santa sees a massive influx of visitors and therefore it is a good idea to pre-book accommodation. Ayacucho is famous as a source of exquisite handicrafts, including pottery, leatherwork, textiles and jewellery.
CUSCO: The capital of the Inca Empire (founded AD 1100), Cusco today is a fascinating mix of Inca and colonial Spanish architecture and was declared a World Heritage Site by UNESCO in 1983. Almost every central street has remains of Inca walls, arches and doorways that serve as the foundation for the colonial and modern buildings. More archaeological sites are abundant in the nearby area and towns. Narrow alleys of whitewashed houses with sky-blue and bottle-green shutters open out onto elegant squares with stone-hewn fountains and elegant restaurants and *posadas* (inns). Colourful murals depicting historical scenes can be seen on countless walls and indigenous women with braids and embroidered shawls set up makeshift stalls selling woven blankets and handmade crafts and jewellery. Shops around the main square are open all week from dawn to midnight, but close for about two hours during lunch. There is a wide array of hotels, hostels, pensions and family houses, as well as restaurants and other services related to tourism. Cusco also has a good choice of nightlife.
The **Church of Santo Domingo** was built on the foundations of the Inca Temple of the Sun, **Qoricancha**, (Quechua for golden courtyard: its walls were covered in solid gold sheets, much to the delight of the gold-hungry Spanish invaders). Heavy doors leading into the cloisters are now adorned with Moorish star- and diamond-shape patterns. The cloisters are lined with oil paintings in heavy gilt frames that depict scenes from the life of St Dominic. Remains of the original Inca temple walls are found inside the main courtyard. The Incas built these walls tapering upwards so that they would withstand earthquake tremors. Huge blocks of green and grey diorite stone were placed together in a perfect fit without mortar, perfectly demonstrating the sophisticated Inca engineering and architectural skills. A further example of Inca skill with polygonal masonry is seen in the **Stone of Twelve Angles**. The elegant **Plaza de Armas**, or main square, is lined with arcades and houses with ornately carved wooden balconies and terracotta tiled roofs. Dominating the square is the **Cathedral**, which is flanked on the left by the **Church of Jesús María**. Its altar is elaborately carved from cedarwood that is covered in gold and silver plate (*plateresco*) and mirrors. In the cathedral there are several notable features, from the 400kg (882lb) main altar fashioned from silver mined in Potosí, Bolivia, to the 1958 silver-plated truck, that carries some 14 statues in the annual Corpus Christi procession. The early 17th-century cedarwood choir stalls bear testimony to the skill of the principal carver, Tomas Tuero Tupac, and are some of the finest in Peru. Marcos Zapata's painting, *La Ultima Cena* (The Last Supper) has the apostles with ghostly white pallor, while Judas is given the darker skin colouring of an Indian and, stretched out in the centre of the table, is a local Inca delicacy – *cuy*, or roast guinea pig. To the right of the cathedral is the **Church of El Triunfo**. Inside, a painting commissioned by Alonso Cortés de Monroy depicts the great earthquake of 1650 with the inhabitants praying to *El Señor de los Temblores* (Lord of the Earthquakes). Underneath the chapel are

Credit: © PromPeru

commemorative plaques to Garcilaso Inca de la Vega, Inca chronicler, whose remains were returned from Spain to Cusco several years ago. Other sites of interest include the **Museo de Arte Religioso**, **Museo Palacio Municipal**, **Museo de Historia Nacional**. Visitors should purchase a Cusco Visitors Card available from the Tourist Information Office on the main square, that allows the bearer entrance to all of the Inca sites surrounding Cusco, including the town's museums.

SACSAYHUAMÁN: Outside Cusco are four nearby Inca ruins, of which Sacsayhuamán is the most impressive (the others are **Puca Pucara**, **Qenko** and **Tambo Machay**). This magnificent ceremonial centre, with its three vast ramparts that run parallel for more than 350m (1148ft), was the site of the famous battle between Manco Inca and Juan Pizarro, Francisco's younger brother, in 1536. The boulders used to construct the walls are immense, weighing up to 360 tons and measuring up to 10m (33ft) in height and 4m (13ft) in depth. On June 24 each year, thousands of locals arrive to celebrate the Inti Raymi festival with a colourful pageant held at Sacsayhuaman. Visitors can explore the sites on horseback; it is easy to hire horses and a guide at the park's entrance.

URUBAMBA: The Urubamba was once the **Sacred Valley of the Incas**. Key sites to visit include the Inca ruins and popular Sunday market at **Pisac**, as well as the extensive complex of ruins at **Ollantaytambo**. Urubamba, the main town in the valley, is a base from which to explore the surrounding region. Worth a detour is the pottery belonging to Pablo Seminario, whose distinctive work shows pre-conquest influences.

SALINERAS DE MARAS: About 10km (6 miles) from here are the salt pans of Maras. These pre-Inca salt pools were constructed during the Chanapata culture between AD 200-300 and AD 900, from a natural salt spring. Terraces were carved from the hillside and through a system of natural irrigation and gravity (still in perfect use today) the water courses along channels to form pools of water, which evaporate in the sun to leave salt deposits. There are over 3000 pools still in use, co-owned by 400 indigenous families. All the salt is scraped by hand from the sides of the pools into sacks and then pulled up the hillside by mules, consensus dictates on which days the water will be diverted along channels to collect in a certain group of pools.

MACHU PICCHU: For most visitors, the Inca city of Machu Picchu is the highlight of their visit. Revealed to the Western world by the American Hiram Bingham on July 24 1911, and declared a World Heritage Site by UNESCO in 1983, it is probably the most important archaeological site in South America and requires at least one day to explore fully. Buried beneath jungle vegetation for centuries, excavations revealed a myriad of staircases, terraces, temples, palaces, towers and fountains. Highlights of the site include the **ceremonial baths**, the **Temple of the Sun**, **Temple of the Three Windows** and the **Intihuatana**, or carved rock pillar used by Inca astronomers to predict the solstices. A 30-minute walk south from the main complex takes the visitor to the **Inca Bridge**, carved into the vertiginous cliff face. Climb the peak of **Huayna Picchu** that towers over the city and from the summit, it is a breathtaking experience to watch the mist roll back to reveal the architectural marvels of the Inca citadel. Visitors should invest in a guide as there is little information for tourists and there is much that is known about the lost city of the Inca. Those interested in trekking the Inca Trail through the Urubamba Valley should organise their treks at home, due to the environmental damage done by unscrupulous local tour operators to the trail. In an effort to minimise the damage caused by visitors, there are currently restrictions on some sections of the Inca Trail.

PUNO: Puno (3827m/12,464ft above sea level) is the centre of Peruvian folklore and hosts some of the best festivals in Peru: *Virgen de la Candelaria* (Feb 2) and *Puno Day* (Nov 5), to name but two. Spaniards were lured to the region by the vast mineral wealth and the area is dotted with both colonial churches and pre-Columbian ruins, such as the **Chullpas de Sillustani**, a complex of tombs in the form of towers built on the banks of Lake Titicaca by the Tiahuanaco people. **Lake Titicaca**, the highest navigable lake in the world, is the home of the *Uros* people who have for centuries built their homes and boats out on the lake using Totora reeds. Extending over a total surface area of 8379 sq km (3235 sq miles), Lake Titicaca is 180km (112 miles) long and 69km (43 miles) across, at its widest point. Around the lake can be found pre-AD 1000 remains from the Pucara and Tiahuanaco cultures. An unforgettable site is the **Yavari Project**, the oldest steamship on Lake Titicaca. The lake forms a natural border between Peru and Bolivia and in this part of Peru the native people are predominantly Aymara and not Quechua speakers.

AREQUIPA: The second-largest city in Peru, Arequipa is also known as the 'white city', since the most important colonial buildings were built of white volcanic rock (ashlar) from a nearby quarry. In 2000, the city was declared a World Heritage Site by UNESCO. Both Spanish colonial and Andalusian influences are visible everywhere. Especially remarkable is the **Santa Catalina Convent** – a beautiful 'city within a city'. Other highlights include the **Casa del Moral** (House of the Mulberry Tree), with its elegant wrought-iron windows and sculptured portico and the **Casa de la Moneda** (the former mint). Arequipa is a great place for hiking and mountaineering expeditions with daily excursions to the **Cotahuasi** and **Colca Canyons**, one of the deepest in the world. **El Misti** is a relatively easy climb and river rafting is becoming popular in the area.

SELVA

IQUITOS: Iquitos is Peru's largest jungle city. Once a booming rubber town in the late 19th century, tourism and oil are now Iquitos' main industries. It is a major base for excursions to the **Amazon basin** and has numerous hotels of varying standards, as well as nearby jungle lodges and camps. The river provides excellent opportunities for travelling down the **Amazon** to Brazil or crossing the river to and from Colombia.

MANU NATIONAL PARK: Located in the rainforests of the Cusco and Madre de Dios regions, Manu National Park is Peru's greatest natural treasure in biodiversity. Extending to some 20,000 sq km (7722 sq miles) of tropical rainforest, the area was first earmarked for protection in 1973, declared a UNESCO Biosphere Reserve in 1977 and a World Natural Heritage Site in 1987. The park is inhabited by indigenous people, including the **Arahuaca**, **Matiguenka**, **Piro**, **Yine** and **Yora** tribes and is divided into three distinct areas. The first section, **Parque Nacional Manu**, can only be entered by scientists and researchers on special permits, while the **Zona Reservada** is accessible to group tours operated by a licensed company, and the **Zona Cultural** consists of a few villages that are outside restricted areas. Tourist infrastructure in the Zona Reservada is rustic and made from sustainable materials such as local timber and woven palm fronds for roofing material. Few of the lodges have hot water or electricity and, as such, are packaged as eco-friendly and follow strict environmental practices. Scientists believe that the park is home to more than 2000 species of plants, 1200 species of butterflies, around 800 types of birds and 200 different mammals. The dense carpet of tropical rainforest is irrigated and dissected by several great rivers, including the **Madre de Dios**, **Manu Panagua** and **Ucayali**. Over time, swamps and cochas (oxbow lakes) have formed, sustaining unique types of flora and fauna. In the Manu region, a whole host of birds can be seen, including the Amazon kingfisher, harpy eagle, hoatzin, orinoco goose and tiger herons. It is possible to spot various primate groups in the dense tree cover, such as the emperor tamarin, spider and howler monkeys, but less common are the lowland tapir, sloth, jaguar or capybaras. For this reason, a stay of seven to eight days is recommended in order to observe a representative sample of the flora and fauna, birds and animals available.

BLANQUILLO ECOLOGICAL RESERVE: Outside the Reserve Zone is the Blanquillo Ecological Reserve, a private reserve that extends to almost 14,000 hectares (34,595 acres). The **Tambo Blanquillo Lodge** owns a floating catamaran hide, which is ideally situated to view the spectacular early morning sight of hundreds of brightly coloured macaws and parrots descending to feed off the 6m- (20ft-) high clay lick, or cliff known as a *collpa*. A 10-minute motorised canoe ride from the lodge connects with a trail that leads to the **Cocha Camunga**, home to a family of giant river otters. Even more opportunities to see wildlife can be enjoyed from a magnificent 40m- (130ft-) high viewing platform, carefully constructed in the boughs of a magnificent Kapok tree.

TAMBOPATA-CANDAMO RESERVED ZONE: The Tambopata-Candamo Reserved Zone is 45km (28 miles) from **Puerto Maldonado** by river. Specialists say that it contains the largest and richest bio-diversity of the world. The flora and fauna within includes more than 2000 flower varieties, 1000 birds and 900 butterflies and dragonflies.

Sport & Activities

Mountain trekking: Practically all of the highlands and some parts of the jungle include trekking circuits, although only a few are being used commercially. Hikes are possible all year round, but the easiest period is the dry season (June to September). Hiking equipment can be bought or hired in Cusco and Huaraz which are the starting points to the most important treks in Peru, listed below.

Inca Trail to Machu Picchu: Probably the most famous trekking route in South America, the trail offers views of snow-capped mountains, high cloud forests and the opportunity to walk past 12 magnificent ancient Inca ceremonial centres, such as those at *Phuyupatamarca* and *Wiñay Wayna*. Completion of the 48km (30 mile) trek takes three to five days, and must be undertaken in a group with an official local leader. The trail fee is approximately US$50 per person, which includes a one-day entrance ticket to Machu Picchu. Due to the popularity of the trail and current restrictions in place to protect it, it is advisable to book your hike at least 30 days in advance, wherever possible.

Cordillera Blanca: The highest tropical mountain range is a 180km- (112.5 mile-) long paradise of snow-capped mountains, glaciers, emerald-green lakes and archaeological sites. It also contains a wide variety of flora and fauna. Practically the entire range is a protected area within the Huascarán National Park. Routes vary from two to 12 days.

Olleros-Chavín Llama Trek: This is a four-day trek between the attractive town of Olleros and the spectacular archaeological site of *Chavín de Huántar*. Llama 2000, as it is known, is an initiative launched by a group of campesino farmers to promote ecotourism while protecting their traditional way of life.

Other trekking areas: These include the *Cordillera Huayhuash* (Huaraz), *Colca Valley* (164km/102 miles north of Arequipa), where major attractions include snow-capped volcanoes; *Mount Ausangate* (south of Cusco), a physically demanding eight- to 12-day walk, which requires climbing through high mountain passes and being exposed to changing weather conditions.

Mountaineering: The Cordillera Blanca (23 summits above 6000m/19,686ft above sea level) and Huayhuash (six summits above 6000m/19,686ft above sea level) are the best-known ranges for mountaineering activities – a unique concentration of mountains and relatively few mountain climbers. There is mild weather almost all year long and relatively easy access to sites that are nevertheless cut off from hectic city life.

Surfing: This is a particular favourite as the beaches of Lima (constant waves from April to September) and the north (heavy seas between October and March) rank alongside the best in Hawaii or California. Top spots include Cabo Blanco, Chicama (or Malabrigo) or Pico Alto.

Fishing: The most renowned spot for **sea fishing** is Punta Sal in Tumbes (North coast). Tuna fish, drums, flounder, pacific croaker, grunts, groupers and large black marlins can be found on the coast of Peru. **Lake** and **river fishing** is good in both the highlands and the jungle.

Whitewater rafting: Rafting in Peru combines amazing landscapes with some tough rapids. Some rivers can be run in one-day trips (mostly on the coast and the highlands), and expeditions lasting from 3 to 12 days can be arranged to run others (mostly in the highlands and the jungle). The Colca River is rated as Peru's premier rafting river.

Mountain biking: Any part of the country, except the coastal desert and the jungle plains, is suitable for mountain biking. Some of the best circuits include those in

the Pachacámac Valley and the Paracas Reserve.
Other: The main sports and activities practised in Peru are **paragliding**, **hang-gliding**, **rock climbing**, **windsurfing**, **horse-riding**, **marathon running** (annual competitions at challenging heights), **snowboarding**, **hot-air ballooning**, **underwater fishing** and **scuba-diving**. **Tennis** facilities are available in Lima. **Golf** facilities are usually available to members only.

Social Profile

FOOD & DRINK: The hot and spicy nature of Peruvian food, created by *ají* and *ajo* (hot pepper and garlic), has become celebrated at home and abroad. Peruvians enjoy a wide variety of vegetables; there are over 2000 kinds of indigenous and cultivated potatoes alone. Tropical fruits are abundant, as are avocados. *Ceviche* is a local speciality (uncooked fish marinated in lemon or lime juice and hot chili pepper, served with fried corn, sweet potatoes, onions and flavoured with coriander). *Escabeche* is a cooked fish appetiser eaten cold, served with peppers and onions. *Corvina* is sea bass, which can be prepared in a variety of ways, and is always an excellent choice. Typical dishes made with scallops (*conchitas*), mussels (*choros*), octopus (*pulpo*) and shrimps (*camarones*) are plentiful and delicious. *Chupe de camarones* is a chowder-type soup made with shrimps, milk, eggs, potatoes and peppers. Other staple dishes include *papa a la huancaina* (yellow potato with cheese and chili sauce), *arroz con choclo* (rice with corn), *cau cau* (tripe cooked with potato, peppers and parsley), *causa rellena* (potato cakes with chicken in the centre, but also cooked with avocado or crabmeat) and *tamales* (boiled corn dumplings filled with meat and wrapped in a banana leaf). Specialities include *sopa criolla* (spicy soup with beef and noodles), *ají de gallina* (shredded chicken in a piquant cream sauce), *anticuchos* (strips of beef or fish marinated in vinegar and spices, then barbecued on skewers) and *lomo saltado* (pieces of beef sautéed with onions and peppers, served with fried potatoes and rice). Rice and potatoes accompany virtually every dish. Traditional desserts are *arroz con leche* (rice pudding), *alfajores* (wafer-thin spirals of shortbread dusted with icing sugar) and served with *manjar blanco* (a caramel sauce), *picarones* (doughnuts served with syrup) and *mazamorra morada* (purple maize and sweet potato starch jelly cooked with lemons, dried fruits, cinnamon and cloves). Table service is the norm in hotels and restaurants and many of them also offer buffet-type lunches.
The most famous drink is *pisco sour*, made from a potent grape brandy. Other pisco-based drinks are *algarrobina* (pisco and carob syrup), *chilcano* (pisco and ginger ale) and *capitán* (pisco and vermouth). *Chicha de jora* (fermented red or yellow corn juice) and *chicha morada* (non-alcoholic purple corn juice) are popular drinks dating from Inca times. Peruvian beers and national wines are good.
NIGHTLIFE: There are many good bars, pubs, discos and casinos in the major towns and tourist resorts. *Peñas* always serve snacks and some serve full meals. Here one can enjoy *criolla* or folk music, especially at weekends. Nightlife in Lima and Cusco has a wide array of choices. Most discos, *peñas*, pubs and karaokes are open until 0300 or 0400 in the morning.
SHOPPING: There are many attractive Peruvian handicrafts such as *alpaca* wool sweaters, *alpaca* and *llama* rugs, Indian masks, weaving, jewellery and much more. Galleries and handicraft shops abound in the Miraflores, Pueblo Libre and downtown districts of Lima. Handicrafts markets are located in Miraflores (Petit Thouars Ave, blocks 52 to 53) and Pueblo Libre (La Marina Ave, blocks 8 to 10). Bargaining is an expected practice with beach vendors and at markets and known as '*regateo*'.
Shopping hours: Mon-Sat 1000-1300 and 1600-2000 (although many shops are open Mon-Sun 0900-2000).
SPECIAL EVENTS: The following is a selection of special events occurring in Peru in 2005; check with the Embassy or Iperú for further details (see *Contact Addresses* section):
Jan *Marinera Dance Festival*, La Libertad. **Feb** *Carnival*, celebrated nationwide, but particularly in Ayacucho, Cajamarca, Iquitos and Puno; *Huanchaco Beach Olympics*. **Feb 1-12** *La Virgen de la Candelaria*, Puno. **Mar** *La Vendimia* (wine festival), Ica; *Holy Week*, celebrated nationwide, but particularly in Ayacucho and Tarma. **Mar-Apr** *Lord of the Earthquakes*, Cusco; *Peruvian Paso Horse Contest*, Pachacámac. **May** *Qoyllur Rit'i - Pilgrimage for the Snow Star* (largest indigenous pilgrimage in the Americas at Quispicanchis), near Cuzco. **Jun** *Corpus Christi Festivities*, Cusco; *Inti Raymi* (Festival of the Sun), Cusco; *San Juan Festival*, Iquitos. **Jul** *Festival of the Virgin of El Carmen*, Paucartambo. **Jul 28** *Independence Day*, celebrated nationwide but with the largest festivals in Lima. **Aug** *Santa Rosa de Lima Day* (Patron Saint of the Americas and The Philippines). **Sep** *International Spring Festival*, Trujillo (parades, handicraft and art exhibits, folk music and gastronomy contests). **Oct** *Procession of the Lord of the Miracles*, Lima. **Nov** *Bullfighting Festival*, Lima. **Nov 1** *All Saints' Day*. **Nov 5** *Puno Day*. **Dec 24** *Santuranticuy Fair* (fair selling images of saints and other crafts), Cusco.

Credit: © PromPeru

SOCIAL CONVENTIONS: Shaking hands is the customary form of greeting. Visitors should follow normal social courtesies and the atmosphere is generally informal. A small gift from a company or home country is sufficient. Dress is usually informal, although for some business meetings and social occasions men wear a jacket and tie. Life is conducted at a leisurely pace. **Tipping:** Service charges of 10 per cent are added to all bills. Additional tips of 5 per cent are expected. Taxi drivers do not generally expect tips.

Business Profile

ECONOMY: The Peruvian economy is divided into two distinct parts: a relatively modern industrial and service economy concentrated on the coastal plain, and a subsistence agricultural economy in the interior. Inevitably, one consequence has been huge migration from the interior to the coastal cities. About one-third of the workforce is engaged in agriculture, producing rice, maize and potatoes for domestic consumption and coffee as the principal cash crop. There is also a substantial illicit economy based on the production of coca (which has grown recently due to the collapse of world coffee prices). Fisheries are also important, and provide substantial export income. Much of the foreign investment of the early 1990s was directed towards Peru's major industry, mining, which accounts for about half of export earnings. Peru is a major producer of copper; in addition, there are sizeable deposits of lead, zinc, silver, gold, and some oil reserves. Manufacturing is concentrated in processed foods, chemicals, metal products, machinery and textiles. In the service sector, tourism has grown considerably during the last two decades, and now brings in almost US$1 billion annually.
During the early- to mid-1990s, Peru implemented important market-oriented reforms, including a drastic overhaul of the fiscal and monetary systems, privatisation of key industries (mining, telecommunications and energy), trade deregulation and measures to attract investment from abroad. The strategy was reasonably successful, boosting exports and government tax revenues while attracting foreign capital. The defeat of the Sendero Luminoso insurgency also served to boost investor confidence. Throughout most of the decade, Peru was among the most dynamic economies in Latin America, with an average annual GDP growth of around 5 per cent. The economy stalled in 1997 – affected by the Asian and Brazilian financial crises, the effects of *El Niño* (especially upon agriculture) and internal politics – but has since recovered. The official unemployment rate is 9.7 per cent, but it is estimated that up to 40 per cent of the workforce are underemployed. During 2004, annual growth was 4 per cent. The inflation rate is 2.3 per cent.
Peru is a member of the Andean Treaty and the Latin American Integration Association, ALADI, which promotes trade and economic development in Latin America. The USA is substantially Peru's largest trading partner; others are China (PR), Chile, Spain and Colombia.
BUSINESS: Although the majority speak Spanish, many businesspeople speak some English. **Office hours:** Mon-Fri 0900-1700.
COMMERCIAL INFORMATION: The following organisation can offer advice: Cámara de Comercio de Lima, Avenida Gregorio Escobedo 396, Jesus Maria, Lima 11 (tel: (1) 463 3434 *or* 8080; fax: (1) 463 2837; e-mail: perured@camaralima.org.pe; website: www.camaralima.org.pe).
CONFERENCES/CONVENTIONS: For further information, contact PromPeru (see *Contact Addresses* section for details).

Climate

Varies according to area. On the coast, winter lasts from June to September. During this period, the mountainous areas are often sunny during the day but cold at night. Heavy rains in the mountains and jungle last from December to April. It never rains in Lima nor most of the coast, except for Tumbes and Piura, which have tropical climates.
Required clothing: Lightweights during summer with warmer clothes worn in upland areas. Mediumweights are advised during cooler months.

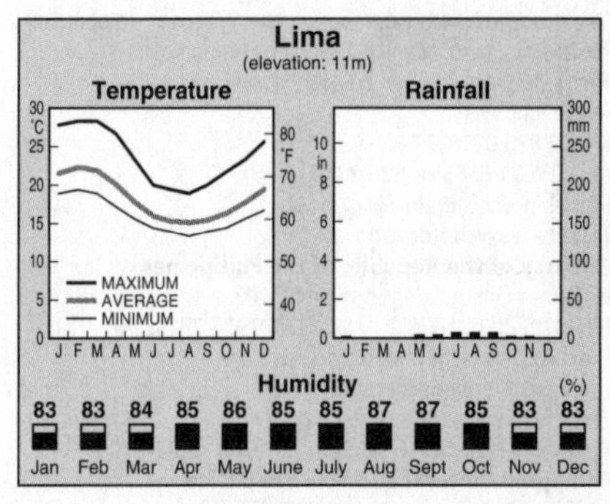

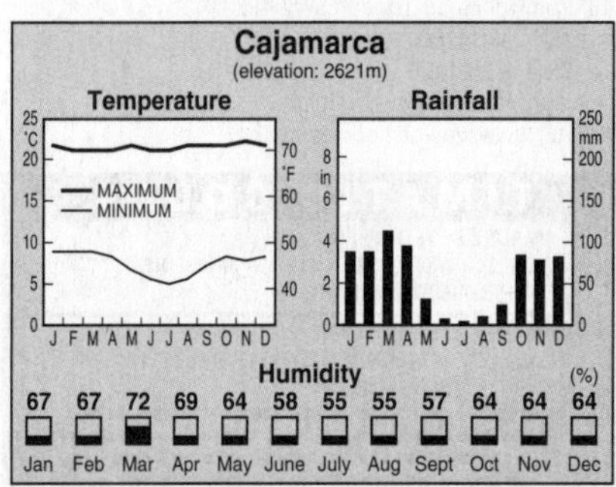

The Philippines

LATEST TRAVEL ADVICE CONTACTS

British Foreign and Commonwealth Office
Tel: (0870) 606 0290 Website: www.fco.gov.uk

US Department of State
Website: http://travel.state.gov/travel

Canadian Department of Foreign Affairs and Int'l Trade
Tel: (1 800) 267 8376 Website: www.dfait-maeci.gc.ca

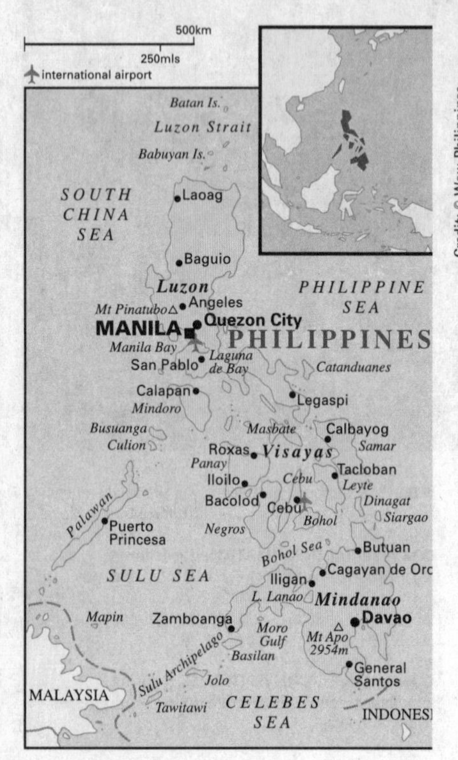

Location: South-East Asia.

Country dialling code: 63.

Philippine Department of Tourism
Room 207, DOT Building, TM Kalaw Street, Ermita, Manila, The Philippines
Tel: (2) 524 2345 *or* 525 6114.
Fax: (2) 521 1088 *or* 524 8321.
E-mail: webmaster@tourism.gov.ph *or* ncr@tourism.gov.ph
Website: www.wowphilippines.com.ph

Philippine Convention and Visitors Corporation (PCVC)
Street address: 4th Floor, Suites 10-17, Legaspi Towers 300, Roxas Boulevard, Manila 1004, The Philippines
Postal address: PO Box EA 459, Manila 1004, The Philippines
Tel: (2) 525 9318-27.
Fax: (2) 521 6165 *or* 525 3314.
E-mail: pcvcnet@dotpcvc.gov.ph
Website: www.dotpcvc.gov.ph

Embassy of the Republic of the Philippines
9A Palace Green, London W8 4QE, UK
Tel: (020) 7937 1600. Fax: (020) 7937 2925.
E-mail: embassy@philemb.org.uk *or* consulars@philemb.org.uk
Website: www.philemb.org.uk
Opening hours: Mon-Fri 0900-1300 and 1400-1700.

Philippine Cultural and Tourism Office
146 Cromwell Road, London SW7 4EF, UK
Tel: (020) 7835 1100.
Fax: (020) 7835 1926.
E-mail: infotourism@wowphilippines.co.uk
Website: www.wowphilippines.co.uk

TIMATIC CODES

Health	AMADEUS: **TI-DFT/MNL/HE** GALILEO/WORLDSPAN: **TI-DFT/MNL/HE** SABRE: **TIDFT/MNL/HE**
Visa	AMADEUS: **TI-DFT/MNL/VI** GALILEO/WORLDSPAN: **TI-DFT/MNL/VI** SABRE: **TIDFT/MNL/VI**

To access TIMATIC country information on Health and Visa regulations through the Computer Reservations System (CRS), type in the appropriate command line listed above.

Credit: © Wow Philippines

British Embassy
Street address: 15-17 Floors, LV Locsin Building, 6752 Ayala Avenue, Makati 1226, Manila, The Philippines
Postal address: PO Box 2927 MCPO, Makati 1226, Manila, The Philippines
Tel: (2) 816 7116 *or* 7348/9 *or* 7271/2 (consular/visa section).
Fax: (2) 819 7206 *or* 810 2745 (visa section) *or* 840 1361 (consular section).
E-mail: uk@info.com.ph (information) *or* uktrade@info.com.ph (commercial).
Website: www.britishembassy.gov.uk/philippines
Honorary Consuls in: Cebu, Olongapo City and Pampanga.

Embassy of the Republic of the Philippines
1600 Massachusetts Avenue, NW, Washington, DC 20036, USA
Tel: (202) 467 9300.
Fax: (202) 467 9417 *or* 466 6288.
E-mail: wdcpe@aol.com *or* consular@philippineembassy-usa.org (consular section).
Website: www.philippineembassy-usa.org
Consulates General in: Chicago, Los Angeles, New York and San Francisco.

Embassy of the United States of America
1201 Roxas Boulevard, Ermita 1000, Manila, The Philippines
Tel: (2) 528 6300 *or* ext 2555 *or* 2246 (consular section).
Fax: (2) 522 4361 *or* 522 3242 (consular section).
Website: http://usembassy.state.gov/posts/rp1/

Embassy of the Republic of the Philippines
130 Albert Street, Suite 606, Ottawa, Ontario K1P 5G4, Canada
Tel: (613) 233 1121.
Fax: (613) 233 4165.
E-mail: embassyofphilippines@rogers.com
Website: http://members.rogers.com/embassyofphilippines

Canadian Embassy
6th-8th Floors, RCBC Plaza Tower 2, 6819 Ayala Avenue, Makati City 1200, The Philippines
Tel: (2) 857 9000. Fax: (2) 843 1082.
E-mail: manil-cs@dfait-maeci.gc.ca (consular section).
Website: www.dfait-maeci.gc.ca/manila

General Information

AREA: 300,000 sq km (115,831 sq miles).
POPULATION: 78,580,000 (official estimate 2002).
POPULATION DENSITY: 261.9 per sq km.
CAPITAL: Manila. **Population:** 1,581,082 (2000).
GEOGRAPHY: The Philippines lie off the southeast coast of Asia between Taiwan and Borneo in the Pacific Ocean and South China Sea. They are composed of 7107 islands and islets (7108 at low tide), 2773 of which are named. The two largest islands, Luzon in the north and Mindanao in the south, account for 65 per cent of the total land area and contain 60 per cent of the country's population. Between the two lie the Visayas Islands.
GOVERNMENT: Republic since 1935. Gained independence from the USA in 1946. **Head of State and Government:** President Maria Gloria Macapagal Arroyo since 2001.
LANGUAGE: Filipino, based on Tagalog, is the national language. English is widely spoken, Spanish less so. There are over 111 cultural and racial groups, each with its own language or dialect; in 1990 there were 988 recorded languages.
RELIGION: Roman Catholic 84 per cent; the rest are made up mostly of Muslims, other Christian denominations, Buddhists and Taoists.
TIME: GMT + 8.
ELECTRICITY: 220 volts (110 volts in Baguio) AC, 60Hz. 110 volts is available in most hotels. Flat and round two- and three-pin plugs are in use.
COMMUNICATIONS: Telephone: IDD is available to main towns. Country code: 63. International calls to the smaller towns must be booked through the operator. Outgoing international code: 00. **Mobile telephone:** GSM 900/1800 network. Operators include *Digitel* (website: www.digitelone.com), *Globe Telecom* (website: www.globe.com.ph), *Islacom* (website: www.innove.com.ph) and *Smart Gold GSM* (website: www.smart.com.ph). Coverage is limited to Manila and other main urban areas. **Fax:** All 3- to 5-star hotels, most government offices and most businesses have facsimile services. **Telegram:** Telegrams can be sent from Eastern Telecommunications Philippines Incorporated offices. **Internet:** ISPs include *Internet Manila* (website: www.i-manila.com.ph) and *Inter.net Phillipines Inc* (website: www.ph.inter.net). Visitors can access their e-mail from Internet cafes across the country **Post:** Airmail to Europe takes at least five days. Post office hours: Mon-Fri 0800-1700. **Press:** There are about 17 daily newspapers. English-language daily newspapers include the *Manila Bulletin*, *Manila Times*, *Philippine Daily Inquirer* and the *Philippine Star*.
Radio: BBC World Service (website: www.bbc.co.uk/worldservice) and Voice of America (website: www.voa.gov) can be received. From time to time the frequencies change and the most up-to-date can be found online.

Passport/Visa

	Passport Required?	Visa Required?	Return Ticket Required?
Full British	Yes	1	Yes
Australian	Yes	1	Yes
Canadian	Yes	1	Yes
USA	Yes	1	Yes
Other EU	Yes	1	Yes
Japanese	Yes	1	Yes

Note: *Regulations and requirements may be subject to change at short notice, and you are advised to contact the appropriate diplomatic or consular authority before finalising travel arrangements. Details of these may be found at the head of this country's entry. Any numbers in the chart refer to the footnotes below.*

PASSPORTS: Passports valid for a minimum of six months beyond intended length of stay required by all.
Note: (a) Holders of Certificates of Identity, Travel Documents ('Titre de Voyage'), Documents of Identity, Taiwanese Passports and all stateless persons *do* require visas. (b) All children of Filipino nationality must hold individual passports. (c) Immigration Officers at ports of entry may admit those with passports only valid for at least 60 days after intended length of stay, at their discretion.
VISAS: Required by all except the following:
(a) **1.** bona fide foreign tourists (including business travellers) for stays of less than 21 days provided holding passports valid for a minimum of six months beyond period of stay and return or onward tickets (except nationals of Afghanistan*, Albania, Algeria*, Bangladesh, Belize, Bosnia & Herzegovina, China (PR), CIS, Croatia, Cuba, East Timor*, Egypt*, Estonia, Georgia, India*, Iran*, Iraq*, Jordan*, Korea (Dem Rep), Latvia, Lebanon*, Libya*, Lithuania, Macedonia (Former Yugoslav Republic of), Nauru, Nigeria*, Pakistan*, Sierra Leone, Serbia & Montenegro, Slovenia, Sri Lanka*, Sudan*, Syrian Arab Republic*, Tonga, Vanuatu, Yemen* and holders of Palestinian* passports who *do* require a visa even if staying less than seven days);
(b) transit passengers continuing their journey to a third

country within 72 hours provided holding onward or return documentation (some nationals are required to leave by the same or first connecting aircraft; enquire at Embassy for details).

Note: (a)* Nationals of these countries must apply for a Temporary Visitor Visa in their country of origin or place of legal residence. (b) All tourists wishing to stay longer than 21 days need a visa.

Types of visa and cost: *Temporary Visitor:* £22 (three month single-entry); £43 (six month multiple-entry); £65 (one year multiple-entry). *Restricted nationals* (three months): £30. Minors must pay P3,120.00 to the Immigration Officer at ports of entry.

Validity: 59 days from date of issue; multiple-entry: between six months and one year from date of issue. Visas normally allow stays of up to 59 days. Extensions are possible at the discretion of the Bureau of Immigration Office, with additional payment to the Emigration Clearance Certificate and corresponding Legal Research Fee.

Application to: Consulate (or Consular section at Embassy); see *Contact Addresses* section.

Application requirements: (a) One application form. (b) One passport-size photo signed on the bottom front, taken in the last six months. (c) Passport valid for at least six months beyond the intended period of stay. (d) Proof of means of support during stay, either by bank statement or letter of employment. (e) Fee, in cash or postal order only. (f) If applying by post, a registered, stamped, self-addressed envelope is required and the application should be signed by a notary or commissioner of oaths. (g) Onward or return tickets. (h) Business travellers also require a letter from the sponsoring Filipino company or from their employer, stating the purpose of the visit. (i) Proof of financial capability, eg latest bank statement, employment certificate etc. (j) Minors (under 15 years) must be accompanied by, or joining, parents to/in the Philippines. They must submit to the Immigration Officer at port of entry, an affidavit of request and consent by either parent/legal guardian (authenticated by relevant Embassy), and a clear photocopy of data page of passport of both minor and their parent(s).

Application for a non-immigrant visa should be made in person.

Working days required: Two. Visas can be collected between 1600 and 1700.

Money

Currency: Philippine Peso (P) = 100 centavos. Notes are in denominations of P1000, 500, 100, 50, 20, 10 and 5. Coins are in denominations of P5, 2 and 1, and 50, 25 and 10 centavos.

Currency exchange: Always use authorised money-changers or banks in Manila. Outside the capital there is a shortage of facilities for changing foreign currency and rates may get progressively worse the further from the city you travel. It is advisable to carry a sufficient amount of Philippine pesos when travelling to other provinces.

Credit & debit cards: American Express, Diners Club, MasterCard and Visa are widely accepted in major establishments throughout the big cities of the Philippines. Check with your credit or debit card company for details of merchant acceptability and other services which may be available.

Travellers cheques: Travellers cheques and major foreign currency may be cashed in all commercial banks and Central Bank dealers. They are also accepted in most hotels, restaurants and shops. To avoid additional exchange rate charges, travellers are advised to take travellers cheques in US Dollars.

Currency restrictions: The import and export of local currency is limited to P10,000; any amount above this must be authorised by the Central Bank of the Philippines. The import and export of foreign currency is unlimited, but must be declared over P10,000.

Exchange rate indicators: The following figures are included as a guide to the movements of the Philippine Peso against Sterling and the US Dollar:

Date	Feb '04	May '04	Aug '04	Nov '04
£1.00=	101.74	99.49	102.63	106.38
$1.00=	55.89	55.70	55.71	56.18

Banking hours: Mon-Fri 0900-1600.

Duty Free

The following items may be imported into the Philippines without incurring customs duty:

400 cigarettes or 50 cigars or 250g of tobacco; 2l of alcoholic beverage of not more than 1l each.

Prohibited items: Firearms, explosives, pornographic material, seditious or subversive material, narcotics and other internationally prohibited drugs (unless accompanied by a medical prescription), gambling articles and machines and misbranded and adulterated foodstuffs.

Public Holidays

2005: Jan 1 New Year's Day. **Mar 24** Maundy Thursday. **Mar 25** Good Friday. **Apr 9** Bataan Day. **May 1** Labour Day. **Jun 12** Independence Day. **Aug 31** National Heroes' Day. **Nov 1** All Saints' Day. **Nov 30** Bonifacio Day. **Nov** Eid Ul Fitr (exact date varies) **Dec 25** Christmas Day. **Dec 30** Rizal Day. **Dec 31** New Year's Eve Bank Holiday.

2006: Jan 1 New Year's Day. **Mar 13** Maundy Thursday. **Mar 14** Good Friday; Bataan Day. **May 1** Labour Day. **Jun 12** Independence Day. **Aug 31** National Heroes' Day. **Nov 1** All Saints' Day. **Nov 30** Bonifacio Day. **Nov** Eid Ul Fitr (exact date varies) **Dec 25** Christmas Day. **Dec 30** Rizal Day. **Dec 31** New Year's Eve Bank Holiday.

Note: Easter is a major holiday in the Philippines and travel may be disrupted.

Health

	Special Precautions?	Certificate Required?
Yellow Fever	No	1
Cholera	2	No
Typhoid & Polio	3	1
Malaria	4	N/A

Note: *Regulations and requirements may be subject to change at short notice, and you are advised to contact your doctor well in advance of your intended date of departure. Any numbers in the chart refer to the footnotes below.*

1: A yellow fever or typhus vaccination certificate is required from travellers over one year of age arriving within six days from infected areas. A certificate is also required by those arriving from small pox or plague infected areas.

2: Following WHO guidelines issued in 1973, a cholera vaccination certificate is not a condition of entry to the Philippines, unless travellers arrive from infected areas. However, cholera is a risk in this country and precautions are essential. Up-to-date advice should be sought before deciding whether these precautions should include vaccination, as medical opinion is divided over its effectiveness; see the *Health* appendix for further information.

3: Vaccination against typhoid is advised.

4: Malaria risk exists throughout the year in areas below 600m, except in the Provinces of Bohol, Catanduanes, Cebu and Manila. No risk is considered to exist in urban areas or in the plains. The malignant *falciparum* strain is present and is reported to be resistant to chloroquine.

Food & drink: Water used for drinking, brushing teeth or making ice should have first been boiled or otherwise sterilised. Milk is unpasteurised and should be boiled. Powdered or tinned milk is available and is advised, but make sure that it is reconstituted with pure water. Avoid dairy products which are likely to have been made from unboiled milk. Only eat well-cooked meat and fish, preferably served hot. Pork, salad and mayonnaise may carry increased risk. Vegetables should be cooked and fruit peeled.

Other risks: *Bilharzia* (schistosomiasis) is endemic in the south. Avoid swimming and paddling in stagnant fresh water; swimming pools that are well chlorinated and maintained are safe. *Dengue fever* and *filariasis* occur and *plague* is carried by insects. *Hepatitis B* is highly endemic. *Hepatitis A* may occur. *Japanese encephalitis* occurs rarely in western Luzon, Mindoro and Palawan from April to November and throughout the year in other areas, with the highest risk from April to January. *Chikungunya fever* is particularly common in urban areas of the central islands, such as Manila. *Gonorrhoea* resistant to penicilin is common in the Philippines, particularly in Manila and Cebu City. *Rabies* is present. For those at high risk, vaccination before arrival should be considered. If you are bitten, seek medical advice without delay. For more information, consult the *Health* appendix.

Health care: There is no reciprocal health agreement with the UK and health insurance is, therefore, essential. Approximately three-quarters of the hospitals are private.

Travel - International

Note: All travel to central, southern and western Mindanao, to Basilan, Tawi-Tawi and the Sulu archipelago is advised against.

AIR: The Philippines' national airline is *Philippine Airlines (PR)* (website: www.philippineairlines.com). Other airlines serving the Philippines include *Air France, British Airways, Cathay Pacific, Gulf Air, Kuwait Airways, Malaysia Airlines, Northwest Airways, Qatar Airways, Royal Brunei Airlines, Silk Air* and *Singapore Airlines.*

Note: The period over Easter, from Good Friday to the following Bank holiday (and sometimes beyond), is a major holiday in the Philippines, as are Christmas and New Year. There may be some difficulty booking a flight during these periods.

Approximate flight times: From Manila to *London* is 20 hours; to *Paris* is 16 hours 30 minutes; to *Los Angeles* is 14 hours 25 minutes; to *New York* is 17 hours 30 minutes; to *Singapore* is three hours 40 minutes; to *Hong Kong* is two hours 35 minutes; to *Bangkok* is two hours 30 minutes; to *Tokyo* is four hours 50 minutes and to *Sydney* is eight hours.

International airports: *Ninoy Aquino (MNL)* is 12km (7 miles) south of Manila. Airport facilities include banks, post office, medical clinic, baggage deposit area, duty free shops and car hire. Bus and taxi services are available to the city (travel time – 60-90 minutes by public bus or 25 minutes by taxi).

Mactan International Airport (CEB) (Cebu Island) is 45km (28 miles) from the city centre. Hotels and tour operators provide their own coaches; taxis can be hired.

Departure tax: P550 for international departures. Children under two years of age and transit passengers are exempt.

SEA: Manila is a major seaport, a crossroads of trade in the Asia-Pacific region. Shipping lines which call at Manila include *American President Lines, Evergreen Lines, Far Eastern Shipping Lines, Lloyd Triestino* and *Premier Shipping Lines.* Schedules and rates are listed in the shipping pages of daily newspapers.

Travel - Internal

AIR: In addition to *Philippine Airlines (PR),* there are several other charter airlines, including *Air Ads, Air Philippines, Asian Spirit, Cebu Pacific Air, Laoag International Airlines, Mindanao Express* and *Seeair* and *Voyager.*

Departure tax: P100 for internal flights from Manila. Children under two years and passengers in transit remaining in the airport are exempt.

SEA: Inter-island ships with first-class accommodation connect the major island ports. For details, contact local shipping lines (Aleson Shipping, tel: (2) 712 0507 *or* WG&A Super Ferry, tel: (2) 528 7000; website: www.wgasuperferry.com).

RAIL: The only railway is on Luzon Island, from San Fernando, Pampagna in the north to Legazpi city, Albay in the south (operated by *Philippine National Railways*). This network runs three trains daily to and from Manila. There is also some air-conditioned accommodation.

ROAD: There are 161,168 km (100,148 miles) of roads spread among the islands, with highways on the Mindanao, Visayas and Luzon island groups. Further roads are currently being constructed. Traffic drives on the right. **Bus:** There are bus services between the towns and also widely available *jeepneys*. These are shared taxis using jeep-derived vehicles equipped to carry up to 14 passengers on bench seats. Fares are similar to buses. **Taxi:** Taxis are available in the cities and in many towns. Make sure meters are used, as some taxi drivers will set an exorbitant and arbitrary rate. **Car hire:** Car rentals are available in Manila and in major cities. The minimum age is 18. **Documentation:** International Driving Permit required, together with a national driving licence.

URBAN: A number of bus routes are operated by *Metro Manila Transport* using conventional vehicles, including double-deckers. Most journeys, however, are made by *jeepneys*, of which there are an estimated 30,000 in Manila alone. The *metro-rail*, a light rail transit link, runs from Baclaran terminal in the south to Caloocan terminal in the north. Tricycles (motorbikes with sidecars) and trishaws are a cheaper alternative for shorter distances around towns.

Travel times: The following chart gives approximate travel times (in hours and minutes) from **Manila** to other major cities/towns in the Philippines.

	Air	Road	Sea
Baguio	0.50	4.00	-
Banaue	0.50*	12.00	-
Batangas	-	2.00	-
Cebu	1.10	-	24.00
Cagayan de Oro	1.25	-	48.00
Davao	1.30	-	48.00
Iloilo	1.00	-	24.00
Laoag	1.25	7.00	-
Palawan	1.10	-	24.00

Note: *As far as Baguio City and then another 8 hours by road.

Accommodation

HOTELS: In Manila there are 11,745 first-class hotel rooms. There are numerous smaller hotels, inns, hostels and pensions. Prices are often quoted both in Philippine Pesos and US Dollars. A complete directory of hotels is available from the Department of Tourism. The majority of establishments belong to the Hotel and Restaurant Association of the Philippines (HRAP), Suite 200, Hotel Intramuros de Manila, Plaza San Luis Complex, Cor. Cabildo and Urdaneta Sts, Intramuros, Manila (tel: (2) 527 5113; fax: (2) 527 9927; e-mail: hrap@info.com.ph). In addition, most regions have their own associations. **Grading:** Hotels are

graded in the following categories based on standards set by the Office of Tourism Services, Department of Tourism, Manila: Economy (43 per cent of all establishments are in this grade), Standard (39 per cent), First Class (9 per cent) and Deluxe (9 per cent).
SELF-CATERING: 'Apartels' are available for minimum stays of one week, and palm *nipa* huts can be rented on some islands.
CAMPING/CARAVANNING: Offered only in a very limited number of places.

Resorts & Excursions

The Philippines is composed of 7107 islands (7108 at low tide), with a total coastline longer than that of the USA. The warm tropical waters offer the attractions of sunbathing and swimming, while divers and snorkellers can explore coral gardens with beautiful marine life and dramatic drop-offs on the sea bed. Charter planes can be hired for reaching some of the more remote islands. Inland, the rich history and culture of the Filipino people, the dramatic landscapes and thriving cities will fascinate the visitor. For the purposes of this guide, this section has been divided into three areas, with the main tourist attractions listed under Luzon, the Visayas, and Mindanao and the South.

MANILA & AREA

Capital and hub of the nation, Manila is situated on the east coast of Luzon. Founded in 1571 on the ruins of a Muslim settlement, Manila has been a port for hundreds of years. The oldest part of the city, the **Intramuros** (Walled City), was protected by a massive wall, some of which still remains today despite savage fighting staged here in World War II. Places of interest include **San Agustin Church** and **Manila Cathedral**, from which there is an excellent view of the 2072 sq km (800 sq miles) of the harbour, and the ruins of **Fort Santiago**. Outside the Intramuros is **Chinatown**, a market in the district of Binondo, crowded with shops, stalls and restaurants. **Luneta Park** contains the **Rizal Monument**, a memorial to the execution of this great Filipino intellectual of the late 19th century. Other places of interest are the **American Cemetery** and **Coconut Palace**.
EXCURSIONS: Manila is a good base from which to make excursions, for instance to **Las Piñas**, situated a little way outside the city, where the famous Bamboo Organ is located and the **Sarao Jeepney factory**, where people are allowed to wander around free of charge.
About one hour's drive away from Manila through coconut plantations, **Tagaytay Ridge** in **Cavite** overlooks a lake that contains **Taal Volcano**, which itself holds another lake. Tagaytay is a popular destination in summer, when all kinds of festivities are celebrated and roadside stalls overflow with flowering plants and fruits in season.
The series of mineral springs of **Hidden Valley** lie secreted in a 90m- (300ft-) deep crater in **Alaminos**, enclosed by rich forests. The pools vary in temperature from warm to cold, and the lush trails end up at a gorge with a waterfall.
Villa Escudero, an 800-hectare coconut plantation in **Quezon Province**, less than two hours by road from Manila, is part of a working plantation, yielding rare glimpses into rural life. Guests are taken on a tour of a typical village on a cart drawn by a **carabao**, or water buffalo.
Corregidor Island, 'The Rock', has a famous memorial to those who were killed during the Japanese invasion, and is accessible by hydrofoil. Day tours include refreshments and guide. A day trip to the town of **Pagsanjan**, 63km (39 miles) southeast of Manila, includes dug-out canoe rides down the jungle-bordered river to the Pagsanjan Falls. This was a location for the filming of *Apocalypse Now*, and is a popular excursion.
Laguna, a short distance from Manila, is a province famous for hot sulphur springs. The 'Towns of Baths', **Cuyab**, **Los Baños** and **Pansol** are situated here.

LUZON

Luzon is the largest and most northerly of the main islands. Its spectacular landscape is made up of mountainous regions in the north, the flat vistas of the central plain, lakes and volcanoes in the southern peninsula, and a coastline dotted with caves and sandy-beached islands. Manila, the capital of the Philippines, lies on the island's east coast (see *Manila & Area*).
BAGUIO: 250km (150 miles) north of Manila is Baguio, 1525m (5000ft) above sea level, a cool haven from the summer heat. It is accessible both by air and land, though the drive up the zigzagging **Kennon Road** is more popular as it offers spectacular views of the countryside. Baguio has a good variety of restaurants, mountain views and walking excursions. Main attractions include **The Mansion**, summer residence of the Philippine president; **Bell Church**; **Baguio Cathedral**; and the **Crystal Caves**, composed of crystalline metamorphic rocks and once an ancient burial site.
BANAUE: Banaue is an eight hour bus ride north of Baguio. A remote mountain community lives here, and tourists can visit their settlements. The beautiful **rice terraces** are the main attraction of this area. A breathtaking sight, they rise majestically to an altitude of 1525m (5000ft), and encompass an area of 10,360 sq km (4000 sq miles). The terraces were hand-carved some 2000 years ago using crude tools cutting into once barren rock, each ledge completely encompassing the mountain. Now listed by UNESCO as World Heritage sites, they offer an unforgettable sight to tourists and trekkers in the area (see also *Sport & Activities*). Banaue has a tourist hotel and many good pensions.
HUNDRED ISLANDS: Lying off the coast of **Pangasinan**, the Hundred Islands group is made up of 400 islets surrounded by coral gardens and white sand beaches. This area is ideal for swimming and fishing. Hundred Islands is the second-largest marine reservation in the world, teeming with over 2000 species of aquatic life. The caves and domes of **Marcos Island** and the **Devil's Kitchen** are worth exploring. The entire province of **Palawan** is a remarkable terrain for adventure and exploration, with its primeval rainforests, **St Paul's Underground River** and **Tubattaha Reef**. Inter-island cruises around northern Palawan are now available.
ELSEWHERE: Mindoro island, reached by ferry from Batangas pier and south of Manila, is a place where the stunning scenery includes **Mount Halcon**, 2695m (8841ft) high, **Naujan Lake** and **Tamaraw Falls**.
La Union, situated on the northwest coast of Luzon, has some of the best beach resort facilities on the island. There are regular buses to La Union from Baguio and Manila.
Bicol Region, situated in the east, is developing as a tourist destination and offers beaches, hotels and sights such as the **Mayon Volcano**, a nearly perfect cone, and the **Kalayukay Beach Resort**.

THE VISAYAS

The Visayas is a group of islands between Luzon and Mindanao. The main islands are **Cebu**, **Leyte**, **Negros**, **Panay** and **Samar**, the latter famous as the island first sighted by the Spanish explorer Ferdinand Magellan in the 16th century and as the landing point for the American liberation forces in 1944. Samar and Leyte are linked by the **San Juanico Bridge**, the longest in the country.
CEBU: Cebu City is the main resort of the Visayas. Cebu is the most densely populated island, a commercial centre with an international harbour, and the Philippines' second city. Sights include **Magellan's Cross**, a wooden cross planted by Magellan himself over 450 years ago to commemorate the baptism into the Christian faith of Rajah Humabon and his wife Juana with 800 followers, and **Fort San Pedro**, the oldest and smallest Spanish fort in the country, which was built on the orders of Spanish conquistador Miguel Lopez de Legazpi in 1565.
Carcar town, south of Cebu City, has many preserved Castillian houses, gardens and churches. The **Chapel of the Last Supper** in **Mandaue City** features hand-carved life-size statues of Christ and his apostles dating back to Spanish times. The **Magellan Monument** on **Mactan Island** was raised in 1886 to mark the spot where Magellan died, felled by the fierce chieftain, Datu Lapu-Lapu, who refused to submit to the Spanish conquerors. There is also a monument to Datu Lapu-Lapu honouring him as the first Filipino patriot. **Maribago** is the centre of the region's guitar-making industry. As well as many historical sites there are popular hotels, beach clubs and resorts.
PANAY: Iloilo on Panay is an agricultural province producing root crops, vegetables, cocoa, coffee and numerous tropical fruits. The attractions include beach resorts and, in **Iloilo City** (reached by air), the 18th-century **Miagao Church**, a unique piece of Baroque colonial architecture with a facade decorated with impressions of coconut and papaya trees. **Sicogon Island** is a haven for scuba divers, and has mountains and virgin forests to explore. **Boracay Island** is another such island paradise, accessible by air via Kalibo, followed by a bus or jeepney ride to Malay, and finally by ferry or pumpboat to Caticlan. A survey considered its powdery-fine white-sand beach to be amongst the best in the world.
BOHOL: Bohol Island, just across the straits from Cebu in Central Visayas, is the site of some of the country's most fascinating natural wonders; hundreds of limestone hills, some 30m (100ft) high, that in summer look like oversized chocolate drops, earning them the name **'Chocolate Hills'**. Covered by thin grass that dries and turns brown in the summer sun, they are a strange spectacle with mounds rising up from the flatlands, and are situated about 55km (34 miles) northeast of **Tagbilaran City**, the island's capital. Bohol also offers handsome white sand beaches and pretty secluded coves, accessible via good roads. The island is a coconut-growing area and its local handicrafts are mostly of woven materials: grass mats, hats and baskets. **Baclayon Church** merits a visit, as it is probably the oldest stone church in the Philippines, dating back to 1595. The island can be reached by plane or ferry. The air journey from Cebu to Tagbilaran takes 40 minutes. Ferries go from Cebu to Tagbilaran or Tubigon, another port north of the capital.

MINDANAO & THE SOUTH

Mindanao is the second-largest and the most southerly island, with a very different feel from the rest of the country. A variety of Muslim ethnic groups live here.
ZAMBOANGA CITY: In the southwestern tip of Mindanao is Zamboanga City, considered by some as the most romantic place in the Philippines and a favourite resort amongst tourists. The city is noted for its seashells, unspoiled tropical scenery and magnificent flowers. Zamboanga was founded by the Spanish, and the 17th-century walls of **Fort Pilar**, built to protect the Spanish and Christian Filipinos from Muslim onslaughts, are still standing. The city has a number of hotels, cars for hire, good public transport and *vintas* (small boats), often with colourful sails, available to take visitors round the city bay. The flea market sells Muslim pottery, clothes and brassware. About 2km (1.2 miles) from Fort Pilar are the houses of the Badjaos, which are stilted constructions on the water. Water gypsies live in boats in this area, moving to wherever the fishing is best. **Plaza Pershing** and **Pasonanca Park** are worth visiting. Nearby Santa Cruz Island has a sand beach which turns pink when the corals from the sea are washed ashore, and is ideal for bathing, snorkelling and scuba diving. There is also an old Muslim burial ground here.
ELSEWHERE: Davao province is the industrial centre of Mindanao, renowned for its pearl and banana exports. Davao City is one of the most progressive industrial cities in the country. The province is the site of **Mount Apo**, the highest peak in the country, while the **Apo Range** has spectacular waterfalls, rapids, forests, springs and mountain lakes.
On the northern coast of Mindanao, **Cagayan de Oro** is the gateway to some of the most beautiful islands in the Philippines. By way of contrast, in **Bukidnon** there are huge cattle ranches and the famous Del Monte pineapple fields, and **Iligan City** is the site of the hydroelectric complex driven by the **Maria Cristina Falls**.
The province of **Lanao del Sur** is characterised by its Muslim community, which has settled along the shores of **Lake Lanao**. Besides the lake, other attractions include **Signal Hill**; **Sacred Mountain**; the native market, **Torongan**; homes of the Maranao royalty; the various Muslim mosques on the shores of the lake; and examples of the famous brassware industry centred in **Tugaua**.

Sport & Activities

Watersports: The Philippines' clear waters, tropical climate, abundant coral reefs and varied marine life make them an excellent location for **scuba diving** and **snorkelling**, with options ranging from resort-based diving to extended trips to unexplored areas. White sandy beaches are ubiquitous. The islands of Batangas, Bohol, Mindoro (particularly *Apo Reef Marine Park*) and Palawan offer some of the country's best dive sites. The detailed and informative pocket map *A Diver's Paradise* is available from the Philippine Department of Tourism (see *Contact Addresses* section). **Boating** enthusiasts can rent traditional canoes (*bancas*) on most beaches. **Surfing** and **windsurfing** are also popular. **Kayaking** and some **rafting** are available in the wet season in the interiors of Luzon and Mindanao.
Fishing: The Philippines' warm waters, incorporating almost 2,000,000 sq km (772,200 sq miles) of fishing grounds, rank 12th in worldwide fish production. These grounds are inhabited by some 2400 fish species, including many game fish such as giant tuna, tanguingue, king mackerel, great barracuda, swordfish and marlin. Local tour operators in Manila will help arrange trips. Game fishing is best from December to August.
Golf: There are approximately 70 courses, but only a handful of these conform to championship specifications. Unfortunately, good golf courses can be difficult to access: all private clubs have security guards with instructions to refuse entry to non-members. Courses that admit visitors tend to be expensive. Some of the best courses open to non-members include: *El Club Intramuros* (in central Manila); *Forbes Park* (in southeastern Manila, where two of three courses are open to visitors); *Canlubang* (one of many spectacular courses in southern Luzon and the only one open to non-members); and *Camp John Hay* (near the Baguio hill resort, in the mountains, where golfers can rent private bungalows). Further courses are on the islands of Mindanao and Visayas (at *Bacolod*, *Cebu*, *Davao* and *Iloilo*), which can be reached by ferry or on an internal flight. Non-members may sometimes be allowed to play at private clubs on a personal invitation; hotels can also make arrangements. For further information, or to request the brochure *Golf in The Philippines*, contact the Philippine Department of Tourism (see *Contact Addresses* section) *or* the Federation of Golf Clubs (Philippines) (website: www.federationgolf.com).
Ecotourism: Various commercial operators offer package adventure tours with an ecological slant, including activities such as **canopy walking** (participants are lifted by pulleys to the canopy on the Philippine rainforest near Cagayan de Oro). The best areas for **trekking** and **mountaineering** include the region around Matulid River, Mount Pulog and Mount Halcon as well as the famous UNESCO World Heritage-listed rice terraces in the Cordillera mountain range in northern Luzon (see also *Resorts & Excursions*).

Whale and **dolphin watching** is popular in the Tanon Strait near Bohol Island.
Other: A traditional game is **Sipa**, played with a small wicker ball, which visitors can watch in Manila at the Rizal Court.

Social Profile

FOOD & DRINK: Unlike a lot of Asian cooking, Filipino cuisine is distinguished by its moderate use of spices. American, Chinese, Japanese, Malay and Spanish influences have all left their mark in a subtle blending of cultures and flavours. Naturally, seafoods feature strongly, freshly harvested and often simply grilled, boiled, fried or steamed and served with *kalamansi* (the local lemon), *bagoong* (a fish paste) or vinegar with *labuyo* (the fiery native pepper). Restaurants specialising in seafood abound, offering crabs, lobsters, prawns, oysters, tuna, freshwater fish, *bangus* (the bony but prized milkfish) and the sweet *maliputo*, found in deep-water lakes. The *lechon* (roasted whole pig) is prepared for fiestas and family celebrations. Other delightful specialities include *kare-kare* (an oxtail stew in peanut sauce served with bagoong), *sinigang* (meat or fish in a pleasantly sour broth) and *adobo* (braised pork and chicken, in tangy soy sauce, vinegar and garlic). Among the regional dishes, the Ilocos region's *pinakbet* (vegetables sautéed with pork and bagoong), Central Luzon's *relleno* (boned and stuffed chicken or fish) and the Visayas' *kinilaw* (raw fish marinated in a spicy vinegar dressing) top the list. Rice is a staple of Filipino cuisine. Fruit is plentiful with mangoes, papayas, bananas, chicos, lanzones, guavas and rambutans. Philippine preserves like *atsara* (a chutney-like vegetable preserve) and the numerous native desserts like the *pili nut brittle* (a crunchy sweet made with the luscious pili nuts found only in the Bicol region) can be purchased in local markets. All the regional dishes are available in Manila's excellent restaurants, which, like the restaurants of all the main towns, offer a varied cuisine. For the less adventurous, there are also European-style restaurants and American fast food. Restaurants are generally informal, with table service.
Alcoholic drinks include locally brewed beer, of which San Miguel is the best known, and the delicious Philippine rum. Waiter service is common in bars and there are no strict regulations regarding the sale of alcohol.
NIGHTLIFE: The choice of entertainment in Manila displays the Filipinos' affinity for music. 5-star hotels offer everything from high-tech discos to lavish cultural songs and dances, as well as superb pop singers and performers, trios, show bands and classical string ensembles. On most evenings there are cultural performances by local artists or foreign groups at the many other venues for the performing arts. Free concerts are offered by several parks every week, and occasionally by banks and other corporations. The Philippines also have some unusual musical groups like the Pangkat Kawayan bamboo orchestra, which uses bamboo musical instruments, and the Rondalla group which uses tiny guitars like the ukelele. Casinos are located in Cebu, Davao, Ilocos Norte, Iloilo, Manila, Pampanga and Zamboanga.
SHOPPING: The Philippines is a haven for shoppers. Countless bargain opportunities for the handicrafts of the different regions are found in the numerous shopping complexes, which range from sleek air-conditioned department stores and malls to open-air bazaars. The chain stores offer everything from the famous *barong tagalog* (hand-embroidered dress shirts for men in delicate *jusi* material) to Tiffany lamps made with capiz shells. For local colour there's nothing like the flea markets where visitors can buy all kinds of cloth weaves, brassware from the south, woodcarvings and other local crafts and souvenirs, like the painted papier-maché horses of Laguna. Some particularly good buys are the silver jewellery from Baguio, coral trinket boxes, rattan furniture, baskets in different designs, woven grass mats (*banig*), antique wooden figurines of saints, ready-to-wear clothes, garments embroidered with the traditional callado, Filipino dresses for women (usually made from banana and pineapple fibres), cigars and *abaca* placemats. Handicraft stores are found everywhere in the country, especially in cities. Large department stores sell both local and foreign manufactured goods. **Shopping hours:** Mon-Sat 0930-2000, but these can vary. Most department stores and supermarkets are open Sunday.
SPECIAL EVENTS: Dozens of colourful festivals are celebrated in the Philippines each year. A comprehensive listing, including all important Muslim festivals and Catholic feast days in honour of patron saints etc, may be obtained from the Department of Tourism. The following is a selection of special events occurring in the Philippines in 2005:
Jan *Philippine Game Fishing Tournament and International Billfish Tournament*, Sta Ana; *Kuraldal* (residents dance to honour St Lucia), Pampanga and Sasmuan. **Jan 9** *Feast of the Black Nazarene*, Manila. **Jan 25-27** *Ati-Atihan*, Kalibo. **Feb** *International Bamboo Festival*, Las Pinas City; *Annual Philippines Poker Run & Motorcycle Rodeo*, Damaguete City. **Mar** *Carabao-Carroza Festival*, Pavia. **Apr** *Moriones* (re-enacting of the beheading of Longinus), Boac, Gasan, Marinduque and Mogpog; Turumba, Laguna and Pakil; *Holy Week Lenten Rituals*, nationwide. **May** *Santacruzan and Flores de Mayo Festival*, nationwide; *Carabao Festival*, Bulacan and Pulilan; *Pahiyas* (parades and flower decorations), Lucban and Sariaya; *Obando Fertility Rites*. **May 30-Jun 1** *Mango Festival 2005*, Manila. **Jun 12** *Independence Day Celebrations*, nationwide, focusing on Manila's Luneta Park. **Jun 24** *Parada Ng Lechon* (roast pig feast), Balayan. **Jul** *Pagoda Sa Wawa*, Balayan; *Sandugo Festival*, Bohol. **Aug** *Aurora Festival*, Tanjay; *Kalibongan Festival*, Kidapawan City; *Tuguegarao City Fiesta*; *Kadayawan Sa Dabaw*, Davao City. **Sep** *Nuestra Senora de Penafrancia*, Naga City. **Oct** *Zamboanga Hermosa Festival*; *Masskara Festival*, Bacolod City; *Lanzones Festival*, Camiguin Island. **Nov** *Feast of San Clemente/Gigantes*, Angono and Rizal. **Nov 1** *All Saints' Day*, nationwide. **Dec** *Giant Lantern Festival*, Pampanga and San Fernando; *Binirayan*, San José. **Dec 16-24** *Misa de Gallo* (Filipino Yuletide Tradition). **Dec 25** *Christmas Festival*, Laoag. **Dec 30** *Rizal Day* (festivities at Luneta Park).

Credit: © Wow Philippines

SOCIAL CONVENTIONS: Government officials are addressed by their titles such as Senator, Congressman or Director. Otherwise, usual modes of address and levels of politeness are expected. Casual dress is acceptable in most places, but in Muslim areas the visitor should cover up. Filipino men may wear an embroidered long-sleeved shirt or a plain white *barong tagalog* with black trousers for formal occasions. The Philippines are, in many respects, more westernised than any other Asian country, but there is a rich underlay of Malay culture. **Tipping:** Usually 10 per cent of the bill. Hotels generally add a 15 per cent service charge, but it is customary to leave small change.

Business Profile

ECONOMY: The agricultural sector produces rice, corn, coconuts, copra, sugar cane and bananas as the main crops. Production of timber, formerly a major export earner, has been suspended due to the effects of deforestation. There is a moderately sized mining industry producing copper, gold, silver, nickel and coal. Offshore oil production is due to begin in the next few years. Most of the Philippines' recent economic development has been industrial, with food processing, oil refining, and the production of chemicals, electrical machinery, metal goods and textiles all having been established during the last 20 years.
Broad financial incentives aimed at attracting foreign investment capital, and the creation of five export processing zones (EPZ) with concessionary tax rates and tariffs, prompted strong growth during the early- and mid-1990s. However, it also produced a somewhat skewed economy in which the Manila area, known as the National Capital Region, now hosts 15 per cent of the population and accounts for one-third of GDP: there are huge income disparities between the capital and the rest of the country. The Philippines' economic growth came to a shuddering halt in late 1997 when the collapse of the region's currencies produced a stock market crash, high inflation, the cessation of foreign investment, and a large budget deficit. *El Niño*, the climatic system which wreaks periodic havoc upon the Philippines, worsened the situation further. The economy has since recovered fairly well. Current annual growth is 4.3 per cent, while industrial production has picked up after several years of decline. Foreign aid (including a US$100 million subvention from the USA in 2002) has helped the country's finances, along with a sharp increase in remittances from the thousands of Filipinos working abroad. Unemployment is still a problem, having grown steadily during the last few years to its current level of 11.4 per cent. The Philippines' longer term economic prospects will depend on the Government's vigour in pursuing essential and overdue reforms to the tax and banking systems, and improvements to the country's shaky infrastructure. The Philippines belong to the Association of South East Asian Nations (the anti-Communist bloc which is now assuming an important economic role) and the Asian Development Bank. The country's major trading partners include The Netherlands, the UK and USA.
BUSINESS: The weather is almost uniformly warm and humid and so short-sleeved shirts, preferably with a tie, can be worn for business visits. However, with most offices being air conditioned, it is best to wear safari suits or a long-sleeved Filipino *barong tagalog* when visiting top business officials and executives. Filipinos have an American business style and English is widely spoken. Best months for business visits are October to November and January to May. Unless you have urgent business matters to attend to, business visits around Christmas and Easter are not recommended as delays tend to be unavoidable. **Office hours:** These vary. Usually Mon-Fri 0800-1200 and 1300-1700. Some private sector offices are open Sat 0800-1200.
COMMERCIAL INFORMATION: The following organisations can offer advice: Philippine Trade and Investment Promotion Centre, 1a Cumberland House, Kensington Court, London W8 5NX, UK (tel: (020) 7937 1898; fax: (020) 7937 2747; e-mail: dtilondon1@aol.com); *or* the Philippine Chamber of Commerce and Industry (tel: (2) 844 5713; fax: (2) 843 4102; email: pcci@philcham.com; website: www.philcham.com).
CONFERENCES/CONVENTIONS: Many establishments are members of the Philippine Convention and Visitors Corporation (PCVC). For further general information, contact the PCVC (see *Contact Addresses* section).

Climate

Tropical climate tempered by constant sea breezes. There are three distinct seasons: the rainy season (June to September), cool and dry (October to February), and hot and mainly dry (March to May). Evenings are cooler. Typhoons occasionally occur from June to September.
Required clothing: Lightweight cottons and linens are worn throughout most of the year, with warmer clothes useful on cooler evenings. Rainwear or umbrellas are advisable for the rainy season.

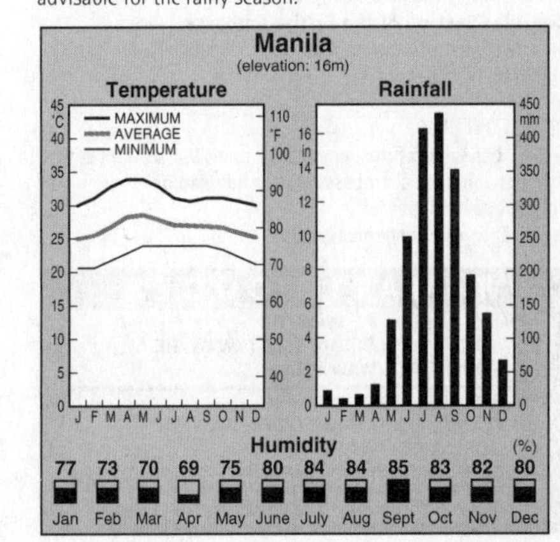

Poland

LATEST TRAVEL ADVICE CONTACTS

British Foreign and Commonwealth Office
Tel: (0870) 606 0290 Website: www.fco.gov.uk

US Department of State
Website: http://travel.state.gov/travel

Canadian Department of Foreign Affairs and Int'l Trade
Tel: (1 800) 267 8376 Website: www.dfait-maeci.gc.ca

Location: Central Europe.

Country dialling code: 48.

Polish Tourism Organisation
4-6 Chalubinskiejo Street, 00-928 Warsaw, Poland
Tel: (22) 630 1736. Fax: (22) 630 1742.
E-mail: pot@pot.gov.pl Website: www.pot.gov.pl

Warsaw Information Centre
Zamkowy Square 1/13, 00-262 Warsaw, Poland
Tel/Fax: (22) 635 1881.
E-mail: wcit@wcit.waw.pl *or* wcit@neostrada.pl
Website: www.wcit.waw.pl

Embassy of the Republic of Poland
47 Portland Place, London W1B 1JH, UK
Tel: (0870) 774 2700. Fax: (020) 7921 3574/5
E-mail: polishembassy@polishembassy.org.uk
Website: www.polishembassy.org.uk
Opening hours: Mon-Fri 0830-1630.

Consulate General of the Republic of Poland
73 New Cavendish Street, London W1W 6LS, UK
Tel: (0870) 774 2800. Fax: (020) 7323 2320.
E-mail: konsulat@polishconsulate.co.uk
Website: www.polishconsulate.co.uk
Opening hours: Mon-Fri 1000-1300 (Wed 1000-1200; Thur 1300-1600).

Polish National Tourist Office
Level 3, Westec House, West Gate, London, W5 1YY, UK
Tel: (0870) 675 012. Fax: (0870) 675 011.
E-mail: info@visitpoland.org Website: www.visitpoland.org

Consular Section of the British Embassy
Warsaw Corporate Centre, 2nd Floor, Ul. Emilii Plater 28, 00-688 Warsaw, Poland
Tel: (22) 311 0000.
Fax: (22)311 0250.
E-mail: consular@britishembassy.pl (consular section) *or* commercial@britishembassy.pl (commercial) *or* info@britishembassy.pl
Website: www.britishembassy.pl

TIMATIC CODES

Health	AMADEUS: **TI-DFT/WAW/HE** GALILEO/WORLDSPAN: **TI-DFT/WAW/HE** SABRE: **TIDFT/WAW/HE**
Visa	AMADEUS: **TI-DFT/WAW/VI** GALILEO/WORLDSPAN: **TI-DFT/WAW/VI** SABRE: **TIDFT/WAW/VI**

To access TIMATIC country information on Health and Visa regulations through the Computer Reservations System (CRS), type in the appropriate command line listed above.

Embassy of the Republic of Poland
2640 16th Street, NW, Washington, DC 20009, USA
Tel: (202) 234 3800-2.
Fax: (202) 328 6271.
E-mail: polemb.info@earthlink.net
Website: www.polandembassy.org

Consular Division of the Embassy of the Republic of Poland
2224 Wyoming Avenue, NW, Washington, DC 20008, USA
Tel: (202) 234 3800.
Fax: (202) 328 2152.
E-mail: polconsul.dc@ioip.com
Consulates also in: Chicago, Los Angeles and New York.

Polish National Tourist Office
5 Marine View Plaza, Suite 208, Hoboken, New Jersey 07030, USA
Tel: (201) 420 9910.
Fax: (201) 584 9153.
E-mail: pntonyc@polandtour.org
Website: www.polandtour.org
Also deals with enquiries from Canada.

Embassy of the United States of America
Aleje Ujazdowskie 29-31, 00-540 Warsaw, Poland
Tel: (22) 504 2000. Fax: (22) 504 2688.
E-mail: publicwrw@state.gov
Website: www.usinfo.pl
Consulate General in: Kraków.

Embassy of the Republic of Poland
443 Daly Avenue, Ottawa, Ontario K1N 6H3, Canada
Tel: (613) 789 0468. Fax: (613) 789 1218.
E-mail: ottawa@polishembassy.ca
Website: www.polishembassy.ca
Consulates General in: Montréal, Toronto and Vancouver.

Canadian Embassy
Ul. Jana Matejki 1/5, 00-481, Warsaw, Poland
Tel: (22) 584 3100. Fax: (22) 584 3192.
E-mail: wsaw@dfait-maeci.gc.ca
Website: www.dfait-maeci.gc.ca/warsaw

General Information

AREA: 312,685 sq km (120,728 sq miles).
POPULATION: 38,610,000 (official estimate 2002).
POPULATION DENSITY: 122.3 per sq km.
CAPITAL: Warsaw. **Population:** 1,609,800 (official estimate 2001).
GEOGRAPHY: Poland shares borders to the east with the Russian Federation, Belarus, Ukraine and Lithuania, to the south with the Czech Republic and the Slovak Republic and to the west with Germany. To the north lies the Baltic Sea. The Baltic coast provides over 500km (300 miles) of sandy beaches, bays, steep cliffs and dunes. Northern Poland is dominated by lakes, islands and wooded hills joined by many rivers and canals. The Mazurian Lake District to the northeast is particularly beautiful. Lake Hancza, the deepest lake in Poland, is located in this district. The River Vistula has cut a wide valley from Gdansk on the Baltic coast to Warsaw in the heart of the country. The rest of the country rises slowly to the Sudety Mountains, which run along the border with the Czech Republic, and the Tatra mountains, which separate Poland from the Slovak Republic. To the west, the River Oder, with Szczecin at its mouth, forms the northwest border with Germany.
GOVERNMENT: Republic since 1918. **Head of State:** President Aleksander Kwasniewski since 1995. **Head of Government:** Prime Minister Marek Belka since 2004.
LANGUAGE: Polish is the official language. There is a small German-speaking community. English and Russian are also spoken.
RELIGION: More than 95 per cent Roman Catholic; other religions include Polish Autocephalous Orthodox, Russian and Greek Orthodox, Protestant, Jewish and Muslim.
TIME: GMT + 1.
ELECTRICITY: 220 volts AC, 50Hz; continental sockets.
COMMUNICATIONS: Telephone: Full IDD is available. Country code: 48. Outgoing international code: 00. Cheap rate on long-distance calls is available from 1600-0600. Telephone cards can be purchased from post offices, newsagents and hotel receptions for local calls. **Mobile telephone:** GSM 900 and 1800 networks cover the whole country. **Internet:** ISPs include *SuperMedia* (website: www.supermedia.com.pl). **Telegram:** Services are provided at all main post offices and by phone. **Post:** Service to Western Europe takes up to four days. *Poste Restante* facilities are available at post offices throughout the country. Post office hours: Mon-Fri 0800-1800. **Press:** Independent publications are flourishing following the changes in the political system; about 100 newspapers are now available. The principal dailies are *Gazeta Wyborcza*, *Rzeczpospolita* and *Wprost*. English-language publications include *The Warsaw Voice* (weekly).
Radio: BBC World Service (website: www.bbc.co.uk/worldservice) and Voice of America (website: www.voa.gov) can be received. From time to time the frequencies change and the most up-to-date can be found online.

Passport/Visa

	Passport Required?	Visa Required?	Return Ticket Required?
Full British	Yes	No/1	No
Australian	Yes	No/2	No
Canadian	Yes	No/2	No
USA	Yes	No/2	No
Other EU	Yes	No/1	No
Japanese	Yes	No/2	No

Note: *Regulations and requirements may be subject to change at short notice, and you are advised to contact the appropriate diplomatic or consular authority before finalising travel arrangements. Details of these may be found at the head of this country's entry. Any numbers in the chart refer to the footnotes below.*

PASSPORTS: Passport valid for at least six months beyond date of arrival required by all.
VISAS: Required by all except the following:
(a) **1.** nationals of the UK for stays not exceeding 180 days and all other EU nationals for 90 days;
(b) **2.** nationals of Andorra, Argentina, Australia, Bolivia, Brazil, Brunei, Canada, Chile, Costa Rica, Croatia, Guatemala, Honduras, Hong Kong (SAR), Iceland, Israel, Japan, Korea (Rep), Liechtenstein, Macau (SAR), Malaysia, Mexico, Monaco, New Zealand, Nicaragua, Norway, Panama, Romania, Salvador, San Marino, Singapore, Switzerland, Uruguay, USA, Vatican City and Venezuela for stays not exceeding 90 days.
Types of visa and cost: *Short-stay* (one to 90 days): £26 (single-entry), £34 (double-entry), £42 (multiple-entry). *Long-validity* (more than 90 days): £51 (single-entry), £59 (double-entry), £68 (multiple-entry). *Transit* (one to five days): £9 (single-entry), £17 (double-entry), £26 (multiple-entry). *Work* (one year maximum, mutiple-entry): £94. Payment is non-refundable even if visa is rejected. Reduced prices are available for students aged under 26 with appropriate identification, and for children.
Concessions are also available for foreigners whose spouse is a Polish citizen. Visas applied for in person can be issued the next day for an express service fee of £22. Contact Consulate (or Consular section at Embassy) for further details.
Validity: Short-stay visas are valid up to 90 days from date of entry. Extensions can be arranged in Poland through the district passport office. Work visas are valid for a maximum of one year. Transit visas are valid for up to five days. Airport Transit visas allow passage through the international zone of an airport and are valid for two days.
Application to: Consulate (or Consular section at Embassy); see *Contact Addresses* section for details.
Application requirements: (a) Passport (must be valid for three months after planned departure from Poland). (b) Completed application form. (c) One passport-size photo. (d) Evidence of immigration status in country of residence, endorsed in current or previous passport (if applicable). (e) Fee, payable by cash or postal order. *Short-stay:* (a)-(e) and, (f) Confirmation of travel itinerary, accommodation booking or invitation from friends or family in Poland. The invitation should be entered in the register of invitations in a Regional Office. *Long-validity:* (a)-(e) and, (f) Letter from applicant's company or organisation and original of a 'Work Promise'. Self-employed persons should produce an invitation from the business partner from Poland. If studying in Poland, an official letter from a college or university must be produced. *Transit:* (a)-(e) and, (f) The visa for country of destination. (g) Transport documentation, such as a rail or aeroplane ticket.
Note: Applications submitted without these requirements will not be considered by the Consular offices and will be returned to the applicant. Holders of Polish visas are still subject to immigration control at the Polish border and are not guaranteed entry. All visitors must possess sufficient funds to cover the cost of their stay.
Working days required: Three. For the following passport holders it may take several weeks (minimum two weeks): Afghanistan, Albania, Algeria, Angola, Armenia, Azerbaijan, Bangladesh, Bosnia and Herzegovina, Burundi, China (PR), Congo (Dem Rep), Congo (Rep), Eritrea, Ethiopia, Georgia, Guinea, India, Iran, Iraq, Jordan, Laos, Lebanon, Libya, Liberia, Morocco, Nigeria, Pakistan, The Phillipines, Rwanda, Serbia and Montenegro, Sierra Leone, Somalia, Sri Lanka, the Syrian Arab Republic, Tanzania, Turkey, Vietnam or holders of travel documents for stateless persons and refugees. Express visas can be processed within 24 hours for a fee of £22. Postal applications may take up to two weeks (no express service available).
Temporary residence: Apply to Consulate.

Money

Currency: Zloty (Zl) = 100 groszy. Notes are in denominations of Zl200, 100, 50, 20 and 10. The new coins are in denominations of Zl5, 2 and 1, and 50, 20, 10, 5, 2 and 1 groszy.

Currency exchange: Foreign currency can be exchanged at all border crossing points, hotels and bureaux de change, some of which are open 24 hours. Cash can also be obtained from Visa credit cards at banks.
Credit & debit cards: American Express, Diners Club, MasterCard and Visa are accepted in larger establishments. Check with your credit or debit card company for details of merchant acceptability and other services which may be available.
Travellers cheques: Readily exchanged. To avoid additional exchange rate charges, travellers are advised to take travellers cheques in Pounds Sterling.
Currency restrictions: The import and export of local currency is prohibited. The import of foreign currency is unlimited, provided declared on arrival. The export of foreign currency is limited to the amount declared on arrival.
Exchange rate indicators: The following figures are included as a guide to the movements of the Zloty against Sterling and the US Dollar:

Date	Feb '04	May '04	Aug '04	Nov '04
£1.00=	7.03	7.11	6.65	6.02
$1.00=	3.86	3.98	3.61	3.18

Banking hours: Mon-Fri 0900-1600, Sat 0900-1300 in main cities. In smaller towns, banking hours are more limited.

Duty Free

The following items may be imported into Poland by persons of 17 years of age and over without incurring customs duty:
250 cigarettes or 50 cigars or 250g of tobacco; 1l of wine and 1l of spirits; goods up to the value of €70.
Prohibited items: The export of all articles of artistic, historical or cultural value is subject to special regulations. Parrots, although in special cases permission is obtainable from the Ministry of Agriculture.

Abolition of duty free goods within the EU: On June 30 1999, the sale of duty free alcohol and tobacco at airports and at sea was abolished in all of the original 15 EU member states. Of the 10 new member states that joined the EU on May 1 2004, these rules already apply to Cyprus and Malta. There are transitional rules in place for visitors returning to one of the original 15 EU countries from one of the other new EU countries. But for the original 15, plus Cyprus and Malta, there are now no limits imposed on importing tobacco and alcohol products from one EU country to another (with the exceptions of Denmark, Finland and Sweden, where limits *are* imposed). Travellers should note that they may be required to prove at customs that the goods purchased are for personal use *only*.

Public Holidays

2005: Jan 1 New Year's Day. **Mar 28** Easter Monday. **May 1** Labour Day. **May 3** National Day. **May 26** Corpus Christi. **Aug 15** Assumption. **Nov 1** All Saint's Day. **Nov 11** Independence Day. **Dec 25-26** Christmas.
2006: Jan 1 New Year's Day. **Mar 17** Easter Monday. **May 1** Labour Day. **May 3** National Day. **Jun 15** Corpus Christi. **Aug 15** Assumption. **Nov 1** All Saints' Day. **Nov 11** Independence Day. **Dec 25-26** Christmas.

Health

	Special Precautions?	Certificate Required?
Yellow Fever	No	No
Cholera	No	No
Typhoid & Polio	No	N/A
Malaria	No	N/A

Note: Regulations and requirements may be subject to change at short notice, and you are advised to contact your doctor well in advance of your intended date of departure. Any numbers in the chart refer to the footnotes below.

Food & drink: Mains water is normally chlorinated, and whilst relatively safe may cause mild abdominal upsets. Bottled water is available and is advised for the first few weeks of the stay. Milk is pasteurised and dairy products are safe for consumption. Local meat, poultry, seafood, fruit and vegetables are generally considered safe to eat.
Other risks: *Hepatitis A* and *B* and *diphtheria* occur. Freshwater fish from the Baltic Sea area could contain fish tapeworm, causing *diphyllobothriasis*. *Tick-borne encephalitis* occurs in forested areas. Vaccination is advisable. Campers and trekkers should wear long trousers when walking near long grass in order to avoid tick bites. *Rabies* is present. For those at high risk, vaccination before arrival should be considered. If you are bitten, seek medical advice without delay. For more information, consult the *Health* appendix.

Credit: © Polish National Tourist Office

Health care: There are reciprocal health agreements with most European countries for hospital treatment and medical expenses. The agreement with the UK allows free emergency medical treatment (including hospital treatment) and some free dental treatment on presentation of an NHS card. UK citizens must, however, pay a call-out charge as well as 30 per cent of the cost of prescribed medicines obtained at a public pharmacy.

Travel - International

AIR: Poland's national airline is *LOT Polish Airlines (LO)* (website: www.lot.com). Other airlines serving Poland include *Aeroflot, Air France, Austrian Airlines, British Airways, Easyjet, El Al, Lufthansa, Ryanair, SAS* and *Swiss*.
Approximate flight times: From Warsaw to *London* is two hours, to *Frankfurt/M* is one hour 50 minutes, and to *Prague* is one hour 20 minutes.
International airports: *Warsaw (WAW)* (Okecie) is 10km (6 miles) southwest of the city (travel time – 20-40 minutes by bus; 20-30 minutes by taxi). Full duty free facilities are available. Airport facilities include post office, banks and bureaux de change, bars and restaurants, left-luggage facilities, tourist information services and car hire (*Avis, Budget, Hertz, National* and *Thrifty*).
Kraków (KRK) (Balice John Paul II) is 16km (10 miles) west of the city centre. Buses and taxis are available. Airport facilities include bar, bureau de change and car hire (Ann, Avis, Budget, Europcar and Hertz). There are duty free facilities in the departure hall.
Wroclaw (WRO) (Strachowice) (website: www.airport.wroclaw.pl) is 8km (5 miles) from the city centre. Airport facilities include a bank, duty free shop, post office, restaurants and shops. Buses, taxis and car hire are also available. There is a daily connection to Frankfurt/M and twice weekly (Thurs and Sun) to Düsseldorf. Katowice (KTW) is 34km (21 miles) from the city. There are connections to Copenhagen, Frankfurt/M and Munich daily. *Gdansk (GDN)* (website: www.airport.gdansk.pl) is the most common entry point into northern Poland.
Departure tax: None.
SEA: *Pol Ferries* operates between Poland and Sweden, Denmark and Finland. For further information, contact the Polish National Tourist Office (see *Contact Addresses* section) *or* Pol Ferries, ul. Chalubinskiego 8, 00-613, Warsaw (tel: (22) 830 0930; fax: (22) 830 0071; e-mail: info@polferries.pl; website: www.polferries.com). Tickets can also be purchased from travel agents or the ferry terminal (tel: (58) 343 1887).
RAIL: *Polish State Railways (PKP)* (website: www.pkp.pl) operates *EuroCity* trains between Poland and a number of major European cities. All services from Western Europe to Poland pass through the Czech Republic, Germany or the Slovak Republic. The main routes link Warsaw with Berlin and Cologne, Budapest, Prague and Vienna. There is a car-sleeper service from the Hook of Holland to Poznan/Warsaw.
ROAD: Poland is best reached from the Czech Republic and Germany or the car-sleeper rail service from the Hook of Holland to Poznan/Warsaw. There are extensive **bus** and **coach** services. *Eurolines*, departing from Victoria Coach Station in London, serves destinations in Poland. For further information contact *Eurolines* (tel: (08705) 143 219; e-mail: welcome@eurolines.co.uk; website: www.eurolines.com).

Travel - Internal

AIR: All internal airlines are operated by *LOT Polish Airlines* (website: www.lot.com) and there is a comprehensive network linking all major cities.
RAIL: Cheap and efficient *InterCity* trains are operated by *Polish State Railways (PKP)* (website: www.pkp.pl) and link all parts of the country in a network radiating from Warsaw. There are two classes of travel. The *Polrailpass* (and *Junior Polrailpass* for travellers under 26) is available for eight, 15, 21 or 30 days. This pass is available from travel agents and international rail ticket outlets, as well as from railway stations and travel agents within Poland. Children under four years of age travel free. Children aged four to 10 pay half fare.
ROAD: Traffic drives on the right. Poland has a dense network of filling stations. Unleaded petrol is available in most of the petrol stations. Most filling stations located along international routes are open 24 hours a day. The Polish Automobile and Motorway Federation *Polski Zwiazek Motorowy (PZM)* can be called on 9637 nationwide for assistance. Starter emergency breakdown service can be called on (0801) 122 222. For further information, contact Polski Zwiazek Motorowy, ul Kazimierzowska 66, 02-518 Warsaw (tel: (22) 849 9361; fax: (22) 848 1951; e-mail: office@pzm.pl; website: www.pzm.pl). **Bus:** There are good regional bus and coach services operated by Polish Motor Communications (PKS) as well as the Polski Express connecting most towns. **Car hire:** Self-drive cars are available at the airport or through various car rental offices in town centres. The minimum age is 21. Charges are usually based on a daily rate plus a kilometre charge. **Regulations:** Speed limit is 60kph (40mph) in built-up areas, 90kph (57mph) on major roads and 110kph (69mph) on motorways. Seat belts and warning triangles are compulsory. Trams have the right of way. From 1 October to 1 April, all vehicles should have their lights switched on at all times. **Documentation:** Tourists travelling in their own cars should have car registration cards, their national driving licence (driving licences of EU nationals are accepted) and valid Green Card motor insurance. An International Driving Permit is also required.
URBAN: Bus: There are good services in all towns, with additional trams and trolleybuses operating in a dozen of the larger urban areas. Warsaw has bus, tramway and rail services. A flat fare is charged and there are pre-purchase tickets and passes. **Tram:** Weekend and seven-day tourist tickets can be purchased. Most public transport operates from 0530-2300. **Taxi:** These are available in all main towns. They are usually found at ranks or can be ordered by phone. There is a surcharge from 2300-0500 and for journeys out of town, as well as at weekends. Taxi drivers may insist on payment in hard currency. **Tipping** is welcomed.
Travel times: The following chart gives approximate travel times (in hours and minutes) from **Warsaw** to other major cities/towns in Poland.

	Air	Road	Rail
Kraków	1.40	4.00	2.35
Poznan	1.00	4.00	3.00
Wroclaw	1.15	6.00	4.35
Gdansk	1.00	6.00	3.40
Szczecin	2.00	8.00	5.40
Katowice	1.30	4.30	2.35
Lódz	-	2.00	1.40

Accommodation

HOTELS: Most major international hotel chains are represented in Poland. International Student Hotels offer better facilities than youth hostels and are inexpensive, comfortable and pleasant. **Grading:** Hotels in Poland are graded in five categories: **luxury**, **4-star**, **3-star**, **2-star** and **1-star**. In addition there are tourist hotels, boarding houses and motels, each graded into three or four categories. For further information, contact the Polish Hotel Association, Ul. Nowogrodzka 44 m 2, 00-695 Warsaw (tel: (22) 622 6991-3; fax: (22) 622 6992; e-mail: hotel@hotel.pl; website: www.hotel.pl).

Credit: © Polish National Tourist Office

GUEST HOUSES: Three categories are available in all towns and run by regional tourist boards. Reservations can be made from local offices.
CAMPING/CARAVANNING: There are many campsites in Poland, nearly 75 per cent of which are fitted with 220-volt powerpoints and several with 24-volt points for caravans. Facilities also include washrooms, canteens and nearby restaurants and food kiosks. The main camping season is June to August. Holders of an international camping card (FICC) qualify for a 10 per cent rebate on rates. **Grading:** There are two categories. Category I sites cover an area of 100 sq m (10,764 sq ft) and have 24-hour reception and lighting. For more information, contact the Polish Federation of Camping and Caravanning (*Polska Federacja Campingui I Caravaningu*), Ul. Grochowska 331, 03-838 Warsaw (tel/fax: (22) 810 6050; e-mail: biuro@pfcc.info; website: www.pfcc.info).
YOUTH HOSTELS: There are about 446 hostels in Poland. Addresses can be found in the *Youth Hostel Handbook* published by the Polish Youth Hostels Association. For further information contact the Polish Youth Hostels Association (*Polskie Towarzystwo Schronisk Mlodziezowych*), Ul. Chocimska 28, 00-791 Warsaw (tel: (22) 849 8128; fax: (22) 849 8354; e-mail: hostellingpol.ptsm@pro.onet.pl).

Resorts & Excursions

Poland is now one of the major destinations for travellers. Its beauty can be admired in both its old cities and in the wild scenery of 22 national parks, about 1200 nature reserves, more than 100 landscape parks and 400 protected areas. The country's regions are largely divided into horizontal bands: the Baltic Coast and the hilly post-glacial lake district. Central Poland is split into northern lowlands and southern uplands, including the Kraków-Wielun Upland with its limestone areas, caves and medieval castles. The Carpathian Mountains, including the Tatras, lie in the extreme south; their mountain scenery, folklore and sports facilities are important parts of their charm.

WARSAW

Spanning both banks of the **River Wisla** (**Vistula**), Poland's capital and largest city was almost completely destroyed during World War II. Following massive and painstaking reconstruction, **Warsaw's Old Town** (**Stare Miasto**) on the west bank was authentically reconstructed from original plans and is now a UNESCO World Heritage Site. The Polish capital plays an important role in the country's cultural life and there are over 20 museums. One of the best is the **Warsaw Historical Museum**, which traces Warsaw's history and shows films shot by the Nazis showing their systematic destruction of the city. The **National Museum** has a superb collection of art and archaeology. **Zamek Królewski**, the reconstructed Royal Castle, is now an important museum of fine and applied arts. The **Wilanów Palace** has a spectacular collection of old paintings and furniture; its **Orangerie** holds the new **Museum of Posters**. The enormous **Palace of Culture and Science** was an unwelcome gift from Josef Stalin; however, it offers wonderful views over the whole city. The **Lazienki Palace** is set in a lovely park with an open-air Greek theatre and a monument to the famous Polish composer Frederic Chopin. The **National** and the **Polish** are the most renowned of the city's many **theatres**. **Zelazowa Wola**, 53km (32 miles) west of Warsaw, is an attractive park in which stands the manor house where Chopin was born. Nature enthusiasts can visit the nearby **Kampinos National Park**, where it is possible to see wild boar and elk.

THE EAST

Lublin is a charming medieval university city 164km (102 miles) southeast of Warsaw. Still further east on the banks of the **River Labunka** is **Zamosc**, founded at the end of the 16th century and once an important centre on the trade route linking Northern and Western Europe to the **Black Sea**. Its **Old Town** has recently been declared a UNESCO World Heritage Site. Its focal point is the **Market Square**; the old and new **Lublin Gates** indicate the city's former role as an important regional fortress. Lublin is given a southern flavour through the many buildings designed by Bernardo Morando of Padua, and by the many Armenians and Greeks who settled here. The **Bialowieza National Park**, an area of primal forest straddling the border with Belarus, is the last major refuge of the European bison as well as being home to many other rare forest-dwelling species.

THE SOUTH

KRAKÓW: Poland's second city also stands on the banks of the River Wisla (Vistula), but far to the south in the wooded foothills of the Tatra Mountains. It still retains its charming medieval air, having largely escaped destruction during World War II; it is one of UNESCO's 12 most significant historical sites. In the middle of the central **Market Square** – the largest in Europe – is the **Cloth Hall**, which was reconstructed in the 19th century from 14th-century merchants' stalls; this houses the art and sculpture galleries of the **National Museum**. Opposite is **St Mary's Church** with its world-famous wooden altar carved by Wit Stwosz. The **Jagiellonian University**, founded in 1364, is one of the oldest in Europe. After many years of neglect, Kraków's former Jewish quarter, **Kazimierz**, is reviving; the **Old Synagogue** (1557) is the oldest surviving in the country. Also in Kazimierz is the country's largest **Ethnographic Museum**. Kraków was Poland's capital until 1596. Overlooking the city is **Wawel Castle**, with its marvellous 16th-century tapestries and, beside it, the Gothic **Cathedral**, where many Polish kings are buried. The **Czartoryski Palace** houses the city's best collection of ancient art, European paintings and crafts.
EXCURSIONS: Another of Poland's UNESCO World Heritage Sites is the cathedral-like salt mines at **Wieliczka**, 13km (8 miles) from Kraków. The subterranean route spans 4.5km (2.8 miles) leading to the oldest part of the mine through 14th- and 15th-century chapels and crystal caves. 70km (43 miles) from Kraków lies the site of the **Oswiecim-Birkenau** (**Auschwitz-Birkenau**) concentration camp in which 4 million people were killed by the Nazis. The camp area has been designated as a memorial monument and a World Heritage Site by UNESCO.
Other important nearby locations include the **Bledowska Desert**, perhaps the only true desert in Europe; **Wadowice**, the birthplace of Pope John Paul II; and the **Icon of the Black Madonna** in the huge Jasna Góra monastery complex at **Czestochowa**, 100km (60 miles) north of Kraków (reputed to have been painted by St Luke).
Bieszczadski National Park is part of the **Carpathian mountain range** and contains the surviving fragments of the **Great Bieszczady Forest**, home to the brown bear, lynx and wildcat.

TATRY (TATRAS MOUNTAINS)

Although the 80km of the Tatras in the extreme south are only a small part of the entire range, they attract over 1.5 million visitors every year, with high peaks for climbing, excellent trails, cable cars and superb wintersports facilities. **Zakopane**, about 112km (70 miles) south of Kraków in the foothills, is a charming resort and wintersports centre. There is a fairytale atmosphere here, with its 'gingerbread' wooden cottages and many inhabitants who still wear national dress. There are four National Parks in the Tatras: **Babiogórski**, **Gorczanski**, **Pieninski** (also with the beautiful mountain gorge of the River Dunajec) and **Tatrzanski**. Camping is not allowed in the parks; climbing is, but only with a guide. Organised trips are available to the **Koscieliska Valley**, through beautiful countryside; the mountain of **Kasprowy Wierch** by means of a cable car offering spectacular views; and **Morskie Oko**, the glacial lake which is one of the Tatras' main attractions.

THE WEST (SILESIA AND WIELKOPOLSKA)

The principal city in the southwest and the capital of Lower Silesia, **Wroclaw** (**Breslau**) can claim to be the cradle of the Polish state: it was here that the Polanie tribe built their first fortified settlement (on **Ostrow Tumski Island**). During the 14th century, the city fell under the rule of Bohemia, followed by the Hapsburgs in the 16th century, and later the Prussians and the German Third Reich. During World War II the town had become a Nazi stronghold, 'Festung Breslau'. But after the war the German population was forced to leave and large numbers of displaced Poles from Lwów (now L'viv) in the Polish Ukraine were encouraged to move there. The mingling of the inhabitants of these two great cities has greatly shaped Wroclaw's culture. The modern city is threaded with 90km (56 miles) of canals and tributaries of the **River Oder** and there are more than 100 bridges. Important sights include the 15th-century **Town Hall**, now the **Historical Museum**; the **Ethnographic Museum** in the **Royal Palace**; and the **Cathedral** on **Ostrow Tumski** (**Cathedral Island**). The 120m (400ft) by 15m (50ft) tall painting, *Panorama of the Battle of Raclawice*, remains the city's best-loved sight; painted in 1894, it celebrates the Russian army's defeat by Tadeusz Krsciuszko's people's militia. Within easy travel from the city are the spas and health resorts of the **Klodzko Valley**, the rugged **Stolowe Mountains**, the ski resorts in the **Karkonosze Mountains** (part of which is a national park) on the border with the Czech Republic, and the many picturesque medieval (and earlier) towns in the region, such as **Boleslawiec**, **Paczkow** and **Swidnica**.
Wielkopolska is the core of the original Polish nation. **Poznan**, the sedate regional capital, stands beside the **River Warta** in the middle of the flatlands north of Silesia. Important sights include the Italianate **Town Hall** in the **Old Market Square**, the **Gorki Palace**, the 12th-century **Church of St John** and **Przemyslaw Castle**, once the seat of the Grand Dukes of Poland. The **National Museum** houses one of the country's few displays of old master paintings. Watersports can be enjoyed in and on the many lakes in the woods surrounding the city. The *Poznan International Trade Fair* is held here every year in June.

THE NORTH

Formerly known as **Danzig**, the important Baltic port of **Gdansk** has had a troubled history. The Order of Teutonic Knights took it from the Poles in the 14th century and later lost it to the Prussians. In the 20th century, it lost its status as a free city when it was attacked and occupied by Nazi Germany in 1939. Its **Lenin Shipyards** were the birthplace of **Solidarnosc** (**Solidarity**) and thus of today's democratic Poland. Almost the entire city was destroyed in World War II, but was restored to its former glory. The city is now a provincial capital at the mouth of the **Wisla** (**Vistula**) and **Motlawa rivers** and a commercial, industrial and scientific centre. The city has the largest Gothic church in Poland – and possibly the largest brick building in the world – the **Church of the Virgin Mary** (**Kosciol Mariacki**). The 17th-century **Golden Gate** and the **Court of the Fraternity of St George** can be viewed along the spectacular **Royal Way**, one of Gdansk's most historic streets. The **National Art Museum** has an excellent collection of Gothic art and sculpture. The beach resort at nearby **Sopot** has Europe's longest pier (500m/1640ft). Within easy reach are the forested **Hel Peninsula**, the **Kashubian Lakeland**, and the Teutonic castles at **Malbork** (**Marienburg**), **Gniew** and elsewhere. There is also a narrow-gauge railway that runs along the **Vistula Spit** offering an attractive way to see part of the Baltic coast.
Spread across the northeast is **Mazuria**, a huge, thinly populated area of lakes, dense forests and swamps. It is rich in wildlife, including wild bison and Europe's largest herd of elks, and offers every form of outdoor pursuit – sailing, canoeing, camping – even mushroom-picking. In the heart of the Mazurian forest, at **Ketrzyn** (Rastenburg), is the site of **Hitler's 'Eagle's Nest'**, the concrete bunker where members of his High Staff attempted to assassinate him in August 1944. The medieval walled town of **Torun**, a UNESCO World Heritage Site on the banks of the River Wisla (Vistula) south of Gdansk, was the birthplace of the astronomer Copernicus (Mikolaj Kopernik). The most notable historic sites include **St Mary's Church**, **St John's Church** (where Copernicus was baptised); the striking Gothic **Town Hall** and the **Granaries** (which helped to make Torun a prosperous trade town). Important museums are the **Town Museum** with the wonderful stained glass for which the town was known, the **Copernicus Museum**, and the **Ethnographic Museum**. **Szczecin**, 60km (37 miles) upstream from the mouth of the **River Oder**, is the largest port on the Baltic Sea. Formerly known as Stettin, it was the capital of Pomerania and its sights include the Pomeranian princes' 14th-century **Palace** and the 12th-century **Cathedral**. The city was largely rebuilt in the last century taking Paris as a model, and has a spacious feel to it with many wide, tree-lined boulevards. It is easy to escape the cities of the north for the beach resorts of the Pomeranian coast, such as **Kolobrzeg** (large and fashionable) or **Leba** (a quiet resort with a beach of fabulous white sand), or the beech woods and islands of the **Wolin National Park**. **Slowinski National Park** is known for its giant 'wandering sand dunes' which can shift several metres each year.

Sport & Activities

Wintersports: The Tatra Mountains are Poland's main **skiing** destination, the most popular resort being Zakopane (see also *Resorts & Excursions* section). The season is from November through to May. The densely wooded *Bieszczady Mountains* in the southeast are highly rated for **cross-country skiing**. Another popular wintersport is **ice-boating** on Poland's frozen waterways. **Sleigh rides** used to be popular with the Polish gentry and 'traditional' rides are available in most resorts.
Watersports: Poland's Baltic coast stretches for some 528km (330 miles), with long sandy beaches. Pollution levels in the Baltic sea are relatively high, particularly in the Bay of Gdánsk. Water temperatures are fairly cold, rising to a maximum of 20°C (68°F) during summer. Cleaner and safer **swimming** is available in the Mazurian Lake District

(consisting of approximately 3000 lakes), also a favourite **angling** destination. Poland's rivers (such as the Parseta, Rega and Stupia) are particularly good for bull trout. Tourists need to buy a fishing licence. For **sailing**, the Augustow, Ilawa and Mazurian lakes are best. **Canoeists** may also head to the Brodnica or Mysliborz lakelands, or the rivers Brda, Czarna Hancza and Obra where canoeing trips lasting up to 12 days can be undertaken. However, the main waterways are pretty polluted.
Hang gliding: Both hang gliding and **paragliding** are popular in the Beskid, Bieszczady and Sudety mountains. The town of Leszno is Poland's main gliding centre.
Other: Poland's national parks and nature reserves offer a variety of **hiking** trails through different types of landscapes ranging from dunes, beaches, rivers and lakes to deep forests and high mountains. Nature and wildlife enthusiasts can observe elks in Poland's marshes and European bison in the Bialowieza forest. Poland is also reputed to have Europe's largest population of storks. All the parks are open to visitors, though some may only be entered on foot and others, such as the *Bialowieza National Park*, may only be toured with a guide. Accommodation and catering facilities are available either within or near all parks. Different types of **cycling** routes are available throughout the country. Special cycling lanes are provided around larger cities. Cycling tours (notably through the Great Mazurian Lake District) are offered by specialist tour operators. **Mountain biking** is popular in the Bieszczady and Karkonosze mountains. Horses have traditionally been popular in Poland and **horseriding** enthusiasts have a large choice of riding schools to choose from. Polish stud farms are internationally renowned and welcome guests; board and lodging is provided and many stables also offer riding instruction. Horse auctions are held at Janów Podlaski, Poznan, Racot and Walewice. The main horseracing tracks are Warsaw (Sluzewiec), Sopot, Raculka (near Zielona Gora), Bialy Bor (near Slupsk) and Ksiaz (near Walbrzych). Inexperienced riders may prefer riding a *Hucul* – a very rare Polish mountain pony.

Social Profile

FOOD & DRINK: Poland has a distinctive cuisine, with typical ingredients being dill, marjoram, caraway seeds, wild mushrooms and sour cream, which is frequently added to soups, sauces and braised meats. The national dish of Poland is *bigos*, made with sauerkraut, fresh cabbage, onions and any variety of leftover meat. Polish meals start with *przekaski* (starters), such as pike in aspic, marinated fish in sour cream, salted and rolled herring fillets with pickles and onions, *kulebiak* (a large mushroom and cabbage pasty) or Polish sausages such as the long, thin and highly spiced *kabanos* or the hunters' sausage (*mysliwska*) made with pork and game. Soups play an important part at mealtimes and are usually rich and very thick. Soups such as *barszcz* (beetroot soup, excellent with sour cream) or *rosol* (beef or chicken bouillon) are often served in cups with small hot pasties stuffed with meat or cabbage. Popular dishes include *zrazy zawijane* (mushroom-stuffed beefsteak rolls in sour cream) served with boiled *kasza* (buckwheat) and pig's knuckles. Poland is also a good country for fish (*ryba*) such as carp served in sweet-and-sour jellied sauce, and poached pike with horseradish in cream. Herring (*sledz*) is particularly popular and is served up in countless different ways. Pastries (*ciastka*) are also very good. Table service is the norm in restaurants.
Vodka (*wódka*), the national drink, is drunk chilled. *Wyborowa* is considered the best standard vodka, but there are many flavoured varieties such as *zubrowka* (bison grass), *tarniowka* (sloe plum), *sliwowica* (prune) and *pieprzowka* (vodka with ground white pepper). Western drinks, such as whisky, gin or brandy, can be obtained in most bars but are expensive. Wine is available but, again, is imported and expensive. The best bottled beer is *zywiec*, a fairly strong lager-type beer. Bars have table and/or counter service. Coffee shops are very popular in Poland and are the favourite places for social meetings from early morning to late at night. They do not close during the day and have the same function as do pubs in the United Kingdom. Alcoholic drinks are available throughout the day.
NIGHTLIFE: Warsaw also reflects the strong theatrical and musical traditions of Poland, with about 17 theatres and three opera companies. Cinemas in Poland show both Polish and foreign films. There are some discos in Poland, as well as a growing number of nightclubs and music bars in Warsaw.
SHOPPING: Special purchases include glass and enamelware, handwoven rugs, silverware, handmade jewellery with amber and silver, dolls in regional costumes, woodcarvings and clay and metal sculptures. **Shopping hours:** Mon-Fri 0600-1800/1900, shorter hours on Saturday and Sunday. 'Night shops' open 2000-0800. Supermarkets and department stores open Mon-Sat 0900-2000. Bookshops open Mon-Fri 1100-1900.
SPECIAL EVENTS: For a full list, contact the Polish National Tourist Office (see *Contact Addresses* section). The following is a selection of special events occurring in Poland in 2005:
Jan 28-30 *Ski-Jumping World Cup*, Zakopane. **Feb** *International Winter Kayaking Trip on the Brda River*. **Mar 15-26** *9th Ludwig van Beethoven Easter Festival*, Warsaw. **Apr 23-May 8** *12th Bydgoszcz Operatic Festival*, Bydgoszcz. **May 1-3** *Podkarpacki Tourist Fair*, Przemyœl. **Jun-Aug** *XIII Warsaw Summer Jazz Days*. **Jul 3-Aug 28** *XI Jazz in the Old Town International Outdoor Festival*, Warsaw. **Sep 28-Oct 24** *Chopin Piano Contest*, Warsaw. **Nov** *Masks International Theatrical Festival*, Poznañ. **Dec** *Nativity Scene Competition*, Kraków.
Note: The Cultural Information Centre publishes *Karnet*, a bilingual cultural monthly publication with details of cultural events. Contact the tourist board for further information.
SOCIAL CONVENTIONS: Poles are friendly, industrious people and foreigners are usually made very welcome. There are vast contrasts between urban and rural life and the Polish peasantry is very religious and conservative, maintaining a traditional lifestyle. Roman Catholicism plays an important role in daily life and criticism or jokes about religion are not appreciated, despite the general good humour of the people. Music and art are also important aspects of Polish culture. Shaking hands is the normal form of greeting. Normal courtesies are observed when visiting private homes and it is customary to bring flowers. Fairly conservative casual wear is the most suitable attire, but dress should be formal when specified for entertaining in the evening or in a smart restaurant. Smoking is restricted in some public buildings. **Photography:** Military installations such as bridges, ports, airports, border points etc should not be photographed. **Tipping:** 10 to 15 per cent is customary in restaurants and cafes. Tipping in self-service restaurants is not expected. Tips for porter's services in hotels and train stations are customary but amounts are at the traveller's discretion.

Business Profile

ECONOMY: As the largest economy in ex-Soviet eastern Europe, the fate of Poland was, and still is, central to that of the whole region. The economic contribution of the agricultural sector declined steadily throughout the 1990s and now accounts for just 3 per cent of the GDP, but still employs one-quarter of the workforce. Livestock and meat are major export earners; rye, wheat, oats, sugar beet and potatoes are the main crops. In the industrial sector, Poland's once substantial coal mining industry – like its counterparts elsewhere in Europe – has been scaled down in recent years. Other important industries are shipbuilding, textiles, steel, cement, chemicals and food processing. Again following the trend across the continent, industry's contribution to the GDP has declined to below 30 per cent, while the service sector has seen rapid growth.
With the collapse of the communist system at the end of the 1980s, Poland adopted the 'big bang' strategy of rapid transition to a market economy: price controls (including subsidies) were removed at a stroke; production, distribution and trade were deregulated; large parts of the economy were privatised using a voucher system; the tax and fiscal systems were overhauled; and the national currency (the Zloty) was made fully convertible. The shock of these measures and the collapse of the Comecon trading system threw the economy into temporary crisis, but it recovered quickly and by the mid-1990s was growing strongly. Many of those parts of the economy still under state ownership – including several important industrial enterprises – were privatised, albeit at a more leisurely pace. By 2000 the private sector accounted for 70 per cent of GDP. Over the next two years the economy suffered mild recession, but by the end of 2003 growth had reached 3.4 per cent and is still rising. Inflation is currently just below 3 per cent. Unemployment, however, has risen consistently since 2000 to its current level of 20.2 per cent, which is one of the highest levels in Europe. This, in turn, has led to the growth of a large informal or 'grey' economy, in which as many as two million people may be engaged.
Poland became a full member of the European Union on May 1 2004, and was one of 10 new entrants. The decision to join was endorsed by 77 per cent of the electorate in a June 2003 national referendum. Within the EU, Poland may be expected to work with its fellow members of the 'Visegrad Group' – Hungary and the Czech and Slovak Republics – who are also joining the EU. Where necessary, they will seek to protect their regional interests against the larger and more powerful Western European economies. Poland's main trading partners are Germany and the 'Visegrad Group' countries. Trade with other members of the EU, including the UK, has already grown substantially during the last decade and is set to increase further.
BUSINESS: In Poland, a formal approach is favoured and it is therefore advisable to give plenty of notice of an intended visit. Employees in state organisations do not take

Credit: © Polish National Tourist Office

a lunch break, but they have their main meal after 1500. **Office hours:** Mon-Fri 0800-1600.
COMMERCIAL INFORMATION: The following organisation can offer advice: Polish Chamber of Commerce (*Krajowa Izba Gospodarcza*), PO Box 361, Trebacka 4, 00-074 Warsaw (tel: (22) 630 9600; fax: (22) 827 4673; e-mail: kigcp@kig.pl; website: www.kig.pl).
CONFERENCES/CONVENTIONS: The most popular conference venues are in Warsaw. Events are also hosted in Kraków, while Gdansk, Wroclaw and other towns are used occasionally.

Climate

Temperate with warm summers, crisp, sunny autumns and cold winters. Snow covers the mountainous area in the south of Poland (mid-December to April). Rain falls throughout the year.
Required clothing: Light- to mediumweights are worn during warmer months. Medium- to heavyweights are needed during winter. Rainwear is advisable all year.

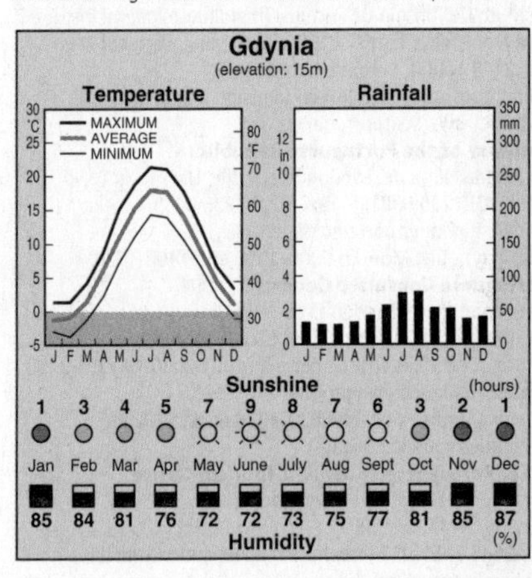

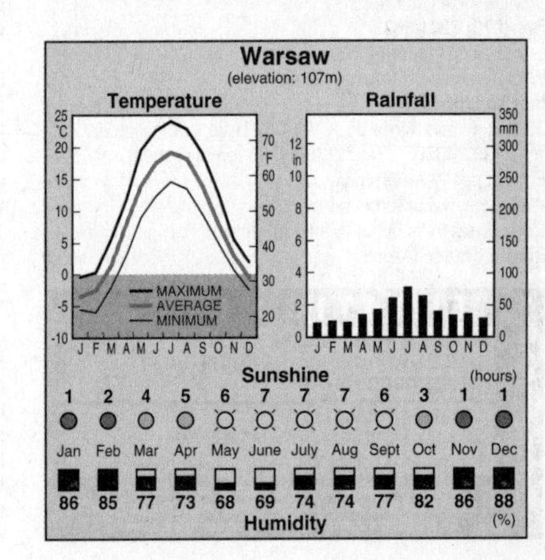

A B C D E F G H I J K L M N O P Q R S T U V W X Y Z

Portugal

LATEST TRAVEL ADVICE CONTACTS

British Foreign and Commonwealth Office
Tel: (0870) 606 0290 Website: www.fco.gov.uk

US Department of State
Website: http://travel.state.gov/travel

Canadian Department of Foreign Affairs and Int'l Trade
Tel: (1 800) 267 8376 Website: www.dfait-maeci.gc.ca

Location: Western Europe.

Country dialling code: 351.

ICEP Portugal (Investimentos, Comércio e Turismo de Portugal)
Instituto De Turismo De Portugal (Portuguese Tourism Institute)
Rua Ivone Silva, Lote 6 - 1050-124 Lisboa, Portugal
Tel: 2178 10000. Fax: 2176 15638/9
Email: turismo@itp.min-economia.pt
Website: www.visitportugal.pt

Embassy of the Portuguese Republic
11 Belgrave Square, London SW1X 8PP, UK
Tel: (020) 7235 5331. Fax: (020) 7235 0739.
E-mail: london@portembassy.co.uk
Opening hours: Mon-Fri 0900-1300 and 1400-1730.

Portuguese Consulate General
3 Portland Place, London W1B 1HR, UK
Tel: (020) 7291 3770 *or* (0906) 550 8948 (recorded visa information; calls cost £1 per minute). Fax: (020) 7291 3799.
E-mail: mail@cglon.dgaccp.pt
Opening hours: Mon-Fri 0830-1330 (closed UK and Portuguese public holidays).

ICEP/Portuguese Trade and Tourism Office
Portuguese Embassy, 11 Belgrave Square,
London SW1X 8PP, UK
Tel: 0845 35512112 (brochure request and information service; local call rate).
Fax: (020) 7201 6633.
E-mail: icep.london@icep.pt
Website: www.visitportugal.com

British Embassy
33 Rua de São Bernardo, 1249-082 Lisbon, Portugal
Tel: 2139 24000. Fax: 2139 24185 (press section).
E-mail: ppalisbon@fco.gov.uk
Website: www.uk-embassy.pt
Consulates in: Funchal (Madeira), Oporto, Portimão and Ribeira Grande (Azores).

TIMATIC CODES

Health	AMADEUS: **TI-DFT/LIS/HE** GALILEO/WORLDSPAN: **TI-DFT/LIS/HE** SABRE: **TIDFT/LIS/HE**
Visa	AMADEUS: **TI-DFT/LIS/VI** GALILEO/WORLDSPAN: **TI-DFT/LIS/VI** SABRE: **TIDFT/LIS/VI**

To access TIMATIC country information on Health and Visa regulations through the Computer Reservations System (CRS), type in the appropriate command line listed above.

Embassy of the Portuguese Republic
2012 Massachussetts Avenue, NW, Washington, DC 20008, USA
Tel: (202) 328 8610. Fax: (202) 462 3726.
E-mail: embportwash@attglobal.net
Consulates General in: Boston, Newark, New Bedford, New York, Providence, San Francisco and Washington, DC.

ICEP/Portuguese Trade and Tourism Office
590 Fifth Avenue, 4th Floor, New York, NY 10036, USA
Tel: (212) 723 0200/99. Fax: (212) 764 6137.
E-mail: tourism@portugal.org
Website: www.portugal.org

Embassy of the United States of America
Avenida das Forças Armadas, Sete Rios 1600-081 Lisbon, Portugal
Tel: 2172 73300.
Fax: 2172 69109 *or* 2172 71500 (consular section).
E-mail: conslisbon@state.gov
Website: www.american-embassy.pt
Consulate in: Ponta Delgada (Azores).

Embassy of the Portuguese Republic
645 Island Park Drive, Ottawa, Ontario K1Y 0B8, Canada
Tel: (613) 729 0883 *or* 729 2922. Fax: (613) 729 4236.
E-mail: embportugal@embportugal-ottawa.org
Website: www.embportugal-ottawa.org
Consulates in: Alberta, Edmonton, Montréal, Toronto, Vancouver and Winnipeg.

ICEP/Portuguese Trade and Tourism Office
60 Bloor Street W, Suite 1005, Toronto, Ontario M4W 3B8, Canada
Tel: (416) 921 7376. Fax: (416) 921 1353.
E-mail: icep.toronto@iceptor.ca
Website: www.visitportugal.com
Only deals with enquiries within Canada.

Canadian Embassy
Avenida da Liberdade 198-200, 3rd floor, 1269-121 Lisbon, Portugal
Tel: 2131 64600. Fax: 2131 64692.
E-mail: lsbon@dfait-maeci.gc.ca
Website: www.dfait-maeci.gc.ca/lisbon
Consulates in: Faro and Ponta Delgada (Azores).

General Information

AREA: 92,345 sq km (35,655 sq miles).
POPULATION: 10,407,000 (offcial estimate 2002).
POPULATION DENSITY: 112.7 per sq km.
CAPITAL: Lisbon. **Population:** 564,657; 1,900,000 in Greater Lisbon
GEOGRAPHY: Portugal occupies the southwest part of the Iberian Peninsula and shares borders in the north and the east with Spain, while to the south and west lies the Atlantic Ocean. The country is divided into various provinces, including the Atlantic islands of Madeira and the Azores; the latter lying some 1220km (760 miles) due west of Lisbon. The Douro, Guadiana and Tagus rivers flow across the border from Spain. North Portugal is mountainous, the highest part being the Serra da Estrela, a popular area for skiing. South of Lisbon stretch the vast plains of the Alentejo region. A range of mountains divides the Alentejo from the Algarve, which runs along the south coast, and is one of the most popular resort areas with wide sandy beaches and attractive bays.
GOVERNMENT: Republic since 1910. **Head of State:** President Jorge Fernando Branco de Sampaio since 1996. **Head of Government:** Prime Minister Pedro Santana Lopes since 2004.
LANGUAGE: Portuguese. English is widely spoken within the business community.
RELIGION: Roman Catholic.
TIME: GMT (GMT + 1 from last Sunday in March to last Sunday in October).
ELECTRICITY: 230 volts AC, 50Hz. 110 volts in some areas and 230 DC in parts of the south. Continental two-pin plugs are in use.
COMMUNICATIONS: Telephone: IDD is available. Country code: 351. Outgoing international code: 00. There are call boxes in most villages and all towns; there are also public telephones in many cafes and bars, from which international calls may be made. **Mobile telephone:** GSM 900/1800 networks. Operators include *Optimus* (website: www.optimus.pt), *TMN* (website: www.tmn.pt) and *Vodafone* (website: www.vodafone.pt). Coverage exists across the whole country. **Fax:** Available at fax bureaux and large hotels in major cities. **Internet:** ISPs include *Esoterica*, which operates an Internet Access Center, and *Comnexo*, *Sonet* and *Telepac*. Internet cafes exist in all urban areas, and some post offices offer Internet facilities. **Telegram:** There are telegram facilities at most major hotels. The public office at Praça dos Restauradores, Lisbon is open daily 0900-1800. **Post:** Post office (*correios*) hours: usually Mon-Fri 0800-2200, Sat-Sun 0900-1800. The post office at Lisbon Airport is open 24 hours a day. Airmail to European destinations from continental Portugal and the Azores takes three days; from Madeira, up to five days. There are *poste restante* facilities at post offices throughout the country.
Press: Each region has its own Portuguese-language dailies. The English-language newspapers published in Portugal include: *Anglo Portuguese News* (Lisbon), and *The News* (Algarve).
Radio: BBC World Service (website: www.bbc.co.uk/worldservice) and Voice of America (website: www.voa.gov) can be received. From time to time the frequencies change and the most up-to-date can be found online.

Passport/Visa

	Passport Required?	Visa Required?	Return Ticket Required?
Full British	Yes	No	2
Australian	Yes	No	2
Canadian	Yes	No	2
USA	Yes	No	2
Other EU	1	No	2
Japanese	Yes	No	2

Note: Regulations and requirements may be subject to change at short notice, and you are advised to contact the appropriate diplomatic or consular authority before finalising travel arrangements. Details of these may be found at the head of this country's entry. Any numbers in the chart refer to the footnotes below.

Note: Portugal is a signatory to the **1995 Schengen Agreement**. For further details about passport and visa regulations in the Schengen area see the introductory section *How to Use This Guide*.
PASSPORTS: Passport valid for at least three months beyond intended departure required by all except:
1. EU nationals and nationals of Iceland, Liechtenstein, Norway and Switzerland holding valid national ID cards.
Note: (a) Passport validity depends on nationality; for nationals of the UK, the passport must be valid for the duration of the stay in Portugal. (b) **2.** A return or onward ticket and funds of €75 plus €40 per day are obligatory for all except nationals of the EU, Iceland and Norway.
VISAS: Required by all except the following for stays of up to 90 days:
(a) nationals referred to in the chart and under passport exemptions above;
(b) nationals of Andorra, Argentina, Bolivia, Brazil, Brunei, Bulgaria, Chile, Costa Rica, Croatia, Cyprus, Czech Republic, El Salvador, Estonia, Guatemala, Honduras, Hong Kong (SAR), Hungary, Iceland, Israel, Korea (Rep), Latvia, Liechtenstein, Lithuania, Macau (SAR), Malaysia, Malta, Mexico, Monaco, New Zealand, Nicaragua, Norway, Panama, Paraguay, Poland, Romania, San Marino, Singapore, Slovak Republic, Slovenia, Switzerland, Uruguay, Vatican City and Venezuela;
(c) transit passengers continuing their journey by the same or first connecting aircraft, provided holding onward or return documentation and not leaving the airport. However, nationals of Afghanistan, Bangladesh, Congo (Dem Rep), Eritrea, Ethiopia, Ghana, Iran, Iraq, Liberia, Nigeria, Pakistan, Senegal, Somalia and Sri Lanka *always* require a transit visa, even when not leaving the airport transit area; contact the Consulate (or Consular section at Embassy) for details.
Types of visa and cost: A uniform type of visa, the *Schengen* visa, is issued for touristic, private or business visits. There are three types of Schengen visa: *Short-stay*, *Transit* and *Airport Transit*. Visa costs are dependent on the tariff charges of the issuing country and prices may vary with exchange rates. Check with your local Embassy for the most up-to-date prices.
Note: A Schengen visa will be issued free of charge to the spouse and children of an EU national, upon presentation of the original marriage or birth certificate and a valid EU passport. For children, original full birth certificates are required.
Validity: Transit visas are valid for single or two entries of maximum five days, including the day of arrival. Visas cannot be extended; a new application must be made each time.
Application to: Consulate (or Consular section at Embassy) responsible for your place of residence; see *Contact Addresses* section. Travellers visiting just one Schengen country should apply to the Consulate of that country; travellers visiting more than one Schengen country should apply to the Consulate of the country chosen as the main destination or the country they will enter first (if they have no main destination).
Application requirements: *Tourism:* (a) Passport or official travel documents accepted by Schengen countries, valid for at least three months longer than the validity of the visa, with blank page for attachment of visa sticker. (b) Application form. (c) One passport-size photo. (d) Proof of purpose of visit in the form of an official letter of invitation from host or business partner, provisional ticket booking and hotel booking where appropriate. (e) Proof of sufficient funds and medical insurance may also be required. (f) Fee (payable in cash or by postal order). (g) For postal applications, a large self-addressed envelope, stamped for registered or recorded delivery. (h) For applicants driving to

Portugal, registration document, proof of legal ownership of the vehicle, driving licence and insurance papers. Applicants entering Portugal by land must register with the Police within three days of arrival. *Business:* (a)-(g) and, (h) Letter from employer or, if self-employed, from solicitor, accountant, bank manager or local Chamber of Commerce stating purpose and duration of the visit. This should be faxed to the relevant Consulate at least 48 hours before submitting an application. References may also be required.
Working days required: From a few days to a few weeks. Apply in plenty of time.
Temporary residence: Contact the Consulate (or Consular section at Embassy) for further details; see *Contact Addresses* section.

Money

Single European currency (Euro): The Euro is now the official currency of 12 EU member states (including Portugal). The first Euro coins and notes were introduced in January 2002; the Portuguese Escudo was still in circulation until 28 February 2002, when it was completely replaced by the Euro. Euro (€) = 100 cents. Notes are in denominations of €500, 200, 100, 50, 20, 10 and 5. Coins are in denominations of €2 and 1, and 50, 20, 10, 5, 2 and 1 cents.
Currency exchange: Many banks offer differing exchange rates depending on the denominations of Portuguese currency being bought or sold. It is common practice for banks to charge 0.5 per cent commission with a minimum charge of approximately £6/€10. However, some banks do not charge any commission on transactions of less than €24.94. Check with banks for details and current rates. Additionally, ATMs are increasingly being installed and tend to be more efficient and only charge 2 per cent commission.
Credit & debit cards: American Express, MasterCard and Visa are widely accepted, as well as Eurocheque cards. Check with your credit or debit card company for details of merchant acceptability and other services that may be available.
Travellers cheques: These are readily exchanged. To avoid additional exchange rate charges, travellers are advised to take travellers cheques in Euros, Pounds Sterling or US Dollars.
Currency restrictions: The import of local or foreign currency in cash or travellers cheques is unlimited. However, there is an obligation to inform the customs authorities if foreign currencies exceed approximately €4987.98/US$6000. The export of local currency is limited to €498.80. There are no restrictions on the export of foreign currency although currency exchange receipts may be requested for amounts over €4987.98. The export of gold, silver, jewellery and other valuables is limited to a value of €149.64 and subject to special conditions. For details, contact the Embassy; see *Contact Addresses* section.
Exchange rate indicators: The following figures are included as a guide to the movements of the Euro against Sterling and the US Dollar:

Date	Feb '04	May '04	Aug '04	Nov '04
£1.00=	1.46	1.50	1.49	1.43
$1.00=	0.80	0.84	0.81	.075

Banking hours: Generally, Mon-Fri 0830-1500 (certain banks in Lisbon are open until 1800). In the Algarve, the bank in the Vilamoura Marina Shopping Centre is open daily 0900-2100.

Duty Free

Visitors 18 years and older arriving from countries outside the EU may import the following duty free goods:
200 cigarettes or 100 cigarillos or 50 cigars or 250g of tobacco; 1l of spirits over 22 per cent or 2l of spirits up to 22 per cent; 2l of wine; 50g of perfume and 250ml of eau de toilette; 500g of coffee or 200g of coffee extract (provided bought in a tax-free shop); 100g of tea or 40g of tea extract (provided bought in a tax-free shop); further goods up to €37.41.
Abolition of duty free goods within the EU: On 30 June 1999, the sale of duty free alcohol and tobacco at airports and at sea was abolished in all of the original 15 EU member states. Of the 10 new member states that joined the EU on May 1st 2004, these rules already apply to Cyprus and Malta. There are transitional rules in place for visitors returning to one of the original 15 EU countries from one of the other new EU countries. But for the original 15, plus Cyprus and Malta, there are now no limits imposed on importing tobacco and alcohol products from one EU country to another (with the exceptions of Denmark, Finland and Sweden, where limits *are* imposed). Travellers should note that they may be required to prove at customs that the goods purchased are for personal use *only*.

Public Holidays

2005: Jan 1 New Year's Day. **Feb 8** Mardi Gras (Carnival). **Mar 25** Good Friday. **Apr 25** Freedom Day. **May 1** Labour Day. **May 26** Corpus Christi. **Jun 10** Portugal Day. **Aug 15** Assumption. **Oct 5** Republic Day. **Nov 1** All Saint's Day. **Dec 1** Restoration of Independence Day. **Dec 8** Immaculate Conception. **Dec 25** Christmas Day.
2006: Jan 1 New Year's Day. **Feb** Mardi Gras (Carnival). **Apr 14** Good Friday. **Apr 25** Freedom Day. **May 1** Labour Day. **Jun 10** Portugal Day. **Aug 15** Assumption. **Oct 5** Republic Day. **Nov 1** All Saints' Day. **Dec 1** Restoration of Independence Day. **Dec 8** Immaculate Conception. **Dec 25** Christmas Day.
Note: Holidays falling on a Sunday are *not* observed on the following Monday.

Health

	Special Precautions?	Certificate Required?
Yellow Fever	No	1
Cholera	No	No
Typhoid & Polio	No	N/A
Malaria	No	N/A

Note: *Regulations and requirements may be subject to change at short notice, and you are advised to contact your doctor well in advance of your intended date of departure. Any numbers in the chart refer to the footnotes below.*

1: A yellow fever vaccination certificate is required from travellers over one year of age arriving in (or going to as a destination) the Azores or Madeira, if coming from infected areas. However, no certificate is required from passengers transiting through Funchal, Porto Santo and Santa Maria.
Health care: There are full state-provided health facilities, but private practices are allowed to co-exist. There are approximately 34,389 doctors and 40,700 hospital beds. There are reciprocal health agreements with most European countries. The agreement with the UK allows free in-patient treatment in general wards of official hospitals to those presenting UK passports (other EU nationals must present form E111). Secondary examinations, X-rays and laboratory tests may have to be paid for. A nominal charge will be made for medical treatment at health centres (*Centro de Saúde*). There may be a charge for prescribed medicines. All dental treatment must be paid for. This agreement is also effective in Madeira and the Azores (although in Madeira a fee must be paid for a GP consultation, which can then be refunded by an appointed bank). Those wishing to take advantage of it should inform the doctor prior to treatment that they wish to be treated under EU social security arrangements. Private treatment must be paid for in full. Medical fees paid whilst in Portugal cannot be reimbursed by the British NHS.

Travel - International

AIR: Portugal's national airline, *TAP Air Portugal (TP)* (website: www.tap.pt), operates direct flights to Faro, Lisbon and Porto from a number of countries, including Canada, France, Spain, the UK and USA. *Portugália Airlines (NI)* (website: www.pga.pt) operates flights from Europe. Other airlines flying to Portugal from the UK are *British Airways, GB Airways* and *Monarch Airlines, Easyjet, bmibaby, Jet 2, MyTravelLite, Flybe, Flyglobespan* and *SATA*.
Approximate flight times: From Lisbon to *London* is two hours 30 minutes and to *New York* is eight hours.
International airports: *Lisbon (LIS)* (Portela de Sacavem) (website: www.ana-aeroportos.pt) is 7km (4.5 miles) north of the city (travel time – 35 minutes). Bus nos. 44, 45 and 83 run every 15 minutes from 0530-0100 to the city centre and main railway station. A special 'Aerobus' departs to the city centre every 20 minutes. Taxi services to the city are available, with a surcharge after 2200. Airport facilities include bureau de change, banks, tourist information, post office, duty free shops and car hire (*Auto Jardim, Avis, Drive Car, Europecar, Hertz, National* and *Sixt*).
Faro (FAO) (website: www.ana-aeroportos.pt) is 4km (3 miles) west of the city (travel time – 30 minutes). Bus nos. 17 and 18 go to the city; taxis are available.
Oporto (OPO) (Oporto Sá Carneiro) (website: www.anaaeroportos.pt) is 20 km (about 7 miles) from the city. Buses and taxis to the city are available.
Faro and Oporto airports both have the following airport facilities: outgoing duty free shop; bank/bureau de change; car hire and a restaurant/bar.
Departure tax: None.
SEA: The principal ports for international passengers are Lisbon, Leixões (Oporto), Funchal (Madeira) and Portimão (Algarve), served by *Cunard, Italia, Linea C, Olympia, P&O* and *Union Castle*. For details, contact shipping lines.
RAIL: Travelling from the UK, the quickest way is to travel by *Eurostar* through the Channel Tunnel to Paris (travel time – three hours) and, from there, to Portugal. The *Sud-Express* runs between Paris and Lisbon, offering first- and second-class seats, sleepers and a restaurant car. For further information and reservations, contact *Eurostar* (tel: (0870) 6000 792 (travel agents) *or* (08705) 186 186 (public; within

Credit: © ICEP Portugal

the UK) *or* (+44 1233) 617 575 (public; outside the UK only); website: www.eurostar.com); *or Rail Europe* (tel: (08705) 848 848). Travel agents can obtain refunds for unused tickets from Eurostar Trade Refunds, 2nd Floor, Kent House, 81 Station Road, Ashford, Kent TN23 1PD, UK. Complaints and comments may be sent to Eurostar Customer Relations, Eurostar House, Waterloo Station, London SE1 8SE, UK (tel: (020) 7928 5163; e-mail: new.comments@eurostar.co.uk). Rail travellers from the UK not using the Channel Tunnel link need to cross the channel via some form of sea crossing, usually by ferry or catamaran; for details on sea crossings, see also the *Sea* section above. The cost of the crossing is usually included in the price of the rail ticket. There is a daily service between London, Paris and Lisbon, taking approximately 26 hours.
ROAD: The only land border is shared with Spain. Major border posts are now open around the clock, but smaller ones may close earlier in winter. From the UK, the quickest routes are via the ferry links from Plymouth to Santander and from Portsmouth to Bilbao in northern Spain (which obviates the need to drive through France). Cars can be imported for up to six months. For information on documentation and regulations, see the *Travel - Internal* section. Travelling from the UK, *Eurotunnel* operates trains 24 hours per day through the Channel Tunnel between Folkestone in Kent (with direct access from the M20) and Calais in France. All vehicles, from motorcycles to campers, can be accommodated. For further information, contact *Eurotunnel Reservations* (tel: (08705) 353 535; e-mail: callcentre@eurotunnel.com; website: www.eurotunnel.co.uk). For further details, see also *Travel – International* in the *France* section. For information on required documentation and traffic regulations, see *Travel – Internal* section. **Coach:** *Eurolines* operates an extensive network of coach services to many destinations throughout Europe, including Coimbra, Faro, Lagos, Lisbon and Oporto. For information on timetables and fares, contact Eurolines (tel: (08705) 143 219; e-mail: welcome@eurolines.co.uk; website: www.eurolines.com).

Travel - Internal

AIR: *TAP Air Portugal* and *Portugália* run services between Lisbon, Faro, Madeira, Porto Santo, Oporto and the Azores. Charter flights are also available. The airline for the Azores is *SATA* (*Sociedade Acoriana de Transportes Aereos*) (website: www.sata.pt), which operates its *Air Açores* service between the various islands.
SEA/RIVER: Transport is available from all coastal ports and along the major rivers. For details, contact local ports.
RAIL: *Caminhos de Ferro Portugueses* (Portuguese Railways) (website: www.cp.pt) provides a rail service to every town. The tourist areas of Cascais and Sintra are connected to Lisbon by frequent express trains. High-speed *Alfa* trains run between Lisbon and Porto via Coimbra and Aveiro. *Fertagus* trains cross the River Tagus in Lisbon, operating between Entrecampus station to Fogueteiro (on the south bank).
Cheap fares: On 'Blue Days', usually Monday afternoon to Thursday, special rates are available. There are also special fares (with 20 to 30 per cent reductions) for groups of 10 or more (*Bilhetes de Grupo*), travelling for a minimum distance of 75km/47 miles (single journey) or 150km/94 miles (return journey). Application should be made four days in advance by the group leader. Tourist Tickets (*Bilhetes Turisticos*) for seven, 14 or 21 days of unlimited travel are also available. The Rail Cheque (*Cheque Trem*), obtainable in four different values, can be in one name or a company's name and has no time limit; it gives a reduction of 10 per cent and can be used both for purchasing tickets and many other railway services.

An International Youth Ticket (*BIJ*) entitles those aged 12 to 26 to a discount (subject to certain conditions) in 25 countries for two months, including Portugal.
Senior citizens are entitled to 50 per cent reduction on production of proof of age. Children under four travel free. Children aged between four and 11 pay half fare.
Euro Domino, Family Card, Inter-Rail Card, Rail Inclusive Tours and *Special Tourist Trips* are amongst other offers from the Portuguese Railways (*Caminhos de Ferro Portugueses*), Calçada do Duque 20, 1249-109 Lisbon Codex (tel: 2132 15700; fax: 2134 73093; website: www.cp.pt). Rail information is also available from ICEP/Portuguese Trade and Tourism Office; see *Contact Addresses* section.
ROAD: Traffic drives on the right. Every town and village can be reached by an adequate system of roads. Petrol stations generally open 0700-2000, although some are open 24 hours. Travel by motorway is subject to a toll according to distance covered and type of vehicle. A small tax may be added to petrol bought with a credit card. **Bus:** There are frequent coach services between all Portuguese cities. For further information, contact *Rede Nacional de Expressos* (website: www.rede-expressos.pt). **Taxi:** Charges are according to distance and taxis are all metered. Taxis are usually painted beige (although some taxis painted in the old colours of green and black still exist). In the city, they charge a standard meter fare; outside the city limits they charge per kilometre and are entitled to charge for the return fare. There is a surcharge for carrying luggage in the cities. **Car hire:** Available from main towns and airports, with or without driver. **Regulations:** Minimum age for driving is 18 (but might be older if hiring a car). Cars may be imported for up to six months. Traffic signs are international. Headlights should be dipped in built-up areas and side lights used when parking in badly lit areas. Children should not travel in the front seat. Seat belts should be worn. Warning triangles are compulsory. It is forbidden to carry cans of petrol in vehicles. Speed limits are 50kph (30mph) in built-up areas, 90kph (56mph) outside built-up areas and 120kph (70mph) on motorways. Visitors who passed their driving test less than one year previously must display a yellow disc with '90' on it on the rear of their vehicle and must not go faster than 90kph (56mph). Permitted speeds will vary if trailers are being used. **Documentation:** International Driving Permits or foreign driving licences are accepted. Third Party insurance is compulsory. Under the requirements of the Portuguese Road Code, those wishing to drive a car must possess a valid national/international driving licence, other official documentation with photograph, log book or rental contract and adequate car insurance. Failure to produce, on request to the authorities, any of the above will result in an on-the-spot cash fine. A Carnet de Passage is needed for a van.
URBAN: Lisbon has an underground (*Metropolitano*) (website: www.metrolisboa.pt), which is currently being expanded. Trams also operate in major Portuguese cities. A tram ride in Lisbon also provides a good opportunity to see the city. There is also an extensive bus network in Lisbon (website: www.carris.pt). **Cheap fares:** In Lisbon, a Tourist Pass is available for either four or seven days travel on trams, buses and the underground. The *Lisboa Card* (for sightseeing) is valid for 24 or 72 hours and offers unlimited bus, tram and underground travel as well as entry to 26 museums and 50 per cent discounts to other cultural attractions.
Travel times: The following chart gives approximate travel times (in hours and minutes) from **Lisbon** to other major cities/towns in Portugal.

	Air	Road	Rail
Faro	0.35	4.00	5.00
Oporto	0.45	5.00	3.00
Funchal	1.30	-	-

Accommodation

There is a wide range of accommodation available all over the country, ranging from luxury hotels, pensions, boarding houses and inns to simple guest houses, manor houses, campsites and youth hostels. *Pousadas* offer very good value and are often situated in places of scenic beauty in converted castles, palaces or old inns.
HOTELS: Most hotels have a private swimming pool and serve international cuisine as well as some typically Portuguese dishes. During the low season, hotels normally grant substantial reductions. There should be an officially authorised list of prices displayed in every bedroom, and children under eight years of age are entitled to a reduction of 50 per cent on the price of full meals and 50 per cent on the price of an extra bed, if sharing parents' room or apartment. Further information can be obtained from the Associação Hotéis de Portugal, Avenida Duque d'Ávila 75, 1000 Lisbon (tel: 2135 12360; fax: 2135 70485; e-mail: ahp.sede@mail.telepac.pt; website: www.hoteis-portugal.pt). **Grading:** Classification of hotels is according to the international **1-** to **5-star** system and their prices are officially approved. Apartment hotels are classified from 2- to 4-star, motels from 2- to 3-star and boarding houses from 1- to 3-star (with 1-star being the best); there are also 4-star *albergarias*.
POUSADAS: The *pousadas* are a network of inns housed in historic buildings, castles, palaces and convents, or sometimes built especially for the purpose. They have often been geographically sited in regions not on the usual tourist itinerary to give people the opportunity to visit the whole country. The architecture and design of the *pousadas* has been carefully studied in order to give visitors a better knowledge of the cultural traditions of the various regions of the country, with particular attention paid to handicrafts, cooking and wines. A guide to *pousadas* can be obtained from Pousadas de Portugal, Avenida de Santa Joana-a-Princesa 10, 1749-090 Lisbon (tel: 2184 42001; fax: 2184 42085; e-mail: guest@pousadas.pt; website: www.pousadas.pt).
PRIVATE HOUSES: Rooms are available in private houses and on farms all over Portugal. Some of the old manor houses are now open to visitors and provide good opportunities for tourists to make contact with Portuguese customs and people. For further information contact your local travel agents tourism information office.
SELF-CATERING: There is self-catering tourist accommodation in deluxe, first- and second-class tourist villages and tourist apartments, particularly on the Algarve. Tour operators can arrange a wide variety of villas for self-catering parties.
YOUTH HOSTELS: Youth hostels are located to give young people the opportunity of visiting towns, countryside, mountains and coastal areas. Tourists can obtain accommodation and meals. For further information, contact MOVIJOVEM, Rua Lucio de Azevedo 29, 1600 Lisbon (tel: 7072 03030; fax: 2172 32101; e-mail: reservas@movijovem.pt; website: www.pousadasjuventude.pt).
CAMPING/CARAVANNING: Portugal provides camping and caravan parks near beaches and in thickly wooded areas. Some have model installations including swimming pools, games fields, supermarkets and restaurants. For further information, check online (websites: www.roteiro-campista.pt *or* www.orbitur.pt). For further information, contact Federação Portuguesa de Campismo, Avenida Coronel Eduardo Galhardo 24D, 1199-007 Lisbon (tel: 2181 26890; fax: 2181 26918; e-mail: campasino@fpcampismo.pt; website: www.fcmportugal.pt).

Resorts & Excursions

Often overshadowed by its much larger eastern neighbour, Spain, Portugal has its own distinct language, identity, customs, landscapes and scenery. Despite the encroachment of tourism, it remains one of the least spoilt corners of Europe. Portugal can conveniently be divided into five regions: Porto and the north, Beiras, Lisbon and the Tagus Valley, Alentejo and the Algarve. Portugal's Atlantic islands, the *Azores* and *Madeira*, are covered separately in this guide. For more information, see their individual entries.

LISBON & THE TAGUS VALLEY

LISBON: Lisbon (Lisboa), the capital of Portugal, enjoys one of the most dramatic settings of any European capital, clinging to a series of steep hillsides at the estuary of the **River Tagus** (Rio Tejo), just 10km (6 miles) from the Atlantic Ocean. Perched above the old Moorish quarter of **Alfama**, characterised by twisting, cobbled streets and whitewashed houses, is the magnificent **Castle of São Jorge**. Founded in the 12th century, its 10 towers crown the hill where the original colony was situated in Phoenician times. **Lisbon Cathedral** (*Sé*) dates from the same period as the castle and was an important element in the fortifications. The downtown **Baixa** district was built on a grid formation following the devastating earthquake in 1755. Today, it is one of Lisbon's best areas for shopping (especially crafts – gold, silver and jewellery). This is a lively area with plenty of cafes and terrace restaurants.
Baixa slopes down towards the River Tagus, Lisbon's main waterway, where visitors can take an interesting boat trip along the estuary and across to the picturesque southern shore. An antiquated elevator operates between Baixa and the aptly named **Bairro Alto** (Upper Town), home of *Fado*, the traditional folk music of Lisbon. Also worth a visit is the **Gulbenkian Foundation**, a cultural centre and museum set in its own park. The museum houses a range of artefacts, from Oriental jewellery to French impressionist paintings.
The exhibition grounds of 'Expo '98' are now known as the **Park of Nations**. Its attractions include the second largest **Oceanarium** in the world, a **Virtual Reality Pavilion**, and the **Vasco da Gama Tower**. The 850m-tower (2788ft) offers excellent views of the city and beyond.
The fin-de-siècle glories of the **Chiado** quarter, traditional haunt of artists and writers, are now re-emerging after a fire in 1988 which destroyed large parts of the city. Also worth seeing is the 2.5km- (1.5 mile-) long suspension bridge over the Tagus which is overlooked by a towering statue of Christ. The riverside suburb of **Belém** is where the ships of Vasco da Gama, Álvares Cabral and other famous explorers were launched in the 15th and 16th centuries. The attractions here include the strikingly beautiful prison tower, known as the **Torre de Belém** (a UNESCO World Heritage Site), the **Monument to the Discoverers**, the **Hieronymite Monastery** – one of the architectural glories of Portugal's Golden Age – and the **Coach Museum**.
ELSEWHERE: There are two famous seaside resorts close to the capital. **Estoril** predates the tourist boom of the 1960s but has adapted well to changing tastes and demands. The elegant hotels, which fringe the glorious **Tamariz Beach**, maintain the standards of the pre-war era. The entertainment on offer includes a casino, restaurants and nightclubs, watersports, golf and riding. **Cascais** has changed even more quickly, from a small fishing village with fine but empty beaches to a lively resort with bars, nightclubs and good-value restaurants. **Sintra** (a UNESCO World Heritage Site), a mountain town 25km (15 miles) from Lisbon, boasts the former summer residence of the Portuguese royal family, the **Monserrate gardens** and a twice-monthly antique market. A classical music festival takes place every July and August. **Colares** is an attractive village, famous for its red wines. **Queluz** has an 18th-century rococo palace, supposedly modeled on Versailles. **Mafra** is home to a Baroque convent built in 1717. **Ericeira** and **Sesimbra** are busy fishing villages with good beaches and developing facilities for tourists. **Tróia** is a modern tourist complex, situated on a peninsula near to the industrial town of **Setubal**, with a casino, marina, good beaches and sports facilities. The village of **Palmela** has a 12th-century castle and monastery, which is now a *pousada* (see the *Accommodation* section). There is a wine festival here in September. The shrine at **Fátima** has been an important centre of Roman Catholic pilgrimage since 1917 when the Virgin Mary appeared to a group of children. Torchlight processions are held annually on May 13 and October 13. **Battle Abbey** (Mosteiro de Santa Maria) in **Batalha** is a UNESCO World Heritage Site. It is a breathtaking example of Portuguese Gothic and Manueline architecture, built to commemorate the victory of King João I over a Castilian army in 1385. **Obidos** is a beautifully preserved fortified town, dating from the Middle Ages. **Leiria**, a quiet country town, is dominated by its 12th-century castle, built on a plateau high above the town. An annual fair takes place here at the end of March. **Santarém** is the capital of a rich agricultural district and the venue for the 'Ribatejo Fair' in June. **Tomar** is a charming town on the **Nabão River** overlooked by a great convent-castle, once occupied by the knights Templar. There are spas at **Caldas da Rainha**, **Cucos** and **Vimeiro**.

PORTO & THE NORTH

This region of Portugal incorporates the historic city of **Porto** (Oporto), famous for Port wine, the remarkably lush coast, the valleys of the **Douro** and the **Minho** and part of Portugal's highest mountain range, the **Serra da Estrêla**.
PORTO: The second-largest city in Portugal was nominated European City of Culture for 2001 and the historical centre is a UNESCO World Heritage Site. Founded by the Romans at the mouth of the **River Douro**, modern Porto (Oporto) is an industrial city with a wonderful atmosphere and plenty to see. The sights of the old town include the **Cathedral** (*Sé*), dating from the 12th to the 18th centuries, the **Church of São Francisco**, famous for its rococo interior, a splendid example of Portuguese gilt-work (*talha dourada*), the 19th century **Stock Exchange** and the **Torre Dos Clérigos**, which offers wonderful views. The old waterfront, known as

the **Cais da Ribeira** (a World Heritage Site), caters for tourists with cafes, restaurants and an open-air market. Across the river, the 18th century Port wine lodges of **Vila Nova de Gaia** are open to the public for tours and tastings.
ELSEWHERE: The **Cathedral** of the ancient Roman town of **Braga** is an important centre of the Roman Catholic church. The best time to visit is during Holy Week when the traditional street processions are impressive. **Guimarães**, a UNESCO World Heritage Site and Portugal's medieval capital, boasts a fine castle, the former palace of the Dukes of Bragança, as well as some attractive squares and churches. **Póvoa de Varzim** retains a small but attractive harbour, a reminder of its days as a fishing port. In recent years, fishing has taken a back seat to tourism, the 8km- (5 mile-) long beach being the main attraction. **Rates** and **Rio Mau** have splendid Romanesque churches. At **Monte São Félix**, the windmills have been converted into houses and there are panoramic views of the coast towards Póvoa de Varzim. **Vila do Conde** is a traditional fishing port and burgeoning resort, famous for its crafts such as 'bone lace' and chocolate-making. **Ofir** presents a vast expanse of sandy beach fringed by pinewoods. **Barcelos** is famous for its handicrafts, particularly ceramics which are on show at the Thursday market. The busy resort of **Viana do Castelo** is noted for its Renaissance and Manueline architecture as well as local products such as ceramics, embroidery, jewellery and filigree. There is a first-class beach across the river at **Praia do Cabedelo**. **Valença** is a 13th-century border town with a flourishing market and ancient fortifications. **Monção**, an attractive old town, is the home of the wine Alvarinho Vinho Verde. The **Peneda-Gerês National Park** comprises 170,000 acres (68,798 hectares) of mountainous countryside near the Spanish border. It is popular with hikers, climbers and naturalists. There are spas at **Caldas de Vizela**, **Gerez**, **Monção** and **Pedras Salgadas**.

BEIRAS

Beiras is a region which includes three provinces (Beira Litoral, Beira Alta and Beira Baixa) but it is the wooded coastal strip that holds most appeal for tourists.
COIMBRA: Portugal's third-largest city, Coimbra boasts one of the oldest universities in the world and is characterised by twisting streets and terraced houses. Worth visiting are the **University**, the magnificent Romanesque **Cathedral** (*Sé*), the **Art Museum** housed in the former Bishop's Palace and the 12th-century **Monastery of the Holy Cross**. Coimbra is also renowned as a centre of *Fado*, traditional Portuguese folk music.
ELSEWHERE: Aveiro, the 'Venice of Portugal', is a fishing port surrounded by salt flats, beaches and lagoons, and dissected by three canals. **Torreira** is a typical fishing village, lying between ocean and lagoon, which can be reached by boat from Aveiro. **Figueira da Foz** is a small but growing resort with an excellent surfing beach and casino. **Anadia**, the centre of the wine-growing region of Bairrada, offers tastings in its cellars. At **Conimbriga**, fine Roman mosaics dating from the first century AD can be seen. **Buçaco** is renowned locally for its 'enchanted forest', cultivated by the Carmelite monks who arrived here in the 17th century. **Pinhal do Rei** is a beautiful pine forest with walking trails and some pristine beaches. **Viseu**, an impressively sited medieval town with a cathedral and bishops' palace (now a museum) lies in a part of the country best known for its *Dão* wine. There are spas at **Curia**, **Luso** and **São Pedro do Sul**. **Serra da Estrêla** is a natural park, with mountain scenery best appreciated from the car.

ALENTEJO

The Alentejo is an agricultural region, renowned for its cork plantations. It also boasts a number of barely discovered historic towns and an extensive coastline of windswept beaches.
EVORA: This beautiful, hilltop town, still protected by a ring of fortified walls enclosing cobbled streets and quaint houses, is a UNESCO World Heritage Site. The sights are numerous and include a splendid medieval **Cathedral** (*Sé*), the **Church of São Francisco**, famous for its grisly ossuary, the 14th-century **Palace of the Dukes of Cadaval** and a ruined **Roman temple**.
ELSEWHERE: Monsaraz is a splendid hilltop village near the Spanish border with traditional whitewashed houses, cobbled streets and fine views of the surrounding countryside. **Marvão** is an impressively sited medieval town, the clifftop location being the main attraction. **Elvas** retains its ramparts, gateways and historic old quarter. **Vila Viçosa** contains the former palace (now a museum) of the Dukes of Bragança.

THE ALGARVE

Portugal's southernmost region looks out onto the Atlantic on two sides. It is one of Europe's favourite package destinations on account of its attractively rocky coastline and excellent sandy beaches. East of the capital, Faro, the beaches are interspersed with mud flats and sandbanks and the resorts are fewer in number and relatively low key. Watersports are one of the main attractions, but it's also home to some world-class golf courses.

Credit: © ICEP Portugal

FARO: The capital of the Algarve, Faro was devastated by the earthquake of 1755, but part of the old town has survived. Sights include the **Cathedral** (*Sé*), rebuilt in the 18th century, an **Archaeological Museum** and the **Carmo Church** and **ossuary**.
LAGOS: A former centre of the slave trade, Lagos was where Henry the Navigator's mariners set sail for West Africa on their voyages of discovery. The main sight is a 17th-century **fort** (now a museum), offering superb views of the town's natural harbour. The pedestrianised town centre is well provided with shops and restaurants and there are boat trips to nearby grottoes and beaches.
ELSEWHERE: Albufeira is a busy market town and well-established resort. **Armação de Pêra** is a fishing village with one of the biggest beaches on the Algarve. **Carvoeiro** is an old fishing village with a picturesque harbour. **Portimão** is one of the largest towns and fishing ports in the Algarve, known for its furniture and wickerwork. Its beach resort is Praia da Rocha. Vilamoura is a modern purpose-built resort with marina and golf courses. **Sagres** is noted for lobster fishing. The village contains the remains of a 15th-century *fort* and there are beaches nearby. **Cape St Vincent** is the most southwesterly point of mainland Europe. **Monte Gordo** is a modern tourist resort with a casino, nightclubs, restaurants and a 20km- (12 mile-) long beach backed by pine forest. **Tavira** is one of the most attractive market towns in the Algarve with cobbled streets, several fine churches and a ruined castle. There are beaches at **Cabanas** and **Pedras da Rainha**. Inland, **Monchique** is set high in the mountains and has a spa. **Silves** is an old walled city with a 12th-century cathedral. **Loulé** is a market town famous for crafts such as leather and copper. The **River Guadiana** forms a natural boundary between Portugal and Spain. There are commanding hilltop views from the ruined fortresses at **Castro Marim**; nearby are the saltpans of the same name, now a nature reserve open for guided tours.

Sport & Activities

Wine tasting: Portugal is renowned for its Port but is also establishing a good reputation for still light wines that use a variety of indigenous grapes. For its size Portugal boasts a surprisingly high number of different styles of wine and vineyards can be found throughout the country. Oporto is famous for port wine, which became a major trade following a 1703 agreement with the United Kingdom, and there are many wine lodges (still bearing English names like Croft or Graham) where visitors are welcome. (For information on Madeira wine, see the *Madeira* section.)
Music and folklore: The melancholic **fado**, said to have originated from 16th-century sailors' songs, is Portugal's best-known musical form. One of the best places to experience it is Lisbon, with many fado clubs located in the **Alfama** and Bairro Alto neighbourhoods. One of the country's main traditional crafts is the making of decorative tiles known as *azulejos*. Visitors wishing to learn the craft should enquire locally. Traditional folk dancing is still practised in rural areas and there are numerous colourful festivals (see *Special Events* in the *Social Profile* section).
Watersports: Portugal's coastline offers excellent beach holidays with all the usual activities – **swimming**, **snorkelling**, **water-skiing**, **sailing** and **windsurfing** – widely available. For information on **diving** contact the Portuguese Federation for Underwater Activities (FPAS), Rua Frei Manuel Cardoso 39, 1700 Lisbon (tel/fax: 2181 41148; e-mail: fpas@fpas.pt; website: www.fpas.pt). The Algarve has a perpetually mild climate, although the tides can be strong in the winter, and **big-game fishing** is popular here. The west coast is best for **surfing**; the **Beiras** in the north has big Atlantic breakers and is still fairly undeveloped, with many deserted beaches. The wetlands around Rio de Aveiro (crossed by numerous canals) offer some interesting **boat trips** in traditional Portuguese *moliceiros* (gondola-like sailing barges). Another good boating destination is the Douro Valley, stretching from Oporto to the Spanish border, where the River Douro is navigable. **Canoeing** is available in the Peneda-Gerês National Park.
Golf: Portugal is a well-known golfing destination and the south in particular has many championship golf courses (there are 19 in the Algarve alone). The climate allows playing all year round. Some of the best-known 18-hole courses include *Estoril*, one of the oldest, close to Lisbon, hosting many major competitions; *Quinta de Marinha*, on the Estoril coast near Lisbon, with good views of the Sintra mountain range; *Golden Eagle*, near Rio Maior, boasting a typically US design, open to non-members; *Ponte de Lima*, a typical mountain course in the northern Minho region, close to vineyards, fruit gardens and mountains; *Estela*, on the coast near Póvoa de Varzim; *Tróia*, in Alentejo, southern Portugal, reputedly the country's most difficult course; and the *Royal Golf Course*, in the Algarve, said to be one of the world's most famous and most photographed courses.
Other: The Peneda-Gerês National Park, a wilderness park in the far north near the Spanish border, has many short-distance **walking** trails with places to **swim** along the way. The dense *Foia* forest in the Algarve highlands also offers good scenic walks. **Horseriding** is also available in the park as well as in many resorts elsewhere. Portugal offers some excellent **cycling** routes, notably in the Minho region in the north, where the most interesting villages and towns are sometimes not accessible by car.

Social Profile

FOOD & DRINK: Seafood is popular, especially in Lisbon, but can be expensive. Soup is a main dish. Typical Portuguese dishes include *sopa de marisco* (shellfish soup cooked and served with wine), *caldo verde* (green soup made with finely shredded green kale leaves in broth) and bacalhau (dried cod, cooked in over 100 different ways). *Caldeirada* is a fish stew with as many as nine kinds of fish, cooked with onions and tomatoes. Also typical is *carne de porco á Alentejana*, in which bits of fried pork are covered with a sauce of clams stewed with tomato and onions. Puddings *include arroz doce* (rice pudding), Madeira pudding and *nuvens* (egg custard). Portugal's sweet pastries (available in most cafes) are also worth a try. Table service is normal.
Portuguese wines have changed beyond recognition over the past 10 years. Many of these new, modern wines are indigenous varieties with distinctive flavours. Sparkling rosé wines are mostly produced for export. *Mateus Rosé* is a famous lightweight rosé. Portuguese brandies are also good; the best are produced around Oporto, where Port wines originate. There are no licensing hours.
NIGHTLIFE: The large towns offer every kind of entertainment. There are many nightclubs, theatres, cinemas, stage shows, folk dancing and music performances. The traditional *Fado* can be heard in many restaurants, and performances begin at about 2200. The theatre season is from October to May. Gambling is authorised and Alvor, Espinho, Estoril, Figueira da Foz, Monte Gordo and Vilamoura have casinos. The elegant Estoril Casino is the most renowned.
SHOPPING: Items include leather goods, copper, ceramics, handcrafted silver and gold, embroidery and tapestry, woodcarving, cork products, porcelain and china, crystal and glassware. **Shopping hours:** Generally Mon-Fri 0900-1300 and 1500-1900, Sat 0900-1300 (and 1500-1900 in December). Shopping centres are usually open Mon-Sun 1000-0000.
SPECIAL EVENTS: Portugal has many festivals – for a complete list, *contact* ICEP/Portuguese Trade and Tourism Office. The following is a selection of special events occurring in Portugal in 2005:
Jan 20 *Festa das Fogaceiras*, Santa Maria da Feira. **Feb 5-8** *Carnival*, Torres Vedras, Sines, Loulé, Sesimbra, Nazaré and Funchal; *Madeira Mardi Gras*. **Feb 21-Mar 7** *Fantasporto*

(International Fantastic Film Festival), Porto. **Mar 21-28** *Holy Week Festivities*, Braga. **Apr 1-4** *Algarve Portuguese Golf Open*, Portimão. **Apr 9-10** *Madeira Flower Festival*. **May 3** *Feast of the Cross/Feast of our Lady of the Castle*, Monsanto. **Jun 1-30** *Atlantic Festival*, Madeira. **Jun 9-11** *Super Bock Super Rock* (music festival), Lisbon. **Jun 12-13** *Feast of St Anthony*, Lisbon. **Jul 4-18** *Almada International Theatre Festival*, Lisbon. **Jul 28-30** *Vilar de Mouros Music Festival*, Porto e Norte. **Aug 17-20** *Paredes de Coura Festival*, Porto e Norte. **Aug 19-21** *Our Lady of Agony Feast*, Viana do Castelo. **Sep 2-4** *Madeira Wine Festival*. **Sep 5** *Portuguese Moto GP*, Estoril. **Sep-Nov** *Porto Jazz Festival*. **Oct-Nov** *National Horse Fair*, Golegã. **Nov 17-20** *2005 Algarve World Cup* (golf tournament).

SOCIAL CONVENTIONS: The Portuguese way of life is leisurely, and old-fashioned politeness is essential. Warm, Latin hospitality is the norm. The country has a deeply individual national character, although each province has its own traditions and folklore. Casual wear is widely acceptable, although beachwear should not be worn in towns. In restaurants, it is usual to smoke only at the end of the meal. Smoking is prohibited in cinemas, theatres and on buses. **Tipping:** Generally 10 to 15 per cent. Taxi drivers are tipped 10 per cent.

Business Profile

ECONOMY: Portugal was traditionally an agrarian economy but since joining the EU in 1986, the industrial and especially the service sectors of the economy have grown considerably by comparison. Agriculture still employs 12 per cent of the workforce – unusually high by Western European standards – and contributes 3 per cent of GDP, producing wheat, maize, tomatoes, potatoes and grapes. Production has undergone a relative decline so that Portugal now imports a sizeable proportion of its foodstuffs after having long been self-sufficient. The manufacturing sector is dominated by the textile and footwear industries and automobiles, which now account for 15 per cent of total exports. Other important products are paper, cork and other wood products, electrical appliances, chemicals and ceramics.

Both foreign and internal investment have been high, attracted by Portugal's relatively low labour costs and the recent modernisation of much of the country's infrastructure. Many former state-owned industries have been sold off under a gradual privatisation programme which began in 1989. During the last five years, unemployment has hovered around 5 per cent while inflation has not risen above 4 per cent; the current figures are 4.4 and 4.1 per cent respectively. Portugal joined the Eurozone upon its inauguration in 1999. Unfortunately since then, the economy has stagnated – growth fell to below 1 per cent in 2001/2 – before contracting by 1 per cent in 2003. The main reasons have been a reduction in domestic demand and government spending cuts – demanded under the terms of Eurozone membership – to tackle the country's large budget deficit.

Although Britain has historically been Portugal's main trading partner, the growth of Anglo-Portuguese trade has failed to keep pace with that of Portugal's other trading partners, particularly Germany, France, Spain and Italy. The Portugal Investment Agency can supply further information (website: www.investinportugal.pt).

BUSINESS: Businesspeople are expected to dress smartly and formal attire is expected in some dining rooms and for important social functions. English is widely spoken in business circles, although when visiting a small family business it is best to check in advance. Visiting cards are generally only exchanged by more senior members of a company. July and August are best avoided. **Office hours:** Mon-Fri 0900-1300 and 1500-1900.

COMMERCIAL INFORMATION: The following organisations can offer advice: Associação Comercial de Lisboa, Câmara de Comércio e Indústria Portuguesa, Rua das Portas de Santo Antão 89, 1169-022 Lisbon (tel: 2132 24050; fax: 2132 24051; e-mail: geral@port-chambers.com; website: www.port-chambers.com); *or* Confederação do Comércio e Serviços de Portugal (CCP), Avenida Dom Vasco de Gama 29, 1449-032 Lisbon (tel: 2130 31380; fax: 2130 31400-1; e-mail: ccp@ccp.pt; website: www.ccp.pt).

CONFERENCES/CONVENTIONS: Lisbon is the main centre for conventions, with venues that can seat up to 1500 people. The Lisbon Convention Centre was founded in 1987, and a major Congress centre, fully integrated with the facilities offered by the Lisbon International Fair, opened in 1989. The fair is a department of the Portuguese Industrial Association, which promotes trade fairs, exhibitions and meetings.

After the EXPO '98 in Lisbon, the North International Area became the new Lisbon Exhibition Centre, with an area of 80,000 sq m (743,200 sq ft), also run by the Portuguese Industrial Association. The Lisbon International Fair will now be the major congress centre in Lisbon, with a capacity for events of up to 3000 delegates. The Lisbon Convention Bureau is a non-profit-making association of companies providing support services to conference organisers. Its services directory includes details of the Congress Centre and hotels with conference facilities. For information, contact the Lisbon Convention Bureau, Rua do Arsenal 15, 1100-038 Lisbon (tel: 2103 12700; fax: 2103 12899). Lisbon opened the Belem Cultural Centre in 1992 to coincide with Portugal's EU Presidency; it features high-quality technical equipment and facilities for meetings of up to 1400 delegates. For further information, contact the Belem Cultural Centre, Praça do Império, 1499-003 Lisbon (tel: 2136 12400; fax: 2136 12500; e-mail: ccb@ccb.pt; website: www.ccb.pt). Additionally, the former site of the EXPO '98 'Utopia Pavillion' has been converted into the multi-purpose Atlantic Pavillion, which can accommodate up to 16,500 seated spectators.

The city of Oporto also has two major international exhibition and congress centres. The Oporto International Exhibition Centre (Exponor) has a total area of 29,500 sq m (274,000 sq ft) with a congress centre that has a capacity for 1000 delegates; the International Congress and Exhibition Centre (Europarque) has a large and flexible exhibition hall that can host receptions for up to 12,000 delegates on a floor space of 7200 sq m (66,890 sq ft). For further information, contact the Porto Convention Bureau, Av Inferior a Ponte D. Luis 1, 53, 1 4050 Porto (tel: 2233 26751; fax: 2233 26752; e-mail: portocvb@portocvb.com; website: www.portocvb.com).

Climate

The northwest has mild winters with high levels of rainfall and fairly short summers. The northeast has longer winters and hot summers. In the south, summers (March to October) are warm with very little rain except in early spring and autumn. High temperatures are moderated by a permanent breeze in Estoril (July to August).

Required clothing: Light- to mediumweights and rainwear are advised.

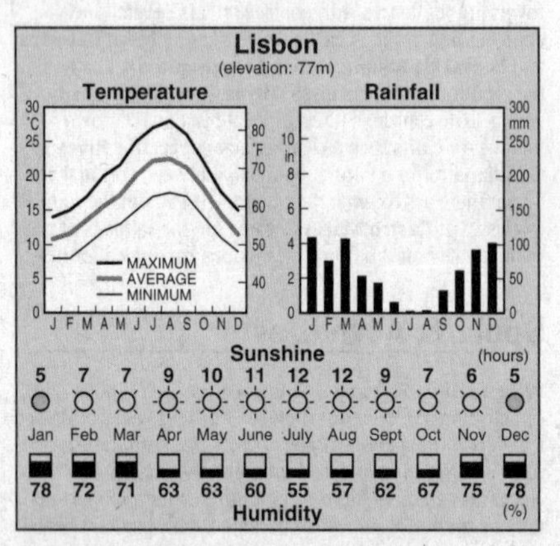

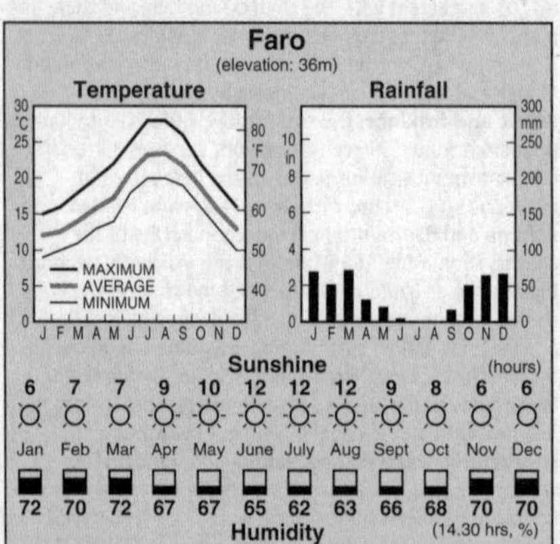

Azores

LATEST TRAVEL ADVICE CONTACTS

British Foreign and Commonwealth Office
Tel: (0870) 606 0290 Website: www.fco.gov.uk

US Department of State
Website: http://travel.state.gov/travel

Canadian Department of Foreign Affairs and Int'l Trade
Tel: (1 800) 267 8376 Website: www.dfait-maeci.gc.ca

Location: Atlantic, 1220km (760 miles) due west of Portugal.

Direcção Regional Turismo Açores
Rua Comendador Ernesto Rebelo 14, 9900-112 Horta, Faial, Azores
Tel: 292 200 500. Fax: 292 200 501.
E-mail: acoresturismo@mail.telepac.pt
Website: www.drtacores.pt

General Information

AREA: 2333 sq km (868 sq miles).
POPULATION: 241,800 (2001).
POPULATION DENSITY: 103.8 per sq km
CAPITAL: São Miguel: Ponta Delgada; **Faial:** Horta; **Terceira:** Angra do Heroismo.
GEOGRAPHY: The Azores are a widely separated group of nine islands in the Atlantic, due west of mainland Portugal. The islands are Corvo, Faial, Flores, Graciosa, Pico, Santa Maria, São Jorge, São Miguel and Terceira. The islands are mountainous in the interior and forested, leading down to long beaches and fishing harbours. There are several hot springs and spas.
TIME: GMT - 1 (GMT from last Sunday in March to Saturday before last Sunday in October).
ELECTRICITY: 230/110 volts AC, 50Hz. Round two-pin plugs are in use.
COMMUNICATIONS: Services are similar to, but less extensive than, those offered on mainland Portugal.
Radio: BBC World Service (website: www.bbc.co.uk/worldservice) and Voice of America (website: www.voa.gov) can be received. From time to time the frequencies change and the most up-to-date can be found online.

Travel - International

AIR: *TAP Air Portugal (TP)* operates flights to the Azores from London via Lisbon to Terceira and Faial. The Azores' local airline, *SATA Air Açores (SP)*, runs interconnecting flights between the islands, and operates from Lisbon to Ponta Delgada.
Approximate flight times: From the Azores to *London* is five hours, plus stopover time in Lisbon of two hours.
International airports: *Ponta Delgada (PDL)* (São Miguel), *Terceira (TER)* (Terceira) and *Faial*.
SEA: *CTC* and *P&O* run cruises to the main port of Ponta Delgada, Horta and Faial.

Accommodation

The main islands have a reasonably good selection of hotel and youth hostel accommodation, and they are rarely full, so although it is a good safeguard, it is not vital to book in advance.

Resorts & Excursions

For more than 500 years the Azores, an archipelago of nine

widely dispersed islands in the middle of the Atlantic, have remained almost completely unspoilt, mainly on account of their remoteness. Volcanic in origin, they are pitted with deep craters, some filled with shimmering lakes, others covered with lush vegetation. Geysers and health-giving sulphur springs abound. The Azores is also characterised by large tracts of arable farmland, sprinkled with tiny settlements of whitewashed houses. The gently sloping hillsides are planted with vineyards and fruit trees. The coastlines tend to be rugged and somewhat forbidding, but there are plenty of bays, and rocky inlets for swimming and sunbathing. Watersports are widely available such as scuba diving and whale watching; equally popular are yachting, horseriding, cycling and hiking. Tourist development throughout is on a modest scale and there are few signs of change.

EASTERN ISLANDS

SÃO MIGUEL: This is the largest island in the group and arguably the most beautiful. One of the most spectacular sights is **Sete Cidades** – a 40 sq km (15 sq mile) volcanic crater with two lakes, one of deep blue, the other emerald green. The former fishing village of **Ponta Delgada** is now the administrative and commercial centre of the archipelago with a population of more than 60,000. The historic centre consists of narrow streets, faced with attractive whitewashed houses, many of which date from the 17th and 18th centuries. The best vantage point is the waterfront promenade. At **Furnas**, visitors can enjoy the **Terra Nostra Park**, a tropical garden created in the 18th and 19th centuries, and bathe in therapeutic sulphurous spring water. **Gorreana** and **Porto Formoso** have what is said to be the only tea plantations in Europe. From the *miradouro* at **Santa Iria**, there are views of almost the entire northern coast. Pineapple products and embroidery are typical souvenirs of the island.

SANTA MARIA: The first island to be discovered, Santa Maria is characterised by vineyards, emerald green fields, palm trees and windmills. **Praia Formosa** has a first-class beach, said to be the best in the archipelago, and is the setting for a music festival in August. The beach at **Bahia de São Lourenco**, is a rockier alternative. **Vila do Porto**, the only settlement of any size, has a 15th-century parish church and the town hall is located in a former 16th-century convent. The island is popular with divers and water-skiers.

CENTRAL ISLANDS

GRACIOSA: This island of vineyards and windmills contains the geological curiosity of **Furna de Enxofre**, a small, warm sulphur lake concealed in a grotto beneath a crater, access to which is via an 80m (270ft) spiral staircase. Graciosa also boasts a subterranean lake (**Caldeira**), and hot springs in the spa village of **Carapacho**. **Santa Cruz**, the major settlement, is an attractive village which converges on a large, irregular square shaded by monkey puzzle trees. It is seen at its best from **Monte da Ajuda**.

TERCEIRA: A gently rural island, Terceira is known as the 'Lilac Isle' because of the distinctive colouring of its sunsets. It is also the home of a specialised kind of bullfight known as **Touradas à Corda**. Terceira is covered with hydrangeas, and along the highways visitors will see the gaily coloured stands that serve as altar stations for the Whitsun procession of the Holy Spirit, one of many festivals on the island. **Angra do Heroismo** was founded in the 15th century and developed into a major commercial outpost for the Portuguese and Spanish empires. Renowned as one of the most beautiful towns of the age, it has now been listed as a UNESCO World Heritage Site. Extending from the harbour is an intricate network of streets, packed with palaces, churches and convents. **Biscoitos** has natural swimming pools among the rocks.

SÃO JORGE: The island is surrounded by sheer, black cliffs, while a profusion of vegetation covers the steep slopes down to the sea. Cedar woods surround the island's capital of **Velas**, which boasts a number of historic buildings including a 17th-century church. São Jorge is the centre for Azores' dairy produce, especially cheeses.

FAIAL: The name means 'beech tree', and blue hydrangea hedges divide the fields. The coast is indented with sheltered bays. **Caldeira** is an immense crater carpeted with greenery and has breathtaking views. **Horta**, the island's main port, is an important yachting harbour and a popular meeting point for trans-Atlantic yachtsmen. Large cruise liners also dock here.

PICO: This island takes its name from its volcano, Portugal's highest peak (2351m/7720ft). The hues of the snow-capped cone vary according to the light, from grey at sunrise to fiery red at sunset. The island is renowned for its vineyards that grow the famous *verdelho* wine of Pico. The largest settlement, **Lajes do Pico**, was until the 1980s the most important whaling centre on the archipelago. Visitors can discover more about the industry at the local museum and by attending the boating festival (*Festa dos Baleeiros*) held every summer.

WESTERN ISLANDS

CORVO: The smallest island, Corvo, has only one village and its few hundred inhabitants are all related to one another. Nobody ever locks their front door and there is no jail or courthouse. Corvo has the living traditions of a pastoral and fishing community.

FLORES: Named after its profusion of flowers. It is often regarded as the prettiest of the islands, with its rugged terrain, flowers growing in the deep canyons, and waterfalls casting hues of blue and green as they splash down into the sea. The island is ideal for watersports. The administrative and commercial centre of Flores is the coastal village of **Santa Cruz**.

Sport & Activities

Watersports: The Azores is a well-known destination for **whale** and **dolphin watching** with over 25 species currently identified in the area. The best time to spot them is from June to September when they feed off the waters around the islands of Faial, Pico and São Jorge. The abundant marine life around the Azores' nine islands offers excellent **diving** and dive centres can be found on a number of islands, particularly Faial and São Miguel. **Surfing** has recently become popular on Santa Maria and São Miguel islands while **sailing** clubs, which can be found on all islands (except Corvo), also provide assistance to **windsurfing** enthusiasts.

Fishing: The Azores is an internationally renowned destination for **deep-sea fishing** and chartered boats are available at many coastal resorts, particularly on Faial and São Miguel where tourist facilities are more developed. **Freshwater fishing** is only allowed in the lakes of the islands of Flores and São Miguel with a licence.

Golf: There are three 18-hole golf courses in the Azores. Two of them (*Furnas* and *Batalha*) are on São Miguel island; the third is on Terceira. The mild climate allows playing all year round.

Flora and fauna: The Azores attract many nature and plant lovers. The lush islands are home to over 50 native plants as well as imported ones, such as the Japanese criptomera or the acacia tree. The flowering hydrangeas and azaleas are particularly widespread. The many species of birds make it an ideal destination for **birdwatching**. For information on special tours and walks, contact the ICEP tourist office (see *Contact Addresses* section).

Volcanoes: The volcanic origins of the archipelago provide interesting material for amateur and professional speleologists as there are numerous craters and other volcanic phenomena to explore. **Caving** enthusiasts can explore the caves and tunnels of Algar do Carvão on Terceira island.

Other: The Azores' rocky landscapes are ideal for **parasailing** and **paragliding**, and operators can be found on Faial, Santa Maria, São Miguel and Terceira.

Social Profile

FOOD & DRINK: Generally the food is Portuguese; seafood and cheese are specialities. Locally produced wines are recommended, as are the brandies distilled on the islands.

SHOPPING: Locally made linens and woollen goods, lace and pottery make good buys.

SPECIAL EVENTS: The following is a selection of special events celebrated annually in the Azores:

Apr *Holy Ghost Festivities*, all islands. **May** *Miraculous Christ*, São Miguel; *Holy Trinity*, all islands. **May-Oct** *Bullfights*, Terceira. **Aug** *Sea Week*, Hosta; *Maré de Agosto Festival*, Santa Maria. **Aug** *Lady of Miracles*, Corvo. **Sep** *Grape Harvest Feast*, Pico and Santa Maria.

Climate

Subtropical due to the Gulf Stream. Very equable and slightly humid climate. The rainy season is from November to March.

Required clothing: Mid-season clothes are best; the temperatures are mild at all times of the year.

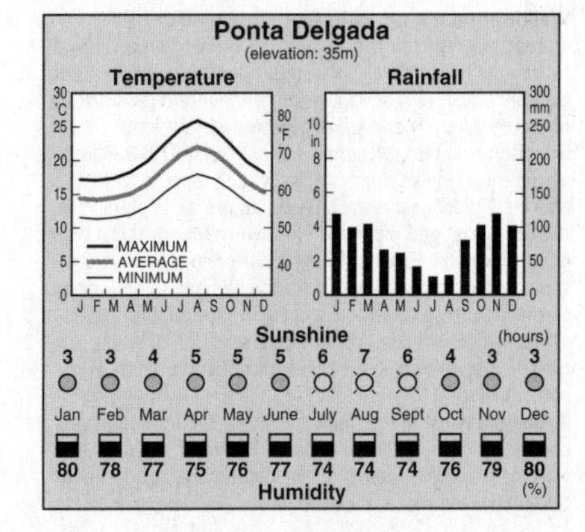

Madeira

LATEST TRAVEL ADVICE CONTACTS

British Foreign and Commonwealth Office
Tel: (0870) 606 0290 Website: www.fco.gov.uk

US Department of State
Website: http://travel.state.gov/travel

Canadian Department of Foreign Affairs and Int'l Trade
Tel: (1 800) 267 8376 Website: www.dfait-maeci.gc.ca

Location: Atlantic Ocean, 990km (619 miles) southwest of Lisbon.

Direcção Regional de Turismo
18 Avenida Arriaga, 9000-519, Funchal, Madeira
Tel: (291) 211 900. Fax: (291) 232 151.
E-mail: info@madeiratourism.org
Website: www.madeiratourism.org

ICEP/Portuguese Trade and Tourism Office
9 Rua do Bom Jesus, 1st Floor, 9050-028 Funchal, Madeira
Tel: (291) 228 555 *or* 229 109. Fax: (291) 232 546.
Website: www.portugal.org *or* www.icep.pt

General Information

AREA: 779 sq km (301 sq miles).
POPULATION: 245,000 (2001).
POPULATION DENSITY: 314.5 per sq km.
CAPITAL: Funchal. **Population:** 126,889 (1991).

GEOGRAPHY: The group comprises the main island of Madeira, the smaller island of Porto Santo, the three uninhabited islets of Ilheu Chao, Deserta Grande and Ilheu de Bugio, and the Selvagens (a group of uninhabited islets located south of Madeira). The islands are hilly and of volcanic origin and the coast of Madeira is steep and rocky with deep eroded lava gorges running down to the sea. These are particularly impressive on the north coast of Madeira island. The largest of a group of five islands formed by volcanic eruption, Madeira is in fact the summit of a mountain range rising 6.5km (4 miles) from the sea bed. At Cabo Girão, west of the capital of Funchal, is the second-highest cliff in the world. Inland, Pico Ruivo is the island's highest point (1862m/6109ft) with the slightly lower Pico de Arieiro (1810m/5940ft) nearby. Both are destinations for sightseeing tours, commanding fine views of the surrounding mountains. Madeira's volcanic origin means that it has no sandy beaches, although there is a small beach, Prainha, near the whaling village of Canical on the extreme east of the island. Madeira itself is 58km (36 miles) long and 23km (14 miles) wide. Porto Santo is much smaller, only 14km (9 miles) long and 5km (3 miles) wide, with a long, golden sandy beach, complementing Madeira.

TIME: GMT (GMT + 1 from last Sunday in March to last Sunday in October).

ELECTRICITY: 230 volts AC, 50Hz. Round two-pin plugs are in use.

COMMUNICATIONS: Services are similar to those offered on the mainland.

Radio: BBC World Service (website: www.bbc.co.uk/worldservice) and Voice of America (website: www.voa.gov) can be received. From time to time the frequencies change and the most up-to-date can be found online.

Travel - International

AIR: The airlines serving Madeira are *GB Airways (GT)* and *TAP Air Portugal (TP). Air Portugal* currently operates two weekly direct flights from London to Madeira, and daily via Lisbon (schedules are subject to changes). There are internal flights between Funchal and Porto Santo.

Credit: © ICEP Portugal

Approximate flight times: From Funchal to *London* is three hours 40 minutes.

International airports: *Madeira Intercontinental (FNC)*, 16km (10 miles) from Funchal, and *Porto Santo (PXO)*, which is served by flights from Funchal and Lisbon. Funchal Airport has a capacity of over 3.5 million passengers per year.

SEA: The main passenger port is Funchal, served by *BI, Costa, CTC, Cunard, Fred Olsen, Lauro, Norwegian American, Norwegian Cruises/Union Lloyd, P&O* and *Polish Ocean*. Ferry services from Madeira to Porto Santo take between two and three hours depending on weather conditions.

Accommodation

There are many luxury hotels on the island along the coast. These tend to be fully booked during the summer and over the Christmas period, therefore early booking is advisable. Most of the hotels compensate for the lack of beaches on the island of Madeira by providing swimming pools.

Resorts & Excursions

Madeira is a singularly beautiful island. The scenery is memorable and remarkably diverse, especially bearing in mind the island's modest size. Madeira has been described as a 'floating garden', reflecting centuries of cultivation. The rich volcanic soil, mild climate and abundant rainfall (especially in the north) have been responsible for contrasting landscapes: lush river valleys, terraced hillsides planted with vines and bananas and dense primeval forest. The most enjoyable way to explore the island is to follow the course of the *levadas* (irrigation channels) which crisscross the countryside. The island's burgeoning coastal resorts are geared to the demands of modern tourism and the expansion of Santa Catarina Airport is expected to lead to a marked increase in the number of foreign visitors over the next decade.

FUNCHAL: Nearly half the island's population of 250,000 lives in the capital, Funchal, a city which enjoys a magnificent setting overlooking a sweeping bay. Most of the sights are conveniently clustered and can easily be visited on foot. The **Cathedral** (*Sé*) was completed in 1514 and is one of the islands oldest buildings. Late Gothic in style, its most remarkable feature is a geometrical wooden ceiling of *Mudejar* (Moorish) design. The **Museum of Sacred Art** in the former Bishops' Palace has a remarkable collection of religious artefacts and paintings by Flemish masters of the 15th and 16th centuries acquired by wealthy sugar merchants. Other sights include the **Botanical Gardens**, 5 hectares (2 acres) of terraced hillside, planted with more than 2000 species from around the globe; the **Blandy Wine Lodge** (**Adegas do São Francisco**) where tours with tastings of Madeira wine are available; the **Mercado dos Lavradores**, a lively flower and vegetable market; and **Quinta das Cruzes**, a former mansion, now a museum with collections of furniture, porcelain, paintings, lithographs and so on from the colonial period. Funchal's **Old Town** (**Zona Velha**) has pastel-painted house fronts, cobbled streets, craft shops, restaurants and bars, some of which stage performances of traditional Portuguese folk music (*Fado*).

THE NORTH COAST: The scenery here is wilder and more dramatic than in the south, with looming cliff faces and swollen seas. The narrow, twisting coast road challenges drivers, but the views are magnificent. **Porto do Moniz** is a lively village, popular with day trippers for its fish restaurants, natural swimming pool and rugged coastal scenery. **São Vicente** is an attractive village, sheltered from the sea. The parish church is worth a look, but the main attractions are the caves (*grutas*), formed by flows of molten lava more than 400,000 years ago. **Santana** lies at the heart of a prosperous agricultural region. Perhaps the most visited village on the island, it is best known for its unusual triangular-shaped houses known as *palheiros*.

CENTRAL MADEIRA: Parts of the mountainous interior can be reached by road. It is possible to drive almost to the summit of **Pico do Arieiro** (1818m/5965ft) where the views are spectacular. The island's highest peak, **Pico Ruivo** (1861m/6106ft), is accessible on foot. **Curral das Freiras** is a hamlet lying at the bottom of a bowl-shaped valley. The dramatic setting is best appreciated from the **Eagle's Nest miradouro** (lookout point). **Monte** became fashionable at the end of the 19th century when a hotel and sanatorium opened to treat consumptives. The hotel grounds are now the **Tropical Gardens**. Monte's church, **Nossa Senhora de Monte** becomes a centre of pilgrimage on 15 August, when worshippers climb the 74 steps on their hands and knees. Monte can now be reached by cable car from Funchal, an alternative to the famous toboggan run. **Quinta do Palheiro Ferreiro** has beautiful gardens laid out by the Blandy family in the 19th century. Nearby is one of Madeira's two championship golf courses.

THE SOUTH COAST: This is the sunniest and most fertile part of Madeira where the terraced hillsides are planted with bananas, vineyards and other crops. Good viewing points include **Cabo Girão**, the second-highest cliff in Europe (580m/1903ft), **Ponta do Sol**, famous for its sunsets and **Ponta do Pargo**, Madeira's westernmost point. **Ribeira Brava** has a fine parish church (**São Bento**), seafront cafes and craft shops. **Câmara de Lobos** is a picturesque fishing village which Sir Winston Churchill painted in the 1950s. To the east of Funchal is the fast-developing resort of **Caniço de Baixo**. The area is well-suited to watersports (especially scuba diving), tennis and golf (Madeira's other championship course is at **Santo da Serra**). **Santa Cruz** is a mini-resort with an attractive promenade, lido and a medieval parish church. **Machico** is Madeira's second-largest town. Worth seeing are the 15th-century parish church, the **Chapel of Miracles** (a place of pilgrimage) and the small but picturesque 18th-century fort. Watersports are available from the stony beach. The only sandy beach on Madeira is at **Prainha**, near the eastern tip of the island. The inland village of **Camacha** is a centre for wickerwork, one of Madeira's traditional cottage industries.

PORTO SANTO: Madeira's much smaller neighbour has noticeably flatter terrain and is famous for its 9km- (5.6 mile-) long beach of golden sand, reputed to have healing properties. The sea is warm enough to swim in all year round. The only sight in the tiny capital, **Vila Baleira**, is the house where Christopher Columbus is said to have once lived.

Porto Santo can be reached from Madeira by plane (15 minutes), catamaran (90 minutes) or ferry (two hours 40 minutes). Advance booking is essential in July and August.

Sport & Activities

Walking and hiking: Paths along the coastline offer dramatic views from the many steep cliffs, often giving way to tranquil terraced valleys further inland. Madeira's interior combines austere moorland, remote mountain passes and forested valleys. The *levadas*, a network of ancient irrigation channels stretching some 2130km (1333 miles) across the island's slopes, are particularly popular with walkers. The longest is the *Lavada do Norte*, beginning in the northwest and meandering down to the southern coast near the capital, Funchal. Walkers suffering from vertigo should check the levada route beforehand as some trails go across very steep mountain slopes. The regional tourist office can provide information on a selection of walks classified according to their level of difficulty, safety and scenic beauty.

Toboggan runs: Before motor vehicles, the toboggan was commonly used in Madeira and a number of special 'runs' were constructed. Today the toboggans carry tourists with two men using ropes to control the wide *carro*, a large wicker basket mounted on wooden runners. The runs are available at the villages of Monte or Terreiro da Luta, down to Funchal.

Wine tasting: The distinctive Madeira wine is renowned throughout the world. The grapes are pressed where they are grown and carried down the hills in goatskin bags by porters. Madeira wine is particularly well known for its high alcohol content and its longevity. The famous *Madeira Wine Festival* takes place annually in September. For further details, contact the Direcçao Regional de Turismo (see *Contact Addresses* section).

Golf: The *Campo de Golfe do Santo da Serra* (27-hole) and *Palheiro* (18-hole) are the two courses on the island, the former offering spectacular panoramic ocean views from its 500m- (1640ft-) high location. Clubs and trolleys are available for hire. The courses are located within 29km (18 miles) of Funchal. For more information, contact Madeira Island Golf (website: www.madeira-golf.com).

Watersports: Madeira's rocky landscape, dominated by cliffs, provides excellent views, but few sandy beaches (the exception being *Porto Santo*). As well as the sea, there are many swimming pools, some on hotel rooftops and others along the seafront. There is also a lido large enough for 2000 people, with pools, shops and restaurants. Arrangements for watersports, including **water-skiing**, **windsurfing**, **snorkelling** and **scuba diving** can be made through some hotels.

Madeira is known for excellent deep-sea **fishing**, particularly blue marlin. A number of companies offer fishing tours to suit all budgets and tastes. Special charters can be arranged for groups.

Social Profile

FOOD & DRINK: Regional dishes include *sopa de tomate e cebola* (tomato and onion soup), *caldeirada* (fish soup), *bife de atum e milho frito* (tuna steak and fried maize), *carne em vinha d'alho* (pickled pork and garlic), *espada* (fresh black sword fish), *espetada* (beef grilled on laurel wood skewers over an open fire) and *bolo de mel* (Madeira honey cake).

Popular wines of Madeira are *malmsey* (Malvasia), a sweet dessert wine, *bual* and the dry *serceal*. Wines, spirits and beers imported from mainland Portugal and Europe are also available. *Galão*, a glass of milky coffee and *bica*, a small cup of black coffee, are also popular.

NIGHTLIFE: Some hotels have excellent nightclubs with music for dancing and international cabaret entertainment. Folk entertainment is also included in the weekly programme of these hotels and, in most cases, non-residents are welcome.

SHOPPING: In Funchal, there is a wide variety of shops selling everyday goods, as well as many souvenirs. Special purchases include Madeira folk art such as embroidery, tapestry and wickerwork. Madeira wine is a popular gift.

SPECIAL EVENTS: Throughout the year, numerous events take place on Madeira and it is a good idea to visit at the time of a specific festival. Around Christmas and New Year, for example, there are some really spectacular celebrations. Cruise ships often stop the night of 31 December in Funchal Harbour so that passengers can appreciate the firework displays, accompanied by church bells and ships' sirens, which herald the New Year. For a complete list of events on Madeira, contact ICEP (see *Contact Addresses* section). The following is a selection of special events celebrated annually in Madeira:

Feb *Carnival*, Funchal. **May** *Flower Festival*, Funchal. **May** *World Championship Triathlon*, Funchal. **Jun** *Cherry Festival*, Jardimda Serra. **Aug** *Our Lady of Grace*; *Our Lady of Pity*. **Sep** *Santíssimo Sacramento*; *Madeira Wine Festival*. **Dec** *Reveillon* (New Years Festival), Funchal; *Switching on the Christmas Illuminations*; *St Silvester Fireworks*.

Climate

Mild subtropical climate with warm summers and extremely mild winters.

Required clothing: Mid-seasonal wear.

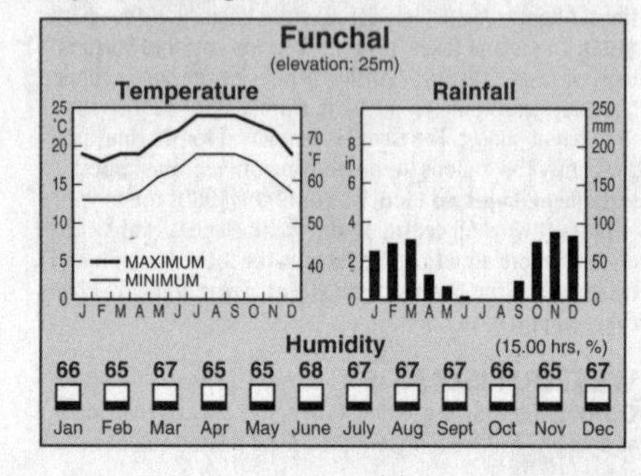

Puerto Rico

LATEST TRAVEL ADVICE CONTACTS

British Foreign and Commonwealth Office
Tel: (0870) 606 0290 Website: www.fco.gov.uk
US Department of State
Website: http://travel.state.gov/travel
Canadian Department of Foreign Affairs and Int'l Trade
Tel: (1 800) 267 8376 Website: www.dfait-maeci.gc.ca

Location: Caribbean.

Country dialling code: 1 787.

Diplomatic representation
As an *estado libre asociado* (a 'commonwealth state') of the USA, Puerto Rico manages its own affairs, but is represented abroad by US Embassies and Consulates. Addresses of these and of US Tourist Offices may be found in the *United States of America* section.

Puerto Rico Hotel and Tourism Association
954 Ponce de León Avenue, Miramar Plaza, Suite 702, San Juan 00907-3605, Puerto Rico
Tel: 725 2901. Fax: 725 2913.
E-mail: info@prhta.org Website: www.prhta.org

Puerto Rico Tourism Company
Street address: 2 La Princesa Building, San Juan 00902, Puerto Rico
Postal address: PO Box 902-3960, San Juan, Puerto Rico
Tel: 721 2400.
Website: www.gotopuertorico.com

Puerto Rico Tourism Company (UK)
67a High Street, 2nd Floor, Walton-on-Thames, Surrey, KT12 1 DJ United Kingdom
Tel: 01932 253 302. Fax: 01932 269 766.
E-mail: puertoricouk@aol.com
Website: www.gotopuertorico.com

British Consulate
Torre Chardon, Suite 1236, 350 Chardon Avenue, San Juan 00918, Puerto Rico
Tel: 758 9828. Fax: 758 9809.
E-mail: btopr1@coqui.net
Website: www.britainusa.com

Puerto Rico Tourism Company (USA)
666 Fifth Avenue, 15th Floor, New York, NY 10103, USA
Tel: (212) 586 6262 *or* (800) 223 6530 *or* 866 7827 (toll-free in the USA). Fax: (212) 586 1212.
Website: www.gotopuertorico.com

Puerto Rico Tourism Company
230 Richmond Street West, Suite 902, Toronto, Ontario M5V 1V6, Canada
Tel: (416) 368 2680. Fax: (416) 368 5350.
E-mail: kerry@prtourismcanada.com
Website: www.gotopuertorico.com

General Information

AREA: 8959 sq km (3459 sq miles).
POPULATION: 3,839,810 (official estimate 2002).
POPULATION DENSITY: 428.6 per sq km.
CAPITAL: San Juan. **Population:** 421,958 (2000).

TIMATIC CODES

Health	AMADEUS: **TI-DFT/SJU/HE** GALILEO/WORLDSPAN: **TI-DFT/SJU/HE** SABRE: **TIDFT/SJU/HE**
Visa	AMADEUS: **TI-DFT/SJU/VI** GALILEO/WORLDSPAN: **TI-DFT/SJU/VI** SABRE: **TIDFT/SJU/VI**

To access TIMATIC country information on Health and Visa regulations through the Computer Reservations System (CRS), type in the appropriate command line listed above.

GEOGRAPHY: Puerto Rico is an island east of the Dominican Republic and west of the British Virgin Islands. Also included are several smaller islands, such as Culebra, Mona and Vieques. The island is comparatively small, 8959 sq km (3459 sq miles), with a central mountain range reaching an altitude of 1338m (4390ft) at Cerro de Punta, and surrounded by low coastal plains. The capital is on the northeast shore. Much of the natural forest has been cleared for agriculture, but the trees in the northeast are protected as a national park. The other main towns are Aguadilla, Arecibo, Bayamón, Caguas, Carolina, Cayey, Farjardo, Guaynabo, Mayagüez and Ponce.
GOVERNMENT: Self-governing US Commonwealth Territory (incorporated). Gained internal autonomy in 1951. **Head of State:** President George W Bush since 2001. **Head of Government:** Governor Sila Maria Calderón since 2001.
LANGUAGE: Spanish and English are the official languages.
RELIGION: Roman Catholic 74 per cent; the remainder are other Christian denominations and Jews.
TIME: GMT - 4.
ELECTRICITY: 110 volts AC, 60Hz.
COMMUNICATIONS: Telephone: IDD service is available. Country code: 1 787. Outgoing international code: 011. **Mobile telephone:** CDMA/TDMA network. Not compatible with GSM handsets (although there are plans to introduce the network soon). **Internet:** ISPs include *Coqui Net* (website: www.coqui.net). Access is available in hotels and business centres. **Post:** Airmail to Western Europe takes up to one week. **Press:** The English-language newspaper published in Puerto Rico is *The San Juan Star*; others include *El Nuevo Día, El Vocero de Puerto Rico* and *Primera Hora*. **Radio:** BBC World Service (website: www.bbc.co.uk/worldservice) and Voice of America (website: www.voa.gov) can be received. From time to time the frequencies change, and the most up-to-date can be found online.

Passport/Visa

As for the USA. See *Passport/Visa* in the *USA* section.

Money

Currency: US Dollar (US$) = 100 cents. For exchange rates and currency restrictions, see the *USA* section.
Currency exchange: Foreign currency can be exchanged at banks and bureaux de change. All major ATM services are also available.
Credit & debit cards: All international credit cards, and many leading debit cards are accepted.
Travellers cheques: Cheques in various currencies are accepted, but US Dollar cheques are preferred.
Banking hours: Mon-Fri 0830-1430. Hours may vary.

Duty Free

As for the USA; see the *USA* section.

Public Holidays

2005: Jan 1 New Year's Day. **Jan 6** Epiphany. **Jan 10** Birthday of Eugenio María de Hostos. **Jan 17** Martin Luther King Day. **Feb 14** President's Day. **Mar 22** Emancipation of the Slaves. **Mar 25** Good Friday. **Apr 15** José de Diego Day. **May 23** Memorial Day. **Jul 4** US Independence Day. **Jul 15** Luis Muñoz Rivera's Birthday. **Jul 25** Constitution Day. **Jul 26** José Celso Barbosa's Birthday. **Sep 5** Labour Day. **Oct 10** Columbus Day. **Nov 11** Veterans' Day. **Nov 19** Discovery of Puerto Rico Day. **Nov 24** Thanksgiving Day. **Dec 25** Christmas Day.
2006: Jan 1 New Year's Day. **Jan 6** Epiphany. **Jan 9** Birthday of Eugenio María de Hostos. **Jan 16** Martin Luther King Day. **Feb 20** President's Day. **Mar 22** Emancipation of the Slaves. **Apr 14** Good Friday. **Apr 21** José de Diego Day. **May 22** Memorial Day. **Jul 4** US Independence Day. **Jul 15** Luis Muñoz Rivera's Birthday. **Jul 25** Constitution Day. **Jul 26** José Celso Barbosa's Birthday. **Sep 4** Labour Day. **Oct 9** Columbus Day. **Nov 11** Veterans' Day. **Nov 19** Discovery of Puerto Rico Day. **Nov 23** Thanksgiving Day. **Dec 25** Christmas Day.
Note: Each town celebrates a festival or fiesta in honour of a local patron saint. These can last up to 10 days.

Health

	Special Precautions?	Certificate Required?
Yellow Fever	No	No
Cholera	No	No
Typhoid & Polio	No	N/A
Malaria	No	N/A

Note: Regulations and requirements may be subject to change at short notice, and you are advised to contact your doctor well in advance of your intended date of departure. Any numbers in the chart refer to the footnotes below.

Food & drink: Water is purified in main areas, although bottled water may be preferable. Mains water is considered safe to drink. Milk is pasteurised and dairy products are safe for consumption. Local meat, poultry, seafood, fruit and vegetables are considered safe to eat.
Other risks: *Hepatitis A* occurs in the northern Caribbean region. The incidence of *dengue fever* has increased in the past few years. *Bilharzia* (schistosomiasis) is present. Avoid swimming and paddling in fresh water; swimming pools which are well chlorinated and maintained are safe. *Rabies* is present. For those at high risk, vaccination before arrival should be considered. If you are bitten, seek medical advice without delay. For more information, consult the *Health* appendix.
Health care: Health services are good but costly; health insurance is recommended.

Travel - International

AIR: Airlines serving Puerto Rico include *American Airlines, American Trans Air, Argentina Airlines, Iberia, KLM, LACSA, Lufthansa, Martinair, Mexicana* and *Northwest Airlines.*
Approximate flight times: From Puerto Rico to *Chicago* is four hours 30 minutes, to *London* is eight hours (direct), to *Los Angeles* is nine hours 30 minutes, to *Miami* is two hours 30 minutes, to *New York* is three hours 15 minutes and to *Washington, DC* is three hours 30 minutes.
International airports: *Luis Muñoz Marín (SJU)* is 14km (9 miles) northeast of San Juan. Buses and taxis are available (travel time - 20 to 30 minutes.) Airport facilities include restaurants, bars, bank, post office, hotel reservations, duty free shops and car hire (*Budget, Dollar* and *Hertz*).
Departure tax: None.
SEA: The main passenger port is San Juan. Cruise lines running services to San Juan include: *Carnival, Celebrity, Cunard, Princess Cruises* and *Radisson Seven Seas Cruises.*

Travel - Internal

AIR: *American Eagle* and *Vieques Air-Link* provide domestic air travel within Puerto Rico.
ROAD: Traffic drives on the right. **Taxi:** A service called a *linea* will pick up and drop off passengers where they wish. Special black and white *Tourist Taxis* exist. **Car hire:** Available at the airport and city agencies: includes *Avis* and *Budget*. **Documentation:** US or foreign licence accepted for first month of stay, after which a national licence will be required.
URBAN: Bus: San Juan has local bus services (*Guaguas*) and there are bus terminals in Bayamón, Catano, Country Club and Rio Piedras, as well as the capital. Buses usually tend not to run after 2100. **Taxi:** *Públicos* (share-taxis) have 'P' or 'PD' at the end of licence plate numbers and run regular routes between established points. They usually operate only during daylight hours and depart from the main *plaza* (central square) of a town. *Públicos* must be insured by law and the Public Service Commission fixes their routes and reasonable rates. Conventional taxis are hired by the hour, and charges are metered except in charter trips outside the usual taxi zones. They can be hailed in the street, or called by telephone. They are available at the airport and at stands at most hotels. Taxi drivers expect a 15 per cent tip.
Travel times: The following chart gives approximate travel times (in hours and minutes) from **San Juan** to other major cities and resorts in Puerto Rico.

	Air	Road	Sea
Ponce	**0.30**	**1.30**	-
Mayagüez	**0.30**	**2.30**	-
Vieques	**0.30**	**0.45***	**2.00**
Fajardo	-	**0.45**	-
Dorado	-	**0.35**	-
Humacao-Palmas	-	**0.45**	-

Note: *As far as Fajardo and then by sea.

Accommodation

HOTELS: San Juan has modern Americanised hotels and there is similar lodging in Ponce. Outside the main urban areas, there are *Paradores* (government-sponsored country inns). These are less modern, but of a good standard. For further information, contact the Puerto Rico Hotel and Tourism Association (see *Contact Addresses* section).
APARTMENTS & CONDOMINIUMS: These are available from a number of companies specialising in renting this type of accommodation and are best around Luquillo Beach to the northeast.

Resorts & Excursions

SAN JUAN

The capital city of San Juan is divided into the old and the new. The old part was founded in 1521 and is now officially declared a National Historic Zone, and many 16th- and

17th-century buildings have been restored and refurbished in the original Spanish style. This part of the city boasts many shops, restaurants, art galleries and museums. The **Pablo Casals Museum** has manuscripts and photographs relating to the work of the famous cellist. **Casa de los Contrafuertes** houses the **African Heritage Museum**. **Casa del Callejón** is a traditional Spanish-style home, which holds the **Museum of Colonial Architecture** and the **Museum of the Puerto Rican Family**. **Casa del Libro** holds a rare collection of early manuscripts and books. The **San Juan Museum of Art and History** was built in 1855 as a market and restored in 1979 as a cultural centre. **Plaza de San José**, at the 'top' of old San Juan and marked by a statue of Juan Ponce de León, is a picturesque area of small museums and pleasant cafes. Other places of interest in Old San Juan include **El Morro** (a 16th-century Spanish fortress) and the 18th-century fort of **San Cristobal**, built in 1771. Both buildings are perched on clifftops at the tip of a peninsula. El Morro has many exhibits documenting Puerto Rico's role in the discovery of the New World and was instrumental in the defence of San Juan in the 16th century and its continuing survival.

Casa Blanca, dating from 1523, was built as a home for Ponce de León, and the **Dominican Convent** (also started in 1523) now houses the **Instituto de Cultura Puertorriqueña**. **La Fortaleza**, completed in 1540, is now the Governor's residence – the oldest of its kind in the Western hemisphere. The old **San Juan City Wall**, dating from the 1630s, was built by the Spanish and it follows the peninsula contour, providing picturesque vantage points for viewing **Old San Juan** and the sea. **San Juan Cathedral**, originally built in the 1520s, was completely restored in 1977. **San José Church** is the second-oldest church in the Western hemisphere – Ponce de León's body was interred here until the early 20th century. The **Alcaldía**, or City Hall, was built between 1604 and 1789. The **Casino** (not a gambling club) is a beautiful building dating from 1917. The rich interior boasts marble floors, exquisite plasterwork and 4.7m (12ft) chandeliers.

Excursions: New San Juan is connected to the old town by a narrow neck of land, and modern architecture has flourished in recent years. The **Botanical Gardens** are worth visiting. A bay cruise is also available, which offers excellent views of the city.

El Yunque, east of the capital, is a 27,000-acre rainforest (with over 240 species of trees) and bird sanctuary. It is the only tropical rainforest in the US National Forest System and is located in the **Luquillo Mountains**.

BEYOND THE CAPITAL

PONCE: The beautiful town of Ponce, on the southern side of the island and connected to the capital by a toll road, is situated near many excellent beaches. It hosts an **Indian Ceremonial Park** and also has several buildings of interest, including a **sugar mill** and **rum museum**. The **Museum of Art** there contains more than 1000 paintings and 400 sculptures, ranging from ancient classical to contemporary art. Its collection of 19th-century Pre-Raphaelite paintings is among the best in the Americas.

Excursions: The Arroyo to Ponce train stops at Guayama, where the station has been restored as a crafts centre.

The **Tibes Indian Ceremonial Centre**, a short drive from Ponce, is an ancient Indian burial ground. A replica of a Taino Indian village has been built near the small museum, reception area and exhibition hall.

LA PARGUERA: The **Phosphorescent Bay**, near La Parguera in the southwest of the island, is a major attraction. Here, marine life, microscopic in size, light up when disturbed by fish, boats or any movement. The phenomenon – especially vivid on moonless nights – is rarely found elsewhere. Boat trips are available at night. There are other phosphorescent bays in **Vieques** and **Fajardo**.

ARECIBO: The **Camuy Caves**, near Arecibo on the north coast, is the third-largest cave system in the world. There are well-paved access roads, a reception area, and electric trains to the entrance of the caves. The **Arecibo Observatory** is the site of the largest radar/radio telescope in the world. Located in the unusual karst country of Puerto Rico, the 20-acre dish is best seen from a small aeroplane flight between San Juan and Mayagüez.

The **Caguana Indian Ceremonial Park**, south of the Arecibo Observatory, was built by Taino Indians as a site for recreation and worship 800 years ago. There is another Ceremonial Park in Ponce.

ELSEWHERE: There are old colonial towns at **San Germán** and **Mayagüez** and a **Tropical Agricultural Research Station** near the Mayagüez division of the University of Puerto Rico, with cuttings of hundreds of tropical plants. Many of the drives through the centre of the island take in spectacular scenery and are to be recommended. The **Espiritu Santo** is a navigable river that flows from the **Luquillo Mountains** to the **Atlantic**, and has 24 passenger launches available for river tours along 8km (5 miles) of the route. Special arrangements can be made for groups (through a tour operator); the boat ride usually takes about two hours.

Sport & Activities

Outdoor activities: Horseriding on mountain trails or beaches is an excellent way to see the island. Puerto Rico prides itself on its *paso fino* horses, a breed noted for its endurance and the comfort it affords the rider. Riding facilities can be found all over the island. Beach riding is particularly recommended at Luquillo in the northeast or Isabela in the northwest. There are many forest reserves with **hiking** trails. Energetic walkers can tackle the mountains in the interior. *Toro Negro*, with its lush forests and marvellous vistas, is recommended, while the highest peak is *Cerro de Punta*. The Guanica dry forest in the southwest or the El Yunque rainforest in the northeast both have visitors' centres where trail maps and advice can be obtained. The *Camuy Caves* in the west of the island are a national park, and visitors need to be escorted by a local guide. **Birdwatchers** will enjoy the Guanica dry forest or the *Cabezas de San Juan* nature reserve. The latter, visits to which must be booked in advance, is run by the Conservation Trust of Puerto Rico, PO Box 9023554, San Juan PR 00902-3554 (tel: 722 5834; fax: 722 5872; website: www.fideicomiso.org).

Watersports: Palmas del Mar rents small- to medium-sized boats for day **sailing** and the resort is headquarters for the annual *Copa del Palmas*, the major 1-design regatta in Puerto Rico. Motorboats and rowing boats are also available. Puerto Rico's shoreline has many areas protected by beautiful coral reefs and cays, and **snorkelling** in shallow reef waters and mangrove areas is an excellent way of seeing the beautiful and colourful underworld of the sea. **Scuba-diving** instruction and equipment rental are available at watersports offices of major hotels and resorts. Recommended areas include the island of Mona, just off Boquerón on the southwest coast, where the marine life is particularly rich. Because this area is a nature reserve, independent divers require government permission to dive there. Desecheo island, off the northwest coast, Parguera and Isabela are also good diving areas. Many beaches cater for **surfing** and **windsurfing**, for example Pine Grove and Condado beaches.

Fishing: Deep-sea fishing is available, with blue and white marlin, sailfish, wahoo, Allison tuna, mackerel, dolphin, tarpon and snook to be found. Fully equipped boats with crew are available for charter all over the island.

Other: There are six **baseball** teams in the league and the San Juan-Santurce stadium seats close to 25,000 people. There are other ball parks at Arecibo, Caguas, Mayagüez and Ponce. There are many **golf** courses, including *Punto Borinquen* at Aguadillo (18 holes), and five 18-hole courses at Dorado. **Tennis** courts are available all over the island, especially at major hotels. In addition, play is available on 17 floodlit public courts in San Juan's Central Park, which is open daily. There are also six courts available at the *Dorado del Mar Country Club* at Dorado. There is **horse racing** at Rio Grande (El Comandante) all year round.

Social Profile

FOOD & DRINK: Puerto Rico (and especially San Juan) abounds with good restaurants, catering for all tastes, from Spanish to Chinese, French, Greek and Italian. The island cuisine is Spanish-based, with rice and beans as the staple diet. *Paella*, chicken dishes, black bean soup, *sancocho* (beef stew), *jueyes* (land crabs) and *pan de agua* (native bread) are all excellent, as is the delicately seasoned *langosta*. Island rums such as *Barrilito* and *Don Q* are not to be missed.

NIGHTLIFE: Puerto Rico's nightlife is abundant and varied. The streets are lively in the evening. Many shops are open late, and the visitor can sit in the squares of old San Juan and indulge in people-watching. A recommended walk is down *La Princesa Promenade*, lined with antique street lamps. Meeting places include a Bogart-style cigar bar and cocktail bars. Hotels provide some of the entertainment, but there are also different types of clubs, both modern and more mainstream. Many Puerto Ricans favour traditional Latin dance clubs with large dance floors, which often have live bands playing *salsa* and *merengue* music. Puerto Ricans are passionate about their nightlife, and often dress up. Casinos are intimate and friendly, generally opening at noon and closing at around 0400 daily. Hotel casinos are open to guests and non-guests alike.

SHOPPING: Special purchases are cigars, coffee, hammocks, straw weavings, sculpture, *santos* (carved religious figures), festival masks and stringed musical instruments. **Shopping hours:** Mon-Wed and Sat 0900-1900, Thurs-Fri 0900-2100, Sun 1100-1700 (shopping malls). Some shops open on Sunday if cruise liners are in port.

SPECIAL EVENTS: 'Fiestas Patronales' celebrations are held in each town's plaza to honour the area's patron saint. These fiestas can last up to 10 days and include religious processions, games, local food and dance. For further details, contact the Puerto Rico Tourism Company (see *Contact Addresses* section). The following is a selection of some of the special events occurring in Puerto Rico in 2005: **Jan** *San Sebastián Street Festival*. **Feb** *San Blás Marathon*; *Coamo*; *Carnival*; *La Virgen de la Candelaria*, Mayagüez; *Ponce Carnival*. **May** *Puerto Rico Heineken Jazz Festival*; San Juan. **Jun** *Casals Festival* (classical music festival), San Juan; *Aibonito Flower Festival*; *San Juan Bautista Day* (begins a week of festivities celebrating San Juan's patron saint). **Jul** *St James Festival*, Loíza. **Aug** *San Juan International Billfish Tournament*. **Sep** *Convention and Hospitality Expo del Caribe*, San Juan. **Oct** *San Juan Cinema Festival*. **Dec** *Bacardi Artisans' Fair*; *Hatillo Mask Fair*. **Dec-Jan** *Navidades* (island-wide Christmas festivities). **Dec 28** *Festival of Innocents*, Hatillo.

SOCIAL CONVENTIONS: Handshaking is the customary form of greeting. Casual dress is acceptable, but shorts should not be worn in hotel dining rooms or casinos, where formal dress is required after 2000. Spanish and American manners and conventions exist side by side on the island. Some hotels require formal dress. **Tipping:** Generally 15 to 20 per cent if not included on the bill.

Business Profile

ECONOMY: Puerto Rico has few natural resources, although some nickel and copper have been located. Manufacturing has overtaken agriculture as the main source of income following an intensive programme of industrialisation by the Government. The main products are pharmaceuticals, electrical and electronic equipment, processed food, textiles, clothing, rum, petrochemicals and refined oil. There is a foreign free-trade zone at Mayagüez. In the agricultural sector, dairy and livestock produce is now more important than sugar cane, the island's main crop. Fresh fruit and vegetables are grown for export.

Tourism is the main service industry and has undergone steady growth in recent years; the sector is now worth more than US$2 billion annually. Another major source of revenue for the territory derived from a US naval base on the island

of Vieques. Although employing over 6000 people and injecting an estimated $300 million annually into the economy, it was widely unpopular with islanders; after sustained pressure, the closure of the base was announced in 2003.

Puerto Rico has observer status at the Caribbean trading bloc, CARICOM. The USA and its corporations dominate both the domestic economy and overall trade patterns, although Puerto Rico has important trading links of its own with Japan, the Dominican Republic and Venezuela. The US government is in the process of removing certain tax exemptions enjoyed by US and foreign investors in Puerto Rico; the economic impact of this is as yet unclear but is causing concern in the territory.

BUSINESS: A knowledge of Spanish (the official language) is very useful, although English is widely spoken; most people in the tourist industry and the greater metropolitan areas are bilingual. Lightweight suits are advised for business meetings. **Office hours:** Mon-Fri 0900-1800. **Government office hours:** Mon-Fri 0830-1630.

COMMERCIAL INFORMATION: The following organisation can offer advice: Chamber of Commerce of Puerto Rico, PO Box 9024033, San Juan (tel: 721 6060/82; fax: 723 1891; e-mail: camarapr@camarapr.net; website: www.camarapr.org).

Climate

Hot tropical climate. The temperature varies little throughout the year. Cooler in the upland areas.

Required clothing: Lightweight tropical clothes. Light rainwear required.

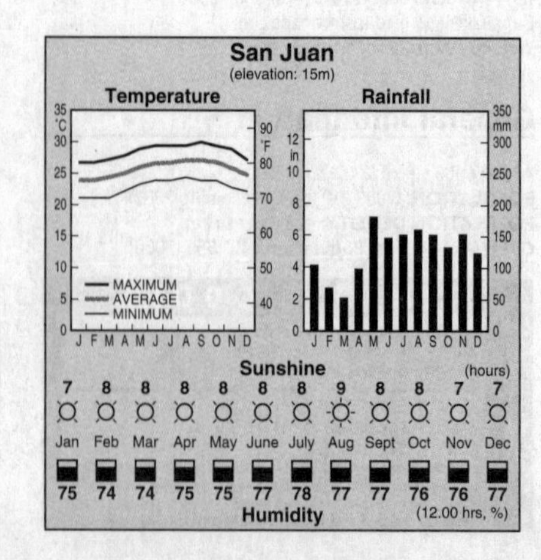

Qatar

LATEST TRAVEL ADVICE CONTACTS

British Foreign and Commonwealth Office
Tel: (0870) 606 0290 Website: www.fco.gov.uk

US Department of State
Website: http://travel.state.gov/travel

Canadian Department of Foreign Affairs and Int'l Trade
Tel: (1 800) 267 8376 Website: www.dfait-maeci.gc.ca

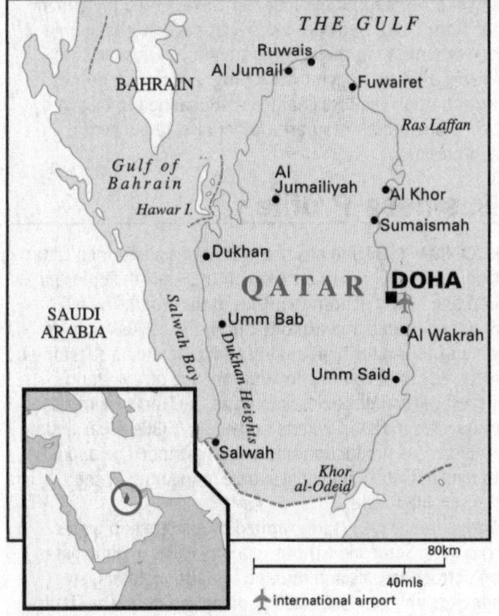

Location: Middle East, Gulf Coast.

Country dialling code: 974.

Qatar Tourism Authority
Postal address: PO Box 24624, Doha, Qatar
Tel: 441 1555. Fax: 437 2993.
E-mail: info@experienceqatar.com
Website: www.experienceqatar.com

Qatar National Hotels Company
Street address: 200 Corniche Street, Doha, Qatar
Postal address: PO Box 2977, Doha, Qatar
Tel: 485 7777. Fax: 483 3328 *or* 8935.
E-mail: info@qnhc.com *or* tm@qnhc.com
Website: www.qnhc.com

Embassy of the State of Qatar
1 South Audley Street, London W1K 1NB, UK
Tel: (020) 7493 2200. Fax: (020) 7493 2661.
Opening hours: Mon-Fri 0930-1600 (1000-1400 during Ramadan); 0930-1230 (visa section).

British Embassy
PO Box 3, Doha, Qatar
Visa section: Ground Floor, AKC Building, Al Saad Street, Doha, Qatar
Tel: 442 1991 *or* 436 4189 (visa section) *or* 435 3543 (commercial section). Fax: 443 8692 *or* 436 4139 (visa section) *or* 435 6131 (commercial section).
E-mail: bembcomm@qatar.net.qa (commercial section) *or* consular@qatar.fco.gov.uk

Qatar Tourism Authority
Kennedy House, 115 Hammersmith Road, London, W14 0QH, UK
Tel: (020) 7371 1571. Fax: (020) 7603 2424.
Email: uk@experienceqatar.com
Website: www.experiencqatar.com

Embassy of the State of Qatar
4200 Wisconsin Avenue, NW, Suite 200, Washington, DC 20016, USA
Tel: (202) 274 1600/3. Fax: (202) 237 0061.
E-mail: info@qatarembassy.org (general enquiries).
Website: www.qatarembassy.net
Also deals with enquiries from Canada.

Embassy of the United States of America
Postal address: PO Box 2399, Doha, Qatar
Tel: 488 4101.
Fax: 488 4298 (general) *or* 4176 (consular section).
E-mail: consulardoha@state.gov *or* PASDoha@state.gov
Website: http://qatar.usembassy.gov

The Canadian Embassy in Kuwait City deals with enquiries relating to Qatar (see *Kuwait* section).

TIMATIC CODES

Health
AMADEUS: **TI-DFT/DOH/HE**
GALILEO/WORLDSPAN: **TI-DFT/DOH/HE**
SABRE: **TIDFT/DOH/HE**

Visa
AMADEUS: **TI-DFT/DOH/VI**
GALILEO/WORLDSPAN: **TI-DFT/DOH/VI**
SABRE: **TIDFT/DOH/VI**

To access TIMATIC country information on Health and Visa regulations through the Computer Reservations System (CRS), type in the appropriate command line listed above.

General Information

AREA: 11,437 sq km (4416 sq miles).
POPULATION: 618,000 (official estimate 2002).
POPULATION DENSITY: 54.0 per sq km.
CAPITAL: Doha. **Population:** 264,009 (1997).
GEOGRAPHY: Qatar is an oil-rich peninsula jutting out into the Gulf between Bahrain and the United Arab Emirates. There are hills in the northwest, but the rest of the country consists of sand dunes and salt flats, with scattered vegetation towards the north.
GOVERNMENT: Emirate since 1971. Gained independence from the UK in 1971. **Head of State:** Crown Prince Sheikh Hamad bin Khalifa al-Thani since 1995. **Head of Government:** Prime Minister Sheikh Abdallah bin Khalifa al-Thani since 1996.
LANGUAGE: Arabic is the official language. Some English is spoken.
RELIGION: Islam.
TIME: GMT + 3.
ELECTRICITY: 220-240 volts AC, 50Hz.
COMMUNICATIONS: Telephone: IDD is available. Country code: 974. There are no area codes. Outgoing international code: 0. **Mobile telephone:** GSM 900 network exists. Main network provider is *Q-tel* (website: www.qtel.com.qa). **Fax:** Available at some major hotels. **Internet:** Main ISPs iclude *Qatar* (website: www.qatar.net.qa). Internet cafes exist in Doha. **Telegram:** The Cable & Wireless office in Doha (0600-2300) and major hotels provide services. **Post:** Airmail to Europe takes up to one week. **Press:** English-language newspapers include the *Gulf Times* and *The Peninsula*. The main dailies are *Al-'Arab*, *Ar-Raya* and *Ash-Sharq*.
Radio: BBC World Service (website: www.bbc.co.uk/worldservice) and Voice of America (website: www.voa.gov) can be received. From time to time the frequencies change and the most up-to-date can be found online.

Passport/Visa

	Passport Required?	Visa Required?	Return Ticket Required?
Full British	Yes	Yes	Yes
Australian	Yes	Yes	Yes
Canadian	Yes	Yes	Yes
USA	Yes	Yes	Yes
Other EU	Yes	Yes	Yes
Japanese	Yes	Yes	Yes

Note: Regulations and requirements may be subject to change at short notice, and you are advised to contact the appropriate diplomatic or consular authority before finalising travel arrangements. Details of these may be found at the head of this country's entry. Any numbers in the chart refer to the footnotes below.

Restricted entry: The Government refuses entry and transit to holders of passports issued by Israel.
PASSPORTS: Passport valid for at least six months required by all.
VISAS: Required by all except the following:
(a) nationals of Bahrain, Kuwait, Oman, Saudi Arabia and United Arab Emirates;
(b) transit passengers whose tickets show they intend to continue their journey from the airport within eight hours.
Note: (a) All visitors require onward or return tickets and sufficient funds for the period of stay. Visa requirements are subject to change, and travellers are strongly advised to contact an Embassy or Consulate of Qatar for up-to-date information. (b) Nationals of Andorra, Australia, Brunei, Canada, EU countries, Hong Kong (SAR), Japan, Korea (Rep), Liechtenstein, Malaysia, New Zealand, San Marino, Singapore, Switzerland and the USA can obtain business and tourist visas upon arrival at the Airport in Doha for 50 Qatari (£10-12).
Types of visa and cost: Prices vary according to nationality. The following prices are for British nationals: *Single-entry*: £36; *Multiple-entry*: £50 (six months), £71 (two years), £130 (five years) (depending on validity).
Note: All children included in the same passport of applicant travelling to Qatar must pay the same fees.
Validity: Single-entry visas permit stays of up to three months. Multiple-entry visas permits stays of up to six months, two years and five years.
Application to: Consulate (or Consular section at Embassy); see *Contact Addresses* section for details. Nationals of countries where Qatar has no diplomatic representation should apply for visas through their hotel in Qatar, which will arrange for the visa to be collected on arrival at the airport. Those wishing to visit friends or relatives in Qatar should ask them to apply to the immigration authorities in Qatar on their behalf for a visa. For longer-period visas apply to the Immigration Department, Ministry of the Interior, PO Box 115, Doha (tel: 465 7802; website: www.e.gov.qa). There is now a facility to book all visas online through the Ministry of Interior's website.
Application requirements: (a) Completed application form. (b) Valid passport. (c) Two passport-size photos. (d) Fee (postal order or company cheque only). (e) Name and address of sponsor in Qatar and for American nationals and EU passport holders except nationals from Ireland and the UK. Business visas need to be accompanied by an invitation letter from company and confirmation of hotel booking. (f) Stamped, self-addressed envelope for postal applications.
Working days required: One, although it could take as long as three weeks depending on nationality. Applications should be made well in advance of the intended departure date.

Money

Currency: Qatari Riyal (QR) = 100 dirhams. Notes are in denominations of QR500, 100, 50, 10, 5 and 1. Coins are in denominations of 50, 25, 10, 5 and 1 dirhams; however, only the 50 and 25 coins are in wide circulation, minting of the rest ceased in the 1970s and smaller denominations are becoming ever-scarcer.
Note: The Qatari Riyal is tied to the US Dollar.
Credit & debit cards: American Express, Diners Club, MasterCard and Visa are widely accepted. Check with your credit or debit card company for details of merchant acceptability and other services which may be available.
Travellers cheques: Widely accepted. To avoid additional exchange rate charges, travellers are advised to take travellers cheques in US Dollars or Pounds Sterling.
Currency restrictions: There are no restrictions on the import or export of either local or foreign currency. Israeli currency, however, is prohibited.
Exchange rate indicators: The following figures are included as a guide to the movements of the Riyal against the Dollar and Sterling:

Date	Feb '04	May '04	Aug '04	Nov '04
£1.00=	6.62	6.50	6.71	6.91
$1.00=	3.64	3.64	3.64	3.65

Banking hours: Sat-Thurs 0730-1330.

Duty Free

The following goods may be imported into Qatar without incurring customs duty:
A reasonable amount of tobacco and perfume for personal use.
Prohibited items: All alcohol is prohibited. Firearms can only be imported with a licence obtained in advance from the Ministry of Defence.

Public Holidays

2005: Jan 21 Eid al-Adha (Feast of the Sacrifice). **Feb 10** Islamic New Year. **Jun 27** Accession of HH The Amir Sheikh Hamad Bin Khalifa Al-Thani. **Sep 3** Independence Day. **Nov 3-5** Eid al-Fitr (End of Ramadan).
2006: Jan 10-13 Eid al-Adha (Feast of the Sacrifice). **Jan 31** Islamic New Year. **Jun 27** Accession of HH The Amir Sheikh Hamad Bin Khalifa Al-Thani. **Sep 3** Independence Day. **Oct 22** Eid al-Fitr (End of Ramadan).
Note: Muslim festivals are timed according to local sightings of various phases of the moon and the dates given above are approximations. During the lunar month of Ramadan that precedes Eid al-Fitr, Muslims fast during the day and feast at night and normal business patterns may be interrupted. Many restaurants are closed during the day and there may be restrictions on smoking and drinking. Some disruption may continue into Eid al-Fitr itself. Eid al-Fitr and Eid al-Adha may last anything from two to 10 days, depending on the region. For more information, see the *World of Islam* appendix.

Health

	Special Precautions?	Certificate Required?
Yellow Fever	No	No
Cholera	No	No
Typhoid & Polio	1	N/A
Malaria	No	N/A

Note: Regulations and requirements may be subject to change at short notice, and you are advised to contact your doctor well in advance of your intended date of departure. Any numbers in the chart refer to the footnotes below.

1: Vaccination against typhoid is advised.
Food & drink: All water should be regarded as being potentially contaminated. Water used for drinking, brushing teeth or making ice should have first been boiled or

otherwise sterilised. Milk is unpasteurised and should be boiled. Powdered or tinned milk is available and is advised, but make sure that it is reconstituted with pure water. Avoid dairy products which are likely to have been made from unboiled milk. Only eat well-cooked meat and fish, preferably served hot. Salad and mayonnaise may carry increased risk. Vegetables should be cooked and fruit peeled.
Other risks: *Typhoid fevers* and *hepatitis A* exist; precautions should be taken. *Hepatitis B* is endemic. *Cutaneous leishmaniasis* occurs.
Rabies is present. For those at high risk, vaccination before arrival should be considered. If you are bitten, seek medical advice without delay.
Note: Certificates proving the visitor to be HIV-negative may be required if planning on staying more than one month in the country. Check with Embassy (see *Contact Addresses* section).
Health care: There are several hospitals in Qatar, the most recent and modern being the Hamad General Hospital. The Poly Clinic has good dentists. Charges are high and health insurance is essential. As a precaution against the intense heat, visitors should maintain a high salt and fluid intake.

Travel - International

Note: There is a high risk of terrorism in Qatar. For further advice, visitors should contact the relevant local government travel advice department.
AIR: *Gulf Air (GF)* and *Qatar Airways (QR)* are the major airlines serving Qatar.
Approximate flight times: From Doha to *London* is eight hours 25 minutes. There are no direct flights from the USA.
International airports: *Doha (DOH)* is 8km (5 miles) southeast of the city (travel time - 25 minutes). Taxis are available to the city with official rates displayed. Facilities include car hire (*Budget* and *Hertz*), banks, restaurant and a duty free shop.
Departure tax: None.
SEA: The main international ports are Doha and Umm Said. The traffic is mostly commercial, but some passenger lines call at Doha.

ROAD: Access is possible via both Saudi Arabia and the United Arab Emirates, but the main international route from Saudi Arabia is unreliable and often impassable during the rainy season.

Travel - Internal

ROAD: The road system is fair, but conditions are poor during the wet season. Driving is on the right. **Bus:** No organised public bus service. **Taxi:** These have black and yellow number plates, are painted orange and white, and are metered. Taxis can be hired on an hourly basis. **Car hire:** Available from local companies at the airport and hotels.
Documentation: An International Driving Permit is required, but a temporary licence can be obtained on presentation of a valid UK licence.

Accommodation

Recent building ensures that Qatar is well served by first-class hotels. There are also a number of **3-** or **4-star** hotels offering reasonable accommodation. Advance booking is strongly advised. All rates are subject to a 15 per cent service charge. For more information, contact the Qatar National Hotels Company (see *Contact Addresses* section).

Resorts & Excursions

DOHA: The capital is a rich mixture of traditional Arabic and modern architecture. The **Grand Mosque** with its many domes and the **Abu Bakir al-Siddiq Mosque** are particularly interesting. There is an excellent **National Museum** in Doha tracing the country's development. The modern town clusters around the Grand Mosque, the **New Amir's Palace** and the **Clock Tower**.
THE NORTH: This area contains most of the historic sites, including **Umm Salal Mohammed**, a relatively large village dominated by the ruins of a 19th-century fort. At **Al Zubara** is the **Qalit Marir Fortress**. **Al Khor** is the second-largest city, situated around a natural shallow harbour. **Gharya** has a golden sandy beach stretching for miles. **Ruwais** boasts a harbour, from where there is an occasional *dhow* service to Bahrain. There are also good beaches at **Fuwairat**, on the northeast coast, and **Ras Abruk**, opposite Hawar Island.
THE WEST COAST: There are beaches at **Umm Bab** ('The Palm Tree Beach'), **Dukhan** and **Salwah**, near the Saudi border.
THE SOUTH: This is a region of sand dunes and beaches, offering opportunities to go pearl hunting, or to practise any number of watersports. The 'inland sea' of **Khor al-Odeid** is the centre of a region of outstanding natural beauty, surrounded by the **Sandi Hills**, accessible only to 4-wheel-drive vehicles.

Sport & Activities

The national sport is **football**. Doha boasts several marinas, sub-aqua clubs and **sailing** facilities, as well as a number of sports clubs which are open to visitors. There are several **camel race** tracks; the main one is found off the road to Dukhan, but spectators need a 4-wheel-drive vehicle to follow the race. The graded track is 18km (11 miles) long through the desert and sometimes more than 250 camels take part with big money prizes and prestige at stake. **Desert excursions** can also be arranged.

Social Profile

FOOD & DRINK: While the best food is generally found in hotels, Chinese, Indian, Persian, Thai, US and Western cuisine is also available. All the major hotels have good public restaurants and most offer outside catering of high quality; waiters, crockery and cutlery will be provided on request. There are a reasonable number of places to eat in Doha, including snack bars serving fast foods, as well as the traditional Levantine *shawarma* and Egyptian *foul* and *taamiyeh*. Restaurants are scarce outside the capital. Alcohol is prohibited and should not be consumed in public, though some international hotels may serve alcohol.
NIGHTLIFE: Public entertainment is rather limited. Doha has a cinema showing English-language films, and there is also the National Theatre. Live entertainment is infrequent, but some international artists do perform in Qatar.
SHOPPING: There are several large modern malls, with cinemas, restaurants and other facilities, as well as brand shops. The old *souks* remain popular for bargains. **Shopping hours:** Generally Sat-Thurs 0800-1200 and 1600-1900 or later, with the malls open until 2100 or 2200. Some shops close on Friday.
SPECIAL EVENTS: Qatar's festivals and events are primarily Islamic celebrations.
The following is a selection of special events occurring in Qatar in 2005:
Jan *Eid al-Adha* (Feast of the Sacrifice). **Mar** *Qatar Masters* (golf), Doha. **Jun-Aug** *Qatar Summer Wonders Festival of Fun*. **Nov** *Eid al-Fitr* (End of Ramadan).
SOCIAL CONVENTIONS: The visitor should be fully aware of Muslim religious laws and customs. Women should always dress modestly. It is also worth noting that, while it is acceptable to cross legs, showing the sole of the foot or unknowingly pointing it at a person is considered an insult. At business and social functions, the traditional Qatari coffee, in tiny handleless cups, will invariably be served. This is a ritual of welcome with strict rules: guests are served in order of seniority - a few drops at first, then, after three or four others have been served, the server returns to fill the first cup; always hold the cup in the right hand; two cups are polite, but never take only one or more than three. For more information, see the *World of Islam* appendix. **Tipping:** Taxi drivers do not expect a tip. A service charge is often added to bills in hotels and most restaurants, otherwise 10 per cent is appropriate.

Business Profile

ECONOMY: Oil and gas reserves have transformed Qatar from an impoverished outcrop on the Arabian Peninsula into one of the richest countries in the world. The oil deposits located and exploited from the 1970s onwards were of unusually high quality and generated a substantial income for the country. In addition, one of the world's largest natural gas fields, known as the North Field, was discovered in Qatari waters in the late 1980s. Measured by revenue, gas production has now outstripped oil and is set to remain Qatar's principal source of income for the foreseeable future.
Agriculture is necessarily limited by climate and water resources. Some indigenous industry exists, mainly based on petrochemicals and refining but also including steel, concrete and cement, plastics, paint and flour. The Qatari government has earmarked US$5 billion for further industrialisation projects over the coming years. Current economic performance is good, with an annual growth of 8.5 per cent and inflation of 2.3 per cent. Qatar is a member of OPEC, the Arab Monetary Fund and the Islamic Development Bank. It also belongs to the World Trade Organization, and hosted the organisation's 2001 round of negotiations. Currently, most of Qatar's oil and gas is sold to Japan and Italy. EU countries, Japan and the USA are the country's main trading partners.
BUSINESS: Politeness and patience in business dealings are needed. **Office hours:** Sat-Thurs 0800-1200 and 1600-1900. **Government office hours:** Sat-Wed 0700-1400.
COMMERCIAL INFORMATION: The following organisation can offer advice: Qatar Chamber of Commerce and Industry, PO Box 402, Doha (tel: 462 2538; fax: 462 1905; e-mail: qcci@qatar.net.qa; website: www.arab.net/qatar/qr_commerce.htm).
CONFERENCES/CONVENTIONS: Several of Doha's largest hotels provide facilities with extensive support services, including simultaneous translation systems and full audio-visual capability. Contact individual hotels for more information.

Climate

Summer (June to September) is very hot with low rainfall. Winter is cooler with occasional rainfall. Spring and autumn are warm and pleasant.
Required clothing: Lightweight cottons and linens are worn during summer months, with warm clothes for cooler evenings and during the winter. Rainwear is advisable during winter.

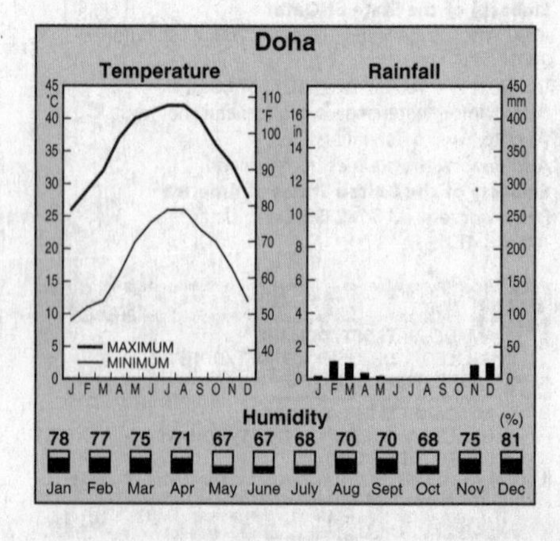

Réunion

LATEST TRAVEL ADVICE CONTACTS

British Foreign and Commonwealth Office
Tel: (0870) 606 0290 Website: www.fco.gov.uk

US Department of State
Website: http://travel.state.gov/travel

Canadian Department of Foreign Affairs and Int'l Trade
Tel: (1 800) 267 8376 Website: www.dfait-maeci.gc.ca

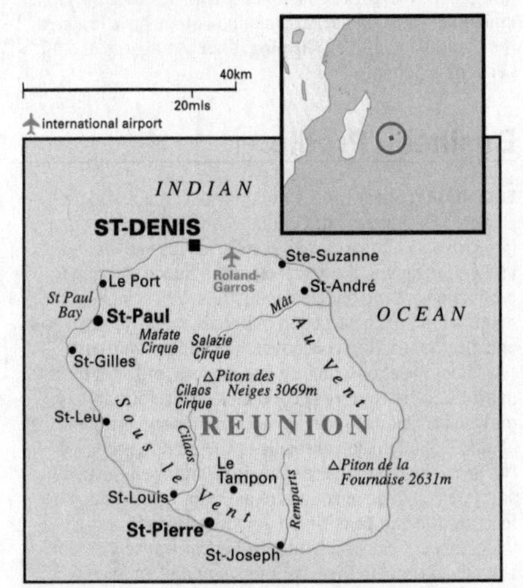

Location: Due east of Madagascar, in the Indian Ocean.

Country dialling code: 262.

Diplomatic representation
Réunion is a *Département d'Outre-Mer* (Overseas Department) of the Republic of France, and is represented abroad by French Embassies – see *France* section.

Comité du Tourisme de la Réunion
Place du 20 Décembre 1848, BP 615, 97472 Saint-Denis, Réunion
Tel: (262) 210 041. Fax: (262) 210 021.
E-mail: ctr@la-reunion-tourisme.com *or* r.barrieu@la-reunion-tourisme.com
Website: www.la-reunion-tourisme.com

Comité du Tourisme de la Réunion
90 rue la Boétie, 75008 Paris, France
Tel: (1) 4075 0279. Fax: (1) 4075 0273.
E-mail: ctr@aol.com *or* ctrparis@aol.com
Website: www.la-reunion-tourisme.com

Maison de la France
178 Piccadilly, London W1J 9AL, UK
Tel: (0906) 824 4123 (consumer information line; calls cost 60p per minute) *or* (020) 7399 3520 (travel trade only).
Fax: (020) 7493 6594.
E-mail: info.uk@franceguide.com
Website: www.franceguide.com

General Information

AREA: 2507 sq km (968 sq miles).
POPULATION: 753,600 (official estimate 2003).
POPULATION DENSITY: 300.6 per sq km.
CAPITAL: Saint-Denis. **Population:** 131,557 (1999).
GEOGRAPHY: Réunion lies 760km (407 miles) east of Madagascar in the Indian Ocean. Running diagonally across the island is a chain of volcanic peaks, separating a green humid eastern zone (*Le Vent*) from a dry, sheltered south and west (*Sous le Vent*). The majority of the population lives along the coast. Sugar cane production accounts for over half the arable land in a country where many basic foodstuffs are imported.
GOVERNMENT: Réunion is an Overseas Department of France and as such is an integral part of the French Republic. **Head of State:** President Jacques Chirac since 1995, represented locally by Prefect Gonthier Friederici since 2001. **Head of Government:** Nassimah Dindar, President of the General Council.

TIMATIC CODES

Health	AMADEUS: **TI-DFT/RUN/HE** GALILEO/WORLDSPAN: **TI-DFT/RUN/HE** SABRE: **TIDFT/RUN/HE**
Visa	AMADEUS: **TI-DFT/RUN/VI** GALILEO/WORLDSPAN: **TI-DFT/RUN/VI** SABRE: **TIDFT/RUN/VI**

To access TIMATIC country information on Health and Visa regulations through the Computer Reservations System (CRS), type in the appropriate command line listed above.

LANGUAGE: French is the official language. Local Creole *patois* is also spoken.
RELIGION: The majority of the population is Roman Catholic, with a Muslim minority.
TIME: GMT + 4.
ELECTRICITY: 220 volts AC, 50Hz.
COMMUNICATIONS: Telephone: IDD is available. Country code: 262. There are no area codes. Outgoing international code: 19. **Mobile telephone:** GSM 900/1800 network available. Network operators include *Orange Réunion* (website: www.orange.re), *Outremer Telecom* and *Société Réunionnaise* (website: www.srr.fr). **Fax:** Most large hotels have facilities. **Internet:** Internet cafes in towns throughout La Réunion provide public access to e-mail and Internet services. **Telegram:** Facilities are available in Saint-Denis. **Post:** Airmail to Western Europe takes up to three weeks. Poste Restante facilities are available in Saint-Denis. **Press:** The two biggest dailies are the *Journal de l'Ile de la Réunion* and the *Quotidien de la Réunion*. Weekly periodicals include *L'Economie de la Réunion* and *Témoignages*. There are no English-language dailies.
Radio: BBC World Service (website: www.bbc.co.uk/worldservice) and Voice of America (website: www.voa.gov) can be received. From time to time the frequencies change and the most up-to-date can be found online.

Passport/Visa

	Passport Required?	Visa Required?	Return Ticket Required?
Full British	Yes	No	Yes
Australian	Yes	No	Yes
Canadian	Yes	No	Yes
USA	Yes	No	Yes
Other EU	Yes/1	No	Yes
Japanese	Yes	No	Yes

Note: Regulations and requirements may be subject to change at short notice, and you are advised to contact the appropriate diplomatic or consular authority before finalising travel arrangements. Details of these may be found at the head of this country's entry. Any numbers in the chart refer to the footnotes below.

PASSPORTS: Passport valid for at least three months beyond applicant's last day of stay required by all except the following:
1. nationals of Belgium, France, Germany, Greece, Italy, Luxembourg, Monaco, The Netherlands, Portugal, Spain and Switzerland, who are holders of national identity cards.
VISAS: Required by all except the following:
(a) nationals of countries referred to in the chart above for stays of up to three months;
(b) nationals of Andorra, Argentina, Bermuda, Bolivia, Brunei, Chile, Costa Rica, Croatia, Ecuador, El Salvador, Guatemala, Holy See, Honduras, Iceland, Israel, Korea (Rep), Liechtenstein, Malaysia, Mexico, New Zealand, Nicaragua, Norway, Panama, Paraguay, Singapore, Switzerland, Uruguay and Venezuela for stays of up to three months;
(c) transit passengers continuing their journey by the same or first connecting aircraft provided holding valid onward or return documentation and not leaving the airport.
Note: (a) Nationals of the EU and EEE, and of the Holy See, Liechtenstein and Monaco do not need a a Long Stay visa (trips exceeding three months). (b) Nationals of Canada, Cyprus, Japan, Korea (Rep), Malaysia, Malta, Mexico, Singapore, USA and Venezuela should apply for a visa if they are to receive a salary, even if their trip is a Short Stay. (c) US nationals need a visa if they are crew members, or journalists on assignments, or students enrolled at schools and universities in any of the French Overseas Departments.
Types of visa and cost: Visas cost £22-26 and must be paid for in cash or with a credit card (certain cards are not accepted). Prices may change due to fluctuation in the exchange rate. In most circumstances, no fee applies to students, recipients of government fellowships and citizens of the EU and their family members.
Validity: *Short-stay* visas (up to 30 days): valid for two months (single- and multiple-entry). *Short stay* visas (31 to 90 days and double- or multiple-entry): valid for a maximum of six months from date of issue. *Transit* visas: valid for single- or multiple-entries of maximum five days per entry, including the day of arrival.
Application to: French Consulate General (for personal visas), or Consular section at Embassy (for diplomatic or service visas); see *Contact Addresses* section for France. All applications must be made in person.
Application requirements: (a) Valid passport with blank page to affix the visa. Minors travelling alone must submit notarised parental authorisation, signed by both parents, plus one copy. (b) Up to two completed application forms. (c) One passport-size photo on each form. (d) Fee, to be paid in cash only if paying by person. If not, fee should be paid by cheque or postal order. (e) Evidence of sufficient funds for stay (two last bank statements, plus copy, or other proof of funds equivalent to US$100 for each day of trip). (f) Letter from employer, or proof of stay in country of residence. (g) Proof of address. (h) Medical insurance. (i) Return ticket and travel documents for remaining journey. (j) Proof of accommodation during stay. (k) Registered self-addressed envelope, if applying by post. (l) Detailed itinerary, including reservations and round trip airline tickets (only required when visa is issued), plus one copy. (m) Proof of employment (eg last payslip or letter from employer). (n) Proof of valid health/travel insurance with worldwide coverage, plus copy. *Business*: (a)-(n) and, (o) Business invitation guaranteeing payment of travel expenses, plus one copy.
Working days required: One day to three weeks depending on nationality.
Temporary residence: If intending to work or stay for longer than 90 days, nationals should contact the Long Stay visa section of the Consulate General or Embassy (tel: (020) 7073 1248).

Money

Currency: Since January 2002 the Euro has been the official currency for the French Overseas Departments (*Départements d'Outre-Mer*) of French Guiana, Guadeloupe, Martinique and Réunion. For further details, exchange rates and currency restrictions, see the France section. US Dollars are also accepted in some places.
Currency exchange: All major currencies can be exchanged at banks and bureaux de change.
Credit & debit cards: American Express, Diners Club and Visa are accepted. MasterCard has limited acceptance. Cards can also be used in ATMs. Check with your credit or debit card company for details of merchant acceptability and other services which may be available.
Travellers cheques: Accepted in most places, and may qualify for discounts on luxury items. To avoid additional exchange rate charges, travellers are advised to take travellers cheques in Euros, US Dollars or Pounds Sterling.
Currency restrictions: Same regulations as France; see *France* section.
Banking Hours: Mon-Fri 0800-1600..

Duty Free

The island of Réunion is an Overseas Department of France, and therefore duty free allowances are the same as those for France; see *France* section.
Prohibited items: All plants, vegetables and vegetable products.

Public Holidays

As for France (see *France* section).

Health

	Special Precautions?	Certificate Required?
Yellow Fever	No	1
Cholera	No	2
Typhoid & Polio	3	N/A
Malaria	No	N/A

Note: Regulations and requirements may be subject to change at short notice, and you are advised to contact your doctor well in advance of your intended date of departure. Any numbers in the chart refer to the footnotes below.

1: A yellow fever vaccination certificate is required from travellers over one year of age arriving from infected areas.
2: A cholera vaccination certificate may be required from travellers arriving from infected areas.
3: There is a risk of typhoid, but not of polio. Immunisation is advised.
Food & drink: All water should be regarded as being potentially contaminated. Water used for drinking, brushing teeth or making ice should have first been boiled or otherwise sterilised. Milk is unpasteurised and should be boiled. Powdered or tinned milk is available and is advised, but make sure that it is reconstituted with pure water. Avoid dairy products which are likely to have been made from unboiled milk. Only eat well-cooked meat and fish, preferably served hot. Pork, salad and mayonnaise may carry increased risk. Vegetables should be cooked and fruit peeled.
Other risks: *Hepatitis A, B* and *E* are present; precautions should be taken.
Rabies is present. For those at high risk, vaccination before arrival should be considered. If you are bitten, seek medical advice without delay. For more information, consult the *Health* appendix.
Health care: There are nine hospitals and many out-patient clinics. The French national health scheme is in force and there is a reciprocal health agreement with the UK (see *France* section). Facilities are limited and full health insurance is advised.

Travel - International

AIR: The main airline to serve Réunion is *Air France (AF)* (website: www.airfrance.com). Other airlines operating to Réunion include *Air Liberté*, *Air Madagascar* and *Corsair International*. *Air Austral* and *Air Mauritius* operate daily flights between Réunion and Mauritius (from Saint-Pierre Pierrefonds Airport). There are often discounts on flights during the periods of March to May and October to November.
Approximate flight times: From Réunion to *London* is 14 hours 40 minutes (via Paris); to *Paris* is 11 hours.
International airports: *Saint-Denis de la Réunion (RUN)* (Roland-Garros) is 10km (6 miles) from the town (travel time – 20 minutes). *Cars Jaunes* (yellow buses) operated by the County Council run 13 times a day between Roland Garros Airport and Saint-Denis bus terminal. Airport facilities include banks/bureaux de change, ATMs, bars, restaurant, post office and car hire (including *Avis*, *Budget* and *Hertz*). *Saint-Pierre Pierrefonds (ZSE)* is 5km (3 miles) from Saint-Pierre. A shuttle bus service operates between Saint Denis and Roland Garros airport bus terminals. Taxi services as well as car hire are available at the airport.
Departure tax: None.
SEA: Both freight and passenger lines (a large number are French) dock at Pointe-des-Galets.

Travel - Internal

AIR: Aero-clubs at Roland-Garros Airport hire planes for flights over the island, which are well worth the price.
SEA: Four shipping lines run services around the island.
ROAD: Roads are fair and there are over 2680km (1665 miles) of roads, 345km (214 miles) of which are main roads. Speed limits are the same as in France. The main road runs on a north–south axis. The island can be easily crossed by bus, taxi or hired car. Car hire is available throughout the island. Further details can be obtained from the Comité du Tourisme de la Réunion. **Bus:** Two types of buses operate on the island: urban buses mainly serve the Saint-Denis area; yellow buses connect main towns. Services are excellent and luxurious, with very comfortable vehicles. Buses stop by request. **Taxis:** Taxi ranks can be found in city centres. Taxis can be hired by telephone (telephone numbers can be obtained from the information points at the airport). There are likely to be extra charges after 2000 Mon-Fri, on Sunday and Bank Holidays. **Car hire:** Available from the airport and from car hire firms in Saint-Denis. Petrol prices are similar to those in France. *Avis*, *Budget* and *Hertz* are among the many car hire companies that are represented at the airports. **Documentation:** An International Driving Permit is recommended, though not legally required.

Accommodation

HOTELS: There is a good range of hotels, inns and *pensions*. Prices are high (and plumbing somewhat basic), but the food is often excellent. Tariffs usually include bed and breakfast, tax and service charges. **Grading:** Hotels range from **1** to **4 stars**.
MOUNTAIN LODGES: Cheap and basic accommodation called *gîtes* favoured by trekkers are available throughout the island. For further information, contact Maison de la Montagne, 9 rue Rontaunay, 97400 Saint-Denis, Réunion (tel: 907 878; fax: 418 429; e-mail: resa@reunion-nature.com; website: www.reunion-nature.com).
YOUTH HOSTELS: For information, contact Les Auberges de Jeunesse de la Reunion, 9 rue Rontaunay, 97400 Saint-Denis (tel: 411 534; fax: 417 217; e-mail: ajoi@wanadoo.fr; website: www.chez.com/fraj).
OTHER ACCOMMODATION: There are many rooms available in guest houses across the island as well as self-catering studio flats and accommodation in farmhouses. For further information, contact Comité du Tourisme de la Réunion (see *Contact Addresses* section).

Resorts & Excursions

SAINT-DENIS: The capital is surrounded by mountains on three sides and has several places of interest, including the **Natural History Museum** and the **Léon Dierx Art Gallery** with its collection of French Impressionist paintings. There are various temples, a mosque and a cathedral, a sign of the cultural and religious variety of the island population. Around town, a good trip to take is the **Plaine d'Affouches** in **La Montagne**, which is lined by lush tamarind trees and calumets, a type of wild fig tree. From **Brûlé**, a footpath leads to the **Roche-Écrite**, a 2227m- (7306ft-) high summit which overlooks the whole of the northern part of the island and slopes down to the **Mafate** and **Salazie Cirques**.
THE CIRQUES: A special feature on Réunion are the so-called *cirques* – large volcanic valleys surrounded by mountains, creating a natural amphitheatre of about 10km (6 miles) in diameter. Day-long sightseeing trips to the cirques may be arranged with travel agents in Saint-Denis. There are over 600km (370 miles) of footpaths leading through the island.
Cilaos, once infamous as a refuge for escaped slaves, is a lovely mountain area rising to about 1220m (4000ft) with impressive views from **Le Bras Sec** and **Îlet à Cordres**. The most beautiful cirque is probably *Salazie*, with its magnificent waterfalls, especially those known as **Le Voile de la Mariée** (The Bride's Veil) near **Hell-Bourg**. There is a day-trip to **Grand-Îlet**, taking in some spectacularly rugged scenery. **Piton des Neiges** is the highest point on the island and is an enjoyable hike from Hell-Bourg.
Mafate is the most secluded of the valleys, unconnected by any road with the outside world.
THE VOLCANO: There are tours to the island's still-active volcano, **La Fournaise**. St Paul also has an interesting street market (Friday afternoons and Saturday mornings) and there are numerous traditional Créole houses.
Nez-de-Boeuf (*'ox's nose'*) affords a splendid view over the **Rivière des Remparts**, 1000m (3300ft) below, the **Plaine des Sables** and the **Belle Combe** pass. The **Enclos Fouque** crater and the highest peak of the 2631m (8632ft) *Fournaise* can both be explored on foot. The still active **Bory** and **Brûlant** craters are also interesting excursions. Réunion abounds with tropical flowers, trees and fruit, and there are tours which aim to show the visitor some of the many species on the island, before returning to the **Botanical Gardens** at Saint-Denis.
THE COAST: Réunion does not have extensive beaches, but those on the leeward west coast are beautiful with yellow, black or white sands. Some of the best beaches are to be found at **Saint-Gilles**, **Saint-Leu** and **Étang-Sale**. These are mostly shallow coral, running out to the reef. The **Corail Turtle Farm** near Saint-Leu is an interesting place. The coral reefs along the west coast are a protected area, but scuba-diving and snorkelling are available. Also on the west coast is the historic town of **Saint-Paul**, Réunion's original capital, and birthplace of Leconte de Lisle.

Sport & Activities

Watersports: Good **swimming** and **diving** are to be found along the *Sous le Vent* coast, especially at Saint-Gilles-des-Bains, which has a reef-protected lagoon. On the more remote beaches, sharks may be a danger, so it is best to enquire locally. **Surfing** can be practised in Saint-Gilles, Saint-Paul and Saint-Pierre. For information on the best beaches, see also the *Resorts & Excursions* section. **Trout fishing** is to be found at the *Takamaka Falls*.
Trekking and mountaineering: There are excellent walking opportunities in the mountains. The National Forestry Office has provided many sign-posted footpaths throughout the island. Good climbing is to be had among the volcanic peaks.
Island tours: One-day tours around the island with stopovers at various locations are available from local operators. Contact the Comité du Tourisme de la Réunion for details (see *Contact Addresses* section).
Spas: Rest cures are available in mountain resorts, such as Cilaos, which is a mountain spa.

Social Profile

FOOD & DRINK: A variety of excellent restaurants, some run by hotels, offer good French cuisine and Creole specialities, notably *rougail* (seafood with sauces) and many unique curries – these include duck, eel and octopus curry (*zourite*). Worth trying is *brèdes*, a delicious local vegetable rather like spinach. Traditional spicy Indian cuisine also appears on the menu, under the heading *massalés*. There are about 10 first-class restaurants in Saint-Denis. Seaside restaurants in particular serve authentic local cuisine – a mixture of African, Chinese and Indian cooking.
Drinks include Arab coffee (*café Bourbon*), French wine and liqueurs, and good local rum such as *rhum arrangé* (white rum with vanilla, orchids, aniseed and cinnamon). Local beer and wine are also very good. A full range of alcoholic drinks are available. Licensing hours are largely unrestricted.
SHOPPING: Local handicrafts include lace and embroidery, coral jewellery and basketwork. Tamarind wood, olive wood and ironwood provide the material for furniture in the traditional 'colonial' style, and are used by sculptors and other craftsmen. Rum, vanilla and extracts of vetiver, geranium and ylang-ylang are also recommended purchases. In Saint-Denis, the main shopping streets are rue du Maréchal-Leclerc, rue Jean-Chatel and rue Juliette-Dodu. **Shopping hours:** Mon-Sat 0830-1200 and 1430-1800, Sun 0800-1200; Mon-Sat 0730-1900, Sun 0800-1200 (department stores).
SPECIAL EVENTS: For further details about festivals and events that occur in La Réunion, contact the Comité du Tourisme de la Réunion (see *Contact Addresses* section). The following is a selection of special events occurring in Réunion in 2005:
Jan *Fire-walking*; *Mango Festival*, Saint-Paul. **Feb** *Pineapple Festival*, Sainte-Clotilde; *The Grape Harvest*, Cilaos; *Cavadee* (Indian sacrificial procession), Saint-André. **Mar** *Fête Tangues* (Festival of Tradition & Nature), Grande-Chaloupe. **May** *Fête du Chouchou et de la Pêche*, Hell-Bourg; *Fête de la Vanille* (Vanilla Festival), Bras-Panon. **Jun** *Fête de la Musique*, nationwide; *The Great Din Carnival*, Saint-Gilles-les-Bains. **Aug** *Fête du Safran* (Saffron Festival), St-Joseph. **Sep** *Tour de L'Îsle* (cycle race). **Oct** *Flower Show*, Le Tampon. **Nov** *International Triathlon*. **Dec** *December 1848 Celebrations*; *Fête des Litchis* (Lychee Festival), Saint-Denis.
SOCIAL CONVENTIONS: The islanders follow French fashion. Normal social courtesies should be observed. The immigrants from India, Pakistan and Europe have retained their cultural identities. **Tipping:** Widely practiced and 10 per cent is normal.

Business Profile

ECONOMY: Sugar cane is the principal crop and export earner in this mainly agricultural economy. Other crops include vanilla, tobacco, and plants such as *vétiver* and *ylang-ylang*, used in tropical essences. Sugar and rum production are the principal industries; others include the manufacture of construction materials, metal goods, textiles and electronics. The service sector, including transport, telecommunications, finance and tourism, provides three-quarters of the country's economic output. Tourism has grown particularly rapidly in recent years, and is now worth about US$300 million annually to the island's economy. However, the Réunion economy is far from self-sustaining and relies on large injections of aid from France and, more recently, the European Union, to cover its trade and budgetary deficits (as an integral part of France, Réunion belongs to the EU). The most pressing problem for the Government is a very high level of unemployment, estimated at 40 per cent. Apart from France, Réunion has important trading relations with Bahrain, Belgium, Italy, Japan and Luxembourg.
BUSINESS: The atmosphere is relaxed and friendly; suits will only be required for the most formal of meetings. A sound knowledge of the French language will be useful, since there are no formal interpreter services available. Prices should be quoted in Euros, and all trade literature should be in French. **Office hours:** Mon-Fri 0800-1200 and 1400-1800.
COMMERCIAL INFORMATION: The following organisations can offer advice: Chambre de Commerce et d'Industrie de la Réunion, 5 bis rue de Paris, BP 120, 97463 Saint-Denis (tel: 942 000; fax: 942 290; e-mail: sg.dir@reunion.cci.fr; website: www.reunion.cci.fr); *or* Délégation Régionale au Commerce, à l'Artisanat et au Tourisme, Préfecture de la Réunion, Avenue de la Victoire, 97400 Saint-Denis (tel: 407 758; fax: 407 701).

Climate

Hot tropical climate. Temperatures are cooler in the hills, occasionally dropping to freezing point in the mountains at night. The cyclone season (January to March) is hot and wet.
Required clothing: Lightweights, with warmer clothes for the evenings.

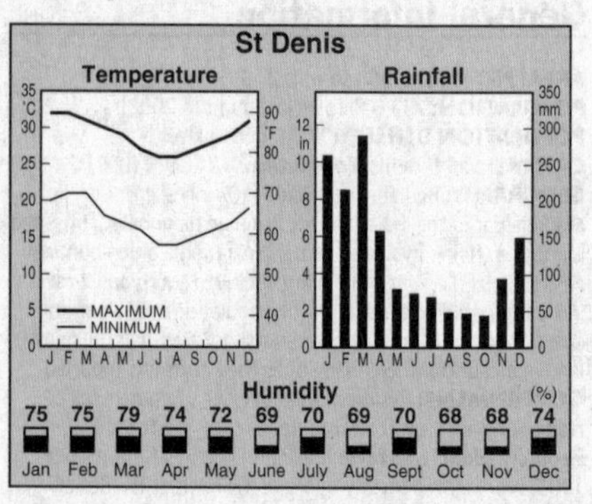

A B C D E F G H I J K L M N O P Q R S T U V W X Y Z

Romania

LATEST TRAVEL ADVICE CONTACTS

British Foreign and Commonwealth Office
Tel: (0870) 606 0290 Website: www.fco.gov.uk
US Department of State
Website: http://travel.state.gov/travel
Canadian Department of Foreign Affairs and Int'l Trade
Tel: (1 800) 267 8376 Website: www.dfait-maeci.gc.ca

Location: Eastern Europe.

Country dialling code: 40.

Ministry of Tourism
Bd. Dinicu Golescu 38, Mezanin 38, 010867 Bucharest, Romania
Tel: (21) 314 9957. Fax: (21) 314 9960.
E-mail: promovare@mturism.ro *or* mturism@terranet.ro
Website: www.mturism.ro *or* www.romaniatourism.com
Embassy of Romania
Arundel House, 4 Palace Green, London W8 4QD, UK
Tel: (020) 7937 9666/7. Fax: (020) 7937 8069.
E-mail: roemb@copperstream.co.uk
Website: www.roemb.co.uk
Opening hours: Mon-Fri 0900-1700; Mon-Thurs 1000-1300 (visa section).
Romanian National Tourist Office
22 New Cavendish Street, London W1M 7LH, UK
Tel: (020) 7224 3692. Fax: (020) 7935 6435.
E-mail: infouk@romaniatourism.com
Website: www.romaniatourism.com *or* www.visitromania.com
British Embassy
Strada Jules Michelet 24, Sector 1, 010463 Bucharest, Romania
Tel: (21) 201 7200 *or* 7300 (consular section).
Fax: (21) 201 7317 (consular section).
E-mail: Consular.Bucharest@fco.gov.uk
Website: www.britishembassy.gov.uk/romania
Embassy of Romania
1607 23rd Street, NW, Washington, DC 20008, USA
Tel: (202) 332 4846/8. Fax: (202) 232 4748.
E-mail: info@roembus.org *or* Consular@roembus.org (consular section).
Website: www.roembus.org
Consulate in: New York.
Romanian National Tourist Office
355 Lexington Avenue, 19th Floor, New York, NY 10017, USA
Tel: (212) 545 8484. Fax: (212) 251 0429.
E-mail: infous@romaniatourism.com
Website: www.romaniatourism.com
Embassy of the United States of America
Strada Tudor Arghezi 7-9, Sector 2, Bucharest 70132, Romania
Tel: (21) 210 4042. Fax: (21) 210 0395.
E-mail: infobuch@usia.gov (information resource centre) *or* bucharest.office.box@mail.doc.gov (US commercial service).
Website: www.usembassy.ro
Consular section: Strada Nicolae Filipescu 26, Bucharest, Romania
Tel: (21) 210 4042. Fax: (21) 211 3360.
E-mail: visasbucharest@state.gov
Embassy of Romania
655 Rideau Street, Ottawa, Ontario K1N 6A3, Canada
Tel: (613) 789 5345/3709/4038. Fax: (613) 789 4365.
E-mail: romania@cyberus.ca
Website: www.cyberus.ca/~romania
Consulates in: Montréal and Toronto.
Canadian Embassy
Strada Nicolae Iorga 36, Sector 1, 010436 Bucharest, Romania
Tel: (21) 307 5000. Fax: (21) 307 5010.
E-mail: bucst@dfait-maeci.gc.ca
Website: www.dfait-maeci.gc.ca

General Information

AREA: 238,391 sq km (92,043 sq miles).
POPULATION: 21,680,974 (2002).
POPULATION DENSITY: 90.9 per sq km.
CAPITAL: Bucharest. **Population:** 1,925,334 (2002).
GEOGRAPHY: Romania is bordered to the north and east by Moldova and Ukraine, the southeast by the Black Sea, the south by Bulgaria, the southwest by Serbia and Montenegro and in the west by Hungary. The country is divided into four geographical areas. Transylvania (a belt of Alpine massifs and forests) and Moldavia compose the northern half of the country, which is divided down the middle by the north–south strip of the Carpathian Mountains. South of the east–west line of the Carpathians lies the flat Danube plain of Walachia with the capital Bucharest, its border with Bulgaria being defined by the course of the Danube. Romania's coastline is along the Black Sea, incorporating the port of Constanta and the Danube Delta.
GOVERNMENT: Democratic Republic since 1991. **Head of State:** President Traian Basescu since December 2004. **Head of Government:** Outgoing Prime Minister Adrian Nastase.
LANGUAGE: Romanian is the official language. Some Hungarian and German are spoken in border areas, while mainly French and some English are spoken by those connected with the tourist industry.
RELIGION: 83 per cent Romanian Orthodox, with Roman Catholic, Reformed/Lutheran, Unitarian, Muslim and Jewish minorities.
TIME: GMT + 2 (GMT + 3 from last Sunday in March to Saturday before last Sunday in October).
ELECTRICITY: 220 volts AC, 50Hz. Plugs are of the two-pin type.
COMMUNICATIONS: Telephone: IDD is available. Country code: 40. Outgoing international code: 00. Public telephones are widely available and can be used for direct international calls. Hotels often impose a high service charge for long-distance calls, but usually do not charge for local calls. **Mobile telephone:** GSM 900/1800 networks. Network operators include *Connex* (website: www.connex.ro), *Cosmorom* (website: www.cosmorom.com) and *Orange* (website: www.orange.ro). **Internet:** *Kappa* and *PC-Net* are two of the largest of the 250-odd ISPs. The former has open-air terminals at Strada Paulescu Nicolae 9, Bucharest, while the latter is at Strada Calderon Jean Louis 1-5, Bucharest. *Sweet Internet Cafe*, Strada Maria Rosetti 7-9, Bucharest (tel: (21) 212 4111) has 24-hour access, as do a couple others of Bucharest's many Internet cafes. **Fax:** Facilities are available at most large hotels. **Telegram:** Facilities at post offices and a night telegram service (2000-0700) is available in Bucharest. Telegrams are an inexpensive and efficient form of international communication from Romania. **Post:** Airmail to Western Europe takes one week. Post offices are open daily, including Saturday mornings. **Press:** English newspapers and publications include *Bucharest Business Week*, *Nine O'Clock* and *Romanian Economic Daily*. There are a great number of daily and weekly newspapers published in Romanian, Hungarian and German.
Radio: BBC World Service (website: www.bbc.co.uk/worldservice) and Voice of America (website: www.voa.gov) can be received. From time to time the frequencies change and the most up-to-date can be found online.

Passport/Visa

	Passport Required?	Visa Required?	Return Ticket Required?
Full British	Yes	No/1	Yes
Australian	Yes	Yes	Yes
Canadian	Yes	No/1	Yes
USA	Yes	No/1	Yes
Other EU	Yes	No/1	Yes
Japanese	Yes	No/1	Yes

Note: *Regulations and requirements may be subject to change at short notice, and you are advised to contact the appropriate diplomatic or consular authority before finalising travel arrangements. Details of these may be found at the head of this country's entry. Any numbers in the chart refer to the footnotes below.*

PASSPORTS: Passport valid for a minimum of six months after return from Romania required by all with at least one blank page.
VISAS: Required by all except the following:
(a) **1.** nationals mentioned in the chart above for up to 90 days, except nationals of Czech Republic, Poland and Slovak Republic who can stay for up to 30 days; and all nationals of Australia who *do* require a visa;
(b) nationals of Andorra, Costa Rica, Iceland, Korea (Rep), Liechtenstein, Malaysia, Monaco, Republic of Moldova, Norway, San Marino, Switzerland and Venezuela for stays of up to 90 days within six months of date of arrival;
(c) nationals of Uruguay for stays of up to 90 days within 12 months of arrival;
(d) nationals of Bulgaria, Croatia and Singapore for stays of up to 30 days;
(e) transit passengers continuing their journey by the same or first connecting aircraft within 24 hours provided holding valid onward or return documentation and not leaving the airport *except for* nationals of Afghanistan, Bangladesh, Congo (Dem Rep), Eritrea, Ethiopia, Ghana, India, Iran, Iraq, Nigeria, Pakistan, Somalia and Sri Lanka who *always* require transit visas.
Note: All other nationals require a visa which must be applied for prior to arrival. There are no visas issued on arrival.
Special requirements: Nationals of the following need an official notarised invitation from a company or individual in Romania, which may be faxed by the Embassy to the Romanian Passport General Directorate or any of the Romania County Passport Authorities for approval (allow at least 30 days):
Afghanistan, Albania, Algeria, Angola, Bangladesh, Benin, Bhutan, Burkina Faso, Burundi, Cambodia, Cameroon, Cape Verde, Central African Republic, China (PR), Chad, CIS (except Moldova, Russian Federation and Ukraine), Comoros, Congo (Dem Rep), Congo (Rep), Côte d'Ivoire, Cuba, Djibouti, Dominican Republic, Egypt, Equatorial Guinea, Eritrea, Ethiopia, Fiji, Gabon, The Gambia, Georgia, Ghana, Guinea, Guinea-Bissau, Guyana, Haiti, India, Iran, Iraq, Jordan, Kenya, Korea (Dem Rep), Laos, Lebanon, Liberia, Libya, Madagascar, Maldives, Mali, Mauritania, Mauritius, Mongolia, Morocco, Mozambique, Myanmar, Nepal, Niger, Nigeria, Pakistan, Palestine, Papua New Guinea, Peru, The Philippines, Rwanda, São Tomé e Príncipe, Senegal, Sierra Leone, Somalia, Sri Lanka, Sudan, Surinam, the Syrian Arab Republic, Tanzania, Togo, Tunisia, Uganda, Vietnam, Yemen and Zambia (if these nationals are married to Romanian nationals the relevant certificate should be produced).
Types of visa and cost: *Single-entry*: £35 (business, conference and family visits or individual tourist). *Transit*: £27 (single-entry); £35 (double-entry). *Multiple-entry*: £60 valid for six months and not renewable. An additional fee of £7 is charged for each person included in the passport if travelling with the owner.
Note: Multiple-entry visas will not be issued to nationals listed under *Special Requirements* above, even if the purpose of their visit is for business.
Validity: *Single-entry*: Six months from date of issue for stays of up to 90 days. *Multiple-entry*: Six months from date of issue for stays of up to 90 days each visit. *Transit*: Five days maximum (for both single- and double-entry).
Application to: Consulate (or Consular section at Embassy); see *Contact Addresses* section. Applicants for Multiple-entry business visas must apply in their own country.
Application requirements: (a) Passport valid for at least six months after visa expires with a blank page to affix visa stamp. (b) One completed application form. (c) Two recent passport-size photos. (d) Fee (paid in cash or by postal order only). (e) Postal applications should be accompanied by a registered, self-addressed envelope. (f) Medical Insurance. (g) Proof of financial means in amount of $100 per day or the equivalent value in convertible currency for the entire period of time. *Tourist* (a)-(g) and, (h) Letter from travel agent or a hotel booking in Romania. *Business*: (a)-(g) and, (h) Letter from employer and invitation from company in Romania. *Student*: (a)-(g) and, (h) Evidence of enrolment on course. *Transit*: (a)-(g) and, (h) Ticket for onward travel with visa if required.
Note: All nationals are advised to check with the Romanian Consulate prior to departure to obtain current details of any further documentation which might be required.
Working days required: Visas take up to a maximum of 30 days to be issued, depending on type of visa and nationality. Travellers are advised to apply for a visa at least a month in advance.
Temporary residence: Enquire at Embassy.

TIMATIC CODES

Health	AMADEUS: **TI-DFT/BUH/HE** GALILEO/WORLDSPAN: **TI-DFT/BUH/HE** SABRE: **TIDFT/BUH/HE**
Visa	AMADEUS: **TI-DFT/BUH/VI** GALILEO/WORLDSPAN: **TI-DFT/BUH/VI** SABRE: **TIDFT/BUH/VI**

To access TIMATIC country information on Health and Visa regulations through the Computer Reservations System (CRS), type in the appropriate command line listed above.

Money

Currency: Leu (plural Lei) = 100 bani. Notes are in denominations of Lei1,000,000, 500,000, 100,000, 50,000, 10,000, 5000 and 1000. Coins are in denominations of Lei5000, 1000, 500 and 100.
Currency exchange: It is recommended that visitors bring hard currency, particularly US Dollars, as this can be easily and even eagerly exchanged by shops, restaurants and hotels. Sterling can be easily exchanged in most resorts. All hard foreign currencies can be exchanged at banks and authorised exchange offices. Rates can vary from one place to another, so visitors are advised to shop around for the best rate of exchange. Exchanges on the black market are made frequently, but visitors are advised to exchange money through proper exchange channels and to receive a currency exchange receipt, as certain services require visitors to show the receipt as proof of having made at least one financial transaction. ATMs (*bancomat*) accepting MasterCard and Visa are becoming more common but should not be relied upon as a sole source of cash.
Credit & debit cards: American Express, Diners Club, MasterCard and Visa are accepted by large hotels, car hire firms and some restaurants. Check with your credit or debit card company for details of merchant acceptability and other services which may be available.
Travellers cheques: Like credit and debit cards, these are usually only useful in hotels and for obtaining cash at the bank or selected exchange offices. To avoid additional exchange rate charges, travellers are advised to take travellers cheques in US Dollars or Euros.
Currency restrictions: The import of local currency is prohibited (unless in possession of a special licence); the export of local currency is prohibited. The import of foreign currency is unlimited; the export of foreign currency is limited to the amount imported.
Exchange rate indicators: The following figures are included as a guide to the movements of the Leu against Sterling and the US Dollar:

Date	Feb '04	May '04	Aug '04	Nov '04
£1.00=	59546.8	60431.5	60807.6	56139.8
$1.00=	32713.5	33834.3	33005.5	29645.6

Banking hours: Mon-Fri 0900-1200 (business matters); Mon-Fri 0900-1200 and 1300-1500 (currency exchange).

Duty Free

The following items may be imported into Romania without incurring customs duty:
200 cigarettes or 200g of other tobacco articles; 1l of spirits; 4l of wine or beer; gifts up to a value of Lei2000; 200g of cocoa; 200g of coffee; and reasonable quantities of perfume, medicines and travel souvenirs.
Prohibited imports: Ammunition, explosives, narcotics, pornographic material, uncanned meats, animal and dairy products.
Prohibited exports: Articles of cultural, historical or artistic value.
Note: Valuable goods, such as jewellery, art, electrical items and foreign currency should be declared on entry. Endorsed customs declarations must be kept, as they must be shown on leaving the country.

Public Holidays

2005: Jan 1-2 New Year. **Jan 6** Epiphany. **May 1** Labour Day. **May 2** Easter Monday (Orthodox). **Dec 1** National Day. **Dec 25-26** Christmas.
2006: Jan 1-2 New Year. **Jan 6** Epiphany. **Apr 24** Easter Monday (Orthodox). **May 1** Labour Day. **Dec 1** National Day. **Dec 25-26** Christmas.

Health

	Special Precautions?	Certificate Required?
Yellow Fever	No	No
Cholera	No	No
Typhoid & Polio	1	N/A
Malaria	No	N/A

Note: *Regulations and requirements may be subject to change at short notice, and you are advised to contact your doctor well in advance of your intended date of departure. Any numbers in the chart refer to the footnotes below.*

1: Vaccination against typhoid is advised.
Food & drink: Mains water is normally chlorinated, and whilst relatively safe, may cause abdominal upsets; visitors are thus advised to drink bottled water. Romania has currently been experiencing water shortages and visitors may find that tap water is only available during certain hours. This is particularly true around Bucharest and other large towns. Visitors in the mountain areas will find it less of a problem as the water is supplied by local mountain springs, full of natural minerals and very safe. Milk is pasteurised and dairy products are safe for consumption. Local meat, poultry, seafood, fruit and vegetables are generally considered safe to eat.
Other risks: *Hepatitis A* and *tuberculosis* occur and *hepatitis B* is endemic. Rare *West Nile Fever* outbreaks have been reported in the southeast. *Brucellosis* occurs sporadically although risk to the traveller is low. Stray dogs may carry *African Typhus* disease.
Rabies is present. For those at high risk, vaccination before arrival should be considered. If you are bitten, seek medical advice without delay. For more information, see the *Health* appendix.
Health care: Medical facilities in Romania are poor and there is a serious shortage of basic medical supplies and qualified personnel. Nationals of countries who do not have a reciprocal health agreement with Romania are expected to pay immediate cash for health services. Health insurance is strongly advised.

Travel - International

AIR: Romania's national airline is *Tarom (RO)* (website: www.tarom.ro). Other airlines that fly to Bucharest include *Air France, Alitalia, Austrian Airlines, British Airways, KLM, Lufthansa* and *Swiss*.
Approximate flight times: From Bucharest to *London* is three hours.
International airports: *Bucharest (BUH)* (Otopeni) (website: www.otp-airport.ro) is 16km (10 miles) north of the city (travel time - 25 minutes). The airport has been greatly modernised in recent years, but some visitors may find it relatively limited compared to Western European or American standards. A bar, snack bar, restaurant, left luggage, first aid, post office, car hire and full duty free facilities are available. There is an express bus service (bus no. 783) which runs every 15 minutes between 0530-2330 Mon-Fri and every 30 minutes Sat-Sun and holidays; the journey takes approximately 40 minutes. Taxis, minibuses and limousines are available 24 hours (travel time - 25 minutes).
There are also international airports at *Arad (ARW), Cluj (CLJ), Constanta (CND)* (Mihail Kogalniceanu), *Sibiu (SBZ)* and *Timisoara (TSR)*.
Departure tax: None.
SEA/RIVER: The main international passenger port is Constanta on the Black Sea. **Sea ferries:** Not running at present. Contact the Romanian National Tourist Office for up-to-date information (see *Contact Addresses* section).
River cruises: Sailings from Passau to Constanta on the Black Sea along the Danube are available; these stop at various places of interest, including Vienna, Bratislava, Budapest, Bazias, Giurgiu, Calafat and Bucharest. The cruises incorporate varied itineraries: historic towns, museums, art collections, monasteries, spas, archaeological sites, folk evenings, nature reserves and of course, the dramatic scenery of Eastern Europe, including the 'Iron Gate' through the Carpathians. With the opening of the Main-Danube Canal, some companies now offer travel as far west as Rotterdam along the Rhine. For further information, contact the Romanian Tourism Promotion Office (see *Contact Addresses* section).
RAIL: The main international train from Western Europe to Romania (Bucharest) is the *Wiener Waltzer*, which runs to Bucharest in summer only (June to September) and includes two nights' travel from Basel, arriving in Bucharest two days later. There are no through carriages from Basel, which means moving to the Bucharest coaches in Vienna. As well as day carriages, there are sleeping cars from Vienna to both Bucharest and Constanta on the Black Sea coast. There are also through trains from other Eastern European cities. *InterRail* allows unrestricted train travel in Romania.
ROAD: The most direct international routes to Romania are via Austria, Germany and Hungary. The best route from Hungary is the E64 from Budapest to Szeged through Arad, Brasov, Campina and Ploiesti. There is also a route from Szeged to Timisoara. A more frequently used route from Hungary to Germany is via the E60 through Oradea. *Eurolines*, departing from Victoria Coach Station in London, serves destinations in Romania. For further information, contact *Eurolines* (tel: (08705) 143 219; e-mail: welcome@eurolines.co.uk; website: www.eurolines.co.uk). For permit regulations, see *Documentation* in the *Travel – Internal* section.

Travel - Internal

AIR: The main airport for internal flights is *Baneasa* (travel time - 20 minutes to Otopeni). *Tarom (RO)* operates regular services from there to Arad, Baia Mare, Cluj-Napoca, Constanta, Iasi, Oradea, Satu Mare, Sibiu, Suceava, Timisoara and Tirgu Mures.
RIVER: The Danube Delta is easily explored by boat. Most trips and cruises depart from the ancient city of Tulcea and sail to Sulina.
RAIL: Bucharest's main station is the Gara de Nord on Calea Grivitei. *Romanian State Railways* (website: www.cfr.ro) runs frequent, efficient and cheap services to most cities, towns and larger villages, some with sleeping and restaurant cars. There are five different types of train, varying in speed from the slow *personal* to the faster *accelerat, rapid* and *express* trains, and the more expensive and comfortable *Inter-City*. Supplements are payable on rapid and express trains, for which seats must be reserved in advance. Express routes run from Bucharest to Timisoara, Cluj-Napoca, Iasi, Constanta and Brasov. Rail Inclusive Tour tickets include transport and hotel accommodation. There are no platforms of any great height in Romania, making entering and alighting a little difficult for the elderly or infirm. There is a discount of 25 to 35 per cent for non-express trains.
ROAD: Traffic drives on the right. The *Romanian Automobile Club (ACR)* has its headquarters in Bucharest (tel: (21) 212 8247 *or* 223 4525) and offers services through all its branches to AA and RAC members. Speed limits are 50kph (30mph) in cities, 60kph (37mph) in built-up areas, up to 90kph (57mph) on main roads and 120kph (75mph) on motorways. Driving under the influence of alcohol is forbidden. **Coach:** Local services operate to most towns and villages. The main coach stations in Bucharest are at 164 Soseaua Alexandriei, 1 Ion Ionescu de la Brad Boulevard, 1 Piata Gării Filarest, 221 Soseaua Chitilei, 141 Pacii Boulevard and 3 Gării Obor Boulevard. **Taxi:** Metered taxis can be hailed in the street or called from hotels. Prices are relatively low, but drivers expect a 10 per cent tip. Although most drivers are honest, prices should be agreed beforehand, especially at the airport. **Car hire:** Available at hotels and at Bucharest Airport. Driving is very erratic, so it might be advisable to hire a car with a driver.
Documentation: National driving licence or International Driving Permit are required, as is Green Card insurance. Most Romanian roads are best suited to 4-wheel-drive vehicles as they are in poor, potholed condition.
URBAN: Good public transport facilities are provided in the main centres. Bucharest has a good bus and tram system and a metro. Tickets are pre-purchased from agents, and there are stamping machines on board buses and trains. There are also daily, weekly and fortnightly passes. A separate minibus network is operated.

Accommodation

HOTELS: Visitors are advised to book accommodation in advance through a travel agency, particularly for summertime visits to coastal resorts. Room prices in lower-end hotels are very reasonable compared to Western European prices, whereas 4- and 5-star hotels are comparable in both standards and price. Breakfast normally costs extra. For further information, contact the Romanian Tourist Office (see *Contact Addresses* section) *or* see online (website: www.rotravel.com). **Grading:** Hotels are classified from **1** to **5 stars**.
BED & BREAKFAST: Accommodation of this type is plentiful in Romania and in smaller towns or villages may be the only options. Private rooms tend to be cheaper than hotel rooms and will be basic but comfortable. For further information, contact the Romanian National Tourist Office (see *Contact Addresses* section).
SELF-CATERING: Addresses of private accommodation and self-catering establishments are available from local tourist offices.
CAMPING/CARAVANNING: There are around 150 campsites in Romania. Prepaid tourist coupons valid from May to September are available from specialised travel agencies.
YOUTH HOSTELS: Most hostels are open in July and August although some are open year-round. Information is available from the Youth Hostel Romania (tel/fax: (264) 586 616; e-mail: office@hihostels-romania.ro; website: www.hihostels-romania.ro).

Resorts & Excursions

BUCHAREST: Bucharest (*Bucuresti*), located midway between the Carpathian Mountains and the Black Sea, in southeastern Romania, has not earned the nickname 'Paris of the Balkans' by accident. Its astonishing range of architecture – from Wallachian wooden and bell-towered mansions to Byzantine-style chapels, neo-classical buildings, striking 1930s modernism and even the post-Stalinist absurdities of Ceaucescu's megalomaniac regime – cannot help but leave the visitor in awe at the varieties of vision that have taken place in this city over the centuries. But Bucharest has also been the epicentre of the country's many upheavals, with the stages of the country's history like vivid tattoos etched across the city's surface, each telling a different chapter of the story. Bucharest now

boasts trendy bars and clubs, some capitalising on the history of Vlad the Impaler, Bucharest's most infamous son, with cobwebs and dank underground dancefloors.
BLACK SEA COAST: This coastline is the principal tourist area of Romania and ideal for family holidays. Its 70km (43 miles) of fine white sandy beaches boasts many resorts, the main ones being **Costinesti**, **Eforie Nord**, **Eforie Sud**, **Jupiter**, **Mamaia**, **Mangalia**, **Neptun-Olimp**, **Saturn**, **Techirghiol** and **Venus-Aurora**. There are boating centres for watersports on the sea and lakes, and both daytime and evening cruises. The curative properties of the salt waters and the mud from **Lake Techirghiol** (whose thermal springs have a year-round temperature of 24°C/75°F), Mangalia, Eforie and Neptun make the Romanian Riviera popular with those seeking spa treatments, especially for rheumatism. The Greek/Byzantine port of **Constanta**, founded in the sixth century BC, merits a visit, and inland there are interesting archaeological sites including the ancient Greek city ruins of **Histria**, **Tomis** and **Callatis**. The area is inhabited by foxes, otters, wildcats and boars and in the migratory periods one can see over 300 species of birds.
DANUBE DELTA: Listed by UNESCO as a World Heritage Site, this vast expanse of protected watery wilderness in the north of the Romanian Black Sea coast comprises three main arms of the Danube with numerous little waterways, wetlands, small patches of forest and a rich and varied wildlife. The backwaters can be explored by fishing boat or floating hotel, and several hotels and campsites welcome visitors. The main town of the Delta is **Tulcea** with its excellent **Danube Delta Museum**.
CARPATHIAN MOUNTAINS: This beautiful and densely forested mountainous area lends itself to many sporting and leisure activities such as skiing, bob-sleighing, horseriding and tennis. Situated in picturesque valleys and on mountain slopes are many health and winter resorts, open all year round and well equipped with ski-hire facilities. The major resorts are: **Borsa**, **Busteni**, **Durau**, **Paltinis**, **Poiana Brasov** and **Predeal** (both of which have illuminated ski slopes), **Semenic** and **Sinaia** (bob-sleigh tracks). All are equipped to cater for a long winter sports season running from December to April. Spectacular mountain lakes are found in the **Fagaras** and **Retezat** ranges, and caves in the **Apuseni**, **Bihor** and **Mehedinti** regions. The **Hurezi Monastery**, in the Vâlcea county, has been listed by UNESCO as a World Heritage site.
BUKOVINA: An area in the northern Carpathian foothills which has unique churches and monasteries with exceptional frescoes dating back 500 years. **Sucevita** is the home of a monastery with the largest number of frescoes in the region. 29km (18 miles) west of Sucevita is **Moldovita**, renowned for its spectacular paintings. The Moldavian region has 48 monasteries in total, nearly all of them built to celebrate victories over the Turks in the 14th and 15th centuries. There are also numerous beautiful old churches, notable for their painted exterior walls decorated with 15th- and 16th-century Byzantine frescoes. Seven of them are now included on the UNESCO World Heritage List.
TRANSYLVANIA: Since Roman times, Romanian spas have been known for their miraculous healing powers. Transylvania holds many well-equipped spa towns, such as **Baile Felix**, **Baile Herculane**, **Covasna** and **Sovata**, some of which have facilities offering acupuncture, acupressure and slimming cures. It is here that the myth of Dracula, immortalised in Bram Stoker's famous novel, originated. The original Dracula was a medieval King known as 'Vlad the Impaler', owing to his unpleasant habits. One of Vlad's original abodes is **Bran Castle**; set in a commanding position, with its thick walls and peaked tower, it offers a dramatic view and a chilling atmosphere (tours are available to Bran Castle from the mountain resort of Poiana Brasov, where it is possible to ski in winter and undertake mountain climbing and walking in summer). From here it's possible to travel to **Sibiu** which has a great market. Transylvania is also known for its numerous Saxon fortified churches, including the **Biertan Church**, which stands on top of a hill overlooking the village of **Biertan** and is a listed UNESCO World Heritage Site.

Sport & Activities

Watersports: Beaches and luxury resorts line the Black Sea coast, which extends for some 245km (153 miles) from the Danube Delta towards the border with Bulgaria in the south. The sea is clean and the absence of tides makes it ideal for **swimming**, **windsurfing** and many other types of waterports. Some of the best-known resorts include the seaport of Constanta; Mamaia, which has a 7km- (4.5 mile-) long beach; and a string of luxury resorts named after women and mythological gods, such as Neptune, Jupiter or Venus (for further details on seaside resorts, see also *Resorts & Excursions* section). **Sailing** is widely practised on the coast, while Romania's many rivers are well-suited for **kayaking**. Tourists wishing to explore the waterways of the protected and UNESCO-listed Danube Delta must comply with strict conservation regulations. Visitors arriving with their own boat must pay a fee at Tulcea Harbour Station and produce their passports, a sailing licence and valid registration papers for their craft.
Fishing: Romania has many easily accessible places for fishing such as the Danube Delta (where there are over 160 fish species including sturgeon, wel, pike and carp) and on lake shores around big cities. For details of legal requirements, contact the Romanian National Tourist Office (see *Contact Addresses* section).
Winter sports: There are numerous facilities for **skiing** with pistes of varying degrees of difficulty found in almost all mountain resorts, the majority of which are equipped with cable cars. The main ski resorts are at Poiana Brasov (13km/8 miles from Brasov) and Sinaia. Facilities are fairly limited in comparison to more established skiing destinations. Locals are very friendly and most ski instructors speak English. National and international skiing and **bob-sleighing** competitions are held annually. **Sledging** tracks, **skating** and **ice hockey** are available at most mountain resorts.
Health spas: Romania has been a renowned spa country since Roman times and there is a choice of 70 health centres as well as 3000 mineral-rich thermal springs. The most renowned health resorts include Baile Herculane in the Cerna Valley (southern Carpathians); Baile Felix (near the city of Ordena in the northwest); and Sovata (in Transylvania near Ursu lake, popular with women). Romanian spas are particularly known for mudbaths (using the sapropelic black mud from Lake Techirghiol) and the Gerovital cure pioneered by Professor Ana Aslan. For further details contact the *National Organisation of Spas*, 2-4 Luterana Street, Sector 1, Bucharest 1 (tel: (1) 312 2993; fax: (1) 314 8097; e-mail: optbr@fx.ro; website: www.spas.ro).
Folklore and culture: Traditional folk music and dancing is still very much alive and shows can be seen in many hotels and restaurants. The renowned Romanian composer Georg Enescu's *Romanian Rhapsody* is world famous. Regional crafts and costumes also play an important part of everyday life: woodcarving, pottery and ceramics, wooden architecture and glass paintings can be found throughout the country. The Dracula myth originated in Romania, where a medieval king known as 'Vlad the Impaler' became the inspiration for Bram Stoker's novel, *Dracula*. One of Vlad's homes, Bran Castle, can be visited in Transylvania.

Social Profile

FOOD & DRINK: Although there are some regional differences between the provinces, there is a definite national culinary tradition. Dishes include *ciorba de perisoare* (soup with meatballs), *ciorba tărănească* (vegetable soup with meat and rice balls served with sour cream), lamb *bors*, giblet soup and a variety of fish soups. The Romanians excel in full-bodied soups, some of the best being cream of mushroom, chicken, beef, vegetable and bean soup. Sour cream or eggs are also added to soups. *Mamaliga* (a staple of mashed cornmeal) is served in many ways. Other national specialities include *tocana* (pork, beef or mutton stew seasoned with onions and served with *mamaliga*), *ghiveci* (over 20 vegetables cooked in oil and served cold), Moldavian *parjoale* (flat meat patties, highly spiced and served with garnishes), *sarmale* (pork balls in cabbage leaves), *mititei* (a variety of highly-seasoned charcoal-grilled meat) and *patricieni* (charcoal-grilled sausages similar to Frankfurters). Fish dishes include *nisetru la gratar* (grilled Black Sea sturgeon), *raci* (crayfish) and *scrumbii la gratar* (grilled herring). Desserts include *placinte cu poale in briu* (rolled cheese pies), Moldavian *cozonac* (brioche) and *pasca* (a sweet cheesecake). Pancakes served with jam, and doughnuts topped with sour cream or jam are also popular desserts. Breakfasts almost always include eggs, either soft-boiled, hard-boiled, fried or scrambled. Omelettes, filled with either cheese, ham or mushrooms, are also frequently served. Vegetarians may have difficulties, as most local specialities are meat-based. Although there are inexpensive self-service snack bars, table service is the norm.
A traditional drink with entrées is *tuică* (plum brandy) which varies in strength, dryness and smell according to locality. *Tuică de Bihor* is the strongest and generally known as palinca. Romanian wines have won international prizes and include *pinot noir*, *cabernet sauvignon*, *riesling*, *pinot gris* and *chardonnay* from the Murfatlar vineyards. *Grasa* and *feteasa* from Moldavia's Cotnari vineyards are also recommended. Many Romanian wines are taken with soda water and hot wine is also popular during winter. Romanian beers are excellent. Romanian sparkling wines, or *methode champagnoise*, are very good and superb value. *Glühwein* (mulled wine) is another popular Romanian drink. There are no licensing hours, but the legal age for drinking in a bar is 18.
NIGHTLIFE: Bucharest has a growing number of discos and nightclubs with entertainment and live dancing. Restaurants at most major hotels double as nightclubs and there are also several Parisian-style cafes. Two casinos operate in the Calea Victoriei. Opera is performed at the Romanian Opera House and the Romanian Athenaeum has two symphony orchestras. Folk entertainment is performed at the Rapsodia Romana Artistic Ensemble Hall and there are a number of theatres.
SHOPPING: Specialist purchases include embroideries, pottery, porcelain, silverware, carpets, fabrics, wool jumpers, woodcarvings, metal, leather goods, rugs, glass paintings and silk dresses. **Shopping hours:** Mon-Sat 0600-2100 for small local shops, while larger stores and department stores open earlier and close later. Some shops open Sun 0600-1200, although these vary according to season.
SPECIAL EVENTS: Folk festivals include dances, music and displays of traditional art. For a full list contact the Romanian National Tourist Office.
The following is a selection of special events occurring in Romania in 2005:
Feb *Secular Winter Customs Festival*, Sfantu Gheorghe. **Apr** *International Festival of Contemporary Theatre*, Brasov; *National Festival of Spring Agricultural Customs*, Hoteni-Maramures District. **May** *Feast of the Daffodils*, Vlahita-Harghita District; *International Jazz Festival*, Brasov. **May-Jun** *Transylvanian International Film Festival*, Cluj Napoca. **Jun** *Traditional Crafts Fair*, Bucharest; *Fundata Fair*. **Jul** *Maiden's Fair*, Gaina Mountain; *Bucharest of Old*. **Jul-Aug** *National Festival of Light Music*, Mamaia; *Medieval Days*. **Aug** *Dance at Prislop*, Prislop Pass; *Medieval Days*, Sighisoara. **Sep** *International Carp Angling Contest*. **Oct** *Halloween in Transylvania*; *Wine Making Festival*. **Dec** *Christmas Traditional Festival*; *De la Colind la Stea Christmas Festival*, Brasov.
SOCIAL CONVENTIONS: Handshaking is the most common form of greeting, but it is customary for men to kiss a woman's hand when being introduced. Visitors should follow normal European courtesies on social occasions. Dress tends to be rather conservative but casual wear is suitable. Beachwear should not be worn away from the beach or poolside. Smoking is prohibited on public transport, in cinemas and theatres. Many Romanians are smokers and gifts of Western cigarettes are greatly appreciated. Other well-appreciated gifts include toiletries and Western clothing. **Photography:** Military installations should not be photographed. Some tourist attractions require visitors to pay a fee of approximately Lei2000 for taking photographs. **Tipping:** A 5 to 10 per cent service tip is customary in restaurants. Porters, chambermaids and taxi drivers expect tips.

Business Profile

ECONOMY: Romania is a major producer of wheat and maize, and grows vegetables, fruit, sugar beet and vegetable oil seeds; wine-making is still widespread and many farms also breed livestock. Communist-era economic policies favoured heavy industry and the agricultural sector has since found it difficult to catch up with European standards. Most land has now been transferred to private ownership. The previously neglected forestry and fishing industries are being developed under long-term programmes. Overall, the contribution of the agricultural sector to GDP has declined from about 33 per cent in 1990 to its present level of 14.8 per cent.
Post-communist industry has undergone a similar contraction, and now accounts for 28 per cent of GDP (down from nearly 60 per cent in 1990). Romanian industry produces industrial and transport equipment, metals, furniture, chemical products and manufactured consumer goods, but the most important sector is oil, natural gas and oil-derived products (petrochemicals, paints and varnishes). The mining industry produces coal, bauxite, copper, lead, zinc and iron ore.
The Romanian economy was crippled under the Ceaucescu regime, not least by its leader's obsession with paying off the whole of the country's national debt (something rarely considered, let alone attempted, by most governments). Since the 1989 revolution, successive governments have concentrated on turning Romania into a market economy.

Progress has been difficult, hampered by the economy's already weak condition and political instability. In the early- and mid-1990s, Romania came close to economic meltdown as the economy contracted by an average of 7 per cent annually and inflation often reached 100 per cent. The situation has improved since 2000, when Romania registered positive growth. GDP is now increasing at an annual rate of 5 per cent; inflation is 22 per cent and official unemployment has fallen to 8 per cent (although there is a large informal economy). IMF and World Bank support have been forthcoming under the usual conditions. Romania has also had access to loans from the European Bank for Reconstruction and Development to which it belongs as a 'country of operation'. The Romanians' ultimate objective is membership of the European Union, with whom it conducts over 60 per cent of its trade (Italy and Germany are the largest individual trade partners). The country originally hoped to join along with the 10 other countries that joined in May 2004. Unfortunately, it was unable to meet the accession criteria in time and now hopes to join, along with neighbouring Bulgaria, in 2007.

BUSINESS: A suit is essential at all business meetings and only on very hot days are shirtsleeves acceptable. English, German and French are used in business circles. Appointments are necessary and punctuality expected. Business cards are widely used. **Office hours:** Mon-Fri 0700-1530.

COMMERCIAL INFORMATION: The following organisation can offer advice: The Chamber of Commerce and Industry of Romania and Bucharest, Bulevardul Octavian Goga 2, Sector 3, 74244 Bucharest (tel: (1) 322 9535; fax: (1) 322 9542; e-mail: ccir@ccir.ro; website: www.ccir.ro).

CONFERENCES/CONVENTIONS: For information, contact the Romanian Convention Bureau, Calea Victoriei 118, 4th Floor, Suite 407, Sector 1, 70179 Bucharest (tel: (21) 314 4100/4102; fax: (21) 314 4101; e-mail: office@conventionbureau.ro; website: www.conventionbureau.ro).

Climate

Summer temperatures are moderated on the coast by sea breezes while inland at sea level it is hot. Winters are coldest in the Carpathian Mountains where there is snow from December through to April. Snow also falls throughout most of the country. Winters are mildest on the coast.

Required clothing: Lightweights are worn in summer on the coast and in low inland areas. Warmer clothes are needed in winter and throughout the year in the uplands. Rainwear is recommended throughout the year.

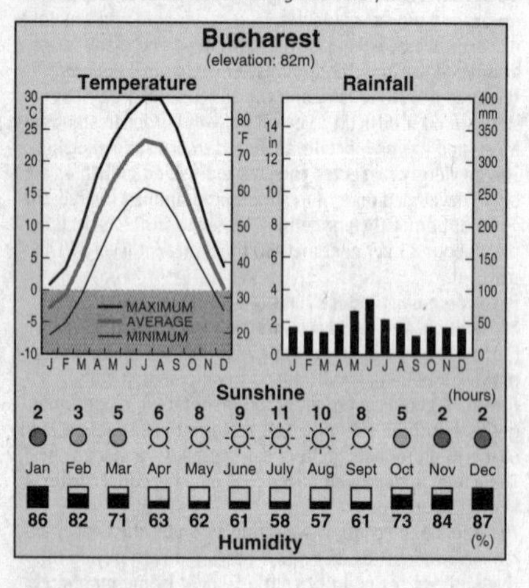

Russian Federation

Location: Eastern Europe/Asia.

Country dialling code: 7. The 0 of the area code should not be omitted when dialling from abroad.

LATEST TRAVEL ADVICE CONTACTS

British Foreign and Commonwealth Office
Tel: (0870) 606 0290 Website: www.fco.gov.uk

US Department of State
Website: http://travel.state.gov/travel

Canadian Department of Foreign Affairs and Int'l Trade
Tel: (1 800) 267 8376 Website: www.dfait-maeci.gc.ca

The State Committee on Physical Culture, Sports and Tourism
18 ul. Kazakova, 103064 Moscow, Russian Federation
Tel: (095) 263 0840.
Fax: (095) 263 0761.
E-mail: info@goskomsport.ru
Website: www.goskomsport.ru

BSI
1 Lize Chaikinoky, Moscow, Russian Federation
Tel: (095) 785 5535. Fax: (095) 785 5536.
E-mail: incoming@bsigroup.ru *or* incoming@russia-tourism.ru
Website: www.russia-tourism.ru
This is a tourism agency that deals with the public.

Russian National Tourist Office
70 Piccadilly, London W1J 8HP, UK
Tel: (020) 7495 7555. Fax: (020) 7495 8555.
E-mail: inntelmoscow@inntel-moscow.co.uk *or* info@visitrussia.org.uk
Website: www.inntel-moscow.co.uk *or* www.visitrussia.org.uk

Embassy of the Russian Federation
13 Kensington Palace Gardens, London W8 4QX, UK
Tel: (020) 7229 2666. Fax: (020) 7229 5804.
E-mail: office@rusemblon.org (press office).
Consular section: 5 Kensington Palace Gardens, London W8 4QS, UK
Tel: (020) 7229 8027. Fax: (020) 7229 3215.
E-mail: info@rusemblon.org
Website: www.rusemblon.org
Opening hours: Mon-Fri 0900-1200, 1400-1800.

Intourist Ltd.
7 Wellington Terrace, Notting Hill, London W2 4LW, UK
Tel: (020) 7727 4100 *or* (0870) 112 1232 (reservation line).
Fax: (020) 7727 8090.
E-mail: info@intourist.co.uk
Website: www.intouristuk.com
Offices also in: Glasgow and Manchester.

British Embassy
Smolenskaya Naberezhnaya 10, Moscow 121099, Russian Federation
Tel: (095) 956 7200. Fax: (095) 956 7201 *or* 7440/1 (visa section) *or* 7430 (press and public affairs).
E-mail: moscow@britishembassy.ru
Website: www.britemb.msk.ru

British Consulate General
Pl. Proletarskoy Diktatury 5, 191124 St Petersburg, Russian Federation
Tel: (812) 320 3200.
Fax: (812) 320 3211.
E-mail: bcgspb@peterlink.ru
Website: www.britain.spb.ru
Consulate in: Ekatarinburg.
Honorary Consulates in: Novorossiisk and Vladivostok.

Embassy of the Russian Federation
2650 Wisconsin Avenue, NW, Washington, DC 20007, USA
Tel: (202) 298 5700. Fax: (202) 298 5735.
E-mail: russianembassy@mindspring.com
Website: www.russianembassy.org
Consular section: 2641 Tunlaw Road, NW, Washington, DC 20007, USA
Tel: (202) 939 8907. Fax: (202) 939 8917 *or* 483 7579.
Consulates General in: Houston, New York, San Francisco and Seattle.

Russian National Group
130 West 42nd Street, Suite 412, New York, NY 10036, USA
Tel: (212) 575 3431 *or* (877) 221 7120 (toll-free in USA).
Fax: (212) 575 3434.
E-mail: info@rnto.org
Website: www.russia-travel.com
Represents the Russian National Tourist Office, Russian Association of Travel Agencies (RATA) and Russian National Olympic Committee.

Embassy of the United States of America
Novinskiy Bulvar 19/23, 121099 Moscow, Russian Federation
Tel: (095) 728 5000. Fax: (095) 728 5112 (administration) *or* 5247 (consular section).
E-mail: consulmo@state.gov
Website: www.usembassy.ru

Consulate General of the United States of America
Furshtatskaya Ulista 15, 191028 St Petersburg, Russian Federation
Tel: (812) 331 2600. Fax: (812) 331 2852.
E-mail: visastpete@state.gov *or* ircpeter@state.gov
Website: www.stpetersburg-usconsulate.ru
Other Consulates in: Vladivostok and Yekaterinburg.

Embassy of the Russian Federation
285 Charlotte Street, Ottawa, Ontario K1N 8L5, Canada
Tel: (613) 235 4341. Fax: (613) 236 6342.
E-mail: rusemb@rogers.com
Website: www.rusembcanada.mid.ru
Consular section: 52 Range Road, Ottawa, Ontario K1N 8J5, Canada
Tel: (613) 236 7220/6215/0920. Fax: (613) 238 6158.
E-mail: ruscons@rogers.com
Consulates in: Montréal and Toronto.

Canadian Embassy
Starokonyushenny Pereulok 23, 119202 Moscow, Russian Federation
Tel: (095) 105 6000 *or* 6070 (visa information line).
Fax: (095) 105 6025 *or* 6090 (visa section).
E-mail: mosco@dfait-maeci.gc.ca
Website: www.dfait-maeci.gc.ca/canadaeuropa/russia

Canadian Consulate General
32 Malodetskoselsky Prospect, 190013 St Petersburg, Russian Federation
Tel: (812) 320 6515.
Fax: (812) 320 6514.
E-mail: spurg@dfait-maeci.gc.ca

TIMATIC CODES

Health	AMADEUS: TI-DFT/SVO/HE GALILEO/WORLDSPAN: TI-DFT/SVO/HE SABRE: TIDFT/SVO/HE
Visa	AMADEUS: TI-DFT/SVO/VI GALILEO/WORLDSPAN: TI-DFT/SVO/VI SABRE: TIDFT/SVO/VI

To access TIMATIC country information on Health and Visa regulations through the Computer Reservations System (CRS), type in the appropriate command line listed above.

General Information

AREA: 17,075,400 sq km (6,592,850 sq miles).
POPULATION: 144,800,000 (official estimate 2001).
POPULATION DENSITY: 8.5 per sq km.
CAPITAL: Moscow. **Population:** 8,297,900 (1999).
GEOGRAPHY: The Russian Federation covers almost twice the area of the USA, and reaches from Moscow in the west over the Urals and the vast Siberian plains to the Sea of Okhotsk in the east. The border between European Russia and Siberia (Asia) is formed by the Ural Mountains, the Ural River and the Manych Depression. European Russia extends from the North Polar Sea across the Central Russian Uplands to the Black Sea, the Northern Caucasus and the Caspian Sea. Siberia stretches from the West Siberian Plain across the Central Siberian Plateau between Yenisey and Lena, including the Sayan, Yablonovy and Stanovoy ranges in the south to the East Siberian mountains between Lena and the Pacific coast, including the Chukotskiy and Kamchatka peninsulas.
Population figures: The following republics are part of the Russian Federation. Population figures were drawn up in 1999.

Republic	Area (sq km)	Population (000's)	Capital
Adygheya	**7600**	**449**	**Maikop**
Altai	**92,600**	**203**	**Gorno-Altaisk**
Bashkortostan	**143,600**	**4110**	**Ufa**
Buryatia	**351,300**	**1053**	**Ulan-Ude**
Chechnyat*	**N/A**	**781**	**Grozny**
Chuvashia	**18,300**	**1362**	**Cheboksary**
Daghestan	**50,300**	**2120**	**Makhachkala**
Ingushetia*	**N/A**	**317**	**Magas**
Kabardino-Balkariya	**12,500**	**786**	**Nalchik**
Kalmykiya	**75,900**	**316**	**Elista**
Karachayevo-Cherkessiya	**14,100**	**434**	**Cherkessk**
Kareliya	**172,400**	**771**	**Petrozavodsk**
Khakassiya	**61,900**	**581**	**Abakan**
Komi	**415,900**	**1151**	**Syktyvkar**
Marii-El	**23,200**	**761**	**Yoshkar-Ola**
Mordoviya	**26,200**	**937**	**Saransk**
Northern Osetiya (Alaniya)	**8000**	**663**	**Vladikavkaz**
Sakha (Yakutiya)	**3,103,200**	**1001**	**Yakutsk**
Tatarstan	**68,000**	**3784**	**Kazan**
Tyva	**170,500**	**311**	**Kyzyl**
Udmurtiya	**42,100**	**1633**	**Izhevsk**

*Until 1992, the territories of the Republic of Chechnya and the Ingush Republic were combined in the Chechen-Ingush autonomous republic (area 19,300 sq km).
GOVERNMENT: Republic since 1991. **Head of Government:** President Vladimir Putin since 2000.
LANGUAGE: Russian. English, French or German are spoken by some people.
RELIGION: Mainly Christian with the Russian Orthodox Church being the largest Christian community. Muslim, Buddhist and Jewish minorities also exist.
TIME: The Russian Federation is divided into 11 time zones. Summer time is + 1 from last Sunday in March to Saturday before last Sunday in October.
Kaliningrad: GMT + 2. **Moscow**, **St Petersburg**, **Astrakhan:** GMT + 3. **Izhevsk** and **Samara:** GMT + 4.
Perm – Nizhnevartovsk: GMT + 5. **Omsk** and **Novosibirsk:** GMT + 6. **Norilsk**, **Kyzyl:** GMT + 7.
Bratsk – Ulan Ude: GMT + 8. **Chita**, **Yakutsk:** GMT + 9.
Khabarovsk, **Vladivostok:** GMT + 10. **Magadan**, **Yuzhno Sakhalinsk:** GMT + 11. **Petropavlosk:** GMT + 12.
ELECTRICITY: 220 volts AC, 50Hz.
COMMUNICATIONS: Telephone: IDD is available. Country code: 7. When dialling the Russian Federation from abroad, the 0 of the area code must *not* be omitted. Outgoing international code: 810. Some Moscow hotels have telephone booths with IDD. For long-distance calls within the CIS, dial 8 then wait for the dial tone before proceeding with the call. Collect calls, calls placed using credit cards and calls from direct dial telephones in hotels can be extremely expensive. The emergency services can be reached as follows: fire – 01; police – 02; ambulance – 03. For enquiries regarding Moscow private telephone numbers, dial 09; for businesses, 927 0009. For national directory enquiries regarding the Russian Federation and the CIS, dial 927 0009. **Mobile telephone:** GSM 900/1800 networks. Network operators include *KB Impuls* (website: www.beelinegsm.ru) and *Mobile Telesystems* (website: www.mts.ru). All major cities are covered by at least one operator. Handsets can be hired from some companies.
Fax: Services are available in numerous business centres and hotels, although the latter option is more expensive.
Internet: ISPs include *Beeonline* (website: www.beeonline.ru) and *Russiaonline* (website: www.online.ru). Public access is available in hotels in larger cities and in Internet cafes. **Telegram:** These may be sent from hotels. **Post:** Airmail to Western Europe takes over 10 days. There are postboxes and post offices in every hotel. *Poste restante* facilities are available at the larger hotels. Inland surface mail is often slow. Post office hours: 0900-1900. **Press:** The main dailies in the Russian Federation are *Izvestiya* and *Komsomolskaya Pravda*, both published in Moscow. Newspapers and magazines are published in some 25 languages. Multilingual editions of the *Moscow News* are available weekly. The *Moscow Times* and *St Petersburg Times* are published in English. There is also a daily Internet newspaper, *Russia Today* (website: www.russiatoday.com).
Radio: BBC World Service (website: www.bbc.co.uk/worldservice) and Voice of America (website: www.voa.gov) can be received. From time to time the frequencies change and the most up-to-date can be found online.

Passport/Visa

	Passport Required?	Visa Required?	Return Ticket Required?
Full British	Yes	Yes	No
Australian	Yes	Yes	No
Canadian	Yes	Yes	No
USA	Yes	Yes	No
Other EU	Yes	Yes	No
Japanese	Yes	Yes	No

Note: Regulations and requirements may be subject to change at short notice, and you are advised to contact the appropriate diplomatic or consular authority before finalising travel arrangements. Details of these may be found at the head of this country's entry. Any numbers in the chart refer to the footnotes below.

PASSPORTS: Valid 10-year passport required by all.
Note: Whilst in the country, visitors must carry ID at all times. Rather than carry original documents, it is advisable to carry photocopies of passports and visas, which will facilitate replacement should either be stolen.
VISAS: Required by all except the following, provided arriving from their country of origin:
(a) nationals of CIS countries (except nationals of Georgia and Turkmenistan who *do* require visas);
(b) nationals of Cuba for stays of up to 30 days;
(c) nationals of Mongolia, provided visiting for purposes of business and holding letter of invitation and return tickets, or travelling as tourists and holding prepaid hotel vouchers;
(d) transit passengers who are continuing their journey

within 24 hours without leaving the transit area.
Types of visa and cost: *Tourist*, *Business*, *Private* and *Transit*: £30, if visa is processed in minimum eight working days. (Processing within three to five days costs £60; next-day processing £80; same-day processing £90; processing within one hour £120.) *Multiple-entry*: £100, standard six working days' processing (same-day processing costs £150).
Note: (a) Nationals of some countries may have to pay a consular fee in addition to the visa processing charges listed. Enquire at the Consulate or Consular section of Embassy for a list of nationals and prices. (b) Transit visas are required by all except passengers remaining in the transit zone of Moscow Sheremetievo airport for less than 24 hours.
Validity: Dependent on purpose of trip. Transit visas are valid for up to three days. Tourist visas are valid for up to one month. Private visas are valid for up to 90 days.
Application to: Consulate (or Consular section at Embassy); see *Contact Addresses* section.
Application requirements: (a) Completed application form. (b) One recent passport-size photo stapled twice to upper-right corner of application form. (c) Passport valid for at least six months after visa expires, with at least one blank page. (d) Fee, payable in cash only or postal orders for postal applications. (e) Postal applications must be accompanied by a large, pre-paid special delivery, self-addressed envelope. *Tourist*: (a)-(e) and, (f) original tourist voucher (exchange order) issued by an authorised travel company stating their reference number, passenger names, dates of entry and exit, confirmation of payment, full itinerary, places to be visited, means of transportation and confirmation in Russian language. The voucher should be stamped and signed by an authorised person. (g) A standard tourist confirmation of acceptance issued by Russian tourist company or hotel accredited by the Ministry of Foreign Affairs in Russia, showing tourist reference number given by Russian Foreign Minister and names of applicants, full itinerary and dates of entry/exit. *Private* (for visiting relations or friends): (a)-(e) and, (f) Official original letter of invitation from Russian Ministry of Internal Affairs. *Business*: (a)-(e) and, (f) An official letter of invitation from company or organisation in the Russian Federation responsible for visit, certified by the local branch of Russian Ministry of Internal Affairs. (g) An introductory letter from applicant's company stating purpose of visit, itinerary, dates of entry and exit, assuming financial responsibility for the visit and stating the companies to be visited. *Transit*: (a)-(d) and, (e) Original and copy of confirmed air ticket to and from the Russian Federation. *Multiple-entry*: (a)-(e) and, (f) Original and a copy of your confirmed air ticket to and from Russia.
Note: (a) Those who are travelling in groups (standard package tours, coach tours, international competitions and cruises) should submit all documentation to the tour operator making the travel arrangements. For visits to relatives/friends in the CIS, enquire at the Consulate for details of application procedures. (b) All travellers staying in the Russian Federation for longer than three days must register their visas through their hotel or sponsor. Private visitors must register with local police on arrival. For travel to Tajikistan, your invitation should be confirmed by the Ministry of Foreign Affairs of the Republic of Tajikistan.
(c) French nationals should also have their previous three months' bank statements, medical insurance and a copy of their tickets. (d) German nationals and all other Schengen country nationals should have travel insurance valid in the Russian Federation. (e) Since February 2003, every foreign citizen is given a migration card free of charge when they cross the Russian border. They must fill in their personal data, terms, purpose of visit and prospective place of residence and present the card when applying for registration within three days of arrival. The migration cards must be handed back upon departure.
Working days required: One to 12, depending on type of visa. Postal applications take at least eight to 12 days to process. Applications for visas may not be made earlier than three months before departure.
Exit visas: Exit visas are required by all passengers who want to leave the country and are normally issued together with the entry visa. If the exit permit has not yet been issued by the representative of the Russian Federation which issued the visa, aliens should obtain it from the Intourist Service Bureau in their hotel two days prior to departure at the latest.
Temporary residence: Enquire at Embassy.

Money

Currency: Rouble (Rbl) = 100 kopeks. Notes are in denominations of Rbl1000, 500, 100, 50 and 10. Coins are in denominations of Rbl5, 2 and 1. The Rouble was devalued by a factor of 1000 in January 1998. The old notes and coins remained legal tender until 2002, although their real value was 1000th of their face value.
Currency exchange: Foreign currency should only be exchanged at official bureaux and authorised banks, and all transactions must be recorded on the currency declaration form which is issued on arrival. It is wise to retain all exchange receipts. Bureaux de change are numerous and easy to locate. Large shops and hotels offer their own exchange facilities. US Dollars in pristine condition are the easiest currency to exchange. It is illegal to settle accounts in hard currency and to change money unofficially.
Credit & debit cards: Major European and international credit and debit cards, including American Express, Diners Club and Visa are accepted in the larger hotels and at foreign currency shops and restaurants, but cash (in Roubles) is preferred. Check with your credit or debit card company for details of merchant acceptability and other services that might be available.
Travellers cheques: Cash is preferred. To avoid additional exchange rate charges, travellers are advised to take travellers cheques in US Dollars.
Currency restrictions: The import and export of local currency is prohibited. The import of foreign currency is unlimited but sums greater than $3000 (or equivalent) must be declared. The export of foreign currency is limited to the amount declared on arrival.
Exchange rate indicators: The following figures are included as a guide to the movements of the Rouble against Sterling and the US Dollar:

Date	Feb '04	May '04	Aug '04	Nov '04
£1.00=	51.93	51.72	53.89	53.62
$1.00=	28.53	28.96	29.25	28.31

Banking hours: Mon-Fri 0930-1730.

Duty Free

Duty free regulations are liable to change at short notice. The following should be used as a guide only, and travellers are advised to contact the Embassy or Consulate for up-to-date information. The following goods may be imported into the Russian Federation by persons of 16 years of age or older without incurring customs duty:
1000 cigarettes or 1kg of tobacco products; 1.5l of spirits and 2l of wine; a reasonable quantity of perfume for personal use; gifts up to the value of US$10,000.
Note: On entering the country, tourists must complete a customs declaration form which must be retained until departure. This allows the import of articles intended for personal use, including currency and valuables which must be registered on the declaration form. Cameras, jewellery, computers and musical instruments should all be declared. Customs inspection can be long and detailed. It is advisable when shopping to ask for a certificate from the shop which states that goods have been paid for in hard currency. Presentation of such certificates should speed up customs formalities.
Prohibited imports: Photographs and printed matter directed against the Russian Federation, weapons and ammunition, narcotics, fruit, vegetables and live animals unless with a special permit.
Prohibited exports: Arms, works of art and antiques (unless permission has been granted by the Ministry of Culture), precious metals and furs.
Note: Up to 280g of caviar per person may be exported, provided a receipt is shown proving that it was bought at a store licensed to sell it to foreigners.

Public Holidays

2005: Jan 1-2 New Year. **Jan 7** Russian Orthodox Christmas Day. **Mar 8** International Women's Day. **May 1-2** Spring and Labour Day. **May 9** Victory in Europe Day. **Jun 12** Independence Day. **Nov 7** Day of Reconciliation and Consent. **Dec 12** Constitution Day.
2006: Jan 1-2 New Year. **Jan 7** Russian Orthodox Christmas Day. **Mar 8** International Women's Day. **May 1-2** Spring and Labour Day. **May 9** Victory in Europe Day. **Jun 12** Independence Day. **Nov 7** Day of Reconciliation and Consent. **Dec 12** Constitution Day.

Health

	Special Precautions?	Certificate Required?
Yellow Fever	No	No
Cholera	No	No
Typhoid & Polio	1	N/A
Malaria	No	N/A

Note: *Regulations and requirements may be subject to change at short notice, and you are advised to contact your doctor well in advance of your intended date of departure. Any numbers in the chart refer to the footnotes below.*

1: Poliomyelitis occurs. Immunisation is advisable.
Food & drink: All water should be regarded as being a potential health risk. Water used for drinking, brushing teeth or making ice should have first been boiled or otherwise sterilised. Contaminated tap water contains a high prevalence of *gastrointestinal* infections. The water supply in St Petersburg especially has been linked to *giardiasis*. Milk is pasteurised and dairy products are safe for consumption. Only eat well-cooked meat and fish, preferably served hot. Pork, salad and mayonnaise may carry increased risk. Vegetables should be cooked and fruit peeled.
Other risks: *Dysentery* is common throughout the country. *Hepatitis A* occurs. Widespread outbreaks of *diphtheria* have been reported. Consult a doctor regarding inoculation before travelling to the Russian Federation. *Tick-borne typhus* has been reported from east and central Siberia. *Tick-borne encephalitis* and *Lyme disease* occur in forested areas throughout the Russian Federation. Vaccination is advisable. Outbreaks of *Japanese encephalitis* have been reported from the southeast. *Leishmaniasis* can occur in the south. Outbreaks of *meningitis* have been reported from Volgograd.
Rabies is present and increasing. For those at high risk, vaccination before arrival should be considered. If you are bitten, seek medical advice without delay. For more information consult the *Health* appendix.
Note: Visitors staying for more than three months must produce a certificate proving they are HIV-negative. The certification requirements are exacting and detailed; a medical examination may also be required. Foreign tests may be acceptable under certain conditions. Check details with the embassy.
Health care: The highly developed health service provides free medical treatment for all citizens. If a traveller becomes ill during a booked tour, emergency treatment is free, with small sums to be paid for medicines and hospital treatment. If a longer stay than originally planned becomes necessary because of the illness, the visitor has to pay for all further treatment. This can be very expensive; air evacuation can cost up to £80,000. All visitors are strongly advised to have full medical cover that includes medical evacuation. It is advisable to take a supply of medicines that are likely to be required (check first that they may be imported legally). A reciprocal health care agreement is in operation between the UK and the Russian Federation, allowing citizens to receive free treatment. Private medical care can be expensive.

Travel - International

Travel warning: Because of the security situation in the North Caucasus, it is strongly advised not to travel to Chechnya, Ingushetia, Dagestan, North Ossetia, Karachai-Cherkessia, Kabardino-Balkaria (including the Elbrus area) and to the eastern and southern parts of Stavropol Krai, particularly where it borders Chechnya and North Ossetia. Chechen militants have threatened further violence in response to the killing of their rebel leader, Aslan Maskhador, on March 8, 2005. It is advised that potential visitors monitor the situation. There is a high threat from domestic terrorism in Russia, including suicide bombings in public places.
AIR: The national airline is *Aeroflot – Russian International Airlines (SU)* (website: www.aeroflot.com). Other airlines serving the Russian Federation include *Air France, Austrian Airlines, British Airways, Czech Airlines, El Al, Finnair, Lufthansa* and *SAS Scandinavian Airlines*.
Approximate flight times: From Moscow or St Petersburg to *London* is three hours 45 minutes. From Moscow to *Almaty* is four hours 40 minutes, to *Baku* is three hours 10 minutes, to *Bukhara* is three hours 40 minutes, to *Kiev* is one hour 45 minutes, to *Minsk* is one hour 20 minutes, to *Odessa* is two hours, to *Samarkand* is three hours 50 minutes and to *Yerevan* is two hours 50 minutes.
International airports: *Moscow (SVO)* (Sheremetyevo) (website: www.sheremetyevo-airport.ru) is 35km (22 miles) northwest of the city. Taxis are available at the airport to the city centre for approximately US$10-15 (travel time – 30 to 40 minutes). 'Autoline' fixed-route taxis and buses are also available. Express coaches depart for the city every 20 minutes (0545-0030). Coaches depart for the airport from the Central Air Terminal in Moscow, 37 Leningradsky Prospekt (travel time – 50 minutes for international flights). Express trains leave every 30 minutes. Airport facilities include outgoing duty free shops, banks/bureaux de change, post office, car hire, restaurants and first aid. Moscow also has three primarily domestic airports: see the *Travel – Internal* section.
St Petersburg (LED) (Pulkovo) is 17km (10.5 miles) south of the city. Buses are available to the city centre 0700-2000 every 10 minutes (travel time – 10 minutes). Taxis are available for roughly US$10 (travel time – 15 minutes). Airport facilities include banks/bureaux de change, flight information, duty free shops, restaurant, bar, snack bar, left luggage and first aid.
Departure tax: None.
RAIL: There are various connections from London. The sleeper coach to Moscow takes about 53 hours. The main route is: London–Brussels–Cologne/Berlin–Moscow. The journey from London to Brussels can be made by a variety

of train and ferry services (including via *Eurostar*), or via the Channel Tunnel. Services from Brussels are daily. There are through trains or coaches from other Western and Eastern European cities, from CIS countries, and from China (PR), Iran, Mongolia and Turkey. See also *Trans-Siberian Express* in the *Travel – Internal* section.

ROAD: Foreign tourists may drive their own cars or may hire cars (see *Travel – Internal*). The speed limit is 60kmph on minor roads, 90kmph on major roads and variable on highways. A road tax is payable upon entry to the country. The following crossing points between Finland and the Russian Federation are available: Vaalima–Torfianovska; Nuijamaa–Brusnichnoye and Rajajooseppi–Lotta. There are also crossing points between the Russian Federation and all neighbouring countries although, at present, there are restrictions on cross-border travel to Azerbaijan and Georgia. Plans to simplify this process are currently underway. Those entering by car should have their visas registered at the hotel, motel or campsite where they will stay for the first night, and must also ensure that the car registration number is recorded in the visa. Travellers should also insure their vehicle with *Ingosstrakh*, which has offices at all crossing points and in most major cities, and to purchase service coupons at the border. Although motorcyclists can enter the Russian Federation, cyclists wishing to cross the Russian border should find out whether this is permissible from the Russian Embassy or their travel agent before departure. *Eurolines*, departing from Victoria Coach Station in London, serves destinations in the Russian Federation. For further information, contact *Eurolines* (tel: (08705) 143 219; e-mail: welcome@eurolines.co.uk; website: www.eurolines.co.uk).

Travel - Internal

AIR: The internal network radiates from Moscow's four airports. *Aeroflot* runs services from Moscow to most major cities. All-inclusive tours are available from specialist tour operators.

Note: In the 1990s, Aeroflot was broken up into many small airlines which led to a catalogue of air disasters earning it a reputation for poor safety. Thankfully, its safety record has improved in recent years.

Domestic airports: *Vnukovo Airport (VKO)* is 29.5km (18 miles) southwest of Moscow. Coaches go to the airport from the Central Air Terminal (travel time - one hour 15 minutes). Outgoing duty free facilities are available at the airport. Taxis are available to the city.

Domodedovo (DME) is 48km (25 miles) southeast of Moscow. A coach goes from the Central Air Terminal to the airport (travel time - one hour 20 minutes).

Bykovo Airport (BKA) is the smallest of Moscow's airports, 35km from the city. Coaches go to the airport from the Central Air Terminal.

Approximate flight times: From Moscow to *Bratsk* is six hours 45 minutes, to *Donetsk* is one hour 30 minutes, to *Irkutsk* is seven hours, to *Khabarovsk* is seven hours 30 minutes, to *Kharkov* is one hour 15 minutes, to *St Petersburg* is one hour 30 minutes, to *Volgograd* is one hour 50 minutes and to *Yalta* is two hours 15 minutes.

SEA: Owing to its geographical position, the Russian Federation has ports on its Pacific and Baltic shores and in the south on the Black Sea. The most important eastern ports are Vladivostok, Magadan, Nakhodka and Petropavlovsk; the most important western ports are St Petersburg and Kaliningrad on the Baltic. The only links to the Atlantic are the ports of Murmansk on the Kola peninsula, which never freezes over and Archangelisk. Major harbours on the Black Sea are Novorossiysk and Sochi. There are plans to build an extension to the St Petersburg harbour at Ust-Luga. Upgrading of facilities at Kaliningrad and Vyborg is also planned. Sea cruises on the Black Sea and the Baltic are popular.

RIVER: Cruises and excursions are available on the Amur, Don, Irtysh, Lena, Ob, Volga and Yenisey rivers. Many companies offer cruises on board comfortable, modern boats. The Volga towns, the Golden Ring and Moscow–St Petersburg are popular routes.

RAIL: The 87,079km (54,109 miles) of track are a vital part of the infrastructure because of the poor road system. The largest and busiest rail network in the world is predominantly for freight traffic. Only a few long-distance routes are open for travel by tourists, and reservations must be made on all journeys. Children under five years of age travel free. Children aged five to nine pay half fare. Rail travellers are advised to store valuables in the compartment under the bed or seat and not to leave the compartment unattended.

The *Trans-Siberian Express*, probably the most famous train in the world, is one of the best ways of seeing the interior of the country. It runs from Moscow to the Pacific coast of Siberia and on to Japan. There is a daily service, but the steamer from Nakhodka to Yokohama only sails approximately once a week. The through journey from Moscow to Yokohama takes 10 days. It is the world's longest continuous train journey, crossing seven time zones and 9745km (5778 miles) from Europe to the Pacific, with 91 stops from Vladivostok to Moscow. Bed linen and towels are provided in the 'Soft Class' (first-class) berths, and there is a toilet and washbasin at the end of each carriage. Attendants serve tea from samovars for a small charge and there is a restaurant car on every train where meals can be purchased (however, no alcohol is available on the train, so passengers are advised to bring their own if desired).

The *Trans-Manchurian Express* follows the same route, before heading southeast into China and down to Beijing. Another, slightly shorter but no less epic journey can be made on the *Trans-Mongolian Railway* to Beijing. It runs from Moscow to Irkutsk (Siberia), skirting Lake Baikal and then entering Mongolia. The journey to the Mongolian capital, Ulaan Baatar, is remarkable for its dramatic scenery. The journey concludes in Beijing.

ROAD: The European part of the Russian Federation depends heavily on its road network, which totals 552,000km (343,000 miles) throughout the Federation. Generally, the few roads in Siberia and further east are impassable during the winter. It is a good idea to arrange motoring holidays through a reputable agency. It is also advisable to pre-plan the itinerary and accommodation requirements. On the majority of tourist routes, signposts are also written in the Latin alphabet. Travellers can take their own car (see *Travel – International*) or hire a vehicle; tariffs include the cost of insurance. Chauffeured cars are available in major cities. Sample distances: Moscow to St Petersburg: 692km (432 miles); Moscow to Minsk: 690km (429 miles); Moscow to Rostov-on-Don: 1198km (744 miles); Moscow to Odessa: 1347km (837 miles).

Bus: Long-distance coach services have only recently become open to foreigners. They are a great way of seeing the country but patience is a necessity and getting lost is commonplace. **Traffic regulations:** Traffic drives on the right. Speeds are limited to 60kph (37mph) in built-up areas and 90kph (55mph) elsewhere. Hooting the horn is forbidden except when to do so might prevent an accident. Motorists should avoid driving at night if possible. It is forbidden to carry unauthorised passengers or pick up hitch-hikers. Driving under the influence of drugs or alcohol is forbidden. Every car must display registration plates and stickers denoting the country of registration and be fitted with seat belts, a first-aid kit, a fire extinguisher and an emergency sign (triangle) or red light. In case of an accident, contact the nearest traffic inspection officer and make sure all participants fill in written statements, to be witnessed by a militia inspector. All repairs will be at the foreign motorist's expense. **Documentation:** An International Driving Permit and a national licence with authorised translations are necessary. Visitors travelling in their own cars must also possess the following documents at all tmes: passport and visa; itinerary card bearing visitor's name and citizenship, car registration number and full details of itinerary presented upon entry to the Russian Federation relating to the route to be taken and the date and place of stopovers; form provided by Customs on arrival guaranteeing that the car will be taken out of the Russian Federation on departure; petrol vouchers purchased at the border; and insurance cover documents. A road tax is payable upon entry to the country (see end of *Travel – International*). Motor insurance for travel within the Russian Federation should be arranged prior to departure, or upon entry to the Russian Federation at the offices of *Ingosstrakh*, the Russian Federation foreign insurance agency. Contact the Embassy or a specialist tour operator for further details.

URBAN: Public transport in the cities is comprehensive and cheap. Many services are electric traction (metro, tramway, trolleybus). Stations on the Moscow and St Petersburg metros are always elegant and often palatial. Entry to the underground is by tokens, which are inserted into the ticket barrier. Fares are standard for the various forms of transport. Taxis are also available; they can be hailed in the street, hired at a rank or booked by telephone. It is safer to use officially marked taxis, which should not be shared with strangers.

Travel Times: The following chart gives approximate travel times (in hours and minutes) from **Moscow** to other major cities/towns in the Russian Federation:

	Air	Rail	Sea
Khabarovsk	7.30	-	-
St Petersburg	1.30	9.00	-
Irkutsk	7.00	88.00	-
Nakhodka	-	-	141.00
Volgograd	1.30	-	-

Accommodation

HOTELS: There are approximately 2500 hotels in the Russian Federation, of which about 100 specialise in accommodating foreign guests. Some hotels meet international standards, whereas others are very basic. Direct reservations by clients are on the increase. Several hotels in Moscow and St Petersburg are run partly as joint ventures, eg the *Aerostar* (**4-star**), the *Olympic-Penta* (all rooms with bathroom, air conditioning, radio, TV, IDD) and the *Novotel* at Moscow airport. The *Pullman Iris* also offers **4-star** comfort. St Petersburg's *Grand Hotel Europe* is one of the first **5-star** hotels in the Russian Federation. The *Hotel Helen* is a Russian-Finnish joint-venture, located 20km (12.5 miles) from St Petersburg airport. Whatever class of accommodation, it is advisable not to leave valuables in hotel rooms and to lock the door before going to sleep.

BED & BREAKFAST: Several companies provide bed & breakfast accommodation with English-speaking families in Moscow, St Petersburg and other cities.

CAMPING/CARAVANNING: Camping holidays are now offered by a number of independent companies.

YOUTH HOSTELS: There are currently two hostels in St Petersburg, three in Moscow and one in Novgorod. Hostels tend to be safer and cleaner than hotels of similar prices. Reservations from outside the Russian Federation should be made at least three to four weeks in advance. Note there is no age restriction. For further information, contact the Russian Youth Hostel Association, St Petersburg International Hostel, 3rd Sovetskaya, 28, St Petersburg 193069 (tel: (812) 329 8018; fax: (812) 329 8019; e-mail: lada_serova@ryh.ru *or* ryh@ryh.ru *or* inquiries@ryh.ru; website: www.ryh.ru/ryha). For postal enquiries, write to the RYHA via Finland at: PO Box 8, SF-53501, Lappeenranta, Finland.

Note: Anyone travelling on a tourist visa to the Russian Federation must (officially at least) have accommodation arranged before arrival.

Resorts & Excursions

MOSCOW

The capital was founded in 1147, but there is evidence that there has been a settlement here since Neolithic times. The focal point of the city is **Red Square**, on one side of which is the **Kremlin** surrounded by a thick red fortress wall containing 20 towers altogether. The **Sobakina Tower**, designed to withstand sieges, contains a secret escape passage. The **Tainitskaya Tower** translates as the 'Tower of Secrets', because it also had a secret subterranean passage leading to the river. The **Trinity Gate** is the tallest of the towers. The **Water-Hoist Tower** conveyed water to the Kremlin. The **Nabatnaya Tower** contained an alarm bell that was rung in times of danger. In the Kremlin grounds, the **Uspensky Cathedral** (1475-79), designed by the Italian architect Aristotle Fioravanti, contains three of the oldest Russian icons. The tsars were crowned here; Ivan the Terrible's throne is situated near the entrance. Also within the Kremlin stand the 14th-century **Grand Kremlin Palace** and the golden-domed **Belfry of Ivan the Great**. **St Basil's Cathedral** (built 1555-60), at another end of the square, is famous for its brightly coloured domes. As the story goes, Ivan the Terrible was so overwhelmed by its beauty that he blinded the architect so that he could never create another building as impressive as this. Opposite St Basil's, the **Spassky (Redeemer's) Gate** is the main entrance to the Kremlin, built in 1491 by Pietro Antonio Solario. The **Blagoveshchensky (Annunciation) Cathedral** was built for Ivan III. It is extravagantly decorated, from its copper domes to its agate- and jasper-tiled floors. It contains 16th-century frescoes and a precious collection of icons. **Our Lady of Kazan Cathedral** has recently been reconstructed and rededicated. The superb murals in the **Faceted Chamber** date from the late 15th century; sadly, the Chamber is not open to the public. The **State Historical Museum** is also located in Red Square. Although there is talk of finally burying Lenin's embalmed body, **Lenin's Mausoleum** is still open to the public on certain days. However, the changing of the guards in front of the Mausoleum, a ritual which used to attract many sightseers, was discontinued in 1993. **Tverskaya Street** near Red Square is one of the main shopping streets. **Arbat Street** is the main thoroughfare of a traditionally bohemian quarter. Today it is a pedestrian zone with crafts and artists' stalls and street performers. The area known as **Kitai-Gorod** lies east of the Kremlin, and is notable for its 16th- and 17th-century churches, especially the five-domed **Cathedral of the Sign**, with its amazing acoustic properties. The splendid **English Estate** dates from the same period, a remnant of the area's former importance as a diplomatic and commercial centre. The nearby **Romanov Apartments** are now a museum. **Zayauzie** is a quiet, attractive district, with its handsome merchants' mansions. The world-famous **Bolshoi Opera and Ballet Theatre** at **Teatralnaya Square** dates from 1824 and has an interior colour scheme of red and gold. **Moscow University** is situated on the southwestern periphery of the city in the **Vorobyevi Hills**. The lookout tower in the park in front of the University complex offers excellent views over the city and the vast **Luzhniki Stadium**. **Novodevichy Convent** near **Sportivnaya** metro station houses a museum of rare and ancient Russian art, and is one of the finest examples of 16th- and 17th-century architecture in the city. The neighbouring **Ostozhenka** and **Prechistenka Streets** feature urban mansions and estates associated with many classic Russian authors, including Tolstoy. The dancer Isadora Duncan shared her studio with her husband, the poet Sergei Yesenin, in the classically designed estate of the millionaire Ushkov in **Prechistenka Street**. **Herzen Street** is one of the oldest in Moscow. It contains the **Moscow State University**, the grand **Tchaikovsky Conservatoire** and the ornate **Mayakovsky Academic Theatre**. The area around **Kuznetzky Most** and **Petrovka Street** is a hub of social and cultural activity, with its popular theatres, fashion shops and business community. One of the most popular new, but macabre attractions is the **KGB Museum** housed in the sinister **Lubyanka** building. The well-preserved **Zamoskvorechye** district was originally a mercantile and artisans' quarter. Many of its churches, warehouses, shops and houses survive. The area is home to the **Tretyakov Gallery**, containing the work of Russian artists and an extensive collection of icons, among them the **Trinity** by Andrei Rublyov. Other places of interest are: the **Pushkin Museum of Fine Arts** with its cosmopolitan collection; the **Moscow Circus**, the original with animal acts and clowns and the newer with more technical wonders; **Izmailovo Park**, formerly the Tsar's estate and the elegant **Tsaritsino** landscaped park; the **Exhibition of Economic Achievements**, where on a large site in the northwest of the city all aspects of Russian life are displayed – such as agriculture, industry, culture and science. The site also contains a zoo and a circus and there is skating and skiing. The nearby **Ostankino TV Tower** is the tallest in Europe, with a revolving restaurant at the top. The **Space Conquerors' Monument**, representing the trajectory of a rocket launch, also dominates the area. The local **Museum of Serf Art** is a reminder of the past. The **Metro** system is a tourist attraction in itself, as well as a cheap and convenient means of travelling around the city. Many stations are sumptuously decorated with marble, glittering chandeliers and works of art. A boat tour on the **Moskva River** is a pleasant way of discovering the city. Excursions start at the **Kutuzovskaya Pier**, accessible from **Kutuzovskaya Metro**. The river is a superb vantage point to view the White House (the Parliament Building), scene of the dramatic siege of 1991, as well as many of the sights listed above.

Excursions: The **State Museum of Ceramics** in **Kuskovo**, 10km (6 miles) from the centre of Moscow, has a fascinating collection of Russian china, porcelain and glass. **Arkhangelskoye Estate**, a museum housed in a palace 16km (10 miles) from Moscow, exhibits European paintings and sculptures, but the main attraction is the grounds which are laid out in the French style. **Zhostovo**, 30km (19 miles) from Moscow, is a centre renowned for its lacquered trays, and **Fedoskino**, 35km (22 miles) from Moscow, produces lacquer miniatures, brooches and other handicrafts. Located near the town of **Tula**, 160km (100 miles) from the capital, **Yasnaya Polyana** is historically significant as the author Leo Tolstoy's estate. The author of *War and Peace* and *Anna Karenina* is buried here and his house, surrounded by landscaped parkland, is now a museum open to the public. Tchaikovsky's home at **Klin**, 90km (56 miles) from Moscow, and Boris Pasternak's home at **Peredelkino** (30 minutes' drive from the capital), are also museums.

Tver, situated 160km (100 miles) from Moscow on the **Upper Volga**, is where Catherine II built a palace in order to take a rest en route from Moscow to St Petersburg. The **Putyevoi Dvorets** (Route Palace) was built by Kazakov in 1763-75. The palace overlooks the river, a convenient location for the tsarina to disembark. The town is also notable for its star-shaped square.

THE GOLDEN RING

Several ancient towns of great historical, architectural and spiritual significance make up the 'Golden Ring', extending northeast from Moscow. They are a rich collection of kremlins (citadels), monasteries, cathedrals and fortresses. All are within easy reach of the capital. Since many were founded on river banks, a cruise is a pleasant way of discovering the region. Modern boats plying the Volga afford comfortable accommodation. As some major sites such as Vladimir and Suzdal are not located near the Volga, a minibus tour with hotel accommodation is a better option for visitors whose primary interest is the region's architectural heritage.

Sergiyev Posad: This small town, formerly known as Zagorsk, is situated on two rivers and is the centre of the handmade toy industry; the **Toy Museum** has a collection beginning in the Bronze Age. The **Trinity Monastery of St Sergius** dates from the Middle Ages and is a major pilgrimage centre. Its **Cathedral of the Dormition** has wonderful blue domes decorated with gold stars. The museum contains examples of Russian ecclesiastical art and crafts.

Sofrin: In nearby Sofrin, the **Icon Workshops** produce ecclesiastical ware. Also near Sergiyev Posad, the literary and artistic museum of **Abramtsevo** houses paintings by Repin, Serov and Vrubel. The museum is surrounded by parkland and birch woods. Ornate traditional Russian huts are dotted around the estate.

Rostov Veliky: Founded in the ninth century, this town has a beautiful **Kremlin** and **Cathedral of the Dormition**. The town overlooks the shores of the **Nero Lake**, and is surrounded by ancient monasteries.

Yaroslavl: Neighbouring Yaroslavl lies on the banks of the Volga, and contains a host of ancient churches, most notably the **Transfiguration of the Saviour Cathedral**, built in the early 16th century.

Kostroma: This town stands at the confluence of the Volga and the **River Kostroma**. It is a renowned cheese-making centre. Its most outstanding building is the **Ipatievski Monastery-Fortress**. Built during the first half of the 14th century, it became the Romanovs' residence three centuries later. The open-air museum features a collection of traditional Russian buildings, including wooden churches, log cabins and windmills brought from all over the Russian Federation.

Suzdal: East of Moscow is Suzdal, perhaps the most important town in the Golden Ring. It boasts 50 well-preserved examples of ancient architecture contained within a relatively small area, providing a wonderfully coherent vision of its past. Historically it was a political and religious centre, and is now a major tourist attraction. The wives of tsars and boyars were exiled to the **Blessed Virgin Convent**.

Vladimir: Less than 32km (20 miles) away is Vladimir, which played a prominent part in the rise of the Russian state. The city's two magnificent cathedrals date from the 12th century. Another notable monument is the **Golden Gate**, a unique example of old Russian engineering skills. The nearby village of **Bogolyubovo** features a 12th-century fortress and **Church of the Protecting Veil**.

Uglich: Another beautiful town on the banks of the Volga, this is notable for its **Kremlin** and the **Chambers of Prince Dmitry**. Prince Dmitry, son and heir of Ivan the Terrible drowned here, after accidentally being dropped in a river by his nurse.

ST PETERSBURG

The Federation's second-largest city, 715km (444 miles)

northwest of Moscow, is known both as a cultural centre and for its elegant buildings. The city is spread over 42 islands in the delta of the **River Neva**. In comparison to Moscow, which tended to be more Eastern in character, St Petersburg has always retained a European flavour and was intended as a 'Window to the West'. It was built by Peter the Great in 1703 and remained the capital for 200 years of Tsarist Russia. Known as Petrograd after the civil war, and Leningrad during the Soviet period, the city reverted to its original name in 1991 by popular demand. Wide boulevards, tranquil canals, bridges and some of the best examples of tsarist architecture gave rise to the epithet the 'Venice of the North'. Although badly damaged in World War II, much of it is now reconstructed. In June and July the city has the famous 'White Nights', when darkness recedes to a brief twilight and the city is imbued with an unusual aura. Many of the most interesting sites, especially those on the left bank of the River Neva, can be explored on foot. The **Palace Square** and the **Winter Palace** are among the most popular attractions for followers of Russian history. Troops fired on demonstrators there in 1905 and the Palace witnessed the capitulation of the provisional government, allowing the Bolsheviks to take the country into eight decades of Communist rule. The **Hermitage** houses the vast private collection of the tsars. The **Museum of the History of the City** gives a comprehensive picture of St Petersburg's history. While exploring the city the visitor will inevitably see the **Alexandrovskaya Column**. **St Isaac's Cathedral** is one of the biggest dome buildings of the world and, like the Kazansky Cathedral, houses a museum. Also worth a visit is the **St Peter and Paul Fortress**, a former prison that is now a popular museum. Members of the Romanov Dynasty are buried in the Cathedral of the same name. The gorgeously decorated **Yusupov Mansion** was built for the Romanovs. Its rooms are sumptuously decorated in mid-19th-century style. The mansion's concert hall is now a venue for recitals, theatrical productions, opera and ballet. A waxwork exhibition commemorates Rasputin, who died in the building. The grand **Nevsky Prospekt**, dominated by the spire of the **Admiralty Building**, is one of the city's main thoroughfares and is lined by opulent buildings. These include the **Kazan Cathedral** and the **Church of the Resurrection**. The collection at the **Russian Museum** covers nearly 1000 years of Russian art history. Nevsky Prospect crosses the **Fontanka River** at **Anichkov Bridge**, and continues to **Palace Square**. Further sights are the **Cathedral of St Nicholas** (Russian Baroque), still a working church; the **Alexander Nevsky Monastery**, the main religious centre in St Petersburg; and the **Museums of Ethnography and Russian Art**. The homes of Dostoyevsky, Pushkin, Anna Akhmatova and Rimsky-Korsakov serve as museums dedicated to their former occupants. The cruiser *Aurora* is berthed on the Neva. A blank shot was fired from her bow to give a signal to start the assault on the Winter Palace in 1917. Lenin also announced the victory of the Revolution from here.

THE SUMMER PALACES: The following palaces beyond the outskirts of St Petersburg are collectively known as the **Summer Palaces**. **Petrodvorets** is a former summer palace of Tsar Peter the Great and is known for its beautiful cascades and fountains. It is located 34km (21 miles) from St Petersburg on the southern shore of the Gulf of Finland. The tsar designed the initial plans himself, and he appointed European and Russian architects to realise his grand project, which was intended to rival Versailles. **Oranienbaum** was built as the summer residence of Alexander Menshikov, Peter the Great's associate. From here, Alexander oversaw the construction of the **Kronstadt** naval fortress on the nearby **Kotlin Island**. Thankfully, the palace and its parkland escaped damage during World War II. Its **Chinese** and **Sliding Hill Pavilions** are exceptionally beautiful. The **Grand Catherine Palace** at **Tsarskoye Selo** was built for Peter the Great's wife. The Scottish architect Charles Cameron designed some of the interiors, although a greater number by Bartholomeo Rastrelli survive. Pushkin spent his formative years in the town. Cameron also designed the subtle buildings at nearby **Pavlovsk**, which were intended to complement the parkland's beauty. The park itself, designed by the Italian Gonzago, is one of the finest landscaped parks in Europe. The estate was originally part of Tsarskoye Selo, but Catherine II gave it to her son Paul. Although she commissioned Cameron to design the estate, Paul, whose relationship with his mother was strained, decided to redecorate the palace.

LAKE LADOGA: Vast and often turbulent, Lake Ladoga is linked to St Petersburg by the River Neva. **Valaam** is the most significant of the islands in the lake's northern archipelago because of its ancient monastery. Its golden domes suddenly rise from the mist that frequently shrouds visiting cruise ships. The founding religious community frequently suffered Swedish and Viking attacks during the Middle Ages. The present buildings date from the late 18th century. As well as being an important pilgrimage centre, the monastery was a noted centre for innovations in crafts and agriculture. Its missionaries brought Orthodox Christianity to the shores of Alaska. A religious community was re-established on the island in 1989, and restoration of the monastery is already under way. Despite years of neglect, Valaam still retains a mysterious air.

THE NORTHWEST

NOVGOROD: South of St Petersburg, Novgorod was founded over 1100 years ago and was one of the most important towns of ancient Russia. Novgorod was the founding city of Rus, the nucleus of modern Russia, although Kiev later became the capital. Picturesquely located on the banks of the River Volkhov, the city is a treasure trove of ancient architecture, with 39 cathedrals and churches. Within the walls of the **Kremlin, St Sophia's Cathedral** (mid-11th century) is the oldest stone structure in the Russian Federation.

KARELIA: Bounded by Finland and the White Sea, Karelia's landscape is a patchwork of lakes, marshes and forests, whose canopies shade abundant mushrooms and berries. The region's capital, **Petrozavodsk**, is a staging post for a variety of holiday activities in the region. The small island of **Kizhi** within **Lake Onega** is easily accessible by hydrofoil from here. The island was an early pagan centre. Its surviving heritage features the 22-domed 18th-century **Church of the Transfiguration**, whose wooden structure was built without a single nail. The open-air museum is a collection of Russian and Karel wooden buildings from the 14th to 19th centuries. The region is ideal for adventure holidays on the **Shuya**, **Suna** and **Vama-Vodla** rivers. Tranquil waters offering spectacular views of the countryside are suddenly interrupted by rapids cascading over glacial boulders. The white waters may be negotiated by kayak or cataraft. The Suna River is excellent for fishing. The **Kivach Waterfall** along its path is especially beautiful. Karel pies called *kalitkas* may be sampled in the local hamlets, often no more than a cluster of sturdy wooden cottages. A real sauna followed by a plunge into a river or lake is an ideal way to unwind at the end of an adventure-packed day.

MURMANSK: Almost due north of St Petersburg, this is the largest city within the Arctic Circle. This important port on the shores of **Kola Bay** is warmed by the waters of the Gulf Stream and is free of ice throughout the year. It was built with British assistance during World War I. The Northern Lights are seen here in November and December and the *Sports Festival of the Peoples of the North* is held in March.

ARKHANGELSK: The largest city in the White Sea area, Arkhangelsk was only opened to tourists in 1990. Before the founding of St Petersburg it was the first and only seaport in Russia. From here, visitors may travel to the nearby village of **Mali Kareli** to view Russian white stone and wooden architecture.

KALININGRAD

The tract of land sandwiched between Lithuania and Poland on the Baltic shoreline is an annexe of the Russian Federation. Its principal town is now called Kaliningrad, although it was known as Königsberg when it was the centre of German East Prussia. The area was ceded to the erstwhile Soviet Union following World War II. The territory's future prosperity depends on the Government's plans to give it special economic status. Architectural remnants which survived the war mark the city's German heritage, such as the **Cathedral**. The philosopher Immanuel Kant, the town's most famous son, is buried near here, and his memory is honoured by the **Kant Museum**. The **Amber Museum**, housed in a restored German fortress tower, celebrates this local precious stone. The town has many attractive parks and gardens, as well as a zoo. Nearby, **Svetlogorsk** is a verdant coastal spa resort which has lost none of its charm. The **Kursche Spit** is a beautiful sand peninsula extending nearly 100km (63 miles) along the coast, and is a rich habitat for plants and animals.

BLACK SEA

Rostov-on-Don: Once an Armenian town, its low buildings still show Armenian influences. Especially interesting is the **Cathedral of the Resurrection**. There are several parks, four theatres, an orchestra, a race-course and a beach. Rostov is the gateway to the Caucasus.

Sochi: A popular resort with a subtropical climate and a famous health spa, it is situated on the Black Sea's eastern coast beneath the dramatic **Caucasus Mountains**. An observation tower on **Mt Bolshoi Akhun**, 23km (14 miles) from the town, provides a spectacular view of the town, almost all of the Caucasian Riviera and the surrounding mountains. There is a large **Riviera Park** with many tourist facilities and a **Botanical Garden**, founded during the last century, with beautiful, interesting trees and shrubs from all over the world. Boat and hovercraft trips on the Black Sea are available from the town's port.

Dagomys: For those who want a resort-based holiday, this new holiday centre lying to the north of Sochi is ideal. Overlooking the Black Sea, it is beautifully located amongst thickly wooded hills and subtropical greenery. Nearby is the **Dagomys State Tea Farm** where visitors can sample the fragrant Krasnodar tea accompanied by the delicious local pastries, jams, fruits and nuts whilst enjoying the spectacular mountain scenery.

RIVER VOLGA

The mighty Volga provides an additional road into the Russian Federation. Travelling by river from Kazan to Rostov-on-Don makes a pleasant tour.

Kazan: The cultural centre of the Tartars, this city boasts a Kremlin dating from the 16th century which, with its towers and churches, is fascinating to visit. The **Tartar State Museum** and the 18th-century **mosque** are also of interest.

Ulyanovsk: Lenin's birthplace; his parents' house situated here used to be a popular museum.

Samara: A major space centre, the city was founded in the 16th century around a fortress surveying the Volga and Samara rivers. The **Old Town** is notable for its fine turn-of-the-century buildings. The Volga shoreline and the nature reserves of the **Zhiguli Hills** are accessible from Samara.

Volgograd: Formerly Stalingrad, the **Victory Museum** celebrates the victory over the Nazis, and the whole city is a monument to the year-long battle that took place there. Tours to the battlefields are available. The town stands at the confluence of the Volga and Don rivers. Boat trips and fishing tours taking in both rivers are possible. Visits to

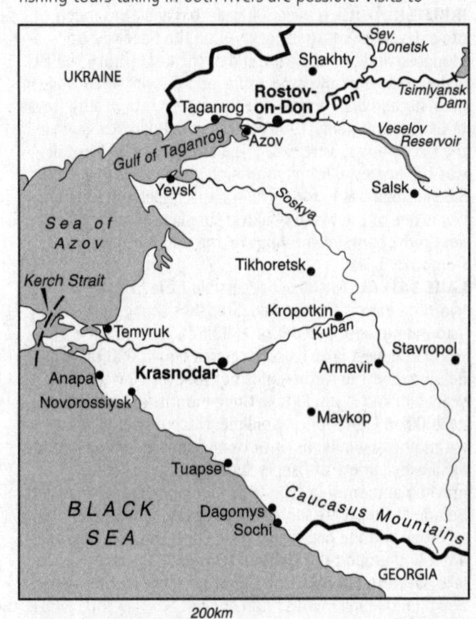

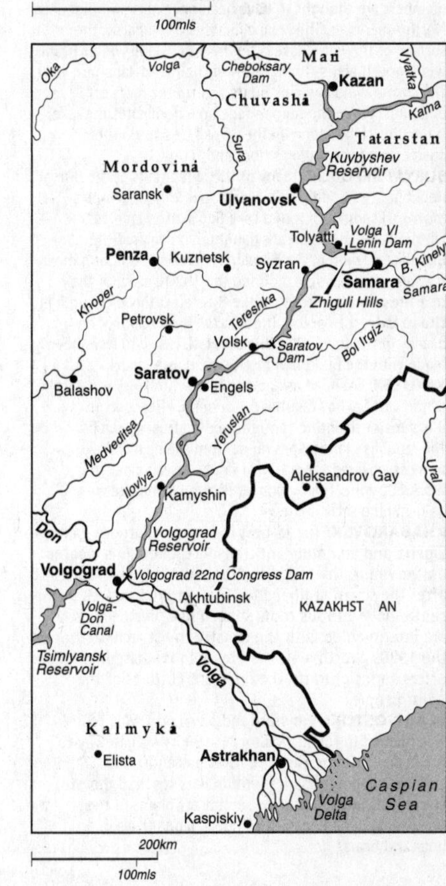

outlying Cossack and Volga-German villages provide a glimpse of the region's history.

THE URALS, SIBERIA & THE FAR EAST

YEKATERINBURG: The birthplace of former Russian President Boris Yeltsin. The city is also historically important as the last resting place of the Romanov royal family, murdered during the Bolshevik revolution.

SIBERIA: Covering an area of over 12,800,000 sq km (4,000,000 sq miles), Siberia contains unimaginably vast stretches of marshy forest (*taiga*). This 'sleeping land', the literal translation of its name, possesses a million lakes, 53,000 rivers and an enormous wealth of natural resources. Although the temperature in winter falls well below freezing point, the weather in summer can be very warm. Tourism is less developed than elsewhere in the Russian Federation and some parts are still not accessible. However, much of the region has been opened up, including **Sakhalin Island** and the **Chukchi Peninsula** just across the Bering Strait from Alaska. The taiga is within easy reach of many of the region's cities. Air-hopping is one way of discovering the wilderness. A famous alternative is the **Trans-Siberian Railway**, the longest continuous railway in the world, a journey which is one of the greatest travel adventures. The line cuts through an area bigger than Western Europe, crossing a landscape which includes arctic wastes, tundra and steppe. The most scenic part of the journey is between Irkutsk and Khabarovsk.

IRKUTSK: Irkutsk is over 300 years old and owes much of its development to its location on the tradeways to Mongolia and China. At the end of the last century, the city began to take on the aspect of a 'boom town' when trade in gold, fur and diamonds suddenly created new wealth. It was to Irkutsk that many 19th-century revolutionaries, such as the Decembrists, were exiled. The **University of Irkutsk** was the first establishment of higher education in eastern Siberia. Today, as in former times, this important Siberian city is one of the world's biggest suppliers of fur. The town lies on the banks of the **Angara**, the only outflowing river from Lake Baikal.

LAKE BAIKAL: The lake is accessible from Irkutsk by hydrofoil during the summer. Statistics about Baikal are astounding; with a depth of 1637m (5371ft) it is the world's deepest lake. Its surface area equals that of Belgium and The Netherlands put together. It is 25 million years old, and it would take three months to walk around its 2000km (1243 mile) shoreline. The purity of its water is maintained by millions of tiny crayfish, providing a habitat for a wide variety of fish, including sturgeon, loach, grayling and *omul* (a type of salmon), one of many species unique to Baikal. Its shores are a feeding ground for wildfowl and the occasional bear. Freshwater seal colonies are found around the **Ushkan Islands** in the centre of the lake. **Olkhon Island** is the site of primitive rock drawings and a unique necropolis of an ancient Siberian tribe whose members are thought to have been ancestors of indigenous North Americans. The local climate is often harsh; the surface of the entire lake often freezes over in winter (trains were moved across the ice during the Russo-Japanese war). The *sarma* wind can sink boats and rip the roofs off buildings. While the human race now dominates the lake, it remains to be seen whether it will be a responsible custodian of the region's flora and fauna.

BURYAT REPUBLIC: Many of the inhabitants of the Buryat Republic are Buddhists. Dozens of picturesque temples (*datsans*) sprang up round Lake Baikal after Empress Elizabeth, Peter the Great's daughter, recognised the Buddhist religion in the Russian Federation. Although most *datsans* were destroyed during the 1930s, many of their treasures were preserved in the Russian Orthodox church in **Ulaan Ude**, the capital. The *Sandalwood Buddha*, on display in the town's **Exhibition Hall**, is said to have been made with the Buddha himself sitting as a model.

YAKUTSK: Founded as a garrison town, Yakutsk is capital of the vast Sakha (Yakutia) Autonomous Republic. Today it is a major scientific centre for permafrost research. The republic's landscapes range from Alpine meadows to moss-covered tundra, with sandy deserts close to the Arctic zone. This is pioneer country, complete with gold-mining settlements.

KHABAROVSK: The largest industrial centre of eastern Siberia and an important transport junction is located on the Amur. The town (founded in 1858) was named after the scientist Khabarov. The red brick houses in the centre have curious roofs shaped like pine needles, and are intermingled with the constructivist architecture of the 1930s. Worth a visit is the regional museum, which offers an insight into the different cultures of the Amur people.

VLADIVOSTOK: A military and naval port, Vladivostok was opened to foreign visitors in 1990. As a gateway to the Pacific and the East, the town has enormous commercial potential. It is within easy reach of the **Ussuriysk taiga**, a unique habitat for plants of the pre-glacial period, as well as tigers, leopard, bison, boar and bears.

Sport & Activities

The increase in tour operators offering the Russian Federation as a destination from Europe now means a wide choice for potential visitors. A bias towards tailor-made holidays has brought added activities and adventures to the traveller's scope. There is a large potential to develop independent adventure tourism and recent years have seen a considerable increase. There are a number of opportunities on offer.

The Russians have also quickly developed some high-tech offerings. It is possible to **fly in a MIG-29 aircraft**, a fighter capable of more than twice the speed of sound, that was once part of the formidable Soviet Air Force. Those interested in Russia's achievements in the field of space travel should visit Star City, just outside Moscow, which is a **cosmonaut training complex** open to visitors. Residential **Russian-language courses** and other short-term study programmes are available. Accommodation is usually with Russian families, and activities are organised. For further information, contact VAO Intourist, 13/1 Milyutinsky per., Moscow 101990 (tel: (095) 923 5089; tel/fax: (095) 923 8575; e-mail: info@intourist.ru; website: www.intourist.ru).

Skiing: This is on offer in the Caucasus, at Teberda-Dombay (west) and at Baksan Elbrus (north), and Kamchatka. As for the big cities, Moscow has a ski jump in the Vorobyevi Hills and days of cross-country skiing, with poles and boots provided, at Suzdal. Cross-country skiing is available outside the city at Olgino on the Gulf of Finland. Downhill skiing enjoys a short season in the Russian Federation and generally lasts from January to March. Skiing in the Russian Federation calls for much fitness and skill, more than the average skier takes with them each year to other European resorts, as facilities in general will take some years to equal those of luxury alpine resorts.

Heli-skiing is now available in the Caucasus and Kamchatka where, it is claimed, the powder snow rivals that of Colorado and there is a guarantee of snow throughout the short season. Amid the wilds of Karelia, north of St Petersburg, cross-country skiing is routed through the taiga and over a terrain of frozen rivers and lakes including Ladoga and Onega.

Outdoor pursuits: Those wishing to go **trekking** can climb to altitudes of 3200m (10,499ft), where the landscape changes en route from alpine meadows of red poppies to snow-capped peaks and scenic plateaux. Until recently, previously unexploited areas of the Fan Mountains, known as Matcha, had never been trodden by Western feet. Perm in the Middle Ural Mountains is home to some of the rarer birds of prey. The Baseguy National Reserve has been created on the Kama River Basin and ornithologists can get glimpses of eagle owls, great grey owls, Ural owls and golden eagles.

The Caucasus Mountains, which stretch from the Black Sea to the Caspian Sea, separate Russia from Armenia and Georgia. Dominating the range is Mount Elbrus, at 5642m (18,510ft), the highest peak in Europe. The jagged peaks overlook a vast vegetation range from palm trees to deciduous forest and flower-carpeted valleys. Elbrus offers a strenuous, though non-technical, climb to its summit. Trekking, again strenuous, is possible across the beautiful scenery of the peak and its neighbours. Six-day Elbrus trekking circuits and three-summit climbs in the Adyl-Su Valley that include the Elbrus peak are also available. Siberia used to be associated with salt mines and permafrost, yet the Altai region of southern Siberia rivals Switzerland for rolling hills, snowy peaks, flowers and pine forests. Undiscovered areas of Siberia, on the borders of Kazakhstan and Mongolia where summer temperatures hit 22°C (71°F), are heady with the scents of its flowers, herbs and trees. Mount Belukha rises to 4506m (14,784ft) over a few scattered villages in an area where the bear population outnumbers the human. Not unsurprisingly, among tours offered are botany itineraries through June and July with safari camp accommodation. There are also **horse-riding** holidays, with routes through the Alpine meadows and coniferous forests of the Sayano Altai Mountains, which also include opportunities for **botany**, **birdwatching** and **river rafting**. Getting around the Pacific peninsula, reminiscent of Alaska just across the Bering Sea, can be done by flying, on all-terrain vehicles or on two sturdily shod feet.

Watersports: Central Asia's Lake Baikal – dubbed the Blue Eye of Siberia – offers canoeing and camping holidays for groups. It is also possible to go **scuba-diving** there.

The Kamchatka River in Russia's Far East has some stiff river-raft tests as well as **canoeing**. Enthusiasts should note that the Veselovskaye Reservoir in the Rostov-on-Don region is noted for **fish**, particularly pike, perch, carp, bream, gudgeon, bullhead and roach. Many towns and cities have artificial **ice-skating** rinks for the summer but during the hard winters frozen lakes and rivers ensure plenty of room for skating. St Petersburg's Central Recreation Park is a favourite among skaters and it also has a ski centre.

Spectator sports: Almost every provincial city has a **football** team and larger cities have several clubs organised within factories, unions and government offices. International events include the *Kremlin Cup* **tennis** tournament and the **Izvestia** *Hockey Prize*. Russia's ethnic diversity is reflected in the wide variety of **local traditional sports**. **Martial arts** are a recent import and are steadily gaining in popularity.

Social Profile

FOOD & DRINK: The kind of food visitors will eat from day to day depends on which city they are visiting and the time of year. Breakfast is often similar to the Scandinavian, with cold meats, boiled eggs and bread served with Russian tea. *Kasha* (porridge) is a staple breakfast dish, made with milk and oats, buckwheat or semolina. For the midday and evening meal the food is often more traditional, again depending on the region. One of the more famous Russian dishes is *borshch*, a beetroot soup served hot with sour cream, and the sister dish of *akroshka*, a kvas soup served cold. Several dishes which are now often seen as international but find their origin in Russia are beef stroganov (beef stewed in sour cream with fried potatoes), *blini* (small pancakes filled with caviar, fish, melted butter or sour cream), *aladyi* (crumpets with the same filling and jam) and especially *ikra* or *krasnaya ikra* (black and red caviar). The local chicken kiev should not be confused with Western imitations. *Tsipleonok tabaka* is another chicken dish: the meat is roasted on a spit. Whole roast suckling pig and roast goose stuffed with buckwheat, roast duck stuffed with apples and shashlik (shish kebab) are served at parties and for special occasions. A vegetable variant of shashlik also exists. Local dishes well worth trying include *kotlyety po Pozharsky* (chicken cutlets), *pirozhky* (fried rolls with different fillings, usually meat), *prostakvasha* (yoghurt), *pelmeni* (meat dumplings), *rossolnik* (hot soup, usually made of pickled vegetables) and *shchi* (cabbage soup). Cabbage leaves and sweet peppers are filled with boiled rice and minced meat. Mushrooms in sour cream are very popular. The great variety of salads available include winter salad and vinegret (made of diced vegetables). Desserts include *morozhenoye* (ice cream), *ponchiki* (hot sugared doughnuts) and *vareniki* (dumplings containing fresh berries, cherries or jam).

One of the most popular drinks is *chai* (sweet tea served without milk). Coffee is generally available with meals and in cafes, although standards vary. Soft drinks, fruit juices and mineral waters are widely available. Vodka is often flavoured and coloured with herbs and spices such as *zubrovka* (a kind of grass), *ryabinovka* (steeped with rowan-tree berries), *starka* (dark, smooth, aged vodka) and *pertsovka* (with hot pepper). *Posolskaya*, *Stolichnaya* and *Rossiskaya* are popular brands. *Krushon* is a highly recommended cold 'punch'; champagne, brandy and summer fruit are poured into a hollowed watermelon and chilled for several hours. This delicious cocktail is traditionally served from a crystal bowl. White wine and cucumber are used to make a drier variant. *Nastoika* is a fortified wine made of herbs, leaves, flowers, fruit and roots of plants with medicinal properties. *Nalivka* is a sweet liqueur made with fruit or berries. The cherry and strawberry flavours are highly recommended. *Ryabin Cognac* ('Ryabina na Konyakye') is made from rowan-tree berries.

Russian champagne is surprisingly good and reasonably priced. Imported wines from Georgia, Moldova and Ukraine, and Armenian Cognac are excellent (for further information, see the separate sections on these countries). *Kvas* is a refreshing and unusual drink, made from a fermented mixture of rye bread, jam, yeast and water, and should be tried on a hot day. Drinks are ordered by grams or by the bottle. City-centre bars close around midnight.

NIGHTLIFE: Theatre, circus, concert and variety performances are the main evening entertainments. Tickets are available in advance or from ticket booths immediately before performances. Visitors should note that prices for foreigners are usually much higher than those paid by Russian nationals. The repertoire of theatres provides a change of programme almost nightly. In the course of one month, 30 different productions may be presented by the *Bolshoi Opera and Ballet Company*. Details of performances can be obtained on arrival. Visitors should apply to the service bureau of their hotel. All of these establishments are open 0600-2200.

SHOPPING: A wide range of goods such as watches, cameras, wines and spirits, furs, ceramics and glass, jewellery and toys may be bought in Moscow and St Petersburg. Shops take payment in roubles and, occasionally, by credit card. It is necessary to allow extra time for souvenir hunting: shopping can be a time-consuming activity, owing to the relatively chaotic state of the retail trade in the Russian Federation. It is also advisable to shop around, as prices vary significantly. A good strategy is to choose your souvenirs in a department store such as *GUM* (on Red Square), and then buy them in a smaller, less centrally located shop. *Kholui* and *Palekh* lacquered boxes make attractive souvenirs. Traditional and satirical *Matryoshka* dolls (wooden dolls within dolls) are widely available. *Khokhloma* wooden cups, saucers and spoons are painted gold, red and black. *Dymkovskaya Igrushka* are pottery figurines based on popular folklore characters. Engraved amber, *Gzhel* porcelain, *Vologda* lace and *Fabergé* eggs and jewellery are highly sought after. A *samovar* makes a good souvenir. Antiquities, valuables, works of art and manuscripts other than those offered for sale in souvenir shops may not be taken out of the Russian Federation without an export licence. **Shopping hours:** Mon-Sat 0900-1900. Most food shops are also open on Sunday. Department stores and supermarkets are open throughout lunchtime. Stores which are open 24 hours a day are becoming more common.

SPECIAL EVENTS: The following is a selection of special events occurring in the Russian Federation in 2005: **Dec 25 2004-Jan 5** *Russian Winter*, Irtutsk, Moscow, Novgorod, St Petersburg, Vladimir/Suzdal. **Jan 7** *Russian Orthodox Christmas*. **Mar** *Spring Festival*. **Mar 7-13** *Maslenitsa Festival*, Moscow. **May** *Moscow Stars*. **Jun 5** *Pushkin Festival*, Pushkinskiye Gori. **Jun 17-26** *Moscow Film Festival*. **Oct 8-16** *Kremlin Cup* (tennis), Moscow. **Dec 25-Jan 5 2006** *Russian Winter*, Irtutsk, Moscow, Novgorod, St Petersburg, Vladimir/Suzdal.

SOCIAL CONVENTIONS: It is customary to shake hands when greeting someone. Company or business gifts are well received. Each region has its own characteristic mode of dress. Conservative wear is suitable for most places and the seasonal weather should always be borne in mind. Smoking is acceptable unless stated otherwise. Avoid ostentatious displays of wealth; it is advisable to keep expensive jewellery, watches and cameras out of sight and take precautions against pickpocketing. **Tipping:** Hotels in Moscow and other large cities include a 10 to 15 per cent service charge. Otherwise 10 per cent is customary.

Business Profile

ECONOMY: The Russian Federaion is blessed by an abundance of natural resources of every description. This includes rich agricultural land from which grain, potatoes and livestock are the main products. Land reform has been one of the most awkward problems facing Russia's post-communist governments: much has been turned over to private ownership but a substantial proportion, especially in the more remote areas, is still owned collectively. Agriculture now accounts for 5 per cent of total economic output while employing 13 per cent of the workforce. Russia has huge deposits of oil and gas – its major export earners – as well as coal and minerals including gold, diamonds, nickel, manganese, copper, iron ore and phosphates. Further unexploited deposits have been located and there are undoubtedly more to be discovered, but they are often in areas (such as the permafrost-covered regions of Siberia and the Russian Far East) where exploitation is technically difficult and transport systems limited.

Energy products and heavy industry – production of vehicles, metal goods, construction materials and machinery – are the kernel of Russia's industrial sector. Textiles and chemicals are other important industries. By contrast, Russia's light industry – especially production of consumer goods– is paltry, accounting for just 2 per cent of total industrial production. The fastest growing part of the economy since 1990 has been the service sector. Here, banking, insurance and property have developed from a base close to nothing, and services now account for just over half of economic output. Both the industrial and service sectors have been hampered by the paucity of small and medium-sized businesses: this is a major flaw in the Russian economy. The sheer size and diversity of the country has made economic reform in the Russian Federation a gargantuan task, especially by comparison with its former East European allies and the other 14 Soviet republics. The economy underwent significant contraction after 1990: Russian economic statistics are notoriously unreliable but, by 1998, it is likely that GDP had declined by between 35 and 50 per cent. That year, a combination of internal and external factors led to the virtual collapse of the economy which was staved off by a large financial injection from the IMF (of the order of US$22 billion). Since then, the economy has undergone a significant recovery with average annual growth of 5 per cent in the last five years (the current figure is 7.3 per cent). The Government has got on top of the hyper-inflation which caused so much damage in the initial stages of the reform process. At 13.7 per cent, current inflation is high by recent Western standards but not unmanageable.

The official unemployment rate is 8.5 per cent, with considerable underemployment. Russia hosts a substantial informal or 'grey' economy in which between 25 and 40 per cent of the workforce are engaged to some extent. But there are some causes for optimism: the success of the Putin government in stabilising the economy has boosted international confidence, especially given the difficult situation inherited from his predecessor, Boris Yeltsin. In what amounted to a firesale, the Yeltsin government sold off the major components of the Russian economy – including the vital oil and gas sector – at knock-down prices to favoured bidders. This process gave rise to the so-called 'oligarchs', a small group of immensely rich individuals who – mostly by virtue of political contacts, good judgement and luck – now own the bulk of the Russian economy. (It is estimated that 20 conglomerates are now responsible for 70 per cent of Russia's GDP.) There is little Putin can do about corporate ownership, but there are other areas where the government can make a difference. Perhaps the most important of these is modernisation of the national infrastructure: the Russian Federation suffers from insufficient and poor-quality transport networks as well as an erratic and antiquated telecommunications system. Moreover, neither commercial law nor the taxation system are functional and effective, with the result that operating conditions for most businesses are difficult. Organised crime thrives in such an environment: billions of dollars of international aid have simply disappeared. Moreover, the removal of exchange controls (as demanded by Western financial donors) has meant that there has also been a large legitimate exodus of money from Russia. In May 2004, five former Soviet bloc states and the three ex-Soviet Baltic republics joined the European Union. This development – unimaginable 15 years ago – presents both opportunities and dangers for the Russian Federation. On balance, the Russian economy will probably benefit from immediate proximity to the EU. Russia's trade patterns have gradually shifted towards Western industrialised nations (not least to meet their high energy demands). Apart from the former Soviet republics of Kazakhstan, Belarus and Ukraine, Russia's main trading partners are Germany, the USA and Japan.

BUSINESS: As a result of recent economic changes which have taken place in the Russian Federation, there are now many thousands of private companies in operation and international business relations have become active. The main business centres are Moscow, St Petersburg, Nizhny Novgorod, Novosibirsk and Vladivostock. **Office hours:** Mon-Fri 0900-1800.

COMMERCIAL INFORMATION: The following organisations can offer advice: The Trade Delegation of the Russian Federation, 32/3 Highgate West Hill, London N6 6NL, UK (tel: (020) 8340 1907 *or* 4491 *or* 3272; fax: (020) 8348 0112; e-mail: info@rustradeuk.org; website: www.rustradeuk.org); *or* Russo-British Chamber of Commerce, 42 Southwark Street, London SE1 1UN, UK (tel: (020) 7403 1706; fax: (020) 7403 1245; e-mail: mail@rbcc.co.uk; website: www.rbcc.co.uk). Moscow Office: Please contact the London office for up-to-date details (information supplied to members only); *or* Ministry for Economic Development and Trade for the Russian Federation – Department for Economic Co-operation with Europe, 18/1 Ovchinnikovskaya nab, 113324 Moscow (tel: (095) 950 1779; fax: (095) 950 1780; e-mail: borisov_ai@gov.ru; website: www.economy.gov.ru); *or* Chamber of Commerce and Industry of the Russian Federation, St. Ilyinka 6, 109012 Moscow (tel: (095) 929 0009; fax: (095) 929 0360; e-mail: dios-inform@tpprf.ru; website: www.tpprf.ru).

CONFERENCES/CONVENTIONS: With every passing year an increasing number of conferences, seminars and symposia (including some for the tourist industry) take place in the Russian Federation. Information on conferences and incentives is available from Intourist Travel Ltd (see *Contact Addresses* section for details).

Climate

Northern & Central European Russia: The most varied climate; mildest areas are along the Baltic coast. Summer sunshine may be nine hours a day, but winters can be very cold. **Siberia:** Very cold winters, but summers can be pleasant, although they tend to be short and wet. There is considerable seasonal temperature variation.

Southern European Russia: Winter is shorter than in the north. Steppes (in the southeast) have hot, dry summers and very cold winters. The north and northeastern Black Sea has mild winters, but heavy rainfall all the year round.

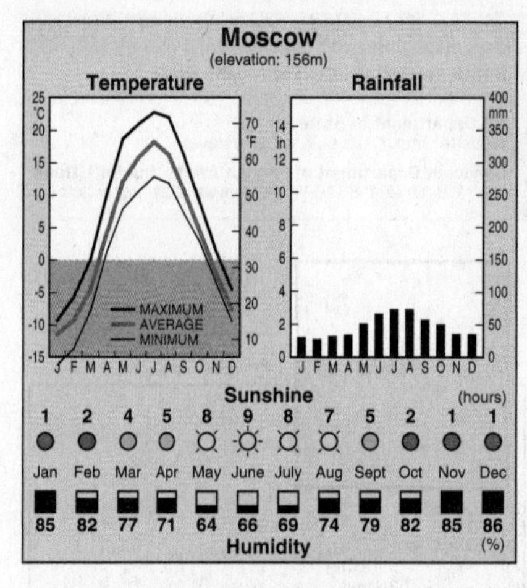

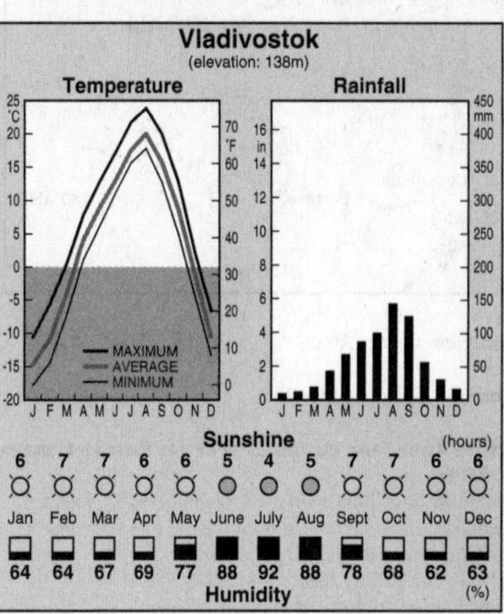

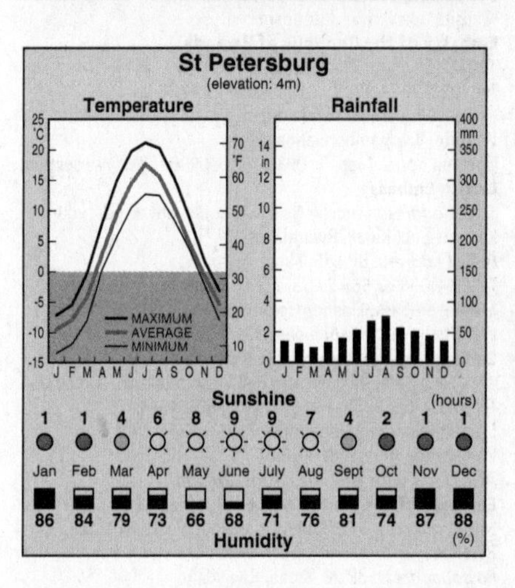

Rwanda

LATEST TRAVEL ADVICE CONTACTS

British Foreign and Commonwealth Office
Tel: (0870) 606 0290 Website: www.fco.gov.uk
US Department of State
Website: http://travel.state.gov/travel
Canadian Department of Foreign Affairs and Int'l Trade
Tel: (1 800) 267 8376 Website: www.dfait-maeci.gc.ca

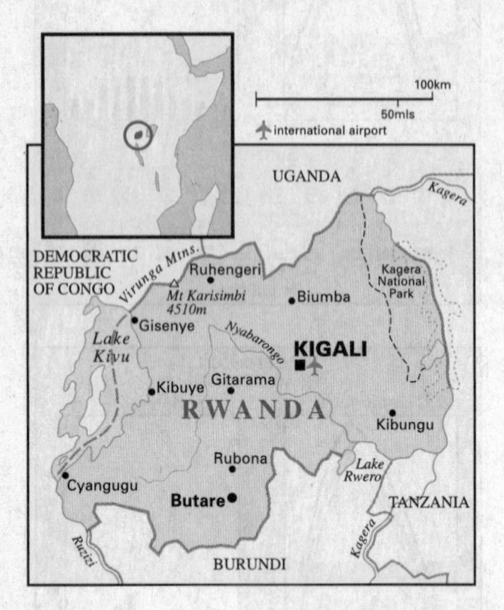

Location: Central Africa.

Country dialling code: 250.

Office Rwandaise du Tourisme et des Parcs Nationaux (ORTPN)
Street address: Boulevard de la Révolution no.1, Kigali, Rwanda
Postal address: BP 905, Kigali, Rwanda
Tel: 576 514 *or* 573 396. Fax: 576 515.
E-mail: reservation@rwandatourism.com
Website: www.rwandatourism.com
Embassy of the Republic of Rwanda
120-22 Seymour Place, London W1H 1NR, UK
Tel: (020) 7224 9832. Fax: (020) 7724 8642.
E-mail: uk@ambarwanda.org.uk
Website: www.ambarwanda.org.uk
Opening hours: Mon-Fri 0930-1730; 0930-1300 (visa section)
British Embassy
Street address: Parcelle No 1131, Boulevard de l'Umuganda, Kacyiru-Sud, Kigali, Rwanda
Postal address: BP 576, Kigali, Rwanda
Tel: 584 098 *or* 585 771/3. Fax: 582 044.
E-mail: embassy.kigali@fco.gov.uk
Website: www.britishembassykigali.org.rw
Embassy of the Republic of Rwanda
1714 New Hampshire Avenue, NW, Washington, DC 20009, USA
Tel: (202) 232 2882-4. Fax: (202) 232 4544.
E-mail: rwandemb@rwandemb.org
Website: www.rwandemb.org
Also deals with enquiries from Canada.
Embassy of the United States of America
Street address: 377 Boulevard de la Révolution, Kigali, Rwanda
Postal address: BP 28, Kigali, Rwanda
Tel: 505 601-3. Fax: 572 128.
E-mail: consularkigali@state.gov
Website: http://usembkigali.net
Office of the Canadian Embassy
Street address: rue Akagera, Kigali, Rwanda
Postal address: BP 1177, Kigali, Rwanda
Tel: 573 210/278. Fax: 572 719.
E-mail: kigali@dfait-maeci.gc.ca
The Canadian High Commission in Nairobi deals with enquiries relating to Rwanda (see *Kenya* section).

TIMATIC CODES

Health	AMADEUS: **TI-DFT/KGL/HE** GALILEO/WORLDSPAN: **TI-DFT/KGL/HE** SABRE: **TIDFT/KGL/HE**
Visa	AMADEUS: **TI-DFT/KGL/VI** GALILEO/WORLDSPAN: **TI-DFT/KGL/VI** SABRE: **TIDFT/KGL/VI**

To access TIMATIC country information on Health and Visa regulations through the Computer Reservations System (CRS), type in the appropriate command line listed above.

General Information

AREA: 26,338 sq km (10,169 sq miles).
POPULATION: 8,272,000 (2002).
POPULATION DENSITY: 314.1 per sq km.
CAPITAL: Kigali. **Population:** 233,640 (1991).
GEOGRAPHY: Rwanda is a small mountainous country in central Africa, bordered to the north by Uganda, to the east by Tanzania, to the south by Burundi and to the west by the Democratic Republic of Congo. The country is divided by great peaks of up to 3000m (9842ft), which run across the country from north to south. The Virunga volcanoes, rising steeply from Lake Kivu in the west, slope down first to a hilly central plateau and further eastwards to an area of marshy lakes around the upper reaches of the A'Kagera River, where the A'Kagera National Park is situated.
GOVERNMENT: Republic since 1962. Gained independence from Belgium in 1962. **Head of State:** President Paul Kagame since 2000. **Head of Government:** Prime Minister Bernard Makuza since 2000.
LANGUAGE: The official languages are Kinyarwanda, French and English. Kiswahili is used for trade and commerce.
RELIGION: Animist (50 per cent), Christian (mostly Roman Catholic) and an Islamic minority.
TIME: GMT + 2.
ELECTRICITY: 220 volts AC, 50Hz.
COMMUNICATIONS: Telephone: Country code: 250. There are no area codes. There is International Direct Dialling but this may be subject to occasional disruptions. **Mobile telephone:** GSM 900/1800 network. Network operators include *MTN Rwandacell* (website: www.mtnrwandacell.co.rw). Handsets can be hired. **Internet:** ISPs include *Rwandatel* (website: www.rwandatel.rw). There are Internet cafes in Kigali. **Telegram:** Facilities are available in Kigali and main hotels. **Post:** Post office hours (Kigali): Mon-Fri 0800-1200 and 1400-1700, Sat 0800-1200. Airmail to Western Europe takes approximately two weeks. **Press:** There is a growing number of English-language newspapers. Publications are also in French or Kinyarwanda and are fortnightly or quarterly. **Radio:** BBC World Service (website: www.bbc.co.uk/worldservice) and Voice of America (website: www.voa.gov) can be received. From time to time the frequencies change and the most up-to-date can be found online.

Passport/Visa

	Passport Required?	Visa Required?	Return Ticket Required?
Full British	Yes	Yes	Yes
Australian	Yes	Yes	Yes
Canadian	Yes	No/1	Yes
USA	Yes	No/1	Yes
Other EU	Yes	Yes	Yes
Japanese	Yes	Yes	Yes

Note: Regulations and requirements may be subject to change at short notice, and you are advised to contact the appropriate diplomatic or consular authority before finalising travel arrangements. Details of these may be found at the head of this country's entry. Any numbers in the chart refer to the footnotes below.

Restricted Entry: The Rwandan Government refuses admission and transit to nationals of Burundi without the proper entry documents.
PASSPORTS: Passports valid for at least six months required by all.
VISAS: Required by all except the following:
(a) 1. nationals of Canada, Germany, Kenya, Tanzania, Uganda and the USA for stays of up to three months;
(b) nationals of China (PR), providing holding Hong Kong (SAR), China passports for stays of up to one month;
(c) transit passengers continuing their journey within 24 hours by the same or first connecting aircraft provided holding onward or return documentation and not leaving the airport.
Types of visa and cost: *Single-entry/Multiple-entry*: £50.
Note: Nationals of Mauritius, South Africa, Sweden and the UK require visas but can obtain them free of charge.
Validity: Three months.
Application to: Consulate (or Consular section at Embassy); see *Contact Addresses* section.
Application requirements: (a) Valid passport. (b) Two passport-size photos. (c) Two completed application forms. (d) Company letters or guarantee for business trips. (e) Fee, payable by company certified cheque, postal order or cash.
Working days required: 24 hours.
Temporary residence: Visas can be extended at the Immigration Office in Kigali.

Money

Currency: Rwanda Franc (FRw) = 100 centimes. Notes are in denominations of FRw5000, 1000, 500 and 100. Coins are in denominations of FRw50, 20, 10, 5, 2 and 1.
Credit & debit cards: Accepted at only a few hotels in Kigali. MasterCard is most widely accepted, with more limited use of Diners Club. Check with your credit or debit card company for details of merchant acceptability and other services that may be available.
Travellers cheques: Generally not recommended although banks accept travellers cheques by the holder.
Currency restrictions: The import and export of local currency is limited to FRw5000. The import and export of foreign currency is unlimited, provided declared on arrival.
Exchange rate indicators: The following figures are included as a guide to the movements of the Rwanda Franc against Sterling and the US Dollar:

Date	Feb '04	May '04	Aug '04	Nov '04
£1.00=	1018.52	997.54	1038.35	1055.89
$1.00=	559.55	558.50	563.60	557.58

Banking hours: Mon-Fri 0830-1230 and 1400-1700, Sat 0830-1130.

Duty Free

The following items may be imported into Rwanda by persons over 16 years of age without incurring customs duty:
Two cartons of cigarettes and 2l of alcoholic beverages.
Note: Game trophies can only be exported with special permission of the Game Department.

Public Holidays

2005: Jan 1 New Year's Day. **Jan 28** Democracy Day. **Apr 7** Genocide Memorial Day. **May 1** Labour Day. **Jul 1** Independence Day. **Jul 4** Liberation Day. **Aug 1** Harvest Festival. **Aug 15** Assumption. **Sep 8** Culture Day. **Sep 25** Republic Day. **Dec 25** Christmas Day. **Dec 26** Boxing Day.
2006: Jan 1 New Year's Day. **Jan 28** Democracy Day. **Apr 7** Genocide Memorial Day. **May 1** Labour Day. **Jul 1** Independence Day. **Jul 4** Liberation Day. **Aug 1** Harvest Festival. **Aug 15** Assumption. **Sep 8** Culture Day. **Sep 25** Republic Day. **Dec 25** Christmas Day. **Dec 26** Boxing Day.

Health

	Special Precautions?	Certificate Required?
Yellow Fever	Yes	1
Cholera	Yes	2
Typhoid & Polio	3	N/A
Malaria	4	N/A

Note: Regulations and requirements may be subject to change at short notice, and you are advised to contact your doctor well in advance of your intended date of departure. Any numbers in the chart refer to the footnotes below.

Note: There is a constant danger of disease, owing to the lack of sanitation. The risk of epidemics is high.
1: A yellow fever vaccination certificate is required from all travellers over one year of age.
2: Following WHO guidelines issued in 1973, a cholera vaccination certificate is not a condition of entry to Rwanda. However, cholera is a serious risk in this country and precautions are essential. Customs officials may demand to see some proof of immunisation. Up-to-date advice should be sought before deciding whether these precautions should include vaccination, as medical opinion is divided over its effectiveness; see the *Health* appendix for further information.
3: Typhoid is a risk, especially in rural areas.
4: Malaria risk exists all year throughout the country. The predominant, malignant *falciparum* strain is reported to be highly resistant to chloroquine and resistant to sulfadoxine-pyrimethamine.
Food & drink: Visitors are advised to bring their own supplies of food, bottled water and vitamins. Clean water is scarce, and all water should be regarded as being potentially contaminated. Water used for drinking, brushing teeth or making ice should have first been boiled or otherwise sterilised. Milk is unpasteurised and should be boiled. Powdered or tinned milk is available and is advised, but make sure that it is reconstituted with pure water. Avoid dairy products that are likely to have been made from unboiled milk. Only eat well-cooked meat and fish, preferably served hot. Pork, salad and mayonnaise may carry increased risk. Vegetables should be cooked and fruit peeled.
Other risks: *Bilharzia* (schistosomiasis) is present. Avoid swimming and paddling in fresh water; swimming pools that are well chlorinated and maintained are safe. *Typhus fever, trypanosomiasis* (sleeping sickness), *onchocerciasis* (river blindness), *hepatitis A* and *E* are widespread; *hepatitis B* is highly endemic. *Menigococcal meningitis* and *TB* occur. *Rabies* is present. For those at high risk, vaccination before arrival should be considered. If you are bitten, seek medical advice without delay. For more information, consult the *Health* appendix.

Health care: Medical facilities are severely limited and extremely overburdened. Almost all medical facilities in Kigali were destroyed during the civil war, but the situation is now improving and most hospitals function to an acceptable level. However, medical insurance, including cover for emergency repatriation, is essential. Visitors are advised to bring their own personal medication.

Travel - International

Travel Warning: All but essential travel to rural areas bordering Burundi and Congo (Dem Rep) is advised against. There remains a risk of indiscriminate attacks on Rwanda from rebel groups operating outside the country in the border regions with those countries.
AIR: There is no direct commercial air service to Rwanda from the UK at present. The national carrier is *Rwandair Express*. Other airlines serving Rwanda include *Air Burundi*, *East African*, *Ethiopian Airlines*, *Kenya Airways*, *SN Brussels Airlines* and *South African Airways*.
Approximate flight times: From Kigali to *London* is 12 hours, including stopovers.
International airports: *Kigali (KGL)* (Kigali International Airport), 12km (7.5 miles) east of Kigali (travel time – 25 minutes). Airport facilities include bar, duty free shop, post office and currency exchange. Bus and taxi services are available.
Departure tax: US$20 or equivalent in Rwanda Francs.
ROAD: International routes are available from the surrounding countries of the Democratic Republic of Congo, Tanzania and Uganda. Visitors are advised to exercise extreme caution, owing to political instability. **Bus:** There are daily services from Kampala in Uganda and Bujumbura in Burundi to Kigali.

Travel - Internal

AIR: Chartered planes are available but are usually expensive.
Departure tax: US$20.
ROAD: Traffic drives on the right. There are three types of road: *National Routes* which are tarmacked, *Provincial Routes* which are in quite good condition and *Local Routes* which are not tarmacked and on which a 4-by-4 vehicle would be advantageous. Extra care should be taken at night, as taxis use full headlights. The network is generally sparse; the roads linking the capital with Butare, Bugarana and the frontier posts are, however, good. Driving is not recommended and visitors are advised to exercise extreme caution. **Bus:** Services are operated by the *Ministry of Transport and Communications* and are classified into three groups: Urban (route numbers prefixed by A, B or C); Suburban (D routes); and Interurban. A timetable and tariff booklet is available in Rwanda. **Taxi:** Available in Kigali and other large towns. Fares should be agreed in advance. Tipping is not expected. **Car hire:** Limited facilities in Rwanda. There are no international car hire firms operating, but there are local companies in Kigali. **Documentation:** An International Driving Permit is required.

Accommodation

HOTELS: Found mostly in Kigali; they are expensive. There are some cheaper new hotels of reasonable standard. Missions with dormitory accommodation are also available, particularly in remote districts and smaller towns. Ruhengeri and Gisenyi mission station hotels are excellent.
GUEST HOUSES: Outside the main towns there are guest houses, which are generally cheaper than hotels. There is a solar-powered house at the edge of the A'Kagera National Park.
CAMPING: At present this is forbidden but facilities are being developed. Rest huts are available on the expedition route in the Virunga Volcanoes.

Resorts & Excursions

Rwanda is a mountainous land in the heart of Africa, split by the **Rift Valley**, and dominated by a mountain range that traverses the country from north to south. The four principal areas of interest are the **Virunga Volcanoes**, the **A'Kagera National Park**, the **Nyungwe National Park** and the region around **Lake Kivu**. The capital city of **Kigali** is mainly a commercial and administrative centre and has little in the way of tourist attractions. For up-to-date information about tours and excursions in the country contact Kiboko Tours & Travel (website: kibokotravels.org.rw) *or ORTPN* in Kigali (see *Contact Addresses* section).
A'KAGERA NATIONAL PARK: Kibungu (Umutara), in the east of the country, is in the centre of a region of lakes and waterfalls, including **Lake Mungesera** and the **Rusumo Falls**. It is also close to the southern tip of the **A'Kagera National Park**, which covers over 2500 sq km (1000 sq miles) of savannah to the west of the A' Kagera River (the frontier with Tanzania). The park has a variety of wildlife and is a habitat for over 500 species of birds. The major

Credit: © Rwanda Tourist Board

point of access is Kabarando; the roads within the park have recently been improved. In the rainy seasons (December, March and April), many of the routes become impassable.
PARC DES VOLCANS: Northwest of A'Kagera is the Parc des Volcans, one of the last sanctuaries of the mountain gorilla. The *ORTPN* bureau and some private companies in Kigali can organise guided tours of the park for small parties; it is advisable to book well in advance. This region is composed of volcanic mountains, of which two, Nyamuragira and Nyiragongo, across the frontier in the Democratic Republic of Congo, are still active.
LAKE KIVU: Gisenyi is the main centre for excursions in the Parc des Volcans. Plane trips can be made from here to view the craters. Situated on the north of Lake Kivu, it also offers many opportunities for water sports or for excursions on the lake. **Kibuye**, further south, is another lakeside resort. Near **Cyangugu**, on the southern shores of the lake, are the spectacular grottoes of **Kaboza** and **Nyenji**, and the thermal waters at Nyakabuye. Nearby, the **Rugege Forest** is the home of many rare species of wildlife.
ELSEWHERE: East of Cyangugu, bordering with Burundi, is **Butare**, the intellectual capital of the country. It boasts an interesting museum, craft shops and a botanical garden. North of Butare is **Gitarama**, which has a good art museum; nearby is the cathedral town of **Kabgayi**; and at **Mushubati**, the grottoes of **Bihongori**.

Sport & Activities

The Parc Nacional des Volcans is most famous for **gorilla tracking** (Dian Fossey spent 18 years studying them here until her murder in 1985). Military units currently guard the park and ensure the safety of visitors, particularly from poachers.
Safaris can be undertaken in A'Kagera National Park at Kabarando; the park is devoted to game preservation and has lions, zebras, antelopes, hippos, buffalo, leopards, apes, impala, crested herons, fish eagles, cormorants, giraffes, elephants, elands and warthogs.
The Virunga Volcanoes between Ruhengeri and Gisenyi are popular with **climbers**. Nyiragongo in the Democratic Republic of Congo is the most commonly climbed from Gisenyi. Rwandan guides are available for two- or three-day expeditions to view the craters.

Social Profile

FOOD & DRINK: Hotels generally serve a reasonable choice of European dishes, while there are Chinese, Greek, Indian, Italian and Middle Eastern restaurants. Some restaurants also serve Franco-Belgian cuisine and African dishes. A fairly good selection of beers, spirits and wines is available. Beer is also brewed locally.
NIGHTLIFE: Apart from the many small bars, there is little in the way of nightlife. There are a few cinemas in Kigali. The *Rwanda National Ballet* is famous for its traditional dancing and singing and can be seen either at national ceremonies or sometimes on request in the villages. There are now several nightclubs, with African, Congolese and Western music; there are also some live music bars with food and dancing available. The French Cultural Centre runs a variety of activities.
SHOPPING: Special purchases include woven baskets with pointed lids, native clay statuettes, masks and charms. Do not buy souvenir gorilla skulls or hands; if they are offered, report the trader to the police. **Shopping hours:** Mon-Fri 0830-1300 and 1400-1730, Sat 0830-1230.
SPECIAL EVENTS: Rwanda celebrates *Easter*, *Christmas* and *New Year*, along with *Democracy Day*, *Republic Day* and *Culture Day* (see *Public Holidays* section for dates).
SOCIAL CONVENTIONS: The traditional way of life is based on agriculture and cattle. The Rwandans settle in the fertile areas, but they do not form villages, each family being surrounded by its own fields. The majority of the population belong to the Hutu tribe. There is a significant Tutsi minority (15 per cent) and a smaller minority of Twa, a mixed race of traditional potters and hunters and said to be the country's first inhabitants. Normal social courtesies apply. **Tipping:** 10 per cent is normal.

Business Profile

ECONOMY: Rwanda's economy, which is based on subsistence agriculture, was devastated by the massacres of 1994, the huge refugee populations that resulted, political upheaval and, since then, ongoing fighting in several parts of the country. Plantains, sweet potatoes, cassava and beans are grown for domestic consumption; tea and coffee are the principal cash crops and there is extensive livestock farming. Some rice and sugar plantations have also been developed. Rwanda has some mineral deposits – principally tin ores, but also several ores containing rare metals such as tungsten and tantalum, which are in heavy demand in the world market.
Extraction of the large natural gas reserves discovered beneath Lake Kivu has begun, although it has been disrupted by local fighting. The industrial sector produces tobacco, metal goods, chemicals, rubber and plastics. In the service sector, the embryonic tourism industry (geared towards ecotourism) has had to restart from scratch as a result of the 1994 genocide and subsequent events. Given the political situation, exacerbated by a series of poor harvests during the late 1990s, it is hardly surprising therefore that Rwanda continues to rely heavily on international aid. A new Structural Adjustment Programme was begun in 1998, followed by an ambitious privatisation programme: both are being conducted under the supervision of the IMF and World Bank. In 2002, telecommunications and government-owned tea plantations were put up for sale. The results so far have been quite good: the economy grew 3.5 per cent in 2004 and inflation was 7.5 per cent. But, like most sub-Saharan African economies, Rwanda is especially vulnerable to commodity price movements; these are presently at a very low level. Aid donors have also promised further assistance conditional on Rwanda pulling its troops out of the Democratic Republic of Congo. The country's principal trading partners are Kenya, The Netherlands, Belgium, Luxembourg, Germany, Switzerland, Tanzania and Uganda. The main regional cooperation mechanism for Rwanda is the Common Market for Eastern and Southern Africa.
BUSINESS: Lightweight suits are advised and appointments are necessary. Best time to visit is from April to October or December to January. A knowledge of French is useful as only a few executives speak English. **Office hours:** Mon-Fri 0800-1230 and 1330-1700.
COMMERCIAL INFORMATION: The following organisation can offer advice: Chambre de Commerce et d'Industrie du Rwanda, BP 319, Kigali, Rwanda (tel: 83538/41; fax: 83532; e-mail: frsp@rwanda1.com).

Climate

Despite its proximity to the Equator, the climate in Rwanda is cooled by the high altitude. It is warm throughout most of the country but cooler in the mountains. There are two rainy seasons: mid-January to April and mid-October to mid-December.
Required clothing: Lightweights are required for most of the year with warmer clothes for cooler upland evenings. Rainwear is advisable.

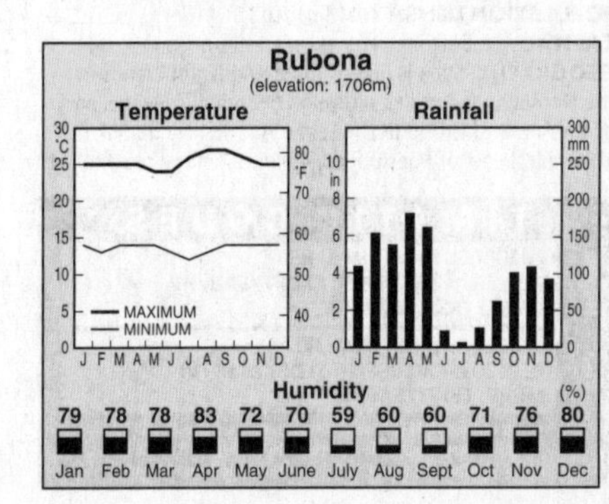

Saba

LATEST TRAVEL ADVICE CONTACTS

British Foreign and Commonwealth Office
Tel: (0870) 606 0290 Website: www.fco.gov.uk

US Department of State
Website: http://travel.state.gov/travel

Canadian Department of Foreign Affairs and Int'l Trade
Tel: (1 800) 267 8376 Website: www.dfait-maeci.gc.ca

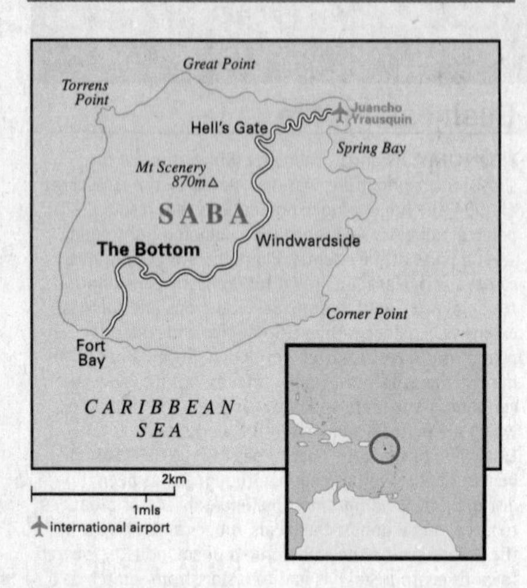

Location: Eastern Caribbean, Leeward Islands.

Country dialling code: 599.

Saba is part of the Netherlands Antilles and is represented abroad by Royal Netherlands Embassies – see *The Netherlands* section.

Saba Tourist Bureau
PO Box 515, Windwardside, Saba, NA
Tel: 416 2231 *or* 2322. Fax: 416 2350.
E-mail: iluvsaba@unspoiledqueen.com
Website: www.sabatourism.com

Office of the Minister Plenipotentiary of the Netherlands Antilles
PO Box 90706, Badhuisweg 173-175, 2597 JP The Hague, The Netherlands
Tel: (70) 306 6111. Fax: (70) 306 6110.
Also deals with tourism enquiries for Saba.

Caribbean Tourism Organisation
22 The Quadrant, Richmond, Surrey, SW1P 1BP, UK
Tel: (020) 8948 0057. Fax: (020) 8948 0067.
E-mail: ctolondon@carib-tourism.com
Website: www.doitcaribbean.com *or* www.onecaribbean.org

British Consulate
Jansofat 38, Curaçao, NA
Tel: (9) 747 3322. Fax: (9) 747 3330.
E-mail: britconcur@attglobal.net

Consulate of the United States of America
Street address: JB Gorsiraweg 1, Willemstad, Curaçao, NA
Postal address: PO Box 158, Willemstad, Curaçao, NA
Tel: (9) 461 3066. Fax: (9) 461 6489.
E-mail: info@amcongencuracao.an
Website: www.amcongencuracao.an

Canadian Consulate
Maduro & Curiels, 2-4 Plaza Jojo Correa, Curaçao, NA
Tel: (9) 466 1115. Fax: (9) 446 1122.

General Information

AREA: 13 sq km (5 sq miles).
POPULATION: 1466 (official estimate 1996).
POPULATION DENSITY: 113 per sq km.
CAPITAL: The Bottom.
GEOGRAPHY: Saba is one of three Windward Islands in the Netherlands Antilles, although geographically it is part of the Leeward Group of the Lesser Antilles, lying 265km (165 miles) east of Puerto Rico, 44km (27 miles) south of St Maarten and 21km (13 miles) west of St Eustatius. Saba is the peak of a submerged extinct volcano. Mount Scenery is thick with forest and rises to almost 900m (3000ft) in less than 2km (1.2 miles). There are four villages, until recently connected only by thousands of steps cut from the rock. A road now links the airport with The Bottom.
GOVERNMENT: Part of the Netherlands Antilles; dependency of The Netherlands. Gained internal autonomy in 1954. **Head of State:** HM Queen Beatrix of The Netherlands, represented locally by Governor Dr Fritz M de los Santos Goedgedrag. **Head of Government:** Prime Minister Miguel A Pourier since 2002. The Netherlands Antilles consist of Aruba, Bonaire, Curaçao, Saba, St Eustatius and St Maarten. The capital of the island group is Willemstad, Curaçao.
LANGUAGE: Dutch is the official language. *Papiamento* (a mixture of Portuguese, African, Spanish, Dutch and English) is the commonly used *lingua franca*. English and Spanish are also widely spoken.
RELIGION: Roman Catholic majority; also Anglican and Wesleyan.
TIME: GMT - 4.
ELECTRICITY: 110/220 volts AC, 60Hz.
COMMUNICATIONS: Telephone: Fully automatic system with good IDD. Country code: 599. Outgoing international code: 00. Calls made through the operator are more expensive and include a 15 per cent tax. IDD is available from hotels and some phone booths. **Mobile telephone:** Analogue networks operated by *Windward Islands Cellular* and digital analogue network (system B) by *East Caribbean Cellular* (website: www.eastcaribbeancellular.com). Compatible with most US handsets but not with GSM handsets. Roaming agreements exist. Handsets can be hired at the company offices in The Bottom. GSM network is being developed and should now be in operation. Most US handsets can be used, and can be activated with a temporary number before or after arrival on the island. Visitors can also register online with ECC. **Internet:** There is currently one Internet cafe on the island, in Windwardside. **Telegram:** Services operated by *Antelecom* and *Lands Radio Dienst*. **Post:** The post office is in The Bottom. Airmail to Europe takes four to six days, surface mail four to six weeks. **Press:** The *Saba Herald* is published monthly in English.
Radio: BBC World Service (website: www.bbc.co.uk/worldservice) and Voice of America (website: www.voa.gov) can be received. From time to time the frequencies change and the most up-to-date can be found online.

Passport/Visa

	Passport Required?	Visa Required?	Return Ticket Required?
Full British	Yes	1	Yes
Australian	Yes	2	Yes
Canadian	Yes	2	Yes
USA	Yes	2	Yes
Other EU	Yes	1/2	Yes
Japanese	Yes	2	Yes

Note: *Regulations and requirements may be subject to change at short notice, and you are advised to contact the appropriate diplomatic or consular authority before finalising travel arrangements. Details of these may be found at the head of this country's entry. Any numbers in the chart refer to the footnotes below.*

PASSPORTS: Passport or official travel documents valid for at least three months after intended return to home country required by all.
VISAS: Required by all except the following:
(a) **1.** nationals of Belgium, Bolivia, Burkina Faso, Chile, Costa Rica, Czech Republic, Ecuador, Germany, Hungary, Israel, Jamaica, Korea (Rep), Luxembourg, Malawi, Mauritius, The Netherlands, Niger, The Philippines, Poland, San Marino, Slovak Republic, Spain, Swaziland, Togo and the UK for touristic stays of up to three months;
(b) most nationals continuing to a third country within 24 hours by the same means of transportation and not leaving the airport and holding tickets with reserved seats and documents for their onward journey.
Note: (a) Nationals of the following countries must apply for a visa *before* entering the country even for touristic purposes: Albania, Bosnia & Herzegovina, Bulgaria, Cambodia, China (PR) (except Hong Kong SAR), CIS, Colombia, Cote d'Ivoire, Croatia, Cuba, Dominican Republic, Estonia, Ghana, Guinea-Bissau, Haiti, Kenya, Korea (DPR), Latvia, Libya, Lithuania, Macedonia (Former Yugoslav Republic), Mali, Nigeria, Romania, Serbia & Montenegro and Vietnam. (b) **2.** All other nationals may enter without a visa for touristic stays of up to 14 days. (c) All stays can be extended locally by the same period that they are valid for.
Types of visa and cost: All visas, regardless of duration of stay or number of entries permitted on visa, cost €35.
Validity: Visas are generally issued for as long as duration of stay, up until a maximum 90 days from date of issue.
Application requirements: (a) Passport or equivalent travel document valid for a minimum of three months after intended return to home country. Passports should contain a blank visa page and endorse residence permit. For minors (18 years and under), an approval of both parents or legal guardians with a copy of each parent's/guardian's passport is required. If passport is new, the old passport must also be submitted. (b) One fully completed application form. (c) One recent passport-size photo per person endorsed on passport, with daytime phone number and address written clearly on the back. More photos may be required. (d) Fee, payable by postal order (to Royal Netherlands Embassy) or cash. Cheques are not accepted. Visa handling fees may be charged on applications handed in, regardless of outcome, depending on Embassy/Consulate. (e) Evidence of sufficient funds amounting to a minimum of £30 for each day of stay (cash not accepted), eg original bank statements, credit card with credit limit statement, traveller's cheques. (f) A recent and original letter from employer, stating commencement date, with last payslip. If self-employed, submit letter from solicitor, accountant or company house. If unemployed, submit social benefit booklet. If in education, submit a recent and original letter from school/college/university, confirming attendance. (g) Valid medical or travel insurance.
Tourist: (a)-(g) and, (h) Invitation from family or proof of accommodation. (i) Return or onward ticket(s), plus necessary documents for returning to country of origin.
Business: (a)-(g) and, (h) Invitation from company that you are visiting.
Application to: Nearest Embassy of the Kingdom of The Netherlands. All further information about visa requirements may be obtained from The Royal Netherlands Embassies which formally represent the Netherlands Antilles; see *Contact Addresses* in *The Netherlands* section.
Working days required: Applications should be lodged at least one month prior to departure.
Temporary residence: Enquire at the office of the Lieutenant Governor of the Island Territory of Saba, The Bottom, Saba. In certain cases, Dutch Europeans may be permitted to reside in the Netherlands Antilles without having to apply for a residence permit. However, it is best to consult the nearest Dutch Embassy/Consulate in advance to ascertain whether this is applicable taking into consideration the individual circumstances of the traveller.

Money

Currency: Netherlands Antilles Guilder or Florin (ANG) = 100 cents. Notes are in denominations of ANG250, 100, 50, 25, 10 and 5. Coins are in denominations of ANG5 and 1 and 50, 25, 10, 5 and 1 cents.
Note: The ANG is linked to the US Dollar.
Currency exchange: There are two banks on the island.
Credit & debit cards: MasterCard and Visa are accepted in larger establishments. Check with your credit or debit card company for details of merchant acceptability and other services that may be available.
Travellers cheques: To avoid additional exchange rate charges, US Dollars are recommended.
Currency restrictions: There are no restrictions on the import and export of foreign or local currency. The import of Dutch or Surinam silver coins is prohibited.
Exchange rate indicators: The following figures are included as a guide to the movement of The Netherlands Antilles Guilder against Sterling and the US Dollar:

Date	Feb '04	May '04	Aug '04	Nov '04
£1.00=	3.25	3.20	3.30	3.39
$1.00=	1.79	1.79	1.79	1.79

Banking hours: Mon-Fri 0830-1130 and 1330-1630.

Duty Free

The following items may be imported into Saba by tourists over 15 years of age only, without incurring customs duty:
200 cigarettes or 50 cigars or 100 cigarillos or 250g tobacco; 2l of alcoholic beverages; gifts to a value of NAG100.
Restricted items: The import of leather goods from Haiti is not advisable. If total value of goods exceeds NAG500, a declaration should be made at customs and cleared at the freight department.

Public Holidays

2005: Jan 1 New Year's Day. **Mar 25-28** Easter. **Apr 30** Queen's Birthday. **May 1** Labour Day. **May 5** Ascension. **Oct 22** Antillean Day. **Dec 5** Saba Day. **Dec 25** Christmas Day. **Dec 26** Boxing Day.
2006: Jan 1 New Year's Day. **Apr 14-17** Easter. **Apr 30** Queen's Birthday. **May 1** Labour Day. **May tbc** Ascension. **Oct 22** Antillean Day. **Dec 4** Saba Day. **Dec 25** Christmas Day. **Dec 26** Boxing Day.

TIMATIC CODES

Health
AMADEUS: **TI-DFT/SAB/HE**
GALILEO/WORLDSPAN: **TI-DFT/SAB/HE**
SABRE: **TIDFT/SAB/HE**

Visa
AMADEUS: **TI-DFT/SAB/VI**
GALILEO/WORLDSPAN: **TI-DFT/SAB/VI**
SABRE: **TIDFT/SAB/VI**

To access TIMATIC country information on Health and Visa regulations through the Computer Reservations System (CRS), type in the appropriate command line listed above.

Health

	Special Precautions?	Certificate Required?
Yellow Fever	No	1
Cholera	No	No
Typhoid & Polio	No	N/A
Malaria	No	N/A

Note: Regulations and requirements may be subject to change at short notice, and you are advised to contact your doctor well in advance of your intended date of departure. Any numbers in the chart refer to the footnotes below.

1: A yellow fever certificate is required from travellers over six months of age arriving within six days of transiting countries with infected areas.

Food & drink: All mains water on the island is distilled from seawater and is therefore safe to drink. Bottled mineral water is widely available. Milk is pasteurised and dairy products are safe for consumption. Local meat, poultry, seafood, fruit and vegetables are generally considered safe to eat.

Other risks: Immunisation against *hepatitis A* is recommended. *TB* and *hepatitis B* might also occur in rural areas.

Health care: There is one hospital in The Bottom plus the University School of Medicine. Medical insurance is essential.

Travel - International

AIR: Airlines serving Saba include *Winair* (website: www.fly-winair.com).

Approximate flight times: All international air travel is via St Maarten. From Saba to *London* (via St Maarten and Amsterdam) is 13 hours, to *Los Angeles* is 10 hours, to *New York* is six hours and to *Singapore* is 34 hours (these will vary considerably, depending on connections).

International airports: *Juancho Yrausquin (SAB)* at Cove Bay. The runway, at 400m (1300ft), is one of the shortest in the world. There are daily STOL turboprop flights to St Eustatius and St Kitts (and thus the airport may be classified as 'international') and thrice daily to St Maarten.

Departure tax: US$7 to Netherlands Antilles, US$22 for all other destinations (due to exchange rates, prices may vary).

SEA: Small boats operate from the Leo A Chance Pier at Fort Bay. There are regular ferry services to St Maarten (travel time – one hour). A weekly cargo boat brings groceries and other supplies from St Maarten. Cruise ships call occasionally.

Travel - Internal

ROAD: Saba has one road, 15km (9.5 miles) long, bisecting the island from the airport to Fort Bay. Traffic drives on the right. **Taxis** are available. Self-drive cars may be hired in Windwardside. **Documentation:** A national driving licence is acceptable.

Accommodation

There are various guest houses including *Caribe Guesthouse, The Cottage Club, Cranston's Antique Inn, Ecolodge Rendez-Vous, The Gate House, Juliana's, El Momo, Queen's Garden Resort, Scout's Place* and *Willard's of Saba*. Most have their own restaurant bar and swimming pool. Some apartments, cottages and villas are also available. A 5 per cent government tax is added to bills.

Resorts & Excursions

Mount Scenery is an extinct volcano rising from the floor of the Caribbean; the 250m (820ft) of it above sea level is known as Saba. With only one road ('The Road') and a population of less than 1500, Saba is the most unspoilt of The Netherlands Antilles; the inhabitants will claim that visitors are so few that each one is something of a celebrity. Until 50 years ago Saba was a secluded oasis, having neither an airport nor a sheltered harbour. From the rocky beach at **Fort Bay**, there was a steep climb of 800 steps hewn out of the rock in order to gain access to the island. The island's four villages are mere clusters of ornate timber cottages perching on the flanks of the mountain. Vegetation becomes increasingly lush towards the summit and the crater itself holds a tropical rainforest scattered with exotic flowers – begonias, giant heliconias and orchids. Tours may be taken by taxi from the airport or pier, or on foot via the forest trails and thousands of stone-cut steps linking the villages. The **Harry L Johnson Memorial Museum** in **Windwardside** is the restored home of a Dutch sea captain. Windwardside also contains the **Tourist Office**, the island's two largest guest houses and most of its shops. The island's capital, **The Bottom**, is situated 250m (820ft) above the ocean on a plateau surrounded by volcanic domes. Here, the **Artisan Foundation** exhibits early examples of 'Saba lace': intricate embroidery on linen that resembles lace. The climate is milder than neighbouring St Eustatius (21km/13 miles away), but the island is subject to sudden downpours.

Sport & Activities

Diving: The waters around Saba have been declared a protected marine park in recognition of the unique opportunities for wall diving they present to experienced divers. Visibility varies from 20 to 30m (75 to 100ft) with a water temperature of 30°C (86°F) in summer, whilst in winter visibility is up to 40m (125ft), with a water temperature of 24°C (75°F). The fragile coral reefs clinging to the submerged mountain slopes are teeming with colourful grazing fish, preyed on by sharks and barracuda. Giant sea turtles and humpback whales are seasonal visitors. Boats and diving equipment can be rented from dive shops. Qualified dive masters can provide tuition at all levels (beginners are confined to the shallow waters of Fort Bay).

Other: The island's few other sports facilities include a concrete **tennis** court at the Sunny Valley Youth Centre in The Bottom and **swimming** pools at all hotels. There are no beaches. Marked **hiking** trails lead up to Mount Scenery.

Social Profile

FOOD & DRINK: Fine local cuisine is offered at the island's guest houses and there are several public restaurants. Local specialities include *calaloo* soup, curried goat, breadfruit, soursop ice cream and exotic fruit grown on the island – mangoes, papayas, figs, bananas and bitter mangoes. Restaurants and bars are usually closed by midnight. Most well-known brands of drink are available and Saba has its own brand of rum – *Saba Spice*, a potent blend of rum, aniseed, cinnamon, orange peel, cloves, nutmeg, spice bush and brown sugar.

NIGHTLIFE: There are few visitors to the island and generally evenings are quiet, but on Friday and Saturday nights there is dancing at some restaurants and some guest houses have lively bars.

SHOPPING: By the middle of the last century, the decline in the world's demand for sugar and indigo had left Saba looking at a very bleak future; the plantations, the only source of employment, reverted to forest. Undaunted, the men built boats and became fishermen, the women stayed at home and embroidered napkins and table cloths using a technique remembered by Mary Gertrude Johnson from her days in a Venezuelan convent. The fishing industry is now marginal but the embroidery has become Saba's chief claim to fame. *The Saba Artisans' Foundation* (founded in 1972 with money from the United Nations' Development Programme) in The Bottom promotes local lacework, silk-screened fabrics and garments printed and handmade by Sabans, as does the *Island Craft Shop* in Windwardside.

Shopping hours: Mon-Sat 0800-1200 and 1400-1800.

SPECIAL EVENTS: For a full list of events, contact the Saba Tourist Bureau (see *Contact Addresses* section); the following is a selection of special events occurring in Saba in 2005:

Apr 30 *Coronation Day & Queen's Birthday*. **Jul** *Saba Summer Carnival Festival*. **Oct 22** *Antillean Day*. **Dec** *Saba Days "Mini Winter Carnival"*.

SOCIAL CONVENTIONS: Dutch customs are still important throughout the Netherlands Antilles, but tourism on neighbouring St Maarten has brought some US influence to Saba (several businesses are US-owned). Dress is casual and lightweight cottons are advised. **Tipping:** A surcharge of 20 per cent is usually added to guest house and restaurant bills to cover government tax and service. Elsewhere, 10 to 15 per cent is expected.

Business Profile

ECONOMY: Economic conditions vary widely between the different islands in the Netherlands Antilles group. Saba has some agriculture, producing sorghum, groundnuts, fruit and vegetables, as well as a modest fishing operation. There is no manufacturing industry other than textiles. Saba has very little of the Netherlands Antilles' recently developed 'offshore' financial services industry; tourism is the most important part of the service sector. Along with Bonaire and St Eustatius, Saba is a net beneficiary of the Netherlands Antilles central treasury. Saba has associate membership of the European Union, as an overseas territory of The Netherlands, and observer status at the Caribbean trading bloc, CARICOM.

BUSINESS: Business is fairly formal and visitors should wear a suit. Appointments should be made and always kept as it is very discourteous to be late. **Office hours:** Mon-Fri 0730-1200 and 1330-1630.

COMMERCIAL INFORMATION: The following organisations can offer advice: Curaçao Chamber of Commerce, PO Box 10, Kaya Junior Salas 1, Curaçao (tel: (9) 461 3918; fax: (9) 461 5652; e-mail: businessinfo@curacao-chamber.an; website: www.curacao-chamber.an); *or* St Maarten Chamber of Commerce and Industry, PO Box 454, C A Cannegieter Street 11, Philipsburg, St Maarten (tel: 542 3590; fax: 542 3512; e-mail: coci@sintmaarten.net).

Climate

Hot, but tempered by cooling trade winds. The annual mean temperature is 27°C (80°F), varying by no more than two or three degrees throughout the year; average rainfall is 1667mm. The temperature can drop to 16°C (60°F) on winter evenings. When climbing Mount Scenery, the temperature will drop by approximately 0.2°C (0.4°F) for each 100m (330ft) gained in altitude.

Required clothing: Lightweights and cottons are worn throughout the year. Umbrellas or light waterproofs are needed for the rainy season.

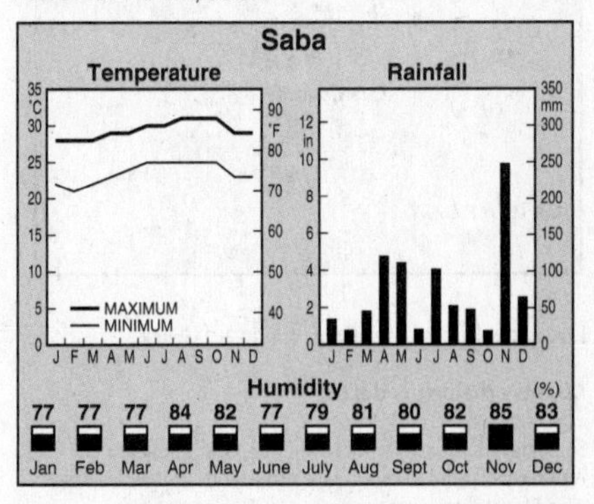

St Eustatius

LATEST TRAVEL ADVICE CONTACTS

British Foreign and Commonwealth Office
Tel: (0870) 606 0290 Website: www.fco.gov.uk
US Department of State
Website: http://travel.state.gov/travel
Canadian Department of Foreign Affairs and Int'l Trade
Tel: (1 800) 267 8376 Website: www.dfait-maeci.gc.ca

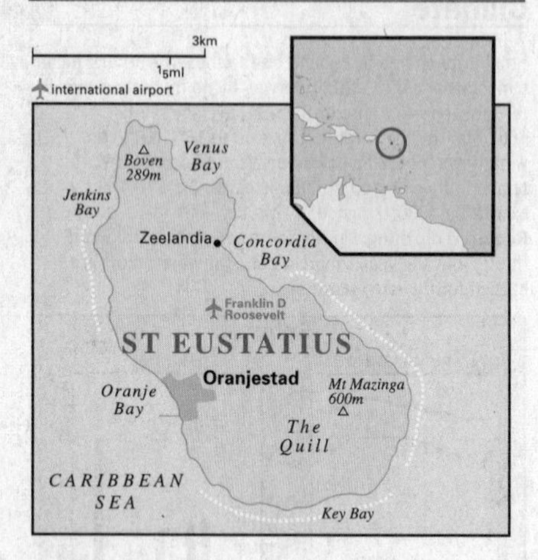

Location: Eastern Caribbean, Windward Islands.

Country dialling code: 599.

St Eustatius is part of the Netherlands Antilles, and is represented abroad by Royal Netherlands Embassies – see *The Netherlands* section.

Statia Tourist Office
Fort Oranje, Oranjestad, St Eustatius, NA
Tel/Fax: 318 2433.
E-mail: euxtour@goldenrock.net
Website: www.statiatourism.com

Office of the Minister Plenipotentiary of the Netherlands Antilles
PO Box 90706, Badhuisweg 173-175, 2597 JP The Hague, The Netherlands
Tel: (70) 306 6111. Fax: (70) 306 6110.

Caribbean Tourism Organisation
22 The Quadrant, Richmond, Surrey, TW9 1BP, UK
Tel: (020) 8948 0057. Fax: (020) 8948 0067.
E-mail: ctolondon@carib-tourism.com
Website: www.doitcaribbean.com *or* www.onecaribbean.org

British Consulate
Jansofat 38, PO Box 3803, Willemstad, Curaçao, NA
Tel: (9) 747 3322. Fax: (9) 747 3330.
E-mail: britconcur@attglobal.net

Consulate of the United States of America
Street address: JB Gorsiraweg 1, Willemstad, Curaçao, NA
Postal address: PO Box 158, Willemstad, Curaçao, NA
Tel: (9) 461 3066. Fax: (9) 461 6489.
E-mail: cgcuracao@attglobal.net
Website: www.amcongencuracao.an

Canadian Consulate
Street address: Maduro & Curiels Bank, NV, Plasa JoJo Correa 2-4, Willemstad, Curaçao, NA
Postal address: PO Box 305, Willemstad, Curaçao, NA
Tel: (9) 466 1115. Fax: (9) 466 1122.

General Information

AREA: 21 sq km (8 sq miles).
POPULATION: 2609 (official estimate 1996).
POPULATION DENSITY: 124 per sq km.
CAPITAL: Oranjestad.
GEOGRAPHY: Politically, St Eustatius is one of three Windward Islands in the Netherlands Antilles; geographically it is part of the Leeward Group of the Lesser Antilles. It lies 286km (178 miles) east of Puerto Rico, 171km (106 miles) east of St Croix, 56km (35 miles) due south of St Maarten and 14km (9 miles) northwest of St Kitts. On the south end of the island is an extinct volcano called The Quill, which has a lush rainforest in the crater. Twice a year, sea turtles clamber up onto the black volcanic sands that rim the island to lay their eggs; giant land crabs hunt on the beaches every night.
GOVERNMENT: Part of the Netherlands Antilles; dependency of The Netherlands since 1630. **Head of State:** Queen Beatrix of The Netherlands, represented locally by Governor Frits Goedgedrag since 2002. **Head of Government:** Prime Minister Etienne Ys since 2004. The Netherlands Antilles consist of Bonaire, Curaçao, Saba, St Eustatius and St Maarten. The capital of the island group is Willemstad, Curaçao.
LANGUAGE: Dutch is the official language. Papiamento (a mixture of African, Dutch, English, Portuguese and Spanish) is the commonly used *lingua franca*. English and Spanish are also widely spoken.
RELIGION: The majority are Protestant with a Roman Catholic minority.
TIME: GMT - 4.
ELECTRICITY: 110 volts AC, 60Hz. Plugs with two flat prongs are in use.
COMMUNICATIONS: Telephone: Fully automatic system with good IDD connections. Country code: 599. Outgoing international code: 00. Calls made through the operator are more expensive and include a 15 per cent tax. **Mobile telephone:** Analogue network operated by *East Caribbean Cellular* (website: www.eastcaribbeancellular.com). Not compatible with GSM handsets but some US handsets can be used. Roaming agreements exist. **Internet:** E-mail provider is *goldenrock.net*. Public access is available in the library. **Telegram:** Services operated by *All American Cables, ANTELECOM* and *TELEM*. **Post:** Airmail to Europe takes four to six days, surface mail four to six weeks. Main post office hours: Mon-Fri 0730-1600. **Press:** No newspapers are published on St Eustatius, but English-language dailies, *Daily Herald* and *St Maarten Guardian* are published on St Maarten. Most other newspapers in The Netherlands Antilles are published in Dutch or Papiamento. **Radio:** BBC World Service (website: www.bbc.co.uk/worldservice) and Voice of America (website: www.voa.gov) can be received. From time to time the frequencies change and the most up-to-date can be found online.

TIMATIC CODES

Health	AMADEUS: **TI-DFT/EUX/HE** GALILEO/WORLDSPAN: **TI-DFT/EUX/HE** SABRE: **TIDFT/EUX/HE**
Visa	AMADEUS: **TI-DFT/EUX/VI** GALILEO/WORLDSPAN: **TI-DFT/EUX/VI** SABRE: **TIDFT/EUX/VI**

To access TIMATIC country information on Health and Visa regulations through the Computer Reservations System (CRS), type in the appropriate command line listed above.

Passport/Visa

	Passport Required?	Visa Required?	Return Ticket Required?
Full British	Yes	1	Yes
Australian	Yes	2	Yes
Canadian	Yes	2	Yes
USA	Yes	2	Yes
Other EU	Yes	1/2	Yes
Japanese	Yes	2	Yes

Note: *Regulations and requirements may be subject to change at short notice, and you are advised to contact the appropriate diplomatic or consular authority before finalising travel arrangements. Details of these may be found at the head of this country's entry. Any numbers in the chart refer to the footnotes below.*

PASSPORTS: Passport valid for at least three months after intended return to home country required by all.
VISAS: Required by all except the following:
(a) **1.** nationals of Belgium, Bolivia, Burkina Faso, Chile, Costa Rica, Czech Republic, Ecuador, Germany, Hungary, Israel, Jamaica, Korea (Rep), Luxembourg, Malawi, Mauritius, The Netherlands, Niger, The Philippines, Poland, San Marino, Slovak Republic, Spain, Swaziland, Togo and the UK for touristic stays of up to three months;
(b) most nationals continuing to a third country within 24 hours by the same means of transportation and not leaving the airport and holding tickets with reserved seats and documents for their onward journey.
Note: (a) Nationals of the following countries must apply for a visa *before* entering the country even for touristic purposes: Albania, Bosnia & Herzegovina, Bulgaria, Cambodia, China (PR) (except Hong Kong SAR), CIS, Colombia, Cote d'Ivoire, Croatia, Cuba, Dominican Republic, Estonia, Ghana, Guinea-Bissau, Haiti, Kenya, Korea (DPR), Latvia, Libya, Lithuania, Macedonia (Former Yugoslav Republic), Mali, Nigeria, Romania, Serbia & Montenegro and Vietnam. (b) **2.** All other nationals may enter without a visa for touristic stays of up to 14 days. (c) All stays can be extended locally by the same period that they are valid for.
Types of visa and cost: All visas, regardless of duration of stay or number of entries permitted on visa, cost €35.
Validity: Visas are generally issued for as long as duration of stay, up until a maximum 90 days from date of issue.
Application requirements: (a) Passport or equivalent travel document valid for a minimum of three months after intended return to home country. Passports should contain a blank visa page and endorse residence permit. For minors (18 years and under), an approval of both parents or legal guardians with a copy of each parent's/guardian's passport is required. If passport is new, the old passport must also be submitted. (b) One fully completed application form. (c) One recent passport-size photo per person endorsed on passport, with daytime phone number and address written clearly on the back. More photos may be required. (d) Fee, payable by postal order (to Royal Netherlands Embassy) or cash. Cheques are not accepted. Visa handling fees may be charged on applications handed in, regardless of outcome, depending on Embassy/Consulate. (e) Evidence of sufficient funds amounting to a minimum of £30 for each day of stay (cash not accepted), eg original bank statements, credit card with credit limit statement, travellers cheques. (f) A recent and original letter from employer, stating commencement date, with last payslip. If self-employed, submit letter from solicitor, accountant or company house. If unemployed, submit social benefit booklet. If in education, submit a recent and original letter from school/college/university, confirming attendance. (g) Valid medical or travel insurance. *Tourist*: (a)-(g) and, (h) Invitation from family or proof of accommodation. (i) Return or onward ticket(s), plus necessary documents for returning to country of origin. *Business*: (a)-(g) and, (h) Invitation from company that you are visiting.
Application to: Nearest Embassy of the Kingdom of The Netherlands. All further information about visa requirements may be obtained from the Royal Netherlands Embassies which formally represent the Netherlands Antilles; see *Contact Addresses* in *The Netherlands* section.
Working days required: Applications should be lodged at least one month prior to departure.
Temporary residence: Enquire at the office of the Lieutenant Governor of the Island Territory of St Eustatius, Oranjestad, St Eustatius. In certain cases, Dutch Europeans may be permitted to reside in the Netherlands Antilles without having to apply for a residence permit. However, it is best to consult the nearest Dutch Embassy/Consulate in advance to ascertain whether this is applicable taking into consideration the individual circumstances of the traveller.

Money

Currency: Netherlands Antilles Guilder or Florin (NAG) = 100 cents. Notes are in denominations of NAG250, 100, 50, 25, 10 and 5. Coins are in denominations of NAG5 and 1 and 50, 25, 10, 5 and 1 cents. The US Dollar is widely accepted. **Note:** The NAG is linked to the US Dollar.
Currency exchange: There are three banks on the island. All major currencies can be exchanged.
Credit & debit cards: MasterCard and Visa are accepted in large establishments. Check with your credit or debit card company for details of merchant acceptability and other services which may be available.
Currency restrictions: There are no restrictions on the import and export of local or foreign currency, except the import and export of amounts of foreign currency exceeding NAG20,000 must declared. The import of Dutch or Surinam silver coins is prohibited.
Exchange rate indicators: The following figures are included as a guide to the movement of the Netherlands Antilles Guilder against the Sterling and the US Dollar:

Date	Feb '04	May '04	Aug '04	Nov '04
£1.00=	3.25	3.28	3.30	3.39
$1.00=	1.79	1.79	1.79	1.79

Banking hours: Mon-Fri 0830-1130 and 1330-1630.

Duty Free

The following may be imported into St Eustatius by tourists over 15 years of age only without incurring customs duty:
200 cigarettes or 50 cigars or 100 cigarillos or 250g tobacco; 2l of alcoholic beverages; gifts to a value of NAG100 (gifts over the value of NAG500 must be declared).
Restricted items: The import of souvenirs and leather goods from Haiti is not advisable.

Public Holidays

2005: Jan 1 New Year's Day. **Mar 25** Good Friday. **Mar 27-28** Easter. **Apr 30** Queen's Birthday. **May 1** Labour Day. **May 20** Ascension. **Jul 25** Carnival Monday. **Oct 21** Antilles Day. **Nov 16** Statia's Day. **Dec 25** Christmas Day. **Dec 26** Boxing Day.
2006: Jan 1 New Year's Day. **Apr 14** Good Friday. **Apr 16-17** Easter. **Apr 30** Queen's Birthday. **May 1** Labour Day. **May 29** Ascension. **Jul 31** Carnival Monday. **Oct 21** Antilles Day. **Nov 16** Statia's Day. **Dec 25** Christmas Day. **Dec 26** Boxing Day.

Health

	Special Precautions?	Certificate Required?
Yellow Fever	No	1
Cholera	No	No
Typhoid & Polio	No	N/A
Malaria	No	N/A

Note: *Regulations and requirements may be subject to change at short notice, and you are advised to contact your doctor well in advance of your intended date of departure. Any numbers in the chart refer to the footnotes below.*

A B C D E F G H I J K L M N O P Q R S T U V W X Y Z

1: A yellow fever certificate is required from travellers over six months of age arriving within six days from infected areas.
Food & drink: Water on the island is considered safe to drink. Bottled mineral water is widely available. Milk is pasteurised and dairy products are safe for consumption. Local meat, poultry, seafood, fruit and vegetables are generally considered safe to eat.
Other risks: *Hepatitis A* and *rabies* occur.
Health care: There is one hospital on St Eustatius. Health insurance is advised.

Travel - International

AIR: The national airline of The Netherlands Antilles is *ALM (LM)*. St Eustatius is served by *Winair* (website: www.fly-winair.com).
Approximate flight times: From St Eustatius to *London* (via St Maarten) is nine hours, to *Los Angeles* is seven hours, to *New York* is three hours 30 minutes and to *Singapore* is 33 hours (these times will vary considerably, depending on connections).
International airports: *FD Roosevelt (EUX)*, 1km (0.6 miles) from Oranjestad, is served by *Winair* which runs scheduled flights from St Kitts & Nevis, from St Maarten six times daily (flight time – 17 minutes) and from Saba. *Golden Rock Airways* runs daily passenger charter flights to St Maarten and elsewhere. The runway is too small for jets.
Departure tax: US$5 to Netherlands Antilles; US$20 for international departures. Prices vary according to the airport. Transit passengers and children under two years of age are exempt.
SEA: There are no ferry services operating on St Eustatius. Plans to develop a service are currently underway. The roll-on, roll-off pier at Oranjestad enables small cruise ships to dock on St Eustatius.

Travel - Internal

ROAD: St Eustatius is a very small island and consequently has very few roads; a road of sorts runs right around the coast and a track leads up to the rim of *The Quill*, the extinct volcano in the south. The entire system can be walked in a few hours, but there are **car hire** and **taxi** companies in Oranjestad. Traffic drives on the right.
Documentation: A national driving licence is acceptable.

Accommodation

There are small hotels offering a total of approximately 50 beds, and several guest houses. There are also several fully equipped apartments available for weekly rental. Advance booking is advised. There is a 7 per cent service charge added to room rates. Information can be obtained from Statia Tourist Office (see *Contact Addresses* section).

Resorts & Excursions

St Eustatius, popularly known as 'Statia', was a thriving transshipment port during the 17th and 18th centuries, becoming known throughout the Caribbean as 'The Golden Rock'. The subsequent decline of the island has only recently been halted by an influx of tourists. Statia is quiet and unhurried, with reminders of its bustling commercial past surviving only in the ruins of old warehouses, the weed-choked **Jewish Cemetery** (connected to **Synagogue Honen Dalim**, the second-oldest synagogue in the New World); colonial houses; **Fort Oranje**, built by the French in 1629 above the town; **Fort Amsterdam** on the Atlantic coast and the foundations of the Dutch sea walls, now sunk beneath the clear waters of the bay.
Other attractions of the island include the newly restored **Old Town**; walking up to **The Quill**, a dormant volcano surrounded by lush tropical rainforest; the **Miriam Schmidt Botanical Garden**; many beautiful and unspoilt beaches with unusual layers of black and tan sand; snorkelling and scuba diving; surfing off the northeast coast; and fishing trips. Contact the Tourist Office for details (see *Contact Addresses* section).

Sport & Activities

Watersports: These predominate, and for many visitors will form the central part of the holiday. **Snorkelling**, **windsurfing** and **water-skiing** are all available with facilities and tuition as necessary, but the island is perhaps becoming best-known as a centre for **scuba-diving**. Many wrecks lie on the black sand amid coral reefs and near the submerged old port just off Oranjestad, and these have long attracted a staggering variety of marine life. The fish have been joined by increasing numbers of expert divers, drawn by a unique combination of first-rate facilities, warm and clear water and coral, and – onshore – comfortable hotels and excellent cuisine. Dive centres on St Eustatius offer complete packages (PADI), resort courses, lessons, equipment hire and snorkel tours.

Social Profile

FOOD & DRINK: Despite the island's small size, there is a good range of restaurants offering different blends of imported and local cuisine. The hotel restaurants are probably the best – indeed the Mooshay Bay Dining Room at The Old Gin House, where Continental food is served on old pewter plates, has been given a 5-star rating by Gourmet Magazine – but the local Creole-style cooking is particularly suited for seafood dishes: pickled conch shell meat, grilled spicy fish and lobster are recommended. The Chinese Restaurant offers authentic Cantonese cuisine; other restaurants also offer Cantonese dishes, together with French, US and local specialities.
There are no licensing hours on the island (although most restaurants and bars are usually closed by midnight), and alcohol is virtually tax-free. Most well-known brand names are available; a 'greenie' is a Heineken.
NIGHTLIFE: Centred on the main hotels and restaurants, including dancing to both taped Western music and live local bands, that might play one of the two different indigenous blends of reggae and calypso – 'Pim Pim' and 'Hippy'.
SHOPPING: The reductions on duty free imports make the purchase of perfume, jewellery or alcohol worthwhile.
Shopping hours: Mon-Sat 0800-1200 and 1400-1800.
SPECIAL EVENTS: For further details, contact the St Eustatius Tourism Development Foundation (see *Contact Addresses* section). The following is a selection of special events occurring in St Eustatius in 2005:
Mar 28 *Easter Monday* (island-wide beach picnics with music, food and drinks). **Apr 30** *Queen's Birthday*. **Jul 1** *Emancipation Day* (celebration of the abolition of slavery). **Jul 17-27** *Antillean Games*; *Statia Carnival*. **Oct 21** *Antillean Day* (celebrations with games and fetes). **Nov 16** *St Eustatius Day* (cultural festivities and celebrations). **Dec 26** *Boxing Day* (local actors parade through the streets depicting recent events).
Note: The *Carnival* sweeps back and forth through the island every year during the month of July; this is of course a popular time to visit and advance bookings are essential.
SOCIAL CONVENTIONS: Dutch customs are still important throughout the Netherlands Antilles, but US influences from the Virgin Islands nearby are dominant on St Eustatius. It is conventional to shake hands on meeting someone. Dress is casual and lightweight cottons are advised. Bathing suits should be confined to the beach and poolside areas only. It is common to dress up in the evening.
Tipping: Hotels add a 5 to 10 per cent government tax and 10 to 15 per cent service charge. Doormen and waiters expect a 10 per cent tip, but taxi drivers are not usually tipped.

Business Profile

ECONOMY: St Eustatius earns a modest income from agriculture and from a major petroleum transshipment programme, but it is tourism that dominates the economy. The island is also a net beneficiary from the central treasury of the Netherlands Antilles. There have been some efforts to develop the fishing industry but for the time being, government employment (in administration for the Netherlands Antilles group) is the most important source of regular employment. The Antilles group as a whole has Overseas Territory status at the EU and observer status at the Caribbean trading bloc CARICOM.
BUSINESS: Office hours: Mon-Fri 0730-1200 and 1330-1630.
COMMERCIAL INFORMATION: The following organisation can offer advice: St Maarten Chamber of Commerce and Industry, PO Box 454, C A Cannegieter Street 11, Philipsburg, St Maarten (tel: 542 3590/5; fax: 542 3512; website: www.sintmaarten.net).

Climate

Hot, but tempered by cooling trade winds. The annual mean temperature is 27°C (80°F), varying by no more than two or three degrees throughout the year; the average rainfall is 1771mm (7 inches).
Required clothing: Tropical lightweights and cottons are worn throughout the year. Umbrellas or light waterproofs are also advisable.

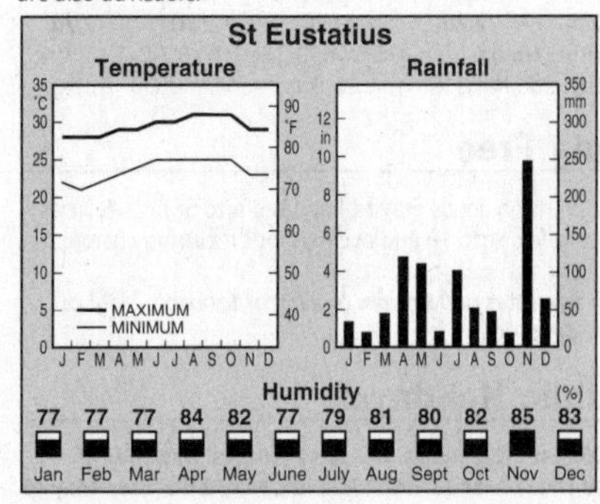

St Kitts & Nevis

LATEST TRAVEL ADVICE CONTACTS

British Foreign and Commonwealth Office
Tel: (0870) 606 0290 Website: www.fco.gov.uk
US Department of State
Website: http://travel.state.gov/travel
Canadian Department of Foreign Affairs and Int'l Trade
Tel: (1 800) 267 8376 Website: www.dfait-maeci.gc.ca

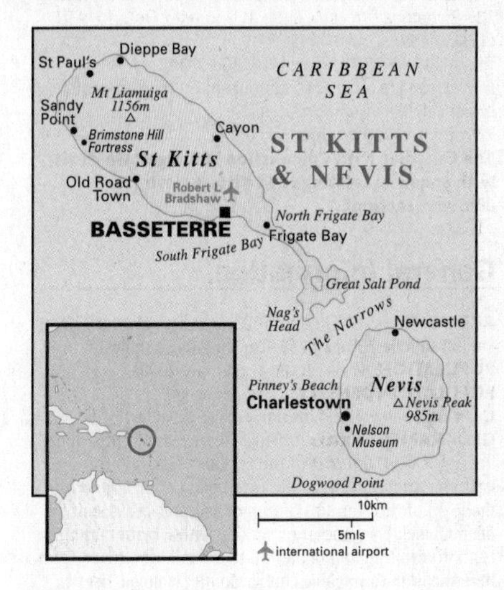

Location: Eastern Caribbean, Leeward Islands.

Country dialling code: 1 869.

St Kitts Tourism Authority
PO Box 132, Pelican Mall, Bay Road, Basseterre, St Kitts
Tel: 465 2620 *or* 4040. Fax: 465 8794.
E-mail: minister@stkittstourism.kn
Website: www.stkittstourism.kn
Nevis Tourism Authority
PO Box 917, Main Street, Charlestown, Nevis
Tel: 469 1042 *or* 7550 *or* (866) 556 3847 (toll-free).
Fax: 469 7551.
E-mail: info@nevisisland.com
Website: www.nevisisland.com
High Commission for St Kitts & Nevis
2nd Floor, 10 Kensington Court, London W8 5DL, UK
Tel: (020) 7460 6500.
Fax: (020) 7460 6505.
E-mail: sknhighcomm@aol.com
Opening hours: Mon-Thurs 0930-1730, Fri 0930-1700.
St Kitts Tourism Authority
Address as for High Commission
Tel: (020) 7376 0881. Fax: (020) 7937 6742.
E-mail: uk-europe.office@stkittstourism.kn
Website: www.stkitts-tourism.com
Caribbean Tourism Organisation
22 The Quadrant, Richmond, Surrey, TW9 1BP, UK
Tel: (020) 8948 0057.
Fax: (020) 8948 0067.
E-mail: ctolondon@carib-tourism.com
Website: www.doitcaribbean.com *or* www.onecaribbean.org
British Honorary Consulate
Office of the Honorary British Council, PO Box 559, Basseterre, St Kitts
Tel: 466 8888. Fax: 466 8889.
E-mail: honbritconsul_skn@hotmail.com
The British High Commission in St John's also deals with enquiries relating to St Kitts & Nevis (see *Antigua* section).
Embassy of St Kitts & Nevis
3216 New Mexico Avenue, NW, Washington, DC 20016, USA
Tel: (202) 686 2636.
Fax: (202) 686 5740.
E-mail: info@embskn.com
Website: www.stkittsnevis.org

TIMATIC CODES

Health
AMADEUS: **TI-DFT/SKB/HE**
GALILEO/WORLDSPAN: **TI-DFT/SKB/HE**
SABRE: **TIDFT/SKB/HE**

Visa
AMADEUS: **TI-DFT/SKB/VI**
GALILEO/WORLDSPAN: **TI-DFT/SKB/VI**
SABRE: **TIDFT/SKB/VI**

To access TIMATIC country information on Health and Visa regulations through the Computer Reservations System (CRS), type in the appropriate command line listed above.

St Kitts Tourism Authority
414 East 75th Street, Suite 5, 5th Floor, New York, NY 10021, USA
Tel: (212) 535 1234 *or* (800) 582 6208 (toll-free in USA).
Fax: (212) 734 6511.
E-mail: nyoffice@stkittstourism.kn
Website: www.stkitts-tourism.com
High Commission for the Eastern Caribbean States
130 Albert Street, Suite 700, Ottawa, Ontario K1P 5G4, Canada
Tel: (613) 236 8952. Fax: (613) 236 3042.
E-mail: echcc@travel-net.com
Office also in: Washington, DC.
Tourism Authority and Consulate of St Kitts & Nevis
133 Richmond Street W, Suite 311, Toronto, Ontario M5H 2L3, Canada
Tel: (416) 368 6707. Fax: (416) 368 3934.
E-mail: canada.office@stkittstourism.kn (tourism enquiries) *or* consulatenevis@rogers.com.
Website: www.stkitts-tourism.com
The Canadian High Commission in Bridgetown deals with enquiries relating to St Kitts & Nevis (see *Barbados* **section).**

General Information

AREA: St Kitts: 176.1 sq km (66.1 sq miles). **Nevis:** 93.3 sq km (36 sq miles). **Total:** 269.4 sq km (104 sq smiles).
POPULATION: 45,841 (official estimate 2000).
POPULATION DENSITY: 170.2 per sq km.
CAPITAL: Basseterre. **Population:** 12,605 (2001).
GEOGRAPHY: St Kitts (officially known as St Christopher) lies in the northern part of the Leeward Islands in the eastern Caribbean. The high central body of the island is made up of three groups of rugged volcanic peaks split by deep ravines. The vegetation on the central mountain range is rainforest, thinning higher up to dense bushy cover. From here the island's volcanic crater, Mount Liamuiga, rises to almost 1200m (4000ft). The foothills, particularly to the north, form a gently rolling landscape of sugar-cane plantations and grassland, while uncultivated lowland slopes are covered with thick tropical woodland and exotic fruits such as papaya, mangoes, avocados, bananas and breadfruit. To the southeast of the island, a low-lying peninsula, on which there are many excellent beaches, stretches towards Nevis.
Some 3km (2 miles) to the south and only minutes away by air or ferry across The Narrows channel is the smaller island of **Nevis**, which is almost circular in shape. The island is skirted by miles of silver-sand beaches, golden coconut groves and a calm, turquoise sea in which great brown pelicans dive for the rich harvest of fish. The central peak of the island, Nevis Peak, is 985m (3232ft) high and its tip is usually capped with white clouds. The mountain is flanked on the north and south sides by two lesser mountains, Saddle Hill and Hurricane Hill, which once served as look-out posts for Nelson's fleet. Hurricane Hill on the north side commands a view of St Kitts and Barbuda. On the island's west side, massed rows of palm trees form a coconut forest. There are pleasant coral beaches on the island's north and west coasts.
GOVERNMENT: Constitutional monarchy since 1983. Gained independence from the UK in 1983. **Head of State:** Queen Elizabeth II, represented locally by Governor General Sir Cuthbert Montroville Sebastian since 1996. **Head of Government:** Prime Minister Dr Denzil Douglas since 1995.
LANGUAGE: The official language is English.
RELIGION: Anglican and other Christian denominations.
TIME: GMT - 4.
ELECTRICITY: 230 volts AC, 60Hz (110 volts available in some hotels).
COMMUNICATIONS: Telephone: IDD is available. Country code: 1 869. Outgoing international code: 1 (Caribbean, Canada and the USA); 011 (elsewhere). **Mobile telephone:** TDMA network not compatible with GSM handsets. Handsets can be hired from the network provider, *C & W Caribbean Cellular* (website: www.caribcell.com). Unregistered roaming is available – visitors with TDMA handsets can make calls without registering, provided they can give a credit card number. **Fax:** This service is available to the public at the offices of *Cable & Wireless* (see below) and at some hotels. **Internet:** ISPs include *Cable & Wireless* (website: www.candw.kn). Public access is available at many hotels and the Internet kiosk at the *Cable & Wireless* offices in Basseterre, St Kitts. **Telegram:** Facilities are available at main hotels and at the offices of *Cable & Wireless* at Cayon Street, Basseterre and Main Street, Charlestown. Opening hours: Mon-Fri 0700-1900, Sat 0700-1400 and 1900-2000, Sun and public holidays 0800-1000 and 1900-2000. **Post:** Airmail to Western Europe takes five to seven days. Post office hours: Mon-Wed, Fri and Sat 0800-1500, Thurs 0800-1100. **Press:** There are three newspapers published in English: *The Democrat* and *The St Kitts and Nevis Observer* (weekly); and *The Labour Spokesman* (twice weekly).
Radio: BBC World Service (website: www.bbc.co.uk/worldservice) and Voice of America (website: www.voa.gov) can be received. From time to time the frequencies change and the most up-to-date can be found online.

Passport/Visa

	Passport Required?	Visa Required?	Return Ticket Required?
Full British	Yes	No	Yes
Australian	Yes	No	Yes
Canadian	1	No	Yes
USA	1	No	Yes
Other EU	Yes	No/2	Yes
Japanese	Yes	No	Yes

Note: *Regulations and requirements may be subject to change at short notice, and you are advised to contact the appropriate diplomatic or consular authority before finalising travel arrangements. Details of these may be found at the head of this country's entry. Any numbers in the chart refer to the footnotes below.*

PASSPORTS: Valid passport required by all except:
1. nationals of Canada and the USA with valid photo ID (for stays of up to six months).
VISAS: Required by all except the following for stays of up to 30 days:
(a) **2.** nationals of countries as indicated in the chart above, except nationals of Cyprus, Czech Republic, Estonia, Hungary, Latvia, Lithuania, Poland, Portugal, Slovak Republic and Slovenia who *do* require a visa;
(b) nationals of Commonwealth countries (except nationals of Cameroon, Mozambique, Namibia and South Africa who *do* require a visa). Nationals of Pakistan can obtain a visa on arrival for up to one month;
(c) nationals of Argentina, Bahrain, Bolivia, Brazil, Chile, Colombia, Costa Rica, Ecuador, Egypt, El Salvador, Guatemala, Honduras, Iceland, Israel, Jordan, Korea (Rep), Kuwait, Liechtenstein, Mexico, Monaco, Nicaragua, Norway, Oman, Panama, Paraguay, Peru, Qatar, Saudi Arabia, Switzerland, Taiwan (China), Turkey, United Arab Emirates, Uruguay and Venezuela;
(d) those continuing their journey to a third country by the same aircraft within 24 hours without leaving the airport.
Types of visa and cost: *Ordinary*. Cost depends on nationality of applicant.
Validity: Usually up to three months.
Application to: Consulate (or Consular section at Embassy or High Commission), *or* British Consulate in countries with no representation; see *Contact Addresses* section.
Working days required: Two to three.
Temporary residence: Apply to the Ministry of Home Affairs, Basseterre, St Kitts.

Money

Currency: Eastern Caribbean Dollar (EC$) = 100 cents. Notes are in denominations of EC$100, 50, 20, 10 and 5. Coins are in denominations of EC$1, and 25, 10, 5, 2 and 1 cents. US Dollars are also legal tender on the islands.
Note: The Eastern Caribbean Dollar is tied to the US Dollar.
Currency exchange: Most major currencies can be exchanged at banks on the islands.
Credit & debit cards: All major cards are widely accepted. Check with your credit or debit card company for details of merchant acceptability and other services that may be available. ATMs are widely available.
Travellers cheques: To avoid additional exchange rate charges, travellers are advised to take travellers cheques in US Dollars.
Currency restrictions: There are no restrictions on the import of local or foreign currency, provided declared on arrival. Export of local and foreign currency is limited to the amount imported and declared.
Exchange rate indicators: The following figures are included as a guide to the movements of the Eastern Caribbean Dollar against Sterling and the US Dollar:

Date	Feb '04	May '04	Aug '04	Nov '04
£1.00=	4.91	4.94	4.97	5.11
$1.00=	2.70	2.70	2.70	2.70

Banking hours: Mon-Thurs 0800-1500, Fri 0800-1700. The St Kitts and Nevis National Bank is open Sat 0830-1130.

Duty Free

The following goods may be imported into St Kitts & Nevis by travellers aged 18 and over without incurring customs duty:
200 cigarettes or 50 cigars or 225g of tobacco; 1.136l of wine or spirits.

Public Holidays

2005: Jan 1 New Year's Day. **Jan 2** Carnival Day. **Mar 25** Good Friday. **Mar 28** Easter Monday. **May 2** May Day. **May 16** Whit Monday. **Jun 12** Queen's Birthday. **Aug 1** August Monday. **Sep 19** Independence Day. **Dec 25** Christmas Day. **Dec 26** Boxing Day.
2006: Jan 1 New Year's Day. **Jan 2** Carnival Day. **Apr 14** Good Friday. **Apr 17** Easter Monday. **May 1** May Day. **Jun 5** Whit Monday. **Jun 12** Queen's Birthday. **Aug 7** August Monday. **Sep 19** Independence Day. **Dec 25** Christmas Day. **Dec 26** Boxing Day.

Health

	Special Precautions?	Certificate Required?
Yellow Fever	No	1
Cholera	No	No
Typhoid & Polio	No	N/A
Malaria	No	N/A

Note: *Regulations and requirements may be subject to change at short notice, and you are advised to contact your doctor well in advance of your intended date of departure. Any numbers in the chart refer to the footnotes below.*

1: A yellow fever vaccination certificate is required from travellers over one year of age arriving within six days from infected areas.
Food & drink: Mains water is chlorinated and safe. Bottled water is available and is advised for the first weeks of stay. Drinking water outside main cities and towns may be contaminated and sterilisation is advisable. Milk is pasteurised and dairy products are safe for consumption. Local meat, poultry, seafood, fruit and vegetables are generally considered safe to eat.
Other risks: *Hepatitis A* and *dengue fever* occur.
Health care: There are large general hospitals in Basseterre and Charlestown, and a smaller public hospital at Sandy Point, St Kitts. There are no private hospitals, but several doctors and dentists are in private practice. Payment upfront will often be required, therefore health insurance is advised.

Travel - International

AIR: Most flights not from the USA are via Antigua, Guadeloupe, Puerto Rico or St Maarten. *American Airlines* has regular flights from the USA. *LIAT (LI)* runs six flights a week from Antigua and offers day-trip charters to St Maarten (for duty-free shopping) and Antigua & Barbuda. Other airlines serving the islands include *American Eagle*, *Caribbean Star* and *Winair*.
Approximate flight times: From *London* to St Kitts is 10 hours, including stopover in Antigua. From *New York* to St Kitts is five hours.
International airports: *St Kitts (SKB)* (Robert Llewellyn Bradshaw, formerly Golden Rock Airport) is 3.2km (2 miles) from Basseterre on St Kitts. Airport facilities include tourist information, restaurant and duty free shop. Taxi fares are regulated; fares from the airport to Basseterre are approximately EC$17 (50 cents is charged on each additional piece of luggage over one).
Newcastle Airfield (NEV) is 11km (5 miles) from Charlestown on Nevis.
Departure tax: EC$54. Children under 12 years of age are exempt. An environment levy fee of EC$5 is also payable on departure.
SEA: Basseterre is a deep-water port capable of berthing ships up to 120m (400ft) and is regularly visited by cruise liners operated by *Carnival, Costa, Cunard, Holland America, Norwegian Cruise Lines, Princess Cruises, Regal Cruises, Royal Caribbean Cruises, Seabourn* and *Sun Cruises*. Regular ferry services operate from St Kitts to St Maarten.

Travel - Internal

AIR: *Nevis Express (VF)* runs a daily round-trip from St Kitts to Nevis (travel time - six minutes). They also offer charter flights to neighbouring islands (tel: 469 9755; website: www.nevisexpress.com).
SEA: There is a regular passenger ferry service between Basseterre (St Kitts) and Charlestown (Nevis) with two to four sailings daily (travel time – 45 minutes). For information, contact the General Manager, St Kitts & Nevis Port Authority, Basseterre.
ROAD: A good road network on both islands makes any area accessible within minutes. Driving is on the left. **Bus:** There are privately run bus services, which are comfortable and make regular, but unscheduled, runs between villages. **Taxi:** Services on both islands have set rates. A schedule of taxi rates is obtainable at the government headquarters. There is a 50 per cent surcharge 2200-0600. Taxi drivers expect a 10 per cent tip. **Car & moped hire:** A selection of cars and mopeds can be hired from several companies. It is best to book cars through the airline well in advance.

Documentation: Before driving any vehicle, including motorcycles, a local Temporary Driver's Licence must be obtained from the Police Traffic Department. This is readily issued on presentation of an International Driving Permit or national driving licence, and a fee of EC$125 for a licence valid for one year, or EC$62.50 for a licence valid for six months.
Travel times: The following chart gives travel times from **Basseterre**, St Kitts (in hours and minutes) to other major towns on the islands:

	Air	Road	Sea
Newcastle, Nevis	0.05	-	-
Charlestown, Nevis	-	-	0.45
Sandy Point	-	0.20	-
Brimstone Hill	-	0.35	-
Frigate Bay	-	0.10	-
Cockleshell Bay	-	0.35	-

Accommodation

In general, prices are considerably reduced in the low season (mid-April to mid-December). Group discounts and package rates are offered by most hotels on request. A government tax of 7 per cent is levied on all hotel bills and the hotels themselves add 10 per cent service charge, although this varies slightly between establishments.
HOTELS: There is a good range of hotels on the two islands, the majority being on St Kitts; most are small and owner-managed, offering a high standard of facilities and comfort. Many are converted from the great houses and sugar mills on the old estates. A full list of hotels can be obtained from the Embassy, High Commission *or* Tourist Board (see *Contact Addresses* section). The majority of hotels belong to the St Kitts & Nevis Hotel & Tourism Association (HTA), PO Box 438, Liverpool Row, Basseterre, St Kitts (tel: 465 5304; fax: 465 7746; e-mail: stkitnevhta@caribsurf.com). **Grading:** Though not a grading structure, many hotels in the Caribbean offer accommodation according to one of a number of plans: **FAP** is Full American Plan: room with all meals (including afternoon tea, supper, etc); **AP** is American Plan: room with three meals; **MAP** is Modified American Plan: breakfast and dinner included with the price of the room plus, in some places, British-style afternoon tea; **CP** is Continental Plan: room and breakfast only; **EP** is European Plan: room only.
GUEST HOUSES: There are several guest houses on both islands. A list is available from the St Kitts & Nevis Department of Tourism.
SELF-CATERING: There are villas and apartments available. A list and full details are available from the St Kitts & Nevis Department of Tourism.

Resorts & Excursions

ST KITTS

BASSETERRE: The picturesque capital, located near the seabord of the west coast, retains the flavour of both French and British occupation, and there are many Georgian buildings surrounding **Independence Square**. Other sights in or near the capital include: **The Circus**, the market, **St George's Church**, **Craft House**, **Brimstone Hill Fortress**, **Black Rocks**, **Romney Manor** and the **Caribelle Batik Factory**, the **Primate Research Centre**, **Frigate Bay Development**, the southeastern peninsula and **Mount Liamuiga**'s volcanic crater.
BRIMSTONE HILL: One of the most impressive New World forts, built on the peak of a sulphuric prominence, known as 'The Gibraltar of the West Indies'. It commands the southern approach to what were the sugar mill plains, and boasts a splendid view of the nearby islands of Saba and St Eustatius. Built in 1690, Brimstone was the scene of a number of Franco-British battles during the 18th century.
FRIGATE BAY: This is the main resort area on the island and has been designated a Tourist Area by the Government. It boasts two fine beaches, hotels, a golf course and a casino.

NEVIS

Since the 18th century, Nevis has been known as the 'Queen of the Caribbean', and over the last 100 years, the island has become one of the world's most exclusive resorts and spas. Most of the original plantation owners lived on the island and it became renowned as a centre of elegant and gracious living. Although Nevis has lived through an earthquake and a tidal wave, which is claimed to have buried the former capital, the island is still dotted, as is St Kitts, with fascinating old buildings and historic sites.
CHARLESTOWN: The capital is a delightful town, with weathered wooden buildings decorated like delicate gingerbread and great arches of brilliantly coloured bougainvillaea. The town contains several reminders of Nevisian history, such as the **Cotton Ginnery**, Alexander Hamilton's birthplace and museum, the **Court House**, the **War Memorial**, the **Alexandra Hospital** and the **Jewish Cemetery**. Some of the plantation houses have now been transformed into superb hotels, such as the famous *Nisbet*. Other sights in or near Charlestown include: **Nevis Philatelic Bureau**, the **Public Library**, the **Market**, **Bath House** (one of the oldest hotels in the Leeward Islands), Eva Wilkin's studio, Eden Brown's Great House, **Fig Tree Church**, **Nelson Museum**, **Bath Hot Springs** and the **Newcastle Pottery**.
ELSEWHERE: North of Charlestown is **Pinney's Beach**, one of the best on the island, an expanse of silver sand, backed by palm trees. Further north still, **Black Sand Beach** and **Hurricane Hill** offer excellent views of both St Kitts and Barbuda.

Sport & Activities

Watersports: Swimming is excellent; most hotels have freshwater pools and some have their own beaches. **Scuba-diving** and **snorkelling** are catered for and beach hotels generally have equipment. Several Basseterre skippers are equipped to take scuba parties. There are dozens of unexplored wrecks around the islands. **Sailing** boats can be hired from beach hotels, although Nevis has very limited facilities. Fast boats and **water-skiing** equipment are available for hire. **Fishing** trips can be organised. Deep-sea fishing is a speciality.
Other: An 18-hole international **golf** championship course is at Frigate Bay and a 9-hole course at Golden Rock, both on St Kitts. There is also an 18-hole championship golf course on Nevis. A number of **tennis** courts are available on both islands, and clubs welcome visitors. Day passes can be purchased. Many of the hotels have their own (mainly hard) tennis courts. Some courts are floodlit for evening play. **Horseriding** in the rainforest or on the beach can be arranged through hotels. There are several **hiking** trails leading into the mountains or through the rainforest. Local guides can be arranged through hotels. Other sports enjoyed and watched include **cricket** and **football**.

Social Profile

FOOD & DRINK: St Kitts & Nevis has built up a widely established reputation for fine food, a reputation which the local restauranteurs guard zealously. Restaurants specialise in Chinese, Continental, Creole, French, Indian and West Indian cuisine. Most restaurants in St Kitts offer a continental menu with island variations. Local dishes include roast suckling pig, spiny lobster, crab back and curries. Restaurants that cater more for locals also offer conch (curried, soused or in salad), turtle stews, rice and peas and goat's water (mutton stew). Christophine, yams, breadfruit and papaya are also served. Nevis is less grand and Charlestown's small restaurants cater more to Nevisians than visitors. Local specialities are native vegetable soup, lobster, mutton and beef. Fruit, including mangoes, papayas and bananas, is sold at the waterfront market.
The locally produced *CSR* (cane spirit) is excellent. A wide range of imported drinks is available.
NIGHTLIFE: Very low key. A number of hotels and inns have string or steel bands to dance to on Saturday nights in the peak season, and there is a disco called *J's Place* at the foot of the Brimstone Hill Fortress in St Kitts. *Reflections Night Club*, also in St Kitts, is open until the small hours. St Kitts has two casinos in Frigate Bay, complete with slot machines, roulette wheels and blackjack tables. In Nevis, *Club Trenim* is recommended. Otherwise, entertainment centres around the pleasant bars of the inns and hotels.
SHOPPING: Local crafts include carvings, batik, wall hangings, leather art and coconut work. Local textiles and designs are also available. Stamp collectors should note the excellent Philatelic Bureaux in Basseterre and Charlestown. Duty free shopping is relatively new to St Kitts and, as yet, only a few shops feature imported merchandise at substantial savings. Nevis' hot pepper sauce, ranked among the Caribbean's best, is a good take-home item and can be bought at the Main Street grocery in Charlestown. Friday and Saturday are the busy market days, and visitors should not miss the chance to witness this abundance of exotic food stalls, accompanied by lively local chatter. **Shopping hours:** Mon-Sat 0830-1200 and 1300-1600; some shops close early on Thursday.
SPECIAL EVENTS: Festivals in St Kitts & Nevis culminate in the annual week-long carnival over Christmas, featuring floats, calypso competitions, masked parades and house parties. Visitors are encouraged to take part. The following is a selection of special events occurring in St Kitts and Nevis in 2005:
Jan 1-2 *Carnival*, Basseterre. **Mar** *Inner-City Festival*, Molineaux. **Apr 14-17** *Easter Celebrations*. **May** *Green Valley Festival*, Cayon. **Jun** *Caribbean Offshore Race*. **Jul** *St Kitts Football Festival*. **Aug 1** *Culturama Day*, Nevis. **Sep** *Newtown Fest*; *Festival de Capisterre*, Newtown Ground. **Sep 19** *Independence Day* (parades, street festivities and dancing). **Oct** *St Kitts Tourism Week* (Caribbean tourism pageant, ocean festival and steel band concerts); *Oceanfest* (sunfish racing, fishing tournament, food, music and dancing). **Nov** *Guy Fest*, Old Town Road. **Dec** *National Carnival* (including Calypso King and Queen competitions, Miss St Kitts beauty pageant and various other youth talent contests). **Dec 26** *Jouvert Morning* (carnival at 0400).
SOCIAL CONVENTIONS: Commercialisation has not yet taken over and the easygoing, quiet way of life of the local people remains almost unspoiled. All visitors to the islands are cordially welcomed; marriages are valid after two days' residence. Islanders maintain traditions of calypso dancing and music and this can be seen particularly during the summer months. Dress is informal at most hotels. Beach attire is not appropriate for around town, in shops or in restaurants. For more formal occasions and functions, a lightweight suit and tie is recommended. **Tipping:** 10 per cent service charge is added to hotel bills. In restaurants, leave 10 to 15 per cent and tip taxi drivers 10 per cent of the fare.

Business Profile

ECONOMY: St Kitts & Nevis has an agricultural economy, the mainstay of which is the sugar industry. As the world sugar price has been very low in the past few years and several sugar crops have been badly damaged by hurricanes and other adverse climatic conditions, St Kitts & Nevis has come to rely on regular injections of foreign aid to prevent economic collapse. The Government has responded by trying to broaden the base of the economy; bananas, yams and sweet potatoes are now important crops and the cultivation of rice and coffee is developing. Fishing is also growing in commercial importance. Manufacturing is dominated by sugar products, and textiles and drinks are also produced. A thriving electronics and data-processing sector is the principal success story from the Government's diversification policy, as is tourism which is developing rapidly, particularly on Nevis, and now brings about US$70 million a year into the economy. More recently, and especially on Nevis, an 'offshore' financial services industry has developed: there are now over 10,000 foreign businesses registered on the island and the government has been obliged to meet new international standards regarding the investigation of money-laundering. The UK and the USA are the islands' main trading partners, as well as other Caribbean states.
BUSINESS: Businesswear for men usually consists of a short- or long-sleeved shirt and tie, or open-neck tunic shirt or, alternatively, safari-type suits. **Office hours:** Mon-Fri 0800-1200 and 1300-1600.
COMMERCIAL INFORMATION: The following organisation can offer advice: St Kitts & Nevis Chamber of Industry and Commerce, PO Box 332, Horsford Road, Fortlands, Basseterre (tel: 465 3967/2980; fax: 465 4490; e-mail: sknchamber@caribsurf.com; website: www.stkittsnevischamber.org).
CONFERENCES/CONVENTIONS: For further information on conferences and convention possibilities, contact the St Kitts & Nevis Hotel & Tourism Association (for address, see *Accommodation* section) *or* St Kitts & Nevis Department of Tourism (see *Contact Addresses* section).

Climate

Hot and tropical climate tempered by trade winds throughout most of the year. The driest period is from January to April and there is increased rainfall in summer and towards the end of the year. The volume of rain varies according to altitude; rain showers can occur throughout the year. The average annual rainfall is about 125cm (50 inches) to 200cm (80 inches) with a wetter season from May to October. Like the other Leeward Islands, St Kitts lies in the track of violent tropical hurricanes which are most likely to develop between August and October.
Required clothing: Tropical lightweights, with light rainwear advisable all year round.

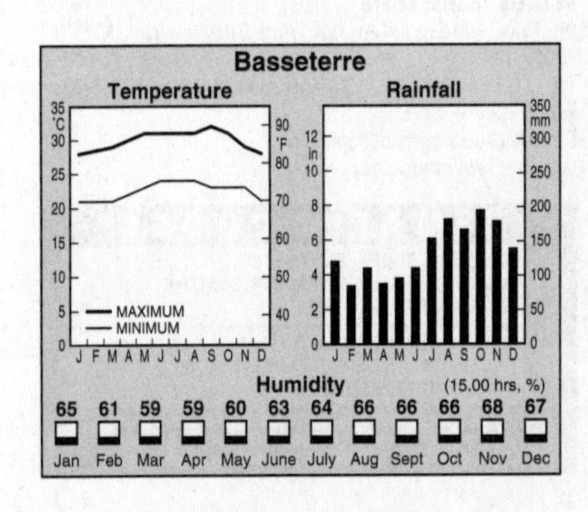

St Lucia

LATEST TRAVEL ADVICE CONTACTS

British Foreign and Commonwealth Office
Tel: (0870) 606 0290 Website: www.fco.gov.uk

US Department of State
Website: http://travel.state.gov/travel

Canadian Department of Foreign Affairs and Int'l Trade
Tel: (1 800) 267 8376 Website: www.dfait-maeci.gc.ca

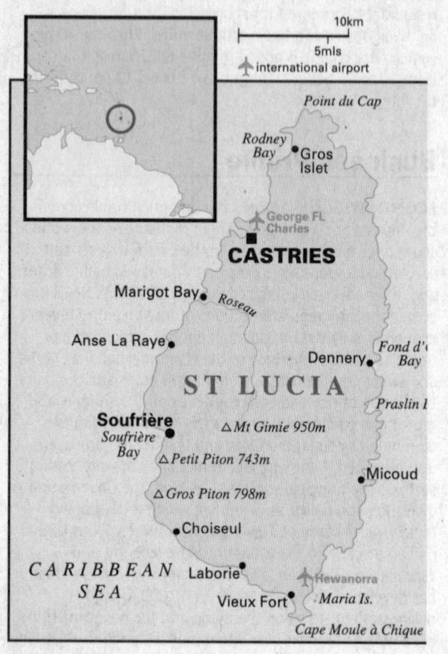

Location: Eastern Caribbean, Windward Islands.

Country dialling code: 1 758.

St Lucia Tourist Board
PO Box 221, Top Floor, Sureline Building, Vide Boutielle Highway, Castries, St Lucia
Tel: 452 4094. Fax: 453 1121.
E-mail: slutour@candw.lc
Website: www.stlucia.org

St Lucia High Commission
1 Collingham Gardens, London SW5 0HW, UK
Tel: (020) 7370 7123. Fax: (020) 7370 1905.
Opening hours: Mon-Thurs 0930-1730, Fri 0930-1700.

St Lucia Tourist Board
1 Collingham Gardens, London SW5 0HW, UK
Tel: (0870) 900 7697. Fax: (020) 7341 7001.
E-mail: sltbinfo@stluciauk.org
Website: www.stlucia.org

British High Commission
Street address: Francis Compton Building, Waterfront, Castries, St Lucia
Postal address: PO Box 227, Castries, St Lucia
Tel: 452 2484/5.
Fax: 453 1543.
E-mail: britishhc@candw.lc *or* postmaster.castries@fco.gov.uk

Embassy of St Lucia
3216 New Mexico Avenue, NW, Washington, DC 20016, USA
Tel: (202) 364 6792.
Fax: (202) 364 6723.
E-mail: eofsaintlu@aol.com
Website: www.sluonestop.com

St Lucia Tourist Board
9th Floor, 800 Second Avenue, Suite 910, New York, NY 10017, USA
Tel: (212) 867 2950 *or* (800) 456 3984 (toll-free in USA).
Fax: (212) 867 2795.
E-mail: stluciatourism@aol.com
Website: www.stlucia.org

TIMATIC CODES

Health	AMADEUS: **TI-DFT/SLU/HE** GALILEO/WORLDSPAN: **TI-DFT/SLU/HE** SABRE: **TIDFT/SLU/HE**
Visa	AMADEUS: **TI-DFT/SLU/VI** GALILEO/WORLDSPAN: **TI-DFT/SLU/VI** SABRE: **TIDFT/SLU/VI**

To access TIMATIC country information on Health and Visa regulations through the Computer Reservations System (CRS), type in the appropriate command line listed above.

The Embassy of the United States in Bridgetown deals with enquiries relating to St Lucia (see *Barbados* **section).**

St Lucia Tourist Board
8 King Street East, Suite 700, Toronto, Ontario M5C 1B5, Canada
Tel: (416) 362 4242 *or* (800) 869 0377 (toll-free in Canada).
Fax: (416) 362 7832.
E-mail: sltbcanada@aol.com
Website: www.stlucia.org

High Commission for the Eastern Caribbean States
130 Albert Street, Suite 700, Ottawa, Ontario K1P 5G4, Canada
Tel: (613) 236 8952. Fax: (613) 236 3042.
E-mail: echcc@travel-net.com

The Canadian High Commission in Bridgetown deals with enquiries relating to St Lucia (see *Barbados* **section).**

Credit: © St Lucia Tourist Board

General Information

AREA: 616.3 sq km (238 sq miles).
POPULATION: 155,996 (official estimate 2000).
POPULATION DENSITY: 253.1 per sq km.
CAPITAL: Castries. **Population:** 62,967 (official estimate 2000).
GEOGRAPHY: St Lucia is the second-largest of the Windward Islands. It has some of the finest mountain scenery in the West Indies, rich with tropical vegetation. For such a small island, 43km (27 miles) by 23km (14 miles), St Lucia has a great variety of plant and animal life. Orchids and exotic plants of the genus *anthurium* grow wild in the rainforests and the roadsides are covered with many colourful tropical flowers. Flamboyant trees spread shade and blossom everywhere. Indigenous wildlife includes a species of ground lizard unique to St Lucia, and the *agouti* and the *manicou*, two rodents, common throughout the island. The Amazona versicolor parrot is another, though more elusive, inhabitant of the deep interior rainforest. The highest peak is Mount Gimie at 950m (3117ft). Most spectacular are Gros Piton and Petit Piton, ancient, volcanic forest-covered cones which rise out of the sea on the west coast. Soufri (vents in a volcano which exude hydrogen sulphide, steam and other gases) and boiling waterpools can be seen here. The mountains are intersected by short rivers which in some areas form broad fertile valleys. The island has excellent beaches and is surrounded by a clear, warm sea.
GOVERNMENT: Constitutional monarchy. Gained independence from the UK in 1979. **Head of State:** Queen Elizabeth II, represented locally by Governor General Calliopa Pearlette Louisy since 1997. **Head of Government:** Prime Minister Kenny Davis Anthony since 1997.
LANGUAGE: English and local French *patois*.
RELIGION: 78 per cent Roman Catholic; also Anglican, Methodist, Seventh Day Adventist and Baptist.
TIME: GMT - 4. **ELECTRICITY:** 220 volts AC, 50Hz.
COMMUNICATIONS: Telephone: IDD is available. Country code: 1 758. Outgoing international code: 011
Mobile telephone: Network operated by *AT&T, Cable & Wireless* and *Digicell*. All phones should now work on the island, although visitors should ensure their telephone settings are correct before travelling. **Internet:** ISPs include *Cable & Wireless* (website: www.candw.lc). Public access is available at the Internet kiosk at Pointe Seraphine. Three Internet cafes are also run by *Cable & Wireless*. **Fax:** Available to the public in Castries at the offices of *Cable & Wireless* and at some hotels. **Telegram:** : Facilities limited to main towns, hotels and *Cable & Wireless*. **Post:** Airmail to Western Europe takes up to one week. *Poste Restante* mail will only be released on presentation of suitable identification. Post office hours: Mon-Fri 0800-1630, Sat 0900-1330. **Press:** The main newspapers are *The Crusader, The Mirror, The Star* and *The Voice of St Lucia. Visions Magazine* is published by the St Lucia Hotel and Tourism Association.
Radio: BBC World Service (website: www.bbc.co.uk/worldservice) and Voice of America (website: www.voa.gov) can be received. From time to time the frequencies change and the most up-to-date can be found online.

Passport/Visa

	Passport Required?	Visa Required?	Return Ticket Required?
Full British	Yes	No/1	Yes
Australian	Yes	2	Yes
Canadian	1	No/1	Yes
USA	1	No/1	Yes
Other EU	Yes	2	Yes
Japanese	Yes	No	Yes

Note: Regulations and requirements may be subject to change at short notice, and you are advised to contact the appropriate diplomatic or consular authority before finalising travel arrangements. Details of these may be found at the head of this country's entry. Any numbers in the chart refer to the footnotes below.

PASSPORTS: Valid passport required by all except:
(a) **1.** nationals of Canada and the USA with valid proof of identity and holding return/onward tickets (for stays of up to six months);
(b) nationals of OECS countries (Antigua & Barbuda, Dominica, Grenada, St Kitts & Nevis and St Vincent & the Grenadines) with a valid National Identity Card;
(c) expired passports accompanied by photo ID issued to nationals of Antigua & Barbuda, Dominica, Grenada, St Kitts & Nevis, St Lucia, St Vincent & the Grenadines and the UK (regardless of endorsement in passport).
VISAS: Required by all except the following:
(a) nationals of Antigua & Barbuda, Dominica, Grenada, St Kitts & Nevis and St Vincent & the Grenadines, at the discretion of the immigration officer upon arrival;
(b) **1.** nationals of Canada, Hong Kong (SAR), the UK and USA for a maximum stay of six weeks;
(c) **2.** nationals of EU countries for stays of up to 28 days except nationals of Czech Republic, Estonia, Hungary, Latvia, Lithuania and Slovak Republic who *do* require a visa;
(d) nationals of American Samoa, Andorra, Argentina, Bermuda, Botswana, Brazil, Brunei, Caricom Member States (except Haiti who have temporary visa restrictions), Cayman Islands, Chile, Costa Rica, Cuba, Ecuador, El Salvador, Faroe Island, French Guiana, French Polynesia, Gibralter, Greenland, Guadeloupe, Guam, Honduras, Israel, Ivory Coast, Korea, Lesotho, Malaysia, Marshall Islands, Martinique, Mayotte, Micronesia, Monaco, Netherlands Antilles, New Caledonia, New Zealand, Northern Marina Islands, Norway, Peru, Reunion, St Helena, St Martin, St Marteen, St Pierre & Miquelon, San Marino, Switzerland, Taiwan, Turks & Caicos Islands, Venezuela and Western Samoa;
(e) those continuing their journey to next destination by the same aircraft without leaving the airport.
Types of visa and cost: *Single-entry Tourist*. Cost depends on nationality of the applicant, but is usually about £35. Postal applications must include an additional £5 postage fee.
Validity: Up to six weeks. Extensions to some visas can be made at the Immigration Department in St Lucia.
Application to: Consulate (or Consular section at Embassy or High Commission); see *Contact Addresses* section.
Application requirements: (a) Valid passport. (b) Completed application form. (c) Passport-size photo. (d) Sufficient funds to cover duration of stay and proof of accommodation. (e) Fee, payable by cash (postal order for postal applications). (f) Valid return or onward ticket.
Working days required: Two to three, depending on nationality of applicant.
Temporary residence: Refer applications or enquiries to Consulate, Embassy or High Commission. Processed through the Ministry of Foreign Affairs, Castries.

Money

Currency: Eastern Caribbean Dollar (EC$) = 100 cents. Notes are in denominations of EC$100, 50, 20, 10 and 5. Coins are in denominations of EC$1, and 50, 25, 10, 5, 2 and 1 cents. US Dollars are also accepted as legal tender.
Note: The Eastern Caribbean Dollar is tied to the US Dollar.
Currency exchange: US Dollars ensure a better exchange rate. Most banks have ATMs.
Credit & debit cards: American Express, Diners Club, MasterCard and Visa are all widely accepted. Check with your credit or debit card company for details of merchant acceptability and other services which may be available.
Travellers cheques: Accepted. US Dollar cheques preferred and will help to avoid additional exchange rate charges.
Currency restrictions: There are no restrictions on the import and export of local or foreign currency.
Exchange rate indicators: The following figures are included as a guide to the movements of the Eastern

Caribbean Dollar against Sterling and the US Dollar:

Date	Feb '04	May '04	Aug '04	Nov '04
£1.00=	4.91	4.71	4.97	5.11
$1.00=	2.70	2.67	2.70	2.70

Banking hours: Generally Mon-Thurs 0830-1500, Fri 0830-1700. Some banks open Sat 0800-1200.

Duty Free

The following items may be imported into St Lucia without incurring customs duty:
200 cigarettes or 250g tobacco products; 50 cigars; 1l of alcoholic beverage.

Public Holidays

2005: Jan 1-2 New Year. **Feb 22** Independence Day. **Mar 25** Good Friday. **Mar 27** Easter Sunday. **Mar 28** Easter Monday. **May 1** Labour Day. **May 16** Whit Monday. **May 26** Corpus Christi. **Aug 1** Emancipation Day. **Oct 3** Thanksgiving Day. **Dec 13** Festival of Lights and Renewal. **Dec 25-26** Christmas.
2006: Jan 1-2 New Year. **Feb 22** Independence Day (25th Anniversary). **Apr 14** Good Friday. **Apr 16** Easter Sunday. **Apr 17** Easter Monday. **May 1** Labour Day. **Jun 5** Whit Monday. **Jun 15** Corpus Christi. **Aug 1** Emancipation Day. **Oct 2** Thanksgiving Day. **Dec 13** Festival of Lights and Renewal. **Dec 25-26** Christmas.

Health

	Special Precautions?	Certificate Required?
Yellow Fever	No	1
Cholera	No	No
Typhoid & Polio	No	N/A
Malaria	No	N/A

Note: *Regulations and requirements may be subject to change at short notice, and you are advised to contact your doctor well in advance of your intended date of departure. Any numbers in the chart refer to the footnotes below.*

1: A yellow fever vaccination certificate is required from travellers over one year of age arriving within six days from infected areas.
Food & drink: Mains water is normally chlorinated, and whilst relatively safe, may cause mild abdominal upsets. Bottled water is available and is advised for the first few weeks of the stay. Milk is pasteurised and dairy products are safe for consumption. Local meat, poultry, seafood, fruit and vegetables are generally considered safe to eat.
Other risks: *Hepatitis A* occurs along with *dengue fever, cutaneous leishmaniasis* and *lymphatic filariasis. Bilharzia* (schistosomiasis) is present. Avoid swimming and paddling in fresh water; swimming pools which are well chlorinated and maintained are safe. Immunisation against *hepatitis B, diphtheria* and *tuberculosis* is sometimes advised.
Health care: Costs of health care are high and full health insurance is essential.

Travel - International

AIR: St Lucia is served by *Air Canada (AC), Air Jamaica, American Airlines, American Eagle, BMI, British Airways (BA), British West Indies Airways (BWIA), Caribbean Star, LIAT* and *Virgin Atlantic.*
Approximate flight times: From Castries to *London* is eight hours, to *Los Angeles* is nine hours, to *New York* is four hours and to *Singapore* is 33 hours.
International airports: *George F L Charles (SLU)* (services inter-island connections and small aircraft from Puerto Rico only) and *Hewanorra (UVF)*, 3km (2 miles) and 67km (42 miles) from Castries respectively. Taxis or buses are available from both airports to Castries. Airport facilities at George F L Charles include a bar/restaurant, a shop and car hire; at Hewanorra there is a bar/restaurant, left luggage and lockers, shops, tourist information, outgoing duty-free shop and car hire (*Avis, Budget, Dollar, Hertz* and *National*).
Departure tax: EC$54. Transit passengers and children under 12 years of age are exempt.
SEA: *L'Express des Iles*, a high-speed catamaran service, operates between St Lucia and Dominica, calling at Martinique and Guadaloupe (travel times: St Lucia–Martinique – one hour 20 minutes; Martinique–Dominica – one hour 20 minutes). St Lucia is also served by a number of cruise lines as well as local passenger/freight lines. Lines include *Cunard, Ocean Village* and *Princess Cruises*. The main ports are Castries, Soufrière and Vieux Fort. The duty-free port at Pointe Seraphine offers two-berth cruise ship facilities, duty-free shopping, restaurants and bars; it may be visited by anyone, although a valid passport and an airline ticket are required to make duty free purchases.

Travel - Internal

AIR: Helicopter transfers operate between George F L Charles and Hewanorra airports.
SEA: Boat charters are easily available at Castries, Marigot Bay and Rodney Bay.
ROAD: All major centres are served by a reasonably good road network. The main cross-island route runs from Vieux Fort in the south of the island to Castries in the north. Traffic drives on the left. Seat belts must be worn at all times. Drinking and driving is against the law. **Car hire:** Cars can be obtained either in Castries, Soufrière and Vieux Fort, or through hotels. Hotels and local tour operators run coach trips for groups. **Documentation:** On presentation of a national driving licence or International Driving Permit, a local licence will be issued by the police or car hire firm. **Bus:** Services connect rural areas with the capital. There is a good service from Castries to Gros Islet in the north of the island with buses departing every 30 minutes during the day. **Taxi:** Hiring a taxi is easy and cheap, with standard trips having fixed rates which should nevertheless be agreed upon beforehand. Tipping is unnecessary.

Accommodation

HOTELS: St Lucia has a range of accommodation to suit every taste and every budget, from deluxe hotels to self-catering apartments. All-inclusive holidays are also proving very popular and several hotels now offer this option. Most hotels provide some form of entertainment in the evening, from calypso music to the ever-popular limbo dancing. Details are available from hotels' reservation desks. A government tax of 8 per cent and service charge of 10 to 15 per cent are added to bills. A leaflet giving hotel and guest house rates is produced by the St Lucia Hotel and Tourism Association, PO Box 545, Castries (tel: 452 5978; fax: 452 7967; e-mail: slhta@candw.lc). The Tourist Board also publishes an accommodation rate sheet. **Grading:** Many hotels in the Caribbean offer accommodation according to one of a number of plans. **AP** is American Plan: room with three meals; **MAP** is Modified American Plan: breakfast and dinner included with the price of the room plus, in some places, British-style afternoon tea; **CP** is Continental Plan: room and breakfast only; **EP** is European Plan: room only. Hotels in St Lucia are also graded on a scale from **3 to 5 stars**.
GUEST HOUSES: A wide range is available; some offer self-catering facilities.

Resorts & Excursions

St Lucia is a beautiful volcanic island with lush rainforests, undulating agricultural land and unspoilt beaches. There is still considerable British and French influence felt on the island. There are several trips and tours available to enable visitors to experience the island. Boat trips offer the visitor an exhilarating day viewing the island from the sea and possibly weighing anchor to picnic at an interesting location. Alternative means of transport include brigs, catamarans and private yachts.
CASTRIES: Castries is one of the most beautifully situated Caribbean cities. Surrounded by hills, its large, safe harbour at the head of a wide bay is a constant hive of activity. Castries is a major port of call for cruise ships, which dock at Pointe Seraphine. The spacious **Derek Walcott Square** features the 19th-century **Catholic Cathedral** standing in the shade of a 400-year-old samaan tree. There is also a colourful, bustling market. **Morne Fortune**, 'hill of good luck', affords the visitor the chance to inspect the fortification which defends Castries. It also provides a magnificent panorama of the city and the surrounding area.
THE NORTH: Gros Islet, on the northwest coast of the island, stages a street party every Friday. Nearby **Pigeon Island National Landmark** has a small museum telling the history of the island. It was from here that Admiral Rodney set sail in 1782 and destroyed the French Fleet in one of the most decisive engagements in European history. This end of the island is now being developed as a centre for tourism. **Anse La Raye**, on the west coast south of Castries, is a colourful fishing village where locals make boats from gum trees; every Friday evening brings the *Friday Night Fish Fry BBQ*. **Marigot Bay**, also on the west coast, is a secluded, palm-fringed yachtsman's paradise. Above Marigot Bay lies **Cul de Sac**, an area of three large banana plantations. From above, they look like gently moving oceans of green leaves. It was here that the original *Dr Doolittle* was filmed.
SOUFRIÈRE: Soufrière is the second-largest settlement on the island and takes its name from the volcano. This deep-water port stands at the foot of two extinct volcanoes, the **Pitons**. Rising to 798m (2619ft) above sea level, these are probably St Lucia's most famous landmarks. The town itself is typically West Indian, a cluster of brightly painted arcaded buildings set hard against the jungle.
THE SOUTH: The road between Soufrière and Fond St Jacques runs eastwards through the rainforest; here are the **Diamond Waterfalls** and **Sulphur Springs** - St Lucia's 'drive-in volcano'.
The picturesque little villages of **Choiseul** and **Laborie** are surrounded by splendid vegetation. The **Morne Coubaril Estate** is also worth a visit.
On the east of the island, the headlands project into the ocean; a visit to the fishing villages of **Dennery** and **Micoud** is highly recommended.

Credit: © St Lucia Tourist Board

Sport & Activities

Watersports: St Lucia is one of the world's breeziest places, where the trade winds blow in from the sea to the southern shore. The sandy beach of *Anse de Sable* offers ideal **windsurfing** conditions for both novice and expert. The west coast, too, offers a selection of resorts and hotels geared to the special needs of the active watersports enthusiast, while elsewhere on the island guests can enjoy **water-skiing** or **scuba-diving**. Enthusiasts' equipment can be accommodated by *British Airways, Virgin Atlantic* and *BWIA*, with windsurfers' boards carried as excess baggage and charged according to size. All west coast beaches have good **swimming**. The Atlantic coast has rugged surf and is not recommended to anyone with little experience and ability, and even an extremely proficient swimmer should not go unaccompanied.
Sailing: Hotels offer hobbycats, dinghies and small speedboats by the hour or half-day; cost is dependent on the board basis of your hotel. From *Marigot Bay* and *Rodney Bay*, the more experienced sailor can hire a variety of craft from comparatively basic, small yachts to larger 12m (40ft) and 18m (60ft) vessels, with crew if required. Tour operators can also arrange for stays of a week or more on the island to be coupled with a 'free floating' holiday on board a chartered yacht visiting the neighbouring islands.
Nature trails and hikes: *St Lucia Forestry Department* and the *National Trust* organise a variety of rainforest, mountain and plantation walks. Local guides are available to help **climbers** tackle the Pitons. The main areas designated for **birdwatching** are the *Bois d'Orange Swamp, Boriel's Pond* and the *Rain Forest*. Arrangements can be made through the St Lucia Forestry Department.
Other: The *International Riding Stables* in Gros Islet offer fully insured **horseriding** for all levels. Another facility, *Trims Riding School*, is located at Cas en Bas.
There are **golf** courses at *Cap Estate*, the northern tip of the island, and at La Toc. All the main hotels have **tennis** courts and arrangements can be made through hotels to play at St Lucia Tennis Club. Sea **fishing** trips are possible, fishing for barracuda, mackerel, kingfish and so on.

Social Profile

FOOD & DRINK: Most hotels have restaurants, in addition to a wide range in the major towns serving many different types of food. Waiter service is the norm. Local dishes include *langouste* (local lobster) cooked in a variety of ways, *lambi* (conch) and other fresh seafood, breadfruit and other local fruit and vegetables. The national dish is green fig and salt fish. Pepper pot and fried plantain are two local specialities worth trying. In general, the food is a combination of Creole with French and West Indian influences.
Many imported spirits are available, but the local drink is rum, often served in punch and cocktails. Caribbean beer, including the locally brewed *Piton* and *Heineken*, and plenty of delicious fresh fruit juices are also available.
NIGHTLIFE: Centres mainly in hotels and some restaurants. On Friday nights, the village of Gros Islet hosts a weekly 'jump up', popular with locals and visitors alike; Anse La Raye hold their *Friday Night Fish Fry BBQ*. Indies and *The Late Lime* are two of St Lucia's most popular nightclubs, both featuring live entertainment. During summer, there is little nightlife, but during the winter the resorts are lively, with plenty of local music and dance.
SHOPPING: Special purchases include unique batik and silkscreen designs made into shifts, sports shirts, table mats, cocktail napkins and shopping bags produced at a studio on the road between Castries and La Toc. Other craft outlets

A B C D E F G H I J K L M N O P Q R S T U V W X Y Z

sell locally made bowls, beads, straw hats, flour-sack shirts, sisal rugs, bags, sandals and woodwork. The recently expanded Pointe Seraphine features over 30 duty free shops (open seven days a week), bars and restaurants placed around an open piazza. Another duty free shopping complex has recently been opened at La Place Carenage. Duty free shopping is available to all visitors, provided they present their passport or airline ticket when purchasing goods. **Shopping hours:** Mon-Fri 0830-1230 and 1330-1600, Sat 0800-1200 and 0900-2100 in shopping malls.

SPECIAL EVENTS: Carnival and the jazz festival are calendar highlights, the latter regularly featuring internationally renowned artists such as Wynton Marsallis and Herbie Hancock. For more detailed information and a full list of events, contact the St Lucia Tourist Board. The following is a selection of special events occurring in St Lucia in 2005:

Jan 13-16 *St Lucia Regatta*. **Mar 26-27** *Caribbean Swim Championships*. **Apr 1** *Earth Day*. **Apr 29-May 8** *St Lucia Jazz Festival*. **Jun** *Festival of Comedy*. **Jun 18-19** *Carnival*. **Aug 30** *Feast of St. Rose De Lima (La Rose)*. **Oct 17** *Feast of La Marguerite*. **Dec** *Market Feast*.

SOCIAL CONVENTIONS: Some French influences still remain alongside the West Indian style of life. The people are friendly and hospitable, and encourage visitors to relax and enjoy their leisurely lifestyle. The *madras* and *foulards* are not often seen in towns, but are sometimes worn at festivals such as the *Feast of St Rose of Lima* in August. Casual wear is acceptable, although some hotels and restaurants encourage guests to dress for dinner. Beachwear should not be worn in towns. **Tipping:** An optional 10 to 15 per cent is sometimes added to bills.

Business Profile

ECONOMY: St Lucia's economy still relies heavily on agriculture but has broadened during the last 15 years. Light industry has been a key part of this process: the establishment of export processing zones and the successful attraction of foreign investment has created a healthy sector producing plastic, textiles and industrial gases and assembling electronic components. There is also a significant construction industry. The main agricultural exports are bananas, coconuts and cocoa. The Government is focusing its efforts on further diversification, principally directed towards the creation of a service sector based on tourism and financial services. It has also effected various deregulation measures and privatisation of a number of major state-owned enterprises. St Lucia is a member of the regional trading bloc, CARICOM, and the region's principal political co-operative grouping, the Organisation of Eastern Caribbean States. The USA and the UK are the main trading partners, the USA for imports and the UK for exports.

BUSINESS: Short- or long-sleeved shirt and tie or a light-weight suit are suitable for most business visits. **Office hours:** Mon-Fri 0800-1630, Sat 0830-1230.

COMMERCIAL INFORMATION: The following organisation can offer advice: St Lucia Chamber of Commerce, Industry and Agriculture, PO Box 482, Vide Bouteille, Castries (tel: 452 3165 *or* 453 1540; fax: 453 6907; e-mail: info@stluciachamber.org; website: www.stluciachamber.org).

CONFERENCES/CONVENTIONS: A number of hotels offer conference and back-up facilities, with seating for up to 200 persons. The St Lucia Tourist Board can provide details. For further information, contact Solar Tours and Travel, 20 Bridge Street, PO Box 1519, Castries (tel: 452 5898; fax: 452 5428; e-mail: solartours@candw.lc; website: www.solartoursandtravel.com).

Climate

Hot, tropical climate tempered by trade winds throughout most of the year. The driest period is from December to May and there is increased rainfall in summer and towards the end of the year (June to November).

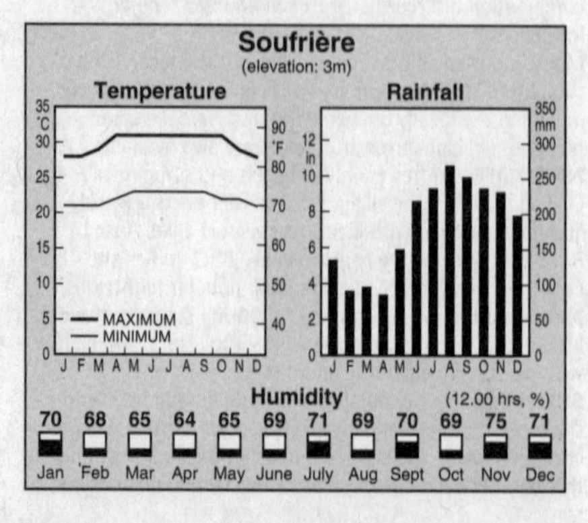

St Maarten

LATEST TRAVEL ADVICE CONTACTS

British Foreign and Commonwealth Office
Tel: (0870) 606 0290 Website: www.fco.gov.uk

US Department of State
Website: http://travel.state.gov/travel

Canadian Department of Foreign Affairs and Int'l Trade
Tel: (1 800) 267 8376 Website: www.dfait-maeci.gc.ca

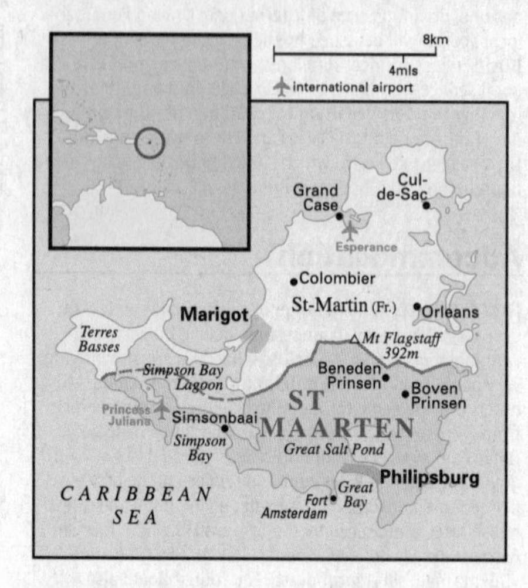

Location: Eastern Caribbean, Windward Islands.

Country dialling code: 599.

St Maarten is part of the Netherlands Antilles represented abroad by Royal Netherlands Embassies – see *The Netherlands* section.

St Maarten Tourist Bureau
Vineyard Park Building, WG Buncamper Road 33, Philipsburg, St Maarten
Tel: 542 2337. Fax: 542 2734.
E-mail: info@st-maarten.com Website: www.st-maarten.com

Office of the Minister Plenipotentiary of the Netherlands Antilles
PO Box 90706, Badhuisweg 173-175, 2597 JP The Hague, The Netherlands
Tel: (70) 306 6111. Fax: (70) 306 6110.

Caribbean Tourism Organisation
22 The Quadrant, Richmond, Surrey, TW9 1BP, UK
Tel: (020) 8948 0057. Fax: (020) 8948 0067.
E-mail: ctolondon@carib-tourism.com
Website: www.doitcaribbean.com *or* www.onecaribbean.org
Opening hours: Mon-Fri 0930-1730.

British Consulate
Jansofat 38, PO Box 3803, Curaçao, NA
Tel: (9) 747 3322. Fax: (9) 747 3330.
E-mail: britconcur@attglobal.net

Consulate General of the United States of America
JB Gorsiraweg 1, Willemstad, Curaçao, NA
Tel: (9) 461 3066. Fax: (9) 461 6489.
E-mail: cgcuracao@attglobal.net
Website: www.amcongencuracao.an

St Maarten Tourist Office
675 Third Avenue, Suite 1806, New York, NY 10017, USA
Tel: (212) 953 2084 *or* (800) 786 2278 (toll-free in Canada and USA). Fax: (212) 953 2145.
E-mail: info@st-maarten.com
Website: www.st-maarten.com

The Canadian Consulate for the Netherlands Antilles deals with enquiries relating to St Maarten (see *Curaçao* section).

St Maarten Tourist Office
c/o Melaine Communications Group, 703 Evans Avenue, Suite 106, Toronto, Ontario M9C 5E9, Canada
Tel: (416) 622 4300. Fax: (416) 622 3431.
E-mail: stmaarten@melainecommunications.com
Website: www.st-maarten.com

TIMATIC CODES

Health	AMADEUS: **TI-DFT/SXM/HE** GALILEO/WORLDSPAN: **TI-DFT/SXM/HE** SABRE: **TIDFT/SXM/HE**
Visa	AMADEUS: **TI-DFT/SXM/VI** GALILEO/WORLDSPAN: **TI-DFT/SXM/VI** SABRE: **TIDFT/SXM/VI**

To access TIMATIC country information on Health and Visa regulations through the Computer Reservations System (CRS), type in the appropriate command line listed above.

General Information

AREA: 34 sq km (16 sq miles).
POPULATION: 36,231 (1996).
POPULATION DENSITY: 1066 per sq km.
CAPITAL: Philipsburg.
GEOGRAPHY: Politically, St Maarten is one of three Windward Islands in the Netherlands Antilles, although geographically it is part of the Leeward Group of the Lesser Antilles, and not strictly an island – it occupies just one-third of an island otherwise under French control (the French sector is called St Martin), lying 8km (5 miles) south of Anguilla, 232km (144 miles) east of Puerto Rico and 56km (35 miles) due north of St Eustatius. St Maarten is the southern sector, an area of wooded mountains rising from white sandy beaches. To the west, the mountains give way to lagoons and salt flats.
For information on the French sector (St Martin), see the *Guadeloupe* section.
GOVERNMENT: Part of the Netherlands Antilles; dependency of The Netherlands since 1630. **Head of State:** Queen Beatrix of The Netherlands, represented locally by Governor General Frits Goedgedrag. **Head of Government:** Prime Minister Etienne Ys since 2004. The Netherlands Antilles consist of Bonaire, Curaçao, Saba, St Eustatius and St Maarten. The capital of the island group is Willemstad, Curaçao.
LANGUAGE: Dutch is the official language. Papiamento (a mixture of African, Dutch, English, Portuguese and Spanish) is the commonly used *lingua franca*. English and Spanish are also widely spoken.
RELIGION: Protestant, with Roman Catholic and Jewish minorities.
TIME: GMT - 4.
ELECTRICITY: 110/220 volts AC, 60Hz.
COMMUNICATIONS: Telephone: Fully automatic system with good IDD. Country code: 599. Outgoing international code: 00. Calls made through the operator are more expensive and include a 15 per cent tax. **Mobile telephone:** TDMA digital network operated by *Telcell* (e-mail: telcell@telem.an). Compatible with most US handsets but not with GSM handsets. Phone hire is available at Telcell's customer care centre in Philipsburg. Roaming exists (member of the Pan American Roaming Corporation). *East Caribbean* Cellular (website: www.eastcaribbeancellular.com) operates digital and analogue networks, system B. Networks cover Saba, St Barthelemy, St Maarten, St Martin and the surrounding waters. Most US handsets can be used, and can be activated with a temporary number before or after arrival on the island. Visitors should register online or dial 0 when in an ECC coverage area. Handsets can be hired from ECC in Philipsburg. **Fax:** Some hotels provide facilities. **Internet:** ISPs include *TelNet* (website: www.sintmaarten.net). **Telegram:** Services operated by *ANTELCOM* and *TELEM*. **Post:** Airmail to Western Europe takes four to six days, surface mail takes four to six weeks. **Press:** English-language dailies include the *Daily Herald* and *St Maarten Guardian*, published on St Maarten. Most other newspapers in the Netherlands Antilles are published in Dutch or Papiamento.
Radio: BBC World Service (website: www.bbc.co.uk/worldservice) and Voice of America (website: www.voa.gov) can be received. From time to time the frequencies change and the most up-to-date can be found online.

Passport/Visa

	Passport Required?	Visa Required?	Return Ticket Required?
Full British	Yes	1	Yes
Australian	Yes	2	Yes
Canadian	Yes	2	Yes
USA	Yes	2	Yes
Other EU	Yes	1/2	Yes
Japanese	Yes	2	Yes

Note: Regulations and requirements may be subject to change at short notice, and you are advised to contact the appropriate diplomatic or consular authority before finalising travel arrangements. Details of these may be found at the head of this country's entry. Any numbers in the chart refer to the footnotes below.

PASSPORTS: Passport or official travel documents valid for at least three months after intended return to home country required by all.
VISAS: Required by all except the following:
(a) **1.** nationals of Belgium, Bolivia, Burkina Faso, Chile, Costa Rica, Czech Republic, Ecuador, Germany, Hungary, Israel, Jamaica, Korea (Rep), Luxembourg, Malawi, Mauritius, The Netherlands, Niger, The Philippines, Poland, San Marino, Slovak Republic, Spain, Swaziland, Togo and the UK for touristic stays of up to three months;
(b) most nationals continuing to a third country within 24

hours by the same means of transportation and not leaving the airport and holding tickets with reserved seats and documents for their onward journey.
Note: (a) Nationals of the following countries must apply for a visa *before* entering the country even for touristic purposes: Albania, Bosnia & Herzegovina, Bulgaria, Cambodia, China (PR) (except Hong Kong SAR), CIS, Colombia, Cote d'Ivoire, Croatia, Cuba, Dominican Republic, Estonia, Ghana, Guinea-Bissau, Haiti, Kenya, Korea (DPR), Latvia, Libya, Lithuania, Macedonia (Former Yugoslav Republic of), Mali, Nigeria, Romania, Serbia & Montenegro and Vietnam. (b) **2.** All other nationals may enter without a visa for touristic stays of up to 14 days. (c) All stays can be extended locally by the same period that they are valid for.
Types of visa and cost: All visas, regardless of duration of stay or number of entries permitted on visa, cost €35.
Validity: Visas are generally issued for as long as duration of stay, up until a maximum 90 days from date of issue.
Application requirements: (a) Passport or equivalent travel document valid for a minimum of three months after intended return to home country. Passports should contain a blank visa page and endorse residence permit. For minors (18 years and under), an approval of both parents or legal guardians with a copy of each parent's/guardian's passport is required. If passport is new, the old passport must also be submitted. (b) One fully completed application form. (c) One recent passport-size photo per person endorsed on passport, with daytime phone number and address written clearly on the back. More photos may be required. (d) Fee, payable by postal order (to Royal Netherlands Embassy) or cash. Cheques are not accepted. Visa handling fees may be charged on applications handed in, regardless of outcome, depending on Embassy/Consulate. (e) Evidence of sufficient funds amounting to a minimum of £30 for each day of stay (cash not accepted), eg original bank statements, credit card with credit limit statement, traveller's cheques. (f) A recent and original letter from employer, stating commencement date, with last payslip. If self-employed, submit letter from solicitor, accountant or company house. If unemployed, submit social benefit booklet. If in education, submit a recent and original letter from school/college/university, confirming attendance. (g) Valid medical or travel insurance. *Tourist*: (a)-(g) and, (h) Invitation from family or proof of accommodation. (i) Return or onward ticket(s), plus necessary documents for returning to country of origin. *Business*: (a)-(g) and, (h) Invitation from company that you are visiting.
Application to: Nearest Embassy of the Kingdom of The Netherlands. All further information about visa requirements may be obtained from The Royal Netherlands Embassies which formally represent the Netherlands Antilles; see *Contact Addresses* in *The Netherlands* section.
Working days required: Applications should be lodged at least one month prior to departure.
Temporary residence: Enquire at the office of the Lieutenant Governor of the Island Territory of St Maarten, Philipsburg, St Maarten. In certain cases, Dutch Europeans may be permitted to reside in the Netherlands Antilles without having to apply for a residence permit. However, it is best to consult the nearest Dutch Embassy/Consulate in advance to ascertain whether this is applicable taking into consideration the individual circumstances of the traveller.

Money

Currency: Netherlands Antilles Guilder or Florin (ANG) = 100 cents. Notes are in denominations of ANG250, 100, 50, 25, 10 and 5. Coins are in denominations of ANG5 and 1, and 50, 25, 10, 5 and 1 cents. There are also a large number of commemorative coins which are legal tender. US Dollars are widely accepted, and prices are usually quoted in both Dollars and Guilders.
Note: The ANG is linked to the US Dollar.
Currency exchange: All major currencies can be exchanged at banks on the island.
Credit & debit cards: All major credit cards are widely accepted.
Travellers cheques: Widely accepted. To avoid additional exchange rate charges, travellers are advised to take travellers cheques in US Dollars.
Currency restrictions: There are no restrictions on the import and export of local or foreign currency, except the import and export of amounts of foreign currency exceeding NAG20,000 must be declared. The import of Dutch or Surinam silver coins is prohibited.
Exchange rate indicators: The following figures are included as a guide to the movement of the Netherlands Antilles Guilder against Sterling and the US Dollar:

Date	Feb '04	May '04	Aug '04	Nov '04
£1.00=	3.25	3.28	3.30	3.39
$1.00	1.79	1.79	1.79	1.79

Banking hours: Mon-Fri 0830-1130 and 1330-1630. Some banks are also open on Saturday.

Credit: © St Maarten Tourist Bureau

Duty Free

The following may be imported into St Maarten by tourists over 15 years of age only without incurring customs duty:
200 cigarettes or 50 cigars or 100 cigarillos or 250g tobacco; 2l of alcoholic beverages; gifts to a value of ANG100.
Restricted items: The import of souvenirs and leather goods from Haiti is not advisable.

Public Holidays

2005: Jan 1 New Year's Day. **Mar 25** Good Friday. **Mar 27-28** Easter. **Apr 29** Carnival. **Apr 30** Queen's Birthday. **May 1** May Day. **May 5** Ascension. **May 8** Celebration of WWII Victory. **Jul 21** Schoelcher Day (Abolition of Slavery). **Nov 1** All Saints' Day. **Nov 11** St Maarten Day. **Dec 15** Kingdom Day. **Dec 25** Christmas Day. **Dec 26** Boxing Day.
2006: Jan 1 New Year's Day. **Apr 14** Good Friday. **Apr 16-17** Easter. **Apr 29** Carnival. **Apr 30** Queen's Birthday. **May 1** May Day. **Jul 21** Schoelcher Day (Abolition of Slavery). **Nov 1** All Saints' Day. **Nov 11** St Maarten Day. **Dec 15** Kingdom Day. **Dec 25** Christmas Day. **Dec 26** Boxing Day.

Health

	Special Precautions?	Certificate Required?
Yellow Fever	No	1
Cholera	No	No
Typhoid & Polio	No	N/A
Malaria	No	N/A

Note: *Regulations and requirements may be subject to change at short notice, and you are advised to contact your doctor well in advance of your intended date of departure. Any numbers in the chart refer to the footnotes below.*

1: A yellow fever vaccination certificate is required from travellers over six months of age arriving within six days of leaving or transiting infected areas.
Food & drink: Water on the island is considered safe to drink. Bottled mineral water is widely available. Milk is pasteurised and dairy products are safe for consumption. Local meat, poultry, seafood, fruit and vegetables are generally considered safe to eat.
Other risks: *Hepatitis A* may occur. *Rabies* occurs.
Health care: There is one general hospital, the St Maarten Medical Centre in Cayhill. Medical care is good. Medical insurance is advised.

Travel - International

AIR: The national airline of the Netherlands Antilles is *ALM (LM)*. The government-owned *Winair (WIA)*, based at Princess Juliana Airport, has scheduled flights to the Lesser Antilles, as well as charter flights to destinations throughout the Eastern Caribbean. Other airlines serving St Maarten include *Air France, American Airlines, BWIA, KLM, LIAT* and *TWA*.
Approximate flight times: From St Maarten to *London* (via Amsterdam) is 12 to 14 hours, to *Los Angeles* is nine hours, to *New York* is four hours 10 minutes, to *St Croix* is 45 minutes and to *Singapore* is 33 hours (all depending on connections).
International airports: *Princess Juliana (SXM)*, 15km (9.5 miles) west of Philipsburg (travel time – 15 minutes), receives regular scheduled flights from other Caribbean islands, Europe and the USA. Taxis are available. Airport facilities include a bank, a restaurant, refreshments, duty free shopping and car hire. In order to protect the livelihood of local taxi drivers, cars hired at the airport are delivered to guests' hotels.
Esperance (SFG), this airport is in the French sector, and is smaller and not equipped for jets.
Departure tax: US$6 to Netherlands Antilles; US$20 for international departures. Prices vary according to the airport. Transit passengers and children under two years of age are exempt.
SEA: St Maarten is a leading port of call for cruise liners. Ferry services operate to Saba, St Barts and St Kitts & Nevis. Cruises operated by *Cunard, Holland America, Prince's Cruise* and *Royal Viking* regularly stop at Philipsburg.

Travel - Internal

SEA: Small boats may be chartered for fishing trips, scuba diving, water-skiing or visits to neighbouring islands. Daily ferries run to and from Anguilla, whilst a catamaran serves St Barts. There are marinas at Oyster Pond, Philipsburg and Simpson Bay Lagoon.
ROAD: Most roads are good. Traffic drives on the right. **Bus:** These run regularly between Philipsburg and Marigot. Minibuses serve the more popular destinations. **Taxi:** There are good services on the island running from the airport, main hotels and towns. Taxis do not have meters but fares are fixed. There is a 50 per cent surcharge after midnight. There is a taxi station at Wathey Square. **Car hire:** There are plenty of car hire firms in the city and at the airport. Chauffeur-driven cars are also available. **Documentation:** A national driving licence is acceptable.

Accommodation

HOTELS: St Maarten has long been a popular holiday destination and is well prepared for the year-round rush, with over 40 hotels offering a total of nearly 9000 beds. Luxury hotels are equipped with everything a visitor could ever need, from casinos to beauty parlours, and have extensive watersports facilities on the premises; even modest beachside establishments usually have their own swimming pool, restaurant and a few skis to lend. A government tax of 5 per cent is levied on all hotel bills and many hotels add a 10 to 15 per cent service charge. Some even add a further 10 per cent as an energy surcharge. For further information, contact the St Maarten Hospitality and Trade Association, PO Box 486, Philipsburg, St Maarten (tel: 542 0108; fax: 542 0107; e-mail: info@shta.com; website: www.shta.com).
GUEST HOUSES: Several guest houses cater for the less demanding; apartments and villas may be rented.

Resorts & Excursions

The most prominent physical feature in St Maarten is the thickly wooded **Mount Flagstaff**, an extinct volcano, but the most important is undoubtedly the excellent beach that follows the south and west coasts. Beach activities and shopping at duty free centres satisfy most tourists but there are several places of interest for the more enterprising visitor.
PHILIPSBURG: The only town of any size, Philipsburg is

A B C D E F G H I J K L M N O P Q R S T U V W X Y Z

Credit: © St Maarten Tourist Bureau

situated on a sand bar that separates **Great Salt Pond**, an *étang* or salt marsh, from the ocean. The entire town consists of two streets, *Voorstraat* (Front Street) and *Achterstraat* (Back Street), running the length of the isthmus and joined by short, narrow alleys. Land has been reclaimed from the marsh for the construction of a ring road; local wits have suggested that this should be called *Nieuwstraat* (New Street) to preserve the Dutch feel of the place. Indeed, many buildings do date back to the early colonial era, and despite the multitude of duty-free shops, Philipsburg retains a predominantly colonial atmosphere. The nine shingled churches and the **Queen Wilhelmina Golden Jubilee Monument** are worth seeing. Nearby is **Fort Amsterdam**, dating from the time of the earliest settlers. Inland are the picturesque ruins of several plantation mansions, set in the wooded hills around Mount Flagstaff, and the **Border Monument**, celebrating 300 years of co-operation between the French and the Dutch. Across the border (no passports are required) is the charming market town of **Marigot**. Small boats are available for various watersports and fishing.

Sport & Activities

Sailing: Enthusiasts are well catered for on St Maarten. The island is one of the Caribbean's leading sailing venues, hosting the *Heineken Regatta* every year. Accommodation for boats is often luxurious. The island has around 12 marinas in beautiful settings, which are well equipped, with some even providing cable television connections. All kinds of vessels can be rented at marinas, from motorboats and yachts to canoes. For those not wishing to pilot their own boat, charter companies offer day trips to other islands, and 'picnic sails' take visitors to secluded bays and nearby uninhabited islands.
Watersports: Expeditions for **deep sea fishing** can be arranged, with half- and full-day charters available all year round. Bareboat charters are also available. Conditions are excellent for **diving**, with coral reefs located close to the shore. One of the most popular dive sites is the wreck of HMS Proselyte, a British man-of-war which sank in 1801. There are also many good sites for **snorkelling**. **Bodyboarding** is popular. Equipment for the full range of watersports can be hired through hotels or at the numerous dive shops on the island.
Other: Both **cycling** and **mountain biking** can be pursued on the coastal road and along the trails around Paradise Peak. There are excellent views. Most large hotels have their own **swimming** pools and **tennis** courts. **Horseriding** expeditions can be arranged for riders of all levels.

Social Profile

FOOD & DRINK: St Maarten's cuisine is as varied as its history, combining Creole, Dutch, English, French and, more recently, international influences. Seafood is, of course, a speciality. Duty on alcohol (and other goods) is low and prices in St Maarten are as cheap as duty-free havens elsewhere. Most well-known brands are available.
NIGHTLIFE: Many of the restaurants and bars have live entertainment and dancing until the early hours. All the large hotels have casinos.
SHOPPING: There is a good range of high-quality duty-free shopping available in Philipsburg. **Shopping hours:** Mon-Sat 0800-1200 and 1400-1800.
SPECIAL EVENTS: For a complete list of events, contact the St Maarten Tourist Office (see Contact Addresses section). The following is a selection of special events occurring in St Maarten in 2005:
Jan 23 *Road Runners CARIB Smalta Fun Run*. **Feb 15-Mar 2** *French Carnival*. **Feb 27** *Bottom Braquette 100k Road Race*. **Mar 4-6** *Heineken Regatta*. **Apr 14-May 2** *Carnival*. **Apr 24-26** *DCME Meets SMART* (Dutch Caribbean Meets Europe, and 4th Annual St Maarten Regional Travel Tradeshow). **May 7-8** *FIAC Marci's Mega Gym Push Paddle*. **Jun 12** *FITAS Evian Netherland Antilles Olympic Distance Triathlon Championship*. **Jul 14** *Avenir Sportif Bastille Day Run*. **Sep 27** *World Tourism Day*. **Oct 1-2** *Eastern Caribbean Golf Championship*. **Nov** *St Maarten Music Festival*. **Dec** *Pan in Paradise, A Folkloric Steel Pan Concert*; *Annual Santa Scramble Golf Tournament*.
SOCIAL CONVENTIONS: Dutch customs are still important throughout the Netherlands Antilles, but tourism has brought increasing US influences and St Maarten is perhaps more easy-going than the southern islands. Dress is casual and lightweight cottons are advised, but it is common to dress up in the evening.
Tipping: Hotel bills always include a government tax of 5 per cent and often a service charge of 10 to 15 per cent. Elsewhere, 10 to 15 per cent is acceptable for doormen, waiters and bar staff. Taxi drivers do not expect a tip.

Business Profile

ECONOMY: Tourism dominates the economy; 70 per cent of all visitors to the Netherlands Antilles visit St Maarten, which results in around half a million tourists annually. Further investment in the tourism infrastructure is under way, including a new major port. Government service provides one of the few alternative sources of employment, while subsistence farming and fishing meet a fair proportion of the islands' domestic needs. St Maarten is the only island in the Antilles group apart from Curaçao which has achieved some success in developing an 'offshore' financial services industry. The Netherlands Antilles group enjoys Overseas Territory status at the EU and observer status at the Caribbean trading bloc CARICOM.
BUSINESS: Formality in business is expected in most of The Netherlands Antilles and lightweight tropical suits should be worn. Appointments should be made in advance and punctuality is taken very seriously. It is customary to shake hands. **Office hours:** Mon-Fri 0730-1200 and 1330-1630.
COMMERCIAL INFORMATION: The following organisation can offer advice: St Maarten Chamber of Commerce and Industry, PO Box 454, C A Cannegieter Street 11, Philipsburg (tel: 542 3590; fax: 542 3512; e-mail: info@sintmaartenchamber.org *or* consult@sintmaartenchamber.org; website: www.sintmaartenchamber.org).

Climate

Hot but tempered by cooling trade winds. The annual mean temperature is 27°C (80°F), varying by no more than two or three degrees throughout the year; average rainfall is 1772mm (70 inches).
Required clothing: Tropicals and cottons are worn throughout the year. Umbrellas or light waterproofs are advisable.

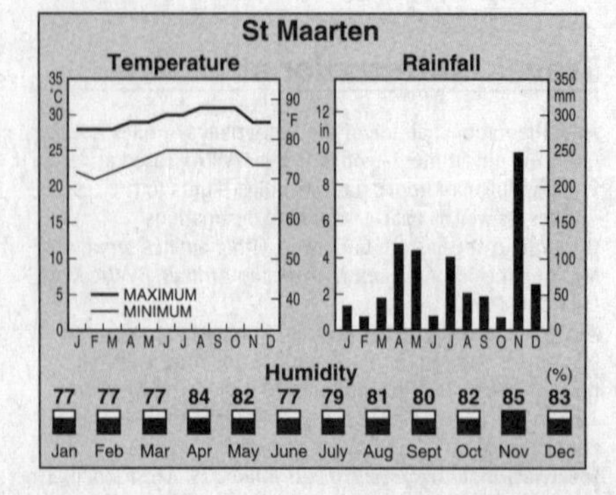

St Vincent & The Grenadines

LATEST TRAVEL ADVICE CONTACTS

British Foreign and Commonwealth Office
Tel: (0870) 606 0290 Website: www.fco.gov.uk
US Department of State
Website: http://travel.state.gov/travel
Canadian Department of Foreign Affairs and Int'l Trade
Tel: (1 800) 267 8376 Website: www.dfait-maeci.gc.ca

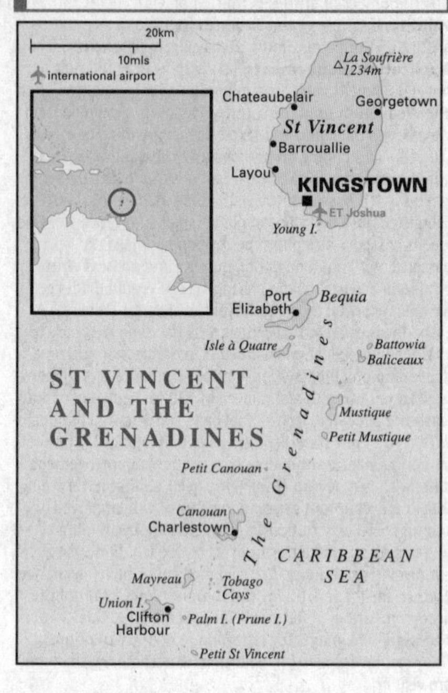

Location: Eastern Caribbean, Windward Islands.

Country dialling code: 1 784.

Ministry of Tourism and Culture
Street address: Cruise Ship Terminal, Harbour Quay, Kingstown, St Vincent
Postal address: PO Box 834, Kingstown, St Vincent
Tel: 457 1502. Fax: 451 2425.
E-mail: tourism@caribsurf.com
Website: www.svgtourism.com
High Commission for St Vincent & the Grenadines
10 Kensington Court, London W8 5DL, UK
Tel: (020) 7565 2874.
E-mail: highcommission.svg.uk@cwcom.net
Opening hours: Mon-Thurs 0930-1730, Fri 0930-1700.
St Vincent & the Grenadines Tourist Office
10 Kensington Court, London W8 5DL, UK
Tel: (020) 7937 6570. Fax: (020) 7937 3611.
E-mail: svgtourismeurope@aol.com
Website: www.svgtourism.com
British High Commission
PO Box 132, Granby Street, Kingstown, St Vincent
Tel: 457 1701. Fax: 456 2750.
E-mail: bhcsvg@caribsurf.com
Embassy of St Vincent & the Grenadines
3216 New Mexico Avenue, NW, Washington, DC 20016, USA
Tel: (202) 364 6730. Fax: (202) 364 6736.
E-mail: mail@embsvg.com
Website: www.embsvg.com
St Vincent & the Grenadines Tourist Office
801 Second Avenue, 21st Floor, New York, NY 10017, USA
Tel: (212) 687 4981 *or* (800) 729 1726 (toll-free in the USA).
Fax: (212) 949 5946.
E-mail: svgtony@aol.com Website: www.svgtourism.com
The United States Embassy in Bridgetown deals with enquiries relating to St Vincent & the Grenadines (see *Barbados* **section).**

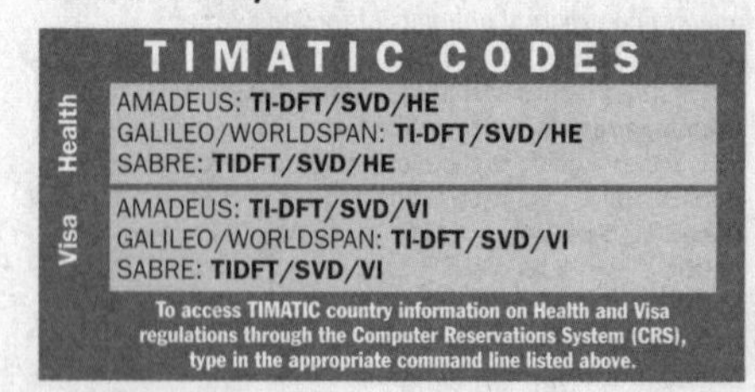
TIMATIC CODES

Health
AMADEUS: **TI-DFT/SVD/HE**
GALILEO/WORLDSPAN: **TI-DFT/SVD/HE**
SABRE: **TIDFT/SVD/HE**

Visa
AMADEUS: **TI-DFT/SVD/VI**
GALILEO/WORLDSPAN: **TI-DFT/SVD/VI**
SABRE: **TIDFT/SVD/VI**

To access TIMATIC country information on Health and Visa regulations through the Computer Reservations System (CRS), type in the appropriate command line listed above.

High Commission for the Eastern Caribbean States
130 Albert Street, Suite 700, Ottawa, Ontario K1P 5G4, Canada
Tel: (613) 236 8952. Fax: (613) 236 3042.
E-mail: echcc@travel-net.com
The Canadian High Commission in Bridgetown deals with enquiries relating to St Vincent & the Grenadines (see *Barbados* section).
St Vincent & the Grenadines Tourist Office
333 Wilson Avenue, Suite 601, Toronto, M3H IT2 Tel: (416) 398 4277. Fax: (416) 398 4199. Email: svgtourismtoronto@rogers.com
Website: www.svgtourism.com

General Information

AREA: St Vincent: 344 sq km (133 sq miles). **Grenadines:** 45.3 sq km (17.3 sq miles). **Total:** 389.3 sq km (150.3 sq miles).
POPULATION: 119,000 (official estimate 2002).
POPULATION DENSITY: 305.7 per sq km (2002).
CAPITAL: Kingstown. **Population:** 13,526 (2001).
GEOGRAPHY: St Vincent & the Grenadines make up part of the Windward Islands and lie south of St Lucia. St Vincent, like all the Windwards, is volcanic and mountainous with luxuriant vegetation and black sand beaches. The highest peak of St Vincent, *La Soufrière* (1219m/4000ft), is volcanic, and deep down in the crater is a lake. The 'tail' of the comet of St Vincent (the Grenadines) is a string of islands and cays that splays south from Bequia (pronounced Beck-Way), Petit Nevis, Isle à Quatre and Pigeon Island to Battowia, Baliceaux, Mustique, Petit Mustique, Savan, Canouan, Petit Canouan, Mayreau and the Tobago Cays, Union Island, Palm Island and Petit St Vincent. All of the Grenadines are famous for their white beaches, clear waters and verdant scenery.
GOVERNMENT: Constitutional monarchy. Gained independence from the UK in 1979. **Head of State:** Queen Elizabeth II, represented locally by Governor General Frederick Ballantyne since 2002. **Head of Government:** Prime Minister Ralph Gonsalves since March 2001.
LANGUAGE: English.
RELIGION: Roman Catholic, Anglican, Methodist and other Christian denominations.
TIME: GMT - 4.
ELECTRICITY: 220/240 volts AC, 50Hz (except Petit St Vincent which has 110 volts AC, 60Hz).
COMMUNICATIONS: Telephone: IDD is available. Country code: 1 784. Outgoing international code: 0. **Mobile telephone:** Providers *Cable & Wireless Caribbean Cellular* and *Digicel*. Visitors from North America can roam on all the islands. **Fax:** Faxes can be sent from most hotels. **Internet:** ISPs include *Caribsurf* (website: www.caribsurf.com). **Telegram:** Facilities are limited to main towns and hotels. **Post:** Airmail to Western Europe takes up to two weeks. Post office hours: Mon-Fri 0830-1500, Sat 0830-1130. **Press:** All newspapers are in English and most are published weekly. The most popular papers are *The News*, *Searchlight* and *The Vincentian*; *The Herald* is published daily.
Radio: BBC World Service (website: www.bbc.co.uk/worldservice) and Voice of America (website: www.voa.gov) can be received. From time to time the frequencies change and the most up-to-date can be found online.

Passport/Visa

	Passport Required?	Visa Required?	Return Ticket Required?
Full British	1	No	Yes
Australian	Yes	No	Yes
Canadian	1	No	Yes
USA	1	No	Yes
Other EU	Yes	No	Yes
Japanese	Yes	No	Yes

Note: *Regulations and requirements may be subject to change at short notice, and you are advised to contact the appropriate diplomatic or consular authority before finalising travel arrangements. Details of these may be found at the head of this country's entry. Any numbers in the chart refer to the footnotes below.*

PASSPORTS: Valid passport required by all except:
1. British subjects and nationals of Canada and the USA holding a driver's licence or birth certificate.
VISAS: Not required. Length of stay is determined by immigration authority on arrival, if necessary. Check with Consulate or High Commission before departure. A return or onward ticket is required by all visitors, as well as proof of accommodation and adequate funds.
Temporary residence: Refer applications or enquiries to the Prime Minister's Office in Kingstown.

Money

Currency: Eastern Caribbean Dollar (EC$) = 100 cents. Notes are in denominations of EC$100, 50, 20, 10 and 5. Coins are in denominations of EC$1, 50, 25, 10, 5, 2 and 1 cents.
Note: The Eastern Caribbean Dollar is tied to the US Dollar.
Currency exchange: All major currencies can be exchanged at banks and at the airport.
Credit & debit cards: All major credit and debit cards are widely accepted. Check with your credit or debit card company for details of merchant acceptability and other services that may be available.
Travellers cheques: To avoid additional exchange rate charges, travellers are advised to take travellers cheques in US Dollars.
Currency restrictions: Free import of local and foreign currency, subject to declaration. Export of local and foreign currency is limited to the amount declared on import.
Exchange rate indicators: The following figures are included as a guide to the movements of the Eastern Caribbean Dollar against Sterling and the US Dollar:

Date	Feb '04	May '04	Aug '04	Nov '04
£1.00=	4.91	4.71	4.97	5.11
$1.00=	2.70	2.67	2.70	2.70

Banking hours: Mon-Thurs 0800-1500, Fri 0800-1700. The bank at *ET Joshua Airport* opens Mon-Sat 0700-1700 with additional extensions during the major festivals.

Duty Free

The following items may be imported into St Vincent & the Grenadines without incurring customs duty:
200 cigarettes or 50 cigars or 225g of tobacco; 1.136l of alcoholic beverage.

Public Holidays

2005: Jan 1 New Year's Day. **Mar 14** National Heroes' Day. **Mar 25** Good Friday. **Mar 28** Easter Monday. **May 1** Labour Day. **May 16** Whit Monday. **Jul 4** Carnival Monday. **Jul 5** Carnival Tuesday. **Aug 1** Emancipation Day. **Oct 27** Independence Day. **Dec 25** Christmas Day. **Dec 26** Boxing Day.
2006: Jan 1 New Year's Day. **Mar 14** National Heroes' Day. **Apr 14** Good Friday. **Apr 17** Easter Monday. **May 1** Labour Day. **Jun 5** Whit Monday. **Jul 3** Carnival Monday. **Jul 4** Carnival Tuesday. **Aug 1** Emancipation Day. **Oct 27** Independence Day. **Dec 25** Christmas Day. **Dec 26** Boxing Day.
Note: If the above dates fall on a Sunday, the following Monday will be taken as a public holiday.

Health

	Special Precautions?	Certificate Required?
Yellow Fever	No	1
Cholera	No	No
Typhoid & Polio	No	N/A
Malaria	No	N/A

Note: *Regulations and requirements may be subject to change at short notice, and you are advised to contact your doctor well in advance of your intended date of departure. Any numbers in the chart refer to the footnotes below.*

1: A yellow fever vaccination certificate is required from travellers over one year of age arriving within six days from infected areas.
Food & drink: Mains water is normally chlorinated, and whilst relatively safe, may cause mild abdominal upsets. Bottled water is available. Milk is pasteurised and dairy products are safe for consumption. Local meat, poultry, seafood, fruit and vegetables are generally considered safe to eat.
Health care: There is one large hospital, the 207-bed Kingstown General Hospital. In addition, there are five district rural hospitals, 38 health centres and one medical laboratory. Visitors can get treatment at primary level, but need a referral for access to the main hospital. As facilities are limited, serious medical problems require evacuation to another island or the USA. Visitors would be expected to pay the full costs for services, therefore health insurance with emergency repatriation is recommended. Visitors with Blue Cross or Blue Shield should have their cards with them and can obtain assistance through the Life of Barbados company.

Travel - International

AIR: Travel to St Vincent & the Grenadines is via Barbados, Grenada, Martinique, St Lucia or Trinidad & Tobago, and then on to St Vincent & the Grenadines in a prop plane. *LIAT (LI)* is the main airline serving St Vincent & the Grenadines. Other airlines include *Air Martinique*, *BWEE Express*, *Caribbean Star*, *Mustique Airways* and *SVG Air*.
Approximate flight times: From St Vincent to *London* (via Barbados) is nine hours, to *Los Angeles* is nine hours, to *New York* is five hours and to *Singapore* is 33 hours.
International airports: *ET Joshua (SVD)* is 3km (2 miles) southeast of Kingstown. Airport facilities include car hire, restaurant, bar and duty free shops. Buses and taxis go from the airport to the city. There are standard fares to a number of major hotels throughout the island. There are also small airports on Bequia, Canouan, Mustique and Union Island for light aircraft.
Departure tax: EC$35 on all international departures; children under 12 years of age and passengers staying for less than 24 hours are exempt.
SEA: Some of the Grenadines are ports of call for a number of cruise lines: *Clipper Cruise Lines, Epirotiki, Festival Cruises, Fred Olsen, Hapag Lloyd, Holland America, Marline Universal, Seabourn* and *Sea Cloud Cruises.*

Travel - Internal

AIR: Local and charter services are available. Small planes can be chartered for inter-island travel. *Mustique Air, SVG Air* and *TIA* run regular services to the Grenadines.
SEA: Yacht chartering is easily arranged and is one of the best ways to explore the Grenadines. Yachts can be hired locally, with or without crew. Two ferries make frequent sailings to Bequia (travel time – 60 minutes). The rest of the Grenadines are served regularly by a mailboat. The Tourist Office can help with all details.
ROAD: Traffic drives on the left. **Bus:** Services run regularly throughout St Vincent. Small minibuses run a shared *route-taxi* service with a standard fare anywhere along the route. Public transport is cheap but crowded. **Taxi:** These are shared and charge standard rates (fixed by the Government). **Car hire:** Easily arranged through a number of national and international firms. **Documentation:** A local driving licence is essential and can be obtained on presentation of a valid national or international licence either at the airport or at the police station in Bay Street, Kingstown, or at the Licensing Authority in Halifax Street, Kingstown (Mon-Fri 0900-1500). The cost is around EC$75.

Accommodation

From casual and economical to elegant and exclusive, lodgings in St Vincent & the Grenadines offer something for every taste and budget. The choice ranges from a rustic cottage on the beach or an historic country hotel in the mountains, to a luxury resort with an island to itself. Young Island, an idyllic small island off the south coast of St Vincent, has a cottage community of separate huts including all modern facilities. All hotels are small and emphasise personal service. A list of rates is available from the St Vincent Department of Tourism and all its overseas offices. All rooms are subject to a 7 per cent hotel tax.
Grading: Many hotels in the Caribbean offer accommodation according to one of a number of plans. **FAP** (Full American Plan): room and all meals supplied (including afternoon tea, supper, etc); **AP** (American Plan): room and three meals supplied; **MAP** (Modified American Plan): breakfast and dinner included with the price of the room plus, in some places, British-style afternoon tea; **CP** (Continental Plan): room and breakfast only; **EP** (European Plan): room only. For further information regarding accommodation, contact the Department of Tourism (see *Contact Addresses* section); *or* the St Vincent & the Grenadines Hotel Association, PO Box 834, Kingston, St Vincent (tel: 458 4379; fax: 456 4456; e-mail: office@svghotels.com; website: www.svghotels.com).

Resorts & Excursions

ST VINCENT

St Vincent is a lush, volcanic island of steep mountain ridges, valleys and waterfalls. The rugged eastern coast is lined with cliffs and rocky shores, while the western coastline dips sharply down to black-sand beaches. To the north, **La Soufrière**, St Vincent's volcano, rises to 1219m (4000ft). St Vincent has frequent rains, and rich volcanic soil which produces an abundance of fruit, vegetables and spices. The interior flatlands and valleys are thickly planted with coconuts, bananas, breadfruit, nutmeg and arrowroot.
Kingstown: The capital of St Vincent is a lively port and market town on the southern coast. The town contains 12 small blocks with a variety of shops and a busy dock area, which is the centre of commerce for the islands. The Saturday morning market, comprising many stalls piled high with fresh fruit and vegetables, brings everyone to town. In the centre of Kingstown, **St Mary's Roman Catholic**

Cathedral, built of grey stone, is a graceful combination of several European architectural styles displaying Romanesque arches, Gothic spires and Moorish ornamentation. Its architecture has led Kingstown to become known as the City of Arches. The ruins of **Fort Charlotte** overlook a 180m (590ft) ridge north of town and offer a magnificent southward view of the Grenadines. The oldest **Botanical Gardens** in the Western hemisphere occupy 8.1 hectares (20 acres) to the north of Kingstown and contain a display of tropical trees, blossoms and plants, including a breadfruit tree descended from the original one brought to the island in 1765 by Captain Bligh.

Elsewhere on St Vincent: The **Falls of Baleine**, at the northern tip of St Vincent, are accessible only by boat. The 18m (59ft) freshwater falls stream from volcanic slopes and form a series of shallow pools at the base. A challenging hike for the more adventurous is the just over 5km (3 miles) journey up **La Soufrière**, St Vincent's northern volcano, which affords a wonderful bird's-eye view of the crater and its islands, and all of St Vincent.

Strung along the western coast are the fishing villages of **Questelles**, **Layou**, **Barrouallie** and **Châteaubelair**, all of which have charming pastel-coloured cottages and excellent black-sand beaches from which fishermen set out daily in small brightly painted boats.

Young Island: Only 180m (590ft) off St Vincent, Young Island rises from the sea, a 10.1 hectare (25 acre) mountain blanketed with tropical foliage and blossoms. Young Island provides an excellent view of the procession of yachts sailing into the harbour of St Vincent. The entire island comprises one resort called *Young Island Resort*, which consists of 29 rustic cottages set on the beaches and hillsides. There is a freshwater pool and tennis courts hidden in the hilltop trees. Adjoining Young Island is the 18th-century **Fort Duvernette**, sculpted from an enormous rock, towering 60m (200ft) above the sea. A ferry, a smaller version of the African Queen, runs regularly between Young Island and St Vincent.

THE GRENADINES

Bequia: This island lies 14km (9 miles) south of St Vincent and is the largest of the Grenadines, measuring 18 sq km (7 sq miles). Little changed by time, it is an island on which life is completely oriented to the sea. It can be reached by boat, although there is an airport, the **JF Mitchell**. Its seclusion has ensured it retained its age-old traditions of boat building and fishing. In the marine park, spearfishing, snares and nets are prohibited. The islanders themselves are the world's last hand-harpooners and their activities do not affect marine stocks, unlike the mechanised fishing of some fleets. The centre of the island is hilly and forested, providing a dramatic backdrop to the bays and beaches.

Admiralty Bay, the island's natural harbour, is a favourite anchoring spot for yachtsmen from all over the world, and here visitors can watch men building their boats by hand on the shores. The attractive region around **Lower Bay** has good opportunities for swimming and other watersports. The quaint waterfront of **Port Elizabeth** is lined with bars, restaurants and craft shops. Bequia is encircled by gold-sand beaches, many of which disappear into coves, excellent for sailing, scuba diving and snorkelling. Lodgings vary from luxurious resort cottages to small, simple West Indian inns. Much of the nightlife centres on the hotels and beachside barbecues, invariably accompanied by a steel band.

Mustique: Heading south, the next port of call is Mustique, a gem in the ocean taking up only 4.5 sq km (2 sq miles). Mustique is privately owned, with a landscape as gentle as its lifestyle – verdant hills roll into soft white-sand beaches and turquoise waters. This island has long been a hiding place for the rich and famous, including members of the British Royal Family. A sprawling 18th-century plantation house has been converted into the island's only resort. Elegant accommodation is available in several stone houses, widely separated for seclusion. The public rooms of the **Main House** are beautifully decorated with antiques, and afternoon tea is served daily on the veranda. There is a hilltop swimming pool with a magnificent panorama, as well as tennis, horseriding, motorcycling and all watersports.

Canouan: The island claims some of the best beaches in the Caribbean – long stretches of powder-white sands, wide shallows and coral. The island stretches over 11 sq km (7.9 sq miles) and has two hotels: the *Canouan Beach Hotel* and *Tamarind Beach Hotel*. There are also three guest houses: the *Anchor Inn*, *Crystal Apartments* and *Rebecca's Place*. The recently established **Carenage Bay** resort is a plush 5-star resort boasting two private beaches and excellent sports facilities including its 18-hole golf club, scuba diving, wind-surfing and tennis.

Tobago Cays: South of Canouan are the Tobago Cays, numerous islets and coves guarded by some of the most spectacular coral reefs in the world. Visitors can sail, snorkel and beachcomb in complete seclusion. The only way to get here is by chartered yacht.

Mayreau: East of the Cays is Mayreau, one of the smaller Grenadines, which has few residents. The island has one hotel, *Salt Whistle Bay Resort*, and can be reached by boat from Union Island. There is one guest house, *Dennis' Hideaway*.

Union Island: Mount Parnassus on Union Island soars 275m (900ft) from the sea – guarding the entrance to the southern Grenadines. The 850 hectare (2100 acre) mountainous island is fringed by superb beaches and is the stopping-off point for yachtsmen and visitors heading to some of the smaller Grenadines. **Clifton Harbour**, the main town, is small and commercial. There are several beachfront inns with a relaxed atmosphere.

Palm Island: The 44.5 hectare (110 acre) flat Palm Island acquired its name from the graceful coconut palms that line the beaches – 8000 in all. This private island has been turned into a resort, the *Palm Island Beach Club*, made up of 20 beachfront stone cottages. Here it is possible to dine in the open air and all watersports take place off the wide, white shores.

Petit St Vincent: The southernmost Grenadine governed by St Vincent is Petit St Vincent, a 45.7 hectare (113 acre) resort set on beaches. The luxuriant foliage and the 22 villas of Petit St Vincent offer guests the ultimate luxury and seclusion, including private patios and seaside vistas. Visitors gather for meals in beachfront pavilions and the ambience is carefree and festive.

Sport & Activities

Watersports: These are a major pastime. Various **sailing** boats head south regularly through the Grenadines. For the novice, professionals are available to handle the sails. Visitors can, of course, bring their own yacht, or charter one, either with or without crew. Yachts are available for charter from Barefoot Yacht Charters (tel: 456 9526 *or* 9334; fax: 456 9238; e-mail: barebum@caribsurf.com; website: www.barefootyachts.com) *or* Sunsail St Vincent at the Lagoon Marina & Hotel (tel/fax: 458 4308; e-mail: sunsailsvg@caribsurf.com; website: www.lagoonmarina.com). Other watersports, particularly **windsurfing** and **scuba diving**, can be arranged through some hotels. Dive sites around St Vincent include *New Guinea Reef*, where sea horses swim around an abundance of black coral; and *Bottle Reef*, so called because the sea bed is dotted with antique gin and rum bottles thrown into the sea from the English fort above in centuries past. **Deep-sea fishing** excursions are available.

Hiking: This can be undertaken in the rainforest. Hiking to the Soufrière volcano (1200m/4000ft) in the north of the island is popular, though strenuous. The trip takes a full day.

Other: Cricket and **football** are very popular. **Tennis** courts are available at Kingstown Tennis Club and facilities may also be arranged through hotels. **Horseriding** can be arranged in Mustique. The only **golf** course is the Carenage Golf Course on Canouan, which is partly on the flat coastal plain and partly carved into the hillside.

Social Profile

FOOD & DRINK: St Vincent is one of the few islands where good West Indian cuisine can almost always be enjoyed in hotels. Specialities include red snapper, kingfish, *lambi* (conch), *callalou* soup, *souse* (pickled meat or seafood) and sea-moss drink. In addition there is plenty of fresh fruit, vegetables and other seafood on offer. Lobster is available in season.

Vincentian beer and rum, a major ingredient in punch and cocktails, are the local drinks, as are a wide variety of local exotic fruit juices.

NIGHTLIFE: Most evening events take place in hotels and it is best to ask at individual hotels for a calendar of events. Nightclubs include the *Aquatic* club and the *Buccama Club* on the Leeward Coast. *The Attic* in Kingstown features a wide variety of music during the week and live entertainment at weekends. There is one casino on the island, at Peniston, on the Leeward side.

SHOPPING: Designs on sea-island cottons can be bought and made up into clothes within a few days at a number of shops. Handicrafts and all varieties of straw-made items, grass rugs and other souvenirs can be bought at a number of workshops and gift shops. **Shopping hours:** Mon-Fri 0800-1200 and 1300-1600, Sat 0800-1200.

SPECIAL EVENTS: For full details, contact the St Vincent & the Grenadines Tourist Office (see *Contact Addresses* section). The following is a selection of special events occurring in St Vincent & the Grenadines in 2005:

Jan 19-Feb 2 *Mustique Blues Festival*. **Jan 28-29** *Blues Fest*, St Vincent. **Mar 24-28** *Easterval*, Union Island; *Easter Regatta*, Bequia. **Apr 1-30** *Gospel Fest Month*. **Jun 21** *Music Day*. **Jun 24-Jul 5** *Vincy Carnival* (street parades, beauty show, King and Queen of Bands and calypso competition). **Aug 1-30** *Emancipation Month - Breadfruit Festival*. **Sep 1-30** *Dance Festival Month*. **Sep 3** *Fashion Caribbean*. **Nov 1-30** *National Drama Festival*.

SOCIAL CONVENTIONS: The Vincentians are fun-loving and easy-going people, and the informal and relaxed lifestyle combines many English influences with West Indian. The Saturday market in Kingstown is bustling with life, seemingly involving all islanders. All visitors are made welcome and casual wear is widely acceptable. Refrain, however, from wearing beachwear or mini shorts on the streets or while shopping. **Tipping:** 10 to 15 per cent service added to the bill. Taxi drivers do not expect tips.

Business Profile

ECONOMY: St Vincent & the Grenadines is poor by Eastern Caribbean standards, with agriculture the main source of income and export earnings. Bananas are the main crop, but St Vincent is also the world's leading producer of arrowroot and grows other exotic fruit, vegetables and root crops. Fishing has also been revitalised and a processing complex has been built with Japanese assistance. Agriculture is especially vulnerable to the unpredictable, often adverse weather patterns of the Caribbean.

Tourism is the other main component of the economy. By regional standards, this was relatively late to evolve and was initially hampered by the lack of a suitable infrastructure. This was addressed with the help of aid from the European Union and the industry is now growing rapidly: the most recent figures record its contribution to the economy at US$90 million. A small manufacturing sector and an embryonic 'offshore' financial services industry complete the country's economic inventory.

St Vincent is a member of the regional trading bloc CARICOM and the Organisation of Eastern Caribbean States, which is assuming a growing economic role. In addition to the USA and the UK, St Vincent's main trade links are with Trinidad & Tobago, Barbados, St Lucia and Martinique.

BUSINESS: Short- or long-sleeved shirt and tie or a safari suit are suitable for most business visits. **Government office hours:** These vary from department to department but generally Mon-Fri 0800-1615, with some opening for a few hours Saturday morning.

COMMERCIAL INFORMATION: The following organisation can offer advice: St Vincent & the Grenadines Chamber of Industry and Commerce, PO Box 134, Coreas Building, Hillsborough Street, Kingstown (tel: 457 1464; fax: 456 2944; e-mail: svgcic@caribsurf.com; website: www.svgcic.com).

CONFERENCES/CONVENTIONS: For information, contact the St Vincent & the Grenadines Tourist Office (see *Contact Addresses* section).

Climate

Tropical, with trade winds tempering the hottest months, June and July.

Required clothing: Lightweights and waterproofs.

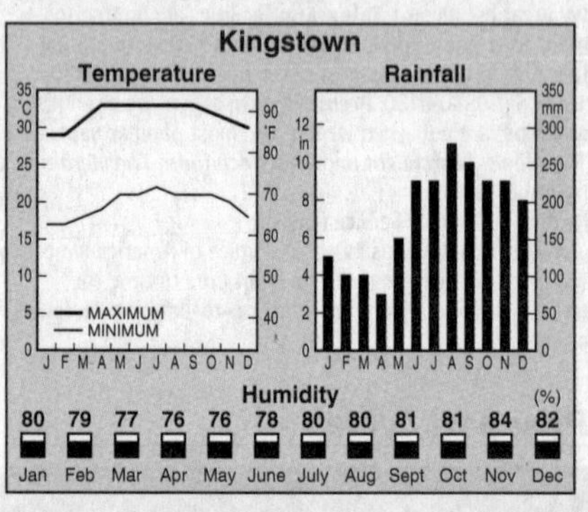

Samoa

LATEST TRAVEL ADVICE CONTACTS

British Foreign and Commonwealth Office
Tel: (0870) 606 0290 Website: www.fco.gov.uk
US Department of State
Website: http://travel.state.gov/travel
Canadian Department of Foreign Affairs and Int'l Trade
Tel: (1 800) 267 8376 Website: www.dfait-maeci.gc.ca

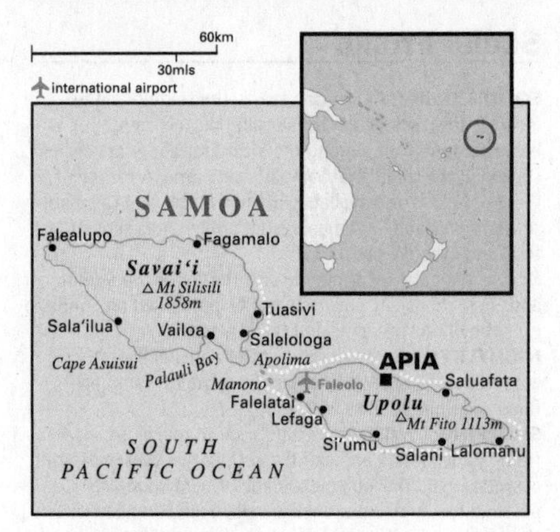

Location: South Pacific.

Country dialling code: 685.

Samoa Tourism Authority
PO Box 2272, Apia, Samoa
Tel: 63500. Fax: 20886.
E-mail: info@visitsamoa.ws
Website: www.visitsamoa.ws
South Pacific Tourism Organisation
Street address: Level 3, FNPF Place, 343-359 Victoria Parade, Suva, Fiji
Postal address: PO Box 13119, Suva, Fiji
Tel: (639) 330 4177. Fax: (639) 330 1995.
Website: www.spto.org
Also deals with enquiries from the UK.
Embassy of Samoa
PO Box 14, 123 avenue Franklin D Roosevelt, B-1050 Brussels, Belgium
Tel: (2) 660 8454. Fax: (2) 675 0336.
E-mail: samoa.emb.bxl@skynet.be
Office of the Honorary British Consul
c/o Kruse, Enari and Barlow Barristers and Solicitors, 2nd Floor, NPF Building, Beach Road, PO Box 2029, Apia, Samoa
Tel: 21895. Fax: 21407.
E-mail: barlowlaw@keblegal.ws
Permanent Mission of Samoa to the United Nations
800 2nd Avenue, Suite 400J, New York, NY 10017, USA
Tel: (212) 599 6196. Fax: (212) 599 0797.
E-mail: samoa@un.int
Also deals with enquiries from Canada.
Embassy of the United States of America
PO Box 3430, Matafele, Apia, Samoa
Tel: 21631 *or* 22696. Fax: 22030.
E-mail: usembassy@samoa.ws
The Canadian High Commission in Wellington deals with enquiries relating to Samoa (see the *New Zealand* **section).**

General Information

AREA: 2831 sq km (1093 sq miles).
POPULATION: 176,848 (official estimate 2001).
POPULATION DENSITY: 62.5 per sq km.
CAPITAL: Apia (Upolu Island). **Population:** 34,126 (1991).
GEOGRAPHY: Samoa consists of nine islands. The largest of these is Savai'i, which covers 1610 sq km (622 sq miles); fertile Upolu, the second largest (1120 sq km/433 sq miles), lies 13km (8 miles) to the southeast across the Apolima Strait. The islands are quiescent volcanoes and reach heights of up to 1858m (6097ft) on Savai'i and 1100m (3608ft) on Upolu. Volcanic activity has not occurred since 1911. The main city, Apia, is located in the north of Upolu.
GOVERNMENT: Constitutional monarchy. Gained independence from New Zealand in 1962. **Head of State:** HH Malietoa Tanumafili II since 1963. **Head of Government:** Prime Minister Tuila'epa Sailele Malielegaoi since 1998.
LANGUAGE: Samoan is the national language. In business and commerce, English is customary.
RELIGION: Congregational Church, Roman Catholic, Methodist and Latter Day Saints.
TIME: GMT - 12.
ELECTRICITY: 240 volts AC, 50Hz (110 volts AC in some hotels). Three-pronged plugs are in use as in Australia and New Zealand.
COMMUNICATIONS: Telephone: Incoming IDD is available. Country code: 685. There are no area codes. Outgoing international calls must be made through the operator. **Mobile telephone:** Samoa has its own analogue mobile phone system operated by Telecom Samoa. Visitors with analogue phones can be assigned a new number for the duration of their stay and calls will be charged to their credit card. **Fax:** Services are available from the main post office in Apia. There are hotels with facilities. **Internet:** Internet and e-mail services are available in Apia and other locations around the islands. **Telegram:** Available from the main post office in Apia. Also in main towns and at major hotels. **Post:** Main post office hours (located on Beach Road, Apia): Mon-Fri 0800-1630. *Poste restante* facilities are also available: enquire at post office. Airmail to Europe takes about three weeks. **Press:** The main English-language newspapers are *Newsline, The Samoa Observer* and *Savali.*
Radio: BBC World Service (website: www.bbc.co.uk/worldservice) and Voice of America (website: www.voa.gov) can be received. From time to time the frequencies change and the most up-to-date can be found online.

Passport/Visa

	Passport Required?	Visa Required?	Return Ticket Required?
Full British	Yes	1	Yes
Australian	Yes	1	Yes
Canadian	Yes	1	Yes
USA	Yes	1	Yes
Other EU	Yes	1	Yes
Japanese	Yes	1	Yes

Note: Regulations and requirements may be subject to change at short notice, and you are advised to contact the appropriate diplomatic or consular authority before finalising travel arrangements. Details of these may be found at the head of this country's entry. Any numbers in the chart refer to the footnotes below.

PASSPORTS: Passport valid for six months beyond the date of departure from Samoa required by all.
VISAS: Required by all except:
1. nationals of any country visiting Samoa as a tourist will be issued with a free 60-day visa on arrival provided they hold confirmed onward tickets, a valid passport and proof of sufficient funds to support the stay. For longer stays, visas should be obtained before arrival or visa extensions can be applied for in Apia.
Types of visa and cost: *Visitor's Permit:* free on arrival. Other types of visa cost from €100-1200 and applicants should enquire directly with the Samoan Embassy.
Validity: Six months from date of issue.
Application to: Nearest Samoan Embassy or Immigration Division of the Prime Minister's Department in Apia.
Application requirements: (a) Two passport-size photos. (b) Completed application form. (c) Fee.
Working days required: Apply at least four weeks in advance.
Temporary residence: Costs from €100 depending on the purpose of your visit. Business and employment visas are 50 per cent cheaper if applied for outside Samoa. Each application is assessed on an individual basis and takes at least four weeks to process.

Money

Currency: Tala or Samoa Dollar (Tala) = 100 sene. Notes are in denominations of Tala100, 50, 20, 10, 5 and 2. Coins are in denominations of Tala1, and 50, 20, 10, 5, 2 and 1 sene.
Currency exchange: Available at the airport or through banks. There are three banks in Samoa: ANZ Bank Samoa Ltd, the National Bank of Samoa and Westpac. These have ATMs at many of their branches throughout Samoa.
Credit & debit cards: American Express, Cirrus, MasterCard and Visa are accepted on a limited basis. Check with your credit or debit card company for details of merchant acceptability and other services which may be available.
Travellers cheques: Accepted in major hotels, banks and tourist shops. To avoid additional exchange rate charges, travellers are advised to take travellers cheques in US Dollars or Pounds Sterling.
Currency restrictions: There are no restrictions on the import of local or foreign currency. Export of local currency is prohibited. Export of foreign currency is limited to the amount imported.
Exchange rate indicators: The following figures are included as a guide to the movements of the Tala against Sterling and the US Dollar:

Date	Feb '04	May '04	Aug '04	Nov '04
£1.00=	4.98	5.04	5.21	4.98
$1.00=	2.73	2.82	2.82	2.63

Banking hours: Mon-Fri 0900-1500, some banks open Sat 0900-1200 and may have slightly longer opening hours.

Duty Free

The following items may be imported into Samoa by persons of 16 years of age or more without incurring customs duty:
200 cigarettes or 250g of cigars or tobacco; 1l of spirits; other goods for personal use up to Tala250.
Prohibited items: Firearms, ammunition, explosives, non-prescribed drugs and indecent publications. Live animals and plants (including seeds, fruit, soil, etc) may not be imported without prior permission from the Director of Agriculture.

Public Holidays

2005: Jan 1-2 New Year. **Mar 25-28** Easter. **Apr 25** ANZAC Day. **May 10** Mothers-of-Samoa Day. **Jun 1** Independence Day. **Aug 1** Labour Day. **Oct 10** Lotu-a-Tamaiti (Day after White Sunday). **Nov 1** Arbor Day. **Dec 25** Christmas Day. **Dec 26** Boxing Day.
2006: Jan 1-2 New Year. **Apr 14-17** Easter. **Apr 25** ANZAC Day. **May 10** Mothers-of-Samoa Day. **Jun 1** Independence Day. **Aug 7** Labour Day. **Oct 9** Lotu-a-Tamaiti (Day after White Sunday). **Nov 1** Arbor Day. **Dec 25** Christmas Day. **Dec 26** Boxing Day.

Health

	Special Precautions?	Certificate Required?
Yellow Fever	No	1
Cholera	No	No
Typhoid & Polio	2	N/A
Malaria	No	N/A

Note: Regulations and requirements may be subject to change at short notice, and you are advised to contact your doctor well in advance of your intended date of departure. Any numbers in the chart refer to the footnotes below.

1: A yellow fever vaccination certificate is required from travellers over one year of age arriving from infected areas.
2: Typhoid is present; polio has not been reported for three years.
Food & drink: Mains water is chlorinated, though bottled water may be preferable. Sterilisation is advisable. Milk is pasteurised and dairy products are safe for consumption. Local meat, poultry, seafood, fruit and vegetables are generally considered safe to eat.
Other risks: *Hepatitis A* occurs and *hepatitis B* is endemic.
Health care: Health insurance, while recommended, is not mandatory. All health services available to locals are accessible to foreigners usually at minimal cost to the traveller. Emergency medical facilities are available at Moto'otua Hospital, in Apia. Private medical and dental treatment is also available.

Travel - International

AIR: Samoa's national airline is *Polynesian Airlines (PH)* (website: www.polynesianairlines.co.nz). Others operating to the islands are *Air New Zealand, Air Pacific* and *Samoa Air*.
International airports: *Apia (APW)* (Faleolo) is 34km (21 miles) from the capital (travel time – 40 minutes). Airport facilities include banks/bureaux de change, post office, duty free shop and car hire (national firms). Buses and taxis operate to the city.
Air passes: The *Polypass* (offered by *Polynesian Airlines*) allows the holder to fly between the Southern Pacific destinations of American Samoa, Fiji, Niue, Samoa, Tahiti and Tonga; Honolulu (Hawaii) and Los Angeles (LA can be replaced with San Francisco, Seattle, Salt Lake City, Oakland, Santa Ana and Las Vegas) in the USA; Brisbane, Melbourne and Sydney in Australia; and Auckland, Christchurch and Wellington in New Zealand. The pass is valid for one year.

TIMATIC CODES

Health	AMADEUS: **TI-DFT/APW/HE** GALILEO/WORLDSPAN: **TI-DFT/APW/HE** SABRE: **TIDFT/APW/HE**
Visa	AMADEUS: **TI-DFT/APW/VI** GALILEO/WORLDSPAN: **TI-DFT/APW/VI** SABRE: **TIDFT/APW/VI**

To access TIMATIC country information on Health and Visa regulations through the Computer Reservations System (CRS), type in the appropriate command line listed above.

Once a reservation has been made and travel begun, all travel must be completed within a maximum of 45 days. Tickets will be issued against the *Polypass* by any Polynesian Airlines office (a valid passport is also required). For further information, contact Polynesian Airlines (website: www.polynesianairlines.com).
The *Visit the South Pacific Pass* is valid for many airlines operating in the South Pacific, including most of the larger ones, such as *Air Caledonie*, *Air Marshall Islands*, *Air Nauru*, *Air Niugingi*, *Air Pacific*, *Air Vanuatu*, *Polynesian Airlines*, *Qantas*, *Royal Tongan Airlines* and *Solomon Airlines*. Offering reductions of up to 40 per cent on normal airfares, this sector-based pass allows for flexible island-hopping between the destinations of the Cook Islands, Fiji, Nauru, New Caledonia, Samoa, Tahiti, Tonga, Vanuatu and the more remote Melanesian and Micronesian islands, together with major cities in Australia (Brisbane, Melbourne and Sydney) and New Zealand (Auckland, Christchurch and Wellington). It is only available for people resident outside of the South Pacific. The journey must be started outside the South Pacific and only one stopover in Australia is allowed. A minimum of two sectors must be bought before departure (extra sectors can be purchased en route). There is a maximum of one pass per person, and passes must be used within six months of the first day of travel. Children under 12 years of age pay 75 per cent of the adult fare. For details and conditions, contact the South Pacific Tourist Organisation (see *Contact Addresses* section).
Departure tax: Tala40 for adults. Transit passengers and children under 12 years of age are exempt.
SEA: The international port is Apia, on Upolu. It is served by both cargo and passenger ships from Australia, Europe, Japan, New Zealand and the USA. There is also a weekly ferry service from Pago Pago on American Samoa.

Travel - Internal

AIR: *Polynesian Airlines (PH)* operates daily flights from Fagali'i or Faleolo on Upolu to Maota and Asau on Savai'i. Charter and sightseeing flights are available.
SEA: There are passenger/vehicle ferries between Upolu (Apia) and Savai'i (travel time - 65 minutes). Check with *Samoa Shipping Corporation* for up-to-date schedules (tel: 20935/6).
ROAD: Traffic drives on the right. Speed limits are 40kph (25mph) within the Apia area and 56kph (35mph) outside the Apia area. Drivers should be alert, especially at night, to the hazard of roaming pigs, dogs and people. **Bus:** Public transport covers most of the islands. There are no timetables; policepeople at the New Market Bus Stand in Apia have information on bus departures. **Taxi:** Cheap and readily available in Apia. They are not metered and prices should be negotiated in advance. There is a minimum charge of Tala2. Longer trips are at a higher rate but are government regulated. **Car hire:** Available from several agencies. Deposit and insurance are usually required. **Bicycles** and **motor scooters** are also available. **Documentation:** An International Driving Permit for drivers over 21 years of age or a valid national licence. The Transport Ministry issues a local licence for a small fee. An International Driving Permit is required for car hire.

Accommodation

There is a government-backed programme to improve and extend facilities for visitors. In recent years, a number of new hotels and resorts have opened, and the choice varies hugely.
HOTELS: There is a good selection of distinctive hotels in Samoa offering high standards at reasonable prices (some inclusive of meals). There are also hotels located in rural areas, including Upolu's south coast and Savai'i. For details, contact the Samoa Visitors Bureau (see *Contact Addresses* section).
SELF-CATERING: A village resort offers the opportunity for self-catering, although, if visitors prefer, a restaurant is also provided. There are many sporting and other facilities for guests. Beach cottages and *fales* are less expensive and offer fewer on-site facilities, though many of them can be found nearby.
ECOTOURISM: Over recent years, the Samoa Visitors Bureau has initiated a National Ecotourism Programme designed to encourage sustainable and environmentally aware tourism by actively involving visitors in their efforts to preserve the natural habitat and national culture. As a result, a number of eco-villages have been established. One resort development that has been recently completed incorporates a number of these aims, and comes complete with composting toilets and outside open-air showers; an on-site work programme and other activities aim to recreate village life, as well as offering interesting trips to other coastal resorts and eco-villages. For further details, contact the Samoa Visitors Bureau (see *Contact Addresses* section).

Resorts & Excursions

A drive anywhere on the two larger islands, Upolu and Savai'i, will inevitably pass through regions of remarkable beauty; ferries sail regularly between them. The smaller islands are more difficult to reach; boat trips and information on island tours and accommodation can be obtained from the Samoa Visitors Bureau (see *Contact Addresses* section). Some hotels and eco-villages (see the *Accommodation* section) also arrange their own trips to neighbouring islands and villages.
UPOLU: The most populous island. **Apia**, the capital and main commercial centre, lies on the beautiful north coast. Nearby at **Vailima** is the house built by the Scottish poet and novelist Robert Louis Stevenson (the local name for him was *Tusitala*, meaning 'teller of tales'), who lived there from 1889 until his death on 5 December 1894. From the lawn you can see his tomb on top of **Mount Vaea**. The house has been restored, and was officially opened as the **Robert Louis Stevenson Museum** in 1994 on the 100th anniversary of his death.
Aleipata district: This is the most beautiful part of Samoa, with a landscape dominated by waterfalls, white-sand beaches and traditional villages. From Apia, a 65km (40 mile) drive leads to the **Falefa Falls**, **Fuipisia Falls** and **Mafa Pass**. Four offshore islands are within accessible distance.
Lefaga Village: On the southwest coast, an attractive village can be reached by a cross-island road. The film *Return to Paradise* was filmed here in 1952.
Manono Island: Just off the coast of Upolu, this island was the inspiration for the legendary 'Bali Hai' in Rodgers and Hammerstein's musical, *South Pacific*.
SAVAI'I: The largest island in the Samoan archipelago, this has been described as 'Polynesia at its truest'. There are scheduled flights and a regular car ferry from Apia on Upolu.
Tafua Peninsula Rainforest Preserve: Ideal for seeing flying foxes and birdwatching, this Preserve is situated near the coastal village of Tafua.
The Tia Seu Ancient Mound: An awe-inspiring 'pyramid' and the largest ancient structure in the whole of Polynesia at 12m (39ft) tall.
Mu Pagoa Waterfall: This, along with the **Alofaaga Blowholes**, **lava caves** and **lava fields**, makes for interesting sightseeing, as does the **Auala Green Turtle Conservation**; a programme managed by the women's committee, where guides show you turtles before they are released back into the wild.

Sport & Activities

Watersports: Samoa offers excellent **snorkelling** and **diving**. Snorkelling is best at high tide, which reduces the need to walk over coral (and damage it). Good locations include the *Palolo Deep Marine Reserve* (open 0800-1800, on Upolu island) and the beaches from Safotu to Manase and between Lesolo Point and Tuasivi (Savai'i island). Diving trips can be arranged via the Samoa Visitors Bureau (see *Contact Addresses* section). **Surfing** has recently become popular although, as the waves break directly on coral reefs, Samoan waters are for experienced surfers only. Currents are often extremely strong as Samoa is located in the middle of the Pacific and ocean swells are not blocked. In some villages, surfing is not allowed on Sundays. On Savai'i island, the villages charge a daily surfing fee to help with school funding. There are currently two surfing resorts; surfing guides are available from the Samoa Visitors Bureau. There are many beautiful beaches and there is excellent freshwater **swimming** at Falefa Falls, Fogaafu Falls, Papase'ea Sliding Rock (a rock slide down a waterfall into a deep, cool, freshwater pool) and Puila Cave Pool. Boats can be hired for net, spear, deep-sea and snorkel **fishing**.
Hiking: There are dozens of routes ranging from coastal walks to mountain treks. Trails tend to grow over rapidly and can sometimes be difficult to get through. Visitors should ask for local advice and permission before heading off or ask for a local guide from the Samoa Visitors Bureau.
Ecotourism: Educational tours to Samoa's stretches of rainforest and conservation areas are available (one popular destination being Tanumapua, close to Apia). There are also several ecological research programmes and eco-lodges on offer (see also the *Accommodation* section). For information, contact the Samoa Visitors Bureau (see *Contact Addresses* section).
Note: Visitors should respect Samoan village traditions (see *Social Conventions* in the *Social Profile* section). Almost all Samoan land (as well as lagoons and bays) is the communal property of a village, family or individual, and visitors should always find out whose land they are accessing (only 20 per cent of the land is not administered by a village). Villagers maintain the beaches, viewing areas and conservation areas and the decision to develop attractions is usually made by a council of chiefs. A small entry fee is payable for most beaches and other attractions. Fees are often indicated, but if no price is given, visitors should ask. In case of doubt, advice can be obtained from other travellers or the Samoa Visitors Bureau (see *Contact Addresses* section).
Other: The 18-hole **golf** course belonging to the Royal Samoa Golf Club at Fagali'i is open to non-members. A type of **cricket** is played locally and is very popular. Traditional cricket matches are played from November to March. The Apia Rugby Union **rugby** season is from March to June and schools also play at this time. Popular matches can be seen on Saturday afternoons at Apia Park. The national team *Manu Samoa* is world famous and the equal of many of the world's best sides.

Social Profile

FOOD & DRINK: At Samoan feasts, the traditional fare includes fresh seafood, roast suckling pig, chicken, breadfruit and fruit. Among the local specialities are dishes cooked in the traditional Samoan oven, *umu*. A variety of Chinese food is also available in a few places and there are several snack and light meal restaurants in Apia serving fast food and other Western food.
Kava is the national drink (see also the *American Samoa* and *Fiji* sections). Alcohol may not be purchased on Sundays except by hotel residents and their guests.
NIGHTLIFE: Several nightclubs offer dancing and other entertainment. Several cinemas show English-language films and Chinese films with subtitles.
SHOPPING: Local items include *siapo* (tapa) cloth, made from mulberry bark and painted with native dyes; mats and baskets; *kava* drinking bowls, made of hardwood and polished to a high gloss; shell jewellery; and Samoan stamps, available from the Philatelic Bureau. **Shopping hours:** Mon-Fri 0800-1200 and 1330-1630, Sat 0800-1230. Some shops remain open during the lunch hour.
SPECIAL EVENTS: For a complete list of events and festivals during 2005, contact the Samoa Visitors Bureau (see *Contact Addresses* section). The following is a selection of special events celebrated annually in Samoa:
Jan *Head of State's Birthday Celebrations*. **Feb** *Annual Marist Samoa Sevens* (golf). **May** *International Game Fishing Tournament*. **Jun** *Independence Day Celebrations*. **Sep** *Teuila Festival*; *Miss Samoa Pageant*. **Oct** *Lotu-a-Tamaiti* (White Sunday). **Nov** *National Environment Week*. **Dec** *13 Days of Christmas*.
SOCIAL CONVENTIONS: Even more than their American Samoan neighbours, Samoans adhere to traditional moral and religious codes of behaviour. According to the Government, the Samoan is the purest surviving Polynesian type, with a reputation for being upright and dignified in character. Life in each village is still regulated by a council of chiefs with considerable financial and territorial power; this 'extended family' social system is intricately and unusually linked with the overall political system. Visitors should avoid walking through villages during evening prayer (usually between 1800 and 1900). Sunday is a day of peace and quiet, and visitors should behave quietly and travel slowly through villages. It is recommended for women to wear a *lavalava* (sarong) rather than shorts and pants; nude or topless bathing is prohibited. When entering a *fale*, shoes should be removed, visitors should never stand when elders are seated, and when sitting down, the soles of your feet should not be shown (the yogic cross-legged style is a good option). Permission should always be asked before taking photographs in a village. Visitors should not offer money to children, even when they ask. For access and fees to certain areas and villages, see the *Sport & Activities* section. **Tipping:** Not customary.

Business Profile

ECONOMY: Most Samoans are involved in subsistence agriculture; some cash crops are also grown for export, the most important of which are coconut, cocoa and bananas. Timber is exported in small quantities. Fishing is another important source of income and employment. There is some small-scale manufacturing industry, mostly concerned with food-processing, textiles, woodworking and light engineering, and some small factories produce consumer goods for the domestic market. The Government has concentrated on tourism and export-oriented manufacturing in its efforts to develop the economy, although aspects of the climate - principally the country's annual cyclones - have made this difficult. Nonetheless, tourism has now expanded to the point where it contributes 17 per cent of GDP, based on the arrival of 90,000 visitors to the island group annually. The Government has also, with some success, sought to promote an offshore financial services industry. Further income comes from the remittances of Samoans working overseas - mostly in New Zealand and, to a lesser extent, in Australia; both these two countries also provide Samoa with a sizeable aid package. Tangible benefits from a 1996 trade

agreement with the Chinese government have become apparent. Meanwhile, a parallel programme of economic reforms won the approval and ensuing financial support of the World Bank, the Asian Development Bank and others. The economy is now growing at 5 per cent annually. Samoa is a member of both the South Pacific Forum and the South Pacific Commission. New Zealand, Australia, Singapore, Fiji, China (PR), Japan and the USA are the major trading partners.
BUSINESS: Shirt and smart trousers will suffice for business visits. Ties need only be worn for formal occasions. Best time to visit is from May to October. **Office hours:** Mon-Fri 0800-1200 and 1300-1630
COMMERCIAL INFORMATION: The following organisations can offer advice: Samoa Chamber of Commerce, Ground Floor, Lotemau Centre, Vaea Street, PO Box 2014, Apia (tel: 21237; fax: 21578; e-mail: info@samoachamber.com; website: www.samoachamber.com); *or* Department of Trade, Commerce and Industry, PO Box 862, Apia (tel: 20471/2; fax: 21646; e-mail: tipu@tci.gov.ws; website: www.tradeinvestsamoa.ws); *or* Samoa Visitors Bureau (see *Contact Addresses* section).

Climate

Samoa has a warm, tropical climate tempered by trade winds between May and September. Temperatures remain relatively constant throughout the year, becoming cooler at night. There are more than 2500 hours of sunshine annually. Rainfall is heaviest between December and April. Sea temperatures rarely fall below 24°C (75.2°F).
Required clothing: Lightweight cottons and linens with warmer clothes for evenings. Rainwear is advisable.

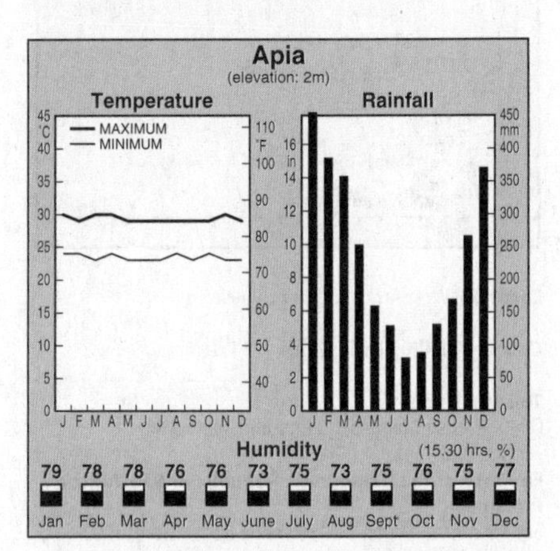

San Marino

LATEST TRAVEL ADVICE CONTACTS

British Foreign and Commonwealth Office
Tel: (0870) 606 0290 Website: www.fco.gov.uk

US Department of State
Website: http://travel.state.gov/travel

Canadian Department of Foreign Affairs and Int'l Trade
Tel: (1 800) 267 8376 Website: www.dfait-maeci.gc.ca

Location: Western Europe, northeastern part of the Italian peninsula.

Country dialling code: 378. The 0 preceding the area code should not be omitted.

Ufficio di Stato per il Turismo (State Tourist Office)
Palazzo del Turismo, Contrada Omagnano 20, 47890
Republic of San Marino
Tel: (0549) 882 914. Fax: (0549) 882 575.
E-mail: statoturismo@omniway.sm *or* customercare@omniway.sm
Website: www.visitsanmarino.com
The British Consulate General in Florence deals with enquiries relating to San Marino (see *Italy* section).
The American Consulate General in Florence deals with enquiries relating to San Marino (see *Italy* section).
The Canadian Embassy in Rome deals with enquiries relating to San Marino (see *Italy* section).

General Information

AREA: 61.2 sq km (23.6 sq miles).
POPULATION: 28,753 (2002).
POPULATION DENSITY: 469.8 per sq km.
CAPITAL: San Marino. **Population:** 2,822 (official UN estimate 2000).
GEOGRAPHY: San Marino is a tiny state bordered by the Italian regions of Emilia-Romagna to the north and east and Marche to the south and west. The landscape is for the most part green with rolling hills, dominated by the three peaks of Mount Titano. Within San Marino lie the capital of the same name and eight villages.
GOVERNMENT: Republic since 1599. **Heads of State and Government:** *Capitani Regenti* for 2004/5 period are Guisppe Arzilli and Roberto Raschi. The Captains Regent are elected by the Great General Council every six months.
LANGUAGE: Italian.
RELIGION: Roman Catholic.
TIME: GMT + 1 (GMT + 2 from last Sunday in March to

TIMATIC CODES

Health	AMADEUS: **TI-DFT/RMI/HE** GALILEO/WORLDSPAN: **TI-DFT/RMI/HE** SABRE: **TIDFT/RMI/HE**
Visa	AMADEUS: **TI-DFT/RMI/VI** GALILEO/WORLDSPAN: **TI-DFT/RMI/VI** SABRE: **TIDFT/RMI/VI**

To access TIMATIC country information on Health and Visa regulations through the Computer Reservations System (CRS), type in the appropriate command line listed above.

Credit: © Ufficio Stampa Turismo

Saturday before last Sunday in October).
ELECTRICITY: 220 volts AC, 50Hz.
COMMUNICATIONS: Telephone: IDD is available. Country code: 378. There are no area codes. Outgoing international code: 00. **Mobile telephone:** GSM 900/1800 networks. Network operators include *Telecom Italia Mobile* (website: www.tim.it) and *Vodafone Omnitel*. **Internet:** Internet cafes can be found in all main towns. ISPs include *Telecom Italia Net* (website: www.tim.it); for further details, see the *Italy* section. **Telegram:** Facilities are available in main hotels. **Post:** Good postal service. Airmail to European destinations takes approximately four days. *Poste Restante* facilities are available at all post offices.
Press: Daily newspapers published in San Marino are *La Tribuna Sanmerinese*, *Nuovo Corriere di Informazione Sammarinese* and *San Marino Oggi*; Italian and foreign newspapers are widely available.
Radio: BBC World Service (website: www.bbc.co.uk/worldservice) and Voice of America (website: www.voa.gov) can be received. From time to time the frequencies change and the most up-to-date can be found online.

Passport/Visa

Travellers will necessarily enter San Marino from Italy. As there are no frontier formalities imposed, any person visiting San Marino must comply with Italian passport/visa regulations; for details, see *Italy* section.

Money

Currency: The first Euro notes and coins were introduced in January 2002. For further information on currency, credit cards, travellers cheques, exchange rates and currency restrictions, see the *Italy* section.
Note: Since the early 1970s, San Marino has increased its production of indigenous gold and silver coins.
Currency exchange: Many banks offer differing exchange rates depending on the denominations of currency being bought or sold. Check with the banks for details and current rates.
Banking hours: Mon-Fri 0830-1330 and 1500-1630.

Duty Free

Visitors must comply with Italian customs regulations; see the *Italy* section.

Public Holidays

2005: Jan 1 New Year's Day. **Jan 6** Epiphany. **Feb 5** Anniversary of the Liberation of the Republic from the Alberoni Occupation and St Agatha's Day. **Mar 25** Anniversary of the Arengo. **Apr 1** Investiture of the new Captains Regent. **May 1** Labour Day. **Jun 10** Corpus Christi. **Jul 28** Anniversary of the Fall of Fascism. **Aug 15** Assumption. **Sep 3** San Marino's Day and Foundation of the Republic. **Oct 1** Investiture of the new Captains Regent. **Nov 1** All Saints' Day. **Nov 2** All Souls' Day. **Dec 8** Immaculate Conception. **Dec 24-26** Christmas. **Dec 31** New Year's Eve.
2006: Jan 1 New Year's Day. **Jan 6** Epiphany. **Feb 5** Anniversary of the Liberation of the Republic from the Alberoni Occupation and St Agatha's Day. **Mar 25**

Anniversary of the Arengo. **Apr 1** Investiture of the new Captains Regent. **May 1** Labour Day. **Jun 15** Corpus Christi. **Jul 28** Anniversary of the Fall of Fascism. **Aug 15** Assumption. **Sep 3** San Marino's Day and Foundation of the Republic. **Oct 1** Investiture of the new Captains Regent. **Nov 1** All Saints' Day. **Nov 2** All Souls' Day. **Dec 8** Immaculate Conception. **Dec 24-26** Christmas. **Dec 31** New Year's Eve.
Note: If any of the above dates fall on a Sunday, the following Monday will be observed as a public holiday.

Health

The health regulations and recommendations are the same as for Italy; for details see the *Italy* section.

Travel - International

AIR: The Italian national airline is *Alitalia (AZ)* (website: www.alitalia.it).
Approximate flight times: From Bologna/Rimini to *London* is two hours 30 minutes.
International airports: *Bologna (BLQ)* is 125km (78 miles) from San Marino and *Rimini (RMI)* is 27km (17 miles) from San Marino. Good bus services are available to San Marino.
RAIL: The nearest station is at Rimini. A funicular serves the capital and Borgo Maggiore. There are no internal railways.
ROAD: Major cities in Italy are within easy reach by car. Rimini is only 24km (15 miles) away and connects to San Marino via the San Marino highway. From San Marino to Urbino is 55km (34 miles), to Ravenna is 70km (44 miles), to Forli is 74km (46 miles), to Ancona is 130km (81 miles), to Bologna is 135km (84 miles), to Florence is 185km (116 miles), to Milan is 330km (206 miles) and to Rome is 350km (219 miles). **Documentation:** See *Italy* section.

Accommodation

All hotels in San Marino are comfortable and of a good standard. Every hotel allows special reductions for groups, children and large families. Full- and half-board arrangements are also available. For more information, contact the State Tourist Office (see *Contact Addresses* section). **Grading:** Hotels in San Marino are classified in four categories, with 1/A category hotels at the luxury end of the market, 1/B category hotels being slightly more modest, and 2 and 3 category hotels for budget travellers.

Resorts & Excursions

Set on the lower slopes of **Mount Titano**, the medieval centre of the city of San Marino has been perfectly preserved and must be explored on foot as cars are banned. The three peaks of the mountain behind are capped with fortified towers, linked by a system of walls and pathways that are accessible from the city below. The city itself is enclosed by three walls containing gateways, towers and ramparts. Inside the walls are narrow, winding streets, churches and medieval houses. Places worth visiting are the **Government Palace**; the **Basilica**; the **State Museum** and **Art Gallery**; **St Francis' Church**, which also has a museum and art gallery; the **Capuccin Friars Church of St Quirino**; and the **Exhibition of San Marino Handicrafts**. Eight villages are scattered around the countryside outside the capital. Places of interest include **Malatesta Castle** at **Serravalle**; the modern church and the stamp and coin museum at **Borgo Maggiore**; the church and convent at **Valdragone**; and the fort at **Pennarossa**. Ancient ruins can be seen throughout the Republic. Attractions outside the city and villages include pine woods, springs, streams, lakes and fishing reserves. There is easy access to Italian beaches on the Adriatic coast nearby

Sport & Activities

There are facilities for **tennis**, **basketball**, **volleyball**, **fishing**, **swimming** and **bowls**. There is a sports club at Serravalle with modern equipment and there are numerous football pitches throughout the Republic. The *24 Ore di San Marino* is the country's main **sailing** regatta (held in July). The *Gran Premio Formula 3000* (Formula One Grand Prix) is one of several annual **motor racing** events. **Stamp-** and **coin-collecting** are popular in San Marino – probably because the country is the only one in the Italian area which issues legal tender gold coins (the famous *Scudi*), and San Marino's philatelic office has been offering information and a new issues and standing order service to collectors for over 40 years. For further information, contact the State Philatelic & Numismatic Office (tel: (0549) 882 365; fax: (0549) 882 363; e-mail: aasfn@omniway.sm; website: www.aasfn.sm).

Social Profile

FOOD & DRINK: Italian cuisine is widely available. Popular first courses include *tortellini*, *passatelli* (broth), *tagliatelle*, *lasagne*, *ravioli*, *cannelloni* and *arbalester's passaduri* (a local speciality). Main dishes include roast rabbit with fennel, devilled chicken, quails, veal escalopes, Bolognese veal cutlets, assorted 'mouthfuls' (three types of tender meat) and Roman veal escalopes. San Marino tart and *cacciatello* (similar to crême caramel) may be ordered for dessert. There is a wide selection of restaurants, both in the capital and in the outlying villages. Table service is customary, although a few restaurants are self-service. San Marino *muscat*, *biancale*, *albana* and *sangiovese* are all good-quality wines produced locally. *Mistra* is the local liqueur.
NIGHTLIFE: Revues, festivals and theatrical productions are popular.
SHOPPING: Special purchases include locally made ceramics; stamps and coins bought from the State Philatelic & Numismatic Office, local wines and liqueurs, local jewellery, playing cards and cigarettes. **Shopping hours:** Mon-Sat 0830-1300 and 1530-1930.
SPECIAL EVENTS: For a list of special events, contact the State Tourist Office (see *Contact Addresses* section). The following is a selection of special events occurring in San Marino in 2005:
Feb 5 *Festival Day of St Agatha.* **Apr 22-24** *San Marino Formula One Grand Prix.* **Jul** *San Marino Etnofestival.* **Sep 3** *Placci Cup* (San Marino Cycling Grand Prix). **Dec 31** *Let's toast the new year together* (New Year's Eve).
SOCIAL CONVENTIONS: Normal European courtesies and codes of conduct should be observed. **Tipping:** Service charges are generally included in hotel bills. A 10 per cent tip is usual.

Business Profile

ECONOMY: San Marino exports wine and cheese. Its other agricultural products are wheat, barley, maize, grapes and olive oil. Industrial production is concerned with cement, synthetic rubber, leather, textiles and ceramics. Light industries have been expanding quickly in recent years as the Government seeks to diversify the economy away from tourism. Nonetheless, tourism continues to provide much of the Republic's income, accounting for about half of GDP from around three million visitors each year. Quarried stone is an arcane though important export. Another unusual source of revenue is the sale of postage stamps and coins: both are popular with collectors and together account for over 10 per cent of government income. Statistical details of San Marino's external trade are included with those of Italy, with whom San Marino has a long-standing customs union. However there are differences in taxation and regulatory structures which have afforded San Marino the status of a tax haven, as a growing number of non-resident deposits have been made in the principality's banks. In 2001 and 2002, the government responded to OECD calls for tax haven economies to institute measures to tackle money-laundering.
BUSINESS: A suit is recommended and prior appointments are absolutely essential. Avoid making appointments early in the morning or straight after lunch. A knowledge of Italian is useful.
CONFERENCES/CONVENTIONS: For information, contact the State Tourist Office (see *Contact Addresses* section).

Climate

Temperate. Moderate snow in winter, some brief showers in summer. The atmosphere is clean, typical of low mountain and hill country with sea breezes.
Required clothing: Light- to mediumweights and rainwear are required.

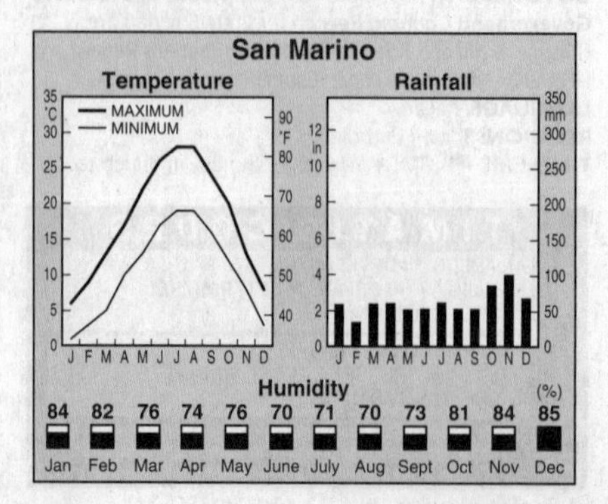

São Tomé e Príncipe

LATEST TRAVEL ADVICE CONTACTS

British Foreign and Commonwealth Office
Tel: (0870) 606 0290 Website: www.fco.gov.uk
US Department of State
Website: http://travel.state.gov/travel
Canadian Department of Foreign Affairs and Int'l Trade
Tel: (1 800) 267 8376 Website: www.dfait-maeci.gc.ca

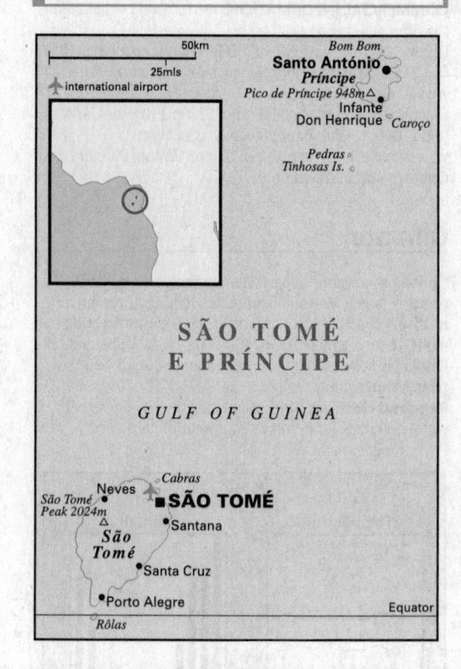

Location: West Africa, Gulf of Guinea.

Country dialling code: 239.

Tourism Office
CP40, Avenue Marginal 12 de Julho, São Tomé
Tel/Fax: (2) 21542.
Embassy of the Democratic Republic of São Tomé e Príncipe
Square Montgommery, 175 Avenue de Tervuren, 1150 Brussels, Belgium
Tel: (2) 734 8966. Fax: (2) 734 8815.
E-mail: ambassade.saotome@fi.be
British Consulate
Residencia Avenida, Avienda da Independencia, CP 257, São Tomé
Tel: (2) 21026/7. Fax: (2) 21372.
Embassy of the Democratic Republic of São Tomé e Príncipe
400 Park Avenue, 7th Floor, New York, NY 10044, USA
Tel: (212) 317 0533. Fax: (212) 317 0580.
E-mail: stp1@attglobal.net *or* wdaf@juno.com
Website: www.saotome.org
Consulates in: Atlanta and Libertyville.
The United States Embassy in Libreville deals with enquiries relating to São Tomé e Príncipe (see *Gabon* section).
The Canadian Embassy in Libreville deals with enquiries from Canadian and Australian citizens relating to São Tomé e Príncipe (see *Gabon* section).

General Information

AREA: 1001 sq km (386.5 sq miles).
POPULATION: 161,000 (official estimate 2003).
POPULATION DENSITY: 137.5 per sq km (census of 2001).
CAPITAL: São Tomé.
GEOGRAPHY: São Tomé e Príncipe comprises two main islands (Saõ Tomé and Príncipe) and the islets Cabras, Gago Coutinho, Pedras Tinhosas and Ilheu dos Rolas (which is

TIMATIC CODES

Health	AMADEUS: **TI-DFT/TMS/HE** GALILEO/WORLDSPAN: **TI-DFT/TMS/HE** SABRE: **TIDFT/TMS/HE**
Visa	AMADEUS: **TI-DFT/TMS/VI** GALILEO/WORLDSPAN: **TI-DFT/TMS/VI** SABRE: **TIDFT/TMS/VI**

To access TIMATIC country information on Health and Visa regulations through the Computer Reservations System (CRS), type in the appropriate command line listed above.

crossed by the Equator line). These lie approximately 200km (120 miles) off the west coast of Gabon, in the Gulf of Guinea. The country is rugged and has a great deal of forest cover and few natural resources. The landscape is varied, combining mountains, tropical forest and beaches.
GOVERNMENT: Republic. Gained independence from Portugal in 1975. **Head of State:** President Fradique de Menezes since 2001. **Head of Government:** Prime Minister Damiao Vaz d'Almeida since 2004.
LANGUAGE: Portuguese is the official language. Creole is also spoken. Some English is spoken, but French is more common.
RELIGION: Roman Catholic majority (82 per cent), with a number of other Christian denominations also represented.
TIME: GMT.
ELECTRICITY: 220 volts AC.
COMMUNICATIONS: Telephone: Very limited IDD is available. **Mobile telephone:** GSM 900. Main network provider is *Companhia Santomense de Telecomunicacoes (SARL)* (website: www.cstome.net). **Internet:** At present there is extremely limited access in the capital. **Telegram:** Facilities are available in the capital and main hotels **Fax:** Services are available from the telephone office and some major hotels (overseas faxes are very expensive). **Post:** Airmail to Europe takes approximately one week to Europe and the USA **Press:** Newspapers are printed in Portuguese. **Radio:** BBC World Service (website: www.bbc.co.uk/worldservice) and Voice of America (website: www.voa.gov) can be received. From time to time the frequencies change and the most up-to-date can be found online.

Passport/Visa

	Passport Required?	Visa Required?	Return Ticket Required?
Full British	Yes	Yes	Yes
Australian	Yes	Yes	Yes
Canadian	Yes	Yes	Yes
USA	Yes	Yes	Yes
Other EU	Yes	Yes	Yes
Japanese	Yes	Yes	Yes

Note: *Regulations and requirements may be subject to change at short notice, and you are advised to contact the appropriate diplomatic or consular authority before finalising travel arrangements. Details of these may be found at the head of this country's entry. Any numbers in the chart refer to the footnotes below.*

PASSPORTS: Valid passport required by all.
VISAS: Required by all except transit passengers continuing their journey to another country by the same or first connecting aircraft within 24 hours provided holding valid onward or return documentation and not leaving the airport.
Types of visa and cost: *Tourist:* single-entry: US$60; mutiple-entry: US$70. *Business:* single-entry: US$80; multiple-entry: US$90. Visas processed immediately are available for an additional fee of US$5. Enquire at the Embassy for further details.
Validity: Three months from date of issue for single-entry; six months from date of issue for multiple-entry. Extensions are possible; apply at the Immigration Department in São Tomé.
Application requirements: (a) Valid passport. (b) Fee, payable by money order only. (c) One passport-size photo. (d) One application form. (e) Stamped addressed envelope to cover international postal charges. (f) Letter stating purpose of travel. (g) Yellow fever immunisation card "copy". *Business:* (a)-(g) and, (h) Company letter.
Application to: Consulate (or Consular section at Embassy); see *Contact Addresses* section. For applications in person, an appointment should be made with the Consulate (or Consular section at Embassy) in advance.
Working days required: Two days (personal application); up to one week (postal applications).
Temporary residence: Enquire at Embassy (see *Contact Addresses section*).

Money

Currency: Dobra (Db) = 100 cêntimos. Notes are in denominations of Db50,000, 20,000, 10,000 and 5000. Coins are in denominations of Db20, 10, 5, 2 and 1, and 50 cêntimos.
Currency exchange: Foreign currencies can be exchanged at banks and some hotels.
Travellers cheques: Limited acceptance by banks and hotels. To avoid additional exchange rate charges travellers are advised to take travellers cheques in US Dollars.
Currency restrictions: The import and export of local and foreign currency is unlimited, provided declared on arrival.
Exchange rate indicators: The following figures are included as a guide to the movements of the Dobra against Sterling and the US Dollar:

Date	Feb '04	May '04	Aug '04	Nov '04
£1.00=	15836.20	15539.1	16185.0	17090.6
$1.00=	8700.00	8700.00	8785.00	9025.00

Banking hours: Mon-Fri 0730-1130.

Duty Free

The following may be imported into São Tomé e Príncipe without incurring customs duty:
Reasonable quantities of tobacco products and perfume (opened).
Prohibited items: Prohibited items: Alcoholic beverages and lottery tickets.

Public Holidays

2005: Jan 1 New Year's Day. **Feb 3** Heroes' Day. **May 1** Labour Day. **Jul 12** Independence Day. **Sep 6** Armed Forces Day. **Sep 30** Agricultural Reform Day. **Nov 26** Argel Accord Day. **Dec 21** São Tomé Day (Catholic). **Dec 25** Christmas Day.
2006: Jan 1 New Year's Day. **Feb 3** Heroes' Day. **May 1** Labour Day. **Jul 12** Independence Day. **Sep 6** Armed Forces Day. **Sep 30** Agricultural Reform Day. **Nov 26** Argel Accord Day. **Dec 21** São Tomé Day (Catholic). **Dec 25** Christmas Day.

Health

	Special Precautions?	Certificate Required?
Yellow Fever	Yes	1
Cholera	2	No
Typhoid & Polio	3	N/A
Malaria	4	N/A

Note: *Regulations and requirements may be subject to change at short notice, and you are advised to contact your doctor well in advance of your intended date of departure. Any numbers in the chart refer to the footnotes below.*

1: A yellow fever vaccination certificate is required from all travellers over one year of age. Travellers arriving from non-endemic zones should note that vaccination is strongly recommended for travel outside the urban areas, even if an outbreak of the disease has not been reported and they would normally not require a vaccination certificate to enter the country.
2: Following WHO guidelines issued in 1973, a cholera vaccination certificate is not a condition of entry to São Tomé e Príncipe. However, cholera is a risk in this country and precautions are essential. Up-to-date advice should be sought before deciding whether these precautions should include vaccination, as medical opinion is divided over its effectiveness; see the *Health* appendix for further information.
3: Vaccination against typhoid is advised.
4: Malaria risk, predominantly in the malignant *falciparum* form exists all year throughout the country. Chloroquine resistance has been reported.
Food & drink: All water should be regarded as being potentially contaminated and therefore unsafe to drink. Water used for drinking, brushing teeth or making ice should have first been boiled or otherwise sterilised. Milk is unpasteurised and should be boiled. Powdered or tinned milk is available and is advised, but make sure that it is reconstituted with pure water. Avoid dairy products which are likely to have been made from unboiled milk. Only eat well-cooked meat and fish, preferably served hot. Pork, salad and mayonnaise may carry increased risk. Vegetables should be cooked and fruit peeled.
Other risks: *Bilharzia* (schistosomiasis) is present. Avoid swimming and paddling in fresh water; swimming pools which are well chlorinated and maintained are safe.
Hepatitis A and *E* are also present; *hepatitis B* is endemic.
Meningococcal disease may occur.
Rabies is present. For those at high risk, vaccination before arrival should be considered. If you are bitten, seek medical advice without delay. For more information, see the *Health* appendix.
Health care: The island has very basic medical facilities, with one hospital. It is important to carry a basic first aid kit. Health insurance is essential.

Travel - International

AIR: The national airline is *Air São Tomé e Príncipe (KY)*, a subsidiary of *TAP Air Portugal*. It operates flights regularly between São Tomé and Libreville (Gabon), where they connect with ingoing or outgoing long-haul flights to or from Europe. *TAP Air Portugal* operates flights from Lisbon and there is also a scheduled flight from Angola.
Approximate flight times: From São Tomé to *London* is six hours 30 minutes (including stopover in Lisbon).
International airports: *São Tomé (TMS)*, 5.5km (3.5 miles) from the town. Transport to the city centre is by airport bus, minibus or taxi. Airport facilities are fairly limited; left luggage, first aid and tourist information are available.
Departure tax: US$20 per adult, payable in cash on departure for all international flights. US$10 must be paid for children, except those under two years who are exempt.
SEA: The main port is São Tomé, but this is not deep-water and few international cruise lines or other passenger ships call there; however, boats do sail there from Libreville and Doula.

Travel - Internal

AIR: *ASTP* (*Air São Tomé e Príncipe*) runs regular flights between São Tomé and Príncipe (flight time - 40 minutes). Panoramic and charter flights are also available.
SEA: A limited ferry service operates between São Tomé and Príncipe.
ROAD: Traffic drives on the right. There are over 380km (236 miles) of roads, although in general these are deteriorating. Some of them are asphalted around São Tomé town, but 4-wheel drive vehicles are necessary to get further afield: animals on the road and potholes may cause problems. There is street lighting only in the capital. There is a **bus** network, and **share taxis** are also in operation. The only public transport on Príncipe is a minibus. **Car hire** can be arranged through the Miramar Hotel (see below). **Documentation:** An International Driving Permit is not legally required but is recommended.

Accommodation

HOTELS: There are currently around 10 hotels in the country offering a total of 200 beds, including the *Miramar Hotel* in the capital São Tomé, the *Marlin Beach* hotel and the *Bom Bom Island Resort* on the northern coast of Príncipe. Apart from the hotels there is also a chain of state-run inns, operated at more modest levels of comfort. Several international hotel chains are currently looking to build high-rise hotels on the islands. But tourism is high on the government's agenda and a push to create more accommodation for this growing market is expected.
CAMPING: This is possible on a number of deserted beaches.

Resorts & Excursions

The islands lie on an alignment of dormant volcanoes, with rugged landscapes, dense forests and virgin, palm-fringed beaches. Only open to tourists since 1987, many of these islands are still almost totally undiscovered by the tourist trade and provide unspoiled beauty and an isolation from the world now rarely found anywhere else. The history of the islands is dominated by the slave trade and slave-worked plantations. These plantations, now mostly nationalised, still remain a major feature of the landscape.
SÃO TOMÉ: The island of São Tomé, with its capital of the same name, represents 90 per cent of the total surface of the country. São Tomé is a picturesque town, with colonial Portuguese architecture and attractive parks. There are a number of *roças* (cocoa plantations) on the island that are worth visiting: **Agostinho Neto**, the largest plantation in the country, is a clear example of São Tomé's colonial past; other *roças* are **Agua Izé**, where visitors can tour the plantation by train, **Monté Café** and **Ribeira Peixe**. Other attractions on the island include the **Boca de Inferno** (Hell's Mouth), a sea water fountain several metres high; the **Cascada São Nicolâu** waterfall near **Pousada Boa Vista**; the **Ilheu da Rolas** (Turtledove Island), a small island off São Tomé crossed by the equator; the **Pico de São Tomé**, the highest mountain in the archipelago (2024m/6800ft); the **Porto Alegre**, on the southern tip of the island; the ancient fishing town of **São João dos Angolares**; and the fortress of **São Sebastião**, which also houses a museum with a collection of religious and colonial art.
PRÍNCIPE: The small island of Príncipe is located 150km (94 miles) from São Tomé and its main town is **Santo Antonio**, which has preserved a distinctive colonial architecture and atmosphere. Dominated by two cocoa plantations, additional attractions for visitors are the **Ilheu Bom Bom**, a tiny island situated off Príncipe's northern coast, where one of the country's few tourist resorts is located; and the **Pico de Principe**, the island's summit (948m/3128ft).

Sport & Activities

Watersports: Saõ Tomé e Principe has some of the clearest waters on the western coast of Africa and is therefore ideal for **swimming**, **snorkelling** and **diving**. Beaches have white as well as black sand. *Lagoa Azul* (Blue Lagoon) on São Tomé is good for snorkelling (but there is only a rocky beach). Individual hotels can arrange diving trips as well equipment hire. Hotels and resorts can also organise deep-sea **fishing** trips, notably on Bom Bom Island.
Other: Visitors can also enjoy excellent **hiking** through São Tomé's rainforest as well as fascinating and varied **birdwatching**.

Social Profile

FOOD & DRINK: There are several restaurants in the capital, augmented by a considerable number of more informal eating establishments patronised by the inhabitants. Reservations are nearly always required, even at the higher profile restaurants, not because of lack of space but to allow the proprietor to obtain sufficient food in advance. Grilled fish and chicken, fried fish and tropical fruit are popular. Most dishes are highly spiced.
SPECIAL EVENTS: Popular theatre has an important place in daily life and each island has its own form of traditional

dance and mime. The *Auto de Floripes* (in São Tomé) and the *Tchiloli* (in Principe) date back to the 16th century and relate the *Tragedy of the Marquis of Mantua and the Emperor Charlemagne*. The roles are passed on from father to son while women usually remain spectators. There are also a number of religious processions dedicated to Catholic saints, and all the main Christian holidays are celebrated. For further information, contact the Embassy in Brussels (see *Contact Addresses* section).
SOCIAL CONVENTIONS: The Portuguese influence is very strong. People are friendly and courteous. Every greeting is accompanied by a handshake. Normal social courtesies should be observed. Alcohol is available and smoking is acceptable. **Photography:** Visitors wishing to photograph local people should ask permission first. **Tipping:** Not always welcomed.

Business Profile

ECONOMY: The economy is based on the export of agricultural products: cocoa, palm oil, bananas, coffee and coconuts. This concentration on cash crops, especially cocoa (most of which is exported) means that the country has to import most of its food. It also means the country's economy is overly dependent on favourable weather conditions and world commodity prices: by and large these have not been kind to São Tomé e Principe's economy in recent years. After the failure to develop an indigenous fishing industry in the 1980s, fishing rights were sold under licence to foreign fleets. Manufacturing industry is confined to a few food-processing plants and factories producing consumer goods for local consumption. A free trade zone has now been established on Principe island in an effort to boost the export economy. Since the late-1990s, economic policy has concentrated on promotion of the private sector and the removal of trade barriers. This has been carried out under the auspices of an IMF Structural Adjustment Programme. The country has also benefited from the IMF's Heavily Indebted Poor Countries Programme, which has eliminated a large slice of the foreign debt; nonetheless, the government still considers elimination of its debt a high priority. It will be able to do this once revenues begin to flow from the oil and gas fields recently discovered (and as yet unexploited) in São Tomé's territorial waters. Exploration bids submitted in 2003 have already resulted in a windfall for the government amounting to hundreds of millions of dollars. With its economy due for a radical transformation, the government is planning to construct a deepwater port and has suggested to the USA that it might consider establishing a naval base (not least to protect the oilfields). The government also hopes to promote the currently minute tourism industry. Economic performance in recent years has been improving and is expected to get even better as revenue from oil starts to come in. Portugal and Angola supply most of the country's imports; The Netherlands is the main export market. São Tomé e Principe is a member of the African Development Bank and the CEEAC trade bloc.
COMMERCIAL INFORMATION: The following organisation can offer advice: Ministry of Foreign Affairs and Co-operation, avenue 12 July, CP 111, São Tomé (tel: (2) 22662; fax: (2) 22597). **Office hours:** Mon-Fri 0800-1200 and 1500-1800, Sat 0800-1200.

Climate

An equatorial climate with heavy rainfall, high temperatures and humidity. The south of the main island, being mountainous, is wetter than the north. The main dry season is from early June to late September. There is another dry season, the 'Pequenha Gravana', from the end of December to the start of February.
Required clothing: Tropicals and lightweight cottons throughout the year. Umbrellas or light waterproofs for the rainy season are advised.

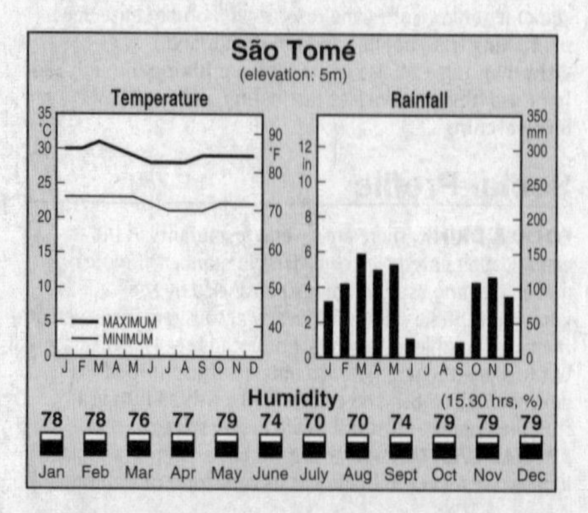

Saudi Arabia

LATEST TRAVEL ADVICE CONTACTS

British Foreign and Commonwealth Office
Tel: (0870) 606 0290 Website: www.fco.gov.uk
US Department of State
Website: http://travel.state.gov/travel
Canadian Department of Foreign Affairs and Int'l Trade
Tel: (1 800) 267 8376 Website: www.dfait-maeci.gc.ca

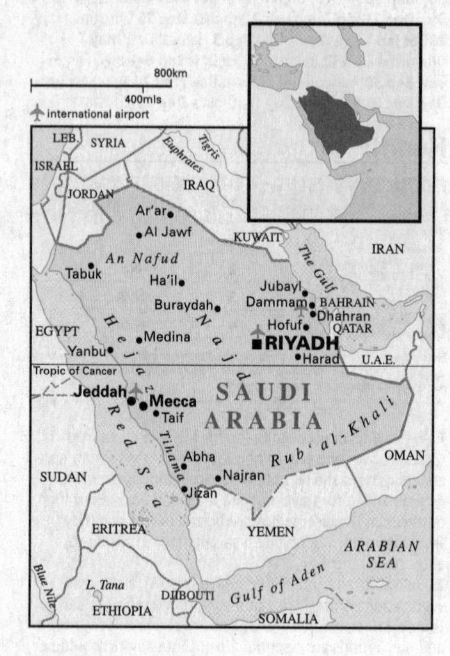

Location: Middle East.

Country dialling code: 966.

Saudi Arabian Ministry of Foreign Affairs
Street address: Nasseriya Street, Riyadh 11544, Saudi Arabia
Postal address: PO Box 55937, Riyadh 11544, Saudi Arabia
Tel: (1) 406 7777 *or* 405 5000.
Fax: (1) 403 0645.
Website: www.mofa.gov.sa
Royal Embassy of Saudi Arabia
30 Charles Street, London W1J 5DZ, UK
Visa section: 30-32 Charles Street, London W1J 5DZ, UK
Tel: (020) 7917 3000.
Fax: (020) 7917 3255.
E-mail: ukemb@mofa.gov.sa
Website: www.saudiembassy.org.uk
Opening hours: Mon-Thurs 0900-1600, Fri 0900-1500.
Consular section: Mon-Thurs 0900-1130 (visa applications); 1400-1530 (passport collection), Fri 1330-1430.
Saudi Arabian Information Centre
18 Seymour Street, London W1H 7HU, UK
Tel: (020) 7486 3470.
Fax: (020) 7486 8211.
E-mail: sair@saudinf.com
Website: www.saudinf.com/main/start.htm
British Embassy
Diplomatic Quarter, PO Box 94351, Riyadh 11693, Saudi Arabia
Tel: (1) 488 0077. Fax: (1) 488 2373 *or* 1209 (consular section).
E-mail: Visa.Riyadh@fco.gov.uk
Website: www.britishembassy.gov.uk/saudiarabia
Consulate in: Jeddah. *Trade Office in:* Al Khobar.
Royal Embassy of Saudi Arabia
601 New Hampshire Avenue, NW, Washington, DC 20037, USA
Tel: (202) 342 3800 *or* 337 4076 (information section) *or* 944 3126 (visa section).
Fax: (202) 337 4084 (consular section).
E-mail: info@saudiembassy.net
Website: www.saudiembassy.net
Consulates in: Houston, Los Angeles and New York.

TIMATIC CODES

Health
AMADEUS: **TI-DFT/RUH/HE**
GALILEO/WORLDSPAN: **TI-DFT/RUH/HE**
SABRE: **TIDFT/RUH/HE**

Visa
AMADEUS: **TI-DFT/RUH/VI**
GALILEO/WORLDSPAN: **TI-DFT/RUH/VI**
SABRE: **TIDFT/RUH/VI**

To access TIMATIC country information on Health and Visa regulations through the Computer Reservations System (CRS), type in the appropriate command line listed above.

Embassy of the United States of America
PO Box 94309, Riyadh 11693, Saudi Arabia
Tel: (1) 488 3800. Fax: (1) 488 3989.
E-mail: USEmbRiyadhWebSite@state.gov
Website: http://usembassy.state.gov/riyadh
Consulates in: Dhahran and Jeddah.
Royal Embassy of Saudi Arabia
99 Bank Street, Suite 901, Ottawa, Ontario K1P 6B9, Canada
Tel: (613) 237 4100-3 *or* 4105 (consular section).
Fax: (613) 237 0567 *or* 7350 (consular section).
Canadian Embassy
PO Box 94321, Diplomatic Quarter, Riyadh 11693, Saudi Arabia
Tel: (1) 488 2288. Fax: (1) 488 1997.
E-mail: ryadh@dfait-maeci.gc.ca
Website: www.dfait-maeci.gc.ca/middle_east/saudi

General Information

AREA: 2,240,000 sq km (864,869 sq miles).
POPULATION: 23,370,000 (official estimate 2002).
POPULATION DENSITY: 10.4 per sq km.
CAPITAL: Riyadh (royal). **Population**: 4,761,000 (UN estimate 2002; including suburbs). Jeddah (administrative). **Population:** 3,192,000 (UN estimate 2001; including suburbs).
GEOGRAPHY: Saudi Arabia occupies four-fifths of the Arabian peninsula. It is bordered to the northwest by Jordan, to the north by Iraq and Kuwait, to the east by the Gulf of Oman, Qatar, the United Arab Emirates and Oman, and to the south by Yemen. To the west lies the Red Sea. Along the Red Sea coast is a narrow coastal strip (*Tihama*) which becomes relatively hotter and more humid towards the south and has areas of extensive tidal flats and lava fields. Behind this coastal plain is a series of plateaux reaching up to 2000m (6560ft). The southern part of this range, *Asir*, has some peaks of over 3000m (9840ft). North of these mountains, in the far north, is *An Nafud*, a sand sea, and further south the landscape rises to *Najd*, a semi-desert area scattered with oases. Still further south the land falls away, levelling out to unremitting desert, the uninhabited 'Empty Quarter' or *Rub al Khali*. Along the Gulf coast is a low fertile plain giving way to limestone ridges inland.
GOVERNMENT: Absolute monarchy since 1932. **Head of State and Government:** King Fahd Ibn Abd al-Aziz Al-Sa'ud since 1982.
LANGUAGE: Arabic. English is spoken in business circles.
RELIGION: The majority of Saudi Arabians follow Islam; around 85 per cent are Sunni Muslim, but Shia Muslims predominate in the Eastern Province.
TIME: GMT + 3.
ELECTRICITY: 127/220 volts AC, 60Hz.
COMMUNICATIONS: Telephone: A sophisticated telecommunications network and satellite, microwave and cable systems span the country. Full IDD is available. Outgoing international code: 00. **Mobile telephone:** GSM 900 band networks are available in over 45 cities. Main network providers are Etihad Etisalat (website: http://etihadetisalat.com.sa) and *Saudi Telecom Company* (website: www.stc.com.sa). **Fax:** Major hotels provide facilities. **Internet:** The Ministry of Post, Telegraph and Telephones provides Internet facilities in most cities. E-mail can also be accessed from many hotels and Internet cafes. Main ISPs include *Arab Net* (website: www.arab.net.sa) and *Shabakah* (website: www.shabakah.net.sa). **Telegram:** Telegrams can be sent from all post offices. **Post:** Internal and international services available from the Central Post Office. Post is delivered to box numbers. Airmail to Europe takes up to one week. Surface mail takes up to five months. **Press:** The main newspapers include *Al-Jazirah*, *Ar-Riyadh* and *Okaz*. English-language dailies include *Arab News*, *Riyadh Daily* and *Saudi Gazette*.
Radio: BBC World Service (website: www.bbc.co.uk/worldservice) and Voice of America (website: www.voa.gov) can be received. From time to time the frequencies change and the most up-to-date can be found online.

Passport/Visa

	Passport Required?	Visa Required?	Return Ticket Required?
Full British	Yes	Yes	Yes
Australian	Yes	Yes	Yes
Canadian	Yes	Yes	Yes
USA	Yes	Yes	Yes
Other EU	Yes	Yes	Yes
Japanese	Yes	Yes	Yes

Note: *Regulations and requirements may be subject to change at short notice, and you are advised to contact the appropriate diplomatic or consular authority before finalising travel arrangements. Details of these may be found at the head of this country's entry. Any numbers in the chart refer to the footnotes below.*

Restricted entry: (a) Holders of an Israeli passport or passports with Israeli stamps in them. (b) Passengers not complying with Saudi conventions of dress and behaviour, including those who appear to be in a state of intoxication, or who display inappropriate affection (especially between men and women) will be refused entry (see *Social Conventions* section). (c) There are special regulations concerning pilgrims entering Saudi Arabia. Contact the Consulate (or Consular section at Embassy) for further information. Members of the Quadyani religious group may be refused entry when travelling for pilgrimage purposes.
Note: (a) Unaccompanied women must be met at the airport by their sponsor or husband and have confirmed onward reservations as far as their final destination in Saudi Arabia. If met by a sponsor, it is worth noting that there are restrictions on women travelling by car with men who are not related by blood or marriage. However it is acceptable for women visiting for business purposes to be accompanied and met at the airport by male business partners: further enquiries can be made at the Information Centre or Embassy. Women and under-aged children should be accompanied by a Moharram (close male family member). (b) No foreign passenger who is working as a domestic servant in Saudi Arabia should be transported to Saudi Arabia unless holding a valid non-refundable return ticket.
PASSPORTS: A passport valid for six months at time of entry is required by all except Muslim pilgrims holding Pilgrim Passes, tickets and other documents for their onward or return journey and entering the country via Jeddah or Medina - although sufficient evidence of Muslim faith must be provided (eg religious authenticated certificate). All passports must be valid for at least six months beyond the estimated stay in Saudi Arabia.
VISAS: Required by all except the following:
(a) nationals of Bahrain, Kuwait, Oman, Qatar and United Arab Emirates;
(b) transit passengers continuing their journey by the same or first connecting aircraft within 18 hours, provided holding valid onward or return documentation, not leaving the airport and making no further landing in Saudi Arabia (except nationals of Burkina Faso, Mali, Niger and Nigeria who *always* require a transit visa);
(c) holders of re-entry permits and 'Landing Permits' issued by the Saudi Arabian Ministry of Foreign Affairs (see *Contact Addresses* section).
Types of visa and cost: *Family Visit*: £39. *Business*: £39; £96 (multiple-entry). *Work*: £10, if paying at Embassy, *or* SR1000 to be paid by employer in Saudi Arabia. *Residency*: £10. *Transit*: £10. *Pilgrim (Ummra)*: no charge (one to three months for a maximum of 30 days).
Note: (a) The Pilgrim (Ummra) visa can only be obtained through an authorised 'Ummra Agency', appointed by the Ministry of Foreign Affairs. Check with Embassy for a full list of appointed agents. Administrative fees may apply. (b) Transit passengers who stay in the King Abdulaziz International Airport, Jeddah Islamic Port or Prince Mohammed bin Abdulaziz Airport in Medina for over 24 hours can perform Ummra or visit a Holy Mosque, provided they withhold a signed agreement with one of the appointed Ummra agencies.
Validity: The visa stay period starts from the first day of entry into Saudi Arabia within the visa's valid dates. Ummra visas are valid for 30 days once in Saudi Arabia.
Application to: Consulate (or Consular section at Embassy); see *Contact Addresses* section. Travellers are advised to apply well in advance.
Application requirements: *Family/Residency:* (a) One application form. (b) One passport-size photo affixed to application form. Children travelling on parents' passport must have photos affixed on passport and endorsed by relevant authorities with photos attached on application form. Copies of birth certificate and marriage certificate of all accompanying children and spouses are also required. (c) Passport valid for at least six months. (d) Prepaid, self-addressed, recorded delivery envelope, if applying by post. If applying by post from Ireland (Rep), enclose a minimum of nine coupons. (e) Fee (payable in cash, by postal order or by banker's draft only for nationals from Ireland (Rep)). (f) Invitation from host or sponsor, with authorisation from the Saudi Ministry of Foreign Affairs. (g) Medical report, authenticated by the UK Foreign Office (for persons over 15 years of age). Applicants from Ireland (Rep) should legalise their medical report at the Irish Foreign Office in Dublin. (h) Authorisation from the Saudi Ministry of Foreign Affairs, obtained by their sponsor in Saudi Arabia. *Business:* (a)-(e) and, (f) Letter of invitation from Saudi host company endorsed by Saudi Chamber of Commerce (original and copy). (g) Letter from company or organisation in own country. *Work:* (a)-(e) and, (f) Letter of introduction from Saudi sponsor and copy of the employment contract. (g) Copies of academic qualifications and work experience in the field of job applied for. (h) Letter of *No Objection* if previously employed in Saudi Arabia. (i) An amount equivalent to SR50 deposited at the Consulate's cashier desk. *Pilgrim:* (a)-(d) and, (e) Airline ticket with confirmed booking (both ways). The point of entry and departure must be Jeddah or Medina. (f) Meningitis immunisation certificate with validity for more than three years and vaccination issued no less than 10 days before travelling. A Yellow Fever certificate may be required, if travelling from an infected area. (g) ID card must be worn on wrist band and luggage must be clearly labelled: 'PILGRIM'. (h) Letter of approval issued by Saudi Ministry of Hajj, confirming that the authorised UK travel agent, tour operator and charities, through which the application for Hajj was submitted, have completed the necessary requirements regarding their pilgrims. (i) Proof of conversion to Islam may have to be submitted. *Transit:* (a)-(e) and, (f) Airline ticket reservation showing proof of leaving Saudi Arabia within 48 hours and visa valid for next destination if applicable.
Note: (a) An Exit Permit is required for most nationals, requiring a passport-size photo and must be issued by the Chief of Police (usually processed within three days after application). It is advised to enquire at the nearest Embassy for further information. (b) There are further requirements for Ummra applications, but these must be submitted by the endorsed travel agent or tour operator.
Working days required: At least 24 hours. At least one week if applying by post. For information on processing time for all other types of visa, contact the Consulate (or Consular section at Embassy).

Money

Currency: Saudi Arabian Riyal (SR) = 100 halala; 5 halala = 20 qurush. Notes are in denominations of SR500, 200, 100, 50, 20, 10, 5 and 1. Coins are in denominations of 100, 50, 25, 10, and 5 halala, and 10, 5, 2 and 1 qurush.
Currency exchange: Most foreign currencies can be exchanged at commercial banks and money-changers, which stay open longer.
Credit & debit cards: American Express, Diners Club, MasterCard and Visa are all widely accepted. Check with your credit or debit card company for details of merchant acceptability and other services which may be available.
Travellers cheques: Widely accepted although they can be hard to change. To avoid additional exchange rate charges, travellers are advised to take travellers cheques in Saudi Riyal, Euros, US Dollars or Pounds Sterling and to carry the purchase receipt.
Currency restrictions: Free import and export of both local and foreign currency. Import of Israeli currency is prohibited.
Exchange rate indicators: The following figures are included as a guide to the movements of the Riyal against Sterling and the US Dollar:

Date	Feb '04	May '04	Aug '04	Nov '04
£1.00=	6.82	6.69	6.90	7.10
$1.00=	3.75	3.75	3.75	3.75

Banking hours: Sat-Wed 0830-1200 and 1700-1900; Thurs 0830-1200. Money-changers stay open longer.

Duty Free

The following items may be imported into Saudi Arabia without incurring customs duty:
600 cigarettes or 100 cigars or 500g of tobacco; a reasonable amount of perfume; a reasonable amount of cultured pearls for personal use.
Note: Duty is levied on cameras and typewriters, but if these articles are re-exported within 90 days, the customs charges may be refunded. It is advisable not to put film into cameras.
Prohibited items: Alcohol, narcotics, pornography, religious books (besides the Qu'ran), pork, contraceptives, firearms, natural pearls, live animals and birds, all types of palm trees, most foods and items listed as prohibited by the Arab League (copy available from the Embassy).

Public Holidays

2005: Jan 21-25 Eid al-Adha (Feast of the Sacrifice). **Sep 23** Saudi National Day. **Nov 3-5** Eid al-Fitr (End of Ramadan).
Jan 10-13 2006 Eid al-Adha (Feast of the Sacrifice). **Sep 23** Saudi National Day. **Oct 22-24** Eid al-Fitr (End of Ramadan).
Note: Muslim festivals are timed according to local sightings of various phases of the moon and the dates given above are approximations. During the lunar month of Ramadan that precedes Eid al-Fitr, Muslims fast during the day and feast at night and normal business patterns may be interrupted. Some disruption may continue into Eid al-Fitr itself. Eid al-Fitr and Eid al-Adha may last anything from two to 10 days, depending on the region. During Hajj (when pilgrims visit Mecca) all government establishments and some businesses will be closed for 10 to 14 days. For more information, see the *World of Islam* appendix.

Health

	Special Precautions?	Certificate Required?
Yellow Fever	No	1
Cholera	No	No
Typhoid & Polio	2	N/A
Malaria	3	N/A

Note: *Regulations and requirements may be subject to change at short notice, and you are advised to contact your doctor well in advance of your intended date of departure. Any numbers in the chart refer to the footnotes below.*

1: A yellow fever vaccination certificate is required from all travellers arriving from countries of which any parts are infected.
2: Vaccination against typhoid is advised.
3: Malaria risk, predominantly in the malignant *falciparum* form, exists throughout the year in most of the Southern region, except the high altitude areas of Asir Province, and in certain rural areas of the Western Province. There is no risk in Mecca or Medina. Resistance to chloroquine has been reported. The recommended prophylaxis is chloroquine plus proguanil. Cerebral Malaria has also occurred, but solely in the Jizan region.
Food & drink: All water should be regarded as being potentially contaminated. Water used for drinking, brushing teeth or making ice should have first been boiled or otherwise sterilised. Milk is unpasteurised and should be boiled. Powdered or tinned milk is available and is advised, but make sure that it is reconstituted with pure water. Avoid dairy products which are likely to have been made from unboiled milk. Only eat well-cooked meat and fish, preferably served hot. Salad and mayonnaise may carry increased risk. Vegetables should be cooked and fruit peeled.
Note: During the *Hajj* (annual pilgrimage to Mecca), Saudi Arabia requires vaccination of pilgrims against *meningococcal meningitis*. Although this applies mainly to pilgrims, other travellers may find themselves affected, especially during the month of August. Vaccination is compulsory all year round, however, for nationals of Burkina Faso, Mali, Niger and Nigeria arriving from the following countries: Burkina Faso, Cameroon, Central African Republic, Chad, Congo (Dem Rep), Ethiopia, The Gambia, Ghana, Guinea, Mali, Niger, Nigeria and Sudan.
Other risks: *Bilharzia* (schistosomiasis) is present. Avoid swimming and paddling in fresh water; swimming pools which are well chlorinated and maintained are safe.
Hepatitis A is common and *hepatitis B* is endemic. *Visceral leishmaniasis* occurs in the southwest of the country. Cases of *Rift Valley Fever* have been reported, mostly in the Jizan area.
Rabies is present. For those at high risk, vaccination before arrival should be considered. If you are bitten, seek medical advice without delay. For more information, consult the *Health* appendix.
Health care: Medical facilities are generally of a high standard, but treatment is expensive. Health insurance is essential.

Travel - International

Note: There is a continuing high threat of terrorism in Saudi Arabia. It is suspected that terrorists are planning further attacks, including against Westerners and places associated with Westerners in Saudi Arabia. All necessary steps to protect safety and to guarantee strict security arrangements should be undertaken. It should also be remembered that Islamic law is strictly enforced in Saudi Arabia.
AIR: Saudi Arabia's national airline is *Saudia (SV)* (website: www.saudiairlines.com).
Approximate flight times: From *London* to Jeddah is five hours 50 minutes, to Riyadh is six hours 25 minutes, and to Dhahran is six hours 45 minutes. From *Los Angeles* to Jeddah is 18 hours 45 minutes and to Riyadh is 21 hours 15 minutes. From *New York* to Jeddah is 13 hours and to Riyadh is 16 hours. From *Singapore* to Jeddah is eight hours 25 minutes.
International airports: *Riyadh (RUH)* (King Khaled International) airport, 35km (22 miles) north of the city.
Dhahran (DHA) (Al Khobar) airport, 13km (8 miles) southeast of Dhahran (travel time - 15 minutes).
Jeddah (JED) (King Abdul Aziz) airport, 18km (11 miles) north of the city (travel time - 30 minutes). Facilities at all the above airports include bus and taxi services, banks/bureaux de change, duty free shopping, car rental, restaurants and tourist information points. From *Jeddah* airport, bus and taxi services are available for Mecca, Medina and Taif.
Dammam (DMM) (King Fahd International) airport, 30km (19) miles northwest of Dammam (travel time - 45 minutes).
Departure tax: SR50. Children, Hajj and Ummra pilgrims

A B C D E F G H I J K L M N O P Q R S T U V W X Y Z

Credit: © Ministry of Information

and passengers accompanying human remains are exempt.
SEA: The main international passenger ports are Dammam (Gulf), and Jeddah and Yanbu (Red Sea).
ROAD: The principal international routes from Jordan are Amman to Dammam, Medina and Jeddah. There are also roads to Yemen (from Jeddah), Kuwait, Qatar and the United Arab Emirates. A causeway links Al Khobar with Bahrain. There are regular international buses between Saudi Arabia and Bahrain, Egypt, Jordan, Qatar, Syrian Arab Republic, Turkey and United Arab Emirates.

Travel - Internal

AIR: There are many domestic airports and air travel is by far the most convenient way of travelling around the country. *Saudia (SV)* connects all main centres. 'Arabian Express' economy class connects Jeddah with Riyadh in just over one hour and Riyadh with Dhahran in just under one hour (no advance reservations). A boarding pass should be obtained the evening before departure. There are special flights for pilgrims arriving at or departing from Jeddah during the *Hajj*.
SEA: Dhows may be chartered for outings on both coasts.
RAIL: Children under four travel free. Children aged four to 11 pay half fare. The main railway line is the 570km-long Riyadh–Dammam line, which links Dhahran, Abqaiq, Hofuf, Harad and Al Kharj. There is a daily service in air-conditioned trains with dining car. An additional line links Riyadh with Hofuf. The railway on the west coast made famous by Lawrence of Arabia's raid has long since been abandoned to the desert.
ROAD: Traffic drives on the right. There are approximately 150,000km (93,000 miles) of roads linking the main towns and rural areas, of which 22,000km (13,600 miles) are paved. The network is constantly being upgraded and expanded (most recently, an expressway has been built from Jeddah to Medina and the trans-peninsula road from Jeddah to Dammam has been upgraded) and on the main routes, much of it is of the highest standard. The corniche that winds down the escarpment between Taif and Mecca is as spectacular a feat of engineering as may be seen anywhere, as is the King Fahed Gateway that links Saudi Arabia to Bahrain. However, standards of driving are erratic, particularly in the Eastern Province, where it is not unknown for lorry drivers to equip their vehicles with hub-knives similar to those seen in the film *Ben Hur*. Criteria for apportioning blame after traffic accidents are also erratic and many driving offences carry an automatic prison sentence. As foreigners are tolerated rather than welcomed in Saudi Arabia, it is best to drive with extreme caution at all times. Women are not allowed to drive vehicles or ride bicycles on public roads. Non-Muslims may not enter Mecca or the immediate area; police are stationed to ensure that they turn off onto a specially built ring road, known amongst expatriates as the 'Christian Bypass'. **Bus:** Services have recently been developed by *SAPTCO* to serve inter-urban and local needs. Modern vehicles have been acquired, including air-conditioned double-deckers. All buses must have a screened-off section for the exclusive use of female passengers. **Taxi:** Available in all cities, but often very expensive. Some have meters, and fares should be negotiated in advance. **Car hire:** The major international car hire agencies have offices in Saudi Arabia. The minimum age is 25. **Documentation:** A national driving licence is valid for up to three months if accompanied by an officially sanctioned translation into Arabic. An International Driving Permit (with translation) is recommended, but not required by law. Women are not allowed to drive. There are also restrictions on women travelling by car with men who are not related by blood or marriage.

Accommodation

There is a good range of hotel accommodation throughout the country. Accommodation is generally easy to find, except during the pilgrimage season when advance reservations are recommended. Service charges are fixed at 15 per cent for deluxe and first-category hotels and at 10 per cent for all others. Hotel charges double in Mecca and Medina during the pilgrimage season, and increase by 25 per cent during the summer months in resort areas such as Abha, Al-Baha, Kamis Mushait and Taif. For further information, contact the Saudi Arabian Ministry of Commerce (see *Contact Addresses* section). **Grading:** There are seven grades of hotel in Saudi Arabia: **deluxe**, **first-class A** and **B**, **second-class A** and **B**, and **third-class A** and **B**.
There are also around 20 youth hostels in Saudi Arabia.

Resorts & Excursions

CENTRAL & EASTERN REGIONS

THE NAJD (CENTRAL REGION): The Najd is a stony desert plateau at the heart of Saudi Arabia, somewhat isolated from the rest of the peninsula. It was from here that Ibn Saud led his tribe of nomads out to create a new kingdom through conquest. Despite oil wealth, some Najdis still lead a semi-nomadic life, tending camels and sheep, but many have settled in the same towns they once milked for tribute with threats of violence. Watchtowers, standing guard on all the high points in Najd, are a reminder of this age-old conflict between nomad and farmer.
Riyadh: The royal capital, Riyadh (Ryad), is a modern city built on the site of the first town captured by Ibn Saud, when he stormed the **Musmat Fort** in 1902 (a spearhead embedded in the main door is said to be the one with which Ibn Saud killed the Turkish governor). Apart from the fort and a few traditional Najdi palaces near **Deera Square**, little trace of the old town remains. The *King's Camel Races* are held near the city in April or May.
Other places of interest in Najd are **Al-Hair**, **Aneyzah**, **Diriya**, **Hail**, **Qassim**, **Shaib Awsat**, **Shaib Laha**, **Towqr**, **Tumair**, **Wadi-al-Jafi** and **Wadi Hanifa**.
HASA (EASTERN REGION): Fertile lowland coastal plains inhabited by the kingdom's Shia minority, who have traditionally lived by fishing, diving for pearls, raising date palms and trading abroad and with the interior. All of Saudi Arabia's vast stocks of oil lie under Hasa or beneath the Gulf, and the locals are now outnumbered by foreign oil-workers from all over the world.
Places retaining some flavour of old Hasa include **Hofuf**, a lively oasis with Turkish influence and a camel market; **Jebel-al-Qara**, where the potteries have been worked by eight generations of the same family; **Abqaiq**, which has a 5000-year-old saltmine, still in operation; the ruined customs house at **Uqair**, once an important Portuguese port and caravan terminus; and **Tarut Island**, site of the oldest town on the peninsula, now a picturesque settlement of fishermen and weavers.

WESTERN & SOUTHERN REGIONS

THE HEJAZ (WESTERN REGION): The west coast is a centre for trade, but of equal importance is the concentration of Islamic holy cities, including Mecca and Medina, which attract pilgrims from all over the world. The region also includes the city of Jeddah, which was until recently Saudi Arabia's diplomatic capital and remains the most important commercial and cultural gateway to the country.
Mecca: The spiritual centre of the Islamic world, forbidden to non-Muslims. Places of significance to Muslims include the **Kaabah Enclosure**, the **Mountain of Light**, the **Plain of Arafat** and the **House of Abdullah Bin Abdul Muttalib**, where Muhammad was born.
Medina: The second-holiest city in Islam and also forbidden to non-Muslims.
Jeddah: Although the city has grown phenomenally, priority is being given to the preservation of the ancient city. The ragged, coral-coloured Ottoman buildings are being renovated. Leisure facilities have increased and the corniche has a 'Brighton' feel about it. There is an amusement park and a wonderful creek allowing both sailing and snorkelling. Its hotels and restaurants are cosmopolitan and there are good fish and meat markets.
Taif: Perched on top of a 900m (3000ft) cliff at the edge of the plateau above Mecca, this resort town enjoys a milder climate than much of the country and was for a long time the official summer capital. It is noted for its pink palaces and for the astounding modern corniche road that winds down the sheer cliffs of the Taif escarpment to the hot coastal plain.
Other important towns in the Hejaz include **Khaybar**, **Hanakiyah**, **Usta**, **Wadi Fatima** and **Yanbu**.
THE ASIR (SOUTHERN REGION): A range of coastal mountains and the only part of the kingdom where there is significant wild vegetation, mostly palms and evergreen bushes. Millet, wheat and dates are grown using largely traditional methods. The inhabitants are darker than other Saudis, being in part descended from African slaves. Baboon, gazelle, leopard, honey badger, mongoose and other 'African' species inhabit remoter areas. Unique to Asir are the ancient **gasaba towers**, phallus-shaped and of unknown purpose.
Places to visit include the ancient caravan city of **Qaryat-al-Fau**, currently being excavated; the great dam and temple at **Najran**; and nearby, amidst orchards of pomegranates, limes and bananas, the ornate ruins of the ancient cities of **Timna** and **Shiban**.

Sport & Activities

Obhir Creek, 50km (30 miles) north of Jeddah, has good facilities for **swimming**, **water-skiing**, **fishing** and **sailing**, and there are similar beaches on the Gulf coast south of Al Khobar. Elsewhere, hotels have swimming pools. The British and US embassies have men-only health clubs as well as swimming pools, **golf** clubs and **squash** and **tennis** facilities. Most companies employing foreign workers also have some sports facilities. The desert terrain provides great opportunities for off-road **motorcycling** but this sport is prohibited from time to time. **Football** is popular and most large towns have modern stadiums.

Social Profile

FOOD & DRINK: Local food is often strongly flavoured and spicy. The staple diet is *pitta* bread (flat, unleavened bread) which accompanies every dish. Rice, lentils, chick peas (*hummus*) and cracked wheat (*burghul*) are also common. The most common meats are lamb and chicken. Beef is rare and pork is proscribed under Islamic law. The main meat meal of the day is lunch, either *kultra* (meat on skewers) or *kebabs* served with soup and vegetables. Arabic cakes, cream desserts and rice pudding (*muhalabia*) also feature in the diet. *Mezzeh*, the equivalent of hôrs d'oeuvres, may include up to 40 dishes. Foreign cooking is on offer in larger towns and the whole range of international cuisine, including fast food, is available in the oil-producing Eastern Province and in Jeddah. Restaurants have table service. There are no bars. Alcohol is forbidden by law, and there are severe penalties for infringement; it is important to note that this applies to all nationals regardless of religion. Arabic coffee and fruit drinks are popular alternatives. Alcohol-free beers and cocktails are served in hotel bars.

NIGHTLIFE: Apart from restaurants and hotels there is no nightlife in the Western sense.

SHOPPING: *Souks* (markets) sell incense and incense burners, jewellery, bronze and brassware, richly decorated daggers and swords, and in the Eastern Province, huge brass-bonded chests. Bargaining is often expected, even for modern goods such as cameras and electrical equipment (which can be very good value). **Shopping hours:** Sat-Thurs 0900-1300 and 1630-2000 (Ramadan 2000-0100). These hours differ in various parts of the country.

SPECIAL EVENTS: Most visitors to Saudi Arabia are Muslim pilgrims and the majority of events celebrated in the country are of a religious nature (see the *World of Islam* appendix). For more information on special events, contact the Saudi Arabian Information Centre (see *Contact Addresses* section). The following is a selection of special events occurring in Saudi Arabia in 2005:

Jan 19-22 *Hajj to Mecca*. **Oct 27-Nov 5** *Saudi International Book Fair*, Jeddah. **Nov 28-Dec 17** *Saudi Motor Show*, Jeddah. **Dec 5-9** *Riyadh Motor Show*.

SOCIAL CONVENTIONS: Saudi culture is based on Islam and the perfection of the Arabic language. The Saudi form of Islam is conservative and fundamentalist, based on the 18th-century revivalist movement of the Najdi leader Sheikh Muhammad Ibn Abdel-Wahhab. This still has a great effect on Saudi society, especially on the position of women, who are required by law only to leave the home totally covered in black robes (*abaya*) and masks, although there are regional variations of dress. The Najd and other remote areas remain true to Wahhabi tradition, but throughout the country this way of life is being altered by modernisation and rapid development. For more information, see the *World of Islam* appendix. Shaking hands is the customary form of greeting. Invitations to private homes are unusual. Entertaining is usually in hotels or restaurants and although the custom of eating with the right hand persists, it is more likely that knives and forks will be used. A small gift either promoting the company or representing your country will generally be well received. Women are expected to dress modestly and it is best to do so to avoid offence. Men should not wear shorts in public or go without a shirt. Visitors should be aware that the norms for public behaviour are extremely conservative and religious police, known as *Mutawwa'in*, are charged with enforcing these standards. Customs regarding smoking are the same as in Europe and non-smoking areas are indicated. During Ramadan, Muslims are not allowed to eat, smoke or drink during the day and it is illegal for a foreign visitor to do so in public. **Tipping:** The practice of tipping is becoming much more common and waiters, hotel porters and taxi drivers should be given 10 per cent.

Business Profile

ECONOMY: Saudi Arabia has the world's largest oil reserves – about 20 per cent of proven deposits – and is also currently the world's largest producer. Oil and natural gas products now account for 35 per cent of Saudi GDP, 75 per cent of government revenue and 85 per cent of export income. The non-oil economy is devoted to agriculture and newly developed industries (considerable effort has been put into ensuring adequate irrigation and industrial water supplies in a country with extremely low rainfall). Agriculture, which supports a little over 10 per cent of the workforce, produces wheat, fruit, vegetables, barley, eggs and poultry, in most of which the kingdom is now self-sufficient. In addition to oil and gas, there are other confirmed and exploitable mineral deposits including limestone, gypsum and marble plus phosphates, bauxite and gold.

The industrial sector produces petrochemicals, steel, engineering and construction materials and a wide range of consumer goods. The service sector is the fastest growing part of the economy at present, with finance and business services, consultancies and property services prominent. The rapid expansion of the Saudi economy from the 1960s onwards stalled during the late 1980s as overstretched finances and persistently low world oil prices forced the Saudi exchequer to rein in its spending plans (government debt is now nearly 100 per cent of GDP – much of which, such as US$40 billion of loans to Iraq, may not be recovered). This has had unfortunate consequences for the large body of foreign labour – an estimated 35 per cent of the workforce – upon which the Saudis rely for much of their technical, managerial and menial labour. Foreigners are now barred from a range of occupations as the government seeks to tackle Saudi unemployment, which is estimated at 25 per cent. Meanwhile, the average Saudi income has fallen by around 40 per cent in the last 20 years. At present, the economy is picking up; annual GDP growth is now 5.3 per cent; inflation is effectively zero. Since the late 1990s, the Saudis have gradually introduced economic reforms. A thriving private sector is viewed as essential to the government's objective of diversifying the economy and reducing reliance on the oil and gas sector. Some state-owned businesses have been sold and a number of measures taken to deregulate the economy and open up domestic markets to foreign competition. To that end, a trade agreement has been signed with the European Union, and Saudi Arabia is expected to join the World Trade Organization in due course. Saudi Arabia is the most influential member of the Organisation of Petroleum Exporting Countries (OPEC) and of the Islamic Development Bank. Japan and the USA are Saudi Arabia's most important trading partners, followed by Korea (Rep), the UK, Singapore and Germany.

BUSINESS: Appointments are necessary. Visiting cards printed in English with an Arab translation are usually exchanged. Men should wear suits for business meetings and formal social occasions. Thursday and Friday are official holidays. **Office hours:** Sat-Thurs 0900-1300 and 1630-2000 (Ramadan 2000-0100), with some regional variation. **Government office hours:** Sat-Wed 0730-1430.

COMMERCIAL INFORMATION: The following organisation can offer advice: Council of Saudi Chambers of Commerce & Industry, PO Box 16683, Riyadh 11474 (tel: (1) 405 3200 *or* 7502; fax: (1) 402 4747; website: www.riyadhchamber.com).

CONFERENCES/CONVENTIONS: Information can be obtained from: Riyadh Exhibitions Company Ltd, PO Box 56010, Riyadh 11554 (tel: (1) 454 1448; fax: (1) 454 4846; e-mail: esales@recexpo.com; website: www.recexpo.com); *or* the Saudi Arabian Ministry of Commerce (see *Contact Addresses* section).

Climate

Saudi Arabia has a desert climate. In Jeddah it is warm for most of the year. Riyadh, which is inland, is hotter in summer and colder in winter, when occasional heavy rainstorms occur. The *Rub al Khali* ('empty Quarter') seldom receives rain, making Saudi Arabia one of the driest countries in the world.

Required clothing: Tropical or lightweight clothing.

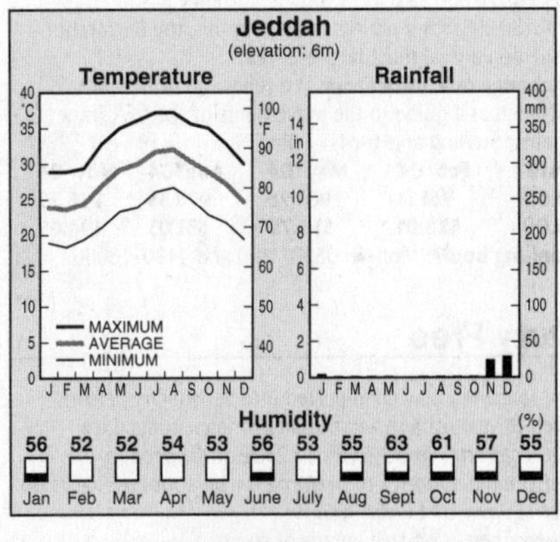

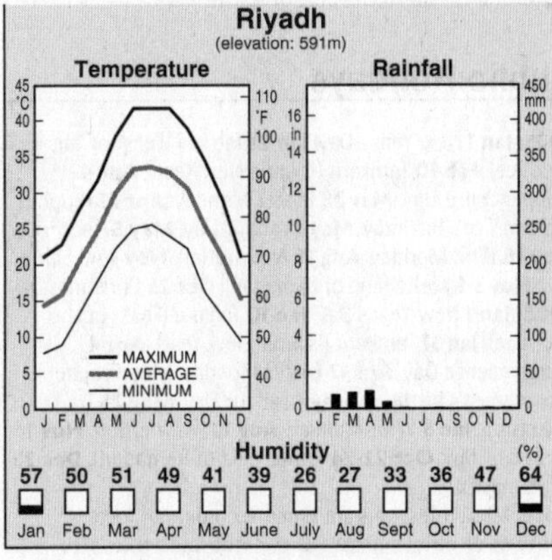

Senegal

LATEST TRAVEL ADVICE CONTACTS

British Foreign and Commonwealth Office
Tel: (0870) 606 0290 Website: www.fco.gov.uk

US Department of State
Website: http://travel.state.gov/travel

Canadian Department of Foreign Affairs and Int'l Trade
Tel: (1 800) 267 8376 Website: www.dfait-maeci.gc.ca

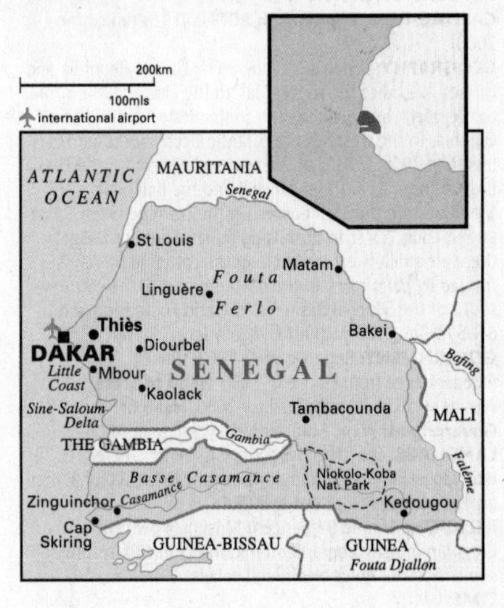

Location: West Africa.

Country dialling code: 221.

Ministère du Tourisme (Ministry of Tourism)
rue Docteur-Camette, BP 4049, Dakar, Senegal
Tel: 821 1126. Fax: 822 9413.

Embassy of the Republic of Senegal
39 Marloes Road, London W8 6LA, UK
Tel: (020) 7937 7237 *or* 7938 4048.
Fax: (020) 7938 2546.
E-mail: mail@senegalembassy.co.uk
Website: www.senegalembassy.co.uk
Opening hours: Mon-Fri 0900-1700; 0930-1300 (visa applications).
Limited tourism services available.

British Embassy
20 rue du Docteur Guillet, BP 6025, Dakar, Senegal
Tel: 823 7392 *or* 9971. Fax: 823 2766 *or* 8415.
E-mail: britemb@sentoo.sn *or* postmaster@britishcouncil.sn

Embassy of the Republic of Senegal
2112 Wyoming Avenue, NW, Washington, DC 20008, USA
Tel: (202) 234 0540-1.
Fax: (202) 332 6315.

Bureau Sénégalais du Tourisme (Senegal Tourist Office)
350 Fifth Avenue, Suite 3118, New York, NY 10118, USA
Tel: (212) 279 1953.
Fax: (212) 279 1958.
E-mail: sentour@aol.com
Website: www.senegal-tourism.com

Embassy of the United States of America
Street address: avenue Jean XXIII, angle Rue Kleber, Dakar, Senegal
Postal address: BP 49, Dakar, Senegal
Tel: 823 4296.
Fax: 822 2991 *or* 5903 (consular section).
E-mail: usadakar@state.gov *or* ConsularDakar@state.gov
Website: http://usembassy.gov/dakar

Embassy of the Republic of Senegal
57 Marlborough Avenue, Ottawa, Ontario K1N 8E8, Canada
Tel: (613) 238 6392.
Fax: (613) 238 2695.
E-mail: info@ambassenecanada.org
Website: www.ambassenecanada.org

TIMATIC CODES

Health	AMADEUS: **TI-DFT/DKR/HE** GALILEO/WORLDSPAN: **TI-DFT/DKR/HE** SABRE: **TIDFT/DKR/HE**
Visa	AMADEUS: **TI-DFT/DKR/VI** GALILEO/WORLDSPAN: **TI-DFT/DKR/VI** SABRE: **TIDFT/DKR/VI**

To access TIMATIC country information on Health and Visa regulations through the Computer Reservations System (CRS), type in the appropriate command line listed above.

Honorary Consulates in: Montréal, Toronto and Vancouver.
Canadian Embassy
Street address: Rue Galliéni x Brière de l'Isle, Dakar, Senegal
Postal address: BP 3373, Dakar, Senegal
Tel: 889 4700. Fax: 889 4720.
E-mail: dakar@dfait-maeci.gc.ca
Website: www.dfait-maeci.gc.ca/dakar

General Information

AREA: 196,722 sq km (75,955 sq miles).
POPULATION: 11,000,000 (estimate 2004).
POPULATION DENSITY: 50.1 per sq km.
CAPITAL: Dakar. **Population:** 2,079,000 (UN projection 2000).
GEOGRAPHY: Senegal is bordered by Guinea Republic and Guinea-Bissau to the south, Mali to the east and Mauritania to the north, and encloses the confederated state of The Gambia. To the west lies the Atlantic Ocean. Most land is less than 100m (330ft) above sea level, except for the Fouta Djallon foothills in the southeast and the Bambouk Mountains on the Mali border. On the coast between Dakar and St Louis is a strip of shifting dunes. South of Dakar there are shallow estuaries along the coastline, which is fringed by palm trees. In the northern part of the country, south of the Senegal Basin, lies the arid Fouta Ferlo, a hot dry Sahelian plain with little vegetation.
GOVERNMENT: Republic since 1963. Gained independence from France in 1960. **Head of State:** President Abdoulaye Wade since 2000. **Head of Government:** Prime Minister Macky Sall since 2004.
LANGUAGE: The official language is French. There are many local languages, the principal one being Wolof. Other groups include Peul, Serer and Diola.
RELIGION: Around 94 per cent Muslim, 4 per cent Christian (mostly Roman Catholic with some Protestants), and a minority holds traditional beliefs.
TIME: GMT.
ELECTRICITY: 230 volts AC, 50Hz.
COMMUNICATIONS: Telephone: IDD is available. Country code: 221. Outgoing international code: 00. Dial 17 (police) *or* 18 (fire brigade) *or* 821 3213 (emergency medical services). **Mobile telephone:** GSM 900. Main network providers are *Sentel* (website: www.millicom.com) and *Sonatel* (website: www.sonatel.sn *or* www.alize.sn). **Fax:** Towns have 'telecentres' from which faxes can be sent. *Sonatel* (responsible for all telecommunications) has fax facilities. Some hotels also have fax machines. **Internet:** ISPs include *Telecom Plus*. There are Internet cafes in Dakar, Saint Louis and other major towns. **Telegram:** There are facilities at main post offices and several hotels. **Post:** Airmail to Europe takes between seven and 10 days, and surface mail between two and six weeks. **Press:** All newspapers are in French and nearly all are controlled directly by political parties.
Radio: BBC World Service (website: www.bbc.co.uk/worldservice) and Voice of America (website: www.voa.gov) can be received. From time to time the frequencies change and the most up-to-date can be found online.

Passport/Visa

	Passport Required?	Visa Required?	Return Ticket Required?
Full British	Yes	No	Yes
Australian	Yes	Yes	Yes
Canadian	Yes	No	Yes
USA	Yes	No	Yes
Other EU	Yes	No/1	Yes
Japanese	Yes	No	Yes

Note: *Regulations and requirements may be subject to change at short notice, and you are advised to contact the appropriate diplomatic or consular authority before finalising travel arrangements. Details of these may be found at the head of this country's entry. Any numbers in the chart refer to the footnotes below.*

PASSPORTS: Passport valid for at least six months after date of entry required by all.
VISAS: Required by all except the following:
(a) nationals of countries referred to in the chart above (except **1.** nationals of Australia, Cyprus, Czech Republic, Estonia, Hungary, Latvia, Lithuania, Malta, Poland, Slovak Republic and Slovenia who *do* require a visa) for stays of up to three months;
(b) nationals of Benin, Burkina Faso, Cape Verde, Côte d'Ivoire, The Gambia, Ghana, Guinea, Guinea-Bissau, Israel, Liberia, Mali, Niger, Nigeria, Sierra Leone, Taiwan (China) and Togo for stays of up to three months;
(c) transit passengers continuing their journey by the same or first connecting aircraft provided holding onward or return documentation and not leaving the airport.
Note: Applications from nationals of the following countries must be referred to the authorities in Dakar and will therefore take longer: Afghanistan, Albania, Angola, Bosnia & Herzegovina, Cambodia, Chile, China (PR), Croatia, Cuba, Cyprus, Equatorial Guinea, Estonia, Guyana, Hong Kong (SAR), Iran, Iraq, Jordan, Korea (Dem Rep), Laos, Latvia, Lebanon, Libya, Lithuania, Maldives, Mozambique, Pakistan, Russian Federation, São Tomé e Príncipe, Serbia & Montenegro, Slovak Republic, Sudan, Syrian Arab Republic, Vietnam and Yemen.
Types of visa and cost: *Entry:* £3.15 (up to 15 days); £7.35 (15 to 30 days); £10.50 (up to 90 days). Cheques are not accepted.
Validity: Three months from the date of issue for stays of up to three months.
Application to: Consulate (or Consular section at Embassy); see *Contact Addresses* section. The visa section at the Embassy of Senegal in London is open 1000-1330 for lodging and 1300-1500 for collection.
Application requirements: (a) Valid passport. (b) Two passport-size photos. (c) Two completed application forms. (d) Letter of invitation or confirmed hotel booking, if applicable. (e) Self-addressed, stamped recorded delivery envelope for postal applications. (f) Evidence of return tickets. (g) Company letter for business trips.
Note: A WHO vaccination card, with current Yellow Fever and Cholera vaccinations, may be required if national is travelling from an endemic area.
Working days required: At least three. Nationals who must submit their applications to the authorities in Dakar prior to travel should submit their visa applications at least 21 days before the intended date of departure.
Temporary Residence: Enquire at Embassy (see *Contact Addresses* section).

Money

Currency: CFA (*Communauté Financiaire Africaine*) Franc (CFAfr) = 100 centimes. Notes are in denominations of CFAfr10,000, 5000 and 1000. Coins are in denominations of CFAfr500, 200, 100, 50, 25, 10, 5 and 1. Senegal is part of the French Monetary Area. Only currency issued by the *Banque des Etats de l'Afrique de l'Ouest* (Bank of West African States) is valid; currency issued by the *Banque des Etats de l'Afrique Centrale* (Bank of Central African States) is not. The CFA Franc is tied to the Euro.
Credit & debit cards: American Express is the most widely accepted, although Diners Club, MasterCard and Visa have limited use. Check with your credit or debit card company for details of merchant acceptability and other services which may be available. Commissions are added for the use of credit cards. There are ATMs in Dakar.
Travellers cheques: Travellers cheques are easy to cash in Dakar. To avoid additional exchange rate charges, travellers are advised to take them in Euros.
Currency restrictions: Import of local currency is unlimited; import of foreign currency is unlimited but subject to declaration. Export of local currency is restricted to CFAfr20,000. Export of foreign currency is limited to CFAfr50,000; for amounts exceeding this, the declaration issued on arrival must be presented.
Exchange rate indicators: The following figures are included as a guide to the movements of the CFA Franc against Sterling and the US Dollar:

Date	Feb '04	May '04	Aug '04	Nov '04
£1.00=	961.13	983.76	978.35	936.79
$1.00=	528.01	550.79	531.03	494.69

Banking hours: Mon-Fri 0800-1100 and 1430-1600.

Duty Free

The following may be imported into Senegal by persons over 18 years of age without incurring customs duty:
200 cigarettes or 50 cigars or 250g of tobacco; a reasonable quantity of perfume for personal use; gifts up to the value of CFAfr5000.
Note: There is no free import of spirits.

Public Holidays

2005: Jan 1 New Year's Day. **Jan 21** Tabaski (Feast of the Sacrifice). **Feb 10** Tamkarit (Islamic New Year). **Apr 4** Independence Day. **Mar 28** Easter Monday. **Apr 21** Prophet Mohammed's Birthday. **May 1** Labour Day. **May 5** Ascension. **May 16** Whit Monday. **Aug 15** Assumption. **Nov 1** All Saints' Day. **Nov 3-5** Korité (End of Ramadan). **Dec 25** Christmas Day.
2006: Jan 1 New Year's Day. **Jan 10** Tabaski (Feast of the Sacrifice). **Jan 31** Tamkarit (Islamic New Year). **Apr 4** Independence Day. **Apr 17** Easter Monday. **May** Prophet Mohammed's Birthday. **May 1** Labour Day. **May 25** Ascension. **Jun 5** Whit Monday. **Aug 15** Assumption. **Nov 1** All Saints' Day. **Oct 22-24** Korité (End of Ramadan). **Dec 25** Christmas Day.
Note: Muslim festivals are timed according to local sightings of various phases of the moon and the dates given above are approximations. During the lunar month of Ramadan that precedes Korité (Eid al-Fitr), Muslims fast during the day and feast at night and normal business patterns may be interrupted. Many restaurants are closed during the day and there may be restrictions on smoking and drinking. Some disruption may continue into Korité itself. Korité and Tabaski (Eid al-Adha) may last anything from two to 10 days, depending on the region. For more information, see the *World of Islam* appendix.

Health

	Special Precautions?	Certificate Required?
Yellow Fever	Yes	1
Cholera	Yes	2
Typhoid & Polio	3	N/A
Malaria	4	N/A

Note: *Regulations and requirements may be subject to change at short notice, and you are advised to contact your doctor well in advance of your intended date of departure. Any numbers in the chart refer to the footnotes below.*

1: A yellow fever vaccination certificate may be required from travellers coming from endemic areas. Enquire at nearest Embassy/Consulate prior to departure.
2: Following WHO guidelines issued in 1973, a cholera vaccination certificate is not a condition of entry to Senegal. However, cholera is a risk in this country and precautions are essential. Up-to-date advice should be sought before deciding whether these precautions should include vaccination, as medical opinion is divided over its effectiveness; see the *Health* appendix for more information.
3: Vaccination against typhoid is advised.
4: Malaria risk, predominantly in the malignant *falciparum* form, exists all year throughout the country; there is a lower risk in the central Western regions from January to June. Resistance to chloroquine and sulfadoxine-pyrimethamine has been reported. The recommended prophylaxis is mefloquine.
Food & drink: All water should be regarded as being potentially contaminated. Water used for drinking, brushing teeth or making ice should first be boiled or otherwise sterilised. Milk is unpasteurised and should be boiled. Powdered or tinned milk is available and is advised, but make sure that it is reconstituted with pure water. Avoid dairy products which are likely to have been made from unboiled milk. Only eat well-cooked meat and fish, preferably served hot. Pork, salad and mayonnaise may carry increased risk. Vegetables should be cooked and fruit peeled.
Other risks: *Bilharzia* (schistosomiasis) is present. Avoid swimming and paddling in fresh water; swimming pools which are well chlorinated and maintained are safe.
Sleeping sickness (trypanosomiasis) is reported. *Hepatitis A* and *E* are widespread; *hepatitis B* is hyperendemic.
Meningococcal meningitis risk exists, particularly during the dry season and in the savannah areas.
Rabies is present. For those at high risk, vaccination before arrival should be considered. If you are bitten, seek medical advice without delay. For more information, see the *Health* appendix.
Health care: In Dakar, doctors are plentiful and most medicines are available. Up-country, however, facilities are minimal. Health insurance is essential.

Travel - International

AIR: Senegal's national airline is *Air Senegal (DS)*. Other airlines serving Senegal include *Air Afrique, Air France, Alitalia* and *Iberia*.
Approximate flight times: From Dakar to *Paris* is five hours 30 minutes, to *London* is seven hours 35 minutes and to *New York* is eight hours 10 minutes.
International airports: *Dakar (DKR)* (Leopold Sedar Senghor) is 17km (10.5 miles) northwest of the city (travel time – 25 minutes). Regular coach and bus services go to and from Dakar. Metered taxis are available. Airport facilities include duty free shop, bar/restaurant, bank/bureau de change, post office and car hire.
Departure tax: None.
SEA: There are regular sailings from the Canary Islands, France, Morocco, Spain and several South American and West African ports. The main port is Dakar.
RAIL: There are two passenger trains (one Senegalese and one Malian) with restaurant and sleeping cars, running from Bamako, Mali, twice a week. The journey can take 30 to 36 hours. It is advisable to travel on the Senegalese train (well up to Western standards), rather than the Malian train (very basic indeed).
ROAD: Roads from Mauritania are tarred and in good condition; the best place to cross the border is at Rosso. Roads from Guinea-Bissau are not yet tarred; there is a border crossing at São Domingo. There is a route from

Senegal to Mali via Tambacounda. There is access across the Sahara by a 5500km (2120 mile) road that runs from Algeria via Mali. The trans-Gambian highway crosses the River Gambia by ferry. There is a good network of **buses** and **taxis** running across the major borders.

Travel - Internal

Note: All road travel in the western Casamance is advised against due to isolated residual rebel activity. Street crime and pick-pocketing is common in parts of Dakar. Most visits to Senegal, however, are trouble-free.
AIR: *Air Senegal* runs services to all the main towns in Senegal. *Gambia Air Shuttle* offers flights from Dakar to Banjul (The Gambia).
There are aerodromes in Ziguinchor, Podor and Tamba.
Departure tax: None.
SEA: It is often quicker to travel by sea than road. There are currently no services from Dakar to Ziguinchor (travel time - 20 hours), following the 2002 Joola Ferry disaster. Sea shuttles depart regularly from Dakar harbour to the Île of Gorée. An excellent new service, *L'Express du Senegal*, links Banjul, Dakar and Ziguinchor. Fares tend to be high.
RAIL: The country has a network of about 1225km (761 miles) of rail track. Trains run from Dakar to towns en route for Bamako in Mali. There is also a service between Dakar and St Louis. There is an ongoing programme of upgrading and expansion. Children under three travel free. Children aged three to nine pay half fare.
ROAD: Traffic drives on the right. There are approximately 3900km (2423 miles) of asphalt roads linking the major towns and the coastal region. The network of roads in the interior is rough (about 10,400km/6460 miles in total) and may become impassable during the rainy season; it is not advisable to drive at night. There are often police checkpoints at the entrance and exit to villages to enforce speed restrictions; fines are paid on the spot. **Bus:** There are many buses available for short distances as well as mini-buses (known locally as *car rapide*), which are cheaper if less efficient. Fares are usually up to CFAfr100. Long-distance services operate subject to demand only. **Taxi:** Available in most towns and fares are metered with a surcharge of CFAfr100. Rates increase after midnight. It is cheaper to hail a taxi in the street than arrange to be collected from the hotel. Bush taxis and estate cars are good for journeys into the interior. **Car hire:** Companies are found in Dakar and the main towns. **Documentation:** A French or International Driving Permit and Green Card are required.
URBAN: Bus and minibus services operate in Dakar.

Accommodation

HOTELS: The government-controlled expansion of tourism has led to an increasing number of hotels. There are several of international standard, and more development is underway, including a number of hotels on the Petite Côte (the stretch of beaches between Dakar and Joal). In Casamance, some luxury resorts have been built. It is advisable to book accommodation in advance, particularly in Dakar where there is an increased demand during the tourist season, which lasts from December to May. Hotels in Dakar generally have air conditioning but tend to be expensive. In addition, visitors may choose the floating hotel in the River Region. **Grading:** Hotels are classified from **1 to 4 stars**.
CAMPING: Government campsites (*campements*) provide a few beds, but no bedding. There are basic facilities for travellers who prefer to wander from the beaten track, although camping independently is strongly discouraged. Sometimes bungalows or grass huts are available; visitors must otherwise provide their own tents.
MISSIONS: Catholic missions will accommodate tourists only in cases of real need.
VILLAGE HUTS: A village will sometimes courteously offer a stranger one of the local huts as living accommodation, but it is necessary for visitors to provide their own bedding.

Resorts & Excursions

DAKAR: A bustling modern city and major port situated at the tip of the Cap Vert peninsula. Dakar's markets include the **Kermel** and the **Sandaga**, the former selling mainly fruit, fabrics, clothing and souvenirs, the latter being the city's main fruit and fabrics market. The main museum is the **Institut Fondemental d'Afrique Noir (IFAN)**, which has a collection of masks, statues and musical instruments from West Africa. Senegal's **Galérie Nationale** is also worth a visit. The **Palais Présidentiel** (presidential palace) is a white building surrounded by luscious gardens. A recent addition to the city is the monument, **La Porte du 3ème Millénaire** (The Third Millennium Gate), which was assembled in order to symbolise Senegal's entry into the third millennium, completed in 2001. The **Grande Mosquée**, the city's most famous mosque (noted for its minaret, which is lit at night), is closed to the public and located in Médina, which is off the tourist map. Dakar's main beaches include the **Plage Bel-Air** and the cleaner and safer **N'Gor** and **Yoff**. Other good beaches within reach are **Toubab Dialao** and **Yenn**, which are well known for their spectacular red cliffs.
EXCURSIONS: About 3km (1.8 miles) from the city lies the UNESCO World-Heritage-listed **Île de Gorée (Gorée Island)**, which used to be a slaving station and was one of the first French settlements on the continent. The island has many colonial-style houses and a small beach, as well as two museums – the **Maison des Esclaves (Slaves' House)** and the **Historical Museum** in the **Fort d'Estrées**. The **Retba Lake** (also called the **Lac Rose** or **Pink Lake** due to its pink colouring) is a popular spot for picnics and weekend excursions. It is also the terminal for the *Paris-Dakar motor rally*.
ST LOUIS: A former slave settlement and once Senegal's capital, St Louis is partly located on the mainland, partly on an island and partly on the **Langue de Barbarie** peninsula at the mouth of the **River Senegal**. The city reached its zenith in 1854, when Faidherbe undertook the unification of the country, which was still divided into small kingdoms at that time. Due to the expansion of Dakar, St Louis inevitably lost some of its importance, but it retains a nostalgic and provincial atmosphere reflected in its narrow streets flanked by beautiful colonial houses, balconies and verandas. The island can be reached via the **Pont Faidherbe**. There are some good beaches and a cruise lasting several days can be made up the River Senegal.
THE PETITE CÔTE: South of Dakar, the **Petite Côte** (Little Coast), which stretches for some 150km (94 miles), is one of Senegal's best beach areas. The main tourist resorts in the area are **Mbour** and, slightly further north, **Saly Portudal**, which is set in a green park and has the highest concentration of luxury hotels as well as its own golf course.
SINÉ-SALOUM DELTA: Further south is the delta formed where the Saloum and Siné rivers flow into the Atlantic Ocean. This wild region of mangrove swamps, dunes and lagoons is also Senegal's main groundnut-growing basin. Located largely within the **Parc National du Delta du Saloum**, the delta's myriad small islands are scattered between so-called *bolongs* (channels). The most popular mode of transport in this beautiful region is the *pirogue* (traditional African boat), which can take visitors to a number of nearby islands: some of the most beautiful include **Betani**, **Guior**, **Guissanor**, the **Île de Mars**, **Palmarin** and **Saloum**. The palm-fringed sandy beaches along the coast give way to dense vegetation populated by small villages of fishermen and groundnut farmers.
BASSE CASAMANCE: This fertile, swampy region borders The Gambia in the north and Guinea-Bissau in the south. However, travellers are advised to avoid this region while political instability continues. The resorts of Cap Skiring and Ziguindor are considered safe at present but check the political situation before visiting. **Cap Skiring**, the region's main tourist hub, has countless hotels along what are generally considered the country's best beaches. The region is well known for its traditional mud houses (also called *impluvium*), the most striking examples of which can be found in **Affinam** (on the north bank of the **Casamance River**) and **Enampor**. On the island of Karaban, the ruins of a Breton church and a colonial settlement are worth visiting.

NATIONAL PARKS

There are six national parks and four reserves in Senegal. The best time for visiting is usually between October and April. The Senegalese Ministry of Tourism advocates a strict nature preservation policy which invites tourists to respect the natural habitat. Accommodation is available, mostly in the form of **campements** or lodges. For further information, contact the Ministère de la Culture, du Tourisme et des Loisirs (see *Contact Addresses* section).
In addition to the national parks, there are also the following natural reserves: Bandia (900 hectares; 2224 acres); Ferlo Nord (a huge 487,000 hectares; 1,203,403 acres); Guembuel (special fauna extending over 720 hectares; 1779 acres); Kalissaye (an ornithological reserve created in 1987 and 16 hectares in size; 40 acres); Ndiael (a fauna reserve); and Popenguine (extending over 1009 hectares; 2493 acres).
Parc National de Niokolo Koba: Occupying a total of 903,150 hectares (2,230,000 acres) and situated in the southeast, this is one of West Africa's greatest reserves for large mammals. The park stretches over two geographical areas: the Sudanese savannah and the Guinea forest. Over 84 species live here, including Africa's largest lions, elephants, panthers, crocodiles, a variety of antelopes and over 300 species of birds. Niokolo Koba can be reached by air (with a flight to Simenti and, from there, a two-hour drive); by road (from Dakar to Tambacounda on the RN1 and from there to the park on the RN7); or by train (two weekly trains from Dakar to Tambacounda). Visitors are not allowed to explore the park on foot. The park headquarters are in Tambacounda.
Parc National des Oiseaux de Djoudj: Situated in the northeast, 60km (37 miles) from St Louis, at the southern edge of the Sahara, this beautiful park has 40,000 acres of water stretches and is one of the most important bird sanctuaries in the world. Its position makes it a favoured gathering place for migrating birds and a number of previously unknown bird species have recently been observed. Numerous organised tours are available from St Louis. It is listed by UNESCO as a World Heritage Site.
Parc National de Basse Casamance: This park is 60km (38 miles) from Ziguinchor in the south and extends over some 4920 hectares (12,300 acres) of forest and mangroves. Situated in a very rainy region, the park benefits from the luxuriance of the Guinea forest with its kapok trees, oil palms and imposing parinarias. Basse Casamance is famous for its tropical vegetation and variety of wildlife. It can be reached by plane or car from Dakar. The park headquarters are in Oussouye.
Parc National Langue de Barbarie: A narrow strip of sandy lands between the Atlantic and the River Senegal, this park is a refuge for birds and sea tortoises who come here to breed. Boat trips from St Louis are available.
Parc National du Delta du Saloum: Situated in the Saloum delta, 80km (50 miles) east of Kaolack, and extending over 72,000 hectares (180,000 acres). The landscape is characterised by small islands, sand dunes and swamps providing a perfect habitat for hundreds of bird species, including pelicans, storks and pink flamingos.
Parc National de l'Île de la Madeleine: Situated west of Dakar, 3km (1.7 miles) from the coast, this small archipelago is a protected marine park of approximately 480 hectares (1200 acres). The rocky nature of the archipelago, thought to be of volcanic origins, has favoured the establishment of numerous colonies of sea birds.

Credit: © Ministry of Information

Sport & Activities

Wildlife: The only place to see large mammals in Senegal is the Parc National de Niokolo Koba, although some species, such as elephants, are now extremely rare. Birdwatchers have more to be excited about - the parks and nature reserves in the coastal regions are renowned bird sanctuaries. Coastal parks often involve boat trips. For further details, see also *National Parks* in the *Resorts & Excursions* section *or* contact the Ministère de la Culture, du Tourisme et des Loisirs (see *Contact Addresses* section). **Watersports:** There are plenty of good beaches, but **swimming** can be hazardous in some places; visitors are advised to enquire with their travel agent before booking a beach holiday. Good areas for swimming include Casamance, Hann Bay, N'Gor Beach and Petite Côte. Many hotels in the main tourist resorts have swimming pools. Underwater enthusiasts will find good **diving** waters all around the Cap Vert Peninsula, with February to April being the best months. **Water-skiing** facilities are available at Dakar alongside the Children's Beach on the lagoon between N'Gor and its island and at the Hanns Bay marinas. **Windsurfing** is possible, and both coastal and river **kayak** trips can be arranged.
Music: West Africa has a strong musical tradition and Dakar is the best place to sample Senegal's vibrant music scene. The capital has numerous established clubs and venues with frequent live performances. Details can be found in the local papers (written in French) or from the Ministère de la Culture, du Tourisme et des Loisirs (see *Contact Addresses* section). Villages also frequently put on musical performances for tourists.
Other: From May through November, Senegal offers excellent **sports fishing**. Organised trips are available from fishing centres and hotels along the coast.
The Senegalese are keen followers of traditional Senegalese **wrestling**. There are matches every Sunday at the Fass arena and in the suburbs or at the Iba Mar Diop Stadium near the Great Mosque. There is a nine-hole **golf** course at Camberene and miniature golf at Dakar-Yoff. **Football** is also very popular, and it is cool enough to **jog**.

Social Profile

FOOD & DRINK: Senegalese food is considered among the best in Africa. The basis of many dishes is chicken or fish, but the distinctive taste is due to ingredients not found outside Africa. This food is served in many restaurants in Dakar. Provincial rest houses serve less sophisticated but delicious variations. Dishes include *dem à la St Louis* (stuffed mullet), *maffe* (chicken or mutton in peanut sauce) and *accras* (a kind of fritter). Suckling pig is popular in the Casamance region.
There are bars in some hotels and clubs. Although Senegal is predominantly a Muslim country, alcohol is available. The traditional drink is mint tea, the first cup drunk slightly bitter, the second with more sugar and the third very sweet. The Casamance drink is palm wine, which is drunk either fresh or fermented.
NIGHTLIFE: There are several nightclubs and music venues in Dakar, playing *mbalakh* (the local modern music), as well as a casino on the route to N'Gor. There are many cinemas showing the latest French films. The Daniel Sorano National Theatre in the Boulevard de la Republique is a popular venue for theatre, concerts and other arts performances.
SHOPPING: Bargaining is customary. At Soumbe-dionne, on the Corniche de Fann, is a craft village where the visitor can watch craftspeople at work and buy their handicrafts. Purchases include woodcarving in the form of African gaming boards, masks and statues; musical instruments; and metalwork, including copper pendants, bowls and statuettes. Most markets and centres sell traditional fabric, embroidery and costume, pottery, necklaces of clay beads and costume jewellery of wood or various seeds. **Shopping hours:** Generally Mon-Sat 0800-1200 and 1430-1800. Some shops open Sunday morning, others are closed Monday.
SPECIAL EVENTS: For more information, contact the Ministère de la Culture, du Tourisme et des Loisirs (see *Contact Addresses* section). The following is a selection of special events occurring in Senegal in 2005:
Jan 1-16 *Paris-Dakar Rally*. **Jun 1-4** *Dakar-Goree Jazz Festival*.
SOCIAL CONVENTIONS: Greetings are appropriate when coming across local people, especially in the bush, and the visitor should make the effort to learn these in one of the local languages. Handshaking on meeting, regardless of how many times a day one meets the person, is normal. When visiting a village, it is polite to call upon the village headman or schoolteacher to explain that you want to spend the night there or visit the area. They will often act as interpreter and will be helpful guides to the customs of the village and also in terms of money, ensuring that a traveller does not find himself in the embarrassing position of paying for hospitality that was given in friendship. Return hospitality with a gift of medicines, food or money for the community. It is not advisable to give money indiscriminately as tourists have encouraged the practice of begging. Casual wear is widely acceptable. Scanty swimwear should be reserved for the beach. Smoking is prohibited in some public places (especially mosques). **Tipping:** A service charge of 10 to 15 per cent is included in all hotel and restaurant bills. Taxi drivers are not normally given a tip.

Business Profile

ECONOMY: In a good year, Senegal is the world's leading producer of groundnuts, which are the country's main export commodity. The farming industry also produces millet, sorghum, maize, rice and vegetables for domestic consumption, but the country's vulnerability to extreme weather conditions have prevented it from reaching self-sufficiency in basic foodstuffs. Fish products have become an important export commodity, accounting for one-third of total export earnings, and the Government also accumulates revenues from the sale of fishing licences to other countries, mostly from the EU. Both farming and fisheries currently face severe problems - the former due to drought, the latter due to over-fishing by foreign fleets.
Senegal is the most industrialised country in French West Africa after Côte d'Ivoire. Exploitable mineral deposits include phosphates (the chemical industry draws on sizeable deposits of lime phosphate and aluminium phosphate within Senegal). Some iron ore and gold deposits have been identified, and there are thought to be oil reserves both on- and offshore. The main industries - which are almost exclusively geared to domestic consumption - involve the processing of agricultural products and phosphates, milling, textiles, commercial vehicle assembly, food and drink, farming materials (implements, fertilisers), paint, asbestos, cement, printing and boat building. There is also, unusually in this part of Africa, a lively information technology sector.
Although the country remains dependent on foreign aid and its finances are weak, it has shown signs of recovery after a stagnant spell in the late 1990s. Current annual GDP growth is 5.5 per cent. In 1998, negotiations with the IMF led to the introduction of a Structural Adjustment Programme in exchange for financial support. Senegal is a member of the CFA Franc Zone and the West African trading bloc, ECOWAS. France is its major trading partner, followed by Côte d'Ivoire, Mali, Spain and the USA.
BUSINESS: A lightweight suit is acceptable for business. French will generally be needed for meetings. Appointments should be made and punctuality is expected, despite the fact that a customer may be slightly late. Visiting cards are essential, preferably in French and English. The right hand should be used for shaking and to pass items. The period from July to October should be avoided for business visits, as many people are on holiday. **Office hours:** Mon-Fri 0800-1230 and 1300-1600. During Ramadan, some offices open 0730-1430.
COMMERCIAL INFORMATION: The following organisations can offer advice: Chambre de Commerce et d'Industrie et d'Agriculture de la Région de Dakar, BP 118, 1 place de l'Indépendance, Dakar (tel: 823 7189; fax: 823 9363).
CONFERENCES/CONVENTIONS: A number of hotels and conference centres offer facilities. Further information can also be obtained from the Embassy of the Republic of Senegal in Washington (see *Contact Addresses* section).

Climate

Senegal is favoured by a warm climate. The dry season runs from December through to May with cool trade winds in coastal areas. Throughout the rest of the year, a hot monsoon wind blows from the south bringing the rainy season and hot, humid weather. Rainfall is heaviest in Casamance and in the southeast and slight in the Sahelian region in the north and northeast, where temperatures tend to be higher.

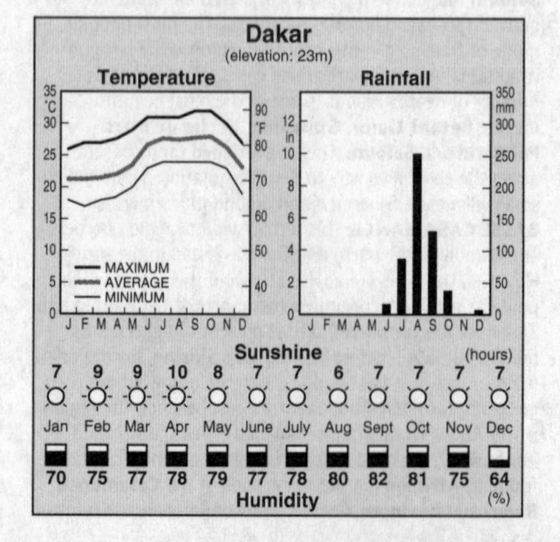

Serbia & Montenegro

LATEST TRAVEL ADVICE CONTACTS

British Foreign and Commonwealth Office
Tel: (0870) 606 0290 Website: www.fco.gov.uk
US Department of State
Website: http://travel.state.gov/travel
Canadian Department of Foreign Affairs and Int'l Trade
Tel: (1 800) 267 8376 Website: www.dfait-maeci.gc.ca

Location: Southern Central Europe.

Country dialling code: 381.

Tourist Organisation of Belgrade
Decanska Street 1, 11000 Belgrade, Serbia and Montenegro
Tel: (11) 322 7834/6154 *or* 324 8310 *or* 8404 (marketing).
Fax: (11) 324 8770.
E-mail: office@belgradetourism.org.yu
Website: www.belgradetourism.org.yu
National Tourism Organisation of Serbia (NTOS)
Decanska 8/V, 11000 Belgrade, Serbia and Montenegro
Tel: (11) 334 2521 *or* 323 2586 *or* 8540 (marketing department). Fax: (11) 322 1068.
E-mail: ntos@yubc.net
Website: www.serbia-tourism.org
National Tourism Organisation of Montenegro
Cetinjski put 66, Trg. Vektre, 81 000 Podgorica, Serbia and Montenegro
Tel: (81) 235 155-8. Fax: (81) 235 159.
E-mail: tourism@cg.yu
Website: www.visit-montenegro.com
Ministry of Tourism of Serbia
Nemanjina Street 22-26, 11000 Belgrade, Serbia and Montenegro
Tel: (11) 323 9993. Fax: (11) 361 0258.
E-mail: kabinet@minttu.sr.gov.yu
Website: www.minttu.sr.gov.yu
Ministry of Tourism of Montenegro
PC Vektra, Cetinjski put bb, 81000 Podgorica, Serbia and Montenegro
Tel: (81) 482 333 *or* 329. Fax: (81) 234 168.
E-mail: lav@mn.yu
Website: www.gom.cg.yu/mintur
Embassy of Serbia and Montenegro
28 Belgrave Square, London SW1X 8QB, UK
Tel: (020) 7235 9049. Fax: (020) 7235 7092.
E-mail: londre@jugisek.demon.co.uk

TIMATIC CODES

Health
AMADEUS: **TI-DFT/BEG/HE**
GALILEO/WORLDSPAN: **TI-DFT/BEG/HE**
SABRE: **TIDFT/BEG/HE**

Visa
AMADEUS: **TI-DFT/BEG/VI**
GALILEO/WORLDSPAN: **TI-DFT/BEG/VI**
SABRE: **TIDFT/BEG/VI**

To access TIMATIC country information on Health and Visa regulations through the Computer Reservations System (CRS), type in the appropriate command line listed above.

Website: www.yugoslavembassy.org.uk
Opening hours: Mon-Fri 1000-1300 (visa section); 1400-1600 (visa telephone enquiries).
British Embassy
Generala Resavska 46, 11000 Belgrade, Serbia and Montenegro
Tel: (11) 264 5055. Fax: (11) 265 9651 *or* 306 1072 (consular/visa section).
E-mail: belgrade.man@fco.gov.uk *or* belgrade.visa@fco.gov.uk (visa enquiries).
Embassy of Serbia and Montenegro
2134 Kalorama Road, NW, Washington, DC 20008, USA
Tel: (202) 332 0333. Fax: (202) 332 3933 *or* 332 5974 (consular section).
E-mail: consular@yuembusa.org (consular section) *or* info@yuembusa.org
Website: www.yuembusa.org
Embassy of the United States of America
Kneza Miloša 50, 11000 Belgrade, Serbia and Montenegro
Tel: (11) 361 9344 *or* 306 4650 (visa section).
Fax: (11) 361 5497 (public affairs section).
Website: http://belgrade.usembassy.gov
Embassy of Serbia and Montenegro
17 Blackburn Avenue, Ottawa, Ontario K1N 8A2, Canada
Tel: (613) 233 6289. Fax: (613) 233 7850.
E-mail: diplomat@embscg.ca
Website: www.embscg.ca
Canadian Embassy
Kneza Miloša 75, 11000 Belgrade, Serbia and Montenegro
Tel: (11) 306 3000 (ext 3341 for consular section).
Fax: (11) 306 3042.
Website: www.canada.org.yu

General Information

As of February 2003, the Yugoslav parliament ceased to be and the Union of Serbia & Montenegro was voted into existence. The Union was agreed in 2002 and will remain unchanged for at least three years after which time the individual states can decide whether to stay united or to separate. At the time of writing, all information is correct and up-to-date, but it may be subject to quick change and new events may alter various aspects of any of the following sections. All information should be double-checked with an official source.
AREA: Serbia and Montenegro comprises Serbia (including the provinces of Kosovo and Vojvodina) with 88,361 sq km (39,449 sq miles) and Montenegro with 13,812 sq km (5331 sq miles). These two were respectively the largest and smallest of the republics which made up the former Yugoslavia. The country officially covers 102,173 sq km (39,448 sq miles), or 40 per cent of the territory of the former federation (255,804 sq km/98,766 sq miles).
POPULATION: Together, Serbia and Montenegro have an estimated total population of 10,664,300 (official estimate 2002).
POPULATION DENSITY: 104.4 per sq km.
CAPITAL: 1,687,000 (UN estimate 2001; including suburbs). Belgrade is the capital of Serbia & Montenegro.
GEOGRAPHY: Roughly rectangular in shape and on a major European communications axis north-west and south-east, Serbia & Montenegro borders Hungary to the north, Romania to the northeast, Bulgaria to the southeast, the Kosovo region and Albania to the south, Bosnia & Herzegovina to the west and Croatia to the northwest. The province of Kosovo, now administered by the UN, is in the south, and shares borders with Macedonia (Former Yugoslav Republic of) and Albania. Serbia is dominated by the flat, fertile farmland of the Danube and Tisza valleys. The scenery varies from rich Alpine valleys, vast fertile plains and rolling green hills to bare, rocky gorges as much as 1140m (3800ft) deep, thick forests and gaunt limestone mountain regions. Belgrade, the capital, lies on the Danube. Montenegro is a small mountainous region on the Adriatic coast north of Albania, bordering Bosnia & Herzegovina to the west. Its small Adriatic coastline comprises the main ports of Bar and those in the Gulf of Kotor.
GOVERNMENT: Union of States since February 2003 (previously Federal Republic since 1992). First gained independence as the 'Kingdom of Serbs, Croats and Slovenes' in 1918 from the Austro-Hungarian Empire; renamed Yugoslavia in 1929. **Heads of State: Union of Serbia and Montenegro:** President Svetozar Marovic since 2003; **Serbia: President:** Boris Tadic since 2004; **Montenegro:** President Filip Vujanovic since 2002. **Heads of Government: Union of Serbia and Montenegro:** Prime Minister Dragisa Pesic since 2001; **Serbia: Prime Minister:** Vojislav Kostunica since 2004; **Montenegro:** Prime Minister Milo Djukanovic since 2003.
The Kosovo region is now administered by the UN.
LANGUAGE: Serbian, which uses the Cyrillic script, Albanian and Hungarian.
RELIGION: Majority Eastern Orthodox Serbs, with a large Muslim ethnic Albanian minority (especially in the province of Kosovo), a Roman Catholic ethnic Serbian minority (mainly located in the province of Vojvodina) and a small Jewish community.
TIME: GMT + 1 (GMT + 2 from last Sunday in March to Saturday before last Sunday in October).
ELECTRICITY: 220 volts AC, 50Hz.
COMMUNICATIONS: Telephone: Telephone: IDD is available. Country code: 381. Outgoing international code: 99. **Mobile telephone:** GSM 900/1800 networks provide coverage in main towns. Network operators are *Mobtel* (website: www.mobtel.com), *Monet* (website: www.monetcg.com), *Promonte* (website: www.promonte.com) and *Telekom Srbija* (website: www.telekom.yu). **Fax:** Transmissions are available to and from Western Europe. **Internet:** ISPs include *Infosky* (website: www.infosky.net). Internet cafes can be found in the main urban centres. **Post:** Postal services within Serbia and Montenegro are reasonably good. **Press:** The main local newspapers and magazines, in decreasing order of circulation (and all based in Belgrade), are *Vecernje Novosti*, *Blic* and *Politika*.
Radio: BBC World Service (website: www.bbc.co.uk/worldservice) and Voice of America (website: www.voa.gov) can be received. From time to time the frequencies change and the most up-to-date can be found online.
Note: *CNN* is also available via satellite (*Astra*) in a number of Belgrade and Montenegrin (Adriatic Coast) hotels.

Passport/Visa

	Passport Required?	Visa Required?	Return Ticket Required?
Full British	Yes	1	No
Australian	Yes	1	No
Canadian	Yes	1	No
USA	Yes	1	No
Other EU	Yes	1	No
Japanese	Yes	1	No

Note: *Regulations and requirements may be subject to change at short notice, and you are advised to contact the appropriate diplomatic or consular authority before finalising travel arrangements. Details of these may be found at the head of this country's entry. Any numbers in the chart refer to the footnotes below.*

Restricted entry and transit: Nationals of Malaysia and Taiwan (China) will be refused admission and transit through the country.
PASSPORTS: Valid passport required by all.
VISAS: Required by all except the following:
(a) nationals of Mexico for up to 180 days;
(b) **1.** nationals mentioned in the chart above and nationals of Andorra, Argentina, Bolivia, Chile, Costa Rica, Croatia, Cuba, Iceland, Israel, Korea (Rep), Liechtenstein, Monaco, New Zealand, Norway, San Marino, Seychelles, Singapore, Switzerland, Tunisia and Vatican City for stays of up to 90 days for touristic purposes only;
(c) nationals of Armenia, Azerbaijan, China (PR), Georgia, Korea (Dem Rep), Kyrgyzstan, Mongolia, Russian Federation, Tajikistan, Turkmenistan and Ukraine for business visits of up to 90 days;
(d) nationals of Macedonia (Former Yugoslav Republic) for stays of up to 60 days;
(e) nationals of Belarus and Bulgaria for stays of up to 30 days;
(f) nationals of Hungary in the territory of the Republic of Montenegro, tourist passes and identity cards issued at the border crossings, for touristic stays of up to 90 days;
(g) nationals of Albania, Bosnia & Herzegovina, Croatia, Macedonia, Russian Federation, Slovenia and Ukraine in the territory of the Republic of Montenegro, tourist passes and identity cards issued at the border crossings, for touristic stays of up to 30 days.
Types of visa and cost: *Visit*, *Business* and *Transit*. Fees vary according to nationality of applicant.
Validity: Visas are valid for one month from date of issue and cannot be postdated. Transit visas are valid for seven days (to be used within six months of issue).
Application to: Consular section at Embassy (see *Contact Addresses* section). Tourist passes can be issued at the border, or on arrival, for all eligible nationals (see above). However, as regulations are subject to change, travellers are advised to check with the Embassy prior to departure.
Application requirements: (a) Completed application form (stating whether single- or double-entry or exit visa is required and giving the length of stay). (b) Valid passport. (c) Letter of invitation or an invitation/receipt or authorised tourist company certifying that the travel arrangement has been paid for, verified by the competent Serbian and Montenegrin authority. (d) Fee payable to Embassy in cash or by postal order. (e) Medical Insurance. (f) Return ticket (g) Proof of sufficient funds. *Business*: (a)-(g) and, (h) Letter of invitation from host company or evidence of self-employment.
Note: Visitors not staying at hotels must register with the police within 24 hours from arrival.
Working days required: 24 hours, unless application needs further referral.
Temporary residence: Enquire at Embassy.

Money

Currency: The official currency in Serbia is the New Yugoslav Dinar. New Yugoslav Dinar (YUM) = 100 paras. Notes are in denominations of YUM5000, 1000, 200, 100, 50, 20 and 10. Coins are in denominations of YUM5, 2 and 1 and 50 paras.
The official currency in Montenegro is the Euro. Euro (€) = 100 cents. Notes are in denominations of €500, 200, 100, 50, 20, 10 and 5. Coins are in denominations of €2 and 1, and 50, 20, 10, 5, 2 and 1 cents.
Currency exchange: As elsewhere in the ex-Yugoslav republics, the only true repositories of value and frequently exchanged currencies are the Euro and the US Dollar (the Pound Sterling is rarely used in the republic). Money should be exchanged through official exchange offices only. There are very few ATMs that accept international bank cards. There are eight money-exchange machines in Belgrade (including one at the airport), accepting Sterling, American dollars and Euros, giving back Dinars. Scottish and Northern Irish pound sterling bank notes are not accepted.
Credit & debit cards: Amex, MasterCard and Visa are sometimes accepted.
Travellers cheques: Although acceptable in theory, in practice these can be very hard to exchange. It is advisable to take hard currency and credit or debit cards.
Currency restrictions: All visitors must complete the customs currency declaration form upon arrival and declare (including travellers cheques) money in excess of €2000 or 120,000 Dinars. Any currency not declared on the form can be confiscated when leaving the country.
Exchange rate indicators: The following figures are included as a guide to the movement of the New Yugoslav Dinar and the Euro against Sterling and the US Dollar:

Date	Feb '04	May '04	Aug '04	Nov '04
£1.00=	101.17	106.31	109.22	111.25
$1.00=	55.58	59.52	59.28	58.75

Date	Feb '04	May '04	Aug '04	Nov '04
£1.00=	1.46	1.49	1.49	1.42
$1.00=	0.80	0.83	0.80	0.75

Banking hours: Mon-Fri 0700-1500, Sat 0800-1400.

Duty Free

The following items may be imported into Serbia & Montenegro without incurring customs duty:
200 cigarettes or 50 cigars or 250g of tobacco; 1l of wine and 1l of spirits; 250ml of eau de toilette and a reasonable quantity of perfume; jewellery and clothing; two photo cameras, one movie camera (up to and including 16mm) and one video camera; one pair of binoculars; one pocket electronic calculator; camping equipment; one bicycle; one engine; sporting requisites (enquire for further details); if portable, one musical instrument, one record player, one radio receiver with or without a cassette recorder, one tape recorder and one typewriter.

Public Holidays

2005: Jan 1 New Year's Day. **Jan 7** Orthodox Christmas Day. **Apr 29** Orthodox Good Friday. **May 2** Orthodox Easter Monday. **Apr 27** Statehood Day. **May 1-2** Labour Days. **May 9** Victory Day. **Nov 29** Republic Day.
2006: Jan 1 New Year's Day. **Jan 7** Orthodox Christmas Day. **Apr 14** Orthodox Good Friday. **Apr 17** Orthodox Easter Monday. **Apr 27** Statehood Day. **May 1-2** Labour Days. **May 9** Victory Day. **Nov 29** Republic Day.
Note: Orthodox Christian holidays may also be celebrated in most parts.

Health

	Special Precautions?	Certificate Required?
Yellow Fever	No	No
Cholera	No	No
Typhoid & Polio	1	N/A
Malaria	No	N/A

Note: *Regulations and requirements may be subject to change at short notice, and you are advised to contact your doctor well in advance of your intended date of departure. Any numbers in the chart refer to the footnotes below.*

1: Vaccination against typhoid is sometimes advised.
Food & drink: Mains water is normally chlorinated and, whilst relatively safe, may cause mild abdominal upsets. Bottled water is available and is advised for the first few weeks of the stay. Milk is pasteurised and dairy products are safe for consumption. Local meat, poultry, seafood, fruit and vegetables are generally considered safe to eat.
Other risks: *Hepatitis A* may occur. *Tularaemia* has been

reported recently in the Kosovo area and travellers are advised to boil all water and be cautious about food preparation. *Crimean congo haemorrhagic fever* is endemic in Kosovo. *Tick-borne encephalitis* and *typhus* occur.
Rabies is present. For those at high risk, vaccination before arrival should be considered. If you are bitten, seek medical advice without delay; for more information, see the *Health* appendix.
Health care: Doctors are well trained but medical facilities are limited. Many medicines and basic medical supplies are often unavailable. Hospitals usually require payment in hard currency. Prescribed medicines must be paid for. Health insurance with emergency repatriation is essential. Visitors may be asked to pay first and seek reimbursement later.

Travel - International

Note: Because of continuing tensions, visitors should exercise caution when travelling to Kosovo and within the Presevo and Bujanovac districts of southern Serbia. Serbia & Montenegro (including Kosovo, which is under UN administration) shares with the rest of the world, including the UK, a risk of indiscriminate terrorist attacks. Visitors should be particularly vigilant in public places, including tourist sites, and keep informed of the latest developments. The Serbia & Montenegro government does not recognise entry points from Kosovo and those on Kosovo's external borders with Albania or Macedonia. Despite the presence of the Kosovo Force (KFOR), there are still some residual mines and unexploded ordnance in some areas of Kosovo. However, the vast majority of travel to Serbia & Montenegro is trouble-free.
AIR: The national airline is *Yugoslav Airlines (JU)* (website: www.jatlondon.com), which flies to destinations including Brussels, Frankfurt/M, London and New York. *Montenegro Airlines* (website: www.montenegro-airlines.cg.yu) flies from Podgorica to Budapest, Frankfurt/M, Ljubljana, Rome and Zurich and from Tivat to Dusseldorf. Airlines which serve Belgrade Airport include *Alitalia, Austrian Airlines* and *Lufthansa*.
International airports: *Belgrade (BEG)* (Surcin) (website: www.airport-belgrade.co.yu) is 19km (12 miles) west of the city. Airport facilities include banks, bars, car hire and post offices. Smaller airports exist elsewhere, such as *Podgorica (TGD)* (formerly Titograd) in Montenegro.
Departure tax: From Belgrade airport: 1000 Dinars, payable at the airport. From Montenegro: €16.
SEA: The principal passenger ports are Bar and Kotor, both in Montenegro. Ferries link the Yugoslav Adriatic coast with Italy, operating between Bar and Bari.
RAIL: Rail services to Belgrade run from Bulgaria, Croatia, Greece, Romania and Turkey. Trains from western Europe travel via Budapest. For up-to-date information, contact *Rail Europe* (tel: (08705) 848 848; website: www.raileurope.co.uk). International trains have couchette coaches as well as bar and dining cars. On some lines, transport for cars is provided.
Note: Train travel should be undertaken with care as assaults and robberies have been reported.
ROAD: The following frontier posts are open for road traffic:
From **Croatia:** Batrovci-Bajakovo.
From **Hungary:** Hercegszanto-Backi Breg (Bezdan); Tompa-Kelebija; Szeged Roszke-Horgos; Bacsalmas-Bajmok; and Tiszasziget-Djala (both crossings for nationals of Yugoslavia and Hungary only).
From **Romania:** Jimbolia-Srpska Crnja; Stamora Moravita-Vatin; Naidas-Kaludaerova (Bela Crkva); and Portile de Fier-(Turnu Severin)-Daerdap (Kladovo).
From **Bulgaria:** Bregovo-Mokranje (Negotin); Kula-Vrska Cuka (Zajecar); Kalotina-Gradina; Otomanci-Ribarci; Kjustendil-Deve Bair (Kriva Palanka); Blagoevgrad-Delcevo; and Petric-Novo Selo.
From **Albania:** Podgradec-Cafa San (Struga); and Kukes-Vrbnica.
From **Macedonia (Former Yugoslav Republic of):** Presevo-Tabanovce; and Djeneral-Jankovic. Nearly all the passes mentioned above are open 24 hours a day.
Bus: Connections are available to Belgrade from destinations including Budapest, Lyon, Munich, Paris, Thessaloniki and Zurich.
See *Travel – Internal* section for information regarding documentation and regulations and *Passport/Visa* section for further information on entry restrictions.

Travel - Internal

AIR: *Montenegro Airlines* and *Yugoslav Airlines (JU)* both offer connections between Belgrade and Podgorica.
Departure tax: From Belgrade airport: 500 dinars. From Montenegro: €8.
RAIL: Internal rail services are generally poor. Services are often overbooked, unreliable and unsafe. Destinations accessible by rail include Bar, Belgrade, Nis, Novi Sad, Pristina and Subotica. For further information, contact Belgrade Coach Station (tel: (11) 644 455).
ROAD: Drivers should not rely on local petrol stations for fuel, owing to shortages of oil, although hard currency might make otherwise rationed and scarce petrol available. Spare parts are very difficult to obtain. Driving at night is not advisable, owing to the poor condition of the roads.
Coach: Efficient and cheap coaches used to connect all towns. The fuel shortages have restricted the services severely. Two notoriously bad roads are the Ibarska Magistrala and the two-lane Moraca Canyon, and these should be avoided when possible. **Taxi:** Main cities have metered taxis. In Kosovo, Pristina is able to provide taxis.
Car hire: Available from airports and main towns.
Regulations: Traffic drives on the right. Speed limits are 120kph (75mph) on motorways and 100kph (62mph) on other roads. Road signs may be poorly marked and new signs are likely to be in Cyrillic script in some areas of the country. **Documentation:** Full national driving licence is accepted. No customs documents are required but car log books, a Green Card (not valid in Kosovo) and vehicle registration/ownership documents and locally valid insurance policy are necessary. Third party insurance can be taken out at the border when travelling to Kosovo.
URBAN: There are good bus services in the main towns, with tramways and trolleybuses in Belgrade. Multi-journey tickets are available and are sold in advance through tobacconists. The passenger punches the ticket in a machine on board. Fares paid to the driver are at double the pre-purchase prices.
Travel times: The following chart gives approximate travel times (in hours and minutes) from **Belgrade** to other major cities/towns in Serbia and Montenegro

.	Air	Road	Rail
Bar	**-**	**7.00**	**6.00**
Podgorica	**0.30**	**6.00**	**5.30**

Accommodation

HOTELS: Deluxe/A-class hotels are confined to Belgrade and a number of Montenegrin Adriatic resorts, most notably the exclusive island of Sveti Stefan. Further down the scale, and particularly in the smaller towns, services are poor. The best hotels are always heavily booked, so advance booking is essential. Prices are very high, and payable in hard currency for visiting foreign nationals. Also, the Montenegrin resorts may be overcrowded, following the closure of the Croatian coastline to all Serbian and Montenegrin nationals. **Grading:** Classification is from **deluxe** to **A**, **B**, **C** and **D class**. **Pensions:** First-, second- and third-class pensions are available throughout the country. **Inns:** Motels are found on most main roads. Prices are set independently according to region, tourist season and the quality of service. There is a N.Din60 per day residence charge.
GUEST HOUSES: Many people offer rooms, often with meals, to visitors in villages without hotels. Discounts are available off-season. Contact tourist offices or travel agencies for details.
SELF-CATERING: Holiday villages are available in many resorts as well as a selection of apartments and villas. Travel agencies and tourist offices have further information.
CAMPING/CARAVANNING: Only available on official sites. A permit from the local tourist office is required for off-site camping. A list is available from the National Tourism Organisation. *Alpine Club* mountain huts are available in all mountain areas. **Note:** Caravans are allowed in duty-free for up to one year.
YOUTH HOSTELS: For information, contact Hostelling International Yugoslavia (website: www.hostels.org.yu) *or* the Ministry of Tourism of Serbia (see *Contact Addresses* section).

Resorts & Excursions

SERBIA

The largest of the republics that made up the former Yugoslavia, Serbia was under Turkish rule and many traces of Muslim influence remain, particularly in the Kosovo-Metohija region. **Belgrade** is the capital of Serbia and the national capital. Its strategic location on the edge of the **Carpathian Basin** near the joining of the **Sava River** and the **Danube**, and also its position on the Stambul Road from Turkey into Central Europe, made it a centre of commerce and communications. Many of the buildings were constructed after World War II. The **Kalemegdan Citadel** straddles a hilltop overlooking the junction of the Sava and the Danube. The **National Museum** is interesting, and there is also the **Museum of Modern Art** and the **Ethnographical Museum**. Well worth a visit is the **Palace of Princess Ljubica** (1831) with a good collection of period furniture. **Skadarlija** is the 19th-century Bohemian quarter with cafes, street performers, art galleries and antique shops. Near **Kraljevo** is the restored **Monastery of Zica**, now painted bright red as it was in Medieval times. It was there that the Kings of Serbia were crowned. The **Kalenic Monastery** is a fine example of Serbian style.

MONTENEGRO

Montenegro is at the southern end of Yugoslavia's coast, an area of spectacular mountain ranges with villages perched like eagles' nests on high peaks. This stands in direct contrast to the republic's coastal region, which extends from the **Gulf of Kotor** to the Albanian border. **Kotor** itself is a bustling port with a picturesque old city quarter. The general architecture is mainly of Venetian origin, as this power dominated the region until 1797. Entering the city through the town gate brings the visitor to the square with the 17th-century **Clock Tower**, overshadowed by the twin towers of the **Cathedral of St Tryphon** (12th century). A visit to the **Naval Museum** and the **Church of St Lucas** (1195) should not be missed.

Sport & Activities

Watersports: Fishing permits are available from hotels or local authorities. Local information is necessary. Fishing on the Adriatic coast is unrestricted, but freshwater angling and fishing with equipment needs a permit. **Sailing** is popular along the coast. Berths and boats can be hired at all ports. Permits are needed for boats brought into the country. The Tara River in *Durmitor National Park* provides excellent facilities for **white-water rafting**.
Other: Both **skiing** and **spa resorts** exist in all regions, but particularly in *Kopaonik* and *Brezovica* (Serbia). The **hiking** is good, particularly in Durmitor National Park. **Football** is a popular spectator sport.

Social Profile

FOOD & DRINK: Cuisine varies greatly from one region to another. On the whole, the meat specialities are better than the fish dishes. National favourites include *pihtije* (jellied pork or duck), *prsut* (smoked ham), *cevapcici* (charcoal-grilled minced meat), *raznjici* (skewered meat), and *sarma* or *japrak* (vine or cabbage leaves stuffed with meat and rice). Desserts are heavy and sweet, including *strukli* (nuts and plums stuffed into cheese balls and then boiled), *lokum* (Turkish Delight) and *alva* (nuts crushed in honey). Table service is usual in hotel restaurants.
Wine is widely available and cheap. *Ljutomer*, *Traminer* and *Riesling* wines from Montenegro are the best known. Varieties include *Dingac*, *Krstac*, *Postup* and *Vranac*. The white *Vugava* produced in Vis is excellent. Popular national spirits are *slivovica* (a potent plum brandy), *loza* and *maraskino* (made of morello cherries). Bars and cafes have counter and table service. Most places serving alcohol close by 2200.
NIGHTLIFE: Cinemas stay open until 2300, restaurants until midnight and nightclubs until 0300.
SHOPPING: Special purchases include embroidery, lace, leatherwork, *Pec* filigree work, metalwork and Turkish coffee sets. **Shopping hours:** Mon-Fri 0800-1200 and 1700-2000, Sat 0800-1500 (many shops are open all day Sat).
SPECIAL EVENTS: The following is a selection of special events occurring in Serbia and Montenegro in 2005:
Feb 26-Mar 6 *Film Festival*, Belgrade. **May** *Sterijino Pozorje Drama Festival*, Novi Sadia. **Jul-Aug** *Festival of Arts*, Budva. **Jul 1-4** *Summer Festival*, Belgrade. **Jul 1-Aug 20** *Theatre City Festival*, Budva. **Aug 19-27** *Sarajevo International Film Festival*.
SOCIAL CONVENTIONS: Hitherto a relatively open, informal and secure society, Serbia & Montenegro is now changing for the worse following the impact of war. Once virtually non-existent, violent crime is now relatively common in the big cities. There are some restrictions on photography. **Tipping:** 10 per cent is expected by hotels, restaurants and taxis.

Business Profile

ECONOMY: Serbia & Montenegro were respectively the largest and smallest of the six constituent republics of the former Yugoslavia. Between 1990 and the overthrow of Slobodan Milosevic in 2000, civil war followed by economic sanctions reduced their economies to less than half their previous output.

Much of their infrastructure and industrial capacity was destroyed. Since 2000, the economic outlook has become much brighter. The lifting of sanctions has restored access to international markets and capital. Annual economic growth since 2000 has been between 10 and 15 per cent. Agriculture is now mainly geared to domestic consumption. Maize, wheat, sugar beet and potatoes are the main crops. Fruit and vegetables are also important. The mining industry – which has proved more resilient than the rest of the industrial economy – produces coal, copper ores and bauxite as well as smaller amounts of iron ore, zinc, oil and natural gas.

However, service industries will be the future of the Union's economy. Tourism, which was the main component of the service sector, has recovered after being all but wiped out; the latest official figures record that Serbia received two million visitors in 2002.

Although the two republics have been formally united since February 2003 in the 'State Union of Serbia and Montenegro', they follow distinct economic policies; there is no customs union or currency alignment. Both governments have, however, embarked on reform programmes which have seen numerous companies privatised and various parts of the two economies opened up to competition. The process has drawn the broad approval of the IMF and the EU, which has supplied a $3 billion aid package to assist the reconstruction process. The policy divisions between Serbia and Montenegro are likely to cause difficulties in the near future, especially as regards the EU, which is firmly opposed to any future schisms in the Balkans. Despite that, Serbia & Montenegro hope to be able to join the group – which currently includes Romania, Bulgaria and Croatia – aiming for full EU membership in 2007.

BUSINESS: As with Croatia, but unlike Slovenia, things go very slowly or not at all on account of the cumbersome bureaucracy and general socio-economic collapse. Communication, however, is not a major problem, as English is popular as a second language. **Office hours:** Mon-Fri 0700/0800-1500/1600.

COMMERCIAL INFORMATION: The EU ban on new investment in Serbia and Montenegro has recently been lifted. The following organisations should be able to offer advice:

Yugoslav Chamber of Commerce and Industry, Terazije 23, 11000 Belgrade (tel: (11) 324 8222 *or* 8123; fax: (11) 324 8754; e-mail: info@pkj.co.yu; *or* Serbia Chamber of Commerce and Industry, Resavska 13-15, 11000 Belgrade (tel: (11) 330 0900; fax: (11) 323 0949; e-mail: kabinet@pks.co.yu; website: www.pks.co.yu); *or* Chamber of Economy of Montenegro, Foreign Economic Relations Sector, ul. Novaka Miloseva 11, 81000 Podgorica (tel: (81) 230 545 *or* 230 714; fax: (81) 230 943; website: www.pkcg.org).

Climate

Serbia has a continental climate with cold winters and warm summers. Montenegro is largely the same, but with alpine conditions in the mountains and a Mediterranean climate on the Adriatic coast.

Required clothing: In winter, mediumweight clothing and heavy overcoat; in summer, lightweight clothing and raincoat required.

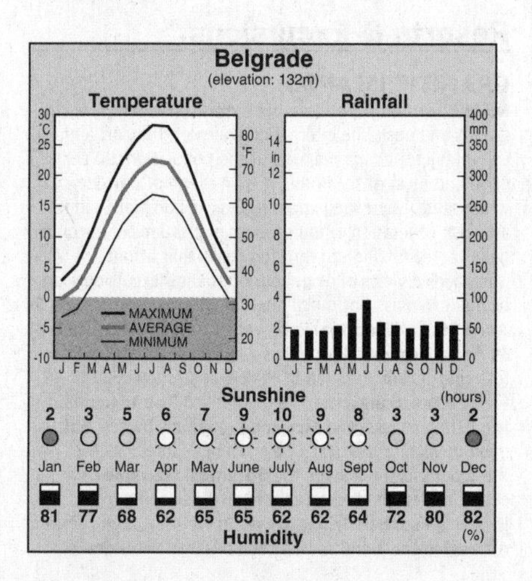

Seychelles

LATEST TRAVEL ADVICE CONTACTS

British Foreign and Commonwealth Office
Tel: (0870) 606 0290 Website: www.fco.gov.uk

US Department of State
Website: http://travel.state.gov/travel

Canadian Department of Foreign Affairs and Int'l Trade
Tel: (1 800) 267 8376 Website: www.dfait-maeci.gc.ca

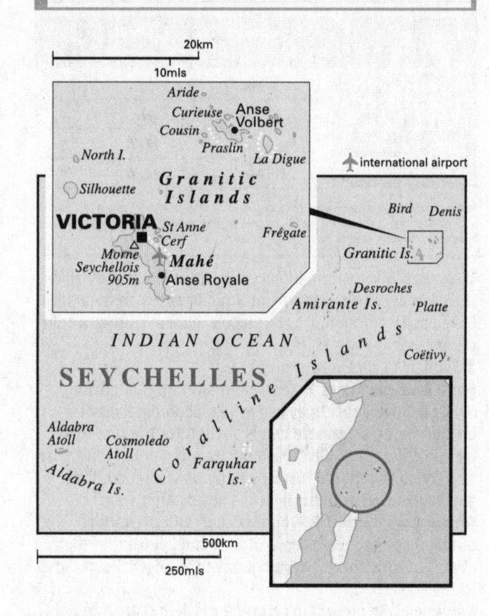

Location: Indian Ocean, 1600km (990 miles) east of Kenya.

Country dialling code: 248.

Seychelles Tourism Marketing Authority (STMA)
PO Box 1262, Bel Ombre, Mahé, Seychelles
Tel: 620 000. Fax: 620 620.
E-mail: seychelles@aspureasitgets.com
Website: www.seychelles.com *or* www.aspureasitgets.com

The High Commission for the Seychelles in *France* **deals with enquiries from UK nationals (51 Avenue Mozart, 75016 Paris; tel: (1) 4230 5747; fax: (1) 4230 5740; e-mail: ambsey@aol.com).**

Seychelles Tourist Office UK
Notcutt House, 36 Southwark Bridge Road,
London SE1 9EU, UK
Tel: (020) 7202 6363. Fax: (020) 7928 0722.
E-mail: seychelles@hillsbalfour.com
Website: www.aspureasitgets.com

British High Commission
Street address: 3rd Floor, Oliaji Trade Centre, Francis Rachel Street, Victoria, Mahé, Seychelles
Postal address: PO Box 161, Victoria, Mahé, Seychelles
Tel: 283 666. Fax: 283 657.
E-mail: bhcvictoria@fco.gov.uk
Website: www.bhcvictoria.sc

Permanent Mission of the Republic of the Seychelles to the United Nations
800 Second Avenue, 4th Floor, Suite 400C, New York, NY 10017, USA
Tel: (212) 972 1785. Fax: (212) 972 1786.
E-mail: seychelle@un.int

United States Consular Agency
Street address: 2nd Floor, Oliaji Trade Centre, Suite 23, Victoria, Mahé, Seychelles
Postal address: PO Box 251, Victoria, Mahé, Seychelles
Tel: 225 256.
Fax: 225 189.
E-mail: usoffice@seychelles.net

The US Embassy in Port Louis deals with enquiries relating to the Seychelles (see *Mauritius* **section).**

The Canadian High Commission in Dar es Salaam deals with enquiries relating to the Seychelles (see *Tanzania* **section).**

TIMATIC CODES

Health
AMADEUS: **TI-DFT/SEZ/HE**
GALILEO/WORLDSPAN: **TI-DFT/SEZ/HE**
SABRE: **TIDFT/SEZ/HE**

Visa
AMADEUS: **TI-DFT/SEZ/VI**
GALILEO/WORLDSPAN: **TI-DFT/SEZ/VI**
SABRE: **TIDFT/SEZ/VI**

To access TIMATIC country information on Health and Visa regulations through the Computer Reservations System (CRS), type in the appropriate command line listed above.

General Information

AREA: 455.3 sq km (175.8 sq miles).
POPULATION: 80,800 (official estimate 2002).
POPULATION DENSITY: 177.5 per sq km.
CAPITAL: Victoria (Mahé). **Population:** 60,000 (1994).
GEOGRAPHY: The Seychelles Archipelago occupies 400,000 sq km (150,000 sq miles) of the Indian Ocean northeast of Madagascar and contains 115 islands and islets. These fall into two groups of markedly different appearance, stemming from their distinct geologies:
Granitic: A dense cluster of 42 islands, the only mid-ocean group in the world with a granite rock formation. Their lush green vegetation is tropical in character, with a profusion of coconut palms, bananas, mangoes, yams, breadfruit and other tropical fruit. Indigenous forest exists on the higher slopes, where cinnamon and tea are planted. All, including the second largest, Praslin, are less than 65km (40 miles) from Mahé.
Coralline: Isolated coral outcrops speckling a vast area of the Indian Ocean to the southwest of the granitic group. They rise only a few feet above sea level but are covered with rich and dense vegetation due to fertilisation by copious amounts of guano. There is no permanent population. Aldabra, the largest atoll in the world, contains one-third of all Seychellois land and is a UNESCO-designated World Heritage Site.
The largest island in either group is **Mahé**, lying 4°S of the equator. It is 27km (17 miles) long by 8km (5 miles) wide and contains Victoria, the capital and main port, and 90 per cent of the population. Mahé is typical of the Granitic Islands, being mountainous and covered with jungle vegetation. Its highest point, indeed the highest point in the Seychelles, is Morne Seychellois (905m/2970ft). The isolated nature of the Seychelles has given rise to the evolution of many unique species of flora and fauna, including the coco-de-mer palm and unique varieties of orchid, giant tortoise, gecko, chameleon and 'flying fox' (fruitbat). National parks and reserves have been set up to protect this heritage. The Seychellois are descended from a mixture of French and British landowners, freed African slaves and a small number of Chinese and Indian immigrants, creating a unique culture.
GOVERNMENT: Republic since 1976. Gained independence from the UK in 1975. **Head of State and Government:** President James Alix Michel since 2004.
LANGUAGE: The official language is Seselwa; Creole, English and French are also spoken.
RELIGION: 92 per cent Roman Catholic with Anglican, Seventh Day Adventist, Muslim, Baha'i and other minorities.
TIME: GMT + 4.
ELECTRICITY: 240 volts AC, 50Hz. British three-pin plugs are in use.
COMMUNICATIONS: Telephone, fax, telegram: *SEYTELS* offers a 24-hour service for telegrams, telephones and faxes via SEYTELS/Cable & Wireless Ltd, Francis Rachel Street, Victoria, Mahé. Phonecards are available. IDD is available. Country code: 248. Outgoing international code: 00. **Mobile telephone:** GSM 900 network. Network operators are *Cable & Wireless* (website: www.cw.com/seychelles) and *Telecom (Seychelles) LTD* (website: www.airtel.sc). **Internet:** ISPs include *Atlas Ltd* (website: http://www.seychelles.net). **Post:** The main post office is in Victoria. Airmail collections are at 1500 weekdays and 1200 Saturdays; airmail to Western Europe normally takes up to one week. Post office hours: Mon-Fri 0800-1500, Sat 0800-1200. **Press:** English-language newspapers include *Seychelles Nation* (morning daily except on Sundays), *The People* (monthly, published by the Seychelles Progressive Front) and *Seychelles Review* (monthly news review).
Radio: BBC World Service (website: www.bbc.co.uk/worldservice) and Voice of America (website: www.voa.gov) can be received. From time to time the frequencies change and the most up-to-date can be found online.

Passport/Visa

	Passport Required?	Visa Required?	Return Ticket Required?
Full British	Yes	No	Yes
Australian	Yes	No	Yes
Canadian	Yes	No	Yes
USA	Yes	No	Yes
Other EU	Yes	No	Yes
Japanese	Yes	No	Yes

Note: *Regulations and requirements may be subject to change at short notice, and you are advised to contact the appropriate diplomatic or consular authority before finalising travel arrangements. Details of these may be found at the head of this country's entry. Any numbers in the chart refer to the footnotes below.*

PASSPORTS: Passport valid for six months from date of arrival in the Seychelles.

VISAS: Visa not required by any nationality as long as they have:
(a) onward or return ticket (if not, onward or return ticket must be purchased on arrival);
(b) proof of sufficient funds (minimum US$150 per day) and organised accommodation for the duration of the stay. A visitor's permit, valid for up to one month, is issued on arrival, subject to possession of (a) and (b) as above; alternatively, a deposit may be made by 'security' bond in lieu. The permit may be renewed, provided the applicant holds a valid open return ticket and applies at least one week before the permit's expiry. For further information, contact the nearest Seychelles Tourist Office.
Transit: Passengers in transit must have tickets with reserved seats for their onward journey.
Temporary residence: Enquire at the High Commission. Additional information about temporary residence and visitor's permits may be obtained from: Immigration Division, 2nd Floor, Independence House, Victoria, Mahé, Seychelles (tel: 611 110; fax: 225 035; e-mail: dgoi@immigration.sc).

Money

Currency: Seychelles Rupee (SRe: singular; SRs: plural) = 100 cents. Notes are in denominations of SRs100, 50, 25 and 10. Coins are in denominations of SRs5 and 1, and 25, 10 and 5 cents. A number of gold and silver coins are also minted (with face values as high as SRs1500), but these are not in general circulation.
Note: Tourists must pay hotel bills in foreign currency (in the form of cash, travellers cheques or credit or debit cards). Payment in local currency is only allowed if an exchange receipt can be shown as proof of the conversion from foreign currency into local currency. The duty-free shop at the airport *only* accepts credit cards or foreign cash.
Currency exchange: Exchange facilities are available at the airport banks, which are open for all flight departures and arrivals. The following banks have branches in the Seychelles and will exchange travellers cheques and foreign currency: *Barclays Bank, Bank of Baroda, Banque Française Commerciale, Central Bank of Seychelles, Development Bank of Seychelles, Habib Bank Ltd, Nouvo Banq* and *Seychelles Savings Bank*. Currency exchange receipts should be kept in order to facilitate re-exchange on departure.
Credit & debit cards: Access, American Express, MasterCard and Visa are widely accepted; Diners Club has more limited use. Check with your credit or debit card company for details of merchant acceptability and other services which may be available.
Travellers cheques: Accepted in most hotels, guest houses, restaurants and shops. To avoid additional exchange rate charges, travellers are advised to take travellers cheques in US Dollars or Pounds Sterling.
Currency restrictions: The import and export of local and foreign currency is unlimited.
Exchange rate indicators: The following figures are included as a guide to the movements of the Seychelles Rupee against Sterling and the US Dollar:

Date	Feb '04	May '04	Aug '04	Nov '04
£1.00=	10.04	9.86	10.17	10.45
$1.00=	5.52	5.52	5.52	5.52

Banking hours: Mon-Fri 0800-1400, Sat 0800-1100.

Duty Free

The following items may be imported into the Seychelles by persons of 18 years or older without incurring customs duty:
400 cigarettes or 500g of tobacco; 2l of spirits or 2l of wine; 200ml of perfume or eau de toilette; food items not exceeding SRs3000; one video camera and one camera; musical instrument; portable electronic or electric equipment; sports requisites and other leisure equipment.
Prohibited items: The import of non-prescribed drugs and all firearms, including air pistols, air rifles and spearfishing guns, and plants and plant products, animals and animal products, radioactive substances and apparatus, dangerous drugs, biological specimens, fireworks and explosives, medicines and poisons are prohibited, unless prior authorisation has been granted. Video tapes must be declared and may be retained for security reasons. The import of animals and food and other agricultural produce is strictly controlled and subject to licensing.
Restricted exports: Shells, unprocessed coco-de-mer, processed or live fish and live tortoises may not be exported.

Public Holidays

2005: Jan 1-2 New Year. **Mar 25** Good Friday. **Mar 28** Easter Monday. **May 1** Labour Day. **Jun 5** Liberation Day (Anniversary of 1977 Coup). **Jun 10** Corpus Christi. **Jun 18** National Day. **Jun 29** Independence Day. **Aug 15** Assumption/La Digue Festival. **Nov 1** All Saints' Day. **Dec 8** Immaculate Conception. **Dec 25** Christmas Day.
2006: Jan 1-2 New Year. **Apr 14** Good Friday. **Apr 17** Easter Monday. **May 1** Labour Day. **Jun 5** Liberation Day (Anniversary of 1977 Coup). **Jun 15** Corpus Christi. **Jun 18** National Day. **Jun 29** Independence Day. **Aug 15** Assumption/La Digue Festival. **Nov 1** All Saints' Day. **Dec 8** Immaculate Conception. **Dec 25** Christmas Day.

Health

	Special Precautions?	Certificate Required?
Yellow Fever	No	1
Cholera	No	No
Typhoid & Polio	2	N/A
Malaria	No	N/A

Note: *Regulations and requirements may be subject to change at short notice, and you are advised to contact your doctor well in advance of your intended date of departure. Any numbers in the chart refer to the footnotes below.*

1: A yellow fever vaccination certificate is required by all travellers over one year arriving from infected areas or who have passed through partly or wholly endemic areas within the preceding six days.
2: Typhoid occurs in rural areas.
Food & drink: Mains water is normally chlorinated and whilst relatively safe, may cause mild abdominal upsets. Bottled water is available and is advised for the first few weeks of the stay. Milk is pasteurised and dairy products are safe for consumption. Local meat, poultry, seafood, fruit and vegetables are generally considered safe to eat.
Other risks: *Hepatitis A* and *B* occur with occasional outbreaks of dengue fever. Visitors should beward of the effects of sunstroke or burning, since the Seychelles is close to the Equator.
Rabies may be present in certain areas. If you are bitten, seek medical advice without delay; for more information, see the *Health* appendix.
Health care: There is a large general hospital in Victoria and there are clinics elsewhere on La Digue, Mahé and Praslin, but medical facilities are limited. Visitors may obtain emergency treatment for a basic consultancy fee. Additional medical insurance is advised.

Travel - International

AIR: The Seychelles' national airline is *Air Seychelles (HM)* (website: www.airseychelles.co.uk). Other airlines flying to the Seychelles include *Aeroflot, Air Europe, Air France, Air Mauritius, British Airways* and *Kenya Airways*.
Approximate flight times: From Mahé to *London* is 12 hours (10 hours direct) and to *New York* is 20 hours and 40 minutes (via London).
International airports: *Mahé Island (SEZ)* (Seychelles International) is 10km (6 miles) southeast from Victoria (travel time – 20 minutes). Some coach services are provided by agents and taxis are available. Airport facilities include an outgoing duty free shop, banking and currency exchange facilities, car hire and restaurant/bar.
Departure tax: US$40 or equivalent, payable in foreign currency or by credit card (local currency is not accepted). Children under 12 years of age are exempt.
SEA: Cruise and cargo ships call at Mahé but there are no scheduled passenger services.

Travel - Internal

AIR: *Air Seychelles* provides an efficient network of scheduled and chartered services from Mahé to Alphonse, Bird, Denis, Praslin, Silhouette and Desroches islands. *Helicopter (Seychelles) Ltd* (tel: 385 858; fax: 373 055; e-mail: info@helicopterseychelles.sc; website: www.helicopterseychelles.com) provides an inter-island shuttle service and scenic flights. Charter flights can be arranged from any heli-stop.
Departure tax: US$40; visitors staying for less than 24 hours pay US$10 and children under 12 years of age are exempt.
SEA: Privately owned schooners provide regular inter-island connections between Mahé, Praslin and La Digue. Boats can be chartered privately to get to the other islands.
ROAD: Traffic drives on the left. There are paved roads only on La Digue, Mahé and Praslin; elsewhere the roads are sandy tracks. Visitors should be aware that Mah is mountainous with narrow, winding roads, rarely with safety barriers. **Bus:** SPTC buses run on a regular basis on Mahé and Praslin from 0530-1900. There are a number of 18-seater coaches for airport transfers and excursions. Prices for buses and coaches are very reasonable. **Taxi:** There are about 135 taxis on Mahé and Praslin with government-controlled rates. There is a surcharge for taxi fares on Praslin between 1900-0600. **Car hire:** There are over 550 cars or *Mini Mokes* for hire on Mahé, and a limited number on Praslin. It is advisable to make advance reservations, especially in the high season. Conditions of hire and insurance should be carefully checked. Hire is on an unlimited mileage basis and the price includes Third Party insurance and tax. Minimum age is 21. Petrol is approximately 30 per cent more expensive than in Europe. **Bicycles** may be hired on La Digue and Praslin. **Traffic regulations:** There is a speed limit of 65kph (40mph) on the open road, decreasing to 40kph (25mph) in built-up areas and throughout Praslin. **Documentation:** A national driving licence is sufficient, for up to three months.
Travel Times: The following chart gives approximate travel times (in hours and minutes) from **Mahé** to other islands in the Seychelles.

	Air	Sea
Praslin	0.15	2.30
La Digue	-	3.15
Bird Is.	0.30	7.00
Denis Is.	0.30	6.00
Round Is.	-	0.15
Frégate Is.	0.15	2.00
Moyenne	-	0.15
Desroches	1.00	-

Note: The ferry from Praslin to La Digue takes approximately 30 minutes.

Accommodation

Although the Seychelles have been a popular tourist destination for more than 10 years and now offer the full range of accommodation from self-catering apartments to luxury hotels, careful planning has ensured that the islands have retained the astonishing beauty and quiet charm that attracted the first tourists. Right from the start, the Government decreed that no new building could be higher than the surrounding palm trees, with the result that big-city levels of comfort and convenience have been achieved in thoroughly Seychellois settings. There are about 4500 hotel beds on the islands and it is advisable to confirm reservations with a deposit, particularly during the high season from December to January and in July and August. For further information, contact the Seychelles Hospitality and Tourism Association, 1st Floor, STMA HQ, Bel Ombre, PO Box 1174, Victoria (tel: 620 210; fax: 620 214; e-mail: sha@seychelles.net; website: www.shta-seychelles.com).
HOTELS & GUEST HOUSES: All recently built hotels come well up to international standards and there are numerous large resort hotels equipped with air conditioning, private bathrooms, swimming pools and full sporting facilities. Older hotels and guest houses on the smaller islands may lack some sophistication, but their charming seclusion has long recommended them to those seeking complete peace and privacy: Somerset Maugham once sought out the quietest so that he could write a novel without interruption. Many hotels and guest houses are former plantation houses modestly modernised and run by the resident owner. Thatched-roof chalets and guest houses, built in the local style, are to be found mainly on outlying islands. The Seychelles Hotel Association comprises some 74 hotels on the islands. More information is available from the Association (see above for address and telephone number). For up-to-date prices, contact the Tourist Office (see *Contact Addresses* section).
SELF-CATERING: Self-catering units are available on the main islands. For details, contact the Tourist Office.
YOUTH AND CAMPING: There are no youth hostels and camping is not permitted.

Resorts & Excursions

GRANITIC ISLANDS

MAHÉ: Surrounded by coral reefs, this is the largest of the islands and hosts the international airport, the port and capital (Victoria), the majority of the population (90 per cent) and most of the hotels. It is an island of powdery white sands (there are almost 70 beaches on Mahé alone) and lush vegetation, rising through plantations of coconut palms and cinnamon to forested peaks that afford unparalleled views of neighbouring islands. Excursions can be made in glass-bottomed boats from Victoria to nearby **St Anne Marine National Park**, which encloses the islands of **St Anne**, **Beacon** (classified as a nature reserve), **Cerf** (offering accommodation in chalets and renowned for Creole food), **Long** (closed to the public), **Round** (reputed for its tuna steaks) and **Moyenne** (privately owned, but open to visiting tourists); or by coach, taking in such attractions as the market, the **Botanical Gardens** (with coco-de-mer, giant tortoises and orchids), and a replica of London's **Vauxhall Bridge Tower** in Victoria, before setting off around the island to visit colonial-style mansions in graceful decline, old plantations of cinnamon and vanilla, and everywhere the greenest of vibrant green jungles. Tourists may also visit the **Morne Seychellois National Park**, occupying the highest part of the island. The **National Museum** in **Victoria** celebrates Seychellois history, folklore and music, and has particularly fine displays depicting the history of spice cultivation.

ELSEWHERE: The other Granitic Islands, 41 of them, are all located within 65km (40 miles) of Mahé. Some of the more notable islands are described below.

PRASLIN: The second-largest island is two to three hours by boat or 15 minutes by air (25 scheduled flights per day) from Mahé. It is famous for the **Vallée de Mai**, another UNESCO World Heritage Site, which contains the double-nutted coco-de-mer palm. Regular excursions are available to smaller islands such as Aride, Cousin, Curieuse and La Digue.

LA DIGUE: Just over three hours by schooner from Mahé or 30 minutes from Praslin, this beautiful island is the breeding ground of the rare black paradise flycatcher. There are very few cars and the ox-cart remains the principal means of transport (although bicycles may be hired). There are beautiful old plantation houses, such as **Château Saint-Cloud**, as well as a vanilla plantation, copra factories and superb beaches.

FREGATE: The most easterly and isolated of the granitic islands, Frégate is associated with pirates (Ian Fleming was obsessed with the notion that a pirate's hoard was buried here). It is also the home of the almost extinct magpie robin. Frégate is 15 minutes by air from Mahé.

THERESE: Notable for its rock-pools and tortoise colony. Accessible from Port Glaud by a 5-minute boat trip.

COUSIN: Two hours by boat from Mahé, Cousin was bought (in 1968) by the International Council for Bird Protection, which operates it as a nature reserve. Amongst the rare bird species thus protected are the brush warbler, the Seychelles toc-toc and the fairy tern. The best time to visit is April or May, when 1.25 million birds nest on the island. All visits to the island must be made as part of an organised tour. Local rangers act as guides; a full tour of the island takes between one and two hours. Local operators can arrange these trips, usually in conjunction with visits to other islands.

ARIDE: Two hours from Mahé, Aride is the most northerly of the granitic islands. Home to vast colonies of seabirds, in 1973 it was bought by Christopher Cadbury, President of the Royal Society for Nature Conservation. It is open to visitors from October to the end of April.

CURIEUSE: Approximately 3km (2 miles) long, Curieuse is covered by lush vegetation and huge takamaka trees. It has been designated a reserve for giant tortoises (imported from Aldabra). Day trips may be arranged from Praslin.

SILHOUETTE: Thought to have been home to one of the Indian Ocean's most notorious pirates, Hodoul, this island may be seen from Beau Vallon Beach on Mahé. It has a population of about 200. Sights include an old plantation house of traditional Seychellois timber construction.

CORALLINE ISLANDS

ALDABRA: The world's largest atoll, home to 150,000 giant land tortoises (reputedly five times more than on the Galapagos Islands) and listed by UNESCO as a World Heritage Site, consists of 13 islands which make up about one-third of the Seychelles' land mass. Until recently Aldabra was only accessible by boat, but **Assumption Island**, in the south of the atoll, now has an airstrip. Aldabra remains under strict supervision of the Seychelles Island Foundation which, nevertheless, intends to open it to a controlled number of visitors.

DENIS: Five to seven hours by boat or 30 minutes by air from Mahé, Denis is also on the edge of the continental shelf and attracts many deep-sea fishermen. Marlin may be caught from October to December. The island's seabird population has, over the years, left rich deposits of guano, which has encouraged the growth of lush vegetation. The minimum stay is two days.

BIRD: Six to eight hours by boat or 30 minutes by plane from Mahé, this island is famous for the millions of sooty terns that migrate here to breed between May and September. Its location at the edge of the Seychelles continental shelf (the sea floor drops rapidly to 2000m/5000ft) also makes it a favoured destination for fishermen. Another claim to fame is Esmeralda, said to be 150 years old and the largest tortoise in the world.

DESROCHES: The largest of the Amirantes archipelago, Desroches is 193km (120 miles) southwest of Mahé (one hour by air). The surrounding coral reef keeps the coastal waters calm and makes it an ideal destination for those seeking watersports. Although Desroches was only recently developed as a resort, there are facilities for water-skiing, windsurfing, sailing, fishing and scuba diving; water scooters may also be hired. The diving is particularly good: there are sea cliffs, tunnels and caves – and, of course, multitudes of fish of many different species. Lessons are available. Visibility is best from September to May. Accommodation is in 20 chalets set amongst casuarina trees and coconut palms.

Credit: © Seychelles Marketing Tourism Authority

PLANTS AND WILDLIFE

As a result of their extraordinary, isolated history, the Seychelles are rich in rare plants which flourish nowhere else on the planet. 81 species are unique survivors from the luxuriant tropical forests that covered the islands until humanity's belated arrival two centuries ago. Outstanding amongst these is the coco-de-mer (sea coconut), native to Praslin, which grows in the Vallée de Mai. Its seed is the largest in nature, and gave rise to many legends when it was washed ashore on the coasts of Africa, India and Indonesia. Since the islands were unknown, the nuts were thought to have grown under the sea – hence the name. Among the many orchids is the vanilla, once widely cultivated for the essence produced from its aromatic pods. Its ornate leaves and lovely flowers make a wonderful display. It is not, however, necessary to travel the length and breadth of the islands to see interesting plants, as many of them can be viewed in Victoria's Botanical Gardens. The Seychelles are also a major attraction for birdwatchers. Millions of terns nest on the islands – among them that most beautiful of seabirds, the fairy tern. Up to two million sooty terns nest on Bird Island, and on Aride can be found the world's largest colonies of lesser noddies, roseate terns and other tropical birds. Some species, on the other hand, are less well represented and are rare almost to the point of extinction. The paradise flycatcher has dwindled to some 30 pairs on one island, La Digue. The Seychelles magpie robin is confined to Frégate, the black parrot to Praslin and the melodious brush warbler to Cousin.

It was only some 20 years ago that active conservation of endangered species began in the Seychelles. Since then, with the establishment of island sanctuaries and nature reserves, much has been done to make the Seychelles a paradise for birds – and for those who love to watch them.

Sport & Activities

Watersports: Coral reef **diving** is possibly the main sporting attraction in the Seychelles. Spearfishing is forbidden and, perhaps as a consequence, the fish are not afraid of people. The clear water makes conditions perfect for **underwater photography**. The coastal waters are a haven for 100 species of coral and over 900 species of fish. The annual *Subios* underwater festival is held in the Seychelles over a three-week period in November and attracts underwater experts from all over the world. **Snorkelling** is also very popular, with many snorkelling spots conveniently close to the beaches; most of the larger hotels rent out snorkelling equipment. A favourite location for snorkelling is the *St Anne National Marine Park*, which encompasses six islands off the coast of Mahé. Details about the Seychelles' best dive sites are also available from the Seychelles Tourist Office (see *Contact Addresses* section). Game **fishing** is a comparatively new sport in the Seychelles, but the abundance of fish has already made the islands popular with enthusiasts. Fishing seasons are governed by weather conditions: from May to September, the trade winds blow from the southeast; and from November to February, from the northwest. Black, blue and striped marlin, sailfish, yellowfish and dogtooth tuna, wahoo and barracuda are just a few of the game fish found in these tropical waters. Power boats, cabin cruisers and yachts are available for charter for anglers and others wishing to explore the islands at their own pace. Vessels may be booked in advance by the day, week or month. Reservations may be made at local agents or through *The Marine Charter Association*, PO Box 204, Victoria, Mahé (tel: 224 679; fax: 322 126; e-mail: mca@seychelles.net; website: www.seychelles.net/mca). The best spots for salt water fly fishing are Alphonse and Desroches island. Windsurfers, canoes and sailing dinghies may be hired on the more popular beaches, such as Beau Vallon Bay on Mahé, and **water-skiing** and **paragliding** are available at many other resort areas. Equipment may be hired.

Other: A new 18-hole **golf** course has recently been opened on Praslin at the Lemuria Hotel (contact the Seychelles Tourist Office for details; see *Contact Addresses* section).

There are also opportunities for **squash**, **tennis** and **badminton**. Organised **hiking** and **walking** tours are available to explore the islands' flora and fauna; some of the best trails are on Aride, Mahé, Praslin and Silhouette.

Social Profile

FOOD & DRINK: Seychellois Creole cuisine is influenced by African, Chinese, English, French and Indian traditions. The careful blending of spices is a major feature and much use is made of coconut milk and breadfruit. Local specialities include *kat-kat banane*, coconut curries, *chatini requin*, *bourgeois grillé*, *soupe de tectec*, *bouillon brède*, *chauve-souris* (fruitbat), *cari bernique*, *salade de palmiste* (made from the 'heart' of the coconut palm and sometimes known as 'millionaire's salad') and *la daube* (made from breadfruit, yams, cassavas and bananas). Breadfruit is prepared in similar ways to the potato (mashed, chipped, roasted and so on) but has a slightly sweeter taste. Other locally produced fruits and vegetables include aubergines, calabashes, choux choutes, patoles, *paw-paws* (papaya), bananas, mangoes, avocados, jackfruits, grapefruits, guavas, lychees, pineapples, melons, limes and golden apples. Lobster, octopus, pork and chicken are used more frequently than beef or lamb, which must be imported. Most restaurants offer a few items of what is termed 'international' cuisine, generally with a bias towards preparations of fresh fish and shellfish, as well as the Creole delicacies mentioned above. There are Italian and Chinese restaurants on Mahé. Some of the main hotels have bakeries and home-baked bread is also a feature of some of the small guest houses and lodges. Waiter service is the norm. All restaurants which are members of the *Seychelles Restaurateurs' Association* quote an average price per person for a three-course meal inclusive of two glasses of wine and coffee. Prior notice should be given in restaurants for groups of four or more and advance bookings should be made for restaurants on Round and Cerf and for *La Réserve* restaurant on Praslin.

A wide range of wines, spirits and other alcoholic beverages is available in the Seychelles. *Seybrew*, a German style lager, is made locally. The same company produces *Guinness* under licence and soft drinks. Local tea is also popular – see below under **Shopping**. A hotel licence permits hotel residents to drink at any time. Alcohol can be sold to anyone between Mon-Fri 1400-1800, Sat 0800-1200 and 1400-1800. Other bars open 1130-1500 and 1800-2200. It is illegal to drink alcohol on any road or in public.

NIGHTLIFE: Largely undeveloped and unsophisticated. There is, however, much to be enjoyed in the evenings, and a speciality is the local *camtolet* music, often accompanied by dancers. Several hotels have evening barbecues and dinner dances. Theatre productions are often staged (in

Creole, English and French) and there are cinemas in Victoria and casinos at *Beau Vallon Bay Hotel* and the *Plantation Club*.
SHOPPING: Local handicrafts include work with textiles (such as batik), fibres (such as basketwares, table-mats and hats) and wood (such as traditional furniture, ornaments and model boats). Pottery and paintings may also be bought. Special souvenirs might include jewellery made from green snail shells. Tea-growing and manufacturing in the Seychelles is done on a small scale. Local tea can be bought in the shops or when visiting the tea factory on Mahé, where many blends of tea may be sampled at the *Tea Tavern*. Vanilla is cultivated as a climbing plant around the base of trees as it can be pollinated by hand. Pods can be bought in shops and used as flavouring. Cinnamon grows wild on all the islands. It can be bought as oil or in quills made from dried bark which can be freshly grated before use. **Shopping hours:** Mon-Fri 0900-1600, Sat 0800-1200. Some shops close weekdays 1200-1300.
SPECIAL EVENTS: For a full list of events, contact the Seychelles Tourist Office (see *Contact Addresses* section). The following is a selection of special events occurring in the Seychelles in 2005:
Jan 25 *Kavadi Thaipoosum*. **Apr** *Rotary Annual Fishing Tournament*; *Seychelles Art Festival*. **May** *FetAfrik: Africa Day Celebrations*. **May 19-22** *SUBIOS*, annual underwater festival. **Jun** *Agricultural and Horticultural Show*, Mahé. **Jul** *Round Table Annual Regatta*, Mahé. **Aug 15** *Feast of the Assumption of the Virgin Mary*. **Sep** *Vinayagar Chadurthi*. **Sep 27** *World Tourism Day*. **Oct** *Festival Kreol*. **Oct 9** *Mahé-Praslin Windsurfing Race*. **Dec** *Christmas Show*, Mahé.
SOCIAL CONVENTIONS: The people live a simple and unsophisticated island life and tourism is carefully controlled to protect the unspoilt charm of the islands. Before the international airport opened in 1971, the islands could be reached only by sea, and since they are miles from anywhere, visitors were few and far between and the people were little influenced by the outside world. They developed their own language and culture which – like so many things on the islands – are unique. Shaking hands is the customary form of greeting. The Seychellois are very hospitable and welcome guests into their homes. When visiting someone's home, a gift is acceptable. A mixture of imperial and metric systems operates. For example, petrol is dispensed in litres, whilst bars sell bottled and draught beer in half-pint measures. Casual wear is essential and formal clothes are only worn by churchgoers. Swimwear should only be worn on the beaches. **Tipping:** Tips in restaurants, hotels, to taxi drivers, porters and so on are usually already included, as 5 to 10 per cent of the bill or fare. All hotel and restaurant tariffs include a service charge, but payment is not obligatory.

Credit: © Seychelles Marketing Tourism Authority

Business Profile

ECONOMY: Tourism is the largest industry in the Seychelles' economy; it now accounts for over 20 per cent of GDP, and draws 70 per cent of foreign exchange earnings. The service sector as a whole covers three-quarters of the Seychelles' economy.
Despite a shortage of fertile land, the agricultural sector produces copra for export, a variety of cash crops including tea and vanilla, and staple foods like cassava and sweet potatoes for domestic consumption. Fishing became increasingly important from the 1980s onwards, both through expansion of domestic operations and the lucrative sale of licences to foreign fleets. Industry comprises a small mining sector which extracts guano (rich in minerals) and some natural gas, plus light and small-scale industries including food and drinks (notably a tuna-canning operation), boat-building, metals, chemicals, wood products and tobacco. There is also a thriving re-export business based on a recently established export-processing zone. Extensive searches for offshore oil and gas reserves have so far been unsuccessful. The economy's heavy dependence on tourism makes it especially vulnerable to external factors (such as the September 11 attacks on the USA), over which it has no control. In 1995, in an attempt to diversify the service economy away from tourism, the Government started to promote the Seychelles as an 'offshore' financial services centre. This has been moderately successful, especially given that this is now a highly competitive and – because of concerns about fraud and money-laundering – controversial field.
After several years of recession, the economy is growing slowly. The main financial problem is the size of the country's external debt. The Seychelles must import many essential products – an expensive process given the islands' location – and this consumes the bulk of the foreign exchange earned from tourism.
The Seychelles is a member of the African Development Bank and the Indian Ocean Commission (which provides for regional economic cooperation). The Seychelles' principal trading partners are the UK, Yemen (the main source of imported oil), Germany and the countries of the South African Customs Union (South Africa, Botswana, Namibia, Lesotho and Swaziland).
BUSINESS: Businessmen do not wear suits and ties, although a smart appearance is advised. Most executives speak English and/or French. **Office hours:** Mon-Fri 0800-1600.
COMMERCIAL INFORMATION: The following organisation can offer advice: Seychelles Chamber of Commerce and Industry, PO Box 599, Ebrahim Building, Victoria, Mahé (tel: 323 812; fax: 321 422; e-mail: scci@seychelles.net).
CONFERENCES/CONVENTIONS: Further information from Mason's Travel, Michel Building, PO Box 459, Victoria, Mahé (tel: 322 642; fax: 225 273); *or* Creole Holidays, Orion Building, PO Box 611, Victoria, Mahé (tel: 280 100; fax: 225 817; e-mail: info@creoleholidays.sc; website: www.creoleholidays.sc); *or* Premier Holidays, Premier Building, PO Box 290, Victoria, Mahé (tel: 225 777; fax: 225 888; e-mail: premier@seychelles.net); *or* Travel Services Seychelles, Mahé Trading Building, PO Box 356, Victoria, Mahé (tel: 322 401; fax: 322 366).

Climate

The islands lie outside the cyclone belt but receive monsoon rains from November to February with the northwest trade winds. This hot and humid season gives way to a period of cooler weather, though the temperature rarely falls below 23°C, and rougher seas when the trade winds blow from the southeast (May to September).
Required clothing: Tropical lightweights, with rainwear advisable during the rainy season. Sun hats and sunglasses essential all year round.

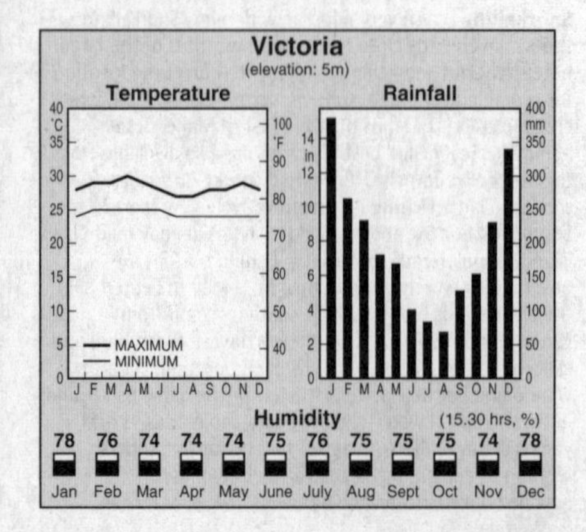

Sierra Leone

LATEST TRAVEL ADVICE CONTACTS

British Foreign and Commonwealth Office
Tel: (0870) 606 0290 Website: www.fco.gov.uk
US Department of State
Website: http://travel.state.gov/travel
Canadian Department of Foreign Affairs and Int'l Trade
Tel: (1 800) 267 8376 Website: www.dfait-maeci.gc.ca

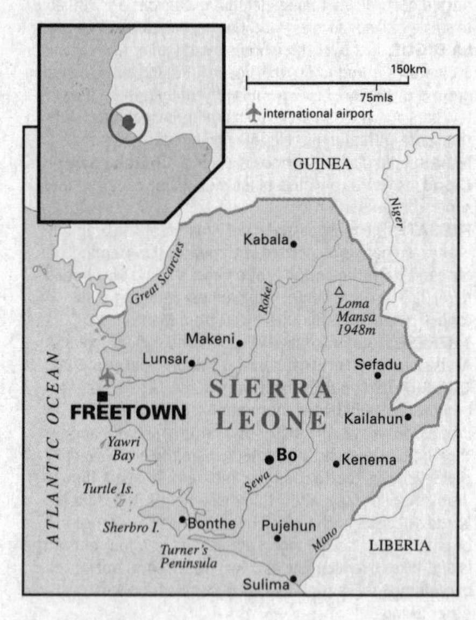

Location: West Africa.

Country dialling code: 232.

National Tourist Board of Sierra Leone
Street address: Cape Sierra Hotel, Room 100, Aberdeen, Freetown, Sierra Leone
Postal address: PO Box 1435, Aberdeen, Freetown, Sierra Leone
Tel: (22) 272 520.
Fax: (22) 272 197.
E-mail: ntbinfo@sierratel.sl *or* ntbslinfo@yahoo.com
Ministry of Tourism and Culture
Ministerial Building, George Street, Freetown, Sierra Leone
Tel: (22) 222 588 *or* 223 772.
High Commission for the Republic of Sierra Leone
Oxford Circus House, 245 Oxford Street,
London W1D 2LX, UK
Tel: (020) 7287 9884. Fax: (020) 7734 3822.
E-mail: info@slhc-uk.org.uk
Website: www.slhc-uk.org.uk
Opening hours: Mon-Thurs 1000-1300 and 1430-1500; Fri 1000-1300.
British High Commission
6 Spur Road, Wilberforce, Freetown, Sierra Leone
Tel: (22) 232 362.
Fax: (22) 232 070.
Embassy of the Republic of Sierra Leone
1701 19th Street, NW, Washington, DC 20009, USA
Tel: (202) 939 9261.
Fax: (202) 483 1793.
E-mail: Sierrale@umbc7.umbc.edu
Website: www.sierra-leone.org
Also deals with enquiries from Canada.
Embassy of the United States of America
Corner of Walpole Street and Siaka Stevens Street, Freetown, Sierra Leone
Tel: (22) 226 481 (ext 249). Fax: (22) 225 471.
E-mail: taylorJB2@state.gov
Website: http://freetown.usembassy.gov
The Canadian Embassy in Conakry deals with enquiries relating to Sierra Leone (see *Guinea* section).

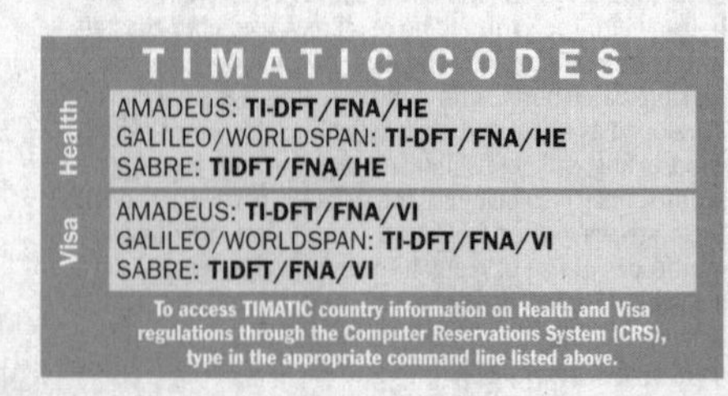
TIMATIC CODES

Health
AMADEUS: **TI-DFT/FNA/HE**
GALILEO/WORLDSPAN: **TI-DFT/FNA/HE**
SABRE: **TIDFT/FNA/HE**

Visa
AMADEUS: **TI-DFT/FNA/VI**
GALILEO/WORLDSPAN: **TI-DFT/FNA/VI**
SABRE: **TIDFT/FNA/VI**

To access TIMATIC country information on Health and Visa regulations through the Computer Reservations System (CRS), type in the appropriate command line listed above.

General Information

AREA: 71,740 sq km (27,699 sq miles).
POPULATION: 4,764,000 (UN estimate 2002).
POPULATION DENSITY: 66.4 per sq km.
CAPITAL: Freetown. **Population:** 837,000 (UN estimate 2001).
GEOGRAPHY: Sierra Leone is bordered to the northwest, north and northeast by Guinea Republic, and to the southeast by Liberia. To the south and southwest lies the Atlantic Ocean. A flat plain up to 110km (70 miles) wide stretches the length of the coast except for the Freetown peninsula, where the Sierra Lyoa Mountains rise to 1000m (3280ft). In some coastal areas, sand bars have formed that stretch out as far as 112km (70 miles). Behind the coastal plain is the central forested area, drained by eight principal rivers, which has been cleared for agriculture. The land rises in altitude eastwards to the Guinea Highlands, a high plateau with peaks rising to over 1830m (6000ft) in the Loma Mountains and Tingi Hills area. The Mende tribe is prominent in the southeast and the Temne in the western and northern areas.
GOVERNMENT: Republic. Gained independence from the UK in 1961. **Head of State and Government:** President Ahmad Tejan Kabbah since 1996.
LANGUAGE: The official language is English. Krio is also widely spoken. Local dialects are Mende, Limba and Temne.
RELIGION: Animist (40 per cent), Islam (40 per cent) and Christian (20 per cent).
TIME: GMT.
ELECTRICITY: 220/240 volts AC, 50Hz. Supply subject to fluctuations.
COMMUNICATIONS: Telephone: IDD is available. Country code: 232. Outgoing international code: 00. **Mobile telephone:** GSM 900/1800 networks available. Operators include *Celtel (SL) Limited* (website: www.msicellular.com), *Comium* (website: www.comium.com), *Lintel (Sierra Leone) Limited* and *Millicom SL* (website: www.buzzsl.com). Coverage limited to Freetown and environs. **Fax:** Facilities are available at SierraTel offices. **Internet:** ISPs include *SierraTel Internet*. Public access outlets are increasingly popping up, especially in Freetown where access is also available through the British Council. **Telegram:** Facilities at Slecom House, 7 Wallace Johnson Street, Freetown. **Post:** Airmail to Western Europe takes about five days. **Press:** Sierra Leone's English-language daily is the *Daily Mail*. Other newspapers are *The New shaft*, *Progress* and *The Vision*.
Radio: BBC World Service (website: www.bbc.co.uk/worldservice) and Voice of America (website: www.voa.gov) can be received. From time to time the frequencies change and the most up-to-date can be found online.

Passport/Visa

	Passport Required?	Visa Required?	Return Ticket Required?
Full British	Yes	Yes	Yes
Australian	Yes	Yes	Yes
Canadian	Yes	Yes	Yes
USA	Yes	Yes	Yes
Other EU	Yes	Yes	Yes
Japanese	Yes	Yes	Yes

Note: *Regulations and requirements may be subject to change at short notice, and you are advised to contact the appropriate diplomatic or consular authority before finalising travel arrangements. Details of these may be found at the head of this country's entry. Any numbers in the chart refer to the footnotes below.*

Restricted entry: Nationals of Liberia need authorisation from the Government of Sierra Leone or they will be refused admission.
PASSPORTS: Passport valid for a minimum of six months required by all.
VISAS: Required by all except the following:
(a) nationals of Benin, Burkina Faso, Cape Verde, Côte d'Ivoire, The Gambia, Ghana, Guinea Republic, Guinea-Bissau, Liberia, Mali, Niger, Nigeria, Senegal and Togo;
(b) transit passengers continuing their journey by the same or first connecting aircraft within 24 hours provided holding onward or return documentation and not leaving the airport transit area.
Types of visa and cost: *Tourist:* £45 (single-entry); £90 (multiple-entry). *Express Tourist* and *Business:* £40 in addition to cost. *Business:* £60 (single-entry); £120 (multiple-entry: six months), £200 (multiple-entry: one year).
Validity: Entry Permits and visas generally are valid for three months and allow a stay of one month in Sierra Leone for single-entry only. An extension is possible by application to the Department of Immigration in Freetown. Multiple-entry tourist and visitor visas are valid for six months; a Business Multiple-entry visa is valid for up to one year.
Application to: Consulate (or Consular section at Embassy or High Commission); see *Contact Addresses* section.
Application requirements: (a) Completed application form. (b) Two passport-size photos. (c) Passport valid for six months. (d) Confirmation of hotel reservation for Tourist visa. (e) Letter of invitation and company letter for *Business* visa. (f) Vaccination against yellow fever, malaria and cholera are required in order to obtain a visa (see *Health* section). (g) Fee in cash or postal order for mail applications. (h) Evidence of sufficient funds.
Working days required: Three. Several weeks are required where referral to authorities in Sierra Leone is necessary. One day for Express visa.

Money

Currency: Leone (Le) = 100 cents. Notes are in denominations of Le5000, 2000, 1000, 500, 100, 50, 20, 10, 5, 2 and 1. Coins are in denominations of Le100 and 50. In June 1986, a system of 'floating' exchange rates was introduced to correct persistent over-valuation of the Leone.
Credit & debit cards: These are not accepted.
Travellers cheques: These are generally not recommended.
Currency restrictions: The import and export of local currency is limited to Le50,000. The import of foreign currency is unlimited subject to declaration; export of foreign currency is limited to the amount declared on arrival (amounts exceeding US$5000 must be authorised by the National Bank of Sierra Leone).
Exchange rate indicators: The following figures are included as a guide to the movements of the Leone against Sterling and the US Dollar:

Date	Feb '04	May '04	Aug '04	Nov '04
£1.00=	4459.62	4375.96	4522.98	4649.05
$1.00=	2450.00	2450.00	2455.00	2455.00

Banking hours: Mon-Thurs 0800-1330, Fri 0800-1400.

Duty Free

The following may be imported into Sierra Leone without incurring customs duty:
200 cigarettes or 225g tobacco; 1.1l of wine or spirits.
Prohibited imports: Narcotics; firearms without a licence from the Commissioner of Police in Freetown.
Abolition of Duty Free Goods within the EU: On June 30 1999, the sale of duty free alcohol and tobacco at airports and at sea was abolished in all of the original 15 EU member states. Of the 10 new member states that joined the EU on May 1 2004, these rules already apply to Cprus and Malta. There are transitional rules in place for visitors returning to one of the original 15 EU countries from one of the other new EU countries. But for the original 15, plus Cyprus and Malta, there are now no limits imposed on importing tobacco and alcohol products from one EU country to another (with the exceptions of Denmark, Finland and Sweden, where limits *are* imposed). Travellers should note that they may be required to prove at customs that the goods purchased are for personal use *only*.

Public Holidays

2005: Jan 1 New Year's Day. **Jan 21** Eid al-Adha (Feast of the Sacrifice). **Mar 25** Good Friday. **Mar 28** Easter Monday. **Apr 21** Maulid-un-Nabi (Birth of the Prophet). **Apr 27** Independence Day. **Nov 3-5** Eid al-Fitr (End of Ramadan). **Dec 25** Christmas Day. **Dec 26** Boxing Day.
2006: Jan 1 New Year's Day. **Jan 10** Eid al-Adha (Feast of the Sacrifice). **Apr 11** Maulid-un-Nabi (Birth of the Prophet). **Apr 14** Good Friday. **Apr 17** Easter Monday. **Apr 27** Independence Day. **Oct 22-24** Eid al-Fitr (End of Ramadan). **Dec 25** Christmas Day. **Dec 26** Boxing Day.
Note: Muslim festivals are timed according to local sightings of various phases of the moon and the dates given above are approximations. During the lunar month of Ramadan that precedes Eid al-Fitr, Muslims fast during the day and feast at night and normal business patterns may be interrupted. Many restaurants are closed during the day and there may be restrictions on smoking and drinking. Some disruption may continue into Eid al-Fitr itself. Eid al-Fitr and Eid al-Adha may last anything from two to 10 days, depending on the region. For more information, see the *World of Islam* appendix.

Health

	Special Precautions?	Certificate Required?
Yellow Fever	Yes	1
Cholera	2	No
Typhoid & Polio	3	N/A
Malaria	4	N/A

Note: *Regulations and requirements may be subject to change at short notice, and you are advised to contact your doctor well in advance of your intended date of departure. Any numbers in the chart refer to the footnotes below.*

1: A yellow fever vaccination certificate is required of travellers arriving from infected areas. Travellers arriving from non-endemic zones should note that vaccination is strongly recommended for travel outside the urban areas, even if an outbreak of the disease has not been reported and they would normally not require a vaccination certificate to enter the country.
2: Following WHO guidelines issued in 1973, a cholera vaccination certificate is not a condition of entry to Sierra Leone. However, cholera is a serious risk in this country and precautions are essential. Up-to-date advice should be sought before deciding whether these precautions should include vaccination, as medical opinion is divided over its effectiveness; see the *Health* appendix for further details.
3: Polio and typhoid both occur.
4: Malaria risk exists, predominantly in the malignant *falciparum* form, throughout the country all year. Resistance to chloroquine has been reported. The recommended prophylaxis is mefloquine.
Food & drink: All water should be regarded as being potentially contaminated. Water used for drinking, brushing teeth or making ice should have first been boiled or otherwise sterilised. Milk is unpasteurised and should be boiled. Powdered or tinned milk is available and is advised, but make sure that it is reconstituted with pure water. Avoid dairy products which are likely to have been made from unboiled milk. Only eat well-cooked meat and fish, preferably served hot. Pork, salad and mayonnaise may carry increased risk. Vegetables should be cooked and fruit peeled.
Other risks: *Bilharzia* (schistosomiasis) is present. Avoid swimming and paddling in fresh water; swimming pools which are well chlorinated and maintained are safe. *Filariasis* and *dengue fever* are present. *Trachoma, hepatitis A* and *E, tungiasis* and *dysentery* are widespread. *Trypanosomiasis* (sleeping sickness) may be present and there is a significant risk of infection for travellers visiting or working in rural areas. *Meningococcal meningitis* and *TB* may occur. *Hepatitis B* is hyperendemic. *Lassa fever* can be contracted in Kenema and the east; the last widely publicised outbreak was in April 2004. There is a high incidence of *HIV/AIDS*.
Rabies is present. For those at high risk, vaccination before arrival should be considered. If you are bitten, seek medical advice without delay. For more information, consult the *Health* appendix.
Health care: Medical facilities are extremely limited and continuing to decline. According to UN estimates, Sierra Leone has the highest death rate and the second-highest infant mortality rate (200 out of every 1000 infants die within one year of birth). Missions and foreign aid organisations provide some medical facilities. Health insurance is essential. It is advisable to take personal medical supplies.

Travel - International

Note: Travel to areas of Sierra Leone bordering Liberia is strongly advised against. British nationals remain potential targets for disaffected groups. Sensible precautions should be taken and a high level of vigilance in public places maintained. However, the threat from terrorism is low.
AIR: Sierra Leone's national airline is *Sierra National Airlines (LJ)*. Other airlines serving Sierra Leone include *Air Guinea Express*and *Ghana Airways* . Owing to political instability, some flights from Europe and the USA are still suspended or disrupted. *SN Brussel* operates. The situation is likely to improve. Check with the relevant airlines, the Embassy or High Commission for up-to-date information.
Approximate flight times: From Freetown to *London* is 10 hours 30 minutes (including transit in Accra).
International airports: *Freetown (FNA)* (Lungi) is 13km (8 miles) north of the city (travel time - 45 minutes). There is a catamaran/ferry link as well as taxi and bus services to the city. A helicopter service is also available (travel time - six minutes). Airport facilities include a post office, bar, shops and currency exchange.
Departure tax: US$20 (payable in hard currency by all except nationals of Sierra Leone). Transit passengers and children under two years of age are exempt.
SEA: The principal port is Freetown which has services to Guinea Republic and Liberia.
RAIL: There are no passenger services at present.
ROAD: There are routes from Guinea Republic and Liberia, but access depends on the prevailing political situation. Contact the Embassy or High Commission for up-to-date information.

Travel - Internal

AIR: *Sierra National Airlines (LJ)* does not operate internal flights. Private airlines can be chartered.
SEA: Ferries connect all coastal ports. For details, contact local authorities or the National Tourist Board of Sierra Leone (see *Contact Addresses* section).

Credit: © Sierra Leone National Tourist Board

ROAD: Traffic drives on the right. Sierra Leone has over 10,000km (6214 miles) of roads. Although the principal highways have a tarred surface, the secondary roads are poorly maintained and often impassable during the rainy season. There are some roadblocks at night on major roads near centres of population. **Bus:** Local and long-distance bus services are operated by the *Sierra Leone Road Transport Corporation*. Buses are fast and cheap and connect all the major centres. **Documentation:** An International Driving Permit is required.
URBAN: Limited bus services in Freetown are operated by the *Road Transport Corporation*, although a substantial part of the city's public transport is provided by minibuses and share-taxis.

Accommodation

There are several hotels in Freetown of international standard with air conditioning and swimming pools. It is always advisable to make reservations in advance. Additionally, there are three luxury hotels located on the peninsula at Lakka and Tokay. The YMCA in Freetown offers clean, cheap accommodation with shared bathroom and kitchen facilities at a reasonable rate. Hotels in the interior are rare, although in Bo there is now a hotel which is of international standard. There are also government rest houses, for which application must be made to the Ministry of the Interior; guests must bring their own linen. For more information, contact the Ministry of Tourism and Culture (see *Contact Addresses* section) *or*, for advice and informal information on this and other aspects of travelling to Sierra Leone, Sierra Leone Tourism Information (website: www.visitsierraleone.org).

Resorts & Excursions

FREETOWN: The most accessible part of Sierra Leone is the **Freetown Peninsula**. From **Leicester Peak**, superb views of the city between the sea and the mountains unfold below, and a narrow, steep road through the mountains leads to the old Creole villages (dating from 1800) of **Leicester**, **Gloucester** and **Regent**. The area was chosen as a resettlement area for liberated slaves who built the villages of **Hastings**, **Kent**, **Sussex**, **Waterloo**, **Wellington** and **York**. Freetown itself, surrounded by thickly vegetated hills, is both a colourful and historic port. Attractions include a 500-year-old cotton tree; the museum; the **De Ruyter Stone**; **Government Wharf** and **'King's Yard'** (where freed slaves waited to be given land); **Fourah Bay College**, the oldest university in West Africa; **Marcon's Church**, built in 1820; and the **City Hotel**, immortalised in Graham Greene's novel *The Heart of the Matter*. The **King Jimmy Market** and the bazaars offer a colourful spectacle and interesting shopping. A boat trip up the **Rokel River** to **Bunce Island**, one of the first slave trading stations of West Africa, makes an interesting excursion.
GAME PARKS: Permits, obtainable from the Ministry of Agriculture and Forestry in Freetown, are necessary for visits to Reserves, and a guide is provided. For more information, contact the Ministry of Tourism and Culture (see *Contact Addresses* section).
The **Outamba-Kilimi National Park** in northern Sierra Leone, which can be reached from Freetown by road or air, offers varied and spectacular scenery; at this and other reserves there are game animals such as elephants, chimpanzees and pigmy hippos. The **Sakanbiarwa** plant reserve has an extensive collection of orchids, which are at their best early in the year.

Social Profile

FOOD & DRINK: Restaurants in the capital serve Armenian, English, French and Lebanese food. African food is served in hotels; local dishes include excellent fish, lobster and prawns, exotic fruit and vegetables.
NIGHTLIFE: Freetown has nightclubs and two casinos and there is music, dancing and local entertainment arranged by the hotels along Lumley Beach in the Cape Sierra district. Some beachside clubs organise concerts by local pop bands.
SHOPPING: Shopping hours: Mon-Sat 0800-1200 and 1400-1700.
SOCIAL CONVENTIONS: The majority of people in Sierra Leone still live a traditional, agricultural way of life, with ruling chiefs, and religions which preserve social stability, as well as local music, dance, customs and traditions. Handshaking is the normal form of greeting. It is usual to be entertained in a hotel or restaurant, particularly for business visitors. Small tokens of appreciation are always welcome. Casual wear is suitable everywhere. Men are rarely expected to wear suits and ties. **Tipping:** Most hotels and restaurants include a service charge of 10 to 15 per cent. Taxi drivers do not expect tips.

Business Profile

ECONOMY: Following what is hopefully a permanent end to the country's debilitating civil war, Sierra Leone can now start to rebuild its shattered economy. With an annual per capita income of just US$140, it is one of the world's poorest countries. It also recorded the lowest figure in the 2004 UN Human Development Index: in other words, it is the worst place in the world to live. The agricultural and mining sectors were particularly badly hit by the fighting. Agriculture employs over two-thirds of the workforce who grow coffee, cocoa, palm kernels, nuts and ginger as cash crops along with rice, bananas and cassava as staples. The fishing industry is also important.
The principal industrial activity is mining: the country has some of the world's most valuable diamond mines, as well as deposits of gold, bauxite and titanium ore. Diamonds have proved as much a curse as a blessing, as much of the civil war fighting was motivated by control of the mines and both the Government and the rebel forces relied on the revenues to sustain their war efforts. The remainder of the industrial sector is devoted to mineral and ore processing, as well as some light manufacturing of consumer goods such as textiles and furniture.
Sierra Leone's other major economic asset is the world's third-largest natural harbour, which the government is hoping to develop as a hub for international and transit trade for the whole of the region.
Since the end of the war, the economy has grown healthily at between 5 and 7 per cent annually. Inevitably, Sierra Leone still depends on large injections of foreign aid to support the economy, and the IMF and World Bank have been involved in the government's reconstruction plans.
Sierra Leone is a member of the African Development Bank and the West African trading bloc ECOWAS. The UK is the country's largest trading partner, followed by the USA, Germany and The Netherlands.
BUSINESS: English is the most common language in business circles. Appointments and punctuality are expected. Visiting cards are essential. September to June are the best months for business visits. **Office hours:** Mon-Fri 0800-1200 and 1400-1700.
COMMERCIAL INFORMATION: The following organisation can offer advice: Sierra Leone Chamber of Commerce, Industry and Agriculture, Guma Building, Lamina Sankoh Street, Freetown (tel: (22) 226 305 *or* 220 904; e-mail: cocsl@sierratel.sl).

Climate

Tropical and humid all year. Between November and April, it is very hot and dry, although the coastal areas are cooled by sea breezes. In December and January, the dry, dusty *Harmattan* wind blows from the Sahara. During the rainy season between May and November, rainfall can be torrential.

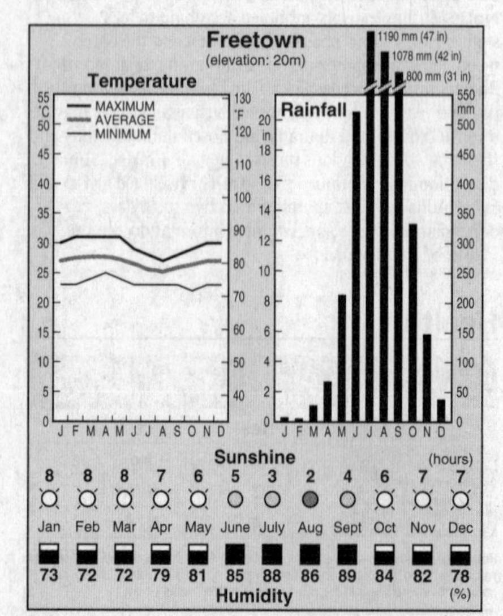

Singapore

LATEST TRAVEL ADVICE CONTACTS

British Foreign and Commonwealth Office
Tel: (0870) 606 0290 Website: www.fco.gov.uk
US Department of State
Website: http://travel.state.gov/travel
Canadian Department of Foreign Affairs and Int'l Trade
Tel: (1 800) 267 8376 Website: www.dfait-maeci.gc.ca

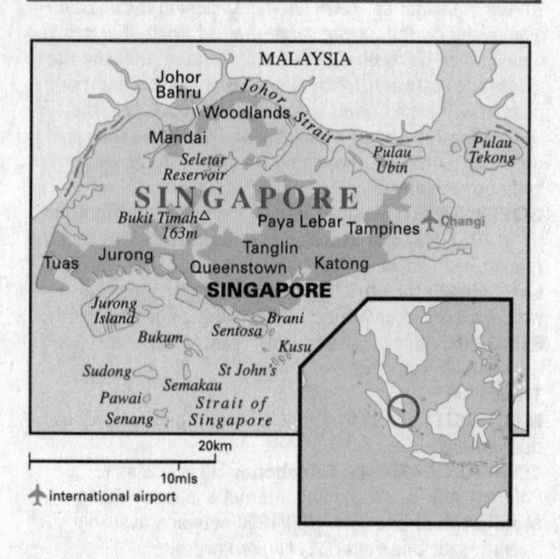

Location: Southeast Asia.

Country dialling code: 65.

Singapore Tourism Board
Tourism Court, 1 Orchard Spring Lane, Singapore 247729
Tel: (65) 6736 6622.
Fax: (65) 6736 9423.
E-mail: stb_visitsingapore@stb.gov.sg
Website: www.stb.com.sg
High Commission for the Republic of Singapore
9 Wilton Crescent, London SW1X 8SP, UK
Tel: (020) 7235 8315.
Fax: (020) 7245 6583 (general) *or* 7235 9850 (consular section).
E-mail: info@singaporehc.org.uk *or* consular@singaporehc.org.uk
Website: www.mfa.gov.sg/london
Opening hours: Mon-Fri 0900-1700; 1000-1230 and 1400-1600 (visa section).
Singapore Tourism Board
1st Floor, Carrington House, 126-130 Regent Street, London W1B 5JX, UK
Tel: (020) 7437 0033 *or* (08080) 656 565 (toll-free in the UK).
Fax: (020) 7734 2191.
E-mail: info@stb.org.uk
Website: www.visitsingapore.com
Also incorporates the Singapore Exhibition & Convention Bureau.
British High Commission
100 Tanglin Road, Singapore 247919
Tel: (65) 6424 4200 *or* 4244 (consular/visa section).
Fax: (65) 6424 4250 *or* 4264 (consular/visa section).
E-mail: commercial.singapore@fco.gov.uk
Website: www.britain.org.sg
Embassy of the Republic of Singapore
3501 International Place, NW, Washington, DC 20008, USA
Tel: (202) 537 3100.
Fax: (202) 537 0876.
E-mail: singemb.dc@verizon.net *or* singembcon.dc@verizon.net (consular section).
Website: www.mfa.gov.sg/washington
Singapore Tourism Board
1156 Avenue of the Americas, Suite 3702, New York, NY 10036, USA
Tel: (212) 302 4861.
Fax: (212) 302 4801.
E-mail: askroc@tourismsingapore.com
Website: http://visitsingapore.com
Office in: Los Angeles.

TIMATIC CODES

Health	AMADEUS: **TI-DFT/SIN/HE** GALILEO/WORLDSPAN: **TI-DFT/SIN/HE** SABRE: **TIDFT/SIN/HE**
Visa	AMADEUS: **TI-DFT/SIN/VI** GALILEO/WORLDSPAN: **TI-DFT/SIN/VI** SABRE: **TIDFT/SIN/VI**

To access TIMATIC country information on Health and Visa regulations through the Computer Reservations System (CRS), type in the appropriate command line listed above.

Embassy of the United States of America
27 Napier Road, Singapore 258508
Tel: (65) 6476 9100.
Fax: (65) 6476 9340 *or* 9232 (consular section).
E-mail: singaporecon@state.gov
Website: http://singapore.usembassy.gov

Consulate General of the Republic of Singapore
999 West Hastings Street, Suite 18200, Vancouver, British Columbia V6C 2W2, Canada
Tel: (604) 669 5115. Fax: (604) 669 5153.
E-mail: singaporeconsul@sprint.ca
Website: www.mfa.gov.sg/vancouver

Canadian High Commission
Street address: 14th and 15th Floors, IBM Towers, 80 Anson Road, Singapore 079907
Postal address: PO Box 845, Robinson Road, Singapore 901645
Tel: (65) 6325 3200. Fax: (65) 6325 3296 *or* 3290.
E-mail: spore-da@dfait-maeci.gc.ca *or* spore-cs@dfait-maeci.gc.ca (consular section).
Website: www.dfait-maeci.gc.ca/singapore

Credit: © Virtually Singapore

General Information

AREA: 659.9 sq km (254.8 sq miles).
POPULATION: 4,185,200 (official estimate 2003).
POPULATION DENSITY: 6,342.2 per sq km.
CAPITAL: Singapore City. **Population:** 3,163,500 (1998).
GEOGRAPHY: The island of Singapore is situated off the southern extremity of the Malay Peninsula, to which it is joined by a causeway carrying a road, railway and waterpipe. The Johor Strait between the island and the mainland is about 1km (0.8 miles) wide. The Republic of Singapore includes some 64 islets. It is a mainly flat country with low hills, the highest being Bukit Timah at 163m (545ft). In the northeast of the island, large areas have been reclaimed, and much of the original jungle and swamp covering the low-lying areas has been cleared.
GOVERNMENT: Republic. Gained full independence from the UK in 1965. **Head of State:** President Sellapan Ramanathan since 1999. **Head of Government:** Prime Minister Lee Hsien Loongsince 2004.
LANGUAGE: The four official languages are Malay (the national language), English, Chinese (Mandarin) and Tamil. Most Singaporeans are bilingual and speak English, which is used for business and administration.
RELIGION: Taoist, Buddhist, Christian, Hindu and Muslim.
TIME: GMT + 8.
ELECTRICITY: 220/240 volts AC, 50Hz. Plug fittings of the three-pin square type are in use. Many hotels have 110-volt outlets.
COMMUNICATIONS: Telephone: Full IDD is available. Country code: 65. Outgoing international code: 001. International calls can be made from public pay phones using a credit card or a phone card (S$2-50) available from Telecom centres and retail outlets. IDD calls made from hotels are free of surcharge. **Mobile telephone:** GSM 900/1800/3G. Network operators include *MobileOne* (website: www.m1.com.sg), *Singapore Telecom* (website: www.singtel.com) and *StarHub* (website: www.starhub.com). **Fax:** There are services at many major hotels and at the Telecoms buildings in Robinson Road and Exeter Road. **Internet:** Internet cafes throughout Singapore

Credit: © Virtually Singapore

provide public access to Internet and e-mail services. Main ISPs include *Cyberway Pte* (website: www.starhub.com) and *Singnet* (website: www.singnet.com). **Telegram:** Telegrams can be sent from post offices, hotels, the Central Telegraph Office at 71 Robinson Road and the Comcentre near Orchard Road. **Post:** Airmail to Europe takes up to one week. There are limited postal facilities at many hotels. Post office hours: Mon-Fri 0830-1700, Sat 0830-1300. The airport and Orchard Point branches are open daily 0700-1900. The General Post Office on Fullerton Road (near the river) and the Comcentre near Orchard Road are open 24 hours. **Press:** The English-language dailies are *The Business Times, The New Paper, The Straits Times* and *Streats.*
Radio: BBC World Service (website: www.bbc.co.uk/worldservice) and Voice of America (website: www.voa.gov) can be received. From time to time the frequencies change and the most up-to-date can be found online.

Passport/Visa

	Passport Required?	Visa Required?	Return Ticket Required?
Full British	Yes	1	Yes
Australian	Yes	1	Yes
Canadian	Yes	1	Yes
USA	Yes	1	Yes
Other EU	Yes	1	Yes
Japanese	Yes	1	Yes

Note: *Regulations and requirements may be subject to change at short notice, and you are advised to contact the appropriate diplomatic or consular authority before finalising travel arrangements. Details of these may be found at the head of this country's entry. Any numbers in the chart refer to the footnotes below.*

Note: (a) Women more than 24 weeks pregnant or more must obtain a letter from a doctor confirming that it is safe for them to travel and a Social Visit Pass for Expectant Mothers prior to arrival; apply at the High Commission or Embassy. (b) Severe penalties are imposed on those found in possession of narcotics; the death penalty is in force for those convicted of trafficking in heroin or morphine.
(c) Regulations are subject to change at short notice and all visitors are therefore advised to check with the High Commission or Embassy before leaving.
PASSPORTS: Passport valid for at least six months beyond date of departure required by all.
Note: There is now a service provided for frequent travellers to Singapore, called the Immigration Automated Clearance System (IACS), through which an Access Card is allocated that holds the individual's unique fingerprint data. This is currently available at Changi Airport, Singapore Cruise Centre, Tanah Merah Ferry Terminal and the bus passenger halls of the Woodlands and Tuas check points. At automated lanes, the Access Card is inserted into a Card Reader and the right thumb is placed onto the fingerprint scanner for verification. Travellers must be six years and older and either Singapore citizens/permanent residents or holder's of a Student's Pass, Employment Pass, Dependent's Pass or Work Permit. Enquire for further details at the nearest Embassy/Consulate.
VISAS: Required *only* by the following:
(a) * nationals of Afghanistan, Algeria, Bangladesh, China (PR), CIS, Egypt, India, Iran, Iraq, Jordan, Lebanon, Libya, Morocco, Myanmar, Pakistan, Saudi Arabia, Somalia, Sudan, Syrian Arab Republic, Tunisia, Yemen and holders of Palestinian Authority passports;
(b) those holding Refugee Travel Documents issued by Middle Eastern countries;
(c) those holding Hong Kong Document of Identity cards, holders of a Macau SAR Travel Permit and Temporary Passports issued by the United Arab Emirates.
Note: (a) *All countries mentioned in (a) (except Macau (SAR)) require a letter from a local sponsor (Singapore registered company, citizen or permanent resident) bearing responsibility for the visitor's stay.
(b) **1.** All other nationals require a *Social Visit Pass*, which is issued on arrival (at the discretion of the Immigration Officer) provided the traveller holds the appropriate application requirements (see below). For nationals holding British and Irish passports, the maximum length of stay is 30 days, for other nationals the maximum length of stay is 14 days. Visitors on a Social Visit Pass are not permitted to work in Singapore. The maximum stay for a tourist is 90 days and an extension must be applied for before the visa's expiry at the Immigration & Checkpoints Authority (ICA) in Singapore. The price of the extension is subject to the immigration officer's discretion (check with immigration on arrival). For stays over three months, applications must be made for a *Long Term Social Visit Pass*, for which a local sponsor (such as a Singapore national aged over 21 years or an organisation) is required.
Types of visa and cost: *Visa, Social Visit Pass* (short- or long-term; S$20), *Professional Visit Pass, Student Pass* and *Transit*. For any extension of pass accumulating to a period of three months or more from the date of entry/issue and for every subsequent extension accumulating to three months or more, the cost is usually S$40. Payment by *NETS* or *CashCard* is preferable. Application packs with instructions and prevailing visa costs at the time of application are obtainable from the High Commission (see *Contact Addresses* section).
Validity: *Social Visit Pass/Student Pass/Professional Visit Pass*: At the discretion of the ICA dependent on the college term dates.
Application to: Consulate (or Consular section at High Commission or Embassy); see *Contact Addresses* section.
Application requirements: *Social Visit Pass*: (a) Valid passport and photocopies of data pages. (b) Valid travel documents including an onward or return ticket (except nationals of Malaysia) and visa entry facilities to onward destinations, if applicable. (c) Sufficient funds. (d) Two completed application forms. (e) Yellow fever vaccination certificate if passing through or coming from an endemic zone within six days of arriving in Singapore. *Student Pass*: (a)-(e) and, (f) Form or letter from college/university in Singapore. (g) Birth certificate. (h) Certified copies of highest educational certificates and results. Depending on nationality, a security deposit from local sponsor may also be required. (i) Proof of registered institution with the Ministry of Education, or has proof of exemption, or is licensed with the Ministry of Community & Sports. *Business/Visitor*: (a)-(e) and, (f) Letter from sponsoring company. (g) For certain nationals, a computer print-out of the Singapore-registered company's detailed business profile, obtainable from the Accounting & Corporate Regulatory Authority (ACRA). *Visa*: (a)-(e) and, (f) Two copies of a letter from local sponsor in Singapore. (g) Two passport-size photos. (h) Letter of introduction for some.
Note: Requirements may vary, especially according to nationality, and according to exact specifications, and travellers should check with the Consulate prior to application.
Working days required: Up to four weeks. However, it is still advisable to allow plenty of time. For those applying for Student visas, allow two to six months.
Temporary residence: Apply to Consulate (or Consular section of High Commission or Embassy), who will forward application to the authorities in Singapore.

Money

Currency: Singapore Dollar (S$) = 100 cents. Notes are in denominations of S$10,000, 1000, 500, 100, 50, 20, 10, 5 and 2. Coins are in denominations of S$1, and 50, 20, 10, 5 and 1 cents.
The currency of Brunei is also legal tender; 1 Brunei Dollar = 1 Singapore Dollar.
Currency exchange: Foreign currencies, travellers cheques and cheques can be changed at most banks and licensed money changers. ATMs are also in operation.
Credit & debit cards: American Express, Diners Club, MasterCard and Visa are widely accepted. Check with your credit or debit card company for details of merchant acceptability and other facilities which may be available.
Travellers cheques: To avoid additional exchange rate charges, travellers are advised to take travellers cheques in Pounds Sterling.
Currency restrictions: There is no restriction on the import and export of local or foreign currency.
Exchange rate indicators: The following figures are included as a guide to the movements of the Singapore Dollar against Sterling and the US Dollar:

Date	Feb '04	May '04	Aug '04	Nov '04
£1.00=	3.08	3.03	3.15	3.10
$1.00=	1.69	1.70	1.71	1.64

Banking hours: Mon-Fri 0930-1500, Sat 0930-1300. Branches of certain major banks on Orchard Road open Sun 0930-1500.

Duty Free

The following goods may be imported into Singapore by passengers of 18 years or older without incurring customs duty:
1l of spirits, 1l of wine and 1l of beer.
Note: These allowances do not apply if arriving from Malaysia.
Restricted items: Chewing gum and tobacco products must be declared upon arrival.
Prohibited items: Firearms, non-prescribed drugs, all pornographic films and literature. Export permits are required for arms, ammunition, explosives, animals, telecommunications equipment, film and video tapes and disks, precious metals and stones, drugs and poisons. Meat and meat products are all strictly forbidden. Duty free cigarettes are prohibited. The penalties for possession of narcotics are severe and visitors not complying with drug regulations do so at the risk of death.

Credit: © Virtually Singapore

Public Holidays

2005: Jan 1 New Year's Day. **Jan 23** Hari Raya Haji (Feast of the Sacrifice). **Feb 9-10** Chinese New Year. **Mar 25** Good Friday. **May 2** Labour Day. **May 23** Vesak (Birth of Buddha). **Aug 9** National Day. **Nov 1** Diwali. **Nov 3-5** Hari Raya Puasa (End of Ramadan). **Dec 25** Christmas Day.
2006: Jan 1 New Year's Day. **Jan 10** Hari Raya Haji (Feast of the Sacrifice). **Jan 28-30** Chinese New Year. **Apr 14** Good Friday. **May 1** Labour Day. **May 13** Vesak (Birth of Buddha). **Aug 9** National Day. **Oct 21** Diwali. **Oct 22-24** Hari Raya Puasa (End of Ramadan). **Dec 25** Christmas Day.
Note: (a) Not all Muslim festivals listed above are national holidays, but all will affect Muslim businesses. Muslim festivals are timed according to local sightings of various phases of the moon and the dates given above are approximations. During the lunar month of Ramadan that precedes Hari Raya Puasa (Eid al-Fitr), Muslims fast during the day and feast at night and normal business patterns may be interrupted. Many restaurants are closed during the day and there may be restrictions on smoking and drinking. Some disruption may continue into Hari Raya Puasa itself. Hari Raya Puasa and Hari Raya Haji (Eid al-Adha) may last anything from two to 10 days, depending on the town. For more information, see the *World of Islam* appendix. (b) Hindu festivals are declared according to local astronomical observations and it is only possible to forecast the month of their occurrence.

Health

	Special Precautions?	Certificate Required?
Yellow Fever	No	1
Cholera	No	No
Typhoid & Polio	No	N/A
Malaria	No	N/A

Note: Regulations and requirements may be subject to change at short notice, and you are advised to contact your doctor well in advance of your intended date of departure. Any numbers in the chart refer to the footnotes below.

1: A yellow fever certificate of vaccination is required from persons over one year of age who have been in or passed through any country classified either partly or wholly as a yellow fever endemic zone within the previous six days. The countries formerly classified as endemic zones are considered by the Singapore authorities to be still infected.
Other risks: *Hepatitis A* and *E* are widespread; *hepatitis B* is hyperendemic.
Rabies is present. For those at high risk, vaccination before arrival should be considered. If you are bitten, seek medical advice without delay. For more information, consult the *Health* appendix.
HIV testing is required for workers who earn less than S$1250 per month and for applicants for permanent resident status. Foreign test results are not accepted.
Health care: Singapore General Hospital receives emergency cases and health care is exceptionally good. There is a large private sector. Health insurance is recommended, as there is no reciprocal health agreement with the UK.

Travel - International

Note: Visitors should not become involved with drugs of any kind: possession of even very small quantities can lead to imprisonment or the death penalty. Singapore shares, with the rest of South-East Asia, a threat from terrorism. Attacks could be indiscriminate and against civilian targets. However, most visits to Singapore are trouble-free.
AIR: Singapore's national airline is *Singapore Airlines (SQ)* (website: www.singaporeair.com). Singapore is a major travel destination served by most major international airlines. There are direct flights to Singapore from a number of cities in Canada, the UK and USA. Airlines flying direct from London include *British Airways*, *Qantas* and *Singapore Airlines*. There are also direct flights from Singapore to all capital cities in South-East Asia.
Approximate flight times: From Singapore to *London* is 13 hours, to *Los Angeles* is 20 hours 25 minutes, to *New York* is 21 hours 55 minutes and to *Sydney* is nine hours 15 minutes.
International airports: *Changi (SIN)* (website: www.changi.airport.com.sg) is 20km (12 miles) east of the city (travel time – 30 minutes). Public transport is readily available to the city centre which is about 16km (10 miles) from the airport. Taxi fare is S$17-22 (there is a surcharge of S$3 for all fares from the airport, increasing to S$5 for fares between 1700-0000, Fri-Sat). There is a regular bus route between the airport and the train station. The Mass Rapid Transit train system now operates from the airport to the city centre and trains depart every 12 minutes. The Maxicab, a six-seater taxi shuttle, operates daily 0900-2300 and tickets cost S$7 (children: S$5); tickets must be bought in advance from the shuttle service counter in the arrivals hall. *Free New Asia – Singapore Tours* are available at no charge for transit passengers with a minimum layover of four hours. Passengers can sign up for a tour at a Free New Asia – Singapore Tour counter located in the airport's transit areas. Singapore Changi Airport's two terminals offer comprehensive facilities ranging from a fitness centre, swimming pool, supermarket, medical clinics and full banking services (including money changing) to business centres and transit hotels with private bathrooms (advance booking is recommended for the hotels). There are left luggage facilities, post offices, bars and restaurants, extensive duty free shops and car hire operators, which include *Avis*, *Budget*, *Hertz* and *Sintat*.
Departure tax: None.
SEA: The international port is Singapore itself, the world's busiest in terms of tonnage. It is served by a growing number of international passenger cruise lines. Cruising is one of the fastest-growing tourist development areas in Singapore and there are plans to considerably expand the already extensive port facilities. There is now also a number of international operators using Singapore as a base for cruises throughout South-East Asia. For further details, contact the Singapore Tourism Board (see *Contact Addresses* section).
RAIL: Trains run to Kuala Lumpur, Johor Bahru and Malacca (Malaysia) on a route which extends to Bangkok (Thailand). Services operate daily between Singapore and Kuala Lumpur; some offer air conditioning and dining cars. There are also overnight trains with sleepers.
ROAD: Singapore is connected to Malaysia and the mainland of Asia by two causeways: one which crosses the Johor Strait; the other linking Tuas in Singapore; bus and coach services operate to the Malaysian town of Johor Bahru and beyond. For required documentation, see *Travel – Internal* section. Buses arriving from Malaysia and Thailand terminate at the Lavender Street terminal.

Travel - Internal

AIR: Sightseeing flights can be arranged locally through the *Republic of Singapore Flying Club*.
SEA: The Singapore Cruise Centre is located at the World Trade Centre, about 10 minutes' drive from the city centre. Harbour cruises and ferry services to Singapore's islands, Malaysia and the Indonesian Riau islands may be boarded at the ferry terminals located at the World Trade Centre and Tanah Merah Ferry Terminal at Changi. A ferry for Sentosa, the most popular offshore island, leaves every 20 minutes starting at 0730.
RAIL: There are regular and well-maintained train services between all major cities and towns.
ROAD: Bus: There is a well-developed system of local services run by two main companies. The service is cheap and efficient and operates 0600-0000 daily. There are additional peak-hours-only shuttle and minibus services. A flat fare system operates on the one-man routes. A timetable and route map are available from bookstores. **Car hire:** There are several car hire/self-drive firms with offices at the airport and in hotels. Traffic drives on the left.
Documentation: A national driving licence is sufficient for stays up to one month. For visits beyond one month, an International Driving Permit is required.
URBAN: Trishaws: This traditional form of chauffeur-pedalled transport is a fun and exciting way to tour the streets of Singapore. **Taxi:** These are numerous and relatively cheap. They can be picked up from outside hotels and official ranks or flagged down in the streets. Taxis are metered. Some surcharges not shown on the metre include: S$1 for all luggage placed in the boot; 50 per cent on the metered fare for journeys between 0000 and 0600; S$3 for all journeys starting at the airport; S$1 for all trips starting in the Central Business District, Mon-Fri 1630-1900 and Sat 1130-1400. It is possible to negotiate hourly rates for round-island tours.
Metro: Singapore has one of the most advanced metro systems in the world. The trains operate 0530-0300 (0600-0000 on Sundays and public holidays) with stations being served on average every six minutes. Fares range from 70 cents to S$1.60. The *Mass Rapid Transit (MRT)* is a modern, comfortable, efficient and cheap way to explore Singapore. Operation hours are 0530-0000 and the train timetables are posted at each station. Over 40 stations link the city centre and suburbs, thus providing an opportunity to visit some of Singapore's attractions along the two main routes, the north-south line and the east-west line. The MRT system also extends out to Changi Airport.

Accommodation

HOTELS: There is a wide variety of accommodation, ranging from budget to modern high-class hotels. These

have extensive facilities, including swimming pools, health clubs, several restaurants, full business services and shopping arcades. It is advisable to make advance reservations. All rooms are subject to 4 per cent tax and 10 per cent service charge. For further information on accommodation in Singapore, contact the Singapore Tourism Board (see *Contact Addresses* section) who can supply the *Singapore Hotels* brochure. The following organisation also offers information: Singapore Hotel Association, 21 Bukit Batok Street 22, Singapore 659589 (tel: 6415 3588; fax: 6415 3510; e-mail: secretariat@sha.org.sg; website: www.sha.org.sg). **Grading:** Some hotels are designated as being 'International Standard' with all modern conveniences such as swimming pools and air conditioning, and prices range from S$100 a night. However, there is no formal star system of grading.
GUEST HOUSES: The majority of the guest houses are situated along Bencoolen Street and Beach Road. Although considerably cheaper than the main hotels, guest houses tend not to be good value for money; the price per night is usually between S$20 and S$30 for a small, ill-equipped room. Discounts are sometimes available when staying a few days.
YOUTH HOSTELS: There are at least a dozen hostel-style establishments offering communal dormitory accommodation; the average price for a night's accommodation is S$10 or less. There is one YMCA International hostel in Singapore.
CAMPING: The few campsites there are in Singapore are inconveniently located, making camping a difficult option. Tents can be rented from the Universal Adventure shop on Pulau Ubin, and can be pitched on open land on the island. The only other option is to go to Sentosa island, where a four-person tent costs S$16 (which includes entrance fee to the island), pitched on a site with toilets and barbecue pits.

Resorts & Excursions

Singapore is truly cosmopolitan, a fascinating mixture of people and culture: officially Chinese, Indian and Malay, but also with a huge foreign resident and transit population of Americans, Burmese, Europeans, Indonesians, Japanese and fellow Asians, making it one of the most diverse centres in Asia. The Singapore Tourism Board publishes a wide range of brochures and booklets giving information on every aspect of the country. This guide lists some of the main attractions in Singapore City itself, including several parks and gardens, and descriptions of the most popular outlying islands.

SINGAPORE CITY

Singapore City was founded in 1819 by Sir Stamford Raffles of the British East India Company, who recommended that different areas of the town be set aside for the various ethnic groups. There are still fascinating pockets where more traditionally exclusive enclaves exist, principally in Chinatown, Arab Street, Serangoon Road (focus of the Indian community) and **Padang Square** with its very strong colonial associations. The best way to experience the remarkable diversity of the city is on foot: the traditional architecture, customs and cuisine of the various ethnic areas are in fascinating contrast to the lavish luxury shopping arcades of Orchard Road and Raffles City.
Orchard Road is the 'Fifth Avenue' or 'Oxford Street' of Singapore, and just as bustling, with its vast luxury malls, shops ranging from megastores to vendors of souvenir tat, as well as cafes and restaurants. The corner bar of the **Singapore Marriott Hotel**, itself a landmark, is the prime spot to watch the world go by.
Arab Street is the centre of the Arabian quarter of Singapore, and a great place for shopping. Other streets with excellent shopping opportunities are **Baghdad Street** and **Bussorah Street**, while **Sultan Plaza** is a centre for cloth traders. The golden domes of the **Sultan Mosque**, Singapore's chief Muslim place of worship, dominate the area; nearby are two historic Muslim burial grounds.
Chinatown, though somewhat overwhelmed by the growth of the Financial District, is a bustling and colourful area with shops, teahouses and restaurants, and also several temples such as the **Fuk Tak Ch'i** in **Telok Ayer Street** and the **Temple of the Calm Sea**. Ancient crafts of calligraphy, papermaking and fortune-telling are practised, and traditional goods and foodstuffs can be bought. The characteristic domestic architecture of Singapore – the shop-house with a moulded front, shuttered upper floor and an arcaded street front – is much in evidence.
Serangoon Road is the centre of **Little India**, the Indian quarter stretching from **Rochar Canal** to **Lavender Street**. The **Zhu Jiao Centre**, at the southern end of Serangoon Road, is a particularly vibrant example of Little India. Other attractions in the area include the **Sri Veeramakalimman Temple**, the **Mahatma Gandhi Memorial Hall** in **Race Course Lane** and **Farrer Park**.
No trip to Singapore would be complete without a visit to the **Raffles Hotel**, one of the most famous hotels in the world. A 'Singapore Sling' in the **Long Bar** is almost *de rigueur*; alternatively, drop into the **Writers' Bar** which provided inspiration for, amongst others, Noel Coward, Somerset Maugham and Joseph Conrad. The **CHIJMES complex** near the Raffles Hotel was developed out of the former **Convent of the Holy Infant Jesus**, whose Gothic shell is the basis for a series of plazas housing chic shops, restaurants and bars. A statue of Sir Stamford Raffles has been erected on the banks of the **Singapore River** on the spot where he is believed to have first set foot in Singapore. Nearby is **Parliament House**, the oldest government building in the country, the core of which dates back to the 1820s. **Boat Quay** and **North Boat Quay**, flanking the river on both banks near the Raffles statue, has now become one of Singapore's most popular bar and recreation areas, with traditional shop-houses converted into restaurants and clubs. **Clarke Quay** forms a triangle defined by a bend in the Singapore River. It is a complex of colonial 'godowns' (eastern term for warehouses) converted into a maze of bars, outdoor eating places, clubs, souvenir shops and mobile stalls that present the 'Old Singapore' tourist experience at its most concentrated, if occasionally tacky. **Riverside Walk**, on the opposite riverbank, extends the zone further, and the whole area is a must-see for visitors. **Mohammed Sultan Road**, west of Clarke Quay, is Singapore's classiest bar and club strip.
PARKS & GARDENS: The **Botanic Gardens**, over 47 hectares (116 acres) of landscaped parkland and primary jungle, are situated to the west of the city (Napier/Cluny roads), and are home to a wide range of animal and plant life. Within the gardens you will find the National Orchid Garden which has the largest collection in the world. Opening hours are Mon-Fri 0500-2300 and until 0000 at weekends and public holidays. Admission is free.
The **Bukit Timah Reserve**, established in 1883 and located northwest of the Botanic Gardens on **Bukit Timah Road**, contains Singapore's last stretches of original and immaculately manicured rain forest. The nature reserve also consists of tropical vegetation with clearly marked trails which lead up to **Bukit Timah**, the highest hill in Singapore. Admission is free.
Fort Canning Park, on **Fort Canning Rise**, was once an ancient fort of the Malay kings covering 2.8 hectares (7 acres). Colonial ruins of the British citadel can still be viewed, as can a 19th-century Christian cemetery. The **Battle Box** in the park is the old command bunker of the World War II defence of Singapore, now a museum open Tues-Sun 1000-1800, with a small admission fee charged.
The **Mandai Orchid Garden** is a commercial orchid farm enshrining Singapore's characteristic horticultural export, with a hillside of exotic orchid species and a spectacular water garden. Opening hours: daily 0900-1730. An admission fee is charged.
The **Kranji War Cemetery and Memorial**, northwest of the **Mandai Orchid Garden**, commemorates the death of all those who fell in the catastrophic campaigns in the defence of Singapore during World War II. The cemetery and landscaped grounds are open daily; no flowers are allowed on the graves.
The **Singapore Zoological Gardens**, towards the north of the island of Singapore, are largely an open zoo, using natural barriers rather than iron bars. Over 170 animals live here, including many rare or endangered species, such as orangutans, Sumatran tigers, Komodo dragons and clouded leopards. Daily attractions include 'wild breakfast' or 'afternoon tea' and 'Animal Showtime'. One special and much publicised attraction is the Night Safari; a combination walking and tram tour of predominantly nocturnal species. The zoo is open daily 0830-1800 and the Night Safari daily 1930-2400.
OTHER ATTRACTIONS: Buddhist and Hindu temples, mosques and Anglican and Catholic cathedrals are all likely to be encountered during a comparatively brief walk around some of the central areas of Singapore. **St Andrew's Cathedral**, the **Cathedral of the Good Shepherd**, the **Al-Abrar Mosque**, the vast and florid **Kong Meng Sang Phor Kark See Temple Complex**, the **Chettiar Hindu Temple** and the **Sri Mariamman Temple** are only a few of these. Other interesting attractions in Singapore City include the **Singapore Art Museum**, the **Asian Civilisation Museum**; the **National Museum & Art Gallery**; **Merlion Park**; the **Thong Chai Medical Institution**; the **Singapore Mint Coin Gallery**; the **Singapore Crocodile House** (feeding time at 1100, crocodile wrestling at 1315 and 1615); and the **Fort Cannings Aquarium** in **River Valley Road**, with over 6000 species of freshwater and marine animals. Also not to be missed is Singapore's **performing arts centre**.

JURONG

Jurong Town is the economic and industrial hub of Singapore, but offers visitors some unusual yet fascinating attractions. The **Singapore Science Centre**, open Tues-Sun 1000-1800, is a remarkable complex which includes hundreds of interactive exhibits, the Aviation Gallery which traces the history of flight, and the Omnitheatre, a cinema with a planetarium-like screen.
Haw Par Villa (formerly The Tiger Balm Gardens) in **Pasir Panjang Road** is a surreal 'Disneyesque' statue park of Chinese mythological and historical figures, created by the Tiger Balm ointment dynasty. The Gardens are open daily 0800-1800.
The **Chinese and Japanese Gardens** are west of the centre by **Jurong Lake**. The two are linked by a 65m (200ft) ornamental bridge, and are fine examples of the skills of oriental landscape gardeners. The gardens are open daily 0900-1800. An admission fee is charged.
The **Jurong Bird Park** on **Jurong Hill** (near the Chinese and Japanese Gardens) covers more than 49.4 acres (20 hectares) and is home to South-East Asia's largest collection of birds. There is also the world's largest walk-in aviary, a nocturnal house and several spectacular bird shows. The park is open Mon-Fri 0900-1800, Sat-Sun 0800-1800. An admission fee is charged.

THE ISLANDS

SENTOSA: The largest and best known of Singapore's offshore islands is also one of the closest to the mainland. Sentosa is a multi-million dollar pleasure resort girdled by a monorail and offering a wide range of activities and attractions. These include the **Underwater World and Dolphin Lagoon**, **Images of Singapore**, the recently upgraded **Musical Fountain Show**, **The Merlion**, the **Butterfly Park & Insect Kingdom Museum**, **Sijori WonderGolf** and the **Carlsberg Sky Tower**. Lovely gardens, beautiful beaches and a plethora of restaurants and eating places all contribute to the island's popularity with tourists and locals alike. Many prefer to skip the theme park attractions and head straight for Sentosa's beaches – **Palawan**, **Siloso** and **Tanjong** – where a wide range of watersports is available. These were built with imported white sand and are often crowded, especially at weekends. There are bus, monorail and tram services linking Sentosa to the city centre, and the causeway bridge is open to foot traffic. An admission fee for entry to the island is charged and composite tickets can also be bought which give admission to some of the attractions; enquire locally for details. Resort hotels, camping and other accommodation are available on the island.
OTHER ISLANDS: St John's Island is large, hilly and tree-shaded with several excellent beaches. There are also several walking trails. There is a regular ferry service from the HarbourFront Centre that takes about 40 minutes.
Kusu Island is noted for two landmarks: the **Keramat** (a Muslim shrine) and the **Chinese Tua Pekong Temple**. There is a regular ferry service from the World Trade Centre that takes about 30 minutes.
Pulau Hantu, **Lazarus Island** and the **Sisters Islands** (the latter being part of the group of Southern Islands) are ideal for fishing, snorkelling and swimming enthusiasts. There are no regular ferry services but boats can be chartered; enquire locally for information.

Credit: © Virtually Singapore

A B C D E F G H I J K L M N O P Q R S T U V W X Y Z

Credit: © Virtually Singapore

Sport & Activities

Golf: Some of the best courses are at the *Raffles Country Club* (which has two 18-hole courses); the *SFRA Resort & Country Club* (three 9-hole courses); the *Sentosa Golf & Country Club* (two 18-hole championship courses); and the *Tanal Merah Country Club* (two 18-hole championship courses). Operating hours are generally 0700-1900 (with some clubs offering night golfing until 2300). In most clubs, non-members are allowed to play for a special fee ranging from S$50-200. Weekends, however, are often strictly reserved for members. Many clubs also require visitors to hold a handicap or proficiency certificate from a recognised club.

Watersports: One of the most popular watersports is **canoeing** round the island and there are a number of operators hiring out canoes at Changi point, East Coast and Sentosa Island. There are also numerous **scuba-diving** schools offering PADI or NAUI recognised courses. Day and night diving in local waters and nearby Malaysia are also available. **Sailing** and **windsurfing** is generally popular on the eastern coast, where most facilities are located. For **water-skiing**, the best locations are Sembawang and Kallang River (a venue for previous world championships). **Fishing** is a year-round sport. Boats and equipment, inexpensive to hire, are available at the Jardine Steps, Changi Park. Singapore offers easy access to numerous offshore islands (see *Resorts & Excursions* section) and Singaporeans drive over to Malaysia to enjoy the watersports off the East coast (see the *Malaysia* section).

Cycling: The cycle paths link many parts of the island and bikes can be rented in many public parks, notably those at Bishan, East Coast Park, Pasir Ris and Sentosa. **Mountain-** or **dirt-biking** is particularly popular in Pulau Ubin.

Horse racing: The *Singapore Turf Club* is responsible for all horseracing meetings. Visitors must observe a strict dress code. Races take place at weekends only; the first race is at 1330, the last race at 1800. **Polo** matches are played regularly at the *Singapore Polo Club*.

Other: Many sports associations and clubs welcome visitors. **Badminton** is almost a national sport, played all year round. **Cricket** is also played in Singapore, the Singapore Cricket Club being one of the oldest sporting associations in the world. It has a sports ground where cricket, **soccer**, **tennis**, **hockey** and **rugby** are played. **10-pin bowling** is also very popular with over 20 centres (each offering more than 20 lanes) catering for the enthusiast. In the Marina South area, some bowling centres are open 24 hours; otherwise, they are generally open 0900-0200.

Social Profile

FOOD & DRINK: Singapore is a gourmet's paradise, ranging from humble street stalls to 5-star restaurants. There are over 30 different cooking styles, including various regional styles of Chinese cuisine, American, English, French, Indian, Indonesian, Italian, Japanese, Korean, Malay, Russian and Swiss. Malay cuisine is a favourite, famed for its use of spices and coconut milk. *Satay* (skewers of marinated meat cooked over charcoal) served with peanut sauce, cucumber, onion and rice is popular. Hot, spicy or sweet Indonesian cuisine includes *beef rendang* (coconut milk beef curry), *chicken sambal* and *gado gado* (a fruit and vegetable salad in peanut sauce). One of the best ways to eat in Singapore is in the open, at one of the ubiquitous street foodstalls. Some are quiet and casual while others are in areas bustling with activity. All have a vast selection of cheap, mouthwatering food. Newton Circus and La Pau Sat are food centres where all types of Asian food can be sampled cheaply. Although there are many self-service establishments, waiter service is more common in restaurants.

Bars/cocktail lounges often have table and counter service. There are no licensing hours. 'Happy hours' are usually from 1700-1900.

NIGHTLIFE: Singapore has a vibrant and exciting nightlife. Entertainment ranges from bars, clubs, discos, karaoke pubs, street opera, night markets, river cruises, multiplex cinemas to theatre productions and international stage shows. Boat Quay and Clarke Quay are popular riverside landmarks that offer exclusive restaurants, alfresco dining and lively bars. Moored Chinese junks have been refurbished into floating bars and restaurants. Bugis Street, Changi Village and Holland Village, known as Holland V, are popular areas for food, drink and entertainment. Muhammad Sultan Road is one of the latest entertainment hubs in Singapore with a wide variety of pubs, nightclubs and wine bars, as is Club Street.

SHOPPING: The vast range of available goods and competitive prices have led to Singapore rightly being known as a shopper's paradise. Special purchases include Balinese, Chinese, Filipino, Indian and Malay antiques; batiks; cameras; Chinese, Indian and Persian carpets; imported or tailored clothing; jewellery and specialised items made of reptile and snake skins, including shoes, briefcases, handbags and wallets. Silks, perfumes, silverware and wigs are other favourite buys. The herding of shop owners from 'Chinatown' into multi-storey complexes lost some of the exciting shopping atmosphere, although these huge centres do provide an air-conditioned environment. Orchard Road is the main shopping street, although many of the large hotel complexes, such as Marina Square, have shopping centres attached. Although most outlets operate Western-style fixed pricing, bargains can still be made in some places but generally only after good research and shrewd negotiating. Electrical equipment of all types can be bought at Sungei Road, but caution is advised as there are many imitation products around. For more information on shopping in Singapore, see the *Singapore Shopping* brochure published by the Singapore Tourism Board.

Shopping hours: Mon-Fri 1000-2100, Sat 1000-2200.

Note: A 3 per cent Goods and Services Tax (GST) is levied on most goods and services purchased from taxable retailers. Tourists whose purchases total S$300 or more from a single retailer participating in the Tourist Refund Scheme are eligible for a refund of the GST paid on goods not consumed in Singapore. Refunds may be received at the airport, prior to departure flights

SPECIAL EVENTS: The cosmopolitan character of Singapore means that a great number of festivals and special events are regularly celebrated; visitors staying for more than a few days would be unlucky not to catch at least one. For more information and for exact dates, see the *Singapore Calendar of Festivals* leaflet published by the Singapore Tourism Board. The following is a selection of special events occurring in Singapore in 2005:

Jan 13-Feb 23 *Spring in the City*. **Jan 15-Feb 28** *Chinese New Year Celebrations*. **Jan 15-29** *Jam X*. **Jan 28-Feb 8** *Hougang Chinatown Spring Festival*. **Feb 7-23** *Singapore River Hongbao*. **Feb 18-19** *Chingay Parade of Dreams*. **Mar 24-Apr 3** *Singapore Fashion Festival*. **Jul 1-31** *Singapore Food Festival*. **Sep 29-Oct 9** *Singapore JewelFest*.

SOCIAL CONVENTIONS: Handshaking is the usual form of greeting, regardless of race. Social courtesies are often fairly formal. When invited to a private home or entering a temple or mosque, remove your shoes. For private visits, a gift is appreciated and, if on business, a company souvenir is appropriate. Dress is informal. Most first-class restaurants and some hotel dining rooms expect men to wear a jacket and tie in the evenings; a smart appearance is expected for business meetings. Evening dress for local men and women is unusual. Each of the diverse racial groups in Singapore has retained its own cultural and religious identity while developing as an integral part of the Singapore community. Over 50 per cent of the population is under 20 years of age. Laws relating to jaywalking, littering and chewing gum are strictly enforced in urban areas. Smoking is widely discouraged and illegal in enclosed public places (including restaurants). Dropping a cigarette end in the street or smoking illegally can lead to an immediate fine of up to S$500. **Tipping:** Officially discouraged in restaurants, hotels and the airport. A 10 per cent service charge is included in restaurant bills.

Business Profile

ECONOMY: Singapore's economy relies on entrepôt trade, shipbuilding and repairing, oil refining, electronics and information technology, banking and finance and, to a lesser extent, tourism. From the late 1970s, the Government promoted export-oriented and service industries with the intention of making Singapore a regional economic hub. Singapore also derived some benefit from the decision of some companies to relocate following the reversion of Hong Kong to Chinese administration in 1997. High-technology manufacturing, particularly computer and telecommunications equipment, and financial services, mainly banking and insurance, form the kernel of the economy. There is also an important oil-refining industry. The newest addition to the economic portfolio is pharmaceuticals: on top of that, the government is promoting Singapore as a centre for biotechnology, especially for stem cell research which has proved so controversial elsewhere. The importance of trade to the economy cannot be overstated: the total value of Singapore's trade is almost three times its GDP (compared with 17 per cent of GDP in the case of Japan). Vibrant economic activity more than compensates for Singapore's lack of natural resources. There is a little agriculture, with the cultivation of plants and vegetables, and some fishing; however, most foodstuffs and raw materials have to be imported. Singapore's only significant natural resource is its superb natural harbour, which is the busiest in the world after Rotterdam. This accounts in part for the high level of Singapore's re-export trade, which accounts for almost half of all trade.

Singapore was less affected than many of its neighbours by the 1997 Asian financial crisis, owing to sound financial management, high savings and investment rates, and massive foreign exchange reserves. However, shortly afterwards the territory was plunged into its worst economic recession for 30 years, largely because of a sudden collapse of international demand in key industries, especially electronics. At the lowest point, Singapore's economy was contracting at an unprecedented rate of 6 per cent per annum. Industrial production fell by over 20 per cent during 2001. GDP growth was a paltry 0.8 per cent in 2003, but that figure rose to a robust 8.6 per cent in 2004. Current inflation is 1.7 per cent. Singapore's principal trading partners are Japan, Thailand, the USA and Malaysia. Singapore is a member of the Association of South East Asian Nations (ASEAN) and of the Asian Pacific Economic Forum (APEC).

BUSINESS: English is widely spoken in business circles. Appointments should be made and punctuality is important. Chinese people should be addressed with their surnames first, while Malays do not have surnames but use the initial of their father's name before their own. Visiting cards are essential, although it is policy for government officials not to use them. **Office hours:** Mon-Fri 0900-1300 and 1400-1700, Sat 0900-1300.

COMMERCIAL INFORMATION: The following organisations can offer advice: Singapore Indian Chamber of Commerce and Industry, 101 Cecil Street, Tong Eng Building, Unit 23-01/04, Singapore 069533 (tel: 6224 6634 *or* 6222 2855; fax: 6223 1707; e-mail: sicci@sicci.com; website: www.sicci.com); *or* Singapore International Chamber of Commerce, 10-01 John Hancock Tower, 6 Raffles Quay, Singapore 048580 (tel: 6224 1255; fax: 6224 2785; e-mail: SA@sicc.com.sg; website: www.sicc.com.sg).

CONFERENCES/CONVENTIONS: Singapore is the top convention city in Asia and ranks among the top 10 meetings destinations in the world. There are many hotels with extensive conference facilities, including the latest audio-visual equipment, secretarial services, translation and simultaneous interpretation systems, whilst Raffles City, a self-contained convention city, can accommodate up to 6000 delegates under one roof. Other popular venues for larger conventions and exhibitions include Suntec Singapore and Singapore Expo, the country's latest addition to conference venues. Full information on Singapore as a conference destination can be obtained from the Exhibition & Convention Bureau within the Singapore Tourism Board (see *Contact Addresses* section). The Bureau is a non-profitmaking organisation with the dual objectives of marketing Singapore as an international exhibition and convention city and of assisting with the planning and staging of individual events.

Climate

Warm and fairly humid summer temperatures throughout the year (approximately 30ºC/86ºF during the day and 23ºC/74ºF in the evening). There is no distinct wet/dry season. Most rain falls during the northeast monsoon (November to January) and showers are usually sudden and heavy.

Required clothing: Lightweight cottons and linens.

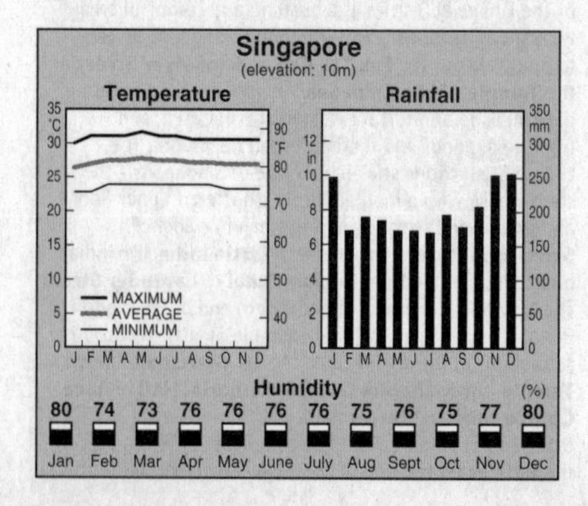

Slovak Republic

LATEST TRAVEL ADVICE CONTACTS

British Foreign and Commonwealth Office
Tel: (0870) 606 0290 Website: www.fco.gov.uk
US Department of State
Website: http://travel.state.gov/travel
Canadian Department of Foreign Affairs and Int'l Trade
Tel: (1 800) 267 8376 Website: www.dfait-maeci.gc.ca

Location: Central Europe.

Country dialling code: 421.

Slovak Tourist Board
Nám. L Štúra 1, PO Box 35, 974 05 Banská Bystrica 5, Slovak Republic
Tel: (48) 413 6146. Fax: (48) 413 6149.
E-mail: sacr@sacr.sk
Website: www.slovakiatourism.sk
Slovak Tourist Board (Bratislava office)
Street address: Zahradnicka 153, 820 05 Bratislava 25, Slovak Republic
Postal address: PO Box 97, 820 05 Bratislava 25, Slovak Republic
Tel: (2) 5070 0801 *or* 5070 0803. Fax: (2) 5557 1649.
E-mail: sacrba@sacr.sk
Website: www.slovakiatourism.sk
Ministry of Economy (Tourism Section)
Mierová 19, 827 15 Bratislava, Slovak Republic
Tel: (2) 4333 0066. Fax: (2) 4854 3321.
E-mail: kuliffany@economy.gov.sk *or* heribanova@economy.gov.sk
Website: www.economy.gov.sk
Embassy of the Slovak Republic
25 Kensington Palace Gardens, London W8 4QY, UK
Tel: (020) 7313 6470/1 *or* 313 6490 (consular section)*or* (09065) 508 956 (recorded visa information; calls cost £1 per minute). Fax: (020) 7313 6481.
E-mail: mail@slovakembassy.co.uk
Website: www.slovakembassy.co.uk
Opening hours: Mon-Fri 1000-1300.
British Embassy
Panská 16, 811 01 Bratislava, Slovak Republic
Tel: (2) 5998 2000. Fax: (2) 5998 2269.
E-mail: bebra@internet.sk.
Website: www.britishembassy.sk

TIMATIC CODES

Health	AMADEUS: **TI-DFT/BTS/HE** GALILEO/WORLDSPAN: **TI-DFT/BTS/HE** SABRE: **TIDFT/BTS/HE**
Visa	AMADEUS: **TI-DFT/BTS/VI** GALILEO/WORLDSPAN: **TI-DFT/BTS/VI** SABRE: **TIDFT/BTS/VI**

To access TIMATIC country information on Health and Visa regulations through the Computer Reservations System (CRS), type in the appropriate command line listed above.

Embassy of the Slovak Republic
3523 International Court, NW, Washington, DC 20008, USA
Tel: (202) 237 1054. Fax: (202) 237 6438.
E-mail: info@slovakembassy-us.org *or* consul@slovakembassy-us.org (consular section).
Website: www.slovakembassy-us.org
Embassy of the United States of America
Street address: Hviezdoslavovo nám 5, 811 02 Bratislava, Slovak Republic
Postal address: PO Box 309, 814 99 Bratislava, Slovak Republic
Tel: (2) 5443 3338 *or* 0861 (consular section).
Fax: (2) 5441 8861 (consular section) *or* 5443 0096.
E-mail: cons@usembassy.sk (consular section).
Website: www.usembassy.sk
Embassy of the Slovak Republic
50 Rideau Terrace, Ottawa, Ontario K1M 2A1, Canada
Tel: (613) 749 4442. Fax: (613) 749 4989.
E-mail: ottawa@slovakembassy.ca
Website: www.ottawa.mfa.sk
The Office of the Canadian Embassy
Carlton Courtyard & Savoy Buildings, Mostova 2, 811 02, Bratislava, Slovak Republic
Tel: (2) 5920 4031. Fax: (2) 5443 4227.
E-mail: brslva@international.gc.ca
Website: www.canada.cz
The Canadian Embassy in Prague deals with enquiries relating to the Slovak Republic (see the *Czech Republic* **section).**
Slovak Association of Travel Agents
Bajkalská 25, 821 01 Bratislava 2, Slovak Republic
Tel: (2) 5341 9058. Tel/Fax: (2) 5823 3385.
E-mail: sacka@ba.sknet.sk *or* sacka@stonline.sk
Website: www.sacka.sk
Association of Information Centres in Slovakia
Nám. Mieru 1, 031 01 Liptovsky Mikuláš, Slovak Republic
Tel: (44) 551 4541. Fax: (44) 5511 4448.
E-mail: infolm@trynet.sk
Website: www.lmikulas.sk *or* www.icm.mikulas.sk
Bratislava Information Service
Klobucnicka Street 2, 814 28 Bratislava, Slovak Republic
Tel: (2) 5443 3715 *or* 16186.
E-mail: bis@bratislava.sk *or* bkis@bratislava.sk
Website: www.bis.bratislava.sk
Cultural and Information Centre
Nám. S. Moysesa 26, 97401 Banská Bystrica, Slovak Republic
Tel: (48) 16186 *or* 415 5085. Tel/Fax: (48) 415 2272.
E-mail: kis@pkobb.sk
Website: www.tis.sk
Poprad Information Agency
Nám. Sv. Egídia 2950/114, Poprad 05801, Slovak Republic
Tel: (52) 16186 *or* 772 1700. Tel/Fax: (52) 772 1394.
E-mail: infopp@ppmsopoprad.sk
Website: www.poprad.sk

General Information

AREA: 49,033 sq km (18,932 sq miles).
POPULATION: 5,378,595 (official estimate 2002).
POPULATION DENSITY: 109.7 per sq km.
CAPITAL: Bratislava. **Population:** 617,049 (2000).
GEOGRAPHY: The Slovak Republic is situated in Central Europe, sharing frontiers with the Czech Republic, Austria, Poland, Hungary and Ukraine. Mountains, lowlands, canyons, lakes, cave formations, forests and meadows provide many examples of the Slovak Republic's year-round natural beauty. The Slovak Republic is a small country but its terrain varies impressively from lowlands to mountain ranges. Almost half of the country is taken up by the Carpathian Arc, a range of mountains stretching across the north. The smaller ranges include the Lesser Carpathians, White Carpathians, Malá (Lesser) Fatra, Vel'ká (Greater) Fatra, High and Low Tatras and the Slovenské rudohorie Mountains (Slovak Ore Mountains).
GOVERNMENT: Republic since 1993. **Head of State:** President Ivan Gasparovic since 2004. **Head of Government:** Prime Minister Mikulájs Dzurinda since 1998.
LANGUAGE: The official language is Slovak. Hungarian, Ruthenian, Ukrainian and German are spoken by ethnic minorities. English is also spoken.
RELIGION: The majority is Roman Catholic. Protestant churches comprise the remainder with Reformed, Lutheran, Methodist and Baptist denominations. There is also a Jewish minority. There is a Greek Orthodox minority in Eastern Slovak Republic.
TIME: GMT + 2 (GMT + 1 from last Sunday in October to last Saturday in March).
ELECTRICITY: Generally 230 volts AC, 50Hz. Round two-pin plugs are in use. Lamp fittings are normally of the screw type.
COMMUNICATIONS: Telephone: IDD is available. Country code: 421. Outgoing international code: 00. There

Credit: © Slovak Tourist Board

Credit: © Slovak Tourist Board

are public telephone booths, including special kiosks for international calls. Surcharges can be quite high on long-distance calls from hotels. Dial 112 for all emergecy services but 18 124 for the emergency road service. **Mobile telephone:** GSM 1800/900/3G. Main network providers include *Eurotel Bratislava* (website: www.eurotel.sk) and *Orange* (website: www.orange.sk). Coverage extends over the whole country, with the exception of remote areas. **Internet:** ISPs include *Euro Web* (website: www.euroweb.sk). There are Internet cafes in main towns. **Telegram:** Facilities are available in all main towns and hotels. Services are available 24 hours at Kolárska 12 (centre of Bratislava) and next to the main railway station in Predstanicné námestie. **Post:** There are Poste Restante services available. Post office hours: Mon-Fri 0800-1800. **Press:** The *Slovak Spectator*, the Slovak Republic's English-language newspaper, is published bi-weekly; *Slovak Foreign Trade* is published monthly by the Slovak Chamber of Commerce. The principal dailies are *Nový Êas, Pravda* and *Šport*.
Radio: BBC World Service (website: www.bbc.co.uk/worldservice) and Voice of America (website: www.voa.gov) can be received. From time to time the frequencies change and the most up-to-date can be found online.

Passport/Visa

	Passport Required?	Visa Required?	Return Ticket Required?
Full British	Yes	No	No
Australian	Yes	No	No
Canadian	Yes	No	No
USA	Yes	No	No
Other EU	1	No/2	No
Japanese	Yes	No	No

Note: Regulations and requirements may be subject to change at short notice, and you are advised to contact the appropriate diplomatic or consular authority before finalising travel arrangements. Details of these may be found at the head of this country's entry. Any numbers in the chart refer to the footnotes below.

PASSPORTS: Passport valid for longer than expiry of visa required by all except:
1. EU nationals, and nationals of Iceland, Liechtenstein, Norway and Switzerland, with a valid national ID card.
VISAS: Required by all except the following:
(a) EU nationals, nationals referred to in the chart above for stays of up to 90 days for touristic or transit purposes only (except full British passport holders, who also do not need visas for business purposes for an indefinite period, and Italy, who are only visa exempt for up to 30 days);
(b) nationals of Andorra, Argentina, Brazil, Brunei, Chile, El Salvador, Guatemala, Honduras, Hong Kong (SAR), Israel, Korea (Rep), Malaysia, Mexico, New Zealand, Nicaragua, Panama, Singapore, Switzerland, Uruguay and Venezuela for stays of up to 90 days;
(c) **2.** nationals of Malta for stays of up to 180 days;
(d) nationals of Monaco for stays of up to three months;
(e) nationals of Bolivia, Bulgaria, Holy See, Romania, San Marino and United Nations passport holders for stays of up to 30 days;
(f) holders of Refugee Travel Documents (Convention of 28 July 1951) are visa exempt provided given refugee status according to the Convention and status of EU states (*except* refugee status from Austria, Cyprus, Estonia, Greece, Hungary, Latvia, Lithuania, Poland, Slovak Republic and Slovenia), and from Iceland, Liechtenstein, Norway and Switzerland.
Note: (a) Visitors should have the equivalent funds of US$50 per person per day for their stay in the Slovak Republic; this may be checked by customs. (b) Further information is available from the Ministry of Foreign Affairs (website: www.foreign.gov.sk).
Types of visa and cost: *Tourist/Transit/Airport Transit*: £24 (single-entry); £55-67 (multiple-entry). *Transit*: £29 (two-way/return).
Note: (a) There is a processing fee of USD$4 per application. (b) Visa cost continually fluctuates according to the exchange rate.
Validity: *Tourist*: *Single-entry*: up to 90 days; *Multiple-entry*: Unlimited number of 90-day stays during a 90-day period. *Transit*: Valid for 90 days for a maximum stay of five days (plus seven reserve days). *Airport Transit*: Three days within airport confines.
Note: *Tourist* visas can be issued a maximum 90 days before the intended start date.
Application to: Consular section at Embassy; see *Contact Addresses* section.
Application requirements: (a) Passport valid beyond requested validity of visa, with one blank page. (b) Completed application form. (c) One passport-size photo. (d) Fee (including processing fee), payable by cash, cheque or postal order. (e) For postal applications include a stamped, self-addressed envelope. (f) Valid health and travel insurance.
Working days required: In most cases, the process will take up to 30 days. However, all visa applications are referred to the Slovak Immigration Headquarters and local embassies can not guarantee the time required for processing.
Temporary residence: Special application form required; enquire at the Embassy.

Money

Currency: Slovenská Koruna (Sk) = 100 halierov. Notes are in denominations of Sk5000, 1000, 500, 100, 50 and 20. Coins are in denominations of Sk10, 5, 2 and 1, and 50 halierov. Further information can be found online (website: www.nbs.sk).
Currency exchange: Foreign currency (including travellers cheques) can be exchanged at bureaux de change, main hotels, all banks, road border crossings, as well as major travel agencies.
Credit & debit cards: Major credit cards (American Express, Diners Club, and MasterCard/Eurocard Visa) and debit cards (Eurocheque cards, Maestro and Visa Electron) may be used to withdraw cash from automatic dispensers and for payments in hotels, restaurants, shops and petrol stations. Credit cards can also be used to obtain currency. Check with your credit or debit card company for details of merchant acceptability and other services which may be available.
Travellers cheques: American Express, Thomas Cook and Visa travellers cheques are accepted in banks and at bureaux de change. Exchange rate charges are at least 1 per cent of the nominal cheque value. To avoid additional charges, travellers are advised to take travellers cheques in Euros, US Dollars or Pounds Sterling.
Currency restrictions: The import and export of local and foreign currency is permitted up to an amount equivalent of SK150,000, which must be declared.
Exchange rate indicators: The following figures are included as a guide to the movements of the Koruna against Sterling and the US Dollar:

Date	Feb '04	May '04	Aug '04	Nov '04
£1.00=	59.88	60.30	60.08	56.37
$1.00=	32.89	33.76	32.61	30.42

Banking hours: Generally Mon-Fri 0800-1700.

Duty Free

The following goods may be imported into the Slovak Republic by visitors 18 years of age or older without incurring customs duty:
200 cigarettes, 100 cigarillos, 50 cigars and 250g of tobacco products; 1l of spirits and 2l of wine; 50g of perfume or 250ml of eau de toilette; gifts up to the value of SK3,000; foodstuffs, fruits and flowers for personal use.
Note: (a) All items of value, such as cameras and tents, must be declared at customs on entry in order to facilitate export clearance on departure. (b) Only half the above quantities are permitted if stay is less than two days. (c) Arms and ammunition require a licence.
Abolition of duty free goods within the EU: On June 30 1999, the sale of duty free alcohol and tobacco at airports and at sea was abolished in all of the original 15 EU member states. Of the 10 new member states that joined the EU on May 1 2004, these rules already apply to Cyprus and Malta. There are transitional rules in place for visitors returning to one of the original 15 EU countries from one of the other new EU countries. But for the original 15, plus Cyprus and Malta, there are now no limits imposed on importing tobacco and alcohol products from one EU country to another (with the exceptions of Denmark, Finland and Sweden, where limits *are* imposed). Travellers should note that they may be required to prove at customs that the goods purchased are for personal use *only*.

Public Holidays

2005: Jan 1 New Year's Day and Independence Day of the Slovak Republic. **Jan 6** Catholic Epiphany. **Mar 25** Good Friday. **Mar 28** Easter Monday. **May 1** May Day. **May 8** Liberation of the Republic. **Jul 5** Day of the Apostles St Cyril and St Methodius. **Aug 29** Anniversary of the Slovak National Uprising. **Sep 1** Day of Constitution of the Slovak Republic. **Sep 15** Our Lady of the Seven Sorrows. **Nov 1** All Saints' Day. **Nov 17** Day of Freedom and Democracy of the Slovak Republic. **Dec 24-26** Christmas.
2006: Jan 1 New Year's Day and Independence Day of the Slovak Republic. **Jan 6** Catholic Epiphany. **Apr 14** Good Friday. **Apr 17** Easter Monday. **May 1** May Day. **May 8** Liberation of the Republic. **Jul 5** Day of the Apostles St Cyril and St Methodius. **Aug 29** Anniversary of the Slovak National Uprising. **Sep 1** Day of Constitution of the Slovak Republic. **Sep 15** Our Lady of the Seven Sorrows. **Nov 1** All Saints' Day. **Nov 17** Day of Freedom and Democracy of the Slovak Republic. **Dec 24-26** Christmas.

Health

	Special Precautions?	Certificate Required?
Yellow Fever	No	No
Cholera	No	No
Typhoid & Polio	No	N/A
Malaria	No	N/A

Note: Regulations and requirements may be subject to change at short notice, and you are advised to contact your doctor well in advance of your intended date of departure. Any numbers in the chart refer to the footnotes below.

Food & drink: Mains water is normally chlorinated and, whilst relatively safe, may cause mild abdominal upsets. Exercise caution in rural areas. Bottled mineral water is available in grocers' shops and restaurants. Milk is pasteurised and dairy products are safe for consumption.
Other risks: *Tick-borne encephalitis* is present in forested areas. Walkers and campers should take precautions against tick bites by wearing long trousers. Vaccination is advisable. *Lyme disease* is present.
Rabies is present. For those at high risk, vaccination should be considered. If you are bitten, seek medical advice without delay; for more information, consult the *Health* appendix.
Health care: Medical insurance is mandatory for nationals of countries with no reciprocal health agreement: without this, entry may be refused. There is a reciprocal health agreement with the UK, but for urgent treatment only. On production of a UK passport, hospital and other medical care will be provided free of charge should visitors fall ill or have an accident while on holiday. Prescribed medicines will be charged for. All international travellers are strongly advised to take out full medical insurance before departure.

Travel - International

AIR: The Slovak Republic is served by *Aeroflot, Aeromist-Kharkiv, Austrian, Air France, Air Slovakia (GM)* (website: www.airslovakia.sk), *British Airways, Czech Airlines, Delta, Hemus Air, Israir, LOT, Lufthansa, Maersk Air, SkyEurope Airlines* and *Slovak Airlines* (website: www.slovakairlines.sk).
Approximate flight times: From Bratislava to *London* is one hour 45 minutes.
International airports: *Bratislava Airport (BTS),* (M R ¡Stefánik) (website: www.letiskobratislava.sk), is 9km (6 miles) from the city. Buses run to the city (travel time – 20 minutes). Taxis are also available (travel time – 20 minutes). Airport facilities include duty free shops, bank, post office, restaurant, bar, snack bar, flight information, left luggage, tourist information, first aid, disabled facilities and car hire (*Avis* and *Hertz*).
Koisice Airport (KSC) is 6km (4 miles) south of the city (website: www.airportkosice.sk). Taxis are available (travel time – 10 minutes). Buses are also available.
Tatry-Poprad Airport (TAT) is 5km (3 miles) from the city.
Vienna International Airport (VIE) (Schwechat) is 50km (31 miles) from Bratislava and can be used as a gateway for intercontinental travellers (website: www.viennaairport.com).
Departure tax: None.
RIVER: International connections from Austria are possible on the Danube which flows into the Black Sea, and is also linked with the Rhine and the Main. Services run as follows: Bratislava–Vienna–Bratislava; Bratislava–Hainburg–Bratislava; and Vienna–Bratislava–Budapest, both ways.
RAIL: The most convenient route to the Slovak Republic from Western Europe is via Prague or Vienna. The Slovak Republic's network also provides direct connections with Berlin, Bucharest, Budapest, Hamburg, Krakow, Kyiv, Lviv, Moscow, St Petersburg, Vilnius and Warsaw.
ROAD: The Slovak Republic can be entered via Austria,

Credit: © Slovak Tourist Board

Czech Republic, Hungary, Poland or Ukraine. There is a motorway from Bratislava via Brno to Prague. There are *Eurolines* bus links from Bratislava and other important towns to major cities such as Cologne, London, Munich, Paris, Venice and Vienna. For further information, contact *Eurolines*, 52 Grosvenor Gardens, London SW1, UK (tel: (08705) 143 219; website: www.eurolines.com *or* www.nationalexpress.com).

Travel - Internal

AIR: The domestic airlines are *Air Slovakia (GM)* (tel: (2) 4342 2742), *Sky Europe Airlines* (tel: (2) 4850 1111; website: www.skyeurope.com) and *Slovak Airlines (9S)* (tel: (2) 4870 4111).
RIVER: There are 2372 km of navigable waterways. The Danube is the main artery for transport by ship which is operated by *Slovenská Plavba Dunajská* (Slovak Danube Shipping Company; website: www.spap.sk), Cruises covering historic and tourist interests are also operated. There is also regular passenger transport on the Danube.
RAIL: The rail network, which has 3662km of track, is operated by *Railways of the Slovak Republic (ZSR)* (website: www.zsr.sk). There are several daily express trains between Bratislava and main cities and resorts. Reservations should be made in advance on major routes. Fares are low, but supplements are charged for travel by express trains. For further information, contact *ZSR*, Klemensová 8, 813 61 Bratislava (tel: (2) 5058 7469).
ROAD: Traffic drives on the right. The major routes run from Bratislava to Prejsov and Kojsice, via Kral'ovany and Poprad. The network of roads and supporting services (garages, petrol stations, restaurants, hotels and motels) is dense and reliable. Roads are standardised as motorways (200km), first- (3000km), second- (3500km) and third-class (11,000km) metalled roads, and are generally in good condition, particularly on the main arteries. Motorways are equipped with emergency telephones every half a mile or less. The *Slovakia* emergency system provides a fast and reliable network of garages, tow trucks and medical services. Road signs comply with European standards. **Bus:** The extensive network covers all areas and is efficient and comfortable. **Car hire:** Self-drive cars may be pre-booked through the tourist office in main towns and resorts. **Traffic regulations:** Seat belts are compulsory and drinking is absolutely prohibited. The speed limit in towns is 60kph (37mph); outside towns, 90kph (56mph); and on motorways, 130kph (81mph). **Documentation:** Most hire companies require a valid international driving licence.
URBAN: Buses, trolleybuses and trams exist in Bratislava and several other towns. All the cities operate flat-fare systems, and pre-purchase passes are available. Tickets should be punched in the appropriate machine on entering the tram or bus. A separate ticket is usually required when changing routes. There is a fine for fare evasion. Blue badges on tram and bus stops indicate an all-night service. **Taxi:** These are available in all the main towns and are metered and cheap; higher fares are charged at night.
TRAVEL TIMES: The following chart gives approximate travel times from **Bratislava** (in hours and minutes) to other major towns in the Slovak Republic.

	Air	Road	Rail
Poprad	0.45	4.00	4.30
Košice	1.00	5.30	5.00
B. Bystrica	-	2.30	4.10
Piešťany Spa	-	0.50	0.50

Accommodation

HOTELS: There are over 1100 hotels in Slovakia. Prices compare very favourably with Western hotels, though services and facilities are often more limited. There is a shortage of accommodation in the peak seasons (May to October, but especially during July and August), and it is wise to pre-book. As yet, a relatively small portion of the hotel network is made up of intermediate and top-class establishments. At present, higher-standard hotels are to be found primarily in Bratislava, in regional towns (such as Banská Bystrica and Kojsice), in spas of national and international significance and in major tourist resorts (such as the High Tatras). Future developments and investment will result in upward reclassification of many establishments. For further information, contact the Slovak Association of Hotels and Restaurants, Námestie Slobody 2, 974 01 Banská Bystrica (tel: (48) 414 4669; fax: (48) 414 3855; e-mail: zhr@zhr.sk; website: www.zhr.sk/ang) *or* Bratislava Hotels (e-mail: info@bratislavahotels.com; website: www.bratislavahotels.com). **Grading:** The international 5-star system has recently been introduced for hotel classification. The present system is: **5-star**, **4-star**, **3-star**, **2-star** and **1-star**. Visitors can expect rooms with a private bath or shower in hotels classified 3-star and upwards.
MOTELS: Motels can be split into four classes. **Grading:** In cheaper motels, every room is provided with central heating and a washbasin with hot and cold water; on every floor there are separate bathrooms and WCs for men and women. The more expensive motels are provided with the following extras: a lift, a bathroom or shower with every room, a radio receiver and, in some cases, a TV set. Car parking facilities are available in both types.
PRIVATE HOUSES: The Slovak Union of Rural Tourism and Agrotourism can arrange stays in private houses in the Slovak Republic throughout the year (Safarikovo nam. 4, 81102 Bratislava; tel/fax: (2) 365 185).
SELF-CATERING: Chalet communities in many parts of the country are available in three categories. **Grading:** The cheaper chalets offer drinking water, WC and heating in winter. Some may provide meals. The more expensive chalets have the following extras: electric lighting, flushing WC, washroom with running water, laundry facilities and an outdoor recreation area.
YOUTH HOSTELS: There are a few hostels (mainly in Bratislava) affiliated to the International Youth Hostel Association in the Slovak Republic (website: www.ckm.sk). Contact Slovakia Youth Hostel Booking, Vysoka 32, 81445 Bratislava (tel: (2) 5273 1024; fax: (2) 5273 1025) for more information.
CAMPING/CARAVANNING: Campsites are split into four classes and have all the usual facilities such as showers, cooking amenities, shops and, in some cases, caravans for hire. For further information, contact the Federation of Camping and Caravanning in the Slovak Republic (tel: (43) 589 8122). Camping outside official sites is limited. **Car camps:** In the lower classes these have a car park, fenced-in campsite, 24-hour service, washroom, WC, drinking water and a roofed structure with cookers and washing-up equipment. Car camps in the higher classes are provided with the following extras: sale of refreshments, toiletries and souvenirs, showers with hot and cold water, flushing WC, laundry facilities, communal sitting room and a reception office.
Note: Visitors can find information about hotels and camping accommodation online (website: www.travelguide.sk).

Resorts & Excursions

Although Slovak history is one of immense Magyar cultural repression, the country emerged from more than a millennium of Hungarian serfdom with its language and identity largely intact. Uniting with the Czechs after World War I was primarily a matter of convenience, thereby thwarting Hungarian plans to retain control. However, the Slovak Republic was definitely the 'junior partner' throughout the 20th century and the country achieved independence in 1993. Modernisation fell well behind that of the Czech Republic and the country is only now opening up to tourism. Despite decades of Communism, Catholicism is almost as strong here as it is in Poland, and many rural communities resisted collectivisation almost completely.
The country divides conveniently into three regions: **Bratislava and the West**, **Central Slovakia** incorporating the mountains, and **The East**. Other than the Alps, the Slovak Republic offers what may be Europe's most exciting landscape – from the Danube plain to towering mountain peaks and quiet valleys, glacial lakes with crystal-clear waters, over 1300 mineral and thermal springs and extensive cave systems. There are seven national parks and 16 protected landscape areas, featuring well-preserved natural environments, the unique Carpathian landscape and remnants of the original virgin forests. Forests cover two-thirds of the country, the rest is agricultural land.

BRATISLAVA & THE WEST

BRATISLAVA: Bratislava, the capital of the Slovak Republic, is the country's political, economic and cultural centre. Located on the **River Danube** (**Dunaj** in Slovak), the city is not, however, another fairytale city like Prague and far more buildings have been destroyed since the last war than were bombed during it. Known for centuries in the German-speaking world as **Pressburg** and in the Hungarian as **Pozsony**, it was the Hungarian capital from the Battle of Mohác (1526) until the Turks were finally driven from the Hungarian plains. Until 1918 the city was largely Hungarian, German and Jewish, rather than Slavic, and it was only renamed **Bratislava** – after the last leader of the Moravian Empire – after World War I.
Matthias Corvinus established the first Hungarian university, the **Academia Istropolitana**, in 1465; however it constantly lost ground to those in Kraków, Prague and Vienna and closed in 1490. The centre of the Old Town (**Stavé Mesto**) is compact with much that is worth seeing near the **Old Town Square**; **Trinity Church** is noted for its magnificent *trompe l'oeil* frescos and the nearby **Corpus Christi Church** (**kaplnka Bozieho tela**) is now a museum packed with icons, jewellery and other aspects of ecclesiastical wealth. The Town Hall (**Stará radnica)** is a delightful mixture of Gothic, Renaissance and 19th-century styles, and the nearby **Jesuit Church** and the wonderful stucco decor of the **Mirbach Palace** are major tourist sites. The 15th-century **hrad** (**Bratislava Castle**), on the hill above the city, was burnt down by its own drunken soldiers in 1811; recently restored, it houses half of the **Slovak National Museum**, but visitors' time is better spent with the wonderful views across the Danube plain. The **Slovak National Gallery** on the waterfront houses Bratislava's most important art. The only other important site near the waterfront is Ödön Lechner's **Modr´y kostolic** (**Little Blue Church**), an Art Nouveau masterpiece dedicated to Bratislava's one important saint, Elizabeth, born in 1207. The controversial **Most SNP** (**Bridge of the Slovak National Uprising**) with its single support column dominates the area; views from the restaurant at the top are superb. Between the Old Town Square and the Bridge is the graceful boulevard, **Hviezdoslavolo námestie**; at the eastern end are the great late-19th-century **Slovak National Theatre** and the more **Sessionist Reduta Theatre**.
THE WEST: Devín with its famous ruined castle is 9km (6 miles) northwest. Near here the Germans were heavily defeated in 864 and 871 and the area is of immense Slovak Nationalist importance. The **Small Carpathians** stretch from Bratislava's northern suburbs to the Váh valley and are a major wine-growing and walking area. **Kamzík** is the first major hill and the cafe, which offers superb views, can be reached either on foot or by chair lift. **Modra** is a major centre for wine and folk pottery. **Trnava** survives with its walled medieval character relatively intact and was the centre for Hungarian church administration from the 16th to the 18th century. **Nitra** is the country's agricultural capital. Along the walk up to the ruined **hrad** (**castle**) are statues of saints, a fine plague column and two enormous gateways. The Gothic **katedrála** (cathedral) at the **castle** contains the remains of two 10th-century saints; next door is the Baroque **Palace of the Bishop of Nitra**. Two important spa towns on the **Váh river** are **Piestany** with its opulent late 19th-century **Thermia Palace Hotel** and **Trencianske Teplice**, best reached by narrow-gauge railway.

CENTRAL SLOVAKIA

The Slovak Republic's greatest tourist sites are its mountains: the **High Tatras** receive the most publicity, but the **Low Tatras** and **Malá Fatra**, although less monumental, are also less developed. Mining and coin minting have played an important part in many of the Central Slovakian towns, with skilled German miners 'imported' in the 13th century. **Banská Bystrica** flourished as the capital of the seven 'Hungarian' (actually German) mining towns and was the centre for the failed 1944 uprising. The **Town Museum** in the Renaissance **Thurso Palace** and the 13th-century **Panna Márie** church with its Gothic altar by Master Pavol of Levoca are the most important tourist sites. **Banská Stiavnica** had the world's first Mining University (1762). The 11 buildings of the **Mining and Forestry Academy**, as well as a number of Renaissance **burghers' houses** are among its chief attractions. The mixed Gothic and Renaissance **hrad** (**town castle**), and the small **gallery houses** of the miners are the major sites in **Kremnica**, once the site of the richest gold seams in Europe.
Although only 26km (16 miles) long, the **High Tatra Mountains** in the north are noted for impressive alpine

features. The **High Tatra National Park** (**TANAP**) has an abundance of wildlife and over 13,000 species of alpine plants – due to the great differences in elevation from 900 to 2655m (2953 to 8710ft). There are more than 85 mountain lakes, of which **Great Hincovo Lake** is the largest. The park has a good selection of accommodation and sporting facilities, climatic spas and 350km (220 miles) of marked hiking trails. **Tatranská Lomnica** makes an ideal starting point for the eastern Tatras. Founded in 1892 as a State climatic spa, it nestles in the foothills of **Skalnaté Pleso** (1751m/5745ft) which boasts the Tatra's best downhill ski and bobsleigh tracks. Other wintersports resorts are **Smokovce** (including a climatic spa), **Strbské Pleso**, and the picturesque Goral village of **Zdiar** lying at the divide of the **Belianske Tatry** and the **Spiisská Magura** mountain ranges. The **Low Tatras National Park** covers the second-highest range within the western Carpathians. The park includes several ski and recreation resorts including **Jasna**, and the **Demänová Valley**, with its extensive ice-cave system. The **Pieniny National Park** is a bilateral national park shared with Poland, 30km (19 miles) northeast of the High Tatras. The Malá Fatra National Park is renowned for the scenic beauty of its valleys and gorges and its abundant wildlife. It is a favourite with hikers in both winter and summer; outside the park, the wooded spa town of **Rajecké Teplice** and the folk painted houses at **Cicmany** are important tourist sites.

THE EAST

The **Spis** (**Zips**) region was resettled by Saxons after the 13th-century Tartar invasions; most villages combine Teutonic (including many Protestant churches) and Slovak traits. The walled town of **Levoca** became the wealthy capital of the Union of Zips Saxons in 1271. The Gothic church of **sv Jakub** (**St James**) houses the world's highest Gothic altar (18.6m/61ft high and 6m/20ft wide) built by Master Pavol and complemented by 12 important side altars. **Kezmarok** is noted for its wooden **Protestant Church**, capable of seating 1500 worshipers. Walled **Spisská Kapitula** was the seat of provosts and later bishops from the 13th century. The Romanesque cathedral of **sv Martin** is featured in many postcards. **Spiis Castle**, dating from the 12th century, is the biggest medieval castle in central Europe.

Southeast of **Poprad**, deep canyons cut through the **Slovensk´y raj** (**Slovak Paradise**) **National Park**. The pine forest landscape is riddled with basins and waterfalls, and the park contains Europe's oldest ice-cave at **Dobsiná** (**Dobsinská l'adová jaskyna**). **Hrabusice-Podlesok** and **Cingov** are ideal starting points for the extensive hiking and biking trails. Further south, the **Slovensky kras** is a karst region at the Hungarian border. The **Andrássy Mausoleum** at **Krásna Hôrka** is the Slovak Republic's finest Art Nouveau building.

Near the Polish border is the **Saris** region (Carpatho-Ruthenia, Podkarpatska Rus), home of the Rusyn minority. **Presov's Uniate Cathedral** (**Grecko-katolica katedrála**), a unique blend of Orthodox and Roman Catholicism, has an enormous Baroque iconostasis. **Bardejov** is an almost perfectly preserved walled medieval German town; the **Rathaus** (**Town Hall**) houses the superb **Saris Museum**. Nearby is the spa town of **Bardehovské kúpele**, once the playground of the Hungarian and Russian nobility; the **open-air folk museum** (**skansen**) is particularly fine.

To the south, **Kosice** is a lively city whose wealth was based on the salt trade; it still retains a strong Hungarian atmosphere. **St Elizabeth's dóm**, the easternmost Gothic cathedral in Europe, is also one of the most beautiful. There are a number of good museums of which the **Technical Museum** is the best. Northeast of Kosice is the **Herl'any Geyser**, which sprays cold mineral water as high as 30m (100ft) every 32 to 34 hours.

Sport & Activities

The mountains, forests and lakes are ideal for outdoor holidaying as well as summer and winter sports. For more detailed information, see the *Resorts & Excursions* section.

Outdoor pursuits: Europe's longest **cycling** route passes through the Slovak Republic, stretching from Passau in Germany along the Danube, through Vienna, Bratislava and on to Stúrovo. Cyclists can then continue their journey by taking a ferry across the Danube into Hungary. There is a very good network of marked trails in all mountain areas, and it is possible to plan a **walking** tour in advance. **Golf** can be played at several courses around the country, including *Bernolakovo* (near Bratislava; website: www.golf.sk), *Koisice*, Tale (near Brezno-Law Tatras) and *Velka Lomnica* (High Tatras; website: www.golfinter.sk). There are also numerous lakes and rivers amidst the glacial landscape, offering excellent **fishing**, **canoeing**, **boating** and **swimming**. The primary watersports areas are at Liptovská Mara, Orava, Sl'nava and Zemplínska Sírava. **Rafting** is particularly good on the *Dunajec* river in the Pieniny national park. Horse riding, hunting and dog cart races are other popular pursuits.

Wintersports: There are popular centres in 30 mountain regions, the best of which are the *Tatra Mountains*, where over 40 ski tows and chairlifts are located. Other popular mountain areas include the *Slovensky raj* range, with its deep canyons, and the *Malá Fatra* range with its neighbouring *Vrátna dolina valley*.

Spas: The country offers a great wealth of curative springs, thermal spas, climatic health resorts and natural mineral waters, renowned throughout the world. There are 23 spa towns officially recognised by the state authorities. *Bardejovské Kúpele* was already established as a health resort in the 13th century. Its healing properties have been said to cure indigestion, disturbed metabolism and various respiratory problems. *Dudince's* spring is rated among the best in the area with a mineral composition suitable for the curing of internal organs, neurological and vascular diseases. The world-famous thermal health resort of *Pieist'any* specialises in rheumatic treatment. *Sliac*, first mentioned in 1244, is regarded as the most important spa for the treatment of cardiovascular disorders. *Trencianské Teplice*, established since 1488, is situated near a sulphuric spring and is suitable for the treatment of the motor neurone system. *Bojnice* is one of the most renowned spas for the treatment of rheumatism.

Social Profile

FOOD & DRINK: Traditional Slovak eating and drinking habits date back to the old Slavic period influenced later by Austrian, German and Hungarian cooking. Slovak food is based on many different kinds of soups, gruels, boiled and stewed vegetables, roast and smoked meats and dairy products. The style of cooking varies from region to region. Slovak specialities include both sweet and savoury dishes made with flour, including dumplings. One such dish is the popular *bryndzové haluisky* (small potato dumplings with sheep's cheese).

Popular drinks include Slovak beer, wine and mineral waters. *Borovicka* (strong gin) and *slivovica* (plum brandy) are particular specialities, as are wine from the Tokay region and sparkling wine from the Bratislava region.

RESTAURANTS: Restaurants and other catering establishments are many and varied, including cafes, buffets, snack bars, inns, ale houses and wine taverns. All restaurants are graded according to quality. The main meal of the day is usually lunch, comprising soup, a main meal and desert. **Tipping:** A 5 to 10 per cent tip is usual.

NIGHTLIFE: Theatre and opera are of a high standard. Much of the nightlife takes place in hotels, although nightclubs are to be found in major cities.

SHOPPING: Souvenirs include pottery, porcelain, woodcarvings, hand-embroidered clothing and food items. There are a number of excellent shops specialising in glass and crystal, while various associations of regional artists and artisans run their own retail outlets (pay in local currency). Other special purchases include folk ceramics from all regions of the Slovak Republic and woodcarvings from the eastern and central parts of the Slovak Republic (Kyjatice, Michalovce and Spijsská Belá). **Shopping hours:** Mon-Fri 0900-1800, Sat 0900-1200.

SPECIAL EVENTS: Most towns have their own folk festivals, with dancing, local costumes and food. These tend to be in the summer months leading up to the harvest festivals in September. For full details, contact the Slovak Tourist Board (see *Contact Addresses* section). The following is a selection of special events occurring in the Slovak Republic in 2005:

Feb *Bratislava Shrovetide*. **Jun 26-Jul 3** *Art Film Festival*, Trencianske Teplice. **Sep 12-20** *Castles Charm & Wine Festival*. **Nov** *International Film Festival*, Bratislava.

SOCIAL CONVENTIONS: Shaking hands is the customary form of greeting. Punctuality is appreciated on social occasions. The minimum drinking age is 18.

Business Profile

ECONOMY: Of all the Soviet bloc economies, the former Czechoslovakia experienced the highest degree of state control. In the late-1960s, after the Prague Spring, the Soviet-backed government revamped the economy to build up heavy industry at the expense of traditional strengths in light and craft-based industries, such as textiles, clothing, glass and ceramics. After the division of Czechoslovakia in 1993, the newly independent Slovak government found these heavy industries to be something of a millstone, but they continue to play a central role in the economy. In a few cases, they have benefited from foreign investment. The other major economic problem was a dearth of natural resources: the most important of these, especially oil, were formerly available cheaply from the ex-Soviet Union but now had to be bought at market rates. The agricultural sector – almost all of which is now privately owned – produces wheat and grains, sugar beet, vegetables and livestock. However, its relative economic contribution (5 per cent of GDP, 8 per cent of the workforce) is not substantial. The bulk of the industrial economy has been transferred to the private sector, including the key areas of machinery and chemical industries, textiles, leather, shoes, glass, electronics, nuclear energy and car manufacturing. Slovak economic policy-makers chose a different path of development from their Czech neighbours, opting for a more gradual transition and retaining certain 'strategic' industries (notably the armaments industry) under state control. An estimated 85 per cent of the economy is now in private hands.

After the initial transition shock, the economy performed fairly well in the mid- and late 1990s, but then went into recession. Growth stagnated while the budget deficit, external debt and unemployment climbed to uncomfortably high levels. Since 2002, however, the situation has been brought under control. Growth has now resumed at between 4 and 5 per cent. Unemployment remains stubbornly high at 17.8 per cent; inflation in 2003 was 8.8 per cent.

Current Slovak economic policy is focused on turning the 15 per cent or so of the economy still controlled by the state over to private ownership, and reforming the republic's still rigid employment code. Both measures are integral to the Slovak Republic's forthcoming accession to the European Union. After signing an association agreement with the EU in October 1993, the country had fulfilled the membership criteria for the EU by the end of 2002. Along with nine other countries (including seven others from East and Central Europe), the Slovak Republic joined on May 1 2004, a decision endorsed by popular referendum during 2003.

Almost two-thirds of Slovak trade is now with the EU's 15 existing members. Otherwise, there remain important links with the other members of the Visegrad Group of central European states (Poland, the Czech Republic and Hungary – all of whom also joined the EU), as well as the Russian Federation and Ukraine.

BUSINESS: Businesspeople wear suits. A knowledge of German and English is useful. Long business lunches are usual. **Office hours:** Mon-Fri 0800-1600 (or longer).

COMMERCIAL INFORMATION: The following organisations can offer advice: Slovak Chamber of Commerce and Industry, Gorkého 9, 816 03 Bratislava (tel: (2) 5443 3291; fax: (2) 5413 1159; e-mail: sopkurad@sopk.sk; website www.scci.sk *or* www.sopk.sk) *or* National Agency for the Development of Small and Medium Enterprises, Prievozská 30, 821 05 Bratislava (tel: (2) 5341 7328; fax: (2) 5341 7339; e-mail: agency@nadsme.sk; website: www.nadsme.sk) *or* the Slovak Investment & Trade Development Agency, Martinèekova 17, 821 01 Bratislava (tel: (2) 5810 0310; fax: (2) 5810 0319; e-mail: sario@sario.sk; website: www.sario.sk).

CONFERENCES/CONVENTIONS: Information can be obtained from the Slovak Chamber of Commerce and Industry (for address, see above). Alternatively, contact the Slovak Tourist Board's Congress & Convention Department (tel: (2) 5070 0801; fax: (2) 5557 1649; e-mail: congress@sacr.sk).

Climate

The Slovak Republic lies in a moderate zone and possesses a continental climate with four distinct seasons. The average daily temperature in Bratislava in winter is -1°C (31 °F), rising to 21°C (70 °F) in the summer. January is the coldest month, the hottest being July and August. The highest peaks are snowcapped 130 days a year.

Required clothing: Mediumweights, heavy topcoat and overshoes for winter; lightweights for summer. Rainwear is advisable throughout the year.

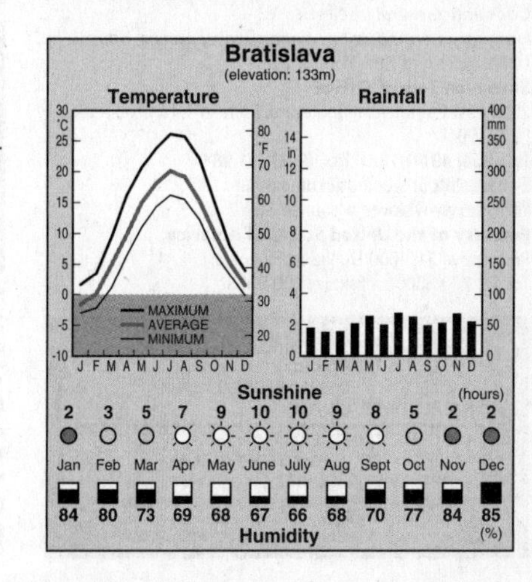

Slovenia

LATEST TRAVEL ADVICE CONTACTS

British Foreign and Commonwealth Office
Tel: (0870) 606 0290 Website: www.fco.gov.uk
US Department of State
Website: http://travel.state.gov/travel
Canadian Department of Foreign Affairs and Int'l Trade
Tel: (1 800) 267 8376 Website: www.dfait-maeci.gc.ca

Location: Southern Central Europe.

Country dialling code: 386.

Slovenska Turisticna Organizacija (Slovenian Tourist Organisation)
Dunajska 156, 1000 Ljubljana, Slovenia
Tel: (1) 589 1840. Fax: (1) 589 1841.
E-mail: info@slovenia-tourism.si
Website: www.slovenia-tourism.si

Embassy of the Republic of Slovenia
10 Little College Street, London SW1P 3SH, UK
Tel: (020) 7222 5400. Fax: (020) 7222 5277.
E-mail: vlo@mzz-dkp.gov.si
Website: www.gov.si/mzz/dkp/vlo/eng
Opening hours: Mon-Fri 0900-1700; 1000-1200 (consular section; for appointments in person).

Slovenian Tourist Office
The Barns, Woodlands End, Mells, Frome, Somerset BA11 3QD, UK
Tel: (0870) 225 5305. Fax: (01373) 813 444.
E-mail: info@slovenian-tourism.co.uk
Website: www.slovenia-tourism.si

British Embassy
4th Floor, Trg Republike 3, 1000 Ljubljana, Slovenia
Tel: (1) 200 3919. Fax: (1) 425 0174.
E-mail: info@british-embassy.si
Website: www.british-embassy.si

Embassy of the Republic of Slovenia
1525 New Hampshire Avenue, NW, Washington, DC 20036, USA
Tel: (202) 667 5363. Fax: (202) 667 4563.
E-mail: slovenia@embassy.org
Website: www.embassy.org/slovenia
Consulate in: Cleveland.
Consulate General in: New York.
Honorary Consulates in: Atlanta, Denver, Florida, Houston, Los Angeles and New York.

Slovenian Tourist Office
2929 East Commercial Boulevard, Suite 201, Fort Lauderdale, FL 33308
Tel: (954) 491 0112. Fax: (954) 771 9841.
E-mail: slotouristboard@kompas.net
Website: www.slovenia-tourism.si

Embassy of the United States of America
Prešernova 31, 1000 Ljubljana, Slovenia
Tel: (1) 200 5500. Fax: (1) 200 5555.
E-mail: email@usembassy.si
Website: www.usembassy.si

Embassy of the Republic of Slovenia
150 Metcalfe Street, Suite 2101, Ottaw a, Ontario K2P 1P1, Canada
Tel: (613) 565 5781/2. Fax: (613) 565 5783.
E-mail: vot@mzz-dkp.gov.si
Website: www.gov.si

Consulate of Canada
c/o Slovenijales Business Centre, Dunajska 22, 1511 Ljubljana, Slovenia
Tel: (1) 430 3570. Fax: (1) 430 3575.
E-mail: canada.consul.ljubljana@siol.net
The Canadian Embassy in Budapest deals with enquiries relating to Canada (see *Hungary* section).

TIMATIC CODES

Health	AMADEUS: **TI-DFT/LJU/HE** GALILEO/WORLDSPAN: **TI-DFT/LJU/HE** SABRE: **TIDFT/LJU/HE**
Visa	AMADEUS: **TI-DFT/LJU/VI** GALILEO/WORLDSPAN: **TI-DFT/LJU/VI** SABRE: **TIDFT/LJU/VI**

To access TIMATIC country information on Health and Visa regulations through the Computer Reservations System (CRS), type in the appropriate command line listed above.

General Information

AREA: 20,273 sq km (7827 sq miles).
POPULATION: 1,995,033 (official estimate 2002).
POPULATION DENSITY: 98.4 per sq km.
CAPITAL: Ljubljana. **Population:** 265,881 (2002).
GEOGRAPHY: This compact and strategically important country is dominated by mountains, rivers and major north–south and east–west transit routes. Slovenia borders Italy to the west, Austria to the north, Hungary to the northeast and Croatia to the southeast, with a 47km- (30 mile-) Adriatic Sea coastline, where the main port is Koper.
GOVERNMENT: Republic since 1991. Gained independence from Yugoslavia (now Serbia and Montenegro) in 1992. **Head of State:** President Janez Drnovsek since 2002. **Head of Government:** Prime Minister Anton Rop since 2004.
LANGUAGE: Slovene, which is closely related to Croat and Czech. Most Slovenes speak German, Hungarian or Italian, with English as a second language.
RELIGION: Most of the population is Roman Catholic (82 per cent), with small communities of other Christians including Eastern Orthodox; there are Muslim and Jewish minorities.
TIME: GMT + 1 (GMT + 2 from last Sunday in March to Saturday before last Sunday in October).
ELECTRICITY: 220 volts AC, 50Hz.
COMMUNICATIONS: Telephone: IDD is available. Country code: 386. Outgoing international code: 00. Calls can be made with magnetic phonecards. For emergencies, dial 112 (ambulance service and fire brigade) or 113 (police). **Mobile telephone:** GSM 1800/900/3G networks cover nearly the whole country. Main network operators are *Mobitel* (website: www.mobitel.si), *SIMobil* (website: www.simobil.si) and *Vega* (website: www.vega070.com). **Fax:** Available to and from countries worldwide. **Internet:** Internet cafes are available. **Telegram:** Facilities are limited. **Post:** Reasonable internal service. Stamps can be bought at bookstalls. Post office hours: Mon-Fri 0800-1800, Sat 0800-1200. The post office at Cigaletova 5, Ljubljana is open 24 hours. **Press:** The main dailies are *Delo* and *Slovenske novice* (both in Ljubljana). The state news agency, *STA*, produces material in English for international distribution on a daily basis. English-language publications include *Ars Vivendi, Slovenia Weekly, Slovenian Business Report* and *Slovenija*. The state TV and radio station *RTS* produces regular news and other broadcasts in English and other West European languages during the tourist season.
Radio: BBC World Service (website: www.bbc.co.uk/worldservice) and Voice of America (website: www.voa.gov) can be received. From time to time the frequencies change and the most up-to-date can be found online.

Passport/Visa

	Passport Required?	Visa Required?	Return Ticket Required?
Full British	Yes	No	No
Australian	Yes	No	No
Canadian	Yes	No	No
USA	Yes	No	No
Other EU	1	No	No
Japanese	Yes	No	No

Note: *Regulations and requirements may be subject to change at short notice, and you are advised to contact the appropriate diplomatic or consular authority before finalising travel arrangements. Details of these may be found at the head of this country's entry. Any numbers in the chart refer to the footnotes below.*

PASSPORTS: Passport valid for three months longer than duration of stay required by all except:
1. nationals of EU countries with a valid national ID card;
VISAS: Required by all except the following:
(a) nationals of countries referred to in the chart above for stays of up to three months;
(b) nationals of Andorra, Argentina, Bolivia, Brazil, Brunei, Bulgaria, Chile, Costa Rica, Croatia, Ecuador, El Salvador, Gibraltar, Guatemala, Honduras, Hong Kong (SAR), Iceland, Israel, Korea (Rep), Liechtenstein, Macau (SAR), Mexico (one month only for business trips), Monaco, New Zealand, Nicaragua, Norway, Panama, Paraguay, Romania, San Marino, Switzerland, Uruguay, Vatican City and Venezuela for stays of up to 90 days;
(c) nationals of Malaysia for stays of up to 30 days;
(d) nationals of Singapore for stays of up to 14 days;
(e) transit passengers continuing their journey by the same or first connecting aircraft, provided holding onward or return documentation and not leaving the airport.
Note: (a) Nationals of the following countries can enter Slovenia without a visa for transit purposes or for stays of maximum 90 days, provided they are in possession of an EU/EFTA residents or work permit that is valid for three months from the date of entry into Slovenia *or* a *Schengen* visa (issued by one of the *Schengen* Member States) that is valid for at least one month beyond their stay in Slovenia: Bosnia & Herzegovina, Macedonia (Former Yugoslav Republic of), Romania (for a maximum of 10 days), Russian Federation, Serbia & Montenegro and Turkey. Nationals of these countries should note that their visa-free stay's duration depends on where they have a valid residence permit/visa, and may be less than 90 days. (b) The following nationals require an airport transit visa if wishing to remain within the international transit area: nationals of Afghanistan, Bangladesh, Congo (Dem Rep), Ethiopia, Eritrea, Ghana, Iran, Iraq, Nigeria, Pakistan, Somalia and Sri Lanka.
Types of visa and cost: All visas, regardless of duration and number of entries, cost €35.
Validity: Visitor (single-, double- and multiple-entry): Either a single uninterrupted stay or collective duration over successive days not exceeding 90 days within a six-month period, starting from the first day of entry. Transit (single-, double- and occasionally multiple-transit): Up to five days.
Application to: Consulate (or Consulate section at Embassy); see *Contact Addresses* section.
Application requirements: (a) Passport valid for at least three months longer than the date of entry into Slovenia. (b) Application form. (c) One passport-size photo. (d) Fee, payable by cash, cheque or postal order. (e) Medical travel insurance testifying the ability to cover urgent medical care whilst in Slovenia. (f) For private visits, an invitation from a person in Slovenia (letter of guarantee) authenticated by a notary, containing data guaranteeing accommodation and support for visit, and other possible costs. The letter must also contain a large amount of other data; please consult the nearest Embassy for further information. (g) For touristic travel, a voucher and confirmation from tourist agency or hotel. (h) For business travel, official invitation from company or organisation in Slovenia. (i) Additional documents, eg return ticket(s) or certificate of employment; contact the nearest Embassy for details. *Transit*: (a)-(e) and, (f) Proof of permitted entry into next destination.
Working days required: Between five and 14 but depends on nationality.
Temporary residence: Enquire at Consulate (or Consulate section at Embassy); see *Contact Addresses* section.

Money

Currency: Slovene Tolar (SIT) = 100 stotins. Notes are in denominations of SIT10,000, 5000, 1000, 500, 200, 100, 50, 20 and 10. Coins are in denominations of SIT10, 5, 2 and 1, and 50 stotins.
Currency exchange: The Tolar is fully convertible within Slovenia, but visitors are advised to exchange surplus amounts to the currency of their choice before leaving Slovenia, as it is not generally exchangeable elsewhere. Foreign currencies can be exchanged at banks and some hotels, supermarkets, petrol stations, tourist agencies and exchange bureaux.
Credit & debit cards: American Express, Diners, EuroCard, MasterCard and Visa are accepted at upmarket establishments; elsewhere cash is preferred. Credit cards can be used to get cash advances from banks.
Travellers cheques: Widely accepted. To avoid additional exchange rate charges, travellers are advised to take travellers cheques in Euros, US Dollars or Pounds Sterling.
Currency restrictions: The import and export of local currency is permitted, although amounts in excess of SIT3,000,000 must be declared to customs.
Exchange rate indicators: The following figures are included as a guide to the exchange rate of the Tolar against Sterling and the US Dollar:

Date	Feb '04	May '04	Aug '04	Nov '04
£1.00=	347.75	357.91	357.98	342.38
$1.00=	191.04	200.39	194.31	184.77

Banking hours: Mon-Fri 0830-1230 and 1400-1700; Sat 0830-1100/1200.

Duty Free

The following goods can be imported into Slovenia by passengers over 17 years of age without incurring customs duty:

200 cigarettes or 50 cigars or 100 cigarillos or 250g of tobacco; 2l of wine and 1l of spirits; 50g perfume and 250ml of eau de toilette; listed items to not exceed €80 in value.

Note: An export licence is required for articles of archaeological, ethnographic, artistic, scientific or cultural value; or for articles over 100 years old.

Abolition of duty free goods within the EU: On June 30 1999, the sale of duty free alcohol and tobacco at airports and at sea was abolished in all of the original 15 EU member states. Of the 10 new member states that joined the EU on May 1 2004, these rules already apply to Cyprus and Malta. There are transitional rules in place for visitors returning to one of the original 15 EU countries from one of the other new EU countries. But for the original 15, plus Cyprus and Malta, there are now no limits imposed on importing tobacco and alcohol products from one EU country to another (with the exceptions of Denmark, Finland and Sweden, where limits are imposed). Travellers should note that they may be required to prove at customs that the goods purchased are for personal use only.

Public Holidays

2005: Jan 1-2 New Year. **Feb 8** Preseren Day (Slovenian Cultural Holiday). **Mar 28** Easter Monday. **Apr 27** Resistance Day. **May 1-2** Labour Day Holiday. **May 15** Pentecost. **Jun 25** National Day. **Aug 15** Assumption. **Oct 31** Reformation Day. **Nov 1** All Saints' Day. **Dec 25** Christmas Day. **Dec 26** Independence Day.

2006: Jan 1-2 New Year. **Feb 8** Preseren Day (Slovenian Cultural Holiday). **Apr 17** Easter Monday. **Apr 27** Resistance Day. **May 1-2** Labour Day Holiday. **Jun 11** Pentecost. **Jun 25** National Day. **Aug 15** Assumption. **Oct 31** Reformation Day. **Nov 1** All Saints' Day. **Dec 25** Christmas Day. **Dec 26** Independence Day.

Health

	Special Precautions?	Certificate Required?
Yellow Fever	No	No
Cholera	No	No
Typhoid & Polio	1	N/A
Malaria	No	N/A

Note: Regulations and requirements may be subject to change at short notice, and you are advised to contact your doctor well in advance of your intended date of departure. Any numbers in the chart refer to the footnotes below.

1: Vaccination against typhoid is advised.

Food & drink: Mains water is considered safe and drinkable. However, bottled water is available and is advised for the first few weeks of the stay. Milk is pasteurised and dairy products are safe for consumption. Local meat, poultry, seafood, fruit and vegetables are generally considered safe to eat.

Other risks: *Hepatitis A* occurs. *Tick-borne encephalitis* is present in forested areas. Walkers and campers should take precautions against tick bites by wearing long trousers. Vaccination is advisable. Immunisation against *hepatitis B*, *diphtheria* and *tuberculosis* is sometimes advised.

Rabies is present. For those at high risk, vaccination before arrival should be considered. If you are bitten, seek medical advice without delay. For more information, consult the *Health* appendix.

Health care: There is a reciprocal health agreement with the UK, allowing free hospital and other medical treatment and some free dental treatment to those presenting a UK passport. Prescribed medicines must be paid for.

Travel - International

AIR: The national airline, *Adria Airways* (website: www.adria-airways.com), operates direct flights from London to Ljubljana. Other airlines serving Slovenia include *Aeroflot, Air France, Austrian Airlines, Lufthansa* and *Malev Hungarian Airlines*.

Approximate flight times: From Ljubljana to *London* is two hour 30 minutes.

International airports: *Ljubljana (LJU)* (Brnik) is 26km (16 miles) northwest of the city. Airport facilities include bank, post office, duty free shop, restaurant, snack bar, shops and car hire (includes *Avis, Budget and Hertz*). Buses are available to Kranj (travel time – 15 minutes) and to Ljubljana (travel time – 45 minutes) every 60 minutes, and every 120 minutes Sat-Sun. Taxis are also available (travel time – 20 minutes). *Maribor (MBX)* and *Portoroz (POW)* also have some international connections.

Credit: © Slovenian Tourism Board

Departure tax: None.

SEA: There are regularly scheduled trips across the Adriatic on the *Prince of Venice* catamaran, which runs between Venice and Izola. There are three marinas (Izola, Koper and Portoroz) to choose from for visitors arriving on private vessels.

RAIL: Connections and through coaches are available from principal Eastern and Western European cities. The *Eurocity Mimara* train connects Ljubljana, Munich, Salzburg and Zagreb. There are direct trains to Slovenia from Austria (Vienna and Villach), Bosnia & Herzegovina, Croatia (Zagreb), Hungary (Budapest), Italy (Rome, Milan, Trieste and Venice) and Macedonia (Former Yugoslav Republic of). International trains have couchette coaches as well as bar and dining cars. On some lines transport for cars is provided.

ROAD: The following are among the frontier posts open for road traffic:

From **Italy**: San Bartolomeo-Lazaret; Albaro Veskova-Skofije; Pesse-Kozina; Fernetti-Fernetici (Sezana); Gorizia-Nova Gorica; Stupizza-Robic; Uccea-Uceja; Passo del Predil-Predel; and Fusine Laghi-Ratece.

From **Austria**: Wurzenpass (Villach)-Korensko Sedlo; Loibltunnel-Ljubelj; Seebergsattel-Jezersko; Grablach-Holmec; Rabenstein-Vic; Eibiswald-Radlji od Dravi; Langegg-Jurij; Spielfeld-Sentilj; Mureck- Trate; Sicheldorf-Gederovci; Radkersburg-Gornja Radgona; and Bonisdorf-Kuzma.

From **Hungary**: Bajansenye-Hodos.

From **Croatia**: Jelsane-Rupa. Nearly all the border crossings mentioned above are open 24 hours a day and are served by buses.

For information regarding **documentation** and **traffic regulations**, see the *Travel – Internal* section.

Travel - Internal

AIR: There are domestic airports at *Maribor (MBX)* in the east of the country and on the Adriatic Coast at *Portoroz (POW)*.

SEA: Slovenia has ports at Izola, Koper, Piran and Portoroz.

RAIL: There are efficient Intercity and stopping services. Train travel is generally inexpensive.

ROAD: Traffic drives on the right. There is a good network of high-quality roads in Slovenia. For further information, contact the national automobile club *Auto-Moto Zveza Slovenjie* (AMZS), Dunajska 128a, 1000 Ljubljana (tel: (1) 530 5300; fax: (1) 530 5402; e-mail: info@center.si; website: www.amzs.si). There is a good **bus** network. The emergency roadside help and information service of AMZS is well organised and can be reached by dialling 1 987.

Traffic regulations: Speed limits are 130kph (80mph) on motorways, 100kph (62mph) on roads reserved to motor traffic and 90kph (56mph) on roads outside residential areas. In cities it is 50kph (31mph). School buses cannot be overtaken. The alcohol limit is 0.05 per cent. Safety belts are compulsory (even in the back, if provided). Dimmed headlights must be turned on at all times while driving (even during the day). **Documentation:** Full national driving licences with a photograph are accepted. An International Green Card for non-EU members can be purchased at the border. International car insurance is mandatory.

URBAN: Ljubljana has bus services and taxis are widely available.

TRAVEL TIMES: The following chart gives approximate travel times from **Ljubljana** (in hours and minutes) to other major cities/towns in Slovenia.

	Road	Rail
Portoroz	1.30	2.30
Maribor	2.00	2.30
Lipica	1.00	-
Bled	0.45	1.15
Murska Sobota	3.00	3.30
Postojna	0.45	1.00
Novo Mesto	1.00	1.30

Accommodation

HOTELS: Slovenia has over 190 hotels with 30,000 beds throughout the country. The hotel categories are **1** to **5 stars**. For instance the stunning Otocec Castle located on an island in the Krka River is just one of many magnificent castle hotels open to visitors. For information about accommodation throughout Slovenia, contact the Hotel Association of Slovenia, Vosnjakova 5, SI-1000, Ljubljana (tel: (1) 430 7820; fax: (1) 433 8659; e-mail: slohotels@ntz-nta.si; website: www.ntz-nta.si/slohotels); *or* the Slovenian Tourist Board (see *Contact Addresses* section).

PRIVATE ROOMS: These can be rented throughout Slovenia through local tourist offices. There are three categories: **I** (en suite), **II** (some en suite facilities – usually shower only) and **III** (shared facilities only). The Slovenian Tourist Board can provide more information (see *Contact Addresses* section).

FARMHOUSES: Visitors can choose between over 270 local farmhouses for an informal and welcoming stay close to nature. For further information, contact the Association of Tourist Farms of Slovenia, Trnoveljska 1, SI-3000 Celje (tel: (3) 491 6481; fax: (3) 491 6480; e-mail: ztks@siol.net).

YOUTH HOSTELS: There are 12 hostels in the country. For details, contact Pocitniska Zveza Slovenije (Hostelling International Slovenia), Gosposvetska 84, 2000 Maribor (tel: (2) 234 2137; fax: (2) 234 2136; e-mail: info@youth-hostel.si; website: www.gaudeamus.si/hostelling). The Youth Hostel International in Ljubljana is open from the end of June to the end of August and is located at Dijafki Pom Tabor, Vidovdanska 7, SI-1000, Ljubljana (tel: (1) 234 8840; fax: (1) 234 1890). There is also a youth hostel in Maribor.

CAMPING: There are sites throughout the country. Most campsites are small but well equipped, with sports facilities and children's playgrounds. Contact the Slovenian Tourist Board for brochures and price lists (see *Contact Addresses* section). Camping is not permitted outside campsites.

Resorts & Excursions

One of the smallest countries in Europe, Slovenia lies in an enviable geographical position between the majestic Alps and the Mediterranean; visitors can thus travel between ski slopes and beach resorts within a matter of hours.

LJUBLJANA: The Slovene capital is the starting point for a wide range of excursions. Situated in the heart of Slovenia, along the banks of the **Ljubljanca River**, the capital is within a two-hour drive of all the state borders. The old part of the town is particularly delightful. There are three bridges crossing the river, one leading directly to the **Town Hall** (1718) with its Baroque fountain and two open courtyards. Towering over the city are the twin towers of **Ljubljana Cathedral** (1708), which house some impressive frescoes.

Credit: © Slovenian Tourism Board

The **Castle**, situated on a hill, overlooks the river. The Castle is currently undergoing repairs and only part of it is open to the public. The tower offers a splendid view of the city. On the eastern bank of the river is the **Town Museum** with an extensive collection of Roman artefacts. Near to the **University** is the **Ursuline Church** (1726) with an altar by Robba. The **National Museum**, the **National Gallery**, the **Municipal Gallery** and the **Modern Art Gallery** with the quiet **Tivoli Gardens** are all interesting.

THE EAST: Maribor, in the east of the country, is Slovenia's second-largest city (population: approximately 100,000). It lies only 16km (10 miles) from the Austrian border and is a three-hour journey by car from Trieste or Vienna. Maribor is a lively cultural, scientific and commercial centre with a **University** and numerous art galleries, museums and theatres. The city is a good starting point for visiting the nearby Alpine region of **Pohorje**, one of Slovenia's main skiing resorts, which hosts major international competitions. Also worth visiting are the nearby wine-growing hills of **Slovenske Gorice**, where a number of Slovenia's excellent white wines are produced. To the south of Maribor, **Ptuj** contains Roman remains, a medieval centre and is the scene of traditional carnivals.

THE JULIAN ALPS: The Julian Alps are a popular skiing area in the winter, particularly the resorts of **Kranjska Gora** and **Bovec**. **Triglav National Park** encompasses the splendour of these mountains, as well as the grassy slopes of the surrounding valleys. It is a great place for keen trekkers and visitors are attracted by the unusual tower on Mount Triglav. **Podkoren** is situated in the mountains near the Austrian border. The fashionable mountain resort of **Bled**, near the Austrian and Italian borders, is set on the idyllic **Lake Bled**, where skating and curling take place in winter, and swimming and rowing in summer. The trout and carp fishing are also very good. Sights include the neo-Gothic **Parish Church** (1904) with its interesting frescoes and **Bled Castle**, the former seat of the bishops of Brixen. Perching above a 100m (328ft) drop, the castle offers magnificent views over the city and lake. Another popular skiing resort is the **Zgornjesavska valley**, which borders Austria and Italy in the northwest. Situated between the Julian Alps and the **Karavanke**, the valley is surrounded by mountain peaks and a number of international skiing and ski jumping competitions take place there every year.

THE COAST: Portoroz is Slovenia's most popular seaside resort, with numerous hotels and pavement cafes. The spectacular 20km cave of **Postojna**, only one hour's drive from the coast, has been deemed one of the greatest sights of natural beauty, and features gigantic stalagmites and a cavernous hall which can hold over 10,000 people.

The port of **Koper** still retains an Italian atmosphere. The old town, entered through **Muda Gate**, is worth exploring. Passing the **Bridge Fountain**, the street widens onto the city's central square. In general, the sights are clustered around the **Town Tower** (1480), which dominates the skyline. Fine examples of the Venetian Gothic style are the 15th-century **Cathedral**, the **loggia** and the **Praetor's Palace**; also of interest is the Romanesque **Carmin Rotunda** (1317). Well worth a visit is the excellent **Provincial Museum**, which houses old maps of the area.

SPAS: Slovenia's natural spas are scattered throughout the country and include the **Radenci Health Resort** (close to the Austrian border) and the **Rogaska Health Resort**, where legend claims that the winged horse Pegasus created curative mineral waters with a magic blow of his hooves.

Sport & Activities

There is a wide range of good **skiing** resorts including those in Bled, Bohinj, Bovec Pohorje, Cerkno, Kranjska Gora, Krvavec, Rogla and Vogel. Health gurus tend to flock to some of Slovenia's 15 natural **spas**. In particular, Radenci spa is renowned for its 'three hearts' mineral water, said to have been served at the imperial court in Vienna and the papal court in the Vatican.

Mountaineering is a traditional Slovene sport – the Julian and Kamnik Alps are particularly popular. The Slovene Mountaineering Association organises adventure holidays (tel: (1) 231 2553; fax: (1) 432 2140; e-mail: info@pzs.si; website: www.pzs.si). Slovenia's location south of the Alps means sport **parachuting**, **paragliding** and **ballooning** are popular. **Hunting** is available. **Sailing** is popular along the coast. Berths and boats can be hired at all ports. Permits are needed for boats brought into the country. The Idrijca, Kolpa, Sava, Sava Bohinjka and Dolinka, Savinja and Soca rivers are all ideal for **kayaking**, **canoeing** and **rafting**. Several specialist agencies can make arrangements and provide equipment; contact the Slovenian Tourist Board for a list of addresses. **Cycling** along bicycle trails, in special mountain bike parks, along the alps and through the spa regions, is becoming an increasingly popular and exciting way of seeing the country. Tours and routes for **trekking** in these regions are also widely available: there are around 7000km of marked trails. For more details, contact the Slovenian Tourist Board. **Fishing** permits are available from hotels or local authorities. Fishing on the Adriatic coast is unrestricted, but freshwater angling and fishing with equipment require a permit. 'Fish-linking' with a local small craft owner is popular. **Basketball** is very popular.

Golf: There are 10 golf clubs in Slovenia. Membership is sometimes open to visitors. For further information, contact the Golf Association of Slovenia, Dunajska 51, 51-1000, Ljubljana (tel: (1) 585 4801).

Thoroughbred horses: Lipica in the west of Slovenia is home to the *lippizaner* horse, bred by the Austro-Hungarian aristocracy of the 18th century. There are currently only 3000 of these horses left in the world. Visitors can take tours of the stud farm, watch performances of classical riding or even ride the horses themselves.

Wine trails: These popular routes for the dedicated connoisseur pass through the three wine regions of Slovenia, where various award-winning wines can be sampled. Contact the Slovenian Tourist Board for further information (see *Contact Addresses* section).

Social Profile

FOOD & DRINK: Slovenia's national cuisine shows an Austro-German influence with sauerkraut, grilled sausage and apple strudel often appearing on menus. The best-known Slovene foods are the breads made for special occasions, which appear in the form of braided loaves or wreathes: the *struklji* stuffed with sweet fillings, meat or vegetables. Another Slovene speciality is *potica*, a dessert prepared with a wide variety of fillings.

The western and northeastern parts of Slovenia are known for their outstanding white wines (*Laski*, *Renski Rizling* and many others). The south is the homeland of the light, russet-coloured *cvicek* wine. The Adriatic Coast and the Karst region have mainly red *karstteran* wine.

SHOPPING: Attractive local gifts include bobbin lace, crystal glass and speciality wines. **Shopping hours:** Mon-Fri 0800-1900 Sat 0800-1300.

NIGHTLIFE: There is a wide selection of theatres, cinemas, casinos and nightclubs in the larger towns. Ljubljana also has a good opera house and the symphony orchestra plays regularly in the Big Hall of the Cultural and Congress Centre.

SPECIAL EVENTS: For a full list of festivals and special events contact the Slovenian Tourist Office (see *Contact Addresses* section). The following is a selection of special events occurring in Slovenia in 2005:

Jan 22-23 *41st Golden Fox Trophy Competitions*, Maribor. **Feb 1** *3rd World Cup in Snowboarding*. **Feb 5** *Carnival*, Maribor; *Carnival for Children*, Razvanje. **Feb 8** *22nd Shrovetide*. **Feb 12** *9th Traditional Plezuh Downhill 2005*. **Mar 11** *The 26th Pruning of the Old Vine*. **Apr 18-23** *The 8th Slovene Book Days*. **May 13-15** *Festival Magdalena*. **Aug 26-27** *12th No Border Jam Festival*, punk music celebration. **Sep 10-30** *Music in September*, Maribor. **Sep 20** *5th Autumn Events Festival in the Embrace of the Old Vine*. **Oct 15-29** *40th Borsnik Meeting*, theatre festival. **Nov 11** *21st Saint Martins Day in Maribor*.

SOCIAL CONVENTIONS: Shaking hands is the normal form of greeting. Usual European social conventions apply and informal dress is widely acceptable. Smoking is prohibited on public transport, in cinemas, theatres, public offices and in waiting rooms. **Tipping:** 10 per cent is generally expected in hotels, restaurants and for taxis.

Business Profile

ECONOMY: Before the disintegration of Yugoslavia (now Serbia and Montenegro) that began in 1991, Slovenia was its richest and most industrialised republic. With few natural resources, Slovenia was initially seriously affected by the civil war and the collapse of the Yugoslav federal market. However, careful economic management enabled a solid recovery. The agricultural sector is fairly small, growing cereals, sugar beet and potatoes, but the large areas of forest, covering about half the country, are an important natural resource. The mining industry is mostly concentrated on coal, but zinc and lead are also extracted along with small quantities of oil, gas and uranium. The manufacturing industry, which accounts for about 30 per cent of GDP, produces electrical equipment, textiles, wood-based products (including paper), chemicals and processed foods. The service sector is dominated by tourism and financial services. The tourism industry was almost annihilated during the early stages of the Yugoslav civil war when Slovenia was most heavily involved; it has since re-emerged, and in 2002 was worth about US$1.5 billion annually.

Financial services are well developed, especially banking and insurance. Successive governments have moved cautiously to reform the economy, introducing market-oriented reforms gradually and - for the most part - successfully. Inflation and unemployment in 2003 were both around 6 per cent, while the economy is growing moderately at 3 per cent annually. Slovenia has joined the IMF, World Bank and the European Bank for Reconstruction and Development, and became a full member of the World Trade Organization in July 1995. Germany, Italy, France and Austria are particularly important trade partners; outside the EU, Croatia is most valuable to Slovenian trade.

Slovenia is the only former Yugoslav republic to have been accepted for membership of the EU, which it joined in May 2004.

BUSINESS: Smart dress is advised. Appointments are usual and visitors should be punctual. Visiting cards are essential. Slovenia is the most efficient and reliable of the ex-Yugoslav republics, being in many respects comparable to Austria and Germany. Executives will generally have a good knowledge of German, English and sometimes Italian. There is a well-developed network of local agents, advisers, consultants and lawyers willing to act for foreign companies. **Office hours:** Mon-Fri 0800-1600.

COMMERCIAL INFORMATION: The following organisation can advise on specific trading organisations: Chamber of Commerce and Industry of Slovenia, Dimiceva 13, SI-1504 Ljubljana (tel: (1) 589 8000; fax: (1) 589 8100; e-mail: infolink@gzs.si; website: www.gzs.si).

CONFERENCES/CONVENTIONS: Slovenia's tradition as a meeting place goes back to 1821, when it played host to the Congress of the Holy Alliance. The main conference locations are Bled, Ljubljana, Portoroz, Radenci and Rogaska Slatina, where there are meeting facilities for up to 2000 participants. For more information, contact Conferences and Conventions Department of the Slovenian Tourist Board (see *Contact Addresses* section); *or* Culture and Congress Centre, Cankarjev dom, Presernova cesta 10, 1000 Ljubljana (tel: (1) 241 7100; fax: (1) 241 7298; e-mail: cankarjev.dom@cd-cc.si; website: www.cd-cc.si).

Climate

Continental climate with warm summers and cold winters (snowfalls in the Alps). Mediterranean climate on the coast.

Required clothing: Mediumweight clothing and heavy overcoats in winter; lightweight clothing and raincoats for the summer, particularly for the higher Alpine north.

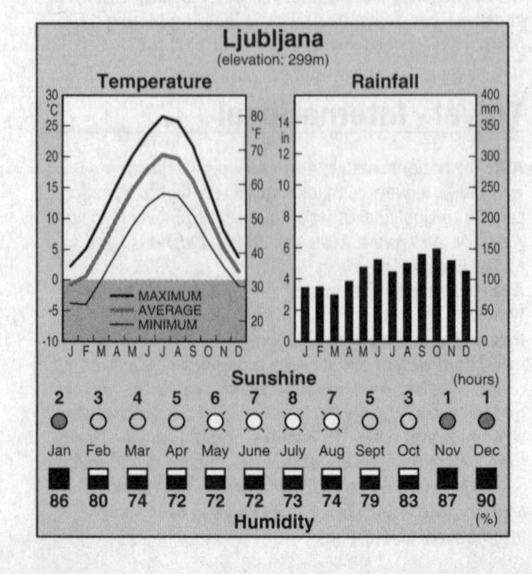

Solomon Islands

LATEST TRAVEL ADVICE CONTACTS

British Foreign and Commonwealth Office
Tel: (0870) 606 0290 Website: www.fco.gov.uk

US Department of State
Website: http://travel.state.gov/travel

Canadian Department of Foreign Affairs and Int'l Trade
Tel: (1 800) 267 8376 Website: www.dfait-maeci.gc.ca

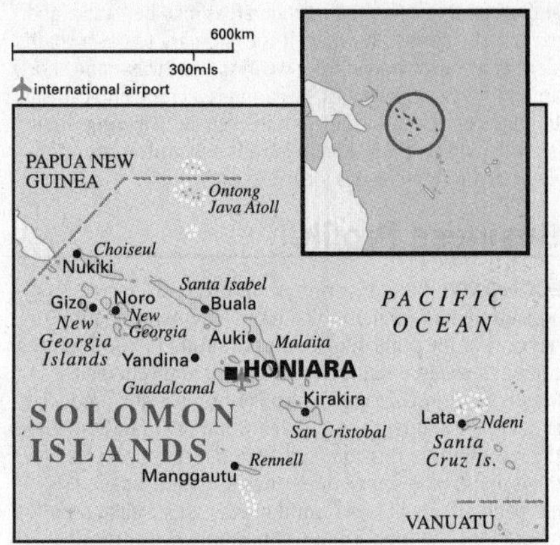

Location: Southwestern Pacific.

Country dialling code: 677.

Solomon Islands Visitors Bureau
Street address: Mendana Avenue, Honiara, Solomon Islands
Postal address: PO Box 321, Honiara, Solomon Islands
Tel: 22442. Fax: 23986.
E-mail: info@svb.com.sb Website: www.visitsolomons.com.sb

South Pacific Tourism Organisation
Street address: Level 3, FNPF Place, 343-359 Victoria Parade, Suva, Fiji
Postal address: PO Box 13-119, Suva, Fiji
Tel: (679) 330 4177. Fax: (679) 330 1995.
Website: www.tcsp.com
Also deals with enquiries from the UK.

Embassy of the Solomon Islands
Avenue Edouard Lacombrt 17, 1040 Brussels, Belgium
Tel: (2) 732 7085. Fax: (2) 732 6885.
E-mail: siembassy@compuserve.com

British High Commission
Street address: Telekom House, Mendana Avenue, Honiara, Solomon Islands
Postal address: PO Box 676, Honiara, Solomon Islands
Tel: 21705/6. Fax: 21549.
E-mail: bhc@solomon.com.sb

Permanent Mission of the Solomon Islands to the United Nations
Suite 400L, 800 2nd Avenue, New York, NY 10017, USA
Tel: (212) 599 6192. Fax: (212) 661 8925.
E-mail: simny@solomons.com
Website: www.solomons.com
Also deals with enquiries from Canada.

US Consular Agent to Solomon Islands
Street address: Blums Building at BJS Agencies Limited, Honiara, Solomon Islands
Postal address: PO Box 439 Honiara, Solomon Islands
Tel: 23426. Fax: 27429.

The American Embassy in Port Moresby deals with enquiries relating to the Solomon Islands (see *Papua New Guinea* **section).**

The Canadian High Commission in Canberra deals with enquiries relating to the Solomon Islands (see *Australia* **section).**

General Information

AREA: 27,556 sq km (10,639 sq miles).
POPULATION: 450,000 (estimate 2001).
POPULATION DENSITY: 16.3 per sq km (2001).

TIMATIC CODES

Health	AMADEUS: **TI-DFT/HIR/HE** GALILEO/WORLDSPAN: **TI-DFT/HIR/HE** SABRE: **TIDFT/HIR/HE**
Visa	AMADEUS: **TI-DFT/HIR/VI** GALILEO/WORLDSPAN: **TI-DFT/HIR/VI** SABRE: **TIDFT/HIR/VI**

To access TIMATIC country information on Health and Visa regulations through the Computer Reservations System (CRS), type in the appropriate command line listed above.

CAPITAL: Honiara. **Population:** 50,000 (2000).
GEOGRAPHY: The Solomon Islands Archipelago is scattered in the southwestern Pacific, east of Papua New Guinea. The group comprises most of the Solomon Islands (those in the northwest are part of Papua New Guinea), the Ontong Java Islands, Rennell Island and the Santa Cruz Islands, which lie further to the east. The larger of the islands are 145 to 193km (90 to 120 miles) in length, while the smallest are no more than coral outcrops. The terrain is generally quite rugged, with foothills that rise gently to a peak and then fall away steeply to the sea on the other side. The capital Honiara is situated on Guadalcanal Island, which also has the highest mountain, Mount Makarakombu, at 2447m (8028ft). There are a number of dormant volcanoes scattered throughout the archipelago.
GOVERNMENT: Constitutional monarchy. Gained independence from the UK in 1978. **Head of State:** HM Queen Elizabeth II, represented locally by Governor-General Nathaniel Waen since 2004. **Head of Government:** Prime Minister Allan Kemakeza since 2001.
LANGUAGE: English is the official language. Pidgin English and over 80 different local dialects are also spoken.
RELIGION: More than 95 per cent of the population are Christian; the rest mostly hold traditional beliefs.
TIME: GMT + 11.
ELECTRICITY: 230/240 volts AC, 50Hz. Australian-type flat three-pin plugs are in use.
COMMUNICATIONS: Telephone: IDD is available. Country code: 677. Outgoing international code: 00. There are no area codes. There are often technical problems with line connections. **Mobile telephone:** GSM 900 network provided by *Solomon Telekom Company* (website: www.solomon.com.sb). Visitors can hire mobile phones on the islands; payment is preferred in cash (US/AUS/NZ currencies are accepted). **Fax:** *Solomon Telekom* provides services at its offices in Honiara (PO Box 148, Honiara; tel: 21576; fax: 23110) and some hotels have facilities. **Internet:** Main ISP is *Solomon Telekom*. Public e-mail facilities are available in Gizo and Honiara. **Telegram:** Services available 24 hours a day administered by Solomon Telekom. **Post:** Airmail to Europe takes approximately seven days. Main post office hours (in Honiara): Mon-Fri 0900-1630, Sat 0900-1100. Other post office hours: Mon-Fri 0800-1630, Sat 0800-1200. **Press:** The main newspapers are the daily English-language *Solomon Star* and *Solomons Voice*.
Radio: BBC World Service (website: www.bbc.co.uk/worldservice) and Voice of America (website: www.voa.gov) can be received. From time to time the frequencies change and the most up-to-date can be found online.

Passport/Visa

	Passport Required?	Visa Required?	Return Ticket Required?
Full British	Yes	No	Yes
Australian	Yes	No	Yes
Canadian	Yes	No	Yes
USA	Yes	No	Yes
Other EU	Yes	No	Yes
Japanese	Yes	No	Yes

Note: *Regulations and requirements may be subject to change at short notice, and you are advised to contact the appropriate diplomatic or consular authority before finalising travel arrangements. Details of these may be found at the head of this country's entry. Any numbers in the chart refer to the footnotes below.*

PASSPORTS: Passport valid for at least six months required by all except nationals of Hong Kong (SAR) with a document of identity.
VISAS: A *Visitor's Permit* will be issued to most nationals on arrival at the airport (including those listed in the chart above). The permit allows stays of up to three months and the cost of the permit varies according to nationality.
Note: Visitors from the following countries need clearance from the Immigration Department and are required to give prior notice in order to obtain a visitor's permit:
(a) all African countries;
(b) all CIS countries (except Belarus);
(c) nationals of Afghanistan, Albania, Angola, Bahrain, Bangladesh, Benin, Bhutan, Bolivia, Bosnia & Herzegovina, Botswana, Bulgaria, Burkina Faso, Cambodia, Cameroon, Cape Verde, Chad, China (PR), Colombia, Comoros Islands, Congo (Dem Rep), Congo (Rep), Costa Rica, Côte d'Ivoire, Croatia, Cuba, Cyprus, Ecuador, El Salvador, Estonia, Guatemala, Haiti, Honduras, India, Indonesia, Iran, Iraq, Jamaica, Jordan, Korea (Dem Rep), Laos, Latvia, Lebanon, Lithuania, Macedonia (Former Yugoslav Republic of), Madagascar, Mauritius, Mexico, Mongolia, Myanmar, Nepal, Nicaragua, Oman, Pakistan, Panama, The Philippines, Qatar, Romania, Saudi Arabia, Seychelles, Sri Lanka, Syrian Arab Republic, Turkey, United Arab Emirates, Venezuela, Vietnam and Yemen.
Application to: Nearest Solomon Islands Consulate, High Commission or Embassy *or* Principal/Director of Immigration, Ministry of Commerce, Foreign Affairs and Tourism, PO Box G26, Honiara (e-mail: immigration@commerce.gov.sb).
Application requirements: *All visitors*: (a) Valid passport. (b) Onward or return tickets. (c) Proof of sufficient funds for the duration of stay. *Visitors requiring prior clearance*: (a)-(c) and, (d) Photocopy of passport. (e) Details of itinerary. (f) Reason for visit.
Working days required: Apply well in advance.
Temporary residence: Apply to the Labour Division, Ministry of Commerce, Foreign Affairs and Tourism (see address above).

Money

Currency: Solomon Islands Dollar (SI$) = 100 cents. Notes are in denominations of SI$50, 20, 10, 5 and 2. Coins are in denominations of SI$1, and 50, 20, 10, 5, 2 and 1 cents.
Currency exchange: Money can be changed at banks, bureaux de change, some hotels, and larger shops and restaurants. Automated foreign exchange machines and three ATMs are available in Honiara.
Credit & debit cards: All major credit cards are widely accepted in hotels and tourist resorts. Check with your credit, or debit, card company for details of merchant acceptability and other facilities which may be available.
Travellers cheques: Can be exchanged at banks, of which there are three in the major towns. To avoid additional exchange rate charges, travellers are advised to take travellers cheques in Australian Dollars or Pounds Sterling.
Currency restrictions: The import of local and foreign currency is unlimited provided declared on arrival. The export of local currency is limited to SI$250; the export of foreign currency is limited to the extent approved by the Solomon Islands' Monetary Authority.
Exchange rate indicators: The following figures are included as a guide to the movements of the Solomon Islands Dollar against Sterling and the US Dollar:

Date	Feb '04	May '04	Aug '04	Nov '04
£1.00=	13.58	13.28	13.76	13.70
$1.00=	7.46	7.43	7.46	7.38

Banking hours: Mon-Fri 0830-1500.

Duty Free

The following items may be imported into the Solomon Islands without incurring customs duty for those aged 18 years and above:
200 cigarettes or 250g cigars or 250g of tobacco; 2l of spirits or equivalent; other dutiable goods up to a total value of SI$400.
Prohibited items: Unlicensed firearms or other weapons (without Police Permit) and offensive literature or pictures. Fruit and vegetables other than from New Zealand need an import permit.

Public Holidays

2005: Jan 1 New Year's Day. **Mar 25-28** Easter. **Jun 10** Queen's Birthday. **Jul 7** Independence Day. **Dec 25** Christmas Day. **Dec 26** National Day of Thanksgiving.
2006: Jan 1 New Year's Day. **Apr 14-17** Easter. **Jun 9** Queen's Birthday. **Jul 7** Independence Day. **Dec 25** Christmas Day. **Dec 26** National Day of Thanksgiving.
Note: Each part of the Solomon Islands has its own Province Day. These are listed below. If a Province Day falls on a Sunday, the following Monday is observed as a public holiday.
Feb 25 Choiseul. **Jun 2** Isable. **Jun 8** Temotu. **Jun 29** Central Island. **Jul 20** Rennell. **Aug 1** Guadalcanal. **Aug 3** Makira/Ulawa. **Aug 15** Malaita. **Dec 7** Western Province.

Health

	Special Precautions?	Certificate Required?
Yellow Fever	No	1
Cholera	No	No
Typhoid & Polio	2	N/A
Malaria	3	N/A

Note: *Regulations and requirements may be subject to change at short notice, and you are advised to contact your doctor well in advance of your intended date of departure. Any numbers in the chart refer to the footnotes below.*

1: A yellow fever vaccination certificate is required for travellers coming from infected areas.
2: Vaccination against typhoid is advised.
3: Malaria risk exists throughout the year except in some outlying islets in the east and south. The malignant *falciparum* strain is present and is reported to be resistant to chloroquine and sulfadoxine-pyrimethamine. The recommended prophylaxis is chloroquine plus proguanil.
Food & drink: All water should be regarded as being a

potential health risk. Water used for drinking, brushing teeth or making ice should first be boiled or otherwise sterilised. Milk is unpasteurised and should be boiled. Powdered or tinned milk is available and is advised, but make sure that it is reconstituted with pure water. Avoid dairy products that are likely to have been made from unboiled milk. Only eat well-cooked meat and fish, preferably served hot. Pork, salad and mayonnaise may carry increased risk. Vegetables should be cooked and fruit peeled.
Other risks: Immunisation against *hepatitis A* is recommended. *Hepatitis B* is endemic. *Filariasis* occurs. *Dengue fever* is now a major health risk. There have also been reports of *Legionnaires Disease* from Auki in the Malaita Province. Coelenterates, poisonous fish and sea snakes are a hazard to bathers.
Health care: Medical facilities are very limited and there are drug shortages. There are eight hospitals, the largest being the Central Hospital in Honiara. Church missions provide medical facilities on outlying islands. Health insurance is essential. There are no decompression facilities.

Travel - International

AIR: The national airline *Solomon Airlines (IE)* (website: www.solomonairlines.com.au) operates flights from Australia. *Qantas* offers three flights a week from Brisbane to Honiara. Other airlines serving the Solomon Islands include *Air Niugini* and *Air Pacific*.
The *Visit the South Pacific Pass* is valid for a number of airlines operating in the South Pacific, including *Air Caledonie, Air Marshall Islands, Air Nauru, Air Niugingi, Air Pacific, Air Vanuatu, Polynesian Airlines, Qantas, Royal Tongan Airlines* and *Solomon Airlines*. Offering reductions of up to 50 per cent on normal airfares, this sector-based pass allows for flexible island-hopping.
Approximate flight times: From Honiara to *London* is 29 hours 45 minutes, excluding stopover in Brisbane.
International airports: *Honiara (HIR)* (Henderson Field) on Guadalcanal Island, 13km (8 miles) east of Honiara (travel time – 20 minutes). Bus and taxi services are available. Facilities include bank/bureau de change, duty-free shops (for scheduled international flights) and car hire (*Avis* and *Budget*).
Departure tax: SI$40. Transit passengers and children under two years are exempt.
SEA: International ports are Honiara (Guadalcanal Island), Yandina (Russel Islands) and Noro (New Georgia). The cargo line *Bank* offers a limited number of passenger places.

Travel - Internal

AIR: Domestic scheduled and charter services are run by *Solomon Airlines* from Henderson Field to most main islands and towns in the Solomons. The *Discover Solomons Pass* is a domestic airpass offering up to eight flights within the Solomon Islands over a period of 30 days. Flightseeing tours can also be arranged.
SEA: Large and small ships, including *Malaita, Ramos, Western Province* and *Ysabel*, provide the best means of travelling between islands. Services are run by the Government and by a host of private operators; some of the Christian missions even have their own fleets. Cruises are also available with *World Discoverer*.
ROAD: Traffic drives on the left. There are over 1300km (800 miles) of roads throughout the islands. About 455km (280 miles) are main roads and a further 800km (500 miles) are privately maintained roads for plantation use. Road maintenance is limited and the general condition of the roads is very poor, as are driving standards. Most of the roads are on Guadalcanal and Malaita; contact the nearest travel department for advice if visiting these areas since some tensions still prevail. **Bus:** There are limited services on the islands. **Taxi:** Available in Auki and Honiara. It is advisable to agree the fare beforehand. **Car hire:** This is available through hotels in Honiara. **Documentation:** A national driving licence will suffice.

Accommodation

HOTELS: There are a number of hotels, motels and lodges in Honiara. Visitors are advised to make advance reservations. Accommodation is also available in Malaita, the Reef Islands and Western Solomons. A number of lodges and resorts on the islands offer a variety of leisure activities. A full list of accommodation and rates is available from the Ministry of Commerce, Employment and Tourism or the Solomon Islands Visitors Bureau (see *Contact Addresses* section).
CAMPING: Camping is rare and is best confined to remoter areas. Permission should always be obtained from the landowner, usually the village chief, before pitching a tent.

Resorts & Excursions

The Solomon Islands are a remote and unspoilt travel destination, with a slowly developing tourist industry. The superb marine life in the surrounding waters makes the islands an excellent destination for diving, cruising and fishing (see also *Sport & Activities* section). **Choiseul, Guadalcanal, Malaita, New Georgia, San Cristobal** and **Santa Isabel** are the main islands. They are up to 200km (120 miles) long and up to 50km (30 miles) wide. Most islands are populated with a range of reptiles (including turtles), as well as marsupials such as 'flying foxes' (fruit bats), *phalangers* and *opossums*. Later introductions included pigs and chickens. Europeans brought cats, horses, cattle and goats. **Honiara**, the capital on Guadalcanal, has a **museum, botanical gardens** and **Chinatown**. There are relics of World War II in and around the town, and notice boards indicate major battles and incidents that took place during the battle for Guadalcanal.
Travel agencies can arrange excursions around Guadalcanal and other islands. Popular tours include the battlefields of World War II, the **Betikama carving centre**, and **Alite** and **Laulasi villages** on the island of Malaita, where shells are broken, rounded and, after further working, strung together. They are used to denote status and as gifts and items of barter in inter-tribal deals. The strings of shells can be worn as bracelets, necklaces, belts and earrings. They may also include animal and fish teeth and, in times past, the teeth of murderers. Collectively, these items are known as 'shell money'.
Carvings for the tourist trade are made on **Bellona** and **Rennell**. Miniature daggers, spears and clubs are very popular. Other carvings show scenes from life on the Solomon Islands, both human and animal. Tourists can organise their own excursions easily, with timetables and information provided by the tourist authority and travel agents.

Sport & Activities

Watersports: The Solomon Islands consist of over 900 volcanic islands and coral atolls spread across the blue tropical waters. **Swimming** is not recommended in the sea around Honiara because of sharks. Facilities for **diving** and **snorkelling** are well developed and, as elsewhere in the South Pacific, diving enthusiasts will find much to marvel at in the waters around the Solomon Islands – coral reefs, a myriad of tropical fish, game fish such as barracudas and sharks and giant clams. Much of the best land-based diving is located in the Western Province on or near the islands of *Gizo* (the capital of the Western Province) and *New Georgia*. Well-known dive sites in the area include *Munda*, on the *Roviana Lagoon*, 15 minutes by plane from Gizo; and *Uepi Island*, on the north side of New Georgia, across the famous *Marovo Lagoon*. Diving tours to the numerous wrecks from World War II are also possible. All resorts offer a full range of diving facilities and most have resident dive instructors. Live-aboard diving tours are also available; for further information, see online (website: www.bilikiki.com *or* www.lalae.com.sb).
Surrounding waters have good **fishing** potential and enquiries may be made at the Point Cruz Yacht Club, which welcomes visitors. A number of resorts now offer a broad variety of sea and other sports.
Ecotourism: Tropical rainforests cover most of the archipelago and there are a number of dormant volcanoes. Exotic orchids, ferns and palms are widespread and butterflies are abundant. There are more than 70 species of reptiles. A variety of trees and shrubs have been introduced along with fruits and vegetables. Educational tours can be organised via the Solomon Islands Visitors Bureau (see *Contact Addresses* section).
Other: There is a nine-hole **golf** course outside Honiara and local tourist agents will make arrangements. **Tennis** courts are at the Supreme Club, arrangements can be made through the hotels. **Bushwalking** and **climbing** are also popular.

Social Profile

FOOD & DRINK: Local recipes include *tapioca* pudding and *taro* roots with *taro* leaves. There are a few restaurants outside the hotels in Honaria. Both Asian and European food is served and the cuisine is generally good. There are two Chinese restaurants in Honiara which are quite popular. Table service is normal. Spirits, wine and beer are available.
NIGHTLIFE: Honiara is a comparatively quiet town, although there are a few clubs with music and dancing, the occasional film show, and snooker and darts. The clubs offer temporary membership to visitors.
SHOPPING: Local purchases include mother-of-pearl items, walking sticks, carved and inlaid wood, copper murals, conch shells and rare varieties of cowrie. New Georgia in the western district is known for carved fish, turtles and birds. Carvings in ebony, inlaid with shell, are unique. Duty-free shopping is available at a number of stores in Honiara. **Shopping hours:** Mon-Fri 0800-1700, Sat 0800-1200.
SPECIAL EVENTS: For a complete list of special events, contact the Solomon Islands Visitors Bureau (see *Contact Addresses* section). The following is a selection of special events occurring in the Solomon Islands in 2005:
Feb 25 *Province Day Choiseul.* **Jun 2** *Province Day Isable.* **Jun 8** *Province Day Temotu.* **Jun 29** *Province Day Central Island.* **Jul 7** *National Independence Celebration.* **Jul 20** *Provine Day Rennell.* **Aug 1** *Province Day Guadalcanal.* **Aug 3** *Province Day Makira/Ulawa.* **Aug 15** *Province Day Malaita.* **Dec 7** *Province Day Western Province.*
SOCIAL CONVENTIONS: A casual atmosphere prevails and European customs exist alongside local traditions. Informal wear is widely suitable although women often wear long dresses for evening functions. Men need never wear ties. Women, in general, should dress modestly and appropriately, noting that certain areas may be 'taboo' and exclusively reserved for men. It is customary to cover thighs. Visitors are discouraged from wearing beachwear and shorts around towns and villages. Swearing is a crime and can lead to huge compensation claims and even jail. **Tipping:** There is no tipping on the Solomon Islands and visitors are requested to honour this local custom.

Business Profile

ECONOMY: The economy depends on subsistence agriculture and fishing, which together employ about 90 per cent of the population. The agricultural sector produces coconuts, sweet potatoes, cassava, fruit and vegetables; livestock rearing has grown steadily. Copra is still produced in commercial quantities, but low world prices have reduced the income from this commodity. As a result, timber is now the islands' main source of revenue although, again, this has been affected by low world prices and a ceiling on production. The timber industry had grown very rapidly during the early-1990s but has been cut back drastically following international pressure (which included suspension of vital financial aid) on the Government to introduce a controlled logging policy. A moratorium of new timber-felling licences was introduced in 1998.
The Solomon Islands' main industrial prospect lies in its mostly undeveloped mineral resources. Gold mining is now important and is set for further expansion; in addition, there are confirmed deposits of copper, lead, zinc, silver, cobalt and other ores. In the service sector, there is a small and – initially – growing tourism industry which brings in around US$15 million annually, but this has been affected by the poor security situation. Despite its narrow economic base, the Government has so far eschewed the choice of some South Pacific neighbours to develop an 'offshore' finance industry. However, it has joined with fellow members of the Pacific Forum in establishing a free trade system in 2002, known as the Pacific Island Countries Trade Agreement (PICTA).
The Solomon Islands continues to receive substantial overseas aid, although much of this is consumed by a large external debt. In 1998, following the Asian financial crisis, the Government also introduced a typical programme of structural reform under the auspices of the IMF. Australia and Japan are the main trading partners, followed by the UK, New Zealand, Korea (Rep), Thailand and Singapore.
BUSINESS: Shirt and smart trousers or skirt will suffice. English and French are widely spoken. The best time to visit is May to October. **Office hours:** Mon-Fri 0800-1200 and 1300-1630, Sat 0730-1200.
COMMERCIAL INFORMATION: The following organisations can offer advice: Ministry of Commerce, Employment and Trade (see *Contact Addresses* section); *or* Solomon Islands Chamber of Commerce and Industry, PO Box 650, Honiara (tel: 39542; fax: 39544; e-mail: chamberc@solomon.com.sb).

Climate

Semi-tropical, mainly hot and humid, with little annual variation in temperature. The wet season (November to April) can bring severe tropical storms.
Required clothing: Tropical, lightweights and cottons are recommended. Rainwear from November to April.

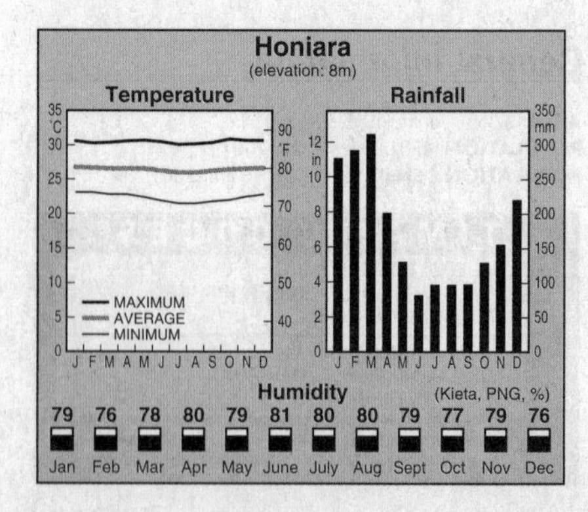

Somalia

LATEST TRAVEL ADVICE CONTACTS

British Foreign and Commonwealth Office
Tel: (0870) 606 0290 Website: www.fco.gov.uk

US Department of State
Website: http://travel.state.gov/travel

Canadian Department of Foreign Affairs and Int'l Trade
Tel: (1 800) 267 8376 Website: www.dfait-maeci.gc.ca

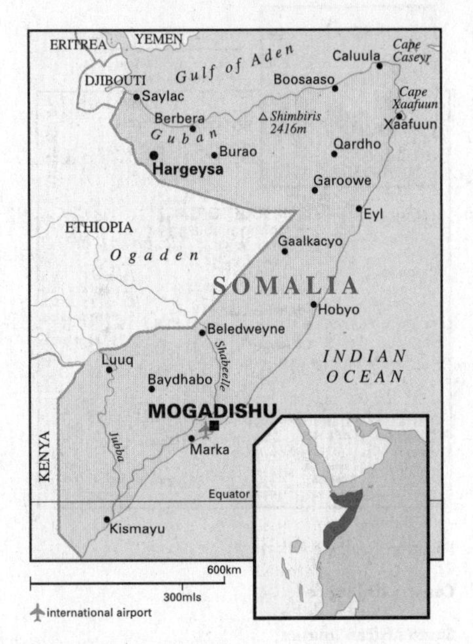

Location: East Africa.

Country dialling code: 252.

United Nations Development Programme for Somalia (UNDP)
Street address: Centenary House, Ring Road, Westlands Lane, Nairobi, Kenya
Postal address: PO Box 28832, Nairobi, 00200 Kenya
Tel: (20) 444 8434. Fax: (20) 444 8439.
E-mail: sandra.macharia@undp.org
Website: www.unsomalia.net *or* www.so.undp.org

European Commission Somalia Unit (ECSU)
Street address: Union Insurance House, Ragati Road, 00100 Nairobi, Kenya
Postal address: PO Box 45119, 00100 Nairobi, Kenya
Tel: (20) 271 2860 *or* 3250. Fax: (20) 271 0997.
E-mail: somalia@cec.eu.int
Website: www.delken.cec.eu.int

The United States Embassies in Nairobi deals with enquiries relating to Somalia (see *Kenya* section).
The Canadian High Commission in Nairobi deals with enquiries relating to Somalia (see *Kenya* section).
The British Embassy in Addis Ababa deals with enquiries relating to Somaliland (see *Ethiopia* section).
The British High Commission in Nairobi deals with enquiries relating to Somalia (see *Kenya* section).

General Information

AREA: 637,657 sq km (246,201 sq miles).
POPULATION: 9,480,000 (UN estimate 2002).
POPULATION DENSITY: 14.9 per sq km.
CAPITAL: Mogadishu. **Population:** 1,219,000 (UN projection 2000, including suburbs).
GEOGRAPHY: Somalia is bordered to the north by the Gulf of Aden, to the south and west by Kenya, to the west by Ethiopia and to the northwest by Djibouti. To the east lies the Indian Ocean. Somalia is an arid country and the scenery includes mountains in the north, the flat semi-desert plains in the interior and the subtropical region in the south. Separated from the sea by a narrow coastal plain, the mountains slope south and west to the central, almost waterless plateau which makes up most of the country. The beaches are protected by a coral reef that runs from Mogadishu to the Kenyan border in the south. They are among the longest in the world. There are only two rivers, the Jubba and the Shabeelle, and both rise in the Ogaden region of Ethiopia. Along their banks is most of the country's agricultural land. The Somali population is concentrated in the coastal towns, in the wetter, northern areas and in the south near the two rivers. A large nomadic population is scattered over the interior, although drought in recent years has led to many settling as farmers or fishermen in newly formed communities.
GOVERNMENT: Somalia gained independence from the UK and Italy in 1960. At the Arta Peace Conference in August 2000, an interim parliament was established.
Executive President: Abdullahi Yusuf Ahmed since 2004.
Prime Minister: Ali Mohamed Ghedi since 2004. The northern part of the country declared itself independent as the Republic of Somaliland with Dahir Riyale Kahin as acting president since 2002.
LANGUAGE: Somali and Arabic are the official languages. Swahili is spoken, particularly in the south. English and Italian are also widely spoken.
RELIGION: The state religion is Islam and the majority of Somalis are Sunni Muslims. There is a small Christian community, mostly Roman Catholic.
TIME: GMT + 3.
ELECTRICITY: 220 volts AC, 50Hz.
COMMUNICATIONS: Telephone: IDD is available. Country code: 252. Outgoing international calls must be made via the operator. **Mobile telephone:** GSM 900 network. Operators are *Hormuud Telecom Somalia Inc*, *Nationlink* (website: www.nationlinks.net) and *Telesom* (website: www.telesom.net). **Internet:** Somalia's *SomaliNet* (website: www.somalinet.com) is one of the country's first ISPs. Internet facilities for visitors are yet to be fully established. **Telegram:** There are limited facilities in the capital, but the main post office in Mogadishu, opposite the Hotel Juba, offers services. **Post:** Airmail to Europe takes up to two weeks. **Press:** No English-language dailies are published. **Radio:** BBC World Service (website: www.bbc.co.uk/worldservice) and Voice of America (website: www.voa.gov) can be received. From time to time the frequencies change and the most up-to-date can be found online.

TIMATIC CODES

Health	AMADEUS: **TI-DFT/MGQ/HE** GALILEO/WORLDSPAN: **TI-DFT/MGQ/HE** SABRE: **TIDFT/MGQ/HE**
Visa	AMADEUS: **TI-DFT/MGQ/VI** GALILEO/WORLDSPAN: **TI-DFT/MGQ/VI** SABRE: **TIDFT/MGQ/VI**

To access TIMATIC country information on Health and Visa regulations through the Computer Reservations System (CRS), type in the appropriate command line listed above.

Passport/Visa

	Passport Required?	Visa Required?	Return Ticket Required?
Full British	Yes	Yes	Yes
Australian	Yes	Yes	Yes
Canadian	Yes	Yes	Yes
USA	Yes	Yes	Yes
Other EU	Yes	Yes	Yes
Japanese	Yes	Yes	Yes

Note: *Regulations and requirements may be subject to change at short notice, and you are advised to contact the appropriate diplomatic or consular authority before finalising travel arrangements. Details of these may be found at the head of this country's entry. Any numbers in the chart refer to the footnotes below.*

Note: The Somali Embassy in London is closed at present owing to civil war in Somalia. Contact the Foreign Office (website: www.fco.gov.uk) for any information regarding entry into Somalia.
PASSPORTS: Valid passport required by all.
VISAS: Required by all except transit passengers continuing their journey by the same or first connecting aircraft, provided holding onward or return documentation and not leaving the airport.
Types of visa: *Tourist*, *Business* and *Transit*.
Validity: Dependent on nationality.
Application to: Contact the Somali Embassy in Addis Ababa, Ethiopia (tel: (1) 635 921/2; fax: (1) 627 847). The British Embassy in Ethiopia can also help with up-to-date information concerning travel to Somalia, available consular services, visa application requirements, visa costs and temporary residence.
Note: Upon arrival, all visitors - except those under 18 years of age - must exchange US$100 or equivalent into local currency. Please note that the exact amount to be exchanged may vary according to region.

Money

Currency: Somali Shilling (SoSh) = 100 cents. Notes are in denominations of SoSh500, 100, 50, 20, 10 and 5. Coins are in denominations of SoSh1, and 50, 10 and 5 cents.
Currency exchange: US Dollar bills are the easiest currency to exchange; hotels are the easiest and safest places. Avoid money changers in crowded areas.
Credit & debit cards: Not accepted.
Travellers cheques: US travellers cheques are preferred but generally not recommended.
Currency restrictions: The import and export of local currency is limited to SoSh200. The import of foreign currency is unlimited provided declared on arrival and exchanged at the national banks within five days after arrival. The export of foreign currency is limited to the amount declared on arrival. All foreign exchange transactions should be recorded on the official currency form which may be required prior to departure from Somalia.
Exchange rate indicators: The following figures are included as a guide to the movements of the Somali Shilling against Sterling and the US Dollar:

Date	Feb '04	May '04	Aug '04	Nov '04
£1.00=	4769.06	4679.58	4952.24	5601.86
$1.00=	2620.00	2620.00	2688.00	3018.00

Banking hours: Sat-Thurs 0800-1130.

Duty Free

The following goods may be imported into Somalia without incurring customs duty:
400 cigarettes or 40 cigars or 400g of tobacco; one bottle of wine or spirits; a reasonable amount of perfume for personal use.

Public Holidays

2005: Jan 1 New Year's Day. **Jan 21** Eid al-Adha (Feast of the Sacrifice). **Feb 19** Ashoura. **Apr 21** Mouloud (Birth of the Prophet). **May 1** Labour Day. **Jun 26** Independence Day. **Jul 1** Foundation of the Republic. **Nov 3-5** Eid al-Fitr (End of Ramadan).
2006: Jan 1 New Year's Day. **Jan 10** Eid al-Adha (Feast of the Sacrifice). **Feb 9** Ashoura. **Apr 11** Mouloud (Birth of the Prophet). **May 1** Labour Day. **Jun 26** Independence Day. **Jul 1** Foundation of the Republic. **Oct 22-24** Eid al-Fitr (End of Ramadan).
Note: Muslim festivals are timed according to local sightings of various phases of the moon and the dates given above are approximations. During the lunar month of Ramadan that precedes Eid al-Fitr, Muslims fast during the day and feast at night and normal business patterns may be interrupted. Many restaurants are closed during the day and there may be restrictions on smoking and drinking. Some disruption may continue into Eid al-Fitr itself. Eid al-Fitr and Eid al-Adha may last anything from two to 10 days, depending on the region. For more information, see the *World of Islam* appendix.

Health

	Special Precautions?	Certificate Required?
Yellow Fever	Yes	1
Cholera	2	No
Typhoid & Polio	3	N/A
Malaria	4	N/A

Note: *Regulations and requirements may be subject to change at short notice, and you are advised to contact your doctor well in advance of your intended date of departure. Any numbers in the chart refer to the footnotes below.*

1: A yellow fever vaccination certificate is required from travellers arriving from infected areas. Travellers arriving from non-endemic zones should note that vaccination is strongly recommended for travel outside the urban areas, even if an outbreak of the disease has not been reported and they would normally not require a vaccination certificate to enter the country.
2: Following WHO guidelines issued in 1973, a cholera vaccination certificate is not a condition of entry to Somalia. However, at the beginning of 2000, an outbreak of cholera was reported, and precautions are recommended for those likely to be at risk. Up-to-date advice should be sought before deciding whether these precautions should include vaccination, as medical opinion is divided over its effectiveness; see the *Health* appendix.
3: Vaccination against typhoid is advised.
4: Malaria risk, predominantly in the malignant *falciparum* form, exists all year throughout the country. Resistance to chloroquine and sulfadoxine-pyrimethamine has been reported. The recommended prophylaxis is mefloquine.
Food & drink: Mains water is normally chlorinated and, whilst relatively safe, may cause mild abdominal upsets. Bottled water is available and is advised for the first few weeks of stay. Drinking water outside main cities and towns is likely to be contaminated and sterilisation is considered essential. Milk is unpasteurised and should be boiled. Powdered or tinned milk is available and is advised, but make sure that it is reconstituted with pure water. Avoid

dairy products which are likely to have been made from unboiled milk. Only eat well-cooked meat and fish, preferably served hot. Pork, salad and mayonnaise may carry increased risk. Vegetables should be cooked and fruit peeled.
Other risks: *Bilharzia* (schistosomiasis) is present. Avoid swimming and paddling in fresh water; swimming pools which are well chlorinated and maintained are safe.
Hepatitis A and *E* are widespread; *hepatitis B* is hyperendemic. *Meningococcal meningitis* may occur.
Rabies is present. For those at high risk, vaccination before arrival should be considered. If you are bitten, seek medical advice without delay. For more information, see the *Health* appendix.
Health care: Medical facilities are very limited and visitors are advised to take their own medicines with them. Health insurance is essential. Medical treatment at government-run hospitals and dispensaries is free for Somalians and may sometimes be free for visitors.

Travel - International

Note: All travel to Somalia, including Somaliland, is not advised because of the dangerous level of criminal activity. There is a high threat from terrorism in Somalia. Strong security precautions should be undertaken by all, especially nationals whose countries have no representation in Somalia, such as the UK.
AIR: The national airline is *Somali Airlines*.
Approximate flight times: From Mogadishu to *London* is 15 hours, flying first to Dubai and then on to London with a stopover in Djibouti.
International airports: *Mogadishu (MGQ)* is 6km (4 miles) west of the city. There is a taxi service to the city centre.
Departure tax: The equivalent of US$20. Transit passengers and children under two years are exempt.
SEA: The principal ports are Berbera, Kismayu, Marka and Mogadishu.
ROAD: There are routes to Somalia from Djibouti and Kenya. There is no border crossing with Ethiopia at present. Roads are underdeveloped, and travel requires suitable 4-wheel-drive desert vehicles.

Travel - Internal

Note: Due to continued civil unrest, travel within Somalia is highly dangerous.
AIR: *Somali Airlines* run regular services to all major towns.
SEA: Modern Somalia is essentially a broad strip of coastal desert. Roads are poor and consequently coastal shipping is an important form of transport, both socially and economically.
ROAD: Traffic drives on the right. It is difficult to travel outside Mogadishu by car. Existing roads run from the capital to Burao and Baidoa and there are sealed roads between Kismayu and Mogadishu, and Hargeysa and Mogadishu. Passenger transport is restricted almost entirely to road haulage. There are few cars and buses, although there are reasonable bus services between the major centres in the south. **Taxi:** These are available in large towns. **Car hire:** Available in Mogadishu. **Documentation:** An International Driving Permit is required.
URBAN: Minibuses and shared taxi-type services run in Mogadishu, but availability may be restricted outside normal working hours (Sat-Thurs 0700-1400).

Accommodation

HOTELS: In the main cities of Hargeisa and Mogadishu, there are international-standard hotels. There are also hotels in Afgoi, Berbera, Borama, Burao, Kismayu and Marka.
REST HOUSES: Government-run rest houses are located in many places with dormitory accommodation for four to 10 people.
LODGES: There are tourist and hunting lodges in national parks at Lac Badana and Bush-Bush, as well as in other areas.

Resorts & Excursions

Note: Due to heightened tension in the region, travel to Somalia is not currently recommended (except Hargeisa). For further information, visitors should seek official advice.
Kismayu National Park, in the southwest, contains many common - and a few rare - East African species. **Hargeisa** in the north contains rarer species. A third park is located outside Mogadishu and there are 10 game reserves in total. Somalia's beaches line the Indian Ocean in the east and are protected by a coral reef running from Mogadishu to the Kenyan border in the south; they are among the longest in the world.

Social Profile

FOOD & DRINK: In peacetime, restaurants in the major cities serve Chinese, European, Italian and Somali food. Local food includes lobster, prawn, squid, crab, fresh tuna, Somali bananas, mangoes and papaya. A traditional Somali meal is roast kid and spiced rice.
NIGHTLIFE: Local bands playing African and European music perform at nightclubs. There are frequent traditional feasts with ritualistic and recreational dance, music and folk songs.
SHOPPING: Traditional crafts include gold, silver jewellery, woven cloth and baskets from the Benadir region, meerschaum and woodcarvings. **Shopping hours:** Sat-Thurs 0800-1230 and 1630-1900.
SOCIAL CONVENTIONS: Traditional dance, music, song and craftsmanship flourish despite gradual modern development. Informal wear is acceptable and there is no objection to bikinis on the beach. Visitors should respect local customs. **Tipping:** 10 to 15 per cent is normal in hotels and restaurants.

Business Profile

ECONOMY: Somalia's economy has been seriously dislocated by years of fighting and political strife, as well as a severe long-term drought which has affected the whole of East Africa. Somalia now ranks among the poorest countries in the world. Subsistence agriculture and livestock rearing occupy most of the working population, although development is hampered by primitive techniques, poor soil and climatic conditions, and a chronic labour shortage. Bananas are the main cash crop and provide nearly half the country's export earnings; cotton, maize, sorghum and other crops are produced for domestic consumption. Animal products, particularly hides and skins, are another key source of revenue, mainly from Saudi Arabia. Fishing has dwindled to the level of individual small boats, but there are provisional plans to restore this to full commercial capacity. Oil and gas deposits have been located but their exploitation has been in abeyance due to the lack of an effective central government. There is little industry other than small-scale operations to meet domestic needs, mainly food-processing and oil refining.
Most economic assets remain in the unstable hands of clan-based militias, with frequent competition for control of particular industries.
Over half the population relies on remittances from abroad as well as large injections of foreign aid, especially from the various United Nations relief organisations. These were disrupted by the closure in 2002 – at the behest of the US government, which claimed links to terrorism – of the al-Barakat finance company which processed a large number of overseas payments; the company also had major interests in other parts of the economy, especially banking and telecommunications. Somalia is burdened by a huge foreign debt and its traditional trade relationships have largely been suspended due to payment problems.
BUSINESS: Wear lightweight suits or safari-style jackets without a tie in hot weather. The best time to visit is October to May. **Office hours:** Sat-Thurs 0800-1400.
COMMERCIAL INFORMATION: The Chamber of Commerce, Industry and Agriculture in Mogadishu is presently closed due to continued civil unrest.

Climate

The *Jilal* starts around January and is the harshest period, hot and very dry. *Gu* is the first rainy season lasting from March to June. *Hagaa*, during August, is a time of dry monsoon winds and dust clouds. The second rainy season is from September to December and is called *Dayr*.
Required clothing: Lightweights and rainwear.

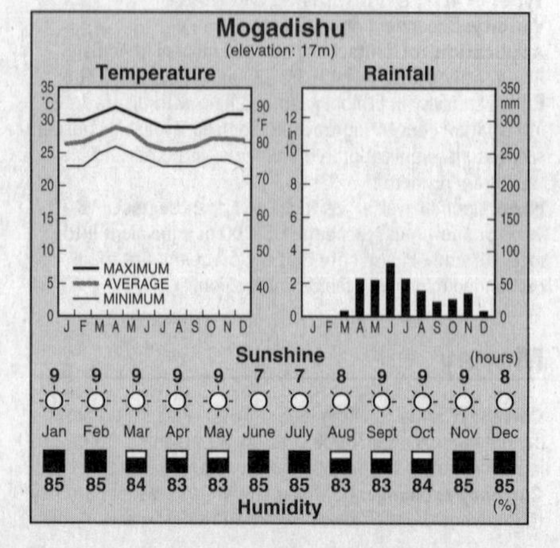

South Africa

LATEST TRAVEL ADVICE CONTACTS

British Foreign and Commonwealth Office
Tel: (0870) 606 0290 Website: www.fco.gov.uk
US Department of State
Website: http://travel.state.gov/travel
Canadian Department of Foreign Affairs and Int'l Trade
Tel: (1 800) 267 8376 Website: www.dfait-maeci.gc.ca

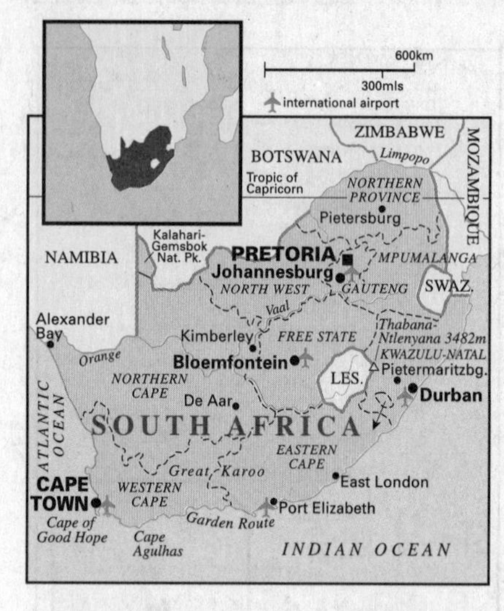

Location: Southern Africa.

Country dialling code: 27.

South African Tourism
Street address: Bojanala House, 90 Protea Road, Chislehurston, Johannesburg 2196, South Africa
Postal address: Private Bag X10012, Sandton 2196, South Africa
Tel: (11) 895 3000. Fax: (11) 895 3001.
E-mail: info@southafrica.net
Website: www.southafrica.net
South African High Commission
South Africa House, Trafalgar Square, London WC2N 5DP, UK
Tel: (020) 7451 7299.
Fax: (020) 7451 7284.
E-mail: general@southafricahouse.com
Website: www.southafricahouse.com
Opening hours: Mon-Fri 0830-1300 and 1345-1700.
Enquiries should be sent by post.
South African Consulate
15 Whitehall, London SW1A 2DD, UK
Tel: (020) 7925 8900/01/10. Fax: (020) 7925 8930/1/2.
E-mail: mailmaster@rsaconsulate.co.uk
Opening hours: Mon-Fri 0845-1245 (personal applications only).
South African Tourism Board (SATOUR)
Street address: 6 Alt Grove, London SW19 4DZ, UK
Postal address: PO Box 49110, London SW19 4DX
Tel: (020) 8971 9364 *or* (0870) 155 0044 (tourism enquiry line and brochure request).
Fax: (020) 8944 6705.
E-mail: info@uk.southafrica.net
Website: www.southafrica.net
British High Commission
255 Hill Street, Pretoria 0002, South Africa
Tel: (12) 421 7733 (general) *or* 421 7500 (main switchboard).
Fax: (12) 421 7555 *or* 7599 (general).
E-mail: media.pretoria@fco.gov.uk
Website: www.britain.org.za
Consular section: Liberty Life Place, Block B, 256 Glyn Street, Hatfield, Pretoria 0083, South Africa
Tel: (12) 421 7801/2.
Fax: (12) 421 7888/77.
E-mail: pta.visaenquiries@fco.gov.uk
British Consulate General

TIMATIC CODES

Health
AMADEUS: **TI-DFT/JNB/HE**
GALILEO/WORLDSPAN: **TI-DFT/JNB/HE**
SABRE: **TIDFT/JNB/HE**

Visa
AMADEUS: **TI-DFT/JNB/VI**
GALILEO/WORLDSPAN: **TI-DFT/JNB/VI**
SABRE: **TIDFT/JNB/VI**

To access TIMATIC country information on Health and Visa regulations through the Computer Reservations System (CRS), type in the appropriate command line listed above.

Five minutes from Johannesburg
International Airport
Two luxurious hotels
Entertainment venues
Trendy bars
Unparalleled gaming venues
Ten till-late nightclub
Restaurants with a world of tastes
Johannesburg's most exciting
destination
CAESARS
GAUTENG
SERVATIONS: +27 (0) 11 928 1928 WWW.CAESARS.CO.ZA INFO@CAESARS.CO.Z

Street address: 15th Floor, Southern Life Centre, 8 Riebeeck Street, Cape Town 8001, South Africa
Postal address: PO Box 500, Capetown 8000, South Africa
Tel: (21) 405 2400. Fax: (21) 405 2448 (administration) *or* 405 2447 (consular) *or* 405 2460 (commercial).
E-mail: Consular.SectionCT@fco.gov.uk
Website: www.britain.org.za
Honorary Consulate also in: Durban.
Embassy of the Republic of South Africa
3051 Massachusetts Avenue, NW, Washington, DC 20008, USA
Tel: (202) 232 4400 *or* 274 7991 (consular section).
Fax: (202) 265 1607.
E-mail: info@saembassy.org *or* Consular@saembassy.org
Website: www.saembassy.org
Consulates General in: Chicago, Los Angeles and New York.
South African Tourism Board (SATOUR)
500 Fifth Avenue, 20th Floor, Suite 2040, New York, NY 10110, USA
Tel: (212) 730 2929. Fax: (212) 764 1980.
E-mail: newyork@southafrica.net
Website: www.southafrica.net
Embassy of the United States of America
Street address: 877 Pretorius Street, Arcadia, 0083, South Africa
Postal address: PO Box 9536, Pretoria 0001, South Africa
Tel: (12) 431 4000 *or* 644 8000 (visa section).
Fax: (12) 342 2299 *or* 646 6916 (visa section).
E-mail: embassypretoria@state.gov *or* consularjohannesburg@state.gov
Website: http://pretoria.usembassy.gov
Consulates General in: Cape Town, Durban and Johannesburg.
High Commission of the Republic of South Africa
15 Sussex Drive, Ottawa, Ontario K1M 1M8, Canada
Tel: (613) 744 0330. Fax: (613) 741 1639.
E-mail: rsafrica@southafrica-canada.ca
Website: www.southafrica-canada.ca
Honorary Consulate in: Vancouver.
Canadian High Commission
Street address: 1103 Arcadia Street, Hatfield, Pretoria, South Africa
Postal address: Private Bag X13, Hatfield 0028, Pretoria, South Africa
Tel: (12) 422 3000 *or* 3090 (visa section) *or* 3014 (consular section).
Fax: (12) 422 3052 *or* 3053 (visa section).
E-mail: pret@dfait-maeci.gc.ca
Website: www.dfait-maeci.gc.ca/southafrica
Consular section: South African Reserve Bank Building, 60 Saint George's Mall, 8001, Cape Town, South Africa.
Tel: (21) 423 5240. Fax: (21) 423 4893.
E-mail: cptown@dfait-maeci.gc.ca

General Information

AREA: 1,219,090 sq km (470,693 sq miles).
POPULATION: 45,454,211 (official estimate 2002).
POPULATION DENSITY: 36.8 per sq km.
CAPITAL: Pretoria (administrative). **Population:** 1,985,983 (2001). Cape Town (legislative). **Population:** 2,893,247 (2001). Bloemfontein (judicial). **Population:** 119,698 (2001).
GEOGRAPHY: The Republic of South Africa lies at the southern end of the African continent. It is bounded by the Indian Ocean to the east and the Atlantic Ocean to the west, and is bordered to the north by Namibia, Botswana, Zimbabwe, Mozambique and Swaziland and totally encloses Lesotho. South Africa has three major geographical regions, namely plateau, mountains and the coastal belt. The high plateau has sharp escarpments which rise above the plains, or *veld*. Despite two major river systems, the Limpopo and the Orange, most of the plateau lacks surface water. Along the coastline are sandy beaches and rocky coves, and the vegetation is shrublike. The mountainous regions which run along the coastline from the Cape of Good Hope to the Limpopo Valley in the northeast of the country are split into the Drakensberg, Nuweveldberg and Stormberg ranges. Following the 1994 elections, South Africa was organised into nine regions. These comprise the Western Cape with its provincial and national capital of Cape Town, the Eastern Cape with its provincial capital of Bisho, the Northern Cape with its provincial capital of Kimberley, KwaZulu-Natal with its provincial capital of Pietermaritzburg, the Free State with its provincial capital of Bloemfontein, the North West Province with its provincial capital of Mmabatho, Limpopo (formerly called the Northern Province) with its provincial capital of Polokwane (formerly called Pietersburg), Mpumalanga with its provincial capital of Nelspruit, and Gauteng with its provincial capital of Johannesburg.
GOVERNMENT: Republic. Gained independence from the UK in 1910. **Head of State and Government:** President Thabo Mvuyelwa Mbeki since 1999.
LANGUAGE: The official languages are Afrikaans, English, isiNdebele, isiXhosa, isiZulu, Sepedi, Sesotho, Setswana, Siswati, Tshivenda and Xitsonga.
RELIGION: Most inhabitants profess Christianity of some form and belong to either Catholic, Anglican and other protestant denominations, Afrikaner Calvinist churches or African independent churches. There are also significant Hindu, Muslim and Jewish communities, and traditional beliefs are still practised widely, sometimes in conjunction with Christianity.
TIME: GMT + 2.
ELECTRICITY: 220/230 volts AC; 250 volts AC (Pretoria), 50Hz. Three-pin round plugs are in use.
COMMUNICATIONS: Telephone: IDD is available. Country code: 27. Outgoing international code: 09. **Mobile telephone:** GSM 900/1800 networks. Operators include *Cell C Ltd* (website: www.cellc.net), *MTN* (website: www.mtn.co.za) and *Vodacom* (website: www.vodacom.co.za). Coverage extends to most urban areas. **Fax:** Most main hotels have this service. **Internet:** ISPs include *I-Africa* (website: www.iafrica.com), *M-Web* (website: www.mweb.co.za) and *Sangonet* (website: http://sn.apc.org). Visitors can access their e-mail from Internet cafes around the country. **Telegram:** Services are available in all towns. **Post:** Airmail to Europe takes up to seven days. Post office hours: Generally Mon-Fri 0830-1630, Sat 0800-1130. Some transactions may not be carried out Mon-Fri after 1530 or Sat after 1100. The smaller post offices close for lunch 1300-1400. *Poste Restante* services are available throughout the country. **Press:** The main newspapers are in English and Afrikaans, and include *Cape Argus, The Citizen, Daily Dispatch, Mercury, The Star* and *Sowetan*.
Radio: BBC World Service (website: www.bbc.co.uk/worldservice) and Voice of America (website: www.voa.gov) can be received. From time to time the frequencies change and the most up-to-date can be found online.

Passport/Visa

	Passport Required?	Visa Required?	Return Ticket Required?
Full British	Yes	No	Yes
Australian	Yes	No	Yes
Canadian	Yes	No	Yes
USA	Yes	No	Yes
Other EU	Yes	No/1/2/3	Yes
Japanese	Yes	No	Yes

Note: *Regulations and requirements may be subject to change at short notice, and you are advised to contact the appropriate diplomatic or consular authority before finalising travel arrangements. Details of these may be found at the head of this country's entry. Any numbers in the chart refer to the footnotes below.*

PASSPORTS: Passport valid for at least 30 days longer than the period covering stay in South Africa required by all.
VISAS: Required by all except the following for business and tourist purposes:
(a) **1.** nationals of Australia, Northern Ireland and the UK;
(b) **2.** nationals of Canada, EU countries (except Northern Ireland and the UK (see above); Cyprus, Hungary, Poland and Slovak Republic for up to 30 days; Estonia, Latvia, Lithuania and Slovenia who *do* require a visa), Japan and the USA for stays of up to 90 days;
(c) **3.** nationals of British Overseas Territories, British Virgin Islands, Guernsey, Isle of Man, Jersey and the Republic of Ireland;
(d) nationals of British Dependent Territories (except Arguilla, Bermuda, British Antarctic Territory, British Indian Ocean Territory, Cayman Islands, Falkland Islands, Gibraltar, Montserrat, Pitcairn Islands, Henderson, Cucie and Oeno Islands, the Sovereign Base Area of Akrotiri and Dhekelia and the Turks & Caicos Islands, who *do* require a visa);
(e) nationals of Andorra, Argentina, Botswana, Brazil, Bulgaria, Chile, Ecuador, Iceland, Israel, Jamaica, Liechtenstein, Mexico, Monaco, New Zealand, Norway, Paraguay, St Vincent & the Grenadines, San Marino, Singapore, Switzerland, Taiwan, Uruguay and Venezuela for stays of up to 90 days;
(f) nationals of Antigua & Barbuda, Barbados, Belize, Benin, Bolivia, Cape Verde, Costa Rica, Gabon, Guyana, Hong Kong (SAR), Jordan, Korea (Rep), Lesotho, Macau (SAR), Malawi, Malaysia, Maldives, Mauritius, Namibia, Peru, Seychelles, Swaziland, Thailand, Turkey, Zambia and Zimbabwe for stays of up to 30 days;
(g) transit passengers continuing their journey by the same or first connecting aircraft provided holding onward or return documentation and not leaving the airport.
Note: (a) Holders of Visitor visas are not allowed to take up employment in South Africa. However, employment can be taken up under certain circumstances and if the requirements for a work permit are complied with, but only if the Embassy/Consulate is contacted in advance. (b) Unaccompanied children under the age of 18 years must hold written consent from their parents when travelling alone. (c) *Study* or *work* permits must be obtained in the country of normal residence before entry into South Africa. However, exceptions may be made. (d) Permits may be extended if done so 30 days prior to expiry of original permit.
Types of visa and cost: *Visitors, Business* and *Transit*: £33. *Study Permits:* £33 (depending on level of education). Nationals of India and Zimbabwe are exempt from visa fees. Other nationals must apply for a visa with the appropriate fee. All fees are subject to change without notice; please check with Embassy or Consulate to confirm costs.
Note: Visa fees will only be requested from nationals of Belize, Benin, Equatorial Guinea, Gabon, Hong Kong (SAR), Korea (Rep), Malaysia, The Philippines, Thailand and Turkey if the intended visit exceeds 30 days.
Application to: Consulate (or Consular section at Embassy or High Commission); see *Contact Addresses* section. Applicants in countries where South Africa is not represented may send their applications to the embassy in the nearest country.
Application requirements: (a) Passport, with at least two blank pages, valid for 30 days longer than the duration of the visit to South Africa. (b) Two passport-size photos. (c) One completed application form (failure to complete the application fully and in detail may result in visa being delayed or refused). (d) Fee (payable by cash, bank draft or postal order). (e) A stamped self-addressed special delivery envelope if applying by post. (f) A valid vaccination certificate, if required by the Act. (g) Proof of sufficient funds to cover visit, in the form of bank statements, bursaries, cash, etc. (h) Onward/return ticket and, if in transit, proof of sufficient documentation for admission to the country of destination. For *Study* permits: (a)-(g) and, (h) Letter, with official letterhead, of admission from a South African education institution, confirming exact period of study and accommodation arrangements. (i) Letter from current place of study, if on a student exchange. (j) Fully completed application form BI-1738. (k) Proof of qualifications. For *Business* permits: (a)-(h) and, (i) Comprehensive business letters from both the UK and South African companies confirming the purpose, nature and duration of the visit, containing written partner agreements with full details of the partners/directors and their residential status in the Republic, if applicable. (j) Certification by a chartered accountant that the applicant will have at least R2,5 m value invested as part of the book value of the business and will comply with at least one of the other criteria stipulated in regulation 24 (contact Embassy/Consulate for further details). This may include audited financial statements proving viability of any future business.
Note: (a) In the case of failure to comply with any of these regulations, visitors may be required to leave a cash deposit with the Immigration Officer. (b) Visitors must be of sound mind and body. (c) Medical insurance is required by all visitors. (d) There is now no single work permit. Each particular work permit has specific application requirements. These specific requirements can be obtained directly from the Embassy/Consulate *or* from the form BI-1738.
Working days required: Applications should be made well in advance. The processing time is 10 days, although visas may be processed quicker if application is submitted directly rather than by post. Nationals applying in the UK for a visa are advised to apply well in advance of their departure date. Work permits may take 12 to 30 calendar days to process.
Temporary residence: Temporary residence permits encompass *Study, Work* or *Workseeker* Permits. Contact the nearest Consulate (or Consular section at Embassy) for further details.

Money

Currency: Rand (R) = 100 cents. Notes are in denominations of R200, 100, 50, 20 and 10. Coins are in denominations of R5, 2 and 1, and 50, 20, 10, 5, 2 and 1 cents.
Currency exchange: Money can be changed at banks, bureaux de change, some hotels, and larger shops and restaurants. Automated foreign exchange machines and ATMs are available at various locations.
Credit & debit cards: MasterCard and Visa are preferred. American Express and Diners Club are also widely accepted. Some ATMs will give cash advances with credit cards. Check with your credit or debit card company for details of merchant acceptability and other facilities which may be available.
Travellers cheques: Valid at banks, hotels, restaurants and shops. To avoid additional exchange rate charges, travellers are advised to take travellers cheques in Pounds Sterling or US Dollars.
Currency restrictions: The import of local currency is limited to R5000 in cash. The export of local currency is limited to R500 in cash. The import and export of foreign currency is unlimited provided it is declared upon arrival or departure.
Exchange rate indicators: The following figures are included as a guide to the movements of the Rand against Sterling and the US Dollar:

Date	Feb '04	May '04	Aug '04	Nov '04
£1.00=	12.87	12.50	11.90	11.17
$1.00=	7.07	7.00	6.46	6.03

Banking hours: Mon-Fri 0830-1530, Sat 0800-1130.

Duty Free

The following goods may be imported into South Africa by passengers over 18 years of age without incurring customs duty:

200 cigarettes and 50 cigars and 250g of tobacco; 1l of spirits or liquor and 2l of wine; 50ml of perfume and 250ml of eau de toilette; other goods up to a value of R3000.

Restricted items: Plants and plant material without import permit, including margarine, honey and other vegetable oils.

Prohibited goods: Narcotics; flick-knives; ammunition, explosives; meat, processed cheese and other dairy products; obscene literature.

Public Holidays

2005: Jan 1 New Year's Day. **Mar 21** Human Rights Day. **Mar 25** Good Friday. **Mar 28** Family Day. **Apr 27** Freedom Day. **May 1** Worker's Day. **June 16** Youth Day. **Aug 9** National Women's Day. **Sep 24** Heritage Day. **Dec 16** Day of Reconciliation. **Dec 25** Christmas Day. **Dec 26** Day of Goodwill.

2006: Jan 1 New Year's Day. **Mar 21** Human Rights Day. **Apr 14** Good Friday. **Apr 17** Family Day. **Apr 27** Freedom Day. **May 1** Workers' Day. **Jun 16** Youth Day. **Aug 9** National Women's Day. **Sep 24** Heritage Day. **Dec 16** Day of Reconciliation. **Dec 25** Christmas Day. **Dec 26** Day of Goodwill.

Note: Holidays falling on a Sunday are observed the following Monday.

Health

	Special Precautions?	Certificate Required?
Yellow Fever	No	1
Cholera	2	No
Typhoid & Polio	3	N/A
Malaria	4	N/A

***Note:** Regulations and requirements may be subject to change at short notice, and you are advised to contact your doctor well in advance of your intended date of departure. Any numbers in the chart refer to the footnotes below.*

1: A yellow fever vaccination certificate is required from travellers over one year of age arriving from infected areas. African countries and the Americas formerly classified as endemic zones are considered by the South African authorities to be infected areas. The yellow fever vaccination certificate only becomes valid 10 days *after* immunisation.

2: Visitors may wish to consider precautions against Cholera, depending on the area in South Africa being visited: a recent outbreak in February 2004 occurred in the Nkomazi area, Mpumalanga Province, which borders Mozambique.

3: Vaccination against typhoid is advised.

4: Malaria risk, predominantly in the malignant *falciparum* form, exists throughout the year in the low altitude areas of Limpopo, Mpumalanga Province (including the Kruger National Park) and northeastern KwaZulu/Natal as far south as the Tugela River. The risk is highest from October to May. Resistance to chloroquine and sulfadoxine-pyrimethamine has been reported. It is strongly recommended that visitors to these areas take anti-malaria tablets before entering these zones (tablets are available from pharmacies without prescription). The recommended prophylaxis is mefloquine (World Health Organization) *or* chloroquine plus pyrimethamine (South African High Commission).

Food & drink: Mains water is considered safe to drink in urban areas but may be contaminated elsewhere and sterilisation is advisable. Milk is pasteurised and dairy products are safe for consumption. Local meat, poultry, seafood, fruit and vegetables are generally considered safe to eat.

Other risks: *Bilharzia* (schistosomiasis) is endemic in the north and east and may be present elsewhere. Avoid swimming and paddling in fresh water; swimming pools that are well chlorinated and maintained are safe. *Hepatitis A* occurs and *hepatitis B* is hyperendemic. *Dengue fever* and *filariasis* are present.

Rabies may be present. For those at high risk, vaccination before arrival should be considered. If you are bitten, seek medical advice without delay. For more information, consult the *Health* appendix.

Health care: Medical facilities are excellent. Health insurance is recommended. A leaflet on health precautions is available from the South African High Commission (see *Contact Addresses* section).

Travel - International

AIR: South Africa's national airline is *South African Airways (SA)* (website: www.flysaa.com). There are frequent direct and indirect flights by numerous major airlines from destinations throughout Europe and North America. For more information regarding airports, contact Airports Company South Africa (tel: (11) 453 9116; fax: (11) 453 9353/4; e-mail: webmaster@airports.co.za; website: www.airports.co.za).

Approximate flight times: From Cape Town to *London* is 11 hours 30 minutes, from Durban is 14 hours and from Johannesburg is 10 hours 30 minutes. From Johannesburg to *New York* is 14 hours 30 minutes.

International airports: *Cape Town (CPT)* (Cape Town International), 22km (16 miles) east of the city. Airport facilities include outgoing duty-free shop, car hire, bank/bureau de change and restaurant/bar. Inter-Cape buses run 24 hours and meet all incoming and outgoing flights. Courtesy buses are operated by some hotels. Taxis are available, with a surcharge after 2300 (travel time - 20 minutes). Car hire is available (includes *Avis*, *Budget*, *Europcar* and *Hertz*).

Bloemfontein (BFN) (Bloemfontein International), 10km (6 miles) east of the city (travel time – 15 minutes). Airport facilities include ATMs, restaurants, car hire and conference facilities. There is an airport shuttle bus to the city centre (leaving from outside the airport building). Taxis are also available.

Durban (DUR) (Durban International), 18km (11 miles) southwest of the city (travel time – 20 minutes). Airport facilities include outgoing duty-free shop, car hire (includes *Avis*, *Budget*, *Hertz* and *Europcar*), bank/bureau de change and bar/restaurant. Airport buses and taxis are available to the city.

Johannesburg (JNB) (Johannesburg International), 22km (14 miles) east of the city (travel time – 35 minutes). Airport facilities include incoming and outgoing duty-free shops, post office, car hire, bank/bureau de change, restaurant and bar. Bus services to Pretoria and Johannesburg are available. Buses link Kempton Park with Johannesburg. Taxis are available. Courtesy coaches are operated by some major hotels.

Port Elizabeth (PLZ) (Port Elizabeth International) is 5km (3 miles) west of the Capital Business District. Airport facilities include Nedbank ATM, conference facilities, information desk (tel: (41) 507 7319), restaurants and pubs, shops, a pharmacy, postal services, car hire. There is an airport shuttle bus to the main international hotels in Port Elizabeth upon request. Taxis are also available.

Departure tax: None.

SEA: The main ports are Cape Town, Durban, East London and Port Elizabeth. *St Helena Steamship Co* Ltd runs a regular passenger service from Avonmouth to Cape Town. Cruises are offered by various companies between South Africa and the Indian Ocean Islands. Cruise lines include

Credit: © South African Tourism

Cunard, Eurocruises, Orient Lines, P&O, Peter Deilmann Cruises, Princess, Radisson Seven Seas and *Silversea Cruises*.

RAIL: The main routes are from South Africa to Zimbabwe, Botswana and Mozambique. Contact *South African Railways (SPOORNET)* (website: www.spoornet.co.za) for further information.

ROAD: There are main routes into South Africa from Botswana (via Ramatlabama), Lesotho, Mozambique (now open after a long war – check with local police about state of road and safety), Namibia, Swaziland and Zimbabwe (via Beit Bridge).

Travel - Internal

AIR: Daily flights link Bloemfontein, Cape Town, Durban, East London, Johannesburg, Kimberley, Port Elizabeth and Pretoria and with other connecting flights to provincial towns. *South African Airways* operates on the principal routes.

Flight discounts: An *Africa Explorer* fare is available to foreign visitors entering South Africa with an IATA airline. It offers a significant saving for anyone planning to use South African Airways' internal network. The fare is valid for a minimum of three days and a maximum of two months: travel may originate and terminate at any point within South Africa that is served by the airline. Travel is not permitted more than once in the same direction over any given sector. There is also a reduction of approximately 30 per cent on some standby fares. South African Airways has various other discount domestic fares including Apex, Slumber, Supersaver and Saver fares.

SEA: *Starlight Cruises* offers links between major ports.

RAIL: The principal intercity services are as follows: the *Blue Train* (website: www.bluetrain.co.za) is a luxury express offering routes between Pretoria, Victoria Falls, Hoedspruit, Port Elizabeth and Cape Town; the *Trans-Oranje* between Cape Town and Durban via Kimberley and Bloemfontein (weekly); and the *Trans-Natal Express* between Durban and Johannesburg (daily). *Rovos Rail* offers luxury (partly steam) safaris to the eastern Transvaal. The *Transnet Museum* also offers various steam safaris around South Africa and Zimbabwe, and the *Trans-Karoo Express* travels between Cape Town, Johannesburg and Pretoria four times a week. All long-distance trains are equipped with sleeping compartments, included in fares, and most have restaurant cars. Reservations are recommended for principal trains and all overnight journeys. There are frequent local trains in the Cape Town and Pretoria/Johannesburg urban areas. All trains have first- and second-class accommodation. Children under two years of age travel free. Children aged two to 11 years pay half fare.

ROAD: There is a well-maintained network of roads and motorways in populous regions. Around a third of roads are paved (with all major roads tarred to a high standard). Traffic drives on the left. In non-residential areas, speed limits are 120kph (75mph). Fines for speeding are very heavy. It is illegal to carry petrol other than in built-in petrol tanks. Petrol stations are usually open all week 0700-1900. Some are open 24 hours. Petrol must be paid for in cash. **Bus/coach:** Various operators, such as *Greyhound, Intercape* and *Translux*, run intercity express links using modern air-conditioned coaches. On many of the intercity routes, passengers may break their journey at any scheduled stop en route by prior arrangement at time of booking and continue on a subsequent coach at no extra cost other than for additional accommodation. **Taxi:** Available throughout the country, at all towns, hotels and airports, with rates for distance and time. For long-distance travel, a quotation should be sought. **Car hire:** Self-drive and chauffeur-driven cars are available at most airports and in major city centres. *Avis, Budget* and *Imperial* are represented nationwide.

Documentation: An International Driving Permit is required. The minimum age is 23 (or 21 on presentation of an American Express/Diners card). Foreign licences in English are valid for up to six months; otherwise, British visitors who are planning to drive in South Africa should check with the *AA* or *RAC* prior to departure that they have all the correct documentation.

URBAN: There are bus and suburban rail networks in all the main towns. Fares in Cape Town and Johannesburg are zonal, with payment in cash or with 10-ride pre-purchase 'clipcards' from kiosks. In Pretoria, there are various pre-purchase ticket systems, including a cheap pass for off-peak travel only. In Durban, conventional buses face stiff competition from minibuses and combi-taxis (both legal and illegal), which are also found in other South African towns. These, although cheap and very fast, should be used with care. For ordinary taxis, fares within the city areas are more expensive than long distances. Taxis do not cruise and must be called from a rank. Taxi drivers expect a 10 per cent tip.

Travel Times: The following chart gives approximate travel times (in hours and minutes) from **Cape Town** to other major cities/towns in South Africa.

	Air	Road	Rail
Johannesburg	**2.00**	**15.00**	**24.00**
Durban	**2.00**	**18.00**	**38.00**
Pretoria	**2.00**	**16.00**	**26.00**
Port Elizabeth	**1.00**	**7.00**	**-**
Bloemfontein	**1.30**	**10.00**	**20.00**

Accommodation

South Africa offers a wide range of accommodation from luxury 5-star hotels to thatched huts (*rondavels*) in game reserves. 'Time-sharing condominiums' are developing in popular resorts. Comprehensive accommodation guides giving details of facilities, including provision for the handicapped, are available at all SATOUR offices and from regional tourist offices. Information covers hotels, motels, farm holidays, game park rest camps, caravan and campsites and supplementary accommodation such as beach cottages, holiday flats and bungalows. Rates should always be confirmed at time of booking. It is forbidden by law to levy service charges, although phone calls may be charged for.

HOTELS: All hotels are registered with the South African Tourism Board, which controls standards. For further information, contact SATOUR (see *Contact Addresses* section). 800 hotels are members of The Federated Hospitality Association of South Africa (FEDHASA), PO Box 71517 (tel: (11) 799 7676; fax: (11) 799 7675; e-mail: fedhasa@fedhasa.co.za; website: www.fedhasa.co.za). FEDHASA has regional offices throughout the country.

Grading: The National Grading and Classification Scheme was introduced in 1994. Participation is voluntary. Hotels are graded **1** to **5 stars** according to the range of facilities on offer, plus an optional classification band grading the level of services and hospitality. The classification band is colour-coded as follows: **Burgundy:** Acceptable standard of services and hospitality in addition to the required facilities. **Silver:** Superior services, hospitality, quality and ambience. Each hotel taking part in the scheme will display a plaque indicating the star-rating and the classification band.

GUEST HOUSES/BED & BREAKFAST: The accreditation programme now applies to guest houses and bed & breakfast establishments. There are very few towns that do not offer this type of accommodation. Advance bookings during the summer season (October to April) are becoming essential, especially in the Western Cape region.

SELF-CATERING: Holiday flats, resorts and health spas are available along main routes, notably the Natal/Cape coasts and in Mpumalanga, limpopo and the Drakenberg. **Grading:** The Accreditation and Classification Programme for self-catering accommodation is part of the National Grading and Classification Scheme which was introduced in 1994. Self-catering accommodation is graded **1** to **5 stars** according to the facilities available and the level of services and hospitality. The classification band is split into three levels.

CAMPING/CARAVANNING: There are over 800 camp and caravan sites in the country; camping is not allowed outside of them. Caravan parks are to be found along all the tourist routes in South Africa, particularly at places favoured for recreation and sightseeing. The standard is usually high. Many caravan parks have campsites. A number of companies can arrange motor camper rentals, with a range of fully-equipped vehicles. Full details can be obtained from SATOUR. **Grading:** Camp and caravan sites are classed as self-catering accommodation (see above).

GAME RESERVES: Game reserve rest camps are protected enclosures within the confines of the park. Accommodation is usually in thatched huts known as *rondavels*, or in small cottages. Some camps have air-conditioned accommodation. Most *rondavels* and cottages are self-contained, with private baths and showers, and sometimes kitchens. Some camps have luxury air-conditioned accommodation. Conservation Corporation Africa (CCA) (website: www.ccafrica.com) was founded in 1990 to develop sustainable wildlife reserves, achieved through low-density, high-quality tourism. Its lodges are bywords for luxury and elegance, but equally important is CCA's work to promote biodiversity, invest in the local rural economies and restore land.

FARM HOLIDAYS: There is a wide range of guest farms open to tourists offering stays in various ecological regions. Opportunities exist for adventure activities such as horse riding, mountain-biking and fishing, as well as agricultural activities like bee-keeping and cattle-ranching. Full details can be obtained from SATOUR (see *Contact Addresses* section).

Resorts & Excursions

South Africa is a stunning country of magnificent landscape, from desert dunes to rolling farmlands, savannah bush, subtropical hardwood forests and superb white sand coast. It has game viewing to equal the best in Africa from Kruger in Mpumalanga to the Zululand area of Kwazulu-Natal, and a host of small parks and reserves in the Northern Provinces and Eastern Capes. Where else can you find penguins and elephants living in the same country? There are over 1000 bird species in the country, and the Western Cape alone has one of the richest floral kingdoms in the world, with over 23,000 plant and flower species and spectacular displays that coat the desert in colour. The country also has a fascinating human and cultural history, stretching back to the aboriginal San (Bushmen) and Khoikhoi, through the black African peoples to the latest arrivals, the Afrikaans and British. It has never been an easy history – tribal wars raged long before the punishing and bitter conflicts between black and white, from the Zulu Wars to the Boer War and the segregation of apartheid society. Archbishop Desmond Tutu named the newly integrated South Africa 'the rainbow nation'. It is a fitting name for a country with 11 official languages and people of all colours, race and creed, living in a vividly coloured and sculpted landscape.

THE WESTERN CAPE

This area of outstanding natural and floral beauty, in the southwestern corner of the country, stretches from the remote rocky outcrops beyond Lambert's Bay in the west to the mountains of the southern peninsula. The first area to be colonised by Europeans, it is particularly famous for its wines.

CAPE TOWN: South Africa's legislative capital is situated at the foot of **Table Mountain**, the famous flat-topped mountain with views out across the peninsula to the Atlantic and Indian Oceans. It is possible to walk up, but for the less intrepid, there is an excellent cablecar. The main hub of the city centre is the **Victoria & Alfred Waterfront**, the beautifully restored old Victorian harbour which offers free entertainment, a wide variety of shops, museums - including the excellent **Aquarium -** taverns and restaurants. Boat trips leave from here for harbour tours or the notorious **Robben Island**, where Nelson Mandela and many other nationalist leaders were imprisoned. The relics of early colonial government are centred on Government Avenue, with many fine old buildings and museums, including the **Parliament Buildings**; **Groote Kerk** (mother

church of the Dutch Reformed faith); the **Cultural History Museum**; **National Museum**; **National Gallery**; **Bertram House**; and **Company's Garden**, planted in 1652 to provide food for passing sailors. Nearby sights of interest include **Bo-Kaap** (the home of the Islamic Cape Malay people, confusingly of mainly Indonesian origin); the **Castle of Good Hope** in Darling Street, built in 1666; the **Old Townhouse** on Greenmarket Square, housing a permanent collection of 17th-century Dutch and Flemish paintings; and the early 18th-century **Koopmans de Wet House**.
Those interested in learning more about black and 'Cape-coloured' culture should visit the **District Six Museum**, Buitenkant Street, and take one of the many excellent guided tours of the outlying townships of **Crossroads**, **Langa** and **Khayelitsha**. It is probably not safe for tourists to venture into these areas on their own.
Cape Town also has excellent sporting and shopping facilities. The **Baxter Theatre** and **Artscape Theatre Complex** offer a mix of local and international fare. Nightlife is concentrated in the **V&A Waterfront**, **Sea Point**, and parts of the central business district, notably around Long Street. Further out, the Cape-Dutch homestead of **Spier** and **Ratanga Junction** theme park both offer a variety of entertainment from classical to jazz concerts.
EXCURSIONS: South of Cape Town, a long peninsula stretches south, lined by fishing villages and holiday resorts, including **Fish Hoek**, **Hout Bay**, **Kommetjie**, **Llandudno**, **Muizenberg** and **Simonstown**, a delightful Victorian town with a couple of interesting museums and the only colony of penguins to live on the African mainland. Inland, the magnificent Cape-Dutch farm, **Groot Constantia**, was one of the first wine farms in the Cape, while the **Kirstenbosch National Botanical Gardens**, created by Cecil Rhodes in 1895 on the lower slopes of **Table Mountain**, is one of the finest botanical gardens in the world. In the summer there are open-air concerts. Nearby **Chapman's Peak** has spectacular views, but the scenic drive from **Hout Bay** is currently closed due to landfalls, and you need to walk the last section to the summit.
About one hour's drive from Cape Town, the **Cape of Good Hope Nature Reserve** covers the southern tip of the Cape peninsula, with a profusion of flowers, birds and animals, culminating in **Cape Point**, where the Indian Ocean meets the Atlantic.
THE WINELANDS: North of Cape Town, the winelands are a stunning region of vineyards, old Cape-Dutch villages and mansions. Many of the vineyards have excellent restaurants; most offer tastings and some provide bed and breakfast.
Stellenbosch, a major centre of wine production, is also one of South Africa's oldest villages with a great many attractive buildings, including the excellent **Village Museum**. The local tourist office provides details for a historic walking tour. Tiny **Franschhoek** originally hosted refugee Huguenots from France, who brought their wine-growing skills to South Africa. It now has an excellent **Huguenot Museum**. **Paarl** is home to several small museums and the **KWV Wine Cellars**. In the **Breede Valley** area, the charming little towns of **Tulbagh**, **Worcester**, **Wellington** and **Ceres** all have fine old buildings, interesting small museums, beautiful scenery, vineyards and fruit orchards.
THE WEST COAST: The fertility of the southern Cape region gradually gives way to the rugged and beautiful West Coast, which has abundant shellfish, and numerous fishing villages, including **Lambert's Bay**, a good surfing spot. Inland, the sculpted sandstone **Cederberg** mountains separate the west coast from the arid **Great Karoo Desert**, which bursts into a mass of flowers every October to November.

THE SOUTH COAST AND GARDEN ROUTE

East from Cape Town, the coastal area known as the **Overberg** includes attractive resort towns such as **Somerset West** and **Hermanus**, probably the best place in South Africa for whale watching; **Cape Agulhas**, the less than inspirational cape which is actually the southerly tip of Africa; the wreck-strewn cliffs around **Arniston**; and **Elim**, a 19th-century Mission village whose principal profession is still growing and drying flowers. **Swellendam**, 215km (130 miles) from Cape Town, is a charming Cape-Dutch village, rich in fine old buildings, several of which make up the excellent **Drostdy** Museum.
From here onwards, the south coast becomes known as **The Garden Route** because of the wealth of forests that used to line the coast. There are a couple of areas of hardwood forest left, but even with so much development, this is a wonderful area for holidays, with excellent beaches, good swimming and plenty of activities on offer.
Mossel Bay was one of the first harbours visited by European sailors and the town now has an excellent museum charting the maritime history of the coast.
Wilderness is a pretty little resort sandwiched between the dunes and the reedy lakes of the **Wilderness Natural Reserve**, an excellent place for birdwatching and canoeing.
Knysna is a comfortable tourist town situated between the lush inland Knysna forests and the horseshoe-shaped **Knysna Lagoon**. It has several interesting small museums and a nearby game farm. South Africa's trendiest resort, **Plettenberg Bay**, has magnificent beaches, the **Robberg Nature Reserve**, where you can usually see seals and dolphins and **Monkeyland**, a sanctuary dedicated to primates of all sorts.
An equally beautiful - but startlingly different - route, called the 'inland route', runs parallel to the coast, on the far side of the mountains. This leaves Cape Town via the Winelands, continuing through market gardening towns, such as **Ashton**, **Robertson** and **Montagu**, well known for wine and olives, into the **Little Karoo**, the scrubby extension of the Great Karoo Desert. Most people choose a mix of the two routes: crossing the **Outeniqua** and **Swartberg Mountains** over a series of dramatically beautiful switchback passes, of which the most beautiful is undoubtedly the **Swartberg Pass** to **Prince Alfred**; and the more common **Outeniqua Pass** from **George** to **Oudtshoorn**, famous for its ostrich farms, as well as the **Cango Caves**.

THE EASTERN CAPE

The Eastern Cape is South Africa's hidden gem, much of it little known and underexplored by tourists, but with an extraordinary variety of cultural history and scenic beauty, ranging from the vast, dry Great Karoo to the fertile agricultural lands of the Little Karoo and the 'Settler Country' around **Grahamstown** and, above all, the magnificent cliffs and coves of the Wild Coast. The Eastern Cape is also home to two of the country's major seaports, **East London** and **Port Elizabeth**, and several excellent small game reserves, including **Addo Elephant Park**. The area around East London is the homeland of the Xhosa people, many of whom, including Nelson Mandela, have played a crucial role in recent South African history.
PORT ELIZABETH: 'PE', as the city is known locally, is unremarkable, being dominated by industry and freeways and subject to strong winds for most of the year. The **City Hall** and **Market Square** are worth a visit, containing a replica of the **Dias Cross**, originally placed by the Portuguese navigator Bartholomew Dias. There are several other interesting buildings, including a memorial to Prester John, the **Campanile Clock Tower** and the **Donkin Lighthouse**, while the old part of town, above the city centre, has some attractive Victorian houses. The **Museum**, **Oceanarium** and **Snake Park** are also on the seafront at **Humewood**. The **King George IV Art Gallery & Fine Arts Hall** has an excellent collection of 19th- and 20th-century art and **Castle Hill Museum**, in the city's oldest house, has a fine collection of Cape furniture. **Settler's Park Nature Reserve** at **How Avenue** abounds with indigenous flora and **St George's Park** has open-air exhibitions and craft fairs, as well as theatrical productions. South of the city are good beaches, such as **King's Beach** and **Humewood Beach**. The latter features the **Apple Express**, one of the few remaining narrow-gauge steam trains, which runs on occasion from Humewood to **Thornhill**.
WEST OF PORT ELIZABETH: The Eastern Cape portion of the **Garden Route** (see also *Western Cape*) notably includes the **Tsitsikamma Coastal National Park**, the remnant of a once-massive indigenous forest, home to immense native trees such as yellowwoods. **Jeffreys Bay** is a world-renowned surfer's paradise. Heading north, miles and miles of sandy beaches run all the way up the coast. The **Alexandria State Forest** is a reserve that runs along the coast and contains a hiking trail along the beach. East from here is **Dias Cross**, the location of one of Bartholomew Dias' stone crosses and a desolate paradise for beach lovers.
Inland, the Karoo is a vast and beautiful upland area with spectacular sunsets: drier, hotter and colder than the coasts. The novelist Olive Schreiner made the area famous and her house at **Cradock** has been restored. The **Mountain Zebra National Park** is worth a visit, on the northern slopes of the **Bankberg range**.
The **Addo Elephant National Park**, 72km (45 miles) north of Port Elizabeth, was created in 1931 to protect the last of the eastern Cape elephants. Recently massively expanded, it offers an excellent range of game, including black rhino, buffalo and antelope and more than 170 bird species. There are also several private reserves nearby, including the excellent **Shamwari** and **Kwandwe**, both of which have very upmarket accommodation and 'Big Five' (elephant, lion, leopard, rhino and buffalo) game viewing.
The town of **Graaff-Reinet**, situated in the heart of the **Karoo Nature Reserve** at the foot of the **Sneeuberg Mountains**, is one of the finest surviving Cape-Dutch towns in South Africa, with many attractive 18th- and 19th-century buildings, as well as parks and museums. Just 5km (3 miles) outside the town, it is possible for visitors to drive into the **Valley of Desolation** along a twisting single-track road that eventually climbs into the mountains. From the viewpoints, it is possible to look down over Graaff-Reinet across towering red and ochre outcrops of rock. The nearby town of **Nieu Bethesda** is worth a visit for the **Owl House**, a remarkable sculpture garden by eccentric artist Helen Martins, subject of a play by Athol Fugard.

Credit: © South African Tourism

SETTLER COUNTRY

East of Port Elizabeth, **Kenton-on-Sea** and **Port Alfred** are pretty little holiday towns, the latter on the mouth of the **Kowie River** - canoeing trips can be undertaken from Port Alfred to **Bathurst**, home of **The Pig and Whistle**, the oldest pub in South Africa (1831).
A short distance inland, Victorian **Grahamstown** is home to one of South Africa's best universities and hosts a giant annual arts festival each July. The town has many fine buildings, amongst which the most interesting are the **Cathedral of St Michael and St George**, situated in the triangular **Church Square**, the 1820 **Settlers Monument** (after the first British to settle the area), **Fort Selwyn**, and rows of shops and houses on Church Square, **Artificers' Square**, **Hill Street** and **MacDonald Street**. The town also has several excellent museums, including the **Albany Museum**, **History Museum**, **Natural Sciences Museum** and the **International Library of African Music**. Local development projects offer traditional Xhosa meals.
Fort Hare University, in the nearby town of **Alice**, was the country's first black university, founded in 1916. **King William's Town** is not only a fine Victorian town, with many beautiful houses and the excellent **Kaffrarian Museum**, but is the birth and burial place of nationalist leader, Steve Biko.
One hour's drive from Grahamstown is the village of **Hogsback**, situated in the striking **Amatola Mountains**. It is an ideal place to walk in the forest of yellowwood, stinkwood and Cape chestnut trees along trails to magical waterfalls – the most spectacular being the aptly-named **Bridal Veil** and **Madonna and Child**.
EAST LONDON AND THE WILD COAST: East London, built on the mouth of the **Buffalo River**, is not only South Africa's fourth-largest port, but a popular seaside resort with a subtropical climate, fine beaches and some of the best surfing in South Africa. There is excellent swimming at **Eastern Beach**, **Nahoon Beach** and **Orient Beach**. The city is not particularly pretty, but it does have some interesting museums and monuments - notably, the **East London Museum** (with the world's only Dodo egg and a stuffed coelacanth); the **Gately House Museum**, built in 1878; the **Anne Bryant Art Gallery**, with an interesting collection of contemporary South African art; an excellent **Aquarium**; fine **Botanical Gardens**; 19th-century **Fort Glamorgan**; and the **Hood Point Lighthouse**. **Latimer's Landing** has a wide range of good shops and restaurants.
Heading west, the **Wild Coast**'s history (as a black 'homeland') and lack of roads have left it gloriously undeveloped. This is a spectacularly beautiful area of wild cliffs and hidden coves, many parts of it inaccessible to normal vehicles. The main road runs inland through the Eastern Cape's uninspiring capital, **Umtata**, with occasional dirt roads winding down to the water's edge. Nelson Mandela was born in and has retired to **Qunu**, 34km (20 miles) west of Umtata on the East London road.
The main tourist town in the area is **Port St Johns**, the closest thing South Africa has to a hippy hangout. Both here and at various coves and rivermouths along the coast are small, hideaway lodges perfect for those who want to relax or fish away from the crowds. Just before the Kwazulu-Natal Border, the **Wild Coast Sun**, with its casino

and waterpark, is an abrupt introduction to the more developed coast near Durban.
To the north is the southern end of the **Drakensberg Mountains**. South Africa's only ski resort, **Tiffendel**, is near the small village of **Rhodes**, where trout fishing, hiking and pony-trekking are all possible.

KWAZULU-NATAL

Perhaps the most diverse province in South Africa, KwaZulu-Natal contains approximately one-quarter of the South African population and ranges from semi-tropical and tropical coastlands to snow-capped peaks in the Drakensberg. In an otherwise arid country, it has the same rainfall as the United Kingdom.
DURBAN: Growing at an alarming rate, Durban is South Africa's third-largest city, a mix of cultures including a large Indian community and a new influx of Africans from countries to the north. Because of the almost tropical climate, swimming is possible all year round, although the city's beaches are becoming increasingly crowded. The central beach area, called the **Golden Mile**, actually stretches for 6km (4 miles) from the **Umgeni River** to the Point. Along it are a wide variety of souvenir stalls and family entertainments, from the excellent **u'Shaka** (aquarium) to funfairs, a **snake park** and mini-golf. This stretch has also increasingly become a target for muggers, and there are safer and quieter beaches north and south. Colonial Durban has its heart in **Francis Farewell Square**, surrounded by a number of fine Victorian and Edwardian buildings, including the **City Hall** (which now contains the **Natural Science Museum** and **Durban Art Gallery**, featuring a fine collection of black South African art and craft). Not far away is the **African Arts Centre**, where much local art is for sale. To the north is **Central Park**. To the west of the centre is the **Indian District**, characterised by markets, mosques, temples and well-preserved buildings from the turn of the century, including the **Juma Musjid Mosque**. At the other end of the **Madressa Arcade** is the **Emmanuel Cathedral**. To the north is the **Victoria Street Market**, filled with spices, curios and fresh produce.
To the north, the **Botanical Gardens** offer cool respite. The other major attractions of Durban lie along the **Victoria Embankment** and beyond, and include the **Yacht Mole**, the **Ocean Terminal Building** (relic of the age of sea travel) and the **Sugar Terminal**, the nexus of KwaZulu-Natal's massive sugar industry. Further out west is the suburb of **Cato Manor**, a fascinating mix of shanties and temples including the **Shree Alayam Second River Hindu Temple**, which has a firewalking festival in autumn. Scattered around the town and suburbs are several other interesting small museums, such as the **Killie Campbell Collection**, an excellent African cultural collection in an old Cape-Dutch mansion, the little **Kwamuhle Museum** of local 20th-century history, the **Natal Maritime Museum** and the **Old Court House**.
EXCURSIONS: Inland: Just north of Durban, the **Valley of a Thousand Hills** is a popular excursion for locals, with plenty of bijou shops and tearooms; the **Assagay Safari Park** and **Phezulu** are basic, child-friendly places offering a crocodile farm, snake park, children's zoo and Zulu dancing. The **Paradise Valley Nature Reserve** is a wonderful place to walk off the beaten track.
THE SOUTH COAST: South of Durban a series of beach resorts, including **Amanzimtoti**, **Scottsburgh**, **Port Shepstone** and **Margate**, have run together to create a ribbon of fun, sea and sand aimed at the family market, with plenty of timeshares, self-catering apartments and fast food. Things to do include a crocodile farm, the **Banana Express railway** and the **Oribi Gorge Nature Reserve**, a scenic collection of forests and steep gorges leading down to the beach, covered in dense forest. The offshore **Aliwal Shoal** and **Protea Banks** are some of the best dive sites in South Africa.
THE NORTH COAST: North of Durban is a similar string of slightly more upmarket resorts. **Umhlanga Rocks** is the home of the **Natal Sharks Board**, which offers audiovisual presentations and shark dissections to those with a taste for gore. **Ballito** offers a wide range of water and land sports, while just to the north, 19th-century Zulu king, Shaka, used to throw his enemies off the cliff at **Shaka's Rock**. Other small towns in the area include **Salt Rock**, which has a small crocodile farm, **Crocodile Creek**, the sugar-cane community of **Tongaat**, and Shaka's capital, **Stanger**, home to an interesting small museum.
THE MIDLANDS AND DRAKENSBERG: Between Natal's coast and the mountains, there is an area of undulating wooded hills and grassy plains with scattered villages and lush farmland, known as the **Natal Midlands**. There are a number of small game reserves with a huge variety of animal and bird life in the Midlands and the foothills of the Drakensberg, while local rivers offer excellent fishing.
Pietermaritzburg, joint state capital (with Ulundi) is the largest city in the area. Although founded by the Voortrekkers, the town's architectural heritage is mostly Victorian, best seen in the area around Church Street. There are several excellent museums including the **Natal Museum**, **Macrorie House Museum**, **Tatham Art Gallery** and **Voortrekker Museum**. The city is particularly attractive in September when the azaleas are in bloom. The **Botanic Gardens** enable visitors to look at a range of indigenous flora. Within easy reach of Pietermaritzburg are the **Howick Falls**, the **Karkloof Falls** and the **Albert Falls Public Resort and Nature Reserve**.
The Drakensberg is South Africa's largest mountain range and the official southern end of the Great Rift Valley, which slices north across Africa for 6000km (3728 miles). Its name, which means 'Dragon Mountains' in Afrikaans, stems from the jagged backbone of saw-toothed peaks. It is a refreshing place with cold mountain streams shaded by ferns and ancient yellowwood trees. The mountains are capped with snow in winter. The area provides good walking, climbing and riding while the peaks are the realm of eagles and bearded vultures. Popular climbs include **Champagne Castle**, **Cathkin Peak** and **Cathedral Peak**.
In the nearby caves are good examples of the rock art of the Bushmen who, until a century ago, inhabited the area. The **Main Caves**, in the **Giant's Castle Game Reserve**, boast more than 500 rock paintings in a single shelter. The reserve, which flanks the border with Lesotho, is dominated by a massive basalt wall incorporating the peaks of **Giant's Castle** (3314m/10,873ft) and **Injasuti** (3459m/11,349ft) and is home to eland, other antelope and a variety of birds, including Cape vulture, jackal buzzard, black eagle and lammergeier.
Just to the north, the **Royal Natal National Park** is one of Natal's most stunning reserves. Its dramatic scenery includes the **Amphitheatre**, an 8km- (5 mile-) long crescent-shaped curve in the main basalt wall. It is flanked by two impressive peaks, the **Sentinel** (3165m/10,384ft) and the **Eastern Buttress** (3047m/9997ft). Even higher is **Mont-aux-Sources** at 3284m (10,775ft). It is the source of the **Tugela River** which plummets 2000m (6562ft) over the edge of the plateau. Hikers should enjoy following the spectacular **Tugela Gorge**.
THE BATTLEFIELDS: The northern part of KwaZulu-Natal is mainly rolling grassland, spiked by occasional rocky *kopjies* (hills) which became the bloody frontline in a whole series of wars between the Zulus, Afrikaans and British (1830–1902).
Ladysmith was the site of a devastating siege during the Anglo-Boer War. The **Town Hall** still shows the scars, while the old **Market Hall** next door is an excellent **Siege Museum**. Behind it, the **Cultural Centre** is dedicated to local cultures and heroes, including former World Boxing Champion, Sugarboy Malinga, and the band, *Ladysmith Black Mambazo*.
There is another excellent museum, the **Talana Museum**, in **Dundee**, site of the first battle of the Boer War. This is also the best place from which to visit **Isandlwana**, **Fugitive's Drift** and **Rorkes Drift**, where a devastating series of battles between the British and Zulus in January 1879 led to the desperate defence of Rorke's Drift mission station by a garrison of 139. Before the battle began, 35 were already wounded. It resulted in the most Victoria Crosses in a single engagement in the history of British warfare and was filmed as *Zulu*, starring Michael Caine. The mission is now an interpretive and arts centre. Also nearby is the battlefield of **Blood River**, scene of a famous victory by the Afrikaaners over the Zulus in 1838.
Further east, the little Afrikaaner town of **Vryheid** (Freedom) was founded in 1884. Today, it is still a pretty little town, with three small museums, the **Lukas Meijer House**, the **Old Carnegie Library** and the **Nieuwe Republiek Museum**. Three major battles of the Anglo-Zulu War were fought nearby.
Just to the south, little-known, but game-rich, **Itala Game Reserve** (29,653 ha/73,243 acres) has spectacular golden grasslands, rocky kopjes and wooded valleys and is home to all major species except lion.
ZULULAND: In the mid-19th century, the **Tugela River** formed the boundary between British Natal and Zululand. **Eshowe** ('the sound of wind in the trees'), now a pretty little farming town, has a Zulu royal pedigree. **Fort Nongqayi** (1883) is now the **Zululand Historical Museum**, while the **Vukani Museum** has the world's largest collection of traditional Zulu arts and crafts. The 200 hectare (494 acre) **Dhlinza Forest** is a small but beautiful patch of indigenous hardwood forest.
In the nearby hills are several Zulu cultural villages, including **Shakaland**, **Pobane**, **KwaBhekithunga**, **Stewart's Farm** and **Simunye**, all providing food and accommodation, a tour of a village, discussion of lifestyle and medicine and dance displays. North of the little market town of **Melmoth**, **Mgungundlovu** ('the place of the great elephant') was the capital of King Dingane (c.1795–1843). The city was destroyed by the Afrikaans, but has now been partially rebuilt as a museum. **Ulundi**, joint capital of KwaZulu-Natal and still home of the Zulu monarchy, has relatively little for the tourist, but the site of the former royal capital, **Ondini**, is now the fascinating **KwaZulu Cultural Museum**.
Much of the northerly part of KwaZulu-Natal is made up of a series of interlinked public and private game reserves that together form one of Africa's finest concentrations of wildlife. In addition, it has a startlingly beautiful coast, with silver sand beaches (shared with turtles), vast sand dunes and offshore coral reefs. The 38,682 hectare (95,545 acre) **Greater St Lucia Wetland Reserve** is a loose collection of wilderness areas around Lake St Lucia, including **Mapelane**, the **St Lucia Game Reserve**, **False Bay Park**, **Sodwana Bay National Park**, **Cape Vidal State Forest**, **Sodwana State Forest**, **St Lucia Marine Reserve** (stretching 5km/3 miles out to sea), the **Maputaland Marine Reserve**, and the **Mkuzi Game Reserve**. It covers five distinct ecosystems varying from dry thorn scrub to tropical forest and bordered by giant dunes, beaches and tropical reefs, has 'Big Five' game viewing, and is the only place in the world where hippos, crocodiles and sharks share the same lagoon. It also has superb birdwatching and diving and, outside the National Park, excellent fishing.
The 96,000 hectare (237,120 acre) **Hluhluwe-Umfolozi National Park** offers a broad range of habitats, from rocky hillside to open savannah grass and thick woodland, supporting some 86 species of mammal and around 425 recorded bird species. This is the Eden of almost all white rhinos in the world, thanks to a carefully controlled breeding programme that has restocked much of the rest of Africa. Between here and St Lucia is the privately owned 17,000 hectare (42,000 acre) **Phinda Resource Reserve**.
In the far north, near the Mozambique border, Lake Sibaya is the largest natural freshwater lake in southern Africa (77 sq km/30 sq miles), offering good bird watching, fishing and hiking. Beyond this, are the **Ndumo** and **Tembe Game Reserves**, with excellent wildlife, including a large rhino population and a variety of birds, and the magnificent coastal and marine **Kosi Bay Nature Reserve**; access is by 4-wheel-drive only.

FREE STATE

The central Free State metamorphoses from grassland interspersed with small granite outcrops in the west to magnificent sandstone hills in the east.
The capital of this province is **Bloemfontein**, an imposing but unattractive town which has some surprisingly good museums, including the **National Museum**, the old **Fourth Raadsaal** (parliament) of the old Free State Republic, the **National Afrikaans Literary Museum**, and the **Oliewenhuis Art Gallery**. By far the most interesting is the **National Women's Memorial and War Museum**, telling the chilling story of the Boer War and the British concentration camps (where 26,370 women and children died) from the Afrikaans perspective.
Outside Bloemfontein, the southern Free State is home to the **Gariep Dam**, a massive 374 sq km (144 sq miles) reservoir, built for irrigation and hydroelectric power. However, the State's most interesting scenery lies in the eastern highlands, on the Lesotho border. From Bloemfontein, hills rise steadily as one heads past **Thaba'nchu**, the old seat of the Basotho kings, to **Ladybrand**, the main route into Lesotho. North from here are **Ficksburg**, which has an annual cherry festival in spring and the new-age settlement of **Rustler's Valley**, which hosts an annual music festival in autumn. Further to the northeast is the **Golden Gate National Park**, verging on the KwaZulu-Natal Drakensberg, characterised by massive weathered sandstone cliffs tinted a multitude of shades of red, yellow and orange.

MPUMALANGA

Mpumalanga (the 'land of the rising sun') covers the highveld plains and mountains from Gauteng to the borders with Swaziland and Mozambique. This is one of the key tourist destinations in South Africa, home, with Limpopo, to the world-famous **Kruger National Park**, a massive reserve the size of Wales and among the best places in Africa to see the 'Big Five', as well as thousands of other species. The park features a wide range of accommodation, from camping (in fenced enclosures to keep lions out) to self-catering huts and cottages.
Surrounding the park, in a series of linked game reserves called **Sabie Sand**, **Manyeleti**, **Klaserie**, **Timbavati** and the **Umbabat**, there are numerous private concessions, less crowded but considerably more expensive than the National Parks camps. These small, luxury camps provide vehicles and guides, and offer facilities such as walks, night drives and off-road game-spotting not allowed within the park proper. As animals wander freely throughout the area, the game viewing is as good as in the main park.
THE ESCARPMENT: The other main area of interest to tourists is the escarpment just to the west of the Kruger boundary. This marks the edge of the African continental plateau with a series of dramatic mountains and plunging cliffs. The road along the rim of the escarpment provides spectacular views of the landscape below, including **The Pinnacle**, a massive, free-standing granite column; **God's Window**, a viewing point over the Lowveld 1000m (3300ft) below; Lisbon Falls and Berlin Falls. It then turns to run along the rim of the **Blyde Canyon** (26km/16 miles long

and 350-800m/1050-2400ft deep), passing **Bourke's Luck Potholes**, a series of strange rock formations created by the swirling action of pebble-laden flood water. There is a spectacular five-day hiking trail along the canyon called the **Blyderivierspoort Hiking Trail**, beginning at God's Window.
The surrounding area has several attractive market towns, such as **Sabie**, situated against the backdrop of **Mauchsberg** and **Mount Anderson**, with an abundance of waterfalls and wild flowers; **Graskop**, a forestry village perched on a spur of the Drakensberg escarpment; and **Pilgrim's Rest**, a gold-rush town with many historic buildings. Nearby, the **Mount Sheba Nature Reserve** embraces 1500 hectare (3705 acres) of ravines and waterfalls. **Nelspruit**, the provincial capital, features the **Lowveld National Botanical Gardens** on the banks of the **Crocodile River**, specialising in Cycads, as well as other semi-tropical Lowveld vegetation.
LIMPOPO (FORMERLY NORTHERN PROVINCE): This province is bordered by Botswana and Zimbabwe to the North and Mozambique to the east, and contains a large section of the Kruger National Park (see the *Mpumalanga* section). This northern section is generally drier and has far fewer tourists than the southern section but still has excellent game viewing. Access is via the copper-mining town of **Phalaborwa**, which has some interesting prehistoric sites, or **Hoedspruit**, home of the **Moholoholo Wildlife Rehabilitation Centre and Cheetah Project**.
Just west of the park, the Letaba area is a lush green farming district with excellent walking, riding and bird-watching amongst the tea plantations and **Magoeboeskloof Mountains**. To the north of Letaba, near the Zimbabwe border, are **Venda** and **Gazankulu**, largely rural peasant communities with a reputation for arts and crafts. The mystical South African artist Jackson Hlungwane, who has pieces of his remarkable sculpture in South African and European galleries, is based here. This is also the home of the Rain Queen, said to have been Rider Haggard's inspiration for *She*, and the **Modjadji Forest**, the world's largest collection of cycads (50-million-year-old palms).
In the west, the **Waterberg mountains** and the **Soutpansberg** provide excellent opportunities for hiking, riding and nature watching, and there are several private game ranches in the area.
In the far south, near the Gauteng border, **Warmbaths** unsurprisingly contains warm mineral springs. In the centre of the province are **Polokwane** (formerly Pietersburg), the provincial capital, notable for the **Bakone Malapa Museum**, and **Potgietersrus**, an attractive old Afrikaaner town, with a rare breeds breeding centre.

GAUTENG

The economic hub of South Africa, Gauteng means 'place of gold' in Sotho. Built on the gold reefs, it is heavily urban, containing the cities of Johannesburg, Pretoria and a scattering of satellite towns, many of them heavily industrial.
JOHANNESBURG AND SOWETO: The discovery of gold near Johannesburg in 1886 turned a small shanty town into the bustling modern city that is today the centre of the world's gold-mining industry and the commercial nucleus of South Africa. The city is currently undergoing a fundamental transformation as planners in the post-apartheid era struggle to integrate wealthy 'white' areas to the north, a decaying inner city, and the poverty-stricken 'black' townships to the south. The city is, as well as being a potentially dangerous place to live and stroll about, the cultural centre of South Africa, with a post-apartheid influx of traders from the north enhancing its cosmopolitan character.
The **Central Business District** (CBD) is characterised by a stark contrast of skyscrapers and bustling street markets; most businesses catering to affluent clients have moved out to the northern suburbs. A spectacular view of the city is available from the **Observatory** on the 50th floor of the **Carlton Centre**. To the west, of some historical interest, is the **Rand Club**, haunt of mining magnates past and present. Also west of the centre, **Newtown** has been the focus of an urban renewal project which includes the excellent **Museum Africa**, several excellent restaurants, the **Market Theatre**, a famous centre of alternative theatre during the apartheid era and after; and the **South African Breweries' Centenary Centre**. More mainstream theatre, music and dance can be seen at the Civic Theatre in **Braamfontein**, also the location of the **Gertrude Posel Gallery**, one of many small, university-run museums, housing a collection of traditional African art.
Just outside the centre is **Hillbrow**, home to, amongst others, large communities of immigrants from the rest of Africa; a landmark is the massive **Ponti** building, dubbed 'petit Kinshasa' by locals. To the north of the CBD lies **Yeoville**, more bohemian and considerably safer. The centre of Yeoville life is **Rockey Street**, lined with cafes and bars where visitors can while away the days in relative peace.
The north of Johannesburg consists of affluent leafy suburbs. Directly north of the city centre, **Parktown** was

Credit: © South African Tourism

the home of the so-called 'Randlords', the 19th-century Gold Rush millionaires, whose houses are still an imposing sight. Nearby is a series of wonderful open spaces containing notable landmarks, such as the **Johannesburg Zoo**, **Zoo Lake** (across the road) and the **South African National Museum of Military History**. North of this are **Rosebank**, teeming with upmarket bars, restaurants and shops; and **Sandton**, probably the wealthiest part of Johannesburg and to all intents and purposes, now the city centre.
Excursions: To the south is the city's only amusement park, **Gold Reef City**, built on the site of a gold mine, with underground tours as part of the attraction.
Soweto, the massive black 'township' to the south, is home to some 4.5 million of the province's poorest people, and also to many *shebeens* (informal bars) and thousands of churches representing hundreds of mainline and independent African denominations. The safest way to visit Soweto is as part of an organised tour. Tourists are welcome and there is plenty to see. As well as shebeens and music venues, tours include visits to nationalist landmarks such as **Freedom Square**, used for rallies, the **Hector Peterson Memorial**, dedicated to the first child to die in the uprisings, and **Nelson and Winnie Mandela's home**, now a small museum.
Further afield, **Heidelberg** is a small town with an interesting **Transport Museum**. North of Sandton, are the **Johannesburg Lion Park**, **Snake Park**, **Rhino and Lion Nature Reserve** and **Lesedi Cultural Village**.
Sterkfontein, in the Magaliesberg mountains, is home to the **Wonder Caves**, one of the world's most important prehistoric sites; 2.5 million-year-old *Australopithecus africanus* was first discovered here.

PRETORIA

Named after the *Voortrekker* leader Andries Pretorius, the town council recently discussed proposals to change the name to Tshwane and award the town city status. Pretoria is the administrative capital of South Africa, known as the 'Jacaranda City' because of the flowering trees lining its streets in October and November. **Church Square** is the centre of the city, and a space of historical importance, while Church Street and its neighbours are lined by some fine 19th-century buildings including **Paul Kruger's House**, the **Groote Kerk**, **Melrose House**, the old **Raadsaal** (parliament) of the Boer republic of Transvaal, and the **State Theatre**, which features a programme of fairly mainstream dance, music and drama. There are also several excellent small museums in the city, including the **Pretoria Art Museum**, the studios of local artists' Coert Steynberg and Anton von Wouw, now both museums, the **Museum of Science and Technology** and the bizarre but fascinating **Correctional Services Museum**.
The **Union Buildings**, overlooking the suburb of **Arcadia**, are one of the pinnacles of British Imperial architecture, designed by Sir Herbert Baker. They are still the administrative seat of the national government and are famous as the site of Nelson Mandela's 1994 inauguration as President. A little further out, the **Voortrekker Monument** is an imposing granite tower built to commemorate the Boer victory over the Zulus at Blood River. Not politically correct these days, it is still a solemn and moving monument, and the little museum beside it is fascinating. **Pretoria Zoo** is definitely worth a visit and has a cable car for a bird's eye view of the big cats.
EXCURSIONS: Just out of town, within easy day-trip distance, are several exceptional sights, including the **De Wildt Cheetah Farm**; **Cullinan Diamond Mine** (book ahead if you want to do the tour); **Pioneer Museum** and **Willem Prinsloo Agricultural Museum** (both 'living' museums with costume-clad characters and displays of farming activities); and two fine old houses, the homes of former president, Jan Smuts, and randlord Sammy Marks.
NORTH-WEST PROVINCE: This province's most famous feature is **Sun City**, gamblers' mecca and host to major golf tournaments and star-studded concerts. Its most spectacular hotel, **The Lost City**, is an H Rider Haggard-like fantasy. Adjacent, the **Pilansberg Game Reserve** covers around 137,000 hectares (338,540 acres). Several farms and an extinct volcanic crater were included in one of the largest rehabilitation exercises ever carried out. This is now an excellent 'Big Five' reserve and the third-largest game park in South Africa. In the far north of the province, on the Botswana border, is the excellent, little known **Madikwe National Park**, which offers excellent walking safaris.
South from Sun City are **Rustenberg**; the **Rustenburg Nature Reserve**, in the **Magaliesberg**, which features antelope and other game, as well as some rare birds of prey such as the black eagle and Cape vulture; and two fairly large and very dull towns, **Klerksdorp** and **Potchefstroom**, the latter home to one of the oldest Afrikaaner universities in South Africa.

THE NORTHERN CAPE

This vast and barren wilderness stretches from the west coast north to the Namibian and Botswana borders and east to the Free State and North-West provinces. The southwest features spectacular carpets of wild flowers in early spring, while the south is part of the Great Karoo and the north intrudes into the **Kalahari Desert**.
In 1866, a boy found a shiny 'pebble' at **Hopetown**, 128km (80 miles) south of Kimberley, allowing a primitive and sparsely populated settlement to become the diamond capital of the world. **Kimberley** is not one of the world's most exciting places, but it does have enough attractions to warrant a stop, chief amongst them the **Big Hole**, which is the largest manmade excavation in the world, and the **Kimberley Mine Museum**, with its replicas of 19th-century Kimberley at the height of the gold rush. The **De Beers Hall Museum** houses a display of cut and uncut diamonds; here can be seen the famous '616' – at 616 carats, the largest uncut diamond in the world – and the 'Eureka' diamond, the first to be discovered in South Africa. Other interesting museums include the **William Humphreys Art Gallery** (fine art), **Duggan-Cronin Gallery** (photography) and **McGregor Museum** (a fine old mansion, with Kimberley's history displayed).
Near Kimberley is the **Vaalbos National Park**, a small reserve containing the extremely rare Black Rhino, and the **Bultfontein Mine**, offering guided tours of a working diamond mine. For those with a military bent, **Magersfontein** lies to the south of Kimberley, site of a catastrophic defeat inflicted on the British by the Boers early in the Boer War.
Northwest of Kimberley, **Kuruman** was a missionary centre used by Robert Moffat and David Livingstone. It has a gushing spring known as the **'Eye of God'** and is near the **Wonderwerk Cave**, an archaeological site of great importance where some of the earliest evidence of the use of fire has been found.
Uppington is a pleasant town on the banks of the **Orange River**, on the way to the **Augrabies National Park**,

centred on a series of dramatic waterfalls plummeting 56m (184ft) into a narrow ravine carved through the desert. The park is home to many interesting species of desert plants while local animals include baboons, vervet monkeys, rhino and antelope.
Further to the north is the vast **Kgalagadi Transfrontier Park**, which is one of Africa's first 'peace parks', administered jointly by South Africa and Botswana. It is the largest nature conservation area in southern Africa and one of the largest unspoilt ecosystems in the world, supporting fauna and flora in bewildering variety. To the west, **Namaqualand** is a vast area of seemingly barren semi-desert, harbouring a treasure-house of floral beauty, appearing after sufficient winter rains: daisies, aloes, lilies, perennial herbs and many other flower species. The flowers are best seen from July to September, depending on when the rains fall. **Calvinia** and **Niewoudtville** are good locations for flowers.
In the far north, on the Namibian border, is the remote and rocky **Richtersveld National Park**, accessible only by 4-wheel drive, with an extraordinary lunar landscape and wide variety of rare desert plants.

Sport & Activities

Wildlife safaris: South Africa's wildlife sanctuaries generally fall into three categories: nature parks, private game reserves and national game reserves. Nature parks are noted more for their scenic beauty and hiking trails than for wildlife. Private game reserves offer a personalised game-viewing programme, while national game reserves are generally explored by tourists in their own vehicles. Further information can be found in the *Resorts & Excursions* section. Besides game viewing from **vehicles**, **walking**, **horseback**, **camel** and **canoeing safaris** are becoming increasingly popular. Safaris on foot follow a network of wilderness trails in the (compulsory) company of an armed ranger. A maximum of eight people between the ages of 12 and 60 may participate per trail (which usually lasts for three nights and two days, with accommodation in designated camps). For reservations and further information, contact the South African National Parks Board (tel: (12) 428 9111; fax: (12) 426 5500; e-mail: reservations@sanparks.org; website: www.sanparks.org); *or* the Wildlife and Environment Society of Southern Africa (tel: (33) 330 3931; fax: (33) 330 4576; e-mail: alisonk@futurenet.co.za; website: www.wildlifesociety.org.za).
Walking and hiking: Nature parks offer marked self-guided trails (with sleeping huts en route) or guided off-the-beaten-track trails (with an experienced, armed ranger providing information about ecology, plants and animals). Some operators also offer **themed walks** with a focus on, for instance, flowers (of which South Africa has nearly 24,000 species). Spectacular flower displays can be seen during August/September in the semi-desert area of Namaqualand.
Wine routes: South Africa's 13 major wine-producing regions have signposted wine routes, of which the best include the *Stellenbosch Wine Route* (the country's first, with all wineries situated within a 12km-/7.5 mile-radius of Stellenbosch); the *Olifants Wine Route* (200km/125 miles long, passing through the Cederberg Mountains, the unspoilt West Coast and Knersvlakte); the *Klein Karoo Wine Trust* (a 300km-/188mile-route through the eastern Cape Winelands); the *Swartland Wine Route* (a 40-minute drive away from Cape Town); the *Orange River Wine Trust* (comprising the northern wine-making regions, irrigated by the Orange, Vaal and Riet rivers); and the *Robertson Valley* (a two-hour drive from Cape Town, known particularly for Chardonnay). Regional wine maps and further details are available from the South African Tourism Board (see *Contact Addresses* section).
Watersports: South Africa has recently gained a reputation for **whale watching** and **shark-cage diving** (with great white sharks) on the Cape. Sharks migrate through the Cape's *False Bay* from June to August and move into the Durban area (KwaZulu-Natal) from October to January. For whale watching fans, the Western Cape Tourism Board has established a *Cape Whale Route* to observe southern right whales, which usually swim very close to the shore. The best time to spot them is from June to September, especially in *Walker Bay*, where a *Whale Festival* is held annually during the last week of September. South Africa's **diving** infrastructure and facilities are well developed. Reef diving is popular in *Sodwana Bay* (on the northern coast of KwaZulu-Natal), while wreck diving is widespread around the Cape. The *Tsitsikamma Coastal Park* offers excellent opportunities for **underwater photography**. Diving certificates are required.
Fishing: One of the country's most popular sports, fishing can be practised along the coast or on the lakes and rivers in the game and nature reserves. One of the world's richest fishing grounds lies around the Cape of Good Hope, where the Atlantic and Indian Ocean currents meet and large shoals of tuna and swordfish draw increasing numbers of **game fishing** enthusiasts. The major **trout fishing** areas are the southern mountain ranges of the Western Cape and the foothills of the Drakensberg Mountains (in KwaZulu-Natal). **Fly fishing** is best in the mountain streams and along the coastline of the Eastern Cape. One highlight on South Africa's fishing calendar is the *Sardine Run*, in June, along the KwaZulu-Natal coast, where hordes of feeding game fish and sharks concentrate.
Golf: South Africa has around 500 courses, often situated in spectacular locations. The best time to play is in the cooler months from May to September. Green fees average £10-20 and a caddie costs around £7. Visitors are welcome on weekdays.
Steam trains: South Africa is one of the few remaining countries where steam locomotives are still widely used. They range from the luxury *Pride of Africa* to small engines on narrow gauge railways like the *Midmar Steam Railway* near Pietermaritzburg. For those looking for a scenic ride, the famous *Outeniqua Choo-Tjoe* runs along the Garden Route on a day-trip from George and Knysna and the Union Limited crosses the famous Kaaimans River Bridge, one of the most photographed railway bridges in the world.
Adventure sports: A changing range of adventure sports is available, the most famous of which probably remains **bungee jumping**, for which South Africa has one of the world's highest drops – the bridge over the Blaukrans River, Western Cape. At 216m (709ft), this jump is more than twice as high as the jump of the bridge linking Zambia and Zimbabwe across the Zambezi River near Victoria Falls.
Spectator sports: South Africans are ardent sports enthusiasts and the success of national teams has been a source of pride and reconciliation for all sections of the community. The South African **rugby** team are world class, the **football** team is one of the best in Africa, while the **cricket** team has proved it is the equal of any in the world. Visitors are made welcome at all these fixtures.

Social Profile

FOOD & DRINK: A thriving agricultural sector yields excellent fresh produce, meat, fruit and wines and the long coastline produces very fresh and cheap seafood. Oysters and linefish (examples of which are Kingklip, Kabbeljou, Cob and Red Roman) are particularly good. Typical South African dishes include *sosaties* (a type of kebab), *bobotie* (a curried mince dish, of which *waterbolmmetjiebredie*, made with a local water plant, is particularly good), *bredies* (meat, tomato and vegetable casseroles), crayfish (or rock lobster) and many other seafood dishes traditional to the Western Cape province. Curries and chutneys are excellent. *Biltong* (seasoned dried meat) is a savoury speciality. *Potjiekos*, a casserole cooked for hours in an iron pot, usually outside, is excellent. *Stywepap* or *Poetoepap*, a sort of polenta made with white maize, is widely eaten with meat. Although there is a wide choice of self-service restaurants, most have table service.
There are excellent local red and white wines, sherries, brandies and some unusual liqueurs. Beer is also very good. Shebeens offer *Umqombothi*, a home-brewed sorghum beer. Bars/cocktail lounges have bartender service. 'Liquor stores' are open weekdays 0900-1800 and Sat 0900-1300, although alcohol is now available in supermarkets outside these hours and under certain circumstances on a Sunday. One can generally buy alcohol at shebeens at any time.
NIGHTLIFE: Cinemas show a variety of international films. In the large cities, there are regular plays, operas and symphony concerts. The local music scene is thriving, and there is a unique South African 'township' jazz style, exponents of which can be seen in all large cities. There are a number of nightclubs and discos open until late. The large hotels usually have live music or cabaret.
SHOPPING: Upmarket boutiques and supermarkets generally coexist with a mass of street traders selling arts, crafts and anything else profitable. Stores are modern. Special purchases include Swakara hand-crafted gold, coats, gold, diamond and semi-precious stone jewellery, leather, suede and fur goods, ceramics and crafts, of which there are now a bewildering variety including many from the rest of the continent. Local wine, brandy and liqueur are cheap and usually excellent. **Shopping hours:** Mon-Fri 0900-1700, Sat 0900-1400, although there is an increasing trend to open later and all weekend in major tourist spots.
SPECIAL EVENTS: For further details, contact South African Tourism (see *Contact Addresses* section). The following is a selection of special events occurring in South Africa in 2005:
Mar 26-27 *Cape Town International Jazz Festival*. **Mar 31-Apr 17** *Gay and Lesbian Film Festival*, Johannesburg and Cape Town. **May 4-7** *Cape Town Waterfront Wine Festival*. **Jul 1-10** *Knysna Oyster Festival*. **Jul 19-31** *Calitzdorp Port Festial*.
SOCIAL CONVENTIONS: Handshaking is the usual form of greeting. Normal courtesies should be shown when visiting someone's home. Casual wear is widely acceptable. Formal social functions often call for a dinner jacket and black tie for men and full-length dresses for women; this will be specified on the invitation. Smoking is prohibited in public buildings and on public transport. **Tipping:** Normally 10 to 15 per cent if service is not included. It is customary to tip porters, waiters, taxi drivers, caddies and room service. By law, hotel rates do not include a service charge.

Business Profile

ECONOMY: The South African economy dominates the southern part of the African continent. Agriculture is strong enough to allow South Africa virtual self-sufficiency in foodstuffs: livestock is reared extensively, and sugar, maize and cereals are produced in large quantities. Specialised products such as wine and fruit are exported in large quantities. The industrial sector has traditionally been based on mining. The country has considerable deposits of common minerals such as coal, but also of valuable metals and ores which are in high demand but are scarce everywhere else except the Russian Federation: these include chromium, manganese, vanadium and platinum. Its most valuable minerals, however, are gold and diamonds, of which South Africa has long been both the world's largest producer and exporter. Gold alone accounts for one-third of the country's entire export income. The only key mineral that South Africa lacks is oil.
Recently, however, the traditional dominance of agriculture and mining has been supplanted by manufacturing and service industries. Manufacturing industry is concentrated in metal-based industries, mainly steel and heavy engineering, with machinery and transport equipment as the principal products. Manufacturing now accounts for around 20 per cent of total economic output. Some advanced technological industries have also emerged in recent years. In the service sector, both financial services and tourism have expanded rapidly and both are now mainstays of the South African economy.
The Mandela government initially committed itself to a gradual economic transition through its Reconstruction and Development Programme, whose principal aim was to tackle the gross inequalities inherited from the apartheid regime. Progress was tempered, however, by the Government's insistence on fiscal restraint. The Government has since designed a scheme under which major economic assets – notably the mines – will be transferred to 'black empowerment entities' over a 10-year period. The economy is currently somewhat sluggish but expected to pick up in 2004. Inflation is currently 9.9 per cent and annual growth a moderate 2 per cent. Few inroads have been made into the high level of unemployment, officially at 26.7 per cent. Perhaps the greatest long-term problem, especially as regards its impact on the workforce, is the very high level of HIV/AIDS infection in the country.
South Africa is the dominant member of the local Southern African Customs Union (with Botswana, Lesotho, Namibia and Swaziland); it has also joined the Southern African Development Community and the Organisation of African Unity. The USA, the UK, Germany and Japan are South Africa's main trading partners.
BUSINESS: Suits are usually expected to be worn for meetings. Appointments are generally necessary and punctuality is expected. Business cards are widely used. **Office hours:** Mon-Fri 0830-1630.
COMMERCIAL INFORMATION: The following organisations can offer advice: South African Chamber of Business (SACOB), 24 Sturdee Avenue, Rosebank, Gauteng (tel: (11) 446 3800; fax: (11) 446 3847/9; e-mail: info@sacob.co.za; website: www.sacob.co.za); *or* the Department of Trade & Industry, Private Bag X84, Pretoria 0001 (tel: (12) 394 9500; fax: (11) 254 9406; e-mail: contactus@thedti.gov.za).
CONFERENCES/CONVENTIONS: There are roughly 815 conference venues in South Africa. The main conference venues are in Pretoria and Johannesburg, though facilities exist in all other major towns, provided mainly by hotels and universities. The Conference and Incentive Promotions Division of SATOUR exists to promote South African venues and to ensure high standards of service and facilities for conference organisers. Contact SATOUR for details (see *Contact Addresses* section); *or* Southern African Association for the Conference Industry (SAACI), PO Box 414, Kloof 3640 (tel: (31) 764 6977; fax: (31) 764 6974; e-mail: admin@contactpub.co.za; website: www.saaci.co.za); *or* Cape Town Regional Chamber of Commerce and Industry, 19 Louis Gradner Street, Cape Town 8000 (tel: (21) 402 4300; fax: (21) 402 4302; e-mail: info@caperegionalchamber.co.za; website: www.capechamber.co.za).

Climate

South Africa's climate is generally sunny and pleasant. Winters are usually mild, although snow falls on the

mountain ranges of the Cape and Natal and occasionally in lower-lying areas, when a brief cold spell can be expected throughout the country.
Required clothing: Lightweight cottons and linens and rainwear. Warmer clothes are needed for winter.

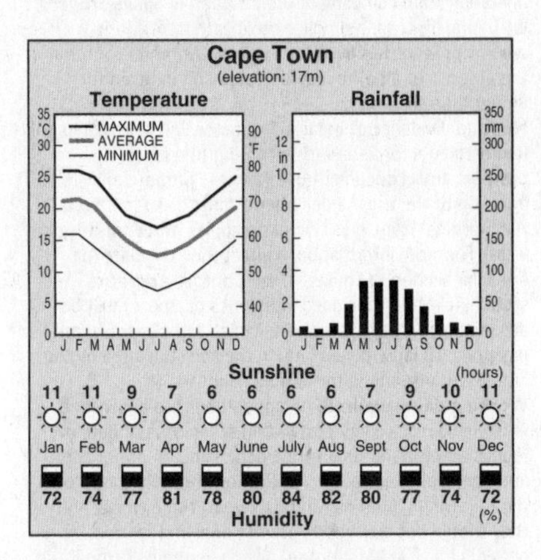

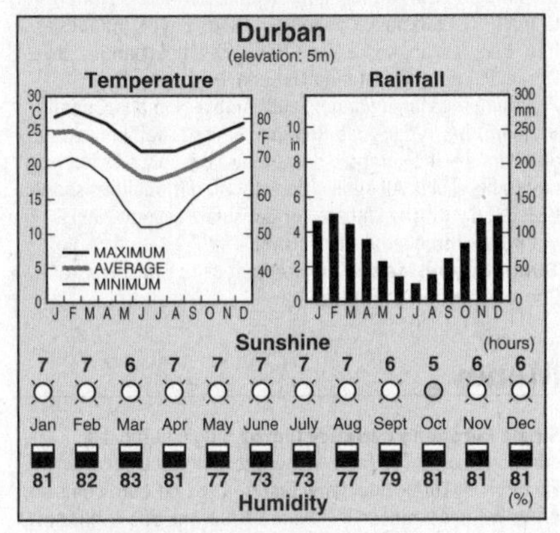

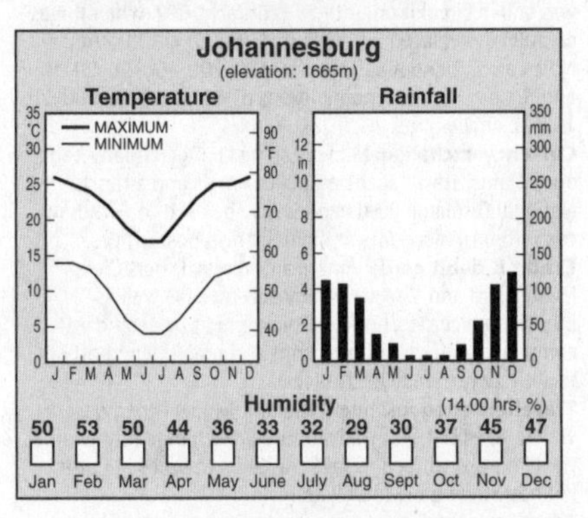

Spain

LATEST TRAVEL ADVICE CONTACTS

British Foreign and Commonwealth Office
Tel: (0870) 606 0290 Website: www.fco.gov.uk
US Department of State
Website: http://travel.state.gov/travel
Canadian Department of Foreign Affairs and Int'l Trade
Tel: (1 800) 267 8376 Website: www.dfait-maeci.gc.ca

Location: Western Europe.

Country dialling code: 34.

Dirección General de Turespaña
Jose Lázaro 6, 28071 Madrid, Spain
Tel: (91) 343 3500. Fax: (91) 343 3446 *or* 3500.
E-mail: infotur.spain@tourspain.es *or* info@spain.info
Website: www.spain.info
Spanish Embassy
39 Chesham Place, London SW1X 8SB, UK
Tel: (020) 7235 5555. Fax: (020) 7259 5392.
E-mail: embespuk@mail.mae.es
Website: www.mae.es
Spanish Consulate
20 Draycott Place, London SW3 2RZ, UK
Tel: (020) 7589 8989 *or* (0906) 550 8970 (recorded visa information; calls cost £1 per minute) *or* (0906) 526 6666 (to order visa applications; calls cost £1.50 per minute).
Fax: (020) 7581 7888.
E-mail: conspalon@mail.mae.es
Opening hours: Mon-Fri 0915-1200 (closed Spanish national holidays; visa information by appointment only), Mon-Fri 0915-1415 (Spanish nationals only), Sat 1000-1200 (Spanish nationals only).
By appointment only.
Consulates in: Edinburgh and Manchester.
Spanish National Tourist Office
2nd Floor, New Cavendish Street, London W1W 6XB, UK
Tel: (020) 7486 8077 *or* (0906) 364 0630 (24-hour brochure request line; calls cost 60p per minute).
Fax: (020) 7486 8034.
E-mail: info.londres@tourspain.es
Website: www.spain.info
Opening hours: Mon-Fri 0915-1615.
British Embassy
Calle de Fernando el Santo 16, 28010 Madrid, Spain
Tel: (91) 700 8200 *or* 319 0200 *or* 524 9700 (consular section) *or* 9727 (visa section). Fax: (91) 700 8210.
E-mail: enquiries.madrid@fco.gov.uk
Website: www.ukinspain.com
British Consulate General
Paseo de Recoletos 7-9, 4th Floor, 28004 Madrid, Spain
Tel: (91) 524 9700. Fax: (91) 524 9730.
E-mail: madridconsulate@ukinspain.com
Website: www.ukinspain.com

TIMATIC CODES

Health	AMADEUS: **TI-DFT/MAD/HE** GALILEO/WORLDSPAN: **TI-DFT/MAD/HE** SABRE: **TIDFT/MAD/HE**
Visa	AMADEUS: **TI-DFT/MAD/VI** GALILEO/WORLDSPAN: **TI-DFT/MAD/VI** SABRE: **TIDFT/MAD/VI**

To access TIMATIC country information on Health and Visa regulations through the Computer Reservations System (CRS), type in the appropriate command line listed above.

Consulates also in: Alicante, Barcelona, Bilbao, Ibiza, Las Palmas (Grand Canaria), Málaga, Palma de Mallorca and Santa Cruz de Tenerife (Canary Islands).
Honorary Consulates in: Benidorm, Cadiz, Menorca, Santander, Seville and Vigo.
Embassy and Consulate of the Kingdom of Spain
2375 Pennsylvania Avenue, NW, Washington, DC 20037, USA
Tel: (202) 452 0100. Fax: (202) 833 5670 *or* 728 2302.
E-mail: embespus@mail.mae.es
Website: www.spainemb.org
Consulates in: Boston, Chicago, Houston, Los Angeles, Miami, New Orleans, New York, Puerto Rico, San Francisco and Washington.
Spanish Tourist Office
666 Fifth Avenue, Btwn 52nd and 53rd Street, 35th Floor, New York, NY 10103, USA
Tel: (212) 265 8822. Fax: (212) 265 8864.
E-mail: oetny@tourspain.es
Website: www.okspain.org
Offices also in: Chicago, Los Angeles and Miami.
Embassy of the United States of America
Serrano 75, 28006 Madrid, Spain
Tel: (91) 587 2200. Fax: (91) 587 2303.
E-mail: amemb@embusa.es
Website: www.embusa.es
Embassy of the Kingdom of Spain
74 Stanley Avenue, Ottawa, Ontario K1M 1P4, Canada
Tel: (613) 747 2252 *or* 7293. Fax: (613) 744 1224.
E-mail: embespca@mail.mae.es
Consulates General in: Montréal and Toronto.
Spanish Tourist Office
2 Bloor Street West, Suite 3402, Toronto, Ontario M4W 3E2, Canada
Tel: (416) 961 3131. Fax: (416) 961 1992.
E-mail: toronto@tourspain.es
Website: www.tourspain.toronto.on.ca
Canadian Embassy
Street address: Calle Nuñez de Balboa 35, 28001 Madrid, Spain
Postal address: Apartado 587, 28080 Madrid, Spain; Apartado 117, 28080 Madrid, Spain (commercial section).
Tel: (91) 423 3250. Fax: (91) 423 3251.
E-mail: mdrid@international.gc.ca
Website: www.canada-es.org
Consulates in: Barcelona and Málaga.

Credit: © Spanish Tourist Office

General Information

AREA: 505,988 sq km (195,363 sq miles); includes Spanish North Africa.
POPULATION: 40,280,8780 (estimate 2004).
POPULATION DENSITY: 84.4 per sq km.
CAPITAL: Madrid. **Population:** 3,092,759 (2003).
GEOGRAPHY: Spain shares the Iberian peninsula with Portugal and is bordered to the north by the Pyrenees, which separate Spain from France. The Balearic Islands (Mallorca, Menorca, Ibiza and Formentera), 193km (120 miles) southeast of Barcelona, and the Canary Islands off the west coast of Africa are part of Spain, as are the tiny enclaves of Ceuta and Melilla on the north African mainland. With the exception of Switzerland, mainland Spain is the highest and most mountainous country in Europe, with an average height of 610m (2000ft). The Pyrenees stretch roughly 400km (249 miles) from the Basque Country in the west to the Mediterranean Sea; at times the peaks rise to over 1524m (5000ft), the highest point being 3404m (11,169ft). The main physical feature of Spain is the vast central plateau, or *Meseta*, divided by

several chains of sierras. The higher northern area includes Castille and León, the southern section comprises Castile/La Mancha and Extremadura. In the south the plateau drops abruptly at the Sierra Morena, beyond which lies the valley of Guadalquivir. Southeast of Granada is the Sierra Nevada, part of the Betic Cordillera, which runs parallel to the Mediterranean, rising to 3481m (11,420ft) and the highest point on the Spanish peninsula (the Pico del Teide on Tenerife in the Canaries is the highest peak in Spain). The Mediterranean coastal area reaches from the French frontier in the northeast down to the Straits of Gibraltar, the narrow strip of water linking the Mediterranean with the Atlantic and separating Spain from North Africa.
GOVERNMENT: Parliamentary monarchy since 1978.
Head of State: King Juan Carlos I since 1975. **Head of Government:** José Luis Rodríguez Zapatero since 2004.
LANGUAGE: Spanish (Castillian), Catalan (in the northeast), Galician (in the northwest) and Basque (in the north).
RELIGION: There is no official religion, but the majority of the population is Roman Catholic.
TIME: Mainland Spain/Balearics: GMT + 1 (GMT + 2 from last Sunday in March to Saturday before last Sunday in October).
The Canary Islands: GMT (GMT + 1 from last Sunday in March to Saturday before last Sunday in October).
ELECTRICITY: 220 or 225 volts AC, 50Hz. Generally, round two-pin plugs and screw-type lamp fittings are in use.
COMMUNICATIONS: Telephone: IDD is available. Country code: 34. Outgoing international code: 00. Emergency calls: 112. Area codes are incorporated within a nine digit number. The following are a selection of codes for major centres: Madrid 91, Alicante 96, Balearic Islands 971, Barcelona 93, Benidorm 96, Bilbao 94, Granada 958, Málaga and Torremolinos 95, Las Palmas 928, Santander 942, Seville 95, Tenerife 922 and Valencia 96 **Mobile telephone:** GSM 900/1800 networks available. Roaming agreements exist with all major networks. Coverage is good throughout most of the country. Main network providers include *Movistar* (website: www.movistar.com), *Retevision Movil* (website: www.amena.com) and *Vodafone* (website: www.vodafone.es). **Fax:** Most post offices have services. Facilities are also generally available at 4- and 5-star hotels, especially those catering for the business and conference traveller. **Internet:** There is a variety of Internet cafes in most urban areas. Main ISPs include *Futurnet* (website: www.futurnet.es), *Ibernet Telematica* (website: www.ibernet.com), *Ozú* (website: www.ozu.es), *Terra* (website: www.terra.es), *Wanadoo* (website: www.wanadoo.es) and *Ya* (website: www.ya.com).
Telegram: Facilities are available at main post offices. A 24-hour service is available in Madrid at Plaza de Cibeles; in Barcelona at Plaza Antonio Lopez; in Bilbao at 15 Calle Alameda Urquijo. **Post:** There are efficient internal and international postal services to all countries. Airmail within Europe usually takes around five days. *Poste Restante* facilities are available at main post offices. **Press:** Local newspapers published in English include the *Costa Blanca News*, *Majorca Daily Bulletin* and the English-language edition of *Sur* (weekly). Spanish dailies with large circulations include *ABC*, *El Marca* (sports only), *El Mundo* and *El País*.
Radio: BBC World Service (website: www.bbc.co.uk/worldservice) and Voice of America (website: www.voa.gov) can be received. From time to time the frequencies change and the most up-to-date can be found online.

Passport/Visa

	Passport Required?	Visa Required?	Return Ticket Required?
Full British	Yes	No	Yes
Australian	Yes	No/2	Yes
Canadian	Yes	No/2	Yes
USA	Yes	No/2	Yes
Other EU	Yes/1	No	Yes
Japanese	Yes	No/2	Yes

Note: *Regulations and requirements may be subject to change at short notice, and you are advised to contact the appropriate diplomatic or consular authority before finalising travel arrangements. Details of these may be found at the head of this country's entry. Any numbers in the chart refer to the footnotes below.*

Note: Spain is a signatory to the 1995 **Schengen Agreement**. For further details about passport/visa regulations within the Schengen area, see the introductory section *How to Use this Guide*.
PASSPORTS: Passport valid for at least three months including 90 days beyond the planned stay required by all except the following:
1. nationals of the EU holding valid national ID cards for stays of up to 90 days.
Note: The requested validity and precise requirements of the passport may vary according to nationality and these are subject to change at short notice; please consult nearest Embassy/Consulate for further details.
VISAS: Required by all except the following:
(a) nationals of EU countries, Iceland, Norway and Switzerland regardless of purpose and/or length of stay;
(b) **2.** other nationals referred to in the chart above for stays of up to 90 days;
(c) nationals of Andorra, Anguilla, Argentina, Bermuda, Bolivia, Brazil, British Virgin Islands, Brunei, Bulgaria, Cayman Islands, Chile, Costa Rica, El Salvador, Falkland Islands, Guatemala, Honduras, Hong Kong (SAR), Israel, Korea (Rep), Liechtenstein, Macau (SAR), Malaysia, Mexico, Monaco, Montserrat, New Zealand, Nicaragua, Panama, Paraguay, Romania, St Helena, San Marino, Singapore, Turks & Caicos Islands, Uruguay, Vatican City and Venezuela for stays of up to 90 days; (d) holders of travel documents issued by the Geneva convention of July 1951, by Belgium, Cyprus, Denmark, Germany, Iceland, Ireland, Liechtenstein, Luxembourg, The Netherlands, Norway, Spain, Sweden, Switzerland and the UK for stays of up to 90 days. Please note that British passports that do not have "European community" on the front page require a visa;
(e) crew members of airlines and merchant navy for stays of up to 90 days;
(f) nationals of any of the *Schengen* member states who hold permanent residency are entitled to re-enter the *Schengen* area without a visa, provided proof of residence and a valid passport are submitted;
(g) transit passengers continuing their journey by the same or first connecting aircraft provided holding valid onward or return documentation and not leaving the airport (except nationals of Afghanistan*, Angola, Bangladesh*, Congo (Dem Rep)*, Cote d'Ivoire, Cuba, Eritrea*, Ethiopia*, Ghana*, Guinea-Bissau, Haiti, India, Iran*, Iraq*, Liberia, Mali, Nigeria*, Pakistan*, Senegal, Sierra Leone, Somalia*, Sri Lanka*, Syrian Arab Republic and Togo who *always* require an airport transit visa if not a permanent resident of Canada, EU countries or the USA; nationals marked * must be permanent residents of Andorra, Canada, Japan, Monaco, San Marino, Switzerland or the USA). As the preceding list is liable to change at short notice, visitors are advised to check transit regulations with the relevant Embassy or Consulate before travelling.
Note: (a) Children of any age holding a valid passport will require a visa. (b) Visas issued to nationals of Turkey are not valid for all *Schengen* member states.
Types of visa and cost: A uniform type of visa, the *Schengen* visa, is issued for tourist, business and private visits. *Short-stay:* £17.25 for up to 30 days, £20.70 for up to 90 days (single-entry); £24.15 for up to 90 days (multiple entries), £34.50 for up to one year (multiple-entry). *Transit:* £6.90. Prices are subject to change and travellers are advised to check with the Consulate before departure. All visas are also subject to an administrative fee.
Note: (a) Spouses and children of EU nationals (providing spouse's passport and the original marriage or birth certificate is produced), and nationals of some other countries, receive their visas free of charge (enquire at Embassy for details). (b) Visa exemptions apply for school children visiting Spain as part of an organised school trip, accompanied by a teacher.
Validity: *Short-stay* (single- and multiple-entry): valid for six months from date of issue for a stay of maximum 90 days per entry. *Transit* (single- and multiple-entry): valid for a maximum of five days per entry, including the day of arrival. Visas cannot be extended and a new application must be made each time.
Application to: In person (strictly only by appointment solicited in writing) to the appropriate Consulate (or Consular section at Embassy) for where applicant lives. Applications may also be conducted through a travel agency or visa agency that may come in person on behalf of the applicant. Postal applications are not accepted. Travellers visiting just one Schengen country should apply to the Consulate of that country; travellers visiting more than one Schengen country should apply to the Consulate of the country chosen as the main destination *or* the country they will enter first (if they have no main destination).
Note: Applicants will be seen by appointment only. Please state number of applicants (immediate family only: wife/husband and descendants) when applying for an appointment. If applying for a family, please send photocopies of passports, plus a self-addressed envelope.
Application requirements: (a) Passport or travel document, valid for at least three months longer than requested visa with one full blank page to affix the visa. (b) Two completed application forms; in the case of minors, the parent or legal guardian may sign. (c) Two passport-size photos (plus three photocopies), preferably stapled to each page of application form; children also require two passport-size photos, to be included in the parent's passport. (d) Fee, payable by cash or postal order only. (e) Proof of purpose of visit (official letter of invitation; return tickets and hotel confirmation). (f) Confirmed accommodation. (g) Evidence of sufficient funds for stay (recent bank statement and photocopies). (h) Formal itinerary, supplied by travel agent or airline. *Business:* (a)-(h) and, (i) Letter from employer; or accountant, solicitor, bank manager or Chamber of Commerce if self-employed. Students should submit proof of attendance. (j) Written invitation from company or organisation in Spain. *Student:* (a)-(i) and, (j) Legalised police certificate from country where applicant has lived for five years or more, confirming the absence of a police record, if studying in Spain for longer than six months.
Note: (a) Evidence of medical insurance will be required. (b) Requirements for visas vary according to nationality, passport, travel document used and the purpose and duration of the trip. All documents must be submitted in their original form, plus two photocopies (three for Business visas). For more information, contact the Consulate (or Consular section at Embassy); see *Contact Addresses* section. (c) Minors included in parent's passport must be accompanied by the parent. The child's right to travel on passport will lapse depending on the age stipulated by the Embassy/Consulate in the issuing country.
Working days required: An appointment to apply for a visa will be received by post within seven days of date of request. Processing time varies, depending on nationality and personal information. Applications from nationals of the following countries will take two to three weeks, and they should not buy tickets prior to applying for and obtaining a visa: Afghanistan, Algeria, Bahrain, Burundi, China (PR), Colombia, Congo (Dem Rep), Egypt, Indonesia, Iran, Iraq, Jordan, Korea (Dem Rep), Kuwait, Lebanon, Libya, Oman, Pakistan, Palestinian National Authority, The Philippines, Qatar, Rwanda, Saudi Arabia, Somalia, Sudan, Surinam, the Syrian Arab Republic, United Arab Emirates and Yemen. Once granted, visas may take only one working day to be issued. All applications for all nationalities should be lodged with the Embassy or Consulate several weeks before the intended date of travel.
Temporary residence: Refer enquiries to Consulate (or Consular section at Embassy).

Money

Single European currency (Euro): Single European currency (Euro): The Euro is now the official currency of 12 EU member states (including Spain). The first Euro coins and notes were introduced in January 2002; the Spanish Peseta was still in circulation until 28 February 2002, when it was completely replaced by the Euro. Euro (€) = 100 cents. Notes are in denominations of €500, 200, 100, 50, 20, 10 and 5. Coins are in denominations of €2 and 1, and 50, 20, 10, 5, 2 and 1 cents.
Currency exchange: Money can be changed in any bank, and at most travel agencies, major hotels and airports. National Girobank Postcheques may be used to withdraw cash from UK accounts at main Spanish post offices.
Credit & debit cards: American Express, Diners Club, MasterCard and Visa are widely accepted, as well as Eurocheque cards. Check with your credit or debit card company for details of merchant acceptability and other facilities which may be available.
Travellers cheques: International travellers cheques are widely accepted. To avoid additional exchange rate charges, travellers are advised to take travellers cheques in Euros, Pounds Sterling or US Dollars.
Currency restrictions: The import and export of local currency is unlimited, but the export of amounts exceeding €6010 (in any currency) per person per journey must be declared. The export of cash notes and bearers-cheques, in any currency, exceeding €3050 per person per journey must also be declared.
Exchange rate indicators: The following figures are included as a guide to the movements of the Euro against Sterling and the US Dollar:

Date	Feb '04	May '04	Aug '04	Nov '04
£1.00=	1.46	1.49	1.49	1.30
$1.00=	0.80	0.83	0.80	0.70

Banking hours: Mon-Fri 0900-1400, Sat 0900-1300 (times may vary).

Duty Free

The following items may be imported into Spain without incurring customs duty by passengers aged 17 years or older arriving from countries outside the EU:
200 cigarettes or 100 cigarillos 50 cigars or 250g tobacco (300 cigarettes, 150 cigarillos, 70 cigars and 400g of tobacco for EU nationals); 1l of spirits if exceeding 22 per cent volume or 2l of alcoholic beverage not exceeding 22 per cent volume and 2l of wine (1.5l exceeding 22 per cent and 3l of up to 22 per cent and 5l of wine for EU nationals); 250ml eau de toilette and 50g of perfume; 500g of coffee or 200g of coffee extract (1000g of coffee and 4000g of coffee extract for EU nationals); 100g of tea or 40g of tea extract; gifts up to the value of approximately €37.26.

Abolition of duty free goods within the EU: On June 30 1999, the sale of duty free alcohol and tobacco at airports and at sea was abolished in all of the original 15 EU member states. Of the 10 new member states that joined the EU on May 1 2004, these rules already apply to Cyprus and Malta. There are transitional rules in place for visitors returning to one of the original 15 EU countries from one of the other new EU countries. But for the original 15, plus Cyprus and Malta, there are now no limits imposed on importing tobacco and alcohol products from one EU country to another (with the exceptions of Denmark, Finland and Sweden, where limits *are* imposed). Travellers should note that they may be required to prove at customs that the goods purchased are for personal use *only*.

Public Holidays

2005: Jan 1 New Year's Day. **Jan 6*** Epiphany. **Mar 19*** San Jose. **Mar 24*** Maundy Thursday. **Mar 25** Good Friday. **May 1** Labour Day. **Aug 15** Assumption. **Oct 12** National Day. **Nov 1** All Saints' Day. **Dec 6** Constitution Day. **Dec 8** Immaculate Conception. **Dec 25** Christmas Day.
2006: Jan 1 New Year's Day. **Jan 6*** Epiphany. **Mar 19*** San Jose. **Apr 13*** Maundy Thursday. **Apr 14** Good Friday. **May 1** Labour Day. **Aug 15** Assumption. **Oct 12** National Day. **Nov 1** All Saints' Day. **Dec 6** Constitution Day. **Dec 8** Immaculate Conception. **Dec 25** Christmas Day.
(a) *These holidays may be replaced by the autonomous communities with another date.
(b) The following dates are also celebrated as regional public holidays (within these regions, there are further public holidays peculiar to the various towns and cities):
Jan 29 Dia de la Convivencia (Ceuta). **Feb 28** Andalucía Day. **Mar 1** Balearic Isles Day. **Apr 23** San Jorge (Aragon) and Day of the Region of Castilla y Leon. **May 2** San Segundo (Castilla y Leon) and Fiesta of the Communidad de Madrid. **May 17** Dia de las Letras Gallegas (Galicia). **May 30** Canaries Day. **May 31** Day of the Region of Castilla-La Mancha. **Jun 9** Day of the Region of Murcia and Day of La Rioja. **Sep 8** Asturias Day, Day of Extremadura and Nuestra la Virgen de la Victoria (Melilla). **Sep 11** National Day of Catalonia. **Sep 15** Nuestra Senora de la Bien Aparecida (Cantabria). **Sep 17** Commemoration of the Spanish Refounding of the City of Melilla. **Dec 26** San Esteban (Balearic Isles and Catalonia).
(c) Catalonia, Navarra, Pais Vasco (Basque Country) and Valenciana also celebrate Easter Monday (**Mar 28 2005** and **Apr 17 2006**).

Health

	Special Precautions?	Certificate Required?
Yellow Fever	No	No
Cholera	No	No
Typhoid & Polio	No	N/A
Malaria	No	N/A

Note: *Regulations and requirements may be subject to change at short notice, and you are advised to contact your doctor well in advance of your intended date of departure. Any numbers in the chart refer to the footnotes below.*

Other risks: *Rabies* is present. For those at high risk, vaccination before arrival should be considered. If you are bitten, seek medical advice without delay. For more information, consult the *Health* appendix.
Health care: There is a reciprocal health agreement with the UK. Medical treatment provided by state scheme doctors at state scheme hospitals and health centres (*ambulatorios*) is free to UK citizens if in possession of form E111. Health insurance is required for private medical care. Prescribed medicines and dental treatment must be paid for by all visitors.

Travel - International

Note: For information on travel to and within the **Balearic Islands** and the **Canary Islands**, see the respective sections.
There is a continuing threat in Spain from both domestic and international terrorism. 192 people died and over 1400 were injured following bomb attacks on three trains in Madrid in March 2004. A group purporting to represent Al-Qaeda claimed responsibility. ETA, the Basque terrorist group, continues to threaten further attacks. However, most visits to Spain are trouble-free.
AIR: Spain's national airline is *IBERIA (IB)* (website: www.iberia.com). Many airlines operate to Spain, including an increasing number of low-cost airlines from the UK.
Approximate flight times: From Barcelona to *London* is two hours; from Ibiza is two hours 20 minutes; and from Málaga is two hours 40 minutes. From Madrid to *Los Angeles* is 13 hours; to *New York* is seven hours 25 minutes; to *Sydney* is 30 hours.

Credit: © Spanish Tourist Office

International airports: Spain boasts over 30 international airports. Information on the major airports follows; information on any of the others can be obtained from AENA (*Aeropuertos Espanoles y Navegación Aérea*) Calle Arturo Soria 109, Madrid 28043 (tel: (90) 240 4704 (customer service line); website: www.aena.es), which is the organisation responsible for running all of the Spanish airports.
Madrid (MAD) (Barajas) is 15km (9 miles) northeast of the city. A bus service departs to the city around every 10 to 30 minutes (0700-2400) and underground services run every four to seven minutes (0600-0130). Taxi service is available. Airport facilities include restaurants and bars, bank, several car hire offices, hotel reservation and tourist information desks, and outgoing duty free shop.
Barcelona (BCN) (del Prat) is 12km (7 miles) southwest of the city. Bus service to the city departs Mon-Fri every 15 minutes, Sat every 30 mins and Sun every 20 mins (0600-2400). Rail service is every 30 minutes (0645-2340). Taxi service to the city is available, costing about €18 (travel time - 30 minutes). Airport facilities include a bank, restaurant, bar, several car hire companies, hotel reservation and tourist information desks and duty free shops.
Alicante (ALC) (Altet) is 12km (7 miles) southwest of the city. Bus service runs to the city (0655-2310) every 10 to 40 minutes, costing €1. A taxi service is available to the city, costing about €12. There is a taxi connection between Alicante and Valencia Airport. Airport facilities include a duty-free shop, bank, bureau de change, car hire, tourist information and restaurant.
Bilbao (BIO) (Sondika) is 10km (6 miles) north of the city. Bus and taxi services to the city are available (travel time - 30 minutes) and cost about €1. Airport facilities include a restaurant, duty-free shop, tourist information desk and car hire.
Málaga (AGP) is 10km (6 miles) southwest of the city. Buses run every 10 to 30 minutes (travel time - 20 minutes). Train service runs every 30 minutes and cost about €1. Taxi service to the city is available, costing €12. Airport facilities include duty-free shop, bank/bureau de change, restaurant and car hire.
Santiago de Compostela (SCQ) is 10km (6 miles) northeast of the city. Buses and taxis are available to the city centre (travel time - 10 to 15 minutes). Airport facilities include bar, banks, car hire and shops.
Seville (SVQ) is 8km (5 miles) from the city. Taxis and buses are available to the city centre (travel time - 20 to 30 minutes).
Valencia (VLC) (Manises) is 8km (5 miles) west of the city. Taxis and buses (0600-2300, every 15 minutes) are available to the city centre (travel time - 60 minutes (bus), 30 minutes (taxi). Airport facilities include several car hire firms, bank/bureau de change, restaurant, bar and duty free shop.
Departure tax: None.
SEA: *Brittany Ferries* (tel: (08703) 665 333; website: www.brittany-ferries.com) operates a service to Santander (on the north coast) from Plymouth (travel time - 18 hours), twice-weekly. *P&O European Ferries* (tel: (08705) 202020; website: www.poportsmouth.com) operates a twice-weekly service from Portsmouth to Bilbao (travel time - 35 hours).
RAIL: There are direct trains between Madrid–Paris and Madrid–Lisbon, as well as Barcelona–Paris, Barcelona–Zürich or Milan and Barcelona–Geneva. These services are called *Estrella*, *Talgo* or *Train-Hotel*. On other international services to and from Spain, a change of train is necessary. However, work on the *AVE* (high-velocity train) route between Madrid and Barcelona is expected to be completed in 2006, after which the French border connection is expected to be fully operational in 2010 and it will be possible to connect with the French *TGV* (high-velocity route) and the rest of the high-velocity routes in Europe.
Motorail services run between Paris and Madrid. For more information, contact the Spanish Rail service (tel: (020) 7224 0345; e-mail: enquiries@spanish-rail.co.uk; website: www.spanish-rail.co.uk). Travelling from the UK, the quickest way is to travel by *Eurostar* through the Channel Tunnel to Paris (travel time – three hours) with a connection to Spain. For further information and reservations contact *Eurostar* (tel: (0870) 600 0792 (travel agents) *or* (08705) 186 186 (public; within the UK) *or* (+44 1233) 617 575 (public; outside the UK only); website: www.eurostar.com); *or* Rail Europe (tel: (08705) 848 848). Travel agents can obtain refunds for unused tickets from Eurostar For Agents, 2nd Floor, Kent House, 81 Station Road, Ashford, Kent TN23 1PD, UK. Complaints and comments may be sent to Eurostar Customer Relations, Eurostar House, Waterloo Station, London SE1 8SE, UK (tel: (020) 7928 5163; e-mail: new.comments@eurostar.co.uk).
ROAD: The main route from the UK is via France. The main motorways to Spain from France are via Bordeaux or Toulouse to Bilbao (northern Spain) and via Marseille or Toulouse to Barcelona (eastern Spain). A number of coach operators offer services to Spain. In the UK, *Eurolines*, departing from Victoria Coach Station in London, serves more than 20 destinations in Spain. For further information, contact *Eurolines*, 52 Grosvenor Gardens, London SW1, UK (tel: (08705) 143 219; website: www.eurolines.com *or* www.nationalexpress.com).
For information on **documentation** and **traffic regulations**, see *Travel – Internal* section.

Travel - Internal

AIR: Domestic flights are run by *IBERIA (IB)* (website: www.iberia.com), *Air Europa* (website: www.air-europa.com), *Binter* (website: www.bintercanarias.es) and *Spanair* (website: www.spanair.com). Scheduled flights connect all main towns as well as to the Balearic and Canary Islands and enclaves in North Africa. Air taxis are available at most airports. Reservations should be made well in advance.
SEA: There are regular hydrofoil and car and passenger ferry sailings from Algeciras to Tangier and Ceuta (North African enclave); Málaga and Almeria to Melilla (North African enclave); Barcelona, Valencia and Alicante to the Balearic Islands; and Cádiz to the Canary Islands. There are also inter-island services, including a catamaran service linking Barcelona and Palma de Mallorca, which takes three hours and runs twice a day. For further information, contact *Trasmediterránea c/o Southern Ferries* (tel: (020) 7491 4968; fax: (020) 7491 3502).
RAIL: The state-owned company *RENFE* (website: www.renfe.es) operates a railway network connecting all the regions on the Iberian peninsula. It is mainly a radial network, with connections between Madrid and all the major cities. There are also some transversal services connecting the northwest coast with the Mediterranean coast, as well as services from the French border down the Mediterranean coast. Principal trains are air conditioned, and many have restaurant or buffet service. Reservations for passenger services in Spain may be made in the UK through the Spanish Rail service (see above), *European Rail Travel* (tel: (020) 7387 0444; fax: (020) 7387 0888; e-mail: sales@europeanrail.com; website: www.europeanrail.com), *Freedom Rail* (tel: (0870) 757 9898; fax: (01253) 595 151; e-mail: sales@freedomrail.com; website: www.freedomrail.com) and *Ultima Travel* (tel: (0151) 339 6171; fax: (0151) 339 9199).
Discount Rail Travel: The Spanish rail system is one of the cheapest in Europe and various discounts are available. Travellers under 26 can purchase a RENFE *Tarjeta*

Explorerail, which allows unlimited travel on all but some regionales and fast trains. It can be bought in Spain, or in the UK from selected travel agents, and is available for seven-, 15- and 30-day periods. Travellers can also enjoy savings by using any one of the European passes available, such as the *Euro Domino Freedom Pass*, which enables holders to make flexible travel arrangements. The pass is available in 19 European countries, but must be bought in the country of residence for which a valid passport or other form of ID has to be shown. In the UK, this pass is available from *Rail Europe*, 178 Piccadilly, London W1, UK (tel: (0870) 837 1371; e-mail: reservations@raileurope.co.uk; website: www.raileurope.co.uk). The tickets are valid for three, four, five, six, seven or eight days within one month. Also available from *Rail Europe*, the *Inter-Rail Pass* (website: www.inter-rail.co.uk) allows up to 50 per cent reductions for second-class rail travel in 28 countries; the pass is now also available for those aged over 26 (at a higher cost). The *Rail Senior Plus* card entitles senior citizens to 30 per cent discount on rail travel into and out of Spain, even during peak hours. This discount does not apply when only travelling internally. The card is available from most British Rail stations.

Note: Seat reservations are required on all intercity trains. This ruling applies to the passes and cards mentioned above.

High-Speed Trains: The *Ave* service averages 300kph and connects Madrid and Seville in two hours 15 minutes, with 12 services each way via Córdoba. Some services also stop at Ciudad Real and Puerto Llano (La Mancha). The stretch from Madrid to Lleida has been in operation for several years. Planned completion of the Madrid to Barcelona leg is due in 2006, and the high-speed border connection with France in 2010. Also, in 2010, the stretches from Cordoba to Malaga, Madrid to Valencia and Madrid to Valladolid should be ready. The *Talgo 200* connects Madrid and Malaga thrice-daily in four hours 35 minutes. Holders of most of the cards and passes mentioned above qualify for discounts, albeit less substantial than the rates quoted above.

Tourist Trains: The *Andalus Express* and *Transcantábrico* offer a pleasant way of discovering their respective regions. There are also a number of privately-run narrow-gauge railways in Spain, located mainly in the north of Spain as well as the Mediterranean coast and the Balearic Islands, which run at a leisurely pace through picturesque scenery. For more information on tourist trains, contact the Spanish National Tourist Office (see *Contact Addresses* section).

ROAD: There are more than 150,000km (95,000 miles) of roads. Motorways are well-maintained and connect Spain north-south. Tolls are in operation on some sections and have to be paid in Euros. Trunk roads between major cities are generally fast and well-maintained. Rural roads are of differing quality. **Bus:** There are bus lines which are efficient and cheap, operating between cities and towns. Departures are generally from a central terminal at which the operators will have individual booths selling tickets. Most places have a bus link of some kind, even the more remote villages. Bus tickets cannot be bought in advance though seats may be reserved locally one or two days in advance. **Car hire:** All major car hire companies are represented in major cities. **Motorcycles:** No person under 18 may hire or ride a vehicle over 75cc. Crash helmets must be worn. **Regulations:** Traffic drives on the right. Side lights must be used at night in built-up areas. Spare bulbs and red hazard triangles must be kept in all vehicles. Traffic lights: two red lights mean 'No Entry'. Parking laws are rigorously enforced. The speed limit for motorways is 120kph (80mph) in general, but for buses and lorries the limit is 100kph (60mph); in built-up areas the limit is 50kph (30mph); for other roads it is 90kph (56mph). **Documentation:** Most foreign licences including Canadian, EU and US are accepted. Third Party insurance is compulsory, plus maybe a Green Card if bringing your own car (available from insurance company).

URBAN: Traffic in Spanish cities is normally heavy, and urban driving takes some time to adjust to. City public transport facilities are generally good. Barcelona, Bilbao, Madrid and Valencia have metros as well as buses. Pre-purchase multi-journey tickets are sold. Other towns and resorts are well served by local buses. Metered taxis are available in most major cities and a 2 to 3 per cent tip is customary.

Travel Times: The following chart gives approximate travel times (in hours and minutes) from **Madrid** to other major cities and towns in Spain.

	Air	Road	Rail
Barcelona	1.00	8.00	8.00
Bilbao	0.50	5.00	6.00
Canary Is.	2.30	-	-
Málaga	1.00	5.00	7.00
Mallorca	1.00	-	-
Palma	1.10	6.00*	5.00*
Santander	0.50	5.00	6.00
Seville	0.55	6.00	7.00
Valencia	0.50	5.00	4.00

Note: *Plus nine hours by boat (three hours by catamaran).

Accommodation

HOTELS & HOSTELS: A variety of hotel-type accommodation is available including apartment-hotels, hotel-residencias and motels. The term *residencia* denotes an establishment where dining-room facilities are not provided, although there must be provisions for the serving of breakfast and a cafe. Further information on accommodation in Barcelona and Madrid can be obtained free of charge online (website: www.barcelona-on-line.com *or* www.madrid-on-line.com). **Grading:** Most accommodation in Spain is provided in hotels, classified from **1** to **5 stars** (the few exceptions have a Gran Lujo, Grande De Luxe category); or hostels and *pensiones*, classified from **1** to **3** stars. The following is an outline of the facilities available in the hotel and hostel categories. **1-star hotels:** Permanently installed heating, lift in buildings of more than four storeys, lounge, 25 per cent of bedrooms with shower, washbasin and WC, 25 per cent with shower and washbasin, the rest have washbasin and hot and cold running water, one common bathroom every seven rooms, laundry and ironing service, telephone on every floor; **2-star hotels:** Permanently installed heating or air conditioning according to climate, lounge, lift in buildings of two or more storeys, bar, 15 per cent of rooms with ensuite bathrooms, 45 per cent with shower, washbasin and WC and the rest with shower, washbasin and hot and cold running water, one common bathroom to every six rooms, laundry and ironing service, telephone in every room; **3-star hotels:** Permanently installed heating or air conditioning according to climate, lounge, lift, bar, 50 per cent of the bedrooms with ensuite bathrooms, 50 per cent with shower, washbasin, WC and hot and cold running water, laundry and ironing service, telephone in every room; **4-star hotels:** Air conditioning in every room, unless climatic conditions require central heating or cooling only, a minimum of two hotel lounges, 75 per cent of the bedrooms with ensuite bathroom and the rest with shower, washbasin, WC and hot and cold running water, laundry and ironing service, telephone in every room, garage parking (in towns), lift and bar; **5-star hotels:** Air conditioning in all public rooms and bedrooms, central heating, two or more lifts, lounges, bar, garage (within towns), hairdressers, all bedrooms with ensuite bathrooms and telephone, some suites with sitting rooms, and laundry and ironing service. **1-star hostels:** All rooms with washbasins and cold running water; one bathroom for every 12 rooms; general telephone; **2-star hostels:** Permanently installed heating, lift in buildings of five storeys or more, lounge or comfortable lobby, one common bathroom to every 10 rooms, all bedrooms with washbasin and hot and cold water, general telephone; **3-star hostels:** Permanently installed heating, lift in buildings of more than four storeys, lounge, 5 per cent of bedrooms with ensuite bathroom, 10 per cent with shower, washbasin and WC, 85 per cent with shower and washbasin and hot and cold running water, one common bathroom to every eight rooms, laundry and ironing service, telephone in every room.

It is always advisable to book accommodation well in advance, particularly during festivals or at popular resorts on the coast from late spring to October. Reservations may be made by writing directly to the hotels, lists of which may be obtained from the Spanish National Tourist Office (see *Contact Addresses* section), or through travel agents or certain hotel booking services. Further information may be obtained from CEHAT (Confederación Espanola de Hoteles y Alojamientos), Calle Orense 32, 28020 Madrid (tel: (91) 556 7112 *or* (90) 201 2141; fax: (91) 556 7361; e-mail: cehat@cehat.com; website: www.cehat.com).

Letters to 5-, 4- or 3-star hotels may be written in English, but it is advisable to write in Spanish to lower categories.

GOVERNMENT LODGES: A chain of lodging places has been set up by the Ministry of Tourism in places of special interest or remote locations. These include attractive modern buildings and ancient monuments of historic interest, such as monasteries, convents, old palaces and castles. Standards are uniformly high, but not at the expense of individual charm and character. Below is a brief description of each type of lodging:

PARADORES: National Tourist Inns, *Paradores*, are hotels with all modern amenities including rooms with private bathroom, hot and cold running water, central heating, telephone in every room, public sitting rooms, garages and complementary services. Advance booking is advised. For further information, contact Paradores de Turismo, Calle Requena 3, Madrid 28013 (tel: (91) 516 6666; fax: (91) 516 6657/8; e-mail: reservas@parador.es; website: www.parador.es); *or* contact the UK representative, Keytel International, 402 Edgware Road, London W2 1ED (tel: (020) 7616 0300; fax: (020) 7616 0317; e-mail: paradors@keytel.co.uk; website: www.keytel.co.uk).

HOSTERIAS: These are traditional restaurants, decorated in the style of the region in which they are situated and serving excellent meals.

GUEST HOUSES: *Pensiones* are common throughout Spain and vary in quality from austere to relatively luxurious. They are usually run by the family on the premises and provide bed and board only.

CAMPING/CARAVANNING: There are around 350 campsites throughout the country, covering a wide quality and price range. Permission from the local police and landowner is essential for off-site camping and there may be no more than three tents/caravans or 10 campers in any one place. Regulations demand that off-site camping is in isolated areas only. For further information, contact ANCE (*Federación Espanola de Empresarios de Cámpings y Ciudades de Vacaciones*), San Bernardo 97-99, 28015 Madrid (tel: (91) 448 1234; fax: (91) 448 1267; e-mail: fedcamping@hotmail.com; website: www.fedcamping.com).

YOUTH HOSTELS: The *Spanish Youth Hostel Network (REAJ)* (e-mail: info@reaj.com; website: www.reaj.com) is the representative in Spain for the International Youth Hostel Federation and there are currently over 200 registered youth hostels throughout the whole of Spain. Most must be booked in Spain, but a couple can be booked from the UK. For further information, contact the *REAJ* central booking network in Barcelona, Turisme Juvenil de Catalunya, C/Rocafort 116-122, 08015 Barcelona (tel: (934) 838 363; fax: (934) 838 350); *or* in Madrid, C/Barquillo 15A, 1G, 28004 Madrid (tel: (91) 522 7007; fax: (91) 522 8067); there is a booking and cancellation charge. The YHA international booking office in England (tel: (01629) 592 600; website: www.yha.org) can offer further advice if required.

Resorts & Excursions

Spain, one of the largest countries in Europe, occupies four-fifths of the Iberian Peninsula. A land of extraordinary geographical and cultural diversity, it has much to offer the tourist. While the Mediterranean beach resorts on the Costa Blanca, Costa Brava and Costa del Sol continue to attract sunseekers, the north coast is gradually gaining in popularity. But there is a great deal more to Spain than the beaches. The terrain is amazingly diverse with a huge variety of landscapes: deciduous and coniferous forests, arid plains, salt marshes, rocky bays and coves, peaks, verdant river valleys and mountain streams.

One of the most pleasurable ways to discover Spain's natural beauty and abundant wildlife is to visit one of the National Parks. Walks, hiking trails and jeep excursions enable visitors to explore marshes and wetlands, coastal dunes, isolated mountain peaks and Atlantic beaches. At certain times of the year the skies are filled with migrating birds heading for North Africa and the parks are also the habitat of a wealth of indigenous flora and fauna. Special mention should be made of rare and endangered species like the royal eagle, the *capercaillie* (woodcock) and the Pyrenean mountain goat. The major national parks in mainland Spain are: **Coto de Doñana** (provinces of Seville and Huelva), **Tablas de Daimiel** (La Mancha), **Ordesa** (Huesca Pyrenees), **Aigües Tortes** (Lleida) and **Montaña de Covadonga** (Picos de Europa).

Over the centuries, Spain's indigenous and conquering peoples have left an indelible legacy. Cromlechs and cave paintings from the prehistoric period, temples and aqueducts from the Roman occupation, Romanesque churches, Moorish baths, mosques and fortresses, medieval cathedrals and castles, Renaissance and Baroque palaces, the modernist architecture of Antoni Gaudí and his contemporaries, as well as present-day masterpieces like the Guggenheim museum in Bilbao and the City of Arts and Sciences in Valencia.

For the purposes of this section, Spain has been divided into eight regions, which do not necessarily reflect political or cultural boundaries: **Madrid**, **Andalucia**, **Ceuta & Melilla**, **Castile/La Mancha & Extremadura**, **Castile/León & La Rioja**, **The Northern Region**, **Navarre & Aragon**, **Valencia & Murcia** and **Catalonia** (including **Barcelona**). Information on the **Balearic Islands** and the **Canary Islands**, both integral parts of Spain, are dealt with separately.

MADRID

The Spanish capital is a vibrant, atmospheric city, short on famous monuments but rich in cultural sights. Pride of place belongs to the city's three superb art museums. The **Prado** has one of the most remarkable art collections in the world, with works by major Spanish and European masters from the Renaissance onwards. The **Museo Nacional Centro de Arte Reina Sofia** is devoted to 20th-century Spanish art with representative works by Miró, Dalí, Juan Gris, and above all by the Cubists, including Picasso. The most famous work on show is his masterpiece from the Civil War period, *Guernica*. The **Museo Thyssen-Bornemisza** is one of the most important private collections of western painting in the world, with more than 800 paintings from the Italian Renaissance to the 20th-century avant garde. The **Royal Palace** dates from the mid-18th century. There are more than 20 rooms open to the public, exhibiting priceless tapestries, paintings, carpets, clocks, furniture, silverware and porcelain. The armoury has one of the most valuable collections in Europe, mainly from the 16th century. Madrid's most historic square, the **Plaza Mayor**, is enclosed by arcades sheltering a variety of craft shops, restaurants and tapas bars. It was completed in 1617 during the reign of Philip III. The popular centre of Madrid is the famous square, the **Puerta del Sol**, the main shopping district and hub of the city's nightlife.

Madrid's most accessible green space is the **Retiro Park**. A former royal retreat, its attractions include a boating lake and summer concerts. The **Botanical Gardens**, a short walk from the Prado, are worth a visit. The **Casa de Campo**, west of the city centre, is a huge open space with a swimming pool, tennis courts, a jogging track and a zoo with aquarium. On the edge of Caso de Campo is the **Parque de Atracciones**, a large amusement park. Southeast of the city is the **Parque Biológico**, a new theme park on bio-diversity with pavilions recreating a variety of ecosystems. There is a 250-hectare Warner Brothers theme park in San Martín de la Vega. Many visitors to the city take the opportunity to see Real Madrid, one of the world's most successful football clubs, at the **Bernabéu Stadium**.

EXCURIONS: There are numerous places of interest within easy reach of the city. The **Monastery of San Lorenzo del Escorial** (49km, 30 miles) was commissioned by Philip II as a mausoleum for Spanish rulers. The highlights are the art museum, with works by Rubens, Tintoretto, Titian and Veronese, the palace, the basilica and the library. Approximately 9km (6 miles) from the Escorial is the **Valle de los Caídos** (Valley of the Fallen), a huge crypt cut into the mountainside surmounted by a stone cross of 152m (500ft). The dictator, General Franco, conceived this dramatic monument as a tribute to those on the Fascist side who died in the Civil War. Franco himself is buried here. **Alcalá de Henares**, a UNESCO World Heritage Site, is the birthplace of the writer Miguel de Cervantes and the English queen, Catherine of Aragon. The main point of interest is the university, founded in the 16th century by Cardinal Cisneros. Other attractions include the 17th-century convent of San Bernardo and the oldest surviving public theatre in Europe – as important to Spain as Shakespeare's Globe is to England. **Aranjuez** is famous for its gardens, an 18th-century **Summer Palace**, built by the Spanish Bourbons and Charles IV's enormously expensive folly, the **Casita del Labrador**, on the banks of the **River Tagus**. Aranjuez is known for strawberries and asparagus. The **Strawberry Train** (**Tren de la Fresa**), complete with steam engine and wooden carriages, operates between Madrid and Aranjuez between mid-April and July and September to mid-October. **Chinchón** is an attractive little town with an atmospheric main square, **Plaza Mayor**, still used for bullfights during the fiesta (August) and for a passion play at Easter. The mountains of the **Sierra de Guadarrama** are easily accessible from Madrid and are an important centre for skiing and winter sports. **Puerto de Navacerrada** and **Valdesquí** are the main resorts.

ANDALUCIA, CEUTA & MELILLA

Andalucia is a mountainous region in the far south of Spain, rich in minerals and an important centre for the

Credit: © Spanish Tourist Office

production of olives, grapes, oranges and lemons. Andalucia (Al-Andalus) was the last stronghold of the Moors who first arrived here from North Africa early in the eighth century and were finally expelled in 1492. The Arab architectural legacy is an important reason for visiting the region, especially the three great cities of Córdoba, Granada and Seville.

SEVILLE (SEVILLA): The regional capital is Seville, one of the largest cities in Spain, bearing numerous traces of the 500 years of Moorish occupation. Seville is the romantic heart of the country, the city of Carmen and Don Juan; its cathedral is the largest Gothic building in the world and has a superb collection of art and period stonework. Christopher Columbus is buried here. The cathedral bell tower, known as the **Giralda** from its crowning weather vane, was originally a minaret and observatory. The climb is worth the effort for the commanding views. Of great importance is the **Alcázar**, the palace-fortress of the Arab kings and one of the finest examples of **Mudéjar** (Moorish) architecture, mostly dating from after the Christian re-conquest. Seville's other sights include the **Alcázar gardens**, the evocative neighbourhood of **Santa Cruz** with its white-washed houses and tiled patios, and the **Torre de Oro**, part of the Arab fortifications and later said to have been covered with gold leaf imported from the Americas.

Holy Week in Seville embodies the religious fervour of the Spanish and is one of the most interesting festivals in the country. Early booking for accommodation at festival time is essential. Holy Week is followed closely by the famous *April Fair*, during which couples parade the fairground mounted on fine Andalucian horses, dressed in the traditional flamenco costume. Drinking, eating, song and dance are the order of the day for the whole week and the fairground with its coloured lanterns and *casetas* bordering the streets is a continuous movement of colour.

CÓRDOBA: Founded by the Romans, Córdoba's heyday was during the early Moorish period when it was reputed to be the most splendid city in Europe. The **Great Mosque** built between 785 and 1002 is the main tourist attraction. Highlights include the **Great Hall**, characterised by delicately carved horseshoe arches of alternating white stone and red brick, the **Patio de Los Naranjas**, the **Ablutions Courtyard** still shaded by orange trees and cooled by fountains, and the **Mihrab** (prayer niche). In the 16th century the mosque was transformed into a Christian church with the building of a Renaissance Choir. Other reminders of Córdoba's history are the old **Jewish Quarter**, which boasts a 14th-century mosque (one of only three in Spain), the **Archaeological Museum** with its substantial Roman and Moorish finds and the area by the river. Just outside town is the ruined palace of **Medina Azaha** – the site is still being excavated.

GRANADA: The last city to fall to the Christians, Granada's outstanding monument is the **Alhambra**, the palace-fortress built by the Nasrid rulers in the 13th to 14th centuries. The most popular tourist attraction in Spain, tickets must be booked at least 24 hours in advance. The highlights include: the **Palacios Nazariés**, its halls, courtyards and loggias decorated with painted enamel tiles, delicately fretted arches, stalactite vaulting, marble sculptures and stucco ornament; the **Alcazába**, an 11th-century hilltop fortress and the **Generalife**, the gardens of the summer palace. Across the river from the Alhambra is the atmospheric Arab quarter of the **Albaicín**. The main sights here are the **Arab baths**, the **Renaissance Casa de Castril** and the **Church of San Nicolás** from where the views of the Alhambra and the surrounding countryside are outstanding. In the town itself, visitors should not miss the

MADRID

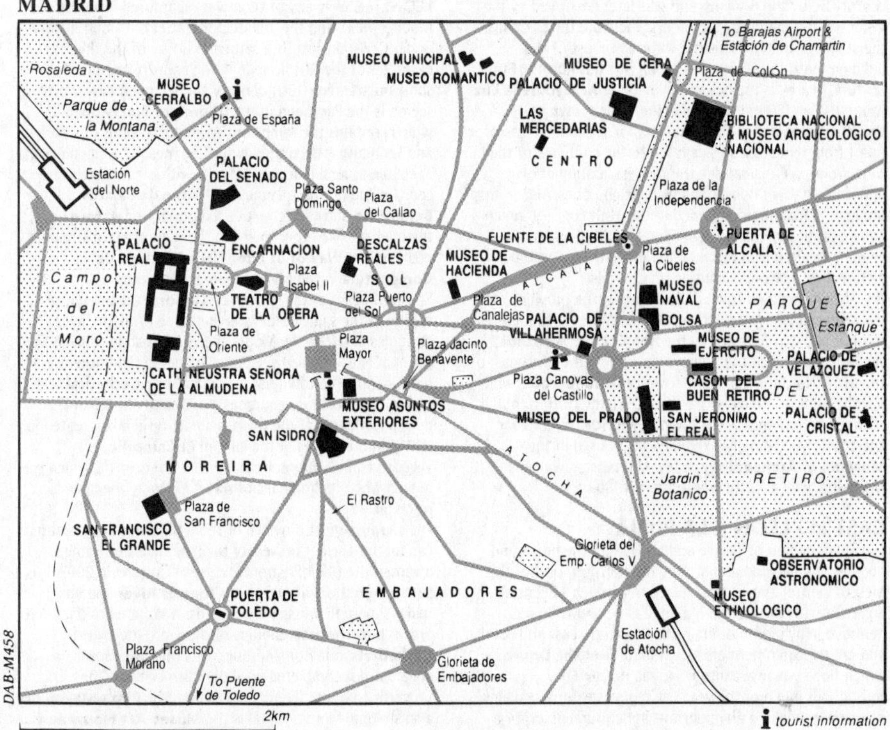

Gothic **Capilla Real** (**Royal Chapel**) built by Ferdinand and Isabella as a mausoleum and a symbol of their triumph over the Moors. The adjoining cathedral, built over several centuries, is impressive mainly in its proportions.
THE SIERRA NEVADA: South of Granada and only about 40km (25 miles) from the coast, is the upland area of the Sierra Nevada, a mountain range running roughly east to west. It contains the highest peaks in Iberia; one of these, the **Pico de Veleta** (over 3400m/11,155ft), is accessible for most of its height by road and coach trips. The region offers the unique opportunity to combine a holiday of winter sports with coastal sunshine and watersports in the Mediterranean (see below). Mountain resorts include **Capileira** (south of the Pico de Veleta), **Borreguiles** and **Pradollano** (both in the Solynieve region). There are also coach excursions from Granada to the picturesquely isolated villages of the **Alpujarra** on the southern fringes of the Sierra Nevada. There are dramatic views of the valleys and ravines from the twisting mountain roads.
Jaén is an ancient town rich in historic buildings and art treasures: the **Provincial Museum**, the **Cathedral**, the **Castle of Santa Catalina** and the 11th-century **Moorish baths** among them. **Baeza** is noteworthy for its aristocratic town houses, mostly dating from the Renaissance period. The most distinguished is the **Palacio de Jabalquinto**, its ornamentation clearly revealing Mudejar influences. Like Baeza, **Ubeda** has many Renaissance palaces, but the outstanding monument here is the **Capilla del Salvador**, a fine example of Plateresque architecture.
COSTA DE LA LUZ: This attractive stretch of coastline extends from the Portuguese border in the west to Tarifa in the east and, while popular with Spanish tourists, is still relatively undeveloped.
Cádiz's heyday as a port was in the 16th century when it traded in gold and silver from the Americas. Today, the town's slightly down-at-heel appearance is part of its charm. Points of interest include the sea fortifications, the 'old' and 'new' **cathedrals** and the tower, **Torre Tavira**, worth the climb for the sweeping rooftop views. The nearest beach is the **Playa de la Victoria**, but there are plenty of alternatives in the direction of **San Lúcar de Barremada**. Less than 30 minutes away is the sherry town of **Jerez de la Frontera**. Several of the **bodegas** (bars), whose links with England began with the importation of 'sherris-sack' in the 16th century, are open to the public for tastings. Other attractions include the splendid Renaissance **cathedral** and a restored 11th-century Moorish **Alcázar** with baths.
Another popular excursion from Cadiz is to the **Sierra de Grazalema National Park** where visitors can enjoy the wonderful mountain scenery. Points of interest along the route include the **Puerto de las Palomas** mountain pass which overlooks **Grazalema** itself, the fortified town of **Zahara de la Sierra** and **Arcos de la Fronteira**, a picturesque village with a commanding cliff top location overlooking the **Rio Guadalete**. The road from Cádiz to **Algeciras** offers spectacular views of the **Straits of Gibraltar**, the North African coastline and the **Atlas Mountains**. From Algeciras, ferries run to Tangier and Ceuta on the north African coast, as well as to the Canary Islands.
In the province of Huelva is the village of **El Rocío** where one of the most important Spanish festivals in honour of the Virgin Mary is held at Whitsun. Also of interest are the beautiful stalactite caves of **Gruta de las Maravillas** in **Aracena** in the north of Huelva province and the national park, **Coto de Doñana**.
COSTA DEL SOL: This densely populated area, popular with tourists on account of its fine beaches and picturesque towns, extends along most of Andalusia's Mediterranean coastline, from **Almeria** to **Tarifa**.
Usually regarded as little more than the gateway to the Costa del Sol, **Málaga** is an attractive and lively city with plenty to interest the passing visitor. The birthplace of Spain's greatest 20th-century artist, Pablo Picasso, it is now home to the newly opened **Picasso Museum** which exhibits an important collection of his paintings. His parents' house is also open to the public. Other sights worth a look are the unfinished **Cathedral** (16th to 18th centuries), the **Tropical Gardens** and two restored Moorish castles, the **Alcazaba** and **Gibralfara**. **Marbella** and **Torremolinos**, the main resorts of the Costa del Sol, are overdeveloped, but it is still possible to find a relatively uncrowded beach further afield. In the same province is **Nerja**, known as the 'Balcony of Europe' on account of its having a promontory look-out which is perched high above the sea with commanding views of the Mediterranean. It is also the home of well-preserved prehistoric caves. An excursion can be made from Málaga to the old mountain town of **Ronda**, spectacularly situated on a gorge in the **Sierra de Ronda**.
COSTA DE ALMERÍA: To the east of the Costa del Sol is the province of Almería, one of the most heavily developed tourist regions of the country. The capital of the same name is a former Roman port, dominated by its Moorish castle, the **Alcazaba**. Attractions here include the 16th-century **Cathedral** and the **Church of Santiago el Viejo**. The main resorts of **Roquetas de Mar, Aguadulce, El Cabo de Gata** and **Mojácar** lie east and west of the town.
THE AFRICAN ENCLAVES: Ceuta is a free port on the north coast of Africa. The city is dominated by the **Plaza de Africa** in the town centre and the cathedral. The promontory has the remains of the old fortress. Bus services are available into Morocco and there are regular car-ferry sailings from Algeciras.
Melilla is also a free port on the north coast of Africa, and is served by car ferries from Málaga and Almería. The town is mainly modern, but there are several older buildings, including a 16th-century church.

CASTILE/LA MANCHA & EXTREMADURA

This inland region lies between Madrid and Andalucia. Bordered by mountains to the north, east and south, it is irrigated by two large rivers, the **Guadiana** and the **Tajo**, both of which flow westwards to Portugal and thence to the Atlantic. Castile/La Mancha, the higher, western part of the region, is also known as **Castilla La Nueva** (New Castile).
CASTILE/LA MANCHA: To the south of Madrid is the ancient Spanish capital of **Toledo**. Rising above the plains and a gorge of the **Rio Tajo**, the city is dominated by the magnificent cathedral and **Alcazar**. The town seems tortured by streets as narrow as the steel blades for which it is famous. Toledo is justly proud of its collection of paintings by El Greco, who lived and painted here. El Greco's most famous painting, *The Burial of the Count of Orgaz*, is preserved in the **Santo Tomé Church**. There are more El Grecos as well as works by Goya and other artists in the **Hospital y Museo de Santa Cruz**, a magnificent Renaissance building with a Plateresque façade. Other reminders of Toledo's rich cultural heritage are its two medieval synagogues and a 10th-century mosque, currently undergoing restoration.
Guadalajara, capital of the province of the same name, is situated northeast of the capital, on the **Rio Henares**. Sights include the 15th-century **Palacio del Infantado** and the **Church of San Gines**.
The provincial capital of **Ciudad Real** is the chief town in the La Mancha region, the home of Don Quixote. There are many places in the surrounding area associated with Don Quixote, including **Campo de Criptana**, believed to be the setting for his fight with the windmills.
Cuenca, also a provincial capital, is famous for its hanging houses. It is one of the most attractive of Spain's medieval towns and the Gothic cathedral is particularly richly decorated. The nearby countryside includes woods, lakes, spectacular caves, towering mountains and valleys, many with fortified towns and villages clinging to their sides.
Albacete is the centre of a wine-producing region. The town witnessed two exceptionally bloody battles during the *Reconquista*, but the considerable rebuilding of the town has left few reminders of its history. More evidence, however, is scattered in the surrounding countryside, where such places as the Moorish castle at **Almansa** and the old fortified towns of **Chinchilla de Monte Aragón** and **Villena** reflect the area's stormy past.
EXTREMADURA: This region consists of the provinces of Cáceres and Badajoz. **Cáceres** was founded in the first century BC by the Romans, and was later destroyed by the Visigoths and rebuilt by the Moors. There are traces of all the stages of the city's history, although most of the buildings date from Cáceres' Golden Age during the 16th century. Nearby is the beautiful village of **Arroyo de la Luz**. Around 48km (30 miles) away is the walled town of **Trujillo**, birthplace of the conquistador, Francisco Pizarro. Apart from two museums devoted to the conquest of the New World, visitors can see the fortress, a number of Renaissance town houses and historic churches. Also in this province is **Plasencia**, founded in the 12th century, which has a beautiful medieval aqueduct, cathedral and a 15th-century convent that has retained much of its original architecture, masonry, painting and murals.
The ancient fortified town of **Badajoz** (in the province of the same name), is situated very close to the Portuguese frontier and was founded by the Romans. The **Alcazaba**, the Moorish part of the town, is on a hill in the northeast of the town. Not far away is the town of **Albuquerque**, which has the ruins of a massive castle and a large Gothic church. In the same province is the town of **Mérida**, famous for ancient Roman ruins; the remains are housed in the **Museum of Archaeology**. A few kilometres away is **Medellín**, where Cortés was born in 1485.

CASTILE/LEÓN & LA RIOJA

The inland region of Castile and León lie to the north and northwest of Madrid and occupy the northern part of the Meseta Central, the plateau that covers much of central Spain. As with the Madrid region, Castile and León are hemmed in by high mountains to the north, east and south and are the catchment area for a large river, the **Douro**, which flows westward into Portugal. Hot and dry throughout much of the year, the region's extensive plains nonetheless make it an important agricultural asset for a country as mountainous as Spain. The small wine region of La Rioja is tucked away to the northeast of Castile and León.
CASTILE LA VIEJA: Superbly situated on a plain overlooked by the **Sierra de Gredos**, **Avila** is the highest provincial capital in the country. A UNESCO World Heritage Site, it is famous for its perfectly preserved 11th-century walls and as the birthplace of the 16th-century mystic, St Teresa. Walking the ramparts is the most obvious attraction. The sights most closely associated with St Teresa are the 17th-century **Convent** now named in her honour (the small museum exhibits items of clothing and other possessions), the **Convento de la Encarnación**, where she served as a nun and the **Convento de San José** which she founded in 1562. The **Cathedral** is a curious hybrid of the Romanesque, Gothic and Renaissance styles.
Segovia is renowned for its 800m-long Roman aqueduct, one of the best preserved structures of its kind in the world. Its other attractions include 18 outstanding **Romanesque churches** and a Gothic **cathedral** by the Arab **Alcazar**. The turrets soaring from its rocky outcrop are said to be the inspiration for Walt Disney's fairytale castles. A short distance from the town is the wonderfully sited **Summer Palace** and gardens of La Granja, built in the first half of the 18th century for Philip V.
The province of **Soria** has a large number of archaeological remains of the Celtiberian and Roman civilisations, many of which can be seen in the **Museo Numantino** in the provincial capital of the same name. Around 9km (6 miles) north of the town is the site of **Numancia**, a fortified Celtiberian town. Attractions in the town of Soria include the 13th-century **Church of San Juan de Duero**, the **Cathedral of San Pedro** and the Renaissance **Palacio de los Condes de Gómara**.
Burgos was the birthplace of the knight El Cid, the embodiment of the chivalric tradition. His tomb, and that of his beloved Doña Jimena, can be seen in the magnificent Gothic cathedral. Palencia, the capital of the province of the same name, was the one-time residence of the Kings of Castile and seat of the Cortes of Castile. The 15th-century **Gothic Cathedral** is the main point of interest, though it can not stand comparison with Burgos. The city has several other late-medieval buildings and an **archaeological museum**. The industrial city of **Valladolid** (population 500,000), capital of a province rich in castles and other ancient buildings, is famous for the *Holy Week Procession* at Easter and the *Ferias Mayores* (Great Fairs) in September. Towards the end of October, the city hosts a major international film festival. Book ahead if a visit is planned at any of these times. The city is associated with some of the most famous names in the history of the Iberian peninsula. Columbus (although not a Spaniard) died here in 1506 – the **Museo de Colon** has objects and artefacts from the Mayan, Aztec and Inca civilisations; the great Spanish poet, Miguel de Cervantes, also had a home here, which is now a museum. The **Museo Nacional de Escultura** has the best collection of polychromatic religious sculpture in the world. There's also a beautiful medieval cathedral and a university. The superb castle at **Peñafiel** houses a **Museum of Wine** of the **Ribera del Duero** region, and commands stunning scenic views.
LEÓN: The lively city of León was recaptured from the Moors in 850, and the architecture reflects its long history under Christian rule. The cathedral is one of the finest examples of the Gothic style in the country and boasts some outstanding 13th-century stained glass. Also worth seeing is the Pantheon in the **Church of San Isidoro**, which contains the tombs of the medieval kings of Castile and León and is decorated with Romanesque wall paintings. There are several places of interest within easy reach of León, including the spectacular **Puerto de Pajares**, **Benavente** and the attractive region around **Astorga**, a town which, like other towns in the region, was a stopping point on the **Way of St James** (see **Santiago de Compostela** in the *Northern Region* section).
South of León is the province of **Zamora**; the provincial capital of the same name was the scene of many fierce struggles between the Moors and the Christians during the Reconquista, in which the Spanish hero El Cid figured prominently. The town has a Romanesque **Cathedral** and several 12th-century churches. Approximately 19km (12 miles) northwest of the town is an artificial lake, created in 1931; on the shores of the lake, in **El Campillo**, is a Visigoth church dating from the seventh century, which was moved when its original site was flooded by the new reservoir.
The southernmost province of León, **Salamanca**, has as its capital the ancient university town of the same name, awarded the title of 'European City of Culture' in 2002. It is situated on the swiftly flowing **Tormes River** and has many superb Renaissance buildings, weathered to a golden-brown hue. The most famous of these are the two **Cathedrals**, one Romanesque, the other late-Gothic in style but not completed until the 18th century. The university and the fine houses around the **Plaza Mayor** are also striking. More unusual is the **Museo Art Nouveau y**

Art Deco, with its fascinating collections of *objets d'art* from the first half of the 20th century. The fiesta in September is very popular and bookings should be made well in advance.

LA RIOJA: This region is famous for its vineyards. The capital, **Logroño**, is in the centre of the region. It is a district with a great historical past; the origins of poetry in the Castilian language lie here and it contains the channel of a European stream of culture – the **Road to Santiago**.

THE NORTHERN REGION

This region comprises northwestern Spain and the northern coast stretching as far as the French frontier. The two outstanding natural features are the **Cantabrian Mountains** and the **Rías Gallegas** estuaries in Galicia. The highest peaks are the **Picos de Europa** (2615m/8579ft) in Asturias, favoured by walkers, climbers and wildlife enthusiasts. There are excellent beaches along the entire coastline, mostly of fine sand, often surrounded by cliffs and crags. Much of the hinterland, however, is green, lush and forested. This is at least partly due to the climate, which is noticeably wetter than in the south.

GALICIA: Galicia is a mountainous region with large tracts of heathland broken by gorges and fast-flowing rivers. The coastline has many sandy bays, often backed with forests of fir and eucalyptus, and deep fjord-like estuaries (*rías*), which cut into the land. The dominant building material is granite. Galicia has its own culture and language (*gallego*, influenced by Portuguese) and many of the roadsigns are in two languages.

La Coruña is one of the largest towns in the region and is said to have been founded by the Phoenicians. Since then it has enjoyed a tempestuous history – the Armada set sail from here in 1588 and Sir John Moore's British Army had to evacuate the town following an ignominious retreat from Napoleon's forces in January 1809. Moore died in the encounter and is buried in the **Jardín de San Carlos**. La Coruña's most attractive feature is the **Ciudad Vieja** (old quarter) on the north spur of the harbour. **Santiago de Compostela** has been a centre of pilgrimage since the early middle ages and is a UNESCO World Heritage Site. The focal point for all visits is the Gothic **Cathedral** completed in 1188. Apart from the revered image of St James, it boasts a magnificent portico and crypt. For further information, see *The Way of St James* section. The Roman town of **Lugo** is noted for having one of the finest surviving examples of Roman walls. **Orense** first attracted the Romans on account of its therapeutic waters. The 13th-century cathedral was built on the site of one dating from the sixth century. **Pontevedra**, the region's fourth provincial capital, is a granite town with arcaded streets and many ancient buildings. Further south is the important port of **Vigo**, the centre of a region of attractive countryside. A good view of the town and the bay can be had from the **Castillo del Castro**.

THE WAY OF ST JAMES: During the Middle Ages, the tomb of St James at Santiago de Compostela was regarded as one of the most holy sites in Christendom and thousands of pilgrims travelled through Spain each year to visit the shrine. This route, the Way of St James, was lined with monasteries, religious houses, chapels and hospices to cater for the pilgrims. Many of these buildings still survive, and any traveller following the route today will find it an uplifting introduction to the religious architecture of medieval Spain. The route began in **Navarre**, at **Canfranc** or **Valcarlos**; from there, travelling west, the main stopping places were **Pamplona**, **Santo Domingo de la Calzada**, **Logroño**, **Burgos**, **León**, **Astorga** and **Santiago de Compostela**. The Saint's feast day, 25 July (the term 'day' is a misnomer since the festival runs for a full week) is celebrated in vigorous style in Santiago de Compostela and accommodation should be booked well in advance. There are several specialist books on the subject of this and other old pilgrim routes that may be followed, both in Spain and elsewhere in Europe.

ASTURIAS: This small, once independent principality is predominantly mountainous although there are also large tracts of forest. The resorts are known collectively as the **Costa Verde** on account of the rich vegetation. **Oviedo**, the capital of Asturias, is an historic town with an outstanding 12th-century Gothic **Cathedral**. The **Camara Santa** has some impressive Romanesque wall paintings and other artistic treasures. Asturias has a remarkably rich legacy of Romanesque churches, several of which can easily be visited from Oviedo. **San Julian de los Prados** dates from AD 830 and is decorated with medieval frescoes. The **Palacio de Santa Maria del Naranco** was also built in the ninth century for Ramiro I as a hunting lodge. The chapel of **San Miguel de Lillo** is nearby. There are many good beaches along the coast, especially around the large fishing village of **Ribadesella** and **Lastres**.

CANTABRIA: The Cantabrian resorts make a convenient base for expeditions to the mountains. Cantabria (and Asturias) are important centres for skiing and winter sports. The main stations are at **Alto Campo**, **San Isidro** and **Valgrande-Pajares**. **Santander** is a busy traditional resort set in a beautiful bay ringed with hills. The Gothic **Cathedral** was destroyed by fire in 1941, but has been carefully restored. The **Municipal Museum** contains a fine collection of paintings by many 17th- and 18th-century artists. Nearby are the fine beaches of **El Sardinero** and **Magdalena**. Santander hosts an impressive music festival throughout August. There are a number of smaller beach resorts to east and west of Santander: **Comillas**, **San Vincente** (an old fishing port with a hill-top Gothic church and ducal palace), **Laredo** and **Castro Urdiales** (an attractive village with a fine harbour, overlooked by a medieval church and the remains of a Knights Templar castle). The **Caves of Altamira** are decorated with wall paintings dating back 13,000 years. Note however that admission is strictly limited and advance applications are essential. 100 metres away is **Neocuerva**, a reproduction of the prehistoric original. Nearby is the well-preserved historic town of **Santillana del Mar** with buildings dating from the 12th to the 18th centuries. **Solares** is noted for the therapeutic qualities of its mineral waters.

THE BASQUE COUNTRY (PAÍS VASCO): Guipúzcoa, **Vizcaya** and **Alava** form the Basque provinces, to the east of the **Cantabrian Mountains**. The economy of this fertile region is based on agriculture, despite having been highly industrialised in the 19th century. The Basques are an ancient pre-Indo-European race and the origins of their language have baffled etymologists for centuries. An independence movement started to make headway around the turn of the 20th century and the separatists still have a following in parts of the region. The Spanish constitution allows the Basques a degree of autonomy, but Nationalist politicians are demanding a greater say in their own affairs. A large though declining port, **Bilbao** is the main city of the region. The city was founded in the early 14th century and the **Old Town** is quite extensive with a Gothic **Cathedral** and an attractive Town Hall. Bilbao's pre-eminent attraction is Frank Gehry's **Guggenheim Museum**, hailed as a masterpiece of 20th-century architecture. The vast exhibition spaces are given over to rotating exhibitions of modern art in all its forms. The **Palacio Euskalduna** is Bilbao's new congress and music centre.

The provincial capital of **San Sebastián**, situated very close to the French frontier, is one of the most fashionable and popular Spanish seaside resorts. Just 7km (4 miles) west of the town is **Monte Ulia**, which offers superb views across the countryside and the **Bay of Biscay**. The art treasures found in the 13th-century **Castle of Butron**, near Bilbao, are also worthy of note.

The third provincial capital of the Basque region, and also the regional capital, is Vitoria, famous as being the site of a British victory during the Peninsula War, an event commemorated in various places in the city. **Vitoria** is remarkable for having two cathedrals; one was completed in the 15th century, whilst the other, on which work commenced in 1907, has yet to be finished.

Credit: © Spanish Tourist Office

NAVARRE & ARAGON

These two medieval kingdoms lie southwest of the French border, with the Pyrenees to the northeast. The landscape offers spectacular views, the mountains contrasting with the lush valleys of the lower ground. This is a popular area for skiing and winter sports. The main resorts include **Astun**, **Candanchú**, **Cerler**, **El Formigal**, and **Panticosa**.

NAVARRE: Pamplona has been inundated with tourists ever since American writer Ernest Hemingway put the town on the map with his novel *The Sun Also Rises* (1927). His fascination was with the *Corrida*, the 'running of the bulls', at the *Festival of San Fermín* (Jul 6-14). During this week, brave or foolhardy visitors join the young men of the town in trying to outrun a large herd of bulls that stampedes through the town's narrow, closed streets. Visitors should book early and expect relatively high prices. Outside the fiesta season, Pamplona's main attractions are its old walled quarter, Renaissance **Cathedral** and imposing **Citadel**.

ARAGON: Aragon rose to prominence in the late 15th century when its kings resided at **Zaragoza**, now the regional capital. Situated on the **River Ebro**, it is a university town with a medieval **Cathedral**, a 17th-century **basilica** dedicated to the Virgin of Pilar (a focus of pilgrimage and celebrations in the second week of October) and the **Aljafería**, a Moorish palace dating from the 11th to the 15th centuries. The **Museo de Zaragoza** has finds dating back to the city's Roman foundations. In the surrounding countryside there are several areas noted for their wine production, such as **Borja** and **Cariñena**, and several castles.

Huesca, situated in the foothills of the **Pyrenees**, is an important market town. There are several attractions within easy reach, including the **Ordesa National Park**, excellent walking and climbing country; the popular summer holiday resort of **Arguis** in the Puerto de Monrepós region; the spa town of **Balneario de Panticosa**; and the high-altitude resort and frontier town of **Canfranc**.

The third and southernmost province of Aragon is **Teruel**. The provincial capital is sited on a hill surrounded by the

BARCELONA

BARRI GOTIC:
1. CATEDRAL
2. PLAÇA DEL REI
3. PLAÇA DE SANT JAIME
4. PALAU DE LA GENERALITAT
5. PALAU EPISCOPAL

FIRA DE BARCELONA:
A. PALAU NUMERO I
B. PALAU DE CINQUATENARI
C. PALAU DE CONGRESSOS
D. PALAU DE LA METAL-LÚRGIA
E. PALAU DE VICTORIA EUGENIA
F. PALAU D'ALFONS XIII
G. PALAU MUNICIPAL D'ESPORTS

1km
½ml

i tourist information

DAB-M453

gorges of the **Rio Turia**. It has a pronounced Moorish influence (the last mosque was not closed until 10 years after the end of the *Reconquista* in 1492), and there are several architectural survivals from its Islamic period. Nearby is the small episcopal city of **Sergobe**, spectacularly situated between two castle-crowned hills.

VALENCIA & MURCIA

VALENCIA: Spain's third-largest city (population 800,000), Valencia is famous for its orange groves, its fruit and vegetable market (one of the largest in Europe) and its lively nightlife. It is also a popular tourist resort with beaches a short bus ride from the town. The newest tourist attraction is Santiago Calatrava's **City of Arts and Science Park**. The **Hemispheric**, an amazing glass structure, houses a planetarium, IMAX dome and laserium. The **Palace of Arts** boasts the largest **oceanarium** in Europe. Valencia's **Cathedral** claims possession of the Holy Grail. The *Fallas* (Mar 15-19) is a major festival culminating in the burning of *papier-mâché* effigies satirising famous Spanish figures and a magnificent fireworks display.

ALICANTE & THE COSTA BLANCA: The **Costa Calida** in the province of Murcia lies to the south of Alicante and is thinly populated except in the areas around the river valleys. Summer temperatures here can be unbearably hot in the resorts but especially inland. **Murcia**, the town, has a **university**, **cathedral** and small **old quarter**. The salt water **lagoon** at **Mar Menor** is good for watersports, while nearby, **La Manga** offers tennis, golf and so on. Other resorts include **Mazarrón**, **La Unión** and **Aguilas**. The best time to visit **Cartagena**, founded, as its name implies, by the Carthaginians in the third century BC, is during *Holy Week*. The **town museum** has a good collection of Roman and pre-Roman artefacts. Space on the beaches around **Torrevieja** is at a premium during the summer.

Further north along the coast is **Alicante**, the most important town on the **Costa Blanca**. The town is dominated by the vast Moorish castle of **Santa Barbara**, which offers superb views of the city. Excursions from Alicante include a run inland to **Guadalest**, a village perched like an eagle's eyrie high in the mountains and accessible in the last stages only by donkey or on foot. Also of great interest are several historical sites, including the castles at **Elda** and **Villena**, and **Elche**, famous for its **forest of a million palm trees**, **Botanical Gardens** and **Basilica**, where a *medieval Mystery play* is performed to celebrate the feast of the Assumption (Aug 14-15).

The Costa Blanca has expanded rapidly in recent years and most of the coastal towns between the Peñón de Ifach and Alicante are primarily tourist resorts. Temperatures are higher than on the Costa Brava and the beaches tend to be more extensive. **Benidorm** is the largest and most intensively developed resort. The new **Terramitica** theme park is proving popular with visitors. One of many places of interest in the area is the **Peñón de Ifach** (Ifach Rock), 5km (3 miles) beyond the walled town of **Calpe**.

THE COSTA DEL AZAHAR: This coastal region extends from **Vinaròs** and the **Gulf of Valencia** to beyond **Denia**. The region has expansive beaches around **Benicàssim**, but its most outstanding feature is, perhaps, the medieval fortress town of **Peñiscola**, a dramatic sight when viewed from a distance. Other places of interest are the ruined castle of **Chisvert**, inland from Peñiscola; the 16th-century **Torre del Rey** at **Oropesa**; and the **Carmelite monastery** at the **Desierto de las Palmas**. North of Valencia is the attractive provincial capital of Castellón, **Castellón de la Plana**. This small town is situated on a fertile plain, and is the centre of a thriving trade in citrus fruits.

CATALONIA (CATALUNYA)

Catalonia is the eastern coastal region, bordering France. It has an ancient culture quite distinct from its neighbours, and many of the inhabitants speak Catalan, a Romance language influenced by medieval French. Catalonia is Spain's industrial and commercial powerhouse but agriculture (olive oil, wine, almonds and fruit) is also important in the region. Catalonia is an important focus of tourism, especially the seaside resorts of the **Costa Brava** and **Costa Dorada**. Skiing and winter sports are on offer for up to six months of the year in the Pyrenees: the resorts include **Baqueira-Beret**, **Espot Esquí**, **Masella**, **La Molina**, **Nuria**, **Port del Compte** and **Rasos de Peguera**.

BARCELONA: Spain's second-largest city (population 2.5 million) is a major commercial and industrial centre and an important Mediterranean port. The **Barri Gótic** (Gothic quarter), as the name suggests, has buildings dating back to the 14th and 15th centuries. Highlights include the **Seu** (old cathedral), the **Episcopal Palace**, the **Palau de la Generalitat** and the **Plaça del Rei**.

The **Museo Picasso** focuses on the artist's formative years, but includes works from the Blue and Rose periods. **Las Ramblas**, Barcelona's main thoroughfare, occupies the site of the ancient city walls and extends from the **Plaça de Catalunya** to the port. Cafes, bookstalls, flower and bird markets and street artists are just some of the attractions of this fashionable avenue. Beyond Plaça Catalunya, the **Eixample** (Extension) boasts a wealth of Art Nouveau and Art Deco architecture. The still incomplete church of the **Sagrada Familia** (Holy Family) is the masterpiece of Spain's greatest 20th-century architect, Antoni Gaudí. Other examples of his work are the **Casa Batlló**, the **Casa Mila** and **Parc Güell**. The funicular to **Tibidabo**, the highest of Barcelona's hills, and the cable car to **Montjuic** in the southern suburbs, offer spectacular views over the city. There are funfairs on both summits. Barcelona's best museums include the Picasso (see above), the **Fundació Joan Miró** with works by another of Spain's most innovative 20th-century artists, the **Museum of Catalan Art**, the **Maritime Museum**, the **Zoological Museum** and the **Monastery of Peldralbes** , which houses part of the Thyssen-Bornemisza art collection.

A popular excursion from Barcelona (40km, 24 miles) is to the famed monastery of **Montserrat** and the **shrine of the Black Madonna**. The mountain setting, 1135m (3725ft) above the **Llobregat River**, is spectacular.

THE COSTA DORADA: The coastline from Barcelona to Tarragona has more fine sandy beaches. **Tarragona** was an important army base in Roman times and visitors can still see the remains of the **forum**, **amphitheatre**, **aqueduct** and **fortified walls**. The city also has an impressive **medieval quarter**. Inland is the town of **Montblanc** with a fine **Gothic church** and the ruins of the 12th-century **Cistercian monastery** at **Poblet**. The two main resorts are **Salou** (the **Port-Aventura Theme Park** is a key attraction) and cosmopolitan **Sitges**.

THE COSTA BRAVA: This coastal strip northeast of Barcelona comprises pine-clad rocks, sandy bays and package resorts. Inland is Lleida, a province that borders the Pyrenees and boasts some of the most spectacular mountain scenery in Spain. Some resorts on the Costa Brava, such as **Tossa de Mar**, remain largely unspoilt despite the massive influx of holidaymakers; others (**Blanes** and **Lloret de Mar** for example) are intensely developed. In summer the crowds can begin to pall but, with persistence, relatively isolated beaches can be found. Coastal ferries operate between the main resorts. **Girona** (Gerona) is one of Catalonia's oldest cities, dating back to the Roman period. The **Gothic Cathedral** has a remarkable collection of medieval religious art. Other attractions include the **Arab baths**, the former **Jewish quarter** and the **fortified walls**. **Figueres** was the birthplace of the artist Salvador Dalí and has a fascinating **Museum** devoted to his work. **Cadaquès** is an enchanting, but touristy, fishing village made famous by Dalí who was a regular visitor. Pals is an intact medieval village, complete with fortifications. **Empúries** (Ampurias) has impressive Graeco-Roman remains.

Sport & Activities

Outdoor pursuits: The many high mountains and the vast central plain or *meseta* offer excellent opportunities for **hiking**, **mountaineering** and **walking**. Particularly suitable for **trekkers** are the mountains in the north of the country. The *Pyrenees*, which cover an area of 450 sq km, feature breathtaking scenery with rocky walls, lakes and ravines. The *Picos de Europa*, just west of Santander, are also wild and dramatic, with some peaks rising to over 2600 metres (8528 feet). Spain's flora and fauna includes the brown bear (found in the Asturias), the *cabra hispánica* or mountain goat (relatively common in the Pyrenees and the Sierra de Gredos, west of Avila) and the rare capercallie or European grouse (in the forests of northern Spain). There are good opportunities for **rock climbing** in the mountains. Well known, challenging climbs include the *Naranjo de Bulnes* in the *Picos de Europa* and *Monte Perdido* in *Ordesa National Park*. **Mountain biking** is becoming increasingly popular, and paths and tracks are plentiful, making most areas accessible. Spain's long equestrian tradition means that **horseriding** can easily be arranged. Mountain trails, river valleys and the wide plains can all be explored on horseback.

Watersports: Swimming, **water-skiing**, and **windsurfing** facilities can be found at nearly all seaside resorts. These can be busy in the summer months. Spain's premier windsurfing resort is *Tarifa*, on the Straits of Gibraltar, where the world championships are held. Inland lakes on the *meseta* in the regions of *Castilla* and *Extremadura* also have good facilities for windsurfing. **Whitewater rafting** and **canoeing** are practised on the rapids in northern Spain. Centres are well equipped and have skilled staff. **Sailing** is very popular, both around the coast and inland. Spain has over 4000km of coastline, and there are many harbours. Over 100 sailing clubs exist, most of which are located near the Mediterranean. **Diving** is also popular; permits can be acquired from the relevent regional authorities.

Fishing: Excellent opportunities exist for all types of fishing. The rivers and streams of the *Pyrenees* and the *Picos de Europa* offer good freshwater game fishing, while trout is abundant throughout the country. The *Asturias* contain the best salmon rivers. Other catches include barbel, perch, pike and tench. Permits must be requested from the regional authorities.

Golf: This is becoming increasingly popular, with both *Costa del Sol* and *La Manga* emerging as two of Spain's premier golfing destinations. At present, Spain has over 200 golf courses, including courses designed by the likes of Robert Trent Jones, Severiano Ballesteros, Jack Niklaus and Jose María Olazabel. The *Valderrama* (near Madrid) is particularly well known. Spain's balmy climate allows for a long golf season. Tuition and equipment hire are widely available.

Wintersports: Spain offers great opportunities for **skiing** and there are many natural ski-runs and winter resorts, equipped with modern facilities, all blessed with the promise of warm sun and blue skies. There is also a wide range of hotels, inns and refuges from which to choose. There are five main skiing regions in Spain; these are the Pyrenean Range, the Cantabrian Range, the Iberian Chain, the Central Chain and the Penibetic Chain. These ranges have diverse characteristics and all are attractive for **mountaineering** in general and for winter sports in particular. For further details, see *Madrid* and the regions of *Cantabria*, *Catalonia* and *Navarre & Aragon* in the *Resorts & Excursions* section.

Spectator sports: A typical and spectacular sport is **pelota vasca**, or **jai-alai**. Most major northern Spanish cities have courts where daily matches are played from October to June. In the towns and cities of the Basque regions, the game is played in summer as well. **Football** is probably the most popular spectator sport, with clubs such as Real Madrid and Barcelona being among the most famous in the world; first-class matches are usually played on Sunday. International matches are also staged from time to time. There is a magnificent **horse racing** track in Madrid with meetings in the autumn and spring; there is racing in San Sebastián in the summer and in Seville in winter. **Motor racing** is a popular spectator sport in Barcelona and Cadiz.

Social Profile

FOOD & DRINK: Eating out in Spain is often cheap and meals are substantial rather than gourmet. One of the best ways to sample Spanish food is to try *tapas*, or snacks, which are served at any time of day in local bars. These range from cheese and olives to squid or meat delicacies and are priced accordingly. Many of the specialities of Spanish cuisine are based on seafood, although regional specialities are easier to find inland than along the coast. In the northern Basque provinces, there is cod *vizcaina* or cod *pil-pil*; *angulas*, the tasty baby eels from Aguinaga; bream and squid. Asturias has its bean soup, *fabada*, cheeses and the best cider in Spain, and in Galicia there is shellfish - especially good in casseroles - and a number of regional seafood dishes such as *hake à la Gallega*.

In the eastern regions, the *paella* has a well-deserved reputation. It can be prepared in many ways, based on meat or seafood. Catalonia offers, among its outstanding specialities, lobster Catalan, *butifarra* sausage stewed with beans, and partridge with cabbage. *Pan amb tomaquet*, bread rubbed with olive oil and tomato, is a delicious accompaniment to local ham and cheese.

The Castile area specialises in roast meats, mainly lamb, beef, veal and suckling pig, but there are also stews, sausages, country ham and partridges. Andalucía is noted for its cooking (which shows a strong Arab influence), especially *gazpacho*, a delicious cold vegetable soup, a variety of fried fish including fresh anchovies, *jabugo* ham from Huelva and many dishes based on the fish that the coast provides in such abundance. Restaurants are classified by the Government and many offer tourist menus (*menu del día*). Restaurants and cafes have table service.

Spain is essentially a wine-drinking country, with sherry being one of the principal export products. Its English name is the anglicised version of the producing town Jerez (pronounced *khereth*), from which the wine was first shipped to England. Today, Britain buys about 75 per cent of all sherry exports. There are four main types: *fino* (very pale and very dry), *amontillado* (dry, richer in body and darker in colour), *oloroso* (medium, full-bodied, fragrant and golden) and *dulce* (sweet). Sanlúcar de Barrameda and Puerto de Santa María are other towns famous for their sherry and well worth visiting. Tourists are able to visit one of the *bodegas* (above-ground wine stores) in Jerez. In the Basque Country, a favourite is *chacolí* - a 'green' wine, slightly sparkling and a little sour, rather than dry.

The principal table wines are the *riojas* and *valdepeñas*, named after the regions in which they are produced. In general, *rioja*, from the region around Logroño in the northeast, resembles the French Bordeaux, though it is less delicate. *Valdepeñas* is a rougher wine, but pleasant and hearty. It will be found at its best in the region where it is grown, midway between Madrid and Cordóba.

In Catalonia, the *ampurdán* and *perelada* wines tend to be heavy and those that are not rather sweet are harsh, with

the exception of the magnificent full-bodied Burgundy-type *penedés* wines. Alicante wine, dry and strong, is really a light aperitif. Nearby, the Murcia region produces excellent wine. Often it makes a pleasant change to try the unbottled wines of the house (*vino de la casa*). It is much cheaper than the bottled wines and, even in small places, is usually good. Similarly, inexpensive supermarket wine is very acceptable. Among the many brands of sparkling wines known locally as *cava*, the most popular are *Codorniú* and *Freixenet*, dry or semi-dry. The majority of Spanish sparkling wines are sweet and fruity.
Spanish brandy is as different from French as Scotch whisky is from Irish. It is relatively cheap and pleasant, although most brandy drinkers find it a little sweet.
Spain has several good mineral waters. A popular brand is *Lanjarón* which comes from the town of the same name. It can be still or sparkling. *Vichy Catalan* is almost exactly like French Vichy. *Malavella* is slightly effervescent and *Font Vella* is still. Cocktail lounges have table and/or counter service. There are no licensing hours.
NIGHTLIFE: Spaniards often start the evening with *el paseo*, a leisurely stroll through the main streets. A cafe terrace is an excellent vantage point to observe this tradition, or enjoy street theatre in the larger cities. The atmosphere is especially vibrant at fiesta time, or when the local football team has won, when celebrations are marked by a cacophony of car horns, firecrackers and a sea of flags and team regalia. *Tapas* bars offer delicious snacks in a relaxed, enjoyable setting and it is fun to try out several bars in one night. The nightclubs of Ibiza, Barcelona and Madrid have attracted the attention of the international media, but the variety on offer caters for most tastes. Things work up to *la marcha* (good fun) relatively late and it is possible to literally dance until dawn. Flamenco or other regional dancing displays provide an alternative for those who prefer to watch dancing.
SHOPPING: In Spain, the shopper can find items of high quality at a fair price, not only in the cities, but in the small towns as well. In Madrid, the Rastro Market is recommended, particularly on Sundays. Half of the market takes place in the open air and half in more permanent galleries, and it has a character all of its own. Catalonian textiles are internationally famous and there are mills throughout the region. Spanish leather goods are prized throughout the world, offering high-fashion originals at reasonable prices. Of note are the suede coats and jackets. In general, all leather goods, particularly those from Andalucía, combine excellent craftsmanship with high-quality design. Fine, handcrafted wooden furniture is one of the outstanding products; Valencia is especially important in this field, and has a yearly international furniture fair. Alicante is an important centre for toy manufacturing. Shoe manufacturing is also of an especially high quality; the production centres are in Alicante and the Balearics. Fine rugs and carpets are made in Cáceres, Granada and Murcia. The numerous excellent sherries, wines and spirits produced in Spain make good souvenirs to take home. **Shopping hours:** Mon-Sat 1000-1300 and 1600-2000. However, most commercial stores and malls stay open from 1000-2200.
SPECIAL EVENTS: Throughout Spain, folklore is very much alive and there is always some form of folk festival occurring. It is almost impossible for a visitor to be anywhere in the country for more than a fortnight without something taking place. The Ministry of Tourism produces a booklet listing and describing Spain's many national and regional feasts and festivals, of which there are over 3000 each year. Fiestas, Saints' Days, *Romerías* (picnics to religious shrines) and *Verbenas* (night festivals on the eve of religious holidays) are all celebrated with great spirit and energy. *Holy Week* is probably the best time of year to visit for celebrations and it is then that the individuality of each region's style of pageantry is best revealed. For further information, contact the Spanish National Tourist Office (see *Contact Addresses* section). The following is a selection of special events occurring in Spain in 2005
Jan 19-20 *Tamborrada*, San Sebastián. **Feb 2-4** *Moors and Christians* (traditional festival), Bocairente. **Feb 3-9** *Carnival in Sitges* (gay carnival), Barcelona. **Feb 8** *Carnival Tuesday*, nationwide. **Mar 15-19** *Las Fallas*, Valencia. **Mar 20-27** *Holy Week* (religious celebrations), nationwide. **Apr 12-17** *Sevilla Fair*. **May** *Festival of the Courtyards and May Fair*, Cordoba. **May 1-3** *Cruces de Mayo*, Granada. **May 1-8** *Feria del Caballo* (horse market), Jerez. **May 15-29** *Fiestas de San Isidro*, Madrid. **Jun** *San Bernabe Fair*, Marbella. **Jun 14-24** *San Juán Festival*, Javea. **Jul 6-14** *San Fermín* (Running of the Bulls), Pamplona. **Jul 11** *San Beneitino de Leire* (traditional festival), Pontevedra. **Jul 16** *Sea Festival*, Fuengirola. **Jul 22-27** *Jazz Festival*, San Sebastián. **Aug 20-28** *Aste Nagusia*, Bilbao. **Aug 31** *La Tomatina*, Buñol. **Sep 24** *La Merced*, Barcelona. **Oct 2-3** *Moors and Christians*, Benidorm. **Oct 6-12** *Fuengirola Fair*. **Oct 28-30** *Saffron Festival*, Consuegra. **Nov** *Benidorm Festival*. **Dec 28** *The Verdiales* (popular music festival), Malaga.
Note: *Carnival* celebrations start around **Feb 8** and last for up to two weeks. Although Carnival is celebrated nationwide, the most famous carnival celebrations are held in the capitals of the Canary Islands - Santa Cruz de Tenerife and Las Palmas de Gran Canaria. For a full list of Carnival events and dates, contact the Spanish National Tourist Office (see *Contact Addresses* section).
SOCIAL CONVENTIONS: Spanish life has undergone rapid change in recent years and many of the stricter religious customs are giving way to more modern ways, particularly in the cities and among women.
Nonetheless, many old customs, manners and traditions have not faded and hospitality, chivalry and courtesy remain important. Handshaking is the customary form of greeting. Normal social courtesies should be observed when visiting someone's home. If invited to a private home, a small gift is appreciated. Flowers are only sent for special celebrations. Conservative casual wear is widely acceptable. Some hotels and restaurants encourage men to wear jackets. A black tie is only necessary for very formal occasions and is usually specified if required. Outside resorts, scanty beachwear should be confined to beach or poolside. Smoking is widely accepted. The evening meal is taken late, generally 2100-2200. The Spanish have two family names; in conversation only the first should be used.
Tipping: Service charges and taxes are usually included in hotel bills, however in addition, a tip should be left for the chambermaid and porters should be tipped per bag. It is also customary to leave a tip for the waiter. Restaurants often include service in the bill so a tip is discretionary. In cafes and bars, it is 5 to 10 per cent. Tip taxis 10 to 15 per cent when metered.

Business Profile

ECONOMY: Until 1975, under the Franco regime, the Spanish economy developed almost in isolation, protected from foreign competition by tight import controls and high tariffs, and gradually evolved from an essentially agrarian economy to an industrial one. Spain joined the (then) European Community in 1986. The transition, which was expected to be very difficult, passed off remarkably well and the Spanish economy now ranks eighth in the world by output. Despite the decline of many of its traditional industries, such as shipbuilding, steel and textiles, Spain achieved the highest average growth rate in the Community during the 1980s and a steady performance throughout the 1990s. This was largely due to the growth of its service sector, which now accounts for two-thirds of economic output.
The only significant legacy of structural weaknesses in the Spanish economy which has not been fully tackled is unemployment, which remains stubbornly high at 11 per cent of the workforce in 2004. However, other economic indicators - such as interest rates and budget deficit - are within the limits that allowed Spain to join the European Monetary Union at the start of 1999. In common with most of its EU partners, the Spanish economy has slowed somewhat since 2000, although annual GDP growth increased in 2004 to 3 per cent.
The agricultural sector produces cereals, vegetables, citrus fruit, olive oil and wine. The processed foods industry has also expanded rapidly. The fishing fleet, although reduced from its peak of a few decades ago, remains one of the world's largest. The relative importance of the agriculture, forestry and fisheries sectors has declined over the last decade and now accounts for less than 4 per cent of GDP. Energy requirements are met by indigenous coal and natural gas, imported oil (mostly from north Africa), and a sizeable nuclear power programme. In the manufacturing sector, the decline of older industries has been offset by rapid expansion in chemicals, electronics, information technology and industrial design. Spain has also become an important producer of motor vehicles; this industry alone accounts for 5 per cent of GDP and 80 per cent of all output is exported. In the service sector, Spain has a vast tourism industry mainly servicing visitors from northern Europe: in 2002, this brought an estimated $40 billion (about 7 per cent of GDP) into the economy. Financial services, transport, media and telecommunications have also undergone substantial growth. The EU countries, the USA and Japan are the country's main trading partners.
BUSINESS: Businesspeople are generally expected to dress smartly. Although English is widely spoken, an interest in Spanish and an effort on the part of the visitor to speak even a few words will be appreciated. Business cards are exchanged frequently as a matter of courtesy and appointments should be made. Punctuality is important. **Office hours:** Tend to vary considerably. Businesspeople are advised to check before making calls.
COMMERCIAL INFORMATION: The following organisations can offer advice: Consejo Superior de Cámaras de Comercio, Industria y Navegación de España, C/Ribera del Loira 12, 28042 Madrid (tel: (90) 210 0096; fax: (92) 528 0007; e-mail: info@cscamaras.es; website: www.camaras.org); *or* Instituo Español de Comercio Exterior (ICEX), 2nd Floor, 66 Chiltern Street, London W1U 4LS, UK (tel: (020) 7467 2330; fax: (020) 7487 5586; e-mail: buzon.oficial@londres.ofcomes.mcx.es; website: www.mcx.es/londres).
CONFERENCES/CONVENTIONS: Most large towns have dedicated convention centres in addition to the facilities provided by hotels. Seating capacity ranges from 540 in Jaca to 4200 in Palma de Mallorca; Madrid can seat up to 2650 persons. Further details can be obtained from the Spain Convention Bureau (FEMP), Calle Nuncio 8, 28005 Madrid (tel: (91) 364 3700; fax: (91) 365 5482; e-mail: secretaria@femp.es; website: www.femp.es); *or* Oficina de Congresos de Madrid, Calle Mayor 69, 28013 Madrid (tel: (91) 588 2900; fax: (91) 588 2930; e-mail: congresos@munimadrid.es; website: www.munimadrid.es/congresos); *or* from the Spanish Tourist Office (see *Contact Addresses* section).

Climate

Spain's climate varies from temperate in the north to dry and hot in the south. The best months are from April to October, although mid-summer (July to August) can be excessively hot throughout the country except the coastal regions. Madrid is best in late spring or autumn. The central plateau can be bitterly cold in winter.
Required clothing: Light- to mediumweights and rainwear, according to the season.

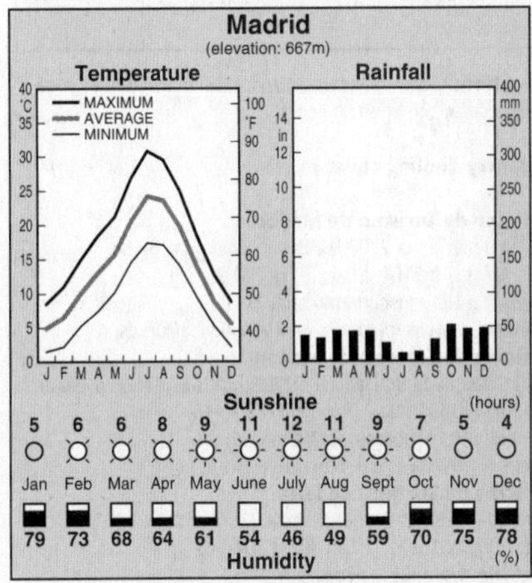

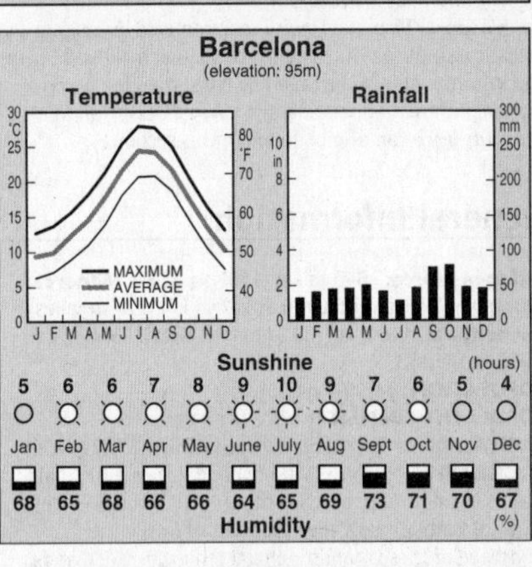

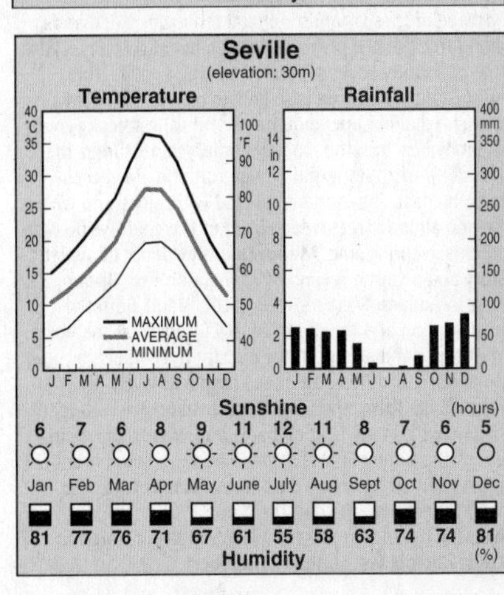

Balearic Islands

LATEST TRAVEL ADVICE CONTACTS

British Foreign and Commonwealth Office
Tel: (0870) 606 0290 Website: www.fco.gov.uk
US Department of State
Website: http://travel.state.gov/travel
Canadian Department of Foreign Affairs and Int'l Trade
Tel: (1 800) 267 8376 Website: www.dfait-maeci.gc.ca

Location: Mediterranean, 240km (150 miles) due east of Valencia on the Spanish coast.

Country dialling code: 34.

Oficina de Turismo de Mallorca
Plaza de la Reina 2, 07012 Palma, Mallorca, Spain
Tel: (971) 712 216. Fax: (971) 720 251.
E-mail: oit@conselldemallorca.net
Website: www.a-palma.es *or* www.illesbalears.es
Oficina de Turismo de Mahón
Calle Rovellada de Dalt 24, 07703 Mahón, Menorca, Spain
Tel: (971) 363 790. Fax: (971) 367 415.
E-mail: infomenorcamao@cime.es
Website: www.e-menorca.org
Oficina de Turismo de Ibiza
Avenida Antonio Riquer 2, Ibiza 07800, Spain
Tel: (971) 301 900. Fax: (971) 301 562.
Website: www.illesbalears.es
The *Passport/Visa* and *Health* requirements for visiting the Balearic Islands are the same as for visiting mainland Spain, and information may be found by consulting the *Spain* section. Information relating to *Money*, *Public Holidays* and *Duty-Free* can also be found in this section.

General Information

AREA: Mallorca: 3640 sq km (1405 sq miles). **Menorca:** 700 sq km (270 sq miles). **Ibiza:** 572 sq km (220 sq miles). **Formentera:** 100 sq km (38 sq miles). **Total:** 5014 sq km (1935 sq miles).
POPULATION: 947,361 (2003).
POPULATION DENSITY: 175.2 per sq km.
CAPITAL: Palma de Mallorca. **Population:** 367,277 (2003).
GEOGRAPHY: Mallorca, Menorca and Ibiza are the main islands in this group, which is situated 193km (120 miles) south of Barcelona off the east coast of Spain. The landscape of these islands is characterised by woodlands, almond trees, fertile plains and magnificent coastlines with numerous sandy coves separated by craggy cliffs. The largest island, **Mallorca** (also known as the 'Isle of Dreams'), has a varied landscape: mountains and valleys, rocky coves and sandy beaches. The main geographical feature is the Sierra del Norte, a mountain range running along the northern coast. The island is covered with pines, and with olive and almond trees, which blanket the countryside with blossoms in springtime. **Menorca** has evidence of ancient history and a strong feeling of connection with Britain, owing to Admiral Nelson's stay on the island. Both the capital Mahón and the old town of Ciutadella at the north end of the island are set at the ends of deep inlets forming natural harbours. There are many bays and lovely beaches on the island. **Ibiza**, the third-largest island, has a rugged coastline with many fruit orchards and woods. The main town of the same name is situated above a busy harbour. A narrow channel separates Ibiza from **Formentera**, the smallest inhabited island in the group.
TIME: GMT + 1 (GMT + 2 from last Sunday in March to Saturday before last Sunday in October).

Credit: © Spanish Tourist Office

Travel - International

AIR: Local flights run by *Iberia (IB)* link all the islands. *Air Europa* and *Spanair* also fly.
Approximate flight times: From *Palma de Mallorca* to London is two hours 15 minutes; from *Menorca* is two hours 20 minutes and from *Ibiza* is two hours 20 minutes.
International airports: *Palma de Mallorca (PMI)* (Son San Juan) is 11km (7 miles) southeast of the city. Buses to the city leave every 30 to 60 minutes (0705-0005; travel time - 30 minutes). Return is from Plaza España. Taxis to the city are also available. The airport has a duty free shop, first aid facilities, bank/bureau de change, bars, car hire, tourist information and post office.
Mahón (MAH) is 6km (4 miles) from Mahón. Coaches or taxis are available to the town.
Ibiza (IBZ) is 8km (5 miles) from the town of Ibiza. Buses to the city leave hourly (0700-2330). Taxis are available to the city.
SEA: The following shipping lines run services to the Balearic Islands: *Balearia Eurolines Maritimes* (website: www.balearia.net); *Buquebus España SA*; *CNAN – Compagnie Nationale Algérienne de Navigation* (car ferry) from Algiers; and *Compañia Trasmediterránea* (car ferry) (website: www.trasmediterranea.es) from Alicante, Barcelona, Valencia and inter-island to Palma, Balearia. The main ports are Palma (Mallorca), Mao and Ciutadella de Menorca (Menorca) and La Savina (Formentera).
Local: There is also a ferry service from Sète (France) to Palma. There are regular ferries from Ibiza to Formentera (travel time - 45 minutes).
RAIL: On Mallorca, narrow-gauge trains run from Palma to Soller five times daily, and to Inca every hour. The Inca-Manacor line reopened in 2003. Inter-Rail passes are not valid. There are no railways on any of the other islands.
ROAD: There are generally good bus services on the islands connecting resorts with main towns. Car and scooter hire is generally available. The steep, narrow inland roads make it difficult for coaches and cars to pass each other (although there are special passing points). On Mallorca, there are over 110km (68 miles) of road, and three toll-free highways lead from Palma to Manova, Cala Blava and Inca. For travel by coach, it is best to check timetables before commencing your journey to avoid difficulties; hotels can often provide this information.

Accommodation

Note: The Balearic government levies an 'eco tax' on people holidaying in the islands. This compulsory fee (equivalent to approximately €1 a day) is to be collected by accommodation providers and is, as yet, not generally included in travel agents'/brochure prices.
HOTELS: Establishments of all categories exist in the Balearics, including hotels catering for around 230,000 visitors, chalets, apartments and bungalows. It is possible to rent furnished or unfurnished chalets for the season, although visitors must book in advance, owing to demand. Rates vary according to season and the standard of accommodation. Numerous packages are available.
CAMPING: There are nine campsites in the Balearic Islands. For further information, contact the Spanish Tourist Office (see *Contact Addresses* in the main *Spain* section).
YOUTH HOSTELS: The Spanish Youth Hostel Network (REAJ) runs a youth hostel in Palma, at Costa Brava 13, 07610 Palma de Mallorca (tel: (971) 260 892; fax: (971) 262 012; e-mail: albergue.platja.de.palma.@bitel.es). There is also a youth hostel in Alcudia, at Ctra. Cap Pinar Km 407400, Alcudia 07400 (tel: (971) 545 823; fax: (902) 111 188; e-mail: lavictoria@bitel.es).

Resorts & Excursions

The Balearics is the name given to the archipelago of four main islands off the Mediterranean coast of Spain (193km/120 miles south of Barcelona). Mallorca, Menorca and Ibiza are all popular tourist destinations, offering remarkably varied scenery as well as beach resorts that provide every kind of amenity. The largest town in the Balearics is Palma (Mallorca). Regular ferry services link Mallorca, Menorca, Ibiza and Formentera.

MALLORCA

Of all the Balearic Islands, Mallorca probably has the most to see and explore, lending itself to a number of half- and full-day excursions, all of which can be made from **Palma**. The best scenery lies in the north of the island. One way to enjoy the mountains of the **Serra de Tramuntana** and the photogenic villages clinging to the lower slopes is to take the antique tourist train to **Sóller** – a tram takes visitors the short distance to the port and coastal resort of the same name. Another worthwhile excursion is to the beautifully sited **Monastery of Valldemossa**, where the composer Frederic Chopin spent the winter of 1838-9, trying, without success, to regain his health. He was accompanied by his mistress, George Sand, who later published a famous account of the disastrous visit. Tourists are also shown the **Formentor Peninsula**, famous for its pinewoods and secluded coves, and the caves of **Hams** and **Drac**, on the eastern coast near **Porto Cristo**. Mention should also be made of the enchanting village of **Deía**, one-time home of the English poet, Robert Graves.
The island's coastline is 300km (186 miles) long and while some stretches have suffered from over-development, many of the beaches retain their natural beauty. The busiest resorts area is the **Bay of Palma** (there are regular bus services from the city). Also popular is the **Bay of Alcúdia** in the northeast of the island. There is a daily boat service during the summer from Port d'Alcúdia to **Menorca** (Ciudadela).
PALMA: The capital clearly demonstrates its long association with maritime commerce and its history as a major Mediterranean port. The old city is beautifully situated on the **Bay of Palma** with modern developments to the east and west. Palma is overlooked by the 14th-century **Castle of Belver**, and other notable buildings include the golden sandstone cathedral (La Seo), the **Archbishop's Palace**, the **Monastery** and **Church of San Francisco** and the **Montesion Church**. Apart from these major buildings, there are many beautiful palaces and churches in the city, many of which were built from the profits of commerce. Palma also offers excellent facilities for holidaymakers, including health care.

MENORCA, IBIZA & FORMENTERA

MENORCA: The second-largest island in the group lies some 40km (25 miles) northeast of Mallorca. The capital, **Mahón**, has many buildings dating from the period of British occupation (1713-83) and is best explored on foot. The attractions include the **Town Hall** (Casa Consistorial), the **Church of Santa Maria** and the **Church of San Francisco**. Trips are available around the harbour. A good highway links Mahón with the older town of **Ciudadela** (the former capital) on the opposite side of the island. It has a **Cathedral**, partly dating from the 14th century, and also boasts several elegant **palacios** and **medieval churches**. Despite the lack of coastal roads, it is possible to explore most points of interest from these two centres, both of which have good beaches within easy reach. Across the island, visitors will encounter prehistoric stone formations from the Talayot civilisation of the second millennium BC. The most important site is **Talatí de Dalt**. Menorca has conserved its stock-farming and leather-working traditions, making its economy less dependent on revenue earned through tourism. Dairy farming centres on **Alaior** where the local cheeses are on sale in the market.
IBIZA: The third-largest island in the group has never been more popular, thanks largely to its frenetic nightlife. The clubs specialising in house music are concentrated in Ibiza Town and San Antonio. Ibiza is much quieter during the October to May period when it retains some of its

traditional atmosphere. There are good sandy beaches south of the capital at **Ses Salines** and **Es Cavallet**. Away from the coast, the island is densely wooded. **Ibiza Town** has a medieval fortress and the **Dalt Vila** (Upper Town) is well worth exploring. Southwest of the town centre is the Punic cemetery **Puig des Molins**. The two other major tourist centres are the coastal towns of **San Antonio Abad** and **Santa Eulalia del Río**.
FORMENTERA: Separated from Ibiza by a 4km- (2 mile-) channel (hourly boat services operate during the summer), the main settlement is the large village of **San Francisco Javier**. Like the other islands in the group, Formentera has no shortage of pinewoods and sandy beaches, and the pace of life is generally more relaxed than on Ibiza.

Sport & Activities

Watersports: Underwater **fishing** is especially popular, with sea bass, sole, dentex, dorado and sea bream all plentiful. It is possible to swim in the sea virtually all year round. Innumerable heated **swimming** pools are also available. There are facilities for different forms of **sailing** in the many sheltered bays. The Balearic Islands are also an arrival point for many Mediterranean **yacht cruises**. Mooring fees in any of the yacht clubs (Palma de Mallorca, Mahón, Ciudadela, Andraitx and Ibiza) are reasonable. Facilities for other watersports, including **water-skiing**, **windsurfing**, **parasailing** and **diving**, are also available. **Other: Tennis** can be played in the Real Club of Palma and in Ibiza, as well as on the private courts of the major hotels of the different towns. There are **golf** courses attached to the big hotels. American **bowling** alleys are available on all the islands. **Horse racing** and **riding** have long been popular. **Bikes** can be hired.

Social Profile

FOOD & DRINK: The varied local cuisine includes rabbit, a wide selection of seafood and pork dishes, Mahón cheeses from Menorca, numerous locally grown fruits and vegetables. Dishes include Mallorcan *ensaimada* (light, sweet pastry roll), Ibizan *flao*, *graixonere de peix*, *tumbet*, *escaldums* of chicken, *sobresada*, Mallorcan soups, and mayonnaise, the famous culinary invention from Menorca. The islands have plenty of good wines and aromatic liqueurs, such as *palo*, which is made from locally grown *St John's bread* (carob beans) and *frigola*. Imported alcoholic and soft drinks are also widely available.
NIGHTLIFE: There are numerous nightclubs and discos (especially in Ibiza), some with open-air dancefloors overlooking the sea, floorshows, live bands and orchestras. There are also many cinemas, theatres, concerts and art exhibitions. Approximately 18km (11 miles) west of Palma, in Magaluf, there is an elegant casino with a large restaurant. For the latest news on the local nightlife, and details of current events, artistic and cultural, consult the local English-language newspaper, *The Bulletin*.
SHOPPING: On the Balearic Islands, there is a strong tradition of craftsmanship. Purchases include furniture, hand embroidered works, handpainted ceramics, carved olive-wood panels, wrought ironwork, glassware, items made from raffia and palm leaves, handmade shoes, the famous pearls made in Mallorca and other costume jewellery from Menorca. **Shopping hours:** Mon-Sat 0900-1300 and 1630-1930.

Climate

The islands enjoy a temperate, Mediterranean climate. The maximum temperatures are not excessive, even in high summer, owing to the cooling influence of the sea. The climate during the winter is mild and dry, and temperatures below zero are practically unknown.

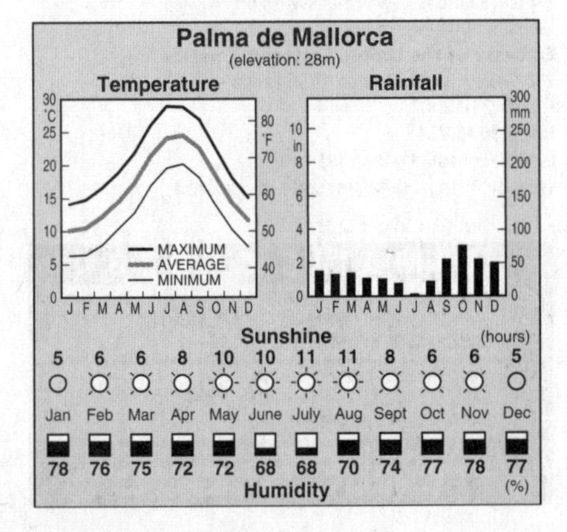

Canary Islands

LATEST TRAVEL ADVICE CONTACTS

British Foreign and Commonwealth Office
Tel: (0870) 606 0290 Website: www.fco.gov.uk
US Department of State
Website: http://travel.state.gov/travel
Canadian Department of Foreign Affairs and Int'l Trade
Tel: (1 800) 267 8376 Website: www.dfait-maeci.gc.ca

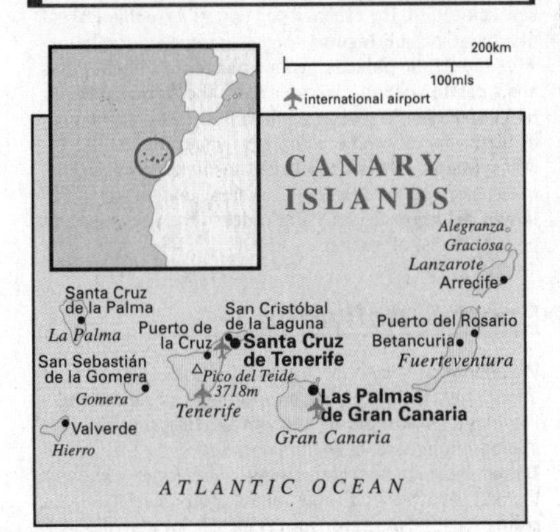

Location: North Atlantic, west of the African coast.

Country dialling code: 34.

Dirección General de Promoción Turistica
Avenida Alcalde Ramirez Bethencorut 7, 35003 Las Palmas de Gran Canaria, Spain
Tel: (928) 306 845.
Fax: (928) 306 813.
E-mail: pturtur@gobiernodecanarias.org *or* comentarios@gobiernodecanarias.org
Website: www.gobiernodecanarias.org
Patronato de Turismo
Leon y Castillo 17, 35003 Las Palmas de Gran Canaria, Spain
Tel: (928) 219 600.
Fax: (928) 219 601.
E-mail: turismo@grancanaria.com
Website: www.grancanaria.com
Saturno
Victor Hugo 60, 35006 Las Palmas de Gran Canaria, Spain
Tel: (928) 293 698.
Fax: (928) 293 738.
E-mail: info@canarias-turismo.com
Website: www.sapromocion.com
The *Passport/Visa* and *Health* requirements for visiting the Canary Islands are exactly the same as for visiting mainland Spain, and information may be found by consulting the *Spain* section. Information relating to *Money, Public Holidays* and *Duty Free* can also be found in this section.

General Information

AREA: 7242 sq km (2796 sq miles).
POPULATION: 1,672,689 (1999).
POPULATION DENSITY: 231.0 per sq km.
CAPITAL: Provincial capitals are Las Palmas de Gran Canaria: **Population:** 377,660 (2003); and Santa Cruz de Tenerife: **Population:** 220,033 (2003).
GEOGRAPHY: The Canary Islands are situated off the northwest coast of Africa and consist of seven islands which are divided into two provinces. **Las Palmas** comprises the islands of Gran Canaria, Fuerteventura and Lanzarote. **Santa Cruz de Tenerife** is made up of Tenerife, La Palma, Gomera and Hierro. All the islands are of volcanic origin and the climate is subtropical. The landscape is varied, and includes mountain ranges, valleys, deserts, cliffs, craters and forests.
TIME: GMT (GMT + 1 from last Sunday in March to Saturday before last Sunday in October).

Travel - International

AIR: Local flights run by *Iberia (IB)* link all the islands.
Approximate flight times: From *Las Palmas* to *London* is six hours 10 minutes (including stopover in Madrid) and from *Tenerife* is six hours 10 minutes (including stopover in Madrid). Direct flights from London to either destination take four hours 15 minutes.
International airports: *Gran Canaria (LPA)* is 22km (14

Credit: © Spanish Tourist Office

miles) south of Las Palmas. Hotel coaches to the city leave every 30 minutes (0630-0200; travel time - 20 minutes). Return journey is from Iberia terminal (Hotel Iberia), Avenida Maritima. Public bus service to the city leaves every 30 minutes, operating a 24-hour service. Return is from the bus station, Parque de San Telmo. Taxis to the city are available. Airport facilities include banks/bureaux de change, post office, chemists, medical service and car hire.
Tenerife-Norte Los Rodeos (TFN), in the north of the island, is 13km (8 miles) from Santa Cruz. Bus service runs every 30 minutes from 0600-2300.
Tenerife-Sur Reina Sofia (TFS), in the south of the island, is used for resorts such as Playa de las Americas. Bus service is scheduled according to flight arrivals. Taxis are available.
La Gomera, 38km northwest of Valle Gran Rey and 34km from San Sebastian, offers regular connections with Gran Canaria and North Tenerife. There are regular bus services to all towns on the island. For further information, contact La Gomera Airport (tel: (34) 9228 73000; website: www.aena.es).
SEA: The majority of cruise ships stop in the Canaries. Further details are available from the Spanish National Tourist Office. *Trasmediterránea* operates a weekly (Saturday) car ferry departing at 1800 from Cadiz-Tenerife-Las Palmas. Contact their UK agent, *Southern Ferries*, 5th Floor, 179 Piccadilly, London W1V 9DB, UK (tel: (020) 7491 4968; fax: (020) 7491 3502; website: www.trasmediterranea.es).
All the islands are linked by regular car and passenger ferries. Day trips to the smaller islands are quickly and easily arranged.
ROAD: There are bus services available. Cars may be hired.

Accommodation

HOTELS: There is a large selection of hotels of all categories. There are also four *paradores* (tourist inns) as well as *pensiones* (guest houses), which are run by the family on the premises and provide bed and board.
CAMPING: There are four campsites, of which three are in Las Palmas and one in Santa Cruz. For further information, contact the Dirección General de Promoción Turistica (see *Contact Addresses* section).
YOUTH HOSTEL: The Spanish Youth Hostel Network (REAJ) (website: www.reaj.com) has a youth hostel in Las Palmas, Avenida de la Juventad, 35450 Santa Maria de Guia, Gran Canaria (tel: (928) 550 685; fax: (928) 882 728).

Resorts & Excursions

The Canary Islands (Islas Canarias) are much closer to the coast of Africa than to mainland Spain and it is the mid-Atlantic location that accounts for the remarkably mild climate. While best known for their white, pristine beaches, the seven islands, all of volcanic origin, offer strikingly diverse landscapes: sub-tropical rainforests, arid plains, pine woods, sand dunes, mountain peaks and remarkable flora. The main tourist resorts are excellent for watersports, windsurfing, sailing, fishing, tennis, golf and so on. The local people take great pride in their folklore traditions and the carnival festivities are famous throughout Spain.
This section follows the administrative division of the archipelago into two provinces: Santa Cruz (Tenerife, La Palma, Gomera and Hierro) and Las Palmas (Grand Canaria, Fuerteventure and Lanzarote).

SANTA CRUZ

TENERIFE: The largest of the islands, Tenerife is dominated by a central mountain range and several spectacular valleys. It has a national park, a gigantic natural crater some 19km (12 miles) in diameter and, to the north, the **Pico del**

A B C D E F G H I J K L M N O P Q R S T U V W X Y Z

Credit: © Spanish Tourist Office

Teide, the highest mountain in Spain. The capital, **Santa Cruz**, is a cosmopolitan city, rich in architecture, notably the **Church of San Francisco**, and has good art and history museums. In the village of **Güimar**, 25km (16 miles) southeast of Santa Cruz, is **Pyramid Park**, where the archaeological digs are worth a visit. **Puerto de la Cruz** is the most important resort and has several buildings dating back to the 17th century. Other places to visit include the second city of **La Laguna**, **La Orotava** (centre of a lush valley), **Garachico** (the 'Pearl by the Sea') and **Los Cristianos**.

LA PALMA: La Palma boasts one of the largest craters in the world, the **Caldera de Taburiente**, best viewed from the **La Cumbrecita** look-out point. The capital of **Santa Cruz** (not to be confused with Santa Cruz de Tenerife) is also worth exploring for its 16th-century architecture and the **Natural History Museum**. Also worth visiting are the woods of **Tilos** near **Los Sauces** (a UNESCO Biosphere Reserve), **Cueva Bonita**, a beautiful natural grotto, and the beaches of **Los Llanos de Aridane**, **Los Cancajos** and **Nogales**.

GOMERA: Gomera is rich in vegetation and is blessed with white sand beaches, particularly **Vallehermoso**. Though not as mountainous as other islands in the group, the terrain is rugged and the most practical method of getting around is often by sea. The capital, **San Sebastián**, is interesting for its connections with the explorer Christopher Columbus, who is commemorated by the **Torre del Conde**, an old fortress and now a national monument. Other noteworthy places on the island are the fishing ports of **Playa de Santiago** and **La Rajita** and the primeval laurel forest of the **Garajonay National Park**. Gomera is famous for its 'whistling' language, used by the islanders to call from mountain to mountain.

HIERRO: The smallest and least-visited island with hardly any beaches, Hierro's coastline mostly comprises sheer cliffs. **Valverde** is the attractive capital. **La Peña** is a look-out point with commanding views and a restaurant. The tiny fishing village of **La Restinga** is the most southern point of the Canaries, and hence Spain, and hence – politically if not strictly geographically – of Europe as well. Surfers head for **Timijiraque**, one of the few sand beaches on the island.

LAS PALMAS

GRAN CANARIA: Gran Canaria is often referred to as a 'miniature continent', as plants usually associated with Europe, Africa and the Americas all flourish here. The splendid beaches include **Playa del Inglés** and **Maspalomas**, nearly 6km (4 miles) long. The capital, **Las Palmas** (not to be confused with the smaller island of La Palma), is a lively city with a magnificent location between two bays. The sights include the **Old Town**, the Gothic **Cathedral of Santa Ana** and several museums. Columbus lived in Las Palmas for a time before setting out on his voyage of discovery. The city has a lively cultural life with opera, dance and music festivals. **Ingenio** is famous for its crafts. **San Bartolomé de Tirajana** is dramatically situated in the crater of a volcano. The fishing ports of **Mogan** and **Sardina del Norte** are worth a visit.

FUERTEVENTURA: The second-largest of the Canary Islands has excellent beaches, particularly around **Jandía** in the south. The island's capital, **Puerto del Rosario**, is home to about one-third of the population and was built in the late 18th century. Other attractions on the island include **Corralejo** in the far north (where straw hats are woven in the traditional manner), and the Norman castle of **Rico Roque**, near **Cotillo**. **Betancuria**, the ancient capital of the island, houses its most important monument, the **Church of Santa María**, noted for its painted ceiling and murals. Camels are a common method of transport on this sandy island.

LANZAROTE: The most easterly of the Canaries is dry and relatively flat. It owes its eerie landscape to the activity of more than 300 volcanoes long since dormant. The ash and craters have been turned to the islanders' advantage for vine cultivation. The capital is the port of **Arrecife**. Places of interest include **Teguise**, the picturesque old capital, with aristocratic **palaces**, historic **convents** and **churches** and a **castle** built on a volcanic cone. The **National Park of Timanfaya** is a spectacular lava flow, awe-inspiring in its barren majesty and covering nearly one-third of the island. **Malpaís de la Corona** has an immense volcanic cave called **Los Verdes**, 6km (3.5 miles) long; nearby is the **Jameo del Agua** lagoon. Camel rides to the volcanoes are a popular tourist attraction.

Sport & Activities

Watersports: The warm, clear sea is excellent for underwater **fishing**, **diving**, **snorkelling** and **swimming**. Facilities for **water-skiing** and **windsurfing** are also available from beaches or from hotels.

Other: There are numerous **tennis** courts (often owned by the hotel or attached to apartments), **golf** courses and **riding** stables. **Spectator sports** include **jai-alai**, the stick game (a sort of fencing with long poles), Canaries **wrestling** and the *garrocha* which is especially practised on the island of La Palma.

Social Profile

FOOD & DRINK: The cuisine of the Canaries offers many dishes based on fish, which are usually served with potatoes and a special sauce called *mojo picón*. The traditional dishes are watercress soup and the popular *sancocho canario*, a fish salad with a hot sauce. Locally grown bananas, tomatoes, avocados and papayas also play an important part in the Canaries' cuisine. Corn meal, wheat flour, pre-roasted corn or barley are eaten instead of bread with certain local dishes. Local pastries include the excellent *tirijalas, bienmesabes, frangollo, bizcochos lustrados, quesadillas, rapaduras y marquesotes*, meat pies and 'nougats' of corn meal and molasses. In the main resorts, restaurants offer the full range of international cuisine, as well as local delicacies. Often restaurants cater for the tastes of particular nationalities.

A full range of wines, spirits and liqueurs from throughout the world is available. Spanish wines and spirits are particularly good value and spirits are slightly cheaper than in the UK. Local beers are pilsner-type lagers and, on the whole, rather weak. Local wines are also produced. Other drinks originating from the islands are rum, honey-rum and Malmsey wine.

SHOPPING: Besides the excellent duty free shopping, there are numerous local items to tempt the visitor. Craftsmanship is represented mainly by skilled open-work and embroidery. Pottery, basket-work based on palm leaves, cane and reed and delicate woodcarvings are also popular. Tobacco produced here is excellent and world famous. Cigars from the Canary Islands are outstanding in quality.

Shopping hours: Mon-Sat 0900-1300 and 1630-1930.

Climate

The climate in the northern islands of the Canaries is subtropical; the south of the islands tends to be hotter and drier, although rainfall is generally low throughout the islands.

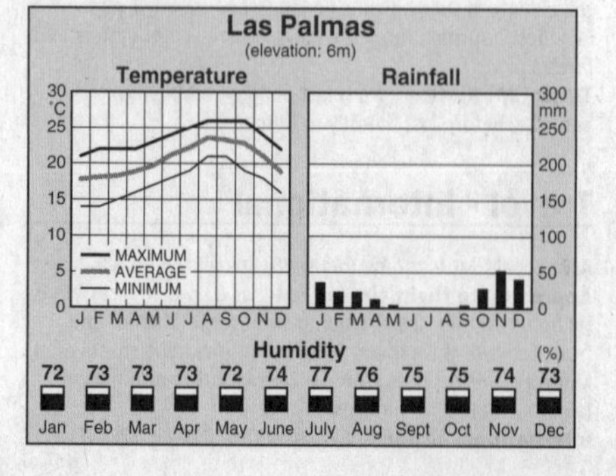

Sri Lanka

LATEST TRAVEL ADVICE CONTACTS

British Foreign and Commonwealth Office
Tel: (0870) 606 0290 Website: www.fco.gov.uk

US Department of State
Website: http://travel.state.gov/travel

Canadian Department of Foreign Affairs and Int'l Trade
Tel: (1 800) 267 8376 Website: www.dfait-maeci.gc.ca

Location: South Asia.

Country dialling code: 94.

Sri Lanka Tourist Board
80 Galle Road, Colombo 3, Sri Lanka
Tel: (1) 243 7759. Fax: (1) 243 7953.
E-mail: tourinfo@sri.lanka.net
Website: www.srilankantourism.org

High Commission of Sri Lanka
13 Hyde Park Gardens, London W2 2LU, UK
Tel: (020) 7262 1841-7. Fax: (020) 7262 7970.
E-mail: mail@slhc.globalnet.co.uk
Website: www.slhclondon.org
Opening hours: Mon-Fri 0930-1700; 0930-1300 (visa section).

Sri Lanka Tourist Board
Clareville House, 26-27 Oxendon Street, London SW1Y 4EL, UK
Tel: (020) 7930 2627. Fax: (020) 7930 9070.
E-mail: srilankatourism@aol.com
Website: www.srilankantourism.org
Opening hours: Mon-Fri 0900-1700.

British High Commission
Street address: 190 Galle Road, Colombo 3, Kollupitiya, Sri Lanka
Postal address: PO Box 1433, Colombo 3, Sri Lanka
Tel: (1) 243 7336-43 *or* 233 5803 (visa section).
Fax: (1) 243 0308.
E-mail: bhc@eureka.lk *or* bhctrade@slt.lk (commercial).
Website: www.britishhighcommission.gov.uk/srilanka

Embassy of Sri Lanka
2148 Wyoming Avenue, NW, Washington, DC 20008, USA
Tel: (202) 483 4025-8. Fax: (202) 232 7181.
E-mail: slembassy@slembassyusa.org
Website: www.slembassyusa.org

Embassy of the United States of America
210 Galle Road, Colombo 3, Sri Lanka
Tel: (1) 244 8007.
Fax: (1) 243 7345.
E-mail: consularcolombo@state.gov
Website: http://usembassy.state.gov/srilanka

TIMATIC CODES

Health	AMADEUS: **TI-DFT/CMB/HE** GALILEO/WORLDSPAN: **TI-DFT/CMB/HE** SABRE: **TIDFT/CMB/HE**
Visa	AMADEUS: **TI-DFT/CMB/VI** GALILEO/WORLDSPAN: **TI-DFT/CMB/VI** SABRE: **TIDFT/CMB/VI**

To access TIMATIC country information on Health and Visa regulations through the Computer Reservations System (CRS), type in the appropriate command line listed above.

High Commission of Sri Lanka
333 Laurier Avenue West, Suite 1204, Ottawa, Ontario K1P 1C1, Canada
Tel: (613) 233 8449. Fax: (613) 238 8448.
E-mail: slhcgen@sprint.ca
Website: www.srilankahcottawa.org
Consulate General in: Toronto.

Canadian High Commission
Street address: 6 Gregory's Road, Cinnamon Gardens, Colombo 07, Sri Lanka
Postal address: PO Box 1006, Colombo 07, Sri Lanka
Tel: (1) 269 5841 *or* 522 6232. Fax: (1) 268 7049.
E-mail: clmbo-cs@international.gc.ca

General Information

AREA: 65,525 sq km (25,299 sq miles).
POPULATION: 19,007,000 (official estimate 2002).
POPULATION DENSITY: 286 per sq km.
CAPITAL: Sri Jayewardenepura Kotte (official). **Population:** 115,826 (2001). Colombo (commercial). **Population:** 642,020 (2001). Sri Jayawardenepura Kotte is only 10km (6 miles) from Colombo.
GEOGRAPHY: Sri Lanka is an island off the southeast coast of the Indian state of Tamil Nadu. It is separated from India by the Indian Ocean, in which lies the chain of islands called Adam's Bridge. Sri Lanka has an irregular surface with low-lying coastal plains running inland from the northern and eastern shores. The central and southern areas slope into hills and mountains. The highest peak is Pidurutalagala (2524m/8281ft).
GOVERNMENT: Democratic Socialist Republic since 1978. Gained independence from the UK in 1948. **Head of State:** President Chandrika Kumaratunga since 1994. **Head of Government:** Prime Minister Mahinda Rajapakse since 2004.
LANGUAGE: Sinhala, Tamil and English.
RELIGION: Buddhist majority (70 per cent), with Hindu, Christian and Muslim minorities.
TIME: GMT + 6.
ELECTRICITY: 230 volts AC, 50Hz. Round three-pin plugs are usual, with bayonet lamp fittings.
COMMUNICATIONS: Telephone: IDD facilities are available to the principal cities. Country code: 94. Outgoing international code: 00. Phone cards are available at post offices and shops. **Mobile telephone:** GSM 900/1800 network. Network operators include *Celltel Infiniti* (website: www.celltel.net), *Dialog GSM* (website: www.dialog.lk), *Hutchison* (website: www.hutchison.lk) and *Mobitel* (website: www.mobitellanka.com). **Fax:** The General Post Office in Colombo (address below) provides a service. Many hotels also have facilities. **Internet:** Internet cafes provide public access to Internet and e-mail services. ISPs include *Pan Lanka Networking PL* (website: www.panlanka.net). **Telegram:** These can be sent from all post offices. **Post:** Overseas mail usually takes 10 to 14 days. The main post office in Colombo is opposite the President's house: General Post Office, Janadhipathi Mawatha, Colombo 1. **Press:** The most popular daily newspapers published in English include the *Daily Mirror*, *Daily News*, *Evening Observer*, *The Island* and *Lankadeepa*.
Radio: BBC World Service (website: www.bbc.co.uk/worldservice) and Voice of America (website: www.voa.gov) can be received. From time to time the frequencies change and the most up-to-date can be found online.

Passport/Visa

	Passport Required?	Visa Required?	Return Ticket Required?
Full British	Yes	No	Yes
Australian	Yes	No	Yes
Canadian	Yes	No	Yes
USA	Yes	No	Yes
Other EU	Yes	No/1	Yes
Japanese	Yes	No	Yes

Note: *Regulations and requirements may be subject to change at short notice, and you are advised to contact the appropriate diplomatic or consular authority before finalising travel arrangements. Details of these may be found at the head of this country's entry. Any numbers in the chart refer to the footnotes below.*

PASSPORTS: Passport valid for at least six months from date of entry required by all.
VISAS: Required by all except nationals of the following countries, who will be issued with visas free of charge for a period of 30 days on arrival at Colombo Airport (for touristic visits only):
(a) nationals of those countries mentioned in the chart above (except **1.** nationals of Malta and the Slovak Republic who *do* require a visa);
(b) nationals of Albania, Bahrain, Bangladesh, Bhutan, Bosnia & Herzegovina, Brunei, Bulgaria, China (PR, including Hong Kong), Croatia, India, Indonesia, Iran, Israel, Korea

Credit: © Marie Peyre

(Rep), Kuwait, Macedonia, Malaysia, Maldives, Nepal, New Zealand, Norway, Oman, Pakistan, The Philippines, Qatar, Romania, Saudi Arabia, Serbia & Montenegro, Seychelles, Singapore, South Africa, Switzerland, Taiwan, Thailand, Turkey and United Arab Emirates;
(c) nationals of CIS countries.
Note: All business visitors require a visa.
Types of visa and cost: *Tourist* and *Business*: £38 (up to three months); fee given is for UK nationals. Fees vary according to nationality; contact the Consulate (or Consular section at Embassy or High Commission); see *Contact Addresses* section. Multiple-entry visas cost £114 (three months) or £189 (12 months).
Validity: As above. Visitors can request to extend their stay by applying to the Department of Immigration & Emigration, 23 Station Road, Colombo 3 (tel: (1) 259 7513; fax: (1) 259 7511). This is issued at the discretion of the authorities who must be satisfied that the applicant has at least US$30 per day for the stay and holds an onward or return ticket for travel.
Application to: Consulate (or Consular section at Embassy or High Commission); see *Contact Addresses* section. British nationals, travelling as tourists, may obtain a visa upon arrival, upon port of entry into Sri Lanka, for up to 30 days.
Application requirements: (a) Valid passport. (b) Completed application form. (c) Two passport-size photos signed on the back by applicant. (d) Visa fee, payable by cash (not if sending by post) or postal order. (e) Self-addressed envelope, with appropriate cost of stamps necessary for returning passport by registered post. (f) Proof of sufficient funds (minimum US$30 per day) for duration of stay. (g) Return or onward ticket. *Business:* (a)-(g) and, (h) A letter from the company or organisation recommending the issue of visa and giving details of the status of the applicant, nature of business, duration of stay, sufficient funds and details of the party, if available in Sri Lanka, with whom the business is to be conducted, along with a letter from that company/organisation in Sri Lanka.
Working days required: At least three.
Temporary residence: Enquire at Embassy or High Commission.

Money

Currency: Sri Lanka Rupee (SLRe, singular; SLRs, plural) = 100 cents. Notes are in denominations of SLRs1000, 500, 200, 100, 50, 20, 10 and 2. Coins are in denominations of SLRs10, 5, 2 and 1, and 50, 25, 10, 5, 2 and 1 cents. There are also large numbers of commemorative coins in circulation.
Currency exchange: Foreign currency must be changed only at authorised exchanges, banks and hotels, and these establishments must endorse such exchanges on the visitor's Exchange Control D form, which is issued on arrival and must usually be returned at the time of departure.
Credit & debit cards: American Express, MasterCard and Visa are widely accepted. Diners Club has more limited acceptance. Check with your credit or debit card company.
Travellers cheques: The rate of exchange for travellers cheques is better than the rate of exchange for cash. To avoid additional exchange rate charges, travellers are advised to take travellers cheques in US Dollars or Pounds Sterling.
Currency restrictions: The import and export of local currency is limited to SLRs1000. The import of notes from India and Pakistan is not allowed, otherwise, the import of foreign currency is not restricted but all amounts over US$5000 are subject to declaration. Export of foreign currency is limited to the amount declared on import.
Exchange rate indicators: The following figures are included as a guide to the movements of the Sri Lanka Rupee against Sterling and the US Dollar:

Date	Feb '04	May '04	Aug '04	Nov '04
£1.00=	177.07	175.93	189.62	196.34
$1.00=	97.28	98.50	102.92	104.94

Banking hours: Mon-Fri 0900-1300. Some city banks close at 1500, whilst some even have night bank facilities.

Duty Free

The following items may be imported into Sri Lanka by visitors aged 18 years and over without incurring customs duty:
200 cigarettes or 50 cigars or 340g of tobacco; two bottles of wine and 1.5l of spirits; a small quantity of perfume and 250ml of eau de toilette.
Prohibited items: Firearms, explosives and dangerous weapons; ivory; antiques, statues and treasures; old books; animals/birds/reptiles (dead or alive) and parts; tea; rubber; coconut plants; dangerous drugs.
Note: (a) Only two members of the same family travelling together are entitled to free import allowances. (b) Valuable personal effects (including jewellery), must be declared on arrival in Sri Lanka. (c) There is no gift allowance.

Credit: © Marie Peyre

Public Holidays

2005: Jan 14 Tamil Thai Pongal Day. **Jan 21** Eid al-Adha (Hadji Festival Day). **Feb 4** Independence Commemoration Day. **Feb 7** Mahasivaratri. **Mar 25** Good Friday. **Apr 13-14** Tamil and Sinhala New Year. **Apr 21** Milad un-Nabi (Birth of the Prophet). **May 1** May Day. **May 23-24** Vesak Poya Days. **Nov 1** Deepavali. **Nov 3-5** Eid al-Fitr (End of Ramadan). **Dec 25** Christmas Day.
2006: Jan 10 Eid al-Adha (Hadji Festival Day). **Jan 14** Tamil Thai Pongal Day. **Feb** *or* **Mar** Mahasivaratri. **Feb 4** Independence Commemoration Day. **Apr 11** Milad un-Nabi (Birth of the Prophet). **Apr 13-14** Tamil and Sinhala New Year. **Apr 14** Good Friday. **May** Vesak Poya Days. **May 1** May Day. **Oct 21** Deepavali. **Oct 22-24** Eid al-Fitr (End of Ramadan). **Dec 25** Christmas Day.
Note: (a) Although not official public holidays, *Poya holidays* are often observed on the day of each full moon. In general, Hindu and Buddhist festivals are declared according to local astronomical observations and it is often only possible to forecast the approximate time of their occurrence. (b) Muslim festivals are timed according to local sightings of various phases of the moon and the dates given above are approximations. During the lunar month of Ramadan that precedes Eid al-Fitr, Muslims fast during the day and feast at night and normal business patterns may be interrupted; however, since Sri Lanka is not a predominantly Muslim country restrictions (which travellers may experience elsewhere) are unlikely to cause problems.

Health

	Special Precautions?	Certificate Required?
Yellow Fever	No	1
Cholera	Yes	2
Typhoid & Polio	3	N/A
Malaria	4	N/A

Note: *Regulations and requirements may be subject to change at short notice, and you are advised to contact your doctor well in advance of your intended date of departure. Any numbers in the chart refer to the footnotes below.*

1: A yellow fever vaccination certificate is required from travellers over one year of age from infected areas.
2: Following WHO guidelines issued in 1973, a cholera vaccination certificate is not a condition of entry to Sri Lanka. However, cholera is a serious risk in this country and precautions are essential. Up-to-date advice should be sought before deciding whether these precautions should include vaccination as medical opinion is divided over its effectiveness; see the *Health* appendix.
3: Typhoid occurs in rural areas.
4: Malaria risk, predominantly in the benign *vivax* form, exists throughout the year, except in the districts of Colombo, Galle, Kalutara and Nuwara Eliya. The malignant *falciparum* strain is also present and is reported to be highly resistant to chloroquine and sulfadoxine-pyrimethamine. The recommended prophylaxis is chloroquine plus proguanil.
Food & drink: All water should be regarded as being potentially contaminated. Water used for drinking, brushing teeth or making ice should have first been boiled or otherwise sterilised. Bottled water and a variety of mineral waters are available at most hotels. Unpasteurised milk should be boiled. Powdered or tinned milk is available and is advised, but make sure that it is reconstituted with pure water. Pasteurised and sterilised milk is available in some hotels and shops. Avoid dairy products made with unboiled milk. Only eat well-cooked meat and fish, preferably served hot. Pork, salad and mayonnaise may carry increased risk. Vegetables should be cooked and fruit peeled.
Other risks: *Hepatitis A, B* and *E* are present and precautions should be taken. *Dengue fever* occurs. *Rabies* is present. For those at high risk, vaccination before arrival should be considered. If you are bitten, seek medical advice without delay. For more information, consult the *Health* appendix.
Health care: Treatment is free at government hospitals and dispensaries; 24-hour treatment is available at Colombo General Hospital. Some hotels also have doctors.

Travel - International

Note: The December 26 2004 tsunami caused extensive damage to the southwestern, southern and eastern coasts. Travellers should seek the latest information prior to travel. All but essential travel to the north or east (other than Trincomalee, Nilaveli and Arugam Bay) is advised against. Much of the north and east of Sri Lanka remains heavily mined, particularly around the A9 road to Jaffna. There is currently heavy flooding in low-lying areas in the north and east, particularly the Jaffna district, and north of Trincomalee (including the road to Nilaveli). There is a threat from domestic terrorism in Sri Lanka. However, most visits to Sri Lanka are trouble-free.
AIR: Sri Lanka's national airline is *SriLankan Airlines (UL)* (website: www.srilankan.lk).
Approximate flight times: From Colombo to *London* is 13 hours 45 minutes, to *Hong Kong* is five hours 10 minutes, to the *Seychelles* is three hours 55 minutes and to *Tokyo* is 12 hours.
International airports: *Colombo Bandaranaike (CMB)* (Katunayake) is 29km (19 miles) north of the city. Buses go to the city regularly and take 45 to 60 minutes. Taxis are available. There are trains to Maradana Station, located 1.6km (1 mile) from the city centre (travel time – 60 minutes). Airport facilities include duty free shop, restaurant, bar, snack bar, bank, post office, tourist information and car hire.
Departure tax: None.
SEA: International ports include Colombo, Galle, Talaimannar and Trincomalee. Passenger services to Sri Lanka are operated by *CIT, Cunard, Holland America, P&O* and *Royal Viking*.

Travel - Internal

AIR: The major domestic airport is *Ratmalana* at Colombo. There are daily flights to smaller airports at Batticaloa, Gal Oya, Palali and Trincomalee. The airport at Jaffna is currently closed.
Departure tax: An embarkation tax of Rs1000 is payable at the Bandaranaike International Airport. Otherwise, none.
Helicopter tours: *Helitours of Ceylon*, with pilots from the Sri Lanka Air Force, offers charter tours of major tourist areas.
RAIL: Trains connect Colombo with all tourist towns, but first-class carriages, air conditioning and dining cars are available on only a few. New fast services operate on the principal routes, including an inter-city express service between Colombo and Kandy, otherwise journeys are fairly leisurely. The total network covers 1500km (900 miles).
Note: Rail services to Jaffna have ceased owing to the violent political disruptions in the northern area.
ROAD: Traffic drives on the left. Most roads are tarred, with a 56kph (35mph) speed limit in built-up areas and 75kph (45mph) outside towns. **Bus:** An extensive network of services of reasonable quality is provided by the *Sri Lanka Central Transport Board*. Private bus drivers are paid according to the number of passengers and can often drive rather dangerously. **Taxi:** These are available in most towns. It is advisable to agree a rate before setting off. **Car hire:** This is available from several international agencies. Air-conditioned minibuses are also available. Chauffeur-driven cars are less expensive and recommended. Avoid remote areas and travelling at night. **Documentation:** In order to avoid bureaucratic formalities in Sri Lanka, an International Driving Permit should be obtained before departure. If not, a temporary licence to drive is obtainable on presentation of a valid national driving licence. This must be endorsed at the AA office in Colombo. The minimum age for driving a car is 18.
URBAN: Bus: The Central Transport Board provides intensive urban bus operations in Colombo, where there are also private buses and minibuses. Fares are generally collected by conductors. Services are often crowded. **Taxi:** These are metered with yellow tops, and red and white plates. Drivers expect a 10 per cent tip. Travel Times: The following chart gives approximate travel times (in hours and minutes) from Colombo to other major cities/towns in Sri Lanka.
Travel Times: The following chart gives approximate travel times (in hours and minutes) from **Colombo** to other major cities/towns in Sri Lanka.

	Air	Road	Rail
Kandy	-	2.30	3.00
Galle	-	3.00	3.00
Bentota	-	1.45	1.45
Matara	-	4.00	4.30
Badulla	-	9.30	9.00
Negombo	-	0.45	0.45
Nuwara Eliya	-	3.30	5.00
Anuradhapura	0.45	5.30	6.00
Polonnaruwa	1.00	6.00	7.00
Trincomalee	1.00	6.00	7.00
Kataragama	-	6.30	-

Accommodation

HOTELS: Sri Lanka offers a wide choice of accommodation. There are seven international-class 5-star hotels with every modern facility. **Grading:** Hotels are classified from **1** to **5 stars**. For further information, contact the Sri Lanka Tourist Hotels Association (see *Business Profile* section); *or* Ceylon Hotels Corporation, 411 Galle Road, Bambalapitiya, Colombo 4 (tel: (1) 250 3497 *or* 259 8923; fax: (1) 250 3504; e-mail: info@ceylonhotels.lk; website: www.ceylonhotels.lk).
GUEST HOUSES: Inns, guest houses and rest houses offer comfortable but informal accommodation.
PRIVATE HOMES: For visitors who would like to get to know the Sri Lankans and see how they live, arrangements can be made to stay in private homes or on a tea or rubber plantation.
PARK BUNGALOWS: There are also many park bungalows run by the Department of Wildlife Conservation, which are furnished and equipped for comfort rather than sophistication.

Resorts & Excursions

Ancient sites include Anuradhapura, Polonnaruwa, Sigiriya, Dambulla, Panduwasnuwara and Yapahuwa. All these places contain the remains of a great civilisation that grew through the centuries under the influence of Buddhism, a gentle faith still preserved in Sri Lanka in its purest form. Vast manmade lakes, large parks, shrines, temples and monasteries speak eloquently of the grandeur of the past and bear testimony to a cultured and imaginative people. The regions in the following guide are used for convenience only and have no administrative significance.

THE INTERIOR

COLOMBO: Sri Lanka's capital is a fascinating city, blending its older culture with modern Western influences. A palm-fringed drive of 34km (21 miles) leads from the Katunayake (Colombo) International Airport to Colombo. Nearby is **Fort**, so-called as it was a military garrison during the Portuguese and Dutch occupation from the 16th to the 18th century, is today the commercial capital of Sri Lanka. **Pettah**, 2km (1 mile) from Fort, is a busy bazaar area. The **Vihara Maha Devi Park**, named after the mother of one of Sri Lanka's greatest kings, is noteworthy for its collection of beautiful flowering trees, a blossoming spectacle in March, April and early May. The park is open daily until 2100 and is well illuminated. The **Parliament Building** is at Sri Jayawardenepura, Kotte. Other attractions include the **Planetarium**, the **National Zoological Gardens** and several museums and art galleries.
SITES OF WORSHIP: There are numerous Buddhist temples scattered around Sri Lanka: **Kelani Rajamaha Viharaya**, 10km (6 miles) from Fort; the **Vajiraramaya** at Bambalapitiya, 6km (4 miles) from Fort; **Dipaduttaramaya** at Kotahena, 5km (3 miles) from Fort; and **Gotami Vihare** at Borella, 7km (4.5 miles) from Fort. Also worth visiting are the **Gangaramaya Bhikkhu Training Centre** and **Sima Malaka** at 61 Sri Jinaratana Road, Colombo, 3km (2 miles) from Fort; the **Purana Viharaya** at Metharamaya, Lauries Road, Colombo 4; and the **Purana Viharaya** at Hendala, 0.8km (0.5 miles) on the Colombo–Negombo road, en-route to the *Pegasus Reef Hotel*. Additionally, there are also some Hindu temples to explore: at Kochikade Kotahena, the **Pettah** and **Bambalapitiya**, Colombo 4; **Sri Siva Subramania Swami Kovil**, Gintupitiya – within walking distance of Sea Street, Colombo 11 (Pettah). Reflecting Sri Lanka's diverse communities, there also mosques worth visiting in the **Davatagaha** mosque at Union Place, Colombo 2; and the **Afar Jumma** mosque in the Pettah.
KANDY & THE HILL COUNTRY: Kandy, a picturesque, naturally fortified town, 115km (72 miles) from Colombo, was the last stronghold of the Kandyan Kings. It withheld foreign conquest until 1815 when it was ceded by treaty to the British. It is now a cultural sanctuary where age-old customs, arts, crafts, rituals and ways of life are well preserved. Good sightseeing trips should take in the **Temple of the Sacred Tooth Relic** (**Dalada Maligawa**); **Embekke Devale**; **Lankatillaka**; **Gadaladeniya**; **Degaldoruwa temples**; museums; **Royal Botanic Gardens**; **Peradeniya**; **Elephants' Bath** at **Katugastota**; the **Kandyan Arts Association**; **Kalapura** (Craftsmen's Village) at Nattarampotha (6.5km/4 miles from Kandy); and **Henawela Village** – famous for its 'Dumbara Mats' (16km/10 miles from Kandy).

THE COAST

Note: Much of Sri Lanka's costline was damaged by the December 26 2004 tsunami. Travellers should seek the latest travel updates prior to travel.

Sri Lanka has approximately 1600km (1000 miles) of beautiful palm-shaded beaches as well as warm, pure seas and colourful coral reefs.

SOUTHWEST COAST: The best time to visit Sri Lanka's southern beaches is from November to April. **Mount Lavinia**, 12km (7 miles) from Colombo, is a good beach resort close to Colombo and the domestic airport. Overlooking the area is what was The Governors House, built in 1805 by Sir Thomas Maitland, and now is the famous **Mount Lavinia Hotel**. **Beruwela**, 56km (35 miles) from Colombo, has good bathing in the bay all year round. **Bentota**, 64km (40 miles) from Colombo, is a pleasant self-contained resort destination, between the sea and the river. The Bentota resort is an interesting diving spot where multi-hued fish can be observed among myriad reef-dwellers. **Hikkaduwa**, 98km (61 miles) from Colombo, is a beautiful coral reef and beach. Regarded as a haven for surfers, watersports enthusiasts and snorkellers, this is a beautiful and colourful marine area, rife for exploration. **Galle**, 116km (72 miles) from Colombo, is famous for its old Dutch fort, and is also a centre for lace-making, ebony-carving and gem-polishing. **Tangale**, 195km (122 miles) from Colombo, is a beautiful bay and there is safe swimming all year round. **Negombo**, 37km (32 miles) from Colombo, near Katunayake International Airport, is Sri Lanka's oldest and best-known fishing village. It stands on a strand separating the sea from a lagoon. The seafood here, particularly the shellfish, is a speciality. The sea and wide sandy expanse always entices a multitude of sun-seeking visitors. At **Unawatuna** in **Galle** is a beach area acclaimed as being among the top 15 beaches in the world, with safe waters within a picturesque setting. For those searching for geological quirks, **Kundawella** is the scene of a large blowhole that operates as a natural spout, gushing water into the air and over the rocks of the beach.

EAST COAST: Visitors are advised to check with the Tourist Board regarding the situation in these areas prior to departure. The best time to visit is from April to September. **Trincomalee**, 257km (160 miles) from Colombo, is the ideal refuge for the beach addict. It boasts one of the finest natural harbours in the world and excellent beaches. All watersports, including fishing, are available here. There are many tempting underwater shipwrecks to explore for the intrepid diver. **Batticaloa**, 312km (195 miles) from Colombo, is famous for its 'singing fish' and the old Dutch fort. **Kalkudah**, 32km (20 miles) from Batticaloa, is ideal for bathing as the sea is clear, calm and reef-protected. **Passekudah**, close to Kaludah, has a fine bay, clear waters and safe swimming. **Nilaveli**, 18km (11 miles) from Trincomalee, is very much a resort centre - all beach and watersports. Whale watching is also one of its special attractions. **Arugam Bay**, 314km (196 miles) from Colombo, 3km (2 miles) from Potuvil, has a beautiful bay and good surfing.

JAFFNA: Jaffna is 396km (240 miles) from Colombo, at the country's northern tip, and is both city and seaport. It was once noted for its Hindu temples, Dutch forts, the **Keerimalai Baths**, the tidal well and the **Chundikulam Sanctuary**. Jaffna has many scenic beaches, the best known of which is **Casuarina Beach**. Check with the Tourist Board, Embassy or High Commission whether the area is off-limits to foreign visitors.

Sport & Activities

Watersports: Operators in the main resorts conduct **diving** expeditions and supply equipment. With over 1600km (1000 miles) of fine beaches and several **swimming** clubs, there is plenty of scope for swimmers. **Water-skiing** and **yachting** are available. **Windsurfing** is a sport that is gaining in popularity and facilities are located in Bentota, Beruwela, Kalutara and Negombo. **Sport fishing** is popular in Sri Lanka and several clubs offer membership to visitors.

Wildlife and flora: There is a number of animal and bird sanctuaries and national parks where protected wildlife can be viewed. Several species are unique to the island, while some others have been introduced. Sri Lanka is well known for its elephants, sizeable numbers of which can be seen in Gal Oya and Udawalawe National Parks and at Handapangala. Other large mammals include leopards, deer and bears. Wild boars, porcupines and monkeys also exist, especially the Grey Langur which is common throughout the island. The native purple-faced Leaf Monkey is to be found in the higher hill regions. Of the 38 species of amphibian, 16 are unique to the island. Reptiles include two native crocodiles, the star tortoise, five species of turtle and many snakes. The five species of poisonous snake are rarely found in towns and villages.

The island's flora varies greatly, ranging from temperate to tropical forests and from arid scrubland and plains to lush hills. There are rhododendron forests as well as tropical rainforests. Orchids and flowering trees can be seen in season.

Other: Rugby, **hockey**, **cricket**, **football**, **tennis**, **squash** and other games are also available. Apply to a local Travel Information Centre. Membership is offered on a temporary basis at several **golf** courses.

Social Profile

FOOD & DRINK: Sri Lankan food tends to be quite spicy. There are many vegetables, fruits, meats and seafoods. Chinese, Continental, Indian and Japanese menus are available in Colombo. A speciality is basic curry, made with coconut milk, sliced onion, green chilli, aromatic spices such as cloves, nutmeg, cinnamon and saffron and aromatic leaves. *Hoppers* is a cross between a muffin and a crumpet with a wafer-crisp edge, served with a fresh egg soft-baked on top. *Stringhoppers* are steamed circlets of rice flour, a little more delicate than noodles or spaghetti. *Jaggery* is a fudge made from the crystallised sap of the kitul palm. The *durian* fruit is considered a great delicacy.

Tea is the national drink and thought to be amongst the best in the world. *Toddy*, the sap of the palm tree, is a popular local drink; fermented, it becomes *arrack* which, it should be noted, comes in varying degrees of strength. Alcohol cannot be sold on *poya* holidays (which occur each lunar month on the day of the full moon).

NIGHTLIFE: Some Colombo hotels have supper clubs with music for dancing. There are theatres in Colombo, cinemas showing films from the USA, ballet, concerts and theatre productions.

SHOPPING: Special purchases include handicrafts and curios of silver, brass, bone, ceramics, wood and terracotta. Also cane baskets, straw hats, reed and coir mats and tea. Batik fabric, lace and lacquerware are also popular. Some of the masks, which are used in dance-dramas, in processions and on festival days, can be bought by tourists. The '18-disease' mask shows a demon in possession of a victim; he is surrounded by 18 faces – each of which cures a specific ailment. Versions produced for the tourist market are often of a high standard. Sri Lanka is also rich in gems. Fabrics include batiks, cottons, rayons, silks and fine lace. **Shopping hours:** Mon-Fri 0900-1730, Sat 0900-1300.

SPECIAL EVENTS: For further information and exact dates, contact the Sri Lanka Tourist Board (see *Contact Addresses* section). The following is a selection of special events occurring in Sri Lanka in 2005:

Jan 14 *Tamil Thai Pongal Day*. **Jan 21** *Hadj Festival*. **Apr 13-14** *Sinhala & Tamil New Year*. **May 1** *May Day Celebrations*. **Jul 29-Aug 13** *Kataragama Festival*. **Aug 11-19** *Esala Perahera (Kandy)*. **Sep 21-25** *'WOMAD' Sri Lanka Festival of Drums*, Colombo, Galle and Kandy. **Nov 1** *Deepavali Festival Day*. **Nov 4** *Ramadan Festival Day*.

SOCIAL CONVENTIONS: Shaking hands is the normal form of greeting. It is customary to be offered tea when visiting and it is considered impolite to refuse. Punctuality is appreciated. A small token of appreciation, such as a souvenir from home or company, is always welcomed. Informal, Western dress is suitable, except when visiting Buddhist temples, whereupon modest clothing should be worn (eg no bare legs and uncovered heads). Visitors should be decently clothed when visiting any place of worship, and shoes and hats must be removed. Jackets and ties are not required by men in the evenings except for formal functions when lightweight suits should be worn. **Tipping:** Most hotels include a service charge of 10 per cent. Extra tipping is optional.

Business Profile

ECONOMY: Although some parts of the economy have suffered severe dislocation as a result of the civil war – especially the once promising tourist industry – Sri Lanka has managed to accommodate the conflict to the extent that the economy performed reasonably well during the last five years. This is reflected in the GDP growth of 5 per cent in 2004. However, inflation rose slightly to 7 per cent in 2004 and unemployment also increased statistically. Agriculture sustains about one-third of the working population and directly contributes around 20 per cent of GDP. The main cash crops are tea, rubber and coconuts, which provide over 75 per cent of export earnings; rice is grown mainly for domestic consumption. Forestry and fishing are also important. The main industrial sectors are mining (gemstones and graphite being the principal minerals), and manufacturing. Iron ore, limestone, clay and uranium ore are also present in commercially exploitable quantities. Hydroelectricity is the main source of power, supplemented by imported oil. Important manufacturing industries include cement and textiles, both of which are valuable export earners.

In the service sector, the growth of tourism has been stunted by the civil war, but banking and insurance have both been performing well. Since the mid-1990s, successive governments have followed the usual prescription of market-oriented policies – privatisation and deregulation – while seeking to build up potential export-earning industries. This strategy was slow to show results at first, but the government persevered and some benefits are now beginning to materialise. The recent peace talks and ceasefire between government and rebels has boosted business confidence both at home and abroad, and alleviated Sri Lanka's chronic shortage of investment capital. The government is now hoping to consolidate its progress by further deregulation, fiscal reform, and privatisation: although it has all but pulled out of manufacturing, the state still owns 90 per cent of the island's land and the bulk of its utilities. India, Japan, the USA and the UK are Sri Lanka's major trading partners.

BUSINESS: Business attire is casual. English is widely

Credit: © Marie Peyre

spoken in business circles. Appointments are necessary and it is considered polite to arrive punctually. It is usual to exchange visiting cards on first introduction. **Office hours:** Mon-Fri 0800-1630.

COMMERCIAL INFORMATION: The following organisation can offer advice: National Chamber of Commerce of Sri Lanka, 450 DR Wijewardena Mawatha, Colombo 10 (tel: (5) 374 801-4; fax: (1) 268 9596; e-mail: sg@nccsl.lk; website: www.nccsl.lk); *or* Ceylon Chamber of Commerce (Sri Lanka Tourist Hotels Association), 50 Navam Mawatha, Colombo 2 (tel: (1) 245 2183 *or* 232 9143; fax: (1) 243 7477 *or* 244 9352; e-mail: info@chamber.lk; website: www.chamber.lk).

CONFERENCES/CONVENTIONS: For further information, contact the Sri Lanka Convention Bureau, Hotel School Building, 4th Floor, 80 Galle Road, Colombo 3 (tel: (74) 713 500/1 *or* (1) 244 0002; fax: (1) 247 2985; e-mail: slcb@sri.lanka.net).

Climate

Tropical climate. Upland areas are cooler and more temperate, and coastal areas are cooled by sea breezes. There are two monsoons, which occur May to July and December to January.

Required clothing: Lightweights and rainwear.

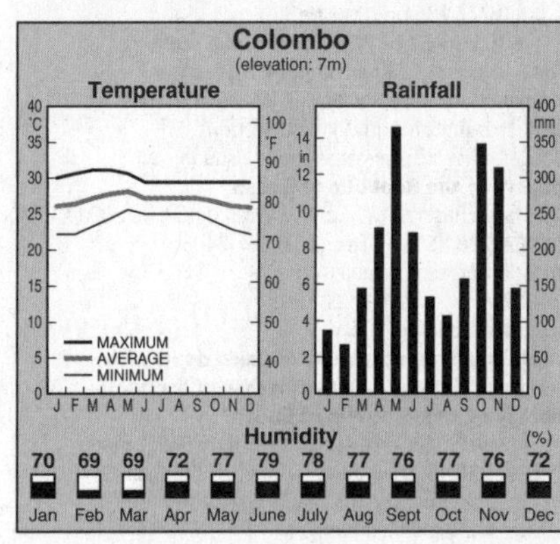

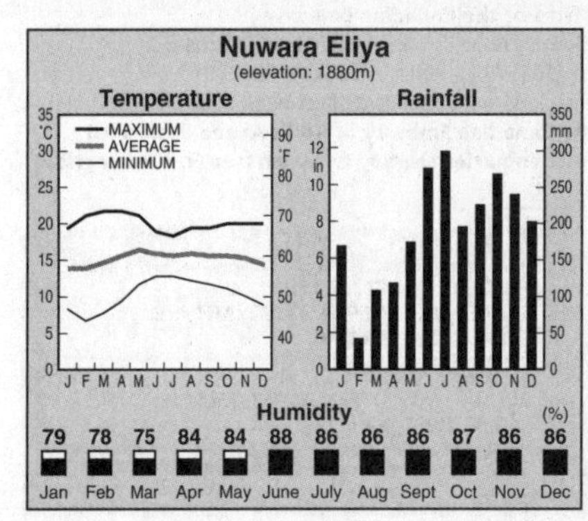

A B C D E F G H I J K L M N O P Q R S T U V W X Y Z

Sudan

LATEST TRAVEL ADVICE CONTACTS

British Foreign and Commonwealth Office
Tel: (0870) 606 0290 Website: www.fco.gov.uk

US Department of State
Website: http://travel.state.gov/travel

Canadian Department of Foreign Affairs and Int'l Trade
Tel: (1 800) 267 8376 Website: www.dfait-maeci.gc.ca

Location: Northeast Africa.

Country dialling code: 249.

Ministry of Environment and Tourism
PO Box 13226, Khartoum, Sudan
Tel: (183) 472 604 *or* 471 329. Fax: (183) 471 437 *or* 473 665.

Embassy of the Republic of Sudan
3 Cleveland Row, St James's, London SW1A 1DD, UK
Tel: (020) 7839 8080.
Fax: (020) 7839 7560 *or* 7839 6009 (visa section).
E-mail: admin@sudanembassy.co.uk
Website: www.sudan-embassy.co.uk
Opening hours: Mon-Fri 0900-1600 (general enquiries); Mon-Fri 0930-1530 (visa section).

British Embassy
Street address: off Sharia Al-Baladiya Street, Khartoum East, Khartoum, Sudan
Postal address: PO Box 801, Khartoum, Sudan
Tel: (183) 777 105 *or* 780 825/56.
Fax: (183) 776 457 *or* 775 562 (consular section).
E-mail: Information.Khartoum@fco.gov.uk *or* Consular.Khartoum@fco.gov.uk (consular section) *or* Visa.Khartoum@fco.gov.uk (visa section).
Website: www.britishembassy.gov.uk/sudan

Embassy of the Republic of Sudan
2210 Massachusetts Avenue, NW, Washington, DC 20008, USA
Tel: (202) 338 8565. Fax: (202) 667 2406.
E-mail: info@sudanembassy.org
Website: www.sudanembassy.org
Consulate General in: New York.

The United States Embassy in Cairo deals with enquiries relating to Sudan (see *Egypt* section).

Embassy of the Republic of Sudan
354 Stewart Street, Ottawa, Ontario K1N 6K8, Canada
Tel: (613) 235 4000 *or* 4999. Fax: (613) 235 6880.
E-mail: sudanembassy-canada@rogers.com
Website: www.sudanembassy.ca

Office of the Canadian Embassy
29 Africa Road, Block 56, Khartoum 1, Sudan
Tel: (183) 790 320/2. Fax: (183) 790 321.
E-mail: david.hutchings@dfait-maeci.gc.ca

The Canadian Embassy in Addis Ababa deals with most enquiries relating to Sudan (see *Ethiopia* section).

TIMATIC CODES

Health
AMADEUS: **TI-DFT/KRT/HE**
GALILEO/WORLDSPAN: **TI-DFT/KRT/HE**
SABRE: **TIDFT/KRT/HE**

Visa
AMADEUS: **TI-DFT/KRT/VI**
GALILEO/WORLDSPAN: **TI-DFT/KRT/VI**
SABRE: **TIDFT/KRT/VI**

To access TIMATIC country information on Health and Visa regulations through the Computer Reservations System (CRS), type in the appropriate command line listed above.

General Information

AREA: 2,505,813 sq km (967,500 sq miles).
POPULATION: 32,878,000 (UN estimate 2002).
POPULATION DENSITY: 13.1 per sq km.
CAPITAL: Khartoum. **Population:** 2,371,000 (UN estimate 2002; including suburbs).
GEOGRAPHY: Sudan is bordered by Egypt to the north, the Red Sea to the northeast, Ethiopia and Eritrea to the east, Kenya, Uganda and the Democratic Republic of the Congo to the south, the Central African Republic and Chad to the west, and Libya to the northwest. There is a marked difference between the climate, culture and geography of northern and southern Sudan. The far north consists of the contiguous Libyan and Nubian deserts which extend as far south as the capital, Khartoum, and are barren except for small areas beside the Nile River and a few scattered oases. This gives way to the central steppes which cover the country between 15°N and 10°N, a region of short, coarse grass and bushes, turning to open savannah towards the south, largely flat to the east but rising to two large plateaux in the west and south, the Janub Darfur (3088m/10,131ft) and Janub Kordofan (500m/1640ft) respectively. Most of Sudan's agriculture occurs in these latitudes in a fertile pocket between the Blue and White Niles which meet at Khartoum. South of the steppes is a vast shallow basin traversed by the White Nile and its tributaries, with the Sudd, a 120,000 sq km (46,332 sq miles) marshland, in the centre. This gives way to equatorial forest towards the south, rising to jungle-clad mountains on the Ugandan border, the highest being Mount Kinyeti, at 3187m (10,456ft).
GOVERNMENT: Islamic Republic since 1986. Gained independence from the UK in 1956. **Head of State and Government:** President Omar Hassan Ahmad al-Bashir since 1989.
LANGUAGE: Arabic is the official language. English and many local dialects are widely spoken.
RELIGION: Muslim in the north; Christian and traditional animist beliefs in the south.
TIME: GMT + 2.
ELECTRICITY: 240 volts AC, 50Hz.
COMMUNICATIONS: Telephone: IDD is available. Country code: 249. Outgoing international calls must go through the operator. **Mobile telephone:** GSM 900 network is operated by *MobiTel* (website: www.sdn-mobitel.com). GSM 900/1800 and 3G networks operated by *Bashair Telecom* (website: www.bashairTelecom.com). Coverage is available in main towns. **Internet:** ISPs include *SudanNet* (website: www.sudanet.net). **Telegram:** The Central Telegraph Office is open at Khartoum (Gamma Avenue) 24 hours a day, including holidays. **Post:** Post office hours: Sat-Thurs 0830-1200 and 1730-1830. Airmail to Europe takes up to one week. **Press:** Censorship is imposed on all press publications, following the 1989 coup. The main dailies are *Abbar al-Youm*, *Al-Rai al-Akhar* and *Al-wan* . The *Sudan Standard* is an English-language daily. There are English-language magazines entitled *New Horizon* and *Sudanow*.
Radio: BBC World Service (website: www.bbc.co.uk/worldservice) and Voice of America (website: www.voa.gov) can be received. From time to time the frequencies change and the most up-to-date can be found online.

Passport/Visa

	Passport Required?	Visa Required?	Return Ticket Required?
Full British	Yes	Yes	Yes
Australian	Yes	Yes	Yes
Canadian	Yes	Yes	Yes
USA	Yes	Yes	Yes
Other EU	Yes	Yes	Yes
Japanese	Yes	Yes	Yes

Note: *Regulations and requirements may be subject to change at short notice, and you are advised to contact the appropriate diplomatic or consular authority before finalising travel arrangements. Details of these may be found at the head of this country's entry. Any numbers in the chart refer to the footnotes below.*

Restricted entry: The Sudanese authorities refuse entry and transit to nationals of Israel and holders of passports that contain visas for Israel (either valid or expired).
PASSPORTS: Passport valid for at least six months required by all.
VISAS: Required by all except:
(a) nationals of the Syrian Arab Republic resident in the Syrian Arab Republic;
(b) those continuing their journey by the same or first connecting aircraft within six hours, provided holding confirmed onward tickets and documents.
Types of visa and cost: *Tourist*, *Business* or *Transit*: £53. Please note that the cost is £23 for Sudanese passport holders.
Validity: *Tourist* or *Business*: One month from the date of issue. *Transit*: One to seven days.
Visits may be extended through the Passport, Immigration and Nationality Office in Khartoum, Sudan.
Application to: Consular section at Embassy; see *Contact Addresses* section.
Application requirements: (a) Three completed application forms (if applying for a transit visa, the country of destination after Sudan should be indicated, together with the anticipated date of arrival and departure from Sudan). (b) Three passport-size photos. (c) Fee, payable by postal order or company cheque only. (d) Letter or invitation from contact in Sudan.* (e) Passport valid for six months from date of entry, with no Israeli visas or immigration stamps affixed (if applying for a transit visa, applicant's passport should be duly endorsed for permission to enter the next country of destination after Sudan). (f) Cholera and yellow fever vaccinations are recommended. (g) A self-addressed envelope, if applicable. (h) Authentic documents from the travel agent proving reservations for a return ticket *or* a bank statement confirming financial capability for the trip *or* if travelling on business, a letter of invitation from the sponsoring company stating purpose of trip, duration of stay, financial responsibility and references in Sudan.
Note: *It is advisable that all business visitors have an invitation letter/fax from the Sudanese government when applying for a visa. A private company inviting an individual to work in Sudan needs to photocopy the first page of their passport and apply on their behalf with it to the Interior Ministry for initial approval. International Organisations need to get approval from the Foreign Affairs Ministry in Sudan. Contact the Consular section at Embassy for further information; see *Contact Addresses* section.
Working days required: Up to four weeks.
Temporary residence: Enquire at Embassy.
Note: Special permits are required for all travel outside Khartoum. These can be obtained from the Passport and Immigration Office, Ministry of Interior, Khartoum. Travellers staying in Sudan for longer than three days must report to the police.

Money

Currency: Sudanese Dinar (sD) = 10 Sudanese Pounds; 1 Sudanese Pound = 100 piastres. Notes are in denominations of sD1000, 500, 100, 50, 10 and 5. There are also a number of commemorative coins in circulation.
Note: The Sudanese Dinar is pegged to the Libyan Dinar. Exchange rates are liable to change significantly and rapidly. There is a black market with a premium of around 5000 per cent over the official rate.
Currency exchange: Currency should be exchanged only at official bureaux de change and banks, and receipts should be retained. There are severe penalties for changing money on the black market.
Credit & debit cards: Check with your credit or debit card company for merchant acceptability and other services which may be available. Due to recent conflicts, it is recommended to bring plenty of cash rather than rely on card transactions in Sudan.
Travellers cheques: These are generally not recommended but should be in a major currency.
Currency restrictions: The import and export of local currency is prohibited. The import and export of foreign currency is unlimited, subject to declaration.
Exchange rate indicators: The following figures are included as a guide to the movements of the Sudanese Dinar against Sterling and the US Dollar:

Date	Feb '04	May '04	Aug '04	Nov '04
£1.00=	474.08	463.23	477.21	472.98
$1.00=	260.45	259.35	259.02	255.96

Banking hours: Sat-Thurs 0830-1200.

Duty Free

The following items may be imported into Sudan by visitors over 20 years of age without incurring customs duty:
200 cigarettes or 50 cigars or 450g of tobacco; a reasonable amount of perfume and eau de toilette for personal use; a reasonable amount of gifts.
Prohibited items: The import of goods from Israel and South Africa is prohibited. Sudan also adheres to the list of prohibited goods drawn up by the Arab League and these include alcoholic beverages. Fresh fruit and vegetables and blank pro-forma invoices may not be imported. Firearms require a permit from the Ministry of Interior. Meat and fish products are prohibited without prior permission from the Ministry of Animal & Fish Resources.

Public Holidays

2005: Jan 1 Independence Day. **Jan 21** Eid al-Adha (Feast of the Sacrifice). **Feb 10** Islamic New Year. **Mar 3** National Unity Day. **Apr 6** Uprising Day. **Apr 21** Al-Mowlid Al Nabawi

(Birth of the Prophet). **May 25** May Revolution Anniversary. **Jun 30** Revolution Day. **Nov 3-5** Eid al-Fitr (End of Ramadan). **Dec 25** Christmas Day.
2006: Jan 1 Independence Day. **Jan 10** Eid al-Adha (Feast of the Sacrifice). **Jan 31** Islamic New Year. **Mar 3** National Unity Day. **Apr 6** Uprising Day. **Apr 11** Al-Mowlid Al Nabawi (Birth of the Prophet). **May 25** May Revolution Anniversary. **Jun 30** Revolution Day. **Oct 22-24** Eid al-Fitr (End of Ramadan). **Dec 25** Christmas Day.
Note: Muslim festivals are timed according to local sightings of various phases of the moon and the dates given above are approximations. During the lunar month of Ramadan that precedes Eid al-Fitr, Muslims fast during the day and feast at night and normal business patterns may be interrupted. Many restaurants are closed during the day and there may be restrictions on smoking and drinking. Some disruption may continue into Eid al-Fitr itself. Eid al-Fitr and Eid al-Adha may last anything from two to 10 days, depending on the region. For more information, see the *World of Islam* appendix.

Health

	Special Precautions?	Certificate Required?
Yellow Fever	Yes	1
Cholera	2	No
Typhoid & Polio	3	N/A
Malaria	4	N/A

Note: *Regulations and requirements may be subject to change at short notice, and you are advised to contact your doctor well in advance of your intended date of departure. Any numbers in the chart refer to the footnotes below.*

1: The risk of yellow fever is primarily in the equatorial south. A yellow fever vaccination certificate is required from travellers over one year of age from infected areas, and may be required from travellers leaving Sudan. Those countries and areas formerly classified as endemic zones are considered by the Sudanese authorities to be infected areas. Travellers arriving from non-endemic zones should note that vaccination is strongly recommended for travel outside the urban areas, even if an outbreak of the disease has not been reported and they would normally not require a vaccination certificate to enter the country.
2: Following WHO guidelines issued in 1973, a cholera vaccination certificate is no longer a condition of entry to Sudan. However, cholera is a serious risk in the country and precautions are essential. Up-to-date advice should be sought before deciding whether these precautions should include vaccination as medical opinion is divided over its effectiveness; see the *Health* appendix.
3: Vaccination against typhoid is advised.
4: Malaria risk, predominantly in the malignant *falciparum* form, exists throughout the year throughout the country. In the north, the risk is seasonal and low. It is higher along the Nile south of Lake Nasser and in the central and southern part of the country. The Malaria risk on the Red Sea coast is very limited. High resistance to chloroquine and resistance to sulfadoxine-pyrimethamine has been reported. The recommended prophylaxis is mefloquine.
Food & drink: All water should be regarded as a potential health risk. Water used for drinking, brushing teeth or making ice should have first been boiled or otherwise sterilised. Milk is unpasteurised and should be boiled. Avoid dairy products which are likely to have been made from unboiled milk. Only eat well-cooked meat and fish, preferably served hot. Pork, salad and mayonnaise may carry increased risk. Vegetables should be cooked and fruit peeled.
Other risks: *Bilharzia* (schistosomiasis) is present. Avoid swimming and paddling in fresh water; swimming pools which are well chlorinated and maintained are safe. *Visceral leishmaniasis* especially occurs in eastern and southern Sudan. Vaccination is strongly recommended. The disease is transferred through sandflies which live mainly on river banks and in wooded areas.
The transmission rate of *trypanosomiasis* (sleeping sickness) is high, with a significant risk of infection for travellers visiting rural areas in the south of the country. *Hepatitis A, B* and *E, diphtheria* and *meningococcal meningitis* are also present. *Dracunculiasis* is prevalent in the south. *Shigellosis* was detected in North Dafur in June 2004, in the Abu Shoak Internally Displaced Persons (IDP) Camp, which has a population of 40,000: there were 11 deaths. *Ebola* was recently detected and contained in Yanbio in south Sudan. *Tetanus* and *Giardia Amoebiasis* also occur. *HIV/AIDS* is becoming an ever-growing problem.
Rabies is present. For those at high risk, vaccination before arrival should be considered. If you are bitten, seek medical advice without delay. For more information, consult the *Health* appendix.
Health care: Medical treatment may be free at certain establishments but health insurance is essential and should include cover for emergency repatriation. Medical facilities are very limited, particularly outside Khartoum.

Travel - International

Note: Travel to the Eritrean border is not advised at present; southern Sudan, Darfur and Kassala should also be avoided, except on essential business or if engaged in relief work. Conflict continues to be a feature of Sudan. Most visits to Khartoum, Port Sudan and other areas in the north are trouble-free. Permits, obtained locally, are required for all travel outside Khartoum. For further advice, contact a local government travel advice department.
AIR: The national airline is *Sudan Airways (SD)*. Other airlines serving Sudan include *British Airways, Lufthansa* and *Syrian Arab Airlines*.
Approximate flight times: From Khartoum to *London* is eight hours, including stopover.
International airports: *Khartoum (KRT)* (Civil) is 4km (2 miles) southeast of the city. Airport facilities include restaurants and duty free shops. Taxi services are available.
Departure tax: US$20 (Sudanese nationals may pay in local currency). Transit passengers are exempt.
SEA: The only sea ports are Port Sudan and Suakin on the Red Sea. Piracy has been reported in the area.
RIVER: There are car ferries from Aswan in Egypt to Wadi Halfa.
RAIL: Rail links run from Cairo (Egypt) to Aswan High Dam and then by riverboat to Wadi Halfa.
ROAD: Entry to Sudan by road is at present only possible at Wadi Halfa on the Egypt/Sudan border.

Travel - Internal

Note: Travel outside of Khartoum is restricted.
AIR: *Sudan Airways (SD)* runs services to 20 airports, including Dongola, Juba, El Obeid and Port Sudan. The most reliable route is Port Sudan to Khartoum. There is also an air-taxi service operating twice weekly to Nyala, available from Khartoum.
Departure tax: sD600.
RIVER: River steamers serve all towns on the Nile but conditions are mostly unsuitable for tourist travel. Services depend on fluctuating water levels. It is wise to take food and water. Destinations include Dongola, Karima, Kosti and Juba. A 320km (200 mile) navigable canal, the *Jonglei*, is under construction in the south.
RAIL: Sudan has an extensive rail network (5500km/3418 miles) but the service is in bad repair, extremely slow and uncomfortable. Travelling first class is advisable; second- and third-class compartments can get very crowded. Sleeping cars are available on main routes from Khartoum to Wau/Nyala, Khartoum to Kassala/Wadi Halfa and Port Sudan to Khartoum. There are a few air-conditioned carriages, for which a supplement is charged.
ROAD: Only major roads are asphalted; road conditions are poor outside towns, roads to the north are often closed during the rainy season (July to September) and street lights are non-existent. Traffic drives on the right. **Bus:** Services run between the main towns and depart from the market places; however they are not entirely safe. *Souk* (market) lorries are a cheap but uncomfortable method of transport. **Taxi:** Also often unsafe, taxis can be found at ranks or hailed in the street. Taxis are not metered, fares must be agreed in advance. **Car hire:** Available in the main towns and at major hotels but charges are high. **Documentation:** *Carnet de Passage*, adequate finance and roadworthiness certificate (from the Embassy) are all needed. An International Driving Permit is recommended, although not legally required. A temporary driving licence is available from local police on presentation of a valid British or Northern Ireland driving licence, for a maximum period of three months. Women *are* allowed to drive in Sudan.
URBAN: Publicly operated bus services in Khartoum have of late become unreliable and irregular which has led to the proliferation of private *bakassi* minibuses, nicknamed *boks*. They pick up and set down with no fixed stops.

Accommodation

HOTELS: Accommodation is scarce outside Khartoum and Port Sudan. Khartoum has around 10 major hotels, including some of international standard, and Port Sudan also has several. There are a few smaller hotels in the main towns and several hostels.
YOUTH HOSTELS: Contact the Youth Hostels Association, PO Box 1705, House no. 66, Street no. 47, Khartoum East (tel: (11) 722 087; fax: (11) 780 308).

Resorts & Excursions

Sudan has only recently been developed as a tourist destination, and communications and facilities are still limited outside Khartoum. Travel restrictions are also in force in much of the country (see *Passport/Visa* section) owing to the presence of separatist insurgents. There is currently a civil war in the south of the country and this, for obvious reasons, has negatively impacted upon the recent attempt to kickstart touristic growth in the country.
KHARTOUM: The capital is situated at the confluence of the Blue and White Niles. With **Omdurman**, the old national capital, and **Khartoum North**, it forms one unit called the 'three-towns capital'. Tourist attractions include the Omdurman camel market and the Arab *souk*.
Particularly noteworthy from a historical and artistic point of view is a visit to the well-organised **National Museum**, which contains archaeological treasures dating back to 4000 BC and earlier. **Khalifa's House Museum** covers Sudan's more recent history, especially the reign of the Mahdi (1881-1899).
EXCURSIONS: A visit to the **Gezira** model farm and a trip along the **Nile** to the dam at **Jebel Aulia**, where the Nile is especially rich in fish, are recommended. The main areas of archaeological interest in Sudan are to be found beside the Nile north of Khartoum. They include **Bajrawiya**, **El Kurru**, **Meroe**, **Musawarat**, **Naga** and **Nuri**.
DINDER NATIONAL PARK: Covering 6475 sq km (2500 sq miles) southeast of Khartoum on the Ethiopian border, the Dinder National Park is one of the largest in the world. Special three-day trips from Khartoum are organised in the high season (December to April).
THE RED SEA: With the transparency of its water, the variety of its fish and the charm of its marine gardens and coral reefs, the Red Sea is one of Sudan's main tourist attractions. The busy **Port Sudan**, **Suakin**, famous during the Ottoman era, and the **Arous Tourist Village**, 50km (30 miles) north of Port Sudan, are just three centres from which to explore the coast. **Erkowit**, 1200m (3930ft) above sea level, is a beautiful resort in the coastal mountains and is famed for its evergreen vegetation.
THE WEST: Jebel Marra, at more than 3088m (10,100ft), is the highest peak in the Darfur region of western Sudan. It is a region of outstanding scenic beauty, with waterfalls and volcanic lakes and a pleasant climate.
THE SOUTH: The Southern Provinces are characterised by green forests, open parkland, waterfalls and treeless swamps abounding with birds and wild animals such as elephant, black and white rhino, common eland, Nile lechwe, lesser kudu, bisa oryx, zebra, crocodile, hippo, hyena, buffalo and the almost extinct shoebill. The **Gemmeiza Tourist Village**, situated in the heart of **East Equatoria**, is considered of special interest, owing to the abundance of game in that area.

Sport & Activities

Note: Civil war and political instability prevent travellers from undertaking these activities at present.
General: There is normally great scope for **watersports** on the Red Sea coast, including **swimming**, **diving** on coral reefs and **fishing** for barracuda, sharks and grey cod. **Wildlife** enthusiasts may head to the *Dinder National Park* while visitors interested in **archaeology** will find much of interest in the region north of Khartoum.

Social Profile

FOOD & DRINK: The staple diet is *fool*, a type of bean, and *dura*, cooked maize or millet, which are eaten with various vegetables. The hotel restaurants in Khartoum and Port Sudan serve international cuisine and there are a few Greek and Middle Eastern restaurants. If invited to a Sudanese home, more exotic food will usually be served. Alcohol is banned by the Islamic *Sharia* code.
NIGHTLIFE: The best entertainment is found in Khartoum and Omdurman, with the national theatre, music hall, cinemas, open-air and hotel entertainment.
SHOPPING: The *souk* has stalls selling food, local crafts, spices, jewellery and silver. Special purchases include basketwork, ebony, gold and silver and assorted handicrafts. Visitors must not buy cheetah skins: the killing of cheetahs is prohibited and they are a protected species under the World Wildlife Act. **Shopping hours:** Sat-Thurs 0800-1330 and 1730-2000.
SPECIAL EVENTS: Events celebrated in Sudan are always Muslim feasts and holy days. The following is a selection of special events celebrated annually in Sudan:
Jan *Eid al-Adha* (Feast of the Sacrifice). **Sep-Oct***Ramadan*. **Oct** *Eid al-Fitr* (End of Ramadan).
SOCIAL CONVENTIONS: In the north, Arab culture predominates, while the people in the more fertile south belong to many diverse tribes, each with their own lifestyle and beliefs. Because Sudan is largely Muslim and operates *Sharia*, women should not wear revealing clothing., although they are not expected to wear a veil or cover their heads. At official and social functions as well as in some restaurants, formal clothes are expected. The Sudanese have a great reputation for hospitality. A curfew operates in major cities from 0000-0400. **Photography:** There are many restrictions on photography: a photography permit can be obtained from the External Information Office at the Ministry of Information in Khartoum. **Tipping:** Not customary.

Business Profile

ECONOMY: Once described as the bread basket of the Arab world, Sudan is a country of high, though largely unrealised, economic potential, which is presently crippled by civil war, a foreign debt of around US$15 billion, and climatic effects which have brought both drought and flooding. Agriculture employs most of the workforce, producing cotton – the major export, wheat, groundnuts, sorghum and sugar cane. Production of gum arabic has declined through the introduction of synthetic substitutes and increasing competition, particularly from West Africa. Livestock breeding has suffered from persistent drought. The manufacturing sector concentrates on processing the country's agricultural output and the production of textiles, cement and some consumer goods. There are some mineral deposits including marble, mica, chromite and gold. There are also some onshore oil deposits: located in the mid-1990s, these came on stream in 1999 and have been of some help in easing Sudan's chronic power shortages. The government has announced a major dam project on the Nile and a new oil refinery that intend to meet electricity demand and the need for planned water distribution. Ultimately, Sudan relies on foreign aid to sustain its economy. Natural phenomena, compounded by the effects of the two-decade-long civil war, have made this more pressing than usual since 2000, as Sudan has needed two large injections of emergency food aid to stave off mass famine. Relations with the IMF have been rocky – Sudan was almost thrown out in the mid-1990s – but the Fund is now providing some financial support in exchange for a standard economic reform programme. Elsewhere, while the political posture of Sudan's Islamic government has alienated Western governments, it can still rely on support from wealthy Arab states, notably Saudi Arabia. Nonetheless, the Islamic government's economic programme has successfully achieved its principal targets of 5 to 6 per cent annual growth and inflation of below 5 per cent. Saudi Arabia is the largest exporter to Sudan, and is also a major recipient of Sudanese exports along with Egypt, Italy and Japan.

BUSINESS: Businessmen should wear a lightweight suit. Visiting businesspeople should respect Muslim customs. It should be clearly stated in advance if the visitor is female. English is widely spoken in business circles although knowledge of a few words of Arabic will be well received. Punctuality is less important than patience and politeness. Personal introductions are an advantage; business cards should have an Arabic translation on the reverse. **Office hours:** Sat-Thurs 0800-1430.

COMMERCIAL INFORMATION: The following organisations can offer advice: Sudan Development Corporation (SDC), PO Box 710, 21 al-Amarat, Khartoum (tel: (11) 472 186 *or* 472 195; fax: (11) 472 148); *or* Sudan Chamber of Commerce, PO Box 81, Gamhoria Street, Khartoum 11114 (tel: (11) 772 346 *or* 776 518; fax: (11) 780 748; e-mail: chamber@sudanchamber.org; website: www.sudanchamber.org).

Climate

Extremely hot (less so November to March). Sandstorms blow across the Sahara from April to September. In the extreme north, there is little rain but the central region has some rainfall from July to August. The southern region has much higher rainfall, the wet season lasting May to October. Summers are very hot throughout the country, whilst winters are cooler in the north.

Required clothing: Tropical clothes all year, warmer clothes for cool mornings and evenings (especially in the desert).

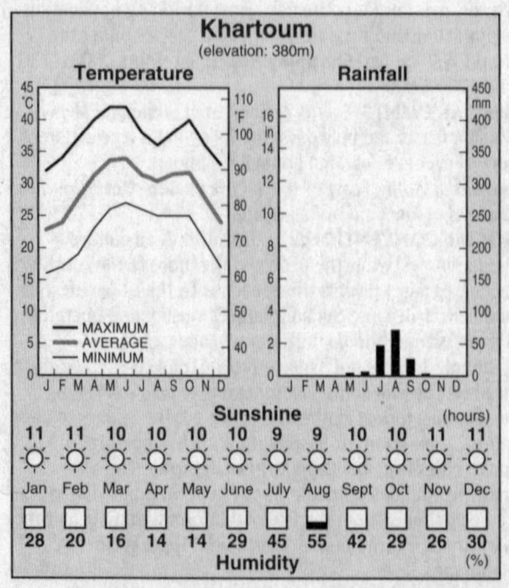

Surinam

LATEST TRAVEL ADVICE CONTACTS

British Foreign and Commonwealth Office
Tel: (0870) 606 0290 Website: www.fco.gov.uk
US Department of State
Website: http://travel.state.gov/travel
Canadian Department of Foreign Affairs and Int'l Trade
Tel: (1 800) 267 8376 Website: www.dfait-maeci.gc.ca

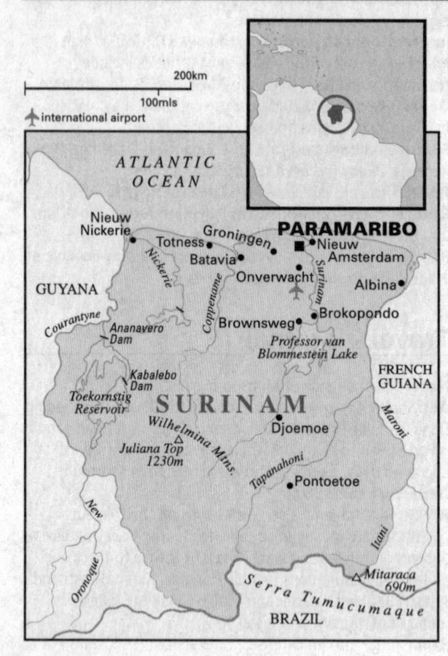

Location: North coast of South America.

Country dialling code: 597.

Ministry of Transport, Communication and Tourism
Prins Hendrikstraat 26-28, Paramaribo, Surinam
Tel: 411 951. Fax: 420 425.
E-mail: tct@tmin.sr

Surinam Tourism Foundation
Street address: Dr JF Nassylaan 2, Paramaribo, Surinam
Postal address: PO Box 656, Paramaribo, Surinam
Tel: 410 357. Fax: 477 786.
E-mail: stsmktg@sr.net (marketing department) *or* stsur@sr.net (secretary's division).
Website: www.suriname-tourism.com

Embassy of the Republic of Surinam
Alexander Gogelweg 2, 2517 JH 3-650844 The Hague, The Netherlands
Tel: (70) 361 7445.

Consulaat-Generaal van de Republiek Surinam
De Cuserstraat 11, 1081 CK Amsterdam, The Netherlands
Tel: (20) 642 6137. Fax: (20) 646 5311.
E-mail: webmaster@suriname.nu
Website: www.suriname.nu

British Honorary Consul
c/o VSH United Buildings, PO Box 1860, Van't Hogerhuysstraat 9-11, Paramaribo, Surinam
Tel: 402 870 *or* 402 558. Fax: 403 515 *or* 403 824.
E-mail: united@sr.net

Embassy of the Republic of Surinam
4301 Connecticut Avenue, Suite 460, NW, Washington, DC 20008, USA
Tel: (202) 244 7488 *or* 244 7590/1/2. Fax: (202) 244 5878.
Website: www.surinameembassy.org
Also deals with enquiries from Canada.
Consulate General in: Miami.

Embassy of the United States of America
Street address: Dr Sophie Redmondstraat 129, Paramaribo, Surinam
Postal address: PO Box 1821, Paramaribo, Surinam PO Box 1821, Paramaribo, Surinam

TIMATIC CODES

Health	AMADEUS: **TI-DFT/PBM/HE** GALILEO/WORLDSPAN: **TI-DFT/PBM/HE** SABRE: **TIDFT/PBM/HE**
Visa	AMADEUS: **TI-DFT/PBM/VI** GALILEO/WORLDSPAN: **TI-DFT/PBM/VI** SABRE: **TIDFT/PBM/VI**

To access TIMATIC country information on Health and Visa regulations through the Computer Reservations System (CRS), type in the appropriate command line listed above.

Tel: 472 900. Fax: 425 788 (consulate) *or* 690. ~
Website: http://usembassy.state.gov/paramaribo

Consulate of Canada
Street address: Wagenwegstraat 50, Boven, 1st Floor, Paramaribo, Surinam
Postal address: PO Box 1449, Paramaribo, Surinam
Tel: 424 527 *or* 424 575. Fax: 425 962.
E-mail: cantim@sr.net

The Canadian High Commission in Georgetown also deals with enquiries relating to Surinam (see *Guyana* section).

General Information

AREA: 163,265 sq km (63,037 sq miles).
POPULATION: 429,000 (UN estimate 2001).
POPULATION DENSITY: 2.6 per sq km.
CAPITAL: Paramaribo. **Population:** 214,000 (2000).
GEOGRAPHY: Surinam is bordered to the north by the Atlantic Ocean, to the east by the Marowijne River (which forms the border with French Guiana), to the west by the Corantijn River (which forms the border with Guyana), and to the south by forests, savannahs and mountains, which separate it from Brazil. In the northern part of the country are coastal lowlands covered with mangrove swamps. Further inland runs a narrow strip of savannah land. To the south, the land becomes hilly and then mountainous, covered with dense tropical forest, and cut by numerous rivers and streams.
GOVERNMENT: Republic since 1987. Gained independence from The Netherlands in 1975. **Head of State:** President Runaldo Ronald Venetiaan since 2000.
LANGUAGE: Dutch is the official language. *Sranan Tongo*, originating in Creole, is the popular language. The main languages are Hindi and Javanese. English, Chinese, French and Spanish are also spoken.
RELIGION: Approximately 48 per cent Christian, 27 per cent Hindu and 20 per cent Muslim.
TIME: GMT - 3.
ELECTRICITY: 127 volts AC, 60Hz. European round two-pin plugs and screw-type lamp fittings are in use.
COMMUNICATIONS: Telephone: IDD is available. Country code: 597. There are no area codes. Outgoing international code: 00. **Mobile telephone:** GSM 900 network. Main operator is *Telesur GSM*. Coverage is mainly limited to Paramaribo. **Fax:** Faxes can be sent from the Telesur offices on Spanhoec Street, Paramaribo, and some hotels. **Internet:** ISPs include *SRNet* (website: www.sr.net). **Telegram:** These can only be sent from offices of *Telesur* (Telecommunicatiebedrijf Surinam) in both Paramaribo and the districts. **Post:** Post office hours: 0700 to mid-afternoon. Airmail to and from Europe usually takes about one week to arrive. **Press:** Dutch-language dailies include *De Ware Tijd* and *De West*.
Radio: BBC World Service (website: www.bbc.co.uk/worldservice) and Voice of America (website: www.voa.gov) can be received. From time to time the frequencies change and the most up-to-date can be found online.

Passport/Visa

	Passport Required?	Visa Required?	Return Ticket Required?
Full British	Yes	Yes	Yes
Australian	Yes	Yes	Yes
Canadian	Yes	Yes	Yes
USA	Yes	Yes	Yes
Other EU	Yes	Yes	Yes
Japanese	Yes	No	Yes

Note: *Regulations and requirements may be subject to change at short notice, and you are advised to contact the appropriate diplomatic or consular authority before finalising travel arrangements. Details of these may be found at the head of this country's entry. Any numbers in the chart refer to the footnotes below.*

PASSPORTS: Passport valid for at least six months after arrival required by all.
VISAS: Required by all except the following:
(a) nationals of Antigua & Barbuda, Barbados, Belize, Brazil, Chile, Costa Rica, Dominica, Ecuador, The Gambia, Grenada, Guyana, Hong Kong (SAR), Israel, Jamaica, Japan, Korea (Rep), Malaysia, Netherlands Antilles (holding valid Netherlands passports), The Philippines, St Kitts & Nevis, St Lucia, St Vincent & the Grenadines, Singapore, Switzerland and Trinidad & Tobago;
(b) transit passengers continuing their journey by the same or first connecting aircraft within 24 hours, provided holding onward or return documentation and not leaving the airport.
Note: Nationals staying for more than 24 hours need to get a transit visa on arrival at the airport.
Types of visa and cost: *Single-entry Tourist*: US$30 (two months). *Multiple-entry Tourist*: US$60 (three to four

A B C D E F G H I J K L M N O P Q R S T U V W X Y Z

months); US$90 (six months); US$175 (12 months). *Business*: US$45 (one month). *Multiple-entry Business*: US$90 (two months); US$270 (six months); US$540 (12 months).
Validity: Single-entry: two months; multiple-entry: up to one year.
Application to: Nearest Embassy (or Consular section at Embassy); see *Contact Addresses* section.
Application requirements: (a) One completed, printed or typed, signed application form. (b) One current passport-size photo (in colour and current, no three-minute photos; for children with no individual passport, a colour photograph should be attached to the application form of the passport holder and their visa must also be paid for). (c) Valid passport. (d) Fee. (e) Self-addressed, stamped envelope with return postage for postal applications. (f) Photocopy of valid return ticket, if applicable. (g) For business trips, letter of invitation from company detailing purpose of trip, name of institute visited with contact details, plus approximate duration of stay, a completed business form and a guarantee or letter of reference.
Note: After arrival in Surinam, visitors are required to report to the Immigration Service within eight days at Police Precinct Nieuwe Haven, Van't Hogerhuysstraat, Paramaribo.
Working days required: At least one week before departure and no earlier than eight weeks. Applicants are encouraged to apply with plenty of time in case the application merits further scrutiny from official bodies. However, some applications may only take one day to be processed if a rush fee is paid of US$50, or equivalent.

Money

Currency: Surinam Dollar (SRD) = 100 cents. Notes are in denominations of SRD100, 50, 20, 10 and 5. Coins are in denominations of 250, 100, 25, 10, 5 and 1 cents.
Note: On 1 January 2004, the Surinam Dollar replaced the Surinam Guilder as the new monetary system. The new currency will enable the Central Bank to re-value the present gulden system to a ratio of 1000 guldens per 1 Surinam Dollar, and not have to differentiate between old and new guldens. The existing gulden coins will not have to be re-issued but will maintain their value and be incorporated into the new system. Surinam Dollars are tied to US Dollars. Old Surinamese bank notes can only be exchanged at the Central Bank.
Early indications show the following exchange rates for the Surinam Dollar against Sterling and the US Dollar:
(Feb '04): £1= SRD$4.98; $1= SRD$2.74. (May '04): £1 =SRD$4.88; $1= SRD$2.73
(Formerly, the monetary system in Surinam was: Surinam Guilder (SG) = 100 cents. Notes are in denominations of SG25,000, 10,000, 5000, 2000, 1000, 100, 25, 10 and 5. Coins are in denominations of 25, 10 and 5 cents.)
Currency exchange: Surinam Dollars are the only legal tender; since the introduction of the new monetary system from the former gulden system, gulden coins are still in circulation, however they have been re-valued to a ratio of 1000 guldens per 1 Surinam Dollar. The Central Bank is authorised to exchange money.
Credit & debit cards: American Express and MasterCard are the most widely accepted credit cards; Diners Club has limited acceptance. Check with your credit or debit card company for merchant acceptability and other facilities which may be available.
Travellers cheques: Must be changed at banks. To avoid additional exchange rate charges, travellers are advised to take travellers cheques in Pounds Sterling or US Dollars.
Currency restrictions: The import of foreign and local currency is unlimited, provided amounts in excess of US$10,000 are declared on arrival. On departure, the imported foreign currency can be exported again, up to the amount declared on arrival. The export of local currency is limited to SRD$1000.
Exchange rate indicators: The following figures are included as a guide to the movements of the Surinam Guilder against Sterling and the US Dollar:

Date	Feb '04	May '04	Aug '04	Nov '04
£1.00=	4717.27	4408.98	4612.42	4736.79
$1.00=	2502.40	2502.40	2502.40	2502.40

Banking hours: Mon-Fri 0730-1400.

Duty Free

The following items may be imported into Surinam without incurring customs duty:
200 cigarettes or 200 cigarillos or 20 cigars or 500g of tobacco; 1l of spirits, 4l of wine and 8l of beer; 50g of perfume and 1l eau de toilette, lotions and eau-de-cologne; *other goods for personal use up to the value of US$500.*
Prohibited items: Fruit (except a reasonable quantity from The Netherlands), vegetables, coffee, plants, roots, bulbs, cocoa, rice, fish, meat and meat products (unless a valid health certificate is shown).

Public Holidays

2005: Jan 1 New Year's Day. **Mar 25*** Holi Phagwa; Good Friday. **Mar 28** Easter Monday. **May 1** Labour Day. **Jul 1** Abolition of Slavery Day. **Nov 3-5** Eid al-Fitr (End of Ramadan). **Nov 25** Independence Day. **Dec 25-26** Christmas.
2006: Jan 1 New Year's Day. **Mar 15*** Holi Phagwa. **Apr 14** Good Friday. **Apr 17** Easter Monday. **May 1** Labour Day. **Jul 1** Abolition of Slavery Day. **Oct 22-24** Eid al-Fitr (End of Ramadan). **Nov 25** Independence Day. **Dec 25-26** Christmas.
Note: (a) In addition, Chinese, Jewish and Indian businesses will be closed for their own religious holidays. (b) Muslim festivals are timed according to local sightings of various phases of the moon and the dates given above are approximations. During the lunar month of Ramadan that precedes Eid al-Fitr, Muslims fast during the day and feast at night and normal business patterns may be interrupted. Many restaurants are closed during the day and there may be restrictions on smoking and drinking. Some disruption may continue into Eid al-Fitr itself, which may last anything from two to 10 days, depending on the region. For more information, see the *World of Islam* appendix. (c) *Hindu festivals are declared according to local astronomical observations and it is only possible to forecast the approximate time of their occurrence.

Health

	Special Precautions?	Certificate Required?
Yellow Fever	Yes	1
Cholera	No	No
Typhoid & Polio	2	N/A
Malaria	3	N/A

Note: *Regulations and requirements may be subject to change at short notice, and you are advised to contact your doctor well in advance of your intended date of departure. Any numbers in the chart refer to the footnotes below.*

1: A yellow fever vaccination certificate is required from all travellers arriving within from infected areas.
2: Typhoid may occur (vaccination is advised); poliomyelitis is not reported.
3: Malaria risk, predominantly in the malignant *falciparum* form, exists throughout the year in the three southern districts of the country. In Paramaribo city and the seven coastal districts, transmission risk is low or negligible. The *falciparum* strain is reported to be resistant to chloroquine, sulfadoxine-pyrimethamine and some decline in sensitivity to quinine has been reported. Mefloquine is therefore the recommended prophylaxis.
Food & drink: Mains water is normally chlorinated and, whilst relatively safe, may cause mild abdominal upsets. Bottled water is available and is advised for the first few weeks of the stay. Drinking water outside main cities and towns is likely to be contaminated and sterilisation is considered essential. The *Melk Centrale* (Government Dairy Company) sells pasteurised milk but otherwise milk is unpasteurised and should be boiled. Powdered or tinned milk is available and is advised, but make sure that it is reconstituted with pure water. Avoid dairy products which are likely to have been made from unboiled milk. Only eat well-cooked meat and fish, preferably served hot. Pork, salad and mayonnaise may carry increased risk. Vegetables should be cooked and fruit peeled.
Other risks: *Bilharzia* (schistosomiasis) is present. Avoid swimming and paddling in fresh water; swimming pools which are well chlorinated and maintained are safe. *Hepatitis A* occurs; *hepatitis B* is highly endemic. *Myiasis* (botfly and screw worm) occurs in rural areas. *Dengue fever* is increasing. There is a high prevalence of the *HIV/AIDS* virus.
Rabies is present. For those at high risk, vaccination before arrival should be considered. If you are bitten, seek medical advice without delay. For more information, consult the *Health* appendix.
Health care: Health insurance is strongly recommended. Medical care is limited: there is only one emergency room in Paramaribo and there are few hospitals in outlying areas.

Travel - International

It should be recognised that burgulary, armed robbery and violent crimes occur with some frequency in Paramaribo and outlying areas. However, most visits to Surinam are trouble-free.
AIR: The national airline is *Surinam Airways (PY)* (website: www.slm.firm.sr). *BWIA West Indies Airways* and *KLM* also fly to Surinam. There are direct flights from Amsterdam three to seven times a week.
Approximate flight times: From Paramaribo to *London* is 10 hours, excluding stopover time in Amsterdam or Miami, which may involve an overnight stay, owing to a lack of connecting flights.
International airports: *Johan Adolf Pengel (PBM)* (Paramaribo) is 45km (28 miles) south of the city. A coach meets all arrivals. There are also buses or taxis to the city (travel time – 45 minutes). Airport facilities include duty-free shop, bank, bar/restaurant and post office.
Departure tax: USD35. Transit passengers and children under two years of age are exempt.
SEA: The main international port is Paramaribo. *Surinam Shipping Line* sails from Mexico and New Orleans monthly. There are coastal services between ports and services to Germany and The Netherlands. The *Royal Netherlands Steamship Company* provides a service from Amsterdam to Surinam with limited passenger accommodation. There are regular car ferry services across the Surinam River and Marowijne River from Albina to St Laurent de Maroni (French Guiana), from Southdrain (Surinam) to Moleson Creek (Guyana), and across the Corantijn River from Nieuw Nickerie to Springlands (Guyana).
ROAD: The coastal road from Paramaribo leads to the borders of French Guiana and Guyana.

Travel - Internal

Note: It is advisable to check the weather conditions before setting out for the interior, as heavy rains can cause delays.
AIR: Domestic flights to towns in the interior are operated from Paramaribo (Zorg en Hoop airfield) by *Surinam Airways (PY)*. They also provide services from Paramaribo to the Nieuw Nickerie district, and maintain a charter service.
RIVER: To visit the interior and some coastal areas, river transport is the least expensive and often most efficient option.
RAIL: There are currently no services in operation.
ROAD: Traffic drives on the left. There is a reasonable, largely paved, road network with some potholes. Drivers using their own cars should make sure they carry a full set of spares. **Bus:** There are services from the capital to most villages, with fixed routes at low prices. Buses tend to be very crowded and chaotic with loud music. **Taxi:** These are not metered, prices should be agreed before departure and tipping is not necessary. They can be hard to find after 2200 and on Sundays or holidays. **Car hire:** Available at the airport and in Paramaribo through main hotels.
Documentation: International Driving Permit required.

Accommodation

HOTELS: Paramaribo has a number of modern hotels with air conditioning, but advance booking is essential owing to the limited number of beds. A 10 per cent service charge is added. There are several small guest houses and pensions in the city and elsewhere, but it is advisable to check with the tourist office for further information. Hotels and restaurants are rare outside the capital, and travellers are advised to bring their own hammock and food. For further information, contact Surinam Tourism Foundation or the Ministry of Transport, Communication and Tourism (see *Contact Addresses* section).
APARTMENTS: Furnished apartments with self-catering facilities can be rented.
CAMPING: Blaka Watra, Cola Kreek, Republiek and Zandery are resorts with picnic grounds and camping/bathing facilities.
YOUTH HOSTELS: There is a YMCA in Paramaribo (Heerenstraat).

Resorts & Excursions

PARAMARIBO: The 17th-century capital is graced with attractive British, Dutch, French and Spanish colonial architecture. The nearby restored Fort Zeelandia houses the **Surinam Museum**. Other attractions include the 19th-century **Roman Catholic cathedral** (made entirely of wood – as is the 17th-century synagogue, which lies in stark contrast to the biggest mosque in the Caribbean), **Independence Square**, the **Presidential Palace** (with an attractive palm garden) and the lively waterfront and market districts. **Palmentuin** is a pleasant park, as is the **Cultuurtuin**, but the latter is a fair distance from the town.
ELSEWHERE: The countryside is sparsely populated, and the scenery and the tropical vegetation and wildlife provide the main attractions: mangrove swamps, rivers and rapids of all sizes, Amazonian rainforest and mountains, and jaguars, tapirs, snakes, tropical birds and giant sea turtles from the **Matapica** and **Galibi beach reserves**, as well as highly endangered species such as the cock of the rock, the harpy eagle, the giant otter and the manatee.

A B C D E F G H I J K L M N O P Q R S T U V W X Y Z

Sport & Activities

Watersports: Beaches are not of the highest standard and only a few are suitable for **swimming** (which is prohibited at some classified beaches within nature reserves). An unusual but popular location for swimming is *Colakreek*, a recreation area 50km (32 miles) south of Paramaribo consisting of numerous creeks with brown water in the small savannah belt behind the coastal plains. There are public pools in Paramaribo, Niew-Nickerie, Moengo and Groningen and most hotels have private pools. There are facilities for **sailing** at *Jachthaven Ornamibo*.
Ecotourism: Nearly 80 per cent of the country is covered with tropical rainforest, which is protected by an efficient system of national parks and protected areas. Guided trips to *Raleighvallen/Voltzberg Nature Park* or *Natuurpark Brownsberg* (Brownsberg Nature Park) can be booked in Paramaribo. Some offer accommodation in lodges. Visits to indigenous village communities can also be organised and frequently involve **river tours**. One of the most popular is the five-day river tour of Kumalu and the Awarra Dam region. **Wildlife** enthusiasts can observe numerous mammals (including jaguars, pumas and ocelots), birds (such as flamingos and eagles), rare flowers (including orchids and *ixora*) as well as the black and blue morpho butterflies. Giant Leatherback sea turtles can be watched laying their eggs in the *Galibi Nature Reserve* (accessible by boat only). Bikes can be hired. Further information can be obtained from the Foundation for Nature Preservation in Surinam, Cornelis Jongbawstraat 14, PO Box 12252, Paramaribo (tel: 427 102/3 *or* 476 597; fax: 421 850; e-mail: webmaster@stinasu.sr; website: www.stinasu.sr).
Golf: An 18-hole golf course is located 5km (3 miles) from Paramaribo on the airport road.

Social Profile

FOOD & DRINK: Owing to the diverse ethnic mixture of the population, Surinam offers a good variety of dishes including American, Chinese, Creole, European, Indian and Indonesian. Indonesian dishes are recommended, usually *rijsttafel* with rice (boiled or fried) and a number of spicy meat and vegetable side dishes, *nasi goreng* (Indonesian fried rice) and *bami goreng* (Indonesian fried noodles). Creole dishes include *pom* (ground tayer roots and poultry), *pastei* (chicken pie with various vegetables) and peanut soup. Indian dishes, such as *roti* (dough pancake) served with curried chicken and potatoes, and Chinese dishes, such as *chow-mein* and *chop suey*, are excellent. *Moksi meti* (various meats served on rice) is a local favourite.
Local drinks include the Indonesian *Dawet* (a coconut drink), *Gemberbier* (Creole ginger drink) and *Pilsener Parbo Bier*. There are some restaurants in Niew-Nickerie and Paramaribo, but they tend to be scarce outside the capital.
NIGHTLIFE: There are several nightclubs in Paramaribo, often attached to a hotel, with live music and dancing. There are also a number of discos and several cinemas, including a drive-in. In general, it is best to stick to the hotels unless accompanied by locals who know the reputations of other nightspots, in particular those out of the town centre. The *Local Events Bulletin* lists all current activities and is usually available in hotels.
SHOPPING: Popular items include Maroon tribal woodcarvings, hand-carved and hand-painted trays and gourds, Amerindian bows and arrows, cotton hammocks, wicker and ceramic objects, gold and silver jewellery, Javanese bamboo and batik, as well as tobacco and liquor products. Chinese shops sell imported jade, silks, glass, dolls, needlework and wall decorations. **Shopping hours:** Mon-Fri 0730-1630, Sat 0730-1300.
SPECIAL EVENTS: For further details, contact the Surinam Tourism Foundation (see *Contact Addresses* section). The following is a selection of special events occurring in Surinam in 2005:

Jan *New Year's Jam/End of Surifesta* (top musicians welcome the New Year). **Feb** *Carnival*. **Mar** *Holi Phagwa Hindu Spring Festival*. **Apr** *Evening March of Folkloric Groups*, Paramaribo. **Nov 1** *Diwali Hindu Light Festival*. **Nov-Jan** *Surifesta* (end-of-year festival). **Nov 4-6** *End of Ramadan*.
SOCIAL CONVENTIONS: Informal dress is suitable for most occasions. Guayabera or safari outfits are increasingly worn in place of jackets and ties. Women should wear long trousers on trips to the interior. Beachwear should be confined to the beach or poolside. **Photography:** It is inadvisable to photograph public places, particularly of a political or military nature (including police stations). There is a general sensitivity about the taking of photographs – it is advisable to seek prior permission before taking photographs to avoid causing offence. **Tipping:** Hotels include 10 to 15 per cent service charge and restaurants may also add 10 per cent to the bill.

Business Profile

ECONOMY: Agricultural products include rice, citrus fruits, sugar and bananas, although this part of the economy is in poor financial condition, compounded by low world prices (the state banana company closed in 2002, although cause for optimism has been bolstered due to a smaller restructured banana company resuming business in March 2004). Shrimp fishing is both important and lucrative. The other main activities in this sector are livestock breeding and, most controversially, logging in Surinam's vast jungle interior. The timber is being exploited under a contract awarded to a Malaysian company, although the Government has come under pressure from the international environmental lobby to restrict the quantity. For the time being the most important industry is still mining, especially bauxite and, more recently, gold. There are also thought to be substantial reserves of iron ore, manganese, copper, nickel and platinum, as well as moderate onshore oil deposits. Apart from processing ores and food products, the industrial sector is largely devoted to the manufacture of cigarettes, drinks and chemicals. Foreign aid, especially from The Netherlands (the former colonial power), has been essential to the economy but political disagreements between The Hague and especially the Bouterse government have meant that it has not always been forthcoming. Surinam became a full member of the Caribbean trading bloc CARICOM in 1995. Economic policy has become more austere since the accession of the Ventiaan administration which has sought to tackle Surinam's long-running fiscal and monetary difficulties under the supervision of the IMF and World Bank. The country's principal trading partners are the USA, The Netherlands, Trinidad & Tobago and Brazil.
BUSINESS: A suit is expected for business. All appointments should be honoured, though punctuality may be difficult owing to unpredictable transport. **Office hours:** Mon-Thurs 0700-1500, Fri 0700-1430.
COMMERCIAL INFORMATION: The following organisation can offer advice: Surinam Chamber of Commerce and Industry, PO Box 149, Dr J C de Mirandastraat 10, Paramaribo (tel: 474 536; fax: 474 779; e-mail: chamber@sr.net).
CONFERENCES/CONVENTIONS: For information, contact the Ministry of Foreign Affairs, Lim A Postraat 25, Paramaribo (tel: 471 209; fax: 410 851; e-mail: biza@sr.net).

Climate

Tropical and humid, cooled by the northeast trade winds. The best time to visit is February to April (short dry season) and August to October (long dry season). The rainy seasons last from November to January and from May to July. Surinam lies outside the hurricane zone and the most extreme weather condition is the *sibibusi* (forest broom), a heavy rain shower.
Required clothing: Lightweights and rainwear.

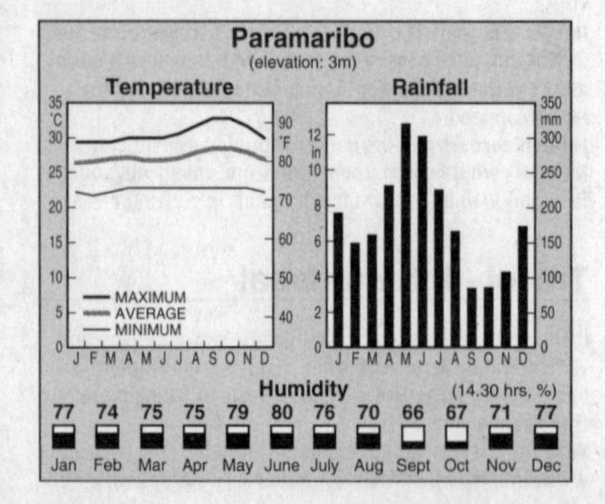

Swaziland

LATEST TRAVEL ADVICE CONTACTS

British Foreign and Commonwealth Office
Tel: (0870) 606 0290 Website: www.fco.gov.uk
US Department of State
Website: http://travel.state.gov/travel
Canadian Department of Foreign Affairs and Int'l Trade
Tel: (1 800) 267 8376 Website: www.dfait-maeci.gc.ca

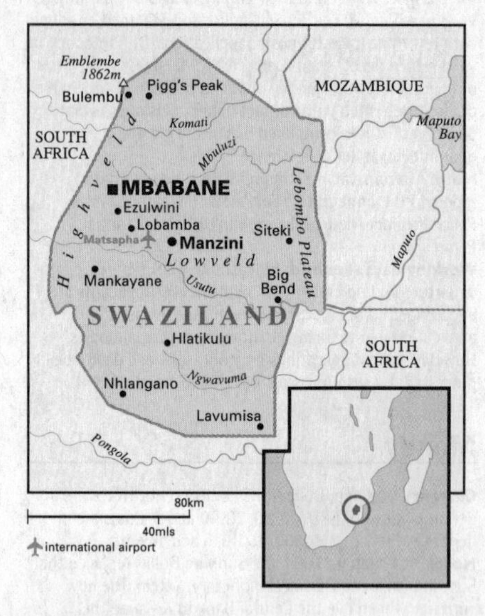

Location: Southern Africa.

Country dialling code: 268.

Ministry of Tourism
PO Box 2652, Mbabane, Swaziland
Tel: (40) 46421 *or* 46556. Fax: (40) 45415.
E-mail: mintour@realnet.co.sz
Website: www.mintour.gov.sz
Kingdom of Swaziland High Commission
20 Buckingham Gate, London SW1E 6LB, UK
Tel: (020) 7630 6611. Fax: (020) 7630 6564.
E-mail: swaziland-swaziland@btinternet.com
Opening hours: Mon-Thurs 0900-1630, Fri 0900-1600.
Embassy of the Kingdom of Swaziland
1712 New Hampshire Avenue, NW, Washington, DC 20009, USA
Tel: (202) 234 5002. Fax: (202) 234 8254.
E-mail: embassy@swaziland-usa.com
Also deals with enquiries from Canada.
Embassy of the United States of America
PO Box 199, 7th Floor, Central Bank Building, Warner Street, Mbabane, Swaziland
Tel: (40) 46441/2 *or* 41695. Fax: (40) 45959.
E-mail: dnmlambo@usembassy.org.sz (commercial section).
Website: http://usembassy.state.gov/mbabane
The Canadian High Commission in Pretoria deals with enquiries relating to Swaziland (see *South Africa* section).

General Information

AREA: 17,363 sq km (6704 sq miles).
POPULATION: 980,722 (1997).
POPULATION DENSITY: 56.5 per sq km.
CAPITAL: Mbabane. **Population**: 73,000 (UN projection 2000).
GEOGRAPHY: Swaziland is surrounded to the north, west and south by the Mpumulanga of South Africa and to the east by Mozambique. There are four main topographical regions: the Highveld Inkangala, a wide ribbon of partly reforested, rugged country including the Usutu pine forest; the Peak Timbers in the northwest; the Middleveld, which rolls down from the Highveld through hills and fertile valleys; and the Lowveld, or bush country, with hills rising

TIMATIC CODES

Health	AMADEUS: **TI-DFT/MTS/HE** GALILEO/WORLDSPAN: **TI-DFT/MTS/HE** SABRE: **TIDFT/MTS/HE**
Visa	AMADEUS: **TI-DFT/MTS/VI** GALILEO/WORLDSPAN: **TI-DFT/MTS/VI** SABRE: **TIDFT/MTS/VI**

To access TIMATIC country information on Health and Visa regulations through the Computer Reservations System (CRS), type in the appropriate command line listed above.

from 170 to 360m (560 to 1180ft). The Lubombo plateau is an escarpment along the eastern fringe of the Lowveld, comprising mainly cattle country and mixed farmland. One of the best-watered areas in southern Africa, Swaziland's four major rivers are the Komati, Usutu, Mbuluzi and Ngwavuma, flowing west-east to the Indian Ocean.
GOVERNMENT: Constitutional monarchy since 1973. Gained independence from the UK in 1968. **Head of State:** King Mswati III since 1986. **Head of Government:** Prime Minister Themba Dlamini since 2003.
LANGUAGE: English and siSwati.
RELIGION: 60 per cent Christian, with most of the remainder adhering to traditional beliefs.
TIME: GMT + 2.
ELECTRICITY: 220/30 volts AC, 50Hz; 15-amp round pin plugs are in use.
COMMUNICATIONS: Telephone: IDD is available. Country code: 268. Outgoing international calls must go through the international operator. Public telephones are available. **Mobile telephone:** GSM 900 network. Network operators include *Swazi MTN* (website: www.mtn.co.sz). **Fax:** Many hotels in Mbabane have facilities. **Internet:** ISPs include *Real Image Internet* (website: www.realnet.co.sz). **Telegram:** Facilities are available in the capital. However, Telex is often a more efficient and cheaper way to send international communications; machines can be found at post offices and major hotels in Mbabame. **Post:** Post offices are in all main centres. Airmail to Europe is unreliable and can take from two weeks to two months. Post office hours: Mon-Fri 0800-1300 and 1400-1700, Sat 0800-1100. **Press:** The English-language newspaper in Swaziland is *The Times of Swaziland*.
Radio: BBC World Service (website: www.bbc.co.uk/worldservice) and Voice of America (website: www.voa.gov) can be received. From time to time the frequencies change and the most up-to-date can be found online.

Passport/Visa

	Passport Required?	Visa Required?	Return Ticket Required?
Full British	Yes	2/3	Yes
Australian	Yes	1	Yes
Canadian	Yes	1	Yes
USA	Yes	1	Yes
Other EU	Yes	2/3	Yes
Japanese	Yes	1	Yes

Note: *Regulations and requirements may be subject to change at short notice, and you are advised to contact the appropriate diplomatic or consular authority before finalising travel arrangements. Details of these may be found at the head of this country's entry. Any numbers in the chart refer to the footnotes below.*

PASSPORTS: Passport valid for at least six months upon entry required by all.
VISAS: Required by all except the following:
(a) **1.** nationals of Australia, Canada, Japan and the USA for stays of up to two months;
(b) **2.** nationals of the EU for stays of up to two months* (except nationals of the Czech Republic, Estonia, Hungary, Latvia, Lithuania, Slovak Republic and Slovenia who *do* require a visa);
(c) nationals of Commonwealth countries for stays of up to two months (except nationals of Antigua & Barbuda, Bangladesh, Belize, Brunei, Cameroon, Dominica, India, Kiribati, Maldives, Mauritius, Mozambique, Nigeria, Pakistan, Sri Lanka, Tuvalu and Vanuatu who *do* require a visa);
(d) nationals of Iceland, Israel, Korea (Rep), Liechtenstein, Norway, San Marino, Turkey, Uruguay and Zimbabwe for stays of up to two months.
Note: * **3.** Nationals of Belgium, Denmark, Greece, Ireland, Luxembourg, The Netherlands and Portugal ca also obtain a visa free of charge upon arrival and may remain in Swaziland longer than two months, at the discretion of the Immigration department. Nationals of the UK may also remain in Swaziland for an undisclosed amount of time.
Types of visa and cost: *Single-entry:* £16. *Multiple-entry:* £24 (three months); £38 (six months); £58 (nine months); £60 (12 months).
Note: Transit passengers should consult their carrying company when making reservations for up-to-date advice on whether a visa is required.
Validity: Three to six months from date of issue for stays of up to two months each. Applications for extensions should be submitted to the Chief Immigration Officer in Swaziland.
Application to: Consulate (or Consular section at Embassy or High Commission); see *Contact Addresses* section.
Application requirements: (a) Application form. (b) Two passport-size photos. (c) Fee. (d) Valid passport. (e) Proof of means of support during stay. (f) Letter on headed paper confirming that the visitor holds return or onward tickets. (g) For all visitors except tourists, a letter of invitation from a Swazi national *or* for business trips, a letter from applicant's company giving details of the business and confirming the financial responsibility for the applicant.
Working days required: One or two unless authorisation is required, in which case the application could take several weeks.
Temporary residence: Apply to Chief Immigration Officer if staying longer than two months in Swaziland.

Money

Currency: Lilangeni (E) = 100 cents. The plural of Lilangeni is Emalangeni. Notes are in denominations of E200, 100, 50, 20 and 10. Coins are in denominations of E5, 2 and 1, and 100, 50, 20, 10, 5, 2 and 1 cents. The South African Rand is also accepted as legal tender (E1 = 1 Rand) although coins are not accepted.
Currency exchange: Visitors are advised to exchange Emalangeni back into their own currency before leaving Swaziland.
Credit & debit cards: American Express, MasterCard and Visa are widely accepted. Check with your credit or debit card company for details of merchant acceptability and other facilities which may be available.
Travellers cheques: Widely accepted. Several banks will exchange travellers cheques, but to avoid additional exchange rate charges, travellers are advised to take them in Euros, Pounds Sterling or US Dollars.
Currency restrictions: The import and export of foreign and local currency is unrestricted.
Exchange rate indicators: The following figures are included as a guide to the movements of the Lilangeni against Sterling and the US Dollar:

Date	Feb '04	May '04	Aug '04	Nov '04
£1.00=	12.87	12.50	11.91	11.06
$1.00=	7.07	7.00	6.46	5.84

Banking hours: Mon-Fri 0830-1430, Sat 0830-1100.

Duty Free

The following items may be imported into Swaziland without incurring customs duty:
400 cigarettes and 50 cigars and 250g of tobacco; one bottle (max 750ml) of alcoholic beverage; 284ml of perfume per person; free export of souvenirs and presents.
Note: Married couples travelling together are allowed free import for one person only.

Public Holidays

2005: Jan 1 New Year's Day. **Mar 25** Good Friday. **Mar 28** Easter Monday. **Apr 19** Birthday of King Mswati. **Apr 25** National Flag Day. **May 1** Labour Day. **May 5** Ascension. **Jul 22** Birthday of the Late King Sobhuza. **Aug/Sep*** Umhlanga, Reed Dance Day. **Sep 6** Somhlolo Day (Independence Day). **Dec/Jan*** Incwala Ceremony. **Dec 25** Christmas Day. **Dec 26** Boxing Day.
2006: Jan 1 New Year's Day. **Apr 14** Good Friday. **Apr 17** Easter Monday. **Apr 19** Birthday of King Mswati. **Apr 25** National Flag Day. **May 1** Labour Day. **May 25** Ascension. **Jul 22** Birthday of the Late King Sobhuza. **Aug/Sep*** Umhlanga, Reed Dance Day. **Sep 6** Somhlolo Day (Independence Day). **Dec/Jan*** Incwala Ceremony. **Dec 25** Christmas Day. **Dec 26** Boxing Day.
Note: *The dates of the Umhlanga and Incwala ceremonies vary according to local sightings of the moon. Contact the Embassy/High Commission for further details.

Health

	Special Precautions?	Certificate Required?
Yellow Fever	No	1
Cholera	Yes	2
Typhoid & Polio	3	N/A
Malaria	4	N/A

Note: *Regulations and requirements may be subject to change at short notice, and you are advised to contact your doctor well in advance of your intended date of departure. Any numbers in the chart refer to the footnotes below.*

1: A yellow fever vaccination certificate is required by travellers over one year of age arriving within six days from infected areas.
2: Following WHO guidelines issued in 1973, a cholera vaccination certificate is no longer a condition of entry to Swaziland. However, cholera is a risk in the country and precautions are essential. Up-to-date advice should be sought before deciding whether these precautions should include vaccination as medical opinion is divided over its effectiveness; see the *Health* appendix.
3: Vaccination against typhoid is advised.
4: Malaria risk exists throughout the year (particularly in the rainy season, from November to February) in all Lowveld areas, particularly Big Bend, Mhlume, Simunye and Tshaneni. The predominant *falciparum* strain is reported to be highly resistant to chloroquine.
Food & drink: Mains water is generally safe but bottled or sterilised water is preferable. Drinking water outside major cities and towns may be contaminated. Milk is pasteurised and dairy products are safe for consumption; exercise caution if milk is of uncertain provenance. Only eat well-cooked meat and fish, preferably served hot. Pork, salad and mayonnaise may carry increased risk. Vegetables should be cooked and fruit peeled.
Other risks: *Bilharzia* (schistosomiasis) is endemic. Avoid swimming and paddling in fresh water; swimming pools which are well chlorinated and maintained are safe.
Hepatitis A is present; *hepatitis B* is highly endemic and precautions should be taken.
Arthropod-borne diseases such as *Crimean-congo haemorrhagic fever, plague, relapsing fever, Rift valley fever* and *tick-bite fever* have been reported.
The humid climate may provoke *asthma* and other respiratory disorders.
Rabies is present.
Health care: Although medical facilities are generally limited in Swaziland, Mbabame Clinic is well-equipped to deal with minor problems. Most international visitors will use private services, frequently attached to the larger hotels. The public sector is improving and treatment is available at low cost. In emergency cases, where specialised treatment is required, the patient may be transported to a South African hospital. Health insurance is recommended. Personal medications may be brought into the country, but a doctor's note is advisable in case of questioning by authorities.

Travel - International

AIR: Swaziland's national airline is *Royal Swazi National Airways Corporation (ZC)*. Comair operates flights to Johannesburg. *Swazi Airlink* runs a regular link between Manzini to Johannesburg.
Approximate flight times: From Manzini to *Johannesburg* is one hour; to *London* is 16 hours (including stopover).
International airports: *Manzini (MTS)* (Matsapha) is 5km (3 miles) northwest of the city. Airport facilities include banks/bureaux de change, restaurants, car hire (*Avis* and *Hertz*) and snack bar. Taxi service to the city centre is available on all arrivals (travel time - 15 minutes).
Departure tax: E20; children under three years or age and direct transit passengers are exempt.
ROAD: There are good roads from Johannesburg, Durban and northern KwaZulu-Natal as well as tourist buses running from KwaZulu-Natal and Mpumalanga. On crossing the border you will be required to show your passport and visa (if required). There is also a token road tax of E5 to be paid. **Bus:** There is a weekly service from Mbabane and Manzini to Johannesburg (travel time - eight hours), and a twice-weekly connection from Mbabane to Maputo.
RAIL: A train service between Durban and Maputo travels through Swaziland stopping at Mpaka, 35km (22 miles) east of Manzini. Departures from Durban are twice weekly (travel time - 16 hours).

Travel - Internal

ROAD: The road system is largely well developed, although there is little street lighting, some roads are winding and roads can be rough in the bush. Small toll charges are set to be introduced on the new highway between Mbabane and Manzini. The maximum speed limit on all roads is 80kph (50mph). The legal blood alcohol limit is 0.15 per cent. Traffic drives on the left. **Bus:** There are numerous (not always entirely safe) buses connecting the different parts of the country, including non-stop buses. Minibus taxis run shorter routes at slightly higher prices than the buses. **Car hire:** There are a number of international car hire companies in Swaziland. **Documentation:** An International Driving Permit is required.
TRAVEL TIMES: The following chart gives approximate travel times (in hours and minutes) from **Mbabane** to other major towns in Swaziland.

	Road
Manzini	0.45
Nhlangano	2.00
Piggs Peak	1.00
Siteki	1.30

Accommodation

There are some good hotels in Swaziland, some of international standard, but it is necessary to book well in advance. Rates quoted are generally per person based on two people sharing. Expect prices to be significantly higher in peak season (December to January, and Easter). There are also smaller motels and inns, campsites and caravan parks outside the city. For further information, contact the Hotel and Tourism Association of Swaziland, PO Box 462, Oribi Court, Allister Miller Street, Mbabane H100 (tel: (40) 42218; fax: (40) 44516). **Grading:** The star-grading system is in use.
CAMPING: Camping is possible near almost every tourist attraction and in all the national parks.

Resorts & Excursions

MBABANE & AREA

Mbabane, the capital of Swaziland, lies at the northern end of the Ezulwini Valley amid the granite peaks and valleys that make up the Dlangeni hills. Mbabane is Swaziland's administrative capital and is small, relaxed and unpretentious. The main attractions in town are the **Mall**, the **New Mall** and **Allister Miller**, the main street, named after the first European to be born there.

EZULWINI VALLEY: The lush Ezulwini Valley is a miracle of nature and the seat of Swaziland's major tourist attractions. Although Swaziland has long been regarded as one of the most beautiful countries in Africa, it was not until an Italian and South African syndicate built southern Africa's first casino hotel on a prime valley site in the early 1990s that Swaziland geared itself towards tourism. In the valley is the magnificent **Royal Swazi golf course**, the **casino**, the **hot mineral spring** – one of eight in the country – known affectionately by locals and guests as the 'Cuddle Puddle', a health studio and a cluster of fine hotels forming the **Holiday Valley** complex.

Lobamba: In the heart of the Ezulwini Valley is Swaziland's royal valley, Lobamba, the spiritual and legislative capital of the kingdom. It is home to the royals' **Embo State Palace**. The **National Museum** is housed here, which offers displays on Swazi culture and has a traditional beehive village beside it.

MANZINI: East across the valley is Swaziland's largest town and its commercial hub, Manzini. On the way here, visitors pass signposts to Swaziland's most famous waterfall, the **Mantenga Falls**, the thriving **Mantenga Arts & Crafts Centre**, the **Mlilwane Game Sanctuary**, Matsapha Airport and the industrial area of **Matsapha**, which produces everything from beer to television sets.

There is an outstanding market every day except Sunday; dawn on Thursdays and Fridays is particularly worth a visit as it is when the rural people bring in their handicrafts to sell to retailers. Manzini's only other point of interest is its original Catholic mission, an elegant stone building opposite the new cathedral; it is not open to casual visitors. Unfortunately the city has little else to offer and is polluted with reckless drivers, city slickers and an ever-growing crime record.

PIGGS PEAK AND THE NORTHWEST

The rolling hills, sparkling streams and countless waterfalls make this one of the most appealing regions of Swaziland. **Piggs Peak**, a small forestry town straggled along the main road, was named after a French prospector called William Pigg, who discovered gold nearby in 1884, where it was mined until the site was exhausted in 1954. Nearby, the **Ngwenya Glass Factory** is the origin of one of Swaziland's best-known exports, Ngwenya glass. Their products, which range from attractive wine glasses to endless trinkets in the shape of rotund animals, are made from recycled glass and are produced by highly skilled workers, who can be watched in action.

THE SOUTH

The scenery, particularly along the drive from Mahamba to Manzini through the Grand Valley, is superb, and the road passes near most of the historical sites of the Swazi royal house. **Big Bend** itself, dominated by a huge sugar mill, is only worth visiting for its hotel, the *New Bend Inn*. It is a slightly run-down colonial establishment with superb views of the valley and well-positioned bars; it is a lively Swazi haunt at weekends, when major parties take place.

The area is currently being developed for tourism, and the first project has been the construction of another casino hotel at **Nhlangano**, about 120km (75 miles) south of Mbabane. The sports facilities, which include a golf course and swimming pool, are excellent. The nearby **Mkondo River** twists its way through gorges and valleys, past waterfalls, pools and rapids and, in the distance, the mountain ranges gleam brown, mauve and blue. Some of Swaziland's finest paintings are found in this area. Other indigenous paintings are located in the mountains north of Mbabane.

NATURE RESERVES & GAME PARKS

The Swaziland National Trust Commission (SNTC) is responsible for the preservation and development of Swaziland's many areas of natural beauty and wildlife. There are currently four SNTC nature reserves, namely **Malolotja**, **Hawane**, **Mantenga** and **Mlawula**, all of which are inhabited by a rich wildlife (including rare species such as the aardwolf or African finfoot) and a wide range of bird species. These reserves are characterised by some of the most beautiful landscapes in southern Africa. In recent years, strong efforts were made to bring back wildlife to the country. As a result, the SNTC has taken a number of once privately run game parks under its wing such as **Mlilwane**, the country's oldest established game sanctuary. Other game sanctuaries that have recently been proclaimed protected areas are **Malolotsha**, in the north near Piggs Peak; **Hlane**, in the shadow of the escarpment in the northeast; and **Mkhaya**. Hlane has wide open spaces supporting big herds of game where the visitor can see the old traditional scenes of Africa. Both Hlane and Malolotsha, which is situated on top of a mountain range and surrounded by steep canyons and waterfalls, are easily reached by road and different types of accommodation and tours are available. For more information, contact the Swaziland National Trust Commission, PO Box 100, Lobamba (tel: (41) 61481/9 *or* 61179; fax: (41) 61875; e-mail: staff@swazimus.org.sz; website: www.sntc.org.sz); *or* the Ministry of Tourism (see *Contact Addresses* section).

MKHAYA GAME RESERVE: Roughly 30km (19 miles) north of **Big Bend** is Mkhaya Nature Reserve, situated along a turn-off from the brilliantly named village of **Phuzumoya** ('drink the wind') in classic lowveld scrubland, filled with acacia and thorn trees. Ted Reilly initially purchased Mkhaya to save the long-horned **Nguni cattle** when white beef-farmers regarded them as too puny and unproductive for their industry, and replaced them with imported stock. Today, the cattle graze alongside zebra, wildebeest and antelope, just as they always used to. Among the other endangered species at Mkhaya are the rare **black rhinos** and the near-extinct **roan antelope**.

MLILWANE WILDLIFE SANCTUARY: This reserve, near Lobamba, is in the heart of the Ezulwini Valley. Its name, **Mlilwane**, refers to the little fire that appears on occasion when lightning strikes the granite mountains. The wildlife is predominantly herbivorous, including antelope, giraffe and zebra, but crocodiles are not uncommon. Over 100km (62 miles) of road enables you to drive through the park to view game, or guided walks and drives can be arranged through the park office.

MLAWULA NATURE RESERVE: The **Lubombo Mountains** that run along the eastern border of Mlawula Nature Reserve provide fantastic views of both Swaziland and the western fringes of Mozambique. Unique species of **ironwood trees** and **cycads** grow on the slopes. There are well-organised trails through the reserve. The **Mlawula stream** and more substantial **Mbuluzi River** both flow through some spectacular valleys in this reserve, and early Stone Age tools over one million years old have been found along their beds.

Sport & Activities

Wildlife safaris: Guided safaris (either by car on on foot) are available in Swaziland's nature reserves and game parks (see *Resorts & Excursions* section). The *Milwane Wildlife Sanctuary* can also be toured on horseback. Despite its small size, Swaziland offers an interesting variety of terrains and animal species. Prices tend to be lower than in neighbouring South Africa. **Whitewater rafting** trips are available on the *Great Usutu River* in the Mkhaya Game Reserve.

Hiking: Popular hikes include the ascent to *Malolotsha Falls* at Piggs Peak; *Sibebe Mountain*, a huge granite outcrop that provides a scenic spot for a picnic; and the climb up *Emlembe*, Swaziland's highest peak.

General: There is an 18-hole **golf** course in the Ezulwini Valley attached to the Royal Swazi Sun Hotel and Spa and the Havelock Golf Course. **Tennis** courts are available at numerous major hotels, notably the Royal Swazi. Several hotels have **swimming** pools and non-residents are generally permitted to use the facilities.

Social Profile

FOOD & DRINK: Restaurants are found mainly in the larger centres and at hotels. Most serve international cuisine: Greek, Hungarian and Indian food is available. Food stalls in the local markets sell traditional Swazi meat stew and maize meal or stamped mealies and roasted corn on the cob (in season).

There is a good selection of spirits, beers and wines. Traditional Swazi beer can be tasted in rural areas. There are no formal licensing hours.

NIGHTLIFE: In the main centres of Mbabane and Ezulwini Valley, there are nightclubs and discos, some with live music and cabaret. The main attraction in Ezulwini Valley is the casino at the Royal Swazi Hotel. There is also a cinema there.

SHOPPING: There is a modern shopping complex in Mbabane but local markets are always interesting places to shop. Purchases from craft centres include beadwork, basketry, grass and sisal mats, copperware, wooden bowls, local gemstone jewellery, wooden and soapstone carvings, calabashes, knobkerries, battleaxes, walking sticks, *karosses* (animal skin mats), drums, woven cloth and batik and tie-dye, which are often incorporated into traditional Swazi garments.

Shopping hours: Mon-Fri 0800-1700, Sat 0800-1300.

SPECIAL EVENTS: The following is a selection of special events celebrated annually in Swaziland:

Jan/Dec Incwala (Fruit Ceremony; every year at a time carefully chosen by astrologers, this four-day ceremony takes place, culminating in a ritual during which the king eats the first fruit of the new season. The ceremony confers the blessing of their ancestors on the nation's consumption of these fruits), nationwide. **Aug/Sep** *Umhlanga* (Reed Dance; an event in which young women pay homage to the Queen Mother), Lombada.

SOCIAL CONVENTIONS: Traditional ways of life are still strong and Swazi culture in the form of religious music, dance, poetry and craftsmanship plays an important part in daily life. Casual wear is normal although more formal wear is customary at the casino and sophisticated hotels. Visitors wishing to camp near villages should first inform the headman. He can normally help with customs.

Photography: Permission to photograph individuals should always be sought. In some cases, a gratuity may be asked for (especially if the subject has gone to some effort to make a show – for example, by wearing traditional regalia). It is prohibited to photograph the Royal Palace, the Royal Family, uniformed police, army personnel, army vehicles or aircraft and bank buildings. Visitors wishing to photograph traditional ceremonies should first contact the Government Information Service, PO Box 451, Mbabane (tel: (40) 42761 *or* 43251; fax: (40) 43953). **Tipping:** 10 to 15 per cent of the bill is customary in restaurants and hotels.

Business Profile

ECONOMY: The economy is dominated by and closely linked with that of South Africa, and the country is a member of the Southern African Customs Union (through which the Government receives around half its total revenue). Agriculture is by far the largest part of the economy, employing over 75 per cent of the working population. Sugar, cotton and fruit are the main cash crops. Tobacco and rice are recent additions to the country's produce, while livestock rearing is traditionally important. The industrial sector, which contributes over 40 per cent of GDP, is mainly concerned with processing agricultural products, largely food and wood products including paper, and also the production of textiles and metal goods. The country's mining industry produces coal, of which there are extensive reserves, and diamonds but the other main products of asbestos and iron ore have been in long-term decline due to falling export demand. The removal of sanctions against South Africa gave a boost to the Swazi economy but the gains have been undermined by a number of factors: drought, low commodity prices, the impact of widespread HIV/AIDS infection on the workforce, the low value of the South African rand (to which the Swazi currency is linked). Moreover, opposition from the business community to King Mswati's autocratic rule has made for a poor commercial environment. Unemployment remains at an estimated 40 per cent. The Government has made efforts to attract foreign capital to fund future development, notably through a number of prestige construction and infrastructure projects. Apart from South Africa, which dominates Swazi trade, the most important trading partners are the UK and France.

BUSINESS: Lightweight suits are generally expected for business. Appointments are necessary and business cards are exchanged. English is widely spoken in business circles. **Office hours:** Mon-Fri 0800-1300 and 1400-1645.

COMMERCIAL INFORMATION: The following organisations can offer advice: Swaziland Industrial Development Co (SIDC), PO Box 886, 5th Floor, Dhlan'ubeka House, Corner Tin & Walker Streets, Mbabane (tel: (40) 44010 *or* 43391; fax: (40) 45619; e-mail: info@sidc.co.sz; website: www.sidc.co.sz); *or* Swaziland Chamber of Commerce and Industry, PO Box 72, Mbabane (tel: (40) 44408; fax: (40) 45442; e-mail: chamber@business-swaziland.com; website: www.business-swaziland.com/chamber).

CONFERENCES/CONVENTIONS: The principal facilities are at the Royal Swazi Convention Centre in the Ezulwini Valley, which has seating for up to 600 people. Several hotels also have facilities for smaller numbers, with back-up services. The Ministry of Tourism (see *Contact Addresses* section) can supply information.

Climate

Due to the variations in altitude the weather is changeable. Except in the lowland, it is rarely uncomfortably hot and nowhere very cold, although frosts occasionally occur in the Highveld which has a wetter, temperate climate. The Middleveld and Lubombo are drier and subtropical with most rain from October to March.

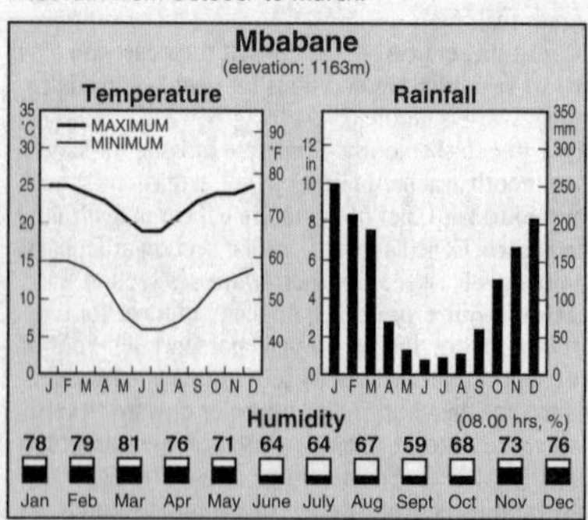

Sweden

LATEST TRAVEL ADVICE CONTACTS

British Foreign and Commonwealth Office
Tel: (0870) 606 0290 Website: www.fco.gov.uk

US Department of State
Website: http://travel.state.gov/travel

Canadian Department of Foreign Affairs and Int'l Trade
Tel: (1 800) 267 8376 Website: www.dfait-maeci.gc.ca

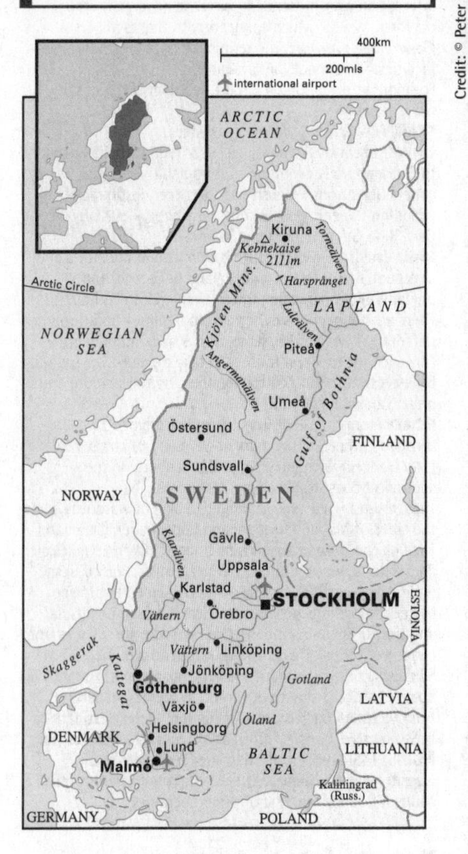

Location: Northeast Europe, Scandinavia.

Country dialling code: 46.

Swedish Travel & Tourism Council
PO Box 3030, 10361 Stockholm, Sweden
Tel: (8) 789 1000. Fax: (8) 789 1031.
E-mail: info@swetourism.se
Website: www.visit-sweden.com

Svenska Turistföreningen (Swedish Tourist Federation)
PO Box 25, 101 20 Stockholm, Sweden
Tel: (8) 463 2100. Fax: (8) 678 1958.
E-mail: info@stfturist.se
Website: www.stfturist.se

Embassy of Sweden
11 Montagu Place, London W1H 2AL, UK
Tel: (020) 7917 6400. Fax: (020) 7724 4174 *or* 7917 6475 (visa section) *or* 6477 (press information).
E-mail: ambassaden.london@foreign.ministry.se *or* ambassaden.london-visum@foreign.ministry.se
Website: www.swedish-embassy.org.uk
Opening hours: Mon-Fri 0900-1230 and 1400-1600 (general enquiries); Mon-Fri 0900-1230 (visa applications).

Swedish Travel & Tourism Council
Sweden House, 5 Upper Montagu Street, London W1H 2AG, UK
Tel: (00800) 3080 3080 *or* 6201 5010 (within Sweden) *or* 7870 5604 (press department). Fax: 6201 5011 (within Sweden) *or* 7724 5872 (press department).
E-mail: emelie@swetourism.org.uk
Website: www.visit-sweden.com

TIMATIC CODES

Health	AMADEUS: **TI-DFT/STO/HE** GALILEO/WORLDSPAN: **TI-DFT/STO/HE** SABRE: **TIDFT/STO/HE**
Visa	AMADEUS: **TI-DFT/STO/VI** GALILEO/WORLDSPAN: **TI-DFT/STO/VI** SABRE: **TIDFT/STO/VI**

To access TIMATIC country information on Health and Visa regulations through the Computer Reservations System (CRS), type in the appropriate command line listed above.

Credit: © Peter Grant

British Embassy
Skarpögatan 6-8, PO Box 27819, 115 93 Stockholm, Sweden
Tel: (8) 671 3000. Fax: (8) 671 9989 *or* 661 9766 (consular and visa section).
E-mail: info@britishembassy.se
Website: www.britishembassy.se

British Consulate General
Södra Hamngatan 23, S-411 14 Gothenburg, Sweden
Tel: (31) 339 3300. Fax: (31) 339 3302.
Website: www.britishembassy.se

Embassy of Sweden
1501 M Street, Suite 900, NW, Washington, DC 20005, USA
Tel: (202) 467 2600. Fax: (202) 467 2699.
E-mail: ambassaden.washington@foreign.ministry.se *or* ambassaden.washington-visa@foreign.ministry.se
Website: www.swedenabroad.se
Consulates General in: Chicago (tel: (312) 781 6262), Detroit (tel: (734) 944 8111), Los Angeles (tel: (310) 473 3350), Minneapolis (tel: (612) 332 6897), New York (tel: (212) 583 2550) and San Francisco (tel: (415) 788 2631).

Swedish Travel & Tourism Council
Council PO Box 4649, Grand Central Station, New York, NY 10163-4649, USA
Tel: (212) 885 9700 (from USA and Canada).
Fax: (212) 885 9764.
E-mail: usa@visit-sweden.com *or* annika.benjes@swetourism.com (press section).
Website: www.swetourism.com
Not open to personal callers.

Embassy of the United States of America
Dag Hammarskjölds Väg 31, SE-115 89 Stockholm, Sweden
Tel: (8) 783 5300. Fax: (8) 660 5879 (consular section) *or* 9181 (commercial service).
E-mail: StockholmWeb@state.gov
Website: www.usemb.se

Embassy of Sweden
377 Dalhousie Street, Ottawa, Ontario K1N 9N8, Canada
Tel: (613) 241 8553. Fax: (613) 241 2277.
E-mail: sweden@bellnet.ca
Website: www.swedishembassy.ca
Consulates in: Alberta, British Columbia, Manitoba, New Brunswick, Nova Scotia, Ontario, Québec City, Saskatchewan and St Johns.

Canadian Embassy
Tegelbacken 4, PO Box 16 129, S-103 23 Stockholm, Sweden
Tel: (8) 453 3000. Fax: (8) 453 3016.
E-mail: stkhm-ag@dfait-maeci.gc.ca *or* stkhm-cs@dfait-maeci.gc.ca (consular/passport section).
Website: www.dfait-maeci.gc.ca/canadaeuropa/sweden

General Information

AREA: 449,964 sq km (173,732 sq miles).
POPULATION: 8,975,670 (official estimate 2003).
POPULATION DENSITY: 19.9 per sq km.
CAPITAL: Stockholm. **Population:** 761,721 (2003).
GEOGRAPHY: Sweden is bordered by Norway to the west and Finland to the northeast, with a long Baltic coast to the east and south. Approximately half the country is forested and most of the many thousands of lakes are situated in the southern central area. The largest lake is Vänern, with an area of 5540 sq km (2140 sq miles). Swedish Lapland to the north is mountainous and extends into the Arctic Circle.
GOVERNMENT: Constitutional monarchy. Gained independence from Denmark in 1523. **Head of State:** King Carl XVI since 1973. **Head of Government:** Prime Minister Göran Persson since 1996.
LANGUAGE: Swedish. Lapp is spoken by the Sámi population in the north; there are also Finnish-speaking minorities. English is taught as the first foreign language from the age of nine.
RELIGION: Around 86 per cent of the population belong to the Church of Sweden (Evangelical Lutheran), separated from the state in January 2000; other Protestant minorities constitute the majority of the remainder.
TIME: GMT + 1 (GMT + 2 from last Sunday in March to Saturday before last Sunday in October).
ELECTRICITY: 230 volts, three-phase AC, 50Hz. Two-pin continental plugs are used.
COMMUNICATIONS: Telephone: Full IDD is available. Country code: 46. Outgoing international code: 00. Coin-operated pay phones no longer exist and they are all now card-operated. Cards are readily available from kiosks and newsagents and instructions in English are displayed in most booths. Credit card phones (indicated by a 'CCC' sign) are widely available. **Mobile telephone:** GSM 900/1800 and 3G networks are available. Main network providers include: *Comviq* (website: www.comviq.se), *Telia AB* (website: www.teliamobile.se) and *Vodafone* (website: www.vodafone.se). Coverage is available across most of the country. **Fax:** An excellent service is widely available throughout the country. **Internet:** Main ISPs include *Dataphone* (website: www.dataphone.net) and *Svenska Internet Centralen* (website: www.sic.se). Internet cafes exist in all main urban areas but are scarcer outside of these areas. **Telegram:** Telegrams can be sent from most hotels and post offices. **Post:** Post office hours: Usually open during normal shopping hours (Mon-Fri 0800-2200, Sat 0900-1500). Some branches may be closed Saturday during July. Post boxes are yellow. Stamps and aerograms are on sale at post offices and also at most bookstalls and stationers. Airmail within Europe takes three to four days. *Poste Restante* facilities are widely available in post offices. **Press:** The provinces have their own newspapers which are widely read in their respective regions; the major dailies are confined largely to the capital and include such titles as *Aftonbladet*, *Dagens Nyheter*, *Expressen* and *Svenska Dagbladet*. Many papers are financed by political parties but independence and freedom of the press is firmly maintained. All papers are in Swedish.
Radio: BBC World Service (website: www.bbc.co.uk/worldservice) and Voice of America (website: www.voa.gov) can be received. From time to time the frequencies change and the most up-to-date can be found online.

Passport/Visa

	Passport Required?	Visa Required?	Return Ticket Required?
Full British	Yes	No	No
Australian	Yes	No	No
Canadian	Yes	No	No
USA	Yes	No	No
Other EU	1/2	No	No
Japanese	Yes	No	No

Note: Regulations and requirements may be subject to change at short notice, and you are advised to contact the appropriate diplomatic or consular authority before finalising travel arrangements. Details of these may be found at the head of this country's entry. Any numbers in the chart refer to the footnotes below.

Note: (a) Sweden is a signatory to the 1995 **Schengen Agreement**. For further details about passport/visa regulations within the Schengen area, see the introductory section *How to Use this Guide*. (b) Sweden does not recognise some Somali passports issued after 31 January 1991; check with Consulate or Consular section at Embassy for further details.
PASSPORTS: Passports, valid for three months after departure from Schengen area, are required by all except the following:
(a) **1.** nationals of EU countries, provided holding a valid national ID card (for stays of up to three months);
(b) **2.** nationals of Denmark, Finland, Iceland and Norway holding travel documents issued for travel between these countries;
(c) nationals of Liechtenstein and Switzerland, provided holding valid national ID cards (for stays of up to three months).
VISAS: Required by all except the following:

A B C D E F G H I J K L M N O P Q R S T U V W X Y Z

(a) nationals of the countries referred to in the chart and listed under passport exemptions above for stays of up to three months;
(b) nationals of Andorra, Argentina, Bolivia, Brazil, Brunei, Bulgaria, Chile, Costa Rica, Croatia, El Salvador, Guatemala, Honduras, Hong Kong (SAR), Israel, Korea (Rep), Liechtenstein, Macau (SAR), Malaysia, Mexico, Monaco, New Zealand, Nicaragua, Panama, Paraguay, Romania, San Marino, Singapore, Switzerland, Uruguay and Venezuela for stays of up to three months;
(c) those continuing their journey, holding tickets with confirmed reservations and required travel documents, arriving and departing from/to a Schengen country and not leaving the transit area.
Note: A transit visa is always required by nationals of the following countries (if holding a visa valid for less than three months): Afghanistan, Bangladesh, Congo (Dem Rep), Eritrea, Ethiopia, Ghana, India, Iran, Iraq, Nigeria, Pakistan, Somalia and Sri Lanka.
Validity: 30 to 90 days.
Types of visa and cost: £24 (price is subject to change depending on the exchange rate). A uniform type of visa, the *Schengen* visa, is issued for tourist, business and private visits. Visa fees are non-refundable and payable on submission of the visa application.
Application to: Consulate (or Consular section at Embassy); see *Contact Addresses* section. Travellers visiting just one Schengen country should apply to the Consulate of that country; travellers visiting more than one Schengen country should apply to the Consulate of the country chosen as the main destination *or* the country they will enter first (if they have no main destination).
Application requirements: (a) Valid passport with at least one blank page. (b) Two recent passport-size photos. (c) Fee, payable in cash or postal order (only if sent by post). (d) Completed, signed application form. (e) Proof of occupation/student status. (f) Proof of purpose of visit (invitation letter from Swedish company/friend for business visas/private-visit visas, or evidence of pre-booked hotel accommodation. (g) Stamped, registered, self-addressed envelope for return of passport. (h) Health insurance. (i) Written consent from parents for minors. (j) Proof of means of support during stay may be required by some nationals.
Working days required: Seven to 60. However, applicants are advised to apply at least 30 days before the date of their intended departure.
Temporary residence: Enquire at Embassy.

Money

Currency: Swedish Krona (SEK) = 100 öre. Notes are in denominations of SEK10,000, 1000, 500, 100, 50 and 20. Coins are in denominations of SEK10, 5 and 1, and 50 öre.
Currency exchange: Currency can be converted at FOREX foreign exchange agencies; these are found in major cities, airports and ferry terminals, etc. ATMs are widely available.
Credit & debit cards: American Express, Diners Club, MasterCard and Visa are all widely accepted, as well as Eurocheque cards. Check with your credit or debit card company for details of merchant acceptability and other facilities which may be available.
Travellers cheques: Widely accepted. To avoid additional exchange rate charges, travellers are advised to take travellers cheques in Euros, Pounds Sterling or US Dollars.
Currency restrictions: There are no restrictions on the import or export of local or foreign currency.
Exchange rate indicators: The following figures are included as a guide to the movements of the Swedish Krona against Sterling and the US Dollar:

Date	Feb '04	May '04	Aug '04	Nov '04
£1.00=	13.49	13.63	13.76	12.73
$1.00=	7.41	7.63	7.47	6.72

Banking hours: Mon-Wed and Fri 0930-1500, Thurs 0930-1500/1730. Some banks in larger cities have longer opening hours and are open at weekends.

Duty Free

The following items may be imported into Sweden without incurring customs duty:
*200 cigarettes or 100 cigarillos or 50 cigars or 250g of tobacco**; *1l spirits over 22 per cent or 2l fortified or sparkling wine, 2l wine and 32l beer**; *a reasonable quantity of perfume; gifts up to a value of SKr1700.*
Note: * Travellers must be over 18 years of age to import any cigarettes or tobacco products; and over 20 years of age to import any alcoholic beverages. These regulations are strictly enforced.
Prohibited items: Narcotics, firearms, ammunition, weapons, most meat and dairy products, eggs, plants, endangered species, fireworks and alcoholic beverages of over 60 per cent alcohol (120° proof).
Abolition of duty free goods within the EU: On 30 June 1999, the sale of duty free alcohol and tobacco at airports and at sea was abolished in all of the original 15 EU member states. Of the 10 new member states that joined the EU on May 1 2004, these rules already apply to Cyprus and Malta. There are transitional rules in place for visitors returning to one of the original 15 EU countries from one of the other new EU countries. But for the original 15, plus Cyprus and Malta, there are now no limits imposed on importing tobacco and alcohol products from one EU country to another (with the exceptions of Denmark, Finland and Sweden, where limits *are* imposed). Travellers should note that they may be required to prove at customs that the goods purchased are for personal use *only*.

Public Holidays

2005: Jan 1 New Year's Day. **Jan 5** Eve of Epiphany.* **Jan 6** Epiphany. **Mar 24** Maundy Thursday. **Mar 25** Good Friday. **Mar 28** Easter Monday. **Apr 30** Valborg's Eve.* **May 1** Labour Day. **May 5** Ascension. **May 16** Whit Monday. **Jun 24** Midsummer's Eve.* **Jun 25** Midsummer Holiday. **Nov 4** All Saint's Eve.* **Nov 5** All Saints' Day. **Dec 24** Christmas Eve.* **Dec 25** Christmas Day. **Dec 26** Boxing Day.
2006: Jan 1 New Year's Day. **Jan 5** Eve of Epiphany.* **Jan 6** Epiphany. **Apr 13** Maundy Thursday. **Apr 14** Good Friday. **Apr 17** Easter Monday. **Apr 30** Valborg's Eve.* **May 1** Labour Day. **May 25** Ascension. **Jun 5** Whit Monday. **Jun 23** Midsummer's Eve.* **Jun 24** Midsummer Holiday. **Nov 3** All Saint's Eve.* **Nov 4** All Saints' Day. **Dec 24** Christmas Eve.* **Dec 25** Christmas Day. **Dec 26** Boxing Day.
Note: * Shops and offices will often close half a day early on the day before an official holiday.

Health

	Special Precautions?	Certificate Required?
Yellow Fever	No	No
Cholera	No	No
Typhoid & Polio	No	N/A
Malaria	No	N/A

Note: *Regulations and requirements may be subject to change at short notice, and you are advised to contact your doctor well in advance of your intended date of departure. Any numbers in the chart refer to the footnotes below.*

Other risks: *Lyme disease* is relatively common in the south of the country, especially during the summer months. *Diphyllobothriasis* occurs rarely along the Baltic coast.
Health care: Health care standards are good. Hospital services are provided at county and regional levels; the latter have a greater range of specialist fields. There are full reciprocal health agreements with other EU countries including the UK. UK nationals should take an E111 form (obtainable from post offices) with them to Sweden in order to take advantage of the agreement. They are then entitled to the same medical services as Swedish citizens. This includes free hospital inpatient treatment (including medicines); children are also allowed free dental treatment. Outpatient treatment at hospitals, all treatment at clinics and general surgeries, most prescribed medicines and ambulance travel must be paid for. To obtain treatment, visit the nearest hospital clinic (*Akutmottagning* or *Vårdcentral*) taking your passport and E111 form with you. Travelling expenses to and from hospital may be partially refunded. If you are taking prescribed medicines, make sure you have an adequate supply before leaving for Sweden. Dental surgeries or clinics are indicated by *Tandläkare* or *Folktandvården* signs and emergency service is available in major cities out of hours. Health insurance is recommended to cover emergency evacuation.

Travel - International

AIR: The national airline is *SAS Scandinavian Airlines System (SK)* (website: www.sas.se). Other airlines serving Sweden include *Air Canada, Air France, Aeroflot, British Airways, Finnair, Lufthansa* and *Ryanair*.
Approximate flight times: From Stockholm to *London* is approximately two hours 30 minutes. From Gothenburg to *London* is one hour 45 minutes. From Stockholm to *Los Angeles* is 14 hours 10 minutes; to *New York* is seven hours 45 minutes.
International airports: *Stockholm (STO)* (Arlanda) (website: www.arlanda.lfv.se) is 42km (26 miles) north of the city. There are frequent bus services operating between the airport and the city from 0625-2305 (travel time - 40 minutes). *Arlanda Express* trains leave for the city every 15 minutes between 0600-2359 (travel time - 20 minutes). Taxi services are also available. Airport facilities include outgoing duty free shop, car hire (*Avis, Budget, Europcar, Hertz*), banks/bureaux de change, cash dispenser, restaurant/bar, coffee shop and tourist information. There is a good selection of hotels within 10km of the airport.
Gothenburg (GOT) (Landvetter) (website: www.landvetter.lfv.se) is 24km (15 miles) east of the city (travel time - 25 minutes). Coach services are frequent between the airport and the Central Station. Buses and taxis are available to the city. Airport facilities include full outgoing duty free shop, car hire (*Avis, Budget, Europcar, Hertz*), bank/bureau de change, restaurant/bar and coffee shop.
Malmö Sturup (MMX) (website: www.sturup.com) is 31km (20 miles) east of the city (travel time - 35 minutes). Bus and taxi services go to the city. Airport facilities include a bureau de change and a duty free shop.
Malmö City Hovercraft (HMA), 200m (650ft) from the Central Station, is now the city's main terminal for international air passengers using the hovercraft service operated by SAS, which connects with flights at *Copenhagen Airport*. The terminal has its own duty free facilities. Taxi services are available.
For more information on airports, contact LFV (website: www.lfv.se).
SEA: *DFDS Seaways ferries* (website: www.dfdsseaways.co.uk) sail all year round from Newcastle to Gothenburg (travel time - 24 hours). There are also ferry connections from Swedish ports to other destinations including Copenhagen, Gdansk, Helsingør, Kiel, Klaipeda, Oslo, Riga, St Petersburg and Tallinn.
RAIL: One UK-Sweden route is from London (Victoria and Liverpool Street) to Hook of Holland or Ostend, and onwards via Copenhagen (travel time - 22 to 25 hours). There are connections by ferry from Denmark and through rail routes from Norway (Oslo, Narvik and Trondheim). However, the quickest route is to take the *Eurostar* train to Brussels, and then to catch a connection to Hamburg and on to Stockholm.
ROAD: From the UK visitors can either drive to Sweden through Europe via Denmark or Germany, or catch a car ferry from Harwich (all year) to Gothenburg on the southwest coast (sailing time - 24 hours).
The Øresund Fixed Link, spanning 15.3km of waterway, joins the cities of Malmö (Sweden) and Copenhagen (Denmark). The link comprises a suspension bridge (7.8km/4.9 miles) and an underwater tunnel (3.5km/2.2 miles), joined in the middle by an artificial island. It was designed to provide better connections between the Scandinavian peninsula and the European continent. **Coach:** There are services from London (Victoria), Dover and Folkstone to a number of Swedish cities throughout the year, taking approximately 30 hours (restricted service in winter). *Eurolines*, departing from Victoria Coach Station in London, serves destinations in Sweden. For further information, contact *Eurolines* (tel: (08705) 143 219; e-mail: welcome@eurolines.co.uk; website: www.eurolines.co.uk). Contact the Swedish Travel & Tourism Council for a list of other operators.

Travel - Internal

AIR: *SAS* serves over 30 local airports. Travel by air is relatively cheap and efficient and there are a number of reduced fares offered by *SAS*; contact the airline for further details.
SEA/LAKE: Unlike Norway and Finland, there are few domestic ferry services in Sweden. The various archipelagos on the southeast coast are served by small ferries, the most comprehensive network being within the Stockholm archipelago, for which you can buy an island-hopping boat pass. The other major link is between the Baltic island of Gotland and the mainland at Nynäshamn and Oskarshamn, which are very popular routes in summer; booking ahead is strongly recommended. There are frequent coastal sailings to all ports and on the hundreds of lakes throughout the country, especially in the north. For details, contact local authorities.
Canal: A canal (served by vintage steamer; website: www.gotakanal.se) connects Gothenburg and Stockholm.
RAIL: The excellent and extensive rail system is run by *Swedish State Railways* (SJ), SE-105 50 Stockholm (tel: 04982 03380; fax: 04982 03391; e-mail: info@swedenbooking.com; website: www.sj.se). The network is more concentrated in the populated south where hourly services run between the main cities, but routes extend to the forested and sparsely populated lake area of the north, which is a scenic and popular holiday destination. Restaurant cars and sleepers are provided on many trains. Reservations are essential for most express services. Motorail car-sleeper services are operated during the summer on the long-distance routes from Malmö, Gothenburg and Västerås to Kiruna and Luleå.
Discount tickets: There are reductions for families and regular passengers, as well as a link-up with other Scandinavian countries via the *Scanrail Pass*, which provides unlimited travel in Denmark, Finland, Norway and Sweden for 21 consecutive days. It also gives free travel on the ferries between Helsingør and Helsingborg. Children aged between four and 11 travel at half the fare or reduced fare. Young people aged 12 to 25 obtain a discount of 25 per cent, and for passengers aged over 60 fares are

discounted by 10 per cent. All passengers may be eligible for discounted tickets, under a scheme known as *raslyst*. This card is valid for two people for one calendar year and entitles travellers to up to 70 per cent off when the booking is made at least seven days in advance. Only a limited number of these tickets are available, so it is advisable to book as far in advance as possible. See online for more details (website: www.scanrail.com).

ROAD: Traffic drives on the right. Sweden's roads are well-maintained and relatively uncrowded, but watch out for animals crossing the road in remote areas. Credit and debit cards are becoming more acceptable as a means of payment at petrol stations. Most petrol stations have 24-hour automatic petrol pumps; they accept SKr100 and 20 notes. **Bus:** Express coach services and local buses are run by *Connex* (website: www.connex.com) and *Swebus* (website: www.swebus.se). Cheap and efficient links are available to all towns. Many coach operators do special offers on tickets on weekends (Friday to Sunday). Information is available in Sweden from local tourist offices. The *Gothenburg, Malmö* and *Stockholm Cards* offer free public transport in those areas, as well as free admission to selected museums and tourist attractions. Cards can be purchased from tourist information centres, camping sites or youth hostels. **Taxi:** Available in all towns and at airports. Intercity taxis are also available. **Car hire:** Available in most towns and cities. All international agencies are represented. **Regulations:** Speed limits outside built-up areas are 110, 90 or 70kph (68, 56 or 43mph) depending on road width and traffic density. In built-up areas the limit is 50kph (31mph) or 30kph (19mph) in school areas. Severe fines and sometimes prison sentences are imposed on drivers over the alcohol limit (0.02 per cent). There are on-the-spot fines for traffic offences. The use of dipped headlights is compulsory in the daytime for cars and motorcycles. Crash helmets are compulsory for motorcyclists. Children under seven may not travel in a car if it is not equipped with a special child restraint or a normal seat belt adapted for the child's use. Emergency warning triangles are obligatory. Studded tyres are only permitted from November 1 to the first Monday after the Easter holiday. **Documentation:** National driving licence is sufficient, but it must include a photo or it will not be recognised. The minimum age for car drivers is 18; for motorcyclists it is 17. The car's log book and written permission must be carried if driving someone else's car. A Green Card is not required by Swedish authorities, but it tops up the cover provided by a domestic policy. It is advisable to check the validity of insurance policies prior to departure.

URBAN: Public transport is efficient, comprehensive and well-integrated. Stockholm has bus, trams, metro (*T-banan*) and local rail services. Pre-purchase multi-tickets and passes are sold, though single tickets can also be obtained on the bus. There are trams in Gothenburg and Norrköping. Taxis are widely available; large taxi companies are cheaper than independents. Several of the main cities, particularly Stockholm, have boat excursions and services; see *Resorts & Excursions* section for further information.

Travel Times: The following chart gives approximate travel times (in hours and minutes) from **Stockholm** to other major cities/towns in Sweden.

	Air	Road	Rail
Gothenburg	**0.50**	**6.00**	**4.30**
Malmö	**1.05**	**8.00**	**6.45**
Östersund	**0.55**	**8.00**	**6.30**
Karlstad	**0.40**	**5.00**	**3.30**
Luleå	**1.15**	**20.00**	**15.00**
Mora	**1.00**	**6.00**	**4.30**

Accommodation

HOTELS AND MOTELS: Hotels are usually of a high standard. Most have a restaurant and/or cafe and a TV lounge, and many include a buffet breakfast in the price. Good first- and medium-class hotels are found in every Swedish town. They are mostly private but are, in many cases, operated by hotel groups and offer special reduced rates for the summer and weekends. Special packages are available throughout the year in Gothenburg, Malmö and Stockholm.

Scattered all over Sweden are country hotels, characterised by good food and attractive settings. Some are renovated and modernised manor houses or centuries-old farmhouses which have frequently been in the same family for generations. They are mostly independently owned and are often located in picturesque surroundings. Others are traditional old inns. During the summer many hotels offer facilities for swimming, fishing, boating, golf and flower-spotting or bird-watching excursions.

There are also a number of mountain hotels which are ideal for those who want a peaceful holiday. They provide a good base for expeditions in the mountains and guided walks are often arranged, as well as other activities such as keep-fit classes, fishing and canoeing. Many are also popular skiing hotels in the winter. A comprehensive list of hotels can be found online (website: www.hotelsinsweden.net).

Grading: There is no formal grading structure, but most first-class hotels display the *SHR* sign indicating that they belong to the *Swedish Hotel & Restaurant Association (SHR)*, Sveriges Hotell & Restaurang Företagare, PO Box 1158, Kammarkargatan 39, 111 81 Stockholm (tel: (8) 762 7400; fax: (8) 215 861; e-mail: info@shr.se; website: www.shr.se).

Hotel discount schemes: Many Swedish hotels offer discounted rates throughout the summer and at weekends during the winter and some of the leading chains have special deals which can be booked in advance, including the *SARA Hotels Scandinavian Bonus Pass*, the *Scandic Hotel Cheque Scheme* and the *Sweden Hotel Pass*. Details of these offers and other (including family) discount schemes are contained in the annual guide *Hotels in Sweden*, obtainable from the Swedish Travel & Tourism Council.

Motels: Sweden has a large number of motels, most of which are new, usually situated on the outskirts of towns or in the countryside. Parking is free. They may have swimming pools, a gymnasium and saunas, restaurants and self-service cafes.

FARMHOUSE ACCOMMODATION: About 100 working farms throughout Sweden offer accommodation, either in the main farmhouse or in an adjoining cottage. Accommodation is normally on a bed & breakfast basis, with self-catering facilities. Some farms offer full board. Accommodation can be booked through local tourist offices. For more information and bookings, see online (website: www.bopalantgard.org).

SELF-CATERING: Forest cabins and chalets are available throughout the country, generally set in beautiful surroundings, near lakes, in quiet forest glades or on an island in some remote archipelago. Purpose-built chalets generally consist of a living room, two or three bedrooms, a well-equipped kitchen and a toilet. They can generally accommodate up to six people, and cooking utensils, cutlery, blankets and pillows are provided. Visitors only need to supply sheets and towels. Log cabins offer a slightly simpler type of accommodation. Renovated cottages and farm buildings are also available, usually in remote spots.

CHALET VILLAGES: Sweden's many chalet villages offer

the advantage of amenities such as a grocery, general shops, leisure facilities, restaurants, swimming pools, saunas, launderette, playgrounds, mini-golf, tennis, badminton or volleyball. Some have programmes of special activities such as music, dancing, barbecues, riding, fishing and walking trails. It is often possible to rent boats or bicycles. Information on rental of holiday cottages or flats can be obtained from specialist agencies, local tourist offices in Sweden or the Swedish Travel & Tourism Council.
CAMPING/CARAVANNING: Family camping holidays are extremely popular in Sweden and there is a tremendous variety of attractive sites. Most are located in picturesque surroundings, often on a lakeside or by the sea with free bathing facilities close at hand. There are about 750 campsites, all officially approved and classified by the Swedish Travel & Tourism Council. Many offer facilities such as boat or bicycle rental, mini-golf, tennis, riding or saunas. Many campsites have facilities for the disabled. Most authorised sites are open with full service Jun 1-Aug 15. Many sites are also open in April or May but the full range of ancillary facilities, such as the post office, may not be. About 200 sites remain open in the winter, particularly in the winter sports areas in central and northern Sweden. All sites open during the winter have electric sockets for caravans.
The price for one night for the whole family plus tent or caravan and use of services is one of the lowest rates in Europe, although at some sites there are small charges for the use of services like showers or launderette.
A *Camping Card Scandinavia* is recommended. It can be bought beforehand and works as a credit card for site fees, allows a quicker check-in time, discounted petrol and provides accident insurance whilst on site. Contact Camping in Sweden for more details (website: www.camping.se).
Camping Cheques, valid at more than 350 sites, can be purchased before the holiday but only as part of a package including a return car-ferry journey. Each cheque is valid for one night's fees for a family with car plus tent or caravan, but does not include additional services. Detailed information about camping in Sweden is contained in a pamphlet which is available free of charge from the Swedish Travel & Tourism Council; an abbreviated list of campsites is also available. Motor homes and caravans can be rented. **Grading:** Standards of facilities and cleanliness at Swedish campsites are probably the highest in Europe. Approved sites are inspected annually by the Swedish Travel & Tourism Council and are awarded a **3-**, **2-** or **1-star** rating according to the facilities provided, as follows: **3-star:** Supervision 24 hours a day, postal service, car wash, cafe, cooking facilities, play and recreational activities and assembly room; **2-star:** Supervision throughout the day, illuminated and fenced-in area, drains for caravans, shaving points, kiosk, grocery shop, telephone and electric sockets for caravans; **1-star:** Daily inspection, a barrier at the entrance, dustbin, drinking water, toilets, washing facilities and hot water for dishwashing, laundering and showers.
Fuel: *Camping Gaz* is not normally available in Sweden and visitors are recommended to take their own supplies. Only propane gas (eg Primus) is obtainable. This is widely available at more than 2000 Primus dealers along with the necessary equipment at reasonable prices. It is important to ensure that equipment designed to burn butane is not refilled with propane; this is both illegal and highly dangerous. It is possible to camp rough in areas away from other dwellings.
Camping Cabins: A useful alternative to tent or caravan camping is to rent one of 4400 camping cabins which are available at 350 sites. These contain bunk beds and kitchen equipment but not sheets.
YOUTH HOSTELS: The 280 hostels range from mansions to a renovated sailing ship, the *Af Chapman*, in the centre of Stockholm, as well as many purpose-built hostels. There are no restrictions on who may use Sweden's hostels. Hostels have two to four beds per room, or family rooms and self-catering facilities. The hostels are run by the *Swedish Tourist Federation (STF)* but members of the UK *Youth Hostels Association* or *Scottish Youth Hostels Association* qualify for a cheaper rate, on production of a membership card. All youth hostels are open during the summer and some for the whole year. They are closed during the day but are open to check in new guests 0800-0930 and 1700-2200. During the summer it is advisable to book in advance. A list of Swedish youth hostels can be ordered from STF (see *Contact Addresses* section for details). The hostels are also listed in the International *Youth Hostel Handbook*, available through the YHA in the UK; see also online (website: www.svenskaturistforeningen.se).
Swedish Tourist Federation: *STF* runs Sweden's youth hostels and several mountain stations in the north of the country and looks after the many mountain huts along the long-distance hiking trails. *STF* also publishes a list of guest harbours and issues guidance to hikers and canoeing enthusiasts.

Resorts & Excursions

STOCKHOLM

Built on a string of islands, Stockholm was founded 700 years ago by King Birger Jarl at the strategic point where the fresh water of **Lake Mälaren** meets the salt water of the **Baltic**. A good starting point for an exploration of the city is the 'Old Town' (**Gamla Stan**), a cluster of old buildings and narrow cobbled streets which formed the original Stockholm. The old buildings are beautifully preserved and the main streets, **Österlånggatan** and **Västerlånggatan**, are pedestrian precincts with a host of boutiques, handicrafts and antique shops. The Old Town has three churches of historic interest, **Storkyrkan** and **Riddarholm Church**, both dating from the 13th century, and the **German Church** with its magnificent Baroque interior. Overlooking the harbour is the **Royal Palace**, which contains the State Apartments, the Crown Jewels, the Hall of State and Chapel Royal, Royal Armoury and **Palace Museum**. Within easy reach of the Old Town, in a magnificent setting on the edge of Lake Mälaren, is Stockholm's elegant **City Hall** (**Stadshuset**), inaugurated about 60 years ago. There is a spectacular view of the capital from the top of the 100m (350ft) tower. Another spot for a magnificent view is the observation platform on the **Kaknäs** communications tower which, at 155m (508ft), is the highest building in Scandinavia.
The island of **Djurgården**, can be reached either by bus from the city centre or by ferry across the busy harbour. The best-known attraction here is the purpose-built **Vasa Museum**, housing the restored 360-year-old wooden warship which was recovered from the depths of Stockholm's harbour in 1961. Also in Djurgården is **Skansen**, an open-air folk museum which celebrated its centenary in 1991. It has about 150 traditional buildings from different regions of Sweden, as well as an open-air zoo and an aquarium. Across the road is **Gröna Lund**, a lively amusement park.
The city boasts over 50 museums. No fewer than eight can be visited in the Djurgården area, including the **Nordic Museum** (**Nordiska Museet**), **Waldemarsudde House**, which was the home of the artist Prince Eugen until 1947, and **Liljevalchs Konsthall**. The **Historical Museum** (**Historiska Museet**) has some priceless treasures and implements from prehistoric Sweden, as well as examples of medieval art. The **National Museum** is Sweden's central museum for the national collections of painting, sculpture, applied arts, printing and drawings.
Every visitor to Stockholm should invest in a special discount card, the 'Stockholm Card' (*Stockholmskortet*) which cuts sightseeing and entertainment costs. Cards of longer validity are available at an extra charge, in Stockholm from the Stockholm Visitor's Board (tel: (8) 508 28500; fax: (8) 508 28510; e-mail: mailto:info@svb.stockholm.se; website: www.stockholmtown.com).
EXCURSIONS: There is a whole armada of boat excursions on offer. 'Under the Bridges of Stockholm' takes a circular tour through part of the harbour as well as Lake Mälaren. A longer trip can be taken out into the archipelago to resorts like **Saltsjöbaden**, **Sandhamn** or **Vaxholm**. Visitors can also take a boat from the City Hall to **Drottningholm Palace**. The **Royal Theatre** has been preserved in its original 18th-century form and plays are still performed there in period costume. There is also a museum depicting the development of the theatre since the Renaissance period.

GOTHENBURG

The history of Sweden's second city **Gothenburg** (*Göteborg*) is closely tied to the sea. The basic pattern of the city owes much to the Dutch architects who designed it; the spacious streets are laid out at right angles and there is a network of canals. The **Nordstaden Kronhuset** area houses the oldest building of the city, built in 1643 and now the **City Museum**. Nearby is **Kronhusbodarna**, an arts and craft workshop centre dating from the 18th century. The **Botanical Gardens** (**Botaniska Trädgården**) contain a rock garden regarded as one of the most impressive in the world, with about 3000 species of Alpine plants. In the city centre is the beautiful **Garden of Trädgårdsföreningen** with its restored **Palm House**, built in the style of London's destroyed Crystal Palace. The **Liseberg Amusement Park** is an ideal spot for children. There are also many museums, such as the **Maritime Museum** (**Sjöfartsmuseet**) which illustrates Sweden's maritime history and the development of its shipbuilding industry.
The *Gothenburg Discount Card* offering free admission to many tourist attractions can be purchased from the Gothenburg tourist office (tel: (31) 612 500; fax: (31) 612 501; website: www.goteborg.com/en).
Excursions: One of the best ways of sightseeing in Gothenburg is on one of the famous **Paddan** boats. Departure is from the terminal at Kungsportsplatsen for an hour-long tour under 20 bridges and out into the busy harbour. Another popular boat trip is to the 17th-century **Nya Elfsborg Fortress** built on an island at the harbour mouth. There are also sightseeing tours of varying duration by bus with an English-speaking guide. A cheap way of travelling around the city is to buy a 24-hour ticket on the tram network. Gothenburg and Stockholm are both starting points for the classic four-day trip through Sweden's great lakes and the historic **Göta Canal**.

THE GOLDEN COAST

This area is situated in the southwest of Sweden and has vast stretches of beaches, warm sea and holiday resorts reaching for 400km (250 miles) from **Laholm** in the south to **Strömstad** in the north. Here there are flat, sandy beaches, bare rocks and fjord-like inlets with meadows stretching down to the seashore and tiny fishing villages.
HALLAND: This is a long, narrow province strung out along the picturesque west coast. Unlike its northern neighbour, Bohuslän (see below), its landscape is gentle, with mile after mile of long sandy beaches, often fringed with pinewoods. Inland, the scenery changes as it meets the tableland of Småland and the landscape is characterised by a series of ridges and valleys. There are also vast forests and heather-covered moors.
Areas of note are **Kungsbacka**, a northern market town and the nearby Onsala peninsula, ideal for bathing, sailing and fishing, and **Fjärås Bräcka**, an unusual gravel ridge formed during the Ice Age. Further south is **Varberg**, one of Halland's main coastal resorts, dominated by the 13th-century **Varberg Fortress**. Other resorts are the port of **Falkenberg** and **Tylösand**, with its long sandy beach sheltered by dunes and pine trees. Halland's capital is the important seaport and industrial town of **Halmstad**. Warmed by the waters of the Gulf Stream, the west coast is a natural choice for seaside holidays.
BOHUSLÄN: The long narrow province of Bohuslän has countless spots where visitors can enjoy an idyllic holiday in the sun. The coastline is deeply indented and there are hundreds of rocky islands. All along the coast are picturesque villages with their typical red-painted huts where the nets are hung out to dry. The province is also one of the most important centres of ancient Swedish civilisation and there are many archaeological relics dating back to the Bronze Age and Viking times.
Excursions: Other towns worth visiting include **Bovallstrand**, **Hunnebostrand**, **Kungshamn**, **Lysekil**, **Smögen** and the islands of **Orust** and **Tjörn**.

SKÅNE

At the southernmost tip of Sweden is the province of Skåne, an area of fertile fields and meadows which was ruled by the Danes until 1658. To this day the Skånians have maintained their own distinctive dialect. As a reminder of the days of Danish rule there are more than 200 castles and manors scattered over the province, often forming part of a farm. This region is famous for its food (in particular the *smörgåsbord*), and the landscape is characterised by rolling fields and pastures and forests but only a few lakes. The best spots for swimming and fishing are along the east, south and west coasts. Inland there are countless small lanes ideal for cycling tours. For golfers, Skåne has some of the finest and most beautifully located courses in Sweden. Other main regional attractions include the medieval town of **Lund** which has a 12th-century cathedral and 14th-century astronomical clock, **Båstad**, **Falsterbo**, **Helsingborg**, **Mölle** and **Ystad**. There is also the **Oresund bridge**, the world's longest single bridge carrying both road and railway traffic, which links Denmark and Sweden.
MALMÖ: Founded in the 13th century, Malmö is Sweden's third-largest city and offers a wealth of parks, gardens, restaurants and a beautiful beach. City sights include the main town squares, **Mamöhus Castle** and **St Petri Church**. **Konsthallen** and **Rooseum museums** are famous for their art collections. Especially recommended is the 'Malmö Card' which can be purchased at the Malmö Tourist Board (tel: (40) 341 200; fax: (40) 341 209; e-mail: malmo.turism@malmo.se; website: www.malmo.se) and entitles visitors to free travel on local buses, free admission to museums and discounts on a wide variety of purchases.

SMÅLAND & BLEKINGE

In the middle of the 18th century, German immigrants established the province of Småland, north of Skåne, as the home of the Swedish glass-making industry. The 'kingdom of crystal' forms only a small part of **Småland**, a very large province that is also a good holiday country with vast forests, pleasant lakes and winding lanes, along which red cottages are dotted. In the province of **Blekinge** there are large oak forests and softer landscapes. This region has many coastal towns that stretch along the Baltic. The **Mörrumsån River** is noted for salmon and sea trout and **Lake Vättern** for char fishing. Boat trips are available to the island of **Visingsö** on Lake Vättern. **High Chaparral** is a reconstructed wild west town.
Three-quarters of the Swedish glassworks are found in the counties of **Kalmar** and **Kronoberg**. They are located off the beaten track surrounded by vast tracts of forest and attract many visitors each year. Each of the 16 glassworks

A B C D E F G H I J K L M N O P Q R S T U V W X Y Z

are open to visitors Mon-Fri 0800-1500, where the craftspeople can be observed and top-quality products can be purchased. Visitors may also be invited to a *hyttsill* – a traditional evening of entertainment including food of fried herrings, sausages and potatoes baked around the glass furnace, served with beer and schnapps. Most of the works have their own shops.

GOTLAND AND ÖLAND

These are Sweden's largest islands, situated off the southeast coast in the Baltic Sea. There is more sunshine here than elsewhere, making it a favourite summer holiday spot with the Swedes and, as a result, the beaches are rather crowded. The islands are of particular interest to ornithologists and botanists and there is a wealth of historic sites – there are Stone, Bronze and Iron Age sites on both islands. Several ferries serve both islands and daily coach trips are available to Öland over one of Europe's longest bridges, starting just outside Kalmar on the mainland. Cycles can be hired on the islands.

Gotland: On Gotland are the **Lummelunda Caves** with their spectacular stalactites and stalagmites and a preserved medieval town at **Kattlundsgård**. **Visby** is the main town.

Öland: On Öland are the royal summer residence at **Solliden**; **Borgholm Castle**; a restored medieval church at **Gärdslösa**; a recently excavated fortified village at **Eketorp**; and many Viking stones and local windmills. **Borgholm** is the main town.

SWEDISH LAKELAND

This region comprises the nine provinces of **Dalsland**, **Värmland** and **Västergötland** in the west, **Dalarna**, **Närke** and **Västmanland** in the north, and **Östergötland**, **Södermanland** and **Uppland** to the east. These form a large part of Sweden with a mixture of open water, vast lakes, plains and meadows and large areas of wild natural scenery. The provinces in the west are dominated by **Vänern**, Sweden's largest lake, while in the north and east are the lakes of **Vättern**, **Mälaren**, **Hjälmaren** and **Siljan** as well as the Baltic Sea. The whole region is considered the cradle of Swedish culture, and it is here that the majority of Swedes live. For visitors there is a wide variety of hotels, campsites and country inns.

Excursions: Västergötland has the castle of **Läckö**, the Trollhättan hydro-electric waterfalls, canoe trips and fishing. **Närke** contains the **Stjerhov Manor**, and a 17th-century inn can be visited at **Grythyttan** in Västmanland. In **Dalarna**, visitors can meet Father Christmas at the **Santaworld** theme park. On the island of **Sollerön** there are Viking graves and in **Kolmården** there is a zoo and safari park. **Gripsholm Castle** is in **Södermanland**. The university city of **Uppsala** boasts Scandinavia's largest **Cathedral** and the Baroque **Castle of Skokloster**, with a vintage car museum.

THE MIDNIGHT SUN COAST

The Midnight Sun Coast is a 1500km (900 mile) stretch of Baltic coastline which runs all the way to the Finnish border. In the south are the spruce forests of the province of **Gästrikland**; immediately to the north of this region is **Hälsingland** with its spectacular views, extensive lakes and typical wood-built mansions. Forestry has traditionally been the dominant industry of **Medelpad**, today one of Sweden's most industrialised areas, although there are plenty of opportunities for visitors who want to fish in unspoilt outback country or rent a cottage in the middle of a countryside rich in prehistoric monuments and relics of ancient cultures.

In the province of **Ångermanland** is some of Sweden's most breathtaking scenery, consisting of forests, lakes, islands, fjords and mountains plunging dramatically to the sea. This magnificent district is called the High Coast. **Västerbotten** offers unspoilt wilderness and the **Norrland Riviera** coastline is ideal for a relaxed holiday. There are also countless clear lakes and rivers teeming with fish, and excellent roads lead inland to the southern part of Lapland. Further north along the coast at **Lövånger** there are hundreds of renovated timber cottages which are rented out to holidaymakers. Nearer the Arctic Circle the air and water temperatures in the summer are much the same as in the Mediterranean and this area has an excellent sunshine record. **Norrbotten** is a fisherman's paradise with plenty of mountain streams and sea fishing.

LAPLAND

The enormous expanse of **Lapland**, one of Europe's last wildernesses, covers a quarter of the area of Sweden but has only 5 per cent of the population. It is both inviting and inhospitable: fell-walkers who leave the marked routes do so at their own risk. The best-known route is **Kungsleden**, which also gives experienced mountaineers the chance to climb Sweden's highest peak, **Kebnekaise**. Other favourite areas for walking are the national parks of **Sarek** and **Padjelanta**. In the west the mountains soar up towards the Norwegian border and the region experiences rapid changes in the weather.

Jämtland, bordering southern Lapland, has plenty of good hiking and fast-flowing rivers for fishermen. It is known for its skiing. Wildlife is abundant in **Härjedalen**, with reindeer, buzzard, beaver, lynx and Sweden's only herd of musk ox.

Excursions: The small northern village of **Jukkasjärvi** has received international reknown for its sculpted **Ice Hotel**, constructed from tonnes of snow and ice from the **Torne River**. It is rebuilt every winter after the summer thaw but attracts a number of tourists eager to experience the 'ice beds' and drinks from the Absolut Icebar. For further information, check online (website: www.icehotel.com). Lapps celebrate their annual church festivals in **Gällivare**. In **Jokkmokk** there are collections of Lapp art and culture, and a **Lapp Staden**, an old village of 70 cone-shaped Lapp huts. **Arjeplog** has an interesting Lapp museum. Iron Age burial grounds and a medieval church are on the island of **Frösö**. The cable-car trip from **Åre** leads up to the summit of **Åreskutan**. Ski resorts include Åre and **Storlien**.

Sport & Activities

Watersports: Sweden has hundreds of miles of beaches, particularly on the west coast, and 96,000 lakes. There are numerous **water-skiing** and **windsurfing** centres on the coast and more accessible lakes. **Skindiving** is mostly confined to the rocky coasts and islets on the west coast both north and south of Gothenburg. Courses are held from June to August. The great number and variety of rapids makes **white-water rafting** a popular sport.

Sailing: There are about 50 centres where canoes are for hire; many campsites also offer a hire service. Sailing boats and motor-cruisers can be hired in more than 25 places in Sweden or visitors can bring their own. Many of Sweden's canals run through beautiful countryside and are well maintained to provide an ideal boating holiday. Short sightseeing trips are available on several canals but the classic journey is by steamer along the Göta Canal. All meals and accommodation are included in the price. Many cruises, some in vintage steamers, are operated from Stockholm out into the archipelago with its 30,000 islands.

Fishing: Sweden has more than 96,000 lakes and visitors can enjoy fishing in most of them. There are also thousands of miles of rivers, streams and brooks and a coastline of 6760km (4200 miles). The salmon season at Mörrum near Karlshamn opens at the beginning of spring. Sea-trout can be caught throughout the year, except in high summer, which is the best time for char and grayling (typical fish from the northern part of the country). Fishing is generally free all along the coastline and in the larger lakes, including Mälaren, Vänern and Vättern, but a special permit is required to fish in other lakes and rivers. Information is available from local tourist offices. **Ice-fishing** is an exciting alternative to try. **Sea-fishing** tours of varying lengths are arranged on the west coast and in the south. Guest harbours are available all round the coast and on lakes Mälaren, Vänern and Vättern. The Swedish Tourist Federation (STF) publishes a list of 330 with some information in English.

Golf: There are excellent golf courses and facilities provided for members and visitors. Sweden has over 400 courses. One situated north of the Arctic Circle enjoys 24-hour daylight during the summer months and many midsummer championships take place at midnight. Clubs and golf carts can usually be rented. For more information, contact the Swedish Golf Federation (website: www.sgf.golf.se).

Wintersports: There are excellent facilities for **skating**, **tobogganing**, **snow-mobiling**, **ice-climbing** and **dog-sledging**. Most skiing takes place in the north, particularly in Dalarna, Härjedalen and Jämtland.

Other: Routes for **hiking** are on well laid-out paths in almost every part of the country. **Cycling** is a popular holiday recreation, particularly in the south. The Swedish Cycling Promotion Institute, in cooperation with regional tourist offices, has scheduled cycling tours in almost every region.

Social Profile

FOOD & DRINK: Swedes like straightforward meals, simply prepared from the freshest ingredients. As a seafaring country with many freshwater lakes, fish dishes are prominent on hotel or restaurant menus. The Scandinavian cold table, called *smörgåsbord*, is traditional. First pickled herring with boiled potatoes, then perhaps a couple more fish courses, smoked salmon or anchovies followed by cold meat, pâté, sliced beef, stuffed veal or smoked reindeer. The hot dishes come next; for instance, another herring dish, small meatballs (*köttbullar*) or an omelette. A fruit salad and cheese with crispbreads round off the meal. Other dishes to look out for are smoked reindeer from Lapland; *gravlax*, salmon that has been specially prepared and marinated; wild strawberries; and the cloudberries that are unique to Scandinavia. Once on the open road the traveller is well catered for with picnic sites on the way, often with

Credit: © Richard Ryan & Stockholm Visitors Board

wooden tables and seats. Top-class restaurants in Sweden are usually fairly expensive, but even the smallest towns have reasonably priced self-service restaurants and grill bars. Many restaurants all over Sweden offer a special dish of the day at a reduced price which includes main course, salad, soft drink and coffee. Waiter service is common although there are many self-service snack bars.

Snapps, the collective name for *aquavit* or *brännvin*, is a Swedish liqueur which is traditionally drunk chilled with *smörgåsbord*. It is made under a variety of brand names with flavours varying from practically tasteless to sweetly spiced. Swedish beers are lager- and pilsner-type brews and come in four strengths. The minimum age for buying alcoholic beverages is 20, although alcohol can be consumed in bars from restaurants from 18 onwards. Wine, spirits and beer are sold through the state-owned monopoly, *Systembolaget*, open during normal shopping hours. Before 1300 on Sundays alcohol cannot be bought in bars, cafes or restaurants. After midnight alcohol can only be bought in nightclubs that stay open until between 0200-0500. In a restaurant or a nightclub, the minimum age for buying alcoholic beverages is 18. Stiff penalties are enforced for drinking and driving.

NIGHTLIFE: Stockholm has pubs, cafes, discos, restaurants, cinemas and theatres. In the more rural areas evenings tend to be tranquil. From August to June, the *Royal Ballet* performs in Stockholm. Music and theatre productions take place in many cities during the summer at open air venues. Outside Stockholm in the 18th-century *Court Theatre of the Palace of Drottningholm*, there are performances of 18th-century opera.

SHOPPING: VAT (*Moms*) is refundable to visitors who are resident in non-EU countries on goods bought at shops participating in the Tax-Free Shopping scheme. The refund is payable to the customer when departing from Sweden at either airports or customs offices at ports. Special purchases include glassware and crystal, ceramics, stainless steel and silver, *hemslöjd* (cottage industry artefacts) and woodcarvings. Women's and children's clothes are good buys, especially handknitted Nordic sweaters. **Shopping hours:** Mon-Fri 0900-1800, Sat 0900-1600. In larger towns, some shops have longer opening hours and are also open Sundays. In rural areas, shops and petrol stations close by 1700/1800.

SPECIAL EVENTS: For details, contact the Swedish Travel & Tourism Council (see *Contact Addresses* section). The following is a selection of special events occurring in Sweden in 2005:

Jan 27-30 *Kiruna Snow Festival*; *The Nordic Antiques Fair*, Stockholm. **Feb 3-6** *Jokkmokks Winter Market*. **Mar 4-13** *Stockholm International Boat Show*. **Mar 16** *World Cup Sprint*, skiing event, Göteborg. **Mar 24-28** *Easter Celebration at Skansen*. **Apr 7-10** *Stockholm Art Fair*, The Nordic Gardens, Stockholm. **Apr 30** *Walpurgis Eve*. **Jun 3-12** *Restaurants Festival - 'A Taste of Stockholm'*. **Jun 4** *Stockholm Marathon*. **Jun 16-18** *Hultsfreds Rock Festival*.

Credit: © Peter Rosen

Jun 24 *Midsummer Eve/Solstice Celebrations.* **Jun 27-Jul 3** *Åre Adventure Festival.* **Jul** *Music at Lake Siljan.* **Jul 8-9** *Hälsinge Hambon.* **Jul 14** *Victoriadagen.* **Jul 16-23** *Stockholm Jazz Festival.* **Jul 17-31** *Skoklosterspelen*, historical event. **Aug 3-7** *Stockholm Pride.* **Aug 5-13** *Göteborgskalaset.* **Aug 19-26** *The Malmö Festival.* **Nov 10-20** *Stockholm International Film Festival.* **Dec 13** *Lucia*, the coronation of Lucia, bearer of light, nationwide.

SOCIAL CONVENTIONS: Normal courtesies should be observed. It is customary for the guest to refrain from drinking until the host makes a toast. The guest should also thank the host for the meal with *Tack för maten.* Casual dress is acceptable for everyday occasions; smarter wear for social occasions, exclusive restaurants and clubs. Evening wear (black tie) will usually be specified when required. Smoking is prohibited on public transport and in most public buildings. **Tipping:** Hotel prices include a service charge. Service in restaurants is not usually included in the bill; around 10 per cent should be added. Late at night the service charge is higher. Taxi drivers should be tipped around 10 per cent.

Business Profile

ECONOMY: Sweden boasts one of Europe's most advanced industrial economies and one of the highest standards of social welfare in the world. It also boasts a relatively large number of world-class multinational companies (Ericsson, Volvo). A prolonged period of peace, which included a policy of neutrality during both World Wars, has contributed much to its economic development. Over half of the country is covered by forest, supplying raw material for the wood-based industries – paper, wood pulp and finished products such as furniture – which account for 20 per cent of Swedish material exports. Most of the country's agriculture is concentrated in the south and central regions and produces dairy products, meat, cereals and vegetables. The agricultural and fisheries sector is, however, fairly insignificant today, accounting for just 2 per cent of GDP. Sweden has a strong industrial sector which produces a number of major exports including vehicles, office and telecommunications equipment, iron and steel, wood products and chemicals. The country is rich in mineral resources, which include 15 per cent of the world's known uranium deposits and large deposits of iron ore, copper, lead and zinc. Lacking fossil fuel deposits, Sweden has large nuclear power and hydroelectric programmes, which meet over 80 per cent of its energy needs.
Sweden was a long-standing member of the European Free Trade Association (EFTA), which linked most Western European economies outside the European Union, before it finally joined the EU in 1995. But there is a strong Euro-sceptic current: so far the Swedes have refused to join the Euro-zone, most recently at a national referendum in September 2003 (despite the endorsement of the national government).
Domestic economic policy has been mainly concerned with making the labour market more flexible and with addressing Sweden's large government debt. The economy was in recession between 1999 and 2002, but is now slowly recovering. Current annual GDP growth is 1.7 per cent, and this is expected to increase during the next two years. Both inflation and unemployment (1.9 and 4.9 per cent respectively) are close to the EU average. Sweden's major bilateral trading partners are Germany, the UK, Norway, Denmark and the USA.

BUSINESS: Businesspeople are expected to dress smartly. English is widely spoken in business circles. Punctuality is important for business and social occasions. Business cards are commonly used. **Office hours:** Flexible working hours are a widespread practice, with lunch between 1200-1300.

COMMERCIAL INFORMATION: The following organisation can offer advice: Stockholm Chamber of Commerce, Box 16050, 10321 Stockholm (tel: (8) 5551 0000; fax: (8) 5663 1600; e-mail: info@chamber.se; website: www.chamber.se).
There are also chambers of commerce for other major towns and regions in Sweden.

CONFERENCES/CONVENTIONS: The main venues are in Stockholm, Gothenburg and Malmö; the Swedish Travel & Tourism Council also lists two in Lapland. The Globe Arena in Stockholm can seat up to 5000 persons and there are other venues in the city catering for up to 3000 persons. Elsewhere in Sweden, most venues have facilities for 200 to 500 persons (although Malmö and Gothenburg have capacity for 1500). Contact the Swedish Travel & Tourism Council for more information (see *Contact Addresses* section); *or* Stockholm Visitors Board, PO Box 16282, SE-103 25 Stockholm (tel: (8) 508 28500; fax: (8) 508 28510; e-mail: info@svb.stockholm.se; website: www.stockholmtown.com); *or* Gothenburg Convention Bureau, Mässans Gata 8, SE-412 51 Gothenburg (tel: (31) 615 200; fax: (31) 811 048; e-mail: info@goteborg.com; website: www.goteborg.com); *or* Malmö Congress Bureau, Centralstationen, SE-21120 Malmö (tel: (40) 342 204; fax: (40) 342 211; e-mail: konferens@malmo.se; website: www.malmo.se).

Climate

In spite of its northern position, Sweden has a relatively mild climate which varies greatly, owing to its length. The summers can be very hot but get shorter further north. The midnight sun can be seen between mid-May and mid-June above the Arctic Circle. Winters can be bitterly cold, especially in the north.
Required clothing: Light- to mediumweights for summer, heavyweights for winter and rainwear all year.

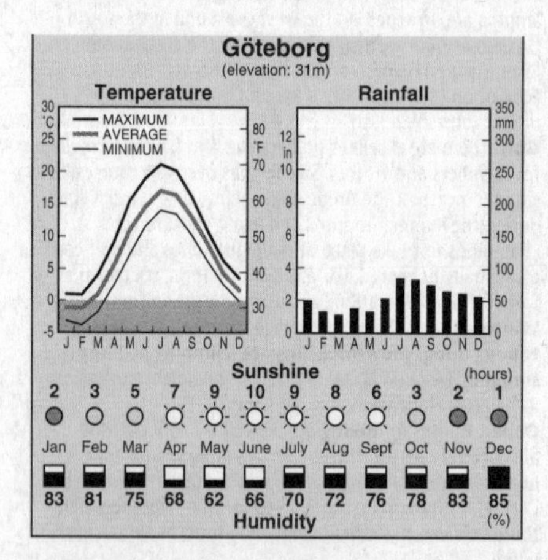

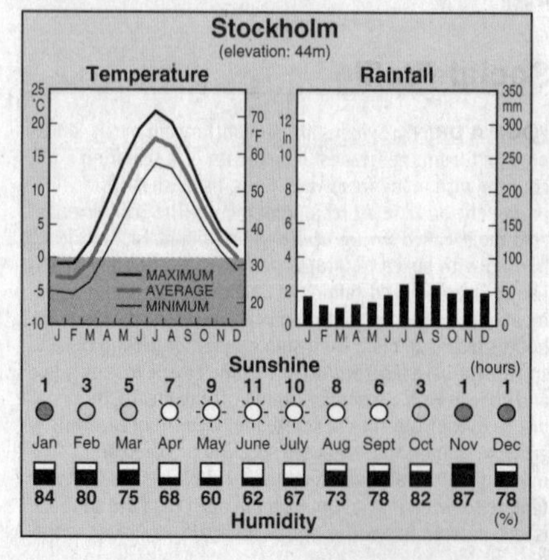

Switzerland

LATEST TRAVEL ADVICE CONTACTS

British Foreign and Commonwealth Office
Tel: (0870) 606 0290 Website: www.fco.gov.uk
US Department of State
Website: http://travel.state.gov/travel
Canadian Department of Foreign Affairs and Int'l Trade
Tel: (1 800) 267 8376 Website: www.dfait-maeci.gc.ca

Location: Western Europe.

Country dialling code: 41.

Switzerland Tourism
Street address: Tödistrasse 7, 8027 Zürich, Switzerland
Postal address: PO Box 2077, 8027 Zürich, Switzerland
Tel: (1) 288 1111. Fax: (1) 288 1205.
E-mail: info@switzerland.com
Website: www.myswitzerland.com

Embassy of Switzerland
16-18 Montagu Place, London W1H 2BQ, UK
Tel: (020) 7616 6000 *or* (09065) 508 909 (recorded visa information).
Fax: (020) 7724 7001 *or* 7723 9581 (visa section).
Website: www.swissembassy.org.uk
Opening hours: Mon-Fri 0900-1200 (for personal visa applications).

Swiss Consulate General
Portland Tower, 6th Floor, Portland Street, Manchester M1 3LD, UK
Tel: (0161) 236 2933. Fax: (0161) 236 4689.
E-mail: vertretung@mch.rep.admin.ch
Website: www.swissembassy.org.uk
Opening hours: Mon-Fri 0900-1200 (personal callers); Mon-Thurs 0800-1230 and 1330-1630; Fri 0800-1230 and 1330-1530 (telephone enquiries).

Switzerland Travel Centre
1st Floor, 30 Bedford Street, London WC2E 9ED, UK
Tel: (00800) 1002 0030 (toll-free in Europe) *or* (020) 7420 4900.
Fax: (00800) 1002 0031 (toll-free in Europe).
E-mail: sales@stc.ch
Website: www.myswitzerland.com
Provides travel advice and information.

British Embassy
Thunstrasse 50, 3000 Bern 5, Switzerland
Tel: (31) 359 7700 *or* 7741 (consular section).
Fax: (31) 359 7765.
E-mail: info@fco.gov.uk
Website: www.britain-in-switzerland.ch

British Consulate General
37-39 rue de Vermont, 6th Floor, 1211 Geneva 20, Switzerland
Tel: (22) 918 2400. Fax: (22) 918 2322.
Website: www.britain-in-switzerland.ch
Honorary Consulates in: Basle, Montreux/Vevey, Ticino, Valais and Zürich.

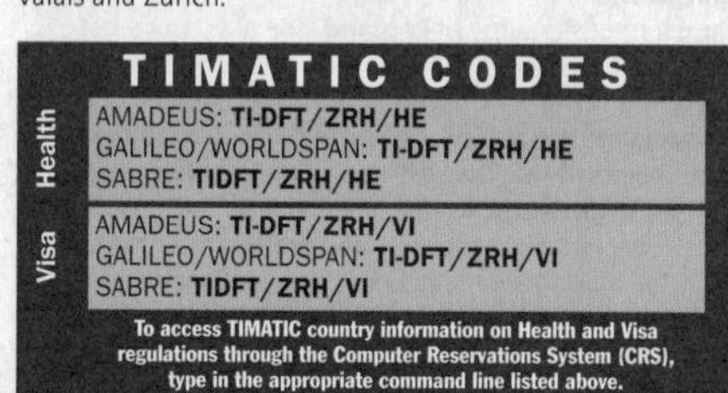
TIMATIC CODES

Health
AMADEUS: **TI-DFT/ZRH/HE**
GALILEO/WORLDSPAN: **TI-DFT/ZRH/HE**
SABRE: **TIDFT/ZRH/HE**

Visa
AMADEUS: **TI-DFT/ZRH/VI**
GALILEO/WORLDSPAN: **TI-DFT/ZRH/VI**
SABRE: **TIDFT/ZRH/VI**

To access TIMATIC country information on Health and Visa regulations through the Computer Reservations System (CRS), type in the appropriate command line listed above.

Embassy of Switzerland
2900 Cathedral Avenue, NW, Washington, DC 20008, USA
Tel: (202) 745 7900. Fax: (202) 387 2564.
E-mail: vertretung@was.rep.admin.ch *or* visa@was.rep.admin.ch (consular section).
Website: www.swissemb.org
Consulate General of Switzerland
633 3rd Avenue, 30th Floor, New York, NY 10017, USA
Tel: (212) 599 5700. Fax: (212) 599 4266.
E-mail: vertretung@nyc.rep.admin.ch
Website: www.swissconsulatenyc.org
Consulates General in: Atlanta, Chicago, Houston, Los Angeles and San Francisco.
Switzerland Tourism
608 5th Avenue, Swiss Center, New York, NY 10020, USA
Tel: (212) 757 5944 *or* (877) 794 7795 (toll-free).
Fax: (212) 262 6116.
E-mail: info.usa@switzerland.com
Website: www.myswitzerland.com
Also in: Los Angeles (trade enquiries only).
Embassy of the United States of America
Street address: Jubiläumsstrasse 93, 3005 Bern, Switzerland
Postal address: PO Box CH 300, Bern, Switzerland
Tel: (31) 357 7011. Fax: (31) 357 7344.
E-mail: bernniv@state.gov
Website: http://bern.usembassy.gov
Embassy of Switzerland
5 Marlborough Avenue, Ottawa, Ontario K1N 8E6, Canada
Tel: (613) 235 1837. Fax: (613) 563 1394.
E-mail: vertretung@ott.rep.admin.ch
Website: www.eda.admin.ch/canada
Consulates General in: Montréal, Toronto and Vancouver.
Switzerland Tourism
926 The East Mall, Toronto, Ontario M9B 6K1, Canada
Tel: (416) 695 3496 *or* (416) 695 3375 (trade enquiries only) *or* (800) 794 7795. Fax: (416) 695 2774.
E-mail: info.caen@switzerland.com
Website: www.myswitzerland.com
Canadian Embassy
Street address: Kirchenfeldstrasse 88, 3005 Bern, Switzerland
Postal address: PO Box 234, 3000 Bern 6, Switzerland
Tel: (31) 357 3200. Fax: (31) 357 3210.
E-mail: bern@dfait-maeci.gc.ca
Website: www.dfait-maeci.gc.ca/switzerland
Visa applications from people residing in Switzerland must be addressed to the Canadian Embassy in Berlin (see *Germany*) or Paris (see *France*).

General Information

AREA: 41,284 sq km (15,940 sq miles).
POPULATION: 7,261,210 (official estimate 2001).
POPULATION DENSITY: 175.9 per sq km.
CAPITAL: Bern. **Population:** 122,500 (2001).
GEOGRAPHY: Switzerland is bordered by France to the west, Germany to the north, Austria to the east and Italy to the south. It has the highest mountains in Europe, with waterfalls and lakes set amid green pastures. The highest peaks are Dufour Peak, 4634m (15,217ft), on the Italian border; the Dom, 4545m (14,912ft); the Matterhorn, 4478m (14,692ft); and the Jungfrau, 4166m (13,669ft).
GOVERNMENT: Federal Republic since 1848. **Head of State and Government:** President Samuel Schmid since 2005.
LANGUAGE: 65 to 70 per cent German in central and eastern areas, 19 per cent French in the west and 8 per cent Italian in the south. Raeto-Romansch is spoken in the southeast by 1 per cent. English is spoken by many. Overlapping cultural influences characterise the country.
RELIGION: Roman Catholic (43 per cent) and Protestant (47 per cent).
TIME: GMT + 1 (GMT + 2 from last Sunday in March to Saturday before last Sunday in October).
ELECTRICITY: 220 volts AC, 50Hz.
COMMUNICATIONS: Telephone: Full IDD is available. Country code: 41. Outgoing international code: 00. Phonecards are available for use in payphones. **Mobile telephone:** GSM 900/1800 networks cover the whole country. Single band networks also in Basle, Geneva and Zurich. Operators include *Orange* (website: www.orange.ch), *Sunrise* (website: www.sunrise.ch) and *Swiss GSM* (website: www.swisscom.com). **Fax:** Facilities are available in all telegraph offices, most major hotels and post offices.
Internet: Internet access is available in phone booths operated by *Swisscom*. Charges are payable by phonecard or credit card. ISPs include *SwissOnline* (website: www.swissonline.ch). **Telegram:** These can be sent from post offices and most hotels or arranged by dialling 110 on the telephone. **Post:** Airmail within Europe takes three days. *Poste Restante* is available at all post offices. Post office hours: Mon-Fri 0730-1200 and 1345-1830. Saturday closing is at 1100 except in major cities. **Press:** The high level of interest in local politics throughout Switzerland has led to a large number of regional newspapers. However, the most popular dailies are *Blick*, *Neue Zürcher Zeitung* and *Tages-Anzeiger Zürich*. European and international newspapers in English, including *The Herald Tribune* and *USA Today*, are also widely available.
Radio: BBC World Service (website: www.bbc.co.uk/worldservice) and Voice of America (website: www.voa.gov) can be received. From time to time the frequencies change and the most up-to-date can be found online.

Passport/Visa

	Passport Required?	Visa Required?	Return Ticket Required?
Full British	Yes	No	No
Australian	Yes	No	No
Canadian	Yes	No	No
USA	Yes	No	No
Other EU	1	No	No
Japanese	Yes	No	No

Note: Regulations and requirements may be subject to change at short notice, and you are advised to contact the appropriate diplomatic or consular authority before finalising travel arrangements. Details of these may be found at the head of this country's entry. Any numbers in the chart refer to the footnotes below.

PASSPORTS: Passport valid for three months after intended period of stay required by all except:
(a) **1.** nationals of Austria, Belgium, Denmark, Finland, France, Germany, Greece, Hungary, Iceland, Ireland, Italy, Liechtenstein, Luxembourg, Malta, Monaco, The Netherlands, Norway, Portugal, San Marino, Slovak Republic, Slovenia, Spain and Sweden holding a valid national identity card;
(b) foreigners holding national Identity Cards issued by the governments of Belgium, France or Luxembourg, provided they are resident in one of these countries.
VISAS: Required by all except the following for stays of up to three months:
(a) nationals of countries referred to in the chart above;
(b) nationals of countries in South and North/Central America, including nationals of Caribbean island states (except nationals of Belize, Bolivia, Colombia, Cuba, Dominican Republic, Ecuador, Haiti and Peru who *do* need a visa);
(c) nationals of Andorra, Brunei, Bulgaria, Croatia, Fiji, Hong Kong (SAR), Iceland, Israel, Kiribati, Korea (Rep), Malaysia, Monaco, New Zealand, Norway, Romania, San Marino, Singapore, Solomon Islands, South Africa, Tuvalu and Vatican City;
(d) nationals of Bahrain, Kuwait, Oman, Qatar, Saudi Arabia, Taiwan (China, PR), Thailand and United Arab Emirates, if in possession of a valid multiple-entry Schengen visa (valid for all Schengen states);
(e) holders of a travel document issued to refugees by the EU with a blue cover and two golden stripes in the top left hand corner and mentioning the agreement of 28 July 1951;
(f) nationals in direct transit travelling within 48 hours, providing they hold all valid documents.
Note: If staying for longer than three months, or if total length of time spent in Switzerland exceeds six months within a 12-month period, a residence permit is required. Visitors holding visas or residence permits must register with the police within eight days of arrival in Switzerland.
Types of visa and cost: *Tourist*; *Visitor*; *Business*; *Transit*. All visas cost £25 for passengers over 18 years of age (children aged under 18 included in a parent's passport are not required to pay a separate visa fee); £12.50 for unmarried passengers aged under 18 with separate passports. Fees can vary due to exchange rates.
Validity: Three months. Transit visas are issued to nationals wishing to pass through Switzerland or continuing on a connecting flight to another country. Holders of transit visas must continue their journey within 48 hours.
Note: Stateless persons require a transit visa at all times. Nationals of Iraq and Somalia do not require a transit visa if they hold a residence permit for an EU country, Canada, Iceland, Norway or the USA. Nationals of Afghanistan, Angola, Bangladesh, Congo (Dem Rep), Ethiopia, Ghana, Guinea, India, Iran, Lebanon, Nigeria, Pakistan, Sierra Leone, Sri Lanka and Turkey do not require a transit visa if they hold a visa or residence permit for an EU country, Canada, Iceland, Norway or the USA.
Application to: Consulate (or Consular section at Embassy responsible for place of residence; see *Contact Addresses* section). UK applicants should note that residents of Northern Ireland, Scotland, Cheshire, Cleveland, Cumbria, Derbyshire, Durham, Greater Manchester, Humberside, Isle of Man, Lancashire, Leicestershire, Lincolnshire, Merseyside, Northumberland, Nottinghamshire, Tyne & Wear and Yorkshire must obtain their visas from the Swiss Consulate General in Manchester (see *Contact Addresses* section). Visa applications must be made in person; postal applications are not accepted.
Application requirements: *Tourist:* (a) Passport or travel document valid for at least three months after intended visit accompanied by valid travel documents. (b) One completed application form (available to download and complete prior to arrival from the Embassy of Switzerland website www.swissembassy.org.uk). (c) One recent, passport-size photo. (d) Fee, payable in cash only. (e) Return/onward ticket. (f) Proof of sufficient funds in the form of a recent bank statement/travellers' cheques (approximately equivalent to £50 per day). (g) Hotel reservation and/or package tour confirmation. *Transit:* (a)-(g) and, (h) Proof of flight with an airline licensed in Switzerland. (i) Visa(s) for ongoing destination(s). *Visitor:* (a)-(f) and, (g) Invitation letter from Swiss residents sent directly to the Embassy, accompanied by a copy of the Swiss resident's Swiss Passport/ID card or Swiss Resident Permit. In special cases, a declaration of guarantee completed by the applicant and the resident may be required, which must then be endorsed by the Aliens Police of the resident's canton. *Business:* (a)-(g) and, (h) Proof of existing business connections or an invitation from Swiss company or business partner sent directly to the relevant Embassy.
Working days required: Visas may be issued immediately, but travellers are advised to apply at least one week prior to departure and no earlier than three months before proposed travel. Some applications may need to be referred to the Swiss authorities, which can take six to eight weeks for approval.
Temporary residence: Nationals of most European and some other countries do not require a visa if they intend to take up employment or residence in Switzerland; however, before entry they must obtain an *Assurance of a Residence Permit* from their employer in Switzerland. Students who wish to attend school, college or university for more than three months must apply for a *Residence Permit* well in advance through their local Embassy or Consulate.

Money

Currency: Swiss Franc (SFr) = 100 rappen or centimes. Notes are in denominations of SFr1000, 500, 200, 100, 50, 20 and 10. Coins are in denominations of SFr5, 2 and 1, and 50, 20, 10 and 5 centimes.
Eurocheques: Eurocheques are no longer guaranteed and and can not be accepted for encashments but may be useable for payments without the guarantee.
Currency exchange: Personal cheques within the Eurocheque system are accepted. ATMs provide a convenient means of obtaining Swiss Francs. There are Bureaux de Change at train stations and banks.
Credit & debit cards: American Express, Diners Club, MasterCard and Visa are widely accepted. Check with your credit or debit card company for details of merchant acceptability and other facilities which may be available.
Travellers cheques: Pound Sterling, US Dollar, Euro or Swiss Franc cheques are accepted at airports, railway stations and banks. To avoid additional exchange rate charges, travellers are advised to take travellers cheques in Pounds Sterling, Euros or US Dollars.
Currency restrictions: There are no restrictions on the import or export of local or foreign currencies.
Exchange rate indicators: The following figures are included as a guide to the movements of the Swiss Franc against Sterling and the US Dollar:

Date	Feb '04	May '04	Aug '04	Nov '04
£1.00=	2.29	2.32	2.28	2.16
$1.00=	1.26	1.29	1.24	1.14

Banking hours: Mon-Fri 0830-1630.

Duty Free

The following items may be imported into Switzerland by persons over 17 years of age without incurring customs duty by:
(a) Visitors from European countries:
200 cigarettes or 50 cigars or 250g of tobacco; *2l of alcohol* (up to 15 per cent) and *1l of alcohol* (over 15 per cent); *gifts up to a value of SFr100.*
(b) Visitors from non-European countries:
400 cigarettes or 100 cigars or 500g of tobacco; *2l of alcohol* (up to 15 per cent) and *1l of alcohol* (over 15 per cent); *gifts up to a value of SFr100.*
Prohibited items: Most meat and processed meat, absinthe and narcotics are prohibited. There are strict regulations on importing animals and firearms.

Public Holidays

2005: Jan 1 New Year's Day. **Jan 2*** Berchtold's Day. **Mar 25*** Good Friday. **Mar 28*** Easter Monday. **May 5*** Ascension. **May 15*** Whit Monday. **Aug 1** National Day. **Dec 25** Christmas Day. **Dec 26** St Stephen's Day.
2006: Jan 1 New Year's Day. **Jan 2*** Berchtold's Day. **Apr 14***

Good Friday. **Apr 17*** Easter Monday. **May 25*** Ascension. **Jun 5*** Whit Monday. **Aug 1** National Day. **Dec 25** Christmas Day. **Dec 26** St Stephen's Day.
Note: (a) * These holidays may not be observed in certain cantons. (b) There are additional regional holidays which are observed in certain cantons only.

Health

	Special Precautions?	Certificate Required?
Yellow Fever	No	No
Cholera	No	No
Typhoid & Polio	No	N/A
Malaria	No	N/A

Note: Regulations and requirements may be subject to change at short notice, and you are advised to contact your doctor well in advance of your intended date of departure. Any numbers in the chart refer to the footnotes below.

Other risks: *Rabies* is present. For those at high risk, vaccination before arrival should be considered. If you are bitten, seek medical advice without delay. For more information, see the *Health* appendix.
Health care: Health care: Health insurance is essential. Medical facilities in Switzerland are among the best in Europe, but treatment is expensive. Various leaflets giving information on health spas and clinics are available from Switzerland Tourism (see *Contact Addresses* section).

Travel - International

AIR: Switzerland's national airline is *Swiss (LX)* (website: www.swiss.com).
Approximate flight times: From Basle, Bern, Geneva or Zürich to *London* is one hour 50 minutes. From Geneva to *Los Angeles* is 17 hours and from Zürich is 14 hours 35 minutes. From Geneva to *New York* is nine hours 45 minutes and from Zürich is seven hours 20 minutes.
International airports: *Zürich (ZRH) (Kloten)* (website: www.flughafen-zuerich.ch) is 11km (7 miles) from the city (travel time – 20 minutes). Trains run every 10 to 15 minutes from under Terminal B. Regional and night buses are available. Passengers arriving in Switzerland by air can purchase a special *Fly-Rail Luggage* ticket from their airport of departure which will enable them to have their luggage delivered directly to a Swiss railway station. With the *Fly-Rail Baggage* service, passengers leaving Switzerland can check their bags in at the railway station up to 24 hours before their flight. Taxis to the city are available (travel time – 15 to 30 minutes).
Geneva (GVA) (website: www.gva.ch) is 5km (3 miles) north of the city. Taxis to the city are available. There is a regular train service to Geneva Cornavin Station (travel time – six minutes). The no. 10 bus runs from the airport to the city centre.
Bern (BRN) (Belp) is 9km (5.5 miles) southeast of the city (travel time – 20 to 30 minutes). Bus services are available to Bern station. A rail service runs from Bern to Zürich Airport. Taxis are also available.
Basle (BSL) (Basel-Mulhouse) is 12km (7 miles) from the city. Bus runs to Basle SBB Luftreisebüro. Taxis are also available.
Departure tax: None.
RAIL: Travelling from the UK, the quickest way is to travel by *Eurostar* through the Channel Tunnel to Paris (travel time – three hours) and, from there, to Switzerland. For further information and reservations contact *Eurostar* (tel: (0870) 0000 792 (travel agents) *or* (08705) 186 186 (public; within the UK) *or* (01233) 617 575 (public; outside the UK only); website: www.eurostar.com); *or Rail Europe* (tel: (08708) 371 371; website: www.raileurope.co.uk). General enquiries and information requests must be made by telephone.
Other connections from London via the main channel crossings are available (minimum travel time of about 14 to 15 hours to Basle and Lausanne, the main points of entry). There are also through trains from many other European cities.
ROAD: Switzerland can be reached by road from Austria, France, Germany and Italy. Some approximate driving times to Geneva and Zürich by the most direct routes are: Calais– Geneva: 12 to 13 hours (747km/464 miles); Dunkirk–Geneva: 12 to 13 hours (732km/454 miles); Calais–Zürich: 13 to 14 hours (790km/490 miles); Dunkirk–Zürich: 14 to 15 hours (880km/ 546 miles).
Coach: There are coach services to Switzerland as well as scheduled coach tour operators. Contact Switzerland Tourism for further details (see *Contact Addresses* section). In the UK, *Eurolines*, departing from Victoria Coach Station in London, serves destinations in Switzerland. For further information, contact Eurolines (tel: (08705) 143 219; e-mail: welcome@eurolines.co.uk; website: www.eurolines.com).

Travel - Internal

AIR: All services are operated by *Swiss*. Domestic air travel is fast but expensive, and with the exception of the Geneva to Zürich flight (travel time – 45 minutes), many businesspeople prefer to travel by rail or road.
RAIL: Rail transport is particularly well developed in Switzerland, with excellent services provided by *Schweizerische Bundesbahnen (SBB)* (website: www.sbb.ch) and many other operators. Use of the *Swiss Pass* (see below) is a superb way to view the scenery, although mainline services are geared to the needs of the hurried business traveller. Trains run at least hourly from the major centres and there is a countrywide timetable of regular services. There are dining cars on many trains, and snacks and refreshments are widely available. Independent railways, such as the *Rhätische Bahn* in the Grisons and the *Berner-Oberland-Bahn*, provide services in certain parts of the country. The *SBB* has introduced specialised cars for disabled people using wheelchairs. Facilities include a lift for wheelchairs, a specially adapted WC and radios adapted for people with hearing difficulties.
There are also a large number of mountain railways which are sometimes the only means of access to winter resorts. Some of these are attractions in their own right: the *Gornergrat-Bahn* in Zermatt is one of the oldest mountain railways and climbs to a height of over 3000m above sea level, offering a spectacular panorama of the Matterhorn and surrounding mountains.
Cheap fares: Available from Switzerland Tourism. The *Swiss Pass* gives unlimited travel on rail services, those of other main regional operators, boats, an extensive network of buses and city trams, as well as reduced price travel on other mountain railways not included in the full scheme. Tickets can be purchased for four, eight, 15, 21 or 28 days. An STS family card allows children up to 16 years of age free travel when accompanied by parents. There are also regional tickets for unlimited travel in different parts of Switzerland at various rates. Other offers include a *Swiss Transfer Ticket* allowing return travel from a Swiss border or airport to a selected destination. A leaflet describing all the schemes is available from Switzerland Tourism. A comprehensive timetable for all Swiss public transport can also be purchased. *InterRail* cards are valid.
ROAD: Traffic drives on the right. Road quality is generally good. Many mountain roads are winding and narrow, and often closed in heavy winter conditions; otherwise chains and snow tyres may be necessary. Rail is often more efficient than driving. **Bus:** Postal motor coaches (website: www.post.ch) provide a service to even the remotest villages, but under the integrated national transport policy few long-distance coaches are allowed to operate. **Taxi:** All taxis have meters for short and long trips, although it is advisable to agree the fare for longer distances out of town. **Car hire:** Available in all towns from hotels and airports and at all manned rail stations. All major European companies are represented. **Regulations:** The minimum driving age is 18. Seat belts are obligatory and children under 12 years must travel in the back of the car. Dipped headlights are compulsory during the day. Drink-driving fines are heavy. **Speed limits:** 80kph (50mph) on country lanes; max 120kph (75mph), min 60kph (37mph) on motorways; and 50kph (31mph) in towns. **Organisations:** The *AA* and *RAC* in the UK are linked with *TCS (Touring Club Suisse)* (website: www.tcs.ch) and *ACS (Automobil Club der Schweiz)*. Contact the *Automobil Club der Schweiz (ACS)*, Wasserwerkgasse 39, CH-3000 Bern 13 (tel: (31) 328 3111; fax: (31) 311 0310; e-mail: acszv@acs.ch; website: www.acs.ch). In emergencies, there is a breakdown service offering assistance throughout Switzerland (tel: 140). **Motorway tax** (*vignette*): An annual road tax of SFr40 is levied on all cars and motorbikes using Swiss motorways. An additional fee of SFr40 applies to trailers and caravans. The *vignette* (sticker) is valid between December 1 of the year preceding and January 31 of the one following the year printed on the vignette. These permits, which are available at border crossings, are valid for multiple re-entry into Switzerland within the duration of the licensed period. To avoid hold-ups at the frontier, however, it is advisable to purchase the vignette in advance: call the Swiss Travel Centre (tel: (00800) 1002 0030) for more details. **Documentation:** A national driving licence is sufficient. Green Card insurance is advised – ordinary domestic insurance policies are valid but do not provide full cover. The Green Card tops the cover up to the level provided by the visitor's domestic policy.
URBAN: Highly efficient and integrated urban public transport systems serve as a model for other countries. There are tramways and light rail services in Basle, Bern, Geneva, Neuchâtel and Zürich. These and a further dozen cities also have trolleybuses. Fares systems are generally automated with machines issuing single or multiple tickets at the roadside. Tickets are also available at enquiry offices. Fares are generally zonal. There is a day ticket for travel in one or more Swiss cities on any given day at a standard fare. Taxis are widely available and drivers expect a 15 per cent tip.

Travel times: The following chart gives approximate travel times (in hours and minutes) from **Zürich** to other major cities/towns in Switzerland.

	Air	Road	Rail
Basle	0.30	1.10	1.05
Bern	-	1.15	1.10
Geneva	0.40	2.45	2.55
Lugano	0.45	3.00	3.00

Accommodation

HOTELS: Hotels are of high quality and in high demand. Advance booking is advised. Bookings cannot be made through Switzerland Tourism. All standards from luxury to family hotels and pensions are available. Most hotels in Switzerland are affiliated to the Schweizer Hotelier Verein (Swiss Hotels Association) (SHV), Monbijoustrasse 130, Postfach 3001 Bern (tel: (31) 370 4111; fax: (31) 370 4444; e-mail: info@swisshotels.ch; website: www.swisshotels.ch). Around 75 per cent of all overnight stays in the country are at SHV member hotels. A service charge of 7.6 per cent is included in hotel bills, and an additional local tax may be payable (depending on the location). **Grading:** The SHV classifies all its hotels according to a 5-star rating system, which stipulates a range of facilities as follows:
1-star (simple): Simple, clean accommodation offering basic amenities. There are approximately 82 SHV-classified 1-star hotels in Switzerland; **2-star (comfortable):** Good standard of comfort and facilities including 30 per cent of rooms with private bath. There are approximately 382 SHV-classified 2-star hotels in Switzerland; **3-star (good middle-class):** Very good standard of comfort and facilities including 75 per cent of rooms with private bath. Minimum size of hotel: 10 rooms. There are approximately 1100 SHV-classified 3-star hotels in Switzerland; **4-star (first class):** High standard of comfort and facilities including all rooms with private bath and 16/24-hour room service. 60 per cent of rooms with colour television. Minimum size of hotel: 25 rooms. There are approximately 436 SHV-classified 4-star hotels in Switzerland; **5-star (luxury):** Very high standard of comfort and facilities including all rooms with private bath, colour television and 16/24-hour room service. Minimum size of hotel: 35 rooms. There are approximately 81 SHV-classified 5-star hotels in Switzerland.
Note: Membership of the SHV is voluntary, and there may be some first-class hotels which do not have a star rating. There are many hotels with no actual star classification that are recognised by, and members of, the SHV as well as Country Inns, Unique hotels, Aparthotels, Mountain Inns/Traveller's Lodges and Low Service hotels.
Any SHV hotel can apply for a maximum of three of the following specialist categories: Family Hotel, Historic Hotel, Bike Hotel, Golf Hotel, Congress Hotel, Eco Hotel, Health Hotel, Drive-in Hotel, Holiday Hotel, Tennis Hotel, Business Hotel, Seminar Hotel and Wellness Hotel. Prices vary slightly according to the popularity of the resort.
The SHV (see above for address) issues an annual guide of around 2500 member hotels and pensions. This shows the rates, addresses, telephone/fax numbers, opening dates and amenities of the various hotels. Also included are lists of spas, resorts, sports facilities and climate. A list of hotels and restaurants catering for Jewish visitors is available from the SHV, as well as a hotel guide for the disabled, the elderly and a list of hotels especially suitable for families. All lists are available from Switzerland Tourism (see *Contact Addresses* section).
CHALETS & APARTMENTS: Information regarding the rental of chalets, houses, flats and furnished apartments is available from local tourist offices and estate agents in Switzerland. A list of contacts is available from Switzerland Tourism.
SPAS: Switzerland has about 22 different mineral springs for the treatment of various health conditions. A guide to Swiss spas, including hotels, is available from Switzerland Tourism.
PRIVATE CLINICS: Details of accommodation in private sanatoria and clinics is included in the publication *Private Clinics in Switzerland*, available from Switzerland Tourism.
CAMPING: There are approximately 450 campsites in Switzerland. Camping on farmland is not permitted. Local area laws and fees vary. It is advisable to make advance reservations in the summer. Camping guides published by the *Swiss Camping Association* and the *Swiss Camping Federation* can be purchased from Switzerland Tourism. The *Swiss Camp Site Owners Association (VSC/ASC)* can be contacted at 3800 Interlaken-Thunersee (tel: (31) 852 0626; fax: (31) 852 0627; e-mail: info@swisscamps.ch; website: www.swisscamps.ch). A list of campsites (produced in conjunction with the Swiss tourist board) is available online (website: www.camping.ch).
YOUTH HOSTELS: Visitors holding membership cards of a national organisation affiliated to the *International Youth Hostels Federation* are entitled to lower prices. To avoid disappointment, wardens of youth hostels should be given prior notice (at least five days) of arrival. An International

Reply Paid Postcard (Youth Hostel Edition) should be used if confirmation is required. For further information, contact Swiss Youth Hostels, Schaffhauserstrasse 14, 8042 Zürich (tel: (1) 360 1414; fax: (1) 360 1460; e-mail: bookingoffice@youthhostel.ch; website: www.youthhostel.ch).
A list of Swiss youth hostels is obtainable from Switzerland Tourism.

Resorts & Excursions

NORTHWEST SWITZERLAND

JURA, NEUCHÂTEL & FRIBOURG: The lakes of **Biel**, **Murten** and **Neuchâtel** are strung along the foot of the **Jura Mountains**. Although not one of the most popular regions for tourists, the rolling hills of the Jura mountains, the **Franches Montagnes** in the Neuchâtel region and the foothills of the **Alps** in the canton of Fribourg to the south of the lakes are excellent for hiking, camping and fishing. The waterfalls of the **Doubs** and the gorges of the **Areuse** in the Jura are very impressive. The area is also famous for its food and wines, and for the production of Swiss precision watches; do not miss the **Horological Museum** at **La-Chaux-de-Fonds**, and the watch-making factories at La-Chaux-de-Fonds and **Le Locle**. The striking yellow stone buildings of medieval Neuchâtel, attractively located beside a lake, were once described by Alexander Dumas as 'carved from butter'. The town itself is celebrated for its cafe culture and first-class cuisine. Worth visiting nearby is the medieval town of **Romont** and the unspoilt lakeside town of **Murten** (known as 'Morat' by its French-speaking minority). The bilingual city of **Fribourg** (or 'Freiburg' to its German-speaking minority), where a Romanesque-Germanic atmosphere prevails, is one of the most interesting historic cities in Switzerland. In the south of the canton of Fribourg, in the foothills of the Alps, lies the **Gruyère** region, famous for its dairy farming which produces one of the best Swiss cheeses: Gruyère. The ancient town of **Gruyères** is still completely surrounded by its old city walls.
BASLE: The ancient university and trading city of Basle (Basel), straddles the Rhine between the Jura, Alsace in France and Germany's **Black Forest**, and is a centre of art and research. During the three days of the *Basler Fasnacht* (a pre-Lenten carnival), no serious sightseeing should or can be done, as visitors are required to take part in grand masked parties and street parades with fancy costumes. There is even a **Fasnacht Fountain** in front of the **City Theatre**. The collection in the **Art Museum** ranges from Cranach and Holbein via Rembrandt to Monet, Picasso and Max Ernst. In the old city centre stands the ancient red sandstone cathedral or **Münster** (parts date from the ninth to 13th century). Its tower affords impressive city vistas. Other sights include the **Spalentor** (1370), one of the original city wall's three remaining towers, and the **Church of St Peter** (15th century). Away from the town, mountain paths zigzag up the Jura mountains.
EXCURSIONS: Although northern Switzerland is not one of the main tourist areas, there are a few well-known holiday resorts beyond Basle, one of which is picturesque **Solothurn** where the prevalent architectural styles are Renaissance and Baroque. Day trips to **Aarau**, **Baden** and the 13th-century moated castle at **Binningen**, are also recommended. During winter months, the main sport in the Jura is cross-country skiing.

SOUTHWEST SWITZERLAND

GENEVA: Geneva is a university town situated on the Rhône-outlet of **Lake Geneva** (**Lac Léman**), at the southern foot of the Jura mountains. Its popularity is, however, not only due to its excellent surroundings. It owes its cosmopolitan nature to the presence of the United Nations, the International Red Cross and numerous other international organisations. Elegant shops, nightclubs, restaurants, fine museums and art galleries and an extensive calendar of cultural activities make it a favourite with many visitors. The old city centre is best explored on foot. One of the finest examples of Romanesque architecture is the **Cathedral de St Pierre**. The flower clock, with over 6,500 blooms, near the lake in the **Jardin Anglais**, pays homage to Geneva's watch industry. A boat trip on the lake is recommended. Dominated by the **Jet d'Eau**, a 145m- (476ft-) high fountain, the lake is generally alive with sailing boats. A crisp breeze known as the *bise* (kiss) blows across the lake and there are facilities for all kinds of watersports, as well as golf and riding nearby. Geneva is also a traditional European centre for health and recuperation, and maintains state-of-the-art sanatoria such as the 100-year-old **Clinique Générale Beaulieu**.
SKI RESORTS: Geneva is the gateway to a variety of ski resorts. One especially extensive area well suited to families but with excellent skiing for all abilities is **Portes du Soleil**, a cluster of small resorts forming a massive skiing circuit which straddles the French-Swiss border. Key Swiss resorts here include the pretty traditional village of **Champéry**, and the tranquil, purpose-built mini resorts of **Champoussin** and **Les Crosets**.
LAUSANNE: The capital of the canton of Vaud, Lausanne is situated on the northern shore of Lake Geneva. The symbol of the city is the **Cathédrale Notre-Dame** in the **Cité**, the old centre, and the **Château St Maire** (1397-1431). A walk along the promenade of the old **Port d'Ouchy** reveals a slower pace of life. A funicular can be taken from Ouchy to the inner city of Lausanne.
EXCURSIONS: Several rivulets and rolling hills dominate the canton Vaud, a famous wine-producing region. Other traditional activities in the region include wood sculpture and cheese-making. Vaud also boasts one of the country's most important historic buildings: the Benedictine monastery **Church of St Pierre** (11th century) in the small town of **Romainmotier**. **Montreux** is renowned for its mild climate and the *International Jazz Festival* in July. At **Villars** there is an 18-hole golf course, while nearby **Château d'Oex**, **Les Diablerets** and **Leysin** are major sporting centres for climbing, mountain-biking, skiing, paragliding and hiking. Each summer there is a rock festival at Leysin and there is summer skiing on the glacier at Les Diablerets (noteworthy for its panoramic views of **Mont Blanc** and the icy peaks and green valleys of the Alps).
Ski resorts: The traditional village resort of **Gstaad** is an upmarket, glamorous destination for skiers with extensive slopes and a thriving après-ski scene. Smaller, more family-oriented winter resorts include Château d'Oex, Leysin and Villars.
VALAIS: Valais ('The valley') stretches all the way from the Rhône Glacier past **Brig**, **Martigny** and **Sion** down to Lake Geneva. Nestling between the northern and the southern side of the Alps is a diverse landscape which will entice every visitor. Glaciers can be found on all peaks of the **Valais Alps** which are the highest in Switzerland: **Dufour Peak** (4634m/15,217ft), **Dom** (4545m/14,917ft), **Weisshorn** (4509m/14,793ft) and the **Matterhorn** (4478m/14,698ft). Small villages of weathered wooden-beamed houses, with flowers pouring out of the windowboxes in summer, perch in clearings high on the slopes. High transverse valleys give access to their resorts at the foot of the alpine giants such as **Saas Fee** in the **Saas Valley** and **Zermatt** in the **Nikolai Valley**; the Matterhorn provides a magnificent backdrop for the latter. In the internationally-known resort of Zermatt, cars are not allowed and transport is either on foot, by electric car or by horse and cart. There are well-posted walks and cablecars, with lifts and tows to the top of the slopes for more ambitious climbing. The highest aerial cablecar in Europe is here at Zermatt, ascending the **Little Matterhorn**. The ski run from here back to the village is the longest in Europe. The historic town of **Brig** boasts the most important Baroque castle in Switzerland, the **Stockalperschloss**. **Sion**, an episcopal town, and **Martigny**, with their castle ruins, are worth a visit and are also ideal starting points for excursions to the surrounding area. Castle enthusiasts should also visit **Leuk**, **Monthey** and **Sierre**. Any visit to the area should also include the **Rhône Glacier** and grotto at **Gletsch**.
Ski resorts: Valais contains some of Switzerland's most celebrated resorts, including the picturesque car-free village of **Zermatt**, which offers excellent skiing for all abilities, lively nightlife and plenty of non-skiing activities. Trendy **Verbier** forms part of the extensive **Les Quatre Vallées** ski area, attracting serious skiers and snow-boarders to its challenging slopes and providing plenty of facilities for young people. The beautiful car-free village of **Saas Fee** has high, snow-sure slopes and is ideal for beginners and intermediates. The popular ski area of **Crans Montana** consists of chic **Crans sur Sierre** with its thriving nightlife, and the more down-to-earth, restrained **Montana**. Smaller, more family-oriented resorts in the region include **Anzère**, **Bettmeralp**, **Riederalp** and **Zinal**.

CENTRAL SWITZERLAND

BERNER OBERLAND: The Berner Oberland, with Interlaken and the Jungfraujoch, as well as Europe's highest railway, is a major tourist area; its spectacular scenery includes famous peaks, mountain lakes, alpine streams and wild flowers. **Adelboden**, **Grindelwald** and **Lenk** were already famous with the European nobility and artists in the 19th century. **Interlaken**, situated between the lakes of **Brienz** and **Thun**, is a renowned climatic health resort and the gateway to the Berner Oberland. From here, a network of roads and mountain railways such as the narrow-gauge **Berner-Oberland-Bahn (BOB)** serve the resorts in the Jungfrau region. **Jungfrau** (4158m/13,642ft), **Mönch** (4099m/13,448ft) and **Eiger** (3970m/13,024ft), whose dangerous, nearly perpendicular northern ascent was first climbed in 1938, are three of the most famous mountains in Switzerland. Their names mean the 'maiden', the 'monk' and the 'ogre'; together they are known as the **Finsteraarhorn Group**. **Finsteraarhorn** (4275m/14,026ft), the highest peak of the **Berner Alps**, is dominated by glaciers which stretch from the upper **Aare** and the **Rhône valley** to Lake Geneva. Also in the region, excursions up the **Schilthorn** mountain by funicular (made famous by James Bond in the movie *Her Majesty's Secret Service*); to the waterfalls at **Giessbach** and **Lauterbrunnen**: to the **Reichenbach Falls** (where Sherlock Holmes fell to his fictional death); and to the **Swiss Open-Air Museum** at **Ballenberg**, with its charmingly preserved houses from all regions of the country displaying traditional crafts and trades, are all recommended. The popular winter resorts of **Adelboden**, **Lenk** and **Zweisimmen** are reached from Spiez on Lake Thun. The castle at **Thun**, with its historical museum located at the top of the **Altstadt** (old town), should not be missed.
Ski resorts: The popular year-round resorts of Grindelwald, Mürren and Wengen thrive during the winter ski and snowboard season (mid-December to late March). **Grindelwald** is quite old-fashioned and quiet in the evenings but with excellent skiing, ideal for intermediates and beginners, and off-piste activities including tobogganing and winter walking trails. The ski network links up with the scenic ski village of **Wengen**, popular with British skiers, and with lots of long, gentle runs, ideal for intermediates. Nearby tiny, traffic-free **Mürren** counts among Switzerland's more rustic resorts, with limited but challenging skiing including the famous **Schilthorn** run where the British invented modern-day skiing. The quiet resort of **Kandersteg** is a good base for cross-country skiing.
BERN: This ancient capital (known as 'Berne' by Switzerland's French-speaking citizens) provides opportunities for sightseeing and shopping in the 11th-century arcaded streets. The backdrop is provided by the Jura in the northwest and the south is dominated by the Alps and their foothills. The medieval city centre is located on the **Aare River** between the 13th-century clocktower (**Zeitglockenturm**) and the striking copper spire of the **Nydegg church** (**Nydeggkirche**). Across the Nyddegg bridge are the ancient medieval **bear pits** (**Bärengraben**), a reminder of the city's ursine emblem seen throughout the town in the form of flags, statues, stained-glass windows and souvenirs. There are daily vegetable and flower markets here in summer, and a celebrated onion market on the fourth Monday of November.
LUZERN: Luzern (known as 'Lucerne' by the country's French-speaking citizens) is located on the edge of a sizeable lake, the **Vierwaldstättersee**. Its medieval old town (**Altstadt**) remains intact; important buildings include the **Hofkirche**, the old **Town Hall** (1602-1606) and the famous **Löwendenkmal**, a memorial to the city mascot the 'dying Lion of Lucerne', carved out of a cliff. Spanning the **River Reuss**, the 170m- (558ft-) long, covered wooden **Chapel Bridge**, was the oldest in Switzerland (1333) until it was destroyed by fire in 1993. It has since been reconstructed. Luzern also houses the **Richard Wagner Museum** and the **Swiss Transport Museum**. An international music festival is held here every year.
EXCURSIONS: The Lucerne region, with its mountains, lakes, pine forests and meadows, is traditionally a very popular tourist area. Ferries on the Vierwaldstättersee service the tiny villages surrounding the lakes and connect with various mountain railways and cableways. Cablecars, passenger lifts and cogwheel railways provide transport to the **Gütsch**, the **Pilatus** and the **Sonnenberg** and other mountains. South of Luzern, near the small town of **Engelberg**, the world's first revolving cable car ascends **Mount Titlis**, the highest lookout-point in central Switzerland. Historians should visit **Schwyz**, one of the three original cantons, the country's namesake and home to the Museum of the **Swiss Federal Charter** and the **Forum of Swiss History**.
SKI RESORTS: The main ski areas near Luzern include the attractive, traditional village of **Andermatt** with reliable snow and challenging skiing, and **Engelberg**, with a small ski area suitable for all abilities.

NORTHEAST SWITZERLAND

ZURICH: Switzerland's largest city is set on its own lake, **Zürichsee**, on the banks of the **Limmat River**, and is the country's main German-speaking business and banking centre. The old part of the town (the **Altstadt**) is especially picturesque. On a walk through the old centre, do not miss the Gothic **Basilica Fraumünster** (11th to 13th century) with its three naves and stained-glass windows by Marc Chagall. Across the river, the skyline is dominated by the **Grossmünster** with its twin towers. Other sights include the impressive **Town Hall**, a fine example from the late Renaissance (17th century), the **Swiss National Museum** and the modern art collections at the **Kunsthaus Zürich**. Zürich also has a full cultural programme. Plays are performed in the **Zürcher Schauspielhaus**, which is considered one of the most prestigious German-speaking theatres.
EXCURSIONS: Zürich is set in the Mittelland ('middle country'), a very lush and picturesque region scattered with small historic towns, villages and vineyards. Local trains and buses provide easy access to the hills, woods and parks that surround Zürich; during the summer, steamer cruises on

A B C D E F G H I J K L M N O P Q R S T U V W X Y Z

Zürich's lake are popular. A day trip to the **Uetliberg**, a hill to the southeast of the city, is also recommended. On clear days, the panorama from the top of the hill includes a bird's eye view of Zurich, with the Valais and Berner Alps to the west and the Black Forest to the east. The medieval castle at **Rapperswil**, on the bank of the lake, is well worth a visit.
WEST AND SOUTH OF LAKE CONSTANCE: This area of northeastern Switzerland rises slowly over the rugged range of the **Churfirsten** near **St Gallen** to the **Glarner Alps**. **Appenzell**, in the northeastern part of Switzerland, with its highest peak, **Säntis** (2504m/8215ft), is ideal for hiking tours. Old traditions remain very much alive in Appenzell and national costume is still worn for village and folk festivals. The Rhine, which springs from **Lake Toma** in the **St Gotthard**, runs through the **Bodensee** (**Lake Constance**) and cascades near **Schaffhausen** into the **Rhine Falls** – one of the largest waterfalls in Europe. On the banks of Lake Constance, **Stein am Rhein** is an especially picturesque small town with cobbled streets, fountains, half-timbered houses and a medieval atmosphere. **St Gallen's** old city centre is dominated by burgher houses from the 17th and 18th century. Not to be missed is the Baroque **Cathedral** and the famous **Abbey Library** (**Stiftsbibliothek**) in the courtyard of the old Benedictine monastery (incunabula and illuminated manuscripts), named a World Heritage Treasure by UNESCO.
EXCURSIONS: Boat trips on Lake Constance to **Konstanz** and **Lindau** in Germany or to **Bregenz** in Austria, and excursions to the **Duchy of Liechtenstein** can easily be arranged from here.

SOUTHEAST SWITZERLAND

GRAUBÜNDEN: There are 150 valleys in the rugged mountainous region of Graubünden (known as 'Grisons' by French-speaking Swiss), the largest, least populated canton of Switzerland, famous for glamorous ski centres, spa resorts and dramatic alpine landscapes. Graubünden also has the longest history of any region of Switzerland with countless castles, fortresses, churches and chapels and, from valley to valley, the local language changes from German to Romansch to Italian.
The climatic health resorts of **Arosa**, **Davos**, **Klosters** and **St Moritz** are renowned the world over, and not only for their winter sports facilities. Typical Engadine stone houses characterise the towns of St Moritz, **Pontresina** and **Zuoz**. The highest peak in the canton is the **Bernina** (4049m/13,284ft), bordering Italy and Austria. **Chur**, the capital of Graubünden and the oldest Swiss settlement, is the hub for many other ski resorts. Sights of the city include the **St Lucius Church**, the **Cathedral** (12th to 13th century) and the **Rhaetic Museum**. In the **Engadine valley**, small villages beyond **Zernez** and the **Swiss National Park** have cross-country skiing and summer walking areas. One-third of the 168 sq km (65 sq mile) Swiss National Park is covered with dense forest and is home to several wildlife species, among them roe deer, eagles, marmot and lizards.
SKI RESORTS: Many of the country's top ski resorts are located in Graubünden including chic, expensive Davos and Klosters, with excellent skiing facilities and lots of varied and sophisticated après-ski, and glamorous St Moritz with its top-notch on- and off-piste activities (snow-polo, horse-drawn sleighs, the Cresta run), glitzy nightlife and luxury hotels. Smaller ski resorts in the area include the beautiful spa town of **Bad Scuol**, the smaller resorts of **Flims** and **Laax**, and beautiful Arosa, popular with downhill skiers of all levels and also for cross-country skiing.
TICINO: The Italian-speaking, southernmost tip of Switzerland is the Ticino, divided from the rest of the country by the Alps but connected by road via the **San Bernadino pass**. Here the climate is subtropical and the atmosphere Mediterranean. From the Alpine valleys the road runs through **Bellinzona** with its three medieval castles, en route to the lake resorts of Southern Ticino. **Locarno**, on the shores of **Lago di Maggiore**, with its narrow streets, pavement cafes and lakeside lido is one of the most popular destinations, with a world-famous film festival in August. Further south, the health and holiday resort of **Lugano** lies on the **Lago di Lugano** between the peaks of **Monte Bré** and **San Salvatore**. The largest city in Ticino, it is a favourite holiday destination for the Swiss. Piazzas, palazzos, palms, the **Cathedral of San Lorenzo** and the promenade along the lakeshore give the city a special flair. Local ferries link Lugano with the scenic lakeside towns of **Gandria** and **Morcote**. During spring the area is in full bloom with fig and olive trees, pomegranates and myrtle. Local buses visit the picturesque villages of the area and funiculars run to the top of **Mount San Salvatore**. Coach excursions to the great passes of **Furka**, **Lukmanier** and **Oberalp**, and to Milan and Venice, can be arranged locally.

Sport & Activities

Hiking: This is a national passion in Switzerland, and hikers are very well catered for. Approximately 50,000km of trails lead through all kinds of terrain in this spectacularly beautiful country. Hiking times are given on the signposts, and trails are graded according to degree of difficulty. The organisation responsible for maintaining the trails and for coordinating local hiking associations is the Swiss Hiking Federation, Im Hirshalm 49, 4125 Riehen (tel: (61) 606 9340; fax: (61) 606 9345; e-mail: info@swisshiking.ch; website: www.swisshiking.ch). The Federation can supply maps and guide books, which may be purchased at a discount by members. Guided walks, weekend trips and holidays are regularly organised by the Federation and the local associations and are open to individuals and groups. Most associations run at least one day's walk per week (usually on Sunday), and these do not need to be booked in advance. All trips are led by qualified volunteer guides. Details of the walks and addresses of local hiking associations are given in the free booklet **Switzerland on Foot**, available from Switzerland Tourism or directly from the Swiss Hiking Federation. Programmes of walks are also published on the Federation's website (see above). In addition to the above excursions, there are also 'Radio Walks', which are announced during the season every Sunday at 0655 on Swiss Radio DRS in the *Guten Morgen* programme. The meeting point, cost, timing and route can be found online (website: www.swisshiking.ch) and on the special telephone line of *Swiss Hiking Trails* (tel: (61) 606 9346). Participants need merely to turn up at the station or meeting point as announced.
Mountain sports: These are widely practised, and include **climbing**, **ice climbing**, **ski touring**, **snow boarding**, **deep-snow skiing**, **heli-skiing** and **glacier walking**. The Swiss Association of Mountain Guides publishes a list of approved mountaineering centres as well as a list of approved guides. Staff at the centres are all qualified, and there are strict rules governing leader-participant ratios. Further information can be obtained from Schweizerischer Bergführerverband, Hadlaubstrasse 49, 8006 Zurich (tel: (1) 360 5366; fax: (1) 360 5369; e-mail: sbv@awww.ch; website: www.4000plus.ch) *or* from Switzerland Tourism. Accommodation is available in the mountains in the form of alpine huts or chalets. As these are open according to season, visitors should check availability with local tourist boards before arriving. It is often necessary to book in advance. For further information on skiing, see *Ski Resorts* in the *Resorts & Excursions* section.
Cycling: There are 3300 km (2046 miles) of well-marked interlinked trails, most of which offer easy cycling. Bicyles can be hired at most railway stations and at many other locations. Those hired at stations can then be returned to any station at the end of the tour. There are also **inline skating** routes throughout the country, varying in difficulty from easy to demanding.
Watersports: Lakes such as Lake Geneva, Lugano, and Neuchâtel offer **sailing**, **water-skiing** and **canoeing**. **Rowing** can be done on Lake Zurich.

Social Profile

FOOD & DRINK: Swiss cuisine is varied. The great speciality is *fondue*, a delicious concoction of *Gruyère* and *Vacherin* cheese, melted and mixed with white wine, flour, Kirsch and a little garlic. Other cheese specialities are *Emmental* and *Tête de Moine*. Regional specialities include *viande sechée* (dried beef or pork) from Valais and the Grisons where it is called *Bündnerfleisch*. The meat is cut wafer thin and served with pickled spring onions and gherkins. *Papet vaudoir* is a delicious dish made from leeks and potatoes. Geneva's great speciality is *pieds de porc* (pigs' feet). Pork sausages or salami come in a variety of local recipes including *Beinwurst*, *Engadinerwurst*, *Kalbsleberwurst* (calf's liver pâté), *Knackerli*, *Landjäger* and *Leberwurst* (pâté). Try *Rösti* (shredded fried potatoes) and *Fondue Bourguignonne* (cubed meat with various sauces). Cakes and pastries are also varied: *Leckerli* are Basle specialities (spiced honey cakes topped with icing sugar, decorated in Bern with a white sugar bear); *Fasnachtküchli* (sugar-dusted pastries eaten during Carnival), *Gugelhopf* (a type of sponge cake with a hollow centre) and *Schaffhausen* (cream-filled cakes) are also popular. Although there are many self-service snack bars, table service is normal.
A great variety of Swiss wines are available throughout the country. There are also spirits made from fruit, the most popular being *Kirsch*, *Marc*, *Pflümli* and *Williams*. Swiss beer of a lager type is also available. Bottled mineral water is an accepted beverage, with local brands including *Henniez* and *Passuger*. Bars/cocktail lounges have table and/or counter service.
NIGHTLIFE: Most major towns and resorts have nightclubs or discos with music and dancing, sometimes serving food. There are also cinemas and theatres, and some bars and restaurants have local folk entertainment.
SHOPPING: Special purchases include embroidery and linen, Bernese woodcarving, chocolate, cheese, Swiss army knives and luxury handmade clocks and watches. **Shopping hours:** Mon-Fri 0800-1200 and 1330-1830, Sat 0800-1200 and 1330-1600. Most shops are closed on Monday mornings.
SPECIAL EVENTS: For more specific details, contact Switzerland Tourism (see *Contact Addresses* section). The following is a selection of special events occurring in Switzerland in 2005:
Jan 3 *Chalandamarz*, traditional event to chase away winter. **Jan 4-5** *Cricket on Ice*, St Moritz. **Jan 17-22** *22nd World Snow Festival*, Grindelwald. **Jan 31-Feb 5** *St Moritz Gourmet Festival*. **Feb 9-12** *Carnival*, Biasca. **Feb 10-12** *Bern Carnival*. **Feb 11-13** *Zurich Carnival*. **Feb 17-19** *Geneva Carnival*. **Mar 11-13** *Easter Egg Market*, Wolfwil. **Mar 13** *Nordic Skiing: Engadine Ski Marathon*, St Moritz. **Mar 19** *La Nuit Blanche - Swiss Winter Sport Night*, Davos. **Apr 3** *International Zurich Marathon*. **Jun 2-5** *European Beer Festival*, Lausanne. **Jun 17-19** *Federal Yodelling Festival & Contest*, Aarau; *Music Festival*, Geneva. **Jun 19** *'Slow Up Hochrhein'*, Laufenburg. **Jun 21** *Fête de la Musique*, Lausanne. **Jun 26** *Alpine Spring Festival*, Grindelwald/Wengen. **Jul 14-24** *'Live at Sunset'*, music festival, Zurich. **Aug 1** *National Day*. **Aug 13** *Street Parade*, Zurich. **Sep 1-17** *La Batie*, Geneva. **Sep 2-4** *Art Air*. **Sep 3-4** *Schubertiade*, Neuchâtel. **Sep 5-11** *Swiss World Festival Vernier*, Geneva. **Sep 23** *Bachfischet*, children's festival and ancient custom. **Oct 12-16** *Lausanne Underground Film & Music Festival*. **Nov 14-20** *Comedy Festival*, Lucerne. **Dec** *Christmas Markets*. **Dec 3** *Course de l'Escalade*, public running through the old town, Geneva. **Dec 10-11** *Fête de l'Escalade*, historical event. **Dec 11** *New Year's Eve Run*, Zurich.
SOCIAL CONVENTIONS: It is customary to give unwrapped flowers to the hostess when invited for a meal. Avoid red roses; never give chrysanthemums or white asters as they are considered funeral flowers. Informal wear is widely acceptable. First-class restaurants, hotel dining rooms and important social occasions may warrant jackets and ties. Black tie is usually specified when required.
Tipping: A service charge is included in all hotel, restaurant, cafe, bar, taxi and hairdressing services by law; further gratuities are not usually required.

Business Profile

ECONOMY: Switzerland has a typical West European mixed economy with a bias towards light and craft-based industries: Swiss precision manufacturing such as watch-making is renowned throughout the world. The country is highly industrialised and heavily dependent on exports of finished goods (in total, exports are equivalent to just under half of Swiss GDP). Lacking raw materials of its own, almost all of these must be imported. In manufacturing, the machinery and equipment industry specialises in precision and advanced technology products: machine tools, printing and photographic equipment, electronic control and medical equipment. There is also a substantial chemical industry, employing 10 per cent of the workforce, which continues to grow steadily. Swiss firms have proved particularly adept at exploiting niche markets across a wide range of industries and products. Although half of the country's food is imported, the agricultural sector is a strong and major employer. The processed foods industry

has a high international profile, particularly in such products as chocolate, cheese and baby foods.
The service sector is dominated by banking, where the particular reputation of the Swiss banking community for discretion has attracted large deposits. The Government has come under some pressure to allow disclosure in the course of criminal and other investigations: recognising the international climate, the Swiss authorities have generally responded more flexibly of late. Switzerland remains one of Europe's major financial centres. Among other service industries, tourism is of growing importance: Switzerland receives around 10 million visitors annually and the industry contributes around $12 billion to the national economy. The economy has been stagnant during the last two years, largely a reflection of conditions throughout continental Europe; the economy contracted slightly during 2003, but is now resuming slow growth.
Switzerland is not a member of the European Union, although nearly two-thirds of its exports are sold to EU countries. The government is in the process of negotiating a new set of bilateral agreements with the EU, but the prospect of it joining the Union is as remote as ever. A referendum rejected even membership of the European Economic Area – a body created to reduce the economic barriers between the EU and the European Free Trade Association (EFTA), to which Switzerland does belong. In May 1992, Switzerland gained admission to the IMF and World Bank.
Switzerland's main trade partners are France, Italy, Germany and the USA.
BUSINESS: Businesspeople are expected to wear suits. Although English is widely spoken, it is always appreciated if a visitor attempts to say a few words in the language of the host. When visiting a firm, a visiting card is essential.
Office hours: Mon-Fri 0800-1200 and 1400-1700.
COMMERCIAL INFORMATION: The following organisations can offer advice: OSEC Business Network Switzerland, Stampfenbachstrasse 85, 8035 Zürich (tel: (1) 365 5770; fax: (1) 365 5221; e-mail: info.zurich@osec.ch; website: www.osec.ch); *or* Economiesuisse Swiss Business Federation, Hegibachstrasse 47, PO Box 1072, 8032 Zürich (tel: (1) 421 3535; fax: (1) 421 3434; e-mail: info@economiesuisse.ch; website: www.economiesuisse.ch). Information can also be obtained from the regional chambers of commerce in each canton.
CONFERENCES/CONVENTIONS: The neutrality, stability and conveniently central location of Switzerland make the country a favourite meeting place for conventions and international organisations. It has an extensive and highly developed network of conference destinations with all the major cities and many of the smaller alpine and lake resorts offering hotels and convention centres which are fully equipped with a complete range of facilities, including interpretation and audio-visual services. Each of Switzerland's main cities has its own Convention Bureau, whilst the Association of Swiss Convention Centres, Swiss Congress, oversees meetings activity throughout the country. The organisation is made up of the 19 leading congress locations in Switzerland and can help with the organisation of a meeting in any region of the country. Contact Switzerland Tourism (see *Contact Addresses* section); *or* Switzerland Convention and Incentive Bureau (SCIB), c/o Switzerland Tourism, Tödistrasse 7, 8027 Zürich (tel: (1) 288 1271; fax: (1) 201 5301; e-mail: scib@switzerland.com; website: www.myswitzerland.com).

Climate

The Alps cause many climatic variations throughout Switzerland. In the higher Alpine regions temperatures tend to be low, while the lower land of the northern area has higher temperatures and warm summers.
Required clothing: Warm clothes and rainwear; lightweights for summer.

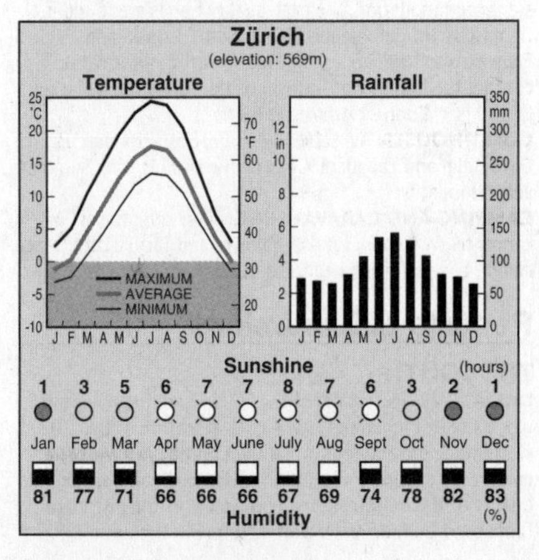

Syrian Arab Republic

LATEST TRAVEL ADVICE CONTACTS

British Foreign and Commonwealth Office
Tel: (0870) 606 0290 Website: www.fco.gov.uk
US Department of State
Website: http://travel.state.gov/travel
Canadian Department of Foreign Affairs and Int'l Trade
Tel: (1 800) 267 8376 Website: www.dfait-maeci.gc.ca

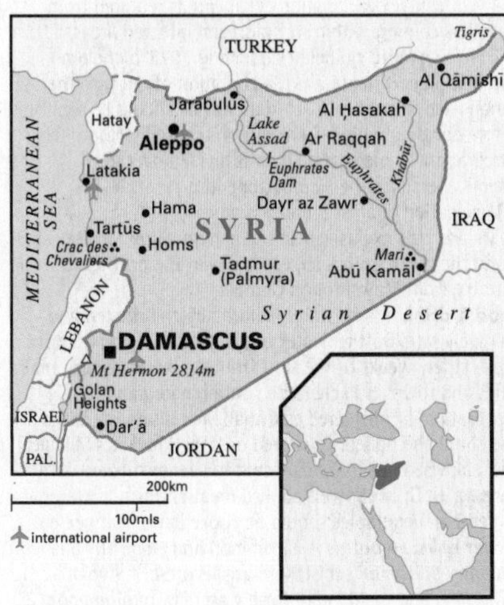

Location: Middle East.

Country dialling code: 963.

Ministry of Tourism
Victoria (Barada) Street, Damascus, Syrian Arab Republic
Tel: (11) 223 3183. Fax: (11) 224 2636 *or* 245 6143.
E-mail: min-tourism@mail.sy
Website: www.syriatourism.org
Embassy of the Syrian Arab Republic
8 Belgrave Square, London SW1X 8PH, UK
Tel: (020) 7245 9012 *or* 7201 8830/8831 (consular).
Fax: (020) 7235 4621.
Opening hours: Mon-Fri 1000-1200 (visa applications); 1400-1500 (visa collection).
E-mail: syrianembassyuk@hotmail.com
Website: www.syrianembassy.co.uk
British Embassy
Kotob Building, 11 Mohammad Kurd Ali Street, PO Box 37, Malki, Damascus, Syrian Arab Republic
Tel: (11) 373 9241/2/3/7. Fax: (11) 373 1600.
E-mail: british.embassy.damascus@fco.gov.uk *or* damascusconsular@fco.gov.uk
Embassy of the Syrian Arab Republic
2215 Wyoming Avenue NW, Washington, DC 20008, USA
Tel: (202) 232 6313. Fax: (202) 234 9548 (general enquiries) *or* 265 4585 (visa section).
E-mail: info@syrianembassy.us
Website: www.syrianembassy.us
Honorary Consulates in: Detroit and Houston.
Embassy of the United States of America
Street address: Abou Roumaneh, rue al-Mansour 2, Damascus, Syrian Arab Republic
Postal address: PO Box 29, Damascus, Syrian Arab Republic
Tel: (11) 333 1342. Fax: (11) 224 7938 *or* 331 9678 (consular section).
E-mail: acsdamascus@state.gov *or* nivdamascus@state.gov *or* ivdamascus@state.gov (consular section).
Website: http://usembassy.state.gov/damascus
Embassy of the Syrian Arab Republic
151 Slater Street, Suite 1000, Ottawa, Ontario K1P 5H3, Canada
Tel: (613) 569 5556. Fax: (613) 569 3800.
E-mail: syrianembassy@on.aibn.com *or* syrianconsulate@on.aibn.com
Website: www.syrianembassy.ca

TIMATIC CODES

Health	AMADEUS: **TI-DFT/DAM/HE** GALILEO/WORLDSPAN: **TI-DFT/DAM/HE** SABRE: **TIDFT/DAM/HE**
Visa	AMADEUS: **TI-DFT/DAM/VI** GALILEO/WORLDSPAN: **TI-DFT/DAM/VI** SABRE: **TIDFT/DAM/VI**

To access TIMATIC country information on Health and Visa regulations through the Computer Reservations System (CRS), type in the appropriate command line listed above.

Canadian Embassy
Street address: Lot 12, Autostrade Mezzeh, Damascus, Syrian Arab Republic
Postal address: PO Box 3394, Damascus, Syrian Arab Republic
Tel: (11) 611 6851 *or* 6692 *or* 6870. Fax: (11) 611 4000 *or* 2761.
E-mail: dmcus-td@dfait-maeci.gc.ca
Website: www.dfait-maeci.gc.ca/syria

General Information

AREA: 185,180 sq km (71,498 sq miles).
POPULATION: 17,800,000 (official estimate 2002).
POPULATION DENSITY: 96.1 per sq km (2002).
CAPITAL: Damascus. **Population:** 2,228,000 (official estimate 2003).
GEOGRAPHY: The country can be divided geographically into four main areas: the fertile plain in the northeast, the plateau, coastal and mountain areas in the west, the central plains, and the desert and steppe region in the central and southeastern areas. The Euphrates flows from Turkey in the north, through the Syrian Arab Republic, down to Iraq in the southeast. It is the longest river in the Syrian Arab Republic, the total length being 2330km (1450 miles), of which 600km (370 miles) pass through the Syrian Arab Republic. The Khabur River supports the al-Khabur Basin in the northeast.
GOVERNMENT: Republic since 1973. Gained independence in 1946. **Head of State:** President Bashar al-Assad since 2000. **Head of Government:** Prime Minister Muhammad Naji al-Otari since 2003.
LANGUAGE: Arabic, French and English. Kurdish is spoken by a small minority.
RELIGION: Over 80 per cent Muslim (mostly Sunni), with sizeable Christian (mostly Orthodox and Catholic) groups and Jewish minorities.
TIME: GMT + 2 (GMT + 3 from 30 March to 30 September).
ELECTRICITY: 220 volts AC, 50Hz. European-style two-pin plugs.
COMMUNICATIONS: Telephone: IDD is available. Country code: 963. Outgoing international code: 00. **Mobile telephone:** GSM 900/1800 network. Network operators include *Mobile Syria* (website: www.syriatel.com) and *Syrian Telecommunications Establishment*. **Fax:** Available at post offices and major hotels. **Internet:** Access to Internet services is available in universities and public offices. *Syrian Telecommunication Establishments* (website: www.ste.net.sy) is the main ISP. **Telegram:** Service available from the main telegraph office in Damascus, most hotels and post offices. **Post:** Airmail to Western Europe takes up to 10 days. Parcels sent from the Syrian Arab Republic should be packed at the post office. There are post offices in virtually all towns. Post office hours: Mon-Fri 0900-1500; larger branches will be open all day. **Press:** The *Syria Times* is published daily in English. All other newspapers are in Arabic (the most important ones being *Al-Baath*, *Ath-Thawra* and *Tishrin*). International papers are also widely available.
Radio: BBC World Service (website: www.bbc.co.uk/worldservice) and Voice of America (website: www.voa.gov) can be received. From time to time the frequencies change and the most up-to-date can be found online.

Passport/Visa

	Passport Required?	Visa Required?	Return Ticket Required?
Full British	Yes	Yes	Yes
Australian	Yes	Yes	Yes
Canadian	Yes	Yes	Yes
USA	Yes	Yes	Yes
Other EU	Yes	Yes	Yes
Japanese	Yes	Yes	Yes

***Note:** Regulations and requirements may be subject to change at short notice, and you are advised to contact the appropriate diplomatic or consular authority before finalising travel arrangements. Details of these may be found at the head of this country's entry. Any numbers in the chart refer to the footnotes below.*

Restricted entry and transit: Holders of Israeli passports will be refused admission; so will any passenger holding a passport containing a visa (valid or expired) for Israel and those holding a stamp indicating an Israel-Jordan border crossing.
PASSPORTS: Passport valid for at least six months required by all except nationals of Lebanon holding valid national ID cards.
VISAS: Required by all except the following:
(a) nationals of Algeria, Bahrain, Egypt, Jordan, Kuwait, Lebanon, Libya, Mauritania, Morocco, Oman, Qatar, Saudi Arabia, Somalia, Sudan, Tunisia, United Arab Emirates and Yemen;
(b) transit passengers continuing their journey by the same or first connecting aircraft within 24 hours, provided

holding onward or return documentation and not leaving the airport.
Types of visa and cost: *Single-entry:* £32. *Multiple-entry:* £50. *Transit.* Payable in cash or by postal order only. These fees are only for nationals of the UK. The cost of visas for other nationalities varies; consult the Embassy for further information.
Validity: Single-entry (three months from date of issue). Multiple-entry (six months from date of issue). Transit (three months from date of issue). Entry visas initially allow stays of up to 14 days. Extensions for up to three months are possible; apply at the Department of Immigration.
Application to: Consulate (or Consular section at the Embassy); see *Contact Addresses* section. In countries where the Syrian Arab Republic does not have diplomatic representation, visitors should apply by post to the nearest Syrian Embassy.
Application requirements: (a) Two completed application forms. (b) Valid passport with at least one blank page. (c) Two passport-size photos. (d) Fee. (e) A stamped, self-addressed envelope for postal applications. (f) For a *business* visa, a company letter stating the nature of the business.
Working days required: Seven.
Temporary residence: Applications to the Department of Immigration in Damascus.

Money

Currency: Syrian Pound (S£) = 100 piastres. Notes are in denominations of S£1000, 500, 200, 100, 50, 25, 10, 5 and 1. Coins are in denominations of S£25, 10, 5, 2 and 1.
Currency exchange: Syrian currency cannot generally be reconverted to hard currency. The country's banking system is state-owned, and there is at least one branch of the Commercial Bank of Syria in every main town. Hard currency can be exchanged for local currency in these branches.
Credit & debit cards: American Express and Diners Club are most readily accepted; some hotels will accept MasterCard. Tickets may be bought with credit cards. Check with your credit or debit card company for merchant acceptability and for other services which may be available.
Travellers cheques: Can be difficult to exchange and are not generally recommended.
Currency restrictions: The import of local currency is unlimited; the export of local currency is limited to S£5000 (when travelling to Lebanon). The import and export of foreign currency is limited to US$5000.
Exchange rate indicators: The following figures are included as a guide to the movements of the Syrian Pound against Sterling and the US Dollar:

Date	Feb '04	May '04	Aug '04	Nov '04
£1.00=	93.87	87.18	87.62	98.82
$1.00=	51.57	48.81	47.56	52.18

Banking hours: Normally Sat-Thurs 0800-1400 (banks tend to close early on Thursdays).

Duty Free

The following items may be imported into the Syrian Arab Republic without incurring customs duty (irrespective of passenger's age):
200 cigarettes or 50 cigarillos or 25 cigars or 250g of tobacco; 30g perfume for personal use; 570ml of spirits; 500ml of lotion and 500ml of eau de cologne; gifts worth up to S£250.
Prohibited items: Firearms and ammunition.

Public Holidays

2005: Jan 1 New Year's Day. **Jan 21** Eid al-Adha (Feast of the Sacrifice). **Feb 10** Islamic New Year. **Mar 8** Revolution Day. **Mar 21** Mothers Day. **Apr 17** Independence Day. **Apr 21** Mouloud (Birth of the Prophet). **May 1** Labour Day. **May 6** Martyrs' Day. **Oct 6** October Liberation War. **Nov 3-5** Eid al-Fitr (End of Ramadan). **Dec 25** Christmas Day.
2006: Jan 1 New Year's Day. **Jan 10** Eid al-Adha (Feast of the Sacrifice). **Jan 31** Islamic New Year. **Mar 8** Revolution Day. **Mar 21** Mothers Day. **Apr 11** Mouloud (Birth of the Prophet). **Apr 17** Independence Day. **May 1** Labour Day. **May 6** Martyrs' Day. **Oct 6** October Liberation War. **Oct 22-24** Eid al-Fitr (End of Ramadan). **Dec 25** Christmas Day.
Note: Muslim festivals are timed according to local sightings of various phases of the moon and the dates given above are approximations. During the lunar month of Ramadan that precedes Eid al-Fitr, Muslims fast during the day and feast at night and working hours are 0900-1400. Many restaurants are closed during the day and there may be restrictions on smoking and drinking. For more information, see the *World of Islam* appendix.

Health

	Special Precautions?	Certificate Required?
Yellow Fever	No	1
Cholera	2	No
Typhoid & Polio	3	N/A
Malaria	4	N/A

Note: *Regulations and requirements may be subject to change at short notice, and you are advised to contact your doctor well in advance of your intended date of departure. Any numbers in the chart refer to the footnotes below.*

1: A yellow fever vaccination certificate is required from travellers coming within six days from infected areas.
2: Following WHO guidelines issued in 1973, a cholera vaccination certificate is not a condition of entry to the Syrian Arab Republic. Up-to-date advice should be sought before deciding whether precautions should include vaccination, as medical opinion is divided over its effectiveness; see the *Health* appendix.
3: Vaccination against typhoid is advised.
4: Malaria risk, exclusively in the benign *vivax* form, exists along the northern border, especially in the northeast of the country, from May through October.
Food & drink: Mains water is normally chlorinated and relatively safe. Bottled water is available and is advised for the first few weeks of the stay. Drinking water outside main cities and towns is likely to be contaminated and sterilisation is considered essential. Milk is unpasteurised and should be boiled. Powdered or tinned milk is available and is advised but make sure that it is reconstituted with pure water. Only eat well-cooked meat and fish, preferably served hot. Vegetables should be cooked and fruit peeled.
Other risks: *Hepatitis A* is common and *Hepatitis B* is endemic. *Bilharzia* (schistosomiasis) is present. Avoid swimming and paddling in fresh water; swimming pools which are well chlorinated and maintained are safe. *Visceral leishmaniasis* occurs in the northwest.
Rabies is present. For those at high risk, vaccination before arrival should be considered. If you are bitten, seek medical advice without delay. For more information, consult the *Health* appendix.
Health care: Health insurance is recommended. There is no reciprocal health agreement with the UK. There are about 200 hospitals and 16,000 doctors; basic medical facilities exist in main cities but there are few outside them. Medical care is provided free of charge to those who cannot afford to pay. For more information, see the *Health* appendix.

Travel - International

Note: There is a continuing risk of terrorism in the Syrian Arab Republic. For further advice visitors should contact the relevant local government travel advice department.
AIR: The Syrian Arab Republic's national airline is *Syrian Arab Airlines (RB)* (website: www.syrian-airlines.co.uk). *British Mediterranean* (a franchise partner of *British Airways*) operates regular services from London to Damascus and two services to Aleppo.
Approximate flight times: From Damascus to *London* is six hours and from Aleppo is four to five hours.
International airports: *Damascus (DAM)*, 25km (18 miles) southeast of the city (travel time – 30 to 40 minutes). Two other international airports, *Aleppo* and *Latakia* offer connections to *Amman* and *Beirut* airports. A bus service runs every 30 mins from 0600-2300.
Facilities include banking, restaurants/snack bars, duty free shop and tourist information.
Aleppo (ALP) (Nejrab), 10km (6.5 miles) from the city (travel time – 20 minutes). Bus and taxi services go to the city. Facilities include banking, restaurants/snack bars and tourist information.
Latakia Airport (LTK) is situated 25km (16 miles) from the city. Although there are no scheduled flights serving this airport, some chartered flights run here.
Departure tax: S£200. Children under 10 years of age and transit passengers (continuing their journey within 24 hours and not leaving the customs zone) are exempt.
SEA: The principal ports are Banyas, Latakia and Tartus. The nearest car ferry sails to Bodrum in western Turkey. Beirut (Lebanon), however, is served – from Alexandria, Cyprus and Greece – and Damascus can then be reached in a couple of hours by road. An attractive alternative is to take a ferry either from Italy (Ancona, Brindisi or Venice) or from Greece (Piraeus) and go as far as Turkey (Bodrum, Izmir or Kusadasi). Three days should be allowed for the sea crossing and another three for the drive from there. Certain lines offer a mixture of cruise and car ferry; the return journey could be made via Bodrum, Heraklion, Rhodes, Santorini and Piraeus.
RAIL: Links go via Ankara (Turkey) and Istanbul. Change at Ankara for the *Taurus Express* to Aleppo.
ROAD: The principal international routes are from Istanbul, via the E5 road to Adana, Ankara and Iskenderun in Turkey. Enter at Bab-al-Hawa for Aleppo, or at Kassab for Latakia. From the south, the best routes are from Aqaba on the Red Sea in Jordan. To enter by car, a customs certificate must be produced; it is obtainable from Automobile Clubs and Touring Clubs against a deposit. **Bus:** Services are available across the desert, with routes from Aleppo and Damascus to Istanbul; Damascus to Amman; Damascus to Beirut and Tripoli; and Damascus to Riyadh.

Travel - Internal

AIR: *Syrian Arab Airlines* fly to Aleppo, Deir ez Zor, Latakia, Palmyra and Qamishly. In general, fares are exceedingly cheap.
RAIL: The railway extends 2200km (1364 miles). A service operates between Damascas-Aleppo-Kamechli. A second line runs between Aleppo-Latakia-Banias-Tartous-Homs-Damascas-Deraa. First-class carriages are air conditioned. There is also a connection from Haleb to the Lebanese border.
ROAD: There are 25,887km (16,086 miles) of roads. Traffic systems are poor and there are numerous accidents. Second-class roads are unreliable during the wet season. The principal route is Aleppo to Damascus and Dar'a (north-south axis). Traffic drives on the right. **Bus:** Services run from Damascus and Aleppo to most towns and are cheap, widely used and efficient. There are orange-and-white air-conditioned *Karnak* (government-operated) buses. Reservations should be made well in advance. Karnak bus routes serve their own terminals, which are usually in or near the city centres. There are also privately-run bus and microbus services which started recently all over the Syrian Arab Republic. **Taxi:** Shared taxis are available to all parts of the country. Service taxis (old limousines) run on major routes and cost 50 to 70 per cent more than Karnak buses. **Regulations:** Speed limits: 20kph (12mph) in the city; 80kph (50mph) on highways.
Documentation: International Driving Permit required. Green Cards are not yet accepted in the Syrian Arab Republic. Insurance is required by law and a customs certificate is needed. These are available from touring and automobile clubs.
URBAN: Publicly owned bus services operate in all major towns and cities. Most buses outside the capital, however, have no signs in a European script to indicate destination or stops, which can make travelling rather difficult. Taxis are widely available. Fares should be agreed in advance and according to the meter in the cities.
Travel times: The following chart gives approximate travel times (in hours and minutes) from **Damascus** to other major cities/towns in the Syrian Arab Republic.

	Air	Road
Aleppo	1.00	5.30
Latakia	1.00	5.00
Deir ez Zor	1.00	8.00
Qamishly	1.00	8.00
Palmyra	1.25	3.00
Dar'a	-	5.00
Al Hasakah	-	8.00
Homs	-	1.30
Hama	-	2.00
Tartus	-	3.00

Accommodation

HOTELS: While accommodation can generally be arranged on arrival from November to March, reservations are highly recommended throughout the year. Particularly during exhibitions, upmarket hotels in Aleppo and Damascus are often fully booked. Tariffs are the same throughout the year. All rates are subject to a 15 per cent service charge.
Grading: Hotels range from fairly low grade to luxurious 5-star accommodation. The best-quality hotels are found in Damascus, though Aleppo, Hama, Homs, Latakia and Palmyra also have luxury hotels. For further information, contact the Ministry of Tourism *or* the Tourist Information Centre (see *Contact Addresses* section).
GUEST HOUSES: Available in Aleppo, Bosra, Damascus, Dar'a, Idlib and Zabadani. *Cités Universitaires* offer summer accommodation.
CAMPING AND CARAVANNING: There are official campsites in Aleppo, Latakia, Palmyra and Tartus. Otherwise, camping is permitted near resorts.

Resorts & Excursions

THE SOUTH

DAMASCUS: The capital of the Syrian Arab Republic is the world's oldest inhabited city. A central feature of this cluttered and clamorous city is the **Ummayyad Mosque**, entered by passing through the **Al-Hamidiyah Bazaar**. The history of the mosque in many ways traces the history of Damascus; built on the site of a temple to the ancient

Aramean god Haddad, the original temple was adapted and enlarged by the Romans and used as a temple to Jupiter. It was later knocked down by the Byzantines, who replaced the pagan temple with the Cathedral of John the Baptist, which was subsequently converted into a mosque to accommodate the Islamic teachings brought by the Arabs in AD 636. The mosque houses the **Tomb of St John the Baptist**. The **Tikiyeh** mosque, built in the mid-16th century, stands out by its two elegant minarets and great dome. The 18th-century **Al Azem Palace** is now a national museum. Situated in old Damascus, a little way off the famous **Via Recta**, or the 'Street called Straight', is the **House of Hanania**, where St Paul hid, using the underground chapel for worship. The church in the **Damascus Wall** from where St Paul escaped in a basket is also still preserved. Also worth seeing is the **Long Souk** (market). Other attractions include the **Sayyida Zainab Shrine** (the granddaughter of the Prophet Mohammad), the **Tomb of Saladin** at the back of the Ummayyad Mosque, and the outskirts of Damascus, especially **Dummar**, with seasonal entertainment and restaurants. **Ghota**, the fruit orchards surrounding Damascus.

BOSRA: Bosra was the first city in the Syrian Arab Republic to become Muslim and has some of the oldest minarets in the whole of Islam. As a stopover on the pilgrimage route to Mecca, Bosra was a prosperous city until the 17th century. By then the region was becoming unsafe and the pilgrims began to take a less dangerous route further west. Bosra's main attraction is a well-preserved Roman **amphitheatre** (with room for 15,000 spectators) in which a musical festival is held every two years. The eastern exit to the town is one of its last surviving vestiges of a pre-Roman civilisation. The remains of an archway dating from the first century – the Nabatean period, of which nearly all traces are now lost – are unique in the Syrian Arab Republic. The **Mosque of Omar** in the centre of the town (called Jami-al Arouss, 'the bridal mosque', by the Bosriots), used to be a pagan temple and now stands as the only mosque surviving from the early Islamic period that has preserved its original facades.

EXCURSIONS: Further interesting sites include **Salkhad**, 23km (14 miles) east of **Bosra**, which has a citadel dating from the time of the Crusades; Al Inat, 26km (15miles) southeast of Salkhad, with its a great reservoir dug out of the rock; and the ruins at **Umm Al Qotein**, near the Jordanian border.

CENTRAL REGION

PALMYRA: This town is set in a desert oasis. The city was ruled by the legendary Queen Zenobia, who stood against the two great empires of the Romans and the Persians. Zenobia was taken captive to Rome when the Emperor Aurelian conquered and destroyed the city in AD 272. The ruins of the **Valley of Tombs**, the **Hypogeum of the Three Brothers**, the **Temple of Baal** and the **Monumental Arch**, now a world UNESCO Heritage Site, are some of the fine remains found over a wide area of the city, prized as containing some of the most famous monuments to the Classical period in the Middle East.

ELSEWHERE: The third-largest city in the Syrian Arab Republic, **Homs** is known for its industry, and is the site of the Syrian Arab Republic's first oil refinery. Of historical interest is the mausoleum of **Khalid Ibn al-Walid**. 65km (40 miles) outside Homs, **Crac des Chevaliers** is the most famous crusader castle in the world. A stronghold of the Hospitallers during the days of the Latin Kingdom of Jerusalem (1100-1290), it maintained a garrison of several thousand soldiers in peacetime. The castle, rising from an altitude of 670m (2200ft), was protected by watchtowers and supplied with food from the surrounding fertile countryside. The crusader castles of **Salaheddin**, near Latakia, and **Markab**, near Banyas, also merit a visit. Situated on the **River Orontes**, 45km (28 miles) from Homs, **Hama** dates back to beyond 5000 BC. The **Norias**, gigantic wooden waterwheels, are a unique feature, still used to provide water for the city and to irrigate the many public gardens. The orchards, the **Great Mosque** and the **Al Azem Palace's Museum** are also of interest.

THE NORTH

ALEPPO: Possibly older than even Damascus, Aleppo's massive **Citadel** stands on the site of a Hittite acropolis. This UNESCO World Heritage Site is one of the most magnificent examples of Islamic Arab military architecture in the Syrian Arab Republic. There are an impressive number of mosques in the city. For the tourist, the **souk** (market), made up of 16km (10 miles) of meandering low corridors lined with shops and bustling with activity, is probably the greatest attraction. The well preserved **hammams**, or public baths, are of interest, as are the ancient **khans** (rest houses).

LATAKIA: This is the Syrian Arab Republic's principal port and the metropolitan city of the country. Set on the Mediterranean coast, Latakia is a major holiday resort. The city stands overlooks the coastal strip on one side and the edge of the **Fertile Plains** (the 'Cradle of Civilisation') on the other. There are a number of antiquities, including the ruined **Temple of Bacchus** and a triumphal arch.

EXCURSIONS: Attractions in the area include the town of **Tartus**, beaches and mountains, and the **Latakia mountain** resorts of **Kassab** and **Slounfeh**. Near Tartus, 10km (6 miles) inland, are the **Drekish Mountains**, famous for the purity of their water.

THE EAST

Ja'bar Citadel is one of the Seleucid fortresses. Situated to the west of Raqqa, it stands on a spit of land and is reflected in the blue waters of the **Euphrates**.

Situated on the left bank of the river, the ancient city of **Raqqa** was built by Alexander the Great in the fourth century BC. Since the construction of the Euphrates Dam, it has played an important economic role in the life of the modern Syrian Arab Republic.

Halabiyé and **Zalabiya** are situated 40km (25 miles) from Deir ez Zor. Their ruins bear witness to their important military role during the reign of Queen Zenobia.

Deir ez Zor, considered to be the 'pearl of the Euphrates', is located on the right bank of the river. The orchards along the banks of the Euphrates harmonise beautifully with the golden desert hues and the silver thread of the river.

Rahba Citadel, near **Mayadin**, was built to ensure the protection of the Euphrates route and to withstand Tatar and Mongol invasions. The ancient city of **Doura Europos** (Salhieh) played an important economic and military role during the time of the Ancient Greeks, Romans, Persians and the Palmyrans.

Mari was built at a strategic point on the trade routes from the Syrian Arab Republic to Mesopotamia. The town's oldest ruins date back 5000 years. Mari's most impressive sight is the extraordinary **Royal Palace**. Built by Zimrilim, ruler of this important city-state 2000 years ago, this enormous palace boasts 300 rooms and halls. It was rediscovered in the course of excavations during the 1930s.

Sport & Activities

The Mediterranean resorts offer **canoeing**, **scuba-diving** and other **watersports**. Inland, there are numerous hotel **swimming** pools and public baths, particularly in Aleppo and Damascus. Many resorts now have facilities for **tennis** and there is a nine-hole **golf** club in Lebanon. **Angling** is most popular in the deep shoreline waters.

Social Profile

FOOD & DRINK: There are numerous restaurants in Aleppo and Damascus serving a variety of Oriental and European dishes. National dishes are *yabrak* (vine leaves stuffed with rice and minced meat), *ouzi* (pastry stuffed with rice and minced meat) and a variety of vegetables cooked with meat and tomato sauce. Among these vegetables are okra, French beans and *malukhiyya*. Table service is the norm and a meal is paid for afterwards.

There are bars serving a wide range of alcoholic drinks. Alcohol is permitted but restrictions are imposed during Ramadan when it is illegal to drink in public from dawn to dusk, even for non-Muslims.

SHOPPING: *Souks* (markets) are the best places for shopping, notably those in Aleppo. Local handicrafts in the Syrian Arab Republic are numerous and precious, including mother-of-pearl items (such as backgammon boards), olive-wood carvings, weaving and embroidery, leather goods and gold and silver jewellery. **Shopping hours:** Sat-Thurs 0930-1400 and 1630-2100 (summer); Sat-Thurs 0930-1400 and 1600-2000 (winter).

SPECIAL EVENTS: The following is a selection of special events occurring in the Syrian Arab Republic in 2005: **Jun** *International Flower Show*, Damascus. **Aug** *Friendship Festival*, Latakia. **Sep** *Cotton Festival*, Aleppo; *International Fair*, Damascus; *Silk Road Festival*; *Festival of Folklore and Music*, Bosra. **Oct** Olive Exhibition, Idleb.

SOCIAL CONVENTIONS: The Syrians are as proud of their modern amenities as their unique heritage and tradition of craftsmanship. Visitors will enjoy the hospitality that is a deep-rooted Arab tradition and sharing the pleasures of an attractive Oriental way of life. It is customary to shake hands on meeting and departure. A visitor will be treated with great courtesy. A souvenir from the visitor's home or company is well received. Conservative casual wear is suitable. Beachwear or shorts should not be worn away from the beach or poolside. Smoking follows Western habits. Smoking is prohibited in public from dawn to dusk during Ramadan. **Photography:** No attempt should be made to photograph anything remotely connected with the armed forces or in the vicinity of defence installations, including radio transmission aerials. **Tipping:** Often expected, especially in more expensive establishments; 10 per cent is generally acceptable.

Business Profile

ECONOMY: The main components of the Syrian economy are agriculture and oil. In the agricultural sector, cotton is the principal commodity and a key export. Wheat, barley, fruit and vegetables are the other main products, the bulk of which are grown for domestic consumption. Oil is the main industry and provides two-thirds of Syrian export earnings, although the future of the sector is limited by the relatively small size of the Syrian Arab Republic's reserves (which are already over half-exhausted). There are also reserves of phosphates (another export earner), iron ore and natural gas. The rest of the industrial economy is divided roughly between three areas: chemicals, rubber and plastics; textiles and leather goods; and food and drink. The service economy is relatively under-developed but expanding rapidly: tourism has seen exceptional growth. A particular problem for the Syrian economy in a very arid region is the availability of water. The Syrians have concluded a long-term agreement with Turkey over use of the northern part of Tigris/Euphrates river system (which also serves Iraq), but this is still a highly sensitive issue.

The government of Basil al-Assad has set a high priority on economic reform. Much of the economy is still state-owned and highly regulated. Some measures have been introduced to promote private enterprise and attract foreign investment; fiscal policy has focused on an overhaul and simplification of the convoluted tax system. The new cabinet installed in May 2003 - and reshuffled again in 2004 - has been tasked to accelerate the economic reform process, although it is likely to encounter many of the same obstacles as its predecessors in the form of well-entrenched vested interests and monopolies. The government must also tackle the problem of unemployment (officially 20 per cent but almost certainly higher). Annual GDP growth is around 0.9 per cent.

The Syrian Arab Republic's trade patterns have shifted since the demise of the Soviet bloc, with which it traded extensively. It is now more vulnerable to attitudes in Washington: under the Bush administration, the Syrian Arab Republic is classed as a 'rogue state' and since November 2003 has been subject to partial economic sanctions. This has a knock-on effect on trade with other countries. At present, the Syrian Arab Republic's main trading partners are Turkey and the main EU economies, particularly Germany, Italy and Spain.

BUSINESS: Formal suits are necessary for business. Businesspeople generally speak English and French. Appointments are necessary and visiting cards are widely used. Arabs often discuss business with more than one person at a time. A list of notarised translators is available from the British Embassy. **Office hours:** Sat-Thurs 0830-1430. All government offices, banks and Muslim firms close Friday and remain open Sunday; Christian firms are generally open Friday and closed Sunday. During the month of Ramadan, government offices start work one hour later than usual.

COMMERCIAL INFORMATION: The following organisations can offer advice: Damascus Chamber of Commerce, PO Box 1040, 126 rue Mou'awiah, Damascus (tel: (11) 211 339; e-mail: dcc@net.sy; website: www.dcc-sy.com); *or* Federation of Syrian Chambers of Commerce, PO Box 5909, rue Mousa Ben Nousair, Damascus (tel: (11) 337 344; fax: (11) 333 1127; e-mail: fscc@fedcommsyr.org; website: www.fedcommsyr.org).

CONFERENCES/CONVENTIONS: Hotels with conference facilities can be found in Damascus (Cham Palace, Ebla-Cham, Omayyad and The Sheraton), in Aleppo (Shahba-Cham), in Latakia (the Cote d'Azure) and in Hama (Apamee-Cham).

Climate

The Syrian Arab Republic's climate is characterised by hot, dry summers and fairly cold winters. Nights are often cool. **Required clothing:** Lightweights are essential in summer with protective headwear. Heavy winter clothing is advisable from November to March.

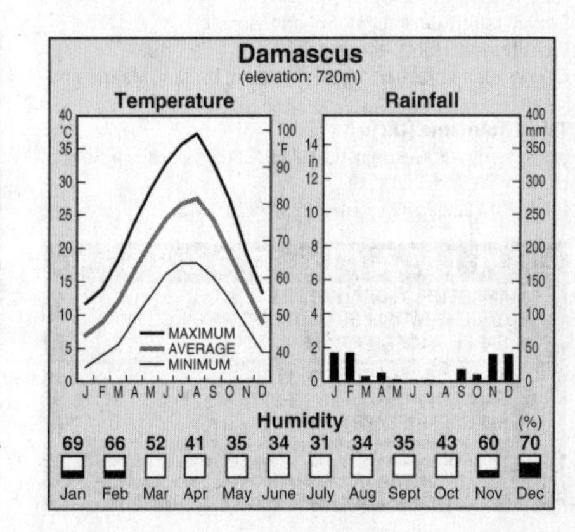

Tahiti and Her Islands

LATEST TRAVEL ADVICE CONTACTS

British Foreign and Commonwealth Office
Tel: (0870) 606 0290 Website: www.fco.gov.uk

US Department of State
Website: http://travel.state.gov/travel

Canadian Department of Foreign Affairs and Int'l Trade
Tel: (1 800) 267 8376 Website: www.dfait-maeci.gc.ca

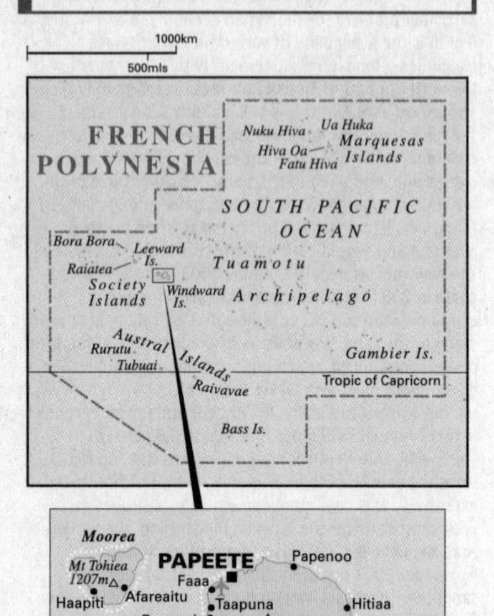

Location: South Pacific.

Country dialling code: 689.

Tahiti and Her Islands are officially known as 'French Polynesia' and constitute a French Overseas Territory; addresses of French Embassies, Consulates and Tourist Offices may be found in the *France* section.

Tahiti Tourisme
Street address: Immeuble Paofai, Batiment D, Boulevard Pomare, Papeete 98713, Tahiti
Postal address: BP 65, Papeete 98713, Tahiti, French Polynesia
Tel: 505 700. Fax: 436 619.
E-mail: tahiti-tourisme@mail.pf
Website: www.tahiti-tourisme.com *or* www.tahiti-tourisme.pf

South Pacific Tourism Organisation (SPTO)
Street address: Level 3, FNPF Place, 343-359 Victoria Parade, Suva, Fiji
Postal address: PO Box 13119, Suva, Fiji
Tel: (679) 330 4177. Fax: (679) 330 1995.
E-mail: info@spto.org
Website: www.spto.org
Also deals with enquiries from the UK.

Tahiti Tourisme Europe
28 boulevard Saint-Germain, 75005 Paris, France
Tel: (1) 5542 6121 (travel trade) *or* 6434 (public).
Fax: (1) 5542 6120.
E-mail: tahititourisme@tahiti-tourisme.fr
Website: www.tahiti-tourisme.fr
Offices also in: Copenhagen, Frankfurt, London, Madrid and Milan.

Tahiti Tourisme (UK)
c/o Synergy, 48 Westminster Palace Gardens, Artillery Row, London SW1P 1RR, UK
Tel: (020) 7222 7282. Fax: (020) 7222 1312.
E-mail: tahiti-tourisme@synergy-umc.com
Website: www.tahiti-tourisme.com

British Honorary Consul
Villa Horizon 6emeKm, Route Fare Rau Ape, PIRAE 98716, Tahiti, French Polynesia
Tel: 706 283. Fax: 420 050.

Tahiti Tourisme North America
300 Continental Boulevard, Suite 160, El Segundo, CA 90245, USA
Tel: (310) 414 8484. Fax: (310) 414 8490.
E-mail: info@tahiti-tourisme.com
Website: www.tahiti-tourisme.com

TIMATIC CODES

Health
AMADEUS: **TI-DFT/PPT/HE**
GALILEO/WORLDSPAN: **TI-DFT/PPT/HE**
SABRE: **TIDFT/PPT/HE**

Visa
AMADEUS: **TI-DFT/PPT/VI**
GALILEO/WORLDSPAN: **TI-DFT/PPT/VI**
SABRE: **TIDFT/PPT/VI**

To access TIMATIC country information on Health and Visa regulations through the Computer Reservations System (CRS), type in the appropriate command line listed above.

General Information

AREA: 4167 sq km (1609 sq miles).
POPULATION: 245,516 (official estimate 2002).
POPULATION DENSITY: 58.9 per sq km.
CAPITAL: Papeete (Tahiti Island). **Population:** 26,181 (2002).
GEOGRAPHY: French Polynesia comprises 120 islands divided into five archipelagos: the Society Archipelago, Tuamotu Archipelago, Marquesas Islands, Austral Islands and Mangreva Islands. The Windward and Leeward Islands, collectively called the Society Archipelago, are mountainous with coastal plains. Tahiti, the largest of the Windward group, is dominated by Mount Orohena at 2236m (7337ft) and Mount Aorai at 2068m (6786ft). Moorea lies next to Tahiti, a picturesque volcanic island with white sand beaches. The Leeward Islands to the west are generally lower in altitude. The largest islands are Raiatea and Bora Bora. Tuamotu Archipelago comprises 80 coral atolls, located 298km (185 miles) east of Tahiti. The Marquesas Islands lie 1497km (930 miles) northeast of Tahiti and are made up of two clusters of volcanic islands divided into a southern and northern group. The grass-covered Austral Islands south of Tahiti are scattered in a chain from east to west over a distance of 499km (310 miles).
GOVERNMENT: French Overseas Territory since 1946. **Head of State:** President Jacques Chirac since 1995, represented locally by High Commissioner Michel Mathieu since 2001. **Head of Government:** Gaston Flosse, President of the Council of Ministers since 1991.
LANGUAGE: The official languages are French and Tahitian. Other Polynesian languages are spoken by the indigenous population. English is widely understood, mainly by islanders accustomed to dealing with foreign visitors.
RELIGION: Approximately 55 per cent Protestant and 34 per cent Catholic.
TIME: Tahiti and Her Islands span three time zones.
GAMBIER ISLANDS: GMT - 9.
MARQUESAS ISLANDS: GMT - 9.5.
SOCIETY ARCHIPELAGO, TUBUAI ISLANDS, TUAMOTU ARCHIPELAGO (EXCEPT GAMBIER ISLANDS), TAHITI: GMT - 10.
ELECTRICITY: 110/220 volts AC, 60Hz. US-style two-pin plugs are in use.
COMMUNICATIONS: Telephone: IDD is available. Country code: 689. Outgoing international code: 00. Operator assistance may be required for international calls. **Mobile telephone:** GSM 900 network. Network operators include *Vini* (website: www.vini.pf). **Fax:** Post offices and some hotels have facilities. **Internet:** There are Internet cafes in Papeete and Moorea. **Telegram:** Facilities are limited to Papeete and Uturoa (Raiatea). Telegrams can be sent from the post office on boulevard Pomare, Papeete. **Post:** Airmail to Western Europe takes up to two weeks. Post office hours (in Papeete): Mon-Fri 0700-1800, Sat-Sun 0800-1000 (outside Papeete, there is a restricted service in the afternoons and at weekends). **Press:** There is an English-language weekly, the *Tahiti Beach Press*.
Radio: BBC World Service (website: www.bbc.co.uk/worldservice) and Voice of America (website: www.voa.gov) can be received. From time to time the frequencies change and the most up-to-date can be found online.

Passport/Visa

	Passport Required?	Visa Required?	Return Ticket Required?
Full British	Yes	No/2	No
Australian	Yes	No/2	Yes
Canadian	Yes	No/3	Yes
USA	Yes	No/3	Yes
Other EU	Yes/1	No/4	No/4
Japanese	Yes	No/3	Yes

Note: *Regulations and requirements may be subject to change at short notice, and you are advised to contact the appropriate diplomatic or consular authority before finalising travel arrangements. Details of these may be found at the head of this country's entry. Any numbers in the chart refer to the footnotes below.*

PASSPORTS: Passport valid for at least three months beyond applicant's last day of stay required by all except the following:
1. nationals of Belgium, France, Germany, Greece, Italy, Luxembourg, Monaco, The Netherlands, Portugal, Spain and Switzerland, who are holders of national identity cards.
VISAS: Required by all except the following:
(a) nationals of countries referred to in the chart above: **2** for stays up to three months; **3** for stays of up to one month; **4** for stays of up to three months unless mentioned under point c below;
(b) nationals of Andorra, Brazil, Bulgaria, Holy See, Hong Kong (SAR), Iceland, Liechtenstein, Macau (SAR), Monaco, Norway, San Marino, Switzerland and Venezuela for stays of up to three months;
(c) nationals of Argentina, Bolivia, Brunei, Chile, Costa Rica, Croatia, Czech Republic, Ecuador, El Salvador, Estonia, Guatemala, Honduras, Hungary, Korea (Rep), Latvia, Lithuania, Malaysia, Mexico, New Zealand, Nicaragua, Panama, Paraguay, Poland, Singapore, Slovak Republic, Slovenia, Uruguay;
(d) transit passengers continuing their journey by the same or first connecting aircraft; provided holding valid onward or return documentation and not leaving the airport.
Types of visa and cost: All visas, regardless of duration of stay and number of entries permitted, cost €35. In most circumstances, no fee applies to students, recipients of government fellowships and citizens of the EU and their family members.
Validity: *Short-stay* (up to 30 days): valid for two months (single- and multiple-entry). *Short stay* (31 to 90 days and double- or multiple-entry): valid for a maximum of six months from date of issue. *Transit* valid for single- or multiple-entries of maximum five days per entry, including the day of arrival.
Application to: French Consulate General (for personal visas), or Consular section at Embassy (for diplomatic or service visas); see *Contact Addresses* section for France. All applications must be made in person.
Application requirements: (a) Valid passport with blank page to affix the visa. Minors travelling alone must submit notarised parental authorisation, signed by both parents, plus one copy. (b) Up to two completed application forms. (c) One passport-size photo on each form. (d) Fee, to be paid in cash only if paying by person. If not, fee should be paid by cheque or postal order. (e) Evidence of sufficient funds for stay (two last bank statements, plus copy, or other proof of funds equivalent to US$100 for each day of trip). (f) Letter from employer, or proof of stay in country of residence. (g) Proof of address. (h) Medical insurance. (i) Return ticket and travel documents for remaining journey. (j) Proof of accommodation during stay. (k) Registered self-addressed envelope, if applying by post. (l) Detailed itinerary, including reservations and round-trip airline tickets (only required when visa is issued), plus one copy. (m) Proof of employment (eg last payslip or letter from employer). (n) Proof of valid health/travel insurance with worldwide coverage, plus copy. *Business*: (a)-(n) and, (o) Business invitation guaranteeing payment of travel expenses, plus one copy.
Working days required: One day to three weeks depending on nationality.
Temporary residence: If intending to work or stay for longer than 90 days, nationals should contact the long stay visa section of the Consulate General or Embassy (tel: (020) 7073 1248).

Money

Currency: French Pacific Franc (CFPFr) = 100 centimes. Notes are in denominations of CFPFr10,000, 5000, 1000 and 500. Coins are in denominations of CFPFr100, 50, 20, 10, 5, 2 and 1. The French Pacific Franc is tied to the Euro. (€1 is worth CFPFr119.331.)
Currency exchange: Exchange facilities are available at the airport, major banks (which may charge up to 5 per cent) and at authorised hotels and shops in Papeete.
Credit & debit cards: American Express, Diners Club, MasterCard and Visa are all accepted. Check with your credit or debit card company for details of merchant acceptability and other services which may be available. ATMs are common on Tahiti, with a few on the smaller islands.
Travellers cheques: The recommended means of importing foreign currency. To avoid additional exchange rate charges, travellers are advised to take travellers cheques in US Dollars or Euros.
Currency restrictions: The import and export of local and foreign currency is unlimited; amounts over €7622 must be declared.
Exchange rate indicators: The following figures are included as a guide to the movements of the French Pacific Franc against Sterling and the US Dollar:

Date	Feb '04	May '04	Aug '04	Nov '04
£1.00=	172.01	175.04	177.86	170.31
$1.00=	94.50	98.00	96.54	89.93

Banking hours: Mon-Fri 0800-1530.

Duty Free

The following items may be imported into Tahiti by passengers 17 years and over without incurring customs duty:
200 cigarettes or 100 cigarillos or 50 cigars or 200g of tobacco; 2l of still wine and 1l of spirits over 22 per cent or 2l of spirits up to 22 per cent; 50g of perfume and 250ml of eau de toilette; goods up to a value of CFPFr5000 (CFPFr2500 for passengers up to 15 years of age).
Prohibited Items: All food products of animal origin.
Note: (a) Plants, fruit, weapons, ammunition and drugs may not be imported. (b) All baggage coming from Fiji and Samoa is collected for compulsory fumigation on arrival in Papeete; allow two hours.

Public Holidays

2005: Jan 1 New Year's Day. **Mar 5** Missionary Day. **Mar 25** Good Friday. **Mar 28** Easter Monday. **May 1** Labour Day. **May 5** Ascension. **May 8** Victory Day. **May 16** Whit Monday. **Jun 29** Anniversary of Internal Autonomy. **Jul 14*** Fall of the Bastille. **Aug 15** Assumption. **Sep 8** Internal Autonomy Day. **Nov 1** All Saints' Day. **Nov 11** Armistice Day. **Dec 25** Christmas Day.
2006: Jan 1 New Year's Day. **Mar 5** Missionary Day. **Apr 14** Good Friday. **Apr 17** Easter Monday. **May 1** Labour Day. **May 8** Victory Day. **May 25** Ascension. **Jun 5** Whit Monday. **Jun 29** Anniversary of Internal Autonomy. **Jul 14*** Fall of the Bastille. **Aug 15** Assumption. **Sep 8** Internal Autonomy Day. **Nov 1** All Saints' Day. **Nov 11** Armistice Day. **Dec 25** Christmas Day.
Note: *Celebrations continue for up to 10 days.

Health

	Special Precautions?	Certificate Required?
Yellow Fever	No	1
Cholera	No	No
Typhoid & Polio	2	N/A
Malaria	No	N/A

Note: *Regulations and requirements may be subject to change at short notice, and you are advised to contact your doctor well in advance of your intended date of departure. Any numbers in the chart refer to the footnotes below.*

1: A yellow fever vaccination certificate is required by travellers over one year of age arriving within six days from infected areas.
2: Vaccination against typhoid is advised.
Food & drink: Mains water is normally chlorinated and, whilst relatively safe, may cause mild abdominal upsets. Bottled water is available and is advised for the first few weeks of the stay. Drinking water outside main cities and towns may be contaminated and sterilisation is advisable. Milk is pasteurised and dairy products are safe for consumption. Local meat, poultry, seafood, fruit and vegetables are generally considered safe to eat.
Other risks: Immunisation against *hepatitis A* and *B* is recommended. *Dengue fever* and *filariasis* occur.
Health care: Medical facilites are good on the major islands. Private medical insurance is recommended.

Travel - International

AIR: *Air Tahiti Nui (TN)* (website: www.airtahitinui.com) is the only Tahiti-based international carrier. Tahiti is served by *Aircalin (Air Calédonie International), Air France, Air New Zealand, AOM French Airlines, Hawaiian Airlines* and *Qantas* for long-haul international flights.
The *Polypass* (offered by Polynesian Airlines) allows the holder to fly between the Southern Pacific destinations of American Samoa, Fiji, Niue, Samoa, Tahiti and Tonga; Honolulu (Hawaii) and Los Angeles in the USA; Brisbane, Melbourne and Sydney in Australia; and Auckland, Christchurch and Wellington in New Zealand. The pass is valid for one year. Once a reservation has been made and travel begun, all travel must be completed within a maximum of 45 days. Tickets will be issued against the Polypass by any Polynesian Airlines office (a valid passport is also required). For further information, contact Polynesian Airlines (website: www.polynesianairlines.com).
The *Visit the South Pacific Pass* is valid for many airlines operating in the South Pacific, including most of the larger ones, such as *Air Caledonie, Air Marshall Islands, Air Nauru, Air Niugingi, Air Pacific, Air Vanuatu, Polynesian Airlines, Qantas, Royal Tongan Airlines* and *Solomon Airlines*. Offering reductions of up to 40 per cent on normal airfares, this sector-based pass allows for flexible island-hopping between the destinations of the Cook Islands, Fiji, Nauru, New Caledonia, Samoa, Tahiti, Tonga, Vanuatu and the more remote Melanesian and Micronesian islands, together with major cities in Australia (Brisbane, Melbourne and Sydney) and New Zealand (Auckland, Christchurch and Wellington). It is only available for people resident outside of the South Pacific. The journey must be started outside the South Pacific and only one stopover in Australia is allowed. A minimum of two sectors must be bought before departure (extra sectors can be purchased en route). There is a maximum of one pass per person, and passes must be used within six months of the first day of travel. Children under 12 years of age pay 75 per cent of the adult fare. For details and conditions, contact the South Pacific Tourist Organisation (see *Contact Addresses* section).
Approximate flight times: From Papeete to *Auckland* is five hours, to *Honolulu* is five hours, to *London* is 19 hours 20 minutes, to *Los Angeles* is seven hours 30 minutes, to *New York* is 16 hours and to *Sydney* is eight hours.
International airports: *Papeete (PPT)* (Faaa), on Tahiti, is 6km (4 miles) from the city (travel time - 15 minutes). Buses run regularly. Metered taxis are also available. Airport facilities include bank/bureau de change, post office, duty free shop, left luggage, news-stand, restaurant, bar, light refreshments, car hire (*Avis* and *Hertz*) and tourist information.
Departure tax: None.
SEA: The international port on Tahiti is Papeete and it's served by *Cunard, Holland America, P&O* and *Radisson Seven Seas*. Other cruise lines serving Tahiti include *Fred Olsen, Princess, Royal Caribbean, Silversea* and *Windstar*.

Travel - Internal

AIR: Domestic flights run by *Air Tahiti (VT)* connect Tahiti with neighbouring islands (Bora Bora, Huahine, Maupiti, Moorea and Raiatea) and remote archipelagos (Tuamotu East and North with Manihi, Rangiroa, Takapoto and Tikehau; Austral Islands of Rurutu and Tubuai; Marquesas Islands of Hiva Oa, Nuku Hiva and Ua Pou).
SEA: There are inter-island connections on the many ferries, catamarans, copra boats and schooners that make regular trips throughout the islands. Daily connections exist between Bora Bora, Huahine, Moorea, Papeete and Raiatea.
ROAD: Traffic drives on the right. **Bus:** Basic buses, known as *trucks*, offer an inexpensive method of travel. They leave from the central market in Papeete town centre travelling to all destinations. No schedule is operated. Bus stops along the way are indicated by blue signs illustrating the *truck*, from where a wave of the hand will prompt them to stop.
Taxi: Available in Bora Bora, Huahine, Moorea, Raiatea and Tahiti. **Car hire:** Major and local agencies, including *Avis, Daniel, Europcar, Hertz* and *Tahiti Rent-A-Car*, hire out cars on the main islands. **Documentation:** A national driving licence is sufficient.

Accommodation

Accommodation varies from air-conditioned, carpeted, deluxe rooms with telephones and room service, to thatched-roofed bungalows (Tahitian *pensions* where the bathroom is shared and may be outdoors with cold showers). In the outer islands, resort hotels normally have individual gardens and over-water bungalows and rooms, many built of bamboo; shows and dance bands are often laid on in the evening. A tax of 7 per cent is added to the cost of all hotel rooms, but this does not apply to pensions or family lodgings. There is a youth hostel in Papeete with 14 rooms; a youth hostel or student card is required. It is possible to rent a room in a family home through GIE Tahiti Tourisme (see *Contact Addresses* section) for a more genuine experience. There are also two campsites on Tahiti.

Resorts & Excursions

TAHITI: The capital, *Papeete*, is located on the island of Tahiti and has in recent years been transformed into a bustling city, very much at variance with the traditional *haere maru* ('take it easy') attitude of the rest of the country. It is, however, still an attractive and colourful port set in magnificent scenery.
To the west of the capital is **Venus Point**, where the first Europeans set foot on the island in 1767. It is overlooked by **Mount Orohena**, the highest point on the island. The Papeete public market, **Le Marché**, is open all week, but really comes to life on Sunday mornings when out-of-town merchants come to sell their wares. Flowers, spices, fabrics and fresh produce are on offer.
The surrounding area is characterised by its spectacular tropical scenery, banana groves, plantations and flowers. Places to see include the **Blowhole of Arahoho**, which throws water skywards; the **Faarumai** and **Vaipahi** waterfalls; the **Paul Gauguin Museum** and **Botanical Gardens** in **Papeari**; the **marae** (open-air temple) of **Mahaiatea**, **Papara Marae Grotto** and **Arahurahu**. The **Lagoonarium de Tahiti** offers four fish parks (including a shark pen) and an amazing underwater display (daily 0900-1700).
MOOREA: Some 17km (11 miles) from Tahiti, and connected to it by a 45-minute ferry service or seven-minute flight, is an island with a simpler and more rustic lifestyle and yet offering plenty of entertainment for the tourist, including traditional-style nightlife. Dominated by volcanic peaks, it also has dazzling white sand beaches and clear lagoons ideal for swimming, diving and snorkelling. Excursions include a visit to the beautiful **Opunohu Valley**, an ancient dwelling place, uninhabited for 150 years, with 500 ancient structures including temples or **marae**, some of which have been restored. **Le Belvédère** is a lookout spot from where the best view of the island may be had.
The nearby island of **Tetiaroa**, recently opened to the public and accessible only by air, is an important seabird sanctuary.
LEEWARD ISLANDS: The Leeward Islands of the Society Group are ancient and unspoilt islands, all less than one hour from Tahiti by plane or ferry. **Huahine**, to the northwest of Tahiti, comprises Huahine-Nui (big Huahine) and Huahine-Iti (little Huahine), which are linked by a narrow isthmus. Sheltered by the surrounding coral reef, the coastal waters and lagoons are good for encountering the local aquatic life. The archaeological site near **Maeva Village** is well worth a visit.
Raiatea is the second-largest island of French Polynesia, 193km (120 miles) from Tahiti, and is the administrative centre for the Leeward Islands. In former times, the island was known as Havai'i, the royal and cultural centre of the region. The ideal conditions make the island a year-round destination for sailing and fishing enthusiasts.
he 'Vanilla Island' of **Tahaa** is surrounded by the same reef as Raiatea, and offers a tranquil and relaxed lifestyle as tourism is only starting here. The breeze constantly carries the aroma of vanilla, from the island's numerous vanilla plantations.
BORA BORA: The most famous of the Leeward Islands is 45 minutes from Tahiti by plane. Excursions include visits to the small villages outside the main town of **Vaitape** and climbs up the two mountains of **Otemanu** and **Pahia**. There are many opportunities for watersports, such as deep-sea fishing, trips by glass-bottomed boat around the lagoons, scuba-diving, snorkelling and swimming on a nearby **motu** (small sandy atoll within the reef of Bora Bora). In common with so many other Polynesian islands, Bora Bora has many ancient temples. There are good hotels on the island.
OTHER ISLANDS: The **Tuamotu** group of islands is largely uninhabited. There are air and ferry links between Tahiti and several of the more popular islands, including **Rangiroa**, which has facilities for all forms of watersports.
The **Marquesas Islands** are less well known among tourists, and as yet they have no first-class hotels. Both Paul Gauguin and Jacques Brel are buried on **Hiva Oa**, and, on **Ua Huka**, it is possible to go horseriding between the numerous valleys. The island of **Fatu Hiva** offers one of Tahiti's most beautiful locations - the valley of **Hanavare**, hidden between volcanic rock on the **Bay of Virgins** - as well as the important archaeological site of *Puamau* with its intact 2.1m- (7ft-) high tiki, the largest on the Marquesas. The islands are four hours from Tahiti by plane. The **Austral Islands** have a generally cooler climate than the rest of French Polynesia. The mutineers of the 'Bounty' attempted to make a settlement on **Tubuai** in 1789. Accommodation is plentiful in the form of bungalows on or near the beach.

Sport & Activities

Watersports: The sea around the South Pacific islands offers excellent **scuba diving**. There are 32 diving clubs in Tahiti which are members of the French Diving Federation and which are open all year round. Equipment can be hired and charter boats can take divers to the best areas. Further details are available from Tahiti Tourisme (see *Contact Addresses* section). **Windsurfing** and **water-skiing** are also well provided for. To supplement the numerous sandy beaches and clear lagoons, there is an olympic-size **swimming** pool at boulevard Pomare, Papeete, as well as pools at many hotels. The largest **yachting** organisation is the Yacht Club de Tahiti. Waters around the islands are ideal for small craft, and several clubs and hotels hire out craft. Fully-equipped deep-sea **fishing** boats are available for charter at Tahiti Actinautic. The Haura (Marlin) Club is a member of the International Game Fishing Association. Other holiday villages and hotels can arrange trips.
Spectator sports: Football is popular throughout the islands and can be seen almost anywhere. *Fautaua Stadium* near Papeete is a major venue on Sunday afternoons. Tahitian-style **horse racing** can be seen at the Hippodrome in Pirae. Races are held 12 to 15 times a year. Other scheduled spectator sports include **archery**, **cycling** and **canoeing**.

Other: Club Alpin in Arue provides information and assistance for **climbing** *Mount Aorai*, with a shelter at 1798m (5900ft), *Mount Diademe* and *Mount Orohena*. Hourly and day-long **horse riding** tours can be arranged through Club Equestre de Tahiti and Centre de Tourisme Equestre de Tahiti, both at the Hippodrome, Pirae, Tahiti. **Tennis** courts are available at Fautaua Tennis Club, which offers temporary membership to visitors. Many of the islands' hotels have courts and some are available to non-residents. There is an 18-hole **golf** course at Atimaono. Mountain bikes and 4-wheel-drive vehicles can be hired to explore the interior. **Paragliding** is available.

Social Profile

FOOD & DRINK: All the classified hotels have good restaurants. Chinese, French, Italian and Vietnamese food is served, as well as the Polynesian specialities; Papeete is noted for Chinese and French cuisine. Tahitian food can be found in some hotels. Popular dishes include smoked breadfruit, mountain bananas, *fafa* (spinach) served with young suckling pig, *poisson cru* (marinated fish, for example, raw tuna served with coconut cream and limes), or *poe* (starchy pudding made of papaya, mango and banana). *Trucks* or lunch wagons parked on the waterfront sell steak, chips, chicken, *poisson cru*, *brochettes* and *shish kebabs*. A key to how expensive a restaurant will be is often indicated by dollar signs; for instance, $$$$ will indicate an expensive restaurant, whereas $ will indicate a budget restaurant.
A full range of alcoholic drinks is widely available.
NIGHTLIFE: Papeete is full of life in the evenings with many restaurants and nightclubs. Most hotels feature Tahitian dance shows, bands and other traditional entertainment.
SHOPPING: Facilities are concentrated in Papeete. Special purchases include Marquesan woodcarvings, dancing costumes, shell jewellery, Tahitian perfumes, *Monoi Tiare Tahiti* (coconut oil scented with Tahiti's national flower), vanilla beans and brightly patterned *pareu* fabrics that make the traditional Tahitian *pareo*. **Shopping hours:** Mon-Fri 0730-1130 and 1330-1700/1800, Sat 0730-1100. Shops will sometimes close for lunch, anytime between 1100-1400. Some shopping centres in the suburbs of Tahiti are open 0730-2000.
SPECIAL EVENTS: For a complete list, contact the GIE Tahiti Tourisme (see *Contact Addresses* section).
The following is a selection of special events occurring in Tahiti in 2005:
Jan *New Year Island Kaina Tour* (island tours in flower buses), Tahiti. **Jan 29** *Chinese New Year Celebrations*, nationwide. **Feb 12** *17th Tahiti Moorea Marathon*. **Feb 14** *St Valentine's Day Celebrations*. **Mar 11-13** *Pearl Regatta*. **Mar-Apr** *Billabong Pro Surfing Tournament*. **May** *Arearea I Tahiti Games* (inter-island games tournaments); *Arrival of the Bounty Commemoration*. **Jun 4-14** *4th Tahiti Nui Cup* (sailing regatta). **Jun 29** *Hiva Vaevae Autonomy Celebration*. **Jul** *Heiva I Tahiti 2005* (Tahiti's largest cultural festival). **Sep 24** *Raid Painapo* (mountain team race), Moorea. **Oct** *Tahiti Carnival*. **Oct-Nov** *Hawaiki Nui Va'a Outrigger Canoe Race*, Bora Bora, Huahine, Raiatea and Tahaa. **Dec 20-31** *Christmas and End of Year Festivities*, countrywide.
SOCIAL CONVENTIONS: The basic lifestyle of the islands is represented by the simple Tahitian fares built of bamboo with *pandanus* roofs. Local women dress in bright *pareos* and men in the male equivalent, but casual dress is expected of the visitor (except in Papeete, where bathing suits and shorts are not considered suitable dress). Traditional dances are still performed mostly in hotels, with Western dance styles mainly in tourist centres. Normal social courtesies are important. **Tipping:** In general not practised but tolerated, since it is contrary to the Tahitian idea of hospitality.

Business Profile

ECONOMY: The traditional Polynesian economy was agricultural, but that sector now accounts for less than 5 per cent of total output and employment. Coconuts are the principal cash crop and vanilla, coffee and citrus fruit are also produced in quantity. There is a substantial fishing industry, based on tuna, most of the income of which is derived from licences granted to foreign fleets.
Manufacturing is mainly devoted to processing agricultural products and a small mining industry has evolved following the recent discovery of phosphate and cobalt deposits. French Polynesia as a whole has suffered from a serious unemployment problem since the end of French nuclear testing in the mid-1990s; although much disliked by local governments and the majority of their peoples, the tests provided many construction and service jobs. As a result, Tahiti now depends heavily on remittances from migrant workers. The Government believes that tourism offers the best, and perhaps the only, prospect for a self-supporting economy. At present, French Polynesia as a whole receives around 230,000 visitors annually, and the industry is worth over US$400 million annually. The territory suffers from a serious trade deficit - imports exceed exports by a factor of 10 - so that considerable aid is needed from the French to balance the country's finances. France dominates the islands' trade; the USA is the other important trade partner.
BUSINESS: Informal in atmosphere. Literature will be in French, but English is understood in some business circles, particularly those connected with tourism. **Office hours:** Mon-Fri 0800-1200 and 1330-1730, Sat 0800-1200.
COMMERCIAL INFORMATION: The following organisation can offer advice: Chambre de Commerce, d'Industrie, des Services et des Métiers Polynésie Française (CCISM), BP 118, Papeete (tel: 472 700; fax: 540 701; e-mail: cci.tahiti@mail.pf.

Climate

Temperate, but cooled by sea breezes. Two main seasons: humid (hot and wet) from November to March, cool and dry from April to October.
Required clothing: Lightweight cottons and linens are worn, with a warm layer for cooler evenings. Rainwear is advisable.

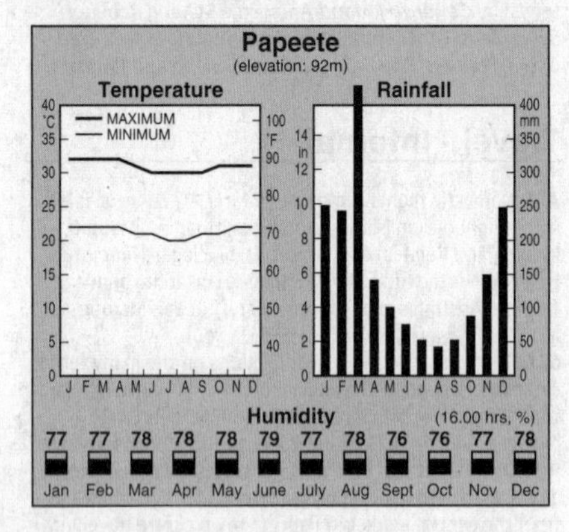

Taiwan (China)

LATEST TRAVEL ADVICE CONTACTS

British Foreign and Commonwealth Office
Tel: (0870) 606 0290 Website: www.fco.gov.uk
US Department of State
Website: http://travel.state.gov/travel
Canadian Department of Foreign Affairs and Int'l Trade
Tel: (1 800) 267 8376 Website: www.dfait-maeci.gc.ca

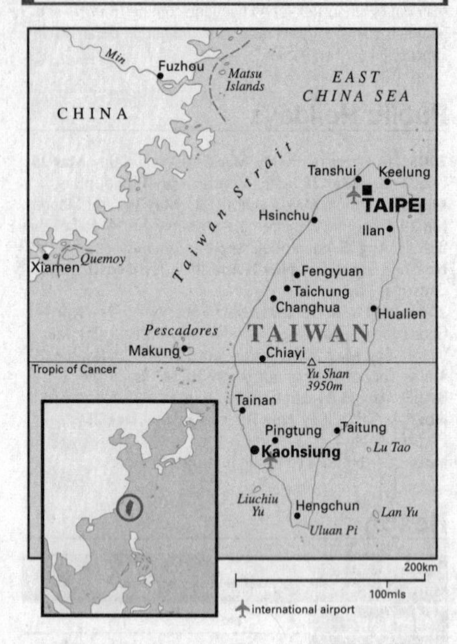

Location: Between the South and East China Seas, off the southeast coast of the People's Republic of China.

Country dialling code: 886.

Tourism Bureau, Ministry of Transportation and Communications
290 Junghsiau East Road, Section 4, Taipei, 106 Taiwan
Tel: (2) 2349 1635 *or* 2717 3737. Fax: (2) 2771 7036.
E-mail: tbroc@tbroc.gov.tw
Website: www.tbroc.gov.tw
Taiwan Visitors' Association
5th Floor, 9F-2, 9 Min Chuan East Road, Section 2, Taipei 104, Taiwan
Tel: (2) 2594 3261 (information hotline).
Fax: (2) 2594 3265.
E-mail: gtva@ms26.hinet.net
Website: www.tva.org.tw
Taipei Representative Office in the UK
50 Grosvenor Gardens, London SW1W 0EB, UK
Tel: (020) 7881 2650 *or* 7881 2654 (visa section).
Fax: (020) 7730 3139.
E-mail: request@tro-taiwan.roc.org.uk *or* tro@taiwan-tro.uk.net
Website: www.tro-taiwan.roc.org.uk
Opening hours: Mon-Fri 0930-1730; 1000-1230 (visa section).
Taipei Economic and Cultural Representative Office (TECRO)
4201 Wisconsin Avenue, NW, Washington, DC 20016, USA
Tel: (202) 895 1800.
Fax: (202) 363 0999 *or* 966 0825.
E-mail: tecroinfodc@tecro-info.org
Website: www.tecro.org
Offices also in: Atlanta, Boston, Chicago, Guam, Honolulu, Houston, Kansas City, Los Angeles, Miami, New York, San Francisco and Seattle.
Taiwan Visitors' Association
37th Floor, 405 Lexington Avenue, New York, NY 10174, USA
Tel: (212) 867 1632. Fax: (212) 867 1635.
E-mail: tvanyc@aol.com *or* tbrocnyc@aol.com
Website: http://taiwan.net.tw
Offices also in: Los Angeles and San Francisco.

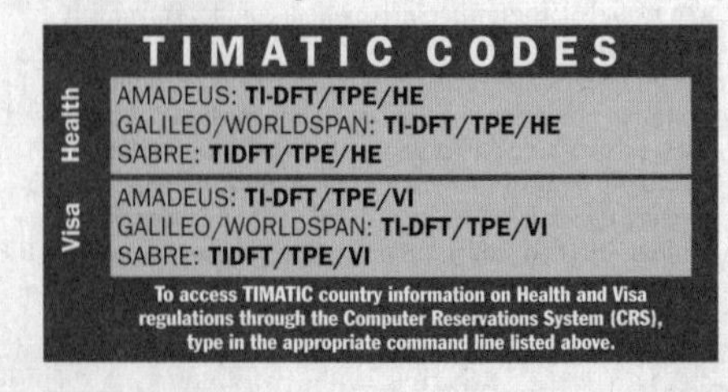

TIMATIC CODES
Health
AMADEUS: TI-DFT/TPE/HE
GALILEO/WORLDSPAN: TI-DFT/TPE/HE
SABRE: TIDFT/TPE/HE
Visa
AMADEUS: TI-DFT/TPE/VI
GALILEO/WORLDSPAN: TI-DFT/TPE/VI
SABRE: TIDFT/TPE/VI
To access TIMATIC country information on Health and Visa regulations through the Computer Reservations System (CRS), type in the appropriate command line listed above.

A B C D E F G H I J K L M N O P Q R S T U V W X Y Z

American Institute in Taiwan (AIT)
7 Lane 134, Hsin Yi Road, Section 3, Taipei 106, Taiwan
Tel: (2) 2162 2000. Fax: (2) 2162 2251.
E-mail: aitarc@mail.ait.org.tw *or* aitvisa@mail.ait.org.tw
Website: http://ait.org.tw
Office also in: Kaohsiung.
Taipei Economic and Cultural Office (TECO)
151 Yonge Street, Suite 1202, Toronto, Ontario M5C 2W7, Canada
Tel: (416) 360 8778 *or* 369 9030 (visa section).
Fax: (416) 360 8765.
E-mail: torgio@bellnet.ca
Website: www.rocinfo.org
Offices also in: Ottawa and Vancouver.

General Information

AREA: 36,188 sq km (13,972 sq miles).
POPULATION: 22,560,000 (2003).
POPULATION DENSITY: 623.6 per sq km.
CAPITAL: Taipei. **Population:** 2,641,856 (2002).
GEOGRAPHY: Taiwan (China) is the main island of a group of 86 islands. It is dominated by the Central Mountain Range covering 69 per cent of its land area and running its full length north to south on the eastern seaboard. Over 200 peaks exceed 3000m (9850ft), the highest being Yu Shan (Jade Mountain) at 3952m (13,042ft), and most are heavily forested. About 31 per cent of the country is alluvial plain, most of it on the coastal strip. The Pescadores (Fisherman's Isles), which the Chinese call Penghu, comprise 64 islands west of Taiwan (China, PR) with a total area of 127 sq km (49 sq miles). The offshore island fortress of Quemoy (Kinmen) and Matsu forms part of the mainland province of Fukien.
GOVERNMENT: Republic since 1912. **Head of State:** President Chen Shui-bian since 2000. **Head of Government:** Premier Frank Hsieh since 2005.
LANGUAGE: The official language is Northern Chinese (Mandarin). Taiwanese is widely spoken, and English is taught as the first foreign language in schools.
RELIGION: Buddhism; also Taoism, Christianity and Islam.
TIME: GMT + 8.
ELECTRICITY: 110 volts AC, 60Hz.
COMMUNICATIONS: Telephone: Full IDD is available. Country code: 886. Outgoing international code: 002. There is an extensive internal telephone system. **Mobile telephone:** GSM 900 and 1800 networks. Network operators include *Far Eastone Telecommunications, KG Telecom* (website: www.kgt.com.tw) and *Taiwan Cellular Corporation* (website: www.twngsm.com.tw). **Fax:** Facilities are widely available. **Internet:** Internet cafes provide public access to Internet and e-mail services. ISPs include *Asia Pacific Online* (website: www.apol.com.tw) and *Chunghwa Telecom/Hinet* (website: www.hinet.net). **Telegram:** Telegrams may be sent from post offices and hotels. **Post:** Airmail to Western Europe takes up to 10 days. *Poste Restante* facilities are available in main cities. **Press:** English-language daily papers include *The China Post* and *Taiwan News*. English-language journals include *Taipei Journal* (weekly) and *Taipei Review* (monthly).
Radio: BBC World Service (website: www.bbc.co.uk/worldservice) and Voice of America (website: www.voa.gov) can be received. From time to time the frequencies change and the most up-to-date can be found online.

Passport/Visa

	Passport Required?	Visa Required?	Return Ticket Required?
Full British	Yes	1	Yes
Australian	Yes	1	Yes
Canadian	Yes	1	Yes
USA	Yes	1	Yes
Other EU	Yes	1	Yes
Japanese	Yes	1	Yes

Note: Regulations and requirements may be subject to change at short notice, and you are advised to contact the appropriate diplomatic or consular authority before finalising travel arrangements. Details of these may be found at the head of this country's entry. Any numbers in the chart refer to the footnotes below.

Restricted entry and transit: Nationals of China (PR) are not currently permitted to enter Taiwan unless on business.
PASSPORTS: Passport valid for at least six months required by all.
VISAS: Required by all except the following, provided they have no criminal record, have a confirmed return air ticket or air ticket and visa for next destination, and seat reservation for departure:
1. nationals of countries referred to in the chart above (except nationals of Cyprus, Czech Republic, Estonia, Hungary, Latvia, Lithuania, Poland, Slovak Republic and Slovenia who *do* require a visa), and nationals of Brunei, Costa Rica, Iceland, Korea (Rep), Liechtenstein, Malaysia, Monaco, New Zealand, Norway, Singapore and Switzerland for stays of up to 30 days (this period cannot be extended).
Note: (a) Nationals of Czech Republic, Hungary and Poland are eligible to apply for a landing visa on arrival at CKS International Airport or Kaohsiung International Airport, on condition that they are holding tickets for an onward destination, and have no criminal record. The Landing visa is valid for 30 days and cannot be extended. They must provide a passport-size photo of themselves with a completed application form and pay a fee of NT$1200, plus a handling fee of NT$800. Nationals from countries who have a reciprocal agreement with Taiwan receive this visa free of charge; (b) Passengers arriving at Kaohsiung International Airport (including passengers arriving from China (PR) may apply for a temporary entry permit at the Kaohsiung Station Aviation Police Bureau. They must convert the permit into a visa at the Bureau of Consular Affairs or its Kaohsiung Office within three days. If they fail to do so, they will be subject to a fine; (c) Nationals holding Hong Kong (SAR), British National (overseas) or Macau (SAR) passports, if born in Hong Kong or Macau or if having previously visited Taiwan, may obtain a visa on arrival, valid for up to 14 days; (d) Passengers arriving at CKS International Airport may apply for a landing visa at the Visa Office at CKS International Airport, Bureau of Consular Affairs *or* the Ministry of Foreign Affairs.
Types of visa and cost: *Single-entry visitor*: £25. *Multiple-entry visitor*: £50. *Landing*: NT$1200, plus NT$800 handling fee. Multiple-entry visas are issued for business purposes only and require a document from employer regarding purpose of visit.
Validity: *Single-entry visitor*: up to three months; up to two extensions of 60 days each may be granted by local police stations for certain applicants, if they have stayed in Taiwan for an initial period of at least 60 days and documents have been submitted that provide evidence for the necessity of an extension. These visas are valid for three months from date of issue. *Multiple-entry visitor*: six months from date of issue. *Landing*: 30 days. A visa is not required by travellers continuing their journey by the same or connecting aircraft on the same day, provided holding confirmed onward tickets and the necessary travel documentation and provided not departing from the transit lounge.
Note: Travellers intending to stay more than three months in Taiwan will be required to take an AIDS test. If the test is positive, they will be required to leave the country.
Application to: Visa section of Taipei Representative Office (see *Contact Addresses* section).
Application requirements: (a) Application form. (b) Two passport-size photos. (c) Passport (valid for at least six months). (d) Documents verifying purpose of visit, or most recent bank statement, or letter from a sponsor in Taiwan (if appropriate). (e) Fee payable in cash, company cheque, by postal order or banker's draft. (f) For a postal application, a registered, stamped, addressed envelope. (g) Confirmed return air ticket and visa for next destination and confirmed seat reservation. (h) Cholera and yellow fever vaccinations are required if arriving from an infected area.
Working days required: One. However, some visa applications may be subject to delay. Applicants who have paid rush handling fees may collect their visas at 1630 on the same day.
Temporary residence: Those wishing to stay more than six months must apply for a Resident visa. Contact the Taipei Representative Office for further information (see *Contact Addresses* section).

Money

Currency: New Taiwan Dollar (NT$) = 100 cents. Notes are in denominations of NT$1000, 500, 200, 100 and 50. Coins are in denominations of NT$50, 10, 5 and 1, and 50 cents.
Currency exchange: All travellers are required to make a currency declaration in writing together with the baggage declaration. Unused currency can be reconverted on departure, on production of exchange receipts.
Credit & debit cards: Accepted in most hotels, restaurants and shops.
Travellers cheques: Accepted in most hotels, restaurants and shops. To avoid additional exchange rate charges, travellers are advised to take travellers cheques in US Dollars.
Currency restrictions: The import and export of local currency is limited to NT$40,000 and a permit from the Ministry of Finance is required for amounts over NT$8000. The import and export of foreign currency is unlimited, although amounts over US$10,000 must be declared on arrival. All exchange receipts must be retained.
Exchange rate indicators: The following figures are included as a guide to the movements of the New Taiwan Dollar against Sterling and the US Dollar:

Credit: Republic of China Government Information Office

Date	Feb '04	May '04	Aug '04	Nov '04
£1.00=	60.70	59.41	62.70	61.02
$1.00=	33.35	33.26	34.04	32.22

Banking hours: Mon-Fri 0900-1530.

Duty Free

The following items may be imported by persons over 20 years of age without incurring customs duty: *200 cigarettes or 25 cigars or 454g of tobacco; One bottle (not more than 1l) of alcoholic beverage; reasonable quantities of perfume; other goods for personal use up to the value of NT$20,000 (NT$10,000 for passengers under 20 years of age).*
Prohibited items: Narcotics, arms, ammunition, gambling articles, non-canned meat products, fresh fruit and toy pistols. Publications promoting communism are prohibited, as are items originating in Albania, Bulgaria, Cambodia, China (PR), Cuba, Korea (Dem Rep), Laos, Romania, Vietnam and members of the CIS. All baggage must be itemised and declared in writing.

Public Holidays

2005: Jan 1-3 Founding of the Republic of China and New Year's Day. **Feb 9-11** Chinese New Year. **Feb 28** Peace Memorial Day. **Mar 29** Youth Day. **Apr 4** Women's/Children's Day and Tomb-Sweeping Day. **May 1** Labour Day. **May 8** Mother's Day. **Jun 11** (5th Day, 5th Moon) Dragon Boat Festival. **Aug 8** Father's Day. **Aug 19** (15th Day, 7th Moon) Ghost Festival. **Sep 3** Armed Forces Day. **Sep 19** (15th Day, 8th Moon) Mid-Autumn Moon Festival. **Sep 28** Teacher's Day (Confucius' Birthday). **Oct 10** National Day. **Oct 25** Taiwan's Retrocession Day. **Nov 12** Birthday of Dr Sun Yat-sen. **Dec 25** Constitution Day.
2006: Jan 1-3 Founding of the Republic of China and New Year's Day. **Jan 29-31** Chinese New Year. **Feb 28** Peace Memorial Day. **Mar 29** Youth Day. **Apr 4** Women's/Children's Day and Tomb-Sweeping Day. **May 1** Labour Day. **May 8** Mother's Day. **May 31** Dragon Boat Festival. **Aug 8** Father's Day. **Sep 3** Armed Forces Day. **Sep 7** Ghost Festival. **Sep 28** Teacher's Day (Confucius' Birthday). **Oct 6** Mid-Autumn Moon Festival. **Oct 10** National Day. **Oct 25** Taiwan's Retrocession Day. **Nov 12** Birthday of Dr Sun Yat-sen. **Dec 25** Constitution Day.

Health

	Special Precautions?	Certificate Required?
Yellow Fever	No	1
Cholera	Yes	2
Typhoid & Polio	3	N/A
Malaria	No	N/A

Note: Regulations and requirements may be subject to change at short notice, and you are advised to contact your doctor well in advance of your intended date of departure. Any numbers in the chart refer to the footnotes below.

1: A yellow fever vaccination certificate is required of travellers arriving from infected areas.
2: A cholera vaccination certificate is a condition of entry if arriving or having passed through an infected area.
3: Vaccination against typhoid is advised.
Food & drink: All water should be regarded as being potentially contaminated. Water used for drinking, brushing teeth or making ice should have first been boiled or otherwise sterilised. Milk is unpasteurised and should be boiled. Powdered or tinned milk is available and is advised, but make sure that it is reconstituted with pure water. Avoid dairy products which are likely to have been made from unboiled milk. Only eat well-cooked meat and fish, preferably served hot. Pork, salad and mayonnaise may carry increased risk. Vegetables should be cooked and fruit peeled.
Other risks: Immunisation against *hepatitis A, B, diphtheria* and *tuberculosis* is recommended. *Japanese encephalitis, dengue fever, influenza* and *visceral leishmaniasis* occur. Rhesus negative blood is rare.
Health care: Health care facilities are good and doctors

Credit: © Republic of China Government Information Office

well trained. Imported medicines are expensive, but locally produced and manufactured medicines are plentiful. Health insurance is recommended.

Travel - International

Travel warning: Earthquakes (mostly minor) occur regularly and typhoons and tropical storms are a risk: visitors are advised to inform themselves about emergency procedures for such events.
AIR: The national airline is *China Airlines (CI)* (website: www.china-airlines.com). *EVA Airways (BR)* offers flights to destinations throughout Asia (excluding China, PR), Australia, Europe, New Zealand and North America. Other airlines serving Taiwan include *British Asia Airways*, *Continental Airlines*, *Singapore Airlines* and *Thai Airways*.
Approximate flight times: From Taipei to *London* is 15 hours 20 minutes including stopover in Hong Kong.
International airports: *Chiang Kai-shek-Taipei (TPE)* is 40km (25 miles) south of the city (travel time - 30 minutes). Airport facilities include an outgoing duty free shop, post office, car hire, bank/bureau de change, bar/restaurant and tourist information. Buses depart every 15 to 20 minutes for both Sung Shan (domestic) airport and the main railway station. Taxis and buses are available to the city centre.
Kaohsiung International (KHH) (website: www.kia.gov.tw) is 9km (4 miles) from the town centre. Airport facilities include an outgoing duty free shop, car hire, taxi rank, bank/bureau de change, post office and bar/ restaurant. A regular bus service is available (travel time - 30 minutes).
Departure tax: None.
SEA: Ferries run regularly between Keelung and Kaohsiung ports (Taiwan) and Okinawa (Japan). There are also sea links between Kaosiung and Macau.

Credit: © Republic of China Government Information Office

Travel - Internal

AIR: *Far Eastern Air Transport*, *Mandarin Airlines*, *Transasia Airways* and *Uni Air* are amongst the domestic airlines that run services to local destinations from Sung Shan Airport, Taipei.
SEA: There are reasonable connections from local ports. For details, contact port authorities.
RAIL: Services are provided to destinations all over the island by the *Taiwan Railway Administration* (website: www.railway.gov.tw). The main tourist routes are Taipei-Taichung-Chiayi-Tainan-Kaohsiung (a top-class service), Taipei-Taichung-Sun Moon Lake (with the last leg of the journey by bus), Chiayi-Alishan (with spectacular mountain scenery) and Taipei-New Hualian-Taitung (scenic coastal route). Air-conditioned electric trains run at least hourly from Taipei to Kaohsiung; some trains have restaurant cars. Children under three travel free; children aged three to 13 pay half fare. Train tickets can be purchased at many major hotels in Taipei, as well as at the main railway station.
ROAD: Traffic drives on the right. There is an adequate road system joining all major cities. A highway links Taipei and Kaohsiung. Some main streets have English signs. Congestion can be a problem, and mudslides may block mountain roads. **Bus:** There are both local and long-distance bus and coach services. **Taxi:** These are plentiful and inexpensive (metered). The destination may have to be written in Chinese for the driver. **Car hire:** This is available in major towns. **Documentation:** An International Driving Permit is required.
URBAN: A number of private bus companies provide extensive services in Taipei. An unfinished Mass Rapid Transit (MRT) system, a monorail train, serves Taipei and its suburbs. Metered taxis are available in Taipei; tipping is not expected, but it is starting to come into practice.
TRAVEL TIMES: The following chart gives approximate travel times (in hours and minutes) from **Taipei** to other major cities/towns:

	Air	Road	Rail
Kaohsiung	0.40	5.30	4.40
Tainan	0.40	4.30	4.10
Taichung	0.30	2.30	2.30
Hualien	0.30	7.00	3.00
Taitung	0.50	10.00	5.30
Sun Moon L.	-	4.30	-
Alishan	-	6.00	-
Kenting	-	6.30	-
Makung	0.40	-	-

Accommodation

HOTELS: There are over 500 tourist hotels in the country offering a broad range of accommodation and services. Prices range from US$30-50 a day for smaller hotels, with US$90-150 a day being average. For details, contact the Press Division of the Taipei Representative Office in the UK or the Taiwan Visitors Bureau. Many hotels belong to the International Tourist Hotel Association of Taipei (tel: (2) 2721 7379). **Grading:** Hotels are rated on a scale of **1 to 5 'Plum Blossoms'**, using a system equivalent to the more familiar 5-star system, with 3 Plum Blossoms being about average:
2 to 3 Plum Blossoms: The 80 hotels in these categories are clean, comfortable and functional.
4 to 5 Plum Blossoms: 50 hotels (half of which are in Taipei) are in these categories. The hotels are luxury class with a range of services and facilities, eg tennis courts, swimming pools and beauty salons.
CAMPING/CARAVANNING: Campsites are available.
YOUTH HOSTELS: Dormitory and non-dormitory rooms are available in major cities and in scenic areas.

Resorts & Excursions

TAIPEI

The principal city in the north, Taipei was designated a 'special municipality' in July 1967, thus acquiring the same status as a province and its mayor the same rank as a provincial governor.
The area of the city has expanded to four times its original size, making it the fastest-growing city in Asia.
The city centre contains the **National Museum of History**, the **Taipei Fine Arts Museum**, the **Taiwan Provincial Museum** and **Chung Cheng** (**Chiang Kai-shek**) **Memorial Hall**, which is a fine example of classical Chinese architecture. The magnificent main entrance is more than 30m (100ft) high. One of Taipei's new attractions is a tour of the **Fu Hsing Dramatic Arts Academy** where traditional Chinese opera and acrobatic performers are trained and where they stage shows. Also new to Taipei is the **City of Cathay**, a replica of an ancient Chinese town which is located within the **Chinese Culture and Movie Centre**.
The **Lungshan** (**Dragon Mountain**) **Temple** is dedicated to Kuan Yin, the Goddess of Mercy, and was built in 1740. The temple, one of more than 5000 temples and shrines in the country, is regarded as the island's finest example of temple architecture.
Among other outstanding buildings of classical Chinese architecture in Taipei are the **Martyrs' Shrine**, the **Sun Yat-sen Memorial Hall** and the **Chungsham Building** in the Yangmingshan district of the metropolis, 40 minutes' drive from the centre of Taipei, where the **National Palace Museum** can also be found; it houses the world's largest and most priceless collection of Chinese art treasures (over 6000 items). **Yangmingshan National Park** is famous for its cherry and azalea trees, and attracts thousands of visitors at blossom time.

BEYOND THE CAPITAL

THE NORTH: Keelung has an imposing hilltop statue of *Kuan Yin*, the Goddess of Mercy. The northeast coastal road offers a spectacular drive, passing the foothills of the Central Mountain Range and overlooking the East China Sea and the Pacific Ocean. The traveller will pass through many small villages, the lifestyles of which have changed little with the advent of high technology. Other outstanding attractions of the area include **Yehliu**, noted for its fantastic rock formations (**Queen's Head**); **Green Bay** and **Chinshan** beaches, with full beach resort facilities; **Shihmen Dam**; and **Wulai**, a mountain resort south of Taipei. Wulai is the site of a hilltop park and of a village inhabited by aboriginals who, besides making and selling artefacts, give song and dance performances for tourists. The **Northeast Coast National Scenic Area**, also with unusual rock formations, is not only good for swimming, diving, surfing, water-skiing and camping, but also the best place for seashore fishing and rock climbing. **Window on China** at **Lungtan**, 53km (33 miles) southwest of Taipei, contains reproductions on a scale of 1:25 of historical and other notable Chinese sites.
CENTRAL TAIWAN: The centre of the island has the most varied landscape. The east-west cross-island highway passes through spectacular mountain passes, most notably the **Taroko Gorge**, a ravine with towering cliffs shot through with extensive marble deposits. **Lishan**, located 1945m (6381ft) up on **Pear Mountain**, is a popular mountain resort. Other popular sights in the mountains include the **Sun Moon Lake**, the **Chitou Forest** recreation area, **Yu Shan** (**Jade Mountain**), and the alpine railway to **Alishan**.
Throughout the central area, there are numerous temples. The region's main towns are **Taichung**, one of the largest ports on the island, and **Hualien** in the east.
THE SOUTH: Kenting National Park is a popular forest recreation area boasting fine beaches, coral lakes, a bird sanctuary and, more recently, facilities for watersports and golf, all set amidst tropical coastal forest. **Kaohsiung** is the main industrial centre and has the island's only other main airport, besides Taipei's Chiang Kai-shek. **Tainan**, the oldest city on the island, is known as the 'City of 100 Temples'; there are in fact 220, amongst them some of the best examples of Confucian temple architecture on the island.
LANYU: Lanyu (**Orchid Island**), one of the smaller islands off the southeast coast, is the home of the aboriginal Yami, one of the world's last surviving hunter-gatherer tribes. **Lotus Lake** in Kaohsiung is the site of the Spring and Autumn pavilions and of the Dragon and Tiger pagodas.

Sport & Activities

Watersports: Taiwan's best **diving** tends to be off the islands around the coast, where the water is clearer and strong sea currents have kept pollution to a minimum. The sites at *Green Island* to the east include *Nanliao*, with beautiful coral; *Chungliao Submerged Reef* (suitable only for advanced divers); and *Tapaisha. Orchid Island* is surrounded by coral reefs and features several recommended dive sites.
The coral reefs of the south and the Pescadores Islands are considered good skindiving areas. Sharks and barracudas are rare in the waters around Taiwan. For further information, contact the Chinese Taipei Diving Association, No 34, Section 2, Chih Shan Road, Taipei (tel: (2) 2883 9466; fax: (2) 2883 9468). Rivers, lakes and the sea are ideal for **swimming**. The best time for swimming on the north coast is May to September; the south coast has warm waters all year round. **Hot springs** abound throughout the country. Some of the sites are easily accessible and provide baths, hot tubs and hotel facilities. Lakes, rivers, fish farms and the sea offer mainly unrestricted **fishing**. Near Taipei, there is good fishing at the Tamsui and Hsintien rivers, Green Lake and Shihmen Reservoir.
Other: There are several year-round **golf** courses. For further information, contact the *Golf Association of the ROC (Taiwan)*, 12F-1, 125 Nanking E. Road, Section 2, Taipei (tel: (2) 2516 5611; fax: (2) 2516 3208; website: www.rocgolf.com). **Ten-pin bowling** alleys and **roller-skating** rinks are quite common in major cities. Tapei also has two **ice skating** rinks. **Hiking** in the numerous parks is also popular.

Social Profile

FOOD & DRINK: The Chinese, never at a loss for vivid description, describe their cuisine as an 'ancient art of ultimate harmony: pleasing to the eye; mouth-watering; and a delight to the palate'. Culinary styles come from all over China including Canton, Hunan, Mongolia, Peking, Shanghai, Szechuan and Taiwan. Cantonese food is more colourful and sweeter than that of other regions. Dishes include fried shrimp with cashews, onion-marinated chicken, beef with oyster sauce and sweet-and-sour pork. Pastries include steamed dumplings stuffed with meat, sweet paste or preserves, buns, deep-fried spring rolls and tarts. Pekinese cooking is mild, combining roast or barbecued meat (often cooked at the table), vegetables and flat pancake wrappers. Dishes include *Peking duck*, carp cooked three ways, steamed prawns, chicken-in-paper, diced chicken in heavy sauce, eels with pepper sauce and ham marrow sauce. Szechuan cooking is hot and spicy, based on red chilli pepper and garlic. Dishes include *Mother Ma's bean curd*, aubergine with garlic sauce, *Gungbao chicken*, fried prawns with pepper sauce, and minced chicken with *Gingko* nuts. Fried breads make a pleasant

change from rice.
Shanghai cooking is mostly seafood with rich salty sauces. Dishes include shark's fin in chicken, mushroom with crab meat, *ningpo* (fried eel), shark's fin soup and West Lake fish. Hunan has both spicy and steamed dishes, including steamed ham and honey sauce, diced chicken with peanuts, steamed silver thread rolls and smoked duck. Mongolian cuisine comprises two basic dishes of *Huoguo* ('firepot' - meat dipped in a sauce based on sesame paste, shrimp oil, ginger juice and bean paste) and barbecue (various slices of meat and vegetables cooked on an iron grill and eaten in a sesame bun).
Taiwanese cooking is mostly seafood with thick sauces. It relies on garlic in the north and soy sauce in the south. Dishes include spring rolls with peanut butter, sweet-and-sour spare ribs, bean curd in red sauce, oyster omelette and numerous excellent seafoods. More information on Chinese cuisine can be found by consulting the corresponding sub-sections in the sections for *China (PR)* and *Hong Kong (SAR)*.
Restaurants almost always have table service although some hotels have buffet/barbecue lunches. Most hotels have restaurants offering both Western and Chinese cuisine and some of the larger hotels offer several styles of Chinese cooking (the Chinese word for hotel, *fan-dien*, means 'eating place'). Most bars have counter service.
There are no set licensing hours and alcohol is widely available.
NIGHTLIFE: Taiwan has an abundance of nightlife, and Taipei in particular is lively at night. Western-style entertainment can be found in hotels, and in the many discos, clubs, restaurants and cinemas in Taipei. Popular amongst local people are KTVs, a type of sing-along club modelled on Japanese karaoke bars; and beer houses, which sell draught beer and snacks. The northern district of Tienmu contains a street of open-air beer houses. The visitor can also sample both traditional and modern tea houses, open all day and in the evening. In the tea-growing countryside around Mucha, it is possible to visit all-night tea houses and sip locally produced teas such as 'iron Buddha' *tiehkuanyin* tea. High-quality meals and snacks are also provided. These tea houses are popular with local families, particularly on special occasions. Back in Taipei, there are night markets selling a variety of items, both modern and traditional. These are bustling with browsers and bargain hunters, whose persistence can be spectacularly rewarded. It is advisable to take a pen and paper to assist in the bargaining process, as most vendors speak only Chinese. Taipei's largest night market is probably *Shihlin Night Market*, famous for its good-value clothing and food. Snacks such as oyster omelettes, pork liver soup and papaya milkshakes are available. Many shops are open at night.
SHOPPING: One of the best ways to shop is to visit the night markets (see above). Purchases include Formosan sea-grass mats, hats, handbags and slippers, bamboo items, Chinese musical instruments, various dolls in costume, handpainted palace lanterns made from silk, lacquerware, ceramics, teak furniture, coral, veinstone and jade items, *ramie* fibre rugs, brassware, handmade shoes, fabrics and chopsticks (decorated, personalised sticks of wood or marble). **Shopping hours:** Mon-Sat 0900-2200.
SPECIAL EVENTS: There are numerous festivals throughout the year, all with variable dates. For an up-to-date list, contact the Taipei Representative Office in the UK or the Taiwan Visitors' Association (see *Contact Addresses* section).
The following is a selection of special events occurring in Taiwan in 2005:
Jan 1-31 *Kending Wind Bell Festival*. **Jan 29** *Chinese New Year*. **Feb 1-28** *Lantern Festival* (various locations). **Feb 23-26** *God of Wealth Festival*. **Apr 5** *Tomb Sweeping Festival*. **May/Oct** *Burning of the Plague God Boats*. **Jun** *Taipei Chinese Food Festival*. **Jun 11** *Dragon Boat Festival*. **Jul-Aug** *Ghost Month Festival*, Quianggu. **Aug 30** *Chung Yuan Ghost Festival*. **Sep 19** *Mid-Autumn Moon Festival*. **Sep 28** *Birthday of Confucius*. **Oct 10** *National Day*. **Nov 12** *Birthday of Dr Sun Yat-Sen*.
SOCIAL CONVENTIONS: Handshaking is common. Casual wear is widely acceptable. Ancient festivals and customs are celebrated enthusiastically and traditional holidays are important. Entertainment is usually offered in restaurants, not at home. Visitors are not expected to entertain. Chinese culture in the form of drama, opera and art is very strong. Despite rapid industrialisation and development, the way of life is very much Chinese, steeped in tradition and old values. **Tipping:** Tipping is not an established custom, although it is on the increase. Taipei hotels and restaurants add 10 per cent service charge and extra tipping is not expected. It is not customary to tip taxi drivers. The standard tip for porters is NT$50 per piece of luggage.

Business Profile

ECONOMY: Taiwan was one of the first 'tiger economies' of the Pacific basin. After phenomenal growth from the 1950s onwards, Taiwan had by 1980 become one of the top-20 trading nations in the world and until the mid-1990s grew at an average annual rate of 8 per cent (much higher than most industrialised countries). Taiwan's success was built on a policy of rapid industrialisation coupled with low overheads and labour costs, which allowed Taiwanese products to compete successfully on world markets. This achievement has been all the more impressive, considering the island's dearth of raw materials (excepting small quantities of coal and marble). Massive foreign currency reserves accumulated over the years have since helped Taiwan to minimise the effects of turbulence in the world economy: this was amply illustrated by the 1997 Asian financial crisis in which Taiwan suffered the least damage of any major economy in the region. However, the crisis drew attention to structural problems in the economy, especially an urgent need for reform of the tax and banking systems. Taiwan's principal industries are textiles, shipbuilding, metals, plywood, furniture and petrochemicals. Agriculture and fisheries, though declining in relative terms, are large enough to allow Taiwan considerable self-sufficiency in basic foodstuffs such as rice, sugar cane, maize and sweet potatoes; fishing is of comparatively minor significance. After a brief recession in 2000/01, the economy is now growing steadily at around 3 per cent annually. Unemployment is manageable at 5 per cent, while inflation is under 0.3 per cent. Export volumes are once again on the increase, and Taiwan runs a healthy trade surplus.
The performance of the Taiwanese economy is significantly affected by external political and economic conditions, especially in China (PR). Despite the 2004 re-election victory of the Sino-Sceptic President Chen, trade volumes with the mainland - already over US$50 billion annually - have increased sharply. Bilateral trade between Taiwan and the mainland rose from $41.01 billion in 2002 to $58 billion in 2003 and is expected to have passed $70 billion in 2004. Taiwan's other major trading partners are the USA, Japan, Germany, Australia and Saudi Arabia (which supplies the bulk of Taiwan's oil requirements). In January 2002, Taiwan was admitted to the World Trade Organization.
COMMERCIAL INFORMATION: The following organisations can offer advice: Ministry of Economic Affairs (ROC), 15 Fu Chou Street, Taipei 100 (tel: (2) 2321 2200; website: http://isc01.moea.gov.tw); *or* China External Trade Development Council (CETRA), 333 Keelung Road, Section 1, Taipei 110 (tel: (2) 2725 5200; fax: (2) 2757 6245; e-mail: taitra@taitra.org.tw; website: www.taiwantrade.com).
CONFERENCES/CONVENTIONS: There is a wide range of convention facilities, including the vast Taipei World Trade Center Complex which houses the Exhibition Hall, the Grand Hyatt Taipei, the International Trade Building and the Taipei International Convention Center. Hotels offer a comprehensive range of facilities and there are some with seating for 1000 and over. For further information, contact Taiwan Convention Association (TCA), 1 Hsin-Yi Road, Section 5, Taipei 110 (tel: (2) 2725 5200; fax: (2) 2723 2590; e-mail: ticc@taitra.org.tw; website: www.ticc.com.tw).

Climate

A subtropical climate with moderate temperatures in the north, where there is a winter season. The southern areas, where temperatures are slightly higher, enjoy sunshine every day, and there is no winter season. The typhoon season is from June to October.
Required clothing: Light- to mediumweights, with rainwear advised.

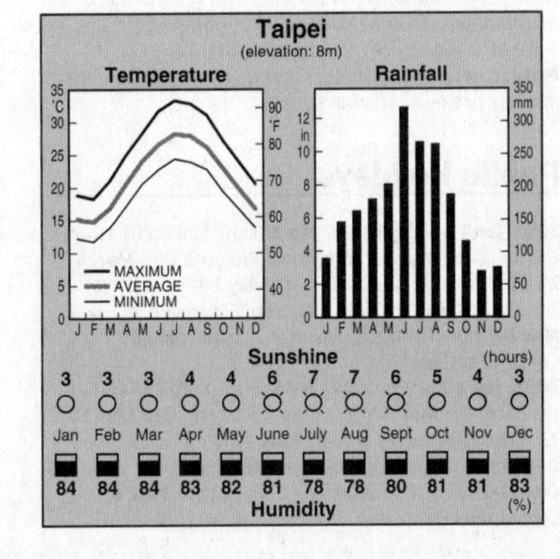

Tajikistan

LATEST TRAVEL ADVICE CONTACTS

British Foreign and Commonwealth Office
Tel: (0870) 606 0290 Website: www.fco.gov.uk
US Department of State
Website: http://travel.state.gov/travel
Canadian Department of Foreign Affairs and Int'l Trade
Tel: (1 800) 267 8376 Website: www.dfait-maeci.gc.ca

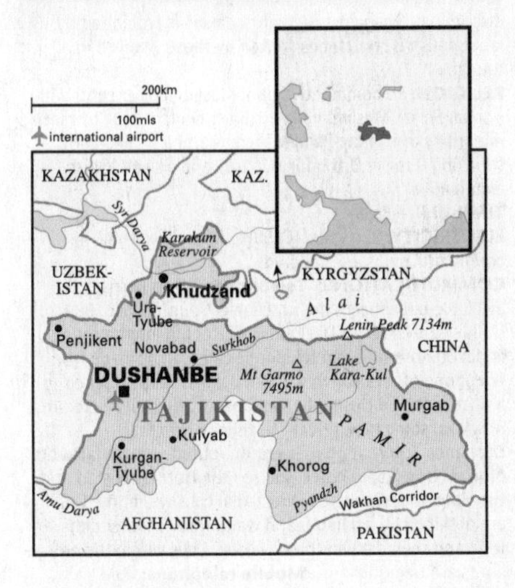

Location: Central Asia.

Country dialling code: 992.

Ministry of Foreign Affairs
Prospekt Rudaki 42, Dushanbe, Tajikistan
Tel: (372) 211 808. Fax: (372) 210 259.
E-mail: mfart@tajik.net
Embassy of the Tajikistan Republic
Otto-Suhr-Allee 84, 10585 Berlin, Germany
Tel: (30) 347 9300. Fax: (30) 3479 3029 *or* 3018.
E-mail: tajemb-germ@embassy-tajikistan.de
Website: www.embassy-tajikistan.de
British Embassy
43 Lutfi Street, Dushanbe 734017, Tajikistan
Tel: (372) 242 221 *or* 241 477 *or* (91) 734 017 (international). Fax: (91) 901 5079.
E-mail: dhm@britishembassy-tj.com
Website: www.britishembassy.gov.uk/tajikistan
Embassy of the Tajikistan Republic
1005 New Hampshire Avenue, NW, Washington, DC 20037
Tel: (202) 223 6090. Fax: (202) 223 6091.
E-mail: tajikistan@verizon.net
Website: www.tjus.org
Embassy of the United States
10 Pavlov Street, Dushanbe, Tajikistan
Tel: (372) 210 348/50 *or* 241 560.
Fax: (372) 210 362 *or* 241 562 *or* 510 029.
The Canadian Embassy in Almaty deals with enquiries relating to Tajikistan (see *Kazakhstan* section).

General Information

AREA: 143,100 sq km (55,251 sq miles).
POPULATION: 6,245,000 (official estimate 2003).
POPULATION DENSITY: 43.6 per sq km.
CAPITAL: Dushanbe. **Population:** 575,900 (2002).
GEOGRAPHY: Tajikistan is bordered by Kyrgyzstan and Uzbekistan to the north, Afghanistan to the south and China (PR) to the east. 93 per cent of the republic is occupied by mountains, most notably by the sparsely populated Pamir Mountains, which include Mount Garmo (formerly Pik Kommunizma; 7495m/24,590ft), the highest point of the former Soviet Union. The mountainous terrain means that in winter it is impossible to reach the east or the north of the country by road without taking a detour

TIMATIC CODES

Health	AMADEUS: **TI-DFT/DYU/HE** GALILEO/WORLDSPAN: **TI-DFT/DYU/HE** SABRE: **TIDFT/DYU/HE**
Visa	AMADEUS: **TI-DFT/DYU/VI** GALILEO/WORLDSPAN: **TI-DFT/DYU/VI** SABRE: **TIDFT/DYU/VI**

To access TIMATIC country information on Health and Visa regulations through the Computer Reservations System (CRS), type in the appropriate command line listed above.

A B C D E F G H I J K L M N O P Q R S T U V W X Y Z

through Uzbekistan and Kyrgyzstan. In the fertile plains of the southwest, cotton dominates the agriculture. In the north, in the Khudzand (formerly Leninabad) region, cotton and silk are the main crops.
GOVERNMENT: Republic. Gained independence from the Soviet Union in 1991. **Head of State:** President Imamali S Rahmonov since 1992. **Head of Government:** Prime Minister Akil Akilov since 1999.
LANGUAGE: Tajik is the official language, an ancient Persian language similar to the languages of Iran and Afghanistan. In the Pamir Mountains, there are at least five different languages, all related to an even more ancient form of Iranian. Russian is widely used (35 per cent of the population speak Russian fluently), and discrimination against Russian speakers is prohibited by law. English is sometimes spoken by those involved in tourism.
RELIGION: Predominantly Sunni Muslim (80 per cent) with a small Shi'ite Muslim minority (5 per cent). A large Ishmaeli minority exists in the Pamirs. There is also a smaller and shrinking Russian Orthodox minority and a small Jewish community.
TIME: GMT + 5.
ELECTRICITY: 220 volts AC, 50Hz. Round, two-pin continental plugs are standard.
COMMUNICATIONS: Telephone: IDD to Tajikistan is available but services are unreliable. Country code: 992 (followed by 372 for Dushanbe). Outgoing International code: 00. International telephone calls can be made from telephone offices which will usually be found attached to a post office (in Dushanbe, on Prospekt Rudaki). There are now also some new, private telephone offices in Dushanbe. International, operator-routed calls can also be ordered from some hotels such as the Hotel Tajikistan and the Hotel Independence. Direct-dial calls within the CIS are obtained by dialling 8 and waiting for another dial tone and then dialling the city code. Calls within the city limits are free of charge. **Mobile telephone:** GSM 900/1800. Network providers include *Indigo Tajikistan* (website: www.indigo.tj), *Josa Babilon Mobile* (website: www.babilon-m.com) and *TT Mobile*. **Fax:** Services are available from the business centre on Prospekt Rudaki in Dushanbe and from major hotels. **Internet:** ISPs include *InterCom* (website: www.tjinter.com) and *Telecom Technology* website: www.tajnet.com). Both these ISPs offer public Internet access at their offices. The *Central Asian Development Agency* (website: www.tajik.net) has public e-mail centres in main towns. Access to the Internet can be problematic owing to the underdeveloped telecommunications network. **Telegram:** Telegram services are available from post offices in large towns. **Post:** Mail to Western Europe and the USA can take between two weeks and two months. Stamped envelopes can be bought from post offices. Addresses should be laid out in the following order: country, postcode, city, street, house number and, lastly, the person's name. Postal services available include registered mail, restricted delivery, special delivery and Express mail (in Dushanbe only). Both surface and air mail are available for parcels. Post office hours: Mon-Fri 0800-1800, Sat: 0900-1700. Visitors can also use the post offices located within the major hotels. **Press:** The press in Tajikistan is censored. All the main newspapers are printed in Dushanbe and include *Narodnaya Gazeta* (Russian), *Sadoi Mardum* and *Tojikiston Ovozi* (Tajik).
Radio: BBC World Service (website: www.bbc.co.uk/worldservice) and Voice of America (website: www.voa.gov) can be received. From time to time the frequencies change and the most up-to-date can be found online.

Passport/Visa

	Passport Required?	Visa Required?	Return Ticket Required?
Full British	Yes	Yes	Yes
Australian	Yes	Yes	Yes
Canadian	Yes	Yes	Yes
USA	Yes	Yes	Yes
Other EU	Yes	Yes	Yes
Japanese	Yes	Yes	Yes

Note: Regulations and requirements may be subject to change at short notice, and you are advised to contact the appropriate diplomatic or consular authority before finalising travel arrangements. Details of these may be found at the head of this country's entry. Any numbers in the chart refer to the footnotes below.

Note: Passport and Visa regulations for all the CIS states are liable to change at short notice. All travellers are advised to contact the nearest Tajikistan Embassy or Consulate for up-to-date details. Countries where Tajikistan has diplomatic representation currently include Austria, China (PR), Germany, Iran and Turkey.
PASSPORTS: Passport valid for at least six months after date of departure required by all.
VISAS: Required by all except nationals of CIS member states (Belarus, Kazakhstan, Kyrgyzstan and the Russian Federation).
Types of visa and cost: *Standard*: €35 for seven days; €45 for 15 days; €50 for 30 days; €70 for 90 days. Express visas (processed on same day) cost double the given fee.
Validity: Dependent on purpose of trip.
Note: An invitation, either official or private, is necessary for visits to Tajikistan. The length of stay should be specified on the invitation, which must be endorsed by the Ministry of Foreign Affairs in Tajikistan. A visa can then be issued by the nearest Tajikistan Embassy. Special visas must also be obtained by those wishing to visit the Gorno-Babakhshan region (the Pamir Mountains). Tourists can apply for a letter of invitation from the State National Travel Agency, 14 Pushkin Street, Dushanbe 734 095 (tel/fax: (372) 231 401).
Application requirements: a) Two completed application forms. (b) Two recent passport-size photos.
(c) Valid passport. (d) A letter, telex, fax or other confirmation of acceptance of invitation (see above) from the Ministry of Foreign Affairs. (e) Fee. (f) Postal applications must be accompanied by a large, stamped, self-addressed envelope.
Note: (a) All visitors are required to register with the authorities within 72 hours of arrival. Hotels will usually arrange this; however, independent travellers will need to go to the Ministry of Foreign Affairs *or* the local OVIR office themselves. (b) An HIV test is required by all foreigners planning to stay longer than 90 days. Foreign tests may be acceptable.
Working days required: 10 (for Standard visas). Express visas are issued on the same day.

Money

Currency: Somoni (S) = 100 dirams. Notes are in denominations of S100, 50, 20, 10, 5 and 1. Dirams, also issued as notes, are in denominations of diram50, 20, 5 and 1.
Currency exchange: The preferred hard currency is the US Dollar, although other hard currencies are in theory also acceptable. All bills are normally settled in cash, and tourists must pay in hard currency for accommodation in hotels, although these are normally included in the price of organised tours. Owing to a shortage of change, a supply of small notes should be carried. International banking services are not available. All money should be changed at the official bureaux de change and the receipts should be kept. However, this law is not rigidly enforced.
Credit & debit cards: Not accepted.
Travellers cheques: Limited acceptance.
Currency restrictions: The import of local and foreign currency is unlimited, subject to declaration on arrival. The export of local currency is prohibited except by Tajikistan residents and the export of foreign currency is limited to the amount declared on arrival. All currency must be declared on arrival and a customs declaration form obtained.
Exchange rate indicators: The following figures are included as a guide to the movements of the Somoni against the US Dollar and the Euro.

Date	Feb '04	May '04	Aug '04	Nov '04
€1.00=	5.06	4.97	5.13	5.27
$1.00=	2.78	2.79	2.79	2.79

Note: Values are given against the Euro rather than Sterling as an accurate exchange rate against Sterling is not available.
Banking hours: Mon-Fri 0800-1700.

Duty Free

Reasonable quantities of goods for personal use may be imported into Tajikistan by persons of 18 years of age or older without incurring customs duty; however, certain items attract a 10 per cent import duty.
Note: A detailed customs declaration form must be filled in and retained by all travellers.

Public Holidays

2005: Jan 1 New Year's Day. **Jan 21** Eid-i-Kurbon (Feast of the Sacrifice). **Mar 8** International Women's Day. **March 20-22** Navrus (Persian New Year). **May 1** International Labour Day. **May 9** Victory Day. **Sep 9** Independence Day. **Nov 3-5** Eid-i-Ramazon (End of Ramadan). **Nov 6** Constitution Day.
2006: Jan 1 New Year's Day. **Jan 13** Eid-i-Kurbon (Feast of the Sacrifice). **Mar 8** International Women's Day. **Mar 20-22** Navrus (Persian New Year). **May 1** International Labour Day. **May 9** Victory Day. **Sep 9** Independence Day. **Oct 22-24** Eid-i-Ramazon (End of Ramadan). **Nov 6** Constitution Day.

Health

	Special Precautions?	Certificate Required?
Yellow Fever	No	No
Cholera	1	No
Typhoid & Pol	2	N/A
Malaria	3	N/A

Note: Regulations and requirements may be subject to change at short notice, and you are advised to contact your doctor well in advance of your intended date of departure. Any numbers in the chart refer to the footnotes below.

1: Following WHO guidelines issued in 1973, a cholera vaccination certificate is not a condition of entry to Tajikistan. However, cholera is a serious risk in this country and precautions are essential. Up-to-date advice should be sought before deciding whether these precautions should include vaccination, as medical opinion is divided over its effectiveness; see the *Health* appendix for more information.
2: Vaccination against typhoid is advised.
3: Cases of malaria, predominantly in the benign *vivax* form, have been reported in some central, western and northern areas of Tajikistan and particularly on the southern border (Khatlon area) between June and October. Those wishing to visit the area should bring suitable medication with them. Resistance to chloroquine is suspected.
Note: Travellers planning to stay in Tajikistan more than 90 days must present a medical certificate indicating that they are HIV-free.
Food & drink: All water should be regarded as being a potential health risk. Water used for drinking, brushing teeth or making ice should have first been boiled or otherwise sterilised. Milk is pasteurised and dairy products are safe for consumption. Only eat well-cooked meat and fish, preferably served hot. Pork, salad and mayonnaise may carry increased risk. Vegetables should be cooked and fruit peeled.
Other risks: There is a *diphtheria* epidemic in Tajikistan and medical advice should be sought before travelling. *Hepatitis A*, *B* and *E* occur. Rare occurrences of *plague* have been reported. *Trachoma* is common, *Crimean Congo haemorrhagic fever*, *typhus*, *leishmaniasis*, *sand-fly fever*, *tick-borne relapsing fever*, *brucellosis*, *plague* and *echinococcosis* all occur but risks to the traveller are low. *Rabies* is present. For those at high risk, vaccination before arrival should be considered. If you are bitten, seek medical advice without delay. For more information, consult the *Health* appendix.
Health care: Standards of health care are low. As the domestic health service is plagued by shortages of medicines and drugs, travellers are advised to take antibiotics and any prescription medicines, contact lens solutions and a first-aid kit containing basic medicines and water treatment tablets. There is no reciprocal health agreement with the UK. Although fees for health services are low, health insurance is recommended.

Travel - International

Note: Travellers are advised to avoid all but essential travel to districts adjoining the Afghan border due to the continuing threat from terrorism and unrest in Afghanistan and to the partly-mined areas bordering Kyrgyzstan and Uzbekistan. Particular care should be taken in the Gorm Valley. The overall security situation in Tajikistan has improved since the end of the civil war in 1997. Visitors should be aware of the continuing threat from terrorism which Tajikistan shares with other countries in Central Asia.
AIR: The national airline is *Tajikistan Airlines* (website: www.tajikistan-airlines.com). Other airlines serving Tajikistan include *Air Kazakstan*, *Eurasia Airlines* and *Samara Airlines*. The UN operates flights for staff and visitors of humanitarian organisations working in Tajikistan.
Approximate flight times: From Dushanbe to *Moscow* is four hours, to *Karachi* is two hours and to *Delhi* is one hour 30 minutes.
International airports: *Dushanbe Airport (DYU)* is 1 mile (2km) south of the city. Bus nos. 3 and 12, and trains 3 and 4, run to the city centre 0600-1800 (travel time - 20 minutes). Taxis are also available 0800-2000 (travel time - five minutes). Airport facilities include first aid, left luggage, chemist, post office, restaurants, snack bars, tourist information and nursery.
RAIL: Trains are the most reliable way of reaching Dushanbe for those not arriving by air. Passenger railways are, however, restricted at present. Dushanbe is connected to a spur of the Trans-Caspian Railway which winds down to the Afghan border in Uzbekistan before heading north towards Dushanbe. Travellers are advised to sit with their back to the engine, as throwing rocks at the windows of passing trains seems to be a popular pastime among local

children. The journey from Tashkent to Dushanbe takes approximately 22 hours; from Moscow it takes approximately four days. Khojand in the north of the country can be reached directly from Samarkand in Uzbekistan. There is also a train service between Dushanbe and Volgograd in the Russian Federation.
ROAD: Tajikistan can be approached by road from Uzbekistan, subject to occasional unannounced border closures and snow. Cars with a Tajik registration, however, are not allowed to enter Uzbekistan, unless the vehicle belongs to a government body. It is not advisable to attempt to cross the border from Kyrgyzstan at present. A new road has recently been built into China (PR). The border between Tajikistan and Afghanistan is officially closed. **Bus:** Services have been severely disrupted by border closures and should not be relied upon. A service normally operates connecting Dushanbe with Tashkent and Samarkand.

Travel - Internal

AIR: The domestic airline is *Tajik Air*, offering internal flights to Khorog in Gorno-Badakhshan (one of the most technically demanding regularly scheduled flights in the world), Khojand and less frequently to Kulyab. All flights are subject to the weather and the endemic fuel shortages of the region. Flights from Dushanbe to Khorog take one hour, to Khojand one hour and to Kulyab 30 minutes. Internal services are subject to cancellations, long delays and overloading of passengers.
RAIL: Passenger railways are restricted at present. There are only three railway lines in Tajikistan: one leading south from Dushanbe through Kurgan-Tyube and Shaartuz to the Uzbek/Afghan border at Termez; one that leads due south from Dushanbe, through Kurgan-Tyube to Tugul on the Afghan border; and one in the northern region which runs from Samarkand, through Khojand to the Fergana Valley. A branch from Kulyab to Kurgan-Tyube is currently under construction.
Note: Travellers are advised to store their valuables in the compartment under the bed/seats, to ensure the door is securely shut from the inside by tying it closed with wire or strong cord, and not to leave the compartment unattended.
ROAD: There is a reasonable road network in Tajikistan, though some parts may be seasonally impassable. During the winter (October to March), three of the four main roads from the capital and the southwest of the country (east to Khorog via Khalaikum, northeast to Osh via the Garm valley, and north to Khojand via the Anzob Pass and Ayni) are all closed by snow. The only way of reaching these areas is through Uzbekistan. The road between Osh (in Kyrgyzstan) and Khorog is kept open all year round and traverses one of the most beautiful and unspoilt regions in the world, the Pamir Mountains. Recent political and economic troubles have meant that road maintenance has been widely neglected. Foreigners are, in theory, allowed to go anywhere except border zones - it is worth noting that the road from Dushanbe to Khorog is in a border zone for much of its length - without having to get special permission (other than an endorsement on their visas). Tourists should inform their tour operator of their plans. If travelling independently, it is worth getting as many official-looking documents as possible in order to negotiate the many checkpoints. Traffic drives on the right. **Bus:** There are services between the major towns when the roads are open. In the south, buses go to Kurgan-Tyrube and Kulyab and as far down as Pyanj and Ayvadaz. Buses to the east reach only around 100km (60 miles), as far as Komsomolabad. Information on timetables and fares can be found at the bus station, or *autovokzal*. **Taxi:** These and chauffeur-driven cars for hire can be found in all major towns. Many are unlicensed and travellers are advised to agree a fare in advance. Officially marked taxis are safe, but sharing with strangers should be avoided. As many of the street names have changed since independence, it is also advisable to ascertain both the old and the new street names when asking directions. **Car hire:** Self-drive car hire is not currently available.
Documentation: It is in theory possible to bring, or buy, one's own transport: drivers should have an International Driving Permit and have arranged insurance before departure.

Accommodation

HOTELS: Tajikistan is not well supplied with hotels. Although there are no restrictions on where visitors may stay, hotels other than the main hotels are unused to accommodating foreigners and all but the most insistent visitors may find it difficult to obtain a room. The main hotels are clean and friendly, although it is difficult to get a room in the Oktyabrskaya, which houses both the US and Russian embassies. Outside the capital, accommodation is very hard to find. For further information, contact Intourist Tajikistan (see *Contact Addresses* section).
DACHAS: It is possible to stay in the government dachas in Khorog, but standards of comfort, amenities and cleanliness vary.

Resorts & Excursions

At present, it is strongly advised for tourists not to travel to Tajikistan due to political unrest and kidnappings. For further information, contact the relevant local government travel advice department. Tajikistan was never well equipped with a comprehensive infrastructure for tourists, and some sites were destroyed in the civil war at the end of 1992. However, there is still much to see.
DUSHANBE: Situated only three hours from the border with Afghanistan is the Tajik capital, Dushanbe, lying in the **Hissar valley** in the southwest of the country. Known primarily for its Monday market (the name Dushanbe is derived from the Tajik word for Monday), it was no more than a village until the Trans-Caspian Railway reached it in 1929. Soviet power had only been established in the region for six years and, somewhat unoriginally, the city was renamed **Stalinabad** and proclaimed capital of the new Soviet Socialist Republic of Tajikistan. It was from here that Brezhnev launched his invasion of Afghanistan in 1979. The main points of interest all lie on or are close to **Prospekt Rudaki**, which runs from the railway station in the south to the bus station in the north. As well as the principal mosque, this area boasts a synagogue that dates back to the late-19th century, a Russian church and a columned opera house. Other features in the city include the **Tajikistan Unified Museum**, situated just north of the railway station in **Ploshchad Aym**, which has stuffed snow leopards and Marco Polo sheep amongst its exhibits. The **ethnographic museum** is on ulitsa Somoni, not far from the **Hotel Tajikistan**.
THE SOUTHWEST: 16km (10 miles) west of Dushanbe lies the **Hissar Port**, a site built between the 16th and 19th centuries which contains, among other things, a ruined **citadel**, two **madrassahs** (Islamic seminaries), a **caravanserai** and a mausoleum. Further west, at **Penjikent** on the Uzbek border, lie the remains of a Sogdian fort that are only now being excavated. The frescoes in Penjikent are reputed to be extremely fine. South of Penjikent lie the **Muragazor Lakes**, a system of seven lakes of differing colours that alter as the light changes. There are remains of Buddhist temples near **Kurgan-Tyube** in the south, from which the biggest Buddha in Central Asia was recovered and is now stored, ignominiously carved up into 60 pieces, in Dushanbe.
THE PAMIRS: The Pamirs are at the hub of Asia. Often described as the **Roof of the World**, these mountains form one of the most unexplored regions on earth. High, cold and remote, they have attracted climbers and hunters from the former Soviet Union for years, but only now are they opening up for the rest of the world. The bulk of the Pamir lies in the semi-autonomous region of Gorno-Badakhshan and visitors should be aware that some elements have been conducting an armed campaign to gain even more autonomy. However, the campaign has been confined to a number of well-defined theatres, most of which are well away from areas likely to interest visitors; the road between Dushanbe and Khorog is the exception.
The only town of any significance on the **Pamir Highway**, which stretches from Dushanbe into Kyrgyzstan, is **Khorog**. The capital of the eastern Tajik region of **Gorno-Badakhshan**, Khorog is a small one-street town with a museum containing stuffed animals and a display of photographs of Lenin. The flight into Khorog from the Tajik capital is said to be the most difficult in the world. **Lake Sareskoye**, in the heart of the Pamirs, was formed in 1911 when the side of a mountain was dislodged by an earthquake and fell into the path of a mountain river. In the north of the Pamirs, **Lake Kara-Kul**, formed by a meteor 10 million years ago, is 3915m (12,844ft) above sea-level and hence too high for any aquatic life. **Pik Lenina** and **Mount Garmo** (formerly Pik Kommunizma) are to the northwest and west respectively of Lake Kara-Kul. At well over 7000m (22,966ft), these two peaks tower over Tajikistan and the neighbouring republic of Kyrgyzstan to the north. Helicopter flights are available for those wishing to climb them. Some people are convinced that **yetis** are alive and thriving in this remote wilderness.
THE SILK ROAD: This ancient trading route was used by silk merchants from the second century until its decline in the 14th century, and is open in parts to tourists, stretching from northern China, through bleak and foreboding desert and mountainous terrain, to the ports on either the Caspian Sea or Mediterranean Sea. For further details of the route, see *Silk Road* in the *China* section.
The main highlight for travellers along the Silk Road in Tajikistan is its stunning natural scenery set against the Pamir and Fan mountains and incorporating lush valleys and turquoise lakes. Trekking trips are best arranged from Samarkand (Uzbekistan).
Travel along the Silk Road can be quite difficult due to the terrain, harsh climate and lack of developed infrastructure. Visitors to the region are advised to travel with an organised tour company or travel agent.

Sport & Activities

Hiking and trekking: Tour operators offer a number of set itineraries, mostly in the southwest of the country and its surrounding mountains, generally during the summer months. The trips generally start in Moscow and include a 14-day trekking trip around the ancient Sogdian lakes such as *Iskander-kul*, north of Dushanbe and the Muragazor Lakes, finishing in Samarkand in Uzbekistan; and a trip to the mountain passes of the *Kara-Tak*, north of Dushanbe, walking 8 to 10km (5 to 6 miles) per day, with baggage being carried by donkeys, and staying in mountain villages. Some operators will organise itineraries to suit individual tastes.
Other: The national sport is **wrestling**, called *Gushtin Geri*. *Bushkashi* is a team game in which the two mounted teams attempt to deliver a headless and legless goat's carcass weighing 30 to 40kg over the opposition's goal line. Players are allowed to wrestle the goat from an opponent, but physical assault is frowned upon. There is **skiing** and **hunting** in the hills behind Dushanbe.

Social Profile

FOOD & DRINK: Traditional Tajik meals start with sweet dishes such as *halwa* and tea and then progress to soups and meat before finishing with *plov*. *Plov* is made up of scraps of mutton, shredded yellow turnip and rice, fried in a large wok, and is a staple dish in all the Central Asian republics. The appetising *shashlyk* (skewered chunks of mutton grilled over charcoal, served with raw sliced onions) and *lipioshka* (round unleavened bread) are often sold on street corners and served in restaurants: the Vastoychny bar restaurant in Dushanbe (on Prospekt Rudaki near the Hotel Tajikistan) serves particularly good *shashlyk*. *Manty* (large noodle sacks of meat), *samsa* (samosas) and *chiburekki* (deep-fried dough cakes) are all popular as snacks. *Shorpur* is a meat and vegetable soup; *laghman* is similar to *shorpur*, but comes with noodles. In the summer, Tajikistan is awash with fruit: its grapes and melons were famous throughout the former Soviet Union. The bazaars also sell pomegranates, apricots, plums, figs and persimmons. Little of the food served in hotels indicates its Tajik heritage: *borcht* is beetroot soup, *entrecote* are well-done steaks, *cutlet* are grilled meatballs, and *strogan* is the local equivalent of beef Stroganoff.
Pirmeni, originating in Ukraine, are small boiled noodle sacks of meat and vegetables similar to ravioli, sometimes in a vegetable soup, sometimes not.
Tea or *chai* is the most widespread drink on offer and can be obtained almost anywhere. Beer, wine, vodka, brandy and sparkling wine (*shampanski*) are intermittently available in many restaurants. If the restaurant is unable to supply it, it is acceptable to bring your own. *Kefir*, a thick drinking yoghurt, is often served with breakfast.
NIGHTLIFE: There are no restaurants operating in the evenings except for the one in the Hotel Oktyabrskaya which shuts at 2200. There is a dollar bar in the basement of the Hotel Tajikistan which is open some evenings. The Ayni opera and ballet theatre on Prospekt Rudaki is still operating, albeit with a reduced programme of matinees. The streets of Dushanbe are deserted after 2000.
SHOPPING: Shortages are the norm in Tajikistan; there is a bazaar and street market behind the Hotel Tajikistan where it is possible to buy food and sometimes handicrafts. Shokhmansur (also known as Zilyoni) Bazaar near Ploshchad Ayni also sells food. There is a souvenir shop on the corner of Prospekt Rudaki and ulitsa Ismail Somoni, under an art gallery which exhibits and sells the work of local artists. **Shopping hours:** Food shops open Mon-Sat 0900-1700.
SPECIAL EVENTS: There is a carnival of *Navruz* (the beginning of the Persian New Year), when a special dish called *sumalak* is prepared from germinating wheat. Many other events celebrated are tied to the Muslim calendar.
SOCIAL CONVENTIONS: *Lipioshka* (bread) should never be laid upside down, and it is normal to remove shoes, but not socks, when entering someone's house. Shorts are rarely seen in Tajikistan and, worn by females, are likely to provoke unwelcome attention from the local male population.

Business Profile

ECONOMY: Tajikistan is the poorest of the five former Soviet Central Asian republics, with an estimated four-fifths of the population living below the poverty line. Basic services and infrastructure are poor to non-existent. Although less than 10 per cent of the country's land can be cultivated, Tajikistan has a sizeable agricultural sector accounting for one-quarter of GDP and employing half the workforce. Large quantities of cotton are produced under ecologically ruinous schemes established during the Soviet era. Grain, fruit and vegetables are also grown. In recent years, the country has been badly hit by a regional drought,

an earthquake and a series of mudslides (caused by poor land use) which forced the Government to make several appeals for international food aid.
Tajikistan's economic prospects lie with exploitation of its mineral resources, which include gold, aluminium, iron, lead, tin and mercury ores. There are coal deposits as well as small amounts of natural gas, which together with hydroelectric schemes meet the bulk of the country's energy needs. There is little heavy industry other than mineral processing (mainly aluminium); light industry is concentrated in food processing and textiles.
The Tajik economy suffered severely during the 1990s from the dislocations caused by the break-up of the Soviet Union followed by two outbreaks of civil war. It has recovered slowly since the 1997 peace accord but some positive results are now showing: the hyper-inflation which blighted the economy during the civil war has now been cut to around 10 per cent. Annual GDP growth in 2002 was a healthy 7 per cent. The Government's economic reform programme, which is now being implemented, comprises a typical recipe of privatisation, deregulation and fiscal reform. Tajikistan secured membership of the IMF and World Bank in 1993; it also belongs to the European Bank for Reconstruction and Development as a 'Country of Operation'. It has received substantial aid from Middle Eastern donors, including Saudi Arabia, Kuwait and the Islamic Development Bank. External donors now supply around 60 per cent of Tajik government income.
Tajikistan now has its own currency, the Somoni, which was introduced in October 2000 to replace the five-year-old Tajik rouble. In April 1998, Tajikistan was admitted to the Customs Union of the Commonwealth of Independent States, a loose federation of former Soviet republics, whose members continue to dominate Tajik trade. Further afield, The Netherlands and the UK are important trading partners. In July 2001, Tajikistan acquired observer status at the World Trade Organisation.
BUSINESS: Tajikistan is looking for foreign investment in a number of sectors, particularly in aluminium processing, which needs extensive modernisation. Foreign businesses are not barred from any economic sphere: although land, livestock and mineral resources are owned by the Government, it is possible to lease them. Foreign concerns are allowed to participate in the privatisation programme. Foreign investments in certain priority areas, which are as yet undefined, are eligible for tax holidays - including import and export duties - although, in effect, each foreign investor negotiates his or her own terms and many are better than the standard laid down in law. All foreign investors must be registered with the Ministry of External Economic Affairs. **Office hours:** Mon-Fri 0800-1700.
COMMERCIAL INFORMATION: The following organisations can offer advice and information: Ministry of Economy and Foreign Economic Relations, 42 Rudaki Street, Dushanbe 734002, Tajikistan (tel: (372) 232 944; fax: (372) 210 404). Information can also be obtained from the US Department of Commerce, Business Information Service for the Newly Independent States, USA Trade Center, Stop R-Binis, 1401 Constitution Avenue, NW, Washington, DC 20230, USA (tel: (202) 482 4655; fax: (202) 482 2293; e-mail: bisnis@ita.doc.gov.

Climate

In Dushanbe, temperatures vary between a minimum -13°C (8°F) in December/January to a maximum 33°C (91°F) in July/August. Humidity is generally low. In the mountains, it can reach -45°C (-49°F) when the wind chill factor is taken into consideration, and rise to 20°C (68°F) in summer. In the Pamir Mountains, the climate is semi-arid to polar.
Required clothing: Warm clothing should be taken by anyone intending to visit the mountains. Those intending to visit the southwest in summer should bring light, loose clothing.

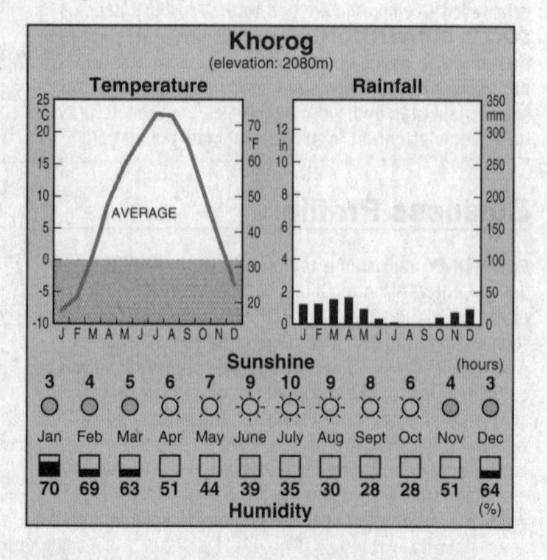

Tanzania

LATEST TRAVEL ADVICE CONTACTS

British Foreign and Commonwealth Office
Tel: (0870) 606 0290 Website: www.fco.gov.uk
US Department of State
Website: http://travel.state.gov/travel
Canadian Department of Foreign Affairs and Int'l Trade
Tel: (1 800) 267 8376 Website: www.dfait-maeci.gc.ca

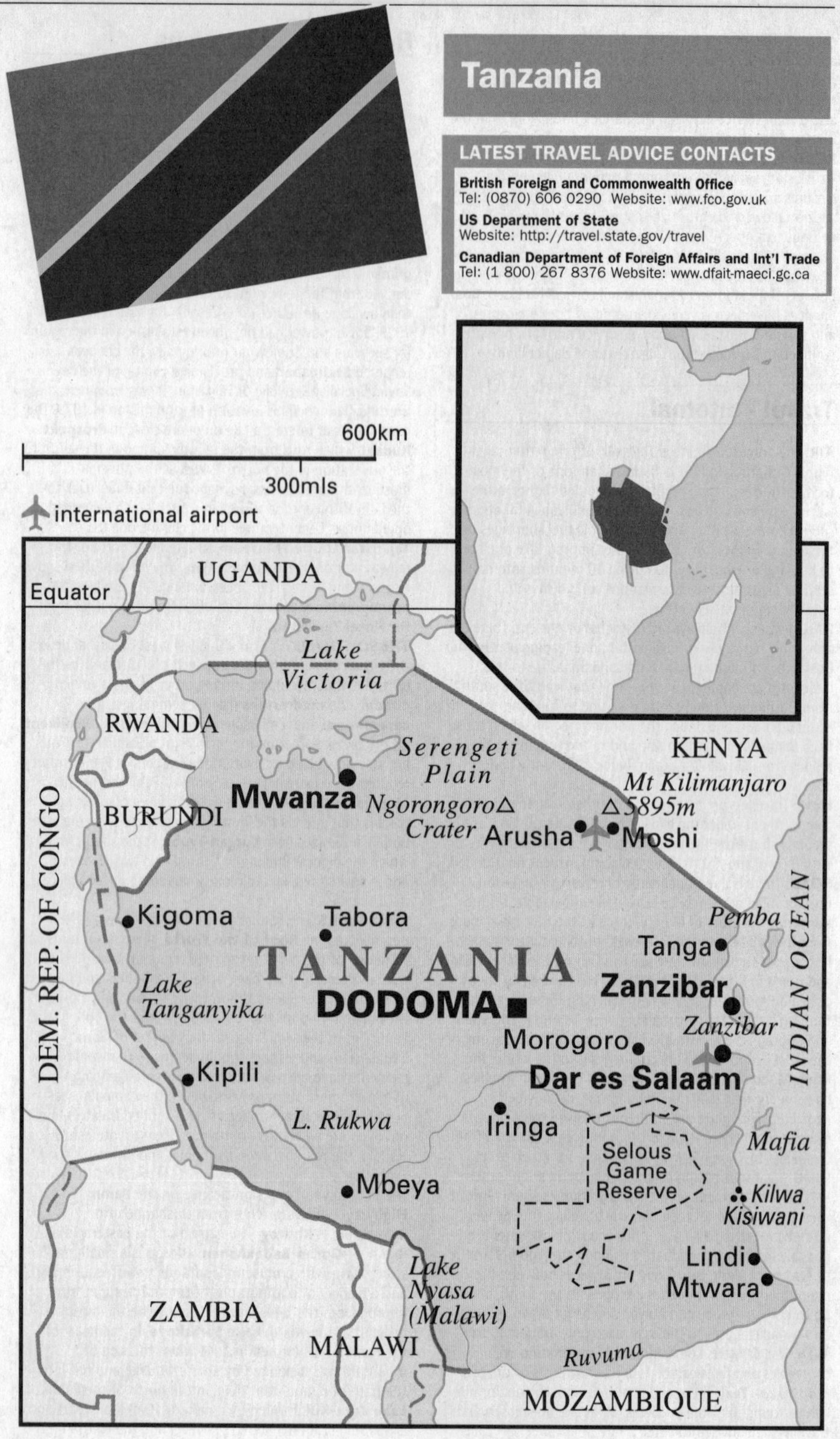

Location: East Africa.

Country dialling code: 255.

Tanzania Tourist Board
Street address: IPS Building, Azikiwe Street, Dar es Salaam, Tanzania
Postal address: PO Box 2485, Dar es Salaam, Tanzania
Tel: (22) 211 1244. Fax: (22) 211 6420.
E-mail: md@ttb.ud.or.tz *or* safari@ud.co.tz
Website: www.tanzaniatouristboard.com

High Commission for the United Republic of Tanzania
3 Stratford Place, London WC1 1AS, UK

TIMATIC CODES

Health	AMADEUS: **TI-DFT/DAR/HE** GALILEO/WORLDSPAN: **TI-DFT/DAR/HE** SABRE: **TIDFT/DAR/HE**
Visa	AMADEUS: **TI-DFT/DAR/VI** GALILEO/WORLDSPAN: **TI-DFT/DAR/VI** SABRE: **TIDFT/DAR/VI**

To access TIMATIC country information on Health and Visa regulations through the Computer Reservations System (CRS), type in the appropriate command line listed above.

British High Commission
Street address: Umoja House, Garden Avenue, Dar es Salaam, Tanzania
Postal address: PO Box 9200, Dar es Salaam, Tanzania
Tel: (22) 211 0101. Fax: (22) 211 0102 (chancery) *or* 0296 (consular) *or* 0297 (visa) *or* 0112 (management) *or* 0080 (commercial).
E-mail: bhc.dar@fco.gov.uk

Embassy of the United Republic of Tanzania
2139 R Street, NW, Washington, DC 20008, USA
Tel: (202) 884 1080 *or* 939 6125. Fax: (202) 797 7408.
E-mail: balozi@tanzaniaembassy-us.org
Website: www.tanzaniaembassy-us.org *or* www.tanzania-web.com

Embassy of the United States of America
Street address: 686 Old Bagamoyo Road, Msasani, Dar es Salaam, Tanzania
Postal address: PO Box 9123, Dar es Salaam, Tanzania
Tel: (22) 266 8001. Fax: (22) 266 8238 *or* 8373.
E-mail: embassyd@state.gov
Website: http://usembassy.state.gov/tanzania

High Commission for the United Republic of Tanzania
50 Range Road, Ottawa, Ontario K1N 8J4, Canada
Tel: (613) 232 1509/0. Fax: (613) 232 5184.

Tanzania
Tanzania
Land of the world famous SERENGETI NATIONAL PARK, SELOUS GAME RESERVE and the astounding annual migration of the wildebeest; of the unique animal paradise of Ngorongoro Crater and legendary Mount Kilimanjaro; of exotic spice drenched Zanzibar and Mafia Island; of the proud, colourful Maasai; of white sands and turquoise sea; of palace ruins and pirate tales. Nowhere else in Africa will you see such wildlife, experience such a fascinating mix of cultures, meet such friendly people or discover such hauntingly beautiful scenery.
TANZANIA
Authentic Africa
Tanzania Tourist Board
P.O. Box 2485, Dar-es-Salaam, Tanzania
Tel: +255 22 2111244/5 Fax: +255 22 2116420
E-Mail: safari@ud.co.tz
Website: http//www.tanzaniatouristboard.com

E-mail: tzottawa@synapse.net
Website: www.tanzania-ottawa.com
Canadian High Commission
Street address: 38 Mirambo Street, off Garden Avenue, Dar es Salaam, Tanzania
Postal address: PO Box 1022, Dar es Salaam, Tanzania
Tel: (22) 211 2831-5 *or* 2865. Fax: (22) 211 6897.
E-mail: dslam@international.gc.ca
Website: www.infoexport.gc.ca/tz

General Information

AREA: 945,087 sq km (364,900 sq miles).
POPULATION: 34,569,232 (2002).
POPULATION DENSITY: 36.6 per sq km.
CAPITAL: Dodoma (administrative capital designate). **Population:** 1,698,996 (2002). Dar es Salaam remains the capital for the time being. **Population:** 2,497,940 (2002).
GEOGRAPHY: The United Republic of Tanzania lies on the east coast of Africa and is bordered by Kenya and Uganda to the north; by Burundi, Rwanda and the Democratic Republic of Congo to the west; by the Indian Ocean to the east; and by Zambia, Malawi and Mozambique to the south. The Tanzanian mainland is divided into several clearly defined regions: the coastal plains, which vary in width from 16 to 64km (10 to 39 miles) and have lush, tropical vegetation; the Masai Steppe in the north, 213 to 1067m (698 to 3500ft) above sea level; and a high plateau in the southern area towards Zambia and Lake Nyasa (Lake Malawi). Savannah and bush cover over half the country, and semi-desert accounts for the remaining land area, with the exception of the coastal plains. Over 53,000 sq km (20,463 sq miles) is inland water, mostly lakes formed in the Rift Valley. The United Republic of Tanzania includes the islands of Zanzibar and Pemba, about 45km (28 miles) off the coast to the northeast of the country.
GOVERNMENT: Federal Republic since 1964. Tanganyika gained independence from the UK in 1961. In 1964, Tanganyika joined with Zanzibar, which had been a British protectorate until 1963, and became Tanzania. **Head of State:** President Benjamin William Mkapa since 1995. **Head of Government:** Prime Minister Frederick Sumaye since 1995.
LANGUAGE: Kiswahili and English are the official languages. The terms Swahili and Kiswahili are used interchangeably, though the term Swahili normally refers to the people while Kiswahili refers to the language. Originating along the coast, Kiswahili is a Bantu language with many words derived from Arabic. Other African languages such as Bantu and those of Nilo-Hamitic and Khoisan origin are also spoken.
RELIGION: Muslim, Christian, Hindu and traditional beliefs.
TIME: GMT + 3.
ELECTRICITY: 230 volts AC, 50Hz. Plugs may be round or square three-pin, fused or unfused.
COMMUNICATIONS: Telephone: IDD is available. Country code: 255. Outgoing international code: 00. In some rural areas, international calls must go through the operator. There are many public call boxes in post offices and main towns. **Mobile telephone:** GSM 900/1800 network. Operators include *Celtel Tanzania Ltd*, *Mobitel* (website: www.mobitel.co.tz), *Tritel* (website: www.tritel.co.tz), *Vodacom Tanzania* and *Zanzibar Telecom*. Coverage is limited to main urban areas. **Fax:** Faxes can be sent from the Tanzanian Telecom Office in Dar es Salaam, and from some hotels. **Internet:** ISPs include *Africa Online* (website: www.africaonline.com), *Cats-net.com* (website: www.cats-net.com) and *TZ Online* (website: www.tzonline.com). E-mail can be accessed in Internet cafes in main urban areas. **Telegram:** Telegrams can be sent from most post offices and major hotels. **Post:** Airmail to Europe takes one week. Courier services take less than 24 hours. **Press:** The English-language newspapers are the *Business Times*, *Daily News*, *The Express*, *The Family Mirror*, *The Guardian* and *Sunday News* printed in Dar es Salaam.
Radio: BBC World Service (website: www.bbc.co.uk/worldservice) and Voice of America (website: www.voa.gov) can be received. From time to time the frequencies change and the most up-to-date can be found online.

Passport/Visa

	Passport Required?	Visa Required?	Return Ticket Required?
Full British	Yes	Yes	Yes
Australian	Yes	Yes	Yes
Canadian	Yes	Yes	Yes
USA	Yes	Yes	Yes
Other EU	Yes	Yes	Yes
Japanese	Yes	Yes	Yes

Note: *Regulations and requirements may be subject to change at short notice, and you are advised to contact the appropriate diplomatic or consular authority before finalising travel arrangements. Details of these may be found at the head of this country's entry. Any numbers in the chart refer to the footnotes below.*

Note: The granting of a visa does not guarantee permission to enter Tanzania. The Immigration Officer reserves the right to grant or deny admission. Visa holders are subject to normal immigration control at the port of entry and should carry with them, for possible presentation to Immigration Officers, the documents submitted with their applications.
PASSPORTS: Passport valid for at least six months required by all.
VISAS: Required by all nationals except the following for stays of up to three months (who are issued with a visitor's pass on arrival): Antigua & Barbuda, Barbados, Belize, Bermuda, Botswana, Brunei, Cyprus, Dominica, Grenada, Guyana, Jamaica, Kenya, Kiribati, Lesotho, Malaysia, Malawi, Maldives, Malta, Mauritius, Namibia, Nauru, St Kitts & Nevis, St Lucia, St Vincent & the Grenadines, São Tomé e Principe, Seychelles, Singapore, Solomon Islands, Swaziland, Tonga, Tuvalu, Uganda, Vanuatu, Zambia and Zimbabwe.
Note: Nationals who do not require visas for stays of up to three months may still need entry permit clearance, except nationals of Kenya and Uganda. All other nationals must obtain visas in advance except nationals coming from a country where there is no Tanzania Embassy, High Commission or Consulate to issue a visa. In this case, these nationals may obtain a visa on arrival at one of the following four main entry points, provided all immigration and health requirements are met: Dar es Salaam International Airport, Kilimanjaro International Airport, Namanga Entry Point (Tanzania-Kenya border crossing) and Zanzibar International Airport.
Types of visa and cost: *Tourist*: £38 (single-entry); £45 (multiple-entry). *Business*: £50 (single-entry); £60 (multiple-entry). Cost of Tourist Visa depends on nationality of applicant. The above prices are for UK nationals; Irish nationals always pay £5. For postal applications, fees are payable *only* by postal order. Please note that once visas are processed, fees are non-refundable.
Validity: Single-entry: Three months from date of issue; Multiple-entry: Six months from date of issue.
Application to: Consulate (or Consular section at High Commission or Embassy); see *Contact Addresses* section.
Application requirements: (a) One completed application form. (b) Two recent passport-size photos. (c) Valid passport. (d) Fee, payable in cash or by postal order, made payable to the Tanzania High Commission (nationals must pay by postal order only for postal applications). (e) Pre-paid self-addressed, stamped envelope for postal applications. (f) For business visitors, a letter indicating the nature of the trip and the business contact in Tanzania.
Note: All nationals may be asked to attend an interview and/or supply further documents.
Working days required: Normally 24 hours. Up to seven days for postal applications.
Temporary residence: Enquire at High Commission or Embassy.

Money

Currency: Tanzanian Shilling (TSh) = 100 cents. Notes are in denominations of TSh10,000, 5000, 1000, 500 and 200. Coins are in denominations of TSh200, 100, 50, 20, 10, 5 and 1, and 100, 50, 20, 10 and 5 cents.
Currency exchange: Money may be changed at banks, authorised dealers and bureaux de change. A receipt should be obtained and kept until departure.
Credit & debit cards: Major credit cards are accepted in larger hotels. Check with your credit or debit card company for details of merchant acceptability and other facilities which may be available.
Travellers cheques: May be cashed with authorised dealers or bureaux de change. To avoid additional exchange rate charges, travellers are advised to take travellers cheques in US Dollars or Pounds Sterling.
Currency restrictions: The import and export of local currency is prohibited. The import of foreign currency is unlimited, subject to declaration. The export of foreign currency is limited to the amount declared on arrival.
Exchange rate indicators: The following figures are included as a guide to the movements of the Tanzanian Shilling against Sterling and the US Dollar:

Date	Feb '04	May '04	Aug '04	Nov '04
£1.00=	2022.84	1994.77	1988.82	2010.16
$1.00=	1111.30	1116.83	1079.50	1061.50

Banking hours: Mon-Fri 0830-1230 (some places are open until 1600), Sat 0830-1300.

Duty Free

The following items may be imported into Tanzania without incurring customs duty:
200 cigarettes or 50 cigars or 250g of tobacco; one bottle of alcoholic beverages; 570ml of perfume.

Public Holidays

2005: Jan 1 New Year's Day. **Jan 12** Zanzibar Revolution Day. **Jan 21** Eid al-Kebir. **Apr 26** Union Day. **May 1** International Labour Day. **Jul 7** Saba Saba (Industry's Day). **Aug 8** Nane Nane (Farmer's Day). **Nov 3-5** Eid al-Fitr (Ramadan). **Dec 9** Independence and Republic Day. **Dec 25** Christmas Day. **Dec 26** Boxing Day.
2006: Jan 1 New Year's Day. **Jan 12** Zanzibar Revolution Day. **Jan 13** Eid al-Kebir. **Apr 26** Union Day. **May 1** International Labour Day. **Jul 7** Saba Saba (Industry's Day). **Aug 8** Nane Nane (Farmer's Day). **Oct 22-24** Eid al-Fitr (Ramadan). **Dec 9** Independence and Republic Day. **Dec 25** Christmas Day. **Dec 26** Boxing Day.
Note: Muslim festivals are timed according to local sightings of various phases of the moon and the dates given above are approximations. During the lunar month of Ramadan that precedes Eid al-Fitr, Muslims fast during the day and feast at night and normal business patterns may be disrupted slightly. Some disruption may continue into Eid al-Fitr itself. Eid al-Fitr and Idd El Haji (Eid al-Adha) may last anything from two to 10 days, depending on the region. For more information, see the *World of Islam* appendix.

Health

	Special Precautions?	Certificate Required?
Yellow Fever	Yes	1
Cholera	Yes	2
Typhoid & Polio	3	N/A
Malaria	4	N/A

Note: *Regulations and requirements may be subject to change at short notice, and you are advised to contact your doctor well in advance of your intended date of departure. Any numbers in the chart refer to the footnotes below.*

1: A yellow fever vaccination certificate is required of all travellers over one year of age travelling from infected areas and travellers coming from countries considered to be endemic by the Tanzanian authorities. The risk of yellow fever is highest in northwestern forest areas.
2: According to 1973 WHO guidelines, a cholera vaccination is no longer required for entry into Tanzania. However, cholera is a risk throughout the country and precautions are essential. Up-to-date advice should be sought before deciding whether these precautions should include vaccination as medical opinion is divided over its effectiveness. For more information, see the *Health* appendix.
3: Vaccination against typhoid is advised.
4: Malaria risk, predominantly in the malignant *falciparum* form, exists all year throughout the country below 1800m (5906ft). The strain is reported to be highly resistant to chloroquine and sulfadoxine-pyrimethamine.
Food & drink: All water should be regarded as being potentially contaminated. Travellers should use bottled water for drinking, brushing teeth, washing vegetables and reconstituting powdered milk. Other food hygiene precautions should be strictly observed.
Other risks: *Bilharzia* (schistosomiasis) is present. Avoid swimming and paddling in fresh water; swimming pools which are well chlorinated and maintained are safe. *Sleeping sickness* (trypanosomiasis) occurs. *Hepatitis A* and *E* also occur; *hepatitis B* is endemic. There has been a recent outbreak of *meningococcal meningitis*. Immunisation against *diphtheria* and *tuberculosis* is sometimes recommended. *Plague* is present in the Tanga region. *Rabies* is present. For those at high risk, vaccination before arrival should be considered. If you are bitten, seek medical advice without delay. For more information, see the *Health* appendix.
Health care: Private health insurance is recommended. There are over 2000 hospitals and clinics and some Christian missions also provide medical treatment; however, facilities are limited and medicines are often unavailable. All treatment must be paid for.

Travel - International

Note: There is a high threat from terrorism in Tanzania, including Zanzibar, as there is in other countries in East Africa. Visitors should be particularly vigilant in public places, including tourist sites and hotels. Armed robberies, especially at remote sites, are increasing. There is no suggestion that these attacks are terrorist-related. Tourists should avoid the area bordering Burundi.
AIR: Tanzania's national airline is *Air Tanzania (TC)*. Other airlines flying to Tanzania include *Air India*, *British Airways*, *Emirates*, *Ethiopian Airlines*, *Gulf Air*, *KLM-Royal Dutch Airlines*, *South African Airways* and *Swiss*.
Approximate flight times: From Dar es Salaam to *London* is 11 hours 15 minutes and from Kilimanjaro is 12 hours 30 minutes (excluding stopover).

TANZANIA

International airports: *Dar es Salaam International (DAR)* is 13km (8 miles) southwest of the city (travel time - 25-30 minutes). A shuttle bus service and taxi services are available to the city. Airport facilities include outgoing duty-free shop, car hire, post office, banking and currency exchange facilities (National Bank of Commerce), a bar and restaurant.
Kilimanjaro International Airport (JRO) and *Zanzibar Airport (ZNZ)*. Shuttle bus services and taxis are available to Arusha from Kilimanjaro. Airport facilities include shops, post office, bar and restaurant.
Departure tax: None.
SEA/LAKE: Dar es Salaam port is served by ocean freighters and passenger liners. Other ports include Mtwara, Tanga, Zanzibar and the Indian Ocean ports of Kilwa, Lindi and Mafia. The *MS Sepideh* runs services between Tanzania and Mombasa (Kenya). Passenger services run on Lake Tanganyika to Bujumbura (Burundi), Congo (Dem Rep of) and Mpulunga (Zambia); Lake Victoria connecting Tanzania with Kenya and Uganda; and Lake Nyasa linking Tanzania with Malawi and Mozambique.
RAIL: There is a twice weekly restaurant car service by Tanzania - *Zambia Railway Authority (Tazara)* from Dar es Salaam to Kapiri Mposhi (Zambia), with a change of train at the border. *Tanzania Railways Corporation (TRC)* provides services between Tanzania, Burundi, Congo (Dem Rep of), Kenya, Rwanda and Uganda. Trains may get very crowded but officials can be readily persuaded to find seats for tourists. Travellers should take special care of their baggage. It is unwise to forward luggage.
ROAD: The tarmac road connecting Tanzania with Zambia is in good condition, as is the road north to Kenya. From Lusaka in Zambia, the Great North Road is paved all the way to Dar es Salaam. Road links from Rwanda and Mozambique are poor.

Travel - Internal

AIR: *Air Tanzania (TC), Coastalair* (website: www.coastal.cc) and *Precision Air* (website: www.precisionairtz.com) run regular services to all main towns. Check with the airline office before leaving for the airport. All national parks have airstrips and there are several charter companies operating single- and twin-engine aircraft to any town or bush airfield or airstrip in the country.
Departure tax: For all departures from Zanzibar to destinations within Tanzania, the tax is TSh2000.
SEA/LAKE: There is a daily speedboat service between Dar es Salaam and Zanzibar which takes 60 to 90 minutes in each direction. Alternatively, the *Sea Express*, a hydrofoil, and the *Flying Horse*, a large catamaran, make this connection. There is also a crossing from Zanzibar to Pemba Island. Timetables and tickets can be obtained at the booking office at the main passenger port. Both Lake Tanganyika and Lake Victoria have steamer services. First-, second- and third-class seating is available on both services; first class has more comfortable seats and is likely to be less crowded. The service on Lake Victoria calls at the ports of Bukoba, Musoma and Mwanza.
RAIL: *Tanzania Railways Corporation (TRC)* provides the principal services, including routes to Northern Tanzania, while those on the route to Zambia are run by *Tazara*. *TRC* runs a daily service from Dar es Salaam to Mwanza on Lake Victoria and Kigoma on Lake Tanganyika with a restaurant car. For further information, contact *TRC*, PO Box 468, Dar es Salaam (tel: (22) 211 0599; fax: (22) 211 6525; e-mail: dgx_dg@trctz.com; website: www.trctz.com).
ROAD: Traffic drives on the left. Tanzania has a good network of tarmac and all-weather roads connecting all major towns. Most minor roads are not all-weather, becoming impassable to all except 4-wheel-drive vehicles during the long rains in April and May. It is not advisable to drive at night because of wild animals, cattle and goats on the road. There are often petrol shortages and spare parts for vehicles can be hard to find. **Bus:** Inexpensive buses connect most places; for example, there are services from Dar es Salaam to Arusha, Morogoro and Moshi. Visitors should avoid travelling by bus during the April/May rains. **Car hire:** Self-drive car hire is available in major cities, although it can be expensive. Vehicles with drivers are also available.
Documentation: An International Driving Permit is required for car hire and must be endorsed by the police on arrival. Otherwise an International Driving Permit is recommended although it is not legally required. A temporary licence to drive is available from the police on presentation of a valid national driving licence.
URBAN: Buses and minibuses operate in Dar es Salaam on a flat-fare basis. Services are often crowded. Taxi services are available. It is advisable to use authorised taxis.

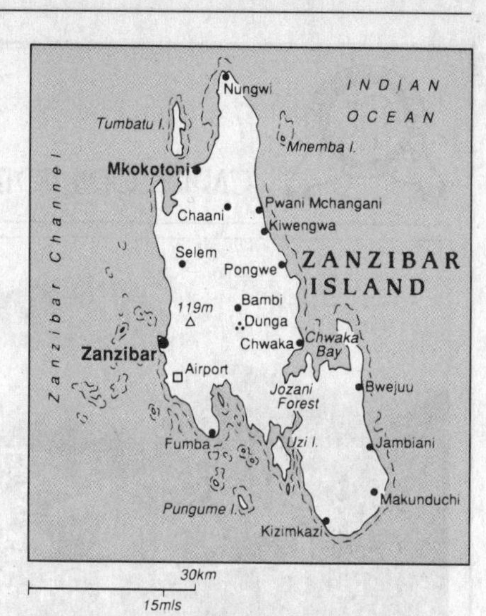

Accommodation

HOTELS: Tanzania has a range of accommodation from very good, expensive hotels to cheaper hotels which, although adequate, lack comfort. Although accommodation is on the expensive side, it is often possible for two people to share a single room except in top hotels. The less expensive hotels are often fully booked. The island of Zanzibar is currently experiencing a major tourism development phase and several new package hotels, many owned by Italian firms, have recently been built on its eastern coast. For more information, contact Tanzania Tourist Board (see *Contact Addresses* section).
WILDLIFE LODGES: There are wildlife lodges in all national parks. Reservations can be made through the Tanzania Tourist Board or by contacting the lodges.
GUEST HOUSES: These are often offshoots of local bars and provide cheap accommodation, but there may be problems with drunken behaviour and theft. Sharing a room is advisable and special attention to possessions should be paid while staying there. These can not be booked in advance. Prices are higher in the larger towns, but in general the quality can be assessed from the tariffs.
CAMPING/CARAVANNING: There are campsites in Arusha, Arusha National Park (four), Kilimanjaro National Park (one), Lake Manyara National Park (two), Mikumi National Park (two), Ngorongoro Conservation Area Authority (two), Ruaha National Park (two), Serengeti National Park (seven) and Tarangire National Park (two). Some have standard facilities, including taps, toilets, bivouac huts and firewood; others are more basic. Permits for entry to each park and also for photography and filming must be obtained before arrival. It is advisable to check the prices and site procedure before arrival. Further information can be obtained from Tanzania National Parks (see *National Parks* section) *or* Wildlife Explorer Ltd in the UK (e-mail: info@wildlife-explorer.com; website: www.wildlife-explorer.co.uk).
YOUTH HOSTELS: There are youth hostels in Lake Manyara National Park (primarily educational groups) and Serengeti National Park, YMCA hostels in Dar es Salaam and Moshi, and a YWCA hostel, which takes couples as well as women, in Dar es Salaam.

Resorts & Excursions

THE COAST

DAR ES SALAAM: Once the capital city (this function has now moved to Dodoma), the major port of Dar es Salaam is the natural starting point for trips in Tanzania. It is near the island of Zanzibar (see below). Parts of Dar es Salaam have a tranquil air that belies industrial and commercial growth. Further attractions include the **National Museum**, housing the skull of Nutcracker Man; **Observation Hill**, which contains the campus and facilities of the University of Dar es Salaam; and the **Village Museum**, with exhibits of traditional housing and crafts.
EXCURSIONS: The fishing village of **Msasani**, 8km (5 miles) from Dar es Salaam, contains tombs dating back to the 17th century. Further south, at **Kilwa Klsiwani**, there are ruins of Portuguese and Arab architecture. Many beautiful beaches are within easy reach of Dar es Salaam, such as those at **Kunduchi**, **Mbwa Maji** and **Mjimwena**. Kunduchi, 24km (15 miles) north of the city, is a fishing village with nearby ruins of Persian tombs and mosques. **Mbudya Island** is an uninhabited island

Credit: © Tanzania Trade Centre

forming part of a protective coral reef which is a good place for diving, snorkelling and fishing. **Sinda Island**, some 14km (9 miles) off Dar es Salaam, also offers facilities for snorkelling and shell fishing.
ELSEWHERE: A 72km (45 mile) drive north of Dar es Salaam is **Bagamoyo**, a one-time slave port and terminus for the caravans. This tiny township is the nearest mainland point to Zanzibar and possesses sandy beaches set in a beautiful bay. Livingstone's body rested in the tiny chapel of the convent here on its way back to London. The town mosque and Arab tombs date from the 18th and 19th centuries. Some 5km (3 miles) to the south is the village of **Kaole**, near which are the ruins of a mosque and pillars believed to be 800 years old. To the north of Bagamoyo, near the Kenyan border, is the country's second port, **Tanga**. From here, the visitor can drive to the beautiful Usambara Mountains and **Moshi** on the slopes of **Mount Kilimanjaro** (see *National Parks* section).

ZANZIBAR & MAFIA ISLAND

ZANZIBAR: The island of Zanzibar, once the metropolis of East Africa, variously ruled by Shirazi Persians, the Portuguese, the Omani Arabs and British colonials, is only 20 minutes' flight from Dar es Salaam (ferries are also available). Otherwise known as the 'Spice Island', Zanzibar's golden age was under the Omani Arabs in the early 19th century. By the middle of the century, it had become the world's largest producer of cloves and the largest slave-trading post on the African eastern coast. Zanzibar's old **Stone Town** is a labyrinth of narrow, winding streets lined with exotic shops, bazaars, colonial mansions, mosques and squares. The visitor can still see the house where Dr Livingstone lived, as well as that used by Burton and Speke. The **Anglican Cathedral Church of Christ** stands on the site of the **Old Slave Market**, off Creek Road, while on the seafront are the palace of the former sultan and the towering **Beit-el-Ajaib** (**The House of Wonders**). Zanzibar is a fascinating place with palaces, forts, stone aqueducts and baths; its history as a cosmopolitan centre of trade gives it a unique atmosphere. The guided **Spice Tours** are recommended (see also *Sport & Activities* section). Within the vicinity lie many offshore islands ringed with coral reefs, the most famous and most visited being **Changuu Island** (also known as 'Prison Island'). There are also many superb beaches, particularly on the east coast, although there are now several package hotels there.
Note: Visitors to Zanzibar should observe Muslim conventions regarding dress when away from the beach. For more information, see the *World of Islam* appendix.
MAFIA: Some 40 minutes' flight south of Dar es Salaam, the island of Mafia is renowned for big-game fish as well as being a unique marine park. Power boats and tackle are available for hire.

NATIONAL PARKS

Tanzania's national parks extend over some 33,660 sq km (13,000 sq miles). In addition, there is the unique Ngorongoro Conservation Area (see below), in which wildlife is protected and where the Masai tribespeople also live and herd their cattle. There are also some 10 game reserves where government-approved hunting safaris operate under licence and about 40 controlled areas where the hunting of game is controlled by a quota system. Further information can be obtained from Tanzania National Parks, PO Box 3134, Arusha (tel: (27) 250 1930 *or* 250 3471; fax: (27) 250 8216; e-mail: tanapa@yako.habari.co.tz). For more information on safaris, see the *Sport & Activities* section.
Mount Kilimanjaro: At 5895m (19,341ft), Africa's highest mountain is a major attraction for mountaineers. Expeditions must be accompanied by a guide and very warm clothes are required for the last section of the climb. The ascent takes about three days, allowing for rests at the three huts and a day or so at the final hut to acclimatise before tackling the final stage to the summit.
Serengeti National Park: This is a plain-dwellers' stronghold of 14,763 sq km (5678 sq miles) reaching up to the Kenyan border and claimed to be the finest in Africa. Here are 35 species of plain-dwelling animals, including wildebeest, zebra, gazelle, cheetah and lion, which feature in the spectacular Serengeti migration, and also an extensive selection of birdlife. Probably the best time to see the migrating herds is from November to May.
Ngorongoro Conservation Area: Rising high above the plains of the Serengeti, this vast protected area stretches from **Lake Natron** in the northeast (the breeding ground for east Africa's flamingoes) to **Lake Enaysi** in the south and **Lake Manyara** in the east. The area includes the still active volcano **Ol Doinyo Lengai** (**Mountain of God**), which last erupted in 1983. The park's centrepiece is the **Ngorongoro Crater**, a collapsed volcano forming a crater that is 610m (2000 ft) deep, 20km (12.5 miles) in diameter, covering an area of 311 sq km (122 sq miles). The crater accounts for just one-tenth of the conservation area, which is home to almost every species of African plains mammal (except for the impala, topi and giraffe) and particularly well known for the endangered black rhino. It also has the densest population of predators in Africa. The rich birdlife includes flamingoes which are attracted by the soda content in **Lake Magadi** on the crater floor.
Lake Manyara National Park: Famous for its elephants and tree-climbing lions. The wall of the **Great Rift Valley** forms a backdrop to the park, before which lies forest, open grassland, swamp and the soda lake. Wildlife includes lions, herds of buffalo, baboons, elephant, rhino, impala, giraffe, leopard, zebra, bushbuck, reedbuck, waterbuck and blue and vervet monkeys. Manyara is also noted for its birdlife, particularly the flamingoes.
Arusha National Park: This park lies within the **Ngurdoto Crater**, a volcano that has probably been extinct for a quarter of a million years. Visitors are able to see buffalo, rhino, elephant, giraffe and warthog.
Mikumi National Park: This park, 1300 sq km (500 sq miles) in area, offers a chance to see lion, zebra, hippo, leopard, cheetah, giraffe, impala, wildebeest and warthog. A popular spot for visitors is the **Kikaboga Hippo Pool**. Although December to March is the ideal time for viewing at Mikumi, there are animals throughout the year.
Tarangire National Park: Only 130km (80 miles) from **Arusha** and 8km (5 miles) off the Great Cape to Cairo road, it is nonetheless an area which compares favourably with the Serengeti in terms of wildlife density.
Ruaha National Park: Tanzania's second-largest and wildest park and the world's largest elephant sanctuary, Ruaha is located 118km (73 miles) from **Iringa** in the Southern Highlands along an all-weather road. The park affords views of unparalleled scenery along the **Ruaha Gorge**, with many sightings of antelope. Iringa is also connected with Dar es Salaam and other centres by air and bus service. The best time to visit is from July to November.
Selous Game Reserve: The Selous Game Reserve in southern Tanzania covers an area larger than Switzerland (about one-sixth of Tanzania's land surface), making it one of the biggest in the world, with a massive elephant population. There is also a high concentration of stalking lions and other game. UNESCO declared the game reserve a World Heritage Site in 1982.
Gombe National Park: This park is near **Kigoma** on the shores of **Lake Tanganyika** and is the home of about 200 chimpanzees, more easily seen here in their natural habitat than anywhere else in the world. This is the place where Jane Goodall devoted her life to recording chimpanzee ethology in a 37-year study.
Other national parks: These include Katavi, Mahale Mountains, Rubondo and Udzungura Mountains. There are also marine parks at Kilwa Reserve, Latham Island Reserve, Rufigi Delta and Tanga Coral Gardens.

Sport & Activities

Safaris: Less busy than neighbouring Kenya, Tanzania's national parks and game reserves provide some of the world's best destinations for viewing wildlife in their natural habitat. Tanzania is home to one of Africa's most magnificent game reserves, the *Selous Game Reserve*, as well as the endless plains of the *Serengeti National Park*, where one of the world's great natural spectacles, the annual migration of some 2 million wildebeest followed by their predators, can be observed. The Selous Game Reserve is inaccessible during the rainy season (from March to May) owing to floods. Numerous tour operators can organise tailor-made safaris, either by vehicle, on foot, on horseback

Credit: © Tanzania Trade Centre

TANZANIA

or by balloon. Some areas, such as the *Mahale Mountains National Park*, are only accessible by plane or boat. In parks such as the *Arusha National Park*, it is possible to drive around without a guide, but those on foot must take an armed guide or ranger. Accommodation is either in luxury lodges or designated camping sites. For details, contact the Tanzania Tourist Board (see *Contact Addresses* section). For further information on national parks and game reserves, see also *National Parks* in the *Resorts & Excursions* section.
Mountaineering: It is possible to climb Africa's highest mountain, *Mount Kilimanjaro*, but it is essential to have the right equipment (such as warm clothing, boots, gloves and a hat) and some experience. All climbers should be aware that guides and porters are essential even for the lower peaks. Organised climbs with food and staff can be arranged at some cost through selected hotels. It is advisable to book well in advance. Alternatively, climbers can bring their own supplies and hire staff and equipment (arctic sleeping bags and extra trousers) at the park gate. Although Kilimanjaro may be attempted by any strong mountain walker, visitors should be aware of the dangers of high altitude sickness which, in extreme cases, can be fatal. There are no known indicators as to who might suffer from altitude sickness (fitness, age and experience are irrelevant) and the only cure is an immediate descent to lower altitudes.
Watersports: Tanzania has 804km (503 miles) of coastline with superb beaches. **Scuba diving** and **snorkelling** are particularly good around the islands of *Mafia* and *Zanzibar*, which have recently gained a high reputation amongst divers. Mafia's *Chloe Bay* is part of a protected marine park, with an unbroken reef running the length of the island. There are also many secluded beaches. Offshore from Zanzibar are several islands ringed with coral reefs. Both Mafia and Zanzibar are also renowned for excellent **deep sea fishing**. There are numerous resorts and operators offering diving and fishing excursions. The main fishing season is from September to March. **Dolphin safaris** and **Dhow trips** are also popular.
Spice tours: Organised tours to Zanzibar's spice and fruit plantations are available all over the 'Spice Island' (as Zanzibar is also known). Along the way, visitors will be invited to taste and buy spices, herbs and fruit. Sadly, because of a decline in world prices, the spice industry and, particularly, its mainstay product - cloves - is now near collapse.

Social Profile

FOOD & DRINK: Most hotels serve local Tanzanian food while the major hotels offer Western and other international food. There is a variety of good seafood such as prawns and lobsters and an abundance of tropical fruit such as coconuts, pawpaws, mangoes, pineapples and bananas. Table service is normal in restaurants. Coffee and tea are of high quality. Tanzania is a secular state and alcohol is not prohibited. A good lager, *Safari*, is produced locally, as is a popular gin called *Konyagi*, a chocolate and coconut liqueur called *Afrikoko* and a wine called *Dodoma*, which comes in red or rosé. Bars generally have counter service.
NIGHTLIFE: In Dar es Salaam, there are several nightclubs, cabarets and cinemas. Generally, the nightlife centres are in the top tourist hotels and restaurants.
SHOPPING: The city and town centres usually have markets which sell curios such as African drums, old brass and copper, carved chess sets, jewellery, and a speciality, large wooden salad bowls carved from a single piece of teak, *mninga* or ebony. Haggling is accepted, indeed often expected. **Shopping hours:** Mon-Fri 0830-1200 and 1400-1800, Sat 0830-1230. Some shops open on Sunday.
SPECIAL EVENTS: The *Sukuma* (or *Bujora*) *Museum*, 15km (9 miles) east of Mwanza, gives approximately weekly performances of traditional dances of the Wasukuma tribe, including the *Bugobobobo* (Sukuma Snake Dance).
The following is a selection of special events occurring in Tanzania in 2005; for more information or exact dates contact the Tanzania Tourist Board (see *Contact Addresses* section):
Jan *Eid al-Hajj* (coincides with annual pilgrimage to Mecca). **Feb 12-13** *Sauti za Busara Swahili Music and Cultural Festival*, Stone Town, Zanzibar. **Mar** *Mwaka Kogwa* (celebration of the Persian New Year), Zanzibar. **Jul** *Zanzibar Cultural Festival*. **Oct 22-24** *Eid al-Fitr* (End of Ramadan), Makunduchi.
SOCIAL CONVENTIONS: When meeting and parting, hands are always shaken; this applies throughout the country in both rural and urban areas. It is the convention to use the right hand, not the left, to shake hands or pass or receive anything. The standard greeting when addressing an individual is *Jambo* to which the reply is also *Jambo*. The greeting for a group is *Hamjambo* to which the reply is *Hatujambo*. People are delighted if visitors can greet them in Kiswahili. There is no fixed protocol to do with hospitality. Dress is smart and a good appearance is highly regarded. Suits and ties or safari suits are worn by men and suits or dresses by women. Ashtrays are usually an indication of permission for a visitor to smoke. Smoking is prohibited in cinemas and on public transport.
Photography: In some places, a charge will be levied on visitors wishing to take photographs; elsewhere a permit may be required. **Tipping:** Not generally encouraged, though waiters and porters in tourist hotels and restaurants may expect to be tipped.

Business Profile

ECONOMY: Agriculture employs around 80 per cent of the working population. Cash crops, including cotton, coffee, tea, sisal, tobacco and cashew nuts, are the country's main export earners, although depressed prices have kept Tanzanian revenues at a static level despite increases in production. There is an expanding mineral sector: diamonds are mined commercially, as are other gemstones and gold. Coal, phosphates, gypsum, tin and other ores are also extracted. Reserves of uranium, nickel, silver and natural gas have been located. The Government granted oil and gas exploration in the mid-1990s, and some small projects are under way, such as natural gas from the Rufiji delta. The industrial sector is small and concentrated in agricultural processing and light consumer goods: sugar processing, brewing, textiles and the manufacture of cigarettes are the most important.
The government had pinned much of its hopes on development of its service industries, especially transport and tourism. Tanzania's relatively poor road network is the subject of a major programme of maintenance and construction, mainly financed by the EU. Tourism, which according to 2002 figures was worth about $1 billion to the Tanzanian economy, has suffered a serious downturn as a result of international terrorism.
The government had privatised several key industries, including the national airline and the main chain of hotels, in anticipation of a growing tourist market (Tanzania received 500,000 visitors in 2002). Both, along with a number of flagship industries, were bought by South African interests which are establishing a strong presence in Tanzania. Of 400 companies earmarked for sale under the original 1995 plan, over 80 per cent have been disposed of (although some have since failed in private hands). Liberalisation of trade and the financial sector were also implemented as part of an IMF-supported structural adjustment programme.
On the whole, the economy has performed fairly well since the mid-1990s. GDP growth in 2002 was over 6 per cent. Tanzania is a recipient of foreign aid from both bilateral and multilateral donors, and some efforts have been made to tackle its large foreign debt. In 2000 the country benefited to the tune of $2 billion from the Heavily Indebted Poor Countries initiative. Total external debt is now just under $7 billion. Tanzania is a member of the African Development Bank, the Southern African Development Community and the East African Community (EAC). Another attempt (the previous one failed in 1977) is being made to establish an East African Customs Union along with Kenya and Uganda. Its principal trading partners are the UK, Japan, Germany, India, Kenya and Congo (Brazzaville).
BUSINESS: Normal courtesies should be shown when visiting local businesspeople. Almost all executives speak English. **Office hours:** Mon-Fri 0800-1200 and 1400-1630, Sat 0800-1230. **Government office hours:** Mon-Fri 0730-1530.
COMMERCIAL INFORMATION: The following organisation can offer advice: Tanzania Chamber of Commerce, Industry and Agriculture, PO Box 9713, Dar es Salaam (tel: (22) 211 9436 *or* 212 1421; fax: (22) 211 9437; e-mail: tccia.hq@cats-net.com *or* tccia.info@cats-net.com; website: www.tccia.co.tz).
CONFERENCES/CONVENTIONS: For information concerning conferences and conventions, contact the Arusha International Conference Centre (AICC), PO Box 3081, Arusha (tel: (27) 250 2593/5 *or* 250 8008; fax: (27) 250 6630; e-mail: md@aicc.co.tz; website: www.aicc.co.tz).

Climate

The climate is tropical and coastal areas are hot and humid. The rainy season lasts from March to June. The central plateau is dry and arid. The northwestern highlands are cool and temperate and the rainy season here lasts from November to December and February to May.
Required clothing: Tropical clothing is worn throughout the year, but in the cooler season, from June to September, jackets and sweaters may be needed, especially in the evenings.

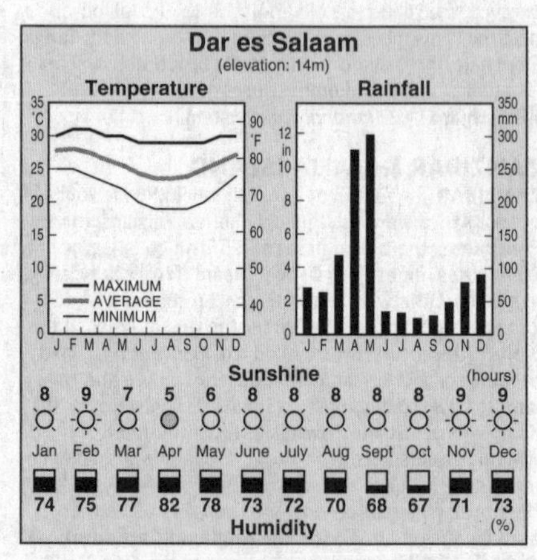

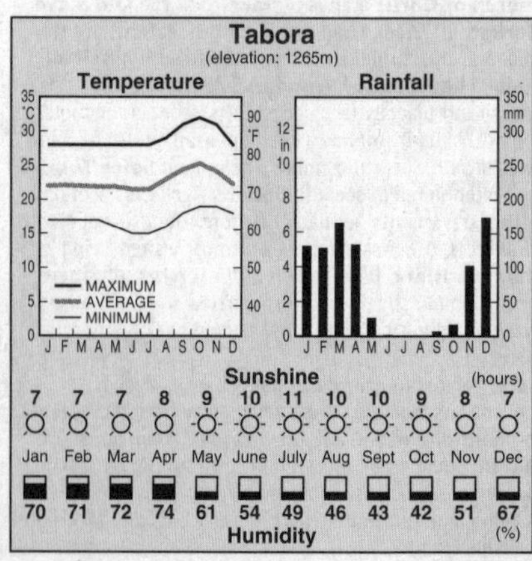

Thailand

LATEST TRAVEL ADVICE CONTACTS

British Foreign and Commonwealth Office
Tel: (0870) 606 0290 Website: www.fco.gov.uk
US Department of State
Website: http://travel.state.gov/travel
Canadian Department of Foreign Affairs and Int'l Trade
Tel: (1 800) 267 8376 Website: www.dfait-maeci.gc.ca

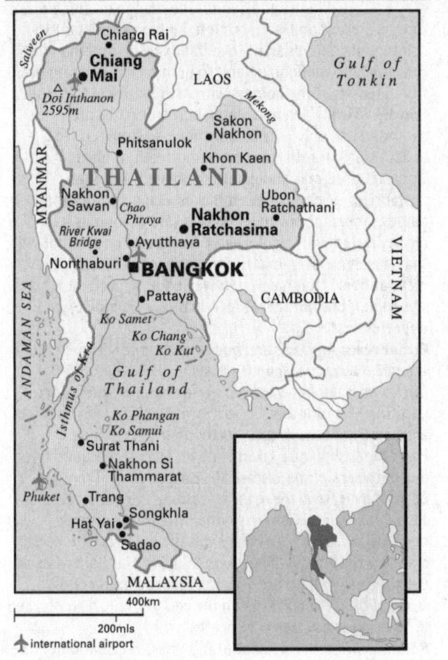

Location: South-East Asia.

Country dialling code: 66.

Tourism Authority of Thailand
1600 New Phetburi Road, Makkasan, Rajatevee, Bangkok 10310, Thailand
Tel: (2) 250 5500. Fax: (2) 250 5511.
E-mail: center@tat.or.tt
Website: www.tourismthailand.org

Royal Thai Embassy
29-30 Queens Gate, London SW7 5JB, UK
Tel: (020) 7589 2944 (ext. 115/119).
Fax: (020) 7823 7492 (visa section).
E-mail: thaiduto@btinternet.com
Website: www.thaiembassyuk.org.uk
Opening hours: Mon-Fri 0930-1230 (consular section); Mon-Fri 1400-1700 (telephone enquiries).
Honorary Consulates in: Birmingham, Cardiff, Dublin, Glasgow, Hull and Liverpool.

Office of Commercial Affairs (Royal Thai Embassy)
11 Hertford Street, London W1J 7RN, UK
Tel: (020) 7493 5749. Fax: (020) 7493 7416.
E-mail: thaicomuk@dial.pipex.com
Website: www.thaicomuk.dial.pipex.com
Opening hours: Mon-Fri 0930-1230 and 1400-1700.

Tourism Authority of Thailand
3rd Floor, Brook House, 98-99 Jermyn Street, London SW1Y 6EE, UK
Tel: (09063) 640 666 (consumer enquiries; calls cost 60p per minute) *or* (0870) 900 2007 (brochure request line) *or* (020) 7925 2511 (trade enquiries). Fax: (020) 7925 2512.
E-mail: info@thaismile.co.uk
Website: www.thaismile.co.uk
Opening hours: Mon-Fri 0930-1700 (personal callers).

British Embassy
1031 Wireless Road, Lumpini, Pathumwan, Bangkok 10330, Thailand
Tel: (2) 305 8333. Fax: (2) 255 8619 (commercial section) *or* 6051 (consular section).
E-mail: visa.bangkok@fco.gov.uk *or* info.bangkok@fco.gov.uk
Website: www.britishembassy.gov.uk/thailand
Consulate in: Chiang Mai.

TIMATIC CODES

Health
AMADEUS: **TI-DFT/BKK/HE**
GALILEO/WORLDSPAN: **TI-DFT/BKK/HE**
SABRE: **TIDFT/BKK/HE**

Visa
AMADEUS: **TI-DFT/BKK/VI**
GALILEO/WORLDSPAN: **TI-DFT/BKK/VI**
SABRE: **TIDFT/BKK/VI**

To access TIMATIC country information on Health and Visa regulations through the Computer Reservations System (CRS), type in the appropriate command line listed above.

Royal Thai Embassy
1024 Wisconsin Avenue, Suite 401, NW, Washington, DC 20007, USA
Tel: (202) 944 3600 *or* 3608 (consular).
Fax: (202) 944 3611.
E-mail: thai.wsn@thaiembdc.org *or* consular@thaiembdc.org
Website: www.thaiembdc.org
Consulates in: Chicago, Los Angeles and New York.
Honorary Consulates in: Alabama, Colorado, Florida, Georgia, Hawaii, Louisiana, Massachusetts, Missouri, Oregon and Texas.

Tourism Authority of Thailand
61 Broadway, Suite 2810, New York, NY 10006, USA
Tel: (212) 432 0433. Fax: (212) 269 2588.
E-mail: info@tatny.com
Website: www.tourismthailand.org

Royal Thai Consulate General
351 East 52nd Street, New York, NY 10022, USA
Tel: (212) 754 1770 *or* 2536-8 *or* 1896. Fax: (212) 754 1907.
E-mail: thainycg@aol.com
Website: www.thaiembdc.org
Offices also in: Chicago and Los Angeles.

Embassy of the United States of America
120 Wireless Road, Pathumwan District, Lumpini Sub-district, Bangkok 10330, Thailand
Tel: (2) 205 4000. Fax: (2) 205 4131.
E-mail: acsbkk@state.gov *or* visabkk@state.gov
Website: www.usa.or.th
Consulate in: Chiang Mai.

Royal Thai Embassy
180 Island Park Drive, Ottawa, Ontario K1Y 0A2, Canada
Tel: (613) 722 4444. Fax: (613) 722 6624.
E-mail: thaiott@magma.ca
Website: www.magma.ca/~thaiott/mainpage.htm
Consulates General in: Calgary, Edmonton, Montréal, Toronto and Vancouver.

Canadian Embassy
Street address: 15th Floor, Abdulrahim Place, 990 Rama IV Road, Bangrak, Bangkok 10500, Thailand
Postal address: PO Box 2090, Bangkok 10501, Thailand
Tel: (2) 636 0540. Fax: (2) 636 0565 (general enquiries) *or* 0555 (consular section) *or* 0568 (trade section).
E-mail: bngkk@dfait-maeci.gc.ca
Website: www.dfait-maeci.gc.ca/bangkok
Consulate in: Chiang Mai.

General Information

AREA: 513,115 sq km (198,115 sq miles).
POPULATION: 62,193,000 (2002).
POPULATION DENSITY: 121.2 per sq km.
CAPITAL: Bangkok. **Population:** 7,527,000, including Thon Buri (UN estimate 2001).
GEOGRAPHY: Thailand is bordered to the west by Myanmar and the Indian Ocean, to the south and east by Malaysia and the Gulf of Thailand, to the east by Cambodia, and to the north and east by Laos. Central Thailand is dominated by the Chao Phraya River.
GOVERNMENT: Constitutional monarchy since 1973. **Head of State:** HM King Bhumibol Adulyadej (Rama IX) since 1946. **Head of Government:** Prime Minister Thaksin Shinawatra since 2001.
LANGUAGE: Thai is the official language. English is widely spoken, especially in establishments catering for tourists.
RELIGION: The vast majority adhere to Buddhism (Theravada form), 4 per cent are Muslim and there are Christian minorities.
TIME: GMT + 7.
ELECTRICITY: 220 volts AC, 50Hz. American- and European-style two-pin plugs are in use.
COMMUNICATIONS: Telephone: IDD is available. Country code: 66. Outgoing international code: 00. **Mobile telephone:** GSM 900/1800/1900 networks. Network operators include *Advanced Info Service* (website: www.ais900.com) and *Total Access Comms Co* (website: www.dtac.co.th). **Fax:** Facilities are widely available in hotels, post offices and travel agencies. **Internet:** Internet cafes provide public access to Internet and e-mail services. ISPs include *Asia Infonet* (website: www.asianet.co.th) and *Internet Thailand* (website: www.inet.co.th). **Telegram:** Telegrams can be sent from hotels, airports and CAT (Communications Authority of Thailand) offices. **Post:** Airmail to Europe takes up to one week. The General Post Office in Bangkok (on Charoen Krung Road) hours: Mon-Fri 0800-2000, Sat-Sun and holidays 0800-1300. Post offices up-country are open Mon-Fri 0800-1630, Sat 0900-1200 . **Press:** Many daily and weekly Thai newspapers are available, most notably *Baan Muang*. Other English-language dailies are *Bangkok Post*, *The Nation* and *Thailand Times*.
Radio: BBC World Service (website: www.bbc.co.uk/worldservice) and Voice of America (website: www.voa.gov) can be received. From time to time the frequencies change and the most up-to-date can be found online.

Credit: © Tourism Authority of Thailand

Passport/Visa

	Passport Required?	Visa Required?	Return Ticket Required?
Full British	Yes	No	Yes
Australian	Yes	No	Yes
Canadian	Yes	No	Yes
USA	Yes	No	Yes
Other EU	Yes	No/1/2	Yes
Japanese	Yes	No	Yes

Note: *Regulations and requirements may be subject to change at short notice, and you are advised to contact the appropriate diplomatic or consular authority before finalising travel arrangements. Details of these may be found at the head of this country's entry. Any numbers in the chart refer to the footnotes below.*

Restricted entry: Nationals of Afghanistan and Iraq will be refused.
PASSPORTS: Passport valid for six months beyond intended length of stay required by all except the following:
(a) holders of a Hong Kong (SAR) certificate of identity bearing a Thai visa issued in Hong Kong;
(b) holders of a Singapore certificate of identity with a visa;
(c) holders of South African temporary passports;
(d) holders of a UN laissez-passer and Macau (SAR) China Travel Permits.
VISAS: Required by all except the following nationals for touristic stays, provided they hold valid passports, sufficient funds and confirmed tickets to leave Thailand within 30 days:
(a) nationals of the countries referred to in the chart above, except **1.** nationals of Cyprus, Czech Republic, Estonia, Hungary, Latvia, Lithuania, Malta, Poland, Slovak Republic and Slovenia, who *do* need a visa;
(b) nationals of Bahrain, Brazil, Brunei, Hong Kong (SAR), Indonesia, Israel, Korea (Rep), Kuwait, Malaysia, New Zealand, Norway, Peru, The Philippines, Qatar, Singapore, South Africa, Switzerland, Turkey, United Arab Emirates and Vietnam;
(c) transit passengers continuing their journey within 12 hours, provided holding confirmed tickets and other documents for an onward journey and they do not leave the transit lounge.

A B C D E F G H I J K L M N O P Q R S T U V W X Y Z

Credit: © Frederik Jurriaanse

Note: (a) **2.** The following nationals can obtain an entry visa on arrival at 23 designated immigration checkpoints throughout Thailand (consult nearest Embassy/Consulate for further information), provided holding a confirmed ticket to leave within 15 days, proof of sufficient funds, application form with recent photo, a valid passport and that their visit is for tourist purposes only: Bhutan, China (PR), Cyprus, Czech Republic, Hungary, India, Kazakhstan, Maldives, Mauritius, Oman, Poland, Russian Federation, Saudi Arabia and Ukraine. The fee for this service is approximately 300 Baht; note that this is subject to frequent change. Travellers should also note that there are normally long queues at the immigration checkpoints.
(b) Anyone intending to stay longer than 15 days *must* obtain a visa prior to arrival.

Types of visa and cost: *Tourist*: £25 (single-entry); *Non-immigrant*: £40 (single-entry), £90 (multiple-entry); *Transit*: £15 (single-entry).

Validity: *Tourist*: 60 days. *Non-immigrant*: 90 days. *Transit*: 30 days. All visas must be used within three months of date of issue, except multiple-entry non-immigration visas which are valid for up to one year. Extensions are available from the Immigration Bureau in Bangkok.

Application to: Consulate (or Consular section at Embassy); see *Contact Addresses* section.

Application requirements: (a) Valid passport. (b) One completed application form. (c) Recent passport-size photo. (d) Fee (cash or postal order only). (e) Proof of sufficient funds to cover stay (Bt20,000 per person, Bt40,000 per family). (f) Confirmed onward or return ticket. (g) Registered, stamped, self-addressed envelope for postal enquiries. *Non-immigrant*: (a)-(g) and, (h) Copy of passport and extra passport photograph. (i) For a business visit, a letter from the employer in country of origin and from the business partner in Thailand explaining the purpose of the visit is required. Other documents may also be required, depending on purpose of visit. *Transit*: (a)-(h) and, (i) Visa for next destination in passport or travel document.

Note: (a) The Royal Thai Embassy in London does not accept visa applications by post. (b) Nationals of Algeria, Bangladesh, Egypt, India, Iran, Iraq, Lebanon, Libya, Nepal, Pakistan, Palestinian Authority passport holders, Sri Lanka, Sudan, Syrian Arab Republic and Yemen must provide additional information. They must also file an application for extension of stay at their Thai Embassy/Consulate General in place of permanent residence, rather than at the Office of Immigration Bureau in Thailand. Contact Consulate for details. (c) Yellow fever vaccination certificates are required for applicants who have visited or come from an affected area. Other vaccinations, such as for Smallpox, may also be requested by the Immigration Doctor and compliance is essential.

Working days required: Two days if submitted in person, approximately one week plus mailing time if applying by post.

Money

Currency: Baht (Bt) = 100 satang. Notes are in denominations of Bt1000, 500, 100, 50, 20 and 10. Coins are in denominations of Bt10, 5 and 1, and 50 and 25 satang. In addition, there are a vast number of commemorative coins which are also legal tender.

Currency exchange: Foreign currencies can be exchanged at banks (which have the best rates), hotels (which charge high commissions) and, in larger towns, bureaux de change (generally open 0800-2000). Outside large towns and tourist areas, notes higher than Bt500 may be difficult to exchange, so visitors are advised to carry small change.

Credit & debit cards: American Express, MasterCard and Visa are widely accepted, while Diners Club has more limited use. Check with your credit or debit card company for details of merchant acceptability and other facilities which may be available.

Travellers cheques: Accepted by all banks and large hotels and shops. To avoid additional exchange rate charges, travellers are advised to take travellers cheques in US Dollars, Euros or Pounds Sterling.

Currency restrictions: The import and export of local currency is limited to Bt50,000 per person or Bt100,000 per family holding one passport. The import and export of foreign currency is unlimited.

Exchange rate indicators: The following figures are included as a guide to the movements of the Baht against Sterling and the US Dollar:

Date	Feb '04	May '04	Aug '04	Nov '04
£1.00=	71.42	71.76	76.51	74.73
$1.00=	39.24	40.18	41.53	39.46

Banking hours: Mon-Fri 0930-1530.

Duty Free

The following goods may be imported into Thailand without incurring customs duty by any person, irrespective of age:
200 cigarettes or 250g of tobacco or equal weight of cigars; 1l of alcoholic liquor; one still camera with five rolls of film or one movie camera with three rolls of 8mm or 16mm film.

Restricted exports: There are restrictions on the export of items of archaeological interest or historical value without a certificate of authorisation from the Department of Fine Arts in Thailand. The export of images of the Buddha and other religious artefacts is also subject to this ruling.

Prohibited items: The import of non-prescribed drugs and all firearms and ammunition is prohibited. Gold bullion must be declared on arrival and can be left at the airport of entry to be retrieved on departure. The import of meat from any country affected by Bovine Spongiform Encephalopathy (BSE) or mad cow and foot and mouth diseases; the measure covers meat from all 15 EU countries and any other infected country.

Warning: Any drug-related offences are severely punished and may result in life imprisonment or even the death penalty.

Public Holidays

Jan 1 2005 New Year's Day. **Feb 17** Magha Bucha Day. **Apr 6** Chakri Day. **Apr 13-15** Songkran (Thai New Year). **May 1** Labour Day. **May 5** Coronation Day. **May 23*** Visakha Bucha. Jul 1 Mid Year Bank Holiday. **July 22*** Khao Phansa Day (Buddhist Lent). **Aug 12** HM The Queen's Birthday. **Oct 23** Chulalongkorn Day. **Dec 5** HM The King's Birthday. **Dec 10** Constitution Day. **Dec 31** New Year's Eve.

2006: Jan-Mar tbc Magha Bucha Day. **Jan 1** New Year's Day. **Apr 6** Chakri Day. **Apr 13-15** Songkran (Thai New Year). **May 1** Labour Day. **May 5** Coronation Day. **May 15*** Visakha Bucha. **Jul-Aug tbc*** Khao Phansa Day (Buddhist Lent). **Jul 1** Mid Year Bank Holiday. **Aug 12** HM The Queen's Birthday. **Oct 23** Chulalongkorn Day. **Dec 5** HM The King's Birthday. **Dec 10** Constitution Day. **Dec 31** New Year's Eve.

Note: * The religious festivals are determined by the Buddhist lunar calendar and therefore are difficult to predict. The dates provided here are estimates.

Credit: © Frederik Jurriaanse

Health

	Special Precautions?	Certificate Required?
Yellow Fever	No	1
Cholera	2	No
Typhoid & Polio	3	No
Malaria	4	No

Note: *Regulations and requirements may be subject to change at short notice, and you are advised to contact your doctor well in advance of your intended date of departure. Any numbers in the chart refer to the footnotes below.*

1: A yellow fever vaccination certificate is required from travellers over one year of age arriving from infected areas. Countries and areas included in endemic zones are considered to be infected areas.

2: Following WHO guidelines issued in 1973, a cholera vaccination certificate is not a condition of entry to Thailand. However, cholera is a serious risk in this country and precautions are essential. Up-to-date advice should be sought before deciding whether these precautions should include vaccination, as medical opinion is divided over its effectiveness; see the *Health* appendix.

3: Vaccination against typhoid is advised.

4: Malaria risk exists throughout the year in rural areas throughout the country, especially in forested and hilly areas and around the international borders. There is no risk in cities and the main tourist resorts, eg Bangkok, Chiang Mai, Pattaya, Phuket and Samui. The malignant *falciparum* form is present and is reported to be highly resistant to chloroquine and resistant to sulfadoxine-pyrimethamine. Resistance to mefloquine and to quinine has been reported from areas near the borders with Myanmar and Cambodia.

Food & drink: Food and water-borne diseases are common. Use only bottled or otherwise sterilised (eg boiled) water for drinking, brushing teeth or making ice. Unpasteurised milk should also be boiled, although pasteurised or homogenised milk is available from some dairies. Tinned or powdered milk is safe as long as it is reconstituted with sterile water. Beware of dairy products that may have been made with unboiled milk. Stick to meat and fish that have been well cooked, preferably served hot, but not reheated. Avoid raw vegetables and unpeeled fruit.

Other risks: *Amoebic* and *bacillary dysentery* and *hepatitis A* and *E* may occur. *Hepatitis B* is highly endemic and *trachoma* is also reported. *Japanese encephalitis* may occur, particularly in rural areas. A vaccine is available, and travellers are advised to consult their doctor prior to departure. Precautions should be taken to guard against mosquito bites due to the risk of this disease and *dengue fever*. There has been an increase in the reported cases of *dengue fever* since January 2005, especially in southern Thailand and areas bordering Malaysia. *HIV* infection is rife in Thailand, especially among prostitutes in Bangkok and Chiang Mai. Rare cases of *Bengal Cholera* have been reported and an outbreak of *leptospiros* in the northeast of the country, following flooding in 1999 caused a number of deaths.
Rabies is present. For those at high risk, vaccination before arrival should be considered. If you are bitten, seek medical advice without delay. For more information, consult the *Health* appendix.

Note: Those suspected or confirmed of carrying AIDS will be refused entry.

Health Care: Health insurance is recommended. Medical facilities are good in main centres. All major hotels have doctors on call.

Travel - International

Travel Warning: On December 26 2004, a tsunami hit areas along Thailand's west coast including Phuket, Krabi, Khao Lak and on Phi Phi Island. The clean up process has been excellent but visitors wishing to travel to affected areas should check with a relevant tour operator, tourist board or embassy for the latest travel advice prior to travel. Visitors are also advised against all but essential travel to the far southern provinces of Pattani, Yala, Narathiwat and Songkhla where there have been attacks by militant separatists in the past.

AIR: Thailand's national airline is *Thai Airways International* (website: www.thaiairways.com).
Bangkok is the main entry point into Thailand, as well as being a major access point for travel to Cambodia, Laos, Myanmar, Nepal and Vietnam.

Approximate flight times: From Bangkok to *London* is 12 hours; to *Manila* is three hours; to *Singapore* is two hours 15 minutes and to *Sydney* is nine hours.

International airports: *Bangkok International (BKK)* (Don Muang) (website: www.airportthai.co.th) is 24km (15 miles) north of the city (travel time - 40 to 60 minutes). There is a 24-hour bus service to the city centre. Trains also run to the city centre (travel time - 30 to 45 minutes). Limousines are available at all hours: service is every 20 minutes depending on flights. Taxis are also available. There is a direct coach service to Pattaya at 0900, 1200 and 1900, returning at 0630, 1400 and 1830. Airport facilities include left luggage, first aid, chemist, duty free shop, banks/bureaux de change, restaurant, bar and snack bars inside the departure lounge, post office situated inside the departure lounge, car hire, accommodation and insurance bureaux.
Chiang Mai International Airport (CNX), 15km (9 miles) southwest of the city (travel time - 20 minutes). Taxi and limousine services are available to the city centre. Airport facilities include car hire, banks/bureaux de change, restaurant, shops and bar.
Phuket International Airport (HKT) is 35km (22 miles) northwest of Phuket. Buses and taxis are available to the city centre. Airport facilities include left luggage, duty free shops, restaurant, car hire and tourist information.
Hat Yai International (HDY) has recently been opened; so

Credit: © Tourism Authority of Thailand
Credit: © Frederik Jurriaanse

far it is only used for Asian destinations and domestic flights. The nearest town is Songkhla (approximately 20km/12.5 miles away). Taxis, bus and train services are available. Airport facilities include duty free shop, restaurant, car hire and post office.
Departure tax: Bt500 for all international departures. Transit passengers and children under two years of age are exempt.
SEA: The main international port is Bangkok. Limited passenger services are available. There are passenger crossings between Thailand and Laos at several points along the Mekong river. Cruise lines calling at Thailand include *Holland America, Orient Lines, Princess, Radisson Seven Seas, Seabourn, Silversea* and *Swan Hellenic*.
RAIL: Through trains operate to Kuala Lumpur, with daily connections to Singapore, Malaysia and to the borders with Cambodia (at Aranyaprathet) and Laos (at Nong Khai). The journey to Singapore takes 48 hours. The opulent Eastern and Oriental Express runs directly from Bangkok to Singapore but it is expensive.
ROAD: There are international roads from Cambodia, Malaysia and Laos. Roads into Myanmar are not officially open to tourist traffic.

Travel - Internal

AIR: *Thai Airways International (TG)* (website: www.thaiairways.com) runs services to all major towns, using a total of 22 airports.
Bangkok Airways (PG) (website: www.bangkokair.com) flies seven additional routes. Discounts are available in off-peak seasons and during special promotional periods.
Departure tax: Bt50 for all domestic flights, Bt400 for domestic flights from Samui Airport. Children under two years are exempt.
RIVER: Thailand has, depending on the season, up to 1600km (1000 miles) of navigable inland waterway. Services operate between Thanon Tok and Nonthaburi, and luxury cruises are available on the *Oriental Queen*. Long-tailed motorboats and taxi-boat ferries also operate. Strong competition on all of the major routes ensures that fares are kept low. Reduced services operate during the monsoon season from May through to October along the east coast and Andaman coast, and from November through until January on the Gulf coast. The more remote spots become inaccessible in these periods.
RAIL: The excellent railway network extends over 4600km (2860 miles), linking all major towns with the exception of Phuket. It is run by *State Railways of Thailand*. It has recently been extended to serve centres on the east coast. There are four main trunk routes to the northern, eastern, southern and northeastern regions, and also a line serving Thon Buri, River Kwai Bridge and Nam Tok. There are several daily services on each route, with air-conditioned, sleeping and restaurant cars on the principal trains. The journeys are leisurely and comfortable, and travelling by train is certainly one of the best ways to get around the country. The *Southern Line Express* stops at Surat Thani for those who wish to continue by bus and ferry to the islands off the east coast. Most railway timetables are published in English.
ROAD: There is a reasonable road network comprising many highways and 52,000km (32,300 miles) of national and provincial roads. All major roads are paved. Traffic drives on the left. **Bus:** There are inter-urban routes to all provinces. Fares are very cheap and buses very crowded. Privately owned air-conditioned buses (seats bookable) are comfortable and moderately priced. **Taxi:** There are plenty of taxis, which operate day and night. There are three types: *taxi-meter*; *taxis* which are unmetered; and 3-wheeled, open-air *tuk-tuks*. Where there is no meter, fares should be agreed before departure. It is sometimes possible to agree fares for longer trips even in taxi-meters. It is also possible to take a *motorbike taxi*. These are especially useful in Bangkok's horrendous rush-hour traffic. Taxi drivers do not always carry change, so it is important to have the correct amount. Passengers are also expected to pay for any motorway tolls. **Car hire:** Available in all main cities. Passports may be held as a form of deposit. **Motorcycle** hire is also available, especially on the larger islands. **Documentation:** International Driving Permit required. IDPs are valid for three months, after which a Thai driving licence is required.
URBAN: Conventional bus services in Bangkok are operated by the *Government Mass Transit Authority*, but there are also extensive private minibus operations and passenger-carrying trucks. Premium fares are charged for air conditioned and express buses. Fares are generally low and are collected by conductors. Ferries and long-tailed motorboats operate on the Chao Phraya River which are a quick and cheap way to get about. Bus maps of the city are available, on arrival, from the tourist office at Don Muang Airport. The *Skyrail*, an elevated mass transit system in Bangkok, runs from 0600-0000.
Travel Times: The following chart gives approximate travel times (in hours and minutes) from **Bangkok** to other major cities/towns in Thailand.

	Air	Road	Rail
Chiang Rai	1.15	12.00	-
Chiang Mai	1.00	10.00	14.00
Hat Yai	1.15	15.00	17.00
Hua Hin	0.40	3.00	4.00
Pattaya	-	3.00	-
Phitsanulok	0.55	5.30	6.00
Phuket	1.20	10.45	-
Samui	1.20	13.00	14.00
Surat Thani	1.00	11.00	12.00
Ubon Ratchathani	1.45	10.00	11.00
Udon Thani	1.00	9.00	10.15

Accommodation

NOTE: A regularly updated list of accommodation availability since the tsunami struck some littoral regions in December 2004 is available from the Tourism Authority of Thailand website (see *Contact Addresses*).
HOTELS: Bangkok has some of Asia's finest hotels, with over 12,000 rooms meeting international standards. Many hotels belong to the large international chains. All luxury hotels have swimming pools, 24-hour room service, air conditioning and a high staff-to-guest ratio. Accommodation styles cover every range, however, and the budget traveller is also well catered for. Bang'lampoo in Bangkok is the main area for cheap accommodation. Hotels outside the capital and developed tourist areas are less lavish but are extremely economical. Member hotels of the Thai Hotels Association can be booked on arrival at the counter of Bangkok's Don Muang Airport, and at similar counters in some provincial airports. For information, contact the Thai Hotels Association (THA), 203-209/3 Ratchadamnoen Klang Avenue, Bowonniwet Bangkok 10200 (tel: (2) 281 9496; fax: (2) 281 4188; e-mail: info@thaihotels.org; website: www.thaihotels.org).
Grading: There is no official system of grading hotels, but prices generally give a good indication of standards. The Tourism Authority of Thailand publishes regional accommodation guides, which give comprehensive details on pricing and facilities.
GUEST HOUSES: Guest houses are cheap and popular with tourists, as are bungalows, which also often have cafes and English-speaking staff.
SELF-CATERING: Holiday villas and flats can be rented. For details, look for advertisements in the English-language newspapers.
CAMPING/CARAVANNING: In general, visitors will find that camping in Thailand is not popular, as other accommodation is available at such reasonable prices. Most of Thailand's campsites are in the area of the National Parks, which are under the management of the Department of Forestry; there are also some private tourist resorts which provide camping facilities. Camping is allowed on nearly all of the islands and beaches, many of which are National Parks in their own rights. Some national parks rent out tents at a reasonable price.
YOUTH HOSTELS: YMCA, YWCA and small, cheap hotels are available all over the country. For further details, contact the Thai Youth Hostels Association, 25/14 Phitsanulok Road, Dusit, Bangkok 10300 (tel: (2) 6287 413-5; fax: (2) 628 7416; e-mail: contact@tyha.org; website: www.tyha.org).

Credit: © Tourism Authority of Thailand

Resorts & Excursions

BANGKOK

Most Thais refer to the capital as 'Krung Thep', the shortened Thai name of a city that actually consists of 32 different words, a fittingly impressive number of monikers for a capital that is one of the world's most eclectic and thrilling. Bangkok is to Thailand what London is to England: the metropole, the hub of business, economic and political affairs. The rapid pace of change and the increasing prosperity that gives the city much of its vibrancy have also caused some problems, with widely reported nightmare traffic congestion and pollution. Over the last few years, the opening of a slick new overland metropolitan railway that enables visitors to glide over the chaotic scenes below, coupled with the cheap and frequent river boats and the reasonably priced air-conditioned taxis, have improved the situation markedly. Through the city flows the **Chao Phraya River**, on the banks of which can be found some of the best hotels in Bangkok. It is also where visitors will find the Grand Palace which, covering a huge area, is one of the major sites. Here also is **Wat Phra Kaeo**, a temple complex which houses the Emerald Buddha. This Buddha statue is not covered in emeralds, as the name suggests, but is made of translucent green jade. Upriver from the Grand Palace are the **Royal Barges**. These richly ornamented barges are still used today for special processions on the Chao Phraya. Within the city limits is a wealth of over 300 Buddhist temple and shrines. Most famous are **Wat Benchamabophit (Marble Temple)**, **Wat Arun (Temple of Dawn)** and **Wat Trimit (Temple of the Golden Buddha)**. One of the largest temple complexes in the country is **Wat Pho**. Altogether, there are over 30 individual temples scattered here, of which the **Temple of the Reclining Buddha** is the largest. The Buddha's statue is enormous, an amazing 47.5m (156ft) long and 15m (49ft) high. The gardens surrounding the temples offer an escape from the hectic pace of the big city. The temple also houses the national school for traditional Thai massage. The **Floating Market** is an interesting place to visit, although it has become more of a tourist attraction than a genuine market for Thais. Other sights include **Lak Muang** (the city stone), the **Erawan Shrine**, where local offerings are made daily, and the **National Museum**. Housed in the **Suan Pakkard Palace** is a collection of precious antiques. Also interesting is the former home of the American silk-dealer Jim Thompson who vanished without a trace in 1967. Today, the house is a craft museum with a shop selling high-quality silks at reasonable prices. Bangkok's burgeoning nightlife is also a major attraction. The ubiquitous 'girlie bars' of **Patpong** are notorious, though these days they are tourist friendly, and, beyond these dens, there are new designer bars and slick modern nightclubs, as well as some of the best restaurants in Asia.

EXCURSIONS: Upriver is the old capital of **Ayutthaya** and the old summer palace at **Bang Pa-In**. Within its confines are striking structures such as a classic Thai **pavilion**, a neoclassical **palace**, a Chinese-style **pagoda** and a Buddhist **temple** that resembles a Gothic church. East of Bangkok lies the **Ancient City**, a vast private park with models, some full sized, some reduced, of most of Thailand's historic monuments and the temple ruins of the Khmer Empire, situated near the Cambodian border. Also just outside the city is the **Rose Garden Country Resort** with daily performances of Thai music, dance, games and ceremonies.

THE INTERIOR

CHIANG MAI: In the far north is Thailand's second-largest city and a centre for excursions to the region's ancient and beautiful temples, the teak forests and their working elephants, caves and waterfalls, and journeys to visit the northern hill tribes. The main attractions are the **Doi Suthep** temple and elephant trekking. Doi Suthep is one of the most famous temples in northern Thailand. Perched high on a hilltop, it offers fine views over the city on clear days. The trip up can either be made via a funicular or a grand staircase with 400 steps. The banisters alone are worth a visit: a giant green-and-red glazed serpent winds its way down to end in a magnificent dragon's head. Elephant trekking in the surrounding countryside has become a big tourist buck earner in the last decade, but visitors should beware that some 'authentic' trips turn out to be just the opposite.

EXCURSIONS: There are many small villages in the area surrounding the city where local handicrafts are produced. In the **Mae Sa Valley**, there is an elephant training school and, nearby, an orchid farm; longer trips can be made to the **Doi Inthanon National Park** and to **Chiang Rai**, from where the **Mekong River** and the **Golden Triangle** can be reached. Another interesting route to take is the road to **Mae-Hong-Son** near the border with Myanmar. It is a good base from which to go trekking or motorcycle touring. On the way round the Mae-Hong-Son loop, it is possible to stop at the small town of **Pai**, a relaxed and friendly place.

CENTRAL PLAINS: The Central Plains, located between Bangkok and Chiang Mai, form the prosperous heart of the country, a rich environment that has seen the rise and fall of great cities and kingdoms. **Phitsanulok** makes a convenient base for excursions into the area. The town is also the site of the **Wat Phra Si Rattana Mahathat**. This important monastery houses the well-known **Phra Buddha Chinnarat**, reputedly one of the most beautiful Buddha images in Thailand. From Phitsanulok, one can visit the ancient city kingdoms of **Kamphaeng Phet** and **Sukhothai**. UNESCO included Sukhothai and its environs on its list of World Heritage Sites. It covers a huge area and includes palaces, temples and pavilions as well as lakes, ponds and canals.

KANCHANABURI: The province of Kanchanaburi is a stunning oasis of jungle-clad hills and sweeping waterways. The town of Kanchanaburi, with its modern hotels and tourist facilities, is the original site of the famous **Bridge Over The River Kwai**, a place where thousands of allied prisoners of war and Thai forced labourers died at the hands of the Japanese. The train trip, whether on the normal scheduled service or the dedicated tourist services, runs along the 'Death Railway' and across the post-war bridge and is a popular activity.

THE NORTHEAST: In the northeast, about three hours by road from Bangkok, is the **Khao Yai National Park & Wildlife Reserve**. The most popular of the country's national parks, it has been developed into a modest resort. As well as the attractions of the wildlife and jungle, the park can be used as a base to visit the many ancient and historical sites in the northeast of Thailand. There are also some excellent Khmer sites in the northeast, including **Lopburi**, **Phanom Rung** and **Pimai**. The northeast also provides its own special festival celebrations, the most exciting being the elephant roundup at **Surin** each November.

THE COAST OF THAILAND

GULF OF BANGKOK: Situated in the Eastern Gulf, **Pattaya**, one of Southeast Asia's most infamous beach resorts, is blighted by excessive development. The quieter nearby resort of **Bang Saen** is a more salubrious choice. A little further away is **Ko Samet**, an idyllic island about a 30 minutes' boat ride from **Rayong**. Two to three hours south of Bangkok are **Cha'am** and **Hua Hin**. The latter was a royal watering place and is currently enjoying a renaissance.

PHUKET: Phuket was one of the regions hit by the tsunami in December 2004. Kamala and Patong beaches suffered the worst damage but the clean up process has been excellent. The island of Phuket (attached by a causeway to the mainland) in the southwest corner of the country is one of several resorts on the Indian Ocean. Phuket is now threatening to outstrip Pattaya as the number one beach resort in Thailand. The main town of **Patong** has a reputation for sex and sleaze, but many of the resort hotels that are dotted around the bountiful beaches of the island are superb. The island is also large enough to accommodate backpacker beach-hut developments alongside the slick luxury hotels. Diving is popular, though visibility can be a problem.

PHANG NGA BAY: Easily reached from Phuket, this bay boasts one of the world's most stunning seascapes; the area was featured in the James Bond film, *The Man with the Golden Gun*. Approximately 3500 islands (**ko**) are scattered in the bay. Though forbidding and seemingly impenetrable from the outside, they harbour a wealth of untouched fauna and flora in their hollow interior. Until recently, they were believed inaccessible from the surrounding sea. There are now canoe trips through tunnels and cracks in the rock, although this is dependent on the prevailing tide.

KO PHI PHI ISLANDS: These idyllic twin islands lie an easy boat trip away from either Phuket or the mainland at Krabi. The largest, **Ko Phi Phi Don**, is a dumbbell shaped slice of paradise, its coastline fringed with white beaches all around, and its interior clad with tropical rainforest. The only town, **Ton Sai**, has been largely ruined by uncontrolled tourist development, but much of the rest of the island is still untouched and a number of upscale hotels and resorts inhibit these better-preserved areas. Neighbouring **Ko Phi Phi Leh**'s main claim to fame was that it was controversially used as the setting for the Hollywood blockbuster, *The Beach*. There is no accommodation on this limestone outcrop, but it makes a perfect day trip.

KO SAMUI: Over the last decade or so, Ko Samui, once a backpacker's haven, has developed into a more sophisticated beach resort, complete with an airport that offers regular flights to and from Bangkok and Krabi. Ko Samui is Thailand's third-largest island, and although tourism is now the main industry, its lingering rustic charm is summed up by the fact that coconut farming is still a major industry. **Chaweng Beach** is the island's largest beach and has a number of good hotels as well as groups of bungalows and bars that are ideal for the budget traveller.

KO PHANGAN: Ko Phangan is still relatively undeveloped and is mainly visited by the more adventurous traveller looking to get away from fast food outlets and chain hotels. Each month it hosts all-night full moon beach parties at **Had Rin** with up to 10,000 revellers frolicking in the moonlit surf in a nefarious festival that attracts everyone from backpackers to the Bangkok young professional set. There are no luxury hotels on the island, but there are plenty of beach hut accommodations dotted in small communities around the island, offering a real escape or the chance to party with other travellers. The only access to Ko Phangan is by boat from Ko Samui or Surat Thani

KO TAO: Ko Tao, which translates as 'Turtle Island', is another less-developed island, but it is becoming increasingly popular as a scuba-diving destination. **Ban Mae Hat** is the only real town, and it is given over to cheap hotels and dive operators. The diving around Ko Tao is excellent with clean water and good visibility.

Sport & Activities

Watersports: Thailand's 2710km (1694 miles) of coastline, on both the Indian and the Pacific Oceans, as well as its many offshore islands, make it a popular destination for watersports, particularly **diving** and **snorkelling**. Two of the largest diving centres are at *Pattaya*, a two-hour drive from Bangkok, and *Phuket*, both of which offer access to numerous offshore islands and coral reefs. The Andaman Sea is particularly good for reef diving, the famous *Similan* and *Surin* islands being the most visited areas. In the Gulf of Thailand, the islands of *Ko Phangan*, *Ko Samui* and *Ko Tao* also attract many divers, while *Ko Chang* and the *Trat* area are amongst the most recent locations to have opened up to sports tourism. The *Burma Banks* and the islands off *Trang Province* have also recently been hailed as new diving destinations. Live-aboard **dive cruises**, equipment rental and certified diving courses are widely available. Several beaches are particularly well-suited for **windsurfing**, particularly *Chaweng*, *Hua Hin*, *Jomtien* (south of Pattaya), *Karon* (on Phuket island), *Kata* and *Lamai* (on Koh Samui). In the Gulf of Thailand, the windiest months are mid-February to April; in the Andaman Sea, the period from September to December has the strongest winds (for further information on beaches, see also the *Resorts & Excursions* section). **Sea canoeing** and **kayaking** have become increasingly popular in recent years, the coastal limestone islands in *Phang Nga Bay*, north of Phuket, being the favourite destination, also offering the chance to explore the half-submerged cave systems known as *hongs*. **Sailing** is a popular way to access Thailand's many islands and the main base for sailing trips in the Andaman Sea is Phuket, which also hosts the annual *Kings Cup Regatta* in December. Sailing cruises in the Gulf of Thailand usually start from Pattaya. Yachts can be chartered either with or without a crew. The presence of big game fish, such as barracuda, tuna, wahoo, swordfish or marlin, attracts many **game fishing** enthusiasts, who can charter fully crewed boats from most major coastal resorts. **Inland raft trips** can be arranged on several rivers.

Trekking: The best trails are in northern Thailand, particularly the remote provinces of *Chiang Mai*, *Chiang Rai* and *Mae Hong Son*. This is also the region of the infamous Golden Triangle, where Thailand, Laos and Myanmar meet and from where much of the world's opium originates. Treks usually run for three or four days through a scenery consisting of forested mountains inhabited by hill tribes whose small villages offer basic overnight accommodation for trekkers. Guides are widely available, but visitors should ensure that, besides English, they speak some of the hill tribe languages and have good contacts with the tribal communities. Although the people are reported to be extremely friendly, trekkers should also be aware that the area is mostly unpoliced and hold ups and robberies have been reported during the last few years.

Meditation: Thailand has dozens of temples and meditation centres specialising in *vipassana* (insight) meditation. Instruction and accommodation is usually free, though donations are expected. Different meditation techniques and dress codes apply to different centres. Upmarket resorts offering **mind, body and spirit** holidays are also available, with various alternative therapies included in the package. Larger retreats are for the serious minded only. Male and female English speakers are welcome, but strict segregation of the sexes is enforced and many places observe a vow of silence.

Thai kick-boxing: Also known as *muay thai*, this traditional sport can be seen every day of the year at the major stadiums in both Bangkok and the provinces. Thai boxing matches are preceded by elaborate ceremonies and accompanied by lively music. Thailand has over 60,000 full-time boxers. Foreigners may enrol at a traditional *muay* training camp, some of which specialise in training westerners. There is a strong spiritual and ritualistic dimension to *muay thai*.

Spectator sports: Horse races are held every two weeks at the Royal Bangkok Sports Club on Saturday and at the Royal Turf Club on Sunday. Another spectator sport is **takraw**, also sometimes called Siamese football, in which a small woven rattan ball is kicked around by players standing in a circle and often performing spectacular moves. The aim of the game is to keep the ball off the ground, and to do this any part of the body can be used except for the hands.

Social Profile

FOOD & DRINK: There are many Asian and European restaurants. Thai food is hot and spicy, but most tourist restaurants tone down the food for Western palates. *Pri-kee-noo*, a tiny red or green pepper, is one of the hot ingredients that might best be avoided. These are generally served on a side plate in a vinaigrette with the main course. Thai dishes include *tom yam* (a coconut-milk soup prepared with makroot leaves, ginger, lemon grass, prawns or chicken); *gang pet* (hot 'red' curry with coconut milk, herbs, garlic, chillies, shrimp paste, coriander and seasoning) served with rice; *kaeng khiaw* ('green' curry with baby aubergines, beef or chicken) served with rice and *gai yang* (barbecued chicken); and *kao pat* (fried rice with pieces of crab meat, chicken, pork, onion, egg and saffron) served with onions, cucumber, soy sauce and chillies. Desserts include *salim* (sweet noodles in coconut milk) and *songkaya* (pudding of coconut milk, eggs and sugar often served in a coconut shell). Well worth trying is sticky rice and mangoes (rice cooked in coconut milk served with slices of mango), a favourite breakfast dish in the mango harvest season (March to May). Other popular fruits are *papaya*, *jackfruit*, *mangosteens*, *rambutans*, *pomelos* (similar to grapefruits) and, above all, *durians*, which *farangs* (foreigners) either love or hate.

Local whisky, either *Mekhong* or *SamSong*, is worth sampling. The local beer comes in varying strengths. Fruit juices and shakes are also worth trying. Coconut milk straight from the shell is available during the harvest season. There are no licensing laws.

NIGHTLIFE: Bangkok offers a wide range of entertainment venues, from nightclubs, pubs, bars, cinemas and restaurants (many of which are open air), to massage parlours, pool halls and cocktail lounges. Performances of traditional religious and court dances can be seen at the Thai Cultural Centre. Elsewhere on the mainland, nightlife takes the form of traditional dances. The islands are renowned for their nightlife, and attendance is almost exclusively foreigners. The *full moon parties* are notorious and continue well into the following morning.

SHOPPING: Good buys include Thai silks and cottons, batiks, silver, pottery with *celadon* green glaze, precious and semiprecious stones, dolls, masks, lacquerware, pewterware, bamboo artefacts and bronzeware. The weekend market at *Chatuchuk Park* in Bangkok is a regular cornucopia with items ranging from genuine antiques to fighting fish. Tailor-made clothes are also good value. **Shopping hours:** Mon-Sun 1000-2100; department stores 1000-2200.

SPECIAL EVENTS: A remarkable number of festivities take place in Thailand throughout the year. For a full list of festivals and events contact the Tourism Authority of Thailand (see *Contact Addresses* section).

The following is a selection of special events occurring in Thailand in 2005:

Jan 13-24 *Bangkok International Film Festival*. **Feb 4-6** *Chiang Mai Flower Festival*. **Feb 9** *Chinese New Year Celebrations*. **Mar 18-20** *Pattaya Music Festival*, Chonburi. **Apr 6-13** *Songkran Festival*, nationwide. **Apr 18-28** *Toh Moh Goddess Shrine Festival*, Narathiwat. **May 13-15** *Rocket Festival*, nationwide. **Jun-Jul tbc** *Samui Carnival*, Samui Island. **Jul 20-21** *Buddhist Lent Candle Procession*, Ubon Ratchatani. **Oct 2-11** *Phuket Ngan Kin Jeh* (Vegetarian Festival). **Sep** *King's Cup Elephant Polo Tournament*, Hua Hin, Prachuab Khiri Khan. **Oct 29-30** *Mekong River Traditional Longtail Boat Race*, Nakhon Phanom. **Nov 11-15** *Sukhothai Loi Krathong Festival*, Sukhothai.

SOCIAL CONVENTIONS: Present-day Thai society is the result of centuries of cultural interchange, particularly with China and India, but more recently with the West. Western visitors will generally receive a handshake on meeting someone. A Thai will be greeted with the traditional closed hands and a slight bow of the head, the *wai*. Buddhist monks are always greeted in this way. The Thai Royal Family is regarded with an almost religious reverence. Visitors should respect this. It is very bad manners to make public displays of anger, as Thais regard such behaviour as boorish and a loss of 'face'. Public displays of affection between men and women are also frowned upon, and it is considered rude to touch anyone on the head or to point one's feet at someone. Shoes should be removed before entering someone's home or a temple. Informal dress is widely acceptable and men are seldom, if ever, expected to wear suits. A traditional Thai shirt is the most suitable attire for men at any official function. Beachwear should be confined to the beach and topless sunbathing is frowned upon. Smoking is widely acceptable. **Tipping:** Most hotels and restaurants will add 10 per cent service charge and 11 per cent government tax to the bill.

Business Profile

ECONOMY: The Thai economy expanded very rapidly during the 1980s and early/mid-1990s; average annual GDP growth between 1990 and 1996 was 8.5 per cent. Nevertheless, certain aspects of its economic performance during this period gave cause for concern, notably the foreign debt, shortcomings in the taxation system and the weakness of the country's financial institutions. The economy was already slowing down when the Asian currency crisis struck in the late summer of 1997. In 1998, the economy contracted by 11 per cent. After a strong initial recovery, the Thai economy stutterd in 2001/2 but has now recovered again and is growing strongly.

Before Thailand assumed its position as one of the Asian tiger economies, agriculture had been the main economic activity: this has declined in relative importance as the industrial and service base expanded and developed. The sector remains important nonetheless: the main crops are rice (of which Thailand is the world's leading exporter), sugar, cassava, maize, rubber, cotton and tobacco. Fishing is also significant, especially for prawns, which have become one of the country's largest exports. Another important natural resource, timber, was highly lucrative until, under international pressure, a logging ban was introduced in 1989. However, illegal logging continues - especially on the Thai-Myanmar border where much of the best quality timber may be found. The country's other principal natural resources are minerals and gemstones are the most lucrative (again, there is much illegal activity in this industry) but there are also major deposits of tin and lead, plus copper, gold, zinc and iron, and rare metal ores containing antimony, manganese and tungsten. Natural gas and oil fields have been located offshore and are now being developed. In the industrial sector, Thailand manufactures cement, electronics, jewellery and refined sugar; there is also an important oil refinery. In the service sector, Thailand has a large tourism industry catering for over 8 million arrivals annually and worth about $7 billion to the economy. Thai companies are also highly active in transport, telecommunications, finance and the media. Thailand is a member of the Association of South East Asian Nations (and as such will participate in the planned Free Trade Area), as well as the Asian Development Bank and the Colombo Plan (a cooperative trading body covering South Asia). Thailand's main trading partners are Japan, Singapore, the USA, Germany and Hong Kong.

BUSINESS: Most people in senior management speak English but in very small companies, or those situated outside the industrial belt of Bangkok, English is not as widely spoken. Most businesses of substantial size prefer visitors to make appointments. Visiting cards are essential. Punctuality is advisable. **Office hours:** Mon-Fri 0800-1700. **Government office hours:** Mon-Fri 0830-1200 and 1300-1630.

COMMERCIAL INFORMATION: The following organisations can offer advice: Department of Export Promotion, 22/77 Rachadapisek Road, Chatuchak, Bangkok 10900 (tel: (2) 511 5066; fax: (2) 512 2670; e-mail: iticdep@depthai.go.th; website: www.thaitrade.com); *or* Thai Chamber of Commerce, 150 Rajbopit Road, 2146, 10200 Bangkok (tel: (2) 622 1860; fax: (2) 225 3372; e-mail: tcc@thaiechamber.com; website: www.thaiechamber.com).

CONFERENCES/CONVENTIONS: The Thailand Incentive and Convention Association has 191 members representing all sectors of business interested in conventions and incentives. Members include hotels, airlines, publishing houses, advertising agencies, cruise operators, travel agents, lawyers, equipment suppliers and banks. The aim of the association is to provide help with every possible query that an organiser may have, as well as providing practical assistance. It publishes a quarterly newsletter, an annual guide, a gift-ideas catalogue and a social programme. The Bangkok Convention Centre is the largest venue in the country, but there are many other venues (including hotels) in Bangkok and elsewhere. The largest markets for delegates in 1988 were Malaysia, Japan, the USA, Taiwan and Australia, though interest from Canada and Germany showed a considerable increase. In October 1991, Thailand hosted the annual meeting of the World Bank and International Monetary Fund attended by 15,000 delegates. Further information can be obtained from the Thailand Incentive and Convention Association (TICA), 99/7 Ladprao Soi 8, Ladyao, Chatuchak, Bangkok 10900 (tel: (2) 938 6590; fax: (2) 938 6594-5; e-mail: info@tica.or.th; website: www.tica.or.th).

Climate

Generally hot, particularly between March and May. The monsoon season runs from June to October, when the climate is still hot and humid with torrential rains. The best time for travelling is November to February (cool season).

Required clothing: Lightweights and rainwear are advised.

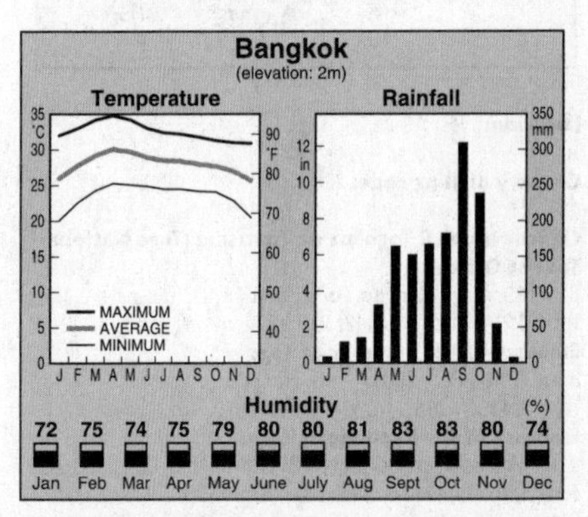

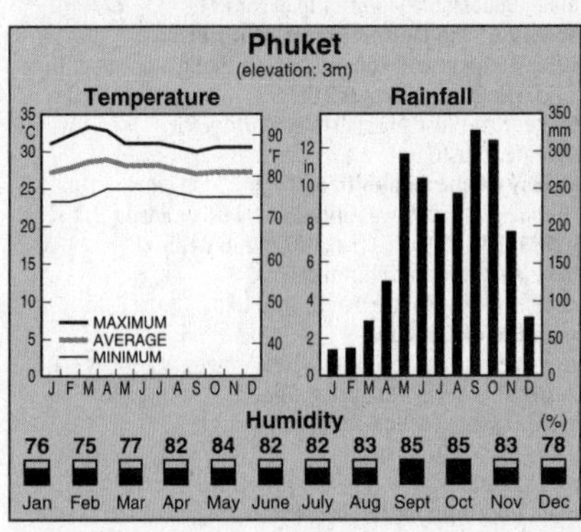

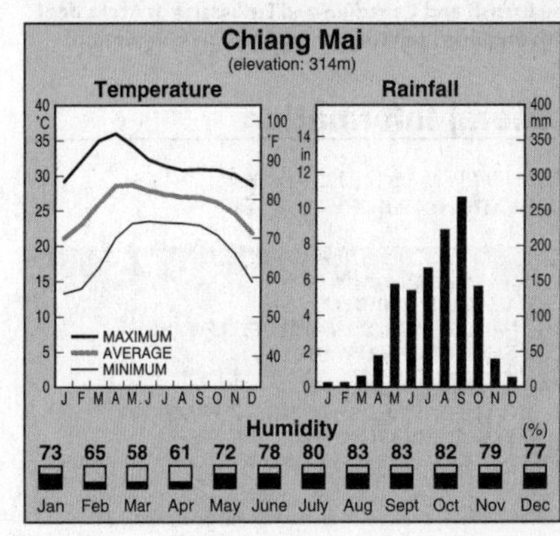

Togo

LATEST TRAVEL ADVICE CONTACTS

British Foreign and Commonwealth Office
Tel: (0870) 606 0290 Website: www.fco.gov.uk
US Department of State
Website: http://travel.state.gov/travel
Canadian Department of Foreign Affairs and Int'l Trade
Tel: (1 800) 267 8376 Website: www.dfait-maeci.gc.ca

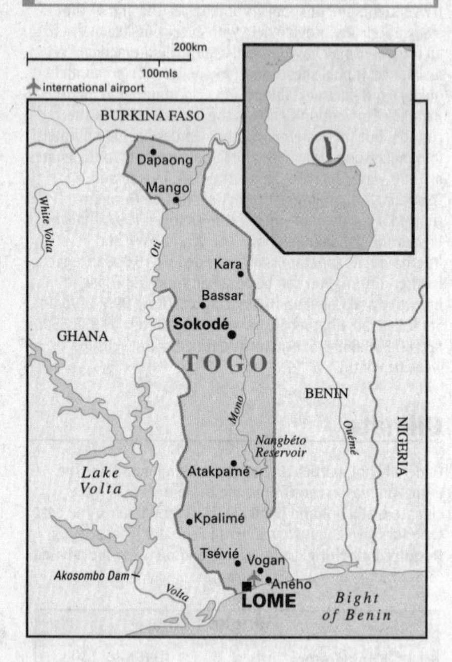

Location: West Africa.

Country dialling code: 228.

Office National Togolais du Tourisme (Togo National Tourist Office)
BP 1289, route d'Aného, Lomé, Togo
Tel: (2) 214 313. Fax: (2) 218 927.
Embassy of the Republic of Togo
8 rue Alfred Roll, 75017 Paris, France
Tel: (1) 4380 1213. Fax: (1) 4380 0605.
Embassy of the Republic of Togo
2208 Massachusetts Avenue, NW, Washington, DC 20008, USA
Tel: (202) 234 4212. Fax: (202) 232 3190.
E-mail: embassyoftogo@hotmail.com
Embassy of the United States of America
BP 852, 15 angle rue Kouenou et rue Béniglato, Lomé, Togo
Tel: (2) 212 994. Fax: (2) 217 952.
Website: http://usembassy.state.gov/togo *or* www.cafe.tg/ustogo
Embassy of the Republic of Togo
12 Range Road, Ottawa, Ontario K1N 8J3, Canada
Tel: (613) 238 5916/7. Fax: (613) 235 6425.
E-mail: ambatogoca@hotmail.com
Consulates in: Montréal and Toronto.
Consulate of Canada
Street address: 101 Boulevard des Armées, Maison N311, Quartier Tokoin Habitat, Lomé, Togo
Postal address: PO Box 1278, Lomé, Togo
Tel: (2) 221 3299.
Fax: (2) 220 3001.
E-mail: honcontogo@laposte.tg
The British and Canadian and Embassies in Accra deal with enquiries relating to Togo (see ***Ghana*** **section).**

General Information

AREA: 56,785 sq km (21,925 sq miles).
POPULATION: 4,801,000 (2002).

TIMATIC CODES

Health	AMADEUS: **TI-DFT/LFW/HE** GALILEO/WORLDSPAN: **TI-DFT/LFW/HE** SABRE: **TIDFT/LFW/HE**
Visa	AMADEUS: **TI-DFT/LFW/VI** GALILEO/WORLDSPAN: **TI-DFT/LFW/VI** SABRE: **TIDFT/LFW/VI**

To access TIMATIC country information on Health and Visa regulations through the Computer Reservations System (CRS), type in the appropriate command line listed above.

POPULATION DENSITY: 84.5 per sq km.
CAPITAL: Lomé. **Population:** 732,000 (official estimate 2001).
GEOGRAPHY: Togo shares borders with Burkina Faso to the north, Benin to the east and Ghana to the west, with a short coast on the Atlantic in the south. The country is a narrow strip, rising behind coastal lagoons and swampy plains to an undulating plateau. Northwards, the plateau descends to a wide plain irrigated by the River Oti. The central area is covered by deciduous forest, while savannah stretches to the north and south. In the east, the River Mono runs to the sea; long sandy beaches shaded by palms characterise the coastline between Lomé and Cotonou in Benin.
GOVERNMENT: Republic since 1967. Gained independence from France in 1960. **Head of State:** President Faure Gnassingbé Eyadéma since February 2005 (succeeded his father after seizing power on his death). **Head of Government:** Prime Minister Koffi Sama since 2002.
LANGUAGE: French is the official language, while Ewe, Watchi and Kabiyé are the most widely spoken African languages. Very little English is spoken.
RELIGION: 50 per cent Traditional or animist, 35 per cent Christian and 15 per cent Muslim.
TIME: GMT.
ELECTRICITY: 220 volts AC, 50Hz single phase. Plugs are square or round two-pin.
COMMUNICATIONS: Telephone: IDD is available to main cities. Country code: 228. There are no area codes. Outgoing international code: 00. **Mobile telephone:** GSM 900 network covers main urban areas. Operators include *Telecel Togo* (website: www.telecel.tg) and *Togo Telecom* (website: www.togotel.net.tg). **Fax:** Available in Internet cafes. **Internet:** ISPs include *Togo Telecom* (website: www.togotel.net.tg). Public access is available in Internet cafes all over the country. **Telegram:** The telegram service is dependable; messages to France and West Africa are less expensive. **Post:** Postal facilities are limited to main towns. *Post Restante* facilities are available and are very reliable. Airmail to Western Europe takes at least two weeks. **Press:** The main newspaper is the government-owned *Togo-Presse*, published in French, *Ewe* and *Kabiyé*. *Les Echos du Matin* is an independent daily. **Radio:** BBC World Service (website: www.bbc.co.uk/worldservice) and Voice of America (website: www.voa.gov) can be received. From time to time the frequencies change and the most up-to-date can be found online.

Passport/Visa

	Passport Required?	Visa Required?	Return Ticket Required?
Full British	Yes	Yes	Yes
Australian	Yes	Yes	Yes
Canadian	Yes	Yes	Yes
USA	Yes	Yes	Yes
Other EU	Yes	Yes	Yes
Japanese	Yes	Yes	Yes

Note: *Regulations and requirements may be subject to change at short notice, and you are advised to contact the appropriate diplomatic or consular authority before finalising travel arrangements. Details of these may be found at the head of this country's entry. Any numbers in the chart refer to the footnotes below.*

PASSPORTS: Valid passport required by all, except nationals of the following with a National Identity Card: Benin, Burkina Faso, Côte d'Ivoire and Ghana.
VISAS: Required by all except the following for stays of up to 90 days:
(a) nationals of Benin, Burkina Faso, Côte d'Ivoire and Ghana;
(b) transit passengers continuing their journey by the same or first connecting aircraft within 24 hours, provided not leaving the airport;
(c) children under 15 if accompanied by their parents.
Note: All nationals can obtain an entry visa on arrival in Togo for a maximum stay of up to seven days. Passports need to be handed in on arrival and collected along with the visa from the police station the following day.
Types of visa and cost: *Entry* and *Residence*: fee depends on nationality. All nationals of the USA will be issued a visa for a maximum stay of 12 months for a fee of approximately US$100.
Validity: Entry visas: Up to 90 days. Visas can be extended on arrival in Lomé at the Direction Générale de la Police Nationale. For stays exceeding 90 days, a residence visa (*visa de sejour*) will be issued.
Application to: Consulate (or Consular section at Embassy); see *Contact Addresses* section.
Application requirements: (a) Two completed application forms. (b) Three passport-size photos. (c) Yellow fever vaccination certificate for travellers over one year of age. (d) Fee. (e) Company letter for business trips.
Working days required: Three.

Money

Currency: CFA (*Communauté Financiaire Africaine*) Franc (CFAfr) = 100 centimes. Notes are in denominations of CFAfr10,000, 5000, 2500, 2000, 1000 and 500. Coins are in denominations of CFAfr250, 100, 50, 25, 10, 5 and 1. Togo is part of the French Monetary Area. Only currency issued by the *Banque des Etats de l'Afrique de l'Ouest* (Bank of West African States) is valid; currency issued by the *Banque des Etats de l'Afrique Centrale* (Bank of Central African States) is not. The CFA Franc is tied to the Euro.
Currency exchange: Foreign currencies can be exchanged at banks and bureaux de change in Lomé and other major cities. The main branch of the Togolese Central Bank in Lomé (BTCI) can give cash withdrawals against a Visa card.
Credit & debit cards: American Express is widely accepted, with more limited use of Diners Club, MasterCard and Visa. Check with your credit or debit card company for details of merchant acceptability and other facilities which may be available.
Travellers cheques: International travellers cheques are accepted in Lomé and other major cities.
Currency restrictions: The import of local currency is limited to CFAfr1 million, the export to CFAfr25,000. The import of foreign currency is limited to the equivalent of CFAfr1 million which should be declared on arrival. The export of foreign currency is limited to the amount declared on entry.
Exchange rate indicators: The following figures are included as a guide to the movements of the CFA Franc against Sterling and the US Dollar:

Date	Feb '04	May '04	Aug '04	Nov'04
£1.00=	961.13	983.76	978.35	936.79
$1.00=	528.01	550.79	531.03	494.69

Banking hours: Mon-Fri 0800-1600.

Duty Free

The following goods may be imported into Togo by persons over 15 years of age without incurring customs duty:
100 cigarettes or 100 cigarillos or 50 cigars or 100g of tobacco; one bottle of spirits and one bottle of wine; 500ml of eau de toilette and 250ml of perfume.

Public Holidays

2005: Jan 1 New Year's Day. **Jan 13** Liberation Day. **Jan 21** Tabaski (Feast of the Sacrifice). **Mar 28** Easter Monday. **Apr 21** Mouloud (Anniversary of Buddha's birthday). **Apr 27** Independence Day. **May 1** Labour Day. **May 5** Ascension. **May 16** Whit Monday. **Jun 21** Day of the Martyrs. **Aug 15** Assumption. **Sep 24** Anniversary of the Failed Attack on Lomé. **Nov 1** All Saints' Day. **Nov 3-5** Eid al-Fitr (End of Ramadan). **Dec 25** Christmas Day.
2006: Jan 1 New Year's Day. **Jan 13** Liberation Day. **Jan 13** Tabaski (Feast of the Sacrifice). **Apr 11** Mouloud (Anniversary of Buddha's birthday). **Apr 17** Easter Monday. **Apr 27** Independence Day. **May 1** Labour Day. **May 25** Ascension. **Jun 5** Whit Monday. **Jun 21** Day of the Martyrs. **Aug 15** Assumption. **Sep 24** Anniversary of the Failed Attack on Lomé. **Oct 22-24** Eid al-Fitr (End of Ramadan). **Nov 1** All Saints' Day. **Dec 25** Christmas Day.
Note: Muslim festivals are timed according to local sightings of various phases of the moon and the dates given above are approximations. During the lunar month of Ramadan that precedes Eid al-Fitr, Muslims fast during the day and feast at night and normal business patterns may be interrupted. Many restaurants are closed during the day and there may be restrictions on smoking and drinking. Some disruption may continue into Eid al-Fitr itself. Eid al-Fitr and Tabaski (Eid al-Adha) may last anything from two to 10 days, depending on the region. For more information, see the *World of Islam* appendix.

Health

	Special Precautions?	Certificate Required?
Yellow Fever	Yes	1
Cholera	2	No
Typhoid & Polio	3	N/A
Malaria	4	N/A

Note: *Regulations and requirements may be subject to change at short notice, and you are advised to contact your doctor well in advance of your intended date of departure. Any numbers in the chart refer to the footnotes below.*

1: A yellow fever vaccination certificate is required from all travellers over one year of age.
2: Following WHO guidelines issued in 1973, a cholera vaccination certificate is not a condition of entry to Togo. However, cholera is a serious risk in this country and precautions are essential. Up-to-date advice should be

sought before deciding whether these precautions should include vaccination, as medical opinion is divided over its effectiveness. See the *Health* appendix for more information.
3: Vaccination against typhoid is advised.
4: Malaria risk exists throughout the year in the whole country. The predominant malignant *falciparum* form is reported to be resistant to chloroquine. The recommended prophylaxis is mefloquine.
Food & drink: All water should be regarded as a potential health risk. Water used for drinking, brushing teeth or making ice should have first been boiled or otherwise sterilised. Milk is unpasteurised and should be boiled. Powdered or tinned milk is available and is advised but make sure that it is reconstituted with pure water. Avoid dairy products which are likely to have been made from unboiled milk. Only eat well-cooked meat and fish, preferably served hot. Pork, salad and mayonnaise may carry increased risk. Vegetables should be cooked and fruit peeled.
Other risks: *Bilharzia* (schistosomiasis) is present. Avoid swimming and paddling in fresh water; swimming pools which are well chlorinated and maintained are safe. *Trypanosomiasis* (sleeping sickness) is reported, as are *hepatitis A, B* and *E* and *meningococcal meningitis*. *Dracuncaliasis* is common in the indigenous population, but unlikely to pose a significant threat to travellers. *Rabies* is present. For those at high risk, vaccination before arrival should be considered. If you are bitten, seek medical advice without delay. For more information, consult the *Health* appendix.
Health care: Limited medical services are provided by the state. Most towns have either a hospital or a dispensary, but these are usually overcrowded and lack adequate supplies. Visitors who get seriously ill are advised to contact their Embassy, which can refer them to a specialist or arrange evacuation. Health insurance and a good supply of personal medical provisions are recommended. There is no reciprocal health agreement with the UK or USA. It is important to carry a basic first aid kit.

Travel - International

AIR: The main airline running services to Togo is *Air Afrique (RK)*, in which Togo is a shareholder. Other airlines operating to Togo include *Air France, Air Gabon* and *Delta Airlines*. Togo has become an important transit point for air travel in Africa. There are frequent flights to major African destinations.
Approximate flight times: From Lomé to *London* is seven hours.
International airports: *Lomé (LFW)* is 6km (4 miles) northeast of the city. Airport facilities include bar, restaurant, snack bar, shops, bank, post office, duty free shop and car hire. Taxis operate from 0600 until the last flight (fare CFAfr2000-5000) to the city centre.
Departure tax: None.
SEA: Ferries from Benin and Ghana call at Lomé and coastal ports. For details, contact the port authorities. *Cunard* and *Princess* cruise lines operate to Togo.
ROAD: There are routes from Benin, Burkina Faso and Ghana (a coastal route runs from Benin through Lomé to Ghana) but conditions are unreliable. The border with Ghana is closed periodically.

Travel - Internal

AIR: *Air Togo* runs services between Niamtougou and Lomé at the weekends.
SEA: Ferries run along the coast. For details, contact the port authorities.
RAIL: There are services between Atakpamé, Blitta and Lomé; Kpalimé and Lomé; and Aného and Lomé. Trains run at least daily on each route.
ROAD: Traffic drives on the right. Tarred roads run to the border countries and the major northern route is called 'The Highway of Unity'. There are roads linking most settlements, but these are largely impassable during the rainy season. Police checkpoints are frequent and may cause delays. It is advisable to keep windows rolled up and doors locked.
Bus/taxi: National bus and taxi systems are reasonably efficient and cheap. Taxis and minibuses are widely available in Lomé and shared taxis are available between towns. There is a surcharge for luggage. Drivers do not expect a tip.
Cycling: Bicycles can be rented in large towns and often incur less delays than cars. **Car hire:** This is available in Lomé; elsewhere the cost of car hire is very high and it is usually better to hire a taxi. **Documentation:** An International Driving Permit is required.

Accommodation

HOTELS: Only Lama-Kara and Lomé have international-class accommodation but there are hotels in all the main towns. There is a severe shortage of accommodation, so it is advisable to book in advance. For further information, contact the Office National Togolais du Tourisme (see *Contact Addresses* section).
CAMPING: This is available free of charge though not recommended. Check with rangers before camping in National Parks.

Resorts & Excursions

Togo's capital, **Lomé**, is the only capital in the world situated right next to a border. The city itself is a mixture of the traditional, especially around the **Grand Marché**, and the modern. The **fetish market**, with its intriguing voodoo charms, lotions and potions, and the **Village Artisanal** are interesting places to wander. The coast is rather disappointing and visitors have to leave the city well behind to find a nice spot.
Other towns of interest include **Togoville**, where the colonial treaty between the Germans and the ruler Mlapa III was signed. The chief still shows copies of the treaty to visitors. In the village itself, there are numerous voodoo shrines and the **Roman Catholic Cathedral**, built by the Germans. The nearby **Lake Togo** is popular with watersports enthusiasts. **Aného**, Togo's colonial capital until 1920, has preserved a distinctively colonial atmosphere, reflected in such attractions as the 19th-century **Peter and Paul Church**, the **Protestant Church** and the **German Cemetery**. The short coastline is home to several small fishing villages, sometimes with examples of colonial architecture. Togo's wildlife parks include the **Fazao National Park** outside **Sokodé**, the **Kéran National Park** near **Kara** and the **Fosse aux Lions** (Lions' Den) southwest of **Dapaong**.

Sport & Activities

Beaches are unsafe for all but the best swimmers, but there are several pools along the beach at Lomé. Hotel pools and the lakeside resort of *Porto Seguro* (a short drive from Lomé) offer safe **swimming**: Hotel Sarkawa has an olympic-sized pool, the biggest in West Africa. There are also **water-skiing** and **sailing** facilities at Porto Seguro. The scenic hill country around Kapilmé offers good opportunities for **hiking**.

Social Profile

FOOD & DRINK: Togon food is particularly good. Most restaurants catering for visitors tend to be French-orientated, although some do serve African dishes. In Lomé in particular, there are many small cafes serving local food. Dishes include meals in *sauce*, soups based on palm nut, groundnut and maize. Meat, poultry and seafoods are plentiful and well prepared, as are the local fruit and vegetables. A popular dish is *riz sauce arachide* - rice with peanut sauce.
A good selection of alcoholic drinks is available - some produced locally such as palm wine and *tchakpallo* (fermented millet).
NIGHTLIFE: There are numerous nightclubs, particularly in Lomé. Most serve food and are open until the early hours for dancing to a mixture of West African and Western popular music. There are also cinemas showing French and English-language films.
SHOPPING: Market purchases include wax prints, indigo cloth, Kente and dye-stamped Adinkira cloth from Ghana, embroideries, batik and lace from The Netherlands, locally made heavy marble ashtrays, gold and silver jewellery, traditional masks, wood sculpture and religious statuettes. Voodoo stalls display an extraordinary range of items used in magic, among them, cowrie shells. **Shopping hours:** Mon-Fri 0800-1730, Sat 0730-1230.
SPECIAL EVENTS: The following is a selection of special events celebrated annually in Togo:
Jul *Evala* (initiation ceremonies, a custom which involves traditional wrestling), Kabiyé region; *Akpema* (girls' initiation ceremonies), Kabiyé region. **Aug** *Kpessosso* (a harvest festival of the Guens); *Ayize* (Bean Harvest Festival celebrated by the Ewe). **Sep** *Agbogbozan* (Ewe Diaspora Festival); *Dipontre* (Yam Festival), Bassar region. **Dec** *Kamou* (Harvest Festival), Kabiyé region.
SOCIAL CONVENTIONS: Music and dance are the most popular forms of culture. The Togolese have had a varied colonial heritage which has resulted in the variety of Christian denominations and European languages; the voodoo religion is a strong influence in the country and many young girls, after fulfilling an initiation period, will devote their lives to serving the religion and the voodoo village priest. Practical, casual clothes are suitable. Beachwear should not be worn away from the beach or poolside. **Tipping:** When not included, a tip of about 10 per cent is customary. Taxi drivers do not usually expect a tip.

Business Profile

ECONOMY: About two-thirds of the working population is employed in agriculture: a wide range of crops are produced, including cotton, cocoa and coffee (the main cash crops) and basic foodstuffs including cassava, maize, yams and sorghum. Togo's other major principal exports are the ores from the country's phosphate mines, although revenues have been hit recently by slack demand and low world prices. Limestone and marble deposits have also been exploited. Togo's mines contain some of the world's richest calcium deposits. Most of Togo's other industry is based on the processing of these agricultural and mineral products, apart from a handful of factories engaged in the production of textiles and consumer goods for domestic consumption. A successful export processing zone, now entering its second decade of operation, has attracted numerous manufacturers from across the world. The service sector is small and tourism negligible.
The country's main economic problems are a huge foreign debt and declining revenues due to low world commodity prices. A typical programme of structural adjustment has been undertaken under the supervision of the IMF and World Bank. Current annual GDP growth is 3.3 per cent while inflation is -1 per cent. Togo is a member of the CFA Franc Zone, the West African trading bloc ECOWAS and various international commodity organisations. Togo's principal trading partners are France, Canada, the USA and Côte d'Ivoire; other important export markets are Bolivia, Indonesia and the The Philippines.
BUSINESS: It is acceptable for visiting businesspeople to wear a safari suit except on very formal business and social occasions. Business is conducted in French, only a few executives speak English. Appointments should be made and business cards should be carried. **Office hours:** Mon-Fri 0700-1730.
COMMERCIAL INFORMATION: The following organisation can offer advice: Chambre de Commerce et d'Industrie du Togo (CCAIT), BP 360, avenue Georges Pompidou, Lomé (tel: 212 065; fax: 214 730; e-mail: ccit@rdd.tg; website: www.ccit.tg).

Climate

From December to January, the *Harmattan* wind blows from the north. The rainy season lasts from April to July. Short rains occur from October to November. The driest and hottest months are February and March.
Required clothing: Tropical lightweights. Rainwear for the rainy season.

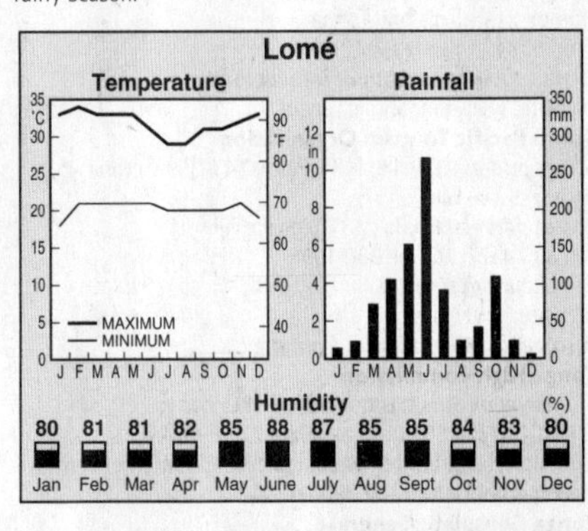

Tonga

LATEST TRAVEL ADVICE CONTACTS

British Foreign and Commonwealth Office
Tel: (0870) 606 0290 Website: www.fco.gov.uk
US Department of State
Website: http://travel.state.gov/travel
Canadian Department of Foreign Affairs and Int'l Trade
Tel: (1 800) 267 8376 Website: www.dfait-maeci.gc.ca

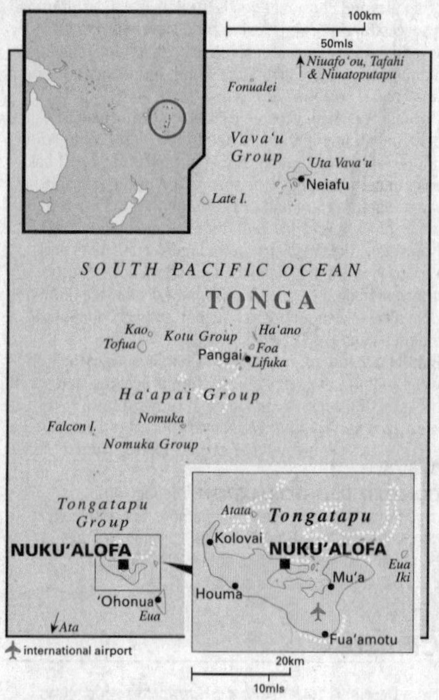

Location: South Pacific.

Country dialling code: 676.

Tonga Visitors' Bureau
PO Box 37, Nuku'alofa, Tonga
Tel: 25334. Fax: 23507.
E-mail: tvb@kalianet.to *or* info@tvb.gov.to
Website: www.tongaholiday.com
South Pacific Tourism Organisation
Street address: Level 3, FNPF Place, 343-359 Victoria Parade, Suva, Fiji
Postal address: PO Box 13119, Suva, Fiji
Tel: 330 4177. Fax: 330 1995.
E-mail: info@spto.org
Website: www.spto.org
Also deals with enquiries from the UK.
Tonga High Commission
36 Molyneux Street, London W1H 5BQ, UK
Tel: (020) 7724 5828. Fax: (020) 7723 9074.
E-mail: vielak@btinternet.com *or* fetu@btinternet.com
Opening hours: Mon-Fri 0900-1700.
Tonga Consulate General
360 Post Street, Suite 604, San Francisco, CA 94108, USA
Tel: (415) 781 0365. Fax: (415) 781 3964.
E-mail: tania@sfconsulate.gov.to (general enquiries).
Website: www.tongaconsul.org
Also deals with enquiries from Canada.
The American Embassy in Fiji also deals with enquiries relating to Tonga (see *Fiji* **section).**
The Canadian High Commission in Wellington deals with enquiries relating to Tonga (see *New Zealand* **section).**

General Information

AREA: 748 sq km (289 sq miles).
POPULATION: 100,281 (official estimate 2000).

TIMATIC CODES

Health	AMADEUS: **TI-DFT/TBU/HE** GALILEO/WORLDSPAN: **TI-DFT/TBU/HE** SABRE: **TIDFT/TBU/HE**
Visa	AMADEUS: **TI-DFT/TBU/VI** GALILEO/WORLDSPAN: **TI-DFT/TBU/VI** SABRE: **TIDFT/TBU/VI**

To access TIMATIC country information on Health and Visa regulations through the Computer Reservations System (CRS), type in the appropriate command line listed above.

POPULATION DENSITY: 134.1 per sq km.
CAPITAL: Nuku'alofa. **Population:** 22,400 (1996).
GEOGRAPHY: Tonga is an archipelago of 172 islands in the South Pacific, most of which are uninhabited, covering an area of 7700 sq km (3000 sq miles). The major island groups are 'Eua, Ha'apai, the Niuas, Tongatapu and Vava'u. Tonga's high volcanic and low coral forms give the islands a unique character. Some volcanoes are still active and Falcon Island in the Vava'u group is a submerged volcano that erupts periodically, its lava and ash rising above sea level, forming a visible island which disappears when the eruption is over. Nuku'alofa, on Tongatapu Island, has a reef-protected harbour lined with palms. The island is flat with a large lagoon, but no running streams, and many surrounding smaller islands. 'Eua Island is hilly and forested with high cliffs and beautiful beaches. The Ha'apai Islands, a curving archipelago 160km (100 miles) north of Tongatapu, have excellent beaches. Tofua, the largest island in the group, is an active volcano with a hot steaming lake in its crater. The Vava'u Islands, 90km (50 miles) north of Ha'apai, are hilly, densely wooded and interspersed with a maze of narrow channels. They are known for their stalagmite-filled caves.
GOVERNMENT: Constitutional monarchy. Gained full independence within the Commonwealth in 1970. **Head of State:** King Taufa'ahau Tupou IV since 1965. **Head of Government:** Prime Minister HRH Prince 'Ulukalala-Lavaka-Ata since 2000.
LANGUAGE: Tongan and English.
RELIGION: Wesleyan Church, Roman Catholic and Anglican. Small denominations of Muslim, Baha'i and Mormon faiths.
TIME: GMT + 13.
ELECTRICITY: 240 volts AC, 50Hz.
COMMUNICATIONS: Telephone: IDD is available. Country code: 676. There are no area codes. Outgoing international code: 00. **Mobile telephone:** GSM 900. Network operators include *Tonga Communications Corporation* (website: www.tcc.to). **Fax:** Services are provided by *Cable & Wireless*. **Internet:** ISPs include *Tonga Communications Corporation*. **Post:** Main post office hours (located in the centre of Nuku'alofa): Mon-Fri 0830-1600. All mail must be collected from the post office. Airmail to Europe takes approximately 10 days. There are branch offices on Ha'apai and Vava'u. **Press:** The *Matangi Tonga, The Times of Tonga* and *Tonga Chronicle* are the English-language newspapers.
Radio: BBC World Service (website: www.bbc.co.uk/worldservice) and Voice of America (website: www.voa.gov) can be received. From time to time the frequencies change and the most up-to-date can be found online.

Passport/Visa

	Passport Required?	Visa Required?	Return Ticket Required?
Full British	Yes	No	Yes
Australian	Yes	No	Yes
Canadian	Yes	No	Yes
USA	Yes	No	Yes
Other EU	Yes	No/1	Yes
Japanese	Yes	No	Yes

Note: Regulations and requirements may be subject to change at short notice, and you are advised to contact the appropriate diplomatic or consular authority before finalising travel arrangements. Details of these may be found at the head of this country's entry. Any numbers in the chart refer to the footnotes below.

PASSPORTS: Passport valid for at least six months required by all.
Note: Ordinary, diplomatic or official Tongan or Tonga National passport holders may enter the Kingdom with passports valid for the date of arrival in Tonga.
VISAS: Visas required by all except the following who can obtain a Visitor's Visa free of charge on arrival, entitling the holder of stays of up to 31 days:
(a) **1.** nationals of countries mentioned in the table above (except nationals of the Czech Republic, Estonia, Hungary, Latvia, Lithuania, Poland, Slovak Republic and Slovenia who *do* need a visa);
(b) nationals of The Bahamas, Barbados, Brazil, Brunei, Cook Islands, Dominica, Fiji, Kiribati, Malaysia, Marshall Islands, Micronesia (Federated States of), Monaco, Nauru, New Caledonia, New Zealand, Niue, Norway, Palau, Papua New Guinea, Russian Federation, St Kitts & Nevis, St Lucia, St Vincent & Grenadines, Samoa, Seychelles, Singapore, Solomon Islands, Switzerland, Tahiti and Her Islands, Turkey, Tuvalu, Ukraine, Vanuatu and Wallis & Futuna, provided holding a valid return ticket to a country where they have citizenship or a valid endorsement in their passport, granting them residency in a country that is not their country of nationality;
(c) those continuing their journey by the same or first connecting flight within less than 24 hours and not leaving the airport.

Note: Visas, valid on arrival and allowing multiple entry into Tonga, are required by all non-Tongan passport holders who are travelling on a one-way ticket, except for the following:
(a) holders of ordinary, diplomatic or official Tongan passports; (b) holders of Tongan National passports; (c) holders of a letter of authority issued by one of Tonga's overseas diplomatic missions and bearing the official stamp of that Tongan diplomatic mission, or a letter of authority issued by the Immigration Division, Ministry of Foreign Affairs of the Government of Tonga, bearing the official stamp of either the Ministry of Foreign Affairs or the Principal Immigration Officer.
Types of visa and cost: *Visitors*: T$40 per month. *Business*: T$200. *Employment*: T$150. *Transit*: If transit period exceeds 24 hours, an airport tax of T$25 is payable by all nationals over two years of age.
Note: Companies and businesses registered and operating in Tonga may bring non-nationals into the country on an employment visa, provided that the said non-citizen holds a specialised skill. Persons undertaking voluntary and charitable work in Tonga are also required to hold an employment visa.
Validity: Visitors are allowed stays of up to 31 days. Extensions for a maximum of three months or, in exceptional circumstances, six months require permission from the Principal Immigration Officer.
Business/employment visas are valid for up to two years and are renewable.
Application to: Applications for visas must be made prior to arrival. For enquiries, contact the Consulate (or Consular section at Embassy or High Commission) *or* the Visa Section, Immigration Division at the Ministry of Foreign Affairs Headquarters in Nuku'alofa (fax: 26970 *or* 23360).
Application Requirements: (a) Valid Passport. (b) Two passport-size photos. (c) Completed application form. (d) Fee, if applicable, accompanied by letter permitting entry into the kingdom and permission to obtain a visa. (e) Onward or return tickets with reserved seats, including valid visa for onward destination if applicable. (f) Proof of adequate funds for duration of stay.
Business/Employment: (a)-(d) and, (e) Medical certificate issued by a doctor specified by the Immigration Division. (f) Two character references. (g) Police certificate from national's own country of residence.
Working days required: Approximately two to three.

Money

Currency: Pa'anga (T$) = 100 seniti. Notes are in denominations of T$50, 20, 10, 5, 2 and 1. Coins are in denominations of 50, 20, 10, 5, 2 and 1 seniti.
Currency exchange: Foreign exchange is available at banks and at major hotels.
Credit & debit cards: Limited use of both Diners Club and Visa.
Travellers cheques: Accepted at banks and at some hotels and tourist shops. To avoid additional exchange rate charges, travellers are advised to take travellers cheques in Australian Dollars or Pounds Sterling.
Currency restrictions: There are no restrictions on the import or export of foreign or local currencies.
Exchange rate indicators: The following figures are included as a guide to the movements of the Pa'anga against Sterling and the US Dollar:

Date	Feb '04	May '04	Aug '04	Nov '04
£1.00=	3.58	3.53	3.62	3.64
$1.00=	1.97	1.97	1.97	1.92

Banking hours: Mon-Fri 0900-1600, Sat 0830-1130.

Duty Free

The following goods may be imported into Tonga without incurring customs duty by persons over 18 years of age only: *200 cigarettes or 250g of cigars or 250g of tobacco; 1l of alcoholic liquor (only for persons 21 years and over); a reasonable quantity of perfume; one camera and personal belongings.*
Note: (a) The import of arms, ammunition and pornography is prohibited. (b) Birds, animals, fruit and plants are subject to quarantine regulations. (c) The export of valuable artefacts and certain flora and fauna is restricted.

Public Holidays

2005: Jan 1 New Year's Day. **Mar 25** Good Friday. **Mar 28** Easter Monday. **Apr 25** ANZAC Day. **May 4** HRH the Crown Prince's Birthday. **Jun 4** Independence Day. **Jul 4** HM King Taufa'ahau Tupou IV's Birthday. **Nov 4** Constitution Day. **Dec 4** Tupou I Day. **Dec 25** Christmas Day. **Dec 26** Boxing Day.
2006: Jan 1 New Year's Day. **Apr 14** Good Friday. **Apr 17** Easter Monday. **Apr 25** ANZAC Day. **May 4** HRH the Crown

Prince's Birthday. **Jun 4** Independence Day. **Jul 4** HM King Taufa'ahau Tupou IV's Birthday. **Nov 4** Constitution Day. **Dec 4** Tupou I Day. **Dec 25** Christmas Day. **Dec 26** Boxing Day.

Health

	Special Precautions?	Certificate Required?
Yellow Fever	No	1
Cholera	No	No
Typhoid & Polio	2	N/A
Malaria	No	N/A

Note: *Regulations and requirements may be subject to change at short notice, and you are advised to contact your doctor well in advance of your intended date of departure. Any numbers in the chart refer to the footnotes below.*

1: A yellow fever vaccination certificate is required from travellers over one year of age arriving from infected areas.
2: Vaccination against typhoid is advised.
Food & drink: Mains water is chlorinated and safe to drink in the main towns. Elsewhere, drinking water should be considered a potential health risk and sterilisation is advisable. Bottled water is available and is advised for the first few weeks of the stay. Milk is pasteurised and dairy products are safe for consumption. Local meat, poultry and seafood are generally considered safe to eat. To prevent serious stomach ailments, wash vegetables and fruit with boiled water and boil any questionable drinking water before use.
Other risks: *Hepatitis A* and *B* occur. Sporadic outbreaks of *Japanese encephalitis* occur; *dengue fever* may also occur.
Health care: The Government provides comprehensive medical and dental facilities for residents and visitors. There are hospitals in Vaiola (Tongatapu), Hihifo (Ha'apai) and Neiafu (Vava'u), which will treat minor ailments and dispense medicines. There are also clinics, dispensaries, chemists and pharmacies. However, serious medical problems should be taken to Australia, Hawaii, New Zealand or Pago Pago (American Samoa). Visitors only pay a token fee for medicines. Health insurance is recommended. For emergency services, dial 911.

Travel - International

AIR: The main airline serving Tonga is *Air Pacific* (website: www.airpacific.com) (*Royal Tongan Airlines* collapsed in 2005). *Air New Zealand* and *Polynesian Airlines* also serve the country.
Air passes: The *Polypass* (offered by Polynesian Airlines) allows the holder to fly between the Southern Pacific destinations of American Samoa, Fiji, Niue, Samoa, Tahiti and Tonga; Honolulu (Hawaii) and Los Angeles in the USA; Brisbane, Melbourne and Sydney in Australia; and Auckland, Christchurch and Wellington in New Zealand. The pass is valid for one year. Once a reservation has been made and travel begun, all travel must be completed within a maximum of 45 days. Tickets will be issued against the Polypass by any Polynesian Airlines office (a valid passport is also required). For further information, contact Polynesian Airlines (website: www.polynesianairlines.com).
The *Visit the South Pacific Pass* is valid for many airlines operating in the South Pacific, including most of the larger ones, such as *Air Caledonie*, *Air Marshall Islands*, *Royal Tongan Airlines* and *Solomon Airlines*. Offering reductions of up to 40 per cent on normal airfares, this sector-based pass allows for flexible island-hopping between the destinations of the Cook Islands, Fiji, Nauru, New Caledonia, Samoa, Tahiti, Tonga, Vanuatu and the more remote Melanesian and Micronesian islands, together with major cities in Australia (Brisbane, Melbourne, Sydney) and New Zealand (Auckland, Christchurch, Wellington). It is only available for people resident outside of the South Pacific. The journey must be started outside the South Pacific and only one stopover in Australia is allowed. A minimum of two sectors must be bought before departure (extra sectors can be purchased en route). There is a maximum of one pass per person, and passes must be used within six months of the first day of travel. Children under 12 years of age pay 75 per cent of the adult fare.
Approximate flight times: From Nuku'alofa to *London* is 20 hours.
International airports: *Fua'Amotu (TBU)* is 13km (8 miles) from Nuku'alofa. Transport by taxi and bus is available. There are car hire services (*Avis*), bars, bank/bureau de change, shops, tourist information and a duty free shop.
Departure tax: T$25 for all passengers; children under 12 years of age and transit passengers are exempt.
SEA: Ports of entry are Neiafu, Niuatoputapu, Nuku'alofa and Pangai. There are no regular passenger services, but berths may be available on cruise ships.

Travel - Internal

AIR: *Royal Tongan Airlines (WR)* provides regular services between Vava'u, Ha'apai, 'Eua, Niuatoputapu and Tongatapu. Bookings and information are available from Royal Tongan Airlines, Nuku'alofa.
SEA: Local ferries sail between all the island groups. There are regular sailings from Faua Wharf in Nuku'alofa to Ha'apai and Vava'u. Ferry schedules are subject to change according to demand or the weather.
ROAD: Traffic drives on the left. There is a good network of metalled roads, although with some potholes. Horses are often used. The low speed limits are strictly obeyed. **Bus:** Minibus services are available throughout Tongatapu. **Taxi:** Saloon-car taxis, minimokes and mini-buses are available. **Car hire:** May be arranged through various agencies. Self-drive or chauffeur-driven cars are available.
Documentation: A current local driving licence is required, available from the Police Traffic Department in Nuku'alofa on production of a valid national or international licence, the fee and a passport. The minimum driving age is 18.
TRAVEL TIMES: The following chart gives approximate travel times (in hours and minutes) from **Nuku'alofa** to other major centres on Tonga.

	Air	Sea
Neiafu (Vava'u)	1.00	24.00
Pangai (Ha'apai)	0.30	18.00
'Eua	0.10	3.00

Accommodation

HOTELS: There are excellent hotels, guest houses, and island and beach resorts made up of Tongan-style houses. Traditional boarding houses are also very popular with tourists. There is a growing selection of accommodation and capacity is expected to increase to 900 rooms. A government tax of 7.5 per cent plus service charge is added to hotel bills. For a complete list of available accommodation, contact the Tonga Visitors' Bureau (see *Contact Addresses* section).
CAMPING: Niu-akalo Hotel offers camping grounds.

Resorts & Excursions

TONGATAPU GROUP

The largest island in the Kingdom of Tonga, **Tongatapu** is home to two-thirds of its people. A roughly triangular shaped island, it measures approximately 34km (21 miles) across from west to east. Most of the island is less than 17m (56ft) above sea level.
NUKU'ALOFA: The capital, home to Tonga's government, is a slow-paced city of 34,000 inhabitants. Sightseeing itineraries should include the white Victorian **Royal Palace** on the waterfront, just beyond **Vuna Wharf**. The Palace was completed in 1867. When HM King Taufa'ahau Tupou is in residence, the royal standard flies from the Palace. The grounds are decorated with tropical shrubs and flowers. While visitors are not allowed to enter the Palace or gardens, there are good views from the low surrounding walls. The **Mala'ekula** (Royal Tombs) are situated in the southern part of the business district along Taufa'ahau Road. The tombs have been a burial place for Tongan royalty since 1893.
THE WEST: One of the most impressive sights in Tonga are the **Blow Holes**, found along the coastline at **Houma**, 14.5km (9 miles) from Nuku'alofa. Waves send sea water spurting some 18m (60ft) into the air through holes in the coral reef. This stretch of coastline is known as the **Mapu 'a Vaea** (the Chief's Whistle) by Tongans because of the whistling sound made by the geyser-like spouts.
At **Kolovai**, 18km (11 miles) west of Nuku'alofa, visitors can find the rare **flying foxes**, dark brown fruitbats, some with wingspans of up to 1m (3ft). The **Ha'atafu** and **Monotapu** beaches are also situated at the western end of the island; they are easily accessible and well protected.
THE EAST: On the eastern end of the island are the **Langi** (Terraced Tombs), 9.5km (6 miles) from the Ha'amonga Trilithon towards Nuku'alofa. The tombs form quadrilateral mounds faced with huge blocks of stone rising in terraces to heights of 4m (13ft), built for the old *Tu'i tonga* (Spiritual Kings). The stones are of coral, built around AD 1200, possibly carried from **Wallis Island** on large canoes known as *lomipeau*.
Ha'amonga Trilithon is a massive stone arch possibly used as a seasonal calendar, erected at the same time as the Terraced Tombs and again made from coral. Each stone is thought to weigh in the region of 40,000kg (about 39 tons). The **Anahulu Cave** is an underground cavern of stalactites and stalagmites near the beach of the same name, about 24km (15 miles) from the capital. **Oholei Beach** is good for swimming.
'EUA: The island of 'Eua, a 10-minute flight away from Tongatapu, has recently been promoted as a tourist destination. It has a blend of modern comfort (the island has one hotel and a motel) and the traditional South Sea island lifestyle. Many species of exotic bird live on the island.

OUTLYING ISLANDS

HA'APAI GROUP: This group of 68 small islands forms the geological and geographical centre of Tonga and is characterised by white sandy beaches, pristine water and spectacular coral reefs. The group's main island, also named **Ha'apai**, has the quaint old town of **Pangai** as its centre. Most of the 68 islands are small, low-lying coral atolls, the exception being the volcanic islands of **Tofua** (whose volcano is still active) and the extinct **Kao** to the West. The famous mutiny on the HMS Bounty in 1789 is said to have taken place in the waters surrounding these islands and it was from here that Captain William Bligh and his loyal men began their epic 6500km (4063 mile) journey to Timor - in a rowing boat. Captain James Cook used these islands as a place of rest and relaxation. In 1995, the entire Ha'apai group was declared a Conservation Area with a view to protect the fragile ecosystems and coral reefs.
VAVA'U GROUP: Lying 240km (150 miles) north of Tongatapu, this cluster of 50 or so thickly wooded islands has one hotel, one motel, one beach resort and four guest houses. There is a daily one-hour flight from the capital and a weekly ferry service; private cruisers and ferries also operate from the harbour at **Neiafu**, the main town. There is excellent diving, with visibility often as much as 30m (100ft). Other attractions include the Fangatongo Royal Residence, the view from **Mount Talau** and **Sailoame Market** in Neiafu.

Sport & Activities

Watersports: Tongan coral reefs provide great beauty and variety for scuba diving and snorkelling; fully-equipped boats, **scuba-diving** and **snorkelling** equipment can be hired. Contact the Tonga Visitors Bureau for information. There are sandy beaches and excellent **swimming** throughout the islands, with pools at some hotels. There is a world-standard **surfing** beach on the island of 'Eua, 11km (7 miles) from Tongatapu. Tongan waters are excellent for **fishing**. There are plentiful game fish including barracuda, tuna, marlin and sailfish. Charter boats are available.
Whale watching: Humpback whales arrive in Tongan waters from around June through to November to calf and to mate. Special speakers for whale watching are plugged into a hydrophone installed on board the Phoenix catamaran based at Neiafu; only the male whales sing.
Horse riding: Horses are still a means of transportation on all the main island groups. Hotels and tour operators can make arrangements for hiring horses. Saddles are not normally available and previous riding experience is strongly recommended.

Social Profile

FOOD & DRINK: Restaurants have table service, and are found mainly in hotels. Local staples are *'ufi* (a large white yam) and *taro*. Other dishes include *lu pulu* (meat and onions, marinated in coconut milk, baked in taro leaves in an underground oven). Tropical fruits and salads are excellent. Feasts play a major role in the Tongan lifestyle. Up to 30 different dishes may be served on a *pola* (a long tray of plaited coconut fronds), and will typically include suckling pig, crayfish, chicken, octopus, pork and vegetables, steamed in an *umu* (underground oven), with a variety of tropical fruits.
NIGHTLIFE: Nightlife is sedate, limited to music and dancing in the hotels, clubs and occasionally at the *Yacht Club*. Floorshows are held on some nights in the main hotels and the Tongan National Centre. Tongan feasts and entertainment are also organised.
SHOPPING: Special purchases are hand-decorated and woven *tapa* cloth, woven floor coverings, *Ta'ovala pandanus* mats, woven *pandanus* baskets, 'Ali Baba' laundry baskets, polished coconut-shell goblets and ashtrays, model outrigger canoes, tortoiseshell ornaments, brooches, earrings, rings and silver-inlaid knives. Tongan stamps and coins are collectors' items; complete sets are on sale at the philatelic section of the Tongan Treasury. There are duty free shops on Tongatapu and Vava'u. A government tax of 5 per cent is added to all bills for goods and services.
Shopping hours: Mon-Fri 0800-1700, Sat 0800-1200.
SPECIAL EVENTS: For a complete list of special events in Tonga, contact the Tonga Visitors' Bureau (see *Contact Addresses* section). The following is a selection of special events occurring in Tonga in 2005:
Jan *New Year Celebrations*. **Feb 19-26** *Vava'u Tuna Fest. HRH Crown Prince Tupouto'a's Birthday Celebrations*. **May** *NZ-Tonga Yacht Regatta*. **Jun 4** *Emancipation Day*. **Jun** *Music Festival*. **Jun-Jul** *Heilala Week Festival*. **Jul 4** *Birthday of His Majesty King Taufa'ahau Tupou IV*. **Jul 4-8**

Heilala Festival Week. **Sep 12-16** *Tonga International Billfish Tournament*, Vava'u. **Oct** *Miss South Pacific Beauty Pageant*. **Dec** *King George Tupou IV Memorial Week*.
SOCIAL CONVENTIONS: Shaking hands is a suitable form of greeting. Although by Western standards Tongan people are by no means rich, meals served to visitors will be memorable. A token of appreciation, while not expected, is always welcome, especially gifts from the visitor's homeland. Casual wear is acceptable, but beachwear should be confined to the beach. It is illegal for both men and women to go shirtless in public. Sunday is regarded as a sacred day, an aspect of Tongan life thrown into sharp relief by the controversy surrounding the so-called 'Tongan loop'. The International Date Line forms a loop around the islands, thereby making them a day ahead of Samoa, even though Samoa is almost due north of Tonga. Members of the Seventh Day Adventist Church therefore maintain that a Tongan Sunday is really a Saturday, and are unwilling to attend church on a day which is only a Sunday because of an apparently arbitrary manifestation of international law. This complex and almost insoluble problem may cause visitors a certain amount of confusion, but travellers to Tonga are advised to respect the religious beliefs of the islanders. **Tipping:** Not encouraged, but no offence is caused if services are rewarded in this way.

Business Profile

ECONOMY: Agriculture is the strongest part of Tonga's economy. The fishing industry was relatively underdeveloped and has been a focus of government plans to expand the economy. Industrial activity is mostly light and small-scale. More recently, these have been joined by enterprises engaged in small manufacturing operations and food processing. The search for oil, which has been licensed to foreign consortia, continues offshore despite lack of success so far. Tonga's own energy requirements are met from renewable sources, principally wave and solar power.
Most of the growth in the economy and the best immediate prospect for Tonga's economic future lie in tourism which has been expanded under a recently completed 10-year development programme. The industry is now worth $10 million annually to the Tongan economy. Nonetheless, the Government is constantly looking for other projects to diversify the island's economy. A further vital source of revenue is remittances from the many thousands of Tongans working abroad, mainly in New Zealand and Australia. Current annual GDP growth is around 3 per cent, but inflation is a staggering 10.3 per cent. Tonga is a member of the South Pacific Forum and the South Pacific Commission. A regional free-trade accord, known as the Pacific Island Countries Trade Agreement, was signed among a group of Pacific governments in 2002. Australia, New Zealand, the USA, Fiji and Japan are Tonga's main trading partners. Some UK exports appear in Tonga as re-exported products from Australia and New Zealand.
BUSINESS: Shirts and ties will suffice for business visits. English is widely spoken followed by French. **Office hours:** Mon-Fri 0830-1630.
COMMERCIAL INFORMATION: The following organisations can offer advice: Ministry of Labour, Commerce and Industries, PO Box 110, Nuku'alofa (tel: 23688; fax: 23887; e-mail: Tongatrade@candw.to); *or* Tonga Chamber of Commerce and Industry, Taufa'ahau Road, PO Box 1704, Nuku'alofa (tel: 25168; fax: 26039; e-mail: chamber@kalianet.to).
CONFERENCES/CONVENTIONS: For advice, contact the Tonga Visitors' Bureau (see *Contact Addresses* section).

Climate

Tonga's climate is marginally cooler than most tropical areas. The best time to visit is from May to November. Heavy rains occur from December to March.

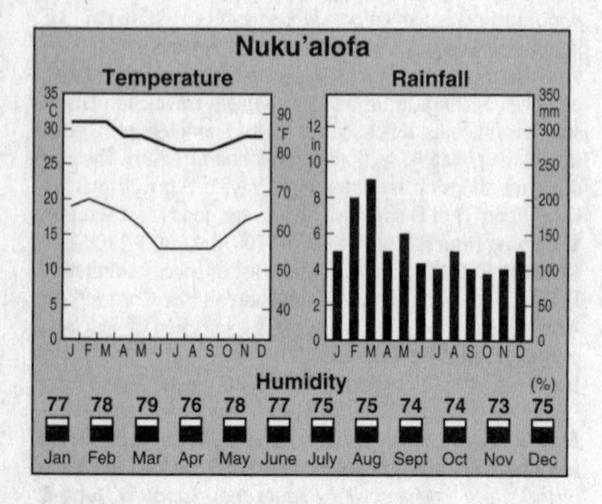

Trinidad & Tobago

LATEST TRAVEL ADVICE CONTACTS

British Foreign and Commonwealth Office
Tel: (0870) 606 0290 Website: www.fco.gov.uk

US Department of State
Website: http://travel.state.gov/travel

Canadian Department of Foreign Affairs and Int'l Trade
Tel: (1 800) 267 8376 Website: www.dfait-maeci.gc.ca

Location: Southern Caribbean, off Venezuelan coast.

Country dialling code: 1 868.

Tourism and Industrial Development Company Ltd (TIDCO)
Level 1, Maritime Centre, 29 Thames Avenue, Barataria, Trinidad
Tel: 675 7034/5/6/7. Fax: 675 7432.
E-mail: tourism-info@tidco.co.tt
Website: www.visittnt.com
Trinidad Hotels, Restaurants and Tourism Association
c/o Trinidad & Tobago Hospitality and Tourism Institute, Airway Road, Chaguaramas, PO Box 243, Port of Spain, Trinidad
Tel: 634 1174/5. Fax: 634 1176.
E-mail: info@tnthotels.com
Website: www.tnthotels.com
High Commission for the Republic of Trinidad & Tobago
42 Belgrave Square, London SW1X 8NT, UK
Tel: (020) 7245 9351. Fax: (020) 7823 1065.
E-mail: tthc@btconnect.com
Website: www.visittnt.com *or* www.tidco.co.tt
Opening hours: Mon-Fri 0900-1700; Mon-Fri 1000-1400 (visa applications).
Trinidad & Tobago Tourism Office
c/o MKI, Mitre House, 66 Abbey Road, Bush Hill Park, Enfield, Middlesex EN1 2QE, UK
Tel: (020) 8350 1009. Fax: (020) 8350 1011.
E-mail: mki@ttg.co.uk
Website: www.visittnt.com
British High Commission
19 St Clair Avenue, PO Box 778, St Clair, Port of Spain, Trinidad
Tel: 622 2748. Fax: 622 4555.
E-mail: ppabhc@tstt.net.tt
Website: www.britishhighcommission.gov.uk/trinidadandtobago
Embassy of the Republic of Trinidad & Tobago
1708 Massachusetts Avenue, NW, Washington, DC 20036, USA
Tel: (202) 467 6490. Fax: (202) 785 3130.
E-mail: embttgo@erols.com
Consulates in: Miami and New York.
Embassy of the United States of America
15 Queen's Park West, PO Box 752, Port of Spain, Trinidad
Tel: 622 6371-6. Fax: 628 5462 *or* 622 0228 (visa).
E-mail: consularportofspain@state.gov
Website: http://usembassy.state.gov/trinidad
High Commission for the Republic of Trinidad & Tobago
200 First Avenue, Ottawa, Ontario K1S 2G6, Canada
Tel: (613) 232 2418/9. Fax: (613) 232 4349.
E-mail: ottawa@ttmissions.com
Website: www.ttmissions.com
Consulate in: Toronto.
Trinidad & Tobago Tourism Office
512 Duplex Avenue, Toronto, Ontario M4R 2E3, Canada
Tel: (416) 485 7827 *or* (888) 535 5617. Fax: (416) 485 8256.
E-mail: andy@thermrgroup.ca *or* tony@thermrgroup.ca
Website: www.visittnt.com
High Commission for Canada
Street address: Maple House, 3-3A Sweet Briar Road, St Clair, Port of Spain, Trinidad
Postal address: PO Box 1246, Port of Spain, Trinidad
Tel: 622 6232. Fax: 628 1830 (general) *or* 2581 (administration) *or* 2619 (immigration) *or* 2576 (trade).
E-mail: pspan@dfait-maeci.gc.ca
Website: www.dfait-maeci.gc.ca/trinidadtobago

TIMATIC CODES

Health	AMADEUS: **TI-DFT/POS/HE** GALILEO/WORLDSPAN: **TI-DFT/POS/HE** SABRE: **TIDFT/POS/HE**
Visa	AMADEUS: **TI-DFT/POS/VI** GALILEO/WORLDSPAN: **TI-DFT/POS/VI** SABRE: **TIDFT/POS/VI**

To access TIMATIC country information on Health and Visa regulations through the Computer Reservations System (CRS), type in the appropriate command line listed above.

General Information

AREA: Total: 5128 sq km (1980 sq miles). **Trinidad:** 4828 sq km (1864 sq miles). **Tobago:** 300 sq km (116 sq miles).
POPULATION: 1,296,000 (official estimate 2001).
POPULATION DENSITY: 252.7 per sq km.

Credit: © Trinidad & Tobago Tourism Office

CAPITAL: Port of Spain. **Population:** 49,031 (2000).
GEOGRAPHY: Trinidad and her tiny sister island of Tobago lie off the Venezuelan coast. Along the north of Trinidad runs the Northern Range of mountains, looming over the country's capital, Port of Spain. South of Port of Spain on the west coast the terrain is low, and the Caroni Swamps contain a magnificent bird sanctuary largely inhabited by the scarlet ibis. On the north and east coasts lie beautiful beaches. Central Trinidad is flat and largely given over to agriculture.
GOVERNMENT: Republic. Gained independence from the UK in 1962. **Head of State:** President Maxwell Richards since 2003. **Head of Government:** Prime Minister Patrick Manning since 2002.
LANGUAGE: The official language is English. French, Spanish, Hindi and Chinese are also spoken.
RELIGION: 30 per cent Roman Catholic, 29 per cent other Christian denominations, 24 per cent Hindu, 11 per cent Anglican, and 6 per cent Muslim.
TIME: GMT - 4.
ELECTRICITY: 110/220 volts AC, 60Hz. US pattern twin plus earth plugs are standard, though variations may be found.
COMMUNICATIONS: Telephone: IDD is available. Country code: 1 868. Outgoing international code: 01. There are no area codes. In Tobago, international telephone calls can be made from the TSTT building on Wilson Road in Scarborough. Many public phone booths take phonecards which can be bought from local shops and the TSTT building. **Mobile telephone:** GSM 1800 operated by *TSTT Cellnet* (website: www.tstt.co.tt). Dual mode handsets are necessary, and can be hired from *TSTT Cellnet* on a short- or long-term basis. Coverage is available in most of Trinidad & Tobago. **Fax:** Widely available in hotels. In Tobago, faxes can also be sent from the TSTT building on Wilson Road in Scarborough. **Internet:** ISPs include *TSTT Internet Services*. There are numerous Internet cafes on the islands. **Telegram:** Port of Spain has good facilities in Independence Square and Edward Street. Cables can also be sent from hotels and the airport. **Post:** The main post office is on Wrightson Road, Port of Spain. Airmail to Western Europe takes up to two weeks; incoming mail can take much longer. The main post office in Tobago is in Market Square,

Scarborough. **Press:** English-language dailies include *Newsday, The Trinidad Guardian* and *Trinidad & Tobago Express*. As well as these dailies and numerous weekly publications, Tobago has its own weekly paper, *Tobago News*.
Radio: BBC World Service (website: www.bbc.co.uk/worldservice) and Voice of America (website: www.voa.gov) can be received. From time to time the frequencies change and the most up-to-date can be found online.

Passport/Visa

	Passport Required?	Visa Required?	Return Ticket Required?
Full British	Yes	2	Yes
Australian	Yes	Yes	Yes
Canadian	Yes	1	Yes
USA	Yes	1	Yes
Other EU	Yes	2	Yes
Japanese	Yes	Yes	Yes

Note: *Regulations and requirements may be subject to change at short notice, and you are advised to contact the appropriate diplomatic or consular authority before finalising travel arrangements. Details of these may be found at the head of this country's entry. Any numbers in the chart refer to the footnotes below.*

PASSPORTS: Valid passport required by all persons aged 16 years and over. Passport must be valid for at least six months from date of return.
Note: All visitors must be in possession of a valid return ticket to their country of residence or citizenship and sufficient funds to maintain themselves whilst in Trinidad & Tobago.
VISAS: Required by all except:
(a) **1.** nationals of Canada and the USA for stays not exceeding three months;
(b) **2.** nationals of EU countries for stays not exceeding three months, except nationals of the Czech Republic, Estonia, Hungary, Latvia, Lithuania, Poland, the Slovak Republic and Slovenia who *always* need a visa;
(c) nationals of Commonwealth countries (except Australia, Cameroon, India, Maldives, Mozambique, Namibia, New Zealand, Nigeria, Papua New Guinea, Samoa, South Africa, Sri Lanka, Tanzania, Tuvalu and Uganda, who *do* require a visa) for stays not exceeding three months;
(d) nationals of Brazil, Iceland, Liechtenstein and Turkey for stays of up to three months;
(e) nationals of Aruba, Colombia, Curacao, French Guiana, Guadeloupe, Israel, Korea (Rep), Martinique, the Netherlands Antilles, Norway, Saba, Surinam, Switzerland and Venezuela.
Types of visa: *Tourist*: £8.50. *Business* (multiple-entry): £8.50 per entry. A non-refundable processing fee of approximately US$15 must be paid at the time of application.
Validity: 90 days.
Application requirements: (a) Completed application form. (b) One passport-size photograph. (c) Valid passport with at least one empty page. (d) Letter of invitation or evidence of hotel booking. (e) Letter from employer. (f) Fee (payable by cash or postal order only). (g) Travel itinerary.
Application to: Consulate (or Consular section at Embassy or High Commission); see *Contact Addresses* section.
Working days required: Tourist visas will normally be issued within 10 working days. Applications from the following nationals may take up to four weeks: Albania, China, Cuba, Korea (Dem Rep), Serbia & Montenegro and Vietnam.
Temporary residence: Enquire at Embassy or High Commission.

Money

Currency: Trinidad & Tobago Dollar (TT$) = 100 cents. Notes are in denominations of TT$100, 20, 10, 5 and 1. Coins are in denominations of TT$1, and 50, 25, 10 and 5 cents.
Currency exchange: Foreign currency can only be exchanged at authorised banks and some hotels. There are ATMs taking cash cards and credit cards in both Trinidad and Tobago (Scarborough only).
Credit & debit cards: American Express, Diners Club, MasterCard and Visa are accepted by most banks, shops and tourist facilities. Many traders charge 5 per cent for the use of credit cards. Check with your credit or debit card company for details of merchant acceptability and other services which may be available.
Travellers cheques: These are very widely accepted and will often prove the most convenient means of transaction. Banks charge a fee for exchanging travellers cheques. Check for the best rates. To avoid additional exchange rate charges, travellers are advised to take travellers cheques in US Dollars or Pounds Sterling.
Currency restrictions: The import of local currency is unlimited, provided declared on arrival. The export of local currency is limited to TT$200. There is free import of foreign currency, subject to declaration. The export of foreign currency is limited to the equivalent of TT$2500 per year.
Exchange rate indicators: The following figures are included as a guide to the movements of the Trinidad & Tobago Dollar against Sterling and the US Dollar:

Date	Feb '04	May '04	Aug '04	Nov '04
£1.00=	11.19	10.98	11.47	11.79
$1.00=	6.15	6.15	6.23	6.23

Banking hours: Mon-Thurs 0800-1400, Fri 0900-1200 and 1500-1700.

Duty Free

The following goods may be imported into Trinidad & Tobago by persons over 17 years of age without incurring customs duty:
200 cigarettes or 50 cigars or 250g of tobacco; 1.5l of wine or spirits in opened bottles; a reasonable quantity of perfume; gifts up to the value of US$200.

Public Holidays

2005: Jan 1 New Year's Day. **Feb 7** Carnival Monday. **Mar 25** Good Friday. **Mar 28** Easter Monday. **Mar 30** Spiritual Baptist Shouters' Liberation Day. **May 30** Indian Arrival Day. **Jun 10** Corpus Christi. **Jun 19** Labour Day. **Aug 1** Emancipation Day. **Aug 31** Independence Day. **Sep 24** Republic Day. **Nov 1** Divali. **Nov 2-4** Eid ul Fitr. **Dec 25-26** Christmas.
2006: Jan 1 New Year's Day. **Feb 27** Carnival Monday. **Mar 30** Spiritual Baptist Shouters' Liberation Day. **Apr 14** Good Friday. **Apr 17** Easter Monday. **May 30** Indian Arrival Day. **Jun 15** Corpus Christi. **Jun 19** Labour Day. **Aug 1** Emancipation Day. **Aug 31** Independence Day. **Sep 24** Republic Day. **Oct 21** Divali. **Oct 22-24** Eid ul Fitr. **Dec 25-26** Christmas.
Note: Hindu festivals are declared according to local astronomical observations and variations may occur.

Health

	Special Precautions?	Certificate Required?
Yellow Fever	No	1
Cholera	No	No
Typhoid & Polio	No	N/A
Malaria	No	N/A

Note: *Regulations and requirements may be subject to change at short notice, and you are advised to contact your doctor well in advance of your intended date of departure. Any numbers in the chart refer to the footnotes below.*

1: A yellow fever vaccination certificate is required from travellers over one year of age arriving from infected areas.
Food & drink: Mains water in Tobago is safe to drink, though bottled water is available in supermarkets. Drinking water outside main cities and towns may be contaminated and sterilisation is advisable. Milk is pasteurised and dairy products are safe for consumption. Local meat, poultry, seafood, fruit and vegetables throughout both islands are generally safe to eat. The authorities advise caution, however, during carnival time when buying food from the 'hawker' stalls in Port of Spain.
Other risks: *Hepatitis A* occurs. Mosquitoes can be inconvenient anywhere just before and after dusk. Visitors are advised to carry insect repellent and bite cream. *Rabies* is present. For those at high risk, vaccination before arrival should be considered. If you are bitten, seek medical advice without delay. Bats are a problem as far as the transmission of rabies is concerned. For more information, consult the *Health* appendix.
Health care: Although there is no reciprocal health agreement with the UK, public sector health care is free. However, health insurance is recommended as Tobago's health care provision is basic, with limited supplies and medication.

Travel - International

AIR: Trinidad & Tobago's national airline is *BWIA (BW)* (website: www.bwee.com), which flies to other Caribbean islands and to several towns on the North and South American coasts. BWIA operates frequent services from London (Heathrow), Miami and New York to Port of Spain. There are weekly flights from London (Gatwick) direct to Tobago on *British Airways (BA)*. Other airlines serving Trinidad & Tobago include *Aeropostal* (from Venezuela), *Air Canada, ALM Antillean Airlines, American Airlines, American Eagle* (from Puerto Rico) and *Condor* (from Frankfurt/M). *Air Caribbean, Caribbean Star* and *LIAT* also offer inter-Caribbean flights.

Credit: © Trinidad & Tobago Tourism Office

Approximate flight times: From Port of Spain to *Barbados* is 50 minutes; to *London* is 10 hours (flying BWIA; with a further 30-minute flight to Crown Point, Tobago); to *New York* is six hours 30 minutes; and to *St Lucia* is two hours 10 minutes (including stop at Barbados).
International airports: *Piarco International Airport (POS)* is 25km (16 miles) east of Port of Spain. Buses are available to the city (travel time - 25 minutes). There are taxis to the city for hotels throughout the island with set fares posted in taxis. Fares increase after midnight. Sharing taxis is an accepted practice. Airport facilities include duty free shops, banks, ATMs, car hire, restaurants, light refreshments, shops and tourist information.
Crown Point (TAB) is 13km (8 miles) from Scarborough and very close to most of the main hotels. Taxis are available (prices for standard journeys are published in the airport arrival lounge). Airport facilities include a bank, shops, restaurant, duty free shop, snack and car hire. For more information on airports, contact the Airports Authority of Trinidad and Tobago (website: www.tntairports.com).
Departure tax: TT$100 (payable in local currency only). Transit passengers and children under five years of age are exempt.
SEA: The main ports are Port of Spain, Point Lisas and Point-à-Pierre. Cruise lines that stop at Port of Spain include *Princess* and *Silversea*.

Travel - Internal

AIR: Every day there are flights every two hours run by *Air Caribbean (C2)* from Piarco (Port of Spain) to Tobago (Crown Point). During peak seasons (especially Carnival time), these are often heavily booked. The service runs until around 2000 in the evening. *Tobago Express* also links Tobago and Port of Spain.
SEA: There is a regular car ferry/passenger service from Port of Spain to Tobago (Scarborough) (travel time - approximately six hours). The day journey (from Port of Spain around 1400) gives a good view of the two islands; the night journey (from Scarborough around 2300) can be uncomfortable. Ferry fares are around TT$160 (return). Return by plane to Port of Spain is recommended.
ROAD: Traffic drives on the left. The road network in Trinidad between major towns is good, but traffic around Port of Spain can be difficult during rush hour and around Independence Square at any time. Two major highways run north-south and east-west. Roads which run off major routes can be very unpredictable, and are susceptible to poor weather conditions. In Tobago, the roads, though narrow in parts, are improving dramatically and most of the island is easy to reach. There is a major highway (Claude Noel Highway) running west-east. Tourists should have no qualms about driving around Tobago at any time of the day or night, although caution should be exercised in more rural areas where chickens and sheep may wander across roads. Hand signals, which may be unfamiliar, are often used. **Bus:** Services are operated by the state *Public Service Corporation (PTSC)*. In the absence of a railway, the main towns are served by bus but although these are cheap, they are crowded and unreliable. The use of shared taxis has increased due to the shortcomings of the bus network; these are available both outside and within Port of Spain. In Tobago, there are regular bus services between Scarborough bus station and Crown Point, Buccoo, Plymouth and Roxborough. **Taxi:** All official taxis have registration 'H'. Hiring a private taxi is much more expensive but gives the

Credit: © Trinidad & Tobago Tourism Office

freedom to go where you like. Though there are fixed rates for certain journeys, it is best to establish this before you start your journey. The quickest and most cost-effective way to get around is by Route taxis and Maxi taxis which serve standard routes within Trinidad, particularly around Port of Spain, starting their route from in or near Independence Square. These have fixed rates. In Tobago, Route taxis (H registered and unregistered) are plentiful along most major routes during the day and can be stopped anywhere along them. Drivers will indicate they have room by sounding their horn. **Car hire:** Cars and motorcycles are available in Port of Spain or Scarborough, and can be arranged via hotels and in Tobago at the airport or through the hotels. Trailbikes are becoming more popular in Tobago, but mopeds are more advisable for the inexperienced rider.
Bicycle hire: In Tobago, there are a number of places in the Lowlands (southeast) where you can hire bicycles.
Documentation: Visitors in possession of a valid driving permit issued in any of the countries listed below may drive in Trinidad & Tobago for a period of up to three months. They are, however, entitled to drive only a motor vehicle of the class specified on their permit. Drivers must at all times have in their possession: (a) their International Driving Permit or equivalent; and, (b) any travel document on which is certified their date of arrival in Trinidad & Tobago. Visitors whose stay exceeds the three-month period are requested to apply to the Licensing Department, Wrightson Road, Port of Spain, for a local Driving Permit. The above information applies to all signatories to the Convention on International Driver's Permits including The Bahamas, Canada, France, Germany, the UK and the USA. *Excluded*: China (PR), South Africa and Vietnam, whose nationals require a passport, International Driving Permit and national licence.
URBAN: Owing to the deterioration of bus services, most public transport journeys in Port of Spain are now made by shared taxis (see above). The Tourism and Industrial Development Company Ltd publishes a list of fares for standard routes (see *Contact Addresses* section).

Accommodation

HOTELS: There are major international chain hotels in Port of Spain, and a number of smaller hotels in the surrounding areas. In Tobago, there is a growing number of international-standard resort hotels, as well as many smaller private hotels, and guest houses. There is a wide range of prices.
For further information, contact the Trinidad Hotels, Restaurants and Tourism Association (see *Contact Addresses* section) or organise your accommodation after arriving in Port of Spain or Tobago. A 10 per cent government room tax and VAT are levied.
GUEST HOUSES: The Tourism and Industrial Development Company Ltd publishes a list of guest houses found throughout Trinidad & Tobago (see *Contact Addresses* section).
HOUSES/APARTMENTS: There is a growing number of apartments and houses available for rent in Tobago, ranging from the very luxurious to the plain and simple. Though many are located in the west in the main tourist part of the island around Crown Point and Shirvan Road, there are many other more secluded and unspoilt areas where there are properties of all standards to rent. Information is available from local sources.
Note: All types of accommodation must be booked well in advance for the *Carnival* (see *Social Profile* section).

Resorts & Excursions

TRINIDAD

PORT OF SPAIN: The home of carnival, steel bands, calypso and limbo dancing, Trinidad & Tobago's blend of different cultures gives them an air of cosmopolitan excitement. Port of Spain, surrounded by the lush green hills of the **Northern Range**, is the capital and business hub of oil-rich Trinidad. The city captures the variety of Trinidadian life, with bazaars thronging beneath modern skyscrapers and mosques rubbing shoulders with cathedrals. The architecture of the city incorporates a mixture of styles: these include Victorian houses with gingerbread fretwork; the German Renaissance **Queen's Royal College**; **Stollmeyer's Castle**, an imitation of a Bavarian Castle; the President of the Republic's residence and the Prime Minister's office at **Whitehall** (both built in Moorish style); and the 19th-century Gothic **Holy Trinity Cathedral**. Places of interest include the shopping district centred on **Frederick Street**; the **Royal Botanic Gardens**; the **Red House** (a stately colonial building, now the seat of government) and the **National Museum** and **Art Gallery**.
EXCURSIONS: The magnificent **Queen's Park Savannah**, to the north of the capital and within walking distance, is spread out at the foot of the Northern Range. A mixture of natural and manmade beauty, with attractive trees and shrubs (including the African Tulip, or 'Flame of the Forest'), it forms a backdrop to playing fields and elaborate mansions, now mostly government offices and embassies. On the outskirts of the city is **Fort George**. Built in 1804, it offers an excellent view of Port of Spain and the mountains of northern Venezuela.
Maracas Bay, **Las Cuevas** and **Chaguaramas** are the nearest beaches to Port of Spain. Maracas tends to be the place to go after Carnival has finished. Approximately 13km (8 miles) to the south of the capital by road and boat is the **Caroni Bird Sanctuary**, home of the Scarlet Ibis. The **Diego Mountain Valley**, 16km (10 miles) from Port of Spain, contains one of the island's most beautiful water wheels.
ELSEWHERE: In the rapidly expanding town of **Chaguanas**, it is possible to sample a wide range of West Indian culinary specialities, particularly East Indian fare. **Arima**, the third-largest town on the island, has an **Amerindian Museum** at the **Cleaver Woods Recreation Centre** in the west of town and the nation's new horse racing track. About 13km (8 miles) north is the **Asa Wright Nature Centre** at **Blanchisseuse**, containing a collection of rare specimens such as the Oilbird or **Guacharo**. The **Aripo Caves** are noted for their stalactites and stalagmites. **Asa Wright** is a must for birdwatching enthusiasts. There is a good hotel there, but rooms are limited and need to be booked well in advance. On the east coast is **Valencia**, a lush tropical forest near the **Hollis Reservoir**. **Cocal** and **Mayaro** are also worth visiting. **San Fernando** is the island's second town and the main commercial centre in the south. Close by is the fascinating natural phenomenon of the **Pitch Lake**, a 36.4 hectare (90 acre) lake of asphalt which constantly replenishes itself.

TOBAGO

Tobago is very different from her sister isle 32km (20 miles) away. It is a tranquil island with calm waters and vast stretches of white sand beaches. In the east, the volcanic part of the island is precipitous and heavily wooded, with the oldest protected rainforest in the western hemisphere. The island is so beautiful and fertile that just about every western European colonial power has fought to have it.
SCARBOROUGH: The capital, Scarborough, has many quaint houses which spill down from the hilltop to the waterside, as well as interesting **Botanical Gardens**. It is overshadowed by the **Fort King George** built in 1779 during the many struggles between the French and the English, an excellent point from which to view the sunset. The **Court House** built in 1825 is today used as the meeting place for the Tobago House of Assembly, while **Tobago Museum** showcases artefacts from Tobago's early American Indian and colonial days.
EXCURSIONS: There are a number of fine beaches throughout the island, each with their own flavour. They include **Pigeon Point** on the northwest coast (admission is charged for use of facilities); **Store Bay** and **Turtle Beach**, where brown pelicans can be seen diving into the waters to catch fish; **Man O'War Bay**, at the opposite end of the island; and **Mount Irvine** and **Bacolet Bays**. It is worth remembering that there is no such thing as a private beach in Trinidad & Tobago, and though some hotels discourage the use of their facilities, most do not mind unless they are very busy, especially if you use their bar and beach restaurants. Many beaches have public facilities. **Buccoo Reef** is an extensive coral reef lying a mile offshore from Pigeon Point. Excursions can be made in glass-bottomed boats and it is an excellent place for snorkelling. These trips run from Store Bay or Pigeon Point, leaving every day at around 1100.
At **Fort James**, there is a well-maintained red brick building, and at **Whim**, a large plantation house. **Arnos Vale Hotel** is a former sugar plantation, now a hotel; a disused sugar mill fitted out with formidable crushing wheels, made in 1857, is still on the grounds. **Englishman's Bay** is an excellent place for a day trip. Birdwatching is a favourite pastime here. The hotel offers tea to non-residents during the late afternoon on the balcony above the gardens. This is a must for birdwatchers and needs to be booked by phone first.
ELSEWHERE: The fishing village of **Plymouth** has a mystery tombstone with inscriptions dating from 1700. **Charlotteville** is a fishing town commanding precipitous views of the headlands. Looming above the town is **Pigeon Peak**, the highest point on the island. There are good swimming beaches, including Pirate's Bay, which can only be reached by boat. **Tobago Forest Reserve** in the east has many trails which provide excellent long hikes for the more active visitor. On the Atlantic (windward) side of the island are many tiny villages including **Mesopotamia** and **Goldsborough**, the town of **Roxborough** and several beautiful bays. **Speyside** is a colourful beach settlement, from which can be seen tiny **Goat Island** and **Little Tobago**, a 182 hectare (450 acre) bird sanctuary. Speyside offers excellent snorkelling and scuba-diving. Windward (Atlantic) beaches are wilder but just as picturesque as those on the Caribbean. On the north coast are the beautiful villages of **Castara** and **Parlatuvier**.

Sport & Activities

Watersports: There are good facilities for all types of watersports, especially at the beaches along the north and east coasts of Trinidad, and all around Tobago. *Buccoo Reef*, just off the southwest coast of Tobago, and *Speyside* offer exciting **scuba-diving** with magnificent coral formations and abundant marine life. Trips in glass-bottomed boats are very popular. Tobago has some of the finest reefs in the Caribbean and many scuba schools located at Speyside and Store Bay.
Fishing: All kinds of fishing - from deep-sea to inland - are widely available and usually rewarding on and off both islands. Kingfish, Spanish mackerel, wahoo, bonito, dolphin fish and yellow tuna are the usual catches, with grouper, salmon and snapper also to be found off the west and north coasts of Trinidad. In Tobago, there is an increasing number of boats available for hire.
Birdwatching and wildlife: These islands have a unique wealth of wild birds and flowers, butterflies and fish, mostly undisturbed, yet accessible. The islands boasts no less than 622 species of butterfly and over 700 species of orchid. The latter are perhaps best seen in Trinidad's *Botanic Gardens* in Port of Spain (along with a wide selection of indigenous trees, shrubs, ferns and cacti). The *Emperor Valley Zoo* has a similarly representative selection of local wildlife - reptile as well as mammal. Birdwatchers on Trinidad should head for the *Nariva Swamp*, the *Aripo Savannah* and the *Asa Wright Nature Centre* and look out in particular for the national bird, the scarlet ibis, conserved in the *Caroni Bird Sanctuary*. The sight of these scarlet birds flying in formation to roost before sundown is a stunning and colourful spectacle. While on Tobago, a visit to *Little Tobago Island* is recommended, particularly if you're keen on birds. Boats leave from Speyside. Hummingbirds are ubiquitous on Tobago; there are 19 recorded species, seven of which are unique to the island. There are specialist birdwatching tours and nature trips available, details of which can be provided by any hotel.
Other: Golf can be enjoyed just outside Port of Spain (Maraval) or in Tobago at the marvellous *Mount Irvine Golf Course*, former host to the *Johnny Walker Pro Am*. **Cricket** is the major spectator sport and the season runs from February to June. The best national and international matches can be seen at the Queen's Park Oval, in Port of Spain. Trinidadians are keen on **racing**, and the *Arima Velodrome* hosts a number of major meetings, particularly around New Year and Easter. It is possible to bet on all English and much US racing in any of the racepools in Port of Spain and Scarborough.

Social Profile

FOOD & DRINK: Bars and restaurants open until late, with a very wide choice of local and Western food and drink. Chinese, Indian and West Indian cooking is available on both islands. Tobago also offers some notable seafood specialities such as lobster, conch and dumplings, crab and dumplings, and all types of fried fish. Local dishes include pilau rice and Creole soups, the best being *sans coche*, *calaloo* and peppery pigeon pea soup. *Tatoo*, *manicou*, pork souse, green salad, *tum-tum* (mashed green plantains), roast venison, *lappe* (island rabbit), *quenk* (wild pig), wild duck and *pastelles* (meat folded into cornmeal and wrapped in a banana leaf - a speciality generally available over Christmas) are also well worth trying if you can. Seafood in Trinidad includes bean-sized oysters and *chip-chip* (tiny shellfish similar in taste to clams). Crab *malete* is excellent, as is the freshwater fish *cascadou*. Indian dishes on both islands include *roti* (dahlpuri bread stuffed with chicken, fish, goat or vegetables), *palhouri* and hot curries. Excellent rums and Angostura bitters are used to make rum punch. The local beers are *Carib* and *Stag*.

NIGHTLIFE: Trinidad has a wide and varied nightlife including hotel entertainment and nightclubs with calypso, limbo dancers and steel bands. During the carnival season (from New Year to Carnival, held two days before Ash Wednesday), both islands are alive with live music in the calypso tents and pan (steel band) yards. In Tobago, the main Calypsonians from Trinidad travel over to perform at Shaw Park, Scarborough and Roxborough. There is something happening most nights of the week at this time - details available from the locals and the *Tobago News*.

SHOPPING: Goods from all over the world can be found in Port of Spain, but local goods are always available. Special purchases include Calypso records, steel drums, leather bags and sandals, ceramics and woodcarvings. Gold and silver jewellery can be good value, as can Indian silks and fabrics. Rum should also be considered. Bright, printed fabrics and other summer garments are available in Trinidad & Tobago, particularly in Port of Spain. **Shopping hours:** Mon-Thurs 0800-1600, Fri 0800-1800 and Sat 0800-1300. Some shops stay open later in Port of Spain, and malls are often open till 2100. Shops close on public holidays, especially during Carnival.

SPECIAL EVENTS: A vast mixture of races has led to a varied cultural life, the diversity of which is reflected in costume, religion, architecture, music, dance and place names. The major event in Trinidad is the *Carnival*, renowned throughout the Caribbean and the rest of the world. The festivities climax at the beginning of Lent, on the two days immediately preceding Ash Wednesday, although the run-up to Carnival starts immediately after Christmas when the Calypso tents open and the Calypsonians perform their latest compositions and arrangements. During Carnival, normal life grinds to a halt and the whole of Trinidad & Tobago is absorbed in the festivities. A week before the Carnival proper, *Panorama* is staged. This is the Grand Steel Drum (pan) tournament; all the big steel bands parade their skills around the Savannah, the large park in the north of Port of Spain. The Panorama preliminaries and local finals in Tobago are worth visiting, as are the pan yards as the bands practise for the big event. *Hosay*, coinciding with the Muslim New Year, sees the Muslim population of Port of Spain, San Fernando and Tunapuna take to the streets in a festival of their own. Contact the Tourism and Industrial Development Company Ltd (see *Contact Addresses* section) for more information and exact dates of the above.

The following is a selection of special events occurring in Trinidad & Tobago in 2005:

Feb 7-8 *Carnival*. **Mar 3-6** *97th Trinidad and Tobago Golf Open*, St Andrews, Moka. **Mar 13** *Jazz Artists on the Greens*, St Augustine. **Apr 2-30** *Festival of Rapso and the Oral Traditions*. **May 8-13** *Angostura Yachting Regatta*. **Jul 27-Aug 1** *Great Fete Weekend*, Pigeon Point. **Jul 28-31** *Tobago Heritage Festival*. **Aug 10-14** *Santa Rosa Festival*, Arima. **Sep 24** *Tobago Festival*. **Nov 1** *Divali Festival of Light*. **Nov** *Eid*. **Dec 31** *National Parang Competition*.

SOCIAL CONVENTIONS: *Liming*, or talking for talking's sake, is a popular pastime, as is chatting about, watching and playing cricket. Many local attitudes are often reflected in the lyrics of the *calypso*, the accepted medium for political and social satire since pre-emancipation days. Hospitality is important and entertaining is commonly done at home. Casual wear is usual, with shirt sleeves generally accepted for business and social gatherings, but beachwear is not worn in towns. **Tipping:** Most hotels and guest-houses add 10 per cent service charge to the bill, otherwise a 10 to 15 per cent tip is usual in hotels and restaurants.

Business Profile

ECONOMY: The oil and gas industry has been the most important in Trinidad & Tobago for some time. It had been in long-term decline from the 1980s due to falling yields and low world prices. More recently, however, new discoveries, increased foreign investment and a steady increase in world prices have reversed the trend. In the summer of 2003, Trinidad signed a landmark agreement with nearby Venezuela, one of the world's largest producers, to collaborate in all aspects of the oil and gas industries. This should ensure the long-term future of the sector for Trinidad. Apart from oil and gas, Trinidad has the world's largest deposits of asphalt.

The non-oil industrial sector is concentrated in relatively new industries established with oil and gas revenues, such as plastics and electronics. The agricultural sector is small, with sugar cane, coffee, cocoa and citrus fruits as the main commodities. Once a net exporter of foodstuffs, Trinidad now imports the bulk of its requirements.

The Government has also sought to address historic under-investment in the tourism industry, a promising part of the economy which has undergone steady growth. The islands now cater to about 400,000 visitors annually; the industry is worth about US$275 million to the Trinidadian economy. Trinidad & Tobago formerly had the most heavily regulated economy in the region but the state-controlled edifice was dismantled during the 1990s as part of an IMF-approved package of privatisation, fiscal and trade liberalisation. The external debt has been substantially reduced while growth and inflation are both close to 5 per cent; unemployment has been cut to 13 per cent from higher levels during the 1990s. As ever, this was achieved at the cost of reductions in social provision and lower than average incomes for the bulk of the population. Trinidad & Tobago is a member of the Caribbean trading bloc, CARICOM. The country's main trading partners are Jamaica, Barbados and Guyana in the region and, further afield, the UK, the USA, Canada, Brazil and Germany.

BUSINESS: Lightweight suits or 'shirt jacks' should be worn. It is normal to shake hands and exchange business cards. The best time to visit is from December to April, except during the Christmas festivities. **Office hours:** Mon-Fri 0800-1600.

COMMERCIAL INFORMATION: The following organisation can offer advice: Trinidad and Tobago Chamber of Industry and Commerce (Inc), Columbus Circle, Westmoorings, Trinidad, PO Box 499, Port of Spain (tel: 637 6966; fax: 637 7425; e-mail: chamber@chamber.org.tt; website: www.chamber.org.tt).

Climate

The tropical climate is tempered by northeast trade winds. The dry season is from November to May, but it is hottest between June and October. The climate in Tobago is pleasant most of the year and although May, June and July can be wet at times, the differentiation between the wet and dry seasons is much less acute.

Required clothing: Tropical lightweights are required. Rainwear is advisable, especially for the wet season.

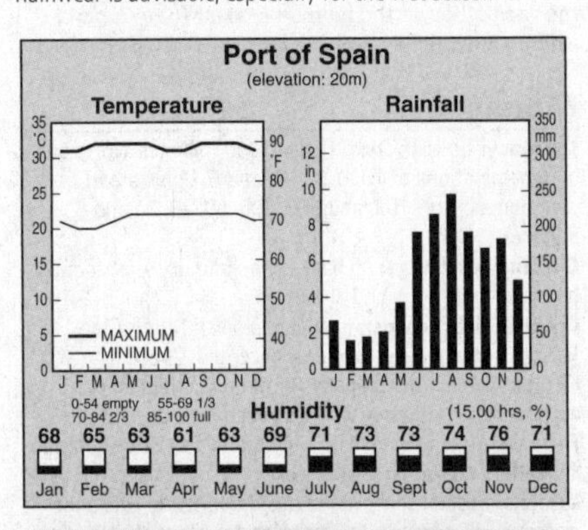

Tunisia

LATEST TRAVEL ADVICE CONTACTS

British Foreign and Commonwealth Office
Tel: (0870) 606 0290 Website: www.fco.gov.uk

US Department of State
Website: http://travel.state.gov/travel

Canadian Department of Foreign Affairs and Int'l Trade
Tel: (1 800) 267 8376 Website: www.dfait-maeci.gc.ca

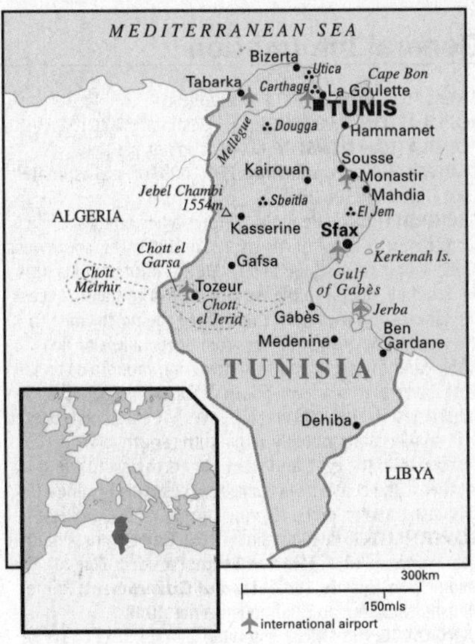

Location: North Africa.

Country dialling code: 216.

Office National du Tourisme Tunisien (ONTT) (Tunisian National Tourist Office)
1 avenue Mohamed V, 1001 Tunis, Tunisia
Tel: (71) 371 044. Fax: (71) 350 977.
E-mail: info@tourism.tunisia.com *or* ontt@Email.ati.tn
Website: www.tourismtunisia.com

Embassy of the Republic of Tunisia
29 Prince's Gate, London SW7 1QG, UK
Tel: (020) 7584 8117 (for enquiries) *or* (09065) 508 977 (24-hour visa information line; calls cost £1 a minute).
Fax: (020) 7225 2884.
Opening hours: Mon-Fri 0900-1700; 0930-1300 (consular section); Mon-Thurs 0930-1300 (visa submissions).

Tunisian National Tourist Office
77A Wigmore Street, London W1U 1QF, UK
Tel: (020) 7224 5561 *or* 5598 (press). Fax: (020) 7224 4053.
E-mail: tntolondon@aol.com
Website: www.tourismtunisia.com

British Embassy
Rue du Lac Windermere, Les Berges du Lac, 1053 Tunis, Tunisia
Tel: (71) 108 700. Fax: (71) 108 749 (management) *or* 769 (press) *or* 779 (visa) *or* 789 (consular).
E-mail: british.emb@planet.tn *or* tvi.tunis@fco.gov.uk *or* tunisconsular.tunis@fco.gov.uk
Website: www.british-emb.intl.tn

Embassy of the Republic of Tunisia
1515 Massachusetts Avenue, NW, Washington, DC 20005, USA
Tel: (202) 862 1850 *or* 680 6006 (tourism enquiries).
Fax: (202) 862 1858.
E-mail: atwashington@verizon.net
Website: www.tunisiaonline.com

Embassy of the United States of America
Zone Nord-Est des Berges du Lac, Nord de Tunis, 2045, La Goulette, Tunisia
Tel: (71) 107 000. Fax: (71) 962 115.
Website: http://tunis.usembassy.gov

Embassy of the Republic of Tunisia
515 O'Connor Street, Ottawa, Ontario K1S 3P8, Canada
Tel: (613) 237 0330. Fax: (613) 237 7939.
Consulate in: Montréal.

TIMATIC CODES

Health	AMADEUS: **TI-DFT/TUN/HE** GALILEO/WORLDSPAN: **TI-DFT/TUN/HE** SABRE: **TIDFT/TUN/HE**
Visa	AMADEUS: **TI-DFT/TUN/VI** GALILEO/WORLDSPAN: **TI-DFT/TUN/VI** SABRE: **TIDFT/TUN/VI**

To access TIMATIC country information on Health and Visa regulations through the Computer Reservations System (CRS), type in the appropriate command line listed above.

Tunisian National Tourist Office
1253 McGill College Avenue, Suite 655, Montréal, Québec H3B 2Y5, Canada
Tel: (514) 397 1182 *or* 0403. Fax: (514) 397 1647.
E-mail: tunisinfo@qc.aira.com
Website: www.tourismtunisia.com

Canadian Embassy
Street address: 3 rue du Sénégal, 1002 Tunis, Tunisia
Postal address: PO Box 31, 1002 Bélvèdere, Tunis, Tunisia
Tel: (71) 104 000.
Fax: (71) 104 191 (administration) *or* 194 (consular).
E-mail: tunis@dfait-maeci.gc.ca
Website: www.dfait-maeci.gc.ca/tunisia

General Information

AREA: 163,610 sq km (63,170 sq miles).
POPULATION: 9,889,900 (official estimate 2002).
POPULATION DENSITY: 60.4 per sq km.
CAPITAL: Tunis. **Population:** 1,927,000 (official estimate 2001 (including suburbs)).
GEOGRAPHY: The Republic of Tunisia lies on the Mediterranean coast of Africa, 130km (80 miles) southwest of Sicily and 160km (100 miles) due south of Sardinia. It is bordered by Algeria to the west and Libya to the southeast. The landscape varies from the cliffs of the north coast to the woodlands of the interior, from deep valleys of rich arable land to desert, and from towering mountains to salt pans lower than sea level. South of Gafsa and Gabès is the Sahara desert. The 1100km (700 miles) of coastline is dotted with small islands, notably Jerba in the south and Kerkennah in the east, and from the northwest to the southeast the coastline is backed successively by pine-clad hills, lush pasture, orchards, vineyards and olive groves.
GOVERNMENT: Republic since 1959. Gained independence from France in 1956. **Head of State:** President Zine Al-Abidine Ben Ali since 1987. **Head of Government:** Prime Minister Muhammad Ghannouchi since 1999.
LANGUAGE: The official language is Arabic. French is the second language, Italian is spoken in major cities, and English and German mainly in tourist resorts.
RELIGION: The principal religion is Islam; there are small Roman Catholic, Protestant and Jewish minorities.
TIME: GMT + 1.
ELECTRICITY: 220/110 volts AC, 50Hz. A two-pin continental plug/adaptor is needed.
COMMUNICATIONS: Telephone: Full IDD is available. Country code: 216. Outgoing international code: 00. Automatic dialling extends to almost every part of the country and covers direct international calls. **Mobile telephone:** GSM 900 network. Operators include *Tunisiana* (website: www.tunisiana.com) and *Tunisie Telecom*. **Fax:** Facilities are available in main towns, hotels and post offices. **Internet:** ISPs include *3S Global Net* (website: www.gnet.tn), *ATI* (website: www.ati.tn) and *Planet Tunisie* (website: www.planet.tn). E-mail can be accessed from Internet cafes in Tunis, Nabeul, Sousse and Tahar ben Amar. **Telegram:** The Telecommunications Centre in Tunis is located at 29 Jamal Abdelnasser. Telegraph facilities are available at the Central Post Office at rue Charles de Gaulle, Tunis; telegrams can also be sent from most hotels. **Post:** Airmail to Europe takes three to five days; an express service guarantees delivery in four days or under. *Poste Restante* facilities are available in main cities. Post office hours: Mon-Sat 0800-1300 (summer, approximately 15 Jun-15 Sep); Mon-Fri 0800-1200 and 1400-1800, Sat 0800-1200 (winter, approximately 16 Sep-14 Jun); Mon-Sat 0800-1500 (during Ramadan). **Press:** Daily newspapers are printed in Arabic or French, the most popular being *As-Sabah* and *La Presse de Tunisie*. The weekly *Tunisia News* is published in English.
Radio: BBC World Service (website: www.bbc.co.uk/worldservice) and Voice of America (website: www.voa.gov) can be received. From time to time the frequencies change and the most up-to-date can be found online.

Passport/Visa

	Passport Required?	Visa Required?	Return Ticket Required?
Full British	Yes	No	Yes
Australian	Yes	Yes/2	Yes
Canadian	Yes	No	Yes
USA	Yes	No	Yes
Other EU	Yes	No/1	Yes
Japanese	Yes	No	Yes

Note: *Regulations and requirements may be subject to change at short notice, and you are advised to contact the appropriate diplomatic or consular authority before finalising travel arrangements. Details of these may be found at the head of this country's entry. Any numbers in the chart refer to the footnotes below.*

PASSPORTS: Passport valid six months after return date required by all.

VISAS: Required by all except the following:
(a) **1.** nationals referred to in the chart above for stays of up to three months, except nationals of Australia who *do* need a visa, and nationals of the Czech Republic, Hungary, Latvia, Lithuania, Poland and the Slovak Republic, who must travel on a recognised package holiday, and nationals of Cyprus and Estonia who *do* need a visa;
(b) nationals of Algeria, Andorra, Antigua & Barbuda, Argentina, Bahrain, Barbados, Bermuda, Bosnia & Herzegovina, Brazil, Brunei, Bulgaria, Chile, Côte d'Ivoire, Dominica, Fiji, The Gambia, Guinea, Honduras, Hong Kong (SAR), Iceland, Kiribati, Korea (Rep), Libya, Liechtenstein, Macedonia (Former Yugoslav Republic), Malaysia, Maldives, Mali, Mauritania, Mauritius, Monaco, Morocco, Niger, Norway, Oman, Qatar, Romania, St Kitts & Nevis, St Lucia, Senegal, Seychelles, Solomon Islands, Switzerland, Turkey and Vatican City;
(c) nationals of the CIS for package holidays only, except nationals of Armenia who *do* need a visa;
(d) transit passengers, provided holding valid onward or return documentation and not leaving the airport or ship.
Note: 2. Nationals of Australia and South Africa, who *do* need a visa, can obtain it on arrival at the point of entry. Check with the Embassy for details of length of stay.
Types of visa and cost: *Short-stay* and *Transit*: £4.
Validity: *Short-stay*: usually up to three months. *Transit*: three days. For up-to-date lengths of stay, contact nearest Consulate.
Application to: Consulate (or Consular section at Embassy); see *Contact Addresses* section.
Application requirements: (a) Valid passport. (b) Photocopy of first five pages of passport and any stamps. (c) Three application forms completed in black ink and capital letters. (d) Two passport-size photos with full name printed on back. (e) Fee (payable by postal order or cash; cheques are not accepted). (f) Registered, stamped, self-addressed envelope for postal application.
Working days required: Approximately 20, for both postal and personal applications.
Temporary residence: For more information, contact the visa section of the Tunisian Embassy (see *Contact Addresses* section).

Money

Currency: Tunisian Dinar (TD) = 1000 millimes. Notes are in denominations of TD30, 20, 10 and 5. Coins are in denominations of TD1, and 500, 100, 50, 20, 10 and 5 millimes.
Currency exchange: All banks change money, as do most hotels of three stars and above.
Credit & debit cards: American Express, Diners Club, MasterCard and Visa are widely accepted. Check with your credit or debit card company for details of merchant acceptability and other services which may be available. There are ATMs in every large town and tourist destination.
Travellers cheques: Readily cashed in banks and the usual authorised establishments; to avoid additional exchange rates, travellers are advised to bring travellers cheques in US Dollars.
Currency restrictions: The import and export of local currency is strictly prohibited. The import of foreign currency is unlimited. The export of foreign currency is limited to the amount imported although re-exchange of local into foreign currency must be only up to 30 per cent of the total imported, up to a maximum of TD100. All currency documentation must be retained.
Exchange rate indicators: The following figures are included as a guide to the movements of the Tunisian Dinar against Sterling and the US Dollar:

Date	Feb '04	May '04	Aug '04	Nov '04
£1.00=	2.23	2.27	2.30	2.30
$1.00=	1.22	1.27	1.25	1.22

Banking hours: Mon-Fri 0730-1130 (summer); Mon-Thurs 0800-1100 and 1400-1615, Fri 0800-1100 and 1300-1600 (winter).

Duty Free

The following goods may be imported into Tunisia by anyone, irrespective of age, without incurring customs duty: *200 cigarettes or 50 cigars or 400g of tobacco; one bottle of alcoholic beverages; a reasonable quantity of perfume; gifts up to a value of TD100.*
Restricted items: The export of antiques is subject to a permit from the Ministry of Cultural Affairs.
Prohibited items: Firearms (unless for hunting), explosives, narcotics, walkie-talkies, obscene publications, any other items which may be regarded as dangerous to public security, health, morality and so on.

Public Holidays

2005: Jan 1 New Year's Day. **Jan 21** Eid al-Idha (Feast of the Sacrifice). **Feb 10** Hegire (Islamic New Year). **Mar 20** Independence Day. **Mar 21** Youth Day. **Apr 9** Martyr's Day. **Apr 21** Mouled (Prophet's Anniversary). **May 1** Labour Day. **July 25** Republic Day. **Aug 13** Women's Day. **Nov 3-5** Eid al-Fitr (End of Ramadam). **Nov 7** New Era Day.
2006: Jan 1 New Year's Day. **Jan 13** Eid al-Idha (Feast of the Sacrifice). **Jan 31** Hegire (Islamic New Year). **Mar 20** Independence Day. **Mar 21** Youth Day. **Apr 9** Martyrs' Day. **Apr 11** Mouled (Prophet's Anniversary). **May 1** Labour Day. **Jul 25** Republic Day. **Aug 13** Women's Day. **Oct 22-24** Eid al-Fitr (End of Ramadan). **Nov 7** New Era Day.
Note: Muslim festivals are timed according to local sightings of various phases of the moon and the dates given above are approximations. During the lunar month of Ramadan that precedes Eid al-Fitr, Muslims fast during the day and feast at night and normal business patterns may be interrupted. Many restaurants are closed during the day and there may be restrictions on smoking and drinking. Some disruption may continue into Eid al-Fitr itself. Eid al-Fitr and Eid al-Idha may last for two days. For more information, see the *World of Islam* appendix.

Health

	Special Precautions?	Certificate Required?
Yellow Fever	Yes	1
Cholera	Yes	2
Typhoid & Polio	3	No
Malaria	No	No

Note: *Regulations and requirements may be subject to change at short notice, and you are advised to contact your doctor well in advance of your intended date of departure. Any numbers in the chart refer to the footnotes below.*

1: A yellow fever certificate is required from travellers over one year of age arriving from infected areas.
2: Following WHO guidelines issued in 1973, a cholera vaccination certificate is no longer a condition of entry to Tunisia. However, sporadic cases of cholera do occur in this region and up-to-date advice should be sought before deciding whether these precautions should include vaccination, as medical opinion is divided over its effectiveness; see the *Health* appendix for further information.
3: Vaccination against typhoid is advised.
Food & drink: Mains water is normally chlorinated, and whilst safe may cause mild abdominal upsets. Bottled water is available and is advised for the first few weeks of the stay. Drinking water outside main cities and towns may be contaminated. Milk should be boiled when unpasteurised (ie if not commercially processed and packed). Powdered or tinned milk is available and is advised but make sure that it is reconstituted with pure water. Avoid dairy products which are likely to have been made from unboiled milk. Only eat well-cooked meat and fish, preferably served hot. Salad and mayonnaise may carry increased risk. Vegetables should be cooked and fruit peeled. These precautions should include western-style buffets.
Other risks: *Dysenteries* and *diarrhoeal diseases* are common in this region. *Hepatitis A* is present and *hepatitis E* is endemic in some areas; precautions should be taken. *Lassa fever* occurs in rural areas. *Mediterranean spotted fever* has been reported. *Tungiasis* is present.
Rabies is present. For those at high risk, vaccination before arrival should be considered. If you are bitten, seek medical advice without delay. For more information, see the *Health* appendix.
Health care: Health insurance is recommended. Tunisia has a well-developed, if somewhat limited, public health service.

Travel - International

AIR: The national airline is *Tunis Air (TU)* (website: www.tunisair.com). There are regular direct flights to Tunisia from all over Europe, but no direct flights from Asia, Australasia, South America or the USA. *Tuniter* also runs services to Hassi Messaoud in Algeria and Malta (see *Travel - Internal* section).
Approximate flight times: From *London* to Tunis is two hours 30 minutes, to Djerba is three hours, to Monastir is three hours and to Sfax is three hours 15 minutes.
International airports: *Tunis (TUN)* (Carthage International) is 8km (5 miles) northeast of the city (travel time - 15 to 30 minutes). An airport-city coach and buses are available. Return is from Hotel Africa Meridien (city air terminal). Taxis are available; a surcharge is levied at night. Airport facilities include a duty free shop and banks/bureau de change.
Djerba (DJE) (*Melita*) is 8km (5 miles) from the city.
Monastir (MIR) (Skanes) is 8km (5 miles) west of the city.

Buses are available to the city centre. *Sfax (SFA)* is 15km (9 miles) from the city.
Tabarka (TBJ) is 2km (1.25 miles) from the city.
Tozeur (TOE) (Nefta) is 10km (6 miles) from the city. All the above airports have bars, restaurants and both incoming and outgoing duty free shops. Taxis are available at all the airports.
Note: A new airport at Enfidha, 100km (62 miles) south of Tunis, is scheduled for completion soon.
Note: Tunisian currency is *not* valid in dutyfree shops.
Departure tax: None for visitors. TD45 for residents and nationals only.
SEA: Tunisia has seven major ports. *SNCM (Ferry Terranée)* runs ferry services from France and Italy to Tunisia. For more information, contact their main office in France (tel: (8) 9170 1801; fax: (4) 9156 3586; e-mail: confo@sncm.fr; website: www.sncm.fr). The major routes are *Marseilles-Tunis* (travel time - 21 to 24 hours) and *Genoa-Tunis* (travel time - 21 to 24 hours). A hydrofoil service is available from Sicily between May and September. *Costa Cruises* offer summer cruises from Genoa to Tunisia.
ROAD: Theoretically, there are several points of entry by road from Algeria, normally served by buses and long-distance taxis: Annaba (in Algeria) to Tabarka (following the coast road); Souk Ahras (in Algeria) to Ghardimaou and El Oued (Algeria) to Gafsa. However, political unrest means that it is difficult for tourists to cross the border. Entry by road from Libya is via the coast road at Gabès, via Ben Gardane and Ras Ajdir.

Travel - Internal

AIR: *Tuninter* runs regular services seven to eight times a day between Tunis and Djerba airports (flight time - approximately one hour). There is a daily flight to Sfax from Tunis, Tuesday to Friday, with two flights on Monday. There are flights to Tozeur on most weekdays. Tuninter is represented internationally by *Tunis Air* (tel: (020) 7734 7644). Prices are reasonable and services are normally heavily subscribed, so it is advisable to book ahead.
SEA: Ferries operate between Sfax and the Kerkennah Islands twice daily, and between Jorf and Jerba Island regularly during the day.
RAIL: Regular trains (run by SNCFT) connect Tunis with major towns. The main route is between Tunis and Gabès, via Sousse, Sfax and Gafsa. It is essential to purchase a ticket before boarding the train or double the fare may be charged. Several daily trains run on each route, many with air-conditioned accommodation and a buffet. The superb views of the Selja Gorge can be seen from the *Lezard Rouge* (Red Lizard), a restored old-fashioned train that runs daily between Metaloui and Redeyef. It is highly advisable to book in advance, if possible, especially for the more popular air-conditioned routes.
ROAD: Tunisia has an extensive road network. In case of breakdown, the *Garde Nationale* (National Guard) will assist free of charge (they usually contact the nearest garage). Traffic drives on the right. **Bus:** The green and yellow coloured national buses, run by SNTRI, are air conditioned and travel daily to most towns across the country. Other services include the intercity buses which are cheap and reasonably comfortable. The destination is written in French and Arabic on the front of the bus. Passengers are allowed 10kg of luggage without additional charge. Each piece of luggage must, however, be registered. **Taxi:** Long-distance taxis (usually large Mercedes or similar), called *louages*, are authorised to carry five passengers. They have no fixed schedule and leave their respective departure points when full. They serve the whole of Tunisia. This is the quickest form of public road transport. There are many *louage* stations and prices are similar to those of buses and trains. **Car hire:** This can be very expensive. To rent a self-drive car, the driver must be over 21 years of age. A full driving licence, which has been valid for at least one year, is acceptable. **Speed limits:** 50kph (30mph) in towns; 100kph (60mph) on major highways. **Documentation:** Log books, valid national driving licences and insurance are essential. Both the AA and RAC are affiliated to the National Automobile Club (NACT) based in Tunis. Insurance valid for up to 21 days can be purchased at the border.
Note: For safety reasons, it is forbidden to drive a car in the Sahara without first contacting the National Guard post at the nearest town, giving the planned itinerary and the expected point of exit from the area. Full provisions, a suitable vehicle and an experienced guide are necessary for any travel in the Sahara.
URBAN: A suburban train line (TGM) links Tunis with the northern suburbs. Tunis and Sousse also have a modern and convenient tram system (*métro léger*). **Taxi:** Within Tunis and other cities, city taxis are numbered and have meters. The price on the meter is what you should pay. There is a 50 per cent surcharge on night fares. **Bicycle:** Bicycles and motorcycles are available for hire in most major towns and do not require a licence.
TRAVEL TIMES: The following chart gives approximate travel times (in hours and minutes) from **Tunis** to other major cities/towns in Tunisia.

	Air	Road	Rail
Hammamet	-	0.45	1.00
Nabeul	-	0.45	1.00
Sousse	-	2.00	2.30
Port el Kantaoui	-	2.00	2.30
Monastir	0.35	3.00	3.00
Sfax	0.50	4.00	4.00
Gabès	-	5.00	6.00
Jerba	0.60	7.00	-
Tozeur	1.10	6.00	-

Note: Travellers to Port el Kantaoui are advised to take the train to Sousse, and travel the remaining 7km (4 miles) by taxi. For Monastir they should change in Sousse for the Metro Leger. For Jerba, they should take the train to Gabès and then the shuttle-bus.

Accommodation

HOTELS: Tunisia has approximately 160,000 hotel beds. There are also several vacation villages within each area. There is a luxury resort in Tabarka which hosts the International Coral Festival of Underwater Photography.
Grading: Hotel accommodation is classified by a star system ranging from deluxe (**5-star**) to clean but simple (**1-star**).
MARHALAS: *Marhalas* are converted caravanserais and often consist of several connected underground houses (in *Matmata* and *Ksars* - ancient granaries), where sleeping quarters and communal bathing and toilet facilities have been installed. They also have their own simple, but clean and adequate, restaurants. There are *Marhalas* at Houmt Souk, Nefta and Kairouan.
CAMPING/CARAVANNING: Tents can be pitched or trailers parked on beaches and in parks with permission from the property owner or from the nearest police or National Guard station. The major campsites are *Le Moulin Bleu* (Blue Mill) at Hammam-Plage, 20km (12 miles) from Tunis; *L'Auberge des Jasmins* (Jasmin Inn) at Nabeul, 65km (40 miles) from Tunis, equipped with showers, wash-basins, toilets, hot and cold running water, shop, restaurant and outdoor theatre in an orange grove; *L'Idéal Camping* at Hammamet, 60km (35 miles) from Tunis, with restaurant facilities; *Sonia Camping & Caravan Site* at Zarzis, 505km (313 miles) from Tunis; and *The Youth Centre of Gabès*, 404km (251 miles) from Tunis (summer only).
YOUTH HOSTELS: Youth Hostels are open to all young people who are members of the *International Youth Hostel Association*. It is recommended to make reservations well in advance, especially for groups. For details, contact the Tunisian National Tourist Office (see *Contact Addresses* section).

Resorts & Excursions

TUNIS

The Tunisian capital - home to one in 10 of the population - combines a modern, European-style city of tree-lined avenues with a vibrant, atmospheric **medina** listed by UNESCO as a World Heritage Site. The main entrance to the medina is through an arched gateway known as the **Bab el Bahr** (or **Porte de France**) on **Place de la Victoire**. To the right is the handsome green and white frontage of the **British Embassy**.
The main thoroughfare through the medina, **rue Djamaa Ez-Zitouna** is often bustling with tourists but more authentic *souks* (markets) can be found in the myriad of surrounding alleys. Originally, each souk specialised in a single trade. Among the oldest is the 13th-century **Souk el Attarine** (the perfume-makers' market), which still sells scents and essential oils.
If you get lost, the major landmark is the **Zitouna Mosque** (Great Mosque) - the largest in Tunisia. It is the only mosque in the city which can be visited by non-Muslims, although access is restricted to a viewing enclosure overlooking a polished marble courtyard.
The **Bardo Museum** is a major tourist attraction, housing one of the world's greatest collections of Roman mosaics. Situated in a former palace belonging to the Husaynid beys who ruled Tunisia in the 18th and 19th centuries, the museum includes archaeological treasures from the Carthaginian, Roman, early Christian and Islamic eras. The Roman section is the undoubted highlight with mosaics covering entire floors and walls, many of them almost completely intact. Common themes include hunting and farming scenes, Greek and Roman gods, sea battles and family life.
Another popular museum - the **National Museum of Carthage** - is located on the outskirts of the city near the airport. It is best visited immediately prior to exploring the ruins of Carthage itself (see *Historic Sites* section).
EXCURSIONS: Close to Carthage, **Sidi Bou Said** is often described as Tunisia's prettiest village. Its cobbled streets and whitewashed houses with light blue window grilles and studded doors has made it a popular stop on any excursion to the Tunis area. Despite its popularity, it has managed to retain its charm. The **Café Sidi Chabanne** is one of the best places in Tunisia to sample the national drink, mint tea, which is served piping hot and topped with pine nuts.
Other suburbs of Tunis include **Gammarth** which has fast become a fully-fledged resort of luxury hotels, including the 5-star *La Residence*, often described as the best hotel in Tunisia.
La Marsa is another upmarket beachfront suburb with a palm tree-lined corniche and long sandy beach.
La Goulette is noted for its excellent fish restaurants which attract crowds from Tunis, especially on warm summer evenings. Once a pirates' stronghold, the town is at the mouth ('the gullet') of the Tunis canal and remains a busy cargo and ferry port. It is linked to Tunis by a suburban rail service, the TGM (travel time - 30 minutes).

NORTHERN TUNISIA

Although bypassed by most British holidaymakers, the area north of Tunis and along the northern coast is a delightful part of the country with dozens of quiet beaches and one of the most fascinating towns in the country.
The region can be quite cold in winter with occasional snow flurries. In summer, it provides a welcome escape from the heat of the capital.
BIZERTE: Easily visited on a day trip from Tunis, Bizerte has been a major port since Phoenician times when it was known as Hippo Zarytus. Under French rule in the late 19th century, it became a naval base and has remained Tunisia's biggest military centre ever since.
At the heart of the town is the wonderfully picturesque **Vieux Port** (Old Port), surrounded by shops and cafes and usually dotted with dozens, of multi-coloured fishing boats. Despite its Byzantine appearance, the **Kasbah** dates mainly from the 17th century. Within its walls is a mini-town of narrow, winding alleys.
On the southwestern approach to Bizerte is the **Monument of the Martyrs** commemorating the Bizerte Crisis of 1961 when French soldiers clashed with Tunisian troops leaving more than 1300 dead.
JEBEL ICHKEUL NATIONAL PARK: About a 40-minute drive from Bizerte, it is one of only two water-based conservation areas in the world to be designated by UNESCO as Wetland World Heritage Sites (the other is the Florida Everglades).
The Park is an important bird sanctuary and between October and February provides a major stopping point for waterfowl migrating between Europe and Africa. It is also home to one of Tunisia's most colourful birds, the purple gallinule, and among its animal life are water buffalo, wild boar, jackals and otters.
TABARKA: Situated in northwest Tunisia close to the Algerian border, Tabarka was supposed to be Tunisia's flagship resort on the north coast.
During the 1980s and early 1990s, the Tunisian government ploughed millions of pounds into creating a purpose-built holiday town with its own international airport. Although it is quite popular in the peak summer months with Continental visitors, it has still to win favour with the British market and is completely dead in autumn and winter. Its future may lie in promoting itself as a diving destination. It offers some of the most exciting dive sites in the Mediterranean including *Tunnels Reef* - an extraordinary complex of caves, caverns and gullies.

CAP BON

Known as the Garden of Tunisia, the Cap Bon peninsula combines sleepy villages, rolling green fields and vineyards with the biggest and most cosmopolitan resort in the country.
HAMMAMET: Situated 64km (40 miles) southeast of Tunis, Hammamet has been attracting package holidaymakers since the 1960s. Known as the Garden Resort for its eucalyptus trees, citrus groves and flowering shrubs, a local bylaw prohibits hotels being built higher than the tallest surrounding palm tree.
A much more relaxed attitude has been taken towards the expansion of the resort. It now extends almost as far as Nabeul in the north, while 8km (5 miles) to the south, a massive new sister resort, Yasmine Hammamet, is being completed.
The focal point of the town is the **Kasbah** which was first built in the 15th century but heavily restored since. It provides the main entry to Hammamet's small medina which is packed with souvenir shops selling leatherware, clothes, pottery, stuffed camels and bird cages.
Hammamet is well served with restaurants to suit all tastes and pockets. Most of the major hotels are set alongside the town's sandy beach - with many also offering indoor and outdoor pools.
Beach activities include sailing, windsurfing and parascending. Most evening entertainment is hotel-based and includes discos and folklore evenings.
Hammamet is a popular centre for golfers with two major

courses, including the **Citrus Golf Complex** which offers two 18-hole championship courses and a 9-hole practice course. Among Hammamet's few tourist sights is the **International Cultural Centre** located in a villa once described by Frank Lloyd Wright as the most beautiful in the world - which perhaps overstates its charms. Guests have included Churchill, Rommel and Anthony Eden. In recent years, it has been the venue for Hammamet's annual summer cultural festival.
NABEUL: Although overshadowed by Hammamet 10km (6 miles) further south, Nabeul has spent the last decade trying to exploit its own tourism potential and now boasts a string of large beachfront hotels. The town's biggest claim to fame is as the centre of Tunisia's pottery industry which dates back to Roman times. The distinctive and very collectable blue and white pottery can be bought all over Tunisia but Nabeul offers one of the widest selections.
Tourists who dislike the idea of haggling can buy items at two official tourist shops in the town where prices are fixed.
Every Friday Nabeul plays host to a so-called *Camel Market* which seems to draw considerably more tourists than it does camels - but it is a good opportunity for shopping and hunting for bargains.
EL HAOUARIA: Best-known for its annual June falconry festival. On the outskirts of the village opposite the island of **Zembra** is a spectacular series of Roman caves. The nearby caves, **Les Grottes des Chauves-Souris**, are home to thousands of bats.
KELIBIA: Kelibia is a picturesque and thriving fishing port which makes a good base for exploring the more rural parts of the Cap Bon region. A massive sixth-century fort overlooks the town and offers spectacular views.

CENTRAL TUNISIA

Includes four of the most popular package-resorts as well as Tunisia's holiest city. Also known as The Sahel, Central Tunisia is a rich agricultural area with hundreds of thousands of olive trees.
PORT EL KANTAOUI: A hugely successful purpose-built resort constructed around a picturesque marina fringed with shops and restaurants. It opened in 1979 and has been expanding ever since.
Its hotels resemble giant, whitewashed palaces and are set in gardens awash with bougainvillaea. Most holidaymakers love the resort because of its familiarity and security. Critics point to its lack of authenticity. Port El Kantaoui offers a 27-hole golf course, home to the *Tunisian Open* and the *PGA Seniors Tour*.
SOUSSE: Tunisia's third-largest city, Sousse lies 8km (5 miles) south of Port El Kantaoui and could not be more different. It is packed with atmosphere and hundreds of years of history. Very much a working city, it has a thriving port and busy fishing harbour which is best viewed early in the morning when the previous night's catch is being unloaded from a flotilla of small boats.
Still emerging as a holiday centre, a string of hotels has been built fronting the city's elegant corniche. Sousse was one of the Phoenicians' great coastal cities but it fell to Arab invaders in the seventh century. In AD 790, the foundations of a new city were laid and several remnants of that time still remain, including the **Great Mosque** and its **Ribat** - one of a chain of fortresses which stretched along the Mediterranean coast. Both are located within Sousse's bustling medina where a cluster of souks sell everything from food and clothes to perfume and jewellery.
The **Kasbah Museum** houses an impressive collection of third- and fourth-century mosaics. It also offers commanding views over the city.
MONASTIR: Like Port El Kantaoui, Monastir is another largely purpose-built tourist town of pristine streets and lavish landscaping. It has an attractive marina and an old fishing port. Most of Monastir's tourist hotels are situated 5 to 6km (3 to 4 miles) west of the town centre at **Skanes** close to Monastir-Skanes Airport - Tunisia's main international gateway for charter flights.
Monastir's most impressive landmark is the golden-domed **Bourguiba Mosque** - the final resting place of the founder of modern-day Tunisia and its first president, Habib Bourguiba.
The town's **Ribat** supposedly dates from the eighth century but it has been restored so many times that little of the original structure is left.
MAHDIA: Mahdia is one of Tunisia's newest tourist towns which has been expanding rapidly since the creation of a tourist zone 5km (3 miles) west of the town centre. It is where the best beaches can be found. While Mahdia struggles to cling to its old way of life which revolved around weaving and a thriving fishing port, nearly every shop and stall in the medina is now geared towards tourism.
The **Great Mosque** may look ancient but it was only built in the 1960s as a replica of the 1000-year-old original.
KAIROUAN: Easily visited on a day trip from Port El Kantaoui, Sousse, Monastir or Mahdia, Kairouan is the most sacred city in Tunisia and Islam's fourth most important centre after Mecca, Medina and Jerusalem.
Within its **medina**, there are more than 50 mosques, the **Great Mosque of Sidi Oqba** being the star attraction. Originally constructed in AD 671, the existing building was built by the Aghlabids in AD 863. Sadly, non-Muslims are barred from entering the prayer hall with its 400 marble pillars and one of the world's oldest pulpits with 250 woodcarved panels.
Rather incongruously, as well as being a spiritual centre, Kairouan is also a frenetic market town and the epicentre of Tunisia's cut-throat carpet-making industry.
KERKENNAH: A small group of islands situated off the coast of **Sfax**, Tunisia's second city which is rarely visited by holidaymakers. There are two main inhabited islands, **Chergui** and **Gharbi** which are joined by a causeway. Regular ferry services operate between Sfax and Kerkennah. The travel time is just less than an hour. Kerkennah makes a pleasant day trip, and for those seeking to get away from it all, it is also worth considering staying several days.

JERBA AND THE SOUTH

Southern Tunisia has much to offer, including the island resort of Jerba and some fascinating towns on the fringes of the Sahara Desert.
JERBA: A popular choice among holidaying Tunisians, Jerba is connected to the mainland by a causeway. There are also ferry services which operate between **Ajim** on Jerba and **Jorf** on the mainland. Although it is only 30km (19 miles) wide by 27km (17 miles) long, Jerba is said to have 354 mosques - one for every day of the Islamic calendar.
The main centre, **Houmt Souk**, is on the island's north coast, only 6.5 km (4 miles) from the airport at **Mellita**. Houmt Souk means 'marketplace' and this remains the town's primary purpose although it also benefits from tourism.
While most tourists stay at the big beach hotels within Jerba's tourist zone 10 to 11km (6 to 7 miles) east of Houmt Souk, accommodation in the town itself includes simple and comfortable fondouk hotels. Most have been built around old courtyards and are very atmospheric.
Midoun - Jerba's second-biggest town - springs to life on Fridays when its sprawling market attracts a large crowd of local people and tourists. It is worth arriving early as everything is over by lunchtime. **Guellala** is a big pottery-producing centre which uses local clay quarried from the hills above the village. Its main street is lined with shops piled high with pots and plates.
The **El Ghriba Synagogue** at **Erriadh** (also known as **Hara Seghira**) is one of the holiest Jewish shrines in North Africa.
THE CHOTT EL JERID: The focal point of Tunisia's desert tourism industry, Chott El Jerid is one of a series of large salt lakes which lie lifeless in summer but evaporate during the winter to create inland seas.
Several oasis towns have sprung up around Chott El Jerid - notably **Tozeur** - now an established resort with a wide range of hotels - most of them situated in a designated tourist zone 3km (2 miles) from the town centre. Tozeur's **Palmery** comprises thousands of date palms watered by 200 springs. The old town district known as **Ouled El Hadef** comprises a network of narrow alleys which have changed little since the 14th century. Their distinctive pale yellow brickwork with geometric motifs is considered a marvel of Islamic art. There is a small airport at Tozeur served from Tunis by the domestic airline Tuninter with up to five flights a week. Nearby, **Nefta** is another oasis town best-known for its **Corbeille**, a deep gully filled with palm trees which can be explored on foot or by donkey.
DOUZ: Sometimes called 'The Gateway to the Desert', Douz is best visited on its Thursday market day, which attracts traders from a wide area, selling everything from dates and spices to sheep and camels.
It is also a major centre for desert trekking - either by camel or in 4-wheel-drive vehicles.
Anyone planning a desert safari needs to inform the National Guard and ensure their vehicle is equipped with a full tool kit and handbook, spare tyres, fuel and water, a compass and emergency rations. It is also advisable to hire a local driver.
The **Douz Museum** explores the history and culture of the Tunisian desert.
Douz also hosts an annual *Festival of the Sahara* (held in November or December each year), which includes camel and greyhound racing, folk dancing and poetry recitals.
MATMATA: Has become a popular stopping point en route between Jerba and Tozeur since the making of the *Star Wars* movies; in the opening sequence of the original *Star Wars* movie, Matmata's troglodyte houses were featured. The cave dwellings, which date from the forth century BC, are built on two levels, consisting of storage rooms above, with living accommodation below. Some are still inhabited and can be visited by arrangement with the owners. One or two have been turned into hotels - which makes for an unusual night's stay.
Another strange type of building found in the deep south of Tunisia are *ksour* - most often seen around **Medenine** and **Tataouine**. Made from mud and stone and three or four stories high, they were built around a courtyard and used as secure storage units for grain. One of the best-preserved is the **Ksar Ouled Soltane**, 24km (15 miles) east of Tataouine. Buildings in its first courtyard are more than 400 years old while the inner complex dates from around 1850.
EXCURSIONS: An interesting day trip from Tozeur or Nefta is exploring the mountain villages of **Tamerza**, **Chebika** and **Mides**. The original village of Tamerza was abandoned after catastrophic flooding in 1969 but visitors can still walk through its eerily empty streets.

HISTORIC SITES

Tunisia has a wide variety of historical settlements - Punic, Roman, Byzantine and Islamic - many of which are in excellent condition.
Holidaymakers staying in the main beach resorts will find organised excursions are available to the most important sites. It is usually possible to reach lesser-known ruins by public transport but hiring a car may be a more practical option.
CARTHAGE: Founded by the Phoenicians in 814 BC, Carthage thrived as a maritime centre and later became the third-largest city in the Roman Empire before being destroyed by the Arabs in AD 692. Although it is Tunisia's best-known archaeological site, it is not particularly easy to navigate. The ruins are scattered over quite a large area in what is now an upmarket commuter suburb of Tunis. Since a complete tour requires a whole day, it is probably more rewarding to make two shorter trips. The best view of the whole site is from **Byrsa Hill** which was the heart of the city in Punic times. Carthage's key attractions include the **Antonine Baths** which - outside of Rome - were once the largest baths in the Roman Empire. Visitors are not allowed to enter the Baths but can study them from a viewing platform. Heat was provided by an underground system of furnaces and - very much like a modern day spa - there were a series of hot rooms, a cold plunge pool and the Roman equivalent of a Jacuzzi.
The **Punic Ports**, now little more than ponds, once provided berths for more than 200 naval vessels. Similarly, little is left of the **Theatre of Hadrian** which was built in the second century.
Tophet was used for child sacrifices. Urns have been unearthed containing the ashes of more than 20,000 boys aged between two and 12 sacrificed by the Carthaginians in the eighth century BC.
EL JEM: This small town 80km (50 miles) south of Sousse would be like dozens of others in Tunisia were it not for its giant amphitheatre - one of the country's truly remarkable sights.
Only slightly smaller than the Colosseum in Rome, it is better preserved and seems much more imposing, partly because it is situated at the end of a street of modern houses.
Built between 230 and 238 in what was then the busy market town of Thysdrus, the amphitheatre could seat crowds of more than 30,000. Even if being built today it would be considered an impressive achievement but without modern construction equipment, the task must have been gargantuan. Blocks of sandstone were transported from quarries 32km (20 miles) away while water was carried 16km (10 miles) through an underground aqueduct. The amphitheatre was used both for festivals and for dawn to dusk gladiatorial contests when petty criminals were pitted against wild animals in fights to the death.
DOUGGA: Tunisia's best-preserved Roman ruins enjoy a lofty setting 96km (60 miles) southwest of Tunis. Formerly known as Thugga under the Numidian king Massinissa in the second century BC, under Roman rule Dougga had a population of up to 10,000. The site's main attraction is its well-preserved Capitol built in 166 BC which is dedicated to Jupiter, Juno and Minerva. Its theatre, which could seat up to 3500, is still used by a summer touring company. Visitors with an earthy sense of humour may be amused by the rather cosy, horseshoe-shaped arrangement of 12 latrines in the **Baths of Cyclops**, while the **House of Trifolium** is thought to have been the town's brothel.
BULLA REGIA: Situated 72km (45 miles) south of Tabarka, Bulla Regia is another impressive Roman site. Its most notable feature is its underground dwellings which were used by wealthy residents to escape the summer heat. The villas were paved with beautiful mosaic floors, some of which remain exactly where they were created, undisturbed for centuries.
THUBURBO MAJUS: Although it was first settled in the fifth century BC, most of the ruins at Thuburbo Majus are from Roman times when the town was an important regional trading centre with a population of around 8000. A sprawling site within an easy day trip of both Tunis and Hammamet, the best-preserved structures include the Forum, Capitol and Winter Baths.
KERKOUANE: Some 8km (5 miles) north of Kelibia are the remarkable remains of a Punic town. Destroyed in 236 BC, it was unearthed in 1952 and is listed by UNESCO as a World Heritage Site. There is an adjoining museum housing pottery, jewellery, wooden carvings and funerary statues.
UTICA: Close to Tunis, Utica was once an important Roman

port but now lies 11km (7 miles) inland. Its ruins include part of a once-massive public baths complex and the **House of the Waterfall** which belonged to a wealthy private citizen.
SBEITLA: The most southerly of Tunisia's major Roman sites, Sbeitla is noted for its massive triumphal arch just before the entrance and for its Forum built in 139 BC. A more modern structure on the site is the sixth-century **Basilica of St Vitalis** with its attractive baptismal font decorated with mosaics.

Sport & Activities

Watersports: Tunisia's clear waters, coral beds and diverse sea life make it a popular destination for **scuba-diving**. Tabarka Yachting Club and the International Diving Centre at Port el Kantaoui are recognised by the World Confederation for Diving and offer fully equipped lessons and trips. Permission must be obtained to dive to the natural reserve islands of Zembra and La Galite. For underwater **fishing**, it is necessary to bring one's own equipment, and obtain details of conservationist underwater fishing restrictions from the National Tourist Office. Visitors who have brought their own equipment can refill their air bottles at the offices of the *Société d'Air Liquide* at Mégrine, 7km (4 miles) from Tunis, and at Sfax. Most hotels on the coast have a heated pool as well as a private beach suitable for **swimming**. Port el Kantaoui is a port of international standard offering mooring for 340 boats, harbour master's office, deep-sea navigation school, **sailing** school, ship-chandler, boat-rental and a dry-docking area with maintenance shops. Prices are competitive, especially for winter careening services. There is a marina at Cap Monastir with similar facilities. Among other sailing (and **water-skiing**) centres is *Le Club Nautique de Sidi-Bou Said*, which has a marina complex. The abundance and great variety of fish makes **fishing** very popular. Catches include mullet, ray, dogfish, groupers, red rock mullet, crayfish and shrimp. A wetsuit is necessary only between November and April. One can watch coral fishing at Tabarka, octopus fishing off the Kerkennah Islands, sponge fishing at Sfax, on the island of Jerba and in the Gulf of Gabès, and tuna fishing by the experts at Sidi Daoud. These 'fishing spectacles' take place in May and June.
Golf: There are excellent courses at *Port el Kantaoui* near Sousse, *Monastir*, *Tabarka*, *Carthage* at *Tunis*, *Tozeur*, *Djerba* and *Hammamet*. Players of all abilities will find very high-quality facilities. The *Open Golf Championships* there have already attracted many leading competitors from all over the world. Created by eminent golf-course architects, the courses are dotted with palm, olive and pomegranate trees, and are next to the sea. Each of the 18 holes is on a different kind of terrain, and treated turf has been imported from California. The courses are well suited to all players. There are luxurious clubhouses, equipment to rent and training/practice grounds with putting green. In Tunis, the golf course at the *Country Club* at La Soukra has recently undergone extension and re-landscaping. More courses are planned for every major resort.
Gliding: The best-known venue for gliding enthusiasts is the *Federal Gliding Centre* at Jebel Rassas, 25km (15 miles) from Tunis, where gliders and qualified instruction in the sport are available to visitors.
Birdwatching: Tunisia has many species of birds, most of which are protected in national parks. The cork-oak forests of Ain Draham, the lake and marshes of Ichkeul near Bizerta, the coastal lagoons round Tunis and Sousse, the rocky hills and steps from Kef to Kasserine, and the oases and deserts of the south all have their characteristic birds. Birdlife also varies with the seasons; in winter, spoonbills, geese, ducks, robins and wagtails seek refuge from the cold further north, while in spring and autumn, migrant swallows and warblers and birds of prey at Cap Bon pass through on their journeys between Africa and Europe. In summer, Mediterranean species like storks, bee-eaters and rollers stay to nest.
Health spas: There are about 100 hot-spring stations throughout Tunisia - mostly in the north of the country. Many of the spas have been used for this purpose since Roman and Punic times. The most important stations are run by personnel specialised in the medical and paramedical fields, and treatments are available for rheumatism, arthritis, a variety of lung and skin complaints, circulatory troubles and gynaecological problems. More information is available from the National Tourist Office.
Film tours: Tunisia's desert near Tozeur has featured in numerous films, most notably in *The English Patient* and *Star Wars*. An increasing number of tour operators now offer desert safaris to the locations where these famous blockbuster movies were shot. For further information, contact the Tunisian National Tourist Office (see *Contact Addresses* section).

Social Profile

FOOD & DRINK: Tunisian food is well prepared and delicious, particularly the authentic lamb or *dorado* (bream) couscous, the fish dishes, *tajine* and *brik* or *brik à l'oeuf* (egg and a tasty filling fried in an envelope of pastry). Tunisian dishes are cooked with olive oil, spiced with aniseed, coriander, cumin, caraway, cinnamon or saffron and flavoured with mint, orange blossom or rose water. Restaurants catering for tourists tend to serve rather bland dishes and 'international' cuisine, and visitors are advised to try the smaller restaurants. Prices vary enormously, and higher prices do not necessarily mean better meals. Tunis and the main cities also have French, Italian and other international restaurants. Self-service may sometimes be found but table service is more common. Moorish cafes, with their traditional decor, serve excellent Turkish coffee or mint tea with pine nuts.
Although Tunisia is an Islamic country, alcohol is not prohibited. Tunisia produces a range of excellent table wines, sparkling wines, beers, aperitifs and local liqueurs, notably *Boukha* (distilled from figs) and *Thibarine*.
NIGHTLIFE: In Tunisia, the theatre season lasts from October to June when local and foreign (especially French) companies put on productions and concerts. International groups appear at the *Tunis Theatre* and in the towns of Hammamet and Sousse. There are numerous cinemas in the larger cities. There are nightclubs in the major tourist resorts and at most beach hotels, as well as in the big city hotels. Belly dancing is a common cabaret feature and lively local bands often play traditional music.
SHOPPING: Special purchases include copperware (engraved trays, ashtrays and other utensils); articles sculpted in olive wood; leather goods (wallets, purses, handbags); clothing (kaftans, jelabas, burnuses); pottery and ceramics; dolls in traditional dress; beautiful embroidery; fine silverware and enamelled jewellery. Among the most valuable of Tunisia's products are carpets. The two major types are woven (non-pile) and knotted (pile). The quality of all carpets is strictly controlled by the National Handicrafts Office, so be sure to check the ONA seal before buying. **Shopping hours:** Mon-Sat 0800-1200 and 1600-1900 (summer); Mon-Sat 0900-1300 and 1500-1900 (winter).
Weekly markets: A source of good purchases are the markets which are set up on certain days in many Tunisian towns and villages. All the products of the region are displayed, including handicrafts, farm produce and secondhand goods. There are ONA workshops and stores throughout the country where visitors can buy items at fixed prices. ONA stores make a reduction of 10 per cent on the price of goods purchased in foreign currency. No duty is payable on articles up to £900 in value which are shipped to EU countries, only if accompanied by an EUR1 form. Visitors who make a purchase of more than TD5, anywhere in Tunisia, should ask for a sales slip and keep all sales slips, along with bank receipts for any currency exchanged, for customs inspection.
SPECIAL EVENTS: A complete list and further information is available from the Tunisian National Tourist Office (see *Contact Addresses* section). The following is a selection of special events occurring in Tunisia in 2005:
May *Lag B'Omer Pilgrimage to La Griba*, Djerba. **Jun-Jul** *Tabarka Jazz Festival*; *Falconry Festival*, Haouaria; *Yasmine Hammamet Festival*. **Jul-Aug** *International Carthage Festival*; *International Sousse Festival*. **Jul 14-Aug 11** *El Jem International Symphonic Festival*. **Jul 15-Sep 15** *Carthage-Byrsa Festival*. **Nov 3-6** *Festival of the Oases* (camel racing), Tozeur. **Nov 8-11** *Sahara Duoz Festival* (desert folklore).
SOCIAL CONVENTIONS: Arabic in culture and tradition, Tunisia is nevertheless one of the more liberal and tolerant Muslim countries. The nomadic Bedouin still follow their traditional way of life in the southern desert. The Tunisians' varied origins are shown in the architecture, crafts, music and regional folk dances. Tunisia has also developed an international reputation as an intellectual and cultural centre. Shaking hands is the usual form of greeting. Hospitality is very important and a small gift in appreciation of hospitality or as a token of friendship is always appreciated. Dress can be informal but should respect the conventions of Islam when visiting religious monuments, ie shoulders and knees must be covered. Outside tourist resorts, scanty beachwear should not be worn. **Tipping:** 10 per cent for all services.

Business Profile

ECONOMY: Tunisia lacks the vast natural resources of its North African neighbours, but careful and successful economic management has brought the country reasonable prosperity. Annual GDP growth is over 5 per cent and current inflation is just under 3 per cent. Only unemployment at 14.3 per cent is a cause for concern. Agriculture and mining are the foundations of the economy. The main agricultural products are wheat, barley, olive oil, wine and fruit, but other foodstuffs have to be imported. Large quantities of phosphate ores are mined along with iron, lead, aluminium fluoride and zinc. Tunisia is also a modest oil exporter, although this industry is in decline; natural gas reserves are likely to last longer. There is a small manufacturing sector involved in processing organic chemicals derived from petroleum and purification of phosphate ore. Other industries produce textiles, construction materials, machinery, chemicals, paper and wood. Tourism dominates the service sector, though the industry is sensitive both to the regional political climate and, more recently, international terrorism: the latter in particular has led to a recent downturn. According to the most recent figures, over five million people visited the country in 2002, contributing nearly US$2 billion to the Tunisian economy.
Government economic policy during the last decade has followed the path of deregulation, including abolition of trade controls, privatisation and making the Tunisian Dinar fully convertible. Tunisia's most important trade links are with the EU whose members (principally France and Germany) account for three-quarters of all the country's trade. Economic relations were strengthened during 1995 by the signing of a free trade agreement with the EU, which is being introduced over a 12-year period ending in 2010. This is similar in content to the association agreements signed by would-be members. Although a considerable diplomatic coup for the Tunisian government, the agreement was part of a wider trend of growing trade links between the southern part of the EU and the rest of the Mediterranean basin. Tunisia is a member of the Union of the Arab Maghreb, the main North African political and economic bloc, and of various pan-Arab economic organisations.
BUSINESS: Arabic and French are the most widely used languages in business circles and a knowledge of either is useful. Interpreter services are available. Appointments are required. **Office hours:** Mon-Fri 0830-1300 and 1500-1745 (winter); Mon-Sat 0830-1300 (summer). Government office opening hours may vary by half an hour.
COMMERCIAL INFORMATION: The following organisations can offer advice: Agence de Promotion de l'Industrie (API), 63 rue de Syrie, 1002 Tunis (tel: (71) 792 144; fax: (71) 782 482; e-mail: api@api.com.tn; website: www.tunisieindustrie.nat.tn); *or* Chambre de Commerce et d'Industrie de Tunis, 1 rue des Entrepreneurs, 1000 Tunis (tel: (71) 359 300; fax: (71) 354 744; e-mail: ccitunis@planet.tn).
CONFERENCES/CONVENTIONS: The following organisation can supply information: Direction du Marketing at the Office National du Tourisme Tunisien (see *Contact Addresses* section).

Climate

Tunisia has a warm climate all year. Best periods are spring and autumn. Temperatures can be extremely high inland. Winter is mild and has the highest rainfall.
Required clothing: Lightweights in summer, mediumweights and rainwear in winter. Sunglasses are advised.

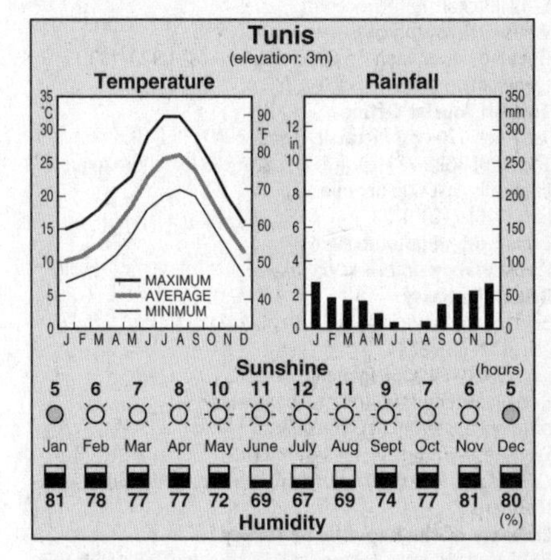

Turkey

LATEST TRAVEL ADVICE CONTACTS

British Foreign and Commonwealth Office
Tel: (0870) 606 0290 Website: www.fco.gov.uk
US Department of State
Website: http://travel.state.gov/travel
Canadian Department of Foreign Affairs and Int'l Trade
Tel: (1 800) 267 8376 Website: www.dfait-maeci.gc.ca

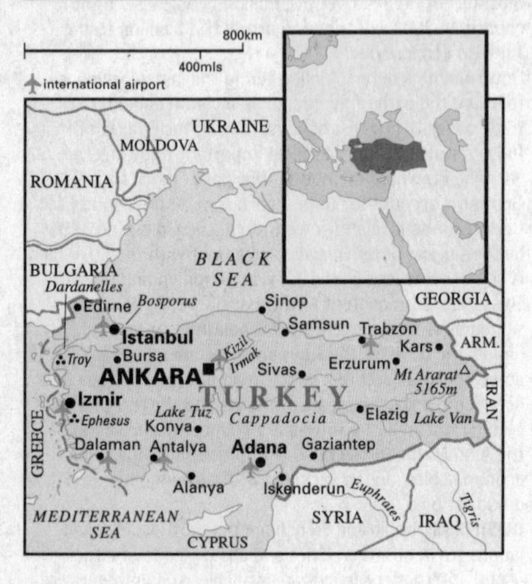

Location: Southeastern Europe/Asia Minor.

Country dialling code: 90.

Ministry of Tourism
Ismet Inönü Bulvar 5, Bahçelievler, Ankara, Turkey
Tel: (312) 212 8360.
Fax: (312) 212 0255.
E-mail: basim@kulturturizm.gov.tr
Website: www.turizm.gov.tr
Embassy of the Republic of Turkey
43 Belgrave Square, London SW1X 8PA, UK
Tel: (020) 7393 0202 *or* 7235 6968 (press office).
Fax: (020) 7393 0066 *or* 7245 9547 (press office).
E-mail: turkish.emb@btclick.com *or* lobm@btconnect.com (press office).
Website: http://turkey.embassyhomepage.com
Opening Hours: Mon-Fri 0900-1700.
Not open to personal callers.
Turkish Consulate General
Rutland Lodge, Rutland Gardens, Knightsbridge, London SW7 1BW, UK
Tel: (020) 7591 6900 *or* (09068) 347 348 (recorded visa information; calls cost 60p per minute).
Fax: (020) 7591 6911.
E-mail: tckons@btclick.com
Website: www.turkconsulate-london.com
Opening hours: Mon-Fri 0930-1230 (visas); 0930-1330 (general enquiries).
Turkish Tourist Office
1st Floor, 170-173 Piccadilly, London W1J 9EJ, UK
Tel: (020) 7629 7771 *or* (09001) 887 755 (brochure request line; calls cost 60p per minute).
Fax: (020) 7491 0773.
E-mail: info@gototurkey.co.uk
Website: www.gototurkey.co.uk
British Embassy
Sehit Ersan Caddesi 46A, Cankaya, Ankara, Turkey
Tel: (312) 455 3344.
Fax: (312) 455 3356 (general) *or* 3353 (consular).
E-mail: britembinf@tnn.net (general) *or* britembcons@tnn.net (consular).
Website: www.britishembassy.org.tr
Consulates in: Antalya, Bodrum, Istanbul, Izmir and Marmaris.
Embassy of the Republic of Turkey
2525 Massachusetts Avenue, NW, Washington, DC 20008, USA
Tel: (202) 612 6700 *or* 6740 (consular section).
Fax: (202) 612 6744.
E-mail: contact@turkishembassy.org (general) *or* consulate@turkishembassy.org.
Website: www.turkishembassy.org
Consulates in: Chicago, Houston, Los Angeles and New York.
Turkish Tourist Office
821 UN Plaza, New York, NY 10017, USA
Tel: (212) 687 2194.
Fax: (212) 599 7568.
E-mail: ny@tourismturkey.org
Website: www.tourismturkey.org
Embassy of the United States of America
Atatürk Bulvar 110, Kavaklidere 06100, Ankara, Turkey
Tel: (312) 455 5555.
Fax: (312) 467 0019.
E-mail: didem@pd.state.gov
Website: www.usemb-ankara.org.tr
Consulates in: Adana and Istanbul.
Embassy of the Republic of Turkey
197 Wurtemburg Street, Ottawa, Ontario K1N 8L9, Canada
Tel: (613) 789 4044.
Fax: (613) 789 3442.
E-mail: turkishottawa@msa.gov.tr
Website: www.turkishembassy.com
Canadian Embassy
Nenehatun Caddesi 75, GOP 06700, Ankara, Turkey
Tel: (312) 459 9200.
Fax: (312) 459 9365 (commercial section) *or* 9363 (consular section).
E-mail: ankra@dfait-maeci.gc.ca
Website: www.dfait-maeci.gc.ca/ankara
Honorary Consulate in: Istanbul.

TIMATIC CODES

Health	AMADEUS: **TI-DFT/ANK/HE** GALILEO/WORLDSPAN: **TI-DFT/ANK/HE** SABRE: **TIDFT/ANK/HE**
Visa	AMADEUS: **TI-DFT/ANK/VI** GALILEO/WORLDSPAN: **TI-DFT/ANK/VI** SABRE: **TIDFT/ANK/VI**

To access TIMATIC country information on Health and Visa regulations through the Computer Reservations System (CRS), type in the appropriate command line listed above.

General Information

AREA: 779,452 sq km (300,948 sq miles).
POPULATION: 69,757,000 (official estimate 2002).
POPULATION DENSITY: 89.5 per sq km.
CAPITAL: Ankara. **Population:** 3,208,000 (official estimate 2002).
GEOGRAPHY: Turkey borders the Black Sea and Georgia and Armenia to the northeast, Iran to the east, Iraq to the southeast, the Syrian Arab Republic and the Mediterranean to the south, the Aegean Sea to the west and Greece and Bulgaria to the northwest. Asia Minor (or Anatolia) accounts for 97 per cent of the country and forms a long, wide peninsula, 1650km (1025 miles) from east to west and 650km (400 miles) from north to south. Two east-west mountain ranges, the Black Sea Mountains in the north and the Taurus in the south, enclose the central Anatolian plateau, but converge in a vast mountainous region in the far east of the country. It is here that the ancient Tigris and Euphrates rivers rise.
GOVERNMENT: Republic since 1923. **Head of State:** President Ahmet Necdet Sezer since 2000. **Head of Government:** Prime Minister Recep Tayyip Erdogan since 2003.
LANGUAGE: Turkish. Kurdish is also spoken by a minority in the southeast. French, German and English are widely spoken in cities and tourist areas.
RELIGION: Muslim with a small Christian minority. Turkey is a secular state which guarantees complete freedom of worship to non-Muslims.
TIME: GMT + 2 (GMT + 3 from last Sunday in March to Saturday before last Sunday in October).
ELECTRICITY: 220 volts AC, 50Hz.
COMMUNICATIONS: Telephone: IDD is available. Country code: 90. Outgoing international code: 00. There is an extensive internal telephone network, but often an interpreter will be needed for more remote areas. To phone from PTT telephone booths, which are found in all areas, telephone cards and tokens are used. Local, intercity and international calls can be made from all PTT offices. **Mobile telephone:** GSM 900 and 1800 band networks exist. Main network providers include *Avea* (website: www.avea.com.tr), *TELSIM Mobil Telekomuniksyon* (website: www.telsim.com.tr) and *Turkcell* (website: www.turkcell.com.tr). Coverage is available in most urban areas. **Fax:** All hotels and PTT offices have facilities. **Internet:** Main ISPs include: *EfesNet* (website: www.efes.net.tr). Internet cafes exist in main urban areas. **Telegram:** These may be sent from all post offices. **Post:** Airmail to Europe takes three days. Turkish post offices are recognisable by their yellow *PTT* signs. Post office hours: major outlets Mon-Sat 0800-2000, Sun 0900-1900; smaller post offices have the same opening hours as government offices. It is also possible to use the 'Valuables Despatch Service' for valuable belongings or important documents. **Press:** The main newspapers are *Hürriyet*, *Milliyet*, *Sabah* and *Zamam*. English-language daily newspapers include *The Turkish Daily News*. **Radio:** BBC World Service (website: www.bbc.co.uk/worldservice) and Voice of America (website: www.voa.gov) can be received. From time to time the frequencies change and the most up-to-date can be found online.

Passport/Visa

	Passport Required?	Visa Required?	Return Ticket Required?
Full British	Yes	4	Yes
Australian	Yes	4	Yes
Canadian	Yes	4	Yes
USA	Yes	4	Yes
Other EU	1	2/4/5	Yes
Japanese	Yes	3	Yes

Note: *Regulations and requirements may be subject to change at short notice, and you are advised to contact the appropriate diplomatic or consular authority before finalising travel arrangements. Details of these may be found at the head of this country's entry. Any numbers in the chart refer to the footnotes below.*

PASSPORTS: Passport valid for at least six months from date of arrival in Turkey required by all, except the following nationals:
1. Belgium, France, Germany, Greece, Italy, Liechtenstein, Luxembourg, Malta, The Netherlands, Spain and Switzerland, who can enter with a national ID card.
VISAS: Required by all except the following:
(a) **2.** nationals of EU countries for stays of up to three months (except those listed under notes **4** and **5** below in *Sticker-type entry visas*, and nationals of Czech Republic and Slovenia who must apply to the Consulate General to obtain a tourist visa a minimum of six weeks prior to departure;
(b) **3.** nationals of Argentina, Bolivia, Bulgaria* (see *Note* below), Chile, Ecuador, El Salvador, Honduras, Hong Kong (SAR), Iceland, Iran, Israel, Japan, Korea (Rep), Liechtenstein, Malaysia, Monaco, Morocco, New Zealand, Nicaragua, San Marino, Singapore, Switzerland, Trinidad & Tobago, Tunisia, Uruguay and Vatican City for stays of up to three months;
(c) nationals of Bosnia & Herzegovina, Croatia and Macedonia (Former Yugoslav Republic) for stays of up to two months;
(d) nationals of Costa Rica, Kazakhstan, Kyrgyzstan and Macau (SAR) for stays of up to one month;
(e) tranist passengers continuing their journey by the same of first connecting aircraft within 24 hours, provided not leaving the airport and in possession of confirmed onward tickets.
Note: Visa exemption for Bulgarians does not apply to those who enter Turkey through certain custom points (contact Consulate for details). Bulgarians must always obtain a visa for transit passages.
Sticker-type entry visas: Tourists and business visitors from the following countries *do* require visas and can obtain a sticker-type entry visa at-the point of entry for a fee. Prices are dependent on nationality (for British nationals, the cost is £10, and for US nationals, the cost is US$45):
(a) **4.** Australia, Austria, Belgium, Brazil, Canada, Ireland, Italy, Malta, The Netherlands, Portugal, Spain, the UK and USA for stays not exceeding three months;
(b) **5.** Armenia, Azerbaijan, Belarus, Estonia, Greek Cypriot Administrative Region, Hungary, Jordan, Latvia, Lithuania, Moldova, Norway, Poland, Romania, Russian Federation, Serbia & Montenegro, Slovak Republic, Tajikistan, Turkmenistan and the Ukraine for stays not exceeding one month;
(c) Georgia and Guatemala for stays not exceeding 15 days.
Types of visa and cost: *Tourist*; *Transit*; *Study*; and *Long Term Business/Multiple-entry*. Prices vary according to nationality. Some visas must be obtained in advance. Contact the Consulate (or Consular section at Embassy); see *Contact Addresses* section.
Validity: Dependent on nationality of applicant.
Application to: Application to: Consulate (or Consular section at Embassy); see *Contact Addresses* section.
Application requirements: (a) Valid passport. (b) One recent passport-size photo. (c) Application form. (d) Latest bank statement and photocopy. (e) Fee (varies for different nationals), payable by postal order and cash only. (f) £5 administrative fee. (g) Registered, pre-paid, self-addressed, special delivery envelope if applying by post. (h) For *business* visas, a letter of invitation from a company in Turkey. For other types of visas, enquire at the Embassy.
Note: Application requirements may vary according to nationality and type of visa sought. Some nationals may also need to show proof of sufficient funds for the duration of their stay; enquire at the Embassy.
Working days required: Minimum of one, dependent on nationality of applicant. Some applications may be referred to the Ministry of Foreign Affairs in Ankara, which may take much longer (minimum six to eight weeks).
Temporary residence: Apply to the Turkish Consulate General (see *Contact Addresses* section) or to the Turkish Diplomatic Mission in the country of residence.

Money

Currency: The New Turkish Lira (YTL) was introduced on January 1 2005 and both this and the old Turkish Lira (TL) will be in circulation throughout 2005. The old Turkish Lira will be withdrawn from circulation from January 1 2006. After this it will only be possible to exchange old Turkish Lira

for New Turkish Lira at the Central Bank for a period of 10 years. 1YTL = 1,000,000TL (ie the new currency has six less zeros than the old currency).
New Turkish Lira (YTL). Notes are in denominations of YTL100, 50, 20, 10, 5 and 1. Coins are in denominations of YTL1 and 50, 25, 10, 5 and 1 New Kuru° (Ykr).
Old Turkish Lira (TL). Notes are in denominations of TL20,000,000, 10,000,000, 5,000,000, 1,000,000, 500,000, 250,000 and 100,000. Coins are in denominations of TL250,000, 100,000, 50,000, 25,000, 10,000 and 5000.
Currency exchange: All exchange certificates and purchase receipts must be retained to prove that legally exchanged currency was used. Money and travellers cheques can be exchanged at all PTT branches. Many UK banks offer differing rates of exchange depending on denominations of Turkish currency being bought or sold. Check with banks for details and current rates.
Credit & debit cards: American Express, Diners Club, MasterCard and Visa are accepted. Check with your credit or debit card company for details of merchant acceptability and other services which may be available.
Travellers cheques: Can be cashed immediately upon proof of identity. However, it may take several days to cash cheques from private accounts. To avoid additional exchange rate charges, travellers are advised to take travellers cheques in Pounds Sterling or US Dollars.
Currency restrictions: There are no restrictions on the import of local or foreign currency, though visitors bringing in a large amount of foreign currency should declare it, and have it specified in their passport upon arrival to avoid difficulties on departure. No more than the equivalent of US$5000 in local currency may be exported. Foreign currency may be exported up to US$5000, but no more than the amount imported and declared.
Exchange rate indicators: The following figures are included as a guide to the movements of the Turkish Lira against Sterling and the US Dollar:

Date	Feb '04	May '04	Aug '04	Nov '04
£1.00=	2,437,314.9	2,701,476.5	2,695,819.1	2,692,842.0
$1.00=	1,339,000.0	1,512,500.0	1,463,250.0	1,422,000.0

Banking hours: Mon-Fri 0830-1230 and 1330-1700.

Duty Free

The following goods may be imported into Turkey without incurring customs duty:
*200 cigarettes and 50 cigars or 200g of tobacco and 200 cigarette papers or 50g of chewing tobacco or 200g of pipe tobacco or 200g of snuff tobacco**; *five bottles (1l) or seven bottles (700ml) of wine and/or spirits; reasonable amounts of coffee and tea; five bottles (up to 120ml each) of perfume; gifts up to a value of €255.65 (or equivalent); electronic articles up to a value of €255.65 (or equivalent).*
Note: (a)* A further 400 cigarettes, 100 cigars and 500g of pipe tobacco may be imported if purchased on arrival at a duty free shop. (b) Very specific amounts and categories of personal belongings may be imported duty free, according to a list available from the Turkish Embassy, Financial and Customs Counsellor's Office.
Prohibited imports: Narcotics, sharp implements, weapons and more than one set of cards.
Restricted exports: (a) The export of souvenirs such as carpets is subject to customs regulations regarding age and value. (b) The export of antiques is forbidden, according to a list available from the Turkish Embassy, Financial and Customs Counsellor's Office. (c) Minerals may only be exported under licence from the General Directorate of Mining Exploration & Research.

Public Holidays

2005: Jan 1 New Year's Day. **Jan 21** Kurban Bayrami (Feast of the Sacrifice). **Apr 23** National Sovereignty and Children's Day. **May 19** Commemoration of Atatürk and Youth and Sports Day. **Aug 30** Victory Day. **Oct 29** Republic Day. **Nov 3-5** Ramazan Bayrami (End of Ramadan).
2006: Jan 1 New Year's Day. **Jan 13** Kurban Bayrami (Feast of the Sacrifice). **Apr 23** National Sovereignty and Children's Day. **May 19** Commemoration of Atatürk and Youth and Sports Day. **Aug 30** Victory Day. **Oct 29** Republic Day. **Oct 22-24** Ramazan Bayrami (End of Ramadan).
Note: Muslim festivals are timed according to local sightings of various phases of the moon and the dates given above are approximations. During the lunar month of Ramadan that precedes Ramazan Bayrami, Muslims fast during the day and feast at night and normal business patterns may be interrupted. Some restaurants are closed during the day and there may be restrictions on smoking and drinking. Generally, centres of tourism are unaffected. Some disruption may continue into Ramazan Bayrami itself. Ramazan Bayrami and Kurban Bayrami may last anything from two to 10 days, depending on the region. For more information, see the *World of Islam* appendix.

Health

	Special Precautions?	Certificate Required?
Yellow Fever	No	No
Cholera	No	No
Typhoid & Polio	1	N/A
Malaria	2	N/A

Note: Regulations and requirements may be subject to change at short notice, and you are advised to contact your doctor well in advance of your intended date of departure. Any numbers in the chart refer to the footnotes below.

1: Outbreaks of typhoid may occur in rural areas.
2: Potential malaria risk (exclusively in the benign *vivax* form) exists from May to the end of October in the Çukorova/Amikova areas and in southeast Anatolia, Adana and Antalya (Side). There is no malaria risk in the main tourist areas in the west and southwest of the country.
Food & drink: Mains water is usually chlorinated in larger towns and cities, but should not be assumed to have been so treated: if used for drinking or making ice it should have first been boiled or otherwise sterilised. If a water source bears the words içilmez, it means that it is not for drinking; sources labelled *içilir, içme suyu* or *içilebilir* are safe to drink. Bottled spring water is widely available. Milk is pasteurised. Eat only well-cooked meat and fish, preferably served hot.
Other risks: *Hepatitis A, B* and *C* are present. *Cutaneous* and *visceral leishmaniasis, meningitis* and *TB* occur. *Rabies* is present. For those at high risk, vaccination before arrival should be considered. If you are bitten, seek medical advice without delay. For more information, see the *Health* appendix.
Health care: Turkey has a large health sector. A great number of Turkish doctors and dentists speak a foreign language, particularly at major hospitals. Private health insurance is recommended; ensure that it covers Asiatic as well as European Turkey.

Travel - International

NOTE: There is a high threat from terrorism in Turkey. There have been a number of small-scale terrorist incidents since the bomb attacks in Istanbul on 15 and 20 November 2003, which caused a large number of deaths and casualties. Extra vigilance is required on the part of visitors, especially in the vicinity of potential terrorist targets.
AIR: Turkey's national airline is *Turkish Airlines (TK)* (website: www.turkishairlines.com).
Other airlines serving Turkey include *Austrian Airlines, Lufthansa* and *Swiss*.
Approximate flight times: From Istanbul to *Frankfurt/M* is two hours 45 minutes, to *London* is three hours 30 minutes and to *New York* is 11 hours.
International airports: *Ankara (ESB)* (Esenboga) is 35km (22 miles) northeast of the city. *THY* buses go from the city one hour 30 minutes before domestic flights and two hours 15 minutes before international flights. There is a taxi service available into the city. Airport facilities include incoming and outgoing duty free shops, bank/bureau de change, and restaurants and bars.
Istanbul (IST) (Atatürk, formerly Yesilkoy) is 24km (15 miles) west of the city (travel time - 30 to 50 minutes). A coach (*THY* bus) goes every 15 minutes to the *THY* terminal. There are taxi services to the city. Airport facilities include incoming and outgoing duty free shop, bank/bureau de change, bar, restaurant, and car hire (*Avis, Budget, Hertz* and *Europcar*).
Izmir (IZM) (Adnan Menderes). A *THY* bus leaves from the city one hour 15 minutes before departure. Airport facilities include bank/bureau de change, bar and restaurant.
Sabiha Gökçen (SAW) is 40km (25 miles) from Istanbul, on the Asian side. There are shuttle bus services to the city (travel time - 30 to 45 minutes) and to Atatürk International Airport (travel time - 60 to 70 minutes). Taxis are available 24 hours a day. Facilities include duty free shops, bank, ATMs, business centre and restaurants/cafes. There are other international airports at *Adana, Antalya, Dalaman* and *Trabzon*.
Departure tax: US$50 is levied only on Turkish nationals, not resident overseas departing from Turkey.
SEA: Major ports are Antalya, Bandirma, Istanbul, Izmir, Marmaris and Mersin. *Turkish Maritime Lines (TML)*, the national shipping organisation, and a number of cruise lines run services to Turkey. Several ferry routes are available: *To/from Italy*: Ferries operate between Venice-Izmir, Venice-Antalya/Marmaris, Venice-Istanbul via Pireaus, and Brindisi-Cesme. *To/from Cyprus*: Three routes exist on which sea buses, together with car and passenger ferries, operate: Alanya-Girne, Tasucu-Girne and Gazimagosa- Mersin. *To/from Greece*: There are privately operated ferry lines between Turkey and the Greek islands: Lesbos-Ayvalik, Chios-Cesme, Samos-Kusadasi, Cos-Bodrum, Rhodes- Marmaris, and Sömbeki-Datça.
Note: All ships, including private yachts, arriving in Turkish waters must go to one of the following ports of entry: Akcay, Alanya, Anamur, Antalya, Ayvalik, Bandirma, Bodrum, Botas (Adana), Canakkale, Cesme, Datca, Derince, Didim, Dikili, Fethiye, Finike, Giresun, Güllük, Hopa (Artvin), Iskenderun, Istanbul, Izmir, Kas, Kemer, Kusadasi, Marmaris, Mersin, Ordu, Rize, Samsun, Sinop, Söke, Tasucu (Silifke), Tekirdag, Trabzon and Zonguldak.
RAIL: Train journeys can be made to Istanbul via some of the major European cities. The journey from London takes three days: *Eurostar* to Paris, *Orient Express* or *EuroCity* to Vienna (overnight), *EuroCity* to Budapest and finally the *TransBalkan* to Istanbul. There is a weekly sleeper from Moscow. *InterRail* tickets are available in the European part of Turkey as far as Istanbul. For more information contact *Turkish Railways (TCDD)* in Istanbul (tel: (212) 527 0050/1 or 520 6575 (reservations); website: www.tcdd.gov.tr).
ROAD: There are roads from Bulgaria, the CIS, Greece and Iran. From London, drivers may either choose the northern route of Belgium-Germany-Austria-Hungary-Romania-Bulgaria, or the southern route through Belgium-Austria-Italy with a car-ferry connection to Turkey. **Coach:** There are regular services between Turkey and Austria, France,

Germany, Greece and Switzerland, as well as Jordan, Iran, Saudi Arabia and the Syrian Arab Republic. *Eurolines*, departing from Victoria Coach Station in London, serves destinations in Turkey. For further information, contact Eurolines (tel: (08705) 143 219; e-mail: welcome@eurolines.co.uk; website: www.eurolines.co.uk).

Travel - Internal

Note: Road conditions and driving standards in Turkey can be poor. Serious road accidents are common. All visitors should be extra careful when travelling around Turkey's road network.
AIR: *Turkish Airlines* provides an important network of internal flights from Istanbul, Ankara, Adana, Antalya, Dalaman, Izmir and Trabzan to all of the major Turkish cities. The airline (tel (UK office): (020) 7766 9300; fax: (020) 7976 1738; website: www.turkishairlines.com) offers reductions to holders of International Student Travel Conference (ISTC) cards.
SEA: *Turkish Maritime Lines* offers several coastal services with their *Adriatic Line* subsidiary, providing excellent opportunities for sightseeing; they also operate a car ferry between Mersin and Magosa. There are services between Istanbul and Izmir, with overnight accommodation and ferry routes along Turkey's northern Black Sea coast. A frequent car ferry crosses the Dardenelles at Gallipoli, from Canakkale to Eceabat and Gelibolu to Lapseki. There are also seabus services. *Turkish Maritime Lines* offers discounts to holders of ISTC cards.
RAIL: Fares are comparatively low. Many trains of the *Turkish Railways (TCDD)* have sleeping cars, couchettes and restaurant cars, but there is no air-conditioned accommodation. Fares are more expensive for express and mail trains, even though express trains are relatively slow, and some routes are indirect. Steam engines, such as the *Anatolia Express*, which traverses eastern Turkey, are retained for tourist trains on some routes; these are often fantastic trips that are the highlight of a visit to Turkey. Tickets can be purchased at *TCDD* offices at railway stations and *TCDD*-appointed agents. *TCDD* offers discounts of 20 per cent to holders of ISTC cards. Children under seven travel free; children aged between seven and 11 pay half fare. Discount fares are available for students, groups, roundtrips and sports teams.
ROAD: There is an extensive road maintenance and building programme; 1400km (900 miles) of motorway is under construction. Traffic drives on the right. In case of an accident, contact the Turkish Touring and Automobile Club (*Turkiye Turing ve Otomobil Kurumu*), Head Office, Sanayi Sitesi Yani, Fort Levent, Istanbul (tel: (212) 282 8140; fax: (212) 282 8042). **Coach:** Many private companies provide frequent day and night services between all Turkish cities. Services are often faster than trains and competition between operators has led to lower fares. Tickets are sold at the bus or coach companies' branch offices either at stations or in town centres. One should shop around for the best prices. Coaches depart from the bus stations (otogar) in large towns and from the town centre in small towns. **Car hire:** Both chauffeur-driven and self-drive cars are available in all large towns. All international companies are represented. **Documentation:** An International Driving Permit is required for visits of over three months. Green Card International Insurance, endorsed for Turkish territory in both Europe and Asia, and Turkish third-party insurance (obtainable from insurance agencies at frontier posts) are also required. Cars can be brought into Turkey for a maximum of six months in one year. On entering, an entry-exit form is filled out. For longer stays, it is necessary to apply to either the Ministry of Finance and Customs or the Turkish Touring and Automobile Club.
URBAN: Bus and trolleybus: Extensive conventional bus (and some trolleybus) services operate in Istanbul, Ankara and Izmir. There are buses in all other large towns. These are generally reliable, modern and easy to use, although publicity is non-existent. Tickets are bought in advance from kiosks and dropped into a box by the driver. **Taxi:** There are many types of taxi, share-taxi and minibus in operation. Taxis are numerous in all Turkish cities and towns and are recognisable by their chequered black and yellow bands. Metered taxis are available. For longer journeys, the fare should be agreed beforehand. A *dolmus* is a collective taxi which follows specific routes and is recognisable by its yellow band. Each passenger pays according to the distance travelled to specific stops. The fares are fixed by the municipality. This is a very practical means of transport and much cheaper than a taxi. Taxis may turn into a *dolmus* and vice versa according to demand. **Ferry:** There are extensive cross-Bosphorus and short-hop ferries between the parts of Istanbul. **Metro:** There are plans to construct a metro system in Ankara.
Travel times: The following chart gives approximate travel times (in hours and minutes) from **Ankara** to other major cities/towns in Turkey (visitors should note that these times are approximate).

	Air	Road	Rail
Istanbul	0.45	6.00	7.00
Izmir	0.50	7.00	10.00
Antalya	1.00	8.00	-
Adana	0.55	6.00	13.00
Erzurum	1.15	11.00	18.00
Van	1.15	15.00	23.00
Trabzon	1.40	3.00	-
Mugla	1.25	10.00	-

Accommodation

HOTELS: In recent years, Turkey has made a considerable effort to develop its hotel facilities. A certain number of hotels throughout the country are registered with the Ministry of Tourism as offering satisfactory facilities. They abide by certain regulations and standards of facilities, and are given the name 'Touristic'. There are other establishments registered with local authorities, and these too correspond to a certain standard in regards to facilities and services. There is also a national hotel association: TUROB, Cumhuriyet Cad., Pak Apt, Kat. 6D, 34437 Istanbul (tel: (212) 294 2464; fax: (212) 296 1739; e-mail: info@turob.com; website: www.turob.org). It is compulsory for establishments to have a book in which guests can register remarks, suggestions and complaints. Complaints can also be made directly to the Ministry of Tourism (see *Contact Addresses* section), *or* to the Ministry of Tourism Directorate of the city concerned. **Grading:** Hotels are graded from **1 star** (1 yildizli) to **5 stars** (5 yildizli). Classification is based on the standard of service and facilities. Motels and holiday villas are **first class** (1 sinif) or **second class** (2 sinif).
GUEST HOUSES: Guest houses (pensions) can be found in holiday resorts and major towns.
SELF-CATERING: Villas and apartments can be rented.
CAMPING/CARAVANNING: There are numerous sites, but facilities are generally limited.
YOUTH HOSTELS: Holders of ISTC cards, International Youth Hostel Federation cards and those registered as 'student' or 'teacher' on their passports can benefit from the youth holiday opportunities available in Turkey. Some Turkish organisations, such as *Turkish Airlines*, recognise the ISTC card and accordingly grant reductions to holders. Further information can be obtained from Yücelt Interyouth Hostel, Caferiye Sok No 6/1, Sultanahmet 34400, Istanbul (tel: (212) 513 6150/1; fax: (212) 512 7628; e-mail: info@yucelthostel.com).

Resorts & Excursions

Straddling Europe and Asia, Turkey has enormously diverse scenery, with rolling central plains, soaring mountains, desert and orchards, white sand beaches and towering sea cliffs. The Hittites, Greeks, Romans, Byzantines, Selçuks, Ottomans, Armenians and a host of smaller civilisations have all added intricate layers of architecture, art and culture, creating a mosaic as rich as any of the gilded Byzantine glories. Today, Turkey's thousands of kilometres of magnificent coast, sunshine and fine food have turned it into a major tourist destination. Much more than that, it is still fascinating culturally - a modern, westernised country, with a largely Muslim population, cautiously spanning the divide between religions and cultures.

ISTANBUL

The only city in the world to span two continents, Istanbul is a bustling, cosmopolitan place, officially founded by Emperor Constantine in AD 326 on the back of a much older village. It remained capital of the Byzantine and Ottoman empires right up until 1923, its illustrious past leaving a rich legacy of mosques, churches, museums and magnificent palaces, coupled with bustling bazaars and a vibrant street life. Istanbul is made up of three distinct cities. The old city of Istanbul is decorated with parks and gardens. Amongst hundreds of fascinating sights, the main attractions include **Topkapi**, the sumptuous palace of the Ottoman sultans overlooking the **Sea of Marmara** and the **Bosphorus**; the delicately decorated **Blue Mosque**, the only mosque in the world with six minarets; the vast dome of **Aya Sophia**, built in 536 as a Byzantine cathedral, later a mosque and now a museum and, underground, the **Yerebatan Sarayi**, a vast Byzantine cistern supported by 336 Corinthian columns. Nearby, the commercial heart of the city, the Grand Bazaar, is still a captivating sight for shoppers and window-shoppers alike, while further along the narrow inlet of the Golden Horn, the **Kariye Camii** has some of the finest Byzantine mosaics to survive today. Across the **Golden Horn**, 'modern' Istanbul, **Beyoglu**, dates back to the foreign cantonments of the 13th century. This is where you find the restaurants, hotels, and modern shops, while the truly modern areas around Taksim are home to cultural centres, exhibition halls and office blocks.
THE BOSPHORUS: The shores of both old and new cities lie along the northern, European bank of the Bosphorous, the narrow strait that divides Europe from Asia. Two massive suspension bridges now span these overcrowded waters, in which tour boats, ferries, supertankers and fishing vessels vie for space in the overcrowded waters. From all of them you see the Istanbul skyline, one of the most dramatic in the world. Tours up the Bosphorous include several notable buildings, including the Sultans' 19th-century **Dolmabahçe Palace**. On the far, Asian shores lie **Uskudar** (Scutari), where Florence Nightingale nursed the sick during the Crimean War; the charming Ottoman summer palace of **Beylerbeyi**; and a whole series of delightful villages full of fish restaurants and fine old mansions, built by the 19th-century aristocracy. Looming at each other across the water are several Byzantine and Ottoman castles, including **Anadoluhisar** and **Rumelihisar**.
THE SEA OF MARMARA: West of Istanbul, the provinces of Thrace and Marmara embrace the Sea of Marmara, while the towns of **Gelibolu** and **Çanakkale** mark the entrance to the **Dardanelles**, the narrow straits leading through to the Mediterranean. This was the site of the infamous **Gallipoli** landings during World War I, which led to the deaths of nearly 250,000 British, Turkish and Anzac troops and shot Turkish General Mustafa Kemal (later known as Ataturk) to fame. Inland, the cities of **Edirne**, in Thrace, and **Bursa**, in Marmara, are both fascinating historic towns with a wide range of magnificent architecture, such as the Selimiye Camii in Edirne, said to be the masterwork of Turkish imperial architect, Mimar Sinan. Just outside Bursa, the **Uludag National Park** is a wonderful forested mountain reserve, with excellent walking in summer and skiing in winter. A short way south of Gallipoli are the ruins of ancient **Troy**. Of the nine levels of the excavated settlement mound, the sixth is supposed to be the Troy depicted in Homer's *Iliad*.

THE AEGEAN COAST

The magnificent coast of ancient Ionia, a crucible of western civilisation, boasts fine beaches and many important historical sites. The attractive tourist towns of **Ayvacik**, **Ayvalik** and **Behramkale** are good places from which to visit the magnificent **Temple of Athena** at **Assos**. Further south lie the ruins of the great city of **Pergamum** (modern **Bergama**), famous in antiquity for its splendid library. It is here that you will find the **Sanctuary of Asclepieion** and two fine temples, the Acropolis and the red-brick **Basilica**. **Izmir**, the birthplace of Homer, is Turkey's third city and an important port. It is a modern metropolis set in a curving bay surrounded by terraced hillsides. As a result of earthquakes and a great fire, there are only a few reminders of old **Smyrna - Kadifekale**, the fourth-century fortress situated on top of **Mount Pagos**. The fortress affords a superb view of the city, and of the **Gulf of Izmir**, the Roman *agora* with some well-preserved porticos and **Statues of Poseidon and Artemis**. **Çesme** is one of the many popular resorts in the Izmir region. It has excellent beaches, thermal springs and a 15th-century fortress. The port of **Sigacik**, the ruins of the ancient Ionian city of **Teos** and the sandy beach at **Akkum** are all between Izmir and Çesme. A short way inland is another fine Graeco-Roman city, **Sardis** (modern **Sart**), with a beautiful **Marble Court**, **Temple of Artemis** and a first-century AD **synagogue**.
The remains of the Hellenistic and Roman city of **Ephesus** (modern **Selçuk**), rumoured to have been founded in the 13th century BC, lie at the foot of **Mount Pion**. Carefully restored and now one of the most spectacular ancient cities in the world, top sights within the huge archaeological area include the **Grand Theatre**, where St Paul preached to the Ephesians, the second-century **Temple of Serapi**, the elegant façades of the **Temple of Hadrian** and the **Library of Celsus**. The site of **Meryemana**, reputed to be the house of the Virgin Mary, lies very close to Ephesus in the small vale of **Mount Bulbul Dagi** (Nightingale Mountain). It has become a world-famous shrine, attracting thousands of pilgrims each year. The nearby town of **Selçuk** is home to the **Ephesus Museum** and **Basilica of St John**, said to be the last home of John the Baptist. The ruins of **Priene**, **Miletus** and **Didyma** are also of great interest and, like Ephesus, are within easy reach of **Kusadasi**, an attractive resort surrounded by sandy bays. Inland are two more fine historic cities, the atmospheric **Heraklea** ad **Latmos**, and **Aphrodisias**.

SOUTHWESTERN TURKEY

This magnificently scenic and historically fascinating area, where the southern Aegean meets the Mediterranean, is known popularly as the Turquoise Coast, due to the intense colour of the sea. Tourism in the region is dominated by several major beach resorts, each with a series of satellite villages, and a great many large hotels. Rocky cliffs are interspersed by lavish white sand beaches. Each small town and fishing harbour has a variety of pleasure boats, fish restaurants, bars and nightlife, while the larger hotels offer a wide range of watersports. And if that is not enough, the area is densely packed with ancient cities, and there is excellent walking in the hills behind the coast. **Bodrum** (birthplace of Herodotus, known as the father of history) is dominated by the magnificent 15th-century crusader **Castle of St Peter**, now home to a fascinating Museum of Underwater Archaeology. Both Bodrum and **Marmaris**, set in a deep fjord-like inlet, have wild, noisy nightlife and a wide variety of boat trips for daytime hangover cures. Destinations include the Greek islands of Kos (from Bodrum) and Rhodes (from Marmaris). From Marmaris, you can also reach the charming fishing village of **Datça**, the ruins of **Knidos**, and the reedy ruins of **Kaunos**, near the small resort of **Dalyan**.

Further along the Mediterranean coast are the small port town of **Fethiye**, with its imposing Lycian rock tombs, and **Ölü Deniz**, a stunning crystal-clear lagoon with a beautiful beach, surrounded by pine-covered mountains. The lagoon is protected from rampant commercial development by its status as a national park, although the surrounding valley is completely overwhelmed by tourist development.

Continuing east along the coast, there are several relatively small and charming resorts such as **Patara**, with its 18km (11 mile) beach; charming little **Kalkan**; **Kas**, one of the most upmarket resorts on the Turkish coast; **Olympos**, a backpacker's paradise and home of the chimaera, a living flame erupting eerily from rock; and **Kemer**, where mass-market all-inclusive hotels hold sway. Between them are a wide range of historic sights, including the ancient cities of **Patara**, **Xanthos**, **Myra** and **Phaselis**.

Inland, there is excellent walking at **Saklikent** and in the **Olympos National Park**. Further away, other worthwhile stops include the pretty old town of **Mugla**, the carpet-making centre of **Milas**; and **Pamukkale**, near **Denizli**, famous for its spectacular calcified waterfall and thermal waters, used since Roman times for their therapeutic powers. Pamukkale also contains the ruins of the Roman city of **Hierapolis**.

THE MEDITERRANEAN COAST

With sunshine for most of the year and a magnificent coastline, the western Mediterranean Coast is a popular holiday area. It is also a region steeped in history and legend, dotted with important sites and great medieval castles. Situated on a cliff promontory, **Antalya** is a popular resort, boasting a picturesque walled old town and harbour, **Kaleiçi**, the monumental **Hadrian's Gate**, **Kesik Minare** and **Yivli Minare** mosques and **Hidirlik Kulesi**, the round Roman tower, and a superb **Archaeological Museum**.

With its mix of charming small guest houses and modern hotels, it is the ideal starting point for tours to the outlying Roman cities of dramatic **Termessos**, in the mountains behind the city; **Perge**, a well-preserved and atmospheric place with tall Hellenistic walls and streets which still bear the marks of chariot wheels; and **Aspendos**, home to a remarkable second-century AD amphitheatre, still used for live performances during the annual festival. Turkey's finest Roman aqueduct lies to the north of the city. **Belek**, 30km (19 miles) east of Antalya, has two championship golf courses, is the habitat of hundreds of species of birds, and one of several local breeding grounds for the rare leatherback turtle. In **Side**, now a thriving seaside resort, the Greek enclosure walls are still virtually undamaged. The town also boasts an exquisite fountain, a theatre, two *agoras* and Roman baths, great beaches and lively nightlife. Nestling at the foot of a rocky promontory and crowned by a Selçuk fortress, the town of **Alanya** has some fine beaches and a great many large resort hotels.

A spectacularly scenic road connects **Anamur**, striking for its wave-swept Selçuk castle and ancient city, and Silifke, dominated by yet another vast fortress. The museum in ancient **Silifke** contains finds from the many archaeological sites in the vicinity. **Mersin**, built on a site dating back to Paleolithic times, is a major port. Nearby, parts of Tarsus date back to biblical times, when St Paul was a child here and Anthony met Cleopatra in the main square. The prosperous city of **Adana**, in the middle of the flat Cukurova plain, is the centre of Turkey's cotton industry, and home to an imposingly huge modern mosque. The massive **Taskopru Bridge**, built by Hadrian in the second century, the ancient covered bazaar and nearby Crusader castles and Hittite settlements are all interesting sites. The road from heavily polluted **Iskenderun** leads through the Belen Pass to **Antakya**, the biblical city of Antioch, where St Peter founded the first Christian community. The grotto where he preached can be seen just outside the town.

THE BLACK SEA COAST

This rugged, mountainous region of Turkey has a wild beauty, but lacks the wealth of historical and climatic attractions of the rest of the country, while the thunderous main road leading west from the CIS destroys much of the local atmosphere. Despite the variable weather, there are several coastal resorts with good, sandy beaches. These include, from west to east, **Kilyos**, **Sile**, **Akcakoca**, **Sinop** (also very interesting historically), **Unye**, **Ordu** and **Giresun**, many of which are sadly tacky, catering to the poorer end of the home-grown tourist market. There are also several fascinating historic towns such as **Safranbolu**, a short distance inland, whose traditional Ottoman architecture has been deemed worthy of UNESCO World Heritage Status; coastal **Amasra** with Hellenistic walls, Roman ruins, Byzantine churches, and 14th-century Genoese fortresses; and **Amasya**, a dramatically sited town which was capital of the short-lived Pontic Kingdom (founded in 120 BC) and has a wide range of ancient, Byzantine and Ottoman buildings, including the rock tombs of the Pontic kings.

Keep to the side roads if you want charm, between the two regional centres of **Samsun** and **Trabzon**. Samsun has an important place in modern history as the War of Independence began here in 1919, which is reflected by one of the finest monuments in Turkey, though little remains to testify to its ancient origins. In Trabzon (the sadly shabby Trebizond of history), the ruins of a Byzantine fortress can still be seen, together with many fine buildings including the **Fatih Camii**, built as a cathedral during the 200-year rule of the Comnene family (11th-century upstarts who overthrew Byzantine rule and carved themselves a small kingdom). The spectacular 14th-century **Monastery of the Black Virgin** at **Sumala**, 54km (34 miles) from Trabzon, is set into the face of a sheer cliff, 300m (1000ft) above the valley floor, and contains some magnificent frescoes.

East of Trabzon, there are few large towns and tourism concentrates on the fascinating lifestyle of the small Laz and Hopa peoples, hiking in the remote, beautiful Kaçkar Mountains and the region of Artvin, once the centre of Turkish Armenian culture and home to several magnificent century churches dating from the ninth to the 11th centuries.

CENTRAL ANATOLIA

The hub of this vast, central plateau - the cradle of the ancient Hittite and Phrygian civilisations - is the modern metropolis of **Ankara**. Kemal Atatürk supervised the construction of Ankara, a capital to replace Istanbul, in this hitherto underpopulated region during the 1920s and 1930s. Since then, it has grown into a thriving, trendy city with a population of nearly three million that has grown to rival Istanbul's sophistication, and is much more interesting than is often imagined. The **Anitkabir**, Atatürk's solemnly imposing mausoleum, dominates the new city. Ankara was, however, built on the site of more ancient settlements and it is fitting that the **Museum of Anatolian Civilisations**, built under the ramparts of the **Citadel**, should house a magnificent collection of Neolithic and Hittite artefacts. There are also reminders of the area's more recent past as part of the Roman and Selçuk empires. More modern additions to the cityscape include the huge, elegant **Kocatepe Mosque** and the **Atakule**, a high tower with a sightseeing platform and restaurant.

Southwest of Ankara are **Afyon**, centre of the legal opium industry, and a fine old Ottoman town; **Yazilikaya** (**Midassehir**), home of the legendary golden king and his giant mausoleum; **Kutahya**, an attractive old city at the centre of the Turkish ceramic trade; and the 'lake district', a pretty, green area of interlocking fresh and brackish lakes that are an excellent birding habitat There are several interesting small towns along the lake shores, such as **Isparta**, famous for its roses, and **Egirdir**, founded by the Hittites, but with a fine collection of Ottoman and Greek houses. Ruined cities of note in the area include **Antioch ad Pisidia**, the recently reconstructed **Sagalassos** and **Kremna**, where the earthworks built by the Roman siege are still clearly visible. Due south of Ankara, past the vast salt lake of **Tuz Gölü**, **Konya** is a former Selçuk capital and one of the great religious centres of Turkey, home of the **Mevlana Tekkesi**, the monastery and mausoleum of Mevlana Celâddin Rumi, one of Islam's most celebrated mystics and founder of the Order of Whirling Dervishes. Other places of interest include the 13th-century **Alâeddin Mosque**, the **Karatay Medrese** (now an excellent Ceramics and Tile Museum) and the **Iplikci Mosque**, Konya's oldest structure.

South of the city, **Catalhöyük** is the second-oldest town in the world, dating back to the sixth millennium BC, while to the east, **Binbirkilise** is an area stuffed with '1001' Byzantine chapels and churches, most now sadly in a desperate state of repair. East of Ankara, the Hittite state archives were found in **Bogazkale** (Hattusas) in 1906, and contained within the Bogazkale-Alacahöyük-Yazilikaya triangle are the most important sites of the Hittite Empire. **Sungurlu** is a good base for visitors to this fascinating but underdeveloped region.

CAPPADOCIA: Southeast of Ankara, Cappadocia is a spectacular, almost surreal landscape of rock and cones, capped pinnacles and fretted ravines. Dwellings have been hewn from the soft, volcanic rock since 400 BC, and the elaborate cave systems have sheltered generations of persecuted settlers. Today, it is a fascinating mix of truly magnificent scenery (as beautiful in the winter snow as in summer), an excellent destination for outdoor activities from mountain biking and hiking to hot-air ballooning, and one of the most compelling historic and artistic regions in this culturally rich country. Many people still live, at least partially, in cave dwellings and in the main tourist centres, there are several charming small hotels with cave rooms. The main towns in the region are **Nevsehir** and **Urgup**. **Göreme** is probably the biggest attraction, with over 30 magnificently frescoed Byzantine rock churches open to the public. **Zelve** has a huge, somewhat eerie underground monastic complex. The villages of **Ortahisar** and **Uchisar**, clustered around rock pinnacles and crowned by citadels, offer excellent views. There are over 400 underground cities in the area; two of the biggest and most exciting are **Kaymakli** and **Derinkuyu**, with up to eight floors and complex systems of apartments, public rooms and streets that could house literally hundreds of people. In the northern part of the area, **Avanos** is a pretty little town with a thriving local ceramics industry.

A short distance west of the main area of Cappadocia, the 10km- (6 mile-) long **Ihlara Canyon** is another Byzantine religious hideout, with around 60 churches, many of them still painted, carved into the walls of an idyllic green Shangri La.

THE EASTERN PROVINCES

The vast, empty expanse of eastern Anatolia differs profoundly from the rest of the country. The landscape has a desolate beauty, with ochre red plains and fertile valleys, lakes, waterfalls, snowcapped peaks and, in the far south, dusty deserts. This again is a fascinating cultural and historic area, stuffed with Biblical and Islamic history, Kurdish and Armenian cultures, fine mosques, palaces and monuments. The region has suffered a degree of political instability and lack of security for several years and is only just reopening to tourists, who should take up-to-date advice before visiting the area. It is far less developed for tourism than western Turkey; accommodation can be very basic and is often hard to find. Eastern Turkey can be said to begin along a rough line from Samsun, on the Black Sea Coast, through the Anatolian towns of **Sivas** and **Tokat**, noted for their Selçuk architecture, to the busy industrial town of **Gaziantep** in the south.

Erzurum, the largest town in the northeast, was one of the eastern bastions of Byzantium for many centuries, and has mosques and mausolea from the Selçuk and Mongol eras, Byzantine walls and two Koranic colleges characterised by minarets and finely carved portals. The frontier town of **Kars**, to the north of Erzurum, is dominated by a formidable 12th-century Georgian fortress. The ruins of the 10th-century **Ani** lie east of Kars.

On the eastern border with Armenia, **Agri Dagri** is the biblical Mount Ararat where, according to legend, Noah's Ark came to rest. Below it lie the imposing palace and mosque of **Ishak Pasha** at **Dogubeyazit**. The walled town of **Van**, on the eastern shore of the immense **Lake Van**, was an important Urartu fortress from 800-600 BC. The citadel dominates the ruins of Selçuk, Ottoman mosques and many rock tombs. On the island of **Akdamar**, in **Lake Van**, is the enchanting 10th-century **Church of the Holy Cross**.

Further south, the twin rivers **Tigris** and **Euphrates**, cradle an agriculturally rich oasis within the desert. This is Biblical Mesopotamia and, some say, the original Garden of Eden. Today, the **GAP Project** is creating an enormous series of interlinked lakes and canals to create hydro-electricity and irrigation, to the fury of neighbouring countries who also rely on the water, and the local Kurkish people who see their homeland slipping from their grasp. Its centrepiece, the Atatürk Dam, is the fourth-largest in the world.

The southeast is filled with ancient cities, traditional cultures and beautiful, if often forbidding, landscapes. Places of note include **Sanliurfa**, site of the ancient pools of Abraham; the beehive houses of **Harran**, from where Abraham decided to move to the land of Canaan; **Nemrut Dagi**, the home of the colossal stone statues erected by King Antiochus I in the first century BC; **Diyarbakir**, built in the fourth century and surrounded by forbidding triple walls of black basalt; and the white-coloured medieval architecture and Roman citadel of **Mardin**.

SKI RESORTS

Turkey may not be the obvious ski destination, but it does have a number of winter sports resorts, generally located in forested mountains of average height. The core season is from January to March. The following ski centres are easily accessible by road or *Turkish Airlines* domestic flights: **Erciyes:** 25km (15 miles) from Kayseri (Cappadocia); **Koroglu:** on the Istanbul-Ankara highway, 50km (30 miles) from Bolu and the Black Sea coast; **Palandoken:** 5km (4 miles) from Erzurum (central-eastern Anatolia); **Saklikent:** 48km (30 miles) north of Antalya, in the Bakirli Dagi mountain range (Mediterranean Coast); **Sarikamis:** near Kars (far eastern Anatolia); **Uludag:** 36km (22 miles) south of Bursa (Marmara).

Sport & Activities

Mountaineering: Turkey has a number of mountain ranges with peaks ranging from heights of 3250m (10,660ft) to the 5165m (16,945ft) of Mount Agri (Ararat), the highest mountain in Anatolia, which provide excellent climbing

possibilities for both novice and expert climbers. Permission is required from the Turkish Mountaineering Club.
Skiing: Winter sports resorts in Turkey are generally located in forested mountains. Ski centres are often easily accessible by road or by *Turkish Airlines* domestic flights. Most resorts are in the north (near Ankara) and the western interior (see *Resorts & Excursions* section).
Watersports: The Mediterranean coast, particularly Izmir, has very warm waters and watersports are widely available.
Trekking: Turkey's vast interior of unspoilt nature, mountains, plateaux, villages and ancient ruins is perfect for exploring on foot.
Golf: There are currently five championship courses in Turkey; one of which is at the Klassis resort close to Istanbul, the other four of which are in the resort of Belek in the Antalya region.

Social Profile

FOOD & DRINK: Turkish food combines culinary traditions of a pastoral people originating from Central Asia and the influences of the Mediterranean regions. Lamb is a basic meat featured on all menus, often as *shish kebab* (pieces of meat threaded on a skewer and grilled) or *doner kebab* (pieces of lamb packed tightly round a revolving spit). Fish and shellfish are very fresh and *barbunya* (red mullet) and *kiliç baligi* (swordfish) are delicious. *Dolma* (vine leaves stuffed with nuts and currants) and *karniyarik* (aubergine stuffed with minced meat) are other popular dishes. Guests are usually able to go into a kitchen and choose from the pots if they cannot understand the names of the dishes. There are also a wide range of Turkish sweets and pastries including the famous *Turkish Delight* (originally made from dates, honey, roses and jasmine bound by Arabic gum and designed to sweeten the breath after coffee). Table service is common. *Ayran* (a refreshing yoghurt drink), tea and strong black Turkish coffee are widely available. Turkey is a secular state and alcohol is permitted, although during Ramadan it is considered polite for the visitor to avoid drinking alcohol. Turkish beer, red and white wines are reasonable. The national drink is *raki* (anisette), known as 'lion's milk', which clouds when water is added. Drinking *raki* is a ritual and is traditionally accompanied by a variety of *meze* (hors d'oeuvres).
NIGHTLIFE: There are nightclubs in most main centres, either Western or Oriental, with music and dancing. There are theatres with concerts in Ankara, Istanbul and Izmir and most towns have cinemas. Turkish baths (*hamam*) are popular.
SHOPPING: Istanbul's *Kapali Carsi Bazaar* has jewellery, carpets and antiques for sale. Turkish handicrafts include a rich variety of textiles and embroideries, articles of copper, onyx and tile, mother-of-pearl, inlaid articles, leather and suede products, jewellery and, above all, carpets and *kilims*. **Shopping hours:** Mon-Sat 0900-1300 and 1400-2000 (closed Sunday). Istanbul covered market: Mon-Sat 0800-1900.
SPECIAL EVENTS: For a detailed list of special events, contact the Turkish Tourist Office (see *Contact Addresses* section). The following is a selection of special events occurring in Turkey in 2005:
Jan *Camel Wrestling Festival*, Aydin and Izmir. **Mar** *Ankara International Film Festival-Ankara; 1915 Sea Victory Celebration-Canakkale.* **Apr** *Traditional Mesir Festival*, Manisa; *International Ankara Music Festival.* **Apr-May** *Ankara International Arts Festival.* **Apr 2-17** *24th International Istanbul Film Festival.* **May 18-Jun 4** *Turkish Theatre Festival*, Istanbul. **Jun 4-Jul 2** *The 33rd International Istanbul Music Festival.* **Jul 7-17** *12th International Instanbul Jazz Festival.* **Aug** *Troy Festival*, Canakkale. **Sep** *Seyh Edibali Commemoration and Culture Festival*, Bilecik; *Grape Harvest Festival*, various locations. **Oct** *International Bodrum Sailing Cup.*
SOCIAL CONVENTIONS: Shaking hands is the normal form of greeting. Hospitality is very important and visitors should respect Islamic customs. Informal wear is acceptable, but beachwear should be confined to the beach or poolside. Smoking is widely acceptable but prohibited in cinemas, theatres, city buses and *dolmuses* (collective taxis). **Tipping:** A service charge is included in hotel and restaurant bills.

Business Profile

ECONOMY: Turkey is self-sufficient in basic foodstuffs including maize, sugar, wheat and barley. Cotton, tobacco, fruit, vegetables and nuts are grown for both domestic consumption and export. A variety of livestock is reared. The agricultural sector still accounts for 15 per cent of total economic output and is a major employer, especially of women in the workforce, 60 per cent of whom work on the land. There is a sizeable mining industry producing copper, chromium, borax and, to a lesser extent, bauxite and coal. Manufacturing has grown significantly during the last 20 years with textiles, food-processing, oil-refining, chemicals and the production of iron and steel having emerged as the most important industries. Tourism dominates the service sector after a phase of rapid expansion and serves as a key source of foreign exchange, although it has suffered from the worldwide downturn following from terrorist attacks (to which Turkey has proven especially vulnerable). In 2002, Turkey received almost 11 million visitors, contributing more than US$11 billion to the economy. Economic performance between 1998 and 2002 was poor with negative GDP growth during most of the period (9 per cent during 2001), while inflation was between 40 and 65 per cent. There was some improvement in 2003: inflation was cut to near 20 per cent and positive growth of 2.5 per cent was recorded. Unemployment was steady at over 10 per cent. Relations with the international financial community have been difficult. Successive governments have agreed reform programmes based on the usual diet of deregulation and privatisation. However, political instability has undermined government attempts to sell utilities and key industries. Turkey has long harboured an aspiration to join the European Union. Poor economic management, the unresolved situation in Cyprus, perennial disputes with Greece and a bad human-rights record have combined to thwart any prospect of EU membership. Nonetheless Europe has increasing influence over the country; Turkish trade patterns have shifted from the Middle East in favour of Europe, and hundreds of thousands of Turkish workers are employed across the EU. Provided that the 2004 expansion of the EU from 15 to 25 countries (including Cyprus) proceeds smoothly, Turkey may harbour a realistic expectation of joining along with Bulgaria and Romania in 2007.
Germany, Italy, France and the UK are now Turkey's principal trading partners. Outside Europe, the USA and Saudi Arabia are also important; to the east, Turkey has built up significant economic links with the former Soviet Republics of Central Asia.
BUSINESS: A formal suit or jacket and tie should always be worn for business. English is widely spoken in business circles, although an effort by the visitor to speak a little Turkish is appreciated. The majority of people in business value punctuality and visiting cards are widely used. **Office hours:** Mon-Fri 0830-1200 and 1330-1730. *Summer:* In the Aegean and Mediterranean regions of Turkey, government offices and many other establishments are closed during the afternoon in the summer months. The summer hours are fixed each year by the provincial governors.
COMMERCIAL INFORMATION: The following organisation can offer advice: Union of Chambers of Commerce, Industry, Maritime Commerce and Commodity Exchanges of Turkey (UCCET), Atatürk Bulvar 149, I
Bakanliklar 06640, Ankara (tel: (312) 413 8000; fax: (312) 418 3268; e-mail: info@tobb.org.tr; website: www.tobb.org.tr).
CONFERENCES/CONVENTIONS: Istanbul and Antalya are the most popular venues, followed by Ankara, Marmaris and Bodrum. There are many 4- and 5-star hotels, which provide facilities and can host conferences and meetings to international standards. Contact UKTAS, International Congress Centre Inc, Harbiye 80230, Istanbul (tel: (212) 296 3055; fax: (212) 224 0878; website: www.icec.org). The Crowne Plaza Istanbul has a conference centre with facilities for up to 1000 people (tel: (212) 560 8110; fax; (212) 560 8158).

Climate

Temperatures in Ankara vary between -4°C (25°F) and 30°C (86°F). Marmara and the Aegean and Mediterranean coasts have a typical Mediterranean climate with hot summers and mild winters.
Required clothing: Light- to medium-weights and rainwear.

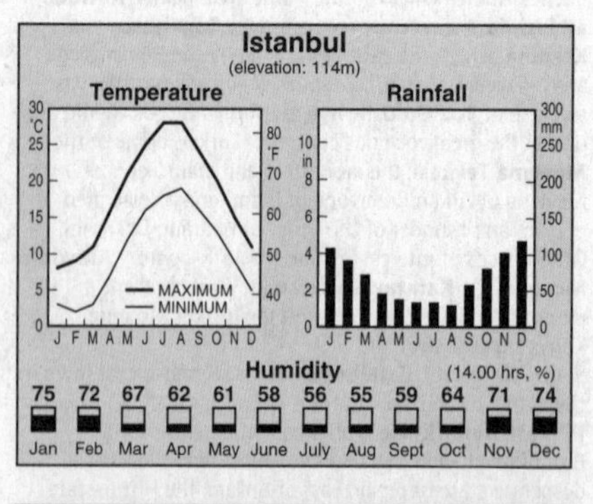

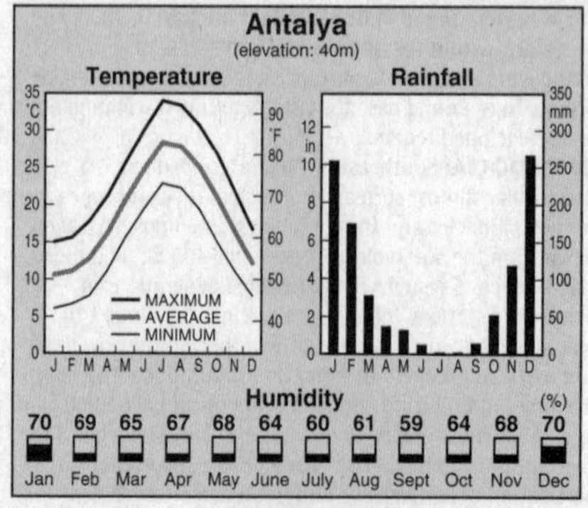

Turkmenistan

LATEST TRAVEL ADVICE CONTACTS

British Foreign and Commonwealth Office
Tel: (0870) 606 0290 Website: www.fco.gov.uk
US Department of State
Website: http://travel.state.gov/travel
Canadian Department of Foreign Affairs and Int'l Trade
Tel: (1 800) 267 8376 Website: www.dfait-maeci.gc.ca

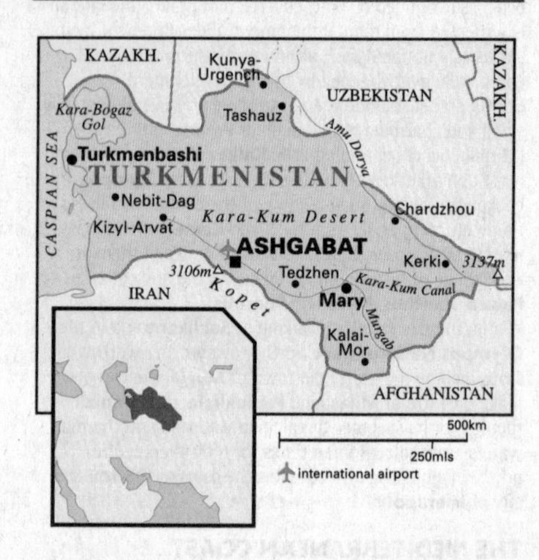

Location: Central Asia.

Country dialling code: 993.

State Committee of Turkmenistan for Tourism and Sport
17 1984/Pushkin Street, 744000 Ashgabat, Turkmenistan
Tel: (12) 354 777 *or* 397 606 *or* 771.
Tel/Fax: (12) 390 065 *or* 396 740.
E-mail: turkmentour@online.tm *or* travel@online.tm
Website: www.tourism-sport.gov.tm
Ministry of Foreign Affairs
83 Makhtumkuli Avenue, Ashgabat, Turkmenistan
Tel: (12) 353 727.
Embassy of Turkmenistan
2nd Floor, St George's House, 14-17 Wells Street, London W1T 3PD, UK
Tel: (020) 7255 1071. Fax: (020) 7323 9184.
Opening hours: Mon-Fri 1000-1800; 1000-1300 (visa section).
British Embassy
PO Box 45, 301-308 Office Building, Four Points Ak Altin Hotel, 744014 Ashgabat, Turkmenistan
Tel: (12) 363 462-4 *or* 498. Fax: (12) 363 465.
E-mail: beasb@online.tm (general) *or* beasbtrade@online.tm (commercial section) *or* beasbppa@online.tm (press and public affairs).
Website: www.britishembassy.gov.uk/turkmenistan
Embassy of Turkmenistan
2207 Massachusetts Avenue, NW, Washington, DC 20008, USA
Tel: (202) 588 1500. Fax: (202) 588 0697.
E-mail: turkmen@mindspring.com
Website: www.turkmenistanembassy.org
Embassy of the United States of America
9 1984/Pushkin Street, 744000 Ashgabat, Turkmenistan
Tel: (12) 350 045.
Fax: (12) 392 614 *or* 350 049 (consular section).
E-mail: irc-ashgabat@iatp.edu.tm
Website: www.usemb-ashgabat.rpo.at
The Canadian Embassy in Ankara deals with enquiries relating to Turkmenistan (see *Turkey* section).

General Information

AREA: 488,100 sq km (188,456 sq miles).
POPULATION: 4,794,000 (official estimate 2002).
POPULATION DENSITY: 9.8 per sq km.
CAPITAL: Ashgabat. **Population:** 605,000 (official estimate 1999).

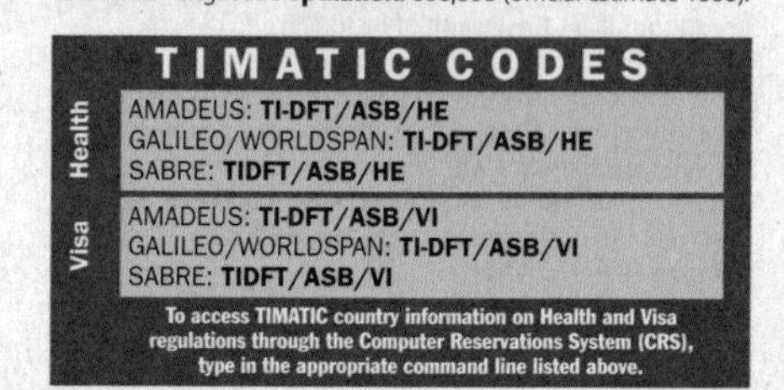
TIMATIC CODES

Health	AMADEUS: **TI-DFT/ASB/HE** GALILEO/WORLDSPAN: **TI-DFT/ASB/HE** SABRE: **TIDFT/ASB/HE**
Visa	AMADEUS: **TI-DFT/ASB/VI** GALILEO/WORLDSPAN: **TI-DFT/ASB/VI** SABRE: **TIDFT/ASB/VI**

To access TIMATIC country information on Health and Visa regulations through the Computer Reservations System (CRS), type in the appropriate command line listed above.

GEOGRAPHY: Turkmenistan shares borders with Kazakhstan to the north, Uzbekistan to the east, Afghanistan to the southeast and Iran to the south. To the west is the Caspian Sea. Nearly 80 per cent of the country is taken up by the Kara-Kum (Black Sand) Desert, the largest in the CIS. The longest irrigation canal in the world stretches 1100km (687 miles), from the Amu-Darya River in the east, through Ashgabat, before being piped the rest of the way to the Caspian Sea.
GOVERNMENT: Republic. Gained independence from the Soviet Union in 1991. **Head of State and Government:** President Saparmyrat Niyazov (Türkmenbashy) since 1992.
LANGUAGE: Turkmen is the official state language, and is closer to Turkish, Azeri and Crimean Tartar than those of its neighbours Uzbekistan and Kazakhstan. The Turkmen script was changed from Latin to Cyrillic in 1940, but the process of changing back to the Turkish version of the Latin script is underway.
RELIGION: Predominantly Sunni Muslim with a small Russian Orthodox minority. Turkmenistan shares the Central Asian Sufi tradition.
TIME: GMT + 5.
ELECTRICITY: 220 volts AC, 50Hz. Round two-pin continental plugs are standard.
COMMUNICATIONS: Telephone: Country code: 993. Area code for Ashgabat: 12. Outgoing international code: 810. **Mobile telephone:** GSM 900/1800 network covers Ashgabat area. Operated by *Altyn Asyr MC* and *BCTI*. **Fax:** Services are available in the main hotels for residents only. **Internet:** ISPs include *Turkmenistan Online* (website: www.online.tm). **Telegram:** Services are available from post offices in large towns. . **Post:** Letters to Western Europe and the USA can take between two weeks and two months. Stamped envelopes can be bought from post offices. Mail addresses should be laid out in the following order: country, postcode, city, street, house number and lastly the person's name. Post office hours: Mon-Fri 0900-1800. The main Post Office in Ashgabat is open until 1900. **Press:** The press in Turkmenistan is still censored. The main newspapers in Ashgabat are *Turkmenistan* and *Vatan* (both in Turkmen) and *Neitralnyi Turkmenistan* (Russian). **Radio:** BBC World Service (website: www.bbc.co.uk/worldservice) and Voice of America (website: www.voa.gov) can be received. From time to time the frequencies change.

Passport/Visa

	Passport Required?	Visa Required?	Return Ticket Required?
Full British	Yes	Yes	No
Australian	Yes	Yes	No
Canadian	Yes	Yes	No
USA	Yes	Yes	No
Other EU	Yes	Yes	No
Japanese	Yes	Yes	No

Note: *Regulations and requirements may be subject to change at short notice, and you are advised to contact the appropriate diplomatic or consular authority before finalising travel arrangements. Details of these may be found at the head of this country's entry. Any numbers in the chart refer to the footnotes below.*

Note: Visa regulations within the CIS are liable to change at short notice. Prospective travellers are advised to contact the nearest Turkmenistan Embassy well in advance of intended date of departure.
PASSPORTS: Valid passport required by all.
VISAS: Visa required by all.
Note: Special permission must be sought by those wishing to visit border zones.
Types of visa and cost: Dependent upon nationality and duration of stay, contact the Embassy for details of prices (see *Contact Addresses* section).
Validity: Subject to the nature of the visit and the discretion of the authorities in Turkmenistan.
Application to: Consulate (or Consular section at Embassy); see *Contact Addresses* section.
Note: a) For those coming from countries without Embassies or Consulates of Turkmenistan, entry visas may be obtained for a maximum of 10 days on arrival, provided holding an invitation from a company in Turkmenistan. (b) Tourists should normally book through a recognised tour operator, who will obtain visas on their behalf. (c) Visitors intending to stay for more than three months must produce a certificate stating that they are HIV-negative.
Application requirements: (a) Two completed application forms. (b) Two passport-size photos. (c) Passport with at least one blank page, valid for six months from date of departure from Turkmenistan. (d) Covering letter explaining purpose of visit. (e) Fee. (f) Stamped, self-addressed envelope. (g) Letter of invitation approved by the Ministry of Foreign Affairs in Turkmenistan (not needed by visitors seeking a transit visa only).
Working days required: Three to seven.
Temporary residence: Applications for temporary residence to carry out business are handled by the Interior Ministry; those wishing to obtain temporary residence for other reasons should apply to the Consular Affairs Office at the Foreign Ministry.

Money

Currency: 1 Manat (TMM) = 100 tenge. Notes are in denominations of TMM10,000, 5000, 1000, 500, 100, 50, 10, 5 and 1. Coins are in denominations of 50, 20, 10, 5 and 1 tenge.
Currency exchange: The preferred hard currency is US Dollars and visitors carrying other currencies may find it hard to change them. It is advisable to take new, clean US Dollar notes in small denominations. Foreign currency can be changed at banks and major hotels. Foreigners are expected to pay all travel and hotel bills in hard currency, and prices bear little relation to what locals are expected to pay. Most packages are all-inclusive and extra payment for accommodation and meals is unnecessary.
Credit & debit cards: Not generally accepted.
Travellers cheques: Should be in US currency, but are generally not accepted.
Currency restrictions: The import and export of local currency is prohibited for foreigners. Import of foreign currency is unlimited subject to declaration, and export is limited to the amount declared on import.
Exchange rate indicators: The exchange rate was US$1 = TMM1000 (official) or TMM3000 (commercial) in April 1996, when it was announced that the official rate would be discontinued. From then on, a unified exchange rate was introduced for all transactions, determined by trading on the Turkmen Interbank Currency Exchange, which commenced operations in 1996.

Date	Feb '04	May '04	Aug '04	Nov '04
£1.00=	8790.24	8760.38	9276.44	9606.00
$1.00=	4973.34	4991.30	5076.45	5140.38

Banking hours: Mon-Fri 0930-1730

Duty Free

Import regulations in Turkmenistan are subject to change at short notice, and travellers should contact the embassy before departure for up-to-date information.
The following goods may be imported into Turkmenistan by passengers aged 16 and over:
200 cigarettes or 200g of tobacco; 2l of any alcoholic beverage (passengers aged 21 and over); personal belongings up to a reasonable value.
Note: On entering the country, tourists must complete a customs declaration form which must be retained until departure. This allows the import of articles intended for personal use, including currency and valuables which must be registered on the declaration form. Customs inspection can be long and detailed. It is advisable when shopping to ask for a certificate from the shop which states that goods have been paid for in hard currency. Presentation of such certificates should speed up customs formalities.
Prohibited items: Military weapons, ammunition and narcotics may not be imported or exported. Works of art and antiques may not be exported (unless permission has been granted by the Ministry of Culture).

Public Holidays

2005: Jan 1 New Year's Day. **Jan 12** Remembrance Day. **Jan 21** Kurban Bairam (Feast of the Sacrifice). **Feb 18** President's Birthday. **Feb 19** National Flag Day. **Mar 8** International Women's Day. **Mar 20** Novruz Bairam (Turkmen New Year). **May 9** Victory Day. **May 18** Constitution Day. **Jun 21** Day of Election of First President. **Oct 6** Remembrance Day (Anniversary of the 1948 Earthquake). **Oct 28** Independence Day. **Nov 3-5** Ramadan Bairam (End of Ramadan). **Dec 12** Neutrality Day.
2006: Jan 1 New Year's Day. **Jan 12** Remembrance Day. **Jan 13** Kurban Bairam (Feast of the Sacrifice). **Feb 18** President's Birthday. **Feb 19** National Flag Day. **Mar 8** International Women's Day. **Mar 20** Novruz Bairam (Turkmen New Year). **May 9** Victory Day. **May 18** Constitution Day. **Jun 21** Day of Election of First President. **Oct 6** Remembrance Day (Anniversary of the 1948 Earthquake). **Oct 22-24** Ramadan Bairam (End of Ramadan). **Oct 28** Independence Day. **Dec 12** Neutrality Day.
Note: Muslim festivals (End of Ramadan and Feast of the Sacrifice) are timed according to the phases of the moon and the dates given are approximations. For more information, see the *World of Islam* appendix.

Health

	Special Precautions?	Certificate Required?
Yellow Fever	No	No
Cholera	No	No
Typhoid & Polio	1	N/A
Malaria	2	N/A

Note: *Regulations and requirements may be subject to change at short notice, and you are advised to contact your doctor well in advance of your intended date of departure. Any numbers in the chart refer to the footnotes below.*

1: Vaccination against typhoid is advised.
2: Malaria risk exclusively in the benign (*P vivax*) form exists from June to October in some villages located in the southeastern part of the country, mainly in the Mary district.
Food & drink: All water should be regarded as a potential health risk. Water used for drinking, brushing teeth or making ice should have been boiled or otherwise sterilised. Milk is pasteurised and dairy products are safe for consumption. Only eat well-cooked meat and fish, preferably served hot. Pork, salad and mayonnaise may carry increased risk. Vegetables should be cooked and fruit peeled.
Other risks: *Diphtheria* and *tuberculosis* outbreaks are reported, and suitable precautions should be taken. *Hepatitis A, B* and *E* occur. *Plague* and *trachoma* occur rarely. Because the climate is very hot and dry, precautions should also be taken against *dehydration*. It is important to drink plenty of (boiled or bottled) water.
Rabies is present. For those at high risk, vaccination should be considered. If you are bitten, seek medical advice without delay. For more information, consult the *Health* appendix.
Health care: Medical insurance, including cover for emergency repatriation, is highly recommended. Medical facilities are poor, high levels of disease have been reported. Travellers are advised to take a well-equipped first aid kit with them containing basic medicines and any prescriptions that they may need.

Travel - International

AIR: The national airline is *Turkmenistan Airlines (T5)*. There are international connections to Abu Dhabi (UAE), Birmingham (UK), Damascus (Syrian Arab Republic), Delhi (India), Istanbul (Turkey), Karachi (Pakistan), Kyiv (Ukraine), London (UK) and Moscow (Russian Federation). There are weekly flights between London and Ashgabat. Ashgabat is also served by *Asseman Airlines* from Tehran, by *Lufthansa* from Frankfurt/M and by *Turkish Airlines* from Istanbul. There are connections within the CIS to Moscow and St Petersburg (Russian Federation), Kyiv (Ukraine) and Tashkent (Uzbekistan). All flight tickets bought by foreigners within Turkmenistan must be paid for in hard currency. The prices tend to be 10 times as much as those that locals pay.
Approximate flight times: From *London* to Ashbagat is six hours 30 minutes, from *Karachi* is four hours 30 minutes, from *Moscow* is three hours 30 minutes, from *Istanbul* is two hours 30 minutes, from *Abu Dhabi* is two hours, from *Tashkent* is two hours, from *Kyiv* is two hours and from *Tehran* is one hour.
International airports: *Ashgabat Airport (ASB)* is approximately 13km (8 miles) northwest of the city centre. A new terminal building has resulted in an increase of capacity. The airport is served by buses and taxis.
Departure tax: US$25. Nationals of CIS countries pay US$15 and nationals of Turkmenistan pay US$5.
SEA: There are ferries to Turkmenbashi (formerly Krasnovodsk) from Baku (Azerbaijan) and an irregular service to Astrakhan (Russian Federation). It is theoretically possible to travel from Moscow to Turkmenbashi via the Volga River and the Caspian Sea without setting foot on dry land.
RAIL: The *Trans-Caspian Railway* connects Turkmenistan with the rest of the Central Asian republics and thence to Moscow and the rest of the CIS. The terminus is in Turkmenbashi on the Caspian Sea, from where it runs through Ashgabat before it crosses into Uzbekistan near the city of Chardzhou.
Approximate rail times: From Turkmenbashi to Tashkent is 24 hours, to Dushanbe is 36 hours and to Moscow is three days. There is a rail link to the Iranian network, enabling train travel from Turkmenistan to Turkey (Istanbul).
ROAD: Turkmenistan is connected by road to Kazakhstan, Uzbekistan and to Mashad and Tehran in Iran. The crossing into Iran is only open to nationals of the CIS and Iran. **Bus:** Services are available to the capitals of the neighbouring republics, and north across the Kara-Kum desert to Kunya-Urgench with connections to Urgench and Khiva in Uzbekistan. A service also runs between Ashgabat and Mashhad (eastern Iran).

Travel - Internal

AIR: *Turkmenistan Airlines* runs regular flights between Ashgabat, Chardzhou, Dashoguz, Mary, Turkmenbashi and Turkmenabat, and once daily flights to Kerki (far east) and Balkanabat. All flight tickets have to be paid for in local currency.
Approximate flight times: From Ashgabat to Chardzhou is one hour 30 minutes and to Mary is one hour.
RAIL: There is a daytime and overnight train between Ashgabat and Turkmenbashi; two daily overnight trains to Turkmenabat, one continuing to Dashgouz; and a daily overnight service between Ashgabat and Gushgi via Mary (although Gushgi is off limits due to its border with Afghanistan). The *Trans-Caspian Railway* runs from Turkmenbashi (formerly Krasnovodsk) in the west, through Ashgabat and Mary to Chardzhou in the east before continuing to Bukhara in Uzbekistan.
ROAD: Traffic drives on the right. Conditions can be dangerous. The main road in Turkmenistan runs along the route of the *Trans-Caspian Railway* (see above). There is also a road that runs north from Ashgabat to Tashauz and Kunya-Urgench before crossing into Uzbekistan. This road crosses 500km (311 miles) of the Kara-Kum desert. **Bus:** Cheap services are available within all the major towns. Modern and comfortable long-distance buses also operate to Dashgouz, Mary, Turkmenabashi and Turkmenabat from Ashgabat. **Taxi:** Taxis and chauffeur-driven cars for hire can be found in all major towns. Many are unlicensed and travellers are advised to agree the fare in advance. As many of the street names have changed since independence, it is also advisable to ascertain both the old and the new street names when asking directions. **Car hire:** Self-drive hire is available from a few large hotels. Traffic regulations: Drinking and driving is strictly forbidden. **Documentation:** An International Driving Permit, or national licence with authorised translation, is required.

Accommodation

HOTELS: There are no restrictions on where foreigners can stay in Turkmenistan. When Turkmenistan gained independence, there was an acute shortage of hotel accommodation, a situation which the Turkmen are working hard to rectify, with feverish hotel construction underway in Ashgabat. A row of luxury hotels has recently been built on the edge of town along a road known locally as the 'Miracle Mile'. These are small hotels with between 15 to 40 rooms that are owned and run by various ministries and governmental organisations. Architectural motifs are mosques, palaces and fortresses. Every provincial centre has at least one hotel, but visitors should not expect Western standards of comfort and amenities. The exception is a new hotel which recently opened in Turkmenbashi; however, as it only has 40 rooms, it is advisable to contact a recognised Turkmen tour company for a reservation. Accommodation and services in hotels are payable in local currency or US Dollars.
REST HOUSES: *Dom Otdykha* (literally 'rest houses') were built on the shores of the Caspian Sea by co-operatives and other concerns for fatigued workers. It is sometimes possible for travellers to obtain accommodation in them.
CAMPING: There are campsites on the shores of the Caspian Sea, and the facilities are gradually improving.

Resorts & Excursions

Turkmenistan's harsh desert conditions and terrain mean that tourism has been relatively undeveloped. Almost all the attractions lie around the fringes of the desert and in ancient ruins such as Merv (now Mary).
ASHGABAT: The capital, on the southern rim of the **Kara-Kum** desert, is a modern city. It replaced the one founded in 1881, which was destroyed in an earthquake in 1948 that measured 10.5 on the Richter scale, killed 30 per cent of the population and razed the city to the ground. Some of the more recent additions to the capital include the **Arch of Neutrality**, a 75m- (246ft-) high monument with a revolving 12m- (39ft-) tall golden statue of President Niyazov at its peak. At the base of the monument, there is a cafe and lifts which can be taken to the viewing platforms. Nearby stands the magnificent white marble **Palace of Turkmenbashi**, decorated with gold-mirrored glass together with an Islamic-motif dome. There are a number of museums, including a fine-art museum and the **National Museum of Turkmenistan**. There is a small carpet museum attached to the carpet factory on Ulitsa Kuragli (formerly Piervomaiskaya), which houses the world's largest handwoven rug. The **Tolkuchka bazaar** (Sunday market) in Ashgabat is the best place anywhere to buy Turkmen carpets, mistakenly called Bukhara carpets in the West.
Excursions: Close to Ashgabat are the remains of **Old Nisa**, the capital of the Parthian kings who ruled from the third century BC to the third century AD over an empire which included Iraq and stretched as far as the Syrian Arab Republic. The national horse stud, **Turkmenbashi Stud Farm**, is 10km (6 miles) from Ashgabat and pure-bred **Akhal-Teke** horses can be viewed here. Trips are best organised through a local travel agency.
The modern town of **Anau**, once the site of the destroyed 15th-century city, is 20km (12 miles) east of Ashgabat. The ruins of the famous mosque (revered for its striking mosaic tiles and 8m- (26ft-) long dragons) can still be seen.
Chuli is a popular mountain resort reached by taxi or private car through a picturesque gorge. Climbing and hiking trips can be arranged, and visitors can stay here.
A pleasant day trip is to **Bakharden**, 90km (56 miles) west of Ashgabat. The underground mineral lake (known in Turkmen as **Kov Ata** which means 'father of lakes') is fed by hot springs and has a constant temperature of 37°C (97°F). Bathing is permitted although there is an admission fee. Accommodation is not available.
MARY: Due east of Ashgabat, Mary is Turkmenistan's second city. A large industrial centre, Mary has little to recommend it other than its interesting **Regional Museum**. However, it lies near the remains of the city of **Merv**, which was once the second city of Islam and known as the 'Queen of Cities' until Ghengis Khan's son, Toloi, reduced it to rubble and reportedly killed a million of its inhabitants in 1221. The ruins of Merv and of the many that both preceded it and succeeded it are spread over a large area. Most of what remains are the brick-built mausolea of rulers and holy men - including the impressive **Mausoleum of Sultan Sanjar**, completed in 1140. Time, weather and invasions have taken their toll on the mud-built cities of the Turkmen.
DASHGOUZ & KONYE-URGENCH: Dashgouz is the largest city in the northern region of Turkmenistan, on a direct train route, 500km (311 miles) from Ashgabat, across the Kara-Kum desert. Although there are a few places to stay and eat, the main sights lie outside the city. The ruins of **Konye-Urgench**, an ancient fortress town with relics dating back to the 14th century, are well worth visiting. Entry is approximately US$2, payable in Manat. Things to see include the **Kutlug Timur Minaret**, one of the tallest minarets in Asia at 67m (220ft) high and built in the 1320s; the **Sultan Tekesh**, **Turabeg Khanym** and **Najm-ed-din Kubra Mausoleums**.
TURKMENBASHI: Situated to the west of Ashgabat, Turkmenbashi was known as Krasnovodsk, but it was renamed in honour of President Saparmurat Niyazov, who has been given the title 'Turkmenbashi' or 'leader of all the Turkmen'. Situated on the shores of the Caspian Sea, it is a Russian creation, built as a bridgehead for the campaign to subdue Central Asia, and later to become the terminal for the **Trans-Caspian Railway**. There are some panoramic views from the mountainside surrounding the town and visitors can enjoy some good beaches and swimming a little further out of town. The **Museum of Regional History and Natural History** makes an interesting visit.

THE SILK ROAD

This ancient trading route was used by silk merchants from the second century AD until its decline in the 14th century, and is open in parts to tourists, stretching from northern China, through bleak and foreboding desert and mountainous terrain to the ports on either the Caspian or Mediterranean Sea. For further details of the route, see *The Silk Road* in the *China* section.
Among the many silk route attractions worth seeing in Turkmenistan are the vibrant Sunday **Tolkuchka market** in Ashgabat (selling such wares as traditional carpets, camels and pistachio nuts), the historical silk road cities of **Konye-Urgench** and **Merv** (including **Kyz-Kala**, a windowless castle known locally as the 'House of the Maiden Tears' and the mausoleum of Mohammed Ibn-Zeida) and the **Kugitang Nature Reserve** which reportedly bears impressions of hundreds of dinosaur footprints. Travel along the silk road can be quite difficult due to the terrain, harsh climate and lack of developed infrastructure. Visitors to the region are advised to travel with an organised tour company or travel agent.

Sport & Activities

Horseriding: Turkmenistan is home to the *Akhal-Teke* horse, a special breed known for its speed and intelligence. These horses occupy a special place in Turkmen culture and are a source of great national pride. An old Turkmen saying goes, 'Getting up in the morning, greet your father and then see your horse'. Rides in the countryside can be arranged through local tour operators or through travel agents specialising in Turkmenistan. The vast open spaces make Turkmenistan very good for riding, though the Akhal-Teke horses are suitable for experienced riders only. Rides can be done just outside Ashgabat through the gorges of the Firuza River and to the local hot springs, and in other parts of the country.
Horse racing: In spring and autumn, horse races are held at the *Hippodrome* in Ashgabat, and 10km (6 miles) south of Ashgabat is the *Turkmenbashi Stud Farm* where the Akhal-Teke horses are bred (see *Resorts & Excursions* section).

Social Profile

FOOD & DRINK: Turkmen food is similar to that of the rest of Central Asia. There are a number of good Western-standard restaurants in Ashgabat, although they rarely have an extensive menu. *Plov* - pronounced 'plof' - is the staple food for everyday (but is also served at celebrations) and consists of chunks of mutton, shredded yellow turnip and rice fried in a large wok. *Shashlyk* (skewered chunks of mutton grilled over charcoal which come with raw sliced onions) and *lipioshka* (rounds of unleavened bread) are served in restaurants and are often sold in the street, but the quality can be variable. Manty are larger noodle dumplings filled with meat. *Shorpa* is a meat and vegetable soup. There are, however, a number of dishes that are particularly characteristic of Turkmenistan: *ka'urma* is mutton deep-fried in its own fat and *churban churpa* is mutton fat dissolved in green tea. *Ishkiykli* are dough balls filled with meat and onion which are traditionally cooked in sand that has been heated by a fire. On the shores of the Caspian Sea, seafood is often substituted for mutton in traditional dishes such as plov. In the west of Turkmenistan, there is a speciality in which mutton is roasted in a clay oven fired with aromatic woods.
In general, hotel food shows strong Russian influence: *borcht* is cabbage soup, *entrecôte* is a well-done steak, *cutlet* are grilled meat balls, and *strogan* is the local equivalent of beef Stroganoff. *Pirmeni*, originating in Ukraine, are small boiled dumplings of meat and vegetables similar to ravioli, sometimes served in a vegetable soup. Green tea is very popular and can be obtained almost anywhere. Beer, wine, vodka, brandy and sparkling wine (*shampanski*) are all widely available in restaurants. *Kefir*, a thick drinking yoghurt, is often served with breakfast.
NIGHTLIFE: Ashgabat has an opera and ballet theatre, which shows both Russian and European works and a drama theatre. There are also a few restaurants offering dancing.
SHOPPING: The Sunday market is the best place in the world to buy the misleadingly named Bukhara rugs, which are actually made in Turkmenistan. There is a shop in the Art Gallery which sells traditional Turkmen handicrafts, silver and costumes including the distinctive Turkmen sheepskin hats. The central bazaar in Ashgabat is a good place to buy food and curiosities. **Shopping hours:** Mon-Fri 0900-1800. Bazaars open at dawn.
SPECIAL EVENTS: A number of festivals in Turkmenistan provide interesting spectacles for visitors. The following is a selection of special events occurring in Turkmenistan in 2005:
Apr 24 *Akilteken Day*, celebration of the Akilteken horse with parades and races. **May 29** *Day of the Turkmen Carpet*. **Nov** *Harvest Festival*.
SOCIAL CONVENTIONS: *Lipioshka* (bread) should never be laid upside down, and it is normal to remove shoes, but not socks, when entering someone's house. Shorts are rarely seen in Turkmenistan and, if worn by females, are likely to provoke unwelcome attention from the local male population.

Business Profile

ECONOMY: Although 90 per cent of the land is occupied by the Kara-Kum desert, agriculture is important to the Turkmen economy. Substantial quantities of cotton - the country is the world's 10th-largest producer - are also produced under ecologically ruinous schemes established during the Soviet era. Grain, fruit and vegetables are widely grown and livestock breeding is an important source of employment. The other mainstay of the economy and its best prospect for the future is an abundance of oil and natural gas deposits, the scale of which rivals anything in the Persian and Mexican Gulfs. New pipelines are planned to supplement the sole existing one, which transports the products via Russia. Other commercially viable reserves include bromine, iodine salts and various other minerals.
Most of Turkmenistan's industry is devoted to processing the country's principal raw materials: textiles are a key export industry and much of the extracted oil is refined within the country. Oil and gas account for 85 per cent of Turkmenistan's export income (under long-term contracts, 80 per cent of the gas goes to the Ukraine while 60 per cent of the oil is bought by Italy).
As one of the poorest republics of the former Soviet Union, Turkmenistan suffered considerable economic disruption and hardship after its demise in 1991 (GDP declined by 10 per cent per year between 1993 and 1998); the increasing

inability of many of its former trade partners to pay for its products has also caused serious difficulties. The Government responded by seeking out new markets. In 1992, Turkmenistan joined the IMF and the World Bank, then the European Bank for Reconstruction and Development (as a 'Country of Operation') and the Islamic Development Bank. The following year a new national currency, the Manat, was introduced. In 1996, the Government introduced an economic reform programme aimed at controlling persistent inflation and promoting foreign investment, especially in the oil and gas sector. This has met with some success; inflation is now 14 per cent, while current annual GDP growth is over 10 per cent. The government has also concentrated resources in developing Turkmenistan's previously poor infrastructure, especially the road network. Some aspects of the reform programme have been delayed, including land reform in which the major role was to be assumed by the private sector. Turkmenistan is a member of the Economic Co-operation Organisation, which brings together the former republics of the southern Soviet Union with Romania, Bulgaria, Albania, Greece and Turkey.

BUSINESS: The Government is particularly interested in encouraging foreign investment in a number of areas, including oil and gas production and refining; agricultural production and processing (particularly in cotton); consumer goods; export-orientated products; research and development; environmental protection and infrastructure. The Turkmen government has put a number of measures in place to encourage foreign investment. Free Enterprise Economic Zones - one in each of the eight *velayat* (regions) - have been created with special incentives for companies that invest in them. These include: no import duties, a three-year tax holiday from the start of production, with a further 13 years of reduced taxes; full-profit repatriation and a swifter licensing procedure. Concerns which are 100 per cent foreign owned must be sited in Free Enterprise Economic Zones, but joint ventures may be set up anywhere. All foreign investments are protected by government guarantee from expropriation. All foreign companies and individuals wishing to invest in Turkmenistan must go through the Commission for International Economic Affairs of the Office of the President of Turkmenistan. Business is conducted formally and smart dress is required. **Office hours:** Mon-Fri 0900-1800.

COMMERCIAL INFORMATION: The following organisation can offer advice: Chamber of Commerce and Industry, B Karryev Street 17, Ashgabat 744000 (tel: (12) 354 717 *or* 355 594; fax: 351 352 *or* 355 381; e-mail: expo@online.tm). Information can also be obtained from the US Department of Commerce, Business Information Service for the Newly Independent States, USA Trade Center, Stop R-Binis, Ronald Reagan Building, 1401 Constitution Avenue, NW, Washington, DC 20230, USA (tel: (202) 482 4655; fax: (202) 482 2293; e-mail: bisnis@ita.doc.gov; website: www.bisnis.doc.gov).

Climate

Turkmenistan has an extreme continental climate: temperatures in Ashgabat vary between 46°C (114°F) in summer and -5°C (23°F) in winter, although it has been known to reach -22°C (-8°F) in extremity. Temperatures in the desert in summer can reach 50°C (122°F) during the day before falling rapidly at night. During the winter, it can reach -10° to -15°C (14° to 15°F).

Required clothing: For those intending to visit the desert in summer, lightweights are vital for the day with warmer clothing for those intending to spend the night in the open. Heavyweights should be taken for winter visits.

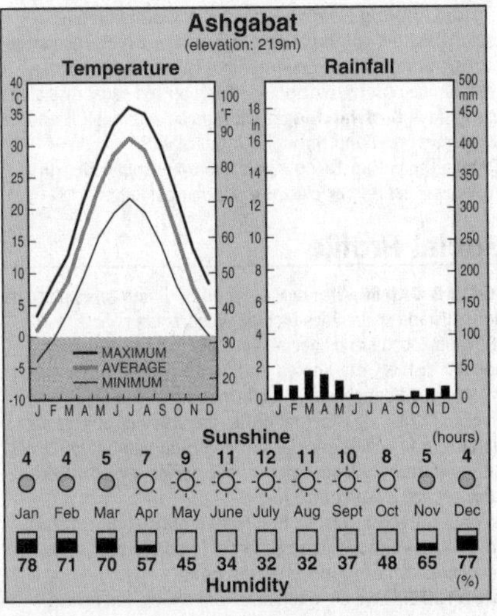

Turks & Caicos Islands

LATEST TRAVEL ADVICE CONTACTS

British Foreign and Commonwealth Office
Tel: (0870) 606 0290 Website: www.fco.gov.uk

US Department of State
Website: http://travel.state.gov/travel

Canadian Department of Foreign Affairs and Int'l Trade
Tel: (1 800) 267 8376 Website: www.dfait-maeci.gc.ca

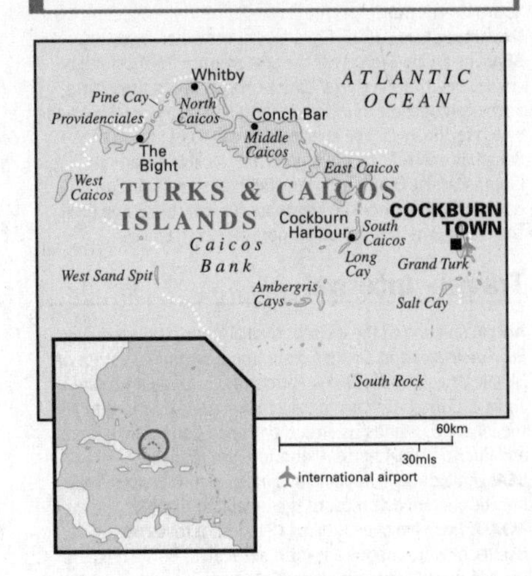

Location: Caribbean, southeast of The Bahamas.

Country dialling code: 1 649.

The Turks & Caicos Islands are a British Overseas Territory and are formally represented abroad by British diplomatic missions.

Turks & Caicos Islands Tourist Board
PO Box 128, Front Street, Grand Turk, Turks & Caicos Islands, British West Indies
Tel: 946 2321. Fax: 946 2733.
E-mail: tci.tourism@tciway.tc
Website: www.turksandcaicostourism.com

Governor's Office
Waterloo, Grand Turk
Tel: (649) 946 2309/2910. Fax: (649) 946 2903/2886.
E-mail: Governor_Office@gov.tc

Overseas Territories Department (Turks & Caicos)
Foreign & Commonwealth Office, King Charles Street, London SW1A 2AP
Tel: (020) 7008 3596 *or* 7798 9342. Fax: (020) 7798 9348.
E-mail: knight_tracyann@yahoo.co.uk

Turks & Caicos Tourist Information Office
Mitre House, 66 Abbey Road, Bush Hill Park, Enfield, Middlesex EN1 2QE, UK
Tel: (020) 8350 1017. Fax: (020) 8350 1011.
E-mail: mki@ttg.co.uk
Website: www.turksandcaicostourism.com

The Canadian High Commission in Kingston deals with enquiries relating to the Turks and Caicos Islands (see *Jamaica* section).

General Information

AREA: 430 sq km (166 sq miles).
POPULATION: 19,000 (official estimate 2001).
POPULATION DENSITY: 44.2 per sq km.
CAPITAL: Cockburn Town (on Grand Turk). **Population:** 2500 (official estimate 1987).
GEOGRAPHY: The Turks & Caicos Islands are an archipelago of more than 30 islands forming the southeastern end of the Bahamas chain. There are two principal groups, each surrounded by a continuous coral reef. Caicos is the larger group and includes Providenciales, Middle (or Grand) Caicos, and the islands of North, South, East and West Caicos, plus numerous small cays, some of which are inhabited. The Turks group, separated by a 35km- (22 mile-) wide channel of water, consists of Grand Turk, Salt Cay and a number of small uninhabited cays.
GOVERNMENT: British Overseas Territory since 1670. Gained internal autonomy in 1962. **Head of State:** HM Queen Elizabeth II, represented locally by Governor Jim Poston since 2002. **Head of Government:** Chief Minister Michael Eugene Misick since 2003.
LANGUAGE: The official language is English. Some Creole is spoken.
RELIGION: Roman Catholic, Anglican, Methodist, Baptist, Seventh Day Adventist and Pentecostal.
TIME: GMT - 5 (GMT - 4 from first Sunday in April to Saturday before last Sunday in October).
ELECTRICITY: 120/240 volts AC, 60 Hz.
COMMUNICATIONS: Telephone: IDD is available. Country code: 1 649. Outgoing international code: 001. There is a good communications network run by *Cable & Wireless Ltd*, with automatic exchange on all the islands. The local telephone directory lists charges for international calls. There is a 10 per cent tax on all calls. Public card-phones are in operation on all the islands; phonecards are available from *Cable & Wireless* and outlets near phone booths. Cheap rates are in operation Mon-Fri 1900-0600 and Sat-Sun all day. **Mobile telephone:** GSM 850 available, operated by *Cable & Wireless West Indies LTD*. **Fax:** All the islands have services. **Internet:** ISPs include *Cable & Wireless* (website: www.cw.tc). Public access is available in Internet kiosks located at the airport and in Internet cafes around the islands. **Post:** The General Post Office is on Grand Turk, with sub-offices in South Caicos, Salt Cay and Providenciales. Airmail to Western Europe takes 5 days. Post office hours: Mon-Thurs 0800-1630, Fri 0800-1600. **Press:** The *Turks & Caicos Free Press*, *Turks & Caicos Press* and *The Turks & Caicos Weekly News* are published weekly, and *The Times of the Islands Magazine* quarterly. *Where, When, How* is a travel magazine which appears monthly.
Radio: BBC World Service (website: www.bbc.co.uk/worldservice) and Voice of America (website: www.voa.gov) can be received. From time to time the frequencies change and the most up-to-date can be found online.

TIMATIC CODES

Health
AMADEUS: **TI-DFT/GDT/HE**
GALILEO/WORLDSPAN: **TI-DFT/GDT/HE**
SABRE: **TIDFT/GDT/HE**

Visa
AMADEUS: **TI-DFT/GDT/VI**
GALILEO/WORLDSPAN: **TI-DFT/GDT/VI**
SABRE: **TIDFT/GDT/VI**

To access TIMATIC country information on Health and Visa regulations through the Computer Reservations System (CRS), type in the appropriate command line listed above.

Passport/Visa

	Passport Required?	Visa Required?	Return Ticket Required?
Full British	Yes	No	Yes
Australian	Yes	No	Yes
Canadian	1	No	Yes
USA	1	No	Yes
Other EU	Yes	No/2	Yes
Japanese	Yes	No	Yes

Note: Regulations and requirements may be subject to change at short notice, and you are advised to contact the appropriate diplomatic or consular authority before finalising travel arrangements. Details of these may be found at the head of this country's entry. Any numbers in the chart refer to the footnotes below.

PASSPORTS: Passport valid for a minimum of six months required by all except:
1. nationals of Canada and the USA, provided holding proof of identity (birth certificate and photo ID).
VISAS: Required by all except the following for stays of up to 90 days:
(a) nationals of countries referred to in the chart above (**2.** except nationals of Estonia, Latvia and Lithuania who *do* require a visa);
(b) nationals of Commonwealth countries;
(c) nationals of Anguilla, Argentina, Bahrain, Bangladesh, Bolivia, Brazil, Bulgaria, Chile, China (PR), Congo (Dem Rep), Costa Rica, Côte d'Ivoire, Ecuador, Hungary, Iceland, Israel, Korea (Dem Rep), Korea (Rep), Kuwait, Liechtenstein, Mexico, Monaco, Nicaragua, Norway, Oman, Panama, Paraguay, Peru, Poland, Qatar, San Marino, Saudi Arabia, Senegal, Surinam, Switzerland, the Syrian Arab Republic, Taiwan (China), Tunisia, Turkey, United Arab Emirates, United States Pacific Territories, Uruguay, Vatican City, Venezuela, Vietnam, Western Samoa and Yemen;
(d) most transit passengers continuing their journey by the same or first connecting aircraft, provided holding onward or return documentation and not leaving the airport.
Nationals of a few countries may require a transit visa. Check with the UK Passport Office before departure.
Note: Nationals of Estonia, Latvia, Lithuania officially still require visas to enter Turks & Caicos; however, if their passport firmly states that they are a national of the European Union, they *may* be permitted visa-free entry, at the discretion of the Immigration Officer.
Types of visa and cost: *Tourist*, *Business* and *Transit*: £28.
Validity: Three months.
Application to: UK Passport Agency; see *Contact Addresses* section.
Application requirements: (a) Passport with six months' remaining validity. (b) Return or onward ticket. (c) Evidence of sufficient funds for the duration of stay.
Working days required: Applications generally have to be

A B C D E F G H I J K L M N O P Q R S T U V W X Y Z

referred to Grand Turk, which takes one month.
Temporary residence: Work and residence permits are required; apply to the Chief Immigration Officer, Government Buildings, Grand Turk.

Money

Currency: US Dollar (US$) = 100 cents. Notes are in denominations of US$100, 50, 20, 10, 5, 2 and 1. Coins are in denominations of 50, 25, 10, 5 and 1 cents.
Credit & debit cards: MasterCard and Visa are widely accepted. Check with your credit or debit card company for details of merchant acceptability and other services which may be available.
Travellers cheques: Accepted by most hotels, shops, restaurants, banks and taxi services.
Currency restrictions: None.
Exchange rate indicators: The following figures are included as a guide to the movements of the US Dollar against Sterling:

Date	Feb '04	May '04	Aug '04	Nov '04
£1.00=	1.82	1.78	1.84	1.89

Banking hours: Mon-Thurs 0830-1430, Fri 0830-1630.

Duty Free

The following items may be imported into the Turks & Caicos Islands without incurring customs duty: 200 cigarettes or 50 cigars; 1.13l of spirits or wine or perfume for personal use.
Restricted items: Spearguns and Hawaiian slings. Firearms require a police permit.
Prohibited items: Drugs and pornography.

Public Holidays

2005: Jan 1 New Year's Day. **Mar 14** Commonwealth Day. **Mar 25** Good Friday. **Mar 28** Easter Monday. **May 30** National Heroes' Day. **Jun 12** HM The Queen's Birthday. **Aug 1** Emancipation Day. **Sep 30** National Youth Day. **Oct 10** Columbus Day. **Dec 25** Christmas Day. **Dec 26** Boxing Day.
2006: Jan 1 New Year's Day. **Mar 13** Commonwealth Day. **Apr 14** Good Friday. **Apr 17** Easter Monday. **May 22** National Heroes' Day. **Jun 12** HM The Queen's Birthday. **Aug 1** Emancipation Day. **Sep 29** National Youth Day. **Oct 9** Columbus Day. **Dec 25** Christmas Day. **Dec 26** Boxing Day.

Health

	Special Precautions?	Certificate Required?
Yellow Fever	No	No
Cholera	No	No
Typhoid & Polio	1	N/A
Malaria	No	N/A

Note: *Regulations and requirements may be subject to change at short notice, and you are advised to contact your doctor well in advance of your intended date of departure. Any numbers in the chart refer to the footnotes below.*

1: A small risk of typhoid exists in rural areas.
Food & drink: All water should be regarded as being potentially contaminated. Water used for drinking, brushing teeth or making ice should have first been boiled or otherwise sterilised. Powdered or tinned milk is available and is advised, but make sure that it is reconstituted with pure water. Only eat well-cooked meat and fish, preferably served hot. Pork, salad and mayonnaise may carry increased risk. Vegetables should be cooked and fruit peeled.
Other risks: A low risk of *dengue fever*. *Hepatitis A*, *B* and *C* occur.
Health care: There is a reciprocal health agreement with the UK. On presentation of proof of residence in the UK (NHS card, driving licence, etc), those under 16 or over 65 receive all medical and dental treatment free of charge. Other UK residents are entitled to free treatment as follows: on *Grand Turk*, dental treatment, prescribed medicines and ambulance travel; on the *outer islands*, medical treatment at Government clinics and prescribed medicines. There are community clinics on all islands. There is a small hospital on Grand Turk and a number of private practitioners, and also an emergency care facility.

Travel - International

AIR: The main airline is *Air Turks & Caicos (QW)* (tel: 946 5481). *American Airlines* offers several daily services. *Air Jamaica* and *Bahamas Air* also operate scheduled flights to and from the Bahamas and Jamaica respectively. *Sky King* offers direct flights. *British Airways* has weekly scheduled flights from Heathrow. *US Airways* offers direct flights from Charlotte, North Carolina and weekly flights from Philadelphia.
Approximate flight times: From Grand Turk to *London*, via the USA or Jamaica, is approximately 13 hours 30 minutes, to *Miami* is one hour 15 minutes, and to *New York* is three hours. From Providenciales to *Miami* is one hour 20 minutes, and to *New York* is five hours 50 minutes (via Miami). It takes three hours 30 minutes to get to Boston. There are direct flights from the UK, Canada, The Bahamas, Jamaica, Dominican Republic and Haiti.
International airports: *Grand Turk (GDT)* is 3.2km (2 miles) south of Cockburn Town (travel time - five minutes). There is a taxi service from Grand Turk to hotels; prices vary. Airport facilities include left luggage, first aid, bars and restaurants. There are international airstrips on *Providenciales (PLS)* and *South Caicos (XSC)*.
Departure tax: US$35. Children under two are exempt.
SEA: The archipelago is off the beaten track for most major cruise lines. However, *Fred Olsen Cruises* sail to the islands, anchoring offshore and transporting passengers to the islands by tender. Boats can be chartered to sail to islands in the Bahamas or Haiti. The main ports are Cockburn Harbour (South Caicos), Grank Turk, Providenciales and Salt Cay. Harbour facilities on South Caicos are currently being improved. There are plans to build a new port on North Caicos.

Travel - Internal

AIR: In addition to the international airports on *Grand Turk*, *Providenciales* and *South Caicos*, there are landing strips on Middle Caicos, North Caicos, Parrot Cay, Pine Cay and Salt Cay. *Turks & Caicos Airways* runs a regular air-taxi service to all the inhabited islands, as well as flights to Cap Haïtien, Nassau and Puerto Plata. Charter flights are also available.
SEA: Limited coast-hopping and inter-island services. Boats may be chartered at most of the inhabited islands.
ROAD: There are over 120km (75 miles) of roads on the islands, of which about one-fifth are sealed. Traffic drives on the left. Speed limits are 20 mph (32 kph) in town and 40 mph (64 kph) elsewhere. If possible, driving at night in Providenciales should be avoided. **Taxi:** Available at most airports, but the supply may be limited and sharing is often necessary. **Car hire:** Available from some local firms on Grand Turk, Providenciales, and North and South Caicos (includes *Avis*, *Budget Rent-a-Car* and *Hertz/Contour*).
Documentation: Local licence available for a fee if holding a national driving licence or an International Driving Permit. A tax of US$10 is levied on all rentals.
Travel times: The following chart gives approximate travel times (in hours and minutes) from **Grand Turk** to other major cities/towns on the islands:

	Air
Salt Cay	0.05
South Caicos	0.15
Middle Caicos	0.20
North Caicos	0.25
Pine Cay	0.30
Providenciales	0.30

Accommodation

There is accommodation on Grand Turk, North, Middle and South Caicos, Salt Cay, Providenciales and Pine Cay, including hotels, inns, a guest house and self-catering apartment complexes. The standard is high, and many have beach frontage, private gardens, swimming pool and extensive watersports facilities. On Providenciales, there is a *Club Med Village*. All rooms are subject to 8 per cent tax and 10 per cent service charge. Advance reservation is necessary. For further details, contact the Turks & Caicos Islands Tourist Board (see *Contact Addresses* section).
Grading: There is a number of standard hotels as well as some luxury and deluxe hotels.

Resorts & Excursions

THE CAICOS GROUP

There are six principal islands and numerous small cays, most of which are uninhabited. They are listed in order from west to east.
West Caicos: The westernmost island has an abrupt coastline leading to deep water that is ideal for fishing and scuba diving. Uninhabited, it is currently only visited by sailors, fishermen and thousands of seabirds.
Providenciales: This island is the centre of the country's major tourist development. The main tourist centre lies around **Turtle Cove**, with its peaceful yacht basin, and **Grace Bay**.
Little Water Cay: Known for its variety of birdlife, this small cay is being developed as a nature resort.
Pine Cay: Pine Cay is inhabited mostly by tropical birds and iguanas, and has one of the most beautiful beaches in the Caicos Islands, if not the whole Caribbean. The northern end has many freshwater lakes with species of saltwater fish brought here by Hurricane Donna in 1960. Part of the **Caicos Cays National Underwater Park** is located here. The reefs of the Caicos bank, with their rich variety of corals and vividly coloured fish, are a must-see.
Parrot Cay: Parrot Cay lies between Providenciales and North Caicos. Once a private island which used to be a hideout for legendary pirates such as Annie Bonnie and Mary Reid, it is now being developed into a modern resort.
North Caicos: Known as the 'Garden Island' of the Caicos, its fertile soils and water provide good farmland. It has miles of deserted white sand beaches, along which hotels provide luxurious and peaceful accommodation. Flamingos, ospreys, iguanas and various other wildlife can be seen at the island's nature reserve.
Middle Caicos: Also known as Grand Caicos, this island is undeveloped. Blessed with a lovely coastline, to the west of Conch Bar the shoreline dips in and out with bluffs and small coves. Visitors should try not to miss the island's spectacular caves.
East Caicos: East Caicos is uninhabited, but when flying to South Caicos, look down for the salmon in the translucent green water. Some of the most beautiful beaches in the Caribbean are to be found here. In the northwest of the island, at **Jacksonville**, there is a series of caves with evidence of early petroglyphs.
South Caicos: The town of **Cockburn Harbour** is situated on a small ridge at the extreme southwest of the island of South Caicos. It was once the chief port for the shipment of salt from the islands.

THE CAICOS GROUP

These are smaller islands, separated from the Caicos Group by the 35km (22 mile) deep-water Columbus Passage channel (formerly the 'Turks Island Passage'), and consist of two main islands and a number of small, uninhabited cays.
Grand Turk: A few minutes from South Caicos by air, with the small metropolis of **Cockburn Town**, Grand Turk is the islands' seat of government and commerce, as well as their historic and cultural centre. The **Turks & Caicos National Museum**, situated on the waterfront, tells the story of the oldest shipwreck discovered in the Americas and exhibits rare prints and manuscripts from all of the islands. **Front Street** has a number of colonial buildings, dating from the early 19th century. They have imposing entrances in the high, whitewashed walls that surround their gardens. There are many delightful bays on the eastern shores of Grand Turk. The island is also a fine base for diving and fishing.
Salt Cay: This is regarded by many as the most charming and atmospheric of all the Salt Islands. There are fine beaches and also still-productive salt ponds. The island is dominated by a great white house, built in the 1830s in solid Bermudian style. Salt Cay also hosts relics of the now defunct whaling industry. In the winter, visitors have the chance to spot gigantic humpback whales.

Sport & Activities

Watersports: With more than 370km (230 miles) of beaches, there is plenty of opportunity for safe **swimming**, supplemented by hotel pools. The spectacular reefs and underwater life surrounding the islands attract **diving** enthusiasts from all over the world. Most clubs and centres have qualified instructors; equipment can be hired and diving trips arranged. There is good **fishing** off all the islands; boats can be hired from most hotels and individual island fishermen can be hired as guides.
Wildlife: During February, March and April, **whale-watching** enthusiasts are able to observe large numbers of the North Atlantic humpback whale population passing through very close to the western shores of Grand Turk and Salt Cay en route to their breeding grounds at Mouchoir Bank nearby. During this period, divers can listen to an underwater concert of whale songs. Encounters with dolphins are also frequent. The friendliness of one **dolphin**, named JoJo, who frequently interacts with humans, has prompted her warden to declare the dolphin a national treasure. The *JoJo Dolphin Project* is one of numerous regional nature conservation programmes, which encourage tourists to respect the environment. Other marine species that can be observed include turtles, spotted eagle rays and manta rays. **Birdwatching** is widespread as rare birds and butterflies are found throughout the islands.
Other: There is an 18-hole **golf** championship course in Providenciales and **cricket** is a popular pastime.

Social Profile

FOOD & DRINK: With rare exceptions, dining takes place in hotels. Island specialities include whelk soup, conch chowder, lobster and special types of fresh fish. Another popular dish is Grits, known locally as *Hominy*; cooked with peas or dried conch, completed by adding vegetables, chicken or fish. Continental dishes are also available as are US/European snacks such as hot dogs and hamburgers. Although some establishments have buffet-style serveries, table service is common.
Alcohol is freely available. Rum-based punch and cocktails are delicious and a wide selection of imported beer, wines and spirits can be found in most bars.
NIGHTLIFE: There are nightclubs and discos, and hotels

arrange beach parties and other entertainments. Events are broadcast in advance on local radio.
SHOPPING: Fairly expensive. The islands' small shops sell locally made baskets, jewellery, ceramics, shells, sponges, hand-screened cloth, souvenir T-shirts and rare conch pearls, allthough the latter is discouraged due to over fishing.
SPECIAL EVENTS: For a complete list, contact the Turks & Caicos Islands Tourist Board (see *Contact Addresses* section). The following is a selection of special events occurring in the Turks & Caicos Islands in 2005:
Jan 1 *Junkanoo Jump-Up* (festivities from midnight to sunrise), Grand Turk and Providenciales. **Jan 30** *Island Network 14th Annual Mini-Triathalon*, Provo. **Feb 11** *Cactus Slam Festival*, Providenciales. **Mar 17** *13th Annual St Patricks Day Pub Crawl*. **Apr** *Earth Day*. **May** *South Caicos Regatta*. **May 30** *National Heroes Day*. **Jun** *Conch Carnival*, Grand Turk; *15th Annual Fools Regatta and Great Raft Race*. **Jun-Jul** *Annual Turks & Caicos Classic Fishing Tournament*, Providenciales. **Jul** *Women's International Festival of Football*, Providenciales; *12th Annual Heineken Game Fishing Tournament*, Grand Turk. **Aug** *Middle Caicos Day Celebrations*. **Sep** *Cultural Week*, various islands. **Oct** *North Caicos Extravaganza*; *10th Annual Oktoberfest*; *Turks and Caicos Music and Poetry Festival*. **Oct 24** *International Human Rights Day*. **Nov** *2nd Annual International Film Festival*, Providenciales. **Dec** *Christmas Tree Light Ceremony*, Grand Turk.
SOCIAL CONVENTIONS: Shaking hands is the normal form of greeting. Hospitality is important and, when visiting someone's home, normal social courtesies should be observed - if possible, a return invitation should be made. A souvenir from home is well received. Informal dress is accepted for most events, but beachwear should be confined to the beach. **Tipping:** There is no tipping in hotels on any of the islands, 15 per cent is added to all bills. In restaurants, tip 15 per cent.

Business Profile

Since salt mining went into decline in the mid-1960s, and finally ceased during the 1990s, the Turks & Caicos Islands have relied on tourism and offshore financial services for most of their income. There is little agriculture but the sizeable fishing industry is both a major contributor to the islands' food requirements and a valuable export earner - particularly from the USA, which buys much of the catch. The only other notable industry is construction, which is largely geared towards improving tourism infrastructure. In the mid-1980s, measures were introduced by the Government to attract an offshore financial services industry and these have met with reasonable success. Unfortunately, it brought laundered money and illicit capital fleeing from elsewhere. Under pressure from London and, more publicly, the Organisation for Economic Cooperation and Development, the Government has now introduced a tighter regulatory structure to prevent fraud and money-laundering. Meanwhile, it has refocused on tourism as the key to the islands' future economic well-being. The sector is now worth about US$500 million to the islands' economy.
Despite receipts from tourism and financial service, some aid from the UK is still needed to balance the budget and fund capital projects. The USA is substantially the largest single trading partner; the remainder of the islands' trade is conducted with the UK and with its Caribbean neighbours.
BUSINESS: The informal relaxed atmosphere prevails even in business circles. A lightweight suit will be the most needed. Best months to visit are from April to October. **Office hours:** Mon-Fri 0800-1300 and 1400-1630.
COMMERCIAL INFORMATION: The following organisation can offer advice: Providenciales Chamber of Commerce, PO Box 361, Providenciales (tel: (649) 946 4583 *or* 231 2110; fax: (649) 946 4582; website: www.provochamber.com).
CONFERENCES/CONVENTIONS: For information, contact the Turks & Caicos Islands Tourist Board (see *Contact Addresses* section).

Climate

Tropical; tempered by trade winds, generally pleasant. Cool nights. Rain in winter. Hurricanes and tropical storms (with flooding) can strike between July to November.
Required clothing: Tropical lightweights. Light sweaters are advised for evenings.

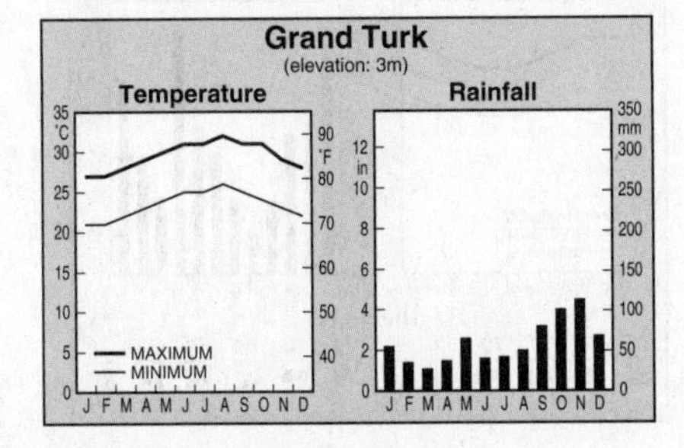

Tuvalu

LATEST TRAVEL ADVICE CONTACTS

British Foreign and Commonwealth Office
Tel: (0870) 606 0290 Website: www.fco.gov.uk
US Department of State
Website: http://travel.state.gov/travel
Canadian Department of Foreign Affairs and Int'l Trade
Tel: (1 800) 267 8376 Website: www.dfait-maeci.gc.ca

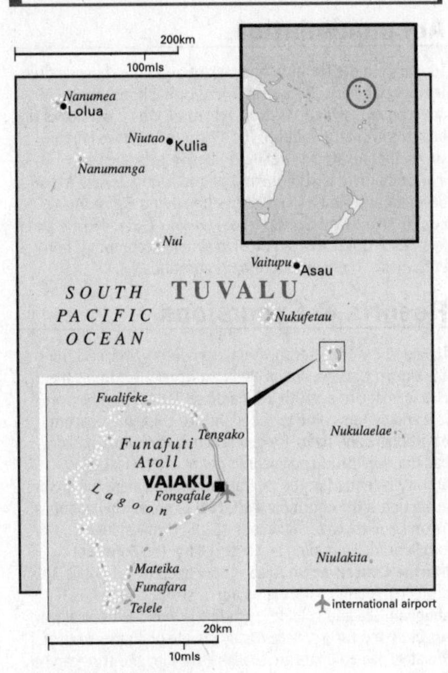

Location: West Pacific.

Country dialling code: 688.

Ministry of Tourism, Trade and Commerce
Private Mail Bag, Vaiaku, Funafuti, Tuvalu
Tel: 20840 *or* 20408.
Fax: 20210.
E-mail: lleneuoti@yahoo.com
Website: www.timelesstuvalu.com
Consulate of Tuvalu
230 Worple Road, London SW20 8RH, UK
Tel/Fax: (020) 8879 0985.
E-mail: tuvaluconsulate@netscape.net
Opening hours: Mon-Fri 0900-1700.
South Pacific Tourism Organisation
Street address: Level 3, FNPF Place, 343-359 Victoria Parade, Suva, Fiji
Postal address: PO Box 13119, Suva, Fiji
Tel: 330 4177.
Fax: 330 1995.
Website: www.spto.org
Also deals with enquiries from the UK.
The British High Commission in Suva deals with enquiries relating to Tuvalu (see *Fiji* section).
The US Embassy in Suva deals with enquiries relating to Tuvalu (see *Fiji* section).
The Canadian High Commission in Wellington deals with enquiries relating to Tuvalu (see *New Zealand* section).

General Information

AREA: 26 sq km (10 sq miles).
POPULATION: 10,880 (2002).
POPULATION DENSITY: 418.5 per sq km.
CAPITAL: Funafuti. **Population:** 4,590 (2000).
GEOGRAPHY: Tuvalu (formerly the Ellice Islands) is a scattered group of nine small atolls in the western Pacific Ocean extending about 560km (350 miles) from north to south. Nearest neighbours are Fiji (to the south), Kiribati (north) and the Solomon Islands (west). The main island, Funafuti, is also the capital and lies 1920km (1200 miles) north of Suva, Fiji.
GOVERNMENT: Constitutional monarchy. Gained independence from the UK in 1978. **Head of State:** HM Queen Elizabeth II, represented locally by Governor-General Faimalaga Luka since 2003. **Head of Government:** Prime Minister Maatia Toafa since 2004.
LANGUAGE: Tuvaluan and English are the main languages.
RELIGION: Approximately 98 per cent Protestant.
TIME: GMT + 12.
ELECTRICITY: 220/240 volts AC, 60Hz (Funafuti only).
COMMUNICATIONS: Telephone: IDD service is available. Country code: 688. There are no area codes. Tuvalu has recently acquired satellite communications technology and international phone calls can be made from most of the islands. **Fax:** Available at the Telecommunication Centre in Funafuti and in hotels. **Internet:** ISPs include *Tuvalu.TV*. **Telegram:** Overseas telegrams may be sent via the Post Office in Funafuti. **Post:** Airmail services to Europe take between five and 10 days to arrive, but can be erratic. Tuvalu stamps are among the most sought after in the world. **Press:** The Government Broadcasting and Information Division publishes *Tuvalu Echoes* (in English, on a fortnightly basis).
Radio: BBC World Service (website: www.bbc.co.uk/worldservice) and Voice of America (website: www.voa.gov) can be received. From time to time the frequencies change and the most up-to-date can be found online.

TIMATIC CODES

Health	AMADEUS: **TI-DFT/FUN/HE** GALILEO/WORLDSPAN: **TI-DFT/FUN/HE** SABRE: **TIDFT/FUN/HE**
Visa	AMADEUS: **TI-DFT/FUN/VI** GALILEO/WORLDSPAN: **TI-DFT/FUN/VI** SABRE: **TIDFT/FUN/VI**

To access TIMATIC country information on Health and Visa regulations through the Computer Reservations System (CRS), type in the appropriate command line listed above.

Passport/Visa

	Passport Required?	Visa Required?	Return Ticket Required?
Full British	Yes	No	Yes
Australian	Yes	No	Yes
Canadian	Yes	No	Yes
USA	Yes	2	Yes
Other EU	Yes	No/1	Yes
Japanese	Yes	Yes	Yes

Note: *Regulations and requirements may be subject to change at short notice, and you are advised to contact the appropriate diplomatic or consular authority before finalising travel arrangements. Details of these may be found at the head of this country's entry. Any numbers in the chart refer to the footnotes below.*

PASSPORTS: Valid passport required by all.
VISAS: Required by all except the following:
(a) **1.** nationals listed in the chart above (except nationals of Cyprus, Czech Republic, Estonia, Hungary, Latvia, Lithuania, Malta, Poland, Slovak Republic and Slovenia who *do* require a visa);
(b) nationals of Commonwealth countries (except nationals of Brunei, Cameroon, Mozambique, Namibia, St Kitts & Nevis and South Africa, who *do* require a visa);
(c) nationals of Iceland, Liechtenstein, San Marino, Switzerland, Tunisia, Turkey and Uruguay;
(d) **2.** nationals of the USA (*only* if the passport is issued by the Marshall Islands);
(e) transit passengers continuing their journey on the same or first connecting aircraft within 24 hours provided holding required travel documents for onward destination and not leaving the airport transit lounge.
Note: Entry permits are issued on arrival providing nationals can provide a valid passport, sufficient funds, proof of accommodation and a return/onward ticket.
Types of visa and cost: Visitor and work permits issued free of charge.
Validity: Visitors are normally permitted to remain in Tuvalu for up to one month, after meeting entry requirements; their visit may then be extended for a maximum of three months at a cost of £10.
Application to: British Consulates, Tuvalu representatives abroad or the Principal Immigration Officer, Office of the Chief of Police, Funafuti, Tuvalu.

Money

Currency: Australian and Tuvaluan currency are both in use, but transactions over AUD$1 are always conducted in Australian Dollars. For details of Australian Dollar denominations and exchange rates, see the *Australia* section.
Tuvaluan Dollar (TV$) = 100 cents. Coins are in denominations of TV$1, and 500, 200, 100, 50, 20, 10 and 5 cents.
Credit & debit cards: Credit cards are not accepted, but MasterCard may be used at the National Bank of Tuvalu for cash advances.
Travellers cheques: Australian Dollars are recommended.
Currency restrictions: There are no restrictions on the import and export of foreign or local currency.
Banking hours: Mon-Thurs 0930-1300, Fri 0830-1200.

A B C D E F G H I J K L M N O P Q R S T U V W X Y Z

Duty Free

The following items may be imported into Tuvalu by visitors without incurring customs duty:
200 cigarettes or 225g of tobacco or cigars (for all visitors irrespective of age); 1l of spirits and 1l of wine (for visitors aged 18 years and over).
Prohibited items: Pornography, pure alcohol, narcotics, arms and ammunition. All plant and animal material must be declared and quarantined. The following items are duty free but must be declared upon arrival: one pair of binoculars, one still camera and six rolls of unexposed film, one cine camera and 200m of unexposed film, one portable radio, one broadcast receiver, one portable tape recorder, one portable typewriter and a reasonable quantity of sports equipment.

Public Holidays

2005: Jan 1 New Year's Day. **Mar 14** Commonwealth Day. **Mar 25** Good Friday. **Mar 28** Easter Monday. **Jun 12** Queen's Official Birthday. **Aug 5** National Children's Day. **Oct 1-2** Tuvalu Days (Anniversary of Independence). **Nov 11** Prince of Wales's Birthday. **Dec 25-26** Christmas.
2006: Jan 1 New Year's Day. **Mar 13** Commonwealth Day. **Apr 14** Good Friday. **Apr 17** Easter Monday. **Jun 12** Queen's Official Birthday. **Aug 5** National Children's Day. **Oct 1-2** Tuvalu Days (Anniversary of Independence). **Nov 11** Prince of Wales's Birthday. **Dec 25-26** Christmas.

Health

	Special Precautions?	Certificate Required?
Yellow Fever	No	No
Cholera	No	No
Typhoid & Polio	No	N/A
Malaria	No	N/A

Note: Regulations and requirements may be subject to change at short notice, and you are advised to contact your doctor well in advance of your intended date of departure. Any numbers in the chart refer to the footnotes below.

Food & drink: All water is stored in tanks and supply is limited so visitors are advised to use water sparingly and take local advice.
Other risks: *Hepatitis A* occurs; *hepatitis B* is endemic. *Dengue fever* and *filariasis* are also present. There is a threat of *tuberculosis*. Poisonous fish and sea snakes can be a potential hazard to bathers.
Health care: Visitors are advised to bring antiseptic cream as cuts are inclined to turn septic but, apart from this precaution, there are no serious health risks. The mosquitoes are non-malarial, but the visitor may nevertheless wish to take protective measures. There are no reciprocal agreements with the UK or USA and travellers are recommended to take out full medical insurance before departure. Tuvalu's only hospital is in Funafuti; the outer islands only have trained nurses. More serious and complicated problems may require medicinal evacuation to Fiji or Australia.

Travel - International

AIR: There are plans to establish a national airline in the near future. Presently *Air Marshall Islands (CW)*, the airline of the Marshall Islands, offers return flights to Funafuti from *Majuro* (Marshall Islands) via *Tarawa* (Kiribati), from Nadi (Fiji) and from *Suva* (Fiji). *Air Fiji* also flies between Suva (Fiji) and Funafuti. It is advisable to book in advance.
The *Visit the South Pacific Pass* is valid for a number of airlines operating in the South Pacific, including *Air Caledonie, Air Marshall Islands, Air Nauru, Air Niugingi, Air Pacific, Air Vanuatu, Polynesian Airlines, Qantas, Royal Tongan Airlines* and *Solomon Airlines*. Offering reductions of up to 50 per cent on normal airfares, this sector-based pass allows for flexible island-hopping between the destinations of the Cook Islands, Fiji, Nauru, New Caledonia, Samoa, Tahiti, Tonga, Vanuatu and the more remote Melanesian and Micronesian islands, together with major cities in Australia (Brisbane, Melbourne, Sydney) and New Zealand (Auckland, Christchurch, Wellington). The journey must be started outside the South Pacific and only one stopover in Australia is allowed. A minimum of two coupons must be bought before departure (a maximum of eight coupons can be purchased en route). For details and conditions, contact the South Pacific Tourism Organisation (see *Contact Addresses* section).
International airports: *Funafuti International (FUN)*. Facilities include a VIP lounge, left luggage and lockers, bank, bureaux de change, restaurant, snack bars, bars, chemist, post office and shops. Buses run 0500-2359 (travel time - 30 minutes). Taxis are also available. There is a pick-up service to the only hotel.
Departure tax: A$10. Children under three years of age and transit passengers are exempt.
SEA: Shipping services operate from Fiji, Australia and New Zealand, calling at the main port of Funafuti. Adventure cruises organised by tour operators also call from time to time.

Travel - Internal

AIR: The only airstrip is at Funafuti. There is no internal air service.
SEA: The islands are served by a passenger and cargo vessel, the *Nivaga II*, based at Funafuti, which occasionally calls at Suva (Fiji).
ROAD: There are a few roads, constructed from impacted coral, and several dirt tracks that span the islands. There are **taxis**, but limited transport service is also provided by privately operated **minibuses**. The usual forms of transport on the islands are small **pick-up trucks**, **motorcycles** and **bicycles**, which can be hired at the hotel.

Accommodation

Tuvalu's remote location and lack of amenities have limited the development of tourism. There is one hotel, the government-owned *Vaiaku Lagi Hotel*, which overlooks the beautiful Funafuti lagoon. The 17 rooms all have lagoon views and private shower. All-inclusive packages are available. There is also one motel, the *Island Breeze Motel*. Several guest houses and lodges (including *Filamona Lodge, Hideaway Guest House, Laisinis Guest House* and *Su's Place Guest House*) provide simple accommodation with meals. There are no camping grounds.

Resorts & Excursions

Tuvalu, the world's second-smallest country and, according to the United Nations, one of the least developed, fulfils the classic image of a South Sea paradise. Tourist numbers are low and visitors come to the islands to enjoy the peaceful atmosphere and palm-fringed beaches. Pandanus, papaya, banana, breadfruit and coconut palms are typical. Most activity is centred in the capital, **Funafuti**, where the greatest attraction is the enormous **Funafuti Lagoon**. The lagoon is 14km (9 miles) wide and about 18km (11 miles) long and is excellent for swimming and snorkelling. The **Funafuti Marine Conservation Area** is now open to the public. This protected marine park, consisting of six tiny islets, has abundant sea and wildlife, including numerous tropical fish, sea birds and turtles. Access is by private or chartered boat. Privately owned boats are available for hire and trips can be made to the many beautiful uninhabited islets in the Funafuti atoll. A short distance from the Vaiaku Lagi Hotel is the **Women's Handicraft Centre**, where locally crafted goods are on sale (see *Social Profile* section). Also worth visiting are the **Philatelic Bureau**, which provides stamps to collectors all over the world, and the **University of the South Pacific Centre**, which sells a range of books relating to Tuvalu and the surrounding region. Another point of interest is the spot that made Tuvalu the focus of international scientific attention almost 100 years ago, when an expedition was sent from London to drill far into the ground to prove Charles Darwin's theory on the formation of coral atolls. The second most populated island in the atoll is **Funafala**, which can be visited by taking the Funafuti Island Council's catamaran (three times a week for a stop of two hours). There are no shops in Funafala, so visitors should take their own provisions. Traditional buildings with thatched roofs can be seen virtually everywhere on the islands.

Sport & Activities

Visitors interested in **watersports** should bring their own equipment as there is little for hire. **Diving** and **game fishing** equipment is available in Funafuti. **Swimmers** should wear sand shoes as stonefish are an occasional hazard. Owing to the strong tide, swimming in the ocean is very dangerous. Swimming in the lagoon is considered fairly safe.
A multi-purpose court for **tennis**, **volleyball** or **basketball** is situated near the Vaiaku Lago Hotel. Visitors who wish to use the hotel's tennis court should bring their own rackets and balls. **Football** is very popular, as is **kilikiti**, a local version of cricket. **Te ano** is a much-loved traditional ball game reminiscent of volleyball.

Social Profile

FOOD & DRINK: The *Vaiaku Lagi Hotel*, *Su's* and *Kai Restaurants* have fully licensed bars and dining facilities, where a good variety of food is served, with an emphasis on fish and local food. In addition, the Vaiaku Lagi Hotel has a barbecue in the courtyard once a fortnight. There is also a number of privately owned snackfood shops and two restaurants on Funafuti's main island with licensed bars and a good variety of food. Beer is imported.
NIGHTLIFE: There are fortnightly discos ('twists') at the *Vaiaku Lagi Hotel*. Groups of entertainers perform traditional dances for a small fee.
SHOPPING: A range of shops, including food, souvenir and clothing shops, are available, mainly on Funafuti. However, the range of merchandise is limited and not designed with the visitor in mind - for example, there is no film-processing service. For local crafts, including Tuvalu weaving, shell jewellery and the traditional lidded wooden boxes (*tulumas*) used by fishermen, the *Women's Handicraft Centre* near the main hotel is excellent. There are no shops on Funafala.
Shopping hours: Mon-Sat 0600-2400.
SPECIAL EVENTS: The following is a selection of special events celebrated annually in Tuvalu:
Aug 3 *National Children's Day*. **Oct 1-2** *Tuvalu Days*.
SOCIAL CONVENTIONS: Traditional values continue to dominate Tuvaluan culture. Footwear should be removed when entering a church, a village meeting house (*manepa*) or private house. Religion plays an important part in daily life. Sunday is a day of rest and church-going for the locals, when visitors are advised to choose activities which do not cause too much disruption. There are limits imposed on the consumption of alcohol outside licensed premises. Whilst dress is usually casual, it is customary for women to keep their thighs covered and beachwear should be confined to the beach or poolside. There are procedures which should be followed by those invited to a feast and visitors should take local advice about this and other matters. It is customary not to speak a foreign language in the presence of a person who does not know it, so apparent indications of a desire to hold a private or confidential conversation should be interpreted as simple courtesy to fellow islanders. Visitors are welcome to join in the numerous local festivals and celebrations with feasting and traditional entertainment. **Tipping:** Optional, but not expected.

Business Profile

ECONOMY: Tuvalu relies on a number of standard and unusual sources of income to sustain its economy. Remittances from abroad, especially Nauru where large numbers of Tuvaluans work in the phosphate industry, are vital. In a less orthodox vein, the sale of stamps (mostly to collectors) is a valuable foreign currency earner. A new source of income was identified when a regional telecommunications operator sought to lease Tuvalu's national telephone code and recover its costs from companies offering 'premium rate' services. The Government agreed and now acquires 10 per cent of its annual budget from this source. It has since made a similar arrangement with its Internet domain suffix, '.tv.' Another important revenue stream comes from the sale of fishing licences to US and Japanese fleets. Fishing is also an important activity in the local economy. Exploration is currently underway to locate mineral resources suspected to lie within Tuvalu's territorial limit. On land, copra is the only significant export: most of the soil is of unsuitable quality for agriculture, which is confined to subsistence activities. There is some small-scale industrial activity producing coconut-based products and handicrafts.
Much of the income from these various sources, plus subventions from the country's major aid donors, has been lodged in a Trust Fund established to generate income for development projects from foreign investment and provide some guarantees against a very uncertain economic future. Tuvalu is a member of the South Pacific Commission and the South Pacific Forum. In 2002, Tuvalu joined the Pacific Island Countries Trade Association (PICTA), a free-trade zone established by the South Pacific Forum. Australia, New Zealand and Fiji are the main trading partners, while the UK provides an aid package mainly to assist the development of the island's infrastructure.
BUSINESS: A high standard of business ethics is to be expected, given that the overwhelming majority of the population is Congregationalist.
OFFICE HOURS: Mon-Thurs 0730-1615 and Fri 0730-1245.
COMMERCIAL INFORMATION: The following organisation can offer advice: Tuvalu Cooperative Society Ltd, PO Box 11, Funafuti (tel: 20634 *or* 20642 *or* 20747; fax: 20748).

Climate

The climate is humid and hot with a mean annual temperature of 30°C (86°F) and comparatively little seasonal variation. March to October tends to be cooler and more pleasant, whilst some discomfort may be experienced during the wet season from November to February.
Required clothing: Lightweight for summer, rainwear for the wet season.

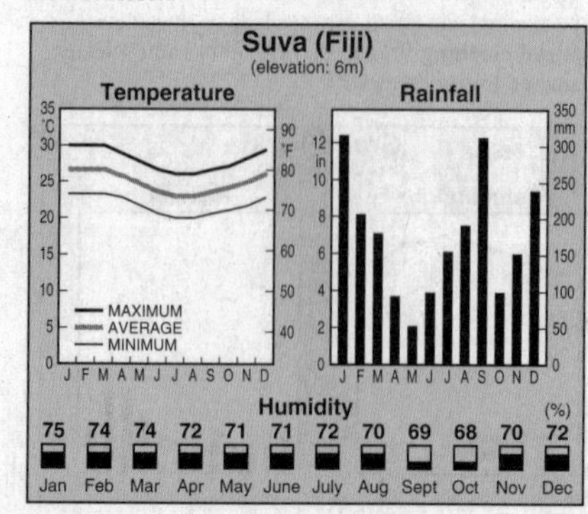

Uganda

LATEST TRAVEL ADVICE CONTACTS

British Foreign and Commonwealth Office
Tel: (0870) 606 0290 Website: www.fco.gov.uk

US Department of State
Website: http://travel.state.gov/travel

Canadian Department of Foreign Affairs and Int'l Trade
Tel: (1 800) 267 8376 Website: www.dfait-maeci.gc.ca

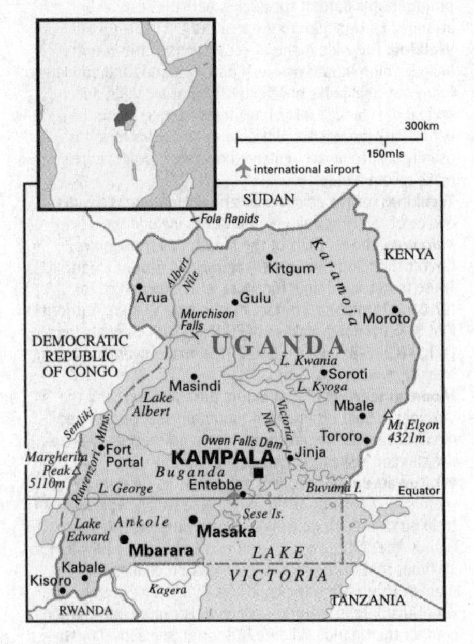

Location: Central/East Africa.

Country dialling code: 256.

Ministry of Tourism, Trade & Industry
PO Box 7103, Farmers House, Parliament Avenue, Kampala, Uganda
Tel: (41) 343 947 *or* 256 395. Fax: (41) 341 247.

Uganda Tourist Board
PO Box 7211, Kimathi Avenue, Ground Floor 13-15, Impala House, Kampala, Uganda
Tel: (41) 342 196/7. Fax: (41) 342 188.
E-mail: ugtb@starcom.co.ug
Website: www.visituganda.com

High Commission for the Republic of Uganda
Uganda House, 58-59 Trafalgar Square, London WC2N 5DX, UK
Tel: (020) 7839 5783. Fax: (020) 7839 8925.
Opening hours: Mon-Fri 0930-1300, 1400-1730; 1000-1300 (visa section).

British High Commission
PO Box 7070, 10-12 Parliament Avenue, Kampala, Uganda
Tel: (31) 312 000.
Fax: (41) 257 304 *or* (31) 312 281 (visa section).
E-mail: bhcinfo@starcom.co.ug (information section) *or* ConsularVisa.Kampala@fco.gov.uk(consular/visa section).
Website: www.britain.or.ug

Embassy of the Republic of Uganda
5911 16th Street, NW, Washington, DC 20011, USA
Tel: (202) 726 7100. Fax: (202) 726 1727.
E-mail: ugembassy@aol.com
Website: www.ugandaembassy.com

Embassy of the United States of America
PO Box 7007, Plot 1577, Gaba Road, Kampala, Uganda
Tel: (41) 259 791 *or* 233 231 *or* 345 422.
Fax: (41) 259 794/5 *or* 250 314.
E-mail: KampalaVisa@state.gov
Website: http://kampala.usembassy.gov

High Commission for the Republic of Uganda
231 Cobourg Street, Ottawa, Ontario K1N 8J2, Canada
Tel: (613) 789 0110 *or* 789 7797. Fax: (613) 789 8909.

TIMATIC CODES

Health	AMADEUS: **TI-DFT/JIB/HE** GALILEO/WORLDSPAN: **TI-DFT/JIB/HE** SABRE: **TIDFT/JIB/HE**
Visa	AMADEUS: **TI-DFT/JIB/VI** GALILEO/WORLDSPAN: **TI-DFT/JIB/VI** SABRE: **TIDFT/JIB/VI**

To access TIMATIC country information on Health and Visa regulations through the Computer Reservations System (CRS), type in the appropriate command line listed above.

E-mail: ugandahighcomm@bellnet.ca
Website: www.ugandahighcommission.ca

Canadian Consulate
Street address: Jubilee Insurance Centre, 14 Parliament Avenue, Kampala, Uganda
Postal address: PO Box 20115, Kampala, Uganda
Tel: (41) 258 141 *or* 348 141 *or* (31) 260 511.
Fax: (41) 349 484.
E-mail: canada.consulate@utlonline.co.ug
Website: www.dfait-maeci.gc.ca/nairobi/uganda_office-en.asp

General Information

AREA: 241,139 sq km (93,104 sq miles).
POPULATION: 24,748,977 (2002).
POPULATION DENSITY: 102.6 per sq km.
CAPITAL: Kampala. **Population:** 1,208,544 (2002).
GEOGRAPHY: Uganda shares borders with Sudan to the north, Kenya to the east, Lake Victoria to the southeast, Tanzania and Rwanda to the south and the Democratic Republic of Congo to the west. Kampala is on the shores of Lake Victoria, and the White Nile flowing out of the lake traverses much of the country. The varied scenery includes tropical forest and tea plantations on the slopes of the snow-capped Ruwenzori Mountains, the arid plains of the Karamoja, the lush, heavily populated Buganda, the rolling savannah of Acholi, Bunyoro, Tororo and Ankole, and the fertile cotton area of Teso.
GOVERNMENT: Republic. Gained independence from the UK in 1962. **Head of State:** President Yoweri Kaguta Museveni since 1986. **Head of Government:** Prime Minister Apolo Nsibambi since 1999.
LANGUAGE: English is the official language, with Luganda and Swahili also widely spoken.
RELIGION: 60 per cent Christian, 32 per cent animist and 5 per cent Muslim.
TIME: GMT + 3.
ELECTRICITY: 240 volts AC, 50Hz.
COMMUNICATIONS: Telephone: IDD is available to and from principal towns in Uganda. Country code: 256. Service for local calls is unreliable. **Mobile telephone:** GSM 900/1800 network. Main network operators are *Cellular Celtel* (website: www.celtel.com), *MTN-Uganda* (website: www.mtn.co.ug) and *Uganda Telecom Ltd* (website: www.utl.co.ug). Coverage extends to all major towns. **Fax:** Service is available at the *Postal & Telecommunications Office*, 35 Kampala Road, Kampala; in central post offices in Jinja and Mbale between 0800-1600; and in some hotels. **Internet:** ISPs include *InfoCom* (website: www.imul.com) and *MTN Uganda* (website: www.mtn.co.ug). There are Internet cafes in Kampala. **Telegram:** Available in main towns. **Post:** Airmail to Europe can take from three days to several weeks. Post office hours: Mon-Fri 0830-1230 and 1400-1730. Some post offices are open Sat 0830-1300.
Press: The English-language papers include *The Economy, Financial Times, Guide, The Monitor, New Vision* and *The Star*.
Radio: BBC World Service (website: www.bbc.co.uk/worldservice) and Voice of America (website: www.voa.gov) can be received. From time to time the frequencies change and the most up-to-date can be found online.

Passport/Visa

	Passport Required?	Visa Required?	Return Ticket Required?
Full British	Yes	Yes	Yes
Australian	Yes	Yes	Yes
Canadian	Yes	Yes	Yes
USA	Yes	Yes	Yes
Other EU	Yes	Yes	Yes
Japanese	Yes	Yes	Yes

***Note:** Regulations and requirements may be subject to change at short notice, and you are advised to contact the appropriate diplomatic or consular authority before finalising travel arrangements. Details of these may be found at the head of this country's entry. Any numbers in the chart refer to the footnotes below.*

Restricted entry: Entry may be refused to passengers not holding sufficient funds, return or onward tickets, and other necessary travel documents.
PASSPORTS: Passport valid past the date of expected departure from Uganda required by all.
VISAS: Required by all except the following:
(a) nationals of Angola, Antigua & Barbuda, The Bahamas, Barbados, Belize, Burundi, Comoros, Cyprus, Eritrea, Fiji, The Gambia, Ghana, Grenada, Jamaica, Kenya, Lesotho, Madagascar, Malawi, Malta, Mauritius, Rwanda, St Vincent & the Grenadines, Seychelles, Sierra Leone, Singapore, Solomon Islands, Swaziland, Tanzania, Tonga, Vanuatu, Zambia and Zimbabwe;
(b) transit passengers continuing to a third country by the same or first connecting flight within 24 hours, provided holding confirmed tickets and travel documents and not leaving the airport.
Note: Some visas may be issued on arrival to Uganda; check with your local Embassy for further details.
Types of visa and cost: *Single-entry*: US$50 (three months). *Multiple-entry*: US$90 (six months), US$190 (one year). *Transit*: US$15. Express processing is available at an additional charge of US$10.
Validity: *Single-entry*: Three months from date of issue; *Multiple-entry*: Six months or one year from date of issue; *Transit*: 24 hours.
Application to: Consulate (or Consular section at High Commission or Embassy); see *Contact Addresses* section.
Application requirements: (a) Passport valid past the date of your expected departure from Uganda. (b) Completed application form. (c) Two recent passport-size photos (with full name printed on the back of one). (d) Fee (cash or postal orders only). (e) Registered self-addressed envelope, if applying by post. *Business*: (a)-(e) and, (f) Letter of invitation/introduction.
Note: Working journalists require a letter of accreditation issued by the Secretary of the Media Council, Dept of Information, PO Box 7142, Kampala (tel: (41) 232 734; fax: (41) 256 888 *or* 342 259).
Working days required: Two.
Temporary residence: Enquire at Embassy or High Commission.

Money

Currency: Uganda Shilling (USh). Notes are in denominations of USh10,000, 5000 and 1000. Coins are in denominations of USh500, 200, 100 and 50.
Currency exchange: Foreign currency may be exchanged at the Central Bank, commercial banks and foreign exchange bureaux.
Credit & debit cards: American Express, Diners, MasterCard
and Visa are accepted but not widely used. Some large hotels, restaurants, travel agencies and shops in urban areas accept credit cards. Check with your credit or debit card company for details of merchant acceptability and other services which may be available.
Travellers cheques: To avoid additional exchange rate charges, travellers are advised to take travellers cheques in US Dollars or Pounds Sterling. It is advised that travellers bring sufficient US dollars in cash in case of emergencies.
Currency restrictions: The import and export of local currency is prohibited. Free import of foreign currency if declared on arrival. Export of foreign currency is unlimited, up to the amount declared on arrival. It is imperative to obtain a currency declaration form on arrival in Uganda. Unspent shillings can be reconverted to foreign currency.
Exchange rate indicators: The following figures are included as a guide to the movements of the Uganda Shilling against Sterling and the US Dollar:

Date	Feb '04	May '04	Aug '04	Nov '04
£1.00=	3472.13	3352.51	3176.21	3308.30
$1.00=	1907.50	1877.00	1724.00	1747.00

Banking hours: Generally Mon-Fri 0900-1500, Sat 0900-1200. Forex bureaus are open until 1700 and able to do electronic transfers to and from overseas.

Duty Free

The following items may be imported into Uganda by visitors over 17 years without incurring customs duty (except from Kenya and Tanzania):
200 cigarettes or 225g of tobacco or a combination thereof; one bottle of spirits or wine; 568ml of perfume.
Restricted exports: A special permit is required to export game trophies.

Public Holidays

2005: Jan 1 New Year's Day. **Jan 21** Eid al-Adha (Feast of the Sacrifice). **Jan 26** Liberation Day. **Mar 8** International Women's Day. **Mar 25** Good Friday. **Mar 28** Easter Monday. **May 1** Labour Day. **Jun 3** Martyrs' Day. **Jun 9** National Heroes' Day. **Oct 9** Independence Day. **Nov 3-5** Eid al-Fitr (End of Ramadan). **Dec 25** Christmas Day. **Dec 26** Boxing Day.
2006: Jan 1 New Year's Day. **Jan 10** Eid al-Adha (Feast of the Sacrifice). **Jan 26** Liberation Day. **Mar 8** International Women's Day. **Apr 14** Good Friday. **Apr 17** Easter Monday. **May 1** Labour Day. **Jun 3** Martyrs' Day. **Jun 9** National Heroes' Day. **Oct 9** Independence Day. **Oct 22-24** Eid al-Fitr (End of Ramadan). **Dec 25** Christmas Day. **Dec 26** Boxing Day.
Note: Muslim festivals are timed according to local sightings of various phases of the moon and the dates given above are approximations. During the lunar month of Ramadan that precedes Eid al-Fitr, Muslims fast during the day and feast at night and normal business patterns may be interrupted. Many restaurants are closed during the day and there may be restrictions on smoking and drinking. Some disruption may continue into Eid al-Fitr itself. Eid al-Fitr and Eid al-Adha may last anything from two to 10 days, depending on the region. For more information, see the *World of Islam* appendix.

Health

	Special Precautions?	Certificate Required?
Yellow Fever	Yes	Yes/1
Cholera	Yes	No/2
Typhoid & Polio	3	N/A
Malaria	4	N/A

Note: *Regulations and requirements may be subject to change at short notice, and you are advised to contact your doctor well in advance of your intended date of departure. Any numbers in the chart refer to the footnotes below.*

1: A yellow fever vaccination certificate is required from travellers over one year of age arriving from infected areas. Travellers arriving from non-endemic zones should note that vaccination is strongly recommended for travel outside the urban areas, even if an outbreak of the disease has not been reported and they would normally not require a vaccination certificate to enter the country.
2: Following WHO guidelines issued in 1973, a cholera vaccination certificate is not a condition of entry to Uganda. However, cholera is a serious risk in this country and precautions are essential. Up-to-date advice should be sought before deciding whether these precautions should include vaccination, as medical opinion is divided over its effectiveness; see the *Health* appendix for more information.
3: Typhoid is widespread and immunisation is advised.
4: Malaria risk, predominantly in the malignant *falciparum* form, occurs all year throughout the country, including the main towns of Fort Portal, Jinja, Kampala, Mbale and parts of Kigezi. Resistance to chloroquine and sulfadoxine-pyrimethamine has been reported. The recommended prophylaxis is mefloquine.
Food & drink: All water should be regarded as being a potential health risk. Water used for drinking, brushing teeth or making ice should have first been boiled or otherwise sterilised. Milk is unpasteurised and should be boiled. Powdered or tinned milk is available and is advised, but make sure that it is reconstituted with pure water. Avoid dairy products which are likely to have been made from unboiled milk. Only eat well-cooked meat and fish, preferably served hot. Pork, salad and mayonnaise may carry increased risk. Vegetables should be cooked and fruit peeled.
Other risks: *Bilharzia* (schistosomiasis) is present. Avoid swimming and paddling in fresh water; swimming pools which are well chlorinated and maintained are safe. Meningitis risk exists, depending on area visited and time of year. *Hepatitis A*, B and *E*, and *tuberculosis* occur. Sleeping sickness (*trypanosomiasis*) is reported. *HIV/AIDS* is widespread. *Rabies* is present. For those at high risk, vaccination before arrival should be considered. If you are bitten, seek medical advice without delay. For more information, consult the *Health* appendix.
Health Care: Visitors should bring personal supplies of medicines that are likely to be needed, but enquire first at the Embassy or High Commission whether such supplies may be freely imported. Comprehensive health insurance is essential and should include cover for emergency air repatriation in case of serious accident or illness. The Ugandan health service has still not recovered from the mass departure of foreign personnel in 1972 and there are medical facilities of a reasonable standard only in large towns and cities.

Travel - International

Note: Travellers are strongly advised against travel to northern and northeastern Uganda because of rebel insurgency and tribal clashes. It is best to contact a local government travel advice department in advance of travel to determine how safe it is to travel to other national parks in Uganda.
AIR: Uganda's main airline, *Uganda Airlines (QU)*, is no longer in operation. Several other airlines are now vying to replace the defunct carrier. Other airlines serving Uganda include *Air Rwanda, Air Tanzania, British Airways, Egyptair, Emirates, Ethiopian Airlines, Gulf Air, Kenya Airways, SN Brussels* and *South Airways*.
Approximate flight times: From Kampala to *London* is eight hours.
International airports: *Entebbe (EBB)* is 40km (22 miles) southwest of Kampala (travel time – 30 minutes). There are bus services to Kampala. Taxis are also available. Airport facilities include duty free shops, restaurants, banks/bureaux de change, post office, car hire and hotel reservations.
Departure tax: No airport tax is levied on passengers upon embarking at the airport (service charge is included in the ticket).
Note: All airline tickets purchased in Uganda must be paid for in hard currency.
LAKE: Between Kampala in Uganda and Mwanza in Tanzania, it is possible to catch a boat on Lake Victoria.
RAIL: Uganda Railways does not operate passenger services at present.
ROAD: There are connections with all neighbouring countries, although borders are not always open. However, travellers should take local advice before crossing the border with Rwanda, and should not attempt to cross the border with the Democratic Republic of Congo. **Bus:** There is a daily bus service between Kampala and Nairobi, Arusha and Dar-es-Salaam.

Travel - Internal

Note: There has been an increase in armed robberies: particular roads to avoid include the main road from Entebbe Airport to Kampala and the roads that leads to Kidepo National Park. The Junjala-Kampala road is also an accident blackspot.
AIR: *Air Commuter, Challenge Air, Eagle Air, Missionary Aviation Fellowship, TMK* and *United Airlines* offer flights from Entebbe to most major towns. Charter flights are also available.
LAKE: Local boat services link Entebbe to the Ssese Islands.
ROAD: Traffic drives on the left. The road network extends over 28,332km (17,605 miles). The roads are of variable quality and radiate from Kampala, although the network is sparse in the north. There are still some army and police check points on roads and railways. The speed limit is 50 mph (80 kph) or 62 mph (100 kmh) on highways. **Bus:** Services run between most parts of Uganda but are unreliable and often very crowded. Scheduled services operate between Entebbe and Kampala (travel time – one hour) and to and from the airport. An extensive network of minibuses, known as *Matatus*, runs to most parts of the country and they are a quick and convenient form of transport, if a little overcrowded. However, there is a law against overloading on buses and if this occurs, the driver and passengers are liable to pay a fine. Post-bus services operate Monday to Saturday from Kampala to main towns. There are also special **taxis**, identifiable by their black and white stripes, which take passengers to wherever they want to go but are more expensive than *Matatas*. **Documentation:** An International Driving Permit and adequate third-party insurance is required. Drivers must carry their vehicle log books and must pay for a temporary road licence.

Accommodation

There are international-standard hotels in Entebbe and Kampala. In smaller towns, hotels are generally of a more limited quality and they may not take travellers cheques or credit cards. Camping, rustic bush camps and guest houses are also available. Information can be obtained from the Uganda Tourist Board (see *Contact Addresses* section). All of the major National Parks offer accommodation in game lodges (see *National Parks* in the *Resorts & Excursions* section). Note that most places will add 10 per cent service charge and 20 per cent VAT to any bill.
CAMPING AND CARAVANNING: Most national parks and major tourist spots have camping sites, but campers should be well prepared and take the necessary precautions.

Resorts & Excursions

Uganda's great natural beauty led Winston Churchill to call it 'the pearl of Africa'. Abundant wildlife (including the famous mountain gorillas) and an excellent climate contribute to the attractions here and, although visitor facilities cannot yet compete with those of neighbouring Kenya, the annual number of tourists to Uganda is rising steadily.
KAMPALA: The capital is set among hills with fine modern architecture, tree-lined avenues, cathedrals, mosques and palaces of the old Kingdom of Buganda, and the **Uganda Museum**. The **Kabaka Tombs** are on **Kasubi Hill**. Shoes must be removed before entering the buildings.
JINJA: The second-largest town in Uganda lies on the shores of **Lake Victoria**. Though somewhat underpopulated, there is a very lively Saturday market. The nearby **Owen Falls Dam** is the source of the **Nile**.
ENTEBBE: The major gateway to Uganda for air travellers, it has fine botanical gardens and a lakeside beach, although bathing is not advisable because of the dangers of *bilharzia* (see *Health* section).
FORT PORTAL: A good base for exploring the **Ruwenzori Mountains**, the hot springs at **Bundibugyo** and the **Semluke Wildlife Reserve**.
KISORO: The starting point for climbing expeditions to **Mounts Muhavura** and **Mgahinga**. There are seven lakes in the vicinity, which offer fishing and possible duck shooting, and the **Bwindi Forest**, where one can see mountain gorillas.
MBALE: Set in fertile and lush country near **Mount Elgon**, this is popular with hikers and inexperienced mountaineers.
NATIONAL PARKS: Uganda has 10 national parks, 10 wildlife reserves and seven wildlife sanctuaries, some of which are acclaimed as being amongst Africa's best. The country's main wildlife attraction for foreign visitors is the rare mountain gorilla, found in **Bwindi Impenetrable National Park** and **Mgahinga Gorilla National Park**, both in the southwest of the country. Many other species of primates can also be seen, including chimpanzees and monkeys. **Kibale National Park** alone contains 12 different types of primate, while **Ruwenzori National Park** is regarded as one of the most spectacular in Africa. Other wildlife is present in abundance (see the *Sport & Activities* section for more details on whitewater rafting, ecotourism, trekking and contact details of Uganda Wildlife Authority). A range of accommodation, from privately run lodges and tented camps to state-run campsites, is available in the parks to suit all tastes and budgets.

Sport & Activities

Uganda's magnificent scenery offers visitors the chance to participate in a range of activities and to view some unforgettable natural spectacles. Activities can all be arranged by Ugandan tour operators.
Walking: The wide range of ecosystems in the country includes high mountains, lush hills, wetlands and arid lands. Many national parks have extensive nature trails, and several of Uganda's lakes have trails leading along the banks. Park rangers are available to advise visitors. It is usually best to be accompanied by a local guide; hotels can make recommendations.
Trekking: For the adventurous traveller, there is a wide choice of trekking trails. Popular treks include the *Karamoja*, the foothills of the mountains (the *Central Circuit* trail) and the *Sasa River Trail* on Mount Elgon. These treks are suitable for those with experience. For further information, contact the Uganda Wildlife Authority, Plot 3, Kintu Road, Nakasero, PO Box 3530, Kampala (tel: (41) 346 287-8; fax: (41) 346 291; e-mail: uwa@uwa.or.ug; website: www.uwa.or.ug).
Mountaineering: Mount Elgon, the Rwenzoris and the Virungas attract experienced mountaineers for easy and medium climbs. Special equipment is not necessary unless the climber wishes to attempt the summit.
Whitewater rafting: Specialist operators take groups of visitors to the rapids of the White Nile which provide thrilling rafting. Huge waves surge around heavily forested islands, the volume of water in this area being equivalent to 10 times that of the Zambezi. Hippos, crocodiles and monkeys are among the creatures that can be seen on the way. Bujagli Falls has grade 5 rapids. For more information, contact the Uganda Wildlife Authority (see above) *or* the Uganda Tourist Board.
Ecotourism: The Uganda Forest Department has set up five forest ecotourism projects at rainforest sites on popular tourist routes around the country. The projects are designed to benefit local communities and to conserve nature in the areas concerned, while giving visitors the opportunity to view wildlife in its natural habitat. They may be visited at any time of year and there is no need to book in advance. Camping facilities or traditional African *bandas* are available to accommodate travellers, and the sites are staffed by rangers and guides who can design programmes and provide information (charges are made for these services). Sites developed so far are the *Budongo Forest Reserve*, the largest mahogany forest in East Africa, situated near Masindi on the road to Lake Albert; the *Mabira Forest*, between Jinja and Kampala; the *Mpanga Forest*, containing abundant birdlife and a drum-making village, situated near Kampala; the *Kasyoha Kitomi Forest*, 1.5km (0.9 miles) from the main Mbarara to Kasese highway, near the Albertine Rift Valley; and the *Kalinzu Forest Reserve*, in the southwest of the country. For further information about these sites, contact the Uganda Tourist Board (see *Contact Addresses* section).
Other: There is excellent **fishing** in numerous inland waters, notably the seven lakes in the vicinity of Kisoro. There are numerous **golf** courses in the country. Lake Victoria has two **sailing** clubs which welcome visitors. Rowing boats and canoes can be hired at Gaba resort beach and at villages near other lakes. Many hotels have **swimming** pools.

Social Profile

FOOD & DRINK: There are restaurants in and around Kampala. Many hotels serve local food. Popular dishes include *matoke* (a staple made from bananas), millet bread, *cassava*, sweet potatoes, chicken and beef stews and freshwater fish. The national drink is *waragi*, a banana gin, popular among visitors as a cocktail base.
SHOPPING: Purchases include bangles, necklaces and bracelets, woodcarvings, basketry, tea, coffee and ceramics.
Shopping hours: Mon-Fri 0800-1700 and Sat 0800-1300.
SPECIAL EVENTS: For more information on special events in Uganda, contact the Uganda Tourist Board (see *Contact Addresses*). The following is a selection of special events occurring in Uganda in 2005:
Jan 26 *NRM Anniversary Day*. **Mar 8** *International Women's Day*. **Jun 3** *Martyr's Day*. **Jun 9** *National Heroes' Day*. **Nov 4-6** *End of Ramadan*.
SOCIAL CONVENTIONS: Shaking hands is the normal form of greeting. Casual dress is usual for most occasions in the daytime or evening. Ugandans have adopted a socially

conservative culture and homosexuality and drug abuse is illegal and widely condemned. **Photography:** Since 1992, photography has been allowed in all areas with the exception of airports or military installations. However, some areas are still sensitive and it is advisable to take local advice. Commercial photographers should consult the Ministry of Information for a permit. **Tipping:** It is customary to give waiters and taxi drivers a 10 per cent tip.

Business Profile

ECONOMY: Agriculture dominates the Ugandan economy, accounting for half of total output and employing over 80 per cent of the workforce. Livestock rearing and a wide range of subsistence crops meet local needs; coffee is the main export commodity. Tobacco, tea, sugar cane and cocoa are also grown for export, and some processing of these is now carried out locally. The industrial sector produces textiles, cement, fertilisers, metal goods and a variety of household items. There are large deposits of copper and cobalt, the mining of which has been disrupted by civil wars and insurgency. In addition, there are known deposits of tin, tungsten, beryllium and tantalum ores. The relatively small tourism industry has suffered from the worldwide downturn since 2002. That year, Uganda received 350,000 visitors; the sector was worth US$250 million to the economy.
The economy recorded fairly steady economic growth throughout most of the last decade (currently over 5 per cent) and, in contrast with much of the rest of Africa, has enjoyed a series of good harvests. The most pressing problem has been the country's debt burden. Uganda has benefited from several cancellations of long-term debt under a programme operated by the Paris Club of major donors and, more recently, the Heavily Indebted Poor Countries relief programme. Its total external debt now stands at just under US$4 billion. In exchange, the Government has been obliged to introduce a series of economic reforms, principally the removal of price controls and trade restrictions and a reduction in government spending. Uganda is a member of the African Development Bank and of the Common Market for Eastern and Southern Africa (COMESA). In 2003, Uganda joined with neighbouring Kenya and Tanzania in a plan to revive the East African Customs Union (a previous attempt folded in 1977). Uganda's principal trading partners are Kenya, the UK, Japan, the United Arab Emirates and India.
BUSINESS: A suit and tie are best worn by men for business meetings. English is used for all business discussions. Appointments should always be made. **Office hours:** Mon-Fri 0800-1300 and 1400-1640.
COMMERCIAL INFORMATION: The following organisation can offer advice: Uganda Investment Authority, PO Box 7418, Investment Centre, Plot 28, Kampala Road, Kampala (tel: (41) 251 562/5 or 251 854/5; fax: (41) 342 903; e-mail: info@ugandainvest.com; website: www.ugandainvest.com); *or* contact the Embassy/High Commission (see *Contact Addresses* section).
CONFERENCES/CONVENTIONS: The Uganda International Conference Centre with its main auditorium and three committee rooms has seating for up to 2000 persons. It is adjacent to the 4-star Nile Hotel and is 3km (2 miles) from the centre of Kampala. The Speke Resort & Country Lodge Munyayo, with 10 state-of-the-art conference rooms with modern facilities, has a capacity of over 3000 people. For further information, contact the Uganda Tourist Board (see *Contact Addresses* section).

Climate

The temperature, usually ranging between 21-25°C, can be quite cool in some parts of the country owing to the country's high altitude, despite its position on the equator. The mountain areas become much cooler and the top of Mount Elgon is often covered with snow. Other parts of the country are much warmer. There is heavy rain between March and May and between October and November.
Required clothing: Lightweights and rainwear, with warm wraps for the evenings are advised.

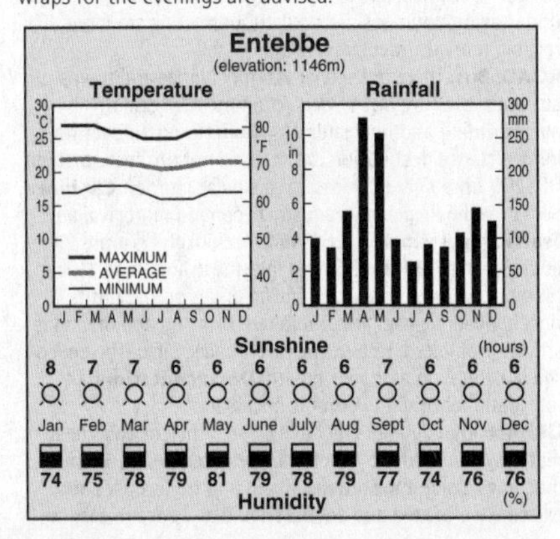

Ukraine

LATEST TRAVEL ADVICE CONTACTS

British Foreign and Commonwealth Office
Tel: (0870) 606 0290 Website: www.fco.gov.uk
US Department of State
Website: http://travel.state.gov/travel
Canadian Department of Foreign Affairs and Int'l Trade
Tel: (1 800) 267 8376 Website: www.dfait-maeci.gc.ca

Location: Central Eastern Europe.

Country dialling code: 380.

Ministry of Foreign Affairs
Mykhailovska Square 1, 01018 Kyiv, Ukraine
Tel: (44) 238 1777. Fax: (44) 238 1888.
E-mail: zsmfa@mfa.gov.ua
Website: www.mfa.gov.ua
Embassy of Ukraine
60 Holland Park, London W11 3SJ, UK
Tel: (020) 7727 6312. Fax: (020) 7792 1708.
Email: emb_gb@mfa.gov.ua
Opening hours: Mon-Fri 0900-1300, 1430-1830.
Not open to personal callers.
Consular section: Ground Floor, 78 Kensington Park Road, London W11 2PL, UK
Tel: (020) 7243 8923 *or* (090) 6550 8955 (information line).
Fax: (020) 7727 3567.
Website: www.ukremb.org.uk
Opening hours: Mon-Fri 0930-1200.
Intourist Travel Ltd
9 Princedale Road, Holland Park, London W11 4NW, UK
Tel: (020) 7792 5240 *or* (0870) 112 1233 (general enquiries).
Fax: (020) 7727 4650.
E-mail: info@intourist.co.uk (reservations only).
Website: www.intouristuk.com
British Embassy
9 Desyatinna Street, 01025 Kyiv, Ukraine
Tel: (44) 490 3660 *or* 494 3400. Fax: (44) 490 3662.
E-mail: ukembinf@sovamua.com
Website: www.britemb-ukraine.net
Consular section: Artyom Business Centre, 4 Glybochytska Street, 04050 Kyiv, Ukraine
Tel: (44) 494 3400. Fax: (44) 494 3418.
E-mail: britvisa.kiev@fco.gov.uk
Embassy of Ukraine
3350 M Street, NW, Washington, DC 20007, USA
Tel: (202) 333 0606.
Fax: (202) 333 0817 *or* 333 7510 (consular).
E-mail: letters@ukremb.com
Website: www.ukremb.com
Consulates in: Chicago and New York.
Embassy of the United States of America
10 Yuriya Kotsiubynskoho Street, 10 Kyiv, Ukraine
Tel: (44) 490 4000. Fax: (44) 490 4085.

TIMATIC CODES

Health
AMADEUS: **TI-DFT/JIB/HE**
GALILEO/WORLDSPAN: **TI-DFT/JIB/HE**
SABRE: **TIDFT/JIB/HE**

Visa
AMADEUS: **TI-DFT/JIB/VI**
GALILEO/WORLDSPAN: **TI-DFT/JIB/VI**
SABRE: **TIDFT/JIB/VI**

To access TIMATIC country information on Health and Visa regulations through the Computer Reservations System (CRS), type in the appropriate command line listed above.

E-mail: acskiev@state.gov (US citizen services) *or* visaskiev@state.gov.
Website: http://kiev.usembassy.gov
Consular section: 6 Mykoly Pymonenka Street, 01901 Kyiv, Ukraine
Tel: (44) 490 4422 (US citizen services).
Fax: (44) 216 3393 (visa appointments) *or* 236 4892 (US citizen services).
Embassy of Ukraine
310 Somerset Street West, Ottawa, Ontario K2P 0J9, Canada
Tel: (613) 230 2961.
Fax: (613) 230 2400 *or* 230 2655 (consular).
E-mail: emb_ca@ukremb.ca *or* consul@ukremb.ca (consular)
Website: www.ukremb.ca
Consulate in: Toronto.
Canadian Embassy
31 Yaroslaviv Val Street, Kyiv 01901, Ukraine
Tel: (44) 464 1144. Fax: (44) 464 0598 (administration) *or* 464 1130 (immigration).
E-mail: kyiv@international.gc.ca
Website: www.kyiv.gc.ca

General Information

AREA: 603,700 sq km (233,090 sq miles).
POPULATION: 47,622,436 (official estimate 2003).
POPULATION DENSITY: 78.9 per sq km.
CAPITAL: Kyiv. **Population:** 2,611,000 (2001).
GEOGRAPHY: Ukraine is bordered by the Russian Federation to the north and east; Belarus to the north; Poland, the Slovak Republic and Hungary to the west; and Romania and Moldova to the southwest. It is a varied country with mountains in the west, plains in the centre and the Black Sea views to the south. The north of the state is dominated by forests. Its other two main features are wooded steppe with beech and oak forests and the treeless steppe. The River Dnieper divides Ukraine roughly in half, and flows into the Black Sea.
GOVERNMENT: Republic. Gained independence from the Soviet Union in 1991. **Head of State:** President Viktor Yuschchenko since 2005. **Head of Government:** Prime Minister Yuliya Tymoshenko since 2005.
LANGUAGE: Ukrainian is the sole official state language. A member of the eastern Slav languages and similar to Russian, it was discouraged for centuries by Tsarist and Soviet authorities. It is still widely spoken in western and central Ukraine, although Russian is spoken by virtually everyone. Russian is the main language spoken in Kyiv, eastern Ukraine and Crimea. The present government uses every opportunity to promote the revival of Ukrainian, particularly in schools. There are 12 million ethnic Russians in Ukraine, 500,000 Jews and more than 250,000 Crimean Tatars.
RELIGION: There are about 35 million Ukrainian Orthodox faithful, although the church is divided into a traditional pro-Moscow and a breakaway pro-Kyiv faction. 5 million Eastern-rite (Uniate) Catholics, subservient to Rome, are concentrated in western Ukraine and it is now several years since a Stalin-era ban on their church was lifted. There are also Protestant and Muslim minorities. Mass emigration has reduced the numbers of Jews, concentrated in Kyiv, Lviv and Odessa.
TIME: GMT + 2 (GMT + 3 from last Sunday in March to Saturday before last Sunday in October).
ELECTRICITY: 220 volts AC, 50Hz.
COMMUNICATIONS: Telephone: Ukraine has reliable communications with the West, and most major cities provide IDD facilities and can be dialled from abroad. Country code: 380. Outgoing international code: 810. Telephone counters in the central post offices of city centres are usually open 24 hours. **Mobile telephone:** GSM 900/1800. Operators are *Kyivstar* (website: www.kyivstar.net), *Ukrainian Mobile Comms* (website: www.umc.ua) and *Ukranian Radio Systems* (website: www.welcome2well.com). GSM 1800 operator is *Astelit*, *Golden Telecom* (website: www.goldentele.com). Coverage is limited to Kyiv and other main urban areas. **Fax:** Facilities are good and are available in most offices and hotels. **Telegram:** These can be sent from central post offices in large cities 24 hours a day. **Internet:** ISPs include *UANet* (website: www.ua.net) and *Ukraine Intercom* (website: www.ukrcom.net.ua). E-mail can be accessed from Internet cafes in Cherkassy, Kyiv, Lyiv and Odessa . **Post:** Services are erratic. Letters to Western Europe can take two weeks or more. The main post office in Kyiv is located at Khreshchatik 22 and is open 24 hours. Post office hours: Generally 0800-1700. **Press:** The most widely read include the daily *Uryadoviy Kuryer*, the parliamentary daily, *Holos Ukrainy*, *Kievskiye Vedomosti*, and the thrice-weekly, *Silski Visti*. The Russian press is also widely available. News from Ukraine is published in English and available in 70 other countries. Western newspapers are now available in Kyiv, but not in other parts of the country.
Radio: BBC World Service (website: www.bbc.co.uk/worldservice) and Voice of America (website: www.voa.gov) can be received. From time to time the frequencies change and the most up-to-date can be found online.

Passport/Visa

	Passport Required?	Visa Required?	Return Ticket Required?
Full British	Yes	Yes	No
Australian	Yes	Yes	No
Canadian	Yes	Yes	No
USA	Yes	Yes	No
Other EU	Yes	Yes	No
Japanese	Yes	Yes/1	No

Note: Regulations and requirements may be subject to change at short notice, and you are advised to contact the appropriate diplomatic or consular authority before finalising travel arrangements. Details of these may be found at the head of this country's entry. Any numbers in the chart refer to the footnotes below.

Note: (a) Ukrainian visas are *not* valid in the Russian Federation, and Russian Federation visas are *not* valid in Ukraine. (b) As a general rule, visitors should apply for a visa before travelling.

PASSPORTS: Passport valid for at least one month beyond return date required by all.

VISAS: Required by all except the following:
(a) nationals of all CIS countries (except nationals of Turkmenistan who *do* need a visa);
(b) nationals of Mongolia, Hungary, Poland and Romania.

Types of visa and cost: *Tourist*: £20 (single-entry); £35 (double-entry). *Business/Private*: £20 (single-entry); £40 (double-entry); £110 (multiple-entry). *Student*: £10 (single-entry). *Transit*: £10 (double-entry); £50 (multiple-entry, business only).

Note: (a) A handling charge of £20 is also required from the Embassy for each application. (b) **1.** For citizens of Japan, visas are free of charge.

Validity: *Single-entry*: Up to six months from date of issue; *Double-entry/Multiple-entry*: Six to 12 months; *Transit*: Five days for each entry.

Application to: Consulate (or Consular section at Embassy); see *Contact Addresses* section.

Application requirements: (a) Valid passport/travel document with at least one blank page. (b) One completed application form. (c) Two recent passport-size photos. (d) Fee (postal order or company cheque only; if applying by post, enclose two separate postal orders or company cheques covering the handling charge and visa fee). (e) A contact telephone number. (f) Recorded, registered, self-addressed envelope for postal applications. *Tourism*: (a)-(f) and, (g) *Tourist voucher with confirmation of hotel booking. *Business*: (a)-(f) and, (g) *Letter of invitation from Ukrainian company or organisation stating purpose of the visit. (h) Copy of registration certificate of company or office in Ukraine. (i) *For *multiple-entry* visas, detailed letters from Ukrainian company and company in home country explaining necessity for multiple-entry visa. *Private*: (a)-(f) and, (g) *Letter of invitation from Ukraine (faxed copy is acceptable) issued by the Passport and Immigration Department of a local Police Station in Ukraine. *Student*: (a)-(f) and, (g) The original invitation letter from the Ministry of Education of Ukraine. *Transit*: (a)-(f) and, (g) Photocopy of the visa (if required) of the country of destination.

Note: *Nationals of EU countries, Canada, Japan, Slovak Republic, Switzerland, Turkey and the USA applying for business or private visas *do not* require a letter of invitation. Nationals of these countries (except nationals of Slovak Republic and Turkey) may also provide a round-trip ticket from a Ukrainian airline company instead of a tourist voucher.

Working days required: 10 if submitted by post; three if submitted in person. This applies only to nationals of the EU, and nationals of Canada, Japan, Slovak Republic, Sweden, Turkey and the USA. For all other nationals, processing will always take approximately 10 days.

Money

Currency: Hryvnya (UAH) = 100 kopiyok (singular: kopiyka). Notes are in denominations of UAH200, 100, 50, 20, 10, 5, 2 and 1. Coins are in denominations of 50, 25, 10, 5, 2 and 1 kopiyok.

Currency exchange: Money should only be changed at currency booths on the street or in banks. It is advisable to keep receipts showing money changed. Changing money with black-market traders is not recommended and can be dangerous.

Credit & debit cards: Not readily accepted. Only a few restaurants and hotels will accept them.

Travellers cheques: Not generally advised. If taken, they should be made out in US Dollars.

Currency restrictions: The import of local currency is up to the amount declared on the Ukrainian Exit Customs Declaration. The export of local currency is limited to UAH85. The import of foreign currency is limited to US$10,000 and any amounts exceeding US$1000 require a special customs form. The export of foreign currency is limited to US$1000. Any higher amounts can be exported with special permission from the National Bank of Ukraine.

Exchange rate indicators: The following figures are a guide to the movements of the Hryvnya against Sterling and the US Dollar:

Date	Feb '04	May '04	Aug '04	Nov '04
£1.00=	9.71	9.51	9.79	10.07
$1.00=	5.33	5.33	5.31	5.32

Banking hours: Mon-Fri 0930-1730.

Duty Free

The following items may be imported into Ukraine without incurring customs duty:
200 cigarettes or 50 cigars or 250g of tobacco products; 1l of spirits and 2l of wine (persons over 20 years of age only); goods for personal use, provided holding proof of their export, or imported under conditions of transit (toiletries and personal effects); gifts up to the value of €200.

Prohibited: Items which can be harmful and dangerous to the health of the population or animals or environment; products containing propaganda or war or racism or genocide; agricultural goods for non-commercial purposes without authorised certificate; high-frequency radio and electronics and communication means; gas; hunting weapons unless permission is given bu authorised relative in Ukraine; dogs and cats (cats, dogs and all birds except pigeons are allowed import if they have veterinarian health certificate not issued over 10 days prior to arrival; rabbits need proof of inoculation done at least 30 days before transportation, or proof of yearly inoculation); pigeons.

Public Holidays

2005: Jan 1 New Year's Day. **Jan 7** Orthodox Christmas Day. **Mar 8** International Women's Day. **May 1-2** Labour Days. **May 9** Victory Day. **Jun 28** Constitution Day. **Aug 24** Ukrainian Independence Day.

2006: Jan 1 New Year's Day. **Jan 7** Orthodox Christmas Day. **Mar 8** International Women's Day. **May 1-2** Labour Days. **May 9** Victory Day. **Jun 28** Constitution Day. **Aug 24** Ukrainian Independence Day.

Health

	Special Precautions?	Certificate Required?
Yellow Fever	No	No
Cholera	No	No
Typhoid & Polio	1	N/A
Malaria	No	N/A

Note: Regulations and requirements may be subject to change at short notice, and you are advised to contact your doctor well in advance of your intended date of departure. Any numbers in the chart refer to the footnotes below.

1: Typhoid may occur in rural areas.

Food & drink: All water should be regarded as a potential health risk. Water used for drinking, brushing teeth or making ice should have first been boiled or otherwise sterilised. Milk is pasteurised and dairy products are safe for consumption. Only eat well-cooked meat and fish, preferably served hot. Pork, salad and mayonnaise may carry increased risk. Vegetables should be cooked and fruit peeled.

Other risks: Widespread outbreaks of *diphtheria* have been reported in recent years. *Tick-borne encephalitis* occurs in forested areas. Visitors are advised to seek medical advice about immunisation and precautionary measures. Good personal hygiene and care with water and food supplies are essential. *Hepatitis A* may occur and precautions should be taken.

Health care: The health service does, in theory, provide free medical treatment for all citizens and travellers who become ill. However, as in most parts of the former Soviet Union, health care is a serious problem. For minor difficulties, visitors are advised to ask the management at their hotels for help. For major problems, visitors are well advised to seek help outside the country. Travel insurance is, in fact, compulsory for all travellers. It is advisable to take a supply of those medicines that are likely to be required (but check first that they may be legally imported) as medicines can prove difficult to obtain. Travellers are advised to contact their Embassy, in the first instance, for advice on where to get medical help.

Travel - International

AIR: *Ukraine International Airlines (PS)*, a Ukrainian alliance with *Aer Fi Group* and *Austrian Airlines/Swiss*, links Kyiv with Amsterdam, Barcelona, Berlin, Brussels, Copenhagen, Frankfurt/M, Helsinki, Lisbon, London, Madrid, Milan, Paris, Rome, Rotterdam, Vienna and Zürich. *Air Ukraine (6U)* serves a smaller number of European points, as well as Moscow and other Russian cities aboard aircraft reclaimed from the former Soviet airline *Aeroflot (SU)*. Flights are also available from Lviv to New York, Warsaw and Washington, from Simferopol to Turkey and from Ivano-Frankivsk to the UK (summer only).

Approximate flight times: From Kyiv to *London* is three hours 30 minutes, to *Moscow* is one hour 15 minutes and to *Vienna* is two hours.

International airports: *Kyiv (IEV)* – Borispol International (KBP) is approximately 34km (21 miles) from central Kyiv. The airport has undergone extensive renovation. Facilities currently include banks/bureaux de change, duty free shops, restaurants, child facilities, post office, left luggage and pharmacy. The bus terminal is located at Ploshcha Peremohy where an airport bus operates services to the city centre every 30 minutes for most of the day (travel time - approximately one hour). The bus fare is around US$2. Taxis usually cost about US$15. The arrival/departure point in central Kyiv is the new entrance to the central railway station.

Departure tax: None.

SEA/RIVER: The main ports are Izmail and Odessa on the River Danube. Services are available to the Russian Federation ports of Novorossiysk and Sochi, Batumi and Sukhumi in Georgia, as well as to a number of cities on the Black Sea and the Mediterranean. A ferry service connects Sevastopol and Istanbul, Turkey. The republic's most important internal waterway is the River Dnieper. Black Sea cruises around the Crimean peninsula are available and well recommended. Most cruises leave from Bulgaria, Romania and Turkey and stop over in Yalta, although there are a few cruises that leave from Yalta.

RAIL: The 22,730km (14,207 miles) of railway track link most towns and cities within the republic and further links extend from Kyiv to all other CIS member states. The main stations are Kyiv and Lyiv. Regular daily services connect these stations with Moscow. There are direct lines to Brest in Belarus, Berlin in Germany, Budapest in Hungary, Warsaw in Poland and Bucharest in Romania. Ukrainian trains are slow. Journeys can range from pleasant to terribly uncomfortable if, for instance, the heating is not working. Security can also be a problem, as many muggings have been reported. If travelling by overnight train, do not leave the compartment unattended. Buying tickets locally can be difficult and it is easier to pre-book through Intourist Travel Ltd before departure (see *Contact Addresses* section). From Kyiv to Moscow takes 16 hours and to St Petersburg is about 36 hours.

ROAD: Of the 172,315km (107,074 miles) of road network, 29,227km (18,161 miles) are main or national roads. Ukrainian roads tend to be in reasonable condition. Border points are at Chop, Mostiska and Uzhgorod. It is recommended to carry a visa to enable a smooth border crossing. Private car-repair garages have recently become available, along with state-owned ones; however, spare parts are still scarce. The biggest problem is availability of suitable petrol (for instance, unleaded petrol is not available). Never set out on a journey without several cans of petrol. Insurance cover can be difficult to arrange. See *Travel – Internal* for information on **traffic regulations** and **documentation**.

Coach: *Eurolines*, departing from Victoria Coach Station in London, serves destinations in the Ukraine. For further information, contact *Eurolines*, 52 Grosvenor Gardens, London SW1, UK (tel: (08705) 143 219; fax: (01582) 400 694; website: www.eurolines.co.uk *or* www.nationalexpress.com).

Bus: A few buses run daily services from Karkiv to Moscow.

Travel - Internal

AIR: Fuel shortages used to result in sharp reductions in flights within Ukraine and erratic timetables. However, the situation has improved recently. *Air Ukraine*'s repainted *Aeroflot* aircraft are far from comfortable and buying tickets is extremely difficult and almost guaranteed to involve complicated negotiations with the local travel agencies. Pre-booking through Intourist Travel Ltd in London is advised (see *Contact Addresses* section). Winter weather frequently grounds aircraft. The most reliable flights are from Kyiv to Donetsk, Lviv and Odessa.

RIVER: Cruises between Kyiv, Odessa and Sevastopol are very popular and can be booked through various tour operators.

RAIL: Again, pre-booking through Intourist Travel Ltd in London is advised, as buying tickets is a difficult undertaking. Journeys are slow, though trains are more reliable than air travel in winter.

ROAD: Bus: There are services to most cities and towns although they are not always recommended due to overcrowding and uncleanliness. **Taxi:** Hiring a driver for a long-distance destination is a realistic option, costing about US$200 from Kyiv to Odessa or a similar journey. **Car hire:** Self-drive hire cars are gradually becoming more available. **Traffic regulations:** Speed limits are 60kph (37mph) in built-up areas, 90kph (55mph) in outside areas and 110kph (69mph) on the motorways. Traffic drives on the right; righthand-drive cars are prohibited. Drinking and driving is strictly prohibited. Heavy fines are imposed if traffic police smell alcohol on a driver's breath. **Documentation:** An International Driving Permit is necessary.

URBAN: Kharkiv and Kyiv have clean, efficient and cheap metro systems, where tickets can be purchased at vending machines inside the stations. Buses and trolleybuses are extremely crowded and are best avoided. Taxis are easy to

A B C D E F G H I J K L M N O P Q R S T U V W X Y Z

find in the cities. State-owned taxis have yellow and black signs on the roof and are metered. Fares should be negotiated in advance for private taxis. Some shared taxis and minibuses exist on fixed routes. Hitchhiking is very common, although not recommended. Travellers can indicate the need for a lift and the driver will take them to their destination cheaply by Western standards, but prices should be agreed in advance. There are no public transport services from 0100-0500.

Accommodation

HOTELS: Standards are lower than in countries where the tourist industry is more developed. The best hotels are in Kyiv, Odessa and the seaside resort Yalta.
PRIVATE ROOMS: A room in a private home is an excellent accommodation option in Ukraine as the people are friendly and hospitable, and prices tend to be far more reasonable. However, there is no organisation as such that arranges rooms in private homes. Visitors can, however, ask around, as the savings and greater comfort may be well worth the effort (as long as due caution is observed).
CAMPING/CARAVANNING: Campsites are available on the outskirts of cities.

Resorts & Excursions

KYIV: The capital of Ukraine is the third-largest city in the CIS. It is also the cradle of Russian civilisation, the origin of the Kyiv Rus State founded in the eighth and ninth centuries and the city from which the Orthodox faith spread throughout Eastern Europe.
Even though many of its buildings were destroyed in World War II, Kyiv still has much to offer. The **Caves Monastery** in the city centre is the focal point of the early Orthodox church. Visitors have to carry candles to see the church relics, which are set in a maze of catacombs. It is the headquarters of the pro-Russian Orthodox church. The 11th-century **St Sofia Cathedral** contains splendid icons and frescoes and is situated in beautiful grounds. The **Golden Gate of Kyiv** is the last remnant of the 10th-century walls built to defend the city. Other attractions include the **Cathedral of St Vladimir** (the headquarters of the rival pro-Ukrainian church), the **Opera House**, the **Museum of Ukrainian Art** (with its collection of the work of regional artists from the 16th century to the present) and the **Historical Museum of Ukraine**. **Andreyev Hill** is a restored cobbled street in central Kyiv now used by artists to sell their wares. There are a lot of cafes and restaurants in this area. **Khreshchatik Street** and **Independence Square** are Kyiv's main thoroughfares. The square is particularly elegant with its chestnut trees and fountains. **Martinsky Palace and Parliament** is the official residence of Ukraine's President. The nearby **Park of Glory** is a war memorial, with a vast and controversial monument of a woman with a sword and shield overlooking the river. Locals go swimming in summer in the **Dnieper River** and climb onto its ice in winter to fish. It is possible to take boat trips on the river. There is a park and a beach on **Trukhaniv Island**.
LVIV: A city of striking Baroque and Renaissance architecture, Lviv is the focal point of Ukrainian national culture. It was the centre of Ukrainian nationalist ambition at the beginning of the Soviet era. The **City Castle** was the first building to fly Ukraine's blue-and-yellow national flag. Lviv is also the headquarters of Ukraine's Greek Orthodox church.
Located by the foothills of the picturesque Carpathians, it is one of the oldest and most unusual cities in Europe. Lviv is 'the city of lions' – the heart and soul of Western Ukraine with a population of over 900,000. Lviv was mentioned in the Volyn chronicle in 1256 when Galycian King Danylo Galytsky founded the city and named it after his son Leo. Thanks to its advantageous location, many important trades and cultures meet in Lviv. Busy trade led to a dramatic increase in prosperity. Secular and religious gentry, rich merchants, artisans and craftspeople lived within the narrow ring of the city walls. As early as the 15th century, the city had its own mint, water supply system and regular international post. The streets were paved with cobbled stones and many new houses were built.
As the centuries passed, the varied heritage led to a wide variety of museum artefacts. The **National Museum**, **Museum of History**, **Art Gallery**, **Antique Armoury** (City Arsenal) and **Museum of Ethnography and Crafts** are famous for their collections. Development of the pharmaceutical trade in Ukraine is represented by the collection of the **Pharmaceutical Museum** – the oldest functioning pharmacy of Lviv (established in 1735). The interiors of these fabulous buildings evoke the atmosphere of times past.
The city itself is often called 'the open-air museum'. The highlight of its architecture is doubtlessly Market Square, connected for more than 600 years with local history. The **Market Square** of the old city performed the function of an economic, political and administrative centre up to the end of the 19th century. The area housed members of the urban nobility and wealthy merchant class, building many mansions and commercial properties. Today, Market Square is the core of the historical and architectural preservation area, consisting of 45 buildings. They reflect elements of many architectural traditions, such as Gothic, Baroque, Renaissance and Rococo.
Several theatre companies perform in Lviv. The **Opera House** of Ivan Franko is a source of great pride to locals. Extravagantly built, with richly decorated façade and interior, its architecture leads Lviv Opera to be classed among the best theatres in Europe.
ODESSA: Odessa is the site of the famous 192 steps of the **Potemkin stairway** from Sergei Eisenstein's film, *Battleship Potemkin*. In addition, Odessa is also a centre of renewal of Jewish culture, with a community of 45,000. There is a vast **Opera House** – one of the world's largest. The ceiling is decorated with scenes from the plays of Shakespeare. Also worth visiting is the **Statue of the Duke of Richelieu**, the **Vorontsov Palace** on the waterfront and the **Archaeological Museum** with exhibits from the Black Sea area and Egypt.
THE CRIMEA: This was once a summer playground for Kremlin leaders. Hotels and services are relatively cheap for Westerners, and the place is a favourite with German tourists. The region's dusty capital of **Simferopol** has few tourist sights. It is **Yalta**, the 'Pearl of the Crimea', which draws visitors. Former Communist Party spas have now been turned into resort centres. The region's vineyards produce good-quality wine which can be tasted locally quite cheaply. The **Wine Tasting Hall** in Yalta is as good a place as any. The **Vorontsov Palace** was designed by Edward Blore, one of the architects of Buckingham Palace. **Nikitsky Gardens**, just outside of Yalta, is a good afternoon's excursion. Industry is centred on **Massandra**, above Yalta. **Livada** is where Roosevelt, Churchill and Stalin met in the **Livada Palace** in 1945. **Foros** is where Gorbachev was held for three days during the 1991 coup.

Sport & Activities

Ukrainians go **skiing** in the Carpathian Mountains in the west, where top resorts are in Vorokhta and Yeremcha near the Romanian border, and Slavsko, close to the Slovak Republic. The most popular spectator sport is **football**, although successes in the international arena for Oksana Baiul, Andrei Medvedev and Sergei Bubka have attracted many to **figure skating**, **tennis** and **athletics**.

Social Profile

FOOD & DRINK: Specialities include *borshch* (beetroot soup), *varenniki* (dough containing cheese, meat or fruit) and *holubtsi* (cabbage rolls). Chicken Kiev exists but is better known in the West. Restaurants still tend to be fairly expensive (around US$40 for a 2- to 3-course meal), but visitors now have a wider choice of cuisines (including French, Indian, Italian, Japanese or Thai), particularly in Kyiv. Crimean wines are excellent, especially dessert wines such as *Krasny Kamen* ('Red Stone'). For those who prefer dry wine, *Abrau* and *Miskhako* are excellent brands of cabernet. Also outstanding are *Artyomov* champagne (bottled in eastern Ukraine) and fortified wines from Massandra, particularly one named 'Black Doctor'.
NIGHTLIFE: Opera is performed in the ornate theatres of Kyiv, Lviv and Odessa. Ukrainians have a deep-rooted musical tradition and singing is very popular. Most cities also have good musical comedy, puppet-theatre and troupes performing theatrical works in Ukrainian and Russian. Tickets are cheap by Western standards and readily available on the day of performance at the box offices. Post-Soviet economics unfortunately mean that many performances are badly attended. Prominent visiting artists most often perform in Kyiv's vast Ukraine Theatre, where prices are higher.
SHOPPING: Artwork is the best buy. Top-quality paintings, ceramics and jewellery may be purchased quite cheaply at galleries or direct from artists on the street. Avoid the state shops, which have dull merchandise. **Shopping hours:** Large state or department stores tend to open Mon-Fri 0800-1900, whereas small boutiques are generally open 0900-1800. Some shops stay open as late as 2000.
SPECIAL EVENTS: The following is a selection of special events occurring in Ukraine in 2005:
Jan 7 *Orthodox Christmas*, nationwide. **Apr 1** *April Fool's Day* (costumes and street dancing), Odessa. **May** *National Virtuoso*, Lviv. **May 28-29** *Kiev Days*. **Aug 24** *Independence Day Celebrations*, nationwide.
SOCIAL CONVENTIONS: Ukrainian people are warm and particularly friendly to visitors. It is not at all uncommon for Ukrainians to invite strangers into their own homes. People on the street are friendly despite the rigours of post-Soviet life. Formal attire is rarely required, though people dress smartly for the theatre. Visitors should avoid ostentatious displays of wealth in public places. **Tipping:** Tips and, if appropriate, small gifts are appreciated. Service is sometimes included in first-class restaurants and hotel bills.

Business Profile

ECONOMY: Ukraine has large areas of very fertile land, which gave it its reputation as the 'bread basket' of the former Soviet Union. Grain, sugar beet and vegetables are the main crops and there is extensive livestock farming. The country is also blessed with mineral resources, particularly coal in the huge Donbass fields, as well as iron ore, manganese and titanium. There are a few reserves of gas and oil but Ukraine has to import over three-quarters of its requirements of these products from elsewhere, mainly from the Russian Federation and Turkmenistan. Much of this is still needed to fuel the heavy industries that dominate the country's manufacturing economy. Metalworking, engineering products (especially machinery and transport equipment) and chemicals are the most important of these. A large proportion of industry was previously devoted to military production but this has sharply declined since the demise of the Soviet Union and drastic cuts in defence budgets.
With some reluctance, Ukraine began to dismantle its highly centralised command economy in 1992 and introduce market mechanisms under the guidance of the IMF, which the country joined, along with the World Bank, in the same year. Key elements of the programme were privatisation, price reform, trade liberalisation and, as a necessary adjunct, the introduction of a fully convertible currency – the Hryvnya – which came into use in 1995. Throughout this period, and for some years after, the Ukrainian economy contracted at about 12 per cent per year, as well as suffering very high inflation which occasionally touched 400 per cent. The reform programme has continued to make slow progress in the face of opposition from entrenched interests, fear of foreign competition and disagreements amongst the pro-reformers over the pace of change. After a difficult first 10 years, the post-Soviet economy is now fairly stable: annual GDP growth is now 9.3 per cent, while inflation has been reduced to a more manageable 12 per cent. Officially, unemployment is 3.7 per cent of the workforce, but a large 'grey' economy has evolved, which some estimates put at half the size of the legitimate economy. Ukraine also belongs to the European Bank for Reconstruction and Development as a 'Country of Operation'. Several of Ukraine's neighbours will be joining the European Union in the near future. Ukraine itself is far from a condition in which it might be accepted for EU membership, but this is bound to have a major impact on the country's economic policy-making.
The Russian Federation still accounts for over one-third of Ukraine's trade; other major trading partners are Germany, Italy, Turkey, Poland and Turkmenistan.
BUSINESS: Suits, and ties for men, are required for official business. Exchange of business cards is extremely common and visitors are advised to bring company cards. **Office hours:** Mon-Fri 0900-1800. Lunch tends to be at least one-and-a-half hours.
COMMERCIAL INFORMATION: The following organisations can offer advice: Chamber of Commerce and Industry, 33 vul. Velyka Zhytomyrska , 01601 Kyiv (tel: (44) 272 2911; fax: (44) 272 3353; e-mail: ucci@ucci.org.ua; website: www.ucci.org.ua); *or* Ministry of Foreign Affairs (see *Contact Addresses* section); *or* Ministry of Foreign Economic Relations, Lvovska pl. 8, 254655 Kyiv (tel/fax: (44) 212 0005).

Climate

Temperate with warm summers; crisp, sunny autumns; and cold, snowy winters.
Required clothing: Lightweight clothes needed in summer, light- to mediumweight in the spring and autumn and heavyweight in the winter.

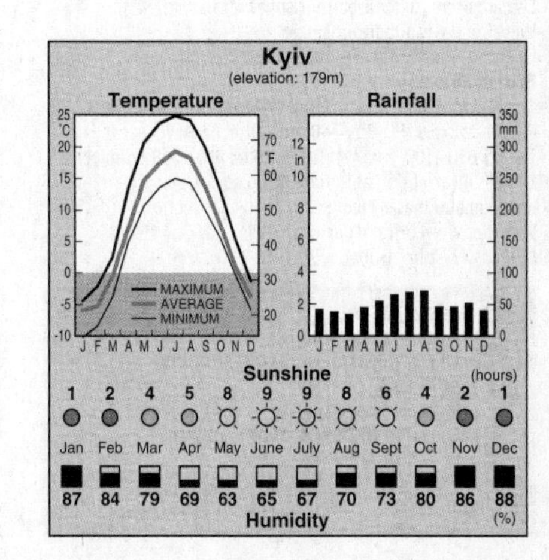

United Arab Emirates

LATEST TRAVEL ADVICE CONTACTS

British Foreign and Commonwealth Office
Tel: (0870) 606 0290 Website: www.fco.gov.uk
US Department of State
Website: http://travel.state.gov/travel
Canadian Department of Foreign Affairs and Int'l Trade
Tel: (1 800) 267 8376 Website: www.dfait-maeci.gc.ca

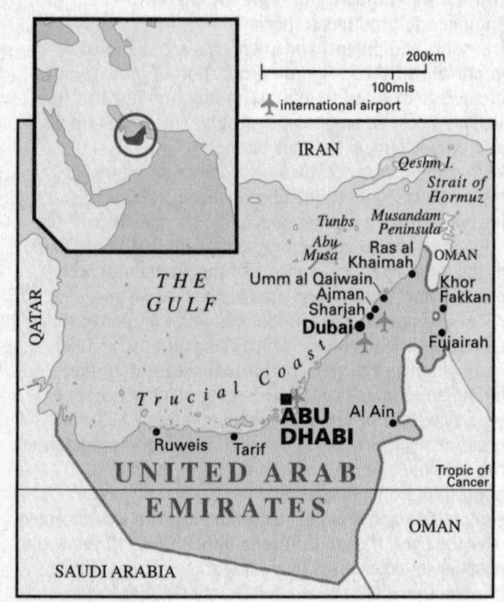

Location: Middle East.

Country dialling code: 971.

Ministry of Information & Culture
Department of External Information, PO Box 17, Abu Dhabi, UAE
Tel: (2) 445 2922 *or* 446 6145.
Fax: (2) 445 2504 *or* 0458.
E-mail: mininfex@emirate.net.ae
Website: www.uaeinteract.com
Department of Tourism & Commerce Marketing
Street address: National Bank of Dubai Building, 10th-12th Floors, Baniyas Road, Deira, Dubai, UAE
Postal address: PO Box 594, Deira, Dubai, UAE
Tel: (4) 223 0000. Fax: (4) 223 0022.
E-mail: info@dubaitourism.ae
Website: www.dubaitourism.ae
Embassy of the United Arab Emirates
30 Prince's Gate, London SW7 1PT, UK
Tel: (020) 7581 1281 or 7808 8302 (consular section).
Fax: (020) 7581 9616.
E-mail: information@uaeembassyuk.net *or* commerce@uaeembassyuk.net (trade and commerce).
Website: www.uaeembassyuk.net
Opening hours: Mon-Fri 0900-1500; 0930-1300 (lodging visa applications); 1300-1400 (visa collection).
Consulate of the United Arab Emirates
48 Prince's Gate, London SW7 2QA, UK
Tel: (020) 7808 8302. Fax: (020) 7581 9616.
Opening hours: Mon-Fri 0930-1300.
Government of Dubai Department of Tourism & Commerce Marketing
1st Floor, 125 Pall Mall, London SW1Y 5EA, UK
Tel: (020) 7839 0580.
Fax: (020) 7839 0582.
E-mail: dtcm_uk@dubaitourism.ae
Website: www.dubaitourism.ae
Opening hours: Mon-Fri 0900-1700.
British Embassy
Street address: 22 Khalid bin Al Waleed Street, Abu Dhabi, UAE
Postal address: PO Box 248, Abu Dhabi, UAE
Tel: (2) 610 1100. Fax: (2) 610 1586 *or* 610 1518 (chancery).
E-mail: information.abudhabi@fco.gov.uk *or* consular.abudhabi@fco.gov.uk (consular section).
Website: www.britain-uae.org
Embassy also in: Dubai.

TIMATIC CODES

Health	AMADEUS: **TI-DFT/JIB/HE** GALILEO/WORLDSPAN: **TI-DFT/JIB/HE** SABRE: **TIDFT/JIB/HE**
Visa	AMADEUS: **TI-DFT/JIB/VI** GALILEO/WORLDSPAN: **TI-DFT/JIB/VI** SABRE: **TIDFT/JIB/VI**

To access TIMATIC country information on Health and Visa regulations through the Computer Reservations System (CRS), type in the appropriate command line listed above.

Credit: © The Government of Dubai, Department of Tourism and Commerce Marketing

Embassy of the United Arab Emirates
3522 International Court, NW, Washington, DC 20008, USA
Tel: (202) 243 2400.
Fax: (202) 243 2432 *or* 2419 (consular section).
Embassy of the United States of America
Al-Sudan Street, PO Box 4009, Abu Dhabi, UAE
Tel: (2) 414 2200.
Fax: (2) 414 2241 (consular).
E-mail: consularabudha@state.gov *or* webmasterabudhabi@state.gov
Website: http://usembassy.state.gov/uae
Consulate General in: Dubai.
Canadian Embassy
Street address: Villa 440, 26th Street (Al Nahayan Street), Abu Dhabi, UAE
Postal address: PO Box 6970, Abu Dhabi, UAE
Tel: (2) 407 1300.
Fax: (2) 407 1399.
E-mail: abdbi@dfait-maeci.gc.ca
Website: www.dfait-maeci.gc.ca/abudhabi
Consulate in: Dubai.
Embassy of the United Arab Emirates
45 O'Connor Street, Suite 1800, World Exchange Plaza, Ottawa, Ontario K1P 1A4, Canada
Tel: (613) 565 7272.
Fax: (613) 565 8007.
E-mail: safara@uae-embassy.com
Website: www.uae-embassy.com

General Information

AREA: 77,700 sq km (30,000 sq miles).
POPULATION: 3,754,000 (official estimate 2002).
POPULATION DENSITY: 48.3 per sq km.
CAPITAL: Abu Dhabi. **Population:** 527,000 (2002).
GEOGRAPHY: The Emirates are bordered to the north by the Gulf and the Musandam Peninsula, to the east by Oman, to the south and west by Saudi Arabia and to the northwest by Qatar. They comprise a federation of seven small former sheikhdoms. Abu Dhabi is the largest Emirate, and the remainder (Ajman, Dubai, Fujairah, Ras al-Khaimah, Sharjah and Umm al Qaiwain) are known collectively as the Northern States. The land is mountainous and mostly desert. Abu Dhabi is flat and sandy, and within its boundaries is the Buraimi Oasis. Dubai has a 16km (10 mile) deep-water creek, giving it the popular name of 'Pearl of the Gulf.' Sharjah has a deep-water port on the Batinah coast at Khor Fakkan, facing the Indian Ocean. Ras al-Khaimah is the fourth emirate in size. Fujairah, one of the three smaller sheikhdoms located on the Batinah coast, has agricultural potential, while Ajman and Umm al Qaiwain were once small coastal fishing villages.
GOVERNMENT: Federation of seven autonomous Emirates. **Head of State:** President Sheikh Khalifa since 2004. **Head of Government:** Prime Minister Sheikh Maktoum bin Rashid Al-Maktoum (Emir of Dubai) since 1990.
LANGUAGE: Arabic is the official language. English is widely spoken and used as a second language in commerce.
RELIGION: Mostly Muslim, of which 16 per cent are Shiite and the remainder Sunni.
TIME: GMT + 4.
ELECTRICITY: 220/240 volts AC, 50Hz. Square three-pin plugs are widespread.
COMMUNICATIONS: Telephone: IDD is available both to and from all states. Country code: 971. Outgoing international code (Abu Dhabi): 00. Main area codes: Abu Dhabi 2; Ajman, Sharjah and Umm al Quwain 6; Al Ain 3; Dubai 4; Fujairah 9; Jebel Ali 4 and Ras al-Khaimah 7. There is a good local telephone network. Telephone calls *within* each state are free. **Mobile telephone:** GSM 900 network. Network operators include *ETISALAT* (website: www.etisalat.co.ae) There is also a GSM Satellite provider, *Thuraya* (website: www.thuraya.com). **Fax:** *ETISALAT* offices at main centres provide a service. All hotels have facilities. **Internet:** Internet cafes provide public access to Internet and e-mail services. ISPs include *Emirates Telecommunication* (website: www.emirates.net.ae). **Telegram:** Services are run by *ETISALAT*, which has offices throughout the Emirates and are also available through main post offices. **Post:** Airmail letters and parcels take about five days to reach Europe.
Press: English-language daily newspapers include *Emirates News, The Gulf Today, Khaleej Times* and *UAE Press Service Daily News*. Foreign newspapers are available in hotel bookshops and supermarkets.
Radio: BBC World Service (website: www.bbc.co.uk/worldservice) and Voice of America (website: www.voa.gov) can be received. From time to time the frequencies change and the most up-to-date can be found online.

Passport/Visa

	Passport Required?	Visa Required?	Return Ticket Required?
Full British	Yes	No/1	Yes
Australian	Yes	No/3	Yes
Canadian	Yes	No/3	Yes
USA	Yes	No/3	Yes
Other EU	Yes	No/2	Yes
Japanese	Yes	No/3	Yes

***Note:** Regulations and requirements may be subject to change at short notice, and you are advised to contact the appropriate diplomatic or consular authority before finalising travel arrangements. Details of these may be found at the head of this country's entry. Any numbers in the chart refer to the footnotes below.*

Restricted entry and transit: The Government of the United Arab Emirates refuses entry and transit to nationals of Israel.
PASSPORTS: Passport valid for a minimum of three months from date of arrival (six months for business travel) required. Often a sponsor will hold a visitor's passport. In these cases a receipt will be issued. This will generally be accepted in place of a passport where a transaction may require one.
VISAS: Required by all except the following:
(a) **1.** nationals of the UK with the endorsement 'British Citizen' for a maximum of 30 days (extendable on request up to 90 days);
(b) **2.** nationals of EU countries (except nationals of Cyprus, Czech Republic, Estonia, Hungary, Latvia, Lithuania, Malta, Poland, Slovak Republic and Slovenia), for a maximum of 30 days (extendable on request up to 90 days);
(c) **3.** nationals of Andorra, Australia, Brunei, Canada, Cyprus, Hong Kong (SAR), Iceland, Japan, Korea (Rep), Liechtenstein, Malaysia, Malta, Monaco, New Zealand, Norway, San Marino, Singapore, Switzerland, the USA and Vatican City for a maximum of 30 days (extendable on request up to 90 days);
(d) nationals of Bahrain, Kuwait, Oman, Qatar and Saudi Arabia;
(e) transit passengers, provided holding valid onward or return documentation and not leaving the airport for up to 12 hours.
Note: The Embassy only issues visas for diplomatic or service visits. For routine travel, visas for tourists and travellers (intending to visit family) and business travellers must be arranged via the *sponsor* (the hotel/package tour operator or UAE resident/company concerned). To obtain approval, the sponsor will require the visitor's proposed flight and passport details in advance. Business visits are made by invitation only and proof of company trading licence is required.
Types of visa and cost: *Visitor* and *Business*: £20. Price given is for UK nationals but price is dependent on nationality. Multiple-entry visas are only issued in very special circumstances. In case of visa being arranged by a sponsor, the request for multiple-entry should be marked clearly.
Validity: 30 days from date of entry and two months from date of issue. It may be possible to extend visas on request for up to a maximum of 90 days at the local immigration office.

Application to: Sponsor (as described above).
Application requirements: (a) Valid passport. (b) One passport-size photo. (c) Duplicate application form. (d) Letter from applicant's company/organisation (with extra copy) stipulating position held and purpose of visit. (e) Letter showing proof of sponsorship. (f) Fee, payable in cash only. (g) Sponsor's name, address, telephone number and occupation (business activity if a company). Contact local sponsor for details of individual requirements.
Working days required: Between one and five when arranged through a sponsor. However, allowances should be made for possible delays in approval procedure. It is strongly advised to apply well in advance of departure date.

Money

Currency: UAE Dirham (Dh) = 100 fils. Notes are in denominations of Dh1000, 500, 200, 100, 50, 20, 10 and 5. Coins are in denominations of Dh1, and 50, 25, 10, 5 and 1 fils.
Note: The Dirham is tied to the US Dollar.
Currency exchange: Most hotels will handle the exchange of foreign currency.
Credit & debit cards: American Express, Diners Club, MasterCard and Visa are widely accepted. Check with your credit or debit card company for details of merchant acceptability and other services which may be available.
Travellers cheques: These are widely accepted. To avoid additional exchange rate charges, travellers are advised to take travellers cheques in US Dollars or Pounds Sterling.
Currency restrictions: The import and export of both local and foreign currency are unrestricted.
Exchange rate indicators: The following figures are included as a guide to the movements of the UAE Dirham against Sterling and the US Dollar:

Date	Feb '04	May '04	Aug '04	Nov '04
£1.00=	6.68	6.56	6.76	6.95
$1.00=	3.67	3.67	3.67	3.67

Banking hours: Sat-Wed 0730-1300, Thurs 0730-1200. Some also open Sat-Wed 1630-1800.

Duty Free

The following items may be imported into the United Arab Emirates without incurring customs duty:
2000 cigarettes and 400 cigars and 2kg of tobacco; 2l of spirits of more than 22 per cent alcohol, and 2l of wine (non-Muslims over 18 years only); a reasonable amount of perfume for personal use (1l of eau-de-toilette and 150g of perfume for those visiting Dubai and/or Sharjah).
Prohibited items: Unstrung pearls except for personal use, raw seafood (only when visiting Dubai and/or Sharjah), fruit and vegetables from cholera-infected areas.

Public Holidays

2005: Jan 1 New Year's Day. **Jan 21** Eid al-Adha (Feast of the Sacrifice). **Feb 10** Al-Hijra (Islamic New Year). **Apr 21** Mouloud (Birth of the Prophet). **Aug 6** Accession of HH Sheikh Zayed. **Sep 1** Leilat al-Meiraj (Ascension of the Prophet). **Nov 3-5** Eid al-Fitr (End of Ramadan). **Dec 2** National Day.
2006: Jan 1 New Year's Day. **Jan 11** Eid al-Adha (Feast of the Sacrifice). **Jan 31** Al-Hijra (Islamic New Year). **Apr 11** Mouloud (Birth of the Prophet). **Aug 6** Accession of HH Sheikh Zayed. **Aug 22** Leilat al-Meiraj (Ascension of the Prophet). **Oct 22-24** Eid al-Fitr (End of Ramadan). **Dec 2** National Day.
Note: Muslim festivals are timed according to local sightings of various phases of the moon and the dates given above are approximations. During the lunar month of Ramadan that precedes Eid al-Fitr, Muslims fast during the day and feast at night and normal business patterns may be interrupted. Many restaurants are closed during the day and there may be restrictions on smoking and drinking. Some disruption may continue into Eid al-Fitr itself. Eid al-Fitr and Eid al-Adha may last anything from two to 10 days, depending on the region. For more information, see the *World of Islam* appendix.

Health

	Special Precautions?	Certificate Required?
Yellow Fever	No	No
Cholera	No	No
Typhoid & Polio	1	N/A
Malaria	2	N/A

Note: Regulations and requirements may be subject to change at short notice, and you are advised to contact your doctor well in advance of your intended date of departure. Any numbers in the chart refer to the footnotes below.

1: Immunisation against polio is sometimes advised; typhoid occurs in rural areas.
2: Malaria is not considered to be a risk in the Emirate of Abu Dhabi nor in the cities of Ajman, Dubai, Sharjah or Umm al Qaiwain. There is, however, a risk of contracting the disease (predominantly the benign *vivax* form) in the valleys and on the lower slopes of mountainous areas of the Northern States. In these areas, chloroquine or proguanil are recommended, plus protection against mosquito bites.
Food & drink: Mains water in major cities is safe to drink, but in small villages it should be filtered, or bottled water should be used. Water used for drinking, brushing teeth or making ice should have first been boiled or otherwise sterilised. Milk is unpasteurised and should be boiled. Powdered or tinned milk is available and is advised, but make sure that it is reconstituted with pure water. Avoid dairy products which are likely to have been made from unboiled milk. Only eat well-cooked meat and fish, preferably served hot. Salad and mayonnaise may carry increased risk. Vegetables should be cooked and fruit peeled.
Other risks: *Cutaneous leishmaniasis* and *tick-borne typhus* may occur; avoid mosquito, sandfly and tick bites. Wear shoes to avoid soil-borne parasites. Take precautions against heat exhaustion and sunstroke. Immunisation against *hepatitis A* is recommended. *Hepatitis B* is endemic.
Rabies is present close to the border with Oman. For those at high risk, vaccination before arrival should be considered. If you are bitten, seek medical advice without delay. For more information, consult the *Health* appendix.
Health care: Medical facilities are of a very high quality but are extremely expensive. Private health insurance is essential.

Travel - International

Note: Foreign nationals visiting the United Arab Emirates are advised to be very vigilant due to a significant terrorist threat to westerners. For further advice, contact the relevant local government travel advice department.
AIR: The national airlines are *Emirates (EK)* (website: www.emirates.com) and *Gulf Air (GF)* (website: www.gulfairco.com). *Emirates* operates international flights to and from Dubai; *Gulf Air* serves all UAE airports. *Emirates* is expanding services to the Far East. Many other airlines operate scheduled services to Dubai.
Approximate flight times: From *London* to Abu Dhabi is six hours 35 minutes and to Dubai is seven hours; from *Frankfurt/M* to Dubai is six hours; from *Hong Kong* to Dubai is eight hours and from *Nairobi* to Dubai is four hours.
International airports: *Abu Dhabi (AUH)* is 32km (20 miles) east of the city (travel time - 40 minutes). Buses and taxis are available at the airport. *Al Ghazal* taxis operate a fixed-rate service. Airport facilities include duty free shop, bank, bar, snack bar, bureau de change, post office and car hire (includes *Avis*, *Budget*, *Europcar* and *Thrifty*).
Al Ain International Airport (AAN) is 13km (8 miles) northwest of Al Ain. *Al Ghazal* taxis operate a fixed-rate service to the city centre. Public buses serve the airport. There is a bank and bureau de change, ATM, two restaurants, coffee shop, 24-hour cafe, duty free complex, children's playground in landscaped gardens, and a medical centre.
Dubai (DXB) (website: www.dubaiairport.com) is 4km (2.5 miles) southeast of the city (travel time - 10 minutes). Taxis and buses are available at the airport. Bus stations are opposite both Terminal 1 and 2. Airport facilities include duty free shop, bank, post office, shops, car hire, restaurant, snack bar and bar. The airport consists of two terminals. Expansion plans are underway to provide a new third Terminal and two new passenger concourses, due to be completed by 2006.
Sharjah (SHJ) is 10km (6 miles) from the city. Taxis are available at the airport. Airport facilities include duty free shop, car hire, bar, restaurant, snack bar and bank (only open restricted hours). *Ras al-Khaimah (RKT)* is 15km (9 miles) from the city. Taxis are available at the airport. Airport facilities include a duty free shop and restaurant/snack bar.
There is also an airport at *Fujairah* with duty free facilities.
Departure tax: None.
SEA: The main international ports are Jebel Ali, Rashid and Zayed (Abu Dhabi), Khalid (Sharjah), Saqr (Ras al-Khaimah) and Fujairah. Cruises call at Abu Dhabi and the cruise terminal in Dubai, and there are passenger/cargo services to the USA, the Far East, Australia and Europe. There are regular sailings between Sharjah and Bandar-é-Abbas (Iran).
ROAD: There is a good road into Oman and a fair one into Qatar that connects with the Trans-Arabian Highway on the overland route to Europe. Buses run daily between Dubai and Muscat (Oman) and also between Dubai or Abu Dhabi to Saudi Arabia.

Travel - Internal

AIR: A daily flight links Abu Dhabi and Dubai. Flights can also be chartered and there are small landing fields throughout the United Arab Emirates.
SEA: Commercial and passenger services serve all coastal ports. A water taxi travels between Dubai and Deira across the creek.
ROAD: There are good tarmac roads running along the west coast between Abu Dhabi and Dubai, Sharjah and Ras al Khaimah; between Sharjah and Dhaid; and linking Dubai with other Northern States and the interior. Traffic drives on the right and the speed limit in built-up areas is 60kph (38mph) and 80 to 100kph (50 to 63mph) elsewhere. **Bus:** Limited services link most towns. However, most hotels run their own scheduled bus services to the airport, city centre and beach resorts. **Taxi:** Available in all towns. In Abu Dhabi and Al-Ain, urban journey fares are metered, whilst fares for longer journeys should be agreed in advance. There is a surcharge for air-conditioned taxis. Many travellers find taxis to be the quickest and most convenient method of travel from Abu Dhabi to Dubai. **Car hire:** Most international car hire companies have offices at airports or hotels. A passport and either a valid international or national licence are necessary. **Documentation:** An International Driving Permit is recommended, although it is not legally required. A local driving licence can be issued on presentation of a valid national driving licence, two photos and a passport.

Accommodation

Accommodation is plentiful and some very reasonable prices can be found, with rates remaining constant all year round. Most of the major international hotel chains are represented, eg Forte, Hilton, Hyatt, Inter-Continental, Marriott, Ramada and Sheraton. There are also top-class beach resort hotels at Jebel Ali and Jumeirah Beach Hotel and a mountain resort hotel at Hatta Fort. Confirmation of reservation by fax is necessary. For more information, contact the Government of Dubai Department of Tourism & Commerce Marketing (see *Contact Addresses* section).

Resorts & Excursions

ABU DHABI

A predominantly modern city, Abu Dhabi nevertheless retains some of its ancient past. The **Diwan Amiri** (White Fort) was built in 1793 and still survives. There are many mosques, from the massive blue mosque on the corner of the **Corniche** to the tiny one in the centre of **Khalifa Street Roundabout**, surrounded by trees. There is also a museum. The oldest part of the town is the **Batin** area, served daily by the fishing *dhows* bringing their catch of Gulf prawns and other fish to the small harbours. The old building yards demonstrate craftspeople's skills that have remained unchanged for centuries. The city has ancient burial mounds at **Um al Nar**.
EXCURSIONS: Al Ain, 100km (60 miles) from Abu Dhabi, is an oasis and former caravan stop, built on a huge fertile plain. There is spectacular scenery along the journey from Abu Dhabi. The resort includes a camel market, zoo and museum containing old and new artefacts and Mesopotamian pottery. There is also a water spring at **Ain Faidha**, 14km (9 miles) from Al Ain. There are important archaeological digs at **Hili**, 10km (6 miles) from Al Ain. The stone tombs, including the famous **Great Sepulchre**, date back 5000 years. South of Al Ain is the **Hafit Mountain**, containing ancient tombs, pottery and swords. There are more ancient sites worth visiting at **Um Al Nar** and **Badi'i Bent Saud**. A fun park is situated at **Al-Hir** and majestic sand seas are to be seen at **Liwa**. Other areas of great scenic beauty include **Qarn Island**, **Belghilam Island** (famous for its gazelle breeding), near to **Sadiyat Island**, and **Abul-Abyadh Island**.

DUBAI

The 'Pearl of the Arabian Gulf' grew up as a seafaring settlement along either side of the Creek, a natural harbour for *dhow* traders, pearl divers and fishermen. **Deira** on the northern bank and Bur Dubai to the south are connected by a tunnel and two bridges and can also be reached by *abra* (water taxi). **Bur Dubai** has substantial areas of old buildings, atmospheric alleyways and **souks** (markets), including the world-famous Gold Souk and colourful Spice Souk. Fascinating glimpses of the past can be gained from **Al Fahidi Fort**, the **Dubai Museum** (which houses, among other things, artefacts recovered from the ancient graves at Al-Ghusais), the traditional windtower houses of the nearby Bastakiya district and, at the mouth of the Creek, the magnificently restored **Sheikh Saeed's Palace**, as well as the diving and heritage villages. The Deira side of the creek is cosmopolitan and lively, with many attractive gardens and first-class shopping facilities, ranging from Western-

style shops to the ancient **souks** where spices, perfume, clothing, antiques, handicrafts and jewels are available. Dubai's thriving tourist industry is based on guaranteed sunshine, a clean and safe environment, bargain shopping and superb sporting facilities, especially for golf and watersports. A long ribbon of development alongside the Gulf, extending south and west of Dubai city to **Jebel Ali**, offers an impressive range of coastal hotels and resorts. The recreation and sporting complex en route to Jebel Ali includes a golf course and an all-grass cricket pitch. Freshwater lakes can also be seen here, full of Japanese carp. The emirate has many well-qualified tour companies offering such activities as desert safaris by 4-wheel drive, sand-skiing, moonlit bedouin barbeques, camel riding and dhow cruises. The *Dubai World Cup* (the world's richest horse race), the *PGA Desert Classic Golf Tournament*, *Dubai Shopping Festival* and more than 80 major trade exhibitions are among the high-profile events attracting business and leisure visitors to the city each year.
EXCURSIONS: The ancient fortressed village of **Hatta** and **Wadi Hatta** is a lush and attractive valley in the foothills of the **Hajar Mountains** with superb desert scenery, on the journey from Dubai.

THE REST OF THE EMIRATES

THE DESERT: A spectacular and varied wilderness of magnificent red dunes and stark mountains with pockets of green oases. It is possible to meet the nomadic *Bedu* folk, whose hospitality is famous, and to watch camel races at dawn.
EXCURSIONS: Includes visits to Bedu villages and to the stunning white sand dunes at **Awir**, where there is a national park. There is a selection of 'safari' holidays available.
THE EAST COAST: This impressive stretch of lush coastline makes a dramatic change after the desert, with steep mountains, unspoilt sandy bays and beaches, ancient fortresses and date palm groves sloping down to the edge of the Indian Ocean with its host of marine life. Scuba diving and snorkelling are very popular here and many forms of watersports are available at the hotels.
EXCURSIONS: Includes visits to the resorts of **Dibba** and **Fujairah**, where there is a museum, a Necropolis, an old fort and, nearby, many small mountain villages.
THE NORTHERN EMIRATES: This region has undergone a dramatic transformation since the discovery of natural gas in 1980 and there has been a considerable amount of expansion in the commercial sector. **Sharjah** is an excellent shopping centre, with its new **souk** containing hundreds of shops. There is also an ancient fort and heritage museum.
EXCURSIONS: Include visits to **Ras al-Khaimah**, where there is an old seaport with spectacular views over the coast and the **Hajar Mountains**; and also visits to the **Dhaid** and **Khatt** oases, the latter with mineral springs. There are also trips available to the natural harbour at **Dibba** and the beautiful **Khor Kalba**, one of the most famous shell beaches in the world. The archaeological site at **Mileiha** (in Sharjah itself) dates back to the 4th century BC; 80-million-year-old fossils are to be seen here. Other archaeological sites include **Dur** at **Umm al-Qaiwain** where Hellenic ruins can be seen (210-100 BC), the **Drabhaniya** ruins in Ras al-Khaimah and the **Zaura** ruins in **Ajman**. Important resort areas are **Khor Fakkan**, which has excellent beaches and watersports facilities and **Khalid Lagoon** (an aquatic park with several islands and a miniature theme park).

Sport & Activities

Golf: Dubai has been declared the number-one golf destination worldwide, by the International Golf Tour Operators Association. The Emirates Golf Club, Dubai, which opened in 1988, was the first grass golf course in the Gulf. In addition, there is also the Abu Dhabi Golf Club (whose facilities include two 18-hole grass courses and a floodlit driving range), Dubai Creek Golf Club and the Nad Al Shiba Golf and Racing Club.
Watersports: Boats and **water-skiing** equipment are available for hire. **Sailing** and **windsurfing** are popular around Dubai and boats are available for hire. The waters off Dubai are considered among the best areas in the world for **diving**. There are sub-aqua clubs in main centres and an extensive range of equipment is available for hire.
Swimming is possible in the many hotel pools or beaches. There is an abundance of game fish in the Gulf. Fully-equipped boats with crew can be hired from the Jebel Ali Hotel marina for deep-sea **fishing** trips.
Spectator sports: Boat racing for about 30 rowers is a traditional sport that is becoming increasingly popular. **Camel** and **horse races** are also held at various race tracks. **Football** has become more popular and can be seen in most large towns and there are three thriving **rugby** clubs in Dubai. **Falconry** is extremely popular among Arabs.
Other: Horse riding is available at several riding centres, and rides through the desert are organised regularly. Many hotels and clubs have **tennis** courts and there are **squash** courts in main centres. **Bowling** alleys can be found in hotels and clubs.

Social Profile

FOOD & DRINK: Specialities of Arab cuisine include *hummus* (chickpea and sesame paste), *tabbouleh* (bulghur wheat with mint and parsley), *ghuzi* (roast lamb with rice and nuts), *warak enab* (stuffed vine leaves) and *koussa mashi* (stuffed courgettes). In the Emirates, *makbous* (spicy lamb with rice) and seafood with spicy rice are also popular. Local fruit and vegetables are increasingly available and there is excellent local fish. Hotels serve both Arab and European food and there is also a number of Chinese, Indian and other restaurants. Frozen foods from all over the world are available in supermarkets.
All the Emirates, with the exception of Sharjah, permit the consumption of alcohol by non-Muslims. It is illegal to drink alcohol in the street or to buy it for a UAE citizen. *Ayran* (a refreshing yoghurt drink) or strong black coffee are served on many occasions.
NIGHTLIFE: There are several nightclubs located in major centres and entertainment ranges from Arabic singers and dancers to international pop stars. Bars are found in all top hotels and range from sophisticated cocktail lounges to English-style pubs. Some hotels also have discos. Traditional dances are performed on public holidays. Most large towns have cinemas showing English-language films.
SHOPPING: Customs duties are low and therefore luxury goods are cheaper than in most countries. The Dubai duty free shop is one of the cheapest in the world. *Souks* sell traditional Emirate leather goods, gold, brass and silverware.
Shopping hours: Daily 0900-2100. Shops close for prayers Fri 1130-1330.
SPECIAL EVENTS: The following is a selection of special events occurring in the United Arab Emirates in 2005:
Jan 7 *Dubai Marathon*. **Jan 15-Feb 14** *Dubai Shopping Festival*. **Feb 17- Mar 3** *Dubai Tennis Championships*. **Mar 3-6** *Dubai Desert Classic* (golf tournament). **Mar 26** *Emirates World Series: Dubai Cup* (horse race). **Jun 17-Aug 27** *Dubai Summer Surprises* (shopping festival). **Dec 1-3** *Dubai Rugby Sevens*. **Dec 2-8** *National Day Festival*.
SOCIAL CONVENTIONS: Muslim religious laws should be observed. Women are expected to dress modestly and men should dress formally for most occasions. Smoking is the same as in Europe and in most cases it is obvious where not to smoke, except during Ramadan when it is illegal to eat, drink or smoke in public. **Tipping:** Most hotels, restaurants and clubs add fairly high service charges to the bill, therefore tipping is not necessary. Taxi drivers are not tipped.

Business Profile

ECONOMY: Oil and gas are the Emirates' main industries, and underpin the country's considerable prosperity. Although average annual revenues have declined in line with low prevailing world oil prices, the Emirates have had sufficient funds to invest in major industrial and infrastructure-related projects. Outside the oil and gas sector, which includes refining and the production of oil-derived chemicals, most economic activity is government sponsored, and designed to diversify the economy and reduce dependence on oil. This strategy has been reasonably successful and the oil sector's contribution to GDP is now down to about 50 per cent. Chemicals, aluminium and steel production are the most important of the new industries. Other newly established industries produce consumer goods for the domestic market. There is some agriculture, mostly livestock rearing, in what is an unfavourable climate; fishing is also significant.
The economy has been fairly sluggish in recent years, again due to declining oil and gas revenues. Current annual GDP growth is around 2 per cent. Most of the country's economic development has been concentrated in the two richest and most powerful of the seven Emirates, Abu Dhabi and Dubai; the remainder are relatively underdeveloped. UAE is a member of OPEC, and of the Gulf Co-operation Council which is increasingly concerning itself with regional economic collaboration. Plans to establish a customs union among the six member states are well advanced, and the GCC has sought advice from the EU on the creation of a single currency. Imports into the UAE are dominated by the Japanese (the main buyer of the Emirates' oil and gas), followed by the USA, the UK, Germany and Korea (Rep).
BUSINESS: Business entertaining will often be lavish. Suits should be worn and prior appointments are essential. English is widely spoken in business circles, but translation services are likely to be available. **Office hours:** Sat-Wed 0800-1300 and 1500/1600-1800/1900 and Thurs 0800-1200. **Government office hours:** Sat-Wed 0730-1330, Thurs 0730-1200. All offices are closed every afternoon during the month of Ramadan.

Credit: © The Government of Dubai, Department of Tourism and Commerce Marketing

COMMERCIAL INFORMATION: The following organisations can offer advice: Federation of UAE Chambers of Commerce and Industry, PO Box 3014, Abu Dhabi (tel: (2) 621 4144; fax: (2) 633 9210; e-mail: fcciauh@emirates.net.ae; website: www.fcci.gov.ae); *or* Dubai Chamber of Commerce and Industry, PO Box 1457, Dubai (tel: (4) 228 0000; fax: (4) 221 1646; e-mail: dcciinfo@dcci.gov.ae; website: www.dcci.gov.ae). In addition, each of the Emirates has its own chamber of commerce.
CONFERENCES/CONVENTIONS: The Dubai International Congress Centre can accommodate 10,000 delegates. At Port Rashid in Dubai, the new cruise terminal has a wide range of facilities including a business centre with Internet access and a conference room. Dubai World Trade Centre hosts a multitude of events (including car rallies and tennis exhibitions). Many hotels in the UAE offer high-standard conference and meeting facilities. For further information on conference and convention facilities, contact the Dubai World Trade Centre, PO Box 9292, Dubai (tel: (4) 332 1000; fax: (4) 331 2173; e-mail: info@dwtc.com; website: www.dwtc.com); *or* Government of Dubai Department of Tourism & Commerce Marketing (see *Contact Addresses* section).

Climate

The best time to visit is between October and May. The hottest time is from June to September with little rainfall.
Required clothing: Lightweights, with mediumweights from November to March; warmer clothes for evening.

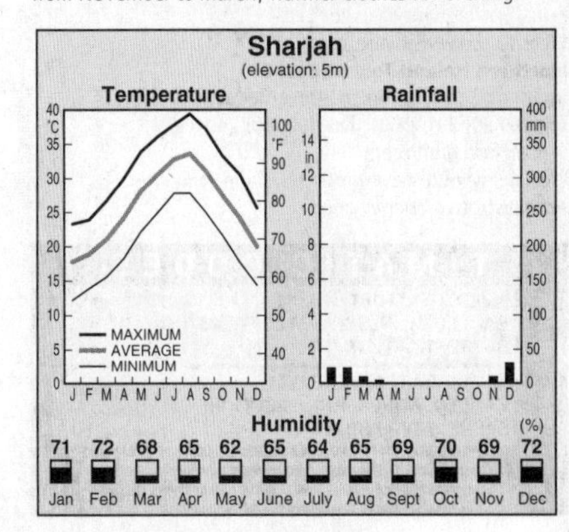

United Kingdom

Credit: © Britain On View & Martin Brent

LATEST TRAVEL ADVICE CONTACTS

British Foreign and Commonwealth Office
Tel: (0870) 606 0290 Website: www.fco.gov.uk

US Department of State
Website: http://travel.state.gov/travel

Canadian Department of Foreign Affairs and Int'l Trade
Tel: (1 800) 267 8376 Website: www.dfait-maeci.gc.ca

Location: Northwest Europe.

Country dialling code: 44.

VisitBritain
Thames Tower, Black's Road, Hammersmith, London W6 9EL, UK
Tel: (020) 8563 3000. Fax: (020) 8563 0302.
E-mail: industryrelations@visitbritain.org (trade enquiries only).
Website: www.visitbritain.com *or* www.visitbritain.com/ukindustry (trade).
Government tourist office that promotes Britain abroad as a tourist destination.

Britain and London Visitor Centre
1 Regent Street, London SW1Y 4XT, UK
Tel: (020) 7808 3807. Email: blvcinfo@visitbritain.org
Personal callers only.

VisitScotland
Fairways Business Park, Deer Park Avenue, Livingston EH54 8AF, UK
Tel: (0845) 225 5121 (within the UK) *or* (01506) 832 121 (outside the UK). Fax: (01506) 832 222.
E-mail: info@visitscotland.com *or* enquiries@visitscotland.com
Website: www.visitscotland.com

Wales Tourist Board/Bwrdd Croeso Cymru
1st and 10th Floors, Brunel House, 2 Fitzalan Road, Cardiff CF24 0UY, UK
Tel: (08701) 211 251. Fax: (08701) 211 259.
E-mail: info@visitwales.com
Website: www.visitwales.com

Northern Ireland Tourist Board
St Anne's Court, 59 North Street, Belfast BT1 1NB, UK
Tel: (02890) 231 221. Fax: (02890) 240 960.
E-mail: info@nitb.com
Website: www.discovernorthernireland.com
Administrative queries only.

TIMATIC CODES

Health
AMADEUS: **TI-DFT/JIB/HE**
GALILEO/WORLDSPAN: **TI-DFT/JIB/HE**
SABRE: **TIDFT/JIB/HE**

AMADEUS: **TI-DFT/JIB/VI**
GALILEO/WORLDSPAN: **TI-DFT/JIB/VI**
SABRE: **TIDFT/JIB/VI**

...cess TIMATIC country information on Health and Visa ... through the Computer Reservations System (CRS), ... the appropriate command line listed above.

Belfast Welcome Centre
47 Donegall Place, Belfast BT1 5AD, UK
Tel: (02890) 246 609. Fax: (02890) 312 424.
E-mail: info@belfastvisitor.com
Website: www.gotobelfast.com

UK Visas
Foreign and Commonwealth Office, King Charles Street, London SW1A 2AH, UK
Tel: (020) 7008 8438.
Fax (020) 7008 8359 *or* 8302 (for those faxing from India, Pakistan, Bangladesh and the Gulf States) *or* 8361 (for those faxing from Africa).
Website: www.ukvisas.gov.uk

British Embassy
3100 Massachusetts Avenue, NW, Washington, DC 20008, USA
Tel: (202) 588 7800 (passports).
Fax: (202) 588 7870 (chancery) *or* 588 7892 (passports).
Website: www.britainusa.com
Consulates General in: Atlanta, Boston, Chicago, Houston, Los Angeles, New York and San Francisco.

VisitBritain
551 Fifth Avenue, Suite 701, New York, NY 10176, USA
Tel: (800) 462 2748 (general information line, toll-free in the USA) *or* (212) 986 2266 (executive offices).
Fax: (212) 986 1188.
E-mail: travelinfo@visitbritain.org
Website: www.visitbritain.com

VisitBritain
625 North Michigan Avenue, Suite 1001, Chicago, IL 60611, USA
Tel: (312) 787 0464 *or* (800) 462 2748 (toll-free in the USA).
Fax: (312) 787 9641.
Website: www.visitbritain.com

Embassy of the United States of America
24 Grosvenor Square, London W1A 1AE, UK
Tel: (020) 7499 9000. Fax: (020) 7495 5012 (visa section).
Website: www.usembassy.org.uk
Opening hours (for telephone enquiries): Mon-Fri 0830-1730.
Consulates General in: Belfast and Edinburgh.

American Embassy Visa Services
Tel: (09068) 200 290 (24-hour visa information line; calls cost 60p per minute; identical information is available on the embassy website at no cost) *or* (09055) 444 546 (operator-assisted visa information; calls cost £1.30 per minute; Mon-Fri 0800-2000, Sat 0900-1600).

British High Commission
80 Elgin Street, Ottawa, Ontario K1P 5K7, Canada
Tel: (613) 237 1530 *or* 1303 (passports) *or* 2008 (visas and immigration). Fax: (613) 237 7980 *or* 232 2533 (visa enquiries).
E-mail: generalenquiries@britainincanada.org (general enquiries) *or* visaenquiries@britainincanada.org (visa and immigration).
Website: www.britainincanada.org
Consulates General in: Montréal, Toronto and Vancouver.

VisitBritain
5915 Airport Road, Suite 120, Mississauga, Ontario L4V 1T1, Canada
Tel: (905) 405 1720 *or* (888) 847 4885 (toll-free in Canada).
Fax: (905) 405 1835.
E-mail: britinfo@visitbritain.org
Website: www.visitbritain.com/ca

Canadian High Commission
Macdonald House, 1 Grosvenor Square, London W1K 4AB, UK
Tel: (020) 7258 6600. Fax: (020) 7258 6333.
E-mail: ldn-cs@dfait-maeci.gc.ca
Website: www.dfait-maeci.gc.ca/canadaeuropa/united_kingdom
Opening hours: Mon-Fri 0900-1700, excluding public holidays.
Consular section: Canada House, Trafalgar Square, Pall Mall East, London SW1Y 5BJ, UK
Tel: (020) 7258 6600. Fax: (020) 7258 6533 *or* 6356.

General Information

The United Kingdom of Great Britain and Northern Ireland consists of *England*, *Scotland*, *Wales* and *Northern Ireland*. Although they form one administrative unit (with regional exceptions), they have had separate cultures, languages and political histories. Within this section are also the *Channel Islands* (excluding *Guernsey* and *Jersey*, which have their own separate entries) and the *Isle of Man* which, although only dependencies of the British Crown, are included for convenience of reference. The *United Kingdom* section consists of a general introduction (covering the aspects that the four countries have in common), sections devoted to the four constituent countries, and sections dealing with the Channel Islands and the Isle of Man.

AREA: 242,514 sq km (93,788 sq miles).

POPULATION: 59,231,900 (official estimate 2002).

POPULATION DENSITY: 244.2 per sq km.

CAPITAL: London. **Population:** 7,188,000 (official estimate, Greater London, 2001).

GEOGRAPHY: The British landscape can be divided roughly into two kinds of terrain – highland and lowland. The highland area comprises the mountainous regions of Scotland, Northern Ireland, northern England and North Wales. The English Lake District in the northwest contains lakes and fells. The lowland area is broken up by sandstone and limestone hills, long valleys and basins such as the Wash on the east coast. In the southeast, the North and South Downs culminate in the White Cliffs of Dover. The coastline includes fjord-like inlets in the northwest of Scotland, spectacular cliffs and wild sandy beaches on the east coast and, further south, beaches of rock, shale and sand sometimes backed by dunes, and large areas of fenland in East Anglia.
More detailed geographical descriptions of the various countries may be found under the respective entries.

GOVERNMENT: Constitutional monarchy. **Head of State:** HM Queen Elizabeth II since 1953. **Head of Government:** Prime Minister Tony Blair since 1997.

LANGUAGE: English. Some Welsh is spoken in parts of Wales, Gaelic in parts of Scotland and Northern Ireland, and French and Norman French in the Channel Islands. The many ethnic minorities within the UK also speak their own languages (eg Cantonese, Greek, Hindi, Mandarin, Turkish, Urdu, etc).

RELIGION: Predominantly Protestant (Church of England), but many other Christian denominations also: Roman Catholic, Church of Scotland, Baptist, Methodist and other free churches. There are sizeable Hindu, Jewish and Muslim minorities.

TIME: GMT (GMT + 1 from last Sunday in March to Saturday before last Sunday in October).

ELECTRICITY: 240 volts AC, 50Hz. Square three-pin plugs are standard and the visitor is unlikely to come across the older round three-pin type..

COMMUNICATIONS: Telephone: IDD is available. Country code: 44. Outgoing international code: 00. There are numerous public call boxes. Some boxes take coins, others phonecards or credit cards. There are a number of suppliers of telecommunication networks, chiefly *British Telecom* and *Cable & Wireless*. **Mobile telephone:** GSM

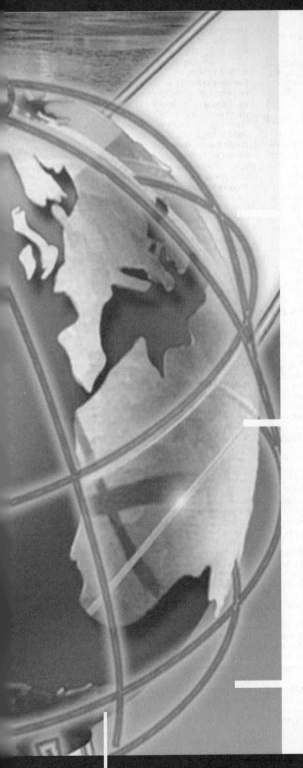

Credit: © Britain On View

900, 1800, 3G and GSM Satellite networks. Network operators include *O2* (website: www.o2.co.uk), *Orange* (website: www.orange.co.uk), *T-Mobile* (website: www.t-mobile.co.uk) and *Vodafone* (website: www.vodafone.co.uk). **Fax:** There are many high-street bureaux in all cities. Most hotels and offices have facilities. **Internet:** There are Internet cafes and centres in most urban areas. ISPs include *AOL* (website: www.aol.com), *BT Internet* (website: www.btopenworld.com) and *Freeserve* (website: www.freeserve.com). Some multimedia phone booths, often located at main railway stations and airports, offer touch-screen access. **Telegram:** These may be sent from a post office or from a private telephone (tel: (0800) 190 190).
Post: Stamps are available from post offices and many shops and stores. There are stamp machines outside some post offices. Post boxes are red. First-class internal mail normally reaches its destination the day after posting (except in remote areas of Scotland), and most second-class mail the day after that. International postal connections are good. Post office hours: Mon-Fri 0900-1730 and Sat 0900-1230, although some post offices are open much longer hours. **Press:** Dominated by about 10 major newspapers, UK circulation figures are amongst the highest in the world. The most influential newspapers are *The Daily Telegraph*, *The Financial Times*, *The Guardian*, *The Independent*, *The Observer* (on Sunday) and *The Times*. The more popular 'tabloid' newspapers are *The Daily Express*, *The Daily Mail*, *The Daily Mirror* and *The Sun*. Most papers have an associated Sunday newspaper, though there are some independents. There are also daily regional newspapers, particularly in Scotland and the north. The London *Evening Standard* is produced in several editions daily, the first being at midday.
Radio: BBC World Service (website: www.bbc.co.uk/worldservice) and Voice of America (website: www.voa.gov) can be received. From time to time the frequencies change and the most up-to-date can be found online.

Passport/Visa

	Passport Required?	Visa Required?	Return Ticket Required?
Full British	Yes	N/A	N/A
Australian	Yes	No	No
Canadian	Yes	No	No
USA	Yes	No	No
Other EU	1	No	No
Japanese	Yes	No	No

Note: Regulations and requirements may be subject to change at short notice, and you are advised to contact the appropriate diplomatic or consular authority before finalising travel arrangements. Details of these may be found at the head of this country's entry. Any numbers in the chart refer to the footnotes below.

PASSPORTS: Passport valid for whole period of the visit to the UK required by all except:
1. nationals of EU countries, Iceland, Liechtenstein, Monaco, Norway and Switzerland with a valid national ID card.
Note: (a) A passport is not required for travel between Great Britain and Ireland, Northern Ireland, the Channel Islands or the Isle of Man. (b) Passengers transiting the UK destined for the Republic of Ireland are advised to hold return tickets to avoid delay and interrogation.
VISAS: Required by all except the following:
(a) nationals listed in the chart above;
(b) nationals of Commonwealth countries (except nationals of Bangladesh, Cameroon, Fiji, The Gambia, Ghana, Guyana, India, Jamaica, Kenya, Maldives, Mozambique, Nigeria, Pakistan, Sierra Leone, Sri Lanka, Tanzania, Uganda and Zambia who *do* need a visa);
(c) nationals of American Samoa, Andorra, Argentina, Aruba, Bolivia, Bonaire, Brazil, Chile, Cook Islands, Costa Rica, Curacao, East Timor, El Salvador, Federated States of Micronesia, French Guiana, Greenland, Guadeloupe, Guam, Guatemala, Honduras, Hong Kong (SAR), Iceland, Israel, Korea (Rep), Liechtenstein, Macau (SAR), Marshall Islands, Martinique, Mexico, Monaco, New Caledonia, Nicaragua, Niue, Norway, Palau, Panama, Paraguay, Puerto Rico, Reunion, Saba, St Eustatius, St Maarten, San Marino, Switzerland, Tahiti and her Islands, Uruguay, US Virgin Islands, Vatican City and Venezuela;
(d) those in transit, provided arriving and departing by air within 24 hours and holding all necessary onward documentation.
Note: *Direct Airside Transit visas* are required by the following countries, even if not entering the UK or changing airports during transit: Afghanistan, Albania, Algeria, Angola, Bangladesh, Belarus, Burundi, Cameroon, China (PR), Colombia, Congo (Dem Rep), Côte D'Ivoire, Ecuador, Eritrea, Ethiopia, Gambia, Ghana, India, Iran, Iraq, Kenya, Lebanon, Liberia, Macedonia, Moldova, Myanmar, Nepal, Nigeria, Pakistan, Palestinian Territories, Rwanda, Senegal, Serbia & Montenegro, Sierra Leone, Somalia, Sri Lanka, Sudan, Tanzania, Turkey, Turkish Republic of Northern Cyprus, Uganda, Vietnam and Zimbabwe.
Note: (a) Entry clearance is required for nationals of the following countries who intend to stay in the UK for more than six months: Australia, Canada, Hong Kong (SAR), Japan, Korea (Rep), Malaysia, New Zealand, Singapore, South Africa and the USA. (b) Nationals not requiring visas are advised to be in possession of either a return ticket or, if arriving on a one-way ticket, proof of sufficient funds to accommodate and support themselves for the duration of stay.
Types of visa and cost: *Standard visit*, *student* and *visitor in transit*: £36. *One-year visit*: £60. *Two-year visit*: £70. *Five-year visit*: £88. *10-year visit*: £150. *Direct Airside Transit*: £27. Fees are usually payable in the local currency and are subject to variation in both price and method of payment. Enquire at nearest High Commission/Embassy. Visa fees are not refundable.
Validity: *Visit visas*: Six months, one year, two years, five years or 10 years; all visit visas are valid for multiple-entries within the period of validity. *Visitor in Transit visas* are not required by those continuing their journey to a third country by the first connecting aircraft within 24 hours, provided possessing confirmed onward travel documentation (except nationals of those countries listed under (c) above). Those in transit to another country, who will remain in the UK for no longer than 48 hours, will need a Visitor in Transit visa. A visit visa is required for any transit stay over 48 hours.
Application to: Nearest British Consulate (or Consular section at Embassy or High Commission); see *Contact Addresses* section.
Application requirements: (a) Passport valid for entire visit. (b) Two recent passport-size photos (some nationals may require three photos). (c) Completed application form (some nationals may be required to fill out an additional form). (d) Fee (postal applications must be accompanied by bank draft, postal or money order only). The supplementary documentation required will vary depending on the type of application, but in all cases it is advisable to also provide: (e) Evidence of funds (bank statements or pay slips). (f) Letter of invitation (if applicable). (g) Evidence of sponsor's funds (if applicable).
Working days required: Dependent on nationality of applicant. Applications usually take between one and 10 working days. Applications that are referred to the Home Office may take up to 13 weeks.
Temporary residence: Enquiries can be made at nearest British Consulate, Embassy or High Commission (see *Contact Addresses* section of your country).

Money

Note: See the individual *Money* sections within the *Jersey*, *Guernsey*, *Isle of Man* and *Northern Ireland* sections for information on currency specific to these regions.
Currency: Pound (£) = 100 pence. Notes are in denominations of £50, 20, 10 and 5. Additional bank notes issued by Scottish banks are legal tender in all parts of the UK. Coins are in denominations of £2 and 1, and 50, 20, 10, 5, 2 and 1 pence.
Currency exchange: Money can be exchanged in banks, exchange bureaux and many hotels. The exchange bureaux are often open outside banking hours but charge higher commission rates. All major currencies can be exchanged. Cash can be obtained from a multitude of ATMs available across the country.
Credit & debit cards: American Express, Diners Club, MasterCard and Visa are all widely accepted. Check with your credit or debit card company for details of merchant acceptability and other services which may be available.
Travellers cheques: Widely accepted. To avoid additional exchange rate charges, travellers are advised to take travellers cheques in Pounds Sterling.
Currency restrictions: There are no restrictions on the import or export of either local or foreign currency.
Exchange rate indicators: The following figures are included as a guide to the movements of Sterling against the US Dollar:

Date	Feb '04	May '04	Aug '04	Nov '04
$1.00=	0.54	0.55	0.54	0.52

Banking hours: Mon-Fri 0930-1630 (there may be some variations in closing times). Some branches of certain banks are open Saturday morning; some all-day Saturday; some are open on Sundays for limited hours; and some offer 24-hour services.

Duty Free

Note: The Channel Islands are treated as being outside of the EU for the Duty Free section.
The following items may be imported into the UK without incurring customs duty by travellers aged 17 years and over arriving from non-EU countries:
200 cigarettes or 100 cigarillos or 50 cigars or 250g of tobacco; 1l of alcoholic beverages stronger than 22 per cent or 2l of still table wine, or fortified or sparkling wine or other liqueurs; 50g of perfume and 250ml of toilet water; other goods including souvenirs up to the value of £145. Goods obtained duty and tax paid in the EU are unlimited.
Prohibited/restricted items: Prohibited items include unlicensed drugs, offensive weapons, indecent and obscene material featuring children, counterfeit and pirated goods, meat, dairy and other animal products and pornography. Restricted items include firearms, explosives and ammunition, live animals, endangered species, certain plants and their produce and radio transmitters.
The UK is one of the few regions of the world completely free of rabies and, until recently, all cats and dogs imported into the country had to spend six months in quarantine. To bring animals and birds into the UK, an import licence must be obtained at least six months in advance. Some animals may now qualify for the PET Travel Scheme (PETS) and can be brought into the UK without being put into quarantine. At present, this is limited to certain travel carriers and animals. *Severe penalties are imposed on persons attempting to smuggle domestic animals into the country. An illegally imported animal is liable to be destroyed.*
For further information about importing animals, contact the Department for the Environment, Food and Rural Affairs, Area 201, 1A Page Street, London SWIP 4PQ (website: www.defra.gov.uk/animalh/quarantine/index.htm); *or* the PETS helpline (tel: (0870) 241 1710; fax: (020) 7904 6206; e-mail: pets.helpline@defra.gsi.gov.uk) *or* the nearest British mission abroad.
Abolition of duty free goods within the EU: On June 30 1999, the sale of duty free alcohol and tobacco at airports and at sea was abolished in all of the original 15 EU member states. Of the 10 new member states that joined the EU on May 1 2004, these rules already apply to Cyprus

and Malta. There are transitional rules in place for visitors returning to one of the original 15 EU countries from one of the other new EU countries. But for the original 15, plus Cyprus and Malta, there are now no limits imposed on importing tobacco and alcohol products from one EU country to another (with the exceptions of Denmark, Finland and Sweden, where limits *are* imposed). Travellers should note that they may be required to prove at customs that the goods purchased are for personal use *only*.

Public Holidays

2005: Jan 1 New Year's Day. **Mar 25** Good Friday. **Mar 28** Easter Monday. **May 2** May Day Bank Holiday. **May 30** Spring Bank Holiday. **Aug 29** Summer Bank Holiday. **Dec 25** Christmas Day. **Dec 26** Boxing Day. **Dec 27** Christmas (forwarded to Monday). **Dec 28** Boxing Day (forwarded to Tuesday).
2006: Jan 1 New Year's Day. **Apr 14** Good Friday. **Apr 17** Easter Monday. **May 1** May Day Bank Holiday. **May 29** Spring Bank Holiday. **Aug 28** Summer Bank Holiday. **Dec 25** Christmas Day. **Dec 26** Boxing Day.
Note: Public holidays are usually referred to as 'bank holidays' in the UK.

Health

	Special Precautions?	Certificate Required?
Yellow Fever	No	No
Cholera	No	No
Typhoid & Polio	No	N/A
Malaria	No	N/A

Note: Regulations and requirements may be subject to change at short notice, and you are advised to contact your doctor well in advance of your intended date of departure. Any numbers in the chart refer to the footnotes below.

Health care: The National Health Service provides free medical treatment (at hospitals and general surgeries) to all who are ordinarily resident in the UK, but requires payment for dental treatment, prescriptions and spectacles. Immediate first aid/emergency treatment is free for all visitors, after which charges are made unless the visitor's country has a reciprocal health agreement with the UK. The following have signed such agreements: all EU countries (but Danish residents of the Faroe Islands are not covered), Anguilla, Australia, Barbados, British Virgin Islands, Bulgaria, Channel Islands (applies only if the visitor is staying less than three months), CIS countries, Czech Republic, Falkland Islands, Hungary, Iceland, Isle of Man, Malta (for visits up to 30 days), Montserrat, New Zealand, Norway, Poland, Romania, Russian Federation, St Helena, Serbia & Montenegro, Slovak Republic and Turks & Caicos Islands. The agreements provide differing degrees of exemption for different nationalities; full details of individual agreements are available from the Department of Health; see also the *Health* appendix.

Travel - International

AIR: The principal national airline is *British Airways (BA)* (tel: (0870) 850 4850; website: www.britishairways.com).
Approximate flight times: From Birmingham to *Amsterdam* is one hour 15 minutes; to *Dublin* is one hour five minutes; to *Düsseldorf* is one hour 20 minutes; to *Frankfurt/M* is one hour 40 minutes; and to *Paris* is one hour 10 minutes.
From Glasgow to *Paris* is two hours 50 minutes via Birmingham.
From Manchester to *Amsterdam* is one hour 25 minutes; to *Brussels* is one hour 35 minutes; to *Dublin* is one hour; to *Düsseldorf* is one hour 25 minutes; to *Frankfurt/M* is one hour 50 minutes; to *Milan* is two hours 25 minutes; to *Nice* is two hours 20 minutes; to *Paris* is one hour 30 minutes; and to *Rome* is two hours 55 minutes.
For approximate durations of international flights from *London*, see the *Travel – International* section of the destination country.
International airports: See *Travel – International* in the relevant country sections for information on UK airports.
Departure tax: None.
SEA: There are many ports offering ferry connections between the UK and mainland Europe, Ireland, the Channel Islands, the Isle of Wight, the Scilly Isles and the Isle of Man. UK ferry operators include: *Brittany Ferries* (tel: (08703) 665 333; website: www.brittany-ferries.co.uk); *Caledonian Macbrayne* (tel: (01475) 650 100; website: www.calmac.co.uk); *Condor Ferries* (tel: (0845) 345 2000; website: www.condorferries.co.uk); *DFDS Seaways* (tel: (08705) 333 111; website: www.dfdsseaways.co.uk); *Fjord Line* (tel: (0191) 143 9669; website: www.fjordline.co.uk); *Hoverspeed* (tel: (0870) 240 8070; website: www.hoverspeed.co.uk); *Irish Ferries* (tel: (08705) 171 717; website: www.irishferries.com); *Isle of Man Steam Packet Co* (tel: (08705) 523 523; website: www.steam-packet.com); *Isles of Scilly Travel* (tel: (0845) 710 5555; website: www.islesofscilly-travel.co.uk); *Norse Merchant Ferries* (tel: (0870) 600 432; website: www.norsemerchant.com); *P&O Ferries* (tel: (08705) 202 020; website: www.poferries.com); *Red Funnel* (tel: (0870) 444 8889; website: www.redfunnel.co.uk); *Stena Line* (tel: (08705) 707 070; website: www.stenaline.com); *Swansea–Cork Ferries* (tel: (01792) 457 1166; website: www.swanseacorkferries.com); and *Wightlink* (tel: (0870) 582 7744; website: www.wightlink.co.uk).
RAIL: Trains meet connecting ferries at Dover, Folkestone, Newhaven, Portsmouth and Weymouth, sailing for Belgium, France, Germany and Spain (board at Victoria Station in London); and at Harwich, sailing for Germany, The Netherlands and Scandinavia (board at Liverpool Street). See also the *Channel Tunnel* and *Eurostar* sections below.
Eurotunnel or the Channel Tunnel: All road vehicles are carried through the tunnel in *Eurotunnel* shuttles running between the two terminals, one near Folkestone in Kent, with direct road access from the M20, and one just outside Calais, with links to the A16/A26 motorway (Exit 13). Each shuttle is made up of 12 single- and 12 double-deck carriages, and vehicles are directed to single-deck or double-deck carriages, depending on their height. There are facilities for cars and motorcycles, coaches, minibuses, caravans, campervans and other vehicles over 1.85m (6.07ft). Bicycles are provided for. Passengers generally travel with their vehicles. Heavy goods vehicles are carried on special shuttles and drivers travel in a separate carriage. Terminals and shuttles are well equipped for disabled passengers, and Passenger Terminal buildings contain a variety of shops, restaurants, bureaux de change and other amenities. The journey takes about 35 minutes from platform to platform and about one hour from motorway to motorway. Services run every day of the year, and there are between two and five an hour, depending on the time of day. There is a reservation system and a turn-up-and-go service. Motorists pass through customs and immigration before they board the shuttle without further checks on arrival. Fares vary according to length of stay, time of day and time of year and whether you have a reservation or not. The price applies to the car, regardless of the number of

passengers or size of the car. The fare may be paid in cash, by cheque or by credit card. There are savings of up to £6 when booking online. For further information, contact *Eurotunnel Customer Services UK* (tel: (08705) 353 535; fax: (01303) 288 786; website: www.eurotunnel.com).
The Eurostar: The direct *Eurostar* train runs through the Channel Tunnel between London and Brussels, Lille or Paris. *Eurostar* is a service provided by the railways of Belgium, France and the United Kingdom, operating direct high-speed trains from London (*Waterloo International*) to Paris (*Gare du Nord*) and to Brussels (*Midi/Zuid*). Due to the opening of Stage 1 of a high-speed rail line in September 2003, it currently takes two hours 35 minutes from London to Paris and two hours 20 minutes from London to Brussels. Trains depart up to 18 times a day from Waterloo to Paris, and up to nine times a day from Waterloo to Brussels. Work on the UK section of the high-speed rail line is being done in two stages. Stage 1 (from the Channel Tunnel through Kent to the outskirts of London) has been completed. Stage 2, to be completed in January 2007, will take the route to a new terminal at St Pancras. When it is completed, the transit times between London St Pancras and Brussels will be just two hours and between London St Pancras and Paris just two hours 15 minutes.
The *Eurostar* trains are equipped with standard-class and first-class seating, buffet and bar, and are staffed by multi-lingual, highly trained personnel. Pricing is competitive with the airlines, and there is a large range of different tickets and prices. Children aged between four and 11 years benefit from a special fare in all classes. Children under four years old travel free but cannot be guaranteed a seat. Wheelchair users and blind passengers together with one companion get a special fare.
For further information and reservations, contact *Eurostar* (tel: (0870) 6000 792 (travel agents) *or* (08705) 186 186 (public; within the UK) *or* (1233) 617 575 (public; outside the UK only); website: www.eurostar.com) *or Rail Europe* (tel: (0870) 837 1371). Travel agents can obtain refunds for unused tickets from Eurostar Trade Refunds, 2nd Floor, Kent House, 81 Station Road, Ashford, Kent TN23 1PD. Complaints and comments may be sent to Eurostar Customer Relations, Eurostar House, Waterloo Station, London SE1 8SE (tel: (020) 7928 5163). General enquiries and information requests *must* be made by telephone. Enquiries in France should be made to Eurostar in Paris (tel: (8) 3635 3539; only available from within France). Information about package deals, inclusive of accommodation and travel on Eurostar can be obtained from *Eurostar Holidays Direct* (tel: (0870) 167 6767).
ROAD: Few formalities are encountered when driving between Northern Ireland and the Republic of Ireland. Eurolines, departing from Victoria Coach Station in London, serves destinations in the United Kingdom. For further information, contact *Eurolines*, 52 Grosvenor Gardens, London SW1, UK (tel: (08705) 143 219; website: www.nationalexpress.com).

Travel - Internal

Note: This section is a general introduction to transport within the UK. Further information is given in the individual *Travel* sections for England, Scotland, Wales, Northern Ireland, the Channel Islands and the Isle of Man.
AIR: *British Airways* operates a shuttle service to Belfast, Edinburgh, Glasgow and Manchester amongst other cities. Other internal operators include: *Aer Lingus (EI), bmi british midland (BD), British European (JY), EasyJet (U2), KLM UK (UK)* and *Ryanair (FR)*.
Approximate flight times: From London to *Aberdeen* is one hour 25 minutes; to *Belfast* is one hour 20 minutes; to *Edinburgh* is one hour 25 minutes; to *Glasgow* is one hour 20 minutes; to *Jersey* is one hour; to *Manchester* is 55 minutes; and to *Newcastle* is one hour and 10 minutes.
From Aberdeen to *Birmingham* is one hour 40 minutes; to *Glasgow* is 55 minutes; to *London* is one hour 25 minutes; to *Manchester* is one hour five minutes; to *Orkney* is 45 minutes; and to *Shetland* is one hour five minutes.
From Belfast to *Birmingham* is one hour; to *Glasgow* is 50 minutes; to *London* is one hour 20 minutes; and to *Manchester* is one hour.
From Birmingham to *Aberdeen* is one hour 40 minutes; to *Belfast* is one hour; to *Edinburgh* is one hour; to *Glasgow* is one hour.
From Edinburgh to *Birmingham* is one hour and to *London* is one hour 25 minutes.
From Glasgow to *Aberdeen* is 55 minutes; to *Belfast* is 50 minutes; to *Birmingham* is one hour; to *Inverness* is 50 minutes; to *London* is one hour 20 minutes; to *Manchester* is one hour five minutes; and to *Stornoway* is one hour five minutes.
From Manchester to *Aberdeen* is one hour five minutes; to *Belfast* is one hour; to *Glasgow* is one hour five minutes; to *Jersey* is one hour 35 minutes; and to *London* is 55 minutes.
SEA: Information on travel to the Channel Islands, Ireland, the Isle of Man and the Scottish islands are given in the relevant *Travel* sections for those countries.
RAIL: The UK is served by an excellent network of railways (16,500km/10,250 miles in total). *Intercity* lines provide fast services between London and major cities, and there are services to the southeast and to major cities in the Midlands, the north and south Wales and between Edinburgh and Glasgow. Some rural areas are less well served (eg the north coast of the west country, parts of East Anglia, Northern Ireland, Northumberland and North Yorkshire, parts of inland Wales, and southern and northern Scotland), although local rail services are generally fairly comprehensive.
Rail passes: There are many discretionary fares, and visitors using trains may like to consider one of the all-line Britrail range of passes giving unlimited travel. This is available to visitors from overseas and is not available in the UK; tickets must be purchased in their home country, although tickets can be collected in the UK. Further details can be obtained from *Network Rail Group* (website: www.networkrail.com). In 2002, the Network Rail Group completed the acquisition of Railtrack Plc. For information about UK train services and fares, contact *National Rail Enquiries* (tel: (08457) 484 950; website: www.nationalrail.co.uk). It can be much cheaper to purchase rail tickets in advance. Disabled travellers are also entitled to discounted train fares; see the *Disabled Traveller* appendix. *InterRail* cards are valid; holders may be entitled to discounts on ferry fares.
ROAD: There are trunk roads ('A' roads) linking all major towns and cities in the UK. Roads in rural areas ('B' roads) can be slow and winding, and in upland areas may become impassable in winter. Motorways radiate from London and there is also a good east-west and north-south network in the north and the Midlands. The M25 motorway circles London and connects at various junctions with the M1, M3, M4, M10, M11 and M40. The only motorway that leaves England is the M4 from London to South Wales. Access to Scotland is by the A1/A1(M) or the A68 to Edinburgh, or the M6 to Carlisle followed by the A74 to Glasgow. Within Scotland, motorways link Edinburgh, Glasgow and Perth. In Northern Ireland, motorways run from Belfast to Dungannon and from Belfast to Antrim. For further information on roads within each country, see the respective *Travel* sections. **Coach:** Every major city has a coach terminus: in London, it is Victoria Coach station, about 1km (0.7 miles) from the train station. There are coach services to all parts of the country. Many coaches have onboard toilets and refreshments. Private coaches may be hired by groups wishing to tour the UK; these can be booked in advance and will visit most major tourist attractions. Many of these destinations now have coach parks nearby. The main carrier is *National Express*. **Traffic regulations:** Traffic drives on the left. Speed limits are 30mph (48kph) in urban areas, 70mph (113kph) on motorways and dual carriageways, elsewhere 50mph (80kph) or 60mph (97kph) as marked. Petrol is graded in a star system: 2-star (90 octane) and 4-star (97 octane). Unleaded petrol is also available at all petrol stations and is sold at a lower price than leaded petrol. Seatbelts must be worn by the driver and front seat passenger. Where rear seat belts have been fitted, they must also be worn. **Documentation:** National driving licences are valid for one year. Drivers must have Third Party insurance and vehicle registration documents. **Automobile associations:** The AA and RAC are able to provide a full range of services to UK members touring the UK. These organisations can also assist people who are travelling from abroad with maps, tourist information and specially marked routes to major events or places of interest.
URBAN: All cities and towns have bus services of varying efficiency and cost. Glasgow, Liverpool, London and Newcastle have underground railways, London and Glasgow's being very old and Newcastle's very new. The urban areas of Birmingham, Cardiff, Glasgow, Liverpool and Manchester are also well served by local railway trains. Manchester has an efficient modern tram service. Licensed taxi operators are generally metered; small supplements may be charged for weekends, bank holidays, excess baggage and late-night travel. In the larger cities, unlicensed operators offer a cheaper (but less efficient and knowledgeable) unmetered service with fares based loosely on elapsed clock mileage; these taxis are called mini-cabs and can be summoned by telephone.

Accommodation

HOTELS: These tend to be much more expensive in large cities, especially London. Different classification schemes are used by the various countries; see the relevant country sections for details. More information is also available from the British Hospitality Association, Queens House, 55-56 Lincoln's Inn Fields, London WC2A 3BH (tel: (0845) 880 7744; fax: (020) 7404 7799; e-mail: info@bha.org.uk; website: www.bha.org.uk), and a selection of some of the finest hotels in the United Kingdom is available online (website: www.distinctionworld.com).
GUEST HOUSES: There are guest houses and bed & breakfast facilities throughout the country.
SELF-CATERING: Cottages can be rented in many areas. For information, contact the local tourist board, or consult the relevant section in local and national papers.
CAMPING AND CARAVANNING: There are camping and caravan sites throughout the UK, for short and long stays. Some sites hire out tents or caravans to those without their own equipment. Most sites offer basic facilities, while some have playgrounds, clubs, shops, phones and sports areas.
HOLIDAY CAMPS: These offer accommodation, food and a full range of leisure activities generally at an all-inclusive price. They provide good holidays for families, and some run babysitting and children's clubs.
YOUTH HOSTELS: There are more than 240 youth hostels in England and Wales. Standards vary greatly, from very basic night-time accommodation for hikers and cyclists, to modern hostels and motels which are often used by families and groups. Prices are very reasonable. For information, contact the Youth Hostel Association of England and Wales, Trevelyan House, Dimple Road, Matlock, Derbyshire DE4 3YH (tel: (01629) 592 600; fax: (01629) 592 702; e-mail: customerservices@yha.org.uk; website: www.yha.org.uk).

Resorts & Excursions

Details of resorts and places of interest throughout the UK may be found by consulting the respective sections for England, Scotland, Wales and Northern Ireland. There are also separate sections for the individual Channel Islands (Alderney, Guernsey, Jersey and Sark & Herm) and for the Isle of Man.

Sport & Activities

The United Kingdom has a wealth of sports and activities to offer visitors – from classic sporting events for spectators, to opportunities for numerous outdoor pursuits. It is well known that many popular sports originated in the UK. Football, cricket, rugby, golf and tennis, to name but a few, were invented here. These sports are still avidly followed and played by many enthusiasts. For more specific information on sport in the different areas of the UK, see the individual country sections.
Spectator sports: Football is the UK's most popular spectator sport. The season lasts from August to May, and matches are played mainly at weekends. Most football clubs sell tickets in advance, though for some clubs (eg Arsenal, Liverpool, Manchester United), games will be sold out months in advance. The main **cricket** (played strictly between April and September) and **tennis** tournaments are held in England, while **rugby** is particularly popular in Wales. **Horse racing** and **motor racing** are very popular throughout the UK, with the chance of making a fortune through the bookmakers being a major attraction. The best-known **rowing** and **sailing** regattas take place in England, and are regarded as important social events.
Golf: There are courses in every corner of the UK, from famous courses to more modest ones. The British Tourist Authority publishes an in-depth guide to 150 courses, containing information on fees and visitor availability called *Golf Britain*.
Outdoor pursuits: Walking, **mountaineering**, **caving**, **climbing** and **cycling** are all easy to arrange. With the UK's countryside ranging from rolling fields and pleasant farmland to austere mountains, all kinds of walks are possible. There are 11 national parks and numerous other protected natural areas in England and Wales. Further information on national parks and specific paths can be

found in the individual country sections. Although nearly all land (including land in national parks) in the UK is privately owned, walkers have access to it along rights of way that are marked on maps and usually signposted. There are also areas where it is permissible to go beyond the rights of way, and these are known as 'open country'. An excellent series of maps is published by the Ordnance Survey, a government agency. Widely available and covering the whole of the UK except Northern Ireland (maps of which are published by the Ordnance Survey of Ireland), these come in different scales (1:50,000 and 1:25,000). There are many outdoor pursuits centres which offer tuition in mountaincraft and watersports and organise trips. Moreover, walking is a very popular activity in the UK, and there are several influential organisations that exist to promote the interests of walkers. The Youth Hostels Association (see *Accommodation* section) provides a network of cheap hostels, and runs courses; The Ramblers' Association, Camelford House, 2nd Floor, 87-90 Albert Embankment, London SE1 7TW (tel: (020) 7339 8500; fax: (020) 7339 8501; e-mail: ramblers@london.ramblers.org.uk; website: www.ramblers.org.uk) produces leaflets and a very useful *Yearbook* (£5.99 plus postage) and organises trips and group walks.
English courses: There are many language schools where foreign students can learn English. More than 370 of these schools are inspected and approved (accredited) by the British Council under their accreditation scheme. A wide variety of courses are available, from business English to courses designed especially for young people and those studying for specific examinations. Many schools organise social programmes and accommodation with local families. Further information and advice about choosing a language course can be obtained from the British Council, Education Information Scheme, 10 Spring Gardens, London SW1A 2BN (tel: (0161) 957 7755; fax: (0161) 957 7762; e-mail: general.enquiries@britishcouncil.org; website: www.britishcouncil.org). The British Council's overseas offices can also provide information and advice.

Social Profile

Each of the countries of the United Kingdom has its own particular national dishes and drinks, festivals and other events of interest, its own attractions for shoppers and its own nightlife and other entertainments. Details may be found by consulting the individual country sections.
SOCIAL CONVENTIONS: The monarchy, though now only symbolic, is a powerful and often subconscious unifying force. Members of the Royal Family are the subject of unceasing fascination, with their every move avidly followed and reported by the popular press, both in Britain and abroad. Handshaking is customary when introduced to someone for the first time. Normal social courtesies should be observed when visiting someone's home and a small present such as flowers or chocolates is appreciated. It is polite to wait until everyone has been served before eating. **Clothing:** A tie, trousers and shoes (as opposed to jeans and trainers) are necessary for entry to some nightclubs and restaurants, otherwise casual wear is widely acceptable. **Use of public places:** Topless sunbathing is allowed on certain beaches and tolerated in some parks. Smoking or non-smoking areas will usually be clearly marked. Cigarettes should not legally be sold to children under 16 years of age. **Tipping:** In hotels, a service charge of 10 to 12 per cent is usual, which may be added to the bill. 10 to 15 per cent is usual for restaurants and it too is often added to the bill, in which case, a further tip is not required. 10 to 15 per cent is also usual for taxi drivers and hairdressers but this is not included in the bill. There is no legal requirement to pay service charges that have been added to bills and if the service has been unsatisfactory, it may be deducted by the customer. Travellers should remember, however, that, in the UK, wage levels for catering staff are set at a deliberately low level in the expectation that tips will make up the difference.

Business Profile

ECONOMY: The UK is a member of the G7 group of the world's leading industrial nations. Since the end of World War II, the UK has followed the trend among all major economies away from industrial production towards service industries, that now account for three-quarters of national income. The transition has often been painful, and although the UK is not unique in this respect - most Western European economies have undergone a similar process during the past 20 years - a worse situation might have occurred without the cushion of revenues from North Sea oil. The UK's traditionally strong agricultural sector has suffered a number of serious setbacks, largely the result of dubious practices that appear to have been rife throughout British agriculture. These undoubtedly contributed to two major outbreaks of disease (BSE and foot-and-mouth) which have caused havoc in the industry and the loss of billions of pounds in export income. Engineering (especially of military products), chemicals, electronics, construction and textiles are the main components of the industrial sector. Among service industries, tourism, media, retail, financial services, telecommunications and computer services are the most important and have undergone rapid growth, while heavy industries have suffered relative decline. The Conservative administration of the 1980s and early 1990s was the first in Western Europe to dismantle the mixed economy of private and state-owned industries that had become the standard model for members of the EU. Many former state-owned industries including oil, telecommunications, gas and electricity, were sold to private shareholders, while the Government imposed tight fiscal controls and enacted pro-business legislation. Controls on trade and on the movement of capital were removed. The model has since been adopted throughout both the industrialised and developing worlds; it has been maintained and then extended by the Labour administration, which took office in 1997.
Britain's economic performance in the last few years has been reasonable, although some cracks are beginning to show as the government has been forced to plan for a much higher level of borrowing than anticipated. A slump in manufacturing industry has pushed unemployment up to 1.5 million (5.2 per cent of the workforce). Both GDP growth (2.1 per cent) and inflation (1.8 per cent) are slightly below the EU averages. The UK's external economic relations are now dominated by the EU (which accounts for 70 per cent of all UK trade), although there are other important trade links with the USA, the Far East and with members of the Commonwealth. Nonetheless, Europe dominates the economic agenda and the overriding issue facing present and future governments is the extent to which they are willing to integrate into the European economy. The argument is now focused on whether Britain should adopt the single European currency, the Euro. Although the economy met the necessary criteria, the Government chose not to join up when the currency was introduced in 1999. The Government has since remained firmly on the fence; while many political and business leaders favour membership, there is huge opposition in the country at large. The conclusion of the debate may be decisive to Britain's economic future.
BUSINESS: Businesspeople are generally expected to dress smartly (suits are the norm). Appointments should be made and the exchange of business cards is customary. A knowledge of English is essential. **Office hours:** Mon-Fri 0900/0930-1700/1730.
COMMERCIAL INFORMATION: The following organisation can offer advice: The British Chambers of Commerce, 65 Petty France, St James's Park, London SW1H 9EU (tel: (020) 7654 5800; e-mail: info@britishchambers.org.uk; website: www.chamberonline.co.uk).
CONFERENCES/CONVENTIONS: The UK conference scene is well organised with several publications comprehensively listing every possible kind of venue (including dedicated centres, hotels, universities, football grounds, race courses, manor houses, castles and theatres). In addition, regional and local tourist boards promote their own areas vigorously. Birmingham and London have an international reputation; there are several excellent conference venues. There are other towns with facilities of near comparable size, and comprehensive back-up services are available everywhere. Bristol, Glasgow, Manchester and Newcastle are among the cities offering a variety of venues, whilst smaller towns such as Chester, Inverness, Llandudno, Salisbury and York offer uniquely attractive environments without sacrificing efficiency. The large political parties of the UK traditionally hold their conferences in seaside towns during the winter; locations include Blackpool (the famous Winter Gardens), Bournemouth and Brighton. Those looking for conventional venues will find the maximum seating capacity (19,000 persons) in London; however, if organisers wished to book Wembley Stadium they could probably do it, so, effectively, there is no upper limit. All parts of the UK are easily accessible by rail and air from London. The *British Conference Destinations Directory* gives brief regional details and is published by the British Association of Conference Destinations, 6th Floor, Charles House, 148-149 Great Charles Street, Birmingham B3 3HT (tel: (0121) 212 1400; fax: (0121) 212 3131; e-mail: info@bacd.org.uk; website: www.bacd.org.uk).

Climate

Owing to it being an island, the UK is subject to very changeable weather. Extremes of temperature are rare but snow, hail, heavy rain and heatwaves can occur. For detailed descriptions, see *Climate* in the respective country sections.
Required clothing: Waterproofing throughout the year. Warm clothing is advisable at all times, and is essential for any visits to upland areas.

England

LATEST TRAVEL ADVICE CONTACTS

British Foreign and Commonwealth Office
Tel: (0870) 606 0290 Website: www.fco.gov.uk

US Department of State
Website: http://travel.state.gov/travel

Canadian Department of Foreign Affairs and Int'l Trade
Tel: (1 800) 267 8376 Website: www.dfait-maeci.gc.ca

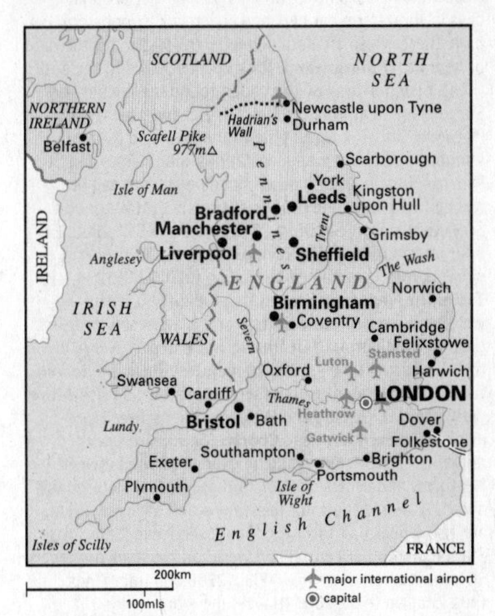

Location: Great Britain.

Visit Britain
Thames Tower, Black's Road, Hammersmith, London W6 9EL, UK
Tel: (020) 8563 3000. Fax: (020) 8563 0302.
E-mail: BLVCinfo@visitbritain.org *or* industryrelations@visitbritain.com (trade enquiries only).
Website: www.visitbritain.com
Promotes Britain abroad.

General Information

AREA: 130,281 sq km (50,356 sq miles).
POPULATION: 49,561,800 (2002).
POPULATION DENSITY: 380.4 per sq km.
CAPITAL: London. **Population:** 7,188,000 (Greater London; official estimate 2001).
GEOGRAPHY: Much of the countryside is relatively flat, consisting of fertile plains and gentle hills. Mountains, moors and steeper hills are found mainly in the north and the west; the Lake District (Cumbria) and the northwest are divided from the Yorkshire Dales, and the northeast, by the (relatively) high-rising Pennines, 'the backbone of England'. The eastern part of the country, particularly East Anglia, is the lowest lying. The coastline is varied, and ranges from long stretches of sandy beaches to steep cliffs and isolated rocky coves.
LANGUAGE: English. The multiplicity of local dialects throughout the country, overlaid with class, and town and country accents makes English a language of astonishing diversity - words and forms of syntax which are obsolete in the southeast may often be found elsewhere. In the larger cities, particularly London, there are many communities who do not speak English as a first language (or who have a *patois* - originating outside of this country - which adds yet more variety to the English language).
For information on Government, time, electricity and communications, see the main *United Kingdom* section.

Public Holidays

Note: Public holidays observed in England are the same as those observed in the rest of the UK (see the main United Kingdom section) with the addition of:
2005: Aug 22 Summer Bank Holiday.
2006: Aug 28 Summer Bank Holiday.

Travel - International

Air: England's principal **international airports** are:
HEATHROW (LHR): Located 24km (15 miles) west of central London. Airport information: tel: (0870) 000 0123; website: www.baa.com/main/airports/heathrow. The airport

has three passenger terminals grouped together in the airport's central area. The fourth terminal is a short distance from the main complex. **Facilities:** Banks (daily) and currency exchange in all terminals; ATMs in all terminals; left luggage in all terminals; post office; a variety of restaurants, bars, cafes and other eating places in all terminals; babycare rooms in all terminals; St George's Chapel, opposite entrance to T2 car park; duty free in all terminals; gift/general shops in all terminals; Travel Care Unit in Queen's Building (tel: (020) 8745 7047, open Mon-Sat 0930-1630); *The Business Centre* Heathrow (tel: (020) 8759 2434, next to T2 emergency medical service); hotel reservation service in all terminals; facilities for the disabled: wheelchairs, telephones, toilets, special parking bays in short-term car park and coach link to long-term car park. There is also an induction loop link system for the hard of hearing. **Underground:** The airport is linked to the entire Greater London area by the underground railway network. Stations for Heathrow Terminals 1, 2, 3 and 4 are on the Piccadilly Line. The travel time to the West End is 47 minutes, and to the mainline stations, King's Cross and St Pancras, 55 minutes. All other mainline stations can be reached with only one change of train in central London. Services run Mon-Sat 0511-2349, and Sun 0557-2330. 24-hour information on the *London Regional Transport* network may be obtained by dialling (020) 7222 1234. **Train:** The *Heathrow Express* (tel: (0845) 600 1515; website: www.heathrowexpress.com) is a fast service from London Paddington to Heathrow. Trains depart every 15 minutes (travel time - 15 to 20 minutes). There is a *Railair* coach, with frequent express services connecting Heathrow with trains at Reading and Woking stations. Details are available in each terminal. **Coach:** *London Transport* operates *Airbuses*, providing an express service between Heathrow and central London. Airbuses call at all terminals and have ample space for passengers and baggage. There are also wheelchair facilities. The A2 service to Kings Cross Station, and other central and west London stops runs every 30 minutes from Heathrow 0530-2208 and from Kings Cross Station 0400-2000 (travel time - one hour 40 minutes). *Speedlink Airport Services' Jetlink* operates every 30 minutes (almost 24 hours a day) to Gatwick (travel time - one hour 10 minutes). The service now runs to Stansted airport twice every two hours (travel time - one hour 25 minutes), operating 0600-0110. *Green Line* coach/bus services (724), run to Watford, St Albans, Hatfield, Welwyn Garden City, Hertford and Harlow. *London Transport*'s 726 bus runs to Kingston, Sutton, Croydon and Bromley. For information on these services, dial (08705) 747 777. *National Express* (tel: (08705) 808 080) runs direct Rapide coach services from Heathrow to most parts of the UK including Manchester 11 times a day (travel time - six hours); Bristol 18 times a day (travel time - two hours); and Birmingham 16 times a day (travel time - two hours 35 minutes). *Speedlink* luxury coaches connect Heathrow with Gatwick (travel time - one hour). Coaches depart every 30 minutes, operating 0440-0040. Many private companies have long-distance coach services linking Heathrow with the rest of the country. West Midlands area: *Flightlink*. East Anglia: *Cambridge Coaches*. For information on schedules, online booking and fares for *Airbus*, *Speedlink*, *Jetlink* and *National Express* services, contact *National Express* (website: www.nationalexpress.com). **Local bus:** *London Transport* (tel: (020) 7941 4500; website: www.londontransport.co.uk) services 81, 105, 111, 140, 222, 285, 555, 556, 557, 726, A10, H30, N105, N140, N285, U3, and its night bus N9 operate from Heathrow Central bus station to various parts of London. The *Oxford Bus Company* (tel: (01865) 785 400) runs the Oxford Express service directly between Heathrow and Oxford at half-hourly intervals during the day and two-hourly intervals throughout the night. *Green Line* also operates local services (see above for coach operations). **Note:** London Transport Travelcheck (tel: (020) 7222 1234) gives up-to-the-minute information on how London services are running. **Taxi:** Available for hire outside each airport terminal. Each terminal has its own taxi rank and the information desk can give an indication of fares. **Car hire:** *Alamo*, *Avis*, *Enterprise*, *Europcar*, *Hertz* and *National* self-drive and chauffeur-driven cars can be hired from desks in each airport terminal. To central London takes 30 minutes to one hour. **Private car:** Heathrow, 38km (24 miles) from central London, is reached either through the tunnel of the M4 motorway spur or from the A4 (Bath) road. It is also close to the M25 orbital motorway, making journeys to virtually all parts of the country relatively simple. It is advisable to avoid the area during peak times (0700-1000 and 1600-1900). Unloading but no waiting is allowed outside terminals. Short- and long-term car parking is available; there are coach connections from the long-term car park to all terminals.

GATWICK (LGW): Located 45km (28 miles) south of central London. Airport information: tel: (0870) 000 2468; website: www.baa.com/main/airports/gatwick. **Facilities:** Banks/currency exchange, ATMs, shops, restaurants, left luggage, duty free shops, chapel, babycare rooms, medical room and facilities for the disabled; all facilities are available 24 hours. There is an executive lounge in the South Terminal. Entry is £19.50. **Train:** *Gatwick Express* (tel: (0845) 850 530; website: www.gatwickexpress.co.uk) operates a nonstop service from Victoria Station at 15-minute intervals from 0500-0030 and also trains at 0330 and 0430 (travel time - 30 minutes). Passengers travelling with *American Airlines*, *British Airways* and *GB Airways* can check in at Victoria Station. There are also regular services to Gatwick from London Bridge Station (travel time - 30 minutes). There are fast and frequent trains from Gatwick, which connect with mainline stations throughout southeast England. There are direct trains daily between Gatwick and many other cities nationwide. For further information, contact National Rail Enquiries (tel: (08457) 484 950). **Coach:** *Flightline* to Victoria Coach Station and Stansted Airport runs hourly 0415-2240 (travel time to Victoria - one hour 25 minutes). *Jetlink* to Heathrow runs every 30 minutes during most of the day and night (travel time - one hour 10 minutes), with extensions to Luton Airport every hour and to Stansted Airport every two hours. The service to Heathrow runs every hour until 0005. *National Express* (tel: (08705) 808 080; website: www.nationalexpress.com) has many direct coach services to most parts of the UK including Birmingham (approximate travel time - four hours); Leicester (approximate travel time - four hours five minutes); and Newcastle (approximate travel time - nine hours 50 minutes). *Flightlink* goes from other cities including Birmingham, Bristol, Cardiff, Manchester, Sheffield and Swansea. Certain charter tour operators also provide coaches from Gatwick for arriving passengers. Check with relevant tour operator. Contact National Express (website: www.nationalexpress) for information on schedules, online booking and fares for Flightlink, Jetlink and National Express services. **Taxi:** Available outside the terminal (travel time to central London - one hour. **Car hire:** *Avis*, *Europcar*, *Hertz*, *National* and *Thrifty* self-drive and chauffeur-driven cars can be hired from desks in the arrivals hall. **Private car:** Gatwick can be reached from London on the A23/M23. It is also close to the M25 orbital motorway, linking all main routes from London. There are ample parking facilities for short and long stays. For fee enquiries, telephone (0870) 000 100.

LONDON CITY AIRPORT (LCY): Located 10km (6 miles) east of the City of London. Airport information: tel: (020) 7646 0088; website: www.londoncityairport.com. This airport, situated at the Royal Docks in the London Borough of Newham, provides frequent scheduled air services linking the City of London with many European cities. Scheduled airlines include *Air France*, *Aer Lingus*, *British European*, *KLM UK*, *Lufthansa*, *Luxair*, *Swiss* and *VLM*. Check-in time is usually about 10 minutes. **Facilities:** Duty free shops, car hire, bank, bureaux de change and ATMs, left luggage, information desk, restaurant and bars, newsagent and bookstore, and business centre with meeting rooms/conference facilities for up to 120 persons.
Train/Underground: Silvertown Station, on the Silverlink Metro line, is 328m (300 yards) from the airport terminal; connections with the Underground are at Highbury and Islington (Victoria Line), Stratford (Central Line and Docklands Light Railway), West Ham (District and Hammersmith and City Lines), West Hampstead (Jubilee Line) and Willesden Junction (Bakerloo Line). Plaistow (District Line) is approximately 3km (2 miles) from the airport; it has its own taxi rank. The Jubilee Line at Canning Town is approximately 1.6km (1 mile) away (travel time by shuttle bus - five minutes). Canning Town is also on the Docklands Light Railway and the Silverlink Metro.
Coach/Bus: A shuttle bus operates every 10 minutes from the terminal to Canary Wharf (Docklands Light Railway); Canning Town (London Underground, Docklands Light Railway and the Silverlink Metro); and Liverpool Street Station (London Underground and mainline trains to the east of England). The service operates approximately Mon-Fri 0600-2220, Sat 0600-1300 and Sun 1005-2220. *London Transport* buses 69 and 473 stop at the terminal, linking it with nearby Docklands Light Railway and Silverlink Metro stations. **Taxi:** Widely available; may be booked in-flight.
Car hire: *Avis*, *Europcar* and *Hertz*. **Private car:** The airport is reached from the City via Commercial Road/East India Dock Road (A13) over the Canning Town Flyover, turning right into Prince Regent Lane, or via Tower Hill along The Highway (A1203) and Silvertown Way (travel time - 30 minutes); from the M25 via the M11 and North Circular (A406) or the A13. Access from the City of London will usually present no problems provided the morning and evening rush hours are avoided. London City Airport has ample car parking space located just outside the terminal building.

STANSTED (STN): Located 48km (30 miles) northeast of central London. Airport information: tel: (0870) 000 0303; website: www.baa.com/main/airport/stansted. **Facilities:** Information desk, executive lounge, lost property, bureaux de change, ATMs, a variety of restaurants and cafes/bars, nursing mothers' room, emergency medical service, duty free shops, fax and photocopying facilities, wheelchairs and toilets for the disabled as well as induction loop system in the international departures lounge. **Train:** The *Stansted Express* runs throughout the day (0430-2330; Sat 0430-2330; Sun 0430-2300) from London Liverpool Street to Stansted (tel: (01223) 453 606; website: www.stanstedexpress.co.uk). Services run every 15 minutes (Mon-Fri 0800-1630 and Sun 0615-2300) and every 30 minutes, evenings and Saturdays (travel time - 45 minutes). There are also services from Stansted to Cambridge and the North. Further information is available from National Rail Enquiries (tel: (08457) 484 950). **Coach:** *Colchester Coach Link* runs services to Stansted from Dunmow, Bradwell and Colchester, daily 0525-2010. *Airbus* connects Stansted with London Victoria Coach Station. Coaches run every 20 minutes during the day and half-hourly throughout most of the night (travel time - one hour 30 minutes). *Jetlink* operates services every two hours, between Gatwick, Heathrow, Luton and Stansted. Jetlink also provides services to Braintree, Cambridge, Ipswich, Milton Keynes, Norwich and Oxford, amongst others. *Flightlink* coaches operate to Gatwick Airport via Victoria Coach Station in London. **Taxi:** To central London takes one hour 30 minutes. **Car hire:** Cars can be hired from desks in the terminal building. For details, contact *Avis*, *Budget*, *Europcar*, *Hertz* or *National*. For air taxis/business aviation services, contact *Artac Air Chartering Service*. **Private car:** Situated 54km (34 miles) northeast of London, the airport is easily accessible by road on M25/M11 from London. The Midlands and the North are reached via the A1, A604 and M11. Long- and short-term car parking space is available.

Luton (LTN): Located 51km (32 miles) northeast of London. Airport information: tel: (01582) 405 100; website: www.london-luton.co.uk. **Facilities:** Bureaux de change, ATMs, general shops, a variety of restaurants and bar/cafes, nursing mothers' room, free play area (two to eight years) in departure lounge, duty free shop, chapel, medical services and facilities for the disabled - wheelchairs, toilets and ambulift. **Train:** Access to Luton Airport is via Luton Airport Parkway station. A courtesy shuttle service operates between the station and airport terminal. Luton is on the *Thameslink* line which runs from Bedford via London (stopping at King's Cross and London Bridge stations) and Gatwick Airport to Brighton. Midland Mainline services connect Luton with the Midlands and the North. Trains run direct to Leicester, Nottingham, Derby and Sheffield. National Rail Enquiries (tel: (08457) 484 950). **Coach:** *National Express* (tel: (08705) 808 080) runs daily services to Birmingham and Manchester. Services also run to most other parts of the UK. *Jetlink* is a direct (limited stop) service connecting Stansted Airport with Luton, Heathrow and Gatwick, which operates hourly from Luton. It runs via Hemel Hempstead and continues on to Brighton. *Greenline* 755 and 757 runs a daily service from the airport to Luton and on to central London. *United Counties* operates directly to Bedford. From Bedford, there are connections to Cambridge, Huntingdon, Northampton, Peterborough and St Neots. Services vary in frequency. *Flightlink* operates direct between the airport and Birmingham, Nottingham and Leicester. **Local bus:** Buses run from the airport to Luton bus and rail stations, with frequent services during the day, and hourly evening services (Mon to Sat). **Taxi:** Can be hired from the rank immediately outside the terminal building. **Car hire:** *Avis*, *Budget*, *Europcar*, *Hertz* and *National Car Rental* have desks at the airport. **Private car:** The airport can be reached on the M1 exiting at Junction 10. Access to the airport from the east is via the A505 dual carriageway from Hitchin. The M25 connects all motorways and the airport can therefore be accessed from the East, South and West via M25, M4, M11 and M23. Travelling from the west also provides several routes from the Dunstable area through Luton. Airport signs should be followed throughout. Long- and short-term car parking is available within the airport boundary.

BIRMINGHAM (BHX): Located 13km (8 miles) southeast of the city centre. Airport information: tel: (0870) 733 5511; website: www.bhx.co.uk. **Facilities:** Bank and foreign exchange services, ATMs, cafes and restaurants, duty free shops, facilities for the disabled, medical centre, nursing mothers' room, shops, spectators' viewing gallery and left-luggage office. **Train:** The main terminal is linked to Birmingham International Station and the National Exhibition Centre (NEC) by the *Air Rail Link* courtesy bus service. Birmingham International is connected to the Intercity network and regional lines and has a fast service to London Euston every 30 minutes (travel time - one hour 20 minutes). Train information: (tel: 08457) 484 950, only available from within the UK). Birmingham New Street Station, in the city centre, is 10 minutes away by Intercity or local services and provides interchange for services throughout the rest of the country. **Coach/Bus:** *Travel West Midlands* operates local services into the suburbs. An Airbus service from the airport to the NEC and various locations around the city centre, operates every 30 minutes (0500-2100). *National Express* offers a frequent, daily service to central Birmingham, Coventry, Lancashire and the

London airports. A service also runs to Birmingham, Cambridge, Chelmsford, Coventry, Northampton and Southend. *Flightlink* operates connections to Gatwick and Heathrow with various collection points along the route. Frequent coaches run to and from Birmingham from London Victoria and most major cities and towns throughout the country. For further information, contact the airport (website: www.bhx.co.uk) *or* National Express (website: www.nationalexpress.com). **Local bus:** Service 900 runs to the city centre Monday to Sunday every 20 minutes from 0322-0031. **Taxi:** Taxis are available outside the Eurohub Terminal (travel time to city centre - 25 minutes). **Car hire:** *Avis, Budget, Europcar, Hertz* and *National Car Rental* have offices at the airport. **Private car:** M1, M5, M6, M40 and M42 are the main routes to Birmingham. The airport is well signposted from the city. There is multi-storey and open-air parking (over 8000 spaces) at the airport. For further details, contact National Car Parks (NCP) (tel: (0870) 606 7050).

MANCHESTER (MAN): Located 17km (10 miles) southwest of the city centre. Airport information: tel: (0161) 489 3000; website: www.manchesterairport.co.uk. **Facilities:** Restaurants/cafes, duty free shops, baby care facilities and play area, shops, banking services, bureaux de change, ATMs, medical centre, post office, conference and banqueting facilities for up to 400 people and full facilities for the disabled. **Train:** Manchester Airport station links the airport to Manchester city centre, with trains departing Mon to Sat every 15 minutes and every 20 minutes on Sunday (travel time - 15 to 20 minutes). Fast trains to all parts of the country leave from Manchester Airport station and there are connections for further services at Manchester Piccadilly and Manchester Victoria (tel: (08457) 484 950, only available from within the UK). **Coach/Bus:** *National Express* (tel: (08705) 808 080) runs daily services to most parts of the UK including Scotland. Skyline buses 43A and 105 operate throughout the week from local villages to Piccadilly rail station and the city centre. Service 500 runs to Bolton and various other stops including the Trafford Centre. For more detailed information on times and frequency of these services, contact *Traveline Manchester* (tel: (0870) 162 0806). **Taxi:** There are taxi ranks situated outside or adjacent to Terminals 1, 2 and 3 (travel time to the city centre - 25 minutes). **Car hire:** *Avis, Budget, Europcar, Hertz, National Car Rental* and *Sixt* have booking offices in Terminals 1, 2 and 3. **Private car:** The airport is at the heart of the country's motorway network and a specially constructed spur from the M56 runs directly into the terminal building. Road connections serve Greater Manchester, Merseyside, Lancashire, Cheshire, the Midlands and West and South Yorkshire. There is car parking space within the airport boundary. *Newcastle (NCL):* Located 10km (6 miles) northwest of the city centre. Airport information: tel: (0870) 122 1488; website: www.newcastleairport.com. **Facilities:** Bureaux de change, bank, ATMs, restaurant/bars, shops, duty free shop, left luggage, baby care facilities, play area, emergency medical services and facilities for the disabled. **Metro:** The Tyneside Metro Rapid Transport system connects the whole of the Newcastle area with the airport. It runs to Newcastle city centre, across the River Tyne to Gateshead and South Shields and to Tynemouth and the coast. For information, call Traveline; tel: (0870) 162 0806). **Train:** Nearest railway station is Newcastle Central, 11km (7 miles) from the airport, linked by buses operated by *Busways*, which run Mon to Sat every 30 minutes, and every hour on Sunday. For further information, contact *National Rail Enquiries* (tel: (08457) 484 950). **Coach:** *National Express* and *Scottish Citylink* operates services to the airport from most major cities in Scotland and the North of England and Midlands. **Local bus:** Services 76, 76A, 77, 77A, 78, 78E, 79 and 79A run from Eldon Square bus concourse, in the centre of Newcastle. These stop on the main road at the airport entrance (travel time - 20 minutes). **Taxi:** A taxi rank is situated outside the railway station, and at the Haymarket near the Eldon Square bus concourse in Newcastle city centre (travel time to city centre - 15 to 20 minutes). Only licensed taxi cabs are allowed to pick up at the airport. **Car hire:** *Avis, Europcar, Hertz* and *National* self-drive agents are located at the airport. **Private car:** The airport can be reached from the south by the A1(M) north, then the A696 Jedburgh trunk road, and from the north by the A1 south, then the A696 Jedburgh trunk road. Open-air long- and short-term parking facilities are available (advance booking recommended during busy periods).

SEA: There are many ports offering ferry connections between England and mainland Europe, Ireland, the Channel Islands, the Isle of Wight, the Channel Isles and the Isle of Man. See *Travel - International* in the main *United Kingdom* section for a list of operators.

RAIL: The *Intercity* network serves all main cities in the UK mainland. All routes radiate from London. For all rail information, call National Rail Enquiries (tel: (08457) 484 950, only available from within the UK). Rail services are operated by numerous private companies. Terminus stations in London serve the following regions:

Southern England and South London: *Charing Cross, London Bridge, Victoria* and *Waterloo*.

East Anglia, Essex, North-East and East London: *Liverpool Street*.

South Midlands, West of England, South Wales and West London: *Paddington*.

East and West Midlands, North Wales, North-West England, West Coast of Scotland and West London: *Euston, Marylebone* and *St Pancras*.

East and North-East England, East Coast of Scotland and North London: *King's Cross*.

There are also many smaller lines that operate less frequently. There are services to the Republic of Ireland via *Fishguard* and *Holyhead*, and to Northern Ireland.

ROAD: England is served by a good network of motorways and trunk roads that connect all the main cities and towns. The main motorways are: **M1:** London, Luton, Leicester, Sheffield, Leeds. **M2/A2:** London to Dover. **M3:** London to Winchester. **M4:** London, Reading, Bristol, Newport, Cardiff, Swansea. **M5:** Birmingham, Gloucester, Bristol, Exeter. **M6:** Coventry, Birmingham, Stoke, Warrington (connecting with the M62 for Liverpool and Manchester), Preston (connecting with the M55 for Blackpool), Morecambe, Carlisle. **M11:** London to Cambridge. **M20/A20**: London to Folkestone. **M25:** London orbital. **M40:** London to Birmingham. **M62:** Liverpool, Warrington, Manchester, Huddersfield, Leeds, Hull. The main trunk roads are: **A1/A1(M)** (motorway in parts): London, Peterborough, Doncaster, Darlington, Newcastle, Edinburgh. **A3:** London, Guildford, Portsmouth. **A5:** London, St Albans, Nuneaton, Birmingham area, Shrewsbury, across inland north Wales to Holyhead. **A6:** London, Bedford, Leicester, Manchester. **A11:** London to Norwich. **A12:** London, Ipswich, Great Yarmouth. **A23:** London to Brighton. **A30:** London, Basingstoke, Yeovil, Exeter, Penzance. **A40:** London, Oxford (M40), Gloucester, Cheltenham, across inland south Wales to Fishguard.

Distances from London (by road): To Birmingham 169km (105 miles), Manchester 299km (186 miles), Liverpool 325km (202 miles), Exeter 278km (173 miles), Penzance 452km (281 miles), Bristol 185km (115 miles), Carlisle 484km (301 miles), Newcastle 441km (274 miles), Sheffield 257km (160 miles), York 311km (193 miles), Cambridge 89km (55 miles), Southampton 124km (77 miles), Dover 114km (71 miles), Oxford 92km (57 miles), Norwich 182km (113 miles), Portsmouth 113km (70 miles) and Harwich 122km (76 miles).

Coach: Many coach companies offer express and stopping services throughout England and the rest of the UK. *National Express* provides nationwide coach information. The head office is at Ensign Court, 4 Vicarage Road, Edgbaston, Birmingham B15 3ES (tel: (08705) 808 080; website: www.nationalexpress.com).

Urban transport in London: The Underground: London has a comprehensive metro service known as the 'Underground' or, colloquially, as the 'tube'. The tube is the oldest and one of the most extensive underground railway networks in the world. There are 13 lines, including the *Docklands Light Railway*, and some - such as the *Central* and the *Metropolitan* - extend well into the surrounding suburbs. Each line has its own colour on the network map, copies of which are widely available. Some lines operate certain sections during peak hours and some stations close altogether in the evenings or at weekends. There is also an extensive network of overground rail services in the London area, particularly in the southeast, many of which connect with Underground services. All of the railway terminus stations connect with at least one Underground line, with the exception of Fenchurch Street (which is, however, virtually adjacent to Tower Hill station on the District Line). Various travel discounts are available. The one-day, weekend or weekly *Travelcard* offers unlimited travel on bus, Underground and overground rail services in one or more zones; it is one of the best methods for visitors to travel throughout London. Monthly and annual Travelcards require a passport-size photograph. For 24-hour enquiries on bus and underground travel, contact London Transport (tel: (020) 7941 4500; website: www.tfl.gov.uk). For enquiries about rail services, contact National Rail Enquiries (tel: (08457) 484 950). Maps and leaflets are widely available, although it should be remembered that the maps of the Underground and overground rail networks are diagrammatic, and do not indicate the relative distances between stations. **Bus:** London is served by an excellent network of buses (about 300 routes), although recent policy has been to cut some of the lesser-used services. Some operate only partial routes at specific times or may discontinue service in the evenings or at weekends. During rush hours, bus travel in central London can become agonisingly slow, although the introduction of bus lanes and 'red routes' on some roads has partly improved this situation. There is a good timetabled network of night bus services, and all routes passing through central London call at Trafalgar Square. **Taxi/Car hire:** Black cabs can be hailed in the street or ordered by phone. Fares are metered but surcharges are levied for extra passengers, large amounts of luggage, travel at night, and on Sundays or public holidays.

Credit: © Britain On View & Martin Brent

Over 3000 new black cabs have facilities for wheelchair-bound passengers. Mini-cabs and cars for hire are also available; numbers are listed in the Yellow Pages telephone directory. **River transport:** Leisure and commuter services on the River Thames are run by a variety of private companies, including *Thames Clippers* (website: www.thamesclippers.com). The main commuter service is between Chelsea Harbour and Embankment. At weekends, there are a variety of cruises and pleasure trips. For further information, contact London Travel Information (tel: (020) 7222 1234; website: www.tfl.gov.uk).

Urban transport: Elsewhere: All towns and cities have bus services. In addition, the areas of Birmingham, Liverpool, Manchester and the cities in South Yorkshire and Newcastle have suburban rail services. Newcastle also has a metro, which consists of a circular line with three branches. It connects with Newcastle Central, Manors and Heworth railway stations and terminates at South Shields (ferry connection to North Shields, also on the metro), St James and Newcastle Airport. Manchester has a fast metrolink tram service running on former railway lines from Bury in the north to Altrincham in the south. There is also a brand new line from Eccles in the west via Salford Quays to the city centre. All cities have taxi services, many using London-type black cabs. Taxi ranks are usually placed near bus stations, railway stations and town centres. Local telephone directories give the numbers of mini-cabs and hire cars.

Accommodation

Accommodation is available at hotels, motels and posthouses, guest houses, farmhouses, inns and self-catering establishments and on campsites.

HOTELS: It is rare to find a town in England, however small, which does not have at least one hotel; in villages, very often doubling as the local pub. Some London hotels, for example the *Savoy*, are famous the world over but there are many newer first-class hotels. In addition, there are many smaller hotels throughout the larger cities; in London, Earl's Court and the area around King's Cross are famous for their many streets of small hotels bearing such names as the *Albany, Apollo* or *Victoria*. For further information, contact the British Hospitality Association, Queens House, 55-56 Lincoln's Inn Fields, London WC2A 3BH (tel: (0845) 880 7744; fax: (020) 7404 7799; e-mail: info@bha.org.uk; website: www.bha-online.org.uk). A selection of some of the finest hotels in England is available (website: www.distinctionworld.com). **Grading:** Over the past three years, the AA, RAC and English Tourism Council have collectively worked towards harmonising inspection standards and ratings of hotels and guest accommodation. The introduction of new quality standards has simplified the rating system. Hotels are classified by use of a star-rating system and guest accommodation by a diamond-rating system. The new classification scheme will apply to all hotels and guest accommodation inspected in England. Although the Scottish and Welsh tourist boards operate separate accommodation classification schemes, the star and diamond ratings will apply to Welsh and Scottish hotels and guest accommodation inspected by the RAC and AA. The hotel classifications are as follows:

1-star: Clean and comfortable accommodation, with a minimum of six bedrooms, three-quarters of which will have ensuite/private facilities. Range of facilities will include a lounge area, alcohol licence, lunch availability option and dining facilities for evening meals; **2-star:** Accommodation offering more extensive facilities including colour TV and private/ensuite facilities in all bedrooms, a lunch availability option and a restaurant serving evening meals; **3-star:** The range of facilities increases and includes a laundry service. More emphasis is placed on the quality and comfort of bedrooms, including remote-control TVs. Staffing levels and quality are of a good standard. Full dinner service, light snacks and lunches are available to residents and non-residents; **4-star:** Includes hotels with extensive accommodation and smaller luxury hotels, which provide high standards of service and wide range of facilities. These include a dry cleaning service and a superior standard of decor, furnishings and fittings in all bedrooms. All ensuite/private facilities will include baths with overhead showers. At least one restaurant will be open daily to residents and non-residents, for all meals. A full lunch service will be available in a restaurant, brasserie or similar; **5-star:** The highest classification, with an extensive range of facilities and services, including excellent staff, high-quality service and a luxurious standard of decor, furnishings and fittings. All rooms have ensuite facilities that include baths fitted with overhead showers, bath robes and bath sheets. All colour TVs offer cable and satellite channels, along with video channels. Additional fax and computer points may be provided. Brochures, booklets and leaflets giving full information on accommodation are available from the English Tourism Council or any of the regional tourist boards.

GUEST HOUSES: There are guest houses and bed & breakfast facilities throughout the country. Under the new quality standards, guest houses, inns and farmhouses providing bed & breakfast services are classified by a diamond-rating system. For listings, contact the appropriate regional tourist board for more information. The classifications are as follows:

1-diamond: Clean and comfortable accommodation. Services include a full-cooked or continental breakfast. Probably no private bathrooms or en suite facilities in bedrooms. Limited range of additional facilities and accessories in bedrooms (eg colour TV, radio, kettle, hairdryer and reading material); **2-diamond:** A higher standard of facilities, comfort and quality, with greater emphasis on guest care; **3-diamond:** An increased standard of comfort and range of facilities, with good levels of customer care. At least 40 per cent of all bedrooms have private bathrooms or en suite facilities; **4-diamond:** Good customer care and facilities. A very good level of quality and comfort; **5-diamond:** Excellent overall level of quality in facilities, accessories, customer care, decor and furnishings and a high standard of maintenance. At least 80 per cent of all rooms have private bathrooms or en suite facilities.

SELF-CATERING: Cottages and bungalows can be rented in many areas. For information, contact the regional tourist board or look in the relevant section in local and national papers. Standards may vary. **Grading:** The English Tourism Council has a 'key' classification system:

1-key: Clean and comfortable, adequate heating, lighting and seating, TV, cooker, fridge and crockery; **2-keys:** Colour TV, easy chairs or sofas for all occupants, fridge with icemaker, bedside units or shelves, plus heating in all rooms; **3-keys:** Dressing tables, bedside lights, linen and towels available, vacuum cleaner, iron/ironing board; **4-keys:** All sleeping in beds or bunks, supplementary lighting in living areas, more kitchen equipment, use of an automatic

1 Durham
2 West Yorkshire
3 South Yorkshire
4 Nottinghamshire
5 Gtr. Manchester
6 Merseyside
7 Cheshire
8 Derbyshire
9 Staffordshire
10 Shropshire
11 West Midlands
12 Warwickshire
13 Leicestershire
14 Northamptonshire
15 Bedfordshire
16 Cambridgeshire
17 Hereford & Worcester
18 Gloucestershire
19 Oxfordshire
20 Buckinghamshire
21 Hertfordshire
22 Greater London
23 Surrey
24 Berkshire
25 Hampshire
26 Wiltshire

washing machine and tumble dryer; **5-keys:** Automatically controlled heating, own washing machine and tumble dryer, bath and shower, telephone, dishwasher, microwave and fridge freezer.

CAMPING/CARAVANNING: There are camping and caravan sites throughout the UK, for short and long stays. Some sites hire out tents or caravans. Most sites offer basic facilities, while some have playgrounds, clubs, shops, phones and sporting areas.

HOLIDAY CAMPS: Offer accommodation, food and a full range of leisure activities generally at an all-inclusive price.

YOUTH HOSTELS: Standards vary greatly, from very basic night-time accommodation for hikers and cyclists, to modern hostels and motels which are often used by families and groups. Prices are very reasonable. For information, contact the *Youth Hostel Association*, Trevelyan House, Dimple Road, Matlock, Derbyshire DE4 3YH (tel: (01629) 592 600; fax: (01629) 592 702; e-mail: customerservices@yha.org.uk; website: www.yha.org.uk).

Resorts & Excursions

England's eventful history and scenic diversity render it one of the world's most popular visitor destinations. Although only united as a single nation little over 1000 years ago, its origins go back to the dawn of civilisation, and the variety of interest it offers reflects this.

From prehistoric Stonehenge to 21st-century attractions like London's Millennium Eye, its inhabitants have (and do) contributed much to the appeal of the UK's largest constituent country. This is not restricted to a material legacy, either – England's cultural mix is rich, thanks to the many invaders, settlers and immigrants who have arrived on her shores through the millennia. Countless others around the globe share aspects of customs, language and history with the English themselves.

England's heritage, and therefore her appeal as a destination, is many faceted and deeply rooted, ranging from the literary genius of Shakespeare to 'everyday' pageantry in the changing of the guard at Buckingham Palace.

The variety and contrast in the nation's countryside is enormous, too, and is often a source of surprise to many visitors venturing beyond the cities for the first time – as is the vast range of visitor attractions, resorts and sights to see and enjoy.

This guide comprises five regional sections, with another highlighting seven of the most popular destinations outside London. These are Bath, Cambridge, The Cotswolds, the Lake District, Oxford, Stratford-upon-Avon and York. The London section covers the capital, while the Southeast includes counties surrounding it, plus East Anglia. The South and Southwest encompasses the remainder of southern England and two sections cover the rest of the country; the Midlands and the North of England. Consult the central website for England's tourist boards (website: www.official-touristboards.co.uk) for further information. Many historic properties and other attractions are administered by the National Trust (tel: (0870) 458 4000; fax: (020) 8466 6824; e-mail: enquiries@thenationaltrust.org.uk; website: www.thenationaltrust.org.uk) and English Heritage (tel: (0870) 333 1181; fax: (01793) 414 926; e-mail: customers@english-heritage.org.uk; website: www.english-heritage.org.uk). The Association of National Park Authorities (website: www.anpa.gov.uk) gives an overview of the 11 National Parks in England (and Wales).

TOP SEVEN DESTINATIONS

Outside London, there are seven places known worldwide as prime attractions. Each has a different appeal, and each lies in a different part of the country – cross-references to the appropriate regional section appear in each entry.

BATH: (website: www.visitbath.co.uk.) Bath first came to prominence as 'Aquae Sulis' in Roman times. It was a fashionable spa resort nearly 2000 years ago, and rediscovered its ancient glories in the 18th century. Much of its beauty dates from the latter period, fine Georgian sandstone architecture dominating the modern cityscape. The original **Roman Baths and Pump Rooms**, though, remain open to visitors. Bath's 500-year-old **Abbey**, built on the site of a Saxon monastery, stands above the **Heritage Vaults**, which tell the story of 1600 years of Christianity in the area. Architectural highlights include John Wood's **Royal Crescent**, a remarkable curving Georgian terrace, and **Pulteney Bridge**, lined with shops and built by Robert Adam in the late 18th century.

CAMBRIDGE: (website: visitcambridge.org – see also the *Southeast and East Anglia* section.) Home of England's second-oldest university, dating from the early 13th century. The individual colleges are the prime attractions of interest in the city, including the oldest, **Peterhouse** (1284), 16th-century **Trinity College**, and **King's College**, whose **chapel** is regarded as one of Europe's finest late-medieval structures. Other attractions include the **Fitzwilliam Museum**, the University's **Museum of Archaeology** and **Museum of Zoology**, and **The Backs**, an area of parkland along the River Cam behind the colleges, where punting is a popular activity. The American War Cemetery at **Madingley** is close to the city, while the **Imperial War Museum Duxford** aviation section lies a short way south of Cambridge. Also near Cambridge is *Grantchester*, home of World War I poet Rupert Brooke.

THE COTSWOLDS: (website: www.visitcotswoldsandseverngale.gov.uk – see also the *South* and *Southwest* and *Midlands* sections.) Covering some 2000 sq km (800 sq miles), primarily in **Oxfordshire** and **Gloucestershire**, this area is famed for its picturesque villages and beautiful rolling hills. Highlights among the villages include **Broadway**, **Bourton-on-the-Water**, **Chipping Campden** and **Moreton-in-Marsh**, part of whose attraction is the distinctive honey-coloured local stone used in their construction. Attractions include England's second-largest parish church, **Tewkesbury Abbey**, Jacobean stately home **Chastleton House**, **Chedworth Roman Villa** near **Cheltenham** and imposing **Sudeley Castle** at **Winchcombe**. The **Cotswold Wildlife Park** at **Burford**, itself another very attractive town, is a popular family outing.

THE LAKE DISTRICT: (website: www.golakes.co.uk – see also the *North of England* section.) England's best-known national park occupies a huge swathe of **Cumbria** and, as its name suggests, there are many large bodies of water. But mountains also feature in this spectacular landscape, among them England's highest, the 978m- (3208 ft-) tall **Scafell Pike**. Visitors flock to the lakes for walking and other outdoor activities, and to trace the roots of literary figures such as Beatrix Potter, Arthur Ransome and William Wordsworth. Wordsworth's former home, **Dove Cottage** at **Grasmere**, is open to visitors – his tomb is in the nearby churchyard. A good starting point is the **National Park Visitor Centre** at Brockhole, while the **World of Beatrix Potter** at **Bowness-on-Windermere** draws people from all over the world. The restored Victorian **Steam Yacht Gondola** plies **Coniston Water** offering pleasure trips.

OXFORD: (website: www.visitoxford.org – see also the *South* and *Southwest* section.) Known as the 'City of Dreaming Spires', Oxford grew around England's oldest university, whose origins lie in the 11th century. Among 36 colleges in the city centre are **Christ Church**, which has an excellent **Art Gallery**, **Trinity College** and **Balliol**. 'The Oxford Story' presents a multimedia introduction to the city, with the help of a 'dark ride' through 800 years of history. St Martin's Church's **Carfax Tower** affords good views of the cityscape. Other major attractions include the **Ashmolean Museum of Art and Archaeology**, the **University Museum**, the **Museum of Modern Art** and the **Bodleian Library**. There is a wide range of themed guided walking tours available.

STRATFORD-UPON-AVON: (website: www.shakespeare-country.co.uk – see also the *Midlands* section.) Once home to William Shakespeare (1564-1616), Stratford draws visitors in their millions. Attractions associated with the Bard include **Shakespeare's Birthplace**, **Anne Hathaway's Cottage**, former home of his wife, **Mary Arden's House**, home of the playwright's mother, and **Holy Trinity Church**, where he and his family lie buried. **The Royal Shakespeare Theatre**, venue for regular RSC (Royal Shakespeare Company) performances, stands on the riverbank. Non-Shakespearean diversions in town include Europe's largest **Butterfly Farm** and the unusual **Teddy Bear Museum**.

YORK: (website: www.york-tourism.co.uk – see also the *North of England* section.) Northern England's most visited city contains a plethora of attractions. Foremost is the massive **York Minster**, northern Europe's biggest Gothic cathedral. The **City Wall** still almost completely surrounds

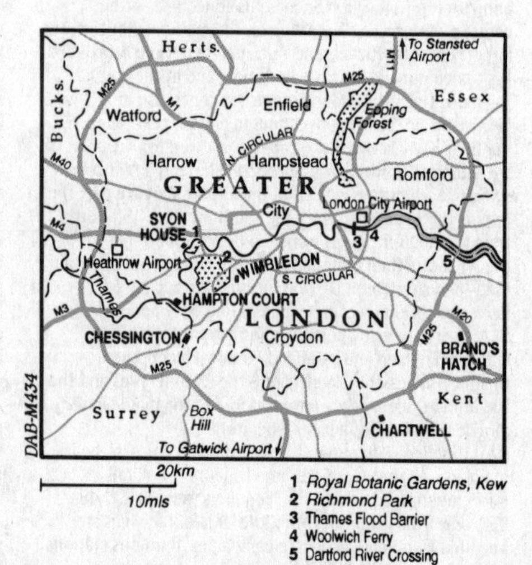

1 *Royal Botanic Gardens, Kew*
2 *Richmond Park*
3 Thames Flood Barrier
4 Woolwich Ferry
5 Dartford River Crossing (tunnel & bridge)

the central area, and **The Shambles** is one of the world's best-preserved medieval streets. York's past as Danish capital of Viking England is explored at the recently refurbished **Jorvik Viking Centre**, while its more recent status as a railway centre is celebrated at the **National Railway Museum**. The extensive **Castle Museum** deals with all aspects of history, including York's associations with chocolate making and Dick Turpin, the notorious 18th-century highwayman. The **Yorkshire Museum** and **City Art Gallery** are also major attractions. Historic buildings, such as timbered **St William's College** and 14th-century **Merchant Venturers' Hall**, abound. Walking tours and sightseeing boat trips on the **River Ouse** are available year round.

LONDON

London Tourist Board & Convention Bureau (tel: (020) 7234 5800; fax: (020) 7378 6225; website: www.visitlondon.com).

London has no obvious centre, because it grew out of two formerly distinct cities. The **City of London** was the site of the original Roman settlement and, later, commercial and trading centre. Meanwhile, **Westminster** became the seat of government after transfer of England's administrative capital from **Winchester** in the 11th century. Over the centuries, they fused, and engulfed surrounding villages and hamlets. Not until 'Green Belt' legislation of the 1950s did expansion slow. Today, 33 London boroughs and the City of London cover an area of nearly 385 sq km (148 sq miles), but contain a great deal of open parkland, common land and even woods. A wide range of guided walking, bus and car tours is available in London. For further details, contact the Tourist Board.

CENTRAL LONDON: Roughly bounded by the Underground Circle Line, this area includes the **West End**, Westminster and the City. The West End contains many of the principal theatres, cinemas, restaurants, cafes, hotels and nightclubs, as well as the best-known shopping areas, like **Oxford**, **Regent** and **Bond Street**, as well as **Covent Garden**.

Places of interest include **Westminster Abbey**, **Big Ben** and the **Houses of Parliament**, the **National Gallery** in **Trafalgar Square**, the **British Museum**, **Buckingham Palace**, the buildings of the **Horse Guards** and **Downing Street** in **Whitehall**, and the **Tate Britain gallery** on **Millbank**. The **London Theatre Museum** is in Russell Street.

The **Royal Opera House**, home of both Royal Ballet and Royal Opera, is in Covent Garden. Backstage tours are available. The **London Transport Museum** is also in this area, whose former fruit and vegetable market is now filled with cafes, pubs, restaurants and shops.

Rock Circus, by **Piccadilly Circus**, brings the story of rock and pop music to life. The **Courtauld Institute** paintings are on display at **Somerset House** (which formerly housed records of births, marriages and deaths).

A short distance to the north is Baker Street, location of **Madame Tussauds**, and the adjacent **London Planetarium**. The **Sherlock Holmes Museum** at 221B Baker Street contains a representation of the fictional detective's apartment.

Further west, in **Kensington** and **Chelsea**, are several other famous shopping streets (**King's Road**, **Knightsbridge** – site of **Harrods** – and **Portobello Road**, with its antiques market). Three of London's largest museums (the **Victoria & Albert**, **Science** and **Natural History**), and the **Royal Albert Hall**, home of the summer Promenade Concerts, are also here. The British **National Army Museum** is in Chelsea's Royal Hospital Road.

Central London also contains four parks: **Hyde Park** (by far the largest), **St James' Park**, **Green Park** and, slightly further north, **Regent's Park**, location of **London Zoo**.

CITY OF LONDON: The City, with a resident population of less than 5000, is, during the day, the workplace of over 500,000 people. It covers just 259 hectares (1 sq mile), hence its nickname of the 'Square Mile'.

Its best-known building is Wren's **St Paul's Cathedral**, completed in 1711. The **Museum of London**, near St Paul's, tells the story of London from prehistoric times to the present day. On permanent display is the famous Lord Mayor of London's coach, which carries the Lord Mayor through the City streets during the annual **Lord Mayor's Show**. Close to the City is the **Tower of London**, built by William the Conqueror in the 11th century. Near here is **Tower Hill Pageant**, which tells London's history in relation to the **River Thames**. The **Bank of England**, the **Stock Exchange**, **Lloyd's of London** (the world's leading insurance market), **Mansion House** (official residence of the Lord Mayor) and the **Central Criminal Court** ('The Old Bailey') all stand within the City boundaries.

Dr Johnson's House is close to **Fleet Street**, former centre of London's newspaper industry. The **Monument** (to the Great Fire of 1666) and the **Royal Exchange** are other famous landmarks; a more recent addition is the **Barbican Centre**, which contains a major arts complex – used by the Royal Shakespeare Company and home to the London Symphony Orchestra.

Tower Bridge, although little over 100 years old, is one of the world's most famous such structures, and it is possible to visit the control room containing the machinery for raising and lowering the central section and to walk along the overhead walkway. Moored on the **South Bank** close to the bridge is World War II battleship **HMS Belfast**, also open to visitors.

SOUTH OF THE THAMES: Immediately at the southern end of Westminster Bridge stands the former **County Hall**, now redeveloped to include the **London Aquarium**, one of Europe's largest.

The **South Bank Arts Centre**, near **Waterloo Station**, is among the most famous attractions south of the river. It comprises the **Royal National Theatre** and the **Royal Festival Hall**.

Nearby is **The Old Vic**, one of London's best known theatres. **Southwark Cathedral**, near London Bridge, is one of the finest Gothic churches in the city. Also in Southwark is an authentic reconstruction of the famous Shakespeare **Globe Theatre**, now open to visitors, and the site of the similar **Rose Theatre**. The brave may also be tempted to visit the ghoulish **London Dungeon**, which dwells upon less pleasant aspects of the capital's history. The redeveloped **Bankside Power Station** houses the **Tate Modern** gallery. Its collection includes major works by Monet, Picasso and Warhol, among many others. For lovers of even more contemporary and controversial artwork, the **Saatchi Gallery** hosts works by modern artists such as Damien Hirst, Tracey Emin and the Chapman Brothers. Also along the South Bank is the **Dali Universe**, a celebration and gallery of the surrealist legend's works. The pedestrianised **Millenium Bridge** by Norman Foster connects the two riverbanks, beginning outside the Tate Modern gallery and ending across the river near to St Paul's Cathedral.

By **Bankside Quay** is **Vinopolis City of Wine**, while another attraction in the area is the overwhelmingly popular **London Eye** ferris wheel which, at 137m (450 ft), is the world's tallest, offering stunning views from its enclosed capsules.

Other attractions near the river include the **Imperial War Museum** in **Lambeth**. Portraying the history of 20th-century conflict, its features include the **Blitz Experience** and a section dedicated to the Holocaust. **Lambeth Palace**, official home of the Archbishop of Canterbury; the **Florence Nightingale Museum**, at St Thomas' Hospital; **Battersea Park**; and the **Design Museum** are all in the vicinity.

A short tube ride to the east is **Greenwich**, with the **National Maritime Museum**, the clipper **Cutty Sark**, the **Royal Naval College** and the **Royal Observatory**, through which runs the Greenwich Meridian, zero degrees longitude. The **Queen's House**, recently restored to its 17th-century glory, is also in Greenwich, as is the **Fan Museum**, with its collection of over 2000 fans.

At the **Woolwich** site of the former **Royal Arsenal**, a new interactive exhibition, **Firepower**, has opened in the **Museum of the Royal Artillery Regiment**.

Further south, London attractions include the **Crystal Palace National Sports Centre** and the **All England Tennis Club and Lawn Tennis Museum** at **Wimbledon**. **Dulwich Village** has England's oldest art gallery, while **Brunel's Engine House** at **Rotherhithe** is site of the world's first underwater tunnel.

Further west are the **Botanical Gardens** (and **palace**) at **Kew**, and **Richmond Park**, where thousands of deer graze freely.

WEST LONDON: London's two major exhibition centres, **Earl's Court** and **Olympia**, stand slightly to the west of the central area. The *Boat Show* and the *Ideal Home Exhibition* are among their principal events. Not far away, **Whiteley's** of **Bayswater** is an Edwardian shopping centre comprising over 80 shops, restaurants and a multi-screen cinema.

Chiswick House in **Chiswick** is a superb Italian-style villa. In **Fulham**, Chelsea Football Club offers tours of its redeveloped **Stamford Bridge** stadium. Further west are **Syon Park** in **Brentford** (which includes a beautiful 16th-century house) and the **London Butterfly House**; nearby is the **Musical Museum**, the **Living Steam Museum** and the **Waterman's Arts Centre**.

South of Brentford and Chiswick is **Hampton Court Palace**, former official royal residence before Buckingham Palace, built by Cardinal Wolsey in the early 16th century and added to by Henry VIII, Charles I, Charles II and William III. Other local houses include the **Orleans House Gallery**, **Ham House** and **Marble Hill House**.

Wembley Arena and Conference Centre is in northwest London, and the new 90,000-seat **Wembley Stadium** is scheduled for completion early in 2006. The late August holiday weekend is marked in the **Notting Hill** area with the famous *Carnival*.

NORTH LONDON: North London contains fashionable **Hampstead**, set on a steep hill. **Hampstead Heath** is one of the largest expanses of parkland in any big city anywhere in the world. Hampstead itself has narrow twisting streets and numerous cafes, restaurants, wine bars and shops. Places to visit include **Burgh House**, **Kenwood House** (a Georgian country house, which contains a fine collection of paintings, set in parkland) and **Keats' House** (the poet's former home, now a museum). To the east, and also on a hill, is **Highgate**, another attractive former village best known for its cemetery which holds the graves of Karl Marx and George Eliot. In **St John's Wood**, visitors can tour **Lords' Cricket Ground**. **Camden Town** is home to a well-known weekend market at Camden Lock – the **Jewish Museum** is also in this area. Further out of town at **Hendon** is the **Royal Air Force Museum** with its collection of historic aircraft.

EAST LONDON: The East End (**Whitechapel**, **Bethnal Green**, **Mile End** and **Bow**) is in many ways the 'real' London, although this part of the capital suffered badly

LONDON

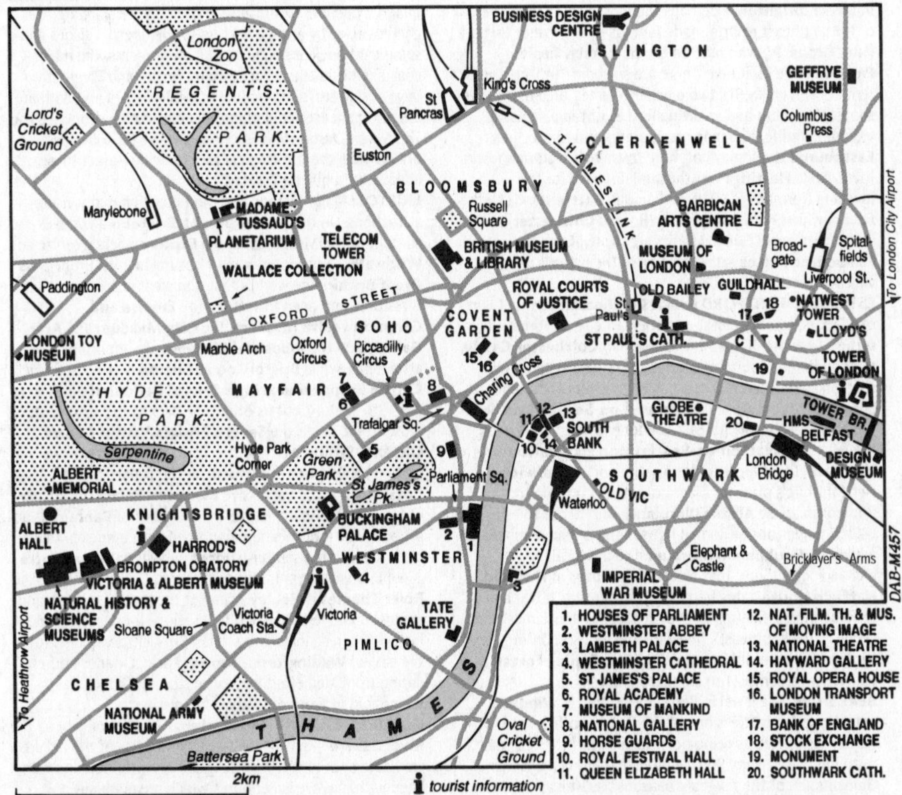

Credit: © Britain On View & Martin Brent

both during the World War II Blitz and at the hands of 1960s urban planners. This is where the Cockneys hail from (it is said that to be a true Cockney, one must be born within earshot of the bells in **Bow Church**).
Cockney traditions linger here: 'Pearly Kings and Queens' make occasional appearances, and there are plenty of 'pie and mash' shops still in evidence.
In the heart of the 'old' East End, the **Whitechapel Art Gallery** is a source of local pride. Another major attraction is the **Bethnal Green Museum of Childhood**, a branch of the Victoria and Albert Museum. Middlesex Street, on the City boundary, is location of **Petticoat Lane Market**. Within walking distance from Petticoat Lane is the lively and trendy **Spitalfields Market** which has an excellent organic food and arts and crafts market on Sundays. Today the City is encroaching on the traditional East End areas. But its success has indirectly led to London's biggest regeneration project – transformation of **Docklands** from 22 sq km (8.5 sq miles) of dereliction to an important business area and leisure attraction.
Renovated **St Katharine's Dock**, close to Tower Bridge, is now an attractive marina surrounded by wine bars and restaurants, and at **Wapping** there are many old warehouses, the majority of which have been converted into homes and leisure amenities – a process underway throughout East London. The **Prospect of Whitby** pub on the Wapping foreshore is a tourist attraction in itself. Nearby **Tobacco Dock** is a large leisure complex with shops, restaurants and entertainment. Moored at the quayside are two replica 18th-century pirate ships.The whole area has undergone intensive redevelopment along its 88km (55 miles) of waterfront, and the **Docklands Light Railway** opened in 1987, providing easy access from the City. The **Canary Wharf** development boasts a 245m- (800ft-) high office tower, Britain's tallest building. **London City Airport** provides quick connections to short-haul destinations. Walks along the river and in the former docks areas are rewarding, offering unexpected glimpses of 18th- and 19th-century London.
The new **Docklands Museum**, which highlights the history of London's river and port industry and communities, occupies a listed warehouse on **West India Quay**.
Elsewhere in East London, **Lea Valley Park** stretches from Hertfordshire to **Bromley-by-Bow** in the East End and offers extensive recreational facilities. Attractions include the 16th-century **Queen Elizabeth's Hunting Lodge** in **Chingford** and the 11th-century **Waltham Abbey**.
Hackney's Victoria Park is another green space in the heart of urban sprawl.
Boat trips are available to the **Thames Flood Barrier**, situated down-river from Greenwich.

SOUTHEAST AND EAST ANGLIA

South East England Tourist Board (tel: (023) 8062 5400; e-mail: enquiries@tourismse.com; website: www.southeastengland.uk.com). East of England Tourist Board (tel: (0870) 225 4800; fax: (0870) 225 4890; e-mail: information@eetb.org.uk; website: www.visiteastofengland.com). Southern Tourist Board (tel: (023) 8062 5400; fax: (023) 8062 0010; e-mail: enquiries@tourismse.com; website: www.southerntb.co.uk).
Covering the 'Home Counties' of Bedfordshire, Berkshire, Buckinghamshire, Hertfordshire, Kent, Surrey, East Sussex, and West Sussex, plus the East Anglian counties of Cambridgeshire, Essex, Norfolk and Suffolk. The Southeast is England's most populous, and prosperous, region. Despite the degree of development, though, there is huge variety of rural and heritage attractions, together with many major coastal resorts. Interests range from the traditional seaside attractions of Brighton, Great Yarmouth and Southend-on-Sea to historic cities like Cambridge, Colchester, Norwich and St Albans. The rural charms of **'Constable Country'**, straddling the Suffolk/Essex border, draw many visitors, as do the more urban attractions of Windsor and Dover, with their mighty castles.
KENT: Known as the **'Garden of England'** for its copious production of fruit, hops and garden produce, Kent is the southeasternmost county in England. **Canterbury** is the major visitor magnet, retaining much of its Medieval charm. **Canterbury Cathedral**, where Thomas à Becket was slain in 1170, is also headquarters of the Anglican Church. Nearby, **St Martin's Church** is one of the oldest churches in use in the country, having held services since AD 500. At Dover, the main cross-channel port, massive Norman **Dover Castle** rises above the famous **White Cliffs**, while the **White Cliffs Experience** portrays a multimedia interpretation of the town's importance over the centuries. **Rochester** is a charming old town with strong Dickensian connections, including **Restoration House**, thought to be the prototype for Miss Haversham's home in 'Great Expectations'.
Tunbridge Wells, in the west of the county, is an elegant 18th-century spa town. Historic highlights in the county include **Hever Castle**, childhood home of Anne Boleyn, and **Leeds Castle**, said to be the world's most beautiful.
SURREY AND EAST/WEST SUSSEX: London now swallows up much of Surrey, but towns like **Guildford** retain a historic charm. Major attractions include **Thorpe Park** and **Chessington World of Adventure**, both theme parks.
In Sussex, **Brighton** is perhaps the most popular and lively of the southeast resorts, made famous by the Prince Regent (later George IV) who ordered the remarkably opulent **Pavilion** to be built here. There are splendid 19th-century terraces and crescents, two piers, the 'Lanes' area of antique shops, a museum and an art gallery. Brighton also has a vibrant nightlife with many restaurants, pubs and clubs.
Eastbourne is a somewhat more restrained Victorian resort town, while **Hastings** was the landing place for the invading Normans in 1066, and nearby **Battle** stands by the field in which Harold I was slain. Roman **Chichester**, to the west of Sussex, is famous for its arts festival and the nearby **Fishbourne Palace** – the remains of the biggest Roman villa yet discovered in Britain.
ESSEX AND HERTFORDSHIRE: Colchester, county town of Essex, is Britain's oldest documented city, continuously settled since pre-Roman times. Norman **Colchester Castle**, built on Roman foundations, has the largest keep of any such building. The Essex coast stretches from the fringes of London in the south, and **Southend-on-Sea** has long been the traditional resort for East Londoners. Further north are the resorts of **Clacton-on-Sea**, **Frinton** and **Walton-on-the-Naze**, together with the historic port of **Harwich**. Hertfordshire's principal places of interest include the Roman city of **St Albans** (**Verulamiam**). Part of the city walls, foundations of Roman houses and a temple remain, while the **Verulamiam Museum** displays local archaeological finds. To the east of St Albans in **Hatfield**, **Hatfield House** dates from the 16th century. It belonged to Robert Cecil, first minister to Elizabeth I and James I, and is one of the southeast's finest historic houses. On the fringes of northeast London is the huge **Epping Forest**, which covers some 24 sq km (9.3 sq miles).
BERKSHIRE: The jewel in Berkshire's crown is **Windsor**, whose massive castle is one of the Queen's official residences as well as being open to visitors. It has been a royal home for nearly 900 years since the time of William I. Guided tours of the town are available, as well as bus tours and river cruises. Nearby is the 19 sq km (7.3 sq miles) **Windsor Great Park**. Some 3km (2 miles) outside the town is **Legoland**, a major family attraction. Elsewhere in Berkshire, **Slough** is the major commercial centre, while **Maidenhead** and **Marlow** are pleasant riverside towns on the banks of the Thames.
BEDFORDSHIRE AND BUCKINGHAMSHIRE: The gently rolling **Chiltern Hills** of Buckinghamshire are within easy reach of London, offering pleasant countryside and quiet villages. At **Amersham**, the **Chiltern Open Air Museum** reflects five centuries of local life. Near **Aylesbury**, **Waddesdon Manor** is an impressive Victorian stately home. The 'new town' of **Milton Keynes** is the county's largest town, with a broad range of shopping and leisure pursuits. Bedfordshire's biggest visitor attraction is **Woburn Abbey**, home of the Dukes of Bedford since the mid-1550s, and surrounded by Britain's biggest **Safari Park**. Close to **Dunstable**, animals are also the focus at **Whipsnade Zoo**.
CAMBRIDGESHIRE: (See also the *Top Seven Destinations* section.) Outside the city of Cambridge, this county largely consists of low-lying agricultural countryside, particularly in the artificially drained **Fenlands** of the north. Highlights include **Ely**, with its huge Cathedral (known as the 'Ship of the Fens'). **Cromwell's House**, home of the former Lord Protector, is open to the public and houses the **Tourist Information Centre**. **Huntingdon** also has strong Cromwellian connections. **Peterborough**, in the northwest of the county, also boasts a fine **Cathedral**, and the **Nene Valley Railway**. Close to the Norfolk border is **Wisbech**, inland port and typical fenland town.
NORFOLK AND SUFFOLK: Norwich, 'capital' of East Anglia and county town of Norfolk, is a delightful city, whose central streets still follow the Medieval pattern. **Norwich Cathedral** is one of England's prettiest, while the **Castle** contains an art gallery, museum and local history exhibitions. Norwich's daily **open-air market** is one of the biggest in the country. East of the city, the **Norfolk Broads** is an extensive network of waterways popular for boating holidays. On the coast beyond the Broads is the major resort of **Great Yarmouth**. In the north and west are resorts such as **Cromer** and **Hunstanton**, plus the former Hanseatic port, **King's Lynn**.
Suffolk, to the south, is a county of quiet, typically 'English' countryside. The main town is **Ipswich**, and the coast is dotted with small resorts like **Aldeburgh** (with its annual arts festival) and **Southwold**.

SOUTH AND SOUTHWEST

Covering Bath, Bristol, and the counties of Cornwall, Devon, Dorset, Gloucestershire, Hampshire, Isle of Wight, Oxfordshire, Somerset and Wiltshire, plus the Isles of Scilly.
Southern Tourist Board (see *Southeast and East Anglia*).
South Western Tourist Board (tel: (01392) 360 050; fax: (01392) 445 112; e-mail: post@swtourism.co.uk; website: www.swtourism.co.uk).
Central Southern England and the Southwest contain many of England's top seaside resort areas, particularly in Devon and Cornwall, the Isle of Wight and along the Dorset coast. Inland, Wiltshire, Oxfordshire and Gloucestershire are characterised by attractive countryside, pretty villages and significant ancient and historical monuments. The major coastal cities, such as Portsmouth, Bristol and Plymouth, have strong seafaring traditions, while Oxford and Bath are among the most popular English cities with visitors (see the *Top Seven Destinations* section). Off the far southwest tip of Cornwall, the sub-tropical Isles of Scilly attract those looking for a quieter holiday.
BRISTOL: Major historic port, and boasting many visitor attractions. On the harbourside, **At-Bristol** is a complex containing an IMAX cinema, the **Explore** science centre and **Wildwalk**, an interpretation of natural history. Brunel's **SS Great Britain**, the world's first iron steam passenger liner, is restored and open to visitors. The **Empire and Commonwealth Museum**, the **City Museum** and **Art Gallery** and the **Industrial Museum** are important attractions, while **Bristol Zoo** at **Clifton** is close to Brunel's **Clifton Suspension Bridge**. **Bristol Cathedral** dates from the 15th century, but its origins lie back in the 12th century. Close to the city is the **Severn Bridges Visitor Centre**.
OXFORDSHIRE: (See also the *Top Seven Destinations* section.) Northwest of **Oxford**, on the fringes of the **Cotswolds**, is the impressive **Blenheim Palace**, birthplace of Sir Winston Churchill. The market town of **Banbury** is an attractive historic location, honoured with a nursery rhyme of its own. To the south is **Didcot**, whose **Railway Centre** is popular with steam train enthusiasts. On the banks of the **River Thames** is **Henley**, scene of the annual regatta, and possessing no less than 300 buildings of architectural and historic interest, including a fine 18th-century bridge. To the east of **Wallingford** is **Stonor Park**, a manor house dating from Medieval times, once a secret Catholic stronghold in times of religious repression.
GLOUCESTERSHIRE: Gloucester is a cathedral city on the **River Severn**. Many of the streets and parts of the old city wall date back to the Middle Ages. The revitalised docks are lined with massive warehouses which are gradually

becoming visitor attractions, among them the *National Waterways Museum*, the **Marina and Tall Ships**, plus the **Opie Collection of Packaging**.
Cheltenham, an elegant Regency spa town, is famous for its **National Hunt Racecourse** and annual music and literature festival. **Malmesbury** contains a fine example of Norman building in its abbey, the ruins of a 12th-century castle, a market square and several attractive 17th- and 18th-century houses. **Cirencester** has extensive Roman remains and is a good centre for exploring the Cotswolds. To the east of the **Wye Valley** is the **Forest of Dean**, 130 sq km (50 sq miles) of ancient hunting forest.
In the hilly countryside east of Gloucester is the village of **Slad**, immortalised by Laurie Lee in his book *Cider with Rosie*.
WILTSHIRE: Even in prehistoric times, the inland county of Wiltshire proved attractive to early settlers, and evidence of this – at places like **Avebury**, **Old Sarum** and **Stonehenge** – makes it ideal for exploring prehistoric remains. In addition, some of England's greatest stately homes are in Wiltshire, including **Corsham**, **Lacock Abbey**, **Longleat**, **Stourhead** and **Wilton**. Longleat is a very grand Elizabethan mansion, famous for its lions, and Stourhead, built in 1722, has particularly fine lakeside gardens.
Salisbury is dominated by its 123m (404ft) cathedral spire, England's tallest. The grounds of **Salisbury Cathedral** contain many notable houses open to the public.
Mompesson House is a perfectly preserved 18th-century home and **Malmesbury House** was once sanctuary for King Charles II, fleeing after the Battle of Worcester in the 17th century. The city has a harmonious blend of gabled houses and historic inns, and offers a good choice of hotels, restaurants and shopping. Open-top bus or horse-drawn omnibus tours are available.
The remains of Old Sarum, ancient city and Norman fortress, are visible 3km (2 miles) away on **Salisbury Plain** but the most important site is the enormous prehistoric stone circle of **Stonehenge**. The site was possibly in use as long ago as 2500 BC. At the western end of Salisbury Plain, **Warminster** is a favourite haunt of UFO spotters.
The former railway works at county town **Swindon** house a new museum, **Steam**, dedicated to Brunel's Great Western Railway.
HAMPSHIRE: This region is one of great natural beauty but also enjoys the benefits of up-to-the-minute shopping, leisure facilities and nightlife. The county is justly famous for the **New Forest**, 376 sq km (145 sq miles) of open heathland, where ponies, deer and cattle roam freely. The New Forest was decreed a Royal Hunting Preserve in 1079 and is a haven for riders and walkers. **Beaulieu**, with its stately home and **Motor Museum**, and **Bucklers Hard** are major attractions.
Southampton is one of the most rapidly expanding cities on the south coast with new marinas, leisure facilities and shopping malls, including the **Bargate**, **Ocean Village** and **Waterfront**.
There is a wealth of maritime history in the neighbouring naval city of **Portsmouth – HMS Victory**, **HMS Warrior**, the **Mary Rose** and the **Royal Naval Museum**. The **D-Day Museum** at **Southsea** tells the story of the 1944 allied Normandy landings.
Former English capital **Winchester**, in central Hampshire, has a magnificent 11th-century **Cathedral. Romsey** is an attractive market town associated with **Broadlands**, 18th-century former home of Lord Mountbatten.
Lymington is an attractive small town lying on the edge of the New Forest, with its own pretty harbour. **Hamble** to the east is a mecca for yachtsmen, the **Hamble River** providing good sheltered moorings, making it an ideal place to start a cruise around its waters or over to the Isle of Wight.
The **Hampshire Borders**, in the north of the county, have some lovely countryside. There are a number of historic houses in the region and lots of military museums.
ISLE OF WIGHT: Only 6km (4 miles) off the mainland, the Isle of Wight has beautiful countryside, unspoilt coastline and many sandy beaches. It has one of the best sunshine records in the country. Craft centres, country parks, historic buildings, sporting and leisure facilities abound. Often described as 'England in Miniature', the island offers rich contrast in scenery and character in its small area.
Cowes, world famous for yachting, also plays host to many national and international events, from sailing to power boating. There are five vineyards on the Isle of Wight, which also stage the unusual annual **Garlic Festival** every summer. **Osborne House**, at **East Cowes**, was Queen Victoria's favourite residence – she died here in 1901. Popular resorts on the southeast coast include **Shanklin**, **Ventnor** and **Sandown**. Parliamentarian forces imprisoned King Charles I at **Carisbrooke Castle**, in the centre of the island near **Newport**, prior to his execution in 1649. To the west, the dramatic **Needles**, chalk outcrops, jut from the sea, while visitors flock to **Alum Bay** to see the remarkable multicoloured sand of its cliffs.
ISLES OF SCILLY: Scilly lies 50km (30 miles) off Land's End – only five (out of a total of around 100) islands are inhabited. They are a popular holiday destination, as the climate is warmer and more temperate than on the mainland. The tourism industry received a boost when former Prime Minister Harold Wilson bought a holiday home there.
Horticulture is now the islands' second-largest industry. Boat trips to visit smaller islands are popular, particularly from **Hugh Town** on **St Mary's**, largest of the islands, where **Star Castle** dominates the skyline. **Tresco**, especially, has the magnificent sub-tropical **Abbey Gardens** and the **Abbey**, which draw many visitors. Air and sea services connect Scilly with the mainland. **Bryher** has two small fortresses and the wild **Hell Bay**.
DORSET: The resort of **Bournemouth** has fine sandy beaches, excellent shopping, top-class entertainment and comfortable hotels and flats, making the town a popular holiday venue.
Nearby, **Poole** has the world's second-largest natural harbour, in which is the island nature reserve of **Brownsea**. Boat trips make the short crossing from **Poole Quay**. The **Tower Park** leisure complex offers varied entertainment and activities. The quayside retains its 18th-century atmosphere – **Poole Pottery** and the **Waterfront Museum** stand on it.
Immediately west of Poole is the **Isle of Purbeck**. The coastline is scenic, also offering the resort of **Swanage**. A little further west is **Weymouth**, with its beach, panoramic bay and historic harbour. There are entertainments and activities for all the family, plus many top attractions and events including the **Brewer's Quay** leisure and shopping development.
Portland, joined to Weymouth by **Chesil Beach** causeway, is a fascinating peninsula. Famous for its stone, it also has several castles, a lighthouse and small, sheltered coves.
Lying inland, northeast of Weymouth, is **Shaftesbury**, Dorset's most ancient hilltop town, characterised by steep cobbled streets. Slightly to the south is the handsome 18th-century **Blandford Forum**. Distinguished by one of the county's most unusual churches is **Wimborne Minster**, a small market town to the southeast.
SOMERSET: Another attractive rural county, Somerset has three fine coastal resorts, **Burnham-on-Sea**, **Minehead** and **Weston-super-Mare**. Much of west Somerset lies within **Exmoor National Park**. Attractions in this region include the tiny **Culbone Church**, the clapper bridge at **Tarr Steps**, the idyllic villages of **Selworthy** and **Dunster**, and **Dunkery Beacon**, the highest point on Exmoor. The town of **Taunton** lies to the west of the county, near the southern end of the wooded **Quantock Hills**. The county's northern boundary is emphasised by the limestone **Mendip Hills**. Along the southern edge are the cave attractions of the **Cheddar Gorge**, **Wookey Hole** and the great cathedral at **Wells**. The southeastern corner of the county around **Yeovil** has many historic houses open to the public. At **Yeovilton**, a short distance north, is the **Fleet Air Arm Museum**. Somerset has mystical connections, notably around the town of **Glastonbury**, where nearby **Glastonbury Tor** has long been a site of pilgrimage.
DEVON: The area, known as the **English Riviera**, comprises **Brixham**, **Paignton** and **Torquay**. The major city is **Plymouth**, seaport for over 500 years and where Sir Francis Drake famously finished his game of bowls in 1588 before defeating the Spanish Armada. In 1620, the Pilgrim Fathers set out for the New World from Plymouth on the **Mayflower**, and parts of the town dating from this period still survive.
Inland on the Cornish border is the stark wilderness of the **Dartmoor National Park**, where wild ponies roam freely across a beautiful landscape dotted with prehistoric remains. The park is popular with walkers. The county town, **Exeter**, has a long history and there are remains of Roman walls, underground passages, a beautiful cathedral and the oldest Guildhall in the Kingdom.
To the north of the county, resorts such as **Ilfracombe** and **Lynton** line the coast, and in the northeast is another National Park, **Exmoor**, which straddles the Devon/Somerset border.
CORNWALL: England's southwesternmost county, Cornwall is a Celtic land of rugged coastline, disused tin mines, attractive fishing villages and small seaside resorts. In the city of **Truro**, the county town, the **Cathedral** and the **Royal Cornwall Museum and Gallery** are the main sights. The nearby south coastline bears the name of the **Cornish Riviera**, and is lined with resorts including **Mevagissey**, **Looe**, **Polperro** and **Falmouth**, where **Pendennis Castle** houses the **National Maritime Museum**'s Cornwall branch.
Close to **St Austell** is one of Britain's most ambitious new tourist developments, the **Eden Project**, whose huge geodesic domes house flora from all over the world.
Cornwall is famous for its gardens, which benefit from the benign effects of the Gulf Stream; highlights among these include the **Lost Gardens of Heligan** and numerous National Trust properties like **Cotehele**, **Lanhydrock** and **Trelissick**.
Newquay, on the Atlantic coast north of Truro, is a mecca for surfers, while, further east, **Bude** offers sweeping sandy beaches. Near here is **Tintagel**, steeped in Arthurian legend, with a castle perched on top of large cliffs, reached only by towering steps.

Credit: © Britain On View & Martin Brent

Outside **Penzance**, in the far west, is **St Michael's Mount**, an island castle which mirrors that of France's **Mont St Michel**. **St Ives**, on the southwestern tip, is also popular, both with families and artists. Both find much to admire in St Ives's large sandy beaches, cobbled streets and plenitude of craft shops and art galleries, including the impressive **Tate Gallery**. **Land's End**, mainland Britain's most westerly point, features a **Heritage Centre** and various other family attractions.

THE MIDLANDS

Heart of England Tourist Board (tel: (01905) 761 100; fax: (01905) 763 450; e-mail: info@visitheartofengland.com; website: www.visitheartofengland.com).
The English Midlands cover a great swathe of the country south of the Humber Estuary and from the Welsh border in the west to the fringes of the Southeast. Counties included in this section are Derbyshire, Herefordshire, Leicestershire, Lincolnshire, Northamptonshire, Nottinghamshire, Rutland, Shropshire, Staffordshire, Warwickshire and the West Midlands.
From the wild moors of the Derbyshire Peak District National Park and major cities like Birmingham to the quiet villages of rural Northamptonshire and Herefordshire, the Midlands is a region of great diversity. The Industrial Revolution began in Shropshire; indeed, industrial heritage is a major feature here: the **Staffordshire Potteries** draw enormous numbers of visitors, while the motor industry has strong links with Warwickshire.
Shakespeare lived in Stratford-upon-Avon (see the *Top Seven Destinations* section), while Nottingham is forever tied to the legend of Robin Hood. Great cathedrals, such as those of Coventry, Lichfield, Lincoln and Worcester, are plentiful. The region's only stretch of coastline, that of Lincolnshire, has an array of seaside resorts, including Cleethorpes, Mablethorpe and Skegness. Canals criss-cross much of the Midlands, and these former industrial supply routes are nowadays an important tourism resource, offering a relaxed way to enjoy the countryside from hired cruisers and narrowboats.
WARWICKSHIRE AND THE WEST MIDLANDS: The industrial heart of Britain is surrounded by lovely countryside. **Birmingham**, Britain's second-largest city, is a centre of both industry and culture. It has a magnificent library, and the **Central Museum & Art Gallery** is one of the finest in the country. Also in the city are the **National Sea Life Centre**, and the **Jewellery Quarter**, whose **Museum** tells the story of this interesting district.
Birmingham has more canals than Venice, most of which are still navigable. **Aston Hall**, to the east of the city centre, is a splendid stately home, while in the southern suburbs at **Bournville**, **Cadbury World** is a popular family attraction in this famous chocolate manufacturing centre.
Birmingham is home to the **National Exhibition Centre**, site of many major exhibitions and trade fairs. Northwest of Birmingham is the **Black Country**, an area extending into southern Staffordshire. Former industrial powerhouse and coal mining centre, the main towns of interest here include **Dudley**, which has a castle and a zoo in the same complex. The town also boasts the open-air **Black Country Living Museum**, from which it is possible to take canal boat trips through the tunnel to the spectacular **Singing Cavern**.
At **Wolverhampton**, **Moseley Old Hall** was once the hiding place of the future King Charles II following his escape from the Battle of Worcester in 1651. The **Walsall Arboretum**, large decorative gardens, stages the

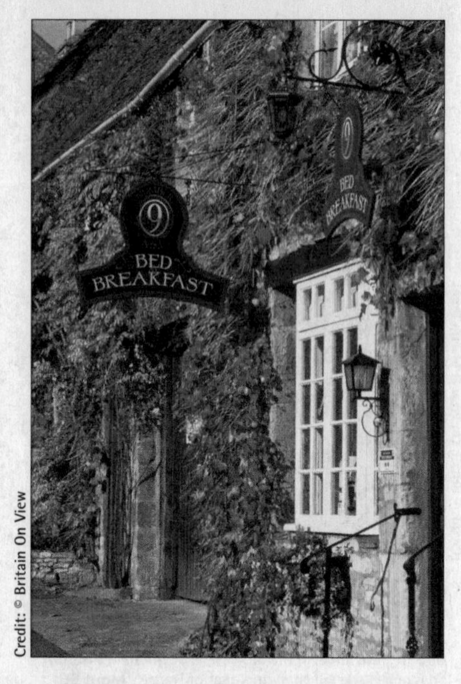

Credit: © Britain On View

immensely popular *Walsall Illuminations* each September and October.
Coventry, city of Lady Godiva and historic centre of the British motor industry, is famous for its modern cathedral, designed by Sir Basil Spence, after destruction of the original during World War II. Warwick contains many historic houses and **Warwick Castle** is one of the region's most popular attractions. In the city's historic **Market Hall**, the **Warwickshire Museum** contains displays of local archaeology and other historic items, while a fine Jacobean mansion houses **St John's Museum**. The **Collegiate Church of St Mary**, the **Doll Museum** and the **Lord Leycester Hospital** are also noteworthy. In the countryside are various stately homes, including 17th-century **Ragley Hall**, near **Alcester**. **Leamington Spa** is an attractive 18th-century spa resort.
HEREFORDSHIRE AND WORCESTERSHIRE: The stretch of country between Worcester and the Welsh border is a rich farming area, with orchards, fields and meadows full of cider apples, hops and white-faced red cattle. Characteristic black and white half-timbered buildings decorate the villages and market towns such as **Ledbury**. The **Wye Valley**, the **Malvern Hills** and the **Teme Valley** all add to the area's beauty.
The Wye Valley is an exceedingly beautiful area, with the river flowing first through gentle countryside but later through spectacular gorges near **Symonds Yat**. The town of **Ross-on-Wye** is a good base for exploring this area. Northwest of Ross is **Hereford**, also on the **River Wye**, an attractive cathedral city, which has a **City Museum and Art Gallery** as well as a **Cider Museum**. Nell Gwynne, actress and mistress of Charles II, was reputedly born here. The medieval **Mappa Mundi** is on view at **Hereford Cathedral**, which also boasts a rare **Chained Library**.
To the west of **Hereford** is **Golden Valley**, a remote region containing many attractive villages. At its northern end on the Welsh border is **Hay-on-Wye**, famous for having one of the world's largest second-hand bookshops.
Worcester, on the banks of the **River Severn**, has a **Cathedral**, the museum and factory of the **Royal Worcester Porcelain Company**, a magnificent **Guildhall** with a Queen Anne facade and a number of streets with overhanging half-timbered houses from the Tudor period. The **Commandery**, once battle headquarters of Charles II, now houses a Civil War audio-visual display.
South of Worcester are the steep **Malvern Hills**, which offer views across the rich agricultural landscape. **Great Malvern** began life as a spa resort in the 18th century. Tastings of the local spring water are available at **St Anne's Well**.
Some 32km (20 miles) north of Worcester is the **Wyre Forest**, ideal for walking and riding. Principal towns in this region are **Bewdley**, **Kidderminster** and **Stourport**, home to the southern terminus of the Severn Valley Railway, England's longest standard-gauge steam railway.
Worcestershire's biggest single visitor attraction is the **West Midlands Safari Park** at Bewdley.
SHROPSHIRE: This is a county of varied landscapes, including moorland, forests, gentle hills and open pasture. Despite this, Shropshire was also birthplace of the Industrial Revolution, evidence of which is visible in the area of **Ironbridge Gorge**. The **Ironbridge Gorge Museum** occupies a number of sites but the area's major landmark is the world's first **Iron Bridge** itself, built in 1779. Ruined **Buildwas Abbey** stands nearby.
On the eastern boundary of this district is the magnificent Restoration house and parkland known as **Weston Park**. Nearby is **Boscobel** where the future Charles II hid in the now famous Royal Oak after the Battle of Worcester.
To the west is the area of **The Wrekin**, a conical-shaped hill that figures in many local tales and legends. The county town, **Shrewsbury**, is one of the finest Tudor towns in England, celebrated for the flower market held every summer. **Shrewsbury Quest** portrays Medieval monastic life at the time of Ellis Peters' 'Brother Cadfael', a fictional 12th-century resident of the town.
South and southwest of Shrewsbury are the **Shropshire Hills**, designated as an area of outstanding natural beauty. **Ludlow** (dominated by the ruins of its castle), **Church Stretton**, **Bishop's Castle**, **Much Wenlock** (13th-century Wenlock Priory is the major attraction here) and **Bridgnorth** (terminus of the steam **Severn Valley Railway**) are all attractive towns.
A large plain with many quiet roads, making it ideally suited to cycling or walking, dominates the north of the county. **Market Drayton**, **Oswestry**, **Wem** (famous for its beer) and **Whitchurch** are the major market towns in this region. **Hawkstone Park**, with its collection of follies, and a cave where Aleister Crowley reputedly held satanic rituals, is an unusual diversion, while the **Roman City** at **Wroxeter** is an important archaeological site.
STAFFORDSHIRE: Both agricultural and industrial, Staffordshire lies partly within the **Peak District National Park** and contains some of the most spectacular countryside, such as **Thor's Cave** and the limestone gorge at **Dovedale** on the Derbyshire border.
Stoke-on-Trent, known worldwide for its pottery industry, has major visitor attractions including the **Wedgwood Story** and the former pottery works now housing the **Gladstone Museum**. Among other famous brands associated with the city, which has some 40 factory shop outlets offering bargain china, are Royal Doulton and Spode.
East of the Potteries are scenic **Churnet Valley** and **Vale of Trent**, the latter containing **Cannock Chase**, an attractive area of heath and woodland. One of the most famous sights in the county is the unusual **Lichfield Cathedral**, which has three spires. Samuel Johnson's birthplace is open to the public. Nearby **Tamworth** has a fine castle, along with Britain's first indoor ski slope using real snow, the **Snowdome**, and **Drayton Manor** theme park.
Staffordshire's numerous stately homes include **Shugborough**, home of photographer Lord Lichfield. To the northeast is **Alton Towers**, the UK's biggest theme park; while in the east is the traditional centre of the English brewing industry, **Burton-upon-Trent**, where the **Bass Museum** tells the story of 'real ale' in the town.
NORTHAMPTONSHIRE: Although major road and rail links traverse Northamptonshire, much of the county remains unspoilt. One of the most attractive regions is the **Rockingham Forest** area in the east of the county, which contains several historic houses and mighty **Rockingham Castle**. There is a Red Kite observatory at the **RSPB Centre**, **Fineshade**, near **Corby**.
Close to **Oundle**, a market town famed for its architecture and major public school, only a mound remains of **Fotheringhay Castle**, where Mary Queen of Scots met her end in 1587. Most other Northamptonshire historic houses are in much better condition, many of them still occupied. Of these, **Althorp** (which has a museum on the grounds commemorating the late Diana, Princess of Wales) and **Sulgrave Manor**, ancestral home of George Washington, are important. Other places of interest include the **Central Museum** in **Northampton** with its fine shoe collection, the **Waterways Museum** at **Stoke Bruerne** and the **Santa Pod** drag racing circuit outside **Wellingborough**.
LEICESTERSHIRE AND RUTLAND: The county of Leicestershire has many castles, manor houses and market towns. **Leicester** itself has Roman remains and a great deal of Medieval architecture, and is nowadays important as a shopping centre. A major visitor attraction is the **National Space Centre**. Other towns of interest in the county include **Market Harborough** (close to which lie **Foxton Locks**, the longest chain of canal locks in England), **Lutterworth** (home of John Wycliffe) and **Melton Mowbray**, famous for Stilton cheese and pork pies. Near Leicester is **Market Bosworth**, the site of one of English history's most famous battles, when Henry Tudor defeated Richard III, the last Lancastrian, in 1485. **Belvoir Castle** near **Melton Mowbray**, is a popular historic attraction.
On the Warwickshire border, **Twycross Zoo** is an important attraction, while at **Coalville**, to the northwest of Leicester, the **Snibston Discovery Centre** is an interactive introduction to the world of technology. **Conkers**, a children's attraction themed on the natural world, is at **Ashby-de-la-Zouch**. **Rutland** has the distinction of being England's smallest county. In the county town of **Oakham**, **Oakham Castle** has a remarkable collection of decorative horseshoes, each presented as a symbolic toll to the borough by monarchs passing through over the centuries.
LINCOLNSHIRE: Lincolnshire, the largest county in the East Midlands and the only one with a coastline, has several seaside resorts, notably **Mablethorpe** and **Skegness**, both of which are towns with good sunshine records. **Grimsby** remains an important fishing port, while nearby **Cleethorpes** is another resort - the **Pleasure Island Theme Park** is a major attraction here.
Inland are the gently rolling hills of the **Lincolnshire Wolds**, where Tennyson spent much of his early life. The area around **Spalding** is among the country's richest farmland, and is famous for growing flower bulbs and its annual *Flower Festival*. The town's **Ayscoughfee Hall Museum** tells the story of surrounding **Fenland**.
During the 12th century, **Boston** was one of the three most important ports in England and, from here many of the Pilgrim Fathers planned to set sail for The Netherlands to find religious freedom, but were betrayed and imprisoned in cells still in **Boston Guildhall**. Boston's unusual church tower, known as the **Boston Stump**, is visible for miles around.
The county town of **Lincoln** is a well-preserved Medieval city and the **Cathedral**, set on a limestone hill, has three towers, a fine Norman west front and a particularly beautiful 13th-century **presbytery**. The aptly named **Steep Hill** has some interesting shops and the **Jew's House**, halfway up the incline, is an unusual attraction. River cruises are available in the city centre.
Stamford, situated at the border of four counties, is another Medieval town, with several fine churches and buildings of mellow stone. Nearby is **Burghley House**, built by one of Elizabeth I's most powerful ministers. The **Medieval Old Hall** at **Gainsborough** in north Lincolnshire is an interesting attraction.
Lincolnshire boasts a number of castles, among them **Bolingbroke Castle** at **Spilsby** and **Tattershall Castle** at **Coningsby**.
NOTTINGHAMSHIRE: Nottinghamshire was the legendary home of Robin Hood, and parts of his **Sherwood Forest** – including the celebrated **Major Oak** – still survive in the **Country Park** north of Nottingham. North Nottinghamshire is a former mining area, in which lies **Eastwood**, birthplace of D H Lawrence. Both his childhood home and the village's **Durban House Heritage Centre** commemorate the controversial author. Closer to Nottingham is **Newstead Abbey**, family seat of Lord Byron. The university city of Nottingham boasts the beautiful neo-Classical **Nottingham Castle**, which overlooks the city and contains a much visited **museum** and **art gallery**, and nearby **Wollaton Hall**, an Elizabethan mansion now housing a **natural history museum**. The **Tales of Robin Hood** (a 'dark ride' attraction), the underground **Caves of Nottingham**, and the **Trip to Jerusalem**, reputedly England's oldest inn, are also of interest in the city centre. Nearby is the **Lace Market** area, where attractions include **Condemned!**, an innovative museum dedicated to crime and often grisly punishment, and **Lace Hall**, which describes the industry from which the area takes its name. **Newark-on-Trent** has a 12th-century castle, and is an important antiques trading centre.
DERBYSHIRE: The spa town of **Buxton**, the highest market town in England, makes a good base from which to explore the **Peak District National Park**, 1300 sq km (500 sq mile) of limestone dales and open moors.
Other places of interest in Derbyshire include **Matlock Bath**, with its cable car ride across the **Derwent Gorge** to the **Heights of Abraham** and **Blue John mine**. **Bolsover**, a small market town with a 17th-century castle, is set in rich farmland. **Creswell Crags** has a **Visitor Centre** at the site of prehistoric archaeological finds. **Chesterfield** is another base for exploring the Peak District and is famous for its crooked-spire church.
At **Bakewell**, **Chatsworth House** is the major attraction; there is also the **Wind in the Willows Visitor Centre**, based on the stories of Kenneth Grahame, at nearby **Rowsley**.
The county town of **Derby** is the home of Royal Crown Derby porcelain, and the city also offers a **cathedral**, museums and the **Assembly Rooms**.
For family outings, the **American Adventure Theme Park** at **Ilkeston** is popular, while at **Crich**, the **National Tramways Museum** offers more specialised interest, as does the **Midland Railway Centre** near **Ripley**.

THE NORTH OF ENGLAND

Cumbria Tourist Board (tel: (01539) 444 444; fax: (01539) 444 041; e-mail: info@golakes.co.uk; website: www.golakes.co.uk). North West Tourist Board (tel: (01942) 821 222; fax: (01942) 820 002; website: www.visitnorthwest.com). Northumbria Tourist Board (tel: (0191) 375 3010; e-mail: ttinfo@onenortheast.co.uk; website: www.ntb.org.uk).
Covering Cheshire, County Durham, Cumbria, Greater Manchester, Lancashire, Merseyside, Northumberland, Teesside, Tyne & Wear and Yorkshire.
In the southern and eastern areas of the region lie sprawling industrial heartlands, but these are surrounded by

some of England's most sparsely populated and, arguably, most beautiful, countryside. The Lake District (see the *Top Seven Destinations* section) is the best known of the English National Parks – but there are three more in the region as well: Northumberland, the North York Moors and the Yorkshire Dales.

The coastline is often spectacular, particularly in north Yorkshire and northern Northumberland, while the North Pennines is as wild as English countryside can get. All this contrasts starkly with the great industrial power-houses of south and west Yorkshire, Greater Manchester, Tyne & Wear and east Lancashire. However, even in the cities, the unique character and heritage of the North Country shines through.

This is also a region containing many reminders of England's convoluted racial and religious heritage. The Romans left 1800-year-old **Hadrian's Wall** to posterity, place names are often of ninth-century Viking origin, and the importance of the Saxon Kingdom of Northumbria to the development of Christianity in England is underlined at Durham City and on Holy Island.

CHESHIRE: Chester, the county town, is famous for being full of pretty black and white timber-framed buildings. The city dates from Roman times, as do parts of its otherwise Medieval city walls. Remains of a 7000-seat Roman amphitheatre stand outside the centre, whose star attraction is **The Rows**, large double-deck buildings housing shops. The city has numerous notable timbered houses, including 17th-century **God's Providence House** and **Bishop Lloyd's House**. **Chester Zoo** is a major attraction, as is the unusual **Cathedral** with its detached bell-tower. The **Deva Roman Experience** recreates Roman life in Chester.

In the surrounding county, significant towns include **Northwich**, where the **Salt Museum** tells the story of Cheshire salt mining, and **Nantwich**, where visitors can descend into the **Hack Green 'Secret' Nuclear Bunker**. Nearby, **Stapely Water Gardens** is the world's biggest attraction of its type. The scenery around **Alderley Edge** is noteworthy, while close to **Macclesfield**, **Jodrell Bank Science Centre and Observatory** is a major visitor attraction. **Quarry Bank Mill**, at **Wilmslow**, is an important industrial heritage site, recreating the 18th-century textile industry of the area.

LANCASHIRE: Lancaster is the main centre in this county – echoes of its Georgian heyday as a major port remain along the historic **St George's Quay**, whose palladian-style **Customs House** is now home to the **Lancaster Maritime Museum**. The city centre architecture reflects the wealth of two centuries ago. **Norman Lancaster Castle**, owned by the Queen in her role as Duke of Lancaster, and still containing a working prison despite being open to visitors, stands beside the attractive **Priory Church of St Mary** on **Castle Hill**. The **Ashton Memorial**, a huge folly, dominates the skyline on the east of the city. Immediately west of Lancaster are traditional seaside resort attractions at **Morecambe**, while in the surrounding countryside, the beautiful **Lune Valley** has inspired artists and poets through the ages, including Turner and Wordsworth. Further inland, the **Pendle Witches Trail** takes visitors on the path of grisly 17th-century events.

Blackpool, further down the Lancashire coast, is one of England's biggest seaside resorts, famous for its Eiffel-like **Tower**, its trams and the **Blackpool Pleasure Beach** amusement park.

GREATER MANCHESTER: Although dominated by one of England's biggest cities, the administrative area of Greater Manchester incorporates rural areas on the western slopes of the **Pennine Hills**, along with smaller industrial towns that grew up during the Industrial Revolution.

In Manchester itself, there are numerous major attractions, including the **Granada Studios Tour**, home of the popular television programme, 'Coronation Street'. There is a new branch of the **Imperial War Museum** beside the **Manchester Ship Canal** in the **Trafford** area of the city. **Manchester United Football Club** is famous around the world, and guided tours of its **Old Trafford** stadium are available. The world's oldest passenger railway station now houses the **Museum of Science and Industry**, while the **Manchester Jewish Museum** occupies a restored 18th-century synagogue. Manchester is also renowned for its vibrant and lively nightlife and abundance of shops, including the enormous **Trafford Centre**, which lies just outside Manchester's city centre.

Outside Manchester, **Wigan** boasts one of the north's most popular attractions in **Wigan Pier** – a recreation of Victorian life based around a large canal basin, and incorporating a number of individual museums and other attractions. Elsewhere in the county, the restored **Elizabethan Old Grammar School** at **Rochdale** is an unusual attraction.

YORKSHIRE: Yorkshire is a region of large industrial cities, beautiful countryside, rugged castles, stately homes and ancient churches. Its prime visitor attraction is, of course, **York** (see the *Top Seven Destinations* section).

In West Yorkshire is the huge Leeds/Bradford conurbation. **Bradford** is famous for its large Asian community, and this (and the food) is an attraction in itself, while **The National Museum of Film, Photography and Television** is the city's prime cultural draw with one of the first IMAX cinema screens. At **Leeds**, the **Royal Armouries** exhibition, **Tetley Brewery Visitor Centre**, **West Yorkshire Playhouse** and the **Thackeray Medical Museum** are all good reasons to spend time in the city. **Wakefield's Caphouse Colliery** houses the **National Mining Museum**. Close by are the wild moors of the **Pennines** where the Brontë sisters lived in **Haworth**. At **Halifax**, **Eureka!** is a major children's attraction. The **Yorkshire Dales National Park** is popular year round. Its landscape is that of the books and TV series featuring vet James Herriot, set at **Askrigg**, in **Wensleydale**. Walking is a popular pastime in this area. Historic castles abound in the region, including the great fortresses of **Middleham** and **Richmond**; the latter associated with Richard III. **Bolton Castle** in **Wensleydale** once imprisoned Mary Queen of Scots, while **Pontefract Castle** in **West Yorkshire** was scene of Richard II's murder in 1400.

Great houses are also a highlight, notably **Castle Howard**, near **Malton**, famous as the setting for the TV adaptation of Evelyn Waugh's *Brideshead Revisited*. Others include **Burton Constable Hall**, **Duncombe Park**, **Harewood House**, **Nostell Priory** and **Sledmere House**.

Maritime East Yorkshire has powerful links with Britain's seafaring traditions. **Hull** is a major working port, recently transformed by waterfront developments, while majestic **Humber Bridge** is an attraction in its own right. Beyond Hull is the gentle lowland area of **Holderness**, which ends in the bird sanctuary at **Spurn Point**. To the north lies the ancient market town of **Beverley**, with Georgian houses in the shadow of the **Minster**. Close by is a racecourse and the **Museum of Army Transport**.

The **North York Moors National Park** has miles of open moorland with picturesque villages nestling in hollows. The **North Yorkshire Moors Railway**, starting at **Pickering**, is just one of several steam railways in Yorkshire – others include the **Embsay Steam Railway** at **Skipton** and the **Keighley** and **Worth Valley Railway**.

On the coast, family resorts include **Bridlington** and **Scarborough**, which have added a number of attractions, such as Bridlington's popular **Leisure World Complex**. There are also many smaller resorts, each with their own special character, like **Whitby** with its busy harbour and ruined clifftop **Abbey**, which inspired Bram Stoker's *Dracula*. **Robin Hood's Bay**, south of Whitby, is a famous beauty spot.

Between the coast and the **Vale of York** lie **The Wolds**, a range of rolling hills with villages and quiet lanes, ideal for walking or cycling. On their fringe is **Malton**, one of many interesting towns in the region – others of note include **Harrogate**, **Ilkley**, **Selby**, **Skipton** and **Thirsk**.

MERSEYSIDE: In the 1960s, The Beatles put **Liverpool** firmly on the tourism map, and their fame still brings visitors from all over the world. Attractions include the **Mersey Ferry**, which plies the river between **Birkenhead** and Liverpool, and the restored **Albert Dock** complex, containing **The Beatles Story**, the **Maritime Museum**, the **Museum of Liverpool Life** and the **Tate Gallery**. Outside the city, the elegant resort of **Southport** lies to the north, **Aintree Race Course** (home of the *Grand National*) is close to **Bootle**, and **Port Sunlight**, an historic model village, is on the **Wirral Peninsula**. The **World of Glass** is **St Helens**' main attraction.

TEESSIDE: An industrial area centred on **Middlesbrough**, whose most famous son was James Cook; the **Captain Cook Birthplace Museum** tells his story. Coastal towns include **Redcar**, **Saltburn** and **Hartlepool**, with its **maritime museum**, restored historic ships and marina. Teesside's industrial history dates from the early-19th century (the world's first passenger train steamed into **Stockton-on-Tees** in 1825). Towns of interest include **Marske**, **Guisborough** and **Upleatham**, with reputedly the smallest church in England.

CUMBRIA: The **Lake District** (see also the *Top Seven Destinations* section) forms the central area of Cumbria. The rest of the county consists of three main sections: the north and east (former Westmorland), which rises with the high North Pennine Hills towards Northumberland and County Durham, the **Irish Sea** coastline and the southern peninsulas. Just south of the Scottish Border is the 2000-year-old cathedral city of **Carlisle**, close to **Hadrian's Wall** and once a Roman camp. Red sandstone **Carlisle Castle** is a major landmark in the city, which has strong associations with the Border Reivers of Medieval times. Their story, along with other local interests, is a central feature of the innovative **Tullie House Museum and Gallery**.

South of Carlisle lies the attractive market town of **Penrith**, to whose east the country rapidly rises across **Alston Moor** to historic **Alston** in the North Pennines, a former lead-mining centre. Set in the heart of an area of outstanding natural beauty, Alston is popular with walkers and cyclists who enjoy spectacular views from nearby **Hartside Crag** (which, in turn, boasts the highest cafe in England). The town also has the country's highest narrow gauge railway, and nearby are the former lead mines of **Nenthead**, now open to visitors.

On the coastline, the once important 18th-century trading port of **Whitehaven** today preserves an echo of former glories in its Georgian buildings. The region also has several coastal resorts such as **Maryport**, **Silloth** and **St Bees**, south of which is the controversial **Sellafield** reprocessing plant, and its **Visitor Centre**. The **Ravenglass and Eskdale** narrow-gauge railway is a pleasant means to reach the Lake District from the coast.

In south Cumbria, the shipbuilding town of **Barrow-in-Furness** has an excellent Docks Museum, while nearby **Ulverston** is famous as the birthplace of comic Stan Laurel, and offers the **Laurel and Hardy Museum**. To the east, **Grange-over-Sands** is a classic seaside resort overlooking **Morecambe Bay** – close to Grange are stately home **Holker Hall** and the preserved **Lakeland** and **Haverthwaite Railway**.

COUNTY DURHAM: Durham, from where Prince Bishops once ruled the North in the King's name, surrounds **Durham City** with its **Castle**, now part of the city's university, and magnificent Norman **Cathedral**. They overlook a horseshoe bend in the **River Wear** from their spectacular position atop a rocky outcrop. The cathedral contains the tombs of two important Northumbrian figures: St Cuthbert and the Venerable Bede. The historic city centre is a UNESCO World Heritage Site.

The surrounding countryside, once a major coalfield, is often very beautiful, with market towns like **Bishop Auckland** and **Barnard Castle** among the highlights. The **Bowes Museum**, **Raby Castle**, and **Beamish**, the **North of England Open Air Museum** attract many thousands of visitors to the county. There are several castles, in varying degrees of preservation. Bishop Auckland is an ancient market town, and there is a 325 hectare (800 acre) deer park close by. **Auckland Castle** is the official residence of the Bishops of Durham. In the nearby village of **Escomb**, seventh-century **Escomb Saxon Church** is one of the oldest such buildings still in use.

Also within the county is part of the wild **North Pennines**, and scenic **Weardale** and **Teesdale**, which contains England's highest waterfall, **High Force**. Close to the Cumbrian border in the North Pennines district is **Killhope Lead Mine**, where visitors can take underground mine tours. **Darlington**, which made its name in the 19th century with the world's first passenger railway to nearby **Stockton**, has a famous railway museum. There are many other attractive towns and villages throughout County Durham, and good walking in the hills and moors.

TYNE & WEAR: Tyne & Wear spans the mouths of the two major rivers in its name. **Newcastle-upon-Tyne** has excellent city centre shopping, museums, theatres, hotels, restaurants and an almost legendary nightlife. There is also **St Nicholas' Cathedral** and the **Norman Castle Keep** from which the city takes its name. Modern attractions include the **Discovery Museum**, the interactive **Centre for Life** and the **Baltic Mill** modern art gallery. Hadrian's Wall began at **Wallsend**, location of the recently opened **Segedunum Roman Fort** attraction, and parts are still visible in the city.

Across the river are **Gateshead** with its massive **Metro Centre** indoor shopping and **South Shields**, home of the late author Catherine Cookson, and the **Arbeia Roman Fort** visitor attraction. **Sunderland** stands at the mouth of the **River Wear** and nearby is **Washington**, famous as the original home of US President George Washington's family. Christian heritage comes to the fore at **Tynemouth Priory** and **Jarrow** (home of the Venerable Bede) where **Bede's World** tells his story.

NORTHUMBERLAND: Northumberland, lying between the Scottish border and Tyne & Wear, is a large, rural county with many attractive villages and market towns. Its most famous landmark is **Hadrian's Wall**. Built in the second century AD, it marks the Roman Empire's northernmost border. Along the wall, numerous Roman forts and settlements are open to public view.

Medieval castles, including massive **Bamburgh**, craggy **Alnwick** and **Dunstanburgh** characterise the countryside, which was long an area of Anglo/Scots conflict. In contrast, ecclesiastical buildings on **Lindisfarne** (Holy Island) and at **Hexham** reflect the important role Northumbria played in establishing English Christianity. Hexham is a good base from which to explore the whole Northumbrian region. Much of the county is a National Park, with rolling moorland stretching from the North Sea to the **Cheviot Hills** on the Scottish border. England's most northerly town, **Berwick-upon-Tweed**, was a regular casualty in border battles, and changed hands between Scotland and England at least 13 times. Its Medieval town walls are among Europe's best preserved. Today, the town is a good base for touring northern Northumberland and the Borders.

Close to the Scottish Border, **Kielder Water** reservoir is Europe's biggest manmade lake and offers a wide range of activity pursuits.

A B C D E F G H I J K L M N O P Q R S T U V W X Y Z

Credit: © Britain On View & Martin Brent

Sport & Activities

Walking: Although England has a high population density, it contains some beautiful and unspoilt countryside, which is ideal for walkers. As a rule, the highest ground is in the north and west of the country, while the east and south tend to be flatter. Just south of the Scottish border is *Northumberland National Park*, featuring moorland and beaches. The *Pennines* ('the backbone of England') stretch for 429km (268 miles) from Kirk Yetholm just over the Scottish border to Edale in Derbyshire, separating Yorkshire in the east from its ancient rival, Lancashire, and from Cumbria in the west. A long-distance footpath, the *Pennine Way*, runs along this range. Relatively demanding, owing to the continual ascents and descents, it is nevertheless very popular. In the northwest, just below Carlisle, lies the spectacular *Lake District*, with England's highest peak, *Scafell Pike* (978m/3207ft), while Yorkshire contains two national parks, the *North York Moors* and the *Yorkshire Dales*. The *Peak District National Park* lies to the south of the Pennines. Gentler hills and farmland are to be found in the 'home counties', the area in the south of England to the west of London. The 'west country' (Cornwall, Devon and Somerset) by contrast, features higher land, moorland, cliffs and a rocky shoreline. The *South West Coast Path* (978km/613 miles) runs around the coast from Minehead in Somerset to South Haven Point near Poole in Dorset. Further information about these areas can be found in the *Resorts & Excursions* section.
Boating: England is threaded with canals and rivers, and there are many lakes and other waterways. Because canals connect urban centres, hiring a canal boat is a good way of visiting towns while still enjoying the countryside. A number of tour operators specialise in hiring out boats; for a list of these, contact the English Tourism Council (see *Contact Addresses* section). Yachts and cabin cruisers can also be hired, and facilities abound in popular sailing areas such as the *Norfolk Broads*.
Cycling: Cyclists are very well catered for in England, and there are many designated cycling routes. Some of these pass through towns and villages and some go through wilder regions. All are signposted and well maintained, and bicycles can be hired all over the country. A list of cycling routes is available from the Tourism Council. East Anglia, its flat terrain sprinkled with picturesque villages, is a good cycling destination.
Spectator sports: English sporting events are often characterised by their traditional atmosphere and valued as much for the social opportunities which accompany them as for the sporting action. Many of the most famous events are patronised by the Royal family, and a certain style of dress is *de rigeur*. The main **horse races** attract a huge following and include *Aintree*, *Ascot* (famous for the extravagant hats worn by women on Ladies' Day) and the *Grand National* (the nation's premier event, prompting bets worth millions of pounds). Many English people are passionate about racing, and there are race courses all over the country. The world-famous **tennis** tournament, *Wimbledon*, takes place in London SW19 in late June and early July. Tickets must be purchased well in advance if good seats are required, while a ballot is held for tickets for the days of the finals. **Rowing** is another traditional sport which provides fans of English culture with a chance to observe some age-old rituals. The year's most prestigious event is the *Henley Regatta*, held at Henley-on-Thames in late June. Boaters and blazers are worn by the men, while women often wear dresses and hats. Rowing eights from all over the world come to compete. The *Oxford vs Cambridge Boat Race* takes place in February. Eights from England's two oldest universities race along the Thames in London from Putney to Mortlake. Nowadays, there are races for women as well as for men. **Cricket**, incomprehensible though it may seem to those unfamiliar with the rules, is popular in England. The most famous ground is Lords in north London. **Football** is enthusiastically followed by all classes of society and, increasingly, by both men and women. Teams such as *Liverpool* and *Manchester United* are known for their skill all over the world. Rugby, which is divided between union and league (amateur and professional), is also popular.
Other: Other sports available include **surfing**, particularly popular in Cornwall; **fishing** (a permit is needed and is available from post offices); **horse-riding**; **climbing**; and other outdoor pursuits.

Social Profile

FOOD & DRINK: Good English cooking is superb and there are some restaurants specialising in old English dishes. In general, the north of the country tends to offer more substantial and traditional food, at more reasonable prices than the south. Every region, however, will have its own speciality; these include roast beef and Yorkshire pudding, game or venison pies, rack of lamb and many fish dishes. Britain is still the home of puddings: *apple crumble* (slices of cooked apple with sweet crumble); *spotted dick* (suet pudding with currants and raisins); and *syllabub* (a Medieval dish consisting of double cream, white wine and lemon juice). The English cream tea is still served in tea rooms, particularly in south-coast seaside resorts. It generally consists of scones, jam, butter, clotted or double cream and, of course, tea. There are many regional varieties in baking: the flat pancake-type scones of the North of England and Scotland; Scottish black bun, a fruit cake on a pastry base; *Bakewell tart*, a pastry base covered with jam, almond filling and topped with icing; and breads of all description. For those who want variety, London and the larger cities offer every type of ethnic food imaginable, Chinese and Indian being particularly popular and good value for money. *Cheddar* and *Stilton* are the most famous British cheeses. Tipping is not compulsory and it is up to the individual whether to pay the 10 to 12 per cent service charge often added automatically to bills. Table service is usual but there are self-service snack bars. Set-price lunches, especially on Sundays, with a choice of about three dishes, are particularly good value, as is pub food.
The British pub is nothing short of a national institution and even the smallest village in the remotest corner of the country will usually have at least one. There are about as many beers in England as there are cheeses in France and the recent revival of real ale has greatly improved the range and qualities of brews available. Look out for the sign 'Free House' outside a pub, meaning that beer from more than one brewery will be sold there. Bitter and lager are the most popular beers, but stout, pale ale, brown ale and cider are also widely drunk. Wine bars and cocktail bars are now common in the larger cities and towns, and the latter will often have a 'happy hour' (when prices are reduced) in the early evening. Under 18s will not be served alcohol and children under 16 are not generally allowed into pubs, although they may sit in the garden. Licensing hours vary between towns, but many pubs, especially in main centres, are open typically 1100-2300; the visitor should not be surprised, however, if they find a pub closing for a period in the afternoon. On Sunday, hours are 1200-2230. Private clubs often have an extension into the early hours.
NIGHTLIFE: The main cities, London in particular, have a vast range to choose from: theatre (including open-air in the summer), opera, ballet, concerts, films, restaurants, nightclubs and discos, as well as, of course, pubs. The weekly magazine, *Time Out*, publishes a comprehensive guide to events in the capital.
SHOPPING: Woollen and woven goods such as *Harris Tweeds* are famous. Printed cottons and silks are to be found, as well as fashionable ready-made clothes. China and porcelain *Wedgwood*, *Crown Derby*, *Royal Doulton* and *Royal Worcester* are good buys, as are luxury food and chocolates. Antiques are to be found all over the country. In London, Charing Cross Road is famous for bookshops, and there are several street markets: Petticoat Lane for clothes and Bermondsey for antiques, to name just two. **Tax-Free Shopping:** Many shops throughout the country now operate a tax-free shopping scheme for overseas visitors. The store will provide a form that should be completed at the time of purchase. Upon arrival at Customs, present the goods and the forms (within three months) to the Customs Officer, who will stamp the vouchers certifying that the goods are being exported, and that you will be entitled to a refund of Value Added Tax (VAT). For further information, contact the British Tourist Office which will be able to supply details. **Shopping hours:** In major cities, Mon-Sat 0900-1730; in London's West End and other large shopping centres, shops stay open to 2000. Many local shops stay open to 1900 or 2000 and some even later; many of these are open on Sunday morning or all day. Larger shops will open Sun 1000-1600. Some towns and areas of cities may have early closing one day a week, usually Wednesday or Thursday.
SPECIAL EVENTS: For a complete list, contact the British Tourist Board. The following is a selection of special events occurring in England in 2005:
Jan 6-16 *London International Boat Show*, London. **Jan 13-16** *West London Antiques and Fine Arts Fair*, Kensington, London. **Jan 15-16** *Motorbike 2005* (motorbike show), Spalding, Lincolnshire. **Feb 11-20** *Comedy Festival 2005*, Leicester. **Feb 13-17** *London Fashion Week*. **Mar 10-13** *Crufts 2005* (dog show), Birmingham. **Mar 14-16** *London Book Fair*, Hammersmith, London. **Mar 28** *Easter Egg Roll*, Hampshire; *Head of the River Race* (Oxford and Cambridge Boat Race), London. **Apr 17** *Flora London Marathon*. **May 1** *May Day Celebrations* (traditional event), Lustleigh, Devon. **May 7-29** *Brighton Festival* (the largest arts festival in England). **May 12-15** *Royal Windsor Horse Show*, Windsor. **May 24-28** *Chelsea Flower Show*, London. **Jun 3-4** *Keswick Beer Festival*, Keswick, Cumbria. **Jun 3-5** *Dickens Festival*, Rochester. **Jun 11** *Trooping the Colour* (official birthday parade of the Queen), London. **Jun 20-Jul 3** *Wimbledon Lawn Tennis Championships*, London. **Jun 22-26** *Glastonbury Festival* (open-air music festival), Glastonbury. **Jun 27-Jul 13** *City of London Festival*. **Jul 5-10** *Hampton Court Palace Flower Show*, Greater London. **Jul 30-Aug 6** *Cowes Week 2005* (yacht-racing regatta on The Solent), Isle of Wight. **Aug 29-Sep 1** *International Beatles Festival*, Liverpool. **Aug 28-29** *Notting Hill Carnival* (West Indian street carnival), London. **Nov 5** *Guy Fawkes* (bonfires and fireworks), nationwide. **Nov 12** *Lord Mayor's Show* (parade), London. **Dec 3-4** *City of Durham Christmas Festival*. **Dec 31** *New Year's Eve Celebrations*, nationwide.

Climate

The climate is temperate with warm wet summers and cool wet winters. Weather varies from day to day and throughout the country as a whole. The west coast and mountainous areas receive the most rain; the east coast, particularly in the north, is colder and windier. The southeast is sunnier than the north with less rain and a climate approaching the continental. The southwest has the mildest climate overall.
Required clothing: European according to season, plus rainwear.

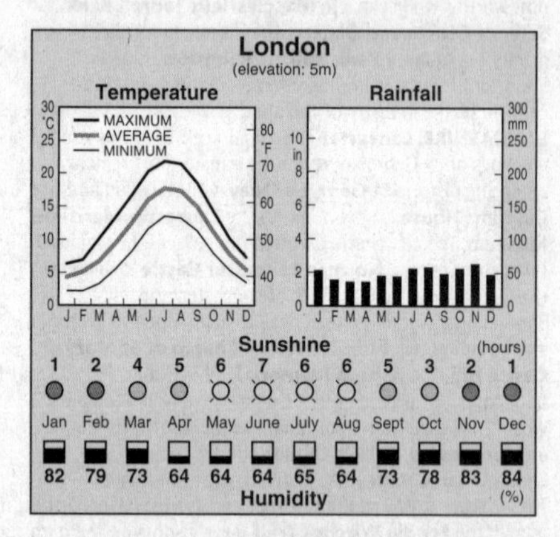

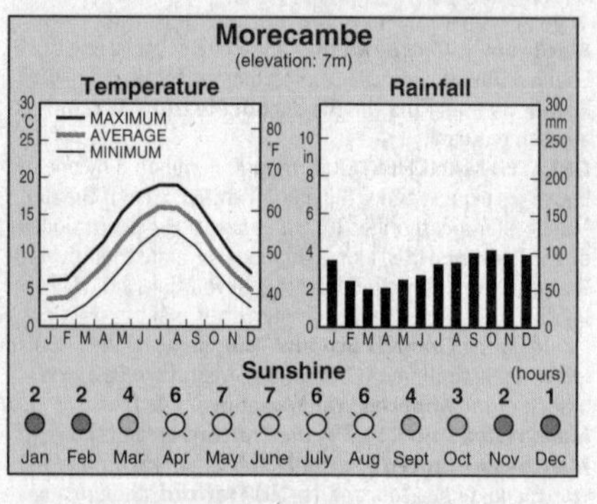

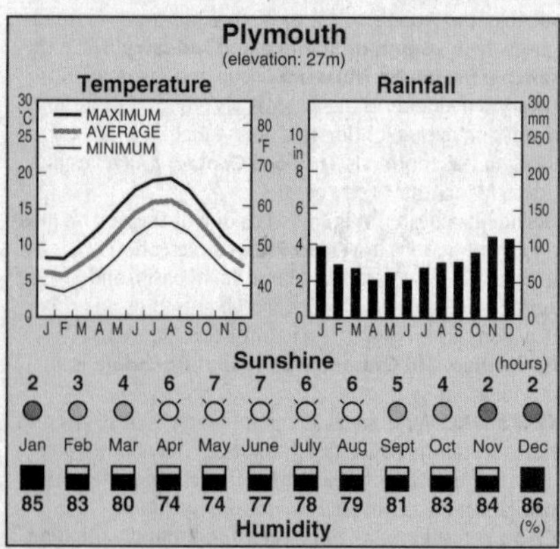

Scotland

LATEST TRAVEL ADVICE CONTACTS

British Foreign and Commonwealth Office
Tel: (0870) 606 0290 Website: www.fco.gov.uk

US Department of State
Website: http://travel.state.gov/travel

Canadian Department of Foreign Affairs and Int'l Trade
Tel: (1 800) 267 8376 Website: www.dfait-maeci.gc.ca

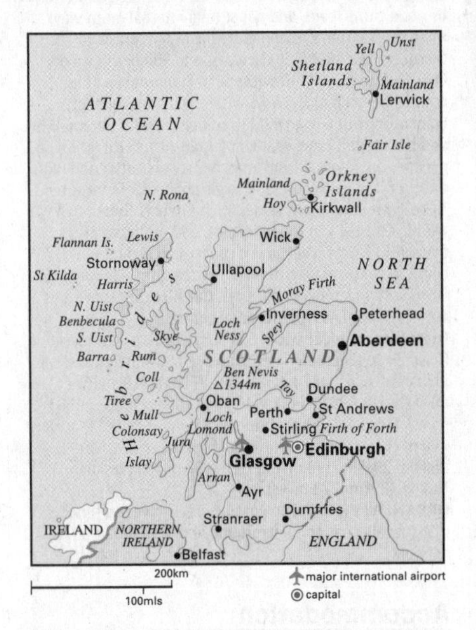

Location: Northern part of Great Britain.

VisitScotland
VisitScotland.com, Fairways Business Park, Deer Park Avenue, Livingston EH54 8AF, UK
Tel: (0845) 225 5121 (within the UK) *or* (01506) 832 121 (outside the UK).
Fax: (01506) 832 222.
E-mail: info@visitscotland.com *or* generalenquiries@visitscotland.com
Website: www.visitscotland.com
Visit Britain in New York deals with enquiries relating to Scotland (see *United States of America* **section).**

General Information

AREA: 77,925 sq km (30,086 sq miles).
POPULATION: 5,054,800 (2002).
POPULATION DENSITY: 64.9 per sq km.
CAPITAL: Edinburgh. **Population:** 449,000 (official estimate 2001).
GEOGRAPHY: The country consists of the southern Lowland area, a region of moorland and pastoral scenery – where most of the population is concentrated – and the northern Highlands, dominated by the Grampian Mountains and Ben Nevis (1344m/4140ft), the highest peak in the British Isles. The whole of the exceedingly beautiful coastline is indented with lochs (particularly in the north and west). Off the west coast there are many islands, the largest of which are Skye and Lewis, the latter being part of the Outer Hebrides. The Orkney and Shetland Islands lie to the northeast of the Scottish mainland, across the Pentland Firth from John O'Groats.
GOVERNMENT: Following elections in May 1999, Scotland was granted its first parliament in 300 years. The new Scottish Parliament has a considerable degree of autonomy, as demonstrated by its tax-raising powers. The UK government maintains control over issues such as defence and foreign policy. **Head of State:** HM Queen Elizabeth II. **Head of Parliament:** First Minister Jack McConnell since 2002.
LANGUAGE: English. Gaelic is still spoken by some, mostly in the West and Highlands.
For information on religion, time, electricity and communications, see the main *United Kingdom* section.

Public Holidays

Public holidays observed in Scotland are the same as those observed in the rest of the UK (see the main *United Kingdom* section) with the addition of:

Credit: © Britain On View & Rod Edwards

2005: Jan 2 New Year Bank Holiday. **Aug 1** Summer Bank Holiday.
2006: Jan 2 New Year Bank Holiday. **Aug 7** Summer Bank Holiday.

Travel - International

AIR: International airports: Scotland's main international airports are *Edinburgh* and *Glasgow*.
Edinburgh (EDI): Located 12km (8 miles) west of the city centre. Airport information: tel: (0131) 333 3181; website: www.baa.co.uk/main/airports/edinburgh. **Facilities:** These include duty free, general and specialist shops, tourist information, hotel reservations service, bureaux de change and ATMs, emergency first-aid facilities, parent and baby room, several coffee and snack bars (both landside and airside) and facilities for the disabled – toilets, wheelchairs, induction loops, telephones and swivel seats in some taxis. **Train/bus:** *Lothian Buses* operate services between the airport and Waverley Bridge (in the city centre, opposite the main railway station), Mon to Sat 0420-0020, every eight to 10 minutes (peak time) and every 15 to 20 minutes (off-peak). Sunday services run 0500-0000 every 15 to 30 minutes. For more information, contact Lothian Buses (tel: (0131) 555 6363; e-mail: mail@lothianbuses.co.uk; website: www.lothianbuses.co.uk). **Taxi:** Available from the rank outside the airport (travel time to city centre – 20 minutes). **Car hire:** *Alamo, Avis, Budget, Europcar, Hertz* and *National* self-drive and chauffeur-driven cars can be hired from desks within the terminal. **Private car:** The A8 runs direct to the airport from the city centre. If coming from the west or north, follow the signs on the M9, M8 and A90.
Glasgow (GLA): Located 14km (9 miles) west of the city centre. Airport information: tel: (0141) 887 1111; website: www.baa.co.uk/main/airports/glasgow. **Facilities:** These include emergency medical services, bureau de change, ATMs, left luggage, general shops, post office, buffet, bar, cafes, restaurants, duty free shop, hotel reservation service and facilities for the disabled – wheelchairs, toilets and telephones. **Train:** Paisley's Gilmour Street station is 3km (2 miles) from the airport. It is easily reached by taxi or bus

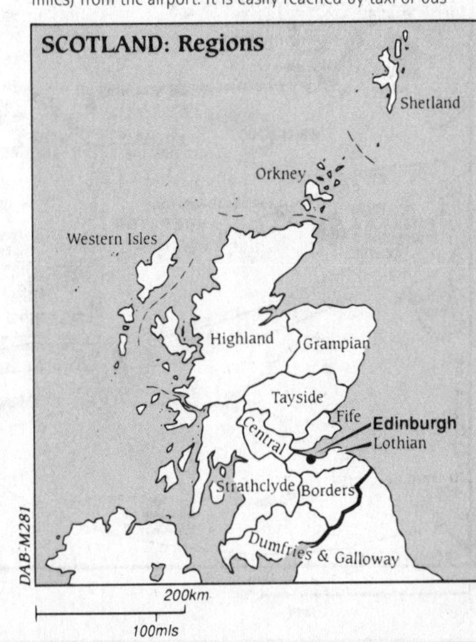

and offers connections to Glasgow Central and other regional stations. For further information, contact *National Rail Enquiries* (tel: (08457) 484 950, UK only). **Bus/Coach:** All buses depart from outside the main airport terminal. *Scottish Citylink* runs regular services to the city centre via Queen Street railway station and Buchanan bus station (bus no. 905), Mon-Fri and Sun 0630-0000, Sat 0600-0000. For more information, contact Scottish City Link (tel: (08705) 505 050; website: www.citylink.co.uk). Scottish Citylink's coach services also operate between the airport, Greenoch and Gouroch. **Taxi:** To the city centre is 20 minutes; to Paisley station is five minutes. Taxis are available from the rank on the terminal forecourt. **Car hire:** *Alamo, Avis, Europcar, Hertz* and *National* have desks next to Domestic Arrivals. **Private car:** The M8 runs direct to the airport from the city centre. Car-parking space is available for 2000 cars.
Other airports: *Aberdeen (ABZ)*: Located 11km (7 miles) northwest of the city centre. Airport information: tel: (01224) 722 331; website: www.baa.co.uk/main/airports/aberdeen. **Facilities:** These include bureau de change, tax-free shopping, restaurants and bars, left luggage, parent and baby room, facilities for the disabled and two airport hotels. **Train:** Aberdeen and Inverness trains stop at Dyce station, which is a short taxi ride from the airport. **Bus:** There are frequent bus services from the city centre to the airport. For details, contact *First* (tel: (01224) 650 000). **Coach:** *Stagecoach Bluebird* services also run to the airport (tel: (01224) 212 266). **Taxi:** Available from the airport (travel time to city centre - 20 minutes). **Car hire:** *Avis, Europcar, Hertz* and *National/Alamo* all have desks at the airport. **Private car:** Signs for the airport should be followed from the A96 Aberdeen to Inverness road.
Inverness (INV): The major airport serving the Highlands, with transfer connections available to airports in the north of Scotland. It is located 14km (9 miles) east of the city centre and is served by taxis and buses. Facilities include an ATM, bar/restaurant and bookshop.

There are several smaller airports in the north of Scotland that are served by flights from Glasgow and, in some cases, from Aberdeen, Inverness and Edinburgh as well. These include *Barra, Benbecula, Kirkwall* (Orkney), *Lerwick* (Shetland), *Stornoway* and *Tiree*. For further information, contact Glasgow Airport (see above).
SEA: Ferry services operate between the mainland and all the Scottish islands but some of these may be infrequent. *Caledonian MacBrayne* operates the largest network of ferries on the river Clyde and west coast, serving many islands, including the Inner and Outer Hebrides. During the summer, services often operate hourly or half-hourly but in the winter they are less frequent. For details of fares, routes and timetables, contact *Caledonian MacBrayne* (tel: (01475) 650 100 (enquiries) or (08705) 650 000 (reservations); fax: (01475) 635 235; website: www.calmac.co.uk). *Northlink Ferries* (tel: (01856) 885 500 (enquiries) *or* (0845) 600 0449 (reservations); fax: (01856) 879 588; website: www.northlinkferries.co.uk) operates services to the Orkneys and Shetlands; from Aberdeen to Lerwick daily, more often in summer (travel time - 12 hours); and from Scrabster to Stromness daily, more often in summer (travel time - 90 minutes).
Other routes include *P&O Irish Sea* ferry service between Cairnryan and Larne up to 12 times a day (travel time - one hour 45 minutes; tel: (0870) 242 4777); and *Stena Line*'s service between Stranraer and Belfast eight times a day (travel time - one hour 45 minutes; tel: (08704) 006 798; fax: (02890) 884 031; website: www.stenaline.com). *The Seacat* (tel: (01624) 661 661 (UK only); website: www.seacat.co.uk) operates between Troon and Belfast Harbour two to three times a day (travel time - two hours 30 minutes). *P&O Irish Sea* and *Stena Line* offer jet boat services from Stanraer to Belfast (travel time - approximately one hour).
RAIL: There are two main-line routes into Scotland from England: from London Euston up the west coast to Glasgow Central and beyond to Perth and Inverness; and from London King's Cross up the east coast to Edinburgh and beyond to Dundee and Aberdeen. For details, contact *National Rail Enquiries* (tel: (08457) 484 950 (UK only); website: www.nationalrail.co.uk). Particularly in the Edinburgh-Glasgow area, there are good services connecting all the main towns. Many of the routes that pass through the Highlands (such as: Perth-Inverness; Inverness-Kyle of Lochalsh; Glasgow-Fort William-Mallaig) are very spectacular. The network extends right up to Thurso and Wick in the extreme north of the country. Sleeper services are available on *Scotrail's Caledonian Sleeper* (which connects London Euston, Edinburgh, Glasgow, Aberdeen, Inverness and Fort William nightly; tel: (0845) 601 5929).
ROAD: Scotland is connected to the main UK road network by good trunk roads, and has several internal motorways. Main access from England is via the M74 (Carlisle to Glasgow), the A696/A68 (Newcastle to Edinburgh via the Cheviots) and the A1 (Newcastle to Edinburgh via the coast). The main motorways within Scotland connect Edinburgh with Glasgow (M8), Edinburgh with Stirling (M9), and the Forth Bridge, near Edinburgh, with Perth (M90). In general, the internal trunk road network is better and more direct on the east coast, and roads north of Inverness tend to be slower and often single track. Snow is common in winter, especially in the Highlands, and motorists are advised to follow local advice concerning weather conditions. The main cross-country road, the A9, connects Perth with Inverness and Thurso. **Car hire:** Self-drive cars are widely available in the major centres.
Distances: *From London*: Edinburgh 663km (412 miles), Glasgow 654km (406 miles), Aberdeen 884km (549 miles), Inverness 923km (573 miles), Fort William 828km (514 miles), Perth 696km (433 miles) and Thurso 1066km (663 miles). *From Edinburgh*: Glasgow 72km (45 miles), Aberdeen 211km (131 miles), Inverness 261km (162 miles), Fort William 231km (138 miles), Perth 69km (43 miles) and Thurso 439km (273 miles).
URBAN: All the major towns and cities have bus services. Glasgow also has an underground and a suburban train network.

EDINBURGH

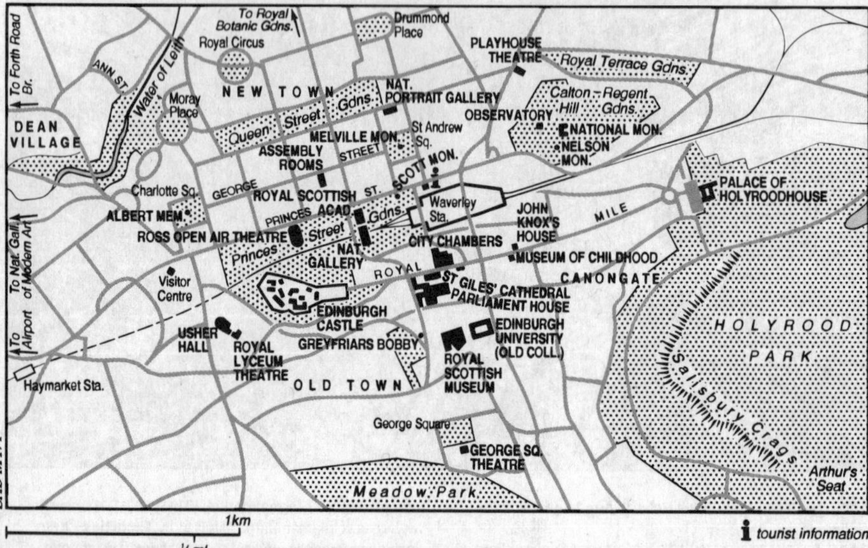

GLASGOW

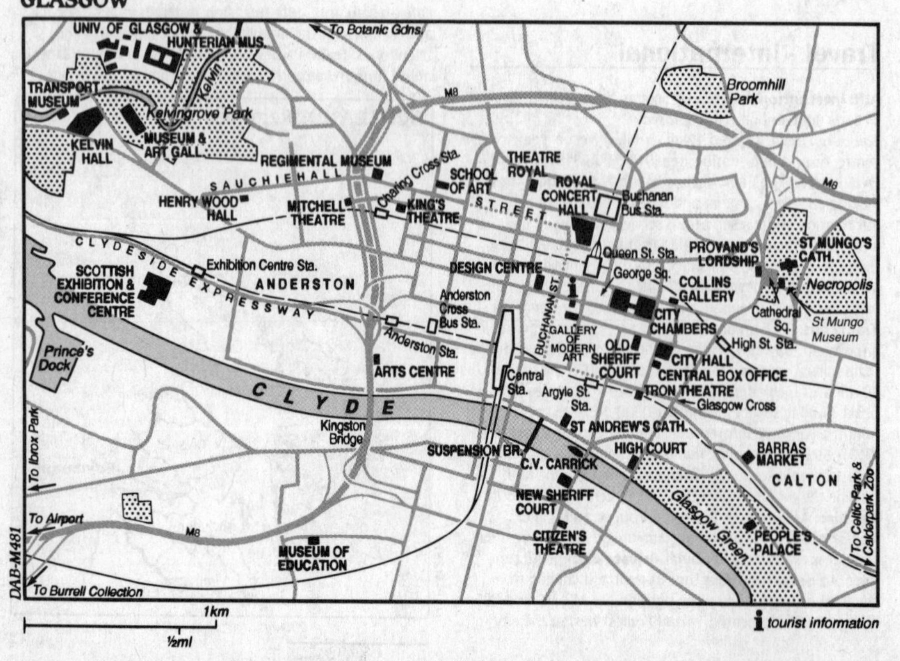

Accommodation

VisitScotland publishes a series of accommodation guides covering hotels and guest houses, bed & breakfast, self-catering and camping and caravanning, for which there is a charge, plus postage and packing.
There is a wide range of accommodation available in Scotland, comprising guest houses, bed & breakfast establishments, hotels, international resort hotels, self-catering, campsites, serviced apartments, lodges, inns, restaurants with rooms and campus accommodation. Many hotels have been built, modernised or refurbished during the last few years, as well as the many guest houses and bed & breakfast premises throughout the country. More than 500 hotels, guest houses and bed & breakfast establishments are members of the 'Walkers Welcome' initiative and make special efforts to meet the needs of walkers.
Grading: VisitScotland has recently introduced a new star system to rate guest accommodation, replacing the Crown System. The ratings are as follows: **1 Star:** Fair and acceptable; **2 Stars:** Good; **3 Stars:** Very good; **4 Stars:** Excellent; **5 Stars:** Exceptional, world-class. For a selection of some of the finest hotels in Scotland, see online (website: www.distinctionworld.com) or, for further information, contact VisitScotland (see *Contact Addresses* section).

Resorts & Excursions

Scotland is one of the world's great tourist destinations, offering a mixture of vibrant cities and beautiful countryside. The nation naturally divides into five main regions: the busy **central belt**, in which both the biggest cities of Edinburgh and Glasgow stand; the **Southwest and Borders**; the long **East Coast**; the mountainous **Highlands and West Coast**; and the many **islands** of the north and west.
Scotland's natural attractions are many, but it also has strong historic and cultural appeal. For more information about the country's legacy of castles and other historic properties, contact the National Trust for Scotland (website: www.nts.org.uk) *or* Historic Scotland (website: www.historic-scotland.gov.uk).

EDINBURGH

(Tourist Board website: www.edinburgh.org.) Known as 'the Athens of the North', Edinburgh is one of the United Kingdom's finest cities. It straddles a deep gorge occupied by newly refurbished **Waverley Station**, and gardens containing the **Scott Monument**. On its south side is **Old Town**, the original city centre, while opposite is the predominantly Georgian **New Town**, with its elegant 18th-century architecture. This is also the main shopping area, centred on **Princes Street**.

Edinburgh Castle, the nation's top tourist attraction, also housing the Scottish Crown Jewels, stands in Old Town at the head of the **Royal Mile**, which extends to the **Palace of Holyrood House**, the Queen's official Scottish residence. **Edinburgh Zoo** is also popular, especially with families. Attractions such as **St Giles' Cathedral**, **John Knox House**, the **Scotch Whisky Heritage Centre**, the **Writer's Museum** and the **Camera Obscura** pepper the Old Town, along with galleries and museums.

Edinburgh is home to many of Scotland's national galleries and museums, including the **Museum of Scotland**, the **National Gallery of Scotland**, a new gallery at the **National Trust for Scotland**, the **National Portrait Gallery**, the **National Gallery of Modern Art** and the **National Museum of Antiquities**. There is also a **National Centre for Dance**.

Edinburgh's cultural life offers a programme of theatre, music and dance unrivalled in the UK outside London. It has Britain's largest stage and largest theatre in the **Festival Theatre** and the **Edinburgh Playhouse**, respectively. These feature during the three-week August *Edinburgh Festival*, the world's largest of its kind. The festival season kicks off with the spectacular *Military Tattoo*, staged outside the Castle. The world's biggest New Year party (known as *Hogmanay* in Scotland) takes place over several days at the end of each year.

Excursions: Attractions close to Edinburgh include the city's port, **Leith**, where the former *Royal Yacht Britannia* is now open to visitors; **Linlithgow**, with its magnificent palace; **Hopetoun House**, one of Scotland's best stately homes at **South Queensferry**; **Deep Sea World**, at **North Queensferry**; and the **Scottish Seabird Centre** at **North Berwick**.

GLASGOW

Glasgow (Tourist Board website: www.seeglasgow.com.) Only 77km (48 miles) west of the capital, Glasgow is a dynamic cultural centre, with a variety of events taking place year-round, and the world-famous **Burrell Collection** and the **Glasgow Royal Concert Hall**. Glasgow has fine parks, and Scotland's only complete medieval cathedral.

Kelvingrove Park's art gallery houses works by top Renaissance and modern painters. The **Royal Exchange Building** houses the **Gallery of Modern Art**.

Hampden Park, the national soccer stadium, incorporates the new **Scottish Football Museum**. On the south bank of the **Clyde**, opposite the **Scottish Exhibition and Conference Centre**, is the new **Glasgow Science Centre** featuring interactive attractions and the 127m (416ft) revolving **Glasgow Tower**. Also on Clydeside is **Clydebuilt**, the Maritime Museum.

Excursions: Southeast of Glasgow is **Lanark**, where the **New Lanark Visitor Centre** is, a complete 200-year-old model village built by social reformer Robert Owen. On a cliff overlooking the Firth of Clyde is **Culzean Castle**, once home to the Kennedy family. Immediately south of the city is **Hamilton**, with 13th-century **Bothwell Castle** and the Robert Adam **Chatelherault Hunting Lodge**. On the way to **East Kilbride** is the newly opened **Museum of Scottish Country Life**, a 68 hectare (170 acre) attraction based on a Georgian farm at **Kittochside**.

CENTRAL SCOTLAND

(Tourist Board website: www.visitscottishheartlands.org.) As well as the country's two major cities, the populous central area of Scotland contains many other places of historic, scenic and general interest. Almost anywhere in this region is within easy excursion distance of either Glasgow or Edinburgh.

Despite the urban nature of much of the central area, attractive countryside is never far away. In the west are the **Firth of Clyde** and the **Dunoon Peninsula**, to the northwest lies **Loch Lomond**, and to the east are the small villages and rugged coastline of the former county of **Berwickshire**.

STIRLING: Huge **Stirling Castle** sits dramatically atop a volcanic promontory above the town. The nearby **Wallace Monument** similarly dominates the surrounding countryside. In the town centre is the **Old Town Gaol**, while close by are the battlefields of **Stirling Bridge** and **Bannockburn**, where William 'Braveheart' Wallace and Robert Bruce respectively inflicted humiliating defeats on the English in the late 13th and early 14th centuries.

Excursions: Blair Drummond Safari Park, the little cathedral city of **Dunblane**, **Doune Castle** and **Callander**, site of the **Rob Roy and Trossachs Visitor Centre**, are all well worth visiting.

SOUTH WEST SCOTLAND AND THE BORDERS

South and west of Glasgow, **Ayrshire** (Tourist Board website: www.ayrshire-arran.com) has an attractive coastline and a number of seaside resorts, including **Prestwick** and **Troon**, site of yet another world-class golf course. Irvine offers the **Scottish Maritime Museum**, and nearby **Dundonald Castle** was childhood home of William Wallace. **Vikingar**, a multimedia visitor centre at **Largs**, highlights Viking influences on the region, while **Alloway**, birthplace of Robert Burns, features a number of attractions dedicated to the poet. Off the Ayrshire coast lies **Arran**, an extremely popular holiday island.

DUMFRIES & GALLOWAY: (Tourist Board website: www.dumfriesandgalloway.co.uk) This region consists of open, rolling countryside, lakes and pine forests. Towns like **Dumfries**, home of Robert Burns; **Kirkcudbright**, a former artist's colony; and **Gatehouse of Fleet** are all popular centres. Country houses, castles, gardens and special interest museums are common in the area. To the far southwest, **Stranraer** is the ferry port for Belfast, and the main town on the subtropical **Rhinns of Galloway Peninsula**.

THE BORDERS: The Borders area (website: www.scot-borders.co.uk) was scene of many Anglo-Scottish battles down the centuries. It is a region of lush green hills and moorland. The area's wealth allowed construction of several outstanding ecclesiastical buildings, notably the abbeys at **Dryburgh**, **Jedburgh** and **Melrose**. The border towns of **Galashiels**, **Hawick**, **Peebles** and **Selkirk** are still centres of the wool, tweed and knitwear industry. **Abbotsford** was home to Sir Walter Scott.

THE EAST COAST

ABERDEEN: (Tourist Board website: www.agtb.org.) Some 56km (35 miles) north of Montrose is the 'Granite City', Scotland's third-largest, built largely, as its nickname suggests, of granite. It is the centre of Britain's North Sea oil industry. The city has a 16th-century cathedral, a university and a 14th-century bridge, the **Brig O'Balgownie**. Visitor attractions include the **Art Gallery**, **Marischal Museum** and **Maritime Museum**. Inland on **Royal Deeside**, **Braemar** is the site of the most famous of the Highland gatherings. There are several National Trust properties within easy reach of Aberdeen, including **Castle Fraser** and **Fyvie Castle**.

DUNDEE: (Tourist Board website: www.angusanddundee.co.uk.) North across the **Firth of Tay** in the former county of Angus is the city of Dundee. A city of printing, jam and jute, Dundee is home to the **Discovery Point Visitor Centre**, based around Captain Scott's exploration ship, **RRS Discovery**, which lies alongside. Another popular attraction is **Sensation**, which offers a hands-on exhibition about the senses. **Verdant Works** traces Dundee's long tradition of jute trading in the **Textile Heritage Centre**.

PERTH: (Tourist Board website: www.perthshire.co.uk.) King James I's own relatives murdered the unpopular monarch here in 1437, and, later, John Knox preached one of his earliest sermons in the town. Nowadays, Perth boasts **Scotland's Garden** and the **National Tartan Centre**, together with two castles and **Scone Palace**, where Scottish monarchs were once crowned.

ELSEWHERE: St Andrews (Tourist Board website: www.standrews.com), northeast of Edinburgh in the 'Kingdom' of Fife, claims to be the home of world golf. In addition, the town has a university, castle and cathedral. The *Lammas Fair* takes place every August. Some 25km (15 miles) to the north is **Glamis**, whose castle features in Shakespeare's *Macbeth*.

West of Dundee is the former county of Perthshire. This area was centre of the Pictish realm, and the northernmost area in Britain occupied by the Romans.

Up the coast from Dundee is **Carnoustie**, famous in golfing circles around the world. Next is **Arbroath**, which has a famous ruined **Abbey** and a strong fishing heritage – the famous 'Arbroath Smokies' (smoked haddock) come from here. Further north, the town of **Montrose** has fine broad streets and sandy beaches.

Continuing north past **Aberdeen** to **Peterhead** and **Fraserburgh**, the coastal trail leads through charming fishing villages, then west along the Moray Firth to the Georgian town of **Banff** and magnificent **Duff House**, where part of the reserve collection of the National Galleries can be seen. Further along this coastline is **Elgin**, which has a ruined cathedral and a well-restored abbey church. There are many highland gatherings and games in this region. Beyond Inverness, the countryside is mainly moorland, glens and forests, and home to some of Britain's rarest fauna, including wildcats and golden eagles.

Most of the towns in this area are small. Highlights include **Dingwall** and **Invergordon**. The towns of **Thurso** and **Wick** mark the end of the railway line. **John O'Groats**, due north of Wick, is the northernmost village on the British mainland.

THE HIGHLANDS & THE WEST COAST

The **Scottish Highlands** (website: www.visithighlands.com) contain some of Britain's most breathtaking scenery. Railway and road traverse the countryside between the capital and Inverness, passing through the **Grampian Mountains** and the **Forest of Atholl**. The lochs of the central highlands feed the **River Tay**, one of the best

Credit: © Britain On View & Rod Edwards

fishing rivers in the British Isles. **Tayside**, and **Speyside** to the north, are Scotland's major whiskey-producing areas, with dozens of distilleries. Also in the Highlands are the **Pass of Killiecrankie**, **Blair Atholl**, **Kingussie** and **Aviemore**, the winter ski resort.

INVERNESS: (Highlands of Scotland Tourist Board website: www.visithighlands.com.) The UK's northernmost city, many of whose buildings date back to the 17th century. Inverness is also famous for its location at the head of Loch Ness, deep-water home of the mythical monster. The site of the **Battle of Culloden** where the government forces, including many of the lowland clans, crushed Bonnie Prince Charlie's forces in 1746.

FORT WILLIAM: One of the best-known towns on the West Coast, as well as the largest resort. Above the town looms Britain's highest mountain, **Ben Nevis** (1343m/4406ft). Attractions in the town include the **Ben Nevis Distillery and Visitor Centre**. Nearby is **Glencoe**, where the Campbells massacred the Macdonald clan in their sleep; when shrouded in mist, Glencoe still has a haunting atmosphere. The **Glencoe Visitor Centre** tells this story, while Celtic myth and legend is the topic of **Highland Mysteryworld** close by.

ELSEWHERE: On the West Coast (Tourist Board website: www.visitscottishheartlands.com) at the mouth of **Loch Linnhe** is **Oban**, gateway to many of the islands and the beautiful region of **Kintyre**. Further north is the town of Mallaig, which, like Oban, is a rail terminus. One of the best ways to reach **Mallaig** is on the **Jacobite Steam Train** from Fort William, which runs through some spectacular scenery. The so-called **'Road to the Isles'**, which also passes through **Glenfinnan** and **Arisaig**, a pretty resort known for its white sands, is the driving alternative.

Ullapool is still an important fishing port, and is also the departure point for car ferries to the **Outer Hebrides**. North of Ullapool, the road passes through **Inverpolly Nature Reserve** into **Sutherland**, and the landscape becomes even wilder, with isolated mountains rising from a rocky plateau. Fishing villages dot the rugged coastline. Inland is one of Europe's last great wildernesses, an area of mountains, moorland, lochs and rivers, rich in wildlife.

THE ORKNEY AND SHETLAND ISLANDS

These two island groups lie northeast of the Scottish mainland – see the *Travel* section for details of air and sea connections. The islands are of particular interest to birdwatchers, sea anglers and rock climbers. Birds are also the main attraction on National-Trust-owned **Fair Isle**, between Orkney and Shetland.

ORKNEY: (Tourist Board website: www.visitorkney.com.) The **Pentland Firth** separates Orkney from the mainland. The islands are fertile, although with very few trees, and enjoy a predominantly mild, variable climate. The main town, situated on **Mainland**, is **Kirkwall**, boasting a cathedral and many other places of interest. Orkney is rich in prehistoric sites, including the Stone Age village of **Skara Brae**, the **Maes Howe** burial mound, and the standing stones at the **Ring of Brogar**. On the other side of **Scapa Flow** is **Hoy**, whose sheer cliffs and windswept sandstone landscape make it one of the most dramatic of the Orkney group. Other islands include **Westray** and **South Ronaldsay**.

SHETLAND: (Tourist Board website: www.visitshetland.com.) This group of 100 (15 inhabited) rugged islands is the most northerly part of Britain. Their climate is surprisingly mild considering their northerly latitude (the same as southern Alaska). The chief town of **Lerwick**, on Mainland, the largest island, relied in former days almost solely on fishing but now benefits from North Sea oil. Places of interest include the **Jarlshof** Bronze Age settlement, the island of Foula, the nature reserve on **Noss**, **Mousa Broch** on uninhabited **Mousa**, and the world's most northerly castle on **Unst**.

THE HEBRIDES

A network of ferry routes from the mainland serves the Inner and Outer **Hebrides**. Many are also reachable by air. Among the inner islands are **Islay** (an important whiskey distilling location with six distilleries open to visitors) and **Jura**. **Iona** is Scotland's Holy Island and first permanent British Christian site, as well as burial place of many Scottish kings and chiefs. A ferry from Oban serves **Mull** and the **Western Isles**. A little further from the mainland are **Coll** and **Tiree**, small communities in the windswept Atlantic.

SKYE: The **Sound of Sleat** and the **Inner Sound** separate world-renowned Skye from the mainland. There are ferry links from **Mallaig**, while the **Skye Bridge** crosses from **Kyle of Lochalsh**. The **Bright Water Visitor Centre** on the Isle of Skye celebrates the history of the island. The island 'capital' is **Portree**, while major attractions include **Talisker Distillery**, **Armadale Castle**, and seal-watching boat trips past the **Cuillin Mountains**.

THE WESTERN ISLES: (Tourist Board website: www.visithebrides.com.) Settled for at least 5000 years, this chain stretches for 200km (130 miles) from north to south in a gentle arc. The northernmost, and largest, islands are **Lewis** and **Harris**, the former containing the Western Isles' capital, **Stornoway** (Steornabhagh). The well-known tweed cloth comes from Harris, at the mountainous southern end of the island. Across the **Sound of Harris** lies **North Uist** (Uibhist a Tuath), further south are **Benbecula** (Beinn na Faoghla), **South Uist** (Uibhist a Deas) and **Barra**, where the 'airport' is the smooth sandy beach. Each island has its own strong character, and all have good beaches. Attractions include the 5000-year-old **Calanais Standing Stones** on **Lewis**; **Barra's Kisimul Castle** and the **Seallam Visitor Centre**, Taobh Tuath, Harris.

Sport & Activities

Golf: Scotland, where golf was invented, is home to some of the world's most famous golf courses, notably the *Old Course* at St Andrews – the historic 'home of golf' (the prestigious *Open Championship* in July 2000 was held here). In total, Scotland has some 500 courses. Further *Open Championship* courses can be found in *Carnoustie*, *Muirfield*, *Royal Troon* and *Turnberry*. In addition, there is an abundance of world-class courses, such as *Blairgowrie*, *Downfield*, *Murcar*, *Nairn*, *North Berwick*, *Royal Aberdeen*, *Royal Dornoch*, *Southerness* and *Western Gailes*. Also available is a fine selection of natural links courses in the outlying areas. For details of golfing holidays, membership and golf courses, contact VisitScotland (see *Contact Addresses* section).

Equestrianism: One of the most popular equestrian activities is **pony trekking** on the native Scottish Highland pony. Beginners can try a one- or two-hour trek, while experienced riders may opt for a full day- or week-long trek. Many riding centres offer unaccompanied children's holidays with the possibility of adopting a pony for a week. In the southeastern Borders area, which is known as 'Scotland's horse country', and where horses play an important part in local festivities, accommodation often comes equipped with stables. Further information can be obtained from The British Horse Society (Scotland), Woodburn Farm, Crieff, Perthshire PH7 3RG (tel: (01764) 656 334; e-mail: chair@bhsscotland.org.uk; website: www.bhsscotland.org.uk).

Cycling: Scotland has an extensive network of signposted cycling routes and off-road trails for **mountain biking**. On small country roads there is often little traffic. Bicycle hire and cycling tours are available throughout Scotland. Bicycle transport facilities are widespread on Scottish trains, notably on *InterCity* services (between London and Scotland), where no extra charge applies (although reservations are compulsory). It is advisable to check in advance if a train will carry bicycles.

Fishing: Visiting anglers must generally have permission, usually in the form of a permit, available from the local tackle dealer, fishing club or estate. Local tourist offices can supply information on fishing in their area, the cost of permits and where to get them. There is no closed season for **coarse fishing**, though the rule is rod only and it is forbidden to fish with two or more rods simultaneously. Scotland is one of the world's best destinations for **salmon fishing**. The statutory closed season for salmon varies from river to river, but is generally from November 1 until February 10-15 (visitors should check with local tourist offices). Fly fishing is the most accepted and traditional method of fishing for salmon. There are also excellent opportunities for **trout fishing**. Glacial lochs are home to the elusive Char, usually found in deep water. Boats and guides can be hired from hotels and angling clubs. The statutory closed season for brown trout is from October 7 until March 14 (both days inclusive). **Sea angling** can be practised along the coast, where boats and bait are supplied by local tourist offices and fishing clubs. More than 50 sea fishing festivals and competitions take place annually. For details, contact the Scottish Federation of Sea Anglers, Unit 28, Evans Business Centre, Mitchelston Industrial Estate, Kikcaldy KY1 3NB (tel: (01592) 657 520).

Watersports: There is 2560km (1600 miles) of coastline and thousands of lochs and rivers. Inland, **canoeing** can be practised on tranquil lochs or **whitewater rafting** on wild river stretches. Along the coast, a well-established **sailing** and **yachting** industry with modern marinas offers a range of sailing and boating facilities. **Canal cruises** are also possible, notably in the Crinan Canal, which links the Clyde and the West Coast of Scotland; and on the 96km- (60 mile-) long Caledonian Canal, with the option to charter a yacht, motor cruiser or stay on a hotel barge. A restoration project, the 'Millennium Link', restored 110km (69 miles) of the canal (from Glasgow to Edinburgh and the Forth to the Clyde). For further information on watersports, marinas, harbours and moorings, contact Sail Scotland Ltd, PO Box 8363, Largs, Scotland KA30 8YD (tel: (01309) 676 757; fax: (01309) 673 331; e-mail: info@sailscotland.co.uk; website: www.sailscotland.co.uk).

Walking and hiking: Scotland's variety of scenery – from rocky peaks, moorland and rolling green hills to lochs, glens, and wild coastlines – makes it ideal for walking. The vast network of trails is steadily growing. Short-distance walks can usually be completed in a day. For advice on the best routes, contact VisitScotland. The best-known long-distance walks include three 'official' trails – the West Highland Way (the busiest, 150km (95 miles) from Milngavie, north of Glasgow, to Fort William, passing through some spectacular Highland scenery, and quite strenuous in the second half); the less demanding Southern Upland Way (Britain's first official coast-to-coast footpath, 340km (212 miles), from Portpatrick to Cockburnspath, passing through moorland, conifer plantations and crossing a few major rivers); and the Speyside Way (a lowland route, 70km (45 miles), from Spey Bay to Tomintoul, running along one of Scotland's most famous salmon-fishing rivers, the Spey). There is free access at all times to areas owned by the National Trust for Scotland (marked 'NTS' and 'FC' on Ordnance Survey maps). Most of the rest of the land is owned privately and, though Scotland is traditionally known for 'free' land access, walkers may be asked to change their routes during the deer stalking and grouse shooting seasons (from mid-August to October 20, and from August 12 to December 10 respectively). The Mountaineering Council of Scotland and the Scottish Landowners' Federation co-publish a useful brochure, *Heading for the Scottish Hills*, with estate maps and telephone numbers for local advice. Visitors camping in the wild are legally required to ask the consent of the landowner. In addition, a respect of the environment and wildlife is essential and visitors may read the Scottish Natural Heritage booklet, *Care for the Hills*, for advice.

Wildlife: Red deer, golden eagles, peregrine falcons and wildcat are some of the creatures inhabiting Scotland's mountainous regions, while the lower slopes of the central Highlands provide a sanctuary for red squirrel, capercaillie, crested tit, Scottish crossbill and pine marten. Wild salmon, trout and otter can be found in Scotland's abundant and spectacular lochs, one of which – Loch Ness – is also the reputed home of 'Nessie', the famously elusive Loch Ness monster.

Wintersports: Scotland has five **ski** resorts: Cairngorm, Glencoe, Glenshee, The Lecht and the Nevis range. Snowfall varies according to the altitude and is most consistent (particularly between November and May) in the Nevis range or Braeriach, in the Cairngorms. **Snowboarding** is possible at all five resorts. **Mountaineering** and **climbing** expeditions (including guides) are also widely available.

Spectator sports: The most popular spectator sports are **rugby** and **football**, while the annual *Highland Games* season (see *Special Events* in the **Social Profile** section) also attracts many visitors.

Social Profile

FOOD & DRINK: In the main cities and towns, a wide variety of British and continental food is available. A traditional Scottish breakfast is *porridge* made from locally grown oats and either milk or water. Other local dishes include *haggis* (chopped oatmeal and offal cooked in the stomach of a sheep), *cullen skink* (fish soup), smoked haddock and salmon and *partan bree* (crab with rice and cream). Baked foods such as cakes and biscuits are exceedingly popular and some of the more famous are flat pancake-type scones, oatcakes and *black bun*, a fruit cake on a pastry base. Scotch whisky is the national drink, and is famous the world over. There are also many local beers as well as lager. Licensing hours are subject to greater variation than in England; some pubs may be open from 1030-2400, others only 1130-1430 and 1830-2300.

NIGHTLIFE: In major cities, such as Edinburgh and Glasgow, there is a vibrant nightlife, with many bars, restaurants, nightclubs and cinemas. These places also offer a fine array of theatre, opera and music concerts. Some of the main venues for drama performances include the *Festival Theatre*, *Playhouse*, *Assembly Rooms* and *Queen's Hall* in Edinburgh, the *Citizen's Theatre* and *Theatre Royal* in Glasgow, as well as many picturesque regional theatres. The SECC building in Glasgow is a popular concert arena for live bands. Nightlife may be more limited in the smaller villages and islands. For more information on musical and theatrical events, contact VisitScotland (see *Contact Addresses* section).

SPECIAL EVENTS: The highlight of the cultural year in Scotland is the *Edinburgh Festival*, which runs during the last two weeks of August and the first week of September. Almost every room in the city large enough to hold an audience is in use during this time, and it is possible to see as many as 10 shows in one day; these might range from a short open-air concert to a full-scale production by the RSC or the LSO. Accommodation in Edinburgh is booked up months in advance at this time. There are also many *Highland Games* during the summer, which include caber-tossing and hammer-throwing competitions. The following is a selection of special events occurring in Scotland in 2005 (for a complete list contact VisitScotland):

Jan 1 *Loony Dook*, Queensferry. **Jan 12-30** *Celtic Connections*, music festival, Glasgow. **Feb** *Glasgow Festival of Love*. **Feb 21-Mar 12** *Inverness Music Festival*. **Mar 10-26** *Glasgow International Comedy Festival*. **Mar 17-20** *StAnza Poetry Festival*, St Andrews, Fife. **May 21-30** *Burns and a' That!* **Jun** *Caledonian Beer Festival*. **Jun 3-12** *Highland Festival*. **Jun 17-26** *Royal Bank Glasgow Jazz Festival*. **Jun 23-26** *Yoral Highland Show*. **Jul 9-10** *T in the Park*, music festival. **Jul 14-17** *Open Golf Championship*, St Andrews. **Jul 22-23** *The Wickerman Festival*. **Jul 29-Aug 7** *Edinburgh International Jazz & Blues Festival*. **Aug 5-27** *Edinburgh Military Tattoo*. **Aug 7-29** *Edinburgh Festival Fringe*. **Aug 13-29** *Edinburgh International Book Festival*. **Aug 14-Sep 4** *Edinburgh International Festival*. **Aug 17-29** *Edinburgh International Film Festival*. **Nov** *Glasgay!* **Dec 29- Jan 1 2006** *Hogmanay*, countrywide. **Dec 31-Jan 1 2006** *Stonehaven Fireball Festival*, traditional event.

Business Profile

BUSINESS: See main *United Kingdom* entry.

CONFERENCES/CONVENTIONS: The Scottish Convention Bureau is the business tourism division of VisitScotland. Enquiries for venues or incentive groups are dealt with swiftly and efficiently, using the network of Area Tourist Boards. They supply a range of publications and guides to help the meeting or incentive planner. For information, contact the Scottish Convention Bureau, 23 Ravelston Terrace, Edinburgh EH4 3EU (tel: (0131) 343 1608; fax: (0131) 343 1844; e-mail: businesstourism@visitscotland.com; website: www.conventionscotland.com).

Climate

Scotland is generally colder than the rest of the UK, especially in the more northerly regions. The west tends to be wetter and warmer than the cool, dry east. In upland areas, snow is common in winter, and fog and mist may occur at any time of year.

Required clothing: Similar to the rest of the UK, according to season. Waterproofing advised throughout the year and warm clothing for the Highlands.

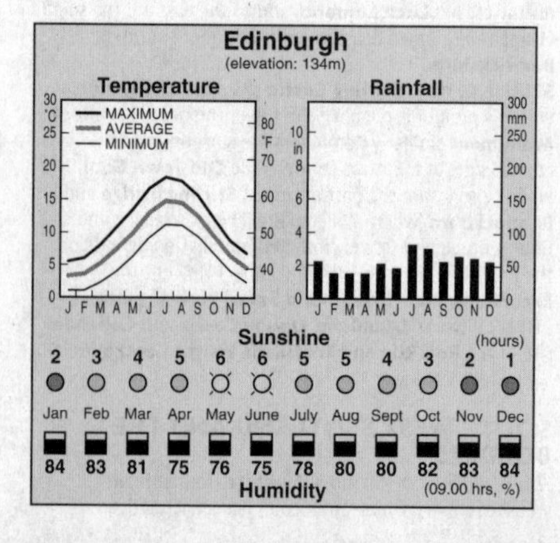

A B C D E F G H I J K L M N O P Q R S T U V W X Y Z

Wales

LATEST TRAVEL ADVICE CONTACTS

British Foreign and Commonwealth Office
Tel: (0870) 606 0290 Website: www.fco.gov.uk

US Department of State
Website: http://travel.state.gov/travel

Canadian Department of Foreign Affairs and Int'l Trade
Tel: (1 800) 267 8376 Website: www.dfait-maeci.gc.ca

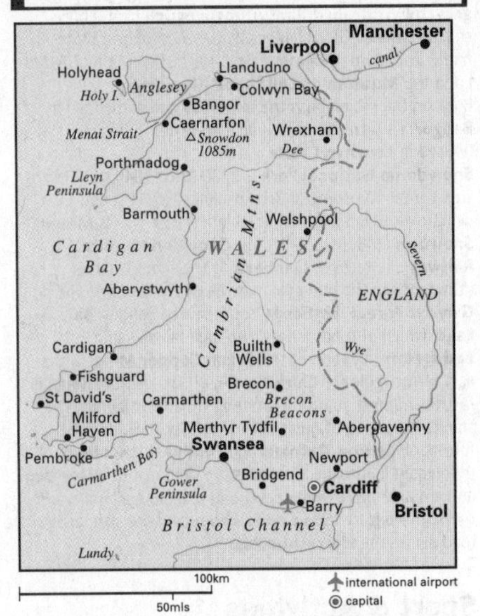

Location: Western Great Britain.

Wales Tourist Board/Bwrdd Croeso Cymru
1st and 10th Floors, Brunel House, 2 Fitzalan Road, Cardiff CF24 0UY, UK
Tel: (08701) 211 251.
Fax: (0870) 211 259.
E-mail: info@visitwales.com
Website: www.visitwales.com

Wales Tourist Board/Bwrdd Croeso Cymru
551 Fifth Avenue, 7th Floor, New York, NY 10176, USA
Tel: (800) 462 2748 (toll-free in the USA) *or* (212) 850 0347.
Fax: (212) 370 6638.
E-mail: walesinfo@visitbritain.org
Website: www.visitwales.com

General Information

AREA: 20,732 sq km (8004 sq miles).
POPULATION: 2,918,700 (2002).
POPULATION DENSITY: 140.8 per sq km.
CAPITAL: Cardiff. **Population:** 305,200 (official estimate 2001).
GEOGRAPHY: Wales is a country of great geographical variation with many long stretches of attractive and often rugged coastline. South Wales is mainly known for its industrial heritage but the western part of the coast between Carmarthen Bay and St David's is similar to that of the more pastoral west country of England, and backed by some equally beautiful countryside. The scenery of mid-Wales includes rich farming valleys, the broad sandy sweep of Cardigan Bay and rolling hill country. North Wales is one of the most popular tourist areas in the British Isles, with many lively coastal resorts. Inland, the region of Snowdonia has long been popular with walkers and climbers. Much of the central inland area of the country is mountainous, with some breathtaking scenery.
GOVERNMENT: Following a referendum in May 1999, Wales was granted its own assembly with a considerable degree of autonomy. The Welsh Assembly does not have a similar level of power and responsibility as that enjoyed by the Scottish Parliament. **Head of State:** HM Queen Elizabeth II. **Head of Government:** First Secretary Rhodri Morgan since 2000.
LANGUAGE: English and Welsh are the official languages. Welsh is taught in all schools, and at least one-fifth of the population speaks it.
For information on time, electricity and communications, see the main *United Kingdom* section.

Public Holidays

Note: Public holidays observed in Wales are the same as those observed in the rest of the UK (see the main United Kingdom section) with the addition of:

Credit: © Wales Tourist Board

2005: Aug 22 Summer Bank Holiday.
2006: Aug 28 Summer Bank Holiday.

Travel - International

AIR: Wales' international airport is *Cardiff International Airport (CWL)* (website: www.cardiffairportonline.com; airport information: tel: (01446) 711 111). Facilities include buffets, snack bar, bars, bureaux de change, ATMs, duty- and tax-free shops, numerous other shops, travel agency, children's play area, executive lounge and facilities for the disabled. **Train:** Local buses link the airport with Cardiff Central station, which is 19km (12 miles) away. The station is served by the InterCity network and regional lines, including a fast service to London Paddington. There are also bus connections to Barry Town Station, 8km (5 miles) from the airport. **Coach:** Regular coach services operate to Cardiff Central Bus Station from London Victoria and other major destinations with connections to the rest of the country. **Local bus:** Bus nos X91, X45 and X35 run from Cardiff bus station to the airport on an hourly basis (Mon to Sat). Service X5 runs from Cardiff bus station every two hours on a Sunday. **Taxi:** Available through local operator *Cardiff Airport Taxis* (tel: (01446) 710 693). **Car hire:** *Europcar* has an office at the airport; *Avis* and *Hertz* also provide services. **Private car:** Cardiff is reached on the M4 from London, exiting at Junction 33 and following the signs. Car-parking facilities are available at the airport for short- and long-term stays.
SEA: The main ports are Fishguard and Holyhead (Anglesey), both of which have ferry connections to the Republic of Ireland.
RAIL: There are two main-line routes into Wales. One runs from London Paddington to Fishguard along the South Wales coast (branching at Whitland to serve Haverford West and Milford Haven), while the other links Holyhead with Chester and northwest England. In addition, the line from Cardiff to Chester (via Newport, Hereford and Shrewsbury) links the south Wales cities with Abergavenny in Gwent and Wrexham in Clwyd. There are also two smaller cross-country lines: these run from Shrewsbury to Welshpool, Barmouth, Harlech, Porthmadog and Pwllheli; from Shrewsbury via Welshpool to Aberystwyth; and from Craven Arms (on the Shrewsbury–Ludlow line) through Llandrindod Wells and Llandovery down to Swansea. There are also a large number of local steam railways, rescued by railway enthusiasts during the Beeching era, known collectively as **The Great Little Trains of Wales**. The most famous of these is the one at Ffestiniog, Porthmadog in Snowdonia, which has lovingly restored locomotives and carriages from the last century. Others include the *Welshpool and Llanfair Railway* (in north Powys), the *Fairbourne and Talyllyn Railways* (both near Barmouth in Cardigan Bay) and the *Bala Lake Railway*. Wanderers' Tickets are available, giving access to all the railways for a specific period. For further information, contact The Great Little Trains of Wales, c/o Talyllyn Railway, Wharf Station, Tywyn, Gwynedd LL36 9EY (tel: (01654) 710 472; fax: (01654) 711 755; e-mail: enquiries@talyllyn.co.uk; website: www.talyllyn.co.uk).
ROAD: The best road approach to Wales from southern England is via the M4 motorway, which runs from west London to Newport, Cardiff and Swansea, almost to Carmarthen. The A5 links London and the Midlands with the ferry port of Holyhead, and the A55 links Holyhead with Chester. The best cross-country road is probably the A44/A470 from Oxford to Aberystwyth. Many of the smaller roads are slow, and in upland areas may become impassable during bad weather. The bilingual Mantais Cymru information line, operated on behalf of the National Assembly for Wales (NAW), offers primary access to the very latest traffic and road user information for travel to, from and within Wales (info line tel: 0845 602 6020; e-mail: info@traffic-wales.com; website: www.traffic-wales.com). **Distances:** From London to *Cardiff* is 249km (155 miles), to *Fishguard* is 425km (264 miles), to *Holyhead* is 476km (296 miles) and to *Aberystwyth* is 394km (245 miles).
URBAN: All the main cities have local bus services. There is a good network of local train services radiating from Cardiff.

Accommodation

HOTELS: Hotels in Wales are subject to the Wales Tourist Board's 'star' classification scheme. The higher the star rating, the greater the range of quality, comfort, equipment, facilities and services on offer. **Grading: 1-star:** Fair to good quality in standards of service, furnishings and guest care; **2-star:** Good quality; **3-star:** Very good quality; **4-star:** Excellent quality; **5-star:** Exceptional quality. The star grading classification scheme also applies to **guest houses, farmhouses, inns** and **hostels**. The star ratings for these types of accommodation reflect the nature of the accommodation and guest expectations (eg inns can achieve 5 stars, as long as the standards of service, facilities and comfort are of the highest quality).
Further information may be obtained from the brochures produced by the Wales Tourist Board (see *Contact Addresses* section). In addition, the Board's north, mid- and south Wales regional tourist companies have lists of accommodation available in their areas.
SELF-CATERING: There is a very wide variety of self-catering accommodation, ranging from holiday villages in or near popular coastal resorts to remote cottages in the mountains of Snowdonia. Contact the regional offices referred to above for an up-to-date list. **Grading:** Accommodation is graded on a scale of 1 to 5 stars, as follows: **1** – Standard; **2** – Approved; **3** – Good; **4** – Very good; **5** – Excellent.
CAMPING/CARAVANNING: There are over 300 caravan parks in the country, both permanent and touring parks, and all sites referred to in accommodation lists or brochures supplied by tourist offices will meet certain minimum requirements. There are many campsites throughout the country. **Grading:** Sites are graded on a scale of **1** to **5 stars** reflecting quality, neatness and cleanliness but not necessarily facilities.

Resorts & Excursions

Populous South Wales incorporates the capital Cardiff, the cities of Swansea and Newport, Carmarthen Bay and two national parks, Pembrokeshire Coast and Brecon Beacons.

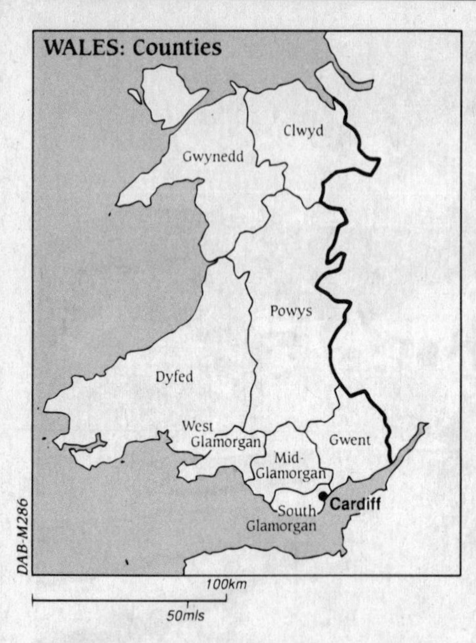

The Cambrian Mountains and the attractive coastal resorts of Cardigan Bay are highlights of mid-Wales, while the North has popular seaside resorts like Llandudno and Rhyl, the island of Anglesey and the scenic delights of Snowdonia National Park.

Wales is an historic land of castles and mountains, sweeping beaches and strong national identity dating back to pre-Norman times. There is an industrial heritage, primarily in the Valleys of the south. It is also famous for its narrow-gauge railways (see *Rail* in the *Travel* section).

SOUTH WALES

CARDIFF (CAERDYDD): The modern city has two parts: the original centre and **Cardiff Bay**, which is now the focus of much leisure and tourism development, as well as home of the **Welsh National Assembly**.

In the city centre, parts of **Cardiff Castle**, despite extensive rebuilding in the 19th century, date back to the Middle Ages. The **National Museum and Gallery**, with Welsh archaeology, arts and crafts, as well as European paintings, is another highlight, as are the many attractive Victorian shopping arcades. The **Millennium Stadium**, new home of Welsh Rugby Union, is an imposing attraction open for guided tours on non-matchdays.

The Cardiff Bay area, about 2km (1.5 miles) south of the centre, offers diverse activities ranging from boat trips to the impressive **Barrage** (which now seals the Bay off from the open sea), to the **Techniquest Science Discovery Centre**. About 8km (5 miles) west of Cardiff is **St Fagans** with its open-air **Museum of Welsh Life**.

SWANSEA (ABERTAWE): The country's second city has over 45 parks, is a popular seaside resort, and is conveniently close to the **Gower Peninsula**. However, it is probably best known as the birthplace of Dylan Thomas (1914-1953). A city centre walking trail begins at the **Dylan Thomas Centre**, and leads visitors around sites associated with the poet and playwright. Elsewhere in the city, the **Swansea Museum** dates from the 1830s. The **Egypt Centre Museum** specialises, as its name suggests, in Egyptology, while pottery, porcelain and modern art feature at the **Glynn Vivian Art Gallery**. At **Parc Tawe**, **Plantasia** is a high-tech tropical hothouse with plants from all over the world. A new Arts Wing was recently opened in Swansea's **Grand Theatre**, the city's main show venue. **Mumbles**, a suburb of Swansea, is also an important resort.

ELSEWHERE: Chepstow, whose castle and town walls date from medieval times, straddles the English/Welsh border. Nearby **Caerwent** is rich in Roman remains. Between Cardiff and the English border is **Newport**, Wales' third-largest town, which has a 15th-century cathedral. South Wales' biggest inland draw is the **Brecon Beacons National Park**, whose main touring bases are **Brecon** and **Abergavenny**. The narrow-gauge **Brecon Mountain Railway** runs through the hills from **Merthyr Tydfil**.

In the Valleys, **Blaenafon** (a UNESCO World Heritage Site) offers industrial heritage attractions in the shape of **Big Pit Mining Museum** and the **Ironworks**. **Caerphilly** has a massive castle, and at nearby **Treharris** is **Llancaiach Fawr Living History Museum**.

Numerous resorts line the coast between Cardiff and Swansea, including **Aberavon**, **Barry** and **Porthcawl**. Others, along the **Gower Peninsula**, include **Oxwich** and **Port Eynon**.

The former county of Pembrokeshire, in the west, has many castles as well as the **Pembrokeshire Coast National Park**. The best-known religious building in the area is the cathedral of **St David's**, Britain's smallest city.

MID-WALES

ABERYSTWYTH: A university town midway round Cardigan Bay, and a popular resort. It is the base for visits to **Devil's Bridge Waterfalls**, one of Britain's most notable beauty spots, linked to the town by the **Vale of Rheidol** narrow-gauge steam railway. There are two other similar railways close by; the **Tal-y-Llyn Railway**, which runs for about 10km (16 miles) from **Abergynolwyn** through beautiful countryside to **Tywyn**; and the **Fairbourne Railway** linking Fairbourne with the Barmouth Ferry. Aberystwyth also has Britain's longest electric cliff railway, and the **Ceredigion Local History Museum**.

MACHYNLLETH: Celtica is a major visitor attraction here, focusing on Wales' Celtic heritage, while underground boat trips and spectacular showcaves feature at **King Arthur's Labyrinth**. The town also boasts the **Centre for Alternative Technology**, which highlights environmental issues and sustainable energy use; **Senedd-Dy Owain Glyndwr** (the 15th-century Welsh parliament building) and the **Y Tabernael** modern art gallery.

WELSHPOOL: To the east of the region, near the English border, this is an attractive town with many Georgian buildings and the **Welshpool and Llanfair** narrow-gauge railway. The **Andrew Logan Museum of Sculpture** is popular, as are cruises on the **Montgomery Canal**. South of the town is the splendid **Powis Castle**, built in the 13th century and modernised 300 years later.

ELSEWHERE: Cardigan, at the southern end of **Cardigan Bay** (*Bae Ceredigion*), is a pleasant market town and a good starting point for exploring western parts of Mid-Wales. Along the bay there are many small resort towns and villages, rocky coves and sandy beaches.

Barmouth was once one of the most popular resorts in the British Isles, frequented by such luminaries as Darwin and Tennyson. There are good beaches, both in the town and near **Dyffryn Ardudwy** to the north.

Towns of interest inland include **Builth Wells**, an important cattle-trading town; **Strata Florida Abbey**; **Lampeter** and **Tregaron** on the **River Teifi**; and **Llandrindod Wells**, Wales' foremost spa resort in the late 18th and early 19th centuries.

On the northern tip of Cardigan Bay is **Harlech**, famous for both its castle that overlooks the peaks of Snowdonia, and for the stirring song, 'Men of Harlech', referring to the 15th-century defence of the castle. South of Harlech is **Llanbedr**, a popular yachting centre.

NORTH WALES

CAERNARFON: Facing the **Isle of Anglesey** across the **Menai Strait** is Caernarfon, whose 13th-century castle and walls dominate the town. Prince Charles' investiture as Prince of Wales took place here in 1969. The **Segontium Roman Fort** is another attraction. Work is currently under way on a 40km- (25 mile-) extension to the narrow-gauge **Welsh Highland Railway**, which will ultimately connect Caernarfon with Porthmadog.

CONWY: With its mighty castle and complete medieval town walls, Conwy is an important historic centre. It also offers the tropical **Butterfly Jungle** and riverbus cruises along the **Conwy River**. The **Royal Cambrian Academy of Art** is also in the town, whose **Visitor Centre** presents a multimedia show about the area. Nearby are the superb **Bodnant Gardens**.

LLANDUDNO: Beneath **Great Orme Head** lies one of the country's busiest resorts. It has almost every possible amenity, as well as being within striking distance of the beautiful hinterland, which includes the **Snowdonia National Park**. The town's attractions include the **Great Orme Mines**, the world's largest prehistoric site of its type, the **Llandudno Cable Car**, which climbs to the summit of Great Orme, and the **North Wales Theatre**, a major arts venue.

RHYL: A town with a 5km- (3 mile-) promenade and extensive leisure and recreation facilities. It is a good base for excursions to **St Asaph**, a city with the smallest medieval cathedral in Britain. Major attractions in Rhyl include the **Sea Life Aquarium**, the **Rhyl Museum and Art Gallery**, as well as the **Pavilion Theatre**.

WREXHAM: Close to the English border, Wrexham is the largest town in North Wales. Attractions such as the **Arts Centre**, the nearby **Minera Lead Mines** and **Bersham Ironworks Heritage Centre** are the main points of interest in an otherwise industrial town. A kilometre south lies **Erddig**, a 17th-century squire's house containing much of the traditional furniture and with many of the outbuildings still in their original condition and in working order.

ELSEWHERE: One of the longest established tourist areas in the British Isles, north coast beach resorts like **Llandudno**, **Prestatyn** and **Rhyl** still remain popular with holidaymakers. The chain of resorts continues almost unbroken for miles; **Abergele**, **Colwyn Bay** (location of the Welsh Mountain Zoo), **Prestatyn** and **Rhos-on-Sea** all have good beaches. Further east lie **Bagillt** and **Flint**, former capital of Flintshire (the modern capital of which is **Mold**).

Porthmadog on **Tremadog Bay** is another resort town – close to here is the village of **Portmeirion**, location for the 1960s *Prisoner* TV series and home of Portmeirion china. The world's oldest independent narrow-gauge railway, the **Ffestiniog Railway**, carries thousands of visitors from Porthmadog to **Blaenau Ffestiniog** each year, many of whom go to see the **Llechwedd Slate Caverns**. West from Porthmadog is the **Lleyn Peninsula**, with its many good beaches, particularly on the south coast, at towns such as **Criccieth** (home of the **Lloyd George Museum**), **Pwllheli**, **Abersoch**, **Aberdaron** and, on the northern coast, **Nefyn** and **Clynnog-Fawr**. **Anglesey**, known as **Ynys Môn** locally, is notable for the remarkable **Menai Bridge**, the **Anglesey Sea Zoo** at **Brynsiencyn**, and **Llanfairpwllgwyngyllgo-gerychwyrndrobwllllantysiliogogogoch** (commonly called Llanfair PG), which boasts the UK's longest place name. The town of **Beaumaris** has a castle built by Edward I and the **Museum of Childhood Memories**.

Back on the mainland is the university and cathedral city of **Bangor**; its attractions include a huge doll collection housed in **Penrhyn Castle**.

Snowdonia National Park is 2200 sq km (840 sq miles) in size, containing some of Britain's finest scenery, and 14 peaks over 915m (3000ft), the highest of which is **Mount Snowdon** (1085m, 3556ft). The **Snowdon Mountain Railway** climbs from **Llanberis** to the summit. Other attractions in the region include **Betws-y-Coed**, in the **Gwydyr Forest**; **Bethesda**, southeast of Bangor; **Bala Lake**, which also has a narrow-gauge railway; and **Beddgelert**, location of the **Sygun Copper Mine**. In the east of the region is **Chirk Castle**, a 14th-century Marcher fortress built to guard the frontier, which it straddles. It stands in an area of great natural beauty, including the forests of **Ceiriog**, **Dyfnant** and **Penllyn**. **Llangollen**, set in forested landscape, overlooks the salmon-rich **River Dee** and a masterpiece of medieval bridge building. Nearby are the 13th-century **Vale Crucis Abbey** and the spectacular road across the **Horseshoe Pass**.

Sport & Activities

Rugby Union: This is the national sport and is played to the very highest level of skill. There are a huge number of local clubs and the international team plays matches at the national venue, the *Millennium Stadium*.

Walking: Wales is a beautiful and mountainous country, ideal for walkers and hikers. There are three national parks: the *Brecon Beacons*, the *Pembrokeshire Coast Path National Park* and *Snowdonia*. The highest peaks are in the north, where the mountains are also more rugged. This area is very popular with climbers, who will find many climbs, scrambles and chimneys of varying degrees of difficulty. There are a lot of outdoor centres and shops where equipment can be hired or bought, and expeditions and tuition for all levels of ability can be arranged. Apart from Mount Snowdon itself (Wales's highest peak at 1085m/3556ft), northern Snowdonia contains the ranges of the *Carnedds*, the *Glyders*, *Moel Hebog* and the *Nantlle Hills*. In southern Snowdonia are the Moelwyns, the Rhinogs, the Arans and Cadair Idris. A classic walk is the 'Snowdon Horseshoe', a 9.5 mile- (15km-) circuit of three glacier-carved valleys near Snowdon. Taking in the knife-edge ridge of Crib Goch on the way to Snowdon's summit, it provides stunning views, but is only suitable for experienced walkers. It is often started at Pen-y-pass, six miles from Llanberis.

The Brecon Beacons offer easier, though still quite challenging, walking while the nearby Wye Valley offers gentle beauty. In the west of the country is the 189 mile- (304km-) 'Pembrokeshire Coast Path', which runs along the coast from Amroth near Tenby to St Dogmaels near Cardigan. The area is of particular interest to birdwatchers, owing to the variety and number of seabirds living on the cliffs there. Other long-distance walks include 'Offa's Dyke Path' (177 miles/285km), which follows the original border between England and Wales. It is strenuous in parts with continual ascents and descents.

Cycling: This can be done all over Wales, though the mountainous terrain can make it strenuous. There are plenty of off-road trails for mountain bikers; the tourist board can provide details of way-marked routes. A new route, the 'Celtic Trail', covers 186 miles, 70 per cent of which is off-road; the trail runs between Newport in the east and Kedwelly in the west. It consists of disused railway lines, canal towpaths and quiet roads, which makes it suitable for all levels of ability. There is also a new high-level route between Pontypridd and Neath.

Watersports: Both the coastal and the inland waters offer endless opportunities for all types of watersports, and there are excellent facilities throughout the country. Wales's three coastlines have no shortage of harbours and marinas, many of them newly developed. Mountain scenery, cliffs, islands and small secluded beaches are some of the attractions for sailors here. Seals, dolphins, basking sharks and porpoise can be seen in offshore waters. West Wales offers some of the best **sea-kayaking** in the world. **Windsurfing** can be done

from beaches in the west (many of which have won European Blue Flag awards – see *Resorts & Excursions* section for further details). The fast tidal streams of the *Menai Straits*, the narrow passage between Angelsey and the mainland, are popular with sailors wishing to test their skills. Boats and tuition are available if necessary from numerous watersports centres. Inland, lakes and rivers offer opportunities for **canoeing**, **sailing** and **dinghy sailing**. Bala Lake is a major centre for these activities, as well as for fishing. **White water** suitable for canoeing and **rafting** can be found nearby. In south Wales, major watersports centres include Llangorse (for windsurfing, canoeing and waterskiing) and Llandegfydd (for windsurfing and sailing).
Other: There are many **golf** courses, **tennis** courts and sports centres throughout the country. Sea **fishing** is good off all coasts and there are also many opportunities for coarse and game fishing inland; Brecon, Snowdonia and the River Teifi (Cardigan) are among the most popular.

Social Profile

FOOD & DRINK: In most major centres, British and continental food is available. Welsh cooking is, in general, simple with abundant fresh local produce, particularly meat and fish. Near the coast, seafood is also widely available. Local dishes include *Welsh rarebit* (cheese on toast), *leek soup, bara brith* (a type of tea bread) and *laver bread*, which is made with seaweed.
NIGHTLIFE: In general, it is similar to that of an English town of comparable size, with bars, restaurants and cinemas being common in the cities and large towns.
SPECIAL EVENTS: *St David's Day* (Mar 1) is dedicated to the patron saint of Wales. Although it is not a public holiday, schoolchildren celebrate and learn about their culture through music, poetry and cookery on this day. Many Welsh villages hold an *Eisteddfod* once a year – a contest for local poets, singers and musicians. All but the largest ones are generally advertised only inside the town itself but visitors are welcome to attend. The following is a selection of special events occurring in Wales in 2005:
Jan 1 *Calennig* (traditional New Year Celebrations), Cardiff. **Jan 6** *Twelfth Night Burning on the Beach*, Saundersfoot. **Jan 7-9** *Saturnalia Roma Festival*, Llanwrtyd Wells. **Apr 2-3** *Gourmet Festival of Fine Food & Drink*, Llanwrtydd Wells. **May 30-Jan 4** *Hay Festival of Literature*, Hay-on-Wye. **Jun 15-26** *Man V Horse Marathon*, Llanwrtyd Wells. **Jul 5-10** *Llangollen International Musical Eisteddfod*. **Jul 18-21** *Royal Welsh Show*. **Jul 24-26** *The Big Cheese*, Caerphilly. **Aug 1-6** *National Eisteddfod of Wales*, Faenol. **Aug 12-14** *Brecon Jazz Festival*. **Oct 1-2** *Apple Festival at Erddig*, Wrexham. **Nov 11-20** *Mid-Wales Beer Festival*, Llanwrtydd Wells.
Note: Accommodation at festival times should be booked well in advance.

Business Profile

BUSINESS: See main *United Kingdom* section.
CONFERENCES/CONVENTIONS: The Wales Tourist Board/Bwrdd Croeso Cymru publishes two brochures on conferences and incentives, as well as a group directory. For information, contact the Business Tourism Unit, Wales Tourist Board, 10th Floor, Brunel House, 2 Fitzalan Road, Cardiff, CF24 0YU (tel: (029) 2047 5202; fax: (029) 2047 5321).

Climate

Wales tends to be wetter than England, with slightly less sunshine. The coastal areas, however, can be very warm in summer. Conditions in upland areas can be dangerous and changeable at all times of the year.
Required clothing: Similar to the rest of the UK, according to season. Waterproofing advised throughout the year, and warm clothes are required for upland areas.

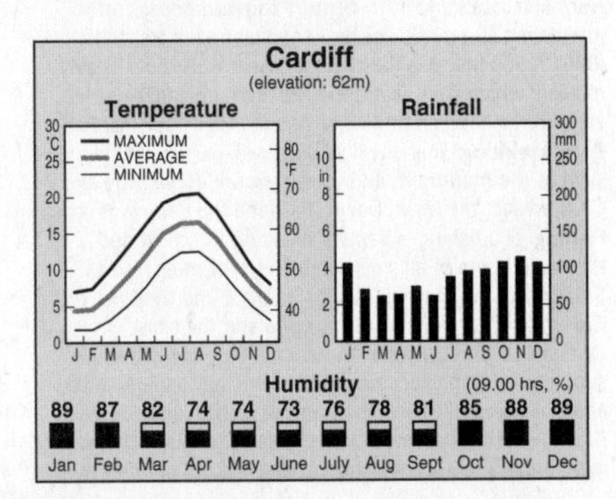

Northern Ireland

LATEST TRAVEL ADVICE CONTACTS

British Foreign and Commonwealth Office
Tel: (0870) 606 0290 Website: www.fco.gov.uk
US Department of State
Website: http://travel.state.gov/travel
Canadian Department of Foreign Affairs and Int'l Trade
Tel: (1 800) 267 8376 Website: www.dfait-maeci.gc.ca

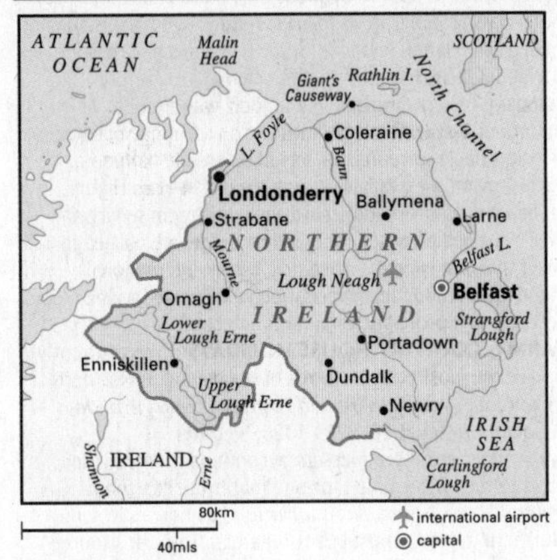

Location: Northern Ireland.

Northern Ireland Tourist Board
St Anne's Court, 59 North Street, Belfast BT1 1NB, Northern Ireland, UK
Tel: (02890) 231 221. Fax: (02890) 240 960.
E-mail: info@nitb.com
Website: www.discovernorthernireland.com
Belfast Welcome Centre
47 Donegal Place, Belfast BT1 5AD, Northern Ireland, UK
Tel: (02890) 246 609. Fax: (02890) 312 424.
E-mail: info@belfastvisitor.com
Website: www.gotobelfast.com
Tourism Ireland
Nations House, 103 Wigmore Street, London W1U 1QS, UK
Tel: (020) 7518 0800 (trade enquiries only) *or* (0800) 039 7000 (brochure request line and enquiries).
Fax: (020) 7493 9065.
E-mail: info.gb@tourismireland.com
Website: www.tourismireland.com
Tourism Ireland
345 Park Avenue, 51st Street, 17th Floor, New York, NY 10154, USA
Tel: (800) 223 6470 (tourist info) *or* (800) 669 9967 (travel agents). Fax: (212) 371 9052.
E-mail: info.us@tourismireland.com
Website: www.tourismireland.com
Tourism Ireland
2 Bloor Street West, Suite 3403, Toronto, Ontario M4W 3E2, Canada
Tel: (416) 925 6368 *or* (800) 223 6470 (consumer enquiries) *or* (866) 477 7717 (travel trade only).
E-mail: info.ca@tourismireland.com
Website: www.tourismireland.com

General Information

AREA: 13,576 sq km (5242 sq miles).
POPULATION: 1,696,814 (official estimate 2001).
POPULATION DENSITY: 125.0 per sq km.
CAPITAL: Belfast. **Population:** 277,100 (official estimate 2001).
GEOGRAPHY: Northern Ireland contains some beautiful scenery, from the rugged coastline in the north and northeast to the gentle fruit-growing regions of Armagh. To the west are the Sperrin Mountains and the lake of Fermanagh, where the winding River Erne provides excellent fishing. The high moorland plateau of Antrim in the northeast gives way to the glens further south and to the Drumlin country of County Down; further south still, the Mountains of Mourne stretch down to the sea.
GOVERNMENT: In 1998, the Good Friday Agreement between Northern Ireland's political parties, the United Kingdom and the Republic of Ireland provided for the transfer of responsibility for the administration of Northern Ireland from the United Kingdom to an elected Northern Ireland Assembly and Executive. **Head of State:** HM Queen Elizabeth II. **Head of Government:** Prime Minister Tony Blair.
LANGUAGE: English. Irish is spoken by a minority.
For information on religion, time, electricity and communications, see the main *United Kingdom* section.

Money

For information on currency, credit cards, travellers cheques, exchange rates and currency restrictions, see the main *United Kingdom* section.
Note: For travelling around and staying at small hotels, cash is needed. Elsewhere, as in England, cheques backed by a banker's card are widely accepted.
Some hotels will change money but *Thomas Cook* (there is one in Belfast, for example) and the banks give the best rate of exchange.
Banking hours: Mon-Fri 0900-1600. In very small villages, the bank may open two or three days a week only, so aim to get cash in the bigger centres.

Public Holidays

Public holidays observed in Northern Ireland are the same as those observed in the rest of the UK (see the main United Kingdom section) with the addition of:
2005: Mar 17 St Patrick's Day. **Jul 12** Battle of the Boyne (Orangemen's Day). **Aug 22** Summer Bank Holiday.
2006: Mar 17 St Patrick's Day. **Jul 12** Battle of the Boyne (Orangemen's Day). **Aug 28** Summer Bank Holiday.

Travel - International

AIR: There are frequent direct flights to Belfast from London's Heathrow, Gatwick, Luton and Stansted airports as well as other major regional UK airports. Airlines that serve Northern Ireland from the UK include *bmibaby, British Airways, EasyJet, Flybe* and *RyanAir*. From North America, *Aer Lingus* operates flights from Atlanta, Ballimore, Boston, Chicago, Los Angeles and New York to Shannon and Dublin. *Continental Airlines* flies from New York (JFK) to Dublin or Shannon. *US Airways* flies from Philadelphia from Dublin or Shannon. Other major airlines operate services from the USA and Canada to Belfast via London, Glasgow and Manchester. There are also direct charter flights from Toronto to Belfast.
Belfast International Airport (BFS): Located 29km (18 miles) northwest of Belfast city centre. Airport information: tel: (028) 9448 4848; website: www.bial.co.uk. Facilities include bureau de change, ATMs, duty free and general shops, a variety of catering facilities, including an international food court, bar and coffee shop, nursing mothers' room, facilities for the disabled, children's play area, and emergency medical services. There is also an executive lounge at the airport, which costs £7-12 to use, depending on your carrier. **Train:** There is at present no direct rail link to Belfast International Airport, but trains run from Londonderry (Derry), Lisburn and Belfast to Antrim (10km/6 miles away) from where a taxi may be hired, or a shuttle bus can be taken to the airport. Trains to and from Dublin are via Belfast Central Station, which has its own *Airbus* stop. A rail timetable is on display at the main exit from the terminal. **Bus:** *Airbus* (Ulsterbus) runs to the city centre Mon to Sat every 30 minutes and Sun every 30 to 60 minutes (tel: (028) 9066 6630). *Airporter Derrydirect* coaches (tel: (028) 7126 9996) travel to the airport from Londonderry (Derry). Coach: The *Antrim Airlink* operates Mon to Fri, £1.40, single fare/£2.50, return fare. It connects with Londonderry, Portrush, Coleraine, Magherafelt and Ballymena. *AIRPorter* operates a direct service to Londonderry every two hours. **Taxi:** Travel time to city centre – 25 minutes. Taxis are available for hire outside the main airport building. Fares are displayed at the exit from the terminal or are available from the information desk. **Car hire:** *Avis, Budget, Cosmo Thrifty, Dan Dooley, Europcar, Hertz* and *National Car Rental* are represented at the airport. **Private car:** The M1 provides the main link with Fermanagh and the west of the Province whilst forming part of the journey to and from Dublin and the east coast of Ireland. The M2 is the airport's main link with the centre of Belfast and to Londonderry (Derry), 116km (72 miles) to the northwest. There is nearby car parking for short and long stays. Access is from the M1 and M2 (parking is available) or by train to Antrim and then taxi.
The small *Belfast City Airport (BHD)* (tel: (028) 9093 9093; website: www.belfastcityairport.com) at *Belfast Harbour* is handy for flights to most regional airports. Regular train and bus services run to the city centre.
Note: For approximate durations of a selection of domestic flights from Belfast, see *Travel* in the main *United Kingdom* section.
Departure tax: None.
SEA: Four ferry companies operate direct services between mainland Europe and Ireland. *Irish Ferries* (tel: (08705) 171 717) operates between between Cherbourg, Roscoff and Rosslare (approximate travel time – 19 hours). *Brittany Ferries* operates the Roscoff-Cork route with one departure per week in each direction from April to September only (travel time – 14 hours). For more information, contact *Brittany Ferries* in Cork (tel: (00353) 2142 77801). *P&O Irish Sea* run ferries between Cherbourg and Rosslare. The *Isle of Man Steam Packet Company's Seacat* (tel: (1800) 805 055; website: www.steam-packet.com) runs a seacat crossing

A B C D E F G H I J K L M N O P Q R S T U V W X Y Z

from Douglas (Isle of Man) to Belfast (travel time – two hours and 45 minutes).

When travelling via Great Britain to Northern Ireland there is a choice of five services across the Irish Sea: *P&O Irish Sea* (tel: (0870) 242 4777) offers frequent daily services between Cairnryan (southern Scotland) to Larne (travel time – one hour 45 minutes), and between Fleetwood and Larne (travel time – eight hours); *Stena Line* (tel: (08705) 204 204) operates frequent daily services between Stranraer (southern Scotland) and Belfast (travel time – one hour 45 minutes). In addition there are frequent crossings between Troon and Larne (travel time – four hours) and Heysham and Belfast (travel time – four hours) by the *Isle of Man Steam Packet Company's Seacat*. An overnight service and daily services are offered on the Liverpool to Belfast route and Liverpool to Dublin route by *Norse Merchant Ferries* (travel time – seven hours 30 minutes; tel: (0870) 600 432). *Irish Ferries* also offer services between Rosslare and Pembroke (travel time – three hours 45 minutes), Rosslare and Cherbourg or Roscoff (France) and also Dublin and Holyhead.

Northern Ireland's only inhabited island is Rathlin, a few kilometres off the north coast. There are frequent passenger boats between Ballycastle and the island. At peak holiday times a sailing/regulation ticket is required as well as a travel ticket. Check when booking. It is always advisable to book a return journey before leaving home.

RAIL: There are four main rail routes from Belfast Central Station: north to Londonderry via Ballymena and Coleraine; north east to the port of Larne; east to Bangor along the shores of Belfast Lough; south to Dublin, in the Irish Republic, via Newry. The Belfast–Dublin non-stop express takes about two hours. There are eight trains daily in both directions (five on Sunday). The busiest times are holiday weekends and the first and last trains on Friday and Sunday, when it is best to reserve seats. Freedom of Northern Ireland passes are available for unlimited travel on trains and buses (costing £12 for one day; £30 for three days and £45 for seven days, to be used within eight days of purchase) and are available from main Northern Ireland railway stations. For information on timetables for *all* rail services, contact *Translink* for *Northern Ireland Railways Information Centre*, Central Station, East Bridge Street, Belfast BT1 3PB (tel: (028) 9066 6630).

ROAD: Bus: Northern Ireland has an excellent bus network and there are particularly good bus links between those towns which are not served by rail. *Translink* operates both *Citylink*, which provides services in Belfast, and *Ulsterbus*, which is responsible for all other services in Northern Ireland. Belfast has three main bus stations: Great Victoria Street, Laganside and Newtonabbey. *Centrelink* buses (service 100) provide links between Belfast's principal rail and bus stations, as well as main shopping centres and the Waterfront Hall. In total, *Citybus* operates over 60 different routes in and around the capital, including two express services between Glengormley and Newtonabbey and the centre, and eight nightlink services that depart from Donegal Square West, Fri to Sat 0100-0200. Ulsterbus operates a comprehensive network of services across the rest of the country, including some scenic routes such as the *Antrim Coaster* (Belfast–Antrim Coast–Portrush–Coleraine), the *Lakeland Express* (Enniskillen–Belfast) and the *Orchard Express* (Belfast–Portadown–Armagh). For more information on any of these services, timetables or prices, contact Translink (tel: (028) 9066 6630; website: www.translink.co.uk).

Traffic regulations: Traffic drives on the left. The speed limit is 30mph (48kph) in towns and cities unless signs show 40mph (64kph) or 50mph (80kph). On country roads, the limit is 60mph (96kph); on dual carriageways, trunk roads and motorways, 70mph (112kph), unless signs show otherwise.

Breakdowns: If the car is rented, contact the rental company. Members of the continental equivalent of the *Automobile Association (AA)* (tel: (0870) 600 0371) can contact their 24-hour breakdown service. The *Royal Automobile Club (RAC)* (tel: (0800) 919 700) provides a similar service. They can be contacted from their roadside phones or from any call box. Non-members should consult the Yellow Pages for breakdown services.

Parking: Permitted where there is a blue 'P' sign, which indicates a car park in towns or a lay-by at the roadside outside towns. Drivers can park elsewhere on the street except when there is a single yellow line, when parking is permitted only at the times shown on the yellow signs nearby; or when there is a double yellow line, which prohibits all parking. Control Zones, which are usually in town centres, are indicated by yellow signs: 'Control Zone. No Unattended Parking'. An unattended car in a Control Zone is treated as a security risk. Never park on zigzag markings near pedestrian crossings. In some towns, the centre may be sealed off at certain times, particularly overnight. Alternative routes will be signposted.

Taxi: Available at main stations, ports and Belfast Airport and are also bookable by telephone in larger towns and cities.

Car hire: The main firms – *Avis*, *Europcar* and *Hertz* – all operate in Northern Ireland and have desks at Belfast International Airport with cars available on the spot. There is also a host of smaller firms.

Accommodation

A wide range of accommodation is available in Northern Ireland. Contact the Northern Ireland Tourist Board for the *Where to Stay in Northern Ireland Guide* and *The B&B Guide*, which give full lists of available accommodation.

HOTELS: Brochures from the Northern Ireland Tourist Board give full details of services. Most establishments belong to the *Northern Ireland Hotels Federation*. For further information, contact the Northern Ireland Hotels Federation, Midland Building, Whitla Street, Belfast BT15 1JP (tel: (028) 9035 1110; fax: (028) 9035 1509; website: www.nihf.co.uk). **Grading:** The Northern Irish Tourist Board operates a 'star' classification system which is used throughout their publications. The main hotel classifications are as follows: **1-star:** Acceptable standards of accommodation and food. Some bedrooms offer ensuite bathroom; **2-star:** Good facilities, offering satisfactory standards of accommodation and food, with ensuite bathroom; **3-star:** Good facilities and a wide range of services in comfortable surroundings, including ensuite bathroom. Refreshments are available during the day; **4-star:** High standard of comfort and service, including room service and well-equipped premises. Food and beverages are obliged to meet the most exacting standards; **5-star:** International standard luxurious accommodation with superb facilities, room service and top-quality restaurants and bars.

FARM & COUNTRY HOUSE HOLIDAYS: This is currently one of the most popular forms of holidaying in Northern Ireland. The *Northern Ireland Farm & Country Holidays Association* (tel: (028) 8284 1325; website: www.nifcha.com) produces an accommodation voucher, valid for bed & breakfast for one night. The *Northern Ireland Town & Seaside Association* has houses in some of Northern Ireland's most beautiful areas, from the Mourne Mountains to the Causeway Coast, and from the Fermanagh Lakes to the Ards Peninsula, each house offering good home-cooking and a traditional Ulster welcome. The Association offers a Tour Operator rate and is happy to arrange 'go as you please' itineraries.

SELF-CATERING: There are self-catering establishments in all of Northern Ireland's six counties. For further information, contact Tourism Ireland offices *or the Northern Ireland Self-Catering Association* (tel: (028) 9077 6174; e-mail: info@nischa.com; website: www.nischa.com). *Rural Cottage Holidays Ltd* also provides a range of self-catering cottages in rural locations (tel: (028) 9024 1100; e-mail: rural.cottages@nitb.com; website: www.cottagesinireland.com).

CAMPING/CARAVANNING: There are over 100 caravan and campsites throughout the six counties of Northern Ireland. Details of the prices and facilities are contained in an information bulletin, *Camping & Caravan Parks*, available from the Northern Ireland Tourist Board. The Northern Ireland Forest Service issues permits for camping in forest areas. Contact *Forest Services*, Department of Agriculture, Dundonald House, Upper Newtownards Road, Belfast BT4 3SB (tel: (028) 9052 4480; fax: (028) 9052 4570; e-mail: customer.forestservice@dardni.gov.uk; website: www.forestserviceni.gov.uk).

YOUTH HOSTELS: There are six youth hostels throughout the six counties of Northern Ireland, including Armagh City youth hostel and Belfast International youth hostel. For further information, contact the Youth Hostel Association of Northern Ireland, 22-32 Donegall Road, Belfast BT12 5JN (tel: (028) 9032 4733; fax: (028) 9043 9699; e-mail: info@hini.org.uk; website: www.hini.org.uk).

Resorts & Excursions

COUNTY ANTRIM: To the northwest lies the **Causeway Coast** with its holiday resorts; the **Giant's Causeway**, 38,000 hexagonal basalt columns formed by cooling volcanic flow (listed by UNESCO as a World Heritage Site); and the **Old Bushmills Distillery**, one of the oldest whiskey distilleries in the world. Nearby, the massive ruined **Dunluce Castle** stands atop the cliffs.

The nine **Glens of Antrim**, and the spectacular coast road running north from **Larne**, are prime draws in the east of the county, as is **Carrickfergus Castle**, on the north shore of **Belfast Lough**. **Castle Gardens** at **Antrim**, on the northeast shore of **Lough Neagh**, exemplify 17th-century horticultural design. Nearby, **Patterson's Spade Mill** at **Templepatrick** is an unusual attraction. Ferries serve **Rathlin Island**, where Robert the Bruce supposedly observed the persistent spider, nowadays a bird sanctuary, from **Ballycastle**.

BELFAST: The capital stands on the **River Lagan** at the head of **Belfast Lough**. It offers excellent shopping and a wide range of visitor attractions. A uniquely Belfast experience is the guided bus tour around focal points of Belfast's recent history, including **Falls Road** and **Shankill Road**, to see the famous murals. The **Ulster Museum**, in the **Botanic Gardens**, covers an eclectic mix of archaeology, art and natural sciences. North of the city centre are **Belfast Zoo**, **Belfast Castle** and **Cave Hill**, a popular lookout point. The **Lagan Lookout** on **Donegall Quay** explains the river's role in Belfast's development. Opposite the refurbished **Grand Opera House** in **Great Victoria Street** is the ornate **Crown Liquor Saloon**, a Victorian public house owned by the National Trust. For younger visitors, the **Dreamworld** indoor theme park is a new venue in the Windsor district.

COUNTY ARMAGH: Northern Ireland's smallest county rises from **Lough Neagh** to rocky **Slieve Gullion**, Cuchulain's mountain, in the south. **Armagh City** is the all-Ireland religious capital, with two cathedrals; the **Armagh County Museum**; **Georgian Mall**; and the **Planetarium/Space Centre**. Outside the City, the **Navan Centre**, built at the site of ancient Ulster capital, **Emain Macha**, offers an exciting multimedia window on the past. At **Craigavon**, the **Lough Neagh Discovery Centre** explains the UK's largest lake. The lough and the **Blackwater River** both offer watersports and angling.

COUNTY DOWN: From **Silent Valley** in the mysterious **Mountains of Mourne**, to **Strangford Lough** (according to legend, St Patrick's landfall when he arrived in Ireland in AD 432) and the resort coast of **Belfast Lough**, this is a county of great variety. At **Holywood**, west of Belfast, the **Ulster Folk and Transport Museum** is a major attraction, while in **Bangor**, the **Castle** and the **North Down Heritage Centre** are highlights. **Mount Stewart House**, near **Newtonards**, is a fine stately home. **Portaferry** offers the **Exploris Aquarium**, while students of St Patrick flock to **Downpatrick**, where his grave reputedly lies in the cathedral grounds, and the **Saint Patrick Centre** tells his story. The linen industry is important to west Down culture, and visitors to **Banbridge** can take appropriately themed guided tours.

COUNTY FERMANAGH: Ulster's **Lakeland** is the predominant feature of the county. **Enniskillen**, the county town, straddles the narrows between **Upper** and **Lower Lough Erne**. Pleasure boats run to **Devenish Island**, an important early monastic site complete with round tower. **Enniskillen Castle** incorporates a **Heritage Centre** and the **Museum of the Royal Inniskilling Fusiliers** regiment. Golf, sailing, water-skiing and even pleasure flying are available nearby. Fishermen make record catches here – the lakes are said to be 'polluted with fish'. Two nearby stately homes, **Florence Court** and **Castle Coole**, are open to the public. Upon entering the **Marble Arch Caves** to the south of Enniskillen, visitors take an underground boat trip to the showcaves. At historic **Belleek Pottery** in the far west of the county, craftspeople demonstrate their skills in fine porcelain manufacture.

COUNTY LONDONDERRY: Massive 17th-century city walls and 'singing pubs' are famous features of **Derry/Londonderry**, on the **River Foyle**. The **Tower Museum** sensitively – and vividly – interprets the city's turbulent history, while the **Fifth Province** celebrates Irish Celtic culture. The **Foyle Valley Railway Centre** focuses on the region's former narrow-gauge network. The wild **Sperrin Mountains** lie south of **Limavady**, near which is the beautiful **Roe Valley Country Park**, where Ulster's first hydroelectric power station, the **Power House**, is open to visitors. At **Draperstown** to the east, the **Ulster Plantation Centre** tells the story of a notorious aspect of Irish history.

COUNTY TYRONE: Between the **Sperrins** in the north and green **Clogher Valley** with its village cathedral in the south lies a region of great historical interest. The **Ulster-American Folk Park** near **Omagh** acknowledges the county's close connections with the USA. The **Ulster History Park** is nearby. **Gray Printers' Museum** at **Strabane** still has its original 19th-century presses. There are forest parks at **Gortin Glen** and **Drum Mano**. **Dungannon**, in the southeast of the county, is home to **Tyrone Crystal** – whose glassworks are open to visitors.

Sport & Activities

Walking: Northern Ireland's scenic beauty and variety of landscapes make it a rewarding country to explore on foot. Forest trails, cliff-top paths and mountain hikes are easily accessible from the widely scattered villages and towns. Lake trails are particularly good around *Lough Neagh* and the *Fermanagh Lakeland*. The *Mourne Mountains* and forest parks in County Down and the *Nine Glens* in County Antrim are also considered excellent for hiking. Archaeological sites, such as stone-age tombs, stone circles (notably in *Beaghmore*), Celtic crosses, monasteries, Norman castles and 17th-century fortified houses offer interesting stopovers. The best known and longest trail (896km/560 miles) is the circular *Ulster Way*, now largely marked, which runs all around Northern Ireland. Another well-known marked trail is the *North Down Coastal Path*.

Pony trekking: This is widely practised, particularly in areas such as the mountains and forests around Newcastle and Castlewellan, the North Down coast and the Causeway coast.

Fishing: Sea fishing is popular all along the coast and skippered boats of all sizes can be hired at most resorts. *Strangford Lough* is famous for its skate and tope. *Carlingford Lough* is nearly as good and the coast of *Belfast Lough* is dotted with sea angling clubs. There are superb waters for river and lake fishing, particularly in the *Mournes* area of Down, the Glens of Antrim and the *River Bann*, which is well known for excellent salmon fishing. In most areas a rod licence and a coarse fishing permit are

necessary. Day permits are available; check at the nearest tackle shop *or* contact the Northern Ireland Tourist Board (see *Contact Addresses* section).
Golf: Some of the best golf courses are situated on the coast – at Whitehead, Bangor, Royal Portrush, Ballycastle, Royal County Down at Newcastle and the Chairndhu Club near Larne. Weekly and daily rates for playing on the courses are available from the club itself or the nearest tourist information centre.
Diving: Northern Ireland can offer the experienced diving enthusiast several areas to explore; these include *Strangford Lough*, some 29km (18 miles) long and averaging 6km (3.5 miles) wide, a fascinating underwater world with many contrasting diving sites. The long history of sea traffic has left a legacy of wrecks in and around the Lough, such as the 'Lees' wreck, an old liberty ship now lying at 12m (39ft), or the remains of the largest vessel wrecked on the Co Down coast, the American troop carrier 'Georgetown Victory'. Also of interest to experienced divers is the rugged, towering coast of *Rathlin Island*, and Northern Ireland's famous north coast.
Cruising: *Loch Erne* has in recent years become very popular for cruising holidays and several tour operators and local companies can arrange holidays; contact the Tourist Board for further details.
Special interest: Northern Ireland offers good opportunities for special interest holidays, from **poetry** and **pottery** to **cooking**, **painting**, **gardening** or **music**. For details of companies offering tailor-made special interest holidays, contact the Northern Ireland Tourist Board (see *Contact Addresses* section).
Other: Both **hang-gliding** and **rock climbing** can be practised in the Mournes, Co Down, Magilligan, Bellarena and Aghadowey, Co Londonderry. The River Bann at Coleraine is good for **water-skiing**, while **canoeing** is widespread at Bangor and Newcastle.

Social Profile

FOOD & DRINK: The best value for money meals in Ulster are to be had at lunchtime (midday), when many restaurants and pubs offer special menus. Most Ulster families have high tea at about 1800 and many hotels and restaurants offer the same. High tea usually consists of a light cooked meal (an Ulster fry – eggs, sausages, ham or fish with chips) and a wide variety of bread, scones and cakes. Dinner is served from about 1900. Typical Northern Ireland foods include shellfish, homemade vegetable soups, potato dishes, dried seaweed, locally grown fruit and home-baked cakes and pastries. A useful booklet is *Where to Eat in Northern Ireland*, available from newsagents and Tourist Information Centres, which lists all the places where food is served, a price indication and brief description of the sort of food. It is advisable to book ahead for the more popular restaurants, especially towards the weekend.
The pubs are open all day Mon-Sat 1130-2300 and Sun 1230-2200 with half an hour 'drinking-up' time. Popular drinks are, of course, *Guinness* – a dark heavy stout with a creamy head – and *whiskey* (Northern Ireland also boasts the world's oldest whiskey distillery at Bushmills). Irish whiskey is often drunk along with a bottle of stout. Real ale fans can try *Hilden*, produced at Lisburn and obtainable locally.
NIGHTLIFE: Northern Ireland has a strong tradition for musical entertainment, from the toe-tapping live folk bands playing in crowded pubs to the soulful lyrics of Van Morrison and the world-famous talent of flautist James Galway. Visitors will be able to find something to suit, from the latest dance music in nightclubs to opera or classical concerts. Traditional Irish music in 'singing pubs' provides a good evening's entertainment in many places, particularly Belfast and Londonderry. Special musical events include the summer *Jazz and Blues Festival* in Londonderry and Limavady and the *October International Guitar Festival* held in Newtownards. Details of bands, concerts and venues are listed in *That's Entertainment* magazine, found in pubs, record stores and bookshops.
There is also a wealth of theatres and art galleries located in and around Belfast, including the famous *Lyric Theatre*, where Liam Neeson started his career. There are summer theatres in Newcastle and Portrush, plus the *Riverside Theatre* at Coleraine. The *Belfast Festival* at Queen's (three weeks in November each year) is Europe's biggest arts festival after Edinburgh. Other main venues for drama performances and concerts are the *Grand Opera House*, *Ulster Hall*, *King's Hall* and the *Crescents Art Centre* (all in Belfast), the *Armagh Theatre and Arts Centre* and the new *Millennium Forum* theatre in Derry and numerous regional theatres. Further information can be obtained from the Northern Ireland's Arts Council's monthly magazine *art.ie* *or* from the Northern Ireland Tourist Board (see *Contact Addresses* section).
SHOPPING: Ulster is well known for its pure Irish linen; cut-glass goblets, decanters and bowls; creamy Belleek pottery; handwoven tweed; pure wool jumpers and cardigans hand-knitted in traditional patterns; hand-embroidered wall hangings; Carrickmacross lace and silver jewellery. **Shopping hours:** Shops are generally open 0900-1730, six days a week (late-night shopping on Thursday in Belfast city centre). Other cities and towns close for a half-day one day a week (it differs from town to town). Modern shopping centres on the outskirts of towns have late-night shopping Thur to Fri to 2100.
SPECIAL EVENTS: For a complete list of festivals and other special events celebrated in Northern Ireland, contact the Northern Ireland Tourist Board. The following is a selection of special events occurring in Northern Ireland in 2005:
Jan 4 *New Year Viennese Gala Ulster Orchestra Concert*, Newtownards; **Feb** *Heart of the Glens Festival*, Lisburn. **Feb 11-20** *Visonic Festival*, Belfast & Derry. **Feb 18-20** *Northern Ireland Motorcycle Festival*, Belfast. **Feb 22-28** *Armagh International Sport & Cultural Week*. **Feb 26-27** *Titanic Urban Challenge*. **Mar 4-5** *Coleraine International Choral Festival*. **Mar 26-Apr 2** *Titanic 'Made in Belfast' Festival*. **Apr 7-16** *Belfast Film Festival*. **Apr 30-May 1** *Northern Ireland Game and Country Fair*. **May 2** *Belfast City Marathon*. **May 11-13** *Balmoral Show*. **Jun 2** *Northern Ireland International Air Show*. **Jul** *12th of July Parades*, countrywide. **Sep 1-3** *Hillsborough International Oyster Festival*. **Sep 22-25** *Aspects Irish Literature Festival*. **Nov 13** *Belfast Book Fair*. **Dec** *The Balance House - Christmas Market*.
SOCIAL CONVENTIONS: Due to the political situation in Northern Ireland, visitors should take care when visiting certain parts of the main cities and the border area. No problems should arise provided the visitor follows local advice and avoids expressing dogmatic opinions on political or religious topics.

Business Profile

ECONOMY: The 25-plus years of the Troubles had a profound impact on the economy of Northern Ireland. Historically, the province's main economic strengths were manufacturing, concentrated on the shipbuilding and aerospace industries in the eastern part of the province, and agriculture, which is prevalent throughout. However, manufacturing has, in common with the rest of the UK, been in long-term decline, although a steady stream of government contracts has enabled it to survive in a reduced form. Agriculture has performed steadily, underpinned by the policies of the European Union. The public sector is now the largest single part of the economy and subventions from the British government in one form or another account for the bulk of the province's income. The political settlement in the province has presented a number of new opportunities for Northern Ireland's economy, as well as a number of problems. The most important of these is tourism, which is particularly sensitive to political circumstances in the province and has been largely depressed since the early 1970s. Similar considerations apply to foreign investment that the province is seeking to attract – especially in view of the success enjoyed by the Irish government during the 1990s. Indeed, the growing economic links between Northern Ireland and the Republic may offer the best prospects for the future development of the province's economy. Along with the rest of the UK, the Republic of Ireland already accounts for the bulk of Northern Ireland's external trade.
COMMERCIAL INFORMATION: The following organisation can offer advice: Northern Ireland Chamber of Commerce and Industry, 22 Great Victoria Street, Belfast BT2 7BJ (tel: (028) 9024 4113; fax: (028) 9024 7024; e-mail: mail@northernirelandchamber.com; website: www.northernirelandchamber.com).
CONFERENCES/CONVENTIONS: Contact Northern Ireland Conference Bureau, St Anne's Court, 59 North Street, Belfast BT1 1NB (tel: (028) 9031 5513; fax: (028) 9031 5544; e-mail: nicb@nitb.com).

Climate

In general the weather is similar to the rest of the UK, but Northern Ireland tends to have less sunshine and more rain. Extremes of temperature are rare but conditions can be changeable.
Required clothing: Similar to the rest of the UK, according to season. Waterproofs are advisable throughout the year.

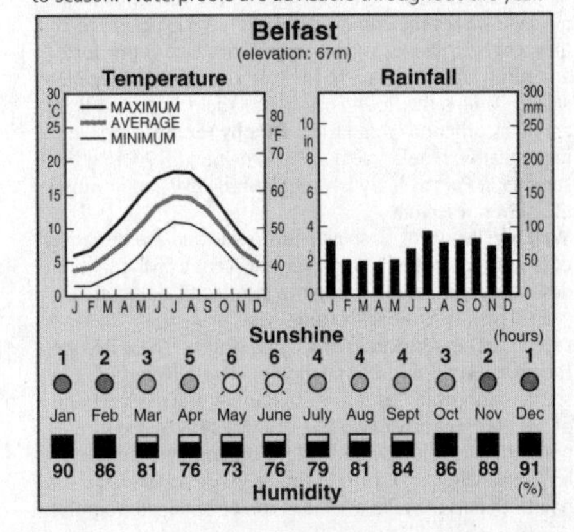

Isle of Man

LATEST TRAVEL ADVICE CONTACTS

British Foreign and Commonwealth Office
Tel: (0870) 606 0290 Website: www.fco.gov.uk

US Department of State
Website: http://travel.state.gov/travel

Canadian Department of Foreign Affairs and Int'l Trade
Tel: (1 800) 267 8376 Website: www.dfait-maeci.gc.ca

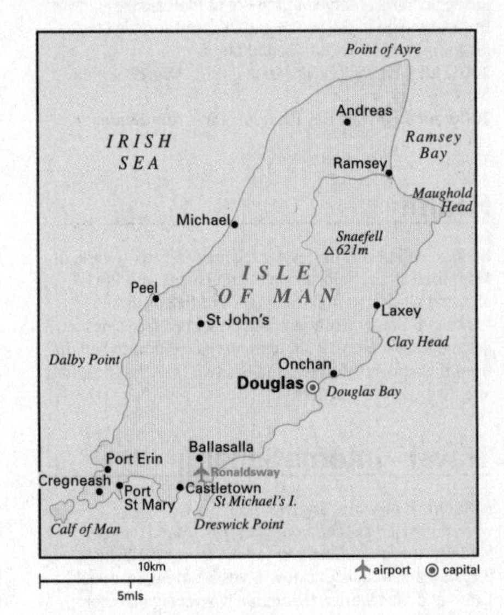

Location: Irish Sea.

Isle of Man Department of Tourism and Leisure
Sea Terminal Buildings, Douglas, Isle of Man IM1 2RG
Tel: (01624) 686 801. Fax: (01624) 686 801.
E-mail: tourism@gov.im
Website: www.visitisleofman.com *or* www.gov.im/tourism

General Information

AREA: 572 sq km (221 sq miles).
POPULATION: 76,315 (2001).
POPULATION DENSITY: 133.4 per sq km.
CAPITAL: Douglas. **Population:** 25,347 (2001).
GEOGRAPHY: The Isle of Man is situated in the Irish Sea, 114km (71 miles) from Liverpool and 133km (83 miles) from Dublin. The island has a mountain range down the middle, the highest peak being *Snaefell* at 620m (2036ft) and a flat northern plain to the Point of Ayre, the most northerly point. The Calf of Man, an islet off the southwest coast, is administered as a nature reserve and bird sanctuary by the Manx Museum and National Trust.
GOVERNMENT: Crown Dependency with own parliament. **Head of State:** HM Queen Elizabeth II, represented locally by Lieutenant-Governor Ian MacFadyen since 2000. **Head of Government:** Chief Minister Richard Corkhill since 2001.
LANGUAGE: Manx Gaelic, the indigenous language, is related to Scots and Irish Gaelic. At one time spoken by all the Manx, the tongue was replaced by English during the last century, and now only 600 or so people speak it to some degree. On Tynwald Day, summaries of the new laws are read out in Manx and English. Manx Gaelic evening classes are regularly held, and a weekly radio programme and newspaper column appear in the language.
TIME: GMT (GMT + 1 from last Sunday in March to last Saturday in October).
ELECTRICITY: 240 volts AC, 50Hz.
COMMUNICATIONS: Telephone: To telephone the Isle of Man from the UK, the STD (area) code is 01624. **Mobile telephone:** See main *United Kingdom* section. Also, *Manx Telecom* (website: www.manx-telecom.com) operates GSM 900 network, with roaming agreements with most European and international providers. **Fax:** Services are available. **Internet:** Internet access is available on the island. Main ISP is *Manx Telecom* (website: www.manx-telecom.com). **Post:** Services are administered by the Isle of Man Post Office Authority which issues its own postage stamps, recognised internationally under the auspices of the Universal Postal Union. Only Isle of Man Post Office Authority stamps are valid for postal purposes on the island. **Press:** There are several local papers published on the island and English papers are widely available.

Money

Currency: The Isle of Man government issues its own decimal coinage, and currency notes of £50, 20, 10, 5 and 1, and coins of £5, 2 and 1, and 50, 20, 10, 5, 2 and 1 pence, all of which are on a par with the UK equivalents. The coins and notes of England, Scotland and Northern Ireland circulate freely on the island.
Banking hours: Mon-Fri 0930-1530. Some are open Sat 1000-1200.

Public Holidays

Public holidays observed in the Isle of Man are the same as those observed in the rest of the UK (see the main *United Kingdom* section) with the addition of:
2005: Jul 5 Tynwald Day (National Day). **Aug 29** Summer Bank Holiday.
2006: Jul 5 Tynwald Day (National Day). **Aug 28** Summer Bank Holiday.

Health

No vaccination certificates are required to enter the Isle of Man. There is a reciprocal health agreement with the UK, allowing all visitors from the mainland free medical treatment. Dental treatment and prescribed medicines must be paid for. No proof of UK residence is required to benefit from the agreement. The island has two first-class hospitals and many dental practices.

Travel - International

AIR: *British Airways (BA)* (website: www.britishairways.com) operates year-round services between the Isle of Man and London Heathrow, Belfast, Birmingham, Dublin, Glasgow, Leeds/Bradford, Liverpool, Luton and Manchester. *Euromanx* (www.euromanx.com), *Flybe (BE)* (www.flybe.com)and *Fly Keenair Shuttle Services* (website: www.flykeen.co.uk) also operate services to the Isle of Man.
International airports: The island's airport is *Ronaldsway (IOM)*, 16km (10 miles) from Douglas. Airport information: tel: (01624) 821 600. Facilities include restaurant, buffet, bar, general shop and newsagents, duty free shop and facilities for the disabled. Airport opening times: Mon-Sat 0615-2045, Sun 0700-2045. A local **bus** operates approximately half-hourly until 1900 and then hourly for the rest of the evening. **Taxis** and **car hire** are also available. Car hire includes *Athol Car Hire*, *Hertz* and *Mylchreests Car Hire*. It is 16km (10 miles) to Douglas by private car. There is one contracted and one public car park.
Departure tax: None.
SEA: Ports include Castletown, Douglas, Peel and Ramsey. Sailings are run by the *Isle of Man Steam Packet* and *Seacat Company* daily from Douglas to Heysham, Belfast, Dublin and Liverpool, although crossings to Belfast are not scheduled in the winter months. Sea cat routes are from Belfast to Heysham or Troon (tel: (08705) 523 523; e:mail: Belfast.Reservations@seacontainers.com; website: www.steam-packet.com).
RAIL: Horse trams run along the 3km (2 miles) of the Douglas Promenade during the summer. The *Steam Railway* operates from Douglas to Port Erin and the *Manx Electric Railway* runs from Douglas to Ramsey. Other services include the unique *Snaefall Mountain Railway*, which runs to the summit of Snaefall mountain, and the *Groundle Glen Railway* (a narrow gauge system), which provides a limited service along a scenic track near Douglas in the summer months.
ROAD: The island is served by *Isle of Man National Transport* **buses** throughout the year. There are also a number of coach operators who operate full- and half-day excursions. Private **taxis** operate all year round and there are a number of **car hire** firms. **Bicycles** are available for hire in the summer months. **Regulations:** Traffic drives on the left. There is no maximum speed limit except in built-up areas. **Documentation:** Full UK driving licence is acceptable.

Accommodation

Hotel, guest house and self-catering accommodation is available, but pre-booking is necessary in the summer months. Grading of accommodation follows UK standards and ranges from basic to deluxe. Camping is only permitted on the official campsite. The importation of caravans is prohibited.

Resorts & Excursions

Viking and Celtic heritage combine to create unusual interest on this charismatic island. Numerous attractions reflect this rich historic mix, branded by Manx National Heritage (website: www.gov.im/mnh) as the **Story of Man**, an umbrella name applied to sites ranging from prehistoric tombs to multimedia exhibitions, and to which English Heritage and National Trust members gain free entry.
Also important are Man's Victorian narrow-gauge railways: the **Steam Railway** linking **Douglas** and **Port Erin**; the **Manx Electric Tramway**, running north to **Ramsey**; and the **Snaefell Mountain Railway**, which climbs 620m (2034ft) above sea level from **Laxey**. A smaller line operates on the cliffs at **Groudle Glen**.
The island also hosts the annual *TT Races* and other motorsport events (see *Sport & Activities* section). Scenic highlights include 17 picturesque **National Glens**, the south coast bays, and **Snaefell** itself, from which England, Scotland, Ireland and Wales are all visible on a clear day.
DOUGLAS: The capital has all the trappings of a seaside resort, with the **Gaiety Theatre**, parks and sweeping beach. **Horse-drawn trams** provide transport along its 3.2km (2 mile) promenade, while pedestrianised shopping areas are close inland. A prime visitor attraction is the **Manx Museum** complex, with its art, archaeological and cartographic galleries, plus a multimedia show introducing the 'Story of Man'.
PEEL: House of Manannan, on **Peel Harbour**, is a high-tech interpretation of the island's history from the earliest times, while ruined **Peel Castle** on **St Patrick's Isle**, reached by a causeway, has Viking origins and incorporates the 13th-century **St German's Cathedral**. Peel is also famous for its kippers, and several smokehouses are open to visitors.
AROUND MAN: Laxey boasts the world's largest working waterwheel at the site of former lead mines. **Cregneash Village**, at the southern tip of the island, is a 'living history' museum recreating Manx life a century and more past, while the **Calf of Man**, a small island nearby, offers bird watching. **Castle Rushen** in **Castletown** is a remarkably complete medieval fortification, while **Rushen Abbey** at **Ballasalla** traces the early roots of Christianity. **Tynwald Hill**, inland from Peel, is the site of the world's oldest continuously running parliament.

Sport & Activities

Motorbike and motor racing: The Isle of Man is regarded by many as the road racing capital of the world, hosting a number of prestigious and unusual events. The most famous of these is the annual *TT* (Tourist Trophy) motorbike festival which takes over the island for two weeks in late May to early June. Competitors from all over the world race around a special circuit on the island's roads, and an atmosphere of celebration prevails. Other road races for motorbikes include the *Ramsey Sprint*, the *Southern 100* in July, and the *Manx Grand Prix* in August. Races and rallies for modern and vintage cars take place throughout the summer on the island's roads, and include the *Manx National Car Rally*, the *Manx International Car Rally* (considered one of the most challenging races in the UK), the *International Hill Climb Championships* and the *Manx Classic* (especially for vintage cars). The varied terrain, sometimes mountainous and with sharp bends, adds to the challenge and excitement of the races.
Sailing: Regarded by sailors as a 'staging post' between Scotland, Ireland, Wales and England, the Isle of Man is well-equipped as a sailing destination. There are four main harbours, plus other good anchorages. The variety of sailing available makes the island suitable for both experienced and inexperienced sailors, with a rugged coastline to the north and south and calm bays to the east and west. The premier sailing event is the *Round the Island Yacht Race*, but there are many other races and trials. **Dinghy racing** is growing in popularity; regular races are held on Sundays during the summer at Port St Mary Bay and Ramsey Bay and in winter at Baldwin reservoir.
Walking: Beautiful, unspoilt countryside and a wide variety of landscapes make the island an excellent walking destination. Sand dunes, marshes, heathland, hills and coastal grassland are all features of its geography. There are several well-marked trails of varying lengths. These include the new 45km (28 mile) *Millennium Way*, which runs south–north from Castletown to Ramsey, tracing the route of the 14th-century *Regia Via*, or Royal Way. While the northern part of the walk is wilder, the southern portion is less demanding, and the trail can be joined at various points. Details of walks and trails can be obtained from the Tourist Board (see *Contact Addresses* section).
Golf: There are eight golf courses on the island and green fees are much cheaper than in the rest of the UK.

Social Profile

FOOD & DRINK: Cuisine is English and Manx. Local specialities include *queenies* (small scallops) and world-famous Manx kippers. A wide variety of alcoholic beverages are available, including Real Manx Ale from the wood and Manx whiskey, gin and vodka. All drinks are cheaper than in the UK. **Licensing hours:** Public houses open Mon-Thurs 1000-2300, Fri-Sat 1000-2400. On Sunday public houses open 1200-2300. Special opening hours apply to the Easter and Christmas/New Year periods.
SHOPPING: VAT is at the same rate as the UK and prices are in general similar to those in the UK. Special purchases include Manx tartan, crafts and pottery. **Shopping hours:** Mon-Sat 0900-1730. Early closing Thursday during the winter months.
Note: For information on people, religion, social conventions, business, tipping and eating and drinking, see the main *United Kingdom* section.
SPECIAL EVENTS: For a complete list, contact the Isle of Man Department of Tourism. The following is a selection of special events occurring in the Isle of Man in 2005:
Jan 1 *Peel New Year Dip* (swim in Peel Beach). **Mar 10-13** *Darts Festival*, Villa Marina. **Mar 19** *Southern Gardener's Spring Show*, Port Erin. **Mar 23-26** *Easter Festival of Sport*. **Mar 26** *Mountain Marathon*, Ramsey to Port Erin. **Mar 31-Apr 4** *Student Festival of Sport*. **Apr 30-May 2** *Round-the-Island Yacht Race*, Ramsey Harbour. **May 6-7** *Roush Rally*. **May 19-22** *Ramsey Angling Festival*. **May 28-Jun 10** *TT Motorcycle Festival*. **May 29** *'Retromobile Isle of Man' & Autojumble*, Kirk Michael. **Jun 23-Jul 2** *Mananan International Festival of Music & the Arts*, Port Erin. **Jul 2-9** *Manx National Week*. **Jul 28-30** *Manx International Rally*, throughout the island. **Jul 31-Aug 13** *British Chess Championships*. **Aug 6** *Manx Angling Festival*. **Aug 12-13** *Royal Manx Agricultural Show*, Sulby. **Aug 12-14** *International Jazz Festival*. **Aug 20-Sep 2** *Manx Grand Prix*. **Dec 2-4** *Winter Mananan Festival*, Port Erin.

Business Profile

ECONOMY: The island's economy relies principally on tourism and financial services attracted by banking secrecy laws that render assets deposited on the island less vulnerable to disclosure requirements than those on the mainland. Taxation rates are also, on the whole, lower than those of the UK. There is a small agricultural sector but very little industry.
BUSINESS: See the main *United Kingdom* section.
COMMERCIAL INFORMATION: The following organisation can offer advice: Isle of Man Chamber of Commerce, 17 Drinkwater Street, Douglas IM1 1PP (tel: (01624) 674 941; fax: (01624) 663 367; e-mail: enquiries@iomchamber.org.im; website: www.iomchamber.org.im).
CONFERENCES/CONVENTIONS: Seating is available for up to 1700 persons, although facilities on the island lend themselves very well to meetings of 100 persons or less. Conferences hosted include those of the National Federation of Young Farmers' Clubs and the Union of Communication Workers. All conference hotels have superb back-up services. For further information, contact the Department of Tourism.

Climate

The climate of the Isle of Man is temperate. There is a considerable variation in rainfall over the island, the driest parts being in the extreme south and over the northern plain, the wettest being the hilly interior. Frost and snow occur much less frequently than in other parts of the British Isles.

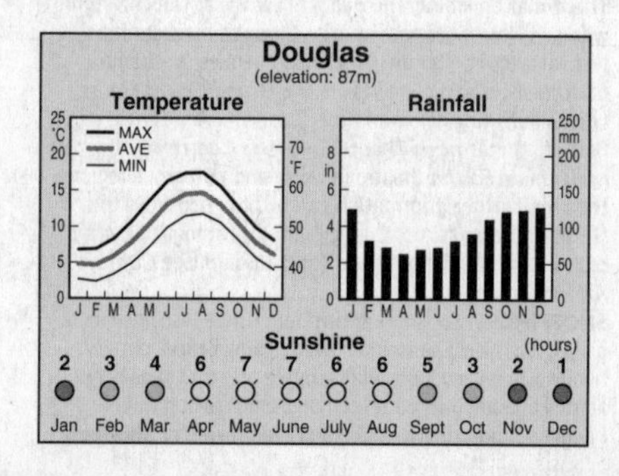

Channel Islands

LATEST TRAVEL ADVICE CONTACTS

British Foreign and Commonwealth Office
Tel: (0870) 606 0290 Website: www.fco.gov.uk

US Department of State
Website: http://travel.state.gov/travel

Canadian Department of Foreign Affairs and Int'l Trade
Tel: (1 800) 267 8376 Website: www.dfait-maeci.gc.ca

Alderney, **Guernsey**, **Jersey**, **Sark** and **Herm**.

There are other, very small islands in the group, but these are not normally open to visitors. Guernsey and Jersey have their own sections.

Alderney

Location: English Channel, the northernmost Channel Island; off the north coast of France.

States of Alderney Tourism Office
Queen Elizabeth II Street, Alderney, Channel Islands, GY9 3AA
Tel: (01481) 823 737 (tourist information) *or* 822 811 (public affairs).
Fax: (01481) 822 436.
E-mail: tourism@alderney.net
Website: www.alderney.gov.gg

General Information

AREA: 7.9 sq km (3.1 sq miles).
POPULATION: 2,294 (2001).
POPULATION DENSITY: 290.0 per sq km.
CAPITAL: St Anne's.
GEOGRAPHY: The most northerly of the Channel Islands, Alderney lies 12km (8 miles) off the coast of Normandy in France and some 32km (20 miles) from Guernsey. The central part of the island is a plateau varying in height from 76 to 90m (250 to 296ft). The land is flat to the edge of the southern and southwestern cliffs, where it falls abruptly to the sea. On the northern, eastern and southeastern sides, it slopes gradually towards rocky and sandy bays and quiet beaches.
GOVERNMENT: Dependency of the British Crown with considerable internal autonomy. **Head of State:** HM Queen Elizabeth II represented locally by Lieutenant-Governor Sir John Foley. **Head of Government:** Sir Norman Browse.
LANGUAGE: English. A Norman *patois* is spoken by some.
TIME: GMT (GMT + 1 from last Sunday in March to last Saturday in October).
ELECTRICITY: 240 volts AC, 50Hz.
COMMUNICATIONS: Telephone: Alderney is linked to the British STD service; the area code is 01481. **Mobile telephone:** GSM 900 and 1800 networks. Network operators include *Guernsey Telecoms* (website: www.guernsey.net). **Internet**: ISPs include *gtonline* and *Guernseynet*. Information is available from *Guernsey Telecoms*. **Post:** Only Alderney and Guernsey stamps will be accepted on outgoing mail. **Press:** Guernsey, Jersey, and British papers are available on the island.

Passport/Visa

No passports are required for travel between the UK, the other Channel Islands and Alderney. See *Passport/Visa* in the main *United Kingdom* section.

Money

Currency: Pound (£) = 100 pence. UK notes and coins are legal tender and circulate together with Channel Islands issue, which are in the same denominations. Channel Islands' notes can be reconverted at parity in UK banks, although they are not accepted as legal tender in the UK.
Banking hours: Mon-Fri 0930-1300 and 1430-1530.

Duty Free

As Alderney falls under the authority of the Bailiwick of Guernsey, customs regulations are the same; see the *Guernsey* section.

Public Holidays

Note: Public Holidays observed in the Channel Islands are the same as those observed in the rest of the UK (see the main *United Kingdom* section) with the addition of:
Aug 22 2005 Summer Bank Holiday. **Aug 28 2006** Summer Bank Holiday.

Health

No vaccination certificates are required to enter Alderney. There is a reciprocal health agreement with the UK, allowing all short-stay visitors (three months maximum) from the mainland free immediate and necessary medical treatment and free emergency dental treatment. Doctor's visits, ambulance services and prescribed medicines must be paid for. Proof of UK residence (driving licence, NHS card and so on) is required to benefit from the agreement. The island has a small hospital, two medical practices and one dental practice. Visitors are advised to obtain health insurance cover prior to their trip.

Travel - International

AIR: *Aurigny Air Services (GR)* offers flights to Guernsey (flight time – 15 minutes), Jersey (flight time – 15 minutes), Southampton (flight time – 45 minutes), Amsterdam and Dinard in France. For further information, contact Aurigny Air Services, Alderney (tel: (01481) 822 886 (reservations); fax: (01481) 823 344). *Le Cocqs Airlink* offers daily flights from Bournemouth (flight time – 35 minutes; tel: (01481) 824 567).
International airports: *The Blaye (ACI)*, with flights to Guernsey, Jersey and Southampton. Airport facilities include buffet, shop and taxis (from rank adjacent to terminal building).
Departure tax: None.
SEA: There is a regular passenger ferry service from Dielette (Normandy) and Guernsey to Alderney, provided by *Victor Hugo Express* (tel: (0233) 610 888). A small ferry service between Dielette and Alderney operates (for details, call (01481) 825 555). For further information, contact the States of Alderney Tourism Office (see *Contact Addresses* section).
RAIL: For information on rail travel, contact *Alderney Railway*, PO Box 75, Alderney.
ROAD: Caravans may not be imported to Alderney. **Bus:** During the summer months, an internal bus service operates on the island running from St Anne's to the five main beaches. **Taxi:** Private taxi companies operate on the island. **Car hire:** There are several car hire companies on the island and two garages which have hire cars. **Bicycle hire:** There are several bike hire firms that rent out bicycles at daily or weekly rates. **Regulations:** Traffic drives on the left. Maximum speed limit is 30mph (48kph). **Documentation:** Full UK driving licence is accepted.

Accommodation

Hotel, guest house and self-catering accommodation is available, but pre-booking is necessary in the summer months. Camping is only permitted on the one official campsite. The import of caravans is prohibited. For further information, contact the States of Alderney Tourism Office (see *Contact Addresses* section).

Resorts & Excursions

The third-largest of the Channel Islands, Alderney is almost treeless and has a heavily indented shoreline with many sandy bays and rugged crags. The island's town, **St Anne**, dates back to the 15th century and has numerous shops and inns lining its cobbled streets. Principal visitor attractions include **St Anne's Church**, often referred to as the 'Cathedral of the Channel Islands' and the **Alderney Society Museum**. Located in the High Street, the museum documents the island's history from neolithic times. It is open daily in summer. The quaint, traditional **Alderney Cinema** is another highlight. Seats are bookable in advance, as are drinks at nearby pubs for the half-time break when the projectionist changes the film reel. Guided tours up a 32m- (96ft-) high **historic lighthouse** are available at the eastern end of the island near **Quesnard Point** at weekends. The lighthouse is accessible either on foot or on the 150-year-old narrow-gauge **Alderney Railway**. The recently formed **Alderney Wildlife Trust** has published a series of recommended walks and also offers guided tours throughout the main season. For details, contact the Alderney Tourism and Wildlife Trust Information Centre in Victoria Street (tel: (01481) 823 737).

Sport & Activities

Sailing: Visitors sailing to Alderney arrive at Braye Harbour (protected by a Victorian breakwater) and those registered with recognised yacht clubs can enjoy the hospitality of the *Alderney Sailing Club* (situated above the harbour). For information on customs and navigational details, contact the *Harbour Master* (tel: (01481) 822 620; fax: (01481) 823 699). Alderney is well located for sailing excursions to the other Channel Islands and France (which is only 12km/8 miles away). The Sailing Club organises several annual events and races, including the *Alderney International Sailing Regatta* (usually held in July). For further details (including boat hire and sailing classes), contact the Alderney Sailing Club, The Harbour (tel: (01481) 822 959).
Watersports: Alderney is surrounded by numerous sandy beaches suitable for **swimming** and **windsurfing**. Surf/sail boards are available for hire on the island. Dogs are banned from most of the islands' beaches between June and September. Some of the best beaches can be found on *Arch Bay*, *Braye Bay* (also popular for water-skiing), *Clonque* (a beach for naturalists), *Corblets* (one of the best swimming beaches), *Longis Bay* (next to Longis Common, which offers good birdwatching), *Platte Saline* (also for naturalists; swimming is not recommended due to strong undercurrents) and *Say* (pronounced 'Soy').
Fishing is well catered for: no permission is needed to fish anywhere from the coastline or the harbour and the local shop offers equipment and advice. The *Angling Festival* is held annually in October. **Sea fishing** enthusiasts are able to charter small boats.
Walking: All parts of the island can be reached on foot and there are some interesting panoramic walks along the cliffs. Every weekend during the main season, the Alderney Society and the States Conservation Officer organise guided walks. Leaflets of recommended walks are available from the States of Alderney Tourism Office (see *Contact Addresses* section).
Other: There is a well maintained 9-hole **golf** course with a bowling green. Green fees are comparatively low compared to the rest of the Channel Islands. For information, contact the *Alderney Golf Club* (tel: (01481) 822 835). Facilities are available on the island for both **squash** and **tennis**.

Social Profile

FOOD & DRINK: Cuisine is largely French influenced. The local speciality is shellfish. A wide variety of alcoholic beverages is available. Spirits, beers and wines are cheaper than on the mainland.
SHOPPING: Alderney has its own duty free retail outlets where visitors can purchase spirits and tobacco at exceptionally low prices prior to their departure. There is no

VAT, but a Guernsey Bailiwick tax is imposed on certain goods such as spirits, wines, beers and tobacco. Prices on luxury goods are lower than in the UK, although the overall cost of foodstuffs is higher. Special purchases include Alderney pullovers, local pottery and crafts. **Shopping hours:** These vary, but the majority of shops open 0930-1230 and 1430-1730. Shops generally close Wednesday afternoons.
SPECIAL EVENTS: For further information, contact the States of Alderney Tourism Office. The following is a selection of special events occurring in Alderney in 2005: **Jan 1** *First Swim of the Year*, Braye Bay. **Mar 25-28** *Easter Weekend*, including *Easter Egg Special*. **Apr 30-31** *Birds & Flowers of Alderney Festival*. **May 1** *Milk-a-Punch Sunday*, traditional event. **May 1-16** *Seafood Festival*. **May 28-30** *Miss Alderney Weekend*. **Jun 3-5** *Men's Open Golf Championships*. **Jun 9-10** *Ladies' Open Golf Championships*. **Jun 28** *Beach Party*, in celebration of the 200th Anniversary of the Battle of Trafalgar, Braye Common. **Jul 8-10** *International Sailing Regatta*. **Jul 30-Aug 7** *Alderney Week*, carnival. **Sep 10** *Half Marathon*. **Oct 18-23** *Annual Angling Festival*. **Oct 1-Nov 11** *TennerFest*.
Note: For information relating to Alderney on people, religion, social conventions, business, tipping and economy, see the *Guernsey* section.

Business Profile

See main *United Kingdom* section.

Climate

The island enjoys a temperate climate with warm summers and milder winter temperatures than those experienced in the UK.

Guernsey

For information on *Guernsey*, see separate section

Jersey

For information on *Jersey*, see separate section

Sark

Location: English Channel.

Sark Tourism Office
Harbour Hill, Sark, Channel Islands GY9 0SB
Tel: (01481) 832 345. Fax: (01481) 832 483.
E-mail: contact@sark.info
Website: www.sark.info
Herm Island Administration Office
Herm Island via Guernsey, Channel Islands GY1 3HR
Tel: (01481) 722 377. Fax: (01481) 700 334.
E-mail: admin@herm-island.com
Website: www.herm-island.com

General Information

AREA: Sark: 5.5 sq km (2.1 sq miles). **Herm:** 2 sq km (0.8 sq miles).
POPULATION: Sark: 550 (1996). **Herm:** 97 (2001, including Jethou).
POPULATION DENSITY: Sark: 100 per sq km. **Herm:** 48.5 per sq km.
GEOGRAPHY: Sark is a 45-minute boat journey east of Guernsey. It is almost two islands, the two parts being joined by a narrow isthmus known as *La Coupée*. The island is a plateau, with a collection of animals and plants unique to Sark. In the spring and autumn, the island becomes home to an unusual selection of migratory birds. The main village is situated at La Collinette. The coastline is rugged, with many cliffs and caves. **Herm** lies between Guernsey and Sark. It has lush and varied scenery, with meadows, unusual wild flowers and steep cliffs overlooking secluded coves and pounding surf. Herm attracts up to 1000 visitors a day during the summer.
GOVERNMENT: Dependencies of the British Crown with considerable internal autonomy. **Head of State:** HM Queen Elizabeth II. **Head of Government:** Seigneur Michael Beaumont. The island of Herm is privately leased by Guernsey. The island of Sark is a personal *fief* held by the Seigneur direct from the British Crown.
LANGUAGE: Local *patois*, a type of old Norman French. English is widely spoken.
COMMUNICATIONS: Telephone: Sark and Herm are connected to the UK STD telephone network; area code: 01481. **Mobile telephone:** GSM 900 and 1800 networks. Network operators include *Guernsey Telecoms* (website: www.guernsey.net). **Internet:** ISPs include *gtonline* and *Guernseynet*. Information is available from *Guernsey Telecoms* (website: www.guernsey.net). **Post:** There is a post office on Sark.
For information on time and electricity, and for further information on communications and money, see the *Guernsey* section.

Passport/Visa

See main *United Kingdom* section.

Money

Currency: Both Sark and Herm use Sterling as currency. UK mainland banks can be found on Sark.

Duty Free

For information on *Duty Free*, *Public Holidays*, *Health*, *Social Profile* and *Business Profile*, see the *United Kingdom* section.

Travel - International

SEA: Sark and Herm can be reached by sea from either Guernsey or Jersey.
Sark: The main harbour is at Maseline. All visitors arriving from the UK must transfer at Guernsey. Sailings from the UK are with *Condor Ferries* departing from Poole or Weymouth. For more details, contact Condor Ferries (tel: (0845) 345 2000; fax: (01305) 760 776). Sailings from France depart from Saint Malo with *Emeraude Lines* (tel: (2) 2318 0180; fax: (2) 2318 1500). The *Isle of Sark Shipping Company* runs daily services between Guernsey and Sark in summer (travel time - 45 to 50 minutes), with a more limited service in winter. For further information, contact Isle of Sark Shipping Company Ltd, Harbour Office, Sark GY9 0SB (tel: (01481) 832 450; fax: (01481) 832 567; e-mail: info@sarkshipping.guernsey.net).
Herm: There is a ferry service daily between Guernsey and Herm (travel time - 20 minutes). Ferries leave every 30 minutes from Guernsey to Herm and faster catamarans can be chartered. Carriers include: *Herm Express Ferry* and *Herm Seaways*, Albert Pier, Weighbridge Clock Tower, St Peter Port, Guernsey (tel: (01481) 724 161; fax: (01481) 714 011); *or Trident Charter Company*, Trident Kiosk, Weighbridge Clock Tower, St Peter Port, Guernsey (tel: (01481) 721 379; fax: (01481) 700 226).
ROAD: No cars are allowed on either island. The Sark 'taxi' is a horse-drawn carriage which takes visitors around the island. Bicycles can also be hired on Sark. Herm has only a few essential tractors and an emergency 4-wheel-drive vehicle.
Note: There is a landing tax for all visitors to Sark.

Accommodation

There are several hotels, many guest houses and self-catering cottages and apartments on Sark. Herm has one hotel, the *White House Hotel*, which has a tennis court, croquet lawn and outdoor swimming pool, and several self-catering cottages. There is also a campsite, the *Seagull* campsite, at the top of the island. For further information, contact the Sark Tourism Office (see *Contact Addresses* section).

Resorts & Excursions

SARK: A feudal state ruled by a *Seigneur*, who is also a member of the autonomous parliament called the Chief Pleas. The island's countryside is characterised by its granite cliffs topped with flowered fields known as *cotils*.
There are several excellent beaches, pools (**Dixcart** and **Grand Greve**) and rock pools, including the **Venus Pool** (a 6.1m/20ft tidal pool) and **Adonis Pool**; most of which are only accessible at low tide. **Creux Harbour** is tiny but picturesque - boat passengers come ashore through cliff-cut tunnels. At the northernmost point of the island lies the *Bec du Nez* or 'Oystercatcher's Rock'- a stretch of rock that juts out to sea, commanding a breathtaking view. At low tide, it is possible to take a boat trip around the coastline of Sark to visit caves including the **Boutique Caves** - according to legend, a past haunt of smugglers. A popular attraction for visitors are the gardens of **La Seigneurie**, which has been the home of Sark's *Seigneurs* since 1730. It has a large Victorian watchtower and is one of the best formal gardens in the Channel Islands. Other attractions include the 19th-century windowless prison (still occasionally used to keep disorderly drunkards for a night or two); **Le Manoir** (an 18th-century manor house built by the first Seigneur of Sark); and the ancient windmill, standing at the highest point in the Channel Islands. **La Coupée**, a very high isthmus (79.2m/260ft above sea level) carrying a narrow road above the sea, links Sark with **Little Sark**. Before it gained railings, people used to cross it on their hands and knees when there were high winds; even now, cyclists and horse carriage passengers must dismount.
HERM: Privately leased, and run as a resort island. Attractions include a **Tom Thumb village** restored from derelict houses, a restored chapel, woods, caves, swimming in rock pools and the shell beach - covered by countless shells deposited by the Gulf Stream, some from as far away as Mexico. There are quite a few pubs on the island, which devise their own opening hours on a rota system; one will almost always be open.

Sport & Activities

Sailing: The islands of Sark and Herm both welcome visiting yachts and boats, though permission should be obtained from the harbour administration offices. Herm Harbour charges no fee for mooring. For details, contact Herm Island Administration Office (see *Contact Addresses* section).
Walking and cycling: Sark and Herm are car-free islands, with the exception of a few farm tractors, which makes walking or cycling around them all the more pleasant. Bicycles are available for hire on both islands. Travel by **horse-drawn carriages** is widespread. The islands offer numerous scenic walks along the cliffs, and a guide with pathways can be obtained from the tourist offices. It is possible to walk around Herm in less than two hours.
Watersports: Sark Island stands high out of the sea and its jagged coast and rocky cliffs occasionally harbour small sandy beaches where **swimming** is possible, notably at *Dixcart Bay*. Herm Island has long sandy beaches on its northern shore which are suitable for swimming and **snorkelling**. **Diving** is also available (a certificate to show proof of qualification is normally required).
Birdwatching: The islands are a treat for birdwatchers.

Climate

These islands enjoy a temperate climate with warm summers and milder winter temperatures than those experienced in the UK.

United States of America

LATEST TRAVEL ADVICE CONTACTS

British Foreign and Commonwealth Office
Tel: (0870) 606 0290 Website: www.fco.gov.uk
US Department of State
Website: http://travel.state.gov/travel
Canadian Department of Foreign Affairs and Int'l Trade
Tel: (1 800) 267 8376 Website: www.dfait-maeci.gc.ca

Location: North America.

Country dialling code: 1.

International Trade Administration, Office of Travel & Tourism Industries
US Department of Commerce, Room 7025, Washington, DC 20230, USA
Tel: (202) 482 0140. Fax: (202) 482 2887.
E-mail: info@tinet.ita.doc.gov
Website: www.tinet.ita.doc.gov

Travel Industry Association of America
1100 New York Avenue, NW, Suite 450,
Washington, DC 20005, USA
Tel: (202) 408 8422. Fax: (202) 408 1255.
E-mail: feedback@tia.org
Website: www.tia.org

Embassy of the United States of America
24 Grosvenor Square, London W1A 1AE, UK
Tel: (020) 7499 9000. Fax: (020) 7495 5012 (visa section).
Website: www.usembassy.org.uk
Opening hours: Mon-Fri 0830-1730.
Consulates in: Belfast and Edinburgh.

American Embassy Visa Services
Tel: (09068) 200 290 (24-hour visa information line; calls cost 60p per minute, UK only; identical information is available on the Embassy website at no cost) *or* (09055) 444 546 (operator-assisted visa information, Mon-Fri 0800-2000, Sat 1000-1600; calls cost £1.30 per minute, UK only).

British Embassy
3100 Massachusetts Avenue, NW, Washington, DC 20008, USA
Tel: (202) 588 6500 or 7800 (passports).
Fax: (202) 588 7866 *or* 7850 (passports).
Visa section: 845 Third Avenue, 51st Street,
New York, NY 10022, USA
Tel: (212) 754 0200. Fax: (212) 754 3062.
E-mail: washi@fco.gov.uk
Website: www.britainusa.com
Consulates in: Atlanta, Boston, Chicago, Dallas, Denver, Houston, Los Angeles, Miami, New York, Orlando, Phoenix, San Francisco and Seattle.

Embassy of the United States of America
490 Sussex Drive, Ottawa, Ontario K1N 1G8, Canada
Tel: (613) 238 5335.
Fax: (613) 688 3080 (general) *or* 3082 (consular section).
Website: www.usembassycanada.gov
Consulates in: Calgary, Halifax, Montréal, Québec City, Toronto, Vancouver and Winnipeg.

Canadian Embassy
501 Pennsylvania Avenue, NW, Washington, DC 20001, USA
Tel: (202) 682 1740. Fax: (202) 682 7689.
Website: www.canadianembassy.org
Consulates in: Anchorage, Atlanta, Boston, Buffalo, Chicago, Dallas, Denver, Detroit, Houston, Los Angeles, Miami, Minneapolis, New York, Pheonix, Raleigh, San Diego, San Francisco and Seattle.

General Information

Information on the USA is provided in two parts: a general overview and individual State profiles, each of which has its own section.
AREA: 9,809,155 sq km (3,787,319 sq miles).
POPULATION: 294,800,000 (official estimate 2004).
POPULATION DENSITY: 30.5 per sq km.
CAPITAL: Washington, DC. **Population**: 565,392 (2004). 20 other cities have a population larger than that of

TIMATIC CODES

Health
AMADEUS: **TI-DFT/JFK/HE**
GALILEO/WORLDSPAN: **TI-DFT/JFK/HE**
SABRE: **TIDFT/JFK/HE**

Visa
AMADEUS: **TI-DFT/JFK/VI**
GALILEO/WORLDSPAN: **TI-DFT/JFK/VI**
SABRE: **TIDFT/JFK/VI**

To access TIMATIC country information on Health and Visa regulations through the Computer Reservations System (CRS), type in the appropriate command line listed above.

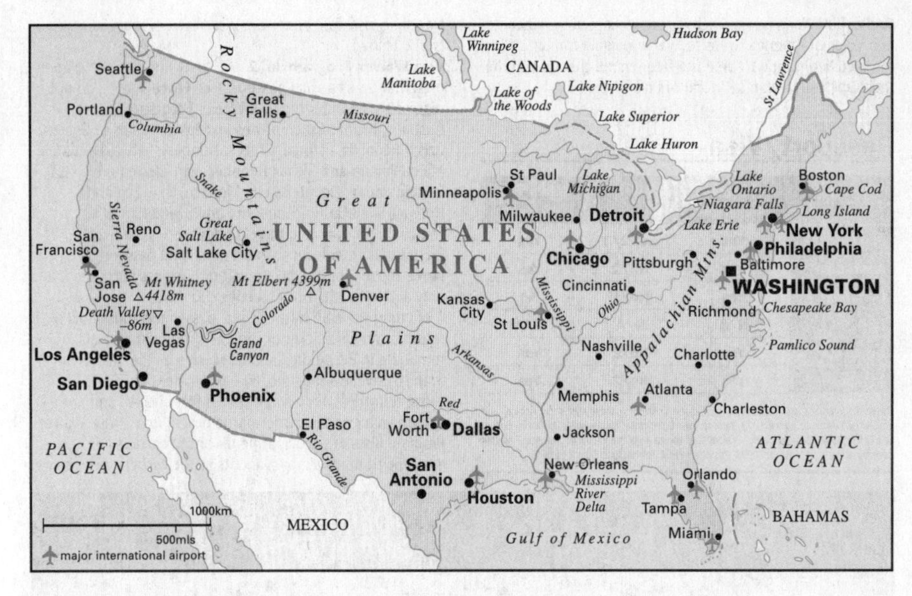

Washington, DC. New York is the largest city, with a population of over 8 million. Chicago, Dallas, Houston, Los Angeles, Philadelphia, Phoenix, San Antonio and San Diego had populations of over 1 million in 2000.

GEOGRAPHY: Covering a large part of the North American continent, the USA shares borders with Canada to the north and Mexico to the south and has coasts on the Atlantic, Pacific and Arctic oceans, the Caribbean Sea and the Gulf of Mexico. The State of Alaska, in the northwest corner of the continent, is separated from the rest of the country by Canada, and Hawaii lies in the central Pacific Ocean. The third-largest country in the world (after the Russian Federation and Canada), the USA has an enormous diversity of geographical features. The climate ranges from subtropical to Arctic, with a corresponding breadth of flora and fauna. For a more detailed description of each region's geographical characteristics, see the individual State sections.

Credit: © South Dakota Department of Tourism

GOVERNMENT: Federal Republic since 1789. Gained independence from the UK in 1776. **Head of State and Government**: President George W Bush since 2001.

LANGUAGE: English, with significant Spanish-speaking minorities.

RELIGION: Protestant majority with Roman Catholic, Jewish and many ethnic minorities. In large cities, people of the same ethnic background often live within defined communities.

TIME: The USA is divided into six time zones:
Eastern Standard Time: GMT - 5 (GMT - 4 from first Sunday in April to last Sunday in October).
Central Standard Time: GMT - 6 (GMT - 5 from first Sunday in April to last Sunday in October).
Mountain Standard Time: GMT - 7 (GMT - 6 from first Sunday in April to last Sunday in October).
Pacific Standard Time: GMT - 8 (GMT - 7 from first Sunday in April to last Sunday in October).
Alaska: GMT - 9 (GMT - 8 from first Sunday in April to last Sunday in October).
Hawaii: GMT - 10.
When calculating travel times, bear in mind the adoption of *Daylight Saving Time (DST)* by most States in summer. From the first Sunday in April to the last Sunday in October, clocks are put forward one hour, changing at 0200 hours local time. Regions not observing *DST* include most of Indiana, all of Arizona and Hawaii.

ELECTRICITY: 110 volts AC, 60Hz. Plugs are of the flat two-pin type. European electrical appliances not fitted with dual-voltage capabilities will require a plug adaptor, which is best purchased before arrival in the USA. The television system is NTSC I/II and is not compatible with the PAL and SECAM systems used in Asia and Europe, although cassettes can be converted.

COMMUNICATIONS: Telephone: Full IDD is available. Country code: 1. Outgoing international code: 011. For emergency police, fire or medical services in major cities, dial 911. The following area codes denote toll-free (freephone) numbers: 800, 855, 866, 877 and 888. Telephone numbers with the prefix 900 are usually expensive. **Mobile telephone:** GSM 1900 network, with a mixture of cellular and digital (especially in major centres) coverage. Most foreign mobile telephones, unless tri-band, do not work in the USA and charges are high. Most visitors choose to hire a mobile telephone. Network operators offering the closest to nationwide coverage include *AT&T Wireless* (website: www.attws.com), *Cingular* (joint venture of *SBC* and *Bell South*; website: www.cingular.com) and *Verizon* (formerly *Bell Atlantic* and *GTE*, now in joint venture with *Vodafone*; website: www.verizonwireless.com). **Fax:** There are bureaux in all main centres, and major hotels also have facilities. Public fax services are widely available; these often require a credit card. **Internet:** There are Internet cafes in most urban areas. ISPs include *America Online* (website: www.aol.com), *AT&T Business Internet Services* (website: www.attbusiness.net), *Cable & Wireless* (website: www.cw.com) and *MSN* (website: www.msn.com). **Telegram:** These can be sent at all Western Union offices by telephone or Internet (website: www.westernunion.com). Check the website for office locations. **Post:** There are numerous post offices throughout the States. Stamps can also be bought at stamp machines in hotels and shops and at ATMs, at an extra cost. Airmail to Europe takes up to one week. Post office hours: Mon-Fri 0900-1700 (24 hours at main offices in larger cities). **Press:** The most influential papers are the *Los Angeles Times*, *The New York Times*, the *Wall Street Journal* and the *Washington Post*. Owing to the high degree of self-government of each State, newspapers tend to be region specific, although recent economic pressures have resulted in large-scale mergers. Even so, the USA publishes more newspapers than any other country, and has perhaps the bulkiest Sunday newspapers in the world, particularly the Sunday edition of *The New York Times*.

Radio: BBC World Service (website: www.bbc.co.uk/worldservice) and Voice of America (website: www.voa.gov) can be received. From time to time the frequencies change and the most up-to-date can be found online.

Passport/Visa

	Passport Required?	Visa Required?	Return Ticket Required?
Full British	Yes	No/2/3	Yes
Australian	Yes	No/2	Yes
Canadian	Yes	No/1	No
USA	N/A	N/A	N/A
Other EU	Yes	No/2	Yes
Japanese	Yes	No/2	Yes

Note: *Regulations and requirements may be subject to change at short notice, and you are advised to contact the appropriate diplomatic or consular authority before finalising travel arrangements. Details of these may be found at the head of this country's entry. Any numbers in the chart refer to the footnotes below.*

Credit: © North Carolina Division of Tourism

Restricted entry: The following are not eligible to receive a USA entry visa:
(a) people afflicted with certain serious communicable diseases or disorders deemed threatening to the property, safety or welfare of others;
(b) anyone who has been arrested (except for very minor driving offences) or who has a criminal record;
(c) narcotics addicts or abusers and drug traffickers;
(d) anyone who has been deported from or denied admission to the USA.
Note: Those who are ineligible may be suitable candidates for a waiver of ineligibility.
PASSPORTS: Valid passport required by all. Validity varies - for most countries, a passport is required for the duration of the stay; check with the Embassy (see *Contact Addresses* section).
Note: (a) For nationals included in the Visa Waiver Program, passports must be valid for at least 90 days from date of entry (except for nationals of Andorra, Brunei and San Marino, who must hold passports valid for at least six months beyond the intended date of departure from the USA). (b) Introduced on October 26 2004, all travellers entering the USA under the Visa Waiver Program now require individual machine-readable passports. Children included on a parent's passport also now require their own machine-readable passport. Travellers not in possession of machine-readable passports will require a valid USA entry visa. (c) Passports issued on or after October 26 2005 will need to have a biometric identifier in order for the holder to travel visa-free under the Visa Waiver Program (VWP).
VISAS: Required by all except the following:
(a) citizens of countries under the Visa Waiver Program (see **2**. below);
(b) **1**. nationals of Bermuda and Canada, provided holding valid passports;
(c) nationals of Mexico, provided holding a valid passport and a US Border Crossing Card.
Note: (a) Landed Immigrants of Canada and British residents of Bermuda who are citizens of, and have valid passports from, Commonwealth countries or Ireland are no longer eligible to enter the USA without a visa.
(b) The Transit Without Visa (TWOV) and International-to-International (ITI) transit programs have been indefinitely suspended as of 2 August 2003. All passengers using US airports for transit purposes are now required to obtain a transit visa. This does not affect qualified travellers travelling visa-free under the Visa Waiver Program (see **2**. below).
Visa Waiver Program: (a) **2**. The following nationals, upon presentation of a valid passport (see **Note** above), do not require a visa under the Visa Waiver Program: Andorra, Australia, Brunei, EU countries (except nationals of Cyprus, Czech Republic, Estonia, Greece, Hungary, Latvia, Lithuania, Malta, Poland and Slovak Republic, who *do* require a visa), Iceland, Japan, Liechtenstein, Monaco, New Zealand, Norway, San Marino, Singapore and Switzerland.
To qualify for visa-free travel under the Visa Waiver Program, nationals must travel on a valid passport (see **Note** above), for holiday, transit or business purposes only and for a stay not exceeding 90 days.
If entering the USA by air or sea, passengers must hold a return or onward ticket or itinerary (if onward tickets terminate in Bermuda, Canada, Mexico or the Caribbean Islands, travellers must be legal permanent residents of those countries), hold a completed form I-94W and enter aboard an air or sea carrier participating in the Visa Waiver Program (lists of participating air or sea carriers are available from most travel agents or the carriers themselves).
If entering the USA by land from Canada or Mexico, hold a completed form I-94W* issued by Immigration at the port of entry and a US$6 fee (only payable in US Dollars).
Note*: (a) Passengers must have the full address and ZIP code of where they are staying in the USA to be able to fully complete the I-94W form. (b) Members of Visa Waiver Program countries who want to work, study or remain more than 90 days in the USA must apply for a visa before travelling, as should those who have been previously refused a visa, have a criminal record, or are in any way ineligible for an unrestricted visa. (c) **3**. Holders of UK passports with the endorsement British Subject, British Dependent Territories Citizen, British Protected Person, British Overseas Citizen or British National (Overseas) Citizen do not qualify for the Visa Waiver Program. Persons unsure about visa requirements (including those defined in 'Restricted Entry' above) should contact the US Consulate General *or* the Visa Department of the US Embassy (see *Contact Addresses* section).
Types of visa and cost: *Tourist, Business, Transit* and *Student*. Other types of visa are also available, contact the US Embassy (website: www.usembassy.org.uk) for further details. The visa application fee is $100 (currently equivalent to £60), regardless of whether the visa is issued or denied and regardless of the duration of the visa or entries required. The Embassy will provide a paying-in slip, which is attached to the application form DS-156. The fee must be paid in cash at a bank prior to submitting a visa application to the US Embassy, and the bank will issue a receipt of payment, which must be attached to the application form. The fee receipt, once paid, is valid for one year. Some nationals may also have to pay a reciprocal visa issuance fee - details are available from the State Department (website: www.travel.state.gov).
Validity: Visas may be used for travel to the USA until the date it expires, or if marked 'valid indefinitely' for up to 10 years. Some visas are valid for multiple entries. The length of stay in the USA is determined by US immigration officials at the time of entry but is generally six months; there is, however, no set time.
Note: (a) The Embassy no longer issues visas valid indefinitely. Any new B-1/B-2 visa issued will be valid for a maximum of 10 years. (b) A visa does not expire with the expiry of the holder's passport. An unexpired, endorsed visa in an expired passport may be presented for entry into the USA, as long as the visa itself has not been cancelled, is undamaged, is less than 10 years old and is presented with a valid non-expired passport, provided that both passports are for the same nationality.
Application to: Visa branches at Consulates General. Those residing in England, Scotland or Wales should apply to the Embassy in London (see *Contact Addresses* section).
Application requirements: (a) Completed visa application form DS-156 and form DS-157, if required. (b) Valid passport (validity dependent upon nationality) and with at least one blank page. (c) One recent passport-size photo. (d) Embassy copy of the fee receipt endorsed by the bank. (e) Evidence of sufficient funds to cover all expenses while in the USA. (f) Documentation of intent to return to country of residence. (g) Supporting documents (such as purpose of visit) and/or issuance fees, where relevant. (h) Stamped self-addressed, special delivery envelope, for return by post. *Business*: (a)-(h) and, (i) Evidence of intended business activities in the USA, such as a letter from employer.
Important Note: All applicants aged 14 to 79 are required to schedule an appointment for an interview. Applicants under the age of 14 and those 80 and over may be eligible to apply for a visa by mail.
Note: Additional processing requirements and information are required for: (a) males aged 16 to 45; (b) nationals of Cuba, Iran, Korea (Dem Rep), Libya, Sudan and the Syrian Arab Republic; (c) nationals of China (PR), Northen Cyprus, the Russian Federation, Somalia and Vietnam. Please note that requirements are subject to change at short notice and any applicant should check with the US Embassy (website: www.usembassy.org.uk).
Working days required: Varies with each Embassy; interview appointment waiting time is usually 25 to 30 days (27 days for London Embassy), and visa processing time is usually five to seven working days (three days for London Embassy). It is important to allow sufficient time for processing the visa, and final travel plans should not be made until a visa has been issued. Applications lodged during the peak travel season may take longer.
Temporary residence: The law in the USA is complex for those wishing to take up residence. More information may be obtained from the Embassy (see *Contact Addresses* section).

Money

Currency: US Dollar (US$) = 100 cents. Notes are in denominations of US$100, 50, 20, 10, 5 and 1. Coins are in denominations of US$1, and 50, 25, 10, 5 and 1 cents.
Currency exchange: Hotels do not, as a rule, exchange currency and only a few major banks will exchange foreign currency, so it is advisable to arrive with US Dollars.
Credit & debit cards: Most major credit cards are accepted throughout the USA, including American Express, Diners Club, MasterCard and Visa. Check with your credit or debit card company for details of merchant acceptability and other services that may be available. Visitors are advised to carry at least one major credit card, as it is common to request prepayment or a credit card imprint for hotel rooms and car hire, even when final payment is not by credit card.
Travellers cheques: Widely accepted in hotels, stores and restaurants, provided they are US Dollar cheques; Sterling travellers cheques are not acceptable and few banks will change these. Change is issued in US Dollars. It should be noted that many banks do not have the facility to cash travellers cheques (the US banking system differs greatly from that of the UK) and those that do are likely to charge a high commission. One or (in some cases) two items of identification (passport, credit card, driving licence) may also be required. To avoid additional exchange rate charges, travellers are advised to take travellers cheques in US Dollars.
Currency restrictions: There are no limits on the import or export of either foreign or local currency. However, amounts in excess of US$10,000 or the equivalent (including foreign currency, travellers cheques, money orders and 'bearer bonds') must be registered with US Customs on Form 4790. Failure to do so may result in civil and criminal prosecution, including seizure of the money. There is an embargo on transactions of US currency with Cuba, Iran, Iraq, Libya and North Korea (Democratic Republic of Korea).
Exchange rate indicators: The following figures are included as a guide to the movements of the US Dollar against Sterling:

Date	Feb '04	May '04	Aug '04	Nov '04
£1.00=	1.82	1.79	1.82	1.86

Banking hours: Variable, but generally Mon-Fri 0900-1500.

Duty Free

The following goods may be imported by visitors over 21 years of age into the USA without incurring customs duty:
200 cigarettes or 50 cigars or 2kg of smoking tobacco or proportionate amounts of each; 0.95l (1qt) of alcoholic

beverage; gifts or articles up to a value of US$100.
Note: (a) Items should not be gift-wrapped, as they must be available for customs inspection. (b) The alcoholic beverage allowance (see above) is the national maximum; certain States allow less and if arriving in those States, the excess will be taxed or withheld. (c) For information about the importation of pets, refer to the brochure *Pets, Wildlife – US Customs*, available at US Embassies and Consulates. (d) Further information on US customs regulations is available online (website: www.customs.ustreas.gov).
Prohibited and restricted items: The following are either banned or may only be imported under licence: (a) Narcotics and dangerous drugs, unless for medical purposes (doctor's certificate required). (b) Absinthe, biological materials, some seeds, fruits and plants (including endangered species of plants and vegetables and their products). (c) Firearms and ammunition (with some exceptions – consult Customs' website). (d) Hazardous articles (fireworks, toxic materials), including matches and match books (unless packed tightly in a closed container). (e) Meat and poultry products – fresh, dried or canned. (f) Any fish (unless certified as disease-free) or their eggs, unless canned, pickled or smoked. (g) Dairy products and eggs. (h) Cuban cigars, brought from any country. (i) Wildlife and endangered species, including crustaceans, molluscs, eggs, game and hunting trophies and crafted articles of any part thereof. (j) Dog and cat fur. (k) Some art and artefacts (such as Pre-Columbian monumental and architectural sculpture and murals from South America). (l) Imports from Iran and leather souvenirs from Haiti (eg drums). (m) Some automobiles. (n) More than one article (limited to once every 30 days) displaying a counterfeit or confusingly similar logo to trademarked and copyrighted articles. (o) Merchandise from embargoed countries: Afghanistan, Cuba, Iran, Iraq, Libya, Serbia & Montenegro and Sudan; information materials (pamphlets, books, tapes, films and recordings) are permitted, except from Iraq.
Note: Gold coins, medals and bullion, formerly prohibited, may be brought into the USA, except from embargoed countries (see above).

Public Holidays

2005: Jan 1 New Year's Day. **Jan 17** Martin Luther King Day. **Feb 21** Presidents' Day. **May 30** Memorial Day. **Jun 14** Flag Day. **Jul 4** Independence Day. **Sep 5** Labor Day. **Oct 10** Columbus Day. **Nov 11** Veterans' Day. **Nov 24** Thanksgiving Day. **Dec 25** Christmas Day. **Dec 31** New Year's Day.
2006: Jan 1 New Year's Day. **Jan 16** Martin Luther King Day. **Feb 20** Presidents' Day. **May 30** Memorial Day. **Jun 14** Flag Day. **Jul 4** Independence Day. **Sep 4** Labor Day. **Oct 9** Columbus Day. **Nov 1** Veterans' Day. **Nov 23** Thanksgiving Day. **Dec 25** Christmas Day. **Dec 31** New Year's Day.

Health

	Special Precautions?	Certificate Required?
Yellow Fever	No	No
Cholera	No	No
Typhoid & Pol	No	N/A
Malaria	No	N/A

Note: Regulations and requirements may be subject to change at short notice, and you are advised to contact your doctor well in advance of your intended date of departure. Any numbers in the chart refer to the footnotes below.

Other risks: *Rabies* may be present in wildlife. For those at high risk, vaccination before arrival should be considered. If you are bitten, seek medical advice without delay. For more information, consult the *Health* appendix.
Health care: Medical insurance providing cover up to at least US$500,000 is strongly advised. Only emergency cases are treated without prior payment and treatment will often be refused without evidence of insurance or a deposit. All receipts must be kept in order to make a claim. Medical facilities are generally of an extremely high standard. Many medications available over the counter in other countries require a prescription in the US. Those visiting the USA for long periods with school-age children should be aware that school entry requirements include proof of immunisation against diphtheria, measles, poliomyelitis and rubella throughout the USA, and schools in many States also require immunisation against tetanus, pertussis and mumps. HIV-positive visitors must apply at the Embassy for a waiver of inadmissibility before entry.

Travel - International

Note: The information to be found immediately below is of a general nature. For more details, consult the individual State sections.
Visitors to the USA should consider that, although all trips to the USA are almost always trouble-free, the US government has maintained its general threat from terrorism as "elevated". All nationals should expect stringent security checks at airports and in other public buildings. The US will also be consequently introducing changes to its entry requirements, with effect from 26 October 2004, for those wishing to enter the US under its Visa Waiver Programme.
AIR: The principal US airlines operating international services are: *American Airlines (AA)* (website: www.americanairlines.com), *Continental Airlines* (website: www.continental.com), *Delta Air* (website: www.delta.com), *Northwest Airlines* (website: www.nwa.com) and *United Airlines* (website: www.ual.com). Many other airlines operate services from all over the world to the USA.
International airports: The busiest airports in the USA include *Atlanta (ATL), Chicago (ORD), Los Angeles (LAX), Dallas/Forth Worth (DFW), San Francisco (SFO), Denver (DEN), Las Vegas (LAS), Minneapolis-St Paul (MSP), Phoenix (PHX)* and *Detroit (DTW)*. For further details, consult the individual State sections.
Approximate flight times: From *London* to Anchorage is eight hours 55 minutes, to Detroit is eight hours 30 minutes, to Los Angeles is 11 hours 20 minutes, to Miami is nine hours 45 minutes, to New York is seven hours 50 minutes, to San Francisco is 11 hours 10 minutes, to Seattle is nine hours 50 minutes and to Washington, DC is eight hours 25 minutes (all times are by non-stop flight).
From *Singapore* to Los Angeles is 18 hours 45 minutes and to New York is 21 hours 25 minutes.
From *Sydney* to Los Angeles is 17 hours 55 minutes and to New York is 21 hours five minutes.
More international flight times may be found in the individual State sections.
Note: Return flights to Europe from the east coast of the USA take approximately 30 to 40 minutes less than outward westbound flights, and from the west coast of the USA approximately 60 minutes less. Visitors arriving in the USA via international airports may be subject to serious delays. A stringent new security system, which requires all visitors with visas to be photographed and fingerprinted upon entry, was put into operation in January 2004, as part of US anti-terrorism measures. Experts warn that this heightened state of alert could prevail for the next few years.
Departure tax: None.
SEA: Numerous cruise lines sail from ports worldwide to both the east and west coasts; contact a travel agent for fares and details.
RAIL: The US and Mexican rail networks connect at Yuma, El Paso and Del Rio, with limited scheduled passenger services. There are several connections with the Canadian network, including New York–Montréal, Chicago–Toronto and Seattle–Vancouver services. For further information, contact *Amtrak* (tel: (800) 872 7245 (toll-free in USA) *or* (212) 582 6875 (New York); website: www.amtrak.com). In the UK, contact *Leisurail* (tel: (0800) 698 7545 *or* (0870) 750 0222).
ROAD: There are many crossing points from Canada to the USA. The major road routes are: New York to Montréal/Ottawa, Detroit to Toronto/Hamilton, Minneapolis to Winnipeg and Seattle to Vancouver/Edmonton/Calgary. There are road links to Mexican destinations from El Paso, San Diego, Tucson and San Antonio. **Bus**: *Greyhound* offers services to many destinations in Canada and some destinations in Mexico (tel: (800) 229 9424 (toll-free in USA); website: www.greyhound.com).

Travel - Internal

AIR: The USA may be crossed within five hours from east to west and within two hours from north to south. Strong competition between airlines has resulted in a wide difference between fares. Categories of fares include first-class, economy, excursion and discount. Night flights are generally cheaper.
Cheap fares: Money-saving schemes for overseas visitors include discounts on internal flights with the *Visit USA (VUSA) Airpass*, offered by the principal US airlines (often in conjunction with *British Airways*) and can be purchased in advance. (Delta offers a similar scheme branded as *Discover America*.) These passes are offered as a minimum of three and a maximum of 10 coupons entitling the passenger to that number of flights within the USA at a discounted fare; price is based on the number of flight segments. A number of restrictions usually apply, including: (a) the pass must be booked in conjunction with a round-trip flight to the USA (although this can, in some cases, be on a different carrier); (b) tickets must be purchased outside North America and are not available to US, Canadian and some Caribbean residents; (c) tickets must often be purchased before a specified time (eg 21 days in advance); (d) the traveller must utilise the first coupon within a specified time period (usually within 60 days of arrival in the USA) and use all the coupons within 180 days of arrival. Agents are advised to contact the offices of individual airlines once a basic itinerary has been organised, as terms may vary.
Note: Baggage allowance is often determined by number and size in addition to weight.
SEA/LAKE/RIVER: There are extensive water communications both along the coastline and along the great rivers and lakes. The Ohio River carries more water traffic than any other inland waterway in the world. Tour ships and passenger and freight lines crisscross all the Great Lakes from ports in Duluth, Sault Sainte Marie, Milwaukee, Chicago, Detroit, Buffalo, Rochester, Cleveland and Toronto.
RAIL: Nearly all the long-distance trains are operated by Amtrak, which serves more than 500 communities in 45 States over a 35,000km (22,000 mile) route system. Even so, rail is not considered the best or fastest way to travel within the USA, as trains can be slow and infrequent, as well as expensive. Some services, however, are popular and reliable. Services along the northeast corridor exist between Boston, New York and Washington. The 'Acela Express' high-speed rail service along the northeast corridor is capable of travelling up to 240kph (150mph), reducing the current three-hour trip between Washington, DC and New York by 30 minutes and the New York to Boston journey from four hours 30 minutes to three hours. Other routes from Washington, DC run south to Miami and New Orleans, and from Boston, New York or Washington, DC to Chicago. From Chicago, daily services radiate to Seattle, Portland, Oakland, San Francisco, Los Angeles, New Orleans and San Antonio (via Fort Worth). Connections also exist between Los Angeles and San Diego, Los Angeles and San Francisco, San Francisco and Bakersfield, San Francisco and Seattle (via Portland), San Antonio and Oklahoma City, New Orleans and Atlanta, and Kansas City and St Louis, amongst others. A coast-to-coast train service is provided between Jacksonville and Los Angeles via Tucson, El Paso, San Antonio, Houston and New Orleans. Prices and timetables are subject to change without notice.
A variety of State and municipal bodies operate short-distance and commuter rail lines around various urban centres, many connected to stops on the Amtrak lines. Amtrak also operates a *Thruway* bus service, which connects to some cities and towns not on the Amtrak grid. A number of independent companies offer short routes,

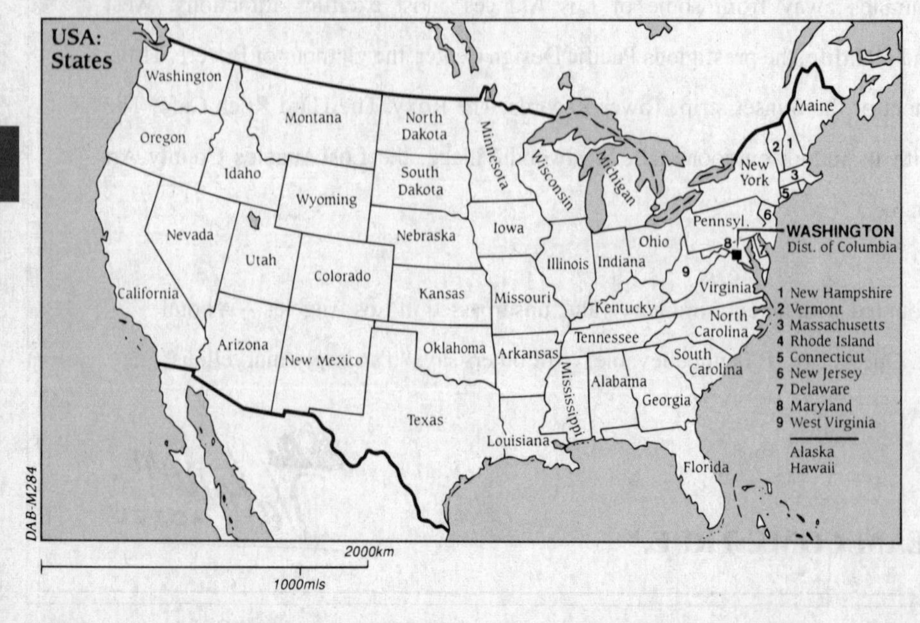

often in scenic locations, onboard vintage trains. These routes are often a good idea for travellers wishing to reach wilderness locations that are off the beaten track.

Amtrak contact details: For up-to-date information, contact *Amtrak* (tel: (800) 872 7245 (toll-free in USA) *or* (212) 582 6875 (New York); website: www.amtrak.com); in the UK, contact *Leisurail* (tel: (0800) 698 7545 *or* (0870) 750 0222). US travel agents can also obtain information on Amtrak train services, schedules and travel packages through the Western Folder Distribution Company Travel Information Network by entering their ARC number online (website: www.travelinfonetwork.com).

Facilities and services: Nearly all trains have coach seating and air conditioning, with a variety of sleeping accommodation available for a supplemental charge. All long-distance trains have waiter-staffed, seated dining facilities. Cafe cars on shorter trips provide snacks and beverages that guests can take back to their seats.

Tour packages: Amtrak offers a variety of tour packages flexible to any budget throughout the USA. Full details are provided in the *Amtrak Travel Planner*, which is widely available. A great deal of the USA's beautiful scenery and historical sites can only be viewed by train. Passenger trains continue to attract a discerning and ever-increasing clientele. Indeed, rail travel in the USA – as in many other countries – has undergone a considerable revival in recent years, and the trend continues. It is therefore advisable for passengers to reserve well in advance, as some routes are often booked out.

Cheap fares: The *USA Rail Pass* is specifically designed for international travellers from outside the USA or Canada and offers 15 or 30 days of unlimited travel either on a national or regional basis.

The *National USA Rail Pass* offers travel on the whole Amtrak network in the USA and Canada (excluding Auto Train, Metroliner and Acela Express between Boston, New York and Washington). It costs US$440 (US$295 off-peak) per person for 15 days and US$550 (US$385 off-peak) for 30 days. The peak season is from 28 May to 6 September and off-peak fares are in effect for the remainder of the year. Children under two years of age travel free and those aged two to 15 pay half the adult fare.

The following *Regional USA Rail Passes* are also available: the *Northeast Rail Pass* is valid on trains from Newport News (Virginia) north to Boston (Massachusetts), Burlington (Vermont) and Montréal (Canada), west from Philadelphia to Harrisburg (both Pennsylvania), west from New York City to Niagara Falls (New York State), and all stations in between; the *East Rail Pass* covers the region east of Chicago (Illinois) and New Orleans (Louisiana) up to Montréal; the *West Rail Pass* covers the region west of Chicago to Seattle (Washington State), Portland (Oregon), San Francisco and Los Angeles (both California); the *Far West Rail Pass* covers the region from Denver (Colorado) to Seattle, San Francisco and Los Angeles; and the *Coastal Rail Pass* covers the west coast and from Seattle to San Diego (California). Prices for these passes vary between US$205 for the 15-day Northeast Rail Pass and US$405 for the 30-day West Rail Pass (with a 20 to 30 per cent reduction during off-peak season). The *Northeast Rail Pass* also provides the option of purchasing a five-day pass for US$149 during the peak and off-peak seasons. Passes can be purchased prior to travel to the USA or at Amtrak stations, upon presentation of a valid passport issued outside Canada or the USA. Passports and passes must be presented for the issuance of rail tickets. The passes cover coach-class travel tickets and seat reservations on Amtrak passenger services. However, rail passes act as a form of payment for seats only – to guarantee a seat on a specific train, a reservation must be made well in advance; cancellation fees may apply. Travellers should contact Amtrak (tel: (800) 872 7245) to find out whether reservations are required on specific journeys they wish to make. For journeys where reservations are required, train times should be reconfirmed 24 hours prior to departure. Travellers planning to travel during peak times should make reservations well in advance. Further information on prices and timetables is available from Amtrak (for contact details, see above). A list of international sales representatives can be found online (website: www.amtrak.com/international/salesreps.html).

ROAD: Driving is a marvellous way to see the USA, although the distances between cities can be enormous (eg 4716km (2930 miles) between San Francisco and New York City). A realistic evaluation of travel times should be made to avoid over-strenuous itineraries. Driving conditions are excellent and the road system reaches every town. Petrol (gas) is cheaper than in Europe. *AAA* (American Automobile Association; website: www.aaa.com) offers touring services, maps and travel advice to affiliate auto club members. Some AAA clubs offer referrals to companies for vehicle insurance policies, which are compulsory in all States, even for hire cars. AAA basic benefits are offered as a courtesy to affiliate auto club members who present their valid membership card (eg AA membership for the UK) while visiting in the USA. For further information, Americans should contact their local AAA club office (listed in the local telephone directory), while visitors to the USA should contact their own national association for information on the AAA before departure.

Bus: *Greyhound* is the main national coach carrier and covers the whole of the USA. This 24-hour service is supplemented by over 11,000 other tour lines, covering the country with reasonably priced and regular services. Some Greyhound services are available to Canada and Mexico. There are express bus services between major cities. Air conditioning, toilets and reclining seats are available on all buses. Meals are not provided, however, food and drink (non-alcoholic) may be consumed on board and there are regular meal stops on longer routes. Unlimited stopovers are allowed for unrestricted fares. Reservations are not accepted (although may be required if connecting to another carrier) and seating is on a first-come, first-served basis; passengers are advised to arrive at the terminal approximately one hour before the scheduled departure. For information on fares and schedules, contact *Greyhound* (tel: (800) 229 9424 (toll-free in USA) *or* (402) 330 8552 (international callers); website: www.greyhound.com).

Cheap fares: Greyhound offers a range of *Discovery Pass* programmes, valid for four to 60 days in the USA and/or Canada, which can be purchased by US, Canadian and overseas travellers. The *International Ameripass* is 10 to 15 per cent cheaper than the domestic version, but must be purchased outside the USA and Canada. The *Ameripass*, which gives seven, 10, 15, 21, 30, 45 or 60 days unlimited travel throughout the USA and some points within Mexico, costs US$219-589 for domestic purchasers (US$209-539 for international). A four-day pass is also available for US$149, but only to overseas visitors. Passes are validated at the ticket counter at the beginning of the trip and identification must be shown; individual tickets are not necessary. The pass is valid for a continuous period (depending on which pass is purchased) starting from validation. Unlimited stops are allowed.

Discounted fares are available for children aged two to 12 years, passengers over 62 years old and students enrolled in undergraduate or postgraduate study. A variety of regional discounts are also available.

For further details, contact Greyhound on one of their *Discovery Pass* numbers (tel: (888) 454 7277 (if purchased in the USA) *or* (888) 661 8747 (if purchased in Canada) *or* (402) 330 8552 *or* 330 8584 (if purchased overseas)).

Car hire: Major international companies have offices at all gateway airports and in most cities. There are excellent discounts available for foreign visitors. US$140 per week is an acceptable budget rate and drivers should make sure that free unlimited mileage is included. A drop-off charge will most likely be added if the car is deposited in a different city from the one in which it was hired. Credit-card deposits and inclusive rates are generally required. As a guide to car sizes, an 'Economy' or 'Compact' refers to a car the size of a standard European car, while a 'Standard' refers to a car nearly the size of a limousine. Minimum ages for hirers vary according to the rental company, pick-up point and method of payment. Agents are advised to contact the individual companies for information on drivers under 25 years of age.

Those looking to hire a car in the USA can save money through fly-drive deals and by booking a car in advance (obtaining written confirmation of the price is recommended).

Drive away: *Auto Driveaway* provides a service enabling the traveller to drive cars to and from a given point, only paying the price of petrol. A deposit is often required and time and mileage limits are set for delivery, which leaves very little time for sightseeing (there are heavy financial penalties for those who exceed the limits). Drivers should also check the car beforehand, so as not to incur any unnecessary repair costs. Some companies allow the driver to finish the journey in Canada. Details are published under *Automobile & Truck Transporting* in the US Yellow Pages. For further information, contact *Auto Driveaway* (tel: (312) 939 3600 *or* (1-800) 346 2277; website: www.autodriveaway.com).

Campers/motorhomes: The hire of self-drive campers or motorhomes, which are called 'recreational vehicles' or RVs in the USA, is easy and provides a good means of getting around. For more information contact *The Recreational Vehicle Dealers Association* (website: www.cruiseamerica.com).

Documentation and insurance: An International Driving Permit is recommended, although it is not legally required (it is often very useful as an additional proof of identity). A full national driving licence is accepted for up to one year. All travellers intending to hire or drive cars or motorhomes in the USA are strongly advised to ensure that the insurance policy covers their total requirements, covering all drivers and passengers against injury or accidental death. A yellow 'non-resident, interstate liability insurance card', which acts as evidence of financial responsibility, is available through motor insurance agents.

Credit: © NYS DED

Additional Collision Damage Waiver covering the car itself is also strongly recommended; in some states this extra insurance is included in hire rates by law.

Traffic regulations: Traffic drives on the right. The speed limit is usually 55mph (89kph) on motorways, but varies from State to State. Speed limits are clearly indicated along highways and are strictly enforced, with heavy fines imposed. Note that it is illegal to pass a school bus that has stopped to unload its passengers (using indicators and warning lights) and all vehicles must stop until the bus has moved back into the traffic stream. It is illegal for drivers not to have their licences immediately to hand. If stopped, do not attempt to pay a driving fine on the spot (unless it is demanded), as it may be interpreted as an attempt to bribe.

Note: There are extremely tough laws against drinking and driving throughout the USA. These laws are strictly enforced.

URBAN: Some US cities now have good public transport services following a 'transit renaissance' after the energy crises of the 1970s. There are numerous underground train systems in operation in major cities including New York (subway), Washington, DC (metro), Boston ('T'), Chicago (train) and San Francisco (BART – Bay Area Rapid Transit); others are being planned or built. There are also several tramway and trolleybus systems, including the much-loved antique trams found in San Francisco.

Note: Many of the underground train systems are dangerous during off-peak hours (the New York subway, in particular, has acquired an almost gothic reputation for violence, although this has been much exaggerated), but they offer cheap, quick and efficient travel during the working day, particularly in New York, Boston and Chicago. Travel by any other means during the day is likely to be slow and arduous.

Accommodation

HOTELS/MOTELS: There are many good traditional hotels. However, the majority are modern and part of national and international chains, often with standard prices. Motels are hotels situated along main roads, away from the city centre and towns. In general, the quality of accommodation is high, with facilities such as televisions and telephones in each room. Hotels expect payment in advance and reservations are held until around 1800, unless a late arrival is requested. For further information, contact the American Hotel & Lodging Association, 1201 New York Avenue, NW, Suite 600, Washington, DC 20005 (tel: (202) 289 3100; fax: (202) 289 3199; e-mail: info@ahla.com; website: www.ahla.com).

Grading: Basic categories fall into **Super**, **Deluxe**, **Standard**, **Moderate** and **Inexpensive**. Prices vary according to standards.

Pre-paid voucher schemes: Several companies offer a pre-paid voucher scheme for use at various hotel and motel chains throughout the USA.

BED & BREAKFAST: This long established tradition in the UK is now spreading across the USA. B&B signs are not generally displayed by individual homes, but most homes offering this service are listed in directories, which may be purchased by interested travellers. 'B&B inns' have up to 20 or so rooms, and are distinguished from 'country inns' in that the latter offer meals in addition to breakfast; further information is available from the Professional Association of Innkeepers International (website: www.paii.org). There are also numerous national and regional B&B associations.
RANCH HOLIDAYS: There are ranches all over the southern and western States offering riding, participation in cattle drives, and activity holidays in mountain and lakeland settings.
CAMPING/CARAVANNING: This is extremely popular, especially in the Rocky Mountains and New England. The camping season in the north lasts from mid-May to mid-September; reservations are recommended if camping during the high season. Camping alongside highways and in undesignated areas is prohibited. For information on campsites, contact KOA (Kampgrounds of America) (tel: (406) 248 7444; fax: (406) 248 7414; website: www.koa.com). The 24,000-plus campsites fall into two general categories:
Public sites: Usually linked with National or State Parks and Forests, offering modest but comfortable facilities from US$8-20 per night. Most of them will have toilet blocks, electricity hook-ups and picnic areas. Campsites are usually operated on a first-come, first-served basis and will often restrict the length of stay. Advance reservations are possible at some national parks.
Privately run sites: These range from basic to resort luxury. Most have laundry and drying facilities, entertainment and information services. Reservations can be made through a central reservation office in the USA. Fees range from around US$15-35. Camping in the **backcountry** (a general term for areas inaccessible by road) requires a permit, available free of charge. Visitors are advised not to drink water from rivers and streams without boiling it for at least five minutes. It is also advisable to check fire regulations and inform a park ranger of the itinerary before setting out to a backcountry area.
YMCA/YOUTH HOSTELS: There are over 2400 YMCA centres throughout the USA. Membership is not necessary but reservations should be made two days prior to arrival via the Head Offices. The YMCA offers centrally located accommodation at attractive rates, coast to coast throughout the USA. Most centres offer single and double accommodation for both men and women and many also have sports facilities. For further information, contact YMCA of the USA, 101 North Wacker Drive, Chicago, IL 60606 (tel: (312) 977 0031; website: www.ymca.net).
Youth hostels offer their members simple, inexpensive overnight accommodation usually located in scenic, historical or cultural places. HI-AYH (Hostelling International - American Youth Hostels) operates some 150 hostels in both urban and rural locations. Membership is open to everyone, with no age limit, with free group and youth (under 18 years) memberships. For further information, contact the national office, 8401 Colesville Road, Suite 600, Silver Spring, MD 20910 (tel: (301) 495 1240; fax: (301) 495 6697; e-mail: hostels@hiusa.org; website: www.hiayh.ekit.com). European visitors should take out membership before travelling (website: www.hihostels.com).
SELF-CATERING: Self-catering facilities, known in the USA as 'apartments', 'condominiums' (or 'condos'), 'efficiencies' or 'villas', are also available.
HOME EXCHANGE: There are several agents who offer home exchange programmes between the UK and USA.

Resorts & Excursions

For details on resorts, excursions, places of interest and tourist attractions in the USA, see the individual State sections.

Sport & Activities

Outdoor pursuits: The vast expanses of wilderness, mountains, forest, canyons and coastlines of the USA lend themselves to a wide range of outdoor pursuits. From **trekking** in the Sierra Nevada Mountains, **whitewater rafting** through the Grand Canyon on the Colorado River, **canoeing** down the Mississippi River, **fishing** on the Great Lakes, **sailing** in Florida, **diving** in Hawaii to **skiing** in the Rocky Mountains, every activity can easily be arranged. The USA's national parks are administered by the National Park Service (NPS; website: www.nps.gov). **Hiking** trails are generally well kept and well marked. The National Park system includes National Monuments, which are smaller than parks and focus on maybe just one archaeological site or geological phenomenon (such as Devil's Tower in Wyoming), National Forests and 170 or so lesser known Parks, which are located away from the cities and highways. State Parks and State Monuments are administered by individual States. Most of the USA's parks and outdoor recreational areas have visitor centres where advice on trails, activities and other practical information (such as weather reports or fishing regulations) can be obtained. Most parks and monuments charge admission fees ranging from US$4-20. A number of passes are available from the NPS: the *National Parks Pass* (US$50) gives one driver and all accompanying passengers a year's unlimited access to nearly all national parks and monuments (users should note that this pass does not reduce fees for facilities such as camping, swimming, parking and boat launching). Only the larger parks have hotel-style accommodation, while almost all parks and monuments have facilities for camping. For further details on camping, see the *Accommodation* section. **Fishing** permits are compulsory and vary from State to State. **Rock climbing** and **mountaineering** are particularly popular in the Sierra Nevada and in the Rocky Mountains. For further information about reservations, permits, regulations and services, visitors should contact the individual parks in advance *or* the National Park Service, 1849 C Street, NW, Washington, DC 20240 (tel: (202) 208 6843; website: www.nps.gov).
Spectator sports: Often called 'the nation's pastime', **baseball** is an important part of the US psyche. The 'boys of summer' play Major League Baseball (tel: (212) 931 7800; website: www.mlb.com) from April to September, 162 games in total, culminating in the post-season *World Series* championships, first contested in 1903. Games are frequent and tickets for regular season games are readily available and can be relatively cheap, starting at around US$9 per seat. **American football** tickets during the September to January National Football League (NFL; tel: (212) 450 2000; website: www.nfl.com) season are not only very expensive but also extremely hard to come by. Many people opt for the popular college games instead. College **basketball** is also surprisingly high profile, although not as big a draw as professional games in the National Basketball Association (NBA) (tel: (212) 407 8000; website: www.nba.com), whose season runs from November to April, with the playoffs often extending to June. The popularity of **ice hockey** has expanded from Canadian and far northern cities to the rest of the USA. Professional teams compete in the National Hockey League (website: www.nhl.com) from October to March, and tickets are sold out quickly. The most popular **tennis** competition in the USA is the *US Open* at Flushing Meadows in New York, held from late August to early September. Individual tickets go on sale during June. For ticket information, write to Customer Service, US Open Ticket Office, USTA National Tennis Center, Flushing Meadows Corona Park, Flushing, NY 11368 (website: www.usopen.org). For general information on tennis, contact the United States Tennis Association (website: www.usta.com). The heart of **horse racing** in the USA is the 'bluegrass country', focused around the State of Kentucky. The most important races of the year, the *Bluegrass Stakes* and the *Kentucky Derby* (on the first Saturday in May), are run at the Churchill Downs racecourse in Louisville, Kentucky. There are also major tracks in New England. **Rodeos**, a legacy of the historical development that resulted from the spread of cattle ranching, are frequently held in Colorado, Oklahoma, Texas and throughout the western States. The USA also hosts the world's largest **motor racing** event, the *Indianapolis 500*, held annually in May.
Wintersports: The USA offers some of the world's best **skiing** runs, particularly in the Rocky Mountains and the Sierra Nevada. The Rocky Mountain States (and Colorado in particular) are good for **downhill skiing**, the best-known resorts including Aspen, Big Sky, Jackson Hole and Vail. In the Sierra Nevada, Lake Tahoe is the major ski destination. **Cross-country skiing** is also well catered for, with backcountry ski lodges scattered around mountainous areas along both coasts (New England and California) and in the Rockies. Minnesota, Wisconsin and Wyoming are also good destinations for cross-country skiing. Information on cross-country skiing can be obtained from the Cross Country Ski Areas Association (website: www.xcski.org). In the past few years, **snowboarding** has become increasingly popular, and plenty of ski resorts now offer half pipes and board rental.
Golf: The American passion for golf is exemplified by the extremely high number of courses found throughout the country, as well as the massive crowds flocking to the United States Golf Association's national championships games. In 2002, the 102nd *US Open* was held on a public course for the first time, at Bethage State Park (Black Course) on Long Island. For further details on courses, fees and competitions, contact the United States Golf Association (USGA), PO Box 708, Far Hills, NJ 07931 (tel: (908) 234 2300; fax: (908) 234 9687; website: www.usga.org).
Watersports: One of the activities that epitomises US sport is **surfing** and Hawaii, with its legendary winter swells at northern Oahu (surfing's spiritual home), Sunset Beach, Waimea and the Banzai Pipeline (situated in the Ehukai beach parks), remains one of the USA's (and the world's) most famous surfing destinations. California also has some good breaks in Malibu, Rincon and Steamer Lane. During winter, southern California is also superb, with swells at Huntingdon Beach and Santa Cruz. **Diving** and **snorkelling** are particularly good in California, Florida, Hawaii and along the East Coast. The Professional Association of Diving Instructors (PADI), the world's largest recreational diving membership organisation, has its headquarters in California, at 30151 Tomas Street, Rancho Santa Margarita, CA 92688 (tel: (800) 729 7234 *or* (949) 858 7234; fax: (949) 858 7264; e-mail: webmaster@padi.com; website: www.padi.com). Other popular watersports include **sailing**, **windsurfing**, **sea kayaking** and **jetskiing**.

Social Profile

FOOD & DRINK: In large cities, restaurants are mostly modern and very clean, offering a vast range of cuisines, prices and facilities. US breakfasts are especially notable for such specialities as pancakes or waffles with maple syrup, home fries and grits (a Southern dish). Foreigners are often perplexed by the common question of how they would like their eggs fried, ie 'over easy' (flipped over briefly) or 'sunny side up' (fried on one side only). Fast food chains serving hot dogs, hamburgers and pizzas are everywhere. Regional specialities range from Spanish and Mexican flavours in the southwest to Creole, French and 'Soul Food' in the Deep South, Tex-Mex tastes in Texas, seafood chowder and Maine lobsters of New England, and the bare edible minimum that is California cuisine. Restaurants come in all shapes and sizes, ranging from fast-food, self-service and counter service to drive-in and table service. The 'diner' is an integral part of the US way of life; consisting of a driveway, neon lights and simple food served from the counter; these are generally located in or just outside smaller towns. Discounts on eating out include *Early Bird Dinners*, where discounts are offered for meals served prior to 1800; *Children's Platters*, selections from a low-cost children's menu; and *Restaurant Specials*, when a different specific meal is offered each day at a discount price or there is an all-you-can-eat menu.
There are also many types of bars, ranging from the smart cocktail lounge, cafe-style, high 'saloon' style bars and imitations of English pubs to the 'regular' bar. Many have 'happy hours' with cheaper drinks and free snacks on the counter. Generally speaking, waiter/waitress service costs more. Drinking laws are set by the individual States, counties, municipalities and towns, although closing time in bars is traditionally between midnight and 0300. The legal age for drinking also varies from 18 to 21 from State to State and the laws on the availability of alcohol run from New Orleans' policy of anytime, anywhere and to anyone, to localities, such as in Utah, where drinking is strictly prohibited. Where the laws are severe, there are often private clubs or a town only a few kilometres away from the 'dry town' where alcohol sales are legal. It is important to be aware of these laws when visiting an area and it is worth remembering that where alcohol is available, visitors may be asked to produce some form of identity that will prove their age. It should also be noted that it is illegal to have an open container of alcohol in a vehicle or on the street. Beer is the most popular and widespread drink and is served ice cold. In some States the alcohol content of beer is restricted to around 3 per cent. The best places to find good beer are micro-breweries and brewpubs, found in most major cities and university towns. Californian wines are very popular; see *Food & Drink* in the individual State sections for further details.
NIGHTLIFE: Clubs generally stay open until the early hours in cities, where one can find music and theatre of all descriptions. Theatre tickets for Broadway, New York's equivalent of London's West End 'Theatreland', can be booked through the Group Sales Box Office, 226 West 47th Street, 10th Floor, New York, NY 10036 (tel: (800) 223 7565 *or* (212) 398 8383; website: www.bestofbroadway.com). Special discounts for group bookings are available. Tickets must be paid for in advance and will be mailed out or kept at the theatre box office for collection on the night of the performance. Gambling is only allowed in licensed casinos and the legal age for gamblers is 21 years of age or over.
SHOPPING: Variety, late opening hours, competitive prices and an abundance of modern goods typify US shopping. Many small stores, specialist food shops and hypermarkets are open 24 hours a day. Clothes and electronic goods can be bought direct from factories. Retail outlets range from flea markets and bargain stores to large chain department stores. Malls are a popular way of shopping in the USA and consist of a cluster of different kinds of shops in one building, often a few storeys high, connected by an indoor plaza. Note that a sales tax is levied on most or all items in most States and the addition is not included on the price label; sales tax can be anywhere from 3 to 15 per cent, depending on the State; some States have no sales tax at all. **Shopping hours**: Mon-Sat 0900/0930-1730/1800. There may be late-night shopping one or two evenings a

week. Some States permit Sunday trading.
SPECIAL EVENTS: The holidays which are closest to the people's hearts are *Thanksgiving* and *Christmas*; see also *Special Events* in the individual State sections.
Mardi Gras: Every year, New Orleans celebrates the weeks leading up to Mardi Gras (Feb 8 in 2005), attracting visitors from all over the USA and abroad. There are parades, dancing in the streets and revellers in masks and costumes all in a spirit of wild abandon.
The Fourth of July: In honour of the USA's victory against the British in the Revolutionary War, this holiday is celebrated throughout the country, with spectacular fireworks displays. US fireworks are among the best in the world and some of the most dazzling shows take place over lakes, rivers or on the coast, where the sky is lit up and the light is reflected in the water.
Hallowe'en: Another holiday celebrated in the USA is Hallowe'en (Oct 31). Children dress up in costumes, often as witches, devils and ghosts and tour the neighbourhood, usually in groups, knocking on the doors of nearby houses and saying 'trick or treat'. The owner of the house is then obliged to give the children some sort of 'treat', usually food or sweets. Failure to comply can result in the 'trick'. The night before Hallowe'en is known as Mischief Night, when children roam their neighbourhoods making a nuisance of themselves with pranks such as ringing doorbells and running away or spreading toilet paper along fences and telephone poles. Both of these nights are somewhat unpopular with adults, but children have a great time and the tradition is probably too ingrained in US psyche to be discontinued.
Thanksgiving: This takes place on the fourth Thursday of November (Nov 24 in 2005). It is a festival celebrated with close family and friends. Blessings are shared and prayers of thanks are said over a meal of roast turkey, bread stuffing, roast potatoes and yams. This holiday originated in the first year after the Pilgrim Fathers arrived in the New World, as a feast to thank the Native Americans for their aid and advice in helping the immigrants come to grips with a new land.
Christmas: Americans celebrate Christmas (Dec 25) in a big way, both religiously and as consumers. Northern regions have the added bonus of wintery weather and snowfall, and a 'White Christmas' (a fairly common event in the New England area and other northern States) always adds to the atmosphere.
SOCIAL CONVENTIONS: The wide variety of national origins and the USA's relatively short history has resulted in numerous cultural and traditional customs living alongside each other. In large cities, people of the same ethnic background often live within defined communities. Shaking hands is the usual form of greeting. A relaxed and informal atmosphere is usually the norm. As long as the fundamental rules of courtesy are observed, there need be no fear of offending anyone of any background. Americans are renowned for their openness and friendliness to visitors. Gifts are appreciated if one is invited to a private home. As a rule, dress is casual. Smart restaurants, hotels and clubs insist on suits and ties or long dresses. Smoking is becoming increasingly unpopular in the US and is often considered offensive; it is essential to ask permission from all present before lighting up. Smoking is forbidden on city transport and often restricted or forbidden in public buildings. There will usually be a notice where no smoking is requested and most restaurants have smoking and non-smoking sections. Smoking is banned in all restaurants in California and New York City.
Tipping: Widely practised, as service charges are not usually included in the bill and waiters depend heavily on tips for their income. Waiters generally expect 15 to 20 per cent, as do taxi drivers and hairdressers. It should be noted that a cover charge is for admission to an establishment, not a tip for service. Porters generally expect US$1 per bag.

Credit: © Tennessee Tourism

Business Profile

ECONOMY: The US economy is the world's largest, most powerful and most diverse. The roots of this lie in the physical expansion and development of the country during the 19th century. As a result, the USA benefited from a unique combination of mass immigration, technological and marketing innovations, exploitation of natural resources, the expansion of international trade, historical fortune (hugely destructive wars that caused immense damage to other world powers but left the USA virtually untouched) and the fostering of a political and economic system well designed to exploit them. The enormous influence of US-based multinational companies in the world economy has not only afforded unique global influence to the US government but also allowed its currency to acquire unique international status. Large areas of the USA, particularly in the Midwest, are under cultivation and produce a wide range of commodities: the most important of these are cotton, cereals and tobacco, all of which are exported on a large scale. The principal mining operations produce oil and gas, coal, copper, iron, uranium and silver. The US manufacturing industry is a world leader in many fields including steel, vehicles, aerospace, telecommunications, chemicals, electronics and consumer goods. Since the late 1970s, however, the biggest employer has been the service sector, particularly finance (including banking, insurance and equities), leisure and tourism. Services now account for three quarters of output and employment. New computer-based industries associated with the Internet, which began revolutionising lifestyles and commerce during the late 1990s, rose quickly, burned brightly and died suddenly. Toward the close of 2000, many of these 'dot-com' industries plunged into bankruptcy. The USA's technology sector went into decline and the country found itself in recession.
Annual growth averaged around 4 to 5 per cent during the late 1990s, but slipped to 2.2 per cent as the economy slowed down. The events of September 2001 added to the pessimistic outlook for the economy, as several industries (notably civil aviation and tourism) suffered a sudden fall in demand. In addition to important IT and telecommunications industries, traditional manufacturing industries, such as steel, were also depressed. Toward the end of 2003, a BSE scare caused a major upheaval in the USA's meat industry, particularly affecting its exports (mainly to Japan). The internationally controversial war on Iraq has also threatened many trade friendships and lowered the value of the US Dollar (US$1 in 1990 had the same buying power as US$1.42 in 2003), although the USA's economic might has been maintained. Unemployment reached 5.2 per cent in February 2005.
The USA's most important trade relationship is with Canada (which accounts for approximately 20 per cent of all US trade). The two countries concluded a free trade agreement in 1989: this accord formed the basis for the North American Free Trade Agreement (NAFTA), to which Mexico became a signatory in 1992. (NAFTA is of similar proportions to the EU in terms of population and economic output.) Other major trading partners are Japan, the UK and Germany, followed by other members of the EU.
BUSINESS: Businesspeople are generally expected to dress smartly, although a man may wear a short-sleeved shirt under his suit in hot weather. Normal business courtesies should be observed, although Americans tend to be less formal than Europeans. Appointments and punctuality are normal procedure and business cards are widely used. Dates in America are written month-day-year: July 4 2005 would thus be abbreviated as 7/4/05. Write out the month in full to avoid confusion. **Office hours**: Mon-Fri 0900-1730.
COMMERCIAL INFORMATION: The following organisations can offer advice: The Partnership for New York City, 1 Battery Park Plaza, 5th Floor, New York, NY 10004 (tel: (212) 493 7400; fax: (212) 344 3344; e-mail: info@pfnyc.org; website: www.nycp.org); *or* The US Chamber of Commerce, 1615 H Street, NW, Washington, DC 20062 (tel: (202) 659 6000 or (800) 638 6583; e-mail: intl@uschamber.com; website: www.uschamber.org); *or* the Trade Information Center, US Department of Commerce (tel: (800) 872 8723; fax: (202) 482 4473; e-mail: tic@ita.doc.gov; website: www.tradeinfo.doc.gov); *or* the National Foreign Trade Council, 1625 K Street, NW, Suite 200, Washington, DC 20006 (tel: (202) 887 0278; fax: (202) 452 8160; e-mail: nftcinformation@nftc.org; website: www.nftc.org); *or* British American Business Inc, 52 Vanderbilt Avenue, 20th Floor, New York, NY 10017 (tel: (212) 661 4060; fax: (212) 661 4074) *or* the UK office at 75 Brook Street, London W1K 4AD, UK (tel: (020) 7467 7400; fax: (020) 7493 2394; website: www.babinc.org).
CONFERENCES/CONVENTIONS: If for no other reason than its role in the world economy, the USA is an important conference destination; there are State, city and regional travel and convention organisations in every part of the country, each actively promoting its own assets. With so much information available, the real problem for the organiser is to find some way of getting through it all. There are several magazines aimed at helping the conference organiser; they include Meeting & Conventions Magazine (website: www.meetings-conventions.com), Successful Meetings Magazine (website: www.successmtgs.com) and Corporate Meetings and Incentive Magazine (website: www.meetingsnet.com). Home to three of the 10 largest convention venues in the USA, Las Vegas was the most popular US trade show venue in 2004, hosting some 174 shows, followed by New York City, Chicago, Atlanta, Dallas, Orlando, New Orleans, San Diego, San Francisco and Washington, DC. Organisers interested in US venues should contact the US Travel Industry Association or one of the travel organisations listed in the individual State sections. In addition to the State organisations, addresses of travel and convention organisations for cities and counties are also included.

Climate

See the individual State sections.

Alabama

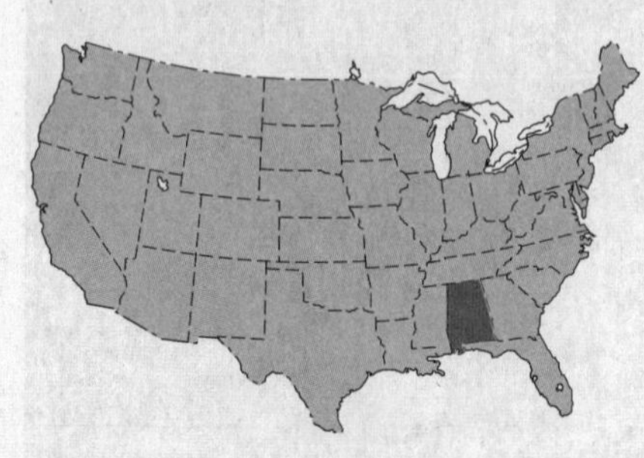

Alabama Bureau of Tourism & Travel
Street address: Suite 126, Alabama Center for Commerce, 401 Adams Avenue, Montgomery, AL 36104
Postal address: PO Box 4927, Montgomery, AL 36103
Tel: (334) 242 4169 *or* (800) 252 2262 (toll-free).
Fax: (334) 242 4554.
Email: info@tourism.state.al.us
Website: www.800alabama.com
Greater Birmingham CVB
2200 Ninth Avenue North, Birmingham, AL 35203
Tel: (205) 458 8000 *or* (800) 458 8085 (toll-free).
Fax: (205) 458 8086.
E-mail: info@birminghamal.org
Website: www.birminghamal.org
Huntsville/Madison County CVB
500 Church Street, Suite 1, Huntsville, AL 35801
Tel: (256) 551 2230. Fax: (256) 551 2324.
E-mail: info@huntsville.org
Website: www.huntsville.org
Mobile Bay CVB
Street address: 1 South Water Street, Mobile, AL 36602 (Mobile Convention Centre).
Postal address: PO Box 204, Mobile, AL 36601
Tel: (251) 208 2000 *or* (800) 566 2453 (toll-free). Fax: (251) 208 2060 *or* 2150 (Mobile Convention Centre).
E-mail: landon-howard@mobile.org
Website: www.mobile.org
Montgomery Area CVB
Convention & Visitor Bureau, 300 Water Street, Montgomery, AL 36104
Tel: (334) 261 1100 *or* (800) 240 9452 (toll-free).
Fax: (334) 261 1111.
E-mail: tourism@montgomerychamber.com
Website: www.visitingmontgomery.com

General Information

NOTE: Alabama means 'tribal town' in the Creek Indian language.
Nickname: The Heart of Dixie
State bird: Yellowhammer (Flicker)
State flower: Camellia
CAPITAL: Montgomery
Date of admission to the Union: 14 Dec 1819
POPULATION: 4,530,182 (official estimate 2004)
POPULATION DENSITY: 33.4 per sq km
2003 total overseas arrivals/US ranking: 72,000/29
TIME: Central (GMT - 6). *Daylight Saving Time* is observed.

THE STATE: Alabama offers mountains, lakes, caverns, woodland and beaches. Birmingham is its largest city. Attractions include the **VisionLand** theme park and **McWane Center** (a hands-on science adventure) and **IMAX theatre**; the **Birmingham Museum of Art**; and the **Alabama Sports Hall of Fame (ASHOF)**, founded in 1967 and dedicated to sporting legends such as Jesse Owens and Joe Louis.
Montgomery was the first capital of the Confederacy, and the **First White House of the Confederacy**, home to Jefferson Davis, first President of the provisional government, is still open to the public. Country music lovers from across the USA make pilgrimages to the **Hank Williams Memorial** in the Oakwood Cemetery Annex. Fans lay flowers next to the huge cowboy hat that lies on his gravestone. The *Alabama Shakespeare Festival*, the fifth-largest Shakespeare festival in the world, attracts around 170,000 visitors every year between August and November, and is staged at the **Carolyn Blount Theatre**. Some 200 years of American art is covered in the **Montgomery Museum of Fine Arts**. Alabama played a key role in the American civil rights movement in the 1950s and 1960s. The Reverend Martin Luther King Jr first preached at the **Dexter Avenue King Memorial Baptist Church** in Montgomery, a National Historic Landmark, and sites commemorating the struggle can be found across the State.

Credit: © Alabama Bureau of Tourism and Travel

These include the statues in Birmingham's **Kelly Ingram Park**, the **National Voting Rights Museum and Institute** in **Selma**, and the **Civil Rights Memorial** in **Montgomery**. In Birmingham, visitors can go on the **Black Heritage Tour** of the city centre and visit the **Birmingham Civil Rights Institute (BCRI)** with its impressive display of African-American history. **Tuskegee** is just an hour's drive from Montgomery. A former slave, Booker T Washington, founded the **Tuskegee Institute** to improve educational opportunities for blacks. Today, visitors can take guided tours of the thriving university and a restored version of Washington's home, another National Historic Landmark. **Mobile** is a major seaport, home to the **Mobile Museum of Art** and a lively *Family Mardi Gras* celebration (Jan 21-Feb 8 2005); carnival costumes are on display in the **Museum of Mobile**. The city is famed for its diverse architecture resulting from English, French and Spanish rule, notably in the **Church Street Historic District**. For children, there is the **Gulf Coast Exploreum** and the **Phoenix Fire Museum**, which includes antique fire engines. Other Alabama tourist destinations and attractions include the **US Space & Rocket Center** in **Huntsville**; the **Robert Trent Jones Golf Trail**; the **Russell Cave National Monument** in **Bridgeport**; and the resort towns of **Gulf Shores** and **Orange Beach**.

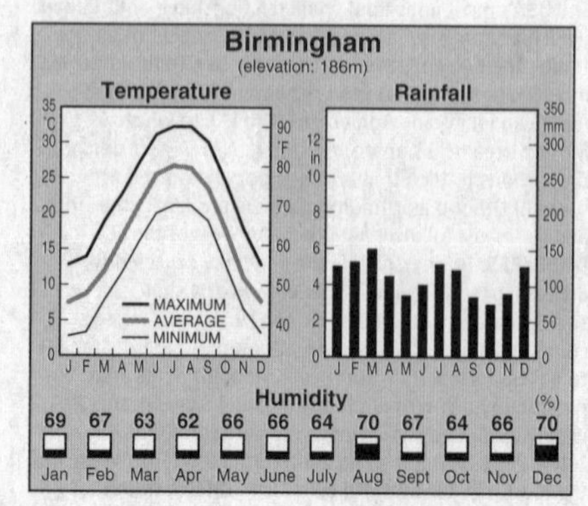

Alaska

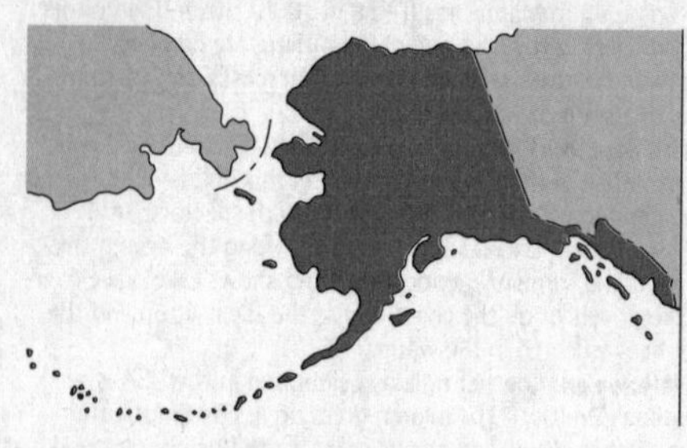

Alaska Travel Industry Association
2600 Cordova Street, Suite 201, Anchorage, AK 99503
Tel: (907) 929 2842. Fax: (907) 561 5727.
E-mail: info@alaskatia.org
Website: www.travelalaska.com *or* www.alaskatia.org
Provides tourist information to visitors and trade.
Alaska Public Lands Information Center
605 West Fourth Avenue, Suite 105, Anchorage, AK 99501
Tel: (907) 271 2737. Fax: (907) 271 2744.
E-mail: anch_web_mail@nps.gov
Website: www.nps.gov/aplic
Other offices in Fairbanks, Ketchikon and Tok.
Anchorage CVB
524 West Fourth Avenue, Anchorage, AK 99501
Tel: (907) 276 4118. Fax: (907) 278 5559.
E-mail: info@anchorage.net
Website: www.anchorage.net
Fairbanks CVB
Log Cabin Visitor Information Centre, 550 First Avenue, Fairbanks, AK 99701
Tel: (800) 327 5774 *or* (907) 456 5774 *or* 4636.
Fax: (907) 452 2867.
E-mail: info@explorefairbanks.com
Website: www.explorefairbanks.com
Juneau CVB
1 Sealaska Plaza, Suite 305, Juneau, AK 99801
Tel: (907) 586 1737 *or* (800) 587 2201 (toll-free).
Fax: (907) 586 1449.
E-mail: info@traveljuneau.com
Website: www.traveljuneau.com
Ketchikan Visitors Bureau
131 Front Street, Ketchikan, AK 99901
Tel: (907) 225 6166 *or* (800) 770 3300 (toll-free).
Fax: (907) 225 4250.
E-mail: info@visit-ketchikan.com
Website: www.visit-ketchikan.com
Southeast Alaska Discovery Center
50 Main Street, Ketchikan, AK 99901
Tel: (907) 228 6220. Fax: (907) 228 6234.
E-mail: r10_ketchikan_Alaska_info@fs.fed.us
Website: www.fs.fed.us/rio/tongass

General Information

Nickname: The Last Frontier
State bird: Willow Ptarmigan
State flower: Forget-Me-Not
CAPITAL: Juneau
Date of admission to the Union: 3 Jan 1959
POPULATION: 655,435 (official estimate 2004)
POPULATION DENSITY: 0.4 per sq km
2003 total overseas arrivals/US ranking: Under 38,000
TIME: Alaska (GMT - 9) in the greater part of the State; Hawaii-Aleutian (GMT - 10) west of 169° 30'. *Daylight Saving Time* is observed in the greater part of the State, but not west of 169° 30'.

THE STATE: The largest state in the USA, Alaska is a sparsely populated land of immense natural beauty. At one-fifth the size of the lower 48 States, Alaska has 3 million lakes, over 3000 rivers, 17 of the USA's 20 highest peaks, 100,000 glaciers and 15 national parks, preserves and monuments.

Travel - International

AIR: *Ted Stevens Anchorage International (ANC)* (website: www.dot.state.ak.us/anc/aiawlcm.html) is served by seven international carriers and 17 domestic carriers.
Fairbanks International (FBK) (website: www.dot.state.ak.us/faiiap) is the state's second-largest airport and has direct services from a number of North American gateways. Ketchikan International (KTN) sits on Gravina Island just across from the city; a small ferry runs from the airport to just above the State ferry dock.
Juneau International (JNU) is located 14km (9 miles) north of Juneau.

Domestic airports: Most in-State flights are on jet or turboprop aircraft. Several airlines, largely based at Anchorage, operate scheduled air-taxi and air-charter services to almost every Alaskan village. *Alaska Airlines* (tel: (800) 252 7522; website: www.alaskaair.com) flies to Alaska's largest cities (Anchorage, Fairbanks, Juneau and Ketchikan), as well as a number of bush communities throughout the state. A number of smaller, regional airlines provide statewide services.
SEA: The *Alaska Marine Highway System* (website: www.dot.state.ak.us/amhs) provides a practical ferry service on four separate routes: inside Passage/Southeast, Southwest, Southcentral and a Cross-Gulf route. Visitors can board the ferry at Bellingham (Washington) and travel up to Skagway on the Inside Passage/Southeast route; the Southwest route connects the Kenai Peninsula and Prince William Sound to the Aleutians Islands; the new Kennicott ferry runs an infrequent Southcentral service (once a month during summer), linking the two routes (running between Juneau and Seward).
RAIL: The scenic, historic and expensive *Alaska Railroad* (website: www.alaskarailroad.com) operates daily between Anchorage, Fairbanks, Grandview, Hurricane and Seward. At the southern end of the rail corridor, connections with the State ferry system can be made at Seward and Whittier. Except for the Anchorage–Seward and Anchorage– Grandview routes, the railway operates all year round, with reduced services from September to May.
ROAD: The famous *Alaska Highway* covers a staggering 2647km (1645 miles) from Delta Junction, near Fairbanks, to Dawson Creek (British Columbia, Canada). Drivers should note that weather conditions can be hazardous, and create visibility and navigational challenges. The road system is in good condition, however, and if drivers use common sense and are prepared for changes in the weather, the Alaska Highway is an ideal way to explore the State. Other roads only reach a quarter of the State's vast area, and treacherous weather conditions can make driving a hazardous option. Further information and suggested itineraries may be found online courtesy of 'North to Alaska' (website: www.northtoalaska.com).
Bus: *Alaska Direct Bus Line* (tel: (907) 277 6652 *or* (800) 770 6652 (toll-free); e-mail: alaskadirect@tokalaska.com) offers bus services from Anchorage to Whitehorse, Canada (travel time – 16 to 18 hours) and from Fairbanks to Whitehorse (travel time - 13 to 15 hours), thrice weekly in summer, weekly in winter. From Whitehorse, *Greyhound Canada* (website: www.greyhound.ca) offers thrice-weekly connections to Vancouver, British Columbia (travel time – 40 hours 30 minutes). The total travel time from Alaska to the lower 48 States can take up to five days and involve a number of connections. *Greyhound Canada* also has daily connections from Prince George, British Columbia to Prince Rupert, British Columbia (travel time - 10 hours 30 minutes), from where a ferry may be taken to Alaska. This trip follows the impressive *Yellowhead Highway* as it heads along to the coast.
URBAN: Cars are available for hire statewide, with major chains featured in most cities.

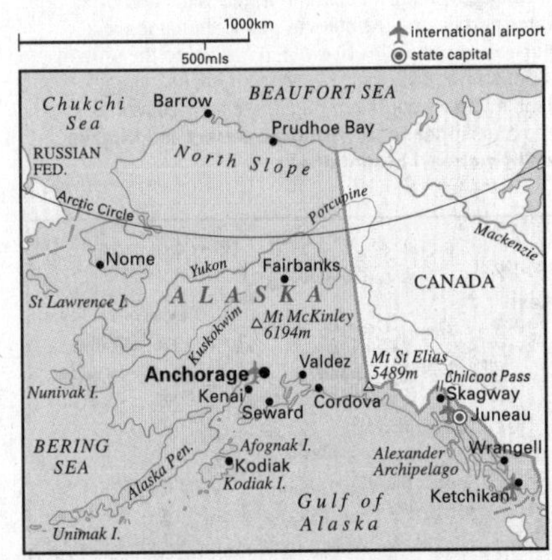

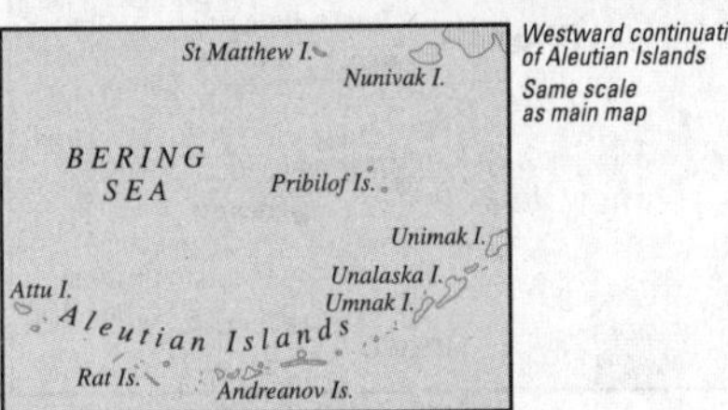

Westward continuation of Aleutian Islands
Same scale as main map

Resorts & Excursions

ANCHORAGE: Alaska's largest city is both a popular tourist destination and the centre of commerce and transportation for the region; 40 per cent of the State's population lives here. Local wildlife museums include the **Alaska Zoo**, the **Imaginarium** and **Potter's Marsh**, where up to 130 species of waterfowl can be viewed from a boardwalk. Geographical reminders of the 1964 Good Friday Earthquake (North America's strongest) can be seen at **Earthquake Park**, while admission to the **Alaska Experience Center** includes a film on this devastating event. A wealth of local history can be seen at the **Heritage Library and Museum**, the **Anchorage Museum of History and Art**, the **Oscar Anderson House Museum**, and the **Alaska Native Heritage Center**, situated some 10km (6 miles) east of the city. A short trip north of town leads to the **Eagle River Visitor Center** and the alpine beauty of **Chugach State Park**. Also north of the city, at **Eklutna Village Historical Park**, highlights include **St Nicholas Russian Church** and the brightly painted 'spirit houses'. South of Anchorage, at Girdwood, visitors can try their luck by panning for gold nuggets at **Crow Creek Mine**.
FAIRBANKS: Alaska's second-largest city, situated at the northern end of the Alaska Highway, is a trade and transportation centre for the Interior and Far North regions. From mid-May through to July, visitors can enjoy more than 20 hours of sunlight a day. Attractions range from the **Alaskaland Theme Park** to the **University of Alaska Fairbanks Museum**.
Throughout the winter, Fairbanks hosts world-class sled-dog races, ice-sculpting competitions and skiing events. The most sought after winter attraction, however, is the **aurora borealis**, which lights up the northern skies (best from December to March). A popular excursion is to the **Chena Hot Springs** resort, some 95km (60 miles) east of the city.
JUNEAU: Juneau, Alaska's third-largest city, is accessible only by sea or air. The city boasts excellent examples of original historic buildings and some fine museums, including the **Alaska State Museum** and the **Juneau-Douglas City Museum**. It is also famed for the great outdoors and its many hiking trails, as well as opportunities to view whales, bears and eagles.
From Juneau, a short flight can be made to view the nearby **Mendenhall Glacier**, located 21km (13 miles) from Juneau.
VALDEZ: Situated on the edge of the Prince William Sound, Valdez is popular for the abundance of outdoor pursuits available (such as hiking, rafting and fishing). The most popular excursion is to **Columbia Glacier**, a 6km- (4 mile-) wide piece of ice, which is the fastest moving glacier in the world; it can be reached via day cruises, charter boat, flight-seeing tours and the State ferry.
DENALI: This stunning region offers a wide variety of activities, including hiking, ice-climbing and wildlife viewing. Denali is an Athabascan name meaning 'the high one'. At 6197m (20,331ft), **Mount McKinley** is the tallest peak in North America, and on a clear day it can be seen from Anchorage, 240km (149 miles) away. **Denali National Park & Preserve** is famous for panoramic views of Mount McKinley and the **Alaska Range**. A popular day excursion takes tourists on a shuttle bus through the wilderness to see caribou, grizzly bears, wolves and moose.
KETCHIKAN: This city is famous for three things: salmon, totem poles and rain. Around 419cm (165 inches) of rain fall each year on this southeastern city. Visitors should not let this put them off, however, as it is here they will find the **Totem Heritage Center**, and the **Saxman Totem Park**, which contains the world's largest collection of standing totem poles. The **Totem Bight State Historical Park**, with its collection of replica totem poles and a tribal house, overlooks the **Tongass National Forest**, the largest in the USA and home to more than 50 species of birds, mountain goats, orca whales and glacier bear. Excursions include a boat or plane trip into the **Misty Fjords National Monument**. The coastal rain forests and glacial fjords shelter many species of land animals and sea life.
KODIAK: The principal town on **Kodiak Island**, this is the home of Alaska's largest fishing fleet. The legacy of Russian influence can be found at the **Baranov Museum**, while the culture of the island's native people can be explored in the little **Alutiiq Museum**. The **Kodiak National Wildlife Refuge** covers two-thirds of the island, offering a protected habitat for Kodiak brown bears, which are the largest carnivores in North America.

Social Profile

FOOD & DRINK: To enjoy Alaskan cuisine one must love fish. Salmon, halibut and trout feature heavily on most menus. The delicious caribou stew is another favourite. Russian dishes, such as borscht, feature in some towns. Alaskan delicacies include smoked salmon, wild berry products and reindeer sausage. The legal drinking age is 21

Credit: © Alaska Travel Industry Association

but Alaska has several 'dry' villages where any possession of alcohol is illegal.
NIGHTLIFE: Live music is very popular in Alaska. Many bars offer a wide choice of late-night sounds, ranging from rock to jazz and blues.
SHOPPING: Unique Alaskan products and crafts include gold nugget jewellery; items carved from ivory and jade; handmade clothing and toys; items made from skin, fur or bone; and woven baskets of beach grass, bark and baleen. Native sea-oil candles, beaded mittens, fur mukluks and miniature hand-carved totem poles are also popular souvenirs. The 'Made in Alaska' logo indicates that an item has been genuinely manufactured in Alaska, and the 'silver hand' logo identifies Native Alaskan handicrafts.
SPORT: Alaska offers some of the most spectacular **fishing** in the world. Rivers, lakes and streams throughout the State provide the chance to hook trout (such as rainbow, cut-throat and steelhead), as well as other, more challenging game fish including arctic grayling and sheefish. **Skiing** is another popular option, but the official sport of Alaska is actually **dog mushing**. Visitors can take a team of spirited huskies on a sled-dog tour or watch the experts at work in one of the many annual sled-dog races.
SPECIAL EVENTS: The following is a selection of special events occurring in Alaska in 2005:
Jan 1 *Annual Polar Bear Swim*, Wrangell. **Jan 7-9** *Traditional Russian Christmas and Starring*, Kodiak Island. **Feb 13** *Yukon Quest International Sled Dog Race*, Fairbanks. **Mar 2-27** *World Ice Art Championships*, Fairbanks. **Mar 5** *Mayor's Cup Cross-Country Snowmachine Race*, Valdez. **Mar 6** *Tour of Anchorage Annual Ski Race*, Anchorage **Mar 18-20** *ACS Open North American Championship Sled Dog Race*, Fairbanks. **Apr 11-17** *31st Annual Alaska Folk Festival*, Juneau. **Apr 14-23** *Whale Fest*, Kodiak Island. **May 20-28** *Juneau Jazz and Classics*. **Jun 3-5** *Celebration 2005 Native Cultural Event*, Juneau. **Jun 11** *Fairbanks Summer Arts Folk Festival*. **Jun 20-21** *Midnight Sun Festival*, Nome. **Jun 26-27** *Gold Rush Days*, Juneau. **Jul 8-10** *Bear Paw Festival*, Chugiak/Eagle River. **Jul 20-23** *World Eskimo-Indian Olympics*, Fairbanks. **Jul 20-24** *Golden Days 2005*, Fairbanks. **Aug 5-7** *59th Golden North Salmon Derby*, Juneau. **Sep 17** *Arts Faire*, Ketchikan. **Dec 3, 10, 17** *Winter Solstice Celebrations*, Fairbanks.

Climate

The climate varies widely throughout the State. Anchorage's summer weather is pleasant and the winters are mild. Fairbanks, the Interior and parts of the Bush region experience Alaska's most extreme weather conditions with average temperatures ranging from 22ºC (72ºF) in high summer to -28ºC (-19ºF) in winter.
Required clothing: In the Anchorage area, a layered wardrobe is the best option, with a light jacket in summer and a warm coat in winter. Elsewhere, very warm winter clothing is required in the coldest months. Lightweight clothing is advisable during the summer.

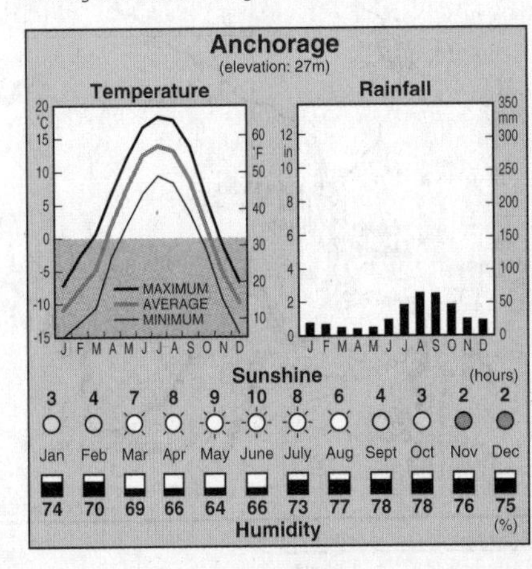

Arizona

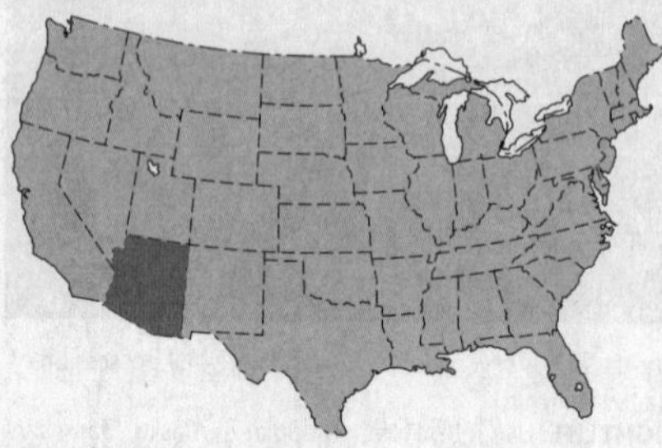

Arizona Office of Tourism
1110 West Washington Street, Suite 155, Phoenix, AZ 85007
Tel: (602) 364 3700 *or* (866) 275 5816. Fax: (602) 364 3702.
E-mail: travel-info@azot.com
Website: www.arizonaguide.com
Arizona Tourism Office (UK Office)
c/o McCluskey International, 4 Vencourt Place, Hammersmith, London W6 9NU, UK
Tel: (020) 8237 7979 *or* (0906) 577 0031 (brochure request line; calls cost £1.50 per minute).
Fax: (020) 8237 7999.
E-mail: info@mccluskey.co.uk
Website: www.arizonaguide.com *or* www.mccluskeyinternational.co.uk
Trade enquiries only.
Lake Havasu CVB
314 London Bridge Road, Lake Havasu City, AZ 86403
Tel: (928) 453 3444 *or* (800) 242 8278 (toll-free).
Fax: (928) 453 3344.
E-mail: info@golakehavasu.com
Website: www.golakehavasu.com
Greater Phoenix CVB
400 East Van Buren Street, Suite 600, Phoenix, AZ 85004
Tel: (602) 254 6500 *or* (877) 225 5749 (toll-free).
Fax: (602) 253 4415.
E-mail: visitors@visitphoenix.com
Website: www.visitphoenix.com
Scottsdale CVB
4343 North Scottsdale Road, Suite 170, Scottsdale, AZ 85251
Tel: (480) 421 1004 *or* (800) 782 1117 (toll-free).
Fax: (480) 421 9733.
E-mail: visitorinformation@scottsdalecvb.com
Website: www.scottsdalecvb.com
Metropolitan Tucson CVB
100 South Church Avenue, Tucson, AZ 85701
Tel: (520) 624 1817 *or* (800) 638 8350 (toll-free).
Fax: (520) 884 7804.
E-mail: info@visittucson.org
Website: www.visittucson.org

General Information

Nickname: Grand Canyon State
State bird: Cactus Wren
State flower: Saguaro Cactus Blossom
CAPITAL: Phoenix
Date of admission to the Union: 14 Feb 1912
POPULATION: 5,743,834 (official estimate 2004)
POPULATION DENSITY: 19.3 per sq km
2003 total overseas arrivals/US ranking: 487,000/12
TIME: Mountain (GMT - 7).
Daylight Saving Time is not observed.

THE STATE: Arizona contains some of the most spectacular scenery in the whole of the USA. The **Grand Canyon**, the **Painted Desert National Park** and **Petrified Forest National Park** (comprising the **Painted Desert** in the north and **Rainbow Forest** in the south) are just some of the highlights. **Phoenix**, the largest city in the State, shares borders with **Scottsdale**, the primary resort destination in Arizona. Both cities have a variety of accommodation and attractions, unique shopping, fine art galleries and many cultural events. Other State attractions include **Tucson**, the second-largest city; **Saguaro National Park**; **Arizona-Sonora Desert Museum**; six national forests, including **Kaibab National Forest** and **Tonto National Forest**; **Monument Valley Navajo Tribal Park**; **Hoover Dam**; **Montezuma Castle National Monument**; and **Tombstone**, site of the infamous shoot-out at the **OK Corral**.

Travel - International

AIR: *Phoenix Sky Harbor International (PHX)* (website: http://phoenix.gov/AVIATION) is 6km (4 miles) from the city centre. In 2003, the airport saw an increase in passenger numbers, which has pushed it up in the rankings to sixth busiest airport in the USA and 11th busiest in the world; over 1 million passengers are international arrivals. The airport is linked by a *Valley Metro* bus service that runs every 25 minutes 0600-1830 (travel time - 22 minutes). Taxis are available 24 hours a day, as is a door-to-door limousine service and a super-shuttle service; the latter departs every 15 minutes (0900-2100), less frequently at night.
Tucson International (TUS) (website: www.tucsonairport.com) is 16km (10 miles) from the city centre. Taxis and shared-ride vans that travel door-to-door run 24 hours a day; a local *Sun Tran* bus service is also available, although these are slow.

Approximate flight times: From Phoenix to *Atlanta* is three hours 30 minutes, to *Chicago* is three hours 20 minutes, to *Los Angeles* is one hour 25 minutes, to *Miami* is four hours 10 minutes and to *New York* is four hours 30 minutes.

RAIL: Three *Amtrak* (tel: (800) 872 7245 (toll-free); website: www.amtrak.com) trains run a weekly service from downtown Tucson, on the 'Sunset Limited' line (Benson-Tucson-Maricopa-Yuma) between Los Angeles and New Orleans. There is no rail link between Tucson and Phoenix, although an *Amtrak* Thruway bus service connects the cities. There is a daily service from Flagstaff on the 'Southwest Chief' line (Winslow-Flagstaff- Williams Junction-Kingman) between Los Angeles and Chicago. The *West Rail Pass* is available for 15 or 30 days unlimited travel between the Pacific Coast and as far east as Chicago and New Orleans. The *Far West Rail Pass* is also available for 15 or 30 days travel, covering the region from the Pacific Coast as far east as Alburquerque (New Mexico) and El Paso (Texas). First-class sleeping cars can be reserved for an additional fee.

ROAD: Most major routes run east-west. **Bus**: Greyhound buses (tel: (800) 229 9424 (toll-free); website: www.greyhound.com) are available to many destinations throughout the USA. Gray Line, with offices in Phoenix and Tucson, offers two-hour to two-day local sightseeing tours.

Approximate driving times: From Phoenix to *Tucson* is two hours, to *Las Vegas* is five hours 30 minutes, to *Los Angeles* is six hours, to *San Diego* is six hours, to *El Paso* is six hours 30 minutes and to *Albuquerque* is nine hours.

Approximate bus journey times: From Phoenix to *Tucson* is two hours, to *Los Angeles* is seven hours, to *El Paso* is seven hours 45 minutes, to *Las Vegas* is eight hours, to *San Diego* is eight hours and to *Albuquerque* is 10 hours.

URBAN: Bus: *Phoenix Valley Metro* buses run every 30 minutes throughout the day and every 10 to 20 minutes during peak traffic hours, although stops are spaced far apart; schedules are available at the downtown terminal, at First Avenue and Washington Street. Tickets for local and costlier express fares are sold in books of 10; daily and monthly local passes are available. A free DASH bus service runs Mon-Fri 0630-2300 between the Arizona Center and the State Capitol (downtown). A bus service links Phoenix and Scottsdale, and special dial-a-ride services operate in both cities Mon-Sat 0630-1000. Tucson also has a local bus network. **Car hire**: Easily available in Phoenix and other major cities, with many car hire firms offering special weekend or weekly rates.

Resorts & Excursions

GREATER PHOENIX AREA: The sixth-largest city in the USA and the capital of Arizona, **Phoenix** has enjoyed a growth in popularity recently, thanks to its improved airport facilities and a large investment in extensive urban redevelopment. Today, it claims to have more 5-star hotels than any other US city. Some of the more recent development projects in the city centre include the extensive remodelling of the **Phoenix Art Gallery**; the downtown **Copper Square** area; the **Arizona Science Center** with its interactive exhibits; **Heritage Square**, with fine buildings from the late 19th century; the US$20-million, 225-suite **Hilton Hotel**, located in the central business district; the **Arizona Center** (an 8-block complex with a 600-room hotel, offices, restaurants, shops and entertainment); **Patriots Square Park**, in the centre of Phoenix, with a sophisticated and spectacular laser light system that is visible for miles around; the restaurants and bars located in restored warehouses near the **Bank One Ballpark (BOB)**; and the lively shops and restaurants of the **Arizona Center**. Sightseeing options include **Encanto Park**, **Pueblo Grande Museum**, **Papago Park** (including the **Phoenix Zoo** and **Desert Botanical Garden**), **South Mountain Park** and the recently expanded **Heard Museum**, devoted to the art, anthropology, history and Native American culture of Arizona.
The metropolitan area, home to over 3 million residents, is the 14th-largest in the USA and offers some 174 golf courses. Founded in 1888 and having a strong Western heritage, **Scottsdale** has matured into a mecca for lovers of relaxed lifestyles. Year-round sunshine makes the outdoors a way of life, with scores of tennis courts, swimming pools and an ever-increasing number of spas. Attractions include a new museum of contemporary art and **Taliesin West**, the home and workshop of the famous architect Frank Lloyd Wright. On the western edge of Phoenix, **Glendale** is known for its antique shops, while in the southeast are **Mesa**, the third-largest city in the State, and **Tempe**, known for the shopping and nightlife on pedestrianised **Mill Avenue**.

LAKE HAVASU CITY: Nestled amidst rugged desert peaks on the **Colorado River**, this city with a small-town feel became the new home of **London Bridge** in 1971. Dismantled stone by stone, the bridge was brought over from England and reassembled in Arizona, where it became the focal point for an array of English-style shops, pubs and lodgings. The city's warm, dry climate ensures that swimming, fishing, jet boating, water-skiing and other watersports along the miles of public shoreline are a year-round possibility. Likewise, it has led to the growth of outdoor activities such as tennis, golf, hiking, rock climbing and mountain biking in the area, as well as jeep tours in the nearby **Sonoran Desert** and **Mojave** or **Chemehuevi Mountains**.

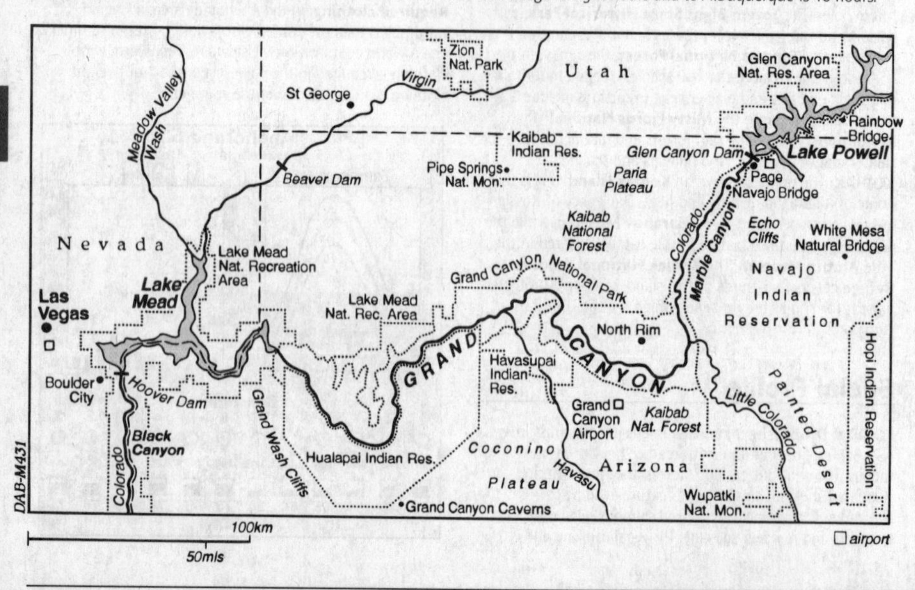

SEDONA: An attractive town nestled in the extraordinary red-rock formations and cliffs at the foot of Oak Creek, Sedona has a strong local arts and New Age scene and some celebrities have second homes here. The beautiful **Oak Creek Canyon** provides lush scenery, and there are prehistoric Native American ruins to be seen nearby. Jeep tours, hiking and mountain biking are also available.

TUCSON: This popular winter resort is one of the fastest-growing resort cities in the USA. Surrounded by a ring of five mountain ranges in the Sonoran Desert, it is known for its constant sunshine; and its location, only 160km (100 miles) from the Mexican border, is apparent in its architecture, cuisine, lively fiestas and cultural festivals. The **Tucson Children's Museum**, with many hands-on exhibitions, is a favourite with children and adults alike, as is the zoo at the **Arizona-Sonora Desert Museum**. Some 48km (30 miles) north of Tucson, visitors to the State can be dazzled, if not alarmed, by the gargantuan bubble that is **Biosphere 2** - a Plexiglas bubble laboratory containing five separate and self-contained ecosystems. It was designed to help scientists colonise Mars but a series of mishaps has plagued this project; even sightseers do not come in their crowds any more (during the early 1990s it was one of the State's most popular attractions). It is nevertheless worth a look, if only from afar. Guided tours are available.

YUMA: As the best site for crossing the Colorado River, Yuma has long been an important transport centre. The **Yuma Territorial Prison**, with cells carved out of the rock, is Arizona's most visited State Historic Park. From 1876 to 1909, it housed many of Arizona's most dangerous and notorious criminals. **Fort Yuma** was built in 1851 during the gold rush to protect settlers and the southern route to California. The **St Thomas Mission**, the **Quechan Indian Museum** and the **Yuma Crossing State Historic Park** are other popular attractions.

APACHE TRAIL: Passing through arid deserts, winding canyons, looming buttes, glistening lakes and the ominous volcanic dome known as **Superstition Mountain**, the Apache Trail is an extraordinary scenic drive. Attractions include **Goldfield Ghost Town and Mine Tours**, **Superstition Mountain Museum**, **Lost Dutchman State Park**, **Tortilla Flat** (an old stagecoach stop offering 'killer' chilli and prickly-pear cactus ice cream), **Roosevelt Bridge** and **Tonto National Monument** (well-preserved cliff dwellings occupied 500 years ago by the Salado Indians and featuring examples of their weavings, jewellery, weapons and tools).

GRAND CANYON: The jewel of the National Park Service and a World Heritage Site, the Grand Canyon's impact is awe-inspiring. This massive rend in the earth may be experienced in a variety of different ways: by aeroplane or helicopter, from the back of a mule, on foot or aboard a raft. For those wanting to catch a memorable sunrise or sunset, it is worth booking accommodation at one of the hotels in and around the canyon. As the area is far from any city, those wanting to save time and see it all can take a 'flightseeing' trip over the canyon. Further information is available from the Grand Canyon Chamber of Commerce (tel: (928) 527 0359; website: www.grandcanyonchamber.org).

The most common way to get there is by car from either Phoenix or Las Vegas (see the *Nevada* section), or to use the town of **Flagstaff** (tel: (800) 842 7293 or (928) 779 7611; website: www.flagstaffarizona.org), on the historic **Route 66**, as a base (travel time – 90 minutes). The planet Pluto was discovered at the **Lowell Observatory** here.

LAKE POWELL: Many tour boats ply the waters of the second-largest manmade lake in the USA. The most popular option, however, is to hire a houseboat and float serenely past the scenic wonderland of red rocks. Well worth seeing is the **Rainbow Bridge**, a spectacular natural stone bridge on the Navajo Reservation (see below), which most visitors travel to by boat. Information is available from Lake Powell Resorts & Marinas (tel: (800) 528 6154 or (602) 278 8888; website: www.visitlakepowell.com).

NATIVE AMERICAN RESERVATIONS: The **Navajo Reservation** spreads over more than 64,750 sq km (25,000 sq miles) and is home to 250,000 Navajos. Once a semi-nomadic people, they are known for their adaptability and have incorporated many skills into their culture from the Spanish and early settlers. They traditionally lived in *hogans* (dome-shaped houses of log and adobe) in small, scattered settlements. Nowadays, visitors are more likely to meet a Navajo as a guide on a horseback ride in the **Canyon de Chelly National Monument** or on one of the jeep tours through **Monument Valley**, where a number of John Wayne films were shot.

In the middle of the Navajo Reservation sits the **Hopi Reservation**, comprising 6475 sq km (2500 sq miles) and accommodating 7000 Hopis. They have lived in the region for 1500 years and are known for their amazing agricultural talents in farming dry and difficult land. The Hopis live in snug pueblo-style villages on top of three mesas. This area is treasured for its outstanding natural beauty.

TOMBSTONE: Tombstone owes its enduring appeal to the brief showdown at the OK Corral, and movies such as *Wyatt Earp* and *Tombstone* mean that it has retained its popularity. This notorious town plays on its past with restored sites and attractions like the **Boot Hill Cemetery**, the **Crystal Palace Saloon**, the **Bird Cage Theatre** and even has its original newspaper, named the *Tombstone Epitaph*. Re-enactments of famous gunfights are played out each day.

Credit: © Arizona Tourism Office

Social Profile

FOOD & DRINK: Most restaurants serve American or American/Continental food but Mexican, Chinese and Italian cuisine is also available, sometimes as a 'Southwest style' fusion using Mexican spices. Drinking is legal in any licensed bar, restaurant, hotel or inn Mon-Sat 0600-0100 and Sun 1200-0100. The minimum legal drinking age is 21. Many supermarkets and drug stores sell alcoholic beverages. Most liquor stores close at 0100. Possession and consumption of alcohol are prohibited on the Navajo, Hopi and other reservations.

THEATRE & CONCERTS: Herberger Theater Center in Phoenix hosts the *Arizona Theatre Company*, *Arizona Opera* and *Ballet Arizona* (all of which are based in Phoenix), as well as the *Actors' Theatre of Phoenix*. Touring Broadway shows can be seen at Phoenix's historic **Orpheum Theatre** (restored for US$14 million over a period of 12 years and completed in 2002) and the circular **Gammage Auditorium**, designed by Frank Lloyd Wright, in nearby Tempe.

NIGHTLIFE: Phoenix and Tucson have various nightclubs, and there is evening entertainment at many resorts in the area. Scottsdale's nightlife is more concentrated, while the university crowd go out in Tempe, where there are good jazz clubs on Mill Avenue.

SHOPPING: Phoenix has excellent shopping facilities, including **Biltmore Fashion Park** and the **Arizona Center**. Other good shopping centres in the metro area are at the **Scottsdale Fashion Square** and the upscale Italian-style **Borgata**, also in Scottsdale, and along pedestrianised **Mill Avenue** and at the **Arizona Mills** mall in Tempe. Special buys in Arizona include Navajo silver and turquoise jewellery, sand paintings, rug weaving, Hopi silver jewellery, kachina carvings, pottery, basketry and paintings. Tucson is a good place to pick up many of these items, as well as reasonably priced goods from Mexican import stores.

SPORT: Home games during the **American football** season are held at the **Sun Devil Stadium** in Tempe between the Arizona Cardinals and other visiting teams. The Arizona Cardinals will move into their new state-of-the-art stadium in Glendale for the 2006 NFL season. A number of Arizona cities provide the training ground for some excellent major-league **baseball** teams every March, although none could match the Phoenix-based Arizona Diamondbacks, who shine at the **Bank One Ballpark**. The Phoenix Suns play **basketball** in the **America West Arena**, where **hockey** games between the Phoenix Coyotes and visiting teams are held in winter.

Horse racing can be seen at **Turf Paradise** in Phoenix and **Rillito Downs** in Tucson. **Car-racing** takes place in Tucson at the **Southwestern International Raceway** and in Phoenix at **Firebird Raceway** and **Phoenix International Raceway**, where NASCAR races are held. **Rodeos** are popular in Arizona and there are over 25 major rodeo sites throughout the state. **Skiing** is available in the winter at **The Arizona Snow Bowl** near Flagstaff, **Mount Lemmon** (one hour outside Tucson) and **Sunrise Ski Area** outside Pinetop/Lakeside. **Other sports** available include archery, horseback riding, bowling, fishing, golf, hiking, hunting, swimming, river tubing, hang-gliding, ballooning and tennis.

SPECIAL EVENTS: The annual *Navajo Nation Fair* is the largest Native American fair in the USA. It takes place in **Window Rock**, capital of the Navajo Nation, for five days in September. It includes lasso competitions, rodeos, horse racing, arts and crafts exhibitions, country & western dances, song and dance competitions, livestock and agricultural exhibits, food and a big parade. The following is a selection of special events occurring in Arizona in 2005: **Jan 14-15** *Sierra Stampede* (all-women's professional rodeo), Sierra Vista. **Jan 22** *Dillinger Days Street Festival*, Tucson. **Feb 18-27** *50th Annual Arabian Horse Show*, Scottsdale. **Feb 20** *Chili Cook-Off and Western Heritage Day*. **Mar 12** *Territorial Days*, Tombstone. **Apr 2-3** *Art Walk*, Tubac. **Apr 9** *Tombstone Rose Festival*. **May 4** *Cinco De Mayo*, Nogales. **May 21-23** *Wyatt Earp Days*, Tombstone. **Jun 29-Jul 4** *Frontier Days and World's Oldest Rodeo*, Prescott. **Aug 27-29** *Apple Harvest Festival*, Willcox. **Sep 14-16** *Gila Valley Cowboy Poetry and Music Gathering*, Safford. **Oct 6-23** *Arizona State Fair*, Phoenix. **Oct 14-16** *Helldorado Days*, Tombstone. **Oct 28-30** *London Bridge Days*, Lake Havasu. **Nov 12-13** *Emmett Kelly Jr Days*, Tombstone. **Nov 25** *32nd Annual Festival of Lights*, Bisbee. **Dec 17** *La Posada*, Ajo.

Climate

Mostly warm and comfortable all year round. Mountainous areas, such as Flagstaff at 2134m (7000ft), are colder, particularly in winter, and in summer, there are cool mountain breezes. Desert temperatures range from hot during the day to cold at night.

Required clothing: Lightweight cotton clothing for all seasons, with a wrap for cool nights. Warmer clothing is needed in the mountains, especially in the ski areas.

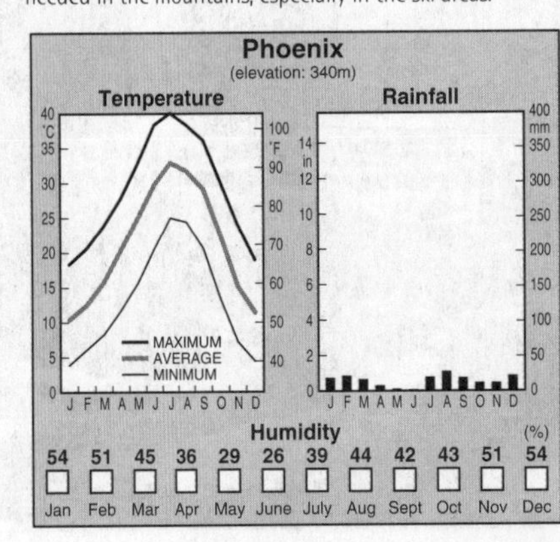

Arkansas

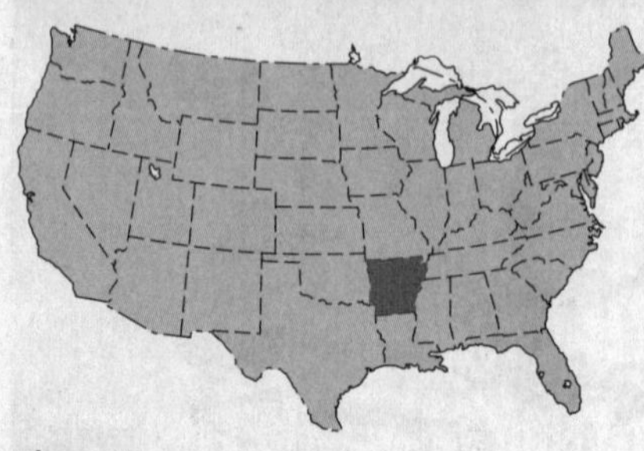

Arkansas Department of Parks & Tourism
1 Capitol Mall, Little Rock, AR 72201
Tel: (501) 682 7777 *or* (800) 628 8725 (toll-free).
Fax: (501) 682 1364.
E-mail: info@arkansas.com
Website: www.arkansas.com

Little Rock CVB
Street address: Robinson Center, Markham, Little Rock, AR 72201
Postal address: PO Box 3232, Little Rock, AR 72203
Tel: (501) 376 4781 *or* (800) 844 4781 (toll-free).
Fax: (501) 374 2255.
E-mail: lrcvb@littlerock.com
Website: www.littlerock.com

Hot Springs CVB
Street address: 134 Convention Boulevard, Hot Springs National Park, AR 71901
Postal address: PO Box 6000, Hot Springs National Park, AR 71902
Tel: (501) 321 2277 *or* (800) 772 2489 (toll-free).
Fax: (501) 321 2136.
E-mail: hscvb@hotsprings.org
Website: www.hotsprings.org

General Information

Nickname: The Natural State
State bird: Mockingbird
State flower: Apple Blossom
CAPITAL: Little Rock
Date of admission to the Union: 15 June 1836
POPULATION: 2,673,400 (official estimate 2004)
POPULATION DENSITY: 19.6 per sq km
2003 total overseas arrivals: Under 38,000
TIME: Central (GMT - 6). *Daylight Saving Time* is observed.

THE STATE: Arkansas has a varied landscape of plains, mountains, forests, rivers, cattle farms, industrial centres and oil wells. The main claims to fame of this State are the beauty of its outdoors and that former President Bill Clinton was the Governor in **Little Rock** before moving to the White House – there are museums and exhibits dedicated to his life. One of Arkansas' earliest settlements, Little Rock is a thriving place filled with museums, art exhibitions and parks. Attractions include the **Decorative Arts Museum**; **River Market District**; **the Governor's Mansion**; **Historic Arkansas Museum**; **Arkansas Arts Center**; and the **Museum of Discovery**. The **William J Clinton Presidential Center and Library** is currently under construction; the grand opening is scheduled for November 2004. The project will incorporate the **Rock Island Railroad Bridge** and the **Choctaw Station**, originally built in 1899, which are also being renovated. The best time to visit Little Rock is during *Riverfest* on the last evening of *Memorial Day* weekend, when the locals celebrate in style at **Julius Breckling Riverfront Park** with bands, dancing and a fireworks display. The glorious **Ozark Mountains** stretch from southern Missouri through northern Arkansas. The village of **Mountain View** is a musical mecca, home to the **Ozark Folk Center** and events such as the *Arkansas Folk Festival* in April and the *Arkansas State Old-Time Fiddle Championships* in September. Fishing in the **White River** is another option, but before casting out, a fishing licence must be obtained from one of the local stores. Excursions can be taken to **Buffalo National River**, which is a great spot for canoeing, or to the **Blanchard Springs Caverns** on the south border of the **Ozark National Forest**, which covers 0.5 million hectares (1.2 million acres) and is home to **Mount Magazine**, the tallest mountain in the State. **Eureka Springs** draws millions of tourists to its *Great Passion Play* outdoor drama and the *Christ of the Ozarks* statue, which stands 1.8m (6ft) high and was completed in 1966. At **Hot Springs National Park**, visitors can soothe their worries away in a choice of bathhouses, cheer on thoroughbreds or fish and swim at three great lakes. **Texarkana** lies on the border with Texas; in the **Museum of Regional History** there is an exhibition devoted to Scott Joplin (the African-American ragtime pianist and composer), a famous former resident of the town. Other State attractions include the **Crater of Diamonds State Park**, where visitors can dig for diamonds, **Fort Smith National Historic Site** and **Toltec Mounds Archaeological State Park**.

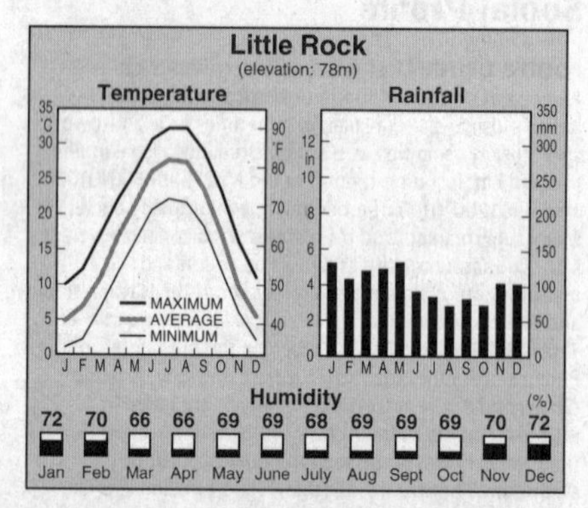

Credit: © Arkansas Department of Parks & Tourism

California

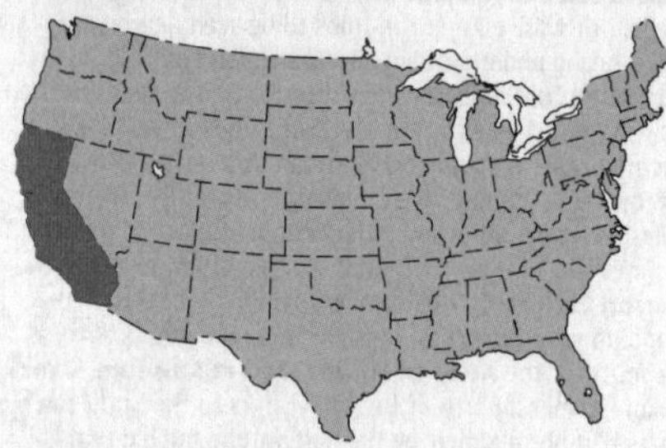

California Travel Industry Association
1414 K Street, Suite 305, Sacramento, CA 95814
Tel: (916) 443 3703. Fax: (916) 447 2984.
E-mail: info@caltia.com
Website: www.caltia.com

California Tourism
980 Ninth Street, Suite 480, Sacramento, CA 95814
Tel: (916) 444 4429 *or* (800) 862 2543 (toll-free).
Fax: (916) 444 0410.
E-mail: caltour@commerce.ca.gov
Website: www.visitcalifornia.com

California Tourism Office (UK Office)
Tel: (020) 8237 7970 *or* (0906) 577 0032 (brochure request line; calls cost £1.50 per minute).
Fax: (020) 8237 7999.
E-mail: california@mccluskey.co.uk
Website: www.visitcalifornia.com *or* www.mccluskeyinternational.co.uk
Trade enquiries only.

California State Parks
PO Box 942896, Sacramento, CA 94296
Tel: (916) 653 6995 *or* (800) 777 0369 (toll-free).
Fax: (916) 654 6374.
E-mail: info@parks.ca.gov
Website: www.parks.ca.gov

Anaheim/Orange County Visitor & Convention Bureau
800 West Katella Avenue, Anaheim, CA 92802
Tel: (714) 765 8888 *or* (888) 598 3200.
Fax: (714) 991 8963.
E-mail: mail@anaheimoc.org

Buena Park Convention & Visitors Office
6601 Beach Boulevard, Suite 200, Buena Park, CA 90621
Tel: (714) 562 3560 *or* (800) 541 3953 (toll-free).
Fax: (714) 562 3569.
E-mail: tourbp@buenapark.com
Website: www.visitbuenapark.com

Calaveras Visitors Bureau
Street address: 1192 South Main Street, Angels Camp, CA 95222
Postal address: PO Box 637, Angels Camp, CA 95222
Tel: (209) 736 0049 *or* (800) 225 3764 (toll-free).
Fax: (209) 736 9124.
E-mail: info@gocalaveras.com
Website: www.gocalaveras.com

California Deserts Tourism Association
37-115 Palm View Road, Rancho Mirage, CA 92270
Tel: (760) 328 9256. Fax: (760) 340 4281.
E-mail: gilzim@earthlink.net

Fresno City and County CVB
848 M Street, 3rd Floor, Fresno, CA 93721
Tel: (559) 233 0836 *or* (800) 788 0836 (toll-free).
Fax: (559) 445 0122.
E-mail: pbfresno@aol.com
Website: www.fresnocvb.org

Greater Bakersfield CVB
515 Truxtun Avenue, Bakersfield, CA 93301
Tel: (661) 325 5051 *or* (877) 425 7353 (toll-free).
Fax: (661) 325 7074.
Website: www.bakersfieldcvb.org

Lake Tahoe Visitors Authority
1156 Ski Run Boulevard, South Lake Tahoe, CA 96150
Tel: (530) 544 5050 *or* (800) 288 2463 (toll-free; reservations only).
Fax: (530) 544 2386.
E-mail: info@ltva.org
Website: www.bluelaketahoe.com

Long Beach Area CVB
1 World Trade Center, 3rd Floor, Long Beach, CA 90831
Tel: (562) 436 3645 *or* (800) 452 7829 (toll-free).
Fax: (562) 435 5653.
E-mail: info@longbeachcvb.org
Website: www.visitlongbeach.com

LA Inc (The CVB)
333 South Hope Street, 18th Floor, Los Angeles, CA 90071
Tel: (213) 624 7300 *or* (800) 228 2452 (toll-free).
Fax: (213) 624 9746.
Website: www.seemyLA.com

Mammoth Lakes Visitors Bureau
Street address: 437 Old Mammoth Road, Suite Y, Mammoth Lakes, CA 93546
Postal address: PO Box 48, Mammoth Lakes, CA 93546
Visitor centre: Mammoth Lakes Visitor Center Ranger Station, Highway 203 (walk-in visitor information)
Tel: (760) 934 2712 *or* (888) 466 2666 (toll-free).
Fax: (760) 934 7066.
E-mail: info@visitmammoth.com
Website: www.visitmammoth.com
Monterey County CVB
Street address: 150 Olivier Street, Monterey, CA 93940
Postal address: PO Box 1770, Monterey, CA 93942
Tel: (831) 649 1770 *or* (888) 221 1010 (toll-free).
Fax: (831) 648 5373.
E-mail: info@mccvb.org
Website: www.montereyinfo.org
Napa Valley CVB
1310 Napa Town Center, Napa, CA 94559
Tel: (707) 226 7459. Fax: (707) 255 2066.
E-mail: info@napavalley.org
Website: www.napavalley.com
Palm Springs Desert Resorts Convention and Visitors Authority
70-100 Highway 111, Suite 201, Rancho Mirage, CA 92270
Tel: (760) 770 9000 *or* (800) 967 3767 (toll-free).
Fax: (760) 770 9001.
E-mail: info@palmspringsusa.com
Website: www.palmspringsusa.com
Pasadena CVB
171 South Los Robles Avenue, Pasadena, CA 91101
Tel: (626) 795 9311 *or* (800) 307 7977 (toll-free).
Fax: (626) 795 9656.
E-mail: info@pasadenacal.com
Website: www.pasadenacal.com
Riverside CVB
3750 University Avenue, Suite 175, Riverside, CA 92501
Tel: (909) 222 4700 *or* (888) 748 7733.
Fax: (909) 222 4712.
E-mail: riversidecb@linkline.com
Website: www.riversidecb.com
Sacramento CVB
1608 I Street, Suite 600, Sacramento, CA 95814
Tel: (916) 808 7777 *or* (800) 292 2334 (toll-free).
Fax: (916) 808 7788.
Website: www.discovergold.org
San Diego CVB
401 B Street, Suite 1400, San Diego, CA 92101
Tel: (619) 232 3101 *or* 236 1212 (visitor information).
Fax: (619) 696 9371.
E-mail: sunshine@sdcvb.org
Website: www.sandiego.org
San Francisco CVB
201 Third Street, Suite 900, San Francisco, CA 94103
Tel: (415) 974 6900 *or* 391 2000 (visitor information).
Fax: (415) 227 2602.
E-mail: vic1@sfcvb.org
Website: www.sfvisitor.org
San José CVB
408 Almaden Boulevard, San José, CA 95110
Tel: (408) 295 9600 *or* (800) 726 5673 (toll-free).
Fax: (408) 295 3937.
E-mail: concierge@sanjose.org
Website: www.sanjose.org
Santa Barbara CVB and Film Commission
1601 Anacapa Street, Santa Barbara, CA 93101
Tel: (805) 966 9222 *or* (800) 549 5133 (toll-free).
Fax: (805) 966 1728.
E-mail: tourism@santabarbaraca.com
Website: www.santabarbaraca.com
Santa Maria Valley Chamber of Commerce and Visitor & Convention Bureau
614 South Broadway, Santa Maria, CA 93454
Tel: (805) 925 2403 (ext 814) *or* (800) 331 3779 (toll-free).
Fax: (805) 928 7559.
E-mail: smvcc@santamaria.com
Website: www.santamaria.com
Santa Monica CVB
520 Broadway, Suite 250, Santa Monica, CA 90401
Tel: (310) 319 6263 *or* (800) 771 2322 (toll-free) *or* (310) 393 7593 (visitor centre) *or* (800) 544 5319 (visitor centre, toll-free). Fax: (310) 319 6273.
E-mail: info@santamonica.com
Website: www.santamonica.com
Shasta Cascade Wonderland Association
1699 Highway 273, Anderson, CA 96007
Tel: (530) 365 7500 *or* (800) 474 2782 (toll-free).
Fax: (530) 365 1258.
E-mail: scwa@shastacascade.com
Website: www.shastacascade.org
West Hollywood CVB
8687 Melrose Avenue, Suite M38, West Hollywood, CA 90069
Tel: (310) 289 2525 *or* (800) 368 6020 (toll-free).
Fax: (310) 289 2529.
E-mail: whcvb@visitwesthollywood.com
Website: www.visitwesthollywood.com

Credit: © California Tourism Office

General Information

Nickname: Golden State
State bird: California Valley Quail
State flower: California or Golden Poppy
CAPITAL: Sacramento
Date of admission to the Union: 9 Sep 1850
POPULATION: 35,893,799 (official estimate 2004).
POPULATION DENSITY: 85.7 per sq km
2003 total overseas arrivals/US ranking: 3,984,000/3
TIME: Pacific (GMT - 8). *Daylight Saving Time* is observed.

THE STATE: 'The Golden State' of California has it all: snow-capped mountains, vast deserts, lush forests and long stretches of golden beach. The most populous State in the USA, California can be divided into 12 tourist regions: the Central Coast, Los Angeles County, Orange County, the North Coast, San Diego County, the San Francisco Bay Area, Shasta Cascade, Gold Country, the Central Valley, the High Sierra, the Deserts and the Inland Empire.
Known as 'the Middle Kingdom', the **Central Coast** extends from the Bay Area to Los Angeles County, along the Pacific coast and to the vineyards of the valleys around **Santa Barbara**. The **Monterey Peninsula** and **Big Sur** are tranquil areas of great natural beauty with some of the most scenic drives in the country. No trip to California is complete without a visit to the second-biggest city in the USA: **Los Angeles**, the 'City of Angels'. It lives up to its reputation as 'the entertainment capital of the world', offering the best in theatre, symphony and ballet, as well as the chance to spot stars in **Hollywood**. Alongside museums, sporting events and some of the country's finest restaurants, Los Angeles County has miles of sunny coastline and an abundance of State Parks and natural recreation areas.
Orange County is home to one of the world's most famous attractions, **Disneyland Resort**. As well as the theme parks, resorts and shopping, the county offers 67km (42 miles) of beaches and the charming rural communities of the **Santa Ana Mountains**. The **North Coast** is a land of rugged shoreline, redwood forests and vineyards. Stretching from San Francisco to the Oregon border, the region includes **Lake**, **Mendocino**, **Napa** and **Sonoma** counties, which boast world-class wineries, and is an attractive mix of rough wilderness and cultivated farmland. The balmy climate and beautiful beaches of **San Diego County** make it a popular destination. The city's Spanish heritage is reflected in numerous buildings and museums. Attractions include the famous San Diego Wild Animal Park, **San Diego Zoo** and **Sea World**.
The **San Francisco Bay Area** is one of the world's most popular destinations. **San Francisco** is a cosmopolitan city, whose cable cars and **Golden Gate Bridge** are instantly recognisable. The **Bay Area** offers world-class museums, restaurants, wineries, shopping and historic sites. Outdoor enthusiasts will love the **Golden Gate National Recreation Area** and the coastal resort area of **Santa Cruz**.
In the northeastern corner of the State lies one of the country's most beautiful and unspoiled regions – the **Shasta Cascade**. The region's waterfalls, whitewater rivers, forests, icy lakes and towering mountains – including the **California Cascade** range – provide stunning vistas. **Gold Country** is where the California Gold Rush, which forever changed the State – and the country – began in 1849. On the western slopes of the **Sierra Nevada**, Gold Country is full of historic mining towns and museums, while California's capital city, **Sacramento**, still shows clear signs of its pioneer beginnings.
Running between the Sierra Nevada and the coastal foothills is the **Central Valley**, California's agricultural heartland. This enormous valley, one of the most productive agricultural regions in the world, is laced with thousands of miles of waterways and dotted with green pastures, orchards and vineyards. **Bakersfield** and **Fresno** are interesting regional centres.
The beautiful wilderness of the **High Sierra**, immortalised in the photography of Ansel Adams, is an outdoor enthusiast's delight. Home to the famous **Yosemite National Park** and the resorts of **Lake Tahoe** and the **Mammoth Lakes**, the region offers a wide range of recreational activities, as well as some spectacular landscapes.
The **Deserts** region, in the southeast, features expansive landscapes, brilliant skies, traces of pioneer history and glittering resort cities. Natural phenomena include the isolated **Death Valley National Monument** and the vast **Joshua Tree National Monument**, while in spring, the desert explodes with displays of wild flowers. Most visitors to the region explore one of the rustic ghost towns or drive along historic **Route 66**.
The **Inland Empire**, centred around the cities of **Riverside** and **San Bernardino**, is the fastest-growing metropolitan region in the USA. Only one hour from Los Angeles, its varied landscape – from snow-capped mountains to sand dunes and farmlands – makes it an ideal film location, and the region is known as 'Hollywood's largest backlot'.

Travel - International

Air: *Los Angeles International (LAX)* (website: www.lawa.org/lax) serves more than 80 passenger airlines. Located on Santa Monica Bay, 24km (15 miles) from the city centre, it is the world's fifth-busiest airport and third-busiest in the USA (2002 total passenger rankings), handling all international arrivals (some 14.8 million) and three-quarters of domestic arrivals to the Southern California region. For information on airline locations, parking and ground transport, contact the airport (tel: (310) 646 5252). The airport is located 26km (16 miles) southwest of downtown Los Angeles; a free 24-hour shuttle service is available to the LAX Transit Center, where there are local buses to the city centre (travel time - 30 to 45 minutes). Coaches provide reasonably priced services to all major locations in the city centre, as well as many surrounding areas such as Hollywood. Various door-to-door shuttle services are also available.
San Francisco International (SFO) (website: www.sfoairport.com) is 25km (15 miles) southeast of the city (travel time - 30 minutes). The airport handles over 7 million international arrivals per year and is ranked 11th busiest in the USA (2002 total passenger rankings). *SamTrans* buses leave every 30 minutes (travel time - 30 minutes to one hour). The *SFO Airporter* bus departs every 15 minutes. Limousine, taxi and various shuttle services are also available.
Oakland International (OAK) (website: www.flyoakland.com) is located across the Bay 32km (20 miles) from central San Francisco and receives international charter flights and US domestic flights. Airporter buses link the airport with central Oakland and San Francisco International Airport. *AirBART* buses connect

A B C D E F G H I J K L M N O P Q R S T U V W X Y Z

with the *BART* rapid transit (underground) system at Coliseum/Oakland International Airport station every 15 minutes, giving access to central San Francisco.
Domestic airports: *The Bob Hope Airport in Burbank (BUR)* (website: www.burbankairport.com) is about 20km (13 miles) from central Los Angeles, and receives US domestic services only. Burbank is the nearest airport for access to Hollywood.
John Wayne (SNA) (website: www.ocair.com) is located approximately 16km (10 miles) from Santa Ana. Buses, taxis and shuttles depart from the Ground Transportation Center.
Long Beach (LGB) (website: www.lgb.org) is about 35km (22 miles) from Los Angeles International.
Ontario International (ONT) (website: www.lawa.org/ont) is located approximately 60km (38 miles) east of central Los Angeles and mainly serves the Orange County area.
Sacramento International (SMF) (website: www.sacairports.org) is located 19km (12 miles) from the city, and mainly receives US domestic services.
San Diego International (SAN) (website: www.san.org), 5km (3 miles) west of San Diego city centre, is primarily a gateway to southern California for domestic traffic.
Approximate flight times: From **Los Angeles** to *Anchorage* is five hours 40 minutes, to *Chicago* is four hours, to *Guatemala City* is four hours 40 minutes, to *Honolulu* is five hours 40 minutes, to *London* is 10 hours 15 minutes, to *Mexico City* is three hours 40 minutes, to *Miami* is four hours 45 minutes, to *New York* is five hours 10 minutes, to *Orange County* is 30 minutes, to *Papeete* (Tahiti) is nine hours 15 minutes, to *San Diego* is 55 minutes, to *San Francisco* is one hour 20 minutes, to *Seattle* is two hours 40 minutes, to *Singapore* is 20 hours 25 minutes, to *Sydney* is 19 hours 30 minutes, to *Vancouver* is three hours and to *Washington, DC* is four hours 40 minutes.
From **San Francisco** to *Anchorage* is five hours 35 minutes, to *Chicago* is four hours, to *Honolulu* is five hours 25 minutes, to *London* is 10 hours 30 minutes, to *Los Angeles* is one hour 20 minutes, to *Mexico City* is four hours 15 minutes, to *Miami* is five hours, to *New York* is five hours 15 minutes, to *Papeete* (Tahiti) is 10 hours 40 minutes, to *San Diego* is one hour 25 minutes, to *Seattle* is two hours five minutes, to *Singapore* is 19 hours 30 minutes, to *Sydney* is 14 hours 25 minutes, to *Vancouver* is two hours 15 minutes and to *Washington, DC* is four hours 50 minutes.
SEA: A ferry service links **San Francisco** with the Bay communities of Sausalito, Larkspur (in Marin County), Tiburon, Vallejo, Oakland and Alameda. San Francisco departure is from Pier 1, adjoining the Ferry Building at the foot of Market Street, or from Fisherman's Wharf. In the **Los Angeles** area, there is a daily, low-fare cruise service from **Long Beach** to **Catalina Island**.
RAIL: The *Amtrak* terminal in **Los Angeles** is Union Station, at 800 North Alameda Street, on the edge of the business district. It is at the western end of several major routes across the southern Rockies, is the southern terminus of the West Coast line to Seattle (although there are frequent shuttle services heading further south to San Diego), and at the western end of east-west routes from Chicago, St Louis and New Orleans. In **San Francisco**, the *Embarcadero BART* station and the *Transbay Terminal*, at 425 Mission Street, are used only for limited suburban services; the *Amtrak Terminal* at Oakland, across the Bay, is the central node on the West Coast line and also the western terminus of a line running across the high Rockies to Salt Lake City and beyond. *Amtrak* provides free shuttles between their Oakland station and the Transbay Terminal.
San Diego is served by *Amtrak* trains from Los Angeles, with a station located downtown, on 4005 Taylor Street. For information on train schedules and reservations, contact *Amtrak* (tel: (800) 872 7245 (toll-free); website: www.amtrak.com).
Approximate rail travel times: From **Los Angeles** on the *Texas Eagle* to *Phoenix* is eight hours, to *El Paso* is 18 hours, to *San Antonio* is 29 hours, to *Austin* is 32 hours, to *Fort Worth* is 37 hours, to *Dallas* is 39 hours, to *St Louis* is 54 hours and to *Chicago* is 61 hours; on the *Southwest Chief* to *Flagstaff* is nine hours, to *Albuquerque* is 16 hours, to *Kansas City* is 32 hours and to *Chicago* is 38 hours; on the *Sunset Limited* to *Houston* is 34 hours and to *New Orleans* is 43 hours; on the *Coast Starflight* to *San José* is nine hours, to *Oakland* is 11 hours, to *Sacramento* is 13 hours, to *Portland* (Oregon) is 29 hours and to *Seattle* is 33 hours.
From **Oakland** on the *California Zephyr* to *Reno* is six hours, to *Salt Lake City* is 16 hours, to *Denver* is 31 hours and to *Chicago* is 50 hours.
ROAD: *Greyhound* (tel: (800) 229 9424 (toll-free); website: www.greyhound.com), runs a reliable and frequent service to and from every major city in the USA, as well as locations in Canada and Mexico. There are six *Greyhound* bus stations in Los Angeles; the main station is at 1716 East Seventh Street. In San Francisco, *Greyhound* buses use the *Transbay Terminal* (see above), while San Diego has a downtown terminal at 120 West Broadway.
Approximate driving times: From **Los Angeles** to San Diego is two hours, to *Las Vegas* is six hours, to *San Francisco* is eight hours, to *Phoenix* is eight hours, to *Reno* is 10 hours, to *Albuquerque* is 16 hours, to *Seattle* is 24 hours, to *Dallas* is 29 hours, to *Chicago* is 44 hours, to *Miami* is 58 hours and to *New York* is 58 hours.
From **San Francisco** to *Reno* is four hours, to *Portland* (Oregon) is 13 hours, to *Albuquerque* is 12 hours, to *Seattle* is 16 hours, to *Dallas* is 36 hours, to *Chicago* is 45 hours, to *New York* is 61 hours and to *Miami* is 65 hours. All times are based on non-stop driving at or below the applicable speed limits.
Approximate bus travel times: From **Los Angeles** to *San Diego* is two hours 30 minutes, to *Las Vegas* is five hours 30 minutes, to *San Francisco* is seven hours 30 minutes, to *Phoenix* is eight hours 30 minutes, to *Yosemite* is 10 hours 15 minutes, to *Sacramento* is 12 hours 30 minutes, to *Albuquerque* is 17 hours 30 minutes and to *Portland* (Oregon) is 22 hours.
From **San Francisco** to *Sacramento* is two hours, to *Lake Tahoe* is five hours, to *Reno* is five hours 30 minutes, to *Los Angeles* is seven hours 30 minutes, to *Yosemite* is seven hours 30 minutes and to *Portland* (Oregon) is 16 hours.
Urban Los Angeles: The distances between the city's various attractions can be intimidating at first but it is a relatively easy city to get around quickly, provided the visitor has a car. The freeways are well marked, though congested during rush hours. Leading car hire and motor camper rental agencies have offices at the airport and in the city centre. Local radio stations broadcast frequent traffic reports from 0600-1000 and 1500-1900. Many southern Californian freeways have designated car-pool lanes, known as HOVs. Do not merge into an HOV lane if your car is not carrying the specified number of passengers as fines are levied. LA County Metropolitan Transit Authority (MTA) buses run approximately every 15 minutes (0500-0200) on major routes, with a reduced service at night. Express buses are also available. The Metrorail train system covers three routes: downtown to Long Beach (blue); between Union Station to North Hollywood (red); and Hawthorne to Norwalk (green).
Travel beyond Los Angeles: Within Los Angeles County, the *Southern California Rapid Transit District (RTD)* provides a good bus service. For trips beyond Los Angeles, the *Orange County Transit District* accepts transfers from *RTD* for services throughout suburban Orange County. Buses are reasonably priced but travellers may have to wait some time to catch one. Though taxis are readily available, the large size of Los Angeles makes them expensive and impractical.
San Diego: The *Metropolitan Transit System* is operated by *San Diego Transit Corporation*, a consortium of companies providing a good and extensive bus service at moderate prices. The *San Diego Trolley* runs a 26km (16 mile) route from the Santa Fe Depot to San Ysidro, on the Mexican border (travel time - 45 minutes). Taxis are expensive. Car hire is readily available, with *Avis*, *Budget*, *Dollar-A-Day*, *Hertz* and *National* all providing services.
San Francisco: Public transport, operated by *MUNI*, is excellent. The network of buses (including night buses), streetcars and cable cars is the most economical way to get to destinations beyond walking distance. The basic fare includes transfers between the different forms of transport, except for cable cars, which have a separate fare structure. Passengers must have exact change when they board as drivers carry no change; the MUNI Passport travel passes (one-, three- or seven-day) are available and allow for travel on all *MUNI* and *BART* systems within the city. Taxis are readily available in most of the central area and other major streets. Because San Francisco occupies a comparatively small area, taxi fares tend to be lower than in most other major cities. All major national car hire agencies are represented in San Francisco; motor campers may also be hired. For information on local companies, look in the San Francisco *Classified Telephone Directory*. Buses and streetcars also provide services from the centre to more distant points in the city, including Golden Gate Park, Twin Peaks, Seal Rocks, Mission Dolores, the Presidio and Golden Gate Bridge. The clean and efficient Bay *Area Rapid Transit (BART)* subway and surface-rail system links San Francisco with communities on the east side of sprawling San Francisco Bay, including Oakland, Alameda, Fremont, Richmond and Berkeley, site of the prestigious University of California campus.

Resorts & Excursions

North Coast

The North Coast of California is a land of rugged coastline, rivers, ancient redwood forests and vineyards. Stretching nearly 645km (400 miles) north of San Francisco to the Oregon border, the region reaches 80km (50 miles) inland to encompass the world-renowned vineyards of Napa County.
NAPA COUNTY: Located less than 80km (50 miles) northeast of San Francisco, Napa County is the USA's best-known wine region. There are over 250 wineries, many offering tours and wine tasting. The valley town of **Calistoga** is famous for its natural springs and attracts mud and mineral bath devotees year-round. It is also home to one of the world's three 'Old Faithful' geysers. There is a petrified forest nearby, with a museum and walking tour. At **St Helena**, the **Silverado Museum** displays memorabilia connected with the author Robert Louis Stevenson. For a bird's-eye view of the valley, adventurers can take to the sky in a hot-air balloon or a glider.
SONOMA COUNTY: The hub of Sonoma County is **Santa Rosa**, with many visitor attractions and a variety of accommodation. To the north is the wine country surrounding the charming town of **Healdsburg**, while to the south is the historic village of **Sonoma**, where a historic plaza is flanked by an 1823 Spanish mission, the last to be founded in California. Nearby, the river city of **Petaluma** features stately Victorian-era homes and steamboat excursions, as well as over two dozen antique shops. On the outskirts is the **Petaluma Adobe State Historic Park**, once part of a sprawling ranchero. To the north is the coastal resort of **Bodega Bay** and historic **Fort Ross**, a 19th-century Russian outpost.
MENDOCINO COUNTY: This is a gateway to the more romantic regions of the North Coast. **Ukiah** is the county seat and the centre for yet another flourishing wine region. The **Grace Hudson Museum and Sun House** feature artifacts and paintings of the Pomo Native Americans. Nearby is **Little River**, with golfing, tennis, whale watching and fine dining. On the coast is the seaport of **Fort Bragg**, now the headquarters for 1885 'Skunk Train' excursions through redwood forests to **Willits**. At Willits, the **Mendocino County Museum** displays local historic exhibits. Nearby is the charming village of **Mendocino**, founded in the 1850s as a logging town and now a thriving artists' colony. Sights here include **Ford House**, the 1854 home of Mendocino's founder, where Pomo Native American artefacts are on display.
LAKE COUNTY: Inland from Mendocino, Lake County is the home of premium wines and an abundance of lakes. **Clear Lake**, with more than 160km (100 miles) of shoreline, is the largest natural freshwater lake in California, known as the 'bass capital of the world'. There are opportunities in Lake County for attending one of the many festivals as well as water-skiing, fishing, swimming, boating, bicycling, birdwatching and rock hounding. The **Anderson Marsh State Historic Park** near Clear Lake, once home to the Pomo tribe, is rich in archaeological history.
DEL NORTE COUNTY: Visitors to this northern county will be welcomed by the towering statues of legendary lumberjack Paul Bunyan and his blue ox, Babe, near **Klamath**. The **Klamath River** and **Smith River** recreational areas attract anglers from around the world. **Crescent City**, the northern gateway to **Redwood National Park**, boasts scenic excursions and the **Battery Point Lighthouse**, the oldest working lighthouse on the Pacific Coast, built in 1856. The revered Redwood National Park covers 110,000 acres of land and includes three State Parks, the world's tallest tree, stunning shorelines and the world's largest free-roaming herd of Roosevelt elk. It also features two of the most scenic panoramas on the West Coast: the **Crescent City Overlook** and the **Klamath River Overlook**.
HUMBOLDT COUNTY: Much of the Redwood National Park is located in the county, as is the **Avenue of the Giants**, a 53km- (33 mile-) scenic route with hiking and picnicking. Along the coast is the 19th-century seaport of **Eureka**, where General Ulysses S Grant was commander of Fort Humboldt (now a State Historic Park) in 1854. The Victorian village of **Ferndale**, the 'Lost Coast' and the King Range Wilderness are other attractions. To the east is high mountain country, ideal for fishing and river rafting. At **Arcata Marsh Wildlife Sanctuary**, guided nature walks and a visitors' centre cater for nature-lovers. **Trinidad** offers a variety of bed & breakfast accommodation set along the coast.
TRAVEL: Redwood Highway 101 connects the region with San Francisco. Scenic and Heritage routes include Avenue of the Giants (Route 254), North Central Coast Heritage Corridor (Highway 1), Route 116, Smith River Scenic Byway (State Route 199), Tahoe-Pacific Heritage Corridor (Route 20, 101, 80 and 89), Trinity River Scenic Byway (Route 299), Valley of the Moon Highway (Route 12). Visitors to Napa County can fly to *Oakland International Airport (OAK)* (website: www.flyoakland.com), which has quick access to the wine country.
SPECIAL EVENTS: Visitors will find a variety of events held in the region throughout the year, including wine tastings, vineyard tours, wine appreciation classes, picnics and markets. The following is a selection of special events occurring in the North Coast in 2005:
Jan 29-Apr 9 *Annual Napa Valley Mustard Festival* (celebration of Wine Country food, wine, art and history), Napa Valley. **May 13-15** *Napa Home and Garden Show*. **Jun 2-5** *25th Annual Napa Valley Wine Auction*. **Jul 21-**

Aug 14 *Wine Country Film Festival*, Napa. **Sep** *Napa River Festival*, downtown Napa. **Nov 25** *Yountville Festival of Lights*.
CLIMATE: Summers are very warm, with cool evenings, while the spring and autumn months are mild, with cool evenings. The winter 'rainy season' is gentle and occurs between January and March.

Shasta Cascade

The Shasta Cascade Region, roughly the size of Belgium, contains some of California's most breathtaking natural wonders. The 'Three Shastas' include the huge **Shasta Dam**, the beautiful **Shasta Lake** and the dramatic, snow-capped **Mount Shasta**, one of the nation's tallest mountains at 4248m (14,162ft). The region contains seven national forests, several national and state parks, six wild and scenic rivers, the State's largest lakes, the **Trinity Alps** and the **California Cascade Range**. It is an outdoor enthusiast's dream, offering an endless range of activities in summer or winter.
REDDING & SHASTA COUNTY: The lively community of Redding, on the **Sacramento River**, is the centre of the Shasta Cascade Region, and with over 2500 hotel rooms, provides the widest variety of lodging choices within the region. **Turtle Bay Exploration Park**, one of Redding's major attractions, is a collection of museums and exhibits that focus on the Sacramento River watershed and the history of far northern California. Current attractions include the new **Turtle Bay Museum**, with permanent interactive exhibits and two exhibition galleries; the **McConnell Arboretum**, some 90 hectares (220 acres) of walking trails; and **Paul Bunyan's Forest Camp**, with the popular summer butterfly house.
The **Sundial Bridge** crosses the Sacramento River and provides a new downtown entrance to **Redding's Sacramento River Trail** system. Additional attractions include the region's best shopping and the **Sacramento River Trail**, suitable for both walkers and cyclists.
The ghost town of old **Shasta** in **Shasta State Historic Park** is 9km (6 miles) from Redding. Known as 'Queen City' in the height of the gold rush, Shasta's jail and general store have been restored. The county courthouse, also restored, houses historical exhibits, including an outstanding collection of historic Californian artwork. Nearby is **Whiskeytown Lake**, a scenic spot for canoeing, fishing, sailing and other watersports. The vivid blue waters of **Shasta Lake** are ideal for houseboating, and with the biggest combined rental fleet of houseboats in the world, holidaymakers are well catered for. The largest lake in the state, it was formed when four powerful rivers were dammed by the **Shasta Dam**, itself a popular attraction, with the highest overflow spillway in the world – three times higher than Niagara Falls. To the northwest lies the **McArthur-Burney Falls Memorial State Park** with its 39m (129ft) waterfall; the rivers and streams in the area offer some of the best fly-fishing in the State. To the west of Redding, **Trinity Alps Wilderness Area** is the second-largest wilderness area in California, with over 55 lakes, and several mountain ridges and deep canyons that offer breathtaking views. The historic gold mining town of **Weaverville** and picturesque **Trinity Lake** are also located here.
MOUNT SHASTA: The second-highest volcano in the lower 48 states, the majestic Mount Shasta dominates the landscape. The mountain provides great hiking in summer and downhill and cross-country skiing in winter; and the alpine village of Mount Shasta makes a good base from which to explore the mountain and surrounding area. Fishing and rafting are popular on the Klamath, McCloud, Sacramento, Salmon, Scott and Shasta rivers. Relics of the area's gold mining heritage are on display at **Siskiyou County Courthouse** in nearby **Yreka**, which has a collection of huge gold nuggets, and the **Siskiyou County Museum**, which includes a miner's cabin and logging and trapping memorabilia. The **Klamath Basin National Wildlife Refuge** at **Tulelake** is renowned for its abundant wildlife, including the country's largest winter population of bald eagles. Also at Tulelake is the **Lava Beds National Monument**, a distinctive and rugged landscape formed when volcanoes erupted in the **Klamath Basin**. Near the picturesque mountain town of **Dunsmuir** is **Castle Crags State Park**, where the ancient granite outcrops resemble the turrets of a castle.
LASSEN VOLCANIC NATIONAL PARK & LASSEN COUNTY: This area is home to the 3137m (10,457ft) volcano of **Lassen Peak**, which last erupted in 1921 and is part of the **California Cascade Range**. Volcanic activity is still evident at sites like **Bumpass Hell**, with its bubbling geothermal mud pools, **Little Hot Springs Valley**, **Boiling Springs Lake**, **Devils Kitchen Sulphur Works** and **Terminal Geyser**. **Eagle Lake**, the second-largest natural lake in California, offers some of the best fishing in the region; anglers flock here hoping to hook the famous Eagle Lake trout.
RED BLUFF: Situated on the Sacramento River, this town hosts the annual *Red Bluff Rodeo*, one of the largest three-

Credit: © California Tourism Office

day rodeos in the western USA. The **Kelly Griggs Museum**, a Victorian house with guided tours, and the **William B Ide Adobe State Historic Park**, a memorial to the only President of the Republic of California, are interesting reminders of the area's rich history.
The town of **Chico**, at the southern end of the Shasta Cascade, contains **Bidwell Park**, where *The Adventures of Robin Hood* was filmed with Errol Flynn in 1937. The park was also the setting for scenes of *Gone With The Wind*. The **Bidwell Mansion State Historic Park** has preserved the mansion and grounds of the town's founding father, John Bidwell, a wealthy gold miner.
SPECIAL EVENTS: The following is a selection of special events occurring in the Shasta Cascade in 2005:
Apr 6-11 *Kool April Nites* (Northern California's largest classic car show), Redding. **Apr 15-17** *Red Bluff Round-Up* (America's largest three-day rodeo), Red Bluff. **May 5-8** *Sacramento County Fair*. **May 25-30** *Silver Dollar Fair*, Chico. **Jun 15-19** *Shasta District Fair*, Anderson. **Jul 4** *Freedom Festival* (one of the five largest fireworks displays in the West), Redding. **Aug 10-14** *Siskiyou Golden Fair*, Yreka; *Plumas-Sierra County Fair*, Quincy. **Aug 12-Sep 5** *California Exposition & State Fair*, Sacramento. **Sep** *Siskiyou Century Bike Ride*, Yreka. **Sep 7-11** *Tulelake-Butte Valley Fair*, Tulelake.

High Sierra

The spectacular High Sierra region is home to the **Yosemite**, **Sequoia** and **Kings Canyon National Parks**, the year-round resort of **Lake Tahoe** and some of the country's best ski resorts. The **Mammoth Lakes** area, including the ski fields of **Mammoth Mountain**, is a major destination for outdoor enthusiasts and boasts some spectacular natural attractions.
LAKE TAHOE: The Washoe Native Americans called it 'The Lake in the Sky' and, situated over 1800m (6000ft) above sea level in a stunning alpine setting, it is not hard to see why. Tahoe has clear blue skies, snow-capped mountains and an array of cultural and historical riches. The 115km (72 mile) drive around the lake affords impressive views of the basin. Lake cruises are also available – the *MS Dixie II* and *Tahoe Queen* paddle-wheelers cruise from **South Shore** to **Emerald Bay**, with views straight into the clear waters. Tahoe's spectacular scenery can also be enjoyed from the Aerial Tram at **Heavenly Ski Resort**, which transports passengers to 600m (2000ft) over the **Gunbarrel Ski Run**. **Emerald Bay State Park**, at the southwest corner of the lake, features Tahoe's only island, **Fannette Island**. Sights here include **Vikingsholm**, a 38-room Scandinavian-style castle, open for guided tours in the summer. On Route US50, the **Lake Tahoe Historical Society Museum** displays the area's most comprehensive collection of early photos. Watersports enthusiasts are amply catered for, as the lake is blessed with excellent beaches at **Emerald Bay**, **Baldwin**, **Regan** and **Timber Cove**, where boating, jet-skiing, para-sailing, scuba-diving and windsurfing are popular activities. The site of the 1960 Winter Olympics, Lake Tahoe has a number of outstanding ski resorts. On the California/Nevada border, the **Heavenly Ski Resort** has the highest elevation in the Tahoe basin. Other resorts include **Kirkwood** and **Sierra-at-Tahoe**.
Gambling has been popular ever since wealthy holidaymakers started flocking to Tahoe at the turn of the century. Some of the biggest names in the casino industry, offering a variety of headline entertainment and 24-hour gaming, are to be found just over the border on the Nevada side of Lake Tahoe.
NORTH LAKE TAHOE: This world-famous skiing destination has a great selection of high-quality resorts, including **Alpine Meadows**, **Diamond Peak**, **Homewood Mountain Resort**, **Northstar-at-Tahoe**, **Squaw Valley USA** and **Sugar Bowl**. There are plenty of activities for non-skiers, ranging from ice skating, swimming, hot tubbing and snow-tubing at Squaw Valley to sleigh rides and snowmobiling at Northstar-at-Tahoe.
EASTERN SIERRA: The **Mammoth Lakes** area is a major resort with spectacular scenery, year-round activities and plenty of sightseeing. In winter, **Mammoth Mountain** has more than 9km (6 miles) of downhill ski runs and great cross-country skiing, while in summer, the same slopes attract thousands of mountain bikers. Natural features include the lakes which were scooped out by glaciers and the remarkable **Devils Postpile Natural Monument**, formed when glaciers flowed over the lava that had erupted and filled a river valley.
Other sights include **Bishop**, where the **Bishop Creek Recreation Area** offers camping, trout fishing, horseriding and boating. **The Inyo National Forest** is home to the oldest living things on earth: bristlecone pines more than 4700 years old. **Bodie** is one of the most authentic ghost towns of the West, preserved in a state of 'arrested decay'. **Mono Lake**, an inland sea with bizarre tufa towers, was formed about 700,000 years ago and is one of the world's oldest lakes. **Hot Creek Canyon**, where volcanic activity heats pools and streams of water, also makes for an interesting visit. Near **Independence** is the infamous internment camp of **Manzanar**, where more than 10,000 Japanese were held during World War II. The Eastern slopes of the Sierra Nevada offer outstanding views of the **Sierra Crest**.
WESTERN SIERRA: On the western slopes of the Sierra are the **Sequoia** and **Kings Canyon National Parks**, famed for their forests of giant sequoia trees, the largest trees on earth. The 2500-year-old **General Sherman Tree** in **Giant Forest** is the largest tree in the world (by volume) with a circumference of 31.1 m (102.6 feet). **Kings Canyon** is the deepest canyon in the USA. **Yosemite National Park** contains the world's best-known glacier-carved valley, spectacular waterfalls and granite monoliths, and the **Mariposa Grove of Giant Sequoias**. **Glacier Point** offers some of the best views of the area. Attractions in **Yosemite Village** include the **Yosemite Museum** with a Native American cultural exhibit, the **Museum Gallery** with historical works of art, and the **Ansel Adams Gallery**, which features many signed photos, prints and posters.
SPECIAL EVENTS: The following is a selection of special events occurring in High Sierra in 2005:
Mar 4-13 *Tahoe Snow Festival* (largest winter carnival in the West), Tahoe City. **Apr 7-10** *Jazzaffair Three Rivers*, Sequoia National Park. **Apr 29-30** *Annual Gates and Wakes Competition*, North Lake Tahoe. **May 13-14** *Reno-Tahoe Wine & Gourmet Food Festival*, Reno Hilton, Reno. **May 20-22** *Lake Tahoe Jazz Festival*. **Jul 12-17** *Celebrity Golf Championship*, Lake Tahoe. **Aug 1-13** *Sierra Summer Festival*, Mammoth Lakes. **Aug 10-11** *Great Gatsby Festival*, Lake Tahoe. **Sep 5** *Labor Day Lake Tahoe*, South Lake Tahoe; **Oct** *Oktoberfest*, North Lake Tahoe. **Dec** *Night of Lights*, throughout the Mountains area.

Gold Country

The western ridges of the Sierra Nevada are home to Gold Country, also known as the 'Mother Lode'. The discovery of gold here in 1848 attracted 300,000 fortune seekers from all over the world. Not everyone struck it rich, but the gold rush changed California forever and left a rich legacy of historic mining towns, railways and museums. The State capital, **Sacramento**, is a sophisticated city with strong ties to its pioneer past. Visitors can follow in the footsteps of the famous '49ers' at the **Columbia**, **Empire Mine** and **Marshall Gold Discovery State Historic Parks**, explore caverns and the wineries of **El Dorado**, **Amador** and **Calaveras** counties, or go white-water rafting on the **American River**.

SACRAMENTO: The Californian capital since 1854, Sacramento is home to more than 32 theatres, galleries and museums, and is full of visible reminders of its past. The state historic park of **Old Sacramento**, on the **Sacramento River**, features 53 historic buildings (the largest collection in the West) and recreates the Sacramento of the gold rush. It includes the **California State Railroad Museum**, which highlights how railways shaped the lives, economy and culture of California and the West. Historic steam train rides run on weekends from April to September. Also in the neighbourhood is the **Crocker Art Museum**. Opened in 1873, it is the oldest art museum in the west and exhibits early Californian paintings, drawings by the Old Masters and contemporary art. In the centre of the city is the Renaissance Revival-style **State Capitol** and **California State Capitol Museum**. Modelled on the capitol in Washington, DC, the building has housed the California Legislature since 1869. Tours are also available of the grand Victorian **Governor's Mansion**, home to 13 of California's governors and filled with historic furnishings. Artefacts from more than 100 Native American tribes are on show at the **California State Indian Museum**, where an exhibit traces the life of Ishi, California's last Yahi Indian. The new **Golden State Museum** tells the ongoing story of California and celebrates what is distinctive about the State. Over 100 species, 40 of them threatened or endangered, are housed at **Sacramento Zoo**, including polar bears, snow leopards and Sumatran tigers. Sacramento is home to professional ballet, opera and theatre companies and has a vibrant nightlife, with dozens of clubs, comedy venues and restaurants offering everything from Moroccan to Vietnamese cuisine.

Excursions: Folsom, 32km (20 miles) east of Sacramento, was one of the largest cities in the state during the gold rush. Today it is home to 60 antique dealers and over 40 artisans' studios, art galleries and working artists, as well as the historic buildings of the **Old Town**. **Lake Nacoma** and **Folsom Lake** offer sailing, water-skiing and windsurfing and a range of other activities for outdoor enthusiasts.

EL DORADO COUNTY: This is the heart of Gold Country, where James Marshall discovered the first Californian gold at **Sutter's Mill** in **Coloma**. Visitors can see where the gold rush began and pan for gold at the **Marshall Gold Discovery State Historic Park**, which has a museum and both original and restored buildings. The South Fork of the American River at Coloma is especially popular with whitewater rafters, offering some of the best rafting in the country. Known as 'Hangtown' in its early days, **Placerville** is full of historic buildings and operates the **Gold Bug Mine**, the only gold mine in the state open to visitors; the mine is on the National Register of Historic Places. Wineries have flourished in the spectacular foothills of the Sierra Nevada since the gold rush, and tours and tastings are available year-round.

CALAVERAS COUNTY: Southeast of Sacramento, Calaveras County is home to forests of giant sequoias at **Calaveras Big Trees State Park**, award-winning wineries and gold rush towns like **Mokelumne Hill**, **Avery** and **Arnold**. Mark Twain became a household name after writing *The Celebrated Jumping Frog of Calaveras County* at **Angels Camp**, where the *Jumping Frog Jubilee* is held annually in May. At the gold rush town of **Murphys**, visitors can explore the **Mercer Caverns**, 10 caverns with rare crystal formations. At **Cave City**, the **Moaning Cavern**, with a main chamber large enough to hold the Statue of Liberty, is open all year round, and the **California Cavern** is open for tours from spring to autumn.

TUOLUMNE COUNTY: Visitors can prospect for gold at **Jamestown**, which has served as a backdrop for films like *Butch Cassidy and the Sundance Kid* and *High Noon*. The nearby **Columbia State Historic Park** is California's best-preserved gold-mining town, with gold panning, stagecoach rides and tours of an active gold mine.

AMADOR COUNTY: Dotted with gold rush towns like **Amador City** and **Sutter Creek**, this region is renowned for its wineries – there are around two dozen of them in **Shenandoah Valley**. An outstanding collection of Sierra Nevada Indian artefacts, as well as a reconstructed Miwok village, can be found at the **Chaw'se Regional Indian Museum** in the **Indian Grinding State Historic Park** near **Jackson**. The spectacular crystal formations and deep lakes of **Black Chasm Cavern** can be seen on guided tours. **Mariposa**, in the south of Gold Country, is home to California's oldest courthouse, built in 1854. The **Mariposa County Museum** features a miner's cabin and a reconstructed Native American village, while the **California State Mining and Mineral Museum** boasts one of the largest gem and mineral collections in the world.

SPECIAL EVENTS: The following is a selection of special events occurring in Gold Country in 2005:

Mar 12-13 *Calaveras Celtic Fair*, Angels Camp. **Mar 19** *Irish Days*, Murphys. **May 5-8** *Sacramento County Fair*. **May 19-22** *Calaveras County Fair and Jumping Frog Jubilee*, Frogtown, Angels Camp. **May 27-30** *Sacramento Jazz Jubilee*. **Jun 16-19** *El Dorado County Fair*, Placerville. **Jul 28-31** *Amador County Fair*, Plymouth. **Aug 12-Sep 5** *California State Fair*, Sacramento. **Sep 2-5** *Mariposa County Fair and Homecoming*. **Oct 1** *Calaveras Grape Stomp and Gold Rush Street Faire*, Murphys.

Central Valley

Sprawling from Bakersfield in the south to the **Mendocino National Forest** in the north, the Central Valley is one of the most productive farming areas in the world. Covered in orchards, fields and vineyards and fed by a network of rivers and lakes – including the 1610km (1000 mile) Delta waterway system – it offers plenty of outdoor recreational opportunities. There is also an abundance of historic sites to explore, and wildlife refuges where visitors can observe native animals in their natural habitat.

BAKERSFIELD: The discovery of gold and oil brought settlers of every nationality to Bakersfield and today it is a proudly multi-cultural city. The history of the region is on show at the **Kern County Museum**, which features 58 historic buildings and **Black Gold: The Oil Experience**, a science, technology and history interactive exhibit, which opened in November 2002. The **California Living Museum** is a zoo, botanical garden and natural history museum featuring exhibits native to California.

In the Bakersfield area are the **Tule Elk State Reserve**, a protected area for native elk, and the **Colonel Allensworth State Historic Park** at **Earlimart**, a town with restored 19th-century buildings built by and for African-Americans. The **Kern National Wildlife Refuge** at **Delano** is a winter home to wildfowl; the best time for birdwatching is from October to March. The **Upper** and **Lower Kern** rivers are popular with whitewater rafters.

FRESNO: The city of Fresno is at the heart of Fresno County, the fifth-largest county in California and the USA's leading agricultural region. The **Kings Canyon**, **Sequoia** and **Yosemite** national parks are all close to the city. The **Fresno Metropolitan Museum** has a permanent exhibition on the life of William Saroyan, the Pulitzer Prize- and Oscar-winning author who grew up in Fresno, as well as a large collection of landscape paintings by Ansel Adams and Maynard Dixon, and Native American baskets. The charming **Chaffee Zoo** features rainforest, orangutan and tiger exhibits and the world's first computerised reptile house, where temperature, humidity and light cycles are controlled to resemble a natural habitat, as well as regular camel rides and hippo feeding. Children also love **Storyland**, with its buildings inspired by fairy tales. The **Meux Home** (1899) and the **Kearney Mansion** (1906) are museums recreating turn-of-the-century lifestyles, while the **Forestiere Underground Gardens**, a 60-room underground maze over 4 hectares (10 acres), is one of the city's more unusual attractions.

MERCED: Known as the 'Gateway to Yosemite', Merced is just a short drive from the **Yosemite National Park** and its spectacular valleys, waterfalls, granite monoliths and giant sequoias. The **Yosemite Wildlife Museum** is a great place to learn about the animals that live in the area. Visitors to Merced can also sample the award-winning wines and beers at the **Red Rock Winery and Brewery** or see cheese being made at the **Hilmar Cheese Company**. The **Castle Air Museum** at **Atwater** displays 43 vintage military aircraft from World War II and the wars in Korea and Vietnam.

THE DELTA: Many visitors see the sights of the Delta by houseboat, but **Stockton** also makes a good base from which to explore the region. Formed by the Sacramento, San Joaquin and Mokelumne rivers, the Delta is the ideal place for boating, fishing, water-skiing and windsurfing. Attractions in nearby **Lodi** include the **The San Joaquin County Historical Society Museum**, which traces the history of the area from the earliest native inhabitants up to the present, the **Micke Grove Park and Zoo** and the **Great Valley Serpentarium**, a living reptile museum. Those with a sweet tooth should take a detour to the **Hershey Visitors' Center** at **Oakdale**, where visitors can watch chocolate being made, or the **Herman Goelitz Candy Company** in **Fairfield**. The inventors of the jelly bean give daily tours of the factory where the famous *Jelly Belly* beans are produced. **Modesto**, south of Stockton, is home to the world's largest winery, *E & J Gallo*. The vintners have preserved the 1883 **McHenry Mansion**, furnished with period antiques, for visitors.

SPECIAL EVENTS: The following is a selection of special events occurring in Central Valley in 2005:

Mar 5-6 *Fresno County Blossom Trail*, Fresno. **Apr 22-24** *Asparagus Festival*, Stockton. **Apr 27-May 1** *Merced County Spring Fair*, Los Banos. **May 5-8** *Dixon May Fair*. **May 12-15** *High Desert Spring Festival*, Ridgecrest. **May 20-21** *Swedish Festival*, Kingsburg. **Jun 15-26** *San Joaquin County Fair*, Stockton. **Jul 9-24** *Merced County Fair*, Merced. **Sep 8-11** *Desert Empire Fair*, Ridgecrest. **Sep 21-Oct 2** *Kern County Fair*, Bakersfield. **Sep 24** *Dixon Scottish Games & Gathering*, Dixon. **Oct 5-16** *Big Fresno Fair*. **Nov 12-13** *Kearney Park Renaissance Faire*, Fresno.

San Francisco Bay Area

The compact region of the San Francisco Bay Area combines the cosmopolitan atmosphere of the big city with the wide open spaces of the country. Here, visitors can hike and explore redwood parks or ocean beaches, and take in opera, ballet and exotic dining experiences.

SAN FRANCISCO: San Francisco is situated on a 120 sq km (46.6 sq mile) peninsula, bounded on the west by the Pacific Ocean, on the north by the **Golden Gate Strait** and from north to east by **San Francisco Bay**. This provides one of the world's finest landlocked harbours. The Bay is spanned by two landmarks, the **Golden Gate Bridge** and the **San Francisco–Oakland Bay Bridge**. It is also graced by four islands – **Alcatraz**, **Angel**, **Yerba Buena** and **Treasure**. The city's history is a mixture of Spanish colonialism and rowdy US romanticism. The first European settlement on the site of the present city was established in 1776. It kept the name Yerba Buena until 1847, when it was officially christened San Francisco. The city is built on a series of hills – more than 40 of them – so that almost every other street points the way to a panoramic view of the Bay. The principal hills, which earned it the Roman sobriquet of the 'City of the Seven Hills', are **Nob Hill**, **Russian Hill**, **Telegraph Hill**, **Twin Peaks**, **Mount Davidson**, **Rincon** and **Lone Mountain**.

One of San Francisco's principal attractions is its network of 130-year-old cable cars, the USA's only mobile National Historic Landmark. In the **San Francisco Cable Car Museum**, visitors can view the actual cable-winding machinery as it reels 17km (11 miles) of steel at a steady pace of 15km (9.5 miles) per hour. Visitors might be surprised that the **Golden Gate Bridge** is not actually gold at all. It is painted orange, is resistant to harsh weather conditions and is at its most visible through fog. The 1017 acres of **Golden Gate Park** encompass meadows, lakes, rose gardens, an arboretum, a rhododendron dell, an open-air music concourse, a children's playground, a buffalo paddock and the tallest artificial waterfall in the West. The park is also home to the **California Academy of Sciences**, which includes the **Natural History Museum**, the **Morrison Planetarium** and the **Steinhart Aquarium**. The **Cartoon Art Museum**, the only one of its kind in the USA, displays rotating exhibitions of art from comic books, with approximately 6000 original pieces in its permanent collection. Most of the city's museums are free at least one day each month. Other sights include **Fisherman's Wharf**, with its bay-view restaurants and **Pier 39**'s resident sea lions; **Alcatraz**, once the site of the USA's toughest maximum security prison, and now a National Park; **Chinatown**, the most concentrated Asian enclave outside Asia; the pagoda-crowned **Japan Center**; **Ocean Beach**; and **North Beach**.

The cultural scene includes the US$44-million **Yerba Buena Center for the Arts**, which is devoted to showcasing the work of artists from the multi-cultural community and features diverse programmes of dance, theatre, music, film, installations and festivals. The new **Rooftop at Yerba Buena Gardens** includes a restored 1906 carousel and **Zeum**, a high-tech, hands-on arts centre for children. The **San Francisco Museum of Modern Art**, designed by Swiss architect Mario Botta, was the first museum on the West Coast solely devoted to 20th-century art. The city offers its own ballet and opera companies, as well as a symphony orchestra and dozens of live theatre groups, including the perennially popular **American Conservatory Theater**. For visitors seeking peace and quiet, San Francisco's Russian Hill, with its historic brown-shingle houses, sweeping views and botanical treasures offers an ideal getaway. Telegraph Hill, crowned by **Coit Tower**, is laced with stairways.

FOOD & DRINK: There is a limitless variety of ethnic, US, health food and international cuisine in San Francisco. For a treat, sample fresh crab and shrimp at the seafood houses that line the famous Fisherman's Wharf. There are also numerous 'fast food' restaurants.

THEATRES & CONCERTS: The **Orpheum Theater** offers light opera. **Geary Theater** is the home of the *American Conservatory Theater*, which also stages special performances at **Marines Memorial Theater**. **Curran** and **Golden Gate Theaters** show major Broadway productions. The **San Francisco Symphony** performs in the magnificent new **Louise M Davies Symphony Hall**, while popular music concerts are given in the **Civic Auditorium** in July. The **San Francisco Ballet** also performs in the **Opera House** during the December holiday season. The San Francisco opera season, one of the most outstanding in the country, runs from mid-September to November.

NIGHTLIFE: This is a great city for nightlife, boasting everything from strip joints to chic piano bars, elegant supper clubs and live music venues. The city also has a lively gay scene.
SHOPPING: The city is noted for its art, jewellery and handcrafted items. The principal shopping district surrounds Union Square in the city centre. Others include Ghirardelli Square and the Cannery (trendy clothes, foods, art, kitchen imports); Union Street (boutiques, antiques, arts and handicrafts in restored Victorian settings); Pier 39, a shopping/restaurant complex on a long pier; Chinatown and Japantown.
SPORT: The city offers major-league baseball (April to September) and professional football US-style (September to December). There is thoroughbred, quarter horse and harness-racing at **Bay Meadows Race Track** and **San Mateo** (September to June) and thoroughbred racing at **Golden Fields**, Albany (winter and spring).
TRAVEL: *San Francisco International Airport (SFO)* (website: www.flysfo.com) is located 15 minutes from the city centre. Car hire is available. The clean and efficient *BART (Bay Area Rapid Transport System)* operates four lines, joining San Francisco with Oakland, Berkeley, Concord and Fremont. *San Francisco Municipal Railway (MUNI)* operates buses, cable cars and a subway/streetcar system. For more detailed information, see *Travel* in the general California section.
SPECIAL EVENTS: The following is a selection of special events occurring in the San Francisco Bay Area in 2005:
Feb 1-28 *San Francisco Crab Festival.* **Feb 19-27** *TulipMania*, Pier 39. **Mar 16-20** *2005 San Francisco Flower and Garden Show*, Cow Palace. **Apr-Sep** *San Francisco Giants' Baseball Season.* **Apr 1-30** *Cherry Blossom Festival*, Japantown. **May** *Wells Fargo Spring Cup 2005 Regatta*, Mission District. **May 1** *Cinco de Mayo Parade & Festival*, Mission District. **May 15** *Bay to Breakers Footrace.* **May 28-29** *Carnival* (one of the largest annual events), Mission District. **Jun 25-26** *San Francisco Lesbian/Gay/Bisexual/Transgender Pride Celebration.* **Jul 4** *Fourth of July Waterfront Festival*, Pier 39. **Jul 31** *San Francisco Marathon.* **Sep** *Chocolate Festival*, Ghirardelli Square. **Sep 7-18** *San Francisco Fringe Festival.* **Sep 16-18** *Monterey Jazz Festival.* **Sep 17** *Viva Las Americas* (part of Hispanic Heritage Month), Pier 39. **Sep 24-25** *San Francisco Blues Festival.* **Oct-Nov** *San Francisco Jazz Festival.* **Oct 2** *Castro Street Fair.* **Oct 8-9** *Fleet Week San Francisco.* **Oct 10** *Columbus Day Celebration.* **Oct 14-16** *San Francisco Harvest From the Sea.* **Oct 30** *Pumpkin Pandemonium*, Pier 39.
CLIMATE: San Francisco's 'automatic air conditioning' (created by a unique combination of waters, winds and topography) makes it one of the coolest spots in California. The weather is spring-like all the year round. The summer fog usually clears by noon. Knitwear and light woollens suffice all year round.

The Bay Area

In the northern Bay Area is **Vallejo**, California's first capital, and a magnet for history buffs, sportspeople and nature lovers. The **Naval Historical Museum** is well worth a visit here, and the annual *Whaleboat Regatta* in October is a colourful calendar highlight. Nearby is **Six Flags Marine World**, a wildlife theme park featuring shows with whales, dolphins and tigers, as well as thrilling rides.
East of the Bay is **Berkeley**, home of the prestigious **University of California**, and cultural attractions such as the **U C Berkeley Art Museum**, **Pacific Film Archive** and **Zellerbach Hall**. A range of independent bookstores, cafes and nightlife caters for students and tourists alike. Moving south, **Oakland** is the centre of many activities in the Bay Area. Miles of waterfront, boating and breathtaking scenery from acres of hilltop parkland make up this charming city. Points of interest include the **Oakland Museum of California**, which retraces local history and colourful **Jack London Square and Village**, with their waterfront dining and shopping facilities.
Further south still, **San Jose** is noted for its year-round golden climate and offers unique visitor attractions, including the **Rosicrucian Egyptian Museum**, the bizarre **Winchester Mystery House** and **The Tech Museum of Innovation**, focused entirely on technology with four main galleries and an IMAX theatre. Just 50 minutes south of San Francisco, in the heart of Silicon Valley, is **Santa Clara**, known as 'The Mission City'. Attractions here include **Paramount's Great America**, an enormous theme park featuring rides and live entertainment. At the southern tip of the Bay Area is **Santa Cruz**, where points of interest include **Felton Covered Bridge** (the tallest covered bridge of its kind, built in 1892), **Roaring Camp** and the **Big Trees Narrow-Gauge Railroad**, which offers steam-train excursions. **Santa Cruz Mission State Historic Park** houses a replica of the original 1791 mission. The **Santa Cruz Boardwalk** features the West Coast's only beach amusement park, with one of the world's top-10 rollercoasters.

Credit: © California Tourism Office

Central Coast

California's Central Coast is a beautiful region, extending from the dramatic coastline visible from Route 1, the **Pacific Coast Highway**, to the inland valleys with their vineyards and wineries. A variety of recreation options are available: surfing at Santa Cruz or Santa Barbara, diving in **Monterey Bay**, horseback riding or driving at **Pismo Beach** or walking on **Pacific Grove**'s oceanfront recreation area. Boating is available on **Lake Casitas** in Ventura County, **Lake Nacimiento** near Paso Robles, **Lake Cachuma** in the Santa Ynez Valley, and the **San Justo Reservoir** in Hollister. Other major attractions include **Hearst Castle**, built by the tycoon William Randolph Hearst, the model for Orson Welles' *Citizen Kane*; the **Monterey Bay Aquarium**; **Goleta Beach**, with its year-round Mediterranean climate; **Montecito**, the luxury residential area east of Santa Barbara; the Danish-influenced town of **Solvang**; the **Carpinteria State Beach Park**, with 1200m (4000ft) of ocean frontage; and the **Santa Cruz Boardwalk**. North of Santa Barbara, the flower fields of **Lompoc Valley** and the ancient **Chumash Cave** and pictographs afford added interest. **Nipomo Dunes Preserve**, the second-largest expanse of dunes in California, stretches from Vandenberg Air Force Base in Santa Barbara County to Pismo Beach. California's historic missions dating from the Spanish Colonial era can also be toured.
SPECIAL EVENTS: The following is a selection of special events occurring in Central Coast in 2005:
Jan 29-Feb 6 *Santa Barbara International Film Festival.* **Feb 17-20** *Annual Masters of Food and Wine*, Carmel. **Apr 15-17** *44th Annual Wildflower Show*, Pacific Grove. **Apr 20-24** *Santa Barbara Fair and Exposition.* **Apr 22-24** *Santa Maria Valley Strawberry Festival.* **Apr 28-30** *Monterey Wine Festival.* **May 12-15** *Salinas Valley Fair*, King City. **May 14-15** *Castroville Artichoke Festival.* **Jun 3** *California Cowboy Show*, Carmel Valley. **Jun 24-26** *Monterey Blues Festival.* **Jul 10** *Summer Jamboree*, Carmel Valley. **Jul 13-17** *Santa Barbara County Fair*, Santa Maria. **Aug 13** *13th Annual Winemakers Celebration*, Monterey. **Aug 16-21** *Monterey County Fair.* **Aug 21** *55th Annual Pebble Beach Concours d'Elegance* (classic car show), Pebble Beach. **Sep** *Beer Festival*, Monterey. **Sep 11** *Carmel TomatoFest 2005.* **Sep 16-18** *Monterey Jazz Festival.* **Oct 1** *Butterfly Parade*, Pacific Grove. **Nov 10-13** *Ninth Great Wine Escape Weekend*, Monterey. **Nov 17-27** *Amateur Horse Show*, Santa Barbara. **Dec 2** *Tree Lighting Ceremony*, Monterey. **Dec 31** *First Night* (music, dance, poetry and exhibitions), Monterey.
CLIMATE: Mild and sunny 12 months a year – there is no 'off season'. Most people wear comfortable sports clothing all year round.

The Monterey Peninsula

The Monterey Peninsula has been called the 'jewel of the Central Coast'. For more than 300 years, it has impressed all who have landed on its shores, from the early Spanish explorers and missionaries to present-day visitors.
The beauty and charm of the Peninsula captured the hearts and imagination of artists and writers such as John Steinbeck, Henry Miller, Robinson Jeffers, Robert Louis Stevenson and Ansel Adams. Each in his own way sought to preserve the magic on canvas, paper or film.
The Monterey Peninsula's dramatic coastline and sunny valleys are the backdrop for the rich cultural and maritime heritage, which is preserved today in the Mexican *adobes*, the **Maritime Museum**, **Cannery Row** and **Fisherman's Wharf** in historic Monterey.
Much of the area's charm stems from the many cultural influences – Native American, Mexican, Spanish, Italian and Asian – which shaped the region's early development. Attractions include the world-class **Monterey Bay Aquarium**, with its spectacular **Outer Bay Wing**. The Aquarium is the perfect spot from which to survey the depths of the **Monterey Bay National Marine Sanctuary**.
The quaint village of **Carmel-by-the-Sea**, a village in a forest, offers over 90 art galleries and the annual *Bach Festival* – testaments to its 100-year reputation as a centre for the visual and performing arts.
Pacific Grove is home to the colourful annual migration of Monarch butterflies, which can be seen in autumn. It also features Victorian architecture, much of which houses bed & breakfast inns and restaurants.
Carmel Valley, a mere 3.2km (2 miles) inland from the coast, is a sunny upland area, which boasts golf courses, horseback riding, a tennis resort and the **Ventana Wilderness Area**, which visitors can explore on foot.
Pebble Beach, home of the *AT&T National Pro-Am Golf Tournament*, is a world-class resort with two full service resort hotels, four golf courses and, of course, the famed 17-Mile Drive on which sits the oft-photographed **Lone Cypress Tree**.
Big Sur offers dramatic coastal scenery, with its **Bixby Bridge** and **Julia Pfeiffer State Park**. Two world-class resorts in the area contribute to the range of lodging options.
TRAVEL: To reach the Monterey Peninsula from Los Angeles or San Francisco, drivers may take State Highway 101 or Scenic Highway 1. *San Francisco* and *Los Angeles* airports offer flights to *Monterey Peninsula Airport (MRY)*. The *Monterey/Salinas Airbus* offers scheduled services between *San José* and *San Francisco* airports and the Monterey/Salinas area.

Santa Barbara

Santa Barbara, on the American Riviera, lies 534km (332 miles) south of San Francisco and 150km (92 miles) north of Los Angeles. Highway 101 runs directly through it. The Santa Barbara scenic tour is an excellent way to see the area. Attractions to look out for along the **Scenic Loop** include the much-admired **Santa Barbara County Courthouse**. The elegant interior includes hand-painted ceilings, wrought-iron chandeliers, giant murals, carved doors and imported tiles. The 24m- (80ft-) high clock tower affords panoramic views of the city. The **Mission Santa Barbara**, the 'Queen of the Missions', was established in December 1786 and boasts unique twin bell towers and a lovely facade. Many of the city's historic adobe houses from the Spanish and Mexican eras are featured in the central area. In the **Hill-Carrillo Adobe**, for example, can be found the city's first wooden floor. The **Santiago de la Guerra Adobe**, now remodelled, is one of the city's oldest structures. The **Fernald Mansion and Trussell-Winchester Adobe** is a well-furnished 14-room Victorian mansion with a handsome staircase and carved decorations. It is one of the finest remaining examples of Victorian architecture in the area. Other attractions include the **Museum of Natural History**, a nationally renowned museum specialising in Californian and North American West Coast history, with 11 exhibit halls and a Lizard Lounge featuring live reptiles and amphibians. Highlights include an **Indian Hall** with a diorama of historic Chumash life and

the giant skeleton of a blue whale, as well as fine art, western saddles, exquisite costumes and picturesque antique toys. The **Santa Barbara Museum of Art** is one of the nation's outstanding regional museums and offers work by O'Keefe, Eakins, Sargent and Hopper. The **Santa Barbara Botanic Garden** is devoted to the study of California's native flora, cacti, redwoods and wildflowers, while the **Andrée Clark Bird Refuge** features a peaceful lagoon, gardens and a variety of freshwater birds. At the **El Presidio de Santa Barbara**, founded in 1782, visitors can view buildings belonging to the last Spanish military outpost in California. The **Presidio Chapel** contains restored 18th-century decorations, while the padre's and commandant's quarters feature authentically reproduced furniture and architecture. The **Santa Barbara Zoological Gardens** offers a botanical area and more than 700 species of animals from around the world, including big cats, elephants and giraffes. **Stearns Wharf**, once part-owned by the film star James Cagney and his brothers, is the oldest active working pier in California. It offers gifts and souvenirs, wine tasting and a seafood market. Views of the mountains and the ocean are spectacular from here.
Moreton Bay Fig Tree, the largest of its kind in the nation, is an Australian import planted in Santa Barbara in 1874. It has a span of 48m (160ft) and provides 6400 sq m (21,000 sq ft) of shade. The **Yacht Harbour and Breakwater** is the departure point for shoreline tours and fishing excursions. Its paved walkway offers a 0.5-mile walking tour with harbour, city and mountain views.
The **Carriage Museum** houses a unique collection of horse-drawn carts and carriages used by the pioneer families of Santa Barbara. The collection includes stagecoaches, buggies, army wagons and a black hearse. The climate makes this area conducive for all types of sports and recreational activities. Santa Barbara County is also noted for its parkland, ranging from small gardens with quiet groves to vast meadows, hills and mountains, each with a unique setting. The **Wine Country** in the Santa Barbara region, with over 43 wineries and nearly 10,000 acres of vineyards, is the fastest-growing region of its kind in the world. Easily accessible from Highways 101, 154 or 246, the area extends from the vineyards of **Santa Maria** and **Santa Ynez Valleys** to the wineries and tasting rooms in downtown Santa Barbara. A variety of micro-climates makes it possible to grow and produce excellent Cabernet Sauvignon, Chardonnay, Pinot Noir, Riesling, Sauvignon Blanc and many other wine grapes.
THEATRES & CONCERTS: Santa Barbara also offers a wide array of cultural and artistic activities. Some of the performing companies and venues include: **The Santa Barbara Symphony Orchestra**; the **Civic Light Opera**; the **Ensemble Theatre**; **Center Stage Theatre**; **Lobero Theatre**; **Granada Theatre**; **Santa Barbara County Bowl** and the **Arlington Theatre** built by Fox West Coast Theatres with a distinctive Moorish spire and a curved *trompe d'oeil* ceiling. It now acts as Santa Barbara's performing arts centre. The **University of California** at Santa Barbara and **Santa Barbara City College** also offer dramatic performances. The **Contemporary Arts Forum**, founded in 1976, is the focal point for contemporary art in Santa Barbara. The facility also includes three exhibition spaces.
SHOPPING: Santa Barbara offers abundant shopping opportunities: *Big Dog*, *Territory Ahead*, *Firenze*, *Isabel Bloom* and the *Santa Barbara Ceramic Design* are based here. Further shopping opportunities are available on **State Street** and at **El Paseo**; **La Arcada Court**; **Paseo Nuevo**; **Victoria Court**; **La Cumbre Plaza**; **Coast Village Road** and **Montecito Village**. **Brinkerhoff Avenue** is a charming one-block street of Victorian houses selling antiques, fascinating memorabilia and other specialities, while **El Paseo** is a unique Old Spanish-style shopping arcade, recently renovated as the site of speciality shops and art galleries. **The Farmers' Market** is a colourful outdoor area where local growers sell fresh fruits, vegetables, flowers and other produce at reasonable prices.
TRAVEL: *Santa Barbara Airport (SBA)* (website: www.flysba.com) is located 12km (8 miles) north of central Santa Barbara. Major airlines servicing Santa Barbara include: *American Eagle*, *America West Express*, *Delta Connection*, *Horizon Air* and *United Express*. Door-to-door shuttles and taxis are available. Car hire companies at the airport include *Avis*, *Budget*, *Hertz* and *National*. *Amtrak* offers daily north and southbound services on two lines (the 'Coast Starlight' from Seattle to Los Angeles and the 'Pacific Surfliner' from San Luis Obispo to San Diego) from their station at 209 State Street. Frequent bus services are provided by *Greyhound*.

Los Angeles

Encircled by four mountain ranges, the city of Los Angeles is oddly isolated, prompting early chroniclers to describe it as 'an island on the land'. To appreciate the city it should be thought of as five distinct regions: **Downtown**, **Hollywood**, **The Valleys**, **Westside** and **The Beaches**. The city of **Santa Monica**, with its beautiful beaches and small town atmosphere, has long been a hideaway for Hollywood stars. The city of Los Angeles was originally christened by wandering Spanish missionaries in 1781 as *'El Pueblo de Nuestra Senora la Reina de los Angeles de Porciuncula'* ('The Town of Our Lady Queen of the Angels by the Porciuncula'), and shortened a few years later to Los Angeles. Most residents simply refer to it by its initials, LA. It has also been called, at varying times, 'The City of Angels', 'The New Eden', 'The New Jerusalem', 'The New Babylon', and 'Lotus Land', as over the decades it grew from a cowtown to a boomtown, then an oiltown to Tinseltown. It was not accidental that the automobile culture and the film and aerospace industries took root in the area, or that almost every conceivable – and a few inconceivable – fads, fashions and styles have at some time or other sprouted in the city's consenting climate and spirit. Basking in a sunny, semitropical climate, and blessed with a diversity of cultures, Los Angeles mixes and matches different settings and scenes with a singular style. The city offers a dizzying array of attractions, from world-famous amusements to a wealth of museums, pop and high culture, Hollywood stars, ethnic enclaves and every cuisine imaginable. The latest hot fashions can be found in bargain centres and boutiques catering for every whim and budget. And one can always simply go native and bike, blade or 'veg' out.
LA is full of renowned museums, including the **Los Angeles County Museum of Art**, with its comprehensive collection of Western, as well as Asian and Near Eastern art, and its striking **Japanese Pavilion**; the **Museum of Contemporary Art (MOCA)**, which has three venues (California Plaza, Pacific Design Center and the Geffen Contemporary) with free entry on Thursdays; and the **Wells Fargo Museum**, featuring 130 years of Western history. Music and dance, classic, contemporary, native, hot and cool, rock, rap, blues and jazz can all be heard in a variety of venues across the city. Jazz fans in particular should head for **5th Street Dick's** in the up-and-coming **Crenshaw District**. As one might expect, LA has a wealth of cinemas showing every conceivable production – foreign, revivals, experimental and classic, as well as the most current films. Comedy clubs, magic shows, blues bars, juice bars, coffee house recitals and poetry readings are among the many diversions on offer when darkness falls in LA. The club scene is very fickle; a must-go night filled with this season's stars can go bust within weeks. The result is a fluid nightlife, so visitors should check out the local listings magazines for an up-to-date guide.
DOWNTOWN: LA's dynamic urban core has undergone a major facelift recently and the construction of new buildings and facilities has reinforced the area's claim to be the Pacific's premier business centre. Downtown attractions include the **Museum of Neon Art (MONA)**, which displays an art collection in electric media and neon signs, and the restored **Angel's Flight**, originally a funicular railway dating from 1901, which met with disaster in 2001, after an accident left one passenger dead and seven wounded. Modern art buffs will want to visit **MOCA** at the **Geffen Contemporary**. One of the world's largest newspapers, the *Los Angeles Times*, is across the street and offers behind-the-scenes tours of the media empire. For the more academically inclined, the **Los Angeles Central Library**, one of the nation's most respected research and resource centres, is also its third-largest public library, following a period of significant expansion. The **El Pueblo de Los Angeles State Historic Park** preserves a number of historically important buildings from the Spanish and Mexican eras. Downtown LA is a cornucopia of cultures; **Chinatown**, **Little Tokyo**, and the Latino-influenced **Olvera Street** and **Broadway** are examples of local communities. Befitting its climate and context, and individualistic spirit, the area has a particularly rich and varied architecture and design heritage. It is where the American Arts and Crafts movement flourished; the Spanish Colonial, Mexican and Mission Revival styles were rediscovered; where the Art Deco style, followed by the Moderne and the machine-like Modern styles took root; and where Frank Lloyd Wright experimented with new materials, forms and theories. There are whimsical, way-out designs, most of which can be seen from the street, along with a variety of public art. Among other things, LA has also been called 'The Mural Capital of the World'; the many examples of this art form are thanks to the city's temperate climate, and ethnic and neighbourhood pride.
Just south of Downtown is **Exposition Park**, site of the **Los Angeles Memorial Coliseum** and the **Sports Arena**. At the park, visitors can see the **Natural History Museum**, the **California African American Museum**, the **California Science Center** and stroll through the campus of the **University of Southern California**.
HOLLYWOOD: Los Angeles is the unabashed film and entertainment capital of the western world; more films are made here, more television shows taped here and more stars and would-be stars live here than anywhere else in the USA. The famous Hollywood sign, nestling in the hills above the city, stands as a constant reminder of the presence of the film industry. The streets and beaches are often used as locations, though most of it happens behind the well-guarded gates of the various studios scattered across the city. Still, in the opulent enclaves that cater to so-called 'industry types' – **Beverly Hills** and **Santa Monica** (see below) – an occasional celebrity can be glimpsed on the streets or in the shops.
For an insider's view of the industry, *NBC*, *Warner Bros* and *Universal Studios Hollywood* all offer tours. The Universal tour is the most popular artificial attraction in America after the Disney theme parks, with the new *Shrek 4-D™* experience now open. The **Hollywood Bowl Museum** features changing exhibits on performing arts in Los Angeles, while The **Hollywood Entertainment Museum** honours the film industry. In the **Griffith Park** area, one of the largest urban parks in the country, one can visit the outstanding **Los Angeles Zoo**, **Griffith Park Observatory**, **Travel Town** and the **Autry Museum of Western Heritage**. Other area attractions include **Hollywood Boulevard**, with its 'walk of fame' etched in the pavement.
WEST HOLLYWOOD: West Hollywood hosts more post-Oscar parties than any other city, and over 70 per cent of all filming in West Hollywood is on the **Sunset Strip**. Major films shot in the area include *Get Shorty*, *Casper*, *Heat* and *Leaving Las Vegas*. West Hollywood is best known for its sophisticated shopping and exciting and varied nightlife. The city is home to illustrious clubs, mostly found along the Sunset Strip, which are frequented by the rich and famous. 'The Creative City' features over 30 art galleries. Both the **Le Montrose Suite Hotel** and the **Wyndham Bel Age Hotel** house original international art collections that are worth millions.
WEST SIDE: LA's West Side is famed for its arty, trend-setting style. This is where the stars live and play. The West Side includes some of the city's most prestigious addresses, including Beverly Hills, Century City, Westwood, Brentwood and Bel Air. Maps of the homes of celebrities are available on street corners for individual exploration, and scheduled tours are also offered. **Beverly Hills** is home to the most famous shopping district in the world and is also home to the LA branch of the **Museum of Television and Radio**, which allows visitors to gain access to 75 years of programming history. Another museum attraction is the **Skirball Cultural Center**, located near the **Getty Center** and featuring original fragments of Ellis Island benches as well as a reconstruction of an archaeological dig. Car fans will flock to the **Petersen Automotive Museum**, which celebrates the history of the motor car with the largest car collection in the country. Theatre also thrives in this area: top Broadway musicals such as Sunset Boulevard draw crowds to the **Schubert Theatre** in **Century City**. The **Groundling Theatre** on **Melrose Avenue** premieres comedy revues. The **UCLA Center for the Performing Arts** shows big-name talent. And for film previews and special screenings, the theatres in **Westwood**, which are frequented by students from the nearby University of California campus, are a popular testing ground for the industry. Blues fans will want to pay a visit to the **House of Blues** on Sunset Boulevard to catch daily live performances of established, as well as up-and-coming blues artists. Another attraction is the **Museum of Tolerance**, featuring high-tech interactive exhibits that tell the history of racism and prejudice as well as the story of the Holocaust.
SANTA MONICA: The first of the fabled Southern Californian beach towns, Santa Monica entices visitors with its coastline, palm-lined cliffs and small town atmosphere. Just 13km (8 miles) from *Los Angeles International Airport*, Santa Monica offers a respite from the big city bustle. It has for decades been a favourite hideaway for Hollywood as well, with Mary Pickford and Douglas Fairbanks Sr, Greta Garbo, Cary Grant, Clark Gable, Bette Davis and Joan Crawford calling it home. Today, Meryl Streep, Michelle Pfeiffer and Ted Danson are just a few of the celebrities who live in Santa Monica. The thriving arts scene and cutting-edge cuisine add an air of European sophistication to this seaside community. A pedestrian-orientated city, Santa Monica's many attractions, hotels, restaurants and shops are within easy walking distance of one another and the beach. Primary beaches include **Santa Monica State Beach** and **Will Rogers State Beach**.
The **Santa Monica Museum of Art** is a design marvel by famed architect Frank O Gehry. The museum displays the work of contemporary and modern artists. In nearby **Malibu**, the famed **J Paul Getty Museum**, an exact replica of a Roman country villa, houses one of the world's largest and most valued art collections. Shopping is another popular pastime. The city has four different shopping areas, each with its own distinct character. **Montana Avenue**, **Main Street**, **Santa Monica Place** and **Third Street Promenade** feature speciality shops, restaurants and exclusive boutiques. In the evening, **Third Street Promenade** is transformed into a lively entertainment centre. Street performers fill the pavements and restaurants push dining tables aside to create dance floors. Home to a lively British population, Santa Monica also sports a dash of Old-World camaraderie with some of the best pubs and tea

A B C D E F G H I J K L M N O P Q R S T U V W X Y Z

rooms outside Great Britain. Santa Monica's most famous landmark is the pier. Having undergone a phased US$45 million restoration, the West Coast's oldest pleasure pier, built in 1908 during the height of the city's popularity as a seaside resort, is now home to **Pacific Park**. The park features a 55ft roller coaster and a giant Ferris wheel, as well as many other rides. The old pier's carousel, with hand-crafted gilt and painted horses, offers rides each day. Additional features here include the newly renovated **Boat House**, pubs, restaurants, shops and a fresh fish market. The 61,000-hectare **Santa Monica Mountains National Recreation Area**, on the city's northern border, offers camping, hiking, backpacking, horseriding, picnicking and birdwatching. **Will Rogers State Historic Park**, the 75-hectare ranch of the late humorist, features stables, polo matches at the weekends and tours of the cowboy/philosopher's ranch house.

THE BEACHES: The Beaches area of Los Angeles is a great place to hang out. One can bask in the sun in a quiet cove in **Malibu**, or bike or rollerblade along a path from **Santa Monica**, past the street performers of **Venice Beach**, the day sailors of **Marina del Rey**, the volleyball players on **Manhattan Beach**, and the surfers and fishermen off **Hermosa** and **Redondo**. This 35km- (22 mile-) oceanfront stretch celebrates the Southern Californian lifestyle, with a diversity of accessible, sandy beaches and picturesque views. Among the more popular spots to catch a wave and check out the local sun-tanning scene are **Will Rogers Beach State Park**, the Santa Monica and Venice piers and **Newport Beach**. For a classic Los Angeles experience, a visit to Venice Beach, where the body-beautiful skate by and street performers attract crowds every day, is a must. Also a part of Venice is **Muscle Beach**, where local hunks flex their pecs for bystanders.

The beach areas offer other diversions besides the fleshly variety. In the canyons of Malibu, for example, is Barbara Streisand's estate which houses her **Center for Conservancy Studies**. Visitors can enjoy the houses and landscaped meadows and orchards to be found here. At **Bergamot Station**, there is a 5.5 acre complex with a dozen galleries offering art-lovers a one-stop shopping experience.

THE VALLEYS: Once known as the notorious hang-out of the Valley Girls, The Valleys comprise three distinct areas, with plentiful shopping and several major annual events. **Mulholland Drive**, situated in the hills above the **San Fernando Valley**, offers panoramic views of the area below. **Ventura Boulevard** is a major shopping thoroughfare that attracts celebrities to its speciality shops and restaurants. Just north, in **Santa Clarita Valley**, is **Six Flags Magic Mountain**, a huge amusement park featuring thrilling rides and six roller-coasters. Adjacent to this is the **Six Flags Hurricane Harbor**, a themed waterpark featuring tube slides, speed slides and a wave pool. **Burbank** is the home of **NBC Studios**, where visitors can see the taping of famous TV shows.

Just east of the San Fernando Valley is the **San Gabriel Valley**, where **Pasadena** is the site of the world's most famous New Year's Day event, the **Tournament of Roses Parade**. Cultural attractions in the city include the **Norton Simon Museum of Art**, the **Huntington Library and Gardens** and **Los Angeles Arboretum**. Nearby Santa Anita is home to one of the most beautiful racetracks in the world and, high above in the **Angeles National Forest**, is **Mount Wilson**, with a small observatory and museum.

FOOD & DRINK: Many cities in the world may claim to cater for all needs or tastes, but LA goes one step further. Food ranges from mainstream, such as Italian or Mexican, to the more quirky, such as Nigerian and Uzbek. Residents and visitors alike believe that LA is much improved by the new Asian influences, which are reflected not only in the wide choice of cuisine on offer, but also in the city's ethnic diversity. Variety is not only available in content, but also in price. LA can boast some of the most expensive restaurants in the world, including **Valentino** in Santa Monica, **Rex II Ristorante** in downtown LA and **Matsuhisa** and **Spago** in West Hollywood. However, even on a more modest budget, many choices are on offer, such as at **La Serenata de Garibaldi** in Boyle Heights. It is even possible for a couple to eat out for less than US$20. **Rosalind's Ethiopian Restaurant**, **La Parilla** and the **Bombay Café** are reputed to be amongst the best. Santa Monica also has some top-class places to dine out, and with nearly 400 restaurants, cafes and pubs, the city boasts one restaurant for every 217 residents.

THEATRES & CONCERTS: Broadway hits can be seen at theatres in the **Music Center** complex, 135 N. Grand Avenue; one of the three largest performing arts centers in the USA. The **Walt Disney Concert Hall** was opened in October 2003 and is the new home of the *Los Angeles Philharmonic*. The complex's **Dorothy Chandler Pavilion** is home to the film industry's annual *Academy Awards* and the *Civic Light Opera*. The world-famous **Hollywood Bowl**, 2301 N. Highland Avenue, stages summer concerts. The **Universal Amphitheater** in the grounds of **Universal Studios** presents major pop and rock concerts. Other top venues include the **Mark Taper Forum** and the **Ahmanson Theater** (both part of the Music Center complex), the **Schubert Theater**, and the outdoor **Greek Theater** in Griffith Park.

NIGHTLIFE: It is no surprise that LA is known for its nightlife, with appearances by top-rate acts and a chance to rub shoulders with the stars. The most exciting and varied nightlife can be found in West Hollywood, where the clubs feature rock, jazz, comedy, pop and R&B. Since the 1920s, the Sunset Strip has been a centre for nightlife, home to some of the world's most illustrious clubs such as **The Roxy**, **Whisky A Go-Go**, **The Viper Room** and **The Comedy Store**. Gay and lesbian nightlife thrives in **Santa Monica Boulevard** with clubs such as **Axis**, **Revolver**, **Rage** and **Mickys**. The **San Fernando Valley** is also lively after dark, and many hotels present star entertainment.

SHOPPING: Smart shops, boutiques and department stores are found in downtown Los Angeles and Beverly Hills. In West Hollywood, **Sunset Plaza** is lined with speciality shops, while **Melrose** showcases the hottest new designer trends. Good value gifts, jewellery and handicrafts are sold in **Little Tokyo** and **Olvera Street**. Serious shoppers can explore the **Fashion District** and the **Jewellery District** downtown, where quality merchandise is sold at discount prices.

SPORT: Horse racing is held at **Santa Anita Park**, Arcadia (October and December to April); and thoroughbred racing (mid-April to late July) and night harness racing (August to early December) at **Hollywood Park**, Inglewood. The area also has professional baseball (August to December), professional basketball and ice hockey.

TRAVEL: Getting around in the 'land of the car' may be easier than most visitors think. Transport in Southern California is made simple from any of the four major airports: *Los Angeles International Airport*, *John Wayne/Orange County Airport*, *Ontario Airport* and *Long Beach Airport*. For more detailed information, see *Travel* in the main *California* section, or visit the website of *Los Angeles World Airports* (website: www.lawa.org).

SPECIAL EVENTS: The following is a selection of special events occurring in Los Angeles in 2005:

Jan 16 *62nd Annual Golden Globe Awards*. **Feb** *Black History Month*. **Feb 12-13** *Chinese New Year Parade and Carnival*. **Feb 27** *77th Annual Academy Awards* (invitation only), Hollywood. **Mar 26** *Blessing of the Animals* (fiesta and animal parade), Olvera Street, Los Angeles. **May 5** *Cinco de Mayo Celebration* (Mexican Festival). **Jun 9-12** *San Fernando Valley Fair*, Burbank. **Jun 19** *Juneteenth Festival* (commemorating the end of slavery). **Jul** *Verizon Music Festival*, Los Angeles. **Jul 4** *Independence Day Celebrations*. **Sep 4** *Los Angeles Birthday Celebrations*, Olvera Street, Los Angeles. **Sep 9-Oct 2** *Los Angeles County Fair*, Pomona. **Sep 15-18** *Annual Route 66 Rendezvous*. **Nov 27** *Hollywood Christmas Parade*. **Dec** *Annual Whittier Christmas Parade*, Uptown Whittier.

CLIMATE: Los Angeles' climate is generally sunny and warm with gentle ocean breezes in the summer. The humidity is low and there is very little rain.

Orange County

Orange County used to be a quiet farming community, but ever since Walt Disney decided to build his first amusement park in Anaheim in 1955, millions of visitors have been descending on the region. The area is now famous for its luxury beach resorts and some of the best family entertainment in the world. Orange County encompasses an area of 2067 sq km (798 sq miles), with 68km (42 miles) of coastline and beaches. There are 31 incorporated cities within its boundaries, including **Huntington Beach**, **Newport Beach**, **Laguna Beach**, **Dana Point** and **Costa Mesa**. **Anaheim** and **Buena Park** host a high concentration of family-oriented attractions. The region offers a variety of accommodation, from family hotels for the budget-conscious to full-service luxury hotels. The region also offers a feast of international and continental cuisine, from five-star restaurants to quaint boardwalk cafes.

ANAHEIM CITY: Anaheim City is 45km (28 miles) south of central Los Angeles and 50km (31 miles) southeast of *Los Angeles International Airport*, 145km (90 miles) north of San Diego and 645km (400 miles) south of San Francisco. There are close to 20,000 hotel rooms in Anaheim and nearly half of them surround the **Anaheim Convention Center** and are within walking distance of Disneyland. Easily the most renowned attraction in Orange County, *Disneyland* continues to be hugely popular. *Tomorrowland* brings a new generation 3-D experience, with a high-speed journey throughout the land upon rocket cars of the future, an interactive pavilion of technology and the landmark *Astro Orbitor* attraction. Other attractions include *Honey, I Shrunk the Audience*, *Innoventions* and the ever-popular *Star Tours*; and the thrill rides, such as *Splash Mountain* and the *Matterhorn*. *Disneyland* is open every day of the year. Also in Anaheim is **Tinseltown Studios**, which allows visitors to attend a two-hour awards show and dinner. As part of the experience, some guests will be presented with a

Credit: © California Tourism Office

Tinseltown statuette for their on-screen performance in a well-known film.

BUENA PARK: Southeast of LA and a stone's throw from Disneyland is Buena Park. Boasting a variety of dining and shopping opportunities, this 1-mile stretch of land is aptly known as the 'Entertainment Corridor'. One of the nation's oldest and most popular theme parks, **Knott's Berry Farm** was founded by Walter and Cordelia Knott and is now in its 79th year. Originally established as a diversion for visitors to the Knotts' rhubarb farm and kitchen cafe, it now has six themed areas, including Ghost Town, complete with cowboys and gunfights, and *Camp Snoopy*, the 6-acre home of *Snoopy and the Peanuts* gang. The park is always offering something new and the latest is *Supreme Scream* on the *Boardwalk*. One of the world's tallest thrill rides, the 254ft vertical ascent is followed by three seconds of weightlessness and a downward plunge at 80kph (50mph). The nearby **Movieland Wax Museum** is home to more than 300 movie and TV stars, all in realistic sets with props and costumes from the shows that made them famous. Guests can walk through replica movie sets with their favourite stars, including John Wayne, Robin Williams, Marilyn Monroe and Julia Roberts. Also nearby is **Ripley's Believe It or Not Museum** which features treasures collected by the journalist, such as a flea circus with fleas in costume, shrunken heads, mummies and more. Also in Buena Park is **Adventure City**, a 2-acre children's theme park offering 11 rides and attractions, live entertainment and programmes designed to educate children about topics ranging from transport to crime prevention.

COSTA MESA: Known as the 'City of the Arts', Costa Mesa is the cultural hub of Orange County. It features the striking **Orange County Performing Arts Center**, which hosts a wide variety of cultural arts, including theatre, ballet, opera and classical music, while the **South Coast Repertory** stages cutting-edge productions and Tony-Award-winning plays. The **Orange County Museum of Art's South Coast Plaza Gallery** has exhibits by artists working in different media. Nearby is the **California Scenario**, an outdoor sculpture garden designed by Isamu Noguchi. The city's fairgrounds host the annual *Orange County Fair* in July.

THE BEACHES: Orange County's 68km (42 miles) of beaches offer pristine stretches of sand and tidal pools, along with some of the finest sunbathing, surfing and sailing anywhere in the USA.

Huntington Beach is known as 'Surf City' and offers surfing aficionados unsurpassed opportunities. The world's largest surfing contest, the *Bluetorch Pro of Surfing Championships*, hits the beach each summer. The **Huntington Beach International Surfing Museum** chronicles the history of the sport through antique surfboards, photographs and memorabilia of both pioneering and modern-day surfing legends. **Newport Beach** used to be an idyllic weekend hideaway for the rich and famous. Today, it is a coastal community of diverse character and unique lifestyles, where a vibrant business culture combines with the intimate atmosphere of charming and distinct enclaves. Newport Beach is surrounded by one of the largest small-boat harbours in the world and bordered by more than 10km (6 miles) of scenic Pacific Ocean coastline, making it a popular vacation spot. The nearby **Balboa Pier**, a 276m- (919ft-) long structure, provides a perfect place for fishing and sightseeing. The **Orange County Museum of Art** has an extensive collection of Californian art. **Laguna Beach**, the 'Riviera of the West Coast', is considered by many to be the jewel of

Southern Californian beach cities. Part of Laguna's charm is its seaside village atmosphere; the strand flows seamlessly into the town, which is filled with bistros, shops and art galleries. Heisler Park, on a bluff overlooking the Pacific, is a great place for a picnic or barbecue and has stairs leading directly down to the beach. Laguna Beach is also home to more than 70 art galleries, including the famous **Laguna Art Museum**.
Dana Point is known for the **Dana Point Marina** and its range of water activities. Whale watching is available from late December through March, when boat excursions take visitors to view hundreds of Californian Gray Whales on their annual migration along the coast. Boats depart from **Balboa Pavilion** as well as Dana Point.
ELSEWHERE: The **Mission San Juan Capistrano** in **San Juan Capistrano**, built in 1776 and recently restored, is the oldest historical attraction in Southern California. It was made famous by the annual return of the swallows on St Joseph's Day (19 March). The **Los Rios District** features some of California's oldest adobe buildings, some still inhabited.
Yorba Linda is home to the **Richard Nixon Presidential Library and Museum**, at the farmhouse where America's 37th President was born and raised. The graves of the President and Mrs Nixon are set among White-House-styled gardens.
An Orange County landmark, the **Crystal Cathedral** is a spectacular US$16 million glass cathedral designed by architect Philip Johnson. The only one of its kind in the world, it is open daily to visitors and free guided tours are available. *The Glory of Christmas* and *The Glory of Easter* theatrical productions, using special effects, live animals and casts of over 200, are presented annually. **Little Saigon** is the largest Vietnamese business district in the USA. The area features a wide variety of French, Vietnamese and Asian shops and restaurants as well as an **Asian Garden**.
Raging Waters, in **San Dimas**, is the largest water theme park west of the Mississippi and features a variety of slides, rides, chutes and lagoons for adults and children and a 12m (40ft) volcano.
Wild Rivers Waterpark offers over 40 rides and attractions, two huge wave-action pools and special features for both kids and adults. The park's attractions include *The Edge*, *The Ledge*, *The Abyss* and *Tugboat Bay*.
Cruises are available to beautiful **Catalina Island**, 40km (26 miles) off the Californian coast. Sightseeing tours include a glass-bottomed boat trip, scenic **Terrace Drive**, kayaking excursions, harbour and coastal boat cruises and a new undersea adventure in a semi-submersible submarine.
Several companies operate speedy luxury passenger vessels to the island. The **Catalina Flyer**, a 500-passenger catamaran, whisks passengers to Catalina Island in less than 75 minutes. Daily trips are offered from March to November, with limited weekend runs during the winter months. Other vessels, operated by *Catalina Channel Express* sail all year round from San Pedro, Long Beach and Dana Point. **Glen Ivy Hot Springs Spa**, only 30 minutes from Anaheim, offers mineral pools, wading pools and saunas, and visitors can treat themselves to a massage, facial or even a eucalyptus wrap. This picturesque day resort has been a popular spot for over 100 years and is famous for its natural hot springs and red clay mud bath.
THEATRES & CONCERTS: Orange County is home to many theatres, including the 3000-seat **Orange County Performing Arts Center**, **South Coast Repertory Theater**, **Fullerton Civic Light Opera Company**, **Goodtime Theater** and **Irvine Meadows Amphitheater**. Dinner theatres in the area include **Medieval Times Dinner and Tournament**, **Wild Bill's Wild West Dinner Extravaganza**, **Comedy Mystery Dinner Theater** and **Wizardz**. Nightclubs range from quiet piano bars to folk and pop.
SHOPPING: Located 15 minutes south of Anaheim is **South Coast Plaza** in Costa Mesa. Its national and international shops offer the greatest variety of world-class shopping and dining in Southern California. Restaurants here offer gourmet food as well as informal Californian dishes. South Coast Plaza is also notable for its range of confectioners. Adjacent to South Coast Plaza is **Crystal Court**, which features some 40 speciality shops. Orange County's largest indoor swapmeet, **Anaheim Indoor Marketplace**, has more than 12,356 sq metres (133,000 sq ft) of space with over 200 variety shops. Many brand-name items can be found here at 50 to 70 per cent below retail price. Overlooking the Pacific Ocean is **Fashion Island Shopping Center**. Orange County's only open-air regional shopping centre, it features 200 shops and services, more than 40 places to eat and a variety of entertainment options. **MainPlace** offers 190 shops and the **MainPlace/MarketPlace**, which showcases international food shops and restaurants, gourmet coffees, and desserts. In addition to a variety of shops, **Triangle Square** offers the sounds of world-renowned and locally acclaimed entertainers and a number of award-winning restaurants. The **Mall of Orange** features major department stores and over 100 fine speciality shops and restaurants. Another shopping expedition is a visit to **Ontario Mills** where visitors will find a 1.7 million sq ft megamall. **The Lab, Anti-Mall** has a variety of unique and alternative shops for those seeking a different shopping experience.
SPORT: The **Edison International Field of Anaheim** is the home of Major League Baseball's Anaheim Angels, whilst the National Hockey League's Mighty Ducks of Anaheim face off at the 17,250-seat **Arrowhead Pond of Anaheim**.
TRAVEL: *Amtrak* has five train stations located throughout Orange County in the cities of Anaheim, Santa Ana, Fullerton, San Juan Capistrano and Irvine. A *Greyhound* bus station is located in Anaheim at 100 West Winston Street. *Greyhound* offers regular departures to almost anywhere in the USA. Scheduled daily shuttles provide transport from the major airports to various Orange County destinations. There are several companies that service the area including *Airport Bus* and *SuperShuttle*. *Airport Bus* offers a complete scheduled coach service to Anaheim from Los Angeles International and John Wayne/Orange County airports at economical fares with no reservations required. *SuperShuttle* is available seven days a week, 24 hours a day and services all hotels. Vans are available at Los Angeles airport on demand, but reservations are required at John Wayne.
Several major sightseeing companies offer a variety of tours and excursions; contact the tourist board for further details (see *Contact Addresses* section). Car hire is an option that allows visitors to explore Orange County at their own pace and according to their own tastes. Several companies are available in the area. *Yellow Cab* and other taxi companies provide transport to all Southern California areas, including the airports.
SPECIAL EVENTS: The following is a selection of special events occurring in Orange County in 2005:
Mar 18-20 *Return of the Swallows Celebration*, San Juan Capistrano. **Apr 21-30** *Newport Beach International Film Festival*. **Apr 29-May 1** *Youth Expo*, Costa Mesa. **Jun** *Huntington Beach Smooth Jazz Series Presents*. **Jul 4** *Independence Day Celebrations and Parade*. **Jul 8-31** *Orange County Fair*, Costa Mesa. **Sep 17-tbc** *35th Annual Summer Surf Contes*, Huntington Beach. **Dec 12-21** *Cruise of Lights*, Huntington Beach.
CLIMATE: The average temperature is 21°C (70°F). Summers are moderate to hot with cool evenings. Winters are mild with a little rain. Rainfall averages 13 inches annually.

Inland Empire

Larger than Rhode Island, Connecticut and Delaware combined, the Inland Empire ranges from the farmlands and orchards of the Santa Ana River Valley to the mountains and ski resorts of the north. The region's varied landscape makes it popular with film makers, giving rise to its nickname, 'Hollywood's largest back lot'. Only an hour east of Los Angeles, the Inland Empire flourished after World War II and is now the fastest growing metropolitan area in the USA. Highlights of the region include California's oldest vineyards in **Rancho Cucamonga** and the country's newest vineyards in **Temecula**, as well as a variety of museums and the mountain resort of **Big Bear Lake**.
SAN BERNARDINO: Known as the 'friendly city', San Bernardino combines big-city facilities with a small-town atmosphere. The **California Theater of Performing Arts** showcases classical music and light opera, while large-scale productions are held at the **Glen Helen Blockbuster Pavilion**. Seating 65,000, it is the country's largest outdoor amphitheatre and attracts world-class entertainment. Held on weekends from May to June, the *Renaissance Pleasure Faire* recreates the festival atmosphere of Elizabethan times, with costume parades, contests and entertainment. The *Route 66 Rendezvous*, held annually in September, attracts 400,000 car buffs and classic vehicles which cruise through town.
Excursions: South of San Bernardino at **Redlands** are the **Marmalade Mansions**, 300 restored Victorian homes built by residents who made their fortunes in the citrus industry, and the **San Bernardino County Museum**. The historic 1830 **Asistencia Mision de San Gabriel**, originally a mission outpost, was later used as a ranch. Northeast of **Barstow** is the **Calico Ghost Town**. Once one of the richest areas in California with more than 500 mines and 22 saloons, the town was deserted when the price of silver plummeted in 1907.
RIVERSIDE: The famous **Mission Inn** in Riverside has long been a favourite with the rich and famous. Bette Davis and Humphrey Bogart were guests, Richard and Pat Nixon were married here, and Ronald and Nancy Reagan began their honeymoon in the hotel's Presidential Suite. This National Historic Landmark contains a museum with paintings, sculpture and furnishings from the Mission Inn collection and traces the development of Riverside since the 1870s. The **Riverside Art Museum**, designed by Julia Morgan, showcases works by Southern Californian artists. At the **University of California, Riverside**, visitors can stroll through the **Botanic Gardens**, 16 hectares (39 acres) of herb, rose and desert gardens, or the **UCR/California Museum of Photography**. The **State Citrus Historic Park** highlights how the citrus industry changed the history of Southern California.
ONTARIO: *Ontario International Airport (ONT)* (website: www.lawa.org/ont) is only 64km (40 miles) from Los Angeles and is serviced by 13 airlines, including *American Airlines*, *Continental*, *Delta* and *United*, and carries over 6.5 million passengers annually. California's largest entertainment and outlet mall, **Ontario Mills**, is found here. Other attractions include the indoor **American Wilderness Zoo and Aquarium** and **Graber Olive House**, an 1894 cannery and museum.
BIG BEAR LAKE: This year-round recreation resort sits 7000ft above sea level. Boating, fishing, hiking, mountain biking and jet-skiing in the summer, and skiing, snowboarding and other snow sports in the winter, make it a popular destination with outdoor enthusiasts. Attractions include the *Alpine Slide* at **Big Bear's Magic Mountain Recreation Area**, a quarter-mile dry track, one of only three in the USA, and **Moonridge Animal Park**, which cares for injured, lost and endangered animals, including grizzly bears. For spectacular views, catch the scenic chair lift to the **Snow Summit Mountain Resort**.
ELSEWHERE: Lake Arrowhead, west of Big Bear Lake, is also great for outdoor activities and water sports. Take a boat trip on the **Arrowhead Queen** to view the landscape and alpine-style homes that surround the lake, or visit the **Ice Castle** skating rink and Olympic training facility in **Blue Jay**.
Northwest of Big Bear Lake at **Victorville** is the **Roy Rogers-Dale Evans Museum**, a frontier fortress full of mementos from the Western stars' films and television shows, and the **Route 66 Museum**, displaying a collection of artefacts and photographs related to the famous highway.
SPECIAL EVENTS: The following is a selection of special events occurring in Inland Empire in 2005:
Apr-May (weekends) *Ramona Pageant* (an early Californian romance play performed on a mountainside), Ramona Bowl, Hemet. **Apr 16-Jun 5** *Renaissance Pleasure Faire*, San Bernardino. **Apr 24-25** *Apple Blossom Festival*, Oak Glen. **Apr 30-May 31** *Arts in the Country Festival*, Temecula. **May 7-15** *San Bernardino County Fair*, Victorville. **May 21-22** *Orange Blossom Festival*, Riverside. **May 26-30** *National Orange Show*, San Bernardino. **Jun** *Redlands Bowl Summer Music Festival*. **Jun 3-5** *Temecula Valley Balloon and Wine Festival*, Temecula. **Jun 25-26** *Annual Lavender Festival*, Temecula. **Jul 4** *Fireworks and Barbecue*, Big Bear Lake. **Sep-Oct** *Oktoberfest*, Big Bear Lake. **Sep 15-18** *Route 66 Rendezvous*, San Bernardino. **Oct** *Grape Harvest Festival*, Rancho Cucamonga. **Oct 7-9** *Calico Days* (Old West celebration), Calico Ghost Town. **Oct 8-16** *Southern California Fair*, Perris. **Oct 28-30** *Ghost Haunt*, Calico Ghost Town. **Nov 25-27** *Calico Heritage Festival*, Calico Ghost Town.

San Diego County

At the southern extreme of southern California is **San Diego County**, home to 2.8 million people. Its beautiful beaches stretch for 113km (70 miles) along the coast. The city of **San Diego** boasts 10,878 sq km (4200 sq miles) of country, which encompasses the metropolitan sophistication of the city itself, the caves of La Jolla, the flowers and wineries of **North County**, the mountain peaks of **East County**, the Mexican flavours of **South Bay** and the **Golden Triangle**, noted for its upmarket shopping and dining. Other temptations include the dazzling array of restaurants in **Coronado**, the sense of heritage and history exemplified by the **Mission Valley**, the vast aquatic playground of **Mission Bay Park** and the duty free border zone of **Tijuana**, Mexico.
San Diego City: America's sixth-largest city is where California's history began. The local climate approaches perfection, but there is more to the city than sun and sand. It is a place of character, rich in art and culture. Central **San Diego** is a vibrant collection of neighbourhoods, restaurants, shops and attractions stretching from the Bay to the Uptown district, including the residential areas of **Hillcrest** and **Golden Hill**. The original centre of commerce here was **Old Town** (the birthplace of California), but by the turn of the century, **New Town**, founded by the New Englander, Alonzo Horton, had taken its place. The **Gaslamp Quarter** is the city's historic district, a 16-block area of shops, galleries, coffee houses, theatre spaces and dozens of restaurants. The **Japanese Friendship Garden** offers a pleasant refuge. It can be explored by horse-drawn carriage, a Ford Model T or on foot with an audio walking tour from the Gaslamp Quarter Foundation.
The **San Diego Maritime Museum**, anchored along Harbour Drive, is a good place to begin an exploration of the waterfront. Here, visitors can look at the **Star of India** (a century-old windjammer), the steam ferry Berkeley, and the luxury yacht **Medea**. The cruise ship terminal is a popular waterfront destination and excursion boats leaving from Pier B can take visitors on a tour of the bay.

The city's maritime past is further commemorated in **Seaport Village**, a 14-acre waterfront shopping and dining complex, which puts the visitor in mind of the days when cargo ships would embark on the perilous journey from New England, rounding Cape Horn before reaching California. The village has 57 shops and galleries, four award-winning restaurants and 13 sidewalk eateries, as well as hosting frequent music events.

Balboa Park is another reminder of the founders' civic vision. It covers 1200 acres and contains some fantastic architecture, including 14 museums, art galleries, the **Reuben H Fleet Space Theater and Science Center**, the **Simon Edison Center for the Performing Arts**, the **San Diego Junior Theater**, **Starlight Bowl**, sports facilities and the **California Tower** with its working 100-bell carillon. The **Spreckels Organ Pavilion** features concerts on Sunday afternoons (and Monday evenings in summer). The Park also houses the world-famous **San Diego Zoo**, which houses 800 different species. The entire zoo is designed as a 100-acre tropical garden which can be visited on foot or on a guided bus tour. Other attractions in Balboa Park include the **Botanical Building**, the **Park Carousel**, the **Miniature Railroad**, the **Spanish Village Art Center** and the **WorldBeat Cultural Center**.

The new **Miramar Speed Circuit** offers indoor high-speed go-kart racing for speed freaks.

CORONADO: This quaint village is set on a peninsula, connected to the mainland on the south by way of a narrow sandbar known as the **Silver Strand**. The fascinating **Hotel del Coronado**, known as 'The Del', boasts turrets, tall cupolas and hand-carved wooden pillars. The central area features dozens of boutiques, shops and restaurants and a large central park with a bandstand where concerts are performed each Sunday throughout the summer. **Silver Strand State Beach** is particularly popular with families and offers camping and RV (Recreational Vehicle) facilities. This place offers a great variety of fine restaurants and seafood is a celebrated attraction.

POINT LOMA: From here, the onlooker is afforded a magnificent panoramic view of San Diego Bay, Shelter Island, Harbour Island, Coronado, the Embarcadero and central San Diego from the **Cabrillo National Monument**. It is also a great place to watch the annual migration of California grey whales. More than 15,000 make the journey from Alaska to Baja each year.

MISSION VALLEY: If San Diego is the birthplace of California, then the **Mission Basilica San Diego De Alcala** is the birthplace of San Diego. It was founded in December 1769 by Father Junipero Serra and the Mission, the **Presidio** and the town that sprung up at the foot of it were the first outposts of the Spanish government in *Alta California*. Today, Mission Valley has major shopping centres, restaurants and sporting facilities. A very popular attraction is the **Old Town**, which served as the heart of San Diego until the 1800s. Many original 19th-century structures in the **Old Town State Historic Park** have been reconstructed or restored and reflect and illustrate the changes since Serra's day. **Heritage Park** is a haven for the restoration and preservation of Victorian dwellings and serves as a transition area between the Mexican and early-American preserve.

MISSION BAY PARK: This is the largest facility of its kind in the world – a monument to the outdoor lifestyle. Swimming, power-boating, fishing and sailing all occupy separate areas. At **Sea World**, orca whales, sea lions, otters and dolphins are featured; the new R.L Stine's *Haunted Lighthouse* attraction is a 4-D adventure adapted from an old fisherman's tale. **Belmont Park** offers two vintage landmarks: *The Plunge*, the largest indoor swimming pool in Southern California, and the *Giant Dipper* rollercoaster, which boasts 792m (2600ft) of stomach-churning track.

NORTH COUNTY: The **Escondido** area is home to the **San Diego Wild Animal Park**, as well as a number of wineries offering tours and wine tasting. The gentle climate has earned the coastal areas of **Encinitas** and **Leucadia** the distinction of 'Poinsetta Capital of the World'. In Encinitas are the **Quail Botanical Gardens**, containing one of the world's most diverse and important plant collections. The seaside village of Carlsbad offers beaches, resorts, fine dining and sporting facilities. In the springtime, the surrounding hills are covered in a lush carpet of ranunculus and other multi-coloured flowers. **Legoland California**, an amusement park based on the world-famous plastic bricks, celebrated its fifth birthday in 2004 with five new attractions, including additions to *Miniland* (featuring replicas of famous sights and real-life city scenes), a new rollercoaster, a 'block of fame' celebrity attraction, an archaeology attraction and an interactive racing ride. Further up the coast, **Oceanside** features one of the longest municipal wooden piers on the West Coast. Oceanside is also the site of the **Mission San Luis Rey**, the largest of California's 21 missions. Nearby is the **Mount Palomar Observatory**, which houses the 200-inch Hale Telescope, one of the country's largest.

SOUTH BAY: This area encompasses **National City**, an important commercial area, **Chula Vista**, **San Ysidro** and **Imperial Beach**. In addition to its marinas, parks and restaurants, Chula Vista is home to the **Arco Olympic Training Center** and **the Nature Interpretative Center** at the **Sweetwater Marsh National Wildlife Refuge**, one of the few remaining Pacific salt marsh habitats.

Credit: © California Tourism Office

TRAVEL: San Diego is about two-and-a-half hours from central Los Angeles via Interstate 5. Interstate 8 serves drivers from Yuma, Arizona and destinations further eastward. *San Diego International Airport (SAN)* (website: www.san.org) is currently served by over 20 airlines, including *AeroMexico, Alaska Airlines, America West, American Airlines, Continental, Delta, Hawaiian Airlines, United Airlines* and *US Airways*. *Amtrak* provides a train service to and from Los Angeles. *Greyhound* provides bus services. *San Diego Transit Corporation* operates an integrated system of buses, which serve the metro area. The *San Diego Trolley* provides services in the city centre and out as far as the Mexican border, as well as to East County.

SPECIAL EVENTS: The following is a selection of special events occurring in San Diego County in 2005:
Jan 1-Mar 15 *Whalefest*. **Mar 5** *Ocean Beach Kite Festival*. **Mar 10-21** *San Diego Latino Film Festival*. **Apr 2-3** *San Diego Classic Crew* (rowing competitions). **Apr 19-May 3** *San Diego International Film Festival*, Price Center Theatre. **Apr 30-May 1** *Fiesta Cinco De Mayo*, Old Town State Park. **May 7** *12th Annual Imperial Beach Chili And Jazz Festival*. **May 28-29** *KIFM Jazz Festival*, Gaslamp Quarter. **Jun 10-Jul 4** *San Diego County Fair*, Del Mar. **Jun 11-12** *19th La Jolla Festival of the Arts and Food Fair*. **Jul 15-17** *US Open Sandcastle Competition*, Imperial Beach Pier. **Sep 9-11** *Traditional Gathering and 16th Annual Pow Wow*. **Sep 10-11** *Annual California Indian Days Celebration*. **Oct** *Oktoberfest in La Mesa*, La Mesa Boulevard. **Oct 26-Nov 2** *Dia de Los Muertos*. **Nov 23-27** *San Diego Thanksgiving Dixieland Jazz Festival*. **Nov 24-Jan 4** *2006 Holiday of Lights at Del Mar*. **Dec 1-31** *San Diego Holiday Jazz & Blues Festival*.

CLIMATE: The mild climate makes the county an ideal and perennial destination. The average daytime temperature is 21°C (70°F) and winter temperatures seldom fall below 4°C (40°F). Humidity is generally low.

The Deserts

Expansive landscapes, brilliant skies, traces of pioneer history and glittering resort cities make the California desert region a year-round retreat. Natural phenomena abound, from the solitude of **Death Valley National Park** to the vast **Joshua Tree National Park**. The quiet pleasures of the back country, where a desert tortoise may be one's only companion, and the excitement of a sunny resort in the **Coachella Valley**, are both equally possible. Other options include trekking across ancient Native American lands, boating down the **Colorado River**, rock hounding, fishing on the **Salton Sea**, watching wildlife, exploring a ghost town or driving down historic **Route 66**.

BARSTOW/JOSHUA TREE AREA: Bustling **Barstow**, originally a railway junction and transport centre, is a good base for exploring the myriad sights in this High Desert area. From Barstow, visitors can make a tour of nearby **Calico Ghost Town**, a restored 19th-century mining town with campsite, shops, mine tours, train rides, gold panning and a melodrama playhouse. The **Mojave National Scenic Preserve** offers a remote slice of the Old West, featuring spectacular natural landscapes and history. Another eerily remote area is the **Joshua Tree National Park** – 220 sq km (850 sq miles) of protected land with many opportunities for hiking and rock climbing. To the south, **Providence Mountains State Recreation Area** offers dramatic eastern Mojave scenery, hiking trails and the limestone **Mitchell Caverns**, primitive camping and a visitor centre. **Rainbow Basin/Owl Canyon** is a colourful natural landmark containing the fossilised remains of numerous animals.

COLORADO RIVER/IMPERIAL VALLEY: River recreations are abundant in **Needles** and **Blythe**, resort towns situated along the Colorado River, which separates Nevada and Arizona from the southeastern portion of California's Deserts Region. Here, water devotees can boat, fish and tube down the lazy river from **Lake Havasu**, which was created by **Parker Dam**. Water from the Colorado River has today transformed the desert lands of Imperial Valley into a fertile farming and recreation area. **El Centro**, an agricultural market centre, is a good base for exploring the valley's wealth of attractions. East of El Centro is the **Imperial Sand Dunes**, popular with off-road vehicle enthusiasts. To the west are the **Coyote**, **Fish Creek** and **Superstition** mountains, which attract rock hounds and fossil collectors. North of El Centro, anglers and boating enthusiasts are lured to buoyant **Salton Sea**, a vast inland lake. Boating, saltwater fishing and hunting are popular recreational activities here. It also offers swimming, nature trails, a variety of campsites, an 18,000-acre boating park, the **Salton Sea National Wildlife Refuge** and the **Imperial Wildlife Area**.

PALM SPRINGS/COACHELLA VALLEY: With 330 days of sunshine, the Coachella Valley is a year-round paradise for lovers of the outdoors. This 19th-century desert resort area now features no less than 10,000 swimming pools, 600 tennis courts and 90 golf courses. Visitors can shop, watch polo matches, tour museums and art galleries, attend the theatre or dance the night away. More adventurous travellers can go horseriding or hiking through the historic **Indian Canyons**, be whisked from sea level to the top of 3300m (10,800ft) **Mount Jacinto** via an aerial tramway or hover above the Coachella Valley in a hot-air balloon.

OTHER ATTRACTIONS: These include **Palm Desert**'s **Living Desert Wildlife and Botanical Park**, which sustains five plant communities and about 250 bird and animal species; and **Moorten's Botanical Garden**, in Palm Springs, which shelters more than 3000 species of desert plants.

TRAVEL: There are direct and non-stop flights and convenient connections for the major airlines serving the *Palm Springs International Airport (PSP)* (website: www.palmspringsairport.com), including *Alaska Airlines, America West, American Airlines, Continental, Delta, Northwest Airlines* and *United*.
Ontario International Airport (ONT) (website:

www.lawa.org/ONT) is a one-hour drive by freeway. *Los Angeles International Airport (LAX)* (website: www.lawa.org/lax) is a two-hour drive. *John Wayne Airport (SNA)* (website: www.ocair.com) in Orange County and *San Diego International Airport (SAN)* (website: www.san.org) are, respectively, two hours and half an hour away by car. *Amtrak* provides daily services to the nearby community of Indio. There is a frequent and convenient bus service with *Greyhound* to the Palm Springs Bus Depot, 311 North Indian Canyon Drive.

SPECIAL EVENTS: The following is a selection of special events occurring in The Deserts in 2005:
Feb 18-27 *Riverside County Fair and National Date Festival*, Indio. **Mar 3-6** *Palm Springs Native American Film Festival*. **Apr 1-3** *13th Annual Joshua Tree National Park Arts Festival*. **May 20-21** *Smooth Jazz Festival*, Palm Springs. **Jun 2-5** *Fifth Annual Film Noir Festival*, Palm Springs. **Aug 27-28** *12th Annual Idyllwild Jazz in the Pines*, Palm Springs. **Sep** *Palm Springs International Festival of Short Films*. **Nov 4-6** *Greater Palm Springs Pride*.

CLIMATE: The area's warm, dry climate is a major attraction, with 354 days of sunshine and less than 5.5 inches of rain each year.

Social Profile

FOOD & DRINK: California has always been a social melting pot, and this is reflected in its modern, cosmopolitan cuisine with an endless variety of ethnic influences. Specialities include steak and seafood and some of the country's top restaurants can be found in centres like Los Angeles, San Francisco and San Diego. California is also renowned for its excellent wines, which rival many of the European vintages. Santa Barbara, and Lake County and the Napa Valley on the north coast, are famous for their wines. Temecula, in the Inland Empire, is the country's newest wine-producing region. Vineyards established on the western ridges of the Sierra Nevada during the gold rush have made wine the new treasure in Gold Country.

THEATRES & CONCERTS: As the entertainment capital of the world, Los Angeles offers a range of concerts and theatre performances year-round, including Broadway hits. San Francisco has its own symphony orchestra and opera and ballet companies, which give outstanding performances throughout the year. San Diego's opera season is just part of the city's colourful arts scene.

NIGHTLIFE: There are few places in the world that can rival California's nightlife. Los Angeles is home to an array of illustrious clubs with rich and famous patrons. San Francisco, with its young, lively population, is known around the world as a great party town.

SHOPPING: Some visitors come to California just for the shopping. Whether they are after the latest fashions or quaint handicrafts, the State's vast range of shops and malls will satisfy any consumer. The boutiques and department stores of Los Angeles are famous worldwide. The city of Ontario, east of Los Angeles, is home to California's largest entertainment and outlet mall. Orange County and Santa Barbara are also known for the quality and variety of their shopping.

SPORT: Sport is an important part of life in California. San Francisco and San Diego have teams competing in the National Football League, and the State's cities are represented by four basketball teams in the National Basketball Association and three Major League Baseball teams. Horse racing and harness racing are popular in Los Angeles and San Francisco, while the rest of the State offers plenty of opportunities for those who enjoy watersports, hiking and skiing. The beaches of Orange County host some of the best surfing anywhere in the world.

Climate

Summers are hot, while the winter months are mild with wetter weather.

Required clothing: Lightweight during the summer with warmer wear for the cooler winter period.

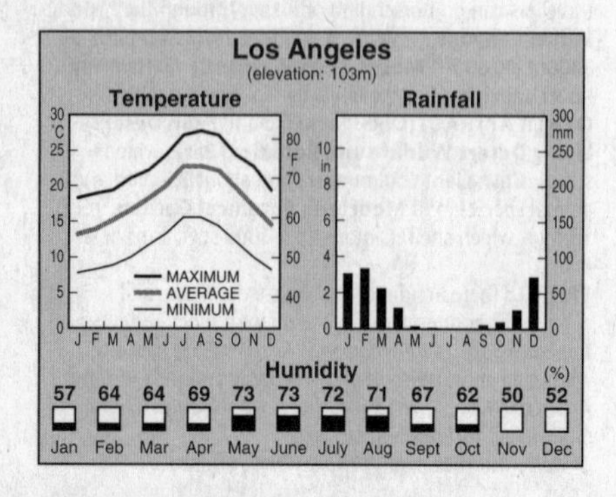

Colorado

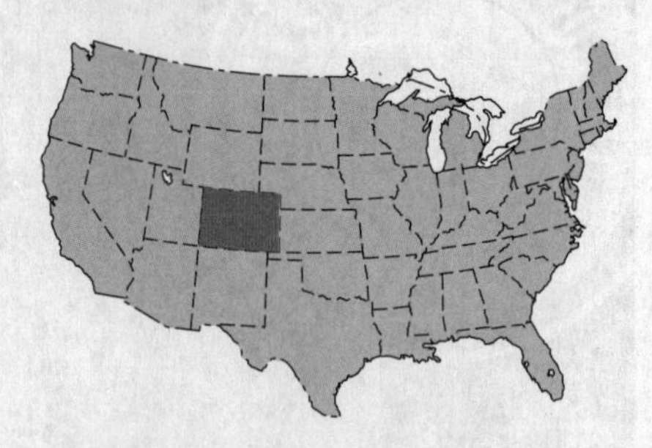

Colorado Tourism Office
1625 Broadway, Suite 1700, Denver, CO 80202
Tel: (303) 892 3885 *or* (800) 265 6723 (toll-free) *or* (303) 892 3850 (international inquiries).
Fax: (303) 892 3848.
E-mail: industry@colorado.com *or* international@colorado.com (international inquiries)
Website: www.colorado.com

Colorado Tourism Office (UK)
c/o Cellet Travel Services Ltd, Brook House, 47 High Street, Henley-in-Arden, Warwickshire B95 5AA, UK
Tel: (01564) 794 999. Fax: (01564) 795 333.
E-mail: info@cellet.co.uk
Website: www.cellet.co.uk *or* www.colorado.com

Colorado Ski Country USA
1507 Blake Street, Denver, CO 80202
Tel: (303) 837 0793 *or* 825 7669 (snow report).
Fax: (303) 837 1627.
E-mail: info@coloradoski.com
Website: www.coloradoski.com

Colorado Springs CVB
515 South Cascade Avenue, Colorado Springs, CO 80903
Tel: (719) 635 7506 *or* (800) 888 4748 (toll-free).
Fax: (719) 635 4968.
E-mail: cscvb@coloradosprings-travel.com
Website: www.coloradosprings-travel.com *or* www.experiencecoloradosprings.com

Denver Metro CVB
1555 California, Suite 300, Denver, CO 80202
Tel: (303) 892 1112 *or* (800) 233 6837 (toll-free).
Fax: (303) 892 1636.
E-mail: visitorinfo@dmcvb.org
Website: www.denver.org

General Information

Nickname: Centennial State
State bird: Lark Bunting
State flower: Rocky Mountain Columbine
CAPITAL: Denver
Date of admission to the Union: 1 Aug 1876
POPULATION: 4,601,403 (official estimate 2004)
POPULATION DENSITY: 17.1 per sq km
2003 total overseas arrivals/US ranking: 288,000/17
TIME: Mountain (GMT - 7). *Daylight Saving Time* is observed.

THE STATE: Colorado is known for its famous **Rocky Mountains** and is a year-round destination that boasts spectacular national parks, forests, gold-rush ghost towns and Native American ruins. The capital, **Denver**, is the gateway to numerous ski resorts and is home to many museums, parks, gardens and a restored Victorian square. State attractions include **Colorado Springs**, **Pikes Peak Ghost Town**, the **Rocky Mountain**, **Black Canyon of the Gunnison** and **Mesa Verde** national parks, the sandstone formations of the **Garden of the Gods**, and **Aspen**, **Vail** and **Breckenridge** ski resorts.

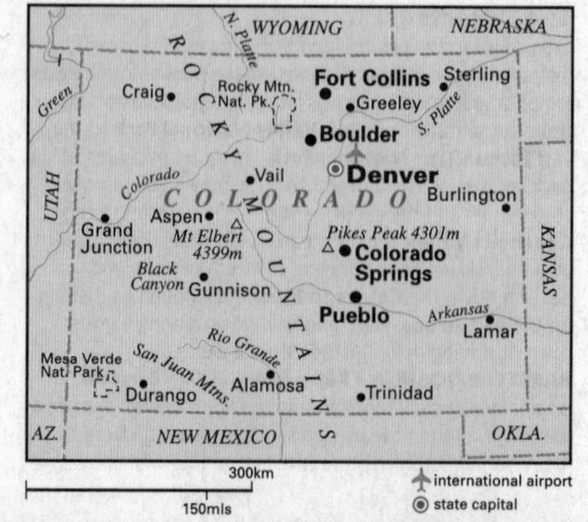

Travel - International

AIR: *Denver International (DEN)* (website: www.flydenver.com), one of the largest airports in the world, will celebrate its 10th anniversary in 2005. It covers 137 sq km (53 sq miles), which is twice the size of Manhattan Island. The airport is located 38km (24 miles) northeast of Denver (travel time – 30 minutes). *British Airways* operates direct flights to Denver from London Heathrow. *SkyRide* buses run to downtown Denver and Boulder. Taxis, shuttle buses, public buses and limousines are available to the city. Car hire is also available. There are also many shuttles that operate services to Colorado's various resorts, such as Aspen, Colorado Springs, Estes Park (Rocky Mountain National Park), Steamboat Springs, Summit County and Winter Park. Advance booking is recommended.

Domestic airports: The major ski resorts are all served by their own airports with domestic flights from many major centres in the USA. Airports include *Aspen/Pitkin County*, *Colorado Springs*, *Durango/La Plata*, *Gunnison County*, *Vail/Eagle County* and *Yampa Valley* (for Steamboat).

Approximate flight times: From Denver to *Atlanta* is two hours 50 minutes, to *Boston* is three hours 45 minutes, to *Chicago* is two hours 20 minutes, to *Dallas* is one hour 50 minutes, to *Houston* is two hours 15 minutes, to *London* is 10 hours, to *Los Angeles* is two hours 30 minutes, to *Miami* is three hours 35 minutes, to *New York* is three hours 40 minutes, to *San Francisco* is two hours 40 minutes, to *Seattle* is two hours 50 minutes and to *Washington, DC* is three hours 40 minutes.

RAIL: Denver's growth is historically linked to its importance as a rail centre. It is a hub on the major *Amtrak* east–west route (tel: (800) 872 7245 (toll-free); website: www.amtrak.com), with daily services to Chicago and San Francisco on the 'California Zephyr'. Westbound trains pass through Glenwood Canyon, which is one of the most beautiful railway routes in the USA. The 'Southwest Chief', which links Chicago with Los Angeles, passes through the southeast corner of the State, where a bus link to Denver is available. The *Ski Train* (tel: (303) 296 4754; website: www.skitrain.com) makes a scenic two-hour journey through the Rockies during the skiing season and on Saturdays in summer.

Approximate rail travel times: From Denver to *Omaha* is 10 hours five minutes, to *Salt Lake City* is 15 hours 30 minutes, to *Chicago* is 20 hours five minutes, to *Los Angeles* is 25 hours 55 minutes (including bus connection) and to *San Francisco* is 33 hours 55 minutes.

ROAD: *Greyhound* (tel: (800) 229 9424 (toll-free); website: www.greyhound.com) has a terminal in downtown Denver, at 1055 19th Street.

Approximate driving times: From Denver to *Albuquerque* is nine hours, to *Salt Lake City* is 10 hours, to *Dallas* is 16 hours, to *St Louis* is 17 hours 10 minutes, to *Minneapolis* is 17 hours 30 minutes, to *Chicago* is 20 hours 20 minutes, to *Los Angeles* is 23 hours 50 minutes, to *Seattle* is 28 hours 30 minutes and to *New York* is 37 hours.

Approximate bus travel times: From Denver to *Cheyenne* is two hours 30 minutes, to *Albuquerque* is nine hours 30 minutes, to *Amarillo* is 10 hours 30 minutes, to *Kansas City* is 13 hours and to *Las Vegas* is 16 hours.

URBAN: Denver is well served with buses and a light rail system run by *RTD* (website: www.rtd-denver.com), as well as taxis. The *16th Street Mall Shuttle* provides free transport at least once every three minutes until 1900, Mon-Fri 0500-0100, along the 1.6km- (1 mile-) long pedestrian mall in the city centre. During summer (June to September), the *Cultural Connection Trolley* takes passengers around Denver's main attractions, departing every 30 minutes, 0930-1750. Car hire is readily available, with *Alamo*, *Avis*, *Budget*, *Dollar*, *Enterprise* and *Hertz* all providing services.

Resorts & Excursions

EXCURSIONS

DENVER: Located at 1609m (5280ft) above sea level, on high rolling plains at the foot of the Rocky Mountains, Denver, known as the **Mile High City**, has a population of 500,000 people and is the largest city within a 1000km (625 mile) radius. Founded as a gold-mining camp in 1859, Denver was the centre of the Old West, filled with wagon trains, cowboys, Native Americans, gamblers and gunfighters.

Today, the city is known for its wonderful museums, architecture, cultural facilities and parks. Denver has an invigorating and sunny climate with four distinct seasons and is compact enough to be enjoyed on foot. The **Colorado State Capitol**, with its spectacular genuine gold roof, enjoys sweeping views over the city and the Rockies. Nearby are the **US Mint**, with the second-largest storehouse of gold bullion in the USA after **Fort Knox** in Alaska. The **Denver Art Museum**, which houses a fine Native American collection, as well as many other exhibits, is currently undergoing a massive expansion project and will double in size by 2006. A new gallery for modern and contemporary art will be a highlight. Other museums in Denver include the **Museum of Nature & Science**, with a state-of-the-art space exhibition, as well as several interactive exhibits; the **Museum of Western Art**, with the third-largest collection of Western art in the USA; and the **Colorado History Museum**, which documents the colourful stories of the Native Americans, cowboys, miners and explorers who have all called Colorado home. **Larimer Square**, a Victorian block of shops and cafes, is the gateway to the **Lower Downtown District** of Denver. Also known as **LoDo**, this area comprises 20 blocks of century-old warehouses and buildings that have been converted to antique shops, galleries, clubs, restaurants and offices. The **16th Street Mall** is a tree-lined promenade in the heart of the city, running between downtown Denver and Union Station. Popular with shoppers, it is always alive with pedestrians, cafes, street performers and fountains. **Ocean Journey**, a maritime theme park in Denver's **Platte River Valley**, is located close to the **Children's Museum** and the **Mile High Stadium**.

Those seeking a refuge from the downtown bustle can head for one of Denver's 205 parks. The City Park is home to the **Denver Zoo**, **City Park Golf Course** and the **Denver Museum of Natural History**, which boasts wildlife art and an IMAX theatre amongst its attractions. The **Denver Botanic Gardens** comprises water gardens, a Japanese garden, a rock alpine garden and a conservatory housing a collection of orchids and bromeliads. The **Centennial Gardens** are inspired by the formal gardens of Versailles.

COLORADO SPRINGS: At 2000m (6562ft) above sea level and one hour south of Denver, Colorado Springs is dominated by the red sandstone pinnacles of the **Garden of the Gods**. Other attractions in or near the city include **Manitou & Pikes Peak Cog Railway**, with views of the Continental Divide; **Manitou Springs**; **Old Colorado City**; **Pikes Peak Ghost Town**; **Royal Gorge Bridge**; **US Air Force Training Center** and the **US Olympic Training Centre**.

SKI RESORTS: With their powdery snow and sparkling blue skies, the **Rocky Mountains** of Colorado, and the ritzy resort of **Aspen** in particular, are renowned the world over for unparalleled skiing.

In recent years, the region has gained considerable popularity with European ski enthusiasts, as well as visitors from within the USA, and the range of facilities and accommodation is unrivalled. Aspen, located 256km (160 miles) west of Denver, attracts the rich and famous from all over the world and is perhaps America's most sophisticated ski resort, offering a full range of winter and summer activities and countless restaurants and shops. **Vail**, two hours west of Denver, is among the top ski destinations in the nation and is built in a Tyrolean style, while **Summit County** is home to the popular ski resorts of **Keystone**, **Arapahoe Basin**, **Copper Mountain** and **Breckenridge**. Other ski resorts in the State include **Tiehack/Buttermilk** (popular with beginners), **Beaver Creek Resort** (suitable for families), **Ski Cooper** (near the historic city of Leadville), **Copper Mountain Resort**, **Crested Butte Mountain Resort**, **Cuchara Valley Ski Resort**, **Eldora Mountain Resort**, **Howelsen Ski Area** (the oldest ski area in Colorado and home to the most complete ski-jumping complex), **Keystone Resort** (with the longest ski season in the State), **Loveland Ski Areas**, **Monarch**, **Powderhorn**, **Wolf Creek**, **Durango Mountain Resort** (an uncrowded ski area in the southwest of the State with the famous **Durango–Silverton** narrow-gauge steam railway), **Silver Creek** (affordable family skiing), **Snowmass Ski Area**, **Steamboat** (with its nickname **Ski Town USA** and its distinctly Western heritage), **Ski Sunlight** (with the world's largest hot springs pool at **Glenwood Springs**), **Telluride** and **Winter Park** (which is also home to the **National Sports Center for the Disabled**). All the resorts offer reliable amounts of snow and an extensive range of accommodation and other facilities.

NATIONAL PARKS & MONUMENTS: The Colorado Rocky Mountains are home to three spectacular national parks. Located in the high plateau country of southwestern Colorado, the 21,044 hectare (52,000 acre) **Mesa Verde National Park** is designated as a World Heritage Site and contains some of the largest and most impressive examples of the dramatic Anasazi culture's cliff dwellings. Built over 700 years ago, these amazing structures have as many as 200 rooms. The park has paved roads offering views over the major ruins. There is a museum that attempts to explain the riddle of why the Native Americans built their villages in caves, and why, by the year 1300, they had completely abandoned the Mesa Verde plateau.

Rocky Mountain National Park is located 104km (65 miles) northwest of Denver, and is Colorado's most popular attraction. Reaching heights of 3736m (12,183ft), **Trail Ridge Road** crosses the park and forms one of the highest continuous highways in North America. Massive peaks, rugged canyons, flower-strewn meadows, peaceful lakes and thundering waterfalls combine to offer the visitor over 640km (400 miles) of spectacular wilderness. With its majestic mountain backdrop and picturesque main street, the resort village of **Estes Park**, on the edge of Rocky Mountain National Park, is very popular with visitors.

Credit: © Colorado Tourism Office

Black Canyon of the Gunnison National Park preserves the most spectacular 19km- (12 mile-) stretch of the 85km (53 mile) gorge carved by the **Gunnison River**. A paved road circles the rim of the canyon, which at some points is nearly half a mile deep. **Colorado National Monument** is an area of fantastic red rock canyons, monoliths, pillars and cliffs, while **Dinosaur National Monument** is a plateau cut by two rivers and is home to one of the world's richest deposits of dinosaur and reptile fossils. At the eastern edge of the San Luis Valley lies the **Great Sand Dunes National Monument**, with some of the highest inland sand dunes in North America. **Hovenweep National Monument** features the ruins of an ancient civilisation, with prehistoric towers, pueblos and cliff dwellings dating back almost 900 years.

Social Profile

FOOD & DRINK: Local specialities include fresh rainbow trout, buffalo and elk steaks and Mexican dishes. There are also restaurants offering Southeast Asian cuisine, innovative *New Southwestern* cuisine and international cuisines in every price range. For a distinctly Colorado-style meal, visit one of the many small breweries and brew pubs in Denver, Boulder and many mountain towns, which offer freshly brewed local beer and delicious food. Colorado brews more beer than any other State in the USA. Many of the 30 locally brewed beers on tap in Denver are not available in any other city, while the internationally known *Coors* beer offers free tours around its brewery, the largest-single brewing facility in the world. Minimum legal drinking age is 21 and ID may be requested in order to purchase or consume alcohol. Bars stop serving alcohol at 0200.

NIGHTLIFE: The **Denver Performing Arts Complex** houses seven theatres including the **Boettcher Concert Hall**. Among the other varied entertainments in the city, there are smaller venues staging theatre, popular music, jazz, dance, comedy and country & western music. For detailed information on scheduled events, visitors can consult The *Denver Post* or the *Rocky Mountain News*. Many of the ski resorts, notably Aspen and Vail, have countless restaurants, bars and other *après-ski* diversions.

SHOPPING: Denver offers extensive shopping facilities. **Cherry Creek Shopping Center**, the **Denver Pavillions** (located on 16th Street Mall), **Park Meadows Center** (the first shopping centre in the USA that resembles a beautiful mountain lodge) and **Larimer Square** all offer a pleasant shopping environment. Denver now has three factory outlet shopping centres: **Castle Rock** (situated 20 minutes south of Denver), **Silverthorne** in Summit County and **Rocky Mountain Factory Outlets** at Loveland. The **Colorado Mills** complex is located in Lakewood, near Denver, and has been described as 'Disneyland meets outlet mall'. Aspen in the Rocky Mountains has an unsurpassed range of shops and upmarket boutiques selling top designer lines. Special buys in Colorado include gold earrings and necklaces, Native American jewellery, Navajo rugs, and handicrafts such as pottery, wind chimes and wildlife sculptures.

SPORT: Colorado truly is a year-round paradise for the sports enthusiast. The Rocky Mountains offer unparalleled **skiing** in winter, as well as every other form of winter sport, while the mountain landscape offers **summer sports**, including whitewater rafting, hiking, mountain biking, horseriding, fishing, golf, tennis and more. Popular **spectator sports** include American football, football, basketball, hockey and baseball – Denver has teams in all of the five professional leagues. The *Colorado Rockies* play at *Coors Field*, the *NBA Denver Nuggets* and *NHL Colorado Avalanche* are both resident at the 20,000-seat *Pepsi Center*, while the *NFL Denver Broncos* play at the *INVESCO Field* at Mile High.

SPECIAL EVENTS: The following is a selection of special events occurring in Colorado in 2005:

Jan 8-23 *National Western Stock Show and Rodeo*, Denver. **Jan 21-23** *Boulder Bach Festival*. **Feb 5-8** *Mardi Gras*, Vail. **Feb 6** *34th Annual Frisco Gold Rush*. **Mar 12** *St Patrick's Day Parade*, Leadville and Denver. **Apr 21-23** *UNC/Greeley Jazz Festival*, Greeley. **May 1-31** *Boulder Creek Festival*, Boulder. **May 2-7** *Cinco de Mayo*, (celebration of Hispanic heritage and culture), Greeley. **May 28-30** *Territory Days*, Colorado Springs. **Jun 10-11** *Colorado State Square Dance Festival*, Greeley. **Jun 17-19** *Gaelic Highland Festival*, Canon City. **Jun 25-26** *Annual Colorado Brewers Festival*, Fort Collins. **Jun 25-27** *Denver International Busker Festival*. **Jul 2-4** *Cherry Creek Arts Festival*, Denver. **Jul 9-10** *AT&T Lo Do Music Festival*, Denver. **Jul 9-11** *Rocky Mountain High*, Denver; *11th Annual Colorado Irish Festival*, Denver. **Jul 29-30** *Royal Gorge Weekende*, Canon City. **Jul 29-31** *Rocky Grass Festival*, Lyons. **Sep 11** *Chili & Frijole Festival*, Pueblo. **Oct 1-31** *Starz Denver International Film Festival*.

Note: The ski resorts all hold their own individual festivals during the winter season, including season opening and closing celebrations, Christmas markets, competition events, carnivals and torchlight parades.

Climate

The capital, Denver, has a mild, dry climate with an average of 300 sunny days a year. Spring is mild with warm days and cool evenings; summer has very warm days with low humidity and cool evening breezes. Denver often enjoys an Indian Summer right into November, while winter is cold, sunny and crisp, with some snowfall. The mountains enjoy warm summer days with cool evenings. Autumn arrives early in the high ground, with abundant snowfall from December to April and temperatures around freezing point.

Required clothing: Warm clothing, especially in the mountains, from November to March/April. Cottons and linens during the summer months

Lakewood, Denver
(elevation: 1719m)

Temperature — Rainfall

Humidity (Cheyenne WY, %)

Jan	Feb	Mar	Apr	May	June	July	Aug	Sept	Oct	Nov	Dec
49	49	49	49	46	42	40	39	40	46	48	51

Connecticut

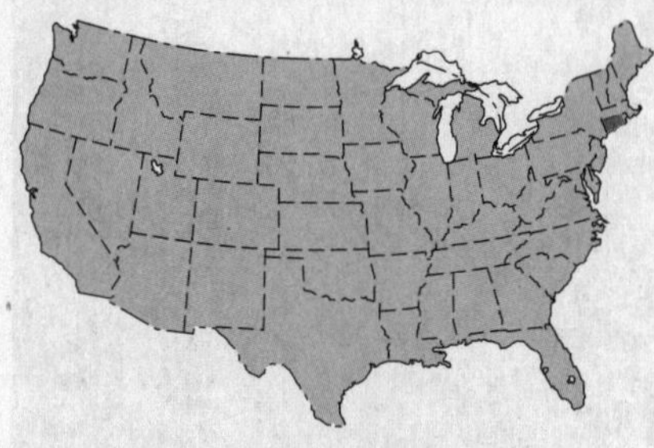

Connecticut Commission on Culture & Tourism
505 Hudson Street, Hartford, CT 06106
Tel: (860) 270 8080 *or* (800) 282 6863 (toll-free).
Fax: (860) 270 8077.
E-mail: robert.damroth@po.state.ct.us
Website: www.ctbound.org
Greater New Haven CVB
59 Elm Street, New Haven, CT 06510
Tel: (203) 777 8550 *or* (800) 332 7829 (toll-free).
Fax: (203) 782 7755.
E-mail: mail@newhavencvb.org
Website: www.newhavencvb.org
Greater Hartford CVB
31 Pratt Street, 4th Floor, Hartford, CT 06103
Tel: (860) 728 6789 *or* (800) 446 7811 (toll-free).
Fax: (860) 293 2365.
E-mail: ghcvb@hartfordcvb.org
Website: www.enjoyhartford.com
Mystic & Shoreline Visitor Information Center
27 Coogan Boulevard, Olde Mistick Village, Mystic, CT 06355
Tel: (860) 536 1641. Fax: (860) 536 0578.
E-mail: mysticinfocenter@yahoo.com
Website: www.mysticinfo.com
Coastal Fairfield County CVB
Gate Lodge, Mathews Park, 297 West Avenue,
Norwalk, CT 06850
Tel: (203) 853 7770 *or* (800) 866 7925 (toll-free).
Fax: (203) 853 7775.
E-mail: info@coastalct.com
Website: www.coastalct.com

General Information

Nickname: Constitution State
State bird: American Robin
State flower: Mountain Laurel
CAPITAL: Hartford
Date of admission to the Union: 9 Jan 1788 (original 13 States; date of ratification of the Constitution)
POPULATION: 3,503,604 (official estimate 2004)
POPULATION DENSITY: 244 per sq km
2003 total overseas arrivals/US ranking: 252,000/18
TIME: Eastern (GMT - 5). *Daylight Saving Time* is observed.

THE STATE: Connecticut is a mixture of town and country; beyond the towns and major cities inhabited by New York commuters are quiet colonial villages set in a rural landscape. The third-smallest State in the USA, Connecticut has a rich literary history. **Hartford** was the home of Mark Twain, and tourists can visit **The Mark Twain House**, at Nook Farm, where he wrote his greatest work, *The Adventures of Huckleberry Finn*, in 1884. Next door is the cottage in which the author of *Uncle Tom's Cabin*, Harriet Beecher Stowe, lived until her death in 1896, also open for tours. For children, there is the delightful **Bushnell Park Carousel**, which was built in 1914 in one of the first public US parks. Other Hartford attractions include the oldest public art museum in the country, **Wadsworth Atheneum**, the **Museum of Connecticut History**, and the **Old State House**, which housed the State government until 1914. **New Haven** is the site of **Yale University**, the **Peabody Museum of Natural History**, the **Center for British Art**, and **Yale University Art Gallery**. The Art Gallery houses a fine collection, including American decorative arts, pre-Colombian pieces and works by European masters such as Van Gogh. More modern fare can be viewed at the **Neon Garage**. The town is also known for its theatre; famous names to have trodden New Haven's boards include Jodie Foster, Glenn Close and Meryl Streep. *The New Haven Symphony Orchestra* and the *Yale Repertory Theater* have their homes here.

Mystic Seaport is a living museum of Connecticut's maritime past. There is a display of wooden ships, a maritime museum, shops, and art and craft collections. Visitors can marvel at the sharks, dolphins and seals at **Mystic Aquarium**. They can also shop and dine in the New England Colonial setting of **Olde Mistick Village**. Some 8km (5 miles) east of Mystic, **Stonington Borough** is a delightful old fishing village, which boasts a number of antique shops and a **Lighthouse Museum**. Other attractions in the State include the entertainment complexes and casinos of **Foxwoods Resort** and the **Mashantucket Pequot Museum and Research Center** in **Mashantucket**, the **Mohegan Sun** in **Uncasville**, the **Haight Vineyards** in **Litchfield** and the **Ocean Beach Park**, with a sand beach and wooden boardwalk, in **New London**.

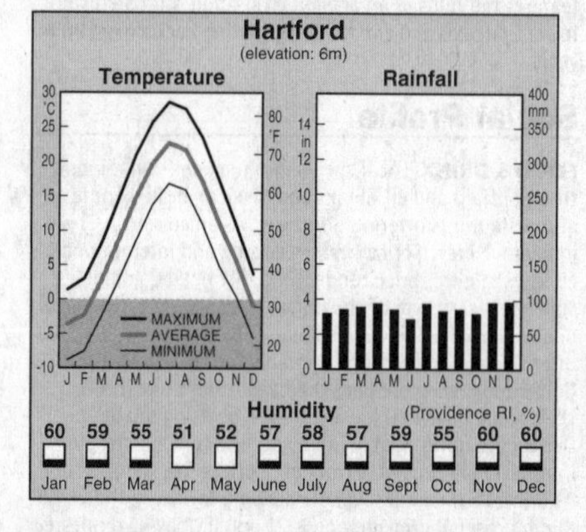

Delaware

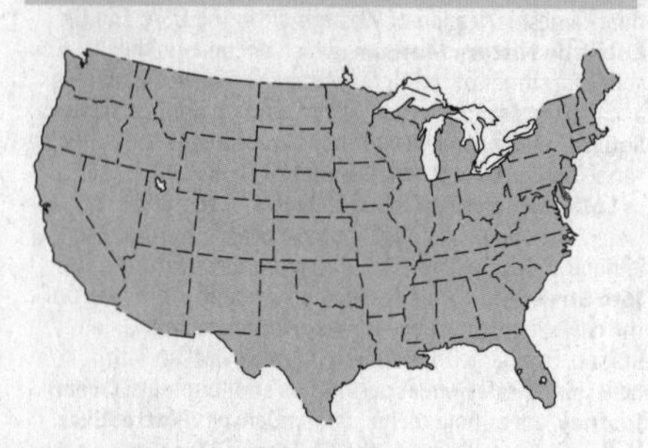

Delaware Tourism Office
99 Kings Highway, Dover, DE 19901
Tel: (302) 739 4271 *or* (866) 284 7483 (toll-free).
Fax: (302) 739 5749.
Website: http://delaware.gov
Greater Wilmington CVB
100 West 10th Street, Suite 20, Wilmington, DE 19801
Tel: (302) 652 4088 *or* (800) 489 6664 (toll-free) *or* (800) 422 1181 (toll-free, after 1700 EST).
Fax: (302) 652 4726.
E-mail: info@wilmcvb.org
Website: www.wilmcvb.org *or* www.visitwilmingtonde.com
Kent County Tourism CVB
435 North DuPont Highway, Dover, DE 19901
Tel: (302) 734 1736 *or* (800) 233 5368 (toll-free).
Fax: (302) 734 0167.
E-mail: kctc@visitdover.com
Website: www.visitdover.com
Southern Delaware Tourism
PO Box 240, Georgetown, DE 19947
Tel: (302) 856 1818 *or* (800) 357 1818 (toll-free).
E-mail: southdel@dmv.com
Website: www.visitsoutherndelaware.com

Credit: © Delaware Tourism Office

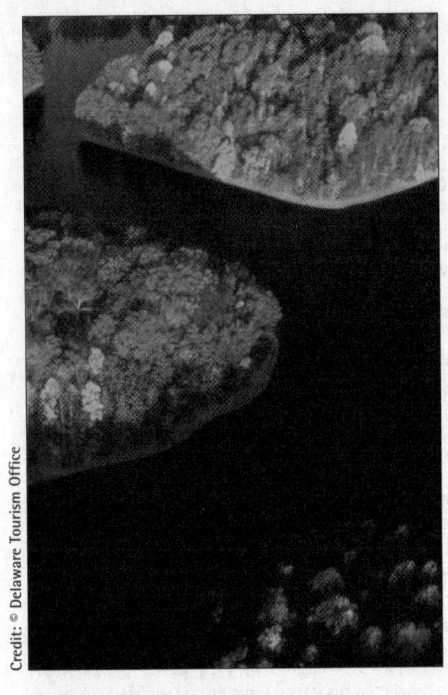

Credit: © Delaware Tourism Office

General Information

Nickname: Diamond State
State bird: Blue Hen Chicken
State flower: Peach Blossom
CAPITAL: Dover
Date of admission to the Union: 7 Dec 1787 (original 13 States; date of ratification of the Constitution)
POPULATION: 830,364 (official estimate 2004)
POPULATION DENSITY: 125.5 per sq km
2003 total overseas arrivals: Under 38,000
TIME: Eastern (GMT - 5). *Daylight Saving Time* is observed.

THE STATE: This small State's administrative and commercial centre is **Wilmington**. Founded in 1638, the city includes museums, galleries, a port and a new trolley car system modelled on the world-famous cable cars in San Francisco. **Fort Christina Historic Park** is the site of Delaware's first permanent settlement, when Finns and Swedes landed here in 1638, while the **Delaware Art Museum** exhibits a permanent collection of 19th- and 20th-century American art and Pre-Raphaelite English art of the 19th century, including works by Edward Hopper, Howard Pyle and Andrew Wyeth. The nearby **Brandywine Valley** is home to the Du Pont mansions, as well as the Hagley Museum, which explains how this powerful family's fortune was made. The capital, **Dover**, is home to numerous museums, including the **Air Mobility Command Museum**, which exhibits planes and military artefacts. The rest of the State is mostly rural. **Lewes** is a quaint seaside historic town with some delightful beaches. East of Lewes is the **Cape Henlopen State Park**, Delaware's largest State Park, with its seabird nesting colony and white sand dunes. Nearby, **Rehoboth Beach** is a seaside resort popular with families for its amusement park, 1.6km- (1 mile-) long boardwalk, fine restaurants and shops. Bargain hunters will be enticed by the retail outlet shopping that is available in the vicinity. **Dewey Beach** is a lively holiday spot with plenty of bars and clubs to keep youthful holidaymakers happy, as well as opportunities for watersports. Historic **New Castle** includes some wonderfully preserved buildings, such as the 1732 **Old Court House**, which served as the first state capitol, and the Colonial style **George Read II House**.

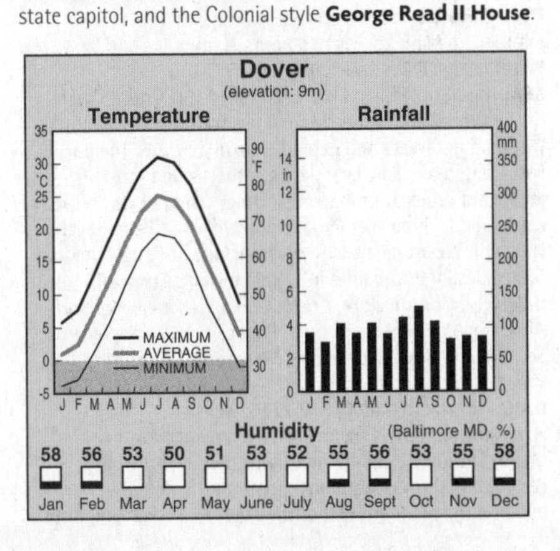

Florida

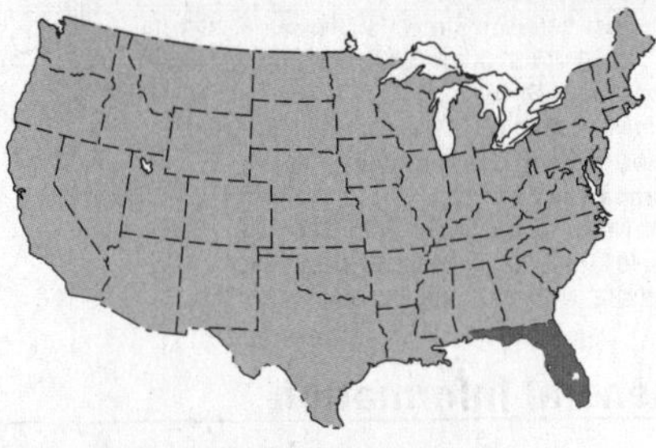

Visit Florida (the Official Tourism Marketing Corporation for the State of Florida)
Street address: 661 East Jefferson Street, Suite 300, Tallahassee, FL 32301
Postal address: PO Box 1100, Tallahassee, FL 32302
Tel: (850) 488 5607. Fax: (850) 224 2938.
Website: www.visitflorida.org or www.visitflorida.com

Visit Florida (UK)
28 Eccleston Square, London SW1V 1NZ, UK
Tel: (020) 7932 2406 *or* (01737) 644 882 (brochure request).
Fax: (020) 7932 2426.
E-mail: visitfloriduk@flausa.com
Website: www.flausa.com/uk
This office is not open to the public.

Beaches of South Walton Tourist Development Council
Street address: 25777 US 331 South, Santa Rosa Beach, FL 32459
Postal address: PO Box 1248, Santa Rosa Beach, FL 32459
Tel: (850) 267 1216 *or* (800) 822 6877 (toll-free).
Fax: (850) 267 3943.
E-mail: florida@beachesofsouthwalton.com
Website: www.beachesofsouthwalton.com

Greater Fort Lauderdale/Broward County Convention Center
1950 Eisenhower Boulevard, Fort Lauderdale, FL 33316
Tel: (954) 765 5900. Fax: (954) 763 9551.
E-mail: sbelidor@ftlauderdalecc.com
Website: www.ftlauderdalecc.com

Central Florida Visitors & Convention Bureau
600 North Broadway, Suite 300, Bartow, FL 33830
Tel: (863) 298 7565 *or* (800) 828 7655 (toll-free).
Fax: (863) 298 7564.
E-mail: info@sunsational.org
Website: www.sunsational.org

Daytona Beach Area CVB
Main Office: 126 East Orange Avenue, Daytona Beach, FL 32114
Welcome Centre: 1801 West International Speedway Boulevard, Daytona Beach, FL 32118
Tel: (386) 255 0415 *or* (800) 854 1234 (toll-free).
Fax: (386) 255 5478.
E-mail: info@daytonabeach.com
Website: www.daytonabeach.com

Emerald Coast CVB
1540 Miracle Strip Parkway, Fort Walton Beach, FL 32548
Tel: (850) 651 7131 *or* (800) 322 3319 (toll-free).
Fax: (850) 651 7149.
E-mail: emeraldcoast@co.okaloosa.fl.us
Website: www.destin-fwb.com

Florida's Gulf Islands (Bradenton CVB/Manatee County)
Street address: 1 Haben Boulevard, Palmetto, FL 34221
Postal address: PO Box 1000, Bradenton, FL 34206
Tel: (941) 729 9177 *or* (800) 462 6283 (toll-free).
Fax: (941) 729 1820.
E-mail: info@flagulfislands.com
Website: www.flagulfislands.com

Florida's Gulf Islands (Bradenton CVB/Manatee County) (UK Office)
c/o Siren PR, Inigo Place, 31/32 Bedford Street, Covent Garden, London WC2E 9SW, UK
Tel: (020) 7257 8886. Fax: (020) 7257 8876.
E-mail: flagulfislands@sirenpr.co.uk
Website: www.flagulfislands.com

Florida Keys & Key West Tourism Development Council
c/o Stuart Newman Associates, 2140 South Dixie Highway, Suite 203, Miami, FL 33133
Tel: (305) 461 3300 *or* (800) 352 5397 (toll-free; visitor information) *or* (800) 771 5397 (toll-free; multilingual tourist assistance).
Fax: (305) 461 3311.
Website: www.fla-keys.com

Florida Keys & Key West Tourism Development Council (UK Office)
c/o Cellet Travel Services Ltd, 47 High Street, Henley-in-Arden, Warwickshire B95 5AA, UK
Tel: (01564) 794 555.
Fax: (01564) 795 333.
E-mail: info@cellet.co.uk
Website: www.fla-keys.com *or* www.cellet.co.uk

Greater Fort Lauderdale CVB
100 East Broward Boulevard, Suite 200, Fort Lauderdale, FL 33301
Tel: (954) 765 4466 *or* (800) 356 1662 (toll-free).
Fax: (954) 765 4467.
E-mail: gflcvb@broward.org
Website: www.sunny.org

Greater Miami CVB
701 Brickell Avenue, Suite 2700, Miami, FL 33131
Tel: (305) 539 3000 *or* (800) 933 8448 (toll-free).
E-mail: visitor@gmcvb.com
Website: www.miamiandbeaches.com *or* www.gmcvb.com

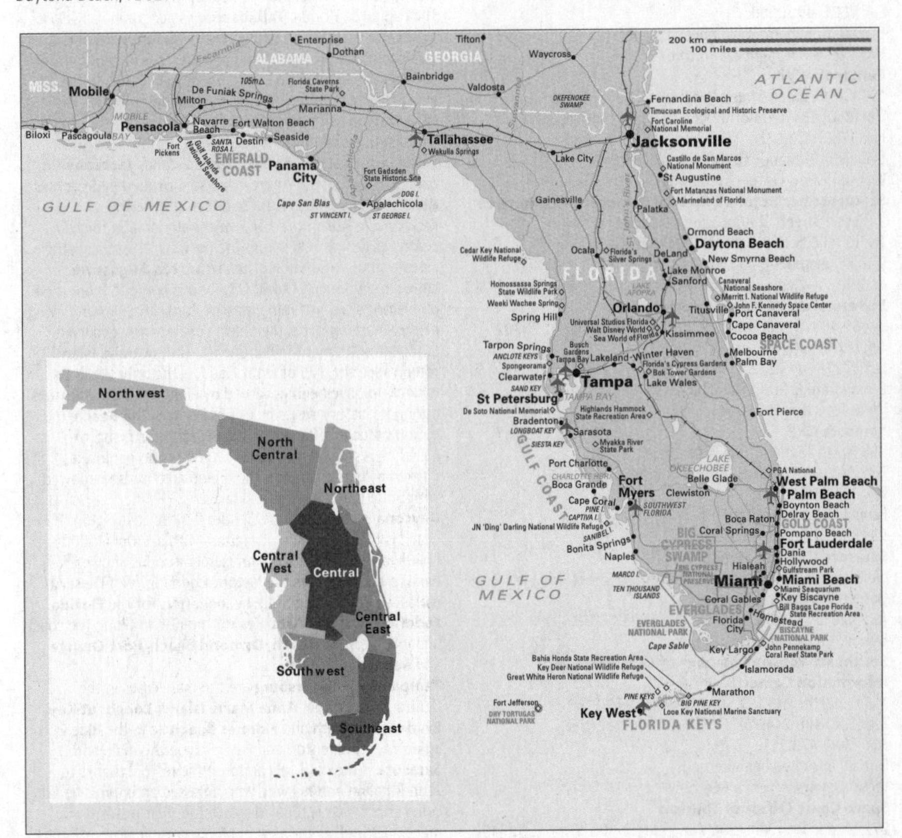

Greater Naples Chamber of Commerce Visitor and Information Center
2390 Tamiamy Trail North, Naples, FL 34103
Tel: (239) 262 6141. Fax: (239) 435 9910.
E-mail: info@napleschamber.org
Website: www.napleschamber.org
Indian River County Chamber of Commerce
1216 21st Street, Vero Beach, FL 32960
Tel: (772) 567 3491. Fax: (772) 778 3181.
E-mail: lburns@indianriverchamber.com
Website: www.indianriverchamber.com
Jacksonville and The Beaches CVB
550 Water Street, Suite 1000, Jacksonville, FL 32202
Tel: (904) 798 9111 *or* (800) 733 2668 (toll-free).
Fax: (904) 798 9103.
E-mail: jaxcvbadmin@jaxcvb.com
Website: www.visitjacksonville.com
Lee County Coast Visitor & Convention Bureau (includes Fort Myers and Sanibel Island)
21800 University Drive, Suite 550, Fort Myers, FL 33907
Tel: (239) 338 3500 *or* (800) 237 6444 (toll-free).
Fax: (239) 334 1106.
E-mail: vcb@leegov.com
Website: www.fortmyers-sanibel.com
Lee Island Coast Visitor and Convention Bureau (UK Office)
The Priory, Suite H, Syresham Gardens, Haywards Heath, Sussex RH16 3LB, UK
Tel: (01444) 414 188 or (01737) 644 722 (brochure request).
Fax: (01444) 414 155.
E-mail: leeVCBUK@aol.com
Website: www.leeislandcoast.com
Marco Island CVB
1102 North Collier Boulevard, Marco Island, FL 34145
Tel: (239) 394 7549 *or* (800) 788 6272 (toll-free in USA).
Fax: (239) 394 3061.
E-mail: info@marcoislandchamber.org
Website: www.marcoislandchamber.org
New Smyrna Beach Area Visitors Bureau
2238 State Road 44, New Smyrna Beach, FL 32168
Tel: (386) 428 1600 *or* (800) 541 9621 (toll-free).
Fax: (386) 428 9922.
E-mail: nsbinfo@nsbfla.com
Website: www.nsbfla.com
Orlando/Orange County CVB
6700 Forum Drive, Suite 100, Orlando, FL 32821
Visitor Centre: 8723 International Drive, Orlando, FL 32819
Tel: (407) 363 5800 *or* 354 5509 (international) *or* (800) 215 2213 (toll-free) *or* 363 5872 (visitor centre).
Fax: (407) 370 5012.
E-mail: info@orlandocvb.com
Website: www.orlandoinfo.com
Palm Beach County CVB
1555 Palm Beach Lakes Boulevard, Suite 800, West Palm Beach, FL 33401
Tel: (561) 233 3000 *or* (800) 833 5733 (toll-free).
Fax: (561) 471 3990.
E-mail: fulfillment@palmbeachfl.com
Website: www.palmbeachfl.com
Pensacola CVB
117 West Garden Street, Pensacola, FL 32502
Tel: (850) 434 1234 *or* (800) 874 1234 (toll-free).
Fax: (850) 432 8211.
E-mail: information@visitpensacola.com
Website: www.visitpensacola.com
St Augustine/St John's County Chamber of Commerce
1 Riberia Street, St Augustine, FL 32084
Tel: (904) 829 5681. Fax: (904) 829 6477.
E-mail: chamber@aug.com
Website: www.staugustinechamber.com
St Petersburg/Clearwater Area CVB
14450 46th Street North, Suite 108, Clearwater, FL 33762
Tel: (727) 464 7200 *or* (877) 352 3224.
Fax: (727) 464 7222.
E-mail: info@floridasbeach.com
Website: www.floridasbeach.com
Sarasota CVB
655 North Tamiami Trail, Sarasota, FL 34236
Tel: (941) 957 1877 *or* (800) 522 9799 (toll-free).
Fax: (941) 951 2956.
E-mail: info@sarasotafl.org
Website: www.sarasotafl.org
Sarasota CVB (UK Office)
c/o Siren PR, Inigo Place, 31/32 Bedford Street, Covent Garden, London WC2E 9SW, UK
Tel: (020) 7257 8886. Fax: (020) 7257 8876.
E-mail: sarasota@sirenpr.co.uk
Southeast Volusia Chamber of Commerce and Information Center
115 Canal Street, New Smyrna Beach, FL 32168
Tel: (386) 428 2449 *or* (877) 460 8410 (toll-free).
Fax: (386) 423 3512.
E-mail: info@sevchamber.com
Website: www.sevchamber.com
Space Coast Office of Tourism
2725 Judge Fran Jamieson Way, Suite B-105, Viera, FL 32940
Tel: (321) 637 5483 *or* (800) 936 2326 (toll-free).
Fax: (321) 637 5494.
E-mail: info@space-coast.com
Website: www.space-coast.com
Tallahassee Area CVB
106 East Jefferson Street, Tallahassee, FL 32301
Tel: (850) 413 9200 *or* (800) 628 2866 (toll-free).
Fax: (850) 487 4621.
E-mail: vic@mail.co.leon.fl.us
Website: www.seetallahassee.com
Tampa Bay CVB
400 North Tampa Street, Suite 2800, Tampa, FL 33602
Tel: (813) 223 1111. Fax: (813) 229 6616.
Website: www.visittampabay.com

General Information

Nickname: Sunshine State
State bird: Mockingbird
State flower: Orange Blossom
CAPITAL: Tallahassee
Date of admission to the Union: 3 Mar 1845
POPULATION: 17,397,161 (official estimate 2004)
POPULATION DENSITY: 102.1 per sq km
2003 total overseas arrivals/US ranking: 4,200,000/1
TIME: Eastern (GMT - 5), in the greater part of the State. *Daylight Saving Time* is observed.

THE STATE: Florida is one of the most popular tourist destinations in the world, with visitors heading to 'The Sunshine State' in search of fun, sun and thrills. **Walt Disney World**, **Magic Kingdom Park** and **Busch Gardens** are just a few of the manmade attractions for which the State is famed. But there is more to Florida than Mickey Mouse and white-knuckle rides. Winding waterways, freshwater lakes, hills, forests, exciting cities, 13,560km (8426 miles) of coast, countless bays, inlets and islands, and a legendary climate make this one of the most popular States in the USA.

Florida is divided into eight geographical regions: Northwest; North Central; Northeast; Central West; Central; Central East; Southwest; and Southeast Florida & the Keys. Situated on the southeastern tip, **Miami** and **Miami Beach** have long been a haunt of the rich and famous, and star-spotting is a popular pastime here. The city also has a well-established Cuban sector called Little Havana. **Palm Beach** scores equally highly in the glamour stakes, thanks largely to Addison Mizner who designed a US$50 million development of mansions and hotels, including one commissioned by the Vanderbilts. **Fort Lauderdale** is a popular spot for families, offering a wide assortment of sports and recreational activities. To the south, the **Florida Keys** are made up of the Upper, Middle and Lower Keys and Key West. A tropical climate, beautiful beaches and clear blue waters attract a steady flow of visitors to the Keys all year round.

The capital of Florida, **Tallahassee**, is geographically closer to Atlanta than Miami and is strictly Southern in tone. It was chosen as the State capital in 1823, as a compromise between Pensacola and St Augustine, which had both been vying for the honour. Today, it is often described as 'The Other Florida' with its rolling hills, oak forests, cool climate and distinctly Southern feel.

In the northeastern corner of Florida stands **Jacksonville**, named after General Andrew Jackson. Divided by **St John's River**, the city boasts futuristic features like the *Jacksonville Automated Skyway*, a monorail in the city centre, as well as relics from the past in its historic district, listed on the National Register. Nearby **St Augustine** is known as 'America's Oldest City' and is home to more than 60 historic sites, including massive forts, missions and living history museums; it is the oldest continuously occupied European settlement in continental USA. **Amelia Island**, often called the 'Isle of Eight Flags', is the only site in the country to have been governed by eight different countries during its history. At its heart lies **Fernandina Beach**, the nation's second-oldest city. The verdant northeastern coastline is shaped by a series of points and peninsulas flanked by barrier islands. The inland area is also endowed with State parks, springs and lakes.

Daytona is located in the slender Central East region. The beach is the city's main attraction, with a 510m (1700ft) boardwalk brimming with amusements, rides and snack bars. To the north lies the historic community of **DeBary**, which is home to the State headquarters for the **Florida Federation of the Arts**. Resorts are dotted along the coast and include **Vero Beach**, **Ormond Beach**, **Port Orange** and **Sebastian**.

Tampa and **St Petersburg** are the main cities in the Central West region. **Anna Marie Island**, **Longboat Key**, **Bradenton Beach** and **Holmes Beach** lie in the Blue Gulf, adjacent to Bradenton and Palmetto on the mainland. **Sarasota** is the cultural capital of the region, thanks to John Ringling and his wife who amassed an impressive art collection, which is today displayed in their restored mansion. **Pinellas** forms a stubby peninsula west of Tampa Bay, linked to Tampa by three bridges. The southwestern region is home to **Naples**, a popular seaside retreat with seemingly endless golfing, shopping and fishing opportunities. Just off the mainland, **Marco Island** stands as a model of ecological preservation. **Charlotte County** is only 27km (17 miles) long, but it boasts an amazing 193km (120 miles) of coastline. *Charlotte Harbor* is protected by a triangular web of land fringed by barrier islands such as **Gasparilla**, a one-time pirates' haven.

Orlando is the face of Florida that most people recognise, with its enormous number of theme parks, movie studios, water parks and entertainment facilities. The northern boundaries of Central Florida are engulfed by a national forest so large that it has to be administered by two separate Ranger districts.

The **Ocala National Forest** covers 153,049ha (378,178 acres) divided into three recreation areas and linked by a 105km (65 mile) trail. Nearby **Silver Springs**, a network of 150 springs, is the world's largest artesian spring; hundreds of thousands of gallons of water bubble through the spongy limestone bedrock each day. There are 1440 lakes in **Lake Country**, which is the setting for the area's vineyards and wine-growing region. Southwest of Orlando is **Polk Country**, which is famed for its beautiful landscape of citrus groves and pine forests.

Travel - International

Air: International airports: *Miami (MIA)* (website: www.miami-airport.com) is 9km (6 miles) west of Miami (travel time - 25 minutes). There is a 24-hour shuttle service to the central bus station and hotels on request. Public buses are also available to the city. Taxi, van and limousine services are also available; fares are fixed. *Greyhound* (tel: (800) 229 9424 (toll-free); website: www.greyhound.com) runs daily services throughout the Florida Keys and to destinations in the north.

Tampa (TPA) (website: www.tampaairport.com) is 8km (5 miles) northwest of Tampa (travel time - 15 minutes). A bus service runs into the city; limousine and taxi services are also available.

Scheduled flights from the UK to Orlando arrive at *Orlando International (ORL)* (website: www.state.fl.us/goaa), which is 15km (9 miles) south of Orlando (travel time - 15 minutes). There is a 24-hour shuttle service available to any hotel in Orlando. Hire cars, coach, bus, taxi and limousine services are available.

Chartered flights from the UK arrive in *Orlando Sanford Airport (SFB)* (website: www.orlandosanfordairport.com), approximately 29km (18 miles) northeast of Orlando. Car hire, coaches, buses, taxi, limousine and shuttle services into the city are available.

Fort Lauderdale-Hollywood (FLL) (website: www.fll.net) is 8km (5 miles) from Fort Lauderdale (travel time - 10 minutes). Hire cars, limousines, taxis and bus services are available, with rail connections to the surrounding counties.

Approximate flight times: From **Miami** to *Atlanta* is one hour 50 minutes, to *Barbados* is three hours 25 minutes, to *Caracas* is three hours 10 minutes, to *Charlotte* is two hours, to *Chicago* is three hours 10 minutes, to *Dallas/Fort Worth* is three hours 20 minutes, to *Freeport* is 40 minutes, to *Grand Turk* is one hour 45 minutes, to *Guatemala City* is two hours 40 minutes, to *Honolulu* is 12 hours 15 minutes, to *Houston* is three hours, to *London* is eight hours 10 minutes, to *Los Angeles* is seven hours, to *Mexico City* is three hours 15 minutes, to *New York* is two hours 40 minutes, to *Orlando* is one hour, to *Panama City* is three hours, to *Port-au-Prince* is 45 minutes, to *Providenciales* is one hour 35 minutes, to *St Croix* is two hours 40 minutes, to *San Francisco* is seven hours 25 minutes, to *San Juan* is two hours 25 minutes, to *Santo Domingo* is two hours 10 minutes, to *Tampa* is 55 minutes and to *Washington, DC* is two hours 20 minutes.

From **Tampa** to *London* is 10 hours (direct flight), to *Miami* is 55 minutes and to *New York* is two hours 40 minutes.

From **Orlando** to *London* is nine hours, to *Miami* is 55 minutes, to *New York* is two hours 30 minutes and to *Washington, DC* is two hours.

SEA: The port of Miami has been called the 'Cruise Capital of the World' and offers ocean liners for business meetings, weekend getaways and extended luxury cruises. The port of Fort Lauderdale, Port Everglades, is the second most important cruise port in Florida. Other cruise ports on the east coast include Port Canaveral and Port of Palm Beach. The main West Coast cruise ports include St Petersburg and Tampa. Major cruise lines in Florida include *Carnival, Celebrity, Commodore, Costa, Cunard, Disney, Holland America, Norwegian, Premier, Princess, Radisson Seven Seas, Regal, Royal Caribbean, Seabourn, Silversea* and *Windjammer Barefoot*.

RAIL: *Amtrak* (tel: (800) 872 7245; website: www.amtrak.com) is the rail service provider. Amtrak's Miami Station is 11km (7 miles) northwest of the city centre. It is the southernmost point on the network, marking the southern end of the main east coast line from

New York (and ultimately Boston). Amtrak also serves Jacksonville, with services running through Orlando to Tampa (a branch line terminates at Sarasota, a few miles south of Tampa on the Gulf of Mexico), and west through Pensacola to New Orleans (Louisiana).

ROAD: The best major routes through Florida are: Daytona Beach to St Petersburg (I-4), Jacksonville to the Alabama border (I-10), St Petersburg to Tampa (I-275), the lower West Coast to Fort Lauderdale (I-75), the North-South highway (I-95) or (I-75) and the East-West cross-state highway from Clearwater to Vero Beach (State 60). The Florida's Turnpike is a 723km (449 mile) system of limited-access toll highways, which passes through 11 counties from north Miami to a junction with I-75 in north central Florida. Most roads are excellent throughout the State.

Approximate driving times: From **Orlando** to *Miami* is four hours 45 minutes, to *Daytona* is one hour, to *Fort Lauderdale* is four hours 30 minutes, to *Jacksonville* is three hours, to *Key West* is eight hours 45 minutes, to *Naples* is four hours, to *Pensacola* is nine hours, to *St Petersburg* is two hours 30 minutes, and to *Tallahassee* is fiive hours 15 minutes. All times are based on non-stop driving at or below the applicable speed limits.

Approximate Greyhound travel times: From **Miami** to *Fort Lauderdale* is one hour to *Orlando* is nine hours, to *St Petersburg* is seven hours 30 minutes, to *Jacksonville* is 11 hours 15 minutes, to *Tampa* is eight hours 15 minutes, and to *Tallahassee* is 14 hours.

Urban: Miami's transport system includes an elevated *Metrorail* system running a north-south route through the city. The *Downtown Metromover* combines the fun of a theme park with the convenience of above-street-level travel. Metrobuses operate frequently through most areas of Greater Miami. Fares are moderate and transfers are available. Taxis can be expensive in the Miami area; one can usually hail them but delays may be encountered at rush hours. Taxis can also be booked by telephone. Most major car hire and motor camper hire firms have offices at the airport or in central Miami. Many provide a drop-off service in other parts of the State. Major hotels can often arrange immediate car hire. Road signs marked with an orange sun on a blue background indicate routes to major tourist attractions.

Credit: © Visit Florida

Resorts & Excursions

North West Florida

The Northwest region of Florida stretches from **Pensacola** on the State's western border to the shores of **Apalachee Bay**. The northwest coastline is the gateway to the Florida peninsula and is easily negotiable. Yet the busy coastal region gives no clue to the items of interest further inland – a geometric pattern of trail systems, secret caverns and bubbling springs – including **Marianna**, where visitors can explore the spectacular labyrinths of **Florida Caverns State Park**.

The earliest European explorers were Spanish and landed at **Pensacola Harbor** in 1540 when Hernando de Soto began his explorations of the Gulf Coast. However, it was not until the 18th century that a permanent settlement was established in the region. Under British rule from 1763, Pensacola was eventually taken by Spain during the American Revolution. The area was again prominent during the Civil War period, thanks to the triangle of fortresses which encircled the 150 sq mile span of barrier islands now known as the Gulf Islands National Seashore. To this day, the area retains its military significance.

PENSACOLA: The flags of Spain, France and England have flown over the city of **Pensacola** during its turbulent past. The *Colonial Archaelogical Trail* leads visitors through the different eras of the city's history, and highlights an ongoing programme of excavation by local archaeologists. The city centre features the **Pensacola Museum of Art**, housed in the old city jail; the **Pensacola Cultural Center**; **Quayside**, the South's largest co-operative art gallery; **Wall South**, a replica of the Vietnam Veterans' Memorial in Washington, DC; and the beautifully restored **Saenger Theatre**, where local and national musical groups regularly perform.

A few miles to the west lies one of the biggest and best air and space museums in the country, the **National Museum of Naval Aviation**. Displays cover the age of aviation from the first flight in a wood and fabric biplane to today's travels in space with the *Skylab Command Module*. East of Pensacola, the **Gulf Breeze Zoo** is home to more than 700 animals and a huge botanical garden, while gorillas and chimpanzees roam free on two large islands. The beauty of Pensacola's beaches is protected by Federal and State reservations, which preserve them from development. **Gulf Islands National Seashore** and **Big Lagoon Park** offer huge areas of untouched beaches, which are easily accessible to the public.

TRAVEL: Approximately 60 flights arrive and depart from *Pensacola Regional Airport* (website: www.flypensacola.com) each day. The city is situated on the Amtrak network and is also accessible from most major interstate highways; the Greyhound station is located 11km (7 miles) north of the city center.

SPECIAL EVENTS: The following is a selection of special events occurring in Pensacola in 2005:
Feb *Black History Month*, University of West Florida, Pensacola. **Apr 9-10** *Pensacola JazzFest*, Selville Square. **May 6-8** *21st Annual Crawfish Creole Fiesta*, Bartram Park, Pensacola. **May** *The Florida Springfest* (three-day music festival), Pensacola. **Jun 2-11** *56th Fiesta of Five Flags*, Pensacola. **Jul-Aug** *Annual Bushwacker and Music Festival*, Pensacola. **Sep 23-25** *Annual Seafood Festival*, Pensacola. **Nov** *Great Gulf Coast Arts Festival*, Pensacola

CLIMATE: Pensacola boasts an average of 343 days of sunshine per year and an average annual temperature of 24°C (75 ºF).

EMERALD COAST: East of Pensacola, visitors will be struck by the glorious coastal scenery. Linked by an impressive bridge network, a long coastal road skirts the mainland and the offshore islands, running from Pensacola to **Fort Walton Beach** and **Santa Rosa Island**. Near Santa Rosa, **Destin**
is known for fine fishing, while the **Beaches of South Walton** embrace the smart prosperous community of **Seaside**, with its white-washed houses, excellent dining and shopping facilities.

South Walton's beaches extend eastward towards **Panama City**, which took its name from the famous canal in 1906. Today, its attractions and nightlife, which extend for 43km (27 miles), are celebrated throughout the State.

DESTIN/FORT WALTON BEACH: Famous for 38km (24 miles) of sugar-white sands and brilliant green waters, these southern sea towns both offer some of the world's finest shells and superb seafood. The **Henderson Beach State Park** offers acres of unspoilt coastal terrain. Hailed as the 'World's Luckiest Fishing Village', Destin's **East Pass** is only 16km (10 miles) from 30m (100ft) depths. Harbouring the largest and most elaborately equipped charter-boat fleet in Florida, more billfish are caught on the Northern Gulf each year than by all the other Gulf ports combined. There is also a wider variety of game fish than elsewhere, from cobia and scampi to triggerfish and king mackerel. Numerous deep-sea excursions are available for both first-time fishers and the more experienced angler.

PANAMA CITY BEACH: Watersports are high on the list of attractions at Panama City Beach, which boasts a network of waterways, bays and lagoons. **St Andrews State Recreation Area** is made up of more than 1000 acres of nature trails and beaches. Visitors can take a shuttle to **Shell Island** from **Treasure Island Marina**. The **Museum of the Man-in-the-Sea** explores the ocean, while other attractions include the **Miracle Strip Amusement Park**, **Shipwreck Island Water Park** and **Alvin's Magic Mountain Mall**, which houses sharks and alligators in a 30,000 gallon tank.

APALACHICOLA: Apalachicola has a rich heritage. Once, it was the third-largest cotton port on the Gulf Coast, serving as a base for the Confederate forces trying to run the Union blockades during the Civil War. Today, this protected region of swamps and springs enjoys acclaim as the centre of Florida's seafood industry. Its large oyster beds are responsible for a high percentage of the State's exports.

TRAVEL: *Destin/Fort Walton Beach Airport* is located 2km (1 mile) east of Destin; *Panama City/Bay County International Airport* (website: www.pcairport.com) lies 6km (4 miles) north of Panama City. The *Panama City Beach Trolley* shuttles along the beach, making various flag stops. Taxis run on a grid system and fares increase as one moves away from Harrison Avenue.

SPECIAL EVENTS: The following is a selection of special events occurring on the Emerald Coast in 2005:
Apr 21-24 *19th Annual Sandestin Wine Festival*, Destin. **May** *Annual Destin Mayfest*, Destin; *Seaside Spring Wine Festival*, Seaside. **Jun 3-6** *Billy Bowlegs Pirate Festival*, Fort Walton Beach/Okaloosa Island. **Oct** *Annual Indian Summer Seafood Festival*, Panama City.

CLIMATE: There are warm temperatures all year round with a summer high of 31°C (88 ºF).

North Central Florida

The North Central region lies between the Gulf of Mexico and Georgia at the base of the Appalachians. This region is bisected by the **Suwannee River**, which was immortalised in Florida's official state song, written by Stephen Foster. **Tallahassee**, the state capital and the only uncaptured Confederate capital east of the Mississippi, has preserved the famous battle site of **Natural Bridge** where the Union forces suffered a defeat in 1865. Today, the city is a wonderful haven of colour – azaleas, dogwoods, daphne, magnolias and camellias are all to be seen in bloom here. The **Museum of Florida History** and the **Black Archives Research Center** can also be found here.

One of the area's most notable natural features is **Wakulla Springs**, which delivers more than 15,000 gallons of water per second.

Seafood was the staple of one of the region's historic sites, **Cedar Key**, which is one of the oldest ports in the State. This island became a major supplier of seafood and timber products for the northeastern States during the Railroad era. Today, it is noted for its shopping, Victorian architecture and artistic flair.

TRAVEL: *Tallahassee Regional Airport (THL)* (website: www.ci.tallahassee.fl.us/citytlh/aviation) is located 10 minutes from the city and served by *AirTran Airways, Air Wisconsin, Continental Express, Delta Air Lines, Delta Connection Services, Northwest Airlink* and *US Airways Express*.

Amtrak's Tallahassee station is situated five minutes away on Railroad Avenue. Tallahassee is also served by *Greyhound* buses. The *Old Town Trolley* provides a free round trip ride from the Civic Center.

SPECIAL EVENTS: The following is a selection of special events occurring in North Central Florida in 2005:
Jan 10-16 *Freedom Blues Festival*, Tallahassee. **Mar** *Tallahassee Jazz & Blues Festival*. **Mar-Nov** *Downtown Marketplace*, every Saturday, Tallahassee. **Apr** *Annual Spring Arts Festival*, Gainesville. **May** *Southern Shakespeare Festival*, Tallahassee. **May 27-29** *Annual Folk Festival*, White Springs. **Aug** *North Florida Fair*, Tallahassee. **Nov 12-13** *Annual Downtown Festival and Arts Show*, Gainesville.

CLIMATE: Tallahassee is mild and moist owing to its close proximity to the Gulf, with an average temperature of 19°C (67ºF).

A B C D E F G H I J K L M N O P Q R S T U V W X Y Z

North East Florida

Straddling the beautiful **St John's River**, **Jacksonville** is located in the northeast corner of Florida on the Atlantic Ocean. The historic districts of **St Augustine** and Fernandina Beach on Amelia Island are situated nearby.

CLIMATE: The Northeast Region offers mild winters, a cool spring and fall, and it is generally warm during the summer months.

JACKSONVILLE & AREA: The **Jacksonville Landing**, on the north bank, is bustling with restaurants, nightclubs and shops, all housed under one giant orange-roofed facility. The **Museum of Science and History** and the nationally acclaimed **Cummer Museum of Art** and its gardens are situated in the city centre, just a few minutes away from the **Jacksonville Museum of Modern Art**.

The First Coast area is one of the few unspoiled areas of the Atlantic Coast. Nature trails and national parks line the seafront, providing opportunities for hiking, kayaking and camping. Just a few minutes northeast of the city is the Timucuan Ecological and Historic Preserve, an 18,500 hectare (46,000 acre) wetland and historic community. The trails and waterways are filled with indigenous and endangered wildlife such as ospreys, herons, bald eagles, sea turtles, manatees and wood storks. The **Talbot Island State Park** provides miles of pristine beaches, dunes, coastal hummocks and marshlands. **Big Talbot Island** boasts spectacular bluffs, 19km (11.5 miles) of untouched beaches, two plantation ruins, sand dunes, salt marshes, tidal creeks and a driftwood forest. South of Big Talbot is **Little Talbot Island**, an undeveloped barrier island. The entire 1000 hectare (2500 acre) island is a protected State Park and has white sand beaches and a popular campsite.

Fort George Island State Cultural Site contains the longest record of civilisation in **Duval County**. The huge oyster shell mounds found on the island are evidence of Timucuan Indian habitation dating back over 7000 years.

Katherine Abbey Hanna Park is Jacksonville's premier 180 hectare (450 acre) beachfront getaway and boasts sunny beaches, freshwater lakes and wooded campsites. Established in 1914 with just one animal, a white-tailed fawn, the **Jacksonville Zoological Gardens** is today alive with more than 800 animals from around the world. At the **Okavango Petting Zoo** children can pet domestic African animals such as pygmy goats, dwarf zebu, miniature horses and Sardinian pygmy donkeys.

TRAVEL: *Jacksonville International Airport (JIA)* (website: www.jaxairports.org) is 20 minutes from the city centre. Jacksonville is served by both *Amtrak* trains and *Greyhound* buses. The Amtrak station, Florida's hub, is located 10km (6 miles) west of downtown Jacksonville. The *Jacksonville Transportation Authority (JTA)* provides a local bus service seven days a week with 50 routes. JTA also operates the *Automated Skyway Express*, a monorail system serving the city centre.

SPECIAL EVENTS: The following is a selection of special events occurring in Jacksonville & Area in 2005:

Apr 7-10 *Jacksonville Jazz Festival*, Metropolitan Park and The Jacksonville Landing. **Apr 28-May 1** *Annual World of Nations Celebration*, Metropolitan Park. **May** *Riverfest*, Jacksonville. **May/Jun** *Sail Jacksonville* (tall ships), Downtown Riverfront. **Nov** *Annual Jacksonville Light Parade*, Jacksonville Waterfront. **Nov 11** *Veteran's Day Parade*, Jacksonville.

ST AUGUSTINE & AREA: The USA's oldest city is a time capsule capturing nearly 500 years of fascinating history. Situated on the uppermost Atlantic Coast of Florida, the water's-edge colonial village has 144 blocks of historic houses listed on the National Register of Historic Places. The **Castillo de San Marcos** endures as the nation's oldest and only remaining 17th-century masonry fort. Now a National Monument, the Spanish-built bastion guarded the mouth of **Matanzas Bay** from British invaders. The **Spanish Quarter Living Museum** is a village where actors portraying Spanish soldiers and settlers in traditional costume re-enact 18th-century crafts.

Other attractions include **Anastasia State Recreation Area**, a 1700 acre bird sanctuary on **Anastasia Island**; the still operational **St Augustine Lighthouse and Museum**; the **Oldest Store Museum**, which recreates a late 19th-century general store; and the USA's first alligator exhibition farm, **St Augustine Alligator Farm**. Just past the beaches of Anastasia Island lies **Marineland of Florida**, the world's first oceanarium. It features 1000 wonders of the deep, including Nelly, the world's oldest known living dolphin, born on 27 February 1953.

SPECIAL EVENTS: The following is a selection of special events occurring in St Augustine & Area in 2005:

Mar *7th Annual San Sebastien Harvest Festival and Grape Stomp*, St Augustine. **Mar 4-6** *Native American Indian Festival*, Francis Field. **Mar 19** *Lighthouse Festival*, St Augustine. **Mar 27** *St Augustine Easter Parade*.

Apr 14-17 *EPIC Celebration of Spring*, St Augustine.

Jul 4 *Fourth of July Fireworks*, St Augustine.

Nov 19-Jan 31 2006 *Nights of Light*, St Augustine.

Central West Florida

The Central West region is dotted with scenic freshwater sources rich in minerals, and there is an especially high concentration of these in the area known as 'The Nature Coast'. There is also an abundance of parkland and a whole series of sophisticated resorts. The region's natural allure and endless beaches betray no hint, however, of its rich and divergent cultural history. **Tarpon Springs**, for example, is a Mediterranean-style sponging village, which was founded in 1895. Sponge docks, Greek foods, festivals and 19th-century architecture still typify the town. On a larger scale, **Ybor City**, in the heart of Tampa, demonstrates the city's Hispanic roots with museums, bakeries and restaurants. A network of bridges, including the striking **Sunshine Skyway Bridge**, connects the scattered islands and peninsulas of the Gulf Coast.

CLIMATE: Central West Florida has a temperate climate with an average temperature of 22°C (71°F). With an average of 361 days of sunshine each year, the St Petersburg/Clearwater area enjoys an average temperature of 23°C (73°F). The annual average water temperature along the beaches is 24°C (75°F).

ST PETERSBURG/CLEARWATER: The St Petersburg/Clearwater area is located on Florida's West Coast, bordered on the east by Tampa Bay and on the west by the Gulf of Mexico. The area is best known for its constant sunshine and 56km (35 miles) of beaches. The **Pinellas peninsula** and its famous beaches are within minutes of Florida's popular attractions – just 30 minutes away is Busch Gardens in Tampa and 90 minutes away are Walt Disney World Vacation Kingdom, EPCOT Center, Sea World, Universal Studios Escape and other Central Florida sites.

St Petersburg is home to world-class museums, including the **Salvador Dali Museum**, which contains the world's most comprehensive collection by this famous Spanish surrealist; the **St Petersburg Museum of Fine Arts**, noted for its display of French Impressionist paintings; the **St Petersburg Museum of History**, which offers historical exhibits; the **Florida International Museum**, which was recently named a **Smithsonian Institution** affiliate and is home to the largest private collection of John F Kennedy memorabilia, including a recreation of JFK's Oval Office; and the relocated and expanded **Florida Holocaust Museum**. A US$12 million renovation of **The Pier** has turned this popular spot on the St Petersburg waterfront into a festival marketplace of shops, restaurants and entertainment, while **Bay Walk** boasts an open-air themed plaza, 20-screen theatre complex, restaurants and retail outlets. The **Florida Botanical Gardens** in **Largo** include Wedding, Tropical, Topiary and Jazz gardens, and are part of a new botanical learning centre where visitors can attend walking tours and workshops. Begun in 1998 and still being developed, the US$16 million, 250-acre project, when complete, will be Florida's largest gardens. The Gardens are adjacent to the **Gulf Coast Museum of Art and Heritage Village** and are the centrepiece of **Pinewood Cultural Park**, where culture, history and botany are combined.

Ideal parks for nature study, fishing, swimming and picnics are **Fort De Soto Park**, south of St Petersburg, plus the **Honeymoon Island State Recreation Area** and **Caladesi Island State Park** near **Dunedin**. All three are undeveloped barrier islands. Fort DeSoto and the Honeymoon Islands are connected to the mainland by causeways. Caladesi Island is ideal for swimming, fishing, picnics, snorkelling and scuba-diving, kayaking and guided nature walks. A 5km (3 mile) nature trail winds through the island's interior. It is accessible only by a ferry service, with departures from Honeymoon Island and **Clearwater**.

The **Pinellas Trail** is a 76km (47 mile) linear park, perfect for cyclists, walkers, joggers and rollerbladers. The **Suncoast Seabird Sanctuary**, in Indian Shores, is the largest wild bird hospital in North America. There are over 500 birds on site, including a large nesting colony of injured brown pelicans. Samples of marine life can be found at the **Clearwater Marine Aquarium**, a research centre that conducts a 'head start' programme for baby sea turtles and includes tanks containing numerous varieties of fish, as well as Sam, the bottlenose dolphin. **Celebration Station** in Clearwater is a mini-theme park and includes go-karts, bumper boats and more. *Clearwater Ferry Service* offers exciting boat trips, including *Dolphin Encounter* and *Caladesi Island Adventure*. The **Sea Screamer**, which is moored in Clearwater, is the world's largest speedboat. The 20 hectare (50 acre) **Moccasin Lake Nature Park** features a lake, upland forest, wetlands and most of the plant and animal species native to the area, as well as an environmental and energy education centre. At **Tarpon Springs**, attractions include the *Inness Paintings* exhibition at the Universalist Church, featuring a large collection of works by American landscape artist George Inness Sr; **Konger Coral Sea Aquarium**; and **St Nicholas Greek Orthodox Church**, a replica of St Sofia's in Constantinople.

TRAVEL: *St Petersburg-Clearwater International Airport (PIE)* is served by the carriers *Air Transat*, *American Trans Air*, *Can Jet*, *Con Quest*, *Jets Go*, *Seacoast*, *Sun Wing* and *USA 3000*, plus other charters from the USA and Canada with *Express One*, *Ryan International* and *US Airways*, especially during the winter season. St Petersburg is served by *Greyhound* bus services.

SPECIAL EVENTS: The following is a selection of special events occurring in St Petersburg and Clearwater in 2005:

Jan 29 *Pinellas Folk Festival*, Heritage Village. **Feb 24-27** *Greek Fest*, Tarpon Springs. **Mar 5-6** *Harbor Sounds Music Festival*, Safety Harbour. **Mar 11-13** *Cajun/Zydeco Crawfish Festival*, St Petersburg. **Mar 18-20** *Tampa Bay Blues Festival*, St Petersburg. **Mar 19** *DaliFest*, Salvador Dali Museum, St Petersburg. **Mar 19-21** *2005 Festival of Baseball*, Clearwater. **Apr 2-13** *Festival of States*, St Petersburg and Clearwater. **Jun 11-12** *Tampa Bay Caribbean Carnival*, St Petersburg. **Oct 13-16** *Clearwater Jazz Holiday* (four days of free concerts), Coachman Park, Clearwater. **Dec 24** *Light up the Bayou*, Tarpon Springs. **Dec 31** *First Night*, St Petersburg.

SARASOTA: The city of Sarasota is the cultural capital of Florida. The **Ringling Museum Complex**, the official **State Museum of Florida**, is a major attraction with superb old masterpieces and a fine contemporary collection. Sarasota's **Downtown Cultural District** contains the Sarasota **Opera House** (also home of the **Sarasota Ballet**) and numerous theatres and nightclubs. **Historic Palm Avenue**, filled with fine art, antiques, jewellery and fashion, was a bustling street in the early-1900s, frequented by Sarasota's founding families. Today, shopping emporia line **Palm Avenue** and the corner of Main Street. **Sarasota Quay** also offers a variety of speciality shops, as well as restaurants and nightclubs located on the water. Just minutes from the Quay and Palm Avenue, dinner cruises and charter boats depart from the stylish city marina.

North Lido Beach is a half-mile stretch of sand shaded by towering Australian pines. The public beach offers a swimming pool, a playground and shops. At the southern end of **Lido Key** are picnic tables, grills, a volleyball court and a playground. **St Armands Key** boasts a circle ringed by restaurants, nightclubs and exclusive shops. The **Circus Ring of Fame**, a sidewalk of circus stars, decorates the central park space.

Located between the waters of the Gulf of Mexico and Sarasota Bay, **Longboat Key** offers an abundance of outdoor activities. Anglers cast lines from Longboat's white sandy beaches, piers and jetties. Boaters can cruise to nearby islands such as **City Island**, which is the setting for the **Mote Marine Aquarium**. Next door to the aquarium, the **Pelican Man's Bird Sanctuary** is a rescue and rehabilitation centre for pelicans and other wild birds.

Siesta Key is best known for its sandy beaches, the widest and most popular in the county. A few miles south of the main beach, snorkellers flock to **Crescent Beach** where sea sponges and fish can be viewed under the Gulf's surface. The southernmost spot on Siesta Key is **Palmer Pointe South**, a popular getaway for boaters and hikers. More than 8 hectares (20 acres) of unspoiled beach make this one of the most beautiful spots in the Key.

Other attractions in Sarasota County include the **Gulf Coast World of Science**, where visitors can dig for fossils, touch live snakes and experiment with static electricity. There are 50 restored antique cars to view at **Bellm's Cars and Music of Yesterday** as well as 1200 music boxes and a penny arcade. **Marie Selby Botanical Gardens** specialises in air plants, orchids and colourful bromeliads. Ten lush tropical acres are filled with winding trails, beautiful gardens and exotic waterfowl at the **Sarasota Jungle Gardens**. There are also shows featuring snakes, turtles, alligators and other reptiles. **Myakka State Park and Wilderness Preserve** covers more than 14,000 hectares (35,000 acres) of wetlands, prairies and dense woodlands along the twisting **Myakka River** and **Upper Myakka Lake**. The park is home to hundreds of species of plants, trees and flowers. For a close-up view, visitors can take the boat or tram leaving from the *Boat Basin*. There are also numerous trails, a small natural history museum and a bird walk. **Oscar Scherer State Recreation Area** boasts streams for canoeing, a swimming lake, campsites, nature trails, cycling paths, a recreation hall and picnic areas. Visitors can discover Sarasota's past on **Little Sarasota Bay**, in **Osprey**. **Spanish Point**, which contains a late Victorian pioneer homestead, a Native American burial mound, a 19th-century chapel, cemetery and remnants of the formal gardens of a turn-of-the-century estate.

TRAVEL: The *Sarasota/Bradenton International Airport (SRQ)* (website: www.srq-airport.com), located 9.6km (6 miles) south of Sarasota and 16km (10 miles) north of Bradenton, is served by six major air carriers and two commuter airlines, including *Air France*, *Alitalia*, *American Trans Air*, *Delta*, *Northwest* and *US Airways*. Sarasota and Manatee counties provide public transport services from the airport approximately 12 hours per day. The buses are located at the west end of the baggage claim wing in the Ground Transportation area. Airport shuttle and taxi services are also available. Airport facilities include ATMs, a conference centre, a post office and car hire. *Greyhound* buses stop in downtown Sarasota, while *Amtrak*'s Thruway bus service connects its Tampa railway station with

Sarasota, stopping at the local bus terminal on Lemon Avenue. Public buses serving the beaches also stop here.
SPECIAL EVENTS: The following is a selection of special events occurring in Sarasota in 2005:
Jan 28-Feb 6 *Sarasota Film Festival.* **Feb 5** *Scottish Highland Games and Heritage Festival*, Sarasota.
Mar 20-26 *Sarasota Jazz Festival.* **Apr 8-10** *Venice Sharks Tooth Festival*, Venice Beach. **Jun 25-Jul 3** *The Suncoast Offshore Grand Prix Festival*, Sarasota. **Nov** *Sarasota Reading Festival; Sarasota Blues Festival.*
TAMPA: Tampa is one of the nation's fastest growing cities and largest ports, with thriving industries and artistic communities. The **Tampa Museum of Art** houses an impressive collection of ancient Greek and Roman items, as well as a series of changing exhibitions. The **Florida Aquarium** features interactive exhibits where visitors can learn about Florida's tropical sea life. Visitors can defy the laws of gravity in the *Challenger Space Experience* or stroll through the free-flying Butterfly Encounter at the **Museum of Science and Industry (MOSI)**. The *Amazing You* exhibition explores the human body, *Our Florida* focuses on environmental issues and *Our Place in the Universe* introduces guests to space travel. **Ybor City State Museum** traces the development of Ybor City, Tampa, the cigar industry and Cuban immigration. The **Henry B Plant Museum** includes Victorian furniture and Wedgwood pottery. **Busch Gardens** is a huge amusement park featuring African wildlife. Giraffes, zebras and antelope roam freely through the park's 24 hectare (60 acre) plain, next to thrilling rides such as the Kumba. There is also a 5 hectare (13 acre) water park, **Adventure Island**, just northeast of Busch Gardens.
TRAVEL: *Tampa International Airport (TPA)* (website: www.tampaairport.com), located west of the city Tampa (travel time - five minutes), and northeast of the St Petersburg/Clearwater area (travel time - 30 minutes), has been rated the nation's best for the past 10 years by the International Passenger Traffic Association. TPA is served by many airlines: *Air Canada, AirTran, American West, British Airways* (to London Gatwick), *Continental, Delta, Frontier, Jet Blue, Midwest Express, Northwest, Song, Southwest, Spirit, United, US Airways* and *US Airways Express*. Public buses to the Tampa are operated by Hillsborough Area Regional Transit (HART). For coaches and charter buses, the passenger pick-up and drop-off points are located in the bus spaces of the Commercial Ground Transportation Quadrants. Limousines, point-to-point shuttles, taxis and car hire are also available.
Amtrak trains stop at the station on Nebraska Avenue. Trains run to Jacksonville, Miami, New York City, Orlando and Philadelphia. A Thruway bus service operates from this station. A *Greyhound* bus service also stops in Tampa. *HART* local bus services make getting around the city and nearby sights and attractions easy.
SPECIAL EVENTS: The following is a selection of special events occurring in Tampa in 2005:
Jan 29 *Gasparilla Pirate Festival*, Downtown Tampa. **Feb 4-6** *Gasparilla Distance Classic* (running events), Tampa. **Feb 10-21** *Annual Florida State Fair*, Florida State Fairgrounds, Tampa. **Mar 5-6** *Gasparilla Festival of the Arts*, Tampa. **Apr 9-10** *AirFest 2005*, MacDill Airforce Base. **May 7-8** *Tomatoe Festival*, Ruskin. **Oct 29** *Guavaween* (parade, costume contest and concerts), Ybor City. **Nov 6-7** *Ruskin Seafood and Arts Festival.* **Nov 19** *Cigar Heritage Festival*, Ybor City.

Central Florida

The central region of Florida, which includes **Orlando**, is home to an enormous number of theme parks, entertainment facilities, resorts, movie studios and water parks. It is the face of Florida that most people recognise instantly. But Central Florida has another side, seen in the majestic **Ocala National Forest** and peaceful **Lake County**.
CLIMATE: Central Florida has warm sunny days and mild nights. The average monthly temperature is 24°C (75°F) in the winter and 35°C (95°F) in the summer. The average rainfall is 50 inches.
ORLANDO: Orlando is the one-stop vacation spot that offers more than 88,000 hotel rooms, 3000 restaurants and 66 attractions, which have established it as one of the world's favourite holiday spots. Orlando's attractions include hair-raising rides, nail-biting adventures and heart-pounding suspense. Thrill-seekers can experience the terrifying attack of a Great White shark on the *Jaws Ride* at **Universal Studios, Florida**, or take a sensual journey to the world's most wonderful seaside cities and discover the 'soul of the sea' at *The Waterfront*, SeaWorld Orlando's newest attraction. **Walt Disney World Resort** is the biggest, and arguably the best, amusement park in the world. It contains four sections: the **Magic Kingdom**, with seven theme regions; **Epcot Center**, a science and world exhibition centre; **Disney MGM Studios**, a movie and theme park; and **Animal Kingdom**, an adventure and safari park featuring wild animals, exotic landscapes and thrill rides. Popular attractions include a 13-storey free-fall plunge on the *Twilight Zone Tower of Terror* at Disney MGM Studios; Epcot's *Mission:SPACE*, which recreates space travel and pushes the boundaries of entertainment technology; and the *Stitch's Great Escape* at *Tomorrowland* in the Magic Kingdom.
Blizzard Beach, Disney's third and largest water park, is set in a faux snow-capped mountain range featuring Florida's only chairlift, which carries guests to the tip of *Mount Gushmore*. A number of water slides challenge visitors, including *Summit Plummet*, the tallest, fastest water slide in the world. More high-speed rides can be found at **Typhoon Lagoon**. *River Country*, in **Disney's Fort Wilderness Resort**, is a relaxing water park where holidaymakers can relax and enjoy the beautiful natural surroundings.
SeaWorld Orlando, southwest of Orlando (travel time - 19 minutes), is one of the country's largest marine parks and features whales, dolphins, sea lions, seals and otters. The most popular shows are the ones starring the killer whales, Shamu and Baby Namu.
Pleasure Island is a high-energy, nighttime entertainment complex featuring seven themed nightclubs, stage shows and live concerts, plus a giant New Year's Eve celebration every night of the week. It is located in an area known as **Downtown Disney**, along with such restaurants as *Wolfgang Puck, House of Blues* and the Cuban-style *Bongo's Cafe*.
Cultural attractions include the **Charles Hosmer Morse Museum of American Art**, which boasts the world's largest collection of Louis Tiffany glass. **Cornell Fine Arts Museum**, located at **Rollins College**, houses one of the largest and most distinguished art collections in Florida. Other popular sights include **Eatonville**, just north of Orlando, which is home to the **Zora Neale Hurston National Museum of Fine Arts**; the **Maitland Art Center**; Orlando Museum of Art; **Orange County Historical Museum**, which includes a renovated **1926 Orlando Firehouse**; and the **Albin Polasek Galleries**.
Other attractions in and around Orlando include **World of Orchids**, the first permanent indoor display of its kind in the world; **Church Street Station**, a block-long entertainment complex in the heart of central Orlando; **Gatorland**, in nearby **Kissimmee**; and **Wet 'n' Wild**, a water park offering numerous adventurous water activities.
TRAVEL: *Orlando International Airport (MCO)* (website: www.state.fl.us/goaa) is located within 24km (15 miles) of the major attractions and central Orlando.
Orlando Sanford Airport (SFB) is located 56km (35 miles) north of Orlando and handles a number of charter airlines. Shuttle buses and vans, taxis, limousines and rental cars are available from both airports.
SPECIAL EVENTS: The following is a selection of special events occurring in Orlando in 2005:
Feb 18-20 *115th Silver Spurs Rodeo*, Kissimmee. **Mar 4-6** *Kissimmee Kiwanis Bluegrass Festival.* **Apr 8-17** *Florida Film Festival*, Orlando. **Apr 2-3** *Spring Fiesta in the Park*, Orlando; *Arts in April* (month-long arts festival), Orlando. **Jul 4** *July Fourth Lakeside Celebrations*, Kissimmee and St Cloud. **Sep 30-Nov 13** *Epcot International Food and Wine Festival*, Orlando. **Oct** *Halloween Horror Nights*, Universal Studios. **Nov 25-Dec 30** *2005 Epcot Holidays around the World* (traditional event featuring daily tree-lighting ceremony, themed storytellers, and culminating in a candlelit procession). **Dec 10** *Kissimmee Holiday Extravaganza.*
ELSEWHERE: Located in the central highlands north of Orlando, **Lake County** boasts more than 1000 lakes offering fishing, boating and swimming opportunities. The area is noted for its scenic beauty of gentle hills dotted with orange groves and quiet country roads and parks framed by antique brick streets. Major attractions include the **Lakeridge Winery and Vineyard** which is open for tours and tastings all year round. The **House of Presidents Wax Museum** features the *White House in Miniature* exhibit. Other popular sights include the **Florida Citrus Tower**, **Uncle Donald's Farm**, **Trout Lake Nature Center** and **Wekia Falls Resort** in **Sorrento**. Recreational activities include water-skiing, in-line skating, swimming and cycling. **Seminole Lake** is home to the largest glider teaching school in Florida and is open to visitors who want to experience the joys of soaring.
The northern boundaries of Central Florida are engulfed by a national forest so large it needs to be administered by two separate ranger districts. The **Ocala National Forest** covers 378,178 acres, divided into three divergent recreation areas linked by a 106km (65 mile) trail. The town of **Ocala** boasts a 19th-century historic district, a major art museum and some 400 horse farms.

Central East Florida

This slender but significant region stretches from **Daytona Beach** in the north to **Stuart** in the south.
CLIMATE: Central East Florida has warm sunny days and mild nights. The average monthly temperature is 24°C (75°F) in the winter and 35°C (95°F) in the summer.

Credit: © Visit Florida

DAYTONA BEACH: The Daytona Beach area covers 37km (23 miles) along the Atlantic coast and at low tide offers a 150m (500ft) expanse of hard white sand. The beach first became well known in the 1930s and 1940s as a testing ground for the early pioneers of high-speed motor cars and it was here that Sir Malcolm Campbell set his 1935 land speed record - an amazing 444kph (276mph) run in his rocket-powered *Bluebird*. For a small charge visitors can still take their cars on part of the beach, but the top speed now allowed is just 16kmph (10mph). Real speed is confined to the **Daytona International Speedway**, which hosts the famous *Daytona 500* race each February. The *Pepsi 400 NASCAR Winston Cup Series* takes place in the summer. The speedway also houses a huge collection of racing memorabilia and early racing films and conducts 30-minute tours on days with no races. Other attractions include the huge **Daytona Flea and Farmers Market**, open Friday to Sunday; the **Harbour Marina**; and the **Ocean Center**, which hosts top entertainers, sporting events and conventions. Historical sights include **The Casements**, the former home of John D Rockefeller; **Gamble Place**, a historical and nature preserve; **Ponce de Leon Inlet Lighthouse**; and **Sugar Mill Gardens**, a large botanical garden and dinosaur park.
TRAVEL: Flights into Daytona arrive at the *Daytona Beach International Airport (DAB)* (website: www.flydaytonafirst.com). *Greyhound* buses come and go from 138 South Ridgewood Avenue, four minutes west of the beach. *Voltran Transit Co* operates local buses in the area.
SPECIAL EVENTS: The following is a selection of special events occurring in Daytona Beach in 2005:
Feb 5-20 *Speed Weeks.* **Mar 14-13** *Bike Week.* **Mar 14-31** *Spring Break.* **Mar 18-20** *Spring Daytona Beach Car Show and Swap Meet.* **Apr 15-17** *Black College Reunion.* **Jul 2** *Pepsi 400 NASCAR Winston Cup.* **Oct 20-23** *Biketoberfest.* **Nov** *Halifax Art Festival.* **Nov 24-27** *Daytona Turkey Run* (car show and swap meet). **Nov 25-26** *Birthplace of Speed Celebration.*
NEW SMYRNA BEACH: South of Daytona Beach is New Smyrna Beach. Billed as the 'World's Safest Bathing Beach', it is also the beach closest to the popular Orlando area and Central Florida attractions and an attraction in itself. Only a short drive from Orlando and Daytona Beach International Airports, New Smyrna Beach lays claim to the best Florida offers - excellent backwater fishing, fresh seafood and seasons of sunshine. As the second-oldest settled city in Florida, **New Smyrna** offers visitors tours of several historical sites and museums. Also named one of the 'Top Small Cities for the Arts', this coastal town houses the **Atlantic Center for the Arts**, an artists-in-residence community, and many other galleries and exhibits. **New Smyrna Beach** is 21.2 km (13.2 miles) of white sand and continues into the largest section of **Canaveral National Seashore Park** and **Mosquito Lagoon** where backwater fishing for giant Redfish have set international angler records. Canaveral Seashore Park offers miles of pristine beaches, bird watching, kayaking and hiking for the adventurous traveller. Affordable accommodations range from motels to oceanfront hotels, condominiums and bed & breakfast inns.
SPACE COAST: South of New Smyrna Beach at Titusville is the start of the '**Space Coast**', a 115km (72 mile) stretch of beach which leads down to **Palm Bay**.
The main attraction here is **Cape Canaveral** in the **Titusville** area - home of the US Space Program. All of NASA's shuttle flights take off from the **Kennedy Space Center**. The **Kennedy Space Center Visitor Complex** runs continuous tours of the complex where visitors see the actual launchpads and astronaut training centres as well as museums and exhibits. IMAX presentations give visitors the illusion of space travel. Tours take in the **Apollo/ Saturn Visitors' Center**, the **Launch Complex 39 Observation Gantry** and the **International Space Station Center**, which highlight the past, present and future of the USA's Space Program. Visitors should plan to spend at least an

Credit: © Visit Florida

hour at each of these facilities.
The **Astronauts' Hall of Fame**, a few kilometres from the Kennedy Space Center offers a self-guided tour through the early days of space exploration, focusing on the *Mercury 7* and *Gemini* astronauts. A virtual reality trainer and shuttle simulator make this a hands-on exhibit. The **Valiant Air Command Warbird Museum** displays historical military aircraft.
The **Canaveral National Seashore** is an unspoilt area of beaches and sand dunes where the giant loggerhead and green turtles come ashore in summer to lay their eggs. The marshy **Merritt Island National Wildlife Refuge** is home to more endangered species than any other refuge in the USA and features deer, sea turtles, alligators, eagles and excellent walking tracks. **Port Canaveral** is America's second-busiest cruise passenger port. The National Historic District of **Main Street Titusville** boasts many fine 18th- and 19th-century buildings. This charming area also contains antique shops, restaurants, a playhouse and more. The 7000-seat **Space Coast Stadium** in **Viera** is the spring training home of Major League Baseball's Florida Marlins; games are played from March to September. **Cocoa Beach** is a popular resort famed for surfing and a lively nightlife. **Cocoa Beach Pier** stretches 256 metres (800ft) into the Atlantic Ocean, offering exceptional fishing and views. The central shopping area has been recreated as **Olde Cocoa Village**. **Astronaut Memorial Hall and Planetarium** features memorabilia, astronomical multimedia programmes on a 360° domed ceiling, and a public-access space telescope.
Brevard Zoo features jaguars, llamas, anteaters, monkeys, exotic birds and other Latin American animals. The **Brevard Museum of History and Natural Science** traces the origins of Brevard County and the **Brevard Museum of Art and Science** hosts major touring art exhibitions. The **Melbourne/Palm Bay** area is near the largest sea turtle nesting area in the USA, which stretches from **Spessard Holland Park**, south to **Sebastian Inlet**. Turtles come ashore from May to August and hatchlings struggle back to the ocean until late October. *Turtle walks* are offered on Space Coast beaches. Perched on the southern tip of the island, the 30m (90ft) **Merritt Island Dragon** is a concrete and steel sculpture inspired by a local legend. Melbourne's historic centre features galleries, boutiques, restaurants and antique stores. The **Henegar Center** is the oldest building in the area, and has varied theatrical offerings throughout the year, while the **Maxwell C King Center** is the hub of area's cultural life.
TRAVEL: *Melbourne International Airport (MLB)* (website: www.mlbair.com) serves Brevard County and the Space Coast. Car hire is available and the airport runs a shuttle service throughout several counties.
SPECIAL EVENTS: The following is a selection of special events occurring in Central East Florida in 2005:
Mar *Florida Marlins Profile Baseball Spring Training*, Space Coast Stadium, Melbourne. **Mar 11-13** *Seafest*, Cape Canaveral. **May-Sep** *Sea Turtle Nesting Season.*

South West Florida

Florida's Southwest coast lies along the shores of the Gulf of Mexico and much of the area's charm and island ambience comes from the multitude of barrier islands sprinkled along the coastline. It has the feel of 'Old Florida', with a relaxed, subtropical, island-style environment. In addition to the many parks and wildlife refuges in the region, there is an abundance of recreational activities: beachcombing, canoeing, golf, windsurfing, biking, tennis, boating, fishing, water-skiing and just plain sightseeing. The first tourist to visit Florida's Lee Island Coast was Spanish explorer Ponce de Leon, who deposited his stone marker on Pine Island in 1513 and was later mortally wounded in these same waters by a Calusa Indian arrow. Shell mounds, which have provided an insight into the lives of these seafaring Native Americans, can still be found on Pine Island.
TRAVEL: *Southwest Florida International Airport (RSW)* (website: www.swfia.com) offers non-stop and connecting flights across the USA and Canada, provided by all the major US and Canadian airlines. Major European destinations are easily accessible via connections through a number of US hubs, and services are available from France, Germany, Sweden and the UK (travel time – approximately eight hours). Airport facilities include long-term and short-term parking, a visitor information centre (provided by the Lee Island Coast Visitor & Convention Bureau) and car rental. *Lee Tran* buses run between 0600 and 2200. Another bus service is provided on an hourly basis to a transfer point located at Daniels Parkway and US State Highway 41. Connections can be made from that point to the remainder of the Lee Tran bus routes.
SPECIAL EVENTS: The following is a selection of special events occurring in Southwest Florida in 2005:
Jan 29-Feb 20 *Edison Festival of Light*, Fort Myers. **Mar 3-5** *68th Annual Sanibel Shell Fair & Show*, Sanibel Island. **Mar 19** *16th Annual Sounds of Jazz*, Cape Coral. **Apr 21-24** *Fort Myers Beach Film Festival*. **Apr 24** *A Taste of the Islands*, Sanibel Island. **May 14-15** *Fort Myers Beach Air Show*. **May 21** *Freedom Fest 2005*, Cape Coral. **Jun 5** *Annual Fort Myers Beach 'Taste of the Beach' Festival*. **Jul 4** *Independence Day Celebrations*, Fort Myers and Sanibel Island. **Aug 6-7** *Fort Myers Beach Offshore Fishing Rodeo*. **Oct 6** *Island Expo 2005*, Fort Myers. **Oct 28-30** *Oktoberfest*, Cape Coral. **Nov 9-13** *19th Annual American Sandsculpting Championship*, Fort Myers.
SANIBEL & CAPTIVA ISLANDS: Unspoiled yet luxurious, **Sanibel Island** is connected to the mainland by a scenic causeway that spans the waters of **Pine Island Sound**. Sanibel is probably best known for the fabulous shells found on its shores, but the reputation of its beaches is growing. Sanibel's main thoroughfare, **Periwinkle Way**, is picturesque, lush with jungle and framed by a canopy of Australian pines. Interesting shops and unique restaurants dot the road from the **Sanibel Lighthouse** to **Tarpon Bay Road**. A variety of eateries offer everything from fine dining to casual seafood bars. Two attractions not to be missed are **Lighthouse Park** and the **J N 'Ding' Darling National Wildlife Refuge**, occupying more than a third of the island. The refuge features delightful footpaths, winding canoe trails and an 8km (5 mile) scenic drive, all of which are surrounded with sea grape, wax and salt myrtles, red mangrove, palms and other native plant varieties. Naturalists will get their best view of the wide variety of fauna and flora from observation towers strategically placed throughout the nature sanctuary.
A short span at Blind Pass joins Sanibel to **Captiva**, an intimate hideaway where Spanish pirate José Gaspar held his female prisoners captive. Several barrier islands are accessible from Captiva by boat. Other excursions include a shelling tour to **Upper Captiva** or a visit to the **Cayo Costa State Island Preserve**.
FORT MYERS & AREA: The city of **Fort Myers** is perhaps best known for its palm-lined boulevards and Thomas Alva Edison's winter home. Edison spent 46 winters in his old-Florida-style home, a tour of which provides an insightful look at this great inventor. His home, laboratory and experimental gardens are located on 14 acres of land on the **Caloosahatchee River**. For 24km (15 miles), McGregor Boulevard is lined on both sides with statuesque royal palm trees, the first 200 of which were imported from Cuba and planted by Thomas Edison.
The Caloosahatchee separates Fort Myers from **Cape Coral**, a boating community with more canals than Venice, Italy. In addition to the Edison Home, visitors to Fort Myers, Cape Coral and the neighbouring towns of **North Fort Myers**, **Lehigh** and **Bonita Springs** can enjoy a visit to **Henry Ford's home**, the **Lee County Nature Center** and **The Shell Factory**.
Fishing is a popular pastime in Southwest Florida. The waters are teeming with fish, from delicious red snappers and grouper to game fish such as snook and tarpon. A short boat ride away, and connected to the mainland by a short causeway near Punta Gorda, is **Boca Grande**, a slice of 'Old Florida' on **Gasparilla Island**. Long known as a playground for the wealthy, this quaint, sleepy town is a favourite spot for sport fishing – tarpon is a popular catch here. Further south are **Estero Island** and **Fort Myers Beach**, ideal for family holidays with its safe, gently sloping shoreline and numerous activities.
Golf aficionados will appreciate the fact that Southwest Florida has more golf holes per capita than any other destination in the USA.
NAPLES: Naples is a charming city with an atmosphere of understated elegance. Home to cosy beach cottages and 5-star resorts, Naples is also known for its pristine shoreline and abundant wildlife.
Both the ambience and the scenery are serene, thanks to the easygoing demeanour of the Neapolitans and the city's meticulously maintained thoroughfares, parks and shopping areas. A stroll along Fifth Avenue South and Third Street South's tree-lined avenues in 'Olde Naples' reveals a variety of gift boutiques, antique emporia, apparel shops and art galleries, as well as a range of cafes and restaurants. The **Old Marine Market Place** at **Tin City** on **Naples Bay** reflects Neapolitan history at a time when the area supplied fresh fish from tin-roofed warehouses. Not far away, **The Village on Venetian Bay** is reminiscent of a Mediterranean plaza with winding waterways and walkways. At **Waterside Shops**, cascading waterfalls are the central point for major retailers, clothiers and galleries. The **Caribbean Gardens Zoological Park** offers 21 hectares (53 acres) of rare, endangered animals and tropical gardens. At the **Teddy Bear Museum**, almost 3000 bears in every shape and size are whimsically arranged.
Naples boasts more than 53 golf courses. Professional tournaments such as the *PGA Greater Naples Intellinet Golf Challenge* and the *Florida Senior Open* take place throughout the year. Tennis is a close second to golf and Naples offers community courts in a park-like setting just blocks away from the beach.
Wildlife is also plentiful in the Naples area. Numerous venues afford ample opportunities to view endangered species such as the manatee, the American bald eagle, and the North American wood stork. Nature lovers will enjoy a real view of Old Florida along two miles of scenic boardwalks in the National Audubon Society's **Corkscrew Swamp Sanctuary**.
South of Naples is **Collier Seminole State Park**, featuring guided boat tours through mangrove forests along the **Blackwater River**.
MARCO ISLAND & THE SOUTHWEST: South of Naples is **Marco Island**, located at the southernmost tip of Florida's **Gulf Coast** and nearly lost amongst the **Ten Thousand Islands**, a maze of mangrove isles that stretch from Naples to the Florida Keys. It is an area of stunning beauty. Marco Island, the largest and only inhabited isle, is a retreat for the wealthy.
Its pampered perfection complements the tangled wildness and sweeping sawgrass prairies of Florida's famous **Everglades National Park**, which lies only an hour away. The Everglades is the USA's third-largest national park. Several excursions offer a glimpse of the country's only subtropical region, by means of airboat tours, nature trails and safari vans. The unassuming fishing hamlets of **Everglades City** and **Chokoloskee Island**, both locked in time, offer visitors an interactive eco-adventure in the inspirational beauty of Florida's final frontier. For information on the eastern areas of the Everglades, see the *Southeast Florida and the Keys* section.

South East Florida and the Keys

Southeast Florida is home to one of the USA's most international cities – Greater Miami – which offers a rich array of exotic cuisine, nightlife, festivals, shopping, attractions, arts and architecture. Once strictly a winter resort, the area is now a year-round holiday destination for tourists from all over the world. The vibrant life of the coastal area provides a startling contrast to the **Everglades National Park**, which stretches across a large portion of southern Florida. The USA's only subtropical region, this expanse of wetlands is within easy reach of the main cities in Southeast Florida (for information on the western areas of the Everglades, see the *Southwest Florida* section).
Stretching from **Key Largo** at the northern end to **Key West** in the south, 45 of the over 800 islands of the **Florida Keys**, once known as the Cayos, are linked by Overseas Highway 1.
CLIMATE: Greater Miami and the Beaches' subtropical climate ensures plentiful sunshine all year round. There is sufficient rainfall during the summer and early autumn. Virtually all buildings are air conditioned. In fact, a light sweater or jacket is advisable to take the chill off the indoor climates. The powerful rays of the sun also make it a good idea to wear a hat or protective sunscreen when planning to be outdoors for long periods.
MIAMI: Today, Greater Miami is an international crossroads of commerce, culture, sports, entertainment, transport and tourism. This cosmopolitan city boasts beautiful beaches, right next to one of the USA's most vibrant urban centres. Often called the 'City of the Future', Miami contains dramatic skyscrapers, modern hotels and an international financial district. Greater Miami is famed for conch fritters, black beans and rice, cowbells and castanets, salsa and compas, jig and rumba. It offers a unique blend of 21st century and Old World architecture, sports facilities and sunbathing opportunities, big-city culture and small-town neighbourhoods.
The **American Airlines Arena**, a distinctive, neon-lit addition to Miami's futuristic skyline, has emerged as a focal point for the city's renaissance. This home for the

Miami Heat basketball team is across from the new **Miami-Dade Performing Arts Center**. Ornamented by a parade of palm trees, **Brickell Avenue**'s towers of mirrored glass and steel command some of the area's most coveted views of the Atlantic Ocean and **Biscayne Bay**. **Bayside Marketplace** is a restaurant, shopping and entertainment complex on the bay. Nearby, the **Metro-Dade Cultural Center** is a Mediterranean-style complex housing the **Center for the Fine Arts**, the **Historical Museum of Southern Florida** and one of the largest libraries in the southeast.

Trips across the half dozen causeways that span Biscayne Bay are short and scenic, connecting mainland Miami to the seaside attractions. **Bal Harbor**, **Surfside**, **Sunny Isles**, **Key Biscayne** and **Miami Beach** are minutes from the heart of the city.

MIAMI BEACH: Renovated hotels along **Ocean Drive** and throughout the **Art Deco District** have captured national praise for the Art Deco, Streamline Moderne and Spanish Mediterranean Revival styles which dominate the 1 sq mile area. Just north of the **Art Deco Historic District**, multi-million dollar restorations have transformed many of the well-known hotels along **Collins Avenue**. The striking new architecture of the recently expanded **Miami Beach Convention Center** makes it an instant landmark. The updated and hip **Lincoln Road Mall** is a hub of the arts and entertainment: the street now houses the **South Florida Arts Center**, the **Colony Theatre** and the headquarters of *MTV Latino*, the *New World Symphony* and *Sony Latin America*.

At the southernmost tip of Miami Beach, **South Pointe Park** offers an ideal vantage point to watch luxury cruise ships make their way out to sea. Boat watching is also a favourite pastime at the **International Yacht Harbor**, one of the largest marinas in South Florida. All year round, the warm sand, azure waters and pleasant breezes of Miami Beach beckon sunbathers, picnickers and outdoor diners.

ELSEWHERE: Biscayne National Park offers glass-bottomed boat rides through mangroves and islands and out to tropical coral reefs rising 8m (25ft). **Miami Metrozoo** represents state-of-the-art zoo design, with exotic animals in habitats very similar to their original homes in the wild. **Miccosukee Indian Village**, west of Miami, shows how this Native American tribe existed (and still exists) in the heart of the Florida Everglades. The **Monkey Jungle** gives visitors the chance to see North America's first colony of wild monkeys in lush tropical jungle surroundings. **Vizcaya**, south of central Miami on Biscayne Bay, is a beautiful 70-room Italian Renaissance-style palace set in 10 acres of picturesque formal gardens. The **Miami Museum of Science & Space Transit Planetarium** has many attractions, including a laser show. With over 3000 exotic animals, 500 species of plants and the largest crocodile in captivity, **Parrot Jungle Island** opened in June 2003, after its US$47 million relocation to Watson Island, mid way between Miami and South Beach, off the MacArthur Causeway.

TRAVEL: *Miami International Airport (MIA)* (website: www.miami-airport.com), located 7 miles from central Miami, ranks 12th in the USA for total passenger traffic, with approximately 30 million travellers passing through its portals annually. Parking at the airport is simplified by a state-of-the-art people-mover system that connects the parking areas to the main airport terminal via moving walkways. Airlines serving the airport include *Air Canada*, *Air France*, *American Airlines*, *British Airways*, *Continental* and *Delta Airlines*. *Miami Air International* is an upmarket charter airline specialising in cruise travellers, and incentive and corporate travel. *Supershuttle* offers easy, door-to-door transport to and from the airport. Customer service representatives are on call 24 hours a day and are located outside the airport baggage claims area. More than 19 of the 63 Dade County routes serve Greater Miami and the Beaches every day, as well as the Miami Seaquarium, the Orange Bowl Stadium, the Cultural Centre and Metrozoo.

SPECIAL EVENTS: The following is a selection of special events occurring in Miami in 2005:
Jan 14-16 *Art Deco Weekend*, Miami Beach. **Feb 4-13** *Miami Film Festival*. **Feb 17-21** *Miami International Boat Show*, Miami Beach. **Feb 19-21** *Coconut Grove Arts Festival*. **Feb 24-27** *Coral Gables Bluefest*, Coral Gables. **Feb 25-27** *South Beach Wine and Food Festival*, Miami. **Mar** *Carnaval Miami*, Little Havana. **Apr 22-May 1** *Miami Gay and Lesbian Film Festival*. **May 8-9** *Great Sunrise Balloon Race and Festival*, Miami. **Jun** *Goombay Festival*, Coconut Grove. **Jun 3-6** *South Florida Boat Show*, Miami Beach. **Nov-Jan 2006** *Santa's Enchanted Forest*, Tropical Park, Miami.

FORT LAUDERDALE: **Greater Fort Lauderdale** is one of the premier tourism destinations in South Florida. During the 1920s, this sleepy outpost boomed when real estate speculators dredged the Everglades, forming irrigation canals and creating the 'Venice of America'. Brick-paved pedestrian promenades, columned porticos and hundreds of new palm trees make the city's famed beachfront strip one of the best in the USA. In total, there are 23 miles of beach front, 300 miles of inland waterways and 3500 restaurants.

Riverwalk, a linear park, links hotels, restaurants and attractions along the banks of the **New River**, leading to the **Broward Center for the Performing Arts**. Water taxis ply Fort Lauderdale's canals and the **Intracoastal Waterway**.

Opportunities to explore the natural world in Greater Fort Lauderdale include **Butterfly World**, dedicated to the study, care and display of beautiful butterflies from all over the globe; **Flamingo Gardens**; the **Water Taxi**; and the **Museum of Discovery & Science**. The **Secret Woods Nature Center** features wetlands, mangrove swamps and numerous plant and animal communities. It is possible to ride an airboat through the Everglades at **Sawgrass Recreation Park** or **Everglades Holiday Park**. The **Old Fort Lauderdale Village & Museum** is a historic village in the centre of Fort Lauderdale, comprising the 1905 **New River Inn** (housing the museum), the 1905 **Philemon Bryan House** (the administrative offices of the Fort Lauderdale Historical Society), the 1907 **King-Cromartie House** (museum) and the **Replica 1899 Schoolhouse**. The new **Hoch Heritage Center** is due to open in 2005. The Society produces exhibits on the area's development, the history of sports in South Florida, regional architecture, Seminole Indian culture and even a silent movie theatre. The **Ah-Tah-Thi-Ki Museum**, on the **Seminole Indian Reservation**, includes profiles of historic leaders, artefacts, traditional crafts, toys and jewellery exhibits.

The **Von D Mizell Library** is just one of several attractions in **Broward County** with important affiliations to the African-American community. Displays feature the black heritage of Broward County, especially authors and artists, as well as memorabilia of Dr Mizell, one of the area's first African-American doctors. **Bonnet House** is a historical estate of 14 hectares (35 acres) that reflects the history of South Florida. The waterfront estate includes a plantation-style house, art gallery, a bamboo bar and shell museum and eight outbuildings.

Other attractions include **Stranahan House**, the home of the area's first ferryman, Frank Stranahan, and the **Graves Museum of Archaeology & Natural History** with exhibits on the Tequesta Indians of South Florida, as well as ancient Egypt and the Near East, marine archaeology, pre-Hispanic Americas and the Carole Jacobs Mineral Collection. Boats can be hired from **Bahia Mar Marina** or visitors can hop aboard *The Jungle Queen*, a paddleboat. Also in the area is Sawgrass **Mills Mall**, the world's largest designer outlet mall, which features over 275 speciality shops.

TRAVEL: *Fort Lauderdale/Hollywood International Airport (FLL)* (website: www.fll.net) is located in Fort Lauderdale. It is served by 24 airlines including *Air Canada*, *Air Jamaica*, *American Airlines*, *Continental*, *Delta*, *TWA* and *United*.

SPECIAL EVENTS: The following is a selection of special events occurring in Fort Lauderdale in 2005:
Feb 4-6 *Fiesta Tropicale* (South Florida's Mardi Gras). **Feb 12-Mar 13** *13th Annual Florida Renaissance Festival*, Deerfield Beach. **Apr** *Fort Lauderdale Seafood Festival*, Smoker Park. **Nov** *19th Annual Sound Advice Blues Festival*, Fort Lauderdale.

PALM BEACH: This is a popular hang-out of the rich and famous, who spend their days buying jewellery in Cartier on **Worth Avenue** or sipping iced-tea at the polo matches. The resort is also home to the **Henry Morrison Flagler Museum**, a tribute to the railroad mogul who established the area as an exclusive holiday destination by laying out the opulent palm-lined boulevards. Other attractions in the area include the **Burt Reynolds Ranch & Film Studios**, a 68 hectare (168 acre) ranch featuring a mini-petting farm, gift shop and museum; the **Rapids Water Park**, with four gigantic waterslides; the **Sailfish Marine and Lion Country Safari Park**, with more than 1000 wild animals, free boat cruises, miniature golf and a dinosaur and reptile park; and the **International Museum of Cartoon Art** has a permanent collection which includes 100,000 original drawings, 10,000 books and hundreds of hours of film and videotape. Other museums in the area are the **Children's Museum of Boca Raton**, **South Florida Science Museum** and **Morikami Museum & Japanese Gardens**.

West of Palm Beach is **Lake Okeechobee**, the second-largest lake in the USA, celebrated for its large-mouth bass fishing.

SPECIAL EVENTS: The following is a selection of special events occurring in Palm Beach in 2005:
Jan 15-30 *South Florida Fair*. **Mar 17-20** *Palm Beach Boat Show*. **Apr 27-May 1** *Sunfest*, West Palm Beach.

THE KEYS: From Miami to **Key West** is only 45 minutes

Credit: © Visit Florida

by air. The first Key from Miami is **Key Largo**, the longest island of the Keys chain and the site where Humphrey Bogart and Lauren Bacall battled with both Edward G Robinson and the elements in the movie *Key Largo*.

Key Largo's star attractions are **John Pennekamp Coral Reef State Park** – the first underwater preserve in the USA – and the adjacent **Key Largo National Marine Sanctuary**. These two refuges feature 55 varieties of delicate corals and almost 500 different species of fish. Key Largo also features the world's only **underwater hotel**, where guests can spend the evening in the midst of the marine life of the Keys. **Islamorada** is the centrepiece of a group of islands called '**The Purple Isles**' that includes **Plantation Keys**, **Windley Key** and both **Upper Matecumbe Key** and **Lower Matecumbe Key**. Known as the 'Sportfishing Capital of the World', Islamorada is famed for its angling opportunities and features the Keys' largest fleet of offshore charterboats and shallow water 'backcountry' boats. The Keys boast more sportfishing world records than any other fishing destination in the world. Anglers can find sailfish, marlin, kingfish, snapper, barracuda and grouper. **Long Key State Park** has nature trails leading to tropical hummocks and **Grassy Key** is the site of the **Dolphin Research Center**. **Marathon**, heart of the Florida Keys, and neighbouring **Key Colony Beach**, boast 18- and 9-hole golf courses respectively. It is also home to **Crane Point Hammock**, a 26 hectare (63.5 acre) land tract that is one of the most important historical and archaeological sites in the Keys. The area contains evidence of pre-Columbian and prehistoric Bahamian artefacts and was once the site of a Native American village. At Crane Point is the **Museum of Natural History of the Florida Keys** and the **Florida Keys Children's Museum**, which explores the islands' rich natural history. **Big Pine Key** is noted for the **Looe Key National Marine Sanctuary**, a national refuge for miniature Key deer, tropical forests and even a few alligators in the **Blue Hole**.

Ernest Hemingway purchased a pre-Civil War mansion in Key West and lived in it for 10 years while writing some of his best-known novels. His legend remains and visitors continue to seek out his home – now a museum – and his favourite bar. In the evening, visitors gather at **Mallory Square** to 'call it a day'. The daily 'Sunset Celebration' is a tradition that Key Westers share with visitors. While musicians, jugglers, mime artists and an occasional fire-eater provide the entertainment, the sun sinks slowly below the horizon.

SPECIAL EVENTS: The following is a selection of special events occurring in The Keys in 2005:
Jan 29-30 *20th Annual Key West Craft Show*. **Feb 12-13** *11th Annual Pigeon Key Art Festival*, Marathon. **Mar 19-20** *32nd Annual Original Marathon Seafood Festival*, Marathon. **Apr 22-May 1** *23rd Conch Republic Independence Day Celebration*, Key West. **Apr 23-24** *Annual 7 Mile Bridge Run*, Marathon. **May 11-15** *Key West Songwriters Festival*. **Jun 13-18** *Cuban American Heritage Festival*, Key West. **Jul 9** *21st Annual Underwater Music Festival*, Big Pine Key. **Jul 18-24** *Hemingway Days Festival*, Key West. **Jul 20-23** *Drambuie Key West Marlin Tournament* (in conjunction with the Hemingway Days Festival). **Oct 21-30** *27th Annual Fantasy Fest*, Key West. **Nov 13-20** *Key West Offshore World Championships* (powerboat racing). **Dec 31** *New Year's Eve Celebrations*, Key West.

Social Profile

FOOD & DRINK: Miami/Miami Beach: There are more than 300 fine restaurants, and most hotels maintain excellent dining rooms. Some gourmet eateries are expensive but many popular restaurants have economy prices. Cuban and Mexican food is very popular in Miami, and because Florida is surrounded almost entirely by water, seafood is a State speciality. Fresh stone crabs are not available anywhere else in the USA. **Orlando**: International Drive is the centre of a variety of restaurants that include Chinese, tapas, Cuban, Asian/Pacific rim and even fondue. **Tampa**: There is a clear emphasis on Latin cuisine in Tampa but all tastes are catered for, with everything from international restaurants to fast food.
NIGHTLIFE: Miami/Miami Beach: Nightclubs exist in most hotels and resorts. The Coconut Grove area, with its trendy nightclubs and cocktail bars, offers a swinging nightlife both inside the clubs and on the streets where many people just come for a stroll, in order to be where the action is. The most lavish and lively clubs are Cuban supper clubs. *Les Folies* and *Les Violons*, both on Biscayne Boulevard, are highly recommended and feature spectacular shows and excellent food. **Tampa:** The best nightlife on the Gulf Coast can be found in Ybor City, which is Tampa's lively and historic Latin quarter. The action centres on Seventh Avenue, which closes to traffic at weekends to allow the party atmosphere to spill out on to the streets.
SHOPPING: Miami: The city's main shopping streets are *Flagler Street*, between Biscayne Bay and Miami Avenue; and *Biscayne Boulevard*, between Flagler Street and north to 16th Street. Luxury and designer shops can be found at *Village of Merrick Park* in Coral Gables, south of Miami. **Miami Beach:** The principal shopping area is *Lincoln Road Mall*. Just north of Miami Beach is the *Bal Harbour Shopping District*. **Fort Lauderdale:** The famous *Sawgrass Mills Factory Outlet Mall* is located on the northwest edge of the city and many boutiques can be found near the waterfront. **Tampa:** The main shopping area is around *Franklin Street Mall*. **Orlando:** Shoppers can take advantage of a huge range of retail outlets from factory outlet malls such as *Lake Buena Vista Factory Stores* to designer malls such as *Orlando Premium Outlets* and the *Mall at Millenia*.
SPORT: Florida's sports opportunities are endless. **Greyhound-racing** is held in Bonita Springs, Daytona Beach, Fort Lauderdale, Jacksonville, the Keys, Miami, Orange Lake, Palm Beach, Pensacola, Sarasota, St Petersburg and Tampa. **Harness-racing** is popular in Pompano and thoroughbred **horse racing** in Fort Lauderdale, Miami and Tampa. Other spectator sports include professional **basketball**, played in Miami at the *American Airlines Arena*; professional **football**, with the *Miami Dolphins* playing at the *Pro Player Stadium* in Miami and the *Tampa Bay Buccaneers* team in Tampa; and **polo**, played at the *Palm Beach Polo and Country Club*. Other sports on offer include **golf**, **tennis**, **fishing**, **boat-racing**, **motorcar-racing**, **rodeo**, **baseball**, **diving** and **sailing**. Hunting and fishing licenses are sometimes required by persons over 16 years of age; check with the Florida Fish and Wildlife Conservation Commission (website: www.floridaconservation.org). For further information and brochures on any of the above-listed sports, contact the Florida Sports Foundation, 2930 Kerry Forest Parkway, Tallahassee, FL 32309 (tel: (850) 488 8347; fax: (850) 922 0482; e-mail: info@flasports.com; website: www.flasports.com).
THEATRE & CONCERTS: Miami/Miami Beach: The best known theatres include the *Theater of Performing Arts* at Miami Beach Convention Center Complex and *Coconut Grove Playhouse*, which plays major Broadway hits. The Concert Association of Florida books many major stars; their shows are usually staged at Dade County or Miami Beach Auditoria. **Fort Lauderdale:** *Parker Playhouse* was created by Zev Buffman, owner of the Coconut Grove Playhouse, and shows usually move on from there to the Parker. The *Sunrise Music Theater* often features big-name performers.

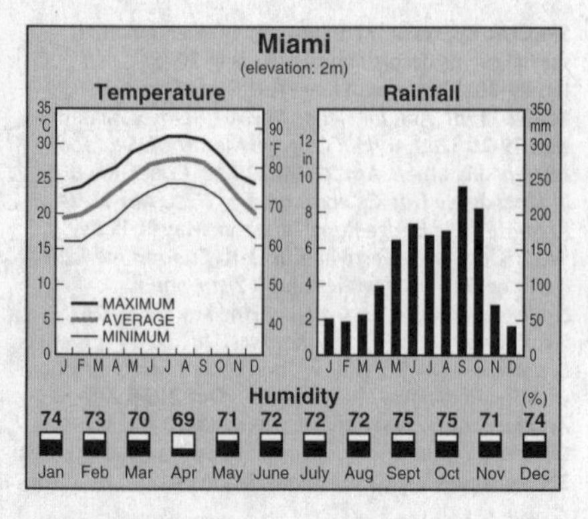

Georgia

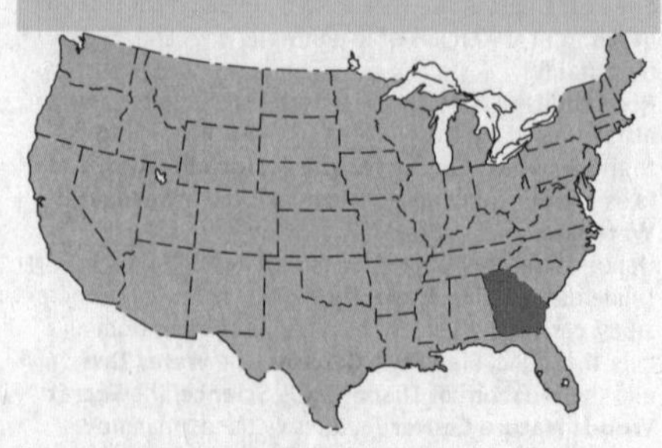

Georgia Department of Economic Development
Street address: Tourism Division, 75 Fifth Street NW, Suite 1200, Atlanta, GA 30308
Postal address: Tourism Division, PO Box 1776, Atlanta, GA 30301
Tel: (404) 962 4000 *or* (800) 847 4842 (toll-free).
Fax: (404) 962 4009.
Website: www.georgiaonmymind.org *or* www.georgia.org
Department of Tourism (UK Office)
c/o Lofthouse Enterprises, 22 Lulworth Close, Bewbush, Crawley, Sussex RH11 8XS, UK
Tel: (01293) 560 848. Fax: (01462) 440 783.
E-mail: anne-young.georgia@virgin.net
Website: www.georgiaonmymind.org
Atlanta CVB
233 Peachtree Street NE, Suite 100, Atlanta, GA 30303
Tel: (404) 521 6600 *or* (800) 285 2682 (toll-free).
Fax: (404) 577 3293.
E-mail: info@atlanta.net
Website: www.atlanta.net
Athens CVB
300 North Thomas Street, Athens, GA 30601
Tel: (706) 357 4430 *or* (800) 653 0603 (toll-free).
Fax: (706) 546 8040.
E-mail: tourinfo@visitathensga.com
Website: www.visitathensga.com
Savannah Area CVB
101 East Bay Street, Savannah, GA 31401
Tel: (912) 644 6401 *or* (877) 728 2662 (toll-free).
Fax: (912) 644 6498.
Website: www.savannahchamber.com

General Information

Nickname: Peach State
State bird: Brown Thrasher
State flower: Cherokee Rose
CAPITAL: Atlanta
Date of admission to the Union: 2 Jan 1788 (original 13 States; date of ratification of the Constitution)
POPULATION: 8,829,383 (official estimate 2004)
POPULATION DENSITY: 57.4 per sq km
2003 total overseas arrivals/US ranking: 451,000/13
TIME: Eastern (GMT - 5). *Daylight Saving Time* is observed.

THE STATE: Georgia is the largest State east of the **Mississippi River**, and was founded in 1735 by James Oglethorpe, an Englishman who landed in **Savannah** and established the 13th colony in the New World. Georgia is the only State to be named after a British monarch. It is a mixture of the Old and New South, and is geographically diverse, with landscapes ranging from mountains in the northeast to the mysterious, low-lying **Okefenokee Swamp** in the south, called the land of the 'trembling earth' by the region's Native American tribes. It was in this State that gold was first struck in North America in the early part of the 19th century, and the gold rush that followed centred around the town of **Dahlonega**. Georgia's varied climate ranges from the low humidity of the **Blue Ridge Mountains** to the subtropical southern coastal region.

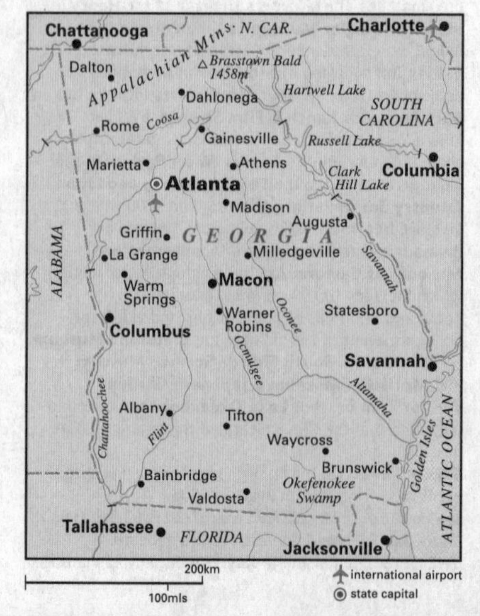

Travel - International

AIR: International airports: *Hartsfield-Jackson Atlanta International (ATL)* (website: www.atlanta-airport.com) is 16km (10 miles) south of the city (travel time – 20 minutes). With almost 80 million passengers using the airport in 2003, the airport is the busiest in the world (2002 passenger rankings), although most of those passengers are domestic. There is a full range of facilities available, including a business centre, and numerous shops and restaurants. The *Metropolitan Atlanta Rapid Transport Authority (MARTA)* operates rapid rail services every 10 minutes (0430-0100), from the airport to the city centre (travel time - 15 minutes) and throughout the metropolitan area. Taxis, shuttle vans, limousines and car hire are also available.
Approximate flight times: From Atlanta to *London* is nine hours, to *Miami* is one hour 50 minutes, to *New York* is two hours 10 minutes and to *Washington, DC* is one hour 40 minutes.
RAIL: The *Amtrak* (tel: (800) 872 7245 (toll-free); website: www.amtrak.com) 'Crescent' service, linking New York City with New Orleans, stops in Atlanta, while the 'Silver Service/Palmetto' service between New York City and Miami stops in Savannah; see the *New York* section for approximate travel times on these lines. Bus 23 runs to the Amtrak station in Atlanta, 1688 Peachtree Street NW; a taxi is required to get to the Amtrak station in Savannah, which is situated some 5 km (3 miles) southwest of the city, at 2611 Seaboard Coastline Drive.
ROAD: *Greyhound* (tel: (800) 229 9424 (toll-free); website: www.greyhound.com) has terminals in Atlanta, Decatur, Hapeville, Marietta and Norcross.
Approximate driving times: From Atlanta to *Birmingham* is three hours, to *Charlotte* is five hours, to *Nashville* is five hours, to *Charleston* (South Carolina) is six hours, to *Dallas* is six hours, to *Tallahassee* is six hours, to *Jacksonville* is seven hours, to *Memphis* is eight hours, to *Cincinnati* is nine hours, to *New Orleans* is nine hours, to *Charleston* (West Virginia) is 10 hours, to *Miami* is 13 hours, to *Chicago* is 14 hours, to *New York* is 17 hours, to *Salt Lake City* is 30 hours, to *Los Angeles* is 45 hours and to *Seattle* is 53 hours. All times are based on non-stop driving at or below the applicable speed limits.
Approximate bus travel times: From Atlanta to *Chattanooga* is two to four hours, to *Birmingham* is three to six hours, to *Charlotte* is four to five hours, to *Mobile* is six to 10 hours, to *Jacksonville* is eight hours, to *St Petersburg* is 12 to 16 hours and to *Miami* is 15 to 21 hours.
URBAN: The public transport system in Atlanta is excellent. The most economical transport is the *Metropolitan Atlanta Rapid Transport Authority (MARTA)* (website: www.itsmarta.com), which consists of 74km (46 miles) of rapid rail and 2373km (1475 miles) of bus lines operating Mon-Fri 0500-0130 and weekends and holidays 0530-0030. Daily and weekly travel passes are available. **Car hire:** Cars and motorcampers can be hired for touring the Atlanta area. Local companies can be contacted through the Atlanta classified telephone directory.

Credit: © Georgia Department of Industry, Trade & Tourism

Credit: © Georgia Department of Industry, Trade & Tourism

Resorts & Excursions

Atlanta & the North

ATLANTA: Now a booming services-industry centre with a population of over 400,000 (and a metro population topping 4 million), Atlanta – known as 'The City in a Forest' – most dramatically expresses the transition from Old South to New. Along its residential streets, magnolia and dogwood trees surround handsome Georgian-style homes, yet only blocks away, some of the country's most dazzling contemporary buildings are rising at record speed to add to Atlanta's ever-growing skyline.

The **Georgia State Capitol** on Washington Street on Capitol Square also houses the **Georgia Hall of Fame** and the **Hall of Flags**. The **Tomb of Martin Luther King** is located at the **Ebenezer Baptist Church**. The 14-storey **CNN Center** houses offices, a hotel, a sports arena and the headquarters of the CNN news agency. **Underground Atlanta**, a restored four-square block shopping and entertainment area, is located near the business centre of Atlanta and is home to the **Zero Mile Post**, which marks the city's birthplace. **Grant Park** contains the **Atlanta Zoo**, the restored **Confederate Fort Walker**, and the **Cyclorama**, a world-famous 123m (406ft) circumference painting of the Battle of Atlanta. **Piedmont Park** has facilities for swimming and tennis.

THE NORTH: 24km (16 miles) east of downtown Atlanta is **Stone Mountain**, where gigantic representations of three Confederate heroes – Robert E Lee, Jefferson Davis and Thomas 'Stonewall' Jackson – have been carved into a cliff-face; a climb takes approximately 45 minutes to one hour, while the cable car is an easier option of getting to the top. Within easy travelling distance of Atlanta are: **Augusta**, home of the *Masters Golf Tournament* every April; **Dahlonega**, an old mining town, where visitors can still pan for gold; and **Madison**, a historic town that was spared from ruin during Sherman's March in 1864. The nearby **Pine Mountain** area is noted for its **Callaway Gardens** and for President Franklin D Roosevelt's **Little White House** at **Warm Springs**. In the old capital of Georgia, **Milledgeville**, there is a trolley tour six days a week around the town's historic district.

Savannah & the Southeast

SAVANNAH: On the Atlantic coast, 400km (240 miles) southeast of Atlanta, Savannah was the USA's first planned city. It has become the greatest urban historic preservation site in the USA. Much of Savannah's original beauty remains, and more than a thousand of its buildings are historically important, including the Regency-style **Owens-Thomas House** designed by William Jay, and **Davenport House**, one of the best examples of Georgian architecture in the New World. **Fort Pulaski**, one of Savannah's five forts open to the public, is named after the Polish hero of the American Revolution. **Tybee Island** features sands, fishing piers and a marine science centre. The city is also home to the celebrated *Savannah Jazz Festival* in September.

THE SOUTHEAST: The **Golden Isles**, south of the city, are known for their leisurely resorts, with beaches, fine golfing, tennis and fishing. **Jekyll Island**, an ideal destination for bird watchers, golfers and history enthusiasts, is located off the Atlantic coastline's marshlands. It can be reached within an hour's drive from either Savannah or Jacksonville, Florida. The resort island is known for its natural beauty and a deep sense of history. From 1886 to 1942, Jekyll was the winter sanctuary of some of the US's wealthiest industrialists, such as William Rockefeller and Richard Crane. The beautifully restored **Victorian Clubhouse** and the historic district are perfect examples of this bygone era. **St Simons** is the largest of the Golden Isles, with vast woodlands and stretches of unspoilt marshes and coastline. **Sea Island** is home to **The Cloister** hotel and superb resort activities, including tennis, golf and a spa. **Waycross** is one of three gateways to the **Okefenokee Swamp**, one of the country's most beautiful wilderness areas. The swamp is a refuge of exotic plant and animal life, including alligators.

Social Profile

FOOD & DRINK: Atlanta offers an extensive choice of food, its restaurants covering a wide variety of cuisine, from Continental to Thai to Ethiopian.

THEATRES & CONCERTS: The **Academy Theater** is a professional outreach theatre. *Alliance Theater Company*, housed in the **Woodruff Arts Center**, presents a main stage season from August to June. The **Fox Theater**, saved from demolition and known as the 'Fabulous Fox', stages concerts and Broadway productions of hit musicals like *The Phantom of the Opera*. The *Atlanta Ballet* performs during spring, autumn and winter, and the celebrated *Atlanta Symphony Orchestra* performs at the **Woodruff Arts Center**, led by music director Robert Spano and principal guest conductor Donald Runnicles.

NIGHTLIFE: Nightlife varies from intimate piano bars and dinner theatres to the underground music clubs of Atlanta. The *Buckhead* and *Virginia-Highlands* communities in Atlanta have a thriving nightlife.

SHOPPING: Lenox Square Mall and **Phipps Plaza**, both shopping centres in Buckhead, can be reached by *MARTA* bus and rail.

SPORT: Georgia is a paradise for outdoor enthusiasts due to its temperate climate. There are around 400 **golf** courses in the State, including the Augusta National Golf Club which is home to the *Masters Golf Tournament*. **Tennis** is also popular across the State, particularly at the *Lincoln Tennis Center* which hosted Olympic matches in 1996. **Other sports** including **mountain biking**, **hiking** and **fishing**.

SPECIAL EVENTS: The following is a selection of special events occurring in Georgia in 2005:

Jan 30 *Celebrating FDR's 124th Birthday*, Warm Springs. **Feb 1-28** *Festival of Camellias*, Fort Valley. **Feb 2** *Annual Groundhog Day Celebration*, Lilburn. **Mar 1-30** *St Patrick's Festival* (the world's longest), Dublin. **Mar 4-6** *Springtime Made in the South*, Augusta. **Apr 4-10** *Masters Golf Tournament*, Augusta. **Apr 16** *Southland Jubilee*, Greensboro. **Apr 23** *Kite Founder's Day Festival*, Wrightsville. **May 5-7** *18th Annual Lewis Family Homecoming & Bluegrass Festival*, Lincolnton. **May 7** *Pine Tree Festival*, Swainsboro. **Jul 2-4** *Fantastic Fourth Celebration*, Stone Mountain. **Jul 9** *Thunder Over Thurmond*, Lincolnton. **Oct 1** *Oliver Hardy Festival 2005*, downtown Harlem. **Dec 3-4** *Victorian Christmas*, Thomasville.

Climate

Hot/humid in summer; mild in winter. Cooler in the northern mountains. Temperatures range from a January high of 10°C (50°F) and a low of 0°C (32°F) to a July high of 33°C (90°F) and a low of 21°C (70°F).

Required clothing: Lightweight cotton clothes and rainwear. Warm clothing for evenings in the spring and autumn, during the winter season and in mountain areas.

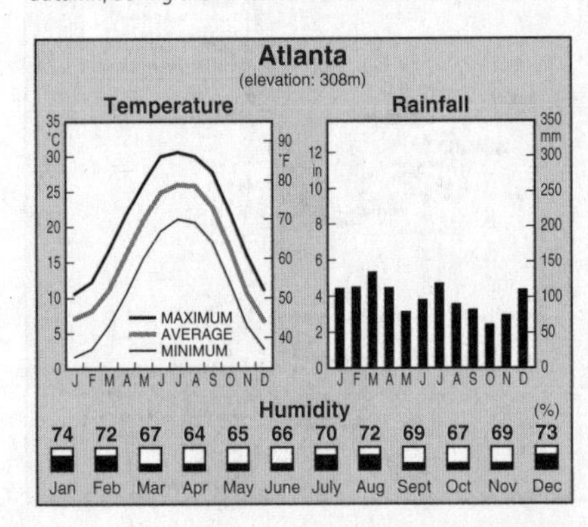

Hawaii

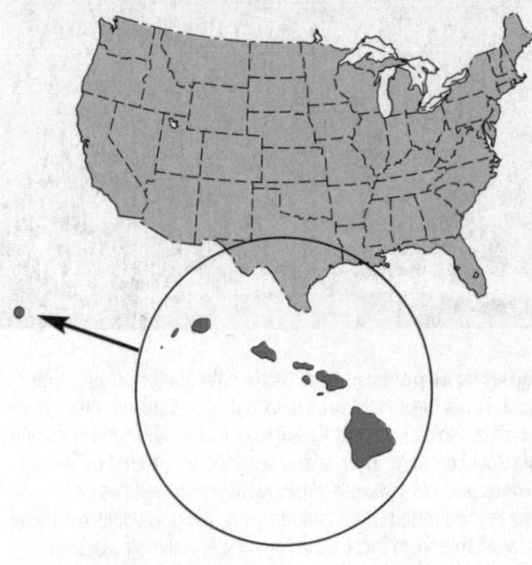

Hawaii Tourism Authority
Hawaii Convention Centre, 1801 Kalakaua Avenue, Honolulu, HI 96815
Tel: (808) 973 2255. Fax: (808) 973 2253.
E-mail: streitas@hawaiitourismauthority.org
Website: www.hawaii.gov/tourism

Hawaii Visitors & Convention Bureau
2270 Kalakaua Avenue, Suite 801, Honolulu, HI 96815
Tel: (808) 923 1811. Fax: (808) 924 0290.
E-mail: info@hvcb.org
Website: www.gohawaii.com

Chamber of Commerce of Hawaii
1132 Bishop Street, Suite 402, Honolulu, HI 96813
Tel: (808) 545 4300. Fax: (808) 545 4369.
E-mail: info@cochawaii.org
Website: www.cochawaii.org

Hawaii Hotel & Lodging Association
2250 Kalakaua Avenue, Suite 404-4, Honolulu, HI 96815
Tel: (808) 923 0407. Fax: (808) 924 3843.
E-mail: hhla@hawaiihotels.org
Website: www.hawaiihotels.org

Oahu Visitors Bureau
733 Bishop Street, Suite 1520, Honolulu, HI 96813
Tel: (808) 524 0722 *or* (877) 525 6248. Fax (808) 521 1620.
E-mail: webmaster@visit-oahu.com
Website: www.visit-oahu.com

General Information

Nickname: Aloha State
State bird: The Nene (Hawaiian Goose)
State flower: Yellow Hibiscus
CAPITAL: Honolulu
Date of admission to the Union: 21st Aug 1959
POPULATION: 1,262,840 (official estimate 2004)
POPULATION DENSITY: 44.6 per sq km
2003 total overseas arrivals/US ranking: 1,947,000/4
TIME: Hawaii-Aleutian (GMT - 10). *Daylight Saving Time* is not observed.

THE STATE: The island group of Hawaii lies 3860km (2400 miles) off mainland USA, comprised of 132 islands and atolls. The state of Hawaii consists of eight islands, of which seven are inhabited and six allow visitors. Oahu contains the capital, Honolulu, and is the most commercialised, while Hawaii is the biggest island. Oahu has two diagonal mountain ranges (the Waianae and Koolau), with many beautiful waterfalls. Hawaii is cloaked in macadamia orchards and coffee plantations. The islands support rainforest, green flatlands and a variety of other climates – in fact, of 13 climatic regions, Hawaii has all but two. Physically and psychologically, Hawaii stands apart from the USA, with an ethnically diverse population and a rich Polynesian heritage.

Travel - International

Air: International airports: *Honolulu International Airport (HNL)* is about 13km (8 miles) northwest of the city (14.5km/9 miles from Waikiki). Almost a quarter of the arrivals at the airport are international. City bus services 19 and 20 run every 30 minutes (travel time – 30 minutes), however large luggage and backpacks with heavy frames are not allowed on city buses. Various shuttles and coaches to Waikiki hotels meet all flight arrivals during the day (travel time – approximately 25 minutes). Taxis are also available (travel time – 20 minutes) and cost about US$25. Other international airports are *Hilo International Airport* and *Kana International Airport*.

Credit: © UDT Hawaii Conference and Exhibitions

Domestic airports: *Hawaii:* Waimea-Kohala. *Kauai:* Lihue. Lanai: Lanai Airport. Maui: Hana, Kahului, Kapalua-West, Maui. *Molokai:* Ho'olehua and Kalaupapa. *Oahu:* Dillingham Airfield, Kalaeloa. Frequent inter-island services are offered by *Aloha Airlines* and *Hawaiian Airlines*, which also sells passes offering unlimited inter-island flying; coupon books for these are available from local travel agents. All-island passes are typically available in increments of five, seven, 10 and 14 days.
Approximate flight times: From **Honolulu** to *Anchorage* is five hours 40 minutes, to *Chicago* is 10 hours, to *London* is 17 to 19 hours (including stopover, and depending on route taken), to *Los Angeles* is five hours 20 minutes, to *Miami* is 10 hours 35 minutes, to *New York* is 11 hours 40 minutes, to *San Francisco* is five hours, to *Singapore* is 18 hours 15 minutes, to *Sydney* is 12 hours 30 minutes, to *Washington, DC* is 11 hours, to the islands of *Kauai* and *Maui* is 20 minutes and to *Hawaii* is 35 minutes.
Air Passes: The *Polypass* (offered by Polynesian Airlines) allows the holder to fly between the Southern Pacific destinations of American Samoa, Fiji, Niue, Samoa, Tahiti and Tonga; Honolulu (Hawaii) and Los Angeles in the USA; Brisbane, Melbourne and Sydney in Australia; and Auckland and Wellington in New Zealand. The pass is valid for one year on *Polynesian Airlines* and its Interline Partners (*Air New Zealand* and *Qantas*). Once a reservation has been made and travel begun, all travel must be completed within a maximum of 45 days. Tickets will be issued against the Polypass by any Polynesian Airlines office (a valid passport is also required) and reservations must be made to ensure a seat. For further information, contact Polynesian Airlines (website: www.polynesianairlines.com).
SEA: Hawaii has 10 commercial harbours. *Hawaii:* Hilo, Kawaihae. *Lanai*: Kaumalapao Harbor. *Kauai*: Nawiliwili, Port Allen. *Maui*: Kahului. *Molokai:* Kaunakakai. *Oahu:* Honolulu, Kalaeloa Barber's Point, Kewalo Basin. Cruise lines running to Hawaii include *Carnival Cruises*, *Celebrity Cruises, Norwegian Cruise Lines*, *P&O Cruises* (Honolulu), *Princess Cruises* and *Royal Caribbean. Norwegian Cruise Lines* also operates inter-island cruises. Ferries run between Maui, Lanai and Molokai.
RAIL: The *Hawaiian Railway Society* on Oahu offers 90-minute journeys on a historical diesel-electric locomotive formerly used to haul sugar cane from Ewa Plantation Village to Ko'olina, available on Sundays. On Maui, the *Lahaina-Kaanapali & Pacific Railroad*, also known as the *Sugarcane Train*, offers daily 30-minute rides between Old Town Lahaina and Kaanapali Beach Resort.
Road: Driving is on the right-hand side of the road. Right-hand turns are permitted in the right lane at a 'stop' light unless otherwise indicated. Pedestrians are given the right of way most of the time. **Bus:** Deluxe modern tour buses operate on all islands. **Taxi:** Metered taxis are available throughout the main islands. **Car hire:** Available through local and international agencies. Drivers must be over 21 years of age for car hire. **Documentation:** Foreign driving licence required.
Urban: Good local bus services are provided on Oahu by *TheBus* (website: www.thebus.org), which covers the entire island with over 60 routes. An exact flat-fare system operates and free transfers are available on request. For further information, telephone the *Bus Information Line* (tel: (808) 848 5555). On other islands, taxis are available and car hire is possible. Limited public bus services operate on Kauai and Hawaii.

Resorts & Excursions

Oahu Island

When Captain James Cook landed here in the 18th century, Oahu had been untouched by the West. It achieved prominence when the volume of Honolulu's commercial traffic increased and the US Navy acquired rights to Pearl Harbor. Oahu has four divisions from a tourist's point of view: Honolulu, the metropolitan centre; Waikiki Beach, 5km (3 miles) from Honolulu's downtown area; Oahu's famous North Shore, stretching from Kahuku to Kaena Point; and the Windward Coast, notable for its beaches. The Leeward Coast, on the western side, is more desolate, though in recent years a certain amount of development has taken place and new residential areas, golf courses, parks, a shopping centre and an amusement park (**Hawaiian Waterways Adventure Park**) have sprung up.

Honolulu

The cultural, commercial and political centre of the island group is the starting point for most visitors. The **Waikiki Beach** area is a particularly popular resort region of the city, and is currently undergoing a US$300 million rejuvenation programme, including construction of new walkways, traffic calming measures, and picnic and entertainment areas. Some of the older high-rise hotels in the district have been demolished and replaced by new low-rise hotels and public walkways, as part of an extensive redevelopment project, which will encompass nearly 3 hectares (8 acres) of Waikiki land. The first phase, which will create the Waikiki Beach Walk and a low-level retail complex, pedestrian areas, meeting space and entertainment areas around an open-air plaza, will be completed in 2005. Some 436 hotel rooms will be lost during phase one alone; phase two, which is slated for commencement in 2006, will spell the end for three of Waikiki's hotels, to be replaced by a single 890-room venue. The old harbour area here (known as **Aloha Tower Marketplace**) is now an attractive and modern waterfront development, and is one of the major attractions in the area, with shopping plazas, restaurants and pavement entertainers. Other attractions include: **Kalakaua Avenue**, **Kilohana Square**, the **Ala Moana Center** and the **Kahala Mall** (all noted for their shopping); the **Honolulu zoo** near **Kapiolani Park** (where the *Honolulu Marathon* is concluded annually); the **National Cemetery of the Pacific**, or **Punchbowl**, a memorial and cemetery for US military veterans; central Honolulu, including **Chinatown**; the fine collection of Asian art at the **Honolulu Academy of Arts**; **Bishop Museum**; the new **Hawaii State Art Museum**; **Iolani Palace** and the spectacular **Nuuanu Pali**.

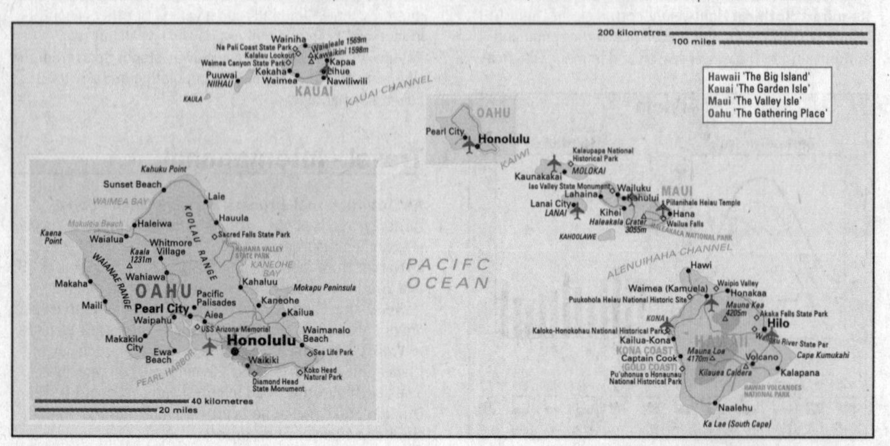

There are also many other parks, plus aquaria, museums and theatres in the city and its environs.
Oahu's most visited attraction is **Pearl Harbor** and the **USS Arizona Memorial** (open daily 0730-1700), the scene of Japan's surprise attack which brought the USA into World War II. Free tours take visitors by boat to the memorial spanning the wreck of the Battleship Arizona where 1177 men died; the last boat leaves at 1500 and arriving early is recommended.
Excursions: A variety of excursions is available. At least a day should be allowed for the **Circle Island Tour**, which takes in the whole of Oahu. Attractions en route include **Waimea Falls Park**, **Pearl Harbor**, the **Polynesian Cultural Centre**, **Sea Life Park**, the **Waialua Coffee Visitors' Center** (on a former plantation), the **Sacred Birthstones** and **Sunset Beach**.

Hawaii

'The Big Island' encompasses over 10,000 sq km (4000 sq miles) and holds more attractions than initially meet the eye. Towns like **Kailua-Kona** and other resorts lie along the Kohala Coast on the west side of the island. Over on the east coast lies the town of **Hilo** as well as **Hawai'i Volcanoes National Park**, one of the natural wonders of the world. At 4103m (13,677ft), **Mauna Loa** is the largest single mountain mass in the world, while at 1200m (4000ft), the still-active **Kilauea**'s steaming vents and frequent eruptions provide an unusual (and safe) spectator sport. The volcano is continuously erupting, and can be seen entering the ocean at sea-level.

Maui

Hawaii's second-largest island is popularly known as 'The Magic Isle' and attracts a multitude of tourists every year. Luxury resorts and budget condos abound, but there are isolated spots of raw beauty. Attractions include the town of **Wailuku**; the more bustling town of **Kahului**; the **Iao Valley**; the historic whaling town of **Lahaina**; **Mount Haleakala**, a massive volcanic crater whose name translates as 'The House of the Sun'; the tranquil beauty of Hana on the Eastern Shore; the East Mountain range with its native ecosystem; the waterfalls at **Wailua Cove**; and **Ka'eleku Caverns**, which are located beneath the **Hana Rainforest**, and now open to the public for guided tours.

Lanai

Once known as 'The Pineapple Isle' (pineapples have dominated the plantation economy since the early 1900s), beautiful Lanai now offers two 5-star resorts. Spectacular natural attractions include the dramatic **Shipwreck Beach** or **Kaiolohia** with its petroglyph rock carvings and the mystical **Garden of the Gods** at **Kanepu'u**. Other attractions include the ruins of **Kaunolu Village** (a complete archaeological site) and the **Munro Trail**, which leads to the **Hauola Gulch**, a truly spectacular view of the neighbouring islands. From November to April, Lanai is the perfect place for whale watching, as humpback whales make the waters around the island their winter breeding and calving grounds.

Molokai

A 15-minute flight east of Honolulu, Molokai, 'Hawaiian by Nature', offers wide open vistas, an easygoing ambience and a lively local community. Attractions include the harbour town of **Kaunakakai**, with its quaint and colourful shops; **Mount Kamakou**; the **Moaulu Falls**; the beautiful **Halawa Valley**; **Molokai Ranch**; and **Father Damien's Community at Kalaupapa**.

Kauai

'Hawaii's Island of Discovery' is breathtakingly beautiful (some say it is the most outstanding in the archipelago), with staggering mountains and miles of sandy beaches. Located at the northwestern end of the curve of islands, Kaua'i is small (1400 sq km or 552 sq miles), with a laid-back pace and discreet tourist facilities; ideal for the visitor who does not care for crowded beaches or high-rise hotels. Local attractions include **Mount Waialeale**; the capital town of **Lihue**; **Waimea Canyon**; the tropical rainforest in the centre of the island; the **Wailua River**; the **Fern Grotto**; the awesome **Na Pali Coast** and the nearby temple of **Holoholoku Heiau**. **Hanakapiai Beach** is 2 miles inland and there is a stupendous waterfall 2 miles up in the **Hanakapiai Valley**.

Social Profile

FOOD & DRINK: Hawaiian food offers the best of 'Pacific Rim' and 'New American' cooking syles, influenced by Chinese, Mediterranean, Mexican and other Asian countries. Many dishes are based on chicken, pork, seafood and local fruit and vegetables cooked using traditional methods. Special condiments and spices are used (see below). Much of the food available on the islands is basically US with Asian influences brought in by the assortment of ethnicities that make up the population.
The classic traditional Hawaiian feast is the *luau* based

around a *puaa kalua* (whole pig) that has been shaved and rubbed with rock salt on the inside. It is then placed on chicken wire, filled with hot stones from the fire, and cooked in an *imu* (pit) along with sweet potatoes, plantains and sometimes *laulau* (pork, butterfish and spinach-like taro shoots wrapped in leaves and steamed). The steam is prevented from escaping by encircling the pig with banana and coconut husks and taro leaves and covering the pit with wet burlap bags. The cooking process takes about six hours. The *kalua* pig is eaten with fingers and is accompanied by the traditional Hawai'ian *poi* (thick paste made from ground taro), *opihi* (a salty, black, clam-like mollusc) and *lomi lomi* salmon (salmon rubbed with an onion and tomato marinade). *Chicken luau* comprises tender chicken pieces cooked with taro tops and coconut cream. Garnishes include *limu* (seaweed), *paakai* rock salt and chopped roasted *kukui* nuts. Local seafood includes *moi* (mullet) *ulua, opakapaka* (pink snapper), lobster and yellowfin tuna. Hawaiian breakfast specialities are macadamia nuts and banana and coconut pancakes with coconut syrup. Fresh fruit and nut ice-creams or sorbets make excellent desserts.
The minimum legal drinking age is 21 years of age. It is illegal to consume alcohol in parks and on beaches.
NIGHTLIFE: Bars and nightclubs abound, especially on Oahu and Maui. Top international stars are booked, whilst *luau* shows (traditional Hawaiian banquets followed by live performances of music and dancing) are in themselves a great attraction. Jazz, big band music, tea dances and hula groups are all available.
SHOPPING: The *Aloha Tower Marketplace, Royal Hawaiian Shopping Center* and the *Ala Moana Shopping Center* in Waikiki Beach, Honolulu, are popular shopping areas. **Opening hours:** Mon-Sat 0900-2100. Some shops may open Sun 0830-1800.
SPORT: Golf courses are numerous and scenic. **Deep-sea fishing** is very popular off Hawaii's Big Island. The Hawai'ian islands are particularly good for **watersports**. One-week **yachting** charters are available, with or without crews. All boats are equipped with Coast-Guard-approved safety equipment and are under Coast Guard supervision. **Surfing** is, of course, a very popular sport – for both participants and spectators. *Waikiki Beach* is probably the most famous surfing beach in the world; learners are welcome here. **Snorkelling** is especially popular near the *Molokini Crater* off Maui, as well as at various sites around each of the islands. Increasingly popular is the hair- and dust-raising sport of **downhill biking**, particularly so on the 64km (40 miles) of Haleakala volcano's slopes in Maui. In addition, there are some exciting international events such as the *Canoe Races*, in which outrigger canoes race against each other. One particularly gruelling race course runs from Molokai to Waikiki.
SPECIAL EVENTS: There is a variety of events and festivals on the different islands; an up-to-date list can be found online (website: www.calendar.gohawaii.com). The following is a selection of special events occurring in Hawaii in 2005:
Jan 10-16 *Sony Open in Hawaii 2005*, Oahu. **Mar 27-Apr 2** *Merrie Monarch Festival*, Hawaii. **Apr 1-2** *12th Annual Hawaii International Jazz Festival*, Maui. **Jul 23-24** *Waikiki Artfest*, Oahu. **Sep 9-17** *Aloha Festivals* (Hawaii's largest multicultural festival), Hawaii. **Sep 24** *Matsuri Kauai 2005*, Haua. **Oct 15** *Ironman Triathalon World Championship*, Hawaii.

Climate

Warm throughout the year, with an average temperature of 24-29° C (75-85° F), and no appreciable difference between 'summer' and 'winter'. Heavy rainfall can occur in some mountainous areas from December to February, but most areas only receive short showers, while others remain totally arid.
Required clothing: Lightweights are advised throughout the year, with warmer clothes for winter. Beachwear is popular, and protection from the midday sun, such as sunglasses and sun hats, is advisable.

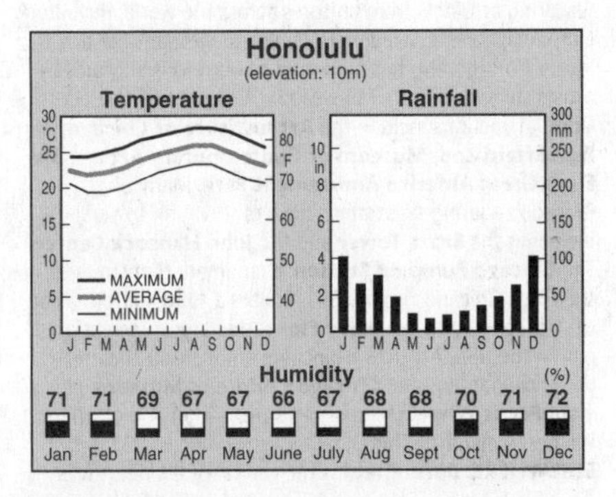

Idaho

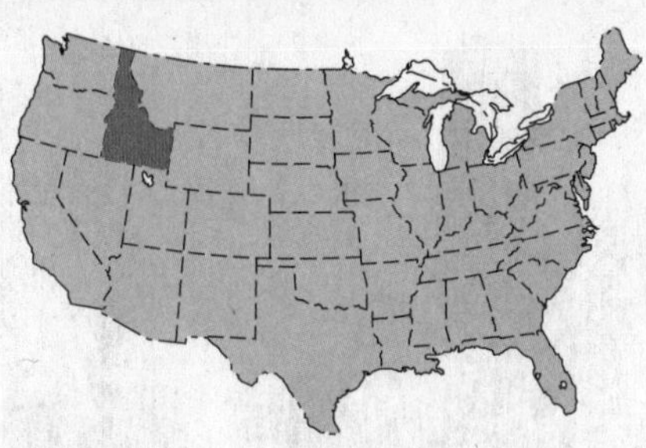

Idaho Department of Commerce, Division of Tourist Development
Street address: 700 West State Street, Boise, ID 83720
Postal address: PO Box 83720, Boise, ID 83720
Tel: (208) 334 2470 *or* (800) 842 5858 (toll-free).
Fax: (208) 334 2631.
E-mail: tourism@visit.idaho.gov
Website: www.visitid.org
Rocky Mountain International (UK Office)
7 Thornton Avenue, Warsash, Southampton, Hampshire SO31 96D, UK
Tel: (01489) 557 533 (trade enquiries only) *or* (09063) 640 655 (customer request line; 60p per minute).
Fax: (01489) 557 534.
E-mail: rmi.uk@btinternet.com
Website: www.rmi-realamerica.com
Boise CVB
Street address: 312 South Ninth Street, Suite 100, Boise, ID 83702
Postal address: PO Box 2106, Boise, ID 83701
Tel: (208) 344 7777 *or* (800) 635 5240 (toll-free).
Fax: (208) 344 6236.
E-mail: receptionist@boisecvb.org
Website: www.boise.org

Credit: © Idaho Commerce & Labor

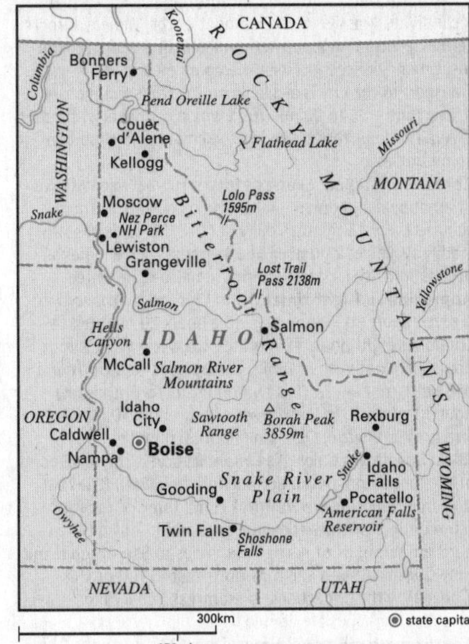

General Information

Nickname: Gem State
State bird: Mountain Bluebird
State flower: Syringa
CAPITAL: Boise
Date of admission to the Union: 3 July 1890
POPULATION: 1,393,262 (official estimate 2004)
POPULATION DENSITY: 6.3 per sq km
2003 total overseas arrivals: Under 38,000
TIME: Mountain (GMT - 7) in the greater part of the State; Pacific (GMT - 8) in the north. *Daylight Saving Time* is observed.

THE STATE: The contrasting terrain of Idaho includes *Hell's Canyon National Recreational Area*, the deepest river gorge in North America and home to the **Snake**, **Salmon** and **Rapid rivers**; **Clearwater National Forest**; and two of the finest big-game hunting areas in the USA – **Chamberlain Basin** and **Selway-Bitterroot Wilderness**. The State capital, **Boise**, comes to life during the summer months with a lively festival and the *Western Idaho Fair* in August. It is also home to the **World Center for Birds of Prey**; the **Basque Museum & Cultural Center** and the **Boise Art Museum**. Attractions to the southeast include the massive **Shoshone Falls**; the **Shoshone Indian Ice Caves**; and historic **Fort Hall**.

Credit: © Idaho Commerce & Labor

The upmarket **Sun Valley** resort area in the centre of the State offers skiing and wintersports, as well as a range of summer activities. In the nearby hills is a wide choice of hot springs, including the **Warfield Hot Spring** and **Russian John Hot Spring**. The **Craters of the Moon National Monument & Preserve** is a huge lava field with a maze of tunnels and caves. There are plenty of campsites available nearby. **Sawtooth National Recreation Area** is home to the **Sawtooth** and **White Cloud mountains** and the **Smokey** and **Boulder ranges**. Further north, the **Lewis and Clark Scenic Byway** offers travellers a chance to trace the 'Corps of Discovery' expedition route along the **Clearwater** and **Lochsa rivers**, in the land of the Nez Perce Indians, who are recalled by the **Nez Perce National Historical Park**.
In the north of the State, the resort town of **Coeur d'Alene** is home to the world's only floating golf green, which is situated on a lake where visitors can also hire canoes or take a boat cruise. The **Wallace District Mining Museum** is situated to the east of Coeur d'Alene. Also on offer in this area is the **Sierra Silver Mine Tour** and the **Oasis Bordello Museum**. Visitors can also ride up **Silver Mountain** on the world's longest single-stage gondola.

Illinois

Illinois Bureau of Tourism
James R Thompson Center, 100 West Randolph Street, Suite 3-400, Chicago, IL 60601
Tel: (312) 814 4733 *or* (800) 2266 6632 (toll-free).
Fax: (312) 814 6175.
E-mail: tourism@commerce.state.il.us
Website: www.enjoyillinois.com

Chicago and Illinois Tourism Office
c/o Cellet Travel Services Ltd, 47 High Street, Henley-in-Arden, Warwickshire, B95 5AA, UK
Tel: (01564) 794 999 *or* (08700) 503 410 (brochure request).
Fax: (01564) 795 333.
E-mail: info@cellet.co.uk
Website: www.gochicago.com

Visit Illinois
27 East Monroe, Suite 300, Chicago, IL 60603
Tel: (312) 658 1047. Fax: (312) 873 4015.
E-mail: info@visitillinois.net
Website: www.visitillinois.net

Chicago Office of Tourism
Chicago Cultural Center, 4th Floor, 78 East Washington Street, Chicago, IL 60602
Tel: (312) 744 2400 *or* (877) 244 2246 (toll-free).
Fax: (312) 744 2359.
E-mail: tourism@ci.chi.il.us
Website: www.cityofchicago.org/tourism

Chicago Convention and Tourism Bureau
2301 South Lake Shore Drive, Chicago, IL 60616
Tel: (312) 567 8500 *or* (877) 244 2246 (toll-free).
Fax: (312) 567 8533.
Website: www.choosechicago.com

Springfield CVB
109 North Seventh Street, Springfield, IL 62701
Tel: (217) 789 2360 *or* (800) 545 7300 (toll-free).
Fax: (217) 544 8711.
E-mail: mailbox@springfield.il.us
Website: www.visit-springfieldillinois.com

General Information

Nickname: Land of Lincoln
State bird: Springfield Cardinal
State flower: Native Violet
CAPITAL: Springfield
Date of admission to the Union: 3 Dec 1818
POPULATION: 12,713,634 (official estimate 2004)
POPULATION DENSITY: 84.8 per sq km
2003 total overseas arrivals/US ranking: 829,000/7

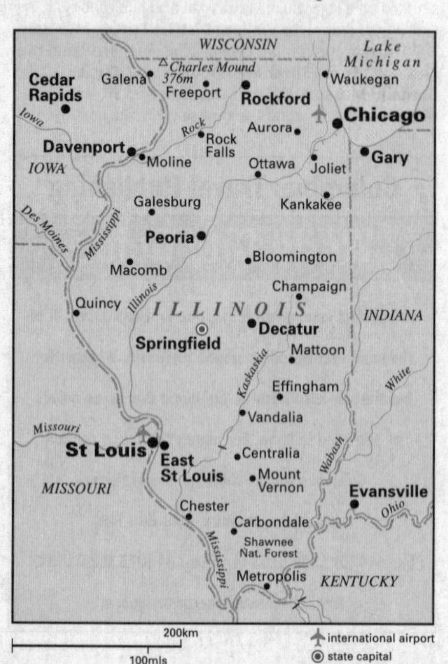

Credit: © Illinois Bureau of Tourism

TIME: Central (GMT - 6). *Daylight Saving Time* is observed.
THE STATE: Illinois, stretching from **Lake Michigan** to the **Mississippi River**, embraces vast, rich farmlands, the giant city of **Chicago**, rolling glacial plains and, to the south, the hills and valleys of the **Illinois Ozarks**. Illinois boasts 6900km (4300 miles) of scenic shoreline, 1100 historic sites and half a million acres of state parks. Abraham Lincoln, the 16th US President, spent most of his professional (he was a lawyer) and political life here.

Travel - International

AIR: International airports: *Chicago O'Hare International (ORD)* (website: www.ohare.com/ohare/home.asp), 27km (17 miles) northwest of downtown Chicago, is the world's second-busiest airport for total passengers, handling over 66 million passengers in 2003. It is also the US headquarters for *American Airlines* and *United Airlines*. Lower-level pedestrian passageways inside the airport terminals lead directly to the *Chicago Transit Authority (CTA)* station; the free *Airport Transit System (ATS)* also links the terminals and station. The CTA Blue Line train provides a 24-hour service between central Chicago and O'Hare (travel time - approximately 40 minutes). Most major car hire firms have offices at the airport. Taxis and limousines are also widely available, as are shuttle buses and buses serving regional destinations.
Connections from O'Hare to *Midway International* (see below) are provided by the *Omega Airport Shuttle bus*, which operates an airport transfer service every hour 0700-2200 (travel time - 30 minutes to one hour), and *Coach USA Wisconsin*, with an hourly service between the airports from 0800-2200.
Domestic airports: Domestic airports: *Midway International (MDW)* (website: www.ohare.com/midway/home.asp), 16km (10 miles) southwest from downtown Chicago, handles regional and local flights. Massive redevelopment of the Midway Airport Terminal, including a new terminal building and a Federal Inspection Services Facility, were completed in 2004. Transport to the city is available on the CTA's Orange Line (travel time - 20 to 30 minutes), which connects with other CTA rail and bus routes serving the city and 40 suburban communities.
Continental Airport Express shuttles run between Midway International and downtown Chicago and the northern suburbs every 15 minutes daily 0600-2330. Taxis are also readily available; a number of other buses serve regional destinations. Major car hire firms are also represented.
Approximate flight times: From Chicago to *Anchorage* is seven hours, to *Honolulu* is nine hours 20 minutes, to *London* is eight hours 40 minutes, to *Los Angeles* is four hours 20 minutes, to *Miami* is three hours, to *Montréal* is two hours, to *New York* is two hours, to *Toronto* is one hour 30 minutes, to *Vancouver* is four hours 30 minutes and to *Washington, DC* is one hour 50 minutes.
RAIL: Downtown Chicago's *Union Station* is the focal point of the Amtrak rail passenger network (tel: (800) 872 7245 (toll-free); website: www.amtrak.com); three of the four transcontinental lines converge here and it is also the northern terminus of north-south lines to San Antonio and New Orleans. A sixth line runs northeast to Toronto (Canada), with connections to Montréal. Services to neighbouring cities are limited.
Approximate rail travel times: From Chicago on the 'Three Rivers'/'Pennsylvanian' to *Pittsburgh* is nine hours 40 minutes, to *Philadelphia* is 18 hours and to *New York* is 21 hours; on the 'Lake Shore Limited' to *Toledo* is four hours 20 minutes, to *Cleveland* is seven hours, to *Buffalo* is 10 hours and to *New York* is 19 hours; on the 'Cardinal' to *Indianapolis* is five hours, to *Cincinnati* is eight hours 35 minutes and to *Washington, DC* is 23 hours; on the 'Capitol' to *Pittsburgh* is nine hours 45 minutes and to *Washington, DC* is 17 hours 45 minutes; on the 'City of New Orleans' to *Memphis* is 10 hours 30 minutes and to *New Orleans* is 19 hours 40 minutes; on the 'International' to *Kalamazoo* is two hours 20 minutes, to *Port Huron* is six hours 20 minutes and to *Toronto* is 12 hours 20 minutes; on the 'Ann Rutledge' to *St Louis* is seven hours and to *Kansas City* is 12 hours; on the 'Empire Builder' to *Minneapolis/St Paul* is eight hours 15 minutes, to *Spokane* is 37 hours 30 minutes, to *Seattle* is 46 hours and to *Portland* is 46 hours. Approximate times for Chicago-Los Angeles and Chicago-Oakland (San Francisco) services may be found in the *California* section.
ROAD: Long-distance bus companies operating in the State include *Greyhound* (tel: (800) 229 9424 (toll-free); website: www.greyhound.com), with services across the USA, and *Trailways* (tel: (703) 691 3052; website: www.trailways.com), with services to neighbouring States. There is a 24-hour bus terminal at 630 West Harrison Street in Chicago.
Approximate driving times: From Chicago to *Milwaukee* is two hours, to *Madison* is three hours, to *Indianapolis* is four hours, to *Detroit* is five hours, to *St Louis* is six hours, to *Des Moines* is seven hours, to *Cleveland* is seven hours, to *Nashville* is nine hours, to *Kansas City* is 10 hours, to *New York* is 16 hours, to *Dallas* is 19 hours, to *Miami* is 27 hours, to *Seattle* is 44 hours and to *Los Angeles* is 44 hours. All times are based on non-stop driving at or below the applicable speed limits.
Approximate bus travel times: From Chicago to *Milwaukee* is two hours, to *Indianapolis* is three hours 30 minutes, to *St Louis* is five to seven hours, to *Detroit* is six to eight hours, to *Cleveland* is seven to eight hours, to *Omaha* is 10 hours, to *Memphis* is 10 to 11 hours and to *New York City* is 17 hours.
URBAN: Bus: A wide network of bus routes run by the *Chicago Transit Authority (CTA)* (tel: (312) 836 7000; website: www.transitchicago.com) covers the city on the major north-south and east-west streets. **Train:** The *CTA* runs both subway trains and elevated trains from 'The Loop' in downtown Chicago to the suburbs. The CTA system uses a transit card system for fare payment, these are available at all elevated train stations. Commuter rail services are run by *METRA*. **Car hire:** Cars and motor campers are available.

Resorts & Excursions

CHICAGO: Nicknamed the 'Windy City', Chicago is one of the world's giant trade, industry and transportation centres and the birthplace of the skyscraper. In contrast, its Lake Michigan shoreline is dotted with sandy beaches, hundreds of parks, harbours, zoos and vast expanses of forest reserve. It is one of the USA's largest cities and the hub of the Midwest, with a population of nearly 3 million (8.5 million in the metropolitan area) and more than 69,000 hotel rooms in the downtown and metropolitan areas alone. The inhabitants in the 'Chicagoland' area speak more than 50 languages, making it the most ethnically diverse city in the USA. It is also known for its distinct neighbourhoods, each with its own unique character. For visitors to the USA, it is the gateway to the farmlands and cities of Illinois and Indiana, and the recreation areas of Wisconsin.
The **Museum of Science & Industry** has more than 2000 exhibits. The pedestrianised **Museum Campus** is the site of three museums surrounded by one continuous park. These are the **Field Museum of Natural History**, which spans the development of the universe from 4.5 billion years ago to the present day; the **John G Shedd Aquarium and Oceanarium**; and the **Adler Planetarium**, which houses the **Sky Dome**. Special events and free activities take place in the park during the summer.
The city has a number of museums and art galleries featuring artefacts from cultures across the world, including Lithuania, Poland, Sweden, Ukraine and Vietnam. For art lovers, Chicago also has a number of outdoor sculptures by artists such as Picasso, Miró, Moore, Chagall and Calder. Other attractions include the **Art Institute of Chicago**, **Brookfield Zoo**, **Museum of Contemporary Art** and **Six Flags Great America Amusement Park**. Many of Chicago's soaring skyscrapers have observation towers, including the **Sears Tower** and the **John Hancock Center**. The **Chicago Pumping Station**, a landmark that survived the Great Chicago Fire of 1871, houses a tourist information centre, open daily. The **Navy Pier** is the largest recreational pier in the USA. Attractions include an open-air theatre, botanical gardens, the **Chicago Children's Museum**, plus a giant **Ferris Wheel** standing 15 storeys high and offering the best view of the famous Chicago skyline.
ELSEWHERE: Springfield is the capital of Illinois. It was

here that Abraham Lincoln married and began his legal career. Attractions include **Lincoln's Tomb** (a State Historical Site) and the **Illinois State Museum**. **New Salem State Park**, nearby, is a recreation of the pioneer community as it was in Lincoln's day. Southern Illinois was one of the first regions of North America to be settled by the French. This colourful heritage is reflected in towns such as **Prairie du Rocher** and **Kaskaskia**. The **Shawnee National Forest**, with its huge areas of wilderness and many tourist sites, stretches across the lower part of Illinois. To the west, **Fort Crevecoeur** is a replica of a French outpost. The **Dickson Mounds** were raised by Mississippian Native Americans many centuries ago. To the north is **Galena**, a Victorian city, with many historic sites and tourist activities. **Starved Rock State Park** has a lodge, hiking trails, picnic areas and excursion boats from May to September. **Cahokia Mounds** is a relic of the most sophisticated prehistoric Native American civilisation community north of Mexico.

Social Profile

FOOD & DRINK: Chicago is known for its prime rib steaks and deep pan Chicago pizza. It is packed with some 7000 restaurants of all types, serving food from around the world.
THEATRES & CONCERTS: Major Chicago theatres include the **Chicago**, **Goodman**, **Chicago Shakespeare Theatre**, **Shubert** and **Arie Crown**. The **Auditorium Theater** stages ballet and musical events. Chicago is now home to the world-renowned *Joffrey Ballet*. The **Civic Center for the Performing Arts** stages performances by the *Lyric Opera Company*. The *Chicago Symphony Orchestra* performs at the new **Symphony Center**.
NIGHTLIFE: Chicago boasts everything from nightclubs, jazz spots, cinemas and discos to belly dancing, rock bands and folk music. It is the home of 'urban blues', a form developed by such greats as Muddy Waters and Elmore James, continued today in Chicago and around the world by performers such as Buddy Guy and Robert Cray.
SHOPPING: The main shopping areas in Chicago include **State Street**, North Michigan Avenue's **Magnificent Mile**, **Woodfield Mall** and the quaint speciality stores in Old Town, Lincoln Avenue and New Town.
SPORT: The *Chicago Bears* play **American football** from September to December at **Soldier Field**. The **baseball** teams, *Chicago Cubs* and *Chicago White Sox*, play during the summer months at **Wrigley Field** and **Comiskey Park**. The *Chicago Bulls* take to the **basketball** court from January to April at the **Chicago Stadium**, which is also home to the ice hockey team, the *Chicago Blackhawks*. Illinois has the highest number of public and championship **golf** courses in the USA; there are 700 of these, 200 of which can be found in the immediate Chicagoland area.
SPECIAL EVENTS: The following is a selection of special events occurring in Illinois in 2005:
Feb 13 *Chinese New Year Parade*, Chicago. **Feb** *Theater Fever*, Chicago. **Mar 4-6** *18th Annual Illinois Horse Fair*, Springfield. **Mar 5** *Ceilidh Festival*, Peoria. **Mar 10-12** *Rootabaga Jazz Festival*, Galesburg. **Mar 12** *St Patrick's Day Parade*, Chicago; *Seventh Annual Storytelling Festival*, Schaumburg. **Apr 23** *Festival of Spring*, Decatur. **Jun 4** *Aquafest*, Sullivan. **Aug 8-10** *Prairieland Bluegrass Festival*, Jacksonville. **Sep 9** *Cajun on Chicago*, Springfield. **Sep 23-25** *Honeybee Festival*. **Oct 1-2** *Scarecrow Festival*, Galesburg. **Nov 19-20** *Winter in the Woods*, Monticello. **Dec 3** *Lights Fantastic Parade*, Carbondale.

Climate

Wide variation between hot summers and freezing winters, especially in the north of the State. The highest humidity is in the summer near the Great Lakes.
Required clothing: Warm winter clothes are needed in the coldest months. Light- to mediumweights are advised for the summer. Rainwear may be useful.

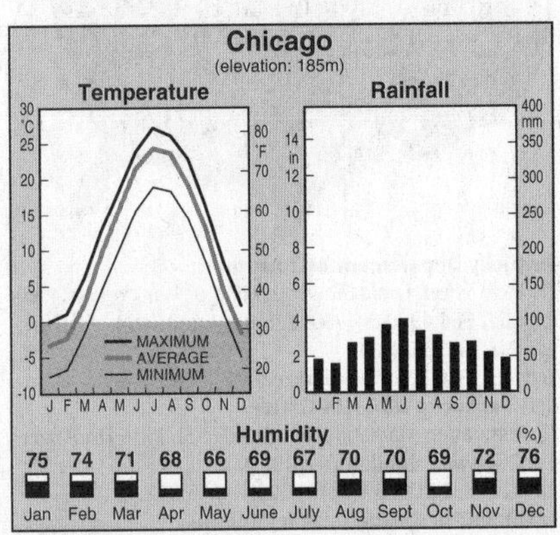

Indiana

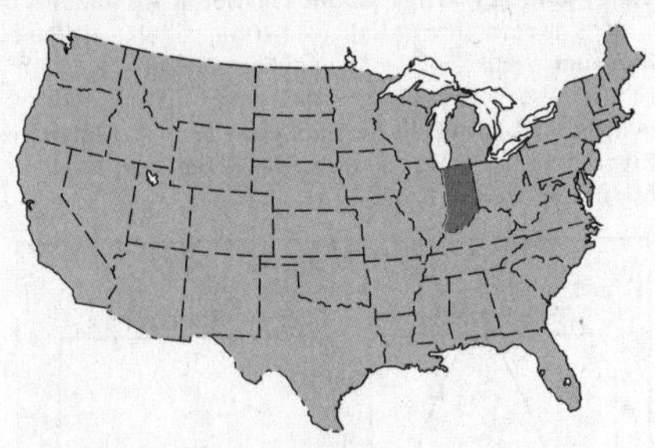

Indiana Tourism Division
Department of Commerce, 1 North Capitol, Suite 700, Indianapolis, IN 46204
Tel: (317) 232 8860 *or* (800) 290 6946 (toll-free).
Fax: (317) 233 6887.
Website: www.enjoyindiana.com
Indianapolis Convention & Visitors Association
One RCA Dome, Suite 100, Indianapolis, IN 46225
Tel: (317) 639 4282 *or* (800) 958 4639 (toll-free; tourism hotline) *or* (800) 556 4639 (toll-free; reservations).
Fax: (317) 684 2598.
E-mail: icva@indianapolis.org
Website: www.indy.org
Greater Lafayette CVB
301 Frontage Road, Lafayette, IN 47905
Tel: (765) 447 9999 *or* (800) 872 6648 (toll-free).
Fax: (765) 447 5062.
E-mail: info@homeofpurdue.com
Website: www.homeofpurdue.com
Bloomington/Monroe County CVB
2855 North Walnut Street, Bloomington, IN 47404
Tel: (812) 334 8900 *or* (800) 800 0037. Fax: (812) 334 2344.
E-mail: cvb@visitbloomington.com
Website: www.visitbloomington.com
Marion/Grant County CVB
217 South Adams Street, Marion, IN 46952
Tel: (765) 668 5435 *or* (800) 662 9474 (toll-free).
Fax: (765) 668 5424.
E-mail: director@jamesdeancountry.com
Website: www.jamesdeancountry.com

General Information

Nickname: Hoosier State
State bird: Cardinal
State flower: Peony
CAPITAL: Indianapolis
Date of admission to the Union: 11 Dec 1816
POPULATION: 6,237,569 (official estimate 2004)
POPULATION DENSITY: 66.1 per sq km
2003 total overseas arrivals/US ranking: 144,000/26

TIME: Eastern (GMT - 5) in the greater part of the State; Central (GMT - 6) in the west; Eastern (GMT - 5) in the east. *Daylight Saving Time* is not observed in the greater part of the State, but is observed in the west and east.
THE STATE: Adjoining Lake Michigan to the north, Indiana features deep valleys, cornfields, foothills and vast farmlands. Amid the rolling plains stands **Indianapolis**, the State capital and national centre for industry, commerce and culture. The business sector lies at the heart of the city, however, many of the tourist attractions are situated on the outskirts. Located downtown are the **Eiteljorg Museum of American Indians and Western Art** and the **Indianapolis Zoo**, which is renowned for its large collection of dolphins and whales. Further out are the **Indianapolis Museum of Art** and the **Krannert Pavillion**, with an extensive display of modern art. A must for families is the **Children's Museum of Indianapolis**. Indianapolis also offers a selection of musical entertainment to suit all tastes: the **Madame Walker Theatre Center** has seen the likes of Louis Armstrong grace its stage, while every June the city hosts the *Indy Jazz Fest*. The *Indianapolis Symphony Orchestra* and *Indianapolis Opera* are other popular options. The most famous sporting event to hit the city is the *Indianapolis 500* speedway race on Memorial Day Weekend; a month of shows, exhibitions and parades in May leads up to the main event. The other big motorsport events are the *Brickyard 400* race in August, and the US *Grand Prix Formula One* race, held in late September.
At **Wolf Park**, an hour northwest of Indianapolis near **Lafayette**, wolves wander freely and, even when they can not be seen, their piercing howls announce their presence. To the south, **Bloomington** reaches bursting point during its *Fourth Street Festival of the Arts & Crafts* in August. Other local highlights are the **Bloomington Antique Mall**, **Indiana University Art Museum** and **Lake Monroe**, which lies just south of the town.
State attractions also include the **Indiana Dunes National Lakeshore**; **Amish Acres**, a restored 19th-century Amish community at Nappanee; the **Conner Prairie Pioneer Settlement**; the **Squire Boone Caves**; the **James Dean Memorial Gallery** in **Fairmount**, 16km (10 miles) south of his birthplace, **Marion**, on 8 Feb 1931; and **Fort Wayne**, Indiana's second-largest city and the scene of many bloody battles. Fort Wayne is home to the **Lincoln Museum**, which depicts the life story of the USA's 16th president.

Credit: © Indiana Tourism Division

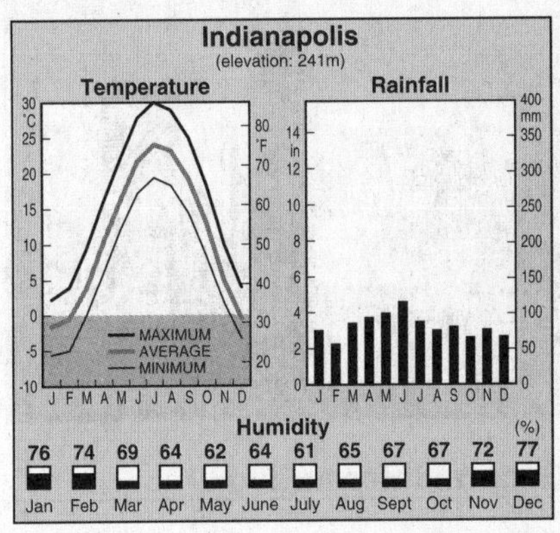

A B C D E F G H I J K L M N O P Q R S T U V W X Y Z

Iowa

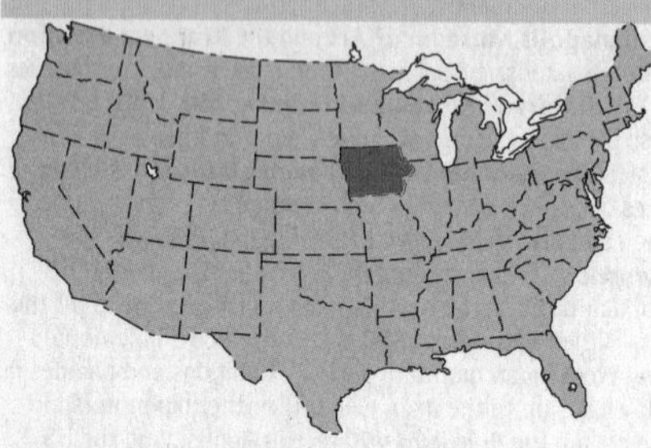

Iowa Tourism Office
200 East Grand Avenue, Des Moines, IA 50309
Tel: (515) 242 4705 *or* (800) 345 4692 (toll-free).
Fax: (515) 242 4718.
E-mail: tourism@iowalifechanging.com
Website: www.traveliowa.com
Greater Des Moines CVB
405 Sixth Avenue, Suite 201, Des Moines, IA 50309
Tel: (515) 286 4960 *or* (800) 451 2625 (toll-free).
E-mail: info@desmoinescvb.com
Website: www.seedesmoines.com
Iowa City/Coralville CVB
408 First Avenue, Coralville, IA 52241
Tel: (319) 337 6592 *or* (800) 283 6592 (toll-free).
Fax: (319) 337 9953.
E-mail: cvb@icccvb.org
Website: www.iowacitycoralville.org

Credit: © Iowa Department of Economic Development

General Information

Nickname: Hawkeye State
State bird: Eastern Goldfinch
State flower: Wild Rose
CAPITAL: Des Moines
Date of admission to the Union: 28 Dec 1846
POPULATION: 2,944,062 (official estimate 2003)
POPULATION DENSITY: 20.2 per sq km
2002 total overseas arrivals: Under 38,000
TIME: Central (GMT - 6). *Daylight Saving Time* is observed.

THE STATE: Almost 95 per cent of Iowa's gently undulating land is given over to agriculture, but dotted across the landscape are many scenic parks, lakes and recreation areas, such as **East Okoboji**, **West Okoboji** (Iowa's deepest natural lake), **Spirit Lake** and **Clear Lake**. Its rich cultural heritage can be seen in the **German Amana Colonies**, with their many historic sites and museums. The tulips of **Pella** reflect the town's Dutch past and **Des Moines**, Iowa's capital, was clearly named by French explorers. Des Moines has a great selection of amusements for children including the **Science Center of Iowa**, which transports visitors out of this world with impressive laser shows and simulated space shuttle flights. Other sights in Des Moines are the **State Historical Museum and Archives**, **Botanical Center**, **Des Moines Art Center** and **Jordan House** in **West Des Moines**. The city also hosts a number of annual events such as the *Iowa State Fair* in August and a *Jazz in July* celebration, with free daily jazz concerts throughout the city. Just out of town, the community of **Indianola** is the setting for the **National Balloon Museum**, which holds the colourful *National Balloon Classic* in August. Iowa City is dominated by the **University of Iowa** campus. The city also boasts the beautiful **Old Capitol** building among the cluster of historic buildings called the Pentacrest. Museums include the **Museum of Natural History** and the **Medical Museum** in the University of Iowa Hospitals and Clinics. The **Amana Colonies** are seven villages situated along the Iowa River. They welcome tourists to the **Museum of Amana History**, **Community Church**, **Communal Kitchen Museum** and the **Cooper Shop Museum**. They are renowned for their friendly nature, and their German heritage is evident in the local restaurants, which serve family-style portions of traditional dishes. The **South Amana Barn Museum** in **South Amana** is an unusual museum that depicts the history of rural USA in miniature.

Other Iowa attractions include the **Boone and Scenic Valley Railroad**; **Effigy Mounds National Monument**, with its relics of ancient Native American culture; and **Fort Museum**, a replica of the town of **Fort Dodge** in the 19th century. Also worth a visit are Iowa's two national scenic byways: the **Loose Hills Scenic Byway** along the **Missouri River** in western Iowa and the **Great River Road** along the **Mississippi River** on Iowa's eastern border.

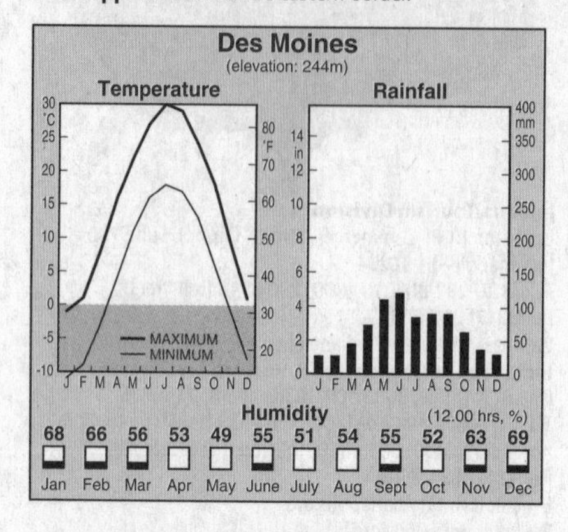

Kansas

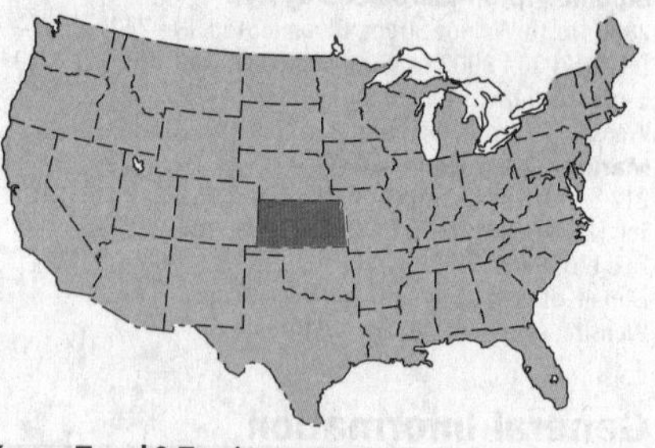

Kansas Travel & Tourism
1000 SW Jackson Street, Suite 100, Topeka, KS 66612
Tel: (785) 296 2009 *or* (800) 252 6727 (toll-free).
Fax: (785) 296 6988.
E-mail: travtour@kansascommerce.com
Website: www.travelks.com
Greater Wichita CVB
100 South Main Street, Suite 100, Wichita, KS 67202
Tel: (316) 265 2800 *or* (800) 288 9424 (toll-free).
Fax: (316) 265 0162.
Website: www.visitwichita.com

General Information

Nickname: Sunflower State
State bird: Western Meadowlark
State flower: Sunflower
CAPITAL: Topeka
Date of admission to the Union: 29 Jan 1861
POPULATION: 2,735,502 (official estimate 2004)
POPULATION DENSITY: 12.9 per sq km
2003 total overseas arrivals: Under 38,000
TIME: Central (GMT - 6) in the greater part of the State; Mountain (GMT - 7) in four Western counties. *Daylight Saving Time* is observed.

THE STATE: The geographical centre of North America, Kansas is a major agricultural area, with vast areas of farmland. As highway signs remind travellers, 'Every Kansas farmer feeds 75 people – and you.'

It was through Kansas that families on the *Oregon* and *Santa Fe Trails* drove their wagons westwards in search of new homesteads, while cowboys on the *Chisholm Trail* drove vast herds of longhorns north in search of the railroads. To cater for the new population, cowtowns like **Abilene** and **Dodge City** were born, and as whites forced Native Americans to move westwards, fierce battles over land erupted. Later, feuds over Kansas's maintenance of slavery gave rise to the term 'Bleeding Kansas'.

Today, the State boasts many monuments to its Old West past, as well as numerous recreation centres, reservoirs and rivers offering all kinds of outdoor pursuits. Attractions include the restored cattle town of Dodge City. Here, it is

Credit: © Kansas Travel & Tourism

worth visiting the **Boot Hill Museum** which recreates the Boot Hill Cemetery and Front Street as they looked in the 1870s. Near Boot Hill is the **Gunfighter Wax Museum**, located in the **Kansas Teachers' Hall of Fame**. In Abilene, the **Eisenhower Center** houses the Eisenhower family home from 1898 to 1946, as well as a museum and library. **Wichita**, the largest city in Kansas, famed today for aircraft manufacture, is home to the **Museums on the River District**, which includes an art museum and a botanical garden. Particularly worth a visit are the **Old Cowtown Museum**, which introduces visitors to the cattle days of the 1870s with an open-air history exhibit, the **Mid-America All-Indian Center Museum**, where traditional and modern works by Native American artists are on display, and **Exploration Place**, with its many fascinating discovery exhibits. Wichita is also home to **Sedgwick County Zoo**, one of Kansas's top tourist attractions. Kansas's capital, **Topeka**, boasts the **Kansas Museum of History**, the **Kansas State Capitol**, dating back to 1866, and the **Topeka Zoological Park**.

For those hungry to be at the centre of the action, a trip to the stone monument 3km (2 miles) northwest of **Lebanon** on the northern border of the State is a must – it is the geographical centre point of the entire USA.

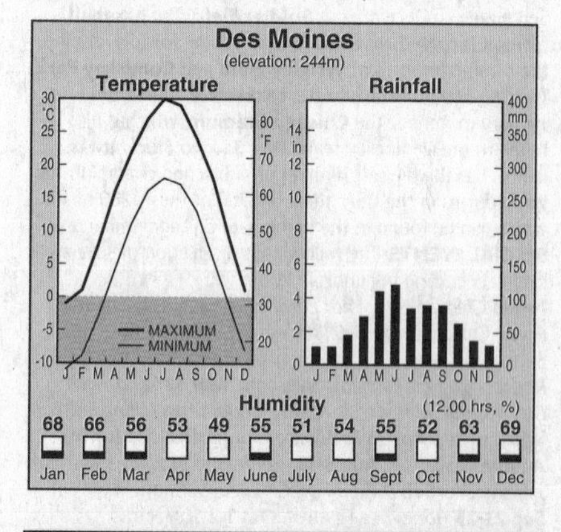

Kentucky

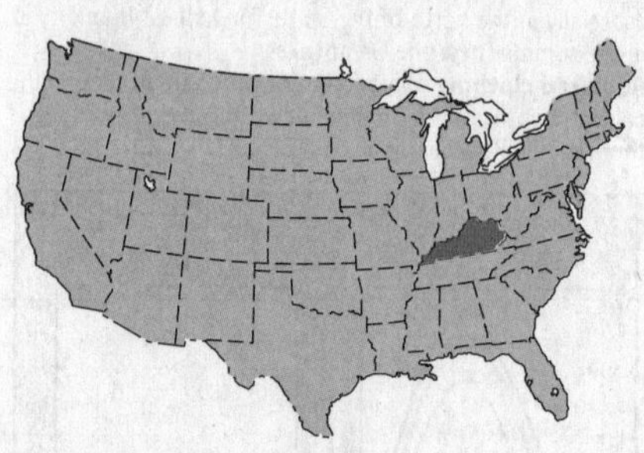

Kentucky Department of Tourism
500 Mero Street, Capital Tower, 22nd Floor, Frankfort, KY 40601
Tel: (502) 564 4930 *or* (800) 225 8747 (toll-free).
Fax: (502) 564 5695.
Website: www.kentuckytourism.com
Visit Kentucky USA (UK Office)
c/o Destination Marketing, Power Road Studios, 114 Power Road, Chiswick, London W4 5PY, UK
Tel: (020) 8994 0978. Fax: (020) 8994 0962.
E-mail: ky@destination-marketing.co.uk

Website: www.kentuckytourism.com
Greater Louisville CVB
1 Riverfront Plaza, 401 West Main Street, Suite 2300, Louisville, KY 40202
Tel: (502) 584 2121 *or* (800) 626 5646 (toll-free).
Fax: (502) 584 6697.
E-mail: info@gotolouisville.com
Website: www.gotolouisville.com
Lexington CVB
301 East Vine Street, Lexington, KY 40507
Tel: (859) 233 1221 *or* 233 7299 *or* (800) 838 1224 (toll-free) *or* (800) 845 3959 (toll-free). Fax: (859) 254 4555.
E-mail: vacation@visitlex.com
Website: www.visitlex.com
Northern Kentucky CVB
50 East River Center Boulevard, Suite 200, Covington, KY 41011
Tel: (859) 261 4677 *or* (800) 447 8489 (toll-free).
Fax: (859) 261 5135.
E-mail: info@nkycvb.com
Website: www.nkycvb.com
Kentucky Tourism Council
1100 US Highway 127 South, Building C, Frankfort, KY 40601
Tel: (502) 223 8687. Fax: (502) 223 5646.
E-mail: ktc@mis.net
Website: www.tourky.com
Southern and Eastern Kentucky Tourism Development Association
2292 South Highway 27, Somerset, KY 42501
Tel: (606) 677 6000/99. Fax: (606) 677 6059.
Website: www.tourseky.net *or* www.tourseky.com

General Information

Nickname: Bluegrass State
State bird: Cardinal
State flower: Goldenrod
CAPITAL: Frankfort
Date of admission to the Union: 1 June 1792
POPULATION: 4,145,922 (official estimate 2004)
POPULATION DENSITY: 39.6 per sq km
2003 total overseas arrivals/US ranking: 72,000/34
TIME: Eastern (GMT - 5) in the eastern part of the State; Central (GMT - 6) in the west.
Daylight Saving Time is observed.

THE STATE: Kentucky is best known for horses, bourbon, fried chicken and bluegrass music. **Lexington** is the horse-breeding centre and many of its surrounding farms welcome visitors on free tours. **Louisville** boasts the famous *Kentucky Derby*, along with historic buildings, top arts venues and steamboat trips. Other attractions include: the **Patton Museum** at **Fort Knox**; the pioneer settlement, **Homeplace 1850s**, at **Kentucky Lake**, one of the largest manmade lakes in the USA; the **Daniel Boone National Forest**; and **Bardstown**, the 'bourbon capital of the world'. **Berea** is the 'crafts capital' of the State.

Travel - International

AIR: International airports: *Cincinnati/Northern Kentucky International (CVG)* (website: www.cvgairport.com) is located in Northern Kentucky, 20km (12 miles) from Cincinnati, Ohio. Buses, shuttles and taxis are available to Cincinnati.
Louisville International (SDF) (website: www.louintlairport.com) is situated 8km (5 miles) south of the city. Buses, taxis, shuttles and limousines provide transportation to the city centre.
Domestic airports: *Blue Grass Field (LEX)* (website: www.bluegrassairport.com) in Lexington serves regional and some national carriers, with connecting flights via commuter carriers to smaller cities in the State.
RAIL: There is a daily *Amtrak* (tel: (800) 872 7245 (toll-free); website: www.amtrak.com) service between Chicago and New Orleans, which stops at Fulton. Three trains a week run between New York Union Station and Chicago, serving Ashland, South Portsmouth and Mayville. There is no service to Louisville, although *Amtrak Thruway* buses connect daily with Chicago.
ROAD: Approximate bus travel times: From Louisville to *Cincinnati* is two hours, to *Indianapolis* is two hours, to *Lexington* is two hours, to *Nashville* is three hours and to *Chicago* is six hours. From Lexington to *Cincinnati* is one hour and to *Knoxville* is three hours. The main service provider is *Greyhound* (tel: (800) 229 9424 (toll-free); website: www.greyhound.com).
URBAN: In Louisville, there is an extensive system of buses serving most of the metropolitan area, and a trolley service from the east side of Fourth Street to the Riverfront Wharf. The Toonville II Trolley serves Third, Fourth and Fifth Street, while the Main Street Trolley has stops on Main Street and Market Street.

Resorts & Excursions

LEXINGTON: The capital of Kentucky's horse country, Lexington has more than 250 horse farms in the area. The **Kentucky Horse Park**, a working horse farm, provides an educational look at the State's equestrian history. Visitors can watch films about horse racing and breeding, and demonstrations of horse shoeing and harness-making. The **International Museum of the Horse** and the **American Saddle Horse Museum** are also located here. **Keeneland Racecourse** is the setting for exciting thoroughbred races in April and October. Standard breeds compete at the nation's oldest existing racetrack, the **Red Mile Harness Track**, throughout the year. Other attractions in Lexington include the **Mary Todd Lincoln House**, the home of Abraham Lincoln's wife. During visits to the Todd home, Lincoln loved to spend time reading in his father-in-law's extensive library. The **Lexington Children's Museum** has a number of exciting exhibits that can be touched and explored by children, including a *Bubble Factory* and the *Science Station X*.
LOUISVILLE: Located at the **Falls of the Ohio River**, Louisville was founded by General George Rogers Clark in 1778 as a base from which to harass British troops during the American Revolution. Today, restored historic sites sit side-by-side with modern structures, and visitors can wander through the quaint streets in **Old Louisville**. The nation's oldest steamboat, the **Belle of Louisville**, still sails along the **Ohio River**. Other highlights in the city are **Glassworks**, a unique facility that includes glass studios, galleries and a cafe; the **Portland Museum of Art**, which includes a sound and light show; the **Falls of the Ohio State Park**, where visitors can walk onto the world's largest exposed Devonian fossil bed; **Louisville Science Center**; and the **Speed Art Museum**.
The two weeks of Derby celebrations lead up to the most important date on Louisville's calendar – the first Saturday in May, when the famous *Kentucky Derby* at **Churchill Downs** provides an exciting climax to the festivities.
ELSEWHERE IN BLUEGRASS COUNTRY: The region gets its name from the variety of grass that produces a small blue flower in early spring. Bluegrass country is famous for horses, tobacco and bourbon.
Shaker Village of Pleasant Hill lies about 30 minutes southwest of Lexington. Members of the 19th-century Shaker religious sect lived a simple life here, and, today, visitors can tour their 2024 hectare (5000 acre) farm and living history museum. Nearby **Harrodsburg** is the oldest permanent English settlement west of the Alleghenies. **Old Fort Harrod State Park** contains a part of the replica 1774 fort. Actors dressed in 18th-century costume demonstrate skills, such as blacksmithing and quilting.
Hodgenville, south of Louisville, is the birthplace of Abraham Lincoln. The Lincoln family lived at the **Sinking Spring Farm** for more than two years before moving to **Knob Creek**. **Lincoln's Boyhood Home** is a reproduction cabin located on the original site where he lived until he was eight years old. The **Abraham Lincoln Birthplace National Historic Site** has 56 steps, one for each year of his life. The 47 hectare (116 acre) park traces the history of the President's humble roots. In **Newport**, in the north of the State, across the river from Cincinnati, Ohio, is the **Newport Aquarium**, open daily, with 66 exhibits of fresh and saltwater fish from around the world, with a new permanent exhibit opened in 2004.
EASTERN HIGHLANDS: The vast **Daniel Boone National Forest**, with its magnificent **Red River Gorge**, runs through the entire region. Two of Kentucky's most beautiful lakes, **Cave Run Lake** and **Laurel River Lake**, lie at each end of the forest. The **Big South Fork National River and Recreation Area**, is a national park wilderness straddling the Kentucky-Tennessee border.
One of the most popular areas is **Cumberland Gap National Park**, with its breathtaking views of the **Appalachian Mountains**. The **Cumberland Falls** are known as the 'Niagara of the South' and this is one of the few places in the world where one can see a 'moonbow' on a regular basis. Canoeing and rafting trips are very popular in this area.
MAMMOTH CAVE NATIONAL PARK: Mammoth Cave is the largest known network of natural caves and underground passageways in the world, with more than 560km (350 miles) of explored passageways. Many species of animals and different types of cave formation can be

Credit: © Visit Kentucky USA

found within the national park. Park rangers lead tours of varying length from 30 minutes to six hours 30 minutes. Above ground, the park offers miles of hiking trails, including a wheelchair access route.

Social Profile

FOOD & DRINK: Kentucky is home to the famous 'Kentucky Fried Chicken', which consists of chicken fried in a secret original recipe involving a blend of 11 herbs. KFC fast food restaurants can be found throughout the USA. In the Bluegrass Region, many menus feature *Country Ham*, which is usually cured for a few years to strengthen its flavour. It is traditionally served with crunchy *Beaten Biscuits*. *Spoonbread* is a corn-based bread, so moist it has to be spooned out of the dish, and *Kentucky Burgoo* is a tasty local stew.
Bourbon is the number one drink in Kentucky. Visitors can take a distillery tour at **Maker's Mark Distillery**, near Loretto, **Labrot & Graham** near Versailles, **Buffalo Trace Distillery** in Frankfort, **Austin Nichols Distilling Company** and **Four Roses Kentucky Bourbon Whiskey Distillery** in Lawrenceburg, **Jim Beam's American Outpost** in Clermont, and **Heaven Hill** in Bardstown. Alcohol can be bought in 30 of Kentucky's 120 counties, and in 15 cities in the remaining 90 counties.
THEATRES & CONCERTS: The **Kentucky Center for the Arts** in Louisville offers a diverse mix of entertainment virtually every night of the year. Also in Louisville, the **Actors Theater** features a Tony Award-winning company which takes part in the successful *Humana Festival of New American Plays* in the spring.
NIGHTLIFE: Country music is very popular in many of the bars and clubs in Kentucky, which is not surprising for a State that has produced stars such as Billy Ray Cyrus, Crystal Gayle, Loretta Lynn and Dwight Yoakam. Jazz performances take place at Glassworks on Market Street, Louisville.
SHOPPING: Berea is Kentucky's arts and craft capital. Local shops sell pottery, woodwork, jewellery, quilts and weaving. The largest hand-weaving studio in the USA, *The Churchill Weavers* produces a quality collection of ladies accessories, blankets and neckties. Louisville is great for antique shopping. Popular antique shops in Louisville include **Den of Steven** and **Joe Ley Antiques**. In Western and Northern Kentucky, there is a variety of outlet malls in which to shop for bargains.
SPORT: Kentucky is called the 'horse capital of the world' and **riding** options range from pony trekking to overnight horse camping. Louisville hosts the annual *Equitana USA*, the world's fair of equestrian sports. Kentucky is a great place for **hiking** and **backpacking**. Two major trails, the *Sheltowee Trace National Recreation Trail* and the *Jenny Wiley National Recreation Trail*, provide routes through the scenic forested highlands of Eastern Kentucky.
Cumberland Gap National Park has 1790km (1112 miles) of trails, including the popular 34km (21 mile) *Ridge Trail*. The 14 major river systems in Kentucky offer a wide choice of **canoeing**, **kayaking** and **rafting** opportunities. *Rockcastle* is one of the most popular whitewater canoe runs in the USA. The **Daniel Boone National Forest** offers excellent **climbing**. The State's quiet, winding roads are ideal for **cycling** and almost 1000km (620 miles) of the *TransAmerica Bicycle Trail* are in Kentucky. For **golf** enthusiasts, Louisville's challenging *Valhalla Golf Course* hosted the 1996 and 2000 *PGA Championship*. The **Kentucky Speedway** is a motor racing circuit located 18km (30 miles) south of the *Cincinnati/Northern Kentucky International* airport.
SPECIAL EVENTS: The following is a selection of special events occurring in Kentucky in 2005:

Mar 12 *Mammoth Cave Hamfest*, Cave City. **Mar 17-20** *My Old Kentucky Home Festival of Quilts*, Bardstown. **Apr 14-16** *Hillbilly Days*, Pikeville. **Apr 15-May 8** *Kentucky Derby Festival*, Louisville. **Apr 20-23** *American Quilter's Society National Quilt Show*, Paducah. **May 7** *131st Kentucky Derby*, Louisville. **May 28-30** *Iberian Horse Weekend*, Lexington. **Jun 11-12** *Great American Brass Band Festival*, Danville. **Jul 6-10** *Shakespeare Festival*, Lexington. **Jul 8-10** *Berea Craft Festival*. **Jul 13-14** *National Corvette Homecoming*, Bowling Green. **Sep 14-18** *Kentucky Bourbon Festival*, Bardstown. **Sep 16-18** *Historic Constitution Square Festival*, Danville; *Spoonhead Festival*, Berea. **Oct 2** *Clog Fest*, Lexington. **Oct 8-9** *Kentucky Guild of Artists and Craftsmen Fall Fair*, Berea.

Climate

Kentucky has a temperate climate. Annual rainfall is 122cm (48 inches), including an average snowfall of 34.8cm (13.7 inches). The wettest seasons are spring and summer, and the driest is autumn.

Required clothing: Spring and autumn usually require light wraps, especially during the evening. Summer can be very warm, but cool evenings are not unusual.

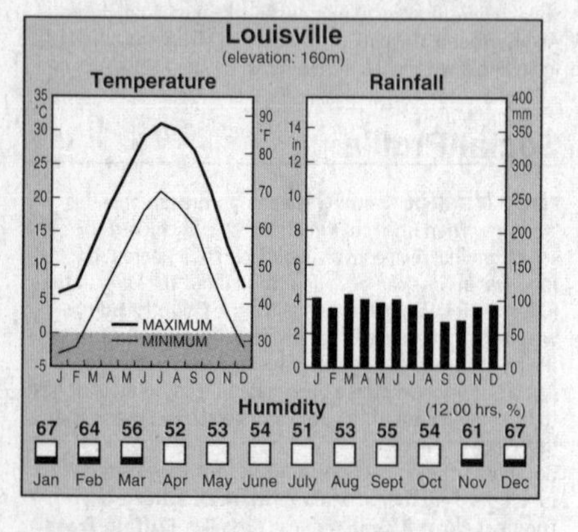

Louisiana

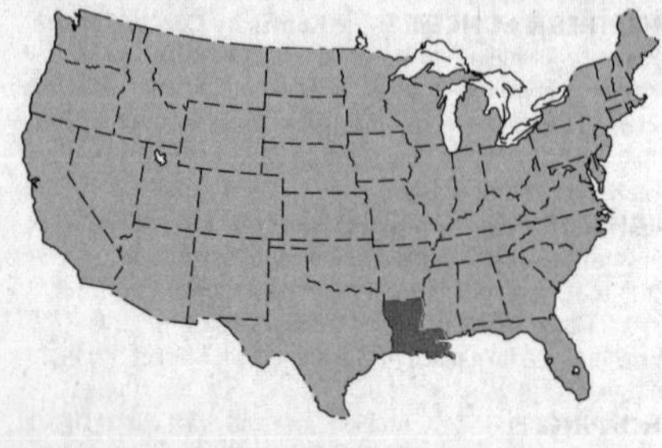

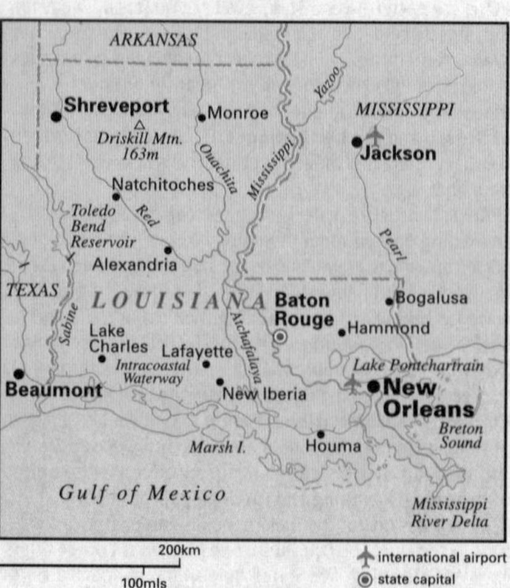

Louisiana Office of Tourism
Street address: 1051 North Third Street, Baton Rouge, LA 70802
Postal address: PO Box 94291, Baton Rouge, LA 70804
Tel: (225) 342 8100 *or* (800) 227 4386 (toll-free; trade only) *or* (800) 677 4082 (toll-free). Fax: (225) 342 8390.
E-mail: free.info@crt.state.la.us
Website: www.louisianatravel.com

Louisiana Office of Tourism (UK Office)
c/o Travel & Tourism Marketing Ltd, 33 Market Place, Hitchin, Hertfordshire SG5 1DY, UK
Tel: (01462) 458 696. Fax: (01462) 455 391.
E-mail: louisiana@ttmworld.co.uk
Website: www.louisianatravel.com

Baton Rouge Area CVB
730 North Boulevard, Baton Rouge, LA 70802
Tel: (225) 383 1825 *or* (800) 527 6843 (toll-free).
Fax: (225) 346 1253.
E-mail: br@bracvb.com
Website: www.visitbatonrouge.com

Lafayette Convention & Visitors Commission
Street address: 1400 NW Evangeline Thruway, Lafayette, LA 70501
Postal address: PO Box 52066, Lafayette, LA 70505
Tel: (337) 232 3737 *or* (800) 346 1958 (toll-free).
Fax: (337) 232 0161.
E-mail: info@lafayettetravel.com
Website: www.lafayettetravel.com

Natchitoches CVB
781 Front Street, Natchitoches, LA 71457
Tel: (318) 352 8072 *or* (800) 259 1714 (toll-free).
Fax: (318) 352 2415.
E-mail: est1714@natchitoches.net
Website: www.natchitoches.net

New Orleans Metropolitan CVB
2020 St Charles Avenue, New Orleans, LA 70130
Tel: (504) 566 5011 *or* (800) 748 8695 (toll-free).
Fax: (504) 566 5046.
E-mail: internet@neworleanscvb.com
Website: www.neworleanscvb.com

Shreveport-Bossier Convention & Tourists Bureau
Street address: 629 Spring Street, Shreveport, LA 71101
Postal address: PO Box 1761, Shreveport, LA 71166
Tel: (318) 222 9391 *or* (800) 551 8682 *or* (888) 458 4748 (toll-free). Fax: (318) 222 0056 *or* 429 0667.
E-mail: info2@shreveport-bossier.org
Website: www.shreveport-bossier.org

Southwest Louisiana CVB
1205 North Lakeshore Drive, Lake Charles, LA 70601
Tel: (337) 436 9588 *or* (800) 456 7952 (toll-free).
Fax: (337) 494 7952.
E-mail: touristinfo@visitlakecharles.org
Website: www.visitlakecharles.org

General Information

Nickname: Pelican State
State bird: Brown Pelican
State flower: Magnolia Grandiflora
CAPITAL: Baton Rouge
Date of admission to the Union: 30 Apr 1812
POPULATION: 4,515,770 (official estimate 2004)
POPULATION DENSITY: 33.6 per sq km
2003 total overseas arrivals/US ranking: 216,000/22
TIME: Central (GMT - 6). *Daylight Saving Time* is observed.

THE STATE: Louisiana's marshy **Mississippi Valley** is one of the most attractive areas of the USA. **New Orleans**, its largest city, is one of the country's major tourist destinations. It is famed for Dixieland jazz, architecture, superb cuisine and its unique French Quarter. The city also boasts a wide choice of museums and galleries. Other places to see in the State include **Lafayette**, a city of magnificent gardens and the start of the 40km (25 mile) **Azalea Trail**; the **Atchafalaya Basin**, the largest and most remote swamp in the USA; the huge salt domes of **Avery**; and **Alexandria**, surrounded by forests and parks. The 138m- (452ft-) high marble and limestone **Capitol Building** is situated in **Baton Rouge**.

Travel - International

AIR: *Louis Armstrong New Orleans International (MSY)* (website: www.flymsy.com) is located 29km (18 miles) from New Orleans' city centre (travel time – 20 to 30 minutes). Public buses run to the city centre every 15 to 20 minutes (weekdays) and every 30 minutes (weekends), daily 0600-1830. *Greyhound* (see below) also has buses from the airport to many destinations. *Mississippi Coast Service (Coastliner)* provides a shuttle service to the Gulf Coast and destinations en route, making several trips 0800-2330 daily. *St Tammany Tours* provides a service between the airport and Lake Pontchartrain (north shore); this 24-hour service requires advance reservation. Taxis are available 24 hours a day, and limousines are also available at the airport. Facilities include a bank, shops, snack bars, restaurant/bar, post office and car hire (*Alamo, Avis, Budget, Hertz, National* and *Thrifty*).

Approximate flight times: From New Orleans to *Atlanta* is one hour 25 minutes, to *Chicago* is two hours 20 minutes, to *Los Angeles* is four hours 10 minutes, to *Miami* is one hour 45 minutes and to *New York* is two hours 50 minutes.

RIVER: The *Delta Queen Steamboat Company* (tel: (504) 586 0631 *or* (800) 543 1949 (toll-free); website: www.deltaqueen.com) runs scheduled paddlewheel cruises up and down the Mississippi River, stopping at several cities. The *New Orleans Steamboat Company* (tel: (504) 586 8777 *or* (800) 233 2628 (toll-free); website: www.steamboatnatchez.com) offers a number of harbour cruise options. Information and tickets are available at booths behind Jackson Brewery and the aquarium in New Orleans.

RAIL: *Amtrak* trains serve New Orleans (tel: (800) 872 7245 (toll-free); website: www.amtrak.com). Services include the 'Sunset Limited', which links Los Angeles with Orlando (Florida) via New Orleans; the 'Crescent', which links New Orleans with New York via Atlanta (Georgia); and the 'City of New Orleans', which heads north from New Orleans to Chicago via Memphis (Tennessee). Trains depart from New Orleans Union Passenger Terminal, located at 1001 Loyola Avenue.

ROAD: *Greyhound* buses connect all Louisiana's major towns and cities with destinations throughout the USA (tel: (800) 229 9424 (toll-free); website: www.greyhound.com). Buses stop at New Orleans Union Passenger Terminal (see above).

Approximate driving times: From New Orleans to *Mobile* is three hours, to *Houston* is six hours, to *Birmingham* is seven hours and to *Memphis* is eight hours. All times are based on nonstop driving at or below the applicable speed limits.

Approximate bus travel times: From New Orleans to *Mobile* is three hours, to *Houston* is eight hours, to *Birmingham* is eight hours and to *Memphis* is 10 hours.

URBAN: Bus: The famous 'Streetcar Named Desire' that Blanche Dubois dreamt of has been replaced, rather prosaically, by a bus. However, bus services are extensive and available throughout the city. The *Regional Transit Authority* offers a *VisiTour* pass allowing unlimited rides on buses and streetcars all day. **Streetcar:** These still run a 24-hour service (with a reduced service at night) on St Charles Avenue and Carrollton in New Orleans, starting from Canal Street. A new streetcar runs every 15 minutes Mon-Fri 0600-2300 and Sat-Sun 0700-2300, along the riverfront between the Convention Center and Esplanade Avenue. **Car hire:** A national driving licence and a major credit card are needed to hire a car. **Horsecab:** Horse-drawn carriages offer a scenic means of transport through the French Quarter.

Resorts & Excursions

New Orleans

New Orleans was founded in 1718 and named after Philippe Duc D'Orléans. Today, this little outpost is called 'The Big Easy', and is a city known worldwide for jazz, Creole cuisine, riverboats and carnivals.

Music plays an integral part in the unique atmosphere of New Orleans. Old-line musicians play classic tunes during brunch and dinner, street musicians huddle in doorways at dusk to perform, and free concerts are offered weekly in the **French Quarter**. Louis Armstrong, Harry Connick Jr, Fats Domino, Pete Fountain, the Neville Brothers and Jelly Roll Morton are all part of the city's rich musical heritage. There is more music in New Orleans than ever before, with Zydeco, rock and roll, rhythm and blues, Dixieland, gospel, Cajun music and country joining the jazz tradition. To hear traditional jazz at its best, one should visit **Bourbon Street** or **Preservation Hall**, where musicians play every evening. Music festivals include the *New Orleans Jazz and Heritage Festival*, which takes place in April and May each year. Stars that have performed at the event include Aretha Franklin, Bob Dylan and Patti LaBelle.

New Orleans' *Mardi Gras* is the biggest party of the year and rocks the whole city during the three weeks leading up to Ash Wednesday. Colourful parades, masquerade balls and street parties make the festival one of the loudest and liveliest celebrations in the world.

There is also a rich cultural side to New Orleans. It was here that the country's first opera house was built. The city boasts an excellent **Museum of Art** and a **Contemporary Arts Center**, while the **Warehouse District** has been revitalised by galleries, restaurants and shops that display the crafts of local artists. The **Louisiana State Museum** on Jackson Square includes exhibitions on Mardi Gras and jazz. The collection of French works at the **New Orleans Museum of Art** is renowned throughout the world. At the **Louisiana Children's Museum**, kids of all ages can pretend to star in their own TV show or shop in a recreated mini-mart. In addition to the opera, ballet and symphony seasons, there are regular Broadway shows and live theatre in almost a dozen locations.

Excursions: There are tours of every description in New Orleans that take in everything from haunted houses to alligator-filled swamps. Also popular are the literary tours of the homes and haunts of famous writers – William Faulkner, Tennessee Williams, Lillian Hellman and Sherwood Anderson all lived and worked here. Bayou/swamp tours offer Cajun

A B C D E F G H I J K L M N O P Q R S T U V W X Y Z

storytellers, food, music and an opportunity to go crawfish harvesting with the locals. Another special tour is one that explores the city's Black Heritage and highlights the contributions of African-Americans to New Orleans.
Ponchatoula (and its antiques), **Mandeville** (on Lake Pontchartrain), **Covington** (with its artists colony) and **Hammond** are just a few of the towns within easy reach of New Orleans. At the **Global Wildlife Center**, visitors can enjoy horseback riding among the exotic animals that roam the 364 hectare (900 acre) park. Nearby, the lush swampland bordering the **Pearl River** is popular with birdwatchers. At **Honey Island Swamp**, boat tours are available. **Kenner** features **Rivertown USA**, which is a combination of historical sites and family attractions in a Victorian setting.
Ferries provide transport across the **Mississippi River**, including one departing from the levée at the foot of Canal Street. One-day cruises are available: *Steamboat Natchez* has harbour, dinner and jazz cruises; *John James Audubon* has a zoo cruise between the **Aquarium** and **Riverfront Park** to the **Audubon Zoo**; and *Louisiana Swamp Tours* offers a selection of special cruises through the Louisiana swamps, including buffet and dinner cruises.

The Rest of the State

BATON ROUGE: The capital of Louisiana is also the heart of the Southern 'Plantation Country' region. The 'Blues' are a large part of the Baton Rouge heritage, sung by slaves as they picked plantation cotton, and the city was the original home of many of the USA's most well-known blues musicians.
The **Capitol Building** is a 34-storey building with a viewing platform overlooking 11 hectares (27 acres) of formal gardens in the Capitol grounds. Other attractions include the **Old Capitol**, with its **Center for Political and Governmental History**; the **Louisiana Governor's Mansion**, with exhibits of art, natural history and anthropology; **Baton Rouge Zoo**, with its 57 hectares (140 acres) of walk-through areas and forest settings for over 400 animals; the **Louisiana Arts and Science Center Riverside**, located in a remodelled railroad station; and the **LSU Rural Life Museum**, an outdoor museum located in the grounds of a former plantation, showing the type of work done in a 19th-century plantation community. Many magnificent old plantation mansions are available for viewing in this area, some offering bed & breakfast facilities as well as tours.
LAFAYETTE: The industrial and cultural hub of 'Cajun' country is home to 100,000 people, many of whom are descended from French-speaking Canadians from Nova Scotia. They settled in the region after 1764, having been deported by the British for refusing to give up the Catholic faith or pledge allegiance to the British crown. These people were originally known as 'Acadians', but the name was eventually shortened to 'Cajuns'. The land is full of swamps and bayous. **Acadian Village** and **Vermilionville** are faithful replicas of early Cajun communities.
Excursions: Houma, a bayou town, is known for its many swamp tours, where alligators, wading birds and myriad other forms of swampife thrive. **New Iberia**, home of world-famous *Tabasco* sauce, offers tours of subtropical gardens, stately antebellum homes, rice mills and the hot sauce and pepper plant farms. **St Martinville** is a quiet and elegant town once known as 'Le Petit Paris' for its luxurious balls, operas and highlife. Its Cajun museum and church are well worth visiting. On the *Creole Nature Trail*, near **Lake Charles**, ducks, geese, alligators, nutria and muskrats run rampant.
NATCHITOCHES: The oldest town in Louisiana, perched on **Cane River Lake**, was first established as a fort and trading post in 1714 to prevent the Spanish from encroaching on French territory. It is now a charming lake town and farm centre. It has numerous historic houses, many offering bed & breakfast, and is surrounded by pecan orchards, cotton farms and 18th-century plantation homes. The region around Natchitoches is known as 'The Crossroads' because it is where the French and Spanish heritage of the south meets the pioneer spirit of the north. It is also a haven for country music, having spawned such luminaries as Jerry Lee Lewis and Mickey Gilley.
Excursions: To the northeast, **Monroe**, another river town, also has many historic houses and a museum; the **Louisiana Purchase Gardens and Zoo** in Monroe is a 40 hectare (100 acre) park with moss-laden oaks, formal gardens and winding waterways. *Dogwood Trail Drive* is a 29km (18 mile) journey over the State's highest hills; it passes among blossoming dogwood trees, revealing the region's particular beauty.
SHREVEPORT: A leading oil and gas centre located close to the Texan border, with a distinctly American West flavour, Shreveport is also renowned as a trade, gaming and entertainment area; the town hosts several major annual events, attracting visitors from far and wide (see *Special Events* section). **Shreve Square** has an attractive cluster of nightclubs, restaurants and shops.
Attractions include the **Louisiana State Exhibit Museum**, featuring dioramas, an art gallery, historical murals and archaeological relics; **RW Norton Museum**, featuring Old West artists Frederic Remington and Charles M Russell; **Pioneer Heritage Center**; and the **American Rose Center**, a famous garden showplace.
Excursions: This region is known as 'Sportman's Paradise' for its many forests and lakes offering opportunities for fishing, hunting, canoeing and hiking. An annual *Fishing Tournament* takes place at *Toledo Bend*. **Louisiana Downs Thoroughbred Racetrack**, across the **Red River** in **Bossier City**, is open for racing from late spring until the autumn. **Poverty Point State Historic Site** is an ancient Native American religious area dating from 1700 BC and one of the most important archaeological finds in the USA.
EUNICE: One of the most charming towns in Louisiana, Eunice has a strong musical tradition, with excellent Cajun music played every weekend at the **Prairie Acadia Cultural Center** in the **Jean Lafitte National Park**. The center also has some exhibits on local life. Another attraction is the **Eunice Museum**. The town celebrates *Mardi Gras* in style, with an annual spectacular that involves horses parading though the downtown and, of course, lots of Cajun music.

Social Profile

FOOD & DRINK: Creole cooking is a speciality in Louisiana, where the mix of cultures has resulted in a cuisine using the best elements of each nationality. The State's location makes it a prime spot for seafood: fresh fish, shrimp, crabs, oysters and crayfish abound. Game meat is also popular in Louisiana cuisine, including rabbit and wild turkey. Tropical fruits, such as bananas and pineapples, are often used in Creole cooking, along with spices such as hot peppers and *filé* (the ground powder for making gumbo). Oyster bars are prevalent, especially along the seaside or riverfront. Creole cafes serve traditional favourites, such as gumbo, red beans and rice. Other Cajun specialities include *étouffée*, *sauce piquante* and *jambalaya*. A meat pie, shaped like a half-moon and filled with a spicy mixture of ground beef and pork, is a speciality of Natchitoches. The town of Henderson on the edge of Atchafalaya Swamp is famous for its Cajun cuisine, and its many restaurants, specialising in seafood, attract visitors from miles away. *Southern Cookin'*, found in the Crossroads region in northern Louisiana, is savoured for its delicious fried chicken, barbecued meat, cornbread and peach pie.
New Orleans is justly renowned for its superb gourmet restaurants which offer Creole specialities, including Oysters Rockefeller, Bananas Foster and *pompano en papillote*. One can savour a breakfast of *beignets* and *café au lait*, dine while overlooking the city or the riverfront, or travel to the seafood houses out by the lake.
Given its southern climate, cold drinks are much relished in this State. Iced tea is a favourite. Alcohol can only be purchased by those over 21 years of age, and is available at supermarkets and liquor stores. Some parts of northern Louisiana do not sell alcohol.
THEATRES & CONCERTS: *Le Petit Théâtre du Vieux Carré* in New Orleans is one of the oldest theatre groups in the country and is highly recommended. Shreveport houses one of the best-known US community theatre groups in its **Little Theater**. Louisiana has engendered a rich black music scene derived from the rhythmic chants of riverboat men, the soulful gospel tunes of field hands and the wild syncopation of jazz greats such as Jelly Roll Morton and Louis Armstrong. Free jazz and brass-band concerts take place in Jackson Square, in New Orleans' French Quarter.
NIGHTLIFE: Nightlife is especially lively in New Orleans. The shows and cabarets of **Bourbon Street** are renowned – every third door on this famous street is a nightclub.
SHOPPING: Louisiana offers tax-free shopping to international visitors for items sold by a participating merchant. A tax refund voucher can be requested from any *Louisiana Tax Free Shopping (LTFS)* participator and the tax can be refunded at the LTFS centre at New Orleans airport on presentation of voucher, receipt, passport and travel ticket. Refunds can also be obtained by mail if sent with voucher, receipts, travel ticket and a notarised statement explaining why vouchers were not redeemed at the airport as well as the present whereabouts of the merchandise.
Among the cities of this State, New Orleans has many excellent shopping opportunities. Souvenirs are plentiful, and other good buys include Creole pecan pralines, Mardi Gras masks, beautifully bottled and hand-mixed perfumes, and various antiques on sale in shops on **Royal Street**. In addition, fine retail shops can be found at **Jackson Brewery**. The **French Market** is the USA's oldest city market and offers a mix of speciality shops, chain stores and restaurants. For second-hand items, the **Community Flea Market** is located nearby. Other excellent shopping areas in New Orleans include the **New Orleans Center**, **Canal Place**, **The Esplanade**, **Riverwalk** and **Uptown Square Shopping Center**. **Northgate Mall** in Lafayette and

Credit: © Louisiana Travel & Tourism Marketing

Lakeside Shopping Center in Metairie are also good options.
SPORT: Fishing, both freshwater and saltwater, is popular all year round. King mackerel, jewfish, marlin, bluefish, cobia, channel bass, pompano, red snapper and amber jack are found in coastal areas and in the Gulf of Mexico. Crayfish (or crawfish) are an inland speciality. The bass fishing is also highly regarded. Tarpon fishing is available near Houma and at Grand Isle. A fishing licence is necessary for non-residents. **Hunting** is available during the winter months with a licence; popular game includes duck, squirrel, deer, turkey and wildfowl. Bear, deer and turkey require a special licence (further information is available from the Wildlife and Fisheries Commission in New Orleans). **Swimming** is available in recreation areas throughout Louisiana and 18-hole golf courses are available in Lafayette (City Park Golf Course), Shreveport (Andrew Querbes Park), Lakeside and New Orleans (Lakewood Country Club, which also sponsors the *Greater New Orleans Open* every spring).
SPECIAL EVENTS: Lousiana's famous New Orleans *Carnival* or *Mardi Gras* comes to a climax every year on Shrove Tuesday. Costumes, dazzling floats, street dancing and general wild abandonment are the order of the day. Mardi Gras country-style celebrations also take place in southern Louisiana towns, with music, dancing and enough gumbo to feed the whole town.
The following is a selection of special events occurring in Louisiana in 2005; for a detailed programme of events, contact the Lousiana Department of Culture, Recreation & Tourism (see *Contact Addresses* section):
Jan 16 Oyster Food Fest, Lafitte. **Feb 8** *Mardi Gras Day*, New Orleans. **Mar 12** *Wearin' of the Green Parade* (St Patrick's Day celebrations), Baton Rouge. **Mar 30-Apr 3** *Tennessee Williams Literary Festival*, New Orleans. **Apr 1-3** *Cajun Hot Sauce Festival*, New Iberia. **Apr 3** *Celebration of the Louisiana Iris*, Lafitte. **Apr 8-10** *French Quarter Festival*, New Orleans; Ponchatoula Strawberry Festival. **Apr 23-May 2** *New Orleans Jazz and Heritage Festival*. **May 6-8** *Crawfish Festival*, Breaux Bridge. **Jul 16-17** *Jean Lafitte Seafood Festival*. **Aug 4-7** *Satchmo Summer Fest*, New Orleans. **Sep 4** *Creole Zydeco Festival*, St Martinsville. **Sep 24-25** *Louisiana Cane Sugar Festival & Fair*, New Iberia. **Aug 18-22** *Delcambre Shrimp Festival*. **Sep 9-11** *Rayne Frog Festival*. **Oct 1-8** *Red River Revel Arts Festival*, Shreveport. **Oct 8** *Fall Festival*, Mooringsport. **Oct 28-Nov 13** *Louisiana State Fair*, Shreveport. **Nov 5-Dec 11** *Louisiana Renaissance Festival*, Hammond. **Nov 19-Jan 6 2006** *Festival of Lights (Christmas celebrations)*, Natchitoches.
In addition, a number of other Cajun music festivals take place throughout the year, including:
Apr 20-24 *Festival International de Louisiane*, Lafayette. **Jun 4-5** *Cajun Music Festival*, Mamou. **Sep 3** *Southwest Louisiana Zydeco Music Festival*, Plaisance. **Sep 16-18** *Festivals Acadiens*, Lafayette.

Climate

Humid and subtropical. Milder in spring, autumn and winter.
Required clothing: Lightweight cotton clothing for summer, with sweaters and jackets for winter. Rainwear or an umbrella is advised for all seasons.

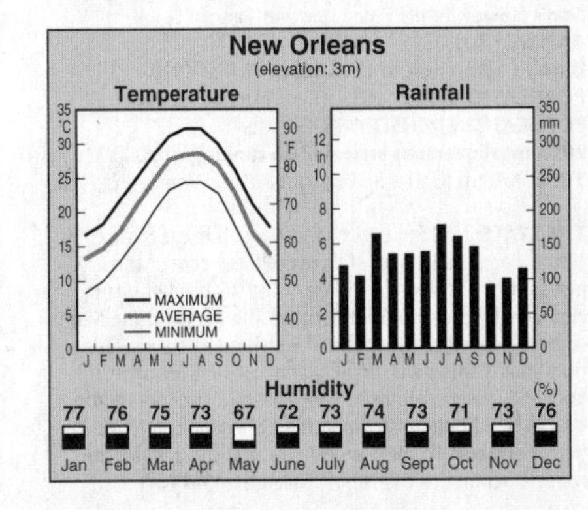

Maine

Maine Office of Tourism
59 State House Station, Augusta, ME 04333
Tel: (207) 624 7483 *or* (888) 624 6345 (toll-free).
Fax: (207) 287 8070.
E-mail: katie.n.woodbury@maine.gov
Website: www.visitmaine.com
Acadia National Park
PO Box 177, Eagle Lake Road, Bar Harbor, ME 04609
Tel: (207) 288 3338. Fax: (207) 288 8813.
E-mail: acadia_information@nps.gov
Website: www.nps.gov/acad
CVB of Greater Portland
245 Commercial Street, Portland, ME 04101
Tel: (207) 772 5800 *or* 4994 (groups).
Fax: (207) 874 9043.
E-mail: info@visitportland.com
Website: www.visitportland.com
Kennebunk & Kennebunkport Chamber of Commerce
Street address: 17 Western Avenue, Kennebunk, ME 04043
Postal address: PO Box 740, Kennebunk, ME 04043
Tel: (207) 967 0857 *or* (800) 982 4421 (toll-free).
Fax: (207) 967 2867.
E-mail: info@visitthekennebunks.com
Website: www.visitthekennebunks.com

Credit: © Maine Officer of Tourism

General Information

Nickname: Pine Tree State
State bird: Chickadee
State flower: White Pine Cone and Tassel
CAPITAL: Augusta
Date of admission to the Union: 15 Mar 1820
POPULATION: 1,317,253 (official estimate 2004)
POPULATION DENSITY: 14.4 per sq km
2003 total overseas arrivals/US ranking: 115,000/31
TIME: Eastern (GMT - 5). *Daylight Saving Time* is observed.

THE STATE: Nothing ever changes much in the State of Maine. Forests and lakes still cover 90 per cent of the land, just as they did when Leif Ericson and his band of Viking explorers first set foot on the coast. The length of the Maine coast from Kittery to Lubec still testifies to two vigorous traditions: fishing and shipbuilding. Lobsters are plentiful here and lobster pounds dot the coastline. Visitors should bear in mind that lobster-poaching is a serious offence here. **Portland**, Maine's largest city, features a Victorian reconstruction in what is now called the **Old Port Exchange**. Ferries run to the nearby **Casco Bay Islands**. **Sebago Lake** provides opportunities for water-skiing, while **Freeport** offers opportunities for budget shopping. A few miles south of Portland and a popular haunt for authors and artists is the town of **Kennebunk**, filled with bookshops and art galleries. To the east is the town's coastal counterpart, **Kennebunkport**, the summer home of former US President George Bush and family.
In the summer, crowds flock to **Camden**, 161km (100 miles) northeast of Portland. The **Camden Hills State Park** offers more than 40km (25 miles) of trails and a harbour view. In **Belfast**, north of Camden, travellers can enjoy antique sales and flea markets. Further along the coast, boating excursions depart from forested **Deer Isle** to **Isle au Haut**, part of **Acadia National Park**, boasting 47,633 acres (19,277 hectares) of lakes, woodlands, ponds and mountains. The pretty village of **Bar Harbor** makes a good base to visit the carriage roads and hiking trails of the park's main sector on **Mount Desert Island**.

Portland, Maine (elevation: 31m)

Temperature — MAXIMUM / MINIMUM (°C / °F)
Rainfall (in / mm)

Humidity (12.00 hrs, %)

Jan	Feb	Mar	Apr	May	June	July	Aug	Sept	Oct	Nov	Dec
62	61	60	57	58	60	63	62	63	60	63	64

Maryland

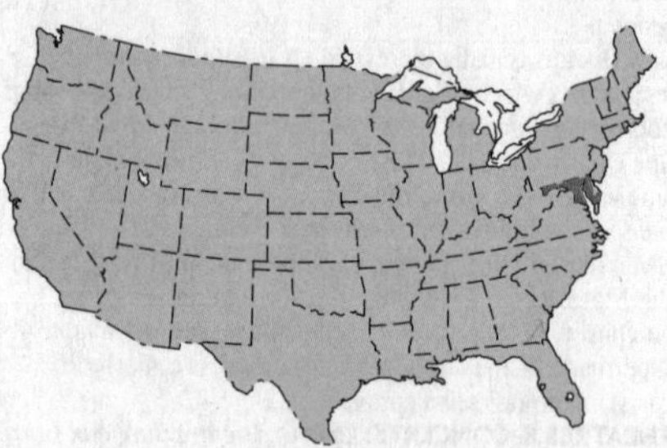

Maryland Office of Tourism Development
217 East Redwood Street, 9th Floor, Baltimore, MD 21202
Tel: (410) 767 3400 *or* (800) 634 7386 (toll-free).
Fax: (410) 333 6643.
E-mail: info@mdisfun.org
Website: www.choosemaryland.org
Annapolis & Anne Arundel County CVB
26 West Street, Annapolis, MD 21401
Tel: (410) 280 0445. Fax: (410) 263 9591.
E-mail: info@visit-annapolis.org
Website: www.visit-annapolis.org
Baltimore Area Convention & Visitors Association
100 Light Street, 12th Floor, Baltimore, MD 21202
Tel: (410) 659 7300 *or* (877) 225 8466 (toll-free).
Fax: (410) 727 2308.
E-mail: vc@baltimore.org
Website: www.baltimore.org

General Information

Nickname: Old Line State *or* Free State
State bird: Baltimore Oriole
State flower: Black-eyed Susan
CAPITAL: Annapolis
Date of admission to the Union: 28 Apr 1788 (original 13 States; date of ratification of the Constitution)
POPULATION: 5,558,058 (official estimate 2004)
POPULATION DENSITY: 173 per sq km
2003 total overseas arrivals/US ranking: 198,000/23
TIME: Eastern (GMT - 5). *Daylight Saving Time* is observed.

THE STATE: Maryland, one of the original 13 States of the USA, was founded by Lord Baltimore in 1634. Its **Atlantic Plain**, divided by **Chesapeake Bay**, rises through the rolling hills and scenic farmland of the State's heartland to the **Allegheny Mountains** of the northwest. Its tourist destinations range from the 16km (10 miles) of white, sandy beaches at **Ocean City** to **Baltimore's** bustling **Inner Harbor**. Chesapeake Bay's 6400km (4000 miles) of shoreline, including its tributaries, separate the **Eastern Shore** area of Maryland from the rest of the State. The twin-spanned **Chesapeake Bay Bridge** is the major link between the two sections. The distance between Baltimore and Washington, DC is only about 60km (40 miles).

Travel - International

AIR: International airports: *Baltimore/Washington International (BWI)* (website: www.bwiairport.com) is 16km (10 miles) south of Baltimore and 40km (25 miles) northeast of Washington, DC. Some 19 million passengers passed through this ultra-modern airport in 2002. MTA light-rail services depart every 17 minutes to Baltimore (travel time - approximately 25 minutes), while airport shuttles run every 20 minutes (travel time - 30 minutes). MARC commuter trains run hourly on weekdays between Washington, DC, and Baltimore Pennsylvania Station via the airport. Fast and frequent shuttle buses and rail services are also available to Washington, DC. Taxis and limousines are available, and *Alamo, Avis, Budget, Dollar, Enterprise, Hertz, National* and *Thrifty* car hire companies are represented.
Approximate flight times: From Baltimore to *London* is seven hours 30 minutes, to *Los Angeles* is five hours 45 minutes and to *New York* is one hour 15 minutes.
RAIL: Baltimore is on the main East Coast *Amtrak* line (tel: (800) 872 7245 (toll-free); website: www.amtrak.com) and consequently receives frequent direct services from as far afield as New Orleans and Miami. There are also frequent shuttles to Washington, DC, New York and Boston. For approximate travel times on this line, see the *New York* section. Trains arrive at Pennsylvania Station, 1515 North Charles Street.
ROAD: *Greyhound* (tel: (800) 229 9424 (toll-free); website: www.greyhound.com) buses stop at the Greyhound Bus Station, 2110 Haines Street, in downtown Baltimore.
Approximate driving times: From Baltimore to *Washington, DC* is 50 minutes, to *Philadelphia* is two hours, to *New York* is four hours, to *Chicago* is 15 hours, to *Miami* is 23 hours, to *Dallas* is 29 hours, to *Los Angeles* is 56 hours and to *Seattle* is 59 hours. All times are based on non-stop driving at or below the applicable speed limits.
Approximate bus travel times: From Baltimore to *Washington, DC* is one hour, to *Philadelphia* is two hours 30 minutes and to *New York* is four hours.
URBAN: The entire Baltimore metropolitan area is covered by the *Maryland Transit Administration* (website: www.mtamaryland.com), which runs buses, light rail and the metro. Services run 0600-0000 (weekdays) and 0700-0000 (weekends); exact change is required on buses. Water taxis provide regular cross-harbour services, including a route between the National Aquarium and Fell's Point. Taxis can be hailed easily on the street in major tourism areas, and in front of major hotels, or ordered by phone. Cars and motorhomes can be hired.

Resorts & Excursions

BALTIMORE: Maryland's major city is one of the USA's busiest ports. Restoration of the city's **Inner Harbor** area has created one of the major tourist destinations in the mid-Atlantic region. Baltimore has a cosmopolitan population of 650,000 (more than 2.5 million in the metro area) and an attractive village-like atmosphere.
The Inner Harbor area contains the **Top of the World Observation Level** at the **World Trade Center**, the **National Aquarium** in Baltimore, the **Maryland Science Center** and two pavilions on the water's edge, filled with shops and restaurants. It is also the site of the **Port Discovery** children's museum. The open-air **Harborplace Amphitheatre** is the site of the annual summer-long street performers' festival. Nearby is the **Charles Center** with 9 hectares (22 acres) of offices, tower blocks, overhead walkways, fountains and plazas, including the **Morris Mechanic Theater**. Also nearby is the **Baltimore Arena**,

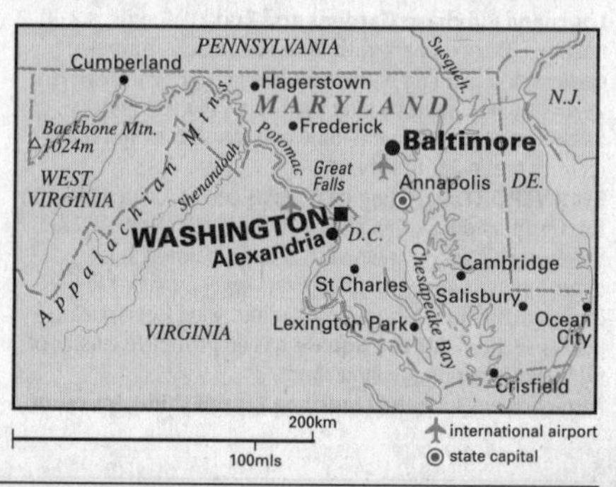

Credit: © Capital Region USA

which is the site for indoor soccer and other special attractions. The beautiful **Pier Six Concert Pavilion**, at the Inner Harbor, hosts concerts during the summer months (June to late September). City art museums include the **Baltimore Museum of Art**, **Walters Art Museum** and the **American Visionary Art Museum**. **Mount Vernon Place** contains 19th-century houses and squares, and various cultural institutions, such as the **Peabody Conservatory of Music**. It also includes the **Washington Monument**, which can be climbed for a panoramic view. A short water-taxi ride or drive away from the Inner Harbor is the star-shaped, brick-built **Fort McHenry National Monument**, whose bombardment in 1814 inspired the writing of 'The Star-Spangled Banner' and where special drills and military ceremonies are performed. The neighbourhoods of **Fell's Point** and **Little Italy** can also be reached by water taxi.

CAPITAL REGION: A town of quaint brick buildings and parks, **Frederick** is an excellent starting point for a tour of Civil War sites, which are found in and around the city. **Gambrill State Park**, just west of the town, offers outstanding panoramic views from the Catoctin peaks. **Camp David Presidential Retreat**, near **Thurmont**, is the traditional retreat for US Presidents. The public is not allowed inside, but visitors can experience the same lovely landscape in **Catoctin Mountain Park**, which surrounds it. **Cunningham Falls State Park** is also nearby.

ANNAPOLIS & THE EASTERN SHORE: The State capital has an attractive harbour, the impressive campus of the US Naval Academy and beautiful period architecture. Annapolis makes a good starting point for a tour of the **Eastern Shore**, since it is just a few miles from the famous **Bay Bridge**. The bridge leads to **St Michaels**, a quaint town that highlights life along **Chesapeake Bay**; **Crisfield** and **Smith Island**, home to huge populations of Maryland blue crabs; **Salisbury**, where visitors will find the **Ward Museum of Wildfowl Art**; and **Ocean City**, a lovely beach resort boasting an expansive white sand beach, a 5km- (3 mile-) long boardwalk, amusements, tram rides, boating and deep-sea fishing.

WESTERN MARYLAND: More rugged than the rest of Maryland, this part of the State extends into the **Blue Ridge** and **Allegheny Mountains**. The forested peaks and valleys offer all manner of summer and winter activities for the outdoor enthusiast.

The **Chesapeake & Ohio Canal National Historic Park**, stretching 295km (184 miles) from Washington, DC to **Cumberland** in Western Maryland, is where the young Lieutenant-Colonel George Washington began his military career. His headquarters can still be seen here. The canal was once a major avenue of commerce. The towpath for mule-drawn barges now serves as a popular hiking and biking trail. **Deep Creek Lake** in **Garrett County** is the State's four-season resort, with skiing, golf and many water-based activities.

Social Profile

FOOD & DRINK: Maryland is well known for its many outstanding restaurants offering fresh seafood caught in Chesapeake Bay. Establishments range from the very expensive to cheap fast food counters.

THEATRES & CONCERTS: The *Baltimore Symphony Orchestra* gives concerts in the **Joseph Meyerhoff Symphony Hall** and at **Oregon Ridge Park** for outdoor summer concerts. The *Baltimore Opera* performs at the **Lyric Theater**. The *Annapolis Symphony Orchestra* plays at the **Maryland Hall for the Creative Arts**. The **Peabody Conservatory of Music** in Baltimore is the oldest music school in the country and visitors can attend concerts and recitals by faculty students and guest artists.

NIGHTLIFE: Baltimore's **Fell's Point** district is a historic waterfront neighbourhood that was once a shipbuilding centre. Today, it is home to a variety of restaurants and pubs known for their lively atmosphere. The nearby neighbourhood of **Canton** is rapidly gaining a similar reputation.

SHOPPING: Shopaholics will want to visit **Harborplace** and **The Gallery**, three buildings filled with clothing shops, gift boutiques and eating places located in the heart of the Inner Harbor. Antique lovers should head to **Howard Street**, better known as **Antique Row**. About 20 minutes outside of Baltimore, there is a huge array of assorted shops along the main street of Ellicott City. **Towson Town Center**, north of Baltimore, is a popular mall. **Arundel Mills**, near Baltimore/Washington International Airport, offers discounted merchandise and entertainment facilities.

SPECIAL EVENTS: The following is a selection of special events occurring in Maryland in 2005:

Feb 25-27 *American Craft Council Baltimore Show*, Baltimore. **Apr 3-May 1** *Spring Festival*, Towsontown. **Apr 28-May 1** *Southern Maryland Spring Festival*, Leonardtown. **May 13-21** *Preakness Festival*, Baltimore. **May 14-15** *Wine in the Woods*, Columbia. **Jun 10-19** *Festival of the Arts*, Columbia. **Jun 11-12** *Great Grapes!* (wine and music festival), Timonium. **Jul 4** *Jamboree in the Park*, Ocean City. **Jul 22-24** *Artscape*, Baltimore. **Aug 1-Oct 31** *Maryland Renaissance Festival*, Annapolis. **Aug 13-14** *Annual Seafood Festival*, Havre de Grace. **Aug 25-Sep 5** *Maryland State Fair*, Timonium. **Sep 2-4** *Hard Crab Derby & Fair*, Crisfield. **Sep 18-25** *Westminster Fall Festival*. **Nov 19** *Thanksgiving Day Parade*, Baltimore.

Climate

Hot, humid summers and mild, damp winters.

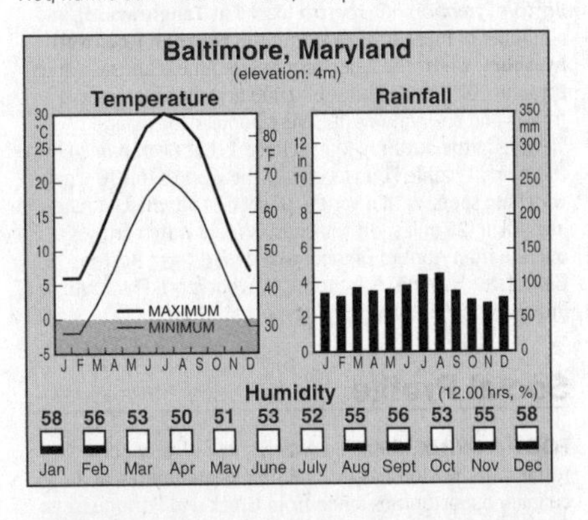

Massachusetts

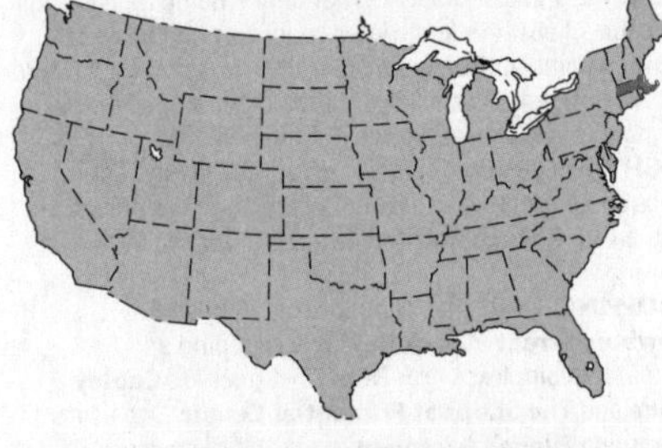

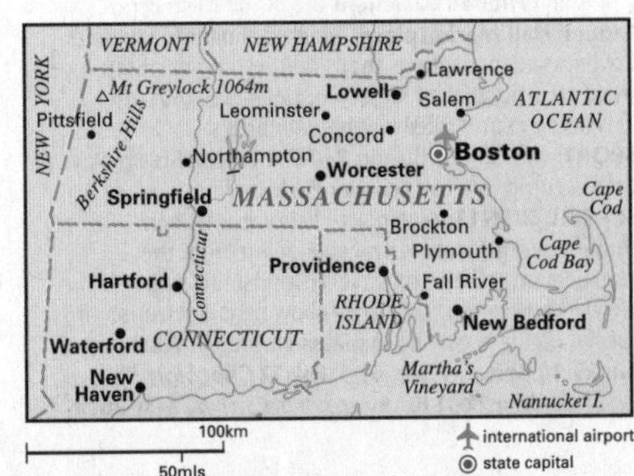

Massachusetts Office of Travel & Tourism
10 Park Plaza, Suite 4510, Boston, MA 02116
Tel: (617) 973 8500 *or* (800) 227 6277 (toll-free).
Fax: (617) 973 8525.
E-mail: vacationinfo@state.ma.us
Website: www.massvacation.com

Massachusetts Office of Travel & Tourism (UK Office)
c/o First Public Relations, Molasses House, Clove Hitch Quay, Plantation Wharf, London SW11 3TN, UK
Tel: (020) 7978 5233. Fax: (020) 7924 3134.
Website: www.massvacation.com

For information on tourist regions not listed below, contact the Massachusetts Office of Travel & Tourism.

Central Massachusetts CVB
30 Worcester Center Boulevard, Worcester, MA 01608
Tel: (508) 755 7400 *or* (800) 231 7557 (toll-free).
Fax: (508) 754 2703.
E-mail: visitorinfo@worcester.org
Website: www.worcester.org

Greater Boston CVB
2 Copley Place, Suite 105, Boston, MA 02116
Visitor centre: 215 Tremont Street, Boston, MA 02116
Tel: (617) 536 4100 *or* (888) 733 2678.
Fax: (617) 424 7664.
E-mail: visitus@bostonusa.com
Website: www.bostonusa.com

Greater Springfield CVB
1441 Main Street, Springfield, MA 01103
Tel: (413) 787 1548 *or* (800) 723 1548 (toll-free).
Fax: (413) 781 4607.
E-mail: info@valleyvisitor.com
Website: www.valleyvisitor.com

Cape Cod Chamber of Commerce
Street address: Junction of Route 6 and Route 132, Hyannis, MA 02601
Postal address: PO Box 790, Hyannis, MA 02601
Tel: (508) 362 3225 *or* (888) 332 2732 (toll-free).
Fax: (508) 362 3698.
E-mail: info@capecodchamber.org
Website: www.capecodchamber.org

Berkshire Visitors Bureau
3 Hoosac Street, Adams, MA 01220
Tel: (413) 743 4500 *or* (800) 237 5747 (toll-free).
Fax: (413) 743 4560.
E-mail: bvb@berkshires.org
Website: www.berkshires.org

North of Boston CVB
17 Peabody Square, Peabody, MA 01960
Tel: (978) 977 7760 *or* (877) 662 9299 (toll-free).
Fax: (978) 977 7758.
E-mail: info@northofboston.org
Website: www.northofboston.org

Plymouth County CVB
32 Court Street, 2nd Floor, Plymouth, MA 02360
Tel: (508) 747 0100 *or* (800) 231 1620 (toll-free).
Fax: (508) 747 3118.
E-mail: info@SeePlymouth.com
Website: www.seeplymouth.com

General Information

Nickname: Bay State
State bird: Chickadee
State flower: Mayflower
CAPITAL: Boston
Date of admission to the Union: 6 Feb 1788 (original 13 States; date of ratification of the Constitution)
POPULATION: 6,416,505 (official estimate 2004)
POPULATION DENSITY: 234.7 per sq km
2003 total overseas arrivals/US ranking: 829,999/7
TIME: Eastern (GMT - 5). *Daylight Saving Time* is observed.

THE STATE: The gateway to New England, Massachusetts was the destination of the *Mayflower* in 1620 and is one of the original 13 States. It is very diverse, offering everything from cobblestoned streets and village greens to space-age technology centres. The **Berkshire Hills** cut across its western corner. To the east the land rolls down to the sea, embracing the state capital, **Boston**, and the beaches of **Cape Cod**.

Travel - International

AIR: International airports: *Boston Logan International (BOS)* (website: www.massport.com), 6km (4 miles) from the city centre, is the largest airport in New England; it received almost 4 million international passengers in 2002. Airport services include a free shuttle bus (marked *Massport*), which runs 0530-0100, stopping at each airline terminal, the Water Transportation Terminal, Satellite Parking and the MBTA subway station, which has a service every eight to 12 minutes to downtown Boston (travel time - 15 minutes). Buses are available to destinations all over the state, and a commuter rail link is available from Boston to various points

A B C D E F G H I J K L M N O P Q R S T U V W X Y Z

in Massachusetts. Taxis, limousines and hire cars are also available (travel time - 20 minutes). *Massport Airport Water Shuttle*, serviced by a separate bus, offers a boat ride from the airport to Rowes Wharf in downtown Boston (travel time – seven minutes).

Approximate flight times: From Boston to *London* is six hours 30 minutes, to *Los Angeles* is six hours 15 minutes, to *Miami* is three hours 30 minutes and to *New York City* is one hour 15 minutes.

RAIL: *Amtrak* (tel: (800) 872 7245 (toll-free); website: www.amtrak.com) links Boston with New York (Pennsylvania Station), Philadelphia and Washington, DC, on the 'Acela Express', and New York City and Chicago on the 'Lake Shore Limited. The 'Federal' line runs daily from Boston to New York City, Philadelphia, Baltimore and Washington, DC, while the 'Regional' line covers many stops between Boston and Newport News (Virginia). There is also a 'Downeaster' service from Boston to Portland (Maine), with four trips daily. There are four stations in Boston, the 'Downeaster' service departs from North Station, 126 Causeway Street, while all other services depart from South Station, Atlantic Avenue and Summer Streets, or Back Bay Station and Route 128 Station. The 'Lake Shore Limited' and 'Regional' services also stop at Worcester. Car hire is available at most stations.

Approximate rail travel times: From Boston to *New York City* is four hours 15 minutes, however, with the *Acela* high-speed train, travel time from Boston to New York City is three hours 30 minutes. *Amtrak* operates around a dozen *Acela Express* roundtrip trains daily between Boston, New York City and Washington, DC.

ROAD: Long-distance bus companies operating in the state include *Greyhound* (tel: (800) 229 9424 (toll-free); website: www.greyhound.com) and *Peter Pan Bus Lines* (tel: (800) 343 999 (toll-free); website: www.peterpanbus.com).

Approximate driving times: From Boston to *Providence* is one hour, to *Hartford* is two hours, to *Portland*, Maine is two hours, to *Albany* is three hours, to *New York City* is four hours, to *Montréal* is six hours, to *Chicago* is 20 hours, to *Miami* is 31 hours, to *Dallas* is 37 hours, to *Los Angeles* is 63 hours and to *Seattle* is 63 hours. All times are based on non-stop driving at or below the applicable speed limits.

Approximate bus travel times: From Boston to *Providence* is one hour, to *Portland*, Maine is two hours, to *Hartford* is two hours 20 minutes, to *New York City* is four hours 30 minutes, to *Chicago* is 22 hours, to *Miami* is 31 hours, to *Dallas* is 42 hours, to *Los Angeles* is 68 hours and to *Seattle* is 74 hours.

URBAN: *Massachusetts Bay Transportation Authority (MBTA)* (website: www.mbta.com) operates Boston's subway system (known as the 'T'), as well as bus, trolleybus and train services throughout the city and surrounding towns. The subway system is the oldest in the USA and runs daily 0500-0100. Fares are moderate and passengers can transfer easily between surface and underground transportation. The *Boston Visitor Pass* allows for daily, three-day or weekly travel on all subway and local buses. Suburban buses and commuter trains extend travel beyond the immediate city, to destinations such as Concord, Ipswich and Salem. Taxis can be hailed throughout the city, but delays can be experienced during rush hours; taxis can also be hired by telephone. Car hire is available.

Resorts & Excursions

BOSTON: Boston is a city of contrasts, a gentle blend of the old and the new. The city has a very 'English' feel about it, with hilly, crooked, cobblestone streets, a grassy common and cosy Victorian townhouses with polished brass door-knockers. It also played a vital role in the opposition to colonial rule that led to the American War of Independence. The **Freedom Trail**, which is marked by signs and a red pavement line, is a 5km (3 mile) walk that passes 16 points of historical interest, some of which are in the **Boston National Historical Park**. The **Skywalk Observatory** at the **Prudential Tower** is a viewing platform on the 52nd floor (open daily 1000-2200), offering a spectacular view over the city; the city's highest observation point, the **John Hancock Observatory**, was closed permanently after the New York terrorist attacks on 11 September 2001. Other attractions include harbour cruises, some of which enable the visitor to see the Boston skyline, the airport and the 1822 USS Constitution at **Charlestown Navy Shipyard**; the **Museum of Fine Arts**; the famous **Museum of Science**; the **John F Kennedy Library and Museum**; the **New England Aquarium**; the **Old North Church**; **Faneuil Hall**; and the **Ball & Finch Pub**, upon which the popular TV series, *Cheers*, was based.

Cambridge lies across the Charles River from Boston. Here stands **Harvard University**, the USA's oldest university (1636). In the south of Boston is **Quincy**, the birthplace of Presidents John Adams and John Quincy Adams.

ELSEWHERE: Salem, north of Boston, is famous for its seafaring history and the 1692 witch trials. Also north of Boston, **Marblehead** is one of the East Coast's premier sailing centres, its old town full of 18th- and 19th-century homes of fishermen, merchants and artisans. Just west of Boston, **Concord** is one of the most historic and beautiful towns in the USA. Its **Old North Bridge** was the site of the 'shot heard round the world' in the opening engagement of the American War of Independence. The engagement commenced on what is now called Battle Road in **Lexington** on 15 April 1775. **Plimoth Plantation**, in **Plymouth**, is an open-air museum recreating a 1627 Pilgrim village. The Mayflower II, also in Plymouth, is a full-scale reproduction of the ship in which the Pilgrims made their harrowing 66-day voyage from England. **Battleship Cove**, in **Fall River**, harbours 20th-century US Navy vessels and is the largest complex of its kind in the country.

New Bedford, a restored whaling community, has the **Seamen's Bethel**, which inspired Herman Melville's description in Moby Dick, and the **New Bedford Whaling Museum**, which displays the skeleton of a rare, 20m (66ft) blue whale. **Cape Cod** has some 400km (250 miles) of beautiful beaches, and 21 seaside towns and fishing villages, making it one of the USA's prime resort areas. The **Cape Cod National Seashore** stretches over 10,927 hectares (27,000 acres), featuring expanses of unspoilt sandy beach and stunning desert-like sand dunes. **Provincetown**, at the tip of the Cape, is where the Pilgrims first landed.

Nantucket Island, once a great whaling port, is now a popular sun resort. Nantucket and **Martha's Vineyard**, a picture-postcard island, both lie off the coast of Cape Cod. They are accessible by air from Boston, Hyannis, New Bedford, New York City and Providence (Rhode Island), and by ferry from Hyannis and Woods Hole – booking well ahead for ferry and air services is strongly advised in the summertime.

Old Sturbridge Village, in central Massachusetts, is a living history museum recreating an 1830s New England town. The **New England Science Center** in nearby **Worcester** has a zoo, various exhibits and a range of lectures, which provide an ideal learning opportunity for all members of the family. The **Higgins Armory** in Worcester, set in a Gothic-style castle, contains the largest on-display collection of medieval and Renaissance armour in the western hemisphere.

Just two hours from Boston are the **Berkshire Hills** and the **Mohawk Trail**. The former is the summer home of the *Boston Symphony Orchestra* (based at **Tanglewood**), and a number of museums, including the **Norman Rockwell Museum**; whilst the legendary Native American trail winds through 202,347 hectares (500,000 acres) of State parks, forests and reservations. It is very popular for foliage viewing in the autumn. Massachusetts has been named by the World Wildlife Fund as one of the world's top 10 whale watching spots, with a variety of species of whales found just 40km (25 miles) off the coast. Whale watch cruises operate from April to October and depart from Boston, Gloucester, Hyannis, Nantucket, Newburyport, Plymouth, Provincetown, Quincy and Rockport.

Social Profile

FOOD & DRINK: There is a wide variety of very good restaurants. Boston has many ethnic communities, and culinary opportunities range from Greek and Portuguese to Chinese and Syrian. Seafood is a speciality throughout Massachusetts, including local lobster, scallops, scrod and delicious clam chowder. The legal age for the purchase of alcohol is 21 (with valid identification).

THEATRES & CONCERTS: Boston is the traditional review town for Broadway shows. The theatrical season is mainly in the autumn and winter. The *Boston Symphony Orchestra*, one of the greatest of all international ensembles, has a full schedule of autumn and winter concerts, and makes its summer home at **Tanglewood** in the Berkshires (in western Massachusetts). 'Boston Pops' concerts are staged in the spring and summer, as well as at Christmas.

NIGHTLIFE: Boston offers a variety of jazz clubs, dance clubs and intimate piano bar lounges, as well as pubs such as the **Bull & Finch Pub**, the inspiration for the TV show *Cheers*.

SHOPPING: The high-fashion district in Boston is **Newbury Street** in **Back Bay**. Two shopping and restaurant complexes near Newbury Street are **Copley Place** and **The Shops at Prudential Center**. Department stores and **Filene's Basement** are in the town centre. **Faneuil Hall Marketplace**, which is similar to London's Covent Garden, contains shops and restaurants. Statewide, there are a number of factory-outlet stores that offer designer and other items at bargain prices.

SPORT: The famous Boston *Red Sox* baseball team plays at the eccentric yet cosy **Fenway Park** stadium.

SPECIAL EVENTS: A complete list of events held throughout the State is available online from the Massachusetts Office of Travel & Tourism (website: www.massvacation.com). The following is a selection of special events occurring in Massachusetts in 2005:

Jan 29-30 *Boston Wine Expo*. **Feb 12** *Chocolate Festival*, Deerfield. **Mar 12-13** *Pembroke Arts Festival*. **Mar 20** *St Patrick's Day Parade*, South Boston. **Apr 18** *Battle of Lexington Green Re-enactment*, Lexington; *Patriot's Day Celebration*, Lexington; *Boston Marathon*. **May 14-22** *Annual Cape Cod Days*. **May 18-22** *Nantucket Wine Festival*, Nantucket Island; *Higgins Faire*, Worcester. **May 21-23** *CraftBoston*, Boston. **May 29-31** *Faneuil Hall Marketplace* (street performers festival), Boston. **Jun 15-19** *Nantucket Film Festival*. **Jun 29-Jul 4** *24th Annual Boston Harborfest*. **Jul 4** *Boston Pops Fourth of July Celebration*. **Jul 9** *Blackstone Valley Celtic Festival*, Sutton. **Jul 15-16** *19th Annual Green River Festival*, Greenfield. **Aug 1** *Chinatown Festival*, Boston. **Aug 7-8** *38th Annual Pembroke Arts Festival*. **Aug 27-28** *Festival of the Lion*, Grafton. **Sep 4-Oct 24** *King Richard's Faire*, Carver. **Sep 8-11** *Franklin County Fair*, Greenfield. **Sep 16-Oct 2** *The Big E/Eastern States Exposition*, West Springfield. **Sep 23-25** *Bourne Scallp Festival*. **Oct 2** *Cape Cod Oyster Festival*, Hyannis. **Oct 17-18** *Head of the Charles Regatta*, Boston/Cambridge. **Nov 24** *Old Sturbridge Village – Thanksgiving Day Celebration*, Sturbridge; *Plymouth Plantation Thanksgiving Celebration*. **Dec 3** *64th Annual Boston Holiday Tree Lighting*. **Dec 12** *Re-enactment of the Boston Tea Party*, Boston. **Dec 31** *First Night*, Boston.

Climate

Warm and sunny from May to October, followed by cold winters. The autumn is spectacular: the climate and variety of hardwoods produce vibrant colours, attracting visitors worldwide. Foliage season begins in mid- to late-September, with peak colour often coinciding with the Columbus Day weekend in mid-October.

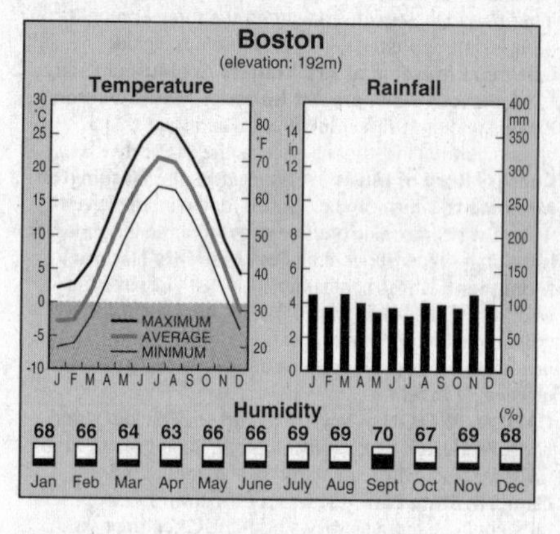

Michigan

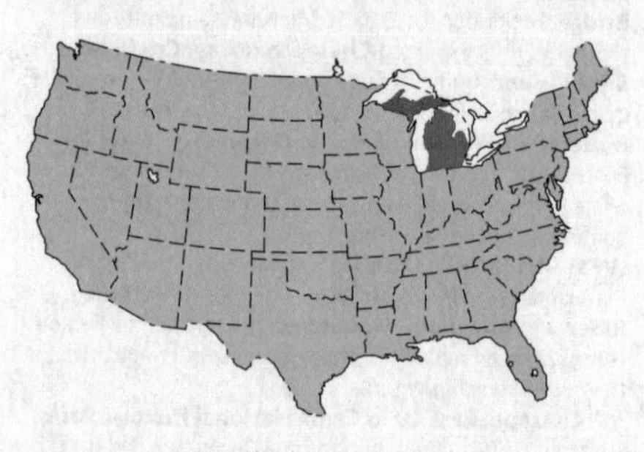

Travel Michigan
300 North Washington Square, 2nd Floor, Lansing, MI 48913
Tel: (517) 373 0670 *or* (888) 784 7328 (toll-free).
Fax: (517) 373 0059.
Website: www.michigan.org

Great Lakes of North America (UK Office)
c/o Cellet Travel Services Ltd, 47 High Street, Henley-in-Arden, Warwickshire B95 5AA, UK
Tel: (01564) 794 999 *or* (0870) 900 0997 (toll-free; brochure request line). Fax: (01564) 795 333.
E-mail: info@cellet.co.uk
Website: www.glna.org *or* www.cellet.co.uk

Detroit Metro CVB
211 West Fort Street, Suite 1000, Detroit, MI 48226
Tel: (313) 202 1800 *or* (800) 338 7648 (toll-free).
Fax: (313) 202 1808 *or* 1833.
E-mail: vic@visitdetroit.com
Website: www.visitdetroit.com

General Information

Nickname: Great Lakes State
State bird: Michigan Robin
State flower: Apple Blossom
CAPITAL: Lansing
Date of admission to the Union: 26 Jan 1837
POPULATION: 10,112,620 (official estimate 2004)
POPULATION DENSITY: 40.4 per sq km
2003 total overseas arrivals/US ranking: 361,000/14
TIME: Eastern (GMT - 5) in the greater part of the State; Central (GMT - 6) in Dickinson, Gogebic, Iron and Menominee Counties. *Daylight Saving Time* is observed.

THE STATE: Michigan comprises two peninsulas. These are divided by **Lake Michigan**, and linked by one of the world's longest suspension bridges across the **Straits of Mackinac**. **Lakes Superior**, **Huron** and **Erie** also form the State's shorelines. The Lower Peninsula, mainly agricultural and industrial, contains inland lakes, meadows and sandy beaches, as well as the 'Motor City' of **Detroit**. The Upper Peninsula is more rugged, and boasts forests, white beaches, trout streams and winter ski resorts.

Credit: © MEDC

Travel - International

AIR: International airports: *Detroit Metro (DTW)* (website: www.metroairport.com) is 32km (20 miles) west of the city centre. The airport is the USA's 10th busiest for total passenger numbers (2002) and also receives a sizeable share of international arrivals (2.7 million in 2003). *Metropolitan* shuttles and taxis are available to downtown areas; car hire is also available.
Approximate flight times: From Detroit to *London* is seven hours 30 minutes, to *Los Angeles* is five hours 10 minutes, to *Miami* is two hours 50 minutes and to *New York City* is one hour 40 minutes.
RAIL: Detroit is on the *Amtrak* 'Michigan Services' Chicago–Toronto line, which runs from Chicago to Toronto, stopping at a number of Michigan locations, including Jackson, Detroit, Royal Oak and Birmingham (tel: (800) 872 7245 (toll-free); website: www.amtrak.com); see the *Illinois* section for approximate travel times. The station is located at 11 West Baltimore Avenue; car hire is available.

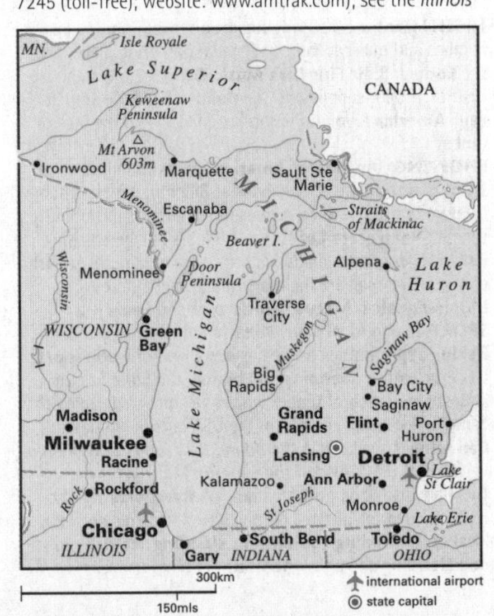

ROAD: *Greyhound* (tel: (800) 229 9424 (toll-free); website: www.greyhound.com) buses are most frequent in the south; only a few buses serve the Upper Peninsula.
Approximate driving times: From Detroit to *Cleveland* is three hours, to *Chicago* is five hours, to *Cincinnati* is five hours, to *Indianapolis* is five hours, to *Toronto* is five hours, to *Buffalo* is six hours, to *New York City* is 13 hours, to *Dallas* is 24 hours, to *Miami* is 27 hours, to *Los Angeles* is 49 hours and to *Seattle* is 49 hours. All times are based on non-stop driving at or below the applicable speed limits.
Approximate bus travel times: From Detroit to *Cleveland* is four hours, to *Cincinnati* is five hours 30 minutes, to *Chicago* is six hours, to *Toronto* is six hours, to *Indianapolis* is eight hours, to *Duluth* is 19 hours 15 minutes and to *Los Angeles* is 32 hours.
URBAN: Most larger communities have bus and taxi services. Detroit also has a city-centre rapid rail system, the *People Mover*, which connects 13 stations in downtown Detroit. *D-DOT* and *SMART* buses serve the city centre and suburbs respectively.

Resorts & Excursions

DETROIT: Industrial Detroit is the nation's car manufacturing centre. The oldest city in the Midwest, founded in 1701, it is now the 10th-largest city in the USA, with a population of just under 1 million (the metro area, with 5.5 million inhabitants, ranks eighth). Detroit is also a major port, linked to the Atlantic Ocean via Lake Erie and the St Lawrence Seaway.
There are many museums, art galleries, zoos and attractions in the city, and cultural events and major league sports are frequent crowd-pullers. A US$220 million urban redevelopment project promises to further enhance the city's cultural attributes; the most recent development is the creation of the **Max M Fisher Music Center**, proudly referred to as **The Max**. The next phase, the creation of the **Detroit High School for the Fine, Performing & Communication Arts**, will be completed in 2005. **Hitsville USA** is a mecca for Motown fans, where the sounds of Diana Ross, The Temptations, and The Four Tops are immortalised. The **Renaissance Center** houses dozens of restaurants, a 1400-room hotel and a variety of shops, as well as being General Motors' world headquarters. **Belle Isle**, the nation's largest urban island park, offers biking, canoeing, an aquarium and a **Great Lakes Museum**. The **Cultural Center** features the **Detroit Historical Museum**, the **Detroit Science Center**, the **Detroit Institute of Arts** (the fifth-largest art museum in the USA) and the **Charles H Wright Museum of African-American History** (the largest museum of its kind). The **Detroit Zoological Park**, containing more than 5000 animals in natural settings, can be toured by tractor-train. **Greektown**, along Monroe Avenue, offers Greek food, entertainment and speciality shops.
Excursions: The **Henry Ford Museum** and **Greenfield Village** can be found at **Dearborn**, a Detroit suburb; the 5 hectare (12 acre) indoor museum focuses on America's industrial development and the 33 hectare (81 acre) village comprises more than 80 buildings, a train and a riverboat. Also in Dearborn are the **Automotive Hall of Fame**, **Spirit of Ford** and **Henry Ford's Fair Lane Estate**.
ELSEWHERE: Michigan's Great Lakes coastline – along with 60,000km (36,000 miles) of rivers and 11,000 inland lakes – offers great boating, canoeing, fishing and watersports opportunities.
Cranbrook Educational Community and **Cranbrook House and Gardens** are located in **Bloomfield Hills**, 40km (25 miles) north of central Detroit. The grounds contain a beautiful country estate and landscaped gardens with an art museum, science museum, nature centre, planetarium, observatory and various educational institutions.
Ann Arbor, to the west of Detroit, is the home of the **University of Michigan** and has a multitude of bookstores and cosy cafes. **Traverse City**, on the west side of the State, is the heart of a recreational haven, featuring sand dunes, resorts, golf and skiing. Located where the Upper and Lower Peninsulas meet, **Mackinac Island** is a well-known summer resort; cars are not allowed and visitors must walk, cycle or use horse-drawn carriages. Attractions include the impressive **Grand Hotel** and **Fort Mackinac**, a restored 18th-century military outpost. **Isle Royale National Park** is a beautiful wilderness island in **Lake Superior**.

Social Profile

FOOD & DRINK: The State has a wide variety of US and ethnic restaurants. Steak and seafood are especially popular.
THEATRES & CONCERTS: In Detroit, the **Fisher Theater** and **Fox Theatre** present Broadway shows. In 2005, the *Detroit Symphony Orchestra* will perform their season

Credit: © MEDC

(April to September) in the new, US$60 million **Max M Fisher Music Center** opened in October 2003, with a beautifully restored and modernised **Orchestra Hall**. The orchestra also performs at the *Meadow Brook Music Festival*, **Oakland University** (June to mid-August). The *Michigan Opera Theater* presents its shows at the restored **Detroit Opera House**. Opera, ballet and drama are also performed at the **Music Hall Center** (October to December). **Cobo Arena** stages rock and soul concerts. Summer theatre is found throughout the State.
NIGHTLIFE: There is a variety of nightlife, including supper clubs with star entertainment. Clubs offer a variety of music, ranging from 'Motown' soul music, which originated in Detroit, to blues (this is the hometown of John Lee Hooker) and classical music.
SHOPPING: Detroit's main shopping areas include the **Renaissance Center**, **Greektown** and suburban malls. Resorts have speciality shops and gallery districts. The nation's first shopping mall, **Northland**, opened in Southfield in 1954.
SPORT: Detroit offers professional **basketball**, **baseball**, **hockey**, **football** and **horse racing**. Michigan has over 800 public-access **golf** courses – more than any other State in the USA.
SPECIAL EVENTS: The following is a selection of special events occurring in Michigan in 2005:
Mar 3-Apr 3 *East Lansing Film Festival*. **Apr 2** *Wheatland Music Jamboree*. **Apr 2-3** *Annual University of Michigan Dance for Mother Earth Pow Wow*, Ann Arbor. **Apr 2-17** *Cereal City's Silly Sunny Circus Day*, Battle Creek. **Jun 2-5** *42nd Annual Birmingham Village Fair*. **Aug 17** *Manitou Music Festival*. **Sep 2-5** *Michigan Bean Festival*, Fairgrove. **Sep 3** *Sailing Festival Craft Show*, St. Joseph. **Sep 29-Oct 2** *Four Flags Area Apple Festival*, Niles. **Oct 1** *Red Flannel Festival*, Cedar Springs. **Nov 18** *Silver Bells in the City*, Lansing.

Climate

Summers are warm with cool nights. Winters are cold, especially around the Great Lakes where conditions can be severe (however, there are good conditions for wintersports).

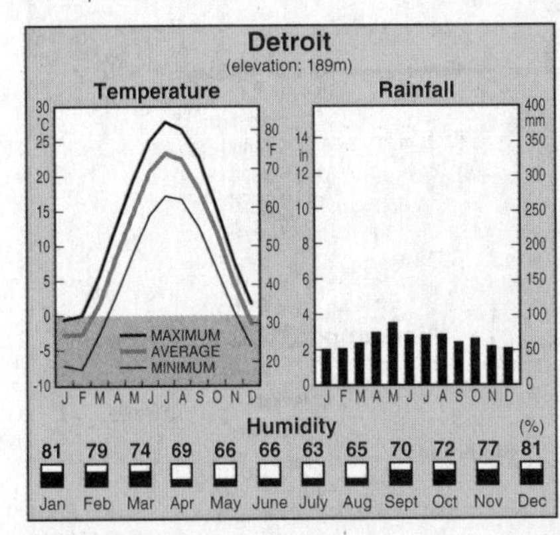

Minnesota

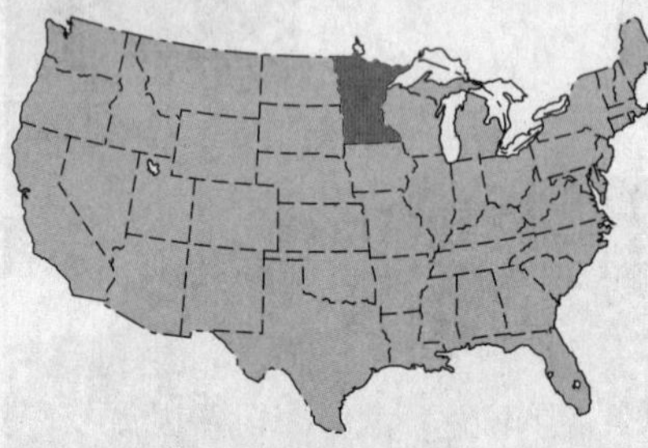

Minnesota Office of Tourism
100 Metro Square, 121 7th Place East, St Paul, MN 55101
Tel: (651) 296 5029 *or* (800) 657 3700 (toll-free).
Fax: (651) 296 2800.
E-mail: explore@state.mn.us
Website: www.exploreminnesota.com
Bloomington CVB
7900 International Drive, Suite 990,
Bloomington, MN 55425
Tel: (952) 858 8500 *or* (800) 346 4289 (toll-free).
Fax: (952) 858 8854.
E-mail: cvb@bloomingtonmn.org
Website: www.bloomingtonmn.org
Greater Minneapolis Convention & Visitors Association
250 Marquette Avenue South, Suite 1300,
Minneapolis, MN 55401
Tel: (612) 767 8000 *or* (888) 676 6757 (toll-free).
Fax: (612) 335 5841.
E-mail: tourism@minneapolis.org
Website: www.minneapolis.org
St Paul CVB
175 West Kellogg Boulevard, Suite 502, St Paul, MN 55102
Tel: (651) 265 4900 *or* (800) 627 6101 (toll-free).
Fax: (651) 265 4999.
E-mail: info@stpaulcvb.org
Website: www.visitsaintpaul.com

General Information

Nickname: North Star State
State bird: Common Loon
State flower: Showy Pink and White Lady's Slipper
CAPITAL: St Paul
Date of admission to the Union: 11 May 1858
POPULATION: 5,100,958 (official estimate 2004)
POPULATION DENSITY: 22.9 per sq km
2003 total overseas arrivals/US ranking: 90,000/29
TIME: Central (GMT - 6). *Daylight Saving Time* is observed.

THE STATE: Minnesota, the second northernmost State in the USA (after Alaska), is one of the nation's leading outdoor tourist destinations, with 68 State parks, 55 State forests and more than 12,000 lakes. The State borders Canada, the upper Midwest States and **Lake Superior**, the largest freshwater lake in the world.

Travel - International

AIR: International airports: *Minneapolis-St Paul International (MSP)* (website: www.mspairport.com) is 16km (10 miles) from the cities (which are contiguous). A

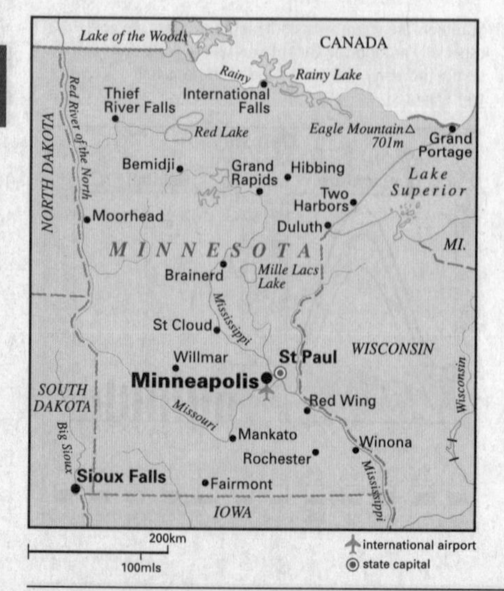

Credit: © Minnesota Office of Tourism

US$2.6 billion expansion plan is underway to accommodate the growing number of passengers, expected to reach 40 million per year by the time the improvements are completed in 2010; the airport currently deals with around 32 million passengers annually and international passenger numbers increased by 10 per cent in 2002. There is a free shuttle bus between terminals, and *Airport Express* shuttles run to hotels in Minneapolis and St Paul, while buses connect with cities in the surrounding area. An airport limousine service and taxis are available, as are all major car hire companies.

Approximate flight times: From Minneapolis/St Paul to *London* is eight hours, to *Los Angeles* is four hours, to *Miami* is three hours 30 minutes, to *New York City* is two hours 40 minutes and to *Salt Lake City* is two hours 50 minutes.

RAIL: Minneapolis/St Paul is on the *Amtrak* Chicago–Seattle line (tel: (800) 872 7245 (toll-free); website: www.amtrak.com); for approximate travel times, see the *Illinois* section. The station is at a location equidistant to Minneapolis and St Paul, at 730 Transfer Road.

ROAD: *Greyhound* (tel: (800) 229 9424 (toll-free); website: www.greyhound.com) provides a long-distance bus service. Terminals are located in both downtown Minneapolis (950 Hawthorne Avenue) and St Paul (166 West University Avenue). **Approximate driving times:** From Minneapolis/St Paul to *Duluth* is three hours, to *Madison* is five hours, to *Fargo* is five hours, to *Sioux Falls* is five hours, to *Omaha* is seven hours, to *Chicago* is eight hours, to *Winnipeg* is eight hours, to *St Louis* is 11 hours, to *Rapid City* is 11 hours, to *Denver* is 17 hours, to *Dallas* is 19 hours, to *New York* is 25 hours, to *Seattle* is 34 hours, to *Miami* is 35 hours and to *Los Angeles* is 41 hours. All times are based on non-stop driving at or below the applicable speed limits.

Approximate bus travel times: From Minneapolis/St Paul to *Duluth* is three hours 20 minutes, to *Fargo* is five hours 30 minutes, to *Milwaukee* is eight hours, to *New York City* is 18 hours, to *Miami* is 43 hours and to *Los Angeles* is 44 hours.

URBAN: Local bus services in Minneapolis/St Paul are operated by *Metropolitan Transit* (website: www.metrotransit.com). Trolleys serve the downtown locations in both Minneapolis and St Paul.

Resorts & Excursions

MINNEAPOLIS: Minneapolis and St Paul adjoin each other on either side of the **Mississippi River** and have a metropolitan area population of nearly 3 million. They are known as the Twin Cities and began as frontier towns, with German, Irish and Scandinavian immigrants. Minneapolis is a modern city with fine theatres, nightclubs, stores, a year-round sports programme and a distinguished symphony orchestra. The city is also the site of one of the world's largest universities, the **University of Minnesota**.

Nicollet Mall is a downtown shopping promenade that includes the 51-storey **IDS** (**Investors Diversified Services**) **Center**, which towers over the downtown area, **Nieman Marcus** and **Saks Fifth Avenue**. Construction on the new **Lake Street Center** started in July 2004. The **Minneapolis Institute of Arts** exhibits major art masterpieces from Europe, the Orient and the Americas. The **Walker Art Center** stages contemporary art exhibitions, concerts and lectures, and also features an **Outdoor Sculpture Garden**, which is the largest of its kind in the USA. It is open all year round and is one of the State's top tourist attractions.

Other highlights include the **Minnesota Landscape Arboretum**; **Valleyfair** amusement park; and **Minnesota Zoo**. **Minnehaha Falls** was made famous in Longfellow's poem, *The Song of Hiawatha*. The **Target Center**, **HHH Metrodome**, **St Anthony Falls**, **St Anthony Main** and the '**Mississippi Mile**', a riverside recreational park, are all notable attractions in downtown Minneapolis. Mississippi River steamboat excursions are also popular.

The **Hennepin Avenue Theater District** and the **Warehouse District** offer evening entertainment.

ST PAUL: Older and perhaps more dignified than Minneapolis, as befits a State capital, the city has abundant parks and lakes. The **Ordway Center for the Performing Arts** offers drama, concerts and art galleries. The **Science Museum** features the **William L McKnight Omnitheater**. The **Landmark Center** now houses the **Minnesota Museum of American Art**. Its distinguished history includes the trials of several famous gangsters in the 1930s, when it was the **Federal Court House**.

The new **Landmark Plaza** hosts a number of festivals and concerts, as well as a farmer's market in August; a bronze statue of cartoonist Charles Shultz honours the cartoonist.

Excursions: Bloomington, 15 minutes from Minneapolis and St Paul, is home to the **Mall of America**. The largest entertainment and retail complex in the USA, it attracts 42 million visitors each year (see *Social Profile* section). The Mall is poised to grow even further, with plans for hotels, new shops, restaurants and entertainment attractions and a fitness and spa facility planned for the future. Attractions at the Mall include **Camp Snoopy** (the largest indoor theme park in the USA), the **LEGO Imagination Center** and **Underwater Adventures**, a 5.4 million-litre (1.2 million gallons) walk-through aquarium. **Stillwater** is a charming, historic town on the St Croix River, 48km (30 miles) northwest of the city.

DULUTH: This scenic port at the western tip of **Lake Superior** receives ships from all over the world (via the St Lawrence Seaway). Attractions include harbour and lake cruises; **Lake Superior Maritime Visitor Center**; the **St Louis Country's Heritage & Arts Center**, known locally as **The Depot**; and the **Skyline Parkway**, high above the city. **Spirit Mountain** is a year-round holiday and outdoor recreation centre, 11km (7 miles) south of Duluth.

ELSEWHERE: The spectacular **North Shore Drive** (US Highway 61) follows the north shore of Lake Superior for 240km (150 miles) from Duluth to the Canadian border and was recently designated an 'All American Road' for its unique, scenic beauty. **Split Rock Lighthouse State Park** preserves one of the most scenically-situated lighthouses in the USA, about 43km (27 miles) north of **Two Harbors**. The **North Woods** region embraces vast wilderness and lakes. Major resort areas include the towns of **Bemidji**, **Brainerd**, **Detroit Lakes** and **Grand Rapids**, as well as the **Lake Mille Lacs** area.

The **Mississippi River** begins in Minnesota, travelling over 1000km (600 miles) within the State. The new **Mississippi River Visitor Center** is a collaboration between the National Park Service and the Science Museum. The **Great River Road** that runs south from the Twin Cities to the Iowa border offers magnificent views of the river and the many bird species, including the American Bald Eagle, that travel this route on their migrations.

Social Profile

FOOD & DRINK: The Twin Cities have many excellent restaurants, notably steakhouses; however, international cuisine as diverse as Greek and Japanese is also widely available, and Minneapolis is home to the newest **Hard Rock Cafe** in the USA. Regional freshwater fish is a speciality.

THEATRES & CONCERTS: The Twin Cities offer more theatres than any other US metropolitan area outside New York City, with more than 100 theatre companies. The **Guthrie Theater** in Minneapolis is dedicated to the innovative presentation of classical drama. Broadway shows and theatrical events are performed at the restored **Historic Orpheum Theatre**, **Historic State Theatre** and the **Historic Pantages Theatre** in the **Hennepin Theater District** in downtown Minneapolis. The *Minnesota Orchestra* performs regularly at **Orchestra Hall** in Minneapolis. The *St Paul Chamber Orchestra's* home is the **Ordway Center for the Performing Arts Theater** in St Paul.

NIGHTLIFE: The State's nightclubs offer rock groups, jazz combos and musical comedy. Popular gathering places are the **Loon** and the **Fine Line Music Cafe** in the Warehouse District of Minneapolis, and the **Dakota Bar & Grill** in St Paul. **America Live!** is a nightclub collective in the Mall of America.

SHOPPING: The **Mall of America** stands 15 minutes south of downtown Minneapolis at Bloomington. It is home to more than 520 stores, dozens of restaurants (including the first **Rainforest Café**), 9 nightclubs, 14 cinemas, an indoor roller coaster and a walk-through aquarium. At each corner of the mall are the major department stores – **Bloomingdale's**, **Macy's**, **Nordstrom** and **Sears**.

SPORT: Owing to its many lakes, Minnesota has plenty of **fishing** opportunities, as well as every kind of **watersport**. It is excellent for **camping** and **hiking**. The State has the largest population of timber wolves, nesting bald eagles and common loons (diver birds) in the USA outside of Alaska. **Canoeing** is available in the *Boundary Waters Canoe Area Wilderness (BWCAW)* in the *Superior Natural Forest*. There are also good **golf** facilities. **Wintersports** are also well provided for, abetted by the State's strategic northern location, and **skiing**, **ice-skating**, **sledding**, **ice fishing**, **dog sledding** and **snowmobiling** are all available.

SPECIAL EVENTS: The following is a selection of events occurring in Minnesota in 2005:
Jan 22 Polar Days Festival, Bemidji. **Jan 28-29** *Third Crossing Sled Dog Rendezvous*, Frazee; Arctic Blast, Canby. **Jan 28-Feb 6** *Winter Carnival*, St Paul. **Jan 29-30** *Cabin Fever Days*, Cannon Falls. **Feb 26** *Grumpy Old Men Festival*, Wabasha. **Jun 26** *Vikingland Band Festival*, Alexandria. **Jul 11** *Rally in the Valley*, Jackson. **Jul 29-30** *25th Annual Blueberry Arts Festival*, Ely. **Aug 13-Sep 25** *Minnesota Renaissance Festival*, Shakopee. **Aug 25-Sep 5** *Minnesota State Fair*, St Paul. **Sep 9-11** *Harvest Moon Festival*, Ely. **Dec** *Hollidazzle Parades*, Minneapolis. **Dec 3** *Holiday Fest*, Jackson.

Climate

Winters are cold with adequate snow for skiing, skating, snowmobiling, ice fishing and sledding. Summers are warm, with adequate rainfall for crop growth, and are conducive to summer sports, including swimming, fishing, camping and hiking. Minnesota only rarely experiences heat waves or drought.

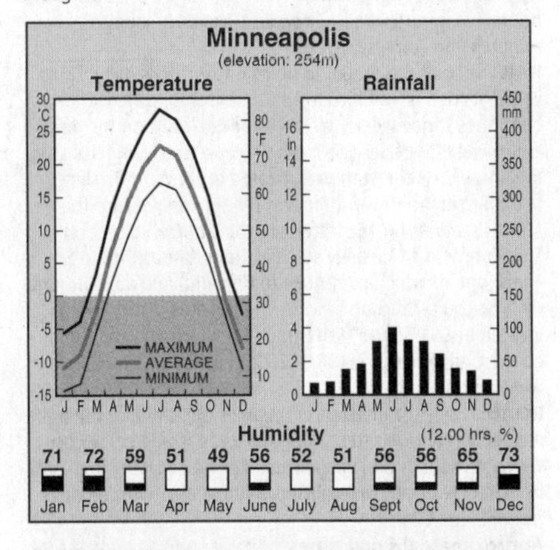

Mississippi

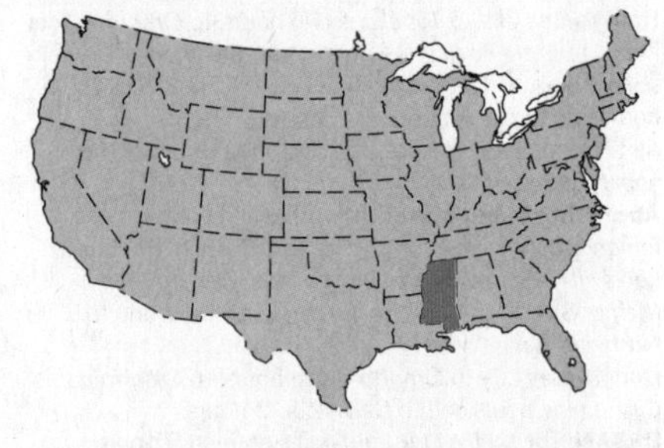

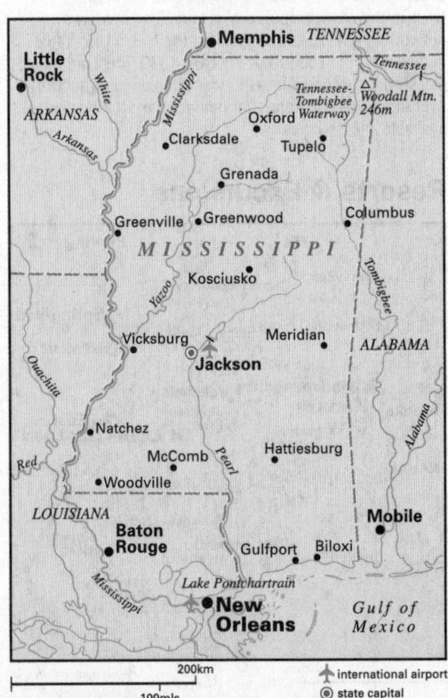

Mississippi Development Authority/Tourism Development Division
Street address: 501 North West Street, Jackson, MS 39201
Postal address: PO Box 849, Jackson, MS 39205
Tel: (601) 359 3449 *or* 3297. Fax: (601) 359 2832.
Website: www.visitmississippi.org *or* www.mississippi.org
Mississippi Tourist Information UK
Lofthouse Enterprises, Woodlands Park Street, Hitchin, Herts SG4 9AH, UK
Tel: (01462) 440 787. Fax: (01462) 440 766.
E-mail: mississippi@david-nicholson.com
Website: www.deep-south-usa.com
Jackson CVB
921 North President Street, Jackson, MS 39202
Tel: (601) 960 1891 *or* (800) 354 7695 (toll-free).
Fax: (601) 960 1827.
E-mail: info@visitjackson.com
Website: www.visitjackson.com
Mississippi Gulf Coast CVB
Street address: 942 Beach Drive, Gulfport, MS 39507
Postal address: PO Box 6128, Gulfport, MS 39506
Tel: (228) 896 6699. Fax: (228) 896 6788.
E-mail: tourism@gulfcoast.org
Website: www.gulfcoast.org
Natchez CVB
640 South Canal Street, Box C, Natchez, MS 39120
Tel: (601) 446 6345 *or* (800) 647 6724 (toll-free).
Fax: (601) 442 0814.
E-mail: info@visitnatchez.com
Website: www.visitnatchez.com
Tupelo CVB
Street address: 399 East Main Street, Tupelo, MS 38804
Postal address: Post Office Drawer 47, Tupelo, MS 38802
Tel: (662) 841 6521 *or* (800) 533 0611 (toll-free).
Fax: (662) 841 6558.
Website: www.tupelo.net
Vicksburg CVB
Street address: 1221 Washington Street, Vicksburg, MS 39181
Postal address: PO Box 110, Vicksburg, MS 39181
Tel: (601) 636 9421 *or* (800) 221 3536 (toll-free).
Fax: (601) 636 9475.
E-mail: mailcvb@vicksburgcvb.org
Website: www.visitvicksburg.com

General Information

Nickname: Magnolia State
State bird: Mockingbird
State flower: Magnolia Blossom
CAPITAL: Jackson
Date of admission to the Union: 10 Dec 1817
POPULATION: 2,902,966 (official estimate 2004)
POPULATION DENSITY: 23 per sq km
2003 total overseas arrivals: Under 38,000
TIME: Central (GMT - 6). *Daylight Saving Time* is observed.

THE STATE: The beautiful 'Magnolia State' is a land of great variety, with wide-open spaces, white sand beaches, bustling cities, quaint little towns and a real feel of the Deep South. This is the State where the key battle of the American Civil War was fought (at Vicksburg in 1863) and where racial strife erupted with terrifying force in the 1960s. It is also the State whose geographical beauty and rich atmosphere have inspired a wealth of artistic talent, from William Faulkner, Eudora Welty and Tennessee Williams to Elvis Presley, Jimmie Rodgers and B B King. As well, the mighty **Mississippi River**, thousands of acres of lush parkland and the Gulf of Mexico coastline combine to make Mississippi a popular outdoor destination.

Travel - International

AIR: International airports: *Jackson International (JAN)* (website: www.jmaa.com) lies to the east of the city. Major car hire companies are represented, and taxis are available.
Domestic airports: There are further airports at Greenville, Gulf Coast (Biloxi), Hattiesburg, Meridian and Tupelo.
RIVER: The *Delta Queen Steamboat Company* (tel: (800) 543 1949 (toll-free); website: www.deltaqueen.com), runs scheduled paddlewheel cruises up and down the Mississippi River, stopping at several Mississippi cities, and travelling as far upriver as Minneapolis/St Paul. A similar journey is available on a European-style hotel barge operated by *RiverBarge Excursion Lines* (tel: (888) 462 2743 (toll-free); website: www.riverbarge.com).
RAIL: Two *Amtrak* (tel: (800) 872 7245 (toll-free); website: www.amtrak.com) lines traverse Mississippi: the 'City of New Orleans' passes through Jackson on its way north to Chicago, and the 'Crescent' cuts through the southeast corner of the State (stopping at Meridian, Laurel, Hattiesburg and Picavune) on its way from New Orleans to Atlanta, Washington, DC and New York City.
Approximate rail travel times: From Jackson to *New Orleans* is four hours 30 minutes, to *Memphis* is four hours 30 minutes, and to *Chicago* is 10 hours 25 minutes.
ROAD: The speed limit on interstate highways in Mississippi is 70mph (112kmph) unless otherwise stated. *Greyhound* buses (tel: (800) 229 9424 (toll-free); website: www.greyhound.com) are frequent along the coast of Mississippi; services north and into the Delta are infrequent.
Approximate bus travel times: From Jackson to *Memphis* is four hours, to *New Orleans* is four hours, to *Montgomery* is seven hours, and to *Dallas* is 10 hours.
Greyhound (tel: (800) 229 9424 (toll free); website: www.greyhound.com) is the major service provider.
URBAN: *Jackson Transit System (JATRAN)* runs buses throughout the city; services run until 1800. Bus schedules and maps are posted at most bus stops and are available at *JATRAN* headquarters, 1025 Terry Road, Jackson (tel: (601) 948 3840).

Resorts & Excursions

NORTH MISSISSIPPI: Starting at the State's northeastern corner, the historic Natchez Trace Parkway winds 640km (400 miles) through Mississippi, ending up at Natchez in the southwest and, as one writer put it, is 'what God meant a highway to be'. Free of billboard advertising and commercial traffic, and with a speed limit of 50mph (80kmph), the parkway provides a scenic introduction to the delights of Mississippi and leads visitors down paths once trekked by buffalo, Native Americans and frontiersmen.
The largest city in north Mississippi, **Tupelo** is best known for its native son, Elvis Presley. Visitors can stop at **Elvis Presley's Birthplace**, the humble two-room house where 'the King' was born, and the adjacent museum **Times and Things Remembered**, which contains rare photos, memorabilia and a statue of 'The King' aged 13. Other attractions include the **Tupelo Automobile Museum** (the first of its kind in the State) with over 100 restored automobiles, and the **Tupelo Buffalo Park**, featuring a herd of buffalo, which can be viewed from aboard the Monster Bison Bus.
Corinth is home to the **Civil War Interpretative Center** as well as a number of lively festivals.
To the west, **Oxford** is the picturesque town captured forever in the writings of William Faulkner. Faulkner's house can be visited today and remains much as the literary giant left it, with the outline of his novel, *A Fable*, scrawled on his study wall. Audio walking tours of the town are available from the tourism council.
Mississippi's vibrant blues tradition can be sampled at the **Delta Blues Museum** in Clarksdale, while the new **Blues Heritage Museum and Gallery** can be found in Greenwood.
CENTRAL MISSISSIPPI: Jackson, Mississippi's political and industrial heart, retains a small-town flavour, with a wealth of cultural attractions. At the **Old Capitol Historical Museum**, exhibits chronicle the Civil Rights movement, while the **Smith Robertson Museum** houses displays on African-American Mississippian history and heritage. Other attractions include the **Museum of Art** and the **Museum of Natural Science**.
The city of **Vicksburg** lies on the Mississippi River west of Jackson and is a prime source of southern history. Some of the bloodiest battles of the Civil War took place on the site of the **Vicksburg National Military Park**. Here, on July 4 1863, the Union victory helped the Yankees gain control of the Mississippi River, a crucial element in winning the war. Living history demonstrations and battle re-enactments every summer provide a fascinating insight into this dramatic period. In addition, dockside casinos offer entertainment on the Mississippi River and many antebellum homes can provide bed & breakfast accommodation. Vicksburg is also home to the delightful new **Great Animal Adventures and Children's Museum**, located in an 1888 stable building.
The childhood of Jim Henson, creator of the *Sesame Street* and *Muppets* characters, can be remembered at **Leland**'s *Birthplace of the Frog* exhibition. Music also plays its part, with the **Highway 61 Blues Museum** in downtown **Leland**.
New attractions in **Canton** include the **Canton Movie Museum** and the **Canton Multi-Cultural Center and Museum**, with topics ranging from slavery and civil rights to family and music. Local Canton residents feature at the oral history kiosk.
SOUTH MISSISSIPPI: Perched atop the bluffs of the Mississippi River, **Natchez** was spared major destruction in the Civil War. Today, over 500 historic buildings still stand, including mansions, churches and public buildings, providing a wonderful glimpse of pre-war life in the Deep South. Many of these graceful mansions contain original furnishings, while a good number offer bed & breakfast accommodation. **Natchez-under-the-Hill**, once notorious for its riverside gambling, is now a colourful area of pubs, gift shops, restaurants and dockside gaming. Natchez is also the starting point for the **Deep South Antique & Wine Trail**, which is a co-operative endeavour between the

A B C D E F G H I J K L M N O P Q R S T U V W X Y Z

States of Mississippi and Louisiana and covers 322km (200 miles) and six counties, with over 100 antique shops en route.

A town that perhaps best typifies the Old South, **Woodville** is the location of **Rosemount Plantation**, the boyhood home of **Confederate President Jefferson Davis**. The town of **Hattiesburg** is famous for the **All-American Rose Garden**, which features 740 patented bushes, and is also home to the **Armed Forces Musuem**.

Located on a Native American reservation, the **Pearl River Resort** in **Choctaw** features gaming and entertainment facilities, two hotels, and a golf club. New additions, slated for completion by 2006 include a recreational complex, a fitness and wellness center, a lake-side hotel, exposition hall, a Choctaw memorial and a labyrinth.

MISSISSIPPI GULF COAST: There are 42km (26 miles) of sun-drenched sandy beaches on the coast, with many points of historic interest. **Biloxi** is the site of many pre-war buildings, including **Beauvoir**, the retirement home of Jefferson Davis. Biloxi is also the point of departure for daily cruises to **Ship Island**, location of **Fort Massachusetts**, a POW camp during the Civil War, as well as excursions to **Back Bay**, on **Deer Island**.

Social Profile

FOOD & DRINK: State favourites include farm-raised catfish, fried chicken, barbecues, and fresh seafood. The tiny Delta town of Belzoni claims to be the catfish capital of the world. The highlight of the year is the *Catfish Festival*, which sees the crowning of the Catfish Queen and a catfish-eating contest.

THEATRE & CONCERTS: Jackson is the only city in the United States to host the *International Ballet Competition* every four years, and its symphony orchestra and opera company offer lively programmes. Phase II of the recently completed **Natchez City Center** project will involve the restoration of the **City Auditorium**.

NIGHTLIFE: Las Vegas-style entertainment casinos abound, especially in Greenville, Natchez, Philadelphia, Tunica, Vicksburg, and along the Mississippi Gulf Coast. Vicksburg has the *Bottleneck Blues Bar*, decorated in a 1930s delta-style.

SHOPPING: Antique shops and malls are plentiful. The *Canton Flea Market*, held in May and October, is ever-popular. In Port Gibson the 'Pieces and Strings' market runs from the last weekend in March to the end of April and features African- and European-American quilts and quilting demonstrations.

SPORT: Hunting and **fishing** are popular. For further details, contact the Mississippi Department of Wildlife, Fisheries & Parks (tel: (601) 432 2400; website: www.mdwfp.com). The *Magnolia Golf Trail* is a new 14-course trail featuring the best of Mississippi's many **golf** courses. The State's finest golf courses can be found in Hattiesburg; the *Cranebrake Golf Club* and the *Timberton Golf Club* have both achieved high acclaim in golfing publications.

SPECIAL EVENTS: Every spring, over 20 cities and towns host 'pilgrimages', the seasonal opening of pre-Civil War and Victorian homes, featuring costumed extravaganzas and candlelit tours. Over 300 festivals take place every year, a great number of which are music-oriented. The following is a selection of special events occurring in Mississippi in 2005:
Feb 4-13 *Dixie National Livestock Show, Parade and Rodeo*, Jackson. **Mar 12-Apr 2** *World Catfish Festival*, Belzoni. **Apr 14-17** *2nd Annual Armory Railroad Festival*. **May 9** *Annual Gum Tree Festival*, Tupelo. **Jun 3-4** *Delta Jubilee & Cooking Contest*, Clarksdale. **Jul** *18th Annual Slugburger Festival*, Corinth. **Jul 13-16** *Choctaw Indian Fair*. **Dec 1-31** *Annual Christmas Tree Festival*, Jackson.

Climate

Mississippi's climate is moderate, with January's temperature reaching 50°F (10°C) and summer's sometimes stretching to 90°F (32°C). The year-round average is 64°F (18°C).

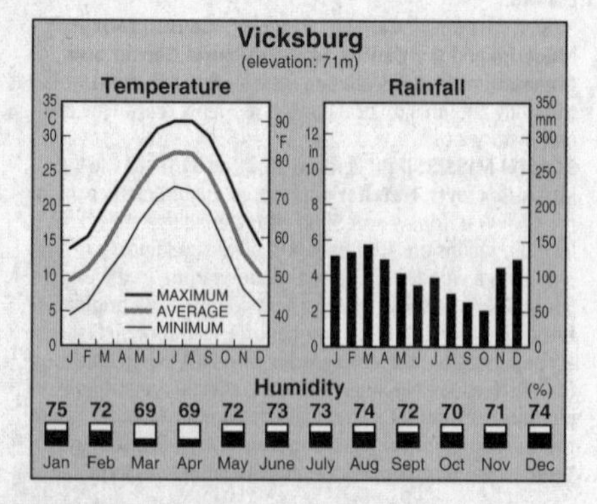

Missouri

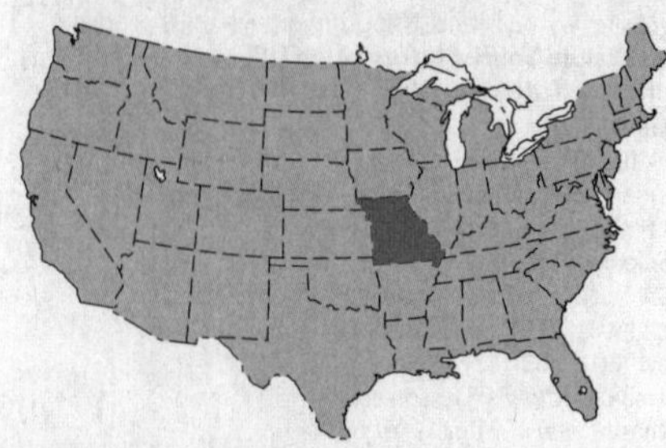

Missouri Division of Tourism
Street address: 301 West High, Jefferson City, MO 65101
Postal address: PO Box 1055, Jefferson City, MO 65102
Tel: (573) 751 4133 *or* (800) 519 2300 (toll-free).
Fax: (573) 751 5160.
E-mail: tourism@ded.mo.gov
Website: www.visitmo.com

Missouri Division of Tourism (UK Office)
c/o Cellet Travel Services Ltd, 47 High Street, Henley-in-Arden, Warwickshire B95 5AA, UK
Tel: (01564) 794 999. Fax: (020) 491 1114.
E-mail: info@cellet.co.uk
Website: www.visitmo.co.uk *or* www.cellet.co.uk

Branson/Lakes Area CVB
PO Box 1897, Branson, MO 65615
Tel: (417) 334 4084 *or* (800) 935 1199 *or* (800) 214 3661 (toll-free). Fax: (417) 334 4139.
E-mail: info@bransoncvb.com
Website: www.explorebranson.com

Cape Girardeau CVB
100 Broadway, Cape Girardeau, MO 63701
Tel: (573) 335 1631 *or* (800) 777 0068 (toll-free).
Fax: (573) 334 6702.
E-mail: visitcape@capegirardeaucvb.org
Website: www.capegirardeaucvb.org

CVB of Greater Kansas City
1100 Main Street, Suite 2200, Kansas City, MO 64105
Tel: (816) 221 5242 *or* (800) 767 7700 (toll-free).
Fax: (816) 691 3805.
E-mail: info@visitkc.com
Website: www.visitkc.com

St Louis Convention & Visitors Commission
1 Metropolitan Square, Suite 1100, St Louis, MO 63102
Tel: (314) 421 1023 *or* (800) 325 7962 *or* 916 8938 (toll-free).
Fax: (314) 421 0394.
E-mail: tourism@explorestlouis.com
Website: www.explorestlouis.com

Springfield CVB
815 East St Louis Street, Springfield, MO 65806
Tel: (417) 881 5300 *or* (800) 678 8767 (toll-free).
Fax: (417) 881 2231 *or* 7201 (sales).
E-mail: cvb@springfieldmo.org
Website: www.springfieldmo.org

General Information

Nickname: Show Me State
State bird: Bluebird
State flower: Hawthorn Flower
CAPITAL: Jefferson City
Date of admission to the Union: 10 Aug 1821
POPULATION: 5,754,618 (official estimate 2004)
POPULATION DENSITY: 31.9 per sq km
2003 total overseas arrivals/US ranking: 90,000/29
TIME: Central (GMT - 6). *Daylight Saving Time* is observed.

THE STATE: Missouri, in the heart of the USA, is a blend of frontier West, gracious South, the sophisticated East and industrial North. The **Missouri Valley** was a major pioneer route, with **St Louis** known as 'The Gateway to the West'. It is bounded by the **Mississippi River** in the east. Prairies lie north of the **Missouri River** (the longest in the USA), with great plains to the west, rolling hills in the south and the Southern-style cotton lands to the southeast. The State's riverboat culture was immortalised by Mark Twain in *Life on the Mississippi* and in his tales of *Tom Sawyer* and *Huckleberry Finn*.

Travel - International

AIR: International airports: *Lambert St Louis International (STL)* (website: www.lambert-stlouis.com) is 21km (13 miles) northwest of central St Louis (travel time - 30 minutes). The **Metro Link** light-rail system connects the airport with downtown St Louis. Taxis, airport limousines and car hire (*Alamo, Avis, Budget, Dollar, Enterprise, Hertz,*

Credit: © Missouri Division of Tourism

National and *Thrifty*) are also available. *Greyhound* buses (see below) stop at the airport, providing a route to further flung destinations. *Kansas City International (KCI)* is 32km (20 miles) northwest from the city centre (travel time - 40 minutes). Shuttle buses run every 30 minutes (0600-0000) to hotels in Kansas City and Westport. Taxis and car hire (*Ace, Alamo, Avis, Budget, Dollar, Enterprise, Hertz, National* and *Thrifty*) are available.

Approximate flight times: From London to *St Louis* is 8 hours five minutes and to *Kansas City* is 13 hours 20 minutes (including stopover).

RAIL: St Louis is a stopping point on *Amtrak's* daily 'Texas Eagle' service from Chicago to San Antonio, which continues thrice weekly to Los Angeles. Trains on the daily 'Southwest Chief Service' from Chicago to Los Angeles stop in Kansas City; the station is located at 30 West Pershing. For approximate travel times on the former line, see the *Illinois* section; for the latter, see the *California* section. There are also twice daily services from Kansas City to St Louis (one of which continues to Chicago) and an additional daily St Louis-Chicago service. The St Louis station is located at 551 South 16th Street. For more information, contact *Amtrak* (tel: (800) 872 7245 (toll-free); website: www.amtrak.com).

ROAD: Long-distance bus companies operating in the State include *Greyhound* (tel: (800) 229 9424 (toll-free); website: www.greyhound.com) and *Jefferson Lines* (tel: (888) 864 2832 (toll-free); website: www.jeffersonlines.com), with services from Kansas City.

Approximate driving times: From St Louis to *Kansas City* is four hours, to *Chicago* is five hours, to *Indianapolis* is five hours, to *Louisville* is five hours, to *Cincinnati* is six hours, to *Memphis* is six hours, to *Nashville* is six hours, to *Des Moines* is seven hours, to *Little Rock* is seven hours, to *Oklahoma City* is 10 hours, to *Minneapolis/St Paul* is 11 hours, to *Dallas* is 13 hours, to *New York* is 19 hours, to *Miami* is 25 hours, to *Los Angeles* is 39 hours and to *Seattle* is 45 hours.

From Kansas City to *Topeka* is two hours, to *Omaha* is four hours, to *Little Rock* is seven hours, to *Oklahoma City* is seven hours, to *Chicago* is 10 hours, to *New York* is 25 hours and to *Los Angeles* is 34 hours.

All times are based on nonstop driving at or below the applicable speed limits.

Approximate bus travel times: From St Louis to *Indianapolis* is five hours, to *Kansas City* is five hours, to *Louisville* is six hours, to *Chicago* is seven hours, to *Memphis* is seven hours, to *Tulsa* is nine hours and to *Nashville* is nine hours.

From Kansas City to *Omaha* is five hours, to *Oklahoma City* is nine hours and to *Denver* is 13 hours.

URBAN: The *Metro Link* light-rail system in St Louis (website: www.metrolouis.org) is complemented by a network of BSTS public bus routes; the Metro Link is free in downtown St Louis Mon-Fri 1100-1330. There are public bus services around Kansas City and surrounding suburbs (website: www.kcata.org). Car hire and taxis are readily available in both cities.

Resorts & Excursions

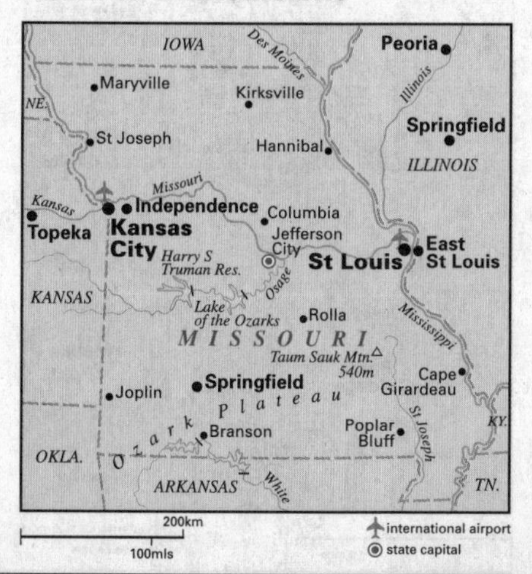

ST LOUIS: The largest city in Missouri and one of the US's largest inland ports, St Louis was once a booming centre for fur traders and explorers opening up 'The West'. It is now a modern communications, commercial, industrial and cultural centre. It still retains its love affair with the **Mississippi River**, on whose banks can be heard ragtime, blues and Dixieland jazz. The influence of the many ethnic groups that created the city can still be seen in the German burgher houses, elegant French mansions (on its south side), and in the Italian 'Hill' neighbourhood and other diverse enclaves.
At 192m (630ft), the Gateway Arch on the riverfront is the nation's tallest memorial. It honours St Louis as the starting point for settlers who began their trek to the western frontier from the city and contains an observation deck and exhibits on the American West. Among the area's 100-plus attractions are: the **Six Flags St Louis** theme park, the **Missouri Botanical Garden**, the **Missouri History Museum**, **The Magic House Children's Museum**, the new **Challenger Learning Center** (with space simulators), sights along **Old Route 66**, **St Louis Zoo** and other cultural attractions in the **Forest Park**, currently undergoing renovation. St Louis celebrates the centennial of the 1904 *World's Fair*.
EXCURSIONS: Hannibal in northeast Missouri was Mark Twain's hometown during the 19th century. Many museums and shows celebrate the author's life and works, including the **Mark Twain Boyhood Home** and the **New Mark Twain Museum**.
KANSAS CITY: Once the eastern terminus for some of the West's most famous trails, such as the *Oregon*, *California* and *Santa Fe*, **Kansas City** is now a major commercial and agricultural centre for the Midwest. Kansas City is situated on the State line between Missouri to the east and Kansas to the west.
The **Worlds of Fun** entertainment complex has more than 120 rides, rollercoasters and live entertainment, with a Spinning Dragons rollercoaster. The **Country Club Plaza**, the nation's oldest shopping centre, was established in 1922. Other attractions include **Oceans of Fun**, a water theme park, and the **Nelson-Atkins Museum of Art**. The **Arabia Steamboat Museum** displays artefacts recovered from a steamboat which sank in the Mississippi with 200 tons of cargo in 1856.
EXCURSIONS: Independence, 16km (10 miles) east of Kansas City, celebrates its association with former resident Harry S Truman at the **Truman Library & Museum**.
St Joseph, north of Kansas City, boasts the **Pony Express National Memorial** and the **Patee House Museum**. The **Lake of the Ozarks** in central Missouri has more than 1600km (1000 miles) of forested shoreline and offers watersports, canoeing, golfing, tennis, caves, shows and museums, as well as the recently renovated **Timber Falls Indoor Water Park**. It is home to three outstanding State parks – **Bennett Springs**, the **Lake of the Ozarks** and **Ha Ha Tonka**. In **Liberty**, the **Jesse James Bank Museum** is the site of the nation's first daylight bank robbery.
BRANSON: Branson first became popular at the turn of the 20th century, when Harold Bell Wright's *The Shepherd of the Hills*, with its colourful depiction of life in the Ozarks, was published. Today, the area is known as a live entertainment capital and for its three picturesque lakes, **Lake Taneycomo**, **Table Rock Lake** and **Bull Shoals Lake**, which provide excellent opportunities for fishing and water activities. Branson's best-known attraction is **Silver Dollar City**, a turn-of-the-century craft village with daily music shows and rides like the *Thunderation Rollercoaster*, the *Lost River Water Ride* and the *Buzz Saw Falls*. Branson offers pop, swing, rock and roll, country and gospel music performances at around 40 theatres, with more than 90 daily shows, and attracts legends of the entertainment world, such as Andy Williams and Mel Tillis.

Social Profile

FOOD & DRINK: Everything from elegant downtown restaurants to more casual eating places serve traditional ethnic fare in St Louis. The Kansas City area is famous for its steaks and barbecues.
THEATRES & CONCERTS: In St Louis, there are performances at the **Opera Theatre of St Louis**, the **Fox Theater** and the outdoor **Muny Theatre**. The *Kansas City Philharmonic* plays at the **Music Hall**. Also in Kansas City, the **Missouri Repertory Theater** performs on the University of Missouri's campus; other venues include the **Lyric Opera** of Kansas City and **Starlight Theater**. Branson has a busy theatre scene, with venues including the **Country Tonite Theater**, **Moon River Theater** and the **Branson Variety Theater**.
NIGHTLIFE: There are many nightclubs and restaurants on the riverfront in St Louis, where jazz and ragtime music is performed nightly and discos can be found in most modern hotels. There are four full-gaming casinos located within 15 minutes of downtown Kansas City, whose historic *Westport* district is home to great blues, jazz and R&B.

Credit: © Missouri Division of Tourism

SHOPPING: Two of the St Louis area's most elegant regional shopping malls are **Plaza Frontenac** and the **St Louis Galleria**. The new **St Louis Mills** mall combines shopping with a NASCAR Speedcar track, a skatepark and an ice rink (the new practice ground for the St Louis Blues NHL ice hockey team). The city's neighbourhoods are also filled with fashionable boutiques, speciality shops, gourmet delicatessens and antique stores.
Soulard Market in south St Louis is a colourful and amusing place to shop on Saturdays. The market was established in 1779 and today offers fresh goods, such as meat and home-baked items, as soon as they arrive in the city. **Union Station**, the city's historic Victorian railroad station, has been redeveloped as a festival marketplace, with more than 100 shops and restaurants, and numerous nightclubs. Branson is also becoming a popular shopping destination, with three outlet malls, and unique craft and gift stores throughout the city. Kansas City has nationally-known stores, plus hundreds of shops and boutiques to be found off the beaten path.
SPECIAL EVENTS: The following is a selection of special events occurring in Missouri in 2005:
Jan 30 *Groundhog Run*, Kansas City. **Feb 12-13** *Missouri Wine Fest*, St Louis. **Feb 18** *Winter Bluegrass Music Festival*, Hannibal. **Feb 20-24** *Soulard Mardi Gras*, St Louis. **Feb 26-27** *Chocolate Wine Trail*, Hermann. **Mar 12** *St Patrick's Day Parade*, St Louis. **Mar 19** *Old Time Fiddlers Content*, Boonville. **Apr 1-2** *13th Annual Big Muddy Fall Festival*, Boonville. **Apr 5-9** *BransonFest*. **Apr 9-10** *Spirit of St Louis Marathon*. **May 6-8** *Valley of Flowers Festival*, Florissant. **May 7** *Ozarks Day Festival*, Eminence; *Truman Day Celebration*, Lamar. **May 8-24** *Renaissance Faire*, Wentzville. **May 14-15** *Lewis & Clark Heritage Days*, St Charles. **May 20-22** *Plumb Nellie Days*, *31st Annual Hillbilly Festival & Craft Show*, Branson. **Jun 4-5** *Strawberry Festival*, Kimmswick. **Jun 10-12** *Festival of the Four States*, Joplin. **Jun 24-26** *Heritage Days*, Boonville. **Jun 25** *Barton Country's 150th Birthday Celebration*, Lamar. **Jun 25-26** *St Louis PrideFest*; *Airfest*, Joplin. **Jul 2-4** *Fair St Louis*. **Jul 13-16** *Prairie Home Fair*, Boonville. **Jul 14-17** *Golden Harvest Days*, Golden City. **Aug 27** *Annual Oldtime Fiddle Contest*, Branson. **Sep 9-11** *St Louis Art Fair*. **Sep 17** *Prairie Days*, Liberal; *Great Forest Park Balloon Race*, St Louis. **Sep 17-18** *Fall Festival*, Rockaway Beach. **Sep 24-25** *Pioneer Days at the Boone Home*, Defiance. **Oct 1** *Apple Days*, Lamar. **Oct 8** *Rodeo Days Arts & Crafts Festival*, Eureka. **Oct 15-16** *Deutsch Country Days*, Marthasville. **Oct 22-23** *Apple Butter Festival*, Kimmswick.

Climate

The region has the most continental climate of any area in the USA. Winters are cold and summers warm, with frequent heatwaves.

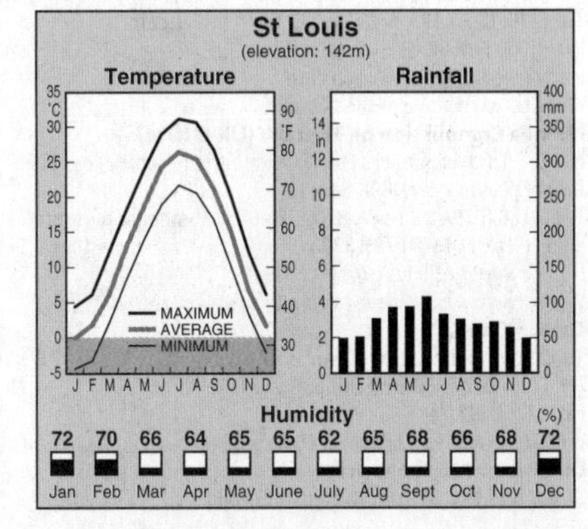

Montana

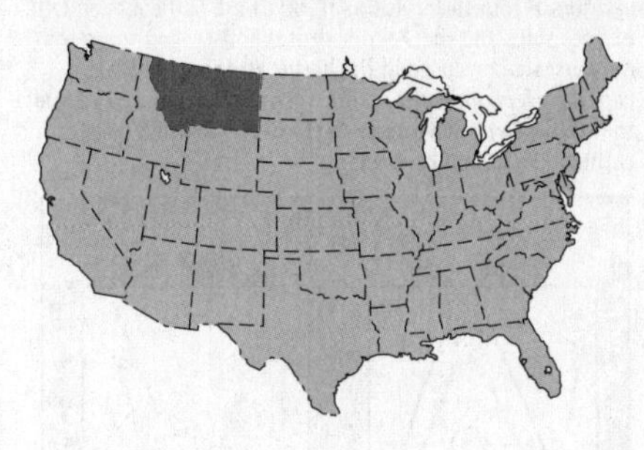

Montana Promotional Division
Street address: Department of Commerce, 301 South Park Avenue, Helena, MT 59620
Postal address: PO Box 200533, Helena, Montana 59620
Tel: (406) 841 2870 *or* (800) 847 4868 (toll-free)
Fax: (406) 841 2871.
E-mail: cwhiting@state.mt.us
Website: www.visitmt.com
Information about Montana's seven convention and visitors bureaux, communities and chambers of commerce is available on the Montana Promotional Division's website or in their free publications, *The Montana Travel Planner* and *Montana Vacation Guide*.
Rocky Mountain International
7 Thornton Avenue, Warsash, Southampton, Hampshire SO31 96D, UK
Tel: (01489) 557 533 (trade enquiries only) *or* (09063) 640 655 (consumer request line; 60p per minute).
Fax: (01489) 557 534.
E-mail: rmi.uk@btinternet.com
Website: www.rmi-realamerica.com

General Information

Nickname: Treasure State
State bird: Western Meadowlark
State flower: Bitterroot
CAPITAL: Helena
Date of admission to the Union: 8 Nov 1889
POPULATION: 926,865 (official estimate 2004)
POPULATION DENSITY: 2.45 per sq km
2003 total overseas arrivals: Under 38,000
TIME: Mountain (GMT - 7). *Daylight Saving Time* is observed.

THE STATE: Montana is the fourth-largest State, after Alaska, Texas and California, covering 38 million hectares (94 million acres). Almost a quarter of Montana is national forest or public lands, with almost 2 million hectares (5 million acres) protected as wilderness areas. Elk, deer, antelopes, wolves and bears are just a few of the 500 species of wildlife that can be seen in Montana. The **National Bison Range**, just north of **Missoula**, was established in 1908 to protect the animal from extinction. Today, around 450 bison roam this high plains refuge. Between May and October, when all the routes are open, there is a small per-vehicle charge to access the range and view the magnificent creatures.
Waterton-Glacier International Peace Park is home to many endangered bears, big horn sheep, mountain goats, moose and grey wolves. The park is divided into two areas: **Waterton Lakes National Park** in Alberta (Canada) and the larger **Glacier National Park** in Montana. The 84km (52 mile) *Going-to-the-Sun Road* crosses the park's spectacular alpine landscape and is one of America's most scenic drives. Hiking is a popular option, with over 1200km (750 miles) of trails to follow, many offering back-country camping opportunities. There are also special routes for cyclists and horses, and many of the larger lakes have tour boat services. Anyone who enters the park is advised to take park rangers' warnings and advice about encounters with bears very seriously. Other recreation areas include the **Bob Marshall Wilderness Area**, the huge **Charles M Russell National Wildlife Refuge** and **Yellowstone National Park**, which is shared with Idaho and Wyoming, and is the oldest national park in the world, dating back to 1872.
Billings, with nearly 100,000 residents, is Montana's largest city and a regional business/service centre. The area around Billings offers great opportunities for fishing, hiking and western adventures, such as guest ranches and cattle drives. The outdoor recreation department at **Montana State University – Billings** offers canoeing classes and other outdoor activities. The highlights of the town's calendar are the *Billings Summer Fair* (third weekend of July), *Big SkyFest* hot air balloon festival (late July/early August) and

the Montana Fair (August), in addition to an active year-round cultural scene. **Little Bighorn Battlefield National Monument** lies an hour southeast of Billings. General George Armstrong Custer and his men made their last stand here on 25 June 1876 against the Sioux and Cheyenne warriors. A tour takes visitors through the battle movements of both sides and the visitors' centre houses a museum that displays weapons used in the battle. **Helena**, the State capital, offers fine 19th-century architecture, museums and the Gothic-style **St Helena Cathedral**, modelled on the cathedral in Cologne, Germany.

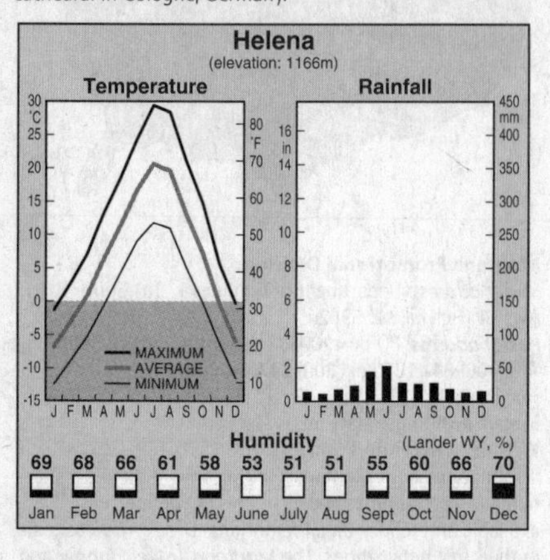

Nebraska

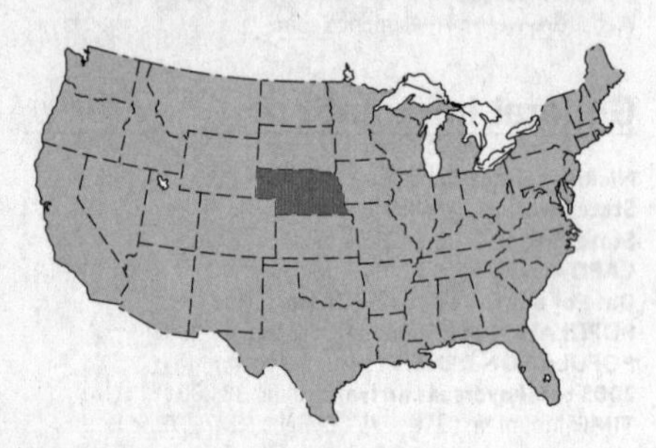

Nebraska Division of Travel & Tourism
PO Box 98907, Lincoln, NE 68509
Tel: (402) 471 3796 *or* (877) 632 7252 (toll-free). Fax: (402) 471 3026.
E-mail: tourism@visitnebraska.org
Website: www.visitnebraska.org

Greater Omaha CVB
1001 Farnham Street, Suite 200, Omaha, NE 68102
Tel: (402) 444 4660 *or* (866) 937 6624 (toll-free). Fax: (402) 444 4511.
Website: www.visitomaha.com

Lincoln CVB
Street address: 1135 M Street, Suite 300, Lincoln, NE 68508
Postal address: PO Box 83737, Lincoln, NE 68501
Tel: (402) 434 5335 *or* (800) 423 8212 (toll-free). Fax: (402) 436 2360.
E-mail: info@lincoln.org
Website: www.lincoln.org

General Information

Nickname: Cornhusker State
State bird: Western Meadowlark
State flower: Goldenrod
CAPITAL: Lincoln
Date of admission to the Union: 1 Mar 1867
POPULATION: 1,747,214 (official estimate 2004)
POPULATION DENSITY: 8.7 per sq km
2003 total overseas arrivals: Under 38,000
TIME: Central (GMT - 6) in the greater part of the State; Mountain (GMT - 7) in the west. *Daylight Saving Time* is observed.

THE STATE: Nebraska rises from the Missouri prairie lands to the Great Plains and foothills of the Rocky Mountains. **Omaha**, its largest city, is one of the State's major tourist destinations. **Girls and Boys Town**, the famous homeless boys' community, is situated nearby. Originally founded as 'Boys Town' by Father Edward Flanagan, the home for unwanted and distressed boys is still thriving, and, today, girls also enjoy the care and protection it offers. The attraction that draws the most visitors through its gates, however, is the **Henry Doorly Zoo**, which contains **Lied Jungle**, the largest indoor tropical rainforest in the world. In contrast to the zoo's popular **Scott Kingdoms of the Seas Aquarium**, where brown sharks swim ominously close to onlookers, the **Desert Dome** houses three distinct desert climates in one biosphere. Located just underneath is the new **The Kingdoms of the Night** nocturnal exhibit, which houses animals that live in dark habitats. Omaha's varied nightlife ranges from punk to opera, while theatre lovers can take advantage of the free *Shakespeare on the Green* (*Nebraska Shakespeare*) festival, which takes place in late June and early July in **Elmwood Park**.

Lincoln is one of the most stunning State capitals in the USA. The **State Capitol Building**, known as the 'Tower on the Plains', is as impressive inside as it looks from the street; for an unsurpassed view of the city, take the elevator to the top floor. Other city sights include the **Museum of Nebraska History**, which has a moving exhibit on the history of the Plains Native Americans; **Mueller Planetarium**; **Sheldon Memorial Art Gallery**, including a collection of Warhol Pop Art; and the **University of Nebraska State Museum**, which boasts the largest mounted mammoth in a US museum. The Strategic Air & Space Museum, near Ashland, features exhibitions and displays of aircraft and missiles, and is regarded as one of the best in the USA.

Nebraska is also home to **Homestead National Monument** of America; the pioneer landmarks of **Scotts Bluff National Monument** and **Chimney Rock**; **Fort Robinson State Park**, where Chief Crazy Horse surrendered in 1877; and the **Buffalo Bill State Park**.

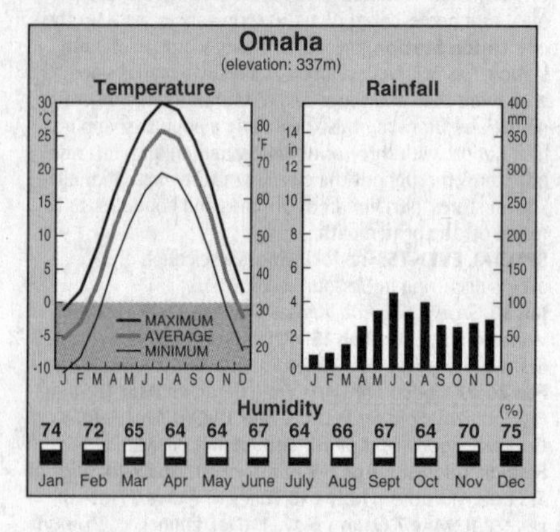

Nevada

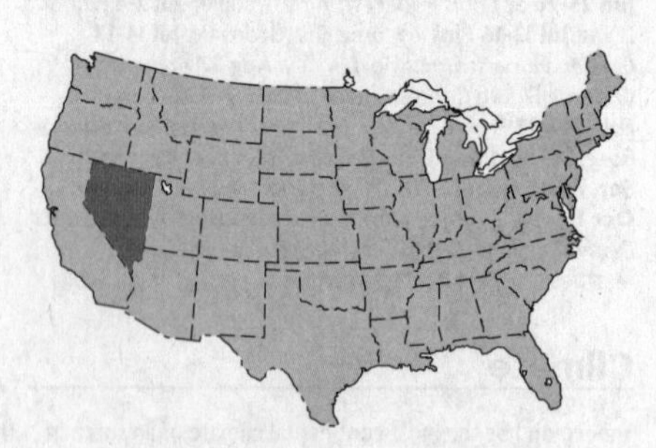

Nevada Commission on Tourism
401 North Carson Street, Carson City, NV 89701
Tel: (775) 687 4322 *or* (800) 237 0774 (toll-free).
Fax: (775) 687 6779.
E-mail: ncot@travelnevada.com
Website: www.travelnevada.com

Nevada Commission on Tourism (UK Office)
c/o Cellet Travel Services Ltd, 47 High Street, Henley-in-Arden, Warwickshire B95 5AA, UK
Tel: (01564) 794 999 *or* (0870) 523 8832 (brochure request line). Fax: (01564) 795 333.
E-mail: info@cellet.co.uk
Website: www.travelnevada.com *or* www.cellet.co.uk

Carson City CVB
1900 South Carson Street, Suite 100, Carson City, NV 89701
Tel: (775) 687 7410 *or* (800) 638 2321 (toll-free).
Fax: (775) 687 7416.
Website: www.visitcarsoncity.com

Duckwater Shoshone Tribe
Street address: 511 Duckwater Falls Road, Duckwater, NV 89314
Postal address: PO Box 140068, Duckwater, NV 89314
Tel: (775) 863 0227. Fax: (775) 863 0301.

Elko Nevada Chamber of Commerce
1405 Idaho Street, Elko, NV 89801
Tel: (775) 738 7135 *or* (800) 428 7143. Fax: (775) 738 7136.
E-mail: chamber@elkonevada.com
Website: www.elkonevada.com

Fallon Convention and Tourism Authority
100 Campus Way, Fallon, NV 89406
Tel: (775) 423 4556 *or* (866) 432 5566 (toll-free).
Fax: (775) 423 8926.
E-mail: falntour@phonewave.net
Website: www.fallontourism.com

Las Vegas Convention Visitors Authority
3150 Paradise Road, Las Vegas, NV 89109
Tel: (702) 892 0711 *or* 7575 *or* (800) 332 5333 (toll-free).
Fax: (702) 386 7818.
E-mail: rab@lvcva.com
Website: www.vegasfreedom.com *or* www.lvcva.com

Las Vegas Convention Visitors Authority (UK Office)
c/o Cellet Travel Services Ltd, 47 High Street, Henley-in-Arden, Warwickshire B95 5AA, UK
Tel: (01564) 794 999. Fax: (01564) 795 333.
E-mail: info@cellet.co.uk
Website: www.lasvegasfreedom.co.uk *or* www.cellet.co.uk

Las Vegas Chamber of Commerce
3720 Howard Hughes Parkway, Las Vegas, NV 89109
Tel: (702) 641 5822 *or* 735 1616 (information service).
Fax: (702) 735 2011.
E-mail: info@lvchamber.com
Website: www.lvchamber.com

Las Vegas Paiute Tribe
1 Paiute Drive, Las Vegas, NV 89106
Tel: (702) 386 3926. Fax: (702) 383 4019.

Mason Valley Chamber of Commerce (for Pioneer Territory)
227 South Main Street, Yerington, NV 89447
Tel: (775) 463 2245. Fax: (775) 463 3369.
E-mail: moreinfo@masonvalleychamber.com
Website: www.masonvalleychamber.com

Mineral County Chamber of Commerce
901 Sierra Way, PO Box 1635, Hawthorne, NV 89415
Tel: (775) 945 5896 or (877) 736. Fax: (775) 945 1257.
E-mail: mceda@gbis.com
Website: www.hawthorne-nveda.org

Reno-Sparks Convention Visitors Authority
Street address: 4590 South Virginia Street, Suite G, Reno, NV 89502
Postal address: PO Box 837, Reno, NV 89504
Tel: (775) 827 7600 *or* (800) 367 7366. Fax: (775) 827 7666.
E-mail: info@visitrenotahoe.com
Website: www.visitrenotahoe.com

Tahoe-Douglas Chamber of Commerce and Visitor Center
Street address: Highway 50 at Roundhill, Lake Tahoe, NV 89449
Postal address: PO Box 7139, Lake Tahoe, NV 89449
Tel: (775) 588 4591. Fax: (775) 588 4598.
E-mail: info@tahoechamber.org
Website www.tahoechamber.org

Washoe Tribe of Nevada & California
919 Highway 395 South, Gardnerville, NV 89410
Tel: (775) 265 4191 *or* (775) 265 8600 (toll-free).
Fax: (775) 265 6240.
Website: www.washoetribe.us

White Pine County Tourism and Recreation Board
150 Sixth Street, Ely, NV 89301
Tel: (775) 289 3720 *or* (800) 496 9350.
Fax: (775) 289 6757.
E-mail: ccmanager@nwpower.net
Website: www.elynevada.net

General Information

Nickname: Silver State
State bird: Mountain Bluebird
State flower: Sagebrush
CAPITAL: Carson City
Date of admission to the Union: 31 Oct 1864
POPULATION: 2,334,771 (official estimate 2004)
POPULATION DENSITY: 8.2 per sq km
2003 total overseas arrivals/US ranking: 1,370,000/5
TIME: Pacific (GMT - 8). *Daylight Saving Time* is observed.

THE STATE: Explorer John C Fremont's 1844/5 expedition with legendary scout Kit Carson opened up the region called Nevada, previously part of Mexico. The name 'Nevada', meaning 'snow-capped' in Spanish, was adopted in 1861 when the territory was established. The State has since been sectioned off into 'territories'. The **Cowboy Country**, found along the I-80 corridor across northern Nevada, was once the main trail across the State, used by thousands of pioneers on horseback and in covered wagons. The **Reno-Tahoe Territory**, situated on the eastern slopes

of the Sierra Nevada, contains many of Nevada's most scenic and historic sights. The **Pony Express Territory**, named after the famous riders, offers one of the last opportunities to experience the Old West. In the **Pioneer Territory**, which encompasses south central Nevada, visitors can trace the story of Nevada's rich mining history.
Las Vegas, Nevada's largest city, is one of the major gambling and entertainment centres of the world. Luxury hotels, casinos and show venues line **The Strip**, a section of Las Vegas Boulevard South; a lower-priced, smaller version is found at the **Downtown Casino Center**, which also features the **Fremont Street Experience**, a four-block canopied street mall with nightly light shows. Outdoor sports, top restaurants and nightclubs are also on offer. Las Vegas is probably the easiest place in the world in which to get married. Around 230 marriage licences are issued per day.
Reno, another entertainment and casino city, is known for its quiet residential areas, and surrounding historic and natural attractions.

Travel - International

Air: International airports: *McCarran International (LAS)* (website: www.mccarran.com) is situated 1.6km (1 mile) from the Strip, 8km (5 miles) from central Las Vegas. The airport is one of the USA's busiest; scheduled airlines include *Alaska Airlines, America West Airlines, American Airlines, Continental Airlines, Delta Air Lines, United Airlines, US Airways* and *Virgin Atlantic*. The *Citizens Area Transit* (*CTA*), a service of the Regional Transportation Commission of Clark County, operates bus services to and from the airport. Routes 108 and 109 have direct access to the airport and stop on Zero Level, directly outside the arrivals and baggage claim area. CAT *Paratransit Services* is a shared public transport service in small buses for persons with disabilities who cannot independently use the regular CAT bus. There is no CAT bus service from the airport to the Strip. *CLS Transportation* and *Gray Line* both provide a reasonably priced service to the Strip and downtown hotels. *Bell Trans* (website: www.belltrans.com) operates a minibus service to the Strip and downtown Las Vegas, with *Las Vegas Limousine* and *Showtime Shuttle* operating similar services. The *Airport Shuttle* provides a door-to-door service. Shuttle/limo companies are located on the east side of baggage claim; hotel shuttles are often free for guests. Shuttle services to and from communities outside Las Vegas are also available; reservations are often required. Taxis are available on the west side of baggage claim. Car hire service booths are located in the centre of the baggage claim area. All off-airport car hire services may be accessed by a bank of free telephones also located in baggage claim. All car hire companies are located outside the terminal area and provide their own airport courtesy shuttle to transport customers to/from their lots.
Reno/Tahoe International (RNO) (website: www.renoairport.com) is located 6.5km (4 miles) southeast of the centre of Reno. Airlines serving the airport include *Alaska Airlines*, **American Airlines**, **Continental Airlines**, **Delta Air Lines** and **United Airlines**. Local bus route 24 takes travellers into the city (travel time - 20 minutes). Taxis and limousines are available, as well as most major car hire companies.
Approximate flight times: From Las Vegas to *Atlanta* is three hours 45 minutes, to *Chicago* is three hours 25 minutes, to *Houston* is three hours, to *Los Angeles* is one hour 10 minutes, to *New York* is five hours, to *San Diego* is one hour 10 minutes and to *Seattle* is two hours 30 minutes.
RAIL: *Amtrak* (tel: (800) 872 7245 (toll-free); website: www.amtrak.com) trains stop at Reno, 245 Evans Avenue, on the 'California Zephyr' line, which links Chicago with Emeryville (California). There is no Amtrak service to Las Vegas, although a Thruway bus service operates from the airport station (from the Charter Bus Area) and the Greyhound Station, 200 South Main Street.
ROAD: There is a total of 79,520km (49,700 miles) of streets and highways, of which 64,830km (40,520 miles) are county roads. *Citizen's Area Transit, Gray Line Tours of Southern Nevada, Greyhound, K-T Services* and *Ray & Ross Transport* offer daily bus services.
Approximate bus travel times: From Las Vegas to *Los Angeles* is six hours, to *San Diego* is nine hours, to *San Francisco* is 14 hours 20 minutes, to *Chicago* is 18 hours, to *New Orleans* is 46 hours 20 minutes and to *Miami* is 60 hours 25 minutes.
URBAN: Buses are operated by the *Citizens Area Transit – CAT* (tel: (702) 228 7433); routes 301 and 302 run to the Strip from downtown Las Vegas. Privately run trolley services are also available. The *Las Vegas Strip Trolley* (tel: (702) 382 1404) runs the length of the Strip every 15 minutes (0930-0130) and costs US$1.75 per journey. The *Downtown Trolley* (tel: (702) 229 6024), serving the downtown casinos, runs every 15 to 20 minutes (0700-2300) and costs US$0.50 per journey. The *Meadows Mall Express Trolley* (tel: (702) 229 6024) runs a downtown route, popular with shoppers, from 1030 to 1700 Monday to Saturday; the fare is US$1.50 per journey. The new *Robert N Broadbent Las Vegas Monorail*, opened in December 2004, takes passengers along the 6km (4 mile) route from the MGM Grand Hotel & Casino to Sahara Avenue, stopping at a number of stations en route (travel time - 15 minutes). The second line, extending to Fremont Street in downtown Las Vegas, will be completed by 2007. Taxis and limousines are also available in Las Vegas, and all major car hire companies are represented.

Resorts & Excursions

Cowboy Country

The beautiful **Jarbidge Wilderness Area** and the surrounding forests, north of Elko, are excellent regions to sightsee by horse. **Wildhorse** and **Southfork Reservoirs** are known for their good fishing, as are the wetlands of the **Ruby Lake National Wildlife Refuge**. The **Ruby Mountains**, where visitors can try their hand at the sport of heli-skiing, also make an excellent hiking ground.
The **Western Folklife Center** in **Elko**, known for the *Cowboy Poetry Gathering*, is dedicated to the preservation of Western ranch culture. Elko's historic **Commercial Casino** (dating from 1869) has reopened after a fire caused its 10-month closure. The casino now includes 72 new machines and 49 new games and various new entertainment areas.
Some 32km (20 miles) along Highway 227 (a *National Scenic Byway*) are the Ruby Mountains, and **Lamoille Canyon**. On the edge of the Bonneville Salt Flats at the Utah-Nevada border is the resort of **Wendover**, and up near the Nevada-Idaho border is **Jackpot**. **Winnemucca**, once a stop on the emigrant trail, now entertains visitors in true cowboy tradition. In Elko, the **Northeastern Nevada Museum** is well worth a visit, featuring exhibits on mining, ranching, railroads, natural history and Native Americans. In **Lovelock**, the **Pershing County Marzen House Museum** has displays of mining equipment, home fixtures, Native American artefacts and a Lovelock Cave exhibition. The *Great Cowboy Cookout* in Wendover offers a horse-drawn wagon ride and a cowboy-style cookout.
SPECIAL EVENTS: The following is a selection of special events occurring in Nevada's Cowboy Country in 2005: **Jan 22-29** *Cowboy Poetry Gathering*, Elko. **Mar 11-13** *Shooting the West XVII* (photography conference), Winnemucca. **May 27-29** *Run-A-Mucca Motorcycle Rally*, Winnemucca. **Jun 7-9** *Silver State Stampede Rodeo*, Elko. **Jul 2-3** *National Basque Festival* (includes dancing, parades, wood chopping and games), Elko. **Jul 29-31** *50s Fever and Good Times Street Drags*, Winnemucca. **Aug 27-Sep 5** *Elko County Fair & Livestock Show*, Elko. **Sep 2-4** *Tri-County Fair and Stampede*, Winnemucca. **Dec 31** *Countdown in downtown*, Elko.
TRAVEL: Elko's airport is the *J C Harris Field*. Scheduled air services are provided by *Delta Connection-Sky West*; chartered services by *El Aero Services*. Amtrak trains stop at Elko on route from Chicago to Emeryville in California (see *Travel - International* section). All major transport facilities are available, including *Greyhound* bus connections and car hire.
CLIMATE: Temperatures reach a summer high of 94°F (35°C) in Lovelock, while winter temperatures can drop below 10°F (-12°C) in Elko and Wells.

Pony Express Territory

Scattered along US Highway 50 are the ruins of old **Pony Express Stations**, as well as the mining towns of **Austin** and **Eureka**. The road also passes through the town of **Fallon** and the lush **Lahontan Valley** – the site of the first reclamation project in the USA. The **Forty-Mile Desert** has been transformed into productive ranchlands. Also on US Highway 50 is the old mining town of Austin, founded by a former Pony Express rider. Eureka was a boomtown of the 1870s lead and silver mining period, and is well preserved to this day. Across nine mountain ranges lies **Ely**, gateway to one of the country's least-crowded National Parks, **Great Basin National Park**. Attractions here include the spectacular rock formations of the **Lehman Caves**; the **East Ely Railroad Depot Museum**, where visitors can learn of the mining and transport heritage of the region; the **Eureka Sentinel Museum**, located in the home of the town's longest-running newspaper, with displays of the lead and silver mining era; **Grimes Point Archaeological Site**, with a trail through boulders covered with petroglyphs; and the **Hidden Cave**, an ancient storage site for local Native Americans, located near Fallon.
SPECIAL EVENTS: The following is a selection of special events occurring in Nevada's Pony Express Territory in 2005: **May 12-15** *Nevada Open Road Challenge* (car rally and show), Ely. **May 13-15** *Spring Wings Festival*, Fallon. **Jul 4-9** *Silver State International Rodeo*, Fallon. **Jul 15-17** *Nevada Indian Days All-Indian Rodeo and Pow Wow* (includes rodeo, parade, pow-wow, Native American hand games, arts and crafts), Fallon. **Aug** *Eureka County Fair; White Pine County Fair*, Ely; *White Pine County Horse Races*, Ely; *Nevada Motorcross Championships*, Fallon. **Sep 2-5** *Heart of Gold Cantaloupe Festival*, Fallon. **Sep 24-25** *Fallon Senior Pro Rodeo*. **Oct** *WNCC Collegiate Rodeo*, Fallon; *Sixth Annual Reining Futurities*, Fallon. **Oct 6-8** *Harvest Days and Nevada State Picnic*, Fallon. **Oct 6-9** *Eighth Annual Stockhorse Spectacular*, Fallon. **Oct 8** *Fourth Annual Mayor's Cup Golf Tournament*, Fallon. **Dec 2** *Christmas Tree Lighting*, Fallon. **Dec 3** *Hometown Christmas* (craft and food vendors), Fallon. **Dec 31** *New Year's Eve Fireworks*, Fallon.
TRAVEL: The regional airport is *Yelland Field Airport* in Ely, which has good connections to destinations throughout the USA.
CLIMATE: The summer weather is hot, reaching temperatures of 92°F (33°C) in Fallon. In winter, temperatures drop below 20°F (-7°C).

Reno Tahoe Territory

The steep eastern slopes of the **Sierra Nevada** rise up to contain **Lake Tahoe**. **Carson City** is only 14.4km (9 miles) away, but is nearly 500m (1500ft) below. The lake not only hangs over the State capital, but also the towns of **Minden** and **Gardnerville**, which are almost directly below it. Reno-Tahoe Territory is geographically compact and Carson City, **Reno** and **Sparks** all make good bases from which to explore. The area is one of the fastest-growing communities in the West and more then US$1 billion will be channelled into Reno and Sparks. South Lake Tahoe will receive US$250 million for redevelopment and improvement of its downtown.
TRAVEL: *Lake Tahoe International Airport (TVL)* (website: www.laketahoeairport.com) is located in the Sierra Nevada mountains at Lake Taho. *Greyhound* buses stop at Carson City, with one service to Los Angeles and a second to Reno. *K-T Services* operate scheduled bus services, while *Frontier Tours* operates chartered services. Car hire is widely available.
CLIMATE: Temperatures range from a high of 89°F (32°C) in the summer months to 30°F (-1°C) and below in the winter.
RENO: Reno was founded at Lake's Crossing, where **Myron Lake's** bridge crossed the **Truckee River**. A new whitewater park on the river is a popular attraction with kayakers and thrill seekers; the park also includes an amphitheatre, picnic facilities and river access for boaters. Many gambling casinos are to be found downtown on **Virginia Street** including **Harrah's**, **Nevada Club**, the **Eldorado**, the **Golden Phoenix**, **Circus Circus**, **Silver Legacy**, **Fitzgerald's** and the **Sands Regency**.
A **River Walk** follows the river east past the Hilton and through Sparks, and westwards past an amphitheatre. The **Sierra Nevada Museum of Art** is located in two sites: the **E L Weigand Museum**, with a variety of travelling exhibitions and shows by local artists; and the neo-Georgian **Hawkins House**, which exhibits 19th- and 20th-century US art. The **Stremmel Gallery** is a thriving showcase for leading artists, as is the **University of Nevada Reno** campus. The **Nevada Historical Society Museum** is excellent for those wishing to learn about Nevada's history. There is also a museum at the **Fleischmann Planetarium**, which features star shows and *SkyDome* films. The **National Automobile Museum** has exhibitions of classic cars throughout the year.
SPECIAL EVENTS: The following is a selection of special events occurring in Reno in 2005: **Jan 17** *Martin Luther King Celebration*, Reno/Sparks. **Apr 21-23** *Reno International Jazz Festival*. **May 7-8** *Cinco de Mayo Celebrations*, Reno. **Jun 16-25** *27th Annual Reno Rodeo* (world-class athletes compete in the 'Wildest Rodeo in the West'). **Jul 1-31** *Arttown 2005* (arts festival), Reno. **Jul 15-17** *Big Easy* (Cajun festival), Sparks. **Jul 30-Aug 7** *Hot August Nights* (a celebration of the USA's love affair with cars and rock 'n' roll), Reno. **Aug 4-11** *33rd Annual Concours d'Elegance & Wooden Boat Week*, Reno. **Aug 17-21** *Reno-Tahoe Open PGA Championship* (golf tournament), Montreux Golf Country Club. **Aug 24-28** *Nevada State Fair*, Reno. **Sep 9-11** *The Great Reno Balloon Races*; *46th Annual Virginia City Camel Races*. **Sep 15-18** *National Championship Air Races*, Reno/ Stead Airport. **Sep 24-25** *Genoa Candy Dance*. **Oct 8-9** *Great Italian Festival*, Reno. **Nov-Dec** *Festival of the Trees and Lights*, Reno. **Dec 3** *Sparks Hometowne Christmas*.
Carson City & Surroundings
The town of **Genoa** began as a log cabin trading post and was Nevada's first white settlement: today, it is a village and a State park. The once-wealthy Comstock mining district comprising **Dayton**, **Silver City**, **Gold Hill** and **Virginia City** was founded by prospectors from California. The period of the Civil War dominates **Carson City**, the State capital; the silver-domed 1894 **Capitol Building**, the State library, the **Nevada State Museum** (all close to each other) and the **Nevada State Railroad Museum** are well worth a visit. **Lake Tahoe** is a top-class skiing resort with a vibrant nightlife, and is home to the *Shakespeare at Sand Harbor*

Credit: © Nevada Commission on Tourism

Festival, which takes place in the summer. The spectacular scenery can be seen from the lake's excursion boats. Another lake, noted for excellent fishing, is the **Pyramid Lake** north of Reno, part of the **Paiute Native American Reservation**.

SPECIAL EVENTS: The following is a selection of special events occurring in Carson City and surrounds in 2005: **Jan 15** *Winter, Wine & All That Jazz*, Carson City. **Mar 12** *12th Annual Cowboy Jubilee & Poetry*, Carson City. **May 5-8** *Spring Fun Fair*, Carson City. **May 15** *10th Annual Multi-Cultural Festival*, Carson City. **Jun 10-12** *Carson City Rendezvous*. **Jun 24-26** *Run What Cha Brung*, (rock and roll weekend, with cars and entertainment), Carson City. **Jul 1-4** *Fourth of July Cavalcade of Spectaculars*, Carson City. **Jul 29-31** *Silver Dollar Car Classic*, Carson City. **Sep 18** *St Theresa's Basque Festival*, Carson City. **Oct 1** *Oktoberfest*, Carson City. **Oct 27-30** *Nevada Day Celebration* (including *Nevada Day Parade*), Carson City. **Dec 1** *Silver and Snowflake Festival of Lights*, Carson City. **Dec 11** *Victorian Home Christmas Tour* (selected homes decorated and open for viewing), Carson City; *Holiday Treat Concert*, Carson City.

Pioneer Territory

To the north of Pioneer Territory, mountain ranges and long narrow valleys rise high above the timberline of Pinon pines. Further south, however, the land descends into the Mojave Desert, with its distinctive Joshua trees and creosote.

The **Toiyabe Range** in the Basin and Range Country provides spectacular mountain scenery (over 3000m/10,000ft). **Walker Lake**, the remains of an ancient inland sea, is now a popular resort for boating and fishing, and nearby **Hawthorne** makes a good base for exploring this region.

Beatty is the gateway to the famous **Death Valley National Park**, where visitors will witness unique geological features in the extremes of the desert. **Scotty's Castle** is a popular, if slightly odd, century-old desert guest ranch. Amongst Nevada's own parks in Pioneer Territory is the *Berlin-Icthyosaur State Park*, home to the well-preserved and greatly detailed ghost town of **Berlin**. The **Cathedral Gorge State Park**, towards the east, is worth visiting to see the spectacular spires and grottoes carved into the clay by natural erosion.

The mining town of **Goldfield** was founded in 1902, and contains the beautiful **Goldfield Hotel** and the **Esmeralda County Courthouse**, as well as the old mining district. The **Lyon County Museum** in **Yerington** has displays of a kitchen, sheriff's office, barbershop, mining artefacts, schoolhouse, blacksmith shop and a 100-year-old general store. The **Belmont Courthouse State Historic Site** is located in the ghost town of **Belmont**, and was the county seat of Nye until 1905. Visitors to the **Pahrump Valley Winery** in **Pahrump** can look forward to free tours, tasting and Saturday evening concerts, as well as a gourmet restaurant. In **Hawthorne**, the **Mineral County Historical Museum** houses animal, bird and fossil exhibitions, mining and fire-fighting equipment, buggies and a 1907 drugstore display.

SPECIAL EVENTS: The following is a selection of special events occurring in Nevada's Pioneer Territory in 2005: **Apr** *Annual Arts & Loon Festival* (celebrates the return of the loons each year and includes guided boat tours), Lake Walker, Hawthorne. **May** *Spring Mother's Day Madness* (women's team roping), Yerington. **Jun** *Spring Fling Car Show*, Yerington; *Portuguese Celebration* (dance parade and 'Sopa'), Yerington. **Aug** *Spirit of Wovoka Days Pow Wow*, Yerington. **Aug 19-22** *Lyon County Fair & Rodeo*, Yerington. **Sep** *Sundae in the Park* (arts and crafts festival), Yerington. **Dec** *County Christmas*, Yerington.

Las Vegas Territory

Las Vegas is becoming an increasingly elaborate holiday destination. Each new hotel-casino tries to outdo the last for sheer spectacle. **Laughlin**, on the Colorado River, has become the second most popular holiday destination in Nevada, owing largely to the reasonably priced accommodation and restaurants, and the fact that it has unusually sunny summers and mild winters considering its location. A US$100 million development on the **Laughlin Bay Marina** opened in 2005 and is the hub of entertainment in the Laughlin area; a plan to add housing to the area is currently underway. **Mesquite** and **Primm**, on the Nevada border with Utah and California respectively, are also becoming popular new resort towns.

CLIMATE: The average temperature is 66°F (19°C) and the average yearly rainfall is 10.7cm (4.2 inches). There are 212 clear days annually, 82 partly cloudy days and 71 cloudy days.

Las Vegas: Las Vegas is Spanish for 'The Meadows'. 'Vegas', as seen today, began after World War II when the idea of large hotels along the brand new Strip was developed. Tourism and gaming are the two major employers. Manufacturing, the **Nellis Air Force Base** and other government agencies, warehousing and trucking are secondary industries. The city proper is an 135,618 sq km (84,272 sq mile) enclave surrounded by **Clark County**. The **Las Vegas Strip** is best seen at dusk when it is lit up in neon lights. Children will enjoy **Wet 'n' Wild**, a water park on the Strip, and the **Lied Discovery Children's Museum**. **Fremont Street Experience** is a pedestrian mall dominated by gaming with a spectacular light show every night. For something different, the **Marjorie Barrick Museum of Natural History** houses exhibitions of the archaeology and natural history of the Mojave Desert, whilst the **Old Las Vegas Mormon Fort Historic Park** is the site of the first settlement of Las Vegas, and the **Nevada State Museum and Historical Society** explains southern Nevada's history. The **Liberace Museum** contains memorabilia from the world-famous pianist. The **Guinness World of Records Museum** is an interesting exhibition based on the famous book. The **Circus Circus – Grand Slam Adventuredome** theme park provides circus acts daily from 1100-2400 (free of charge) and thrilling theme park rides. Not to be missed is the stunning *Fountains of Bellagio* display of over 1000 fountains, choreographed with light and sound at the **Bellagio Resort** (Mon-Fri every 30 minutes 1500-1900 and every 15 minutes 1900-2400; Sat and Sun every 30 minutes 1200-1900, and every 15 minutes 1900-2400). Bellagio also boasts a **Botanical Garden**.

HOTEL-CASINOS: The 3044-room **Mirage Hotel-Casino** displays a man-made volcano. Nearby, the **Treasure Island** features Buccaneer Bay with a full-scale pirate ship and British frigate engaged in battle. The **MGM Grand Hotel & Theme Park** is the largest resort hotel in the world. The recently opened **New York, New York** duplicates the Big Apple's skyline, while the **Las Vegas Hilton Hotel & Casino** offers an interactive Star Trek experience with virtual reality stations, a themed bar and Star Trek memorabilia. There is also **The Excalibur**, with 4008 rooms, built in the style of a medieval castle, and the Egyptian-themed **Luxor**, a full-scale pyramid watched over by a sphinx.

GETTING MARRIED: More than 45 wedding chapels operate throughout the metropolitan area, including some in major hotels in the city. The **Little White Chapel**, 1301 Las Vegas Boulevard South, where Joan Collins was married, has a 24-hour drive-through window.

FOOD & DRINK: Las Vegas is becoming world-renowned for its restaurants and every conceivable taste is catered for, from a seven-course gourmet meal to a custom hamburger. Diners can choose from seafood, steak, southwestern, Brazilian, Chinese, Continental, Italian, Japanese and Mexican cuisines. The ultimate eating experience is the Las Vegas buffet: the *Golden Nugget Buffet*, the *Las Vegas Hilton Buffet*, the *Palatium Buffet* at **Caesars Palace**, and the *World's Fare Buffet* at **The Riviera** are all worth trying. **Picasso** at the **Bellagio** and **Renoir** at **The Mirage** have been ranked among the top 17 restaurants in the world. **Roxy's Diner** is a 1950s-style diner, serving thick milkshakes in tall, frosted glasses, sandwiches, burgers and a selection of blue-plate specials. The **Stage Deli of Las Vegas** is at the **Forum Shops** at **Caesars**. Speciality items are flown in from the world-famous New York Stage Deli, offering a full line of breakfast, lunch and dinner. **Spago** features celebrity chef Wolfgang Puck's 'California Cuisine', which emphasises fresh, locally produced ingredients incorporating the cuisines of Europe, the Orient, Latin America and the USA to create an eclectic menu. The themed **Harley-Davidson Cafe**, **Star Trek: The Adventure** and **Motown Cafe** provide a fun atmosphere for dining.

SHOPPING: Vast malls display a wide range of products: the Forum Shops at **Caesars**, the **Fashion Show Mall**, the **Desert Passage** at the Aladdin Resort, the **Grand Canal Shoppes** at the Venetian Resort (includes a reproduction of Venice's Grand Canal – complete with gondolas), the **Boulevard Mall** (the largest shopping centre in Nevada), the **Meadows Mall** (with 140 shops and restaurants), and the **Belz Factory Outlet World** are all popular. The **Fashion Outlet Stores** (south of Belz Factory Outlet World) recently opened in Primm.

SPECIAL EVENTS: The following is a selection of special events occurring in Las Vegas in 2005: **Jan 30** *Las Vegas Marathon*. **Apr 1-2** *Big League Weekend* (baseball tournament), Cashman Field. **Apr 7-10** *Clark County State Fair and Rodeo*, Logandale. **Apr 20-24** *Laughlin River Run*. **May-Jun** *Laughlin River Days* (powerboat racing). **May 6-7** *Cars, Stars and Guitars Motorhead Festival*, Las Vegas. **Jul 4** *Rockets over the River*, Laughlin. **Sep** *Laughlin Professional Bull Riders Series*. **Sep 24** *Las Vegas Triple – NASCAR Craftsman Truck Series Night Race*. **Dec 2-11** *National Finals Rodeo*, Thomas and Mack Center, Las Vegas. **Dec** *The NFR Experience* (rodeo festival), Las Vegas.

TRAVEL: *McCarran International (LAS)* (website: www.mccarran.com), with slot machines in the terminal, is 1.6km (1 mile) from the Strip, and 8km (5 miles) from central Las Vegas. There are more than 965 taxis, 325 limousines and 16 bus and/or charter firms serving the district. The *Citizens Area Transit* (CAT) is a public transportation company that operates 31 routes throughout the Las Vegas metropolitan area, and one route in Laughlin.

Outside the city

There is plenty to see in the Las Vegas Territory outside Las Vegas itself. The **Spring Mountains** offer back-country adventure, while **Mount Charleston** is good for winter sports and is home to the **Las Vegas Ski and Snow Board Resort**. **Lake Mead** and **Lake Mohave** are contained in the vast (600,000 hectare/1.5 million acre) **Lake Mead National Recreation Area**. **Hoover Dam** has a new visitor centre, where tourists can see right over the edge of the **Black Canyon** precipice. At the north of Lake Mead is the **Valley of Fire State Park**, with its fascinating landscape of naturally carved red sandstone. The **Desert National Wildlife Refuge** complex, incorporating the **Pahranagat National Wildlife Refuge**, **Ash Meadows National Wildlife Refuge** and **Moapa Valley National Wildlife Refuge**, is the largest wildlife refuge in the USA. **Moapa Valley** was the site of Nevada's first city.

In **Boulder City**, the **Black Canyon River Raft Tour** is a 19km (12 mile) rapid-free raft trip, beginning at Hoover Dam. Hoover Dam itself was completed in 1935, and is the highest dam in the western hemisphere. The **Hoover Dam Museum** houses historical artefacts relating to the workers, and construction of the dam and Boulder City. The **River Mountain Hiking Trail** is an 8km (5 mile) round-trip route with spectacular views of Lake Mead and Las Vegas Valley. The **Ethel M Chocolate Factory & Cactus Garden** in **Henderson** shows how chocolates are made; the cactus garden includes 350 species of cactus. The **Davis Dam** in Laughlin is a 61m- (200ft-) high earth-filled dam. The **USS Riverside** is a luxury casino cruiser which has been designed to pass under the Laughlin Bridge. **Bonnie Springs** in **Old Nevada** is an old Western town. The **Lost City Museum** in **Overton** houses exhibitions featuring the Anasazi Indians and early Moapa Valley settlers.

SPECIAL EVENTS: The following is a selection of special events occurring in the Las Vegas Territory in 2005: **Apr 1-3** *Native American Arts Festival*, Henderson. **May 7-8** *Spring Jamboree and Craft Fair*, Boulder City. **Jul 4** *Annual Fireworks Display and Boulder City Damboree*, Boulder City. **Oct** *Nevada Heritage Festival and Gem & Mineral Fair*, Henderson.

Climate

Nevada is basin and range country, with about 250 mountain ranges running north–south. Base elevation ranges from 1365m (4500ft) to 1880m (6200ft); altitudes vary from over 3945m (13,000ft) to less than 152m (500ft). The climate in Nevada is arid with abundant sunshine, light rainfall and snow. Average temperatures vary from about 70°F (21°C) in the south to 45°F (7°C) in the north.

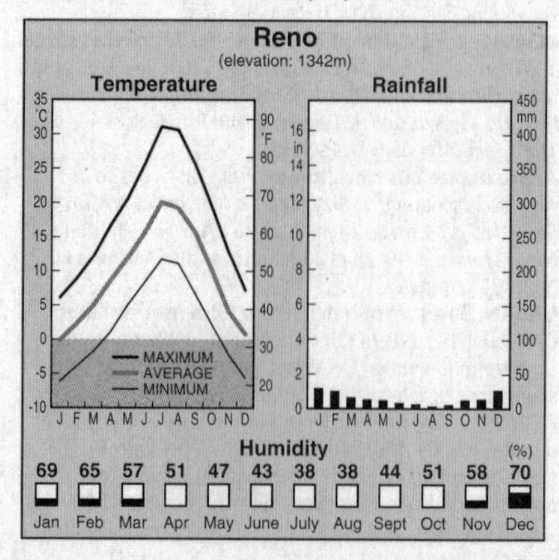

New Hampshire

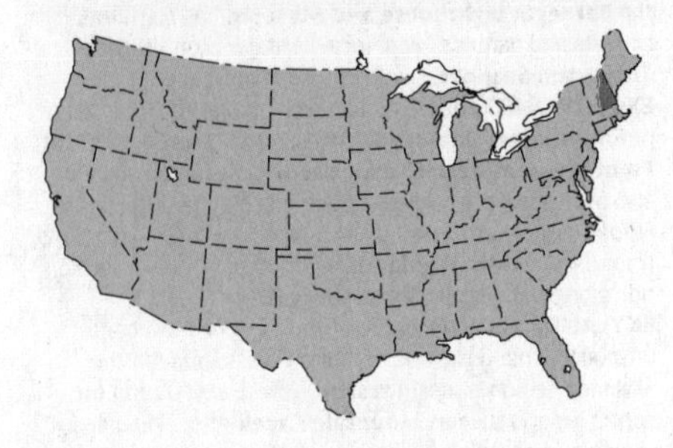

New Hampshire Division of Travel and Tourism Development
172 Pembroke Road, PO Box 1856, Concord, NH 03302
Tel: (603) 271 2665 *or* (800) 386 4664 (toll-free).
Fax: (603) 271 6870.
E-mail: travel@dred.state.nh.us
Website: www.visitnh.gov
New Hampshire Lodging & Restaurant Association
Street address: 14 Dixon Avenue, Suite 208,
Concord, NH 03302
Postal address: PO Box 1175, Concord, NH 03302
Tel: (603) 228 9585. Fax: (603) 226 1829.
E-mail: nhlra@nhlra.com
Website: www.nhlra.com

General Information

Nickname: Granite State
State bird: Purple Finch
State flower: Purple Lilac
CAPITAL: Concord
Date of admission to the Union: 21 June 1788 (original 13 States; date of ratification of the Constitution)
POPULATION: 1,299,500 (official estimate 2004)
POPULATION DENSITY: 53.7 per sq km
2003 total overseas arrivals/US ranking: 90,000/28
TIME: Eastern (GMT - 5). *Daylight Saving Time* is observed.

THE STATE: New Hampshire is noted for its scenic beauty, from **Mount Washington** in the northern **White Mountains** to the ocean beaches near **Hampton**. The *Cog Railway* ride to the top of Mount Washington affords panoramic views of Canada and the neighbouring States. The **Mount Washington Observatory** has played an important part in recording and researching weather for more than 50 years, and at the new **Weather Discovery Center** in **North Conway**, visitors can use hands-on, interactive exhibits to learn about the weather and its effects. More adventurous visitors can climb to the top along **Tuckerman Ravine Trail**. At the summit, there is a museum, information centre and a snack bar where visitors can sit down and rest their weary feet. **Franconia Notch State Park**, a dramatic 13km (8 mile) gorge nearby, is one of New England's most acclaimed beauty spots. It was formed by glacial movements that began during an ice age 400 million years ago. Franconia is best known for the 'Old Man of the Mountain', a huge human profile formed by five ledges of stone. **The Basin Waterfall** is another of the park's most popular attractions. Major ski resorts in Franconia include **Cannon Mountain**, **Loon Mountain** and **Waterville Valley**. New Hampshire also attracts visitors for its tax-free outlet shopping. In North Conway, most major clothing labels can be snapped up for a fraction of the normal price at one of the many factory outlet shops. The town of **Laconia**, between **Lake Winnipesaukee** and **Lake Winnisquam**, is another popular tourist destination.

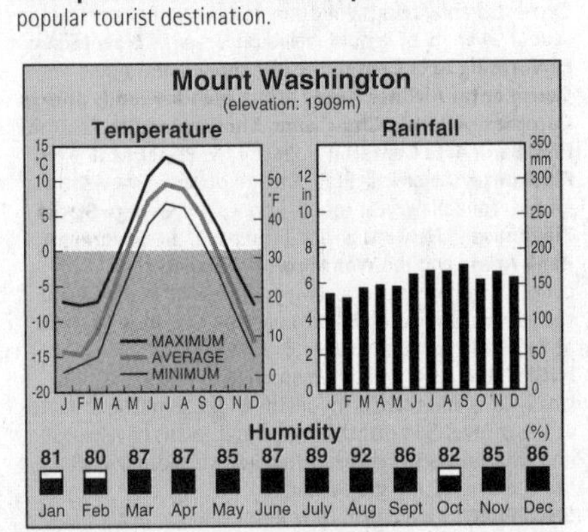

New Jersey

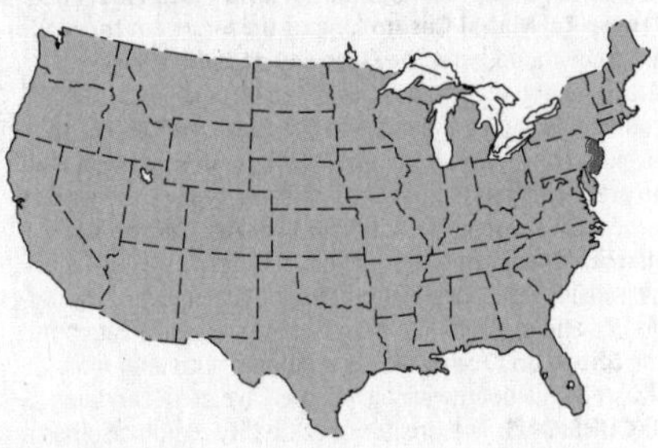

New Jersey Commerce & Economic Growth and Tourism
Postal address: PO Box 820, Trenton, NJ 08625
Street address: 20 West State Street, Trenton, NJ 08608
Tel: (609) 292 2470 *or* (800) 847 4865 (toll-free).
Fax: (609) 633 7418.
Website: www.visitnj.org
Atlantic City Convention & Visitors Authority
2314 Pacific Avenue, Atlantic City, NJ 08401
Tel: (609) 348 7100 *or* (888) 228 4748 (toll-free).
Fax: (609) 345 2200.
Website: www.atlanticcitynj.com
Cape May County Department of Tourism
4 Moore Road, Cape May Court House, NJ 08210
Tel: (609) 463 6415 *or* (800) 227 2297 (toll-free).
Fax: (609) 465 4639.
E-mail: tourism@co.cape-may.nj.us
Website: www.thejerseycape.com
Greater Wildwoods Tourism Improvement & Development Authority
4501 Boardwalk, Wildwood, NJ 08260
Tel: (609) 729 9000 *or* (800) 992 9732 (toll-free).
Fax: (609) 846 2631.
E-mail: info@wildwoodsnj.com
Website: www.wildwoodsnj.com
Skylands Regional Tourism Council
360 Grove Street, Bridgewater, NJ 08807
Tel: (908) 725 1582 *or* (800) 4759 5263.
Fax: (908) 722 7823.
E-mail: info@skylandstourism.org
Website: www.skylandstourism.org

General Information

Nickname: Garden State
State bird: Eastern Goldfinch
State flower: Purple Violet
CAPITAL: Trenton
Date of admission to the Union: 18th Dec 1787 (original 13 States; date of ratification of the Constitution)
POPULATION: 8,698,879 (official estimate 2004)
POPULATION DENSITY: 385.1 per sq km
2003 total overseas arrivals/US ranking: 685,000/10
TIME: Eastern (GMT - 5). *Daylight Saving Time* is observed.
THE STATE: New Jersey, one of the Mid-Atlantic States, is bordered by the Atlantic Ocean to the east and the Delaware River to the west. Small in size, the State nonetheless features hundreds of miles of rolling countryside and natural parkland set amidst mountains, lakes and forests. In increasing numbers, tourists from around the world are discovering that New Jersey is more than just a gateway to the United States – it is America in miniature, with an abundance of tourist attractions to suit every taste. These include beautiful beaches, exciting nightlife and many award-winning cultural attractions. While sections of the State such as **Atlantic City** and the **Jersey Shore** are world-renowned, there is also a wealth of lesser-known historic landmarks, national parks and cultural events on offer.

Travel - International

AIR: International airports: *Atlantic City International Airport (ACY)* (website: www.acairport.com) is 16km (10 miles) from Atlantic City. A regular shuttle service runs to Atlantic City (cost: US$20) and taxis are available to the city for around US$30. Limousine services and car hire (*Avis, Budget* and *Hertz*) are also available at the terminal building.
Philadelphia International Airport (PHI) is one hour's drive from Atlantic City via the Atlantic City Expressway (see the *Pennsylvania* section).
Newark International Airport (EWR) (website: www.newarkairport.com), 27km (16 miles) southwest of midtown Manhattan, is the major hub for international arrivals to the State, although many travellers head to nearby Manhattan, which is connected by bus services (travel time - 30 minutes). The airport has extensive facilities, including banks, shops and duty free shops, restaurants, bars and coffee shops, a nursery and car hire (*Avis, Budget, Dollar, Hertz* and *National*). Taxis, buses (both local and those serving regional destinations), shuttles and limousines are available at all three terminals. *NJ Transit* operates bus routes to and from the airport; buses 37 and 62 stop at Newark Airport Terminal B. Newark is linked to Princeton by the *Princeton Airporter*, which runs an hourly service 0700-2200 (cost US$23). Taxi fares to the city of Newark are determined by zone, and cost US$11-15. The *Newark Airport AirTrain* is a monorail service that connects the airport terminals with the *Newark International Airport Station*, serviced by Amtrak and NJ Transit trains, which travel to Newark Penn Station (with connections to buses, trains to southern New Jersey, and the PATH rapid-transit system (website: www.pathrail.com) to Manhattan), Hoboken (connections to northern and western New Jersey) and New York Penn Station in Midtown Manhattan. For further information, contact the New Jersey Transit Information Center (tel: (973) 762 5100 *or* (800) 772 2222; website: www.njtransit.com).
TRANSPORT TO NEW YORK CITY: Rail services to Manhattan are available at Newark Airport International Station and Newark Penn Station (see above). *Olympia Airport Express* runs frequent bus services 0400-2345 to Midtown Manhattan, stopping at the Port Authority Bus Terminal and Grand Central Station Terminal (both of which are also served by New York Airport Service express buses running to JFK and La Guardia airports – see *New York* section) and Penn Station (travel time – 30-60 minutes); the fare is US$13. *NJ Transit* buses from Newark arrive at the Port Authority Terminal in Manhattan. Shared minibuses that stop on demand are run by *Express Shuttle USA*, which serves the area between 23rd and 63rd Streets (0600-2300) for US$14 per person, and *SuperShuttle Manhattan*, which stops anywhere south of 227th Street (24 hours) for US$15-19. *Gray Line Air Shuttles* run from Newark to Manhattan 0700-2330 and cost around US$15-20. Taxis to downtown and midtown Manhattan cost US$34-55, plus tolls. **Inter-airport transfers:** There are direct bus services from Newark to JFK 0600-2030 on the Princeton Airporter for US$23, and to La Guardia on the ETS Air Shuttle for US$28. There is a scheduled helicopter service between the airports, and limousine service is also available. The flat-rate taxi fare from Newark to JFK is US$60 plus tolls; to La Guardia, the fare is US$65 plus tolls.
Inter-airport transfers: Inter-airport transfers: There are direct bus services from Newark to JFK 0600-2030 on the *Princeton Airporter* for US$23, and to La Guardia on the *ETS Air Shuttle* for US$25. There is a scheduled helicopter service between the airports, and limousine service is also available. The flat-rate taxi fare from Newark to JFK is US$60 plus tolls; to La Guardia, the fare is US$50 plus tolls.
Approximate flight times: See flight times in *New York* section, as they are almost exactly the same.
SEA: *Circle Line Tours* operates a year-round ferry service to the Statue of Liberty and Ellis Island from Liberty State Park in Jersey City. *Hoboken Ferry Service, TNT Hydrolines* and *Port Imperial Ferry* operate services to and from New York City. *Cape May-Lewes Ferry* operates a service to and from Cape May to the State of Delaware.
RAIL: Penn Station in Newark serves *NJ Transit* trains as well as most *Amtrak* (tel: (800) 872 7245 (toll-free); website: www.amtrak.com) services along the New

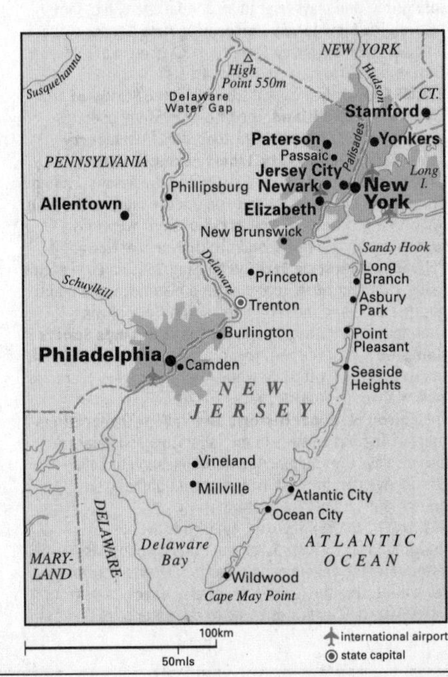

Credit: © New Jersey Commerce & Economic Growth Commission Office of Travel & Tourism

York–Philadelphia–Washington corridor, including high-speed Acela Express trains. For train times on these routes, see the *New York* section; trains from Newark to New York take 15 to 20 minutes. Trains between Atlantic City and Philadelphia are operated by *NJ Transit* and *Amtrak*.
ROAD: Travel from New Jersey to New York City is across the George Washington Bridge or through the Lincoln and Holland Tunnels. Bridges connecting to Philadelphia are the Walt Whitman Bridge, Betsy Ross Bridge and the Benjamin Franklin Bridge. The Delaware Memorial Bridge connects New Jersey with Delaware. The New Jersey Turnpike runs north and south through the State, while the Garden State Parkway takes travellers to the shore points. **Bus:** Penn Station (McCarter Highway/Market Street, Newark) handles long-distance and regional buses. *Greyhound* (tel: (800) 229 9424 (toll-free); website: www.greyhound.com) is the main long-distance carrier.
Approximate driving times: From Newark to *Philadelphia* is one hour 30 minutes, to *Hartford* is two hours 30 minutes, to *Albany* is three hours 30 minutes, to *Baltimore* is three hours 30 minutes, to *Boston* is four hours 30 minutes, to *Washington, DC* is four hours 30 minutes, to *Pittsburgh* is six hours, to *Portland* (Maine) is six hours 30 minutes, to *Montréal* is seven hours 30 minutes, to *Buffalo* is seven hours, to *Toronto* is eight hours, to *Cleveland* is nine hours, to *Indianapolis* is 14 hours, to *Chicago* is 15 hours, to *Miami* is 26 hours 30 minutes, to *Dallas* is 32 hours 30 minutes, to *Los Angeles* is 57 hours, to *San Francisco* is 60 hours, and to *Seattle* is 60 hours. All times are based on non-stop driving at or below the applicable speed limits.
Approximate bus travel times: From New Jersey to *Philadelphia* is one hour 40 minutes, to *Albany* is three hours, to *Washington, DC* is four hours 40 minutes, to *Boston* is four hours 45 minutes, to *Montréal* is eight hours 30 minutes, to *Buffalo* is nine hours, to *Pittsburgh* is nine hours, and to *Cleveland* is nine hours 30 minutes.

Resorts & Excursions

NEWARK: The northeastern portion of New Jersey offers an eclectic mix of culture, heritage, sports and shopping. Newark is the third-oldest of the major US cities and the largest in New Jersey. It is a hub of transport connections, arts and culture, and fast city life. The **Newark Museum** is considered one of the nation's most comprehensive fine arts museums and the largest museum complex in the State, with 80 galleries of art (ancient and modern) and science, a planetarium and a mini-zoo. **Branch Brook Park** has more cherry blossoms than Washington, DC in the springtime, and plays host to an annual cherry blossom festival. The **New Jersey Performing Arts Center** is the home of the *New Jersey Symphony Orchestra* and features performances from international artists.
EXCURSIONS: Just east of Newark lie the **Statue of Liberty** and **Ellis Island**. The *Circle Line* ferry operates services to these important historic sites from **Liberty State Park** in **Jersey City**. **Liberty Science Center**, located in Liberty State Park, is one of New Jersey's leading attractions, and offers a hands-on science museum with an IMAX Dome Theater, as well as exhibits on inventions, technology, environment and health. North of Newark is **Palisades Interstate Park**, comprising 2500 acres of scenic roads, stunning views, picnic areas, a historic museum and nature sanctuary, and hiking and skiing trails, plus an enormous children's fun park. The **Meadowlands Sports Complex** in East Rutherford, northwest of Newark, is home to professional football, basketball and ice hockey teams, as well as a world-class racetrack.
The **Edison National Historic Site** in West Orange offers tours of Thomas Edison's home, laboratory and library. It also displays the equipment and chemicals with which Edison invented the first incandescent lightbulb, photograph and motion picture.
ATLANTIC CITY: Known as 'America's Favorite Playground', it features 12 casino hotels, world-class entertainment, championship sporting events, gourmet restaurants and the famous boardwalk, which dates from 1870. Atlantic City is also home to saltwater taffy, numerous trade shows and conventions, and the annual Miss America Pageant.
The **Atlantic City Boardwalk** is an attraction in itself, lined with dazzling casinos, amusement rides, games and shops on one side and by 10km (6 miles) of sand beach and surf on the other. The notorious **Trump Plaza Hotel** and **Trump Taj Mahal Casino** (one of the largest in the world) are to be found here. The **Gateway at Bally's** has new shopping and dining facilities on an elegant walkway connecting the casino hotel to the **Claridge Casino**, as well as extra convention and meeting space. **Convention Hall**, an art deco architectural extravaganza, houses the world's largest pipe organ. The **Atlantic City Art Center and Historic Museum** traces the city's history as a 150-year-old seaside resort and entertainment centre, and includes photos and memorabilia from the Miss America Pageant. The **Shops on Ocean One** is a modern shopping mall situated on a boardwalk pier shaped like an ocean liner.
EXCURSIONS: The Greater Atlantic City region also has a quieter side. The **Towne of Historic Smithville**, an authentic 18th-century village filled with shops, is worth a visit. Coastal wildlife is preserved at the **Edwin B Forsythe National Wildlife Refuge**, due north of Atlantic City in **Brigantine**, where the **Sea Life Museum** can also be found. The **Gardner's Basin** area is home to the **Ocean Life Center**, a marine education attraction with aquariums and a 'touch tank'. The **Noyes Museum** in **Oceanville** is known for its large collection of American fine and folk art. The region is also home to one of the oldest vineyards in the USA – the **Renault Winery** (which also features the **Glass Museum**) **in Egg Harbor**.
DELAWARE RIVER REGION: This area of pristine wilderness is richly steeped in history and natural beauty. American history buffs can visit battlefields and barracks that tell the story of New Jersey's important role in the birth of the USA. Arts and culture can be experienced at the many museums and theatres in the region.
Trenton is home to the second-oldest **State House** in continuous use in the USA. Other attractions include the **Trenton Battle Monument** and **Trenton City Museum**. Evening entertainment ranges from a Trenton Thunder minor league baseball game (during the summer) to a night at the theatre in Princeton.
The **Old Barracks Museum** on **Barracks Street** is the site of the famous day-after-Christmas battle during the Revolutionary War and includes restored soldiers' quarters, 18th-century period rooms and antiques. The **New Jersey State Planetarium and Museum**, which examines New Jersey history back to 500 BC, and **William Trent House** are also worth visiting.
Princeton, 18km (11 miles) north of Trenton, is a charming, historic town, home of the world-renowned **Princeton University**. The town offers excellent art exhibitions and music, as well as dance and theatre performances, exclusive shops and restaurants. Walking tours take visitors to Princeton University and the battlefield where Washington's army defeated the British in 1777. Other attractions include **Einstein's House** (he was a Princeton University lecturer), **Princeton University Art Museum**, **Bainbridge House**, **Clarke House** on the **Princeton Battlefield**, and **Drumthwacket**, a stately Greek-revival Southern-style mansion that is now the Governor's official residence.
Camden, a town 43km (27 miles) south of Trenton in the Delaware River region, has **Walt Whitman's House** and the **New Jersey State Aquarium**, which combines entertainment, science and cutting-edge technology with some 5000 aquatic animals and over 80 individual fresh and salt water exhibits. Next door is the 25,000-seat **Tweeter Center**, which presents a wide range of headliner entertainment. New to the Camden Waterfront is the **USS New Jersey Museum**, aboard one of the most decorated battleships in US naval history.
Historic **Salem**, 53km (33 miles) south of Camden on Route 45, has 60 18th-century buildings along **Market Street**, museums, exhibits and the 500-year-old **Salem Oak**, near the court house. The *Cowtown Rodeo*, in nearby **Pilesgrove**, is the oldest rodeo on the east coast and has competitions every Saturday from May to September and a large flea market every Tuesday and Saturday.
Camping, canoeing, swimming, fishing, horseriding and hiking can be enjoyed in a venture out to the **Pine Barrens**, the largest wilderness area east of the Mississippi River. Designated the **New Jersey Pinelands National Reserve** in 1978, it was the first national reserve to be created in the USA, and was recognised by UNESCO as a Biosphere Reserve in 1983.
SHORE REGION: Home to rock stars Bruce Springsteen and Jon Bon Jovi, the Shore Region boasts white sandy beaches, rolling farmland, quaint seaside resort towns and historic sites. Dotting the shore are exciting towns like **Seaside Heights** and **Point Pleasant**, which are home to boardwalk amusement rides and games, while quieter towns like **Spring Lake** and **Ocean Grove** offer charming bed & breakfast inns. Exciting amusement rides and the world's largest safari park are located at **Six Flags Great Adventure and Wild Safari** in **Jackson**, along with the **Hurricane Harbor** waterpark. **Allaire State Park** in **Farmingdale** is a restored 18th-century bog-iron mining village offering period shops, bakeries and churches, as well as the **Pinecreek Railroad** train, craft and antique shows and square-dancing at weekends. On **Long Beach Island**, the **Barnegat Lighthouse and Museum** has maritime exhibits and gardens. More local heritage is on show at **Tuckerton Seaport**, a working maritime village.
EXCURSIONS: Cruises can be taken aboard the *River Belle* or *River Queen*, large stern-wheelers that ply the waters off **Point Pleasant Beach**, where deep-sea fishing boats are also available. Party cruises can be taken aboard the *Sandy Hook Lady*, an authentic paddle-wheel steamer which runs from the **Atlantic Highlands** harbour and offers a scenic ride along the historic **Shrewsbury River**.
SKYLANDS REGION: Some of the most beautiful and unspoiled land in the northeastern USA is found in the Skylands Region of northwestern New Jersey. During the winter, resorts such as **Mountain Creek** offer skiing and snowboarding for all skill levels; while in summer, camping, hiking and watersports can be enjoyed at numerous State and National Parks, such as the **Delaware Water Gap National Recreation Area**. Revolutionary War historic sites, wineries, museums, antique stores and bed & breakfast inns are scattered throughout the region.
The **Clinton Historical Museum** and **Spruce Run Reservoir** in Clinton are accompanied by quaint shops and charming restaurants. **Waterloo Village**, in **Stanhope**, is a restored 18th-century village of colonial craft shops and homes, and hosts a summer series of jazz and bluegrass festivals. **Morristown National Historic Park** was the site of George Washington's winter encampments and the **Ford Mansion**, now a museum. Battle re-enactments take place throughout the year. The 30 acre **Land of Make Believe**, in **Hope**, fulfils childhood fantasies, as do the life-size animated characters in the **Fairy Tale Forest**, in **Oak Ridge**.
Hiking, canoeing, fishing and river rafting on the **Delaware River** can be organised during the summer, and ice-skating, tobogganing, snowmobiling, skiing and ice fishing are available during the winter. The **Frelinghuysen Arboretum**, in **Morris Township**, offers 125 acres of self-guided trails, including a Braille Trail. **Liberty Village Premium Outlets** in **Flemington** is a high-quality shopping complex with Early American-style architecture and landscaping. Also in Flemington is the **Black River** and **Western Railroad**, where visitors can take a one-hour ride on a steam- or diesel-powered train.
SOUTHERN SHORE REGION: Located along the southeastern tip of New Jersey on the Atlantic Ocean is a region for those who enjoy seaside culture and heritage, boardwalk amusements, fishing and birdwatching. The **Wildwoods** and **Ocean City** boardwalks buzz with excitement, in contrast to the quieter retreats of **Stone Harbor** and **Avalon**. **Cape May**, a National Historic Landmark, is a popular Victorian seaside town with many bed & breakfast inns, trolley tours and the superb **Cape May County Zoo**. **Wheaton Village**, in **Millville**, is the world's largest museum of American glass, with a 7000-item collection ranging from paperweights to Tiffany masterpieces. **Cold Spring Village** is a recreation of an old farm village, with period shops and restaurants. Visitors can stroll through 25 different gardens at **Leaming's Run Gardens and Colonial Farm** in **Swainton**.

Social Profile

FOOD & DRINK: New Jersey offers everything from gourmet cuisine to 'home-cooking' country food, in settings ranging from restaurants to diners. In addition to the staple US fare of steaks, seafood and hamburgers, cuisines from around the world can be found throughout New Jersey.
THEATRE & CONCERTS: There are numerous theatres scattered throughout New Jersey that offer productions ranging from Shakespeare to contemporary works. Concerts and special performances by the *New Jersey Symphony Orchestra* and famous entertainers are held throughout the year at a variety of venues including Newark's **New Jersey Performing Arts Center**, the symphony's new home; **Continental Airlines Arena** at the **Meadowlands Sports Complex**; **Atlantic City Casino Showrooms**; and the **PNC Bank Arts Center** in Holmdel. The **Paper Mill Playhouse**, the official State theatre of New Jersey, shows musicals and plays year round, as does the **George Street Playhouse** in New Brunswick. In Trenton, the **Sovereign Bank Arena** and the **War Memorial Theater** host concerts and other events. Live performance is also held in the various casino hotels, including the new **Blue Martini** at Bally's, on the Atlantic City Boardwalk.
NIGHTLIFE: Atlantic City's nightclubs are open until the small hours and there is round-the-clock gambling available at the casinos. Some of the oceanfront towns have clubs and entertainment centres with a lively atmosphere along the boardwalks into the evenings.
SHOPPING: Shopping in New Jersey appeals to all tastes

and budgets. *Jersey Gardens Mall* in Elizabeth is the State's largest outlet shopping mall, while upmarket shopping malls feature the famous department stores of *Macy's*, *Bloomingdales* and *Saks Fifth Avenue*. Bargains on brand-name merchandise can be found at the *Secaucus Outlet Center* in Secaucus. *Liberty Village* and *Turntable Junction* outlet centres in Flemington offer equally attractive deals. Antique stores fill small New Jersey towns like Chester, Haddonfield and Mullica Hill, while outdoor flea markets offer an eclectic array of jewellery, clothing, housewares, furniture and more. There is no sales tax on clothing in New Jersey.

SPECIAL EVENTS: Dozens of festivals and events are celebrated throughout the State each year, including the annual Miss America Pageant in Atlantic City. The following is a selection of special events occurring in New Jersey in 2005:

Feb 18-20 *United States Super 8 Film and Digital Video Festival*, New Brunswick. **Mar 12** *St Patrick's Day*, Morristown. **Mar 19-20** *Atlantic City Spring Festival* (largest indoor art, antique and collectibles show in the world). **Apr 9-13** *35th Annual Monmouth Festival of the Arts*, Tinton Falls. **Apr 23-May 1** *Cape May Spring Festival*. **Apr 29-May 1** *Trenton Film Festival*. **May 7-8** *Mystic Realms Fantasy Festival*, Pine Hill. **May 21-22** *Cruisin River Festival*, Red Bank. **Jun 5** *New Jersey's 14th Annual Gay Pride Festival*, Asbury Park. **Jun 17-19** *150th Anniversary Baseball Festival*, Hoboken. **Jul 27-31** *Monmouth County Fair*, Freehold. **Jul 29-31** *Quick Chek NJ Festival of Ballooning*, Readington. **Aug 1-6** *Warren County Farmers Fair & Hot Air Balloon Fest*, Belvidere. **Sep** *Miss America Pageant*, Atlantic City. **Dec** *16th Annual Festival of Trees*, New Brunswick.

Climate

The State's temperature ranges from a July average of 23°C (74°F) to -1°C (30°F) in January, with a more pronounced difference between north and south in the winter. There is moderate rainfall throughout the year.

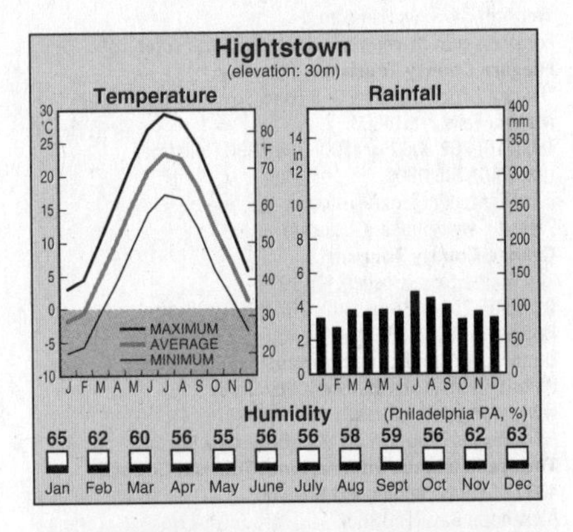

New Mexico

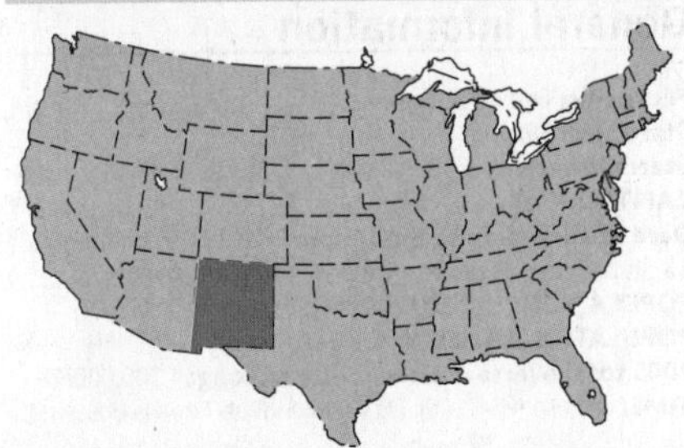

New Mexico Department of Tourism
Street address: 491 Old Santa Fe Trail, Santa Fe, NM 87501
Postal address: PO Box 20002, Santa Fe, NM 87503
Tel: (505) 827 7400 *or* (800) 733 6396 (toll-free).
Fax: (505) 827 7402.
E-mail: enchantment@newmexico.org
Website: www.newmexico.org

Albuquerque CVB
Street address: 20 First Plaza, NW, Suite 601, Albuquerque, NM 87102
Postal address: PO Box 26866, Albuquerque, NM 87125
Tel: (505) 842 9918 *or* (800) 733 9918 (toll-free).
Fax: (505) 247 9101.
E-mail: info@itsatrip.org
Website: www.itsatrip.org

Carlsbad CVB/Chamber of Commerce
Street address: 302 South Canal Street, Carlsbad, NM 88220
Postal address: PO Box 910, Carlsbad, NM 88221
Tel: (505) 887 6516 *or* (800) 221 1224 (toll-free).
Fax: (505) 885 1455.
E-mail: chamber@caverns.com
Website: www.carlsbadchamber.com

Gallup CVB
Street address: 201 East Highway 66, Gallup, NM 87301
Postal address: PO Box 1270, Gallup, NM 87305
Tel: (505) 863 3841 *or* (800) 242 4282 (toll-free).
Fax: (505) 726 1278.
E-mail: genuine@gallupnm.org
Website: www.gallupnm.org

Santa Fe CVB
Street address: 201 West Marcy, Santa Fe, NM 87501
Postal address: PO Box 909, Santa Fe, NM 87504
Tel: (505) 955 6200 *or* (800) 777 2489 (toll-free).
Fax: (505) 955 6222.
E-mail: scenter@santafe.org
Website: www.santafe.org *or* www.santafenm.gov

Taos County Chamber of Commerce and Visitor Centre
1139 Paseo Del Pueblo Sur, Taos, NM 87571
Tel: (505) 758 3873 *or* (800) 732 8267 (toll-free).
Fax: (505) 758 3872.
E-mail: taos@taoschamber.com
Website: www.taoschamber.com

General Information

Nickname: Land of Enchantment
State bird: Roadrunner
State flower: Yucca Flower
CAPITAL: Santa Fe
Date of admission to the Union: 6th Jan 1912
POPULATION: 1,903,289 (official estimate 2004)
POPULATION DENSITY: 60.04 per sq km
2003 total overseas arrivals/US ranking: 90,000/29
TIME: Mountain (GMT - 7). *Daylight Saving Time* is observed

THE STATE: New Mexico is graced with deserts, forests, cities, lakes and mountains. Its Pueblo Native American and Spanish cultures are still very much alive. **Albuquerque**, the largest city, has an international airport, and its Old Town, museums and cultural centres make it an important tourist destination and a good base for travelling through the State. **Santa Fe**, with its adobe architecture, is the USA's oldest State capital. Other attractions include the **Sandia Peak** area and ski runs; the **Carlsbad Caverns**; the mountain resort of **Ruidoso**; the Spanish colonial village of **La Mesilla**; prehistoric Native American sites; and **the Navajo Native American Reservation** near **Farmington**.

Travel - International

AIR: International airports: *Albuquerque International Airport (ABQ)* (website: www.cabq.gov/airport) is located 6km (4 miles) southeast of the city centre. Taxis, limousines and shuttle buses are available to Albuquerque and Santa Fe (travel time - 70 minutes) and regional buses serve other destinations in the State. Car hire agencies at the airport include *Alamo*, *Avis*, *Budget*, *Dollar*, *Hertz*, *National* and *Thrifty*.

El Paso Airport (ELP) (website: www.elpasointernationalairport.com) also serves as a gateway into southern New Mexico - see the *Texas* section.

RAIL: *Amtrak* (tel: (800) 872 7245 (toll-free); website: www.amtrak.com) serves New Mexico on two routes. The

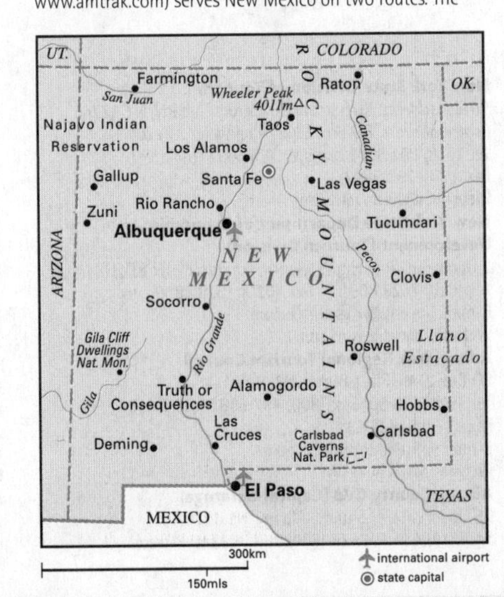

Credit: © New Mexico Department of Tourism

Southwest Chief, connecting Chicago to Los Angeles, stops daily at Raton, Las Vegas (New Mexico), Lamy, Albuquerque and Gallup. The thrice-weekly *Sunset Limited*, connecting Orlando and New Orleans to Los Angeles, stops at Lordsburg and Deming in the State's southwest corner, as well as at El Paso (Texas).

ROAD: The main **bus** companies operating in New Mexico are *TNM&O* and *Greyhound* (tel: (800) 229 9424 (toll-free); website: www.greyhound.com). There are four daily buses to Santa Fe and Taos from the modern bus terminal in Albuquerque, 300 Second Street SW.

Approximate bus travel times: From Albuquerque to *Santa Fe* is one hour 15 minutes, to *Taos* is three hours, to *El Paso* is six hours, to *Flagstaff* is six hours 45 minutes, to *Phoenix* is nine hours, to *Denver* is 10 hours, to *Oklahoma City* is 12 hours, and to *Los Angeles* is 18 hours. From Santa Fe to *Taos* is one hour 35 minutes.

URBAN: In Albuquerque, most buses run Mon-Sat 0600-1800. Santa Fe has seven routes running throughout the city.

Resorts & Excursions

ALBUQUERQUE: Situated near the centre of the State, Albuquerque nestles in the **Rio Grande** valley below the majestic **Sandia Mountains**. One-third of New Mexico's population lives in the city, but it manages to retain some small-town qualities. The cultural influences of both the Native American and Hispanic early settlers is evident in everything from food to architecture. Visitors can explore the **Coronado State Monument** where Spanish explorer, Coronado, and his men stayed while searching for the seven cities of gold. The **Indian Pueblo Cultural Center** traces the history of the State's 19 Native American Pueblos. Exhibits feature contemporary works by pueblo artists and seasonal and traditional dances are performed. The **National Hispanic Cultural Center of New Mexico** is located in the historic **Barelas** district. The complex features a newly opened theatre and amphitheatre, as well as art galleries and a genealogical research center. The **Sandia Peak Aerial Tramway** takes tourists 4.3km (2.7 miles) above the deep canyons of Albuquerque. It is the world's longest single-span tramway and should be avoided by those who do not have a head for heights. Back on terra firma, visitors can walk through an active volcano, tour an ice-age cave and gaze up at the huge dinosaurs in the **New Mexico Museum of Natural History & Science**, or visit the new *S&S DoubleShot* ride at **Cliff's Amusement Park**.

Excursions: Along the popular **Turquoise Trail** are former mining towns such as **Madrid** and **Golden**, which were left deserted when supplies of gold, turquoise and coal mines ran dry. On Interstate 25 at **Budaghers**, between Albuquerque and Santa Fe, the Traditions festival marketplace is dedicated to selling products and services made in New Mexico. Performances and exhibitions in the outdoor plaza and gazebo showcase New Mexico culture.

SANTA FE: The 'City of the Holy Faith' is the oldest and highest capital in the country. It boasts more than 150 art galleries, most of which are within easy walking distance of the city centre. These include the **Museum of New Mexico**; **Santa Fe Children's Museum**, with interactive exhibits; **Institute of American Indian Arts Museum**; **Wheelwright Museum of the American Indian**, which includes displays of jewellery, weavings, pottery and paintings of Native American cultures; and the **Museum of International Folk Art**. Along the **Santa Fe Trail** are **San Miguel Mission**, one of the oldest churches in the country, and **Loretto Chapel**

with its 'Miraculous Stairway'. Further down the trail is the **State Capitol**, one of the newest capitol buildings in the country. Its unique design is modelled after the Zia sun symbol on the State flag.

TAOS: Visitors to Taos can see the ancient **Taos Pueblo**, home to the Taos people long before the arrival of Columbus. Spanish colonisers arrived 400 years ago and examples of their craft and culture can be found at **Millicent Rogers Museum** and the 200-year-old **Martinez Hacienda**. The Old West also lives on at the home of 19th-century scout, Kit Carson, and in the nearby house where Carson's brother-in-law and governor of New Mexico Territory was murdered. The governor's wife and children escaped by digging through the wall of their adobe home with kitchen utensils.

NORTHWEST REGION: The northwest region is home to the oldest surviving Pueblo, **Acoma**, the newest, **Laguna**, and the largest, **Zuni**. Some Pueblos are open to the public daily, others only on feast days. The region also includes part of the country's largest reservation – the Navajo. The **Navajo** are noted for their beautiful silver and turquoise jewellery, sand paintings and other crafts.

Nestling on a high plateau in the foothills of the **Rocky Mountains**, Aztec stretches along the **Animas River**. The **Aztec Ruins National Monument** is the main attraction with its restored **Great Kiva**, which was once used for religious ceremonies. The nearby **Animas** and **San Juan rivers** provide some of the best trout fishing in the nation.

SOUTHERN NEW MEXICO: White Sands National Monument in the **Tularosa Basin** contains the world's largest gypsum sand dunes. They were formed when rainwater dissolved gypsum in a nearby mountain and then collected in the basin's **Lake Lucero**. As the desert weather evaporated the lake water, the gypsum crystals were left behind and eventually formed the continually growing sand dunes.

Carlsbad is home to the **Pecos River**, **Living Desert State Park** and the **Presidents Park Amusement Village**. The world-famous **Carlsbad Caverns** were explored in 1922 and declared a national monument by President Calvin Coolidge a year later; they were re-designated as part of **Carlsbad Caverns National Park** in 1930. Visitors can descend 250m (830ft) into the caverns down a steep, slippery path, before touring the many chambers and passages. The surrounding area also features the **Guadalupe Mountains**, where the rugged wilderness of the American West has been preserved.

Attractions in the southwest corner of the State include **Gila Cliff Dwellings National Monument**, with more than 40 stone and timber rooms carved into the cliff's natural caves, and **Silver City**, a beautiful mountain retreat.

Social Profile

FOOD & DRINK: Most menus feature *tortillas*, which are flat discs of Mexican bread made of wheat flour or cornmeal and baked on a hot dry griddle. Native American *fry-bread* is deep-fried wheat bread, often eaten with honey or served as the base of a Navajo *taco*. Another speciality, the *sopaipilla*, is a piece of wheat bread that puffs when deep fried. An *enchilada* is meat and cheese, spread on or rolled in a corn tortilla and smothered with green or red chilli sauce. *Burritos* are meat, beans and diced potatoes wrapped in a flour tortilla, sometimes smothered in hot sauce and cheese. *Chile rellenos* are whole green chiles, stuffed with cheese, battered and fried.

THEATRE & CONCERTS: Santa Fe has an active theatre scene and lively music venues with top-class acts. The *Santa Fe Opera* performs beneath the stars against a beautiful mountain backdrop. In Albuquerque, performing arts range from ballet to Spanish folk operetta, and from medieval music to barbershop choruses.

SHOPPING: Silver jewellery is a great buy. Native American craftspeople often use turquoise streaked with threads of silver or gold. Other popular gemstones include coral, *lapis lazuli* (dark blue), *malachite* (green), jet and pink shell. A small animal shape carved from stone is called a 'fetish', and may be strung with beads on a necklace. Each pueblo has characteristic styles and colours of pottery ranging from brightly coloured pots to plain clay ones. Other special buys include Navajo rugs; wooden dolls; *retablos*, which are wooden boards painted with an image of Christ or a saint; and painted carvings called *bultos*.

SPORT: The high mountains and dry air make for great downhill and cross-country **skiing**. There are nine major skiing areas in the State. **Horseracing** is also popular and six racetracks offer up to 300 days of races each year. For those who enjoy **horse riding**, there are many dude ranches and riding stables located across New Mexico. **Hiking** or exploring underground caverns are other options, as is **whitewater rafting** on the *Rio Grande* or *Rio Chama*. Mountain streams and well-stocked lakes are perfect for **fishing**.

SPECIAL EVENTS: The following is a selection of special events occurring in New Mexico in 2005:

Jan 10-30 *19th Annual Wine Festival*, Taos. **Feb 3-8** *Mardi Gras in the Mountains*, Red River. **Feb 17-20** *White Sands Film Festival*, Alamogordo. **Feb 18-20** *Klezmerquerque 2005* (Jewish music and dance from Eastern Europe), Albuquerque. **Mar 11-13** *National Fiery Foods Show*, Albuquerque. **Mar 31-Apr 3** *Taos Picture Show*. **May 1-31** *Spring Arts Celebration*, Taos. **May 3** *Santa Cruz Dance*, Taos Pueblo. **May 21** *Third Annual Folk Life Festival*, Taos. **May 27-29** *10th Annual Blues Festival*, Silver City. **Jun 13** *San Antonio Feast Day*, Taos Pueblo. **Jul 1-4** *2005 UFO Festival*, Roswell. **Jul 8-10** *Old Timers' Festival*, Magdalena. **Aug 6-8** *84th Annual Inter-Tribal Indian Ceremonial*, Gallup. **Aug 21-22** *Indian Market*, Santa Fe. **Aug 26-28** *Taos Country Fair*, Taos. **Aug 27-29** *Duck Races*, Deming. **Sep 4-6** *Hatch Chile Festival*. **Sep 9-25** *New Mexico State Fair*, Albuquerque. **Sep 21-25** *Wine & Chile Fiesta*, Santa Fe. **Sep 25-26** *Whole Enchilada Fiesta*, Las Cruces. **Oct 2-10** *Balloonfiesta 2005*, Albuquerque. **Nov 16-21** *Festival of the Cranes*, Socorro. **Dec 1-5** *Santa Fe Film Festival*.

Climate

Before 'Land of Enchantment' became the official State description, New Mexico was known as 'The Sunshine State' because it receives well above the average national levels of sunshine each year. But with a State as large and varied as New Mexico, the climate differs considerably from one place to the next. In villages and cities such as Angel Fire and Las Vegas, which are 1.5km (1 mile) above sea level, temperatures above 100°F (37.7°C) are not uncommon. In winter, snow falling in the lowlands frequently melts by midday, but ski areas maintain good bases from late November into mid-April.

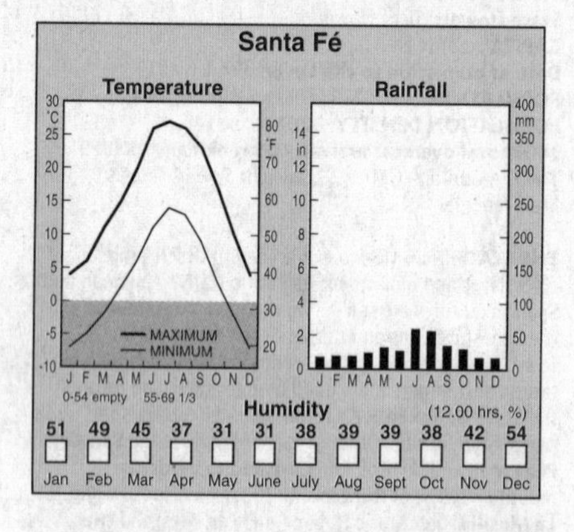

New York

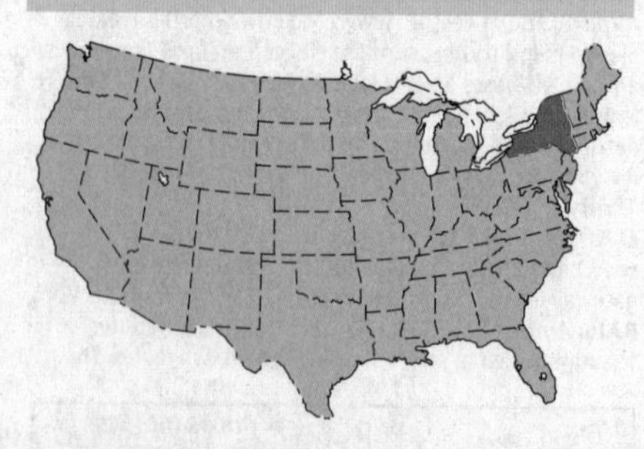

New York State Division of Tourism
Street address: 30 South Pearl Street, Albany, NY 12245
Postal address: PO Box 2603, Albany, NY 12220
Tel: (518) 292 5361 *or* (800) 225 5697 (toll-free).
Fax: (518) 292 5802.
Website: www.iloveny.com

New York State Department of Economic Development (Tourism Division)
3 Dyers Building, High Holborn, London EC1N 2JT, UK
Tel: (020) 7629 6891. Fax: (020) 7629 8359.
E-mail: iloveny@nyseurope.com
Website: www.iloveny.com

Adirondack Regional Tourism Council
PO Box 2149, Plattsburgh, NY 12901
Tel: (518) 846 8016 *or* (800) 487 6867 (toll-free).
Fax: (518) 846 8018.
E-mail: info@adirondacks.com
Website: www.adk.com

Albany County CVB (Capital-Saratoga)
25 Quackenbush Square, Albany, NY 12207
Tel: (518) 434 1217 *or* (800) 258 3582 (toll-free).
Fax: (518) 434 0887.
E-mail: accvb@albany.org
Website: www.albany.org

Greene County Tourism (Catskill Region)
PO Box 527, Catskill, NY 12414
Tel: (518) 943 3223 *or* (800) 355 2287 (toll-free).
Fax: (518) 943 2296.
E-mail: tourism@discovergreene.com
Website: www.greenetourism.com

Chautauqua County VB
Street address: Chautauqua Institution Welcome Center, Route 394, Chautauqua, NY 14722
Postal address: PO Box 1441, Chautauqua, NY 14722
Tel: (716) 357 4569 *or* (800) 242 4569 (toll-free).
Fax: (716) 357 2284.
E-mail: andrewnixon@tourchautauqua.com
Website: www.tourchautauqua.com

Finger Lakes Tourism Alliance
309 Lake Street, Penn Yan, NY 14527
Tel: (315) 536 7488 *or* (800) 530 7488.
Fax: (315) 536 1237.
E-mail: info@fingerlakes.org
Website: www.fingerlakes.org

Long Island CVB and Sports Commission
330 Motor Parkway, Suite 203, Hauppauge, Long Island, NY 11788
Tel: (631) 951 3440 *or* (877) 386 6654 (toll-free).
Fax: (631) 951 3439.
E-mail: tourism@funonli.com
Website: www.funonli.com

NYC & Company
810 Seventh Avenue, New York, NY 10019
Tel: (212) 484 1222 *or* (800) 692 8474 (toll-free).
Fax: (212) 245 5943.
E-mail: nytourism@nycvisit.com
Website: www.iloveny.com
Provides information on New York City.

NYC & Company CVB (UK Office)
c/o Hills Balfour, Notcutt House, 36 Southwark Bridge Road, London SE1 9EU, UK
Tel: (020) 7202 6368. Fax: (020) 7928 0722.
E-mail: nycvisit@hillsbalfour.com
Website: www.nycvisit.com
For press and travel trade assistance and sales only.

Niagara County Tourism
Niagara Office Building, 345 Third Street, Suite 605, Niagara Falls, NY 14303
Tel: (716) 282 8992 *or* (800) 338 7890 (toll-free).
Fax: (716) 285 0809.
E-mail: ntcc@niagara-usa.com
Website: www.niagara-usa.com

Orange County Tourism
124 Main Street, Goshen, NY 10924
Tel: (845) 291 2136 *or* (800) 762 8687 (toll-free).
Fax: (845) 291 2137.
E-mail: tourism@co.orange.ny.us
Website: www.travelhudsonvalley.org *or* www.orangetourism.org
Provides information on Hudson Valley Region.

Thousand Islands International Tourism Council
43373 Collins Landing, PO Box 400, Alexandria Bay, NY 13607
Tel: (315) 482 2520 *or* (800) 847 5263 (toll-free).
Fax: (315) 482 5906.
E-mail: info@visit1000islands.com
Website: www.visit1000islands.com

General Information

Nickname: Empire State
State bird: Bluebird
State flower: Rose
CAPITAL: Albany
Date of admission to the Union: 26th July 1788 (original 13 States; date of ratification of the Constitution)
POPULATION: 19,227,088 (official estimate 2004)
POPULATION DENSITY: 136.3 per sq km
2003 total overseas arrivals/US ranking: 4,200,000/1
TIME: Eastern (GMT - 5). *Daylight Saving Time* is observed.

THE STATE: New York State can be divided into 11 holiday regions: The Adirondacks, Capital-Saratoga, The Catskills, Central-Leatherstocking, Chautauqua-Allegheny, Finger Lakes, Greater Niagara, Hudson Valley, Long Island, New York City and Thousand Islands-Seaway.

There is only one **New York City**. No other US metropolis even comes close to it in terms of population, diversity of culture, entertainment, business and commerce. Yet within a day's drive, visitors can find fine beaches and seascapes; quiet, forested mountains; quaint, small towns; and plenty of historical sightseeing.

Long Island, a short train ride east of Manhattan, is the largest island adjoining the continental USA. A popular destination for native city dwellers, Long Island has recently been discovered by everyone else. It boasts some beautiful white sand beaches, as well as the celebrated seaside resort of **Hamptons**.

To the north of the city lie the **Hudson River Valley** and the resort area of **The Catskills**. Many visitors have compared the Hudson River with the Rhine – both feature busy boat traffic, dramatic cliffs, green hills and magnificent mansions. The Catskills, situated almost in New York City's backyard, are among the State's leading resort areas. A haven for outdoor enthusiasts, the region offers a range of activities including fishing and skiing, as well as some fascinating historical buildings.

New York State's capital, **Albany**, lies in the **Capital-Saratoga** region, north of the Hudson Valley. Its fine museums are among the oldest in the country. **Saratoga Springs** has been a leading spa and horseracing centre since the late-19th century and is the 'summer home away from home' for the *New York City Opera/Ballet* and *Philadelphia Orchestra*.

The **Finger Lakes** region in Central New York is dotted with resorts, campsites, water recreation areas, fine lakes and woodland scenery. Gouged into the land by the action of prehistoric glaciers, 11 slender lakes extend from north to south like the fingers of a hand. The area used to be famous for the quality of its glass, and today is known as the State's prime wine-producing region.

The **Greater Niagara** region is home to the State's second-largest city, **Buffalo**, a major industrial centre with a strong sense of history. It is a good base from which to plan an excursion to the most celebrated natural attraction in New York State, the 56m (184ft) **Niagara Falls**, which can be visited on foot, by boat or by helicopter. The Niagara River flows north from **Lake Erie** to **Lake Ontario**, plunging down to form the celebrated falls in the process.

The lakes and rivers of the **Chautauqua-Allegheny** region offer a range of outdoor recreational activities. Visitors can also tour Amish communities, Native American reservations and wineries; the region is the largest grape-growing area outside California. The **Adirondacks** region is where James Fenimore Cooper set the action of his legendary novel, *The Last of the Mohicans*. **Adirondack Park** is the largest State park in the USA at 2.4 million hectares (6 million acres). The region is known for its woodland cabins, luxurious lakeside resort hotels and the prospect of canoeing, salmon fishing and big-game hunting. The adjacent **Thousand Islands-Seaway** region offers a host of summer activities, including cruises among the many picturesque islands. More than 320km (200 miles) of spectacular coastline can be seen from the famous *Seaway Trail* byway, a scenic route stretching 700km (454 miles) past Lake Erie, the **Niagara River**, Lake Ontario and the **St Lawrence River**.

The **Central-Leatherstocking** region was once the USA's western frontier, but is known today for its Native American memorials and sporting museums, including the **National Baseball Hall of Fame** at **Cooperstown**.

Travel - International

AIR: The three airports serving New York City are operated by the *Port Authority of New York and New Jersey* (website: www.panynj.gov).

International airports: *John F Kennedy (JFK), La Guardia (LGA)* and *Newark International (EWR)*; all of these airports handle domestic and international flights, but most international flights into New York arrive at *JFK*. Flights from or via London *Heathrow* to New York land at *JFK*, and flights from London *Gatwick* land at *JFK* and *EWR*. Some transfer connections via continental Europe land at *LGA*, but the airport's primary function is to handle internal US flights. For further information on timetables, transport and details of travel to New York City, contact the New York Port Authority. Travellers from Europe arriving at *JFK* will generally make their onward connection from there. Connections to smaller locations, and connections for travellers arriving at *EWR*, may have to be made by transferring to *LGA*.

John F Kennedy International (JFK): The airport (website: www.panynj.gov/aviation/jfkframe.HTM) is located in Queens, 24km (15 miles) southeast of midtown Manhattan (travel time – 50-60 minutes). The airport receives the most international passengers in the USA (15.3 million in 2002), over half of its total passenger count. For transport into the city, a free *Airport Shuttle Bus* labelled *'Long Term Parking Lot'* takes travellers to Howard Beach Station; from there, a subway connection on the 'A' train (which runs every 10 to 15 minutes) takes approximately 90 minutes to central Manhattan, stopping at a number of stations with further connections on the way. An express bus service, the *New York Airport Service Express Bus*, is offered by New York Airport Service to the Port Authority Bus Terminal (Manhattan West Side) or Grand Central Station (Manhattan East Side). A single fare is US$15; buses operate every 15 to 30 minutes from 0600-0000 (travel time 45-90 minutes depending on traffic). *Gray Line Air Shuttle* (tel: (212) 315 3006) operates a shared minibus service on demand between 0700-2330, which goes anywhere between Battery Park and 125th Street (travel time – 40-60 minutes, including stops at all major hotels). The *Super Shuttle Manhattan* (tel: (212) 258 3826), available on demand 24 hours a day, is a shared door-to-door service going anywhere between 23rd and 96th Streets. Taxis cost US$45 plus tolls and tips for all destinations on Manhattan island. Travellers are advised not to travel with a taxi driver who approaches them first. Always find out the standard rate as unscrupulous drivers may overcharge. Uniformed taxi dispatchers (recommended) are available during peak hours and provide information on fares.

Transport to other destinations: Limousine services are available to some cities in Connecticut, Long Island and upstate New York. Coach services are available to New Jersey and Pennsylvania.

La Guardia (LGA): The airport (website: www.panynj.gov/aviation/lgaframe.HTM) is located in Queens, 13km (8 miles) east of midtown Manhattan (travel time – 30-45 minutes). For transport into the city, the M-60 MTA bus goes over Triborough Bridge and intersects with all subway lines as it crosses to the Upper West Side of Manhattan; exact change (US$2) or a 'MetroCard' (an electronic fare card in use on all MTA buses and most subway stages) is required plus an additional US$2 if changing to the subway. The 24-hour *Triboro Coach* services Q33 and Q47 run from the airport to Manhattan and Queens, connecting with local buses and various subway lines. Frequent express bus services are provided by *Gray Line Bus Services, New York Airport Services* and *Super Shuttle*. Private limousines and vans are available. There is also a ferry service, the *Delta Water Shuttle*, which departs from the Marine Air Terminal to 34th Street on the East River or to Pier 11 on Wall Street in downtown Manhattan (travel time – 30-45 minutes). Yellow taxis are readily available from designated taxi stands.

Newark International Airport (EWR): The airport (website: www.newarkairport.com) is located across the river in New Jersey. For details, see the *New Jersey* section. *Olympia Airport Express Service* offers links between EWR and Manhattan.

Inter-Airport transfers: Regular helicopter transfers are available on *New York Helicopter (HD)* between New York airports and to Newark Airport Terminal 'C'. Coach transfers are available between all three New York airports, though it may be necessary to change at Port Authority Bus Terminal in Manhattan. *New York Airport Express Service* offers links between JFK and LGA (journey time – 45 minutes), as well as services between Manhattan and the airports. The *Princeton Airporter* offers a frequent service between JFK and EWR; *Olympia Trails* provides links between all three airports, 0600-2400. A limousine service is available to Newark Airport. Taxis are also available.

Approximate flight times: From New York to *Anchorage* is eight hours 30 minutes, to *Atlanta* is two hours 40 minutes, to *Baltimore* is one hour 20 minutes, to *Barbados* is four hours 40 minutes, to *Bermuda* is two hours, to *Boston* is one hour 10 minutes, to *Buenos Aires* is 10 hours 15 minutes, to *Buffalo* is one hour 50 minutes, to *Caracas* is four hours 55 minutes, to *Chicago* is two hours 50 minutes, to *Cincinnati* is two hours 10 minutes, to *Cleveland* is one hour 45 minutes, to *Dallas/Fort Worth* is four hours, to *Detroit* is two hours, to *Frankfurt* is seven hours 30 minutes, to *Hartford* is one hour, to *Honolulu* is 12 hours, to *Houston* is four hours, to *London* is six hours 50 minutes, to *Los Angeles* is six hours, to *Mexico City* is five hours 10 minutes, to *Miami* is three hours 10 minutes, to *Minneapolis/St Paul* is three hours 10 minutes, to *Montréal* is one hour 25 minutes, to *Moscow* is eight hours 50 minutes, to *Nassau* is three hours, to *New Orleans* is three hours 25 minutes, to *Norfolk* is one hour 30 minutes, to *Orlando* is two hours 50 minutes, to *Philadelphia* is 50 minutes, to *Pittsburgh* is one hour 30 minutes, to *Providence* is one hour, to *Rio de Janeiro* is nine hours 15 minutes, to *Rome* is eight hours 10 minutes, to *St Croix* is four hours, to *St Maarten* is three hours 50 minutes, to *St Thomas* is three hours 50 minutes, to *San Francisco* is six hours 10 minutes, to *San Juan* is three hours 50 minutes, to *Santo Domingo* is three hours 50 minutes, to *Shannon* is si x hours, to *Singapore* is 21/22 hours, to *Sydney* is 26 hours, to *Tampa* is three hours, to *Tel Aviv* is 12 hours 30 minutes, to *Toronto* is one hour 30 minutes and to *Washington, DC* is one hour 10 minutes.

SEA/LAKE: The *Staten Island Ferry* (departing from Battery Park) operates between Lower Manhattan and Staten Island. The *Circle Line Ferry* (departing from Battery Park) sails to the Statue of Liberty and Ellis Island. *Circle Line Sightseeing Cruises* provide guided tours around Manhattan Island and along the Hudson River (departing from Pier 83, West 42nd Street). Frequent ferry services also run from Manhattan to Brooklyn, New Jersey and Queens. Operators include *NY Waterway* (website: www.nywaterway.com) and *Seastreak* (website: www.seastreakusa.com). *Lake Champlain Ferries* provide several crossings on Lake Champlain, between New York State and Vermont. Routes include: Plattsburg NY-Grande Isle; Port Kent NY-Burlington and Essex NY-Charlotte. Wolfe Island, Ontario, is connected to Cape Vincent in New York by a ferry service which operates daily during the summer (website: www.wolfeisland.com). A service from Wolfe Island to Kingston, Ontario, operates daily throughout the year.

Credit: © NYS DED

RAIL: Pennsylvania Station, at Seventh Avenue and 32nd Street, serves both the *Long Island Railroad*, with routes to Long Island and New Jersey, and *Amtrak*, nationwide (tel: (800) 872 7245 (toll-free); website: www.amtrak.com). Grand Central Station, at 42nd Street and Park Avenue, is the terminus for services to upstate New York (*Metro North*) and Connecticut. There are two daily trains to Montréal and one to Toronto.

Approximate rail travel times: From New York on the 'Adirondack' to *Montréal* is 14 hours 30 minutes; on the 'Keystone' to *Philadelphia* is one hour 30 minutes and to *Harrisburg* is 16 hours; on the 'Maple Leaf' to *Buffalo* is eight hours, to *Niagara Falls* is nine hours and to *Toronto* is 12 hours; on the 'Silver Service/Palmetto' to *Baltimore* is three hours, to *Washington, DC* is three hours 30 minutes, to *Jacksonville* is 18 hours, to *Orlando* (Disney World) is 21 hours, to *Tampa* is 23 hours and to *Miami* is 26 hours; and on the 'Crescent' to *Charlotte* is 10 hours, to *Atlanta* is 16 hours, to *Birmingham* is 19 hours and to *New Orleans* is 27 hours. There are frequent shuttles to *Washington, DC* and *Boston*, taking three hours 15 minutes and four hours 30 minutes respectively. The new *ACELA Express* takes two and half hours to *Washington, DC* and three hours to *Boston*.

ROAD: Travel from Manhattan to New Jersey is across George Washington Bridge or through the Lincoln or Holland Tunnels. The Verrazano-Narrows Bridge connects Brooklyn with Staten Island. Queensborough Bridge links Manhattan and Queens. Take Triborough Bridge for upstate New York and the New England Thruway and Bruckner Expressway to New England. Bus: The Port Authority Bus Terminal, at 42nd Street and Eighth Avenue, handles long-distance and regional buses, including *Greyhound* services (tel: (800) 229 9424 (toll-free); website: www.greyhound.com).

Approximate driving times: From New York on the 'Adirondack' to *Montréal* is 14 hours 30 minutes; on the 'Pennsylvanian' to *Philadelphia* is one hour 30 minutes and to *Harrisburg* is 16 hours; on the 'Maple Leaf' to *Buffalo* is eight hours, to *Niagara Falls* is nine hours and to New York to *Philadelphia* is two hours, to *Hartford* is two hours, to *Albany* is three hours, to *Boston* is fpur hours, to *Baltimore* is four hours, to *Washington, DC* is five hours, to *Portland* (Maine) is six hours, to *Montréal* is seven hours, to *Buffalo* is eight hours, to *Pittsburgh* is eight hours, to *Toronto* is nine hours, to *Cleveland* is 10 hours, to *Indianapolis* is 15 hours, to *Chicago* is 16 hours, to *Miami* is 27 hours, to *Dallas* is 33 hours, to *Los Angeles* is 58 hours, to *San Francisco* is 61 hours and to *Seattle* is 61 hours. All times are based on non-stop driving at or below the applicable speed limits.

Approximate bus travel times: New York (tel: (800) 231 2222; toll-free) to *Philadelphia* is two hours 20 minutes, to *Albany* is three hours, to *Washington, DC* is four hours 40 minutes, to *Boston* is four hours 45 minutes, to *Montréal* is eight hours 30 minutes, to *Buffalo* is nine hours, to *Pittsburgh* is nine hours and to *Cleveland* is nine hours 30 minutes.

Urban: Public transport (buses and subway) in New York is run by *Metropolitan Transportation Authority (MTA) – New York City Transit* (tel: (718) 330 1234; website: www.mta.nyc.ny.us), whose services are cheaper and more efficient than those of the private companies also operating. **Subway:** Despite its reputation, the New York City subway is fast, air conditioned, cheap and runs 24 hours a day, seven days a week. Moreover, the latest statistics show that crime on the subway has declined considerably. Express trains run between major stops and local trains stop at every station. Subway maps are posted in each subway car and pocket maps are available from token booths. Prepaid MetroCards can be purchased from subway booths, vending machines or some newsagents and can be used on buses. There are reduced fares for senior citizens and the disabled. For further information, contact the *Metropolitan Transportation Authority – New York City Transit (MTA)* (tel: (718) 330 1234). **Bus:** Services are extensive and are run mostly by the *New York City Transit Authority*. MetroCards are valid, or one may pay the driver; the exact fare is required, change will not be given. Three-quarters of the city's buses are equipped with wheelchair lifts at the rear door. **Taxi:** The standard yellow cab is metered and reasonably cheap. There is no charge for extra passengers, but there is a 50-cent surcharge between 2000 and 0600. **Hansom cabs:** Horse-drawn carriages line up at 59th Street and Fifth Avenue, just outside the *Plaza Hotel*. **Car hire:** All the major national car hire companies are represented in New York City and many have offices at the city's airports.

Resorts & Excursions

New York City

New York, the 'city that never sleeps', is one of the world's great metropolises, offering visitors everything from the ethnic flavours of **Chinatown** and **Little Italy**, to the galleries of **SoHo**, the cafes of **Greenwich Village**, the glitz of the **Theater District**, the shopping on **Fifth Avenue** and the affluence of **Park Lane** and the **Upper West Side**. New York City is made up of five boroughs and is laid out on a grid of avenues and streets. Most tourist sights are found on **Manhattan Island**, the city's entertainment and business centre. The remaining four boroughs are primarily residential – the **Bronx** to the north, **Queens** to the east, **Brooklyn** to the southeast and **Staten Island** to the southwest. Each has wealthy and salubrious districts alongside working-class neighbourhoods – demonstrating New York's varied social mix. The total area of all five boroughs is 780 sq km (301 sq miles). New York's location at the mouth of the Hudson River on the Atlantic Ocean is reflected in the city's importance as a port, and as the point of disembarkation for millions of immigrants to the USA. Vibrating with the energy of over 7 million inhabitants, New York is a constantly evolving, growing and changing organism. The sheer volume of things to do – theatre, ballet, opera, museums – is astonishing. Many of the city's 18,000-plus restaurants are reporting boom times, while several new hotels have emerged over the past few years. Renovations of historic theatres in the area – such as the Victory, the Lyric or the Academy/Apollo – have been followed by a flood of restaurateurs and prospective retail tenants signing up for space on or near Times Square. The terrorist attacks on Manhattan's famous Twin Towers on 11 September 2001 has had a detrimental effect on the city's tourism. However, New York's JFK airport still enjoys its status as the USA's busiest airport for international arrivals, with over 15 million international tourists (many of them from the UK) using the airport in 2002. On the whole, however, numbers are down, with Newark International and La Guardia reporting a 4 per cent and 6 per cent decrease in international arrivals respectively. Crime, on the other hand, is plummeting, following the introduction of 'zero tolerance' policing; according to FBI crime statistics, the city is the safest large city in the USA. The **New York City Police Museum**, at 100 Old Slip at South Street, shows just how this is done. Visitors with disabilities will now find wheelchair access to 99 per cent of New York City buses and 40 per cent of subway stations. Public telephones for the deaf are also widespread. Two brochures for disabled people are available from New York City Transit (see contact number above).

MANHATTAN: The Manhattan skyline is an instantly recognisable sight, immortalised in countless films and television programmes. One of the best views of it can be obtained from the **Staten Island Ferry** (see below). Following the terrorist attacks of 11 September 2001, the famous landmark of the World Trade Center with its twin towers was completely destroyed, forever altering both the skyline and the history of America. The decision has recently been made to build a memorial at the 'Ground Zero' site. The Lower Manhattan Development Corporation announced in January 2004 that Michael Arad and Peter Walker's design for a grove of trees above two reflecting pools, named 'Reflecting Absence', would be chosen to immortalise that infamous event. The design was chosen over 5000 submitted ideas. Also in the planning is the ambitious **Freedom Tower** skyscraper, designed by David M Childs, which could have a unique turbine tower as a feature, creating one-fifth of the energy used by the building and doubling as somewhat unorthodox Buddhist prayer wheels.

The first European settlement on Manhattan was by the Dutch in the 1620s, who named the city New Amsterdam. In 1664, the British took over and renamed it New York, and settlement continued from south to north along the island. Skyscrapers, such as the art-deco **Empire State Building**, offer spectacular views of the city by day or night.

Statue of Liberty and Ellis Island: New York's most famous image is the 46.5m- (151ft-) high **Statue of Liberty**, located on Liberty Island, which may be reached by boat from **Battery Park** on Manhattan's southern tip. A lift and staircase inside the Statue take visitors up to an observation platform. The Liberty/Ellis Island Ferry departs from the historic **Castle Clinton** at Battery Park every 30 minutes and also stops at **Ellis Island**, the gateway for the massive numbers of immigrants arriving in New York between 1892 and 1954. On the island, the **Wall of Honor**, the world's longest wall of names, commemorates over 600,000 immigrants, and the **Ellis Island Immigration Museum** offers an interesting insight into the lives of New York's early immigrants. In Battery Park City, the new **Skyscraper Museum** celebrates the architectural style so intrinsic to the city's history and psyche.

Lower Manhattan: The oldest part of the city is at the southern end of Manhattan. East of Battery Park is the **Financial District**, containing the famous **Wall Street** and the **New York Stock Exchange**, where visitors have access to a public gallery to catch a glimpse of the frenetic trading action. The historic **South Street Seaport**, located at the end of Wall Street, offers great views of **New York Harbor**. The seaport is a thriving waterfront community with a world-class maritime museum and more than 100 shops, cafés and restaurants. To the northeast of the seaport is the famous **Brooklyn Bridge**, leading to Brooklyn. **Chinatown**, Manhattan's most thriving ethnic neighbourhood extends from Canal Street into **Little Italy** and east into the **Lower East Side**. This labyrinth of narrow streets, crammed with Chinese stores and restaurants, is home to over 100,000 residents. While Chinatown has expanded in recent years, neighbouring Little Italy has dwindled somewhat, and few of the original Italian immigrants remain, though Little Italy's restaurants, delis and bakeries remain as tempting as ever. East of Little Italy, the Lower East Side has traditionally been New York's Jewish area, owing to a flow of Jewish immigrants to the area in the late 19th and early 20th centuries. The recently revamped **Museum of Jewish Heritage** is located here. In addition to its other two Manhattan venues, the **Guggenheim Foundation** is adding a new waterfront museum on the East River. The area is also known for its **Orchard Street Market**, an open-air bazaar, and its numerous delis. To the northwest, **Greenwich Village** has been a melting pot for art, literature and music for decades, though its legendary bohemian feel has partly been replaced by upmarket beatnik chic. South of Greenwich Village is **SoHo** (*So*uth of *Ho*uston), which has become synonymous with art since the 1960s, and retains its arty, avant-garde character, with plenty of galleries, cafes, boutiques and loft spaces fronted by interesting cast-iron façades. Still further south is **TriBeCa** (*Tri*angle *Be*low *Ca*nal Street), once a deserted warehouse district, and now a growing residential area.

Midtown Manhattan: The heart of the city is located between 34th Street south and 59th Street north and contains several of New York's landmark buildings, including the 102-storey **Empire State Building** (completed in 1931). Worth visiting here are **Bryant Park** and the beautiful **New York Public Library** nearby; the 1930s art-deco **Chrysler Building** (New York's first skyscraper); the **United Nations Building** (the organisation's world headquarters); **Grand Central Station**, which has been completely restored, with special attention paid to its magnificent constellation ceiling; **Fifth Avenue**, the city's most glamorous thoroughfare, filled with luxury shops and department stores; the Chelsea neighbourhood, home of the landmark **Chelsea Hotel** and also centre for New York's gay community as well as a new magnet for art galleries and commercial developers; the **Rockefeller Center**, famous for its (winter-only) ice skating rink and also the home of NBC Studios, which can be visited; and the new **American Folk Art Museum**. A few blocks away, the highly celebrated **Museum of Modern Art** underwent a massive US$650 million expansion, which was completed in spring 2004. The **Carnegie Hall** now also includes the **Judy and Arthur Zankel Hall**. At the heart of Midtown is the Broadway theatre district near the recently revamped, once seedy but now 'family-friendly' **Times Square**, with its recently reopened **Biltmore Theater**, and the world's largest toy store, home to a 60ft Ferris wheel and life-size Barbie house.

Uptown Manhattan: Uptown Manhattan covers the area north of 59th Street and is split roughly in the middle by **Central Park** (see below). To the northwest of the park is **Columbia University** and the **Cathedral of St John the Divine**, the world's largest Gothic cathedral, which is still under construction (begun in 1812); the cathedral was recently designated a landmark by the New York City Landmark Preservation Commission. The new US$115 million **Jazz at Lincoln Center** opened in autumn 2004; the venue is part of the new **AOL Time Warner Center**, which contains luxury retail outlets, restaurants, office space, condominiums and a 249-room hotel. The **Alvin Ailey American Dance Theater** also opened its new facility in autumn 2004. The **Joan Weill Center for Dance** will be the largest facility dedicated exclusively to dance in the USA. Further north, **Harlem** is noted for its rich African-American community. Good examples of classic New York brownstones can be seen in Harlem's **Sugar Hill**. Several decayed and crime-ridden areas in Harlem are now being redeveloped.

BROOKLYN: Brooklyn is best reached via **Brooklyn Bridge**, which is particularly striking at night, and usually bustling with people during the day. Having crossed the bridge, visitors arrive in **Brooklyn Heights**, a good area to walk around. The **Jewish Children's Museum** is a new attraction to the area. Further southeast lie **Prospect Park** and the adjacent **Brooklyn Botanic Gardens**; the **Brooklyn Academy of Music**, home to the interesting *Next Wave Festival*; and the historic **Park Slope** district, notable for its old brownstones. Downtown Brooklyn is home to the recently renovated **New York Transit Museum**, located in a decommissioned subway station, with over 200 trolleys on display. **Coney Island** and **Brighton Beach**, the latter full of Russian shops and restaurants, are at the south/southeastern end of the borough.

THE BRONX: Major attractions include the world-famous **Bronx Zoo** and **New York Botanical Garden**; **Yankee Stadium**, home to the *Yankees* baseball team; **Poe Cottage**, former home of the writer Edgar Allan Poe; and **Woodlawn Cemetery**, where several famous musicians, including Miles Davis, are buried. This area of New York is currently good at breaking records. The 19,200-seat **Randall's Island Pavilion** opened in May 2003 and was the first major new live stage venue to be built in the city in 30 years, while the **Ferry Point Park Golf Course**, designed by Jack Nicklaus, will open later this year as the first golf course to be built in the city for 35 years.

QUEENS: Major attractions in the borough include the **Astoria Movie Studios** with the (attached) **American Museum of the Moving Image**, close to La Guardia airport; and **Shea Stadium** (home to the *New York Mets* Major League Baseball team), with the nearby **Flushing Meadows-Corona Park**. The southern half of Queens includes a portion of the **Gateway National Recreation Area** which, despite its location next to JFK International Airport, provides a refuge to hundreds of bird species.

STATEN ISLAND: Visitors to the island often do so mainly to enjoy the view of the classic New York skyline from the **Staten Island Ferry**, which operates from Battery Park (downtown) past the Statue of Liberty and Ellis Island to Staten Island. The **Verrazano-Narrows Bridge** connects Staten Island with Brooklyn.

PARKS & BEACHES: New York's most famous park, **Central Park**, was created in 1856, when officials set aside 341 hectares (843 acres) of land between Fifth and Eighth Avenues and 59th and 110th Streets. John Lennon fans may pay their respects at **Strawberry Fields**, the area of the park dedicated to his memory. Also within the park is the **Central Park Wildlife Center**, a small but interesting zoo. During summer, the park hosts afternoon and evening concerts. Additions to the park include the **Dana Discovery Center** and fishing pond (with free poles and bait). Visitors should note that it is not advisable to visit Central Park after dark. The recently restored **Bryant Park**, behind the New York Public Library, has been a great success with businesspeople and visitors on lunch, especially as it offers free outdoor concerts and comedy shows. Reminiscent of Paris, with gravel pathways, green folding chairs and a manicured lawn, it's a great place for sunbathing, reading or enjoying a sandwich or salad bought from kiosks in the park. The fountain at the western end is a good place for a romantic rendez-vous. Other parks include the world-famous **New York Botanical Garden** in the Bronx, which has 100 hectares (250 acres) of woods, waterways and gardens and whose centrepiece is the newly restored **Enid A Haupt Conservatory**. **Riverside Park**, running alongside the Hudson River; **Battery** and **Washington Square** parks in Lower Manhattan; the **Brooklyn Botanical Gardens**, **Marine Park** and **Prospect Park** in Brooklyn; and **Cunningham**, **Flushing Meadows/Corona**, **Jacob Riis** and **Kissina** parks in Queens. **Clove Lake Park** and **Fort Wadsworth** on Staten Island boast impressive views of New York harbour. There are several fine beaches to the east of New York City. Nearest to Manhattan are **Brighton Beach**, **Coney Island** and **Manhattan Beach**. Other beaches include **Orchard Beach** in Pelham Bay Park, **South Beach** and **Wolfe's Pond Park** on Staten Island.

SPECIAL EVENTS: The following is a selection of special events occurring in New York City in 2005; for further events, contact NYC & Company CVB (see *Contact Addresses* section):

Mar 17 *St Patrick's Day Parade*, Manhattan. **Jun-Aug** *Celebrate Brooklyn Performing Arts Festival*, Brooklyn. **Jul 4** *Macy's 4th of July Fireworks*, near East River. **Aug**

Harlem Week, citywide. **Aug 29-Sep 11** *US Open Tennis Tournament*, Flushing. **Nov 6** *New York City Marathon*. **Nov 24** *Macy's Thanksgiving Day Parade*, Manhattan. **Dec 31** *New Year's Eve at Times Square*.

Greater Niagara

Located in western New York State between Lake Erie and Lake Ontario, **Niagara Falls** is one of the most outstanding spectacles on the North American continent. There are three main waterfalls, **American**, **Bridal Veil** and **Canadian** (**Horseshoe**) **Falls**, each in a different stream of the Niagara River. Other attractions in the region include **Letchworth State Park**, **Buffalo**, **Lake Erie** and **Lewiston**.

NIAGARA FALLS: Ten million tourists visit Niagara Falls each year, making it one of the most popular tourist destinations in America. The **Niagara River** rapids, just above the Falls, and the **Niagara Gorge**, below the Falls, offer beautiful scenery and many opportunities for sightseeing. The price of most merchandise is lower in Niagara Falls than in most other parts of the USA and Canada. Within the city of Niagara there are two large factory outlet malls, a large shopping mall and several retail districts. The region offers good antique shopping. Niagara's hotels are near to the Falls, attractions and shopping. Many of them are only a short walk from the edge of the Falls themselves.

The **New York State Park** that surrounds the Falls is the oldest State Park in the nation and has been restored to its original 19th-century design. Created by Frederick Olmstead to provide a natural setting for the Falls, it became a model for the uniquely American style of park. It includes many woodland islands in the rapids just above the Falls and a new visitor centre. The **Viewmobile** is a coach that tours the park. The **Great Lakes Gardens** outside the centre use grass, flowers and shrubs to depict the Great Lakes. Visitors can take the **Maid of the Mist Boat Tour** that travels into the spray of the Falls, or explore the **Cave of the Winds**, on Goat Island, in the middle of the river above the Falls.

The **Niagara Whirlpool**, on the river beneath the Falls, can be visited by jet boat. North of the Falls is **Old Fort Niagara** – a restored fortress and park containing military buildings, including the 1726 **French Castle**, one of the oldest European-designed buildings on the continent. Other attractions in the area include the **Daredevils Hall of Fame** with photographs, contraptions and memorabilia of the swimmers, tightrope walkers and others who braved the Falls (sometimes fatally); the **Aquarium of Niagara**, with more than 1500 aquatic animals including sharks, piranhas and sea lions; the **Niagara Aerospace Museum**, and the **Amherst Museum** at **Amherst**, which recreates life on the 19th-century Niagara Frontier.

TRAVEL: The *Buffalo/Niagara Falls International Airport* is only a 25-minute drive from the Falls and is served by many airlines, domestic and international. Shuttles to all major hotels are available. The *Niagara Falls International Airport* is just seven minutes away by coach or taxi. It can accommodate the largest jumbo jets and is available for charter flights. For people arriving by coach, Niagara Falls is located on a major Interstate Highway, less than one day's drive from New York City and the eastern USA. The Falls are also accessible by rail. Amtrak offers two trains per day, which arrive from New York City bound for Toronto; the station is 3km (2 miles) south of downtown Niagara Falls. *Greyhound* (tel: (800) 229 9424 (toll-free); website: www.greyhound.com) provides a direct service from New York to Niagara, with a conveniently central bus terminal at Fourth Street and Niagara Street.

Buffalo & Area

Standing at the eastern extremity of **Lake Erie** on the border with Canada, **Buffalo** is the State's second-largest city, the gateway to Niagara Falls and the Finger Lakes, and within easy reach of Lake Ontario and Toronto. It is home to the State's most important museum outside New York City, the **Albright-Knox Art Gallery**, which contains works by Picasso, Renoir, Van Gogh and Monet, among others. The **Buffalo and Erie County Historical Society** displays the inventions of Niagara Frontier residents, including *Cheerios*, cold remedies and pacemakers.

Allentown Association is among the largest historic preservation sites in the USA. The area includes arts and crafts, Victorian-style homes, international food and galleries. The graves of President Millard Fillmore and Seneca Indian Chief Red Jacket can be found at the **Forest Lawn Cemetery**. Other attractions include the Burchfield Arts Center, with the largest collection of watercolours by American artist Charles F Burchfield; **the Buffalo Museum of Science** with a children's discovery room; **CEPA Gallery**, devoted to photographic art; and the **Naval and Military Park**, where the World War II destroyer, *USS Sullivans*, is docked. **Buffalo Zoo** in **Delaware Park** has large enclosures with natural features and is home to Siberian tigers, gorillas and elephants. The **Six Flags Darien Lake** is a popular waterpark, with new attractions in the pipeline.

EXCURSIONS: Artpark, in the historic village of **Lewiston**, is the only State Park in the nation dedicated to the visual and performing arts. The 80 hectare (200 acre) park includes a 2300-seat theatre, nature trails, free outdoor performances and workshops. **Letchworth State Park** is known as the 'Grand Canyon of the East' and offers visitors magnificent views of the **Genesee River Gorge**. Outdoor activities on offer include camping, hiking and picnicking. The only socialised wolf pack in the eastern USA lives at the **Institute for Environmental Learning** in **Lyndonville**, which also houses bald eagles and cougars. Full of houses and shops from the 1820s, **Lockport** is known for its five enormous locks on the **Erie Canal**. The **Lockport Cave Tour** takes visitors along the locks, through a tunnel blasted out of rock in the 19th century, and ends in an underground boat ride.

TRAVEL: There are limousine services from *Greater Buffalo Airport (BUF)* to the city, 14.5km (9 miles) away, or direct to Niagara Falls. Taxis are also available. There are *Amtrak* rail links from Buffalo to Niagara Falls, on the Toronto-Niagara Falls line; trains to Chicago stop at the Depew station, some 13km (8 miles) from downtown Buffalo. *Empire Trailways*, *Greyhound* and long-distance bus services both stop at the downtown bus terminal at Ellicott Street and Church Street (the hub for Metro Bus and Metro Rail city services); bus route 40 runs hourly to the Niagara Falls.

SPECIAL EVENTS: The following is a selection of special events occurring in Greater Niagara in 2005:

Mar 13 *St Patrick's Day Celebrations*, Buffalo. **Aug 3-7** *Niagara County Fair*, Lockport. **Aug 13-14** *Annual Lewiston Outdoor Fine Arts Festival*, Lewiston. **Sep 17-25** *Greater Niagara Fish Odyssey* (angling competition), public waterways of Niagara and Erie. **Sep 25-Oct 31** *Pumpkin Farm Fall Festival*, Clarence. **Nov 20** *Light Up the Night Parade and Tree Lighting Ceremony*, Niagara Falls.

Each spring, the *Festival of Gold* celebrates the blooming of daffodils all over Niagara County. The flowers can be seen at **Artpark**, **New York Power Authority** and **Old Fort Niagara**, as well as in extensive areas along the **Robert Moses Parkway** from Rainbow Boulevard North to Lewiston. The *Festival of Gold* began in 1992, when volunteers planted 405,000 daffodil bulbs across the county. From **Nov 23-Jan 3 2006**, the *23rd Annual Winter Festival of Lights* in Niagara Falls attracts more than 8.5 million visitors. Billed as 'Niagara's Holiday Gift to the World', the festival is one of the nation's premier winter attractions, combining hundreds of thousands of colourful lights, animated displays, professional and community entertainment and almost two months of events.

Hudson Valley

The **Hudson River Valley** spans 225km (140 miles) from the **Battery** in Manhattan to New York's **State Capitol** in Albany, encompassing New York City and a 10-county region to the north (Westchester, Rockland, Orange, Putnam, Duchess, Ulster, Columbia, Greene, Albany and Rensselaer counties). As the Hudson River flows northwards, its landscape becomes more subdued and turns from rugged shorelines to gentle, rolling hills. The **Catskill Mountains**, located to the west, provide a stunning backdrop. Away from the river itself, the Valley contains rich, fertile lands that were originally farmed by the many Native American Algonquin tribes and the early Dutch settlers. Although some of it is being converted to non-agricultural uses, these lands remain the largest agricultural area in the State.

The Hudson River Valley was originally inhabited by Native Americans over 3000 years ago, before being settled by the Dutch in the early 17th century. Important decisions involving the early development of the USA were made throughout the region and it was the centre of the Revolutionary War. Today, approximately 3 million people live in the Hudson Valley. The Hudson River Valley corridor serves as a major transport and commercial link between the ports of New York City and Albany. The Erie Canal, constructed in 1852, linked New York City to Chicago before the development of the railway in the late-1880s made barges obsolete.

The scenery of the Hudson Valley inspired the works of early US writers, artists and designers and contributed to an appreciation of the natural environment. The Valley was the birthplace in the mid-19th century of the Hudson River School of painting – the largest, longest and most influential movement in American art history. James Fenimore Cooper (*The Leatherstocking Tales*) and Washington Irving (*The Legend of Sleepy Hollow*) used the unique landscape and folklore of the Hudson Valley as the backdrop to their literary works. The Hudson Valley is also scattered with the works of famous landscape architects: Andrew Jackson Downing, Frederick Law Olmsted and Calvert Vaux, as well as a wide array of historic and archaeological sites and museums associated with Native Americans, the Dutch and English settlements, the Revolutionary War and the Hudson River School.

The Hudson Valley has a long tradition as a holiday destination. In the mid- to late-19th century, it served as a retreat for wealthy industrialists from New York City such as

Credit: © NYS DED

the Vanderbilts and Rockefellers, who built the elaborate estates along the shores of the Hudson known as 'Millionaires' Row'. City dwellers have also sought refuge at the many resorts located in the western mid-to-upper Hudson Valley region. Today, the area continues to offer year-round opportunities for many outdoor activities such as boating, camping, hiking, hunting, skiing, bicycling, rock climbing and canoeing. Tourism is the Valley's largest employer.

WESTCHESTER COUNTY: Known as the 'Golden Apple of New York State', Westchester is located just 24km (15 miles) north of Manhattan and is the gateway to the Hudson Valley. With ties to both areas, Westchester benefits from the two different worlds. The county is bordered on the west by the Hudson River and on the east by the **Long Island Sound**, offering plenty of opportunities for boating, sailing and watersports. The county is home to 40 private and public golf courses and top-name department stores, discount malls and exclusive boutiques. The city's historic roots go deep and are reflected in the many museums, historic sites and other attractions. These include the **Hudson River Museum** in **Yonkers**, where paintings by the famous Hudson River School of artists are on display. At **Tarrytown** is the restored home of writer Washington Irving, and nearby is **Lyndhurst**, the estate and Gothic-style mansion formerly owned by the 19th-century tycoon, Jay Gould. Visitors can also tour the Rockefeller estate, **Kykuit**, or spend some time at the historic **Playland Park**, built in 1928 as a family amusement park and a National Historic Landmark, with new attractions for 2004.

ORANGE COUNTY: This is the only county in the State located between two rivers, the **Delaware River** on the west and the **Hudson** on the east. Founded in 1683, Orange County was named after England's House of Orange, and the county has played a major role in US history. George Washington lived and had his headquarters here until the Revolutionary War ended.

Today, Orange County has the greatest number and the most diverse assortment of attractions in New York outside Manhattan: **West Point**, where visitors can observe impressive military parades by cadets at the United States Military Academy; **Storm King Art Center** (the largest sculpture park in the USA); **Woodbury Common** (the largest discount designer outlet in the world); West **Point Museum Village** (the largest living history museum in New York); **Sugar Loaf Art and Craft Village**, with working craftspeople and more than 60 shops, and the **New York Renaissance Faire**. At **Washingtonville** is the **Brotherhood Winery**. The country's oldest winery, it also boasts the largest wine cellars in the USA. Orange County is also known for the beauty of its rolling farmland, and features apple orchards and picking farms that have farm stores, hay rides and seasonal events throughout the year. With 56km (35 miles) of the **Appalachian Trail** and several large State Parks, hiking is popular in Orange County, as is canoeing or rafting the **Delaware River**, one of the 10 most ecologically healthy rivers in the USA.

DUCHESS COUNTY: Named for Mary, Duchess of York and later Queen of England, this county was home to Franklin D Roosevelt, who is buried with his wife, Eleanor, at **Hyde Park**. Here, on the Hudson River, is the **Vanderbilt Mansion**, a striking 54-room Italian Renaissance structure, furnished elegantly in marble and mahogany. The **Culinary Institute of America**, 3 miles north of Poughkeepsie, is one of the world's great cookery schools. Visitors can sample the cuisine at one of the three restaurants on its campus, the **American Bounty Restaurant**, **Caterina de Medici** or **Escoffier Room**, as well as two cafes. At **Rhinebeck**, the **Old Rhinebeck Aerodrome** houses an extensive museum of native warplanes, including several World War I models.

SPECIAL EVENTS: The following is a selection of special events occurring in Hudson Valley in 2005:
Jan 1-Mar 6 *Open Air Ice Rink*, Bear Mountain State Park. **Feb 19-21** *George Washington's Birthday Celebrations*, Newburgh. **Mar 13** *St Patrick's Parade*, Tarrytown. **May** *Native American Pow Wow*, Bear Mountain State Park; *Blessing of the Animals*, North Salem. **Jun 5** *25th Annual Times Herald Orange Classic 10K*, Middletown. **Jul 20-31** *Orange County Fair*, Middletown. **Aug 23-28** *Duchess County Fair*, Rhinebeck. **Sep** *Cheese Festival*, Monroe. **Sep 8-11** *Yorktown Grange Fair*, Yorktown Heights. **Sep 24-25** *Hudson Valley Garlic Festival*, Saugerties. **Oct** *Oktoberfest*, Bear Mountain State Park; *Applefest*, Warwick. **Oct 2** *Support Connection 11th Annual Support-A-Walk*, Yorktown Heights. **Dec** *Holiday Festival*, Bear Mountain State Park. **Dec 31** *First Night*, Middletown.

Finger Lakes

Located midway between New York City and Niagara Falls in west central New York State, the Finger Lakes represent one of the truly unspoiled vacation areas in the USA. Well known for its picturesque lakes, wineries and lush forests, the region offers many opportunities for recreational activity. It is home to 25 State Parks and a variety of museums and historic homes.
The Native Americans believed the Finger Lakes were formed when the Great Spirit reached out to bless the region and left behind the imprint of his hand. Geologists report instead that the unique features of the area – the 11 long narrow lakes lying side by side, the wide valleys and the deep gorges with rushing waterfalls – were formed by the grinding action of Ice Age glaciers. These geographical features are found nowhere else in the world.
Jesuit missionaries, the first Europeans to arrive in the region, found it controlled by the Cayuga, Onondaga and Seneca Native Americans, part of the powerful Iroquois Confederacy. The area's Native American heritage is still apparent today in the names of communities and landmarks throughout the region. Although the Finger Lakes area is known primarily for its natural beauty and abundant recreational opportunities, it has also played a significant role in US social, economic and political history and is the home of famous statesmen, inventors and businesspeople.
From west to east, the six largest lakes are: **Canandaigua**, **Keuka**, **Seneca**, **Cayuga**, **Owasco**, and **Skaneateles**. There are many fine lodges and small resorts on the lakes' shores, where visitors can take in the outstanding scenery and make the most of recreational opportunities, especially boating and fishing.
SYRACUSE: The city flourished after the opening of the **Erie Canal** in 1825, and the **Erie Canal Museum**, a restored 1850s canal-boat-weighing station set along the canal, celebrates the waterway's importance to the region. Other attractions include the **Milton J Rubenstein Museum of Science and Technology**, which has a planetarium and a terrarium with live lakeshore creatures, and **Rosamond Gifford Zoo** in **Burnet Park**, with 14.5 hectares (36 acres) and more than 1000 animals in their natural habitat. The **Everson Museum of Art** features the nation's largest display of US ceramics. Life in the 17th century is recreated at the **Sainte Marie Among the Iroquois Living History Museum**; the Sainte Marie mission was built by the French in 1657 at the invitation of the Iroquois people. The **Canal Center** has a canoe launch and facilities for biking, hiking and picnicking, while visitors to the **Cedarvale Maple Syrup Company** can see how maple syrup is made.
ROCHESTER: The third-largest urban area in New York State, Rochester has more sites on the National Register of Historic Places than any other city its size. Known for its beautiful parks and gardens, the city hosts the celebrated *Lilac Festival* each May. The **Raging Rivers Waterpark**, **Seabreeze Amusement Park** and **Seneca Park Zoo** are all popular entertainment spots. George Eastman, inventor in 1892 of roll film and the Kodak camera, lived here. The **George Eastman House** is a national historical landmark and its outstanding **International Museum of Photography** details the development of the art from the time of Daguerre to the satellite photos of the space age. At the **Rochester Museum and Science Center**, visitors can learn about the Seneca Native Americans through exhibits and artefacts that date from 1550 to 1820. The **Laser, Light & Fireworks Spectacular** in the High Falls District includes interactive 3-D exhibits, including a model flour mill. At nearby **Victor**, the 'capital' of the Seneca people from 1650 to 1687 is preserved at the State Historic Site of **Ganondagan**.
WINE REGION: Viticulture has flourished in the Finger Lakes region for more than a century, and today it is one of the world's leading wine districts. Many wineries offer free guided tours and tasting. All of the area's vineyards and wineries lie on the **Cayuga Wine Trail**, located between **Seneca Falls** and **Trumansburg**, centred around the **Cayuga**, **Keuka** and **Seneca** lakes. The **Greyton H Taylor Wine Museum** in **Hammondsport** details the history and the process of winemaking, while dinner cruises are offered on the **Keuka Maid** and sunny afternoons can be enjoyed at the nearby **Keuka Lake State Park**.
ELSEWHERE: The Finger Lakes region was renowned for the quality of its glass, and the newly renovated **Corning Museum of Glass** in **Corning** has exhibits spanning 3500 years of glass-making. Visitors can still observe craftspeople shaping exquisite glass objects. **Ithaca** is home to the **Sciencenter**, a hands-on science museum and outdoor science playground, the **Herbert F Johnson Museum of Art**, which houses a collection spanning 40 centuries and six continents, and the **Sapsucker Woods Bird Sanctuary**. North of Ithaca, the **Taughannock Falls State Park** features a waterfall higher than Niagara. At **Watkins Glen**, visitors will find the **Hall of Fame** and the **National Motor Racing Museum**. At the north end of **Cayuga Lake** is the **Montezuma National Wildlife Refuge**, a resting and feeding area for more than 235 species of migratory birds.
SPECIAL EVENTS: The following is a selection of special events occurring in Finger Lakes in 2005:
Feb 18-27 *Winterfest 2005*, Syracuse. **Mar 12** *23rd Annual St Patrick's Parade*, Syracuse. **May 13-22** *Lilac Festival*, Rochester. **Jun 4-5** *Fairport Canal Days*, Fairport. **Jul 2-Aug 14** *Sterling Renaissance Festival*. **Jul 15-17** *Finger Lakes Wine Festival*, Watkins Glen. **Jul 16-17** *Rochester MusicFest*. **Aug 14-21** *Seneca Lake Whale Watch Festival*, Geneva. **Aug 25-Sep 5** *New York State Fair*, Syracuse. **Sep 2-4** *New York State Festival of Balloons*. **Nov** *Annual Art Mart*.

The Adirondacks

The Adirondacks region is full of natural attractions – dense forests, craggy mountains, streams, rivers and spring-fed lakes – and historic sites. The region saw many critical skirmishes during the American Revolution and French and Indian Wars. Visitors may choose to tour these battlegrounds, walk in the footsteps of Hawkeye from *The Last of the Mohicans* or meditate in the solitude of a remote Adirondack lake as Ralph Waldo Emerson and Albert Einstein did. The area has long been home to artisans, and local products, known as *Adirondackana*, include the famous Adirondack chair, birch bark picture frames, authentic North Country maple syrup and hand-woven pack baskets.
ADIRONDACK PARK: The Park is the USA's largest wilderness reserve outside Alaska and one of the most successful conservation efforts in history. Created in 1882 to preserve the **Great North Woods** of New York State, the 2.5 million hectare (6 million acre) natural sanctuary is protected under the State Constitution. Roughly the size of Vermont and bigger than the Grand Canyon and Yellowstone national parks combined, the park stretches over nearly one-third of New York State. This rugged land, which looks today very much like it did more than 10,000 years ago, is less than one day's drive from northeastern USA and eastern Canada.
It is the abundance of water – nearly 2500 lakes and ponds and more than 48,000km (30,000 miles) of rivers and streams – that makes the Adirondacks so distinct among the world's great wilderness areas. As recently as the late-19th century, these waters were virtually the only mode of transport in the Adirondacks. Today they are a source of recreation, attracting canoeists, kayakers and whitewater rafters. There are miles of sandy beaches and thousands of secluded swimming holes, broad lakes for windsurfing and boating, and nearly every species of freshwater fish to challenge fishing enthusiasts.
ADIRONDACK MOUNTAINS: The Adirondacks region is home to some of the tallest and most dramatic mountains in the eastern USA. With names like **Giant**, **Skylight** and **Upper Wolfjaw**, the 46 highest Adirondack mountains, known as 'the High Peaks', are situated in the northeastern part of the park. Here, on the summit of the majestic **Mount Marcy**, is the highest point in New York State. Traversing the mountains and surrounding wilderness are more than 3200km (2000 miles) of marked trails for hiking, mountain biking and horseback riding, and extreme pitches off the beaten path to challenge rock climbers.
The Adirondacks are a winter playground, with more than nine different ski areas and thousands of trails for cross-country skiing and snowshoeing. Opportunities for winter camping attract the robust of spirit and there are bob-sleigh rides for those wishing to experience the 'champagne of thrills'. Snowmobilers consistently put the Adirondacks high on their list for its extensive network of trails and great pit stops. There are also dog-sleigh rides and hundreds of frozen lakes on which to skate or go ice-fishing, and several Olympic venues to visit in **Lake Placid**. Other attractions in Lake Placid include the **Adirondack Craft Center** and the **Lake Placid Center for the Arts**. Boat cruises are available from the Marina, while the **Adirondack Scenic Railroad** takes passengers on a 32km- (20 mile-) round trip between Lake Placid and Saranac Lake. Scenic flights over the Adirondack High Peaks are also available.
At the base of the mountains lies **Lake Champlain**, considered the most historic body of water in North America.
SPECIAL EVENTS: The following is a selection of special events occurring in the Adirondacks in 2005:
Feb 4-13 *Winter Carnival*, Saranac Lake. **Feb 25-27** *Empire State Winter Games*, Lake Placid. **Apr 24** *Spring Blossom Fiddle Jamboree*, Long Lake. **Jun 23-26** *Lake Placid Film Festival*. **Jun 28-Jul 10** *Lake Placid Horse Shows*. **Jul 4** *Independence Day Celebrations*, Tupper Lake. **Jul** *HSBC Ironman USA*, Lake Placid. **Aug 12-14** *Lake Placid Art and Craft Festival*. **Sep 9-11** *Canoe Classic*, Old Forge to Saranac Lake. **Sep** *Battle of Plattsburgh Celebration*. **Sep 22-25** *33rd Annual Adirondack Hot Air Balloon Festival*, Queensbury. **Oct 1-2** *'The World's Largest Garage Sale'*, Warrensburg.
All year round, the towns and villages of the Adirondacks are bustling with activity. Throughout the region there are art and craft exhibitions, music festivals, and theatrical performances. There are also good old country fairs, holiday celebrations and sports events of all kinds, including international athletic competitions. Full details can be obtained from the Adirondack Regional Tourism Council (see *Contact Addresses* section).

The Catskills

From the lush greenery of the southern Catskills to the dramatic, unspoiled peaks of the north, there is plenty to occupy visitors, whether they are seeking excitement or the perfect spot for a tranquil stay. The four-county region offers opportunities for a wide range of outdoor activities, from ballooning to rafting and from fishing to skiing. The region lies just 145km (90 miles) north of New York City, and around 30 minutes from *Stewart International Airport*, which is served by five major airlines.
GREENE COUNTY: The home of Washington Irving's legendary Rip Van Winkle, picturesque Greene County is popular with families and offers top-quality skiing in the winter. The **Catskill Game Farm**, open from May to October, is home to more than 2000 animals, including endangered species. It has a petting zoo where visitors can feed animals, and hosts the only chimpanzee act in the USA. Giant waterslides, rafting and swimming pools will keep children entertained at the **Zoom Flume**, the Catskills' largest water park. Just two hours from New York City, the **Hunter Mountain** ski resort is known as 'the snowmaking capital of the world', ensuring plenty of snow throughout the winter. With 53 trails on three mountains, the resort caters for everyone from beginners to experienced skiers. In the summer months, a 1.5km (1 mile) chairlift takes visitors up to a summit lodge. Night skiing is one of the attractions at the resort of **Ski Windham**. Other resorts include **Bobcat**, **Ski Cortina** and **Ski Plattekill**.
SULLIVAN COUNTY: In the south of the region, Sullivan County, along with Ulster County, hosts most of the Catskills' famous resort hotels, where Broadway entertainment and sumptuous dining are staples. Sullivan is noteworthy as the site of the most famous rock concert in history – the 1969 *Woodstock Music and Arts Festival*, commemorated at the **Bethel Woodstock Museum** at **Kauneonga Lake**. Today, **Woodstock** is a haven of art and craft galleries and shops. The **Onteora Trail**, part of Highway 28 which skirts the **Ashokan Reservoir**, makes a good scenic drive to the town. The county is the cradle of modern fly fishing, and the **Catskill Fly Fishing Center and Museum** at **Livingston Manor** is dedicated to preserving the USA's fly-fishing heritage and protecting its environment. The scenic **Delaware River** is also home to the largest wintering population of bald eagles in the northeastern USA.
ULSTER COUNTY: Located where the Catskill Mountains meet the Hudson River, Ulster County is home to a hefty slice of US history. It boasts the largest collection of old stone houses in the USA, built by Dutch and French Huguenot settlers three centuries ago. **Kingston**, New York State's first capital and third-oldest city, features buildings that in 1777 hosted the first State Senate, Assembly and Constitutional Convention. The **1676 Senate House** is the oldest public building in the USA. The maritime heritage of the Hudson River is preserved at the **Hudson River Maritime Museum**, which runs boat rides to the nearby historic **Rondout Lighthouse**. At **Phoenicia**, in the 1899 **Ulster and Delaware Station**, the **Empire State Railway Museum** houses an exhibit relating to the history of the railway in the region. **Esopus Creek** is noted for its fine trout fishing. The ski resort of Belleayre operates a summer chairlift to picnic areas over 1000m (3285ft) high. In the winter, it offers good cross-country skiing and is close enough to New York City for a weekend or even day ski trip.
DELAWARE COUNTY: The Catskills are bordered to the west by Delaware County, which offers excellent antique shopping and is dotted with 19th-century covered bridges. **Hanford Mills Museum**, a vintage water-powered mill, is on the National Register of Historic Places. The **Delaware-Ulster Rail Ride** at **Arkville** takes a scenic route through the Catskill Mountains and allows passengers to experience the thrills of the days when rail was the chief means of cross-country transport and train robberies were not unusual. In **Delhi**, the **Gideon Frisbee Homestead**, built in the 1790s for a local judge, is an outstanding example of early federal architecture.

SPECIAL EVENTS: The following is a selection of special events occurring in the Catskills in 2005:
Apr 1 *Opening of the Trout Season*, Catskill Region. **Apr 23-14** *Annual Hudson Valley Beer and Food Festival*, Hunter Mountain. **Aug 2** *Ulster County Fair*, New Paltz. **Aug 13-14** *German Alps Festival*, Hunter. **Aug 15-20** *Delaware County Fair*, Walton. **Aug 20-21** *International Celtic Festival*, Hunter. **Sep** *Microbrew and Wine Festival*, Hunter. **Oct 2-3** *Oktoberfest*, Hunter.

Capital – Saratoga

The capital of New York State, **Albany**'s attractions include museums, art exhibitions and 19th-century architecture. **Saratoga Springs** is one of the northeast's more accessible resorts, 30 minutes north of Albany and only three hours from Boston, Montréal and New York City. The region is renowned for top-class horse racing and the **Saratoga Race Course** draws thousands of visitors from around the world each year.
ALBANY: The city of Albany stands beside the Hudson River north of New York City and makes a good base from which to explore 'upstate New York'. Albany is dominated by the US$2 billion **Rockefeller Empire State Plaza**, a striking 10-building complex that includes the 44-storey **Corning Tower**, the venerable **State Capitol** and the city's performing arts theatre (nicknamed 'The Egg' for its unusual shape). The **New York State Museum**, the country's oldest and largest State Museum, portrays the urbanisation of New York City and has lifelike dioramas among the exhibits on Native Americans, gems and birds. The **Albany Institute of History and Art** is the oldest museum in the State; its permanent collection of 15,000 objects relate to the art, history and culture of Albany and the Upper Hudson Valley. **St Peter's Church**, notable for its stained glass and floor mosaics, is well worth visiting.
SARATOGA SPRINGS: Saratoga Springs has been a leading spa and horse racing centre since the late-19th century and the streets are lined with regal Victorian mansions. Walking tours of the city's historic districts are available from the *Saratoga Urban Cultural Park Visitors Center*.
Popular attractions include the **Saratoga Raceway** and the **Saratoga Race Course**. The raceway is known as the world's most beautiful harness track and features races nine months a year. The race course hosts the country's most prestigious thoroughbred racing during late July and August. Spectators are welcome at the polo matches held during the summer. Racing fans will appreciate the **National Museum of Racing**, which features hands-on exhibits, while the **Saratoga Harness Hall of Fame** houses a varied collection of harness racing memorabilia.
For those in the mood for something other than horses, a drive over to nearby **Saratoga Spa State Park**, with its 890 hectares (2200 acres) of woods, manicured lawns, Georgian architecture and pavilions, mineral bathhouses and recreational facilities is recommended. The *New York City Opera/Ballet* and the *Philadelphia Orchestra* perform here in the summer at the **Saratoga Performing Arts Center**, which is also the venue for the *Newport Jazz Festival*. In winter, the park offers cross-country skiing and snow shoeing. Also located in the park is the **National Museum of Dance**, the only one of its kind in the country. The **Saratoga National Historic Park** is the site of two important battles which proved to be a turning point in the American Revolution.
Activities on offer include sunrise and sunset hot-air balloon flights. Disney's newest venture, the **Saratoga Springs Resort & Spa** opens with the theme of 'upstate New York - late 1800s'. The resort is opening in phases and when completed, will be the largest Disney Vacation Resort.
ELSEWHERE: Canoeists will enjoy the **Fulton Chain of Lakes**. **Lake George** is the most popular resort region in the southeastern corner of the park. Flower lovers can visit the gardens of **Yaddo**, a legendary artists' retreat. Open to the public every day during daylight hours, some 20,000 people visit the gardens annually.
SPECIAL EVENTS: The following is a selection of special events occurring in Saratoga in 2005:
Feb 4-6 *Winterfest*, Saratoga Springs. **Feb 4-6** *The Albany American Wine Festival*. **Feb 6-27** *Winter Carnival*, Lake George. **Mar 18-20** *Capital District Garden & Flower Show*, Troy. **May 6-8** *Annual Tulip Festival*, Albany. **Jun 25-26** *Jazz Festival*, Saratoga Springs. **Jul** *Fleet Blues Fest*, Albany. **Jul 4** *Independence Day Celebration*, Albany. **Jul 12-17** *Saratoga County Fair*, Ballston Spa. **Aug 16-21** *Altamont Fair* (agricultural exhibit and carnival), Altamont. **Aug 12-14** *Great Northern Catskills Balloon Festival*, Greenville. **Sep 8-10** *Saratoga Global Wine and Food Festival*, Springs Spa State Park. **Sep** *Adirondacks National Car Show*, Lake George. **Sep 10** *Riverfront Jazz Festival*, Albany. **Oct 1-2** *Capital District Apple Festival & Craft Fair*, Altamont. **Oct 9** *Columbus Parade and Italian Festival*, Albany. **Nov-Dec** *Capital Holiday* (over 100 events take place throughout the Capital – Saratoga Region). **Dec** *Victorian Stroll*, Troy. **Dec 5-9** *Northeast Holiday Art & Craft Show*, Albany. **Dec 31** *First Night*, Albany.

Long Island

Located just east of New York City, Long Island is the largest island adjoining the continental USA, stretching 190km (118 miles) into the Atlantic Ocean. Long Island has been the chosen vacation resort of savvy New Yorkers for 100 years and is just being discovered by everyone else. The region is famous for the **Hamptons**, celebrated seaside resorts and fishing villages, and the mansions described in the books of F Scott Fitzgerald. Whale watching and deep-sea fishing, wineries and 'pick-your-own' produce stands are guaranteed to keep visitors occupied. Each region of Long Island – the North Shore, South Shore, South Fork, North Fork and Central Suffolk – offers something special.
For culture seekers, Long Island has 140 museums and historic sites. Sports enthusiasts can watch horse racing, horse jumping and polo, motor racing, hockey, lacrosse, major league baseball, tennis and golf. Sports participants can play golf and tennis, ride horses, hang glide, sky dive, sail and surf. Long Island offers a variety of ever increasing shopping opportunities – from indoor shopping malls such as **Roosevelt Field** in **Garden City**, the East Coast's largest shopping centre, to quaint visitor-oriented shopping villages on historic main streets in places like **Huntington**, **Sea Cliff**, **Stony Brook** and **Syosset**.
NORTH SHORE: The North Shore is known as the 'Heritage Trail', with areas dating back to colonial times, the Revolutionary War era and the earliest days of the nation. Tycoons like the Vanderbilts, Chryslers and Guggenheims spent their summers here in opulent *Great Gatsby*-era mansions and gardens, many of which are open to the public today. **Port Jefferson** offers a historical village, waterside dining and numerous antique shops. Walt Whitman was born on Long Island, and his 19th-century farmhouse, now a State Historic Site, stands in **West Hills**, **Huntington Station**. It includes an interpretive centre with 130 portraits of the poet, original letters, manuscripts and artefacts. Also on the North Shore are the **Museums at Stony Brook**. This 9-acre site includes an art museum with 19th- and 20th-century US works; a **Carriage Museum**, with 90 renowned horse-drawn carriages; and a history museum with changing exhibits on historical themes and 15 miniature period rooms. The **Nassau County Museum of Art**, located in a mansion on the former Frick estate at **Roslyn Harbor** has four major art exhibitions annually, while the **Heckscher Museum of Art** in **Huntington** has a collection spanning 500 years of European and American art.
SOUTH SHORE: The South Shore is a seaside haven, with 80km (50 miles) of ocean beaches, including the beautiful white sand of the **Fire Island National Seashore** and **Jones Beach**. Long Island has an island of its own, the famous Fire Island seaside resort with its restored lighthouse. Cars are forbidden along its 50km- (32 mile-) stretch of communities. This part of the island also features numerous museums, including the **Long Island Maritime Museum**; the **Long Island Children's Museum** with hands-on exhibits and the **Long Island Reptile Museum** with a huge variety of live reptiles and amphibians. The US$34 million world-class **Long Island Aquarium** will be opening in 2005, featuring a six-storey glacier under a glass skylight.
NORTH FORK: The North Fork has preserved the tranquillity of its 17th-century farming and fishing heritage, and features miles of lush farm land with 'pick-your-own' produce stands and acres of vineyards. There are whales to watch far out in the ocean, coastal nature trails to hike and beaches to explore. **Shelter Island**, reminiscent of a peaceful New England village, is located on the North Fork and is perfect for exploring by bicycle. The **Railroad Museum of Long Island** at **Greenport** commemorates the region's railways.
SOUTH FORK: Known as **The Hamptons**, the South Fork offers a mix of culture, restaurants, historic sites, nightlife, shops and recreational activities. Long Island's Native American heritage can be explored in **Southampton**, where the Shinnecock Indians maintain a reservation and present a public pow-wow in early September. The region features the seaside resort of **Montauk**, fishing villages and beaches, one of which, in **East Hampton**, was rated the second most beautiful in the northeastern USA. At **Southampton** is the **Parrish Art Museum**, housing a collection of American and regional art. The **Pollock-Krasner House and Study Center**, the home and studio of abstract expressionist painters Jackson Pollock and Lee Krasner, is also in East Hampton.
CENTRAL SUFFOLK: In the centre of Long Island, Central Suffolk is a favourite with outdoor enthusiasts and features the Pine Barrens, 40,470 hectares (100,000 acres) of preserved forest. The area's rivers flow through wildlife refuges and are ideal for canoeing and kayaking. Other attractions include the new **Atlantis Marine World**, the **SplishSplash Water Park** at **Riverhead** and the **Animal Farm Petting Zoo** at **Manorville**.
SPECIAL EVENTS: The following is a selection of special events occurring in Long Island in 2005:

Credit: © NYS DED

Jan 29 *Teen Night*, Riverhead. **Jun 16-19** *Annual Strawberry Festival*, Mattituck. **Jun 11** *Belmont Stakes* (thoroughbred racing), Belmont Park. **Jul-Aug** *Northville Long Island Golf Classic*, Jericho. **Aug** *Polish Town Festival*, Riverhead; *Norstar/Hamlet Cup Tennis Tournament*, Commack. **Aug-Sep** *Shinnecock Pow Wow*, Shinnecock Indian reservation, Southampton. **Aug 6-8** *Balloon Festival*, Long Island. **Aug 27** *Long Island Scottish Games*, Old Westbury Gardens. **Aug 28-Sep 4** *Hampton Classic Horse Show*, Bridgehampton. **Sep** *Bellmore Street Fair*. **Sep 10** *25th Annual Country & Western Day*, Riverhead. **Oct** *Long Island Fair*, Old Bethpage Restoration Village. **Oct 9** *Country Fair*, Riverhead. **Oct** *Oyster Festival*, Oyster Bay.
There are more than 300 annual festivals and events, such as the maritime and harvest festivals celebrating Long Island's nautical and agricultural heritage, throughout the year.

Thousand Islands – Seaway

The lakes, rivers, islands and forests of this scenic corner of New York State offer the visitor four seasons of fun. The **Thousand Islands** are actually 1870 islands which extend along an 80km- (50 mile-) stretch of the **St Lawrence River** between New York State and Ontario. Attractions include an Amish community, State Parks and sights such as the Thousand Islands, the **Eisenhower Lock** and the **Erie Canal**.
Visitors should not miss a trip to romantic **Boldt Castle** on **Heart Island**. Begun by the owner of the Waldorf-Astoria as a gift for his wife, work on the castle was abandoned after her untimely death. The historic lighthouses at Oswego, Port Ontario, Sackets Harbor, Cape Vincent and Ogdensburg mark the way along **Lake Ontario** and the St Lawrence River. Historic battlefields at **Fort Ontario**, **Little Sandy**, **Ogdensburg** and **Sackets Harbor** commemorate the defence of the frontier of the nation.
The **Minna Anthony Common Nature Center** on **Wellesley Island** offers bird walks, hiking trails, a butterfly house, canoeing and cross-country ski trails in winter. Visitors can tour the **Antique Boat Museum** in **Clayton** and see 150 North American freshwater craft, 250 engines and other nautical memorabilia. Other attractions include the **St Lawrence-FDR Power Project Visitors Center** in **Massena** and the **Frederick Remington Museum** in **Ogdensburg**.
Thousand Islands-Seaway offers a huge choice of accommodation – spectacular resorts, modern hotels and motels, quaint bed & breakfast facilities, cabins and campsites. Visitors can dine, dance and enjoy evenings of nightclub entertainment at the major resorts, complete with luxurious rooms, swimming pools and boat-dockage. There are both public and private campsites, most of which are equipped to serve both tents and recreational vehicles, and many include facilities for swimming, hiking and boating. Tourists can choose from a selection of golf courses or tennis courts, tour the Islands or the Erie Canal on a cruise boat, and watch spectacular sunsets over the St Lawrence River and Lake Ontario. The region is full of opportunities for people who love the outdoors. Sailing, scuba diving and whitewater rafting are popular, as are skiing and snowmobiling in the winter. Some of the best sports fishing in the nation can be found here all-year-round. It's not unusual to see a professional bass or salmon tournament underway on the Lake Ontario, **Oneida Lake** or St Lawrence River.
SPECIAL EVENTS: The following is a selection of special events occurring in Thousand Islands-Seaway in 2005:
Mar 8-10 *Watertown Home Show*. **Apr 8-10** *1000 Islands Annual Spring Boat Show*, Recreation Park Arena Clayton. **Jul 1-5** *Oswego County Fair*, Sandy Creek. **Jul 28-31** *Harborfest 2005*, Oswego. **Oct** *Oktoberfest*. **Dec 2-3** *1000 Islands Christmas Festival*; *Country Home Christmas Tour*.
Summers are enlivened by a wide variety of festivals, old-fashioned county fairs, fishing derbies, regattas, and many high-energy events.

Chautauqua-Allegheny:

Located in the western corner of the State, Chautauqua-Allegheny's natural beauty has made it a popular tourist destination for over a century. The region's many lakes and rivers offer a wide range of outdoor recreational opportunities, complemented by a variety of cultural and historical attractions and the influence of Amish and Native American communities.

CHAUTAUQUA: Chautauqua County, on the southeastern shore of **Lake Erie**, is home to the largest and finest grape-growing region in the East, where local wineries conduct tours of their facilities and offer tastings. Fishing, boating, sailing and water-skiing are popular pastimes at the region's lakes and waterways. From May to September, visitors can enjoy **Chautauqua Lake** aboard the *Chautauqua Belle*, an 1890s replica steam-powered paddle-wheel boat. The **Chautauqua Institution** is a lakeside community occupying 300 hectares (750 acres) in a Victorian setting. Its nine-week summer season, from June to August, offers visitors the best in fine and performing arts, education, recreation and religion. The institution's covered amphitheatre has played host to many outstanding musicians and lecturers including Tony Bennett, Barbara Bush, President Clinton and Anne Murray.

LILY DALE: The *Lily Dale Assembly*, established in 1879 by the 'Free Thinkers', is a community dedicated to the science, philosophy and religion of Spiritualism. A short drive from Lily Dale will lead visitors to Amish country. A society within a society, the Amish community is well known for woodwork, leathercraft, carpentry and rug-making. A variety of Amish handmade crafts are available at local shops, and area restaurants offer a taste of Amish foods.

JAMESTOWN: Birthplace of the world's most famous ornithologist, Roger Tory Peterson, Jamestown is home to the **Roger Tory Peterson Institute of Natural History**, dedicated to informing visitors about the natural world. An art gallery (and its collection of Roger Tory Peterson prints), library, gift shop, butterfly garden and the Institute's headquarters are situated on 11 hectares (27 acres) of woods and meadows. **Fenton Historical Society** is also located nearby. Set in a Civil War-period mansion, the museum includes Victorian memorabilia, Swedish and Italian rooms and early Jamestown genealogy. The **Lucille Ball – Desi Arnaz Museum**, a tribute to the town's most famous daughter, has two annual festivals in late-May and early-August.

SALAMANCA: Salamanca is the only city in the world situated on a Native American reservation. The **Seneca-Iroquois National Museum** highlights the cultural and contemporary heritage of the Seneca and five other tribes that make up the Iroquois Confederacy. The **Salamanca Rail Museum** is a restored passenger depot constructed in 1912 by the Buffalo, Rochester and Pittsburgh Railway. Historic photographs, video representations and artefacts are reminders of a time when rail was the primary means of transport.

The largest State Park in New York, **Allegheny State Park** occupies 26,000 hectares (64,000 acres) and offers excellent facilities for both summer and winter recreation including camping, hiking, fishing and cross-country skiing. The **Allegheny Reservoir** provides excellent canoeing and watersports.

ELSEWHERE: Other attractions in the region include **Griffis Sculpture Park** in **Ashford Hollow**, with 200 pieces of sculpture in a 400-acre woodland setting; **Rock City Park** in **Olean**; **Dunkirk Historical Lighthouse Veterans Park**; **Panama Rocks** with caves, cliffs and wild flowers; the 1891 **Opera House** in **Fredonia**; and **Webb's Candy Factory Tour** in **Mayville**.

SPECIAL EVENTS: The following is a selection of special events occurring in Chautauqua-Allegheny in 2005: **Feb 18** *Ice Castle Extravaganza/Winter Fest*, Mayville. **May** *Maple Syrup Festival*, Gerry. **Jun 8-10** *Great Blue Heron Music Festival*, Sherman. **Jun 27-Aug 29** *Chautauqua Institution Summer Season 2005*. **Jul 4** *Annual Lights over the Lake*, Silver Creek. **Aug 10-14** *61st Annual Gerry Rodeo*; *Nature Art Festival* (view artists at work in their 'studios away from home'), Roger Tory Peterson Institute, Jamestown Audubon Nature Center and the Jamestown Armory. **Sep** *Festival of Grapes*, Silver Creek. **Oct 8-9** *Ellicottville Fall Festival* (one of the largest autumn festivals in the region), Ellicott. **Nov 24** *Thanksgiving with the Birds*, Jamestown.

Central – Leatherstocking

Once considered to be America's western frontier, the Central-Leatherstocking region now ranks in the forefront of world-encompassing sports and Native American memorials. The area is famed for hidden caverns such as **Howe Caverns**, with its massive stone formations and stunning underground lake.

COOPERSTOWN: For more than 50 years the name Cooperstown has been synonymous with baseball. Home of the **National Baseball Hall of Fame and Museum**, **Doubleday Field** and numerous trading card and memorabilia shops, this vibrant village on the shore of **Otesgo Lake** contains some popular museums. The **Farmers' Museum and Village Crossroads** graphically recreates life in the 1880s. Costumed guides work at looms, on the printing press and make brooms on the farm. Meanwhile, ox-carts carry visitors through the complex of buildings. Across the road, two golf courses are laid out along the lake by **Fenimore House**, headquarters of the *New York Historical Association*. Each summer, **Gallery 53 Artworks** mounts a show of 'baseball as art' with paintings, sculpture, wood and metal works defining the athleticism and agility of players as well as historic moments and places associated with the game. The *Glimmerglass Opera* stages productions at the **Alice Busch Opera Theater** throughout July and August.

ONEONTA: A few miles from Cooperstown, the city of Oneonta is home to the **National Soccer Hall of Fame**. Soccer tournaments are held at the **Wright Soccer Campus**, the **State University** facility and the fields of **Harwick College**. The college's **Yager Hall** displays changing exhibitions in addition to artefacts, pottery and baskets from the local Susquehanna River Valley archaeological digs.

HOWES CAVE & AREA: In the heart of the Leatherstocking region at the town of **Howes Cave** are the famous **Howe Caverns**. Visitors to the 10-million-year-old caves, which feature magnificent limestone formations, travel 48m (156 feet) under the earth. Tours of the caverns include a boat ride on the underground **Lake of Venus**. Other attractions in the area include the **Iroquois Indian Museum**, which has exhibits of Native American arts, history and archaeology and includes a **Children's Museum and Nature Park**, and the living museum at the 1743 **Palatine House** at **Schoharie**. The **Howe Caverns Animal Farm** is a favourite with children.

ONEIDA INDIAN NATION: Just off the NY State Thruway (1-90) at exit 3, the Oneida Indian Nation operates a 24-hour, seven-day-a-week gaming facility, the only casino in the State. Four elegant restaurants, no-smoking blackjack areas and slotless games are among the amenities on offer. **Vernon Downs**, a nearby harness (standardbred) racing facility, features a new hotel on its grounds. *Traditions with a Future* examines the heritage, artefacts and culture of the nation at its white pine log **Shakowi Cultural Center**. At exit 34 stands the **International Boxing Hall of Fame**, a storehouse of gloves, robes and other mementos of pugilists from around the world. Each year in early June, new members are initiated into the hall with a weekend of ceremonies, exhibition bouts and public meetings. The **Canal Museum** depicts how this impressive cross-state waterway was constructed. A side trip to the **Chittenango Landing Canal Boat Museum** shows where packet boats were dry-docked for repair and upkeep.

ROME: The **Erie Canal Village** in Rome is where construction of the canal actually began. Some 20 buildings were moved here to create a replica of a canal-side town, complete with church and tavern. On a section of the 1825 waterway, visitors can ride on a packet boat pulled by mules. Travellers can also rent their own packet boats at **Troy** and **Skaneateles** for self-steered trips on the canal. Several communities on the route provide tour-boat trips on the enlarged, turn-of-the-century canal.

Outside Rome is **Delta Lake**, a new 2000m- (6500ft-) long rowing course.

SPECIAL EVENTS: The following is a selection of special events occurring in Central - Leatherstocking in 2005: **Mar 6-27** *Sugaring Off* (Sundays only - traditional maple-sugaring activities), Cooperstown. **Jul-Aug** *Honor America Days Celebration*, Rome. **Aug** *Canal Fest*, Sylvan Beach. **Aug 19-21** *Annual New York State Woodsmen's Field Days*, Boonville. **Sep** *Remsen Barn Festival*. **Oct 10** *Columbus Day Parade*, Rome.

Climate

The climate is changeable with moderate rainfall throughout the year. During the summer, heatwaves are common, with temperatures staying at over 99°F (37°C) for several days.

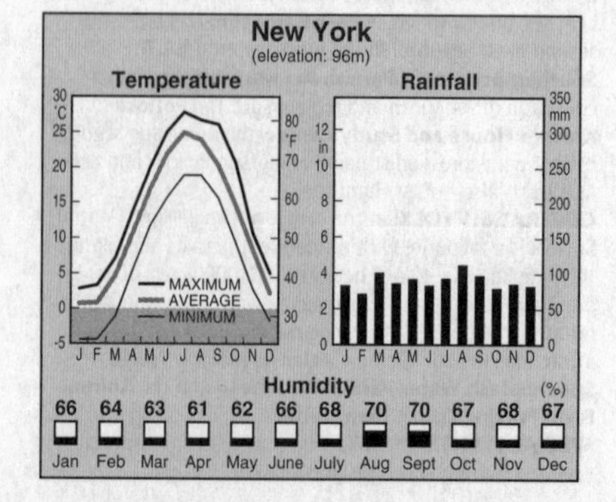

North Carolina

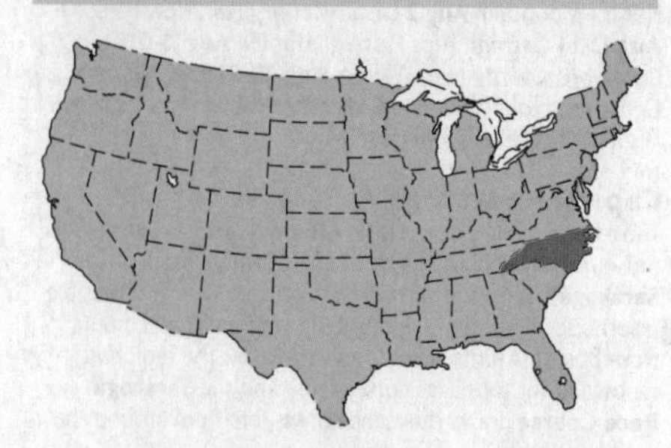

North Carolina Division of Tourism, Film and Sports Development
301 North Wilmington Street, Raleigh, NC 27601
Tel: (919) 733 4171 *or* (800) 847 4862 (brochure requests; toll-free). Fax: (919) 715 3097.
Website: www.visitnc.com

North Carolina Division of Tourism (UK Office)
c/o Hills Balfour, Notcutt House, 36 Southwark Bridge Road, Lonson SE1 9EU, UK
Tel: (020) 7202 6368. Fax: (020) 7928 0722.
E-mail: northcarolina@hillsbalfour.com
Website: www.visitnc.co.uk

Greater Raleigh CVB
421 Fayetteville Street Mall, Suite 1505, Raleigh, NC 27602
Tel: (919) 834 5900 *or* (800) 849 8499 (toll-free).
Fax: (919) 831 2887.
E-mail: visit@visitraleigh.com
Website: www.visitraleigh.com

Asheville CVB
Street address: 151 Haywood Street, Asheville, NC 28801
Postal address: PO Box 1010, Asheville, NC 28802
Tel: (828) 258 6102 *or* (800) 257 5583 (toll-free; visitor information). Fax: (828) 254 6054.
E-mail: visit@exploreasheville.com
Website: www.exploreasheville.com

Charlotte CVB
500 South College Street, Suite 300, Charlotte, NC 28202
Tel: (704) 334 2282 *or* (800) 722 1994 (toll-free).
Fax: (704) 342 3972.
E-mail: info@visitcharlotte.com
Website: www.visitcharlotte.com

Durham CVB
101 East Morgan Street, Durham, NC 27701
Tel: (919) 687 0288 *or* (800) 446 8604 (toll-free).
Fax: (919) 683 9555.
E-mail: visitorinfo@durham-cvb.com
Website: www.durham-nc.com

General Information

Nickname: Tar Heel State
State bird: Cardinal
State bird/flower: Flowering Dogwood
CAPITAL: Raleigh
Date of admission to the Union: 21 Nov 1789 (original 13 States; date of ratification of the Constitution)
POPULATION: 9,541,221 (official estimate 2004)
POPULATION DENSITY: 68.4 per sq km
2003 total overseas arrivals/US ranking: 252,000/18
TIME: Eastern (GMT - 5). *Daylight Saving Time* is observed.

THE STATE: Natural attractions in North Carolina range from sandy beaches in the east to high mountain ranges in the west. Fringed by 480km (300 miles) of beaches, islands and inlets, the North Carolina coast is renowned for its fishing, boating and other recreational opportunities. The **Heartland**, often referred to as 'the Piedmont', is composed of gently rolling plains that host picturesque golf courses, lakes and farmland, as well as the State's largest urban areas. **Charlotte**, the largest city, is a thriving convention and entertainment centre. The **Outer Banks Barrier Islands** along the coast include resorts, fishing villages and stretches of national seashore. **Cape Hatteras National Seashore** also boasts areas of undeveloped beach. Western North Carolina is bounded by two ranges of the southern **Appalachians**, the **Blue Ridge Mountains** and the **Great Smoky Mountains**, with peaks exceeding 1800m (6000ft). Other attractions include **Raleigh**, with its fine architecture and cultural centres, and the **Qualla Boundary Cherokee Indian Reservation**.

Travel - International

AIR: International airports: *Charlotte/Douglas International (CLT)* (website: www.charlotteairport.com), 13km (8 miles) west of Charlotte, offers direct domestic and international services to more than 150 cities, with over 500

daily flights. The *Carolina Transportation Airport Express* shuttle service operates to the uptown area, major hotels and most business districts. Car hire and fixed-fare taxis are also available.
Raleigh-Durham International (RDU) (website: www.rdu.com) is situated 6km (4 miles) from the Research Triangle Park. The *Raleigh/Durham Shuttle* leaves every 30 minutes to the city centre (travel time - 15 minutes). Taxis are also available.
RAIL: A number of *Amtrak* (tel: (800) 872 7245 (toll-free); website: www.amtrak.com) routes pass through the State, including a daily New York–Miami (via Orlando) 'Silver Service' trains (stopping in Raleigh) and the New York–New Orleans 'Crescent', which stops at Charlotte. The 'Piedmont' provides a daily passenger train service from Raleigh to Charlotte, while the 'Carolinian' runs a daily service from Charlotte to Raleigh. The latter train continues on to Washington, DC and New York City. Transfers to the Silver Service trains are possible in Raleigh, Wilson and Rocky Mount. The station in Raleigh is located at 320 West Cabarrus Street, while the Charlotte station can be found at 1914 North Tryon Street.
ROAD: North Carolina has a good road network of highways and scenic byways allowing easy access to all parts of the State. *Interstate 40* is the major east–west artery, crossing the State from Wilmington on the Atlantic Coast to the Great Smoky Mountains, via Raleigh, Durham and Winston-Salem; the I-85 links it with Charlotte. A State-wide system of designated Bicycling Highways covers 4830km (3000 miles) of roads. There are many bus companies serving the area, including *Greyhound* (tel: (800) 229 9424 (toll-free); website: www.greyhound.com) services, with stops at many destinations within the State, including Chapel Hill, Charlotte, Durham, Raleigh and Winston-Salem.
Approximate bus travel times: From Raleigh to *Durham* is 35 minutes, to *Chapel Hill* is one hour 20 minutes, to *Richmond* is three to fpur hours and to *North Charleston* is eight hours. From Durham to *Chapel Hill* is 35 minutes and to *Washington, DC* is six hours. From Asheville to *Charlotte* is three hours, to *Knoxville* is three hours and to *Atlanta* is seven hours.
URBAN: The *Triangle Transit Authority* (website: www.ridetta.org) provides a bus service between the metropolitan areas of Raleigh, Durham, Cary and Chapel Hill.

Resorts & Excursions

OUTER BANKS REGION: This region was selected as the site for the first English colony in the USA, but the attempt failed. This important part of North Carolina's history is recreated every year in an outdoor play, The *Lost Colony*, performed from June to August. Outer Banks was also where the Wright brothers made the first powered flight in 1903, commemorated at the **Wright Brothers Memorial** at **Kitty Hawk**. Today, the Outer Banks offers beach resorts and magnificent wildlife reserves in the south. Attractions along the **Cape Hatteras National Seashore** include the Outer Banks ponies, **Bodie Island** and the Hatteras lighthouses which are among the oldest in the country. A few miles inland, the USA's past is revealed in the historic **Albemarle** region, in which the towns of **Bath**, **Edenton**, **Halifax** and **Washington** are located.
New Bern is the State's first capital and second-oldest town. The restored **Tryon Palace** and surrounding buildings transport visitors back to the 18th century. Also in New Bern is the **Fireman's Museum**, formed by the two oldest continuously operated fire companies in the USA. Included in the exhibits is 'Fire Horse Fred', who pulled the fire-hose wagon for 17 years. He died in 1925 while pulling the fire wagon to a false alarm. A 40-minute drive from New Bern is the **Crystal Coast** area, which includes the deep-sea port of **Morehead City**, the historic waterfront town of **Beaufort** and many beautiful beaches.
Wilmington is North Carolina's largest seaport. The **Cotton Exchange**, a 19th-century structure converted into shops and boutiques, once exported more cotton than any other port in the world. Across the river sits the **USS North Carolina Battleship Memorial**, a World War II battleship. Her story is told on summer nights in 'The Immortal Showboat', a spectacular sound and light show.
HEARTLAND REGION: The State capital, **Raleigh**, is a relaxed, historic town with a thriving arts community. It is the home of the nation's first State symphony and museum of art: the **North Carolina Museum of Art** has eight galleries with works by Botticelli, Monet, Raphael and Rubens. Other attractions include the **North Carolina Museum of History**, the **Museum of Natural Sciences** and the **Exploris Center and IMAX Theatre**. **Chapel Hill** is the setting for the **University of North Carolina**, the oldest State-supported institution in the country. **North Carolina Botanical Gardens** contain almost every plant found in the State, and the **Morehead Planetarium** is where more than 100 of the USA's astronauts trained before venturing into space. A new convention centre is currently being built in downtown Raleigh, slated to open in early 2007.
Durham, known as 'The City of Medicine', is the home of the world-famous **Research Triangle Park** and **Duke University** with its lovely chapel and gardens. Other attractions include **Bennett Place**, site of the largest surrender of the Civil War, the **Tobacco Museum** and the historic **Stagville Center**.
Charlotte is the State's largest city and is rich in commerce and industry. **Discovery Place** features hands-on exhibits of science and technology for all ages. The State's biggest theme park, **Carowinds**, lies 10 minutes south of Charlotte. It pays tribute to the film *Wayne's World* with a white-knuckle ride called *Hurler*. Located northeast of Charlotte, **Old Salem** is a preserved and restored 18th-century Moravian village. Attractions include the new US$10 million **Old Salem Visitor Center** offering tours of the districts, the **St Philips Moravian Church** (the oldest extant African-American church in North Carolina), the **Old Salem Toy Museum** and the restored **Herbst House**.
CAROLINA MOUNTAINS: To the west are the magnificent North Carolina Mountains, including **Mount Mitchell** (2040m/6684ft), the highest peak in Eastern America. 200 peaks in the **Appalachian Mountain chain** reach more than 1.6km (1 mile) high. A great way to see the area is along the scenic **Blue Ridge Parkway** which winds along the spine of the **Blue Ridge** and **Great Smoky Mountains**. Within easy reach of the parkway are numerous small mountain towns. **Tweetsie Railroad** has a steam locomotive that carries passengers through mountain passes and a frontier village. The parkway also leads to **Asheville**, where George Vanderbilt's elaborate 225-room **Biltmore Estate** is located. The estate includes a winery with a visitor centre, tasting room and shop where bottles of the local vintage are sold. **Grove Park Inn Resort** is also situated nearby. The list of people who have stayed at this high-class hotel includes Thomas Edison, F Scott Fitzgerald, Henry Ford, Franklin D. Roosevelt and Woodrow Wilson.

Social Profile

FOOD & DRINK: Numerous festivals are held annually in North Carolina in honour of favourite foods, including apples, watermelons, seafood, turkey, pickles and collard greens. (See *Special Events* below for further details of food festivals.) Local specialities include sweet potato pie, fried okra and buttered lima beans. Other dishes that regularly feature on menus in North Carolina include roast chicken with pecans, country ham with red-eye gravy and chocolate pecan torte with whipped cream. Seafood lovers should head for Calabash, which locals boast is 'the seafood capital of the world'. Barbecues are also very popular, particularly in Lexington, North Carolina's barbecue capital, which has more barbecue restaurants *per capita* than any other area in the country. Barbecue sauce is an often keenly debated subject. Eastern Carolina barbecue features a vinegar-based sauce, while western Carolinians use a tomato-based sauce. Barbecue is often served with coleslaw, hush puppies and baked beans.
THEATRE & CONCERTS: North Carolina's State theatre, the **Flat Rock Playhouse**, is the oldest professional summer theatre in the State and its *Vagabond Players* are rated as one of the best summer stock theatre companies in the country. The **Brevard Music Center**, near Flat Rock, offers a summer season in which guest artists perform more than 50 different concerts. Raleigh is home to the **BTI Center of Performing Arts**, with the **Fletcher Opera Theatre**, **Kennedy Theatre**, **Memorial Auditorium** and **Meymandi Concert Hall**. The *Broadway South*, *Carolina Ballet*, *NC Symphony*, *NC Theatre* and *Off-Broadway South* all perform here.
NIGHTLIFE: Student bars dominate the university towns of Chapel Hill, Durham and Raleigh; top rock bands appear at the **Cat's Cradle** club in Carrboro. Charlotte offers a wide range of entertainment, including nightclubs and bars around the **Uptown Entertainment District**.
SHOPPING: North Carolina's aquariums offer workshops for coastal crafts and include shops selling unusual gifts. They are located in Manteo on Roanoke Island, Kure Beach

Credit: © North Carolina Division of Tourism

and Pine Knoll Shores. Brevard is also popular for its many craft centres and shops. The world's largest furniture market is located in High Point near Winston-Salem. **Concord Mills**, just north of Charlotte, has over 200 outlet and speciality shops, restaurants and a 24-screen cinema.
SPORT: The 21,000-seat multi-purpose **RBC Center in Raleigh** is home to the popular ice hockey team, the *Carolina Hurricanes*, and hosts other sporting events, such as football and motorcross racing, as well as popular music events and other acts. The dirt-track racing in **Wayne County**, sports car racing at the **Chimney Rock Hill Climb**, drag racing at **Fayetteville International Dragway**, and NASCAR races at **Charlotte Motor Speedway**, are just some of the exciting motorsports events in the State. **Pinehurst** is recognised as the centre of **golf** in North Carolina, but there are more than 600 courses spread across the State, including **Brick Landing**, **Lockwood Folly**, **Marsh Harbor**, **Oyster Bay**, **The Pearl** and **Sea Trail**. Other popular sporting activities include **cycling**, **horse riding**, **tennis**, **watersports** and **archery**.
SPECIAL EVENTS: The following is a selection of special events occurring in North Carolina in 2005:
Feb 2 *Groundhog Day Celebration*, Raleigh. **Feb 13** *25th Annual Run of the Roses*, Raleigh. **Feb 18** *14th Annual Native American Powwow*, Durham. **Apr 1-2** *27th Annual Newport Pig Cookin' Contest*, Raleigh. **Apr 22-24** *North Carolina Pickle Festival*, Faison. **Apr 28-May 1** *Merle Fest*, Wilkesboro. **Jun 18** *2005 US Open*, Raleigh; *Bluegrass Experience*, Raleigh. **Aug 20** *Shindig on the Green*, Asheville. **Sep 22-25** *Festival in the Park*, Charlotte. **Oct 8-9** *John Blue Cotton Festival*, Larinburg. **Oct 15** *Yodkin Valley Pumpkin Festival*, Elkin. **Oct 22** *Barbecue Festival*, Lexington. **Nov 15** *Veteran's Celebration*, Kenansville. **Dec 2-4** *Festival of Lights*, Greensboro. **Dec 3** *Winterfest*, Jacksonville.

Climate

North Carolina has a moderate climate with an average year-round temperature of 61°F (16°C). The climate varies sharply with altitude, with the State's Atlantic coastline naturally warmer than the mountains in the west.

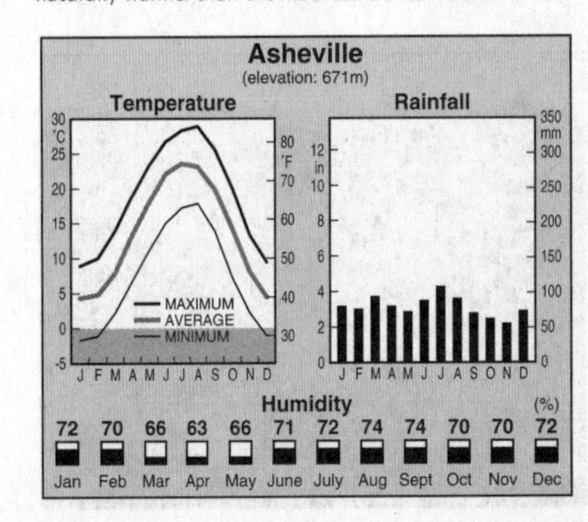

North Dakota

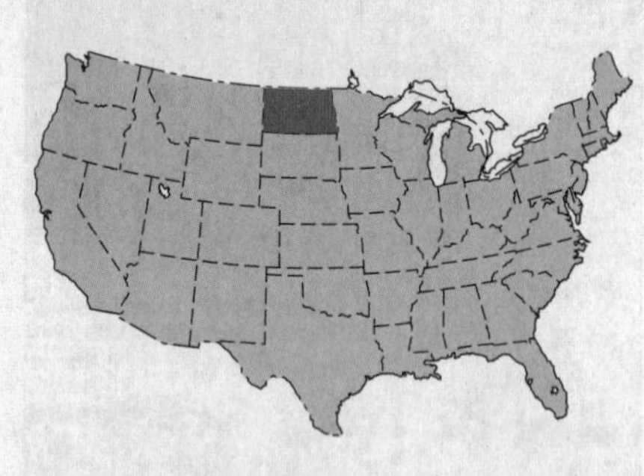

North Dakota Tourism Division
Street address: Century Center, 1600 East Century Avenue, Suite 2, Bismarck, ND 58503
Postal address: PO Box 2057, Bismarck, ND 58502
Tel: (701) 328 2525 *or* (800) 435 5663 (toll-free).
Fax: (701) 328 4878.
E-mail: tourism@state.nd.us
Website: www.ndtourism.com
Fargo-Moorhead CVB
2001 44th Street, SW, Fargo, ND 58103
Tel: (701) 282 3653 *or* (800) 235 7654 (toll-free).
Fax: (701) 282 4366.
E-mail: info@fargomoorhead.org
Website: www.fargomoorhead.org

General Information

Nickname: Peace Garden State
State bird: Western Meadowlark
State flower: Wild Prairie Rose
CAPITAL: Bismarck
Date of admission to the Union: 2 Nov 1889
POPULATION: 634,366 (official estimate 2004)
POPULATION DENSITY: 3.7 per sq km
2003 total overseas arrivals: Under 38,000
TIME: Central (GMT - 6) in the greater part of the State; Mountain (GMT - 7) in the west. *Daylight Saving Time* is observed.

THE STATE: North Dakota, one of the most rural States in the USA, is famous for its scenery and Old West heritage. **Fargo**, on the eastern border, is the State's largest city. The metropolitan area of Fargo-Moorhead is a prime tourist destination, with attractions such as **Plains Art Museum**, **Red River Zoo**, **Fargo Air Museum**, **Children's Museum at Yunker Farm** and **Bonanzaville** (a restored pioneer village). The **Reineke Fine Arts Center**, at the North Dakota State University, has music, theatre and other events, while the nearby **FargoDome** hosts the NDSU football team, as well as other sporting events and popular music acts.
The 28,329 hectare (70,000 acre) **Theodore Roosevelt National Park** set in the Badlands of western North Dakota offers spectacular views and includes the restored cow-town of **Medora**. The park takes its name from Theodore Roosevelt, who bought **Elkorn Ranch** here after his wife and his mother died on the same day on 14 Feb 1884. He found inspiration among the quiet canyons of 'rough-rider country', famously declaring 'I never would have been President if it weren't for my experiences in North Dakota'. The **South Unit** of the park features a 58km (36 mile) scenic automobile loop, an excellent way to see this area. On the loop itself, **Wind Canyon** is a constantly evolving site, formed by winds blowing against the soft clay. Still in the park, **Peaceful Valley Ranch** offers a variety of horseback excursions, while **Maltese Cross Cabin**, Roosevelt's first cabin in the State, is still open to the public today.

Credit: © North Dakota Tourism Division

Fort Abraham Lincoln, south of Mandan, was the final command and home of Lt Colonel George Custer, where he and his Seventh Cavalry departed for the Battle of Little Bighorn. On 25 June 1876, Custer's entire command of 265 men was wiped out in a 20-minute battle with the Sioux, led by Sitting Bull, Gall and Crazy Horse. It is still possible to see Custer's house and inspect the commissary and barracks of this famous fort. The **On-A-Slant Indian Village** nearby traces the area's history from the first Native American settlements. Other North Dakota attractions include the recreation areas around **Lake Sakakawea** and the **Little Missouri River**; the **Fort Union Trading Post** and **Knife River Indian Villages National Historic Sites**; the **Custer House**, **Fort Lincoln**; and the **Lewis and Clark Interpretive Center**.

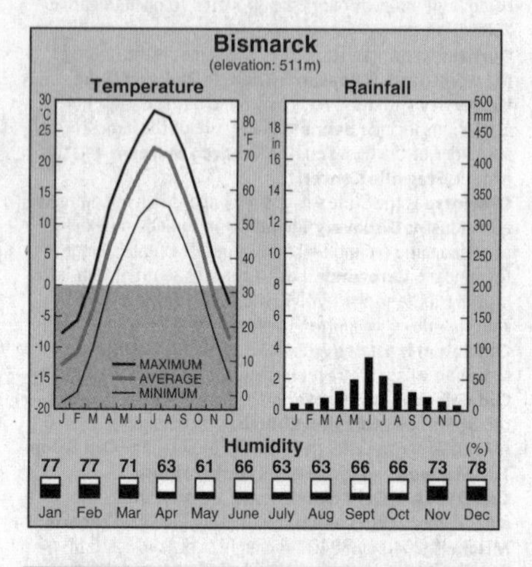

Ohio

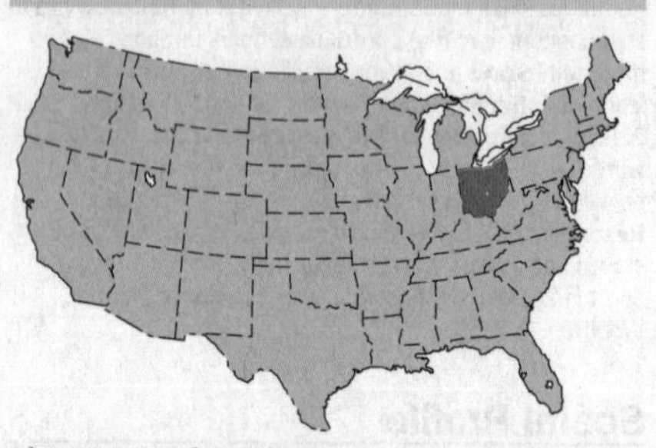

Ohio Division of Travel & Tourism
Street address: 77 South High Street, 29th Floor, Columbus, OH 43216
Postal address: PO Box 1001, Columbus, OH 43216
Tel: (614) 466 8844 *or* (800) 282 5393.
Fax: (614) 466 6744.
E-mail: tbrown@odod.state.oh.us
Website: www.ohiotourism.com *or* www.discoverohio.com
Experience Columbus
90 North High Street, Columbus, OH 43215
Tel: (614) 221 6623 *or* (800) 354 2657 (toll-free).
Fax: (614) 221 5618.
Website: www.experiencecolumbus.com
Greater Cincinnati CVB
300 West Sixth Street, Cincinnati, OH 45202
Tel: (513) 621 2142 *or* (800) 543 2613 (toll-free).
Fax: (513) 621 5020.
Website: www.cincyusa.com
CVB of Greater Cleveland
50 Public Square, 3100 Terminal Tower, Cleveland, OH 44113
Tel: (216) 621 4110 *or* (800) 321 1001 (toll-free).
Fax: (216) 621 5967 *or* 623 4499 (tourism).
E-mail: cvb@travelcleveland.com
Website: www.travelcleveland.com

General Information

Nickname: Buckeye State
State bird: Cardinal
State flower: Scarlet Carnation
CAPITAL: Columbus
Date of admission to the Union: 1st Mar 1803
POPULATION: 11,459,011 (official estimate 2004)
POPULATION DENSITY: 98.7 per sq km
2003 total overseas arrivals/US ranking: 324,000/16
TIME: Eastern (GMT - 5). *Daylight Saving Time* is observed.
THE STATE: Ohio, birthplace of eight US Presidents, is located in the heart of the Midwest. The sandy shores of **Lake Erie** mark the State's northern border and the long and winding **Ohio River** marks its southern border. The State's expanse of fertile farmland is dotted with industrial centres, but also embraces the rolling hills overlooking the **Scioto River Valley** in the north, which become wilder and steeper as they reach the foothills of the **Appalachian mountain chain**, and the thick forest lands full of waterfalls and sandstone cliffs in the south, which include **Hockings Hills State Park** and the vast **Wayne National Forest**. The **Cuyahoga Valley National Recreation** area in the northeast near **Cleveland** has rugged terrain with river valleys and steep, forested hills. The State also has 40,869km (25,543 miles) of waterways, including the **Mohican** and **Tuscarawas rivers**. **Columbus** is Ohio's capital and is the largest city in both area and population – it is the 15th-largest city in the USA.

Travel - International

AIR: International airports: *Cincinnati/Northern Kentucky (CVG)* (website: www.cvgairport.com) is 19km (12 miles) southwest of the city centre (travel time - 15 minutes). In addition to the national carriers, Comair, a Cincinnati-based regional airline, offers flights. *Air France* and *Delta Air Lines* both offer non-stop services to Paris, France (travel time - eight hours). *TANK* public buses (website: www.tankbus.org) run between the airport and downtown Cincinnati and Covington daily (0500-0000; travel time - 30 minutes); buses stop outside Terminals 1 and 3. *Airport Executive Shuttle* buses serve the city centre and the Kentucky side of the river; drop-offs at various points en route can be arranged. Taxis, limousine services and car hire from *Alamo*, *Avis*, *Budget*, *Dollar*, *Hertz*, *National* and *Thrifty* are also available.
Cleveland Hopkins International Airport (CLE) (website: www.clevelandairport.com) is 18km (10 miles) southwest of the city centre (travel time – 20 minutes). The *Greater Cleveland Regional Transit Authority (RTA)* offers a rapid transit service departing every 15 minutes between the airport and Tower City Center (travel time – 20 minutes), where connections to other bus and rail services are available. Taxis, limousines and car hire (*Alamo*, *Avis*, *Budget*, *Dollar*, *Enterprise*, *Hertz*, *National* and *Thrifty*) are also available.
Port Columbus International Airport (CMH) (website: www.port-columbus.com) is located 11km (7 miles) northeast of downtown Columbus. Taxis, limousines and shuttle buses to the city centre are available, as is the *Capital City Flyer* bus, operated by *Central Ohio Transit Authority (COTA)*.
Approximate flight times: From Cincinnati to *London* is nine hours, to *New York* is one hour 30 minutes, to *Los Angeles* is four hours 15 minutes, to *Miami* is two hours 15 minutes, and to *Washington, DC* is one hour.
From Cleveland to *Cincinnati* is one hour 15 minutes, and to *New York* is one hour 40 minutes.
RIVER: There are over 1600km (1000 miles) of canals in Ohio and there are many canal boat excursions available.
RAIL: A number of *Amtrak* (tel: (800) 872 7245 (toll-free); website: www.amtrak.com) services run west-east across the State, emanating from Chicago. The line through Toledo splits at Cleveland, with one line travelling to New York City and Boston (via Buffalo) and the other passing through Pittsburgh en route to Washington, DC or Philadelphia and New York City. A parallel line from Chicago to Pittsburgh passes through Akron daily. The Chicago to Washington, DC service via Indianapolis and Cincinnati only runs three days a week. For journey times, see the *Illinois* section. Ohio also offers a number of scenic railway excursions run by private operators, often on historic trains.
ROAD: Bus: *Greyhound* (tel: (800) 229 9424 (toll-free); website: www.greyhound.com) offers services throughout the State.
Approximate bus travel times: From Cincinnati to *Louisville* is two hours, to *Columbus* is two hours, to *Indianapolis* is two hours 30 minutes, to *Cleveland* is five hours, to *Detroit* is six hours, to *Pittsburgh* is six hours, to *Knoxville* is six hours 30 minutes, to *Chicago* is seven hours, to *St Louis* is eight hours, to *Atlanta* is 12 hours, to *Washington, DC* is 12 hours, and to *New York* is 15 hours.
From Cleveland to *Pittsburgh* is three hours, to *Detroit* is four hours, to *Buffalo* is four hours, to *Toronto* is seven hours, to *Chicago* is seven hours 30 minutes, to *Washington, DC* is nine hours, and to *New York* is nine hours 30 minutes.
From Columbus to *Cleveland* is three hours, to *Pittsburgh* is four hours, to *Indianapolis* is four hours, to *St Louis* is nine hours, to *Washington, DC* is 10 hours, and to *New York* is 13 hours.
URBAN: The Cincinnati bus system offers services throughout Hamilton County and portions of Clermont County. In addition to numerous bus routes, Cleveland's *Regional Transit Authority* has three rapid-transit lines that meet at downtown's *Tower City Center Station*. Taxis are available in the major cities.

Resorts & Excursions

Major Cities

CINCINNATI: Cincinnati offers a variety of museums and galleries, fine dining and excellent shopping. The **National Underground Railroad Freedom Center** focuses on the struggle for freedom experienced by runaway slaves and opened in August 2004. It is the first of its kind in the USA and features five history galleries, a changing exhibits gallery, a theatre, and research and education centres, as well as the **Underground Railroad Children's Exhibit and Slave Jail**. The **Contemporary Arts Center** (painting, sculpture, photography and other media) moved to its current home, the **Lois & Richard Rosenthal Center for Contemporary Art**, fairly recently, and the **Cincinnati Art Museum** (masterpieces and African-American art) gained a wing and a free admission policy. The **Cincinnati Zoo & Botanical Garden** also boasts new attractions for 2005, while the **Taft Museum of Art** underwent its grand reopening in May 2004 after a US$22 million renovation and expansion. Cincinnati's museums include the **Behringer-Crawford Museum** (archaeology, palaeontology, wildlife, history and art); **Harriet Beecher Stowe House** (home of the author of *Uncle Tom's Cabin*); the **Skirball Museum** (Jewish history, artefacts, ceremonial objects and paintings); and the **Museum Center at Cincinnati Union Terminal**, where the **Cincinnati Historical Museum** and the **Cincinnati Museum of Natural History** are housed in an Art Deco train station; a 'Baseball as America' exhibition will delight sports fans. Other attractions include riverboat and steamboat cruises on the **Ohio River**; the **Basilica of the Assumption**, with the largest stained-glass window in the world; the **Kentucky Horse Center**, an escorted tour of a working thoroughbred-training facility; **Kentucky Horse Park**, a museum celebrating the horse (where horse riding is also available); and the **William Howard Taft National Historic Site**, the birthplace of the former US President.

CLEVELAND: Cleveland is a city of turn-of-the-century architecture and grand public monuments, with diverse neighbourhoods and miles of lakefront park and beaches. Cleveland's museums include the **African-American Museum**; the **Crawford Auto-Aviation Museum** (with over 200 vintage cars and aircraft); **Hower House** (a 28-room Victorian mansion); the **Kent State University Museum** (a fashion museum); the **Temple Tifereth-Israel Museum**; and **Trolleyville** (a streetcar and locomotive museum). Other attractions include the **Cleveland Botanical Garden** (with a flower show modeled on London's famous Chelsea Flower Show, showing May 27-30 2005) and the **HealthSpace Cleveland** (formerly the *Health Museum of Cleveland*), in the Fairfax neighbourhood, housing both permanent and temporary exhibits, as well as containing an education centre, two laboratories, an auditorium and a kitchen (for culinary courses).

The **Steamship William G Mather** (a floating steamship museum), the **Great Lakes Science Center** (with over 375 hands-on exhibits), and the **Rock'n'Roll Hall of Fame and Museum** are among the highlights in the North Coast Harbor area. **The Flats**, once the centre of heavy industry, is the primary entertainment district. The **Historic Warehouse District** is on the National Register of Historic Places and has some of Cleveland's finest architecture, as well as art galleries, restaurants and shops. **University Circle**, 8km (5 miles) east of downtown, is the cultural centre of Cleveland, thanks to the **Cleveland Museum of Art** (Asian, medieval and 19th-century European art), the **Cleveland Museum of Natural History** and the **Cleveland Children's Museum**.

The **Nathan and Fannye Shafran Planetarium** and the **Ralph Perkins II Wildlife Center & Woods Garden**, with a massive outdoor gallery with live animals and birds, are situated within the **Museum of Natural History**. Located in the terminal lobby of the **Burke Lakefront Airport**, in downtown Cleveland, the **International Women's Air & Space Museum** focuses on women's achievements in these fields, with an **OMNIMAX Theater** to enhance the experience. The **African Safari Wildlife Park** is the Midwest's only drive-through safari, while **Cleveland Metroparks Zoo** and the **Rainforest**, south of the city centre, is the seventh-oldest zoo in the country, with more than 3300 animals. The Rainforest features animals and insects in realistic habitats, with simulated tropical thunderstorms and an 8m- (25ft-) high waterfall. Visitors are able to see vets at work when the new Zoological Medicine facility opens. Also in the Metroparks are the **Ohio & Erie Canal Reservation** and **Cuyahoga Valley National Recreation Area** facilities.

East of the city, the **Holden Arboretum** is the largest in the USA.

COLUMBUS: Columbus, the largest city in Ohio, is home to the **Children's Museum**, the excellent **Ohio Historical Center** (exploring the history of the Ohio region along with exhibitions of decorative arts); **Ohio Village** (a recreated pre-Civil War town); the **Wexner Center for the Arts**; the **Columbus Museum of Art** (European Impressionist, post-Impressionist and German Expressionist masterpieces); **Ohio's Center of Science and Industry**; and the restored boyhood home of the writer/cartoonist James Thurber. Two of the most interesting neighbourhoods are the lavishly restored **German Village**, with superb architecture, fine restaurants and taverns, and the 27-acre **Brewery District**, the vintage beer-making factories of which now contain restaurants, speciality shops and taverns. The **Columbus Zoo & Aquarium** also contains **The Roadhouse**, featuring Australian, Indonesian and Southeast Asian Island wildlife. Other attractions include **Wyandot Lake Amusement and Water Park**, with 13 water slides and a wave pool; a replica of the **Santa Maria**, moored on the **Scioto River**; **Franklin Park Conservatory**, a crystal palace with tropical plants and recreations of seven ecosystems; and the **Short North Gallery District**, with contemporary galleries and shops selling everything from glass sculpture to secondhand clothing.

The Rest of the State

THE SOUTHEAST: With its high hills, steep ravines and beautiful **waterfalls**, this region is known as Ohio's outback and can be observed in **Wayne National Forest** and from **Archer's Fork Loop**, a 15km- (9.5 mile-) hiking trail. **Hocking Hills State Park** is home to **Ash Cave** (Ohio's largest recess cave, with a 27m- (90ft-) high waterfall), **Cedar Falls**, **Rock House** (a series of large rooms mysteriously carved into the side of a cliff), the 46m- (150ft-) high **Cantwell Cliffs** and **Hocking Forest**, where rock climbing is permitted.

Chillicothe, Ohio's first capital, is surrounded by historical sites such as the **Hopewell Culture National Historical Park**, one of the greatest concentrations of Hopewell Native American burial sites. The town also offers the **Adena State Memorial**, built in 1807, and **Ross County Historical Society Museum**. The town of **Marietta** was the first organised American settlement in the Northwest Territories. Historical sites include **Campus Martius Museum** (the site of the first government and the fortification that protected the settlers during the Ohio Native American Wars in 1790-94), the **Ohio River Museum** and theatre performances on the **Showboat Becky Thatcher**. **Zanesville** offers a narrated ride on a sternwheeler and the **National Road/Zane Grey Museum**, with information about the building of America's first highway and Zanesville's famous Western writer. 24km (15 miles) south of Zanesville is **The Wilds**, a 9000-acre nature reserve.

Athens has a college-town atmosphere with a four-block area of narrow brick streets, historic buildings and interesting shops. The **Bob Evans Farm** in **Rio Grande**, the former home of a famous Ohioan sausage-maker, includes a 19th-century stagecoach stop, an authentic log-cabin village, a farm museum, horseriding and canoeing excursions.

The town of **Pomeroy** is perched on the edge of a sandstone cliff high above the **Ohio River** and the 1848 **Meigs County Courthouse** is one of the most picturesque buildings in southern Ohio. A scenic drive along the river leads to **Gallipolis**, originally settled by the French and possessing an interesting historic district and French art-colony galleries at **Riverby**, a historic Federal-style home.

THE NORTHEAST: The world's largest Amish population resides in the northeast's **Holmes**, **Stark**, **Tuscarawas** and **Wayne** counties, a haven of country shops selling everything from handwoven baskets, handmade quilts and antiques to homemade cornmeal. For a glimpse into the Amish lifestyle, the **Yoder's Amish Home** in Holmes County offers two reproduction Amish farmhouses and buggy rides for children. The **Western Reserve Historical Society**, which aims to preserve and protect the people of northeast Ohio, is the largest privately supported regional history society in the USA and regularly features exhibitions highlighting aspects of life in this part of Ohio.

The town of **Canton** has a museum complex that includes the **McKinley National Memorial** (with memorabilia on the assassinated president), the **National Inventors Hall of Fame**, **Discover World** and the **Museum of History, Science and Industry**. The **Pro Football Hall of Fame** is also located here. In **Mansfield**, there is the **Richland Carrousel Park** and **Kingwood Center**, a mansion and flower park with English gardens, landscaped ponds and strutting peacocks. **Youngstown** features the **Butler Institute of American Art** and **Youngstown Historical Center of Industry and Labour**, which highlights the steel industry that made the city famous. The 65-room Tudor-style **Stan Hywet Hall**, in **Akron**, is the largest private residence in Ohio and has formal English and Japanese gardens. Outside the city, **Six Flags World of Adventure** is an amusement park that includes the former **Sea World of Ohio** featuring Shouka the killer whale, no less than 10 rollercoasters, a water fun park, and tigers prowling on **Tiger Island**, as well as 14 new attractions such as the **Hurricane Mountain** and **Shark Attack** water slides and **The Thrill Bee** and **Starfish** rides.

Credit: © Ohio Division of Travel & Tourism

The 33,000-acre **Cuyahoga Valley National Recreation Area** encompasses a 35km- (22 mile-) long river surrounded by steep, forested hills, sandstone gorges and hidden waterfalls popular with birdwatchers and hikers. Within this area is also the Hale Farm and Village, a living-history museum depicting life in the mid-19th century.

THE CENTRAL AREA: In the Columbus area is a circle of historic small towns, such as **Granville**, with its 19th-century shops, museums, landmark inns and fine restaurants. **Lancaster** has **Square 13** (one of America's most beautiful and well-preserved residential blocks), **The Sherman House Museum** (with memorabilia on this famous political family) and **The Georgian Museum** (a restored mansion with period furniture). **Circleville** has outstanding architecture and numerous antique shops. The **Ohio Caverns** are the State's largest caves, while the **Zane Caverns**, 8km (5 miles) east of **Bellefontaine**, contain amazing pearl-like deposits. Also in the area is the **Mad River Mountain Resort** ski hill.

Sites which give an insight into the Native American culture in the region are **Flint Ridge State Memorial and Museum** in **Brownsville**, built over a flint pit used by the Hopewell, with exhibits on how they made weapons; and **Moundbuilders State Memorial** in Newark, great circular earthworks, 366m (1200ft) in diameter with 2-4m (8-14ft) walls, created over 2000 years ago by Hopewell Native Americans; the adjacent **Moundbuilders Museum** is the first museum in the USA exclusively devoted to prehistoric Native American art.

Situated in the picturesque north central region, **Ashland** is Ohio's apple country. The **Johnny Appleseed Heritage Center & Outdoor Historical Drama**, featuring an outdoor amphitheatre seating 1600 to host this musical drama and a research and education centre, will open in 2005. There is also an orchard, garden and nature trail.

THE NORTHWEST: Lake Erie is the main attraction in this area, with boating, fishing and tours of the islands offered by a number of operators. On **South Bass Island**, the Victorian-style village of **Put-in-Bay** offers plenty of gift shops, vintage saloons and fine restaurants. The 97m- (317ft-) high observation deck of **Perry's Victory and International Peace Memorial** offers fine views. **Middle Bass Island** is dominated by the Gothic castle of the **Lonz Winery**, established in 1860 and still making wine – tours and tastings are available. **Kelleys Island** is on the National Register of Historic Places. Along with old, picturesque homes, it offers historical sights such as **Inscription Rock**, an exceptionally large Native American pictograph.

Geneva State Park opened its new US$16.7 million **Geneva State Park Lodge** (Ohio's ninth state park lodge) in 2004. With breathtaking views of Lake Erie, this promises to be a popular destination for nature lovers, although luxuries (a restaurant, lounge and indoor swimming pool) have not been excluded. Scattered along **Sandusky Bay** are the towns of **Lakeside**, known for its Victorian architecture and summertime concerts, **Marblehead**, with its lighthouse and lakefront shops and artists' studios, and **Port Clinton**, home to fine restaurants and fishing. Sandusky is the largest town, full of gardens and historic homes (such as the 1834 stone mansion housing the **Follett House Museum** of Lake Erie memorabilia), as well as the **Merry-Go-Round Museum** (with a working carousel inside it). But the town is most famous for **Cedar Point Amusement**

Park, one of the largest in the USA and celebrated for its rollercoasters, most notably the *Top Thrill Dragster*, the highest in the world. In the park's popular **Soak City** water park, the **Splash Zone** includes waterslides, chutes, geysers and over 100 watery gadgets to enjoy. A giant bucket, 48-feet high, continuously douses visitors to the zone. An Indoor Waterpark Resort for winter water fun called **Castaway Bay** opened in November 2004. The park has been named 'Best Amusement Park in the World' by the National Park Historical Association for four consecutive years and is currently undergoing a US$10 million expansion. **Toledo**, on the **Maumee River**, is the northwest's largest city and is famous for its glass-making, available at **Libbey Glass Factory Outlet Store**. The century-old **Toledo Museum of Art** and adjacent **University of Toledo Center for the Visual Arts** are among the top 10 art museums in the USA. **Toledo Zoo** has recently completed its ambitious expansion project, introducing its *Africa!* attraction, unveiling a host of African animals, including termites (albeit simulated ones), and a hand-carved *African Animal Carousel*. Upriver, the restored riverfront towns of **Grand Rapids** and **Waterville** feature train and riverboat excursions.
Other attractions in the northwest include the **Neil Armstrong Air & Space Museum** in **Wapakoneta**; **Sauder Farm and Craft Village** in **Archbold** (a pioneer village with a museum); and the **Edison Birthplace Museum and Historical Museum** in **Milan**.
THE SOUTHWEST: Just north of Cincinnati, **Paramount's Kings Island Theme Park** offers Broadway-style shows and big-name stars, as well as a 15-acre water park and thrill rides. Most exciting, however, is the unveiling of the *Boomerang Bay 'Down Under'* resort, featuring over 50 wet and wild activities and 30 slides. The **Jack Nicklaus Sports Center** has two golf courses designed by the man himself. Once a large spa resort, **Yellow Springs** is still one of Ohio's most scenic towns, with an interesting historic district and the **Glen Helen Nature Preserve**, adjacent to the **Antioch College** campus. Nearby is the spectacular 31m (100ft) waterfall at **Clifton Gorge**, and **Clifton Mill**, one of the USA's largest operating gristmills.
The **Carillon Historical Park** in the city of **Dayton** is an 18-building complex with authentic recreations of 19th-century homes, businesses and industries; one of the planes flown by the Wright brothers; and one of the largest carillons in Ohio. Near here is the **Aviation Trail**, with many historical sites relating to the Wright brothers. The **Paul Laurence Dunbar State Memorial** was the house of the famous African-American author and is now a museum. **SunWatch Archaeological Park** is a prehistoric Native American village offering visitors close-up looks at ongoing digs, reconstruction daub-and-thatch lodges. 10km (6 miles) northeast of Dayton is the **US Air Force Museum**, the world's largest and oldest military aviation museum. Other sites in the southwest include the **National Afro-American Museum and Cultural Center** in **Wilberforce**; **Rankin House** (where abolitionist Reverend John Rankin hid more than 2000 slaves from 1825 to 1865) in **Ripley**; **Serpent Mound State Memorial** (a giant snake, one-quarter of a mile long and 6m/20ft wide, created by the Adena Native Americans over 2000 years ago) near **Locust Grove**; **Fort Ancient State Memorial** (an archaeological site displaying evidence of the Hopewell and Fort Ancient Native American tribes), southeast of **Lebanon**; and the **Piqua Historical Area**, offering restored 19th-century architecture and rides on a canal boat down a stretch of the **Miami & Erie Canal**.

Social Profile

FOOD & DRINK: Ohio is farm country, with fresh local produce and big wholesome meals. Pork and beef are common, and fried chicken features on many menus in the State, especially in the south. Corn is a staple of Amish cooking, featuring in *cornmeal mush* (a breakfast dish made with cracked corn, eggs and milk, then fried) and *hominy* (made from the kernels of white corn). Desserts usually centre around homemade fruit – apple pie is particularly popular, almost always served *à la mode* (with ice cream). The Amish people offer some regional specialities such as hand-cranked ice cream, homemade granola and maple-cinnamon rolls.
Tomato juice is the state beverage and Kentucky bourbon is a popular alcoholic drink. Spirits are sold only at state stores, while beer and wine are available in grocery stores and drug stores. Drinking hours in restaurants and bars are determined by the type of liquor licence held by the establishment; the minimum age to consume alcohol is 21.
THEATRES & CONCERTS: The *Cincinnati Opera* (the second-oldest opera company in the USA) and *The Cincinnati Pops Orchestra* perform at **Music Hall** (the *Pops Orchestra* has a summer season at **Riverbend Music Center**). Theatres include **Cincinnati Playhouse in the Park** and the **Ensemble Theater of Cincinnati**.
A series of more than 100 concerts is presented annually at the *Cleveland Institute of Music* by the *Institute's Symphony and Chamber Orchestras*, *Opera Department* and *Contemporary Music Ensemble*. The acclaimed *Ohio Ballet* performs at a variety of venues and festivals. The *Cleveland Ballet* performs at **Playhouse Square**, one of the largest performing arts centres in the country and home to five restored theatres (the **Allen**, **Hanna**, **Ohio**, **Palace** and **State Theaters**). The *Ohio Chamber Orchestra* performs in the **Little Theater** at the **Cleveland Convention Center**, and the *Cleveland Orchestra* at **Severance Hall** from September to May and at the newly remodelled **Blossom Music Center** during the summer. Theatre can be seen at the **Cleveland Public Theater**, the **Cleveland Play House** (the first regional theatre in the USA), **Playhouse Square Center** and **Karamu House** (a multi-racial arts centre). **Cain Park** has dance, theatre and music concerts (ranging from jazz to classical) in the summer.
The **Wexner Center for the Arts** in the Short North district in Columbus has an excellent programme of classical music, dance and jazz. The *Martin Luther King Jr Performing and Cultural Arts Complex* has performances by a variety of African-American artists. The *Jazz Arts Group of Columbus* also has an excellent programme. Elsewhere in the State are the *Ohio Light Opera Company* in **Wooster**, **Center for the Arts** in Canton and the **Ariel Theater** in **Gallipolis**.
NIGHTLIFE: *The Flats* in Cleveland is a popular nightlife entertainment area. The *Short North District*, *German Village* and the *Brewery District* in Columbus have excellent nightlife. Nightlife areas in Cincinnati include *The Wharf* at Covington Landing and the *Oldenberg Brewery Complex*. Dayton is known for its jazz clubs, while the blues can be enjoyed at Cleveland's new *House of Blues* venue.
SHOPPING: Major outlet shopping centres include *Ohio Factory Shops*, 58km (36 miles) south of Columbus; *Jeffersonville Outlet Center* in Jeffersonville; *Aurora Farms Factory Outlets*; *Lake Erie Factory Outlet Center* in Milan, and *JC Penney Outlet Store* and *Brice Outlet Mall* in Columbus. The *Easton Town Centre* in Columbus features shops, restaurants and a 30-screen cinema. The towns of Lebanon and Waynesville are known as the 'Antiques Capital of the Midwest'. For speciality Amish buys, the best areas for shopping are the 8km- (5 mile-) radius around Fredericksburg in Wayne County and the area between Charm and Farmerstown in Holmes County.
SPORT: The State's pro **baseball** teams are the *Cincinnati Reds* and the *Cleveland Indians*. The Indians play at Jacobs Field. The new *Great American Ball Park* is a welcome addition to Cincinnati's thriving sporting scene. The **American football** team is the *Cincinnati Bengals*. **Skiing** is also available: the major resorts are *Alpine Valley Ski Area* and *Boston Mills/Brandywine Ski Resort*, both near Cleveland; *Clear Fork Ski Area and Snow Trails Ski Resort* near Mansfield; and Mad River Mountain Ski Resort east of Bellefontaine.
Cleveland Metroparks has 19,000 acres of **walking** and **hiking** trails, nature centres and **golf** courses (boats, canoes and cross-country skis are available for hire in appropriate seasons). The *Firestone Country Club* is an excellent golf course, which holds the World Golf Championship NEC Invitational in August. **Fishing**, **swimming**, **watersports** and **boating** can be enjoyed on Lake Erie; **canoeing** on the Mohican and Tuscarawas rivers; fishing and **sailing** on the *Muskingum Watershed Conservancy District* lakes; hiking and rock climbing in *Hocking Hills State Park* and *Wayne National Forest*. Other State parks offer a variety of activities on land and water.
SPECIAL EVENTS: The following is a selection of special events occurring in Ohio in 2005:
Feb 5-13 *National City Cleveland Home & Garden Show*, Cleveland. **Feb 6** *Annual Black Heritage Concert*, Cleveland. **Feb 26-27** *Maple Syrup Weekend at Caesar Creek State Park*, Waynesville. **Feb 26-Mar 6** *Fifth Third Bank Home & Garden Show*, Cincinnati. **Mar 3-Sep 5** *Blooms and Butterflies*, Columbus. **Mar 4-6** *Arnold Fitness Weekend*, Columbus. **Mar 5** *National Cambridge Collectors' All Cambridge Glass Auction*, Cambridge. **Mar 13** *Maple Fest*, Republic. **Mar 17** *St Patrick's Day*, Cleveland. **Mar 19** *Early Spring Woodcock Walk at Maumee State Park*, Oregon; *St Patrick's Day*, Dublin; *Trinket or Treasure*, Columbus. **Mar 26** *Hayes Easter Egg Roll*, Fremont. **Apr 20-24** *Cincinnati Flower Show*. **May 27-29** *Cleveland Botanical Gardens Flower Show*. **May 27-30** *Great American Rib Cook-Off*, Cleveland; *Greek Heritage Festival*, Tremont. **May 28** *Ye Olde Mill Ice Cream Festival*, Utica. **May 30-Jun 5** *Memorial Golf Tournament*, Dublin. **Jun 2-5** *Columbus Arts Festival*. **Jun 8-10** *Toledo Harbor Lighthouse 101 Year Festival*, Oregon. **Jun 17-18** *Festival Latino*, Columbus. **Jun 18-25** *Great Ohio Bicycle Adventure*, Findlay. **Jun 22-25** *London Strawberry Festival*. **Jul 29-30** *Queen City Blues Festival*, Cincinnati. **Aug 3-14** *Ohio State Fair*, Columbus. **Aug 5-6** *Ohio Mennonite Relief Sale & Auction*, Kidron; *Vintage Ohio Festival*, Cleveland. **Aug 5-7** *Irish Festival*, Dublin. **Aug 6-7** *Twins Day Festival*, Twinsburg. **Aug 20-21** *Coshocton Canal Festival*. **Aug 27-Oct 23** *Ohio Renaissance Festival*, Harveysburg. **Sep 3-5** *Cleveland National Air Show*. **Sep 9-10** *Marion Popcorn Festival*. **Sep 30-Oct 1** *Ohio Swiss Festival*, Sugarcreek. **Oct 8-9** *Ashtabula County Covered Bridge Festival*, Jefferson. **Oct 9-10** *Apple Butter Days & Fall Foliage Tour*, Gnadenhutten. **Oct 14-16** *35th Bob Evans Farm Festival*, Rio Grande; Apple Butter Stirrin', Coshocton. **Oct 15** *Fall on the Farm*, Archbold. **Dec 3-5** *Ashtabula County Christmas*, Austinburg.

Climate

Mild to cold winters and hot summers.
Required clothing: Lightweights for the summer and heavyweights for the winter.

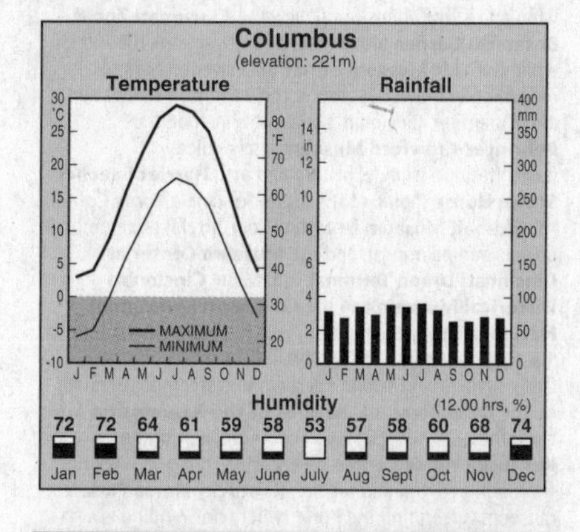

Oklahoma

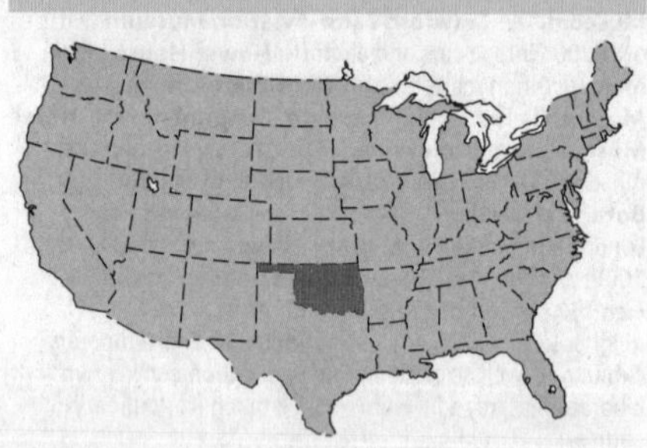

Oklahoma Tourism & Recreation Department (Travel & Tourism Division)
Street address: 15 North Robinson, Suite 100, 6th Floor, Oklahoma City, OK 73102
Postal address: PO Box 52002, Oklahoma City, OK 73152
Tel: (405) 521 2406 *or* (800) 652 6552 (toll-free).
Fax: (405) 521 3992.
E-mail: information@travelok.com
Website: www.travelok.com
Oklahoma City CVB
189 West Sheridan, Oklahoma City, OK 73102
Tel: (405) 297 8912 *or* (800) 225 5652 (toll-free).
Fax: (405) 297 8888.
E-mail: okccvb@okccvb.org
Website: www.visitokc.com
Tulsa CVB
2 West Second Street, Williams Center Tower II, Suite 150, Tulsa, OK 74103
Tel: (918) 585 1201 *or* 560 0263 *or* (800) 558 3311 (toll-free).
Fax: (918) 592 6244.
E-mail: sheilasimmons@tulsachamber.com
Website: www.visittulsa.com

General Information

Nickname: Sooner State
State bird: Scissor-tailed Flycatcher
State flower: Mistletoe
CAPITAL: Oklahoma City
Date of admission to the Union: 16 Nov 1907
POPULATION: 3,523,553 official estimate 2004)
POPULATION DENSITY: 19.5 per sq km
2003 total overseas arrivals: 38,000/38
TIME: Central (GMT - 6). *Daylight Saving Time* is observed.

THE STATE: Oklahoma is home to more Native American tribes than any other State except California, with 39 tribal headquarters and members of at least 67 tribes. While Native Americans have lived in Oklahoma for thousands of

A B C D E F G H I J K L M N O P Q R S T U V W X Y Z

years, many tribes were forcibly relocated to this land (many dying from starvation and disease along the way on the infamous 'trails of tears') when it was established as Indian Territory in the early 19th century. Today, visitors will find Native American art galleries, museums, historic sites, pow wows, dances and festivals. The **Cherokee Heritage Center** (outside Tahlequah), the **Cheyenne Cultural Center** (in Clinton), the **Five Civilized Tribes Museum** (in Muskogee), and numerous other sites all provide insight into Native American culture. Oklahoma is home to the longest driveable stretch of **Route 66**, with nearly 643km (400 miles) of 'America's Main Street'. Along an older route, the State saw cowboys and cattle drives on the **Chisholm Trail**. A life-size statue of a cattle drive, entitled 'On the Chisholm Trail', is located outside the **Chrisholm Trail Heritage Center**, in **Duncan**, as a monument to the US cowboy. The center itself has just undergone a massive renovation and upgrade, with lots more to discover about the cowboy way of life. Cattle are still transported along the Chrisholm Trail route, nowadays in trucks, headed for the largest cattle auction in the USA, located in **Oklahoma City's Stockyards City**. Here, visitors will find shops selling authentic western wear and gear. Oklahoma City is also home to the **National Cowboy & Western Heritage Museum**, showcasing Western and Native American art and artefacts, the **Oklahoma City National Memorial Museum**, and the **Myriad Botanical Gardens & Crystal Bridge Tropical Conservatory**. The annual *Red Earth Native American Cultural Festival*, held each spring, is an enormous celebration of art, music and dance. Other aspects of the State's heritage are apparent at the **Oklahoma Prison Rodeo** in **McAlester** to the east, the **Oklahoma International Bluegrass Festival** in **Guthrie** to the north, and in many unique rural festivals, such as the *Okra Festival*, the *Rattlesnake Roundups*, the *Kolache Festival*, *Strawberry Festival* and the *Watonga Cheese Festival*.

Fortunes made in oilfields left a legacy in northeastern Oklahoma that includes mansions, museums, art galleries and Art Deco architecture. The **Gilcrease Museum** in **Tulsa** contains the world's most comprehensive collection of art of the American West. The Rodgers and Hammerstein musical *Oklahoma!* is still running at **Discoveryland**, in **Sand Springs** (outside Tulsa). Some 50 State parks and many other natural havens showcase Oklahoma's 11 distinct ecoregions and plentiful unspoilt beauty, including **Robbers Cave State Park**, **Greenleaf State Park**, **Beavers Bend State Resort Park**, **Roman Nose State Park**, the **Wichita Mountains National Wildlife Refuge**, **Alabaster Caverns State Park**, the **Tallgrass Prairie Preserve** and the **Talimena Scenic Drive** through the **Ouachita National Forest**.

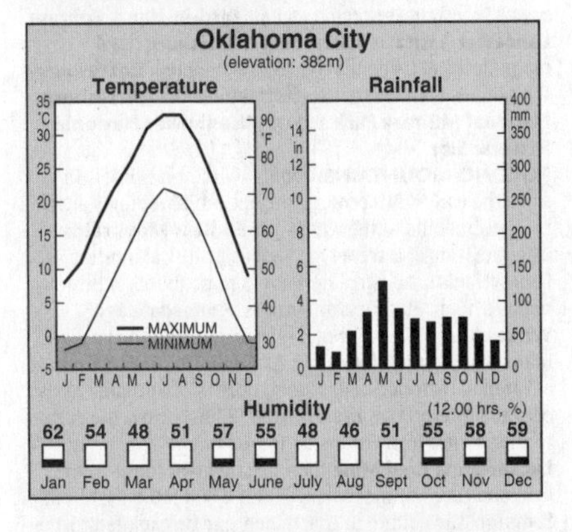

Oregon

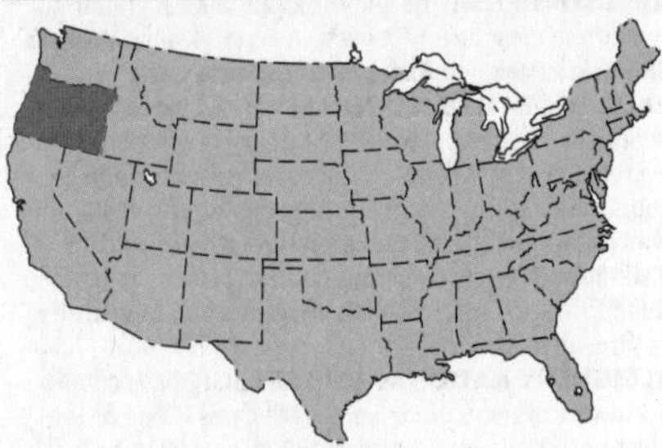

Oregon Tourism Commission
670 Hawthorne Avenue, SE, Salem, OR 97301
Tel: (503) 378 8850 *or* (800) 547 7842 (toll-free).
Fax: (503) 378 4574.
E-mail: infotourism@traveloregon.com
Website: www.traveloregon.com

Portland Oregon Visitors Association
1000 South West Broadway, Suite 2300, Portland, OR 97205
Tel: (503) 275 8355 (visitor information) *or* (503) 275 9750 (administration) *or* (800) 962 3700 (toll-free) *or* (877) 678 5263 (toll-free; hotel reservations).
Fax: (503) 275 8351.
E-mail: info@pova.com
Website: www.travelportland.com

Convention & Visitors Association of Lane County Oregon
Street address: 754 Olive Street, Eugene, OR 97401
Postal address: PO Box 10286, Eugene, OR 97440
Tel: (541) 484 5307 *or* (800) 547 5445 (toll-free).
Fax: (541) 343 6335.
E-mail: info@cvalco.org
Website: www.visitlanecounty.org

General Information

Nickname: Beaver State
State bird: Western Meadowlark
State flower: Oregon Grape (Holly Grape)
CAPITAL: Salem
Date of admission to the Union: 14 Feb 1859
POPULATION: 3,594,586 (official estimate 2004)
POPULATION DENSITY: 14.1 per sq km
2003 total overseas arrivals/US ranking: 162,000/24
TIME: Pacific (GMT - 8) in the greater part of the State; Mountain (GMT - 7) in most of Malheur county. *Daylight Saving Time* is observed.

THE STATE: Thousands of visitors each year are drawn to the scenic beauty of this State. In the northeast, deep gorges vie for attention with the craggy beauty of the towering **Wallowa Mountains**. Outdoor types will also be drawn to the southeast's huge and desolate **Steens Mountain Wilderness Area**, as well as the **Oregon Dunes National Recreation Area** along the coast.

Salem is the capital of Oregon and the State's third-largest city; it boasts many fine museums, gardens and parks, including the **Mission Mill Museum**, **Old Aurora Colony Museum**, **Bush House Museum** and **Oregon Garden**, which recently opened the new **Frank Lloyd Wright House**.

The more urbane should consider **Portland**, the 'City of Roses', which boasts gardens, restaurants, shops, concerts, jazz festivals, theatres and first-class hotels. It is possible to see the best of the city's vibrant dramatic and visual arts scene on the first Thursday of each month when the small galleries in the Southwest and Northwest districts remain open until 2100. The **Portland Art Museum** houses paintings and sculptures from the 1350s to the 1950s. The city also boasts the **American Advertising Museum**, the **Oregon Museum of Science and Industry**, **Pittock Mansion**, **Oregon Zoo** and the recently renovated **PGE Park**.

An hour from Portland is the stunning **Columbia River Gorge**. Here, the Columbia furrows its way through a canyon 300m- (1000ft-) deep, plunging between hills and sheer cliff faces. The **Columbia River Maritime Museum** can be found in **Astoria**. The **Vista House**, completed as a memorial to Oregon's pioneers, acts as the visitors centre in **Crown Point State Park**. East of Crown Point, a string of waterfalls, including the mighty **Multnomah Falls**, attracts 2 million visitors per year. The towns of **Hood River** and **The Dalles** offer visitor services in the gorge; whilst the **Columbia River** itself, with its 50kph (30mph) winds, is a windsurfing paradise.

On the Idaho border lies North America's deepest gorge – **Hells Canyon**. In some places, the walls drop 1650m (7900ft) to the **Snake River** below. A quick flit through on a jet boat or a leisurely drift by raft are two ways of viewing this mighty wonder. Oregon breaks another record by boasting the nation's deepest lake, located in southern Oregon. It forms the centrepiece of **Crater Lake National Park**, plunging from an 1800m- (6000ft-) elevation to a depth of nearly 600m (1932ft). Skiing is offered in the **Willamette Pass** and **Hoodoo Ski Areas**, which have recently undergone improvements to their existing facilities. For those heading coastwards, the renowned **US Highway 101** hugs the Pacific shore with a stretch lying between the coastal towns, where hundreds of miles of State parks offer direct connections with the beach. Some of Oregon's most famous cheeses are nurtured on the shore of **Tillamook Bay** and those who hunger for a hunk should visit the **Tillamook Cheese Visitor's Center**. **Newport** offers the sights and smells of a classic seaport, including an **Aquarium**, whilst connoisseurs of ale can sample local favourites across the bay bridge at the **Rogue Ale Brewery**. Both the **Oregon Coast Aquarium** and **Oregon State University Hatfield Marine Science Visitor Center** are located here, providing unique and educational views of coastal wildlife and the environment.

Other attractions in the State include **Bend**, home to the **High Desert Museum**; **Eugene**, with the newly renovated **Hult Center for the Performing Arts**; and **Baker City**, offering the **National Historic Trail Interpretive Center**. A Calendar of Events can be obtained from the Oregon Tourism Commission (website: www.traveloregon.com).

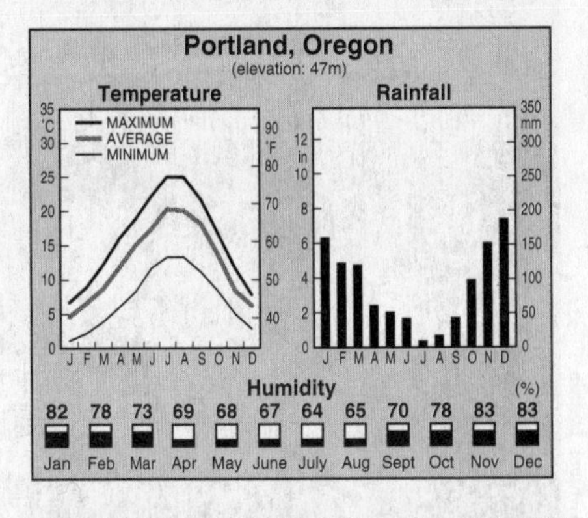

Pennsylvania

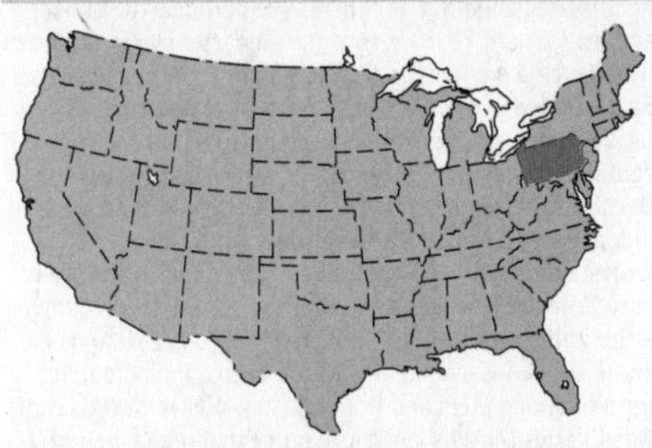

Office of Tourism, Film and Economic Development Marketing
Department of Community & Economic Development, 4th Floor, Commonwealth Keystone Building, 400 North Street, Harrisburg, PA 17120
Tel: (717) 787 5453 *or* (800) 847 4872 (toll-free, brochure request). Fax: (717) 787 0687.
E-mail: info@visitpa.com Website: www.visitpa.com

Pennsylvania Tourism
c/o Destination Marketing, Power Road Studios, 114 Power Road, Chiswick, London W4 5PY, UK
Tel: (020) 8994 0978. Fax: (020) 8994 0962.
E-mail: pa@destination-marketing.co.uk
Website: www.visitpa.com

Gettysburg CVB
PO Box 4117, Gettysburg, PA 17325
Tel: (717) 334 6274 *or* (800) 337 5015 (toll-free).
Fax: (717) 334 1166.
E-mail: info@gettysburgcvb.org
Website: www.gettysburgcvb.org

Philadelphia CVB
1700 Market Street, Suite 3000, Philadelphia, PA 19102
Tel: (215) 636 3300 *or* (800) 225 5745. Fax: (215) 636 3327.
E-mail: info@pcvb.org Website: www.pcvb.org

Greater Pittsburgh CVB
Regional Enterprise Tower, 425 Sixth Avenue, 30th Floor, Pittsburgh, PA 15219
Tel: (412) 281 7711 *or* (800) 359 0758 (toll-free).
Fax: (412) 644 5512.
E-mail: info@gpcvb.org
Website: www.visitpittsburgh.com

Valley Forge CVB
600 West Germantown Pike, Plymouth Meeting, PA 19462
Tel: (610) 834 1550 *or* (800) 441 3549 (toll-free).
Fax: (610) 834 0202.
E-mail: info@valleyforge.org
Website: www.valleyforge.org

General Information

Nickname: Keystone State
State bird: Ruffed Grouse
State flower: Mountain Laurel
CAPITAL: Harrisburg
Date of admission to the Union: 12th Dec 1787 (original 13 States; date of ratification of the Constitution)
POPULATION: 12,406,292 (official estimate 2004)
POPULATION DENSITY: 104 per sq km
2003 total overseas arrivals/US ranking: 613,000/11
TIME: Eastern (GMT - 5). *Daylight Saving Time* is observed.

Credit: © Pennsylvania Tourism

THE STATE: Pennsylvania is a region steeped in colourful history. It started out as the 'Holy Experiment' of Quaker activist William Penn, Jr. Granted a charter by King Charles II to develop a colony in the New World, Penn selected a lush wooded portion of the countryside, where he vowed to welcome anyone who believed in God. Less than a century later, the country's Founding Fathers signed the Declaration of Independence and the Constitution at Independence Hall in **Philadelphia** – now one of the largest cities in the USA – and the American nation was born. A revolution of a very different nature soon followed – the Industrial Revolution. Rich in iron ore, coal and crude oil, Pennsylvania had all the necessary ingredients for a booming steel and iron industry. 'Hell with the lid off' was Charles Dickens' description of Pittsburgh when he visited a city so polluted that street lamps had to be kept on during the day to improve visibility. Today, Pittsburgh is known as a 'Renaissance city'; what remains of that area is a wealth of cultural and historical landmarks, and the visitor can breathe freely in bright urban landscapes, bustling city sophistication and a great outdoors. Pennsylvania boasts 20 State and 1 National Forest, 116 State Parks, 1 Great Lake (Lake Erie), 50 other natural lakes, 2500 man-made lakes, along with thousands of miles of rivers and streams. The state is also something of a cultural mecca, with many world-class museums, while its citizens represent a rich mix of cultural and ethnic backgrounds.

Travel - International

AIR: *Philadelphia International Airport (PHL)* (website: www.phl.org) is 13km (8 miles) southwest of the city (travel time – 25 minutes). The cheapest way to reach the city centre is the *SEPTA Airport Express Train*, running every 30 minutes to all three city centre stations, 0600-2400 daily. Taxis, car hire and limousine services are also available. *Pittsburgh International Airport* (website: www.pitairport.com) is 22.5km (14 miles) west of the city centre. *Port Authority Transit* public buses run approximately every 20 minutes daily 0500-2400 to Oakland via Robinson and downtown Pittsburgh. The *Airlines Transportation* shuttle runs every hour daily 0700-2200 to downtown Pittsburgh and Oakland. Limousine services, taxis and car hire are also available.
Approximate flight times: From *London* to *Philadelphia* is eight hours 20 minutes, and to *Pittsburgh* is eight hours 55 minutes.
LAKE/RIVER: Pennsylvania has three of the country's busiest ports within its borders. Philadelphia is the largest freshwater port in the world. Erie is one of the major Great Lakes ports and Pittsburgh is one of the nation's largest inland ports, providing access to the extensive 1400km- (900 mile-) US inland waterway system.
RAIL: Pennsylvania has dozens of passenger railroads (website: www.parailways.com) in addition to mainline *Amtrak* (tel: (800) 872 7245 (toll-free); website: www.amtrak.com) services. Philadelphia is home to one of *Amtrak*'s busiest stations, at 30th Street, which is served by the 'Acela Express' service linking Washington, DC (travel time – one hour 35 minutes) with New York City (travel time – one hour 10 minutes) and Boston (travel time – five hours). It also receives *Amtrak* trains from Chicago, Miami and New Orleans, and *NJ Transit* trains from Atlantic City. Free transfers to the urban transportation system, run by *SEPTA*, are available to *Amtrak* passengers (request upon ticket purchase). Pittsburgh has daily *Amtrak* services to Chicago, New York City, Philadelphia and Washington, DC. See the *Illinois* and *New York* sections for examples of travel times on several services passing through these cities.
ROAD: Bus: *Greyhound* (tel: (800) 229 9424 (toll-free); website: www.greyhound.com) is the main service provider.
Approximate driving times: From Philadelphia to *Baltimore* is two hours, to *New York* is two hours, to *Washington, DC* is three hours, to *Pittsburgh* is six hours, to *Chicago* is 14 hours, to *Miami* is 25 hours, to *Dallas* is 31 hours, to *Los Angeles* is 56 hours and to *Seattle* is 59 hours. From Pittsburgh to *Niagara Falls* is four hours, to *Washington, DC* is four hours, and to *Chicago* is eight hours. All times are based on non-stop driving at or below the applicable speed limits.
Approximate bus travel times: From Philadelphia to *New York* is two hours, to *Washington, DC* is three hours, to *Pittsburgh* is seven hours, to *Chicago* is 18 hours, to *Miami* is 30 hours, to *Dallas* is 37 hours, to *Los Angeles* is 65 hours, and to *Seattle* is 74 hours.
URBAN: In Philadelphia, the *Southeastern Pennsylvania Transportation Authority (SEPTA)* (tel: (215) 580 7800; website: www.septa.org) has interconnecting buses, trolleys (streetcars), subways and elevated railways. From May-November, the distinctive *PHLASH* buses connect most of the city's major attractions. Exact change is required on all services. Pittsburgh has an efficient network of buses serving the various districts. The *PAT* subway service is rather modest but is free in downtown Pittsburgh.

Resorts & Excursions

PHILADELPHIA: Situated on the **Delaware River**, Philadelphia is the fifth-largest city in the USA and a vibrant national centre of commerce, industry, medical education, research and the arts, while still preserving quiet pockets of some of the nation's most historic territory. In 1776, the Declaration of Independence and the Constitution were signed in **Independence Hall**, which stands in the centre of **Independence National Historical Park**. The new **National Constitution Center** is the first museum in the world dedicated to honouring the US Constitution. The glass **Liberty Bell Center** houses the bell that was sounded at the first public reading of the Declaration of Independence and features indoor and outdoor areas with interpretive exhibits. **Franklin Court**, where Franklin's home once stood, houses an underground museum. Other places of interest include the **Old City Hall**, early home of the US Supreme Court; **Christ Church**, where Franklin and George Washington once worshipped; the **Philadelphia Museum of Art & Rodin Museum**; **Penn's Landing**, where State founder William Penn first arrived in 1682; and **Valley Forge National Historical Park**, just west of the city, one of the most revered shrines of the American Revolution. **Fairmount Park**, by the **Schuylkill River**, is one of the USA's largest city parks; visitors can learn all about the river in the neo-classical **Fairmount Water Works Interpretive Center** on **Waterworks Drive**.
PITTSBURGH: The second-largest city in the State, Pittsburgh was once the USA's centre for steel production; however, the steel mills have been replaced by a dramatic skyline of dazzling skyscrapers. With its traditional ethnic spirit, close-knit neighbourhoods, vibrant culture and burgeoning business community, Pittsburgh consistently ranks highly in the listings of America's most liveable places. The **Point State Park Fountain** in the **Golden Triangle** area of central Pittsburgh symbolises the creation of the **Ohio River** at the meeting of the **Monongahela** and **Allegheny rivers**. Other attractions include the **Carnegie Science Center**, with its **Museum of Natural History**; the **University of Pittsburgh**'s 42-storey 'Cathedral of Learning'; and the **Heinz History Center**, which celebrates west Pennsylvanian history. The **Andy Warhol Museum** houses over 7000 works of this Pittsburgh-born pop artist.
LAUREL HIGHLANDS: Once a retreat of wealthy Pittsburgh industrialists, the Laurel Highlands feature major ski resorts, trout fishing, hiking and biking trails. With its Class III and IV rapids, the **Youghiogheny River** provides some of the best whitewater rafting in the East. **Old Bedford Village** offers a living history of the pioneer era, with costumed guides, crafts demonstrations and 40 authentic buildings. The area is also home to two of Frank Lloyd Wright's masterpieces: **Kentuck Knob** and the spectacular **Fallingwater**.
PENNSYLVANIA DUTCH COUNTRY: This farmland is home to the world-renowned Amish and Mennonites, the 'plain people' who fled religious persecution in Germany ('Deutschland' – hence the misnomer 'Dutch country') for a simple pastoral life without modern conveniences. The town of **Lancaster** is closely associated with the Pennsylvania Dutch but the centre of tourism is the town of **Intercourse**, where, at **The People's Place**, films, crafts and interpreters weave the story of these settlers. Detours down side roads are rewarded with glimpses of horse-drawn ploughs and buggies, auctions, antique shops and the occasional private home where the exquisite Amish quilts and crafts are sold. In nearby **Hershey** is the world's largest chocolate factory, 'Chocolatetown USA', with a visitor's centre, shopping outlets and an amusement park. Other towns to visit in the region include **Bird-in-Hand**, **Ephrata**, **Lancaster**, **Lititz** and **Strasburg**. **Harrisburg** has a magnificent 650-room State Capitol building. **Gettysburg**, the famous Civil War battle site, features the **Gettysburg National Military Park** and the **Eisenhower National Historic Site**.
POCONO MOUNTAINS: Popular with honeymooners since the early-19th century, the Pocono Mountains and their neighbours to the west – the **Endless Mountains** – offer breathtaking scenery as well as historical interest. Pennsylvania's industrial heritage is to be found in this region's many museums and towns. **Honesdale** and **Wilkes-Barre** played pivotal roles in building the coal and railroad industries of America. At **Scranton**, **Steamtown** is a National Historic Site featuring dozens of antique railroad cars and interpretive displays. 76m (250ft) below the earth, former miners lead visitors on tours through the **Lackawanna Coal Mine** for a first-hand account of the lives and times of the miners. About 64km (40 miles) from Scranton, the culture of coal miners can be explored further at **Eckley Miners' Village**, an authentic coal-mining town. More of the wealth of the Industrial Revolution is preserved in the Victorian village of **Jim Thorpe**, nestled along winding roads in the shadow of the Pocono Mountains. The region also includes freshwater lakes, excellent shad fishing, whitewater rafting and Pennsylvania's section of the **Appalachian Trail**. The Endless Mountains are home to two of the most beautiful parks in Pennsylvania: **World's End State Park** and **Ricketts Glen State Park**.
VALLEYS OF THE SUSQUEHANNA: Outdoor activities abound in this region, with 19 State parks offering everything from swimming, hiking, horse-riding and cross-country skiing. Boating and fishing can be enjoyed in the many tributaries of the **Susquehanna River**, which is distinguished by its numerous covered or 'kissing' bridges. Quaint river towns, such as **Selinsgrove** and **Lewisburg**, dot the area.
ALLEGHENY NATIONAL FOREST REGION: Located northwest of the Susquehanna Valley, this is one of the most unspoiled areas of Pennsylvania, protected from settlers by rugged terrain and harsh weather conditions. **Elk County** is home to one of only two wild elk herds east of the Mississippi. The entire region sports more big game than any other part of Pennsylvania. The **Allegheny National**

Forest offers a vast area of woodlands, virgin timber, rivers and beautiful vistas. Wintersports enthusiasts can explore 480km (300 miles) of snowmobiling trails and seven cross-country ski trails. The **Pennsylvania Grand Canyon**, a 300m- (1000ft-) deep gorge that twists along 80km (50 miles) of **Pine Creek** and embraces 300,000 acres of forest, can be explored on foot, horseback, canoe or river raft. For quaint country charm, **Wellsboro** offers a slower pace and a picturesque **Main Street**, complete with authentic gas street lamps. Connected by the mighty **Kinzua Bridge**, the towns of **Kane** and **Smethport** boast fine country inns.
LAKE ERIE REGION: Bordering Lake Erie, one of the Great Lakes, the northwestern corner of the State features 32,000 acres of lakes, as well as hundreds of miles of rivers for fishing, boating and swimming.

Social Profile

FOOD & DRINK: Various regions in Pennsylvania have their own specialities. In the Pocono Mountains area, superb local mountain trout is featured in many restaurants. Pennsylvania Dutch food is a unique variation of German cuisine, including pickles, relishes, apple butter, dumplings, pretzels, molasses and shoo-fly pie (a sweet dessert made with molasses). Seven sweet and seven sour dishes are served in a type of smorgasbord. A variety of sausages and cold cuts originate from this region, such as the delicious Lebanon bologna and dried beef. The best restaurants for this unique cuisine can be found around Lancaster. The legal age for drinking is 21 in Pennsylvania and bottled liquor is only sold in State stores.
THEATRES & CONCERTS: In Philadelphia, summer performances in the round are staged at the *John B Kelly Playhouse*. The city's opera house and concert hall is at the *Academy of Music*, the home of the *Philadelphia Orchestra*. The huge *Mann Music Center* in *Fairmount Park* stages summer concerts. Visitors can see Broadway musicals in Pittsburgh's *Benedum Center*, while the ornate *Heinz Hall* is home to the *Pittsburgh Symphony Orchestra*. In large cities and many smaller towns throughout Pennsylvania, visitors will find orchestras, playhouses and dance troupes.
NIGHTLIFE: There are numerous dinner theatres, nightclubs, jazz clubs and ethnic entertainment throughout Pennsylvania's towns and cities.
SHOPPING: Philadelphia and Pittsburgh have always been famous for antiques and handicrafts. The main shopping areas in Philadelphia include the *Bourse*, *Head House Square* and *New Market*. The second-largest shopping complex in the USA, *The Plaza & The Court at King of Prussia*, lies to the north of the city. For budget shoppers, *Franklin Mills* (just outside Philadelphia), *Grove City* (north of Pittsburgh) and Reading have hundreds of factory outlets, offering the chance to pick up name-brands at reduced prices. In addition, there is no sales tax on clothing and shoes in Pennsylvania. Antiques buffs should stop in Adamstown, where over 1500 dealers display their wares every Sunday.
SPORT: The new *Lincoln Financial Field* is home to the *Philadelphia Eagles* football team.
SPECIAL EVENTS: The following is a selection of special events occurring in Pennsylvania in 2005:
Feb 5-13 *Philadelphia International Auto Show*, Punxsutawney. **Feb 18-20** *Greater Philadelphia Mid-Winter Scottish and Irish Music Festival and Fair*, King of Prussia. **Feb 19** *11th Annual Tobyhanna Ice Harvesting Festival*. **Feb 27** *17th Annual Ice Tee Golf Tournament*, Lake Wallenpaupack. **Feb 13-15** *Greater Philadelphia Mid-Winter Scottish and Irish Music Festival and Fair*, King of Prussia. **Mar 6-13** *Philadelphia Flower Show*, Philadelphia. **Mar 12** *St Patrick's Day Celebrations*, Blakeslee. **Mar 19-20** *Reggae Festival Weekend*, Tannersville. **Apr 23** *Native American Heritage Day*, Horsham. **May 14-15** *32nd Annual Mercer Museum Folk Fest*, Doylestown. **Jun 9-12** *Wind Gap Bluegrass Festival*, Philadelphia. **Jul 12-Aug 1** *Under the Stars Movie Series*, Doylestown. **Sep 3** *McLain Celtic Festival*, Carlisle. **Oct 7-9** *Applefest*, Franklin.

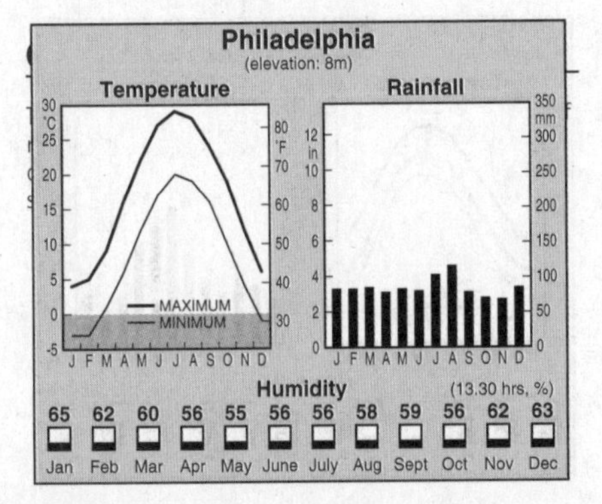

Rhode Island

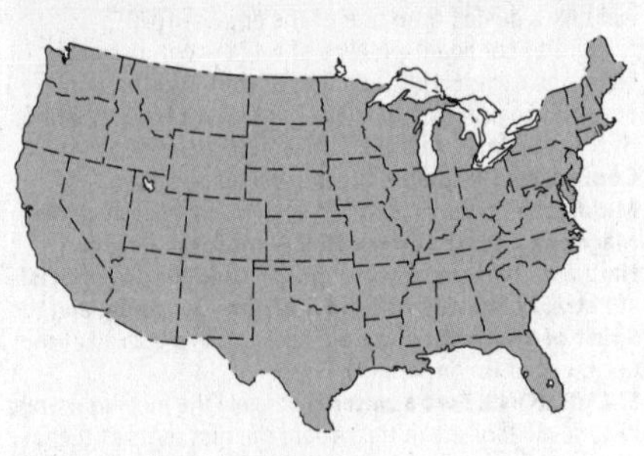

Rhode Island Tourism Division
1 West Exchange Street, Providence, RI 02903
Tel: (401) 222 2601 *or* (800) 556 2484 (toll-free; 24 hours).
Fax: (401) 273 8270.
E-mail: visitrhodeisland@riedc.com
Website: www.visitrhodeisland.com
Block Island Tourism Council
Block Island Chamber of Commerce, PO Box D, Block Island, RI 02807
Tel: (401) 466 5200 *or* (800) 383 2474 (toll-free).
Fax: (401) 466 5286.
E-mail: info@blockislandchamber.com
Website: www.blockislandchamber.com
Newport County CVB
23 America's Cup Avenue, Newport, RI 02840
Tel: (401) 849 8048 *or* 845 9123 (visitor information) *or* (800) 976 5122 (toll-free) *or* (800) 326 6030 (toll-free).
Fax: (401) 849 0291.
E-mail: jbailey@gonewport.com
Website: www.gonewport.com
Blackstone Valley Tourism Council
175 Main Street, Pawtucket, RI 02860
Tel: (401) 724 2200 *or* (800) 454 2882 (toll-free).
Fax: (401) 724 1342.
E-mail: info@tourblackstone.com
Website: www.tourblackstone.com
Providence Warwick CVB
1 West Exchange Street, 3rd Floor, Providence, RI 02903
Tel: (401) 274 1636 *or* (800) 233 1636 (toll-free).
Fax: (401) 351 2090.
E-mail: information@goprovidence.com
Website: www.goprovidence.com

General Information

Nickname: Ocean State
State bird: Rhode Island Red
State flower: Violet
CAPITAL: Providence
Date of admission to the Union: 29 May 1790 (original 13 States; date of ratification of the Constitution)
POPULATION: 1,080,632 (official estimate 2004)
POPULATION DENSITY: 270 per sq km
2003 total overseas arrivals: 72,000/34
TIME: Eastern (GMT - 5). *Daylight Saving Time* is observed.

THE STATE: Although it takes just 45 minutes to drive from one end of Rhode Island to the other, the smallest State offers more than 640km (400 miles) of coastline, broad sandy beaches, parks, cities and a wealth of historic attractions. It was also the first State to declare independence from Great Britain on 4 May 1776 and the first that passed laws against slavery in 1774. **Providence** underwent a major facelift in the 1990s that has resulted in the renaissance of Rhode Island's capital city. The revitalisation project included the rerouting of two rivers and the building of beautifully landscaped pedestrian walkways and Venetian-style footbridges. At the hub of the project is **Waterplace Park**, a 1.6 hectare (4 acre) urban park that surrounds a tidal basin. The **East Side** is filled with many fine restored homes, and **Brown University** includes several 18th-century buildings. The **Museum of Natural History and Planetarium** is one of a kind in the State, with collections containing over 24,000 archaeological and ethnographic specimens, with the focus on Native American and Pacific Island heritage. Other highlights include the **RISD Museum**, an art museum which houses 80,000 works of art and boasts an interesting Japanese collection; while in the adjacent city of **Pawtucket**, the **Slater Mill Historic Site**, the birthplace of the American Industrial Revolution, is also open for tours.
Newport, a top sailing spot, is an all-seasons resort offering a beautiful harbour that is rich in colonial history, as well as white beaches and some splendid scenery. Newport was the setting for the marriage of John F Kennedy to Jacqueline Bouvier and hosted the Americas Cup race for 53 years. Many of its magnificent mansions (including those built by the Vanderbilts and the Astors) are open to the public. Other sights include the **Touro Synagogue**, which has been restored to its former glory, and the **White Horse Tavern**, built in 1673 by a pirate. A summer season of jazz and folk festivals is a major part of its appeal: classical music takes centre stage in July during the *Newport Music Festival*, while the following month sees the arrival of the *Apple & Eve Newport Folk Festival*. Also in August, the *JVC Jazz Festival* in Newport, one of the oldest and best known in the country, draws music-lovers to **Fort Adams State Park**.
A popular excursion is the one-hour ferry trip from **Point Judith** to **Block Island** to see the **National Wildlife Refuge** and the magnificent 60m- (200ft-) high **Mohegan Bluffs**. The State's scenic centrepiece, **Narragansett Bay**, is home to yachting regattas as well as a thriving fishing industry.

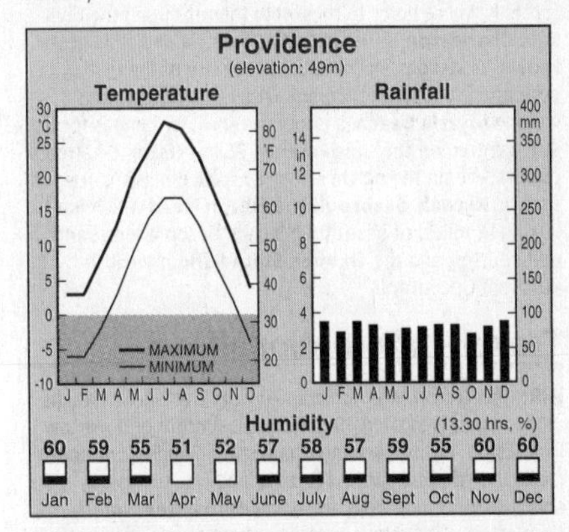

South Carolina

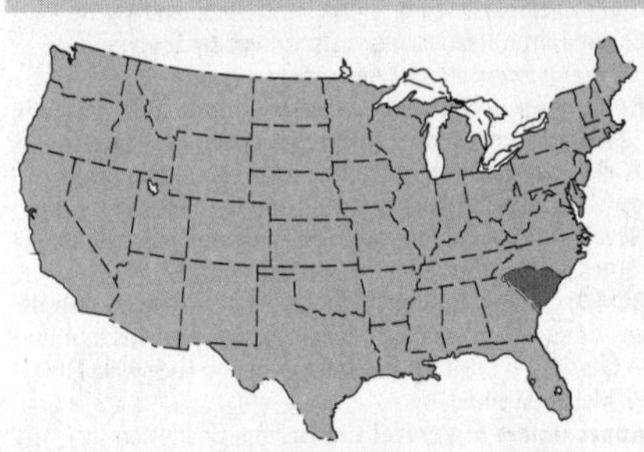

South Carolina Department of Parks, Recreation & Tourism
1205 Pendleton Street, Columbia, SC 29201
Tel: (803) 734 1700 *or* (888) 727 6453 (toll-free).
Fax: (803) 734 1163.
Website: www.discoversouthcarolina.com
Charleston Area CVB
423 King Street, Charleston, SC 29403
Tel: (843) 853 8000 *or* (800) 868 8118 (toll-free).
Fax: (843) 853 0444.
Website: www.charlestoncvb.com
Columbia Metropolitan CVB
1101 Lincoln Street, Columbia, SC 29201
Tel: (803) 545 0000 *or* (800) 264 4884.
Fax: (803) 545 0013.
E-mail: visit@columbiacvb.com
Website: www.columbiacvb.com
Greater Greenville CVB
Street address: 631 South Main Street, Suite 301, Greenville, SC 29601
Postal address: PO Box 10527, Greenville, SC 29603
Tel: (864) 421 0000 *or* 233 0461 (visitor centre) *or* (800) 351 7180 (toll-free) *or* (800) 717 0023 (toll-free; visitor centre).
Fax: (864) 421 0005.
E-mail: cityinfo@greatergreenville.com
Website: www.greatergreenville.com
Hilton Head Island Visitor & Convention Bureau
Street address: 1 Chamber Drive, Hilton Head Island, SC 29928
Postal address: PO Box 5647, Hilton Head Island, SC 29938
Tel: (843) 785 3673 *or* (800) 523 3373 (toll-free; US only).
Fax: (843) 785 7110.
Website: www.hiltonheadisland.org
Myrtle Beach Area Chamber of Commerce and Information Center
Street address: 1200 North Oak Street, Myrtle Beach, SC 29577
Postal address: PO Box 2115, Myrtle Beach, SC 29577
Tel: (843) 626 7444 *or* (800) 356 3016 (toll-free).
Fax: (843) 483 3010.
Website: www.myrtlebeachinfo.com

General Information

Nickname: Palmetto State
State bird: Carolina Wren
State flower: Carolina Yellow Jasmine
CAPITAL: Columbia
Date of admission to the Union: 23rd May 1788 (original 13 States; date of ratification of the Constitution)
POPULATION: 4,198,068 (official estimate 2004)
POPULATION DENSITY: 50.6 per sq km
2003 total overseas arrivals/US ranking: 144,000/26
TIME: Eastern (GMT - 5). *Daylight Saving Time* is observed.

THE STATE: From the rolling hills of the Upcountry to the glistening lakes of the midlands to the wide, white sandy beaches of the 320km- (200 mile-) Atlantic coastline, South Carolina has beautiful scenery and a rich history documented by attractive plantations and the northwestern foothills where fierce battles were fought during the Civil War. **Charleston**, situated on the coast, is one of its best-known tourist destinations, being the site of the first permanent English settlement. Other State attractions include **Myrtle Beach**, a popular resort city famous for its golf, centred on the sun-drenched 95km- (60 mile-) stretch of coastline on the northern border; peaceful island resorts such as **Kiawah**, **Seabrook** and **Hilton Head** which has 20km (12 miles) of beautiful beaches, unspoilt forest and golf courses; and the **Oconee State Park** in the lush northern Upcountry.

Travel - International

AIR: *Charleston International Airport* (website: www.chs-airport.com) is located 19km (12 miles) north of downtown Charleston. Airlines serving Charleston include *Continental*, *Delta*, *Northwest*, *United Express* and *US Airways*. A shuttle service and taxis are available to downtown Charleston. The State is accessible from several international gateways, including Atlanta, Charlotte, Cincinnati, New York, Philadelphia and Raleigh/Durham airports, with connecting services to domestic airports (see below).
Domestic airports: A number of national and regional carriers serve the airports in Charleston, Columbia, Florence, Greenville/Spartanburg, Hilton Head Island and Myrtle Beach. Hilton Head Island is also served by *Savannah (Georgia) International Airport*.
RAIL: Rail service through America's *Amtrak* (tel: (800) 872 7245 (toll-free); website: www.amtrak.com) system is available to Charleston and Columbia on the main New York–Washington–Miami routes, and to Greenville on the New York–Washington–New Orleans route. Trains on these routes also stop at a number of smaller centres.
ROAD: *Greyhound* (tel: (800) 229 9424 (toll-free); website: www.greyhound.com) is the main carrier, with bus terminals in Charleston (3610 Dorchester Road) and Greenville (100 W. Mcbee Avenue).
Approximate bus travel times: From Charleston to *Savannah* is three hours, and to *Charlotte* is six hours. From Columbia to *Savannah* is two hours, to *Washington, DC* is 10 hours, and to *Miami* is 13 hours.
URBAN: The *Coastal Rapid Public Transit Authority* serves Myrtle Beach and Conway. In Myrtle Beach, the *Great American Trolley* travels from the central beach area to Broadway at the Beach via Myrtle Square Mall. *CARTA* runs a reliable bus service within Charleston, while *Downtown Area Shuttles (DASH)* operates a frequent service from the tourist information point.

Resorts & Excursions

CHARLESTON: This aristocratic colonial port boasts beautifully restored antebellum homes, quaint old churches and lovely hidden gardens. So many churches dot the streets of Charleston that the city has been nicknamed 'The Holy City'. Some of the most historic among them include the **First Baptist Church**, **French Huguenot Church**, **St Philip's Episcopal Church** and the **Unitarian Church**. Popular attractions include **Cabbage Row**, which was the inspiration for America's first opera, *Porgy & Bess*. **Charles Towne Landing** is an unusual park located on the first permanent English settlement in South Carolina. Visitors can take a guided tram tour of the original 1670 fortification or board a replica of a 17th-century trading ketch and explore 11km (7 miles) of pathways through beautiful English park gardens. The **Market Hall**, a National Historic Landmark in a Greek Revival style, houses the **Confederate Museum**. Other attractions include **Middleton Place**, America's oldest formal English garden; **Magnolia Garden**; **Boone Hall Plantation**; **Drayton Hall**; the **Charleston Museum**; the **Cold War Memorial** at **Patriot's Point Naval and Maritime Museum**; and the **Spirit of South Carolina**, a replica tall ship docked at the north end of Union Terminal Pier.
EXCURSIONS: Fort Sumter is possibly the most important historic military site in the nation; the first shots of the Civil War were fired at Fort Sumter from Fort Johnson in 1861. Boat tours to Fort Sumter leave from **Liberty Square** and **Patriots Point Maritime Museum**. Charleston beach resorts include **Fairfield Ocean Ridge** at **Edisto Island**, **Seabrook Island Resort**, **Wild Dunes Resort** on the **Isle of Palms**, and **Kiawah Island**.
COLUMBIA: Columbia is the seat of State government and the hub of the arts, education and history in South Carolina. Attractions include the **Columbia Museum of Art**, where contemporary art shares the spotlight with masterpieces of the Baroque and Renaissance. Ranked among the top10 zoos in the nation, **Riverbanks Zoo and Garden** uses water and light to create the illusion of privacy and wild, unlimited space for the 2000 animals. The **Confederate Relic Room and Museum** features weapons and memorabilia, including flags, newspapers, clothing, pictures and money. The **Fort Jackson Museum** traces the history of the American soldier and a special exhibit focuses on the life and times of President Andrew Jackson. Other sights include **Robert Mills Historic House and Park**, **Millwood Plantation Ruins**, the **South Carolina State Museum**, **Riverfront Park** and **Historic Columbia Canal**.
GRAND STRAND AND MYRTLE BEACH: Stretching 96km (60 miles) from **Little River** near the North Carolina border to the tidelands of historic **Georgetown**, the Grand Strand is a long area dotted with beaches and tourist resorts. Popular attractions for children include the **Myrtle Beach National Wax Museum**; **Myrtle Beach Pavilion Amusement Park**, which boasts a giant **German Pipe Organ** dating from 1900; **NASCAR Speedpark**; and **Ripley's Aquarium**. Fun water rides can be found at **Myrtle Waves Water Park** and **Wild Water and Wheels** in **Surfside Beach**. **Family Kingdom Amusement Park** boasts *Swamp Fox*, a legendary wooden rollercoaster. There is also an array of family entertainment complexes offering professional stage and music programmes.
Other sights include **Brookgreen Gardens**, a showplace of art and nature developed in the 1930s by Archer and Anna Hyatt Huntington on the site of four colonial rice plantations. Amongst the 2000 species of plants, visitors can view around 550 of America's finest 19th- and 20th-century sculptures by artists such as Frederic Remington and Daniel Chester French, as well as many by Anna Hyatt Huntington herself. Across the street is the oceanfront **Huntington Beach State Park**, which is also home to **Atalaya**, once the castle-like studio of Mrs Huntington. The park offers a visitors' centre, boardwalk nature trails, camping, picnicking, sunbathing and nature programmes. **Myrtle Beach State Park** is one of the most popular parks in the State with cabins, camping swimming and pier fishing. The **South Carolina Hall of Fame** in **Myrtle Beach** has interactive video displays that salute outstanding citizens of South Carolina. The story of rice and indigo is told through dioramas and artefacts at the **Rice Museum** inside the **Old Market Building** in Georgetown.
PAWLEY'S ISLAND: One of the oldest resorts on the Atlantic Coast, the island was once a refuge for colonial rice planters' families wishing to avoid malaria. Many of the old beach houses can be rented. The original Pawley's Island rope hammocks have long been handmade in this area.
THE BLUE RIDGES: The Cherokees called this range 'the Great Blue Hills of God'. This was Cherokee country when the first traders came here. By the late-1820s, all that was left of the Lower Cherokee Nation were place and river names, such as Jocassee, Seneca and Tokeena. Today, Upcountry attractions include the **Anderson Arts Center**, the **Anderson County Museum**, **Greenville Zoo**, **Hollywild Animal Park**, **Campbell's Covered Bridge** and the **Irma Morris Museum of Fine Art**. The lively town of **Spartanburg** has several attractions, including **Cleveland Park**; **Hatcher Garden and Woodland Preserve**; the **Zimmerli Amphitheater**; the **Motor Sports Museum of the South**; and a new **Cultural Arts Facility** for the arts, science and heritage, including a 500-seat theatre.
The falls of **Whitewater** cascade over the Blue Ridge, down a drop of 275m (900ft). The top of **Raven Cliff Falls** in **Caesars Head State Park** offers a bird's-eye view encompassing the great sweep of the Blue Ridge. **Chattooga National Wild and Scenic River**, which separates South Carolina from Georgia, is a popular spot for whitewater rafting, canoeing and kayaking. **Table Rock State Park** is one of the State's oldest and most popular parks. Camping, boating, fishing, swimming, nature trails and summit hikes have drawn record numbers of visitors.

Social Profile

FOOD & DRINK: Charleston boasts a number of fine seafood restaurants, where specialities include shrimp with grits and *Charleston She-Crab Soup*. There are more than 1700 restaurants on the Grand Strand in Myrtle Beach, offering every type of food imaginable. The legal age for drinking is 21. Alcohol cannot be served after midnight on Saturday and all day Sunday, except in establishments with special permits in Charleston, Columbia, Edisto Beach, Hilton Head, the Myrtle Beach area and Santee.
THEATRE & CONCERTS: *Alabama Theater* and *Caroline Opry* in Myrtle Beach are popular venues for country music acts. Nearby, *Broadway at the Beach* offers 12 theatres with famous stars and a wide array of entertainment.
NIGHTLIFE: The liveliest spot in South Carolina is Myrtle Beach, where the nightclubs are open for business every night of the week. Choices range from country music venues to high-energy dance clubs. In Charleston, fun-seekers should head for the trendy new *Terrace* at *Merion Square* or the eclectic *Tristan* in the city's French Quarter. There is now also the massive *Mall of South Carolina* in Myrtle Beach.
SHOPPING: Popular places to shop for bargains include the *Waccamaw Outlet Park*, the *Factory Outlet Shops*, the variety of shops at *Barefoot Landing* and numerous golf and sporting goods shops. A popular purchase is the Pawley's Island hammock, which visitors can watch being made at the *Hammock Shop* on Pawley's Island. Myrtle Beach also offers good shopping opportunities at the new *Tanger Outlet Center*.
SPORT: There are over 335 **golf** courses statewide, and the Low Country offers more than 100 championship courses, several of which are frequented by renowned master players – the recently renovated *Kiawah Island Resort* is ranked as one of the top courses in the USA. **Tennis** is another big outdoor attraction, while **cycling** is well catered for with the creation of a network of cycle paths in *Litchfield Beach* and *Pawley's Island*; expansions to the network are planned for the future. Other activities include **watersports**, **hiking** and **fishing**. Hiking and **biking** are both possible on the *Palmetto Trail*, which opened after almost 10 years in the planning. The trail runs through Santee Cooper County from the coast to Manchester Forest in Sumter County.
SPECIAL EVENTS: The following is a selection of special events occurring in South Carolina in 2005:
Feb 11-20 *Budweiser Lowcountry Blues Bash*, Charleston. **Mar 12** *Hilton Head Island Shamrock Run*, Hilton Head. **Mar 17-19** *Patchwork Tales Storytelling Festival*, Rock Hill. **Mar 26** *Aiken Spring Steeplechase*, Aiken Spring; *Ebony Festival*, Argent Square. **Apr 1-3** *Spring Festival*, Cheraw. **Apr 2** *Peach Blossom Festival*, Johnston. **May 27-29** *Iris Festival*, Sumter. **May 27-Jun 12** *Spoleto Festival USA* (performing arts festival), Charleston. **Jun 18** *Art in the Park*, Myrtle Beach. **Jul 15-17** *Pageland Watermelon Festival*, Pageland. **Aug 6** *Little Mountain Reunion*. **Sep 17** *Harvest Hoe-Down Festival*, Aynor. **Sep 23-Oct 3** *Gastor Fest*, Olanta. **Sep 24** *Fire Fest*, Camden. **Oct 6-16** *South Carolina State Fair*, Columbia. **Nov 5** *Catfish Festival*, Society Hill. **Nov 5-6** *Revolutionary War Field Days*, Camden. **Nov 26** *Chitlin' Strut*, Salley. **Dec 2-4** *Christmas in the Village*, Pendleton. **Dec 4** *Christmas Parade*, Simpsonville.

Climate

South Carolina has a temperate climate. Spring and fall are the most pleasant seasons. In winter, temperatures generally average 40-45°F (5°-7°C) in inland areas, and 55-60°F (12°-15°C) by the shore. Summer temperatures, modified by mountains in some areas and by sea breezes in others, range from 75-85°F (24°-29°C), and can reach as high as 90°F (32°C) and above.

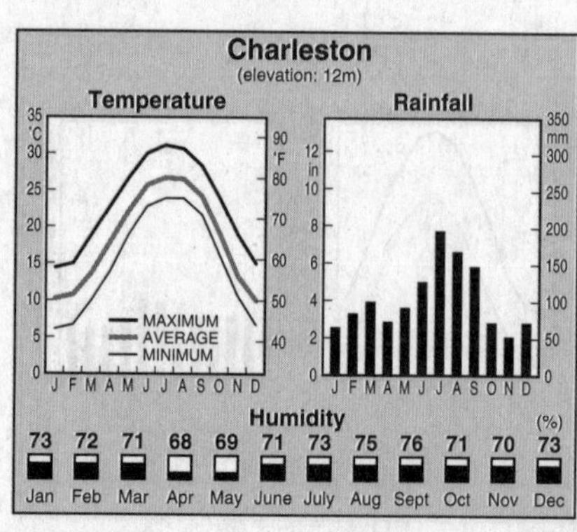

South Dakota

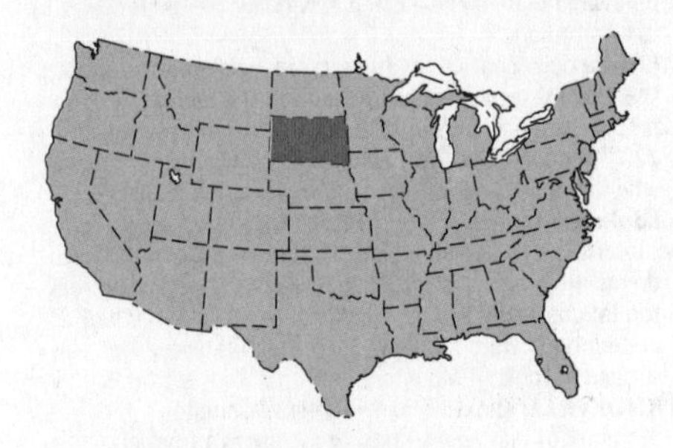

South Dakota Department of Tourism
711 East Wells Avenue, Pierre, SD 57501
Tel: (605) 773 3301 *or* (800) 732 5682 (toll-free).
Fax: (605) 773 3256.
E-mail: sdinfo@state.sd.us
Website: www.travelsd.com
Rocky Mountain International (UK Office)
7 Thornton Avenue, Warsash, Southampton, Hampshire SO31 9GD, UK
Tel: (01489) 557 533 (trade enquiries only) *or* (09063) 640 655 (customer request line; calls cost 60p per minute).
Fax: (01489) 557 534.
E-mail: rmi.uk@btinternet.com
Website: www.rmi-realamerica.com
Rapid City CVB
Street address: 444 Mount Rushmore Road, Rapid City, SD 57701
Postal address: PO Box 747, Rapid City, SD 57709
Tel: (605) 343 1744 *or* (800) 487 3223 (toll-free).
Fax: (605) 348 9217.
E-mail: tourist@rapidcitycvb.com
Website: www.rapidcitycvb.com
Sioux Falls CVB
200 North Phillips Avenue, Suite 102, Sioux Falls, SD 57104
Tel: (605) 336 1620 *or* (800) 333 2072 (toll-free).
Fax: (605) 336 6499.
E-mail: sfcvb@siouxfalls.com
Website: www.siouxfallscvb.com

Credit: © South Dakota Department of Tourism

General Information

Nickname: Mount Rushmore State
State bird: Ring-necked Pheasant
State flower: American Pasque Flower
CAPITAL: Pierre
Date of admission to the Union: 2 Nov 1889
POPULATION: 770,883 (official estimate 2004)
POPULATION DENSITY: 17 per sq km
2003 total overseas arrivals: Under 38,000
TIME: Central (GMT - 6) in the eastern part of the State; Mountain (GMT - 7) in the west. *Daylight Saving Time* is observed.

THE STATE: Tucked into the heart of the USA, the 'Mount Rushmore State' offers untouched nature in abundance, vast stretches of fertile prairies and early pioneer towns. Near the eastern border, **Sioux Falls** is the largest city in the region, and boasts its namesake waterfall, as well as the **Center for Western Studies**, the **Old Courthouse Museum**, **St Joseph's Cathedral** and the **Washington Pavilion of Arts and Science**. On the opposite side of the State, **Rapid City** is the gateway to the **Black Hills**, with mountains, caves, forests and lakes; **Wind Cave National Park**; and **Custer State Park**, with its herd of over 1500 bison. **Jewel Cave National Monument**, the third-longest cave in the world, is also located at **Custer**.
Also in South Dakota's southwest corner is its biggest tourist attraction by far, the **Mount Rushmore National Memorial**, where the 18m- (60ft-) high heads of four US presidents (George Washington, Thomas Jefferson, Theodore Roosevelt and Abraham Lincoln) have been blasted and carved out of the mountain. Work began on this massive 'Shrine of Democracy' in 1927 and took 14 years to complete. In the Black Hills, the **Crazy Horse Memorial**, a privately funded monument, is the world's largest mountain sculpture in progress. The upper half of the 22-storey high horses head is a memorial honouring the North American Indian, standing 171m- (563ft-) high and 195m- (641ft-) long. The excellent **Indian Museum of North America** is located at Crazy Horse Memorial and is well worth a visit. Just to the south, the community of **Hot Springs** is home to **Evans Plunge**, the world's largest naturally heated swimming pool and **The Mammoth Site**, the world's largest concentration of Columbian and woolly mammoth bones discovered in their primary context (ie where they died). **Badlands National Park** encompasses 98,785 hectares (244,000 acres) of striking rock formations – steep canyons, jagged spires, bands of colourful rocks – blended with mixed-grass prairies. Campgrounds and cabins are available to visitors. **Pierre**, the capital of South Dakota, is home to numerous attractions, including the **South Dakota Cultural Heritage Center**, **South Dakota National Guard Museum**, **South Dakota State Capitol** and the **South Dakota World War II Memorial**. Some 48km (30 miles) north of **Fort Pierre** is **Triple U Buffalo Ranch**, the location of many scenes in the film *Dances with Wolves*.

Pierre (elevation: 526m)
Temperature — Rainfall
MAXIMUM / AVERAGE / MINIMUM
Humidity (Bismarck ND, %)

Jan	Feb	Mar	Apr	May	June	July	Aug	Sept	Oct	Nov	Dec
77	77	71	63	61	66	63	63	66	66	73	78

Tennessee

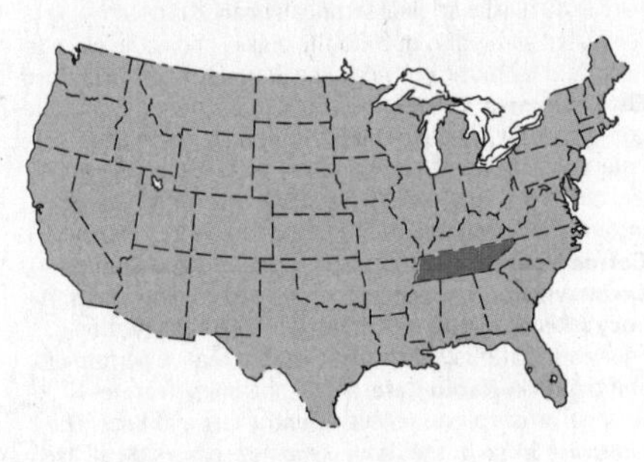

Tennessee Department of Tourism Development
312 8th Avenue North, 25th Floor, Nashville, TN 37243
Tel: (615) 741 2159 *or* (800) 462 8366 (toll-free).
Fax: (615) 741 7225.
E-mail: tourdev@state.tn.us
Website: www.tnvacation.com *or* www.tntourism.com
Tennessee Tourism (UK)
Lofthouse Enterprises, Woodlands Park Street, Hitchin, Herts SG4 9AH, UK
Tel: (01462) 440784. Fax: (01462) 440783.
E-mail: tennessee@david-nicholson.com
Website: www.deep-south-usa.com
Chattanooga Area CVB
2 Broad Street, Chattanooga, TN 37402

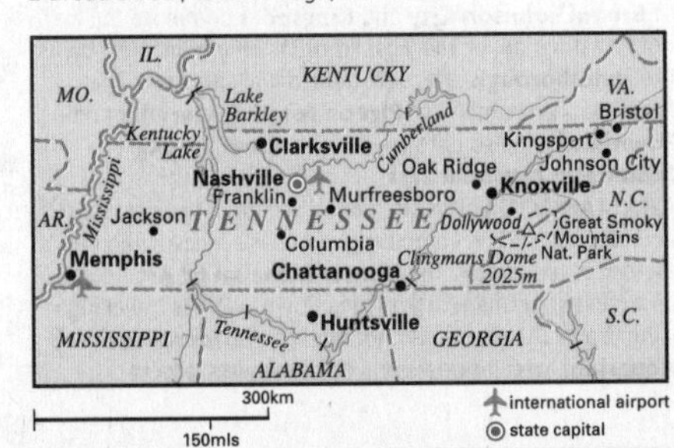

Tel: (423) 756 8687 *or* (800) 322 3344 (toll-free).
Fax: (423) 265 1630.
Website: www.chattanoogafun.com
Knoxville CVB
301 South Gay Street, Knoxville, TN 37902
Tel: (865) 523 7263 *or* (800) 727 8045 *or* (866) 790 5373 (toll-free). Fax: (865) 673 4400.
Website: www.knoxville.org
Memphis CVB
47 Union Avenue, Memphis, TN 38103
Tel: (901) 543 5300 *or* (800) 873 6282 (toll-free).
Fax: (901) 543 5350/1.
E-mail: vic1@mcvb.org
Website: www.memphistravel.com
Nashville CVB
140 Fourth Avenue North, Suite G250, Nashville, TN 37219
Tel: (615) 259 4730 *or* 259 4700 *or* (800) 657 6910 (toll-free).
Fax: (615) 259 4126.
E-mail: nashcvb@musiccityusa.com
Website: www.musiccityusa.com

General Information

Nickname: Volunteer State
State bird: Mockingbird
State flower: Iris
CAPITAL: Nashville
Date of admission to the Union: 1st June 1796
POPULATION: 5,900,962 (official estimate 2004)
POPULATION DENSITY: 54.1 per sq km
2003 total overseas arrivals/US ranking: 162,000/24
TIME: Eastern (GMT - 5) in the eastern part of the State; Central (GMT - 6) in the west. *Daylight Saving Time* is observed.

THE STATE: Located in the southeast region of the USA, Tennessee is unique in that it shares a border with eight States. Tennessee has always been a melting pot of musical styles. From the eastern mountains came Appalachian folk songs and Bluegrass, while Country music flowered in Nashville. Gospel, Blues, Rockabilly, and ultimately, Rock 'n' Roll, all stemmed from the Mississippi belt. As well as being able to investigate the roots of major popular music traditions, travellers will also find the world's largest Bible-producing business.
Nashville is a major music performance and recording centre and also boasts a host of fine colleges and churches. To the southwest is **Memphis**, home of the blues and the birthplace of Rock 'n' Roll, near the Mississippi border. Tennessee's largest city and a major trading centre, Memphis is known chiefly for being the location of *Graceland*, the home of Elvis Presley. Historic *Beale Street*, featured in so many blues songs, is also in Memphis. Barbecues reign supreme in this city, and the annual *World Championship Barbecue Cooking Contest* takes place here every May.
Over on the southeastern side of the State, perched next to the Tennessee River, is **Chattanooga**. This bustling city, with its train made famous by Glenn Miller's song 'Chattanooga Choo Choo', is also home to the **Hunter Museum of Art**, and the **Tennessee Aquarium**, the largest freshwater aquarium in the world.
More than half of Tennessee is forested, and great tracts have been set aside as State and National parks, forests, wilderness areas and game preserves. **Gatlinburg** and **Pigeon Forge** are the starting points for trips into the **Great Smoky Mountains National Park**, as is the pleasant city of **Knoxville**, a former State capital.

Travel - International

AIR: International airports: *Memphis International Airport (MEM)* (website: www.mscaa.com) is 16km (10 miles) southeast of the city (travel time – 20 minutes). Most major car hire firms are represented. Taxis, limousines and hotel shuttles are available to the city centre, as is the hourly *Memphis Area Transit Authority (MATA)* local bus, which departs near Terminal C. An out-of-town shuttle bus

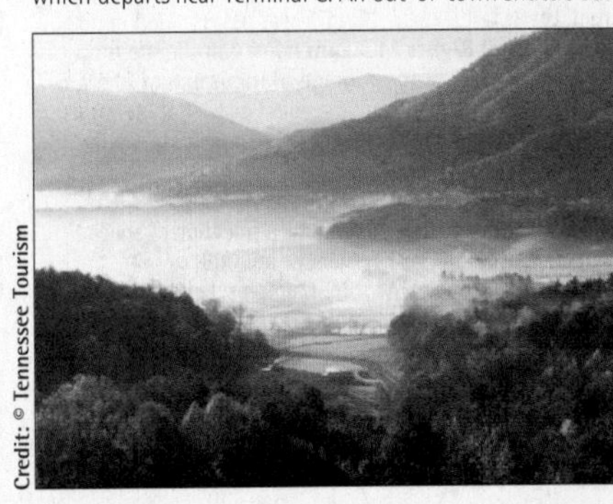

Credit: © Tennessee Tourism

A B C D E F G H I J K L M N O P Q R S T U V W X Y Z

operates from the airport to Arkansas (Little Rock and Jonesboro) and to Mississippi (Oxford).

Nashville International Airport (BNA) (website: www.nashintl.com *or* www.flynashville.com) is located 13km (8 miles) southeast of the city. The *Metropolitan Transit Authority (MTA)* bus no. 18 leaves the airport nine times a day (Mon-Fri) and four times a day at the weekend. The *Anytime-Transport Shuttle Service* (website: www.anytimetransportshuttleservice.com) runs to destinations in suburban Nashville, Middle Tennessee, and Bowling Green (Kentucky). Limousine services, car hire and taxis are widely available. *Gray Line* operates a van service to hotels in central Nashville every 15 minutes 0500-2300 (travel time – 30 minutes). *Greyhound* operates services to Fort Campbell, Knoxville and Memphis several times a day; the *Express Shuttle* service travels to Chattanooga seven times a day; and the *K-Town Shuttle* serves Knoxville four times a day.

Domestic airports: *Chattanooga Metropolitan Airport (CHA)* (website: www.chattairport.com), 5km (3 miles) east of the city, serves the greater Chattanooga area including southeast Tennessee, north Georgia, and northeast Alabama. Car hire, taxi and limousine services are also available.

McGhee Tyson Airport (TYS) (website: www.tys.org) is located 7.5km (12 miles) south of central Knoxville. Car hire companies, limousines and taxis are available at the airport; the *Airport Express Shuttle* provides connections to the city centre.

RAIL: Memphis and Newbern-Dyersberg, on the Chicago-New Orleans line, are the only stations on the national Amtrak rail network (tel: (800) 872 7245 (toll-free); website: www.amtrak.com). Nashville and Chattanooga have connecting Thruway bus services (operated by *Greyhound*) to Atlanta, which is on the New Orleans–Washington, DC–New York City route. Car hire from *Hertz* is available at the Memphis station. The Tennessee Valley Railroad runs a 10km (6 mile) round trip from Chattanooga.

ROAD: Bus: *Greyhound* (tel: (800) 229 9424 (toll-free); website: www.greyhound.com) is the main service provider, with bus terminals at Chattanooga, Knoxville, Memphis and Nashville.

Resorts & Excursions

West Tennessee

The land between the **Tennessee** and **Mississippi** rivers is fertile territory for exploration, especially as the homes of heroes and icons – Davy Crockett, Alex Haley, Casey Jones and Buford Pusser – are open to the public. Nature lovers will enjoy the bald eagles at **Reelfoot Lake**, the recreational opportunities of **Kentucky Lake** or the quiet, sombre atmosphere of the battlefields at **Shiloh National Military Park**. A visit to the **West Tennessee Delta Heritage Center** in **Brownsville**, showcasing the region's heritage, provides a good introduction to the area. Its five major exhibitions include the **Tennessee Room**, which highlights West Tennessee towns and attractions, the **West Tennessee Music Museum**, the **Scenic Hatchie River Museum**, the **Cotton Museum**, and **Sleepy John Estes' House**, a tribute to this big man of the blues.

MEMPHIS: Memphis enjoys a well-deserved reputation among music-lovers all over the world. Critics claim that the Blues were born here on **Beale Street** and a legendary piece published by the 'Father of the Blues', W C Handy, in 1912, successfully proclaimed its power and authenticity. Beale Street includes restaurants, gift shops, boutiques, parks and nightclubs, as well as the **Beale Street Police Museum** and **A Schwab's Dry Goods Store**, a small department store which has been in the same family since 1876 and still offers old-fashioned bargains.

For many, though, the only reason to come to Memphis is to pay respect to the King – Elvis Presley. His beloved home, **Graceland**, is a mecca to the pilgrims of Rock 'n' Roll. The impressive **Trophy Room** effectively documents his impact on the music industry as a singer and entertainer.

Aside from its musical heritage, Memphis' legendary past as a Delta city and a civil rights centre should not be forgotten. It was at the Lorraine Motel at 450 Mulberry Street, that Martin Luther King Jr was assassinated and the **National Civil Rights Museum** housed at the site is an effective reminder of the courage of thousands of African-Americans. In the downtown business district of Memphis, cotton, the 'white gold' of the Delta region, is still hand-graded in a century-old warehouse and decorative paddle wheelers still churn their way up the Mississippi.

SPECIAL EVENTS: The following is a selection of special events occurring in West Tennessee in 2005:

Feb 1-28 *Black History Month*, Memphis. **Feb 21-22** *Beale Street Zydeco Festival*, Memphis. **May 12** *World Championship Barbecue Contest*, Memphis. **Jun 3-4** *Memphis Italian Festival*. **Jun 18-20** *Juneteenth Festival*, Memphis **Aug 8-14** *Elvis Week*, Graceland Mansion, Memphis. **Nov-Jan 2006** *Christmas at Graceland*, Graceland Mansion, Memphis.

Central Tennessee

The heartland of the state was a crucial theatre of operations during the American Civil War. At **Carter House**, in **Franklin**, the bullet-pocked walls bear witness to one of the deadliest battles of the campaign. For those with a taste for military history as well as the macabre, the **Tennessee Antebellum Trail** offers daily tours to seven historic sites, including the blood-stained floors of **Carnton Mansion**, where, after the battle at **Franklin**, the bodies of five Confederate generals once lay. Starting in Nashville, this 145km- (90 mile-) loop drive also takes in the **Rippavilla Plantation**, dating from 1852, where the five generals ate their last breakfast.

Aside from its martial past, this beautiful and lively region also boasts a musical and entertainment heritage. Country music is alive and well at the **Grand Ole Opry** and the **Ryman Auditorium**. Connoisseurs of bourbon should note that the famous **Jack Daniel Distillery** offers daily guided tours (0900-1630) and much insight into Mister Jack's famous distilling process.

Visitors with a passion for open countryside should visit the area where the **Tennessee Walking Horses** graze or the ancient **Cumberland Plateau**, which forms a natural boundary between Middle and East Tennessee. Waterfalls, deep river canyons, parks and resorts characterise this historic region.

NASHVILLE: The home of Country music, Tennessee's capital is known as 'Music City USA'. The centre of Nashville's music industry is **Music Row**, around Division and Demonbreun streets. Spanning an entire city block, the **Country Music Hall of Fame** is located in the revitalised entertainment district of central Nashville.

Nashville has a reputation as the 'Athens of the South', and boasts a life-sized replica of the Parthenon in **Centennial Park**. It features **Athena**, the 'tallest indoor statue in the Western World', and the celebrated **Cowan Collection of American Paintings**. In central Nashville, **Union Station Hotel** at 1001 Broadway has a magnificent arched ceiling of stained glass, whilst the **District** area features the cast-iron and masonry of its late 19th-century commercial buildings, as well as numerous restaurants and clubs.

Galleries and museums, many of which reflect Tennessee's Antebellum and plantation history, include the **Carl Van Vechten Gallery**, exhibiting collections by Cézanne, Picasso and Renoir as well as displays of work by Georgia O'Keeffe and Alfred Steiglitz. Another popular attraction is the **Hermitage**, President Andrew Jackson's manor house. Admission includes a visit to nearby **Tulip Grove Mansion**. The **Bicentennial Mall** was built to honour the State's founding in 1776. The award-winning **Opryland Hotel and Convention Center** features **The Delta**, an indoor, quarter-mile river, complete with four 25-passenger flatboats.

ENTERTAINMENT: The **Grand Ole Opry** is the setting for the nation's longest-running live radio show, which moved here in 1976 (the original setting, Ryman, has been renovated and is also open to the public) and is the place to hear Country music on Friday and Saturday nights. **Gaylord Entertainment Center** hosts concerts, sporting events and conventions while **Opry Mills** is a new shopping and entertainment resort covering more than 750 acres on the site of former Opryland USA. Good venues for live music include **Caffé Milano** (jazz, bluegrass and rock), **Henry's Coffee House** with acoustic performances and **Canyon Country Saloon**, which features up and coming artists. **Lucy's Record Shop** sells music during the day, but on Friday and Saturday hosts the latest alternative performers, and the funky **Radio Cafe**, an old pharmacy, features national artists playing Blues, Country, Jazz and Rock. *The Nashville Scene* or the *Tennessean* newspapers list all live music events.

SPECIAL EVENTS: The following is a selection of special events occurring in Central Tennessee in 2005:

Feb 10-13 *Antiques and Garden Show*, Nashville. **Mar 15** *President Andrew Jackson's Birthday Celebrations*, Nashville. **Apr 4-9** *Tin Pan South*, Nashville. **Apr 11** *CMT Music Awards*, Nashville. **Apr 23** *Latin Music Street Fair*, Nashville. **May 27-Sep 5** *Music City Summer Festival*, Nashville. **Sep 9-18** *Tennessee State Fair*, Nashville.

East Tennessee

This region was America's major frontier crossing. Thousands of settlers followed in Daniel Boone's footsteps westwards through the **Cumberland Gap**. The three cities of **Bristol**, **Johnson City** and **Kingsport** dominate the northeast region, or the 'First Frontier', where historic towns like **Jonesborough** offer self-guided walking tours. The family tourism centres of **Pigeon Forge**, **Sevierville** and **Townsend** are also gateways to the **Great Smoky Mountains National Park**.

CHATTANOOGA: This city began as a trading post in 1815 and has retained its commercial emphasis by evolving into a factory outlet centre. The **Hunter Museum of Art** houses an excellent permanent art collection as well as travelling exhibitions. The city is also notable for the **Tennessee Aquarium**, which houses one of the world's largest collections of freshwater marine life. A US$129 million expansion project for Chattanooga, completed in May 2005, encompasses the **Creative Discovery Museum**, the **Tennessee Aquarium** and the **Hunter Museum of Art**. It improves the current facilities of Ross Landing, including a renovated marina and a brand new public pier and riverfront park.

Chattanooga contains another record-holding installation – the world's steepest passenger railway, the **Incline**, which propels its passengers up a stomach-churning gradient of 72.7°. The journey is worthwhile, especially on a clear day, when the territories of seven States are visible from **Lookout Mountain**. Here, at **Rock City Gardens**, subterranean black-lit gnome dioramas and Mother Goose theme areas are constructed around several interesting rock formations. **Ruby Falls**, a spectacular 44m- (145ft-) high underground waterfall flows 341m (1120ft) below the surface of Lookout Mountain.

KNOXVILLE: Knoxville, named after Washington's Secretary of War, Henry Knox, began life as a frontier outpost after the Revolutionary War. Bordered by huge lakes created by the Tennessee Valley Authority, Knoxville offers some eclectic sightseeing. A stroll through the **World's Fair Park** leads to the **Knoxville Museum of Art**, while **Blount Mansion**, a National Historic Landmark, was the 1792 frame house of governor William Blount. Nearby, the **James White Fort** still exhibits portions of the original stockade built in 1786 by Knoxville's founder.

The **Farmer's Market**, 24km (15 miles) from the downtown area, offers an authentic taste of Appalachia. The pavilion sells local produce, plants, jams, jellies, arts and crafts. The **Museum of Appalachia**, in Norris, is a huge village replete with authentic houses, barns and cells.

GREAT SMOKY MOUNTAINS: The largest wilderness area in the USA, this national park extends over half a million acres of the **Appalachian Mountains**, bordered by North Carolina and the Tennessee valleys. The park is home to bears, white-tailed deer, wild turkeys and more than 1500 species of flowering plants. Conifer forests are to be found at elevations of more than 1800m (6000ft). The mountains are beautiful in all seasons, but perhaps the best time to see them is in October when they are showered in colour. The park has three visitor centres, *Cades Cove*, *Oconaluftee Visitor Centre* and *Sugarlands*. There are also 10 campgrounds, each with tent sites, trailer space, water and tables. There are over 1400km (900 miles) of hiking trails and 270km (170 miles) of road throughout the park. Rangers at the visitor centres can assist with trip planning.

DOLLYWOOD: Die-hard Country fans will want to visit this all-American attraction in the Tennessee hills, created by the Queen of Country herself – Dolly Parton. Dollywood is usually open between May and October 1000-1800, and in winter for Christmas Specials. The park's newest attraction is **Thunderhead**, a US$7 million wooden rollercoaster. Dollywood is located in the city of **Pigeon Forge**, which has major shopping outlet malls and celebrates the culture of the East Tennessee mountains. Craftspeople show their skills and Country stars perform.

SPECIAL EVENTS: The following is a selection of special events occurring in Tennessee in 2005:

Feb 26 *Fifth Annual Saddle Up*, Pigeon Forge. **Mar 9-Jun 10** *Springfest*, Gatlinburg. **Apr 6-24** *Dogwood Arts Festival*, Knoxville. **Apr 21** *Fifth Annual Gatlinburg Rib Fest*. **Jul 3-4** *Fourth of July Midnight Parade*, Gatlinburg. **Sep 23-24** *Townsend Fall Festival and Old Timer's Day*.

Climate

Located in the Temperate Zone, Tennessee has a generally mild climate year round, but still enjoys four distinct seasons. The average high temperature in winter is 9.4°C (49°F) and the average low is -1°C (30°F). In the summer, the average high temperature is 31.7°C (89°F) and the average low is 19.4°C (67°F). The average annual rainfall in Tennessee is 124.7cm (49.7 inches).

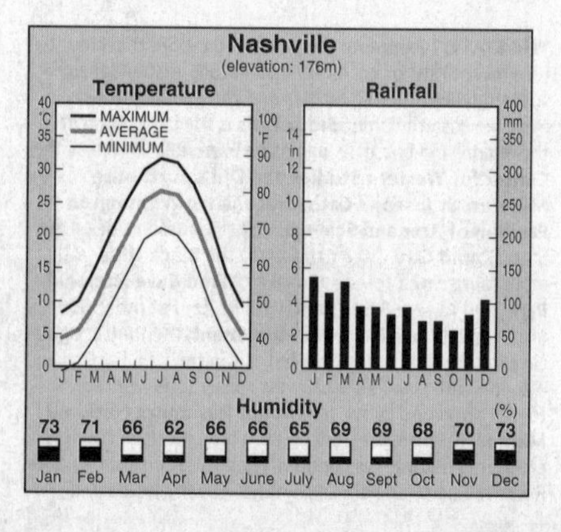

Texas

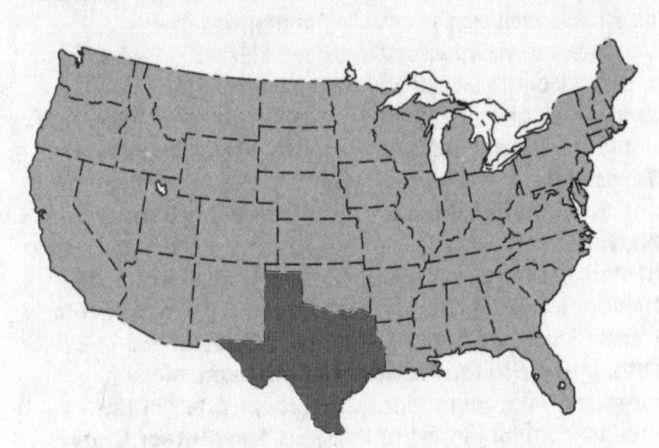

Texas Economic Development, Tourism Division
Street address: 221 East 11th Street, 4th Floor, Austin, TX 78701
Postal address: PO Box 12428, Austin, TX 78711
Tel: (512) 936 0101. Fax: (512) 936 3030.
Website: www.traveltex.com
State of Texas Tourism Office (UK)
c/o First Public Relations, Molasses House, Clove Hitch Quay, Plantation Wharf, London SW11 3TN, UK
Tel: (020) 7978 5233. Fax: (020) 7924 3134.
E-mail: fiona@firstpr.co.uk
Website: www.firstpr.co.uk
Amarillo Convention and Visitors Council
1000 South Polk Street, Bivins Mansion, 2nd Floor, Amarillo, TX 79101
Tel: (806) 374 1497 *or* (800) 692 1338 (toll-free).
Fax: (806) 373 3909.
E-mail: amarcvb@arn.net
Website: www.visitamarillotx.com
Arlington CVB
1905 East Randol Mill Road, Arlington, TX 76011
Tel: (817) 265 7721 *or* (800) 433 5374 (toll-free).
Fax: (817) 265 5640.
Website: www.arlington.org
Austin CVB
301 Congress, Suite 200, Austin, TX 78701
Tel: (512) 474 5171 *or* (800) 926 2282 (toll-free).
Fax: (512) 583 7282.
E-mail: tourism@austintexas.org
Website: www.austintexas.org
Bandera CVB
PO Box 171, Bandera, TX 78003
Tel: (830) 796 3045 *or* (800) 364 3833 (toll-free).
Fax: (830) 796 4121.
E-mail: bandera@hctc.net
Website: www.banderacowboycapital.com
Corpus Christi CVB
1201 North Shoreline, Corpus Christi, TX 78401
Tel: (361) 881 1888 *or* (800) 678 6232 *or* 766 2322 (toll-free).
Fax: (361) 887 9023.
Website: www.corpuschristicvb.com
Dallas CVB
325 North St Paul, Suite 700, Dallas, TX 75201
Tel: (214) 571 1000 *or* 1300 (tourist information) *or* (800) 232 5527 (toll-free). Fax: (214) 571 1008 *or* 1350.
E-mail: inform@dallascvb.com
Website: www.visitdallas.com
El Paso CVB
1 Civic Center Plaza, El Paso, TX 79901
Tel: (915) 534 0600/1 *or* (800) 351 6024 (toll-free).
Fax: (915) 534 0687.
E-mail: info@elpasocvb.com
Website: www.visitelpaso.com
Fort Worth CVB
415 Throckmorton Street, Fort Worth, TX 76102
Tel: (817) 336 8791 *or* (800) 433 5747 (toll-free).
Fax: (817) 336 3282.
Website: www.fortworth.com
Galveston Island CVB
2504 Church Street, Galveston, TX 77550
Tel: (409) 763 6564 *or* (866) 505 4456 (toll-free).
Fax: (409) 765 8611.
E-mail: info@galvestoncvb.com
Website: www.galveston.com
Greater Houston Convention and Visitors Bureau
901 Bagby, Suite 100, Houston, TX 77002
Tel: (713) 437 5200 *or* (800) 4468 7866 (toll-free).
Fax: (713) 227 6336.
E-mail: houtour@ghcvb.org
Website: www.visithoustontexas.com
McAllen Chamber of Commerce
Street address: 1200 Ash Avenue, McAllen, TX 78501
Postal address: PO Box 790, McAllen, TX 78505
Tel: (956) 682 2871 *or* (877) 622 5536 (toll-free).
Fax: (956) 631 8571.
Website: www.mcallen.com
Odessa CVB
700 North Grant, Suite 200, Odessa, TX 79761
Tel: (432) 333 7871 *or* (800) 780 4678 (toll-free).
Fax: (432) 333 7858.
E-mail: info@odessacvb.com
Website: www.odessacvb.com
San Antonio CVB
203 South St Mary's Street, International Center Building, 2nd Floor, San Antonio, TX 78205
Tel: (210) 207 6700 *or* (800) 447 3372 (toll-free).
Fax: (210) 207 6782.
E-mail: sacvb@sanantoniovisit.com
Website: www.sanantoniovisit.com
Waco CVB
Street address: Waco Convention Center, 100 Washington Avenue, Waco, TX 76702
Postal address: PO Box 2570, Waco, TX 76702
Tel: (254) 750 5810 *or* (800) 321 9226 (toll-free).
Fax: (254) 750 5801.
E-mail: visitus@wacocvb.com
Website: www.wacocvb.com

General Information

Nickname: Lone Star State
State bird: Western Mockingbird
State flower: Bluebonnet
CAPITAL: Austin
Date of admission to the Union: 29th Dec 1845
POPULATION: 22,490,022 (official estimate 2004)
POPULATION DENSITY: 32.3 per sq km
2003 total overseas arrivals/US ranking: 829,000/7
TIME: Central (GMT - 6). *Daylight Saving Time* is observed.

THE STATE: Texas, the 'Lone Star State', is the second-largest state in the USA, covering more than 695,676 sq km (268,600 sq miles). Spain was the first European power to lay claim to Texas; the State also flew the flags of France and Mexico before gaining its independence in 1836. Texas borders Mexico along the **Rio Grande** and embraces vast mountain ranges and canyons to the west; lakes, plantations and pine forests to the east; broad plains to the north; citrus groves, **Gulf of Mexico** beaches and low-lying alluvial plains to the south; and rolling hill country and clear natural springs at its heart. Its great wealth stems from its vast oil reserves. It has several booming cities: **Dallas**, **El Paso**, **Fort Worth**, **Houston**, **San Antonio**, and its capital city, **Austin**.

Travel - International

AIR: International airports: *Dallas/Fort Worth International (DFW)* (website: www.dfwairport.com) is 27km (17 miles) from both cities (travel time - 35 minutes). The airport is the fourth-busiest in the USA and sixth-busiest in the world (2003 passenger rankings), annually serving over 52 million passengers. The airport itself is the size of Manhattan. Passenger shuttle vans provide a free transit link between terminals, while *American Airlines* and *American Eagle* passengers can use the Skylink High-Speed Train that connects Terminals A, B, C, E and DFW's future international Terminal D. Opened early in 2005, the new system keeps average ride times to five minutes, with a maximum ride time of nine minutes between the farthest distances. In addition, passengers wait an average of two minutes for the trains to arrive in the spacious stations that were contructed just for Skylink. The *Dallas Area Rapid Transit (DART)* no. 202 express bus runs from the North Shuttle Parking Lot to downtown; a free shuttle service is provided to the North Shuttle Parking Lot from all terminals. There are also free shuttles to the *Trinity Railway Express* commuter line, which links Dallas, Fort Worth and the airport. The *Yellow Checker Shuttle Co.* Airporter van runs to the city every 30 minutes. Taxis, shared-ride shuttles, limousines, courtesy cars and car hire are also available.
George Bush Intercontinental Airport Houston (IAH) (website: www.houstonairportsystem.org) is 32km (20 miles) north of the city (travel time - 30 minutes). The *Airport Express* shuttle travels to the Galleria and downtown hotels (travel time - 45 minutes). Metro bus routes 101 and 102 operate every 30 minutes approximately 0500-2400 daily, dropping passengers off in downtown Houston. Taxis are also available, but expensive.
El Paso International Airport (ELP) (website: www.elpasointernationalairport.com) is 13km (8 miles) east of the city; it serves as a gateway to western Texas, southern New Mexico, and northern Mexico. Sun Metro runs daily bus services to the airport on route 33. Many hotels offer a complimentary shuttle service.
San Antonio International Airport (SAT) (website: www.sanantonio.gov/airport) is 14km (8.5 miles) from the city, with flights from Latin America and major US cities. Public buses and the more expensive *SA Trans Shuttle* run to the city centre (travel times - one hour and 20 minutes respectively). Taxis are also available.

Credit: © Texas Tourism

Domestic airports: *Dallas Love Field (DAL)* is 9.5km (6 miles) from Dallas city centre. The airport is a hub for *Southwest Airlines*. *DART* bus 39 travels to downtown Dallas; shuttles and taxis are also available. Other primarily domestic airports include *Amarillo International Airport*, *Austin Bergstrom International Airport*, *Corpus Christi International Airport*, *Laredo International Airport*, *Lubbock International Airport* and *William P Hobby Airport* in Houston.
Approximate flight times: From Dallas/Fort Worth to *Austin* is 50 minutes, to *London* is nine hours, to *Miami* is two hours 40 minutes, and to *New York* is three hours 30 minutes. Flight times from Houston are similar.
RAIL: *Amtrak* (tel: (800) 872 7245 (toll-free); website: www.amtrak.com) journeys between main cities are difficult and (except for Dallas to Fort Worth) can only be made on the long-distance trains. The daily *Texas Eagle* service from Chicago passes through Dallas and Fort Worth on its way to San Antonio, where transfers to Los Angeles are possible on the thrice-weekly *Sunset Limited*, which arrives from Orlando via New Orleans and Houston. The daily *Heartland Flyer* links Oklahoma City and Fort Worth.
ROAD: *Greyhound* (tel: (800) 229 9424 (toll-free); website: www.greyhound.com) runs frequent services connecting Dallas, Fort Worth, Houston, San Antonio and other major towns and cities in Texas and further afield. Bus services off the main routes are not highly developed.
Approximate bus travel times: From *Dallas/Fort Worth* to *Oklahoma City* is four hours 30 minutes, to *Houston* is four hours 30 minutes, to *San Antonio* is six hours, to *Tulsa* is seven hours, to *Amarillo* is eight hours, to *Memphis* is 13 hours 30 minutes, to *New Orleans* is 13 hours and to *El Paso* is 13 hours.
From Houston (tel: (713) 759 6581) to *San Antonio* is four hours, to *Dallas* is four hours 30 minutes and to *New Orleans* is eight hours 30 minutes.
Approximate driving times: From Dallas/Fort Worth to *Oklahoma City* is four hours 30 minutes, to *Houston* is four hours 30 minutes, to *San Antonio* is six hours, to *Little Rock* is seven hours, to *Amarillo* is seven hours, to *Kansas City* is seven hours, to *Jackson* is eight hours, to *New Orleans* is 10 hours, to *El Paso* is 12 hours, to *St Louis* is 13 hours, to *Denver* is 16 hours, to *Chicago* is 19 hours, to *Mexico City* is 24 hours, to *Miami* is 28 hours, to *Los Angeles* is 29 hours, to *New York* is 33 hours, and to *Seattle* is 44 hours.
From Houston to *San Antonio* is four hours, to *Brownsville* is seven hours, to *New Orleans* is seven hours, to *El Paso* is 15 hours, to *Chicago* is 24 hours, to *Miami* is 25 hours, and to *Los Angeles* is 31 hours. All times are based on non-stop driving at or below the applicable speed limits.
URBAN: *Dallas Area Rapid Transit (DART)* (website: www.dart.org) provides a convenient light-rail service with two north-south lines passing through the city centre. *DART* also runs the *Trinity Railway Express* commuter rail line between Dallas and Fort Worth; buses between the cities are operated by *Greyhound* (see above). *DART* also operates the city's local bus network, which is well run and reasonably priced. DART services run daily 0500-0030. The *McKinney Trolley* runs a route between the *Dallas Museum of Art* in downtown Dallas to the West End Historic District. In Fort Worth, *The T* operates both the bus

Credit: © Texas Tourism

network and the *Longhorn Trolley* service, which runs between various tourist attractions and hotels. Most major car hire companies have offices in both cities and motor campers are available for hire. Houston's *Metropolitan Transport Authority of Harris County*, Texas *(METRO)* (website: www.ridemetro.org) provides reasonably priced bus services. The *METRORail* light-rail system, running 12km (7.5 miles) from downtown Houston to south of Reliant Park, opened in January 2004. The train serves 16 stations with transfers to *METRO* buses available. This new system is a massive step forward for Houston and will hopefully relieve some of the congestion in the city, although there have been complaints about the slow speed of the trains and the short distance covered. Taxis are readily available, but can be impractical and expensive for short distances. Car hire is the best way to get around, but visitors are advised to make advance reservations as the demand is high.

Resorts & Excursions

DALLAS: Originally a trading post, Dallas has grown into an important centre for commerce and fashion. It has a glittering high-rise skyline, elegant stores, fine restaurants and a rich cultural life. Located in the Prairies and Lakes region, Dallas is a modern sophisticated city, yet still possesses the much-renowned Texan hospitality and southwestern charm. It is increasingly recognised for its cosmopolitan spirit and entrepreneurial flair.

Dallas is a city rich in historical sites and futuristic sights. The downtown area features shimmering glass towers and angled spires, whereas in the **West End Historic District** there are hundred-year-old buildings now occupied by lively shops, restaurants and museums. The **McKinney Avenue Trolley** rolls down red-brick streets. **Old City Park** is a pioneer community featuring homes, a church, a schoolhouse and Main Street as it was in the days of the original settlers. The 50-storey **Reunion Tower** has a glass-elevator ride to observation terraces and a revolving restaurant with night-time dancing.

Dealey Plaza is the site of President John F Kennedy's assassination and there is a dramatic exhibit of the event at the **Sixth Floor Museum**. The **John F Kennedy Memorial** at Main and Market Streets is open all year round. Popular attractions are the **DeGolyer Estate**, built by a rich oil baron and relocated to the grounds of the **Dallas Arboretum and Botanical Garden**, and **Southfork Ranch**, the home of the famous TV series' Ewing clan. The **Center for World Thanksgiving** is a tranquil meditation garden with fountains and a contemporary chapel.

Amongst the city's many other attractions is **Fair Park**, home to the **Age of Steam Museum**; **Dallas Aquarium**; the **Museum of Natural History**, with a superb dinosaur exhibition; the **Texas Hall of State**; and **The Women's Museum: An Institute for the Future**. Favourite family activities include **Six Flags Over Texas** theme park, the **Farmer's Market** and the **Dallas Zoo**, featuring 'the Wilds of Africa'. Recreational facilities available in Dallas include paddleboating among the ducks on **Bachman Lake** and horse riding through the backwoods of a real Texan ranch.

FORT WORTH: Much more 'Western' in spirit, Fort Worth started as a military outpost and then became a cow town where cattlemen brought their herds to be shipped. Much of the Old West is preserved in Fort Worth today and it continues to be a centre for the cattle industry.

The **Historic Stockyards** retain the flavour of the Old West. Daily cattle drives take place along **Exchange Avenue** in the Historic Stockyards. **Sundance Square**, located in downtown Fort Worth, is a vibrant entertainment district with a fine collection of hotels, shops, restaurants, live music clubs, theatres, movies and an exciting nightlife. There is also a log-cabin village, a zoological park and a Japanese garden. Museums include the **Amon Carter Museum of Western Art**, the **Sid Richardson Collection of Western Art**, the **Fort Worth Art Museum**, the **National Cowgirl Museum and Hall of Fame** and the **Kimbell Art Museum**. The **Fort Worth Zoo** highlights wildlife from different regions of the State in its 'Texas Wild' exhibit.

AUSTIN: The State capital, 128km (80 miles) northeast of San Antonio, is the gateway to the Texas Hill Country and the chain of Highland Lakes. It is one of the most beautiful cities in the USA and a popular golfing destination. The city features the **Capitol Building**, the 1856 **Governor's Mansion**, nine historical districts, the **Bob Bullock Texas State History Museum** (offering an interactive tour of the unique history of Texas) and the **Texas Spirit** theatre. The 300 acre **University of Texas** campus offers the **Lyndon B Johnson Presidential Library**. Other attractions include the **Lady Bird Johnson Wildflower Center** and the **Sixth Street Entertainment District**, where all types of live music are played.

EXCURSIONS: The 240km (150 miles) chain of **Highland Lakes**, to the northwest of the city, are excellent for fishing, boating and swimming. A day trip into the scenic hill country, where several award-winning wineries are located, is well worthwhile.

HOUSTON: The fourth-largest city in the USA and the largest in Texas, Houston has a population of more than 1.9 million (its metro population of 4.7 million falls short of the 5.2 million in the Dallas/Fort Worth area, however). Houston has been the centre of the US oil industry ever since 'black gold' was discovered at nearby **Beaumont** in 1901. The city is named after Texas hero General Sam Houston, the first President of the Republic of Texas. It is also the space headquarters of the USA and a thriving international port, being connected to the Gulf of Mexico by the 80km (50 miles) **Houston Ship Channel**. Houston's towering skyscrapers reflect its booming economy. The **Museum District** is home to 11 institutions, including the **Museum of Fine Arts**, **Contemporary Arts Museum**, **The Menil Collection**, **Holocaust Museum**, **Children's Museum of Houston** and **Houston Museum of Natural Science**. Downtown attractions include **Sam Houston Historical Park**, **Tranquility Park** and the **Old Market Square**. The **Houston Zoo**, in **Hermann Park**, is popular with children. The veteran, pre-World War I battleship, *Texas*, is moored on the **San Jacinto River** near the **Battleground Monument**, which marks the 1836 battle for Texan independence. The **Lyndon B Johnson Space Center** has exhibitions of space technology and stages regular film shows explaining the US space programme. **Six Flags AstroWorld** is a family entertainment park with live shows, restaurants and rides; whilst next door is **Six Flags WaterWorld**, a water recreation park.

SAN ANTONIO: This modern, prosperous city retains much of its Spanish heritage with its fiestas, buildings and lifestyle and is the number one visitor destination in Texas. The city's **Paseo del Rio** (Riverwalk) shopping and entertainment area is unique.

In 1836, the **Alamo** was the site of a furious battle between a handful of independence-seeking Texans (led by Davy Crockett) and a large Mexican army. Today it is a shrine to Texan courage and patriotism. The six-storey-high *IMAX Theater* tells the whole story of the Alamo in a gripping film. The city's Spanish heritage is visible at the **San Antonio Missions National Historic Park**, which comprises four Spanish missions, while the **Institute of Texan Cultures** tells the story of the region's multicultural heritage. San Antonio is becoming a popular golf destination and is also home to two major theme parks – the world's largest marine-life park, **Sea World of Texas**; and **Six Flags Fiesta Texas**, with what was until recently the world's highest and fastest wooden rollercoaster.

EXCURSIONS: Working ranch holidays are widely available in the hill country to the west of San Antonio, near **Bandera**, the 'Cowboy Capital of the World'. **New Braunfels**, between Austin and San Antonio, was founded by German immigrants in the 1840s. Today their descendants celebrate their heritage with traditional German festivals.

THE GULF COAST: Corpus Christi, south of San Antonio on the Gulf of Mexico, was an ideal pirates' hideaway in the 19th century and is now a major seaport and resort, famous for its fishing and windsurfing competitions. Just off the coast is **Padre Island**, a narrow 170km (95 miles) barrier island with watersports, fishing centres and an impressive expanse of protected National Seashore, wildlife refuges and birdlife sites; it is connected to Corpus Christi by a causeway. **McAllen**, in the far south of the State, is noted for its Mexican flavour and shopping facilities. Nearby **Santa Ana National Wildlife Refuge** is one of the top 10 birding sites in the USA, boasting a record count of bird species. **Galveston Island**, further up the coast near Houston, is rich in history and pirate lore and noted for its sandy beaches, fishing, watersports and turn-of-the-century architecture.

THE NORTH & WEST: Abilene, 242km (151 miles) west of Fort Worth, is home to the reconstructed frontier settlement **Buffalo Gap Historic Village**. **Palo Duro Canyon State Park**, near **Amarillo** in the far north of the State, has startling scenery and facilities for hiking, picnicking, camping and horseriding. The **Panhandle-Plains Museum**, in the nearby city of **Canyon**, charts the region's development from early Native American life to modern farming and ranching. The State's westernmost city, **El Paso**, stands beside the **Rio Grande** in the dramatic **Franklin Mountains**. The largest US city on the Mexican border, it is actually closer to the metropolitan areas of New Mexico, Arizona and southern California than it is to any major Texan cities. The city's aerial tramway gives breathtaking views across Texas and Mexico. El Paso offers a wide variety of cultural and sporting activities, including symphony concerts, theatre, museums, libraries, horse- and hound-racing and many other sports. The **University of Texas El Paso**, known for its Bhutanese-style architecture, and **Sun Bowl stadium** are located here. **Big Bend National Park**, south of El Paso, boasts spectacular views of stark desert, forests, mountains and canyons carved by the Rio Grande. Hiking and rafting, especially in the Santa Elena canyon, are popular. The city of **Odessa**, east of El Paso, is home to the **Presidential Museum**, the only museum in the country dedicated to the office of the President. 10 miles west of Odessa is **The Meteor Crater**. Approximately 168m (550 feet) in diameter, it is the second-largest meteor crater in the USA and was created when a barrage of meteors crashed to the earth between 20,000 and 30,000 years ago. The city of **Midland** is home to the **Commemorative Air Force Museum** and the **Petroleum Museum**.

Social Profile

FOOD & DRINK: Beef features widely in Dallas/Fort Worth – this being cattle country – but there is also a great variety of international cuisine including Chinese, French, Italian, Mexican and Spanish. Dallas has more AAA 5-diamond-rated restaurants than any other US city; they include *The French Room* at the Adolphus Hotel and *The Mansion* on Turtle Creek. In all, Dallas boasts more than 5000 restaurants. Country cooking is popular and includes such local specialities as chicken-fried steak and catfish fried in cornmeal batter. There are several dinner theatres where visitors can eat and see a show.

A great variety of restaurants serves many different types of food in Houston. Specialities include Mexican and Spanish cuisine and Gulf seafood. In Austin, approximately 1500 restaurants offer a variety of cuisine including Texan-style steaks and barbecues, typical American, Italian, Mediterranean, Mexican and many others. Tex-Mex was practically invented in San Antonio, and this native cuisine can be found throughout the city, along with everything from down-home barbeque specialities to fine French cuisine.

THEATRES & CONCERTS: The **Dallas Music Hall** in **Fair Park** stages concerts, musicals and operas. The **Dallas Theater** presents a wide range of drama. The downtown arts district houses the **Morton H Meyerson Symphony Center**, **Dallas Museum of Art** and the **Arts District Theater**. Avant-garde theatres can be found in Deep Ellum. In Fort Worth, the **William Edrington Scott Theater** presents plays, musicals and films. **Casa Mañana Theater** stages Broadway musicals during the summer. The **Nancy Lee and Perry R Bass Performance Hall** is home to the city's renowned symphony, opera and ballet companies, as well as the **Van Cliburn International Piano Competition** and productions of Casa Mañana.

The **Jesse H Jones Hall for the Performing Arts** is the home of the *Houston Symphony Orchestra*, while the **Wortham Performing Arts Center** houses the *Houston Ballet* and the *Houston Grand Opera*. Other Houston venues include the renowned **Alley Theater**, the **Hobby Center for the Performing Arts**, the open-air **Miller Theater** in **Herman Park** and the **Music Hall**.

In Austin, the **Paramount Theater** presents top name entertainers in musicals, comedies, concerts and dramas. The **Zachary Scott Theater** presents musicals and plays, and the **Zilker Hillside Theater** has outdoor musicals and plays. The **Frank Erwin Center** is known for its major recording artist concerts. The **University of Texas Bass Concert Hall** is home to the *Austin Lyric Opera*, *Austin Symphony*, *Austin Ballet* and travelling Broadway productions.

The **Majestic Theater** hosts the *San Antonio Symphony*, as well as travelling Broadway shows and concerts. The unique **Arneson Theater** is an outdoor theatre on the banks of San Antonio's Paseo del Rio, and the recently opened **Verizon Amphitheater** hosts national touring acts.

NIGHTLIFE: Dallas has clubs, cabarets, discos, singles bars and corner pubs, with music ranging from classical to jazz and from country to contemporary rock. Some clubs are listed as 'private' – they are located in a 'dry' area and membership (usually available for a nominal fee) is required to be served alcohol. There are also some comedy clubs sprinkled throughout the city and others offer comedy and drama while customers dine. Fort Worth also has a number of nightclubs, but the musical emphasis here is on country & western music. *Billy Bob's Texas*, the world's largest honky-tonk nightclub, with a 6000-person capacity, plays

host to some of the biggest names in country music in addition to having live bull riding. For an authentic Old West experience, the *White Elephant Saloon* offers live western entertainment.
Houston's many nightspots range from big-name entertainment to supper club revues, pavement cafes, discos and singles bars. *Bayou Place* in downtown Houston is a popular night spot. Austin is noted for its nightly live music venues. Historic 6th Street takes on a lively atmosphere in the evenings as people go pub-crawling between venues catering for country & western, soul, R&B, rock 'n' roll and jazz music. San Antonio offers all sorts of musical entertainment, including traditional 'Tejano' sounds, Dixieland jazz, symphony concerts, country & western and college music. The *Paseo del Rio* is the centre for much of the city's nightlife.
SHOPPING: Dallas has more shopping centres per capita than any other US city and some of the largest shopping malls in the southwest. The elegant and original *Neiman Marcus* department store is now a popular tourist attraction. *Dallas Market Center* is one of the world's largest wholesale trade shopping centres and also offers fine restaurants. Both Dallas and Fort Worth have fine speciality shops. Nearby *Grapevine Mills Outlet Mall* sells discounted merchandise. World-class shopping is available in more than 300 stores at the *Galleria* shopping centre in Houston. The best buys are Western-style clothes, hats, boots, saddles and riding equipment. *Katy Mills Outlet Mall* carries discount name-brand fashions. Authentic Mexican folk art can be found throughout San Antonio, especially at *El Mercado*, patterned after an authentic Mexican market. Between San Antonio and Austin lies San Marcos, where the *Prime Outlet Mall* and *Tanger Outlet Mall* offer plenty of bargains.
SPORT: The *Dallas Cowboys* (**American football**) play at the Texas Stadium and the *Houston Texans* began their inaugural season in 2002 under the new, retractable-roofed Reliant Stadium. The *Dallas Burn* (**soccer**) play at the Frisco Soccer & Entertainment Center, opened in 2005 while the *Dallas Sidekicks* play indoor soccer at the Reunion Arena (although they aren't playing for the 2004/5 season). The *Texas Rangers* play **baseball** at Americquest Field in Arlington and the *Houston Astros* play baseball at Minute Maid Park. The *Dallas Stars* play **hockey** at Dr Pepper Star Centre. The *Dallas Mavericks* play professional **basketball** at the American Airlines Center. Other pro basketball teams are the *Houston Rockets*, who play in the new Houston Toyota Center, and the *San Antonio Spurs*, who play at SBC Center. **Golf** courses are available in and around Austin, Houston, Fort Worth, Dallas, Irving and San Antonio. The major cities also have many facilities for **tennis**, **softball**, **running**, **cycling** and **polo**.
SPECIAL EVENTS: Various livestock shows and rodeos take place throughout the year. The following is a selection of special events occurring in Texas in 2005:
Jan 29-Feb 20 *Washington's Birthday Celebration*, Laredo. **Feb 5** *Carnaval Brasileiro*, Austin. **Feb 12-13** *Eagle Fest*, Emory. **Mar 4-6** *North Texas Irish Festival*, Dallas. **Mar** *Annual Dallas Morning News Golf Expo*. **Mar 12-14** *Rattlesnake Roundup*, Sweetwater. **Mar 12-Apr 3** *Excalibur Fantasy Faire*, Smithville. **Apr 1-3** *Shanghai Days Cowboy Gathering*, Wharton. **Apr 1-3** *North Texas Jazz Festival*, Addison. **Apr 9-May 30** *Scarborough Faire* (renaissance festival), Waxahachie. **Apr 30-May 1** *Cinco de Mayo*, San Marcos. **Apr 28-May 1** *Mayfest*, Fort Worth. **May 27-30** *Official Texas State Arts and Crafts Fair*, Kerrville. **Jun 3-5** *Scottish Festival and Highland Games*, Arlington. **Jul 9** *Parker County Peach Festival*, Weatherford. **Oct 2-Nov 20** *Texas Renaissance Festival*, Plantersville. **Oct 7-9** *Celtic Heritage Festival*, Bedford.

Climate

Average temperatures are: 34-36°C (93-96°F) during summer; 12-14°C (54-57°F) during winter; and 19-22°C (66-72°F) for coastal winter temperatures.

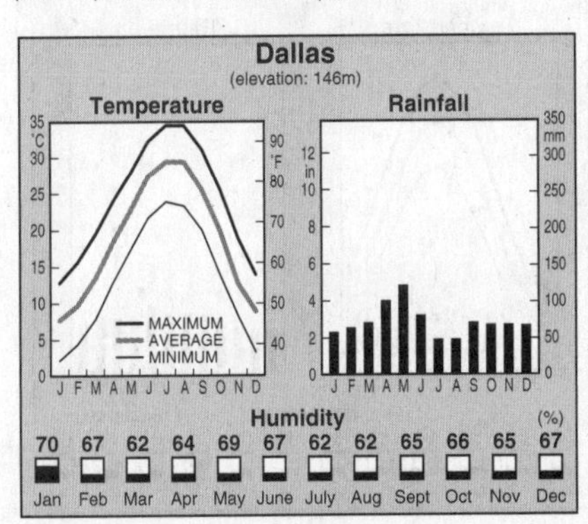

Utah

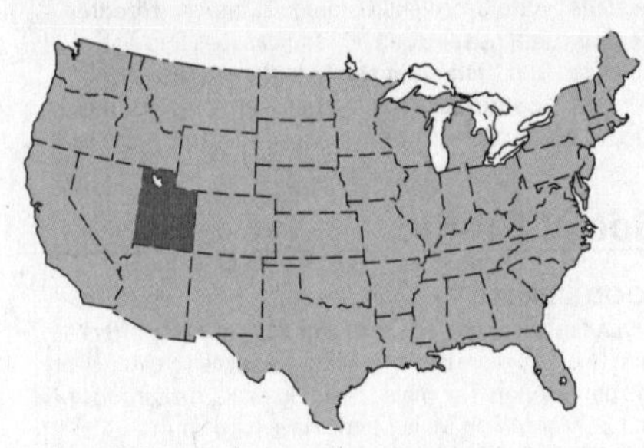

Utah Travel Council
Street Address: Council Hall, 300 North State Street, Capitol Hill, Salt Lake City, UT 84114
Tel: (801) 538 1030 *or* (800) 200 1160 (toll-free).
Fax: (801) 538 1399.
E-mail: travel@utah.com
Website: www.utah.com
Foremost West – USA
770 East South Temple, Suite B, Salt Lake City, UT 84102
Tel: (801) 532 6666. Fax: (801) 532 1921.
E-mail: foremostw@aol.com
Utah State Parks and Recreation
Street address: 1594 West North Temple, Suite 116, Salt Lake City, UT 84114
Postal address: PO Box 146001, Salt Lake City, UT 84114
Tel: (801) 538 7220 or (800) 322 3770 (toll-free; reservations).
Fax: (801) 538 7378.
E-mail: parkcomment@utah.gov
Website: www.stateparks.utah.gov
Cache Valley Tourist Council
160 North Main Street, Logan, UT 84321
Tel: (435) 752 2161 *or* (800) 882 4433 (toll-free).
Fax: (435) 753 5825.
E-mail: tourism@tourcachevalley.com
Website: www.tourcachevalley.com
Canyonlands North Travel Region
Street address: 89 East Center, Moab, UT 84532
Postal address: Moab Area Travel Council, PO Box 550, Moab, UT 84532
Tel: (435) 259 1370 *or* (800) 635 6622 (toll-free).
Fax: (435) 259 1376.
E-mail: info@discovermoab.com
Website: www.discovermoab.com
Canyonlands South Travel Region
Street address: 117 South Main Street, Monticello, UT 84535
Postal address: San Juan County Community Development, PO Box 490, Monticello, UT 84535
Tel: (435) 587 3235 *or* (800) 574 4386 (toll-free).
Fax: (435) 587 2425.
E-mail: info@sanjuancountry.org
Website: www.utahscanyoncountry.com
Dinosaurland Travel Region
55 East Main, Vernal, UT 84078
Tel: (435) 789 6932 *or* (800) 477 5558 (toll-free).
Fax: (435) 789 7465.
E-mail: dinomaster@dinoland.com
Website: www.dinoland.com
Mountainland Association of Governments (Tourism)
586 East 800 North, Orem, UT 84097

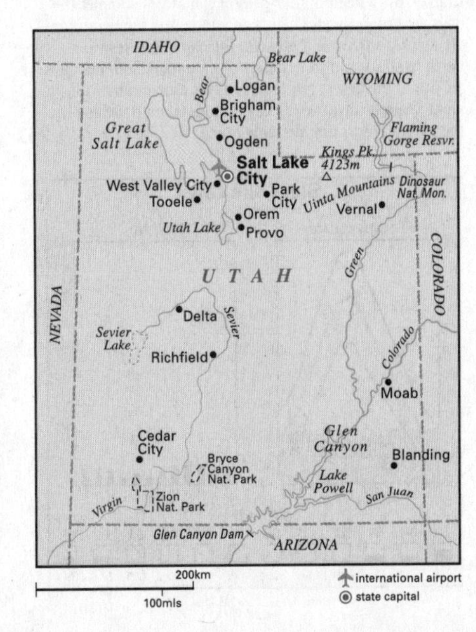

Credit: © Utah Travel Council

Tel: (801) 229 3800. Fax: (801) 229 3801.
Website: www.mountainland.org
Ogden/Weber County CVB
2501 Wall Avenue, Suite 201, Ogden, UT 84401
Tel: (801) 627 8288 *or* (866) 867 8824 (toll-free).
Fax: (801) 399 0783.
E-mail: info@ogdencvb.org
Website: www.ogdencvb.org
Salt Lake CVB
90 South West Temple, Salt Lake City, UT 84101
Tel: (801) 521 2822 *or* (800) 541 4955 (toll-free).
Fax: (801) 534 4927.
E-mail: slcvb@saltlake.org
Website: www.visitsaltlake.com

General Information

Nickname: Beehive State
State bird: California Gull/Sea Gull
State flower: Sego Lily
CAPITAL: Salt Lake City
Date of admission to the Union: 4th Jan 1896
POPULATION: 2,389,039 (official estimate 2004)
POPULATION DENSITY: 10.9 per sq km
2003 total overseas arrivals/US ranking: 252,000/18
TIME: Mountain (GMT - 7). *Daylight Saving Time* is observed.

THE STATE: Utah's attractions include canyons, colourful towns and breathtaking national parks. **Salt Lake City** is the world centre of The Church of Jesus Christ of Latter-day Saints. Utah, surrounded by the **Wasatch Mountains**, boasts historic buildings, churches, museums, science exhibitions and arts festivals. Other State attractions include **Zion National Park** around the **Virgin River Canyon**, with its temple-like rock formations; **Canyonlands**, **Arches** and **Capitol Reef** national parks; **Timpanogos Cave** and the **Dinosaur National Monument** near **Vernal**. Utah has five National Parks.

Travel - International

AIR: International airports: The *Salt Lake City International Airport (SLC)* (website: www.ci.slc.ut.us/airport) is located 6km (4 miles) west of the city centre and four minutes west of Temple Square. The *Utah Transit Authority* (website: www.utabus.com) operates a daily service (route 50) between the city centre and South and West Temple via the airport; other bus services are also available: Route 53 runs between the city centre and Tooele/Grantsville via the airport, while route 56 runs from the airport to West Valley. *Redtail Aviation* offers flights into Moab from the surrounding areas. Taxis, limousines and vans are readily available. There are Ground Transportation Information desks in both terminals, where hotel courtesy cars can be arranged.
RAIL: Salt Lake City is on Amtrak's daily *California Zephyr* line (tel: (800) 872 7245 (toll-free); website: www.amtrak.com), which links Chicago with Emeryville (California). The station is located at 340 South 600 Street West; car hire from *Hertz* is available. Other Utah destinations on this service are Green River, Helper and Provo.
ROAD: Approximate bus travel times: From Salt Lake City to *Las Vegas* is eight hours 30 minutes, and to *Los Angeles* is 15 hours 30 minutes. From Cedar City (near Zion National Park) to *Las Vegas* is three hours, to *Provo* is four hours, to *Salt Lake City* is five hours, and to *Los Angeles* is 10 hours. *Greyhound* (tel: (800) 229 9424 (toll-free); website: www.greyhound.com) is the main carrier.

URBAN: In Salt Lake City, the *Utah Transit Authority (UTA)* (website: www.utabus.com) offers frequent bus services to the University of Utah campus, to Ogden, the suburbs, the airport and east to the mountain canyons and Provo. Journeys within downtown areas are free. Maps are available at libraries and the Visitors' Bureau. *UTA* also runs the *TRAX* tram system. Taxi companies include *City Cab*, *Ute Cab* and *Yellow Cab*.

Resorts & Excursions

GOLDEN SPIKE EMPIRE: This is the best area for viewing the **Great Salt Lake**, the largest lake west of the Mississippi River. One of the most unusual rock formations in the west can be seen at the **Devil's Slide**, which resembles a gigantic children's slide. Among the natural scenic wonders are the **Wasatch-Cache National Forest**, the **East Canyon State Park**, the **Willard Bay State Park**, the **Lost Creek State Park**, and the **Antelope Island State Park**.
BRIDGERLAND: On the western edge of Bridgerland in **Cache Valley** are the **Wellsville Mountains**. The **Wellsville Cone** and **Box Elder Peak** are the highest peaks in this range. The 1500-year-old **Jardine Juniper**, the oldest juniper in the **Rocky Mountains**, is 19km (12 miles) from **Logan** in **Logan Canyon** and a short hike from **Wood Camp Campground**. Cultural attractions include the **American West Heritage Center**, which includes the **Man and His Bread Museum** and the **Ronald V Jensen Living Historical Farm**, an authentic Mormon pioneer farm. Daily activities here are performed exactly as they would have been in 1917. The centre is currently a massive 65 hectares (160 acres) and intends to add another 71 hectares (175 acres). Other popular sights include the **Nora Eccles Art Museum**, **Chase Fine Arts Centre**, the **Mormon Temple** and **Rendezvous Beach**.
GREAT SALT LAKE COUNTRY: The **Great Salt Lake** is the second saltiest body of water in the world, after the Dead Sea. It stretches 148km (92 miles) north to south and is about 77km (48 miles) wide. **Salt Lake City** is a thriving modern city whose proximity to the mountains and lakes makes it a popular base for outdoor enthusiasts. The city is also the spiritual centre of The Church of Jesus Christ of Latter-day Saints and home to the **Salt Lake Temple** and the *Mormon Tabernacle Choir*. The **Museum of Church History and Art** houses Mormon historical memorabilia, fine art sculptures and paintings. The **Utah State History Museum** houses State historical exhibits, featuring hundreds of photographs, some 3500 artefacts and other works of art. Other attractions include the **Marmalade Historic District**, where many of the original pioneer homes can be found; the **Pioneer Memorial Museum**; and the **Utah Museum of Natural History** at the **University of Utah**. Southeast of the city, the year-round **Snowbird Tram** rises 870m (2854ft) to the top of the 3300m (10827ft) **Hidden Peak** with a 360-degree view of Utah's mountain ranges and valleys. Among the natural attractions are the **Great Salt Lake Park**, **Jordan River State Park** and **This Is The Place Park**.
MOUNTAINLAND: The **Timpanogos Cave National Monument** is on the north slope of **Mount Timpanogos**. The **Alpine Scenic Loop** is one of Utah's most popular summer drive destinations. Lying across Utah's northern border, the **Flaming Gorge National Recreation Area** stretches from **Ashley National Forest** to the south Wyoming desert. Recreational activities available include fishing, boating and hiking.
DINOSAURLAND: Sheep Creek Canyon Geological Area offers spectacular rock formations. The **Drive-Through-the-Ages Geological Area** has rock layers that were laid down during a period of more than a billion years. **Dinosaur National Monument** sprawls across eastern Utah and into Colorado. Pittsburgh palaeontologist Earl Douglass began scouring the area for bones in 1908 and the quarry he excavated lies at the west end of the park.
PANORAMALAND: Fish Lake offers cabins and other facilities on the shoreline. Views of the unusual cliffs of **Thousand Lake Mountain** to the north and **Boulder Mountain** to the south are offered near **Teasdale** and **Torrey**. **Big Rock Candy Mountain** in **Marysvale Canyon** is the only formation of its kind. **Little Sahara Recreation Area** has more than 20,000 acres of free-moving sand dunes.
COLOR COUNTRY: Attractions include **Lake Powell** at **Glen Canyon National Recreation Area**; the **Cedar Breaks National Monument**; **Mammoth Cave**; and the **Boulder Mountain Scenic Byway**. Southeast of **Cedar Breaks** is picturesque **Navajo Lake** and the 1040-acre **Joshua Tree Natural Area** near the Arizona border. **Bryce Canyon National Park** shows thousands of delicately carved spires rising in brilliant colours from amphitheatres. **Capitol Dome**, **Hickman Bridge**, the **Waterpocket Fold** and **Cathedral Valley** are sandstone formations. **Zion National Park** is one of the nation's oldest national parks and offers miles of trails.
CANYONLANDS: Moab is a great base for exploring Utah's southeast. The town boasts the **Hole 'n the Rock**, a 14-room house carved out of a sandstone cliff, the **Dan O'Laurie Museum** and **Pale Creek Ranch** which offers trail rides into the **La Sal Mountains**. The **Navajo Tribal Reservation** covers 64,750km (25,000 sq miles) in three States. **Canyonland National Park** is divided into three sections by the Green and Colorado rivers: the **Needles Region** contains spires, arches and canyons and Native American ruins; **Island in the Sky** offers breathtaking views of the surrounding mountains and canyons; the rugged **Maze** area is the most remote district of the park.

Social Profile

FOOD & DRINK: Hotels and restaurants sell alcoholic beverages and wine. The centre of Salt Lake City offers a variety of ethnic restaurants, with inexpensive eateries on the outer fringe. The main shopping malls, *Crossroads Mall* and *ZCMI Mall* on Main Street, have food courts.
THEATRES & CONCERTS: In 1899, the third Legislature authorised the nation's first publicly funded arts council. It supports the *Utah Symphony*, the *Ballet West*, the *Utah Opera Company* and *Repertory Dance Theatre*, among others. The State has many theatres and art galleries. Cedar City hosts the nationally acclaimed *Shakespearean Festival*, and Salt Lake City boasts two professional theatre companies. In Logan, the *Festival Opera Company* performs in a restored theatre. Utah is also home to the *Sundance Film Festival*, the *Gina Bachauer International Piano Competition* and the *Mormon Tabernacle Choir*.
SPORT: Skiing is a popular sport in Utah. The *2002 Olympic Winter Games* took place in Utah during February and the public can enjoy most of these winter facilities. The State has 14 ski resorts, seven of which are less than an hour's drive from Salt Lake City. These include *Alta Ski Resort*, *Beaver Mountain*, *Snowbird Ski and Summer Resort*, *Park City*, *The Canyons Ski Area* and *Deer Valley Resort*. Seven snowmobile complexes are located across the State, linking hundreds of miles of trails systems. Several ski resorts now offer summer chairlifts and **mountain biking**. **Boating** is also a popular sport in Utah – the State offers the sixth-largest area of navigable water in the USA. Colorado, Green and San Juan Rivers are renowned for their rapids and the possibility of **whitewater rafting**. Utah's **golf** courses are famous for their scenery, conditions and variety.
SPECIAL EVENTS: The following is a selection of special events occurring in Utah in 2005:
Jan 20-30 *Sundance Film Festival*, Park City. **Feb 17-19** *Crescent Jazz Festival*, Orem. **Apr 7-9** *Baby Animal Days*, Wellsville. **May 28-29** *Annual Moab Arts Festival*. **Jun 9-11** *Great American West Rodeo*, Logan. **Jun 16-18/21-26** *Mormon Miracle Pageant* (Utah's biggest outdoor pageant), Manti. **Jun 18** *Pony Express Day*, Clarkston. **Jun 23-25** *Utah Arts Festival*, Salt Lake City. **Jul 1-4** *American Freedom Festival*, Provo. **Jul 14-16** *Annual Ute Stampede*, Nephi. **Jul 16-24** *Ogden Pioneer Days*. **Jul 24** *Days of '47 Pioneer Day Celebration*, Salt Lake City. **Jul 29-Aug 6** *Utah Festival of the American West*, Logan. **Aug 26-27** *Trout & Berry Days*, Paradise. **Sep 2-17** *Moab Music Festival*. **Sep 17** *Top of Utah Marathon*, Blacksmith Fork Canyon to Merlin Olsen park. **Sep 25** *Fall Harvest Festival*, Wellsville. **Oct 30** *Pumpkin Day*, Wellsville. **Nov 25-Jan 2 2006** *Christmas Lighting of Temple Square*, Salt Lake City.

Climate

Utah enjoys a distinct four-season climate. In summer the days are hot, with cool nights. In winter, the temperatures are low with snow in the north. The climate varies from north to south and from desert to mountain. Summer days are hot in the desert but temperatures drop dramatically at night. Travellers will need extra clothes when travelling in the mountains in summer or winter.

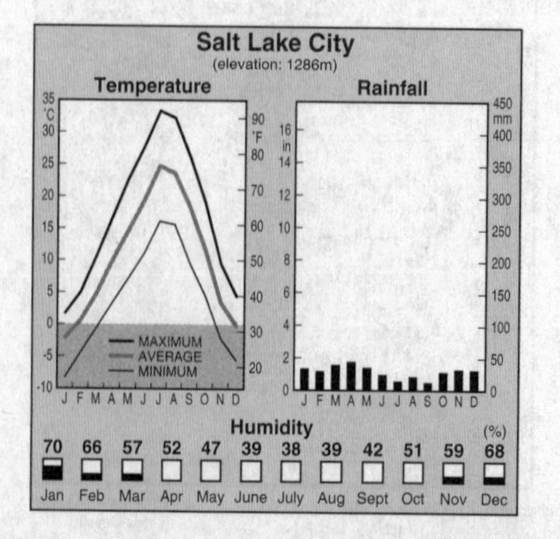

Vermont

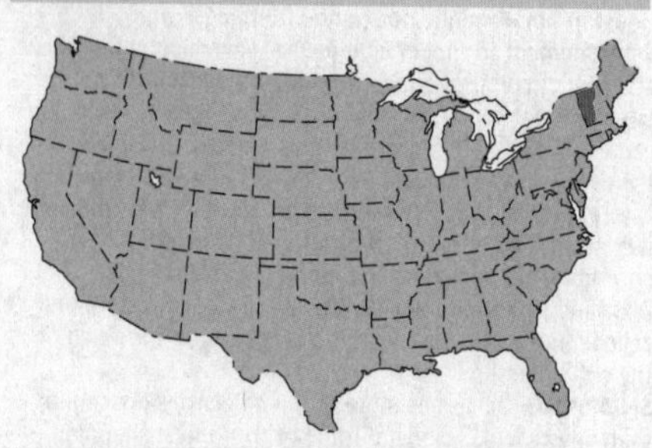

Vermont Department of Tourism and Marketing
Street address: 6 Baldwin Street, Montpelier, VT 05633
Postal address: Drawer 33, Montpelier, VT 05633
Tel: (802) 828 3676 *or* (800) 837 6668 (toll-free).
Fax: (802) 828 3233 *or* 5900.
E-mail: info@vermontvacation.com
Website: www.vermontvacation.com
Discover New England
c/o Cellet PR, 16 Dover Street, London, W15 4LR, UK
Tel: (020) 7491 1112 *or* (01564) 794 999 (brochure request).
Fax: (020) 7491 1114.
E-mail: info@celletpr.co.uk
Website: www.discovernewengleand.org *or* www.vermont-uk.com
Lake Champlain Regional Chamber of Commerce and CVB
60 Main Street, Suite 100, Burlington, VT 05401
Tel: (802) 863 3489 *or* (877) 686 5253 (toll-free).
Fax: (802) 863 1538.
E-mail: vermont@vermont.org Website: www.vermont.org

General Information

Nickname: Green Mountain State
State bird: Hermit Thrush
State flower: Red Clover
CAPITAL: Montpelier
Date of admission to the Union: 4 Mar 1791
POPULATION: 621,394 (official estimate 2004)
POPULATION DENSITY: 25 per sq km
2003 total overseas arrivals: Under 72,000/36
TIME: Eastern (GMT - 5). *Daylight Saving Time* is observed.

THE STATE: Vermont is a State that is best enjoyed outdoors. Although it is the only New England State without a seashore, its border with **Lake Champlain** more than compensates. The largest city, **Burlington**, affords magnificent views of the water, and has many sporting and recreation areas. There are three different *Lake Champlain Ferries* crossing from points in Vermont to New York and back departing two to three times per hour each day.
Missisquoi National Wildlife Refuge and **Burton Island State Park** lie at the northern end of the lake and offer great camping and hiking opportunities. The best views, however, are to the south at **Mount Philo State Park**, Vermont's oldest State park, which is just 15 minutes from the city centre. Vermont is the USA's third-largest ski State, with 16 alpine resorts and just under 30 for cross-country skiing. In the summer, skis are exchanged for mountain bikes and hiking boots. Fishing is also a hugely popular pastime. At **Brattleboro**, in southeast Vermont, the sporting action revolves around the **West** and **Connecticut rivers**. Canoeing is the best way to explore the lush green countryside. Other less energetic attractions include the **Brattleboro Museum & Art Center**, and the **Shelburne Museum**, heading back up lake towards Burlington. Vermont is also home to **Shelburne Heritage Park**, with its early New England buildings; **Green Mountain National Forest**, with its historical trails and drives; and various ski destinations.

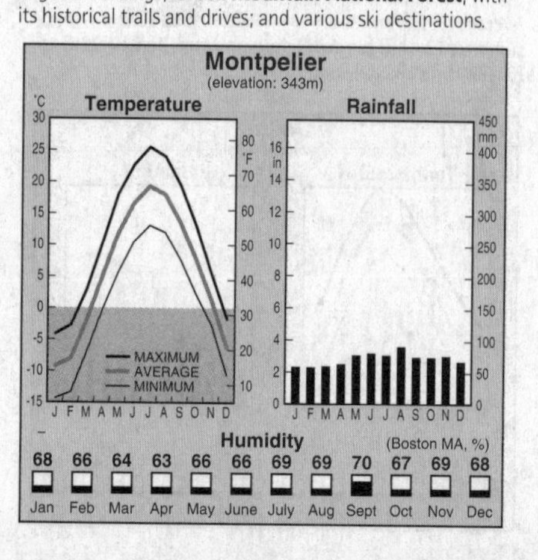

Virginia

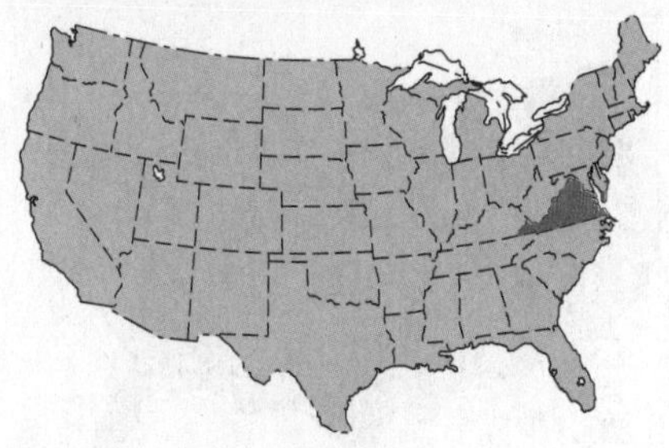

Virginia Tourism Corporation
901 East Byrd Street, 19th Floor, Richmond, VA 23219
Tel: (804) 786 2051 *or* (800) 847 4882 (toll-free).
Fax: (804) 786 1919.
E-mail: vainfo@helloinc.com
Website: www.virginia.org
Virginia Tourism Corporation (UK Office)
1st Floor, 182-184 Addington Road,
South Croydon, Surrey CR2 8LB
Tel: (020) 8651 4743. Fax: (020) 8651 5702.
E-mail: geoff@ttmi.demon.co.uk
Website: www.virginia.org
Alexandria Convention & Visitors Association
421 King Street, Suite 300, Alexandria, VA 22314
Tel: (703) 838 4200 *or* (800) 388 9119 (toll-free).
Fax: (703) 838 4683.
E-mail: acva@funside.com
Website: www.funside.com
Norfolk CVB
232 East Main Street, Norfolk, VA 23510
Tel: (757) 664 6620 *or* (800) 368 3097 (toll-free).
Fax: (757) 622 3663.
E-mail: dallen@norfolkcvb.com
Website: www.norfolkcvb.com
Virginia Beach Convention & Visitors Bureau
Suite 500, 2101 Parks Avenue, Virginia Beach, VA 23451
Tel: (757) 437 4700 *or* (800) 700 7702 (toll-free).
Fax: (757) 437 4747.
E-mail: vabvc@vbgov.com (visitor centre).
Website: www.vbfun.com

Credit: © Capital Region USA

General Information

Nickname: Old Dominion State
State bird: Cardinal
State flower: Dogwood
CAPITAL: Richmond
Date of admission to the Union: 25th June 1788 (original 13 States; date of ratification of the Constitution)
POPULATION: 7,459,827 (official estimate 2004)
POPULATION DENSITY: 67.3 per sq km
2003 total overseas arrivals/US ranking: 234,000/21
TIME: Eastern (GMT - 5). *Daylight Saving Time* is observed.

THE STATE: Virginia stretches from the Atlantic Ocean to the **Blue Ridge** and **Allegheny Mountains**. It is one of the country's most historic and scenic States. Some of its leading attractions are located along the **Potomac River: Arlington National Cemetery**, with the grave of John F Kennedy; **Old Town Alexandria**; and **Mount Vernon**, George Washington's country estate.
Driving trails link more than 250 Civil War sites across Virginia. **Richmond**, the capital of the Confederacy in the Civil War, has many fine old buildings and cultural options. **Williamsburg**, **Yorktown** and **Jamestown** (the birthplace of the USA) are three of its most historic sites, situated further east.
Shenandoah Valley, with its caverns, waterfalls and popular resorts, is to the west. Other attractions include **Virginia Beach**, **Shenandoah National Park**, **Blue Ridge Parkway**, **Luray Caverns**, **Cumberland Gap** and **Great Falls Park**. **Norfolk** is an important Atlantic seaport and home to the world's largest naval base. Virginia boasts nearly 60 wineries offering tastings and tours.

Travel - International

AIR: International airports: There are flights from US and major European cities into Virginia's *Washington Dulles International Airport (IAD)* (website: www.metwashairports.com) and *Maryland's Baltimore/Washington International Airport (BWI)* (website: www.bwiairport.com). Washington, DC is also served by North American flights via its *Ronald Reagan Washington National Airport*; see the *Washington, DC* section for airport details and flight times.
Norfolk International Airport (ORF) (website: www.norfolkairport.com) is located 8km (5 miles) northeast of downtown Norfolk with domestic departures to a number of cities throughout the USA.
RAIL: *Amtrak* (tel: (800) 872 7245 (toll-free); website: www.amtrak.com) rail service passes through Virginia on two main north–south routes, linking New Orleans (via Atlanta and Charlottesville) and Miami (via Richmond) with Washington, DC and New York City. A couple of services (originating in Newport News) continue on to Boston.
Approximate rail travel times: From Richmond to *Williamsburg* is one hour 15 minutes, to *Washington, DC* is two hours 10 minutes, to *Virginia Beach* is three hours 30 minutes (including bus transfer), to *Philadelphia* is four hours 45 minutes, to *New York* is six hours 30 minutes, and to *Boston* is 10 hours 20 minutes.
ROAD: Located mid-way between New York and Miami, Virginia boasts well-maintained major highways as well as some of the nation's oldest and most scenic byways.
Bus: *Greyhound* (tel: (800) 229 9424 (toll-free); website: www.greyhound.com) buses run from most larger towns to destinations across the USA. A number of East Coast routes are run in partnership with *Carolina Trailways*.
Approximate bus travel times: From Richmond to *Williamsburg* is one hour, to *Charlottesville* is one hour 30 minutes, to *Washington, DC* is two hours 15 minutes, to *Norfolk* is two hours 30 minutes, to *Baltimore* is three hours 45 minutes, and to *Philadelphia* is four hours 45 minutes.

Resorts & Excursions

NORTHERN VIRGINIA: The region of Northern Virginia has historic ties to both the Revolutionary and Civil War eras and is also the State's horse and wine country, where visitors enjoy steeplechase, polo events and wine tasting in the rolling countryside.
Well-known attractions include **Arlington National Cemetery**, where an eternal flame burns at the gravesite of John F Kennedy; the **Iwo Jima Marine Memorial**; George Washington's **Mount Vernon Estate** and **Robert E Lee's Arlington House**; and historic plantations such as **Oatlands**, **Morven Park**, **Kenmore**, **Gunston Hall** and **Woodlawn**. **Carlyle House**, **Christ Church** and **Gadsby's Tavern** are well-preserved public buildings in **Old Town Alexandria**. **Potomac River** cruises afford scenic views of Alexandria, Washington, DC and the Mount Vernon Estate. The **Newseum** in Rosslyn is dedicated to US and international newsmakers. **Wolf Trap Farm Park** is America's only national park for the performing arts.
CENTRAL/SOUTHSIDE: Richmond is the State capital and was also the Capital of the Confederacy. This compact city is ideal for walking tours of historic districts and is ringed by Civil War battlegrounds. Among its numerous restored homes and museums are the **Virginia Museum of Fine Arts**, the intriguing **Edgar Allan Poe Museum**, the **Science Museum and Universe Planetarium**, the **White House of the Confederation**, the **Virginia Historical Society** and **Paramount's Kings Dominion** theme park.
Many of the nation's greatest founders lived in Central Virginia. Thomas Jefferson's beloved **Monticello**, the graceful, domed mansion he lived in for 40 years, can be visited at **Charlottesville**. Minutes away is **Ash Lawn**, the 535-acre plantation which belonged to President James Monroe. The mansion and grounds of **Montpelier**, where James Madison, 'Father of the US Constitution', lived with his wife, Dolly, can be found in Orange County.
SHENANDOAH VALLEY: Here, travellers will find glorious mountains, a spectacular valley and some of the most beautiful scenery in America. **Skyline Drive** runs through Shenandoah National Park and travels across the crests of the **Blue Ridge Mountains**. A wide range of outdoor activities, from hiking and canoeing to horseback riding and special naturalist programmes, are on offer in and around the park. In **Roanoke**, Shenandoah's largest city, there is a zoological park, the **Transportation Museum of Virginia** and one of Virginia's finest farmers' markets. Several

museums, a planetarium, and a theatre can be found at the 'Center in the Square'. **Explore Park** recreates Native American settlements and portrays life in pioneer days. At the northern end of the valley, **Winchester**, 'Apple Capital of the Nation', plays host each year to the *Shenandoah Apple Blossom Festival*. In **Staunton**, a recreation of **Shakespeare's Blackfriar's Theatre** is a popular draw, as is the **Frontier Culture Museum**, with its reconstructions of early farmsteads. The wonders of nature are visible everywhere in this region, from the 65m- (215ft-) high vaulted **Cathedral of Stone** outside **Lexington** at **Natural Bridge**, to the seven castle-like rock towers of the **Natural Chimneys**, west of **Harrisonburg**. The largest of the five limestone caverns open for tours is at Luray. Harrisonburg also boasts the new **Court Square Theater**. Refined **Barboursville** is another favourite destination, with the focus on fine wine and international cuisine and events including visiting chef programmes and an opera season.

SOUTHWEST: The **Allegheny**, **Blue Ridge** and **Cumberland** mountains offer many country roads, hiking trails, clear creeks, cascading waterfalls, well-maintained parkland and picnic areas. On the border with **Kentucky** are two breathtaking parks: **Breaks Interstate Park**, with its 480m- (1600ft-) deep **Grand Canyon of the South** and **Cumberland Gap National Historical Park**. Here, the adventurous Daniel Boone travelled the famous pass to the west. **Bristol** is home to the **Birthplace of Country Music Alliance Museum**, a good introduction to the rich musical heritage of this region heard in local barns and rural music sheds such as the **Carter Family Fold** in **Hiltons**. The **Blue Ridge Parkway**, one of America's most scenic roadways, takes visitors through lush farmland. **Wytheville** is home to **Wolf Creek Indian Village**, while **Abingdon** has a thriving local arts scene. **Mount Rogers**, 32km (20 miles) to the east, is the highest peak in Virginia.

TIDEWATER & HAMPTION ROADS: This is the oldest part of America and features historic cities, unspoilt beaches and colonial taverns. At the **Colonial National Historical Park** and archaeological dig at **Jamestown**, visitors will see the remains of the first permanent English settlement, established in 1607. At nearby **Jamestown Settlement**, a full-scale replica of **James Fort** is on display, along with reproductions of three 17th-century ships that brought the English settlers to Virginia. In **Hampton**, the **Virginia Air and Space Center** houses full-size air- and spacecraft. Formerly the State capital, **Williamsburg** is the largest restored 18th-century town in America and is home to **William and Mary**, the second-oldest college in the USA. In Norfolk, visitors will find the **Chrysler Museum**, **Nauticus**, the **National Maritime Center** and the upscale **MacArthur Center**. To the north, the **Chesapeake Bay Bridge-Tunnel** leads to Virginia's **Eastern Shore**, a 112km- (70 mile-) long peninsula that is bordered by the Atlantic on one side and **Chesapeake Bay** on the other.

East of Norfolk, **Virginia Beach** is a popular seaside town offering a range of attractions and facilities. The **First Landing/Seashore State Park** has miles of seashore, picnic areas, camping and a beautiful biking trail. Other attractions in Virginia Beach include the **Cape Henry Lighthouses**, **Old Coastguard Station** (built in 1903 and now a museum), the **Contemporary Art Center of Virginia** and the **Virginia Marine Science Museum** (featuring an 800,000-gallon aquarium). Two annual festivals offer fresh oysters, steamed clams, crabs and seafood chowder.

Further south, the **Back Bay National Wildlife Refuge** has a 7700-acre beach and is a refuge for a large variety of migratory birds. The nearby **False Cape State Park** is an ocean-to-freshwater bay habitat, accessible only by boat or an 8km (5 mile) bike ride, and offering excellent opportunities for walking and camping.

Social Profile

FOOD & DRINK: The region excels in local seafood, including oysters and blue crabs, and in the traditional cuisine of the cities. Local wines have become increasingly well known. Richmond, both an old Southern capital and a college town, offers cheap student eateries, thoughtfully-prepared regional cuisine and every type of ethnic food. Visitors can pick up their own fresh fruit and vegetables at the *Farmers' Markets*. At Williamsburg, the *Williamsburg Shopping Center* offers a colonial culinary experience, fast-food places and many pancake houses. There are many fast-food restaurants along the boardwalk at Virginia Beach, where outstanding seafood restaurants can also be found.

THEATRES & CONCERTS: Theatres abound in Virginia and many have historic and outdoor settings. The *Richmond State Ballet and Virginia Opera* offer a rich and varied programme of events. Traditional mountain music and dance is popular, and the world's largest fiddlers' convention is held every August in the small town of Galax. Top-name folk musicians play at the **Birchmere** in Alexandria. Jazz and rock music are on offer in Charlottesville and Richmond.

NIGHTLIFE: Richmond's comedy clubs, theatres, rock and jazz venues and pubs offer a diverse nightlife. In Virginia Beach, *Peabody's* and *Hot Tuna* are popular clubs.

SHOPPING: Among the top attractions for visitors to Virginia are the quality and the quantity of its shopping, particularly in the discount and outlet categories. A wide range of shops is found in the malls throughout Virginia, notably at *The Fashion Center at Pentagon City* in Arlington, *Tysons Corner Center* and the *Potomac Mills* outlet mall in Woodbridge.

SPORT: The whole eastern coastline of the region is lined with long golden sand beaches – at Virginia Beach alone, these stretch for 45km (28 miles) – with plentiful **watersports** opportunities. Buggs Island Lake and Smith Mountain Lake are Virginia's largest **boating** lakes. **Whitewater canoeing** is popular on the Shenandoah, Maury and James rivers; rapids as high as Class IV are found along urban Richmond's stretch of the James River. Virginia is one of the richest saltwater sport **fishing** areas in the world. More than 25 species of freshwater fish are found in the State's waters, although a licence is required to fish. **Cycling** is popular: one of the longest US rails-to-trails bikeways (72km/45 miles) is located in Northern Virginia. For **hikers**, the *Appalachian Trail* offers 720km (450 miles) of winding pathways through Virginia. *Bryce Mountain, The Homestead, Massanutten* and *Wintergreen* are the four **downhill ski** areas in Virginia. The *Massanutten Resort* now offers year-round attractions, with swimming, fishing, horseriding and golf offered in the warmer months. These resorts offer accommodation ranging from the rustic to the luxurious with skiing to cater for all levels. **Grass skiing** is available at *Bryce Resort*.

SPECIAL EVENTS: The following is a selection of special events occurring in Virginia in 2005:

Feb 5 *Annual Cherry Jubilee*, Dumfries. **Feb 20** *Revolutionary War Encampment and Skirmish*, Alexandria. **Feb 21** *George Washington Birthday Parade*. **Mar 5** *Mardi Gras Celebration*, Wintergreen; *St Patrick's Celebration and Parade*, Alexandria. **Mar 9-12** *Williamsburg Film Festival*. **Mar 12** *Manassas St Patrick's Day Parade*. **Mar 19** *March Muster*, Fredericksburg; *St Patrick's Day Parade and Festival*, Roanoke. **Mar 19-20** *Whitetop Mountain Maple Festival*. **Mar 27** *Easter on Parade*, Richmond. **Apr 1** *Black Maria Film and Video Festival*, Richmond. **Apr 2** *Daffodil Festival*, Gloucester; *Heart of Virginia April Fools Festival*. **Apr 15-17** *Honaker Rdebud Festival*. **Apr 16-17** *Virginia Fly Fishing Festival*, Waynesboro. **Apr 23** *Celtic Celebration*, Big Island. **Apr 23-24** *Graves Mountain Spring Fling Festival*, Syria; *Victorian Festival*, Staunton; *Virginia Hot Glass Festival*, Staunton. **Apr 26-May 1** *Shenandoah Apple Blossom Festival*, Winchester. **Apr 30** *Coal Heritage Festival*, Pocahontas. **May 4-8** *Birds and Blossom Festival*, Norfolk. **May 6** *Fiesta del Pueblo*, Culpeper. **May 7** *Culpeper Days; Mayfest XVIII*, Fredericksburg. **Aug 19-20** *Fries Fiddlers Convention*. **Aug 26-Sep 3** *Shenandoah Country Fair*, Woodstock. **Sep 2-5** *Labor Day Spectacular*, Woodstock. **Sep 3** *Taste of the Mountains Main Street Festival 2005*, Madison. **Sep 5** *Labor Day Festival and Coal Miners Reunion*, Pocahontas. **Sep 9-10** *Apple butter Festival in Shenandoah National Park*, Luray; Neptune Wine Festival, Virginia Beach. **Sep 9-11** *Hampton Bay Days*. **Sep 10** *Dock Boggs Memorial Festival*, Wise. **Sep 12-17** *Washington County Fair and Burley Festival*, Abingdon. **Sep 24** *Harvest Jubilee and Wine Festival*, Altavista. **Sep 25** *Appalachian Folk Festival*, Roanoke. **Nov 1-Jan 1 2006** *100 Miles of Lights* (light shows and holiday events), Hampton, Newport News, Richmond, Virginia Beach and Williamsburg. **Nov 11-13** *Mistletoe Market*, Abingdon.

Climate

Generally speaking, Virginia enjoys pleasantly hot summers and relatively mild but crisp winters, with moderate rainfall throughout the year. Average coastal temperatures in July and August rarely exceed 90°F (32°C), while in winter there is often snow. The mountainous areas in the west of the region provide welcome respite from the higher temperatures of summer.

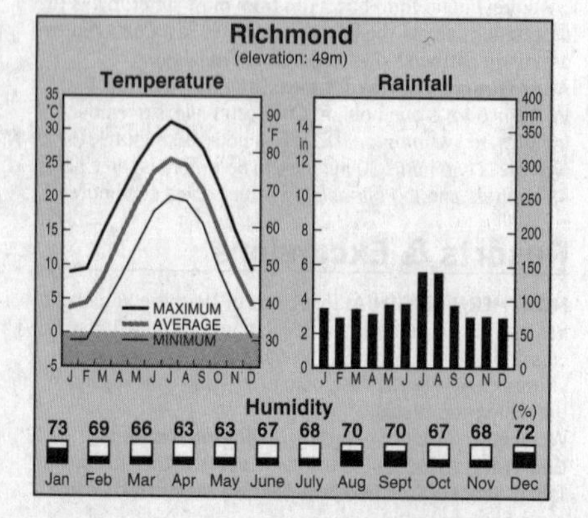

Washington, DC

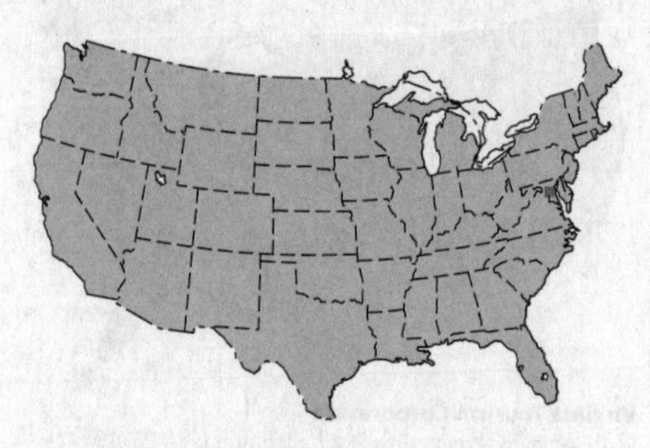

Washington, DC Convention & Tourism Corporation
901 Seventh Street NW, 4th Floor, Washington, DC 20001
Tel: (202) 789 7000 *or* (800) 422 8644 (toll-free).
Fax: (202) 789 7037.
Website: www.washington.org

General Information

Nickname: None
State bird: Wood Thrush
State flower: American Beauty Rose
CAPITAL: N/A
SENATE APPROVAL DATE OF THE FEDERAL CITY: July 1 1790
POPULATION: 565,392 (official estimate 2004)
POPULATION DENSITY: 3298.6 per sq km
2003 TOTAL OVERSEAS ARRIVALS: 1,049,000
TIME: Eastern (GMT - 5). *Daylight Saving Time* is observed.

THE DISTRICT: "DC" stands for 'District of Columbia', not a state but an administrative district created specifically to avoid having the capital city in any one state. Washington, DC is a city of green parks, wide tree-lined streets, white marble buildings and, surprising for a US city, no skyscrapers, which gives it a more European air. It is the centre for visiting diplomats and has one of the largest concentrations of hotel and motel rooms in the country. Tourism is the leading private industry and business interests are increasingly attracted by the many light-industrial, high-tech and research companies now moving into the region. The 'Metro area' refers to the District of Columbia and surrounding counties and cities in Maryland and Virginia.

Following the terrorist attack on the **Pentagon** of September 11 2001 and subsequent anthrax alerts, as well as the sniper attacks in 2002, which left 10 people dead and three wounded, security throughout the capital is on heightened alert. Travellers may experience extensive waits or cancellations of tours around sensitive public buildings. General information can be obtained from the nearest US embassy or from the Foreign Commonwealth Office (website: www.fco.gov.uk); the Washington, DC Convention and Tourism Corporation (website: www.washington.org) and online from the District of Columbia's (website: www.dc.gov), which highlights specific closure of federal buildings and the status of different tours.

Travel - International

AIR: International airports: *Washington-Dulles International (IAD)* (website: www.metwashairports.com) is 43km (27 miles) from the city (in Virginia; travel time – 50 minutes). The *Washington Flyer Coach Service* operates every 30 minutes daily 0545-2215 (with a reduced service at the weekend) between the airport and the West Falls Church *Metrorail* (subway) station. Tickets may be purchased from the airport's Ground Transportation Center ticket counter; the bus departs from the Main Terminal (door 4). A *Metrobus* service is available at the station to areas not served by Metrorail. Taxis are also available.

Baltimore-Washington International Airport (BWI) (website: www.bwiairport.com) is located 48km (30 miles) from Washington, DC (travel time – 38 minutes). A frequent shuttle train service is provided by between the airport terminal and the airport's own rail station (BWI Rail Station), where *Amtrak* and *MARC* services to the city are available. *MARC* trains also run to a number of other destinations. A *SuperShuttle* bus departs every hour from the lower level; tickets can be bought from the Ground Transportation Desk; services to other destinations are also available. *Metrobus* express route B30 runs every 40 minutes daily to Green Belt *Metrorail* station for US$3. The Greenbelt *Metrorail* station

connects to other stations throughout the city, as well as Virginia, Montgomery and Prince George Counties. A daily light-rail service is available to downtown Baltimore and Hunt Valley. The *Airport Shuttle* offers a door-to-door service in the State of Maryland. Taxi services are available on the lower level near each exit; average fares are US$63 (to Washington, DC) and US$103 (to Washington-Dulles International Airport).
Limousines and luxury sedans are also available at the airport.
Domestic airports: *Ronald Reagan Washington National (DCA)* (website: www.metwashairports.com) receives transfer connections from other US gateways. It is 5km (3 miles) southwest of the city. *Metrorail*, the region's rapid transit system, operates frequent subway trains from its National Airport station (opposite terminals B and C) to a variety of stops in both the city and the Maryland and Virginia suburbs. *Metrobus* services are also available at the *Metrorail* station, to areas not served by the train. *SuperShuttle* operates a service to Union Station. Taxi, limousine and car hire services are also available.
Approximate flight times: From Washington, DC to *Anchorage* is 10 hours 25 minutes, to *Atlanta* is one hour 40 minutes, to *Chicago* is two hours 10 minutes, to *Frankfurt/M* is seven hours 40 minutes, to *Honolulu* is 13 hours 40 minutes, to *London* is six hours 50 minutes, to *Los Angeles* is five hours 40 minutes, to *Miami* is two hours 30 minutes, to *Montréal* is two hours, to *New York* is one hour, to *Orlando* is two hours 10 minutes, to *Paris* is eight hours 20 minutes, to *San Francisco* is seven hours 10 minutes, to *Singapore* is 25 hours 45 minutes, and to *Toronto* is two hours 20 minutes.
RAIL: *Amtrak* (tel: (800) 872 7245 (toll-free); website: www.amtrak.com) operates long-distance services through Washington, DC. The principal corridor is the New York–Philadelphia–Baltimore–Washington, DC route, with frequent fast trains. There are also routes to Chicago via Pittsburgh or Cincinnati; New Orleans via Charlotte and Atlanta; and Miami via Raleigh or Charleston. There are also local trains to the Philadelphia area. The travel time to New York is 3 hours by *Metroliner* or 2 hours 45 minutes on the *Amtrak Acela Express*. The main station is Union Station, 50 Massachusetts Avenue NE.
ROAD: *Greyhound* (tel: (800) 229 9424 (toll-free); website: www.greyhound.com) services arrive and depart from the modern bus terminal at 1005 First Street NE. **Approximate driving times:** From Washington, DC to *Baltimore* is one hour, to *Richmond* is two hours, to *Norfolk* is four hours, to *New York* is five hours, to *Pittsburgh* is five hours, to *Charleston* (West Virginia) is seven hours, to *Charlotte* is eight hours, to *Cincinnati* is 10 hours, to *Chicago* is 14 hours, to *Miami* is 22 hours, to *Dallas* is 28 hours, to *Los Angeles* is 55 hours, and to *Seattle* is 58 hours. All times are based on non-stop driving at or below the applicable speed limits.
Approximate bus travel times: From Washington, DC to *Richmond* is two hours, to *Philadelphia* is three hours 30 minutes, to *New York* is four hours 30 minutes, to *Pittsburgh* is five hours 30 minutes, and to *Knoxville* is 12 hours 30 minutes. The main service provider is *Greyhound* (tel: (800) 229 9424 (toll-free); website: www.greyhound.com).
URBAN: The *Washington Metropolitan Area Transit Authority (WMATA)* (website: www.wmata.com) provides bus and rail transit service in Washington, DC and neighbouring communities. The Metro (subway) system offers quick and comfortable transport within the city centre; fares are zonal with a surcharge during peak hours. Lines extend into the suburban areas of Maryland and northern Virginia. There are also suburban and central bus services. It is possible to transfer from Metro to bus without additional charge (except during rush hour), but not from bus to Metro. Taxis are available within the city area; fares are again zonal (and comparatively cheap by big-city standards). Most major car hire and motor camper hire agencies have offices in Washington, DC.

Credit: © WCTC

Resorts & Excursions

As befits a capital city, the rectangular grid of streets is cut by long diagonals (named after States) radiating from important sites such as the **Capitol** and the **White House**. Aligned with the grid is a grand formal vista, the **National Mall**, which extends from **Capitol Hill** to **Potomac Park** on the river of the same name. A second rectangular garden runs northwards, at right angles to the Mall, as far as the **White House**, which has been the home of every US President since 1800 and is visited by more than one million people every year. The **Tidal Basin**, a beautiful lake famous for its Japanese cherry trees, lies just to the southwest. The **National Mall** contains many of Washington, DC's most important monuments and institutions, including the **Lincoln** and **Jefferson Memorials**; the **Washington Monument** (at 169m/555ft, the tallest masonry structure in the world); the **Smithsonian Institution**, including the old **Museum of Natural History**; the modern **National Gallery of Art**, with its stunning East Building designed by the world-famous architect I M Pei and its beautiful six acre sculpture garden; and, of course, the **Capitol**, where Senators and Representatives meet under a magnificent 55m (180ft) dome to shape US legislative policy.
Many recreational activities are available, including boat trips on the **Potomac River** (the jetty is to the south of the **Lincoln Memorial**). **Arlington National Cemetery**, on the other side of the river, contains the graves of 175,000 US soldiers who fought in wars from the American Revolution onwards.
Other sights include **Chinatown**, where many of the city's Asian shops and restaurants are centred; **Constitution Gardens**, with more than 50 acres of trees and lawns; the **J Edgar Hoover Building** (the FBI's headquarters) at Ninth Street; Pennsylvania Avenue and the nearby recently opened **International Spy Museum**; the **Pentagon** (at present tours have been cancelled indefinitely owing to the terrorist attacks of September 2001); and the **US Supreme Court**, the highest court in the country. Picturesque **Georgetown**, in the area of Wisconsin and M Streets, is one of DC's liveliest spots, and the cobblestone streets, cafes and lovely riverside walk make this a pleasant area in which to wander.

Social Profile

FOOD & DRINK: Washington, DC has a renowned selection of excellent restaurants and almost any national cuisine can be found.
THEATRES & CONCERTS: Pennsylvania Avenue houses the **National** and **Ford Theaters**. The **John F Kennedy Center for the Performing Arts** stands at the foot of New Hampshire Avenue, overlooking the Potomac River. Here there are four theatres for live performances of opera, concerts, musical plays, drama and festival occasions; free performances are held every day of the year from 6pm at the **Millennium Stage**. A fifth theatre houses the **American Film Institute**. Open-air concerts are held at the **Jefferson Memorial** in the summer, and the **National Gallery of Art** has Sunday evening concerts in the West Building, West Court Garden. US military bands play free concerts at the Washington Monument, the Capitol, and the Navy Memorial during the summer.
NIGHTLIFE: Washington enjoys a growing number of nightclubs with live entertainment. There are, however, numerous bars and discos in central Washington, Adams-Morgan, Georgetown and the suburbs.
SHOPPING: There are several shopping areas in Washington, DC. A collection of self-contained shops known as the 'Shops at National Place' can be found off

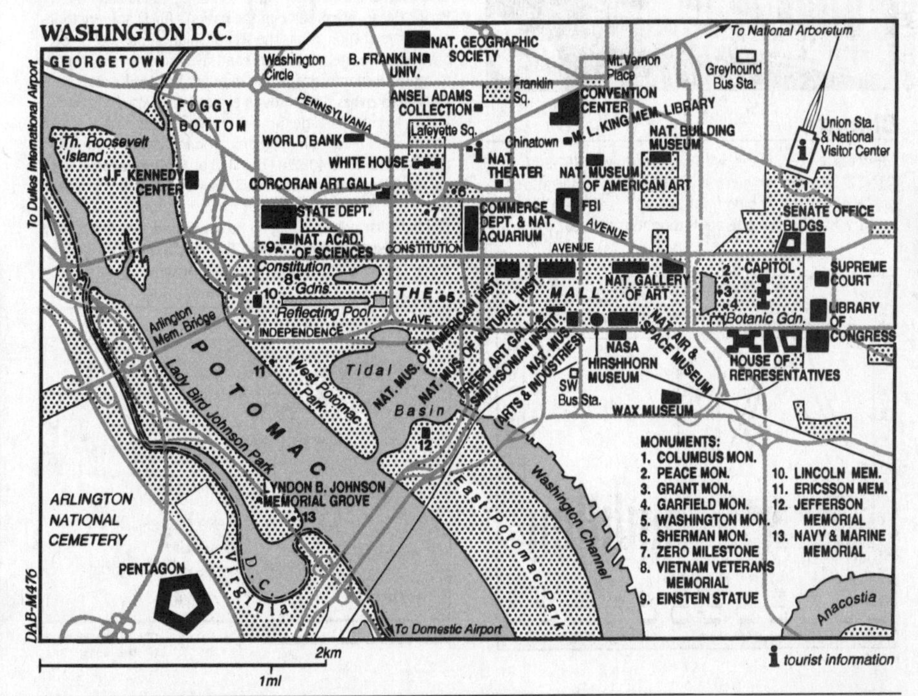

A B C D E F G H I J K L M N O P Q R S T U V W X Y Z

Credit: © WCTC

F Street, between 11th and 15th Streets; Connecticut Avenue (between K Street and Dupont Circle) has many speciality shops; and Georgetown offers a wide range of boutiques, bookshops, antique dealers, arts and crafts shops, and pavement stalls as well as a very attractive mall on M Street. More traditional malls include the Pentagon City Mall, located in Arlington, VA (15 minutes by Metro from the downtown area), and the Mazza Gallerie, at the corner of Wisconsin and Western Avenues. Some of the government buildings offer unique souvenirs in giftshops open to the public.

SPECIAL EVENTS: The following is a selection of special events occurring in Washington, DC in 2005; for further details see online (website: www.washington.org):
Feb 9-13 *44th Annual Washington Boat Show*, Washington Convention Center. **Mar-Apr** *AmericArtes* (Mexican and Andean music festival), John F. Kennedy Center for the Performing Arts. **Mar 12** *Washington Marathon*. **Mar 13** *St Patrick's Day Parade*, Constitution Avenue. **Mar 17-20** *The Washington Home & Garden Show*, Washington Convention Center. **Mar 26-Apr 11** *National Cherry Blossom Festival*, Constitution Avenue. **Apr** *White House Easter Egg Roll*, South Lawn, White House. **Apr 13-24** *Filmfest DC International Film Festival*. **May 28-30** *Taste of DC*, Historic Pennsylvania Avenue. **Jun 5-12** *Capital Pride* (gay pride festival), Dupont Circle and Pennsylvania Avenue. **Jun 23-Jul 4** *Smithsonian Folklife Festival*, National Mall. **Jun** *DC Caribbean Festival*. **Jun 25-26** *National Capital Barbecue Battle*, Pennsylvania Avenue. **Jul 4** *National Independence Day Celebration*, Constitution Avenue. **Jul 30-Aug 7** *Tennis Classic*, William HG Fitzgerald Tennis Center. **Aug 30-Sep 19** *Prelude Festival*. **Oct 4** *National Book Festival*, National Mall. **Nov** *Washington Craft Show*, Washington Convention Center. **Nov 11** *Veterans Day Celebrations*. **Dec-Feb 2006** *Holiday Homecoming* (ongoing festive celebrations).

Credit: © WCTC

Climate

Summers are very warm, with highs in July of 75°-90°F (21°-32°C). Although generally mild, winter temperatures can be quite low, ranging from 24°-40°F (-4° to +4°C) in January. Rainfall is moderate throughout the year.

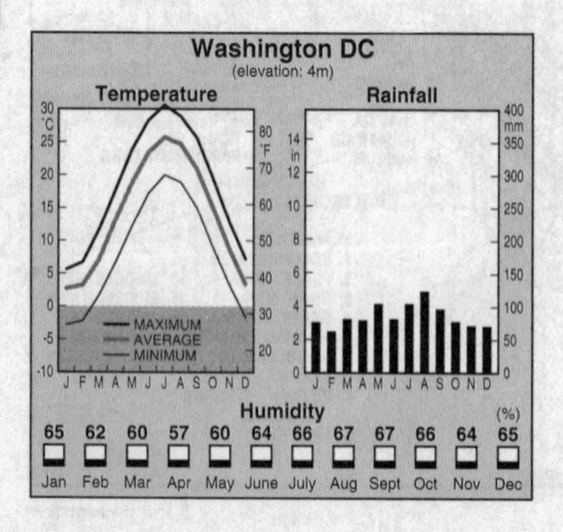

Washington State

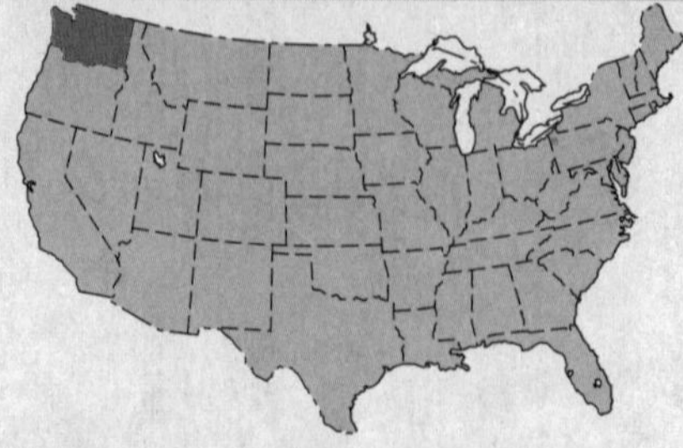

Washington State Tourism
PO Box 42525, Olympia, WA 98504
Tel: (360) 725 4028 *or* (800) 544 1800 (toll-free).
Fax: (360) 786 1451.
E-mail: tourism@cted.wa.gov
Website: www.experiencewashington.com

Washington State Information (UK Office)
c/o First Public Relations, Molasses House, Clove Hitch Quay, Plantation Wharf, London SW11 3TN, UK
Tel: (020) 7978 5233. Fax: (020) 7924 3134.
E-mail: eve@firstpr.co.uk
Website: www.firstpr.co.uk

Washington State Hotel & Lodging Association
13540 Linden Avenue North, Seattle, WA 98133
Tel: (206) 306 1001 *or* (877) 906 1001 (toll-free).
Fax: (206) 306 1006.
E-mail: admin@wshla.com
Website: www.stayinwashington.com or www.wshla.com

Seattle's CVB
1 Convention Place, 701 Pike Street, Suite 800, Seattle, WA 98101
Tel: (206) 461 5800 (administration) *or* 461 5840 (visitor information) *or* (800) 535 7071 (toll-free, hotel information).
Fax: (206) 461 5855.
E-mail: travel@seeseattle.org
Website: www.seeseattle.org

Spokane Regional CVB
801 West Riverside, Suite 301, Spokane, WA 99201
Tel: (509) 624 1341 *or* (800) 662 0084 (toll-free).
Fax: (509) 623 1297.
E-mail: conventions@visitspokane.com
Website: www.visitspokane.com

General Information

Nickname: Evergreen State
State bird: Willow Goldfinch
State flower: Coast Rhododendron
CAPITAL: Olympia
Date of admission to the Union: 11th Nov 1889
POPULATION: 6,203,788 (official estimate 2004)
POPULATION DENSITY: 33.6 per sq km
2003 total overseas arrivals/US ranking: 342,000/15

TIME: Pacific (GMT - 8). *Daylight Saving Time* is observed.
THE STATE: Washington State, bordering Canada and the Pacific Ocean, offers some of the nation's finest scenery for outdoor recreation. It has the second-highest population of any western State, yet visitors can travel from any city centre to peaceful countryside within minutes. The **Snake** and **Columbia rivers** flow through eastern Washington before joining to cut a passage through the **Cascades**, the north–south mountain range that dominates the centre of the State, rising to 4392m (14,411ft) at **Mount Rainier**. There are many fine beaches and small resorts on the Pacific coast. Much of the State is covered by coniferous forest. Holiday highlights include yachting on **Puget Sound**, hiking along the **Pacific Crest National Scenic Trail** and mountain climbing in the Cascades and the **Olympic Mountains**.

Travel - International

AIR: International airports: *Seattle-Tacoma International (SEA)* (website: www.portseattle.org/seatac) is 22km (14 miles) south of the city (travel time - 20 minutes). Shuttles and buses link the airport to points throughout the city, running continuously 24-hours; a door-to-door service is available from *Shuttle Express*, serving a variety of destinations, including Seattle and Tacoma. The *Airport Express Gray Line* departs twice an hour to downtown Seattle hotels. *Metro Transit* offers a public bus service to Seattle, while *Sound Transit* has regional services. Beginning September 24 2005, the *Downtown Seattle Transit Tunnel* will be closed for two years to build *Link* light rail between SeaTac and downtown Seattle. All buses currently operating in the tunnel will move to surface streets in downtown Seattle. Taxis are available. The airport Ground Transportation Information desk is located on the third floor of the parking garage.
Approximate flight times: From Seattle to *London* is nine hours five minutes, and to *San Francisco* is one hour 50 minutes.
SEA: *Washington State Ferries* (website: www.wsdot.wa.gov/ferries) link Seattle with the Olympic Peninsula, Bainbridge Island and other points in the region. The *Victoria Clipper* (website: www.victoriaclipper.com) links Victoria and Vancouver (British Columbia, Canada) to Seattle via high-speed catamarans.
RAIL: Three *Amtrak* (tel: (800) 872 7245 (toll-free); website: www.amtrak.com) lines cross the State. The daily *'Empire Builder'* from Chicago splits at Spokane, with onward services to Seattle and Portland (Oregon). There are four trains daily from Seattle to Portland; the *'Coast Starlight'* continues on to Los Angeles, while the daily *'Amtrak Cascades'* service comes from Eugene-Springfield (Oregon) and heads north to Vancouver, British Columbia via Tacoma (travel time - four hours); see the *California* and *Illinois* sections for other travel times. The Seattle station is located at 303 South Jackson Street; car hire is available (*Budget*, *Hertz* and *National*).
ROAD: *Greyhound* (tel: (800) 229 9424 (toll-free); website: www.greyhound.com) is the main carrier.
Approximate driving times: From Seattle to *Vancouver* is three hours, to *Portland* is three hours, to *Spokane* is six hours, to *Boise* is 10 hours, to *Calgary* is 15 hours, to *Los Angeles* is 24 hours, to *Chicago* is 44 hours, to *Dallas* is 45 hours, to *New York* is 61 hours, and to *Miami* is 69 hours. All times are based on non-stop driving at or below the applicable speed limits.
Approximate bus travel times: From Seattle to *Vancouver* is four hours, to *Portland* is four hours and to *Spokane* is seven hours. *Greyhound* (tel: (800) 229 9424; website: www.greyhound.com) is the main carrier.
URBAN: Seattle has an excellent bus system. An underground bus tunnel operates through central Seattle from the International District to the *Convention Center*, with stops at Pioneer Square, the financial district and the *Westlake Center*. A high-speed monorail links the city centre with the *Seattle Center*. Public transport is free in the centre of downtown. Taxis and car hire are also available.

Resorts & Excursions

SEATTLE: The 'Emerald City' is the primary international and domestic gateway to Washington State and the Pacific Northwest. The State's largest city is surrounded by the waters of **Lake Washington** and **Puget Sound** and enjoys spectacular views of **The Cascades** and the **Olympic Mountains**. The waterfront area is known for its seafood restaurants, shops and water excursions.
The **Seattle Center**, built for the 1962 World Fair, is the city's cultural heart, the home of opera, symphony, ballet and repertory theatre companies. It also contains the 185m- (605ft-) tall **Space Needle**, with an observation deck, restaurant and cocktail bar. **Pioneer Square** is a 17-square-block National Historic District showcasing Seattle's early history with shops, art galleries, restaurants and a unique underground tour. **Chinatown** offers arts, crafts and cuisine from China and Japan. **Pike Place Public Market** situated just above the waterfront, is the oldest continually operating farmers' market in the USA, featuring abundant seafood and produce, as well as handcrafted items from the Pacific Northwest. Harbour tours and fishing excursions are easily available, and the excursion to **Tillicum Village** is highly recommended. Other major attractions include **Woodland Park Zoo**, **Seattle Aquarium** and the **Japanese Garden**.
ELSEWHERE: Olympic National Park, west of Seattle, has glacier-studded mountains, rainforests, lakes, streams and miles of unspoiled coastline. **Tacoma**, south of Seattle, is the State's third-largest city. Its **Point Defiance Park** is one of the finest urban parks in the Pacific northwest. **Mount Rainier National Park**, southeast of Tacoma, offers

breathtaking views and skiing and other wintersports.
Mount St Helens, in **Gifford Pinchot National Park** in southwest Washington, is the site of the infamous volcanic eruption of 1980, which left a gigantic crater in the mountain's north flank. It is possible to take short trips by light aircraft over the summit.
Ellensburg, located in the central part of the State, features the famous *Ellensburg Rodeo*, which is held every Labor Day weekend. **Kennewick**, **Pasco**, **Richland** and **Yakima** are at the heart of the region's wine country.
Spokane, near the border with Idaho in eastern Washington, is the State's second-largest city; it boasts the outstanding **Riverfront Park**.

Social Profile

FOOD & DRINK: Seattle is noted for its seafood, and has more than 2000 restaurants serving many different types of cuisine. Restaurant/bars can stay open until 0200 all week. Beer and wine are available in grocery stores and spirits in State stores, usually every day 1000-2000, except Sunday. Stores in big cities have later closing hours. The minimum drinking age is 21.
THEATRES & CONCERTS: The *Seattle Opera*'s season runs from September to May. The *Seattle Symphony Orchestra* plays from September to June. Both the *Pacific Northwest Ballet* and the *Seattle Repertory* have seasons that run from October to May.
NIGHTLIFE: Jazz spots, nightclubs and discos are scattered throughout Seattle.
SHOPPING: *Westlake Center*, *Nordstrom*, the *Bon Marché* and *Pacific Palace* are among the major malls and department stores located in the heart of Seattle's retail district. Other interesting shopping areas include *Pioneer Square*, the *Waterfront* and *Pike Place Market*.
SPORT: Seattle has a number of professional sport teams, although none matches the fervour with which the *Seattle Mariners* **baseball** team, who play at the new Safeco Field, are followed. The *Seattle Seahawks* is the major American **football** team, who play in Qwest Field. The other big-league team is the Seattle Supersonics, who play basketball in the Key Arena. The *Seattle Thunderbirds* play **ice-hockey** in the US-division Western Hockey League.
SPECIAL EVENTS: The following is a selection of special events occurring in Washington State in 2005:
Feb 24-27 *Wintergrass Bluegrass Festival*, Tacoma. **Mar 4-6** *Spring Arts and Crafts Show*, Spokane. **Mar 11-13** *Gem, Mineral & Jewelry Show*, Spokane. **Mar 12** *27th Annual St Patricks Day Parade*, Spokane. **Mar 18-20** *Eighth Annual Othello Sandhill Crane Festival*. **Apr 2** *Fourth Annual Unity in Spirit Pow Wow*, Spokane. **Apr 14-17** *Puyallup Spring Fair*. **Apr 15** *Rainfest*, Forks. **Apr 16-24** *Japan Week*, Spokane. **May 6-8** *Maritime Festival*, Seattle. **May 8-22** *Lilac Festival*, Spokane. **Jun 4-6** *Mule Days*, Reardan. **Jun 9-12** *11th Annual Dixieland Jazz Festival*, Spokane. **Jun 25-26** *Seattle Pride*. **Jul 4** *Family Fourth at Lake Union*, Seattle; *Fourth of July Splash*, Kent; *Freedom Fest*, Fort Lewis; *Kinderfest*, Leavenworth; *Tacoma Freedom Fair*. **Jul 20-24** *King County Fair*, Enumclaw. **Aug 6** *Scottish Highland Games*, Spokane. **Aug 12-14** *A Taste of Edmonds*. **Aug 26-27** *Eighth Annual Outdoor Quilt Show*, Reardan. **Sep 2-5** *Bumbershoot* (arts and music festival), Seattle. **Sep 9-11** *Puyallup Pro Rodeo*. **Sep 15-18** *Wenatchee River Salmon Festival*, Leavenworth. **Sep 17** *Pirate Jamboree*, Ocean Shores. **Oct 14-16** *Bird Fest*, Ridgefield. **Nov 4-6** *Dixieland Jazz Festival*, Ocean Shores. **Nov 11** *Spokane Cork and Keg Festival*. **Nov 25-27** *Winter Fan-ta-sea* (arts and crafts festival), Ocean Shores. **Dec 31** *First Night*, Spokane.

Climate

Washington has two distinct climate zones. Summer days west of the Cascades rarely rise above 79°F (26°C), and winter days seldom drop below 46°F (8°C) while the east of the State has warm summers and cool winters.

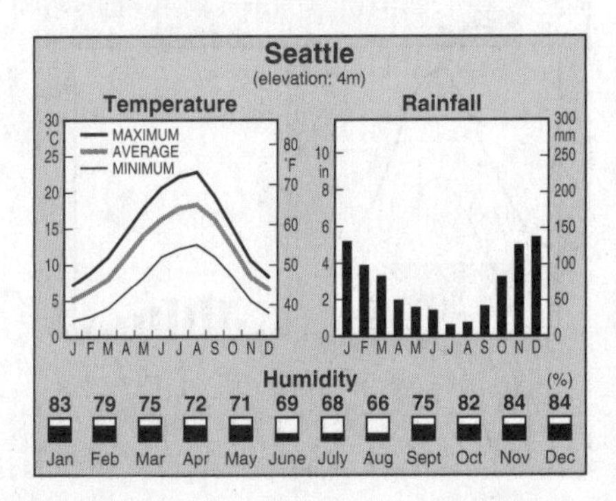

West Virginia

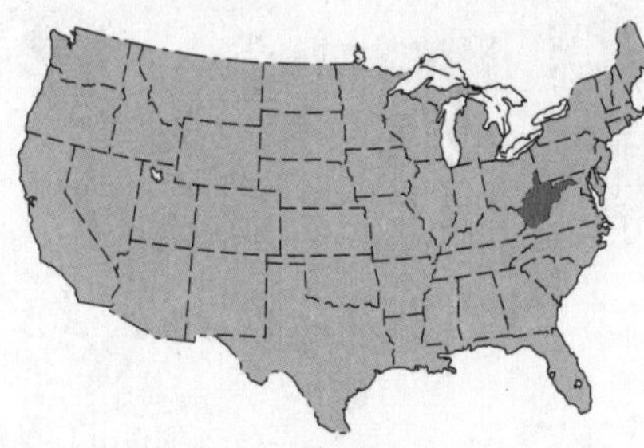

West Virginia Division of Tourism
90 MacCorkle Avenue, SW, South Charleston, WV 25303
Tel: (304) 558 2200 *or* (800) 225 5982 (toll-free).
Fax: (304) 558 2956.
E-mail: info@callwva.com
Website: www.callwva.com
West Virginia Tourism (UK Office)
c/o Destination Marketing, Power Road Studios, 114 Power Road, Chiswick, London W4 5PY, UK
Tel: (020) 8994 0978. Fax: (020) 8994 0962.
E-mail: wv@destination-marketing.co.uk
Website: www.callwva.com
Charleston CVB
200 Civic Center Drive, Charleston, WV 25301
Tel: (304) 344 5075 *or* (800) 733 5469 (toll-free).
Fax: (304) 344 1241.
E-mail: visitorinfo@charlestonwv.com
Website: www.charlestonwv.com
Greater Morgantown CVB
201 High Street, Suite 3, Morgantown, WV 26505
Tel: (304) 292 5081 *or* (800) 458 7373 (toll-free).
Fax: (304) 291 1354.
E-mail: info@tourmorgantown.com
Website: www.tourmorgantown.com

General Information

Nickname: Mountain State
State bird: Cardinal
State flower: Rosebay Rhododendron
CAPITAL: Charleston
Date of admission to the Union: 20 June 1863
POPULATION: 1,815,354 (official estimate 2004)
POPULATION DENSITY: 28.9 per sq km
2003 total overseas arrivals: Under 38,000
TIME: Eastern (GMT - 5). *Daylight Saving Time* is observed.

Credit: © Destination Marketing

THE STATE: Surrounded by the Appalachians, the mountain State of West Virginia has a history of poverty and physical isolation. Today, however, tourists flock to this beautiful region to enjoy historic sightseeing and an abundance of recreational sports, including skiing and other wintersports, mountain-biking, whitewater rafting, hiking and fishing. At the historic town of **Harper's Ferry**, the site of John Brown's rebellion in 1859, numerous fine museums run exhibits on slavery and the Civil War. More than 200 festivals, fairs, special events, tournaments and races celebrate and showcase the culture and heritage of West Virginia.
Whitewater rafting is a favourite activity at the **New River Gorge National River**, which winds its way through the Appalachians. The **Monongahela National Forest** occupies a vast area in the eastern part of the State and includes the **Spruce Knob-Seneca Rocks National Recreation Area**. Home to bears and deer, Monongahela offers over 500 campsites and miles of hiking trails. West Virginia also boasts some of the nation's best State parks, with good naturalist programmes and recreational facilities. These include four resort State parks, complete with lodges, cabins, swimming pools, championship golf courses, restaurants and additional amenities. Other attractions include the **State Capitol** in **Charleston**, one of the finest Italian Renaissance buildings in the USA.

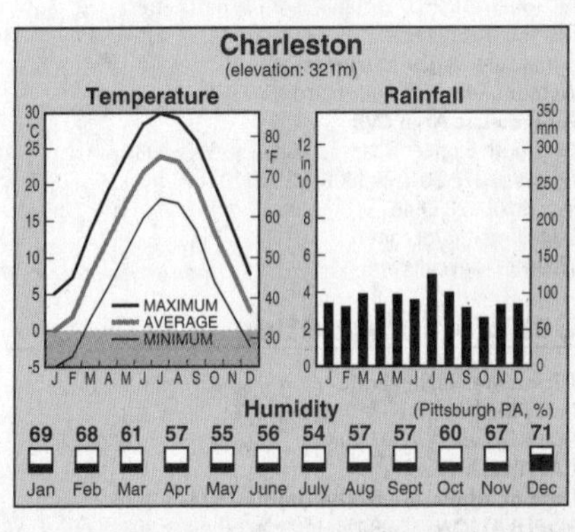

Credit: © Destination Marketing

Wisconsin

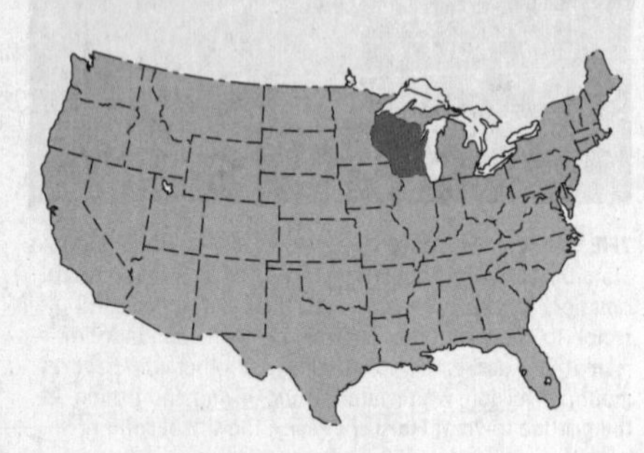

Wisconsin Department of Tourism
Street address: 201 West Washington Avenue, Madison, WI 53703
Postal address: PO Box 8690, Madison, WI 53708
Tel: (608) 266 2161 *or* (800) 432 8747 (toll-free).
Fax: (608) 266 3403.
E-mail: tourinfo@travelwisconsin.com
Website: www.travelwisconsin.com
Greater Milwaukee CVB
101 West Wisconsin Avenue, Suite 425, Milwaukee, WI 53203
Tel: (414) 273 7222 (visitor information) *or* (800) 554 1448 (toll-free; visitor information).
Fax: (414) 273 9707 (visitor center).
E-mail: visitor@milwaukee.org
Website: www.milwaukee.org
Greater Madison CVB
615 East Washington Avenue, Madison, WI 53703
Tel: (608) 255 2537 *or* (800) 373 6376 (toll-free).
Fax: (608) 258 4950.
E-mail: gmcvb@visitmadison.com
Website: www.visitmadison.com
Fond du Lac Area CVB
171 South Pioneer Road, Fond du Lac, WI 54935
Tel: (920) 923 3010 *or* (800) 937 9123 (toll-free).
Fax: (920) 929 6846.
E-mail: visit@fdl.com
Website: www.fdl.com

General Information

Nickname: Badger State
State bird: Robin
State flower: Wood Violet
CAPITAL: Madison
Date of admission to the Union: 29 May 1848
POPULATION: 5,509,299 (official estimate 2004)
POPULATION DENSITY: 32.5 per sq km
2003 total overseas arrivals/US ranking: 108,000/28
TIME: Central (GMT - 6). *Daylight Saving Time* is observed.

THE STATE: Located in the Great Lakes Region, Wisconsin is bordered to the east by **Lake Michigan** and separated from Canada in the north by **Lake Superior**. This is a beautiful State, with over 15,000 lakes and thousands of miles of rivers and streams. Its varied countryside also includes sandstone cliffs, sandy beaches, northern forests and rich, southern farmland. Wisconsin is famed for its hospitality and friendly atmosphere and is known as the beer capital of the nation. **Milwaukee**, on the southeast shores of Lake Michigan, is the State's largest city. Well known for its German heritage and beer industry, the city boasts over 1500 bars and taverns. Many festivals are held throughout the summer, the most lavish of which is the *Summerfest* in late-June. The **Charles Allis Art Museum** and the lakefront **Milwaukee Art Museum** offer fine collections of art.
West of Milwaukee, **Madison**, the State capital, is located on an isthmus between **Lake Mendota** and **Lake Monona**. This gracious city is the site of the **University of Wisconsin**, and student culture thrives, with lively coffee shops, secondhand (thrift) shops and bicycle paths. Also here is the impressive **State Capitol**, with its outstanding ceiling frescoes, and, in nearby **Baraboo**, the **Circus World Museum**, former home of the Ringling Brothers' Circus.
Wisconsin's **Door County** is a peninsula comprising 403km (250 miles) of beautiful coastline that extends into Lake Michigan. The scenery here is breathtaking, with lighthouses, picturesque villages, art galleries and miles of sandy beaches. Camping is plentiful, as is Door County cuisine, such as 'fish boils' and cherry pie. Other State attractions include the 21 **Apostle Islands** on Lake Superior, home to the largest collection of lighthouses in the USA, as well as fine sandy beaches, caves, forests, black bears and bald eagles. Especially popular is **Madeline Island**, with its fine beaches and unspoilt landscape.

Wyoming

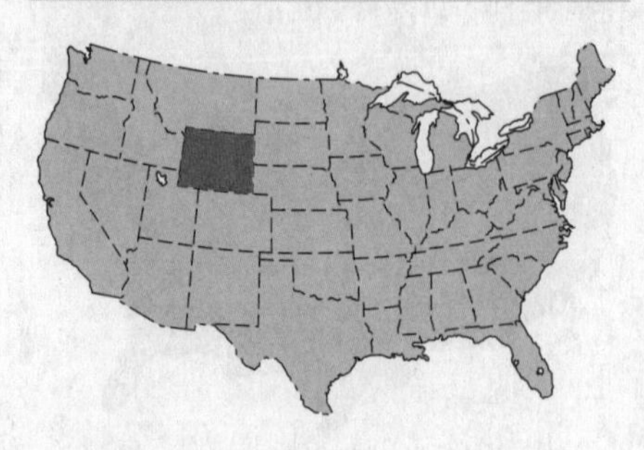

Wyoming Business Council – Tourism Office
I-25 at College Drive, Cheyenne, WY 82002
Tel: (307) 777 7777 *or* (800) 225 5996 (toll-free).
Fax: (307) 777 2877.
E-mail: tourism@state.wy.us
Website: www.wyomingtourism.org
The Tourism Office has a full list of local visitors' offices on their website.
Rocky Mountain International
7 Thornton Avenue, Warsash, Southampton, Hampshire SO31 9FL, UK
Tel: (01489) 557 533 (trade enquiries only) *or* (09063) 640 655 (customer request line; 60p per minute).
Fax: (01489) 557 534.
E-mail: rmi.uk@btinternet.com
Website: www.rmi-realamerica.com
Cheyenne Area CVB
121 West 15th Street, Suite 202, Cheyenne, WY 82001
Tel: (307) 778 3133 *or* (800) 426 5009 (toll-free).
Fax: (307) 778 3190.
E-mail: helpdesk@cheyenne.org
Website: www.cheyenne.org
Jackson Hole Chamber of Commerce
Street address: 990 West Broadway, Jackson, WY 83001
Postal address: PO Box 550, Jackson, WY 83001
Tel: (307) 733 3316. Fax: (307) 733 5585.
E-mail: info@jacksonholechamber.com
Website: www.jacksonholechamber.com

General Information

Nickname: Equality State/Cowboy State
State bird: Western Meadowlark
State flower: Indian Paintbrush
CAPITAL: Cheyenne
Date of admission to the Union: 10 July 1890
POPULATION: 506,529 (official estimate 2004)
POPULATION DENSITY: 2.0 per sq km
2003 total overseas arrivals: Under 57,000/37
TIME: Mountain (GMT - 7). *Daylight Saving Time* is observed.

THE STATE: In the heart of the Rockies, Wyoming is known as the 'Cowboy State' and was the home of 'Buffalo Bill' Cody. It is the ninth-largest State in the USA and has the smallest population. The spirit of the Wild West is alive and kicking in Wyoming, with its open spaces, rugged country and breathtaking scenery. Ranching is still a major industry here, and one of the world's largest rodeos – *Cheyenne*

Credit: © Wyoming Travel & Tourism

Credit: © Wyoming Travel & Tourism

Frontier Days, held annually in July – has drawn visitors to the State capital since 1897. Visitors to Wyoming can also choose to spend time at one of the many guest or working ranches and experience at first hand Wyoming's special frontier heritage. Geographical attractions include 11 major mountain ranges, prairies, grasslands, parks, forests, lakes and rivers. The world's first national park, the huge **Yellowstone National Park** (website: www.nps.gov/yell), is located on top of one of the earth's few 'hot spots' – a place where the earth's crust is so thin that the hot, molten core can influence surface conditions.
Yellowstone's violent volcanic history has resulted in a unique environment of geysers, bubbling hot pools, alpine lakes and great canyons. **Old Faithful Geyser**, the park's most famous attraction, erupts almost hourly, sending jets of boiling water into the air. Just south of Yellowstone is the beautiful **Grand Teton National Park**, with ample hiking, cycling and horseriding opportunities; and the mountain valley town of **Jackson**, which in winter becomes one of the world's premier ski spots. South of Jackson is **Bridger-Teton National Forest**. The Shoshone and Arapaho Native American tribes live east of this forest, on the **Wind River Indian Reservation**.

Credit: © Wyoming Travel & Tourism

Heading northeast, **Cody**, Buffalo Bill's hometown, is best known for the **Buffalo Bill Historical Center** – often called 'The Smithsonian of the West'. Cody is also home to **Old Trail Town**, a collection of pioneer buildings and relics of the Big Horn Basin area. Further east are the dramatic **Big Horn Mountains**, with the charming towns of **Buffalo** and **Sheridan** nestled at the base of the range. At Buffalo, the **Jim Gatchell Museum of the West** offers fascinating insights into frontier history. In the northeast, the majestic **Devil's Tower National Monument** rises over 360m (1200ft) from the valley and attracts thousands of climbers. Back towards the centre of the State, the **National Historic Trails Interpretative Center**, which chronicles the great westward emmigration of the 19th century, is located in **Casper**.

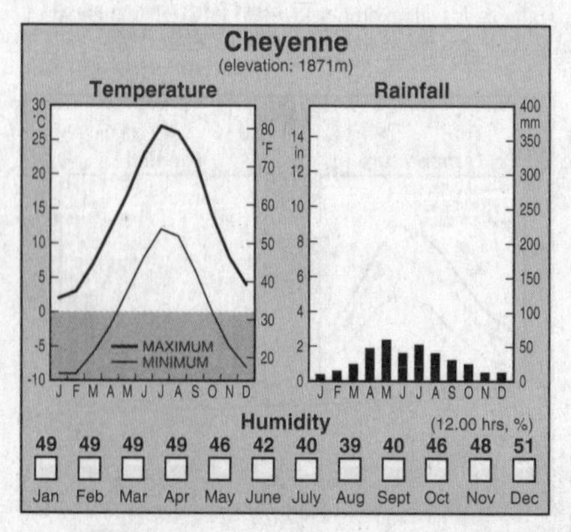

US External Territories

LATEST TRAVEL ADVICE CONTACTS

British Foreign and Commonwealth Office
Tel: (0870) 606 0290 Website: www.fco.gov.uk

US Department of State
Website: http://travel.state.gov/travel

Canadian Department of Foreign Affairs and Int'l Trade
Tel: (1 800) 267 8376 Website: www.dfait-maeci.gc.ca

This section includes basic facts on a number of the US External Territories: Baker & Howland Islands, Jarvis Island, Johnston Atoll, Kingman Reef, Midway Islands, Navassa Island, Palmyra and Wake Island. For more information on these islands, contact a US Embassy; see *USA* section.

Resorts & Excursions

BAKER & HOWLAND ISLANDS AND JARVIS ISLAND

US Fish & Wildlife Service – Pacific Islands
PO Box 50088, Room 5-231, 300 Ala Moana Boulevard, Honolulu, Hawaii, HI 96850, USA
Tel: (808) 792 9550. Fax: (808) 792 9586.
Website: www.fws.gov/pacific

Location: Central Pacific Ocean. **Population:** Currently uninhabited. **Geography:** Baker & Howland Islands are two low-lying coral atolls located about 2575km (1600 miles) southwest of Honolulu, Hawaii. There are no lagoons on the islands. Jarvis Island is a low-lying coral island about 2090km (1300 miles) south of Hawaii. **Time:** GMT - 12. **History:** The Islands were originally settled by the USA in 1935, but were subsequently evacuated during World War II. In 1974, the Islands were registered as national wildlife refuges to be administered by the US Fish & Wildlife Service and visitors wishing to land on the islands must seek permission from this organisation (for address, see above). In 1990, Congress passed legislation for the Islands to be included within the boundaries of the State of Hawaii.

JOHNSTON ATOLL

US Department of the Interior
1849 C Street, NW, Washington, DC 20240
Tel: (202) 208 3100.
E-mail: webteam@ios.doi.gov
Website: www.doi.gov

US Department of Defense
Commander, Johnston Atoll (FCDNA),
APO San Francisco, CA 96035, USA
Website: www.defenselink.mil

Location: Pacific Ocean. **Area:** 2.6 sq km (1 sq mile). **Population:** Uninhabited. **Geography:** Located 1319km (820 miles) west-southwest of Honolulu, Johnston Atoll consists of Johnston Island, Sand Island and two manmade islands, East (Hikina) and North (Akua). **Time:** GMT - 10. **History:** The USA began a chemical disposal facility on Johnston Atoll in 1985, but it was not until 1989 that it gained the world's attention when the USA agreed to destroy 400 tons of nerve gas here after transporting it from the Federal Republic of Germany. Complaints were lodged by the South Pacific Forum nations and various environmental groups, which resulted in the USA sending a group of scientists to monitor the safety of the disposal facility's activities. Today the Atoll is no longer a storage or disposal site for chemical weapons; by 2004, the site was completely cleaned and closed. An oasis for reef and birdlife, nowadays, the Atoll is jointly administered by the Department of the Interior, US Fish and Wildlife Service (for address, see above) and the US Department of Defense.

KINGMAN REEF

US Fish & Wildlife Service – Pacific Islands
PO Box 50088, Room 5-231, 300 Ala Moana Boulevard, Honolulu, Hawaii, HI 96850, USA
Tel: (808) 792 9550. Fax: (808) 792 9586.
Website: www.fws.gov/pacific

Location: Pacific Ocean. **Geography:** Located 1500km (925 miles) southwest of Hawaii, Kingman Reef consists of a reef and shoal measuring 8km (5 miles) by 15km (9.5 miles). **History:** The reef is closed to public access and was a Naval Defense Sea Area and Airspace Reservation administered by the US Department of Defense. In 1990, Congress passed legislation for the reef to be included within the boundaries of the State of Hawaii. In January 2001, the waters around the reef were designated a National Wildlife Refuge.

TIMATIC CODES

Health	AMADEUS: **TI-DFT/HNI/HE** GALILEO/WORLDSPAN: **TI-DFT/HNI/HE** SABRE: **TIDFT/HNI/HE**
Visa	AMADEUS: **TI-DFT/HNI/VI** GALILEO/WORLDSPAN: **TI-DFT/HNI/VI** SABRE: **TIDFT/HNI/VI**

To access TIMATIC country information on Health and Visa regulations through the Computer Reservations System (CRS), type in the appropriate command line listed above.

MIDWAY ISLANDS

US Fish & Wildlife Service – Pacific Islands
PO Box 50088, Room 5-231, 300 Ala Moana Boulevard, Honolulu, Hawaii, HI 96850, USA
Tel: (808) 792 9550. Fax: (808) 792 9586.
Website: www.fws.gov/pacific

Midway Atoll National Wildlife Refuge
PO Box 29460, Honolulu HI 96820, USA
Tel/Fax: (808) 674 8237.
E-mail: Michael_R_Johnson@fws.gov
Website: http://midway.fws.gov

Location: Northern Pacific Ocean. **Area:** 5 sq km (2 sq miles). **Population:** 40 (2002). **Geography:** Located 1850km (1150 miles) northwest of Hawaii, the Midway Islands consist of Sand Island, Eastern Island and several small islets within the reef. **Time:** GMT - 11. **History:** The Islands' administration transferred from the US Department of Defense to the Department of the Interior in 1996 (for address, see above). Limited tourism is now permitted; the Islands are a national wildlife refuge. In 1990, Congress passed legislation for the Territory to be included within the boundaries of the State of Hawaii.

NAVASSA ISLAND

Location: Caribbean Sea. **Area:** 5.2 sq km (2 sq miles). **Population:** Uninhabited. **Geography:** Navassa Island is a raised coral island with a limestone plateau and lies 160km (100 miles) south of Guatánamo Bay, Cuba and 65km (40 miles) west of Haiti. **Time:** GMT - 5. **History:** In 1857, Navassa became a US Insular Area and was mined for guano until operations ceased in 1898. In 1997, the Office of Insular Affairs, under the control of the US Department of the Interior, took responsibility of the island. Reports in 1998 showed that a variety of unique plant and animal species existed on Navassa and visits to the island were subsequently prohibited. The US Department of the Interior, US Fish and Wildlife Service (see address in *Midway Islands* section) took command in 1999 and it became a National Wildlife Refuge.

PALMYRA

Location: Pacific Ocean. **Area:** 100 hectares (247 acres). **Population:** Uninhabited. **Geography:** Palmyra is made up of approximately 50 low-lying islets about 1600km (1000 miles) south of Honolulu. **Time:** GMT - 11. **History:** Administered by the US Department of the Interior since 1961, Palmyra was included within the boundaries of the State of Hawaii after legislation in 1990. In 1996, it became known that the Hawaiian owners of the islands were to sell the atoll to a US company which was allegedly planning to establish a nuclear waste storage facility. The Government of Kiribati protested at these moves and reiterated its attempts to include the atoll within its own national boundaries. However, the original designs for the island were abandoned and, in November 2000, the atoll was sold to the Nature Conservancy (website: http//nature.org) for approximately US$30 million. The lagoons and surrounding waters were later transferred to the US Fish and Wildlife Service (see address for *Midway Islands* section) in January 2001, and it was designated a National Wildlife Refuge.

WAKE ISLAND

US Department of Defense
Department of the Air Force, The Pentagon, Washington, DC 20330, USA
Tel: (703) 545 6700.
Website: www.defenselink.mil

Location: Pacific Ocean. **Area:** 8 sq km (3 sq miles). **Population:** 124 (2002). **Geography:** Wake Island lies in the Pacific Ocean and consists of three islets, Wake, Wilkes and Peale, approximately 2060km (1280 miles) east of Guam and 500km (310 miles) north of the Marshall Islands. The location (not the size) of this island makes it of major importance to the US government. **Time:** GMT + 12. **History:** A protectorate island of the USA, the US flag having been formally raised over the island in 1898, its strategic location has led in the past to its use as a trans-Pacific telegraph relay station and a stopover for flights in the days before jet flight became universal. From 1941-44, it was occupied by the Japanese. In 1990, Congress proposed that the islands should be included within the boundaries of Guam. This sparked off a reaction from the Republic of the Marshall Islands, which also claimed rights to the island. The island has been a military air force base since 1972 and is administered by the US Department of Defense (for address, see above).

Note: The following countries all have their own sections in the *World Travel Guide*:
AMERICAN SAMOA, **GUAM**, **US VIRGIN ISLANDS**. For **PALAU** and the **NORTHERN MARIANA ISLANDS**, see the **PACIFIC ISLANDS OF MICRONESIA** section.

US Virgin Islands

LATEST TRAVEL ADVICE CONTACTS

British Foreign and Commonwealth Office
Tel: (0870) 606 0290 Website: www.fco.gov.uk

US Department of State
Website: http://travel.state.gov/travel

Canadian Department of Foreign Affairs and Int'l Trade
Tel: (1 800) 267 8376 Website: www.dfait-maeci.gc.ca

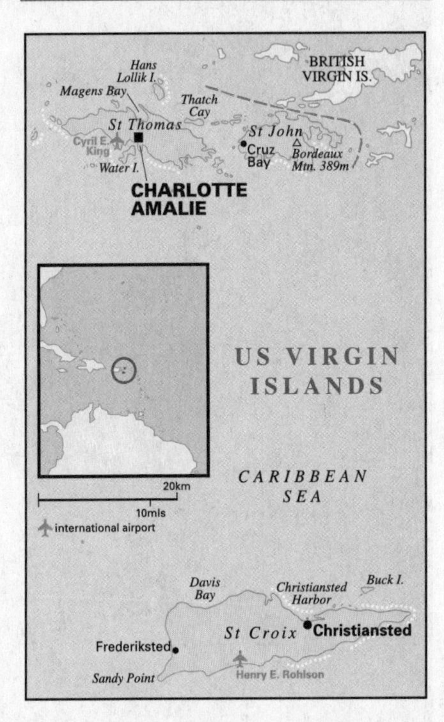

Location: Caribbean, Leeward Islands.

Country dialling code: 1 340.

Diplomatic representation
The US Virgin Islands are a United States External Territory represented abroad by US Embassies. For addresses, see the *USA* section.

US Virgin Islands Department of Tourism
Street address: 78 Constant 1-2-3, St Thomas, USVI 00802
Postal address: PO Box 6400, St Thomas, USVI 00804
Tel: 774 8784 *or* (800) 372 8784 (toll-free).
Fax: 774 4390.
E-mail: info@usvitourism.vi
Website: www.usvitourism.vi

US Virgin Islands Department of Tourism
c/o Destination Marketing, Power Road Studios, 114 Power Road, Chiswick, London W4 5PY, UK
Tel: (020) 8994 0978.
Fax: (020) 8994 0962.
E-mail: usvi@destination-marketing.co.uk
Website: www.usvitourism.vi

US Virgin Islands Department of Tourism
1270 Avenue of the Americas, Suite 2108,
New York, NY 10020, USA
Tel: (212) 332 2222.
Fax: (212) 332 2223.
E-mail: usviny@aol.com
Website: www.usvitourism.vi
Offices also in: Atlanta, Chicago, Los Angeles, Miami and Washington, DC.

US Virgin Islands Division of Tourism
703 Evans Avenue, Suite 106, Toronto,
Ontario M9C 5E9, Canada
Tel: (416) 622 7600. Fax: (416) 622 3431.
E-mail: usvi@travmarkgroup.com
Website: www.usvitourism.vi

TIMATIC CODES

Health	AMADEUS: **TI-DFT/STT/HE** GALILEO/WORLDSPAN: **TI-DFT/STT/HE** SABRE: **TIDFT/STT/HE**
Visa	AMADEUS: **TI-DFT/STT/VI** GALILEO/WORLDSPAN: **TI-DFT/STT/VI** SABRE: **TIDFT/STT/VI**

To access TIMATIC country information on Health and Visa regulations through the Computer Reservations System (CRS), type in the appropriate command line listed above.

A B C D E F G H I J K L M N O P Q R S T U V W X Y Z

Credit: © US Virgin Islands Department of Tourism

General Information

AREA: 347.1 sq km (134 sq miles).
POPULATION: 110,000 (UN estimate 2001).
POPULATION DENSITY: 312.9 per sq km.
CAPITAL: Charlotte Amalie (St Thomas). **Population:** 11,044 (2000).
GEOGRAPHY: The islands are situated 64km (40 miles) east of Puerto Rico and comprise some 50 islands covered with lush tropical vegetation. St Thomas is long and narrow, rising abruptly to a ridge with an excellent deep-water harbour. St John is covered partly in bay forests. St Croix consists of 215 sq km (83 sq miles) of rolling ex-plantation land.
GOVERNMENT: US External Territory (Unincorporated). Gained a measure of self-government in 1954. **Head of State:** President George W Bush since 2001. **Head of Government:** Governor Thomas Macan since 2002.
LANGUAGE: English is the official language. Spanish and Creole are also widely spoken.
RELIGION: Christian, mainly Protestant.
TIME: GMT - 4.
ELECTRICITY: 110 volts AC, 60Hz.
COMMUNICATIONS: Telephone: IDD is available. Country code: 1 340. There are no area codes. Outgoing international code: 001. The USA (including most toll-free numbers) can be dialled directly from the islands. Efficient overseas cable and telephone services are in operation. **Mobile telephone:** GSM 1900 network. **Fax:** Services are available. **Internet:** ISPs include *VIAccess* (website: www.viaccess.net). Internet cafes exist on St Thomas. **Post:** Airmail to Europe takes up to one week. The postage is the same as in the USA. First-class post to the USA automatically travels by air through the US postal service. Post office hours: Mon-Fri 0900-1700, Sat 0900-1200.
Press: The daily newspapers are *St Croix Avis* and *Virgin Islands Daily News*.
Radio: BBC World Service (website: www.bbc.co.uk/worldservice) and Voice of America (website: www.voa.gov) can be received. From time to time the frequencies change and the most up-to-date can be found online.

Passport/Visa

Immigration requirements for the US Virgin Islands are the same as for the USA; see the *USA* section.

Money

Currency: US Dollar (US$) = 100 cents. See the USA section for information on currency exchange, exchange rates, credit and debit cards and so on.
Travellers cheques: To avoid additional exchange rate charges, travellers are advised to take travellers cheques in US Dollars.
Currency restrictions: Import and export of amounts in excess of US$10,000 must be declared.
Banking hours: Mon-Thurs 0900-1430, Fri 0900-1400 and 1530-1700.

Duty Free

Duty must be paid on all gifts and alcohol brought in from abroad. Other customs regulations, duty free exemptions and prohibitions are as for the USA; see *Duty Free* in the *USA* section.

Public Holidays

Jan 1 2005 New Year's Day. **Jan 6** Three Kings' Day. **Jan 19** Martin Luther King Day. **Feb 14** Presidents' Day. **Mar 24** Holy Thursday. **Mar 25** Good Friday. **Mar 28** Easter Monday. **May 23** Memorial Day. **Jul 3** Danish West Indies Emancipation Day. **Jul 4** US Independence Day. **Jul 25** Hurricane Supplication Day. **Sep 5** Labor Day. **Oct 11** Columbus Day. **Oct 17** Virgin Islands Thanksgiving Day. **Nov 1** D Hamilton Jackson Day. **Nov 11** Veterans' Day. **Nov 24** US Thanksgiving Day. **Dec 25** Christmas Day. **Jan 1 2006** New Year's Day. **Jan 6** Three Kings' Day. **Jan 19** Martin Luther King Day. **Feb 13** Presidents' Day. **Apr 13** Holy Thursday. **Apr 14** Good Friday. **Apr 17** Easter Monday. **May 22** Memorial Day. **Jul 3** Danish West Indies Emancipation Day. **Jul 4** US Independence Day. **Jul 25** Hurricane Supplication Day. **Sep 4** Labor Day. **Oct 9** Columbus Day. **Oct 17** Virgin Islands Thanksgiving Day. **Nov 1** D Hamilton Jackson Day. **Nov 11** Veterans' Day. **Nov 23** US Thanksgiving Day. **Dec 25** Christmas Day.

Health

	Special Precautions?	Certificate Required?
Yellow Fever	No	No
Cholera	No	No
Typhoid & Polio	1	N/A
Malaria	No	N/A

Note: Regulations and requirements may be subject to change at short notice, and you are advised to contact your doctor well in advance of your intended date of departure. Any numbers in the chart refer to the footnotes below.

1: Vaccination against typhoid and poliomyelitis is advised.
Food & drink: Water precautions are advised outside the main centres. Mains water is considered safe to drink. Milk is pasteurised and dairy products are safe for consumption. Local meat, poultry, seafood, fruit and vegetables are generally considered safe to eat.
Other risks: *Bilharzia* (*schistosomiasis*) may be present in some fresh water; swimming pools that are well chlorinated and maintained are safe. Visitors should enquire locally. Immunisation against *hepatitis A* should be considered.
Health care: Medical costs are very high and health insurance is essential. Medical facilities are of a similar standard to those in the USA. There are hospitals on St Croix and St Thomas; a clinic is located on St John.

Travel - International

AIR: *USAir (US)* has daily direct flights to St Thomas and St Croix. *American Airlines (AA)* offers daily, direct services from New York (*JFK*) and Miami to St Thomas and St Croix. Other airlines that fly to the US Virgin Islands include *Britannia Airways*, *Continental Airlines*, *Delta* and *United Airlines*. Services from the US mainland to the Virgin Islands are available through *Air Sunshine*, *American Eagle* and *Cape Air*. Seaplanes connect St Thomas and St Croix several times a day. For schedules of these and other operators' routes to the US Virgin Islands, contact the airlines directly.
Approximate flight times: From St Croix to *London* is 14 hours (including stopover), to *New York* is three hours 45 minutes, to *Miami* is two hours 30 minutes, to *St Maarten* is 45 minutes, to *St Thomas* is 30 minutes and to *San Juan* is 30 minutes.
International airports: *St Thomas (STT)* (Cyril E King) is 5km (3 miles) west of Charlotte Amalie.
St Croix (STX) (Henry E Rohlsen) is about 14km (9 miles) southwest of Christiansted.
Departure tax: None.
SEA: The main passenger ports are Charlotte Amalie (St Thomas) and Frederiksted on St Croix. Regular ferries sail between St Thomas and St John and the British Virgin Islands and Fajardo (Puerto Rico). Ferries leave from Charlotte Amalie and Red Hook Dock on St Thomas, for Cruz Bay on St John. A number of cruise lines operating out of Miami and San Juan includes the US Virgin Islands in their itineraries around the Caribbean. Cruise lines include *Carnival*, *Celebrity*, *Norwegian Cruise Lines*, *Princess* and *Royal Caribbean*. For more information on cruise ships to the US Virgin Islands, contact the US Virgin Islands Department of Tourism (see *Contact Addresses* section) *or* consult the 'Cruise Ship Schedules' online (website: www.ships.vi).
ROAD: Well-maintained roads connect all main towns. Speed limit is 35kph (20mph) in towns and 55kph (35mph) elsewhere. Driving is on the left. **Bus:** Public services operate on St Thomas from Charlotte Amalie to Red Hook and Bordeaux, and St Croix has a taxi-van service between Christiansted and Frederiksted. St John has a bus service running from Cruz Bay to Salt Pond. **Taxi:** Available on all the islands. These follow standard routes between various points, and the fares for these are published. Sharing taxis is

a common practice. **Car hire:** There are several international car hire agencies at the airports and in the main towns on St Croix, St John and St Thomas. Jeeps or mini-mokes are popular modes of travel and these too can be hired. **Documentation:** National licences are accepted; an International Driving Permit is not required.
Travel Times: The following chart gives approximate travel times (in hours and minutes) from **Charlotte Amalie** to other major cities/towns in the US Virgin Islands.

	Air	Road	Sea
Chris'sted, SC	0.25	-	-
Cruz Bay, SJ	-	-	0.45
Magens Bay	-	0.20	-
Coral World	-	0.40	-

Note: SC = St Croix; **SJ** = St John.

Accommodation

HOTELS: The islands have more hotels per square mile than anywhere in the Caribbean. Costs vary according to standard, but are generally quite high compared to other Caribbean islands. The islands' hotel association has a counter at the airport to assist with reservations. The following organisations can give further information: St Thomas & St John Hotel & Tourism Association, PO Box 2300, St Thomas, VI 00803 (tel: 774 6835; fax: 774 4993; e-mail: stsjhta@vipowernet.net; website: www.sttstjhta.com *or* www.virgin-islands-hotels.com); *or* St Croix Hotel & Tourism Association, PO Box 24238, Gallows Bay, St Croix, VI 00824 (tel: 773 7117; website: www.stcroixhotelandtourism.com). A variety of guest houses, condominiums and villas are also available in St John and St Thomas.
CAMPING: There are two main campsites, all on the island of St John. One of the main sites, Cinnamon Bay Camp, is located inside the 11,560 acre St John National Park. Inexpensive bare plots, plots with tents already set up and cottages are available for a maximum stay of two weeks. The site is very popular, so reservations should be made well in advance by contacting Cinnamon Bay Camp, PO Box 720, Cruz Bay, St John, VI 00831 (tel: 776 6330; fax: 776 6458; website: www.cinnamonbay.com). The other campsite is at Maho Bay near a beautiful beach. Contact Maho Bay Camp, PO Box 310, Cruz Bay, St John, VI 00830 (tel: 715 0501; e-mail: mahobay@maho.org; website: www.maho.org). So-called 'eco-tents', which are part of the tourist authorities' wish to encourage 'sustainable tourism' and rustic cabins are also available.

Resorts & Excursions

ST CROIX

St Croix is the largest of the US Virgin Islands.
Christiansted is one of the two major towns showing early Danish influence. **Fort Christiansværn** (dating from 1774), **Government House**, the **Old Custom House and Art Gallery** and the **wharf** area are among its historic sites. Outside of Christiansted, on **West Airport Road**, is the **Cruz Rum Distillery** where visitors can taste the islands' rum and watch it being made. On the way to **Frederiksted** is **Whim Greathouse**, portraying plantation life in the 18th century. Frederiksted is also of Danish origin and has a 15 acre tropical rainforest nearby.

EXCURSIONS

Offshore Attractions: The much smaller **Buck Island** can easily be reached by sailing the 10km (6 mile) channel that separates it from Christiansted. Offshore is one of the world's most impressive marine gardens, maintained by the National Park Service as an underwater protected reef.
ST THOMAS: St Thomas is the second-largest and the most cosmopolitan of this chain of islands. Like St Croix, it has many associations with the Danes and retains much Danish influence. The main town, **Charlotte Amalie**, is the group's capital. Imported goods from all over the world make it a marvellous shopping centre and stores tucked into remodelled Danish warehouses line each side of the picturesque **Main Street**.
Cobblestoned alleys with numerous boutiques lead down to the waterfront. **Blackbeard's Castle** is the earliest fortification in the US Virgin Islands. Other attractions include **Fort Christian**, built in 1672; the **Coral World Observatory**; the **Frederick Lutheran Church** of 1850; **Government House** on **Government Hill** (1866); **Venus Pillar** on **Magnolia Hill**; **Bluebeard's Tower**, the 19th-century pirate's one-time abode; and the **Synagogue** on **Crystal Gade**, one of the oldest in the western hemisphere. On the northern coast is **Magens Bay**, claimed to be one of the world's top 10 beaches.
ST JOHN: St John is the most 'unspoilt' of the islands. It has no airport, and two-thirds of the island's deep valleys and most of its shoreline have been set aside as the **Virgin Islands National Park**. **Cruz Bay** is a small town offering excellent gift shops and dive centres. **Trunk Bay** is a beautiful beach, and the diving is very good. Accommodation on the island is limited. **Caneel Bay** is a luxurious resort. **Cinnamon Bay** and **Maho Bay** have campsites. Cottages can also be rented.

Sport & Activities

Sailing: Enthusiasts wishing to explore the myriad islands scattered around the territory can hire sailing boats or powerboats, with or without a skipper, either for afternoon or evening trips or for an all-inclusive week on a charter yacht. A list of operators can be obtained from the US Virgin Islands Department of Tourism (see *Contact Addresses* section). **Boat races** take place all year round, including the *Rolex Cup Regatta* (on St Thomas) and the *Mumm's Cup Regatta* (on St Croix). Guided **kayak** tours through Mangrove Lagoon and St Thomas' Marine Sanctuary provide the opportunity to see egrets, herons and other wildlife.
Watersports: The US Virgin Islands are an established **diving** and **snorkelling** destination with well-developed facilities. Coral reefs, warm and calm seas, a rich marine life and excellent visibility are the main attractions for divers of all abilities. Beginners without certification may enrol on an open-water training course (usually completed in three days). However, local instructors recommend learners to complete basic pool work at home and finish their four open-water dives after arrival. The diving season is busiest from December through April, when advance booking on dive packages is recommended. Some of the best dive sites include *Andreas Reef* (on St Thomas, known for its variety of tropical fish); *Buck Island Reef National Monument* (a protected area on St Croix with markers describing marine life); *Carval Rock* (for advanced divers, on St John); *Salt River Canyon* (one of the most popular sites, also on St Croix); and *Submarine Alley* (an advanced dive site, also on St Thomas, with large coral islands).
Fishing: Sport fishing is excellent, particularly for blue and white marlin, sailfish and wahoo, with the *North Drop* (accessible from St John or St Thomas) being the best-known spot. Sport fishing charters with experienced skippers are widely available. Local fishermen are keen to encourage the 'catch-and-release' method in order to preserve fish species. Fishing competitions, such as the *Bastille Day Kingfish Tournament* or the *Open Atlantic Blue Marlin Tournament* attract amateurs and professionals from all over the world.
Other: There are two 18-hole **golf** courses on St Croix, at Buccaneer Hotel and at Carambola Resort. A 9-hole course is located at the Reef. St Thomas has an excellent 18-hole course at Mahogany Run. There are many **tennis** courts available on St Croix and St Thomas and a few on St John. **Horse riding** is available in Frederiksted and Christiansted on St Croix.

Social Profile

FOOD & DRINK: High-quality restaurants serve everything from French and Italian to Chinese cuisine. Island specialities include fresh fish and lobster. Dining out is casual and there is an increasing number of eateries on the main islands offering seafood, burgers, steaks and local fare. *Cruzan* rum is strong and distinctive.
NIGHTLIFE: Steel bands, folk singing, calypso and limbo dancing are popular. Discos are also available. St Thomas has several nightclubs; many hotels also offer entertainment. Cinemas on St Croix and St Thomas show English-language films.
SHOPPING: All luxury items up to US$1200 are cheap as they are duty free. Charlotte Amalie on St Thomas is the best shopping centre. Best buys include watches, cameras, fine jewellery, china, leather goods, perfume, spirits and designer clothing. **Shopping hours:** Mon-Sat 0900-1700. When cruise ships are in port, some shops open on Sunday.
SPECIAL EVENTS: For a full list, contact the US Virgin Islands Department of Tourism (see *Contact Addresses*). The following is a selection of special events occurring in the US Virgin Islands in 2005:
Jan 1 *3rd Annual St Croix Millennium Marathon VI Pace Runners*. **Jan 6** *Festival Village Grand Finale* (fireworks to mark the end of the Crucian Christmas Festival), St Croix. **Jan 8** *Adults Parade*. **Feb 19-21** *Agriculture & Food Fair*, St Croix. **Mar 25-27** *International Rolex Regatta*. **Apr 4-May 1** *St Thomas' Annual Carnival*. **Apr 15** *Sunset Jazz in Frederiksted*. **May 1** *St Croix Half-Ironman Triathlon*. **May 29** *Beach-to-Beach Power Swim Fundraiser*. **May 30** *Memorial Day 2-Mile Run*. **Jul 1-7** *St John Cultural Celebration*. **Jul 23-24** *Arts & Crafts Fair*, St Thomas. **Oct 23** *St Croix Coral Reef Swim*. **Dec** *Crucian Christmas Festival*, throughout the islands.
SOCIAL CONVENTIONS: The US Virgin Islanders are overwhelmingly friendly and helpful and the pace of life is very relaxed. Shaking hands is the normal form of greeting and the appropriate time of day (good morning/afternoon/evening) is usually uttered at every encounter. Politeness and courtesy is expected. Dress is informal for most occasions apart from the formal requirements of some hotels. **Tipping:** All hotels add 8 per cent room tax and 10 to 15 per cent service charge. Restaurants will either add a 10 to 15 per cent service charge or expect the equivalent tip.

Business Profile

ECONOMY: When Denmark sold the islands to the US government in 1917, they insisted that the existing privileges of the inhabitants be respected. A result of this is that the Virgin Islands are not part of the Federal Customs Area, a state of affairs that affords various advantages. This, in turn, has allowed the islands to support a high standard of living that they are naturally reluctant to relinquish. Tourism is a key industry, contributing around US$1.2 billion annually to the economy. The manufacturing industry is relatively new and thriving, producing pharmaceuticals, electronics and textiles. In addition, the islands have one of the world's largest oil refineries and a thriving trade in rum. Agriculture is confined to producing for local consumption; there are no significant natural resources. Transhipment and financial services are the islands' other main sources of revenue.
COMMERCIAL INFORMATION: The following organisations can offer advice: St Croix Chamber of Commerce, PO Box 3009, Orange Grove, Suite 12, Christiansted, VI 00820 (tel: 773 1435; fax: 773 8172; e-mail: stcroixchamber@vipowernet.net; website: www.stxchamber.org); *or* St Thomas–St John Chamber of Commerce, PO Box 324, 6-7 Main Street, St Thomas, VI 00804 (tel: 776 0100; fax: 776 0588; e-mail: chamber@islands.vi; website: www.usvichamber.com).
CONFERENCES/CONVENTIONS: The US Virgin Islands are an idyllic place to hold a conference or convention. In St Croix, facilities are available in four major hotels for up to 200 people and in two beach resorts for up to 125. In St John, facilities are available at the Hyatt Regency for up to 350 persons and in the National Park for 50 persons. St Thomas has meeting facilities in two hotels for up to 300 persons and in seven beach resorts for up to 850 persons. For further information on conference/convention facilities in the US Virgin Islands, contact the US Virgin Islands Department of Tourism (see *Contact Addresses* section).

Climate

Hot throughout the year, cooled by the eastern trade winds. Lowland areas have fairly evenly distributed rainfall, with August to October being the wettest time.
Required clothing: Lightweight clothes throughout the year. Umbrella or light waterproof clothing is useful.

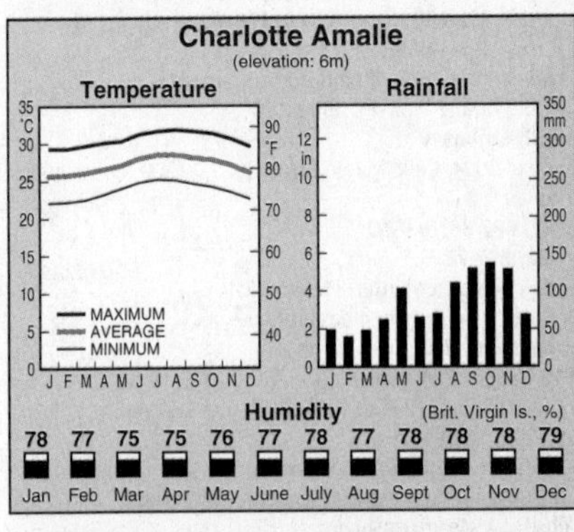

Credit: © Steve Simonsen

Uruguay

LATEST TRAVEL ADVICE CONTACTS

British Foreign and Commonwealth Office
Tel: (0870) 606 0290 Website: www.fco.gov.uk
US Department of State
Website: http://travel.state.gov/travel
Canadian Department of Foreign Affairs and Int'l Trade
Tel: (1 800) 267 8376 Website: www.dfait-maeci.gc.ca

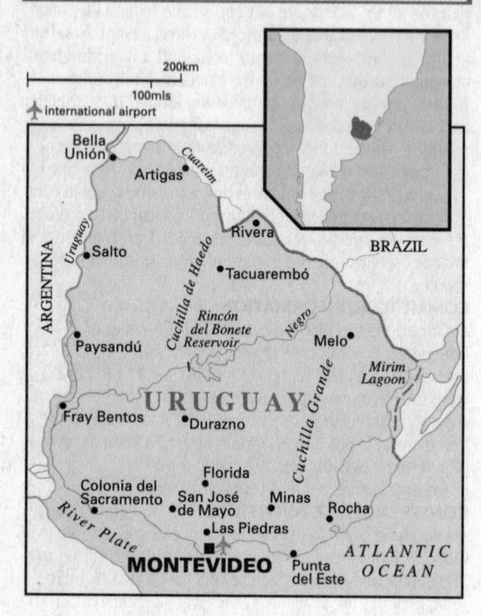

Location: South America.

Country dialling code: 598.

Ministerio de Turismo del Uruguay (Ministry of Tourism)
Rambla 25 de Agosto de 1825 esq, Yacaré, S/N (plano), Montevideo, Uruguay
Tel: (2) 188 5100.
Fax: (2) 916 2487.
E-mail: borvaberry@mintur.gub.uy *or* secretariaministerio@mintur.gub.uy
Website: www.mintur.gub.uy
Embassy of Uruguay
2nd Floor, 140 Brompton Road, London SW3 1HY, UK
Tel: (020) 7589 8835 *or* 7589 8735 (visa section).
Fax: (020) 7581 9585.
E-mail: emburuguay@emburuguay.org.uk
Opening hours: Mon-Fri 0900-1700.
British Embassy
PO Box 16024, Calle Marco Bruto 1073, 11300 Montevideo, Uruguay
Tel: (2) 622 3630/3650.
Fax: (2) 622 7815.
E-mail: bemonte@internet.com.uy
Website: www.britishembassy.org.uy
Embassy of Uruguay
1913 I Street, NW, Washington, DC 20006, USA
Tel: (202) 331 1313-6 *or* 4219 (consular section).
Fax: (202) 331 8142.
E-mail: uruwashi@uruwashi.org *or* conuruwashi@uruwashi.org (consular section).
Website: www.uruwashi.org
Consulates General in: Chicago, Los Angeles, Miami and New York.
Honorary Consulates in: Boston, Chicago, Honolulu, Nevada, New Orleans, San Francisco, San Juan, Seattle and Utah.
Embassy of the United States of America
Lauro Muller 1776, 11200 Montevideo, Uruguay
Tel: (2) 418 7777.
Fax: (2) 418 8611.
E-mail: webmastermvd@state.gov
Embassy of Uruguay
Suite 1905, 130 Albert Street, Ottawa, Ontario K1P 5G4, Canada
Tel: (613) 234 2727 *or* 234 2937 (consular section).
Fax: (613) 233 4670.
E-mail: uruott@iosphere.net
Website: www.iosphere.net/~uruott
Canadian Embassy
Plaza Independencia 749, Suite 102, 11100 Montevideo, Uruguay
Tel: (2) 902 2030.
Fax: (2) 902 2029.
E-mail: mvdeo@dfait-maeci.gc.ca
Website: www.dfait-maeci.gc.ca/uruguay

TIMATIC CODES

Health	AMADEUS: **TI-DFT/MVD/HE** GALILEO/WORLDSPAN: **TI-DFT/MVD/HE** SABRE: **TIDFT/MVD/HE**
Visa	AMADEUS: **TI-DFT/MVD/VI** GALILEO/WORLDSPAN: **TI-DFT/MVD/VI** SABRE: **TIDFT/MVD/VI**

To access TIMATIC country information on Health and Visa regulations through the Computer Reservations System (CRS), type in the appropriate command line listed above.

General Information

AREA: 176,215 sq km (68,037 sq miles).
POPULATION: 3,385,000 (2002).
POPULATION DENSITY: 19.2 per sq km.
CAPITAL: Montevideo. **Population:** 1,329,000 (UN estimate 2001).
GEOGRAPHY: Uruguay is one of the smallest of the South American republics. It is bordered to the north by Brazil, to the southeast by the Atlantic, and is separated from Argentina in the west and south by the River Uruguay, which widens out into the Rio de la Plata estuary. The landscape is made up of hilly meadows broken by streams and rivers. There is a string of beaches along the coast. Most of the country is grazing land for sheep and cattle. Montevideo, the most southern point of the nation, accommodates more than half of the population. About 90 per cent of the land is suitable for agriculture, although only 12 per cent is used in this way. Uruguay is known as the 'Oriental Republic' because it stands on the eastern bank of the Rio de la Plata.
GOVERNMENT: Republic since 1967. Formerly declared independence from Spain in 1825 and officially recognised in 1928. **Head of State and Government:** President Tabare Vazquez since 2004.
LANGUAGE: Spanish. Some English is spoken in tourist resorts.
RELIGION: Roman Catholic is the predominant religion.
TIME: GMT - 3.
ELECTRICITY: 220 volts AC, 50Hz. Continental flat three-pin or round two-pin plugs.
COMMUNICATIONS: Telephone: IDD is available to Uruguay, but callers from Uruguay may experience difficulty, although direct dialling is possible. Country code: 598. Outgoing international code: 00. The local telephone service, which is operated by the Government, is good. **Mobile telephone:** GSM 1900 network operated by AM Wireless Uruguay. GSM 1800 network operated by ANTEL (website: www.antel.com.uy). **Fax:** Facilities are widely available. **Internet:** ISPs include *Movinet* (website: www.movinet.com.uy) and *Uruguay Net* (website: www.uruguaynet.com.uy). There are Internet cafes in main urban areas. **Telegram:** These can be sent worldwide through *Italcable, ITT Comunicaciones, Mundiales SA* and *Western Telegraph Co Ltd.* **Post:** Post office hours: 0800-1800 (main post office in the old city, Montevideo: 0900-1900). Airmail to Europe takes three to five days. **Press:** All newspapers are in Spanish; the most popular dailies include *La Mañana, El Observador, El País* and *Ultimas Noticias.* **Radio:** BBC World Service (website: www.bbc.co.uk/worldservice) and Voice of America (website: www.voa.gov) can be received. From time to time the frequencies change and the most up-to-date can be found online.

Passport/Visa

	Passport Required?	Visa Required?	Return Ticket Required?
Full British	Yes	No	Yes
Australian	Yes	No	Yes
Canadian	Yes	No	Yes
USA	Yes	No	Yes
Other EU	Yes	No/1	Yes
Japanese	Yes	No	Yes

Note: Regulations and requirements may be subject to change at short notice, and you are advised to contact the appropriate diplomatic or consular authority before finalising travel arrangements. Details of these may be found at the head of this country's entry. Any numbers in the chart refer to the footnotes below.

PASSPORTS: Valid passport required by all except:
(a) nationals of Uruguay who arrive from Argentina, Brazil, Chile or Paraguay with a national identity card;
(b) nationals of Argentina, Bolivia, Brazil, Chile, Colombia, Costa Rica, Dominican Republic, Ecuador, Guatemala, Honduras and Paraguay with a national identity card for stays of up to 90 days.
VISAS: Required by all except the following:
(a) nationals of countries referred to in the chart above, except **1.** nationals of Estonia and the Slovak Republic who *do* need a visa (please note that nationals of Canada, Ireland, Malta and the USA are only permitted visa-free stays of up to three months);
(b) nationals of Argentina, The Bahamas, Barbados, Belize, Bolivia, Brazil, Chile, Colombia, Costa Rica, Croatia, Ecuador, El Salvador, Guatemala, Honduras, Hong Kong (SAR), Iceland, Israel, Jamaica, Korea (Rep), Malaysia, Mexico, New Zealand, Nicaragua, Norway, Panama, Paraguay, Peru, Romania, Switzerland, Trinidad & Tobago and Venezuela;
(c) nationals of Dominican Republic, Liechtenstein and Turkey for stays of up to three months;
(d) nationals of Malaysia for up to 30 days;
(e) holders of a re-entry permit issued by Uruguayan officials.
Types of visa and cost: *Tourist*: £27. *Business* and *Tourist*: Enquire at Consulate (or Consular section at Embassy) for cost as it may vary with the exchange rate.
Validity: Visas are for stays of up to three months, except for visas issued to Malaysian nationals which are valid for one month. Extensions for a further three months are possible; apply at the Immigration Office in Uruguay.
Application to: Consulate (or Consular section at Embassy); see *Contact Addresses* section.
Application requirements: (a) Valid passport. (b) One passport-size photo. (c) Completed application form. (d) References in Uruguay (name, address and phone number) or hotel booking confirmation. (e) Return ticket and travel documentation (including the flight number and the dates of arrival and departure). (f) Postal applications should be accompanied by a stamped, self-addressed envelope. (g) For business visits, a letter from the company in the country of origin.
Working days required: 14.
Temporary residence: Enquire at Embassy.

Money

Currency: Peso Uruguayo (urug$) = 100 centécimos. Notes are in the denominations of urug$1000, 500, 200, 100, 50, 20, 10 and 5. Coins are in denominations of urug$10, 5, 2 and 1.
Currency exchange: Visitors are advised to buy local currency at banks and exchange shops, as hotels tend to give unfavourable rates. Inflation in Uruguay, though less severe than in other Latin American countries, leads to frequent fluctuations in the exchange rate.
Credit & debit cards: American Express, Diners Club, MasterCard and Visa are the most commonly used. Check with your credit or debit card company for details of merchant acceptability and other services which may be available. ATMs may reject European or US credit cards.
Travellers cheques: Sterling travellers cheques can only be changed at The Bank of London & South America; visitors are therefore advised to carry US Dollar travellers cheques (US$50 and US$100 denominations only).
Currency restrictions: There are no restrictions on the import or export of either local or foreign currency.
Exchange rate indicators: The following figures are included as a guide to the movements of the Peso Uruguayo against Sterling and the US Dollar:

Date	Feb '04	May '04	Aug '04	Nov '04
£1.00=	53.53	52.91	53.30	50.72
$1.00=	29.41	29.62	28.93	26.78

Banking hours: Mon-Fri 1300-1700.

Duty Free

The following items may be imported into Uruguay without incurring customs duty (50 per cent of these allowances for persons under 18 years of age):
(a) Residents of Uruguay arriving from Argentina, Bolivia, Brazil, Chile or Paraguay (maximum four times a year):
200 cigarettes or 25 cigars or 250g of tobacco; 1l of alcohol; 2kg of foodstuffs.
Total value of exempted imports not to exceed US$30.
(b) Residents of Uruguay arriving from other countries (once a year):
400 cigarettes or 50 cigars or 500g of tobacco; 2l of alcohol; 5kg of foodstuffs.
Total value of exempted imports not to exceed US$150.
(c) All other nationals:
400 cigarettes or 50 cigars or 500g of tobacco; 2l of alcohol; 5kg of foodstuffs; two articles of the following electrical, optical and electronic equipment: portable radio, photo camera, movie camera, movie projector, typewriter and slide projector.
Restricted: All plants and plant derivatives must be accompanied by a sanitary certificate.

Public Holidays

2005: Jan 1 New Year's Day. **Jan 6** Epiphany. **Feb 7-8** Carnival. **Mar 24** Maundy Thursday. **Mar 25** Good Friday. **Apr 19** Landing of the 33 Patriots. **May 1** Labour Day. **May 18** Battle of Las Piedras. **Jun 19** Birth of General Artigas. **Jul 18** Constitution Day. **Aug 25** National Independence Day. **Oct 12** Discovery of America. **Nov 2** All Souls' Day. **Dec 25** Christmas Day.
2006: Jan 1 New Year's Day. **Jan 6** Epiphany. **Feb** Carnival. **Apr 13** Maundy Thursday. **Apr 14** Good Friday. **Apr 19** Landing of the 33 Patriots. **May 1** Labour Day. **May 18**

Battle of Las Piedras. **Jun 19** Birth of General Artigas. **Jul 18** Constitution Day. **Aug 25** National Independence Day. **Oct 12** Discovery of America. **Nov 2** All Souls' Day. **Dec 25** Christmas Day.
Note: Many businesses close during Carnival Week and during Tourist Week (Easter).

Health

	Special Precautions?	Certificate Required?
Yellow Fever	No	No
Cholera	No	No
Typhoid & Polio	1	N/A
Malaria	No	N/A

Note: Regulations and requirements may be subject to change at short notice, and you are advised to contact your doctor well in advance of your intended date of departure. Any numbers in the chart refer to the footnotes below.

1: There is a slight risk of typhoid fever but no cases of polio have been reported in Uruguay in recent years; vaccination against typhoid is advised.
Other risks: In January 2004, a Methicillin-resistant bacteria appeared, which killed seven people - although this bacteria is mostly confined to shanty towns surrounding Montevideo.
Food & drink: Mains water is considered safe to drink. Drinking water outside main cities and towns may be contaminated and sterilisation is advisable. Milk is pasteurised and dairy products are safe for consumption. Local meat, poultry, seafood, fruit and vegetables are generally considered safe to eat.
Health care: Uruguay has an excellent medical service. Private health insurance is recommended.

Travel - International

AIR: Uruguay's national airline is *Primeras Líneas Uruguayas de Navegación Aérea (PLUNA)* (PU) (website: www.pluna.com.uy), which operates flights to various destinations in Argentina and Brazil.
Approximate flight times: From Montevideo to *London* is 15 hours 15 minutes (including one hour 30 minutes' stopover in Madrid) and to *New York* is 14 hours.
International airports: *Montevideo (MVD)* (Carrasco) is 19km (12 miles) from the city (travel time – 35 minutes). There is an airport bus to the city centre. Taxis are also available. Facilities include a duty free shop, post office, restaurants, car hire and a bank/bureau de change.
Air passes: *The Mercosur Airpass*: Valid within Argentina, Brazil, Chile (except Easter Island), Paraguay and Uruguay. Participating airlines include *Aerolineas Argentinas (AR)* (however, flights on this airline cannot be combined with any others, as it has no agreements and its tickets are not accepted by other airlines), *Austral (AU)*, *LAN-Chile (LA)*, *Pluna (PU)*, *TAM (PZ)*, *Transbrasil Airlines (TR)*, *VARIG (RG)* and *VASP (VP)*. The pass can only be purchased by passengers who live outside South America, who have a return ticket. Only eight flight coupons are allowed with a maximum of four coupons for each country and are valid for seven to a maximum of 30 days. At least two countries must be visited (to a maximum of five) and the flight route cannot be changed. A maximum of two stopovers is allowed per country.
The *Visit South America Pass*: Must be bought outside South America in country of residence and allows unlimited travel to 36 cities in the following countries: Argentina, Bolivia, Brazil, Chile (except Easter Island), Colombia, Ecuador, Paraguay, Peru, Uruguay and Venezuela. Participating airlines include *LanChile*, *LanPeru* and *American Airlines*. A minimum of three flights must be booked, with no maximum; the maximum stay is 60 days, with no minimum, and prices depend on the amount of flight zones covered. For both air passes, children under 12 years of age are entitled to a 33 per cent discount and infants (under 2 years old) pay only 10 per cent of the adult fare. For further details, contact one of the participating airlines.
Departure tax: US$12 is levied on international departures (US$6 to Buenos Aires), if departing from Carrasco International Airport. All other airports to all other destinations levy US$6.
SEA: Montevideo, the main international port, is served by cargo lines from the USA and Europe. There is a night-ferry service from Buenos Aires to Montevideo (travel time – 10 hours). High-speed ferries (called 'planes' due to their speed) also operate between Montevideo and Buenos Aires (travel time – two hours 30 minutes; website: www.buquebus.com). There are also services from Colonia (160km/100 miles west of Montevideo) to Buenos Aires by ferry and a thrice-daily hydrofoil service. A port departure tax may be levied.
ROAD: Coaches and buses travel regularly between Brazil and Uruguay – these are modern coaches with bar, TV, WC and radio. The travel time between Montevideo and Porto Alegre (Brazil) is 14 hours; to Rio de Janeiro (Brazil) is 59 hours. Buses run by *COT* depart weekly for Asunción and Iguazú Falls in Paraguay, while other services, also weekly, link Montevideo with Florianópolis, Rio de Janeiro and Santiago in Brazil and with northern and southern regions of Argentina.

Travel - Internal

AIR: The only internal flights available since *TAMU*, a branch of the Uruguayan Air Force, suspended its services, are the domestic legs of international flights from Punta del Este via Montevideo to Brazil.
SEA/RIVER: There are no scheduled boat services along the principal rivers but the River Uruguay is navigable from Colonia to Salto, and the Río Negro (flowing across the country from northeast to northwest) is navigable as far as the port of Mercedes.
RAIL: A few local services run between villages. These are not usually used by tourists and are under threat of closure.
ROAD: Traffic drives on the right. There are 45,000km (28,000 miles) of roads in Uruguay, 90 per cent of which are paved or otherwise improved for all-weather use. However, the conditions of roads varies. Traffic is often disorganised. **Bus:** The bus service is good: two main bus lines (*COPSA* and *COT*) provide services throughout the country, connecting all towns and the Brazilian border points. **Car hire:** Available in Montevideo. **Documentation:** An International Driving Permit or UK license is required. A temporary licence to drive in Uruguay, valid for 90 days, must be obtained from the Town Hall (*Municipio*).
URBAN: Extensive bus services operate in Montevideo and the suburbs. There are flat fares for the central area and suburban services. Metered taxis are available in all cities and from the airport. Drivers carry a list of fares. A surcharge is made for each item of baggage and between 2400-0600. Within city limits, taxis may be hired by the hour at an agreed rate.

Accommodation

HOTELS: There are numerous first-class hotels in Montevideo and along Uruguay's coastal resorts, where rates are usually a little higher. It is essential to book during the summer and during carnival week in Montevideo. There are several lower-priced hotels in the city for more basic accommodation. For more information, contact the Asociación de Hoteles y Restaurantes del Uruguay (AHRU), Gutierrez Ruiz 1215, Montevideo (tel: (2) 902 3990 *or* 908 0141; fax: (2) 908 2317; e-mail: ahru@montevideo.com.uy; website: www.ahru.org). **Grading:** Three categories according to price and standard. Prices tend to be higher during the tourist season. There is a 23 per cent value-added tax in Montevideo. At the beaches, many hotels offer only US-plan terms (full board).
CAMPING: Allowed at numerous designated sites throughout the country; elsewhere it is necessary to get police permission.
YOUTH HOSTELS: Uruguay is a member of the International Youth Hostel Federation and there are several youth hostels throughout Uruguay offering cheap accommodation, run by Asociacion de Alberguistas del Uruguay (Hostelling International Uruguay), Canelones 935, PO Box 10680, CP 11100, Montevideo (tel: (2) 900 5749; fax (2) 901 3587; website: www.hosteluruguay.org).

Resorts & Excursions

Uruguay is drawing increasingly more visitors each year, and for good reason. The country enjoys 500km (300 miles) of fine sandy beaches on the Atlantic and the Río de la Plata, woods, hills, hot springs, hotels, casinos, art festivals and numerous opportunities for sport and entertainment.
MONTEVIDEO: The capital contains more than half of Uruguay's population and is the country's natural trading centre. There are nine major bathing beaches, the best of which are **Carrasco**, **Malvin**, **Miramar**, and **Pocitos**. The suburbs have restaurants, nightclubs and hotels. Montevideo's architecture combines colonial, European and modern influences. The old inner city, known as the **Ciudad Vieja** (Old Town), is a small peninsula surrounded by the sea near the metropolitan port. The **Cabildo** (the old town council hall), the **Cathedral**, the **Plaza Matriz**, the **Plaza Zabala** and the **Port Market** are fine examples of Uruguay's colonial past. The Old Town, also a centre for antique shops, contrasts dramatically with the rising number of modern buildings and office blocks surrounding the area. The most interesting entrance to the city is via the **Puerta de la Ciudadela** (Door to the Citadel), part of the old wall that still surrounds Montevideo leading on, via the **Plaza Independencia**, to the popular and lively city centre.
ELSEWHERE: To the west of Montevideo is **Colonia Suiza** ('The Swiss Colony'), reached by hydrofoil from the capital. It has a delightful old quarter. Other beach resorts along the Uruguayan coast include **Atlántida**, **Piriápolis** and the fishing port of **Paloma**. **Carmelo** on the **River Uruguay** and **Mercedes** on the **Río Negro** (a tributary) are amongst the many picturesque river ports; further up Uruguay is **Salto**, one of the country's largest cities. **Fray Bentos**, near Mercedes, gave its name to the famous processed meat company. The journey north through **Florida** and **Durazno** to **Tacuarembó** on the Brazilian border takes one through the heart of the country's agricultural lands. The beautiful hills surrounding the town of **Minas** are well worth a visit, as is **Colonia del Sacramento**, which has been rebuilt in its original 18th-century style.
Resorts: The Atlantic coast resorts are popular from December to April, and have fine beaches. Most fashionable of these is **Punta del Este**, 145km (90 miles) from Montevideo. It has two main beaches and offers water-skiing, fishing, surfing and yachting; there is also a golf course. Villas and chalets can be rented in the wooded area on the edge of town. Two nearby islands, **Gorniti** and **Lobos**, are worth a visit.

Sport & Activities

Watersports: Windsurfing and **water-skiing** are popular along the coast. **Boating** is a favourite Uruguayan pastime. Santiago Vazquez on the St Lucia River is one of several popular centres. Arrangements can be made for hire of motor or sailing boats in Montevideo and elsewhere. There are plenty of places to swim when the weather permits. The 'metropolitan' beaches (from Ramírez and including Pocitos) tend to be dirty and unsuitable for bathing. Those along the Atlantic coast are, however, clean and are suitable for **swimming**. Many of the resort areas in the interior have swimming pools. The mineral baths at Minas are worth a visit.
Fishing: There are three fishing areas: along the Rio de la Plata from Colonia to Piriápolis for surf-casting; from Piriápolis to Punta del Este (considered one of the best fishing areas in the world); and along the Atlantic Coast towards the Brazilian border. Boats and tackle can be hired in fishing clubs in Fray Bentos, Montevideo, Mercedes, Paysandú, Punta del Este and Salto.
Golf: There is a municipal course in Montevideo, plus clubs at the Punta del Este Country Club and Victoria Plaza Hotel.
Spectator sports: There are two main **horseracing** tracks: Hipodromo de Maronas (Saturday and Sunday afternoon); and Las Piedras (Thursday, Saturday and Sunday). **Football** is the most popular spectator sport; matches are played regularly throughout the country.
Dune walking is increasingly popular in Cabo Palonia.

Social Profile

FOOD & DRINK: The majority of Uruguayan restaurants are *parrilladas* (grill-rooms), which specialise in the country's most famous traditional dish, the *asado* (barbecued beef). Beef is part of most meals and comes in many forms, including the *asado de tira* (ribs), *pulpa* (boneless beef), *lomo* (fillet steak) and *bife de chorrizo* (rump steak). *Costillas* (chops) and *milanesa* (a veal cutlet) are also popular, usually eaten with mixed salad or chips. *Chivito* is a sandwich filled with slices of meat, lettuce and egg. Other local dishes are *puchero* (beef with vegetables, bacon, beans and sausages), pizza, pies, barbecued pork, grilled chicken in wine, *cazuela* (stew), usually served with *mondongo* (tripe), seafood, *morcilla dulce* (sweet black sausage made from blood, orange peel and walnuts) and *morcilla salada* (salty sausage). Desserts include *dulce de leche* (milk sweets), *chaja* (ball-shaped sponge cake filled with cream and jam), *mossini* (cream sponge), lemon pie and *yemas* (crystallised egg yolk). Table service is usual in restaurants. Cafes or bars have either table and/or counter service.
Uruguayan wines are of good quality. A popular drink is *medio-medio* (half dry white wine and half champagne). Beers are very good. Imported beverages are widely available. Local spirits are *caña*, *grappa* and locally distilled whisky and gin. There are no set licensing hours.
NIGHTLIFE: Theatre, ballet and symphonic concerts are staged in Montevideo from March to January. Tango is nearly as popular as in Argentina, and the 'La Cuparsita' club in Montevideo fills up quickly. There are discos in the Carrasco area. There are several dinner-dance places in Montevideo. Large Montevideo hotels have good bars. When there is music for dancing, the price of drinks increases quite considerably. There are also several casinos.
SHOPPING: Special purchases include suede jackets, amethyst jewellery and paintings. The Tristan Narvaja Market is famous for its antiques and there are many antique shops in the Old Town. **Shopping hours:** Mon-Fri 0900-1200 and 1400-1900, Sat 0900-1230.
SPECIAL EVENTS: The principal festival is the national *Carnival Week* (starting **Feb 7** in 2005). Although this 'fiesta' is officially only for the Monday and Tuesday preceding Ash Wednesday, most shops and businesses close for the entire week. Houses and streets are appropriately decorated and humorous shows are staged at open-air

A B C D E F G H I J K L M N O P Q R S T U V W X Y Z

theatres. *La Semana Criolla*, or *Holy Week* (**Mar** in 2005), offers traditional activities like *asados* (barbeques), folk music and horseriding/cowboy stunt riding. For a complete list of special events, contact the Ministerio de Turismo (see *Contact Addresses* section).
SOCIAL CONVENTIONS: Shaking hands is the normal form of greeting. Uruguayans are very hospitable and like to entertain both at home and in restaurants. Normal courtesies should be observed. Smoking is not allowed in cinemas or theatres or on public transport. **Tipping:** Ten per cent when no service charge is added. Taxi drivers expect a tip.

Business Profile

ECONOMY: Uruguay is one of the more prosperous Latin American countries. The economy has a traditionally strong agricultural sector, with beef and wool being the most important products; dairy exports to other Latin American countries are substantial. Crop farming is widespread, producing mostly cereals, rice, fruit and vegetables. Manufacturing is concentrated in oil and coal-derived products, chemicals, textiles, transport equipment and leather products. The oil and coal, both for manufacturing and energy consumption (the latter supplemented by Uruguay's own hydroelectricity stations), are imported. Mining is confined to small-scale extraction of building materials, industrial minerals and some gold. The tourism industry brings in just under US$1 billion annually. Uruguay's economic health depends heavily on that of its two large neighbours, Argentina and Brazil. Both Latin American giants have been in the doldrums since the turn of the millennium, then, in August 2002, both Argentina and, to a lesser extent, Brazil were gripped by financial crises. This led to a collapse in the cross-border trade upon which Uruguay is heavily dependent. The government was forced to take emergency measures in the form of currency devaluation, loan rescheduling and, in an unusually drastic move, closing down the country's entire financial system as it approached meltdown. It also appealed for support from the IMF, which responded with a US$3 billion package. With the worst of the crisis past, Uruguay is now returning to something approaching economic health. Uruguay is a member of Mercosur, the principal regional trade bloc, as well as the Asociación Latinoamericana de Integración (ALADI) and the Inter-American Development Bank. The country's main trading partners are Brazil, Argentina, the USA and Germany.
BUSINESS: Businessmen should wear conservative suits and ties. As far as communication is concerned, some knowledge of Spanish will prove invaluable, although English may be spoken by many in business and tourist circles. Appointments are necessary and punctuality is expected. Visiting cards are essential and it would be an advantage to have the reverse printed in Spanish. Avoid visits during Carnival week. **Office hours:** Mon-Fri 0830-1200 and 1430-1830.
COMMERCIAL INFORMATION: The following organisations can offer advice: Cámara Nacional de Comercio y Servicios del Uruguay, Rincón 454, Piso 2, CP 11000, Codigo Postal 1000, Montevideo (tel: (2) 916 1277; fax: (2) 916 1243; e-mail: gerencia@cncs.com.uy; website: www.cncs.com.uy); *or* Uruguayan American Chamber of Commerce, 1710 First Avenue, Suite 333, New York, NY 10128, USA (tel: (212) 722 3306; fax: (212) 996 2580; e-mail: gateway@uruguaychamber.com; website: www.uruguaychamber.com).

Climate

Uruguay has an exceptionally fine temperate climate, with mild summers and winters. Summer is from December to March and is the most pleasant time; the climate during other seasons offers bright, sunny days and cool nights.
Required clothing: Mediumweight clothing for winter; lightweight clothing and raincoat required.

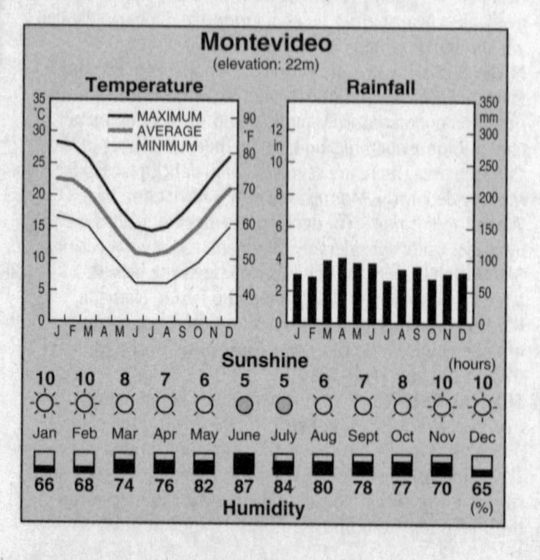

Uzbekistan

LATEST TRAVEL ADVICE CONTACTS

British Foreign and Commonwealth Office
Tel: (0870) 606 0290 Website: www.fco.gov.uk
US Department of State
Website: http://travel.state.gov/travel
Canadian Department of Foreign Affairs and Int'l Trade
Tel: (1 800) 267 8376 Website: www.dfait-maeci.gc.ca

Location: Central Asia.

Country dialling code: 998.

National Company Uzbektourism
47 Khorezm Street, Tashkent 700047, Uzbekistan
Tel: (71) 133 5414 *or* 136 7954. Fax: (71) 136 7948.
E-mail: marketing@uzbektourism.uz
Website: www.uzbektourism.uz
Ministry of Foreign Affairs
9 Uzbekistan Street, Tashkent 700029, Uzbekistan
Tel: (71) 133 6475. Fax: (71) 139 1517.
E-mail: letter@mfa.uz Website: www.mfa.uz
Embassy of the Republic of Uzbekistan
41 Holland Park, London W11 2RP, UK
Tel: (020) 7229 7679. Fax: (020) 7229 7029.
E-mail: info@uzbekembassy.org
Website: www.uzbekembassy.org
Opening hours: Mon-Fri 1000-1700; Mon-Wed and Fri 1000-1300 (consular section).
Uzbekistan Airways
3-4 Picton Place, London W1U 1BJ, UK
Tel: (020) 7935 1899 *or* 2810. Fax: (020) 7935 9554.
E-mail: lon@uzbekistan-airways.com
Website: www.uzairways.com
British Embassy
67 Gulyamov Street, Tashkent 700000, Uzbekistan
Tel: (71) 120 6288 *or* 7852/3/4 *or* 6451.
Fax: (71) 120 6549 *or* 6430 (visa section).
E-mail: brit@emb.uz
Website: www.britain.uz
Embassy of the Republic of Uzbekistan
1746 Massachusetts Avenue, NW, Washington, DC 20036, USA
Tel: (202) 887 5300. Fax: (202) 293 6804.
E-mail: embuzbekistan@uzbekistan.org *or* info@uzbekistan.org
Website: www.uzbekistan.org
Consulate General of the Republic of Uzbekistan
801 2nd avenue, 20th Floor, New York, NY 10017, USA
Tel: (212) 754 7403/4718.
Fax: (212) 838 9812.
E-mail: info@uzbekconsulny.org
Embassy of the United States of America
82 Chilanzarskaya Street, Tashkent 700115, Uzbekistan
Tel: (71) 120 5450 *or* 4718/9 (consular section).
Fax: (71) 120 6335 *or* 5448 (consular section).
E-mail: personnel@usembassy.uz *or* consular@usembassy.uz (consular section)
Website: www.usembassy.uz

TIMATIC CODES

Health	AMADEUS: **TI-DFT/TAS/HE** GALILEO/WORLDSPAN: **TI-DFT/TAS/HE** SABRE: **TIDFT/TAS/HE**
Visa	AMADEUS: **TI-DFT/TAS/VI** GALILEO/WORLDSPAN: **TI-DFT/TAS/VI** SABRE: **TIDFT/TAS/VI**

To access TIMATIC country information on Health and Visa regulations through the Computer Reservations System (CRS), type in the appropriate command line listed above.

The Canadian Embassy in Moscow deals with enquiries relating to Uzbekistan (see *Russian Federation* section).
Consulate of Canada
Centre 5, House 64, Apartment 21, Tashkent 700017, Uzbekistan
Tel: (71) 120 7270 *or* 137 6728. Tel/Fax: (71) 120 7270.
United States of America United Tours Corporation
150 West 55th Street, New York, NY 10019, USA
Tel: (212) 245 1100. Fax: (212) 245 0292.
E-mail: oyachny@aol.com

General Information

AREA: 447,400 sq km (172,740 sq miles).
POPULATION: 26,093,000 (UN estimate 2003).
POPULATION DENSITY: 58.3 per sq km.
CAPITAL: Tashkent. **Population:** 2,157,000 (UN estimate 2001; including suburbs).
GEOGRAPHY: Uzbekistan is bordered by Afghanistan to the south, Turkmenistan to the west, Kazakhstan to the north, Kyrgyzstan to the northeast and Tajikistan to the east and has a colourful and varied countryside. The south and east are dominated by the Tien-Shan and Pamir-Alai mountain ranges and the Kyzyl Kum Desert lies to the northeast. The northwestern autonomous region of Karakalpakstan is bordered by the Aral Sea and the sparsely populated Ustyurt Plateau with its vast cotton fields.
GOVERNMENT: Republic. Declared independence from the Soviet Union in 1991. **Head of State:** President Islam Karimov since 1991. **Head of Government:** Prime Minister Shavkat Mirzoyoev since 2003.
LANGUAGE: The official language is Uzbek, a Turkic tongue closely related to Kazakh and Kyrgyz. There is a small Russian-speaking minority. Many people involved with tourism speak English. The Government has stated its intention to change the Cyrillic script to the Latin.
RELIGION: Predominantly Sunni Muslim, with Shia (15 per cent), Russian Orthodox and Jewish minorities.
TIME: GMT + 5.
ELECTRICITY: 220 volts AC, 50Hz. Round two-pin continental plugs are standard.
COMMUNICATIONS: Telephone: Country code: 998. Area code for Tashkent: 71. IDD is available, but calls from hotel rooms still need to be booked either from reception or from the floor attendant. International calls can also be made from main post offices (in Tashkent on Prospekt Navoi). Direct-dial calls within the CIS are obtained by dialling 8 and waiting for another dial tone and then dialling the city code. Calls within the city limits are free of charge. **Mobile telephone:** GSM 900 network provided by *Coscom* (website: www.coscom.uz). GSM 900/1800 network provided by *Daewoo* (website: www.daewoounitel.com) and *Uzdunrobita* (website: www.uzdunrobita.uz). Coverage is limited to certain areas around Tashkent. **Fax:** Services are available from major hotels for residents only. **Internet:** ISPs include *Eastlink* (website: www.eastlink.com). Internet cafes exist in Tashkent. **Telegram:** Services are available from post offices in large towns. **Post:** Letters to Western Europe and the USA can take between two weeks and two months. Stamped envelopes can be bought from post offices. Addresses should be laid out in the following order: country, postcode, city, street, house number and, lastly, the person's name. Post office hours: Mon-Fri 0900-1800. The Main Post Office in Tashkent (see above) is open until 1900. Visitors can also use the post offices situated in the major hotels. There are a number of international courier services based in Tashkent. **Press:** There are no independent daily newspapers in Uzbekistan. The main editions are published in Tashkent and include *Khalk suzi* and *Narodnoye Slovo* (in Russian and Uzbek), and *Soliqlav va Bojhom Habarlari/Nalogovie I Tamojennie Vesti* and *Uzbekistan ovizi*.
Radio: BBC World Service (website: www.bbc.co.uk/worldservice) and Voice of America (website: www.voa.gov) can be received. From time to time the frequencies change and the most up-to-date can be found online.

Passport/Visa

	Passport Required?	Visa Required?	Return Ticket Required?
Full British	Yes	Yes	No
Australian	Yes	Yes	No
Canadian	Yes	Yes	No
USA	Yes	Yes/1	No
Other EU	Yes	Yes	No
Japanese	Yes	Yes	No

Note: Regulations and requirements may be subject to change at short notice, and you are advised to contact the appropriate diplomatic or consular authority before finalising travel arrangements. Details of these may be found at the head of this country's entry. Any numbers in the chart refer to the footnotes below.

PASSPORTS: Passport valid for six months after departure date required by all.
VISAS: Required by all except the following:
(a) nationals of the CIS (except nationals of Kyrgyzstan, Tajikistan and Turkmenistan who *do* require a visa);
(b) transit passengers continuing their journey within 24 hours by the same or first connecting aircraft provided holding valid onward or return documentation and not leaving the transit area.
Types of visa and cost: *Tourist* and *Business*. *Single-entry*: US$40 (seven days); US$50 (15 days); US$60 (30 days); US$80 (three months); US$120 (six months); US$160 (one year). *Multiple-entry*: US$60 (one month); US$150 (six months); US$250 (one year). *Group*: US$15 per person (15 days); US$25 per person (30 days). *Transit*: US$20 (24 hours); US$25 (48 hours); US$30 (72 hours); US$40 (double-entry).
Note: (a) **1.** US nationals can obtain multiple-entry business or tourist visas issued for up to four years for a cost of US$100. (b) Visa applications are subject to a US$20 service charge (US$10 for transit visas). (c) Visa regulations within the CIS are liable to change at short notice.
Validity: Tourist visas are normally single-entry/exit and are valid for the duration of the tour. Business visas are multiple-entry, valid for six months in the first instance and extendable. Nationals of Austria, Belgium, France, Germany, Italy, Japan, Spain, Switzerland and the UK can obtain a multiple-entry visa for touristic/business stays of up to one month; nationals of the USA can achieve such visas for stays of up to four years. Visas should be used within one month of date of issue.
Application to: Uzbek Embassies where they exist.
Application requirements: (a) Valid passport with at least one blank page to affix the visa. (b) Two completed and signed application forms. (c) Two passport-size photos. (d) Fee, payable in US$ or a cheque in pounds sterling on collection of visa. (e) Pre-paid, stamped, self-addressed envelope, if applying by post. *Tourist*: (a)-(e) and, (f) Letter of invitation from inviting partners in Uzbekistan. Applications are usually made through a travel agent. *Business*: (a)-(e) and, (f) Business invitation from Uzbekistan giving details of activities to be undertaken and length of stay in Uzbekistan. This letter can be sent directly to the Ministry of Foreign Affairs in Uzbekistan, who will then contact the Embassy directly, giving permission for the stay. *Private visits*: (a)-(e) and, (f) Letter of invitation from friends/relatives endorsed by the immigration department of the Ministry of Internal Affairs in Uzbekistan. *Transit*: (a)-(e) and, (f) Air ticket to onward destination.
Note: (a) Tourists (other than nationals of Austria, Belgium, France, Germany, Italy, Japan, Spain, Switzerland, the UK and USA, who also do not need to submit letters of invitation as part of their visa application requirement) must have booked a tour with a recognised tour company. (b) Visitors staying longer than three days must register with the Ministry of Internal Affairs within three working days. However, most hotels will automatically do this on behalf of the visitor.
Working days required: 10. For nationals of Austria, Belgium, France, Germany, Italy, Japan, Spain, Switzerland, the UK and USA, allow two days.
Temporary residence: It is possible to apply for temporary residence. The government of Uzbekistan officially requires visitors to carry a medical certificate proving they are free of HIV, but this is rarely enforced.

Money

Currency: Uzbek Sum (Sum) = 100 tiyn. Notes are in denominations of Sum1000, 500, 200, 100, 50, 25, 10, 5, 3 and 1. Coins are in denominations of 50, 20, 10, 5, 3 and 1 tiyn.
Currency exchange: Tourists and businesspeople without special status have to pay for hotels, hotel services and transport in hard currency; US Dollars are the most widely acceptable. All bills are normally settled in cash. It is illegal to change money on the black market and penalties can be harsh. Banks and the currency exchange bureaux in major hotels will change at the official rates.
Credit & debit cards: Acceptable in some of the major hotels in tourist centres. Uzbekistan has said that it intends to introduce its own Visa card in the near future.
Travellers cheques: Limited acceptance.
Currency restrictions: The import of foreign currency is unlimited, but should be declared on arrival. Travellers importing sums in excess of US$1000 may be subject to a body search. The export of foreign currency is permitted. Travellers who have imported sums in excess of US$2000 are required to provide proof of lawful exchange into Sum, otherwise a fine of 30 per cent of the amount imported will be payable. The import and export of local currency is unlimited.
Exchange rate indicators: The following figures are included as a guide to the movements of the Sum against Sterling and the US Dollar:

Date	Feb '04	May '04	Aug '04	Nov '04
£1.00=	1792.24	1799.48	1895.80	1990.32
$1.00=	984.61	1007.49	1029.01	1051.02

Banking hours: Mon-Fri 0930-1730.

Duty Free

The following goods may be imported into Uzbekistan by passengers aged 16 and older without incurring customs duty:
1000 cigarettes or 1kg of tobacco products; 1.5l of alcoholic beverages and 2l of wine; a reasonable quantity of perfume for personal use; other goods for personal use up to a value of US$10,000.
Note: All valuable items such as jewellery, cameras and computers should be declared on arrival.
Prohibited imports: Firearms, ammunition, drugs, photographs and printed matter directed against the country, live animals (without special permit) and fruit or vegetables.
Prohibited exports: Items more than 100 years old and those of special cultural importance require special permission for export. When buying items that may be more than 100 years old, ask for a certificate stating the age of the item(s). Precious metals, stones, furs, arms and ammunition, antiquities and art objects (subject to duty and special permit from the Ministry of Culture) are also prohibited.

Public Holidays

2005: Jan 1 New Year's Day. **Jan 21** Kurban Khait (Feast of the Sacrifice). **Mar 8** International Women's Day. **Mar 20-22** Navrus. **Apr 21** Prophet's Birthday. **May 1** Labour Day. **May 9** Day of Memory and Respect. **Sep 1** Independence Day. **Nov 3-5** Ramadan Khait (End of Ramadan). **Nov 18** Flag Day. **Dec 8** Constitution Day.
2006: Jan 1 New Year's Day. **Jan 10** Kurban Khait (Feast of the Sacrifice). **Mar 8** International Women's Day. **Mar 20-22** Navrus. **May 1** Labour Day. **Apr 11** Prophet's Birthday. **May 9** Day of Memory and Respect. **Sep 1** Independence Day. **Oct 24-26** Ramadan Khait (End of Ramadan). **Nov 18** Flag Day. **Dec 8** Constitution Day.
Note: Muslim festivals are timed according to local sightings of various phases of the moon and the dates given above are approximations. For further information, consult the *World of Islam* appendix.

Health

	Special Precautions?	Certificate Required?
Yellow Fever	No	No
Cholera	Yes	1
Typhoid & Polio	2	N/A
Malaria	No/3	N/A

Note: *Regulations and requirements may be subject to change at short notice, and you are advised to contact your doctor well in advance of your intended date of departure. Any numbers in the chart refer to the footnotes below.*

1: Following WHO guidelines issued in 1973, a cholera vaccination certificate is not a condition of entry to Uzbekistan. However, cholera is a serious risk in this country and precautions are essential. Up-to-date advice should be sought before deciding whether these precautions should include vaccination, as medical opinion is divided over its effectiveness; see the *Health appendix* for more information.
2: Vaccination against typhoid is advised.
3: Although Malaria is not considered a problem, there has been a confirmed case of Malaria contracted in the Termez region. It may be necessary to consult a doctor about the - albeit unlikely - need for anti-malarial drugs if travelling to this area.
Food & drink: All water, particularly outside main centres, should be regarded as being a potential health risk. Water used for drinking, brushing teeth or making ice should have first been boiled or otherwise sterilised. Milk is pasteurised and dairy products are safe for consumption. Only eat well-cooked meat and fish, preferably served hot. Pork, salad and mayonnaise may carry increased risk. Vegetables should be cooked and fruit peeled.
Other risks: Immunisation against *hepatitis A* and *meningococcal meningitis* is advised. *Hepatitis B* and *E* occur. *Trachoma* is quite common. *Tickborne encephalitis* and *diphtheria* also occur.
Rabies is present. For those at high risk, vaccination before arrival should be considered. If you are bitten, seek medical advice without delay. For more information, consult the *Health* appendix.
Health care: Emergency health care is available free of charge for visitors although, as in most parts of the former Soviet Union, medical care in Uzbekistan is inadequate and there are extreme financial problems. Doctors and hospitals often expect cash payment for health services. There is a severe shortage of basic medical supplies, including disposable needles, anaesthetics, antibiotics and vaccines. Travellers are therefore advised to take a well-equipped first-aid kit with them containing basic medicines and any prescriptions that they may need. For minor difficulties, visitors are advised to ask the management at their hotel for help. In case of emergency, travellers should get a referral from either the Tashkent International Medical Clinic or from the appropriate Embassy, since foreigners are strongly advised not to approach local health care facilities without somebody who knows local conditions and the language. For major problems, visitors are well advised to seek help outside the country. Travel insurance is essential.

Travel - International

Travel Warning: Uzbekistan's borders are potential flashpoints and some are mined. All but essential travel to areas bordering Afghanistan, Tajikistan and Kyrgyzstan is advised. There is also a high threat from terrorism in Uzbekistan. The last significant attack was in July 2004, near the US and Israeli embassies and at the Uzbek Prosecutor's Office, which killed four people and injured at least eight.
AIR: The national airline, *Uzbekistan Airways (HY)*, currently flies from London (four flights a week), Amsterdam, Athens, Bangkok, Bahrain, Beijing, Birmingham, Delhi, Dhaka, Frankfurt/M, Hoshemin, Istanbul, Jeddah, Kiev, Kuala Lumpur, Moscow, New York, Osaka, Paris, Riyadh, Rome, Seoul, Sharjah and Tel Aviv. It also flies to most destinations within the CIS. Tashkent is also served by a number of other international carriers: *Lufthansa*, *Pakistan International Airlines*, *Turkish Airlines* and *Xinjiang Airlines*. Flights to Tajikistan have been suspended since the Tajik civil war at the end of 1992. For further information, contact *Uzbekistan Airways* in Tashkent (tel: (71) 254 8529). HY Travel in London are agents for *Uzbekistan Airways* (see *Contact Addresses* section).
Approximate flight times: From Tashkent to *London* is seven hours (direct), to *Bangkok* is six hours 30 minutes, to *Frankfurt/M* is six hours, to *Beijing* is five hours 30 minutes, to *Tel Aviv* is four hours 30 minutes, to *Delhi* is three hours 30 minutes, to *Istanbul* is three hours 30 minutes and to *Moscow* is three hours 30 minutes.
International airports: *Tashkent International Airport (TAS)* is in the south of the town, about 11km (7 miles) from the centre. Facilities include left luggage, bureau de change, duty free shops, restaurants and bars. It is served by buses that run every 10 to 20 minutes (travel time - 30 to 60 minutes). Trains connect the airport with the centre (travel time - 10 to 20 minutes) and taxis are readily available (travel time - 15 to 20 minutes).
Departure tax: US$10.
RAIL: Tashkent is the nodal point for rail services from Central Asia. Lines lead west to Ashgabat (Turkmenistan), south to Samarkand and on to Dushanbe (Tajikistan), east to Bishkek (Kyrgyzstan) and Almaty (Kazakhstan) and north to Moscow (Russian Federation). From Tashkent, along the *Saratov-Syr Darya Line*, the journey to Moscow takes nearly three days. There is also a spur line to the Fergana Valley in the east of the country, which leads to Osh in Kyrgyzstan. It is possible to connect to China through Almaty; and to Iran and the Middle East (via Turkmenistan). Foreigners have to pay for rail tickets in hard currency, preferably US Dollars, but it is still a cheap option by Western standards.
ROAD: Uzbekistan has road connections to all its neighbours. The border between Afghanistan and Uzbekistan is closed to all except Uzbek and Afghan nationals. Travellers should exercise caution around the Kyrgyz-Uzbek border as some violent incidents have occured. It is not advisable to bring your own car. Contact your local Embassy for details. **Bus:** There are services to all the neighbouring countries, although the occasional border closures between Uzbekistan and Tajikistan make this route unreliable. Long-distance buses leave from the Tashkent bus station near the metro station. Foreigners have to pay for tickets in hard currency. **Car hire:** It is possible to hire cars with drivers for long journeys; they will normally ask to be paid in US Dollars. The best place to look for these is at the long-distance bus and train stations.

Travel - Internal

AIR: *Uzbekistan Airways (HY)* flies to all the major towns and cities in Uzbekistan on a regular basis. Destinations include Andijan, Karshi, Namangan, Navoi (which is 45 minutes by bus from Bukhara), Nukus, Samarkand, Tashkent and Termez. Tickets can be bought at the *Uzbekistan Airways* ticket agency opposite the Hotel Russia on Shota Rustaveli in Tashkent or at the departure terminal of the

airport. International flights booked in Tashkent should be paid for in US Dollars although some credit cards are accepted. It is preferable to pay for domestic flights in Sum.
Approximate flight times: From Tashkent to *Termez* is one hour 20 minutes, to *Nukus* is two hours, to *Samarkand* is 40 minutes, to *Navoi* is one hour and to *Namangan* is one hour 40 minutes.
RAIL: There are 3400km (2113 miles) of railways linking Termez, Samarkand, Bukhara, the Fergana Valley and Nukus. There are two railway stations in Tashkent – North and South. The *Trans-Caspian Railway* traverses the country from Chardzhou in Turkmenistan via Kagan (near Bukhara), Samarkand and Dzhizak, where the railway branches off to serve the capital, Tashkent. Passengers should store valuables under the bed or seat, and should not leave the compartment unattended. Tickets can be bought on the ground floor of the Hotel Locomotif or at the OVIR office at the station.
ROAD: The Republic of Uzbekistan is served by a reasonable road network. Traffic drives on the right. **Bus:** Services connect all the major towns within Uzbekistan and are cheap and fairly reliable. **Taxi:** Taxis and cars for hire can be found in all major towns. It is safer to use officially marked taxis, although many taxis are unlicensed. Travellers are advised to agree a fare in advance, and not to share taxis with strangers. As many of the street names have changed since independence, it is also advisable to ascertain both the old and the new street names when asking directions. Cars can be hired by the trip, by the hour or by the day or week.
Documentation: An International Driving Permit will be required when car hire facilities have been introduced.
URBAN: Tashkent is served by taxis, buses, trolleybuses, trams and the only underground in Central Asia. The underground network was expanded in 1991, making it 31km (19 miles) long, with 23 stations. Public transport is cheap and generally reliable. There are regular bus services to all major towns in Uzbekistan.

Accommodation

HOTELS: Tourists are still required to stay in hotels that are licensed by Uzbekourism, and most hotels are run by them. However, a growing number of independent hotels are now being licensed. It is necessary for visitors to have a slip of paper stamped by the hotel to prove that they have stayed there. Services and facilities are not generally up to Western standards, but efforts are being made to improve them and there is a growing number of western-style hotels owned by foreign companies. Most tourist hotel rooms have a shower and WC ensuite, although supplies of soap and toilet paper can be unreliable. All regional capitals have at least one Uzbektourism hotel that will accept foreigners. Many tourists will have booked tours which include accommodation, others will have to pay in US Dollars, unless they have special exemptions.
BED & BREAKFAST: There are a few bed & breakfast hotels springing up, but they are small and can be difficult to get into. A new association of bed & breakfasts is being created by the Government.
CAMPING: Uzbektourism runs a number of temporary campsites in the mountains.

Resorts & Excursions

Uzbekistan lies astride the **Silk Road**, the ancient trading route between China and the West (for more details, see **Silk Road** in the *China* section). The country boasts some of the finest architectural jewels among the Silk Road countries, featuring intricate Islamic tile work, turquoise domes, minarets and preserved relics from the time when Central Asia was a centre of empire and learning. Good examples of this architecture can be found in the ancient walled city of Khiva in Urgench, the winding narrow streets of the old town of Bukhara and Samarkand, known locally as the 'Rome of the Orient'. The Ferghana Valley, surrounded by the Tian Shan and Pamir mountains, still produces silk and is well worth visiting for its friendly bazaars and landscape of cotton fields, mulberry trees and fruit orchards.
Uzbektourism will arrange tours to suit taste and budget. An increasing number of Western tour companies offer packages that take travellers to Bukhara, Samarkand and Tashkent, with all accommodation and travel paid before leaving. Owing to the difficulties of touring independently, travellers with limited time are advised to buy a package and make use of the services of a recognised tour company.
TASHKENT: The capital lies in the valley of the **River Chirchik** and is the fourth-largest city in the CIS. Tashkent has always been an important international transport junction. Unfortunately, it preserves only a small proportion of its architectural past. A massive earthquake in 1966 flattened much of the old city and it was rebuilt with broad, tree-lined streets and the new buildings are of little architectural interest. The earlier buildings lie in the old town to the west of the centre. A myriad of narrow winding alleys, it stands in stark contrast to the more modern Tashkent. Of interest among the older buildings are the 16th-century **Kukeldash Madrasa**, which is being restored as a museum, and the **Kaffali-Shash Mausoleum**. Many of the Islamic sites in Tashkent are not open to non-Muslims, and visitors should always ask permission before entering a mosque or other religious building. Tashkent houses many museums of Uzbek and pre-Uzbek culture. These include the **State Art Museum**, which houses a collection of paintings, ceramics and the Bukharan royal robes. The **Museum of Decorative and Applied Arts** exhibits embroidered wall hangings and reproduction antique jewellery. As important historical figures, such as Amir Timur – better known as Tamerlane in the West – are being given greater prominence, the exhibits and perspective of the museums are also changing.
SAMARKAND: Samarkand is the site of Alexander the Great's slaying of his friend Cleitos, the pivot of the Silk Road and the city transformed by Timur in the 14th century into one of the world's greatest capitals. Founded over 5000 years ago, the city flourished until the 16th century before the sea routes to China and the rest of the East diminished its importance as a trading centre. Much of its past glory survives or has been restored. The centre of the historical town is the **Registan Square**, where three huge madrasas (Islamic seminaries) – including **Shir-Dor** and **Tillya-Kari** – built between the 15th and 17th centuries, dominate the area. Decorated with blue tiles and intricate mosaics, they give some idea of the grandeur that marked Samarkand in its heyday.
The **Bibi Khanym Mosque**, not far from the Registan, is testimony to Timur's love for his wife. Now it is a pale shadow of its former self, having been partly destroyed in the 1897 earthquake, and seems permanently under repair. However, it is still possible to see the breadth of vision of the man who conquered so much of central and south Asia. Timur himself is buried in the **Gur Emir**. On the ground floor, under the massive cupola, lie the ceremonial graves of Timur and his descendants. The stone that commemorates Timur is reputed to be the largest chunk of Nephrite (jade) in the world. The actual bodies are situated in the basement, which unfortunately is not open to the public.
The **Shah-i-Zinda** is a collection of the graves of some of Samarkand's dignitaries. The oldest date from the 14th century as Samarkand was starting to recover from the depredations of the Mongol hordes of the 13th century. Other sites of interest in Samarkand include the **Observatory of Ulug Beg**, Timur's grandson, which was the most advanced astronomical observatory of its day. There is also the **Afrasiab Museum**, not far from the observatory, containing a frieze dating from the sixth century, which shows a train of gifts for the Sogdian ruler of the day.
BUKHARA: West of Samarkand, Bukhara was once a centre of learning renowned throughout the Islamic world. It was here that the great Sheikh Bahautdin Nakshbandi lived. He was a central figure in the development of the mystical Sufi approach to philosophy, religion and Islam. In Bukhara, there are more than 350 mosques and 100 religious colleges. Its fortunes waxed and waned through succeeding empires until it became one of the great Central Asian khanates in the 17th century.
The centre of historical Bukhara is the **Shakristan**, which contains the **Ark**, or palace complex of the Emirs. Much of this was destroyed by fire in the 1920s, but the surviving gatehouse gives an impression of what the whole must have been like. Near the gatehouse is the **Zindan** or jail of the Emirs, which has a display of some of the torture methods employed by the Emirs against their enemies. Not far from the Ark, the 47m- (154ft-) high **Kalyan Minaret**, or tower of death, was built in 1127 and, with the **Ishmael Samani Mausoleum**, is almost the only structure to have survived the Mongols. It was from here that convicted criminals were thrown to their deaths.
Other sites of interest in Bukhara include the **Kalyan Mosque**, which is open to non-Muslims, the **Ulug Beg Madrasa** – the oldest in Central Asia – and, opposite, the **Abdul Aziz Madrasa**. Bukhara, with the narrow, twisting alleyways of its old quarter, is full of architectural gems.
ELSEWHERE: Khiva, northeast of Bukhara, is near the modern and uninteresting city of **Urgench**. Khiva is younger and better preserved than either Samarkand or Bukhara. The city still lies within the original city walls, and has changed little since the 18th century. Part of its attraction is its completeness; although it has been turned into a museum town and is hardly inhabited, it is possible to imagine what it was like in its prime when it was a market for captured Russian and Persian slaves.
The **Art Gallery** in **Nukus**, the capital of Karakalpakstan, in the west of the country, has the best collection of Russian avant-garde art outside St Petersburg.
The **Chatkalsky Reserve** in the western Tian-Shan is a narrow unspoilt gorge and contains snow tigers, the rare Tian-Shan grey bear and the Berkut eagle.

Sport & Activities

Mountaineering: The mountains in the south of the country offer good **trekking**. There are high peaks for those wanting a challenge, while easier treks can be done in the foothills and on the plateaux. The best time to go is between March and November. There are many opportunities for serious **mountaineering**, and Uzbekistan contains some of the world's highest peaks, including *Peak Pobeda* (7439m/24,399ft), *Peak Korzhenevskaya* (7105m/23,304ft) and *Peak Khan-Tengri* (6995m/22,943ft). Equipment can be transported to base camps by helicopter. Recommended sites for **ice climbing** include the *Gissar*, *Matcha* and *Turkestan* ridges. Vertical rock faces for **rock climbing** can be found in the Fan mountains (at *Bodkhana*, *Chapdara*, *Maria-Mirali* and *Zamok*) and on the Matchi Ridge (at *Aksu*, *Asan-Usan* and *Sabakh*).
Cycling: Tours are available for cyclists of all levels. Easier rides can be done in the Ferghana Valley and around Tashkent, where lake and mountain scenery can be enjoyed. The more experienced cyclist might prefer to take the *Silk Road* from Tashkent via Lake Aidarkul to Khiva.
Other: There is **skiing** in the mountains above Tashkent. The deepest **caves** in Asia are in Uzbekistan at *Boi-Bulok* (1415m/4641ft) and *Kievskaya* (990m/3247ft). These are suitable for experienced cavers only. Beautiful gypsum formations can be seen at the *Kugitang* cave, while the caves of *Baisuntau* contain mummified bears and those in western *Tian Shan* feature underground rivers and lakes. The **martial arts**, particularly *Taekwon-Do*, are also popular. **Rafting** and **kayaking** are possible on the Angren, Chatkal, Pskem, Syr Darya and Ugen river, the best time being September to October.

Social Profile

FOOD & DRINK: Uzbek food is similar to that of the rest of Central Asia. *Plov* is the staple food for both every day and celebrations, and usually consists of chunks of mutton, shredded red and yellow carrot and rice fried in a cast iron or aluminium pot. There are dozens of variations of this dish. *Shashlyk* (skewered chunks of mutton barbecued over charcoal – kebabs – served with sliced raw onions) and *lipioshka* (rounds of unleavened bread) are served in restaurants and are often sold on street corners and make an appetising meal. Uzbeks pride themselves on the quality and variety of their bread. *Samsa* (samosas) are also sold in the street, but the quality is variable. *Manty* are large boiled dumplings stuffed with meat and *shorpa* is a meat and vegetable soup. During the summer and autumn, there is a wide variety of fruit: grapes, pomegranates, apricots – which are also dried and sold at other times of the year – and, dwarfing them all, mountains of honeydew and watermelons. In general, hotel food shows a strong Russian influence: *borcht* is a beetroot soup, *entrecote* is well-done steak, *cutlet* are grilled meat balls and *strogan* is the local equivalent of Beef Stroganoff. *Pirmeni* originated in Ukraine and are small boiled dumplings of meat and vegetables, similar to ravioli, sometimes served in a vegetable soup. There are a number of restaurants that serve both European and Korean food (Stalin transported many Koreans from their home in the east of the former Soviet Union, believing them to be a security threat). There is a hard-currency restaurant at the top of the Hotel Uzbekistan that serves Chinese and Korean food.
Tea is the staple drink of Central Asia, and *chai-khanas* (tea houses) can be found almost everywhere in Uzbekistan, full of old men chatting the afternoon away with a pot of tea in the shade. Beer, wine, vodka, brandy and sparkling wine (*shampanski*) are all widely available in restaurants. *Kefir*, a thick drinking yoghurt, is often served with breakfast.
NIGHTLIFE: Tashkent has a variety of theatres that show everything from European operas to traditional Uzbek dancing and music. The Navoi theatre, opposite the Tashkent Hotel, shows opera and ballet. The prices are low by Western standards; shows generally start at 1800. There is also a number of themed Western-style bars, restaurants and discos.
SHOPPING: The best place to experience Central Asia is in the bazaars. The bazaars of Tashkent and Samarkand offer goods ranging from herbs and spices to Central Asian carpets. In the Alaiski Bazaar in Tashkent, it is possible to buy decorated Uzbek knives. Silk is still produced in the country and well-priced silks can be bought at large department stores. Many museums have small shops which sell a variety of modern reproductions and some original items. It is possible to buy carpets and embroidered wall hangings. Bukhara is famous for its gold embroidery, and visitors can buy elaborately embroidered traditional Uzbek hats. Visitors should be aware that it is illegal to export anything more than 100 years old or items which have a cultural significance. **Shopping hours:** Food shops open 0800-1700, all others open 0900-1900.
SPECIAL EVENTS: For further information on events in Uzbekistan, contact the National Company Uzbektourism (see *Contact Addresses* section). The following is a selection of special events occurring in Uzbekistan in 2005:
Mar 20-22 *Navrus* (Spring Festival), nationwide.
Dec *Pakhta-Bairam Harvest Festival*, Karakalpak.
SOCIAL CONVENTIONS: *Lipioshka* (bread) should never be laid upside down and should never be put on the ground, even if it is in a bag. It is normal to remove shoes but not socks when entering someone's house or sitting down in a *chai-khana*. Shorts are rarely seen in Uzbekistan and, worn by women, are likely to provoke unwelcome attention from the local male population. Avoid ostentatious displays of wealth (eg jewellery) in public places. Homosexuality is illegal. **Photography:** Photography near airports, military barracks and police stations can upset the authorities.

Business Profile

ECONOMY: Agriculture is the main component of Uzbekistan's economy. Livestock is reared in the steppes while a variety of crops, including grains, fruit and vegetables, are grown in the more fertile valleys. In addition, vast quantities of cotton are produced in formerly arid areas fed by artificial irrigation schemes. Uzbekistan continues to consume over three-quarters of the water available to the ex-Soviet Central Asian Republics. The result of this ill-conceived plan has been one of the world's greatest ecological catastrophes in the Aral Sea, once among the world's largest inland seas, which has been deprived of the bulk of its river sources and has consequently contracted to one-third of its original size. The country has substantial natural resources – especially natural gas, which is an important export earner – and oil. Uzbekistan also boasts the world's largest opencast gold mine and has deposits of silver, uranium, copper, lead, zinc and tungsten. Machinery and vehicles account for the bulk of manufacturing output.
Self-sufficiency in food and energy products meant that Uzbekistan did not suffer as badly as other republics from the collapse of the Soviet Union and its economic system. In principle, this made reform a somewhat easier prospect than for many of Uzbekistan's neighbours. In 1992, Uzbekistan joined the IMF, the World Bank, and the European Bank for Reconstruction and Development (as a 'Country of Operation'). A new currency – the Sum – was introduced in 1996. Economic reform began in earnest in 1994 but the Government has since blown hot and cold over putting it into effect. Much of the economy has now been transferred into private ownership, but key sectors remain under state control and the financial crises of 1997/98 in Asia and the Russian Federation persuaded the Government to put many reform plans on hold. Currency and export controls were introduced in an attempt to insulate the economy, as far as possible, from external influence (although the Government now plans to make the Sum fully convertible in the near future). The lack of reform has also deterred many potential foreign investors. Uzbekistan's recent economic performance has been patchy. Current annual GDP growth is 4.2 per cent, while inflation is around 20 per cent. Uzbekistan has joined the Economic Co-operation Organisation of ex-Soviet republics and former socialist countries. Its main trading partners are the Russian Federation, Kazakhstan and Tajikistan, along with Switzerland (the largest export market after the Russian Federation), Germany, Korea (Rep), the UK and Turkey.
BUSINESS: Uzbekistan's government is actively encouraging foreign investment, particularly in the processing industries for its raw material output. The January 1994 decree puts into law a number of tax incentives for foreign investors, formally lays out guarantees for property protection, and promises a faster and less bureaucratic method of registration for foreign concerns. Other areas in which the Uzbeks would like to encourage foreign investment include the financial sector, energy production, extraction and processing of mineral raw materials, textiles, telecommunications, tourism and ecology. All foreign companies currently have to be registered with the Ministry of Foreign Economic Relations.
Office hours: Mon-Fri 0900-1800.
COMMERCIAL INFORMATION: The following organisations can offer advice: Agency for Foreign Economic Relations, ul. T Shevchenko 1, 700029 Tashkent (tel: (71) 138 5000 *or* 5123/5; fax: (71) 138 5200/5100/5252; e-mail: secretary@mfer.uz; website: www.mfer.uz); *or* Uzbekistan Exhibition Centre, 107 Amir Temur St, 700084 Tashkent (tel: (71) 134 4545 *or* 135 0973; fax: (71) 134 5440/4088; e-mail: info@uzexpocentre.uz; website: www.uzexpocentre.uz). Information can also be obtained from the Business Information Service for the Newly Independent States, US Department of Commerce, USA Trade Center, Stop R*BISNIS, 1401 Constitution Avenue, NW Washington, DC 20230, USA (tel: (202) 482 4655; fax: (202) 482 2293; e-mail: bisnis@ita.doc.gov; website: www.bisnis.doc.gov).

Climate

Uzbekistan has an extreme continental climate. It is generally warmest in the south and coldest in the north. Temperatures in December average -8°C (18°F) in the north and 0°C (32 °F) in the south. However, extreme fluctuations can take temperatures as low as -35°C (-31°F). During the summer months, temperatures can climb to 45°C (113°F) and above. Humidity is low. The best time to visit is during the spring and autumn.

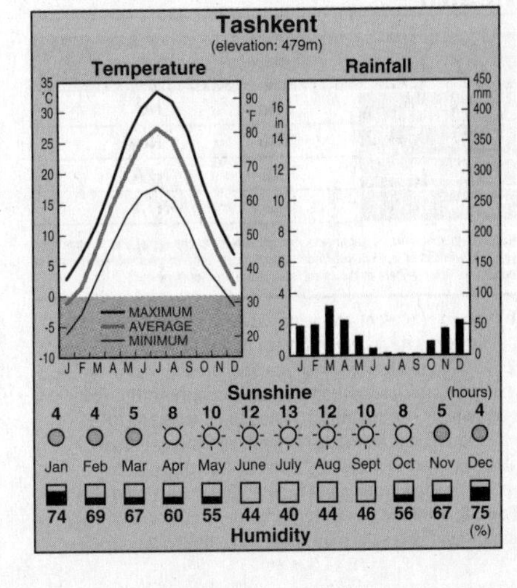

Vanuatu

LATEST TRAVEL ADVICE CONTACTS

British Foreign and Commonwealth Office
Tel: (0870) 606 0290 Website: www.fco.gov.uk
US Department of State
Website: http://travel.state.gov/travel
Canadian Department of Foreign Affairs and Int'l Trade
Tel: (1 800) 267 8376 Website: www.dfait-maeci.gc.ca

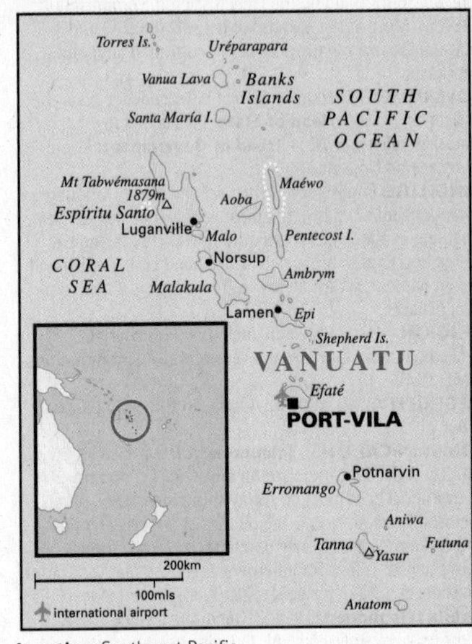

Location: Southwest Pacific.

Country dialling code: 678.

Vanuatu National Tourism Office
PO Box 209, Ground Floor, Pilioka House, Port Vila, Vanuatu
Tel: 22515 *or* 22685 *or* 22813. Fax: 23889.
E-mail: tourism@vanuatu.com.vu
Website: www.vanuatutourism.com
British High Commission
Street address: La Casa d'Andrea e Luciano, Rue Pierre Lamy, Port Vila, Vanuatu
Postal address: PO Box 567, Port Vila, Vanuatu
Tel: 23100. Fax: 23651.
E-mail: bhcvila@vanuatu.com.vu
Website: www.britishhighcommission.gov.uk/vanuatu
The High Commission is scheduled for closure at the end of 2005.
South Pacific Tourism Organisation (SPTO)
Street address: Level 3 FNPF Place, 343-359 Victoria Parade, Suva, Fiji
Postal address: PO Box 13119, Suva, Fiji
Tel: (679) 330 4177. Fax: (679) 330 1995.
Website: www.spto.org
Also deals with enquiries from the UK.
Permanent Mission of the Republic of Vanuatu to the United Nations
42 Broadway, 12th Floor, Suite 1200-18, New York, NY 10004, USA
Tel: (212) 425 9600. Fax: (212) 422 3427.
E-mail: vanunmis@aol.com
The American Embassy in Moresby deals with enquiries relating to Vanuatu (see *Papua New Guinea* **section).**
The Canadian High Commission in Canberra deals with enquiries relating to Vanuatu (see *Australia* **section).**

General Information

AREA: 12,190 sq km (4707 sq miles).
POPULATION: 202,200 (official estimate 2002).
POPULATION DENSITY: 15.8 per sq km.
CAPITAL: Port-Vila (Island of Efaté). **Population:** 30,139 (1999).

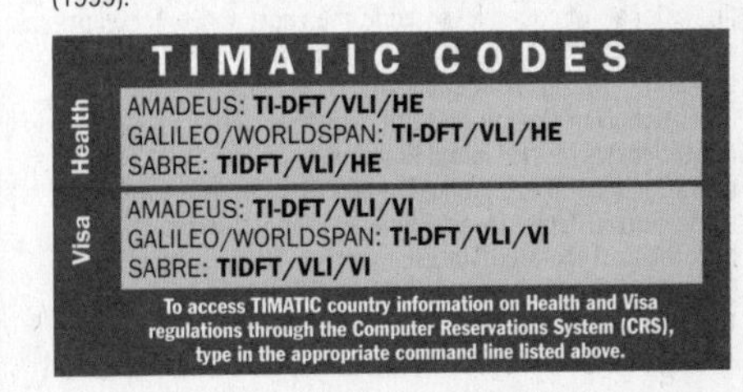

TIMATIC CODES

Health	AMADEUS: **TI-DFT/VLI/HE** GALILEO/WORLDSPAN: **TI-DFT/VLI/HE** SABRE: **TIDFT/VLI/HE**
Visa	AMADEUS: **TI-DFT/VLI/VI** GALILEO/WORLDSPAN: **TI-DFT/VLI/VI** SABRE: **TIDFT/VLI/VI**

To access TIMATIC country information on Health and Visa regulations through the Computer Reservations System (CRS), type in the appropriate command line listed above.

GEOGRAPHY: Vanuatu, formerly called the New Hebrides, forms an incomplete double chain of islands stretching north to southeast for some 900km (560 miles). They are situated approximately 2250km (1407 miles) northeast of Sydney, Australia, and 800km (500 miles) west of Fiji. Together with the Banks and Torres islands, the chains comprise about 40 mountainous islands and 40 islets and rocks. The islands are volcanic in origin and there are five active volcanoes. The Ambrym and Lopevi volcanoes are permanently active and highly dangerous. Lopevi was extinct for many years but became active 50 years ago. Further to the south, on the island of Tanna, is Yasur, cited as the most accessible active volcano in the world and a major tourist attraction. Geophysical activity is under constant monitoring by the French scientific organisation, ORSTOM. Most of the islands are densely forested and mountainous with narrow bands of cultivated land along the coasts.
GOVERNMENT: Republic. Gained independence from the UK/France in 1980. **Head of State:** President Kalkot Mataskelekele since 2004. **Head of Government:** Prime Minister Han Lini since 2004.
LANGUAGE: English and French are the official languages. Bislama (Pidgin English), the most widely used day-to-day language, is a Melanesian mixture of French and English. French and English are widely spoken and both English and French names exist for all towns. There are more than 115 local dialects.
RELIGION: Mostly Christian, including Presbyterian, Anglican, Roman Catholic and several other denominations.
TIME: GMT + 11.
ELECTRICITY: 240 volts AC. Australian three-pin plugs are in use.
COMMUNICATIONS: Telephone: IDD is available. Country code: 678. There are no area codes. Outgoing international calls must go through the international operator. There are public telephones at airports and post offices. Phone cards can be purchased in local currency from the post office. For emergency services, dial: 22333 for fire services; 22222 for police; 22100 for an ambulance. **Mobile telephone:** GSM 900. Operators include *Smile* (website: www.smile.com.vu). *TVL* also operates an analogue cellular network compliable with AMPs. Coverage is nationwide. **Fax:** Most hotels and post offices have facilities. **Internet:** ISPs include *Vanuatu.Com* (website: www.vanuatu.com.vu). There is an Internet cafe in Port-Vila. **Telegram:** Available at the Central Post Office in Port-Vila and at main hotels. **Post:** Post offices are located on the main streets in Port-Vila and Luganville, on Espiritu Santo. Airmail to Europe takes about seven days. Post office hours: Mon-Fri 0730-1630. **Press:** *Port Vila Presse* is published daily in English and French, the *Vanuatu Daily Post* in English and the *Vanuatu Weekly* in English, French and Bislama. The monthly *Pacific Island Profile* is published in English and French. For tourist information, see the quarterly publication, *Hapi Tumas Long Vanuatu*.
Radio: BBC World Service (website: www.bbc.co.uk/worldservice) and Voice of America (website: www.voa.gov) can be received. From time to time the frequencies change and the most up-to-date can be found online.

Passport/Visa

	Passport Required?	Visa Required?	Return Ticket Required?
Full British	Yes	No	Yes
Australian	Yes	No	Yes
Canadian	Yes	No	Yes
USA	Yes	No	Yes
Other EU	Yes	No/1	Yes
Japanese	Yes	No	Yes

Note: Regulations and requirements may be subject to change at short notice, and you are advised to contact the appropriate diplomatic or consular authority before finalising travel arrangements. Details of these may be found at the head of this country's entry. Any numbers in the chart refer to the footnotes below.

PASSPORTS: Passport valid for a minimum of four months beyond date of arrival required by all.
VISAS: Required by all except the following, provided they are in possession of confirmed onward travel documents, for stays of up to 30 days:
(a) nationals of countries listed in the chart above, **1.** except nationals of the Czech Republic, Estonia, Hungary, Latvia, Lithuania, the Slovak Republic and Slovenia;
(b) nationals of Commonwealth countries, and dependencies of the United Kingdom;
(c) nationals of Brazil, Chile, China (PR), Cuba, Hong Kong (SAR), Korea (Rep), Kuwait, Marshall Islands, Mexico, Micronesia (Federated States), Morocco, Norway, Peru, The Philippines, Russian Federation, Switzerland, Taiwan, Thailand, Tunisia, United Arab Emirates, Vatican City and Zimbabwe;
(d) transit passengers continuing their journey by the same or first connecting aircraft, provided holding valid onward or return documentation and not leaving the airport.
Types of visa and cost: *Visitor* (for tourist and business purposes): Vt2500.
Validity: A maximum of 30 days with the possibility of extensions of up to four months in any period of one year.
Application to: Principal Immigration Officer, Private Bag 092, Port Vila (tel: 22354; fax: 25492).
Application requirements: (a) Valid passport. (b) Two passport-size photos. (c) Proof of sufficient funds and/or accompanying business letter. (d) Return or onward tickets, and other necessary documents for onward destination.

Money

Currency: Vatu (Vt) = 100 centimes. Notes are in denominations of Vt5000, 1000, 500 and 200. Coins are in denominations of Vt100, 50, 20, 10, 5, 2 and 1. Australian Dollars are also accepted in some shops and restaurants.
Currency exchange: Exchange facilities are available at the airport and trade banks. It is advisable to exchange foreign currency after arriving in Vanuatu. Australian Dollars are accepted by many shops, restaurants and hotels in Port-Vila, but rarely outside major towns. There are ATMs at the ANZ Bank and supermarket.
Credit & debit cards: MasterCard and Visa are quite widely accepted, American Express and Diners Club less so. Check with your credit or debit card company for details of merchant acceptability and other services which may be available.
Travellers cheques: These are widely accepted.
Currency restrictions: There are no restrictions on the import or export of either local or foreign currency.
Exchange rate indicators: The following figures are included as a guide to the movements of the Vatu against Sterling and the US Dollar:

Date	Feb '04	May '04	Aug '04	Nov '04
£1.00=	210.37	203.67	209.60	201.39
$1.00=	111.60	115.60	113.77	106.35

Banking hours: Generally Mon-Fri 0800-1500, except Westpac Bank: Mon-Fri 0830-1600. Bureaux de change open Mon-Fri 0800-1730/1800, Sat-Sun 0830-1600.

Duty Free

The following items may be imported into Vanuatu by passengers aged 15 and over without incurring customs duty: *Personal effects and wearing apparel, used or worn and for own use; 200 cigarettes or 100 cigarillos or 50 cigars or 250g of tobacco; 1.5l of spirits and 2l of wine; 250ml of eau de toilette and 100ml of perfume; other articles up to a value of Vt20,000.*

Public Holidays

2005: Jan 1 New Year's Day. **Feb 21** Father Lini Day. **Mar 5** Custom Chief's Day. **Mar 25** Good Friday. **Mar 28** Easter Monday. **May 1** Labour Day. **May 5** Holy Thursday (Ascension). **Jul 24** Children's Day. **Jul 30** Independence Day. **Aug 15** Assumption. **Oct 5** Constitution Day. **Nov 29** Day of Unity. **Dec 25** Christmas Day. **Dec 26** Family Day.
2006: Jan 1 New Year's Day. **Feb 21** Father Lini Day. **Mar 5** Custom Chief's Day. **Apr 14** Good Friday. **Apr 17** Easter Monday. **May 1** Labour Day. **May 25** Holy Thursday (Ascension). **Jul 24** Children's Day. **Jul 30** Independence Day. **Aug 15** Assumption. **Oct 5** Constitution Day. **Nov 29** Unity Day. **Dec 25** Christmas Day. **Dec 26** Family Day.

Health

	Special Precautions?	Certificate Required?
Yellow Fever	No	No
Cholera	No	No
Typhoid & Polio	1	N/A
Malaria	2	N/A

Note: Regulations and requirements may be subject to change at short notice, and you are advised to contact your doctor well in advance of your intended date of departure. Any numbers in the chart refer to the footnotes below.

1: Typhoid is present and vaccination is advised. No cases of poliomyelitis have been reported in recent years.
2: A low to moderate risk of malaria, predominantly in the malignant *falciparum* form, exists throughout the year everywhere. The strain is reported to be resistant to chloroquine and sulfadoxine-pyrimethamine. The *vivax* strain is, in some cases, resistant to chloroquine. The recommended prophylaxis is chloroquine plus proguanil.
Food & drink: Mains water is normally chlorinated and, whilst relatively safe, may cause mild abdominal upsets. Bottled water is available and is advised for the first few weeks of the stay. Milk is pasteurised and dairy products are safe for consumption. Local meat, poultry, seafood, fruit and vegetables are generally considered safe to eat.
Other risks: *Hepatitis A*, *dengue fever* and *typhoid fever* exist throughout the islands. *Hepatitis B* is endemic. Poisonous fish and sea snakes can be a hazard to bathers.
Health care: There are hospitals in Aoba, Epi, Espiritu, Malekula, Port Vila, Santo, Tanna and smaller clinics and medical dispensaries on the smaller islands. Health insurance is advised.

Travel - International

AIR: The national airline is *Air Vanuatu (NF)*, Rue de Paris, PO Box 148, Port-Vila, Vanuatu; tel: 23848; fax: 25626; e-mail: reservation@airvanuatu.com.vu; website: www.airvanuatu.com), which offers daily services between Port-Vila and Brisbane, Melbourne and Sydney (Australia), and Auckland (New Zealand).
Approximate flight times: From Vanuatu to *London* is 30 hours.
International airports: *Port-Vila (VLI)* (Bauerfield) is 6km (4 miles) from Port-Vila (travel time – 15 minutes). Buses and taxis are available. Facilities have been upgraded and currently include bank/bureaux de change, left luggage, duty free shops and bars.
Air passes: The *Visit the South Pacific Pass* is valid for many airlines operating in the South Pacific, including the larger ones, such as *Air Caledonie*, *Air Nauru*, *Air Niugingi*, *Air Pacific*, *Air Vanuatu*, *Polynesian Airlines*, *Qantas* and *Solomon Airlines*. Offering reductions of up to 40 per cent on normal airfares, this sector-based pass allows for flexible island-hopping between the destinations of the Cook Islands, Fiji, Nauru, New Caledonia, Samoa, Tahiti, Tonga, Vanuatu and the more remote Melanesian and Micronesian islands, together with major cities in Australia (Brisbane, Melbourne and Sydney) and New Zealand (Auckland, Chirstchurch and Wellington). It is only available for people resident outside of the South Pacific. The journey must be started outside the South Pacific and only one stopover in Australia is allowed. A minimum of two sectors must be bought before departure (extra sectors can be purchased en route). There is a maximum of one pass per person, and passes must be used within six months of the first day of travel. Children under 12 years of age pay 75 per cent of the adult fare. For details and conditions, contact the South Pacific Tourist Organisation (see *Contact Addresses* section).
Departure tax: Vt2800. Children under 12 years of age are exempt. The departure tax must be paid in cash and in local currency (Vatu) only.
Note: The departure tax is often included in airfares: please check with your travel agent when booking.

Travel - Internal

AIR: Domestic services are provided by the government-owned *Vanair* (tel: 22643; fax: 23910; e-mail: sales@vanuatu.com.vu; website: www.vanair.vu). It offers scheduled services to 29 destinations within the archipelago. However, it is very expensive and is an occasionally unreliable air service. The privately owned *Dovair* airline also offers domestic flights.
Departure Tax: Vt400. Children under 12 years of age are exempt. The departure tax must be paid in cash and in local currency (Vatu) only.
Note: The departure tax is often included in airfares: please check with your travel agent when booking.
SEA: Inter-island ferries infrequently operate from Port-Vila and Espiritu Santo to the northern and southern islands. *Coral* and *Hibiscus Tours* operate boats to various islands.
ROAD: Traffic drives on the right. Of the 1130km (702 miles) of road, 54km (32 miles) are paved. Roads are either compacted coral or dirt tracks. The road around the island of Efate is currently open but it should be checked with the visitor's hotel or police whether the road is open before attempting to drive around the island. There is no public transport. **Bus:** Private buses serve the town centre and the airport in Port-Vila. **Minibus:** Frequent services available. As there are no timetables, the most common way to catch a minibus is to flag one down and tell the driver where to go. **Taxi:** These are plentiful and all are metered, although a fixed rate can be agreed. **Car hire:** Major car hire operators have offices in Port-Vila. Cars, 4-wheel drive vehicles and jeeps are available. **Documentation:** A national driving licence is acceptable.

Accommodation

Vanuatu has several international-standard resorts based in Port-Vila, including luxury/superior resorts such as *Chantillys on the Bay*, *Mangoes Resort*, *Erakor Island*

Resort, and luxury/superior hotels such as *Breakas Beach Resort, Harbour Villa* and *The Melanesian Port Vila*. There are also plenty of standard hotels and adventure lodges on Port-Vila. A number of smaller resorts with simpler facilities are located on Efaté, Espiritu Santo, Malekula, Tanna and other islands. Conventional hotel-style accommodation as well as self-contained studio apartments, bungalows, guest houses and lodges are available in all resorts. There is no hotel tax or service charge. Full details are available from the Vanuatu National Tourism Office (see *Contact Addresses* section) *or* the Vanuatu Hotel and Resort Association, PO Box 230, Port Vila (tel: 23388; fax: 23880; e-mail: bryan@iririki.com).

CAMPING/CARAVANNING: Camping is available on Efate and some of the outer islands. For a complete list of campsites, contact the Vanuatu National Tourism Office (see *Contact Addresses* section).

Credit: © South Pacific Tourism Organisation

Resorts & Excursions

Vanuatu's unspoilt landscape and rich cultural heritage make it an attractive destination for adventurous visitors. Tourism is centred on the islands of Efaté, Tanna and Espiritu Santo, but there are plans to develop facilities on more of the islands. The capital, **Port-Vila**, is on **Efaté Island**; its **Cultural Centre** has one of the most extensive Pacific artefact collections in the world. There are also plenty of opportunities for active visitors, especially those interested in watersports.

Tanna Island has the world's most accessible active volcano, **Yasur**. Visitors can drive to the summit and peer into the crater at a seething mass of bubbling lava. The village of the **John Frum** cargo cult can also be visited; it began with the arrival of an American soldier in World War II and believers wait for him to return with great riches.

Espiritu Santo Island inspired James A Michener to write *South Pacific*. Here, scuba divers can see where the liner *President Coolidge* and the destroyer *USS Tucker* rest on the seabed.

On **Pentecost Island** during April and May visitors can, for a fee, see men performing the **Naghol** (a ritual leap) to ensure a bountiful yam harvest; they tie vines to their ankles and leap from a 30m (100ft) tower, falling head first. Only the vine saves them from death. Only recently, this ceremony was opened to the public and the fee goes towards local projects. Visitors who are interested should contact the National Tourism Office of Vanuatu well in advance. There are a number of tours available in Vanuatu, including trips to see volcanoes (by air), harbour cruises, sailing trips, fishing trips, cultural tours and visits to World War II relics.

Sport & Activities

Watersports: The good visibility and warm temperature of Vanuatu's waters ensure excellent conditions for **scuba diving**, which can be practised all year round. Most dive operators are located in Port-Vila, on the island of Efaté, and on Espiritu Santo, Vanuatu's largest island. Dive cruises depart from within walking distance of the town centres and many dive sites are located close to the shore. Internationally recognised certification courses are available, with special provisions for beginners. Dive stores stock a wide range of equipment, which can also be hired easily. Numerous World War II shipwrecks, usually in fairly deep waters, lie scattered around the islands, one of the most famous being the *SS President Coolidge*. The *Million Dollar Point*, where military equipment was dumped at the end of the war, can also be visited by divers. The seabed around the offshore islands of North Efaté is renowned for its deep canyons. There is a diving recompression chamber operated by ProMedical Vanuatu at the ProMedical Vanuatu facility, Port-Vila. For further information on diving, contact the *Vanuatu Scuba Association (VSA)*, Tranquility Island Dive Base, PO Box 991, Port-Vila, Vanuatu (tel: 22209; fax: 23304). There are many beautiful beaches suitable for **swimming** and most hotels have pools. **Kayaking**, **game fishing**, **sailing**, **windsurfing** and **water-skiing** are also popular.

Ornithology: Birdlife is prolific and varied, particularly in the southern islands during the breeding season (September to January).

Other: There is a **tennis** club at Port-Vila and at the resorts. There are also several 9- to 18-hole **golf** courses; visitors can arrange rounds through hotels or the Vanuatu National Tourism Office (see *Contact Addresses* section). **Horse riding** is available, and it is possible to go **hiking** through the rainforest and in the mountains.

Social Profile

FOOD & DRINK: There are many restaurants in the main tourist areas. Seafood features strongly on hotel and restaurant menus in Port-Vila and the main towns. The numerous ethnic backgrounds of the inhabitants of Vanuatu are reflected in different styles of cooking. Chinese and French influences are the strongest. Food is generally excellent everywhere. French cheese, pâtés, bread, cognac and wine are available in Port-Vila's two major shops. Local fruit is excellent.

NIGHTLIFE: Port-Vila has several nightclubs with music and dancing. There is also a cinema. Evening cruises are organised with wine, snacks and island music. Traditional music and dancing take place at various island festivities to which visitors are welcome, and some hotels put on evening entertainment and dancing. Details are available from the National Tourism Office of Vanuatu (see *Contact Addresses* section).

SHOPPING: Special purchases include grass skirts from Futuna and Tanna, baskets and mats from Futuna and Pentecost, carved forms and masks from Ambrym and Malekula, woodwork from Tongoa and Santo, and pig tusks and necklaces made of shells or colourful seeds from villages near Port Vila. Duty free shops sell a selection of luxury items. **Shopping hours:** Mon-Sat 0700-2000. Chinese stores open Sunday mornings from 0800 and in the evenings. Most shops close from 1130-1330 (except restaurants, banks, supermarkets and the Post Office). The market in the town centre is open every day (except Sunday) for flowers, fruit, vegetables and handicrafts.

SPECIAL EVENTS: For a complete list of special events, contact the National Tourism Office of Vanuatu (see *Contact Addresses* section). The following is a selection of special events occurring in Vanuatu in 2005:

Feb 15 *John Frum Day*, Tanna. **Mar 20** *Fete de la Francophonie*. **Apr 19, 22, 26, 29/May 7, 14, 21, 28** *Naghol*, Pentecost Island (see *Resorts & Excursions* section). **Jun 25** *Ocean Swim*. **Aug** *Vanuatu Golf Open*; *Vanuatu Agriculture Show*. **Sep** *Toka* (large clan alliance dance), Tanna; *Twin Waterfall Festival*, West Vanualava, Banks Islands. **Oct 13-16** *Fest Napuan Music Festival*.

SOCIAL CONVENTIONS: Informal wear is suitable for most occasions. Some establishments appreciate men wearing long trousers in the evenings. Life goes at its own pace and while modern influences can be seen in the main centres, in the hill villages and outlying islands, age-old customs continue. Those hiking or exploring must be aware that Vanuatu has strict and sensitive land ownership regulations. **Tipping:** Not expected or encouraged, as it goes against local tradition.

Business Profile

ECONOMY: Agriculture and fishing occupy 40 per cent of the working population. Fruit and vegetables are grown for domestic consumption while coffee, coconuts, copra, beef and fish are the main export commodities. The sale of fishing licences to foreign fleets is another important source of revenue. There is also a sizeable timber industry, originally encouraged by the Government but now strictly regulated in the wake of international pressure. The industrial sector is mostly concerned with food processing and construction. Identified mineral resources, including manganese, gold and copper have yet to be exploited on a commercial scale.

While mineral deposits may be of future value to the Vanuatu economy, the Government's recent efforts to diversify the economy have been focused on the service sector. The most important of these is tourism – backed by the construction of new hotels and airport improvements, allied to a focus on 'ecotourism' – and 'offshore' financial services. Tourism is worth about US$55 million to the economy annually. A 'flag of convenience' shipping register was also created. Despite these efforts, the economy is still vulnerable to its geographical circumstances; a severe earthquake followed by a tsunami in late 1999 caused considerable damage to several islands. Meanwhile, offshore finance has run into trouble. In April 2002, Vanuatu was one of seven countries 'named and shamed' by the Organisation for Economic Cooperation and Development (OECD) and threatened with sanctions for its failure to take adequate measures against money-laundering. Since then, the Vanuatu authorities have tightened their financial services regulatory regime. Foreign aid remains essential to sustain the economy, which is currently growing at 2 per cent annually. In 2002, Vanuatu signed up to the newly-established regional trade bloc created under the Pacific Island Countries Trade Agreement (PICTA). Australia, New Zealand, Japan, the UK and France are the principal donors. These countries, plus Bangladesh, are also the country's principal trading partners.

BUSINESS: A casual approach to business prevails. Shirts and smart trousers will suffice – ties are only necessary for the most formal occasions. Business is conducted in Pidgin English or French. **Office hours:** Mon-Fri 0730-1130 and 1330-1630.

COMMERCIAL INFORMATION: The following organisations can offer advice: Vanuatu Chamber of Commerce, PO Box 189, Port Vila (tel: 27543; fax: 27542; e-mail: atarivile@vanuatu.gov.vu); *or* Vanuatu Investment Promotion Authority, 1st Floor, Pilioko House, Port-Vila (tel: 24096; fax: 25216; e-mail: cde@vanuatu.com.vu; website: www.investinvanuatu.com).

Climate

Subtropical. Trade winds occur from May to October. Warm, humid and wet between November and April. Rain is moderate. Cyclones are possible between December and April.

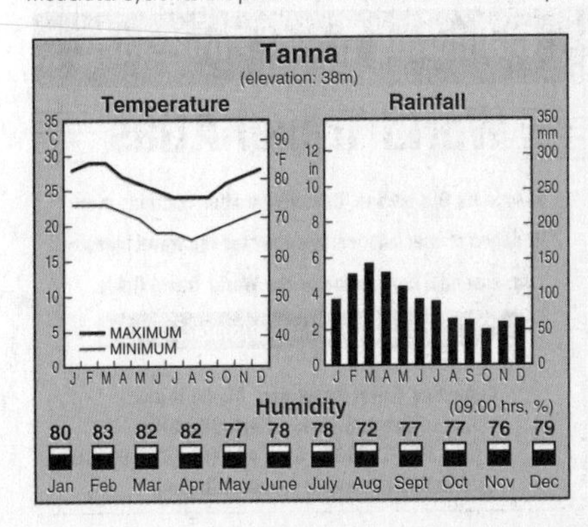

Vatican City

LATEST TRAVEL ADVICE CONTACTS

British Foreign and Commonwealth Office
Tel: (0870) 606 0290 Website: www.fco.gov.uk
US Department of State
Website: http://travel.state.gov/travel
Canadian Department of Foreign Affairs and Int'l Trade
Tel: (1 800) 267 8376 Website: www.dfait-maeci.gc.ca

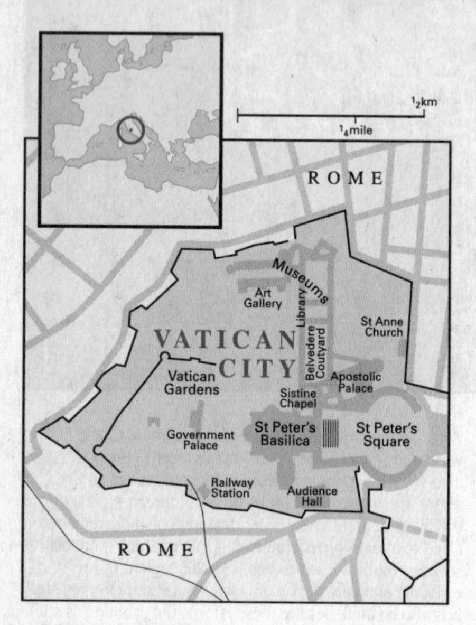

Location: Europe, Italy (Rome).

Country dialling code: 39 followed by the area code for Rome, 06. The 0 of Italian area codes should not be omitted when dialling from abroad.

Italian State Tourist Offices can provide advice and information on visiting the Vatican City. For addresses, see *Italy* section.

Holy See Press Office
Via della Conciliazione 54, 00193 Rome, Italy
Tel: (06) 698 921. Fax: (06) 6988 5178.
Website: www.vatican.va

Apostolic Nunciature
54 Parkside, Wimbledon, London SW19 5NE, UK
Tel: (020) 8944 7189. Fax: (020) 8947 2494.
E-mail: nuntius@globalnet.co.uk
Opening hours: Mon-Fri 1000-1700.

British Embassy to the Holy See
Via dei Condotti 91, 00187 Rome, Italy
Tel: (06) 6992 3561. Fax: (06) 6994 0684.

Apostolic Nunciature
3339 Massachusetts Avenue, NW, Washington, DC 20008, USA
Tel: (202) 333 7121. Fax: (202) 337 4036.

Embassy of the United States of America to the Holy See
Via delle Terme Deciane 26, 00153 Rome, Italy
Tel: (06) 4674 3428. Fax: (06) 575 8346.
Website: http://vatican.usembassy.it

Apostolic Nunciature
724 Manor Avenue, Ottawa, Ontario K1M 0E3, Canada
Tel: (613) 746 4914. Fax: (613) 746 4786.
E-mail: nuntius@bellnet.ca

Canadian Embassy to the Holy See
Palazzo Pio, 00193 Rome, Italy
Tel: (06) 6830 7316. Fax: (06) 6880 6283.
E-mail: vatcn@international.gc.ca
Website: www.dfait-maeci.gc.ca/canadaeuropa/holysee

General Information

AREA: 0.44 sq km (0.17 sq miles).
POPULATION: 900 (2002).
POPULATION DENSITY: 2045.5 per sq km.
GEOGRAPHY: The Vatican City is situated entirely within the city of Rome, sprawling over a hill west of the River Tiber, and separated from the rest of the city by a wall. Vatican City comprises St Peter's Church, St Peter's Square, the Vatican and the Vatican Gardens.
GOVERNMENT: The State of the Vatican City came into existence in 1929. **Head of State and Government:** His Holiness Pope John Paul II died in April 2005, and Cardinals are, as we go to press, soon to enter the conclave (a centuries-old ritual) in order to elect a successor.
LANGUAGE: Italian and Latin are the official languages, though most international languages are spoken to some extent.
TIME: GMT + 1 (GMT + 2 from last Sunday in March to Saturday before last Sunday in September).
ELECTRICITY: 220 volts, 50Hz.
COMMUNICATIONS: Telephone: IDD is available. The international dialling code is that for Italy (39), plus 06. Outgoing international code: 00. The Vatican has its own telephone network. **Telegram:** Vatican City has its own telegraph service. **Post:** Stamps issued in the Vatican City are valid only within its boundaries. **Press:** The daily newspaper published in the Vatican City is *L'Osservatore Romano*, with weekly editions in English and other international languages.
Radio: *Vatican Radio* broadcasts worldwide on a daily basis. Programmes are offered in 34 languages and are sent out from the Vatican on short wave, medium wave, FM, and satellite. For frequencies, see online (website: www.vatican.va).

Passport/Visa

There are no formalities required to enter the Vatican City, but entry will always be via Rome, and Italian regulations must therefore be complied with (see *Italy* section).
There is free access only to certain areas of the Vatican City; these include St Peter's Church, St Peter's Square, the Vatican Museum and the Vatican Gardens. Special permission is required to visit areas other than those mentioned.

Money

Currency: Vatican coins are similar in value, size and denomination to those of Italy, although the monetary system is separate from that of Italy; the Euro is, however, legal tender in the Vatican City (see *Money* in the *Italy* section). Vatican coins are the Gold Lire 100 (nominal); Silver Lire 500; 'Acmonital' Lire 100 and 50; 'Italma' Lire 10, 5 and 1; and 'Bronzital' Lire 20.
The first Euro coins and notes were introduced in January 2002 (see *Money* in the *Italy* section).

Duty Free

There are no taxes and no customs/excise in the Vatican City. For Italian duty free allowances, see *Italy* section.

Public Holidays

See *Italy* section.

Health

See *Italy* section.

Travel - International

The Vatican City has its own small railway, which runs from the Vatican into Italy. For travel in Rome, see the *Italy* section. There is a speed limit of 30kph (20mph) in the Vatican City.

Accommodation

Board and lodging is not available to members of the general public in the Vatican City itself; for information on accommodation in Rome, see the *Italy* section.

Resorts & Excursions

The Vatican City is best known to tourists and students of architecture for the magnificent **St Peter's Basilica**. Visitors are normally admitted to the dome, 0800-1700. **The Museum & Treasure House** is open 0845-1300 in winter and 0845-1600 during the summer months. Leading up to it is the 17th-century **St Peter's Square**, a superb creation by Bernini. On either side are semicircular colonnades, and in the centre of the square is an Egyptian obelisk hewn in the reign of Caligula.
It is also possible to visit the **Necropoli Precostantiniana**, the excavations under St Peter's, although permission has to be obtained in advance and is usually granted only to students and teachers with a professional interest in the work being carried out. Contact the Tourist Information Office in St Peter's Square.
The **Vatican Gardens** can only be visited by those on guided tours or bus tours. Tickets are available from the Tourist Information Office in St Peter's Square; it is advisable to apply two days in advance. There is a restaurant in the museum and a bar and cafeteria on the roof of St Peter's.
To the right of St Peter's stands the **Vatican Palace**, the Pope's residence. Among the principal features of the Palace are the **Stanze**, the **Sistine Chapel**, the **Garden House** or **Belvedere**, the **Vatican Library** and the **Vatican Collections**, containing major works of art and valuable pictures. The **Museum & Treasure House** includes the **Collection of Antiquities**, **Museo Pio-Clementino**, the **Egyptian Museum**, the **Etruscan Museum** and the **Museum of Modern Religious Art**.

Social Profile

SPECIAL EVENTS: Mass is said daily in the Vatican. When the Pope is in residence, he usually gives a public audience on Wednesday mornings. Special events are held at key times throughout the liturgical year (*Advent*, *Christmas*, *Lent*, *Easter* and *Pentecost*). For more information about events occuring throughout the year, contact the Holy See Press Office (see *Contact Addresses* section) *or* the Vatican's Central Reception (*Servizio Accoglienza Centrale SAC*), Piazza San Marcello 4, 00187 Rome (tel: (06) 6982; fax: (06) 6988 5255).

Business Profile

ECONOMY: The Vatican has three main sources of income: the *Instituto per le Opere di Religione* (IOR, Institute of Religious Works), voluntary contributions known as 'Peter's Pence' and the interest on the Vatican's investments. The IOR – the Vatican Bank – has attracted some controversy in recent years through the emergence of huge debts and allegations of corruption. Nonetheless, as the heart of a worldwide entity with millions of adherents, the Vatican continues to wield immense financial influence. The Vatican produces little other than religious artefacts, and its material requirements are largely met from Italian sources.
COMMERCIAL INFORMATION: The following organisations can offer advice: Prefecture of the Economic Affairs of the Holy See, Palazzo delle Congregazioni, Largo del Colonnato 3, 00120 Rome (tel: (06) 6988 4263; fax: (06) 6988 5011); *or* Instituto per le Opere di Religione (IOR), 00120 Città del Vaticano, Rome (tel: (06) 6988 3354; fax: (06) 6988 3809).

Climate

See *Italy* section.

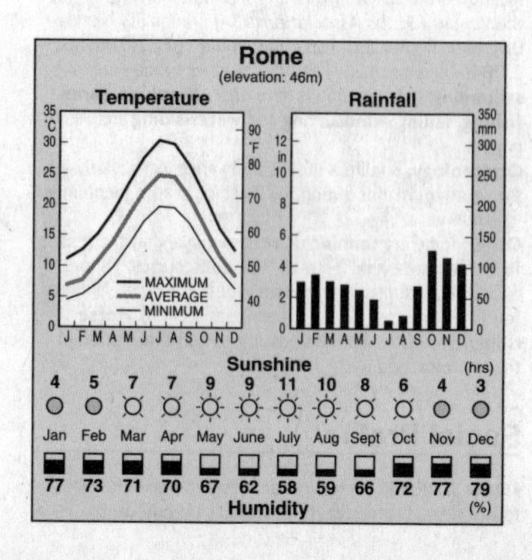

Venezuela

LATEST TRAVEL ADVICE CONTACTS

British Foreign and Commonwealth Office
Tel: (0870) 606 0290 Website: www.fco.gov.uk

US Department of State
Website: http://travel.state.gov/travel

Canadian Department of Foreign Affairs and Int'l Trade
Tel: (1 800) 267 8376 Website: www.dfait-maeci.gc.ca

Location: South America.

Country dialling code: 58.

INATUR (Nacional Instituto de Turismo)
Mexico Avenue, Caracas Hilton Hotel, South Tower, Floors 1 and 2, Caracas, Venezuela
Tel/Fax: (212) 576 1193 *or* 9032.
E-mail: promocionymercadeoinatur@yahoo.com

Embassy of the Republic of Venezuela
1 Cromwell Road, London SW7 2HW, UK
Tel: (020) 7581 2776 *or* 7584 4206. Fax: (020) 7589 8887.
E-mail: info@venezlon.co.uk
Website: www.venezlon.co.uk
Opening hours: Mon-Fri 0900-1700.

Embassy of the Republic of Venezuela (Consular section)
56 Grafton Way, London W1T 5DL, UK
Tel: (020) 7387 6727. Fax: (020) 7383 3253.
Website: www.venezlon.co.uk
Opening hours: Mon-Fri 1000-1300.

British Embassy
Street address: Torre La Castellana, Piso 11, Avenida Principal, La Castellana, Caracas 1060, Venezuela
Postal address: Apartado 1246, Caracas 1010A, Venezuela
Tel: (212) 263 8411. Fax: (212) 267 1275.
E-mail: britishembassy@internet.ve
Website: www.britain.org.ve
Consulates in: Maracaibo, Mérida and Porlamar.

Embassy of the Bolivarian Republic of Venezuela (Consular Section)
1099 30th Street, NW, Washington, DC 20007, USA
Tel: (202) 342 2214. Fax: (202) 342 6820.
E-mail: apaiva@embavenez-us.org
Website: www.embavenez-us.org

Venezuelan Consulate General
7 East 51st Street, New York, NY 10022, USA
Tel: (212) 826 1660. Fax: (212) 644 7471.
E-mail: info@consulado-ny-gov.ve
Website: www.newyork.embavanez-us.org
Other consulates in: Boston, Chicago, Houston, Miami, New Orleans, San Francisco and San Juan (Puerto Rico).

Embassy of the United States of America
Calle F con Calle Suapure, Urb. Colinas de Valle Arriba, Caracas 1080, Venezuela
Tel: (212) 975 6411 *or* 7831 (consular section). Fax: (212) 975 6710 *or* 8991 (consular section).
E-mail: consularcaracas@state.gov *or* embajada@state.gov
Website: http://caracas.usembassy.gov

Embassy of the Republic of Venezuela
32 Range Road, Sandy Hill, Ottawa, Ontario K1N 8J4, Canada
Tel: (613) 235 5151. Fax: (613) 235 3205.
E-mail: info.canada@misionvenezuela.org
Website: www.misionvenezuela.org
Consulates in: Montréal and Toronto.

Canadian Embassy
Street address: Avenida Francisco de Miranda con Avenida Sur de Altamira, Altamira, Caracas 1062, Venezuela
Postal address: Apartado Postal 62302, Caracas 1060A, Venezuela
Tel: (212) 600 3000. Fax: (212) 261 8741.
E-mail: crcas@dfait-maeci.gc.ca
Website: www.dfait-maeci.gc.ca/caracas/

TIMATIC CODES

Health	AMADEUS: **TI-DFT/CCS/HE** GALILEO/WORLDSPAN: **TI-DFT/CCS/HE** SABRE: **TIDFT/CCS/HE**
Visa	AMADEUS: **TI-DFT/CCS/VI** GALILEO/WORLDSPAN: **TI-DFT/CCS/VI** SABRE: **TIDFT/CCS/VI**

To access TIMATIC country information on Health and Visa regulations through the Computer Reservations System (CRS), type in the appropriate command line listed above.

General Information

AREA: 916,445 sq km (353,841 sq miles).
POPULATION: 25,549,084 (official estimate 2003).
POPULATION DENSITY: 27.9 per sq km.
CAPITAL: Caracas. **Population:** 1,975,787 (official estimate 2000).
GEOGRAPHY: Venezuela is bordered to the north by the Caribbean, to the east by Guyana and the Atlantic Ocean, to the south by Brazil, and to the west and southwest by Colombia. The country consists of four distinctive regions: the Venezuelan Highlands in the west; the Maracaibo Lowlands in the north; the vast central plain of the Llanos around the Orinoco; and the Guiana Highlands, which take up about half of the country.
GOVERNMENT: Republic. Gained independence from Spain in 1830. **Head of State and Government:** President Hugo Chávez Frías since 2000.
LANGUAGE: Spanish is the official language. English, French, German and Portuguese are also spoken by some sections of the community.
RELIGION: 86 per cent Roman Catholic.
TIME: GMT - 4.
ELECTRICITY: 110 volts AC, 60Hz. US-style two-pin plugs are the most commonly used fittings.
COMMUNICATIONS: Telephone: IDD is available. Country code: 58. Outgoing international code: 00. **Mobile telephone:** GSM 900 network. Operators include *Corporación Digitel* (website: www.digitel.com.ve), *Digital Cellular* and *Infonet*. Coverage is limited to around Caracas and major cities. **Fax:** Available at the larger hotels. **Internet:** ISPs include *CantvNet* (website: www.cantv.net), *Compuserve Venezuela* (website: www.csi.com.ve) and *Internet Venezuela* (website: www.internet.ve). E-mail can be accessed from Internet cafes in most urban areas. **Telegram:** Services are available from public telegraph offices. **Post:** There is an efficient mail service from Venezuela to the USA and Europe. Airmail to Europe takes three to seven days. Internal mail can sometimes take longer. Surface mail to Europe takes at least one month. **Press:** The English-language daily newspaper is *The Daily Journal*, published in Caracas. Spanish-language dailies include *El Nacional*, *El Universal*, *Meridiano* and *Ultimas Noticias*.
Radio: BBC World Service (website: www.bbc.co.uk/worldservice) and Voice of America (website: www.voa.gov) can be received. From time to time the frequencies change and the most up-to-date can be found online.

Passport/Visa

	Passport Required?	Visa Required?	Return Ticket Required?
Full British	Yes	No/2	Yes
Australian	Yes	No/2	Yes
Canadian	Yes	No/2	Yes
USA	Yes	No/2	Yes
Other EU	Yes	No/1/2	Yes
Japanese	Yes	No/2	Yes

Note: *Regulations and requirements may be subject to change at short notice, and you are advised to contact the appropriate diplomatic or consular authority before finalising travel arrangements. Details of these may be found at the head of this country's entry. Any numbers in the chart refer to the footnotes below.*

PASSPORTS: Passport valid for at least six months (if entering with a visa) or for the duration of stay (if entering with a Tourist Entry Card) required by all.
VISAS: Required by all except the following, who *do*, however, require a Tourist Entry Card (TEC), which is issued free of charge by an authorised air carrier on presentation of valid air tickets (including return or onward ticket) for stays of maximum 90 days:

Credit: © INATUR

(a) nationals of countries mentioned in the chart above, except **1.** nationals of Cyprus, Estonia, Latvia and Malta who *do* need a visa;
2. (b) nationals of Andorra, Antigua & Barbuda, Argentina, Barbados, Belize, Brazil, Bulgaria, Chile, Costa Rica, Croatia, Grenada, Guatemala, Hong Kong (SAR), Iceland, Jamaica, Liechtenstein, Malaysia, Mexico, Monaco, Netherlands Antilles, New Zealand, Norway, Panama, Paraguay, Romania, San Marino, St Kitts & Nevis, St Lucia, St Vincent & the Grenadines, South Africa, Switzerland, Taiwan, Trinidad & Tobago and Uruguay.
Types of visa and cost: *Tourist Entry Card*: Free of charge (single-entry). *Tourist*: £22 (multiple-entry). *Business*: £44 (multiple-entry). *Transit*: £22 (single-entry).
Validity: *Tourist*/Tourist Entry Cards: 90 days (tourist visas are valid for up to one year but only permit entry for 90 days in any one period). *Business*: 180 days. *Transit*: up to 72 hours.
Application to: Consulate (or Consular section at Embassy); see *Contact Addresses* section. Tourist Entry Cards are available at the airport check-in desk prior to departure.
Application requirements: *Tourist*: (a) Completed and signed application form. (b) Two recent colour passport-size photos. (c) Passport with at least six months' validity at time of visa application. (d) Fee (postal order). (e) Self-addressed, stamped envelope for postal applications. *Business*: (a)-(e) and, (f) Employer's reference and letter confirming purpose of visit. (g) Reference from company to be contacted in Venezuela. *Student*: (a)-(e) and, (f) Letter of admission from educational institution. (g) Proof of academic degrees/attestations. *Transit*: (a) Ticket confirming you will be continuing to a third country. (b) Name of airline carrier. (c) Flight number. (d) Date you will be entering and departing Venezuela. (e) Name of entry and departing Venezuelan port or airport.
Working days required: Three.
Temporary residence: Special authorisation is required from the Ministry of Internal Affairs in Caracas.

Money

Currency: Bolívar (Bs) = 100 céntimos. Notes are in denominations of Bs50,000, 20,000, 10,000, 5000, 2000, 1000, 500, 100, 50, 20, 10 and 5. Coins are in denominations of Bs500, 100, 50, 25, 5, 2 and 1, and 50, 20, 10 and 5 céntimos.
Currency exchange: Banks will change cheques and cash, and *cambios* will change cash only; as will hotels, although often at a less favourable rate.
Credit & debit cards: American Express, MasterCard and Visa are widely accepted; Diners Club has more limited acceptance. Check with your credit or debit card company for details of merchant acceptability and for other facilities which may be available.
Travellers cheques: Widely accepted, although one may

be asked to produce a receipt of purchase when changing them in Venezuela. Exchange is more difficult in some places than others. Some kinds of travellers cheques are not accepted; seek advice before travelling. To avoid additional exchange rate charges, travellers are advised to take travellers cheques in US Dollars.
Currency restrictions: The import and export of local and foreign currency is unlimited.
Exchange rate indicators: The following figures are included as a guide to the movements of the Bolívar against Sterling and the US Dollar:

Date	Feb '04	May '04	Aug '04	Nov '04
£1.00=	2940.27	3351.03	5030.53	4740.52
$1.00=	1600.00	1915.20	2730.50	2503.31

Note: The above rates are the official rates for non-commercial transactions. 'Essential Import' and 'Preferential' rates are also used.
Banking hours: Mon-Fri 0830-1530.

Duty Free

The following items may be imported into Venezuela without incurring customs duty:
200 cigarettes and 25 cigars; 2l of alcoholic beverages; four small bottles of perfume; new goods up to a value of US$1000.
Prohibited Items: Flowers, fruit, meat and meat products, live plants and birds or bird products or bird by-products from Chile.

Public Holidays

2005: Jan 1 New Year's Day. **Feb 7-8** Carnival. **Mar 24** Holy Thursday. **Mar 25** Good Friday. **Apr 19** Declaration of Independence. **May 1** Labour Day. **Jun 24** Battle of Carabobo. **Jul 5** Independence Day. **Jul 24** Birth of Simón Bolívar. **Oct 12** Columbus Day. **Dec 25** Christmas Day. **Dec 31** New Year's Eve.
2006: Jan 1 New Year's Day. **Feb** Carnival. **Apr 13** Holy Thursday. **Apr 14** Good Friday. **Apr 19** Declaration of Independence. **May 1** Labour Day. **Jun 24** Battle of Carabobo. **Jul 5** Independence Day. **Jul 24** Birth of Simón Bolívar. **Oct 12** Columbus Day. **Dec 25** Christmas Day. **Dec 31** New Year's Eve.
Note: There are some additional regional holidays; enquire at the Embassy *or* the Corporación de Turismo de Venezuela (see *Contact Addresses* section).

Health

	Special Precautions?	Certificate Required?
Yellow Fever	Yes	1
Cholera	2	No
Typhoid & Polio	3	N/A
Malaria	4	N/A

Note: *Regulations and requirements may be subject to change at short notice, and you are advised to contact your doctor well in advance of your intended date of departure. Any numbers in the chart refer to the footnotes below.*

1: A yellow fever vaccination certificate is required from travellers over one year of age arriving from infected areas. The last outbreaks of yellow fever were in September 2004, when one person died in the municipality of Sucre, Merida State. Sporadic cases are, however, under control due to a countrywide vaccination and surveillance programme.
2: Cases of autochthonous cholera were reported in 1996. Visitors are advised to take necessary precautions. Up-to-date advice should be sought before deciding whether these precautions should include vaccination as medical opinion is divided over its effectiveness. See the *Health* appendix for more information.
3: Vaccination against typhoid is advised.
4: Malaria risk in the benign *vivax* form exists throughout the year in some rural areas of Apure, Amazonas, Barinas, Bolívar, Sucre and Táchira states. The malignant *falciparum* form is restricted to certain jungle areas of Amazonas (Atabapo), Bolívar (Cedeño, Gran Sabana, Raul Leoni, Sifontes and Sucre) and Delta Amacuro (Antonia Diaz, Casacoima and Pedernales) states and is reported to be highly resistant to chloroquine in the interior of Amazonas state. The recommended prophylaxis is chloroquine in *vivax* risk areas and mefloquine in *falciparum* risk areas.
Food & drink: Mains water is not drinkable and should be boiled or filtered. Bottled water is available and is advised for the first few weeks of the stay. Drinking water outside main cities and towns may be contaminated and sterilisation is advisable. Milk is pasteurised and dairy products are safe for consumption. Local meat, poultry, seafood, fruit and vegetables are generally considered safe to eat.
Other risks: *Bilharzia* (schistosomiasis) is present in north-central Venezuela. Avoid swimming and paddling in fresh water; swimming pools that are well chlorinated and maintained are safe. *Paragonimiasis* (oriental lung fluke) and *dengue fever* have been reported. *Hepatitis A* also occurs; *hepatitis B* and *D* (delta hepatitis) are highly endemic. *Cutaneous* and *mucocutaneous leishmaniasis* occur in rural areas. *Visceral leishmaniasis* is rarer. In the southeast, some deaths have been caused by mercury in the river water. *Dengue fever* is increasingly common and there are epidemics of *viral encephalitis* at times.
Rabies has been reported. For those at high risk, vaccination before arrival should be considered. If you are bitten, seek medical advice without delay. For more information, consult the *Health* appendix.
Health care: The best-equipped hospitals are in the state capitals. Emergency treatment is free and most hospitals have intensive care units. However, private hospitals are of a much higher standard, and although health insurance is not mandatory, it is recommended.

Travel - International

Travel Warning: Although Venezuela remains politically polarised, the mood has subdued since the presidential recall referendum on August 15 and the regional elections on October 31 in 2004. Nevertheless, political demonstrations may occur at any time, withholding the possibility of localised violence. Street crime is also rising and visitors are warned to be on their guard at all times. There have been reported muggings by bogus taxi operators at Caracas International Airport (Maiquetia).
AIR: Venezuela's national airlines are *Aeropostal (Alas de Venezuela) (VH)*, and *Avensa and Servivensa (VC)*, which no longer flies to Europe. Other airlines serving Venezuela include *British Airways*, *Lufthansa* and *United Airlines*.
Note: On December 14 2004, the Venezuelan National Civil Aviation Institute suspended all international flights to six airports: Caracas (Metropolitan), Chorallave, Coro, Cumaná, Maturin and Puerto Cabello.
Approximate flight times: From Caracas to *London* is nine hours, to *Los Angeles* is nine hours and to *New York* is five hours.
International airports: *Caracas (CCS)* (Simon Bolivar) is 22km (14 miles) from the city (travel time - 30 to 45 minutes). There is a coach service to the city every 60 minutes (0530-2359). Buses (*littoral*) are available to the city every 60 minutes (0600-1800). Taxis to the city are available on ranks. Airport facilities include duty free shop, bank/bureau de change, bar/restaurant, tourist information and car hire (*Avis*, *Budget* and *National*).
Departure tax: Bs58,200 (adults) or Bs38,800 (children aged two to 15) leaving Venezuala on international flights from all international airports. Transit passengers and children under two years are exempt.
The Visit South America Pass: This must be bought outside South America in country of residence and allows unlimited travel to 36 cities in the following countries: Argentina, Bolivia, Brazil, Colombia, Chile (except Easter Island), Ecuador, Paraguay, Peru, Uruguay and Venezuela. Participating airlines are *American Airlines*, *LanChile* and *LanPeru*. A minimum of three flights must be booked, with no maximum; the maximum stay is 60 days, with no minimum; and prices depend on the amount of flight zones covered. Children under 12 years of age are entitled to a 33 per cent discount and infants (under two years old) only pay 10 per cent of the adult fare. For further details, contact one of the participating airlines.
SEA: The principal Venezuelan ports are La Guaira, Puerto Cabello, Maracaibo, Guanta, Porlamar and Ciudad Bolívar (on the Orinoco River). The principal shipping lines operating to Venezuela are: from the USA: *Venezuelan Line*; from European ports: *Columbus Line*, *French Line*, *Hapag Lloyd*, *Polish Ocean Lines* and, the Spanish ships, 'Cabo San Juan' and 'Cabo San Roque'. *Cunard* offers Caribbean cruises from San Juan that include a stop in Caracas. Other cruise lines include *Celebrity Cruises* and *Costa*.
Departure tax: Exit tax on all air and sea departures, regardless of nationality, of Bs13,200.
RAIL: There are no international rail links with neighbouring countries.
ROAD: Road access is from Colombia (Barranquilla and Medellin) to Maracaibo, and from the Amazon territory of Brazil (Manaus) to Caracas.

Travel - Internal

AIR: Almost all large towns are connected with scheduled services operated by domestic airlines, including *Aeropostal* (website: www.aeropostal.com), *Aerotuy* (website: www.tuy.com) and *Avensa and Servivensa*. There are various discount tickets offered by *Avensa and Servivensa*, including special student and family prices. For further information, contact your local travel agency. Air travel is the best means of internal transport but services are often overbooked and even confirmation does not always ensure a seat. Travellers are advised to arrive at the airport well before the minimum check-in time in order to obtain confirmed seats. Schedule changes and flight cancellations with no advance warning are also likely.
Departure tax: Bs600.
SEA: Ferries link Puerto La Cruz with Margarita Island (travel time - two hours 45 minutes).
RAIL: The only railway runs between Barquisimeto and Puerto Cabello, with no air conditioning. There are plans for a considerable extension to the rail network. There are ambitious plans in progress for a 1400km (870 mile) national network to be constructed in the near future.
ROAD: Traffic drives on the right. Internal roads between principal cities are of a high standard, with 17,050km (10,595 miles) of paved motorways, 13,500km (8400 miles) of macadam highways and 5850km (3635 miles) of other roads. All vehicles must carry a spare tyre, wheel block, jack wrench and special reflector triangle. The quality of roads is variable but the main roads in Caracas and to the interior are good. In the event of an accident, both vehicles must remain in the position of the accident until a Traffic Police Officer arrives, otherwise insurance companies will be unable to pay claims. Drivers routinely ignore red lights. **Bus:** There are fairly cheap interurban bus services; quality of travel varies a lot, however. **Car hire:** Self-drive cars are available at the airport and in major city centres but are expensive.
Documentation: National driving licences are valid for one year. International Driving Permits are also valid.
URBAN: Caracas has a 35-station metro, which is comfortable and inexpensive. Conventional **bus** services have badly deteriorated in recent years and there has been a rapid growth in the use of *por puestos* (share-taxis). These are operated by minibus companies and tend to serve as the main form of public transport in Caracas and major cities. Fares charged are in general similar to those on the buses, although they are higher during the evenings and at weekends. **Taxis** in Caracas are metered but the fare can nonetheless be negotiated with the driver. It is customary not to use meters after midnight; the fare should be agreed before setting out. Taxi fares double after 2000. Taxi rates are posted at the airport. Motorcycles may not be used in Caracas after 2200.
Travel times: The following chart gives approximate travel times (in hours and minutes) from **Caracas** to other major cities/towns in Venezuela.

	Air
Porlamar	**0.45**
Los Roques	**0.50**
Mérida	**1.00**
Canaima	**1.15**
Cumana	**0.45**
Maracaibo	**1.00**
Ciudad Bolívar	**0.50**

Accommodation

HOTELS: There are many excellent hotels in Caracas. Numerous smaller hotels are open throughout the country but it is essential to make reservations at both these and the larger international hotels well in advance. It normally follows that the more expensive the hotel, the better the facilities. Hotels do not add a service charge, and generally there is no variation in seasonal rates. Hotels outside the capital tend to be cheaper and the standard may not be as high. A useful guide is the *Guía Turistica de Caracas Littoral y Venezuela*, published by the Corporación de Turismo de Venezuela, available at local tourist offices.
Grading: Hotels in Venezuela have been graded into three categories; **3-star** (65 hotels), **4-star** (22 hotels) and **5-star** (15 hotels).
YOUTH HOSTELS: For further information, contact: Hostelling International, Av Lecuna Partque Central, Edif. Tajamar, Nivel OFC 1, Of. 107, Caracas (tel: (212) 576 4493; fax: (212) 577 4915; e-mail: hostellingven@cantv.net); *or* Idiomas Vivos s.r.l., Resd. La Hacienda, Local 1-4T, Final Av. ppal. de las Mercedes, Apdo. 80160, Caracas 1080 (tel: (212) 993 6082; fax: (212) 992 9626 *or* 993 2412; e-mail: info@ividiomas.com; website: www.ividiomas.com).
CAMPING/CARAVANNING: Camping in Venezuela can involve spending a weekend at the beach, on the islands, in the Llanos or in the mountains. Camping can also be arranged with companies who run jungle expeditions. As in much of South America, however, good facilities are not widespread and camping is not used by travellers as a substitute for hotels on the main highways. No special campsites are yet provided for this purpose.

Resorts & Excursions

Venezuela offers a great variety of landscapes - tropical beaches, immense plains, enormous rivers, forests, jungle, waterfalls and great mountains. Unfortunately, the flash floods and mudslides which hit Venezuela in 1999 severely damaged the country's infrastructure; some of which may still not have been fully restored. Travellers should check prior to departure, particularly if planning to visit Vargas State.

CARACAS

Nestling in a long narrow valley in the coastal mountain range 16km (10 miles) from the north coast, Caracas is

A B C D E F G H I J K L M N O P Q R S T U V W X Y Z

typical of the 'new Venezuela', despite being one of the oldest established cities in the country (founded in 1567). The city is constantly growing and changing but, among the new developments, there are still areas of the old towns intact – **San José** and **La Pastora**, for example. Other periods of the country's history have left substantial monuments; these include the **Plaza Bolívar**, flanked by the old cathedral and the Archbishop's residence, the **Casa Amarilla** and the **Capitol** (the National Congress) building, erected in 1873 in just 114 days, which has a fine mural depicting Venezuelan military exploits. Other places worth visiting include the **Panteon Nacional** (which contains the body of Simon Bolívar), the **Jardín Botánico**, the **Parque Nacional del Este**, and, for recreation, the **Country Club**. Museums in the capital include the **Museo de Bellas Artes**, the **Museo del Arte Colonial**, the **Museo del Arte Contemporáneo**, the **Museo de Transporte** and the **Casa Natal del Libertador** (a reconstruction of the house where Bolívar was born; the first was destroyed in an earthquake). Next door is a museum containing the liberator's war relics. There is a large number of art galleries, as well as daily concerts, theatrical productions, films and lectures. The city also has a wide range of nightclubs, bars and coffee shops, especially along the **Boulevard de Sabana Grande**.

Excursions: Mount Avila gives a superb view across the city and along the coast. There are several beaches within 30km (20 miles) of the capital, with excellent 'taverns' and restaurants. For further information on these and other coastal resorts, see the following section.

THE NORTH COAST

The 4000km (2800 miles) of Caribbean coastline represents the major tourist destination in the country. The area has numerous excellent beaches and resorts ranging from the comparatively luxurious to the unashamedly opulent, which stretch along the coastline. **Maiquetia** is one of the best and most popular, offering wide beaches, an extensive range of watersports and some of the best fishing (including an international competition for the giant blue sailfish). There are daily air-shuttles from **Maiquetia** to **Porlamar**, on **Margarita Island**, a popular tourist resort with beautiful beaches, good hotels and extensive shopping centres. Also to the west of Caracas are **Macuto**, **Marbella**, **Naiguata**, **Carabelleda**, **Leguna** and **Oriaco**, all of which boast excellent beaches. To the north of Maiquetia are the idyllic islands of **Los Roques**.

La Guaira is the main port for Caracas. Although now heavily industrialised, the winding hilltop route from the city and the old town are worth visiting. Further west along the Inter-American highway is **Maracay** with its opera house, bullring and **Gomez Mausoleum**. Excursions run to **Lake Valencia** and Gomez's country house, the **Rancho Grande**.

The coastal resorts of **Ocumare de la Costa** and **Cata** can be reached by way of the 1130m (3710ft) **Portachuelo Pass** through the central highlands. The coastline is dotted with fine beaches and islands, many inhabited only by flamingos and scarlet ibis. Most can be reached by hired boat. **Morrocoy**, off the coast from **Tucacas**, is the most spectacular of these – hundreds of coral reefs with palm beaches ideal for scuba diving and fishing. **Palma Sola** and **Chichiriviche** are also popular. Ferries run from **La Vela de Coro** and **Punto Fijo** to the islands of Aruba and Curaçao. Journeys take about four hours and delays are to be expected.

Puerto la Cruz is a popular coastal resort with bars and restaurants and good beaches. It is also a good centre for travelling to remoter beaches. There is the Morro marina development in the Lecherías area adjacent to Puerto la Cruz, and the attractive town of **Pueblo Viejo** with 'old' Caribbean architecture and a Venetian lagoon layout – boats are the only means of transport. The attractiveness of the Puerto la Cruz area means that there has been an increase of foreign investment here in recent years.

CENTRAL & WESTERN VENEZUELA

The **Llanos** is an expansive, sparsely populated area of grassland east of the **Cordillera de Mérida** and north of the **Orinoco**, reaching up to the north coast. The area is the heart of the Venezuelan cattle country and the landscape is flat and only varied here and there by slight outcrops of land. It is veined by numerous slow-running rivers, forested along their banks. The swamps are the home of egrets, parrots, alligators and monkeys. The equestrian skills of the plainsmen can be seen at many rodeos throughout the Llanos, as well as exhibitions of cattle roping and the **Joropo**, Venezuela's national dance.

Barquisimeto, one of the oldest settlements in Venezuela, is now the country's fourth-largest city and capital of the Llanos. Its cathedral is one of the most famous modern buildings in the country.

Along the Colombian border is the Cordillera de Mérida and, to the east of this range, the **Cordillera Oriental**. Set in the area between these two ranges are the city of **Maracaibo** and **Lake Maracaibo**. Windless and excessively humid, the city and its environs are dominated by the machinery of oil production from the largest oil fields in the world, discovered in 1917. Sightseeing tours are available from here to the peninsula of **Guajira** to the north, where the Motilone and Guajiro Indians live.

Their lifestyle has changed little since the days of the first Spanish settlers. Their houses are raised above the lake on stilts and are in fact the original inspiration for naming the country Venezuela, or 'Little Venice'.

The **Cordillera de Mérida** are the only peaks in the country with a permanent snowline. Frosty plateaux and lofty summits characterise the landscape and many cities have grown up at the foot of the mountains, combining tradition with modern ways of life, as well as diversified rural and urban scenery. The scenery in this area is extremely varied – lagoons, mountains, rivers, beaches, ancient villages, historical cities, oil camps, sand dunes and Indian lake dwellings on stilts. The **Sierra Nevada National Park** offers opportunities to ski between November and June but, at an altitude of 4270m (14,000ft), this is recommended only for the hardiest and most dedicated.

Mérida, to the south, is today a city of wide modern avenues linking mainly large-scale 20th-century developments, although, wherever possible, relics of the colonial past have been allowed to stand. A university town and tourist centre, it nestles in the **Sierra Nevada**, overshadowed by **Bolívar Peak** (5007m/15,260ft) and **Mirror Peak** (where the world's highest cable car climbs to an altitude of 4675m/14,250ft). Mérida has modern and colonial art museums and much more worth seeing, including the **Valle Grande**, the **Flower Clock**, **Los Chorros de Milla**, the **Lagoons of Mucubaji**, **Los Anteojos**, **Tabay**, **Pogal**, **Los Patos**, **San-say** and the famous **Black Lagoon**. A mountain railway runs from the town to **Pico Espejo**. The view from the summit looks over the highest peaks of the Cordillera and the Llanos. The **Andean Club** in Mérida arranges trips to **Los Nervados**, the highest village in the mountains. Again, this is only recommended for the hardy. Other excursions from Mérida include **San Javier del Valle**, a relaxing mountain retreat, and **Jaji**, which has some fine examples of colonial architecture.

EASTERN VENEZUELA

The coastal regions to the north of the Guiana **Highlands** have some fine tourist beaches and resorts. These include **Higuerote**, **La Sabana** and also **Lecheria**, where the *San Juan Drum Festival* is held during late June.

The **Guiana Highlands** lie to the south of the Orinoco River and constitute half the land area of the country. Their main value is as a source of gold and diamonds. The Orinoco and its delta have been developed as major trade centres.

Ciudad Bolívar, formerly known as Angostura, and the home of Angostura bitters, is an old city on the south bank of the Orinoco and still bears traces of its colonial past, although it is currently the centre of modern developments. The **Gran Sabana National Reserve** is the largest of the Venezuelan plateaux and has an extraordinary array of wildlife. **Santa Elena**, **Guri Dam** (a hydroelectric complex supplying electricity to most of Venezuela) and **Danto Falls** are all worth a visit. **Santa Elena de Uairén** is a rugged frontier town which holds a Fiesta in August. **Mount Roraima**, suggested as the site of Conan Doyle's *Lost World*, can be climbed on foot. A fortnight's supplies and full camping equipment should be taken as the trip can take up to two weeks. The nearest village to the mountain is **Peraitepin**. **Tepuy Peak** is also worth a visit. Trips can be arranged to the diamond mines at **Los Caribes**. In **Icaban**, after a heavy rainfall, it is common to see children searching the slopes for gold nuggets washed down from the slopes.

It is possible to arrange trips by boat up the Orinoco River delta to **La Tucupita**. **Canaima** (one of the world's largest national parks, comprising 7,400,000 acres/3,000,000 hectares) is the setting for the spectacular **Angel Falls**, which carry the waters of the **Churum River** into an abyss. At 979m (3212ft), they are the highest in the world, a sight no visitor should miss. Trips can be arranged which take in the waterfalls and other nearby attractions, including many rare plants – Canaima has over 500 species of orchid alone. Overnight accommodation is available on the shores of the lagoon.

Other national parks in Venezuela are to be found in Bolívar State and the Amazonas Federal Territory, for example, **El Cocuy** and **Autana**.

Sport & Activities

Hiking and trekking: Venezuela has 42 national parks and around 20 nature reserves (*monumentos naturales*) which, together, cover some 15 per cent of the total land mass. All types of walks, ranging from signposted trails to mountain climbing and jungle paths, are possible. Visitors should note that a permit, issued by central or regional *Inparques* offices, is required to visit the parks. The well-developed tourist facilities at the *Parque Nacional El Avila* include around 200km (125 miles) of fairly easy, signposted trails, as well as numerous camping grounds. Most serious trekkers head up to the Venezuelan Andes, stretching some 400km (250 miles) from Táchira on the Colombian border north-eastwards, and offering everything from snow-capped peaks to lush rainforests. The most popular area for **mountain trekking** and **rock climbing** is the *Sierra Nevada de Mérida*, where several of the country's highest peaks (such as the *Pico Bolívar* or the *Pico Humboldt*) and the magnificent *Parque Nacional Sierra Nevada* are located. Experienced guides (who are strongly recommended for mountaineering) and equipment can be hired in Mérida, the regional tourist hub. Other popular trekking destinations in the area include *Los Nevados* (reached via an easy trek along a beautiful mountain track); *Pico El Aguila* (accessible from Valera, which can be reached on a bus ride from Mérida along Venezuela's highest road); and the *Sierra de la Culata* (particularly known for its desert-like landscapes). The Mérida region is also noted for its **cable car** (*teleferico*), the world's longest and highest, which runs for 12.6km (7.9 miles) from Mérida to the top of *Pico Espejo* (4765m/15,629ft), and provides easy access to starting points for mountain treks. Another popular trekking destination is Guyana, in the southeast, a region dotted with Venezuela's characteristic *tepuis* (flat-topped mountains with vertical flanks) and home to the country's most famous natural attraction – *Angel Falls* (called *Salto Angel* in Spanish), the world's highest waterfall (with an uninterrupted drop of 979m/3212ft, which is about 16 times the height of Niagara Falls). Access to the falls is fairly difficult (there is no road link) and involves a flight to Canaima (the main tourist base, some 50km/31.5 miles northwest of the falls), followed by either another **scenic flight** in a light aircraft, or a motorised **canoe trip** to the foot of Angel Falls (which only operates from June to November, the rainy season, and takes approximately two days).

Watersports: One of the most popular destinations for water-based activities is the *Isla de Margarita*, which lies some 40km (25 miles) off the mainland north of Cumaná (from where a twice-daily ferry provides access to the island), and whose Caribbean climate and 167km- (105-mile) long shoreline (with white sandy beaches) draw increasing numbers of **swimming**, **surfing**, **snorkelling** and **diving** enthusiasts. These activities are available all along the Caribbean coast (in the northeast of the country), with one destination, the *Parcque Nacional Mochima*, standing out: it consists of a wealth of islands and islets some of which, such as the *Isla de Plata* (the most developed), are surrounded by coral reefs. In the northwest, the coastal strip and the numerous offshore islands and coral reefs forming the *Parque Nacional Morroy* provide ideal snorkelling and diving. **Boat trips** through the mangrove *caños* (channels) and to several of the park's islands (notably to *Cayo Sombrero* and *Chichiriviche*, two of the best known) are available. The **fishing**, both fresh- and salt-water, is good.

Other: Mountain biking and **paragliding** are widely practised in the Mérida region, while **caving** enthusiasts may head to the *Cueva del Guácharo*, the most spectacular of Venezuela's many cave systems, located three hours by bus from Cumaná. Caracas has South America's largest and most modern **horse racing** track – *La Rinconada* – open Saturday and Sunday. **Horse riding** can be arranged at most tourist spots. **Boxing**, **baseball** and **football** are the most popular spectator sports in Venezuela and can be seen all year round. The indigenous *lucha libre* **wrestling** is a weekly event.

Note: All forms of hunting are prohibited.

Social Profile

FOOD & DRINK: Cumin and saffron are used in many dishes but the distinctive and delicate flavour of most of the popular dishes comes from the use of local roots and vegetables. Some local specialities are *tequenos*, a popular hors d'oeuvres (thin dough wrapped around a finger of local white cheese and fried crisp); *arepas* (the native bread), made from primitive ground corn, water and salt; and *tostadas*, which are used for sandwiches (the mealy centre is removed and the crisp shell is filled with anything from ham and cheese to spiced meat, chicken salad or cream cheese). *Guasacaca* is a semi-hot relish used mostly with grilled meats. *Pabellón criollo* is a hash made with shredded meat and served with fried plantains and black beans on rice. *Hallaca* is a local delicacy, eaten at Christmas and New Year; cornmeal is combined with beef, pork, ham and green peppers, wrapped in individual pieces of banana leaves and cooked in boiling water. *Parrilla criolla* is beef marinated and cooked over a charcoal grill. *Hervido* is soup made with chunks of beef, chicken or fish and native vegetables or roots. *Purée de apio* is one of the more exotic local roots (boiled and puréed, with salt and butter added, it tastes like chestnuts). *Empanadas* (meat turnovers), *roast lapa* (a rare, large rodent) and *chipi chipi* soup (made from tiny clams) are excellent. Table service is the norm and opening hours are 2100-2300.

A B C D E F G H I J K L M N O P Q R S T U V W X Y Z

There is no good local wine, although foreign wines are bottled locally. There are several good local beers, mineral waters, gin and excellent rum. Coffee is very good and a *merengada* (fruit pulp, ice, milk and sugar) is recommended. *Batido* is similar but with water and no milk. *Pousse-café* is an after-dinner liqueur. Bars have either table or counter service. A *lisa* is a glass of draught beer and a *tercio* a bottled beer. Most bars are open very late and there are no licensing laws.

NIGHTLIFE: There are many nightclubs and discos in the major cities of Venezuela. The National and Municipal Theatres offer a variety of concerts, ballet, plays, operas and operettas. There are other theatres - some of which are open-air - in Caracas, as well as several cinemas.

SHOPPING: There are many handicrafts unique to Venezuela that are made by local Indian tribes. Good purchases are gems and jewellery, *cacique* coins, gold, pearls, pompom slippers, seed necklaces, shoes and handbags, Indian bows, arrows, mats, pipes and baskets, *alpargatas* (traditional local footwear of the Campesinos), *chinchorros* (local hammocks) and many other Indian goods. **Shopping hours:** Mon-Sat 0900-1300 and 1500-1900.

SPECIAL EVENTS: Most national celebrations are tied to the Christian calendar. As well as Christmas, Easter and Corpus Christi, every village and town in Venezuela celebrates the feast of its patron saint. It is during these provincial festivals that the tourist can enjoy the colourful folklore that is a mixture of the cultures of pre-Columbian Indians, African slaves and Spanish colonists. For further information on special events, contact the Corporación de Turismo de Venezuela (see *Contact Addresses*). The following is a selection of special events occurring in Venezuela in 2005:
Jan 14 *Procesion de la Divina Pastora* (religious procession), Santa Rosa to Barquismeto. **Feb** *Carnaval*, nationwide (but especially in Carúpano). **Mar 27** *Burning of Judas* (Easter ritual), nationwide. **Jun** *Los Diablos Danzantes* (dancing in celebration of Corpus Christi), nationwide; *Festival of St John* (religious festival celebrated with drumming), nationwide.

SOCIAL CONVENTIONS: Shaking hands or using the local *abrazo*, a cross between a hug and a handshake, are the normal forms of greeting. In Caracas, conservative casual wear is the norm. Men are expected to wear suits for business, and jackets and ties are usual for dining out and social functions. Dress on the coast is less formal but beachwear and shorts should not be worn away from the beach or pool. Smoking follows European habits and in most cases it is obvious where not to smoke. Some public buildings are also non-smoking areas. **Tipping:** Tips are discretionary but in the majority of bars and restaurants 10 per cent is added to the bill and it is customary to leave another 10 per cent on the table. Bellboys and chambermaids should be tipped and, in Caracas, tips are higher than elsewhere. Taxi drivers are not tipped unless they carry suitcases. Petrol pump attendants expect a tip.

Business Profile

ECONOMY: Venezuela was a primarily agricultural country until the discovery and extraction of oil began in the 1920s. Oil is now dominant, providing one-quarter of GDP, one-third of government revenues and 80 per cent of export earnings. The national oil corporation, *PDVSA*, is one of the world's largest companies. Venezuela has some of the largest known reserves in the world. There are long-term plans to introduce greater diversity into the economy but little change in its basic structure may be expected in the near future.

Agriculture's share of the workforce has now fallen to 5 per cent of GDP, but the sector remains important by providing a non-oil export income in the form of its dairy and beef produce. Some cash crops – mostly rice, sugar and coffee – are grown. Most of the other farming activity is devoted to staple crops for domestic consumption. As well as oil, Venezuela has substantial deposits of iron and aluminium ores, plus gas, coal, diamonds, gold, zinc, copper, titanium, lead, silver, phosphates and manganese. The processing of these ores and the country's agricultural products account for the bulk of the industrial sector. However, over-dependence on oil income has meant that Venezuela's industries are suffering from a historic failure to modernise.

Venezuela was a prominent founding member of the Organisation of Petroleum Exporting Countries (OPEC) and the current president, Hugo Chávez, has played a leading role in the revival of the organisation's fortunes since the late 1990s. Since the beginning of 2002, Venezuela's recent economic performance has been severely affected by the turbulent political situation. After the currency crisis of February 2002 came an attempted coup. Then in December large parts of the economy – including the all-important oil industry – were affected by a two-month-long strike. This had a devastating impact: the economy is believed to have contracted by around 10 per cent during 2003. In 2004, this is estimated to have improved slightly, but is still forecasted as an annual contraction of 8 per cent.

Venezuela belongs to the *Asociación Latinoamericana de Integración* (ALADI), which seeks to promote a common market for Latin America, and to the Inter-American Development Bank. The USA accounts for 40 per cent of Venezuela's trade; Brazil and Colombia are its other key trading partners.

BUSINESS: English is becoming more widely spoken in business circles, particularly at executive level. Nevertheless, Spanish is essential for most business discussions. Appointments are necessary and a business visitor should be punctual. It is common to exchange visiting cards. **Office hours:** Mon-Fri 0800-1800 with a long midday break.

COMMERCIAL INFORMATION: The following organisations can offer advice: CONAPRI, Consejo Nacional de Promoción de Invensiones (National Council for Investment Promotion), Edificio Forum, Local LC-A (planta baja), Calle Guaicaipuro, El Rosal, Caracas 1060 (tel: (212) 951 6507 *or* 3692 *or* 953 4732; fax: (212) 953 3915; e-mail: conapri@conapri.org; website: www.conapri.org); *or* *FEDECAMARAS*, Federación Venezolana de Cámaras y Asociaciones de Comercio y Producción (Federation of Chambers of Commerce and Industry), Apartado 2568, Edificio Fedecámaras, Pent-House 2, Avenida El Empalme, El Bosque, Caracas (tel: (212) 731 1711; fax: (2) 730 2097; e-mail: secgeneral@fedecamaras.org.ve; website: www.fedecamaras.org.ve).

CONFERENCES/CONVENTIONS: Larger hotels have facilities. For further information, contact the Corporación de Turismo de Venezuela (see *Contact Addresses* section).

Climate

The climate varies according to altitude. Lowland areas have a tropical climate. The dry season is from December to April and the rainy season from May to December. During the rainy season, there is the possibility of flooding in certain low-lying areas, such as the Llanos and in some valley of the Andes. Various parts of Venezuela, including Caracas and the eastern part of Sucre, are vulnerable to earthquakes, although there have been no serious earthquakes for many years. The best time to visit is between January and April.

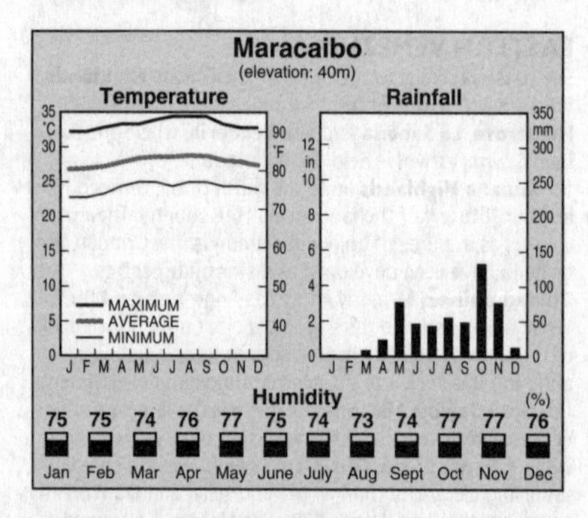

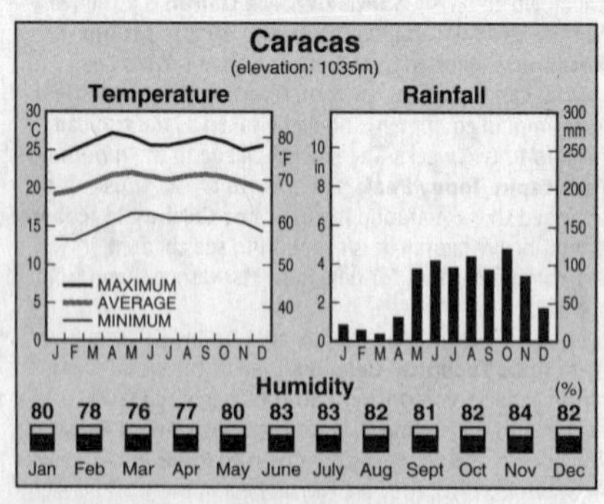

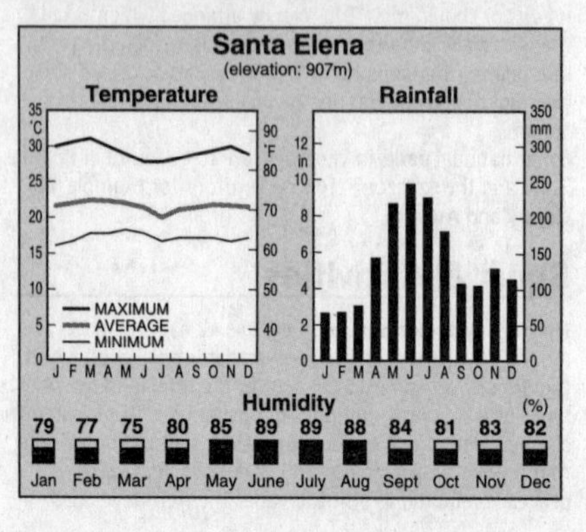

Vietnam

LATEST TRAVEL ADVICE CONTACTS

British Foreign and Commonwealth Office
Tel: (0870) 606 0290 Website: www.fco.gov.uk

US Department of State
Website: http://travel.state.gov/travel

Canadian Department of Foreign Affairs and Int'l Trade
Tel: (1 800) 267 8376 Website: www.dfait-maeci.gc.ca

Location: South-East Asia.

Country dialling code: 84.

Vietnam Tourism
30A Ly Thuong Kiet Street, Hanoi, Vietnam
Tel: (4) 826 4089/154 (English speaking) *or* 825 7532 (French speaking). Fax: (4) 825 7583.
E-mail: vntourism2@hn.vnn.vn
Website: www.vn-tourism.com

Embassy of the Socialist Republic of Vietnam
12 Victoria Road, London W8 5RD, UK
Tel: (020) 7937 1912. Fax: (020) 7937 6108.
E-mail: consular@vietnamembassy.org.uk
Website: www.vietnamembassy.org.uk
Opening hours: Mon-Fri 0900-1730; 0930-1230 (visa section).

Adventure World
Street address: Level 3, 73 Walker Street, North Sydney, NSW 2060, Australia
Postal address: PO Box 834, North Sydney, NSW 2059, Australia
Tel: (2) 8913 0755. Fax: (2) 9956 7707.
E-mail: info@adventureworld.com.au
Website: www.adventureworld.com.au

British Embassy
4th and 5th Floors, Central Building, 31 Hai Ba Trung Street, Hanoi, Vietnam
Tel: (4) 936 0500 *or* 0546 (visa/consular section).
Fax: (4) 936 0561/2.
E-mail: behanoi@hn.vnn.vn
Website: www.uk-vietnam.org

Embassy of the Socialist Republic of Vietnam
1233 20th Street, Suite 400, NW, Washington, DC 20036, USA
Tel: (202) 861 0737 *or* 2293 (consular).
Fax: (202) 861 0917.
E-mail: info@vietnamembassy-usa.org *or* consular@vietnamembassy-usa.org
Website: www.vietnamembassy-usa.org

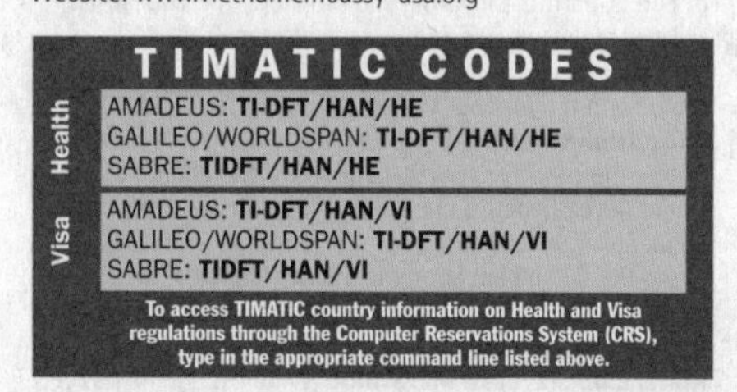
TIMATIC CODES

Health
AMADEUS: **TI-DFT/HAN/HE**
GALILEO/WORLDSPAN: **TI-DFT/HAN/HE**
SABRE: **TIDFT/HAN/HE**

Visa
AMADEUS: **TI-DFT/HAN/VI**
GALILEO/WORLDSPAN: **TI-DFT/HAN/VI**
SABRE: **TIDFT/HAN/VI**

To access TIMATIC country information on Health and Visa regulations through the Computer Reservations System (CRS), type in the appropriate command line listed above.

Embassy of the United States of America
7 Lang Ha Street, Ba Dinh District, Hanoi, Vietnam
Tel: (4) 772 1500. Fax: (4) 772 1510.
Website: http://hanoi.usembassy.gov
Consular section: Rose Garden, 6 Ngoc Khanh Street, Hanoi, Vietnam (tel: (4) 831 4590; fax: (4) 831 4578; e-mail: visahanoi@state.gov).
Embassy of the Socialist Republic of Vietnam
470 Wilbrod Street, Ottawa, Ontario K1N 6M8, Canada
Tel: (613) 236 0772 *or* 236 1398 (consular).
Fax: (613) 236 2704 *or* 0819 (consular section).
Canadian Embassy
31 Hung Vuong Street, Hanoi, Vietnam
Tel: (4) 734 5000. Fax: (4) 734 5049.
E-mail: hanoi@international.gc.ca
Consulate General in: Ho Chi Minh City.

General Information

AREA: 329,247 sq km (127,123 sq miles).
POPULATION: 78,685,800 (official estimate 2001).
POPULATION DENSITY: 239 per sq km.
CAPITAL: Hanoi. **Population:** 3,751,000 (UN estimate 2000; including suburbs).
GEOGRAPHY: Vietnam shares borders to the north with the People's Republic of China and to the west with Laos and Cambodia. The South China Sea lies to the east and south. The land is principally agricultural with a central tropical rainforest.
GOVERNMENT: Socialist republic since 1980. Gained independence from France in 1954. **Head of State:** Chairman Tran Duc Luong since 1997. **Head of Government:** Prime Minister Phan Van Khai since 1997.
LANGUAGE: Vietnamese is the official language. English, French, Chinese and occasionally Russian and German are spoken.
RELIGION: Buddhist majority. There are also Taoist, Confucian, Hoa Hao, Caodaist and Christian (predominantly Roman Catholic) minorities.
TIME: GMT + 7.
ELECTRICITY: 220/110 volts AC, 50Hz; plugs are mostly flat pin.
COMMUNICATIONS: Telephone: IDD is available. Country code: 84. Outgoing international code: 00. **Mobile telephone:** GSM 900 network. Operators include *Vietnam Posts & Communications Telecom Service (GPC)* (website: www.vnpt.com.vn) and *Viettel Mobile* (website: www.vietel.com.vn). Coverage is largely limited to main urban areas. **Fax:** Available in most post offices, hotels and businesses. **Internet:** ISPs include *Internet Vietnam* (website: www.vnn.vn). E-mail can be accessed from Internet cafes in Hanoi and Ho Chi Minh City. **Telegram:** Facilities are available in most towns. **Post:** Postal services can be slow. Airmail to Europe can take up to three weeks. **Press:** Daily and weekly newspapers in Vietnam include *Lao Dong, Nhan Dan* (The People) and *Quan Doi Nhan Dan*. The *Vietnam Economic Times, Vietnam Investment Review, Saigon Times, Vietnam Courier* and *Vietnam News* are published in English.
Radio: BBC World Service (website: www.bbc.co.uk/worldservice) and Voice of America (website: www.voa.gov) can be received. From time to time the frequencies change and the most up-to-date can be found online.

Passport/Visa

	Passport Required?	Visa Required?	Return Ticket Required?
Full British	Yes	Yes	No
Australian	Yes	Yes	No
Canadian	Yes	Yes	No
USA	Yes	Yes	No
Other EU	Yes	Yes	No
Japanese	Yes	No/1	No

Note: Regulations and requirements may be subject to change at short notice, and you are advised to contact the appropriate diplomatic or consular authority before finalising travel arrangements. Details of these may be found at the head of this country's entry. Any numbers in the chart refer to the footnotes below.

PASSPORTS: Passport valid for at least one month after expiration of visa required by all.
VISAS: Required by all except:
(a) nationals of Bulgaria, Cuba, Korea (Dem Rep) and Romania;
(b) nationals of the Russian Federation (if possessing invitation in Russian from Russian host detailing specific 'mission' involved, in which case, a visa can be obtained after seven days);
(c) nationals of China (PR) (if with passport stamped AB and visiting for specific purposes), Mongolia (if with passport stamped AB, AC or AO, and visiting for specific purposes) and Ukraine (stamped AB);

Credit: © Buffalo Tours

(d) nationals of Indonesia, Laos, Malaysia, Singapore and Thailand for stays of up to 30 days;
(e) nationals of The Philippines for stays of up to 21 days;
(f) **1.** nationals of Japan and Korea (Rep) for stays of up to 15 days;
(g) transit passengers continuing their journey within 24 hours, provided holding valid return or onward tickets. At present visas can be issued for either groups or individuals.
Note: For security reasons, it is advisable to carry copies of documents rather than originals when in Vietnam.
Types of visa and cost: *Tourist*: £38 (single-entry); £55 (express service); £70 (multiple-entry). *Single-entry Business*: £40 (one month). *Multiple-entry Business*: £70 (one month); £90 (three months); £120 (six months or more).
Validity: Tourist visas are valid for one month from proposed date of entry. Visas can usually be extended for another month, at extra cost, in the larger towns.
Note: All regulations, including those concerning which counties require visas, cost of visas and validity of visas, are very complex and subject to frequent change. It is therefore advisable to contact the Consular section at the Embassy before any travel to Vietnam.
Application to: Consulate (or Consular section at Embassy); see *Contact Addresses* section.
Application requirements: (a) Completed application form. Additional forms must be filled out by those who have never visited Vietnam before (or not within the last 36 months), and foreigners accompanying spouses, children or parents of Vietnamese nationals. (b) One passport-size photo. (c) Valid passport. (d) Fee (non-refundable), payable by cash, bank draft or postal order. To have your passport returned by post, please add £5 and include a stamped self-addressed envelope. *Business*: (a)-(d), and (e) Approval obtained through a Vietnamese sponsor.
Working days required: Two (Tourist visa express application); five (Tourist visa). Entry visas can be applied for in person up to six months prior to date of travel.

Money

Currency: New Dông (D). Notes are in denominations of D100,000, 50,000, 20,000, 10,000, 5000, 2000, 1000, 500, 200 and 100. Coins are not used.
Currency exchange: The US Dollar is the most favoured foreign currency. Australian, British, Japanese, Singaporean and Thai currency, as well as the Euro, can usually be changed in the larger cities; great difficulty may be encountered in trying to exchange any other currencies. There is a charge for changing money in banks.
Credit & debit cards: An increasing number of outlets accept MasterCard and Visa. However, outside main centres, it is wise to carry cash. Check with your credit or debit card company for details of merchant acceptability and other services which may be available.
Travellers cheques: These are widely accepted in hotels and banks. To avoid additional exchange rate charges, travellers are advised to take travellers cheques in US Dollars or Euros.
Currency restrictions: Import and export of local currency is prohibited. Import and export of foreign currency over US$3000 is subject to declaration. Proof of all expenses should be kept.
Exchange rate indicators: The following figures are included as a guide to the movements of the New Dông against Sterling and the US Dollar:

Date	Feb '04	May '04	Aug '04	Nov '04
£1.00=	30548.0	28662.6	29017.0	29886.4
$1.00=	16205.0	16268.0	15750.0	15782.0

Banking hours: Mon-Fri 0800-1630, Sat 0800-1200.

Duty Free

The following items may be freely imported into Vietnam by foreign visitors without incurring customs duty:
400 cigarettes; 100 cigars or 500g of tobacco; up to 5kg of tea and up to 3kg of coffee; 1.5l of liquor at 22 per cent and above, and 22.2l of liquor below this amount, and 3l of all other alcoholic beverages; a reasonable quantity of perfume and personal belongings; other goods not exceeding D5 million.
Prohibited items: The importation of non-prescribed drugs, firearms and pornography is prohibited.

Public Holidays

2005: Jan 1 New Year's Day. **Feb 9-11*** Têt, Lunar New Year. **Apr 30** Liberation of Saigon. **May 1** May Day. **Sep 2** National Day.
2006: Jan 1 New Year's Day. **Jan 29-31*** Têt, Lunar New Year. **Apr 30** Liberation of Saigon. **May 1** May Day. **Sep 2** National Day.
Note: *Check with the Embassy for the exact date. Visitors may experience difficulties during this period as shops, restaurants and public services close and prices tend to go up in the few shops that remain open.

Health

	Special Precautions?	Certificate Required?
Yellow Fever	Yes	1
Cholera	Yes	2
Typhoid & Polio	3	N/A
Malaria	4	N/A

Note: Regulations and requirements may be subject to change at short notice, and you are advised to contact your doctor well in advance of your intended date of departure. Any numbers in the chart refer to the footnotes below.

1: A yellow fever vaccination certificate is required from travellers over one arriving from infected areas.
2: Following WHO guidelines issued in 1973, a cholera vaccination certificate is not an official condition of entry to Vietnam. However, cholera is a serious risk in this country and precautions are essential. Up-to-date advice should be sought before deciding whether these precautions should include vaccination, as medical opinion is divided over its effectiveness. For more information, see the *Health* appendix.

Credit: © Buffalo Tours

3: Vaccination against typhoid is advised.
4: Malaria risk exists, predominantly in the *falciparum* form, throughout the year everywhere except urban areas, the Red River delta and the coastal plains of Central Vietnam. The risk is highest in the three central highlands provinces of Dak Lak, Gia Lai and Kon Tum, as well as the southern provinces of Ca Mau, Bac Lieu and Tay Ninh. The malignant *falciparum* form is reported to be highly resistant to chloroquine and sulfadoxine-pyrimethamine. The recommended prophylaxis is mefloquine.
Food & drink: All water should be regarded as being potentially contaminated. Water used for drinking, brushing teeth or making ice should have first been boiled or otherwise sterilised. Milk is unpasteurised and should be boiled. Powdered or tinned milk is available and is advised, but make sure that it is reconstituted with pure water. Avoid dairy products that are likely to have been made from unboiled milk. Only eat well-cooked meat and fish, preferably served hot. Pork, salad and mayonnaise may carry increased risk. Vegetables should be cooked and fruit peeled.
Other risks: *Bilharzia* (schistosomiasis) is present in the delta of the Mekong River. Avoid swimming and paddling in fresh water; swimming pools which are chlorinated and well maintained are safe.
Japanese encephalitis is a risk in Hanoi and in rural areas. A vaccine is available and travellers are advised to consult their doctor prior to departure. *Hepatitis A*, *B* and *E* occur; precautions should be taken. *Dengue fever* can be epidemic and *filariasis* is endemic in some rural areas. *Typhoid fever, amoebic* and *bacillary dysentry* can occur. *Trachoma* and *plague* occur rarely. Diagnoses of *avian influenza* have once again increased since December 2004, although the number infected is still minimal. All visitors are advised against close contact, and under-cooked consumption of, poultry.
Rabies is present. For those at high risk, vaccination before arrival should be considered. If you are bitten, seek medical advice without delay. For more information, consult the *Health* appendix.

Credit: © Buffalo Tours

Health care: There are hospitals in major towns and cities, and health care centres in all provinces, but facilities are limited everywhere and there is a lack of medicines. Health insurance is essential and should include cover for emergency repatriation by air. Immediate cash payment is expected for services.

Travel - International

Note: Penalties for illegal drug importation and use are severe and can include the death penalty.
There have been renewed outbreaks of avian influenza (bird flu) throughout Vietnam. Coming into contact with poultry should be avoided and care should be taken when consuming poultry dishes that the meat is sufficiently cooked.
AIR: Vietnam's national airline is *Vietnam Airlines (VN)* (website: www.vietnamairlines.com.vn). The most usual routes to Vietnam are from Bangkok, Hong Kong, Kuala Lumpur, Manila, Paris, Singapore and Taipei. Most Asian carriers have flights to Vietnam, as do *Air France* and *Qantas*.
Approximate flight times: From Hanoi to *London* is approximately 17 hours, including two hours' stopover in Bangkok.
International airports: *Noi Bai International Airport (HAN)* at Noi Bai is 45km (28 miles) north of Hanoi. Buses and metered taxis are available. The airport has basic facilities.
Tan Son Nhat International Airport (SGN) is 7km (4.5 miles) from Ho Chi Minh City. Buses and metered taxis are available.
Departure tax: US$12 (Ho Chi Minh City and Hanoi) and US$8 (Da Nang), payable in US Dollars or New Dông.
SEA: The major ports are Ho Chi Minh City, Vung Tau, Haiphong, Da Nang and Binh Thuy. International cruise facilities are available.
RAIL: It is possible to cross into China by rail from Lao Cai to Kunming in the Yunnan province of China or through Lang Son to Nanning. There are trains from Beijing-Dong Dang-Hanoi and back twice weekly.
ROAD: There are routes to Guangxi, China through Lang Son, Cambodia through Moc Bai and also to Laos at Lao Bao and Cau Trieu.
Note: It is important to remember that all Vietnamese visas are issued with a specified exit point. If this exit point needs to be altered, it must be done so at an immigration office or through a travel agent in Hanoi or Ho Chi Minh City.

Travel - Internal

AIR: *Vietnam Airlines (VN)* operates daily flights between Hanoi, Ho Chi Minh City, Hue, Da Nang and Nha Trang. Regular services are also provided between Hanoi and Ho Chi Minh City to Buon Ma Thuot, Dalat, Na San, Phu Quoc, Pleiku, Qui Nhon and Vinh. *The Northern Airport Flight Service Company* operates flights by helicopter to Halong Bay from Hanoi.
Departure Tax: D20,000 from Hanoi, Ho Chi Minh City, Hai Phong and Da Nang. D10,000 from other airports.
SEA: A local network operates between ports. Cruise facilities are available. Contact the Embassy before departure.
RAIL: Visitors may use the rail transport system independently or as part of a rail tour. Long-distance trains are more expensive but are faster, more reliable and more comfortable. Although a few carriages now have air conditioning, facilities are still short of international standards, and foreigners' rates are comparable to the air fares. The main rail route connects Hanoi and Ho Chi Minh City and the journey can take between 30 and 40 hours. There are also services from Hanoi to Haiphong, Dong Dang, Lao Cai, Thai Nguyen and from Yen Vien to Ha Long. Contact Vietnam Railways (website: www.vr.com.vn) for more information.
ROAD: There is a reasonable road network. Traffic drives on the right. Roads, especially in the north, are often in a bad state of repair and may be impassable during the rainy season. Driving in Vietnam can be a hair-raising experience as the normal rules of highway discipline are rarely followed by the majority of drivers. There is a good highway from Hanoi to Ho Chi Minh City. **Bus:** Services are poor and overcrowded. Minibuses often run between tourist hotels in the major towns. **Car hire:** It is possible to hire chauffeur-driven cars. **Documentation:** An International Driving Permit and a test (taken in Vietnam) are required.
URBAN: There are local bus services in Ho Chi Minh City and in Hanoi, which also has a tramway. It is also possible to travel by taxi, motorbike or *cyclo* (cycle rickshaw; motorised version also exists); the last of these options can leave the traveller vulnerable to theft from opportunistic passers-by and the government is trying to phase them out. When travelling by taxi, it is advisable to note down the driver's registration number (displayed on rear side of taxi) for security reasons.

Accommodation

Tourist facilities have vastly improved in the last few years and most towns have small hotels and guest-houses. In the major towns, there is a full range of accommodation to suit all budgets. For information, contact a travel operator that specialises in Vietnam *or* the Department for Hotel Management of the Vietnam National Administration of Tourism, 80 Quan Su Street, Hanoi (tel: (4) 942 1061; fax: (4) 822 4714; e-mail: vnat@vietnamtourism.com; website: www.vietnamtourism.com).

Resorts & Excursions

HANOI & THE NORTH

HANOI: The capital, Hanoi, sprawls on the banks of the **Red River**. It is a beautiful city that retains an air of French colonial elegance with pretty yellow stucco buildings lining leafy streets. Hanoi is also a city of lakes, which adds to its air of sleepy grace. At present there are relatively few cars – many people travel by bicycle or moped. Although the streets are busy, there is little congestion and pollution is not yet a problem. It is a city that appears lodged in a bygone age. In the middle of the city lies the peaceful **Hoan Kiem Lake** (Lake of the Restored Sword) with the 18th-century **Ngoc Son Temple** (Jade Mountain Temple) sitting on an island in its centre. The temple can be reached by **The Huc Bridge** (Rising Sun Bridge). To the north of Hoan Kiem Lake is the **Old Quarter**, a fascinating maze of small antiquated streets lined with markets and pavement restaurants and cafes. West of the Old Quarter and south of the West Lake is the former **Ville Française**. This is the old French administrative centre and is characterised by enormous colonial-era châteaux and wide spacious boulevards. It also houses Hanoi's most popular attraction, the **Ho Chi Minh Mausoleum**. When visiting the Mausoleum, it is important to be respectful both in dress and attitude. Ho Chi Minh was the father of the modern state and is still held in reverential regard. His house, built in 1958, is also on public view. Other museums in Hanoi include the **Bao Tang Lich Su** (History Museum), the **Bao Tang Quan Doi** (Army Museum), **Ho Chi Minh Museum**, **Bao Tang My Thuat** (Fine Arts Museum), **Bao Tang Cach Manh** (Revolutionary Museum) and **Independence Museum**. There are a number of interesting pagodas in Hanoi. The **One Pillar Pagoda**, first constructed in 1049 (subsequently destroyed by the French just before they were ejected from the city and then rebuilt by the new government), was built to resemble a lotus flower – the symbol of purity rising out of a sea of sorrow. The **Temple of Literature** built in 1076 was the first university in Vietnam. It is a graceful complex of small intricate buildings and peaceful courtyards. To the northwest of the **Citadel** is the **West Lake**, which is about 13km (9 miles) in circumference. The shores of the lake are popular amongst the Hanoians for picnics and there are a number of cafes. The lake also contains the wreckage of a crashed American B52 bomber.
ELSEWHERE: About 160km (100 miles) from Hanoi, near the port of **Haiphong**, is **Ha Long Bay**. This is an amazing complex of 3000 chalk islands rising out of the South China Sea. The area is strange, eerie and very beautiful. Many of the islands contain bizarre cave formations and grottoes. Near Ha Long Bay is **Catba Island**, a designated National Park and a rich repository of plants and wildlife.
About 250km (155 miles) north of Hanoi, high in the **Hoang Lien Mountains**, is the old hill station of **Sapa**. This area is inhabited by the Hmong and Zhao hill tribes. Every weekend there is a market when the local tribespeople come into town to trade. In the evening, they celebrate with huge amounts of potent rice alcohol. It is absolutely vital that when visiting this area tourists are sensitive to local culture and traditions. If one follows the road from Sapa 200km (125 miles) further into the mountains (this can only realistically be attempted by jeep), one reaches **Dien Bien Phu**, scene of the humiliating defeat of the French by the Viet Minh that finally put paid to French colonial occupation in Indochina. This is a wild, beautiful and remote region.

CENTRAL VIETNAM

HUE: Midway between Hanoi and Ho Chi Minh City lies the city of Hue. The former capital of the emperors of Vietnam, it is known for its beautiful imperial architecture, although a great deal of this was destroyed during the Tet offensive in 1968. **The Perfume River** forms the border between the city itself and the former 'Forbidden Purple City', the mighty **Citadel**. This 'city within a city' with its tombs, pagodas and lakes covered in lotus flowers was largely destroyed during the Vietnam War, but one can still see evidence of its former magnificence. Within easy reach of the city are the tombs of several of Vietnam's emperors. Most interesting, perhaps, are the **Tomb of Minh Mang** and the **Tomb of Tu Duc**. The city also houses fine examples of Buddhist pagodas and other temples, such as the **Thien Mu Pagoda**.
ELSEWHERE: Near Hue is **Da Nang**, city of **China Beach**, the **Marble Mountains** and the **Cham Museum**, which houses magnificent examples of the art of the Indianised Cham civilisation. Approximately 20km (12 miles) from Da Nang is **Hoi An**. This is a delightful small riverine town replete with temple and pagodas.
A day's drive from Hoi An, through some of Vietnam's most breathtaking scenery, is **Nha Trang**. This is a pleasant resort with a good beach. From here it is easy to reach the town of **Da Lat** in the Central Highlands, evocative of a typical French town, which is popular among domestic tourists for its cool climate and alpine scenery.

HO CHI MINH & THE SOUTH

HO CHI MINH CITY: Set back from the delta formed by the Mekong River, Ho Chi Minh City (formerly Saigon) is the main commercial centre of the southern part of Vietnam, receiving its name in honour of the leader who successfully led the nation against both France and the USA. Locals still like to refer to it as Saigon. More modern than other Vietnamese cities, Ho Chi Minh City has also retained its French colonial influences. Its vibrancy is maintained by the ever-entrepreneurial Saigonese who have taken the Government reforms to heart and re-embraced the capitalist ethic with unrestrained enthusiasm. The streets are jam-packed with mopeds and scooters, often carrying whole families. The markets are chaotically busy. There is a lot to see in Ho Chi Minh City. The colourful **Emperor of Jade Pagoda** is an excellent example of a Chinese temple. Inside, there are elaborate woodcarvings decorated with gilded characters and sculptures depicting local deities. The hustle and bustle of trading is best observed in the markets of **Cholon**, the ancient Chinese quarter. The **Hôtel de Ville** is a wonderful example of French colonial architecture. The **War Crimes Museum** bears witness to the suffering inflicted on the Vietnamese people during the Vietnam War in the 1960s and 1970s. Other sites relevant to that era are **Re-Unification Hall** and the former US Embassy. An interesting excursion from Saigon is a visit to the **Cu Chi Tunnels** in which the South Vietnamese Communists concealed themselves and from which they launched attacks on US soldiers.
ELSEWHERE: Northwest of Ho Chi Minh City, **Tay Ninh** is an interesting destination as it is the home of the Caodai religion. This is a purely Vietnamese sect formed this century which takes teachings and precepts from most of the world's major religions. Tay Ninh is the site of the largest Caodaist temple in Vietnam. This structure is colourful and unique.
South of Ho Chi Minh city are the flat, verdant planes of the **Mekong Delta** where much of Vietnam's rice crop is grown. There are several towns in this region from which the visitor can take boat trips on the many tributaries of the Mekong.

Sport & Activities

Cycling: Vietnam is ideal for long-distance cycling as much of the country is flat and the shortage of vehicles makes for light traffic. Caution is needed, however, especially on busier roads as traffic can be very undisciplined. Bicycle hire is widely available.
Watersports: In total, Vietnam has 3260km (2021 miles) of coastline. The most popular beaches are *Vung Tau*, just north of the Mekong Delta; and *Nha Trang*, near Da Lat, where the clear, turquoise waters offer good **snorkelling** and **scuba diving**. Snorkelling and diving equipment can be hired at most beach resorts. Other good beaches can be found at *Phan Thiet* (southcentral coast); *Mui Ne* (noted for its large sand dunes); and the magnificent *Ha Long Bay*, where some 3000 islands, covered in lush vegetation and dotted with beaches and grottoes, rise out of the Gulf of Tonkin. Access to the islands is by boats, which can be hired in Ha Long City.

Hiking: There is good hiking and **horse riding** in the beautiful countryside around Da Lat. Guides are recommended and can be hired locally. Generally, the northwest is the best region for hiking. Other good destinations include *Bach Ma National Park*, *Cuc Phuong National Park* (near Hanoi) and *Lang Bian Mountain* (in Da Lat), where guides are compulsory. In the north, *Ba Be Lake National Park* (which contains several lakes, waterfalls and caves) and *Cat Ba National Park* on Cat Ba Island also offer beautiful scenery.
Other: Caving enthusiasts may head for the spectacular *Pong Nha* river caves, northwest of Dong Hoi. **Boat trips** are particularly popular in the *Mekong Delta*, Vietnam's southernmost region, which consists of an intricate network of rice paddies, swamps and forests interlaced with canals and rivers. River cruises also operate on the *Saigon River* (a good way to see Saigon) or the *Perfume River* (near Hue). There are opportunities for visitors to see some of the **Vietnam War sights**. It is possible to walk part of the *Ho Chi Minh Trail*, a series of roads, trails and paths used as supply routes by the North Vietnamese during the war. It ran from North Vietnam southward through the Truong Son mountains and into western Laos. The claustrophobic network of tunnels used by villagers and guerrillas during the war at Cu Chi (35km/22 miles from Ho Chi Minh City) and Vinh Moc can also be visited.

Social Profile

FOOD & DRINK: Vietnamese cooking is varied and usually very good. It is a mixture of Vietnamese, Chinese and French traditions, with a plethora of regional specialities. As in all countries of the region, rice or noodles usually provide the basis of a meal. Not surprisingly, fish is plentiful. Breakfast is generally noodle soup locally known as *pho* (pronounced 'fur'). French-style baguettes are available throughout Vietnam. Local specialities include *nem* (pork mixed with noodles, eggs and mushrooms wrapped in rice paper, fried and served hot) and *banh chung* (glutinous rice, pork and onions wrapped in large leaves and cooked for up to 48 hours, to be eaten cold at any time). Vietnamese dishes are not complete without *nuoc mam* (a fish sauce) or *mam tom* (a shrimp sauce). Western-style cooking is on offer wherever tourists or business people are found in any numbers.
Green tea is refreshing and available everywhere. Apart from baguettes, the French culinary legacy also embraces rich, fresh, filter coffee, usually brewed on the table in front of the customer. Vietnamese often have a fondness for beer; it is possible to get both local and imported brands. When in Hanoi, it is worth trying the local draught beer available at street stalls. It is called *Bia Hoi* and is not only cheap, but free of additives. *Rice wine* is also a favourite throughout the country. It is generally extremely potent.
SHOPPING: Local specialities include lacquer painting, reed mats, embroidery, tailor-made *ao dais* (female national costume) and mother-of-pearl inlay on ornaments and furniture, not to mention the ubiquitous conical hat. **Shopping hours:** Mon-Sun 0730-1200 and 1300-1630.
SPECIAL EVENTS: Most regions, particularly where the minority groups live, have their own traditional festivals incorporating music, opera and dance. *Têt* (Lunar New Year) and important Buddhist festivals are celebrated during February and March each year. Although celebrated, Buddhist and Christian festivals are not considered national holidays. The following is a selection of special events occurring in 2005:
Feb 1-3 *Têt Festival* (Lunar New Year celebrations), nationwide. **Feb 9-11** *Mai Dong Festival*, Hai Ba Trang. **Feb 27-May 18** *Perfume Pagoda Festival*, Juong Son Village. **Apr 28-May 8** *Elephant Races*, Don Village. **Jun 2** *Buddha's Birthday*. **Jun 10-12** *Ba Chua Xu Temple Festival*, Chau Doc. **Sep 1-10** *Kate Festival*. **Sep 22-23** *Do Son Buffalo Fights*, Haiphong. **Sep 28** *Mid-Autumn Festival*, nationwide. **Oct 26-28** *Keo Pagoda Festival*, Thai Binh.
SOCIAL CONVENTIONS: Handshaking and a vocal greeting is normal. Clothing should be kept simple, informal and discreet. Avoid shorts if possible as they are usually only worn by children. Footwear should be removed when entering Buddhist pagodas. Vietnamese people should not be touched on the head. **Photography:** There are restrictions at ports, airports and harbours, and in similar areas elsewhere. It is courteous to ask permission first before taking photographs of people. **Tipping:** Officially prohibited but widely practised, especially in the south. Discretion is advised.

Business Profile

ECONOMY: The economy of Vietnam was devastated by 30 years of war up to 1975, after which, policy errors and a USA-enforced trade boycott combined to stifle development. Since the end of the boycott in 1994, and the introduction of liberalising and deregulating measures by the Government, the Vietnamese economy underwent significant growth of around 8 to 9 per cent annually. The 1997 Asian financial crisis put a temporary brake on the economy but annual growth has since recovered to 7.2 per cent in 2003; inflation was 5.5 per cent in the first quarter of 2004, and unemployment estimated at 7 per cent. Agriculture remains the principal employer in Vietnam and produces 25 per cent of total output. Rice, of which Vietnam is the world's second-largest exporter (after Thailand), is the staple crop. Other cash crops include sugar cane, coffee, rubber, tea, cotton and groundnuts. Timber was once exploited on a large scale but the industry was cut back throughout the 1990s prior to a total ban in 1997. Oil, coal and natural gas are present in significant quantities, along with deposits of tin, zinc, antimony, chromium and gold. The oil and gas fields are mostly offshore and of relatively low quality, but after steady growth during the 1990s, it now accounts for 16 per cent of Vietnam's industrial output. The remainder of the industrial sector is devoted to the production of textiles, chemicals, processed foods and machinery. The industrial sector, whose annual growth has averaged over 10 per cent since 1995, now accounts for 25 per cent of GDP.
The ending of the US embargo in 1994 allowed Vietnam to join institutions such as the World Bank and IMF, as well as giving access to the wider international financial system. The banking and finance sector has undergone rapid growth in the last few years, and the government has belatedly realised the importance of modernising what is a fairly primitive system. Similar considerations apply to Vietnam's relatively poor infrastructure and the archaic condition of many of its state-owned industries. A recent trade agreement with Washington is likely to boost foreign investment in Vietnam. Vietnam is a member of the Asian Development Bank and has signed the ASEAN Free Trade Agreement. Japan, Singapore and Hong Kong are Vietnam's principal trading partners, followed by France and Germany.
BUSINESS: Smart lightweight casuals would usually be worn for meetings as suits are needed for only the most formal occasions. English is not spoken by all officials and a knowledge of French will be useful. Business cards should have a Vietnamese translation on the back. **Office hours:** Mon-Sat 0730-1200 and 1300-1630.
COMMERCIAL INFORMATION: The following organisation can offer advice: Vietcochamber (Chamber of Industry and Commerce of Vietnam), 4th Floor, 9 Dao Duy Anh Street, Hanoi (tel: (4) 574 3985; fax: (4) 574 3063; e-mail: vbfhn@hn.vnn.vn *or* vcci@fmail.vnn.vn; website: www.vcci.com.vn).

Climate

Because of its geography, the climate in Vietnam varies greatly from north to south. Tropical monsoons occur from May to October. It is almost totally dry throughout the rest of the year.
Required clothing: Tropicals and washable cottons are worn all year. Rainwear is essential during the rainy season.

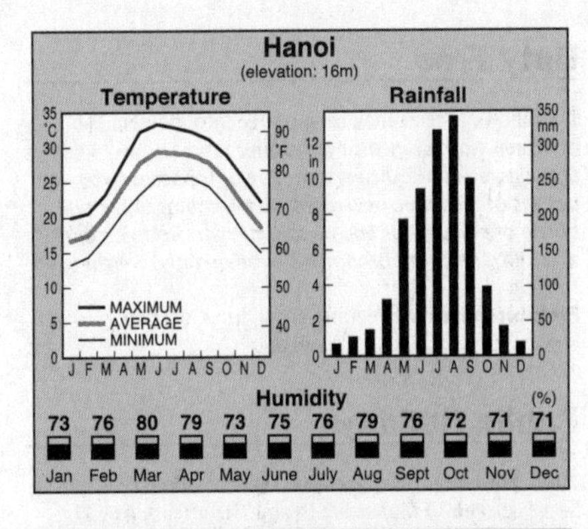

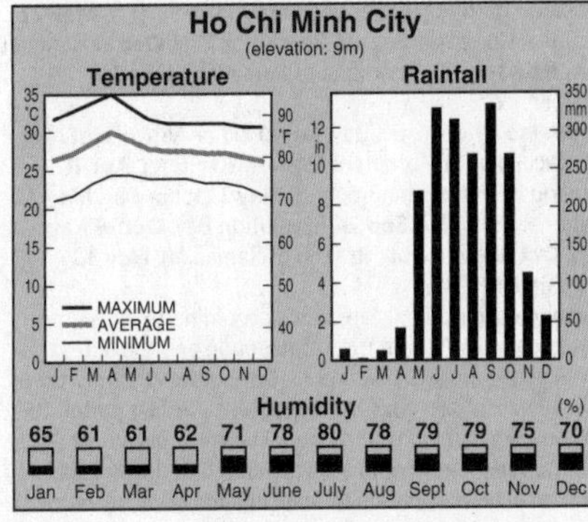

Republic of Yemen

LATEST TRAVEL ADVICE CONTACTS

British Foreign and Commonwealth Office
Tel: (0870) 606 0290 Website: www.fco.gov.uk
US Department of State
Website: http://travel.state.gov/travel
Canadian Department of Foreign Affairs and Int'l Trade
Tel: (1 800) 267 8376 Website: www.dfait-maeci.gc.ca

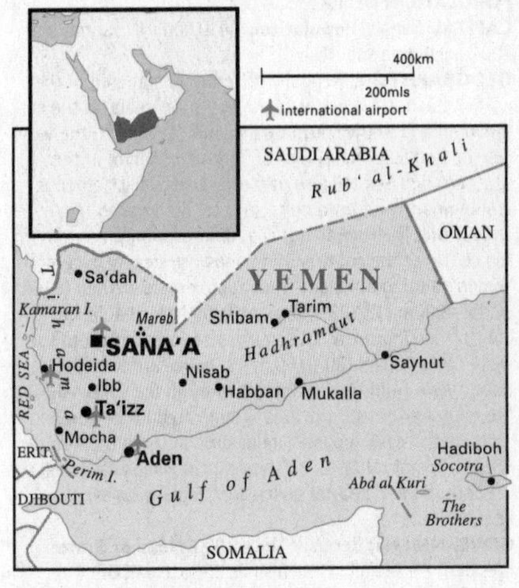

Location: Middle East, Arabian Peninsula.

Country dialling code: 967.

General Authority of Tourism, Yemen
PO Box 129, Sana'a, Republic of Yemen
Tel: (1) 252 319. Fax: (1) 252 316.
E-mail: mkt@yenet.com *or* info@gtda.gov.ye
Yemen Tourism Promotion Board
48 Hadda Street, PO Box 5607, Sana'a, Republic of Yemen
Tel (510) 794 1516. Fax: (510) 794 447.
E-mail: yementpb@y.net.ye
Website: www.yementourism.com
Embassy of the Republic of Yemen
57 Cromwell Road, London SW7 2ED, UK
Tel: (020) 7584 6607 *or* 7581 4039 (consular section).
Fax: (020) 7589 3350.
Website: www.yemenembassy.org.uk
Opening hours: Mon-Fri 0900-1600; 1000-1400 (visa section).
British Embassy
Street address: Abu-al-Hasan-al-Hamadani Street (Hadda Street), Sana'a, Republic of Yemen
Postal address: PO Box 1287, Sana'a, Republic of Yemen
Tel: (1) 264 081/2/3/4. Fax: (1) 263 059.
E-mail: visaenquiries.sanaa@fco.gov.uk *or* BritishEmbassySanaa@fco.gov.uk
Website: www.britishembassy.gov.uk/yemen
British Consulate General
Street address: 20 Miswat Road, Khormaksar, Aden, Republic of Yemen
Postal address: PO Box 6304, Khormaksar, Aden, Republic of Yemen
Tel: (2) 232 712/3/4/5. Fax: (2) 231 256.
E-mail: consularenquiries.sanaa@fco.gov.uk
Embassy of the Republic of Yemen
2319 Wyoming Avenue, NW, Washington, DC 20008, USA
Tel: (202) 965 4760.
Fax: (202) 337 2017.
E-mail: information@yemenembassy.org
Website: www.yemenembassy.org
Embassy of the United States of America
Street address: Sa'awan Street, Sheraton Hotel District, Himyar Zone, Sana'a, Republic of Yemen
Postal address: PO Box 22347, Sana'a, Republic of Yemen
Tel: (1) 303 155-9.
Fax: (1) 303 160-5.
Website: http://yemen.usembassy.gov

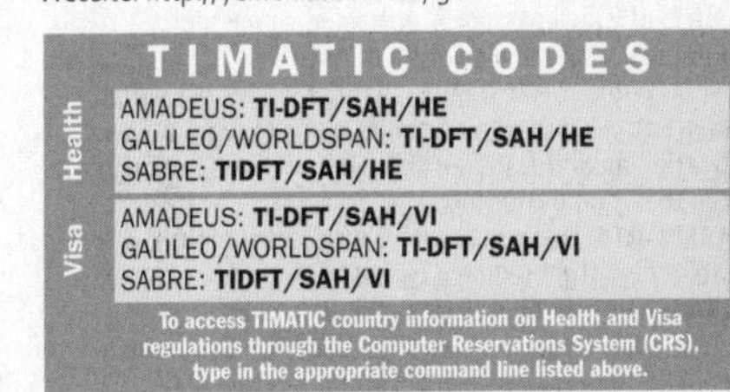

TIMATIC CODES

Health	AMADEUS: **TI-DFT/SAH/HE** GALILEO/WORLDSPAN: **TI-DFT/SAH/HE** SABRE: **TIDFT/SAH/HE**
Visa	AMADEUS: **TI-DFT/SAH/VI** GALILEO/WORLDSPAN: **TI-DFT/SAH/VI** SABRE: **TIDFT/SAH/VI**

To access TIMATIC country information on Health and Visa regulations through the Computer Reservations System (CRS), type in the appropriate command line listed above.

Embassy of the Republic of Yemen
788 Island Park Drive, Ottawa, Ontario K1Y 0C2, Canada
Tel: (613) 729 6627. Fax: (613) 729 8915.
E-mail: info@yemenincanada.ca *or* consular@yemenincanada.ca (consular section).
Website: www.yemenincanada.ca
The Canadian Embassy in Riyadh normally deals with enquiries relating to Yemen (see *Saudi Arabia* section).

General Information

AREA: 536,869 sq km (207,286 sq miles).
POPULATION: 19,000,000 (official estimate 2003).
POPULATION DENSITY: 36 per sq km
CAPITAL: Sana'a. **Population:** 1,410,000 (UN estimate 2001; including suburbs).
GEOGRAPHY: The Republic of Yemen is bordered in the northwest, north and northeast by Saudi Arabia, in the east by Oman and in the south by the Gulf of Aden. To the west lies the Red Sea. The islands of Perim and Karam in the southern Red Sea are also part of the Republic. Yemen is predominantly mountainous, supporting terraced agriculture. The Hadramaut is a range of high mountains in the centre of the country. Highlands rise steeply in central Yemen, ranging in height from approximately 200m (656ft) to the 4000m (13,123ft) peak of Jabal Nabi Shauib. In contrast is *Tihama*, a flat semi-desert coastal plain to the west, 50 to 100km (30 to 60 miles) wide. Surface water flows down from the mountains through the valleys during the rainy season and the area is cultivated for cotton and grain. In the east, the mountains drop away to the *Rub al-Khali* or 'Empty Quarter' of the Arabian Peninsula, a vast sea of sand. The arid coastal plains are fringed with sandy beaches.
GOVERNMENT: Republic since 1990. **Head of State:** President Ali Abdullah Saleh since 1990. **Head of Government:** Prime Minister Abdul Bajammal since 2001.
LANGUAGE: Arabic. English is widely spoken as a second language.
RELIGION: Sunni Muslim (especially in the north) and Shia Muslim, with some small Christian and Hindu communities. There is also a small Jewish minority.
TIME: GMT + 3.
ELECTRICITY: 220/230 volts AC, 50Hz.
COMMUNICATIONS: Telephone: IDD is available in parts of the country. Country code: 967. Outgoing international code: 00. **Mobile telephone:** GSM 900 network. Operators include *Spacetel* and *Yemen Mobile Phone Company*. **Fax:** Some hotels have facilities. **Internet:** ISPs include *TeleYemen* (website: www.y.net.ye). There are Internet cafes in Mukalla and Sana'a. **Telegram:** Facilities are available. *Yemen Telecommunications Company* has offices at Steamer Point (24 hours) and at Crater. **Post:** Airmail to Western Europe from Sana'a takes about four days; mail to and from other towns may take longer. Post office hours: Sat-Thurs 0800-1400 and 1600-2000. **Press:** Daily and weekly Arabic newspapers include *26 September*, *Al-Jumhuriaya* and *Ath-Thawra*. *The Yemen Observer* and *The Yemen Times* are published in English. **Radio:** BBC World Service (website: www.bbc.co.uk/worldservice) and Voice of America (website: www.voa.gov) can be received. From time to time the frequencies change and the most up-to-date can be found online.

Passport/Visa

	Passport Required?	Visa Required?	Return Ticket Required?
Full British	Yes	Yes	No
Australian	Yes	Yes	No
Canadian	Yes	Yes	No
USA	Yes	Yes	No
Other EU	Yes	Yes	No
Japanese	Yes	Yes	No

Note: *Regulations and requirements may be subject to change at short notice, and you are advised to contact the appropriate diplomatic or consular authority before finalising travel arrangements. Details of these may be found at the head of this country's entry. Any numbers in the chart refer to the footnotes below.*

Restricted entry and transit: The Government of the Republic of Yemen refuses entry and transit facilities to holders of Israeli passports, or holders of passports containing visas valid or expired for Israel or any indication, such as entry or exit stamps, that the holder has visited Israel. Entry is also refused to nationals of Algeria, Egypt, Libya, Sudan and Tunisia if their journey does not originate from their home country.
PASSPORTS: Passport valid for at least six months after date of departure required by all.
VISAS: Required by all except the following:
(a) nationals of Egypt, Iraq, Jordan and the Syrian Arab Republic;
(b) transit passengers continuing their journey by the same or first connecting aircraft, provided holding valid onward or return documentation and not leaving the airport within 48 hours.
Types of visa and cost: *Tourist/Visitor* (Single-entry): £40. *Business*: £50 (Single-entry); £120 (six month Multiple-entry); £220 (one year Multiple-entry). *Transit*: £40.
Validity: *Single-entry*: two months from date of issue for stays of up to one month; *Mutiple-entry*: six months *or* one year from date of issue for stays of up to one month each.
Application to: Consulate (or Consular section at Embassy); see *Contact Addresses* section.
Application requirements: (a) Two completed application forms. (b) Two passport-size photos. (c) Return air ticket. (d) Valid passport. (e) Fee (if applying in the UK, the fee must be paid at a branch of HSBC and proof of payment must be presented with visa application). (f) An airline ticket in and out of Yemen. (g) Stamped, self-addressed envelope for postal applications. (h) For tourist visits, letter from travel company organising the trip. Group travel must be organised through a travel company in Yemen. (i) For business visits, an invitation from the applicant's company explaining the purpose of the visit and the nature of the business. (j) For multiple-entry visas, a letter from a company in Yemen.
Working days required: Three. If applying by post, processing will normally take five days.

Money

Currency: Yemeni Riyal (YR) = 100 fils. Notes are in denominations of YR1000, 500, 200, 100, 50, 20 and 10. Coins are in denominations of 10 and 5 fils.
Currency exchange: Local currency can easily be reconverted. There are very few ATMs. US dollars in cash are the easiest convertible currency.
Credit & debit cards: Cards generally have limited acceptance; American Express and Diners Club are the most widely accepted. Check with your credit or debit card company for details of merchant acceptability and other services which may be available.
Travellers cheques: Can be exchanged at some banks and hotels. To avoid additional exchange rate charges, travellers are advised to take travellers cheques in Pounds Sterling.
Currency restrictions: Import and export of local currency up to YR2000 for residents, and prohibited for non-residents. There are no restrictions on the import of foreign currencies but amounts exceeding US$3000 should be declared on arrival. Export of foreign currency is permitted up to the amount imported and declared.
Exchange rate indicators: The following figures are included as a guide to the movements of the Yemeni Riyal against Sterling and the US Dollar:

Date	Feb '04	May '04	Aug '04	Nov '04
£1.00=	335.56	325.19	340.44	350.86
$1.00=	178.01	184.57	184.79	185.28

Banking hours: Sat-Wed 0830-1200, Thurs 0800-1130.

Duty Free

The following items may be imported into the Republic of Yemen without incurring customs duty:
600 cigarettes or 60 cigars or 450g of tobacco; two bottles of alcoholic beverages (non-Muslims only); one bottle of perfume or eau de toilette; gifts up to a value of YR100,000; gold ornaments (women only) weighing up to 350g.
Prohibited items: Firearms, illegal drugs, obscene literature, all products of Israeli origin.

Public Holidays

2005: Jan 1 New Year's Day. **Jan 21** Eid al-Adha (Feast of the Sacrifice). **Feb 10** Muharram (Islamic New Year). **Apr 21** Mouloud (Birth of the Prophet. **May 1** Labour Day. **May 22** National Unity Day. **Sep 26** Revolution Day. **Oct 14** National Day. **Nov 3-5** Eid al-Fitr (End of Ramadan). **Nov 30** Independence Day.
2006: Jan 1 New Year's Day. **Jan 10** Eid al-Adha (Feast of the Sacrifice). **Jan 31** Muharram (Islamic New Year). **Apr 11** Mouloud (Birth of the Prophet). **May 1** Labour Day. **May 22** National Unity Day. **Sep 26** Revolution Day. **Oct 14** National Day. **Oct 22-24** Eid al-Fitr (End of Ramadan). **Nov 30** Independence Day.
Note: Muslim festivals are timed according to local sightings of various phases of the moon and the dates given above are approximations. During the lunar month of Ramadan that precedes Eid al-Fitr, Muslims fast during the day and feast at night and normal business patterns may be interrupted. Many restaurants are closed during the day and there may be restrictions on smoking and drinking. Some disruption may continue into Eid al-Fitr itself. Eid al-Fitr and Eid al-Adha may last anything from two to 10 days, depending on the region. For more information, see the *World of Islam* appendix.

Health

	Special Precautions?	Certificate Required?
Yellow Fever	No	1
Cholera	No	No
Typhoid & Polio	2	N/A
Malaria	3	N/A

Note: *Regulations and requirements may be subject to change at short notice, and you are advised to contact your doctor well in advance of your intended date of departure. Any numbers in the chart refer to the footnotes below.*

1: A yellow fever vaccination certificate is required from travellers over one year of age arriving from infected areas.
2: Vaccination against typhoid is advised.
3: Malaria risk, almost exclusively in the malignant *falciparum* form, exists throughout the year (but mainly from September through February) in the whole country below 2000m. However, there is no risk in Sana'a City. Resistance to chloroquine has been reported. Chloroquine plus proguanil is recommended.
Food & drink: Where mains water is chlorinated, it may cause mild abdominal upsets; supplies in Sana'a are said to be safe. Bottled water is available and is advised for the first few weeks of the stay. Drinking water outside main cities and towns is likely to be contaminated and sterilisation is considered essential. Water used for drinking, brushing teeth or making ice should have first been boiled or otherwise sterilised. Milk is unpasteurised and should be boiled. Avoid dairy products that are likely to have been made from unboiled milk. Only eat well-cooked meat and fish, preferably served hot. Salad and mayonnaise may carry increased risk. Vegetables should be cooked and fruit peeled.
Other risks: *Cutaneous leishmaniasis* exists throughout the area and *visceral leishmaniasis* may occur in the west of Yemen. *Bilharzia* (schistosomiasis) is present. Avoid swimming and paddling in fresh water; swimming pools which are well chlorinated and maintained are safe. *Typhoid fever*, *dracunculiasis*, *onchocerciasis* and *hepatitis A* occur; *hepatitis B* is endemic. The altitude may cause health problems.
Rabies is present. For those at high risk, vaccination before arrival should be considered. If you are bitten, seek medical advice without delay. For more information, see the *Health* appendix.
Health care: Health care facilities are relatively poor, especially outside major cities. The major hospitals in Sana'a are: Al Jumhuriyya, Al Kuwait and Al Thawra. In Aden, there is the Al Jumhuriyya, the Saudi Hospital and the Refinery Hospital. Most large cities have a general hospital. There is no reciprocal health agreement with the UK. Medical insurance is essential.

Travel - International

Travel warning: All travel to the area around Saada in northern Yemen is advised against, primarily due to heavy fighting that has occurred there since June 20 2004. The Yemen Tourist Police are discouraging individual travel outside Sana'a and require all such travellers to apply for permission. There is still considered to be a continuing high threat from terrorism and that, in particular, international terrorists are targeting western - including British - interests in Yemen.
AIR: The Republic of Yemen's national airline is *Yemen Airways (Yemenia) (IY)* (website: www.yemenia.com).
Approximate flight times: From London to *Sana'a* is 10 hours (direct) and to *Aden* is nine hours, excluding stopover time.
International airports: *Sana'a (SAH)* (El-Rahaba) is 13km (8 miles) north of the city (travel time – 30 minutes). Transport to the city centre is by taxi. Airport facilities include a bank/bureau de change, duty free shop, baggage facilities and restaurants, as well as car hire.
Taiz (TAI) (al-Janad) is 4km (2.5 miles) from the city (travel time – 10 minutes). Taxis, buses and car hire are available.
Hodaidah (HOD) is 8km (5 miles) from the city. Taxis, buses and car hire are available.
Aden (ADE) (Khormaksar) is 11km (7 miles) from the city (travel time – 20 minutes). Limited bus and taxi services available.
Departure tax: None.
SEA: The main international ports are Aden, Hodaidah, Mokha, Mukalla and Nashton. Cargo vessels with passenger berths call at Hodeida.
ROAD: Driving to Yemen is not recommended but there are routes from Jeddah, Mecca and Riyadh (in Saudi Arabia) to Sana'a.

Travel - Internal

AIR: *Yemen Airways (IY)* operates services between Sana'a, Ta'izz and Hodeida. There are also flights from Aden. It is advisable to double-check flight reservations and times before departure.
Departure tax: None.
SEA: Local ferries connect local ports. For details, contact port authorities.
ROAD: There are approximately 5000km (3125 miles) of asphalt roads and 20,000km (12,500 miles) of feeder roads. Road conditions and driving standards are quite poor and many roads are in a state of disrepair, with mountain roads particularly hazardous. The Ministry of Housing, Construction and Urban Planning is now supervising a redevelopment and reconstruction plan for Yemen's road network. Within Sana'a and from Ta'izz to Mokha, the roads are reliable. From Aden to Ta'izz is three to five hours' driving time. A road links Aden and Sana'a, otherwise the road network is mainly limited to desert tracks. Use of 4-wheel drive vehicles and a guide is recommended. There is a road from Aden to Mukalla of 500km (310 miles). Traffic drives on the right. **Bus:** There are regular intercity bus services. The General Authority of Tourism (see *Contact Addresses* section) runs landcruisers and tourist coaches to all towns. **Taxi:** Recognisable by yellow licence plates. Taxi-sharing is the cheapest transport between cities. There are minimum charges within main cities but fares should be negotiated beforehand for intercity journeys. **Car hire:** Available in main towns; 4-wheel drive is recommended. Chauffeur-driven cars are also available. **Documentation:** An International Driving Permit is required. A temporary licence valid for three months is available from local authorities on presentation of a valid national licence.
TRAVEL TIMES: The following chart gives approximate travel times (in hours and minutes) from **Sana'a** to other major cities/towns in the Republic of Yemen.

	Air	Road
Ta'izz	**0.45**	**3.30**
Hodeida	**0.40**	**3.00**
Aden	**0.45**	**4.30**

Accommodation

HOTELS: Accommodation varies from ancient palace hotels and modern luxury hotels to *funduks* and tribal huts. It is necessary to book in advance and to receive a written confirmation. Winter and summer rates are the same. All bills are subject to a 10 to 15 per cent service charge. Standards range from basic to 5-star. The best hotels are located in Hodeida, Mareb, Sana'a, Ta'izz and Tawahi (Aden). There are also hotels at Jaar, Mukalla (al-Shaab), Mukheiras, Seiyyum (al-Salaam) and Shihr (al-Sharq). Outside the main centres, facilities are limited. Contact a travel agent *or* the General Authority of Tourism for further details (see *Contact Addresses* section).
CAMPING: Khokha and Mokha have campsites; details may be obtained from local travel agents in Sana'a.

Resorts & Excursions

The Republic of Yemen is the least known and, in many ways, the most spectacular region of all Arabia. As much of the Central Highlands rise over 3000m (10,000ft), travellers should be prepared for the high altitudes. The attraction of the Republic of Yemen for the visitor is largely its striking scenery, spectacular Islamic and pre-Islamic architecture and the deep sense of the past. Tours are available within and around the major cities; enquire at local travel agents for details.

SANA'A & AREA

SANA'A: This area has been intensely cultivated for centuries and is the site of many of the major towns. **Sana'a**, the modern capital and long an important citadel along the trade route between Aden and Mecca, dates back to the first century and, according to popular legend, to early biblical days. The citadel, **Qasr al-Silah**, was rebuilt after the arrival of Islam in the seventh century and is still intact. The old centre is surrounded by the remains of the city walls, which can be seen in the south along **Zuberi Street** before **Bab al-Yemen**, in the east along **Mount Nugum** starting from the walls of the citadel, and in the north on the road from **Bab Sha'oob** to **Taherir Square**. The 1000-year-old **Bab al-Yemen Market** is divided into 40 different crafts and trades. The spice market is one of the best to visit, standing out from the rest by the rich aroma of incense and famed Arabian spices. Other markets include the **Souk al-Nahaas**, once the copper market, now selling embroidered head-dresses, belts and **jambias** (curved daggers). The **Great Mosque of Sana'a** is the oldest and largest of the mosques in Sana'a and one of the oldest in the Muslim world, constructed in the lifetime of the Prophet and enlarged in AD 705. The layout is typical of early Islamic architecture, with an open, square courtyard, surrounded by roofed galleries. The **National Museum** is located in Taherir Square in **Dar al-Shukr** (or the 'Palace of Gratefulness'); it contains engravings of pre-Islamic times, bronze statues, a beautiful **mashrabia** (cooling place for water) and several examples of folk art. It offers a good view of Taherir Square and the **Muttawakelite Estate** from the roof.
ELSEWHERE: Some 8km (5 miles) north of Sana'a is **Rawdha**, a garden city famous for its sweet grapes, the mosque built by Ahmed ibn al-Qasim and the **Rawdha Palace**, now used as a hotel. **Amran**, north of Rawdha, lies on the edge of the fertile basin of **al-Bawn**. The city is surrounded by the old clay city walls of pre-Islamic, Sabean origin. **Hajjah** is a day's journey to the west of Sana'a. The countryside is made up of high mountains and large valleys, including the **Wadi Sherez**, 1000m (3280ft), and **Kohlan**, 2400m (7875ft). Hajjah itself is a citadel, situated on the central hill of Hajjah, famous for underground prison cells used by the Imams. **Hadda Mountain**, south of Sana'a, is dotted with villages and orchards growing apricots, peaches, walnuts and almonds. The village of Hadda has two old Turkish mills. **Wadi Dhar**, 10km (6 miles) from Sana'a, is an idyllic valley filled with grapes, pomegranates and citrus fruits, surrounded by a barren plateau. **Shibam**, 36km (22 miles) from Sana'a, is a pre-Islamic settlement, protected by the great fortification of **Koukaban**.

THE WEST & SOUTHWEST

TA'IZZ: The city of Ta'izz lies in the south at an altitude of 1400m (4590ft). The old city has been all but swallowed up by the fast-growing modern city around it but beautiful old houses and mosques remain within the line of the 13th-century city wall, which is still intact along the southern side. To the north, only the gates of **Bab Musa** and **al-Bab al-Kabir** remain. The southern wall offers a splendid view of Ta'izz. **Al-Qahera**, within the city walls, is the fortress and the oldest part of the city. **Al-Ashrafiya** and **al-Mudhaffar** are two of the most beautiful mosques in Yemen. The museum in the **Palace of Imam Ahmed** contains the personal effects of the last Imam, and has preserved the spirit of Yemen from before the beginning of the Republic. The **Salah Palace**, to the east just outside the city, is another museum of the royal family. The **Souk Ta'izz** sells a variety of goods, including silverware and carpets. **Mount Saber** is 18km (11 miles) from Ta'izz and offers a breathtaking view of the city and the Ta'izz basin. A heavy-duty vehicle is needed to drive to the top. The mountain rises to an altitude of 3000m (9840ft) and the weather can be very cold.
THE RED SEA COAST: Mokha is an old Himyarite port on the Red Sea. In the 17th and 18th centuries, Mokha enjoyed a boom period exporting coffee, which was becoming fashionable in Europe (particularly Amsterdam and Venice, where the first coffee houses were opened). Coffee was later cultivated elsewhere and Mokha fell into decline. In recent years, the Government has improved the harbour and communications within Mokha in an attempt to resurrect this once-prosperous city. **Hodeida** is reached via the mountains of **Manakha**. A modern city port on the **Red Sea**, the harbour itself was completed in 1961. There is little here of historical interest apart from the fish market, where fishing boats have been built from wood in the same way for hundreds of years.
ELSEWHERE: The **Tihama** in the west has a negligible rainfall and is predominantly hot, humid and sparsely populated. The road south from Sana'a to Ta'izz runs through extremely mountainous countryside and passes the towns of **Dhofar**, the ancient capital of the Himyarites (115 BC–AD 525), and **Ibb**, a once-important stopping point on the Sana'a to Ta'izz road. Remains of the city walls and an aqueduct can still be seen. The **Sumara Pass**, at an altitude of 2700m (8860ft), gives a spectacular panoramic view over the **Yarim** and **Dhamar** basins.
Along another route, running roughly parallel to the Red Sea coast, **Beit al-Faqih**, 60km (37 miles) inland from Hodeida, has a good craft market. **Manakha**, once a road station for the Ottoman Turks, is situated on a saddle of the **Haraz Mountains**. Traditional Ismaeli villages lie to the east. This area is exceptionally good for hiking.

THE NORTH

SA'DAH: The walled city of Sa'dah was once an iron mining and tanning centre and an important station along the Himyarite Sana'a–Mecca trade route. Later, Sa'dah was chosen as the capital of the Zaydi state and became the centre of Zaydi learning. The **al-Hadi Mosque** is still an important institution for education in Zaydism. It is possible to walk along the top of the city walls, which afford good views of the city. The **Najran Gate** in the north is the most interesting of the gates, protected by an alleyway leading to the doors. The **Great Mosque** is the central building in the city. The market sells traditional stone necklaces and some fine silverware. The **Sa'dah Fortress** is the seat of the provincial government, thickly walled, and once the Imam's residence. Outside the city is the **Zaydi Graveyard**, filled with some of the most beautiful gravestones in Yemen. The **Sad'ah Basin** is strikingly fertile, providing Yemen's early crops of grapes, and is excellent for walking and hiking.
MAREB: Once the capital of the kingdom of Sheba, Mareb is now largely in a state of disrepair. Blocks of stone with Sabean writing bear testament to the history of the city. Southwest of Mareb is the ancient **Mareb Dam**, used thousands of years ago to irrigate the surrounding land. The dam fell into disuse around AD 570, after which large numbers of people emigrated northwards. The stonework is impressive, measuring 600m (1968ft) wide and 18m (60ft) deep.
ELSEWHERE: Between Sana'a and Sa'dah in the north lies the **Wadi Wa'aar**. The climate here is subtropical, and mangoes, papayas and bananas grow freely. Out of this rises the **Shahara**, a huge mountain massif, the highest point being nearly 3000m (9840ft) above sea level. This can be climbed by foot or by 4-wheel drive car; **Shahara City** offers overnight accommodation. **Shahara Bridge**, built in the 17th century, connects two mountains and can still be crossed by foot.
The **Eastern Mountains** (al-Mashrik) slope down from an altitude of 3000m to 1100m (9840ft to 3610ft). The landscape gradually turns to sand dunes where the population decreases; agriculture is concentrated around wadies.

ADEN

The history of **Aden** as a port goes back a long way; it is mentioned in the Biblical *Book of Ezekiel* (c. 6th century BC). There is a collection of pre-Islamic artefacts in the **National Museum of Antiquities** near Tawahi Harbour. **Crater**, the oldest part of the city, lies in the crater of an extinct volcano and is where the most ancient constructions in Aden may be seen. These are the **Aden Tanks**, manmade reservoirs, partly cut out of the rock, with a storage capacity of 50,000,000 litres. When it rains, the upper basins fill up first and then overflow into the lower basins. Also in Crater may be found the **Ethnographical Museum** and the **Military Museum**. The 14th-century **Mosque of Sayyid Abdullah al-Aidrus** commemorates the patron saint of Aden. In **Ma'allah**, the visitor can see traditional Arab boats. To the south of Aden is **Little Aden**, also in the crater of an extinct volcano; this is an area of small fishing villages in sheltered bays, with several superb beaches fringing the Indian Ocean.

Sport & Activities

General: The Haraz Mountains and al-Mahwit are good **trekking** locations. **Diving** is increasingly popular in the Red and Arabian seas, as is **sailing**. **Fishing** is also a possibility.

Social Profile

FOOD & DRINK: Hotel restaurants serve both Oriental and Western dishes, particularly Chinese and Indian. There are a few independent restaurants serving international and Arab cuisine. Seafood is particularly recommended, as is *haradha* (a mincemeat and pepper dish). Also *marag lahm* (meat soup), *hanid* (lamb meat cooked in typical oven with spices) and *kabsa* (rice with lamb meat) should not be missed. Alcohol is not generally available but may be served in hotels. It is illegal to buy alcohol for a Yemeni citizen. Tourists are advised to respect Muslim customs and traditions.
NIGHTLIFE: This is generally centred on the major hotels.
SHOPPING: *Souks* (markets) are interesting places to shop and buy handicrafts. Purchases include *foutah* (national costume), leather goods, *jambia* (daggers), candlesticks, scarves (woven with gold thread), amber beads, brightly coloured cushions and ceramics. Other items include gold- and silverwork, spice, perfume, *bukhur* incense with charcoal and pottery containers in which to burn it, coloured mats and sharks' teeth. **Shopping hours:** Sun-Thurs 0800-1300 and 1600-2100.
SPECIAL EVENTS: Most special events in Yemen are religious holidays, which are tied to the Islamic Hijra calendar; therefore, the dates vary each year. For details of special events and festivals held in Yemen, contact the General Authority of Tourism (see *Contact Addresses* section).
SOCIAL CONVENTIONS: Traditional values are still very much part of everyday life and visitors will be treated with traditional courtesies and hospitality. Many of the population work in agriculture, with several thousand dependent on fishing. The rest live and work in towns and there is a small nomadic minority living along the northern edges of the desert. Guns become more noticeable further north, slung over the shoulder and carried in addition to the traditional *jambia*. In towns, women are veiled with black or coloured cloth, while in the villages such customs are not observed. Yemenis commonly chew *qat*, a locally

A B C D E F G H I J K L M N O P Q R S T U V W X Y Z

grown shrub bearing shoots that have a stimulant effect (similar to caffeine), chewed in markets and cafes but more stylishly sitting on cushions in a guestroom or *mafrai* at the top of a multi-storeyed Yemeni house. For the visitor, conservative casual clothes are suitable; visiting businesspeople are expected to wear suits. Men need to wear a jacket and tie for formal occasions and in smart dining rooms. Women are expected to dress modestly and beachwear and shorts should be confined to the beach or poolside. Smoking is forbidden during Ramadan. Foreigners are requested not to smoke, eat or drink in public. **Tipping:** The practice of tipping is becoming more common. Waiters and taxi drivers should be tipped 10 to 15 per cent.

Business Profile

ECONOMY: Yemen is one of the poorest countries in the Arab world, and among the principal motivations behind the unification of Yemen in 1990 was the prospect of economic transformation and expansion. However, it is only in the last few years that the economy has started to show sporadic signs of improvement. Under IMF auspices, the government has implemented a programme of structural reforms involving privatisation and an overhaul of the financial system. In exchange, the Yemenis received financial support and some relief of Yemen's US$5 billion foreign debt. The economy is now growing at around 5 per cent, and inflation eased to 11 per cent, after a rapid increase in previous years. Large-scale unemployment persists; an estimated 30 per cent of the workforce are out of work and there is serious under-employment.
Agriculture is concentrated in the fertile northern part of the country. The principal cash crops are cereals, cotton, coffee, fruit, vegetables and *qat* (a narcotic leaf); sorghum, potatoes, wheat and barley are grown for local consumption. Livestock rearing and fishing, both of which occur throughout the country, are also important. The manufacturing industry is mainly involved in the production of construction materials, processed foods, tobacco, drinks and chemicals. However, the most important industrial activity is oil and gas production. Yemeni reserves are modest by regional standards but since the opening of the refining complex at Aden in 1994 and new fields coming on stream, the sector accounts for the majority of export earnings. Aden also hosts a newly established free-trade zone. Other mineral deposits, which are concentrated in the south, include copper, gold, lead, zinc and molybdenum.
Yemen's main trading partners are the United Arab Emirates, the Republic of Korea, Saudi Arabia, Japan, Egypt and the USA.
BUSINESS: Businesspeople are expected to dress smartly for meetings and formal social occasions. English is commonly used in business circles. Appointments are needed and visitors should be punctual. Visiting cards are often exchanged. Do not be surprised during a meeting if Yemeni businessmen chew *qat*. **Office hours:** Sat-Wed 0800-1500.
COMMERCIAL INFORMATION: The following organisation can offer advice: General Investment Authority (website: www.giay.gov.ye).

Climate

The climate varies according to altitude. The coastal plain is hot and dusty throughout most of the year. The highlands are warm in summer and, during winter, from October to March, nights can be very cold in the mountains. Annual rainfall is extremely low and temperatures, particularly in summer, are very high. The most pleasant time is from October to April.
Required clothing: Lightweight clothes are worn in the coastal plain all year. Warmer clothes are needed from November to April in the highlands.

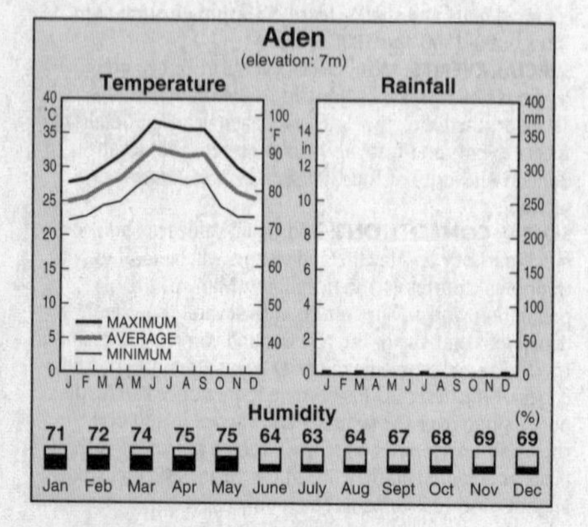

Zambia

LATEST TRAVEL ADVICE CONTACTS

British Foreign and Commonwealth Office
Tel: (0870) 606 0290 Website: www.fco.gov.uk
US Department of State
Website: http://travel.state.gov/travel
Canadian Department of Foreign Affairs and Int'l Trade
Tel: (1 800) 267 8376 Website: www.dfait-maeci.gc.ca

Location: Central southern Africa.

Country dialling code: 260

The Tourism Council of Zambia
Street address: Holiday Inn, Ridgeway, Lusaka, Zambia
Postal address: PO Box 36561, Lusaka, Zambia
Tel: (1) 251 666. Fax: (1) 251 501.
E-mail: tcz@zamnet.zm
Website: www.zambiatourism.com
Zambia National Tourist Board
Street address: 4th Floor, Century House, Cairo Road, Lusaka, Zambia
Postal address: PO Box 30017, Lusaka, Zambia
Tel: (1) 229 087/88/89/90. Fax: (1) 225 174.
E-mail: zntb@zamnet.zm
Website: www.zambiatourism.com
Zambia National Tourist Board
Street address: Tourist Centre, Musi-oa-Tunya Road, Livingstone, Zambia
Postal address: PO Box 60342, Livingstone, Zambia
Tel: (3) 321 404 *or* 097 897 790/097 417 389 (mobile).
Tel/Fax: (3) 321 487.
E-mail: zntblive@zamnet.zm
Website: www.zambiatourism.com
High Commission for the Republic of Zambia *and* **Zambia National Tourist Board**
2 Palace Gate, London W8 5NG, UK
Tel: (020) 7589 6655. Fax: (020) 7581 1353 *or* 0546.
E-mail: immzhcl@btconnect.com (immigration) *or* zntb@aol.com (tourism).
Website: www.zhcl.org.uk *or* www.zambiatourism.com
Opening hours: Mon-Fri 0930-1300 and 1400-1700; Mon-Fri 1000-1300 (visa section).
British High Commission
Street address: Independence Avenue 5210, 15101 Ridgeway, Lusaka, Zambia
Postal address: PO Box 50050, Lusaka, Zambia
Tel: (1) 251 133. Fax: (1) 253 798 *or* 252 842 (visa section).
E-mail: BHC-Lusaka@fco.gov.uk
Website: www.britishhighcommission.gov.uk/zambia
Embassy of the Republic of Zambia
2419 Massachusetts Avenue, NW, Washington, DC 20008, USA
Tel: (202) 265 9717. Fax: (202) 332 0826.
E-mail: info@zambiainfo.org
Website: www.zambiaembassy.org
Also deals with enquiries from Canada.

TIMATIC CODES

Health
AMADEUS: **TI-DFT/LUN/HE**
GALILEO/WORLDSPAN: **TI-DFT/LUN/HE**
SABRE: **TIDFT/LUN/HE**

Visa
AMADEUS: **TI-DFT/LUN/VI**
GALILEO/WORLDSPAN: **TI-DFT/LUN/VI**
SABRE: **TIDFT/LUN/VI**

To access TIMATIC country information on Health and Visa regulations through the Computer Reservations System (CRS), type in the appropriate command line listed above.

Embassy of the United States of America
Street address: Corner of Independence and United Nations Avenues, Lusaka, Zambia
Postal address: PO Box 31617, Lusaka, Zambia
Tel: (1) 250 955 *or* 252 230/318. Fax: (1) 252 225.
E-mail: paslib@zamnet.zm *or* consularlusaka@state.gov
Website: http://zambia.usembassy.gov
Canadian High Commission
Street address: 5199 United Nations Avenue, Longacres, Lusaka, Zambia
Postal address: PO Box 31313, Lusaka, Zambia
Tel: (1) 250 833. Fax: (1) 254 176.
E-mail: lsaka@dfait-maeci.gc.ca
Website: www.dfait-maeci.gc.ca/africa/zambia-contact

General Information

AREA: 752,614 sq km (290,586 sq miles).
POPULATION: 10,698,000 (UN estimate 2002).
POPULATION DENSITY: 14.2 per sq km.
CAPITAL: Lusaka. **Population:** 1,640,000 (official estimate 2000).
GEOGRAPHY: Zambia is a vast plateau bordered by Angola to the west, the Democratic Republic of Congo to the north, Tanzania to the northeast, Malawi to the east, Mozambique to the southeast, Zimbabwe and Botswana to the south and the Caprivi Strip of Namibia to the southwest. The Zambezi River together with Lake Kariba forms the frontier with Zimbabwe. Victoria Falls, at the southern end of the manmade Lake Kariba, is one of the most spectacular sights in Africa (if not the world). In the east and northeast, the country rises to a plateau 1200m (3937ft) high, covered by deciduous savannah, small trees, grassy plains or marshland. The magnificent Luangwa and Kafue National Parks have some of the most prolific animal populations in Africa.
GOVERNMENT: Republic. Gained independence from the UK in 1964. **Head of State and Government:** President Levy Patrick Mwanawasa since 2002.
LANGUAGE: English is the official language, but there are over 73 local dialects. The main languages are Bemba, Kaonde, Lozi, Lunda, Luvale, Nyanja and Tonga.
RELIGION: Around 30 per cent of the population is Christian (Protestant and Roman Catholic), a smaller number are Muslim and Hindu, and a small minority have traditional animist beliefs.
TIME: GMT + 2.
ELECTRICITY: 230 volts AC, 50Hz.
COMMUNICATIONS: Telephone: IDD is available. Country code: 260. Outgoing international code: 00. There are public telephones and most calls are made through a post office. **Mobile telephone:** GSM 900 network. Operators include *Celtel* (website: www.msi-cellular.com), *Telecel* (website: www.telecel.co.zm) and *Zamtell* (website: www.zamtel.zn). Coverage is limited to some areas around Lusaka and near the coast. **Internet:** ISPs include *Coppernet* (website: www.coppernet.zm), *Zamnet* (website: www.zamnet.zm) and *Zamtel* (website: www.zamtel.zm). E-mail can be accessed from Internet cafes in Livingstone and Lusaka. **Fax/telegram:** There are public fax facilities at the central post office in Lusaka and at principal hotels. Telegrams may be sent from telegraph offices in main centres, open Mon-Fri 0800-1700, Sat 0800-1300 (closed Sunday and public holidays). **Post:** Airmail to Western Europe takes 7 to 14 days. **Press:** *National Mirror*, *The Sportsman*, *The Sun*, *Sunday Times of Zambia* and *Zambia Daily Mail* are published in English. **Radio:** BBC World Service (website: www.bbc.co.uk/worldservice) and Voice of America (website: www.voa.gov) can be received. From time to time the frequencies change and the most up-to-date can be found online.

Passport/Visa

	Passport Required?	Visa Required?	Return Ticket Required?
Full British	Yes	Yes	Yes
Australian	Yes	Yes	Yes
Canadian	Yes	Yes	Yes
USA	Yes	Yes	Yes
Other EU	Yes	1	Yes
Japanese	Yes	Yes	Yes

Note: *Regulations and requirements may be subject to change at short notice, and you are advised to contact the appropriate diplomatic or consular authority before finalising travel arrangements. Details of these may be found at the head of this country's entry. Any numbers in the chart refer to the footnotes below.*

PASSPORTS: Passport valid for six months from the date of entry required by all.
VISAS: Required by all except the following for stays of up to 30 days:
(a) **1.** nationals of Ireland (all other EU nationals *do* require a visa);
(b) nationals of Romania and Serbia & Montenegro;

(c) nationals of Commonwealth countries (except nationals of Australia, Bangladesh, Canada, The Gambia, Ghana, India, Mozambique, New Zealand, Nigeria, Pakistan, Papua New Guinea, Sierra Leone, Sri Lanka and the UK who *do* require a visa);
(d) transit passengers continuing their journey by the same or first connecting aircraft within 24 hours provided holding valid onward or return documentation and not leaving the airport.
Note: A *Bonafide Tourist*, who is travelling on a pre-arranged package tour with a foreign tour operator, or in conjunction with a local tour operator in Zambia, will be issued a fee-waived visa for a stay of no longer than 14 days. The fee-waived visa will be issued at any port of entry to Zambia. The Bonafide Tourist will also be exempt from submitting a letter of invitation, photocopy of flight details and proof of funds.
Types of visa and cost: *Tourist*, *Business*, *Private* and *Transit*. The cost depends on nationality. For UK citizens: £33 (single-entry); £45 (double- and multiple-entry). Payable in cash in person or by postal order payable to the Zambia High Commission.
Validity: Six months from date of issue for a stay of maximum 30 days; transit visa valid for seven days. Daytripper visas are valid for tourists entering Zambia for no more than 24 hours.
Application to: Consulate (or Consular section at High Commission or Embassy); see *Contact Addresses* section.
Application requirements: (a) One completed application form. (b) Two recent passport-size photos. (c) Valid passport. (d) Fee (payable in cash or by postal order). (e) Self-addressed stamped envelope for postal applications. (f) Letter of invitation confirming purpose of visit from host in Zambia, for all trips. (g) Proof of the Zambian host's immigration status. (h) Proof of return journey to home country. (i) Proof of sufficient funds during length of stay in Zambia.
Working days required: Three.
Temporary residence: For stays in excess of 90 days, apply to the Chief Immigration Officer (CIO), Kent Building, PO Box 50300, Lusaka (tel: (1) 252 622 *or* 252 629; tel/fax: (1) 252 008; fax: (1) 251 725).

Money

Currency: Kwacha (K) = 100 ngwee. Notes are in denominations of K10,000, 5000, 1000, 500, 100, 50 and 20. Coins are in denominations of K1, and 50, 20, 10, 5, 2 and 1 ngwee.
Currency exchange: Exchange of foreign currency is carried out at authorised banks and bureaux de change. ATMs are available within Lusaka and some of the major towns in Zambia.
Credit & debit cards: American Express is widely accepted, with more limited use of Diners Club, MasterCard and Visa. Check with your credit or debit card company for details of merchant acceptability and other services which may be available.
Travellers cheques: Widely accepted. To avoid additional exchange rate charges, travellers are advised to take travellers cheques in US Dollars, Euros or Pounds Sterling.
Currency restrictions: The import and export of local currency is limited to K100. Free import of foreign currency subject to declaration on arrival. The export of foreign currency is limited to the amount declared on import. All passengers entering or departing from Zambia must declare all currency notes exceeding US$5000 or equivalent.
Note: Currency declaration forms and exchange receipts must be shown if purchasing airline tickets in Zambia.
Exchange rate indicators: The following figures are included as a guide to the movements of the Kwacha against Sterling and the US Dollar:

Date	Feb '04	May '04	Aug '04	Nov '04
£1.00=	8952.80	8325.27	8739.00	8945.13
$1.00=	4750.00	4730.00	4742.50	4817.50

Banking hours: Vary from bank to bank, but most are open Mon-Fri 0815-1430. Some banks are open 0815-1030 on the first and last Saturday of the month.

Duty Free

The following items may be imported into Zambia by persons over 18 years without incurring customs duty:
200 cigarettes or 450g of tobacco; one opened bottle of alcoholic beverage.

Public Holidays

2005: Jan 1 New Year's Day. **Mar 12** Youth Day. **Mar 25** Good Friday. **Mar 28** Easter Monday. **May 1** Labour Day. **May 25** African Freedom Day (Anniversary of the OAU's Foundation). **Jul 4** Heroes' Day. **Jul 5** Unity Day. **Aug 1** Farmers' Day. **Oct 24** Independence Day. **Dec 25** Christmas Day.
2006: Jan 1 New Year's Day. **Mar 12** Youth Day. **Apr 14** Good Friday. **Apr 17** Easter Monday. **May 1** Labour Day. **May 25** African Freedom Day (Anniversary of the OAU's Foundation). **Jul 3** Heroes' Day. **Jul 4** Unity Day. **Aug 7** Farmers' Day. **Oct 24** Independence Day. **Dec 25** Christmas Day.
Note: It is advisable to verify exact dates in advance.

Health

	Special Precautions?	Certificate Required?
Yellow Fever	No	No
Cholera	1	No
Typhoid & Polio	2	N/A
Malaria	3	N/A

Note: *Regulations and requirements may be subject to change at short notice, and you are advised to contact your doctor well in advance of your intended date of departure. Any numbers in the chart refer to the footnotes below.*

1: Following WHO guidelines issued in 1973, a cholera vaccination certificate is no longer a condition of entry to Ghana. However an outbreak of cholera occurred in Lusaka District in 1999 and cholera is still prevalent, particularly in the rainy season.
2: Vaccination against typhoid and polio is advised.
3: Malaria risk (including cerebral malaria), predominantly in the malignant *falciparum* form, exists throughout the year in the whole country. The malignant form is reported to be highly resistant to chloroquine and sulfadoxine-pyrimethamine. The recommended prophylaxis is mefloquine.
Food & drink: Water used for drinking, brushing teeth or making ice should have first been boiled or otherwise sterilised. Milk is pasteurised and dairy products are generally safe for consumption. Only eat well-cooked meat and fish, preferably served hot. Pork, salad and mayonnaise may carry increased risk. Vegetables should be cooked and fruit peeled.
Other risks: *Bilharzia* (schistosomiasis) is present. Avoid swimming and paddling in fresh water; swimming pools that are well chlorinated and maintained are safe. *Human trypanosomiasis* (sleeping sickness) is reported in the north. *Trachoma* is widespread, as are *hepatitis A* and *E. Hepatitis B* is hyperendemic. *Dysentery* is endemic. Epidemics of *meningococcal meningitis* may occur, particularly in the savannah areas during the dry season. *HIV/AIDS* affects a high proportion of the population. *Plague* occurs very rarely. *Rabies* is present. For those at high risk, vaccination before arrival should be considered. If you are bitten, seek medical advice without delay. For more information, consult the *Health* appendix.
Health care: There is no reciprocal health agreement with the UK. Health service is not free and health insurance is advisable. Adequate health care cannot be assured outside main towns. It is advisable to carry basic medical supplies as they are limited in Zambia.

Travel - International

Note: All but essential travel to areas of Zambia bordering the Democratic Republic of Congo and Angola is advised against. There are also landmines in both these areas and also on the border with Mozambique. Care should be ensured when driving, since car-hijacking and armed robbery are on the increase. Road safety and driving standards are poor.
AIR: Zambia's airlines are *Aero Zambia (Z9)* and *Zambian Airways (Q3)*. Other airlines serving Zambia include *Air Zimbabwe*, *British Airways*, *Ethiopian Airlines*, *Kenya Airways* and *South African Airways*. *Zambian Airways* can be contacted at PO Box 310277, Lusaka (tel: (1) 271 230; fax: (1) 271 054; e-mail: roanhq@zamnet.zm *or* roanair@zamnet.zm; website: www.zambianairways.co.zm).
Approximate flight times: From *London* to Lusaka is 10 hours.
International airports: *Lusaka (LUN)* is 26km (16 miles) east of the city (travel time - 30 minutes). Airport and city bus services are available. Taxi service is also available to the city. Return is by prior arrangement with taxis (taxi fares are negotiable). Airport facilities include outgoing duty free shop, car hire, bank/bureau de change, restaurant and post office.
Mfuwe (MFU) is situated in the South Luangwa National Park, one hour 15 minutes' flight from Lusaka International Airport. Lodges and camps within the park provide airport transfers by prior arrangement.
Departure tax: US$20 (payable in cash). Transit passengers and children under two years are exempt.
RIVER/LAKE: There are ferry crossings from Mpulungu across Lake Tanganyika to Kigoma in Tanzania and to Bujumbura in Burundi; and a service across the Zambezi from Kazungula to Botswana.
RAIL: There are two major rail routes linking Zambia with Zimbabwe and Tanzania. *Zambia Railways* serves Livingstone and has a connection across the Victoria Falls to Bulawayo and Harare in Zimbabwe. There are two trains daily in either direction (travel time - nine to 12 hours depending on whether the ordinary or express service is used). The trains have first-, second- and third-class carriages. *Tanzania–Zambia Railways Authority (TAZARA)* operates trains from Kapiri Mposhi to Dar es Salaam in Tanzania. Services are often suspended and it is advisable to check at the tourist office in Lusaka for details.
ROAD: Coach and bus services are available to Botswana, Malawi, South Africa, Tanzania and Zimbabwe. The main routes are from Zimbabwe via Chirundu or Kariba and Livingstone; from Botswana via Kasane and Kazungula; from Mozambique via Villa Gambito and Zumbo; from Tanzania via Nakonde and Mbala; from Malawi via the Mchinga/Chipata border or further north at Nyika Plateau; and from the Democratic Republic of Congo via Kashiba, Mwenda, Sakania, Mokamba, Kasumbalesa and Kapushi. Opening hours for road borders are from 0600-1800 (except for Victoria Falls which closes at 2000). As yet, there is no border crossing from Angola. A Temporary Import Permit is needed to bring a vehicle into Zambia.

Travel - Internal

AIR: *Aero Zambia*, *Zambia Skyways*, *Zambian Airways* and charters operate domestic routes to destinations including Chipata, Kasaba Bay, Kasama, Kitwe, Livingstone, Lusaka, Mangu, Mfuwe, Ndola and Victoria Falls. There are over 120 other airports, aerodromes and airstrips in the country.
Departure tax: K12,000 (US$5).
RIVER/LAKE: Local ferries operate on all waterways. Contact local authorities for details.
RAIL: Zambia has three main internal train lines, one from Livingstone to Lusaka, from Lusaka to the Copperbelt, and from Kapiri Mposhi to the Northern border with Tanzania. The main train station is in Dedan Kamathi Road, in central Lusaka, one road east of Cairo Road. There is a daily Kitwe - Lusaka - Lir stopping train. There is also an express train (*The Zambezi Express*) leaving Livingstone on Sundays, Tuesdays and Thursdays, arriving in Lusaka the next morning.
Children under three years of age travel free, children between three and 15 years pay half price. There is first- and second-class accommodation and light refreshments are available on some services.
ROAD: Traffic drives on the left. There is a fairly good network of roads (38,763km/24,087 miles in total, of which 8200km/5095 miles is tarred), although they are often in poor condition. **Bus:** The network of intercity bus services is run by private operators and *Zambia Telecommunications (Zamtel)*. The service used to be unreliable but it is much better nowadays. The buses provided are clean, cheap and frequent. *CR coach*, linking Lusaka with Livingstone, Chipata, Ndola and Mongu (twice a day, leaving from *ShopRite* in Cairo Road) should be booked well in advance. Other coach services are available, including *Giraffe*. **Car hire:** Several firms operate in main centres. Information is available from the Zambia National Tourist Board (see *Contact Addresses* section) *or* the *Lusaka Bus Terminus* on Dedan Kimathi Road, Lusaka. *Avis*, *Hertz*, *Taiwo*, *Zungulila* and other car-hire firms can provide chauffeur-driven cars. **Documentation:** An International Driving Permit is required. UK driving licenses may be used for up to 90 days.
URBAN: Bus services in Lusaka are provided by private minibuses and shared taxis. The buses are somewhat basic, and can become very crowded. Taxis are not metered and fares should be agreed in advance. It is also advisable to negotiate a fare.

TRAVEL TIMES: The following chart gives approximate travel times (in hours and minutes) from **Lusaka** to other major cities/towns in Zambia.

	Air	Road	Rail
Livingstone	1.20	6.30	11.00
Ndola	1.00	4.00	6.30
Kitwe	1.00	4.30	7.00
Mfuwe	1.30	-	-

Accommodation

Accommodation in Zambia may be divided into four main categories: hotels, motels, lodges and camps; and two minor categories: Government (GRZ)-hostels and camping/caravan sites. Zambia is a large, wild and, as yet, largely undeveloped country. Only the major tourist sites are fully prepared to cater for the needs of the visitor and payment is in hard currency, except at smaller establishments.

HOTELS & MOTELS: Hotels are concentrated around Lusaka, Livingstone and the Copperbelt region. Others are widely dispersed around the country along principal roads or near towns. It is advisable to book in advance and to obtain confirmation in writing. All bills are subject to a 10 per cent service charge in lieu of tips and 23 per cent sales tax. Tipping in hotels is not permitted by law. **Grading:** Hotels are graded according to a 5-star system and range from an ungraded class to one 5-star hotel. For further information, contact the Hotel and Catering Association of Zambia, PO Box 30815, Lusaka (tel: (1) 252 779; website: www.zambiatourism.com).

NATIONAL PARKS: All lodges and many camps in the parks are offered on a fully catered basis. As the quality of accommodation and associated facilities varies enormously from one place to another, visitors intending to stay should contact the relevant tour operator/tourist office for detailed information.

LODGES: These are generally stone buildings with thatched roofs designed to complement the natural environment, housing a maximum of 40 beds.

CAMPS: The most common and most widely used type of accommodation for safaris. In general, standard facilities include hot and cold running water, electricity and waterborne sanitation plus the basic accoutrements for comfortable living. For instance, Luangwa's camps have beds, clean linen, refrigerators, crockery, cutlery, mosquito nets, lamps, toilets and showers. At non-catered camps, visitors must bring their own food and drink. Some are open all year round while others open from June to October or November.

GRZ-HOSTELS: These are available throughout the provinces. They have a small capacity, rising in exceptional cases to 24 rooms. Government rest houses are available in many centres but they are very basic.

CAMPING/CARAVANNING: Sites are available at most of the tourist centres, including several national parks. It is best to make reservations well in advance. If booking is more than four weeks in advance, some operators charge a 15 per cent deposit. Prices may increase during peak periods. For further information, contact the Zambia National Tourist Board, who can supply a list of Zambian tour operators.

Resorts & Excursions

LUSAKA: Attractions in the capital include nightclubs, restaurants, cinemas, the **Kabwata Cultural Village** (devoted to the preservation of indigenous arts and crafts and displays of traditional dancing), the **Cathedral of the Holy Cross**, the **Munda Wanga Botanical Gardens and Zoo** and the **Lusaka National Museum** (opening hours: daily 0900-1630).

NATIONAL PARKS: The Zambian government has long recognised the economic importance of its wildernesses and is acutely aware of environmental concerns: almost one-third of the country is given over to national parks and game reserves. Tourism is mostly concentrated in eight of the 19 parks – Kafue, Kasanka, Lochinvar, Lower Zambezi, Luangwa, Mosi-oa-Tunya, Sioma Ngwezi and Sumbu (described below) – the remainder, as yet, having fewer facilities. The Zambia National Tourist Board also recommends the following national parks: **Blue Lagoon**, **Nyika** and **Sioma Ngwezi**.

All the main national parks are accessible by car and plane. National parks require an entry permit bought from the main gate during opening hours. For further detailed information about safaris, see also the *Sport & Activities* section *or* contact the Zambia National Tourist Board (see *Contact Addresses* section).

Note: Most tourist organisations are controlled by tour operators and prices of tours need to be fixed well in advance.

Kafue National Park: Situated in the centre of the southern half of the country, Kafue encompasses a huge area (22,500 sq km/8687 sq miles) and is one of the biggest game sanctuaries in Africa. Noted for its beauty, the park is bisected by the **Kafue River**, which attracts hundreds of species of birds and offers good game fishing. Eight-day walking and driving tours are available. The principal attraction is the prolific wildlife. Accommodation is provided throughout the year at **Mukambi Lodge** (no guided safaris during the rainy season, November to April), and the **Musungwa Lodges**, and at **New Kalala Camp** (full catering) and others. There are also several seasonal non-catered camps.

South Luangwa Valley National Park: Regarded as one of the most exciting game reserves in the world, the **Luangwa Valley** is home to a huge variety of animals: among many others, elephants, hippo, lions, zebras, giraffes, antelopes, buffaloes, monkeys and wild dogs. Blossoming trees and exotic flowers set the scene. The main rainy season runs from November/December to May. There are lodges at **Chichele**, **Kapani**, **Mfuwe** (all year) and **Tundwe** (dry season), and catered camps at **Chibembe**, **Kaingo Camp**, **Tena Tena** (dry season) and **Chinzombo** (all year). There are also several seasonal non-catered camps. Facilities in the park include luxury double rooms in chalets, private baths and toilets, full three-course meals, bar facilities and swimming pools.

Lochinvar National Park: Exceptional diversity of birdlife (over 420 recorded species). The park is situated on the southern edge of the **Kafue Flats**, a wide floodplain of the Kafu river, famous for its large herds of lechwe, an antelope unique to the Kafue Flats. There is one lodge, open throughout the year.

Sumbu National Park: The sandy shorelines of **Lake Tanganyika** provide the setting for three all-year beach resorts: at **Kasaba**, **Ndole** and **Nkamba** bays. There is also a small non-catered camp at Ndole Bay. Activities include swimming, sunbathing, boat rides and freshwater big-game fishing for the Goliath tigerfish (up to 35kg), giant catfish and the Nile perch (both up to 50kg and more). It is possible to arrange visits into the surrounding bush to watch game. **Kasaba Lodge** boasts an afternoon tea service, a bar and beach barbecues. **Nkamba Bay Lodge** offers exactly the same facilities as Kasaba but facilities are housed in rondavels. The park's spectacular sunsets are not to be missed.

Victoria Falls/Mosi-oa-Tunya National Park: Located on the southernmost edge of Zambia bordering Zimbabwe, the astonishing **Victoria Falls** are the mightiest cataracts in the world – the 2.5km- (1.5 mile-) wide Zambezi River drops 100m (330ft) into a narrow chasm at a rate of 550 million litres every minute. The spray can be seen 30km (20 miles) away. The **Mosi-oa-Tunya National Park** nearby is small by Zambian standards but is home to most of Zambia's more common wild animals. Also nearby is **Livingstone**, 'Tourist Capital of Zambia', with several luxury hotels, a casino, and the **National Museum**, housing Livingstone memorabilia and anthropological exhibits. The **Railway Museum** is also situated in Livingstone.

Kasanka National Park: This is one of Zambia's smallest parks, with an area of 390 sq km (150 miles). It encompasses eight lakes and four rivers, the largest being the beautiful Luwombwa. Kasanka is an attractive and diverse park with forest and swamps, home to specialised mammals and birds. Animals include elephant, hippo, reedbuck, waterbuck, hyena, warthog, baboon, jackal, leopard and the rare blue monkey, which can be found in the forests that flank Kasanka's rivers.

Lower Zambezi National Park: This lies along the **Zambezi River**, 100 km (62 miles) downstream of the Victoria Falls. It has abundant wildlife, including elephant, hippo, buffalo, zebra, lion and leopard together with a great variety of birds. Game drives and walks will often reveal big cats and, on occasion, the cheetah. Canoe safaris, fishing for tiger fish, bottle-nose fish or bream and birdwatching activities are available.

North Luangwa National Park: This is one of Africa's most spectacular surviving wilderness areas. It covers 4636 sq km (1790 sq miles) of primarily woodland park with numerous small rivers, including the beautiful Mwaleshi which all play an important role. The park is particularly noted for its huge herds of buffalo. Walking safaris here will also reveal elephants, leopards, wildcat, hyena, puku, impala, zebra, baboon and velvet monkey. Over 350 bird species are found here, including the crested leorie, crowned crane, carmine bee-eater and giant eagle owl.

Sport & Activities

Safaris: For information on Zambia's national parks and wildlife reserves, see the *Resorts & Excursions* section. The usual method of animal watching is from an open-topped Land Rover, but walking and canoeing tours are also available. In general, safaris are limited to six to eight persons per vehicle (with experienced guides provided). As a precaution, no more than six may make up a walking party and the guide will be armed. Nocturnal safaris are also possible. Native wildlife includes buffalo, elephant, antelope, lion, zebra, rhino, hippo and crocodile. **Birdwatching** enthusiasts may head to *Lochinvar*, where 400 different species have been recorded.

Adventure sports: Zambia's centre for adventure sports is Livingstone, whose proximity to the grandiose Victoria Falls ensures a steady increase in the range (and cost) of the thrill-inducing activities now available in the area. In addition to **bungee jumping** off the 111m- (364ft-) bridge linking Zambia and Zimbabwe across the River Zambezi, enthusiasts can now **abseil** down the gorge or **high-wire** across it – the latter involving a gravity-defying trip in a body harness attached to a cable spanning the chasm. Scenic flights in **micro-light aircraft** offering aerial views of the falls are also available. **Whitewater rafting** trips on the Zambezi are considered particularly wild. Longer and quieter river trips lasting from one to seven days usually follow the Victoria Falls–Lake Kariba itinerary, with Lake Kariba also offering the possibility to relax for a week on a luxurious **houseboat**. **Rock climbing** and **hiking** are also popular.

Social Profile

FOOD & DRINK: Owing to the liberalisation of the economy, there is now plenty of food in the shops. Local specialities include bream from the Kafue, Luapula and Zambezi rivers, and Nile perch, lake salmon and other freshwater fish.

Mosi, *Rhino* lager and imported beers and assorted soft drinks are available. Spirits are also available.

NIGHTLIFE: Lusaka has dancing and floorshows in the main hotels, cinemas and theatres. The Copperbelt and Livingstone areas offer a variety of entertainments including casinos and nightclubs. Very popular among travellers are boat trips on the river with a few drinks (also called 'booze' cruises).

SHOPPING: Lusaka has modern shops, supermarkets and open-air markets. Special purchases include African carvings, pottery and copperware, beadwork and local gemstones. **Shopping hours:** Mon-Fri 0800-1700 and Sat 0800-1300.

SPECIAL EVENTS: There are many traditional ceremonies and festivals that take place throughout Zambia. The following is a selection of special events occurring in Zambia in 2005:

Jan *Kwanga* (traditional festival), Lake Bangweulu. **Feb** *Livingstone City's 100th Birthday Celebrations*; *N'cwala* (the chief of the Ngoni people tastes the first fresh fruit of the year). **Mar** *Ku-omboka* (the Lozi chief or *Litunga*, together with his entire household, is paddled up a natural canal flood plain, from Leaului to Limulunga, his residence in the rainy season); *Zambia National Fishing Competition*, Lake Tanganyika. **May** *Annual African Queen Celebrations*, Livingstone; *Livingstone Arts and Drama Festival*. **Aug** *Livingstone Carnival*. **Sep** *World Tourism Week*. **Sep/Oct** *Shimunenga* (a traditional ceremony of the Ba-Ila people), Maala on the Kafue Flats. **Oct** *Women in Music* (music festival), Lusaka. **Nov** *150 Year Anniversary Victoria Falls*.

SOCIAL CONVENTIONS: African culture and traditions remain prominent and there are various customs, folklore and traditional crafts in the different regions. Traditional dancing is popular and there are many colourful annual ceremonies that take place throughout the country. Visitors to the outlying areas should expect to be met with curiosity. Shaking hands is the normal form of greeting. Gifts are often offered to visitors as a sign of gratitude, friendship or honour. One should never refuse a gift but accept it with both hands. **Photography:** Visitors are able to take photographs in most places but are advised to avoid military installations. **Tipping:** A 10 per cent sales tax is added to all bills. Tipping in hotels has been abolished by law but a 10 per cent tip may be expected or included in bills elsewhere.

Business Profile

ECONOMY: The Zambian economy relies heavily on the country's mineral wealth, particularly copper (of which Zambia is one of the world's largest producers), and also cobalt and zinc. These account for the bulk of export earnings and provide essential raw materials for Zambia's manufacturing industry, which accounts for over one-third of national output. Apart from raw material processing, the manufacturing sector includes vehicle assembly and oil refining as well as the production of fertilisers, textiles, construction materials and a variety of consumer products. Despite the role played by industry (unusually high by African standards), export earnings were steadily declining throughout the 1990s, mainly as a result of persistently low commodity prices. One stark illustration of the trend was the closure in 2002 of the Konkola copper mine – the country's largest and a major source of government revenue – as being no longer viable. Agriculture produces 30 per cent of GDP and employs two-thirds of the population. Maize and cattle are the main earners; other crops (cassava, millet, sorghum and beans) are produced mainly for domestic consumption but have to be supplemented by substantial food imports. Zambia's hydroelectric projects have allowed it self-sufficiency in energy.
Economic policy changed radically during the 1990s when the Government sought the backing of the IMF in tackling Zambia's serious financial problems. With some difficulty, many of the IMF-imposed measures were put into effect. More recently, Zambia has been a beneficiary of the Heavily Indebted Poor Countries programme to reduce the external debts of the world's poorest countries, but still owes over US$6 billion. The IMF is still involved with Zambia, although the current Zambian administration has proved reluctant to implement some of its demands, particularly privatisation of remaining state assets. The economy has been growing (5.1 per cent in 2004) but inflation (21 per cent) and unemployment (estimated at 50 per cent) remain high. Zambia is a member of the Southern African Development Council (SADC). Its main trading partners are Japan, the UK, South Africa, the USA and China.
BUSINESS: Formal dress is acceptable for people at business meetings. English is widely used in business circles. **Office hours:** Mon-Fri 0800-1300 and 1400-1700.
COMMERCIAL INFORMATION: The following organisations can offer advice: Ministry of Commerce, Trade and Industry, PO Box 31968, Kwacha Annex, Cairo Road, Lusaka (tel: (1) 228 301; fax: (1) 226 673; e-mail: comtrade@zamnet.zm); *or* Zambia Chamber of Commerce and Industry, PO Box 1968, Lusaka (tel: (1) 223 617; fax: (1) 222 650 *or* 226 727); *or* Zambia Investment Centre, PO Box 34580, Lusaka (tel: (1) 255 241; fax: (1) 252 150; e-mail: invest@zamnet.zm; website: www.zic.org.zm).
CONFERENCES/CONVENTIONS: For further information, contact the Mulungushi International Conference Centre, PO Box 33200, Lusaka (tel: (1) 290 506 *or* 291 229; fax: (1) 291 991; e-mail: micc@zamtel.zm).

Climate

Although Zambia lies in the tropics, the height of the plateau ensures that the climate is seldom unpleasantly hot, except in the valleys. There are three seasons: the cool, dry winter season from May to September; the hot, dry season in October and November; and the rainy season, which is even hotter, from December to April.
Required clothing: Lightweights or tropical with rainwear.

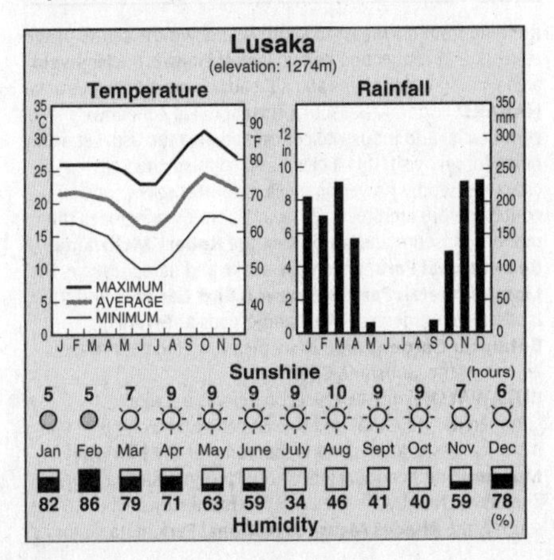

Zimbabwe

LATEST TRAVEL ADVICE CONTACTS

British Foreign and Commonwealth Office
Tel: (0870) 606 0290 Website: www.fco.gov.uk
US Department of State
Website: http://travel.state.gov/travel
Canadian Department of Foreign Affairs and Int'l Trade
Tel: (1 800) 267 8376 Website: www.dfait-maeci.gc.ca

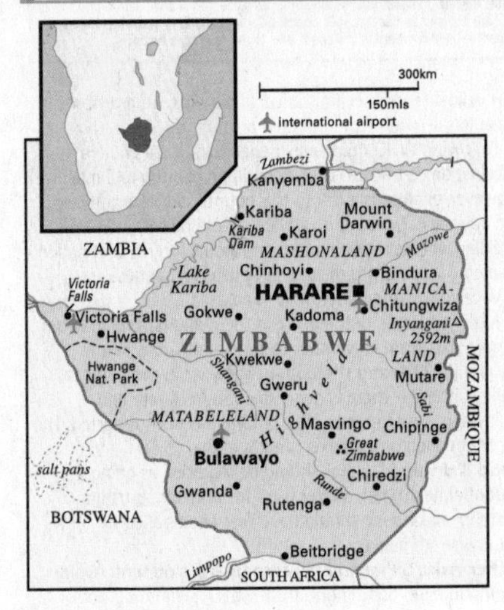

Location: Southern Africa.

Country dialling code: 263.

Zimbabwe Tourism Authority (ZTA)
Street address: 65 Samora Machel Avenue, Tourism House, Harare, Zimbabwe
Postal address: PO Box CY286, Causeway, Harare, Zimbabwe
Tel: (4) 752 570. Fax: (4) 758 826/8.
E-mail: info@ztazim.co.zw
Website: www.zimbabwetourism.co.zw/destzim
Embassy of the Republic of Zimbabwe
Zimbabwe House, 429 Strand, London WC2R 0JR, UK
Tel: (020) 7836 7755. Fax: (020) 7379 1167.
E-mail: zimlondon@yahoo.com
Website: http://zimbabwe.embassyhomepage.com
Opening hours: Mon-Fri 0900-1700; 0900-1230 (visa section).
Zimbabwe Tourism Office
Address as Embassy.
Tel: (020) 7240 6169. Fax: (020) 7240 5465.
E-mail: zta.london@btclick.com
Website: www.zimbabwetourism.co.zw
British Embassy
Street address: Corner House, 7th Floor, Samora Machel Avenue/Leopold Takawira Street, Harare, Zimbabwe
Postal address: PO Box 4490, Harare, Zimbabwe
Tel: (4) 772 990 *or* 774 700. Fax: (4) 774 605.
E-mail: bhcinfo@zol.co.zw *or* british.info.harare@fco.gov.uk (general information) *or* consular.harare@fco.gov.uk (consular information).
Website: www.britishembassy.gov.uk/zimbabwe
Embassy of Zimbabwe
1608 New Hampshire Avenue, NW, Washington, DC 20009, USA
Tel: (202) 332 7100. Fax: (202) 483 9326.
E-mail: zimemb@erols.com
Website: www.zimbabwe-embassy.us
Zimbabwe Tourism Office
128 East 56th Street, New York, NY 10022, USA
Tel: (212) 486 3444. Fax: (212) 486 3888.
Website: www.zimbabwetourism.co.zw
Deals with enquiries from all of North America.
Embassy of the United States of America
172 Herbert Chitepo Avenue, Harare, Zimbabwe
Tel: (4) 250 593/4.
Fax: (4) 796 488 *or* 722 618 (consular section).
E-mail: consularharare@state.gov
Website: http://harare.state.gov

TIMATIC CODES

Health
AMADEUS: **TI-DFT/HRE/HE**
GALILEO/WORLDSPAN: **TI-DFT/HRE/HE**
SABRE: **TIDFT/HRE/HE**

Visa
AMADEUS: **TI-DFT/HRE/VI**
GALILEO/WORLDSPAN: **TI-DFT/HRE/VI**
SABRE: **TIDFT/HRE/VI**

To access TIMATIC country information on Health and Visa regulations through the Computer Reservations System (CRS), type in the appropriate command line listed above.

Embassy of the Republic of Zimbabwe
332 Somerset Street West, Ottawa, Ontario K2P 0J9, Canada
Tel: (613) 237 4388/9. Fax: (613) 563 8269.
E-mail: zim.embassy@sympatico.ca
Website: www.zimbabweembassy.ca
Canadian Embassy
Street address: 45 Baines Avenue, Harare, Zimbabwe
Postal address: PO Box 1430, Baines Avenue, Harare, Zimbabwe
Tel: (4) 252 181-5. Fax: (4) 252 186 (general).
E-mail: hrare@dfait-maeci.gc.ca
Website: www.dfait-maeci.gc.ca/zimbabwe

General Information

AREA: 390,757 sq km (150,872 sq miles).
POPULATION: 12,835,000 (UN estimate 2002).
POPULATION DENSITY: 32.8 per sq km.
CAPITAL: Harare. **Population:** 1,868,000 (UN projection 2001; including suburbs).
GEOGRAPHY: Zimbabwe is bordered by Zambia to the northwest, Mozambique to the northeast, South Africa to the south and Botswana to the southwest. The central zone of hills gives rise to many rivers, which drain into the manmade Lake Kariba to the northwest, the marshes of Botswana to the west or into the Zambezi River to the northeast. The *highveld* landscape is dotted with *kopjes* (massive granite outcrops). Along the eastern border for some 350km (220 miles) is a high mountainous region of great scenic beauty, rising to 2592m (8504ft) at Mount Inyangani, the country's highest point. Zimbabwe offers some of the best wildlife parks in southern Africa, notably Hwange (southwest), Matopos (south) and Nyanga (northeast) national parks. These, together with the Victoria Falls and Great Zimbabwe, are the principal attractions for visitors.
GOVERNMENT: Republic. Gained independence from the UK in 1980. **Head of State and Government:** President Robert Mugabe (Head of Government since 1980 and Head of State since 1987).
LANGUAGE: The official language is English, with Shona and Ndebele dialects.
RELIGION: Christianity, with traditional beliefs in rural areas, and some Hindu, Muslim and Jewish minorities.
TIME: GMT + 2.
ELECTRICITY: 220/230 volts AC, 50Hz.
COMMUNICATIONS: Telephone: Full IDD is available. Country code: 263. Outgoing international code: 110. **Mobile telephone:** GSM 900 network. Operators are *Econet* (website: www.econet.co.zw), *Net*One Cellular* (website: www.netone.co.zw) and *Telecel Zimbabwe*. Coverage is limited to a few urban areas. **Fax:** Widely available. **Internet:** ISPs include *Africa Online* (website: www.africaonline.com), *Data Control*, *InterData* and *M-web Zimbabwe* (website: www.mweb.co.zw). E-mail can be accessed from Internet cafes in Harare and in Mashonaland. **Telegram:** Available at post offices and major hotels. **Post:** Airmail to Europe takes up to one week. **Press:** The main English-language newspapers are *The Chronicle*, *The Financial Gazette*, *The Herald*, *The Sunday Mail* and *The Sunday News*. Visitors should note that the carrying of the main independent newspapers (*The Financial Gazette*, *The Independent* and *The Standard*) can provoke a hostile reaction from *ZANU (PF)* supporters.
Radio: BBC World Service (website: www.bbc.co.uk/worldservice) and Voice of America (website: www.voa.gov) can be received. From time to time the frequencies change and the most up-to-date can be found online.

Passport/Visa

	Passport Required?	Visa Required?	Return Ticket Required?
Full British	Yes	2	Yes
Australian	Yes	2	Yes
Canadian	Yes	2	Yes
USA	Yes	2	Yes
Other EU	Yes	1/2	Yes
Japanese	Yes	2	Yes

Note: *Regulations and requirements may be subject to change at short notice, and you are advised to contact the appropriate diplomatic or consular authority before finalising travel arrangements. Details of these may be found at the head of this country's entry. Any numbers in the chart refer to the footnotes below.*

PASSPORTS: Passport valid for at least six months beyond date of departure required by all.
VISAS: Required by all except the following:
(a) **1.** nationals of Cyprus, Ireland and Malta;
(b) nationals of Aruba, The Bahamas, Barbados, Belize, Bermuda, Botswana, Cayman Islands, Fiji, Grenada, Guyana, Hong Kong (SAR), Jamaica, Kenya, Kiribati, Leeward Islands, Lesotho, Malawi, Malaysia, Maldives, Mauritius, Montserrat, Namibia, Nauru, New Zealand, Norway, St Kitts & Nevis, St Lucia, St Vincent & the Grenadines, Singapore, Solomon Islands, Swaziland, Tanzania, Tonga, Trinidad & Tobago, Turks & Caicos Islands, Tuvalu, Uganda, Vanuatu, Western Samoa and Zambia;

(c) passengers continuing their journey to a third country within 6 hours by the same or connecting flight, provided holding tickets with reserved seats and documents for onward travel and not leaving the transit area.

Note: 2. Nationals of the following countries may obtain visas valid for up to 90 days on arrival in Zimbabwe, provided holding tickets and documents for return or onward travel and sufficient funds for their stay: Argentina, Australia, Austria, Belgium, Brazil, Brunei, Canada, Cook Islands, Denmark, Dominican Republic, Egypt, Finland, France, Germany, Ghana (gratis visa; free-of-charge), Greece, Iceland, Indonesia, Israel, Italy, Japan, Korea (Rep), Kuwait, Liechtenstein, Luxembourg, Monaco, The Netherlands, New Zealand, Norway, Palau, Palestinian Authority Region (State Of), Papua New Guinea, Poland, Portugal, Puerto Rico (USA), Seychelles, South Africa (gratis visa; free-of-charge), Spain, Sweden, Switzerland, United Arab Emirates, United Kingdom, Uruguay, USA, US Virgin Islands and Vatican City.

Types of visa and cost: Visa at port of entry: cost dependent on nationality, British nationals £36, contact consular section at Embassy or High Commission for further details. Cost of visa from Embassy: single-entry £40; double-entry £50. Multiple-entry visas only issued when in Zimbabwe.

Validity: Six months from date of issue.

Application to: Consular section at Embassy or High Commission; see *Contact Addresses* section. For Multiple-entry visas, travellers must apply direct to the Chief Immigration Officer in Harare, Zimbabwe.

Application requirements: (a) Completed application form. (b) Passport valid for at least six months beyond date of departure. (c) Fee, payable by cash, postal order or banker's draft (cheques are not accepted). (d) Two passport photographs. (e) Return ticket and proof of sufficient funds (this requirement applies to all visitors, including those who may enter visa-free).

Note: All visitors to Zimbabwe must be in possession of return tickets (or funds in lieu) and sufficient funds to support themselves. The granting of a visa is not a guarantee of entry.

Working days required: Usually seven; minimum of 48 hours from receipt of application.

Temporary residence: Apply to Chief Immigration Officer, Private Bag 7717, Causeway, Harare.

Money

Currency: Zimbabwe Dollar (Z$) = 100 cents. Notes are in denominations of Z$500, 100, 50, 20, 10, 5 and 2. Coins are in denominations of Z$5, 2 and 1, and 50, 20, 10, 5 and 1 cents.

Currency exchange: Major foreign currencies can be exchanged at banks and major hotels at the official exchange rate.

Credit & debit cards: American Express, Diners Club and Visa are widely accepted, whilst MasterCard has more limited use. Some ATMs accept credit cards. Check with your credit or debit card company for details of merchant acceptability and other services which may be available.

Travellers cheques: Banks and major hotels will exchange these. To avoid additional exchange rate charges, travellers are advised to take travellers cheques in US Dollars or Pounds Sterling.

Currency restrictions: The import and export of local currency is limited to Z$50,000. The import of foreign currency is unlimited. The export of foreign currency is unlimited as long as supported by the visitor's currency declaration form.

Exchange rate indicators: The following figures are included as a guide to the movements of the Zimbabwe Dollar against Sterling and the US Dollar:

Date	Feb '04	May '04	Aug '04	Nov '04
£1.00=	1502.86	9356.87	10233.0	10715.0
$1.00=	827.20	5316.10	5554.32	5658.22

Banking hours: Mon-Tue and Thurs-Fri 0800-1500, Wed 0800-1300 and Sat 0800-1130.

Duty Free

The following items may be imported into Zimbabwe without incurring customs duty:

Goods up to a value of US$250 per person, inclusive of tobacco, perfume and gifts; for persons of 18 years of age or older, 5l of alcoholic beverages (up to 2l of which may be spirits).

Note: (a) The import of drugs, honey, pornographic or obscene literature, toy firearms, flick knives and lockable knives is prohibited. (b) Permits are issued on arrival for firearms and ammunition. (c) Agricultural products including seeds and bulbs require an import licence.

Public Holidays

2005: Jan 1 New Year's Day. **Mar 25** Good Friday. **Mar 28** Easter Monday. **Apr 18** Independence Day. **May 1** Workers' Day. **May 25** Africa Day. **Aug 8** Heroes' Day. **Aug 9** Defence Forces Day. **Dec 22** Unity Day. **Dec 25-26** Christmas.

2006: Jan 1 New Year's Day. **Apr 14** Good Friday. **Apr 17** Easter Monday. **Apr 18** Independence Day. **May 1** Workers' Day. **May 25** Africa Day. **Aug 7** Heroes' Day. **Aug 8** Defence Forces Day. **Dec 22** Unity Day. **Dec 25-26** Christmas.

Health

	Special Precautions?	Certificate Required?
Yellow Fever	No	1
Cholera	Yes	2
Typhoid & Polio	3	N/A
Malaria	4	N/A

Note: *Regulations and requirements may be subject to change at short notice, and you are advised to contact your doctor well in advance of your intended date of departure. Any numbers in the chart refer to the footnotes below.*

1: A yellow fever vaccination certificate is required from travellers arriving from infected areas.

2: Following WHO guidelines issued in 1973, a cholera vaccination certificate is not a condition of entry to Zimbabwe. However, cholera is a risk in this country and precautions are advisable. Up-to-date advice should be sought before deciding whether these precautions should include vaccination, as medical opinion is divided over its effectiveness.

3: Vaccination against typhoid is advised.

4: Malaria risk, predominantly in the malignant *falciparum* form, exists from November to June in all areas below 1200m (3937ft) and throughout the year in the Zambezi Valley although there is negligible risk in Harare and Bulawayo. Resistance to chloroquine has been reported. The recommended prophylaxis is mefloquine.

Food & drink: All water should be regarded as being a potential health risk. Water used for drinking, brushing teeth or making ice should have first been boiled or otherwise sterilised.

Other risks: *Bilharzia* (schistosomiasis) is present. Avoid swimming and paddling in fresh water; swimming pools which are well chlorinated and maintained are safe. *Human trypanosomiasis* (sleeping sickness) has been reported. *Trachoma* and *Hepatitis A* and *E* are widespread. *Hepatitis B* is hyperendemic. Epidemics of *meningococcal meningitis* may occur, particularly in the savannah areas during the dry season. There may be a small risk of plague in rural areas, especially Matabeleland.

Rabies is present. For those at high risk, vaccination before arrival should be considered. If you are bitten, seek medical advice without delay. For more information, consult the *Health* appendix.

HIV/AIDS is a high risk throughout the country (around 25 per cent of the adult population are infected) and precautions should be taken.

Health care: Medical facilities are good in the major towns and there are well-equipped clinics in most outlying areas, although medical costs can be high. There may be drugs shortages in public hospitals. There is no reciprocal agreement with the UK. Health insurance is essential; adequate medical provision is often only provided privately, especially in urban areas. Private hospitals may require health insurance or a cash payment before admission.

Travel - International

Note: Visitors to Zimbabwe should exercise caution at all times and remain aware of recent developments in the country. It is recommended that visitors to the country travel only with organised tour operators to well-established destinations. There has been an increase in violent crime at political destinations but main tourist areas remain largely unaffected. High-density suburbs have been the target of particularly fierce political clashes and should therefore be avoided.

AIR: Zimbabwe's national airline is *Air Zimbabwe (UM)* (tel: (4) 575 021; website: www.airzim.co.zw). Other airlines serving Zimbabwe include *Aeroflot, Air Botswana, British Airways, Egyptair, KLM, Lufthansa, Majestic Air, South African Airlines* and *Zambia Airways*.

Approximate flight times: From Harare to *London* is nine hours 50 minutes. There are direct flights connecting London with Victoria Falls. Connections from the capital to Bulawayo take approximately one hour.

International airports: *Harare (HRE)* is 14km (9 miles) southeast of the city. Coaches run at regular intervals to the city (travel time – 20 minutes). Taxis are available. Airport facilities include post office, restaurant, duty free shop and bank/bureau de change.

Bulawayo (BUQ) is 24km (15 miles) from the city. Limited bus and taxi services are available.

Victoria Falls (VFA) is 22km (13 miles) from the town. Bus and taxi services are available.

Departure tax: US$20 (non-residents); US$20 or equivalent in local currency (residents). Children under two years and transit passengers are exempt.

RAIL: There are train connections from South Africa through Botswana to Bulawayo. There is a link to Zambia via Victoria Falls.

ROAD: There are roads from Botswana, Malawi, Mozambique, South Africa, Tanzania and Zambia. Off the main routes (Beitbridge and Victoria Falls), travel conditions are often difficult during heavy rains. Border posts are generally open from 0600-1800, although the more popular routes through Beitbridge, Plumtree and Victoria Falls are open from 0600-2000.

Travel - Internal

Note: Carjacking, street crime, rape and credit card fraud are on the increase due to high rates of unemployment and deteriorating economic conditions. US citizens and other foreigners are perceived to be wealthy and therefore could be targeted by criminals who operate in the vicinity of hotels, restaurants and shopping malls in Harare and in the major tourist areas, such as Victoria Falls. Caution should be exercised at all times. Travellers are also encouraged to make two photocopies of the biographic page of their passport; leave one copy at home with friends or relatives and carry the second copy for identification and sightseeing purposes.

AIR: Connections to Buffalo Range, Bulawayo, Gweru, Hwange, Kariba, Masvingo and Victoria Falls are run by *Air Zimbabwe* and other airlines. There are also special light-aircraft services at Kariba and Victoria Falls offering sightseeing and game-viewing flights.

RAIL: There are daily trains between Bulawayo, Chiredzi, Harare, Labatse, Mutare, Plumtree, Triangle and Victoria Falls run by *National Railways of Zimbabwe* (website: www.planet.nu/sunshinecity/nrz). The rail system is under-developed and poorly maintained.

ROAD: There is an excellent road network, with paved roads connecting all major towns and many rural areas. Traffic drives on the left. There are often fuel shortages, particularly outside the main cities, and therefore it is wise to drive with a full tank of petrol when possible.

Bus/coach: There are a number of buses, minibuses and coach services serving most of the country. However, buses are not recommended since they are often overcrowded and inadequately maintained. *Blue Arrow Luxury Coaches* provides bus services to principal destinations including Harare-Bulawayo (via Chivhu and Kwe Kwe). For more details, contact the Zimbabwe Tourism Authority (see *Contact Addresses* section) or, for ground handlers, contact Zimbabwe Tourism Office in London (see *Contact Addresses* section). **Car hire:** Available at airports and main hotels. **Documentation:** International Driving Permit or national licence; if not in English, it must be accompanied by a certificate of authority or translation of text.

URBAN: A reasonable bus service is provided in Harare by a subsidiary of the *Zimbabwe Omnibus Company*. Tickets are bought in advance from booths. There is also a local bus network in Bulawayo.

WATER: Ferries run on Lake Kariba from Kariba to Binga and Mlibizi.

Accommodation

HOTELS: There are hotels and lodges (which are similar to guest houses and provide bed and breakfast). A list of registered hotels is available from the Zimbabwe Tourism Authority (see *Contact Addresses* section). Non-residents must pay hotel bills in foreign currency (usually US$) or by credit card. Local currency is not acceptable, even on presentation of exchange certificates. **Grading:** All hotels are graded on a 5-star system, with those classified 1-star or above being registered with the Zimbabwe Tourism Authority. Over 70 hotels are registered. Further information can be obtained from the Hospitality Association of Zimbabwe (HAZ), PO Box CY 398, Causeway, Harare (tel: (4) 733 211 *or* 792 919; fax: (4) 708 872; e-mail: hazim@ecoweb.co.zw; website: www.haz.co.zw).

CAMPING/CARAVANNING: Most centres and tourist areas have caravan parks and campsites.

Resorts & Excursions

Running from northeast to southwest down the centre of the country, and connecting its two largest cities, is the **Highveld**, a chain of low mountains and Zimbabwe's most populous area.

HARARE: Formerly Salisbury, the capital is Zimbabwe's commercial and industrial centre and also the usual starting point for any visit. It is a clean and sophisticated city, characterised by flowering trees, colourful parks and contemporary architecture. Local sightseeing includes the modern museum and art gallery, the **Robert McIlwaine Recreational Park**, which has a lake and game reserve, the **Lion & Cheetah Park**, the **Larvon Bird Gardens** and the landscaped gardens of aloes and cycads at **Ewanrigg Botanical Gardens**. Due to its pleasant climate, Harare is known as the 'Sunshine City'.

BULAWAYO: Zimbabwe's second city is a major commercial, industrial and tourist centre. The city is rich in historical associations and is the home of the **National Museum** and headquarters of the National Railways of Zimbabwe. Nearby are the ancient **Khami ruins**, while to the south is the **Rhodes Matopos National Park**, notable for its

Appendices

Appendices

Travel Trade Associations

ABTA

In 2004, visits abroad by UK residents rose by 4 per cent to reach a total of 63.6 million, according to national statistics conducted by Census (website: www.statistics.gov.uk). Such statistics augment sustained growth in UK travel and tourism over the last few years, hinting at the overcoming of global deterrents, such as 9-11 in New York and the subsequent 'War on Terror', which initially blighted UK confidence in overseas travel. To summarise, more UK nationals are travelling abroad than ever before. All of which puts a big responsibility on the organisation that represents the vast majority of tour operators and travel agents in Britain – the Association of British Travel Agents (ABTA). Indeed, ABTA recently announced record data for online searches in January 2005: its website logged over 100,000 searches, a figure that doubles the amount recorded the previous year. January is a notorious peak period for people researching holidays, but it appears that more people are choosing to research their holidays through recognized and trusted Associations, and ABTA's profile continues to expand, particularly since the appointment of its new President, Martin Wellings, in 2004. It is for all these reasons that the Association strives so hard to ensure consistently high standards of trading practice for the benefit of consumers and the travel industry. ABTA's principal duties are to create as favourable a business environment as possible for its Members, while ensuring that standards of service and business throughout its Membership are of the highest calibre. This is all good news for the holidaymaker, to whom ABTA's famous symbol has come to represent choice, value and protection.

ABTA was formed in 1950 with just 100 Members, at a time that coincided with the dawn of a new era for British travellers. World War II had set in motion huge advances in aviation technology, and the advent of the jet aircraft brought foreign travel within the scope of a far wider group than ever before. Foreign travel came to be seen as a temporary escape from the drabness of post-war Britain and the mass-market holiday boom began. So how does ABTA work?

- ABTA is a self-regulatory body that is run by its Membership. The Board of Directors and Committees, appointed by Members, make up the policy-making and enforcing machinery of the Association and help to ensure that ABTA remains in close touch with the whole of its Membership, plus dealing with the many areas of specific interest to the industry.

  As well as their year-round work to raise standards and improve conditions throughout the industry, ABTA's Board and Committees are also active behind the scenes. This action takes the form of liaison and negotiation with other trade bodies and representatives of government in the UK and overseas – for example, to reduce delays at airports, put pressure on governments to avert air traffic control strikes, improve insurance cover recommended by ABTA travel agents and protest at the ever-increasing range of taxes on travellers.
- ABTA shall continue to lobby, on behalf of its Members and general public, for the abolition of the Air Passenger Duty tax (holiday poll tax) throughout 2005. ABTA is also expected to continue parliamentary lobbying regarding issues such as airport expansion and advance passenger information being required by overseas governments. ABTA has also just overseen successful lobbying of the review of US entry procedure; the necessity for biometric passport data requirements has now been delayed until October 2005.
- The Members of ABTA are required to adhere to strict rules that govern their business practice. These are contained in ABTA's Code of Conduct that regulates all aspects of tour operators' and travel agents' relationships with their customers (and between themselves), and which have been drawn up by specialists in the travel industry in conjunction with the Office of Fair Trading. One of the principal aims of the Code is to promote the best interests of the consumer and, at the same time, maintain high standards and beneficial trading conditions within the industry.
- The Code of Conduct lays down in detail the minimum standards on brochures, requiring that they contain clear, comprehensive and accurate descriptions of such things as the type of travel, destination, nature of accommodation and meal facilities offered. It details rules that govern booking conditions in brochures as they relate, for example, to the cancellation or alteration of tours, holidays or other travel arrangements by the tour operator. It also contains strict rules about dealing with complaints promptly and efficiently. The Code also regulates the conduct between tour operators and travel agents. The Code regulates all aspects of Members' relationships with their customers, and covers their responsibility with regard to the standard of service they provide and the information they are responsible for giving – for example, regarding insurance facilities, passport, visa and health requirements or alterations to travel arrangements. It also lays down rules concerning Members' trading relationships with each other.
- Members of ABTA are required to adhere to precise financial specifications monitored by ABTA's Financial Services Department, which regularly checks all Members' accounts. ABTA's wholly owned subsidiary, TTC Training, works to ensure high standards of training for the industry, and therefore high standards of service to the consumer, which is a logical and important responsibility. The TTC runs a series of comprehensive courses for all levels of experience and for all age groups, which are respected throughout the travel trade.
- ABTA administers a comprehensive system of financial protection, the purpose of which is to ensure that if an ABTA Member fails financially, ABTA is able to arrange for customers whose holidays or other travel arrangements are in progress at the time of the failure to continue their holidays, as far as possible as originally planned, and, in any event, to make certain that customers abroad are returned to the UK. ABTA also reimburses customers whose holidays have not yet started to enable them to make alternative holiday arrangements.
- Tour operator- and travel agent-Members of ABTA are required to provide bonds or other suitable protection to secure their customers in the event of financial failure. In addition, there are funds which cover all Members and provide a 'second line of defence' to back up the extensive bonding system.
- There are one or two exceptions to this wide-ranging protection scheme. It should be noted that it does not apply in the event of financial

failure of a non-ABTA company or firm, even if the booking was made through an ABTA travel agent. Completed holidays or contracts that have been terminated or broken at the time of financial failure are also not covered by this financial protection.

- In addition to a comprehensive advice service offered to pre- and post-departure queries, the Association provides a low-cost independent arbitration service to Members' clients who have failed to get their dispute settled. It is administered by the Chartered Institute of Arbitrators, and the costs are subsidised by ABTA. The scheme provides for a simple and inexpensive method of arbitration on documents alone, with the ruling of the Arbitrator being legally binding. A client may elect against using this service and may prefer to resolve a dispute through the courts.

For further information, contact: ABTA, 68-71 Newman Street, London W1T 3AH, UK (tel: (020) 7637 2444 or (0901) 201 5050 (travel information line; UK callers only; 50p per minute) or (020) 7307 1900 (press enquiries); fax: (020) 7637 0713; e-mail: information@abta.co.uk or consumer.affairs@abta.co.uk (post-holiday enquiries only) or corporate@abta.co.uk (press enquiries); website: www.abta.com). Contact: Keith Betton/Frances Tuke.

ACTA

The Association of Canadian Travel Agencies (ACTA) is a national non-profit trade association, which was established in 1977.

ACTA's mission is to represent the interests of its members - primarily retail travel agents - to the public, to governments, to suppliers and other bodies, assisting them in maximising their economic objectives. ACTA's core functions include advocacy, information and research, public relations and the development of membership for the purposes of strengthening the association's effectiveness as the voice of the industry.

ACTA's board of directors consists of 10 travel professionals, working to improve the industry and assist ACTA members in reaching their professional objectives. ACTA's seven regional offices are critical to the national association's success as they work diligently at serving the needs of members at the grassroots level. As members of Canada's largest, not-for-profit retail travel association, members benefit from the following:

- Information on travel industry developments;
- Input into the association's advocacy agenda;
- Invitations to regional and national events, conferences and tradeshows;
- International industry representation through alliances with affiliated associations in other countries;
- Member-discounted rates for various products and services;
- Research and information on consumer and market trends.

For further information, contact: ACTA, Suite 1705, 130 Albert Street, Ottawa, Ontario, Canada K1P 5G4 (tel: (613) 237 3657; fax: (613) 237 7052; e-mail: pbeauparlant@acta.ca or tlambert@acta.ca; website: www.acta.ca).

AFTA

The Australian Federation of Travel Agents Limited (AFTA) is the representative body for Australia's travel agents with its Head Office located in Pitt Street, Sydney, and was founded in 1957. AFTA represents the majority of travel agents in Australia.

AFTA provides financial, legal and marketing benefits, education and training, and develops policies and strategies critical to the retail travel sector. AFTA also has affiliated membership with the Universal Federation of Travel Agents Associations (UFTAA), ensuring that AFTA is listened to at international forums.

AFTA's role as industry watchdog ensures that the viewpoint of the agent is transmitted through media outlets and through lobbying activities. AFTA policies are established by a national Board of Directors in conjunction with the Chief Executive, and AFTA provides a unique forum of industry networking through its Chapter Meetings and Conferences.

Major Activities:

- The Australian Travel Professionals Program (ATPP), established by AFTA to "enhance professionalism through education", has over 2900 members from both retail and wholesale sectors of our industry. The Program helps meet the needs of consumers and the travel industry for professional standards and quality service.
- The AFTA Travel & Tourism Colleges are owned and operated by AFTA. Support for the colleges is given by the travel and tourism industry through on-the-job training and employment of graduates. The AFTA Colleges produce graduates of exceptionally high calibre. Colleges are located in five major cities: Adelaide, Brisbane, Melbourne, Perth and Sydney. There is also an External Studies program for those wishing to gain entry into the industry.
- AFTA Travel Insurance.
- AFTA Traveller Magazine is the official magazine of AFTA, published quarterly.
- AFTA Business Insurance for AFTA travel Agents.
- Credit Card Fee Rates: AFTA has negotiated various Merchant Fee Rates on behalf of AFTA Members.
- Annual Conventions.
- Domestic Tourism Educational (DTE) – held in all major Australian capital cities, these workshops allow principals and agents to discuss travel and tourism developments in Australia.
- Industry and Government relations.
- Consumer grievance and ethics service.
- Conciliation process for industry disputes.

For further information, contact: AFTA Limited, 3rd Floor, 309 Pitt Street, Sydney NSW 2000, Australia (tel: (02) 9264 3299 or (1300) 326 416; fax: (02) 9264 1085; e-mail: afta@afta.com.au; website: www.afta.com.au).

ANTOR

ANTOR, the Association of National Tourist Office Representatives in the United Kingdom, has a membership of more than 90 National Tourist Offices representing countries from all over the world, with vastly different attractions, resources, geographical features and cultural heritages. This voluntary non-political organisation has been established since the early 1950s. It serves the dual role of a forum for the exchange of views and experiences of its members, and of a driving force for joint promotional activities aimed at both the trade and the consumer.

Drawing on broad knowledge and experience, ANTOR brings a fully international approach to problems affecting all aspects of the travel industry, with which ANTOR works in close partnership. It maintains contact with the media and other organisations in the travel industry, such as ABTA, AITO, CIMTIG, FTO and ITT, and is frequently called on for its views on matters relating to the industry as a whole.

ANTOR thus aims, through mutual cooperation, to coordinate and improve services that government tourist offices offer to the UK travel industry and to the consumer. ANTOR's regular business meetings for its members are also often addressed by leading tourism experts.

For further information, contact: ANTOR, PO Box 5017, Hove, East Sussex BN23 3ZD, UK (tel: (0870) 241 9084; e-mail: secretary@antor.com; website: www.antor.com).

ASTA

The international travel and tourism industry transcends borders. Business colleagues and customers are situated all over the world. The challenge is often to find a way to expand the focus beyond the community and promote services to those colleagues on the other side of the world. The American Society of Travel Agents (ASTA) aims to provide that opportunity. Members of ASTA gain access to the following international membership benefits:

Industry Integrity and Consumer Awareness:

- Asta Logo: Consumers and US travel agents look for the ASTA logo because they prefer to do business with firms they can trust. ASTA members adhere to the strong Code of Ethics and Bylaws, thus assuring that ASTA members are reputable companies. Members receive exclusive use of the ASTA logo on their letterhead, storefronts, websites, etc.
- International Photo ID Membership Card: US suppliers and travel agents worldwide recognize the international Photo Membership Card as a sign of professionalism and "integrity in travel".

ASTAnet:

- Industry Information: ASTAnet is a major information resource available 24 hours. ASTAnet contains information on business practices, commission levels, and up-to-the-minute industry information.
- Web Exchange: A new service on ASTAnet, the Web Exchange is similar to a virtual bulletin board listing travel and supplier specials, important commission notices and other needs by ASTA agents and suppliers. Many postings concern the need for receptive agents all over the world.
- Directory Listing: ASTA members receive a free listing on ASTAnet's online member directory. The listing will include a link to the member's e-mail address and an optional link to their website, providing exposure to other members and consumers worldwide.
- Trip Request Service: ASTA's Trip Request Service offers members exclusive access to potential business from consumers. Anywhere from US$500,000 to US$1,000,000 in business awaits each day.

Education and Business Service:

- World Travel Congress: Meet international and US agents and suppliers who are looking for business partners across borders at this world-class event, scheduled for November 6-11 in Montréal in Quebec, Canada.
- Global Discussion Groups: An automated e-mail tool for interactive discussions on topics of common interest with travel agents around the world.

For more information, contact: ASTA, 1101 King Street, Ste. 200, Alexandria, Virginia 22314, USA (tel: (703) 739 2782; fax: (703) 684 8319; e-mail: askasta@astahq.com; website: www.astanet.com).

ITT

The Institute of Travel & Tourism (ITT) was inaugurated in 1956 when the package tourism industry was in its infancy. Its original members were a handful of professionals who recognised the need for an organisation to set, maintain and improve standards within the travel and tourism industry.

The aim of ITT is "to develop the professionalism of its members within the industry". This may seem a high ideal for an industry that is fragmented and has traditionally prided itself on its entrepreneurial spirit. There are many in the travel industry who, with no formal training, are justifiably proud of their achievements, earned by hard work on the job. However, today's travel market is sophisticated, highly competitive and requires the use of complex information technology. Imagination and common sense are not always enough, and everyone involved in the travel business needs to be competent and well trained – in short, a professional. Consequently, ITT aims to help practising and potential managers develop and maintain their professional knowledge and skills. The awarding of a recognised professional qualification entitles members to use designatory letters within their title: A Inst TT, M Inst TT, F Inst TT. ITT ensures that these designations are recognised as a mark of professional achievement.

ITT acknowledges the importance of education and training at every level of experience and seniority. Many young people follow full-time courses of study at colleges around the UK. ITT accredits college courses that offer comprehensive and high-quality teaching, equipment and facilities. Students attending Institute-approved colleges are assured of the highest-quality education and preparation for a career in the travel industry. This accreditation process has now been extended to include in-company skills training courses. The accreditation of in-house management-level training will be developed in the near future.

Formal qualifications are essential in establishing a minimum level of knowledge and expertise, but ITT recognises that continuing professional development is crucial. To this end, ITT runs a series of one-day seminars each year, on subjects as diverse as travel legislation and the law, brochure production, technology, time management, presentation skills, negotiating skills, sales skills, management skills, business development and financial management and control. These seminars are offered both as open courses or in-house courses for companies, which can be tailored or developed to meet the specific needs of individual firms.

ITT arranges regular meetings for members, providing a forum for discussion of current issues, such as market conditions and legislation. ITT also organises an annual conference, which gives members the opportunity to probe issues affecting the industry, and to hear the views of senior industry figures and opinion formers. In 2005, *the annual conference takes place 13 to 15 June in Barbados*. ITT is also hosting its second annual conference for aspiring travel professionals, ASPIRE 05, in Liverpool, UK. Product knowledge is essential too, and educational tours to destinations such as Disneyland Paris, The Gambia and India have been organised for members in recent years.

ITT is managed by a Chief Executive reporting to a Board of Directors, comprised of senior travel industry professionals.

For further information, contact: ITT, Mill Studio, Crane Mead, Ware, Hertfordshire SG12 9PY, UK (tel: (0870) 770 7960; fax: (0870) 770 7961; e-mail: enquiries@itt.co.uk; website: www.itt.co.uk).

UFTAA

UFTAA, founded in 1966, is the United Federation of Travel Agents' Associations and the highest world body representing the travel industry. In 2003, UFTAA became a Confederation comprising nine regions worldwide. The national associations are thus members through their respective regions. In addition to the National Associations, UFTAA highly values the individual membership and support of a large number of individual travel agents, tour operators, wholesalers, travel partners and others allied to the tourist industry. UFTAA represents some 100 national associations which, together with additional affiliate members, cover a total of 118 countries. The 2005 UFTAA Congress is to be held from 24 to 28 October in Mauritius.

The Federation's objectives are:

- To provide an international forum where worldwide travel issues are addressed.
- To unite and reinforce national associations of travel agents and thereby encourage the establishment of associations in countries where they do not exist.
- To represent and promote the interests of the trade to governments, suppliers and other international bodies and take any initiative that can help, stimulate and develop the travel and tourism sector throughout the world.
- To serve, help and advise members, to see to their protection and development within economic, legal and social spheres, and take the necessary steps to standardise norms of professional ethics.
- To encourage and maintain efficient communication between members.
- To preserve human and natural environments and a harmonious co-existence of all sectors of travel and tourism.
- To study and disseminate legislation relating to travel trade activities, particularly those that overlap national borders.

UFTAA also operates in cooperation with IATA, a Professional Travel Agents' ID-Card Programme offering reduced travel benefits and added values at national level, as well as travel accident insurance minimising the risks for travel agents at an affordable cost. Additionally, UFTAA offers professional assistance through the Travel Agency Commissioners, as well as legal and litigation services.

For further information, contact: UFTAA, 1 avenue des Castelans, Stade Louis II, Entrée H, MC-98000 Monaco (tel (377) 9205 2829; fax: (377) 9205 2987; e-mail: uftaa@uftaa.org; website: www.uftaa.org).

WATA

WATA, the World Association of Travel Agencies, is a non-profit-making organisation created by independent travel agents for the benefit of all travel agencies around the world. It helps locally respected agencies combine their personal touch with the influence gained by global recognition. Since its foundation in 1949, WATA has become a truly well-respected name in the travel industry worldwide. With over 100 members in 50 countries, WATA has today established an international network of travel agents who enjoy some unique privileges and benefits. WATA's basic idea is to bring local (preferably privately owned) travel agencies into an international network, so that every member is offered all the facilities and advantages of being associated with an international body – in addition to enjoying local prominence. As a consequence, a substantial increase in the volume of business to the agency's turnover can be expected.

By becoming a WATA member, a travel agency/tour operator can rely on:

- Business opportunities: WATA insures business increase visibility of the member's products and business support.
- Exclusivity: Striving for recognition and credibility on the market.
- Dynamism: Members are proactive, exchanging ideas, experience and expertise.
- Prestige and quality: Assurance of a high quality of service.

In addition to having 100 members worldwide and respectability within the tourism industry, WATA is launching a full E-Business platform to promote and sell the incoming services of its members worldwide.

Membership of WATA is open to any travel agency, preferably privately owned, which can prove a sound financial structure, and that adheres to the highest professional standards expected in the industry, enjoying a prominent standing in the local community. WATA membership is exclusive on a per-city basis so a strong selection is made.

Please apply for an application form and a copy of the Articles of Association.

For further information, contact: Administrative Manager, WATA, 11 rue Riant Coteau, 1196 GLAND, Switzerland (tel: (22) 995 1545; fax: (22) 995 1546; e-mail: wata@wata.net; website: www.wata.net).

International Organisations

Listed below are major international organisations concerned with economics and trade.

Asia-Pacific Economic Co-operation – APEC

35 Heng Mui Keng Terrace, Singapore 119616

Tel: (65) 6775 6012.

Fax: (65) 6775 6013.

E-mail: info@apec.org

Website: www.apec.org

Members: Australia, Brunei, Canada, Chile, China (PR), Chinese Taipei, Hong Kong (SAR), Indonesia, Japan, Korea (Rep), Malaysia, Mexico, New Zealand, Papua New Guinea, Peru, The Philippines, Russian Federation, Singapore, Taiwan (China), Thailand, USA, Vietnam.

Asociación Latinoamericana de Integración – ALADI

(Latin American Integration Association – LAIA)

Cebollati 1461, Montevideo 11200, Uruguay

Tel: (2) 410 1121.

Fax: (2) 419 0649.

E-mail: sgaladi@aladi.org

Website: www.aladi.org

Members: Argentina, Bolivia, Brazil, Chile, Colombia, Cuba, Ecuador, Mexico, Paraguay, Peru, Uruguay and Venezuela.

Association of Southeast Asian Nations – ASEAN

70A Jalan Sisingamangaraja, Jakarta 12110, Indonesia

Tel: (21) 726 2991 or 724 3372.

Fax: (21) 739 8234 or 724 3504.

E-mail: public@aseansec.org

Website: www.aseansec.org

Members: Brunei, Cambodia, Indonesia, Laos, Malaysia, Myanmar, The Philippines, Singapore, Thailand and Vietnam.

Caribbean Community & Common Market – CARICOM

Street Address: 3rd Floor, Bank of Guyana Building, 1 Avenue of the Republic, Georgetown, Guyana

Postal Address: PO Box 10827, Georgetown, Guyana

Tel: (22) 69280-9. Fax: (22) 67816.

E-mail: carisec2@caricom.org

Website: www.caricom.org

Members: Antigua & Barbuda, The Bahamas, Barbados, Belize, Dominica, Grenada, Guyana, Haiti, Jamaica, Montserrat, St Kitts & Nevis, St Lucia, St Vincent & The Grenadines, Surinam and Trinidad & Tobago.

Associate Members: Anguilla, Bermuda, British Virgin Islands, Cayman Islands and Turks & Caicos Islands.

Observers: Aruba, Colombia, Dominican Republic, Mexico, The Netherlands Antilles, Puerto Rico and Venezuela.

The Colombo Plan for Co-operative Economic & Social Development in Asia and the Pacific

13th Floor, Bank of Ceylon, Merchant Tower, 28 St Michael's Road, Colombo 3, Sri Lanka

Tel: (11) 2564 448. Fax: (11) 2564 531.

E-mail: info@colombo-plan.org

Website: www.colombo-plan.org

Members: Afghanistan, Australia, Bangladesh, Bhutan, Cambodia, Fiji, India, Indonesia, Iran, Japan, Korea (Rep), Laos, Malaysia, Maldives, Mongolia, Myanmar, Nepal, New Zealand, Pakistan, Papua New Guinea, The Philippines, Singapore, Sri Lanka, Thailand, the USA and Vietnam.

Commonwealth

Commonwealth Secretariat, Marlborough House, Pall Mall, London SW1Y 5HX, UK

Tel: (020) 7747 6500. Fax: (020) 7930 0827.

E-mail: info@commonwealth.int

Website: www.thecommonwealth.org

Members: Antigua & Barbuda, Australia, The Bahamas, Bangladesh, Barbados, Belize, Botswana, Brunei, Cameroon, Canada, Cyprus, Dominica, Fiji, The Gambia, Ghana, Grenada, Guyana, India, Jamaica, Kenya, Kiribati, Lesotho, Malawi, Malaysia, Maldives, Malta, Mauritius, Mozambique, Namibia, Nauru, New Zealand, Nigeria, Pakistan, Papua New Guinea, St Kitts & Nevis, St Lucia, St Vincent & The Grenadines, Samoa, Seychelles, Sierra Leone, Singapore, Solomon Islands, South Africa, Sri Lanka, Swaziland, Tonga, Trinidad & Tobago, Tuvalu, Uganda, United Kingdom, United Republic of Tanzania, Vanuatu and Zambia.

Dependencies & Associated States: Australia: Ashmore & Cartier Islands, Australian Antarctic Territory, Christmas Island (Pacific), Cocos (Keeling) Island, Coral Sea Islands Territory, Heard & McDonald Islands and Norfolk Island; New Zealand: Cook Islands, Niue, Ross Dependency and Tokelau Islands; United Kingdom: Anguilla, Bermuda, British Antarctic Territory, British Indian Ocean Territory, British Virgin Islands, Cayman Islands, Channel Islands, Ducie & Oeno Islands, Falkland Islands, Gibraltar, Henderson, Isle of Man, Montserrat, Pitcairn, St Helena and Dependencies (Ascension Island and Tristan da Cunha), South Georgia, South Sandwich Islands and Turks & Caicos Islands.

Commonwealth of Independent States – CIS

17 Kirov Street, 220050 Minsk, Belarus

Tel: (17) 222 3517. Fax: (17) 227 2339.

E-mail: postmaster@www.cis.minsk.by

Website: www.cis.minsk.by

Members: Armenia, Azerbaijan, Belarus, Georgia, Kazakhstan, Kyrgyzstan, Moldova, Russian Federation, Tajikistan, Turkmenistan, Ukraine and Uzbekistan.

Co-operation Council for the Arab States of the Gulf

Tel: (1) 482 7777 (ext 1245).

Fax: (1) 482 9109.

Members: Bahrain, Kuwait, Oman, Qatar, Saudi Arabia, United Arab Emirates.

Council of Arab Economic Unity

Street Address: General Secretariat, 1113 Cornishe El-Nil Street, 4th Floor, Cairo, Egypt

Postal Address: PO Box (1) Mohammed Farid 11518, Cairo, Egypt

Tel: (2) 575 5321 or 575 4252 or 575 5045.

Fax: (2) 575 4090.

E-mail: caeu@idsc.net.eg

Website: www.caeu.org.eg

Members: Egypt, Iraq, Jordan, Kuwait, Libya, Mauritania, Palestine National Authority, Somalia, Sudan, the Syrian Arab Republic and Yemen (Rep).

Council of Europe

Avenue de l'Europe, 67075 Strasbourg CEDEX, France

Tel: (3) 8841 2000 (general) or 8841 2033 (information point). Fax: (1) 8841 2745.

E-mail: infopoint@coe.int or media@coe.int

Website: www.coe.int

Economic Community of West African States – ECOWAS

60 Yakubu Gowon Crescent, Asokoro District, PMB 401, Abuja, Nigeria

Tel: (9) 314 7647-9.

Fax: (9) 314 3005 or 314 7646.

E-mail: info@ecowas.net

Website: www.sec.ecowas.int

Members: Benin, Burkina Faso, Cape Verde, Côte d'Ivoire, The Gambia, Ghana, Guinea, Guinea-Bissau, Liberia, Mali, Niger, Nigeria, Senegal, Sierra Leone and Togo.

European Union – EU

Brey 12th Floor, Office 100, B-1049 Brussels, Belgium

Tel: (2) 299 1559. Fax: (2) 295 8532.

Website: www.europa.eu.int

Meetings of the principal organs take place in Brussels, Luxembourg and Strasbourg.

Members: Austria, Belgium, Denmark, Finland, France, Germany (Federal Republic of), Greece, Ireland, Italy, Luxembourg, The Netherlands, Portugal, Spain, Sweden and the United Kingdom.

The following new members joined the EU on May 1 2004: Cyprus, Czech Republic, Estonia, Hungary, Latvia, Lithuania, Malta, Poland, the Slovak Republic and Slovenia.

European Central Bank – ECB
Street Address: Kaiserstrasse 29, D-60311, Frankfurt-am-Main, Germany
Postal Address: Postfach 16 0319, D-60066, Frankfurt-am-Main, Germany
Tel: (69) 13440.
Fax: (69) 1344 6000.
E-mail: info@ecb.int
Website: www.ecb.int

European Free Trade Association – EFTA
9-11 rue de Varembé, CH-1211 Geneva 20, Switzerland
Tel: (22) 332 2626.
Fax: (22) 332 2699.
E-mail: mail.gva@efta.int
Website: www.efta.int
Members: Iceland, Liechtenstein, Norway and Switzerland.

Franc Zone
Direction Générale des Services Etrangers (Service de la Zone Franc), Banque de France, 31 rue Croix-des-Petits-Champs, BP 75001, Paris Cedex 01, France
Tel: (1) 4292 4292 or 6480 2020. Fax: (1) 4292 3988.
Website: www.banque-france.fr
Members: Benin, Burkina Faso, Cameroon, Central African Republic, Chad, Comoros, Congo, Côte d'Ivoire, Equatorial Guinea, Gabon, Guinea-Bissau, Mali, Niger, Senegal and Togo.

League of Arab States
Arab League Building, PO Box 11642, Medan, Tahrir Square, Cairo, Egypt
Tel: (2) 575 0511. Fax: (2) 574 0331.
Website: www.arableagueonline.org
Members: Algeria, Bahrain, Comoro Islands, Djibouti, Egypt, Iraq, Jordan, Kuwait, Lebanon, Libya, Mauritania, Morocco, Oman, Palestine National Authority, Qatar, Saudi Arabia, Somalia, Sudan, Syrian Arab Republic, Tunisia, United Arab Emirates and Yemen (Rep).

Nordic Council
Store Strandstræde 18, DK 1255, Copenhagen, Denmark
Tel: (33) 960 400.
Fax: (33) 111 870.
E-mail: nordisk-rad@norden.org
Website: www.norden.org
Members: Denmark (with the autonomous territories of the Faroe Islands and Greenland), Finland (with the autonomous territory of the Åland Islands), Iceland, Norway and Sweden.

Organisation for Economic Co-operation & Development – OECD
2 rue André Pascal, F-75775, Paris Cedex 16, France
Tel: (1) 4524 8200.
Fax: (1) 4524 8500.
Website: www.oecd.org
Members: Australia, Austria, Belgium, Canada, Czech Republic, Denmark, Finland, France, Germany (Federal Republic of), Greece, Hungary, Iceland, Ireland, Italy, Japan, Korea (Rep), Luxembourg, Mexico, The Netherlands, New Zealand, Norway, Poland, Portugal, Slovak Republic, Spain, Sweden, Switzerland, Turkey, United Kingdom and the USA.

African Union - AU
Street Address: Roosevelt Street (Old Airport Area) W21 K19, Addis Ababa, Ethiopia
Postal Address: PO Box 3243, W21 K19, Addis Ababa, Ethiopia
Tel: (1) 517 700.
Fax: (1) 517 844.
Website: www.africa-union.org
Members: Algeria, Angola, Benin, Botswana, Burkina Faso, Burundi, Cameroon, Cape Verde, Central African Republic, Chad, Comoros, Congo (Dem Rep), Congo (Rep), Côte d'Ivoire, Djibouti, Egypt, Equatorial Guinea, Eritrea, Ethiopia, Gabon, The Gambia, Ghana, Guinea, Guinea-Bissau, Kenya, Lesotho, Liberia, Libya, Madagascar, Malawi, Mali, Mauritania, Mauritius, Mozambique, Namibia, Niger, Nigeria, Rwanda, Saharan Arab Democratic Republic, São Tomé & Príncipe, Senegal, Seychelles, Sierra Leone, Somalia, South Africa, Sudan, Swaziland, Tanzania, Togo, Tunisia, Uganda, Zambia and Zimbabwe.

Organisation of American States – OAS
17th Street & Constitution Avenue, NW, Washington, DC 20006, USA
Tel: (202) 458 3000.
Fax: (202) 458 3967.
Website: www.oas.org
Members: Antigua & Barbuda, Argentina, The Bahamas, Barbados, Belize, Bolivia, Brazil, Canada, Chile, Colombia, Costa Rica, Cuba*, Dominica, Dominican Republic, Ecuador, El Salvador, Grenada, Guatemala, Guyana, Haiti, Honduras, Jamaica, Mexico, Nicaragua, Panama, Paraguay, Peru, St Kitts & Nevis, St Lucia, St Vincent & the Grenadines, Surinam, Trinidad & Tobago, Uruguay, the USA and Venezuela.
Note: *The Cuban government was suspended from OAS activities in 1962.

Organisation of the Petroleum Exporting Countries – OPEC
Obere Donaustrasse 93, A-1020 Vienna, Austria
Tel: (1) 21112 279.
Fax: (1) 21498 27.
Website: www.opec.org
Members: Algeria, Indonesia, Iran, Iraq, Kuwait, Libya, Nigeria, Qatar, Saudi Arabia, United Arab Emirates and Venezuela.

Secretariat of Central American Economic Integration – SIECA
Secretaria de Integración Económica Centroamericana, formerly known as MCCA – Mercado Común Centroamericano
4a Avenida 10-25, Zona 14, Apartado Postal 1237, 01901 Guatemala City, Guatemala
Tel: (3) 682 151/4.
Fax: (3) 681 071 or 373 750.
E-mail: info@sieca.org.gt
Website: www.sieca.org.gt
Members: Costa Rica, Guatemala, El Salvador, Honduras and Nicaragua.

South Pacific Forum
c/o Pacific Islands Forum Secretariat, Ratu Sukuna Road, Private Mail Bag, Suva, Fiji
Tel: 331 2600. Fax: 330 5573.
E-mail: info@forumsec.org.fj
Website: www.forumsec.org.fj
Members: Australia, Cook Islands, Fiji, Kiribati, Marshall Islands, Micronesia (Federated States of), Nauru, New Zealand, Niue, Palau, Papua New Guinea, Samoa, Solomon Islands, Tonga, Tuvalu and Vanuatu.

Southern African Development Community – SADC
SADC House, Private Bag 0095, Gaborone, Botswana
Tel: 395 1863. Fax: 397 2848.
E-mail: registry@sadc.int
Website: www.sadc.int
Members: Angola, Botswana, Congo (Dem Rep), Lesotho, Malawi, Mauritius, Mozambique, Namibia, South Africa, Swaziland, Tanzania, Zambia and Zimbabwe.

Union of the Arab Maghreb
14 Rue Zalagh, Agdal, Rabat, Morocco
Tel: (37) 671 274/8 or 280.
Fax: (37) 671 253.
Website: www.maghrebarabe.org
The location of the Union's Secretariat rotates with the chairmanship.
Members: Algeria, Libya, Mauritania, Morocco and Tunisia.

United Nations
United Nations Headquarters, First Avenue at 46th Street, New York, NY 10017, USA
Tel: (212) 963 7112 or 963 4475 (public enquiries).
Fax: (212) 963 4879.
E-mail: inquiries@un.org
Website: www.un.org
Members: The UN currently has 191 Member States.

United Nations Conference on Trade and Development – UNCTAD
Palais des Nations, 8-14 Avenue de la Paix, 1211 Geneva 10, Switzerland
Tel: (22) 917 5809. Fax: (22) 907 0051.
E-mail: info@unctad.org
Website: www.unctad.org

UN International Monetary Fund (IMF)
700 19th Street, NW, Washington, DC 20431, USA
Tel: (202) 623 7000. Fax: (202) 623 4661.
E-mail: publicaffairs@imf.org
Website: www.imf.org

World Bank Group
1818 H Street, NW, Washington, DC 20433, USA
Tel: (202) 477 1000. Fax: (202) 477 6391.
Website: www.worldbank.org

World Trade Organization
Centre William Rappard, 154 rue de Lausanne, CH-1211 Geneva 21, Switzerland
Tel: (22) 739 5111. Fax: (22) 731 4206.
E-mail: enquiries@wto.org
Website: www.wto.org

Calendar of Events

April 2005 - March 2006

APRIL 2005

1-4	ITEX 2005, Abu Dhabi, United Arab Emirates
1-9	IFWTO (International Federation of Women's Travel Organisation) 36th Annual Conference, San Diego, Mexico
7-9	AITF 2005 (Azerbaijan International Tourism Fair), Baku, Azerbaijan
7-10	ASTA Cruisefest, Miami, USA
7-10	2nd Great Lakes Hospitality & Tourism Educators Conference, Indianapolis, USA
8-10	5th Global Travel & Tourism Summit, New Delhi, India
13-16	27th International Fair of Tourism, Belgrade, Serbia & Montenegro
17-21	54th PATA Annual Conference, Macau
17-28	WTO Practicum, Madrid, Spain
19-21	IMEX 2005 (Worldwide Exhibition for Incentive Travel, Meetings & Events), Frankfurt, Germany
20-23	The Beijing International Travel & Tourism Market, Beijing, China
21-23	The International Tourism Exhibition – Fair of the Silk Road Countries, Tbilisi, Georgia
26-29	7th Caribbean Conference on Sustainable Tourism Development, Tobago
28-30	KITF 2005 (Kazakhstan International 'Tourism & Travel'), Almaty, Kazakhstan
30- May 3	2nd International Conference on Culinary Tourism, California, USA

MAY 2005

3-6	Arabian Travel Market (ATM), Dubai, United Arab Emirates
7-11	Indaba 2005, Durban, South Africa
12-15	IGLTA (International Gay & Lesbian Travel Association) World Convention, Cologne, Germany
12-15	Marché Méditerranéen International du Tourisme, Tunis, Tunisia
15-20	ATA 30th International Congress, Nairobi, Kenya
16-17	EyeforTravel: Revenue Management & Pricing in Travel, Miami, USA
19-21	1st Kyrgyzstan International Travel & Tourism Exhibition, Bishke, Kyrgyzstan
25-28	Environmental Tourism Exhibition, Kiev, Ukraine
26-28	3rd Asia-Pacific Travel Conference 2005, Kuala Lumpur, Malaysia

JUNE 2005

7-8	EyeforTravel: Travel Distribution Summit Europe, London, UK
9-12	19th International Travel Expo, Hong Kong (SAR), China (PR)
13-15	ITT Annual Conference, Barbados
18-24	Australia Tourism Exchange, Perth, Australia
22-24	Beijing International Tourism Expo, Beijing, China (PR)
21-24	Turinfo 2005, Havana, Cuba
22-25	LACIME 2005: Latin America & Caribbean Incentive & Meetings Exhibition, Sao Paulo, Brazil
23-24	4th International Symposium on Aspects of Tourism, Brighton, UK

JULY 2005

6-9	Border Tourism & Community Development, Xishuangbanna, Yunnan, China

AUGUST 2005

3-6	IACVB 91st Annual Convention, California, USA
13-16	ESTO 2005, Idaho, USA
14-17	37th NBTA Convention & Trade Show, San Diego, USA
28-Sep 1	AIEST 2005 (55th Congress), Gull Lake, USA

SEPTEMBER 2005

1-2	The NSW Tourism Conference 2005, Wollongong, NSW, Australia
6-8	Mediterranean Travel Fair (MTF), Cairo, Egypt
6-8	Business Travel Show, Dusseldorf, Germany
7-9	La Cumbre, The Americas Summit, Houston, USA
12-16	50th Annual IFEA Convention & Expo, San Antonio, USA
22-24	Top Resa Deauville: Travel & Tourism Trade Show, Deauville, France
22-24	13th International Travel Show, Warsaw, Poland
22-24	JATA World Travel Fair, Tokyo, Japan
25-28	APTA Expo, Dallas, USA
27	World Tourism Day
27-28	PATA Travel Mart, Kuala Lumpur, Malaysia
29-Oct 2	AWTTE 2005 (Arab World Travel & Tourism Exchange), Beirut, Lebanon

OCTOBER 2005

1	ICCA Exhibition, Cape Town, South Africa
2-5	3rd International Institute for Peace through Tourism Summit, Pattaya, Thailand
3-4	EyeforTravel: Travel Distribution Summit USA, Chicago, USA
4-6	CIS Travel Market, St Petersburg, Russia
8-10	Envie De Partir, Paris, France
10-16	World Youth & Student Travel Conference, Toronto, Canada
16-21	Skal International World Congress, Zagreb, Croatia
17-19	The International Hotel Conference, Monte Carlo, Monaco
18-20	Seatrade International Maritime Convention, London, UK
19-22	Tour Salon 2005 (International Exhibition of Tourism), Poznan, Poland
26-30	ABAV 2005 (The Fair of Americas), Rio de Janeiro, Brazil

NOVEMBER 2005

1-2	Seatrade Europe Cruise, Ferry & River Cruise Convention, Hamburg, Germany
2-4	12th ATLAS Annual Conference 2005, Barcelona, Spain
4-8	NTA Annual Convention, Detroit, USA
3-6	Philoxenia 2005, Thessaloniki, Greece
6-9	44th ICCA Congress & Exhibition, Montevideo, Uruguay
6-11	ASTA World Travel Congress, Montreal, Canada
8-9	10th Adventure & Backpacker Industry Conference, Sydney, Australia
8-10	MADI Travel Trade, Prague, Czech Republic
11-13	11th Backpacker & Adventure Travel Expo, Sydney, Australia
11-13	SITV Travel & Tourism Fair, Comar, France
14-17	World Travel Market (WTM), London, UK
22-25	ASTA's World Travel Congress, Montreal, Canada
24-27	ABTA Convention, Marrakech, Morocco
26-28	Arabian Tourism Bureau 2005 (ATB3), Damascus, Syria
29-Dec 1	EIBTM, Barcelona, Spain
30-Dec 3	Nigerian International Travel & Tourism Exhibition (NITTEX), Abuja, Nigeria

DECEMBER 2005

5-8	International Golf Travel Market (IGTM), Maspalomas, Spain
6-8	International Luxury Travel Market (ILTM), Cannes, France

JANUARY 2006

1	International Fair for Holidays, Travel & Leisure, Vienna, Austria
10-16	Vakantiebeurs, Utrecht, The Netherlands
13-15	Adventure Travel & Sports Show, London, UK
25-29	FITUR International Tourism Trade Fair, Madrid, Spain
26-29	FESPO, Zurich, Switzerland
29-30	Intourfest Moscow, Moscow, Russian Federation
31-Feb 2	Business Travel Show, London, UK
TBC	ITF Slovakia Tour (International Travel Fair), Bratislava, Slovak Republic
TBC	BTL (Lisboa Travel Market), Lisbon, Portugal

FEBRUARY 2006

2-5	DESTINATIONS Holiday & Travel Exhibition, London, UK
8-12	Reisen Hamburg 2005, Hamburg, Germany
TBC	Vacances, Sport et Loisirs (Travel Trade Fair), Geneva, Switzerland
TBC	AIME, Melbourne, Australia

MARCH 2006

8-11	ITB 2006, Berlin, Germany
TBC	BTTF (British Travel Trade Fair), Birmingham, UK
TBC	Salon Mondial du Tourism, Versailles, France

Weather

The following gives an indication of the way in which weather conditions affect people. The comfort or discomfort felt in different conditions depends on temperature, humidity and wind. For information on specific weather conditions in each country, see the relevant country entry.

Humidity

Humidity, expressed as a percentage, is the amount of moisture in the air. A relative humidity of 100 per cent is the maximum possible moisture content held at any given temperature. As air can hold more moisture at greater heat, so 100 per cent humidity at 26°C (79°F) holds more moisture than 100 per cent humidity at 10°C (50°F). Low humidity results in rapid evaporation; perspiration evaporates easily and wet clothes dry quickly. Such conditions prevail in hot and dry climates, where one experiences far less discomfort and can endure relatively high temperatures. In a hot climate with high humidity conditions, perspiration cannot evaporate easily and clothes dry slowly. One feels hot and uncomfortable as heat loss through perspiration is minimised. A breeze can sometimes relieve the discomfort associated with high humidity. Below freezing point the air can hold very little moisture and humidity has little effect. Although damp (raw) cold is less pleasant than dry cold in temperatures above freezing point, wind is a more important factor.

Wind

One feels cooler in wind because air movement around the body has the effect of carrying body heat away. In hot weather the body temperature is regulated chiefly by the evaporation of perspiration. When the air temperature exceeds normal skin temperature (about 34°C; 93°F), in a dry climate, the cooling power of wind becomes critical. In low temperatures, the wind speed is equally critical. A temperature of 0°C (32°F) with a wind speed of 50kmph (30mph) feels colder than the lower temperature of -20°C (4°F) in calm conditions. High wind speeds can increase the risk of frostbite.

Many regions have particular winds which occur at certain times of the day or seasons of the year, and there are general rules; for instance, winds generally drop at night and increase by day (especially on the coast). Wind speed almost always increases with altitude. However, average wind statistics are almost impossible to supply, although forecasts are given in some countries, such as the USA, on TV and radio or in newspapers.

Wind-chill factor

Wind-chill factor does not indicate actual temperature; rather, it gives an indication of outdoor conditions by estimating the temperature a suitably dressed person would feel outside. It can be deduced from wind speeds and average temperatures. In less extreme conditions, a sunny day will produce extra warmth. The rate of heat loss from the body can be measured in kilogram calories per square metre of body surface per hour. The wind-chill factor is often given in weather bulletins.

Temperature range

This can be estimated by measuring the difference between the maximum and minimum temperatures, which usually occur just after midday and just before dawn. In cloudy, rainy areas, the range may be quite small, but in very sunny, dry climates such as deserts or mountainous regions, there may be a large range with surprisingly cold nights. As a general rule, the greatest range is inland and the lowest on the coast.

Precipitation

Precipitation includes all forms of moisture falling on the ground (rain, snow, sleet, hail or fog drip). Generally, this is rain, but on high mountains, or in countries with very cold winters such as Canada, the Russian Federation and parts of China (PR), Scandinavia and the USA, it may well fall as snow. All forms are measured as the melted equivalent of rain, with one foot of snow being roughly equivalent to one inch of rain. Generally, below 2°C (36°F), snow or sleet are as likely as rain. At freezing point or below, snow is most likely. Rain falling below freezing point, although rare, is very dangerous, especially on roads.

Precautions

Height above sea level: The general fall in temperature is at the rate of 0.6°C for every 100m (1°F for every 300ft), especially in cloud. Higher altitudes can also mean a wide range of day and nighttime temperatures. Atmosphere becomes thinner over 1800m (6000ft), the sun's rays are more powerful, and breathing and exertion become more difficult. Adequate clothing should always be taken when walking or climbing.

Heat

In high temperatures the body keeps cool by sweating. However, if the humidity is too low or evaporation is increased by wind, the body may not sweat fast enough to match the rate of evaporation. In such conditions the risk of heat exhaustion or heatstroke increases.

Heat exhaustion: Symptoms are loss of appetite, lassitude and general discomfort, with possible hallucinations and vomiting. The sufferer should be moved to a cool place and made to drink salty water to replace moisture and salt lost in perspiration.

Heatstroke: When the body's cooling mechanism stops, the body becomes dry and temperature rises. The symptoms are burning sensations and dry skin followed by feverishness, sometimes developing into headache and confusion. Immediate medical attention is essential as heatstroke may be fatal. The patient should be cooled as fast as possible, preferably put in a cool place, splashed with cold or iced water, wrapped in a wet sheet with a fan directed onto the body; vigorous massage can also help. Prevention: In a very hot country, do not over-exert until after about a week's acclimatisation, especially after air travel. (Air conditioning delays the process of acclimatisation.) Drink plenty of liquids (not too much alcohol) and take salt. Avoid sunburn and wear light, comfortable clothing.

Cold

Body heat can be generated by physical activity and maintained by wearing suitable clothing. The danger occurs if one stops moving, becomes tired or if one remains in a strong wind below freezing point.

Hypothermia: Also known as 'exposure'. The body temperature falls, which can be fatal. Risks of hypothermia usually occur through lack of adequate clothing in mountainous regions or at sea, especially at night and if clothes become wet (evaporation from wet clothing causes the body to lose heat more rapidly). Rain and snow with a strong wind increases the danger; old people are particularly susceptible. Hypothermia becomes critical at a very low level of body temperature, around 25°-28°C (77°-82°F). The body should be re-warmed rapidly, preferably in a bath of 40°-45°C (104°-113°F). Artificial respiration and cardiac massage are required if breathing has stopped.

Frostbite: Affects flesh exposed to extreme cold, usually the face, hands and feet. The flesh freezes and this can result in a loss of limbs. The affected parts should be re-warmed slowly as soon as possible, preferably in water no hotter than 40°-44°C (104°-111°F). Do not bandage, massage or rub frostbitten skin.

Climate Graph Conversions

Easy-to-use and informative climate charts are provided at the end of each country's entry.

Health

The health of travellers abroad may not be protected by services and legislation well-established at home. Changes in food and water may bring unexpected problems, as may insects and insect-borne diseases, especially in hot countries. Few have at their fingertips the current detailed knowledge needed to advise those travelling to a particular country, and personal reminiscences may not always reflect current or common problems. A danger of generalising is that it may be forgotten, for example, that malaria is a risk in Turkey, poliomyelitis occurs in Europe, and hepatitis A virus occurs worldwide and is not destroyed by many methods of purifying drinking water. Specific advice on which diseases are present in countries to be visited is likely to be complicated. A practical starting point for the traveller seeking advice is to consider which diseases can be prevented by immunisation, prophylactic tablets, or other measures, and decide whether it is appropriate to do so.

An unpredictable environment is especially a problem for the overland traveller who plans their own journey and needs greater knowledge of disease prevention and management than the traveller in an aeroplane or on a sea cruise, whose environment, food and drink are largely in the hands of the operator. Unforeseen changes in timetables may lead to stays in accommodation that are not of the expected standard. Delays at airports can take place in overcrowded and unhygienic conditions, where the facilities have not kept pace with increased demand and insect-borne diseases may also be contracted. Jet lag and exhaustion may prompt a traveller to take risks with food and drink. More experienced travellers tend to have fewer health problems. Better planning, immunisation and experience in prevention may all play a part, as well as salutary lessons learnt on previous occasions.

A questionnaire survey of returning travellers (most of whom had been to Europe, especially the Mediterranean countries) showed that half had had diarrhoea or respiratory symptoms while abroad. Excessive alcohol, sun and late nights can add to the problems. About one in 100 package holidaymakers who take out a health insurance policy make a claim. Diarrhoea and sunburn are principal reasons but accidents are also common. Injuries occur especially in and around swimming pools, to pedestrians forgetting that traffic drives on the opposite side to home, and from unfamiliar equipment such as gates on lifts. Sexually transmitted diseases are a big problem in certain destinations and cases could require urgent treatment.

Long-stay travellers may adapt to these initial problems but then find themselves suffering from diseases endemic in their chosen country, such as malaria, hepatitis, diarrhoea and skin problems. 2 per cent of British Voluntary Service overseas personnel contract hepatitis A within eight months if they are not protected. Car accidents occur while driving on non-metal roads, and some emotional problems may be resolved only by an early return home.

The traveller should be insured against medical expenses and most policies include the cost of emergency repatriation where appropriate. Such insurance, however, rarely covers a service overseas that is similar to that available at home. Language and administrative differences are likely to present problems. Leaflet T6, issued annually by the Department of Health, describes the free or reduced-cost medical treatments available in other countries and the documents (passport, NHS medical card, form E111) that the traveller has to have with them. Reciprocal arrangements between countries differ and fees may have to be paid and then reclaimed in the visited country itself, which can be time-consuming. Extra provision should be made for such emergencies. Any reciprocal arrangement between the UK and a country is mentioned in each country's entry. Form E111, counter stamped in post offices, is needed in some countries of the European Union. Travellers should note that the E111 will be replaced by the European Health Insurance Card in December 2005. Only a 'small' supply of medicines for personal use may be taken out of the UK, unless Home Office permission is obtained.

Immunisation

Yellow Fever

This disease is caused by a virus that circulates in animals indigenous to certain tropical forested areas. It mainly infects monkeys, but if a person enters these areas the virus may be transmitted to them by mosquitoes whose normal hosts are monkeys: this is jungle yellow fever. It occurs haphazardly and is clearly related to a person's habits. If, from an animal source, the virus begins to circulate between a person and his own mosquitoes, primarily Aedes aegypti, epidemics of urban yellow fever result. Immunisation protects the individual and is effective in preventing the spread of the virus to countries where Aedes aegypti is prevalent. It is therefore reasonable for such countries to request a certificate of vaccination from all travellers from areas where human cases are occurring. Many national administrations, however, require immunisation of all travellers over one year of age from all countries, or else all travellers over one year from countries where endemic (enzootic) foci occur. A map indicating yellow fever endemic zones can be found on p919. Immunisation is clearly not required when travelling outside the enzootic zones. Within the zones, if it is not compulsory, it is not always necessary. For instance, in the absence of an epidemic of yellow fever, a business trip within the confines of Nairobi would be perfectly safe. Nevertheless, local and current knowledge of cases is required for such decisions to be made, so, in practice, immunisation is recommended to all travellers within enzootic zones. Immunisation in the UK is undertaken only at recognised yellow fever vaccination centres. A current list of vaccination centres within the UK can be found online: (website: www.info.doh.gov.uk/doh/yellcode.nsf/pages/Help?open). Once immunised (a single vaccination is used), the vaccination certificate becomes valid for 10 years after 10 days. It is not recommended for pregnant women and children under nine months of age.

Cholera

In 1973, the World Health Organization (WHO), recognising that immunisation cannot stop the spread of cholera among countries, deleted the requirement of cholera immunisation as a condition of admission to any country from the International Health Regulations. In 1990, the WHO stated that immunisation against cholera was ineffective and not recommended. In 1991, the WHO confirmed that certification was no longer required by any country or territory. For a small number of countries, however, a cholera vaccination certificate is still a condition of entry; in this case, advice should be sought from a medical professional.

Typhoid Fever

Typhoid fever is endemic worldwide and is usually spread faecal-orally. The risk of infection is increased in areas of high carriage rates and poor hygiene. The risk is not significantly increased for the traveller to areas with public health standards similar to those of the UK – namely Australia, Canada, northern Europe, Japan, New Zealand and the USA – and immunisation for these areas is not necessary. Outside these areas the risks reflect not only local hygiene and carriage rates but also lifestyle. Travelling or living rough, living in rural areas, or 'eating out' makes transmission more likely. The risks are therefore small for the air traveller with full board at a reputable hotel, and immunisation is unnecessary. On the other hand, overland travel to Australia would be a clear indication for immunisation. Between these extremes there are many circumstances for which risks cannot be precisely defined. Typhoid vaccination is now no longer routinely recommended for the millions of tourists to southern Europe each year, although it may still be advisable, not only for those whose lifestyle or occupation increase the risk of such exposure, but also during local outbreaks.

Hepatitis A

The hepatitis A virus is endemic worldwide and spread faecal-orally. Protection from symptomatic infection can be provided by active immunisation or passively acquired immunoglobulin. The virus circulates freely in our own population however, and many travellers will be immune already. Protection should be offered to the same groups as are offered typhoid immunisation, as exposure to one infection would imply the risk of exposure to the other. The recurrent tropical traveller may have his antibodies against hepatitis A checked. If antibodies are present, that person is immune. If antibodies are absent, inactivated hepatitis A vaccine should be given. Hepatitis A in children is usually mild and more often asymptomatic, so immunisation is not essential. Hepatitis A vaccine is available for use in children over the age of 12 months.

Poliomyelitis

A survey undertaken in Scotland in 1989 showed that 20 per cent of the tested population did not have antibodies to all three serotypes of poliovirus. Hence a consultation about travel abroad is an opportunity to complete primary courses or boost immunisations that are nationally recommended. Although the number of polomyelitis cases has fallen greatly worldwide, some vaccine-derived outbreaks have recently developed and immunisation is still advised. Oral poliomyelitis vaccine is given, but supplies of inactivated polio vaccine are available if oral vaccine is contraindicated.

Tetanus

As with poliomyelitis, all individuals should gain or maintain immunity to tetanus. It is firmly recommended for life in the UK, as well as for travel abroad. A preparation combined with low-dose diphtheria toxoid is recommended for travellers when immunity requires boosting.

Special Rare Diseases

Avian Flu

In February 2005, the World Health Organisation (WHO) issued its strongest warning yet about the possibility of global bird flu pandemic. In the same month, Cambodia recorded its first human casualty of avian influenza A (H5N1). As of March 2005, Cambodia, Vietnam and Thailand had all recorded human deaths caused by avian influenza with the number of confirmed cases standing at 55, 42 of which were fatal. In a bid to prevent the spread of the virus, approximately 140 million birds in the affected countries were culled.

WHO is now very concerned that the disease may mutate into a form that is more easily transmitted between humans. Governments around the world are being urged to prepare contingency plans in case of an outbreak.

SARS

Severe Acute Respiratory Syndrome (SARS) is a respiratory illness caused by a novel coronavirus (SARS-CoV). It began in Guangdong Province, China (PR), in November 2002. The disease was first recognised in Asia in February 2003, and spread to more than two-dozen countries in Asia, Europe and North and South America over the following months. There were over 8000 confirmed cases of the disease and international travel was a significant factor in the worldwide spread of the disease. There have been no reported cases since early in 2004 and experts announced in February 2005 that another SARS outbreak on the scale of that in 2002-03 is highly unlikely. Nevertheless, travellers should pay attention to reports of any further outbreaks. Additionally, it would be prudent for travellers to China to avoid visiting live food markets and avoid direct contact with civets and other wildlife from these markets.

SARS is an airborne illness and can be transmitted from person to person. The incubation period for SARS is typically two to seven days. The illness generally begins with a prodrome of fever. The fever is often high, sometimes associated with chills and rigors and might be accompanied by other symptoms such as headache, malaise, and muscle pain. At the onset of illness, some persons have mild respiratory symptoms. After three to seven days, a lower respiratory phase begins with the onset of a dry, non-productive cough. In 10 to 20 per cent of cases, the respiratory illness is severe enough to require hospitalisation and mechanical ventilation. The severity of illness is highly variable, ranging from mild illness to death.

To date, there is no available immunisation against the coronavirus/SARS.

BSE

Bovine Spongiform Encephalopathy (BSE) is an illness caused by an unconventional transmissible agent, causing fatal brain disease with unusually long incubation periods, measured in years. Strong evidence has accumulated indicating a causal relationship between BSE or 'mad cow disease' and a disease in humans called variant Creutzfeldt-Jakob disease (vCJD). BSE in cattle caused a huge epidemic in the UK, with over 180,000 cases reported since 1987, with a peak in 1992. Bioassays have identified the BSE agent in the brain, spinal cord, retina, distal root ganglia, ileum and bone marrow of cattle experimentally infected orally. To reduce any risk of acquiring vCJD from food, travellers to Europe, the UK, and other areas with indigenous cases of BSE, may consider avoiding beef and beef products altogether.

The current risk of acquiring vCJD from eating beef (muscle meat), and beef products produced from cattle in countries with a possible increased risk of BSE, cannot be determined precisely. Sporadic cases of BSE were reported in many countries in Europe and the UK in 2004.

Rabies

Most doctors do not think it necessary to immunise the average traveller visiting areas where rabies is endemic, although this may be advisable for those in remote areas who would be many days' travel away from a source of vaccine and rabies immunoglobulin if infected. However, all travellers should avoid contact with animals, especially cats and dogs. If they do get bitten, wounds should be promptly washed with copious soap and water followed by the application of alcohol (spirits like gin and whisky can be used). If the animal's owner is available, ask whether the animal has been vaccinated against rabies (check certification). A forwarding address or telephone number should be left to enable contact should the animal become unwell over the next two weeks. Seek local medical advice promptly and give details of the incident to local police. On return, the traveller's medical practitioner should be informed and further check-ups and treatment may be necessary.

Diphtheria

Diphtheria is endemic worldwide. Most morbidity and mortality occur in children and they should be immunised as nationally recommended (initial primary course and booster on school entry and school leaving). Adult travellers with a high risk of infection are those in contact with children in poorer areas – for example, health workers and teachers. Travellers may have their immunity boosted by a low-dose preparation of diphtheria toxoid. A preparation combined with tetanus toxoid is now also available.

Meningococcal Meningitis

Although the bacteria responsible for this illness circulates widely throughout the world, certain areas, like the dry areas bordering the southern Sahara, are renowned for recurrent epidemics and many areas suffer occasional epidemics, as in Brazil, India and Nepal. Following a recent outbreak during the pilgrimage to Mecca, a quadrivalent vaccine is now required for travel to the Haj in Mecca. Immunisation is recommended for travellers to such areas with outbreaks, particularly those staying long-term. Travellers heading to remote areas should check for the latest disease outbreaks.

Tick-borne Encephalitis

Tick-borne encephalitis is caused by an arbovirus, transmitted by the bite of an infected tick. Its distribution is confined to warm and low-forested areas in parts of Central Europe and Scandinavia, particularly Austria, Czech Republic, Germany, Slovak Republic and throughout all the republics of the former Yugoslavia (Bosnia & Herzegovina, Croatia, Macedonia, Serbia & Montenegro and Slovenia). The forests are usually deciduous with heavy undergrowth. Those normally at risk are foresters and those clearing such areas, but increasing contact will occur with increased recreational use, such as camping and walking. Most human illness occurs in late-spring and early-summer. Tick bites are best avoided by limiting contact with such areas, wearing clothing to cover most of the skin surface and using insect repellents on outer clothes and socks. Where prolonged contact is necessary, a killed vaccine is essential.

Japanese B Encephalitis

This virus infection is transmitted by mosquitoes in certain rural areas of eastern Asia, the Indian subcontinent and a few Pacific islands. Occasional larger outbreaks develop and this infection tends to have a higher mortality rate than the many other similar viruses that can cause encephalitis. If planning to sleep in rural areas with a high risk or an active outbreak, immunisation should be considered; this is available from Aventis Pasteur (tel: (01628) 785 291; website: www.apmsd.co.uk). Considerable protection is offered by avoiding mosquito bites (see the Malaria Prophylaxis section) and staying indoors at night in rural areas where known cases are occurring.

West Nile Virus

West Nile Virus is a rare infection spread by the bite of an infected mosquito. It can affect people, horses, many types of birds and some other animals. There is no evidence to suggest that West Nile Virus can be spread from person to person or directly from an animal to person.

There was a severe outbreak of the virus in the US in 2003, when there were 1764 reported human cases of West Nile Virus in 34 states. 31 of these cases were fatal.

It is best evaded by avoiding mosquito bites; use an insect repellent - preferably one containing DEET - on clothes or exposed skin.

Plague

Plague is an infection of wild rodents transmitted by fleas. It exists in many rural areas of Africa, Asia and the Americas. The risk to the traveller from the bite of an infected flea is low. Routine immunisation is not recommended. In enzootic areas (usually rural and hilly), contact with rodents should be discouraged by preventing their access to food and waste, avoiding dead rodents and rodent burrows. Fleas can be discouraged by insect repellents. The most recent outbreak was in the Democratic Republic of Congo in 2005. There is an incubation period of between three and seven days and persons usually show 'flu-like' symptoms. Early diagnosis and treatment is essential.

Hepatitis B

Vaccination should be considered for groups such as medical, nursing and laboratory staff planning to work among populations with high HBsAg carriage rates. The recommended regimen consists of three doses, the boosters given at one month and six months after the initial dose. Immunity is predicted to last about five years but those at high risk should have antibodies checked three months after completion of course. Quicker regimens are used but are less effective and should be boosted again at six to 12 months. A combined hepatitis A and B vaccine is available.

Other Considerations

HIV

People infected with HIV (human immunodeficiency virus), who may appear perfectly well, pass on the infection by sexual intercourse or if their blood is inoculated into other people, as in the sharing of needles by drug users, the transfusion of untested blood, or the reuse of injection needles without sterilisation between patients. Certain areas of the world, such as parts of tropical Africa, Asia and South America have a higher number of carriers of HIV. However, the potential for infection exists worldwide and precautions should always be taken, whether at home or abroad. The use of condoms and spermicidal cream during sexual intercourse should reduce the level of risk.
Thought must also be given to the need for blood transfusions, where blood is not tested for HIV antibodies, and the need for injections where there is doubt about the sterility of the needles (these may be sterilised by placing in boiling water for 20 minutes). Kits containing appropriate needles and syringes are available. Travellers should know their blood group. The World Health Organization (WHO) is vigorously opposed to any country requiring travellers to present a certificate stating that they are free from HIV infection. Besides being against International Health Regulations, it is both clinically unsound and epidemiologically unjustifiable as a means of limiting infection. However, at least 40 countries have introduced restrictions, such as compulsory HIV testing or refusal of entry for 'suspicious' visitors, though mostly those planning to stay, work or study long-term.

Malaria Prophylaxis

Malaria is widespread in tropical and subtropical areas of the world and is spread by the bite of a female anopheline mosquito that has been infected by the malaria parasite.
The increasing mobility of the population, especially through air travel, brings a further hazard since travellers may be bitten by mosquitoes at airports en route as well as in the countries where they stay. The speed of travel means that first symptoms may occur in a country and in a context where the disease will not be immediately considered.
Mosquitoes may even be brought by aeroplanes to non-endemic areas and infect, for example, airport staff or travellers' relatives. Infection also occurs through blood transfusion (cold storage does not destroy the parasites) and the sharing of needles by drug users.
The life-threatening form of malaria is caused by Plasmodium falciparum. Because of the travelling habits of those living in the UK, this form of malaria is usually imported from Africa, but also from Asia. Prevention is primarily aimed at this parasite. Nevertheless, the same advice is given to those likely to be exposed to the less dangerous P vivax, P malariae and P ovale, partly to prevent an unpleasant illness but also because P falciparum infection can never be presumed to be absent in any malarious area. There is no immediate prospect of an effective vaccine, so regular ingestion of prophylactic tablets is necessary. This requires habits that some find difficult or even distasteful, and because of increasing resistance to these tablets, they can no longer guarantee protection from illness. Bites must be avoided or reduced (see below) and any flu-like illness with fever and shivers lasting more than two days should be promptly diagnosed. If such symptoms develop after return, even months afterwards, the attending doctor should be reminded of the date and place of travel.
Note: A map showing areas of malarial risk and areas where chloroquine resistance has been reported is printed on p919 (source: WHO, Geneva).

Personal precautions against malaria:

- Avoid mosquito bites, especially after sunset, when the anopheline mosquitoes responsible for transmitting malaria are most active. Long trousers, sleeves and dresses, netting on windows, and mosquito nets over beds help to prevent mosquito bites.
- Insect repellents may be used on exposed skin, and insecticides inside buildings or on breeding sites. Repellent-impregnated wrist and ankle bands, and electrical insecticide vaporisers may also be used.
- Mosquitoes should not be encouraged to breed by leaving stagnant water – for example, in blocked drains or around plant pots.
- Prophylactic tablets are necessary because the above measures, although valuable, are unlikely to be fully effective.

Precautions against malaria before travel:

- Start most tablets two weeks before departure to confirm tolerance and obtain adequate blood concentrations before exposure.
- Take the tablets with absolute regularity, according to the doctor's instructions. Prophylactic doses of drugs are not normally curative should infection get established.
- Prophylaxis is usually continued for four weeks after leaving an endemic area, though the new antimalarial, Malarone, only needs to be taken for one week after leaving such areas. All forms of the parasite develop first in the liver and only later re-enter the blood, where most prophylactic drugs take effect.
- Seek advice on which type of tablet to take from an advice centre (see table).

Deep Vein Thrombosis (DVT)

Travelling which involves any long periods of inactivity, either by land or air, can cause deep vein thrombosis (DVT) in predisposed individuals. This is when a blood clot (thrombus) forms within a vein that accompanies an artery (deep vein) and remains there. This, in turn, leads to a risk of pulmonary embolus (PE), where the clot travels from its original site to another part of the body, which can be potentially life threatening.
There are some identifiable groups of people who are at an increased risk of DVT. These include people who have:

- A previous history of DVT/PE
- Obesity
- Recently had major surgery
- Congestive heart failure
- Malignant disease
- Paralysis of the legs
- Pregnant women
- Women taking oral contraception

The risks can be reduced by frequently exercising the lower limbs and walking whenever possible, taking deep-breathing exercises and preventing dehydration by drinking lots of water and avoiding excess alcohol or caffeine.

Children

As children begin to crawl and walk they become more vulnerable to faecal-oral infections and hazards such as bites, accidents and burns. Open wounds should be kept clean and covered with dressings until healed. Deaths from scorpion bites are unusual but mostly occur in children under two years of age. Allowing toddlers to play outside unattended can be particularly hazardous.
Taking adequate malarial prophylaxis should not encourage the traveller to ignore the risks from other mosquito-borne diseases such as dengue fever, which can be more severe in children. Protection from mosquito bites is also important in those children who are strongly allergic to them. Appropriate clothes and bed or window netting at night are usually more valuable in the long term than insect repellents.

Pregnancy

Live vaccinations are best not given during pregnancy, although if someone unprotected against yellow fever is going to live in a high-risk area, the theoretical risk of vaccination is outweighed by the serious nature of the illness. If the vaccine is not given, a doctor's letter endorsed with a health board or authority stamp to say the inoculation is contraindicated is usually accepted. Inactivated poliomyelitis vaccine may be used instead of oral live vaccine.
A mother immunised against tetanus passes on protection to her baby over the neonatal period and a booster can be given during pregnancy if necessary. Hepatitis A in pregnancy may be more severe and also result in premature labour.
Prevention is generally encouraged for those at risk. Malarial prophylaxis should be maintained throughout pregnancy but the risks of some drugs have to be balanced against the type of malaria and likelihood of its transmission in different areas; specialist advice should be sought.

Contraception

Those using oral contraceptives should be aware that absorption could be affected during gastrointestinal illnesses, that some brands may not be available locally, and that they may be continued over the usual break in the cycle if menstruation is going to occur at an inconvenient time, such as during a long journey. They may contribute to the fluid retention that some people experience in hot climates.
Reliable condoms are not available in all localities abroad.

QUICK GUIDE TO VACCINATION/PROPHYLAXIS
Requirements & Programmes

When time permits, immunisation should be started well in advance so that adequate intervals between doses can be maintained. If notice to travel is short, a rapid course or single dose may be given but the immunity provided will not be as effective. Children should be up-to-date with the routine UK vaccination schedule. Extra consideration should be given to the need for vaccinating pregnant women. If it is known that a full initial (primary) course of any of these vaccines has been given, then only single booster doses are necessary.

Against	No. of injections in primary course (inc. period of protection)	Validity of certificate	Revaccination	Other details
Yellow Fever	1 injection gives protection for 10 years.	10 days after inoculation for 10 years.	Every 10 years validity taking immediate effect.*	Reactions to vaccination are rare, although some discomfort might be experienced. Not for infants under 9 months or pregnant women.
Diphtheria	If over 10 years, 3 doses of low-dose vaccine at monthly intervals. Usually given as DTP to children under 10 years.	Not applicable.	Low-dose booster combined with tetanus toxoid every 10 years.	Only mild reactions expected.
Typhoid Fever				
(a) Vi vaccine	1 injection.	Not applicable.	Single booster every 3 years.	Only mild local and systemic reactions. Not for children under 18 months of age. A combined preparation with Hepatitis A vaccine is now available.
(b) Oral	1 capsule on alternate days for 3 doses.	Not applicable.	Annual 3-dose booster for recurrent travellers.	Only mild reactions expected. To be kept refrigerated. Do not use with antibiotics within 12 hours of mefloquine, in pregnant or immuno-compromised, or concurrent oral polio vaccine. Not for children under 6 years of age. More expensive.
Hepatitis A	1 injection will provide protection for 6 months to 1 year	Not applicable.	Single booster at 6 months to 1 year can be expected to provide 10 years' protection.	Half-dose preparation now available for ages 1 to 15 years. Combined preparation vaccines are now available with Typhoid Vi or hepatitis A.
Poliomyelitis	3 oral doses given at 4 weekly intervals.	Not applicable.	Single booster every 10 years.	Different (inactivated) vaccine available for pregnant women.
Tetanus	3 injections given at 4 weekly intervals.	Not applicable.	Single booster every 10 years. Now combined with low-dose diphtheria toxoid to boost both.	Local tenderness, swelling and redness may occur.
Malaria	Tablets should be taken 2 weeks prior to departure and continued regularly while in malarial zone. It is essential to continue taking tablets for 4 weeks after leaving zone – except Malarone.	Not applicable.	Not applicable.	Pregnant women and newborn infants require special consideration. Marone is effective when given for 2 days before, during, and only 7 days after travel. It is expensive and not licensed for trips longer than 4 weeks.

* If vaccination is recorded on a new certificate, travellers are advised to retain their old certificate until their new certificate is valid.

Publications

The following list is selective, but includes sources that are readily available and frequently updated.

HEALTH ADVICE FOR TRAVELLERS (T6) – DEPARTMENT OF HEALTH
Available free from post offices, by dialling (0800) 555 777 (toll-free) or online (website: www.dh.gov.uk/PolicyAndGuidance/HealthAdviceForTravellers/fs/en). If more than 10 copies are required, they can be ordered from the Department of Health, PO Box 777, London SE1 6XH, UK (tel: (08701) 555 455; fax: (01623) 724 524).
This is a yearly publication containing advice on how to reduce health risks, with a list, by country, of compulsory and recommended immunisations. It advises about travel insurance and entitlement to reduced-cost medical treatment for UK nationals in other countries.

INTERNATIONAL TRAVEL AND HEALTH – WORLD HEALTH ORGANISATION, GENEVA
This lists, by country, compulsory immunisations and malaria risk, and gives the distribution by geographical area of other health risks with appropriate advice. Previously published as a handbook (last published 2005), the information is now available and frequently updated online (website: www.who.int/ith).

ABC OF HEALTHY TRAVEL (FIFTH EDITION)
E Walker, G Williams, F Raeside & L Calvert, British Medical Journal, 1997.
An easy-to-read guide to the health problems of travel, intended for the general practitioner and informed lay person.

HEALTH INFORMATION FOR INTERNATIONAL TRAVEL 2003-2004
Available from the Public Health Foundation, PO Box 753, Walford MD 20604, UK (tel: (877) 252 1200 (toll-free); website: http://bookstore.phf.org).
Although written primarily for healthcare providers, this book contains information that could be useful for any traveller.

ROUGH GUIDE TO TRAVEL HEALTH
2004, Rough Guides (website: www.roughguides.com).
Contains pre-planning information, safety tips for active travel and an A-Z Health section.

THE TRAVELLERS' GOOD HEALTH GUIDE
T Lankester, Sheldon Press.
Contains clear, concise information on all you need to know to stay healthy abroad.

UNDERSTANDING TRAVEL AND HOLIDAY HEALTH
B Carroll & G Lea, Family Doctor Publications, 1997; revised 2003. Available to purchase online (website: www.familydoctor.co.uk).
Explains potential hazards and offers practical advice on how to keep risk to a minimum whilst travelling.

YOUR CHILD'S HEALTH ABROAD – A MANUAL FOR TRAVELLING PARENTS (2ND EDITION)
Dr J W Howorth & Dr M Ellis, Bradt Publications, 2004.
A down-to-earth guide for anyone travelling overseas with children.

TRAVEL WITH CHILDREN (4TH EDITION)
Cathy Lanigan, 2002, Lonely Planet (website: www.lonelyplanet.com).
Contains practical information and tips for travelling with children.

LONELY PLANET HEALTHY TRAVEL GUIDES
Destination-specific pocket guides offering practical advice; see online (website: www.lonelyplanet.com).

STAYING HEALTHY IN ASIA, AFRICA AND LATIN AMERICA
D G Schroeder ScD, MPH, Moon Publications, 1995; updated 2000.
An informative handbook providing information on staying healthy whilst visiting, or living in, developing countries.

Advice Centres

Note: *Members of the public should be aware that personal medical advice cannot necessarily be obtained from organisations listed in this section. In many cases their own medical practitioner will be in the best position to take account of relevant personal factors. Where specialist advice is supplied to members of the public (very often for a fee), this has been noted. Some addresses, however, are provided to particularly assist professionals in the travel trade who wish to keep abreast of developments in the rapidly changing medical world.*

UNITED KINGDOM

DEPARTMENT OF HEALTH
Public Enquiries Office: Richmond House, 79 Whitehall, London SW1A 2NL
Tel: (020) 7210 4850. Minicom: (020) 7210 5025.
E-mail: dhmail@dh.gsi.gov.uk. Website: www.dh.gov.uk.
Public Health Laboratory Service: Website: www.phls.co.uk.

LONDON SCHOOL OF HYGIENE AND TROPICAL MEDICINE
Keppel Street, London WC1E 7HT
Main Switchboard: Tel: (020) 7636 8636.
Malaria Information Healthline: Tel: (09065) 508 908 (24 hours; calls cost £1 per minute).
Website: www.lshtm.ac.uk.

MEDICAL ADVISORY SERVICE FOR TRAVELLERS ABROAD –(MASTA)
Masta Travellers Healthline: Tel: (0906) 8224 100 (calls cost 60p per minute).
Validated by the London School of Hygiene and Tropical Medicine, this is a 24-hour, regularly updated advice line (with interactive technology) for travellers seeking information about vaccinations etc, in most countries and regions.

HOSPITAL FOR TROPICAL DISEASES (HTD)
Mortimer Market Centre, 2nd Floor, Capper Street, London WC1E 6AU
Tel: (020) 7387 9300 or 4411. Fax: (020) 7383 7645. Website: www.thehtd.org.
Travellers Healthline Advisory Service: Tel: (09061) 337 733 (calls cost 50p per minute, which also links to a fax-back service costing £1.50 per minute). Fax: (09061) 991 992 (no fax modems; ordinary fax machines only).

MASTA TRAVEL LOCATION LINE
26 clinics nationwide. Tel: (01276) 685 040. Website: www.masta.org/travel-clinics/clinic-locator.asp.

SCOTTISH CENTRE FOR INFECTION AND ENVIRONMENTAL HEALTH
Part of Health Protection Scotland (HPS).
Clifton House, Clifton Place, Glasgow G3 7LN
Travel Medicine Clinic: Tel: (0141) 300 1100. Fax (0141) 300 1170.
E-mail: eric.walker@scieh.csa.scot.nhs.uk (travel health enquiries).
Website: www.show.scot.nhs.uk/scieh/.

LIVERPOOL SCHOOL OF TROPICAL MEDICINE
Pembroke Place, Liverpool L3 5QA
Tel: (0151) 708 9393. Fax: (0151) 705 3370. E-mail: emt@liv.ac.uk (personnel). Website: www.liv.ac.uk/lstm.

NHS WALK-IN CENTRE
Manchester Airport, walkway between Terminal 1 and 3, Manchester N90 1QZ
Tel: (0161) 489 2109. Fax: (0161) 489 2280.

DIABETES UK
10 Parkway, London NW1 7AA
Tel: (020) 7424 1000. Fax: (020) 7424 1001.
E-mail: info@diabetes.org.uk. Website: www.diabetes.org.uk.
Issues leaflets and travel guides to the more popular countries with advice pertinent to the diabetic.

ROYAL ASSOCIATION FOR DISABILITY AND REHABILITATION (RADAR)
12 City Forum, 250 City Road, London EC1V 8AF
Tel: (020) 7250 3222. Minicom: (020) 7250 4119. Fax: (020) 7250 0212.
E-mail: radar@radar.org.uk. Website: www.radar.org.uk.
A wide range of leaflets and services are available to help disabled people arrange, insure and enjoy their travels. (See separate appendix in The Disabled Traveller.)

SWITZERLAND

WORLD HEALTH ORGANIZATION (WHO)
Avenue Appia 20, 1211 Geneva 27
Tel: (22) 791 2111. Fax: (22) 791 3111. E-mail: info@who.int. Website: www.who.int.

USA

US DEPARTMENT OF HEALTH AND HUMAN SERVICES
200 Independence Avenue, SW, Washington, DC 20201
Tel: (202) 619 0257 or (1877) 696 6775 (toll-free in the USA). Fax: (202) 690 7203.
Website: www.os.dhhs.gov.

INTERNATIONAL ASSOCIATION FOR MEDICAL ASSISTANCE TO TRAVELLERS (IAMAT)
1623 Military Road, #279, Niagara Falls, NY 14304-1745
Tel: (716) 754 4883. E-mail: info@iamat.org. Website: www.iamat.org.
A non-profit organisation dedicated to the gathering and dissemination of health and hygiene information worldwide.

CENTER FOR DISEASE CONTROL AND PREVENTION (CDC)
National Center for Infectious Diseases: Mailstop C-14, 1600 Clifton Road, Atlanta, GA 30333.
Tel: (404) 639 3311 (information line) or 3534 (public enquiries) or (800) 311 3435.
Website: www.cdc.gov.
Travellers Health Section: Contact via online form;
Website: www.cdc.gov/travel/contactus2.htm.
Website: www.cdc.gov/travel (general information).

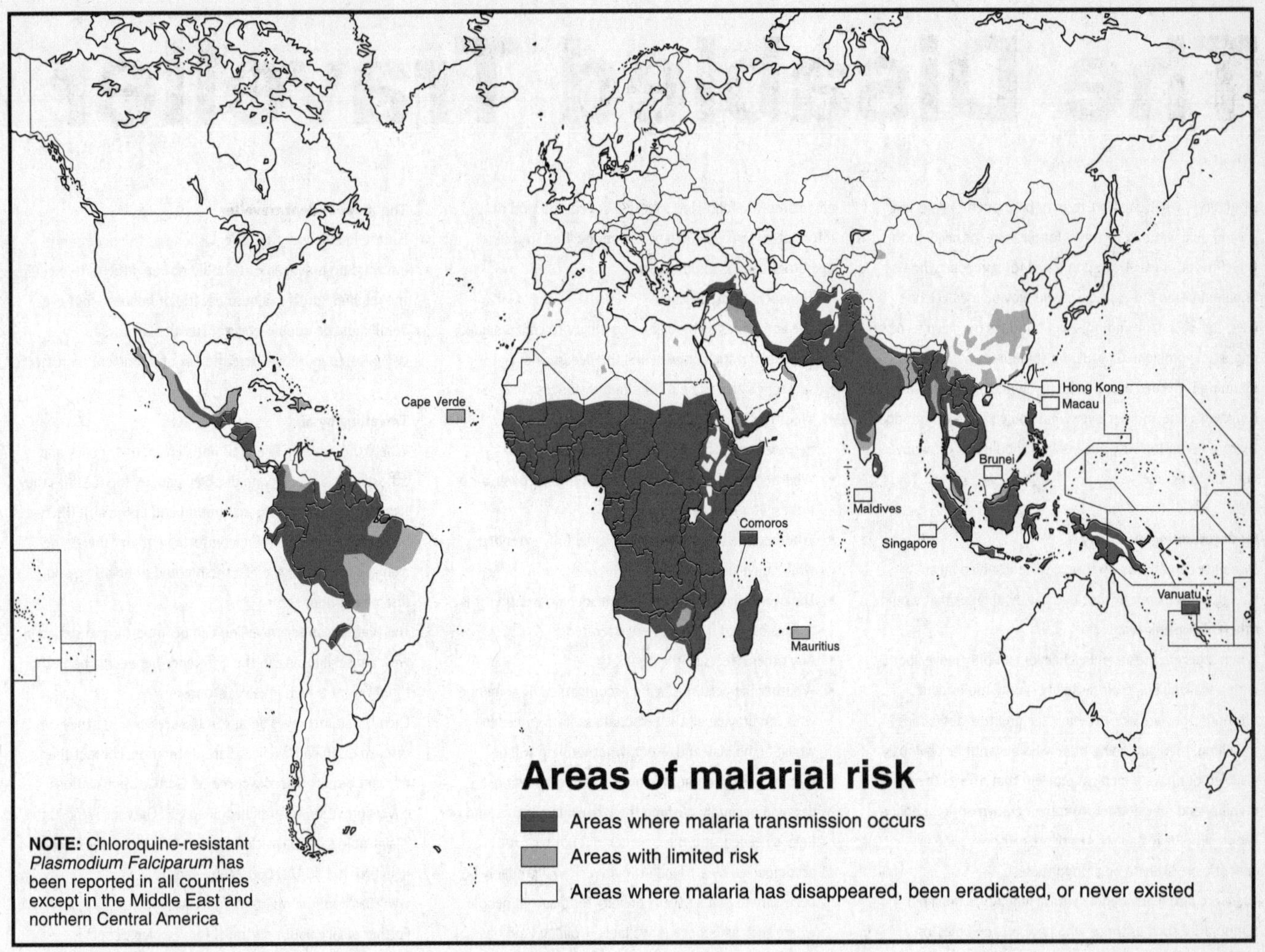
Cape Verde
Hong Kong
Macau
Brunei
Maldives
Comoros
Singapore
Vanuatu
Mauritius
Areas of malarial risk
Areas where malaria transmission occurs
Areas with limited risk
Areas where malaria has disappeared, been eradicated, or never existed
NOTE: Chloroquine-resistant Plasmodium Falciparum has been reported in all countries except in the Middle East and northern Central America

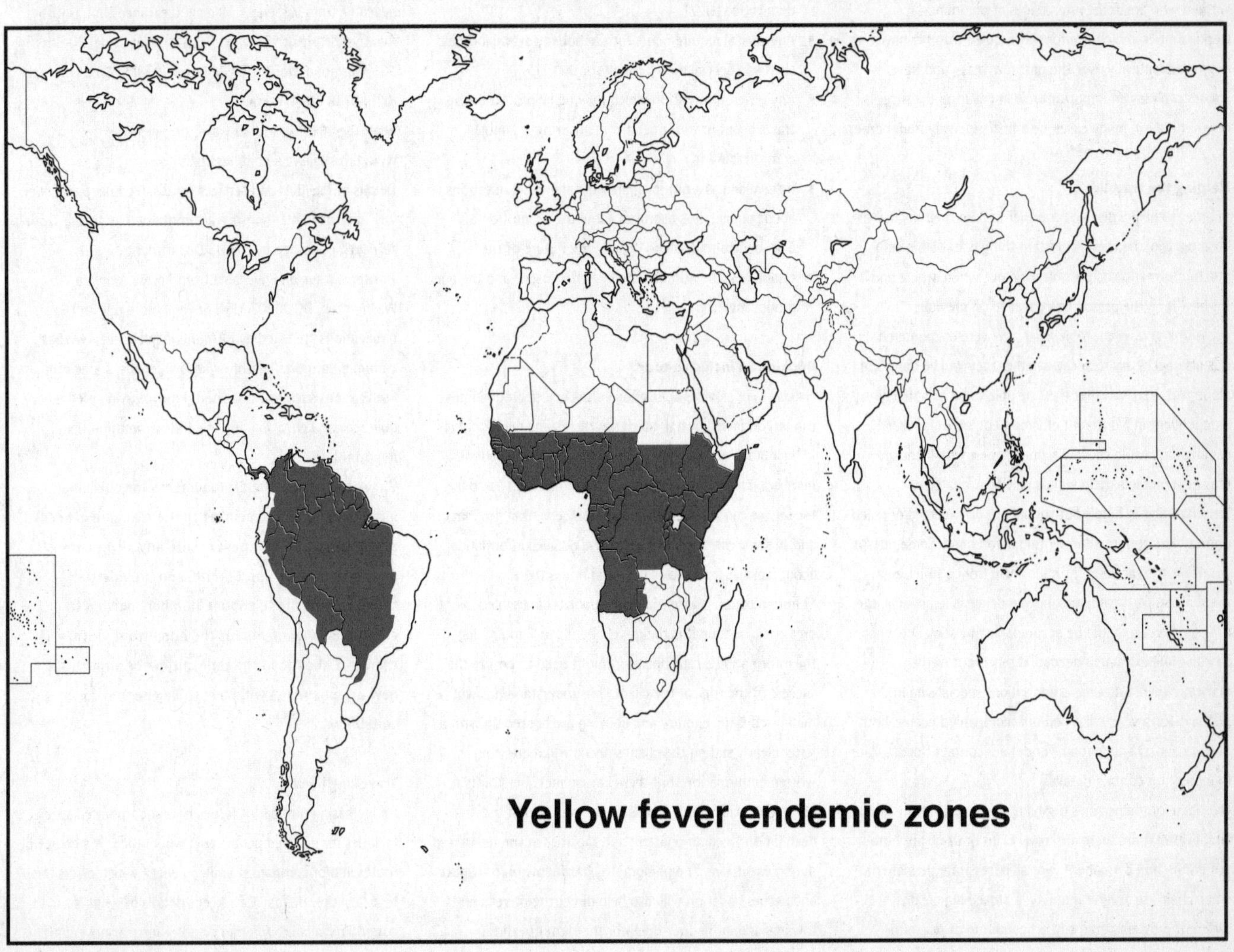
Yellow fever endemic zones

The Disabled Traveller

Disability - whether short term or permanent - does not stop people wanting to travel for pleasure, or needing to travel for business. Arranging travel for someone who has impaired vision or hearing, or who may be a wheelchair user, can be a daunting prospect but does not need to be an impossible problem. Careful and sometimes painstaking planning is needed, but provided you and your client are frank with one another over what you can and cannot do, there is no reason why both of you should not be happy with the outcome.

Understanding disability

Disability can take many forms: to be disabled means having an impairment that takes away abilities that would otherwise be enjoyed.

When a person uses a wheelchair, or can only move about with a walking aid, their disability is only too evident. Although they are likely to have the greatest difficulties in travelling, there are many more who may not be obviously disabled but have a medical problem that affects their mobility and may detract from their enjoyment of a holiday. People who have had strokes or are arthritic, blind or epileptic are likely to be among these.

There are also many people whose mobility is impaired temporarily, such as those who have broken limbs, or women who are in the later stages of pregnancy.

Opportunities and choice for the disabled traveller have grown dramatically over the past few years, and travel agents can play an important role in ensuring the success of what may, in many cases, be a first trip away from home.

Helping the traveller

In order to help a disabled traveller to plan their holiday or business trip, the most important thing is to obtain as much information as possible. Find out when, where and for how long the person has travelled on previous occasions, and what problems, if any, were encountered.

It is also necessary to know whether they will be travelling alone and, if so, whether they are able to be completely independent in a different environment, an unfamiliar climate that could cause discomfort, or where language may be a problem. Help will usually be available at terminals and in hotels but should not be expected or relied upon unless confirmed in writing beforehand. Sometimes it is sufficient to arrange for minor help from a hotel, eg a ramp for steps. If complete independence is impossible, the disabled person should be accompanied by someone who can give the extra help needed. If this is out of the question, there are some organisations specialising in holidays for severely disabled unaccompanied people, both in this country and abroad. For details, contact Holiday Care (see p922 for contact details).

The name of the person's disability and its effects are also vital information. There are many kinds of disability, both temporary and permanent. Not all necessitate permanent wheelchair use or limit mobility; a broken leg creates different problems than a heart condition or respiratory complaint. The following checklist covers the kind of information that needs to be communicated to tour operators, carriers and hoteliers:

- The name of the disability
- The limitations to mobility - eg ability to walk unaided, the use of a stick or crutches, the need to hold someone's arm to help over long distances
- Whether the use of a wheelchair is permanent, necessary most of the time, or for distance only
- Whether transfer from a wheelchair into a coach, air or train seat is easy or difficult
- Whether one or both legs need to be fully extended whilst travelling
- The overall dimensions of the wheelchair, whether it is collapsible and if it is battery operated
- Any other effects of the disability
- Whether the person is being accompanied by someone who can provide all the personal assistance needed whilst on holiday and, if not, whether help will be required with feeding, washing, bathing, toileting, dressing or simply pushing the wheelchair. If this kind of help is needed, and the traveller will not be accompanied by a friend or relative, it will probably be necessary to join a special holiday for disabled people where such assistance is available: Holiday Care has details (see p922)
- Any special requirements for the holiday or the journey, such as a special diet, oxygen or other aids
- Any other information which may be helpful to the travel agent or tour operator in ensuring the most comfortable trip
- If travelling as a group, apart from the usual questions about budget, it is useful to know the proportion of able-bodied to disabled people; the nature of the disabilities; the number of wheelchair users; and the age groups involved

Booking an inclusive tour

Holiday Care provides a list of operators whose programmes can be considered by a disabled traveller (some mention this in their brochures and give a contact name and telephone number). If a particular country or resort has been asked for, the service can tell you which operators serve that destination and, in some cases, will be able to give detailed information about facilities for disabled people in hotels there.

Communication is essential when booking a disabled client on a package tour. It is the travel agent's task to provide all the information a tour operator might need to ensure the success of the trip for the client. Misunderstandings will be minimised if the enquiry and booking are backed up with a letter clearly stating the client's needs and requesting written confirmation that these can be met. The points to be covered will include transport to, from and at the destination; accommodation; and facilities at the resort and during excursions. The paragraphs that follow on transport and accommodation will also help direct the travel agent towards asking the tour operator the right questions.

The independent traveller

For the independent traveller, as long as the necessary information is available, it should not be difficult to meet the requirements for a business trip or holiday - but every detail must be double-checked, particularly on a complicated journey where the risk of a problem is greater.

Travelling by air

Where there is a choice of airlines, check their policy and attitude towards carrying disabled people; the facilities they have for them (both on the ground and in the air); the type of aircraft (some are more comfortable than others); the availability of special diets; the method of boarding and disembarkation; etc.

The time of day for travelling can be important to someone with a disability, as can the difference between a non-stop flight or one which involves stopovers.

Each UK airport gives details of the services that they can offer to disabled travellers. For information, contact the relevant airport. The *Welcome to Gatwick* publication covers provision for disabled people at Gatwick Airport; this is available from Gatwick Airport Ltd, Gatwick, West Sussex RH6 0NP (tel: (0870) 000 2468; website: www.baa.com/main/airports/gatwick).

Further advice about air travel for disabled people is available from Passenger Medical Clearance Unit, British Airways Plc, Health Services (HMAG), Waterside, PO Box 365, Harmondsworth UB7 0GB (tel: (020) 8738 5444; fax: (020) 8738 9644; e-mail: health.services@britishairways.com; website: www.britishairways.com/health).

Details of facilities and services for disabled people at over 280 airports in 40 countries are contained in *Access Travel; Airports*, published by the US Department of Transportation, and available from Access America, Washington, DC 20202, USA. Several more relevant publications are listed by BAA online (website: www.baa.com/main/airports/heathrow/special_needs_frame.html).

Publications such as these should only provide preliminary guidance and checking any specific information is still important.

Check to confirm the arrangements for checking in and boarding and remember that equal care is needed at the end of the journey; ensure any airport transfer arrangements are appropriate, and provide the traveller with the telephone numbers needed to confirm arrangements for the homeward journey. If there is a change in the time, airline or airport, the new arrangements will have to be checked for suitability.

Travelling by sea

An increasing number of ferries have incorporated special facilities for disabled people and, where there is a choice of routes and/or companies, you can check which offers the best facilities. Holiday Care keeps details of what is currently available; whether or not a ferry or hovercraft offers special facilities, it is still crucial that the company is informed in advance that someone is disabled. When booking a crossing for a disabled passenger, ensure the company knows the nature of the disability and the sort of help needed during the journey.

Cruises can be especially attractive to older and disabled people, and most shipping lines offering cruises or fly/cruises are used to carrying disabled passengers. However, the following potential problems should be considered:

- A cruise may not be feasible for someone who cannot walk at all and is unaccompanied
- Shore excursions may not be possible, especially if tendering is involved and passengers have to board launches
- Coaches on shore excursions are unlikely to have any special facility for a disabled person
- Bad weather can be distressing for everyone, but especially so for someone not too steady on their feet or a wheelchair user

When booking a wheelchair user on a cruise, obtain the following information before making definite reservations:

- Width of lift floors and whether they offer access to all parts of the ship
- Width of cabin and toilet/bathroom doors; whether the doors open outwards and, if not, whether they block the plumbing; whether any existing steps at the doorways can be ramped temporarily
- Whether any cabins have an extra basin in the room to save some trips to the bathroom; where they are located; how much they cost; and their location in relation to lifts, etc
- Whether a wheelchair user is excluded from any part of the ship because of stairs, narrow doorways or other obstacles
- Which excursions ashore require a launch to be used and whether help would be available if the stairs down to the launch cannot be used; whether the gangplank used by passengers is too steep for a wheelchair user; and whether the one used by the crew is any lower and could be used instead
- What special arrangements might be needed at the beginning and end of the cruise
- Any restrictions on the type of wheelchair used
- Availability of laundry and/or launderette facilities

Travelling by road and rail

The provision of facilities for disabled travellers in coaches, taxis, hire cars and trains varies considerably from country to country. Even where there are specially adapted vehicles, as in the UK, these may not be available on all routes or at more than a few locations; check with the relevant carrier for further information. However, rail companies in the UK have recently done much to improve the service offered to disabled passengers.

The Disabled Person's Railcard gives discounts to holders and is available to people with a variety of disabilities; for information, ask for the Disabled Person's Railcard leaflet at stations, travel centres and post offices, which gives details and includes an application form. Application forms can also be obtained online (website: www.nationalrail.co.uk).

Visually impaired travellers who do not have a Disabled Person's Railcard (website: www.disabledpersons-railcard.co.uk) are entitled to discounts on standard and season tickets. Disabled travellers may be accompanied by one companion, who will be entitled to the same discounts. Guide dogs accompanying blind people are always conveyed free of charge.

Rail companies can give various types of assistance to disabled travellers, provided it is arranged in advance. Disabled travellers can contact their local station or ring National Rail Enquiries (tel: (08457) 484 950). For full details, ask for the Rail Travel for Disabled Passengers leaflet, free from all stations and travel centres. The leaflet can also be obtained by post from the Association of Train Operating Companies (ATOC), 40 Bernard Street, London WC1N 1BY.

Note: All new licensed London cabs have been equipped to carry wheelchairs. There are now approximately 4000 cabs that are capable of this and it is hoped that soon all cabs in service will be able to take wheelchairs on board. These cabs are available from cab ranks at stations, airports and hotels across London and can be hailed in the normal way.

The Disability Discrimination Act stipulates that all trains, trams and tube trains brought into use after 31 December 1998 should be accessible to disabled people and allow them to travel in safety and reasonable comfort. The Act, passed in 1995, should mean that travel for disabled people on all types of public transport shall gradually become easier.

Where there are no special facilities, it may still be possible for a disabled person to travel by road or rail, always ensuring that prior notification is given to the operator, giving precise details of route and timing. Where appropriate, help may then be provided.

Car hire

Some international car hire firms have cars equipped with hand controls for drivers with lower-limb disability. For further details, contact individual car hire companies.

Accommodation

The nature and degree of the disability will dictate the type of accommodation required. The points covered are important and particularly relevant to wheelchair users; however, when booking, ask what facilities will be needed for minimum and maximum comfort, request these facilities, back up your request with a letter and ask for confirmation in writing that they are available.

Access

For wheelchair access, entrance or side doors need to be ramped or level, with a minimum width of 80cm (32in). Interior doors also need to be at least this width, with no steps leading into public rooms (restaurant, lounge, bar, toilets, etc). There are many disabled people who do not use wheelchairs but are unable to use steps or stairs. A number of accommodation guides - details of which can be obtained from Holiday Care - show where there are ground-floor bedrooms. Most of these also show where there is a lift available, so even if there are no ground-floor bedrooms, access may be just as feasible due to the lift. If making enquiries about a hotel or guest house with a lift, ensure that the bedroom is as near to the lift as possible, and do ask whether there are any steps in the corridor between the lift doors and the bedroom.

General facilities

If ground-floor bedrooms are not available, there should be a lift large enough to take a wheelchair, ie at least 140cm (55in) deep by 1100cm (43in) wide.

Bedroom

The door should be at least 80cm (32in wide); there should be sufficient turning space for a wheelchair, ie 140cm (55in) by 140cm (55in), and free width of at least 80cm (32in) to one side of the bed.

Bathroom

The door should be at least 80cm (32in) wide; enough room is needed to enter in a wheelchair and close the door, with space beside the WC for a wheelchair to enable sideways transfer; support rails near the bath and WC are also needed.

Outside

There should be a route without steps and with a firm smooth surface which wheelchairs can use; this would ideally facilitate access to the swimming pool or beach without needing to negotiate steps; the availability (or otherwise) of a swimming pool hoist should be indicated; the accommodation should be in a central position with shopping and entertainment facilities within easy reach, since otherwise, specially arranged transport would be needed to enable disabled travellers to go on trips or excursions.

The Accessible Symbol

The Hotel and Holiday Consortium, made up of 21 organisations, including the Association of British Travel Agents, the BTA and the British Hospitality Association, has drawn up a range of minimum standards that must be met by an establishment before the Accessible Symbol can be awarded. Requirements for the new symbol are as follows:

- A public entrance to the building must be accessible to disabled people from a setting-down or car-parking point
- Where an establishment has a car park, a parking space must be reserved for a disabled guest on request
- Disabled people must have access to the following areas (if provided): reception, restaurant or dining room, lounge, TV lounge (unless TV is provided in the bedroom) and bar
- A minimum of one guest room with bath or shower and WC facilities en suite, which is suitable for a wheelchair user, should be provided. Where these facilities are not en suite, a unisex WC compartment and a bath or shower room suitable for a wheelchair user must be provided on the same floor level

Useful Publications

Flying High, published by the Disabled Living Foundation
Access to Air Travel, available from RADAR
Door to Door – A Guide to Transport for Disabled People, available from RADAR

Useful Contacts

Disabled Living Foundation, 380-384 Harrow Road, London W9 2HU (tel: (020) 7289 6111 (main switchboard) or (0845) 130 9177 (helpline, open Mon-Fri 1000-1600); minicom: (020) 7432 8009; e-mail: dlfinfo@dlf.org.uk; website: www.dlf.org.uk).

Organisations

Holiday care

7th Floor, Sunley House, 4 Bedford Park, Croydon, Surrey CR0 2AP.

Tel: (0845) 124 9971 (information) or 124 9974 (admin) or 124 9973 (reservations; UK only) or (208) 760 0072 (outside UK). Minicom: (0845) 124 9976. Fax: (0845) 124 9972 (admin).

E-mail: info@holidaycare.org. Website: www.holidaycare.org.uk.

Holiday Care, which was established as a registered charity in 1981, is the UK's central source of holiday information for people whose disability makes it difficult for them to find a holiday. An entirely non-commercial organisation, it provides details of accommodation, transport, facilities or publications that are most appropriate to the person's needs. At present, the following areas of information are covered by the service; new topics are continually being added.

UK holidays for disabled people: Specialist commercial and voluntary operators; access, accommodation and catering guides; self-catering accommodation; hotels and guest houses; special interest and activity holidays; farm holidays; specially-adapted accommodation; group facilities; university and college accommodation; holiday camps and centres; accommodation where personal or nursing care is provided; boating holidays; coach, rail, taxi and ambulance information; car hire; non-smoking accommodation; holidays suitable for those with epilepsy; holidays for people with learning difficulties; opportunities for those with mental health needs; escorts; financial assistance; information for deaf and/or blind people; various holidays for physically, mentally and/or sensorily disabled children; use of oxygen on holiday.

It is vital that adequate insurance cover is arranged. One of the biggest problems disabled people have faced in the past has been the inclusion in policies of a 'pre-existing medical condition' exclusion clause. These still appear in the policies offered by quite a number of tour operators. Do check very carefully that the policy offered does not have this clause. Even those who exclude nothing often require that a 'fitness to travel' certificate is obtained from a doctor beforehand. Holiday Care offers information on insurance for disabled travellers. Recommended companies include VentureSure (tel: (0800) 181 532; website: www.venturesure.co.uk) which can provide travel insurance for disabled or terminally ill people.

RADAR

(Royal Association for Disability and Rehabilitation) 12 City Forum, 250 City Road, London EC1V 8AF.

Tel: (020) 7250 3222. Fax: (020) 7250 0212. Minicom: (020) 7250 4119. E-mail: radar@radar.org.uk. Website: www.radar.org.uk.

RADAR is a national organisation run by and for disabled people. It acts as a pressure group to improve the environment for disabled people, campaigning for their rights and needs and challenging negative attitudes and stereotypes. Information and advice is given on a variety of subjects that affects the daily lives of disabled people. The organisation publishes Holidays in Britain & Ireland – A Guide For Disabled People.

BREAK

Davison House, 1 Montague Road, Sheringham, Norfolk NR26 8WN.

Tel: (01263) 822 161. Fax: (01263) 822 181. E-mail: office@break-charity.org. Website: www.break-charity.org.

BREAK provides holidays, short breaks and respite care for children, adults and families with special needs at two centres on the picturesque North Norfolk coast, so that while guests enjoy a seaside holiday, those who regularly care for them can have a much needed rest. There is also a wheelchair-friendly self-catering chalet in the West Country for families on low incomes.

British Red Cross

44 Moorfields, London EC2Y 9AL

Tel: 0870 170 7000. Fax: 020 7562 2000. E-mail: information@redcross.org.uk. Website: www.redcross.org.uk.

The British Red Cross can provide regional contact addresses and telephone numbers for local organisations that are able to offer help and support. The British Red Cross also has international offices where people can obtain useful equipment, such as wheelchairs, whilst on holiday. An information pack can be supplied on request.

Tripscope

The Vassall Centre, Gill Avenue, Bristol BS16 2QQ.

Tel/Minicom: (0845) 758 5641 (helpline; from within the UK) or (117) 939 7782 (from outside the UK). Fax: (0117) 939 7736. E-mail: enquiries@tripscope.org.uk. Website: www.tripscope.org.uk.

Tripscope is a travel and transport information service for disabled and elderly people, and can advise on planning local, long-distance and international journeys.

Access Travel

6 The Hillock, Astley, Manchester M29 7GW.

Tel: (01942) 888 844. Fax: (01942) 891 811. E-mail: info@access-travel.co.uk. Website: www.access-travel.co.uk.

Access Travel was founded in 1991 and is a tour operator that deals specifically with disabled travellers - in particular, wheelchair users. The company personally inspects accommodation and can therefore recommend suitable lodgings according to the traveller's individual needs. They can also assist with consumer protection; quotes and discounts on airfare; special aids; nursing and care services; adapted vehicles; and disabled-friendly car hire.